DATE DUE

DEMCO 38-296

Who's Who
among
Asian
Americans
1994/95

R

Who's Who
among
Asian
Americans
1994/95

◯

AMY L. UNTERBURGER, EDITOR

FOREWORD BY

CHANG-LIN TIEN, CHANCELLOR

UNIVERSITY OF CALIFORNIA

BERKELEY

Gale Research Inc. · DETROIT · WASHINGTON, D.C. · LONDON

Staff

Editor: Amy L. Unterburger

, Motoko Fujishiro Huthwaite, Julie K. Karmazin, Karen D. Kaus, Terrance W. Peck

nt Editors: Christopher M. McKenzie, Kelly Sprague

ors: Miranda H. Ferrara, Shirelle Phelps, Paula K. Woolverton

Senior Editor: Peter M. Gareffa

Research Manager: Victoria B. Cariappa

Research Supervisor: Mary Rose Bonk

Editorial Associates: Reginald A. Carlton, Frank Vincent Castronova, Andrew Guy Malonis, Norma Sawaya

Editorial Assistants: Laurel Sprague Bowden, Dawn Marie Conzett, Eva Marie Felts, Shirley Gates, Doris Lewandowski, Sharon McGilvray, Dana R. Schleiffers, Amy B. Wieczorek

Production Director: Mary Beth Trimper

Art Director: Cynthia D. Baldwin

Desktop Publishers/Typesetters: C.J. Jonik, Yolanda Y. Latham

Cover design by Somberg Design, Ann Arbor

Data Entry Services Manager: Benita L. Spight

Data Entry Supervisor: Gwendolyn S. Tucker

Data Entry Associates: Renee L. Aleksa, LySandra C. Davis, Edgar C. Jackson, Frances L. Monroe

Editorial Data Systems Supervisor: Theresa Rocklin

Programmers: Lan Campeau, Ida M. Wright

The paper used in this publication meets the minimum requirements of American National Standard for Information Sciences—Permanence Paper for Printed Library Materials, ANSI Z39.48-1984. ∞™

No part of this book may be reproduced in any form without permission in writing from the publisher, except by a reviewer who wishes to quote brief passages or entries in connection with a review written for inclusion in a magazine or newspaper.

Printed in the United States of America
Published simultaneously in the United Kingdom
by Gale Research International Limited
(An affiliated company of Gale Research Inc.)

The trademark ITP is used under license.

Who's Who among Asian Americans
Advisory Board

Contents

Foreword ix

Introduction xi

Key to Biographical Information xiii

Abbreviations Table xv

Biographies 1

Obituaries 709

Geographic Index 713

Occupation Index 735

Ethnic/Cultural Heritage Index 765

Foreword

More than 150 years ago, the first modern-day wave of Asians settled in the United States. Yet Asian Americans continue to be widely regarded as foreigners and sojourners. It is not by chance this view is so prevalent. Until recently, history books have remained silent about the contributions of Asian Americans.

This first edition of *Who's Who among Asian Americans* is a powerful tool for breaking the silence. Students and scholars will be able to use this resource to further understanding about the role of Asian Americans.

Women and men of Asian descent helped to forge this great nation. Chinese laborers helped build the transcontinental railroad and joined the California Gold Rush. Japanese, Filipino, and Korean immigrants toiled on Hawaiian sugar plantations and transformed barren California fields into fertile farmland. The lucky ones eventually leased and owned farms of their own. Filipinos found employment in service industries and in Alaskan salmon fisheries, while Asian Indians turned to the railroad and lumber industries. Numerous Japanese businesses blossomed in California in the early twentieth century.

As the United States expanded westward in the unrelenting drive to fulfill its manifest destiny, it looked to Asia as a source of labor. Yet the nation was reluctant to allow full participation of the Asians who were eager to make America their home.

The Naturalization Law of 1790 denied naturalized citizenship to all non-whites until the 1940s. Other laws followed that specifically excluded Asians. The Chinese Exclusion Act of 1882 banned the entry of Chinese laborers. Some states passed laws that prohibited Asians from leasing and owning farms. The signing of Executive Order 9066 at the start of World War II led to the internment of 110,000 Japanese Americans whose only crime was their heritage. The numbers of Asian immigrants remained low until 1965 when Congress enacted an immigration act that abolished discrimination against Asians.

Despite efforts to block participation of Asian Americans, our ancestors persevered. Their contributions to America are profound. As Ronald Takaki notes in *Strangers from a Different Shore: A History of Asian Americans*, Japanese farmers produced most of California's short-term crops in the first decades of this century. They grew 70 percent of California's strawberries, 95 percent of fresh snap beans, 67 percent of fresh tomatoes, and 95 percent of spring and summer celery. A Chinese immigrant named Ah Bing was responsible for developing the Bing cherry.

In World War II, more than 50,000 Filipino-American, Chinese-American and Japanese-American soldiers served their country. Japanese-American soldiers helped to free prisoners from the horrors of Dachau. Korean Americans who were fluent in Japanese translated Japanese secret documents and taught the Japanese language. Chinese Americans worked in defense industries and gave full support to the war effort.

As soon as the United States opened the door to Asian Americans, we became leaders in all fields. Asian Americans are distinguished scholars, dedicated state and federal representatives, Nobel Prize-winning scientists, successful entrepreneurs, and stellar athletes. Asian-American community activists, lawyers, doctors, and public servants are improving the quality of life in communities around the nation. Asian Americans have made dazzling contributions to arts, entertainment and architecture — from Yo-Yo Ma to Seiji Ozawa, from Maxine Hong Kingston to Yoshiko Uchida, from I.M. Pei to Minoru Yamasaki, from Wayne Wang to Amy Tan, from Connie Chung to Le Ly Hayslip.

The timing of the first *Who's Who among Asian Americans* is significant. This volume reflects the remarkable achievements of a population that was marginalized until just three decades ago.

The force of Asia Americans will burgeon in coming years. We are the fastest growing minority group in the United States. In the 1970s and 1980s, the number of people of Asian descent increased by more than 200 percent. Today, the 7.2 million Asian Americans in the United States represent 2.9 percent of the population. Projections indicate that by the turn of the twenty-first century, Asian Americans will represent 4 percent of the population.

Our increasing diversity enriches the nation as well. Vietnamese, Thai, Mien, Laotian, Cambodian, and Hmong immigrants are transforming entire neighborhoods.

The publication of *Who's Who among Asian Americans* is just the first step. This volume, along with other reference sources, must be used widely to tell the story of Asian Americans. The interpretation of history is vital to our future, not just for Asian Americans, but for the entire nation. People's views and actions are shaped by their understanding of history.

If history books continue the old practice of overlooking ethnic minorities, the future looks bleak. By the year 2056, people of color are projected to be the majority in the United States. Many cities already reflect the America of tomorrow. In urban centers, African Americans, Latinos, whites, Chicanos, Asian Americans and Native Americans attend school together, work together, eat at restaurants together, and shop together.

Yet we do not always get along together. Outbreaks of ethnic strife from Brooklyn's Crown Heights (1991) to South Central Los Angeles (1992) are stark reminders of what the future will hold unless we build understanding and respect about the many races and cultures that make up our nation.

Diversity is a handicap only if we allow it to be. Each one of us is responsible for making sure the history of our multicultural nation is told. Each one of us is responsible for making sure that future generations learn about the contributions of all people. Only then will the promise of a diverse America be realized.

Chang-Lin Tien
Chancellor, University of California, Berkeley

Introduction

*W*ho's *Who among Asian Americans* (*WWAA*) is a new, distinctive endeavor — the first listing of contemporary Asian-American leaders from all occupations and ethnic and cultural subgroups. *Who's Who among Asian Americans* gives you key biographical facts on nearly 6,000 men and women who have changed today's world and are shaping tomorrow's.

The Asian-American population is growing at a faster pace than any other segment of the U.S. population. The biographical entries you will find on these pages reflect the diversity of Asian-American achievement by documenting the contributions of leaders in all fields of endeavor. Together these entries make *WWAA* the single most comprehensive publication devoted to recording the dynamic growth of Asian-American accomplishment. It serves as a single reference point for information that will help you stay up-to-date on the scope of Asian-American achievement.

Compilation Methods

The selection of *Who's Who among Asian Americans* listees is based primarily on reference value. In order to identify noteworthy achievers, the editors contacted more than 2,000 associations, businesses, government offices, and colleges and universities for suggestions. The editorial staff also continuously scans a wide variety of books, magazines, newspapers, and other material. The *WWAA* Advisory Board members provide recommendations for listees, as well.

Candidates become eligible for inclusion by virtue of positions held through election or appointment to office, notable career achievements, or significant community service. For the purposes of this book, the term Asian American is used to describe a U.S. resident or citizen whose ancestry is Asian or Pacific Islander. This definition includes more than 20 major nationalities and ethnic groups, including:

Bangladeshi	Indonesian	Nepalese
Bhutanese	Japanese	Pacific Islander
Bruneian	Korean	Pakistani
Cambodian (Kampuchean)	Laotian	Singaporean
Chinese	Malaysian	Sri Lankan
Indian	Mongolian	Thai
Filipino	Myanmar (formerly	Vietnamese
Hmong	Burmese)	

Please note that "Indo-American" refers to those of Indian ethnicity and is used rather than the term "Indian American" to prevent confusion with those of Native American ethnic background. The term Pacific Islander includes the following islands: Fiji, Guam, Hawaii, Northern Marianas, Palau, Samoa, Tahiti, and Tonga. Hmong are an ethnic group from Laos, Thailand, Vietnam, and southern China.

Asian persons who are not American citizens are considered eligible if they live or work in the United States and contribute significantly to American life. Such broad coverage makes *Who's Who among Asian Americans* the logical source to consult when gathering facts on a distinguished leader or a favorite celebrity, locating a colleague, contacting an expert, recruiting personnel, or launching a fund-raising effort.

Once identification is complete, we attempt to secure information directly from biographees. Potential new listees receive a questionnaire asking them to furnish the data that forms the basis of an entry. Those candidates whose achievements merit inclusion proceed through the remaining stages of entry compilation.

Sometimes potential listees decline to furnish biographical data or are unavailable to the editors at press time. In these cases, we have compiled selected entries from a variety of secondary sources to help ensure that *WWAA* is as comprehensive as possible. These entries are marked by an asterisk (*), indicating that the listees have not personally provided or reviewed the data.

Important Features

To complement its thorough coverage, *Who's Who among Asian Americans* uses these important features to help you quickly locate the information you need:

- **Boldface rubrics** allow quick and easy scanning for specifics on personal data, educational background, career positions, organizational affiliations, honors and awards, special achievements, military service, other biographical sources, home address, business address, and telephone number.

- **Obituaries section** provides you with entries on recently deceased newsworthy Asian Americans. This section provides a full entry plus date and place of death when available.

Indexing

Who's Who among Asian Americans features three indexes to help you easily locate entries in a variety of ways:

- **Geographic Index**—This index allows you to locate biographees by specific city, state, and country of residence and/or employment. (Only those listees who agree to allow their addresses to be printed will appear in this index.)

- **Occupational Index**—This index allows you to identify listees working in more than 200 fields ranging from accounting to zoology.

- **Ethnic/Cultural Heritage Index**—This index identifies listees by their ethnic or cultural background. (Only those listees who indicated their ethnic/cultural heritage will appear in this index.)

Availability in Electronic Formats

- **Diskette/Magnetic Tape.** *WWAA* is available for licensing on magnetic tape or diskette in a fielded format. Either the complete database or a custom selection of entries may be ordered. The database is available for internal data processing and nonpublishing purposes only. For more information, call please 800-877-GALE.

- **Online.** *WWAA* is available online through Mead Data Central's NEXIS Service in the NEXIS, PEOPLE and SPORTS Libraries in the GALBIO file.

Acknowledgments

The editors wish to thank the Advisory Board members whose names appear on page v for their advice and encouragement as we compiled this first edition of *Who's Who among Asian Americans*.

We would also like to thank the many individuals and organizations who nominated achievers for consideration in this volume.

Suggestions Welcome

Comments and suggestions from users on *Who's Who among Asian Americans* are welcome. Also, if there is someone you think should be included in the next edition, please let us know. Address correspondence to:

The Editor
Who's Who among Asian Americans
Gale Research Inc.
835 Penobscot Building
Detroit, Michigan 48226-4094

Key to Biographical Information

[1] **LEE, GUS CHIEN-SUN**

[2] Attorney, author, lecturer. [3] Chinese American. [4] **PERSONAL:** Born in San Francisco, CA; son of Tsung-Chi Lee & Da-Tsien Tsu; married Diane; children: Jena, Eric. [5] **EDUCATION:** USMA West Point; University of California, Davis, 1969, JD, 1976. [6] **CAREER:** University of California, Davis, assistant dean, 1969-74; US Army, command judge advocate, 1977-80; Sacramento, California, Office of the DA, deputy DA, 1980-85; California District Attorneys Association, deputy director, 1985-89; State Bar of California, senior executive, legal education, 1989-; author, currently. [7] **ORGANIZATIONS:** Boys & Girls Club, board member, 1991-; Main Library Campaign, literary luminary, 1991-; West Point Association of Graduates, 1984-; UCD Alumni Association, 1977-; Asian Pacific American Alumni Association, UCD, 1993. [8] **HONORS/AWARDS:** University of California, Davis, Alumni Citation for Excellence, 1991; New York Times, Best 100 Book List, 1991; California District Attorneys Association, Service/Top Instructor, 1988, 1989; Office of the DA, Sacramento, Order of the Silk Purse, 1984; State Bar of California, service, 1993. [9] **SPECIAL ACHIEVEMENTS:** Author of: China Boy, 1991; Honor & Duty, 1994; one-page article on California, Time magazine, November 18, 1991, p99; SBC Instructors Manual, 1993; SBC Videos: Law & Mr Finnegan, 1990-93. [10] **MILITARY SERVICE:** US Army, cpt, 1964-68, 1977-80, Parachutist Wings; Meritorious Service Medal w/oak leaf cluster, ARCOM; AAM. [11] **BIOGRAPHICAL SOURCES:** New York Times, Washington Post, SF Chronicle/Examiner, Denver Post, San Diego Times, Chicago Times, CNN, Good Morning America, etc. [12] **BUSINESS ADDRESS:** PO Box 791, Colorado Springs, CO 80901.

[1]   Name of biographee
[2]   Ethnic/cultural heritage
[3]   Occupation
[4]   Personal data
[5]   Educational background
[6]   Career information
[7]   Organizational affiliations
[8]   Honors/awards
[9]   Special achievements (publications, works of art, language proficiency, etc.)
[10] Military service
[11] Sources for more information
[12] Home and/or business address and telephone number (at listee's discretion)

Biographees are listed alphabetically by surname. In cases where the surnames are identical, biographees are arranged first by surname, then by first and middle names, and finally by suffixes such as Jr., Sr., or II, III, etc. Surnames beginning with a prefix (such as De, De La, or Van), however spaced, are listed alphabetically under the first letter of the prefix and are treated as if there were no space. Surnames with punctuation (Chin-Lee) are treated as if there were no punctuation. Names with more than one possible filing element (Paul De La Cruz Blanco) are listed according to the main element indicated by the biographee. Diacritics appear in names when indicated by the listees.

Abbreviations Table

AK	Alaska	MO	Missouri
AL	Alabama	MS	Mississippi
Apr	April	MT	Montana
AR	Arkansas	NC	North Carolina
Aug	August	ND	North Dakota
AZ	Arizona	NE	Nebraska
CA	California	NH	New Hampshire
CO	Colorado	NJ	New Jersey
CT	Connecticut	NM	New Mexico
DC	District of Columbia	Nov	November
DE	Delaware	NV	Nevada
Dec	December	NY	New York
Feb	February	Oct	October
FL	Florida	OH	Ohio
GA	Georgia	OK	Oklahoma
HI	Hawaii	OR	Oregon
IA	Iowa	PA	Pennsylvania
ID	Idaho	PR	Puerto Rico
IL	Illinois	RI	Rhode Island
IN	Indiana	SC	South Carolina
Jan	January	SD	South Dakota
Jul	July	Sep	September
Jun	June	TN	Tennessee
KS	Kansas	TX	Texas
KY	Kentucky	UT	Utah
LA	Louisiana	VA	Virginia
MA	Massachusetts	VI	Virgin Islands
Mar	March	VT	Vermont
MD	Maryland	WA	Washington
ME	Maine	WI	Wisconsin
MI	Michigan	WV	West Virginia
MN	Minnesota	WY	Wyoming

BIOGRAPHIES

A

ABARQUEZ-DELACRUZ, PROSY
State official. Filipino American. **PERSONAL:** Born Aug 11, 1952, Manila, Philippines; daughter of Eleazar Abarquez & Asuncion Castro Abarquez; married Enrique B Delacruz, Jan 4, 1979; children: Corina, Carlo. **EDUCATION:** BS, food technology, 1972, JD, 1982. **CAREER:** LA County Dept of Public Social Services, eligibility worker, 1976-78; California DHS, supervising investigator, 1986-92, regional administrator, 1992-. **ORGANIZATIONS:** Asian Pacific Americans for New Los Angeles, founding member, steering committee, 1993-; Alliance for Philippine Concerns, national vice chair, 1991-; International Women's Support Group, founding member, 1990-; Philippine Network, 1990-; Gabriela Network, 1992-. **HONORS/AWARDS:** Philippine Women's Network, Recognition Award for Excellence, 1992; City of Los Angeles Human Relations Commission, Recognition Award for Cross-Cultural Understanding, 1991; California Dept of Health Services Food & Drug Branch, Recognition Award for Excellence, 1979, 1980, 1984-85. **SPECIAL ACHIEVEMENTS:** Author, "Is It Because I Am A Filipino?," Los Angeles Times, Nov, 1992; "LA's Rainbow Revolt-From Ashes to Multicultural Unity," LA Filipino Bulletin, Nov, 1992; proficient in English and Tagalog. **BIOGRAPHICAL SOURCES:** "Filipina Appointed to State Food & Drug," LA Filipino Bulletin, Dec 1992; "State Food & Drug Appoints First Asian," California Examiner, Dec 1992. **BUSINESS ADDRESS:** Regional Administrator, Food & Drug Branch, California Dept of Health, 1449 West Temple St, Suite 224, Los Angeles, CA 90026, (213)620-2965.

ABBAS, MIAN M.
Scientist. Pakistani American. **PERSONAL:** Born Jun 22, 1933, Nawanshehr, India; son of Mian Ataullah; married Adiba, Jul 24, 1960; children: Hamid, Rashida, Sheerin, Omar. **EDUCATION:** Panjab University, BS, 1955; Laval University, MS, 1960; University of Rhode Island, PhD, 1967. **CAREER:** Ohio University, assistant professor, 1968-70; University of Kentucky, associate professor, 1970-74; University of Maryland, senior research associate, 1974-79; Drexel University, associate professor, research professor, 1979-87; NASA/Marshall Space Flight Center, astrophysicist, 1987-. **ORGANIZATIONS:** American Geophysical Union; American Association for Advancement of Science. **HONORS/AWARDS:** National Research Council, National Academy of Science, senior fellow, 1974-76; National Research Council of Canada, fellow, 1958-60. **SPECIAL ACHIEVEMENTS:** Over 60 publications in professional scientific journals, 1967-; numerous chapters in books; Remote Sensing of Atmospheres and Oceans, Ed Deepak, Academic Press, 1980. **BIOGRAPHICAL SOURCES:** Citation Index, Philadelphia, in volumes, 1968-. **HOME ADDRESS:** 1604 Chandler Rd, Huntsville, AL 35801-1482, (205)880-2360. **BUSINESS ADDRESS:** Astrophysicist, NASA/Marshall Space Flight Center, Huntsville, AL 35812, (205)544-7680.

ABE, MAKOTO
Educator. Japanese American. **PERSONAL:** Born Jan 24, 1961, Tokyo, Japan. **EDUCATION:** MIT, BS, 1984, MS, 1984, PhD, 1991. **CAREER:** University of Illinois, Chicago, Marketing Department, professor, 1991-. **HONORS/AWARDS:** Tau Beta Pi. **BUSINESS ADDRESS:** Professor, Dept of Marketing, University of Illinois, Chicago, 601 S Morgan St, Rm 2331 UH, m/c 243, Chicago, IL 60607, (312)996-7326.

ABHYANKAR, SHREERAM SHANKAR
Educator. Indo-American. **PERSONAL:** Born Jul 22, 1930, Ujjain, Madhya Pradesh, India; son of Shankar Keshav & Uma Tamhankar Abhyankar; married Yvonne M Abhyankar, Jun 5, 1958; children: Hari, Kashi. **EDUCATION:** Bombay University, BS, 1951; Harvard University, AM, 1952, PhD, 1955. **CAREER:** Visiting professor at numerous schools, 1956-91; Purdue University, professor of industrial engineering & computer sciences, 1963, Marshall Distinguished Professor of Mathematics, 1967-. **ORGANIZATIONS:** American Mathematical Society, 1953-; Mathematical Association of America, 1953-; Indian Mathematical Society, 1967-; Maharashtra Academy of Sciences, 1976-; International Journal of Mathematics and Mathematical Sciences, editorial board, 1978-; Journal of the Indian Mathematical Society, editorial board, 1978-; Journal of the Indian Academy of Mathematics, editorial board, 1978-; Indian Journal of Pure and Applied Mathematics, editorial board, 1987-; Ulam Quarterly, editorial board, 1989-. **HONORS/AWARDS:** Alfred P Sloan Foundation, Research Fellow, 1958-60; Purdue University, Herbert Newby McCoy Award, 1973; MAA, Lester R Ford Prize, 1977, Chauvenet Award, 1978; Phi Beta Kappa, 1984; Indian National Science Academy, fellow, 1987; Indian Academy of Sciences, fellow, 1988; University of Valladolid, Spain, Medal of Honor, 1990. **SPECIAL ACHIEVEMENTS:** Generalized Rodeletive Correspondence Between Multitableaux & Multimonomials, Discrete Mathematics, vol 93, p 1-17, 1991; Galois Theory on the Line in Nonzero Characteristics, Bulletin of the American Mathematical Society, vol 27, p 68-133, 1992; Generalized coinsertion & standard multitableaux, Journal of Statistical Planning & Inference, vol 34, p 5-18, 1993; numerous others. **HOME ADDRESS:** 111 Waldron St, West Lafayette, IN 47906, (317)743-2440. **BUSINESS ADDRESS:** Marshall Distinguished Prof of Math, Math Dept, Purdue University, West Lafayette, IN 47907.

ABO, RONALD K.
Architect. Japanese American. **PERSONAL:** Born Jul 10, 1946, Rupert, ID; son of Isamu Abo and Ameria Abo; divorced; children: Tamiko N, Reiko D. **EDUCATION:** University of Colorado, BArch, 1969. **CAREER:** Seracuse Lawyer Partners, draftsman, 1967-71; ABR Partnership, associate, 1971-76; ABO Architects, president, 1976-. **ORGANIZATIONS:** Private Industry, board member, vice chair allocations comm, 1990-; AIA Denver, board member, 1985-92, past pres, 1992, president, 1991, 1st vice president, 1990, secretary, 1989; AIA Colorado, board member, 1991; University of Colorado at Denver, Alumni Assoc board member, 1990-91. **HONORS/AWARDS:** Colorado AIA, Universal Design, 1990; National Assn of Remodelers, Commercial Design, 1990; Western Mountain Region AIA, Award of Excellence, 1984; Colorado AIA, Award of Excellence, 1984; WOOD, Merit Award, 1985. **SPECIAL ACHIEVEMENTS:** AIKIDO, 3rd degree black belt, 1988; Denver Community Leadership Forum, Graduate, 1985; Architectural Registration, Colorado, 1972; University of Colorado at Denver, Excellence and Diversity, 1991. **MILITARY SERVICE:** Colorado National Guard, sp-5, 1969-75. **BUSINESS ADDRESS:** President, Abo Architects PC, 1448 Pennsylvania, Denver, CO 80203, (303)830-0575.

ABRAHAM, JOHN
City official, community activist. Indo-American. **PERSONAL:** Born Mar 19, 1946, Trivandrum, Kerala, India; son of K V Abraham & Sosamma Abraham; married Mary Abraham, May 15, 1972; children: John Jr, Thomas, Matthew. **EDUCATION:** Institute of Textile Technology, BS, 1967; Philadelphia College of Textiles & Science, 1972-73; Stevens Institute of Technology, MS, 1990. **CAREER:** Duralite Co, manager; US Postal System, engineer, letter carrier, supervisor; Bergen County, supervisor; Township of Teaneck, mayor, currently. **ORGANIZATIONS:** Bergen County Human Relations Comm, founding cochair; B C Christian Fellowship, founding president; Kerala Cultural Forum, trustee; Indian Republican Club, founding chairman; Republican county committeeman; Democratic county committeeman; NAACP, life member; UJW, life member. **HONORS/AWARDS:** B C Christian Fellowship, Man of the Year, 1990-92; KCF, Man of the Year, 1992; Indian Republican Club, Man of the Year, 1993; many organizations in US & India, honored as first

Indian-born mayor in USA to be elected. **HOME ADDRESS:** PO Box 24, Teaneck, NJ 07666, (201)836-3300.

ABRAHAM, THOMAS

Industry and market analyst. Indo-American. **PERSONAL:** Born Sep 11, 1948, Pathanamthitta, Kerala, India; son of T G Abraham & Aleyamma Abraham; married Susy T Abraham, Sep 22, 1980; children: Nitya, Jay T. **EDUCATION:** Columbia University, MS, 1975, industrial engineer, 1980, DEngSci, 1981. **CAREER:** Denver Research Institute, research metallurgist, 1981-83; Business Communications, project analyst, 1984-85; Brookhaven National Lab, assistant metallurgist, 1985-86; Business Communications Co, Ceramics Group, director, 1986-. **ORGANIZATIONS:** American Ceramic Society, 1986-; Global Org of People of Indian Origin, convener, 1989-; National Federation of Indian Assns, chairman, 1988-92, president, 1980-88; Federation of Indian Assns, president, 1976-81; India Club of Columbia University, president, 1975-76. **HONORS/AWARDS:** National Federation of Indian Associations, Outstanding Service, 1988; Federation of Indian Associations, Outstanding Service, 1981; Indian American Kerala Cultural and Civic Center, 1992; Council of Indian Associations, Outstanding Service, 1989; India Tribune, Gandhi Community Service Award, 1983. **SPECIAL ACHIEVEMENTS:** Published: technical papers in Ceramic Society Bulletin, The Material Society (TMS) Journal, and the Ceramic Industry. **HOME ADDRESS:** 60 Bradley Place, Stamford, CT 06905, (203)329-8010.

ACHAR, NARAHARI B. N.

Educator. Indo-American. **PERSONAL:** Born Jan 5, 1939, Chikkellur, Karnataka, India; son of Bangalore Narasimhamurthy Achar and Rukmini Bai; married Kusuma K Achar, Jul 3, 1973; children: Pramod, Chandrika. **EDUCATION:** University of Mysore, India, BSc (honors), 1960; Pennsylvania State University, MS, 1965, PhD, 1968. **CAREER:** Argonne National Lab, res associate, 1969-72; Penn State University, res associate, 1973-80; Bucknell University, visiting assistant professor, 1980-84; Memphis State University, professor, 1984-. **HONORS/AWARDS:** Mysore University, Siddloghatta Rama Rao Gold Medal, 1960; Government of Mysore, Physical Sciences Prize, 1960; Penn State University, fellowship, 1966. **SPECIAL ACHIEVEMENTS:** Author of over 60 published articles in journals. **BUSINESS ADDRESS:** Professor, Dept of Physics, Memphis State University, Manning Hall, RM 336, Memphis, TN 38152.

ADVANI, SURESH GOPALDAS

Educator. Indo-American. **PERSONAL:** Born Aug 19, 1959, Pune, Maharashtra, India; son of Kamla and Gopaldas Advani; married Yolanda Chetwynd, Dec 29, 1987; children: Madhu. **EDUCATION:** Indian Institute of Technology, Bombay, BTec, 1982; University of Illinois at Urbana-Champaigh, PhD, 1987. **CAREER:** University of Illinois, research assistant, 1984-87, teaching fellow, 1986-87; University of Delaware, assistant professor, 1987-92, associate professor, 1992-. **ORGANIZATIONS:** ASME, Polymer Committee, chair; CADCOMP, symposium organizer; Society of Rheology; Polymer Processing Society; Polymer Technical Committee, chair. **HONORS/AWARDS:** Society of Plastic Engineers, Best Paper; International Travel Award. **SPECIAL ACHIEVEMENTS:** Edited book on flow and rheology in composites manufacturing; developed models for manufacturing with composites. **BUSINESS ADDRESS:** Associate Professor, Dept of Mechanical Eng, University of Delaware, 126 Spencer Laboratory, Newark, DE 19716, (302)831-8975.

AGARWAL, ARUN KUMAR

Educator. Indo-American. **PERSONAL:** Born Mar 17, 1944, Lucknow, Uttar Pradesh, India; son of Ram Das Agarwal and Champa Devi Agarwal; married Prabha Vati Agarwal, Feb 5, 1967; children: Anju, Amit K. **EDUCATION:** Lucknow University, India, BSc, 1960, MSc, 1963, PhD, 1967. **CAREER:** West Virginia University, postdoctoral fellow, 1968-69; AT&T Bell Lab, member of tech staff, Summers, 1982-84; Grambling State University, professor, 1969-. **ORGANIZATIONS:** American Mathematical Society, 1993; Mathematical Association of America, 1993; Bharat Ganita Parishad, life member, 1993-. **SPECIAL ACHIEVEMENTS:** Certificate of proficiency, French, 1964; published research papers in entire functions, 1965-; reviewer for Math Reviews and Zentral Blatt Fur Mathematik, 1970-. **BUSINESS ADDRESS:** Professor, Grambling State University, PO Box 679, Grambling, LA 71245, (318)274-2422.

AGARWAL, GYAN CHAND

Educator. Indo-American. **PERSONAL:** Born Apr 22, 1940, Baghwanpur, Saharanpur, Uttar Pradesh, India; son of Hari Chand & Ram Rati Agarwal; married Sadhna Agarwal, Jul 7, 1965; children: Monika Agarwal-Punjabi, Mudita. **EDUCATION:** Agra University, India, BSc, 1957; University of Roorkee, India, BE electrical, 1960; Purdue University, MSEE, 1962, PhD, 1965. **CAREER:** Purdue University, graduate teaching assistant, 1960-62, instructor of electrical engineering, 1962-65; University of Illinois, Chicago, assistant professor, 1965-69, associate professor, 1969-73, professor, 1973-; Indian Institute of Science, India, visiting professor, 1971; Indian Institute of Technology, India, visiting associate professor, 1972. **ORGANIZATIONS:** Institute Electrical & Electronics Engineering, 1961-, fellow, 1986; American Association for Advancement of Science, 1968-, fellow, 1990; American Institute for Medical and Biological Engineering, founding fellow, 1992; Society for Neuroscience, 1978-; Sigma Xi, 1964-; Phi Kappa Phi, 1969-; Eta Kappa Nu, 1986-. **HONORS/AWARDS:** University of Roorkee, Merit Scholarship, 1958-60; Khosla Gold Medal for best student in BE final examination; Thomson Memorial Gold Medal for best Engineering Design Project; University of Roorkee, General Maclagan Prize for Electrical Engineering, 1960; Engineering Foundation, NY, Certificate of Appreciation, 1982; FDA, Certificate of Appreciation, 1985. **SPECIAL ACHIEVEMENTS:** L Stark and GC Agarwal, Biomaterials, Plenum Press, NY, 1969; co-author, over 100 journal papers in engineering and medical journals; over 20 book chapters; over 200 conference papers and presentations. **BUSINESS ADDRESS:** Professor, Dept of Electrical Engineering & Computer Science, University of Illinois, Chicago, 851 South Morgan St, Rm 1120 SEO, (mc-154), Chicago, IL 60607-7053, (312)996-8679.

AGARWAL, RAMESH KUMAR

Educator, aerospace company executive. Indo-American. **PERSONAL:** Born Jan 4, 1947, Mainpuri, Uttar Pradesh, India; son of Radha Kishan & Parkash Vati Agarwal; married Sugita Agarwal, Oct 26, 1978; children: Vivek, Gautum. **EDUCATION:** Indian Institute of Technology, Kharagpur, BTech, 1968; University of Minnesota, MS, 1969; Stanford University, PhD, 1975. **CAREER:** Rao and Associates, principal engineer, 1975-76; NASA Ames Research Center, NRC research associate, 1976-78; McDonnell Douglas, program director/MDC fellow, 1978-. **ORGANIZATIONS:** American Institute of Aeronautics & Astronautics, fellow, 1993; American Society of Mechanical Engineers; American Physical Society; American Heliocopter Society; American Academy of Mechanics; Sigma Xi; Sigma Gamma Tau. **HONORS/AWARDS:** Society of Automotive Engineers, Best Paper, 1988. **SPECIAL ACHIEVEMENTS:** Author of over 100 scientific publications, including book chapter, 1978-; short courses in supercomputing and computational fluid dynamics. **HOME ADDRESS:** 2358 Sterling Pointe Dr, Chesterfield, MO 63005-4510, (314)532-2174. **BUSINESS ADDRESS:** Program Director, McDonnell Douglas Fellow, McDonnell Douglas Aerospace Corporation, PO Box 516, St. Louis, MO 63166, (314)233-2528.

AGARWALA, VINOD SHANKER

Materials scientist. Indo-American. **PERSONAL:** Born Aug 9, 1939, Sitapur, Uttar Pradesh, India; son of Bhagwati Prasad Agrawal & Ramkatori Devi; married Asha Varma, Feb 12, 1987; children: Veena V, Vinay. **EDUCATION:** Banaras Hindu University, India, BSc, 1959, MSc, 1961; Massachusetts Institute of Technology, MS, 1966; Banaras Hindu University, PhD, 1968. **CAREER:** MIT, research assistant, 1965-67; Colonial Board Co, develop chemist, 1967; Canadian Department of Energy, Ottawa, Mineral and Resources, research fellow, 1967-69; Superior Steel Ball Co, metallurgist, 1970-72; University of Connecticut, senior research associate, 1972-76; Wright-Patterson AFB, Ohio, NRC research associate, 1976-77; Naval Air Warfare Center, scientist, group leader, 1977-. **ORGANIZATIONS:** National Association of Corrosion Engineers, committee chairperson; American Society for Testing of Materials, committee officer; Electrochemical Society; ASM International; National Geographic Society; DOD Triservice Panel on Corrosion. **HONORS/AWARDS:** Department of the Navy, Scientific Achievement Award, 1984, Best Independent Research Award, 1984; Air Force/Navy, Best Research Paper Award, 1986; NACE International, Romanoff Best Paper Award, 1989; Department of the Navy, Best Independent Research Award, 1992. **SPECIAL ACHIEVEMENTS:** Navy expert, corrosion and corrosion control in aircraft systems; recognized international authority in corrosion science; published over 100 research papers in the field of corrosion science, electrochemistry, metallurgy and tribology; several patents in corrosion sensors, lubricants, and corrosion resistant coatings.

AGGARWAL, ANIL K.
Company executive. Indo-American. **PERSONAL:** Born Apr 5, 1947, Batala, Punjab, India; son of Paras and Sukhwanti Aggarwal; married Madhvi Aggarwal, Aug 8, 1976; children: Payal, Sameer. **EDUCATION:** Baring College, AA, 1965; Punjab Engineering College, BS, 1969; Indian Institute of Science, MS, 1971; Rice University, PhD, 1974. **CAREER:** Amcomp Corp, president, currently.

AGGARWAL, BHARAT BHUSHAN
Educator, researcher. Indo-American. **PERSONAL:** Born Feb 22, 1950, Batala, India; son of Sita Ram Aggarwal; married Uma Aggarwal, Aug 29, 1989; children: Rishi, Manoj. **EDUCATION:** University of Delhi, India, BS, biochemistry; Benares Hindu University, India, MS, biochemistry; University of California, Berkeley, PhD, biochemistry, 1977. **CAREER:** University of Louisville Medical Center, national research scholar, 1973-74; University of California, San Francisco Medical Center, postdoctoral fellow, 1977-80; Genentech, scientist, group leader, 1980-89, senior scientist, group leader, 1984-89; University of Texas, Health Science Center, Houston, professor, gen instruction, 1989-, M D Anderson Cancer Center, professor of medicine, biochemistry, 1989-. **ORGANIZATIONS:** American Society for Biochemistry & Molecular Biology, 1989-; American Assn for the Advancement of Science, 1989-; American Endocrine Society, 1980-86; Intl Society for the Interferon Research, 1981-85. **HONORS/AWARDS:** Rockefeller University, Postdoctoral Fellowship, 1977-79; University of California, Chancellor's Patent Fund Award for Scholarly, 1977; Ministry of Education Government of India, National Performance Scholarship for Study Abroad, 1973; Advanced Research Center, fellowship, 1973; University Grant Commission, Research Fellowship, 1972. **BUSINESS ADDRESS:** Professor, Dept of Clinical Immunology, Cytokine Research Section, University of Texas, M D Anderson Cancer Center, 1515 Holcombe Blvd, Box 041, Houston, TX 77030, (713)792-3503.

AGGARWAL, ISHWAR D.
Federal official, scientist. Indo-American. **PERSONAL:** Born May 18, 1945, Delhi, India; married Shail Aggarwal, Jun 8, 1969; children: Puneet, Anjali. **EDUCATION:** Indian Institute of Technology, Bombay, India, BS, 1968; Catholic University of America, MS, 1971, PhD, 1974. **CAREER:** Corning Glass Works, senior scientist, 1974-75; Galileo Electro-Optic Corp, associate director of research, 1975-78; Valtec Corp, vice president, 1978-84; Lasertron Inc, vice president, 1984-86; Naval Research Labs, section head, 1986-. **ORGANIZATIONS:** Optical Society of America, 1974-; American Ceramic Society, 1974-; Material Research Society, 1989-. **SPECIAL ACHIEVEMENTS:** Published more than 60 papers on fiber optics and materials glass engineering; editor, book, Fluoride Fiber Optics, Academic Press; contributor, chapters in two books; obtained general patents. **HOME PHONE:** (703)323-0173. **BUSINESS ADDRESS:** Section Head, Infrared Materials and Chemical Sensors, Naval Research Labs, Code 5603, Washington, DC 20375-5338, (202)767-9316.

AGGARWAL, LALIT KUMAR
Educator. Indo-American. **PERSONAL:** Born Oct 10, 1944, New Delhi, India; son of Pritam Lal Aggarwal and Krishna Devi; married Alice Beatriz Pappalardo, Feb 1, 1974; children: Vashali Maria, Lakshmi Cristina. **EDUCATION:** University of Washington, BArch, 1966; Rensellaer Polytechnic Institute, MArch, 1968; University of Washington, MUP, 1970; University of Pennsylvania, MA, peace science, PhD, 1976. **CAREER:** Naramore, Bain, Brady & Johanson, architect, 1968-69; Delaware Valley Regional Planning Commission, analyst, 1970-73; LaSalle University, assistant professor, 1977-78; Drexel University, associate professor, 1980-. **ORGANIZATIONS:** International Peace Policy Research Institute, board of trustees, 1986-; Operations Research Society of America, member, 1992-; Peace Science Society International, 1973-; Decision Science Institute, 1986-; American Statistical Association, 1982-. **SPECIAL ACHIEVEMENTS:** Co-author, "Multivariate Imagestatistics and Discriminant Analysis," Proceedings of Northeast Decision Science Institute, pp 360-366, 1993; co-author, "Power of Goodness-of-Fit Tests in Detecting Balanced Mixed Normal Distributions," Educational & Psychological Measurement, vol 51, no 2, pp 253-270, 1991; co-author "A Survey on Nuclear Weapons and International Law," Peace and Change, vol 15, no 2, pp 195-204, April 1990; "Imagestatistics: A General Method and an Application," Statistical Graphics Section, Proceedings of the American Statistical Association, pp 53-59, 1988; "Precontractual Bargaining," Mid-Atlantic Journal of Business, vol 25, no 1, pp 1-20, 1988. **HOME ADDRESS:** 5869 Overbrook Ave, Philadelphia, PA 19131, (215)477-2188.

AGGARWAL, MANMOHAN D.
Educator. Indo-American. **PERSONAL:** Born Sep 17, 1947, Ambala Cantt, Haryana, India; son of Benarsi Dass & Shanti Devi; married Saroj B, Jan 16, 1974; children: Manish. **EDUCATION:** Panjab University, BS (hons in math), 1966; Roorkee University, MS, 1968; Calcutta University, PhD, 1974. **CAREER:** Kurukshetra University, research associate, 1975-76, assistant professor of physics, 1976-80; Pennsylvania State University, postdoctoral scholar, 1980-81; Alabama A&M University, research associate, 1981-83, assistant professor of physics, 1983-86, associate professor of physics, 1986-93, professor of physics, 1993-. **ORGANIZATIONS:** Materials Research Society, 1990-; American Association of Crystal Growth, 1988-; Electrochemical Society, 1992-; Huntsville India Association, president, 1992-93; North American Thermal Analysis Society, 1989-. **HONORS/AWARDS:** NASA, First International Microgravity Laboratory, Appreciation Award, 1992, New Technology Innovation Award, 1983. **SPECIAL ACHIEVEMENTS:** 69 research publications in research journals of physics; 2 patents. **HOME ADDRESS:** 2204 Noel Drive, Huntsville, AL 35803, (205)883-7691. **BUSINESS ADDRESS:** Professor, Alabama A&M University, Meridian St, PO Box 428, 124 Chambers Hall, Normal, AL 35762-0285, (205)851-5308.

AGGARWAL, RAJ
Consultant, educator. Indo-American. **PERSONAL:** Born Jun 27, 1947, Jagraon, Punjab, India; son of N R and P V Aggarwal; married Karen L Aggarwal, May 15, 1976; children: Sonia R. **EDUCATION:** Indian Institute of Technology, BTech, mechanical engineering, 1963-68; Kent State University, DBA, MBA, 1968-72; University of Chicago, postdoctoral, 1972-74. **CAREER:** University of Toledo, professor & chair of finance, 1976-87; University of Michigan, professor of finance, 1980-82; John Carroll University, Mellen Chair and Professor in Finance, 1987-; Manco Inc, board member, 1989-; Harvard University, professor of international business, 1990; International University of Japan, Tokyo, professor of finance, 1991; consultant to Fortune 100 companies and US Government. **ORGANIZATIONS:** Academy of International Business, vice president, 1986-88; Eastern Finance Association, vice president, 1989-91, director, 1992-. **HONORS/AWARDS:** US Government, Senior Fulbright Research Fellowship to Singapore, 1984. **SPECIAL ACHIEVEMENTS:** Published 14 books & over 100 papers. **BUSINESS ADDRESS:** The Edward J & Louise E Mellen Chair and Professor in Finance, John Carroll University, 20700 N Park Blvd, Cleveland, OH 44118-4520, (216)397-4584.

AGGARWAL, RAJESH
Educator. Indo-American. **PERSONAL:** Born Jun 30, 1959, Delhi, India; son of Bhagwat S Aggarwal and Kailashwati Aggarwal; married Rita Aggarwal, May 24, 1991. **EDUCATION:** Indian Institute of Technology, Delhi, India, BS, tech, 1981; University of Texas, Arlington, MS, computer sci, 1985, PhD, 1987. **CAREER:** University of Southern Mississippi, assistant professor, 1987-90; Middle Tennessee State University, assistant professor, 1990-. **ORGANIZATIONS:** American Institute of Decision Sciences, 1985-; American Institute of Certified Public Accountants, 1992-. **HONORS/AWARDS:** American Institute of Certified Public Accountants, CPA, 1993. **SPECIAL ACHIEVEMENTS:** Author of articles in numerous publications. **BUSINESS ADDRESS:** Professor, Dept of Computer Information Systems, Middle Tennessee State University, Murfreesboro, TN 37130, (615)898-2375.

AGGARWAL, ROSHAN LAL
Educator, physicist. Indo-American. **PERSONAL:** Born Feb 15, 1937, Salala, Punjab, India; son of Chet Ram & Lila Vati Aggarwal; married Pushap Lata Aggarwal, Oct 13, 1958; children: Rajesh, Achal. **EDUCATION:** Punjab University, BSc (honors), 1957, MSc (honors), 1958, Purdue University, PhD, physics, 1965. **CAREER:** Punjab University, India, lecturer, physics department, 1958-60; MIT, Francis Bitter National Magnet Lab, staff member, 1965-70, associate director, 1977-84, group leader, 1984-86; MIT, Physics Dept, sr research scientist, 1975-89, senior lecturer, 1989-; MIT Lincoln Laboratory, staff member, 1986-. **ORGANIZATIONS:** American Physical Society, fellow, 1970-; Optical Society of America, 1985-; Sigma Xi, 1965-. **SPECIAL ACHIEVEMENTS:** Publications: over 200 articles in scientific journals such as Physical Review, Physical Review Letters, Solid State Communications, Applied Physics Letters, Journal of Applied Physics, Optics Letters, etc, 1963-. **BUSINESS ADDRESS:** MIT Lincoln Laboratory, 244 Wood St, Rm SR-116, Lexington, MA 02173-9108, (617)276-6709.

AGNIHOTRI, NEWAL K.
Publisher, editor. Indo-American. **PERSONAL:** Born Jan 3, 1941, Balrampur, Uttar Pradesh, India; son of Shree Ganesh Agnihotri and Brijkishori Devi Agnihotri; married Sukhda Agnihotri, Jun 1, 1963; children: Anupam, Amita. **EDUCATION:** Illinois Institute of Technology, MS, electrical engineering, 1974. **CAREER:** Heavy Electricals, Ltd, India, manufacturing engineer, 1962-71; Sargent & Lundy Engineers, project engineer, 1971-81; EQES, Inc, senior publisher and editor, 1981-. **ORGANIZATIONS:** Chicago Council on Foreign Relations; United Nations Association of the USA; American Nuclear Society; Institute of Electrical and Electronics Engineers; American Society of Mechanical Engineers. **SPECIAL ACHIEVEMENTS:** Toastmasters Club, public speaking; editor, Presidents & Prime Ministers magazine. **BUSINESS ADDRESS:** Senior Publisher and Editor, EQES Inc, 799 Roosevelt Rd, Bldg 6, Suite 208, Glen Ellyn, IL 60137-5925, (708)858-6161.

AGRAWAL, BRIJMOHAN
Quality control supervisor. Indo-American. **PERSONAL:** Born Nov 27, 1938, Ramnagar, Uttar Pradesh, India; son of Ramnarian Agrawal and Satyawati Agrawal; married Sushma Agrawal, Nov 21, 1965; children: Ratna Gupta, Deepak. **EDUCATION:** Lucknow University, BSc, biology, 1958, BSc, geology, 1960; Punjab University, Chandigarh, BPharm, 1964; State of Illinois, Applied Food Service Sanitation License, Approved Apprentice Pharmacist. **CAREER:** Van Den Berghs Foods Co, quality control supervisor, currently. **HOME ADDRESS:** 926 Glenmore Lane, Elgin, IL 60123-2301.

AGRAWAL, DHARMA PRAKASH
Educator. Indo-American. **PERSONAL:** Born Apr 12, 1945, Balod, Madhya Pradesh, India; son of Saryoo P Agrawal (deceased) and Chandrakanta Agrawal; married Purnima Agrawal, Jun 7, 1971; children: Sonali, Braj P. **EDUCATION:** Federal Institute of Technology, Switzerland, DScTech, 1975; Roorkee University, India, ME (with honors), 1968; Ravisharkar University, India, BE, 1966. **CAREER:** MNR Engineering College, India, lecturer, 1968-72; University of Roorkee, India, lecturer, 1972-73; Federal Institute of Technology, Switzerland, assistant, 1973-75; University of Technology, lecturer, 1976; Southern Methodist University, post-doctoral/instructor, 1976-77; Wayne State University, assistant/associate professor, 1977-82; NC State University, associate professor, professor, 1982-. **ORGANIZATIONS:** IEEE, Tech Committee on Computer Architecture, chair, 1992-94; J of Parallel & Distribution-Computing, editor, 1984-; Intl Symposium on Computer Architecture, program chair, 1984; Intl Conference on Parallel & Distributed Processing, general chair, 1993; Assn for Computing Machinery, Lectureship Committee, 1992-; Intl Symposium on Computer Architecture, Steering Committee, 1994; Intl Conference on Parallel Processing, program chair, 1994. **HONORS/AWARDS:** IEEE, Fellow, 1987, Certificate of Appreciation, 1984, Meritorious Service Award, 1990; US Jaycees, Montgomery, Outstanding Young Men of America, 1981; Intl Tech Info Service, Japan, World Researcher's Award, 1981. **SPECIAL ACHIEVEMENTS:** Author, Advanced Computer Architecture, IEEE-CS Press, 1986; co-author, Advances in Distributed System Reliability, IEEE-CS Press, 1990; co-author, Distributed Computing Network Reliability, IEEE-CS Press, 1990; Self-study Guide on Parallel Processing, IEEE Press, 1991; contributor, Macmillan Encyclopedia of Computers, Computer Architecture, 1991. **BUSINESS ADDRESS:** Professor of Electrical & Computer Engineering, North Carolina State University, 232 Daniels Hall, Raleigh, NC 27695-7911, (919)515-3984.

AGRAWAL, KRISHNA CHANDRA
Educator. Indo-American. **PERSONAL:** Born Mar 15, 1937, Calcutta, W. Bengal, India; son of Prasadi Lal Agrawal and Asharfi Devi Agrawal; married Mani, Dec 2, 1960; children: Sunil, Lina, Nira. **EDUCATION:** Andhra University, India, BS, 1959, MS, 1960; University of Florida, PhD, 1965. **CAREER:** Yale University, School of Medicine, research associate, 1966-69, instructor, 1969-70, assistant professor, 1970-76, associate professor, 1976; Tulane University, School of Medicine, associate professor, 1976-81, professor, 1981-. **ORGANIZATIONS:** American Association for Cancer Research, 1966-; American Chemical Society, 1967-; American Society for Pharmacology and Experimental Therapeutics, 1973-; Radiation Research Society, 1980-; International Society for Antiviral Research, 1991-; American Society of Hematology, 1993-; American Cancer Society, Scientific Advisory Committee, 1980-84, 1986-88; National Institutes of Health, Study Section on AIDS and Related Research, 1990-94. **HONORS/AWARDS:** Andhra University, India, Pantulu Gold Medal, 1959; Sigma Xi, 1965; American Institute of Chemists, Fellow, 1971. **SPECIAL ACHIEVEMENTS:** Published 80 scientific papers in peer-reviewed journals; 10 chapters in several scientific books; 120 scientific abstracts. **BUSINESS ADDRESS:** Professor, Dept of Pharmacology, SL83 Tulane University School of Medicine, 1430 Tulane Ave, New Orleans, LA 70112, (504)588-5444.

AGRAWAL, PRADEEP K.
Engineering educator. Indo-American. **PERSONAL:** Born Jan 25, 1954, Rampur, Uttar Pradesh, India; son of Rameshwar Prasad Agrawal and Parvati Devi Agrawal; married Kanchan P Agrawal, Dec 15, 1991; children: Sanjay P. **EDUCATION:** University of Roorkee, India, BChE, 1974; University of Delaware, MChE, 1977, PhD, 1979. **CAREER:** Georgia Institute of Tech, assistant professor of chem eng, 1979-85, associate professor of chem eng, 1985-. **HOME ADDRESS:** 2367 Doreen Court NE, Atlanta, GA 30345-2607, (404)636-4781. **BUSINESS ADDRESS:** Professor, School of Chemical Engineering, Georgia Institute of Technology, Atlanta, GA 30332-0100, (404)894-2826.

AHLUWALIA, BALWANT S.
Educator. Indo-American. **PERSONAL:** Born Mar 12, 1932, Lahore, India; son of Harbans Singh Ahluwalia; married S Jane Ahluwalia, Mar 1, 1962; children: David, Raj. **EDUCATION:** UP Veterinary College, India, DVM, 1957; University of Minnesota, MS, 1959, PhD, 1963. **CAREER:** Hormel Institute, scientist, 1963-66; Worcester Foundation Exp Biology, scientist, 1966-68; Natl Institutes of Health, scientist, 1968-71; Howard University, professor, 1971-. **ORGANIZATIONS:** Society of Andrology, Public Relations Committee, chairman, 1984-88; Endocrine Society, Public Relations Committee, 1982-84. **HONORS/AWARDS:** Howard University College of Medicine, Best Researcher Award, 1979. **SPECIAL ACHIEVEMENTS:** Natl Institutes of Health, review committee. **BUSINESS ADDRESS:** Professor, College of Medicine, Howard University, 520 W St NW Box 23, Washington, DC 20059, (202)865-1662.

AHLUWALIA, BRIJ MOHAN SINGH
Physician, educator. Indo-American. **PERSONAL:** Born Oct 22, 1939, India; married Satwant; children: Sandeep, Samita. **EDUCATION:** Hindu College Delhi University, India, premedical, 1955-56; Punjab University, India, BS, MB, 1961, MD, 1966. **CAREER:** Westchester Co Medical Center, director of neurology, 1986-; New York Medical College, neurology, acting co-chairman, 1987-90, professor of clinical neurology, 1988-, department of neurology, vice chairman, 1991-. **ORGANIZATIONS:** Association for Research in Nervous & Mental Diseases Inc; Neurovascular Society of North America, founding member; American Heart Association, Westchester/Putnam Chapter; American Academy of Clinical Neurophysiology; Medical Advisory Board of the Amyotrophic Lateral Sclerosis Assn, Hudson Valley Support Group; American Academy of Neurology, fellow; American Heart Association, director, Stroke Council, fellow; Assn of University Professors of Neurology; Hudson Valley Association of Physicians from India, president. **HONORS/AWARDS:** Punjab University, Medal in Obstetrics & Gynecology for Second Position in Final MB, BS Examination; Indian Council of Medical Research, Research Fellowship, Endemic Fluorosis, 1963-67; Doctor I Fund Foundation, Doctor of the Year Award, 1992. **SPECIAL ACHIEVEMENTS:** Coauthor: Neurological Complications of Human Recombinant Tumor Necrosis Factor, under preparation; Nosocomial Stroke, J Stroke Cerebrovasc Dis, vol 3, pp112-114, 1993; How Important Is Transesophageal Echo for Patients with Suspected Embolic Events?, American Heart Assn Scientific Sessions, Nov 1992; presentation: with others, Superiority of Transesophageal Echocardiography in the Detection of Interatrial Communication, American Society of Echocardiography, Boston, 1992. **BUSINESS ADDRESS:** Professor of Clinical Neurology, Dept of Neurology, New York Medical College, Munger Pavilion, 4th Fl, Valhalla, NY 10595.

AHLUWALIA, DALJIT SINGH
Educator, researcher. Indo-American. **PERSONAL:** Born Sep 5, 1932, Dist Sialicot, Punjab, India; son of Santokh Singh Ahluwalia and Labh Kaur Ahluwalia; married Devinder K Ahluwalia, Mar 28, 1960; children: Gurprect Singh, Jasjit Singh, Gurrioder Singh, Muninder Kaur. **EDUCATION:** Punjab University, India, BA, 1952, MA, math, 1955; Indiana University, MS, physics, 1965, PhD, math, 1965. **CAREER:** Indiana University, assistant professor, 1965-66; Courant Institute NYU, visiting member, 1966-68, assistant professor, 1968-69, associate professor, 1969-81, professor, 1981-86; New Jersey Institute of Technology, mathematics dept, chair, 1986-89, Center for Applied Math & Statistics, director, 1989-; National Science Foundation, applied mathematics program, director, 1993-94. **ORGANIZATIONS:** Overseas Indian Congress of North America, founder/president, 1979-83; Heart & Hands for

Handicapped Children, executive committee, 1978-82; Sikh Renaissance Institute, president, 1980-81, executive committee, 1975-80; Liaison Committee for Legislation, 1975-76; National Advisory Council for South Asian Affairs, 1978-85; Society of Industrial & Applied Methods, 1965-; American Math Society, 1965-88; International Scientific Radio Union, 1970-. **HONORS/AWARDS:** Indiana University, Graduate School fellow, 1962-65; Courant Institute of Math & Science, visiting member, 1966-68; National Institute of Finance, Ambassador of Goodwill, 1982; Outstanding Educator of America Award, 1971. **SPECIAL ACHIEVEMENTS:** Book: Ordinary Differential Equation with Applications, Holt, Rinehart, Winston, 1976; published more than 24 research papers in international journals on Elastic-Plastic flow in material, asymptotic solutions in wave propagation, underwater acoustics. **BUSINESS ADDRESS:** Professor of Mathematics, Director, Center for Applied Mathematics & Statistics, New Jersey Institute of Technology, University Heights, Cullimore Hall, #618, Newark, NJ 07102, (201)596-5784.

AHLUWALIA, HARJIT SINGH
Educator. Indo-American. **PERSONAL:** Born May 13, 1934, Bombay, Maharashtra, India; son of Sewa Singh Ahluwalia and Jaswant Kaur Ahluwalia; married Manjit Kaur Pal, Nov 29, 1964; children: Suvinder Singh, Davinder Singh. **EDUCATION:** Panjab University, BSc (honors), 1953, MSc, 1954; Gujarat University, PhD, 1960. **CAREER:** Physical Research Lab, senior research fellow, 1954-62; UNESCO, Paris, France, technical assistance expert, 1962-63; SW Center for Advanced Studies, research associate, 1963-64; IAEA, Vienna, Austria, visiting professor, 1965-67; Pan American Union, visiting professor, 1967-68; NASA Headquarters, visiting senior scientist, 1987-88; University of New Mexico, professor of physics, 1968-. **ORGANIZATIONS:** Cosmic Ray Commission of IUPAP, national representative of Bolivia, 1966-69; COSPAR, national representative of Bolivia, 1966-69; SPARMO, national representative of Bolivia, 1966-69; Middle Atmosphere Program of Universidad Mayor de San Andres, La Paz, Bolivia, SCOSTEP, steering committee member,representative of IUPAP, 1984-89; Laboratorio de Fisica Cosmica, scientific director, 1965-67, member of working group-2, 1990-95; High Energy Cosmic Ray Group in STIP, general secretary, 1976-86; Solar-Terrestrial Energy Program of ICSU. **HONORS/AWARDS:** Panjab University, Merit Scholar, 1948-53; NSF, research grants, 1963-65, 1968-81; USAF, research grants, 1962-68; Sandia Corporation, research grants, 1969-72; NASA, research grants, 1972-77, 1988-. **SPECIAL ACHIEVEMENTS:** Over 200 scientific papers in refereed journals, conference proceedings; transactions of societies, etc; three books. **BUSINESS ADDRESS:** Professor, Dept of Physics and Astronomy, The University of New Mexico, 800 Yale Blvd, NE, Albuquerque, NM 87131-1156, (505)277-2941.

AHLUWALIA, RASHPAL S.
Educator, engineer. Indo-American. **PERSONAL:** Born Oct 1, 1946, New Delhi, India; son of Mr K S Ahluwalia; married Meena Ahluwalia, Dec 13, 1975; children: Rohit, Tina, Priya. **EDUCATION:** Ravi Shanker University, India, BSc, 1967; University of Western Ontario, MSc, 1973, PhD, 1977. **CAREER:** Bell Northern Research, Canada, 1976-78; Bowling Green State University, assistant professor, 1979-80; Ohio State University, assistant professor, 1980-85; West Virginia University, professor, 1985-. **ORGANIZATIONS:** Institute of Industrial Engineers, senior member; Society of Mfg Engineers, senior member; Institute of Electrical & Electronics Eng, senior member, local chapter, director, vice president development; American Society of Quality Control; Morgantown Lions Club. **HONORS/AWARDS:** College of Eng, Outstanding Leadership Award, 1989; Wright-Patterson AF Base, summer fellow, 1986. **SPECIAL ACHIEVEMENTS:** Several publications; examiner, Malcolm Baldrige Quality Award, 1991. **HOME ADDRESS:** 220 Jaco Drive, Morgantown, WV 26505, (304)599-4722. **BUSINESS ADDRESS:** Professor, Industrial Engineering Dept, West Virginia University, PO Box 6101, Room 521, ESB, Morgantown, WV 26506-6101, (304)293-4607.

AHMAD, JAMEEL
Educator. Pakistani American. **PERSONAL:** Born May 22, 1941, Mianwali, Punjab, Pakistan; son of Naseer Bakhsh & Iftikhar Begum Bakhsh; married Rosalba Ahmad, Mar 31, 1983; children: Sidney, Monica. **EDUCATION:** Punjab University, Pakistan, BSc, 1962; University of Hawaii, MS, 1964; University of Pennsylvania, PhD, 1967. **CAREER:** Wiedner University, assistant professor of engineering, 1967-68; Cooper Union College, assistant professor of civil engineering, 1968-72, associate professor of civil engineering, 1972-79, professor of civil engineering, 1979-, director of research, 1983-. **ORGANIZATIONS:** Society of Asphalt Technologists, trustee, 1990-93; American Society of Civil Engineers, 1969-93; Chi Epsilon, 1971. **HONORS/**

AWARDS: University of Pennsylvania, University Fellow, 1965-1966; East-West Center, University of Hawaii, exchange scholar, 1962-65; Cooper Union, Rossi Prize, 1971; American Society of Civil Engineers, Award for Distinguished Service, 1984. **SPECIAL ACHIEVEMENTS:** "No-linear Acoustic Response of Cylindrical Shells," Journal of Franklin Institute, 1975; "Post-Buckling Dynamic Response of a Circular Plate," Journal of Franklin Institute, 1972; 2 US Patents, 1991, 1992. **BUSINESS ADDRESS:** Research Director/Civil Engineering Professor, Cooper Union for Advancement of Science & Art, 51 Astor Pl, New York, NY 10003, (212)353-4294.

AHMED, A. RAZZAQUE
Educator. Indo-American. **PERSONAL:** Born Oct 27, 1948, Hyderabad, India; son of A Salam Ahmed. **EDUCATION:** All-India Institute of Medical Sciences, MBBs, 1972; UCLA, MD, 1976; Harvard University, DSc, 1988. **CAREER:** UCLA, assistant professor, 1978-86; Harvard University, associate professor, 1988-93; Boston University, professor, 1993-. **HONORS/AWARDS:** Red Cross, Individual Ivestigator, 1985; NIH, RD1, 1989. **SPECIAL ACHIEVEMENTS:** Author of 110 original publications; 4 books. **BIOGRAPHICAL SOURCES:** Index Medicus. **BUSINESS ADDRESS:** Professor, Dept of Dermatology, Boston University, School of Medicine, 80 E Concord St, Boston, MA 02118.

AHMED, SHAIKH SULTAN
Physician, educator. Pakistani American. **PERSONAL:** Born Sep 13, 1937, Delhi, India; son of M Rafee and Sughra Jan; married Shaheen, Mar 18, 1967; children: Salman, Sohaib. **EDUCATION:** DJ Science College, Pakistan, BSc, 1958; Dow Medical College, Pakistan, MB, BS, MD, 1963; Samaritan Hospital, MD, 1966; Tucson Hospitals Medical Ed Program, MD, 1968; UMDNJ-New Jersey Medical School, MD, 1969. **CAREER:** UMDNJ-NJMS, instructor in medicine, 1970-72, assistant professor of medicine, 1972-75, associate professor of medicine, 1975-80, Stress Testing Laboratory, UH, director, 1975-, Vascular Catheterization Laboratory, UH, co-director, 1976-, professor of medicine, 1980-, Medical Services, Firm C, University Hospital, chief, 1983-91. **ORGANIZATIONS:** American Federation of Clinical Research, 1969; American Heart Association, NJ & NY, 1970; American College of Cardiology, fellow, 1970; American Association of University Professors, president, UMDNJ Chapter, 1991-92; Royal College of Physicians of Canada, fellow, 1972; Royal Society of Medicine of UK, fellow, 1974; Islamic Association of North America, 1977; Association of Pakistani Physicians of NA, 1979; Sigma Xi, 1987. **HONORS/AWARDS:** American College of Physicians, Fellow, 1973; UMDNJ-New Jersey Medical School, Faculty Org, president, 1987-88; Pakistan Academy of Medical Sciences, Fellow, 1988; President of Pakistan, Sitara Quide Azam, 1992; American Biographical Institute, Life Achievement Award, 1992. **SPECIAL ACHIEVEMENTS:** 20 research grants; 124 publications; 9 books and chapters; 192 presentations. **HOME ADDRESS:** 40 Greentree Terrace, Tenafly, NJ 07670, (201)568-4604. **BUSINESS ADDRESS:** Professor of Medicine, Co-director, Cardiac Catheterization Lab, Director, Stress Testing Laboratory, University of Medicine & Dentistry of NJ, New Jersey Medical School, 185 South Orange Ave, MSB I-534, Newark, NJ 07103-2714, (201)982-4736.

AHMED, WASE U.
Geologist. Pakistani American. **PERSONAL:** Born Sep 27, 1931, Moradabad, Uttar Pradesh, India; son of Riazuddin Ahmed & Shahjahan Begum; married Carol L Ahmed, Feb 15, 1962; children: Tahmina, Leila, Mona, Rena. **EDUCATION:** BS, agriculture, 1956; BS, geology, 1961. **CAREER:** Buehler Ltd, geologist, currently. **ORGANIZATIONS:** American Society for Metals; American Metallographic Society; International Cement Microscopy Association; American Society for Histotechnology. **SPECIAL ACHIEVEMENTS:** Published articles in Practical Metallography, Industrial Research, Microstructural Science, International Cement Microscopy, Industrial Research World Cement, Industrial Diamond Review; US patent. **HOME ADDRESS:** 720 Newport North, Roselle, IL 60172.

AHN, HO-SAM
Pharmacologist. Korean American. **PERSONAL:** Born Feb 25, 1940, Seoul, Republic of Korea; son of Dae-Sun Ahn and Do-Nam Kwon; married Young-Hee Im, Aug 11, 1969; children: Mary Miwon, Katherine Misook. **EDUCATION:** Seoul National University, BS, zoology, 1963, MS, physiology, 1965; Princeton University, MA, cell biology, 1967; Rutgers University Graduate School, PhD, zoology, 1972. **CAREER:** Merck & Co Inc, research biochemist, 1970-73; Albert Einstein College of Medicine, postdoctoral fellow, 1973-77, associate, 1977-78; Schering-Plough Corp, senior scientist, 1978-82, principal

scientist, 1982-92; Schering-Plough Research Institute, senior prinicpal scientist, 1992-. **ORGANIZATIONS:** Korean Bioscience Club of New York, coordinator, 1983-84; Korean Scientists & Engineers Association in America, Inc, chapter president, 1983-84; UN Industrial Development Organization, expert on mission, 1987, 1989; American Society for Pharmacology & Experimental Therapeutics, 1990-; New York Academy of Science, 1973-; Wesearch Toastmaster, founding member, 1983-87, educational vice president, 1987. **HONORS/AWARDS:** National Institute of Mental Health, Individual Postdoctoral Fellowship, 1974-77; Wesearch Club, Toastmaster International Chapter, Service Award, 1987. **SPECIAL ACHIEVEMENTS:** Contributor, Growth, Nutrition & Metabolism of Cell in Culture, V4, 1977; first author of a paper presented at an international symposium on dopamine receptors, 1978; contributor, New Cardiovascular Drugs 1985, 1985; co-discoverer of Claritin, a new non-sedating antihistamine, 1982; first author of an article in The Biology of Phosphodiesterase, 1992. **MILITARY SERVICE:** Republic of Korea Army Infantry, private first class, 1960-62. **BUSINESS ADDRESS:** Senior Principal Scientist, Schering-Plough Research Institute, 2015 Galloping Hill Rd, K-15-3 3600, Kenilworth, NJ 07033, (908)298-3230.

AHN, JAEHOON
Journalist. Korean American. **PERSONAL:** Born May 13, 1941, Republic of Korea; son of Heung Yul Ahn and Eun Rae Park Ahn; married Soonhoon L Ahn, Feb 22, 1969; children: Soomie L, Yoomie L. **EDUCATION:** Various graduate schools. **CAREER:** Washington Post, online editor, currently. **ORGANIZATIONS:** Sigma Delta Chi, Society of Professional Journalists; Asian American Journalists Association. **SPECIAL ACHIEVEMENTS:** MBC-Radio, 750th broadcast of Ahn Jaehoon's News & Commentary from Washington, 1991-93. **MILITARY SERVICE:** Army, Republic of Korea, PFC, 1961-62. **BUSINESS ADDRESS:** Online Editor, News Dept, Washington Post, 1150 15th St NW, Washington, DC 20071, (202)334-6756.

AHN, STEVE FITZGERALD
Legal assistant, translator, interpreter. Korean American. **PERSONAL:** Born Jul 6, 1933, Hansan-Myun, Chungnam-Do, Republic of Korea; son of Jin Ho Ahn and In-Pil Park; married Sook-Ja Choi, May 30, 1967; children: Bi-Rang Tamashiro, Hui-Young, Bi Bi, Bo Bi. **EDUCATION:** Sangji University, Korea, LLB, 1969; Jones College, real estate, 1984-91. **CAREER:** Interpreter, translator: Denver City & County Courts; Aurora City Court; Arapahoe County Court; Littleton City Court; Colorado, all courts; Immigration and Naturalization Service; Captain's Office, owner, 1990-; AIM Realty Co, sales associate, 1992-. **SPECIAL ACHIEVEMENTS:** Officially certified by all courts, State of Colorado. **MILITARY SERVICE:** Korean Air Force, training in USA, captain. **BUSINESS ADDRESS:** Owner/Legal Assistant, Real Estate, Captain's Office, #1450 S Havana St, Suite 332-A, Aurora, CO 80012, (303)752-3483.

AHUJA, SATINDER
Chemist. Indo-American. **PERSONAL:** Born Sep 11, 1933, Jehlum, Punjab, India; son of Jawahar Lal & Sushil Vati; married Fay Ahuja, Nov 1962; children: Jay, Paul. **EDUCATION:** Banaras University, BPharm, 1955, MPharm, 1956; Philadelphia College of Pharmacy & Science, PhD, 1964. **CAREER:** Lederle Labs, Assay development chemist, 1964-66; Ciba-Geigy Corp, senior scientist, 1966-74, senior staff scientist, 1974-91, senior research fellow, 1991-; Pace University, adjunct faculty, professor, currently. **ORGANIZATIONS:** American Chemical Society, councilor, 1991-93, NY Section, chairman, 1990, Chromatography & Separation Chemistry Subdiv, chairman, 1983-84; Rho Chi. **HONORS/AWARDS:** Rockland Chemical Society, Distinguished Chemist, 1989; American Association for Advancement of Science, Panel of Experts; UN Committee on African Chairs of Technology. **SPECIAL ACHIEVEMENTS:** 60 publications, presentations; author/editor, 7 books; speaks 4 languages fluently. **BUSINESS ADDRESS:** Senior Research Fellow, Ciba-Geigy Corp, Old Mill Rd, Suffern, NY 10901.

AIKAWA, JERRY KAZUO
Physician, educator. Japanese American. **PERSONAL:** Born Aug 24, 1921, Stockton, CA; son of Genmatsu Aikawa & Shizuko Yamamoto; married Chitose Aihara, Sep 20, 1944; children: Ronald K. **EDUCATION:** University of California, AB, 1942; Wake Forest College, MD, 1945. **CAREER:** Bowman Gray School Medicine, assistant professor of medicine, 1948-53; University of Colorado School Medicine, assistant professor to professor of medicine, 1953-88, Clinical Affairs, associate dean, 1983-, Allied Health Programs, associate dean, 1983-, professor emeritus, currently. **ORGANIZATIONS:** US Atomic Energy Commission, postdoctoral fellow, 1948-50; American Heart

Association, established investigator, 1952-58; University Hospital, Laboratory Services, director, 1961-83, Medical Board, president, 1983-. **HONORS/AWARDS:** American Heart Association, Medical Research Grant-in-Aid, 1952-58; US Atomic Energy Comm, Medical Research, Grant-in, 1958-70. **SPECIAL ACHIEVEMENTS:** Research publications include monographs on: myxedema, Rocky Mountain Spotted Fever, computerization of the clinical laboratory, and magnesium in clinical medicine, 1948-85. **HOME ADDRESS:** 7222 E Gainey Ranch Rd, #115, Scottsdale, AZ 85258-1530, (602)991-3849.

AKAKA, DANIEL KAHIKINA
US senator. Pacific Islander American. **PERSONAL:** Born Sep 11, 1924, Honolulu, HI; son of Kahikina Akaka and Annie Kahoa Akaka; married Mary Mildred Chong, May 22, 1948; children: Millanie K Mattson, Daniel K Jr, Gerard K, Alan L, Nicholas K. **EDUCATION:** University of Hawaii, bachelor of education, 1952, certificate, secondary education, 1953, certificate, school administration, 1961, master of education, 1966. **CAREER:** Hawaiian Electric Co, welder, 1942; US Army Corps of Engineers, welder-mechanic, 1943-44; schools in Hawaii, teacher, 1953-60; Ewa Beach Elementary School, vice principal, principal, 1960-64; Pohakea Elementary School, principal, 1964-65; Kaneohe Elementary Sch, principal, 1965-68; Hawaii Compensatory Education, program specialist, 1978-79; Hawaii Office of Economic Opportunity, director, 1971-74; Office of the Governor of Hawaii, human resources, special asst, 1975-76; US Congress, representative, 1977-90; US Senate, senator, 1990-, committees include: Committee on Energy & Natural Resources, Subcommittee on Mineral Resources Development & Production, chairman; Committee on Veterans' Affairs; Committee on Governmental Affairs; Committee of Indian Affairs; Democratic Policy Committee. **ORGANIZATIONS:** NEA; Musicians Association of Hawaii; Hanahauoli School, board of directors; Act 4 Educational Advisory Council; Library Advisory Council. **SPECIAL ACHIEVEMENTS:** Asian Pacific American Committee for Clinton/Gore, honorary co-chair, 1992. **MILITARY SERVICE:** US Army Corps of Engineers, 1945-47. **BUSINESS ADDRESS:** Senator, US Senate, SH-720 Hart Senate Office Bldg, Washington, DC 20510-1103, (202)224-6361.

AKI, KEIITI
Educator. Japanese American. **PERSONAL:** Born Mar 3, 1930, Yokohama, Japan; married 1956; children: two. **EDUCATION:** University of Tokyo, BS, 1952, PhD, geophysics, 1958. **CAREER:** California Institute of Technology, Fulbright research fellow, geophysics, 1958-60, visiting associate professor, geophysics, 1962-63; Earthquake Research Institute, University of Tokyo, research fellow, seismology, 1960-62, associate professor, seismology, 1963-65; Intl Institute Seismol and Earthquake Eng, lecturer, UNESCO, 1960-65; National Center Earthquake Research, US Geological Survey, geophysicist, 1967-; Massachusetts Institute of Technology, professor, geophysics, 1966-84; University of Chile, visiting professor, 1970, 1972; Sandia Labs, Los Alamos Science Labs, consultant, 1976-79; Japan Society for the Promotion of Science, visiting scholar, 1978; National Research Council, committee on seismology, chairman, 1978-82; University of Alaska, distinguished visiting professor, 1981; Intl Assn Seismol and Earth's Interior, lecturer, 1981; NSF, consultant, 1981; University of Paris, visiting professor, 1983; University of Southern California, Wm Keck Professor of Geology, 1984-. **ORGANIZATIONS:** National Academy of Science; American Geophysical Union; Seismological Society of America, president, 1979-80; Society of Exploration Geo-physicists; American Academy of Arts & Science, fellow. **HONORS/AWARDS:** Seismol Society of America, medal, 1987. **BUSINESS ADDRESS:** William Keck Professor of Geological Science, University of Southern California, Los Angeles, CA 90089.*

AKIYOSHI, MIKE M.
Pooltable manufacturing company executive. Japanese American. **PERSONAL:** Born Jun 5, 1940, Fukuoka, Japan; married Joann E, Jan 30, 1965; children: Sachiko, Michiko, Teruko, Michael. **CAREER:** CSA Pool Table Manufacturing Company, owner. **BUSINESS ADDRESS:** Owner, CSA Pool Table Mfg, 627-19th Ave, San Francisco, CA 94121, (415)752-6838.

AKKAPEDDI, PRASAD RAO
Research director. Indo-American. **PERSONAL:** Born Dec 23, 1943, Masulipatam, Andhra Pradesh, India; son of Hanumanth Reo Akkapeddi and Suseela Akkapeddi; married Suguna, Jul 24, 1971; children: Prasanth, Sirisha. **EDUCATION:** University of Southern California, PhD, EE, 1973, MS, EE, 1971. **CAREER:** Perkin-Elmer Corp, assoc director of research, 1984-87, Technical Advisory Committee, chairman, 1987-89, director of research, 1987-89; Hughes Danbury Optical Systems Inc, director of research, 1989-. **ORGA-**

NIZATIONS: Hughes Technology Networks, leader & member, 1989-; Telugu Association of Connecticut, secretary, 1991-93. **HONORS/AWARDS:** Perkin-Elmer, Manager of the Year, 1987. **SPECIAL ACHIEVEMENTS:** Graduated from Babson School of Executive Management, 1988. **BUSINESS ADDRESS:** Director of Research, Hughes Danbury Optical Systems Inc, 100 Wooster Heights Rd, MS 848, Danbury, CT 06810, (203)797-6470.

ALBANO, ALFONSO M.
Educator. Filipino American. **PERSONAL:** Born Aug 2, 1939, Laoag, Ilocos Norte, Philippines; son of Pedro G Albano and Eliza Madamba Albano; married Concepcion San Jose, Aug 5, 1967; children: Maria Teresa, Sarah Eliza. **EDUCATION:** University of the Philippines, BS, 1959; University of Iowa, MS, 1964; SUNY-Stony Brook, PhD, 1969. **CAREER:** University of the Philippines, assistant instructor, 1960-62; SUNY Stony Brook, instructor, 1969-70; Bryn Mawr College, lecturer, 1970-71, assistant professor, 1971-77, associate professor, 1977-84, professor, 1984-85, Marion Reilly professor, 1985-; Lorenz Institute, University of Leiden, visiting physicist, 1974-75, 1978-79. **ORGANIZATIONS:** American Physical Society; American Association of Physics Teahcers; Phillipping-American Academy of Science & Engineering, president, 1989; Sigma Xi; Sigma Pi Sigma; Phi Kappa Phi. **SPECIAL ACHIEVEMENTS:** Co-author, "Physics: Principles & Applications," Houghton-Mifflin, Boston, 1977; co-editor, "Measures of Complexity & Chaos," Plenum, New York, 1990; co-editor, "Complexity and Chaos," World Scientific, Singapore, 1994. **BUSINESS ADDRESS:** Professor, Dept of Physics, Bryn Mawr College, 101 N Merion Ave, Bryn Mawr, PA 19010-2899.

ALCANTARA, LARRY JAMES
City government manager. Filipino American. **PERSONAL:** Born Nov 10, 1947, Silverton, OR; son of Juan A Alcantara & Ann Marie Carey; divorced; children: Damien, Nicole. **CAREER:** State of Washington, employment interviewer, 1972-73; City of Seattle, assistant personnel analyst, 1973-77, personnel analyst, 1977-79, personnel transactions manager, 1979-80, employment services manager, 1980-82, recruiting services manager, 1992-. **ORGANIZATIONS:** Filipino-American City Employees of Seattle, president, 1990-; Filipino Youth Activities, board vice president, 1991-; Filipino Political Action Group of Washington, chair, political endorsement, 1993-; Filipino Cultural Heritage Society of Washington, board, Independence Celebration, chair, 1992-; Pista SA Nayon, Filipino Community Seafair Festival, chair, venue, 1991-. **HONORS/AWARDS:** Filipino National Historical Society, Very Impressive Pinoy, 1992; Leadership Tomorrow, Class of 1994; City of Seattle, Advanced Management Program, Graduate, 1986. **SPECIAL ACHIEVEMENTS:** 1000 + hours, formal training in leadership, management, human resources, computers. **MILITARY SERVICE:** US Marine Corps, e-4, 1965-68; Vietnam 1967-68. **HOME ADDRESS:** PO Box 4334, Seattle, WA 98104, (206)328-3354. **BUSINESS ADDRESS:** Recruiting Services Manager, Personnel Dept, City of Seattle, 710 2nd Ave, Ste 1200, Dexter Horton Bldg, Seattle, WA 98104, (206)684-7971.

ALEJANDRO, REYNALDO GAMBOA
Business executive. Filipino American. **PERSONAL:** Born Oct 11, 1947, Manila, Philippines; son of Jacinto Pablo Alejandro and Arsenia Gamboa. **EDUCATION:** Ateneo de Manila University, AB, 1963; New York Restaurant School, certificate, cooking & mgt, 1981; University of the Philippines, MLS, 1967. **CAREER:** New York Public Library, librarian, 1969-75, research librarian, dance collection, 1975-81, curator, culinary collection, 1985-89; Philippine Dance Co of New York, artistic director/choreographer, 1969-81; Center for Wine & Food Studies, director of food program, 1989-92; Cuisine Unlimited Corp, president, currently. **ORGANIZATIONS:** Dance Perspectives Foundation, trustee, 1991-; Filipino American Natl Historical Soc, trustee, 1988-; Natl Restaurant Assn, 1982-; Assn for Asian Studies, 1975-; Culinary Historians of New York, 1987-; Culinary Historians of Boston, 1987-; Lions Club, 1992-. **HONORS/AWARDS:** University of the Philippines Alumni Assn of America, Outstanding Alumnus, 1987; Pride of the Malay Race, Perlas ng Silangan Award, Alice Tully Hall, Lincoln Ctr, 1989; Natl Commission on Culture & the Arts, research grant, 1992-93; Ateneo Eastern States Foundation, Inc, "A Man for Others" Award, 1993. **HOME ADDRESS:** 160 Bleecker St, New York, NY 10012, (212)674-0673.

ALI, MIR MASOOM
Educator. Bangladeshi American. **PERSONAL:** Born Feb 1, 1937, Patuakhali, Bangladesh; son of Mir Muazzam Ali and Azifa Ali; married Firoza Ali, Jun 25, 1959; children: Naheed Hossain, Fahima, Farah Gosnell, Mir Ishtiaque. **EDUCATION:** University of Dhaka, Bangladesh, BSc (with honors), 1956,

MSc, 1957; University of Toronto, MSc, 1967, PhD, 1969. **CAREER:** University of Dhaka, Socio-Economic Board, field officer, 1957; Government of Pakistan, research officer, 1958-66; University of Toronto, teaching assistant, 1966-69; visiting professor: Yeungnam University, S Korea, 1993, Dhaka University, Bangladesh, 1983-84, Jahangirnagar University, Bangladesh, 1983-84, 1991; Ball State University, assistant professor, 1969-74, associate professor, 1974-78, professor, 1978-. **ORGANIZATIONS:** Royal Statistical Society, fellow, 1970-; Institute of Statisticians, fellow, 1990-; North America-Bangladesh Statistical Association, founding president, 1989-; Institute of Math Stat, 1970-; American Statistical Association, 1970-; International Statistical Institute, 1989-; Islamic Society of Statistical Science, 1990-; Bangladesh Statistical Society, life member, 1989-. **HONORS/AWARDS:** Bangladesh Stat Association, Qazi Motahar Husain Gold Medal, 1991; Ball State University, Outstanding Researcher Award, 1985; Midwest Biopharm Statistical Workshop, Meritorious Service Award, 1987; American Statistical Association, COC Governing Board, vice chair, 1992-84, Central Indiana Chapter, president, 1989-91; Ball State University, Outstanding Faculty Award, 1992-93. **SPECIAL ACHIEVEMENTS:** Over 80 articles in national and international professional statistical journals; over 110 reviews of articles and books published; over 95 papers presented at national and international statistical conferences and universities, 1970-; chaired sessions at international conferences; Parisamhyan Samikkha, editor; Journal of Statistical Studies, overseas executive editor; editorial board: Aligarh Journal of Statistics, Pakistan Journal of Statistics, Journal of Statistical Research. **BUSINESS ADDRESS:** Professor, Dept of Mathematical Sciences, Ball State University, Muncie, IN 47306-0490, (317)285-8640.

ALI, YUSUF
Pharmaceutical company executive. Indo-American. **PERSONAL:** Born Dec 8, 1953, Dohad, Gujarat, India; son of Zehrabai and Kurbanhusen; married Zahera, Nov 8, 1985; children: Arif. **EDUCATION:** M S University, Baroda, India, BS, 1976; Polytechnic Institute of New York, MS, 1978; University of Florida, PhD, 1984. **CAREER:** Alcon Labs Inc, post-doctoral associate, 1984-85, Ophthamalic Product Development, senior scientist, 1985-89, manager, 1990-92, associate director, 1993-. **ORGANIZATIONS:** American Association of Pharmaceutical Scientists; American Chemical Society. **HONORS/AWARDS:** Alcon Labs Inc, Technical Excellence Award, 1992. **HOME ADDRESS:** 6904 Wicks Trail, Fort Worth, TX 76133, (817)346-3459.

ALLEN, SUSAN AU
Attorney, association executive. Chinese American. **PERSONAL:** Born Nov 1, 1946, China; daughter of Mabel & Sanjoe Au; married Paul S Allen, Aug 1975; children: Mark, Edward. **EDUCATION:** Antioch School of Law, JD, 1983; Georgetown University Law Center, LLM, 1989. **CAREER:** Paul Shearman Allen & Associates, partner, 1983-. **ORGANIZATIONS:** Administrative Conference of the US, council member, 1989-; US Pan Asian American Chamber of Commerce, president, 1984-; Excellence 2000 Awards, chair, 1988-; The Washington Committee, executive council, 1992-; District of Columbia Minority Bus Opportunity Comm, commissioner, 1989-; National Minority Suppliers Development Council, development comm, 1993-; Washington Performance Arts Society, director, 1990-; Kennedy Center for the Performing Arts, director, 1992-. **HONORS/AWARDS:** District of Columbia Chamber of Commerce, Rising Star, 1992. **SPECIAL ACHIEVEMENTS:** Language proficiency: read and write Chinese. **BUSINESS ADDRESS:** President, US Pan Asian American Chamber of Commerce, 1625 K St, NW, Ste 380, Washington, DC 20006, (202)638-1764.

ALOTA, RUBEN VILLARUEL
Naval officer. Filipino American. **PERSONAL:** Born Oct 23, 1952, Bantayan, Cebu, Philippines; son of Josefa V Alota; married Teresita P Alota, Oct 16, 1976; children: Jairus Benjamin. **EDUCATION:** University of the City of Manila, AA, 1972; Embry-Riddle Aeronautical University, BSPA, 1982. **CAREER:** US Navy, enlisted, 1972-83, ensign, 1983-85, lieutenant junior grade, 1985-87, lieutenant, 1987-. **ORGANIZATIONS:** Filipino-American Assn of Brevard County, president, 1993-; Knights of Rizal Space Coast, Florida, chapter commander, 1993-; Epsilon Delta Mu Fraternity, 1970-. **MILITARY SERVICE:** US Navy, numerous awards. **HOME ADDRESS:** 1895 Whispering Oaks Cir, Melbourne, FL 32934, (407)254-8049.

ALVARES, ALVITO P.
Educator. **PERSONAL:** Born Dec 25, 1935, Bombay, India; son of Amancio B Alvares (deceased) and Diva Alvares; married Joy Ann Alvares, Aug 30, 1969; children: Christopher, Kevin. **EDUCATION:** University of Bombay, India,

BSc, 1955, BSc, tech, 1957; University of Detroit, MS, 1961; University of Chicago, PhD, 1966. **CAREER:** Burroughs Wellcome & Company, senior research biochemist, 1967-70; The Rockefeller University, research associate, 1970-71, assistant professor, 1971-75, associate professor, 1975-77; Uniformed Services University, School of Medicine, associate professor, 1977-78, professor, 1978-. **ORGANIZATIONS:** New York Academy of Sciences; American Society for Pharmacology & Experimental Therapeutics; American Society for Biochemistry & Molecular Biology; American Society for Clinical Pharmacology & Therapeutics; Society for Toxicology; Society for Experimental Biology and Medicine; International Society for the Study of Xenobiotics; American Association for the Advancement of Science. **HONORS/AWARDS:** FASEB Visiting Scientist for Minority Institutions, 1987, 1991, consultant, Life Sciences Research Office, 1991-92; NIH, Career Development Award, 1975-78; editorial boards: Clinic Pharmacology & Therapeutics, Pharmacology, Drug Metab & Disposition; Lucknow and Chandigarh, UNDP/CSAR Tokten Visiting Scientist, 1990. **SPECIAL ACHIEVEMENTS:** Author of 116 scientific articles in journals & books; Henry M. Jackson Foundation, scientific review board, 1989-90; National Institutes of Health Ad Hoc Study Sections; Irma T Hirscl Scholar, New York, 1974-78; Uniformed Services University, faculty senate, 1978-80, 1983-86. **HOME ADDRESS:** 7547 Heatherton Lane, Potomac, MD 20854-3221, (301)299-8457. **BUSINESS ADDRESS:** Professor, Dept of Pharmacology, Uniformed Services University, School of Medicine, 4301 Jones Bridge Rd, Bethesda, MD 20814-4799, (301)295-3226.

AMPHAVANNASOUK, ENG
Social work case manager. Laotian American. **PERSONAL:** Born Oct 6, 1935, Vientiane, Lao People's Democratic Republic; son of Saythong & Pong; married Khamlang Amphavanasouk, Nov 15, 1988; children: Five. **CAREER:** Intercultural Mutual Assistance Association, case manager, currently. **MILITARY SERVICE:** Royal Laotian Army, Lt Col, 1954-75; Medaille Merite Civique, 1962, Medaille Commemorative, 1965, US Military Meritorious Medal, 1969. **BUSINESS ADDRESS:** Laotian Case Manager, Lao Assistance Center of MN, 1015 Olson Memorial Hwy, Minneapolis, MN 55405, (612)374-4967.

AN, MYOUNG HEE
Researcher. Korean American. **PERSONAL:** Born Dec 17, 1958, Seoul, Republic of Korea; divorced; children: Benjamin Shenefelt. **EDUCATION:** Polytech of New York, BS, 1983; CUNY, Graduate Center, PhD, 1986. **CAREER:** York College/CUNY, associate professor, 1989-91; Aware, Inc, technical staff, consultant, 1991-. **ORGANIZATIONS:** IEEE; ACA. **SPECIAL ACHIEVEMENTS:** Author: Algorithms for Discrete Fourier Transform and Convolution, Springer-Verlag, 1989; Mathematics of Multidimensional Fourier Tranform Algorithms, Springer-Verlag, 1993; "Discrete Fast Fourier Transform Algorithms: A Tutorial Survey," in ADV Inc, Electronics and Electron Physics, v 80, Academic Press, 1991. **BUSINESS ADDRESS:** Consultant, Technical Staff, AWARE, Inc, One Memorial Drive, Cambridge, MA 02142, (617)577-1700.

AN, NACK YOUNG
Educator. Korean American. **PERSONAL:** Born Jan 25, 1936, Pyongyang, Pyungan-Namdo, Republic of Korea; son of Joon-Myung An and Hyung-Bok Chung; married Rose Jungja Lee An, Dec 22, 1961; children: Millie, Eunice, Dorothy. **EDUCATION:** Berea College, BA, 1961; University of Virginia, PhD, 1964. **CAREER:** Virginia Polytechnic Institute & State University, assistant professor of political science, 1964-68; Trenton State College, assistant professor, 1968-70; Georgia State University, dean of graduate school, 1970-72, professor of political science, 1972-. **ORGANIZATIONS:** American Political Science Association, 1964-; Southern Political Science Association, 1964; Journal of Politics, ed board, book review ed, 1974-78; Diplomacy, editorial board, 1968-; Asian Studies Center, advisory board, 1980-; Pacific/ Asian Mental Health Research Center, chair, adv bd, 1973-80. **HONORS/ AWARDS:** Omicron Delta Kappa, 1972; Pi Sigma Alpha, 1983; Republic of Korea, Presidential Achievements Citation, 1990. **SPECIAL ACHIEVEMENTS:** Vincent Auriel and External Affairs, 1969; National Democratic Party of Germany, 1970; Comparative Politics of Education, 1978. **MILITARY SERVICE:** US Army, sgt, 1950-53; Purple Heart, Combat Infantry Badge. **BUSINESS ADDRESS:** Professor, Department of Political Science, Georgia State University, University Plaza, Atlanta, GA 30303-3044, (404)651-3153.

ANAND, A. ANGELA
Health care administrator. Indo-American. **PERSONAL:** Born in Amritsar, Punjab, India; daughter of Bawa J Singh Bhalla & Harbans K Bhalla; married Rajen S Anand; children: Sunjay, Bobby (Shabeen). **EDUCATION:** Delhi University, India, BA; New Delhi Polytechnic, India, diploma, journalism; CORO Foundation, certificate, public affairs; California State University, Long Beach, MBA, currently; Punjab University, India, MEcon. **CAREER:** Freelance consulting and writing; California State University, Long Beach, administrative assistant, 1975; East Long Beach Neighborhood Center, administrative assistant, 1975-76; City of La Habra, manpower specialist, 1977-78; City of Long Beach, assistant community services analyst, 1977-85; California Museum of Science & Industry, education specialist, 1985; City of Garden Grove, public relations assistant, 1986; Complete Medical Care, Inc, administrator, 1986-. **ORGANIZATIONS:** Asian Indian Women's Network, president; Asian Pacific Womens Network, board member; Women in Communications, Inc, past president; Asian Advertising and Public Relations Association; Round Table Women of Orange County. **SPECIAL ACHIEVEMENTS:** Published several articles for print media; made appearances on television; proficient in Hindi, Punjabi, and Urdu. **HOME ADDRESS:** 8391 Satinwood Circle, Westminster, CA 92683, (714)894-2608. **BUSINESS PHONE:** (714)751-0995.

ANAND, CHARANJIT S.
Sales executive. Indo-American. **PERSONAL:** Born May 29, 1956, New Delhi, Delhi, India; son of Jagjit S Anand and Amrit K Anand; married Manleen Anand, Jan 16, 1983; children: Jasleen K, Amar S. **EDUCATION:** Clark University, MBA, 1982. **CAREER:** Omni Resources Corp, vice president of sales, currently. **BUSINESS ADDRESS:** Vice President of Sales, Omni Resources Corporation, 50 Howe Ave, Millbury, MA 01527.

ANAND, RAJEN S.
Educator. Indo-American. **PERSONAL:** Born Apr 27, 1939, India; son of Dial Singh Anand (deceased) & Daya Kaur (deceased); married Angela Anand, Oct 29, 1969; children: Sunjay, Shabeen. **EDUCATION:** University of California, Davis, PhD, 1969, DVM, 1969. **CAREER:** University of California, Davis, research physiologist, 1963-69; California State University, Long Beach, department chair, 1985-90, Dept of Communicative Disorders, department chair, 1990-92, Dept of Biological Sciences, professor of physiology, 1970-. **ORGANIZATIONS:** American Physiological Society, 1980-; Federation of Indo-American Associations, secretary, 1981-84, president, 1984-86, chairman, 1986-88; Indo-American Political Association, chair, 1989-; Asian & Pacific Islander Caucus, chair, 1991-93; California Democratic Party, executive board, 1990-. **HONORS/AWARDS:** California State University, Long Beach, Outstanding Professor Award, 1981, Meritorious Performance & Professional Award, 1986, 1988; University of California, Davis, Outstanding Student Award, 1967, 1968, Hertzendorf Memorial Award, 1969. **SPECIAL ACHIEVEMENTS:** Over 350 publications in various newspapers and magazines; over 36 scientific publications; delegate to Democratic National Conventions, 1988, 1992. **HOME PHONE:** (714)894-2608. **BUSINESS ADDRESS:** Professor, Dept of Biological Sciences, California State University, 1250 Bellflower Blvd, Long Beach, CA 90840, (310)985-4816.

ANAND, RAKESH
Physician. Indo-American. **PERSONAL:** Born Nov 11, 1955, Punjab, India; son of P C Anand and San Tosh; married Meena, Jun 30, 1980; children: Ravi, Rishi. **EDUCATION:** Armed Forces Medical College, MD, 1980. **CAREER:** Pontiac Medical Center, physician, currently. **HOME ADDRESS:** 9018 Linden Dr, Tinley Park, IL 60477, (708)614-9539.

ANAND, SATISH CHANDRA (SAM)
Researcher. Indo-American. **PERSONAL:** Born Aug 9, 1930, Delhi, India; son of Bhagat Singh Anand and Vidya Vati Anand; married Sushma, Jan 27, 1958; children: Ajay, Alka, Sanjay. **EDUCATION:** Delhi University, BS, 1951; Banaras Hindu University, MS, 1954; NC State University, master's, 1959; University of Wisconsin, PhD, 1962. **CAREER:** University of Illinois, research associate, 1962-63; Punjab Agricultural University, associate professor, 1964-71, senior geneticist, 1972-73; McNair Seed Company, soybean breeder, 1973-79; University of Missouri, associate professor, 1979-85, professor, 1986-. **ORGANIZATIONS:** American Society of Agronomy, national soybean certifying agent, 1988-92; University of Missouri, crop valley review committee, 1980-92, seed policy committee, 1978-92; Indian Society of Genetics, fellow, 1966; American Society of Agronomy, 1973-; Crop Science Society of America, 1973-; Society of Nematologists, 1982-; US Department of Agriculture, ad hoc reviewer, 1990-. **HONORS/AWARDS:** Progressive

Farmer Magazine, Man of the Year, 1990; Missouri Seed Improvement Association, Honor, 1991; Missouri Soybean Association, Research Award, 1992; American Soybean Association, Production Research Award, 1993. **SPECIAL ACHIEVEMENTS:** Developed & released Hartwig, a soybean variety resistant to all races of cyst nematodes, 1991; developed & released soybean varieties Delsoy 4500, Delsoy 4900, Delsoy 4710, Delsoy 4210, Avery, Bradley, Pershing, Rhodes & McNair, seed company varieties, 1975-92; published over 100 research papers in scientific journals. **BUSINESS ADDRESS:** Professor, University of Missouri, Columbia, Delta Center, Portageville, MO 63873, (314)379-5431.

ANANDAN, MUNISAMY
Scientist. Indo-American. **PERSONAL:** Born Mar 15, 1940, Perampattu, NA, Tamil Nadu, India; son of Ramasamy Munisamy and Sali; married Visalakshi Anandan, May 10, 1967; children: Sharadamani, Yesheswini. **EDUCATION:** Voorhees College, India, BSc, 1960; Annamalai University, India, MSc, 1963; Indian Institute of Technology, Bombay, MTech, 1966; Indian Institute of Science, Bangalore, PhD, 1979. **CAREER:** Bhaba Atomic Research Center, scientific officer, 1963-64; Bharat Electronics Ltd, India, manager, displays, 1967-87; Bell Communications Research, visiting scientist, 1987-88; Thomas Electronics Inc, research scientist, 1988-. **ORGANIZATIONS:** Society for Information Display, Mid Atlantic Chapter, vice chairman, 1992-93; IEEE, senior member, 1991-; American Physical Society, 1991-; Illumnination Engineering Society, 1991-. **HONORS/AWARDS:** Electronic Componet Industries Association, India, R&D Excellence 1st Prize, 1984; R&D Magazine, Chicago, R&D 100 Award, 1992. **SPECIAL ACHIEVEMENTS:** Five patents; 18 research publications. **BUSINESS ADDRESS:** Research Scientist, Thomas Electronics Inc, 100 Riverview Dr, Wayne, NJ 07470, (201)696-5200.

ANDERSON, WANNI W.
Educator, educational administrator. Thai American. **PERSONAL:** Born Jan 17, 1937, Bangkok, Thailand; daughter of Song Wibulswasdi and Lamom Wibulswasdi; married Douglas D Anderson, Sep 8, 1963. **EDUCATION:** Chulalongkorn University, Bangkok, Thailand, BA (honors), 1959; Brown University, MA, 1962; University of Pennsylvania, PhD, 1973. **CAREER:** Chulalongkorn University, lecturer in English, 1959-63; Harvard University, lecturer in education, 1976-77, 1983-84; Silpakorn University, visiting professor, 1985-86; Brown University, Dept of Anthropology, assistant professor of research, 1988-91, adjunct assistant prof, 1991-93, adjunct associate prof, 1993; Brown University Center for the Study of Race and Ethnicity in America, associate director, 1991-. **ORGANIZATIONS:** Assoc of Asian American Studies, 1991-; Southern New England Consortium on Race and Ethnicity, steering committee, 1992-; American Anthropological Assoc, 1974; Association for the Study of Play, editorial board, 1991-, executive committee, 1982-84; Soc for Folklore Studies, 1964-; Asian Folklore Studies, 1980-; Save the Children Fund, Krabi, Thailand, founder, 1987. **HONORS/AWARDS:** National Science Foundation, research grant, 1991-94; NIMH, postdoctoral research award, 1982-83; NICHD, postdoctoral research award, 1981-82; East-West Center, Professional Associate Award, 1984, 1983, 1978; Inter Folklore Assoc, Chicago Folklore Prize, 1974. **SPECIAL ACHIEVEMENTS:** Author, "The Making of Laotian American Women," The Dilemmas of Ethnic Adolescents, 1994; "The Social World & Play Life of Thai Muslim Adolescents," Asian Folklore Studies, 1988; guest editor of special volume "Folklore & Folklife of Thailand," Asian Folklore Studies, 1989; associate director, The Many Faces of Play, Human Kinetics, 1986; language proficiency: Thai, English, French, Russian. **BUSINESS ADDRESS:** Associate Director, Center for the Study of Race & Ethnicity in America, Brown University, Box 1886, Providence, RI 02912, (401)863-3041.

ANDO, KOICHI
Educator. Japanese American. **PERSONAL:** Born Jun 30, 1950, Nagano, Nagano-Prefecture, Japan; son of Takeshi & Masako Ando; married Shirley Ando, Jun 21, 1978; children: Mayumi, Sen. **EDUCATION:** Meiji University, Japan, BA, 1974; San Francisco State University, MA, 1982. **CAREER:** San Francisco Unified School District, instructional aide, 1977-79; United Japanese Community Services, counselor, 1979-81; Kimochi Inc, Senior Services, case worker, 1981-83; Asian Community Mental Health Services, case manager, 1984-87; University of Hawaii, instructor, 1988-89; Western Oregon State College, assistant professor, director of international education, 1989-. **ORGANIZATIONS:** NAFSA International Educators, Oregon state representative, 1991-93; Japan Pacific Resource Network, president/board of directors, 1985-87; Nobiru-Kai, Japanese Newcomers Services, president/board of directors, 1981-84; Nihonmachi Legal Outreach, board of directors, 1981-83;

Nihonmachi Little Friends, board of directors, 1985-87. **HONORS/ AWARDS:** International Institute, Immigrant of the Year, 1985; International Student Inc, Foreign Student Advisor of the Year, 1991; NAFSA International Educators Region I, NAFSAn of the Year, 1992. **SPECIAL ACHIEVE-MENTS:** Bilingual/biliterate in Japanese and English; San Francisco Japantown New Year Festival chairman, 1981-83; "New Immigration Law," Japan Resource Network, 1987; "Everyone Is Minority," Japan Resource Network, 1991. **BUSINESS ADDRESS:** Assistant Professor/Director of International Education, Western Oregon State College, Office of International Education & Services, 345 N Monmouth Ave, Monmouth, OR 97361, (503)838-8425.

ANDRADA, WILMER VIGILIA
Health care manager, real estate executive. Filipino American. **PERSONAL:** Born Jan 7, 1948, Guimba, Nueva Ecija, Philippines; son of Hermenigildo Andrada and Carmelita Andrada. **EDUCATION:** Manila Central University, BS, medical technology, 1969; Methodist Medical Center, School of Medical Technology, 1970; Central Michigan University, health services administration, 1984. **CAREER:** Medical Center Laboratory, chief tech, 1980-92; Methodist Medical Central, pm supervisor, 1972-; Property Management, owner, 1980-; Morton Medical Laboratory, owner, manager, 1993-. **ORGANIZATIONS:** American Heart Assn, board of directors, 1990-93; Methodist Men, 1989-. **HOME ADDRESS:** 1602 Moss Ave, Peoria, IL 61606, (309)637-3628. **BUSINESS ADDRESS:** Owner, Property Management, 1602 Moss Ave, Peoria, IL 61606-1641.

ANG, CHARLES C.
Engineer. Chinese American. **PERSONAL:** Born Aug 4, 1927, Fuzhou, Fujian, China; son of Ban Jin Ang & Sui Chu Tang; married Loraine G Ang, Apr 19, 1986; children: Veronica D, Eileen D Yuen, Charles G Jr. **EDUCA-TION:** University of Santo Tomas, BSCE, 1949; Lehigh University, MSCE, 1950. **CAREER:** Pennsylvania Department of Transportation, project engineer field, 1950-51, Rust Engineering Co, structural engineer, 1951-53; Lehigh University, graduate assistant, 1953-54; Modjeski & Masters, senior structural engineer, 1954-57; Edward Kelcey & Beck, structural squad leader, 1957-60; Dorfman Bloom Inc, Ammann & Whitney, senior structural engineer, 1960-63; D'Ambly Inc, chief structural engineer, 1963-78; Ang Associates Inc, president, 1977-. **ORGANIZATIONS:** American Society of Civil Engineers, 1962-; American Concrete Institute; International Bridge & Structural Engineering; National Society of Professional Engineers; Pennsylvania Society of Professional Engineers; Philadelphia Chinatown Development Corp, advisory board; City of Philadelphia, minority business enterprise council, 1982-85; Minority Architects & Engineers Alliance, director. **HONORS/AWARDS:** James F Lincoln Arc Welding Foundation, certificate of award, 1964; Pennsylvania Department of Transportation, Excellence in Highway Design Award, 1988; Concrete Construction Committee, Award of Excellence, 1990; American Institute of Steel Construction, AISC Architectural Award of Excellence, 1990; Construction Management Association of America, Project of the Year Award, 1991. **SPECIAL ACHIEVEMENTS:** Author, "Squire Column with Double Eccentricities Solved by Numerical Method," ACI Journal, 1961; co-lecturer, "Structural Steel Design, Fabricator & Erection," 4-week seminar sponsored by Institute of Chinese Engineers, Taipei, China, 1978; structural designer, wind connections for Verazano Narrows Bridge, 1960. **BUSINESS ADDRESS:** Professional Engineer, President, Ang Associates Inc, 444 N Third St, Ste 200, Philadelphia, PA 19123, (215)923-7010.

ANNAMALAI, NAGAPPAN K.
Military research engineer. Indo-American. **PERSONAL:** Born Aug 29, 1936, Shanmughanathapuram, Tamil Nadu, India; son of Ramanathan Nagappan and Valliammai Achi; married Solai Annamalai, Apr 29, 1963; children: Pari Nagappan, Angayurkanni. **EDUCATION:** Annamalai University, BS, 1959; Indian Institute of Technology, Kharagpur, MTech, 1963; Rutgers State University, MS, 1971, PhD, 1974. **CAREER:** Annamalai University, asst professor, 1959-66, associate professor, 1966-69; Rutgers University, research/teaching assistant, 1969-74; West Virginia University, asst professor, 1974-77; Clarkson University, associate professor, 1977-85; Northeastern University, honorary faculty, part-time faculty, 1985-; USAF, research electronics engineer, 1985-. **ORGANIZATIONS:** Institute of Electronic Engineers, 1969-; Electrochemical Society, 1979-; Sigma Xi, 1974-. **HONORS/AWARDS:** Walter C Russell, scholarship, 1971-73; Ford Foundation, fellowship, 1972-74. **SPECIAL ACHIEVEMENTS:** Published: over 50 papers in technical journals, a book in Tamil: Basic Electrical Engineering; 2 patents, 1985, 1993. **BUSINESS ADDRESS:** Research Electronics Engineer, US Air Force, Phil-

lips Laboratory, PL/VTER, 80 Scott Rd, Bldg 1128, Rm 27, Hanscom AFB, MA 01731-2909, (617)377-3047.

AOKI, BRENDA JEAN (BRENDA WONG)
Theater artist. Japanese American/Chinese American. **PERSONAL:** Born Jul 29, 1953, Salt Lake City, UT; daughter of Dave & Boots Aoki; married Mark George Izu, Dec 4, 1991. **EDUCATION:** University of California, Santa Cruz, BA (honors), 1976; San Francisco State University, multiple subjects teaching credential, K-12 early childhood development certificate, 1981. **CAREER:** Self-employed touring artist, 1985-. **ORGANIZATIONS:** National Endowment for the Arts, panelist, special projects, 1993, presenting commissioning, 1992; California Arts Council, panelist, touring roster, 1988-94; Western States Arts Federation, touring artist, 1992-95; North Carolina Touring Roster, 1992-94. **HONORS/AWARDS:** Dramalogue, Best Performance, Best Writing, 1992; Rockefeller Foundation, Multi-Arts Production Grant, 1991, 1992; National Association of Independent Record Distributors, Best Spoken Word Album, 1990; San Francisco Nikkei in Education, Nikkei in Education Award, 1990; San Francisco Bay Guardian, Goldie Award, 1990. **SPECIAL ACHIEVEMENTS:** Theater commissions: The Queen's Garden; Ballad of the Bones; San Jose Taiko Collaboration; Long Beach Video Annex; Tokyo Form and Spirit Exhibition; Chinese Myths and Rebuses Exhibition; film, TV & radio: Living on Tokyo Time; Peggy Sue Got Married; "No Way Out, Music Video"; "Layin' It on the Line"; "State of the Heart". **BUSINESS ADDRESS:** Touring Artist, 41 A Parsons St, San Francisco, CA 94118, (415)567-9546.

AOKI, GUY MIKI
Radio writer/producer, association executive. Japanese American. **PERSONAL:** Born May 12, 1962, Hilo, HI; son of Herbert and Janet Aoki. **EDUCATION:** University of Hawaii-Manoa, 1982-83; Occidental College, 1980-81, 1983-84; Dick Grove School of Music, 1985-86. **CAREER:** ABC Watermark/"American Top 40," production asst, 1984-85, researcher, 1985-88, music assembly producer, 1986-88; Los Angeles Times, reporter, 1988-89; Dick Clark Productions, "Countdown America," writer/co-producer, 1989-. **ORGANIZATIONS:** Media Action Network for Asian Americans, co-founder, president, 1992-, Rising Sun, fundraising, chair, press relations committee, chair; Natl Coalition for Redress & Reparations, 1984-, Japanese American internment video, chr, press & public relations, chr, Multi-Media Day of Remembrance Program, chr, 50th Anniversary of Pearl Harbor "Counter-Programming" Committee, chr, Coordinating Committee; Asian Pacific Students Union, Southern California Steering Committee, co-chair, 1984-88; Occidental College Asian Alliance, 1980-81, 1983-84, vp, 1984; Psi Chi, 1984. **HONORS/AWARDS:** Billboard Magazine, Best Syndicated Radio Program-Adult Contemporary Field, "Countdown America," writer, 1991. **SPECIAL ACHIEVEMENTS:** Columnist: "Into the Next Stage," Rafu Shimpo, 1992-; pop music critic, features writer, publications include: Los Angeles Times; Goldmine; Music Connection; Rock Scene; Tozai Times; BAM; Creem; Rice Magazine; Asi-Am; The Occidental; artwork published: Honolulu comic zine, 1983; keyboardist, additional scorer: Aesop's Falables, musical, Hawaii, 1979. **BIOGRAPHICAL SOURCES:** Rafu Shimpo, Fall 1991; Hilo Tribune Herald, 1990, fall 1991. **BUSINESS ADDRESS:** President, Co-Founder, Media Action Network for Asian Americans, PO Box 1881, Santa Monica, CA 90406-1881, (213)486-4433.

AOKI, HARUO
Educator. Japanese American. **PERSONAL:** Born Apr 1, 1930, Kunsan, Cholla-Pukto, Republic of Korea; son of Akira Aoki and Yae Aoki; married Ann, Apr 2, 1981; children: Kanna, Akemi, Mieko. **EDUCATION:** Hiroshima University, Japan, BA, 1953; University of California, Los Angeles, MA, 1958; University of California, Berkeley, PhD, 1965. **CAREER:** University of California, Berkeley, professor emeritus, currently. **HONORS/AWARDS:** Shinmura Foundation, Shinmura Izuru Prize, 1989. **HOME ADDRESS:** 1501 Elm St, El Cerrito, CA 94530. **BUSINESS PHONE:** (510)642-3480.

AOKI, KATHRYN KIKU
Journalist. Japanese American. **PERSONAL:** Born Dec 15, 1960, Oakland, CA; daughter of Yasuhiko Aoki and Margaret Mitsuye Aoki. **EDUCATION:** Contra Costa College, associate degree (with honors), 1982; San Franciso State University, journalism, 1985. **CAREER:** Nichi Bei Times, reporter, 1985-, assistant editor, 1987-92. **ORGANIZATIONS:** Japanese Cultural and Community Center of Northern California, board member, 1988-; Asian American Journalists Association, 1985-; Society of Professional Journalists, 1985-; Kimochi, Inc, volunteer, 1986-; Asian American Bar Association of Greater

Bay Area, 1990-; Asian Business League of San Francisco, 1993; Buddhist Church of Oakland, Dharma School teacher, 1979-; Japanese American Citizens League, Contra Costa Chapter, 1979-. **HONORS/AWARDS:** Contra Costa College, Journalism Dept, Advocate Award, 1981; Contra Costa JACL, Scholarship, 1979; Soroptimist International of El Pinablo, Scholarship, 1982; Delta Kappa Society International, 1982. **SPECIAL ACHIEVEMENTS:** Young America Sings, National Poetry Press, 1979. **BUSINESS ADDRESS:** Reporter, Nichi Bei Times, 2211 Bush St, San Francisco, CA 94115, (415)921-6822.

AOKI, ROCKY (HIROAKI)
Restaurateur. Japanese American. **PERSONAL:** Born 1940, Japan; married Chizuru Kobayashi; children: Kevin, Grace. **EDUCATION:** CCNY, School of Hotel Management. **CAREER:** Benihana Steakhouses, founder, president, 1963-; Benihana of Tokyo Inc, Benihana Natl Corp, chairman of the board, currently. **HONORS/AWARDS:** Asian Pacific Coalition, Mainstream America Business Award, 1992; Japanese Olympic Games, flyweight wrestler, 1960; Benihana Grand Prix, First Place, 1982. **SPECIAL ACHIEVEMENTS:** Broadway play producer; movie producer; boxing promoter; Benihana Grand Prix powerboat race, sponsor, participant; first balloon crossing of the Pacific Ocean, team member, 1981. **BIOGRAPHICAL SOURCES:** Newsmakers, 1990. **BUSINESS ADDRESS:** Founder/CEO, Benihana National Corp, 8685 NW 53rd Terrace, Miami, FL 33166, (305)592-1129.*

AOKI, THOMAS T.
Educator, physician. Japanese American. **PERSONAL:** Born Jun 12, 1940, Oakland, CA; son of Joseph S Aoki and Esther A Aoki; married Susan K Aoki, Aug 3, 1963; children: Elizabeth N, Katherine H, Carolyn M. **EDUCATION:** University of California, Berkeley, 1958-61; Yale University School of Medicine, MD, 1965; Harvard University School of Medicine, 1969-72. **CAREER:** Yale University School of Medicine, Internship in Medicine, 1965-66, resident in medicine, 1968-69; United States Public Health Service, surgeon, 1966-68; Joslin Diabetes Center, research fellow, investigator, 1965-75, investigator, 1980-84; Howard Hughes Medical Institute, investigator, 1975-80; University of California, Davis, chief, div of endocrinology, professor of medicine, 1984-; Aoki Diabetes Research Institute, director of research. **ORGANIZATIONS:** American Diabetes Association, 1977-; Endocrine Society, 1980-; Western Association of Physicians, 1984-; Sacramento Center for Blood Research, board of directors, 1991-94; American Federation for Clinical Research, 1979-. **HONORS/AWARDS:** The Medical Foundation, Fellowship, 1973-75; Yale University School of Medicine, Moseley Award for Scholastic Excellence, 1965. **SPECIAL ACHIEVEMENTS:** Over 100 original articles in the field of hormone fuel metabolism and diabetes research. **BUSINESS ADDRESS:** Chief, Div of Endocrinology, Professor of Medicine, University of California, 4301 X St, FOLB II-C, Sacramento, CA 95817, (916)734-3739.

AONO, ISAMU
Economic adviser, consulting company executive. Japanese American. **PERSONAL:** Born Mar 19, 1944, Tokyo, Japan; son of Shotaro Aono and Hisako Aono; married Kathy Aono, Sep 30, 1979. **EDUCATION:** Keio University, Tokyo, Japan, BS, economics, 1966; MIT, MS, management, 1972. **CAREER:** Small Business Corp. of Japan, chief economic adviser, currently; PRC Inc, president, CEO, currently. **ORGANIZATIONS:** Stanford University, Asian Pacific Research Center; MIT Enterprise Forum; Commonwealth Club of Northern California; Japan Society of Northern California; World Affairs Council. **HONORS/AWARDS:** Keio University, Dean's List, Distinguished Economist Award. **SPECIAL ACHIEVEMENTS:** Publications include: "Late 90's Technological Change," JETRO; "93's Economical Condition," Key Person Magazine; "Disaster of Hurricane Andrew," JR Railroad Corp; "US Small Business," SBA, Japan. **BIOGRAPHICAL SOURCES:** US Japan Business News, Nov 1990; Key Person, Dec 1991. **BUSINESS ADDRESS:** President, CEO, PRC Inc, 432 N Canal St, Unit 12, South San Francisco, CA 94080.

AOYAMA, CALVIN TAKEO
Insurance broker. Japanese American. **PERSONAL:** Born Oct 16, 1942, Reno, NV; son of Fred Aoyama and Hana Aoyama; married Emily Aoyama, May 3, 1969; children: Lisa, Douglas. **EDUCATION:** San Francisco State University, BA, 1965; The American College of Life Underwriters, CLU, 1975. **CAREER:** Alexander & Baldwin, claims adjuster, 1965-66; California Casualty, vice president, 1966-. **ORGANIZATIONS:** Buddhist Temple of Alameda, 1976-; Boy Scouts of America, Alameda, events chairman, 1987-90; American Society of Chartered Life Underwriters, 1975-83; National Assn of Life Under-

writers, 1973-83. **MILITARY SERVICE:** Army Reserves, e-4, 1960-63. **BUSINESS ADDRESS:** Vice President, California Casualty Group, 2000 Alameda de las Pulgas, Suite 144, San Mateo, CA 94403, (415)572-4617.

AOYAMA, YASUTAKA BARRON
Brokerage firm executive. Japanese American. **PERSONAL:** Born Aug 31, 1962, New York, NY; son of Tetsuji Aoyama and Akiko Aoyama. **EDUCATION:** Brown University, AB (magna cum laude), 1985; Harvard University, MPA, 1987. **CAREER:** Bankers Trust Co, mergers and acquistions, associate, 1988-89; Pacific Arts Center, managing director, 1991; Cohig and Associates, options principal, 1992-. **ORGANIZATIONS:** Co-Motion Dance Co, treasurer, 1990-. **HONORS/AWARDS:** Harvard University, Kennedy Fellow, 1985; Alfred P Sloan Foundation, Sloan Fellow, 1983. **HOME ADDRESS:** PO Box 9006, Aspen, CO 81612. **BUSINESS ADDRESS:** Options Principal, Cohig & Associates, Inc, 600 E Hopkins, Aspen, CO 81611, (303)920-2505.

ARAI, TOMIE
Visual artist. Japanese American. **PERSONAL:** Born Aug 16, 1949, New York, NY; daughter of Tim Arai & Tomoe Arai; married Legan Wong; children: Masai Glushanok, Akira Wong. **EDUCATION:** Philadelphia College of Art, 1968, Intaglio, The Printmaking Workshop, 1985-87; Intaglio, Teachers College Printmaking Department, 1987. **CAREER:** PS 1 Museum/ Institute for Contemporary Art, artist, instructor; New York Foundation for the Arts, artist-in-residence, 1992-93; Children's Book Press, illustrator, 1993-. **ORGANIZATIONS:** Chinatown History Museum, board of trustees, 1993; Printed Matter Inc, board of directors, 1993; Godzilla-Asian American Visual Artists Network, steering committee, 1991-93; Coast-to-Coast National Women Artists of Color Organization, org comm, 1990-93; Lower East Side Printshop, board of directors, 1992-93; District 1199 Bread and Roses Cultural Project, advisory board. **HONORS/AWARDS:** New York Foundation for the Arts, Artist's Residency Grant, 1992-93, fellowship in printmaking, 1992; National Endowment for the Arts, Interarts Grant, 1992, Visual Artist Fellowship for Works on Paper, 1994; PS 1 Museum/Institute for Contemporary Art, studio residency, 1991; New York State Council on the Arts, artists residency, 1988. **SPECIAL ACHIEVEMENTS:** Prints are currently in the collections of the Washington State Arts Commission, the Museum of Modern Art, Library of Congress Pennell Print collection and YWCA Offices of the National Board; Public Art Commission, NYC Department of Cultural Affairs, Per Cent for Art Program, 1992-93; China's Bravest Girl, illustrator, Children's Book Press, 1992; Framing an American Identity, solo installation, Alternative Museum, 1992; committed to print; group exhibition at the Museum of Modern Art, NYC, 1988. **BIOGRAPHICAL SOURCES:** Lucy Lippard, Mixed Blessings: New Art in Multicultural American, Pantheon Books, 1990; The Decade Show, Frameworks of Identity in the 1980's, catalogue, New Museum of Contemporary Art, 1990. **HOME ADDRESS:** 245 W 107th St, 12H, New York, NY 10025, (212)749-2259.

ARAKAWA, EDWARD TAKASHI
Physicist. Japanese American. **PERSONAL:** Born Apr 8, 1929, Honolulu, HI; son of Wilfred S Arakawa and Otsugi Arakawa; married Harue Yamashiro Arakawa, Jul 15, 1955; children: Sandra Kay Henry, David Ken, Paul Edward, Carolyn Ann Livengood. **EDUCATION:** Samford University, BS, 1951; Louisiana State University, MS, 1953, University of Tennessee, PhD, 1957. **CAREER:** Union Carbide, research scientist, 1957-80; Martin Marietta, senior research scientist, 1980-. **ORGANIZATIONS:** European Space Research Organization, surface physics consultant, 1975; Atomic Bomb Casualty Committee, radiation research consultant, 1958-60. **HONORS/AWARDS:** American Physical Society, fellow, 1982; Optical Society of America, fellow, 1974; Martin Marietta, Inventor Award, 1986; Industrial Research, Research and Development 100 Award, 1981, 1986. **SPECIAL ACHIEVEMENTS:** Vacuum Ultraviolet Radiation Physics; Surface Plasmon Phenomena; Resonance Ionization Mass Spectroscopy; Optical Materials in Planetary Research. **HOME ADDRESS:** 111 Amherst Ln, Oak Ridge, TN 37830, (615)483-4904. **BUSINESS ADDRESS:** Senior Research Scientist, Oak Ridge Nat Lab, Bldg 4500S, H-160, Oak Ridge, TN 37831-6123, (615)574-6218.

ARAKAWA, KASUMI
Physician, educator. Japanese American. **PERSONAL:** Born Feb 19, 1926, Toyohashi, Japan; son of Masumi Arakawa and Fuyako Arakawa; married June H Arakawa, Aug 25, 1955; children: Jane R Fowler, Kenneth L, Amy K. **EDUCATION:** Tokyo Medical College, MD, 1953; Showa University School of Medicine, PhD, 1985. **CAREER:** University of Kansas Medical Center, Dept of Anesthesiology, professor, chairman, 1977-. **HONORS/AWARDS:**

Fulbright Scholarship, 1954; Sharing Corporation, scholarship, 1956. **HOME ADDRESS:** 7917 El Monte, Prairie Village, KS 66208.

ARAKAWA, MINORU
Computer software company executive. Japanese American. **PERSONAL:** married. **CAREER:** Nintendo of America, president, 1980-. **BUSINESS ADDRESS:** President, Nintendo of America, 4820 150th Ave NE, Redmond, WA 98052, (206)882-2040.*

ARAKI, MINORU S.
Aeronautics company executive. Japanese American. **CAREER:** Lockheed Missiles & Space System Co, Inc, exec vp, 1988-. **ORGANIZATIONS:** National Academy of Engineering. **BUSINESS ADDRESS:** Executive Vice President, Lockheed Missiles & Space Syst Co Inc, Dept 100 Bldg 101 PO Box 3504, Sunnyvale, CA 94088-3504.*

ARIF, SHOAIB
Chemist. Pakistani American. **PERSONAL:** Born May 28, 1950, Karachi, Sind, Pakistan; son of Mohammed Arif & Shahjahan Begum; married Nasreen Arif. **EDUCATION:** University of Karachi, BS, chemistry, 1969, MS, chemistry, 1971. **CAREER:** Private Formulations, chemist, 1977-78; City of New York, Department of Water Res, chemist, 1978-80; Cameo Inc, chief chemist, 1980-83; Go-Jo Industries, associate dir of research, 1983-85; Sani-Fresh International, development chemist, 1985-87; Jeri-Jacobus Laboratories, tech director, 1987-89; Olin Chemicals, application specialist, 1989-. **ORGANIZATIONS:** Society of Cosmetic Chemists, secretary, 1983-85; American Chemical Society, 1990-92; Chemical Specialties Manufacturing Association, chairman, testing committee, 1989-; Cosmetic Toiletries & Fragrance Association, 1983-85; American Association of Textile Colorists & Chemist, 1990-; American Oil Chemist Society, 1990-. **SPECIAL ACHIEVEMENTS:** Published paper regarding acid dye leveling agents, 1992; paper on hard surface cleaners, 1993; 3 patents filed. **BUSINESS ADDRESS:** Chemist, Olin Chemicals, 350 Knotter Dr, Cheshire, CT 06410, (203)271-4121.

ARIKAWA, NORMAN
Port authority financial executive. Japanese American. **PERSONAL:** married; children: one daughter. **CAREER:** Port Authority of Los Angeles, chief accountant, currently. **ORGANIZATIONS:** Los Angeles/Nagoya Sister City Program; Nisei Week Festival; Pacific American Ballet Theater. **BUSINESS ADDRESS:** Chief Accountant, Port Authority of Los Angeles, PO Box 151, San Pedro, CA 90731, (310)519-3400.*

ARIMURA, AKIRA
Research administrator, educator. Japanese American. **PERSONAL:** Born Dec 26, 1923, Kobe, Japan; son of Jojiro & Kiyoko Arimura; married Katsuko Arimura, Jul 31, 1957; children: Jerome Jiko, Makoto Mark, Mika Margaret. **EDUCATION:** Nagoya University, Japan, medicine, MD, 1951, Dept Physiology, PhD, 1957. **CAREER:** Tulane University, professor of medicine, 1973-, adjunct professor of anatomy, 1979-, Clinical RIA Lab, director, 1980-87, Lab for Molecular Neuroendocrinology and Diabetes, director, 1980-85, USJBRL, director, 1985-, Dept of Physiology, adjunct professor, 1989-; Kelo University, visiting professor, 1990-. **HONORS/AWARDS:** Fulbright Exchange Scholarship, 1956; Yale University, James Hudson Brown Fellowship, 1956-58. **SPECIAL ACHIEVEMENTS:** Honorary member of Japan Endocrine Society; over 800 papers & abstracts; many invited speeches, lecturer; editorial board, journal reviewers, more than 10 journals; establishment of US-Japan Biomedical Research Lab & Clinical RIA Lab at Tulane; initiated student exchange program between 2 countries; organized national & international symposiums; one of the 300 most-cited authors & 17 most-cited physiologists, 1961-75, 28 among the top 50 researchers & the most-cited scientist in Japan, 1965-78; 35th among the top 50 researchers in the world, 1973-84. **BIOGRAPHICAL SOURCES:** Nobel Duel, by Wade. **BUSINESS ADDRESS:** Dir, US-Japan Biomedical Research Labs, Tulane University, Hebert Center, 3705 Main St, Bldg 30, Belle Chasse, LA 70037, (504)394-7199.

ARIZA, YASUMI
Landscaper (retired). Japanese American. **PERSONAL:** Born Jul 18, 1927, Montebello, CA; married Miyoko Ariza, Mar 10, 1957. **CAREER:** Yas Landscape and Gardening Service, Inc, president, retired. **ORGANIZATIONS:** Japan-America Society of Phoenix; City of Phoenix, Park, Recreation and Library Dept, Matsuri Committee. **HOME ADDRESS:** 3325 W Orangewood Ave, Phoenix, AZ 85051-7452, (602)841-0968.

ARORA, MADAN LAL
Physician. Indo-American. **PERSONAL:** Born Mar 10, 1950, Mohnyin, Burma; married Neelam Dutt, Jan 27, 1978; children: Shagun, Sonal, Salonee. **EDUCATION:** Arya College, India, pre-med, 1971; Dayanand Medical College, India, MBBS, 1977; PGI Chandigarh, MD, 1981; Wayne State University, 1987. **CAREER:** Michigan State University School of Medicine, asst prof, currently; McLaren Regional Cancer Center, hematologist, oncologist, currently. **HOME PHONE:** (517)791-3417. **BUSINESS ADDRESS:** Assistant Professor, Medicine, Michigan State University School of Medicine, McLaren Regional Cancer Center, 4100 Beecher Rd, Flint, MI 48532, (313)235-8568.

ARORA, SAMIR CHANDRA
Investments analyst. Indo-American. **PERSONAL:** Born Nov 26, 1961, New Delhi, India; son of P C Arora (deceased) & Prema Arora; married Rohini Arora, Jan 3, 1990. **EDUCATION:** Indian Institute of Technology, New Delhi, BTech, 1983; Indian Institute of Management, Calcutta, MBA, 1985; University of Pennsylvania, Wharton School, MA, finance, 1991. **CAREER:** Rank Xerox Ltd, UK, assistant to the controller; Alliance Capital Management Corp, vice president, 1991-. **HONORS/AWARDS:** University of Pennsylvania, Wharton School, Dean's Fellowship for Distinguished Merit, 1988-91; Indian Institute of Management, Gold Medalist, overall first rank, 1985. **BUSINESS ADDRESS:** Vice President, Alliance Capital Management Corp, 1345 Ave of the Americas, 37th Fl, New York, NY 10105.

ARORA, VIJAY K.
Educator. Indo-American. **PERSONAL:** Born Nov 13, 1945, Multan, Pakistan; son of Hari Chand Arora & Chander Bhagan Arora; married Rashmi Arora, Dec 2, 1976; children: Vineeta, Namita. **EDUCATION:** Kurukshetra University, BSc (honors), 1965, MSc, 1967; University of Colorado, MS, 1970, PhD, 1973; Western Michigan University, MS (honors), 1976. **CAREER:** University of Colorado, lecturer, 1968-74; Western Michigan University, assistant professor, 1974-76; King Saud University, professor, 1976-85; University of Illinois, visiting associate professor, 1981-82; Wilkes University, professor of electrical engineering, 1985-; University of Tokyo, visiting professor, 1989-91; National University of Singapore, visiting professor, 1991-93. **ORGANIZATIONS:** Institute of Electrical and Electronics Engineers, senior member; American Physical Society, life member; American Association for Engineering Education. **HONORS/AWARDS:** Kurukshetra University, University Medal, 1965, National Scholarship, 1965-67; US Dept of Commerce, Citation for International Cooperation in Sci & Tech, 1974; IEEE, Singapore, Appreciation Award, 1993; Wilkes University, Outstanding Faculty, 1989-91. **SPECIAL ACHIEVEMENTS:** Over 110 publications in international journals and conference proceedings; international lectures; visited several institutions on short term assignments; active in Asian community; proficient in Arabic, Hindi, Urdu. **HOME PHONE:** (717)868-3625. **BUSINESS ADDRESS:** Professor, Dept of Electrical & Computer Engineering, Wilkes University, Wilkes Barre, PA 18766, (717)831-4813.

ASAHARA, DAVID J.
Business owner. Japanese American. **PERSONAL:** Born Nov 25, 1952, Tacoma, WA; son of Joe & Reyko Asahara; married Barbara A Mizoguchi-Asahara, Oct 20, 1984. **EDUCATION:** Washington State University, BA, 1975. **CAREER:** Oriental Garden Center, vice president, 1975-89, president, currently. **HONORS/AWARDS:** Boy Scouts, Eagle. **BUSINESS ADDRESS:** President, Oriental Garden Center Inc, 30650 Pacific Hwy S, Federal Way, WA 98003.

ASANO, IZUMI
Accountant. Japanese American. **PERSONAL:** Born Aug 31, 1951, Maki, Niigata, Japan; son of Masayoshi Asano and Chii Asano; married Margaret J Vanbuskirk, Feb 19, 1982; children: Taiyo V. **EDUCATION:** Waseda University, BA, 1975; CUNY, Baruch College, MBA, 1989. **CAREER:** SEC International, chief of president's office, manager; KPMG Peat Marwick, tax specialist; Arthur Andersen & Co, Japanese practice director, currently. **ORGANIZATIONS:** AICPA; MACPA; JASW; JVS; JCA; JBAM; JAFS. **SPECIAL ACHIEVEMENTS:** Articles in English journals and others in Japan, written in Japanese. **BUSINESS ADDRESS:** Japanese Practice Director, Arthur Andersen & Co, 1666 K St NW, Washington, DC 20006, (202)862-7457.

ASHTEKAR, ABHAY VASANT
Educator. Indo-American. **PERSONAL:** Born Jul 5, 1949, Shirpur, India; son of Vasant D Ashtekar & Vimala Nandrekar Ashtekar; married Christine M Clarke, Jul 10, 1989. **EDUCATION:** Bombay University, India, BS (w/ honors), 1969; University of Chicago, PhD, 1974. **CAREER:** Universite' de Paris VI, professeur, chair de Gravitatior, 1983-85; Syracuse University, distinguished professor of physics, 1984-93; Pennsylvania State University, Eberly professor of physics, director, Center for Gravitational Physics a Geometry, 1993-. **ORGANIZATIONS:** NSF Institute of Theo Phys, co-ordinator of 6 month workshop, 1986; Classical & Quantum Gravity, editor of International Journal, 1988-91; NSF Oversight Committee, 1988; NSF Panel to Select Young Presidential Investigators, 1989; Xanthopoulas International Award Committee, 1991-; United Nations Development Program, consultant, 1991; Intl-Society for General Relativity, Governing Council, 1989-; Intl Journal of Modern Physics, managing editor, 1992-. **HONORS/AWARDS:** Sloan Foundation, Alfred P Sloan Research Fellowship, 1981-85; Syracuse University, Chancellor's Citation for Academic Excellence, 1987, Wasserstrom Award for graduate teaching, 1992; Gravity Foundation, First Prize, Annual International Competition, 1977; Govt of India, National Merit Scholarship, 1965-69. **SPECIAL ACHIEVEMENTS:** Author or co-author of 5 scientific books, 1986-91, 102 scientific papers, 1974-93. **BIOGRAPHICAL SOURCES:** Discover Magazine: Beyond Einstein, p 60-68, April, 1993; Sciences: The Quantum Loop, p 32-36, Nov/Dec, 1989. **BUSINESS ADDRESS:** Eberly Chair in Physics, Dir, Ctr for Gravitational Physics & Geometry, Pennsylvania State University, 320 Osmond Hall, University Park, PA 16802-6300, (814)863-0117.

ASLAM, NASIM MOHAMMED
Registered nurse. Indo-American. **PERSONAL:** Born Jan 4, 1946, Dar-Es-Salaam, United Republic of Tanzania; daughter of Nurbanu Rajan and Kassamali Rajan; married Mohammed Aslam, Jul 27, 1973; children: Shabana, Shazia. **EDUCATION:** General Council for England & Wales, SRN, 1967, SCM, 1968, 1970; State Board of Texas, RN, 1987. **CAREER:** Harefield Hospital, Harefield, Middlesex, England, registered nurse, 1963-68; Harris Hospital, 1970-71; Parkland Hospital, registered nurse, 1971-73; Dallas Osteopath Hospital, registered nurse, 1975-77; Mary Sheils Hospital, 1977-78; RHD Memorial Hospital, 1978-92; Presbyterian Hospital of Plano, registered nurse, currently. **ORGANIZATIONS:** Girl Scouts of America, leader, currently; Foriegn Nurses Assn, president, 1971-73; Health Dallas, Ismaili Sect, 1987-89. **HONORS/AWARDS:** Girl Scout Troop #563, 5 Years Service Award, 1993. **SPECIAL ACHIEVEMENTS:** Opened a health clinic for the underprivileged, 1987. **HOME ADDRESS:** 10917 Damon Ln, Dallas, TX 75229, (214)350-8029.

ASUNCION, ALFREDO, JR.
Physician. Filipino American. **PERSONAL:** Born Apr 17, 1963, New Iberia, LA; son of Alfredo Asuncion Sr and Shizue Osakabe Asuncion; married Vanessa Oviedo Asuncion, Mar 28, 1987; children: Erika Yumi. **EDUCATION:** University of Santo Tomas, BSMT, 1983; Lyceum-Northwestern College of Medicine, MD, 1987. **CAREER:** US Army, biomedical research assistant, 1988-92; SUNY-HSC, Dept of Pathology, resident physician, 1992-. **ORGANIZATIONS:** College of American Pathologist; American Medical Assn. **SPECIAL ACHIEVEMENTS:** Co-author, abstracts: "Albumin Transport across the Blood Brain Barrier," Microcirculatory Society, 1990; "Elevated NE and E Levels Attenuate Cardiac Performance following Brain Injury," FASEB Meeting, 1992. **MILITARY SERVICE:** US Army, s sgt, 1988-92; Army Commendation Medal, 1992. **HOME ADDRESS:** 111 Linwell Terr #3, Syracuse, NY 13206-2040, (315)424-8579.

ASUNCION, GARY RAYMOND ESPEJO
Environmental scientist. Filipino American. **PERSONAL:** Born May 10, 1965, Manila, Philippines; son of Immaculata Espejo Asuncion and Mariano Villarosa Asuncion. **EDUCATION:** University of Minnesota, pre-med undergraduate studies, 1983-85; University of Florida, College of Agriculture, BS, food resource economics, 1990. **CAREER:** Environmental Science & Engineering, Inc, staff scientist, 1990-. **ORGANIZATIONS:** Florida Chapter of the National Asbestos Council, 1992-; Univ of Florida, Filipino Student Assn, 1989-90; University of Florida Minorities in Agriculture, Natural Resources and Related Sciences, 1989-90. **BIOGRAPHICAL SOURCES:** St Paul Dispatch/Pioneer Press, sports section, 1982; District 1 Newspaper, Battle Creek, MN, 1983. **BUSINESS ADDRESS:** Staff Scientist, Environmental Science & Engineering, Inc, 6280 Hazeltine National Dr, Orlando, FL 32822, (407)240-1288.

ATOJI, MASAO
Research scientist, editor. Japanese American. **PERSONAL:** Born Dec 21, 1925, Higashiosaka, Japan; son of Yoshinoyu Atoji and Kiyo Atoji; married Iris, May 18, 1957; children: Naomi Jean Atoji-Walker, Cynthia Ann Szubzda, David Masao. **EDUCATION:** Osaka University, BS 1948, PhD, 1956. **CAREER:** University of Minnesota, research associate, 1951-56; Iowa State University, assistant professor, 1956-60; Argonne National Laboratory, associate chemist, 1960-69, senior chemist, 1969-81; Litton Systems, Inc, senior staff chemist, 1981-83; Motorola Inc, senior staff chemist, 1984-87; Northwestern University, research scientist, 1988-90; American Chemical Society, Chemical Abstracts Service, associate editor, 1990-. **ORGANIZATIONS:** American Physical Society, life fellow, 1957-; Physical Society of Japan, life member, 1960-; American Chemical Society, 1957-; American Association for the Advancement of Science, 1958-; American Crystallographic Association, 1954-; Society for Applied Spectroscopy, 1984-; American Association of Crystal Growth, 1981-; Sigma Xi, life member, 1957-; American Translators Association, 1993. **HONORS/AWARDS:** American Physical Society, fellow, 1962; Osaka University, Yukawa Fellow, 1952; National Research Council, senior fellow, 1988; Phi Lambda Upsilon, 1953-. **SPECIAL ACHIEVEMENTS:** Fluent in Japanese; research in material science, neutron and x-ray diffraction, crystal and magnetic structure, semiconductor crystal growth and fabrication, metallurgy, superconductors; over 120 research publications quoted in over 3000 publications, 1950-. **HOME ADDRESS:** 702 86th Pl, Downers Grove, IL 60516, (708)985-1248. **BUSINESS ADDRESS:** Associate Editor, Chemical Abstracts Service, American Chemical Society, 2540 Olentangy River Rd, Columbus, OH 43210, (614)447-3600.

AU, ANDREW T.
Computer sales manager. Hong Kong American. **PERSONAL:** Born Mar 16, 1964, Hong Kong. **EDUCATION:** Western Illinois University, BBA, 1986. **CAREER:** Atlantic Computer Inc, computer sales manager, currently. **HOME ADDRESS:** 4002 Maxson Rd, #10, El Monte, CA 91732, (818)350-0228.

AU, CALVIN K.
Wholesale company executive. Hong Kong American. **PERSONAL:** Born Jan 8, 1948, Hong Kong; son of To-Sang Au and Ching-Yin Lee. **EDUCATION:** University of London, LLB, 1971. **CAREER:** Zabin Industries, Inc, vice president, currently.

AU, CHI-KWAN
Educator. Chinese American. **PERSONAL:** Born Jan 21, 1946, Macao; son of P C Au and Y H Wong; married Bernadette Au, Jul 31, 1970; children: Irene, Benjamin. **EDUCATION:** Hong Kong University, BSc, 1968; Columbia University, MA, 1970, PhD, 1972. **CAREER:** University of Illinois, research associate, 1972-74; Yale University, research associate, lecturer, 1974-75; University of South Carolina, professor, 1975-. **ORGANIZATIONS:** American Physical Society, 1970. **HONORS/AWARDS:** Am Physical Society, fellow, 1990; University of South Carolina, Education Foundation Award in Science & Engineering, 1985. **SPECIAL ACHIEVEMENTS:** Over 70 publications in refereed journals, 1972-. **BUSINESS ADDRESS:** Professor, Dept of Physics, University of South Carolina, S Main St, Columbia, SC 29208-0001.

AU, LEO YUIN
Bank executive. Chinese American. **PERSONAL:** Born Mar 15, 1949, New York, NY; son of Harry K Au and Yat Lai Au; married May S Au, Jun 18, 1977; children: Constance K, Christopher H. **EDUCATION:** Wesleyan University, BA, 1971; University of Chicago, AM, 1974; Harvard Business School, MBA, 1976. **CAREER:** Mellon Bank, vice president, 1982-84, portfolio and funds management, manager, senior vice president, 1984-. **HOME ADDRESS:** 2547 Longmount Dr, Wexford, PA 15090. **BUSINESS ADDRESS:** Senior Vice President, Mellon Bank, NA, One Mellon Bank Center, Rm 410, Pittsburgh, PA 15258.

AU, PATRICK SIU-KEE
Engineering firm executive. Chinese American. **PERSONAL:** Born Dec 10, 1941, Kowloon, Hong Kong; son of Chi-Ping Au and Yuen-Ching Wong; married Millie Lee Au, May 30, 1970; children: Angela Lee, Olivia Lee. **EDUCATION:** University of Illinois at Urbana-Champaign, BSCE, 1967; Rider College, MBA, 1973. **CAREER:** Parsons, Brinckerhoff, Quade & Douglas Inc, civil engr, 1967-72; Funk, Fletcher & Thompson Inc, project engr, 1972-76; Ewell, Bomhardt & Associates, sr project engr, 1976-77; Transviron Inc, vice pres, 1977-78; Kennedy, Porter & Associates, chief engr, 1978-79; Pullman Swindell Inc, project mgr, 1979-82; Pittsburgh Engineering Consul-

tants Inc, founder, president, 1982-. **ORGANIZATIONS:** American Society of Highway Engineers, dir, 1990-; Institute of Transportation Engineers, 1979-; American Society of Civil Engineers, 1967-; American Consulting Engineers Council, 1982-; The Bourse at Virginia Manor Assn, dir, 1987-; American Arbitration Assn, 1987-. **HONORS/AWARDS:** American Society of Highway Engineers, Distinguished Service Award, 1991; American Society of Civil Engineers, Distinguished Service Award, 1988. **SPECIAL ACHIEVEMENTS:** Licensed professional engineer in: New Jersey, Maryland, Pennsylvania, West Virginia. **BUSINESS ADDRESS:** President, Pittsburgh Engineering Consultants Inc, 2275 Swallow Hill Rd, Bldg 400, Pittsburgh, PA 15220, (412)276-8200.

AU, TUNG
Educator. Chinese American. **PERSONAL:** Born Sep 8, 1923, Hong Kong; son of Tung C Au & Fuk K Leung; married Isabel Szeto, Jun 18, 1955; children: Thomas P, Yolande Au Petersen. **EDUCATION:** St John's University, China, BS, civil engineering, 1943; University of Illinois, Urbana-Champaign, MS, civil engineering, 1948, PhD, civil engineering, 1951. **CAREER:** Engineering Consultants, Detroit, structural engineer, 1951-55; University of Detroit, assistant professor of engineering mechanics, 1955-57; Carnegie-Mellon University, associate professor of civil engineering, 1957-64, professor of civil engineering, 1964-92, professor of civil engineering emeritus, 1992-. **ORGANIZATIONS:** American Society of Civil Engineering, honorary member, 1990; American Society for Engineering Education; American Society for Testing Materials. **HONORS/AWARDS:** ASCE, Civil Engineering State-of-Art Award, 1973; ASEE, Western Electric Award, 1979, Centennial Medallion, 1993; Carnegie-Mellon University, Robert E Dougherty Award for Education Leadership, 1990. **SPECIAL ACHIEVEMENTS:** Coauthor, with Paul Christiano, Fundamentals of Structural Analysis, Prentice Hall, 1993; co-author with Thomas P Au, Engineering Economics for Captial Investment Analysis, second edition, Prentice Hall, 1992; co-author with Chris Hendrickson, Project Management for Construction, Prentice Hall, 1989. **HOME ADDRESS:** 1301 Stanley Dollar Dr, Apt 2, Walnut Creek, CA 94595.

AU, WILKIE WAI KEE
Priest, educator, counselor. Chinese American. **PERSONAL:** Born Jan 12, 1944, Honolulu, HI; son of T H Au and Violet Au. **EDUCATION:** Gonzaga University, BA, 1968; University of Southern California, MS, ed, 1972; University of California, Santa Barbara, PhD, 1976. **CAREER:** Loyola Marymount University, professor, 1988-, Jesuit Collegiate Program, 1976-81; Jesuit Novitiate, director, rector, 1982-88; Spiritual Development Services, director, 1992-. **HONORS/AWARDS:** College Theology Society, Book Award, 1990. **SPECIAL ACHIEVEMENTS:** Author, By Way of the Heart: Toward a Holistic Christian Spirituality, 1989. **HOME ADDRESS:** 7101 W 80th St, Los Angeles, CA 90045.

AULAKH, KAY
Engineering and construction company exective. Indo-American. **PERSONAL:** Born in Zeeburg, West Coast Demerara, Guyana; daughter of Ganesh Balbahadur; married Dave Aulakh, Nov 6, 1969; children: Vic, Nikki. **EDUCATION:** Catholic University of America, BS, 1986. **CAREER:** SMS Inc, pres, 1982-85; EMS Travel Inc, pres, 1990-93; Engineering Management Services, pres, 1985-. **ORGANIZATIONS:** ARTA, Natl. Cap Area Chap president, 1992-; National Association of Women Business Owners, county chair, 1990-; ASTA; CTO; IATA. **BUSINESS ADDRESS:** President, Engineering Management Services, Inc, 9905 Georgetown Pike, Ste #202, Great Falls, VA 22066, (703)759-1614.

AVIADO, DOMINGO M.
Pharmacologist. Filipino American. **PERSONAL:** Born Aug 28, 1924, Manila, Philippines; son of Domingo Gatus Aviado & Sevirina Ong Mariano; married Asuncion Guevara Aviado, Aug 15, 1953; children: Maria Cristina Gentile, Carlos Guevara, Domingo Guevara, Maria Asuncion. **EDUCATION:** University of Pennsylvania Medical School, MD, 1948. **CAREER:** University of Pennsylvania, instructor to professor of pharmacology, 1948-77; Allied Chemical Inc, senior research director, 1977-79; Atmospheric Health Sciences, research director, 1980-. **ORGANIZATIONS:** International Union of Pharmacology, treasurer, 1959-65; Academy of Medicine of New Jersey, fellow, 1971-; 10 professional organizations. **HONORS/AWARDS:** Guggenheim Foundation, fellow, 1962-63. **SPECIAL ACHIEVEMENTS:** Author of 7 books on pharmacology and toxicology; over 300 publications on pharmacology and toxicology. **BUSINESS ADDRESS:** Research Director, Atmospheric

Health Sciences, 225 Hartshorn Dr, Short Hills, NJ 07078-3225, (201)564-9156.

AWAKUNI, GENE I.
Educational administrator. Japanese American. **EDUCATION:** University of Hawaii at Manoa, BA, political science, MSW; Harvard University, EdD, EdM, counseling and consulting psychology. **CAREER:** VA Hospital in Hawaii, psychiatric social worker; Salem State College, counselor; Tufts University, Asian American Center, director; University of California Irvine, Counseling Center, director; University of California Santa Barbara, Student Academic Services, asst vice chancellor; California State Polytechnic University, Pomona, Student Affairs, vice president, 1993-. **ORGANIZATIONS:** University of California's Student Affirmative Action Committee. **BUSINESS ADDRESS:** VP for Student Affairs, California State Polytechnic University, Pomona, 3801 W Temple Ave, Pomona, CA 91768, (909)869-3418.*

AZIZ, KHALID
Educator. Pakistani American. **PERSONAL:** Born Sep 29, 1936, McLeod G Road, Bahwalpur, Pakistan; son of Aziz Ul Hassan and Rashida Hassan; married Mussarrat Aziz, Nov 12, 1962; children: Natasha, Imraan. **EDUCATION:** University of Michigan, BSE, 1955; University of Alberta, BSc, 1958, MSc, 1961; Rice University, PhD, 1966. **CAREER:** University of Calgary, professor of chem & petroleum eng, 1965-82; Stanford University, earth sciences, associate dean, 1983-86, chairman of petroleum eng, 1986-91, professor of petroleum eng, 1982-. **ORGANIZATIONS:** Society of Petroleum Engineers; Society for Industrial and Applied Mathematics; American Institute of Chemical Engineers; Association of Professional Engineers, Geologists and Geophysicsts. **HONORS/AWARDS:** Chemical Institute of Canada, fellow, 1974; Petroleum Society of CIM, Distinguished Service Award, 1975; University of Calgary, Killam Resident Fellow, 1977; Society of Petroleum Engineers, Ferguson Award, 1979, Distinguished Member, 1983, Reservoir Engineering Award, 1987, Lecter C Uren Award, 1988; Stanford University, Otto N Miller Professorship, 1989; SPE, Distinguished Achievement Award for Petroleum Engineering Faculty, 1990; Pi Epsilon Tau, Diploma of Honor, 1991. **SPECIAL ACHIEVEMENTS:** Over 170 publications; Petroleum Reservoir Simulation, Applied Science, 1979; Flow of Complex Mixtures in Pipes, Van Nostrand, 1972; Petroleum Society of CIM, Gradient Curves for Well Analysis and Design, 1979. **BUSINESS ADDRESS:** Professor of Petroleum Engineering, Stanford University, Green Earth Sciences Building, Stanford, CA 94305-2170, (415)723-9116.

AZUMANO, GEORGE ICHIRO
Travel agency executive. Japanese American. **PERSONAL:** Born Jun 9, 1918, Portland, OR; son of Hatsutaro Azumano and Satsuki Azumano; married Nobuko Azumano, Mar 21, 1976; children: Loen, Dozono, James Forest, Bette Jo Orazio. **EDUCATION:** University of Oregon, BS, 1940. **CAREER:** Azumano Insurance Agency, partner, 1946-93, Azumano Travel Service, Inc, chairman of the board, 1949-93. **ORGANIZATIONS:** American Society of Travel Agents, 1960-94; Independent Insurance Agents of Oregon, past board member, 1955-; Japanese American Citizens League, past president, 1947; Japanese Ancestral Society of Portland, past president, 1976-78; Rotary Club of Portland, past board member, 1965-; United Methodist Church, Conference, lay leader, 1991-; United Methodist Church, general board of pensions, 1980-88; Willamette University, board of trustees, 1988-94; St Vincent Hospital & Medical Center, advisory board, 1991-94; Small Business Administration, Oregon State Advisory Board, 1976-79; Japanese American National Museum, board of trustees, 1990-94; Oregon Museum of Science and Industry, bd of trustees, 1991-94. **HONORS/AWARDS:** Govt of Japan, Fourth Class Order of Rising Sun, 1983. **MILITARY SERVICE:** Infantry, private 1st class, 1941-42. **HOME PHONE:** (503)774-0609. **BUSINESS ADDRESS:** Chairman of the Board, Azumano Travel Services, Inc, 320 SW Stark, Ste 600, Portland, OR 97204, (503)223-6245.

AZUMAYA, GORO
Mathematician. Japanese American. **PERSONAL:** Born Feb 26, 1920, Yokohama, Japan; son of Soshichi Azumaya and Haruko Azumaya; married Mutsuko Azumaya; children: Hidehiko. **EDUCATION:** Tokyo University, Japan, BS, rigakushi, 1942; Nagoya University, Japan, PhD, rigaku-hakushi, 1949. **CAREER:** Nagoya University, Japan, research assistant, 1942-45, lecturer, 1945-48, assistant professor, 1948-53; Hokkaido University, Japan, professor, 1953-68; Indiana University, professor, 1968-90, professor emeritus, currently. **ORGANIZATIONS:** Mathematical Society of Japan, 1946-; American Mathematical Society, 1959-. **HONORS/AWARDS:** Chubu News Paper

Co, Japan, Chunichi Cultural Prize, 1949. **SPECIAL ACHIEVEMENTS:** Author, "Corrections and Supplementaries to My Paper Concerning K-R-S Theorem," Nagoya Math Journal, vol 1, 1950; "On Maximally Central Algebras," Nagoya Math Journal, vol 2, 1951; "A Duality Theory for Injective Modules," American Journal of Math, vol 81, 1959; "Completely Faithful Modules and Self-Injective Rings," Nagoya Math Journal, vol 27, 1966; "Separable Rings," Journal of Algebra, vol 63, 1980; "Exact and Serial Rings," Journal of Algebra, vol 85, 1983; "F-Semi-perfect Modules," Journal of Algebra, vol 136, 1991; "A Characterization of Semi-perfect Rings and Modules," Ring Theory, Proceedings of Ohio State Conference, World Scientific, 1993. **BIOGRAPHICAL SOURCES:** "The Brauer Group of a Commutative Ring," by M Auslander & O Goldman, Trans AMS, vol 97, p 368, 1960; "Algebra II Ring Theory," by C Faith, Springer-Verlag, 191, chapter 21, p 142, 1976; Rings and Categories of Modules, by W Anderson & K R Fuller, Springer-Verlag, second edition, pp 144, 327, 331, 1991. **BUSINESS ADDRESS:** Professor Emeritus, Dept of Mathematics, Indiana University, 3rd St, Rawles Hall, Bloomington, IN 47405.

B

BACHO, NORRIS V.
Government official. Filipino American. **PERSONAL:** Born Mar 29, 1954, Seattle, WA; son of Vincent de la Victoria Bacho & Remedios Abella Bacho. **EDUCATION:** University of Washington, BA, 1978, Graduate School, research and teaching assistantship, 1980; Seattle University, MBA program, 1990-. **CAREER:** Seattle City Council, legislative intern, 1979-80; City of Seattle, Comm & Human Dev Housing Neighborhood Dev, community planner, 1980-83, Finance Econ Dev Retail Business Improvement, project mgr, 1983-88; Westlake Center, The Rouse Company, manager of retail operations, 1988-91; City of Tacoma, planning and development services director, 1991-. **ORGANIZATIONS:** Harborview Medical Center, board of trustees, 1983-, vice president, 1990-91, president, 1992, past president, 1993, 1994; Washington State Downtown Association, 1987-88; Seattle Crisis Clinic, 1983-87; Seattle Emergency Housing Service, 1983-86; King County Airport Noise Advisory Commission, 1982-83; Municipal League of Seattle Candidate Evaluation Committee, 1981; University of Washington, board of control, 1973; International District Improvement Association, 1973. **HONORS/AWARDS:** The Rouse Company, Volunteer Recognition Program, 1990; State of Washington, Governor's Award, 1985; Filipino Youth Activities Monondanao Raya, Youth of the Year, 1970; Serra Club, 1968. **SPECIAL ACHIEVEMENTS:** US Department of Housing and Urban Development, Comm Fellows Graduate School Fellowship, 1978; Harborview Medical Center Board of Trustees, president, 1992; completed Athens, Greece, International Marathon, 1983; climbed Mt Rainier, 14,426 ft, 1986. **BUSINESS ADDRESS:** Director, Planning and Development Services, City of Tacoma, 747 Market St, Rm 1036, Tacoma, WA 98402-3768.

BACHO, PETER
Author, educator, attorney. Filipino American. **CAREER:** Teacher, journalist, attorney. **HONORS/AWARDS:** Before Columbus Foundation, American Book Award, 1992; San Francisco Bay Area Book Festival, 1992. **SPECIAL ACHIEVEMENTS:** Author, Cebu, University of Washington Press, 1991; a collection of stories, forthcoming. **BUSINESS ADDRESS:** Author, Cebu, University of Washington Press, PO Box 50096, Seattle, WA 98145-5096, (206)543-4050.*

BAGASAO, PAULA Y.
Government official. Filipino American. **EDUCATION:** UCLA, BA, cultural geography, MEd. **CAREER:** University of California-Systemwide, Academic Affirmative Action, director; Dept of Education, Culture and Sports, Dept of Foreign Affairs, Dept of Science and Technology, adviser in Philippines, 1991-92; PYB Associates, consultant, principal, currently; Office of Presidential Personnel, personnel manager, currently. **ORGANIZATIONS:** TOKTEN Program, UNDP consultant; New York Science and Technology Advisory Council; American Assn for Higher Education, Asian Pacific American Caucus, former chairperson. **SPECIAL ACHIEVEMENTS:** Institute for Education Leadership, first Asian American woman fellow; former President Jimmy Carter's Presidential Administration, Natl Institute of Education, appointed special asst to deputy director, 1980-81; Filipino Intercollegiate Networking Dialogue third annual conference, speaker. **BUSINESS ADDRESS:** Manager, Office of Presidential Personnel, White House Personnel Office, 1600 Pennsylvania Ave NW, Washington, DC 20500, (202)647-1835.*

BAGASRA, OMAR
Physician, scientist. Indo-American. **PERSONAL:** Born Oct 9, 1948, India; son of Amina Habib & Habib Ahmed; married Theresa R Bagasra, May 22, 1977; children: Alexander Umar, Anisah Beth. **EDUCATION:** University of Karachi, Pakistan, BSc, microbiology, 1968, MSc, biochemistry, 1970; University of Louisville, PhD, 1979; Univ of Autonoma de Cid Juarez, MD, 1985. **CAREER:** Hahnemann University, assistant professor, associate professor, 1980-87; Agha Khan University, Pakistan, visiting professor, 1987; University of Medicine & Dentistry of New Jersey, associate professor of microbiology, 1987-90; St Christopher's Hospital for Children, associate director of clinical immunology, 1990-91; O'Brien-Kreitzberg Research & Development, chief molecular biology consultant, 1990-; Temple University School of Medicine, research associate professor, 1990-91, adjunct associate professor, 1991-; Thomas Jefferson University, associate professor, director, molecular retrovirology lab, 1991-. **ORGANIZATIONS:** American Association of Immunologists, 1983-; American Society for Advancement of Science, 1985-; American Society for Clinical Immunology, 1987-; International AIDS Society, 1988-; Research Society of Alcoholism, 1989-; Academy of Medicine of New Jersey, 1989-; American Board of Medical Lab Immunology, diplomate, 1993-. **HONORS/AWARDS:** University of Louisville, Graduate Student Fellowship. **SPECIAL ACHIEVEMENTS:** Animal model of human venereal and congenital syphilis, Am J Path, vol 126, p 599-601, 1987; Anti-human immunodeficiency virus activity of dextran sulfate and other polysaccharides, J Inf Diseases, vol 158, p 1084-87, 1988; Tar-independent replication of HIV-1 in glial cells, J Virology, vol 66, p 7522-28, 1992; numerous others. **BUSINESS ADDRESS:** Director, Molecular Retrovisology Labs, Thomas Jefferson University, 1020 Locust St, Jefferson Hall, #328A, Philadelphia, PA 19107.

BAGGA, K. JAY SINGH
Educator. Indo-American. **PERSONAL:** Born Nov 8, 1952, Dehradun, Uttar Pradesh, India; son of Sunder Singh Bagga and Lajwanti Bagga; married Daljit Kaur Bagga, Nov 27, 1974; children: Amrita K, Jasdeep S. **EDUCATION:** Bombay University, BS, 1972; Purdue University, MS, 1977, PhD, 1984; Ball State University, MS, 1989. **CAREER:** Indiana-Purdue University, asst professor, 1984-88, associate professor, 1988-89; Ball State University, Dept of Computer Science, professor of computer sciences, 1989-. **ORGANIZATIONS:** Assn of Computing Machinery, 1989-; Math Assn of America, 1984-; IEEE Computer Society, 1990-. **HONORS/AWARDS:** Office of Naval Research, Research Grants, 1986-89, 1991-93; Ball State University, Summer Grant, 1990. **SPECIAL ACHIEVEMENTS:** Publications: in journals, Discrete Math, 1992; Congressus Numerantium, 1988-92; in conference proceedings, 1984-92; presentations at national and international conferences, 1984-93. **BUSINESS ADDRESS:** Professor, Dept of Computer Science, Ball State University, Muncie, IN 47306.

BAHAL, SURENDRA MOHAN
Research scientist. Indo-American. **PERSONAL:** Born Jul 1, 1935, Lyallpur, India; son of S N Bahal & S D Bahal; married Chander Kanta Bahal, May 5, 1961; children: Neeta Bahal O'Mara, Neelam. **EDUCATION:** University of Bombay, India, BS (w/ honors), 1954, BScTech, pharmacy, 1956, MScTech, pharmacy, 1959; Temple University, PhD, pharmacy, 1965. **CAREER:** Wyeth Ayerst Research, 1964-88; E I Du Pont de Nemours & Company Inc, 1988-90; Du Pont Merck Pharmacy Company, research manager, 1991-. **ORGANIZATIONS:** American Association of Pharmaceutical Scientists; Parenteral Drug Association, 1988-; Philadelphia Pharmaceutical Forum; Rho Chi Society, 1964-. **HONORS/AWARDS:** Lunsford Richardson Pharmacy Award, Eastern Region, 1965; Pharmaceutical Research Discussion Group, Outstanding Research Industrial Pharmacy Publication, 1970. **SPECIAL ACHIEVEMENTS:** Author, "Kinetic Analysis of Complex Formation between Penicillin and Sucrose," Journal of Pharm Science, vol 62, p 267, 1973; "Binding of Salicylate to Crystalline Bovine Serum Albumin and to Fraction V Bovine Serum Albumin," Journal of Pharm Science, vol 59, p 1047, 1970; "Effect of the pH of Precipitation on the Antacid Properties of Hydrous Aluminum Oxide," Journal of Pharm Science, vol 59, p 317, 1970; "Kinetics of Hydrous Aluminum Oxide Conversion in Mixtures of Amorphous Alumina Gels of Various Acid Reactivities," Journal of Pharm Science, vol 59, p 376, 1970; various other publications; several US patents. **BUSINESS ADDRESS:** Research Manager, Du Pont Merck Pharmaceutical Company, Experimental Station, E400/1243, Wilmington, DE 19880-0400, (302)695-7566.

BAHL, OM PARKASH
Educator. Indo-American. **PERSONAL:** Born Jan 10, 1927, Lyallpur, Punjab, India; son of Daulet R Bahl and Hira D Tejkaur Bahl; married Nirmal Nanda,

Oct 8, 1952; children: Vinita, Vikram, Meanakshi. **EDUCATION:** Govt College, India, BS, 1942; Punjab University, India, MS, 1950; University of Minnesota, PhD, 1962. **CAREER:** Arya College, India, chemistry lecturer, 1950-52; Govt College, India, chem lecturer, 1952-57; University of Minnesota, res assoc, 1962-63; UCLA, res assoc, 1963-64; University of Southern California, Dernham Fellow, American Cancer Soc, asst prof, biochem, 1965-66; SUNY, Buffalo, Dept of Biochem, asst prof, 1966-68, assoc prof, 1968-71, prof, 1971-74, Div of Cell & Molecular Biology, prof, 1974-77, Dept of Biol, chairman, prof, 1976-86, prof, 1983-. **ORGANIZATIONS:** American Soc Biol Chemists, 1968-; Amer Chemical Soc, 1966-; British Biochem Soc, 1963-; NY Academy of Sciences, 1963-; Endocrine Soc, 1968-; Amer Soc Cell Biology, 1980-. **HONORS/AWARDS:** Indian Govt, Presidential Medal (Padam Bhushan), 1973; Pres U Liege, Medal, 1971; Natl Council Asian Indian Orgs in N America, Med & Life Sci Award, 1982; NIH, grants, 1966-; WHO, grants, 1977-83; Amer Chemical Soc, Schoelkopf Award, 1978. **SPECIAL ACHIEVEMENTS:** Research program involves structure & function relationships in human hCG & its receptor; aims of program are studies on structure & function relationships of gonadotropins, including preparation & characterization of recombinant selenomethionyl hCG on large scale to obtain x-ray diffraction grade crystals for 3-dimensional structural analysis; recombinant unglycosylated hCG, & its alpha & beta subunits to resolve questions of carbohydrate role in function of hCG & selenomethionyl unglycosylated hCG; polypeptide & carbohydrate chains of rhCG & its subunits; rhCG, alpha and beta, on large scale for further evaluation of their in vivo biological properties; carbohydrate mutants of hCG alpha & beta in baculovirus expression system to evaluate contribution of individual N-linked carbohydrate to function of hCG; over 110 publications. **HOME ADDRESS:** 110 Heritage West, Williamsville, NY 14221, (716)688-2379. **BUSINESS ADDRESS:** Professor, Dept of Biological Sciences, State University of NY at Buffalo, 347 Cooke Hall, Buffalo, NY 14260, (716)645-2525.

BAI, SHEN HUM
Engineer. Chinese American. **PERSONAL:** Born Nov 1, 1932, Soochow, Kiangsu, China; son of Youyu Bai and Chung Ing Suen; married Woo Jok Yong Bai, 1958; children: Frederico N, Peter. **EDUCATION:** University of Toledo, BSME, 1974. **CAREER:** Doehler Jarvis, DHQ, manager, equipment engineering; Doehler Jarvis, Pottstown, engineering manager; Doehler Jarvis, DHQ, manager of advanced engineering, director advanced engineering, currently. **ORGANIZATIONS:** SAE; NADCA; AFS; SME. **SPECIAL ACHIEVEMENTS:** Fluent in Chinese, Portuguese, and English. **HOME ADDRESS:** 1771 Sandoval Ln, Huntington Beach, CA 92647, (714)841-5473.

BAI, TAEIL ALBERT
Research scientist. Korean American. **PERSONAL:** Born Jul 16, 1945, Chung-Chun-Li, Chollanamdo, Republic of Korea; son of Jong-hun Bai and Soo-bong Suh Bai; married Sue; children: Samuel, Jean, Helen. **EDUCATION:** Kyung Hee University, Korea, BS, 1967; University of Maryland, MS, 1974, PhD, 1977. **CAREER:** University of Maryland, research associate, 1977-78; University of California, San Diego, post graduate scientist, 1978-81, assistant research scientist, 1981-82; Stanford University, senior research scientist, 1982-. **ORGANIZATIONS:** American Physical Society; American Astronomical Society; American Geophysical Union, American Association for Advancement of Science. **HONORS/AWARDS:** University of Colorado, Donald E Billings Award, 1978. **SPECIAL ACHIEVEMENTS:** Discovery of the Solar Fundamental Period of 25.5 Days, 1992; Discovery of Hot Spots for Solar Activity, 1988; Foundation of the Northern California Korean Coalition, 1991; publication of more than 40 professsional papers, 1975-. **BUSINESS ADDRESS:** Senior Scientist, Center for Space Science & Astrophysics, Stanford University, ERL Bldg, Stanford, CA 94305, (415)723-1386.

BAJAJ, HARJIT SINGH
Travel agency executive. Indo-American. **PERSONAL:** Born Mar 19, 1956, New Delhi, Delhi, India; son of Jaswant S Bajaj and Raj Kaur Bajaj; married Harinder Bajaj, May 23, 1992. **EDUCATION:** Delhi University, BCom, 1978, PG, tourism, 1980. **CAREER:** Sita World Travel, travel supervisor, 1981-83; Travel Center, manager, 1983-87; Shoppers Travel Inc, president, 1987-. **ORGANIZATIONS:** American Society of Travel Agents, 1990-; International Assn of Travel Agents, 1989-. **BUSINESS ADDRESS:** President, Shoppers Travel Inc, 303 Fifth Ave, Suite 705, New York, NY 10016, (212)779-8800.

BAJPAI, PRAPHULLA KUMAR
Educator. Indo-American. **PERSONAL:** Born Sep 24, 1936, Charkhari, Uttar Pradesh, India; son of Tarak Nath Bajpai and Eshwar Devi Bajpai; married

Robin Ann Bodiker, May 28, 1966; children: Raina, Kiran, Malia. **EDUCATION:** Agra University, India, BVSc, AH, 1958, MVSc, AH, 1960; Ohio State University, MSc, 1963, PhD, 1965. **CAREER:** University of Michigan, research associate, 1972-73; Wright State University, adjunct associate professor, 1975-78, adjunct professor, 1978-; University of Dayton, instructor, 1964-66, assistant professor, 1966-70, associate professor, 1970-78, professor, 1978-. **ORGANIZATIONS:** Rocky Mountain Bioengineering Symposium, board of directors, 1993; Academy of Surgical Research, chairman/program committee, 1991, 1992; Society for Biomaterials & Artificial Organs, India, executive council, 1990-; Southern Biomedical Engineering Conference, steering committee, 1991-; Academy of Surgical Research, board of directors, 1986-92; Society for Biomaterials, Awards Committee, US chairman, 1984-86; Society for Study of Reproduction, Placement Service Committee, 1983-85; Ohio Academy of Sciences, medical program committee, chairman, 1969; Trends in Biomaterials & Artificial Organs, editorial board, 1990-. **HONORS/AWARDS:** Academy of Surgical Research, Andreas F von Recum Award, 1993; Society for Biomaterials & Artificial Organs, India, C P Sharma Award, 1992; Southern Biomedical Engineering Conference, C William Hall Research Award, 1990; National Research Council, Senior Research Associate Award, 1990-91; Engineering and Science Foundation, Dayton, OH, Outstanding Engineers & Science Award, 1987. **SPECIAL ACHIEVEMENTS:** Journal of Applied Biomaterials, assistant editor, 1986-; Trends in Biomaterials & Artificial Organs, associate editor, 1986-90; Journal of Investigative Surgery, associate editor, 1991-; Journal of Biomedical Materials Research, editorial board, 1981-. **BUSINESS ADDRESS:** Professor, University of Dayton, 300 College Pk, Sherman Hall, Dayton, OH 45469-2320, (513)229-3029.

BAJPAI, RAKESH KUMAR

Educator. Indo-American. **PERSONAL:** Born Dec 24, 1950, Kanpur, Uttar Pradesh, India; married Sunita Bajpai, Mar 10, 1977; children: Ambareesh, Ashish. **EDUCATION:** Harcourt Butler Technological Institute, BS, chemical engineering, 1969; Indian Institute of Technology, MTech, chemical engineering, 1972, PhD, 1976. **CAREER:** Indian Institute of Technology, Kanpur, research assistant, 1970-76; Indian Institute of Technology, New Delhi, lecturer, 1976-78; Institute fuer Garungsgewerbe und Biotechnology, wissenschaftlicher mitarbeiter, 1979-82; University of Missouri, assistant professor, 1982-86, associate professor, 1986-93, professor, 1993-. **ORGANIZATIONS:** American Chemical Society, 1980-; American Institute of Chemical Engineers, 1983-. **HONORS/AWARDS:** UNESCO/WHO, postgraduate fellowship, 1973; Eth-Zurich, postdoctoral fellowship, 1978. **SPECIAL ACHIEVEMENTS:** Author of over 40 refereed publications; 100 publications; editor/co-editor of 2 books; member editorial board for the Journal of Microbial Biotechnology. **BUSINESS ADDRESS:** Professor, University of Missouri, W 2030 Engineering Building East, Columbia, MO 65211, (314)882-3708.

BAK, CHAN SOO

Scientist. Korean American. **PERSONAL:** Born Jun 15, 1936, Kangjin, Chunnam, Republic of Korea; son of Jong Suk Bak and Sam Yang Choi; married Kyung Ja Bak, Jun 15, 1966; children: James H, David H. **EDUCATION:** Seoul National University, BS, 1959; University of Pittsburgh, PhD, 1970. **CAREER:** State University of New York, Stony Brook, research associate, 1970-72; University of Massachusetts, research associate, 1972-73; Temple University, research associate, 1973-76; Spectro-Systems, Inc, senior physicist, 1976-80; Hughes Aircraft Company, technical staff, 1980-. **ORGANIZATIONS:** Materials Research Society; Society for Information Display; Society of Phot-Optical Instrumentation Engineers; American Physical Society; Sigma Xi. **HONORS/AWARDS:** Hughes Aircraft Company, 13 Invention Awards, 1980-92, 5 Patent Application Awards, 1989-92. **SPECIAL ACHIEVEMENTS:** Patent, "Thermal Indicator for Wells," US 4390291, 1983; "Method of Fabricating Anisometric Metal Needles and Birefringent Suspension Thereof in Dielectric Fluid," US 5179993, 1993; 4 patents pending; 18 publications. **MILITARY SERVICE:** Korean Air Force, first lieutenant, 1960-64. **HOME ADDRESS:** 641 N Lois Avenue, Newbury Park, CA 91320, (805)498-2518.

BALACHANDRAN, KASHI RAMAMURTHI

Educator. Indo-American. **PERSONAL:** Born Jun 16, 1941, Madras, Tamil Nadu, India; son of K S Ramamurthi and Rukmani Ramamurthi; married Rajini Sarma Balachandran, Jul 13, 1969; children: Siddharth Kashi, Sumitra Kashi. **EDUCATION:** University of Madras, India, BE (honors), 1962; University of California, Berkeley, MS, 1964, PhD, 1968. **CAREER:** The National Cash Register Co, research analyst, 1967-68; University of Wisconsin-Milwaukee,

assistant professor, 1968-72; Georgia Institute of Technology, associate professor, 1972-76; University of Kentucky, associate professor, 1976-79; New York University, professor and doctoral program director, 1979-. **ORGANIZATIONS:** Wisconsin Governor's Commission on Education, 1969-70; Opsearch Journal, associate editor, 1973-84; Journal of Accounting, Auditing and Finance, associate editor, 1986-. **SPECIAL ACHIEVEMENTS:** Author of more than 50 articles in professional and scholarly journals, 1968-. **HOME ADDRESS:** 4 Tracy Rd, East Brunswick, NJ 08816, (908)390-1795. **BUSINESS ADDRESS:** Prof of Operations Mgmt & Acctg Info, New York University, 40 W 4th St, 434 Tisch Hall, New York, NY 10003, (212)998-0029.

BALAGURU, PERUMALSAMY N.

Educator. Indo-American. **PERSONAL:** Born Mar 26, 1947, Tamil Nadu, India; son of Perumal Samy & Gengammal; married Surya Prabha Balaguru, Jun 6, 1974; children: Balasoundhari, Balamuralee. **EDUCATION:** University of Madras, BE (with honors), 1968; Indian Institute of Science, ME, 1970; University of Illinois, Chicago, PhD, 1977. **CAREER:** University of Madras, associate lecturer, 1970-73; Rutgers The State University of New Jersey, professor, 1977-. **ORGANIZATIONS:** American Society of Civil Engineers, 1978-; American Concoret Institute, 1977-; Tau Beta Pi; Xi Epsilon. **HONORS/AWARDS:** Rutgers Parents Association, Outstanding Teacher, 1993; Civil Engineering Students, Teacher of the Year, 1981. **SPECIAL ACHIEVEMENTS:** Book, Fiber Reinforced Cement Composites, McGraw Hill, 1992; edited book on computers for Quality Control of Concrete, ACI; author, 9 book chapters, 60 journal papers, 40 proceeding papers, 30 reports, 70 presentations; ACI Committee 549 on Ferrocement, chairman; member of four other technical committees on concrete. **BUSINESS ADDRESS:** Professor, Dept of Civil Engineering, Rutgers The State University, Box 909, Piscataway, NJ 08855-0909, (909)932-2232.

BALDONADO, ARDELINA ALBANO

Educator. Filipino American. **PERSONAL:** Born in Ilocus Norte, Philippines; daughter of Jovita Acosta Albano & Rosalino Albano; married Alfredo Baldonado, Jan 2, 1963; children: Rozelda, Mark, Erika. **EDUCATION:** BS, nursing, 1959, MS, 1965, PhD, 1982. **CAREER:** Northwestern University, nursing faculty, 1965-70; James Ward Throne School of Nursing; St Francis Hospital School of Nursing, nursing faculty chairman, 1971-73; University of Illinois, Chicago, nursing faculty, 1973-76; Loyola University, chairperson, medical surgical nursing, 1990-92, assistant dean, director of undergraduate program, 1984-88, associate professor, 1976-. **ORGANIZATIONS:** Philippine Nurses Association of Chicago, vice president, board of directors; American Nurses Association; American Educational Research Association; Midwest Nursing Research. **HONORS/AWARDS:** University of the Philippines, MS Scholar; Santo Tomas University, college scholar; Sigma Theta Tau. **BUSINESS ADDRESS:** Associate Professor, School of Nursing, Loyola University, Chicago, 6525 N Sheridan Rd, Damen Hall, Rm 435-D, Chicago, IL 60626, (312)508-3258.

BALDOZ, GERALD L.

Public administrator. Filipino American. **PERSONAL:** Born Nov 10, 1948, Yakima, WA; son of Primo D Baldoz and Helen I Baldoz; married Deborah A Baldoz, Feb 14, 1992; children: Angelina T. **EDUCATION:** Yakima Valley Community College, 1975-76. **CAREER:** Hotel Roosevelt, food & beverage manager, 1969-72; Hotel Sorrento, food & beverage manager, 1972-75; self employed, farmer, 1980-82; Yakima County Courthouse, asst director, 1975-80, contract manager, 1982-. **ORGANIZATIONS:** Yakima County Homeless Coalition, board of directors, 1990-93; Washington State Dept of Social & Health Services Advisory Committee, board member, 1989-93; Fil-American Intercommunity Council of Pacific NW, vice president, 1986-87; Fil-American Community of Yakima Valley, president, 1986-87, board of directors, 1985, 1988, 1990. **BUSINESS ADDRESS:** Contracts Manager, Yakima County Courthouse, 630 E Yakima Ave, Yakima, WA 98901, (509)575-4252.

BALIGA, JAYANT

Educator, educational administrator. Indo-American. **PERSONAL:** Born Apr 28, 1948, Madras, India; son of B Vittal Baliga and Sanjivi Baliga; married Pratima Baliga, Dec 25, 1975; children: Avinash, Vinay. **EDUCATION:** Indian Institute of Technology, Madras, BTech, 1969; Rensselaer Polytechnic Institute, MS, 1971, PhD, 1974. **CAREER:** GE-CRD, staff member, 1974-79, Power Device & IC Programs, manager, 1979-88; NCSU, Elec & Comp Engineering, professor, 1988-, Power Semiconductor Research Center, director, 1991-. **ORGANIZATIONS:** IEEE, fellow, 1983-; ISPSD, chairman, 1993, vice chairman, 1992, technical program chairman, 1991. **HONORS/**

AWARDS: National Academy of Engineering, elected to membership, 1993; IEEE, Morris Liebman Award, 1993, William Newell Award, 1991; BSS, Pride of India Award, 1992; Science Digest Magazine, Among 100 Brightest Young Scientists in America, 1985. **SPECIAL ACHIEVEMENTS:** Author/editor of 5 books; co-author, more than 300 publications; more than 60 patents; contributed chapters to 12 books/encyclopaedias. **BUSINESS ADDRESS:** Director, Power Semiconductor Research Center, Professor, North Carolina State University, Capability Drive, Research II, Room 200, Raleigh, NC 27695-7924, (919)515-6169.

BANADA-TAN, LETICIA
Reference librarian. Filipino American. **PERSONAL:** Born Oct 29, 1950, Cagayan, Philippines; daughter of Catalino Bugan Banada and Geronima Casauay Banada; married Cleofer Go Tan, Mar 31, 1977. **EDUCATION:** University of the East, BSE, library science, 1971; University of the Philippines, MLS, 1978. **CAREER:** University of the Philippines, library aide, 1971-74; Mindanao State University, Philippines, reference librarian, 1974-82; FIDM, reference librarian, 1989-91; Los Angeles County Public Library, Norwalk Regional Library, reference librarian, 1991-. **ORGANIZATIONS:** American Library Association; California Library Association. **HONORS/AWARDS:** Mindanao State University, Philippines, Staff Development Program, 1976-78. **BUSINESS ADDRESS:** Reference Librarian, Norwalk Regional Library, 12350 E Imperial Highway, Norwalk, CA 90650, (310)868-0775.

BANAKAR, UMESH VIRUPAKSH
Educator. Indo-American. **PERSONAL:** Born Dec 4, 1956, Solapur, Maharashtra, India; son of Virupaksh T Banakar and Asha V Banakar; married Suneeta U Banakar, May 4, 1984; children: Kapil U. **EDUCATION:** Sangameshwar College, Solapur, India, int science, 1975; Goa College of Pharmacy, Bombay University, India, BPharm, 1978; Duquesne University, PhD, 1985. **CAREER:** Roussel Pharmaceuticals Ltd, Bombay, India, product chemist, 1978-79; JN Medical College, School of Pharmacy, Belgaum, India, lecturer, 1980; Duquesne University, School of Pharmacy, instructor, 1981-84; Creighton University, School of Pharmacy, assistant professor, 1985-87, associate professor, 1988-90; St Louis College of Pharmacy, director of research, 1990-, associate professor, 1990-. **ORGANIZATIONS:** AAPS, 1988-; APhA, 1985-; AACP, 1985-; Controlled Release Society, 1990-; International Society of Technology Assessment in Healthcare, 1991-; Phi Beta Alpha, 1990-; Rho Chi, chapter adviser, 1986-; Sigma Xi, 1986-. **HONORS/AWARDS:** International Executive Service Corps, service to country, 1992; Creighton University, School of Pharmacy, Achievement in Research & Scholastic Activity, 1990; Health Futures Foundation, Faculty Development Award, 1986, 1989; Rho Chi, Excellence in Teaching, 1988; Kappa Psi, Dr Ellerbeck Memorial Award, 1988. **SPECIAL ACHIEVEMENTS:** Specialized Drug Delivery Systems, Pharm Press of Slovenia, 1993; Pharmaceutical Dissolution Testing, Marcel Dekker, Inc, New York, 1992; Pharmaceutics I & II, Varsity Press, Omaha, NE, 1986. **HOME ADDRESS:** 803 Barbara Ann Ln, Ballwin, MO 63021, (314)256-2494. **BUSINESS ADDRESS:** Director of Research, Associate Professor of Pharmaceutics, St Louis College of Pharmacy, 4588 Parkview Pl, St Louis, MO 63110, (314)367-8700.

BANERJEE, AMIYA KUMAR
Research scientist. Indo-American. **PERSONAL:** Born May 3, 1936, Rangoon, Burma; son of Phanindra N & Bibhati Banerjee; married Sipra Banerjee, Jan 23, 1965; children: Antara, Arjun. **EDUCATION:** Presidency College, India, BSc (honors), chemistry, 1955; Calcutta University, India, MSc, biochemistry, 1958, PhD, biochemistry, 1964, DSc, science, 1970. **CAREER:** Roche Institute of Molecular Biology, Dept of Cell Biology, staff associate, 1969-71, assistant member, 1971-74, associate member, 1974-80, full member, 1980-87; Cleveland Clinic Foundation, Dept of Molecular Biology, chairman, 1987-, Research Institute, vice chairman, 1990-; Case Western Reserve University, Dept of Physiology & Biophysics, professor, 1991-. **ORGANIZATIONS:** Virology, associate editor, 1983-; Journal of Virology, editorial board, 1985-; Journal of Cellular and Molecular Biology Research, editorial board, 1982-; National Institutes of Health, virology study section, 1982-86, experimental virology study section, 1992-96; American Cancer Society, Cuyahoga Unit, study section, 1988-92; American Society for Virology, membership committee, 1988-; Public and Scientific Affairs Board, medical microbiology, 1989-. **HONORS/AWARDS:** Phoebe Weinstein Award on Negative Strand Virus Research, 1977; Professor S C Roy Commemoration Medal, 1983; Thomas Lord Endowed Chair of Molecular Biology, 1990; Wellcome Foundation Visiting Professorship, 1992. **SPECIAL ACHIEVEMENTS:** Recipient

of four grants; participant in national & international meetings, 1987-92; 234 publications including: "Immunological Characterization of the VSV Nucleocapsid N Protein Expressed by Recombinant Baculovirus in Spodoptera exigna Larva: Use in Differential Diagnosis between Vaccinated and Infected Animals," Virology, vol 192, p 207-216, 1993; "Expression of the Vesicular Stomatitis Virus Nucleocapsid Protein Gene in E Coli: Analysis of its Biological Activity in vitro," Virology, vol 193, p 340-347, 1993. **BUSINESS ADDRESS:** Chairman, Dept of Molecular Biology, Research Institute, Cleveland Clinic Foundation, 9500 Euclid Ave, NC 20, Cleveland, OH 44195, (216)444-0625.

BANERJEE, CHANDRA MADHAB
Educator. Indo-American. **PERSONAL:** Born Aug 28, 1932, Calcutta, W. Bengal, India; son of Nihar Banerjee & Sukumar Banerjee (deceased); married Janet Banerjee, Jul 23, 1966; children: Kyle, Aaron, Dean, Neal. **EDUCATION:** University of Calcutta, MBBS, 1955; Virginia Commonwealth University, PhD, 1967. **CAREER:** Jefferson Medical College, associate professor of physiology, 1967-76; Southern Illinois University School of Medicine, professor of physiology, 1974-. **ORGANIZATIONS:** American Physiological Society, 1967-; American Heart Association, council member, 1967-. **HONORS/AWARDS:** Southern Illinois University, Master Teacher, 1989. **SPECIAL ACHIEVEMENTS:** Over 50 scientific publications including book chapters. **BUSINESS ADDRESS:** Professor of Physiology, Southern Illinois University School of Medicine, Lindegreen Hall, Carbondale, IL 62901, (618)453-1564.

BANERJEE, DEBASISH
Educator. Indo-American. **PERSONAL:** Born Jun 21, 1951, Ranchi, Bihar, India; son of S K Banerjee (deceased) and Anurupa Banerjee; married Ruby M Banerjee, Feb 18, 1992; children: Aurobindo. **EDUCATION:** St Xavier's College, India, BSc (honors), 1968; Patna University, India, MSc, 1971; University of Arkansas, MBA, 1987, PhD, 1992. **CAREER:** Ranchi University, assistant professor, 1972-73; United Commercial Bank, probationary officer, officer, 1974-85; University of Arkansas, graduate assistant, 1985-91; Northwestern State University, assistant professor, 1991-. **ORGANIZATIONS:** Decision Sciences Institute, 1988-; Decision Sciences Institute (Southwest), 1988-; Southwestern Small Business Institute Association, 1993-. **HONORS/AWARDS:** Texas Instruments, Author Award, 1993. **SPECIAL ACHIEVEMENTS:** Author: "A Formal Methodology for Subject Area Identification in IEF Re-engineering Projects," J of Computer Information Systems, 1994; "On Altman's Failure/Nonfailure Model: A Comparison of Discriminant, Logit, Nearest Neighbor and Neural Net Models," J of Business & Entrepreneurship, 1994; "Softlifting: A Model of Motivating Factors," J of Business Ethnics, 1994. **BIOGRAPHICAL SOURCES:** Computer World; Shreveport Times; Natchitoches Times. **HOME ADDRESS:** 709 Royal St, Natchitoches, LA 71457, (318)352-6685. **BUSINESS ADDRESS:** Assistant Professor, CIS, Northwestern State University, Division of Business, #107B, Natchitoches, LA 71497, (318)357-5713.

BANERJEE, JAYANTA KUMAR
Educator. Indo-American/Bangladeshi American. **PERSONAL:** Born Aug 29, 1941, Malda, Bengal, India; son of Monica Banerjee and Kiran Kumar Banerjee; married Eligia Briceno De Banerjee, Jan 10, 1975; children: Kumar, Anyana, Nayan. **EDUCATION:** Jadaupvr University, India, BEng, 1961; University of Waterloo, Canada, MASc, 1966, PhD, 1969; Queen's University, Canada, MEd, 1987. **CAREER:** Haarmann KG, Germany, design trainee, 1962-63; Maschinenfabrik, Germany, mechanical designer, 1963-64; Universidad Del Valle, Colombia, assistant professor, 1969-72; Universidad de Los Andes, Venezuela, associate professor, coordinator, 1973-76; Universidad Nacional, Venezuela, research professor, 1977-86; University of Vermont, professor, 1986-89; University of Puerto Rico, professor, 1989-. **ORGANIZATIONS:** American Soc for Engineering Education, 1971-; American Soc of Mechanical Engineers, 1974-; Verein Deutscher Ingenieure, Germany, 1965-; Assn of Professional Engineers, Ontario, 1966-; Rotary Club Intl, Tariba, Venezuela, 1979-84; Deutsch-Indische Gesellschaft, Germany, 1962-64; University of Waterloo, India-Canada Assn, 1964-70; University of Puerto Rico, South Asia Club, founding member, 1993-. **HONORS/AWARDS:** Govt of India, Undergraduate Student Award, 1957-61; Govt of Ontario, Canada, Graduate Student Award, 1967-68, 1986-87; Queen's University Canada, Plaque of Appreciation, 1983-84; Universidad de Los Andes, Venezuela, Plaque of Honor, 1976; Universidad Nacional, Venezuela, Plaque of Honor, 1984. **SPECIAL ACHIEVEMENTS:** Over 70 technical & educational pubs, 1965-; newspaper & magazine articles, poems & literary critiques published in Bengali, English & Spanish, 1956-; traveled extensively in Asia, Europe, & in

North, Central & South America; fluent in English, Spanish & German; Asian languages: Bengali, Hindi, Sanskrit. **BIOGRAPHICAL SOURCES:** "New UF Prof a Polyglot," Gainesville Sun, 1986, Feb 2, 1986; "Esto Debe Saberse," La Nacion, Venezuela, Aug 29, 1983. **HOME PHONE:** (809)265-3319. **BUSINESS ADDRESS:** Professor, Dept of Mechanical Engineering, University of Puerto Rico, Mayaguez, Luccetti Bldg, Rm L-214, Mayaguez, PR 00681-5000, (809)832-4040.

BANERJEE, MUKUL R.
Educator. Indo-American. **PERSONAL:** Born Jan 3, 1937, Dacca, India; son of Chuni Lal Banerjee and Snehalata Banerjee; married Gita, Dec 4, 1968; children: Amit, Sumita. **EDUCATION:** Calcutta University, BVSc, 1957; Louisiana State University, PhD, 1964. **CAREER:** Indiana University, research associate, 1965, instructor, 1966-67, assistant professor, 1968-72; University of Florida, NIH research fellow, 1973-74; Tennessee State University, associate professor, 1975-76; Meharry Medical College, associate professor, 1977-79, professor, 1980-. **ORGANIZATIONS:** American Physiological Soc, educ committee; Intl Biometeorological Soc; Sigma Xi, secretary, Meharry Chapter, 1988-; New York Academy of Sciences; Health Sciences Consortium, peer review board; Meharry Medical College: Institutional Policy Review Committee, 1992; 43rd Intl Science & Engineering Fair, Nashville, TN, judge, 1992; School of Graduate Studies, Appointments, Promotions & Tenure Committee, chair, 1992-; Graduate School, faculty council, 1992-; Faculty, Student Fellowship, steering committee, 1992; Faculty Development Committee, 1991-; Committee on Scientific Misconduct, 1990-; Space Allocation Commitee, Basic Science Bldg, 1989-; Curriculum Council, First year Preclinical Subcommittee, 1986-88. **HONORS/AWARDS:** National Heart, Lung and Blood Institute, research grant, 1988-93; Outstanding Basic Science Instructor, 1986, 1989, 1992; Kaiser-Permanente Teaching Excellence Award, 1989. **SPECIAL ACHIEVEMENTS:** 20 publications, including: Circ Res, co-contributor, vol 68, p 352-358, 1991; Am J Physiol, vol 263, p H660-H663, 1992; J Appl Physiol, vol 74, p 460-465, 1993. **BUSINESS ADDRESS:** Professor of Physiology, Meharry Medical College, 1005 D B Todd Blvd, Basic Sciences Building, Nashville, TN 37208-3501, (615)327-6288.

BANERJEE, PRITHVIRAJ
Educator. Indo-American. **PERSONAL:** Born Jul 17, 1960, Khartoum, Sudan; son of Sunil Chandra Banerjee and Anima Banerjee; married Swati, Oct 28, 1984; children: Siraj. **EDUCATION:** Indian Institute of Technology, BTech, EE, 1981; University of Illinois, MS, EE, 1982, PhD, EE, 1984. **CAREER:** University of Illinois, assistant professor, 1985-89, associate professor, 1989-93, professor, 1993-. **ORGANIZATIONS:** Institute of Electronics & Electrical Engineering, senior member, 1989-; Association of Computing Machinery, 1985-. **HONORS/AWARDS:** University of Illinois, University Scholar, 1992; Xerox, Senior Xerox Award, 1992; National Science Foundation, Presidential Young Investigator, 1987; IBM, Faculty Development Award, 1986; Indian Institute of Technology, President's Gold Medal, 1981. **SPECIAL ACHIEVEMENTS:** Author, Parallel Algorithms for VLSI CAD, Prentice-Hall, 1994; published 120 papers in journals and proceedings of conferences on parallel processing computers. **BUSINESS ADDRESS:** Professor, Dept of Electrical and Computer Engineering, University of Illinois, 1406 W Green St, Urbana, IL 61801-2918.

BANERJEE, SANJAY K.
Educator. Indo-American. **PERSONAL:** Born Feb 24, 1958, Khartoum, Sudan; son of Sunil Chandra Banerjee and Anima Mukherjee Banerjee; married Jaba Chatterjee Banerjee, Jun 18, 1983; children: Anupam, Anurag. **EDUCATION:** Indian Institute of Technology, Kharagpur, BTech (honors), 1979; University of Illinois, Urbana-Champaign, MS, 1981, PhD, 1983. **CAREER:** University of Illinois, graduate research asst, 1979-83; Texas Instruments, technical staff, 1983-87; University of Texas, Austin, assistant professor, 1987-90, associate professor, 1990-93, professor, 1993-. **ORGANIZATIONS:** Institute of Electrical & Electronics Engineers, senior member, 1983-; American Physical Society, 1991-; Electrochemical Society, 1991-; Materials Research Society, 1991-; American Society for Engineering Education, 1991-; Phi Kappa Phi, 1981-. **HONORS/AWARDS:** National Science Foundation, Presidential Young Investigator, 1988; University of Texas, Engineering Foundation Award, 1991, Texas Atomic Energy Fellowship, 1991; IEEE, Best Paper Award, ISSCC, 1986. **SPECIAL ACHIEVEMENTS:** Author of over 150 refereed journal publications; holder of 4 US patents, plus 4 pending; served on various conference committees; reviewer of IEEE, APS and other journals. **BUSINESS ADDRESS:** Professor of Electrical & Computer Engineering, University of Texas, MER 2.606B/79950, Austin, TX 78712-1100, (512)471-6730.

BANERJI, RANAN BIHARI
Educator. Indo-American. **PERSONAL:** Born May 5, 1928, Calcutta, W. Bengal, India; son of Bijan Bihari Banerji and Setabja Chatterji Banerji; married Purnima Purkayastha Banerji, Jul 8, 1954; children: Anindita Spielberg, Sunandita Banerji Ogawa. **EDUCATION:** Patna University, BSc, 1947; University of Calcutta, MSc, 1949, DPhil, 1956. **CAREER:** University of Calcutta, lecturer, 1956-57; Indian Statistical Institute, maintenance engineer, 1957-59; Case Institute of Technology, research associate, 1958-59; University of New Brunswick, assistant professor, 1959-61; Case Western Reserve University, assistant professor, professor, 1961-73; Temple University, professor, 1974-82; Saint Joseph's University, professor, 1982-. **ORGANIZATIONS:** IEEE, 1961-; ACM, national lecturer, editor, 1961-; Pattern Recognition Society, associate editor, 1968-; MAA, 1974-; Religious Society of Friends, Worship Ministry, committee, 1974-. **HONORS/AWARDS:** University of Patna, Gold Medals, 1947; University of Calcutta, Gold Medal, 1949; Fulbright Commission, Travel Fellowship, 1991. **SPECIAL ACHIEVEMENTS:** Formal Techniques in Artificial Intelligence, North Holland, 1990; Artificial Intelligence: A Theoretical Approach, North Holland, 1980; with editor, Artificial and Human Intelligence, North Holland, 1984; Theory of Problem Solving, North Holland, 1969; about 100 scientific articles and reports. **HOME ADDRESS:** 7612 Woodlawn Ave, Melrose Park, PA 19126. **BUSINESS PHONE:** (215)660-1567.

BANIK, SAMBHU NATH
Foundation executive. Indo-American. **PERSONAL:** Born Nov 7, 1935, Joypara, Dacca, India; son of Padma & Kadambzni Banik; married Promila Banik, Nov 16, 1968; children: Sharmila, Kakali. **EDUCATION:** Vidyasasar College, BSc, 1954; Calcutta University, BSc, 1956, MSc, 1958; Bristol University, PhD, 1964. **CAREER:** University Hospital, Saskatoon, director, 1968-71; Government of DC, mental health center, chief, 1981-84, youth services, chief, 1984-88, clinical administrator, 1988-90; US Health and Human Services, executive director, 1990-93; Third World Foundation, chairman, 1993-; Family Diagnostic and Therapeutic Center, director, currently. **ORGANIZATIONS:** Indian American Forum for Political Education, chairman, 1986-90; Association of Indians in America, president, 1982-86; India Cultural Coordination Council, vice president, 1978-81; Prabashi, founder, president, 1973-78; Asian Pacific American Heritage Council, 1983-86; Asian American Council, vice president, 1991-; American Psychological Association, 1991-; American Association of Mental Retardation, 1991-. **HONORS/AWARDS:** Maharishi University, Maharishi Award, 1985; City of New Jersey, Mayoral Citation, 1988; National Indian Chamber of Commerce, Community Service Award, 1992; Mayor of Baltimore, Honorary Citizenship, 1992; Government of DC, Human Services Award, 1985; other community services awards. **SPECIAL ACHIEVEMENTS:** Author, cookbook, Samplings: the Cuisine of India, 1986; published over 25 articles and papers in professional journals; yoga instructor; appointed as a member to National Advisory Council on Drug Abuse; World Congress on Mental Handicap, international chairman, 1994; cooking instructor; proficient in Bengali language. **BIOGRAPHICAL SOURCES:** Federal Staff Directory, p 916, 1991-92. **BUSINESS ADDRESS:** President, Family Diagnostic and Therapeutic Center, 4400 MacArthur Blvd NW, Ste 305, Washington, DC 20007.

BAPATLA, KRISHNA M.
Pharmaceutical company executive. Indo-American. **PERSONAL:** Born in Prattipadu, Guntur District, Andhra Pradesh, India; son of B V Hanumantha Rao and B Nagaratnam; married Anjani, Aug 1967; children: Arun. **EDUCATION:** Andhra University, Waltair, India, MPharm, 1959; University of Southern California, PhD, pharm chemistry, 1966; Fairleigh Dickinson University, MBA, marketing, 1976. **CAREER:** South Dakota State University, assistant professor, 1966-70; Syntex Research Institute, research fellow, 1969-70; SUNY, Buffalo, research associate, 1970-71; Warner-Lambert Co, Production Development, senior scientist, 1971-76; Cooper Labs Inc, Formulations, section head, 1976-78; Alcon Labs Inc, Pharm Tech Affairs, director, 1978-. **ORGANIZATIONS:** American Association of Pharmaceutical Scientists, Regulatory Affairs Section, vice chair, 1993, chair-elect, 1994, chair, 1995; American Pharmaceutical Association, 1966-; American Institute of Chemists, fellow; Rho Chi, Nomination Committee, 1967; Sigma Xi; Lions Club, India Association of North Texas, vice president. **HONORS/AWARDS:** J N Tata Endowment Fellowship, Travel Grant to USA from India; Andhra University, Waltair, Gold Medal Winner, 1st place graduation. **SPECIAL ACHIEVEMENTS:** "Pharmaceuticals in Dosage Forms," "Ophthalmic Suspensions and Ointments," Disperse Systems, Marcel Dekker, 1989; "Development of Ophthalmic Dosage Forms," Pharmaceutical Dosage Forms, Sterile Products,

1992; US Patent 4,120,949: Ophthalmic Solutions for Dry Eyes, 1978. **BUSINESS ADDRESS:** Director, Pharmaceutical Technical Affairs, Alcon Laboratories Inc, 6201 S Freeway, Mail Code R1-14, Fort Worth, TX 76134, (817)551-8121.

BARAT, KAHAR
Turkologist. Chinese American. **PERSONAL:** Born Aug 27, 1950, Urumchi, People's Republic of China; son of Barat Kurban; divorced; children: Shurman. **EDUCATION:** Central Institute for Minorities, diploma, 1980; Harvard University, PhD, 1993. **CAREER:** Xinjiang Academy, assistant researcher, 1980-82; Xinjiang University Hist, lecturer, 1982-86; Harvard GSAS, practical trainee, 1986-93. **HONORS/AWARDS:** Harvard Yenching Institute, Dissertation Grant, 1992-93, Fellowship, 1986-90. **SPECIAL ACHIEVEMENTS:** Translated the tenth century Uygur translation of seventh century Chinese Xuanzang biography. **BIOGRAPHICAL SOURCES:** Journal Asiatique, no 1-2, Paris, 1990; American Asian Review, vol 5, no 2, New York, 1987. **HOME ADDRESS:** 161 Beacon St, Somerville, MA 02143, (617)576-6539.

BARNABAS, MATHEWS MAR
Cleric. Indo-American. **PERSONAL:** Born Aug 8, 1924, Vengola, Kerala, India. **EDUCATION:** Madras University, India, Madras Christian College, BSc, 1949; Osmania University, Hyderabad, India, MSc, 1954; Serampore University, Calcutta, India, BD, 1960. **CAREER:** Orthodox Seminary Kottayam, professor, 1967-72; Kolenechery MM Hospital, chaplain, 1972-78; Martha Mariam Samajam, manager of corporate colleges, president, 1978-92; Malankara Sabha, president, editorial board, until 1992; Temperance Movement, president, until 1992; Iduki Diocese, metropolitan, 1982-; Malankara Orthodox Syrian Church, India, bishop, currently. **SPECIAL ACHIEVEMENTS:** Author of religious books. **BUSINESS ADDRESS:** Metropolitan, Malankara Orthodox Syrian Church, India, Indian Orthodox Church Center, 80-34 Commonwealth Blvd, Bellerose, NY 11426.

BAROT, NAVNIT MANILAL
Construction company executive. Indo-American. **PERSONAL:** Born Apr 8, 1944, Nar, Gujarat, India; son of Manilal Prahladji Barot and Nirmalaben Manilal Barot; married Geeta Navnit Barot, May 17, 1967; children: Shveta N, Sneha S Dixit, Shreya N. **EDUCATION:** MG Science Institute, SYBSc, 1964; Gujarat University, BCE, 1967; Occupational Safety & Hazard Assn, seminar, 1976; Govt of US, fallout shelter design/analyst, 1977-78. **CAREER:** Tishman Construction Co, estimator, 1970; DM&L Construction Co, estimator, project manager, 1970-73; Inland Construction Co, estimator, project manager, 1973-80; Colt Construction Co, project director, 1980-83, chief estimator, vice president, 1983-87; Steinberg & Crane, chief estimator, project manager, 1987-89; Ben A Borenstein & Co, chief estimator, 1989-. **ORGANIZATIONS:** Bochasanwasi Swanimarayan Sanstha, Chicago Chapter, founder, president, 1970-80, honorary member, committee member, 1980-; Shveta & Sagar Corp, president, 1980-; Manav Corp, president, 1980-; Cultural Festival of India, 1991. **SPECIAL ACHIEVEMENTS:** Language proficiency: Hindi, Marathi, Gujarati. **HOME ADDRESS:** 3850 N Bernay Ln, Hoffman Estates, IL 60195-1662, (708)934-1422. **BUSINESS ADDRESS:** Chief Estimator, Ben A Borenstein & Co, 1723 Howard St, Evanston, IL 60202-3767, (708)869-3030.

BARRON, PURIFICACION C.
Nurse, educator, administrator. Filipino American. **PERSONAL:** Born Jan 24, 1932, Minalin, Pampanga, Philippines; daughter of Alfonso E Capulong & Lucia N Capulong; married Rodrigo I Barron, Jul 7, 1968; children: Joseph Rodney. **EDUCATION:** St Luke's Hospital, Philippines, RN, 1951; Mt Sinai Hospital, postgraduate pediatric nursing, 1956; Columbia University, Teacher's College, BS, 1960; Philippine Women's University, Philippines, MA, 1966. **CAREER:** Teaching experience, Philippines, 1960-66: Luzon Colleges, School of Nursing; St Catherine Hospital, School of Nursing; Central Luzon School of Nursing; Martinez Memorial Hospital, School of Nursing; Ortanez General Hospital, School of Nursing; University of Ottawa, School of Nursing, 1966-71; Ottawa General Hospital, School of Nursing, 1966-71; Lorraine School of Nursing; Indiana State University, 1971-74; administrative experience: Ortanez General Hospital, School of Nursing, principal, chief nurse, 1961-62; St Catherine Hospital, chief nurse, 1964; Luzon Colleges School of Nursing, principal, 1965; Holiday Home, nursing director, 1974-75; Pine Knoll Nursing Home, supervisor, nursing director, 1992-. **ORGANIZATIONS:** American Nurses Association, 1971-; Philippines Nurses Association, life member, 1951-; Professional Placement, asst director, 1965-66; St Luke's Alumni Association, life member, 1966-; St Lukes Alumni Nursing Foundation, 1992-. **BIOGRAPHICAL SOURCES:** "RN Honored as a Human

Services Professional," Philippine News, p 15, Aug 26-Sep 1, 1992. **HOME ADDRESS:** 103 Kristy Ln, Carrollton, GA 30117, (404)832-8937.

BARVE, KUMAR P.
State legislator. Indo-American. **PERSONAL:** Born Sep 8, 1958, Schenectady, NY; son of Prabhakar R Barve and Neera S Gokhale Barve. **EDUCATION:** Georgetown University, BA, 1980. **CAREER:** Various campaigns: Bruce Adams and Ike Leggett for County Council, 1986, Bainum for Congress, 1986, Barnes for Senate, 1986, Franchot for Congress, 1988, Dukakis for President, 1988; Montgomery County Young Democrats, treasurer, currently; Dist 17, Democratic Caucus, precinct chairman, currently; Maryland State Legislature, delegate, district 17, 1991-. **ORGANIZATIONS:** Maryland State Legislature, Economic Matters Committee, subcommittee on Bi-County Agencies, currently; Maryland National Abortion Rights Action League, treasurer and board; GCI Consumer Co-op, delegate; Montgomery County Dem Action Committee, founding board member; Gaithersburg and Upper Maryland County Chamber of Commerce; Indian American Democratic Coalition, chairman, 1993-. **BUSINESS ADDRESS:** Assemblyman, Maryland General Assembly, 224 Lowe House Office Bldg, Annapolis, MD 21401, (301)841-3046.*

BASU, ASIT PRAKAS
Educator. Bangladeshi American. **PERSONAL:** Born Mar 17, 1937, Jessore, Bangladesh; son of Haripada and Himangshu Prabha Basu; married Sandra Basu; children: Amit K, Shunit K. **EDUCATION:** Presidency College, Calcutta University, BSc (with honors), 1956, MSc, 1958; University of Minnesota, PhD, 1966. **CAREER:** University of Wisconsin, Madison, assistant professor, 1966-68; IBM Research Center, research staff member, 1968-70; Northwestern University, assistant professor, 1970-71; University of Pittsburgh, associate professor, 1971-74; University of Missouri, professor of statistics, 1974-. **ORGANIZATIONS:** International Stat Inst. **HONORS/AWARDS:** American Association for Advancement of Science, elected fellow; Institute of Mathematical Statistics, fellow; American Statistical Association, fellow; Royal Statistical Society, fellow. **SPECIAL ACHIEVEMENTS:** Edited two books: Advances in Reliability, 1993, Reliability and Quality Control, 1986; consulting and research in statistical reliability theory; published over 80 papers; associate editor, two journals. **BUSINESS ADDRESS:** Professor, Dept of Statistics, University of Missouri, 222 Math Science Building, Columbia, MO 65211.

BASU, SUTAPA
Educational administrator. Indo-American. **PERSONAL:** Born May 4, 1957, Calcutta, India. **EDUCATION:** Evergreen College, BA, 1978; Antioch, MA, 1983; University of Washington, pursuing PhD, anthropology, currently. **CAREER:** Central Area Motivation Program, intake counselor; Indochinese Refugee Employment Program, until 1981; Outreach Center for Seattle Rape Relief, program manager, until 1984; North Seattle Community College, Women's Studies, director, 1984-87; Bellevue Community College, Women's Studies, director, 1987-93; University of Washington, Women's Information Center, director, 1993-. **HONORS/AWARDS:** Asian American Weekly, Woman of the Year, 1991; Soroptomist International, Women Helping Women Award, 1993; United Nations, Human Rights Award, 1988. **BUSINESS ADDRESS:** Director of Women's Information Center, University of Washington, Seattle, WA 98195, (206)685-1090.*

BATRA, RAJEEV
Engineer, government official. Indo-American. **EDUCATION:** Punjab Engg College, India, BS, civil engineering, 1975, MS, civil engineering, 1977. **CAREER:** Irrigation Dept, India, asst engr, 1977-80; Bala & Strandgaard, civil engr, 1980-83; City of San Jose, assoc civil engr, 1983-88, sr civil engr, 1988-90, division mgr, transportation division, 1990-. **ORGANIZATIONS:** ASCE, 1986-; APWA; City of Fremont, planning commissioner, 1991-. **SPECIAL ACHIEVEMENTS:** Represents city of San Jose at various local, regional and state transportation committees. **BIOGRAPHICAL SOURCES:** India West, Aug 1991. **BUSINESS ADDRESS:** Manager, Transportation Division, City of San Jose, 151 W Mission St, #203, San Jose, CA 95110, (408)277-4217.

BATRA, RAVI
Educator, writer. Indo-American. **PERSONAL:** Born Jun 27, 1943, Punjab, India; son of Kusum Thakur & Harish C Batra; married Diane J Spiegel, Feb 21, 1970 (divorced 1981); children: Marlo Sheila; married Sunitra, 1986. **EDUCATION:** Punjab University, BA, 1963; Delhi School of Economics, MA, 1965; Southern Illinois University, PhD, 1969. **CAREER:** Hindu College, Economics, assistant lecturer, 1965-66; Southern Illinois University, Eco-

nomics, assistant professor, 1969-70; University of Western Ontario, Economics, assistant professor, 1970-72; Southern Methodist University, associate professor, 1972-73, Economics, professor, department head, 1973-. **ORGANIZATIONS:** American Economic Association. **HONORS/AWARDS:** Canadian Council, Fellowship, 1971-72. **SPECIAL ACHIEVEMENTS:** Author: Studies in Pure Theory of Intl Trade, 1973; Pure Theory of Intl Trade under Uncertainty, 1975; Downfall of Capitalism and Communism: A New Study of History, 1979, second revised edition, 1990; Muslim Civilization and the Crisis in Iran, 1980; Prout: The Alternative to Capitalism and Marxism, 1980; Regular Cycles of Money, Inflation, Regulation, and Depression, 1985, reprinted as: Regular Economic Cycles: Money, Inflation, Regulation, and Depression, 1989; Great Depression of 1990: Why It's Got to Happen—How to Protect Yourself, 1985; Surviving the Great Depression of 1990: Protect Your Assets and Investments—And Come Out on Top, 1988; Prout and Economic Reform in the Third World, 1989; numerous articles. **BIOGRAPHICAL SOURCES:** New York Times Book Review, Jul 27, 1987, Oct 23, 1988, Oct 29, 1989. **BUSINESS ADDRESS:** Professor, Head, Dept of Economics, Southern Methodist University, Dallas, TX 75275-0496, (214)768-2559.*

BATRA, ROMESH CHANDER
Educator. Indo-American. **PERSONAL:** Born Aug 16, 1947, Dherowal, Punjab, India; son of Amir Chand Batra & Dewki Bai Dhamija; married Manju Dhamija, Jun 26, 1972; children: Monica Rani, Meenakshi Rani. **EDUCATION:** Thapar College of Engineering, India, BS, mechanical engineering, 1968; University of Waterloo, MS, mechanical engineering, 1969; The Johns Hopkins University, PhD, 1972. **CAREER:** The Johns Hopkins University, postdoctoral fellow, 1972-73; McMaster University, research associate, 1973-74; University of Alabama, assistant professor, 1976-77; University of Missouri, assistant professor, 1974-76, associate professor, 1977-81, professor, 1981-. **ORGANIZATIONS:** American Society of Mechanical Engineers, 1976-, fellow, 1990-; American Academy of Mechanics, 1975-, fellow, 1991-; American Society of Engineering Education, 1976-, fellow, 1992-; Society of Engineering Science, 1976-, director, 1990-96; Society of Natural Philosophy, 1972-, treasurer, 1987-90; Society of Rheology, 1976-; American Association of Computational Mechanics, 1990-. **HONORS/AWARDS:** Alexander von Humboldt Award for senior scientists; University of Missouri, Faculty Excellence Award, 1987-92; Indian Geotechnical Society, Jai Krishna Award, 1988; University of Missouri School of Engineering, Halliburton Award, 1986. **SPECIAL ACHIEVEMENTS:** 100 publications in refereed journals, 1972-; co-edited 5 volumes, 1982, 1991, 1992, 1993; NSF Grant, 1981-84, 1987-; ARO, 1985-; 84 presentations at natl & intl conferences. **BUSINESS ADDRESS:** Professor, University of Missouri, Rolla, 125 Mech Eng Annex, Rolla, MO 65401-0249, (314)341-4589.

BAUTISTA, VELTISEZAR BAL
Writer, publisher. Filipino American. **PERSONAL:** Born Oct 31, 1933, Manila, Philippines; son of Amado R Bote & Oliva P Bal; married Genoveva B Abes, Jan 28, 1962; children: Hubert, Lester, Melvin, Ronald, Janet. **EDUCATION:** University of Santo Tomas, BA, literature, journalism, 1951-55. **CAREER:** Bagong Buhay, reporter, deskman, 1952-55; Chronicle Broadcasting Network, news staff writer, 1956-57; Manila Chronicle, reporter, deskman, magazine writer, 1957-65; Newsman's Publishing House, publisher, 1965-76; private and government worker, 1977-85; Bookhaus Publishers, publisher, owner, 1985-. **ORGANIZATIONS:** Publishers Marketing Association, 1985-; Cosmep, International Association of Independent Publishers, 1988-; Michigan Publishers Association, former vice president, 1992-93; Nuevo Ecijanos of Michigan, 1990-. **HONORS/AWARDS:** Quality Books Inc, Small Press Publisher of the Year, 1990; Publishers Marketing Association, Benjamin Franklin Book Award, 1991, Benjamin Franklin Book Award, 1993; Mid-America Publishers Association, Best Cover Design, Best Interior Design, Best Illustrations & Graphics, 1990. **SPECIAL ACHIEVEMENTS:** Author, The Book of US Postal Exams, Bookhaus Publishers, 1985-; Improve Your Grades, Bookhaus Publishers, 1989-; How to Teach Your Child, Bookhaus Publishers, 1990-; The Book of $16,000-$60,000 PO Jobs, Bookhaus Publishers, 1990-; How to Build a Successful One-Person Business, Bookhaus Publishers, 1994. **HOME ADDRESS:** 28091 Hickory Dr, Farmington Hills, MI 48331-2954. **BUSINESS ADDRESS:** Publisher, Bookhaus Publishers, 28091 Hickory Dr, PO Box 3277, Farmington Hills, MI 48333-3277, (810)489-8640.

BAWA, MOHENDRA S.
Electronics company engineer. Indo-American. **PERSONAL:** Born Jun 10, 1931, Jagraon, East Panjab, India; married Ofir, Jul 4, 1963; children: Sandy Kanakis, Pamela Dearen. **EDUCATION:** East Panjab University, BSc, 1949;

Calcutta University, India, MSc, 1954; University of Houston, PhD, 1965. **CAREER:** Central Fuel Research Institute, senior scientific officer, 1955-61; Texas Instruments Inc, senior member technical staff, 1965-. **ORGANIZATIONS:** American Institute of Chemical Engineers; The Electrochemical Society; American Association of Crystal Growers; Sigma Xi. **HOME ADDRESS:** 3313 Steven Dr, Plano, TX 75023.

BEDI, SANDEEP
Computer scientist. Indo-American. **PERSONAL:** Born Jun 10, 1966, India; son of Sushil Bedi & Sudha Bedi. **EDUCATION:** Delhi University, India, 1984-87; University of Massachusetts, BS, accounting, 1991, MBA, computer science, currently. **CAREER:** Tanden Group Management Corp, junior accountant, 1990-91, staff accountant, 1992-93; Thomson Financial Services, summer intern, 1993; Price Waterhouse, summer intern, 1993. **ORGANIZATIONS:** Indian Students Association, 1989-91; Sigma Iota Epsilon Honor Society, 1989-91; University of Massachusetts, Lowell, student senator, 1990-91, accounting society, volunteer work, 1989-90; US Table Tennis Association, 1989-91; US Mens Field Hockey Association, 1989-91. **HOME ADDRESS:** 617 Rutland St, Carlisle, MA 01741, (508)369-7682.

BEHL, WISHVENDER K.
Scientist, inventor. Indo-American. **PERSONAL:** Born Dec 26, 1935, Dhariwal, Punjab, India; son of Amar Nath Behl & Vidya Wat Trehan; married Ravi Kiran Sharma, Feb 15, 1977; children: Vikas, Renuka. **EDUCATION:** University of Delhi, India, BS (w/honors), 1955, MS, 1957, PhD, 1962. **CAREER:** Government Test House, Alipore, India, junior chem assistant, 1957-58; New York University, post-doctoral research scientist, 1962-64; Brookhaven National Laboratory, post-doctoral research associate, 1964-67; US Army Research Laboratory, research chemist, 1967-. **ORGANIZATIONS:** The American Chemical Society, 1965-; Monmouth County Section of American Chemical Society, executive comm, 1971-74; Electrochemical Society, 1969-; American Institute of Chemists, fellow, 1970-; New York Academy of Science, 1971-77; American Association for the Advancement of Science, 1971-77; Schussboower Ski Club, treasurer, 1972-73, president, 1974-75. **HONORS/AWARDS:** University of Delhi, University Merit Scholarship, 1955-57, Science Exhibition Prize, 1955; US Army Research Laboratory, Superior Performance Awards, 1990-93, Certificates of Achievement, 1974-84, Exceptional Performance Awards, 1981, 1983. **SPECIAL ACHIEVEMENTS:** Author of 40 professional publications in professional journals, 1961-; 15 patents in the field of lithium batteries and high temperature molten salt batteries, 1959-; 12 US patents, 2 Canadian patents, and 1 Indian patent. **HOME ADDRESS:** 18 Cambridge Way, Ocean, NJ 07712. **BUSINESS ADDRESS:** Res Chemist, Electronics & Power Sources Directorate, US Army Research Laboratory, Attn: AMSRL-EP-PB, Fort Monmouth, NJ 07703, (908)544-4232.

BELBIS, MANUEL EMUSLAN
Company executive. Filipino American. **PERSONAL:** Born Apr 10, 1941, Pangasinan, Philippines; son of Alejandrino A Belbis and Felicidad E Belbis; married Rebecca C Belbis, Sep 30, 1967; children: Mario, Brian, Jennifer. **EDUCATION:** Mapua Institute of Technology, Philippines, BS, chemistry, 1961. **CAREER:** Feati University, chemistry instructor, 1961-63; Upjohn (PHIL) Inc, sales rep, 1963-66; Industrial Adhesives Co, research chemist, 1966-71; Armour Industrial Products, research chemist, 1971-73; Bostik-USM Corp, technical sales rep, 1973-74; Thiokol Corp, technical sales rep, 1974-76; Industrial Adhesives Co, president, 1976-. **ORGANIZATIONS:** American Chemical Society, 1969-; Packaging Institute, USA, 1977-; The Construction Specifications Institute, 1975-; Adhesive Manufacturers Association, 1977-93; TAPPI-Technical Association of Pulp & Paper, 1977-; Chicago Rubber Group, 1975-76; Lions Club, director, 1992-; Association of Management & Industrial Engineers, 1968-. **HONORS/AWARDS:** America Institute of Chemists, Fellow, 1986; Economic Development Business Council, State of Illinois, Award of Excellence, 1988; University of Illinois, Small Business Award, 1983. **SPECIAL ACHIEVEMENTS:** Thesis: Adhesives from Soybeans, 1961; soloist, church choir, Philippines Performing Arts of Chicago, 1990-93. **BUSINESS ADDRESS:** President, Industrial Adhesives Co, Bond-Plus Division, 130 N Campbell Ave, Chicago, IL 60612, (312)666-2686.

BENAVIDES, VIDA
Political activist. Filipino American. **PERSONAL:** Born Mar 9, 1964. **CAREER:** Democratic National Committee, Constituencies for Asian Pacific American, director, 1993-. **SPECIAL ACHIEVEMENTS:** Active member of the Bill Clinton Campaign for Presidency and the Clinton transition team.

BUSINESS ADDRESS: Director of Constituencies for APA, Democratic National Committee, 430 S Capitol, Washington, DC 20003, (202)863-8000.*

BERSSENBRUGGE, MEI-MEI
Poet, author, educator. Chinese American. **PERSONAL:** Born Oct 5, 1947, Peking, China; daughter of Robert J Berssenbrugge and Martha W Berssenbrugge. **EDUCATION:** Reed College, BA, 1969; Columbia University, MFA, 1973. **CAREER:** Basement Workshop, artist-in-residence; Arts Alaska, artist-in-residence; New Mexico Arts Division, poet-in-schools, 1977-; Institute of American Indian Art, English instructor, 1983-; works include: Fish Souls, Greenwood Press, 1971; Summits Move with the Tide, Greenfield Review Press, 1974; Pack Rat Steve, 1983; Random Possession, Reed Cannon, 1979; contributor, American Born and Foreign: An Anthology of Asian American Poetry, Sunbury, 1979; editor, Walking Ink III, 1983; The Heat Bird, Reed Books, 1986; Hiddeness, 1987; Empathy, Station Hill Press, 1988; Mizu, Chax Press, 1990. **ORGANIZATIONS:** New Mexico Arts Commission, literary panel member, 1980-83; Segue Foundation, board of directors; Tooth of Time Press, board of directors; Center for Contemporary Arts of Santa Fe, advisory board, 1983-; Institute of American Indian Art Press, advisory board, 1983-; PSA; Rio Grande Writers Assn. **HONORS/AWARDS:** Before Columbus American Book Award; NEA Grants for Literature, 1976, 1981; American Book Award, 1980, 1984; Yaddo Colony, Fellow, 1984, 1985, 1987. **BUSINESS ADDRESS:** Poet/Author, Mizu, Chax Press, 5200 16th S, Minneapolis, MN 55417-1814.*

BERTRAND, MIEKO
Business executive. Japanese American. **PERSONAL:** Born Feb 21, 1949, Shimizu, Shizuoka, Japan; married Dennis L Bertrand, Jan 2, 1992; children: Tara M Sarff, Chris K Stevens. **EDUCATION:** Spokane Falls Community College, advertising. **CAREER:** Diamond Press, president, 1985-. **BUSINESS ADDRESS:** President, Diamond Press, 317 Monroe St, Spokane, WA 99201, (509)325-4513.

BHADA, ROHINTON KHURSHED (RON)
Educator, manager, educational administrator. Indo-American. **PERSONAL:** Born Mar 23, 1935, Bombay, India; son of Khurshed A Bhada & Goola K Press Bhada; married Patricia Ann Bergman Bhada, Jan 18, 1959; children: John, James, Sarah, Naomi, Jenny, Nikki. **EDUCATION:** University of Bombay, int sci, 1953; University of Michigan, BS, 1955, MS, 1957, PhD, 1968; University of Akron, MBA, 1974. **CAREER:** University of Michigan, research assistant, 1955-59; Babcock & Wilcox Co, research engineer, 1959-64, group leader, 1964-72, section manager, 1972-77, department manager, 1977-88; New Mexico State University, department head & professor, 1988-90, associate dean & director, 1990-. **ORGANIZATIONS:** American Institute of Chem Eng, 1959-, research comm chair, 1992-; National Society of Professional Engrs, 1990-; NM Society of Professional Engrs, 1990-; Chemical Research Council, 1988-; Oak Ridge Assoc University, council representative, 1992-; Las Cruces Environmental Quality Board, board of directors, 1991-; WM Symposia Inc, board of directors, 1992-. **HONORS/AWARDS:** American Academy of Environmental Engineers, diplomate; US Jaycees, Outstanding National Director, 1970; Ohio Jaycees, Outstanding State President, 1968; National Society of Prof Engs, Outstanding Engineering Achievement, 1991. **SPECIAL ACHIEVEMENTS:** Over 40 publications and papers presented on energy conversion, combustion, waste management, thermodynamics, management techniques and innovative teaching methods; various technical journals, over 100 papers, 1959-; US Patent Office, US patent, 1972. **HOME ADDRESS:** 2228 Cimarron Dr, Las Cruces, NM 88001, (505)522-2115. **BUSINESS ADDRESS:** Associate Dean/Dir, Waste-Management Education & Research Consortium, New Mexico State University, PO Box 30001, Dept WERC, Academic Research Complex C, Las Cruces, NM 88003-0001, (505)646-1510.

BHAGAT, HITESH RAMESHCHANDRA
Research manager. Indo-American. **PERSONAL:** Born Mar 16, 1961, Surat, Gujarat, India; son of Rameshchandra C Bhagat & Hansaben R Bhagat; married Anupama M, Jul 19, 1988; children: Dhruti M Bhagat. **EDUCATION:** The Bombay University, BS, pharmacy, 1981; Massachusetts College of Pharmacy, MS, 1984, PhD, 1988. **CAREER:** University of Maryland, assistant professor of pharmaceutics, 1988-92; Oravax, Inc, head, formulations research, 1993-. **ORGANIZATIONS:** American Association of Pharmaceutical Scientists, 1987-; Controlled Release Society, 1989-;American Association of Colleges of Pharmacy; Rho Chi; American Association of Indian Pharmaceutical Scientists, secretary, 1991-92. **SPECIAL ACHIEVEMENTS:** Co-author: "Evaluation of a Novel, Non-aqueous Technique for the Preparation of Biodegradable

Polymeric Microspheres," (abstract) Pharm Res, 8, S-150, 1991; "Stability Indicating Analysis of Levothyroxine by Capillary Electrophoresis," (abstract) Pharm Res, 9, S-56, 1992; consultant; referee; presenter at professional meetings, etc. **BUSINESS ADDRESS:** Head, Formulations Research, Oravax, Inc, 230 Albany St, Cambridge, MA 02139, (617)494-1339.

BHAGAT, NAZIR A.
Government official. Indo-American. **PERSONAL:** Born Feb 22, 1944, Bombay, India; son of Abdul Bhagat and Zohra Bhagat; married Ashraf, Jan 12, 1980; children: Alisha, Zohar. **EDUCATION:** Indian Institute of Technology, 1963-64; MIT, chemical engineering, BS, 1966, MS, 1967; Harvard Business School, DBA, 1975. **CAREER:** American Cyanamid, systems analyst, 1967-69; Rutgers Graduate School of Business, assistant professor, 1975-80; US Department of Commerce, senior policy analyst, 1980-. **ORGANIZATIONS:** Harvard Business School Club; MIT Club of Washington, board member; Federal Executive Institute Alumni Association, policy committee; International Policy Institute, board member. **HONORS/AWARDS:** US Department of Commerce, Selected for FEI, 1991, Commerce Science Fellowship, 1983, Certificate of Merit, 1981; Cyanamid, Man of the Year Award, 1970, 1971. **SPECIAL ACHIEVEMENTS:** Assists in analyzing and developing the American trade policy. **HOME ADDRESS:** 3411 Fiddler's Green, Falls Church, VA 22044, (703)354-9080. **BUSINESS ADDRESS:** Senior Policy Analyst, Intl Trade Administration, US Dept of Commerce, 14th and E, NW, HCHB, Rm 2224, Washington, DC 20230, (202)482-3855.

BHAGAVATULA, VIJAYAKUMAR (B. V. K. VIJAYA KUMAR)
Educator. Indo-American. **PERSONAL:** Born Aug 15, 1953, Porumamilla, Andhra Pradesh, India; son of Ramamurthy Bhagavatula and Saradamba Bhagavatula; married Latha Bayya, 1982; children: Ramamurthy, Madhusudan, Chandrasekhar. **EDUCATION:** Indian Institute of Tech, Kanpur, India, BTech, elec engrg, 1975, MTech, elec engrg, 1977; Carnegie Mellon University, PhD, elec engrg, 1980. **CAREER:** Carnegie Mellon University, research associate, 1980-82, assistant professor, 1982-87, associate professor, 1987-91, professor, 1991-. **ORGANIZATIONS:** IEEE, senior member, 1980; Optical Society of America, fellow, 1993; Pgh Chapter, president, 1982; Society of Optical Engineering, fellow, 1991; International Neural Networks Society, 1987-; Sigma Xi, Pittsburgh Chapter, vice president, 1992-93; Applied Optics, topical editor, 1990-; Asia-Pacific Engineering Journal, editorial panel member, 1992-; Sri Venkateswara Temple, Pittsburgh, president, 1991-92, secretary, 1993-. **HONORS/AWARDS:** Government of India, Merit Scholarship, 1970-75. **SPECIAL ACHIEVEMENTS:** Author or co-author of 150 technical papers on optical pattern recognition, neural networks, data storage systems and error control coding for conferences and journals; published 4 book chapters. **BUSINESS ADDRESS:** Professor, Dept of Elec and Computer Engineering, Carnegie Mellon University, Pittsburgh, PA 15213, (412)268-3026.

BHALLA, VIPAN KUMAR
Engineer. Indo-American. **PERSONAL:** Born Sep 17, 1945, Amritsar, Punjab, India; son of Benarsi Das Bhalla and Shakuntla Devi Bhalla; married Anita Bhalla, Jul 26, 1973; children: Vendna, Archena, Puja, Ish Prasad. **EDUCATION:** Thapar College of Engineering, India, BSBE, 1967; University of Arkansas, MBME, 1972; McGill University, Montreal, Canada, diploma in management, 1977; Winthrop University, E-MBA, 1990. **CAREER:** Amin Chand Pyare Lal; H K Porter & Co; Stanley Works of Canada Ltd; Rockwell Intl, Troy, MI, Rock Hill, SC, Kenton, OH, manufacturing engineering, manager, currently. **ORGANIZATIONS:** American Society of Quality Control; Institute of Industrial Engineers; Order of Engineers, Quebec, Canada; Indian Standards Institution, New Delhi. **HOME ADDRESS:** 440 Lynshire Lane, Findlay, OH 45840-7120, (419)423-3626. **BUSINESS ADDRESS:** Manager, Manufacturing Engineering, Rockwell International, State Route 68 South, Kenton, OH 43326, (419)674-5250.

BHANDARI, SANJIV
Architect. Indo-American. **PERSONAL:** Born Mar 10, 1959, Chandigarh, India; son of Om Parkash Bhandari (deceased) and Krishna Bhandari; married Arti Bhandari, Mar 10, 1985; children: Nipun, Nakin. **EDUCATION:** Punjab University, B Arch, 1979; Institute for Housing Studies, Holland, Post Graduate Diploma, 1982. **CAREER:** Virender Khanna & Associates, India, intern architect, 1977; Planners Group, India, assistant architect, 1979; PCP Ltd, Iraq, project architect, 1980-84; Brown/McDaniel Inc, San Francisco, senior vice president, 1985-. **ORGANIZATIONS:** Council of Architecture, registrant, 1982; American Institute of Architects, 1986-; Smithsonian Institution, asso-

ciate, 1992; Asian Indian Architects Association, founder, president, 1993; Indian Institute of Architects, associate member, 1993-. **HONORS/ AWARDS:** Punjab University, Merit Scholarship, 1978-79; PCP Ltd, Iraq, Outstanding Performance, 1981-82; National Library of Poetry, Editor's Choice Award, 1993. **SPECIAL ACHIEVEMENTS:** Thesis on Film Studio, Punjab, India, 1979; thesis on Evolutionary Housing for Urban Poor, 1982; published poem in company magazine, PCP Ltd, 1981; contributor, Where Dreams Begin, Anthology, 1993; contributor, Arcadia Poetry Anthology, 1993; contributor, Outstanding Poets of 1994, Anthology, 1994. **BUSINESS ADDRESS:** Senior Vice President, Brown/McDaniel Inc, 650 California St, Ste 2205, San Francisco, CA 94108.

BHANDARKAR, SUHAS D.
Engineer. Indo-American. **PERSONAL:** Born Oct 8, 1964, Coondapur, India; son of D V Bhandarkar and M D Bhandarkar; married Karen Bhandarkar, Oct 11, 1991; children: Steven. **EDUCATION:** Mangalore University, BE, 1986; University of Rhode Island, MS, 1988, PhD, 1990. **CAREER:** AT&T Bell Labs, MTS, research engineer, 1990-. **ORGANIZATIONS:** AIChE, 1987-91; ACerS, 1991-; MRS, 1993-. **SPECIAL ACHIEVEMENTS:** 8 publications. **BUSINESS ADDRESS:** Research Engineer, AT&T Bell Labs, 600 Mountain Ave, IF 202, Murray Hill, NJ 07974-2070, (908)582-2040.

BHAPKAR, VASANT P.
Educator. Indo-American. **PERSONAL:** Born Apr 8, 1931, Kolhapur, Maharashtra, India; married Suhasini. **EDUCATION:** University of Bombay, India, BSc, 1951, MSc, 1953; University of North Carolina, PhD, 1959. **CAREER:** University of Poona, India, lecturer, 1954-60, reader, 1960-68, professor, 1968-72; University of Kentucky, associate professor, 1969-73, professor, 1973-. **ORGANIZATIONS:** Inst of Math Statistics, 1970-; American Statistical Association, 1970-; Indian Statistical Association, 1987-. **HONORS/ AWARDS:** American Statistical Association, Fellow, 1974; International Statistical Institute, elected member, 1983. **SPECIAL ACHIEVEMENTS:** More than 50 research publications, 1954-. **BUSINESS ADDRESS:** Professor, Dept of Statistics, University of Kentucky, 875 Patterson Office Tower, Lexington, KY 40506-0027, (606)257-3610.

BHARGAVA, ASHOK
Educator. Indo-American. **PERSONAL:** Born Jul 1, 1943, Agra, Uttar Pradesh, India; son of Mahabir Prasad Bhargava and Kanti Bhargava; married Devi, Jun 11, 1970; children: Amit, Kamini. **EDUCATION:** University of Delhi, BA (with honors), 1963, MA, 1965; University of Wisconsin, Madison, MS, 1969, PhD, 1975. **CAREER:** University of Wisconsin, Madison, assistant, 1967-70; Siri Ram College, Delhi, lecturer, 1965-66; Marquette University, visiting professor, 1987-; University of Wisconsin-Whitewater, director, Center for Business & Management Services, 1989-91, professor of economics, 1970-. **ORGANIZATIONS:** Association of Indian Economic Studies, chairperson, 1989-91, secretary-treasurer, 1981-89; Association of Managerial Economics, secretary, 1986-; Eastern Economic Association, area representative, 1987-92; Bulletin of Concerned Asian Scholars, editorial board, 1978-; Combat Blindness Foundation, treasurer, 1986-; Minority Business Development Finance Board, 1989-; Wisconsin Governor's Council on Asian Affairs, secretary, 1987-; India Development Service, director at large, 1978-. **HONORS/ AWARDS:** University of Wisconsin, Whitewater, University Service Award, 1992; University of Wisconsin, Madison, Ford Foundation Fellowship, 1968-70; Poverty Eradication Foundation, 1st Prize Essay Competition, with Rashmi Luthra, 1987; University of Delhi, Best Under-graduate Student in Economics, 1963. **SPECIAL ACHIEVEMENTS:** Editor, Studies in the Indian Economy, 1984; editor, Indian Economic Studies, 1985; ''Plan for Poverty Eradication in India,'' 1991; India's ''New'' Business & Economic Policy, 1990; Multinationals and Developing Countries: Lessons from Bhopal, 1988. **HOME ADDRESS:** 4806 Waukesha St, Madison, WI 53705, (608)238-6302. **BUSINESS PHONE:** (414)472-5583.

BHASKAR, SURINDAR NATH
US Army officer (retired). Indo-American. **PERSONAL:** Born Jan 7, 1923, Rasul, Punjab, India; son of Jagan Nath Bhaskar and Maya Devi Bhaskar; married Norma Zeigle Bhaskar, Jan 7, 1950; children: William C, Philip B, Thomas A. **EDUCATION:** Northwestern University Dental School, DDS, 1946; University of Illinois, MS, 1948, PhD, 1951. **CAREER:** University of Illinois, research fellow, Graduate Sch, faculty, Dental Sch, assoc prof of pathology; University of Chicago, research fellow; Armed Forces Inst of Pathology, Oral Tumors Branch, chief, 1958-60; Walter Reed Army Inst of Pathology, Dept of Oral Pathology, chief, 1960-61; US Army Inst of Dental

Research, Walter Reed Army Med Ctr, Div of Oral Pathology, chief, 1961-69, director; US Army, Med Dept, director of personnel, asst surgeon general for dental services; Georgetown University, Sch of Med & Dentistry, prof; US Army Dental Corps, chief, major general; periodontics practice, currently. **ORGANIZATIONS:** American Dental Assn; California Dental Assn; AAAS; Intl Assn for Dental Research; American Acad of Oral Pathology; American Acad of Periodontics; Sigma Xi; Oral Pathology Journal, Oral Surgery, Oral Medicine, assoc editor. **HONORS/AWARDS:** Henry Spenadel Award, 1971; Assn of Military Surgeons of the US, Founders Medal, 1973; Acad of General Dentistry, Albert L Borish Memorial Award, 1979. **SPECIAL ACHIEVEMENTS:** Author of 5 books; over 200 contributions to journals. **MILITARY SERVICE:** US Army, major general; 1955-78; Distinguished Service Medal, 1978; Legion of Merit, 1973; Meritorious Service Medal, 1972. **BUSINESS ADDRESS:** 333 El Dorado St, Monterey, CA 93940, (408)372-0440.

BHAT, K. RAMACHANDRA
Educator. Indo-American. **PERSONAL:** Born Sep 22, 1941, Paivalike Village, Kerala, India; son of K Krishna and Haimavathi Bhat; married Susheela, Jul 8, 1972; children: Haimavathi. **EDUCATION:** Mysore University, India, BSc, 1961; Banaras Hindu University, India, MSc, 1964; Ohio State University, Columbus, MS, 1969; Rutgers University, PhD, 1974. **CAREER:** University of Southern California, post doctoral fellow, 1974-76; University of Maryland, research associate, 1976-78; Johns Hopkins University, research associate, 1978-85; Lincoln University, assistant professor, 1986-. **ORGANIZATIONS:** American Chemical Society; American Association for Advancement of Science; American Association for Cancer Research; Sigma Xi; New York Academy of Sciences; Council on Undergraduate Research. **HONORS/AWARDS:** Environmental Protection Agency, research grant, 1987-91; National Institute of Health, research grant, 1988-92. **SPECIAL ACHIEVEMENTS:** Author of several papers published in refereed scientific journals. **BUSINESS ADDRESS:** Assistant Professor, Lincoln University, Wright Hall, Rm B-7, Lincoln University, PA 19352-0299, (215)932-8300.

BHAT, SHANKAR U.
Researcher, engineer. Indo-American. **PERSONAL:** Born May 13, 1955, Kerala, India; son of Rama U & Honnamma U Bhat; married Jaya, May 21, 1981; children: Radhika, Maya, Savita. **EDUCATION:** Indian Institute of Technology, India, BS, 1978; Massachusetts Institute of Technology, MS, 1982, 1984, ScD, 1986. **CAREER:** Amoco Production Co, senior research engineer, 1985-. **ORGANIZATIONS:** Society of Naval Architects & Marine Engineers, 1982-. **SPECIAL ACHIEVEMENTS:** More than a dozen publications in scientific journals; three presentations in international conferences. **HOME ADDRESS:** 6510 S 110 E Ave, Tulsa, OK 74133, (918)250-8075. **BUSINESS ADDRESS:** Sr Research Engineer, Amoco Production Co, 4502 E 41st St, Rm 3H33, Tulsa, OK 74145, (918)660-4348.

BHATHENA, SAM JEHANGIRJI
Government official. Indo-American. **PERSONAL:** Born Sep 18, 1936, Bombay, Maharashtra, India; son of Jehangirji Pallonji Bhathena and Pirojbai Jehangirji Bhathena; married Pauruchisty K Kias, Jul 14, 1975. **EDUCATION:** University of Bombay, Institute of Science, BSc, 1961, Seth G S Medical College, MSc, 1964, Institute of Science, PhD, 1970. **CAREER:** National Institute of Health, postdoc fellow, 1971-73, Fogarty Intl Fellow, 1974; Georgetown University, assistant prof, 1979-82; VA Medical Center, res biochemist, 1974-82; University of Maryland, assoc prof, 1989-; US Dept of Agriculture, research chemist, 1983-. **ORGANIZATIONS:** American Institute of Nutrition, 1989-; The Endocrine Society, 1976-93; American Diabetes Association, 1975-; AAAS, 1972-; American Chemical Society, 1990-; New York Academy of Science, 1976-93; Society for Exp Biol Med, 1980-; Association of Scientists of Indian Origin, 1984-, secretary treasurer, 1990-91; Association of Indians in American, Washington Chapter, 1973-, president, 1990-94; American Society for Clinical Nutrition, 1989-. **HONORS/AWARDS:** University of Bombay, P Dube Scholarship, 1965-70; Beltsville Human Nutr Research Ctr USDA, Outstanding Research Scientist, 1988; Toastmasters Intl, Distinguished Toastmaster, 1992. **SPECIAL ACHIEVEMENTS:** Over 180 publications including articles in scientific journals, reviews, book chapters and abstracts; presented papers and chaired sessions at more than 50 national and international meetings, 1971-. **HOME ADDRESS:** 11912 Judson Ct, Wheaton, MD 20902-2022, (301)949-5207. **BUSINESS ADDRESS:** Research Chemist, Carbohydrate Nutrition Laboratory, Beltsville Human Nutrition Research Center, US Dept of Agriculture, Bldg 307, Rm 324, Beltsville, MD 20705, (301)504-8422.

BHATIA, RAMESH
Manufacturing company executive. Indo-American. **PERSONAL:** Born Jan 10, 1944, Patna, Bihar, India; son of Lajpat Rai Bhatia (deceased) and Shakuntala Bhatia (deceased); married Kalpana, Oct 15, 1971; children: Anita, Niraj. **EDUCATION:** Bihar College of Engineering, India, BSME, 1965; University of Dallas, MBA, 1981. **CAREER:** Government Polytechnic, India, asst professor, 1965-68; M B Gardner & Co, mech engr, 1969-70; Frederic R Harris Inc, project engr, 1970-77; Atco Rubber Products, president, chief executive officer, 1978-. **ORGANIZATIONS:** National Association of Manufacturers. **HONORS/AWARDS:** Arthur Anderson, Tarrant County Export Award, 1989, 1990, 1991, 1992. **BUSINESS ADDRESS:** President/CEO, Atco Rubber Products, Inc, 7101 Gumm Lane, Fort Worth, TX 76118.

BHATIA, SALIM A. L.
Telecommunication executive. Indo-American. **PERSONAL:** Born Apr 3, 1950, Mombasa, Kenya; son of Akber & Gulbanu Bhatia; married Yasmin, Dec 11, 1971; children: Nadiya, Rafiq. **EDUCATION:** University College, London, BS, eng, 1971; Harvard University, MBA, 1976. **CAREER:** Esso Petroleum Co, UK, engineer, 1971-74; Corning Inc, manager, planning, 1976-81; Siecor, vice president, sales & marketing, 1981-88; BroadBand Technologies Inc, president and CEO, 1988-. **ORGANIZATIONS:** Council for Entrepreneurial Development, former director, 1988-; American Entrepreneurs for Economic Growth, executive committee, 1993; His Highness Prince Aga Khan Shia Imami Ismaili Council for the USA, 1979-, vice president, 1990-; North Carolina Electronics and Information Technologies Association, board member, 1993-. **HONORS/AWARDS:** Council on Entrepreneurial Development. **BIOGRAPHICAL SOURCES:** "The Venture Experience-Three Local Companies That Are Cashing In," Small Business Quarterly, February 1, 93; "The Clinton Push on Technology," Nation's Business, pp 29-32, May 1993; "The Power of Patience," Fortune Magazine, p 130, Nov 15, 1993. **BUSINESS PHONE:** (919)405-4606.

BHATIA, SHARMILA
Archivist. Indo-American. **PERSONAL:** Born Aug 8, 1964, Washington, DC; daughter of Anand Kumar & Bijoya Bhatia; married Stephen Francis Heon, Oct 3, 1992. **EDUCATION:** University of Maryland, BA, 1986; University of South Carolina, MLIS, 1990, MA, 1990. **CAREER:** South Carolina Department of Archives and History, state records archivist I, currently. **ORGANIZATIONS:** Archives and Special Collections Roundtable of SCLA, secretary, 1992, vice-chair, 1993, chair, 1994; South Carolina Library Association, 1992-; American Library Association, 1990-; Society of American Archivists, 1990-. **HONORS/AWARDS:** Phi Alpha Theta History Honor Society, 1984. **BUSINESS ADDRESS:** State Records Archivist I, South Carolina Department of Archives and History, 1430 Senate St, PO Box 11669, Reference, Columbia, SC 29211, (803)734-8596.

BHATIA, TEJ K.
Educator. Indo-American. **PERSONAL:** Born Oct 19, 1945, Multan, Pakistan; son of Parma Nand Bhatia and Krishna Wanti Bhatia; married Shobha K, Sep 18, 1977; children: Kanika K, Ankit K. **EDUCATION:** University of Delhi, India, BA (with honors), 1965; University of Illinois, Urbana-Champaign, MA, 1972, PhD, 1978. **CAREER:** University of Chicago, University of California, University of Wisconsin at Madison, visiting positions, 1974-85; University of British Columbia, Vancouver, instructor, 1976-78; Syracuse University, Linguistic Studies Program, director, 1985-89; Cognitive Science Program, acting director, 1992-, associate professor, 1979-. **ORGANIZATIONS:** Linguistic Soc of America, 1974-; New York State Council on Linguistics, secretary, treasurer, 1981, 1985; American Assn for Applied Linguistics, 1980-; American Assn for Computational Linguistics, 1984-90; Linguistic Soc of India, 1974-80; secretary, co-organizer, dir, fellow of other organizations. **HONORS/AWARDS:** Syracuse University, Special Service Award, 1988; NRI Welfare Society of India, Hind-Ratna, 1991; Phi Kappa Phi Honor Society, 1973; University of Illinois, Consistently Outstanding Instructor, 1973-76; Syracuse University, fellow, Institute for Applied Linguistics, 1979-82. **SPECIAL ACHIEVEMENTS:** Author, Punjabi: A Cognitive-Typological Grammar, 1993; A History of the Hindi Grammatical Tradition, 1987; co-author: Code-Mixing: English Across Language, 1989; Handbook of Language Acquisition, forthcoming; Progression in Second Language Acquistion, 1985; also articles & book chapters; languages: Hindi-Urdu, Punjabi, Siraiki/Multani, Bengali, Nepali, Marathi, Kannada, Kashmiri, Sanskrit. **BUSINESS ADDRESS:** Professor, Syracuse University, 312 HBC, Syracuse, NY 13244-1160, (315)443-5374.

BHATNAGAR, DEEPAK
Research scientist. Indo-American. **PERSONAL:** Born Aug 5, 1949, Bikaner, Rajasthan, India; son of Madan Mohan Bhatnagar & Chander Vati Bhatnagar; married Madhu Kohli Bhatnagar, Jul 20, 1978; children: Deepa. **EDUCATION:** University of Udaipur, India, BS (with honors), agriculture, 1972; Indian Agricultural Research Institute, New Dehli, MS, agricultural physics, 1974, PhD, agricultural physics, 1977. **CAREER:** Indian Agricultural Research Institute, junior research fellow, 1972-74, senior research fellow, 1974-77; International Crops Research Institute for Semi-Arid Tropics, trainee, 1974; India Institute of Medical Sciences, research scientist, 1977-78; Purdue University, research associate, 1979-81; LSU School of Medicine, senior research associate, 1981-85; USDA-ARS, Southern Regional Research Center, research geneticist, gs-12, 1985-88, gm-13, 1988-92, gm-14, 1992-; Tulane University, adjunct professor, 1991-. **ORGANIZATIONS:** American Society for Biochemistry and Molecular Biology; American Chemical Society; American Society of Plant Physiologists; American Society for Microbiology; American Association for the Advancement of Science; Sigma Xi; New York Academy of Sciences. **HONORS/AWARDS:** American Society for Biochemistry and Molecular Biology, High School Teacher Fellowship Award, 1993; USDA Certificate of Merit, 1989, 1991, 1992; USDA-ARS, PMRS Awards, 1989-92; USDA Certificate of Appreciation, 1990; American Heart Association-Louisiana, Dr George S Bel Memorial Research Award, 1982-84; numerous others. **SPECIAL ACHIEVEMENTS:** Appointed to the editorial boards of Mycopathologia, 1990-, Applied and Environmental Microbiology, 1991-; senior editor of 2 books, Handbook of Applied Mycology, vol V, Mycotoxins in Ecological Systems, Marcel Dekker Inc, 1991, Molecular Approaches to Improving Food Quality and Safety, Van Nostrand Reinhold, 1992; panel member, National Research Council, National Academy of Sciences, report published as a book entitled, Neem: A tree for solving global problems, 1992; co-editor, Mycopathologia, vol 107, nos 2-3, 1989; tutor, Operation Mainstream, an adult literacy program, 1988-. **BUSINESS ADDRESS:** Research Geneticist, USDA Agricultural Research Service, Southern Regional Research Center, 1100 Robert E Lee Blvd, New Orleans, LA 70124.

BHATNAGAR, KUNWAR P.
Educator. Indo-American. **PERSONAL:** Born Mar 21, 1934, Gwalior, Madhya Pradesh, India; son of Narayan Swaroop Bhatnagar and Bhagwati Devi Bhatnagar; married Indu Bhatnagar, Apr 28, 1961; children: Divya B Rouben, Jyoti B Burruss. **EDUCATION:** Agra University, India, BSc, 1956; Vikram University, India, MSc, 1958; State University of New York, Buffalo, PhD, 1972. **CAREER:** University of Louisville, School of Medicine, assistant professor, 1972-78, associate professor, 1978-85, professor, 1985-. **ORGANIZATIONS:** American Association of Anatomists; American Society of Mammalogists, life member; Sigma Xi; Bat Research News; Chiropterological Society of India, patron. **HONORS/AWARDS:** Max Planck Institute for Brain Research, Frankfort, Germany, visiting scientist, 1978, 1986; University of Essen Klinikum, Essen, Germany, visiting scientist, 1979. **SPECIAL ACHIEVEMENTS:** Scientific articles in journals, book chapters, 1965-; Bat Research News, former editor, 1982-86; Microscopy Research & Technique, guest editor, 1992. **BUSINESS ADDRESS:** Professor, Dept of Anatomical Sciences & Neurobiology, University of Louisville, School of Medicine, HSC, Louisville, KY 40292.

BHATNAGAR, YOGENDRA MOHAN
Educator. Indo-American. **PERSONAL:** Born Feb 5, 1945, Gorakhpur, Uttar Pradesh, India; son of Ved Bhatnagar and H M Bhatnagar; married Sheela P Bhatnagar, Aug 30, 1974; children: Pooja. **EDUCATION:** University of Lucknow, Lucknow, India, BSc, MSc, 1960-66; University of Copenhagen, 1966-67; Boston College, PhD, 1968-74; Harvard University, School of Medicine, 1974-77. **CAREER:** Boston College, instructor, 1973-74; Harvard University, research fellow, 1974-76, research associate, 1976-77; EIC Corporation, senior scientist, 1977-79; University of South Alabama, assistant professor, 1979-84, associate professor, 1984-. **ORGANIZATIONS:** American Academy for the Advancement of Sciences, 1974-; Society for the Study of Reproduction, 1986-; American Society of Biochemistry & Molecular Biology, 1984-. **HONORS/AWARDS:** National Institutes of Health, Research Career Development Award, 1985-90. **BUSINESS ADDRESS:** Associate Professor, Dept of Structural & Cellular Biology, University of South Alabama, College of Medicine, MSB 2042, Mobile, AL 36688, (205)460-6769.

BHATT, GITA
Mental health administrator. Indo-American. **PERSONAL:** Born Nov 14, 1945. **CAREER:** New York City Board of Education, Asian advisory council;

State of New York, office of mental health. **ORGANIZATIONS:** Asians in Women's Group, founder, 1979-; Queens Child Guidance, board of directors, currently. **SPECIAL ACHIEVEMENTS:** Asian Indian Delegation to the White House, 1985. **BUSINESS PHONE:** (718)920-0808.*

BHATT, GUNVANT R.
Mechanical contractor. Indo-American. **PERSONAL:** Born Jun 22, 1942, Morvi, Gujarat, India; son of Ratilal D Bhatt; married Rita (Tara), Jan 1970; children: Shephali, Sangini. **EDUCATION:** North Dakota State University, MS, mechanical engineering. **CAREER:** SBS Mechanical Inc, president, currently. **ORGANIZATIONS:** American Society of Heating Refrigeration & Air Conditioning. **HONORS/AWARDS:** State of Minnesota, professional engineer. **BUSINESS ADDRESS:** President, SBS Mechanical Inc, 7160 Madison Ave W, Golden Valley, MN 55427, (612)544-3471.

BHATT, JAGDISH J. (JACK)
Educator, author. Indo-American. **PERSONAL:** Born Feb 17, 1939, Umreth, Gujarat, India; son of Jeyshanker & Kamala M Bhatt; married Jan 22, 1970; children: Amar, Anita. **EDUCATION:** University of Baruda, India, BSc (with honors), 1961; University of Wisconsin, Madison, MS, 1963; University of California, Santa Barbara, postgraduate studies, 1968-69; University of Wales, Cardiff, PhD, 1972. **CAREER:** Wisconsin State Geol Survey, assistant geologist, 1961-63; Jackson Community College, instructor, 1964-65; Oklahoma State A&M University, instructor, 1965-66; University of Wales, Wolfson Research Fellow, 1969-79; Stanford University, res scientist, 1971-72; SUNY, Buffalo, assistant professor, 1972-74; Community College of Rhode Island, professor, 1974-. **ORGANIZATIONS:** Pacific Congress on Marine Science & Tech, Tokyo, sci advisory committee, 1990; Interinstitutional Arti & Credit Transfer, Higher Ed, RI State; Marine Science & Tech Program, CCRI, chair, 1978-79; State of Rhode Island, Governor's Ocean Task Force, 1975-76; Geocean Society, CCRI, faculty advisory, 1974-; Panel on Marine Paraprofessional Education, Southern New England Section, Marine Tech Soc, chair, 1979. **HONORS/AWARDS:** Phi Theta Kappa, CCRI, Instructor Excellence Award, 1989-90; Bowling Green State University, archives: custodian of Bhatt's original marine science papers; University of San Diego, Marine Science Program, NSF Fellow, summer 1993. **SPECIAL ACHIEVEMENTS:** Author, 55 scientific, educational, literary publications, including ten books; Oceanography-Year 2000 & Beyond, 1989-90; Oceanography-Concepts & Applications, 1994; Geology and Geochemistry of South Wales Main Limestone Series, Lower Carboniferus; Odyssey of the Damned, sci-fiction, 1992; Spinning Mind, Spinning Time, C'est la vie, poems, 1993; Universe, Mind & Brahman, 1994-95. **BIOGRAPHICAL SOURCES:** Contemporary Authors, V 77-80, 1979. **BUSINESS ADDRESS:** Professor, Community College of Rhode Island, 400 East Ave, Warwick, RI 02886, (401)825-2178.

BHATT, KIRAN CHANDRAKANT
Civil engineer, consultant. Indo-American. **PERSONAL:** Born Nov 19, 1940, Baroda, Gujarat, India; son of Chandrakant V Bhatt and Bhanumati C Bhatt; married Renu K Bhatt, Mar 8, 1969; children: Anita K, Suneet K. **EDUCATION:** MS University, India, BE, civil, 1963; Cornell University, MS, struct, 1965; Widener University, MBA, finance, 1974. **CAREER:** United Engineers & Constructors, supervising structural engr, 1969-86; private practice, financial planner, 1986-88; United Engineers & Constructors, supervising project controls engr, 1988-91; Raytheon Engineers & Constructors, consulting engr, 1991-. **ORGANIZATIONS:** Pennsylvania State, PE, 1974-; New Hampshire State, PE, 1978-. **HOME ADDRESS:** 23 Roberts Place, Somerdale, NJ 08083, (609)627-2402.

BHATTACHARJEE, JNANENDRA KUMAR
Educator. Indo-American/Bangladeshi American. **PERSONAL:** Born Feb 1, 1936, Digli, Sylhet, Bangladesh; son of Gobinda Kumar Bhattacharjee and Kumud Kamini Bhattacharjee; married Tripti Bhattacharjee, Aug 20, 1969; children: Gourab, Mala. **EDUCATION:** M C College, Sylhet, BS, 1957; Dacca University, MS, 1959; Southern Illinois University, PhD, 1966. **CAREER:** Albert Einstein Medical Center, research associate, 1965-66, assistant member, 1966-68; Miami University, Microbiology, associate professor, 1968-72, professor, 1973-. **ORGANIZATIONS:** American Society for Microbiology; Genetics Society of America; Sigma Xi; Ohio Academy of Science; Kiwanis Club of Oxford. **HONORS/AWARDS:** President's Award of Pakistan, 1961; Fulbright Award, 1961; Sigma Xi Mu Chapter, Research Scientist, 1983; American Academy of Microbiology, Fellow, 1985. **SPECIAL ACHIEVEMENTS:** Research on lysine biosynthesis and molecular studies of lysine genes of yeast, 1964-; published many research papers and reviews.

BUSINESS ADDRESS: Professor, Dept of Microbiology, Miami University, Biological Science Building, Oxford, OH 45056, (513)529-4727.

BHATTACHARYA, PRADEEP KUMAR
Educator. Indo-American. **PERSONAL:** Born Jan 12, 1940, Dacca, East Bengal, India; son of Debendra Kumar & Manorama Bhattacharya; married Anuradha Tiruvury, Jun 28, 1978; children: Jyotsna. **EDUCATION:** Banaras H University, India, ISc, biology, 1953, BS, biology, 1955, MS, botany, 1959; University of Saskatchewan, PhD, 1966. **CAREER:** MLK Degree College, India, lecturer in botany, 1959-61; University of Saskatchewan, PhD candidate in Biology Department, 1961-66, post doctoral fellow, 1966-67; University of Western Ontario, post doctoral fellow, 1967-69; University of Wisconsin, research associate, 1969-70; Rockford College, assistant professor, 1970-73; Indiana University Northwest, associate professor, 1973-. **ORGANIZATIONS:** American Society for Cell Biologists, 1970-; American Institute of Biological Sciences; AAAS; AAUP; Sigma Xi; Illinois Academy of Sciences; Indiana Academy of Sciences. **SPECIAL ACHIEVEMENTS:** Author of 15 research articles published in journals in the fields of physiology of plant host-parasite relations and cellular aging; language proficiency: Hindi, Bengali. **HOME ADDRESS:** 2626 N Lakeview, #3608, Chicago, IL 60614. **BUSINESS ADDRESS:** Associate Professor, Indiana University Northwest, 3400 Broadway, Marram Hall, Gary, IN 46408, (219)980-6717.

BHATTACHARYA, PURNA
Bank executive. Indo-American. **PERSONAL:** Born Jul 17, 1946, Jiaganj Pt Murshidabad, W. Bengal, India; son of Satya Brata Bhattacharya and Radha Rani Bhattacharya; married Krishna, Jul 9, 1970; children: Dabica, Sanjeeb. **EDUCATION:** University of Calcutta, India, BCom, 1965, MCom, 1968; Long Island University, MBA, 1975. **CAREER:** Merrill Lynch & Co, accountant, 1970-74; Carver Federal S&L, vice pres, controller, 1974-81; Safra Bank of NY, vice pres, controller, 1984-87; Republic National Bank of NY, vice pres, controller, 1981-84, first vice pres, 1987-. **BUSINESS ADDRESS:** First Vice President, Republic National Bank of New York, 452 Fifth Ave, New York, NY 10017.

BHATTACHARYA, RABI SANKAR
Research scientist. Indo-American. **PERSONAL:** Born Feb 19, 1948, Silchar, Assam, India; son of Ranajit Krishna Bhattacharya & Sucharu Bhattacharya; married Kabita Bhattacharya, Mar 13, 1979; children: Ratnesh, Debanjana. **EDUCATION:** Gauhati University, BSc, 1967; Indian Institute of Technology, Kharagpur, MSc, 1969; Saha Institute of Nuclear Physics, associateship, 1970; Calcutta University, PhD, 1975. **CAREER:** Saha Institute, Calcutta, research fellow, 1969-75; Fom-Institute, Amsterdam, visiting scientist, 1975-77; University of Giessen, W Germany, visiting professor, 1977-78; Max-Planck Institute, visiting scientist, 1978-79; McMaster University, Canada, senior research associate, 1979-80; University of Florida, senior research associate, 1980-81; UES Inc, principal research scientist, 1981-. **ORGANIZATIONS:** American Physical Society, 1981-; Materials Research Society, 1985-; American Society of Metals, 1985-; Society of Tribologists & Lubrication Engineers, 1989-; American Ceramic Society, 1985-; Bohmische Physical Society, elected member, 1992. **SPECIAL ACHIEVEMENTS:** Over 90 articles published in refereed journals, 1972-93; holder of a US patent, 1990. **HOME ADDRESS:** 2125 Matrena Dr, Dayton, OH 45431, (513)426-7561. **BUSINESS PHONE:** (513)426-6900.

BHATTACHARYYA, ASHIM KUMAR
Educator. Indo-American. **PERSONAL:** Born Jul 9, 1936, Kanpur, Uttar Pradesh, India; son of A Bhattacharyya and V N Bhattacharyya (deceased); married Bani Chatterjee, Jul 10, 1966; children: Rupa, Gopa. **EDUCATION:** Calcutta University, BSc, 1957, MSc, 1959, PhD, 1965, DSc, 1989. **CAREER:** University of Iowa, associate research scientist, 1970-74, research scientist, 1974-75; LSU Medical Center, assistant prof of pathology & physiology, 1975-80, associate prof of pathology & physiology, 1980-89, professor of pathology & physiology, 1989-. **ORGANIZATIONS:** American Heart Assoc, council on Arteriosclerosis, fellow; American Physiological Society; American Society for Clinical Nutrition; American Institute of Nutrition; Society for Experimental Biology & Medicine; New York Academy of Sciences; Louisiana State University Medical Center, New Orleans Sigma Xi, secretary, treasurer, 1992-94. **SPECIAL ACHIEVEMENTS:** Published approx 60 research articles in scientific journals; 3 review articles in scientific journals, wrote 1 book chapter. **BUSINESS ADDRESS:** Professor, Dept of Pathology, LA State University Med Ctr, 1901 Perdido St, New Orleans, LA 70112-1393, (504)568-6073.

BHATTACHARYYA, GOURI KANTA
Educator. Indo-American. **PERSONAL:** Born Jan 12, 1940, Hooghly, W. Bengal, India; son of Jagadish Kumar Bhattacharyya and Bivarani Bhattacharyya; married Jogamaya Bhattacharyya, Apr 17, 1962; children: Mitali Lebeck, Shuvra Shikhar. **EDUCATION:** Presidency College, Calcutta, ISc, 1956, BSc (with honors), 1958; Calcutta University, MSc, 1960; University of California, Berkeley, PhD, 1966. **CAREER:** R K Mission College, lecturer, 1960-61; River Research Institute, Calcutta, research officer, 1961-63; Indian Institute of Management, Ahmedabad, professor, 1969-70; Indian Statistical Institute, Calcutta, visiting associate professor, 1975-76, visiting professor, 1987-88; Syracuse University, visiting professor, 1979-80; Calcutta University, visiting professor, 1983; University of Wisconsin, assistant professor of statistics, 1966-69, associate professor of statistics, 1970-75, professor of statistics, 1975-, Department of Statistics, chairman, 1977-79, 1984-87. **ORGANIZATIONS:** American Statistical Association, associate editor, Journal of American Statistical Association, 1980-85. **HONORS/AWARDS:** American Statistical Assn, fellow, 1979; Institute of Mathematical Statistics, fellow, 1983. **SPECIAL ACHIEVEMENTS:** Over 55 papers published in professional research journals; two books published by John Wiley, New York. **BUSINESS ADDRESS:** Professor, Dept of Statistics, University of Wisconsin, 1210 W Dayton St, Madison, WI 53706, (608)262-3851.

BHATTACHARYYA, SHANKAR P.
Educator, educational administrator. Myanmar American. **PERSONAL:** Born Jun 23, 1946, Rangoon, Myanmar; son of Nil Kantha Bhattacharyya (deceased) and Hem Nauni Bhattacharyya (deceased); divorced; children: Krishna Lee, Mohadev, Shona Lee. **EDUCATION:** Indian Institute of Technology, Bombay, BTech (with honors), 1967; Rice University, MS, 1969, PhD, 1971. **CAREER:** Federal University, Rio de Janeiro, professor, 1971-80, electrical eng dept, chairman, 1978-80; 1978-80; Marshall Space Flight Center, NASA, NRE, research associate, 1974-75; Texas A&M University, elect eng, associate professor, 1980-84, professor, 1984-, Telecommunications and Control Systems Lab, director, 1990-92, Systems and Control Institute, director, 1992-. **ORGANIZATIONS:** IEEE Control Systems Society, associate editor, 1985-86, board of governors, 1986. **HONORS/AWARDS:** IEEE, fellow, 1989; Fulbright Association, Senior Lecturer, 1990; Halliburton Foundation, Award of Excellence, 1990; Dresser Industries, Dresser Professorship, 1992; TEES, fellow, 1990. **SPECIAL ACHIEVEMENTS:** Over 100 papers and 3 books in the field of control systems; 8 PhD and 15 masters degree students graduated. **HOME ADDRESS:** 3214 Westchester, College Station, TX 77845, (409)693-9320. **BUSINESS PHONE:** (409)845-7484.

BHATTI, RASHID A.
Tumor immunologist. Pakistani American. **PERSONAL:** son of G M Bhatti & Razia Sultana; married; children: Lubna. **EDUCATION:** University of Karachi; Eastern Illinois University; Harvard Medical School. **CAREER:** Pakistan Council of Scientific & Industrial Research, scientific officer, 1963-65; University of Illinois College of Medicine, research assistant, professor of surgery, 1986-; Cook County Hospital, urology research labs, director, 1973-. **ORGANIZATIONS:** Association of Pakistan Scientists and Engineers of North America, national president; Pakistan Academy of Medical Sciences, vice president, senior fellow; America Association for Cancer Research; European Association for Cancer Research; New York Academy of Sciences. **HONORS/AWARDS:** Mayor of Chicago, Outstanding Citizen Award, 1992; Fulbright Scholar, 1966; recipeint of two international awards for amateur photography; Cambridge, England, Distinguished Services to Medicine Award. **SPECIAL ACHIEVEMENTS:** Author, more than 130 scientific publications, including: original papers, review articles, abstracts and papers published in the proceedings of Intl Cancer Conferences and chapters in books. **BUSINESS ADDRESS:** Urology Research Labs Director, Professor of Surgery, Cook County Hospital, 1835 W Harrison St, Chicago, IL 60612, (312)633-7239.

BHAVNANI, PRATAP GAGUMAL
Journalist, community activist. Indo-American. **PERSONAL:** Born Mar 4, 1914, Hyderabad, Sind, Pakistan; son of Gagumal M & Shami Bhavnani; married Savitri, Apr 22, 1939; children: Nalini Thakrar, Deepak. **EDUCATION:** University of Bombay, BSc, 1936, MA, 1942. **CAREER:** India Tribune, Chicago, managing editor, 1981-88. **ORGANIZATIONS:** Indo-American Center, executive director, 1990-. **HONORS/AWARDS:** India Tribune "Man of the Year," 1988; Sindhi Association of Metropolitaqn Chicago, April 1989; Kala Akademi Award for Community Service, 1989; Hindi Literary Assoc & Sindhi Association, Journalistic Services, June 1985. **HOME ADDRESS:** 3205 Greenleaf, Wilmette, IL 60091, (708)256-7271.

BHOJWANI, RAM J.
Computer scientist. Indo-American. **PERSONAL:** Born Nov 3, 1942, Karachi, Sindh, Pakistan; son of J B Bhojwani and L J Bhojwani; married Asha; children: Rajesh, Shaan. **EDUCATION:** Vikram University, India, BS, 1964; University of Missouri, MS, 1967; University of Pennsylvania, PhD, 1977. **CAREER:** DuPont, methods analyst, 1967-70; Unisys, sr computer scientist, 1971-77; Federal Judicial Center, sr research computer scientist, 1977-91; AT&T Bell Labs, mem of technical staff, 1991-. **HONORS/AWARDS:** Alpha Pi Mu, 1966. **SPECIAL ACHIEVEMENTS:** Publication: Technological Changes & Machine Replacement Policy, 1966. **BUSINESS ADDRESS:** Member of Technical Staff, AT&T Bell Laboratories, 200 Laurel Ave, IF-325, Middletown, NJ 07748, (908)957-2934.

BHOWN, AJIT SINGH
Educator. Indo-American. **PERSONAL:** Born Mar 19, 1934, Jaipur, Rajasthan, India; son of Durga Prasad Bhown (deceased) and Chand Devi Bhown (deceased); married Meera Bhown, Apr 18, 1958; children: Sonchita Chakrabarty, Abhoyjit Singh. **EDUCATION:** University of Rajasthan, Jaipur, MSc, 1957, PhD, 1965. **CAREER:** Government of Rajasthan, reader, until 1974; University of Alabama at Birmingham, professor, 1974-. **ORGANIZATIONS:** ASBMB, 1986-; Protein Society. **HOME ADDRESS:** 2509 Brookwater Circle, Birmingham, AL 35243, (205)970-0960.

BHUYAN, BIJOY KUMAR
Cancer researcher. Indo-American. **PERSONAL:** Born Aug 30, 1930, Calcutta, W. Bengal, India; son of Mahendra N Bhuyan and Tillottoma Bhuyan; married Janet J; children: Shanti, Leela. **EDUCATION:** Utkal University, BSc, 1948; Calcutta University, MSc, 1950; University of Wisconsin, PhD, 1956; Western Michigan University, MA, 1984. **CAREER:** University of Wisconsin, postdoctoral, 1956-57; Saskatchewan Regional Research Lab, postdoctoral, 1957-59; Hindustan Antibiotics, senior scientific officer, 1959-60; Upjohn Co, scientist, 1960-. **ORGANIZATIONS:** American Association Cancer Research, 1960-93; Cell Kinetics Society, 1960-93; Kalamazoo Consultation Center, voluntary service, 1989-93; Couselling Center, volunteer. **SPECIAL ACHIEVEMENTS:** Cancer Research Journal, associate editor. **BUSINESS ADDRESS:** Senior Scientist, Cancer Research Dept, Upjohn Co, Kalamazoo, MI 49002.

BIJLANI, CHANDUR KISHINCHAND
Electrical engineer. Indo-American. **PERSONAL:** Born May 17, 1943, Karachi, India; son of Kishinchand Bijlani and Indira Bijlani; married Ratna, Jun 2, 1969; children: Akash. **EDUCATION:** College of Engineering, India, BSEE, 1965; DeVry Institute of Technology, diploma, automobile engineering, 1982. **CAREER:** Siemens, electrical engr, 1965-. **ORGANIZATIONS:** State of Illinois, professional engineer, 1973-. **SPECIAL ACHIEVEMENTS:** Language proficiency: Hindi, Sindhi, German. **HOME ADDRESS:** 431 Cedarcrest Dr, Schaumburg, IL 60193. **BUSINESS PHONE:** (608)276-3000.

BIRADAVOLU, KALESWARA RAO
Educator. Indo-American. **PERSONAL:** Born Sep 23, 1956, Hyderabad, Andhra Pradesh, India; married Madhavi, Aug 26, 1992. **EDUCATION:** University of New Haven, 1990. **CAREER:** Connecticut State Department of Transportation, programmer, 1990; Monroe College, professor, 1990-. **HONORS/AWARDS:** UNH, Dean's List, 1989. **SPECIAL ACHIEVEMENTS:** Published a book about CTT programming in India. **BUSINESS ADDRESS:** Professor, Monroe College, 29 Fordham E, Bronx, NY 10468.

BISWAS, DIPAK R.
Engineer. Indo-American. **PERSONAL:** Born Feb 3, 1949, India; son of Debendranath & Swarnalata; married Bharati, Mar 10, 1978; children: Minakshi, Mitali. **EDUCATION:** University of Calcutta, BSc, chemistry, 1968, BTech, 1970, MTech, 1971; University of California, Berkeley, MS, 1974, PhD, 1976. **CAREER:** ITT EOPD/Alcatel, manager, 1981-88; Spectran Corp, director, research & development, 1988-91; Fiberguide Industries, director, research & development, 1991-. **ORGANIZATIONS:** American Ceramic Society, life member; Electronics Industry Association, 1988; Society of Photo-optical Instrumentation Engineers, conference co-chairman, 1989-. **HONORS/AWARDS:** University of California, research assistantship, 1972-76; Rockwell Intl, postdoctoral fellowship, 1976-78; ITT EOPD, engineering award, 1983; ITT Corp, Fox Awards, 1985. **SPECIAL ACHIEVEMENTS:** More than 80 publications in different technical journals, magazines, 1975-; 10 US patents, 2 applied. **HOME ADDRESS:** 166 Thoreau Dr, Plainsboro, NJ 08536,

(609)936-9158. **BUSINESS ADDRESS:** Director, Research & Development, Fiberguide Industries, One Bay St, Stirling, NJ 07980, (908)647-6601.

BISWAS, NRIPENDRA NATH
Educator. Indo-American. **PERSONAL:** Born Aug 1, 1930, Lahiri, Dinajpur, India; married Lieselotte, May 14, 1959; children: Indira Benbow, Arun. **EDUCATION:** University of Calcutta, PhD, 1955. **CAREER:** University of Notre Dame, Department of Physics, professor, currently. **BUSINESS ADDRESS:** Professor, Dept of Physics, University of Notre Dame, Notre Dame, IN 46556, (219)631-6458.

BISWAS, RENUKA
Educator, social worker. Indo-American. **PERSONAL:** Born May 6, 1928, Chittagong, India. **EDUCATION:** University of Calcutta, India, BA, 1948, BT, 1949, MA, 1951; University of Pennsylvania, MSW, 1959; Columbia University, DSW, 1971. **CAREER:** Kamala Girls High School, Calcutta, India, senior teacher, 1949-51; Ballygunge Siksha Sadan, Calcutta, India, senior teacher, 1951-57; Hudson Guild, Children's Program, director, 1960-62; Planning & Research Action Institute, Lucknow, India, Women's Program, director/specialist, 1963-68; Greater New York Board of Education, consultant, 1977; Bellevue Hospital Center, senior supervisor, 1969-76; Lock Haven University, Department of Sociology, Anthropology, Social Work & Geography, chairperson, 1986-93, professor, 1977-. **ORGANIZATIONS:** Assn of Asian American Social Work Educators, pres, 1983-90; Commission on Minority Concerns, treasurer, 1988-90; PA Assn of Social Work Educators, 1977-; Natl Assn of Social Workers, 1968-; Council on Social Work Education, 1968-; Assn of Indians in America, life member, 1968-, bd of trustees, 1975-78, exec member, 1968-77; Assn of Asian Indian Women in America, founding member, 1980-, exec member, 1980-85; NOW, 1977-; Southern Poverty Law Center, 1985-; Public Citizen, 1980-; Ross Library, life member, 1987-; Indian Cultural Center, bd of directors, 1973-; Clinton County Children & Youth Services, bd member, 1981-85; Centre Home Care Inc, bd member, 1992-. **HONORS/AWARDS:** Clinton Cty, Children & Youth Festival Committee, Community Service Award, 1993; Monimela (natl youth organization in India), Distinguished Alumni Award, 1992; Jaycees, Distinguished Service Award, 1983; PEO, scholarship, 1960; World Church Organization, scholarship, 1961; Northern PA Chapter of Assn of Indians in America Inc, Distinguished Service Award, 1988; Cultural Association of Bengal and Los Angeles Banga Saamelan, Lifelong Achievement Award, 1993. **SPECIAL ACHIEVEMENTS:** Banti, translation of a Hindi novel of Mannu Bhandari, Sree Publishing Co, 1993; Social Work Practice with Asian Americans, Sage Publications Inc, 1992; Songs of Tagore, Tagore Society of New York Inc, 1991; On Tagore, Tagore Society of New York Inc, 1984; Slum Clearance in Kanpur, Sree Publishing Co, 1981; Hemanter Holi, Sree Pub Co, 1991; Shei Meyeta, Sree Publishing Co, 1981. **HOME ADDRESS:** 200 N Highland Street, Lock Haven, PA 17745. **BUSINESS ADDRESS:** Prof/Chairperson, Dept of Sociology, Anthropology, Social Work & Geog, Lock Haven University, Thomas Field House Annex 103, Lock Haven, PA 17745.

BLANCO, PAUL DE LA CRUZ
Community worker, county official. Filipino American. **PERSONAL:** Born Jul 2, 1944, Echague, Isabela, Philippines; son of Rufino A Blanco (deceased) & Leoncia De La Cruz Blanco (deceased); married Miriam A Blanco, Jan 15, 1972; children: Paulyne B Jalique, Michelle A. **EDUCATION:** Philippine Christian University, BA, psychology, 1965; University of Phoenix, master of arts, organizational mgt, currently. **CAREER:** YMCA of Philippines, executive director, 1967-75; World Alliance of YMCA's, associate director for development, 1976-77; Filipino Caucus, community developer, 1978-84; United Methodist Church, parish worker among Filipinos, 1979-83, director; Long Beach District Filipino Parish, 1983-87; Filipino Outreach Center, executive director, 1980-84; County of LA, DMH, senior community worker II, 1987-; Federation of Filipino-American Associations, Inc, president, CEO, currently. **ORGANIZATIONS:** Citizen Police Complaint Commission, commissioner, 1990-; Long Beach, Bacolod Sister City Committee, chairman, 1992-; International Business Association, director, 1993; Long Beach Community Holding Co, director, 1993; Long Beach Community Partnership; Filipino-American Republican Voters of SB, Chairman, 1990-; Filipino-American Republican Council of CA, vice chair, 1990-; Filipino-American Voters Alliance, honorary chair, 1990-; South Coast Ecumenical Council, vice president, 1990-92; Dateline Brokers, Inc, chairman, 1993. **HONORS/AWARDS:** Virgo Promotions, Ten Outstanding Filipino Americans, 1993; Office of National Service, Outstanding Community Service in Political Affairs, 1989; House of Representatives, Congressional Record of Service, 1989; US Senate,

Outstanding Dedication to Filipino-American Community, 1989; Office of the Governor, Outstanding Contribution to Many Projects, 1989; White House, Office of National Service, Outstanding Community Service. **SPECIAL ACHIEVEMENTS:** Co-author, Under an Iron Heel, Filipino-American WWII, 1993; US Presidential Delegation to the Philippines, 1992; city rep of Long Beach to Bacolod City, Phil, tie-up, 1992; only Asian police commissioner in Long Beach City, 1990-; involved in church, and community, local, and national government, 1978-. **BIOGRAPHICAL SOURCES:** California Asian Courier, vol 1, no 2, p 1, 5, May 1985; California Examiner, p 1, 9, April 8-14, 1992. **HOME ADDRESS:** 2811 Canal Ave, Long Beach, CA 90810.

BLAZ, BEN
Congressman. Pacific Islander American. **PERSONAL:** Born Feb 14, 1928, Agana, Guam; married Ann Evers; children: Mike, Tom. **EDUCATION:** University of Notre Dame, BS, 1951, George Washington University, MA, business administration, 1963. **CAREER:** University of Guam, Mangilao, professor, 1983-84; US Congress, delegate from Guam, 1985-. **HONORS/AWARDS:** Freedoms Foundation, Medal of Freedom, 1969; University of Notre Dame, Distinguished Alumnus Award, 1988; Asian-American Award for Public Service, 1992; US Pan Asian American Chamber of Commerce, Excellence 2000 Award, 1992. **MILITARY SERVICE:** US Marine Corps, brigadier general, 1951-80; Legion of Merit, Bronze Star with Combat V, Vietnamese Cross of Gallantry, Navy Commendation Medal. **BUSINESS ADDRESS:** Congressman, US Congress, 1130 Longworth, Washington, DC 20515-5301, (202)225-1188.*

BLOCH, JULIA CHANG
Bank executive, former US ambassador. Chinese American. **PERSONAL:** Born Mar 2, 1942, Chefoo, China; daughter of Fu-yun Chang and Eva Yeh Chang; married Stuart Marshall Bloch, Dec 21, 1968. **EDUCATION:** University of California, Berkeley, BA, 1964; Harvard University, MA, 1967, postgrad work in management, 1987. **CAREER:** US Senate Select Committee on Nutrition and Human Needs, minority staff, 1971-76, chief minority counsel, 1976-77; US Intl Communications Agency, Office of African Affairs, deputy director, 1977-80; Bureau for Food for Peace and Voluntary Assistance, asst administrator, 1981-87; Bureau for Asia and Near East, asst administrator, 1987-88; Presidential appointee, US Ambassador to Kingdom of Nepal, 1989-93; Bank of America, Corporate Relations, Corporate Communications and Governmental Affairs, group executive vice president, 1993-. **ORGANIZATIONS:** Intl Center for Research on Women, executive board, 1974-81; Executive Women in Government, founder, chair, 1977-; Organization of Chinese American Women, founder, chair, 1977-; Natl Women's Political Caucus, 1978-84; Experiment in Intl Living, natl advisory council, 1981-93; US Natl Committee for Pacific Economic Cooperation, 1984-93; Intergovernmental Group on Indonesia, US delegate, The Netherlands, 1987; World Bank Consultative Group Meeting, US delegate, Paris, 1987; Natl Peace Corps, counsel, 1988-89; presidential advisory council member on Peace Corps, 1988-89; Asia Society, 1989. **HONORS/AWARDS:** Natl Institute for Women of Color, Outstanding Woman of Color, 1982; Organization of Chinese American Women, Woman of the Year, 1987; Peace Corps, Leader for Peace Award, 1987; AID, Humanitarian Service Award, 1987; Asian American Leadership Award, 1989; Natl Assn of Professional Asian Pacific American Women, Distinguished Public Service Award, 1989; Rotary Intl, Paul Harris Award, 1992. **SPECIAL ACHIEVEMENTS:** Chinese Home Cooking, co-author, 1986; A US-Japan Aid Alliance, author, 1991. **BUSINESS ADDRESS:** Group Executive VP, Corporate Relations, Bank of America, 555 California St, Ste 5175, San Francisco, CA 94104, (415)953-9310.*

BOLEN, JEAN SHINODA
Author, educator, psychiatrist. Japanese American. **PERSONAL:** Born Jun 29, 1936, Los Angeles, CA; daughter of Joseph and Megumi Yamaguchi Shinoda; married James Grayson Bolen, May 21, 1966; children: Melody Jean, Andre Joseph. **EDUCATION:** University of California, Los Angeles, 1954-55; Pomona College, 1955-57; University of California, Berkeley, BA, 1958; University of California, San Francisco, MD, 1962. **CAREER:** Los Angeles General Hospital, intern, 1962-63; University of California Medical Center, San Francisco, Langley Porter Neuropsychiatric Institute, psychiatry residency, 1963-66, clinical instructor, psychiatry, 1967-69, asst clinical professor, 1969-77, associate clinical professor, beginning 1977, clinical professor, 1984-; C G Jung Institute of San Francisco, analyst, diplomate, 1966; San Francisco, private practice, 1967-; University of California Hospital, San Francisco, staff member; New Realities Mag, vp, 1968-, ed advisory board, chairman, 1969-. **ORGANIZATIONS:** American Psychiatric Association, Council on National

Affairs, 1974-; N California Psychiatric Society; Royal Society of Medicine. **SPECIAL ACHIEVEMENTS:** Author: The Tao of Psychology: Synchronicity; Ring of Power: The Abandoned Child, the Authoritarian Father, and the Disempowered; Gods in Everyman: A New Psychology of Men's Lives and Loves; Goddesses in Every Woman: A New Psychology of Women. *

BORA, SUNDER S.
Lab director. Indo-American. **PERSONAL:** Born Oct 6, 1938, Almora, Uttar Pradesh, India; son of Himat Singh Bora & Bhawni Devi Bora; married Leela Bora, Jun 22, 1967; children: Renu, Bina. **EDUCATION:** Lucknow University, India, PhD, 1967. **CAREER:** Columbia Medical Center, research associate, 1968-70; Clinical Analysis Service, lab director, 1970-72; NW Hospital Center, assistant lab director, 1972-74, technical director, 1974-, program director, 1975-. **ORGANIZATIONS:** American Association for Clinical Chemistry, 1970-; American Society of Clinical Pathologists, 1979-; Indian Alumni For Clinical Chemistry, board of directors, 1985-89, secretary, 1991-. **SPECIAL ACHIEVEMENTS:** Co-author, IgM in toxic goitar, nontoxic nodular goiter and endemic goiter, Clinical Research, April 1970; IgM concentration in endemic and sporadic nontoxic nodular goiter, The 6th International Thyroid Conference, 1970; Circulating Immunoglobulin M: Increased Concentration in Endemic and Sporadic Hoiter, Science, vol 170, p 1201, 1970; An Evaluation of Total Creatinine Kinase Method for Du Pont ACA, June 1974; numerous others. **HOME ADDRESS:** 70 Crescent Terrace, Bedford Hills, NY 10507, (914)666-4861. **BUSINESS ADDRESS:** Technical Director, Northern Westchester Hospital Center, 400 E Main St, Mount Kisco, NY 10549, (914)666-1674.

BORGAONKAR, DIGAMBER SHANKARRAO
Geneticist, educator. Indo-American. **PERSONAL:** Born Sep 24, 1932, Hyderabad, India; son of Shankarrao Apparao and Kumudinibai Jatar Borgaonkar; married Manda Purandare, Dec 27, 1963; children: Rajendra, Sonya. **EDUCATION:** College of Agriculture, Osmania University, BSc, 1953; Indian Agricultural Research Institute, assoc, IARI, 1955; University of Minnesota, 1959; Oklahoma State University, PhD, 1963. **CAREER:** University of ND, assistant professor, 1963-64; Johns Hopkins University, Chromosome Lab, faculty, head, 1964-78; North Texas State University, professor, Research Center director, 1978-80; University of Delaware, life & health sciences, adjunct professor, 1981-; Thomas Jefferson Medical College, research professor, pediatrics, medical genetics, 1981-; Medical Center of Delaware, Cytogenetics Lab, director, 1980-. **ORGANIZATIONS:** Sigma Xi, 1960; American Association for the Advancement of Science, 1964; Peruvian Society of Medical Genetics, honorary member, 1989; Indian Society of Prenat Diag & Therapy, honorary member, 1990; American College Medical Genetics, affiliate member, 1992. **HONORS/AWARDS:** Hyderabad State Research, Scholar, 1955; National Institutes of Health, Baltic States Exchange Program, 1992; Bionaturalists, Haldane Award, 1988. **SPECIAL ACHIEVEMENTS:** Chromosomal Variation in Man, 7th edition, 1993; Repository of Human Chromosomal Variants & Anomalies, 14th edition, 1993. **BUSINESS ADDRESS:** Director, Cytogenetics Laboratory, Medical Center of Delaware, 4755 Ogletown Station Rd, PO Box 6001, Cytogenetics Laboratory, Newark, DE 19718, (302)733-3550.

BOSE, BIMAL KUMAR
Educator. Indo-American. **PERSONAL:** Born Sep 1, 1932, Calcutta, W. Bengal, India; son of Rajendra and Nirmala; married Arati, Jun 26, 1961; children: Papia, Amit. **EDUCATION:** Calcutta University, BE, 1956, PhD, 1966; University of Wisconsin, MS, 1960. **CAREER:** Bengal Engineering College, electrical engineering, associate professor, 1960-71; Rensselaer Polytechnic Institute, electrical engineering, associate professor, 1971-76; General Electric Corporate Research & Development, professor, electrical engineer, 1976-87; University of Tennessee, Condra Chair of Excellence in Power Electronics, 1987-. **ORGANIZATIONS:** IEEE, fellow, 1989-, Industrial Electronics Society, chairman of power electronics council, 1991-, chairman of power electronics track, 1987-, IEEE Industrial Electronics Transactions, associate editor, 1987-91, Industry Application Society, chairman of industrial converter committee, 1990-91, Power Electronics Society, program co-chairman, 1992; Asia-Pacific Engineer Journal, associate editor, 1993-; National Power Electronics Committee, 1989-. **HONORS/AWARDS:** IEEE Industry Applications Society, Outstanding Achievement Award, 1993; Shanghai University of Technology, Honorary Professor, 1991; Calcutta University, Mouat Gold Medal, 1970; General Electric Company, Silver Patent Medal, 1985. **SPECIAL ACHIEVEMENTS:** Author: Power Electronics and AC Drives, Prentice-Hall, 1986; Modern Power Electronics, IEEE Press, 1992; Adjustable

Speed AC Drive Systems, IEEE Press, 1982; Microcomputer Control of Power Electronics and Drives, 1987; 18 US patents; 105 papers. **MILITARY SERVICE:** National Cadet Corps, India, 2nd Lieutenant, 1961-62. **HOME ADDRESS:** 404 Dixie View Road, Knoxville, TN 37922. **BUSINESS ADDRESS:** Condra Chair of Excellence in Power Electronics, University of Tennessee, 419 Ferris Hall, Knoxville, TN 37996, (615)974-8288.

BOSE, PRATIM
Chemical plant manager. Indo-American. **PERSONAL:** Born Nov 17, 1956, Patna, India; son of Nalini Bose and Uma Bose; married Bijaya Bose, Dec 24, 1980; children: Priya, Neeva. **EDUCATION:** University of Waterloo, BSE, 1979. **CAREER:** Shell Canada, process engineering supervisor, 1987-89; supply & trading coordinator, 1989-90; Westlake Group, production manager, 1990-. **HOME ADDRESS:** 1518 N Covey Lane, Lake Charles, LA 70605, (318)478-1071.

BOWMAN, KIMIKO O.
Research scientist, educator. Japanese American. **PERSONAL:** Born Aug 15, 1927, Tokyo, Japan; daughter of Tuneshiro Osada and Fumiko Osada; divorced. **EDUCATION:** Radford University, BS, 1960; Virginia Polytechnic Institute & State University, MS, 1961, PhD, 1963; University of Tokyo, doctor of engineering, 1987. **CAREER:** ORNL, research scientist, 1963-84, senior research scientist, 1984-; UT, research professor of mathematics, 1990-. **ORGANIZATIONS:** American Statistical Association, fellow, 1963-; Institute of Mathematical Statistics, fellow, 1963-; Biometric Society, 1963-; American Association for the Advancement of Science, fellow, 1966-; International Statistical Institute, elected member, 1978-; Sigma Xi, 1963-; International Association for Statistics Computing, 1978-; Foundation for Science & Disability, president elect, 1988. **HONORS/AWARDS:** Radford University, Outstanding Alumnus, 1978; AWIS, Distinguished and Sustained Contributions to Science, 1988; Martin Marietta Energy Systems Inc, Technical Achievement Award, 1988; Institute for Scientific Information, Citation Classics, 1989; ASA, fellow 1976; AAAS, fellow, 1970; IMS, fellow, 1987. **SPECIAL ACHIEVEMENTS:** Author: Maximum Likelihood Estimation in Small Samples, Charles Griffin & Company Ltd, England, 1977; Properties of Estimators for the Gamma Distribution, Marcel Dekker Inc, 1988; Continued Fractions in Statistical Applications, Marcel Dekker Inc, 1989; Sample Size Requirement: Single and Double Classification Experiments, AMS and IMS, 1975; over 150 technical publications in Biometrika, JRSS, JASA, numerous others. **BUSINESS ADDRESS:** Senior Research Scientist, Oak Ridge National Laboratory, Building 6012, PO Box 2008, Oak Ridge, TN 37831-6367, (615)574-3126.

BRAHMA, CHANDRA SEKHAR
Educator. Indo-American. **PERSONAL:** Born Oct 5, 1941, Calcutta, W. Bengal, India; son of Nalini Kanta Brahma (deceased) and Uma Rani Brahma (deceased); married Purnima Brahma, Feb 18, 1972; children: Charanjit, Barunashish. **EDUCATION:** University of Calcutta, India, BE, 1962; Michigan State University, MSc, 1965; Ohio State University, PhD, 1969. **CAREER:** Frank H Lehr Associates, project engr, 1969-70; John G Reutter & Associates, sr geotechnical engr, 1970-72; Worcester Polytechnic Institute, asst prof, 1972-74; Daniel, Mann, Johnson & Mendenhall, chief geotechnical engr, 1974-79; Sverdrup Corp, sr engr, project mgr, 1979-80; private practice, consultant, 1980-; California State University-Fresno, professor, civil engineering, 1980-. **ORGANIZATIONS:** California Society of Professional Engineers, Fresno Chapter, vp, 1991-92, president, 1992-93; American Society of Civil Engineers, Fresno Branch, vp, 1983-84, president, 1984-85, secretary, 1981-83, San Francisco Section, dir, 1985-86, Committee on Minority Programs, chmn, 1988-89, Awards Committee, chmn, 1993-. **HONORS/AWARDS:** California Society of Professional Engineers, California Central Valley Outstanding Engineer Award, 1993; American Society of Civil Engineers, Edmund Friedman Professional Recognition Award, 1993, Outstanding Professor Award, 1985, Outstanding Civil Engineer Award, 1985, Distinguished Service Award, 1986; Halliburton Services, Inc, Halliburton Award for Teaching Excellence, 1991; California State University-Fresno, Outstanding Professor Award, 1989, Claude C Laval Innovative Technology and Research Awards, 1991, 1992; American Society for Engineering Education, AT&T Foundation Award, 1991; Council for Intl Exchange of Scholars, Fulbright Award, 1984. **SPECIAL ACHIEVEMENTS:** Author: "Computer-Aided Design of Shallow Foundations," 1992; "Ground Characterization of Expansive Soils," 1992; "Value Engineering Analysis of Excavation Support System," 1987; "Stochastic Simulation of Creep Behavior," 1983; "Fundaciones y Mechanica de Suelos," vols 1-3, 1986. **BUSINESS ADDRESS:** Professor,

Civil Engineering, California State University, Fresno, 2320 E San Ramon Ave, East Engineering Bldg, Rm 131, Fresno, CA 93740-0094, (209)278-2579.

BRIGGS, TRACEY WONG
Copy editor. Chinese American. **PERSONAL:** Born Nov 20, 1961, Boulder City, NV; daughter of Morton M & E Elizabeth Wong; married Robert H Briggs, Jun 23, 1984. **EDUCATION:** University of Texas, BJ (highest honors), 1983. **CAREER:** Reno Gazette Journal, reporter, 1983-85; USA Today, reporter, 1986-88, copy editor, 1988-. **ORGANIZATIONS:** Asian American Journalists Association, 1987-; Potomac Valley Track Club, 1988-, past board member, newsletter editor. **HONORS/AWARDS:** University Texas, Lorene Rogers Scholar/Athlete Award, 1983; Potomac Valley Seniors Track Club, President's Award, 1990. **SPECIAL ACHIEVEMENTS:** Co-author, Walking Women: The First Steps, 1993; qualifier, US Olympic Track & Field Trials, 10K racewalk, 1992; former school record holder, 10,000-meter run, University Texas, 1981-83. **BUSINESS ADDRESS:** Copy Editor, USA Today, 1000 Wilson Blvd, 15th Fl, Arlington, VA 22229, (703)276-6580.

BRILLANTES, HERMOGENES BILGERA
Debt and equity financing executive, insurance and securities broker. Filipino American/Chinese American. **PERSONAL:** Born Jan 15, 1944, Lucena City, Quezon, Philippines; son of Felix Chan Brillantes and Cleo B Brillantes; married Teresita, Dec 28, 1969. **EDUCATION:** University of the Philippines, BS business administration, 1966; New York University, graduate studies in business, 1971; American College, currently. **CAREER:** Sacred Heart College, economics and marketing lecturer, 1967-68; USV Pharmaceutical Corp, senior corporate accountant, 1970-72; H B Brillantes & Company, managing director, 1972-; Retirement Investments Portfolio, speaker. **ORGANIZATIONS:** Binhi Kultural Arts Society Inc, president, 1991-; Pan Xenia Intl Foreign Trade Fraternity, governor, 1966, associate member, 1990-; United Philippine Appeal, 1993; Univ of the Philippines, executive committee, 1966. **HONORS/AWARDS:** National Assn of Life Underwriters, Life Insurance Research & Marketing Assn, National Sales Achievement Award, National Quality Award, NJ Leaders Club, 1972-; New York Life Insurance & Securities Co, President's Council, 1982-86, Executive Council, 1987-; Million Dollar Round Table. **SPECIAL ACHIEVEMENTS:** Produced, as president of Binhi Kultural Society, the first Filipino opera on Broadway and in the USA, 1992; published: Philippine Foreign Trade Guideline Manual, 1966; Effects of the Telecommunications Industry on the Economic Development of the Philippines, 1966; The Politics of Foreign Aid in the Philippines, 1965. **BUSINESS ADDRESS:** President, H B Brillantes & Company, Park 80 W Plaza 2, 5-NYL, Saddle Brook, NJ 07662, (201)845-9341.

BROWN, JULIE (NGYUEN NGOE THAN AHN JULIE)
Manufacturing company executive. Vietnamese American. **PERSONAL:** Born 1949, Saigon, Vietnam; married Jim Brown; children: 2. **EDUCATION:** Tulane University, computer science degree. **CAREER:** Ford Motor Co, body engineering dept, warranty analyst; Plastech Engineered Products Inc, president, CEO, 1988-. **SPECIAL ACHIEVEMENTS:** Purchased 2 nearly bankrupt auto parts companies and made them profitable in less than 2 months. **BUSINESS ADDRESS:** President & CEO, Plastech Engineered Products Inc, 33195 Harper Ave, St Clair Shores, MI 48082, (313)294-9440.*

BULSARA, ARDESHIR RATAN (ADI)
Physicist. Indo-American. **PERSONAL:** Born May 15, 1951, Bombay, India; son of Ratan Bulsara and Roshan Bulsara; married Marcia Rutan Bulsara, Jul 8, 1978; children: Cyrus, Nicole. **EDUCATION:** University of Bombay, BSc, 1970; SUNY at Stony Brook, MA, 1973; University of Texas, Austin, PhD, 1978. **CAREER:** University of California, San Diego, post doctoral fellow, 1978-80; Titan Corp, scientist, 1981-83; Naval Command Control & Ocean Surveillance Ctr, scientist, 1983-. **HONORS/AWARDS:** Govt of India, National Scholarship, 1970. **SPECIAL ACHIEVEMENTS:** Publications: over 50 professional papers in peer-reviewed journals. **BIOGRAPHICAL SOURCES:** Nature, vol 352, no 6335, p 469, Aug 1991. **BUSINESS ADDRESS:** Scientist, Naval Command Control & Ocean Surveillance Ctr, San Diego, CA 92152-5000, (619)553-1595.

BULUSU, SURYANARAYANA
Research scientist. Indo-American. **PERSONAL:** Born Aug 21, 1927, Ellore, Andhra Pradesh, India; son of Subrahmanyadutt & Chellayamma Bulusu; married Lakshmi S, Dec 18, 1958. **EDUCATION:** Andhra University, Waltair, BS, (honors), 1948; University of Bombay, BS, tech, 1950, PhD, 1954. **CAREER:** Yale University, research associate, 1954-56; Brookhaven National

Lab, research associate, 1956-58; University of Wisconsin, research associate, 1958-60; US Army Ardec, research scientist, 1960-. **ORGANIZATIONS:** American Chemical Society, 1960-; American Society for Mass Spectroscopy, 1965-; Sigma Xi, 1957-. **HONORS/AWARDS:** Army Research & Development Awards, 1968, 1974, 1990, 1992. **SPECIAL ACHIEVEMENTS:** Editor, Chemistry and Physics of Energetic Materials, Kluwer, 1989; many research publications in Journal Physical Chemistry, Organic Magnetic Resonance, Organic Mass Spectrometry. **HOME ADDRESS:** 22 Skyview Terrace, Morris Plains, NJ 07950.

C

CABANA, VENERACION GARGANTA
Educator, researcher. Filipino American. **PERSONAL:** Born Jan 9, 1942, Lopez, Quezon, Philippines; daughter of Angel Cabana (deceased) and Irene Garganta. **EDUCATION:** Philippine Union College, BS, 1964; University of Chicago, cytotech certificate, 1969; University of Illinois, MS, 1972, PhD, 1980. **CAREER:** Philippine Union College, instructor, 1964-68; University of Washington, research associate, 1972-75; Rush Presbyterian St Lukes Medical Center, instructor, assistant professor, 1980-83, assistant professor, 1987-89; University of Chicago, senior research technician, supervisor, 1969-70, research associate, assistant professor, 1983-87, senior research associate, 1989-. **ORGANIZATIONS:** Chicago Association of Immunologists, 1980-, secretary-treasurer, 1983-85; American Heart Association, arteriosclerosis, fellow, 1983-; American Association of Clinical Chemists, 1983-; American Association of Immunologists, 1980-. **HONORS/AWARDS:** Philippine Union College, most outstanding alumni, 1989. **SPECIAL ACHIEVEMENTS:** Publications: co-author, "The Acute-Phase Response and Associated Lipoprotein Abnormalities Accompanying Lymphoma," J Intern Med, 233: 201-4, 1993; "Abnormal HDL Generated During the Acute Phase Response," Role in HDL Metabolism, 1993; "Development and Application of an Antibody Specific for Apolipoprotein B48," 1993; abstracts: co-author, "Endotoxin-Induced Lipoprotein Alterations in Baboons," American Heart Association 66th Scientific Sessions, 1993; "Transformation of HDL by Free Fatty Acid," American Heart Association 66th Scientific Sessions, 1993. **HOME ADDRESS:** 504 N Richmond St, Westmont, IL 60559, (708)850-7425. **BUSINESS ADDRESS:** Senior Research Associate, Dept of Pathology, University of Chicago, 5841 S Maryland Ave, MC 6079, Chicago, IL 60637, (312)702-6740.

CABANTING, GEORGE PAUL
Business manager. Filipino American. **PERSONAL:** Born Dec 19, 1953, New York, NY; son of Ann Cabanting and Honorio Cabanting; married Patricia Cabanting; children: Ryan, Steven. **EDUCATION:** Bronx Community College, 1971-75; Bergen Community College, business administration, 1980. **CAREER:** AT&T, records retention analyst, 1971-72; World-Wide Volkswagen, technician, test technician, supervisor warranty testing, service training instructor, warranty auditor, 1972-76; Volkswagen of America, warranty specialist, technical analyst, product field support supervisor, compliance engineer, 1976-82; Volvo Cars NA, warranty expense analyst, 1982-84; Porsche Cars NA, manager, warranty and service systems, 1984-. **ORGANIZATIONS:** Society of Automotive Engineers, associate, 1976-; Automotive Service Excellence, master technician, 1974-; Volvo Master Technician, master technician, 1982-84; Volkswagen, Porsche, Audi, Master Technician, master technician, 1977-82; Volvo Cars North America, chairman, expense control committee, 1982-84; Porsche Cars North America PC Users Group, 1987-88. **SPECIAL ACHIEVEMENTS:** Numerous Porsche publications: training manuals, policy manuals, users guides, customer warranty booklets, brochures, 1984-; executive producer: 4 warranty training video tapes, Porsche Cars North America, 1990; musical album: Rise and Fall of Flood, Maple Records, 1970. **HOME ADDRESS:** 13765 Rancho Verde Drive, Reno, NV 89511. **BUSINESS ADDRESS:** Manager, Warranty & Service Systems, Porsche Cars, NA, 100 W Liberty St, Reno, NV 89501, (702)348-3000.

CABRERA, CESAR TRINIDAD
Association administrator. Filipino American. **PERSONAL:** Born Mar 3, 1935, Pasay, Philippines; son of Agapito Cabrera and Paulina Cabrera; married Conchita Tan Cabrera, Jun 23, 1963; children: Cecilia. **EDUCATION:** Cavite Vocational School, 1954-56. **CAREER:** US Navy, MCPO, 1958-88; NASA, GS 9 admin support, 1988-92; Mrs Philippines Home for Senior Citizens, board of directors, 1989-. **ORGANIZATIONS:** The Travelers of WDC, president, 1989-; Zambaleneos Inc, Internal Affairs, vice president, 1993-; Cavite Assoc of Metro Wash DC, special assistant to the president. **HONORS/AWARDS:**

Zambaleneos Inc, Presidential Award, 1989-90; Navy Achievement Award, 1970-72, Navy Commendation Award, 1982-86. **HOME ADDRESS:** 7901 Claudia Dr, Oxon Hill, MD 20745.

CAI, JIN-YI
Educator. Chinese American. **PERSONAL:** Born Jan 23, 1961, Shanghai, People's Republic of China; son of Pu Cai and Ju Zhang; married Gabriele E Meyer, Nov 27, 1987; children: Elizabeth Y, Walter Z. **EDUCATION:** Fudan University, Shanghai, China, 1977-81; Temple University, MA, 1983; Cornell University, PhD, 1986. **CAREER:** Yale University, association professor, 1986-89; Princeton University, assistant professor, 1989-. **ORGANIZATIONS:** Association of Computing Machinery, 1986-. **HONORS/AWARDS:** National Science Foundation, Presidential Young Investigation, 1990-95. **SPECIAL ACHIEVEMENTS:** With Probability One, a random article separates PSPACE from the Polynomial Hierarchy, 1986. **BUSINESS ADDRESS:** Association Professor, Princeton University, 35 Olden St, Computer Science Bldg, Rm 407, Princeton, NJ 08544-2087, (609)258-6314.

CAI, SHELTON XUANQING
Medical scientist. Chinese American. **PERSONAL:** Born Feb 10, 1954, Shanghai, People's Republic of China; son of Zhe-Gao Cai and Li-Ying Wong; married Bing Zhou Cai, Jan 8, 1982; children: David Zhen. **EDUCATION:** Shanghai Medical University, School of Medicine, MD, 1979, MS, 1982; UCLA, School of Public Health, MPH, 1988, PhD, 1991. **CAREER:** Shanghai Medical University, asst professor, 1982-85; Leuven University, Belgium, research fellow, 1985-86; Tyler Medical Clinic, embryologist, 1986-91; UCLA Medical Center, research associate, 1989-91; Olympia Women's Health, lab director, 1991-. **ORGANIZATIONS:** European Society of Human Reproduction and Embryology, 1986-87; American Fertility Society, 1988-89. **HONORS/AWARDS:** Belgium Education Ministry, ABDS Fellowship, 1985; UCLA, Graduate Fellowship, 1988. **SPECIAL ACHIEVEMENTS:** Publications, with others, on human infertility: "Andrology," 22: 539-542, 1990; "Fertility and Sterility," 51: 719-721, 1989; "Reproduction and Contraception," 7: 6-10, 1987; "Acta Genetica Sinica," 11: 230-236, 1984. **BUSINESS ADDRESS:** Medical Scientist, Olympia Women's Health, 403-E Black Hills Lane SW, Olympia, WA 98502, (206)786-1515.

CALDITO, GLORIA CRUZ
Educator, biostatistician. Filipino American. **PERSONAL:** Born Aug 30, 1944, Lingayen, Pangasinan, Philippines; daughter of Tomas Caldito & Ursula Caldito. **EDUCATION:** University of Santo Tomas, Manila, Philippines, BS (magna cum laude), mathematics, physics 1965; University of the Philippines, Quezon City, MS, statistics, 1981; University of Pittsburgh, MA, applied statistics, 1986, PhD, biostatistics, 1990. **CAREER:** University of the Philippines, instructor of mathematics and statistics, 1968-74, assistant professor of statistics, 1975-80, associate professor of statistics, 1981-84; University of Pittsburgh, teaching assistant, 1984-90; Northeastern Ohio Universities College of Medicine, assistant professor of biostatistics, 1990-. **ORGANIZATIONS:** American Statistical Association, 1989-; Biometric Society, 1989-; American Public Health Association, 1991-; Ohio Public Health Association, 1991-. **HONORS/AWARDS:** Australian National University, Colombo Plan Scholarship, Graduate Fellowship in Statistics, 1967. **SPECIAL ACHIEVEMENTS:** Co-author, Social Survey Research Design, Phil Social Science Council, 1981; co-author, Data Analysis and Interpretation, PSSC, 1982; co-author, Sample Survey Procedures, Agricultural Development Council, 1977. **BUSINESS ADDRESS:** Northeastern Ohio Universities College of Medicine, 4209 State, Rt 44, PO Box 95, Rootstown, OH 44272, (216)325-2511.

CAMPBELL, PHYLLIS J. TAKISAKI
Banker. Japanese American. **PERSONAL:** Born in Spokane, WA; married. **EDUCATION:** Washington State University, BA, business administration; University of Washington, MBA, Pacific Coast Banking School, graduate; Stanford University, marketing management program. **CAREER:** Old National Bank, management trainee, 1973, branch manager, senior vice president, manager of all Spokane branches, 1981; US Bank of Washington, senior vice president, area manager for Eastern Washington, executive vice president, manager of the distribution group, 1989-92, Seattle-King County division, president, 1992-93, president, chief executive officer, 1993-. **ORGANIZATIONS:** Spokane Valley Chamber of Commerce, president, 1987-88; Washington State Growth Strategies Commission, 1990; Washington Roundtable and Greater Seattle Chamber of Commerce, board member; Association of Washington Business, vice-chair; Washington State University, regent; Success by 6, Puget Sound youth organization, chair, 1993; Puget Sound Power &

Light, director, 1993. **HONORS/AWARDS:** Puget Sound Matrix Table, Woman of Achievement Award, 1992. **BUSINESS ADDRESS:** President and CEO, US Bank of Washington, PO Box 720, Seattle, WA 98111, (206)344-4553.

CAO, HOANG-YEN THI
Programmer analyst. Vietnamese American. **PERSONAL:** Born Jul 9, 1960, Binh Thuan, Vietnam; daughter of Duc Cao and Mui Thi Phan; married Francis Ly, Jul 8, 1989 (deceased). **EDUCATION:** Los Angeles City College, AA; California State University, Los Angeles, BS. **CAREER:** Gilbraltar Savings & Loan, bank teller, 1985-87; Mandex, programmer analyst, 1987-89; South West Savings & Loan, programmer analyst, 1989-90; Security Pacific State Trust Co, programmer analyst, 1990-92; Aratex Services, programmer analyst, 1992-.

CAO, LE THI
Educator. Vietnamese American. **PERSONAL:** Born Jun 26, 1934, Thudaumot, Vietnam; daughter of Cao Van Vang & Neuyen Thi Hien. **EDUCATION:** Public administration, BS (honors), 1965; MBA, 1975; DBA, 1975. **CAREER:** VN Glass Co, assistant to the chief executive officer, 1969-71; George Mason University, associate professor, 1974-; National Institute of Administration, assistant professor, 1975; School of Economics, assistant professor, 1976-78. **ORGANIZATIONS:** American Accounting Association, 1979-; Institute of Management Accounting, coordinator, 1985-; Vietnamese NIA Alumni Associations, chairman of the board, 1986-; Vietnamese Community in the Metropolitan of Washington DC, Virginia, & Maryland, advisor, 1990-92; Nguyen Ngoc Huy Foundation, board of directors, 1992-. **SPECIAL ACHIEVEMENTS:** Publications in: Journal of Accounting Education; Journal of Business Education; Journal of Education for Business; International Journal of Public Administration; Akron Business and Economic Reviews; IDEA, The Journal of Law & Technology; and Public Budgeting and Financial Management. **BUSINESS ADDRESS:** Professor, School of Business Administration, George Mason University, 4400 University Drive, Robinson Hall, Rm 417, Fairfax, VA 22030, (703)993-1761.

CAOILE, GLORIA T.
Union administrator. Filipino American. **CAREER:** American Federation of State, County, and Municipal Employees, special assistant to the president, currently. **ORGANIZATIONS:** Filipino-American Political Association, Capitol District, chairwoman, currently; Association of Philippine American Women, first vice president; Foundation For Aid to the Philippines, founder, past president, chairwoman of the board; Philippine Heritage Federation and the Progressive Alliance of Filipinos and Americans Inc, past executive vice president, past vice president; Asian Pacific American Heritage Council, past treasurer. **BUSINESS ADDRESS:** Special Assistant to the President, American Federation of State, County, & Municipal Employees, 1625 L St NW, Washington, DC 20036, (202)452-4800.*

CAOILE, JOHN ANTHONY
Hydrogeologist. Filipino American. **PERSONAL:** Born Mar 16, 1948, San Antonio, TX; son of Juan J Caoile and Pauline L Caoile; married Anna Margaret Semler Caoile, Dec 23, 1971. **EDUCATION:** University of Missouri-Kansas City, BS, geology, 1971. **CAREER:** General Testing Laboratories, mgr, soils lab, 1971-80; Ecology and Environment Inc, asst mgr, 1980-. **ORGANIZATIONS:** Assn of Engineering Geologists, 1972- past secretary, Kansas City-Omaha Section, treasurer; American Institute of Professional Geologists #6214, 1983; State of Indiana, professional geologist, 1982-; State of Iowa, ground water professional, 1992-; State of Alaska, professional geologist, 1992. **SPECIAL ACHIEVEMENTS:** Co-author: "Geology of Kansas City Missouri and Kansas," Bulletin of Assn of Engineering Geologists, Aug 1988; "Utilization of Shallow Geophysical Sensing at Two Abandoned Municipal Industrial Waste Landfills on the Missouri River Floodplain," National Water Well Assn, Apr 1984; performed hundreds of site investigations for US Environmental Protection Agency in the midwest, including: remedial project manager, remedial investigation, Des Moines TCE ground water site; project director, North U Drive site, Springfield, MO; performed environmental studies for the Federal Aviation Agency at remote locations in Alaska; well installation for compliance monitoring at Sandia National Laboratories in Albuquerque, NM. **BUSINESS ADDRESS:** Assistant Manager, Ecology and Environment, Inc, 6405 Metcalf, Ste 404, Overland Park, KS 66202, (913)432-9961.

CAPOOR, ASHA
Company executive. Indo-American. **PERSONAL:** Born Jul 24, 1941, Ajmer, Rajasthan, India; daughter of Kailash Mehra & Jagrani Mehra; married Madan Capoor, Jan 19, 1964; children: Anjali Barz, Vineeta Kohorst. **EDUCATION:** Government College, BA, 1960, MA, 1962; Pratt Institute, MLS, 1972. **CAREER:** New York University, research assistant, 1968-69; R R Bowker, editorial coordinator, 1973-76; Baker & Taylor, manager, 1976-81, director, 1981-91, group director, 1991-. **ORGANIZATIONS:** NJLA, Technical Services Section, president, 1981-82; institute & lib development comm, 1993-; Library of Congress, CIP advisory comm, 1987-; ASIS, chair, 1989-91; NISO/SISAC, chair sub comm #DD, 1984-90; ALA/LITA, Vendor Use Interest Group, chair, 1987-88; ALA/APALA, chair, 1986-87; ANSI, sub comm Z39 U, 1981-82. **HONORS/AWARDS:** People to People, invited to visit China, 1985; Rajasthan University, doctoral fellowship, 1963-65. **SPECIAL ACHIEVEMENTS:** London Society of Arts, diploma in fine arts, 1963. **BUSINESS ADDRESS:** Group Director, Baker & Taylor, 652 E Main St, Bridgewater, NJ 08807, (908)218-3976.

CASTRO, MARISSA BARBERS
Political aide. Filipino American. **PERSONAL:** Born Nov 19, 1959, Manila, Philippines; daughter of Enrique J Castro & Lulu B Castro. **EDUCATION:** University of California, 1983. **CAREER:** UCLA, information director, 1982-83; Councilwoman Joy Picus, government intern, 1982-83; Landau Partnership, Inc, executive asst , 1983-85; Councilman Gilbert Lindsay, media & communications secretary, 1985-86; California Campaign '88, deputy press secretary, 1988; Assembly Speaker Pro Tempore Mike Roos, press deputy & field deputy, 1986-89; Office of Asian & Pacific Affairs, Assembly Speaker Willie L Brown, director, 1989-93; Assemblyman Curtis Tucker, Jr, legislative aide, 1993-. **ORGANIZATIONS:** Asian Pacific Women's Network, 1989-, executive vp, 1989-90, president, 1990-92, ex-officio, 1992-93, advisory council, 1994-; Planned Parenthood, Los Angeles, board of directors, 1991-; Coalition for Family Equity, 1990-; Philippine American Los Angeles Democrats, 1987-, president, 1989-91, founding corresponding secretary, 1987-89; Retired Senior Volunteer Program 1987-, advisory board, 1986-87, secretary, 1987-88, first vp, 1991-; Intl Visitors Council, board of directors, 1993-; Junior League, advisory board, 1992-; Search to Involve Philippine Americans, board of directors, 1992-; Women's Advisory Council for the LA Police Commission, 1992-; Natl Women's Political Caucus, 1990-; Asian Pacific Community Fund, founding board member, 1990-91, first vp, 1991-; numerous others. **HOME ADDRESS:** 211 N Kingsley Dr, Los Angeles, CA 90004. **BUSINESS ADDRESS:** Legislative Aide, California Assemblyman Curtis Tucker Inglewood City Hall, 1 Manchester Blvd Box 6500, Inglewood, CA 90306, (310)412-6400.

CAUTHORN, JAMES DANIEL
Contractor. Korean American. **PERSONAL:** Born Oct 25, 1955, Seoul, Republic of Korea; married Cindy, Feb 1, 1973; children: Kyrie, Trisha, Andrew. **EDUCATION:** OSU, 1991. **CAREER:** Pok Wan Contracting Inc, owner, currently. **ORGANIZATIONS:** AGC. **HOME ADDRESS:** 1992 NW Lantana, Corvallis, OR 97330. **BUSINESS PHONE:** (503)753-2020.

CAYETANO, BENJAMIN J.
State official. Filipino American. **PERSONAL:** Born Nov 14, 1939, Honolulu, HI; son of Bonifacio & Eleanor Cayetano; married Lorraine, Sep 20, 1958; children: Brandon, Janeen, Samantha. **EDUCATION:** University of California, Los Angeles, BA, 1968; Loyola University School of Law, JD, 1971. **CAREER:** Private attorney, 1971-; State of Hawaii, House of Representatives, 1974-78, state senator, 1978-86, lieutenant governor, 1986-. **ORGANIZATIONS:** Hawaii Housing Authority, 1972; House Energy and Transportation Committee, chairman, 1975-78; Senate Ways and Means Committee, chairman, 1979-80; senate majority policy leader, 1981-82; Senate Health Committee, chairman, 1981-82; Senate Investigative Committee on Heptachlor, chairman, 1982-83; Senate Economic Development and Public Utilities Committee, chairman, 1983; Task force on Educational Governance, chairman, 1991. **HONORS/AWARDS:** UCLA Alumni Association, Excellence in Public Service Award, 1993; Asia-Pacific Academic Consortium for Public Health, Excellence in Leadership Medallion, 1991. **BIOGRAPHICAL SOURCES:** "Hawaii's Benjamin Cayetano," Rice Magazine, pp 77-80, Dec/Jan 1989; "The Odds Against Ben Cayetano," Honolulu Magazine, p 45, 1979. **BUSINESS ADDRESS:** Lieutenant Governor, State of Hawaii, State Capitol, Honolulu, HI 96813, (808)586-0255.

CHA, CHANG-YUL
Educator. Korean American. **PERSONAL:** Born Apr 8, 1939, Dukdongri Kokummyun, Republic of Korea; son of Il-Sun Cha; married Songhee Cha, Nov 18, 1963; children: Suk-Bae, Suk-Jin, Mijin. **EDUCATION:** Seoul National University, BS, 1961; University of New Brunswick, MS, 1968; University of California, PhD, 1970. **CAREER:** University of California, Davis, 1970-71; McMaster University, post doctoral fellow, 1971-72; Occidental Research Corporation, group leader, 1972-75; Occidental Exploration and Production Co, senior scientist, 1975-77; Occidental Oil Shale, Inc, Process Development, manager, 1977-79; Science Applications, Inc, assistant vice president, 1979-83; Panaho Development Corp, vice president, 1983-85; Western Research Institute, Process Development, manager, 1985-90; University of Wyoming, Chem & Petroleum Engineering Dept, professor and head, currently. **ORGANIZATIONS:** American Institute of Chemical Engineers; Society of Petroleum Engineers; Phi Kappa Phi. **HONORS/AWARDS:** Corrosion Science, T P Hoar Prize for Outstanding Paper, 1981; U W Mortarboard Society, Top Professor, 1982. **SPECIAL ACHIEVEMENTS:** Chemical Engineering Kinetics, J M Smith, Solutions Manual, 1970; Oil Shale Processing Technology, chap 11, 1981; more than 70 technical papers in coal, oil shale, tar sand, heavy oil, flue gas clean-up, corrosion, and transport phenomena; 30 US patents. **MILITARY SERVICE:** Korean Air Force, first lt. **HOME ADDRESS:** 3807 Reynolds St, Laramie, WY 82070, (307)745-7734. **BUSINESS ADDRESS:** Professor/Head, Chem & Petroleum Eng Dept, University of Wyoming, PO Box 3295, University Station, Laramie, WY 82071, (307)766-2837.

CHA, SOYOUNG STEPHEN
Educator. Korean American. **PERSONAL:** Born Jun 25, 1944, Inchon, Republic of Korea; son of Sang O Cha and Sook S Cha; married Young Won Cha, Sep 4, 1974. **EDUCATION:** Seoul National University, BS, mechanical engineering, 1967; Michigan State University, MS, mechanical engineering, 1976; University of Michigan, PhD, mechanical engineering, 1980. **CAREER:** Kolon Engineering Co, project engineer, 1969-74; Northrop Corp, research engineer, 1980-84; University of Illinois, professor, currently. **ORGANIZATIONS:** Society of Photo-Optical Instrumentation Engineers, 1982-; American Society of Mechanical Engineers, committee member, 1977-; American Institute of Aeronautics and Astronautics, 1986-; Society of Experimental Mechanics, 1992-. **HONORS/AWARDS:** University of Michigan, Rackham Graduate Fellow, 1977, Distinguished Achievement Award, 1978, Phi Kappa Phi, 1978; NASA, DOD, DOE, Research Fellow. **SPECIAL ACHIEVEMENTS:** Organizer of SPIE International Conferences, 1991, 1993; guest editor of Optics and Lasers in Engineering, 1992; Organization Committee of Inverse Problems in Engineering, Michigan State University, 1990-92; more than 50 technical articles; numerous lectures and seminars, consultant to companies. **MILITARY SERVICE:** Army, lt, 1967-69. **HOME ADDRESS:** 25W 716 Grange Ct, Wheaton, IL 60187, (708)510-9207. **BUSINESS ADDRESS:** Professor, University of Illinois, Chicago, PO Box 4348, M/C 251, 2017 ERF, Chicago, IL 60680, (312)996-9612.

CHA, SUNGMAN
Educator, researcher. Korean American. **PERSONAL:** Born Mar 1, 1928, Sinsang, Republic of Korea; son of Hak-Ro and Tae-in Cha; married Chung-Ja Mo Cha, Aug 22, 1960; children: Jang-Ho, Mih-Ho, Jih-Ho Donovan. **EDUCATION:** Yonsei University, MD, 1954; University of Wisconsin, PhD, 1963. **CAREER:** Brown University, assistant professor, professor, 1963-93, professor emeritus, currently. **SPECIAL ACHIEVEMENTS:** Sixty publications, mainly on enzyme kinetics and cancer chemotherapy; two US patents on antimetabolites. **MILITARY SERVICE:** Navy, Republic of Korea, lt cdr, 1954-59. **HOME ADDRESS:** 15 Oriole Avenue, Providence, RI 02906, (401)751-5176. **BUSINESS ADDRESS:** Professor Emeritus, Brown University, Bio Med Center, Meeting and Brown Streets, Providence, RI 02912, (401)863-3114.

CHACKO, GEORGE KUTTICKAL
Educator, consultant. Indo-American. **PERSONAL:** Born Jul 1, 1930, Trivandrum, India; son of Geevarghese Kuttickal Chacko and Thankamma Mathew Chacko; married Yo Yee, Aug 10, 1957; children: Rajah Yee, Ashia Yo Chacko Lance. **EDUCATION:** Madras University, MA, econ/political philosophy, 1950; St Xavier's College, 1950-52; Calcutta University, B, commerce, 1952; Princeton University, 1953-54; New School for Social Research, PhD, econometrics, 1959; UCLA, 1961. **CAREER:** Indian Fin, asst editor, 1951-53; Times of India, comml corr, 1953; royal Metal Mfg Co, director, mktg & mgt research, 1958-60; Hughes Semiconductor, mgr, dept of operations research, 1958-60; consultant, 1961-62; UCLA, asst prof, bus admin, 1961-62;

Union Carbide, operations research staff consultant, 1962-63; Research Analysis Corp, member technical staff, 1963-65; MITRE Corp, mts, 1965-67; TRW Systems Group, sr staff scientist, 1967-70; University of Southern California, visiting prof, 1970-71, prof, systems mgt, 1971-83, prof, systems science, 1983-. **ORGANIZATIONS:** Intl Journal of Forecasting, assoc editor, 1982-85; AAAS, fellow; American Astronautical Society, fellow; Operations Research Society of America; New York Acad Sciences. **HONORS/AWARDS:** Natl Science Foundation, intl sci lectures award, 1982; USIA sponsored US Sci emissary to Egypt, Burma, India, Singapore, 1987. **SPECIAL ACHIEVEMENTS:** Author of 23 books, including: Operations Research/Management Science, 1992; editor of 19 books, including: Expert Systems: First World Congress Proceedings, 1992. **BUSINESS ADDRESS:** Professor, University of Southern California, 5510 Columbia Pike, Arlington, VA 22204-3123.

CHACKO, HARSHA E.
Educator. Indo-American. **PERSONAL:** Born Dec 30, 1952, Mankotta, Kerala, India; son of E John Jacob and Saramma Jocob; married Elen K Chacko, Jul 11, 1983; children: Diya, Ayesha. **EDUCATION:** Loyola College, BSc, 1972; University of Massachusetts, BS, 1980, MS, 1981; University of New Orleans, PhD, 1987. **CAREER:** Oberoi Hotels, various positions, 1974-78; Caneel Bay, assistant manager, 1981-82; University of New Orleans, associate professor, 1982-. **ORGANIZATIONS:** Council on Hotel Restaurant & Institutional Education, 1982-; Hospitality Sales and Marketing Association, 1984-; National Restaurant Association, 1985-; Travel and Tourism Research Association, 1990-. **HONORS/AWARDS:** American Hotel/Motel Association, certified hotel admn, 1990; University of New Orleans, outstanding faculty, 1986. **SPECIAL ACHIEVEMENTS:** Author of numerous publications in hospitality journals. **BUSINESS ADDRESS:** Associate Professor, School of Hotel, Restaurant and Tourism Administration, University of New Orleans, New Orleans, LA 70148-0001, (504)286-6385.

CHACKO, KURIAN
Gem and jewelry company executive. Indo-American. **PERSONAL:** Born Dec 5, 1949, Chengannur, Kerala, India; son of Koshy Chacko and Aleyamma Chacko; married Mary, Nov 17, 1974; children: Silvi, Sofi. **EDUCATION:** Kerala University, BBA, 1969. **CAREER:** ACX Corporation, president; Balogh, president, currently. **BUSINESS ADDRESS:** President, Balogh, Inc, 798 Madison Ave, New York, NY 10021, (212)517-9940.

CHACKO, MARIAM RENATE
Physician. Indo-American. **PERSONAL:** Born Feb 24, 1950, New Delhi, India; daughter of Arthur W Chacko and Dorian R Chacko; married Kenneth VI Rolston, May 6, 1984; children: Zahrin. **EDUCATION:** Christian Medical College, India, MBBS, 1974; Baltimore City Hospitals, pediatric residency, 1976-79; University of Maryland, Baltimore, Adolescent Medicine Fellowship, 1979-82. **CAREER:** University of Maryland Hospital, Baltimore, assistant professor of pediatrics, 1982-84; Baylor College of Medicine, Houston, TX, assistant professor of pediatrics, 1984-92, associate professor of clincial pediatrics, 1992-. **ORGANIZATIONS:** Society for Adolescent Medicine, abstract review committee, 1991-93, awards committee, 1991-; North American Society for Pediatric and Adolescent Synecology, abstract review committee, 1991-92, awards committee, 1992; Texas Pediatric Society, chair committee on adolescence, 1991-; American Academy of Pediatrics. **HONORS/AWARDS:** Christian Medical College, Punjab, India, Second Prize, Internal Medicine, 1973. **SPECIAL ACHIEVEMENTS:** Clinical Research: Sexually Transmitted Diseases in Adolescents, 1981-; publications in pediatric and gynecology journals. **BUSINESS ADDRESS:** Associate Professor, Clincial Pediatrics, Baylor College of Medicine, One Baylor Plaza, Houston, TX 77030-3411, (713)770-3440.

CHACKO, RANJIT C.
Educator. Indo-American. **PERSONAL:** Born Jul 23, 1948, Colombo, Sri Lanka; son of Koppara Chandy Chacko & Grace Sarah Chacko; married Danuta Chacko, Apr 15, 1978; children: Kristina, Marissa. **EDUCATION:** St Thomas' College, GLE level, 1966; University of Ceylon, MB, BS, 1971; Mount Sinai Hospital Services, psychiatry, 1977. **CAREER:** Methodist Hospital, deputy chief of psychiatry, 1988-; Baylor College of Medicine, assistant professor, 1977-85, associate professor, 1985-92, professor, 1992-. **ORGANIZATIONS:** American College of Psychiatrists, 1991; American Association of Geriatric Psychiatrists, 1979; Texas Society of Psychiatric Physicians, 1977; Harris County Medical Society, 1977. **HONORS/AWARDS:** American Psychiatric Association, fellow, 1987. **SPECIAL ACHIEVEMENTS:** Several articles published in refereed journals. **BUSINESS ADDRESS:** Professor,

Dept of Psychiatry, Baylor College of Medicine, 1 Baylor Plaza, Houston, TX 77030, (713)798-4880.

CHACKO, VARKKI P.
Securities analyst. Indo-American. **PERSONAL:** Born Sep 21, 1956, Hyderabad, India; son of P C Chacko and T Chacko; married Madhura Kirloskar, Aug 29, 1982; children: Vikram, Ravi. **EDUCATION:** Birla Institute of Technology & Science, India, BE (with honors), 1977, MS, 1978; University of Massachusetts, Amherst, PhD, 1982; New York University, MBA, 1987. **CAREER:** Allied Corp, research engineer, 1982-85; Hoechst-Celanese, group leader, 1985-87; Salomon Brothers, vice president, 1987-. **ORGANIZATIONS:** New York Society of Chemical Analysts. **SPECIAL ACHIEVEMENTS:** Awarded multiple patents, both US & international; published 8 research papers in professional magazines. **BUSINESS ADDRESS:** Director, Salomon Brothers, 7 World Trade Center, 40th Fl, Corporate Bond Research, New York, NY 10048, (212)783-3077.

CHADHA, KAILASH CHANDRA
Scientist, educator. Indo-American. **PERSONAL:** Born Jul 1, 1943, Churu, Rajasthan, India; son of Ralla Ram & Budhwanti Devi Chadha; married Anju Chadha, May 22, 1971; children: Sonia, Priya, Kunal. **EDUCATION:** University of Rajasthan, Jaipur, India, BS, 1962; India Agricultural Research Inst, New Delhi, India, MSe, 1964; University of Guelph, Guelph, Ontario, Canada, PhD, 1968. **CAREER:** National Research Council, Canada, Post Doctoral, 1968-70; Cancer Research Science, Roswell Park Cancer Inst, 1970-74, Senior Cancer Research Science, 1974-; SUNY at Buffalo, associate research prof, 1978-; New York State Dept Health, cancer research scientist 1974-. **ORGANIZATIONS:** WNY-American Society of Microbiology, vice president, 1988-90, president, 19 90-91; International Society for Interferon Research; New York Academy of Sciences; American Association for Advancement of Sciences; European Cancer Society; Research Society on Alcoholism. **HONORS/AWARDS:** Journal of Medicine, editorial board, 1988-. **SPECIAL ACHIEVEMENTS:** Over 60 publications in leading scientific journals, 8 book chapters. **HOME ADDRESS:** 106 Summerview Rd, Williamsville, NY 14221, (716)689-7817. **BUSINESS ADDRESS:** Cancer Research Scientist & Associate Research Professor, Roswell Park Cancer Inst, Elm & Carlton Sts, Cell & Virus Build, Rm 316, Buffalo, NY 14263, (716)845-3101.

CHAE, YONG SUK
Educator, educational administrator. Korean American. **PERSONAL:** Born Jul 29, 1930, Chochiwon, Chung-nam, Republic of Korea; married Mee Soon, Sep 6, 1962; children: Sonia, Claudia, Michael. **EDUCATION:** Dartmouth College, AB, 1956, MS, 1957; University of Michigan, PhD, 1964. **CAREER:** Howard, Needles, Tammen and Bergendoff, staff engineering, 1958-60; Rutgers University, assistant professor, associate professor, professor, 1964-81, professor, associate dean, 1981-86, professor, chairman, civil engineering, 1986-. **ORGANIZATIONS:** American Society of Civil Engineers, fellow, 1964-; American Society for Engineering Education, 1969-; American Society for Testing Materials, 1989-; International Society of Soil Mechanics and Foundation Engineering, 1968-. **HONORS/AWARDS:** National Science Foundation, NATO Senior Fellow in Science. **BIOGRAPHICAL SOURCES:** Who's Who in Technology. **BUSINESS ADDRESS:** Professor & Chairman, Dept of Civil & Environmental Engineering, Rutgers University, PO Box 909, Piscataway, NJ 08855, (908)932-2232.

CHAI, AN-TI
Scientist. Chinese American. **PERSONAL:** son of Tsang-Lu Chai and Shwu-Bo Kao Chai; married Shwu-Chen Wu Chai, 1971; children: Shuann Chih-Tien, Chendy Chih-Han. **EDUCATION:** National Taiwan University, BS, physics, 1961; Kansas State University, MS, physics, 1966, PhD, physics, 1968. **CAREER:** Michigan Technological University, assistant professor, 1968-72; University of California, Bakersfield, lecturer, 1974; University of Florida, interim assistant professor, 1974-76; Case Western University, adjunct associate professor, 1981-83; NASA-Lewis Research Center, physicist, aerospace engineer, 1976-. **ORGANIZATIONS:** National Research Council, advisor, 1980-; NASA-Asian Pacific Islander Working Group, 1990-; NASA-Lewis Research Center, Asian American Advisory Board, 1980-. **HONORS/AWARDS:** NASA, Certificates of Recognition, 1981, Incentive Award, 1983, 1989. **SPECIAL ACHIEVEMENTS:** Five patents; research publications. **BUSINESS ADDRESS:** Physicist, Engineer, NASA-Lewis Research Center, 21000 Brookpark Rd, Mail Stop 500-327, Cleveland, OH 44135, (216)433-2073.

CHAI, DAVID
Company executive. Chinese American. **PERSONAL:** Born Jun 15, 1937, Nanjing, China; married Audrey H Chai, Jul 1, 1961; children: Michael, Christopher, Jennifer. **EDUCATION:** Purdue University, BSEE, 1959; University of Michigan, MS, 1962, PhD, comm science, 1966. **CAREER:** International Business Machines, engineer, 1959-60; Bunker-Ramo Corp, principal researcher, 1967-69; Bell Telephone Laboratories, supervisor, 1969-83; Bell Communications Research, director, 1984-92; Global Synergy, Inc, president, 1992-. **ORGANIZATIONS:** Holmdel Township Planning Board, 1988-91; Monmouth United Chinese Organization, rally leader for Chinese Student Democratic Movement, 1989; Asian Americans for Affirmative Action, president, 1986-90. **HONORS/AWARDS:** Partnership of New Jersey, Leadership New Jersey Fellow, 1992; China Night of Monmouth County, New Jersey, Community Service Award, 1990, 1992; Asian Americans for Affirmative Action of Bellcore and AT&T Bell Labs, Outstanding Contributor, 1992. **SPECIAL ACHIEVEMENTS:** Managing Today for Future Success: the Untapped Resources, a presentation to senior management of Bell Communication Research, 1989. **BIOGRAPHICAL SOURCES:** The Character Wayne Lee in Differences Do Make a Difference, by Roosevelt Thomas, Jr., pp 59-67, 1992. **HOME ADDRESS:** 11 Old Farm Rd, Holmdel, NJ 07733, (908)846-8249. **BUSINESS PHONE:** (908)946-8249.

CHAI, JAY
Business executive. Korean American. **PERSONAL:** Born 1935?, Taegu, Republic of Korea. **EDUCATION:** University of Southern California, MBA. **CAREER:** C Itoh & Co (America) Inc, New York Office, 1961-92, dba ITOCHU International Inc, chairman, CEO, 1992-. **BIOGRAPHICAL SOURCES:** Transpacific, May 1993, p42-43. **BUSINESS ADDRESS:** Chairman, CEO, ITOCHU International Inc, 335 Madison Ave, New York, NY 10017, (212)818-8000.*

CHAKRABARTI, SUBRATA KUMAR
Construction company research director. Indo-American. **PERSONAL:** Born Feb 3, 1941, Calcutta, W. Bengal, India; son of Asutosh & Shefali Chakrabarti; married Prakriti Chakrabarti, Jul 23, 1967; children: Sumita, Prabal. **EDUCATION:** Jadavpur University, Calcutta, India, BSME, 1963; University of Colorado, Boulder, MSME, 1965, PhD, mechanics, 1968. **CAREER:** Kuljian Corp, assistant engineer, 1963-64; Simon Carves Ltd, assistant engineer, 1964; University of Colorado, instructor, 1965-66; Chicago Bridge & Iron Co, hydrodynamicist, 1968-70, head, analytical gp, 1970-79; US Naval Academy, visiting NAVFAC professor, summer 1986, 1988; CBI Technical Services Co, Marine Research, director, 1979-. **ORGANIZATIONS:** American Society of Civil Engineers, fellow, associate ed JWN division, 1975-80; American Society of Mechanical Engineers, fellow, editor, JOMAE, 1987-; American Association for Advancement of Science, fellow, 1975-; National Academy of Science, Marine Research Board, CMS, 1989-; Sigma Xi, 1986-87; State of Illinois, registered professional engineer, 1972-. **HONORS/AWARDS:** American Society Mechanical Engineers, Ralph James Award, 1984, OMAE Achievement Award, 1988; US Patent 4559817, 1985; Jadavpur University, Gold Medal, 1963; University of Colorado, scholastic citation, 1968; American Society Civil Engineers, James Croes Medal, 1974, Freeman Scholar, 1979; State of Illinois Organizers, Outstanding New Citizen, 1981. **SPECIAL ACHIEVEMENTS:** Over 150 publications in journals; books: Hydrodynamics of Offshore Structures, CML Publications, GB, 1988; Nonlinear Methods in Offshore Engineering, Elsevier, W Germany, 1990; Modeling of Offshore Structures, chapter, Applications in Coastal Modeling, 1989; Offshore Structures, chapter, Civil Engineering Practice, Technomic Pub, 1988; Wave-Structure Interaction, chapter, Offshore Structures, Krieger Publishing, 1991; Offshore Structure Modeling, 1994. **HOME ADDRESS:** 191 E Weller Dr N, Plainfield, IL 60544, (815)436-4863. **BUSINESS ADDRESS:** Director, Marine Research, Chicago Bridge and Iron Technical Services Co, 1501 N Division St, Plainfield, IL 60544-8929, (815)439-6237.

CHAKRABARTI, SUPRIYA
Educator. Indo-American. **PERSONAL:** Born Jun 22, 1953, Howrah, W. Bengal, India; son of Chiraranjan Chakrabarti and Ranu Chakrabarti; married Joanne, Dec 17, 1983; children: Misha. **EDUCATION:** University of Calcutta, Bachelors, eng, 1975; University of California, Berkeley, MS, 1980, PhD, 1982. **CAREER:** University of California, Berkeley, senior fellow, 1983-92, assistant research physicist, 1982-92; Boston University, associate professor, 1992-. **ORGANIZATIONS:** American Geophysical Union, life member, 1980-; American Institute of Physics, 1991-. **SPECIAL ACHIEVEMENTS:** Over 80 publications covering planetary atmospheres, ultra violet

insrumentation and space/ground based observational techniques, 1980-. **BUSINESS ADDRESS:** Professor, Boston University, Center for Space Physics, 725 Commonwealth Ave, Boston, MA 02215, (617)353-5990.

CHAKRABORTY, JOANA (JYOTSNA)
Educator, educational administrator. Indo-American. **PERSONAL:** Born Jun 1, 1934, Calcutta, India; daughter of Mohadev Mukherjee and Nilima Mukherjee; married Ajit Chakraborty; children: Mala. **EDUCATION:** City College, Calcutta, BS, 1954; Science College, Calcutta, MS, 1956; Institute of Nuclear Physics, Calcutta, PhD, 1962. **CAREER:** Institute of Nuclear Physics, biophysics, lecturer, research assistant, 1960-69; Medical College of Ohio, physiology, research associate, 1970-72, electron microscopy laboratory, director, 1970-89, assistant professor of physiology, 1972-75, associate professor of physiology, 1975-82, professor of physiology, 1983-, interim chairman of physiology, 1991-. **ORGANIZATIONS:** Association of Chairmen of Departments of Physiology; Society for the Study of Reproduction; Electron Microscopy Society of America; American Society of Andrology; American Society of Cell Biology; New York Academy of Science; Ohio Physiological Society; American Association for the Advancement of Science. **HONORS/ AWARDS:** University of Calcutta, First Class First Zoology, MS, 1956, University Book Prize, 1956; Saha Institute of Nuclear Physics, Research Training Scholar, 1957-60; UCLA and Harbor UCLA, Two Postdoctoral Diplomas, 1970; Cambridge University, Visiting Scholar, 1977. **SPECIAL ACHIEVEMENTS:** Contributor: Testicular Development Structure and Function, 1980; Occupational Toxicology, 1988; over 60 articles in peer-reviewed journals: scientific talks, All India Radio, Calcutta, 1957-69, 1986; regional coordinator, Hands to Clinical Labs of Third World Countries, 1987-. **BUSINESS ADDRESS:** Professor, Interim Chairman, Dept of Physiology, Medical College of Ohio, Health Science Bldg, 3000 Arlington Ave, Toledo, OH 43614, (419)381-4144.

CHAKRAVARTHY, BALAJI SRINIVASAN
Educator, management consultant. Indo-American. **PERSONAL:** Born Jul 16, 1947, Madras, Tamil Nadu, India; son of V S Vijaya Raghavan & Sushila V Raghavan; married Kiran Chakravarthy, Sep 3, 1976. **EDUCATION:** IIT, Madras India, BTech, 1968; IIM, Ahmedabad India, MBA, 1970; Harvard University, DBA, 1978. **CAREER:** Tata Engineering (TELCO), assistant manager, 1970-76; Tulane University, assistant professor of management, 1978-81; Wharton School, associate professor of management, 1981-86; University of Minnesota Carlson School of Management, professor of strategic management, 1986-; INSEAD, France, professor of strategic management, 1992-. **ORGANIZATIONS:** Strategic Management Society, founding member, 1980-; Academy of Management, 1978-; The Institute of Management Science, 1978-. **HONORS/AWARDS:** North American Society of Corporate Planners, best article, Planning Review, 1984; Wharton School, Anvil Award for the Top Teacher, 1986; Carlson School, Rosebowl Award and Carlson Cup, 1991.

CHAKRAVARTHY, SRINIVASARAGHAVAN
Educator. Indo-American. **PERSONAL:** Born Aug 28, 1953, Madras, Tamil Nadu, India; son of P S Srinivasaraghavan & P S Rajalakshmi; married Jayanthi, Jun 10, 1982; children: Arvind. **EDUCATION:** Vivekanandra College, India, BSc, 1973; Presidency College, India, MSc, 1975; University of Delaware, PhD, 1983. **CAREER:** GMI, assistant professor, 1983-86, associate professor, 1986-90, professor, 1990-. **ORGANIZATIONS:** ORSA, 1981-; MAA, 1981-; Sigma Xi, 1981-. **HONORS/AWARDS:** GMI Alumni, Outstanding Teacher Award, 1990; GMI, RI/I Research Grant, 1990; Lilly Endowment, Faculty/Industry Exchange Fellowship, 1988; NSF, research award, 1993. **SPECIAL ACHIEVEMENTS:** Published a number of research articles in leading refereed international journals, 1982-. **BUSINESS ADDRESS:** Professor of Mathematics, GMI Engineering & Management Institute, 1700 West 3rd Ave, Room 2-121 AB, Flint, MI 48504-4898, (810)762-7906.

CHAKRAVARTHY, UPENDRANATH SHARMA
Educator. Indo-American. **PERSONAL:** Born Jan 13, 1952, Bangalore, Karnataka, India; son of Ananthachar Chakravarthy & Jayamma Chakravarthy; married Shubha Chakravarthy, Jan 19, 1983; children: Tejas. **EDUCATION:** Indian Institute of Science, Bangalore, BE, 1973; Indian Institute of Technology, Bombay, MTech, 1975; University of Maryland, MS, 1981, PhD, 1985. **CAREER:** Tata Institute of Fundamental Research, Bombay, scientific officer, 1975-78; University of Maryland, TA, RA, instructor, 1979-85; Computer Corporation of America, computer scientist, 1985-88; Xerox Advanced Information Technology, technical staff, 1988-89; University of Florida, associate

professor, 1989-. **ORGANIZATIONS:** ACM, 1979-; IEEE, 1979-; AAAI, 1990-. **HONORS/AWARDS:** Ministry of Education, India, National Scholarship, 1979, Commonwealth Scholarship, 1979. **SPECIAL ACHIEVEMENTS:** Published over 45 refereed conference/journal papers and book chapters on graphics, image processing, active deductive databases, distributed databases, temporal databases and query optimization. **HOME ADDRESS:** 4049 NW 30th Place, Gainesville, FL 32606, (904)376-9321. **BUSINESS ADDRESS:** Associate Professor, Computer and Information Sciences Dept, University of Florida, 470 CSE, Gainesville, FL 32611-2024, (904)392-2697.

CHAKRAVARTY, INDRANIL
Computer scientist. Indo-American. **PERSONAL:** Born Jan 7, 1954, Delhi, India; son of Sunil K Chakravarty and Monica Bagchi Chakravarty; married Sveta Davé Chakravarty, Jan 7, 1989. **EDUCATION:** New York University, BE, 1974; Rensselaer Polytechnic Institute, M Eng, 1976, PhD, computer & syst eng, 1982. **CAREER:** Schlumberger-Doll Research, member, professional staff, 1981-85, program leader, 1986-88; Schlumberger Ltd, program manager/senior research scientist, 1989-; University of Texas at Austin, adjunct assoc prof, computer science, 1992-. **ORGANIZATIONS:** Sigma Xi, 1981-; New York Academy of Sciences, 1983-; IEEE, 1981; ACM, 1976-; ACM, category editor, computing reviews, pattern recognition/image processing. **SPECIAL ACHIEVEMENTS:** Over 40 publications in computer graphics, image processing, and parallel computing. **BUSINESS ADDRESS:** Sr Research Scientist, Schlumberger Ltd, 8311 North RR 620, PO Box 200015, Austin, TX 78720, (512)331-3721.

CHAN, ADRIAN
Educational administrator, educator. Chinese American. **PERSONAL:** Born Jan 3, 1941, San Francisco, CA; son of Ernest & Flora Chan; married Diedre E Chan, Jun 6, 1974; children: Jennifer Smith Spinelli, Christopher A. **EDUCATION:** Westminster College, BA, 1962; University of Utah, MS, 1964, PhD, 1968. **CAREER:** University of Wisconsin, Milwaukee, professor of educational psychology, 1968-, asst vice chancellor, 1991-; University of Wisconsin System, administrative associate, 1990. **ORGANIZATIONS:** American Psychological Assn, counseling psychology, community psych, 1968-; Asian American Psychological Assn; Kochman Communication Consultants Inc, associate, 1989-; American Assn for Counseling & Development, 1987-. **SPECIAL ACHIEVEMENTS:** Coauthor, "Inclusion and Exclusion: Dual Realities in American Education," University of Wisconsin System, American Ethnic Studies, Ethnicity and Public Policy Series; coauthor, "The Indochinese in Wisconsin," Wisconsin Counselor, vol 6, no 1, p 8-16, 1982; coauthor, "The Education of the Chinese and Indochinese in America," Theory into Practice, 20, winter, 1, 35-44, 1981; coauthor, "Advocate Counseling and Institutional Racism," O A Barbarin, et al, eds, Institutional Racism & Community Competence, Dept of Health & Human Services, NIMH, Govt Printing Office, Pub #ADM 81-907, 1981. **HOME ADDRESS:** 4443 N Stowell Ave, Shorewood, WI 53211, (414)962-2271. **BUSINESS ADDRESS:** Asst Vice Chancellor, Academic Affairs, University of Wisconsin, Milwaukee, PO Box 413, Chapman Hall 301, Milwaukee, WI 53201, (414)229-6518.

CHAN, ALBERT
Educator. Chinese American. **PERSONAL:** Born Mar 28, 1949, Canton Province, People's Republic of China; son of Kin-Man Chan and Tuen-Nga Chang Chan. **EDUCATION:** University of California, Berkeley, BA, 1972; California State University, Long Beach, MS, 1975; University of Nebraska Medical Center, PhD, 1980. **CAREER:** University of Texas Health Science Center, Dallas, NIH Postdoctoral Fellow, 1980-83; University of Mississippi Medical Center, associate professor, 1983-. **HONORS/AWARDS:** National Institutes of Health, Post-doctoral Fellowship, 1981; University of Nebraska, Regents Fellowship, 1978-80; University of California, Berkeley, Luke Kavanagh Scholarship, 1969, WH Wheeler Scholarship, 1968; State of California, California State Scholarship, 1978-72. **BUSINESS ADDRESS:** Associate Professor, Dept of Pharmacology and Toxicology, University of Mississippi Medical Center, 2500 North State St, Jackson, MS 39216-4505, (601)984-1607.

CHAN, ANGELA
Bank administrator, corporate secretary. Hong Kong American/Thai American. **PERSONAL:** Born Dec 15, 1968, San Francisco, CA; daughter of Arthur Y M Chan and Amphorn Chan. **EDUCATION:** San Francisco State University; Golden Gate University, currently. **CAREER:** Winston Oriental Foods Inc, corporate treasurer, 1989-; US Import Export corp, corporate secretary, 1988-; Gateway Bank, FSB, loan administration manager, 1991-. **ORGANIZA-**

TIONS: The National Dean's List, 1988-89, 1990-91. **BUSINESS ADDRESS:** Loan Administration Manager, Gateway Bank, FSB, 3557 Geary Blvd, San Francisco, CA 94118, (415)751-8125.

CHAN, ANTHONY BERNARD (TONY)
Educator, filmmaker. Chinese American/Vietnamese American. **PERSONAL:** Born Jun 25, 1944, British Columbia; son of Steven Chan and Rosy Chan. **EDUCATION:** University of Victoria, BA, 1967; Bowling Green State University, MA, 1969; University of Arizona, MA, 1973; Beijing Language Institute, diploma, 1975; York University, PhD, 1980. **CAREER:** University of Saskatchewan, lecturer in sociology, 1981-82; China Project Office, Saint Mary's University, assistant professor, Chinese history, 1979-80, assistant coordinator, 1982-83; University of Alberta, assistant professor of Chinese history, 1980-81; Canadian Broadcasting Corporation, television reporter, anchor, filmmaker, 1983-85; City Productions, Toronto, producer/writer, 1985; Television Broadcasts Ltd, Hong Kong, senior producer, anchor, television correspondent, 1985-87; California State University, Hayward, associate professor of television studies and production, 1987-90; University of Washington, associate professor & head, broadcast journalism, 1990; Lindca Enterprises, independent producer/director, 1985-. **ORGANIZATIONS:** Commonweal Institute, 1993-; Asianadian Resource Workshop, editor, 1979-85. **HONORS/AWARDS:** Hiroshima Film Festival, Honorable Mention Award for American Nurse, 1993. **SPECIAL ACHIEVEMENTS:** Publications: Gold Mountain: The Chinese in the New World, New Star Books, 1983; Arming the Chinese: The Western Armaments Trade in Warlord China, 1920-28, University of British Columbia, 1982. **BIOGRAPHICAL SOURCES:** "Chan's Plan—To Pull Plug on Asian TV News," South China Morning Post, Hong Kong, p 6D, July 3, 1987; "China Rally Due Friday at Cal State," by Rich Riggs, The Daily Review, Hayward CA, p 7E, June 8, 1989. **BUSINESS ADDRESS:** Associate Professor, Head of Broadcast Journalism, University of Washington, School of Communications, CMU 229, DS-40, Seattle, WA 98195, (206)685-3992.

CHAN, ANTHONY KIT-CHEUNG
Educator. Hong Kong American. **PERSONAL:** Born Jun 21, 1960, Hong Kong; son of Yat & Yuen Yim-Hing Chan; married Grace Chan, Mar 24, 1990; children: Nathan Kar-Ming. **EDUCATION:** California State University, Los Angeles, BA (with honors), 1983, MA, 1985; Claremont Graduate School, MA, 1988. **CAREER:** Dun & Bradstreet, Hong Kong, Ltd, financial analyst, 1987; Woodbury University, assistant professor of economics and finance, 1989-. **ORGANIZATIONS:** Omicron Delta Epsilon, 1983-84, vice president, 1984-85; American Economic Association, 1986; Chinese Zion Baptist Church, officer, 1980-. **HONORS/AWARDS:** California State University, Los Angeles, Department of Economics and Statistics, John Norby Book Scholarship, 1983. **SPECIAL ACHIEVEMENTS:** Author: "Macroeconomics Policy: Expansionary," McGillis Survey of Social Science, Economic Set, pp 1325-1330, 1991; "Monetary Policy Exchange Rate," McGillis Survey of Social Science, Economic Set, p 1496-1550, 1991. **HOME ADDRESS:** 1924 Sunny Heights Dr, Los Angeles, CA 90065, (213)221-2714.

CHAN, ARTHUR H.
Economist. Hong Kong American. **PERSONAL:** Born 1950?, Hong Kong; married Barbara Zeppel; children: Sebastian. **EDUCATION:** University of Nebraska, BEcon, MEcon, MPolSc, DEcon. **CAREER:** New Mexico State, Economics, instructor, 1986-92; Boston University, instructor; US General Accounting Office, senior economist, 1992-; House Committee on Public Works and Transportation, chief economist, 1993-. **BUSINESS ADDRESS:** Chief Economist, US General Accounting Office, 441 G St NW, Washington, DC 20548, (202)275-5067.*

CHAN, ARTHUR WING KAY
Research scientist, educator. Hong Kong American/Chinese American. **PERSONAL:** Born Jun 24, 1941, Hong Kong; married Shirley Pou, Feb 27, 1967; children: Alvin Mark. **EDUCATION:** Australian National University, BSc (1st class honors), 1966, PhD, 1969. **CAREER:** Research Institute on Addictions, research scientist III, 1974-76, research scientist IV, 1976-79, research scientist V, 1979-; State University New York at Buffalo, research assistant professor, 1974-81, research associate professor, 1982-92, research professor, 1993-. **ORGANIZATIONS:** Amer Soc Pharmacology & Experimental Therapeutics, 1978-; Inter Soc for Biomedical Res on Alcoholism, 1986-; Res Soc on Alcoholism, 1976-. **HONORS/AWARDS:** Amer Soc Pharmacology & Experimental Therapeutics, Travel Award, 1987; NATO, Travel Award, 1990; NIAA, Research Grants, 1986-93. **SPECIAL ACHIEVEMENTS:** Numerous publications, book chapters, and presentations, 1966-. **BUSINESS ADDRESS:**

Senior Research Scientist, Research Professor, Research Institute on Addictions, 1021 Main St, Buffalo, NY 14203, (716)887-2529.

CHAN, BILL. *See* **CHAN, CHONG B.**

CHAN, CARL CHIANG
Librarian. Chinese American. **PERSONAL:** Born Jan 23, 1950, San Francisco, CA; son of Robert & Dora Chan. **EDUCATION:** Brown University, AB, 1971; Eastern New Mexico University, 1979-83; University of Chicago, MA, 1987. **CAREER:** Fort Ord Libraries, Durham Branch, head, 1987; AISO Library, Defense Language Institute, head of cataloging, 1987-90, head of public services, 1990-; independent library consultant, 1993-. **ORGANIZATIONS:** Chinese American Librarians Assn, president, 1992-93, vice president/pres elect, 1991-92, board of directors, 1987-90, California chapter president, 1990; Chinese American Citizens Alliance, 1987-, Salinas Lodge, vice pres, 1992, pres, 1993-94; American Library Assn, 1985-; American Indian Library Assn, 1991-; Asian Pacific American Librarians Assn, 1987-; Bibliotecas Para La Gente/REFORMA, 1990-. **HONORS/AWARDS:** Beta Phi Mu, library science honor society, elected to membership, 1987. **SPECIAL ACHIEVEMENTS:** Guest lecturer on multilingual librarianship, University of California, Berkeley, Grad Sch of Library and Info Sci, 1993; guest lecturer on multilingual librarianship, Foothill College, Los Altos Hills, California, 1992; Multicultural Review, Editorial Advisory Board, 1991-; Multicultural Publishers Exchange Conference, guest speaker, 1992, 1993. **MILITARY SERVICE:** US Air Force, capt, 1971-84; Air Force Commendation Medal. **HOME ADDRESS:** 30 Monte Vista Dr #1212, Monterey, CA 93940, (408)649-0373. **BUSINESS ADDRESS:** Head of Public Services, Aiso Library, Defense Language Institute Foreign Language Center, Bldg 617, Presidio of Monterey, CA 93944-5007, (408)647-5572.

CHAN, CARLYLE HUNG-LUN
Psychiatrist, educator. Chinese American. **PERSONAL:** Born Jul 4, 1949, Clarksdale, MS; son of Henry Howe Chan & Jennie Wong Chan; married Patricia M Chan, Jun 18, 1977; children: Christopher Mun-Jit Meyer, Diana Elizabeth Mung-Jun. **EDUCATION:** University of Wisconsin-Madison, BS, 1971; Medical College of Wisconsin, MD, 1975; University of Chicago Hospitals & Clinics, psychiatry residency, 1975-78; Yale University School of Medicine, Robert Wood Johnson Clinical Scholars Program, postdoctoral fellow, 1978-80. **CAREER:** Medical College of Wisconsin, assistant professor, 1980-87, associate professor, director of residency education, 1987-. **ORGANIZATIONS:** American Association of Directors of Psychiatric Residency Training, program chair, treasurer, executive committee, 1989-93; Association for Academy Psychiatry, director, regional coordinator, executive committee, 1993; American Psychiatric Association, fellow, 1990-, Asian American Psychiatry Committee, 1981-84; Wisconsin Psychiatric Association, president, Milwaukee chapter, 1990-91. **SPECIAL ACHIEVEMENTS:** Psychiatry-Medical Examination Review, co-editor with Harry Prosen, 1992. **BUSINESS ADDRESS:** Director of Residency Education, Dept of Psychiatry, Medical College of Wisconsin, 8701 Watertown Plank Rd, Milwaukee, WI 53226, (414)257-5995.

CHAN, CHEUNG M.
Association executive. Chinese American. **PERSONAL:** Born Feb 5, 1917, Canton, Kwongdong, China; son of Kong Jan Chan and Zong Gong Lee; married Qung Jang Loo, Aug 15, 1949; children: Y Sung, Y Yung, Y Kong. **EDUCATION:** Chig-Nanz, BA, 1940. **CAREER:** Self-employed, owner, mgr, 1967-83. **ORGANIZATIONS:** KMT of China (ROC), Baltimore Region, president, 1970-; Chinese Merchant Assn of Baltimore, president, 1970-; Gee How Oat G Assn of Baltimore, president, 1970-; Oversea Chinese Council, adviser, 1987-; Chinese Benevolent Assn of America, president, adviser, 1992-. **HONORS/AWARDS:** Oversea Chinese Council, Best Contribution Award, 1978, Best Adviser Award, 1978. **HOME ADDRESS:** 3620 Greenmount Ave, Baltimore, MD 21218, (410)243-3277.

CHAN, CHIU SHUI
Educator. Chinese American. **PERSONAL:** Born Jun 19, 1950, Taishan, Kwang Tung, People's Republic of China; son of Tit-Chee Chan and Wing-Shau Tam; married Hung-Ching Wang Chan, Aug 20, 1983; children: Dexter Yuan-Jong, Virginia Jia-shin. **EDUCATION:** Chinese Culture University, BS, 1974; University of Minnesota, MArch, 1982; Carnegie-Mellon University, PhD, 1990. **CAREER:** ChunLi Architects & Engineers, Taipei, architect, 1973-74, 1976-77; Miller & Dunwiddie Architects, consultant, 1981; Rasch & Au Architects, Toronto, architect, 1983; University Computation Center, Car-

negie Mellon University, PC consultant, 1985-86; Iowa State University, adjunct assistant professor, 1989-92, assistant professor, 1992-. **ORGANIZATIONS:** Association for Computer-Aided Design in Architecture, 1990-. **HONORS/AWARDS:** Iowa State University, Foreign Travel Grant, 1992, Instructional Development Grant, 1991-92, Design Research Fellowship, 1990-91; Association of Collegiate Schools of Architecture, Computer Institute Fellowship, 1990; Carnegie Mellon University, R K Mellon Fellowship, 1983-84. **SPECIAL ACHIEVEMENTS:** Author, "Operational Definitions of Style," Environment and Planning B: Planning & Design, in press; "How an Individual Style Is Generated," Environment and Planning B: Planning & Design, vol 20, pp 391-423, 1993; "Exploring Individual Style in Design," Environment and Planning B: Planning & Design, vol 19, pp 503-523, 1992; "Exploring Individual Style through Wright's Design," Journal of Architectural and Planning Research, vol 9, pp 207-238, 1992; "Cognitive Processes in Architectural Design Problem Solving," Design Studies, vol 11, pp 60-80, 1990. **BIOGRAPHICAL SOURCES:** Inside Iowa State, volume 11, Number 16, page 3, March 12, 1993; Iowa State University, College of Design Newsletter, volume V, p 2, Fall 1989. **BUSINESS ADDRESS:** Asst Professor, Dept of Architecture, Iowa State University, 482 College of Design, Ames, IA 50011, (515)294-8326.

CHAN, CHIU YEUNG
Educator, educational administrator. Hong Kong American. **PERSONAL:** Born Feb 28, 1941, Hong Kong; son of Hak Tan Chan and Ching Yuen Chan Lam; married Mui Lai Tania Chan, May 6, 1970; children: Andy Sung-Kin, Gary Sung-Hong. **EDUCATION:** University of Hong Kong, BSc (honors), 1965; University of Ottawa, MSc, 1967; University of Toronto, PhD, 1969. **CAREER:** Florida State University, assistant professor, 1969-74, associate professor, 1974-81, professor, 1981-83; University of Southwestern Louisiana, professor, graduate coordinator, 1982-. **ORGANIZATIONS:** American Mathematical Society, 1966-; Society for Industrial and Applied Mathematics, 1976-. **HONORS/AWARDS:** University of Southwestern Louisiana Foundation, Distinguished Professor, 1988. **SPECIAL ACHIEVEMENTS:** Over 60 research publications in various international journals in mathematics. **BUSINESS ADDRESS:** Professor, Graduate Coordinator, Director, Computational Research Lab, University of Southwestern Louisiana, Lafayette, LA 70504-1010, (318)231-5288.

CHAN, CHO LIK
Educator. Chinese American. **PERSONAL:** Born Dec 19, 1955, Hong Kong; married Joanna Yip; children: Charlotte On, Jasmine Hei. **EDUCATION:** University of Hawaii at Manoa, BS, 1979, MS, 1980; University of Illinois-Urbana Champaign, PhD, 1986. **CAREER:** University of Arizona, assistant professor, 1987-93, associate professor, 1993-. **ORGANIZATIONS:** ASME, 1987-; TSM, 1987-. **HONORS/AWARDS:** Pi Tau Sigma, 1977-; Phi Kappa Phi, 1977. **SPECIAL ACHIEVEMENTS:** Numerous journal publications about laser materials processing and boundary element method. **BUSINESS ADDRESS:** Associate Professor, Aero & Mech Engineering Dept, University of Arizona, Aero Bldg #16, Tucson, AZ 85721-0001, (602)621-2503.

CHAN, CHONG B. (BILL CHAN)
Electronics supply company executive. Chinese American. **PERSONAL:** Born Sep 24, 1951, Xieman, Fukien, People's Republic of China; married Sandra Q. Chan, May 26, 1979. **EDUCATION:** University of Texas at Austin, BS, 1974; Carnegie-Mellon University, PhD, 1979. **CAREER:** Halliburton, engineering, 1981-85; Schlumberger, senior engineer, 1985-89; A & M Electronics Supply, president, currently. **ORGANIZATIONS:** AIChE; SPE. **BUSINESS ADDRESS:** President, A & M Electronics Supply, Inc., 6245 Corporate Dr, Houston, TX 77036, (713)777-5600.

CHAN, CHUN KIN
Engineer. Chinese American. **PERSONAL:** Born Jan 21, 1953, Hong Kong; son of Ming Yam Chan and Lau Fong Chan; married Rowena Pik-Lo Chan, Nov 17, 1984; children: Andrea June-Yee, Richard Jon-Holm. **EDUCATION:** Chinese University of Hong Kong, BSc (1st class honors), 1975; Arizona State University, PhD, 1980. **CAREER:** Arizona State University, post-doctoral research assoc, 1981-84; AT&T Teletype, sr engr, 1984-85; AT&T Bell Laboratories, member of technical staff, 1986-. **ORGANIZATIONS:** American Physical Society, life mbr; IEEE, 1990-; American Society for Quality Control, certified reliability engr, 1990-. **HONORS/AWARDS:** Hong Kong Government, Government Scholar, 1970. **SPECIAL ACHIEVEMENTS:** Author of 25 publications included in Physical Review, IEEE Transactions, 1978-. **HOME ADDRESS:** 69 Hazel Avenue, Livingston, NJ 07039, (201)740-9172.

CHAN, DAVID S.
Chemicals engineering manager. Hong Kong American. **PERSONAL:** Born Jul 23, 1940, Hong Kong; son of Sin Yu Chan and Siu Chiu Lo; married Susanne Chan, Jul 26, 1975; children: Clifford, Marcus. **EDUCATION:** San Jose State University, BA, 1964, MS, 1970; University of Southern Mississippi, PhD, 1973. **CAREER:** Stanford Research Institute, biochemist, 1968-70; McLean Hospital, biochemist, 1972-75; Kennedy Shriver Institute, research associate, 1975-78; Beckman Instruments, chemicals process development and chemical engineering manager, 1978-. **ORGANIZATIONS:** American Society of Quality Control, 1983-90; American Society of Neurochemistry, 1972-85; American Assn for the Advancement of Science, 1978-82; Asian Americans for Community Involvement, 1992-. **HONORS/AWARDS:** Harvard University, Fellow of Biological Chemistry, 1972-77. **BUSINESS ADDRESS:** Chemicals Process Development & Chemical Engineering Manager, Beckman Instruments Inc, 1050 Page Mill Rd, Palo Alto, CA 94304, (415)859-1470.

CHAN, DAVID SO KEUNG
Research engineer. Chinese American. **PERSONAL:** Born Jun 6, 1951, Tsuen Wan, New Territories, Hong Kong; son of Konyil Chan and Maureen Chan; married Stella Y S Chan, Oct 12, 1979; children: Jonathan, Benjamin, Heather, Emily. **EDUCATION:** Massachusetts Institute of Technology, SB, 1972, SM, 1972, PhD, 1978. **CAREER:** Bell Laboratories, technical staff, associate member, 1972; Schlumberger-Doll Research, professional staff, 1978-83; ARCO Exploration & Production Research, senior research engineer, 1983-86; GE Corporate Research & Development, project leader, 1986-. **ORGANIZATIONS:** Inst of Electrical & Electronic Engineers, senior member, 1978-; Society of Photo-Optical Inst Engineers, 1989-; GE Elfun Society, 1990-; Sigma Xi, 1972-; Tau Beta Pi, 1972-; Eta Kappa Nu, 1972-. **HONORS/AWARDS:** Massachusetts Institute of Technology, MIT National Scholar, 1968. **SPECIAL ACHIEVEMENTS:** "Analysis of Quantization Errors...," in Selected Papers in Digital Signal Processing II, ed by DSP Committee of IEEE ASSP Society, New York: IEEE Press, pp 373-385, 1976; "Vector Radix Fast Fourier Transform," in Two-Dimensional Digital Signal Processing, vol 20 of Benchmark Papers in Elec Engineering and Computer Science, PA: Dowden, Hutchingon & Ross, 1978. **BUSINESS ADDRESS:** Electrical Engineer, R&D Staff, GE Corporate Research and Development, 1 River Rd, KW-C415, Schenectady, NY 12309, (518)387-7058.

CHAN, DONALD P. K.
Orthopedic spine surgeon, educator. Chinese American. **PERSONAL:** Born Jan 21, 1937, Rangoon, Burma; son of Charles Y C Chan & Josephine Chan; married Dorothy S L Chan, Jul 31, 1966; children: Joanne, Elaine. **EDUCATION:** Univ of Rangoon, Burma, BS, 1944, MD, 1960; Univ of Hong Kong, intern, medicine 1960-61, resident, surgery and orthopaedics, 1961-68. **CAREER:** University of Virginia Health Sciences Center, professor and head, div of spine surgery, currently; University of Vermont, resident orthopaedic surgery, 1968-71; Strong Meml Hospital, Rochester, NY, associate orthopaedist, 1972-80, sr associate orthopaedist, 1980-86, attending orthopaedist, 1986-; University of Rochester, assistant professor, 1972-80, associate professor, 1980-87, professor, 1987-93; Orthopaedic Clinical Services, Rochester, Goldstein Fellowship, dir, chief, Spine Surgery Dept. **ORGANIZATIONS:** Rochester Chinese Association, board of directors, 1991; American Orthopaedic Association, Scoiliosis Research Society; AMA; North American Spine Society; American Spinal Injury Association; EA Orthopeadic Association; Amer Acad of Orthopaedic Surgeons. **HONORS/AWARDS:** Traveling fellow Scoliosis Research Society, Fellow ACS. **SPECIAL ACHIEVEMENTS:** Contributed articles on clinical research related to the spine. **BUSINESS ADDRESS:** Orthopedic spine surgeon, University of Virginia Health Sciences Center Dept of Orthopaedics, Box 159, Charlottesville, VA 22908, (804)982-4242.

CHAN, EDWIN Y.
Architect. Chinese American. **PERSONAL:** Born Apr 23, 1960, Hong Kong; son of Benny P Chan and Esther Poon-Chan. **EDUCATION:** University of California, Berkeley, AB, architecture, 1982; Harvard University, MArch, 1985. **CAREER:** Frank Gehry and Associates, project designer, 1985-. **ORGANIZATIONS:** Licensed architect in state of California, 1991. **HONORS/AWARDS:** Progressive Architecture Award, 1991; Progressive Architecture Citation, 1991; Architecture League NY, Youth Architects Forum, 1986; Japan Architects, International Design Competition, 1981; Terra, International Design Competition, 1991. **SPECIAL ACHIEVEMENTS:** Publications: Now-time, issue 2, 1992; Oz, vol 9, 1987; Transformation, vol 1, 1987, vol 2, 1988; language proficiency: English, Chinese, French. **BUSINESS ADDRESS:** Project Designer, Frank Gehry & Associates, 1520-B Cloverfield Blvd, Santa Monica, CA 90405, (310)828-6088.

CHAN, GARY M.
Physician, educator. Chinese American. **PERSONAL:** Born Mar 8, 1947, Oakland, CA; son of Viola and Hart Chan; married Marilyn Chan; children: Ben, Melissa, Tim. **EDUCATION:** UC, Berkeley, BS, 1968; USC, MD, 1972; UCLA, residency, 1975; University of Cincinnati, fellowship, 1977. **CAREER:** University of Cincinnati, dept of neonatology, fellow, 1975-77; University of Utah, dept of pediatrics, professor, physician, 1977-. **ORGANIZATIONS:** Society for Pediatric Research, 1984-; American Society for Clinical Nutrition, 1983-; American Institute of Nutrition, 1983-; American Society for Bone & Mineral Research, 1982-; American College of Nutrition, fellow, 1979-; National Academy of Clinical Biochemistry, 1984-; American Academy of Pediatrics, 1977-. **HONORS/AWARDS:** American College of Nutrition, Carnation Award, 1992; University of Utah, College of Nursing Award, 1988; National Dairy Council, visiting professor, 1985-91. **SPECIAL ACHIEVEMENTS:** Over 50 journal publications concerning pediatric nutrition, 1977-. **BUSINESS ADDRESS:** Professor, University of Utah Medical School, 50 N Medical Dr, Salt Lake City, UT 84132.

CHAN, GLENN
Cleric. Chinese American. **PERSONAL:** Born Oct 2, 1934, Canton, Kwong Doung, China; son of Chan Monk Kun and Ng Kam Heung; married Helen Chan, Mar 5, 1963; children: Henry. **EDUCATION:** Canton College, BA, 1960; Hong Kong Baptist Seminary, ThM, 1975. **CAREER:** Truth Gospel Church, pastor, 1978-86; Chinese Church of Christ in Oakland, pastor, 1986-. **SPECIAL ACHIEVEMENTS:** Author: The Organization of a Church, 1989; The Study of Revelation, 1992. **BUSINESS ADDRESS:** Pastor, Chinese Church of Christ in Oakland, 2542 MacArthur Blvd, Oakland, CA 94602, (510)530-3936.

CHAN, HARVEY THOMAS, JR.
Food technologist. Chinese American. **PERSONAL:** Born Mar 5, 1940, Astoria, OR; son of Harvey T Chan Sr & Flora M Chan; married Doreen Chan, Dec 26, 1964; children: Baron, Dwight, Teruko. **EDUCATION:** Oregon State University, BS, 1963, University of Hawaii, MS, 1965; Oregon State University, PhD, 1968. **CAREER:** USDA-ARS, research food technologist, 1968-92, research leader, 1992-. **ORGANIZATIONS:** Institute of Food Technologists, 1961-, Hawain Section, chairman, 1977-78; American Chemical Society; American Horticultural Society; Boy Scouts of America, 1979-. **HONORS/AWARDS:** USDA-ARS, Certificate of Merit, 1982, 1992. **SPECIAL ACHIEVEMENTS:** Author: Handbook of Tropical Foods, Marcel Dekker Pub Co, 1983; author: Tropical Fruit Processing, Academic Press, 1988; 70 scientific publications; 2 patents. **HOME ADDRESS:** 932 Komomala Dr, Hilo, HI 96720. **BUSINESS ADDRESS:** Research Leader, US Dept of Agriculture, ARS, Waiakea Experiment Station, PO Box 4459, Hilo, HI 96720, (808)959-4343.

CHAN, HENRY Y. S.
Educator. Chinese American. **PERSONAL:** Born Apr 28, 1947, Hong Kong, Hong Kong; son of Yu Kwan-oi. **EDUCATION:** University of Hong Kong, BA, 1968; Indiana University, Bloomington, MA, 1976, PhD, 1987. **CAREER:** Indiana University, instructor, 1979-87; Lewis and Clark State College, assistant professor, 1987-89; Moorhead State University, assistant professor, 1989-93, associate professor, 1993-. **ORGANIZATIONS:** American Historical Association, 1987-; Association for Asian Studies, 1987-; Asian Research Service, Hong Kong, fellow, 1988-; Association of Asian American Studies, 1993-; World History Association, 1988-; Moorhead Central Lions Club, first vice president, 1993-94; Indiana University Alumni Association. **SPECIAL ACHIEVEMENTS:** Articles in historical journals such as Chinese Studies in History, Asian Profile, Pacific Historical Review; reading knowledge of French and Japanese, fluent in spoken and written Chinese. **BUSINESS ADDRESS:** Professor, Dept of History, Moorhead State University, MacLean Hall, Moorhead, MN 56560, (218)236-4665.

CHAN, JACK-KANG
Anti-submarine warfare engineer, mathematician. Chinese American. **PERSONAL:** Born Oct 20, 1950, Toyshan, Kwangtung, People's Republic of China; son of David En-Shek Chan and Yip-Ching Yuen Chan; married Suet-Fong Chan, Jun 3, 1982; children: Me-Fun, Kang-Ray. **EDUCATION:** University of London, BSc, mathematics, 1974; Chinese University of Hong Kong, BSc, electronics, 1975; Polytechnic University, MS, electrical engineering,

1976, PhD, electrical engineering, 1982, MS, appl math, 1983, PhD, mathematics, 1990. **CAREER:** Sedco Systems, microwave engineer, 1980; Norden Systems, senior member- technical staff, currently. **ORGANIZATIONS:** Institution of Electrical Electronic Engineers, Long Island Signal Processing Chapter, vice-chairman, 1992; American Mathematical Society; Mathematical Association of America; Institution of Electrical Engineers, England, associate member. **SPECIAL ACHIEVEMENTS:** Published papers: Signal Processing (EURASIP), 1990, 1991; International Journal of Mathematics & Mathematical Science, 1992; IEEE Transactions on Reliability, 1993. **HOME PHONE:** (718)961-3113. **BUSINESS ADDRESS:** Senior Technical Staff Member, Norden Systems, United Technologies, 75 Maxess Rd, Melville, NY 11747, (516)845-2560.

CHAN, JAMES C.
Educator, researcher. Hong Kong American. **PERSONAL:** Born Nov 20, 1937, Hong Kong; son of Y C Chan and Betty K Chan; married Grace, Aug 28, 1964. **EDUCATION:** International Christian University, Tokyo, Japan, BS, 1961; University of Rochester School of Medicine, PhD, 1966. **CAREER:** Squibb Inst Med Res, sr research scientist, 1966-68; Indiana University School of Med, asst prof, 1968-71; Baylor College of Medicine, asst prof, 1971-72; University of Texas, M D Anderson Cancer Ctr, assoc professor, 1972-; US Public Health Service, graduate fellowship, 1962-66. **HONORS/AWARDS:** United Board for Christian Higher Education, four year full scholarship to study in Japan, 1957-61. **SPECIAL ACHIEVEMENTS:** Author & co-author of over 150 articles on cancer research & virology. **HOME ADDRESS:** 1542 Searls Blvd, Sugar Land, TX 77478-3916, (713)242-7930.

CHAN, JAMES C. M.
Physician. Hong Kong American. **PERSONAL:** Born Dec 27, 1937, Hong Kong; married Winnie M Y, Jun 25, 1968. **EDUCATION:** University of Hong Kong, 1958-62; McGill University, Montreal, Canada, MD, 1964. **CAREER:** Mayo Clinic, fellow, 1965-67; University of Oregon, fellow, 1967-68; Columbia-Presbyterian Hospital, 1968-70; Childrens Hospital, LA, CA, 1970-73, Wash, DC, 1973-76; NIH, 1976-77, 1987-88; Medical College of Virginia, Nephrology Div, professor, chairman, 1977-. **HONORS/AWARDS:** Best Teacher Awrd, Medical College of Virginia, 1979, Alpha Omega Alpha, 1987; Kidney International, editorial board, Nephrology Ucology, 1991-. **BUSINESS ADDRESS:** Professor, Chairman, Nephrology Division, Children's Medical Center, Virginia Commonwealth University, Medical College of Virginia, 1011 E Marshall St, Richmond, VA 23298-0498, (804)786-9608.

CHAN, JOHN
Corporate finance manager. Chinese American. **PERSONAL:** Born Jan 5, 1964, New York, NY; son of Yick Chun Chan and Shook Ying Chan. **EDUCATION:** Boston University, BS, aerospace engineering, 1985; The Wharton School of the University of Pennsylvania, MBA, 1992. **CAREER:** Skyline Communications, Inc, general manager/owner, 1985-86; CorpAir, Inc, general manager/owner, 1986-90; Small Business Development Center, consultant, 1991-92; Danzi Capital Group, senior associate, 1992-93; Daedalus Partners, partner, 1993-. **SPECIAL ACHIEVEMENTS:** Language proficiency in Chinese. **BUSINESS ADDRESS:** Partner, Daedalus Partners, 4675 MacArthur Ct, Ste 730, Newport Beach, CA 92660, (714)261-0800.

CHAN, JOHN G.
Educator. Chinese American. **PERSONAL:** Born Aug 15, 1938, Oakland, CA; son of Shue Jeong Chan and Yonsin Gee Chan; married Mary Jean Fong, Jan 24, 1964; children: James K, Lisa M. **EDUCATION:** San Francisco State University, BA, biology, 1962, MA, microbiology, 1964; University of Washington, School of Fisheries, PhD, 1970. **CAREER:** University of Hawaii, Hilo, department of biology, chair, 1987-89, division of natural sciences, chair, 1990-92, professor of biology, currently. **ORGANIZATIONS:** American Society for Microbiolgy; AAAS; Sigma Xi; Hawaii Academy of Sciences; Chinese Civic Association of Hawaii. **HONORS/AWARDS:** University of Hawaii, Board of Regents, Award for Excellence in Teaching, 1991; University of Hawaii, Hilo, Outstanding Teacher Award, 1970-71. **BUSINESS ADDRESS:** Professor of Biology, Division of Natural Sciences, University of Hawaii, Hilo, 523 W Lanikaula St, Hilo, HI 96720-4091.

CHAN, KAI CHIU
Educator. Chinese American. **PERSONAL:** Born May 16, 1934, Canton, China; married Kuen Kuen Chan, Aug 17, 1966; children: Alisa C, David C. **EDUCATION:** Tokyo Medical and Dental University, DDS, 1962; University of Iowa, MS, 1964, DDS, 1967. **CAREER:** University of Iowa, instructor,

1964-67, assistant professor, 1967-71, associate professor, 1971-76, professor, 1976-. **BUSINESS ADDRESS:** Professor, Operative Dept, College of Dentistry, The University of Iowa, Iowa City, IA 52242, (319)335-7210.

CHAN, KAM CHUEN
Educator. Hong Kong American. **PERSONAL:** Born Oct 27, 1959, Hong Kong; son of Ngau Chan and Shiu Ping Ko; married Pikki Lai, Jun 8, 1986; children: Jesse. **EDUCATION:** Chinese University of Hong Kong, BSS, 1984; University of Alabama, MA, 1987, PhD, 1990. **CAREER:** Moorhead State University, asst prof, 1990-. **SPECIAL ACHIEVEMENTS:** Research articles in Financial Review, 1992, Journal of Eco & Business, 1993. **BUSINESS ADDRESS:** Asst Prof of Finance, Moorhead State University, 7th Ave S, Moorhead, MN 56563, (218)236-4664.

CHAN, KAWEI
Nuclear engineer. Chinese American. **PERSONAL:** Born Mar 13, 1934, Hong Kong; son of Chun-Choi Chan and Kiu Cheung Chan; married Wenyin Li Chan, Jul 19, 1969; children: Sharon. **EDUCATION:** Army Ordnance Engineering College, Taiwan, BS, 1958; Tsing Hua University, Taiwan, MS, 1962; Purdue University, PhD, 1970. **CAREER:** Tsing Hua University, professor, 1971-80; Bechtel Power Corp., staff engineer, 1981-86; Sargent & Lundy Engineers, principal engineer, 1988-. **ORGANIZATIONS:** American Nuclear Society, 1976-. **HONORS/AWARDS:** Korea Power Engineering Corp., Service Award, 1990. **SPECIAL ACHIEVEMENTS:** Numerous publications in nuclear engineering & design & nuclear science and engineering, 1971-80; work in the field of thermal hydraulic of nuclear power plants, 1980-; read & write Chinese; speak Mandarin and Cantonese. **BUSINESS ADDRESS:** Principal Engineer, Sargent and Lundy, 55 E. Monroe St., Chicago, IL 60603, (312)269-6855.

CHAN, KENYON S.
Educator, educational administrator. Chinese American. **PERSONAL:** Born Apr 18, 1948, Oakland, CA; son of Eugene Chan and Martha Chan. **EDUCATION:** UCLA, BA, 1979, MA, 1972, PhD, 1974. **CAREER:** UCLA, assistant professor; National Center for Bilinguial Research, social policy and education coordinator; California State University, Northridge, professor and chair, 1990-. **ORGANIZATIONS:** Association for Asian American Studies, president, 1994-96, regional rep, 1992-94; American Psychological Association, 1974-; American Educational Research Association, 1974. **SPECIAL ACHIEVEMENTS:** Approximately 25 journal articles and book chapters. **BUSINESS ADDRESS:** Professor and Chair, Asian American Studies Dept., California State University, Northridge, 18111 Nordhoff St, Northridge, CA 91330-8251, (818)885-4966.

CHAN, KWAN M.
Educator. Hong Kong American. **PERSONAL:** Born Jul 30, 1935, Hong Kong; son of Check F and Sau Y Chan; married Karen. **EDUCATION:** Hong Kong University, BSc, 1959; University of Liverpool, PhD, 1966. **CAREER:** Huntington Beach Chinese School, principal, 1990-; Woods Hole Oceanographic Institution, scientist, 1969; Fisheries Research Station, 1961-68; California State University, professor, 1969-. **ORGANIZATIONS:** Hong Kong University Alumni Association of Southern California, president, 1993. **SPECIAL ACHIEVEMENTS:** Author of over sixty publications in environmental science, analytical chemistry; language: Chinese. **BUSINESS ADDRESS:** Professor, California State University, 1250 Bellflower Blvd, Long Beach, CA 90840-0004, (310)985-4817.

CHAN, KWOK HUNG (DANIEL)
Educator. Hong Kong American. **PERSONAL:** Born Jul 26, 1954, Canton, People's Republic of China; son of Yim-tin Chan and Wai-fong Lam; married Shuk-fong Lau, Dec 28, 1984. **EDUCATION:** Chinese University of Hong Kong, BA, 1979, MPhil, 1981; University of Western Ontario, PhD, 1986. **CAREER:** National University of Singapore, lecturer, 1987-89; Memphis State University, assistant professor, 1989-. **SPECIAL ACHIEVEMENTS:** Area of specialization: artificial intelligence. **BUSINESS ADDRESS:** Assistant Professor, Dept of Mathematical Sciences, Memphis State University, Memphis, TN 38152, (901)678-2693.

CHAN, LAURENCE KWONG-FAI
Physician. Hong Kong American/Chinese American. **PERSONAL:** Born Oct 6, 1947, Hong Kong; son of Joseph T S Chan and Sau-Lin Tong Chan; married Cynthia Chi-Shin Cheung Chan, Jul 19, 1977; children: Joseph M. **EDUCATION:** University of Hong Kong, MD, 1972; Royal College of Physicians,

London, MRCP, UK, FRCP, 1977; University of Oxford, PhD, 1983; University of Colorado. **CAREER:** University of Edinburgh, Nuffield Transplant Unit, senior house officer, 1976-77; University of Oxford, Churchill Hospital, Renal Transplant Unit, 1977-79, clinical lecturer in medicine, 1980-83; University of Colorado, assistant professor of medicine, 1983-88, School of Medicine, associate professor of medicine, 1983-, Transplant Nephrology, director. **ORGANIZATIONS:** Chinese American Society of Nephrology, president, 1991-; Magnetic Resonance in Medicine, student stipends committee, 1993-, abstract selection committee, 1990-; American Society of Nephrology, abstract selection committee, 1990; American Society of Transplant Physicians, education committee, 1989; Transplantation Society, 1977-; International Society of Nephrology, fellow, 1977-. **HONORS/AWARDS:** Oxford University, Green College, William Gibson J R Fellow, 1981; Royal College of Physicians of Edinburgh, fellow, 1987; Royal College of Physicians of London, fellow, 1988. **SPECIAL ACHIEVEMENTS:** Clinical studies in kidney transplantation, 1979, 1980; Magnetic resonance in medicine, 1980. **BUSINESS ADDRESS:** Professor of Medicine, University of Colorado School of Medicine, 4200 East Ninth Ave, Box C281, Health Sciences Center, Denver, CO 80262, (303)270-6735.

CHAN, LEE-NIEN LILLIAN

Educator. Chinese American. **PERSONAL:** Born Sep 28, 1941, Hong Kong; daughter of Shao-Wen Ling and Yao-Chung Chiang Ling; married Teh-sheng Chan, May 3, 1969; children: Ming, Irene, Mark. **EDUCATION:** Acadia University, BSc, 1963; University of Wisconsin-Madison, MSc, 1966; Yale University, PhD, 1970. **CAREER:** Yale University, research associate; MIT, research associate; University of Connecticut Health Center, assistant prof; University of Texas Med Branch, associate prof, currently. **ORGANIZATIONS:** American Society of Cell Biology; American Society of Molecular Biology & Biochemistry; American Society of Hematology; International Society of Developmental Biology; American Soc for the Advancement of Science. **HONORS/AWARDS:** NIH, Research Career Development Award; March of Dimes, Basil O'Connor Starter Grant. **SPECIAL ACHIEVEMENTS:** Numerous publications in scientific journals. **BUSINESS ADDRESS:** Associate Professor, Dept of Human Biological Chem & Genetics, University of Tex Med Branch, 515 Basic Science Bldg, Galveston, TX 77555.

CHAN, LO-YI C. Y.

Architect, foundation executive. Chinese American. **PERSONAL:** Born Dec 1, 1932, Canton, China; son of Wing-tsit Chan and Wai Hing Chan; married Mildred Chan, Sep 1, 1957; children: Christopher, Leighton, Leicia. **EDUCATION:** Dartmouth College, BA, 1954; Harvard University, MArch, 1959. **CAREER:** IM Pei, architect, 1960-65; Columbia University, architecture instructor, 1963-67; Cornell University, architecture instructor, 1965-68; Harvard University, architecture instructor, 1976, 1978, 1980, 1981; Prentice & Chan, Ohlhausen, partner, 1965-. **ORGANIZATIONS:** American Institute of Architects, 1963-, fellow, 1977; New York City Art Commission, commissioner, 1992-; Henry Street Settlement, trustee, 1979-; Lingnan Foundation, chairman, 1986-; Berkshire School, trustee, 1992-; Committee of 100, director, 1991-; New York State Council on the Arts, 1993-. **HONORS/AWARDS:** Harvard University, Appleton Fellow, 1960; NEA, Design Fellow, 1975-76; AIA, Design Award, 1993. **MILITARY SERVICE:** US Army, sp3, 1955-57. **HOME ADDRESS:** 270 Riverside Dr, New York, NY 10025. **BUSINESS ADDRESS:** Partner, Prentice & Chan, Ohlhausen, 14 E 4th St, New York, NY 10012, (212)420-8600.

CHAN, LOIS MAI

Educator, librarian. Chinese American. **PERSONAL:** Born Jul 30, 1934, Nanking, China; daughter of Kar K and Sau N Mark; married Shung-Kai Chan, Jun 21, 1963; children: Jennifer M, Stephen Y. **EDUCATION:** National Taiwan University, AB, foreign languages, 1956; Florida State University, MA, English, 1958, MS, library science, 1960; University of Kentucky, PhD, comparative literature, 1970. **CAREER:** University of Minnesota, Library School, visiting lecturer, 1979; University of Hawaii, Graduate School of Library Studies, visiting professor, 1982; OCLC Online Computer Library Center, DDC Online Project, project consultant, 1983-86; University of Michigan, CLR, LCSH Project, consultant, 1988-89; Purdue University Libraries, assistant order librarian, 1960-61, assistant cataloger, 1961-63; Northwestern University Libraries, serials acquisition librarian, 1963-64; Lake Forest College Library, assistant librarian, 1964-66; University of Kentucky Libraries, serials cataloger, 1966-67, College of Library Science, assistant professor, 1970-74, associate professor, 1974-80, School of Library and Information Science, professor, 1980-. **ORGANIZATIONS:** American Library Association, 1960-,

Decimal Classification Editorial Policy Committee, 1975-93, vice chair, 1980-84, chair, 1986-91, International Relations Committee, resources and technical services division, 1981-82, Melvil Dewey Award Jury, 1976-77. **HONORS/AWARDS:** American Library Association, Margaret Mann Citation, 1989; Council on Library Resources, grant for preparation of a new edition Immroth's Guide to the Library of Congress Classification, 1989-91; University of Kentucky Alumni Association, Great Teacher Award, 1980; Council on Library Resources, fellowship, 1978. **SPECIAL ACHIEVEMENTS:** Author, Cataloging and Classification: An Introduction, 2nd edition, McGraw-Hill, 1994; Library of Congress Subject Headings: Principles of Structure and Policies for Application, Cataloging Distribution Service, Library of Congress, 1990; Immroth's Guide to the Library of Congress Classification, 4th edition, Libraries Unlimited Inc, 1990. **BUSINESS ADDRESS:** Professor, School of Library and Information Science, University of Kentucky, Lexington, KY 40506-0039.

CHAN, LUNG S.

Educator. Hong Kong American. **PERSONAL:** Born Dec 25, 1955, Hong Kong; son of Wai Nam Chan and Kit Ching Lam; married Lily Chan, Jul 13, 1985; children: Calvin, Clarice. **EDUCATION:** Wah Yan College, Kowloon, Hong Kong, diploma; Chinese University, Hong Kong, BSSc; UC Berkeley, MA, PhD. **CAREER:** UC Berkeley, research assistant, 1980-82, teaching associate, 1982-84; University of Wisconsin, assistant prof, 1984-90, associate prof, 1990-. **ORGANIZATIONS:** American Geophysical Union, 1980-; Geological Society of America, 1980-; Geological Society of Hong Kong, 1984-. **HONORS/AWARDS:** Chung Chi College, Chinese University of HK, Valedictorian, 1978; US Chamber of Commerce/Mobil, HK, Bicentennial Scholarship, 1978. **SPECIAL ACHIEVEMENTS:** Research in geophysics, tectonics and structures. **BUSINESS ADDRESS:** Associate Professor, Geology Dept, University of Wisconsin-Eau Claire, Park St, Phillips Hall, Eau Claire, WI 54701-4800, (715)836-4982.

CHAN, MARSHA J.

Educator. Chinese American. **PERSONAL:** Born Jan 10, 1952, Oakland, CA; daughter of Raymond & Ida R Chan; married Terry Zhenyong Yang, Jun 11, 1986; children: Tiffany Yang, Bryan Yang. **EDUCATION:** Stanford University, BA, 1973, MA, 1976; San Jose State University, cred sec educ, 1976; University of California, Berkeley, 1978. **CAREER:** De Anza College, Occupational Training Institute, ESL instructor, 1977-80; Chongging Institute of Architectual Engineering, China, English instructor, 1980-81; Graduate School of the Academy of Sciences, China, English instructor, 1981-82; Mission College, English as a second language, 1983-. **ORGANIZATIONS:** US-China People's Friendship Association, president, 1982; TESOL: Teachers of English to Speakers of Other Languages, convention presenter, 1975-; CATESOL: California Association of Teachers of English to Speakers of Other Languages, frequent conference presenter, conference treasurer, 1974-; Asian Americans for Community Involvement, 1974-; Asian/Pacific Americans Action Committee, 1980-; Stanford Asian Pacific American Alumni Club, 1991-. **HONORS/AWARDS:** Mission College, Presidents Award, 1989; Mission College, Academic Senate Award for Service, 1992, Academic Senate Award for Development of Sexual Harassment Policy & Procedures, 1993. **SPECIAL ACHIEVEMENTS:** Language proficiency: English, Mandarin, Cantonese, Spanish, French, Italian; publications: Phrase by Phrase: Pronunciation and Listening in American English, Prentice Hall, 1987; textbook, audiotapes, 50 articles in TESOL Journal, CATESOL Journal, CATESOL News, ESP Journal, The Forum, Mission Messenger, ESL News; videotape productions on English language learning; consultant to corporate executives in accent reduction. **HOME ADDRESS:** 463 Liquidambar Way, Sunnyvale, CA 94086. **BUSINESS ADDRESS:** Professor, English as a Second Language, Mission College, 3000 Mission College Blvd, Santa Clara, CA 95054-1897, (408)988-2200.

CHAN, MASON C.

Educator. Chinese American. **PERSONAL:** Born Sep 2, 1937, Kwong-Tung, China; married Karen Chan, Jun 2, 1964; children: Kalia, Tracy. **EDUCATION:** Chu Hai College, Hong Kong, BA, education, 1961; Wayne State University, MEd, 1963; University of Oregon, EdD, 1968. **CAREER:** Fontana Schools, Special Education, learning specialist, 1968-85, high school teacher, 1985-91; Fontana Unified School District, Office of Traffic Safety, director, special projects, 1991-. **ORGANIZATIONS:** California Assn of Safety Education; NEA, CTA; AAMD. **HONORS/AWARDS:** Fontana Schools, Teacher of the Year, 1982. **SPECIAL ACHIEVEMENTS:** Mentoring Apprenticeship Program, Tobacco Prevention Program, Drop-Out Recovery Program, coordintator, 1992-94. **HOME ADDRESS:** PO Box 878, Twin Peaks, CA 92391, (909)336-2851.

CHAN, MEI-MEI

Journalist. Chinese American. **PERSONAL:** Born Oct 29, 1959, Canton, People's Republic of China; daughter of Yuen Ding Chan & Soo Kam Chan; married Randy Kirk, Jul 25, 1982; children: Aaron Kirk, Regan Chan-Kirk. **EDUCATION:** University of Illinois, Champaign-Urbana, BA, 1981. **CAREER:** Commercial News, Danville, Illinois, features reporter, 1981-82; USA Today, Arlington, VA, cover story reporter, life reporter, 1982-87; USA Weekend, Arlington, VA, associate editor, assistant editor, 1988-90; Chicago Sun-Times, acting deputy features editor, assistant metro editor, 1990-93; Northwestern University, graduate studies, adjunct instructor, 1992; Post Register, Idaho Falls, executive editor, 1993-. **ORGANIZATIONS:** Asian American Journalists Association, print national vice president, 1985-91, Washington DC chapter, founding president, 1985-89; Institute for Journalism Education, 1992-; New Directions for News, participant, 1988, 1993. **HONORS/AWARDS:** Asian American Journalism Association, scholarship to Northwestern Management Training Center, at Northwestern University, fellow, 1992. **BUSINESS ADDRESS:** Executive Editor, Post Register, PO Box 1800, Idaho Falls, ID 83403, (208)522-1800.

CHAN, PENG S. (PENN)

Educator. Chinese American. **PERSONAL:** Born Sep 13, 1957, Penang, Malaysia; son of Ka Sing Chan and Swee Lan Ng (deceased). **EDUCATION:** University of Malaya, Malaysia, LLB (with honors), 1980; University of Texas, Austin, MBA, 1983, PhD, 1986. **CAREER:** Louisiana State University, assistant professor, 1987-89; Global Management Group, president, 1987-; California State University, Fullerton, associate professor, 1989-. **ORGANIZATIONS:** International Franchise Association, educational affiliate, 1989-; American Association of Professional Consultants, registered professional consultant, 1992. **HONORS/AWARDS:** Phi Beta Delta, Distinguished Scholar in International Business, 1992. **SPECIAL ACHIEVEMENTS:** Author, "Franchise Management in East Asia," 1990; author, "Training for Franchise Management," 1991; author of over 60 articles in strategic management, franchising, and international management. **BUSINESS ADDRESS:** Associate Professor, California State University, Fullerton, School of Business Administration & Economics, Fullerton, CA 92634, (714)773-3944.

CHAN, PHILLIP PAANG

Educator, graphic designer, painter. Chinese American. **PERSONAL:** Born Jul 11, 1946, Canton, China; son of Wei-fen Woo. **EDUCATION:** San Jose State University; University of California, Berkeley, BA, 1971, MFA, 1976. **CAREER:** Indiana State University, assistant professor of art, 1984; Oberlin College, visiting assistant professor of art, 1984-85; University of Texas, Austin, visiting lecturer of art, 1985; Pennsylvania State University, assistant professor of art, 1986-88; State University of New York, Oswego, assistant professor of art, 1988-89; University of Wisconsin, Milwaukee, assistant professor of design, 1989-92; Youngstown State University, assistant professor of art & design, 1992-; Cultural Exchange Show: Guadalajara Ministry of Cultural Affairs, 1993; Artist, exhibitions include: 34th Annual Juried Exhibition, San Diego Art Institute, 1988; University of Akron, China Traveling Show: Fine Universities & Art Schools in China, 1992-93; At the Edge II: Laguna Gloria Museum, Austin, TX, 1990; Earth View: Galleria Mesa, Arizona, 1989. **HONORS/AWARDS:** National Endowment for the Arts, Individual Artist Award, 1978. **SPECIAL ACHIEVEMENTS:** National Endowment for the Humanities, summer seminars, 1979, 1983, 1990. **HOME ADDRESS:** 3831 Cook Rd, Rootstown, OH 44272.

CHAN, PO CHUEN

Biologist, toxicologist. Chinese American. **PERSONAL:** Born May 13, 1935, Ichong, Hupeh, China; son of Tin Wa Chan and Pui-Wa Ho; married Lillian Chan, Oct 16, 1961; children: Yola, Vella. **EDUCATION:** International Christian University, BA, 1960; Columbia University, MA, 1963; New York University, PhD, 1967. **CAREER:** Sloan-Kettering Institute for Cancer Research, research associate, 1967-69; Naylor Dana Institute for Disease Prevention, American Health Foundation, associate member, 1970-78; Roswell Park Memorial Institute, cancer research scientist IV, 1978-83; National Institute Environmental Health Science, sr study scientist, 1983-. **ORGANIZATIONS:** American Association for the Adv of Science, fellow, 1965; American Association for Cancer Research, 1977; American Physiological Society, 1977; New York Academy of Science, 1965; Society of Chinese Bioscientists in America, 1987; North Carolina Governor's Task Force Against Racial Religious and Ethnic Hate and Intimidation, 1988-92. **HONORS/AWARDS:** NIH, US Public Health Service, grants, 1973-83; US exchange scientist to France, NCI-INSERM, 1977; Columbia University, Eugene Higgins Fellow, 1960-61. **SPE-**

CIAL ACHIEVEMENTS: Published more than 100 articles in professional journals. **HOME ADDRESS:** 7909 Hollander Place, Raleigh, NC 27606, (919)362-8463. **BUSINESS ADDRESS:** Senior Study Scientist, National Institute of Environmental Health Sciences, PO Box 12233, Research Triangle Park, NC 27709, (919)541-7561.

CHAN, PUI KWONG

Educator. Chinese American. **PERSONAL:** Born Mar 1, 1946, China; married Fung Yuk Leung, Aug 8, 1975; children: Grace, Raymond. **EDUCATION:** Chinese University of Hong Kong, BSc, 1971, MPhil, 1973; University of Toronto, PhD, 1978. **CAREER:** Baylor College of Medicine, associate professor of pharmacology, 1990-. **BUSINESS ADDRESS:** Associate Professor of Pharmacology, Baylor College of Medicine, One Baylor Plaza, Houston, TX 77030, (713)798-7902.

CHAN, ROBERT T. P.

Educator. Chinese American. **PERSONAL:** Born Jan 25, 1943, Foochow, Fuckin, China; son of Cornelius and Ruth Chan; married Gloria C Chan, Dec 20, 1970; children: Timothy, Titus. **EDUCATION:** Pittsburg State University, MS, 1972; University of Georgia, 1972-73; North Carolina State University, 1973-80; California Coast University, PhD, 1984. **CAREER:** California State University, Fullerton, lecturer, 1980-83; California State University, Long Beach, assistant professor, 1980-94; Rancho Santiago College, lecturer, 1988-94; Orange Coast College, lecturer, 1991-94; RTT Institute, president, currently. **ORGANIZATIONS:** The Mathematical Association of America, 1993; National Geographic Society, 1993; American Mathematical Society. **MILITARY SERVICE:** Air Force, lt. **BUSINESS ADDRESS:** President, RTT Institute, 15333 Culver Drive, Ste 420, Irvine, CA 92714, (714)552-7795.

CHAN, SAMUEL H. P.

Educator. Chinese American. **PERSONAL:** Born Aug 1, 1941, Nanking, China; children: Lydia S, Albert R. **EDUCATION:** International Christian University, Japan, BS, 1964; University of Rochester, PhD, 1970; Cornell University, postdoctoral, 1971. **CAREER:** University of Rochester, teaching assistant, 1964-66; Cornell University, postdoctoral research associate, 1969-71; Syracuse University, professor of biochemistry, 1971-. **ORGANIZATIONS:** American Chemical Society; American Society of Biochemistry & Molecular Biology; Sigma Xi; AAAS. **SPECIAL ACHIEVEMENTS:** Proficient in English, Japanese, Mandarin and Cantonese Chinese. **BUSINESS ADDRESS:** Professor of Biochemistry, Syracuse University, 130 College Place, Syracuse, NY 13244, (315)443-3182.

CHAN, SHAM-YUEN

Research scientist. Hong Kong American. **PERSONAL:** Born Sep 8, 1949, Hong Kong; son of K Y Chan & M S Chan; married W Nancy, Jun 30, 1975; children: Eric, Ashley. **EDUCATION:** H K Baptist College, BS, 1973; University of Notre Dame, PhD, 1978. **CAREER:** University of Notre Dame, research assistant professor, 1982-86; Miles Inc, principal staff scientist, manager, 1992-. **ORGANIZATIONS:** American Society for Microbiology, 1981-93; National Registry of Microbiology, 1981-93; NY Academy of Science, 1981-82; Sigma Xi, 1972-73. **HONORS/AWARDS:** Bayer AG, Otto-Bayer Medal, 1992; Miles Inc, Corporate Science Award, 1988. **BUSINESS ADDRESS:** Principal Staff Scientist, Manager, Miles Inc, 4th and Parker, Berkeley, CA 94701, (510)420-5200.

CHAN, SHIH-HUNG

Educator. Taiwanese American. **PERSONAL:** Born Nov 8, 1943, Chang-Hwa, Taiwan; son of Pin Chan; married Shirley S Chan, Jun 14, 1969; children: Bryan, Erick. **EDUCATION:** National Taipei Institute of Technology, diploma, 1963; University of New Hampshire, MS, 1966; University of California, Berkeley, PhD, 1969. **CAREER:** New York University, assistant and associate professor, 1969-73; Polytechnic University of New York, associate professor, 1973-74; Argonne National Laboratory, research staff, 1974-75; University of Wisconsin, Milwaukee, professor, 1976-79, chairman, 1979-89, Wisconsin Distinguished Professor, 1989-, director, 1990-. **ORGANIZATIONS:** American Society of Mechanical Engineers, chairman of aerospace heat transfer committee, 1989-92; American Society of Mechanical Engineers, fellow, 1990-; American Chinese Civic Club, president, 1986-87; State of Wisconsin American Nuclear Society, chairman, 1982-83; Pacific Center of Thermal-Fluids Engineering, advisory board member, 1991-; Annual Review of Numerical Fluid Mechanics and Heat Transfer, editorial advisory board member, 1985-89; ASME Journal of Heat Transfer, associate editor, 1994-. **HONORS/AWARDS:** University of Wisconsin, Milwaukee, Outstanding Research Award, 1983; Outstanding Teaching Award, 1993; National Taipei Institute of Technology, Outstanding Alumni Award, 1991; Yuan-Ze Institute of Technology, Honor Chair Professorship, 1993; State Assembly of Wisconsin, Outstanding Citation, 1984. **SPECIAL ACHIEVEMENTS:** Published over 100 technical publications in journals in the field of combustion, multiphase flows, radiative transfer, heat transfer, nuclear reactor safety analysis, and alternate energy; published 3 chapters in 3 different books. **MILITARY SERVICE:** Marine, 2nd lt, 1963-64. **BUSINESS ADDRESS:** Wisconsin Distinguished Professor, Dept of Mechanical Engineering, University of Wisconsin, Milwaukee, PO Box 784, Milwaukee, WI 53201-0784, (414)229-5001.

CHAN, STEPHEN W.
Educator. Chinese American. **PERSONAL:** Born Jul 28, 1942, Wuchow, Kwangsi, China; married Betty W; children: Audrey S, Stephanie. **EDUCATION:** University of Hong Kong, BSc, 1966, MSc, 1968; University of Hull, UK, PhD, 1970. **CAREER:** Rutgers University, assistant professor, 1972-77; SUNY Brockport, associate professor, 1977-. **ORGANIZATIONS:** Rochester Chinese Association, president, 1993-94. **SPECIAL ACHIEVEMENTS:** Over 40 scientific publications, 1969-89. **BUSINESS ADDRESS:** Associate Professor, Dept of Biological Sciences, SUNY Brockport, Brockport, NY 14420, (716)395-5754.

CHAN, STEVEN D.
Dentist. Chinese American. **PERSONAL:** Born Dec 11, 1951, Los Angeles, CA; son of Daniel Chan and Evelyn Chan; married Suzanne, Jul 25, 1975; children: Scott, Tracy. **EDUCATION:** UCLA, AB, 1973; Georgetown University, DDS, 1978. **CAREER:** Private practice, pediatric dentist, currently. **ORGANIZATIONS:** Southern Alameda County Dental Society, president, 1986-87; California Dental Assn, trustee, 1990-93, Council on Dental Health, 1988-91; California Society of Pediatric Dentists, director, 1990-93; South Bay Chinese Service Club, Scholarship Committee, chmn, 1990-93; Fremont Chamber of Commerce Scholarship Foundation, trustee, 1992-93; City of Fremont Library Commission, commissioner, 1993-97; Citizens For A Better Community, director, 1993-. **HONORS/AWARDS:** American College of Dentists, Fellow, 1990; American Academy of Pediatric Dentists, Fellow, 1991; Academy of Dentistry International, Fellow, 1991; Pierre Fauchard Academy, Fellow, 1992; International College of Dentists, Fellow, 1993. **SPECIAL ACHIEVEMENTS:** Author: "Financing a Dental Practice," Journal of California Dental Assn, Jun 1990; Loan Proposal and Business Plans for a Dental Office - A Workbook, California Dental Assn, 1991; Trademarks and Logos for a Dental Practice - A Guide to Design, 1993. **BUSINESS ADDRESS:** Owner, Steven Chan, DDS, Pediatric Dentist, 1895 Mowry Ave, Ste 121, Fremont, CA 94538.

CHAN, SU HAN
Educator. Malaysian American/Chinese American. **PERSONAL:** Born Jan 7, 1956, Penang, Malaysia; daughter of Ka Sing Chan & Swee Lan Ng (deceased); married Ko Wang, Nov 28, 1989. **EDUCATION:** University of Malaya, BSc, education, 1980; Louisiana Tech University, MBA, 1982; University of Texas, Austin, PhD, 1988. **CAREER:** California State University, Fullerton, associate professor, 1989-93, professor, 1993-. **ORGANIZATIONS:** American Finance Association, 1985-; Financial Management Association, 1985-. **HONORS/AWARDS:** American Association of Individual Investors, Best Paper on Investments, 1990; University of Texas, Austin, Eugene and Dora Bonham Memorial Fund, 1987, Beta Alpha Phi, 1987, Phi Kappa Phi, 1983; Louisiana Tech University, Beta Gamma Sigma, 1982. **SPECIAL ACHIEVEMENTS:** Publications appear in the following journals: Journal of Financial Economics, vol 31, p 381-410, 1992, vol 26, p 255-276, 1990; Journal of Real Estate Research, vol 7, p 493-501, 1992, vol 5, p 231-246, 1990; Journal of Applied Corporate Finance, p 59-66, 1992. **BUSINESS ADDRESS:** Professor, Dept of Finance, California State University, Fullerton, School of Business Administration and Economics, Fullerton, CA 92634, (414)773-2217.

CHAN, SUCHENG
Educator, educational administrator. Chinese American. **PERSONAL:** Born Apr 16, 1941, Shanghai, China; daughter of Kock K Chan & Dora Chan; married Mark Juergensmeyer, Sep 21, 1969. **EDUCATION:** Swarthmore College, BA, 1963; University of Hawaii, MA, 1965; University of California, Berkeley, PhD, 1973. **CAREER:** University of California, Berkeley, asst professor, associate professor, 1974-84; University of California, Santa Cruz, professor, provost, 1984-88; University of California, Santa Barbara, professor, chair, 1988-. **ORGANIZATIONS:** Org of American Historians, Rawley Book Award Committee, 1992-; Immigration History Soc, exec bd, 1991-94; Agri-

cultural History Soc, Saloutos Book Award Comm, 1990-93; UC, Santa Barbara Div, Faculty Legislature, 1989-91, Academic Senate, Comm on Educational Policy & Academic Planning, 1990-92; UC Humanities Research Institute, bd of governors, 1991-95. **HONORS/AWARDS:** Association for Asian American Studies, Outstanding Book Award, for Quiet Odyssey, 1991; California Historical Society, J S Holliday Award, for scholarly contributions to California history, 1991; Gustavus Myers Center for the Study of Civil Rights, Outstanding Book Award, for Asian Americans: An Interpretive History, 1992. **SPECIAL ACHIEVEMENTS:** Author, "Chinese Livelihood in Rural California, 1860-80," Pacific Historical Review LIII:3, pp 273-307, 1984; This Bittersweet Soil: The Chinese in California Agriculture, 1860-1910, 1986; "European & Asian Immigration into the United States in Comparative Perspective, 1820s to 1920s," Immigration Reconsidered: History, Sociology, Politics, 1990; Asian Americans: An Interpretive History, 1991; Asian Californians, 1991; editor, Entry Denied: Exclusion & the Chinese Community in America, 1882-1943, 1991; Quiet Odyssey: A Pioneer Korean Woman in America, 1990; co-editor, Peoples of Color in the American West, DC Heath & Co, 1993.

CHAN, SUITAK STEVE
Educator. Chinese American. **PERSONAL:** Born Oct 10, 1949, Shanghai, People's Republic of China; son of Kaning Chan and Pancy Chan; married Jennifer Chan, May 10, 1985; children: Andrew. **EDUCATION:** Tulane University, BA, 1970; University of Minnesota, MA, 1974, PhD, 1976. **CAREER:** University of Colorado, professor, 1984-. **HONORS/AWARDS:** USIA, Fulbright Awards, 1984-85, 1992; Harvard, Pew Faculty Fellowship, 1991-92; International Studies Assoc, Karl Deutsch Award, 1988. **BUSINESS ADDRESS:** Prof, Dept of Pol Science, University of Colorado, Campus Box 333, Boulder, CO 80309, (303)492-7904.

CHAN, TAT-HUNG
Educator. Chinese American. **PERSONAL:** Born Aug 21, 1951, Hong Kong; son of Yu-Kui Chan & Wah-Yau Pong. **EDUCATION:** Dartmouth College, AB, 1974; Cornell University, MS, 1980, PhD, 1980. **CAREER:** Asiadata Ltd, Hong Kong, programmer, 1975-76; University of Minnesota, Twin Cities, assistant professor, 1980-82; University of Hong Kong, lecturer, 1985-88; SUNY, Fredonia, assistant professor, 1982-85, associate professor, 1988-. **ORGANIZATIONS:** Association for Computing Machinery, 1977-; Institute of Electrical & Electronic Engineers, affiliate member, 1982-; Society for Industrial & Applied Mathematics, 1980-. **BUSINESS ADDRESS:** Associate Professor, Dept of Math & Computer Science, SUNY at Fredonia, 224 Fenton Hall, Fredonia, NY 14063, (716)673-3193.

CHAN, TED W.
Attorney. Chinese American. **PERSONAL:** Born Nov 20, 1960, Hong Kong; son of Gock Yue Chan and Fay Lan Chan; married Greta Louise Helm, Aug 10, 1991. **EDUCATION:** University of California at Berkeley, BA, mathematics, 1983; Santa Clara University, JD, 1987. **CAREER:** Censtor Corporation, corporate counsel, 1990-. **ORGANIZATIONS:** MENSA, 1982-; Triple Nine Society, 1982-; American Bar Assn, 1987-; California Bar Assn, 1990-. **BUSINESS ADDRESS:** Corporate Counsel, Censtor Corporation, 530 Race St, San Jose, CA 95126, (408)298-8400.

CHAN, THOMAS O.
Produce company executive. Chinese American. **PERSONAL:** Born Jun 9, 1954, Sacramento, CA; married Patty Jang. **EDUCATION:** Chinese University of Hong Kong, 1975-76; University of California, Berkeley, BS, 1976; Lincoln Law School, 1982-84. **CAREER:** Kellogg Sales Co, sales, 1977-78; S E Rykoff & Co, sales, 1978-79; General Produce Co Ltd, president, 1979-. **ORGANIZATIONS:** Produce Marketing Association, food service board of directors, 1991-93, bd of directors, 1993-. **BUSINESS ADDRESS:** President, General Produce Co, Ltd, PO Box 308, Sacramento, CA 95812-0308, (916)441-6431.

CHAN, TIMOTHY T.
Real estate broker. Chinese American. **PERSONAL:** Born Aug 31, 1945, Hong Kong; son of Yadsun Cheng and Lai Ching Cheng; married Evelyn Chan, Jul 26, 1969; children: Alvina, Stephanie, Andrew. **EDUCATION:** San Francisco Conservatory of Music, BMus, 1970; San Francisco State University, MA, 1972. **CAREER:** San Francisco Conservatory of Music, violin instructor, 1969-71; San Francisco State University, asst conductor, 1971-73; San Francisco Ballet Orchestra, violinist, 1976-77; Oakland Symphony Orchestra, violinist, 1972-84; Scandia Realty Inc, realtor, associate, 1975-81; Comfort Re-

alty, broker, manager, owner, 1982-; Feher Young & Associates, vice president, 1993-. **ORGANIZATIONS:** National Assn of Realtors; California Assn of Realtors; San Francisco Assn of Realtors; North San Mateo County Assn of Realtors; National Notary Assn. **SPECIAL ACHIEVEMENTS:** National Assn of Real Estate Appraisers, Certified Real Estate Appraiser. **BUSINESS ADDRESS:** Owner, Broker, Comfort Realty, 2742 Judah St, San Francisco, CA 94122, (415)566-8556.

CHAN, TING Y.
Educational administrator (retired). Chinese American. **PERSONAL:** Born May 17, 1932, Canton, China; married Yuet Fong Chan, Aug 19, 1955 (deceased); children: Edward, Henry, Ira. **EDUCATION:** National Chung-Sing University, Taiwan, BA, 1956; San Francisco State College, MA, 1960; Columbia University, Teachers College, 1960-61; Harvard Graduate School of Education, CAS, 1968. **CAREER:** Community School Districts 1 & 2, administrator of curriculum, 1969-71; Manhattan Community College, college coordinator of remediation, 1971-72; Public Schools 42Q, 108M & 63M, assistant principal, 1972-81; Division of Special Education, NYC Board of Education, field supervisor, 1981-89. **ORGANIZATIONS:** Phi Delta Kappa, 1969-93; CSA, 1969-93; Association of Asian Culture & Education, vice president, 1987-93. **HONORS/AWARDS:** CSA, Certificate of Distinguished Service, 1990. **SPECIAL ACHIEVEMENTS:** Chinese translations of books: Teaching in a World of Change, by Robert Anderson; Comparative Education, by Robert Ulich & Edward J King; Social Psychology, by Theodore M Newcomb; Child Psychology-Children & Other People, by Robert S Stewart; A Collection of Ting Y Chan's Novels, by Rutz Press, A Collection of Ting Y Chan's Classical Poems, by Si-Teh-Ciao-Bao, Munchen, W Germany. **BIOGRAPHICAL SOURCES:** Discipline in El Bario, by Francis Clines, New York Times, March 26, 1977; Excerpted biography of Ting Y Chan, Education & Culture, by Ministry of Education, Taiwan. **HOME ADDRESS:** 55-11 97th St, Elmhurst, NY 11368, (718)699-0035.

CHAN, TSZE HAU
Researcher. Hong Kong American. **PERSONAL:** Born May 27, 1954, Hong Kong; son of Pun-Chung Chan. **EDUCATION:** University of Guelph, BA, 1976; University of Windsor, MA, 1979; University of Pittsburgh, MA, 1982, PhD, 1987. **CAREER:** University of Maryland, faculty researcher, 1986-93; National Association of Equal Opportunity, applied research specialist, 1988-93; University of Maryland, lecturer, currently, Pelavin Associates, research analyst, currently. **SPECIAL ACHIEVEMENTS:** Panelist, C-Span, 1992; panelist on LA riots & Black/Korean relations, Radio WAL, Washington DC, 1992; numerous presentations at professional meetings. **BUSINESS ADDRESS:** Research Analyst, Pelavin Associates, 2030, M Street, Suite 800, Washington, DC 20036, (202)785-3308.

CHAN, WAI-YEE
Educator. Hong Kong American/Chinese American. **PERSONAL:** son of Kui Chan and Fung Hing Wong; married May-Fong Sheung, Sep 4, 1977; children: Connie Hai-Yee, Joanne Hai-Wei, Victor Hai-Yue, Amanda Hai-Pui, Bessie Hai-Lui. **EDUCATION:** Chinese University of Hong Kong, BS (honors), 1974; University of Florida, PhD, 1977. **CAREER:** University of Oklahoma, staff research associate, 1978-79, assistant to associate professor of pediatrics, 1979-89; Oklahoma Children's Hospital, scientific director/Biochemical Genetics Lab, 1980-87; VA Medical Center, Oklahoma City, consultant, medical service, 1981-87; University of Washington, Seattle, visiting scientist of biochemistry, 1982; Oklahoma Medical Research Foundation, associate member, 1987-89; Georgetown University, professor of pediatrics, biochemistsry & anatomy, 1989-; Rockville Cantonese Chinese School, vice principal to principal, 1990-93. **ORGANIZATIONS:** American Association of Immunologists, 1990-; American Society for Biochemistry and Molecular Biology, 1982-; American Institute of Nutrition, 1980-; Society for Pediatrics Research, 1980-; American Society of Human Genetics, 1977-; American Coal Assist Ment Prog, advisory board, 1992-; Minority Student Education Advisory Committee, Montgomery County Public Schools, 1993-95; Organization of Chinese Americans, 1993; Chinese American Medical Association, honorary member, 1992. **HONORS/AWARDS:** Chinese University of Hong Kong, Scholarship for Chemistry, 1972-74; Chinese University of Hong Kong, Tak Shing Investment Co Prize for Biochemistry, 1974; Oklahoma Medical Research Foundation, Merrick Award for Outstanding Biomed Res, 1988; University of Oklahoma, Service Award, 1989. **SPECIAL ACHIEVEMENTS:** US Patent on Pregnancy Specific Proteins Applications, 1992; 3 books; 16 chapters in books; over 70 research articles in peer-reviewed journals; over 80 research abstracts. **HOME ADDRESS:** 10708 Butterfly Court, North Potomac, MD 20878,

(301)762-4962. **BUSINESS ADDRESS:** Professor, Dept of Pediatrics, Georgetown University, Children's Medical Center, 3800 Reservoir Rd, NW, 2-PHC, Washington, DC 20007, (202)687-8996.

CHAN, YEUNG YU
Engineer. Hong Kong American/Chinese American. **PERSONAL:** Born Apr 18, 1962, Hong Kong; son of Kit Sam Chan and Wai Sum Ting; married Peggy Chan, Jul 25, 1988. **EDUCATION:** Columbia University, BS, 1984; Rensselaer Polytechnic Institute, MS, 1986; City University of New York, PhD, 1990. **CAREER:** City College of New York, graduate assistant, adjunct lecturer, 1986-90; Bristol-Myers Squibb, research investigator, 1990-. **ORGANIZATIONS:** American Institute of Chemical Engineers, 1984-; American Chemical Society, 1990-. **SPECIAL ACHIEVEMENTS:** Publications include: "Heavy Metal Removal in a Rapid Infiltration Sand Column," Particulate Sci & Tech, vol 6, p 467-481, 1988, presented, 6th Intl Conference of Heavy Metals in the Environment, Sep 1987; "Mass Transfer and Reaction in Microemulsion Systems," PhD thesis, CUNY, 1990. **BUSINESS ADDRESS:** Research Investigator, Bristol-Myers Squibb, One Squibb Dr, Bldg 48, PO Box 191, New Brunswick, NJ 08903-0191, (908)519-3435.

CHAN COSTA, VIVIAN RHODA
Graphic designer, art director. Chinese American. **PERSONAL:** Born in British Columbia; daughter of Rosy Chan (deceased) and Steven Chan; divorced; children: Thoreau Moy, Ibsen Moy; married. **EDUCATION:** Fashion Institute of Technology, New York, AAS, apparel design; Parsons School of Design; School of Visual Arts, New York, BFA, advertising. **CAREER:** Mademoiselle Magazine, fashion illustrator; Dell Publishing Inc, asst art director; Estee Lauder, graphic designer; Seligman & Latz, art director; Elizabeth Arden, art director (free lance); Lord & Taylor, art director (free lance); Warren Gorham Lamont, graphic designer, 1984-93. **ORGANIZATIONS:** The One Club, 1984. **HONORS/AWARDS:** Solar Printer, Best Package Design, 1988.

CHAND, NARESH
Scientist. Indo-American. **PERSONAL:** Born May 10, 1951, Dhikana, Uttar Pradesh, India; son of Mathura Prasad; married Rekha Naresh, Jan 24, 1977; children: Himani, Pallavi, Ravi. **EDUCATION:** Birla Institute of Technology & Science, MTech, 1974; University of Sheffield, MEng, solid state electronics, 1980, PhD, electrical engineering, 1983. **CAREER:** AT&T Bell Laboratories, member of technical staff, 1985-. **ORGANIZATIONS:** IEEE, senior member, 1987-. **SPECIAL ACHIEVEMENTS:** Author of numerous publications. **HOME ADDRESS:** 461 Park Ave, Berkeley Heights, NJ 07922, (908)771-0673.

CHANDAN, RAMESH CHANDRA
Scientist. Indo-American. **PERSONAL:** Born Jul 5, 1934, Lahore, Punjab, Pakistan; son of Shiv Kumar Chandan and Padma Vasishta; married Premila Chandan, Jun 11, 1960; children: Mridula Langlie, Rohini Rowe, Anupama. **EDUCATION:** Punjab University, India, BSc, 1953, BSc (hons school), 1955, MSc (hons), 1956; University of Nebraska-Lincoln, PhD, 1963. **CAREER:** University of Nebraska, research associate, 1963-66; Unilever, Ltd, scientist, 1967-69; Dairylea Inc, R&D, manager, 1969-74; Purity Cheese Co, vice-president, 1974-76; Michigan State University, associate professor, 1976-82; Land'o Lakes, associate director, 1982-84; General Mills, Inc, principal scientist, 1984-. **ORGANIZATIONS:** Am Inst of Chemists, life fellow; Am Chemical Soc; Inst of Food Technol; Am Dairy Sci Assn. **HONORS/AWARDS:** Am Cultured Dairy Prod Inst, Nordica Intl Award, 1982: State of Minn, Governor's Award, 1989. **SPECIAL ACHIEVEMENTS:** Edited one book, five book chapters, 57 refereed research papers, 24 non-refereed articles, two patents. **HOME ADDRESS:** 3257 Rice Creek Rd, New Brighton, MN 55112, (612)631-1535. **BUSINESS PHONE:** (612)540-2864.

CHANDERSEKARAN, ACHAMMA C. (ACHAMMA CHANDER)
Government official. Indo-American. **PERSONAL:** Born in Kerala, India; daughter of Cochuvava Mapillai Coilparampil & Florentine Cochuvava Coilparampil; married C S Chandersekaran, Apr 4, 1970; children: Ashok. **EDUCATION:** Barat College, Lake Forest, Illinois, BA, 1966; University of Illinois, Urbana, MA, 1968; Drexel University, Philadelphia, MBA, 1977. **CAREER:** Burlington County Planning Board, senior planner, 1971-73; US Department of Commerce, financial analyst, 1978-90, program analyst, beginning 1990, international trade specialist, currently. **ORGANIZATIONS:** Asian American Voters Coalition, chairperson, 1992-; Indian American Forum for Political Education, national president, 1986-88; Toastmasters International, area governor, Area 36, 1983; Kerala Association of Greater Washing-

ton, secretary, 1982; University of Illinois, International Student Association, president, 1968. **HONORS/AWARDS:** IAFPE, Massachusetts chapter, Leadership Award, 1992, Distinguished Service Award, 1988; AAVC, Outstanding Contribution Award, 1991; AT&T, 4A Club, Special Recognition Award, 1988; Toastmasters Club, Area Governor Award, 1983; outstanding service awards, cash awards and certificates, 1990-91. **SPECIAL ACHIEVEMENTS:** "Where Do We Go From Here?" Darshan, pp 3-4, Dec 1987; "Asian American Heritage Month: An Opportunity to Let Others Know Who We Are," Asian American Focus, p 2, Summer 1991; "The Strength of Unity," Today's Asian American, p 10, May-June 1993. **HOME ADDRESS:** 8911 Tuckerman Lane, Potomac, MD 20854, (301)983-2587. **BUSINESS PHONE:** (202)482-1316.

CHANDRA, ABHIJIT
Educator. Indo-American. **PERSONAL:** Born Jan 4, 1957, Calcutta, W. Bengal, India; son of Ramesh Kumar and Sandhya Chandra; married Dolly Day, Jun 4, 1984; children: Koushik, Shoma. **EDUCATION:** IIT, Kharagpur, BTech (with honors), 1978; University of New Brunswick, MS, 1980; Cornell University, PhD, 1983. **CAREER:** General Motors Corporation, senior research engineer, 1983-85; University of Arizona, assistant professor, 1985-89, associate professor, 1989-. **ORGANIZATIONS:** ASME, 1980-; Sigma Xi, 1983-. **HONORS/AWARDS:** NSF, Presidential Young Investigator, 1987; Lincoln Arc Welding Foundation, Arc Welding Achievement Award, 1989; Alexander von Humboldt Foundation, Humboldt Fellowship, 1991. **SPECIAL ACHIEVEMENTS:** 50 technical publications in manufacturing; author, "Boundary Element Method in Manufacturing," Oxford Univ Press, 1994. **BUSINESS ADDRESS:** Professor, Dept of Aerospace & Mech Eng, University of Arizona, Bldg 16, Tucson, AZ 85721, (602)621-2080.

CHANDRAMOULI, S. (CHANDRA)
Business consultant. Indo-American. **EDUCATION:** Ferguson College, BSc (with honors), 1973; Indian Institute of Management, Ahmedabad, post-graduate diploma, management, 1976; University of Chicago, MBA, 1980; State of Illinois, CPA, 1983. **CAREER:** Associated Cement Companies, India, officer, 1976-77; University of Bombay, KC College of Management, visiting faculty member, 1976-77; The World Bank, consultant, researcher, 1979-80; American Management Systems Inc, vice pres, 1980-. **ORGANIZATIONS:** AICPA, 1983-; Illinois Society of CPAs, 1983-; Beta Gamma Sigma Society, University of Chicago Chapter, 1980. **HONORS/AWARDS:** Govt of India, National Merit, 1969, 1970, Open Merit Scholarship, 1973; University of Chicago, Price Waterhouse Fellowship in Accounting, 1978, Institute of Professional Accounting Fellowship, 1979, Dean's List, 1979, 1980; University of Poona, Ferguson College, RP Paranjpye Prize in Mathematics, 1972, 1973, Kher Prize in Physics/Chemistry, 1972, 1973. **SPECIAL ACHIEVEMENTS:** Business/System Consultant: Aminoil, RJ Reynolds & Co, 1980-82; State of South Dakota, 1982; State of Ohio, 1983; Santa Fe Energy Co, 1983-85; CEPE, Ecuador, 1985-86; INEMIN, Ecuador, 1986; Commonwealth of Massachusetts, 1986; Dept of Health and Welfare, Canada, 1987; State of Arizona, 1987-88; NY City Bd of Education, 1988-89; State of Colorado, 1989-; State of New Mexico, 1991-; State of Utah, 1993-; State of Minnesota, 1993. **BUSINESS ADDRESS:** Vice President, American Management Systems, Inc, 66 S Van Gordon St, Lakewood, CO 80228, (303)989-7065.

CHANDRAN, KRISHNAN BALA
Educator. Indo-American. **PERSONAL:** Born May 16, 1944, Madurai City, India; son of R Krishna Ayyar and M Krishna Ayyar; married Vanaja, Jun 22, 1972; children: Aruna, Anjana. **EDUCATION:** American College, Madras University, BS, 1963; Indian Institute of Technology, BTech, 1966; Washington University, MS, 1969, DSc, 1972. **CAREER:** Hindustan Motors Ltd, tool try-out engr, 1966-67; Washington University, research assistant, 1969-72; Tulane University, NOLA, research associate, 1972-74, assistant professor, 1974-78, associate professor, 1978; Southern University, adjunct assistant professor, 1977-; University of Iowa, associate professor, 1978-84, professor, 1984-. **ORGANIZATIONS:** American Academy of Mech; American Society of Biomech; American Heart Association; American Society of Eng Edu; American Society of Mech Eng, fellow; Biomedical Engineering Society; Cardiovascular Systems Dynamics Society; American Society of Civil Eng. **HONORS/AWARDS:** American College, Madras University, first prize in physics, 1963; Indian Institute of Tech, Merit Scholarship, 1964; NATO, Advanced Study Institute on Cardiovascular Fluid Dynamics, Fellow, 1975; University of Iowa, Old Gold Fellow, 1979. **SPECIAL ACHIEVEMENTS:** Prosthetic Heart Valves in Blood Compatible Materials and Devices: Perspectives towards the 21st Century, co-author, 1991; Cardiovascular Biomechanics,

1992; "A finite element analysis of artery-graft anastomosis," co-author, Med Biol Eng and Computing, 1992; "A Doppler guided retrograde catheterization system," co-author, Catheterization and Cardiovascular Diagnosis, 1992; "Numerical simulation of steady flow in a two-dimensional total artificial heart model," co-author, J Biomech Eng, 1992; "Flow dynamics across end-to-end vasxular bypass graft anastomoses," co-author, Annals of Biomedical Engineering, 1992; "Dynamic behavior analysis of mechanical monoleaflet heart valve prostheses in the opening phase," J Biomechanical Engineering, 1992. **BUSINESS ADDRESS:** Professor, Dept of Biomedical Engineering, University of Iowa, 1202 EB, Iowa City, IA 52242, (319)335-5640.

CHANDRAN, RAVI
Certified public accountant. Indo-American. **PERSONAL:** Born Aug 28, 1954, Tanjore, Tamil Nadu, India; son of Srinivasan Krishnaswamy and Rajalaxmi Krishnaswamy; married Usha Chandran, Jul 13, 1981; children: Raghu Ram, Maya Laxmi. **EDUCATION:** University of Madras, BS, 1974; Butler University, MBA, 1976. **CAREER:** Goodwill Industries, internal auditor, 1976-78; LANP Water Conditioning, controller, 1978-80; Montgomery Ward, accounting manager, 1980-. **ORGANIZATIONS:** Illinois CPA Society, 1992-; Indiana CPA Society, 1978-91; American Institute of CPAs, 1978-. **SPECIAL ACHIEVEMENTS:** Bilingual: Tamil and English; amateur painter. **HOME ADDRESS:** 595 Cleaveland, Bolingbrook, IL 60440. **BUSINESS PHONE:** (312)467-4999.

CHANDRAN, SATISH RAMAN
Educator. Indo-American. **PERSONAL:** Born Oct 6, 1938, Quilon, Kerala, India; son of Raman Pillai & Ponnamma; married Judith, Oct 1, 1966; children: Pamela, Anjali. **EDUCATION:** University of Kerala, India, BS, 1955, MS, 1958; University of Illinois, PhD, 1965. **CAREER:** University of Illinois, Chicago, professor of biology, 1966-72; Kennedy King College, professor of biology, 1972-. **ORGANIZATIONS:** Human Anatomy & Physiology Society, 1988-; American Association for the Advancement of Science, 1982-88; National Association of Biology Teachers, 1972-80. **SPECIAL ACHIEVEMENTS:** Published more than 20 articles on insectan musculature, microsomal oxidases and mammalian cell culture. **HOME ADDRESS:** 1648 Western Ave, Flossmoor, IL 60422-1837, (708)957-9780. **BUSINESS ADDRESS:** Professor of Biology, Kennedy-King College, 6800 S Wentworth Ave, 3E33, Chicago, IL 60621, (312)602-5211.

CHANDRASEKARAN, BALAKRISHNAN
Educator. Indo-American. **PERSONAL:** Born Jun 20, 1942, Lalgudi, Tamil Nadu, India; son of Srinivasan and Nagamani Balakrishnan; married Sandra Mamrak, Oct 21, 1978; children: Mallika. **EDUCATION:** Madras University, BEng (honors), 1963; University of Pennsylvania, PhD, electrical engineering, 1967. **CAREER:** Smith Kline Instruments, developmental engineer, 1964-65; Philco-Ford Corp, research specialist, 1967-69; Ohio State University, Dept of Computer and Info Science, asst professor, 1969-71, associate professor, 1971-77, professor, 1977-. **ORGANIZATIONS:** Lawrence Livermore Natl Lab, visiting scientist, consultant, 1981; MIT Computer Science Lab, visiting scientist, 1983; NIH Artificial Intelligence in Medicine Workshop, director, 1984; ASME, Artificial Intelligence and Engineering, panel discussion organizer, 1985; Artificial Intelligence in Engineering, associate editor, 1986-; Stanford University, Knowledge System Lab, visiting scholar, 1990-91. **HONORS/AWARDS:** Pattern Recognition Society, Outstanding Paper Award, 1976; University of Pennsylvania, Moore Fellow, 1964-67; IEEE, fellow, Expert Journal, editor-in-chief, 1990-; Ohio University, Morton Distinguished Scholar, 1982; Ohio State University, Senior Research Award, 1983, Distinguished Scholar Award, 1988; American Association for Artificial Intelligence, fellow, 1991-. **SPECIAL ACHIEVEMENTS:** Author of numerous articles in professional journals and texts, including: "Models Versus Rules, Deep Versus Compiled, Content Versus Form," IEEE Expert, p 75-79, April 1991; "Design Problem Solving: A Task Analysis," in Japanese, Nikkei Artificial Intelligence Quarterly, p 142-154, Summer 1991; co-author, "Task Structure Analysis for Knowledge Modeling," Communications of the ACM, p 124-136, Sept 1992; co-editor, Computer Program Testing, Morth Holland, 1981. **BUSINESS ADDRESS:** Professor, Dept of Computer & Info Science, Ohio State University, 2036 Neil Ave Mall, Columbus, OH 43210.

CHANDRA SEKHAR, HOSAKERE K.
Physician, educator. Indo-American. **PERSONAL:** Born Mar 28, 1932, Narasimharajapura, Karnataka, India; son of Hosakere Kapinipathi & Geethamma Bhatta; married Sree Devi, Feb 5, 1961; children: Sunjana Chandra Sekhar Ramanthan, Sumana Chandra Sekhar Rangachar, Sucharita. **EDUCA-**

TION: Mysore University, India, BSc, 1951, MB, BS, 1957; London University, UK, DLO, 1963; Edinburgh University, UK, FRCS, 1965; New York University, DABO, 1973. **CAREER:** British Hospitals, house officer, 1962-65; Government of Karnataka, assistant professor, 1965-68; Suburban Hospital, Bethesda, MD, intern, 1969-70; New York University Medical Center, residency, 1970-73; New York University, Otolaryngology, assistant professor, 1973-77, associate professor, 1977-; Cabrini Medical Center, NY, director otolaryn, 1978-. **ORGANIZATIONS:** American Academy of Otolaryngology, fellow, 1974-; American College of Surgeons, fellow, 1977-; New York Academy of Medicine, fellow, 1980-; New York County Medical Society, 1973-; New York University, Pharmacy & Therapeutics Committee, 1980-; Cabrini Medical Center, cancer committee, 1982-; New York City Mayor's Ethnic Advisory Council, 1982-89; responsible for installation of Gandhi Statue in New York City; Hindu Temple Society, trustee, vice president, NA, 1991; Indian-American Federation of Political Education, vice chair, 1984-88; Governor Cuomo's Asian American Council, New York State, 1989-. **HONORS/ AWARDS:** Federation of Indian Associations, Outstanding Service, 1986. **BIOGRAPHICAL SOURCES:** Amerikannada Literary Magazine, Aug 1988. **HOME ADDRESS:** 630 First Ave, Apt 6B, New York, NY 10016. **BUSINESS ADDRESS:** Associate Professor, Otolaryngology, New York University Medical Center, 530 First Ave, Ste 3C, Faculty Practice Offices, New York, NY 10016, (212)263-7345.

CHANDRASEKHAR, SUBRAHMANYAN

Educator, scientist. Indo-American. **PERSONAL:** Born Oct 19, 1910, Lahore, India; married Lalitha Doraiswamy, Sep 1936. **EDUCATION:** Presidency College, Madras, MA, 1930; Trinity College, Cambridge, PhD, 1933, ScD, 1942; University of Mysore, India, ScD, 1961; Northwestern University, 1962; University of Newcastle Upon Tyne, England, 1965; Ind Inst Tech, 1966; University of Michigan, 1967; University of Liege, Belgium, 2967; Oxford University, 1972; University of Delhi, 1973; Carleton University, Canada, 1978; Harvard University, 1979. **CAREER:** Government of India, Cambridge, scholar in theoretical physics, 1930-34; Trinity College, Cambridge, 1933-47; Yerkes Obs, Williams Bay & University of Chicago, research assoc, 1937, asst prof, 1938-41, assoc prof, 1942-43, prof, 1944-47, Distinguished Service prof, 1947-52, Morton D Hull Distinguished Service prof, 1952-86, prof emeritus, 1986-. **ORGANIZATIONS:** Royal Soc, London, fellow,; Natl Acad Scis; American Phys Soc; American Philos Soc; Cambridge Philos Soc; American Astron Soc; Royal Astron Soc. **HONORS/AWARDS:** Astron Soc Pacific, Bruce Medal, 1952; Royal Astron Soc, Gold Medal, 1953; American Acad Arts & Scis, Rumford Medal, 1957; Royal Soc, Royal Medal, 1962, Copley Medal, 1984; Natl Medal of Sci, 1966; Natl Acad Scis, Henry Draper Medal, 1971; American Phys Soc, Dannie Heineman Prize, 1974; Nobel Prize in physics, 1983; Dr Tomalla Prize Eidgenossiches Technische Hochschule, Zurich, 1984. **SPECIAL ACHIEVEMENTS:** Author: An Introduction to the Study of Stellar Structure, 1939; Principles of Stellar Dynamics, 1942; Radiative Transfer, 1950; Hydrodynamic and Hydromagnetic Stability, 1961; Ellipsoidal Figures of Equilibrium, 1969; Mathematical Theory of Black Holes, 1983; Eddington: The Most Distinguished Astrophysicist of His Time, 1983; Truth and Beauty: Aesthetics and Motivations in Science, 1987; Selected Papers, 6 vols, 1989-90. **BUSINESS ADDRESS:** Professor Emeritus, Laboratory for Astrophysics and Space Research, University of Chicago, 933 E 56th St, Chicago, IL 60637.

CHANDY, VARUGHESE KUZHIYATH

Company executive. Indo-American. **PERSONAL:** Born Jan 16, 1946, Kottayam, Kerala, India; son of Chandy and Mariamma; married Annamma, Jan 17, 1974; children: Marie, Jerry (deceased). **EDUCATION:** BCom; MCom; completed course for Chartered Accountants of India. **CAREER:** Zachariah & Zachariah, CPA, auditor, 1967-73; Manorajya Chain of Publications, general manager, 1973-74; Transway International, internal auditor, 1974-75; New York State Attorney General, senior criminal investigative auditor, 1975-77; New York City Health and Hospitals Corp, deputy comptroller, 1977-86; Interfaith Hospital Center, asst vp, finance, 1986; Master Group of Companies, vp, 1986-90; Empire Blue Cross Blue Shield, senior appeal specialist, 1990-. **ORGANIZATIONS:** Kerala Samajam of Greater New York, treasurer, 1974-75; St. Thomas Mar Thoma Church, NY, auditor, 1977-78; Federation of Kerala Association in NA, natl vp, 1990-; Federation of Indian American Associations (national), board member, 1990-; Federation of Indian Association (local), board member, 1989-, treasurer, 1978-81; Heart and Hand for Handicapped, treasurer, 1979-80; Kerala Cultural Forum (local), president, 1989-; Bergen Co Malayalee Christian, board member, 1989-; Westchester Malayalee Association, vp, 1978-79; St. Peter's Mar Thoma Church, vp, 1990-;

Kerala Center, board of advisory, 1990-; Rajiv Gandhi Mem, board member, 1990-; Indian American Nurses Association, natl, chmn, adv bd, 1992-; Karuna Charities Inc, adv bd member, 1993-; Kerala Center of NJ, founding member, 1993-. **HOME ADDRESS:** 56 West Lawn Dr, Teaneck, NJ 07666, (201)833-4089.

CHANG, ALBERT

Educator. Chinese American. **PERSONAL:** Born Jun 7, 1941, Ling-ling, Hunan, China; son of Simon K H & Mei Chang; married Yvonne Huang Chang, Oct 17, 1970; children: Jeffrey Chimin, Nicholas Yunmin. **EDUCATION:** Harvard College, BA (cum laude), 1963; University of Rochester, School of Medicine, MD, 1968; University of California, Berkeley, School of Public Health, MPH, 1972. **CAREER:** Baltimore City Health Department, director of preschool health services, 1972-74; University of California, Berkeley, assistant professor, 1974-80; UCLA, associate professor, 1980-91; San Diego State University, professor of public health, 1991-, Div of Maternal and Child Care, head, currently. **ORGANIZATIONS:** American Public Health Association, Child Care Standards Project, Central Steering Committee, co-chair, 1988-92; American Public Health Association, MCH Section, chair, 1992-; American Academy of Pediatrics, Committee on Early Childhood, Adoptions & Dependent Care, 1988-93; Association of Teachers of Maternal and Child Health, president, 1991-93. **HONORS/AWARDS:** American Public Health Association, Young Professional Award, 1981. **SPECIAL ACHIEVE-MENTS:** Publication: Caring for Our Children: Health and Safety Guidelines for Out of Home Child Care Programs. **BUSINESS ADDRESS:** Professor and Head, Division of Maternal and Child Health, San Diego State University, Graduate School of Public Health, 6505 Alvarado Rd, Ste 205, San Diego, CA 92120, (619)594-4493.

CHANG, ALICE CHING

Administrator, state official. Chinese American. **PERSONAL:** Born Dec 3, 1914, Peking, Hopei, China; daughter of Shu Sen Chang and Tsai Ching Chao Chang; married Peter Chi-Pan Tsou Sr, Dec 25, 1938 (deceased); children: Peter Tsou Jr, George Tsou, Paul Tsou. **EDUCATION:** National Cheng-Chi University, China, BA, 1938; Worden School of Social Service, MSW, 1964. **CAREER:** Taipei 2nd Girls High, Taiwan, vice principal, 1950-52; Catholic Welfare Bureau, Los Angeles District, case worker, 1954-63; LA County, Dept of Adoption, adoption worker, 1964-70, Dept of Health Services, Social Worker Unit, service supervisor, 1970-80; Chinese Community Service Center Inc, volunteer executive director, 1970-90; California Senior Legislative, elected sr assembly woman, 1980-; Central Adult Day Health Care Center, administrator, 1986-. **ORGANIZATIONS:** Chinese Committee on Aging, Health Committee, chair, 1976-91; National Association of Social Workers, 1964-80; Congress of California Seniors, board of directors, 1986-88; Yi-Chung Association of Senior Citizens, 1980-; Chinese Community Service Center Inc, executive diretor, 1970-90; City Dept of Aging, Council on Aging, mayor-appointed member, 1983-; California Senior Legislature, assembly woman, 1980-93, senior senator, 1993-. **HONORS/AWARDS:** California Senior Legislature, 10 Year Award, 1993, Legislative Award, 1990; California Senior Legislature, Recognition of Membership, 1990; Governor of the State of California, Outstanding Senior Volunteer, 1989; Presidential Roundtable Senatorial Commission, Full & Honorable Senatorial Commission; Republican Party, Republican Presidential Advisory Commission, Award for Outstanding Dedication. **SPECIAL ACHIEVEMENTS:** Author: Transplanted Plum Flower, in Chinese, 1992; "National Health Care Plan," which became CA Law, 1990; "Elder Abuse Law," 1984; started Elder Abuse Hot-Line of Los Angeles County, 1-800-992-1660, 1986; founded, Central Adult Day Health Care Center, 1987. **BIOGRAPHICAL SOURCES:** "A Fighter for Senior Rights," Los Angeles Times, Page J5, Jan 7, 1993; "Crusade for Seniors Home Typifies A Career," Los Angeles Times, Jan 7, 1993; "Debate Continues over Senior Housing Project," Los Angeles Independent, Dec 9, 1992; "Senior Housing Vote Delayed," Los Angeles Times, page J2, Aug 27, 1992. **BUSINESS ADDRESS:** Administrator, Central Community Service Inc, 1348 Kellam Ave, Los Angeles, CA 90026, (213)250-7778.

CHANG, AMY LEE

Association executive. Chinese American. **PERSONAL:** Born Jul 24, 1952, Vincennes, IN; daughter of Pei Wen Chang & Pei Feng Fu; married Robert Young, May 24, 1980; children: William Young, Andrew Young. **EDUCATION:** University of Rhode Island, BS, 1974; University of Vermont, MS, 1978. **CAREER:** University of Vermont, assistant, 1976-78; Montgomery College, instructor, 1978-90; American Society for Microbiology, manager, 1990-, education director, currently. **ORGANIZATIONS:** American Society of Association Executives, currently; Council of Engineering and Scientific Society Executives, currently. **BUSINESS ADDRESS:** Education Director, American Society for Microbiology, 1325 Massachusetts Ave NW, Washington, DC 20005.

CHANG, ANDREW C.
Educator. Chinese American. **PERSONAL:** Born Jan 28, 1940, China; son of C Y Chang and Josephine Chang; married Linda Lin, Sep 21, 1967; children: Edith, Joseph. **EDUCATION:** National Taiwan University, BS, 1962; Virginia Polytechnic Institute, MS, 1966; Purdue University, PhD, 1971. **CAREER:** University of California, assistant professor, 1971-77, associate professor, 1977-82, professor, 1982-, Kearney Foundation of Soil Science, director, 1991-. **ORGANIZATIONS:** International Water Pollution Control Association; California Water Pollution Control Association; American Society of Agronomy; Soil Science Society of America. **HONORS/AWARDS:** US Department of Agriculture, Distinguished Service, 1991; US Environmental Protection Agency, National First Place Award, Outstanding Research Contribution to Enhance Beneficial Use of Municipal Waste Water Sludge, 1991. **SPECIAL ACHIEVEMENTS:** Published over 100 technical articles in professional journals and monographs, 1971-. **BUSINESS ADDRESS:** Professor and Director, Kearney Foundation of Soil Science, University of California Riverside, 900 University Avenue, Riverside, CA 92521-0001, (909)787-5325.

CHANG, ANN HAN-CHIH
Librarian. Taiwanese American. **PERSONAL:** Born Aug 4, 1963, Taipei, Taiwan; married Joyn Yi-Chang Lin, Jul 22, 1987; children: Connie Grace Lin. **EDUCATION:** National Taiwan University, BA, 1985; State University of New York at Buffalo, MLS, 1989. **CAREER:** Taiwan Provincial Handicraft Research Institute, cataloging librarian, 1985-87; Prairie View A&M University, Bibliographic Access, head, 1989-. **ORGANIZATIONS:** American Library Association; Association of College and Research Libraries. **BUSINESS ADDRESS:** Head, Bibliographic Access, John B. Coleman Library, Prairie View A&M University, 3rd St, Prairie View, TX 77446, (409)857-4886.

CHANG, ANTHONY K. U.
State senator. Chinese American. **PERSONAL:** Born Sep 5, 1944, Honolulu, HI; son of Hoo Kin Chang and Ethel Chew Chang; married Lisa Madelon Konove, 1979; children: Ahnya Heaoonohilani, Cymri Teuila. **EDUCATION:** University of Hawaii, BBA, 1969; Richardson School of Law, JD, 1976. **CAREER:** Honolulu, attorney, 1976-; Governor's Office, Hawaii, prog planner, 1977-78; Hawaii State Const Conv, delegate, 1978; Hawaii State Senate, district 17, 1982-, committees include: Ecology, Environ & Recreation, chairman, 1982-84, senate Judiciary, 1983-86, Business Develop and Pac Relations, 1986-88. **ORGANIZATIONS:** Hawaii State Bar Assn; Chinese Chamber of Commerce; Gook Doo Sam Heong Soc; Natl Conf State Legis, Intl Trade Task Force Subcommittee; Port Authority, gen dir. **BUSINESS ADDRESS:** State Senator, Hawaii Legislature, State Capitol, Honolulu, HI 96813, (808)586-6930.*

CHANG, BEN
Business executive. Taiwanese American. **PERSONAL:** Born Jan 1, 1950, Taichung, Taiwan; son of Pu-Chi Chang and Jean Chang; married Kei; children: Ray, Elaine. **EDUCATION:** University of Houston, MBA. **CAREER:** Lanex Corporation, vice president, currently. **BUSINESS ADDRESS:** Vice President, Lanex Corporation, 2460 Mariondale, Los Angeles, CA 90032, (213)227-9779.

CHANG, BENJAMIN TAI-AN
Engineer. Chinese American. **PERSONAL:** Born Feb 28, 1949, Chia-Yi, Taiwan; son of Lin-Shaw Chang and Shwu-Wen Chang; married Anne S K Chang, Jun 5, 1976; children: Evelyn T, Christopher R. **EDUCATION:** National Taiwan University, BS, 1971; University of Rochester, MS, 1975, PhD, 1980. **CAREER:** Shell Development, sr research engr, 1980-93. **ORGANIZATIONS:** Association of American-Chinese Professionals Foundation, president, 1991-92, 1993, vice president, 1989-91, board director, 1987-89. **HONORS/AWARDS:** National Taiwan University, Top Student Awards, 1968-70; Nan-Hai Textile Co, Best Student Awards, 1967-71; Rep of China, Excellent Community Leader Award, 1993. **SPECIAL ACHIEVEMENTS:** Editor, Proceedings of Science, Eng and Technology Conf, 1986-87; 20 technical papers in the areas of materials science. **MILITARY SERVICE:** Ordance Army, 2nd lt, 1971-73. **HOME PHONE:** (713)493-3243. **BUSINESS ADDRESS:** Sr Research Engineer, Shell Development Co, PO Box 1380, Houston, TX 77251-1380, (713)544-7332.

CHANG, BRIANKLE G.
Educator. Chinese American. **PERSONAL:** Born Apr 9, 1954, Taipei, Taiwan; son of Jing-Gao Chang and I-Ming Chang; married Mary Ann Murphy, Apr 1989. **EDUCATION:** Fu Jen Catholic University, Taipei, Taiwan, BA, 1976; University of Illinois, AM, 1981, PhD, 1991. **CAREER:** Rutgers University, lecturer, 1986-88; University of Alabama, assistant professor, 1988-93; University of Massachusetts, assistant professor, 1993-. **ORGANIZATIONS:** International Communication Assn; Speech Communication Assn. **HONORS/AWARDS:** Rotary Intl, Rotary Fellow, 1976; Lilly Endowment Inc, Lilly Teaching Fellow, 1991-92. **BUSINESS ADDRESS:** Professor, Dept of Communications, University of Massachusetts, 407 Machiner Hall, Amherst, MA 01003.

CHANG, BYUNG JIN
Optical company executive. Korean American. **PERSONAL:** Born Sep 26, 1941, Danyang, Chungbook, Republic of Korea; son of Young S and Azie Chang; married Sharon O Chang, Dec 27, 1969; children: Jane, Michael. **EDUCATION:** Seoul National University, BSEE, 1967; Wayne State University, MSEE, 1970; University of Michigan, PhD, electrical engineering, 1974. **CAREER:** Environmental Research Institute of Michigan, research engr, 1971-79; Kaiser Optical Systems, chief scientist, vice pres, 1979-91; General Scientific Corp, chmn, chief executive officer, 1992-. **ORGANIZATIONS:** Optical Society of America, 1973-; SPIE, 1974-; IEEE, 1974-. **SPECIAL ACHIEVEMENTS:** Published over 30 technical papers in professional journals; organized technical conference sessions; taught several tutorial courses at technical conferences. **HOME ADDRESS:** 5521 Overbrook Dr, Ann Arbor, MI 48105. **BUSINESS ADDRESS:** Chairman & CEO, General Scientific Corporation, 77 Enterprise Dr, Ann Arbor, MI 48103, (313)996-9200.

CHANG, CARL KOCHAO
Educator. Chinese American. **PERSONAL:** Born Mar 5, 1952, Taichung, Taiwan; son of Yeh-Hsiu Chang and Lin-Whe Lee; married Jean Chang, Nov 12, 1978; children: Kathy, Wilson. **EDUCATION:** National Central University, BS, 1974; Northern Illinois University, MS, 1978; Northwestern University, PhD, 1982. **CAREER:** Northern Illinois University, teaching assistant, 1977-78; GTE Automatic Electric, systems analyst, 1978-79; Northwestern University, research assistant, 1979-82; AT&T Bell Laboratories, member of technical staff, 1982-84; University of Illinois, associate professor, director, 1984-. **ORGANIZATIONS:** IEEE Computer Society, publications board member, 1991-94; IEEE Software, editor-in-chief, 1991-94; Chinese Academic & Professional Association in Mid-America, president, 1993-94. **HONORS/AWARDS:** CAPAMA, Distinguished Accomplishment Award, 1985, Outstanding Service Award, 1988. **SPECIAL ACHIEVEMENTS:** Established the Industry Advisory Board for IEEE Computer Society/Software; co-founder, IEEE International Conference on Computer Languages & International Conference on Requirements Engineering; co-author: "INTEGRAL-A Petri Net Approach to Distributed Software Development," Information & Software Technology, pp 535-545, December 1989; "Joint Software Research between Industry and Academia," IEEE Software, pp 71-77, Nov 1990; "A Petri Net Based Platform for Developing Communications Software Systems," IEICE, Trans on Fundamentals, Vol E75-A, No 10, Oct 1992. **BUSINESS ADDRESS:** Professor & Director, International Center for Software Engineering, University of Illinois, 851 South Morgan, 1120 SEO, M/C 154, Chicago, IL 60607, (312)996-4860.

CHANG, CAROLINE J.
Government official. Chinese American. **PERSONAL:** Born Dec 13, 1940, Boston, MA; daughter of Reginald Wong and Mahr Jane Wong; married Gene Chang, Nov 11, 1967. **EDUCATION:** Boston University, BA, 1962; Suffolk University Law School, JD, 1977. **CAREER:** AVCO Corp, associate scientist, 1962-70; City of Boston, Chinatown Little City Hall, manager, 1970-74; US Dept of HHS, equal opportunity spec, supv equal opportunity spec, 1974-79, Program Rev & Mgmt Supp Div, director, 1979-82, office for Civil Rights, regional manager, 1982-. **ORGANIZATIONS:** Am Soc Pub Admin, MA Chapter, council member, 1991-; United Way of Mass Bay, board member, 1990-; Asian Comm Dev Corp, board member, 1987-; Asian American Lawyers Association, 1985. **HONORS/AWARDS:** Am Soc Pub Admin, Outstanding Public Administrator, 1993; Massachusetts Women's Political Caucus, Abigail Adams Award, 1993; Women's Educ & Ind Union, Amelia Earhart Award, 1989; Center for Women Pol Stud, Wise Women Award, 1989; Asian American Lawyers Association of Massachusetts, Community Service Award, 1990. **SPECIAL ACHIEVEMENTS:** South Cove Community Health Center, founder, 1972; Chinese Golden Age Center, founder, 1971. **BIOGRAPHI-**

CAL SOURCES: Newsweek Magazine, "Unsung Hero," July 4, 1987. HOME ADDRESS: 133 Gallivan Blvd, Dorchester, MA 02124, (617)298-0811. BUSINESS ADDRESS: Regional Manager, Office for Civil Rights, US Dept of Health & Human Services, Region I, J F Kennedy Bldg, Rm 1875, Boston, MA 02203, (617)565-1340.

CHANG, CHARLES HUNG
Research chemist (retired). Chinese American. PERSONAL: Born Apr 1, 1922, Nanchung, Sichuan, China; married Hsin-Lan W Chang, Sep 11, 1956; children: John Julius, Joyce. EDUCATION: National Central Polytechnic College, China, diploma, 1945; University of Montana, MA, 1955; Wayne State University, PhD, 1959. CAREER: Taiwan Fertilizer Co, assistant chemical engineer, 1947-54; Wayne State University, research associate, 1959-61; GAF Corp, research chemist, 1961-65, research specialist, 1965-73; Crompton & Knowles Corp, research associate, 1973-80, senior research associate, 1980-91, senior scientist, 1991-93. ORGANIZATIONS: American Chemical Society, 1961-; Chinese American Chemical Society, 1980-; American Association of Textile Chemist and Colorist, 1982-. SPECIAL ACHIEVEMENTS: Three technical papers in Journal of Organic Chemistry; twelve US patents; one British patent; one German patent. HOME ADDRESS: 521 Elizabeth Dr, Norristown, PA 19403.

CHANG, CHAWNSHANG
Educator. Taiwanese American. PERSONAL: Born Nov 26, 1955, Taichung, Taiwan; son of Su-in Chang and Tsuhon Chang-Ko; married Amly Chang, Jun 10, 1980; children: Eugene, Philip. EDUCATION: University of Chicago, PhD, 1985. CAREER: University of Wisconsin-Madison, associate professor, 1988-. ORGANIZATIONS: The Endocrine Society; American Society for Biochemistry & Molecular Biology; American Association for Cancer Research. HONORS/AWARDS: Andrew Mellon Outstanding Young Faculty Member, 1989; Cancer Research Foundation, Young Investigator Award, 1989; Milheim Foundation, Young Investigator Award, 1989; American Cancer Society, Junior Faculty Award, 1990-93. SPECIAL ACHIEVEMENTS: Isolation of androgen receptor gene, 1988; total of 62 papers published in journals. HOME ADDRESS: 209 Acadia Drive, Madison, WI 53717, (608)833-6634. BUSINESS ADDRESS: Associate Professor, Dept of Human Oncology, University of Wisconsin-Madison, 600 Highland Ave, K4-632, Madison, WI 53792, (608)263-0899.

CHANG, CHE-GIL
Librarian. Korean American. PERSONAL: Born Sep 20, 1932, Kwangju, Republic of Korea; married Jungsook Choi, Jan 9, 1964; children: Charles, Robert. EDUCATION: Seoul National University, BA, 1955, MA, 1959; George Peabody College, Vanderbilt University, MLA, 1971. CAREER: Chim-myung Girls High School, instructor, 1955-64; Choong-ang University, lecturer, 1964-67; Han-yang University, instructor, 1967-70; Denison University, catalog librarian, 1971-89, adjunct instructor of Japanese, 1983-88, deputy director, 1989-. ORGANIZATIONS: Academic Library Association of Ohio. HONORS/AWARDS: Fulbright Scholarship, Seoul National University, Korea, 1979. SPECIAL ACHIEVEMENTS: Fluent in Japanese & Korean; community service, teaching Tai Chi, 1979-; planning & implementation of Innovative Interfaces Library automation system, 1991-93. MILITARY SERVICE: Korean Military Army, pfc, 1959. HOME ADDRESS: 1049 Burg St, Granville, OH 43023. BUSINESS PHONE: (614)587-6620.

CHANG, CHEIN-I
Educator. Taiwanese American. PERSONAL: Born May 20, 1950, Taipei, Taiwan; son of Hsun Chang (deceased) and Kuei-Lan Kuo Chang. EDUCATION: Soochow University, BS, 1973; National Tsing Hua University, MS, 1975; State University of New York at Stony Brook, MA, 1977; University of Illinois at Urbana-Champaign, MS, 1980, MSEE, 1982; University of Maryland, College Park, PhD, 1987. CAREER: Soochow University, teaching assistant, 1973-75; National Tsing Hua University, teaching assistant, 1973-75; State University of New York at Stony Brook, teaching assistant, 1975-77; University of Illinois at Urbana-Champaign, teaching assistant, 1977-80, research assistant, 1980-82; University of Maryland at College Park, research assistant, 1982-86; University of Maryland Baltimore County, visiting assistant professor, 1987, assistant professor, 1987-93, associate professor, 1993-. ORGANIZATIONS: Institute of Electrical and Electronics Engineers, 1980-; Society of Photo-Optical Instrumentation Engineers, 1991-; International Neural Network Society, 1990-; New York Academy of Science, 1988-. HONORS/AWARDS: IEEE, senior member, 1992; Eta Kappa Nu, 1982; Phi Kappa Phi, 1986; National Collegiate Inventors Program Competition, Finalist,

Honorable Mention, Faculty Advisor, 1993. SPECIAL ACHIEVEMENTS: Set up a remote sensing signal and image processing within UMBC, 1992; disclosure of invention on "Tricognitron": handwritten character recognition, 1992; disclosure of invention on "Multistage Predictive Coding Systems," 1993; disclosure of invention on "A Technique for Arbitrary Signature Detection and Discrimination," 1993. BUSINESS ADDRESS: Associate Professor, Dept of Electrical Engineering, University of Maryland, Baltimore County, 201B Engineering/Computer Science Building, 5401 Wilkins Avenue, Baltimore, MD 21228-5398, (410)455-3502.

CHANG, CHENG-HUI (KAREN)
Educator, physicist. Chinese American. PERSONAL: Born Nov 18, 1948, Tainan, Taiwan; daughter of Wei-C Chang and H C Yeh. EDUCATION: Chung Yuan University, BS, 1971; University of Arkansas, MS, 1975, PhD, 1978. CAREER: Northeastern Oklahoma State University, asst professor, physics, 1981-83; University of Texas Health Sciences Center at Dallas, med phys research fellow, med physicist, 1983-86; West Virginia University, asst professor, 1986-87; North Shore University Hospital, medical physicist, 1988-89; Baylor College of Medicine, asst professor, 1989-90; Moncrief Radiation Center, medical physicist, 1990-92; University of Texas Southwestern Medical School, asst professor, radiation oncology, 1992-. ORGANIZATIONS: American Assn of Physicists in Medicine, 1984-; American Board of Radiology, diplomate; American Society for Therapeutic Radiology and Oncology, 1993-. HONORS/AWARDS: Physics Honor Society, 1976; University of Arkansas, Aubrey E Harvey Graduate Research Award, 1978; Sigma Xi, 1978. SPECIAL ACHIEVEMENTS: Author: "Characteristics of the 18MV Photon Beam Produced by a Dual Energy Linear Accelerator," Med Phy, 1987; "Digital Tomosynthesis: Technique Modifications and Clinical Applications for Neurovascular Anatomy," Radiology, 1984; "Na + Xe Collisions in the Presence of Two Non-resonant Lasers," Chem Phys Lett, 1980; "Comparison of the Born and Glauber Generalized Oscillator: Strengths for the 2s - 3p Transition of Atomic Hydrogen," Phys Rev A, 1978; "Glauber e-Li Elastic Scattering Amplitude," Phys Rev A, 1976. BUSINESS ADDRESS: Assistant Professor, Dept of Radiation Oncology, University of Texas-Southwestern Medical Center, 5323 Harry Hines Blvd, Dallas, TX 75235-9122, (214)648-2296.

CHANG, CHIA-CHEH
Educator. Taiwanese American. PERSONAL: Born Sep 10, 1938, Taiwan; married Patricia Y Chang, Jun 8, 1968; children: Eric W, Hubert W. EDUCATION: Tunghai University, BS (highest honor), 1961; University of Southern California, MA, 1966, PhD, 1968. CAREER: Stanford University, research associate, 1969-72; University of Maryland, senior research associate, 1972-74, assistant professor, 1974-80, associate professor, 1980-86, professor, 1986-. ORGANIZATIONS: American Physical Society, 1972-; MIT, Users Group, board of directors, 1986-87; CEBAF, Hall A, co-manager, 1989, steering committee member, 1989-, coordinator committee member, 1991-93, Users Group, board of directors, 1992-. SPECIAL ACHIEVEMENTS: Over 60 publications in refereed journals. BUSINESS ADDRESS: Professor, Dept of Physics, University of Maryland, Rm 2214, College Park, MD 20742, (301)405-6107.

CHANG, CHIA-NING
Educator. Chinese American. PERSONAL: Born Dec 24, 1950, Shanghai, People's Republic of China; married. EDUCATION: University of Hong Kong, BA, 1972, MPhil, 1978; Hokkaido University, Shushi, 1978; Stanford University, PhD, 1985. CAREER: University of California, Davis, Department of Chinese and Japanese, assistant professor, 1987-. ORGANIZATIONS: Association of Asian Studies, 1984-; Association of Teachers of Japanese, 1984-. HONORS/AWARDS: University of California, Humanities Institute, fellow, 1989-90; Stanford University, Japan Fund recipient, 1983-84; Japan Foundation, dissertation fellow, 1981-82; Japanese Government, Mombusho Scholar, 1974-78; University of Hong Kong, Sir Robert Black College Scholar, 1972-74. SPECIAL ACHIEVEMENTS: Articles in English and Japanese on Japanese literature and cultural history; fluency in Chinese and Japanese; translator of Japanese literature including A Sheep's Song, the autobiography of prominent literary and cultural critic Shuichi Kato. BUSINESS ADDRESS: Professor, Dept of Chinese & Japanese, University of California, Davis, Davis, CA 95616, (916)752-4995.

CHANG, CHIN HAO
Educator. Chinese American. PERSONAL: Born 1926, Haining, Chikiang Province, China; son of Foukaung Chang and Quapao Tang; married Kathy

Chun-Er Chang, 1962; children: Yu-Yang. **EDUCATION:** National Taiwan University, BS, civil engineering; Virginia Polytechnic Institute, MS, engineering mechanics; University of Michigan, PhD, engineering mechanics. **CAREER:** National Taiwan University, Civil Engineering, visiting professor, 1965-66; University of Alabama, Eng Mechanics, assistant professor, 1960-64, associate professor, 1964-76, professor, 1976-88, professor emeritus, 1988-. **ORGANIZATIONS:** American Society of Mechanical Engineering, 1965-88; Academic Society of Mechanics, 1967-88; Research Society of Sigma Si, 1955-82; American Society of Engineering Education, 1964-88. **HONORS/AWARDS:** College of Engineering, Best Research Award, 1978. **SPECIAL ACHIEVEMENTS:** Twenty technical papers were published in American and English technical journals; four papers were presented at national technical conferences. **MILITARY SERVICE:** Engineering Corps of Army of ROTC in Taiwan, second lieutenant, 1952-53. **HOME ADDRESS:** 5180 Courton Street, Alpharetta, GA 30202, (404)751-7426.

CHANG, CHING-JER
Educator. Taiwanese American. **PERSONAL:** Born Oct 17, 1942, Hsinchu, Taiwan; son of Ting-liang & Awei Chang; married Shu-fang Kuo, Dec 25, 1978; children: Philip, Sylvia. **EDUCATION:** National Taiwan Cheng Kung University, BS, 1965; Indiana University, PhD, 1972. **CAREER:** National Taiwan University, research assistant, 1965-67; Indiana University, research, teaching assistant, 1968-72; Purdue University, postdoctoral research associate, 1972-73, assistant professor, 1973-78, associate professor, 1978-84, professor, 1984-. **ORGANIZATIONS:** American Society of Pharmacognosy, executive committee; American Chemical Society; American Association for Cancer Research; North American Phytochemical Society; American Association of College of Pharmacy; American Association for Pharmaceutical Scientists. **HONORS/AWARDS:** Purdue University Cancer Research Award, 1983; Phi Lamda Upsilon, 1969; Sigma Xi, 1973. **SPECIAL ACHIEVEMENTS:** Bioorganic and Natural Products Study Section, National Institutes of Health, 1987-91; Journal of Natural Products, Editorial Advisory Board, 1992-; American Society of Pharmcognosy, executive committee, 1993-97; publications: 150 journal articles, 100 abstracts, 1970-; National Institutes of Health, 4 current active research grants. **MILITARY SERVICE:** Army, 2nd lt, 1965-66. **BUSINESS ADDRESS:** Professor, Dept of Medicinal Chemistry & Pharmacognosy, Purdue University, West Lafayette, IN 47907, (317)494-1373.

CHANG, CHUAN CHUNG
Scientist. Taiwanese American. **PERSONAL:** Born Nov 28, 1938, Tainan, Taiwan; son of Shiang Hua Chang & Ching Hua Chang; married Merry Chang, Aug 17, 1963; children: Eileen, Sue-Lynn. **EDUCATION:** RPI, BS, 1962; Cornell University, PhD, 1967. **CAREER:** Bell Telephone Labs, 1967-84; Bellcore, sceintist, 1984-. **HONORS/AWARDS:** Bell Telephone Labs, distinguished member of technical staff, 1983. **SPECIAL ACHIEVEMENTS:** 205 publications in scientific journals; 7 patents. **BUSINESS ADDRESS:** Distinguished Member of Technical Staff, Bellcore, 331 Newmain Springs Rd, 3X259, Red Bank, NJ 07701, (908)758-2843.

CHANG, CHUN-HAO
Educator. Taiwanese American. **PERSONAL:** Born Aug 18, 1956, Taipei, Taiwan; son of Chin-Tin Chang; married Wenchyi W Chang, Mar 24, 1984; children: Christopher L. **EDUCATION:** National Taiwan University, BA, 1978; University of Houston, MA, 1983; Northwestern University, PhD, 1988. **CAREER:** Oak Ridge National Lab, research associate, 1987-88; Florida International University, assistant professor, 1988-. **ORGANIZATIONS:** American Economic Assn, 1988-; American Finance Assn, 1988-; Econometric Society, 1989-91. **SPECIAL ACHIEVEMENTS:** Publications, coauthor: "Information Acquisition as Business Strategy," Southern Economic Journal 58 (3), pp 750-761, 1992; "Prepayment Risk & the Duration of Default-Free Mortgage-Backed Securities," Journal of Financial Research XVI (3), pp 1-10, Spring 1993; "Profit, Profit-Sharing, & Productivity," in Journal of Economics & Finance, Spring 1993: 103-114; "Comparative Working Capital Management Practices: US Versus Asian Countries," forthcoming in Financial Markets & Economic Integration in Asia, JAI Press; "Optimal Pricing Strategy in Marketing Research Consulting, " 1994. **MILITARY SERVICE:** Taiwanese Army, lieutenant, 1978-80. **HOME PHONE:** (305)434-9010. **BUSINESS ADDRESS:** Assistant Professor, Dept of Finance, Florida International University, University Park, BA 225 A, Miami, FL 33199, (305)348-2680.

CHANG, CLAUDIA
Educator. Chinese American. **PERSONAL:** Born Jan 23, 1952, Worcester, MA; daughter of Min Chueh Chang & Isabelle C Chang; married Perry A

Tourtellotte, May 18, 1982; children: Laura Ann Chang Tourtellotte. **EDUCATION:** Prescott College, BA, 1974; State University of New York, Binghamton, Anthropology, MA, 1977, PhD, 1981. **CAREER:** University of HI, assistant professor, 1988-89; Sweet Briar College, associate professor, 1981-. **ORGANIZATIONS:** American Anthropological Association, fellow, 1993, 1977; Society for American Archaeology, 1977; Society for Visual Anthropology, 1992. **HONORS/AWARDS:** Wenner Gren Foundation for Anthopological Research, small grants, 1988-89; National Academy of Science Interacademy, fellowship, 1992. **SPECIAL ACHIEVEMENTS:** Editor with Harold A Kosler, Pastoralists at the Peryshery: Hedus in a Apitalis World, University of Arizonia Press, 1994; articles in Journal of Field Archaeology, American Antiquity, and American Anthropologist, 1981. **BUSINESS ADDRESS:** Professor, Dept of Anthropology-Sociology, Sweet Briar College, Sweet Briar, VA 24595-1056.

CHANG, CLEMENT C.
Educator, educational administrator. Chinese American. **PERSONAL:** Born Jun 1, 1935, Shanghai, China; married Min Lih Chang; children: Jeff, Grace. **EDUCATION:** National Cheng-Chi University, Taiwan, bachelor's, journalism, 1959; University of Minnesota, master's, journalism, 1967; University of Minnesota, master's, educational technology, 1969. **CAREER:** University of Minnesota, College of Education, instructor, 1969-71, research fellow, 1971-72; North Hennepin College, AV coordinator, 1972-81; Anoka-Ramsey Community College, AV director, 1981-. **ORGANIZATIONS:** Association of Educational Communications & Technology; Minnesota Community College Faculty Association. **HONORS/AWARDS:** Minnesota Community College System, Bush Grant, 1989; Anoka-Ramsey Community College, Entrepreneurship Grant, 1987. **SPECIAL ACHIEVEMENTS:** China Maze, unpublished book; fluent in English & Chinese. **HOME ADDRESS:** 12220 101st Ave N, Maple Grove, MN 55369, (612)425-7114. **BUSINESS ADDRESS:** Audio Visual Director, Anoka-Ramsey Community College, 11200 Mississippi Blvd NW, L118A, Coon Rapids, MN 55433, (612)422-3374.

CHANG, CLIFFORD WAH JUN
Educator. Chinese American. **PERSONAL:** Born Jul 25, 1938, Honolulu, HI. **EDUCATION:** University of Southern California, BS, 1960; University of Hawaii, PhD, 1964. **CAREER:** University of Georgia, research associate, 1964-68; University of West Florida, assist professor, 1968-73, associate professor, 1973-79, professor, 1979-. **ORGANIZATIONS:** American Chemical Society, 1960-; The Chemical Society, London, 1962-; New York Academy of Sciences, 1966-; Sigma Xi, 1964-. **SPECIAL ACHIEVEMENTS:** Published chapters and papers in books and scientific journals; review panelist, National Science Foundation, 1990-91; consultant, Monsanto, Pensacola, 1987-90. **BUSINESS ADDRESS:** Professor, Chemistry Dept, University of West Florida, 11000 University Parkway, Pensacola, FL 32514, (904)474-2745.

CHANG, CRAIG
Financial executive. Chinese American. **PERSONAL:** Born Sep 29, 1943, Chun King, China; son of Mr and Mrs Shou Shien Chang; married Rose, Dec 23, 1967; children: Christopher. **EDUCATION:** Tam Kang College, Taipei, Taiwan, BBA, 1966; University of Bridgeport, MBA, 1978. **CAREER:** Esso, Taipei, Taiwan, accountant, 1967-70; Valley Cable Vision Inc, controller, 1972-74; Akerman Inc, controller, vice president, 1974-82; Highfield Manufacturing Company, vice president, finance, 1982-. **ORGANIZATIONS:** Institute of Management Accounting, 1978-. **BUSINESS ADDRESS:** Vice President, Finance, Highfield Manufacturing Company, 380 Mountain Grove St, Bridgeport, CT 06605, (203)384-2281.

CHANG, DARWIN
Educator. Taiwanese American. **PERSONAL:** Born Jun 29, 1954, Taichung, Taiwan; married Shu-Duan Chang, Dec 31, 1987; children: Lee, William. **EDUCATION:** National Taiwan University, BS, 1976; Carnegie Mellon University, MS, 1980, PhD, 1983. **CAREER:** University of Maryland, research associate, 1983-86; Northwestern University, assistant professor, 1986-. **ORGANIZATIONS:** American Physical Society, 1979-83; Oversea Chinese Physicists Association, 1989-. **HONORS/AWARDS:** Department of Energy, Outstanding Junior Investigator, 1987. **BUSINESS ADDRESS:** Assistant Professor, Dept of Physics and Astronomy, Northwestern University, Sheridan Rd, Evanston, IL 60208.

CHANG, DAVID HSIANG
Educator, engineer, businessman. Chinese American. **PERSONAL:** Born May 4, 1929, Nantung, Kiangsu, China; son of Chia-Ping Chang and Shu-ê Sha;

married Shu-Liang Feng, Aug 22, 1959; children: Edward Kuo-Shu, Eve Kuo-I, Ellen Kuo-Chien. **EDUCATION:** Shanghai Institute of Technology, BS, 1949; Pennsylvania State University, 1954-55; Massachusetts Institute of Technolgy, MS, 1974. **CAREER:** Provincial Taipei Institute of Technology, instructor, 1950-53; Provincial Taiwan Normal University, associate professor, 1953-61; US Agency for International Development, senior specialist, 1961-63; Tai Yuen Textile Co, Ltd, vice-general mill manager, 1961-71; Hsin-Pu Institute of Technology, professor, 1969-70; Yuen-Sun Textile Company, general mill manager, 1971-73; Metricom, Inc, board director, 1992-; Tai Yuen Textile Co, Ltd, NY, managing director, 1974-. **ORGANIZATIONS:** National Civil Service Examination Association, 1950-; Chinese Educational Testing Association, 1956; Chinese Mechanical Engineers Association, 1952-; Chinese Society of Engineers, 1953-; Iota Lambda Sigma, 1954-; Chinese Industrial-Education Association, 1955-. **HONORS/AWARDS:** ROC National Ministry of Examinations, certified scholar in ME, 1950; ROC Ministry of Education, Outstanding Achievement Award for Associate Professor, 1960; International Cotton Advisory Committee, delegate of plenary meetings, 1970, 1985; IAFEL World Congress, delegate, 1985; various states in USA, honorary citizenships, 1976-86; ROC National Development Seminar Delegate on International Trade, 1982; Massachusetts Institute of Technology, Sloan Fellow, 1974. **SPECIAL ACHIEVEMENTS:** Developed 13 complete sets of teaching materials, job sheets, operation sheetings, and information sheets on machinist, electrician, electronics, auto-mechanics, carpentry, foundry, welding, sheetmetal and plumbing, cabinet & pattern making, printing & drafting trades, for 13 trade courses in Taiwan, 1957-60; expanded Tai Yuen's spinning mills facilities, 1961-71; increased annual sales value tenfold, 1975-87; helped Taiwan Cotton Spinning Mills to purchase US cotton, 1980-89; expert in: industrial school teachers training, cotton blending and spinning. **BUSINESS ADDRESS:** General Manager, Managing Director, Tai Yuen Textile Co, NY, Ltd, 990 Avenue of the Americas, Suite 23H, New York, NY 10018, (212)279-6093.

CHANG, DAVID W.
Educator. Chinese American. **PERSONAL:** Born Aug 7, 1951, Canton, People's Republic of China; son of Tsung-Yuin Chang; married Bonnie U Chang, Oct 15, 1977; children: Michelle A, Jennifer M, Michael D. **EDUCATION:** University of Northern Iowa, BA, 1975; University of Chicago Medical Centers, RRT, 1976; Columbus College, MEd, 1984; Nova University, EdD, 1992. **CAREER:** Covenant Memorial Hospital, respiratory technician, 1974-75; Des Moines General Hospital, respiratory therapist, 1976; Broadlawns Medical Center, respiratory therapist, 1976-78; Northeast Iowa Community College, program director, 1978-81; Columbus College, program director, professor, 1981-. **ORGANIZATIONS:** American Association for Respiratory Care, research committee member, 1990-92, educational program committee member, 1989, 1993-94; Georgia Society for Respiratory Care, education committee member, 1991-92, continuing education committee chair, 1994; Georgia Composite Board of Medical Examiners, continuing eduation committee member, 1986-91; Iowa Society for Respiratory Care, board of directors, 1978, 1980-81. **HONORS/AWARDS:** National Board for Respiratory Care, exam writer, 1986-94, perinatal/pediatric specialist, 1991, pulmonary function technologist, 1984, respiratory therapist, 1979; Georgia Society for Respiratory Care, Outstanding Service Award, 1982-83. **SPECIAL ACHIEVEMENTS:** Author of Respiratory Care Calculations, Delmar Publisher, 1994; Medical Terminology, Williams & Wilkins, 1994; ''Microbiology for Respiratory Care,'' AARC, 1989; ''Respiratory Care,'' AARC Journal, 1989, 1990, 1993. **BUSINESS ADDRESS:** Director, Respiratory Therapy, Columbus College, 4225 University Ave, Columbus, GA 31907, (706)568-2130.

CHANG, DAVID WEN-WEI
Educator. Chinese American. **PERSONAL:** Born Jul 1, 1929, Xian, Shaanxi, China; son of Ying Chang and Wei-Ze Chang; married Alice G Chang, Aug 11, 1962; children: Christopher, Victor. **EDUCATION:** Beijing University, Law School, 1948-49; Tamkang University, Rhodes College of Memphis, BA, 1955; University of Minnesota, Minneapolis, MA, 1957; University of Illinois, Urbana, PhD, 1960. **CAREER:** National Cheng-Chi University, visiting chair, 1969-71; Chinese Social Science Academy, visiting lecturer, 1984, 1985; Chinese People's University, Beijing, Fulbright professor, 1992; University of Wisconsin, Oshkosh, coordinator for Asian studies, assistant professor, 1960-62, chairman of political science department, associate professor, 1962-64, professor, coordinator for Asian studies, 1964-. **ORGANIZATIONS:** American Political Science Association; Mid-West Political Science Association; Association for Asian Studies; Wisconsin Political Science Association; Rotary Club; Candlelight Club; Chinese Political Science Association; Chinese Social

Scientist Association in North America. **HONORS/AWARDS:** University of Wisconsin, Oshkosh, University Rosebush Professor, Merit Competition, 1985; Distinguished Educator, 1972; Dr Sun Yat-Sen Scholar Award; Research Scholarship Grants, University of Wisconsin, Regents, 1963, 1970, Pacific Cultural Foundation, 1984, 1991-. **SPECIAL ACHIEVEMENTS:** Book: China Under Deng Xiaoping in Political and Economic Reform, Macmillan Press, London, 1988; book: Zhou Enlai and Deng Xiaoping in Leadership Succession, University Press of America, 1994; book in Chinese language: Chinese Communities in Southeast Asian Countries, Commercial Press, Taipei; chapters, research articles in various academic journals. **HOME PHONE:** (414)231-0160. **BUSINESS ADDRESS:** Professor, Dept of Political Science, University of Wisconsin, Oshkosh, WI 54901-3551, (414)424-3456.

CHANG, DEANNA BAUKUNG
Educator. Chinese American. **PERSONAL:** Born Oct 9, 1946, Honolulu, HI; daughter of Walter Chang and Lorraine Chang. **EDUCATION:** University of Hawaii, Manoa, BA, 1969, MA, 1973, PhD, 1994. **CAREER:** University of Hawaii, Manoa, College of Continuing Education and Community Service, Dept of Sociology, lecturer, 1987-; University of Hawaii, Hilo, Department of Sociology, visiting assistant professor, 1993-94. **ORGANIZATIONS:** American Sociological Association, state liaison, 1994, membership committee, regional rep, Hawaii & the Pacific, 1993-96; Sociologists for Women in Society, mentoring award selection committee, 1993-96; Alpha Kappa Delta-Alpha Hawaii, secretary-treasurer, 1991-94; Domestic Violence Coordinating Council Hawaii, 1993; Hawaii Sociological Association, vice president, 1990-91. **HONORS/AWARDS:** American Sociological Association, minority fellow and dissertation award, 1988-91; Phi Beta Delta-Alpha Zeta, 1991; Phi Beta Kappa, 1967; Phi Kappa Phi, 1967; Pacific Sociological Association, Distinguished Student Paper-First Prize, 1988. **SPECIAL ACHIEVEMENTS:** Amer Soc Association Honors Program, first student from Hawaii, 1988; co-editor, Social Process in Hawaii: Social Control in Law & Health, 1992; author, An Abused Spouse's Self-saving Process: A Theory of Identity Transformation, 1990. **BIOGRAPHICAL SOURCES:** Am Sociological Association Minority Affairs Progr Newsletter, pp 6-7, 1992. **BUSINESS ADDRESS:** Dept of Sociology, University of Hawaii, Hilo, Hilo, HI 96720-4091.

CHANG, DEBORAH I-JU
Health policy adviser. Chinese American. **PERSONAL:** Born Feb 14, 1962, Boston, MA. **EDUCATION:** Massachusetts Institute of Technology, BS, 1984; University of Michigan, MPH, 1987. **CAREER:** Massachusetts State House, intern, 1981-82; Procter and Gamble Co, regulatory affairs engineer, 1984-85; El Paso County Health Department, policy fellow, 1986; University of Michigan, Department of Public Health Policy, research assistant, 1985-87; Office of Legislation and Policy, Health Care Financing Administration, Presidential Management Internship, Medicaid and long-term care analyst, 1987-89; Senator Donald W Riegle, health policy fellow, 1988; Urban Institute, policy research fellow, 1988-89; Senator Donald W Riegle, chairman, Finance Subcommittee on Health for Families and the Uninsured, health policy adviser, 1989-. **ORGANIZATIONS:** American Public Health Association. **HONORS/AWARDS:** National Association of Community Health Centers, Congressional Staff Recognition Award, 1992. **SPECIAL ACHIEVEMENTS:** Publications, co-author with John Holohan, Medicaid Spending in the 1980's: The Access-Cost Containment Trade-Off Revisited, Urban Institute Press, 1990; co-author with A Zappolo, P Doty & T Gustafson, Prospective Payment for Medicare Skilled Nursing Facilities, Dept of Health & Human Services, Report to Congress, 1988; co-author with B Kay, I Butter, K Houlihan, ''Women's Health and Social Change: The Case of Lay Midwives,'' Intl Journal of Health Services, vol 18-1, pp 223-236, 1988. **BIOGRAPHICAL SOURCES:** The Almanac of the Unelected Staff of the US Congress, 1990, 1991, p 659, 1992, p 675, 1993, p 658, Congressional Staff Directory, 1990-94.

CHANG, DOUGLAS HOWE
Film/video producer. Chinese American. **PERSONAL:** Born Aug 30, 1962, New York, NY; son of Victor Chang and Lily C Y Chang. **EDUCATION:** Swarthmore College, BA, English literature, 1984; NYU, Tisch School of the Arts, MA, cinema studies, 1990. **CAREER:** Meta Five Inc, production assistant, 1988-90; Children's Television Workshop, new show projects assistant, 1990; Michael Camerini Inc, associate producer, 1991-92; WGBH-TV, associate producer, 1992-93; self-employed, producer, currently. **ORGANIZATIONS:** New York Film/Video Council, board of directors, 1993. **SPECIAL ACHIEVEMENTS:** Film/video work includes: contributor: ''Art on Film/Film on Art,'' video guide, 1992; associate producer: ''Sites of Recollection,'' video, Williams College Museum of Art, 1992; ''Becoming the Buddha in

LA," 1-hr documentary, WGBH-TV, 1993. **HOME ADDRESS:** 108 W 69th St, New York, NY 10023.

CHANG, EDMUND Z. (ZHI MENG ZHANG)
Educator. Chinese American. **PERSONAL:** Born Oct 20, 1935, Beijing, China; son of Pei Ju Brown Chang and Sheng Ying Dai; married Sheila T Chang, Jul 17, 1974; children: Grace M. **EDUCATION:** Peking University, Beijing, BS, 1961, MS, 1963; Stanford University, PhD, 1985. **CAREER:** Chinese Academy of Geological Sciences, senior researcher, 1963-80; British Petroleum, senior geologist, 1986-90; Stanford University, Dept of Geology, post doctoral researcher, 1985-86, associate professor, 1990-. **ORGANIZATIONS:** Geological Society of America, 1982; American Geophysics Union, 1983; American Assn of Petroleum Geologists, 1990. **SPECIAL ACHIEVEMENTS:** Language proficiency: reads, writes, speaks: Chinese, English; reads: Russian, German; field work and paper presentations include: Reconstruction of Paleo-ocean in Asia, Novosberisk, Russia, IGCP 283, 1993; Intl Geologic Congress, Kyoto, Japan, 1992; publications include: Evolution and Extinction of a Paleo-ocean in Central China, 1993; "Change from Transform to Active Continental Margin of Eastern China," Fukuoka Conference, Monograph, 1992. **BUSINESS ADDRESS:** Associate Professor, Dept of Geology, Stanford University, Palo Alto, CA 94305, (415)723-9170.

CHANG, EDWARD C.
Educator, educational administrator. Chinese American. **PERSONAL:** Born Jul 6, 1936, Kwangtung, China; married Mimi Chang, Sep 1, 1965; children: Norman, Emily. **EDUCATION:** Taiwan Normal University, BA, 1960; Northeast Missouri State University, MA, 1965; University of Oklahoma, PhD, 1969. **CAREER:** Chinese Student Weekly, editor, 1954-56; Albany State College, associate professor, professor of psychology, 1967-, Department of Psychology & Special Education, chairman, 1971-85, Dept of Psychology, Sociology & Social Work, chairman, 1985-93. **HONORS/AWARDS:** University of Oklahoma, Lewenz Scholarship, 1966-67; US Department of Education, Grant Awards, 1988-94. **SPECIAL ACHIEVEMENTS:** Author, Knocking at the Gate of Life, 1985. **BIOGRAPHICAL SOURCES:** American Psychological Association Directory. **HOME ADDRESS:** 125 Red Bud Rd, Albany, GA 31705.

CHANG, EDWARD SHIH-TOU
Educator. Chinese American. **PERSONAL:** Born Jul 6, 1940, Swatow, Kwang Tung, China; son of Thomas Chang and Jessie Chang; married Angela, Jan 12, 1980; children: Cary, Remington, Redford. **EDUCATION:** Chaffey College, AA, 1959; university of California, Riverside, BA, 1961, MA, 1964, PhD, 1967. **CAREER:** University of Chicago, postdoctoral fellow, 1969-70; Science Research Council, senior fellow, 1977-78; University of Kaiserslautern, visiting professor, 1983-84; Institute Theoretical Atomic & Molecular Physics, visiting scientist, 1990-91; University of Massachusetts, professor, 1970-; Smithsonian Institution, visiting scientist, 1991-. **ORGANIZATIONS:** American Physical Society, 1965-; Institute of Physics, fellow, 1976-84. **HONORS/AWARDS:** University of California, Riverside, fellowship, 1959; National Academy of Science, National Research Council Fellow, 1967-69; University of Massachusetts, Faculty Research Grant, 1978. **SPECIAL ACHIEVEMENTS:** Over 50 articles in physics & astrophysical journals such as: The Physical Review, Journal of Physics, The Astrophysical Journal, etc. **BUSINESS ADDRESS:** Professor, University of Massachusetts, Hasbrouck Lab 223, Amherst, MA 01003, (413)545-0586.

CHANG, EDWARD TAEHAN
Educator. Korean American. **PERSONAL:** Born May 6, 1956, Inchon, Republic of Korea; son of Ho Chang and Kum Cho Chang; married Janet C Chang, Aug 10, 1985; children: Angie Y. **EDUCATION:** UC, Berkeley, BA, sociology, 1982; UCLA, MA, Asian American studies, 1984, PhD, ethnic studies, 1990. **CAREER:** California Polytechnic University, assistant professor, 1990-92; UC, Riverside, assistant professor, 1992-. **ORGANIZATIONS:** Korean Community Center of the East Bay, board of directors, 1984-88; Black-Korean Alliance, 1987-92; Association for Asian Studies, 1987-92; National Association for Ethnic Studies, executive council, 1989-90; Association for Asian American Studies, 1984-. **HONORS/AWARDS:** UC Humanities Institute, Residential Fellowship, 1993; Rockefeller Foundation, Humanities Fellowship, 1991; Assn for Asian Studies, Small Grant Award, 1988. **SPECIAL ACHIEVEMENTS:** Author: "Who African Americans Are," in Korean, 1993; actor, consultant: "Lost Angeles," bilingual play, 1993; "Los Angeles: A Struggle Toward Multi Ethnic Community"; Amerasia Journal, guest editor, 1993. **MILITARY SERVICE:** Army, specialist 4, 1975-78. **BIOGRAPHI-**

CAL SOURCES: Los Angeles Times, Editorial Section, Apr 29, 1993; LA Times Calendar Section, F1, Aug 17, 1993; Press Enterprise, Living Section, E1, Apr 25, 1993; Pasadena-Star News, Apr 26, 1993. **BUSINESS ADDRESS:** Assistant Professor of Ethnic Studies, University of California, Riverside, 101 University Office Building, Riverside, CA 92521, (909)787-2144.

CHANG, ELDEN T.
Company executive. Chinese American. **PERSONAL:** Born Jun 30, 1965, Cincinnati, OH; son of Bin Chang and Susan Yu Chang. **EDUCATION:** Harvard, BA, 1987. **CAREER:** Donaldson Lufkin & Jenrette, securities analyst; Diamondhead Enterprises, vice president, currently. **BUSINESS ADDRESS:** Vice President, Diamondhead Enterprises, 4299 Pleasant Run Rd, Irving, TX 75038, (214)257-0432.

CHANG, ERIC CHIEH
Educator. Chinese American. **PERSONAL:** Born Mar 28, 1951, Taipei, Taiwan; son of Shyh Rong Chang; married Ting-Ting Chang, Dec 23, 1977; children: Christina, Sarah, Heidi. **EDUCATION:** National Cheng Kung University, Taiwan, BS, 1974; National Cheng Chi University, Taiwan, 1976; Wright State University, MBA, 1979; Purdue University, PhD, 1982. **CAREER:** University of Iowa, Department of Finance, assistant professor, 1982-86; University of Maryland, Department of Finance, assistant professor, 1986-89; Commodity Futures Trading Commission, USA, visiting financial economist, 1990-92; University of Maryland, Department of Finance, associate professor, 1992-; Hong Kong University of Science & Technology, Department of Finance, deputy head, 1992-. **HONORS/AWARDS:** Chartered Financial Analyst, 1986. **SPECIAL ACHIEVEMENTS:** Co-author, "Tests of the Nominal Contracting Hypothesis Using Stocks and Bonds of the Same Firms," Journal of Banking and Finance, vol 16, pp477-496, 1992; paper presentations: "The Performance and Market Impact of Dual Trading: CME Rule 552," American Finance Association Conference, 1993; "Empirical Testing of Multi-Good Consumption Based Asset Pricing Models," Western Finance Association Conference, 1991. **BUSINESS ADDRESS:** Deputy Head, Dept of Finance, Hong Kong University of Science & Technology, 2412 Academic Bldg, Clear Water Bay, Kowloon, Hong Kong, (852)358-7675.

CHANG, ERNEST SUN-MEI
Educator. Chinese American. **PERSONAL:** Born Dec 7, 1950, Berkeley, CA; son of Shu-Chi Chang and Helen Fong Chang; married Sharon Chang, Nov 8, 1986. **EDUCATION:** University of California, Berkeley, AB, 1973, Los Angeles, PhD, 1978. **CAREER:** University of California, Los Angeles, instructor, 1977; University of Chicago, post doctoral fellow, 1978; University of California, Davis, professor, 1978-. **ORGANIZATIONS:** Jenner Vol Fire Dept, chief, 1978-; American Soc of Zoologists, 1978-; American Assn for the Advancement of Science, 1978-; World Aquaculture Soc, 1978-. **HONORS/AWARDS:** American Cancer Soc, Post Doctoral Fellow, 1978; National Institutes of Health, Post Doctoral Fellow, 1978; University of California, Los Angeles, Graduate Research Award, 1978. **SPECIAL ACHIEVEMENTS:** Over 70 publications in scientific journals. **BUSINESS ADDRESS:** Professor, University of California, Bodega Marine Laboratory, PO Box 247, Bodega Bay, CA 94923, (707)875-2061.

CHANG, FARLAND H.
Broadcast journalist. Chinese American. **PERSONAL:** Born Apr 8, 1963, Walnut Creek, CA; son of Street and Chi Hing Chang. **EDUCATION:** Cornell University, BS, government, 1984; Columbia Graduate School of Journalism, MSJ, 1985; Bristol University, postgrad certificate, radio/film/TV, 1985. **CAREER:** WTKO Radio, reporter, anchor, 1982-84; AP Radio, reporter, 1984-85; Lt Governor S B Woo, press secretary, intl trade specialist, 1986-88; WMDT-TV, ABC, producer, 1988; KGMB-TV, CBS, news reporter, 1989; Guam Cable News, TV news anchor, reporter, 1989-91; WTXF-TV, Fox, news reporter, 1991-. **ORGANIZATIONS:** AFTRA, 1989; Rotary Intl, rotary scholar, 1986; Sigma Delta Chi, Society of Professional Journalists, 1983-; Asian American Journalists Assn, 1991-; NATAS, 1991-. **HONORS/AWARDS:** Columbia Graduate School of Journalism, Outstanding Broadcast Journalist; NATAS, Emmy Award, Spot News Team Coverage, 1991; Associated Press, Spot News Team Coverage, 1992. **BIOGRAPHICAL SOURCES:** Asian Americans in American Politics, Columbia University, 1985. **BUSINESS ADDRESS:** Reporter, WTXF Fox-29, 330 Market St, Philadelphia, PA 19106, (215)923-6397.

CHANG, GENE HSIN

Educator. Chinese American. **PERSONAL:** Born Feb 22, 1952, Shanghai, People's Republic of China; son of Huaisheng Chang and Jiahui Huang; married Jinmei Jiao; children: Elaine, Emily. **EDUCATION:** Fudan University, China, BA, Chinese literature, 1984; University of California, MA, Asian studies, 1986; University of Michigan, PhD, economics, 1989. **CAREER:** Zhejiang Asia-Pacific Research Institute, China, professor, 1992-; University of Toledo, assistant professor, 1989-. **ORGANIZATIONS:** Chinese Economist Society, president, 1990-91, director, 1986-88; Association for Asian Studies, Inc, 1986-; American Economic Association, 1985-; Association for Comparative Economic Studies, 1989-; Univ of Michigan Center for Chinese Studies, 1984-; University of California, Group of East Asian Studies, 1982-84; Young Economist Society, Shanghai, director, 1979-81. **HONORS/AWARDS:** University of Michigan, Rackham Fellow, 1988-89; University of California, Wheeler Fellow, 1983-84. **SPECIAL ACHIEVEMENTS:** "The Inconsistencies Among Disequilibrium Aggregates," Journal of Comp Economics, 1993; "Asymmetric 'Min' Conditions and Estimations for Disequilibrium in Centrally Planned Economies," Comparative Economic Studies, Dec 1992; "The 1982-83 Overinvestment Crisis in China," Asian Studies, 1984; about 30 articles and books in English and Chinese. **BIOGRAPHICAL SOURCES:** "Chinese Academic Associations in the US: Bridges for Scholarly Discourse," China Exchange News, Washington, DC, vol 19, no 1, pp 8-13, Spring 1991. **BUSINESS ADDRESS:** Assistant Professor, University of Toledo, Toledo, OH 43606, (419)537-4677.

CHANG, GORDON H.

Educator. Chinese American. **PERSONAL:** Born Jun 19, 1948, Hong Kong; son of Shu-chi Chang and Helen Fong Chang. **EDUCATION:** Princeton University, BA, 1970; Stanford University, MA, 1972, PhD, 1987. **CAREER:** Laney College, instructor, 1972-82; University of California, Irvine, professor, 1989-91; Stanford University, professor, 1991-. **ORGANIZATIONS:** Organization of American Historians, 1987-; Association for Asian American Studies, 1987-; Chinese Historical Society, 1985-; Chinese Progressive Association, 1972-. **HONORS/AWARDS:** Society for Historians of American Foreign Relations, Bernath Book Award, 1991; Organization of American Historians, Pelzer Award, 1987; Stanford University, Dept of History, Potter Prize, 1986. **SPECIAL ACHIEVEMENTS:** Book: Friends and Enemies: The United States, China, and the Soviet Union, 1948-1972. **BUSINESS ADDRESS:** Professor, Dept of History, Stanford University, Stanford, CA 94305, (415)723-2651.

CHANG, HELEN KUANG

Public relations director. Taiwanese American. **PERSONAL:** Born Jan 1, 1962, Chang-Hua, Taiwan; daughter of Mary Mei-Hwa & Jonah Jui-Hsiong Chang; married Chuck B Goodman, Aug 20, 1988. **EDUCATION:** University of California, Berkeley, BA, (cum laude), mass communications, 1984. **CAREER:** United Methodist Board of Church & Society, communications assistant, 1985-88; San Francisco Convention & Visitors Bureau, Public Relations & Publications, coordinator, 1989-90, acting manager, 1991, assistant manager, 1990, 1991-92; San Jose Convention & Visitors Bureau, Public Relations & Publications, director, 1992-. **ORGANIZATIONS:** San Francisco Bay Area Publicity Club, first vp of programs, 1992; United Methodist Commission of Communications, secretary, 1992-96; Public Relations Society of America; Women in Communications Inc; National Association of Female Executives; Asian American Journalists Associations, associate member. **HONORS/AWARDS:** Publicity Club, Award of Excellence, 1990. **SPECIAL ACHIEVEMENTS:** Los Angeles Publicity Club Pro Awards, Printed Materials, judge, 1991; Women in Communications National Clarion Awards, Crisis Communications, judge, 1991, Membership Recruitment Materials, judge, 1992. **BUSINESS ADDRESS:** Director, Public Relations and Publications, San Jose Convention & Visitors Bureau, 333 West San Carlos, Ste 1000, San Jose, CA 95110, (408)295-9600.

CHANG, HELEN T.

City official. Chinese American. **PERSONAL:** Born Nov 12, 1943, ChungKing, China; daughter of Mr & Mrs Long Jim Tarn; married James C Chang, Jun 8, 1968; children: Andrew C, Audrey M. **EDUCATION:** National Chung Hsing University, BA, economics, 1964; Auburn University, MBA, 1967. **CAREER:** Taipei Institute of Business, instructor, 1964-65; University of Washington, statistician, 1967-69; Baylor College of Medicine, administrative associate, 1969-91; City of Houston, assistant to the mayor, 1992-. **ORGANIZATIONS:** American Public Health Association, Public Health Education & Health Promotion Committee; Community Health Planning & Policy Development, 1993-; US Conference of Local Health Officers, advisory group member; Selective Service System, board member; Red Cross, Houston, board member; Sheltering Arms, Houston, board member; Houston Community College System Foundation, trustee; Greater Houston Coalition for Educational Excellence, trustee, board member; International Festival, country selection committee member; Houston Boy Choir, board member; Chinese Writers Association, USA, board member; Minority Health Coalition, executive committee member; Asian American Coalition, board member. **HONORS/AWARDS:** Foundation for National Political Leadership, 1993; National Republican Asian Assembly, 1992; The Association of American Chinese Professionals, 1987. **SPECIAL ACHIEVEMENTS:** Organized various national conventions; promoted Asian Americans into Houston mainstream politics; first Asian American to serve as the assistant to the mayor in city of Houston; first Asian-American to serve as the transition team member for the mayor of the city of Houston; Asian community liaison to the mayor; promoted international trading with Pacific rim countries. **BUSINESS ADDRESS:** Assistant to the Mayor, City of Houston, 901 Bagby, Mayor's Office, Houston, TX 77002, (713)247-2200.

CHANG, HENRY C.

Library administrator. Chinese American. **PERSONAL:** Born Sep 15, 1941, Canton, China; son of Ih-ming Chang; married Marjorie L Chang, Oct 29, 1966; children: Michelle C. **EDUCATION:** National Chengchi University, BLL, 1962; University of Missouri, Columbia, MA, 1966; University of Minnesota, MALS, 1968; University of Maryland, library administration certificate, 1972; University of Minnesota, PhD, 1974. **CAREER:** University of Minnesota, instructor, 1968-72; University of Minnesota Libraries, assistant head, 1972-74; University of Virgin Islands, chief librarian, lecturer, 1974-75; US Department of Education, project director, 1981-83; Government of US Virgin Islands, director of libraries, museums, archaeological services and territorial librarian, 1975-87, special assistant, 1987-88; HCM Corporation, president, library consultant, 1988-; Braille Institute, director of library services, 1990-. **ORGANIZATIONS:** Caribbean Archives Association, executive board member, 1984-88; Association of Caribbean University & Research Libraries, chair, 1984-86; American Library Association, president's committee, 1984-86, ALA, councilor-at-large, 1980-84; National Commission on Libraries & Information Services, committee chair, 1980-83; VI Historical Records Advisory Board, chair, 1976-87; Asian Pacific American Librarians Association, committee chair, 1980-87, 1992-; Chinese American Librarians Association, board of directors, 1978-84. **HONORS/AWARDS:** International Lions Club, certificate of appreciation, 1992; Virgin Islands Governor's Library Council, commendation, 1987; Government of US Virgin Islands, certification of appreciation, 1986; American Library Association, distinguished service award, 1984; Fort Frederik Commission, service award, 1978. **SPECIAL ACHIEVEMENTS:** Developed, established and implemented Virgin Islands Library & Information Network, 1976-87; author, "Equity at Issue: Library Services & the Nation's Major Minority Groups," 1985; "The Development of Automation in the Cataloging Process," ACURIL, 1984; report on the learning resources center facilities at the University of Turabo, 1984; Needs-Assessment Study of Asian Americans, 1982. **MILITARY SERVICE:** China, 2nd lt, 1962-63. **HOME ADDRESS:** 7839 SVL Box, Victorville, CA 92392, (619)243-2051. **BUSINESS ADDRESS:** Director of Library Services, Braille Institute of America, 741 N Vermont Ave, Los Angeles, CA 90029, (213)663-1111.

CHANG, HOWARD F.

Educator. Chinese American. **PERSONAL:** Born Jun 30, 1960, Lafayette, IN; son of Joseph J Chang and Mary H Chang. **EDUCATION:** Harvard College, AB, 1982; Princeton University, MPA, 1985; Harvard Law School, JD, 1987; Massachusetts Institute of Technology, PhD, 1992. **CAREER:** Harvard Law Review, supervising editor, 1986-1987; Honorable Ruth B Ginsburg, US Court of Appeals for the DC Circuit, law clerk, 1988-89; University of Southern California, assistant professor of law, 1992-. **ORGANIZATIONS:** New York State Bar, 1989-; District of Columbia Bar, 1989-; American Economics Association, 1991-; American Law & Economics Association, 1991-; Asian Pacific American Legal Center, 1992-; Harvard Law Review, editor, 1985-86, supervising editor, 1986-87. **HONORS/AWARDS:** John M Olin Fellowship in Law & Economics, 1987, 1990, 1991; National Merit Scholarship, 1978. **SPECIAL ACHIEVEMENTS:** "Bargaining and the Division of Value in Corporate Reorganization," Journal of Law, Economics & Organization, Vol 8, 1992; "Essays in Law and Microeconomic Theory," PhD dissertation, MIT Department of Economics, 1992. **HOME ADDRESS:** 324 Idaho Avenue, #402, Santa Monica, CA 90403. **BUSINESS ADDRESS:** Assistant Professor of

Law, University of Southern California Law Center, University Park, Los Angeles, CA 90089-5502, (213)740-0145.

CHANG, HSU HSIN
Educator. Chinese American. **PERSONAL:** Born Jan 1, 1934, Wuchang, Hubei, China; son of Chang Chung-ning and Hwang Wen-jane; married Elaine Pardue Chang; children: Chi-chung, Chi-tung. **EDUCATION:** National Taiwan University, BA, 1956; University of Missouri, MA, 1959; Florida State University, MS, 1961; University of Wisconsin, PhD, 1967; Harvard University, postdoctoral, 1969-70. **CAREER:** University of Wisconsin, teaching assistant, 1964-66; California State University at Fresno, assistant professor, 1966-69, associate professor, 1969-73; professor, 1973-. **ORGANIZATIONS:** American Historical Association; Association for Asian Studies. **HONORS/AWARDS:** Wisconsin Ford Area Fellow, American Philosophical Foundation, research grant, 1963-65, 1967, 1969; Sun-Yat-sen Foundation, research grant, 1986; CSUF, Meritorious Performance and Professional Promise Award, Spring 1990; Pacific Cultural Foundation, research grant, 1992; nominated for Joseph Levenson Prize, Best English Language Book on 20th-Century China, 1991. **SPECIAL ACHIEVEMENTS:** Co-editor, Bibliography of Sun Yat-sen in China's Republican Revolution, 1885-1925, Lanham, Maryland, University Press of America, 1990; The Storm Clouds Clear Over China: the Memoir of Ch'en Li-fu, 1900-1993, Hoover Institution Press, Stanford University, 1994; co-author, All Under Heaven: Sun Yat-sen and His Revolutionary Thought, Hoover Institution Press, Standford University, 1991. **BUSINESS ADDRESS:** Professor, Dept of History, California State University, Cedar and Shaw, Fresno, CA 93740, (209)278-2152.

CHANG, HUI-CHING
Educator. Taiwanese American. **PERSONAL:** Born Apr 8, 1962, Taipei, Taiwan; daughter of Ou-Jen & Jua-Hwa Chou Chang; married George Richard Holt, Nov 6, 1990. **EDUCATION:** National Taiwan University, BL, 1984; Semester at Sea, 10 countries, 1985; University of Illinois, MA, 1988, PhD, 1994. **CAREER:** University of Illinois, research assistant, 1987-89, teaching assistant, 1989-90; University of Louisville, instructor, 1990-91; University of South Dakota, assistant professor, 1991-. **ORGANIZATIONS:** Intl Communication Assn, 1990; Speech Communication Assn, 1992; Society for Applied Anthropology, 1992; American Anthropological Assn, 1992; Chinese Communication Assn, 1991; Central States Communication Assn, 1993. **HONORS/AWARDS:** China Marine Corp, Scholarship, 1985; Speech Communication Assn, Peace Communication Interest Group, Top Paper, 1989; Intl Communication Assn, Intercultural Communication Div, Top Paper, 1990; Central States Communication Assn, Organizational Communication Div, Top Panel Paper, 1993; University of South Dakota, University Faculty Development Grant, 1991, Bush Mini-grant, 1992, 1993. **SPECIAL ACHIEVEMENTS:** Co-author: "Debt-repaying Mechanism in Chinese Relationships," Research on Language and Social Interactions, 1994; "Chinese Perspective on Face as Inter-relational Concern," Challenge of Facework, State University of New York Press, 1993; "Phases and Changes: Using Metaphors from I Ching to Teach Small Group Discussion," Journal of Creative Behavior, vol 52, p 95-106, 1992. **BUSINESS ADDRESS:** Asst Prof, Dept of Speech Comm, University of South Dakota, 414 E Clark, 301 Noteboom Hall, Vermillion, SD 57069, (605)677-6199.

CHANG, HYONG KOO
Shoe company executive. Korean American. **PERSONAL:** Born Jun 25, 1957, Seoul, Republic of Korea; son of Jung Yong Chang and Ik Joo Chang; married Won Ju Chang, May 11, 1985; children: Deborah, Daniel. **EDUCATION:** SUNY at Binghamton, BS, accounting, 1982. **CAREER:** Kumkang Shoe Mfg Co Ltd, vice president, currently. **HOME ADDRESS:** 248 Riveredge Rd, Tenafly, NJ 07670, (201)568-1019. **BUSINESS PHONE:** (212)249-5252.

CHANG, JACK CHE-MAN
Research manager. Chinese American. **PERSONAL:** Born Nov 19, 1941, Shanghai, China; son of Chang Tse-Liang and Chang Tyen Ho-Chen; married Elizabeth Chang, Nov 23, 1965; children: Clara, Anthony. **EDUCATION:** Asbury College, BA; University of Illinois, MS, PhD; MIT, post-doctoral. **CAREER:** Eastman Kodak Company, research chemist, 1967-73, research associate, laboratory head, 1973-78, special assignment, 1978-79, Analytical Science Division, assistant director, 1979-81, Electrophotography Division, assistant director, 1981-84, Copy Products Division, manager, 1984-85, Chemistry Division, director, 1985-86, Corporate Research Laboratories, director, 1986-93, Imaging Research Laboratory, division director, 1993-. **ORGANIZATIONS:** American Chemical Society; The Electrochemical Society; Chi-

nese American Chemical Society, board of directors, 1989-1992; Chemical Council of Research, governing board, executive board, 1990-92. **HONORS/AWARDS:** Chemical Council of Research, Malcolm Pruitt Award, 1992. **BUSINESS ADDRESS:** Division Director, Imaging Research Laboratory, Eastman Kodak Company, B-59, Rochester, NY 14610, (716)722-2883.

CHANG, JACK H. T.
Pediatric surgeon. Chinese American. **PERSONAL:** Born Mar 8, 1942, Shanghai, China; son of Frank Chang and Molly Chang; married Laura, Aug 12, 1967; children: Kenneth, Jeffrey, Rebecca. **EDUCATION:** Duke University, BA, 1965, School of Medicine, MD, 1969. **CAREER:** Children's Hospital, Dept of General Pedatric Surgery, chairman, 1976-80; Pediatric Surgery Assoc, surgeon, 1976-80, 1985-92; University Texas Southwestern Medical School, associate professor of surgery, 1980-85; Rocky Mountain Pediatric Surgery, surgeon, 1992-; P/SL Medical Center, director, pediatric surgery, 1992-. **ORGANIZATIONS:** American Pediatric Surgical Association, 1978-; British Association of Pediatric Surgeons, 1988-; International Society for the History of Pediatric Surgery, 1988-; American Association for the History of Medicine, 1983-; History of Science Society, 1990-. **HONORS/AWARDS:** British Association of Pediatric Surgeons, International Society for the History of Pediatric Surgery, 1990. **SPECIAL ACHIEVEMENTS:** Organized Liver Transplant Program, University of Texas Southwestern Medical School, 1st successful liver transplantation in Texas, 1983; first successful open intrauterine surgery in Colorado, 1992; coauthor, "Necrotizing Enterocolitis," Journal of Pediatric Surgery, 24:998, 1989; author, "Paediatric Thoracic Surgery, Historical Aspects," Prog Pediatric Surg, 27:5, 1991; author, "A Practical Treatise on the Diseases of Children, Paediatric Surgery, London 1846," Pediatric Surg Intl, 6:412, 1991. **BUSINESS ADDRESS:** Rocky Mountain Pediatric Surgery, PC, 1601 E 19th Ave, Ste 3200, Denver, CO 80218, (303)839-6001.

CHANG, JAMES C.
Educator. Chinese American. **PERSONAL:** Born Aug 8, 1930, Shanghai, China; married Betty, Oct 10, 1970; children: Tatiana. **EDUCATION:** Mount Union College, BS, 1957; University of California, Los Angeles, PhD, 1964. **CAREER:** E R Squibb & Sons, analytical research chemist, 1959-62; University of Northern Iowa, Department of Chemistry, professor, 1964-. **ORGANIZATIONS:** American Chemical Society, 1957-; Sigma Xi, 1964-; Iowa Academy of Science, fellow, 1964-; IUPAC, affiliate, 1986-. **HONORS/AWARDS:** Chemical Rubber Company, Freshman Chemistry Award, 1954; American Chemical Society, Akron Section Junior Award, 1956; American Inst of Chemists, Senior Award, 1957; Pi Gamma Mu, 1957; Mount Union College, Psi Kappa Omega, 1957. **BUSINESS ADDRESS:** Professor, Dept of Chemistry, University of Northern Iowa, Cedar Falls, IA 50613-0423, (319)272-2059.

CHANG, JAMES WAN CHIE
Attorney. Chinese American. **PERSONAL:** Born Jul 19, 1965, Austin, TX; son of Margaret S Chang. **EDUCATION:** University of Texas, Austin, BBA, 1988; University of Houston, JD, 1991. **CAREER:** Winstead Sechrest & Minick PC, attorney/associate, 1991-. **ORGANIZATIONS:** Houston Bar Association, 1991-; Texas Bar Association, 1991-; Houston Young Lawyers Association, 1991-; Asian American Bar Association, 1991-; Houston Chinatown Council, 1992-; Rotary Club of River Oaks, 1992-; Houston Youth Leadership Council, 1992-. **HONORS/AWARDS:** University of Texas, Presidential Scholar, 1983. **BUSINESS ADDRESS:** Attorney, Winstead, Sechrest & Minick PC, 910 Travis Building, Ste 1700, Houston, TX 77002, (713)650-2787.

CHANG, JANE YUEH
Educator. Taiwanese American. **PERSONAL:** Born Dec 18, 1961, Keelung, Taiwan; married Joe T Chao, Jun 15, 1984. **EDUCATION:** Chang-Yuan University, BS, 1983; The Ohio State University, PhD, 1989. **CAREER:** National Central University, associate professor, 1989-91; The Ohio State University, instructor, 1991; Ohio Wesleyan University, assistant professor, 1991-92; Idaho State University, assistant professor, 1992-. **ORGANIZATIONS:** American Statistical Association. **SPECIAL ACHIEVEMENTS:** Co-author, "A Method for Constructing Universally Optimal Block Designs with Nested Rows and Columns," Utilitas Mathematica 38, p 263-76, 1990; co-author, "Optimal Designs for Multiple Comparison with the Best," Journal of Statistical Planning and Inference 30, p 45-62, 1992. **BUSINESS ADDRESS:** Assistant Professor, Mathematics Dept, Idaho State University, Physics Sciences Bldg, Rm 439, Pocatello, ID 83209, (208)236-3983.

CHANG, JEFFREY CHIT-FU
Educator. Chinese American. **PERSONAL:** Born Jan 10, 1928, Canton, China; son of Chin Mao Chang (deceased) and Tui-Ying Chih Chang (deceased); married Frances Hung-Wen Lin Chang, Aug 22, 1946; children: Paul W, Margaret J Henkel, John W. **EDUCATION:** Western Illinois University, BS, 1965, MS, 1966; University of Georgia, PhD, 1973. **CAREER:** Gardner-Webb University, assistant professor, 1966-73, associate professor, 1973-86, professor of math and computer sciences, 1986-. **ORGANIZATIONS:** Association of Computing Machinary, 1973-; American Statistical Association, 1963-. **SPECIAL ACHIEVEMENTS:** Internal Multi-Dimensional Scaling of Categorical Variables. **HOME ADDRESS:** 143 Woodhill Drive, Boiling Springs, NC 28017.

CHANG, JENNIE C. C.
Scientist. Chinese American. **PERSONAL:** Born Feb 27, 1951, Taipei, Taiwan; daughter of Yung Kay Chang and Chiou Yen Cheng; married Jung Fu Wu, Jan 2, 1977; children: Efan Wu. **EDUCATION:** National Taiwan University, BS, plant pathology, 1972, MS, plant pathology, 1974; University of Texas, Denton, MS, microbiology, 1976; Cornell University, PhD, immunology, 1980. **CAREER:** Cornell University, postdoctoral fellow, 1980-82; University of Colorado Med Ctr, postdoctoral fellow, 1982-84, instructor, 1984-86; University of Kentucky Med Ctr, assistant professor, 1986-90; The Immune Response Corp, scientific investigator, 1990-. **ORGANIZATIONS:** American Association of Immunologists, 1986-. **HONORS/AWARDS:** Tobacco and Health Research Institute, pulmonary immunology grant, 1986-91; NIH, biomedical research support grant, 1988-89; Leukemia Society of America, special fellow grant, 1983-85; NIH, National Research Service Award, postdoctoral, 1980-82; NCI, pre-doctoral fellowship, 1977-80. **SPECIAL ACHIEVEMENTS:** Preferential TcR usage in psoriasis, 1994; Insulinoma Antigen Specific T Cell Clones in Human IDDM, submitted, 1993; Molecular Cloning of Rat Cytokine Synthesis Inhibitory Factor IL-10, published, 1993; Characterization and Function of CD3-CD4-CD8-TcR-alpha beta Bearing Cells, published, 1991; THI Clones Express Higher Cytotoxic Activity to APC Than TH2 Clones, published, 1990; Tobacco Smoke Suppressed T But Not APC in the Lung Draining Lymph Node, published, 1990. **BUSINESS ADDRESS:** Scientific Investigator, The Immune Response Corporation, 5935 Darwin Ct, Carlsbad, CA 92008, (619)431-7080.

CHANG, JERRY LESLIE
State representative. Chinese American/Japanese American. **PERSONAL:** Born Sep 15, 1947, Hilo, HI; son of Leslie Ahana & Alma Kuuleialoha Chang; divorced; children: Jensen, Ren, Jade. **EDUCATION:** Mauna Olu College, AA, 1967; University of Hawaii, Hilo, BA, 1978; Realtors Institute. **CAREER:** Puueo Poi Factory, Inc, general manager, secretary-treasurer, 1979-92; Pacific Homes Unlimited, president, 1982-84; Seawind Realty Inc, realtor, vice president, 1987-; State Rep Andrew Levin, legislative aide, 1988; JC marketing, independent sales, consultation, 1991-; House of Reps, State of Hawaii, rep 1st district, 1989-92, rep 2nd district, 1992-94. **ORGANIZATIONS:** Hawaii County Economic Opportunity Council, director; Big Island Substance Abuse Council, director; Hawaii Island YWCA Community Youth Network, director; Steadfact Housing, director; Hawaii Island Chamber of Commerce; Japanese Chamber of Commerce; Pacific Rim Foundation; Exchange Club of Hilo. **MILITARY SERVICE:** US Army 7th Special Forces Group, Airborne, sergeant, medical specialist, 1967-70. **HOME ADDRESS:** 218 S Wilder Rd, Hilo, HI 96720. **BUSINESS ADDRESS:** Representative, Hawaii State Legislature, House of Representatives, 235 S Beretania St, Rm 1203, Honolulu, HI 96813, (808)586-6120.

CHANG, JHY-JIUN
Educator. Chinese American. **PERSONAL:** Born May 29, 1944, China; married. **EDUCATION:** National Taiwan University, BS, 1966; Case Western Reserve University, MS, 1969; Rutgers-The State University, PhD, 1973. **CAREER:** University of California, Santa Barbara, research assistant professor, research associate, 1973-76; California Institute of Technology, senior fellow, research, 1977; IBM Thomas Watson Research Center, visiting scientist, 1983; Institute of Theoretical Physics, visiting associate professor, 1984; Superconductor Technology Inc, consultant, 1988-; Wayne State University, assistant professor, beginning 1977, associate professor, professor, currently. **ORGANIZATIONS:** American Physics Society, 1973-. **SPECIAL ACHIEVEMENTS:** Many articles published in Physical Review, Physical Review Letters, Low Temperature Physics, 1972-. **BUSINESS ADDRESS:** Professor, Dept of Physics and Astronomy, Wayne State University, Detroit, MI 48202, (313)577-3386.

CHANG, JOSEPH J. C. *See* **CHANG, JUANG-CHI.**

CHANG, JUANG-CHI (JOSEPH J. C. CHANG)
Engineer. Chinese American. **PERSONAL:** Born Apr 24, 1936, Nanking, China; son of Chien-Lieh Chang & Shu-Ming Lin Chang; divorced; children: Jean L S, James J Y. **EDUCATION:** National Taiwan University, BS, 1959; University of British Columbia, Canada, MASc, 1961; Iowa State University, PhD, 1965. **CAREER:** University of Alabama Research Institute, assistant professor, 1964-66; Lockheed Georgia Co, specialist, 1966-67; Lockheed Electronics Co, staff engineer, 1967-74; The Aerospace Corp, project engineer, MTS, 1974-. **ORGANIZATIONS:** IEEE, senior member, 1965-; Registered PE of Texas, 1972-; Sigma Xi, 1964-; Eta Kappa Nu, 1964-. **HONORS/AWARDS:** US Air Force Space Division, Excellence Award, 1987; The Aerospace Corp, Outstanding Accomplishment Award, 1985; Lockheed Electronics Co, Outstanding Achievement Award, 1969. **SPECIAL ACHIEVEMENTS:** IEEE MILCOM Conference Record, Session C5, "A High-Gain, High-Resolution Nulling MBA Using Auxiliary Apertures," October 1992, Session C-11, "Auxiliary Aperture High Resolution SHF Nulling Antenna," Nov 1991, Session 33-4, "Receive MBA Phase Correction Algorithm," Oct 1990, Session 33-3, "Measurement of Temperture Effects on DSCS III Receive MBA," Oct 1990; IEEE Transaction on AES, "The Response of Hard-Limiting Bandpass Limiters to PM Signals," vol AES-6, p 398-400, May 1970. **HOME ADDRESS:** 2434 W 239th St, Torrance, CA 90501, (310)326-0754. **BUSINESS ADDRESS:** Project Engineer, MTS, The Aerospace Corp, 2350 E El Segundo Blvd, MS M8-691, El Segundo, CA 90245, (310)336-3378.

CHANG, KAI
Educator. Chinese American. **PERSONAL:** Born Apr 27, 1948, Canton, China; married Suh-jan; children: Peter, Nancy. **EDUCATION:** National Taiwan University, BS, 1970; State University of New York, Stony Brook, MS, 1972; University of Michigan, PhD, 1976. **CAREER:** University of Michigan, research assistant, 1972-76; Shared Applications Inc, consulting engineer, 1976-78; Hughes Aircraft Co, supervisor, 1978-81; TRW, section head, 1981-85; Texas A&M University, associate professor, 1985-88, professor, 1988-89, E-Systems Endowed professor, 1990-. **ORGANIZATIONS:** IEEE, fellow, 1991-; Electromagnetics Academy, 1990-. **HONORS/AWARDS:** TRW, Special Achievement Award, 1984; Texas A&M University, Halliburton Award of Excellence, 1988, Distinguished Teaching Award, 1989, Distinguished Research Award, 1992. **SPECIAL ACHIEVEMENTS:** Editor, Handbook of Microwave and Optical Components, 4 vols, 1989-91; editor, "Microwave and Optical Technology Letters," Monthly Journal, 1988-; editor, Wiley Book Series on Microwave and Optical Engineering, 1988-; publications: over 200 technical papers. **BUSINESS ADDRESS:** Professor, Dept of Electrical Engineering, Texas A&M University, MS 3128, College Station, TX 77843-3128, (409)845-5285.

CHANG, KAI-HSIUNG
Educator. Taiwanese American. **PERSONAL:** Born Jan 24, 1958, Hualien, Taiwan; son of Tien-Lai Chang and Lian-Yin Chang; married Hsiu C Chang, 1981; children: Cynthia, Samuel. **EDUCATION:** Taipei Institute of Technology, diploma, 1977; University of Cincinnati, MS, 1983, PhD, 1986. **CAREER:** Pan-Asia Electronics, engineer, 1979-81; University of Cincinnati, research assistant, 1981-86; Auburn University, assistant professor, 1986-91, associate professor, graduate program officer, 1991-. **ORGANIZATIONS:** Institute of Electrical and Electronics Engineers, 1984-; American Association for Artificial Intelligence, 1984-. **HONORS/AWARDS:** Auburn University, Outstanding Engineering Faculty, 1989, 1992; University of Cincinnati, Summer Research Fellowship, 1983-84; Taipei Institute of Technology, Outstanding College Student, 1977. **SPECIAL ACHIEVEMENTS:** Published more than 40 journal papers, book chapters, conference papers and technical reports. **MILITARY SERVICE:** Chinese Army, Taiwan, 2nd lieutenant. **BUSINESS ADDRESS:** Associate Professor, Dept of Computer Science & Engineering, Auburn University, 107 Dunstan Hall, Auburn, AL 36849-5347, (205)844-6310.

CHANG, KANG-TSUNG (KARL)
Educator. Taiwanese American. **PERSONAL:** Born Jan 30, 1943, Taitung, Taiwan; son of Ching-tu Chang & Yeh Yang Chang; married Lillian R Chang, Aug 30, 1971; children: Gary C, Mark C. **EDUCATION:** National Taiwan University, BS, 1965; Clark University, MA, 1969, PhD, 1971. **CAREER:** California State University, Northridge, assistant professor, 1971-74; Clark University, assistant professor, 1974-76; University of Minnesota, visiting associate professor, 1980; University of North Dakota, associate professor,

1976-81, department chairman, 1981-84, professor, 1982-86; University of Idaho, professor, 1986-. **ORGANIZATIONS:** Association of American Geographers, 1969-; American Congress on Surveying and Mapping, 1974-; Sigma Xi, 1978-. **SPECIAL ACHIEVEMENTS:** 30 articles on geographic information systems, cartography, and economic geography, 1971-. **HOME ADDRESS:** 1016 Virginia Ave, Moscow, ID 83843, (203)882-1634.

CHANG, KELVIN YAU-MIN
Research manager. Taiwanese American. **PERSONAL:** Born Mar 25, 1944, Chiayi, Taiwan; son of Shue-Lung Chang and Lan-Ying Wang; married Celia Hui-Fen Chang, Aug 2, 1971; children: Kevin Jeffrey, Kenneth Norman. **EDUCATION:** Chung Hsing University, Taiwan, BS, 1968; University of Detroit, MS, 1971; Louisiana State University, PhD, 1975. **CAREER:** University of Alberta, postdoctoral fellow, 1975-76; McMaster University, teaching fellow, 1976-78; Aerospace Institute, research associate, 1978-79; Quatic Chemicals Ltd, laboratory manager, 1979-84; Dexter Corporation, research manager, 1984-92; FMC Corporation, senior research associate, 1992-. **ORGANIZATIONS:** National Association of Corrosion Engineers, technical committee, vice chairman, 1980-; American Society for Testing & Materials, technical committees, 1984-; American Chemical Society, 1975-; International Union of Pure and Applied Chemistry, 1990-; Cooling Tower Institute, water treatment committee, 1984-; North American Taiwanese Professors' Association, environmental protection committee, 1985-; Taiwanese Association of Greater Cleveland, vice president, 1989-90, Chemical Specialties Manufacturers Association, 1992; Association of Water Technologies, 1993. **HONORS/AWARDS:** Dexter Corporation, Outstanding Technical Innovation Award, 1989; David L Coffin Patent Award, 1991, 1992. **SPECIAL ACHIEVEMENTS:** 20 technical presentations and publications; 5 US patents; international technical advisor on water treatment. **HOME ADDRESS:** 35 Amaryllis Lane, Newtown, PA 18940-1248, (215)860-6323. **BUSINESS PHONE:** (609)951-3318.

CHANG, KERN K. N.
Electron physicist. Chinese American. **PERSONAL:** Born Sep 9, 1918, Shanghai, China; married Emily; children: Joseph, Eugene, Ellen. **EDUCATION:** National Central University, BSEE, 1940; University of Michigan, Ann Arbor, MSEE, 1948; Polytechnic Institute, PhD, 1954. **CAREER:** Office of Strategic Services, radio instructor, 1941-42; Central Radio Manufacturing, engineer, 1940-48; RCA Laboratories, technology staff member, 1948-54, group head, 1954-70, fellow, 1970-87; KNN Chang Technologies Inc, chairman, president, currently. **HONORS/AWARDS:** CIE Society, New York, Achievement Award, 1964; RCA Labs, Outstanding Award for R&D in Electron Devices, 1962, 1964, 1967, David Sarnoff Outstanding Award in Science, 1967, Achievement Award for Microwave Research, 1969, fellow, 1967; Shanghai Jiao Tong University, Honorary Professor, 1985, Xian Jiaotong University, 1986; Southeast University, Honorary Professor, 1987; Academy of Science, 1988. **SPECIAL ACHIEVEMENTS:** Author, "Coherent Light Radiation by a Lorentz Field in Gaas," Physical Review Letters, vol 15, no 10, p 453, Sept 1965; author, Parametric and Tunnel Diodes, Prentice Hall; 44 original technical papers; 54 US issued patents; guest speaker at prestigious institutes; microwave tubes, semiconductor devices, picture TV tubes. **BIOGRAPHICAL SOURCES:** Hawaii Shanghai Mingrenlu, "Shanghai Overseas Famous People," p 226. **HOME ADDRESS:** 91 Adams Dr, Princeton, NJ 08540, (609)924-1552.

CHANG, KOW-CHING
Educator. Taiwanese American. **PERSONAL:** Born Jan 11, 1952, Taiwan; married Chiu Ie Chang, Jul 29, 1977; children: Wuen-E, Eileen, Nelly. **EDUCATION:** Chinese Culture University, Taiwan, BS, 1973; University of Nebraska, MS, 1977, PhD, 1980. **CAREER:** University of Nebraska, research assistant, 1976-80, research associate, 1980-81, Chinese Culture University, professor, 1981-1984; University of Arizona, research associate, 1984; North Dakota State University, associate professor, food science, 1984-. **ORGANIZATIONS:** Chinese American Food Society, president, 1992-93, president elect, 1991-92; Institute of Food Technologists, professional member, 1980-; American Association of Cereal Chemists, 1985-92. **HONORS/AWARDS:** NDSU College of Agriculture, Research Excellence, 1991-93; American Heart Association, fellowship, 1984; National Science and Development Council, Research Award, 1982, 1983; Chinese Culture University, Distinguished Alumni, 1980. **SPECIAL ACHIEVEMENTS:** Have 32 full length publications and 34 presentations at the national level; proficient in Chinese, Taiwanese, English, and some Japanese. **BUSINESS ADDRESS:** Associate Pro-

fessor, North Dakota State University, 14CC Computer Center, Room 322, Fargo, ND 58105, (701)237-7485.

CHANG, KWANG-CHIH
Educator. Chinese American. **PERSONAL:** Born Apr 15, 1931, Peking, China; son of Wo-chün and Hsin-hsiang Chang; married Hwei Li Chang, May 19, 1957; children: Julian, Nora. **EDUCATION:** National Taiwan University, BA, 1954; Harvard University, PhD, 1960. **CAREER:** Harvard University, lecturer on anthropology, 1960-61; Yale University, instructor, assistant professor, associate professor, professor in anthropology, 1961-77; Harvard University, professor of anthropology, 1977-84, John E Hudson Professor of Archaeology, 1984-. **ORGANIZATIONS:** American Anthropological Association, fellow, 1960-; Association for Asian Studies, 1960-. **HONORS/AWARDS:** Academia Sinica, 1974; US Natl Academy of Sciences, 1979; American Academy of Arts and Sciences, fellow, 1980; University of Pennsylvania, Lucy Wharton Drexel Medal of Archaelogy, 1987; Chinese University of Hong Kong, honorary doctorate, 1990. **SPECIAL ACHIEVEMENTS:** Various monographs, books, and journal articles in the fields of anthropological archaeology and Chiniese archaeology, 1953-, icnluding: The Archaelogy of Ancient China, Yale, 1963, 1968, 1977, 1986, Shang Civilization, Yale, 1980, The Chinese Bronze Age, Chinese, 1982, 1991, others.

CHANG, KWANG-POO
Educator. Chinese American. **PERSONAL:** Born Nov 12, 1942, Taipei, Taiwan; son of Wo-chung Chang; married Chin Shen Chang, Apr 12, 1972; children: Patrick P. **EDUCATION:** National Taiwan University, BSc, 1965; University of Guelph, MSc, 1968, PhD, 1972. **CAREER:** Rockefeller University, assistant professor, 1976-79, associate professor, 1979-83; Chicago Medical School, professor, 1983-. **ORGANIZATIONS:** American Society Microbiology, 1976-; American Society Tropical Medicine and Hygiene, 1977-; American Society Parasitologists, 1975-; American Society Cell Biology, 1977-; Society Protozoologists, 1976-. **HONORS/AWARDS:** Society Protozoologists, Semour Hutner Prize, 1982; Chicago Medical School, Morris E Parker Award, 1985; Irma T Hirschl Foundation, Career Science Award, 1977; Ontario Entomology Soc, President Prize, 1968. **SPECIAL ACHIEVEMENTS:** Author of approximately 80 scientific papers, 1969-; editor, Leishmaniasis, Elsvier, 1985; NATO Symposium volume, 1987. **BUSINESS ADDRESS:** Professor, University Health Sci, Chicago Medical School, 3333 Green Bay Rd, North Chicago, IL 60064, (708)578-3230.

CHANG, LOUIS WAI-WAH
Educator. Chinese American. **PERSONAL:** Born Jul 1, 1944, Hong Kong; son of Ernest Y P Chang and Jeanne M W Ma-Chang; married Jane Chih-Chun Wang, Sep 26, 1988; children: Michael, Jennifer Michelle. **EDUCATION:** University of Massachusetts, Amherst, BA, chemistry, 1966; Harvard University Medical School, MS, anatomy & histochemistry; Tufts University Medical School, MS, anatomy & histochemistry, 1969; University of Wisconsin-Madison Med School, PhD, pathology, 1972. **CAREER:** University of Wisconsin Med School, assistant professor of pathology, 1972-77; University of Arkansas College of Med, professor of pathology, 1977-. **ORGANIZATIONS:** Am Assoc of Pathologists, 1972-; Am Assoc of Neuropathology, 1972-; Society of Toxicology, 1977-; Society of Neuroscience, 1977-; Society of Toxicopathologists, 1980-; Am Assoc of Advancement of Sci, 1972-; Am Chinese Toxicology Society, 1986-, president, 1988-90; Society of Chinese Bioscientists in America, 1989-. **HONORS/AWARDS:** Am Histotech Society, Golden Forcep Award, 1975. **SPECIAL ACHIEVEMENTS:** US Congress Advisory Panel on Neuroscience, 1988; assoc editor, Neurotoxicology & Teratology, 1982-90; managing editor, Biomedical & Environ Sciences, 1992-; organizer & chairman, Asian Toxicology Conferences, 1990-; editor, 4 vol of Neurotoxicology, 2 vol of Risk Assessment; 2 vol, Metal Toxicol, 1993-94. **BUSINESS ADDRESS:** Professor, Depts of Pathology, Pharmacology & Toxicology, University of Arkansas, Medical Sciences, 4301 W Markham St, Slot 517, Shorey Bldg, Little Rock, AR 72205, (501)686-6400.

CHANG, MABEL LI
Educator. Hong Kong American. **PERSONAL:** Born in Hong Kong; daughter of Mr & Mrs H C Li; married T Timothy Chang, Nov 23, 1957; children: Robert T. **EDUCATION:** National Central University, BA, 1945; Manhattanville College of the Sacred Heart, BA, 1948; New York University, MA, 1948, PhD, 1956. **CAREER:** Nankai University Library, China, translator, 1943-44; Yu Fung Mills, China, executive staff, English teacher, 1944-45; United China Relief, Shanghai, assistant to chief accountant, 1945-46; Catholic Interracial Council of New York, Claver Index Project, head, 1948-60; CUNY,

Bernard Baruch School of Business Administration, lecturer, 1960-65; HEW, Health Insurance Benefits Advisory Council, consultant, 1974-78; Bronx Community College, CUNY, instructor to professor, 1962-92, professor emerita, currently. **ORGANIZATIONS:** Chinese American Scholars Association, trustee, 1990-; Asian American Higher Education Council, trustee, 1991-; Professional Staff Congress, CUNY Retiree Chapter, 1992-; Association for Comparative Economics, charter member, 1960-; American Economic Association, 1947-; Allied Social Sciences Association, 1970-; History of Economics Society, 1974-. **HONORS/AWARDS:** Bronx Community College, Student Government Awards, 1978, 1984; Foundation for Economic Education, Fellowship, 1967; University of Chicago, Seminar on Applied Economics, GE Foundation Grantee, 1964; New York University, Founders Day Award, 1957; United Board for Christian Higher Education in Asia, Fellow, 1955-56. **SPECIAL ACHIEVEMENTS:** MIT, Certificate in Urban Economics, 1973; co-author: Economics for Hong Kong, Longmans Publishing, 1970; author: Exercises in Microeconomcis, BCC Printing, 1976; Workbook in Microeconomics, Avery Press, 1978; Basic Concepts in Microeconomics, BCC Printing, 1991. **HOME PHONE:** (212)864-5910. **BUSINESS ADDRESS:** Professor Emerita, Social Sciences Dept, Bronx Community College of CUNY, University Ave & 181 St, Bronx, NY 10453, (718)220-6350.

CHANG, MARIA HSIA
Educator. Hong Kong American. **PERSONAL:** Born Mar 17, 1950, Hong Kong; daughter of Chang Pao-en & Huang Lu; married A James Gregor, Dec 22, 1987; children: Charles Elmo. **EDUCATION:** University of California, Berkeley, BA, 1973, MA, 1975, PhD, 1983. **CAREER:** Washington State University, visiting assistant professor, 1980-82; University of Puget Sound, assistant professor, 1983-89; University of Nevada, Reno, associate professor, 1989-. **ORGANIZATIONS:** American Association of Chinese Studies, board of directors, 1990-92. **HONORS/AWARDS:** Hoover Institution, National Fellow, 1984-85. **SPECIAL ACHIEVEMENTS:** The Chinese Blue Shirt Society, University of California, Berkeley, East Asian Studies Institute, 1985; Human Rights of the People's Republic of China, Westview, 1988; The Iron Triangle: A US Security Policy for NE Asia, Hoover Institution, 1984; Ideology and Development: Sun Yat-sen and the Economic History of Taiwan, University of California, Berkeley, East Asian Studies Institute, 1981. **BUSINESS ADDRESS:** Associate Professor, Political Science Dept, University of Nevada, Reno, Reno, NV 89557-0060, (702)784-4323.

CHANG, MARIAN S.
Filmmaker, composer, choreographer. Korean American. **PERSONAL:** Born Aug 19, 1958, Atlanta, GA; daughter of C H Joseph Chang & C S Chun. **EDUCATION:** Harvard University, BA, music, 1981; MIT, Experimental Music Studio, computer music, 1985-86; Columbia University, MFA, film, 1993. **CAREER:** Boston-based composer/choreographer for experimental theater, dance, 1981-88; Performing Arts Ensemble, composer for modern dance company, 1986-88; Theatre S, choreographer, co-director, performer for experimental theater co, 1987-88; independent producer, director, screenwriter, 1991-. **ORGANIZATIONS:** Shy Artists Productions, founder, producer for theater, performances & film, 1988-. **HONORS/AWARDS:** Massachusetts Artists Fellowship Program, award recipient, finalist in music composition, 1988, award recipient, finalist in choreography, 1987; Kansas City Music Scholarship Competition, first prize, 1976. **SPECIAL ACHIEVEMENTS:** My Ego Floats in the Secretarial Pool, writer, director, producer of original musical 16mm film, 1993; first creative artist in the history of the Massachusetts Artists Fellowship Program to be recognized in both music composition and choreography for performed works, including: Beach Episode, from An Acquired Taste, 1986, Study in Light, 1985, Down the Path by Sparkling Streams-Gently for 2,000 Years, 1987, I Heard Sad Angels' Voices, 1988. **HOME ADDRESS:** 220 East 27th St, #7, New York, NY 10016.

CHANG, MERVIN HENRY
Educational administrator. Chinese American. **PERSONAL:** Born Sep 11, 1946, Honolulu, HI; son of Henry K C & Rita Y Chang; married Karen J Chang, Dec 20, 1975. **EDUCATION:** Porterville Junior College, AA, 1966; Fresno State College, BA, 1968, standard teaching credential, 1969. **CAREER:** Lompoc Unified School District, industrial arts, teacher, 1969-80; University of Hawaii, drafting tech, associate professor, 1981-92, assistant dean of instruction, 1992-. **ORGANIZATIONS:** National Tech Prep Network, 1991-; Hawaii Joint Apprenticeship Committee, 1991-. **SPECIAL ACHIEVEMENTS:** Lompoc Flower Festival, multi-media acrylic/watercolor, 1st place, 1976; Honolulu Community College, implemented computer-aided drafting and design, 1982. **BUSINESS ADDRESS:** Assistant Dean of

Instruction, Honolulu Community College, 874 Dillingham Blvd, Administration Bldg, 2nd Fl, Honolulu, HI 96817, (808)845-9229.

CHANG, MICHAEL
Tennis player. Chinese American. **PERSONAL:** Born Feb 22, 1972, Hoboken, NJ; son of Joe Chang and Betty Chang. **CAREER:** Professional tennis player, currently; tournaments include: French Open, Wimbledon, Canadian Open, US Open. **ORGANIZATIONS:** US Davis Cup Team, 1990. **HONORS/AWARDS:** Tournaments won include: USTA Boys 18, Junior Hardcourts, 1987, Nationals, 1987, San Francisco, 1988; French Open, 1989; London Indoor, 1990; Canadian Open, 1990; Birmingham, 1991; Association of Tennis Professionals, Salem Open, China, 1993. **BUSINESS ADDRESS:** Professional Tennis Player, c/o Tom Ross, Advantage, 1025 Thomas Jefferson St NW, Ste 450E, Washington, DC 20007, (202)333-3838.*

CHANG, MICHAEL S.
Educator, school board member. Chinese American/Hong Kong American. **PERSONAL:** Born Feb 6, 1957, Hong Kong; son of Coolidge K L Chang & Bette Owen; married Barbara; children: Jonathan, Jacquelyn. **EDUCATION:** San Francisco University, BA, 1980, BS, 1980; Stanford University, MA, 1984, MA, 1985, PhD, 1988. **CAREER:** Stanford University, program associate, 1981-88, resident fellow, 1985-90; San Francisco State University, lecturer, 1987-89; UC Berkeley, research associate director, 1988-89; De Anza College, chair, Asian/Asian American Studies, 1989-. **ORGANIZATIONS:** Asian Americans for Community Involvement, chairman of the board, 1993-; American Educational Research Association; Association for Asian American Studies; Association for Asian Studies; Comparative and International Education Society. **HONORS/AWARDS:** Fulbright Scholar Group to China, 1985; Stanford University, Shaw Fellowship, 1981-86; San Francisco State University, Beta Gamma Sigma, 1980, Beta Alpha Psi, 1979. **SPECIAL ACHIEVEMENTS:** "Education and Socioeconomic Progress: Immigrant and Native-Born Chinese Americans," 1989; "Economic Choices: China After Mao," 1988; "Rural Development in China," 1987; "Chinese Americans and San Francisco Chinatown," 1984; "China Resources: A Guide for the Classroom," 1986. **BUSINESS ADDRESS:** Department Chair, Asian/Asian American Studies, De Anza College, 21250 Stevens Creek Blvd, Cupertino, CA 95014, (408)864-8878.

CHANG, MING
Banker, port commissioner. Chinese American. **PERSONAL:** Born 1952?. **EDUCATION:** Georgetown University, School of Foreign Service, BS. **CAREER:** Swiss Bank Corporation, vice president, currently. **ORGANIZATIONS:** San Francisco Port Commission, commissioner, 1992-; University of San Francisco Center for the Pacific Rim, executive advsiory board, 1992-. **BUSINESS ADDRESS:** Vice President, Swiss Bank Corporation, 101 California, San Francisco, CA 94111, (415)693-8814.*

CHANG, MINGTEH
Educator. Chinese American. **PERSONAL:** Born Jan 18, 1939, Fui-Aun, Fukien, China; married Connie; children: Benjamin, Rebecca, Solomon. **EDUCATION:** National Chung-Hsing University, BS, 1960; Penn State University, MS, 1968; West Virginia University, PhD, 1973. **CAREER:** West Virginia University, Water Research Institute, research associate, 1973-75, Division of Forestry, assistant professor, 1974-75; Stephen F Austin State University, assistant professor, 1975-81, associate professor, 1981-88, professor, 1988-. **ORGANIZATIONS:** American Geophysical Union, 1973-; American Water Resources Association, committee member, 1982-; Soil/Water Conservation Society of America, 1973-; IUFRO, 1982; Texas Forestry Association, 1975-; Chinese Soil/Water Conservation Society, 1984; Chinese Forestry Association, 1984-. **HONORS/AWARDS:** American Institute of Hydrology, certified professional hydrologist, 1984; Xi Sigma Pi; Gamma Sigma Delta. **SPECIAL ACHIEVEMENTS:** More than 60 technical papers published in professional journals; published one textbook at college senior level. **MILITARY SERVICE:** Chinese Army, surveying official, 2nd lt, 1961-62. **BUSINESS ADDRESS:** Professor, College of Forestry, Stephen F Austin State University, Box 6109, SFA Station, Forestry Laboratory, #108, Nacogdoches, TX 75962.

CHANG, MOON K.
Educator. Korean American. **PERSONAL:** Born May 11, 1941, Pusan, Republic of Korea; son of Yonghan Chang and Pogil Park Chang; married Ahn Hyee S Chang, Dec 29, 1972; children: JeUn, JeSuk. **EDUCATION:** Pusan National University, Korea, BA, 1963, MA, 1967; University of Tennessee, Knoxville, MS, 1976, EdD, 1982. **CAREER:** Nicholls State University, associate profes-

sor, 1987-90; Alabama State University, associate professor, 1990-. **ORGANIZATIONS:** Americans with Disabilities Task Force, 1991-; Cultural Diversity Task Force, 1989-91; Council for Exceptional Children, Mental Retardation Division, president, 1990-91; Society of Test Anxiety Research, 1983-; International Council of Psychologists, 1990-; National Teachers Association, 1992-; International Speacial Education Association, 1990-; Kapper Delta Pi, 1983-. **SPECIAL ACHIEVEMENTS:** Integracio escalar, in I Puigdelivol et al, editors, Universitat de Barcelona, Temps d'Educacio, p 27-38, 1991; "Advance organizers, memory tasks and anxiety of children with mild handicaps," Reading Improvement, vol 29, no 1, p 56-57, 1992; "Integration: An American Perspective," REACH, Dublin, Ireland, vol 5, no 1, p 35-40, 1991; "Reach on Down Syndrome: A Review," Looking up at Down Syndrome, Freund, London, 1990; "Logo Research in General and Special Education," Teaching and Learning in Logo-based Environments, Gent, Netherlands, IOS, 1990. **HOME ADDRESS:** PO Box 240972, Montgomery, AL 36117, (205)260-0091.

CHANG, MOU-HSIUNG
Educator. Chinese American. **PERSONAL:** Born Nov 6, 1944, Tainan, Taiwan; son of Mr & Mrs Kings Chang; married Yuen Chang, Jan 24, 1971; children: Dennis, Jeffrey, Pamela. **EDUCATION:** National Chung-Hsing University, BS, applied mathematics, 1967; University of Rhode Island, MS, mathematics, 1971, PhD, mathematics, 1974. **CAREER:** Massachusetts Institute of Technology, visiting scientist, 1984-85; University of Alabama, Huntsville, assistant professor, 1974-78, associate professor, 1978-85, professor of mathematical sciences, 1985-, chairman of mathematical sciences, 1993-. **ORGANIZATIONS:** American Mathematical Society, 1972-; Society for Industrial & Applied Mathematics, 1980-. **SPECIAL ACHIEVEMENTS:** Published more than 30 papers on mathematics in professional journals. **BUSINESS ADDRESS:** Professor, Chairman, Dept of Mathematical Sciences, University of Alabama, Huntsville, 4701 University Dr, Huntsville, AL 35899-0100, (205)895-6470.

CHANG, MYRON N.
Educator. Chinese American. **PERSONAL:** Born Jan 12, 1941, China; son of Shen C Chang and Mei L Chang; married Vivian T Chang, Feb 18, 1972; children: Diane, Debbie, Danielle C. **EDUCATION:** University of Maryland, College Park, MS, 1981, PhD, 1984. **CAREER:** Mayo Clinic, research associate, 1984-86; University of Florida, assistant professor, 1966-91, associate professor, 1991-. **ORGANIZATIONS:** American Statistical Association; Biometric Society; Institute of Mathematical Statistics. **HONORS/AWARDS:** Merck & Co, first Stanley S Schor Visiting Scholar, 1992. **SPECIAL ACHIEVEMENTS:** Publications have appeared in the Annuals of Statistics, Journal of the American Statistical Association, Biometerics, Technometrics, Nonparametric Statistics, Communications in Statistics, Mathematical Biosciences, Statistics in Medicine, Controlled Clinical Trials, Journal of Clinical Oncology, Cancer, Cancer Treatment Reports, and Head and Neck Surgery. **BUSINESS ADDRESS:** Professor, Dept of Statistics, University of Florida, 103 Griffin Floyd Hall, Gainesville, FL 32611, (904)392-1941.

CHANG, NANCY SIU. *See* SIU, NANCY.

CHANG, NELSON
Commodities company executive. Chinese American. **PERSONAL:** Born Jul 17, 1923, Shanghai, China; son of Nai Chi Chang and June Zee Chang; married Edith Hsi, Apr 3, 1954; children: Phyllis, Edmund, Laurence. **EDUCATION:** Wharton School of Finance, 1947; MIT, BS, 1948. **CAREER:** American Cyanamid Co, sales engineer, 1948-51; Orvis Bros & Co, commodity futures broker, 1952-57; Reynolds Securities, Commodity Dept, eastern sales manager, 1957-63; Hayden Stone Inc, commodity futures broker, 1963-71, Commodity Research and Training, vp, director, 1971-73, Shearson, Hayden Stone, senior vp, director, 1973-80, Shearson Amex, Commodity Research and Strategic Planning, senior vp, director; Hayden Commodities, president, 1982-89; Shearson Amex Asia Ltd, board of directors, 1980-89; Shearson Lehman Amex, adv director, 1985-89; Lehman Brothers, vp, 1990; Chang Crowell Management Corp, chairman, 1990-. **BUSINESS ADDRESS:** Chairman, Chang Crowell Management Corp, 800 Connecticut Ave, Norwalk, CT 06854.*

CHANG, NGEE-PONG
Educator. Singaporean American. **PERSONAL:** Born Dec 24, 1940, Singapore; married Mabel, Jun 6, 1965; children: Belinda, Eugene. **EDUCATION:** Ohio Wesleyan University, BA, 1959; Columbia University, PhD, 1963. **CAREER:** Columbia University, research associate, 1962-63; Institute for Advanced Study, research fellow, 1963-64; Rockfeller University, research associate, 1964-65; City College of CUNY, visiting professor, 1965-66, professor of physics, 1966-. **ORGANIZATIONS:** American Physical Society, fellow; Phi Beta Kappa; Sigma Xi; Japan Society for Promotion of Science, fellow, 1974; Asian American Higher Education Council, council member, 1992-; Overseas Chinese Physics Association, president, 1990-92; CCNY China Exchange, director, 1981-. **HONORS/AWARDS:** CCNY Alumni Association, Service Award, 1984; Conference of Minority Public Administrators, New York Chapter, Honoree, 1986; CCNY Chinese Alumni Group, Honoree, 1986; Asian American Higher Education Council, Honoree, 1993. **SPECIAL ACHIEVEMENTS:** Over 65 publications in such refereed professional journals as Physical Review, Physical Review Letters, Physics Letters, etc. **BUSINESS ADDRESS:** Professor, City College of CUNY, 138th St & Convent Ave, Room J311, Science Bldg, New York, NY 10031, (212)650-6884.

CHANG, PATRICIA W.
Women's rights activist. Chinese American. **CAREER:** Children's Hospital Foundation, director of trusts and bequests; Commission on the Status of Women, appointed member, 1992-; Women's Foundation, executive director, currently. **HONORS/AWARDS:** Fresno-Merced Counties Legal Services, Reginald Heber Smith Community Law Fellow. **BUSINESS ADDRESS:** Executive Director, Women's Foundation, 3543 18th St, #9, San Francisco, CA 94110, (415)431-1290.*

CHANG, PAUL KEUB
Educator, engineer. Korean American. **PERSONAL:** Born Apr 8, 1913, Inchon, Kyongi, Republic of Korea; son of Kibin Chang and Lucca Huang; married Frances W S Miu, Nov 26, 1955; children: Sophia W S Chang Lowe, Teresa W S. **EDUCATION:** Technische Hochschule, Berlin, dipl, ing, 1940; New York University, MAE, 1948; Harvard University, MS, 1949; University of Notre Dame, ScD, 1951; Technische universitat Berlin, Dr, Ing, 1963. **CAREER:** Daimler Benz Motoren, Germany, aeronautical engineer, 1941-42; Brown Boveri and Cie, Switzerland, mech engineer, 1946-47; Ainearch Manufacturing Co, prel design engineer, 1952-54; Lockheed Aircraft Corp, research specialist, 1954-58; Catholic University of America, professor, 1958-79, professor emeritus, 1979-; US Naval Ship Research & Development Center, consultant, 1958-63; US Naval Research Laboratory, consultant, 1963-68; US Naval Research Station, consultant, 1968-71; US Naval Ordnance Laboratory, consultant, 1971-76; Korea Advanced Institute of Science & Technology, professor, 1979-88; Comsat General Corp, consultant, 1983; Korea Aerospace Research Institute, consultant, 1993-. **ORGANIZATIONS:** American Institute of Aeronautics & Astronautics, associate fellow; Tau Beta Pi; Sigma Si. **HONORS/AWARDS:** Council for International Exchange of Scholars, Fulbright-Hays, 1963-65, 1990-91; National Research Council, Research Aeronautics, 1986-87; National Cheng Kung University, visiting professor, 1985; National Defense Academy, Yokosuka, visiting professor, 1984; National Academy of Sciences, exchange scholar, 1977-78, 1982; Organization of American States, visiting professor, 1973. **SPECIAL ACHIEVEMENTS:** Books: Separation of Flow, Pergamon Press, 1970; Control of Flow Separation, McGraw Hill, 1976; Otnivnie Techenia (Russian), MIR Publishers, 1972-73; Recent Development in Flow Separation, Pan Hau Pub Co, Seoul, 1985; World Scientific Journey (Korean), 1986; over 50 scientific and technical papers and reports; Upralinie OPtrivom Potoka (Russian), MIR Publishers, 1976. **HOME ADDRESS:** 8005 Falstaff Rd, Mc Lean, VA 22102, (703)356-1135.

CHANG, PAUL PENG-CHENG
Engineering consulting company executive. Chinese American. **PERSONAL:** Born Aug 19, 1931, Jiangtu, Jiangsu, China; son of Su-An Chang and Hwei-Lin (Lou) Chang; married Kristina H Chang, Aug 19, 1968; children: Conway C, Tina C. **EDUCATION:** Taiwan Chen-Kung University, BS, 1956; University of Oklahoma, ME, 1966. **CAREER:** Taiwan Power Company, engr, 1958-64; Sargent & Lundy Engineers Inc, engr, 1966-68; Bechtel Power Corp, supervising engr, 1968-74; Kaisar Engineers Power Corp, principal engr, 1974-80; Gibbs & Hill Inc, asst chief engr, 1980-85; Dravo Engineering Co Inc, chief engr, 1985-88; PPC Consulting Engineers, president, owner, 1988-. **ORGANIZATIONS:** Chinese Engineering Assn, 1960-64. **HONORS/AWARDS:** Taiwan Power Company, Best Underground Pressure Grouting Inspection Performance, 1963. **MILITARY SERVICE:** Air Force Base Service, Taiwan, ROTC, 1956-58. **BUSINESS ADDRESS:** President, Owner, PPC Consulting Engineers, 44577 Parkmeadow Dr, Fremont, CA 94539, (510)659-1425.

CHANG, PAUL STEVEN

Military physician. Chinese American. **PERSONAL:** Born Sep 5, 1956, Carmel, CA; son of Jason Chang and Rhea Kuo Chang; married Mary Clark Chang, Oct 23, 1991; children: Elizabeth Sarah. **EDUCATION:** United States Military Academy, BS, 1978; Chicago College of Osteopathic Medicine, DO, 1991; Walter Reed Army Medical Center, 1991-92. **CAREER:** US Army, platoon leader/company executive officer, 1979-81, 10th Special Forces Group, team leader, 1982-84, staff officer, 1984-85; US Army Intelligence Center, company commander, 1985-86, aide-de-camp commanding general, Ft. Devens, MA, 1986-87, intern class president, 1991-92, emergency room physician, 1992-. **ORGANIZATIONS:** Professional Ski Instructors of America, 1976-. **HONORS/AWARDS:** United States Military Academy, Community Service Award, 1978;. **SPECIAL ACHIEVEMENTS:** Walter Reed Army Medical Center, intern class president, 1991. **MILITARY SERVICE:** Medical Corps, Special Forces, Military Intelligence, major, 1974-; Army Achievement Medal, 1992, Meritorious Service Medal, 1987, Army Commemoration Medal, 1981, 1984, National Defense Service Medal, 1975, 1991. Richard S Weiner, Community Service Award, 1974; US Military Academy, Community Service Award, 1978.

CHANG, PEI K.

Scientist. Chinese American. **PERSONAL:** Born Jan 9, 1936, ChingZao, Shandong, China; son of Wen Hwa Chang and Hsu C Chang; married Charlotte, Sep 2, 1966; children: Michael. **EDUCATION:** National Taiwan University, BS, 1960; Colorado State University, MS, 1964; University of Wisconsin, PhD, 1969; NY Institute of Technology, MBA, 1982. **CAREER:** Stauffer Chemical, research associate, 1968-83; Food Science Associates, senior associate, 1983-85; Modern Maids, R&D, director, 1985; General Foods, technical supervisor, 1985-87; Pepsico, principal scientist, 1987-. **ORGANIZATIONS:** Institute of Food Technologists, 1968-; American Association of Cereal Chemists. **SPECIAL ACHIEVEMENTS:** Holder of 13 food related patents; author of six publications. **BUSINESS ADDRESS:** Principal Scientist, Pepsico, 100 Stevens Ave, Valhalla, NY 10595.

CHANG, PETER ASHA, JR.

Attorney. Korean American. **PERSONAL:** Born Feb 1, 1937, Honolulu, HI; son of Peter A Chang Sr and Helen Lee; divorced; children: Peter III, Catherine, Christopher. **EDUCATION:** Stanford University, AB, 1958, LLB, 1961. **CAREER:** Monterey County, CA, assistant district attorney, 1962-66; Santa Cruz County, CA, district attorney, 1966-75; USA Dept of Justice Strike Force, attorney, 1975; Law Offices of Perz A Chang Jr, owner, 1975-. **ORGANIZATIONS:** National Association of Criminal Defense Lawyers, director, 1991-94; American Board of Criminal Lawyers, fellow, 1990. **HONORS/AWARDS:** California District Attorneys Association, Prosecutor of the Year Award, 1972; National Association of Criminal Defense Lawyers, President's Commendation, 1992. **SPECIAL ACHIEVEMENTS:** Author: "History, Literature and Analogy: A New Perspective on an Old Technique," Mercer Law Review, Fall, 1991; "The Sixth Amendment Right to Counsel," Champion Magazine, Bicentennial Bill of Rights Series, June, 1992; "Reflections on Final Argument," National Association of Criminal Defense Lawyers Publication, 1992; admitted to practice: California; Federal Bar of the Northern, Central, Eastern, Southern Districts of California, Hawaii; US Court of Appeals for 9th, 7th and 5th Circuits & US Supreme Court. **BUSINESS ADDRESS:** Attorney at Law, 331 Soquel Ave, Ste 100, Santa Cruz, CA 95062, (408)429-9191.

CHANG, PETER C.

Educator. Hong Kong American. **PERSONAL:** Born May 3, 1955, Hong Kong; married Suely Chang. **EDUCATION:** Texas A&M University, BS, 1975; University of Illinois, Urbana-Champaign, MS, 1978, PhD, 1982. **CAREER:** University of Maryland, associate professor, currently. **ORGANIZATIONS:** American Society of Civil Engineering, structural analysis committee member; American Society of Engineering Educators. **BUSINESS ADDRESS:** Associate Professor, Dept of Civil Engineering, University of Maryland, College Park, MD 20742, (301)405-1957.

CHANG, PING

Educator. Chinese American. **PERSONAL:** Born Oct 22, 1960, Wuhan, People's Republic of China; son of Xian Zheng Chang and Bi Xia Mi; married Zheng Ye Yang, Aug 18, 1987; children: Lulu. **EDUCATION:** East China Engineering Institute, Nanjing, BS, 1982; City College of New York, ME, 1984; Princeton University, MA, 1986, PhD, 1988. **CAREER:** University of Washington, postdoctoral research associate, 1988-90; Texas A&M University, assistant professor, 1990-. **ORGANIZATIONS:** American Geophysical

Union, 1988-; American Meteorological Society, 1990-. **HONORS/AWARDS:** National Science Foundation, Young Investigator Award, 1993. **SPECIAL ACHIEVEMENTS:** With G Philander, "Rossby Wave Packets in Baroclinic Mean Current," Deep Sea Res, 1989; "Oceanic Adjustments in the Presence of Mean Current in a Reduced Gravity Ocean," J Geophy Res, 1990; "Coastal Kelvin Waves in the Presence of a Slowly Varying Topography," J Fluid Mech, 1991; "Solitary Waves along Potential Vorticity Fronts on an f-plane," J Oceanogr, 1992; "Seasonal Cycle of Sea Surface Temperatures and the Mixed Layer Heat Budget," Geophys Res, 1993. **BUSINESS ADDRESS:** Assistant Professor, Dept of Oceanography, Texas A&M University, College Station, TX 77843-3146, (409)845-8196.

CHANG, REN-FANG

Government lab research scientist. Chinese American. **PERSONAL:** Born Jan 14, 1938, China; married Elizabeth, Apr 27, 1968. **EDUCATION:** National Taiwan University, BS, 1960; University of Maryland, PhD, 1968. **CAREER:** University of Maryland, 1962-78; National Institute of Standards and Technology, government lab research scientist, 1978-. **ORGANIZATIONS:** APS; AAAS; Sigma Xi. **HONORS/AWARDS:** NASA, Apollo II Achievement Award, 1969. **SPECIAL ACHIEVEMENTS:** Numerous publications in professional journals. **BUSINESS ADDRESS:** Government Lab Research Scientist, National Institute of Standards & Technology, Bldg 221, Rm A105, Gaithersburg, MD 20899.

CHANG, RICHARD

Orthodontist. Taiwanese American. **PERSONAL:** Born Jul 29, 1962, Gaoshiung, Taiwan; son of Hong Li and Jean. **EDUCATION:** Kalamazoo College, BA, 1984; Harvard University, DMD, 1989; St Louis University, MSD, 1993. **CAREER:** Private practice, orthodontist, 1992-. **ORGANIZATIONS:** American Assn of Orthodontists, 1991-; American Dental Assn, 1985-; American Board of Orthodontics, certified member, 1992. **HONORS/AWARDS:** American Board of Orthodontics, Board Certification, 1992. **SPECIAL ACHIEVEMENTS:** Publications: Mapping the Visual Cortex of Macaque Monkey, 1984; Hairy Oral Leukoplakia Associated with AIDS, 1988; Baby Bottle Tooth Decay in Native American School Children, 1989. **HOME ADDRESS:** 16929 Glen Oak Run, Rockville, MD 20855, (301)926-2219. **BUSINESS PHONE:** (301)424-0136.

CHANG, ROBERT C.

Educator. Chinese American. **PERSONAL:** Born Jan 3, 1928, Tsingtao, China; son of Chang Shou-yu & Liang Mou-fan; married Sonia Chang, Sep 5, 1959; children: Anthony, Wesley. **EDUCATION:** University of San Francisco, BS, 1951; New York University, MBA, 1954, PhD, 1964. **CAREER:** Consultant to various businesses; University of Bridgeport, associate professor of accounting, currently. **HOME ADDRESS:** 81 Kent Ln, Trumbull, CT 06611, (203)261-6326.

CHANG, ROBERT HUEI

University library director. Chinese American. **PERSONAL:** Born Feb 20, 1932, Tai-an, Shandong, China; son of Yung Chian Chang & Lung Gui Liu; married Helen H P Chang, Dec 16, 1967; children: Edward, Annie. **EDUCATION:** National Chengchi University, Taipei, BA, 1960; University of Missouri-Columbia, MA, 1966; Western Michigan University, MLS, 1967; University of Iowa, PhD, 1975. **CAREER:** United Daily News, reporter, 1960-63; Pittsburg State University, document librarian, 1967-68; East Tennessee State University, acquisition librarian, 1968-69; University of Tennessee, Chattanooga, head book orderer, 1969-70; Upper Iowa University, assistant professor, 1970-71; University of Missouri-Columbia, IMC, assistant professor, director, 1975-77; University of Houston-Downtown, director of library services, 1977-. **ORGANIZATIONS:** AECT, 1977-; ALA, 1977-; Beta Phi Mu, 1967-; CALA, board member, PR committee, award committee chair, 1978-; TLA, 1978-; US Shandong Fellowship Association, president, 1993-; Phi Delta Kappa, 1975-; APALA, 1978-. **HONORS/AWARDS:** National Chengchi University, Journalism Scholarship Award, 1957-60; University of Houston-Downtown, CJ Center, Service Award, 1989. **SPECIAL ACHIEVEMENTS:** Author, "System Approach to Your PR Program," Audiovisual Instruction, April 1977; Journal of Educational Media and Library Science: "The Impact of LRC Concept on Media Education," fall 1982, "An Integrated Library System for the University of Houston Libraries," summer 1983, "To Classify or Not to Classify? A New Look at an Old Problem," winter 1989; "A Proposal for Developing Community Colleges in Taiwan," National Development Seminar—Section of Culture and Education: Written Recommendations and Papers, Taipei Ministry of Education and Commission on Culture Development, part II, p 1-11, 1989; columns and editorial writing for several Chinese newspapers; hundreds of articles published in several Chinese newspapers. **HOME ADDRESS:** 5414 Whisper Ridge Dr, Sugar Land, TX 77479. **BUSINESS PHONE:** (713)221-8011.

CHANG, SEN-DOU
Educator. Chinese American. **PERSONAL:** Born Aug 16, 1928, Zhejiang, China; son of Songding Chang; married Angela W L Chang, Oct 1981; children: Stanley, Victor. **EDUCATION:** Chi-nan University, China, BA, 1949; University of Wisconsin, MA, 1955; University of Washington, PhD, 1961. **CAREER:** California State University, Northridge, assistant professor, 1962-66; University Washington, visiting lecturer, 1966-67; Chinese University of Hong Kong, chair, professor, 1980-82; University of Hawaii, associate professor, 1967-71, professor, 1971-. **ORGANIZATIONS:** Association of American Geographers, 1962-; American Geographical Society, 1968-; American Society for Photogrammetry and Remote Sensing, 1971-; Association for Asian Studies, 1972-. **HONORS/AWARDS:** Fulbright Committee, Fulbright Scholar, 1977-78. **SPECIAL ACHIEVEMENTS:** Author, ''Peking,'' in Encyclopaedia Britannica (Macropaedia), Vol 14, 1974 edition, p 1-14; contributed articles to: Geographical Review Annals, Association of American Geographers, Professional Geographer, China Geographer, Urban Geography; contributed chapters to: The City in Late Imperial China, Stanford University Press, 1977; China's Coastal Cities, University of Hawaii Press, 1992, several other volumes. **BUSINESS ADDRESS:** Professor of Geography, University of Hawaii, 2424 Maile Way, Porteus Hall 445, Honolulu, HI 96822, (808)956-7157.

CHANG, SHAU-JIN
Educator, educational administrator. Chinese American. **PERSONAL:** Born Jan 7, 1939, Kiangsu, China; son of Nai-Fan Chang and Ti-Chen Tsao; married Ying-Ying Chang, Aug 29, 1964; children: Iris Chang Douglas, Michael. **EDUCATION:** Taiwan University, BS, physics, 1959, Tsing Hua University, MS, physics, 1961; Harvard University, PhD, physics, 1967. **CAREER:** Institute for Advanced Study, member, 1967-69; University of Illinois, assistant professor, 1969-71, associate professor, 1971-74, professor, 1974-, associate head, physics department, 1993-. **ORGANIZATIONS:** American Physical Society, fellow, 1976-; Physical Society of ROC, editor, Chinese Journal of Physics, 1992-. **HONORS/AWARDS:** Dept of Education, ROC, Chinese Natural Science Fellowship, 1955-59; Tsing Hua University, Chow's Fellowship, 1959-61; Harvard University, Parker Fellow, 1964-67; Sloan Foundation, Sloan Fellow, 1972-74. **SPECIAL ACHIEVEMENTS:** Author, Introduction to Quantum Field Theory, World Scientific, 1990. **MILITARY SERVICE:** Nuclear Engineer Corp, ROC Army, 2nd lieutenant, 1961-62. **HOME ADDRESS:** 309 Sherwin Dr, Urbana, IL 61801, (217)367-1746. **BUSINESS ADDRESS:** Associate Head and Professor of Physics, University of Illinois, 1110 W Green St, 317 Loomis Lab, Urbana, IL 61801, (217)333-4360.

CHANG, SHEN CHIE (WILLIAM CHANG)
Educator. Chinese American. **PERSONAL:** Born Apr 4, 1931, Nantong, Jiang-Su, China; son of Tung Wu Chang; married Margaret Kwei Chang, Nov 26, 1955; children: Helen N, Hugh N, Hedy N. **EDUCATION:** University of Michigan, BSEE, 1952, MSEE, 1953; Brown University, PhD, 1957. **CAREER:** Stanford University, lecturer, 1957-59; Ohio State University, associate professor, 1959-65; Washington University, professor, 1965-79; University of California, San Diego, professor, 1979-, dept of electrical and comp engineering, chair, 1993-. **ORGANIZATIONS:** IEEE, fellow; OSA, fellow; AIP; University of California MICRO Executive Committee, chair, 1989-92. **HONORS/AWARDS:** University of Michigan, Distinguished Professional Achievement Award, 1978; Washington University, Samuel Sachs Chair, 1976. **SPECIAL ACHIEVEMENTS:** Author, Principles of Quantum Electronics, Addison-Wesley, 1969; more than 100 papers published in IEEE, OSA, and AIP journals. **BUSINESS ADDRESS:** Professor, Chair, Dept of Electrical & Computer Engineering, University of California at San Diego, 9500 Gilman Dr, EBU1 3609, La Jolla, CA 92093-0407, (619)534-2737.

CHANG, SHIH-GER (TED)
Scientist. Taiwanese American. **PERSONAL:** Born Oct 24, 1941, Taipei, Taiwan; son of Tsu-Yin Chang and Yu-Ching T Chang; married; children: Stephanie, Joseph Jarwen, Edward Jarzone. **EDUCATION:** National Taiwan Cheng Kung University, BS, 1964; University of Detroit, MS, 1968; University of California, Berkeley, PhD, 1972. **CAREER:** Lawrence Berkeley Lab, University of California, senior scientist, 1972-. **ORGANIZATIONS:** American Chemical Society; American Institute of Chemical Engineering; Air Pollution

and Waste Management Association. **HONORS/AWARDS:** Federal Laboratory Consortium, USA, Excellence in Technology Transfer, 1992. **SPECIAL ACHIEVEMENTS:** More than fifty professional publications in environmental chemistry; more than ten patents on air pollution control technology; Academia Sinica, China, lectureships, 1981, 1987; National Science Council, Taiwan, lectureships, 1987. **BUSINESS ADDRESS:** Principal Investigator, Lawrence Berkeley Laboratory, University of California, 1 Cyclotron Road, M/S 70-193A, Berkeley, CA 94720, (510)486-5125.

CHANG, SHIN-JYH FRANK
Operations research analyst. Chinese American. **PERSONAL:** Born Jan 3, 1956, Taipei, Taiwan; son of Chih-Gong Chang and Ai-Chin Chu Chang; married Shiouh-Lin Wung Chang, Jul 7, 1981; children: Mingli, Minghan. **EDUCATION:** National Tsing-Hua University, BS, 1977; Michigan State University, MS, 1983; Columbia University, PhD, 1989. **CAREER:** Caliper Corp, sr operations research analyst, 1989-90; GTE Labs Inc, sr member, technical staff, operations research analyst, 1990-. **ORGANIZATIONS:** Operations Research Society of America, 1987-; IEEE, 1991-. **HONORS/AWARDS:** GTE Laboratories, Superior Performance Award, 1993. **HOME ADDRESS:** 7 Independence Rd, Bedford, MA 01730. **BUSINESS ADDRESS:** Senior Member, Technical Staff, GTE Laboratories, Inc, 40 Sylvan Rd, MS-17, Waltham, MA 02254, (617)466-2884.

CHANG, SHING I.
Educator. Taiwanese American. **PERSONAL:** Born Mar 15, 1961, Taipei, Taiwan; son of Yun Chang and Li-Ming Tseng; married Chih-Ching Ma, Jun 1, 1986; children: Michelle. **EDUCATION:** Tsong University, BS, 1983, Arizona State University, MS, 1987; Ohio State University, PhD, 1991. **CAREER:** Kansas State University, assistant professor, 1991-. **ORGANIZATIONS:** IIE, 1991-; ASQC, 1991-. **MILITARY SERVICE:** Army, 2nd lt, 1983-85; Best Service Awards. **BUSINESS ADDRESS:** Asst Prof, Industrial Engineering, Kansas State University, 228 Durland Hall, Manhattan, KS 66506-5101, (913)532-5606.

CHANG, SHIRLEY LIN (HSIU-CHU)
Educator, librarian. Taiwanese American. **PERSONAL:** Born Jun 22, 1937, Chiayi, Taiwan; daughter of Chu-kung Lin & Ying Chang Lin; married Parris H Chang, Aug 3, 1963; children: Yvette Y, Elaine Y, Bohdan P. **EDUCATION:** National Taiwan University, BA, 1960; Columbia University, MLA, 1963; Penn State University, MA, 1988. **CAREER:** Yale University, catalog assistant, 1963; Columbia University, catalog assistant, 1964; Penn State University, ref librarian, 1970-75; Lock Haven University, catalog reference librarian, 1979-. **ORGANIZATIONS:** Chinese American Librarians Association; ALA. **HOME ADDRESS:** 1221 Edward St, State College, PA 16801, (814)237-0538. **BUSINESS ADDRESS:** Catalog/Reference Librarian, Associate Professor, Lock Haven University, Stevenson Library, Lock Haven, PA 17745, (717)893-2312.

CHANG, SIMON
Computer company executive. Chinese American. **CAREER:** CNet Technology Inc, president, currently. **BUSINESS ADDRESS:** President, CNet Technology Inc, 2199 Zanker Rd, San Jose, CA 95131-2109, (408)954-8000.*

CHANG, SOOKYUNG
Research scientist. Korean American. **PERSONAL:** Born Dec 18, 1957, Suwon, Kyung-gi, Republic of Korea; daughter of Sunghoon Chang and Kumjae Chang; married Daniel G Sullivan, Jul 23, 1983; children: Christopher, Kathryn, Kevin. **EDUCATION:** University of California-Los Angeles, 1976-77; University of Chicago, BA, 1980, MS, 1981. **CAREER:** University of Chicago, senior research assistant, 1981-82; Princeton Biomedix, chemist, 1982-85; E M Diagnostic Systems Inc, clinical chemist, 1985; Northwestern University, research technician, 1986-89; Grace/Dearborn Chemical, research scientist I, 1991-. **ORGANIZATIONS:** American Assn for the Advancement of Science, 1992-; California Scholastic Federation, life member. **HONORS/AWARDS:** Edmunson Foundation, Summer Research Fund, 1979. **HOME ADDRESS:** 2025 Sherman, #207, Evanston, IL 60201, (708)328-1918.

CHANG, STEPHEN S.
Educator (retired), consulting company executive. Chinese American. **PERSONAL:** Born Aug 15, 1918, Beijing, China; son of Zie H Chang and Hui F Yuang Chang; married Lucy D Chang, Jun 2, 1952. **EDUCATION:** National Chi-Nan University, BS, 1941; Kansas State University, MS, 1949; University of Illinois, PhD, 1952. **CAREER:** Swift & Company, research chemist, 1955-

57; A E Staley Company, Decatur, senior research chemist, 1957-60; Rutgers State University, professor, 1962-73, professor II, 1973-88, Food Science Department, chairman, 1977-86, professor emeritus, 1988-; Cathay Food Consulting Company Inc, president, chairman of the board, 1983-. **ORGANIZATIONS:** American Oil Chemists' Society, president, 1970-71; Institute of Food Technologists, fellow; American Chemical Society. **HONORS/AWARDS:** American Oil Chemists' Society, Lipid Chemistry Award, 1979, Achievement Award, 1970, A E Bailey Award, 1974; Institute of Food Technologists, Distingushed Food Scientist Award, 1977, fellow, 1974, Nicholas Appert Medal, 1983, International Award, 1989; Japan Oil Chemists' Society, Certificate of Appreciation, 1993; Republic of China, citation from the Prime Minister, 1989, Achievement Award, 1972; Rutgers University, medal, 1988, Award for Excellence in Research, 1984. **SPECIAL ACHIEVEMENTS:** Contributed over 130 articles to scientific journals; patents in lipid chemistry, flavor chemistry and food technology: 24; advisory capacity in the development of food industry in China. **BIOGRAPHICAL SOURCES:** Flavor Chemistry of Lipid Foods, The Stephen S Chang Symposium of the AOCS Honored Scientist Series. **HOME ADDRESS:** 29 Gloucester Court, East Brunswick, NJ 08816, (908)254-5962.

CHANG, SUKJEONG J.
Educator. Korean American. **PERSONAL:** Born Dec 24, 1949, Seoul, Republic of Korea; son of Ki-Ok and Ok-Chung Chang; married Kyunghee Ahn Chang, May 13, 1978; children: Suzie Heejeong, Michael Keeson. **EDUCATION:** Seoul National University, College of Law, Seoul, BA, 1972; Cornell University, Johnson School of Management, MBA, 1981; University of Maryland, PhD, 1986. **CAREER:** Korea Development Bank, assistant manager, 1972-79; University of South Alabama, asst professor, 1986-89; Illinois State University, assoc profesor, 1989-. **ORGANIZATIONS:** American Finance Assn, 1985-; Financial Management Assn, 1986-; Midwest Finance Assn, 1989-; Korea-America Finance Assn, 1987-. **HONORS/AWARDS:** Ministry of Finance, S Korea, Citation, 1975; Korean Government, Korean Honor Scholarship, 1982; Korea Development Bank, Scholarship, 1979; University of S Alabama, Finance Professor of the Year, 1988; Illinois State University, Outstanding Finance Research Award, 1991, 1994. **SPECIAL ACHIEVEMENTS:** A Book of Economic Essays, in Korean, 1993; 35 articles in academic and practical journals, 1988-; journal referees and professional meeting committee, 1988-. **BIOGRAPHICAL SOURCES:** Bibliography of Finance, MIT Press, pp 367, 461, 1991; Illinois Register of Expert Witness, p 55, 1991. **BUSINESS ADDRESS:** Associate Professor of Finance, Illinois State University, Williams Hall, Coll of Business, 5480, Normal, IL 61790-5480, (309)438-2826.

CHANG, SUNG-SHENG YVONNE
Educator. Taiwanese American. **PERSONAL:** Born May 10, 1951, P'ingtung, Taiwan; daughter of Wen-tse & Yu-lan Sun Chang; married Fred P Wang, Aug 31, 1981; children: Eric Y Wang. **EDUCATION:** University of Michigan, MA, 1975; University of Texas, Austin, PhD, 1981; Stanford University, PhD, 1985. **CAREER:** National Taiwan University, visiting lecturer, 1981-82; University of Kansas, assistant professor, 1983-84; University of Texas, assistant professor, 1984-93, associate professor, 1993-. **ORGANIZATIONS:** Association for Asian Studies, 1982-. **SPECIAL ACHIEVEMENTS:** Modernism and the Nativist Resistance: Contemporary Chinese Fiction from Taiwan, Duke University Press, 1993; Bamboo Shoots After the Rain: Contemporary Stories by Women of Taiwan, The Feminist Press, 1991. **HOME ADDRESS:** 9205 Amberwood Cove, Austin, TX 78759. **BUSINESS ADDRESS:** Professor, University of Texas, Austin, 2601 University Ave, UNI 202, Austin, TX 78712, (512)471-1365.

CHANG, SUNG SOOK. *See* **CHOI, SUNG SOOK.**

CHANG, SYLVIA TAN
Health services administrator, educator. Chinese American. **PERSONAL:** Born Dec 18, 1940, Bandung, Java, Indonesia; daughter of Philip H Tan & Lydia S Tan; married Belden S Chang, Aug 30, 1964; children: Donald S, Janice M. **EDUCATION:** Rumah Sakit Advent, School of Nursing, diploma, 1960; Philippine Union College, BS, 1962; Loma Linda University, MS, 1967; Columbia Pacific University, PhD, 1987. **CAREER:** Rumah Sakit Advent, Indonesia, head nurse, 1960-61; White Memorial Medical Center, critical care nurse, team leader, 1963-64; Loma Linda University Medical Center, nursing coordinator, team leader, 1964-66, administrative supervisor, 1967-; Pomona Valley Hospital Medical Center, team leader, head nurse, 1966-67; Columbia Pacific University, faculty mentor, 1986-; La Sierra University, director, health

service, 1988-. **ORGANIZATIONS:** American College Health Association, 1988-; Sigma Theta Tau, 1990-; American Association of Critical-Care Nurses, 1985-; Pacific Coast College Health Association, 1988-; Adventist Student Personnel Association, 1988-; Association of Seventh-day Adventist Nurses, 1967-; Columbia Pacific University Alumni Association, 1987-; Loma Linda University Alumni Association, 1967-. **HONORS/AWARDS:** YWCA, Chamber of Commerce, Press Enterprise, Woman of Achievement, 1991; International Hall of Fame, Distinguished Administrative Service to Profession, 1989; International Roll of Honor, Distinguished Servie to Teaching Profession, 1989. **SPECIAL ACHIEVEMENTS:** Language proficiency: Chinese Mandarin, Indonesian, English; La Sierra University, blood drive coordinator, 1988-; Health Fair Expo site coordinator, 1988-90; workshop speaker, 1992. **BUSINESS ADDRESS:** Director, Health Service, La Sierra University, 4700 Pierce St, Riverside, CA 92515, (909)785-2200.

CHANG, TE-WEN
Physician. Chinese American. **PERSONAL:** Born Oct 12, 1920, Nanchang, China; married Diana, Jun 22, 1952; children: Lynn, Frank, Joseph, Jannet, Catherline. **EDUCATION:** National Central University, MB, 1945; University of Kansas, 1950-52. **CAREER:** Boston University School of Medicine, assistant instructor, 1952-57; Tufts University School of Medicine, senior instructor, associate professor in microbiology, medicine and community health, 1958-92, professor emeritus, 1992-. **ORGANIZATIONS:** Infectious Disease Society of America; American Association for the Advancement of Sciences; New York Academy of Sciences; American Society of Public Health; American Society of Microbiology; American Academy of Microbiology; American Federation for Clinical Research; Sigma Chi; US Army Medical Research Institute, advisor, 1985-86. **HONORS/AWARDS:** Chinese American Medical Society, Achievement Award, 1985. **SPECIAL ACHIEVEMENTS:** Quest editor, Clinical Dermatology, 1984-89; scientific publications in professional journals: 215 articles, 73 abstracts; editor of 2 books; reviewer for 11 medical journals. **MILITARY SERVICE:** Chinese Army, 1945-47, captain. **BUSINESS PHONE:** (617)956-5583.

CHANG, TIEN-CHIEN
Educator. Taiwanese American/Chinese American. **PERSONAL:** Born Jan 3, 1954, Tao Yuan, Taiwan; son of Hsin and Li-Fan Chang; married Li-Fen, Jan 2, 1982; children: David, Joseph. **EDUCATION:** Chung Yuan Christian University, BSIE, 1976; Virginia Polytechnic Institute and State University, MSIE, 1980, PhD, 1982. **CAREER:** Virginia Polytechnic Institute, instructor, 1981-82; Purdue University, assistant professor, 1982-87, associate professor, 1987-91, professor, 1991-. **ORGANIZATIONS:** Institute of Industrial Engr, 1978-; Society of Manufacturing Engr, 1980-; American Society of Mechanical Engr, 1984-. **HONORS/AWARDS:** NSF, Presidential Young Investigator Award, 1986; IIE, Outstanding Young Industrial Engineer of the Year, 1988, Book of the Year, 1992; SME, Outstanding Manufacturing Engineer, 1986, Mfg Textbook of the Year, 1992. **SPECIAL ACHIEVEMENTS:** Author, Expert Process Planning for Manufacturing, Addison-Wesley, 1990; co-author, An Intro to Automated Process Planning Systewms, Prentice Hall, 1985; Computer-Aided Manufacturing, Prentice-Hall, 1991; more that 90 technical papers. **BUSINESS ADDRESS:** Professor, School of Industrial Engineering, Purdue University, West Lafayette, IN 47907-1287, (317)494-5436.

CHANG, TIM P.
Attorney. Chinese American/Japanese American. **PERSONAL:** Born Mar 16, 1965, New York, NY. **EDUCATION:** University of California-Berkeley, College of Engineering, BS, 1987; University of the Pacific, McGeorge School of Law, JD, 1992. **CAREER:** Patterson, Ritner, Lockwood, Zanghi & Gartner, associate attorney, 1993-. **ORGANIZATIONS:** Southern California Chinese Lawyers Assn, 1993-; Phi Delta Phi, 1989-. **BUSINESS ADDRESS:** Associate Attorney, Patterson, Ritner, Lockwood, Zanghi, & Gartner, 3580 Wilshire Blvd, Suite 900, Los Angeles, CA 90010.

CHANG, TIMOTHY S.
Educator. Chinese American. **PERSONAL:** Born May 30, 1925, Shaowu, Fujian, China; son of Chen-Yao Chang and Jin-Feng Li Chang; married Annabelle Y Chang, Nov 5, 1955; children: Cynthia Rynalski, Jonathan, Pamela Rupp, David. **EDUCATION:** Fukien Christian University, Fuzhou, China, BA, 1946; Duke University, MDiv, 1951; North Carolina State University, BS (w/honors), 1952; Ohio State University, MS, 1953, PhD, 1957. **CAREER:** Fujian Shaowu High School, chemistsry teacher, 1946-48; Ohio State University, Ohio Poultry Pullorum diagnosis research assistant, 1952-57; Whitmoyer Laboratories, Inc, dir of microbio, res lab, 1957-66; Norwich

Pharmacal Company, Vet Micro Res Section, chief, 1957-66; CPC (S B Penick Company), dir of animal technology, res & tech, 1969-71; Michigan State University, poultry path & micro, professor, 1971-. **ORGANIZATIONS:** American Society for Microbiology; American Poultry Science Association; World Poultry Science Association; American Association of Poultry Pathologists; Michigan Poultry Allied Industry; Rotary Club; Sigma Xi; Gamma Sigma Delta; Chinese Association of Animal Sci and Vet Science, life membership; MSU Asian Pacific American Faculty and Staff Association, president. **HONORS/AWARDS:** Fukien Christian University, Highest Honor Scholarship; North Carolina State University, High Honor. **SPECIAL ACHIEVEMENTS:** Discovery of the function of the bursa of Fabricius of Chicken in antibody production; Contribution to USDA's Pullorum Eradication program; Introducing white feather turkeys to China; Preventing Marek's Disease mortality, a viral disease in chickens with a chemical compound. **BUSINESS ADDRESS:** Professor, Michigan State University, 114 Anthony Hall, East Lansing, MI 48824, (517)355-8413.

CHANG, TONY H.
Librarian. Chinese American. **PERSONAL:** Born Dec 28, 1951, Shanghai, People's Republic of China; son of Jimmy Chang and Julia Song Chang; married May S Chang, Oct 1982; children: Nancy M, Lucy M. **EDUCATION:** University of California, Berkeley, MLIS, 1983. **CAREER:** Ohio State University, Chinese cataloger, 1985-89; Washington University, Chinese catalog librarian, bibliographer, 1989-. **ORGANIZATIONS:** Association for Asian Studies, 1985-; American Library Association, 1985-; Committee on East Asian Libraries, 1985-. **SPECIAL ACHIEVEMENTS:** "OCLC CJK ho Mei-Kuo Chung wen t'u shu pien mu kuan Li tzu tung hua," T'u shu kuan hsueh yen chiu, August 1988, pp 74-76. **BUSINESS ADDRESS:** Chinese Catalog Librarian/Bibliographer, Washington University, Campus Box 1061, One Brookings Drive, St Louis, MO 63130-4899.

CHANG, TSAN-KUO
Educator. Taiwanese American. **PERSONAL:** Born Nov 18, 1950, Taichung, Taiwan; married Chung-Linn Kao, May 24, 1981; children: James A, Alex L. **EDUCATION:** National Kaohsiung Normal University, BA, 1973; National Chengchi University, MA, 1976; University of Texas, Austin, PhD, 1986. **CAREER:** United Daily News, Taipei, Taiwn, reporter, 1978-80; Cleveland State University, assistant professor, 1986-90; University of Minnesota, associate professor, 1990-. **ORGANIZATIONS:** Association for Education in Journalism and Mass Communication, 1982-; International Communication Association, 1982-; Chinese Communication Association, secretary/treasurer, 1990-. **HONORS/AWARDS:** The Honor Society of Phi Kappa Phi, 1983; Kappa Tau Alpha, 1982. **SPECIAL ACHIEVEMENTS:** Author, The Press and China Policy: The Illusion of Sino-American Relations, 1950-84; articles in Communication Research, Public Opinion Quarterly, Journalism Quarterly, Gazette, Newspaper Research Journal, Communicaion Yearbook. **BUSINESS ADDRESS:** Assoc Professor, School of Journalism and Mass Communication, University of Minnesota, Twin Cities, Minneapolis, MN 55455, (612)626-7754.

CHANG, WARREN W.
Music director. Chinese American. **PERSONAL:** Born Oct 2, 1956, Shanghai, Zhi-Jiang, People's Republic of China; son of Mr & Mrs Jing Tang Chang; married Buyun Chang; children: Linda T. **EDUCATION:** Shanghai Conservatoire, PRC. **CAREER:** Seattle Chinese Orchestra, music director, currently; Warren Chang Music Ensemble, director, currently; Chinese Arts and Music Association, president, currently; Washington Chinese Youth Orchestra, currently.

CHANG, WAYNE WEI
Civil engineer. Chinese American. **PERSONAL:** Born Aug 3, 1963, Taipei, Taiwan; son of Howard H Chang and Tao Tao Chang. **EDUCATION:** University of California, Berkeley, BS, 1986; Massachusetts Institute of Technology, SM, 1988. **CAREER:** Nasland Engineering, senior design engineer, 1988-90, project engineer, 1990-91, project manager, 1991-. **ORGANIZATIONS:** American Society of Civil Engineers, 1983-; Chi Epsilon, 1985-; Sigma Xi, 1988-; Asian Business Association, 1993. **SPECIAL ACHIEVEMENTS:** Experimental analysis of a structural model under dynamic loads, 1988. **HOME ADDRESS:** PO Box 9492, Rancho Santa Fe, CA 92067, (619)756-9051. **BUSINESS ADDRESS:** Project Manager, Nasland Engineering, 4740 Ruffner St, San Diego, CA 92111, (619)292-7770.

CHANG, WEILIN P.
Educator, educational administrator. Chinese American. **PERSONAL:** Born May 26, 1947, Mukden, Manchuria, China; son of Chien-chung Chang and Chien-min Chen; married Lily Y Chang, Oct 20, 1973; children: Howard, Cynthia. **EDUCATION:** National Taiwan University, BSc, 1969; State University of New York at Buffalo, MSc, 1973, PhD, 1975. **CAREER:** Chung Yuan College of Science & Engineering, assoc prof, 1975-77; National Taiwan University, assoc prof, 1977-78; King Abdul Aziz University, assistant prof, 1978-80; United Taiwan Construction, general mgr, 1978-82; Chung-Yuan Christian University, professor, 1982-86; Mesa State College, assoc prof, 1986-87; University of Florida, professor/school director, 1987-. **ORGANIZATIONS:** International Council of Construction Research and Documentation, coordinator of Working Commission 89, 1993-; Am Council for Construction Education, board of trustees, 1992-; Am Institute of Constructors, board of directors, 1991-; National Institute of Building Sciences, subcommittee chair of fire research, 1989-90; Am Society of Civil Engineers, 1977-; Sigma Lambda Chi, 1989-; Phi-Tau-Phi, 1982-. **HONORS/AWARDS:** University of Florida, Teacher of the Year, 1989; Halliburton Education Foundation, Teaching Excellence, 1990; University of Florida, Teaching Excellence, 1988. **SPECIAL ACHIEVEMENTS:** More than 75 professional publications in the area of solid mechanics, fire protection and construction management. **MILITARY SERVICE:** Chinese Marine Corps, 2nd lieutenant, 1969-70. **BUSINESS ADDRESS:** Director, M E Rinker Sr School of Building Construction, University of Florida, FAC 101, Gainesville, FL 32611-2032, (904)392-5965.

CHANG, WILLIAM. *See* **CHANG, SHEN CHIE.**

CHANG, WILLIAM WEI-LIEN
Pathologist, educator. Taiwanese American/Chinese American. **PERSONAL:** Born Feb 7, 1933, Taipei, Taiwan; son of Symonds Tung-Lan Chang and Grace Yun-Huei Chang; married Delphine Li-Fen Chang, Oct 23, 1965; children: Phyllis Shou-Wen Tong, Bernice Shou-Hua, Albert Shou-Yen. **EDUCATION:** National Taiwan University, MD, 1958; Ohio State University, Department of Pathology, resident training, 1962-66, MSc, 1966; McGill University, Montreal, Canada, PhD, 1970. **CAREER:** Mt Sinai School of Medicine, Dept of Anatomy, assistant professor, 1970-73, associate professor, 1973-79; West Virginia University, Department of Pathology, associate professor, 1979-85, professor, 1985-, vice chairman, 1989-93. **ORGANIZATIONS:** American Association of Investigative Pathology, 1982-; American Association of Anatomists, 1971-; US and Canadian Academy of Pathology, 1980-; American Society for Cell Biology, 1973-; American Association for Advancement of Science, 1980-. **HONORS/AWARDS:** Mt Sinai School of Medicine, Excellence in Teaching, 1976. **SPECIAL ACHIEVEMENTS:** Publications in medical journals in the following areas: epithelial cell types and their renewal kinetics in mouse colon, 1969-75; cell population kinetics of developing salivary glands in rodents, 1973-79; histogenesis and multistep process of experimental colonic cancer, 1978-86; histogenesis of colonic polyps in man, including adenomas, 1986-89; proficient in English, Chinese and Japanese. **MILITARY SERVICE:** Chinese Air Force, 2nd lt, medical officer, 1958-60. **BIOGRAPHICAL SOURCES:** N A Wright and M Alison, "The Biology of Epithelial Cell Populations," vol 1 & 2, Clarendon Press, 1984. **BUSINESS ADDRESS:** Professor, Dept of Pathlology, West Virginia University, School of Medicine, Medical Ctr Dr, Health Science Center N, Rm 2105A, Morgantown, WV 26506-9203, (304)293-2093.

CHANG, WILLIAM Y. B.
Government official, educator, researcher. Chinese American. **PERSONAL:** Born Jun 1, 1948, Amoy, China; son of Shan Chang; married Linda Stockton Chang, Mar 26, 1977; children: Chris, Aileen. **EDUCATION:** University of the Pacific, MS, 1973; Indiana University, MA, 1975, PhD, 1979. **CAREER:** Indiana University, Eigenmann Fellow, 1978; Wiley and Sons, book series, co-editor, 1982-; National Academy Sciences, research fellow, 1984-85; Environmental Protection Agency, distinguished visiting scientist, 1990-93; University of Michigan, assistant research scientist, professor, 1979-88, associate research scientist/professor, 1988-93; National Science Foundation, program manager, 1989-. **ORGANIZATIONS:** Freshwater Initiative Coordination Council, executive secretary, 1992-; US-Asia Environmental Partnership, NSF representative, 1992-; NSF Task Group on International Environment, chairperson, 1990-; NSF/AID Steering Committee on Biodiversity, 1991-93; US Scientific Committee on Problem of the Environment, NAS, managing officer, 1990-92; US Man & the Biosphere/Human Systems, 1989-91; AID Title XII, CRSP/Technical Advisory Committee, 1985-90; Yunnan/Hubei Provincial Government, science advisor, 1988-. **HONORS/AWARDS:** Cultural University, Aca-

demic Award, 1969; Indiana University, Eigenmann Fellow Award, 1978; USEPA, Distinguished Visiting Scientist Award, 1990; NOAA, Cooperative Institute for Limnology and Ecosystems Research, fellow. **SPECIAL ACHIEVEMENTS:** More than 70 publications on environmental & natural resources; leading US scholar on Asian environmental issues, in particular, dealing with China; language proficiency in Chinese. **BIOGRAPHICAL SOURCES:** Fisheries, v 12 (3), p 11, 1987. **BUSINESS ADDRESS:** Program Manager, National Science Foundation, 4201 Wilson Blvd, Arlington, VA 22230, (703)306-1704.

CHANG, WINSTON WEN-TSUEN
Educator. Taiwanese American. **PERSONAL:** Born Aug 1, 1939, I-lan, Taiwan; son of Tsan-chin Chang and Shiu-feng Chen; married Shanyong Kuo, Jun 11, 1966; children: David T, Jacqueline D. **EDUCATION:** National Taiwan University, BA, 1962; University of Rochester, MA, 1966, PhD, 1968. **CAREER:** State University of New York, assistant professor of economics, 1967-70, associate professor of economics, 1970-78, professor of economics, 1978-. **ORGANIZATIONS:** American Economic Association, 1967; American Biographical Institute, research board of advisers, 1988-. **HONORS/AWARDS:** State University of New York Chancellor's Award for Excellence in Teaching, 1975. **SPECIAL ACHIEVEMENTS:** Professional articles published in American Economic Review, Econometria, Quarterly Journal of Economics, Review of Economics and Statistics, Review of Economic Studies, Journal of International Economics, International Economic Review, Oxford Economic Papers, Public Choice, etc. **MILITARY SERVICE:** Taiwan Marine Corps (ROTC Program), 2nd lt, 1962. **BUSINESS ADDRESS:** Professor, Dept of Economics, State University of New York at Buffalo, Amherst Campus, 615 O'Brian Hall, Buffalo, NY 14260-0001, (716)645-2116.

CHANG, WON HO
Educator. Korean American. **PERSONAL:** Born Aug 10, 1937, Umsong, Republic of Korea; married Young S Chang, May 6, 1962; children: Susan, Anthony, Eugene. **EDUCATION:** Korea University, BA, political science, 1961; University of Oregon, BA, journalism, 1968; University of Southern California, MA, journalism, 1970; University of Iowa, PhD, mass communications, 1972. **CAREER:** Korea University, Fulbright senior professor, 1987-88; University of Missouri, School of Journalism, Advertising Department, chairman, 1989-90, associate dean of graduate studies, 1991-92, Stephenson Research Center, director, 1992-. **ORGANIZATIONS:** Kappa Tau Alpha; International Communication Association; Association for Education in Journalism and Mass Communication; Korean American Communication Association, president, 1983-86. **HONORS/AWARDS:** University of Missouri, O O McIntyre Distinguished Professor, 1992-. **SPECIAL ACHIEVEMENTS:** Mass Media in China, Iowa State University Press, 1989; Mass Communication and Korea, 1988; editor, Sungkok Journalism Review, 1989-. **BUSINESS ADDRESS:** Prof and Dir, Stephenson Research Center, University of Missouri, School of Journalism, PO Box 838, Columbia, MO 65203, (314)882-7867.

CHANG, YANG-SHIM
Educator. Korean American. **PERSONAL:** Born Jul 26, 1943, Seoul, Republic of Korea; daughter of Seung-Ha Chang & Suck-Soon Kim. **EDUCATION:** Northern Arizona University, DEd, 1981. **CAREER:** Pasadena City College, counselor, 1981-, instructor, 1984-. **ORGANIZATIONS:** American Pyschological Association; California Association for Counseling and Development; American Association for Counseling and Development; Association for Multicultural Counseling and Development; Asian/Pacific Family Center. **BUSINESS ADDRESS:** Professor/Counselor, Social Science, Pasadena City College, 1570 E Colorado Blvd, Pasadena, CA 91106-2003, (818)585-7895.

CHANG, YEN FOOK
Risk management company executive. Chinese American. **PERSONAL:** Born Dec 25, 1949, Penang, Malaysia; son of Chang Fei Seng and Shiu Yit Lian; married Gloria Chang, Sep 6, 1986; children: Katherine, Grace. **EDUCATION:** University of Malaya, BS (with honors), 1971; Southern Illinois University, MS, 1974; Iowa State University, PhD, 1978. **CAREER:** Iowa State University, instructor, 1977-78; Towson State University, asst professor, 1979-81; Fair Isaac Companies, vice pres, dir of analytic products, 1982-. **HONORS/AWARDS:** Iowa State University, Henry Theilman Award, 1977. **HOME ADDRESS:** 135 Nottingham Dr, Alameda, CA 94501. **BUSINESS PHONE:** (415)491-5114.

CHANG, YI-CHIEH
Educator. Taiwanese American. **PERSONAL:** Born Sep 14, 1957, Hsing-Jou, Taiwan; son of Chung-Wei Chang and Shiou-ing Chang; married Shinyir Chang, Jun 24, 1984; children: Emily. **EDUCATION:** National Taiwan University, BS, electrical engineering, 1979, MS, electrical engineering, 1984; University of Michigan, PhD, electrical and computer engineering, 1991. **CAREER:** University of Texas, El Paso, assistant professor, 1991-. **ORGANIZATIONS:** IEEE, 1983; ACM, 1989. **HONORS/AWARDS:** University of Michigan, first award in VLSI design competition, 1989. **SPECIAL ACHIEVEMENTS:** Publication in IEEE Transactions on Computers, 1989. **BIOGRAPHICAL SOURCES:** IEEE Transaction on Computers, vol 38, no 8, pp 1124-1142, August 1989; International Symposium on Fault-Tolerant Computing, pp 188-195, June 1991. **HOME PHONE:** (915)833-4974. **BUSINESS ADDRESS:** Professor, Electrical Engineering Dept, University of Texas, El Paso, 500 University Ave, E-309, El Paso, TX 79968-0523, (915)747-6960.

CHANG, YIA-CHUNG
Educator. Taiwanese American. **PERSONAL:** Born Nov 20, 1952, Taiwan; married Josephine, Apr 29, 1979; children: Steven Sao-hwa, Eric Sao-Yu. **EDUCATION:** Cheng-Kung University, Taiwan, BS, 1974; California Institute of Technology, MS, 1978, PhD, 1980. **CAREER:** California Institute of Technology, teaching assistant, 1976-79, research assistant, 1979-80; University of Illinois, research assistant professor, 1980-82, assistant professor, 1982-86, associate professor, 1986-91, professor, 1991-. **ORGANIZATIONS:** American Physical Society, 1978-; Materials Research Society, 1993-; International Conference Superlattice & Microstructures, program committee, 1992. **HONORS/AWARDS:** Ministry of Education, Taiwan, Chinese Culture Scholarship, 1972-74; Sharp Inc, Sharp Scholarship, 1973; C S Wu, Dr C S Wu Scholarship, 1972, 1974. **SPECIAL ACHIEVEMENTS:** Co-author, 160 papers in journals, including Physcial Review, Journal of Applied Physics, Journal of Vacuum Science & Technology; World Scientific, Journal of Modern Physics, editor, 1992-. **BUSINESS ADDRESS:** Professor, University of Illinois, 1110 W Green St, 224 Materials Research Lab, Urbana, IL 61801, (217)333-4142.

CHANG, YOON IL
Nuclear engineer. Korean American. **PERSONAL:** Born Apr 12, 1942, Seoul, Republic of Korea; son of Paul K Chang; married Ok Ja Chang, Dec 19, 1966; children: Alice, Dennis, Eugene. **EDUCATION:** Seoul National University, BS, 1964; Texas A&M University, ME, 1967; University of Michigan, PhD, 1971; University of Chicago, MBA, 1983. **CAREER:** Nuclear Assurance Corporation, Special Project, manager, 1971-74; Argonne National Laboratory, group leader, 1974-76, section head, 1977-78, associate division director, 1978-83, IFR Program, general manager, 1984-. **ORGANIZATIONS:** American Nuclear Society, 1965-. **HONORS/AWARDS:** University of Chicago, Medal for Distinguished Performance at Argonne National Laboratory, 1985; E O Lawrence Award in Nuclear Technology, 1993. **BUSINESS ADDRESS:** General Manager, IFR Program, Argonne National Laboratory, 9700 S Cass Avenue, Argonne, IL 60439, (708)252-4856.

CHANG, YU LO CYRUS
Educator. Taiwanese American. **PERSONAL:** Born Jun 5, 1958, Tainan, Taiwan; son of Hen Chang & Yung Wu; married Wen Hsia A Ho, Nov 8, 1958; children: Ching Tzer Christopher, Wei Chi Catherine, Wei Yuh Alexandra, Ching Hua Anthony. **EDUCATION:** National Taipei Institute of Technology, BSEE, 1982; SUNY, Binghamton, MSCS, 1985, PhD, 1991. **CAREER:** SUNY, Binghamton, Department of Computer Science, lecturer, 1990-. **ORGANIZATIONS:** IEEE, 1985-. **SPECIAL ACHIEVEMENTS:** Publications include: co-author, "An inference design for fault location in real-time control systems," Journal of Systems and Software, Apr 1994; "Classical inference methods for fault location in homogeneous systems," Technical Report #CS-TR-91-16, SUNY Binghamton, Intl Conference on Reliability, Quality Control, & Risk Assessment, Intl Assn of Science & Technology for Development and IEEE Reliability Society, p 57-61, Nov 4-6, 1992; "Bayesian inference for fault diagnosis in real-time distributed systems," Second Asian Test Symposium, IEEE Computer Society, Academia Sinica of China & Natl Natural Science Foundation of China, Nov 16-18, 1993; "A visual simulation tool for design for diagnosability of dependable systems," ISSAT/IEEE Intl Conf on Reliability and Quality in Design, Mar 1994. **MILITARY SERVICE:** Army, 1st lt, 1982-84. **BUSINESS ADDRESS:** Professor, Dept of Computer Science, State University of New York, Binghamton, Watson School of Engineering, PO Box 6000, Binghamton, NY 13902-6000, (607)777-4162.

CHANG, YUNG-FENG (ALEX)
Educator. Taiwanese American. **PERSONAL:** Born Nov 15, 1935, Heng-Chung, Taiwan; son of Kung-Ling Chang and Ging-Bao Dung; married Su-Ling Chang; children: Candice, Craig. **EDUCATION:** National Taiwan University, BS, 1958, MS, 1960; University of Pittsburgh, PhD, 1966. **CAREER:** National Taiwan University, research assistant, 1961; University of Pittsburgh, research assistant, 1962-66; University of Maryland, research associate, 1966-70, assistant professor, 1970-74, associate professor, 1974-79, professor, 1979-. **ORGANIZATIONS:** American Chemical Society; American Society of Biochemistry and Molecular Biology; American Society of Pharmacology & Experimental Therapeutics; American Society of Neurochemistry; American Association of Dental Schools. **HONORS/AWARDS:** Environmental Protection Agency, Certification of Appreciation, 1977. **SPECIAL ACHIEVEMENTS:** Environmental Protection Agency: Effect of Chronic Exposure to Low Levels of Pollutants on Immune Response, 1973; National Institute of Neurological Disorders & Stroke: Metabolism and Inhibition of Lysine Related to Brain Disorders, 1974, Metabolism and Neurochemistry of Lysine in the Brain, 1977, 1982, 1987, Antiseizure Activity of Lysine Metabolites, 1987; National Institute of Dental Research: Cariostatic Effects of Amino Acids on Cell Wall Biosynthesis, 1976; NIH, grant application reviewer, 1985, 1991; March of Dimes Birth Defect Foundation, grant application reviewer, 1989. **MILITARY SERVICE:** Army Republic of China, 2nd lieutenant. **BUSINESS ADDRESS:** Professor, University of Maryland, 666 W Baltimore St, Dental School, Rm 4-G-29, Baltimore, MD 21201-1586, (410)706-7917.

CHANG-DIAZ, FRANKLIN RAMON
Astronaut. Chinese American. **PERSONAL:** Born Apr 5, 1950, San Jose, Costa Rica; divorced; children: Jean, Sonia. **EDUCATION:** University of Connecticut, BSME, 1973; MIT, PhD, 1977. **CAREER:** NASA, astronaut, beginning 1980, senior mission specialist astronaut, currently. **HONORS/AWARDS:** Hispanic Engineer National Achievement Awards, Outstanding Technical Achievement, 1993. **BUSINESS ADDRESS:** Sr Mission Specialist Astronaut, NASA, Astronaut Office/JSC, Houston, TX 77058.*

CHAO, ALLEN Y.
Pharmaceutical company executive. Chinese American. **PERSONAL:** Born Sep 13, 1945, Shanghai, China; son of Hsi-Hsiung Chao and Hsu-Hwa Chao; married Lee-Hwa Chao, Dec 30, 1972; children: Michael C. **EDUCATION:** Taipei Medical College, BS, 1967; West Virginia University, MS, 1970; Purdue University, PhD, 1973. **CAREER:** Searle Laboratories Inc, Pharmaceutical Technology, director, 1978-93; Watson Laboratories Inc, founder, 1984, president, 1984-91; Watson Pharmaceuticals Inc, president, 1991-. **SPECIAL ACHIEVEMENTS:** Led Watson Pharmaceutical through initial public offering (zpo), 1993. **BUSINESS ADDRESS:** CEO, President, Watson Laboratories Inc, 311 Bonnie Circle, Corona, CA 91720, (909)270-1400.

CHAO, BEI TSE
Engineer. Chinese American. **PERSONAL:** Born Dec 18, 1918, Soochow, China; son of Tse Yu and Yin T Yao Chao; married May Kiang, Feb 7, 1948; children: Clara, Fred Roberto. **EDUCATION:** National Chiao-Tung University, China, BS (highest honor), elec engineering, 1939; Victoria University, Manchester, England, PhD, 1947. **CAREER:** Central Machine Works, China, Tool & Gage Division, asst engineer, 1939-41, associate engineer, 1941-43, manager, 1943-45; University of Illinois, Urbana, research assistant, 1948-50; University of Illinois, Dept of Mechanical Engineering, assistant professor, 1951-53, associate professor, 1953-55, professor, 1955-87, Thermal Science Division, head, 1971-75, Mechanical and Industrial Engineering Dept, head, 1975-87, professor emeritus, 1987-; consultant, 1950-; University of California, Berkeley, Russell S Springer Professor, 1973. **ORGANIZATIONS:** Natl Academy of Engineering; Aircraft Gear Corp, board of directors, 1989-; Academia Sinica; Chiao-Tung University Alumni Association; Tau Beta Pi; Pi Tau Sigma. **HONORS/AWARDS:** Tau Beta Pi, Daniel C Drucker Eminent Faculty Award, 1985; AAAS, fellow; ASME, fellow, Tech Award, 1992; American Society for Engineering Education, Centennial Medallion, 1993. **SPECIAL ACHIEVEMENTS:** Author, Advanced Heat Transfer, 1969; editorial board: Numerical Heat Transfer, 1977-; International Journal Heat and Mass Transfer, 1987-; International Communications in Heat and Mass Transfer, 1987-. **BUSINESS ADDRESS:** Professor Emeritus, University of Illinois at Urbana-Champaign, 264 Mechanical Engineering Bldg, 1206 W Green St, Urbana, IL 61801.*

CHAO, CHIANG-NAN
Educator. Chinese American. **PERSONAL:** Born Apr 26, 1949, Heihe, Heilongjiang, People's Republic of China; son of Tien Ye Zhao; married Lily Hong Li Wang, Oct 10, 1980. **EDUCATION:** Ji Lin University, BA, 1975; Lamar University, MBA, 1984; Arizona State University, PhD, 1989. **CAREER:** Ji Lin University, instructor, 1975-80; St John's University, assistant professor, 1990-. **ORGANIZATIONS:** Chipa International Law Association, 1979-80; Academy of Management, 1988-; Decision Sciences Institute, 1988-; National Association of Purchasing Management, 1986-. **HONORS/AWARDS:** National Association of Purchasing Management, fellowship, 1988; St John's University, research grants, 1991-93. **SPECIAL ACHIEVEMENTS:** Author, China Foreign Trade Decision Making, 1988; Purchasing Productivity Measurement, 1991; Purchasing Performance Evaluation, 1993; chapter 10, Developing Knowledge-Based Systems, 1992; Chinese Purchasing Decision Making, 1992; various other publications. **BIOGRAPHICAL SOURCES:** Decision Making in Chinese Foreign Trade Administration, p 35-40; The Columbia Journal of World Business. **HOME PHONE:** (718)539-1133. **BUSINESS ADDRESS:** Assistant Professor of Management, St John's University, Jamaica, NY 11439-1001, (718)990-6161.

CHAO, CHING YUAN
Educator. Chinese American. **PERSONAL:** Born Dec 5, 1921, Shaoshing, Chekiang, China; son of Jin Ho Chao and Wang Shih Chao; married Nelly ChuKu Chin Chao, Sep 28, 1947; children: Amy Hsiao Ming Chao Chang, Hsiao Lin. **EDUCATION:** National Ying-Shih University, BS, 1945; Iowa State University, MS, 1961, PhD, 1963. **CAREER:** Fukien Provincial Agriculture College, teaching asst, 1945-46; Natl Taiwan University, professor, 1946-63; Dalhousie University, visiting associate professor, 1964-68; Saint Mary University, associate professor, 1968-69; Michigan Technological University, associate professor, 1969-72; Jackson State University, professor, 1972-. **ORGANIZATIONS:** Citizen Ambassador Program, American Delegate in Ag Econ to USSR, 1989; Midsouth Academy of Economics & Finance, editorial board member, 1986-, area coordinator of annual program 1986-; Bureau of Business & Economic Research at JSU, editorial advisor, 1986-; SW Society of Econ & SW Econ Assn, chair & discussant at sessions, 1987-; JSU, Departmental Seminar Committee, chair, 1991-; Mississippi Assn of Chinese, treasurer, 1992; American Economic Assn; American Ag Economic Assn; MAEF; SWSE; SWEA; Phi Tau Phi, 1965-. **HONORS/AWARDS:** Mutual Security Agency of State Dept, study & observation in USA, 1953-54; Council on Economic & Cultural Affairs of Rockefeller Foundation, fellowship, 1959-62; Natl Nanking Ag, University & Ministry of Forest of China, visiting scholar, 1980; Jackson State University, Researcher of the Year Award, 1993, Natl Alumni Assn, Meritorious Citation in Recognition of 20 Years Distinguished Service, 1992. **SPECIAL ACHIEVEMENTS:** Author, Agricultural Production Economics, Natl Compilation Committee, Taiwan, 1960; editor, papers of First Annual Economic Research Symposium at JSU, 1993; paper presented, "Recent Agri Reforms in China," at Research & Development Institute of Plant Protection in Kishinew of Soviet Union, 1989; paper presented, "System of Agri Production Responsibility in China," American Agri Economics Association, 1984; numerous papers in Chinese & Russian Agri Reforms published in American Journal of Ag Economics, MJEF, JSWSE, SWJEA, Journal of Ag Economics; delegate to Soviet Union & World Agri, 1981-. **BIOGRAPHICAL SOURCES:** American Economic Review, p 96, Dec 1989. **HOME PHONE:** (601)372-1931. **BUSINESS ADDRESS:** Professor of Economics and Statistics, Dept of Economics, Finance & General Business, Jackson State University, Lynch St, Jackson, MS 39217-0560, (601)968-2451.

CHAO, EDWARD C. T.
Geologist. Chinese American. **PERSONAL:** Born Nov 30, 1919, Soochow, Jiangsu, China; married Mar 27, 1941; children: Kathy Smith, Evelina, Daniel K H. **EDUCATION:** University of Chicago, PhD, 1948. **CAREER:** Geological Survey, Szechuan Province, China, geologist, 1941-45; US Geological Survey, research geologist, 1949-. **ORGANIZATIONS:** Mineralogical Society of America, fellow, currently; Geological Society of America, fellow, currently; Geochemical Society, secretary, 1965-67; American Geophysical Union, currently. **HONORS/AWARDS:** Franklin Institute, Wetherill Medal, 1965; NASA, medal for exceptional scientific achievement, 1973; Alexander von Humboldt Foundation, senior US Scientist Award, 1975; US Dept of Interior, meritorius award, 1982; Society of Ries Culture, Germany, Ries Culture Award, 1983; Meteoritical Society, Barringer Medal, 1992; discovered an asteroid named (3906) China, 1987. **SPECIAL ACHIEVEMENTS:** Co-author, Mineralogical Approaches to Geological Investigations, Science Press, Beijing, 1990; language proficiency: Chinese. **BIOGRAPHICAL**

SOURCES: Don Wilhelm, The Rocky Moon, University of Arizona Press, 1993. BUSINESS ADDRESS: Research Geologist, US Geological Survey, US Dept of Interior, MS 954 Branch of Eastern Mineral Resources, USGS, Rm 3B-114, Reston, VA 22091, (703)648-6460.

CHAO, ELAINE LAN
Charity executive. Chinese American. PERSONAL: Born in China; daughter of James S C Chao and Ruth M L Chao; married Mitch McConnell, Feb 6, 1993. EDUCATION: Columbia University, 1972; Dartmouth College, 1974: Mt Holyoke College, AB, 1975; Massachusetts Institute of Technology, 1979; Harvard University, MBA; 1979. CAREER: Citicorp, international banker, 1979-83; The White House, White House Fellow, 1983-84; BankAmerica Capital Markets Group, vice president syndications, 1984-86; Maritime Administration, deputy administrator, 1986-88, Federal Maritime Commission, chairman, 1988-89; US Department of Transportation, deputy secretary, 1989-91; Peace Corps, director, 1991-92; United Way of America, president, CEO, currently. ORGANIZATIONS: Council on Foreign Relations, 1988-; American Council Young Political Leaders, board of directors, 1983-; Harvard Business School, vis com, 1989-; Harvard Club, NYC; Harvard Business School Club, Wash, DC, board of directors; Dole Foods Inc, board of directors. HONORS/AWARDS: Harvard Business School, Alumni Achievement Award, 1993; National Conference for College Women Student Leaders, Women of Distinction, 1993; Niagara University, Honorary Doctorate of Humane Letters, 1992; Drexel University, Honorary Doctorate of Humanities, 1992; Sacred Heart University, Honorary Doctorate of Law, 1991; St John's University, Honorary Doctorate of Humane Letters, 1991; Villanova University, Honorary LLD, 1989; National Council Women, US Inc, Young Achiever Award, 1986. BUSINESS ADDRESS: President & Chief Executive Officer, United Way of America, 701 N Fairfax St, Alexandria, VA 22314-2045, (703)683-7100.

CHAO, GEORGIA TZE-YING
Educator. Chinese American. PERSONAL: Born in Washington, DC; daughter of Shou-Ting Chao and Anna Wen Chao; married. EDUCATION: University of Maryland, BS, psychology (honors), 1975; Pennsylvania State University, MS, industrial, organizational psychology, 1978, PhD, industrial, organizational psychology, 1982. CAREER: GMI Engineering & Management Institute, Dept of Management, asst professor, 1982-85; Michigan State University, Dept of Management, associate professor, 1985-. ORGANIZATIONS: Academy of Management Assn, Careers Div, steering committee, 1993-96, Organizational Behavior Div, Human Resources Div, executive committee, 1993-96; Midwest Academy of Management, bd of directors, 1991-92; American Psychological Society; American Psychological Assn; Society of Industrial & Organizational Psychology Inc, Continuing Education Workshops Committee, co-chair, 1991-93; Assn of Asian Pacific American Faculty and Staff of MSU. HONORS/AWARDS: Selected to represent USA at Intl Seminar on Human Resources Development, Japan, 1993. SPECIAL ACHIEVEMENTS: Author and co-author of numerous publications pertaining to the field of psychology, including, coauthor, "Organizational Downsizing," Intl Review of I/O Psychology, p263-332, 1993. BUSINESS ADDRESS: Associate Professor, Dept of Management, Michigan State University, N435 North Business Center, East Lansing, MI 48824, (517)353-5418.

CHAO, JOWETT
Educator. Chinese American. PERSONAL: Born Nov 16, 1915, Mei Xie, Zhejiang, China; son of Chien Chung & Mien; married Cherie Chao, Jul 11, 1939 (deceased); children: Victoria. EDUCATION: National Central University, China, MS, agriculture; Cornell University, PhD, 1949. CAREER: Ministry of Agriculture and Forestry, entomologist, 1942-44; University of California, Los Angeles, research professor of biology, 1948-68. ORGANIZATIONS: Associationsof Soochow, Yenching and National Central University, office of alumni. HONORS/AWARDS: NIH, 20 years support on malaria parasites research, 1948-68; Academy of Science of China, lecturer to Institute of Virology, 1979; US Academy of Sciences, exchange scholar to Czechoslovakia, 1978. SPECIAL ACHIEVEMENTS: Articles: Host-parasite-vector Relationships; Arthropod Cell Culture; Invitro Culture of Blood Parasites; publications in Science, The Journal of Parasitology, Journal Tropic Medicine and Hygiene, J Invertebrate Pathology, and other international journals; contributions to international conferences and conference monographs. HOME ADDRESS: 228 South Palm Dr, Beverly Hills, CA 90212, (310)271-7713.

CHAO, KWANG-CHU
Educator. Chinese American. PERSONAL: Born Jun 7, 1925, Chongqing, Sichuan, China; son of Chungpu Chao and Juipu Chou Chao; married Jiun-Ying Chao, May 2, 1953; children: Howard, Albert, Bernard. EDUCATION: National Chekiang University, BS, 1948; University of Wisconsin, Madison, MS, 1952, PhD, 1956. CAREER: Chevron Research Corp, research engineer, 1957-63; Illinois Institute of Technology, associate professor of chemical engineering, 1963-64; Oklahoma State University, associate professor of chemical engineering, 1964-68; Purdue University, professor of chemical engineering, 1968-, Harry Creighton Peffer Distinguished Professor, 1989-. ORGANIZATIONS: American Institute of Chemical Engineers, 1957-; American Chemical Society, 1957-; International Union of Pure and Applied Chemistry, 1990-; American Association of University Professors, 1970-. HONORS/AWARDS: American Institute of Chemical Engineers, fellow, 1976-; Beijing Institute of Chemical Technology, Honorary Professor, 1984; Zhejiang University, Honorary Professor, 1988; National Science Council, Taiwan, International Scientist Lecturer, 1989. SPECIAL ACHIEVEMENTS: Author, "Thermodynamics of Fluids," Dekker, 1975; "Equations of State-Theory and Applications," Am Chem Society, 1985; "Equations of State in Engineering and Research," Am Chem Society, 1979; "Applied Thermodynamics," Am Chem Society, 1968; 160 publications in technical and scientific journals. HOME ADDRESS: 2909 Henderson Ave, West Lafayette, IN 47906. BUSINESS ADDRESS: Harry C Peffer Distinguished Professor of Chem Eng, Purdue University, School of Chemical Engineering, CHME Bldg, West Lafayette, IN 47907-1283, (317)494-4088.

CHAO, LIN
Educator. Chinese American. PERSONAL: Born May 31, 1950, Hong Kong; son of Tsin Chao & Don Sung Shen. EDUCATION: Cornell University, BA, 1972; Mount Holyoke College, MA, 1975; University of Massachusetts, PhD, 1979. CAREER: Princeton University, post-doctoral fellow, 1979-80; Northwestern University, assistant professor, 1980-87; University of Maryland, associate professor, 1987-. ORGANIZATIONS: Sigma Xi, 1974-77; Society for the Study of Evolution, associate editor, 1983-85; American Association for the Advancement of Science, 1990-. HONORS/AWARDS: Northwestern University, Teaching Award, 1983; University of Maryland, university fellow, 1990. SPECIAL ACHIEVEMENTS: Numerous publications in professional journals; over $500,000 in grants from the National Institutes of Health to study population genetics of microbes and viruses. BUSINESS ADDRESS: Associate Professor, Zoology, University of Maryland, College Park, MD 20742, (301)405-6945.

CHAO, PAUL W. F.
Educator. Chinese American. PERSONAL: Born May 26, 1950, Fukien, Taiwan; son of I Hu Chao & Shu O Chao; married Alice Liu Miin Chao, Jun 10, 1980; children: Caleb, Daniel. EDUCATION: University of Canterbury, BS, chemistry and math, 1974, MS, chemistry, 1977; Washington State University, MBA, 1981; University of Washington, PhD, marketing, 1986. CAREER: Oakland University, assistant professor, 1984-89; University of Northern Iowa, associate professor, 1989-. ORGANIZATIONS: American Marketing Association, 1980-; Academy of International Business, 1987-; Academy of Marketing Science, 1992-; America Chinese Management Educators Association, program committee, 1991-. HONORS/AWARDS: AACSB, Beta Gamma Sigma, 1979; International Marketing Review, Best Paper Award for Consumer Profiles and Perceptions: Country-of-Origin Effects, 1993. SPECIAL ACHIEVEMENTS: Image Variables in Multi-Attribute Product Evaluation: Country-of-Origin Effects, 1984; Implications of Prospective Payment Under DRGs for Hospital Marketing, 1988; Export and Reverse Investment: Strategic Implications for Newly Industrialized Countries, 1989; The Impact of Country Affiliation on the Credibility of Product Attribute Claims, 1989; Partitioning Country-of- Origin-Effects: Consumer Evaluations of a Hybrid Product, 1993. BUSINESS ADDRESS: Associate Professor, Dept of Marketing, University of Northern Iowa, Business Bldg, Cedar Falls, IA 50614-0126, (319)273-2135.

CHAO, ROSALIND
Actress. Chinese American. CAREER: Film, theater and television actress, works include: M*A*S*H; Star Trek: The Next Generation; Memoirs of an Invisible Man; The Big Brawl; Chinese Web; The Terry Fox Story; Twirl; White Ghost; Green Card, Mark Taper Forum, 1986; Last Flight Out, 1990; Against the Law, 1990; Thousand Pieces of Gold, 1991; The Joy Luck Club, 1993. BUSINESS ADDRESS: Actress, Paradigm Talent Agency, 10100 Santa Monica Blvd, 25th Fl, Los Angeles, CA 90067, (310)277-4400.*

CHAO, STANLEY K.
Electronics executive. Chinese American. **PERSONAL:** Born in Kunming, China; married. **EDUCATION:** MIT, MS, EE, 1949. **CAREER:** GT&E, Sylvania, manager, 1958-70; Interdigit Inc, president, 1970-76; Advanced Electronics Inc, president, 1976-. **ORGANIZATIONS:** IEEE. **SPECIAL ACHIEVEMENTS:** Wrote a technical paper on instrumentation; patents on electronic keyboards. **BUSINESS ADDRESS:** President, Advanced Electronics Inc, 112 Beach St, Boston, MA 02111.

CHAO, TIM
Educator. Chinese American. **PERSONAL:** Born Aug 24, 1925, Deh Zhou City, Shandong, China; married Helen, Mar 30, 1952; children: Grace, Victor, Henry. **EDUCATION:** Chung Kuo University, Beijing, BL, 1948; Normal University, Beijing, BEd, 1956; University of Pittsburgh, MEd, 1965. **CAREER:** Chi-Lung High School, Taiwan, instructor, 1949-51; Political Staff College, Taiwan, assistant profesor, 1951-53; Taipei Cheng Kung High School, instructor, 1953-56; Taipei American High School, instructer, 1956-64; Central Queens YMCA, associate dir of phys ed, 1965-67; University of Pittsburgh, graduate assistant, 1964-65; Queensborough Community College/CUNY, associate professor, 1967-. **ORGANIZATIONS:** American Red Cross, Water Safety Committee for Queens Chapter, chairperson, 1967-87; Chinese American Athletic Association in Greater New York, chair, 1982-; Greater New York Chinese American Table Tennis Association, chairman of the board, 1993. **HONORS/AWARDS:** American Red Cross, Certificate of Recognition, 1990. **SPECIAL ACHIEVEMENTS:** American Red Cross Water Safety, instructor, trainer, 1968-. **BUSINESS ADDRESS:** Professor, Dept Health Physical Education & Dance, Queensborough Community College/CUNY, Springfield Blvd, RFK-GYM, Bayside, NY 11364, (718)631-6322.

CHAO, XIULI
Educator. Chinese American. **PERSONAL:** Born Apr 15, 1964, Zibo, Shandong, People's Republic of China; married Helena Hua Wu, Jun 18, 1991. **EDUCATION:** Shandong University, BS, 1983; Chinese Academy of Sciences, MS, 1985; Columbia University, PhD, 1989. **CAREER:** Columbia University, research assistant, 1985-89; New Jersey Institute of Technology, assistant professor, 1989-. **ORGANIZATIONS:** Operations Research Society of America, member; The Institute of Management Science, member; Operation Research, associate editor; IIE Transactions, associate editor. **HONORS/AWARDS:** National Science Foundation, Research Initiation Award, 1992; Shandong University, Best Paper Award, 1983. **SPECIAL ACHIEVEMENTS:** Published more than 25 research papers in professional refereed journals. **HOME ADDRESS:** 77 Orange Road, Apt 40, Montclair, NJ 07042. **BUSINESS PHONE:** (201)596-3658.

CHAO, YUH J.
Educator. Taiwanese American. **PERSONAL:** Born May 9, 1953, Hwalien, Taiwan; married Hsin-Lan L Chao, Jul 1977; children: Isaac E, Adam P. **EDUCATION:** National Cheng-Kung University, Taiwan, BS, 1975; National Tsing-Hwa University, Taiwan, MS, 1977; University of Illinois at Urbana-Champaign, PhD, 1981. **CAREER:** Stubbs, Overbeck and Associates, mechanical engineer, 1981-82; Southern Illinois University, assistant professor, 1982-83; University of South Carolina, assistant professor, 1984-89, associate professor, 1989-93, professor, 1993-. **ORGANIZATIONS:** Society of Experimental Mechanics; American Society of Mechanical Engineers. **HONORS/AWARDS:** Alexander von Humboldt Foundation, Germany, Research Fellowship Award, 1991. **SPECIAL ACHIEVEMENTS:** More than 40 publications on pressure vessel & piping design and analysis, fracture of solids, and experimental mechanics. **MILITARY SERVICE:** Army ROTC, Taiwan, 2nd lieutenant, 1977-79. **HOME ADDRESS:** 225 Char Oak Drive, Columbia, SC 29212. **BUSINESS ADDRESS:** Professor, Dept of Mechanical Engineering, University of South Carolina, Columbia, SC 29208, (803)777-5869.

CHAPATWALA, KIRIT D.
Educator. Indo-American. **PERSONAL:** Born Dec 17, 1948, Surat, Gujarat, India; son of Dhirajlal T & Hansaben D Chapatwala; married Sherry Ann Melton, Jun 11, 1977; children: Heather K, Kendra K, Marah K. **EDUCATION:** Gujarat University, BSc, 1970; Mississippi State University, MS, 1973, PhD, 1978. **CAREER:** Selma University, professor, chairman of division, currently. **BUSINESS ADDRESS:** Professor, Chairman of Division, Selma University, 1501 Lapsley St, Selma, AL 36701, (215)872-4599.

CHATTERJEE, LATA ROY
Educator. Indo-American. **PERSONAL:** Born Feb 11, 1938, Calcutta, W. Bengal, India; daughter of Binode Bhusan Roy & Suneela Roy; married T R Lakshmanan, Jun 24, 1979; children: Srobona, Indira Lakasmanan. **EDUCATION:** Calcutta University, MA, 1960, PhD, 1969; Johns Hopkins University, PhD, 1973. **CAREER:** Loreto College, lecturer, 1967-69; Rutgers University, assistant professor, 1973-75; Johns Hopkins University, assistant professor, 1975-78; Boston University, professor, 1978-. **ORGANIZATIONS:** Oxfam-America, secretary, board of trustees, 1988-; Regional Science Association, 1978-; Association of American Geographers, 1973-; National Trust for Historical Preservation, 1989-; Amnesty International; Nature Conservancy. **HONORS/AWARDS:** Fulbright Association, Senior Research Award, 1985; Cambridge University, visiting scholar, 1984; governments of Sweden, Netherlands, USA, India, Nigeria, Yugoslavia, various research awards, 1975-92; Calcutta University, Sudhira Roy Gold Medal, 1969. **SPECIAL ACHIEVEMENTS:** Author: 2 books, 25 book chapters, 30 journal articles, 17 research reports and discussion papers. **HOME ADDRESS:** 83 Condy Rd, Peterborough, NH 03458. **BUSINESS ADDRESS:** Professor, Boston University, 675 Commonwealth Ave, Rm 457 A, Boston, MA 02215, (617)353-2525.

CHATTERJEE, MONISH RANJAN
Researcher, educator. Indo-American/Bangladeshi American/Myanmar American. **PERSONAL:** Born Jan 2, 1959, Calcutta, W. Bengal, India; son of Suranjan Chatterjee & Lilabati Bhattacharya Chatterjee; married Joyoti Choudhury Chatterjee, Jan 15, 1990. **EDUCATION:** Indian Institute of Technology, Kharagpur, BTech (honors), 1979; University of Iowa, MSEE, 1981, PhD, 1985. **CAREER:** University of Iowa, EE, research assistant, 1980-85, visiting lecturer, 1985, visiting assistant professor, 1985-86; SUNY, Binghamton, EE, visiting assistant professor, 1986-88, assistant professor, 1988-92, associate professor, 1992-. **ORGANIZATIONS:** IEEE, 1980-89, senior member, 1989-; Optical Society of America, 1988-; Sigma Xi, 1989-; ASEE, 1991-; Smithsonian Associates, 1984-; Society Indian Academics Am, 1993; IEEE, Binghamton Section, executive board, vice chair, seminars, 1989-. **HONORS/AWARDS:** Government of India, National Scholarship, 1974; Bharatiya Vidyarthi Parishad, All India Essay Competition, first prize, 1974; Indian Institute of Technology, Merit-Means Scholarship, 1974-79. **SPECIAL ACHIEVEMENTS:** Author of research papers appearing in: IEEE Proceedings, 1981, IEEE Transactions, 1985, 1991, JOSA A and B, 1986, 1989, 1991, Applied Optics, 1989, 1992; author, Kamalakanta, Rupa & Company, 1992. **MILITARY SERVICE:** India Air Force NCC, flight cadet, 1974-77; passed C certificate exam, 1975. **BUSINESS ADDRESS:** Associate Professor of Electrical Engineering, SUNY, Binghamton, P12/EB, Watson School, Engineering Bldg, Binghamton, NY 13902-6000, (607)777-4014.

CHATTERJEE, PRANAB
Educator. Indo-American. **PERSONAL:** Born Oct 15, 1936, Behah, Bihar, India; son of Paritosh Chatterjee and Uma Chatterjee; married Marian, Dec 31, 1991; children: Manjirnath, Sraboni. **EDUCATION:** Viswa Bharah University, BA, 1959; University of Tennessee, MSSW, 1961; University of Chicago, MA, 1963, PHD, 1967. **CAREER:** Case Western Reserve University, professor of social work, currently. **BUSINESS ADDRESS:** Professor of Social Work, Case Western Reserve University, Bellflower & Ford Roads, Mandel - SASS, Cleveland, OH 44106, (216)368-2248.

CHATTERJEE, PRONOY KUMAR
Scientist. Bangladeshi American/Indo-American. **PERSONAL:** Born Oct 26, 1936, Varanasi, Uttar Pradesh, India; son of Rameshwar Chatterjee and Nanibala Chatterjee; married Swapna Chatterjee, Dec 24, 1962; children: Gargi, Partha. **EDUCATION:** Banaras H University, Varanasi, India, BSc, 1956, MSc, 1958; Calcutta University, Calcutta, India, PhD, 1962, DSc, 1974. **CAREER:** Indian Association for the Cultivation of Science, research assistant, 1958-63; Southern Reg Res Center, USDA, post doctoral res associate, 1963-65; Princeton University, post doctoral res associate, 1965-66; Personal Prod, Div of Johnson & Johnson, sr res chemist, 1966-74, manager of material research, 1974-87; Johnson & Johnson, research fellow, 1987-. **ORGANIZATIONS:** American Institute of Chemists, fellow, currently; American Association for Adv of Sci, currently; Tech Assoc for Pulp & Paper Ind, currently; American Chemistry Society, currently; Fiber Society, currently; International Confed of Thermal Assoc, currently; Sigma Xi, currently. **HONORS/AWARDS:** Johnson & Johnson, PB Hoffman Res Sci Award, 1973; Plast Institute of America, Educational Service Award, 1974; National Academy of Sci, USA, Resident Associateship, 1963-65. **SPECIAL ACHIEVEMENTS:** Book Absorbency, Elsevier Sci Publ, 1985; chapters in various books, 1969-92;

45 scientific articles in journals, 1959-93; 15 US patents, patents from 35 countries, 1969-92; short stories in Bengali, published in books & magazines, 1980-92. **BUSINESS ADDRESS:** Research Fellow, Johnson & Johnson, 2351 US Rte 130, Dayton, NJ 08810, (908)274-3026.

CHATTERJEE, SANKAR

Educator, curator. Indo-American. **PERSONAL:** Born May 28, 1943, Calcutta, W. Bengal, India; son of Prafulla K Chatterjee and Biva Chatterjee; married Sibani Chatterjee, Feb 4, 1971; children: Soumya, Shuvo. **EDUCATION:** Jadaupur University, BS, 1962, MS, 1964; Calcutta University, MS, 1964; Smithsonian Institution, postdoctoral fellow, 1978. **CAREER:** Indian Statistical Institute, Calcutta, senior lecturer, 1968-75; University of California, Berkeley, visiting professor, 1976; George Washington University, assistant professor, 1976-78; University of Tubiagen, Germany, visiting professor, 1991-92; Texas Tech University, assistant professor, 1979-84; associate professor, 1984-87; professor, curator, 1987-. **ORGANIZATIONS:** Society of Vertebrate, paleontology, 1976-; Geological Society of America, 1986-; Sigma-Xi, 1986-; Antarctican Society, 1982-. **HONORS/AWARDS:** Texas Senate Proclamation for Important Scientific Contribution, 1991; Women in Communications, Headliner Award, 1992; Field Museum of Natural History, Chicago, Robert Bass Fund, 1990; American Museum of Natural History, NY, Teddy Roosevelt Memorial Fund, 1990. **SPECIAL ACHIEVEMENTS:** Author of 50 scientific publications; co-editor, "New Concepts in Global Tectonics". **BIOGRAPHICAL SOURCES:** Dinosaur Discoveries, by Don lessem, 1993; Discovery, Time, Life, New York Times, featured in Nova Series "The Case of a Flying Dinosaur.". **BUSINESS ADDRESS:** Professor of Geology & Curator of Paleontology, Museum of Texas Tech University, 4th Indiana Avenue, Box 43191, Lubbock, TX 79409.

CHATTERJEE, SATYA N.

Physician. Indo-American. **PERSONAL:** Born Dec 31, 1934, Calcutta, W. Bengal, India; son of Radanath Chatterjee & Jyotirmoyee Chatterjee; married Patricia Ann, Sep 26, 1964; children: Sharmila, Shalini Chatterjee Miller, Arun. **EDUCATION:** University of Calcutta, MBBS, 1957; Royal College of Surgeons, fellow, England and Edinburgh, FRCS, 1963, 1964. **CAREER:** USC, clinical & research fellow, 1973-75; UCLA, assistant professor of surgery, 1975-77; UC, Davis, associate professor of surgery, 1977-84, professor of surgery, 1984-88; physician, currently. **ORGANIZATIONS:** International Transplant Society; American Society of Transplant Surgeons; Western Association of Transplant Surgeons; Sacramento County Medical Society; California Medical Association; Western Association of Transplant Surgeons, president, 1979; Organizing Comm, International Conference on Monoclonal Antibodies, 1983; International College of Surgeons, vice regent, 1984, 1990. **HONORS/AWARDS:** University of Calcutta, First Certificate of Honors, 1954; A K Banerjee Scholarship, 1955; Deutcher Akadamischer, scholarship, 1985. **BUSINESS ADDRESS:** 2600 Capitol Ave, Ste 307, Sacramento, CA 95816, (916)447-6466.

CHATTERJEE, SAYAN

Educator, educational administrator. Indo-American. **PERSONAL:** Born Jun 21, 1951, Calcutta, W. Bengal, India; married. **EDUCATION:** Jadavpur University, BSc, 1971; Indian Institute of Management, PGDM, 1978; University of Michigan, PhD, 1985. **CAREER:** Price Waterhouse & Co, accounts trainee, 1972-74; Bank of India, officer, 1974-76; Calcutta Electric Supply Corp, revenue officer, 1978-80; Purdue University, assistant professor, 1985-89; Case Western Reserve University, associate professor, 1989-. **ORGANIZATIONS:** Academy of Management; Strategic Management Society. **HONORS/ AWARDS:** Academy of Management, Best Paper, 1992, 1988; Weatherhead School of Management, Lewis-Progressive Faculty Fellowship, 1991-92; University of Michigan, Beta Gamma Sigma, 1986; National Science Development Fund, India, National Science Scholarship, 1968. **SPECIAL ACHIEVEMENTS:** Author, "The link between excess resources, transfer costs and mode of entry," Academy of Management Journal, December, 1990; "Sources of Value in Takeovers: Synergy or Restructuring," Strategic Management Journal, May, 1992, "Issues in Corporate Development," Handbook of Business Strategy, H E Glass, ed, Warren, Gorham, Lamont, December, 1992; "Enterprise Analysis: RPM Inc," Cleveland Enterprise, Summer, 1992. **BUSINESS ADDRESS:** Assoc Professor, Policy Division Head, Case Western Reserve University, Weatherhead School of Management, Cleveland, OH 44106-7235, (216)368-5373.

CHATTOPADHYAY, KALLOL (KAL CHATTO)

Pharmaceutical company administrator. Indo-American. **PERSONAL:** Born in India; married Mitra; children: Suman, Orin. **EDUCATION:** College of Pharmacy, BHU, India, BS, pharmacy, 1975; A&M College of Pharmacy, MS, pharmacy, 1988. **CAREER:** University of California, San Francisco, pharmacy assistant, 1979-80; Glaxo Inc, Hospital Division, manager, 1980-88; Amgen Inc, director of pharmacy affairs, 1988-. **ORGANIZATIONS:** Federation of Intl Pharmacy, executive member, 1992-; American Society of Hospital Pharmacy, 1980-; American Assn of College of Pharmacy, executive com industry, 1990-; American Management Assn, 1988-; American Pharmaceutical Assn, honorary member, 1991; American College of Clinical Pharmacy, associate member, 1990; New York Society of Hospital Pharmacist, chair education com, 1988. **HONORS/AWARDS:** Federation of Intl Pharmacy, Grand Prix Allign, 1992; Lifetime TV Medical Intl Film Festival, Freddie Award, 1992; Glaxo, President CLub, 1985. **SPECIAL ACHIEVEMENTS:** Co-author: Introduction of Pharmaceutical Biotechnology, University of Wisconsin, 1989; ACSF and Other CSF, University of California, San Francisco, 1991. **BIOGRAPHICAL SOURCES:** International Pharmacy Journal, vol 6, no 5, p 260, Oct 1992; Genetic Engineering News, p 3, Dec 1992. **HOME PHONE:** (818)991-2373. **BUSINESS ADDRESS:** Director, Pharmacy Affairs, Amgen Inc, 1840 DeHavilland Dr, Amgen Center, Thousand Oaks, CA 91320, (805)447-3283.

CHATURVEDI, ARVIND KUMAR

Biochemistry researcher. Indo-American. **PERSONAL:** Born Jul 29, 1947, Azamgarh, Uttar Pradesh, India; son of Vijai Narain Choubey & Sursari Devi Pandey; married Mira Shukla, Jun 14, 1970; children: Priyanka, Vivek. **EDUCATION:** Gorakhpur University, India, BS, 1966; Banaras Hindu University, India, MS, 1968; Lucknow University, India, PhD, 1972. **CAREER:** Lucknow University Medical College, India, research fellow, 1968-74; Vanderbilt University Medical School, research associate, 1974-77, research instructor, 1977-78; North Dakota State University, Fargo, assistant professor, 1978-82, associate professor, 1982-90; State Toxicology Laboratory, Fargo, assistant toxicologist, 1978-90; University of Oklahoma, adjunct professor, 1990-; Federation Aviation Administration, OK, supervisor, biomechem research section, 1990-. **ORGANIZATIONS:** Society for Experimental Biology and Medicine, 1982-92; Indian Pharmacological Society, life member; Indian Academy of Neurosciences, life member; International Society for Biochemical Pharmacology; American Society for Pharmcology and Experimental Therapeutics; Society of Toxicology; Aerospace Medical Association; numerous others. **HONORS/ AWARDS:** Grants received: American Cancer Society, 1979; National Institute on Drug Abuse, 1980-82; NDSU, NIH, Biomedical Research Support Grant, 1983, 1984; North Dakota Water Resources Research Institute, 1987-89. **SPECIAL ACHIEVEMENTS:** Proficiency in French; co-author, "A death due to self-administered fentanyl," 1990; co-author, "Comparison of toxicity rankings of six aircraft cabin polymers by lethality and by incapacitation," 1992; "Biochemical and toxicological studies on the mixtures of three commonly used herbicides in mice," 1993; numerous others. **BUSINESS ADDRESS:** Supervisor, Biochemistry Research Section, FAA Civil Aeromedical Institute, PO Box 25082, (AAM-613), Oklahoma City, OK 73125-5066, (405)954-4866.

CHATURVEDI, RAM PRAKASH

Educator. Indo-American. **PERSONAL:** Born Dec 15, 1931, Chandikara, Uttar Pradesh, India; son of Satyavati & Totaram; married Saroj Kumari Chaturvedi, May 13, 1964; children: Anjali & Anupama. **EDUCATION:** Agra University, BS, 1953, MS, 1955; University of British Columbia, PhD, 1963. **CAREER:** Agra College, lecturer in physics, 1955-59; University of British Columbia, teaching assistant, 1959-63; Panjab University, lecturer in physics, 1963-64; State University of NY, distinguished service professor, 1965-. **ORGANIZATIONS:** American Physical Society, Sigma Xi, local club president, American Association of Physics Teachers; American Association of Physics Teachers, president, N.Y. section zone councillor; Student Physics Society; Brookhaven National Lab, research scientist. **HONORS/AWARDS:** 30 grants from NSF, D.O.E. Suny Research Foundation & SUNY Cortland Faculty Research. **SPECIAL ACHIEVEMENTS:** 20 publications in Physical Review and Nuclear Inst & Methods; 30 presentations at professional meetings. **BUSINESS ADDRESS:** Distinguished Service Professor, State University of NY, Grahm Ave, Bowers Hall, Cortland, NY 13045, (607)753-2914.

CHATURVEDI, RAMA KANT

Educational administrator. Indo-American. **PERSONAL:** Born Jul 7, 1933, Kanker, Madhya Pradesh, India; son of Chaturbhuj S Chaturvedi & Asarfi D

Chaturvedi; married Veena Chaturvedi, May 28, 1958; children: Sanjiv, Kalpana Gustavson, Seemant. **EDUCATION:** Agra University, Agra, India, BSc, 1954, MSc, 1956, PhD, 1960. **CAREER:** H B Tech Institute, Kanpur, India, Chemistry, lecturer, 1960-64; Saint Stephen's College, Delhi, India, Chemistry, lecturer, 1964-65; Indiana University, Chemistry, research associate, 1965-66; Yale University, Biochemistry, research associate, 1966-70; Greater Hartford Community College, Chemistry, associate professor, 1970-76, Science Department, chairman, 1977-82; Capital Community-Technical College, SMPE Division, director, 1982-. **ORGANIZATIONS:** American Association for Advancement of Science, 1970-87, 1992-; American Association of University Professors, 1980-; American Chemical Society, 1967-84; India Association of New Haven, CT, founder, president, 1966-67. **HONORS/AWARDS:** Connecticut Board of Trustees for Community Colleges, Merit Service Award, 1990; US Education Foundation, Fulbright Grant, 1965-68; Government of India, senior research scholarship, 1957-60. **SPECIAL ACHIEVEMENTS:** 28 research papers in bioorganic chemistry, chemical kinetics and reaction mechanism, 1958-78; sabbatical research project: role of community colleges in international education, 1992. **BUSINESS ADDRESS:** Dir, Div of Science, Mathematics, Psychology & Educ, Capital Community-Technical College, 61 Woodland St, Hartford, CT 06105, (203)520-7836.

CHAU, HENRY CHUN-NAM
Business analyst. Hong Kong American/Chinese American. **PERSONAL:** Born Aug 9, 1961, Hong Kong; son of Kwai Chau Chow and Muk Ying Ng; married Anita Chan, Sep 30, 1990. **EDUCATION:** MIT, BS, 1984; Purdue Univ, MSM, 1994. **CAREER:** Dow Chemical Pacific Ltd, production engr, 1984-85, pharmaceutical technical specialist, 1985-88, business analyst, 1988-90; The Dow Chemical Co, business specialist, 1991-92, senior business specialist, 1992-. **HOME ADDRESS:** 5813 Lantern Lane, Midland, MI 48642, (517)631-0333. **BUSINESS ADDRESS:** Senior Business Specialist, The Dow Chemical Company, 2020 Dow Center, Midland, MI 48674, (517)636-2570.

CHAU, PETER
Financial analyst. Hong Kong American. **PERSONAL:** Born Apr 20, 1950, Hong Kong; married May Chin, Sep 18, 1989. **EDUCATION:** California Institute of Technology, BS, 1972; Cornell University, 1972-75; Columbia University, 1975-76; San Francisco State University, MS, BA, 1988. **CAREER:** East/West Newspaper, publisher, 1982-84; One Step Data, president, 1985-88; Capital Market Technology, chief financial officer, 1988-90; San Francisco State University, instructor, 1989-; Wells Fargo Bank, financial analyst, 1990-. **ORGANIZATIONS:** Assciation for Investment Management & Research; American Urban Economics & Real Estate Association. **HONORS/AWARDS:** Wall Street Journal, Outstanding Graduate Student, 1988. **SPECIAL ACHIEVEMENTS:** Author, How to Play Black Jack, published in Chinese, 1981. **BUSINESS ADDRESS:** Financial Analyst, Wells Fargo Bank, 343 Sansome St, MAC 0163-023, San Francisco, CA 94163-8871, (415)396-4618.

CHAUDHARI, ANSHUMALI
Research scientist. Indo-American. **PERSONAL:** Born Jun 22, 1947, Allahabad, Uttar Pradesh, India; son of Krishna Sahai Chaudhari and Shanti Devi Chaudhari; married Suman Lata Chaudhari, Feb 7, 1973; children: Swetanshu, Shruti. **EDUCATION:** University of Lucknow, India, BSc, 1966, MSc, 1968, PhD, 1976. **CAREER:** University of Lucknow, India, junior research fellow, 1969-75, senior research fellow, 1972-75; National Institute Environmental Health Science, visiting fellow, 1975-77; Wayne State University, research associate, 1977-80; UCLA Center for Health Sciences, adjunct assistant professor of medicine, 1980-85; UC Irvine, associate adjunct professor of medicine, 1985-89; US Army Dental Research Detachment, WRAIR, Walter Reed Army Medical Center, Biochemistry Section, chief, 1989-. **ORGANIZATIONS:** American Society for Pharmacology & Experimental Therapeutics, 1982-; Control Release Society, 1992-; Indian Academy of Neurosciences, 1983-; American Society of Nephrology, 1982-89; American Federation for Clinical Research, 1981-89; Society of Experimental Biology and Medicine, 1993-; Assn of Scientist of Indian Origin in America Inc, secretary-treasurer, 1991-92; Lucknow University Alumni Assn, president, 1990-92; Chitragupta Samaj Inc, president, 1992-; Professor S S Parmar Research Foundation, secretary/treasurer, 1987-. **HONORS/AWARDS:** American Heart Association, GLAA, senior investigatorship, 1984, advance research fellowship, 1979; National Institutes of Health, visiting fellowship, 1975; Indian Council of Medical Research, senior research fellowship, 1974. **BUSINESS ADDRESS:** Chief, Biochemistry Section, US Army Dental Research Detachment, Bldg T-2832, Fort George G Meade, MD 20755, (301)677-2279.

CHAUDHARI, PRAVEEN
Scientist. Indo-American. **PERSONAL:** Born Nov 30, 1937, Ludhiana, Punjab, India; son of Hans Raj Chaudhari and Ved Kumari Chaudhari; married Karin Romhild, Jun 13, 1964; children: Ashok, Pia. **EDUCATION:** Indian Institute of Technology, India, BS (honors), 1961; Massachusetts Institute of Technology, MS, physical metallurgy, 1963, ScD, physical metallurgy, 1966. **CAREER:** MIT, research associate, 1966; IBM Corp, Thomas J Watson Research Center, research staff member, 1966-70, manager, 1970-80, director of physical sciences, 1981-88, science vp, 1982-90, research staff, 1990-. **ORGANIZATIONS:** Hoechst-Celanese, science advisory board; Stanford Synchrotron Radiation Lab, science policy board; Brookhaven Natl Lab Physics; AAAS; NAE. **HONORS/AWARDS:** American Physical Society, George Pake Prize, 1987; AIME, Leadership Award, 1986; IEEE, Liebmann Prize, 1992. **SPECIAL ACHIEVEMENTS:** Presidential Wise Men Commmittee on Super Conductivity, executive secretary, 1988; Presidential Commission on Super Conductivity, 1989. **BUSINESS ADDRESS:** Director, IBM Research Div, Thomas J Watson Research Center, PO Box 218, Rte 134, Yorktown Heights, NY 10598, (914)945-3000.*

CHAUDHARI, SHOBHANA ASHOK
Physician, educator. Indo-American. **PERSONAL:** Born Jul 13, 1950, Nagpur, Maharashtra, India; daughter of Damodar Tukaram Kolte and Sushila Kolte; married Ashok P. Chaudhari, Nov 20, 1975. **EDUCATION:** University of Poona, MBBS, 1972; College of Physicians & Surgeons, Bombay, India, DCH, 1975; University of Bombay, India, MD pediatrics, 1977; American Board of Internal Medicine, 1988, (with added qualifications in geriatrics) 1992. **CAREER:** Lincoln Hospital/New York Medical College affiliate, Department of Medicine, attending physician, 1987-; director student clerkship, 1991-, associate program director, 1992-. **ORGANIZATIONS:** APDIM, 1992-93; American Geriatric Society, 1991-. **SPECIAL ACHIEVEMENTS:** Paper presented in International Congress of Pediatrics on Epidemiology of Leprosy in Children, 1977. **HOME ADDRESS:** 87 Main St., B4, Tarrytown, NY 10591, (914)332-0014.

CHAUDHARY, VED P.
Research administrator. Indo-American. **PERSONAL:** Born Jan 5, 1942, Etawa, Uttar Pradesh, India; married Rajni, Jun 1, 1970; children: Suneal, Ranee. **EDUCATION:** University of Allahabad, India, BSc, 1961; Rutgers State University, MS, 1967; University of Nebraska, PhD, 1970. **CAREER:** Govt Training Center, India, vice principal, 1962-63; UP Agricultural University, India, assistant professor, 1964-65; Brunswick Corporation, Defense Dept, senior engineer; AT&T Bell Laboratories, member of technical staff, 1970-77, supervisor, 1980-83; ITT Europe, manager, 1977-79, Bell Communications Research, director, 1984-. **ORGANIZATIONS:** Sigma Xi, 1969-75; American Institute of Aeronautics & Astronautics, 1970-77; Association for Computing Machinery, 1979-85; New York Academy of Sciences, 1980-85; IEEE Communications Society, 1990-; Asian Americans for Affirmative Action, chairperson, 1984-88, 1993-; Indian American Forum for Political Education, chairperson, 1988-91; Equal Opportunity Task Force, chair, 1989-; Rutgers University, board of trustees, 1993-; US Commission on Civil Rights, NJ State advisory committee, 1992-; Partnership for NJ, Leadership NJ Fellow, 1991; US Dept of Defense, procurement advisory council 1992-. **HONORS/AWARDS:** Governor of NJ, Ethnic Advisory Council, 1991-93. **SPECIAL ACHIEVEMENTS:** US Patent on "Rural Area Interface," Cross-Connection Device, 1975; US Patent on "Dynamic Routing," at five minute intervals, 1992; National Conference on Equal Opportunity, chairman, 1990; Indian American Leadership Conference, chairman, 1991; Asian American Conference on Glass Ceiling, chairman, 1993. **BIOGRAPHICAL SOURCES:** India Abroad, page 8, May 18, 1990; India West, page 39, April 16, 1993; News India, Aug 10, 1990; India Today, July 1993. **BUSINESS ADDRESS:** Director, Bell Communications Research, 33 Knightsbridge Rd, Room PY4J229, Piscataway, NJ 08854, (908)699-2035.

CHAUDHRI, RAJIV JAHANGIR
Securities analyst. Indo-American. **PERSONAL:** Born Dec 21, 1957, New Delhi, India; son of Hari Mohan Chaudhri and Preamvada Chaudhri. **EDUCATION:** Delhi University, St Stephen's College, BA (with honors), 1978; Indian Institute of Management, Ahmedabad, MBA, 1980; Harvard University, Kennedy School, MPA, 1983. **CAREER:** Reckitt & Coleman, regional sales mgr, 1980-81; Goldman, Sachs & Co, vice president, 1984-. **ORGANIZATIONS:** New York Society of Security Analysts, 1987-. **HOME ADDRESS:** 110 Riverside Dr, #11D, New York, NY 10024, (212)787-5287.

CHAUDHRY, G. RASUL
Educator. Pakistani American. **PERSONAL:** Born Jun 6, 1948, Multan, Pakistan; son of Abdul M Chaudhry and Sakeena B Chaudhry; married Zeenat F Chaudhry, Dec 30, 1982; children: Sadia, Saad, Sarah, Sophia. **EDUCATION:** University of Agriculture, Pakistan, BS (honors), 1969, MS (honors), 1972; University of Manitoba, Canada, PhD, 1980. **CAREER:** Punjab Agricultural Research Institute, Pakistan, research officer, 1972-77; University of Manitoba, Canada, teaching assistant, 1977-80; Georgetown University, Medical School, research associate, 1980-82; National Institutes of Health, visiting fellow, 1982-86, senior staff fellow, 1984-85; University of Florida, Gainesville, assistant professor, 1985-89; Oakland University, associate professor, 1989-. **ORGANIZATIONS:** American Society for Microbiology, 1980-; American Association for Advancement of Science, 1985-; American Society for Biochemistry and Molecular Biology, 1992-; American Public Health Association, 1992-; NIH Alumni Association, 1988-; Sigma Xi, 1986-; American Association of University Professors, 1989-. **HONORS/AWARDS:** US Department of Agriculture, Research Grant, 1986-88; National Science Foundation, Research Grants, 1991-9; Florida Department of Environmental Regulation, Research Grants, 1986-92. **SPECIAL ACHIEVEMENTS:** Editor, Biological Degradation and Bioremediation of Toxic Chemicals, 35 research papers, 5 book chapters, 6 research reports. **BIOGRAPHICAL SOURCES:** NIHAA, update, vol 4, no 2, p 9; 92nd General Meeting Journal, American Society for Microbiology, vol 13, no 3, p 1, 1992. **BUSINESS ADDRESS:** Assoc Prof, Dept of Biological Sciences, Oakland University, Dodge Hall, Room 340, Rochester, MI 48309, (313)370-3350.

CHAUDHURI, TAPAN K.
Physician. Indo-American. **PERSONAL:** Born Nov 25, 1944, Calcutta, W. Bengal, India; son of Taposh K Chowdhury and Bulu R Chowdhury; married Chhanda Chaudhuri, Mar 4, 1980; children: Lakshmi, Madhu, Krishna, Deboki. **EDUCATION:** University of Calcutta, premedical, 1961, medical, 1966. **CAREER:** University of Iowa School of Medicine, associate, 1970-71, assistant professor, 1971-74; Eastern Virginia Medical School, associate professor, radiology, 1974-77, professor, radiology, 1977-; VA Medical Center, chief, nuclear medicine, 1974-. **ORGANIZATIONS:** American College of Nuclear Medicine, board of representatives; Society of Nuclear Medicine, academic council; American College of Nuclear Physicians, speakers bureau; Radiological Society of North America; Biophysical Society; American Physiological Society. **HONORS/AWARDS:** American College of Nuclear Medicine, fellow, 1991; American College of Physicians, fellow, 1977; American College of Gestroenterology, fellow, 1977. **SPECIAL ACHIEVEMENTS:** More than 100 publications in national & international scientific and medical journals. **HOME PHONE:** (804)850-2677. **BUSINESS ADDRESS:** Professor/Chief, Nuclear Medicine, Eastern Virginia Medical School & VA Medical Center, 100 Emancipation Dr, Hampton, VA 23667, (804)722-9961.

CHAVAN, SANGITA D.
Fashion designer. Indo-American. **PERSONAL:** Born May 13, 1965, Bombay, India; daughter of Digambar Chavan and Suchita Chavan. **EDUCATION:** Parsons School of Design, BFA, 1987. **CAREER:** Stan Herman Studio, asst designer; Erez Fashions, designer, 1983-87; Adolfo II, designer, 1990-91, 1992-93; Dakota Blue, designer, 1991-92; free-lance designer, 1993-.

CHEE, CHENG-KHEE (JINYI XU)
Artist, educator. Chinese American. **PERSONAL:** Born Jan 14, 1934, Sianyou, Fujian, China; son of Yajie Xu and Xiang-chun (Zheng); married Sing-Bee (Ong) Chee, Aug 28, 1965; children: Yi-Hung, Yi-Min, Wan-Ying, Yen-Ying. **EDUCATION:** Nanyang University, Singapore, BA, 1960; University of Minnesota, MA, 1964. **CAREER:** Nanyang University, Singapore, assistant librarian, 1961-62; University of Minnesota, Minneapolis, teaching assistant, 1963-64; University of Minnesota, Duluth, librarian, 1965-68, instructor, 1968-81, assistant professor, 1981-88, associate professor, 1988-. **ORGANIZATIONS:** American Watercolor Society, signature member, 1981-; Allied Artists of America, signature member, 1981-; Knickerbocker Artists, New York, signature member, 1989-; National Watercolor Society, signature member, 1983-; Midwest Watercolor Society, signature member, 1977-; Sumi-e Society of America, 1979-; Georgia Watercolor Society, signature member, 1981-; Kentucky Watercolor Society, signature member, 1980-. **HONORS/AWARDS:** American Watercolor Society, Silver Medal of Honor, 1991; Allied Artists of America, Gold Medal of Honor, 1980; Knickerbocker Artists, New York, Gold Medal of Honor, 1989; Midwest Watercolor Society, Skyledge Award, 1987; Sumi-e Society of America, Best in Show, 1984, 1986. **SPECIAL ACHIEVEMENTS:** Illustrator, Old Turtle, by Douglas Wood;

which sold over 100,000 copies during the first year, and received the following awards: 1992 Minnesota Book Award for Best Children's Book, 1992 Midwest Children's Book Award, 1993 International Reading Association Children's Book Award, 1993 American Booksellers Association Children's Book of the Year Award, ABBY Award. **BIOGRAPHICAL SOURCES:** Brown, Marcia: "The Eastern Mountain Walks on Earth," 1987-88, China Exhibition Catalog. **HOME ADDRESS:** 1508 Vermilion Rd, Duluth, MN 55812, (218)724-2554. **BUSINESS ADDRESS:** Associate Professor, University of Minnesota, Duluth, 10 University Dr, Library Rm 205, Duluth, MN 55812.

CHELLAPPA, RAMA
Educator. Indo-American. **PERSONAL:** Born Apr 8, 1953, Tanjore, Tamil Nadu, India; son of M Ramalingam and R Kamakshi; married Vishnu P Chellappa, Jun 16, 1983; children: Vivek R, Deepa K. **EDUCATION:** College of Engineering, Guindy, BE, 1975; Indian Institute of Science, ME, 1977; Purdue University, PhD, 1981. **CAREER:** Purdue University, graduate assistant, 1977-81; University of Southern California, associate professor, 1981-91; University of Maryland, professor, 1991-. **ORGANIZATIONS:** Institute for Electronics and Electrical Engineers, fellow, 1981-; American Association for Artificial Intelligence, 1987-; Optical Society of America, 1992-; American Statistical Association, 1992-. **HONORS/AWARDS:** National Science Foundation, Young Investigator Award, 1985; IBM, Faculty Development Award, 1985; University of Southern California, Best Teacher Award, 1991; International Association for Pattern Recognition, Best Paper Award, 1992. **SPECIAL ACHIEVEMENTS:** Published more than 130 technical papers; co-editor and co-author of three books and collected works; co-author of 20 book chapters; presented more than 50 invited talks. **BUSINESS ADDRESS:** Professor, University of Maryland, College Park, A V Williams Bldg, 2365, College Park, MD 20742, (301)405-3656.

CHEN, ALAN KEITH
Educator, attorney. Chinese American. **PERSONAL:** Born Jul 10, 1960, Durham, NC; son of Ronald and Emily Chen; married Alison Brill, Apr 28, 1990; children: Hannah Lesley. **EDUCATION:** Case Western Reserve University, BA, 1982; Stanford University, JD, 1985. **CAREER:** US District Court, Hon Judge Marvin E Aspen, law clerk, 1985-87; ACLU Inc, Roger Baldwin Foundation, staff counsel, 1987-92; University of Denver College of Law, asst professor, 1992-. **BUSINESS ADDRESS:** Assistant Professor, University of Denver College of Law, 1900 Olive St, Denver, CO 80220, (303)871-6283.

CHEN, ALICE WU. *See* **CHEN, YUNG.**

CHEN, AMY L.
Radio producer. Chinese American. **PERSONAL:** Born Mar 22, 1957, Pittsfield, MA; daughter of Franklin & Virginia Chen. **EDUCATION:** Oberlin College, BA, 1979. **CAREER:** The New Museum of Contemporary Art, director of finance and administration; WBAI, producer, currently. **ORGANIZATIONS:** Radio Bandung, producer; Women's International Film, president; Media Network, treasurer; National Asian American Telecommunications Association. **HONORS/AWARDS:** National Federation of Community Broadcasters, Special Achievement Award, 1992; National Endowment for the Arts, media grant, 1993; New York State Council on the Arts, media award, 1992; New York Foundation for the Arts, fellowship, 1991; Harvest Works, artist-in-residence, 1993; Corporation for Public Broadcasting, media award, 1991. **HOME ADDRESS:** 220 Manhattan Ave, #5R, New York, NY 10025, (212)316-3121.

CHEN, ANDREW HOUNG-YHI
Educator, financial administrator. Chinese American. **PERSONAL:** Born Jun 14, 1937, Puli, Taiwan; son of Ching-Son Chen (deceased) and Sang-chu Chen; married Elaine T Chen, Jun 25, 1966; children: Michelle, Mark, Marjorie. **EDUCATION:** National Taiwan University, BA, economics, 1960; University of California, Berkeley, MA, economics, 1964, PhD, finance, 1969. **CAREER:** State University of New York, Buffalo, assistant professor of finance, 1968-71, associate professor of finance, 1971-73, associate professor of finance, 1974-75; University of California, Berkeley, visiting associate professor of finance, 1973-74; Ohio State University, professor of finance, 1975-83; Southern Methodist University, distinguished professor of finance, 1983-. **ORGANIZATIONS:** American Finance Assn; Asian Pacific Finance Assn, founding member; Society of Economic and Financial Management in China, director; Intl Assn of Financial Engineers, board of advisors; Financial Management Assn; Western Finance Assn; Dallas Economists Club. **HONORS/AWARDS:** Kai-

ser Aluminum & Chemical Corp, University of California, Berkeley, grant in aid, 1966-68; Dean Witter Foundation, University of California, Berkeley, research grant, 1974; Center for Research in Public Utilities Finance, University of Texas, Dallas, research grant, 1985-86; Herbert V Prochnow Foundation, research grant, 1986-87; CBOT Educational Research Foundation, research grant, 1989-90. **SPECIAL ACHIEVEMENTS:** Co-author, *Innovations in Dequity Financing,* Quorum Books, 1991; editor, *Research in Finance,* JAI Press, vol 6-11, 1986-93. **BUSINESS ADDRESS:** Professor of Finance, Southern Methodist University, Edwin L Cox School of Business, Bishop Blvd, Fincher Bldg, Dallas, TX 75275-0001, (214)768-3179.

CHEN, ANGELA TZU-YAU
County government official, real estate broker. Taiwanese American. **PERSONAL:** Born Mar 31, 1958, Taipei, Taiwan; daughter of Lai I-Hsin Virginia Chen and Yun-Zang Chen; married Jerry C Chang, Aug 3, 1986; children: Amy Chang. **EDUCATION:** National Taiwan University Medical College, BSN, 1980; George Washington University, MA, 1988. **CAREER:** George Washington University, registered nurse, 1983-86; TLC Nursing Services, registered nurse, owner, 1986-88; ReMax Dynamic Realty, real estate agent, 1989-92; Style Realty Inc, broker, owner, 1992-; County of Fairfax, senior public health nurse, 1993-. **ORGANIZATIONS:** Northern Virginia Board of Realty, 1988-; Board of Nursing, registered nurse, 1982-. **HONORS/AWARDS:** Northern Virginia Assn of Realtors Inc, Million Dollar Sales Club Membership, 1989, CCIM Commercial Realtors Award, 1990. **SPECIAL ACHIEVEMENTS:** Translator: *Emotional Care of Hospitalized Children,* 1981; *Behavioral Concepts and Nursing Throughout the Life Span,* English to Chinese translation, 1984; *Nursing Care to Meet Human Need,* 1985. **HOME ADDRESS:** 6804 Sprucedale Ct, Annandale, VA 22003, (703)642-8845. **BUSINESS PHONE:** (703)533-9181.

CHEN, ANNE CHI
Scientist. Chinese American/Taiwanese American. **PERSONAL:** Born May 10, 1962, Ann Arbor, MI; daughter of Sow-Hsin Chen and Ching-Chih Chen; married Don DiMasi, May 19, 1990. **EDUCATION:** Massachusetts Institute of Technology, BS, 1984; University of California, Los Angeles, PhD, 1990. **CAREER:** Dana Farber Cancer Institute, Harvard Medical School, postdoctoral fellow, 1990-91; Cornell University Medical College, postdoctoral fellow, 1991-. **ORGANIZATIONS:** AAAS, 1988-; AACR, associate member, 1990-; ASCB, associate member, 1993-. **HONORS/AWARDS:** National Institutes of Health, NRSA Postdoctoral Fellowship, 1991, Predoctoral Training Grant, 1984. **SPECIAL ACHIEVEMENTS:** Author of five publications in scientific journals, 1984-90; consultant to World Health Organization, 1985. **HOME ADDRESS:** 16 Whispering Ct, Bardonia, NY 10954.

CHEN, AUDREY HUEY-WEN
Educator. Taiwanese American. **PERSONAL:** Born Oct 27, 1964, Louisville, KY; daughter of Boris Chen & Linda Chen. **EDUCATION:** University of Kentucky, BA, 1986; San Diego State University/University of California, San Diego, joint doctoral program, 1987-89, 1991-. **CAREER:** Carrier Foundation, research associate, 1990-91. **ORGANIZATIONS:** American Psychological Association, student affiliate, 1985-; Society of Behavioral Medicine, student affiliate, 1992-. **HONORS/AWARDS:** University of Kentucky, Orchestra Grant, 1984-85. **SPECIAL ACHIEVEMENTS:** Publications: "The Effects of Numbering Signals on Reading & Recall''; "Voting in Ignorance: The Effects of 'Smooth-Sounding' Names''; "Cognitive-Behavioral Interventions.'' **BUSINESS ADDRESS:** Psychology Graduate Student, SDSU/UCSD Joint Doctoral Program in Clinical Psychology, 6330 Alvarado Ct, Ste 208, San Diego, CA 92120, (619)594-4819.

CHEN, AUGUSTINE CHENG-HSIN
Educator. Chinese American. **PERSONAL:** Born May 28, 1927, Shanghai, China; son of Kan-Tong Chen & Lien-Fong Chang; married Ann P Chen, Jun 20, 1959; children: Frederick T, Grace Y. **EDUCATION:** St John's University, Shanghai, China, BS, civil engineering, 1949; Luther College, Iowa, BA, physics, 1955; University of Nebraska, MS, physics, 1957; New York University, PhD, physics, 1964. **CAREER:** St Vincent College, Pennsylvania, instructor, 1958-59; University of California, San Diego, visiting research physicist, 1970-71; St John's University, assistant professor, 1964-72, associate professor, 1972-, chair, physics department, 1990-93. **ORGANIZATIONS:** American Physical Society, 1964-; Queens Historical Society, trustee, 1993-96; Community Board 7, Queens, City of New York, board member, 1992-94; Chinese Caring Foundation, vice president, 1992-94; Coalition for a Planned Flushing, board member, 1992-93, third vice president, 1993-95; Democratic

Club of Flushing, executive vice president, 1992-94; Chinese Immigrants Services, adviser, 1992-93; Chinese American Voters Association, president, 1990-91. **HONORS/AWARDS:** St John's University, Faculty Outstanding Achievement Medal, 1991; Courvoisier, Leadership Award, 1991; Chinese American Voters Association, Appreciation, 1991; Flushing Chinese Business Association, Outstanding Contribution, 1990; Chinatown Planning Council, Distinguished Service, 1987. **SPECIAL ACHIEVEMENTS:** Author of 27 papers published in Physical Review, Journal of Mathematical Physics, 1962-87, Journal of Physics, American Journal of Physics, Nuovo Cimento, Journal of Theoretical Biology and Advances in Atomic and Molecular Physics; testified before NYC Districting Commission contributing to the 1991 adoption of city council districts which are more representative of Asian Americans. **BUSINESS ADDRESS:** Professor, Physics Dept, St John's University, 8000 Utopia Parkway, B 34, St Albert Hall, Jamaica, NY 11439.

CHEN, BANG-YEN
Educator, researcher. Taiwanese American. **PERSONAL:** Born Oct 3, 1943, Ilan, Taiwan; son of Li-Zen Chen & Ten-Len Wu Chen; married Pi-Mei Chen, Sep 5, 1968; children: Bonny, Emery, Beatrice. **EDUCATION:** Tamkang University, Taiwan, BS, 1965; National Tsinghua University, Taiwan, MS, 1967; University of Notre Dame, PhD, 1970. **CAREER:** Tamkang University, instructor, 1966-68; National Tsinghua University, instructor, 1967-68; Michigan State University, research associate, 1970-72, associate professor, 1972-76, professor, 1976-90, University Distinguished Professor, 1990-. **ORGANIZATIONS:** Bulletin of Mathematics, Academia Sinica, editorial board; Soochow University, editor, Soochow Journal of Mathematics; Algebras, Groups and Geometry, editor; Academia Peloritana of Italy, corresponding member, 1989. **HONORS/AWARDS:** Science University of Tokyo, Doctor of Science, 1981; Tamkang University, Distinguished Alumni, 1991. **SPECIAL ACHIEVEMENTS:** Creator of submanifolds of finite type; founder of Chen surfaces; co-founder of (M+, M-) theory in compact symmetric spaces; author of 300 research articles; author of 5 books. **BUSINESS ADDRESS:** Professor, Dept of Mathematics, Michigan State University, Wells Hall, East Lansing, MI 48824-1027, (517)353-4670.

CHEN, BENJAMIN YUN-HAI
Ocean engineer, naval architect. Chinese American. **PERSONAL:** Born May 3, 1951, Taipei, Taiwan; son of Pon-Hwa Chen & Shieh-Vee Ha Chen; married Sheam-Pey H Chen, Sep 1, 1979; children: Daniel Y, Vincent Y. **EDUCATION:** National Taiwan University, Taipei, Taiwan, BS, civil engineering, 1974; University of Delaware, MS, PhD, ocean and coastal engineering program, 1978, 1982. **CAREER:** University of Delaware Ocean & Coastal Eng Prog, research assistant, 1976-82, Coastal & Offshore Eng & Research, engineering consultant, 1982-83; Naval Ocean Res & Dev Activity, research ocean engineer, 1983-84; David Taylor Model Basin, research naval architect, 1984-. **ORGANIZATIONS:** American Society of Mechanical Engineers, 1987; Sigma Xi, 1990. **HONORS/AWARDS:** University of Delaware, Unidel Fellowship, 1976; David Taylor Model Basin, Outstanding & Sustained Superior Performance, 1988, Performance Management Awards, 1990-93. **SPECIAL ACHIEVEMENTS:** Registered professional engineer in Maryland, 1987; 16 publications in Wave Mechanics & Ocean Engineering, 1978-86; 23 publications in Advanced Propulsor Technology, 1988-93. **MILITARY SERVICE:** Army of Republic of China, 2nd lieutenant, 1974-76. **BUSINESS ADDRESS:** Research Naval Architect, Propulsor Technology Br, David Taylor Model Basin, Carderock Div, Naval Surface Warfare Center, Propulsor Technology Branch, Bethesda, MD 20814, (301)227-1450.

CHEN, BERNARD SHAO-WEN
Banking manager. Chinese American. **PERSONAL:** Born Sep 25, 1960, Boston, MA; son of Tze-Ning Chen and Joan Chen; married Lisa Ruderman Chen, Oct 24, 1992. **EDUCATION:** Massachusetts Institute of Technology, BSME, 1982, MSME, 1984; Columbia Business School, MBA, 1989. **CAREER:** General Electric, manufacturing mgmt program trainee, 1984-86, manufacturing engineer, 1986-87; Bankers Trust, management consultant/assistant vp, 1989-92, project mgr/vp, 1992-. **ORGANIZATIONS:** MIT Alumni Association, 1985-; Columbia Business School, NY Alumni Chapter, 1993-; Pi Tau Sigma, 1981; Beta Gamma Sigma, 1988. **HONORS/AWARDS:** Beta Gamma Sigma Award, 1989. **HOME ADDRESS:** 55 W 14th St Apt 10K, New York, NY 10011. **BUSINESS ADDRESS:** Vice President, Bankers Trust, 4 Albany St, 7th floor, New York, NY 10006.

CHEN, BESSIE B.
Physician. Chinese American. **PERSONAL:** Born Mar 17, 1958, Taipei, Taiwan; daughter of Edward W Chen and Jean J Chen; married Raymond Schettino, Sep 30, 1987; children: Amy Schettino. **EDUCATION:** Johns Hopkins University, BA, 1980; Johns Hopkins Medical School, MD, 1983. **CAREER:** Johns Hopkins University, assistant professor, 1988-90; Piedmont Anesthesia Associates, staff anesthesiologist, 1990-. **ORGANIZATIONS:** AMA, 1985-; AMWA, 1985-; ASA, 1984-; ASRA, 1990-; IARS, 1984-; SCA, 1986-. **BUSINESS ADDRESS:** Physician, Piedmont Anesthesia Associates, 1984 Peachtree Street NW, Suite 515, Atlanta, GA 30309, (404)351-1745.

CHEN, BINTONG
Educator. Chinese American. **PERSONAL:** Born May 11, 1964, Nantong, Jiangsu, People's Republic of China; son of Jinsong Chen & Meiling Ni; married Yubei Zhang, Jun 18, 1987; children: Helen. **EDUCATION:** Shanghai Jiao Tong University, Electrical Engineering Dept, BS, 1985, Dept of Naval Architecture and Ocean Engineering, BS, 1985; University of Pennsylvania, Dept of Systems, MS, 1987, Wharton School, Decision Sciences Dept, PhD, 1990. **CAREER:** University of Pennsylvania, teaching assistant, 1986-90; Washington State University, assistant professor, 1990-. **ORGANIZATIONS:** ORSA, associate member, 1986-; SIAM, associate member, 1990-. **HONORS/AWARDS:** Washington State University, grant-in-aid, 1993; University of Pennsylvania, University of Pennsylvania Fellowship, 1987-88; Shanghai Jiao Tong University, President's List, 1982-85. **SPECIAL ACHIEVEMENTS:** Team member of research project, developed train scheduling & evaluation system for Burlington Northern Railroad & Natl Science Foundation; referee of professional journals; refereed pubs: coauthor, "A Non-interior Continuation Method for Monotone Variational Inequalities," to appear in Mathematical Programming; "A Non-interior Continuation Method for Linear Complementarity Problems," to appear in SIAM Journal of Matrix Analysis & Applications; author, "Finite Convergence of B-differentiable Equation Based Methods for Affine Variational Inequalities," Applied Mathematics Letters 5, p 19-24, 1992. **BUSINESS ADDRESS:** Asst Professor, Dept of Management & Systems, Washington State University, College of Business and Economics, Pullman, WA 99164, (509)335-4458.

CHEN, C. L. PHILIP
Educator. Taiwanese American. **PERSONAL:** Born Jul 4, 1959, Puli, Nan-Tou, Taiwan; son of Cheng-Kuan & Liu-Yu Chen; married Chien-Chiu Chien, Jul 2, 1986; children: Oriana I, Melinda Y. **EDUCATION:** National Taipei Institute of Technology, BS, 1979; University of Michigan, MS, 1985; Purdue University, PhD, 1988. **CAREER:** University of Michigan, teaching assistant, research assistant, 1984-85; Purdue University, research assistant, 1985-88, visiting assistant professor, 1988-89; Wright State University, assistant professor, 1989-. **HONORS/AWARDS:** National Science Foundation, Research Initiation Award, 1989. **SPECIAL ACHIEVEMENTS:** Language proficiency: English, Chinese, Japanese, Taiwanese; publications: "A Systematic Approach for Design and Planning of Mechanical Assemblies," Artifical Intelligence for Engineering, Design, Analysis, and Manufacturing, vol 7, no 1, p 19-36, 1993; with Y H Pao, "An Integration of Neural Network and Rule-Based System for Design and Planning of Mechanical Assemblies," IEEE Trans on Systems, Man, and Cybernetics, no 23, 1993; book chapter, "Setup Generation and Feature Sequencing using Unsupervised Learning Algorithm," edited by Y Takefuji & J Wang, World Scientific Publishing Co Pte Ltd, 1993. **MILITARY SERVICE:** Taiwan Navy Officer, 2nd lt, 1979-81. **BUSINESS ADDRESS:** Assistant Professor, Dept of Computer Science & Engineering, Wright State University, Dayton, OH 45435, (513)873-5107.

CHEN, CARL WAN-CHENG
Engineer. Taiwanese American/Chinese American. **PERSONAL:** Born Feb 22, 1936, Tainan, Taiwan; son of Wen-Ho Chen and Li-Pei Chen; married Nora F, Aug 28, 1965; children: Connie Len, Peter Wen. **EDUCATION:** National Taiwan University, Taipei, Taiwan, BS, 1958; University of California, Berkeley, MS, 1963, PhD, 1968. **CAREER:** Taiwan Public Works Bureau, asst engr, 1960-62; University of California, Berkeley, 1963-68; Water Resources Engineers, engineer, 1968-73; Tetro Tech Inc, vice president, 1973-93; Systech Engineering Inc, president, 1993-. **ORGANIZATIONS:** ASCE, 1968-. **HONORS/AWARDS:** ASCE, 1993 Samuel Arnold Greeley Award for best paper in Tour of Environmental Engineering, 1993; Chinese Engineers and Scientists Assn of So California, Achievement Award, 1978. **SPECIAL ACHIEVEMENTS:** US patent 4,863,083. **BUSINESS ADDRESS:** President, Systech Engineering Inc, 3744 Mt Diablo Blvd, Lafayette, CA 94549, (510)284-7544.

CHEN, CATHERINE W.
Educator, educational administrator. Chinese American. **PERSONAL:** Born Sep 19, 1938, Chengdu, China; daughter of S C Wang and Y T Chia; married Hsuan S Chen, Sep 10, 1966; children: James, John. **EDUCATION:** National Taiwan University, BA, 1960; University of Minnesota, MA, 1966, PhD, 1975. **CAREER:** University of Minnesota, instructor, 1966-69; University of Michigan, lecturer, 1970-71; Northwood University, library director, 1974-85, director of libraries, 1985-89, academic dean, 1989-. **ORGANIZATIONS:** American Association of Higher Education, 1989-, Women's Caucus, Minority Caucus; Red Cross, Midland Chapter, board member, 1992-95; Valley Library Consortium, board member, 1993-. **HOME PHONE:** (517)631-9724. **BUSINESS ADDRESS:** Academic Dean, Northwood University, 3225 Cook Rd, Midland, MI 48640-2311, (517)837-4371.

CHEN, CHAO
Educator. Chinese American. **PERSONAL:** Born Jan 22, 1953, Taiwan; son of Chen-Po Chen and Yen-Ping Chen; married Ping Peng Chen, Mar 29, 1980; children: Jerry J, Andrea J. **EDUCATION:** University of Maryland, PhD, 1988. **CAREER:** California State University, Northridge, professor, 1988-. **ORGANIZATIONS:** Financial Management Association, 1985-; American Finance Association, 1985-; American Accounting Association, 1989-; Western Finance Association, 1986-; Academy of Financial Services, 1992-. **HONORS/AWARDS:** California State University, Northridge, Meritorious Performance and Professional Promise Award, 1990, School of Business Research Grant, 1989-93, University Research Grant, 1989-90; Beta Gamma Sigma, 1988. **SPECIAL ACHIEVEMENTS:** "Triple Witching Hour, Regulatory change and Stock Market Reaction," Journal of Futures Markets, 1994; "Choices among Long-Term Financing for Public Utilities," Financial Review, 1992; "Structural Changes on International Diversification," 1993; "Risk and Return in Copper, Platinum and Silver," Journal of Futures Markets, 1990; "Public Disclosure of Bank Loan Accounting Information," Journal of Accounting and Public Policy, 1989. **MILITARY SERVICE:** Air Force, 1976-78. **BUSINESS ADDRESS:** Professor, Dept of Finance, School of Business Administration, California State University at Northridge, 18111 Nordhoff St, Northridge, CA 91330, (818)885-2459.

CHEN, CHAO LING (DAVID)
Educator. Taiwanese American. **PERSONAL:** Born Sep 28, 1937, Tsaotan, Taiwan; married Virginia; children: Stephen. **EDUCATION:** National Taiwan University, DVM, 1960; Iowa State University, MS, 1966; Michigan State University, PhD, 1969. **CAREER:** Kansas State University, assistant professor, 1969-74, associate professor, 1974-76; University of Florida, associate professor, 1976-81, professor, 1981-, associate chairman, 1988-. **ORGANIZATIONS:** The Endocrine Society; American Physiological Society; Society for Study of Reproduction; International Society of Neuroendocrinology; AAAS; Sigma Xi; New York Academy of Sciences. **HONORS/AWARDS:** Beecham, Best Researcher, 1990. **MILITARY SERVICE:** Chinese Infantry, 2nd lt, 1960-61. **BUSINESS ADDRESS:** Professor and Associate Chairman, Dept of LACs, University of Florida, College of Veterinary Medicine, PO Box 100136, Gainesville, FL 32610, (904)392-4700.

CHEN, CHARLES T. M. *See* **CHEN, TSONG-MING.**

CHEN, CHEYENNE. *See* **SHEN, XIAO-YAN.**

CHEN, CHI HAU
Educator, business executive. Chinese American. **PERSONAL:** Born Dec 22, 1937, Fuchow, Fukien, China; married Wanda Wanchun Chen; children: Ivan Iwen, Christopher Iming. **EDUCATION:** National Taiwan University, BSEE, 1959; University of Tennessee, MSEE, 1962; Purdue University, PhD, 1965. **CAREER:** AVCO Systems, senior research engineer, 1965-68; University of Massachusetts, Dartmouth, senior professor, 1968-; Information Research Laboratory Inc, president, 1983-. **ORGANIZATIONS:** IEEE, elected fellow, 1987-. **SPECIAL ACHIEVEMENTS:** Editor: Computer Engineering Handbook, McGraw-Hill, 1992; Signal Processing Handbook, Marcel-Dekker, 1988; 15 other books and 200 journal publications. **BUSINESS ADDRESS:** Professor, Electrical & Computer Engineering Dept, University of Massachusetts, Dartmouth, Old Westport Road, North Dartmouth, MA 02747, (508)999-8475.

CHEN, CHI-YUN
Educator. Chinese American. **PERSONAL:** Born May 5, 1933, Guangzhou, Guangdong, China; married Yvonne Chen, 1962; children: Donna, Davina.

EDUCATION: Taiwan Normal University, BEd, 1956; Harvard University, AM, 1962, PhD, 1967. **CAREER:** University of Malaya, Chinese Studies, lecturer, 1963-67; Harvard University, visiting associate professor, 1973-74; University of California, History Dept, asst professor, 1967-73, associate professor, 1974-80, professor, 1980-. **ORGANIZATIONS:** Association for Asian Studies, 1967-. **SPECIAL ACHIEVEMENTS:** Book, Hsun Yueh (AD 148-209), Cambridge University Press, 1975; book, Hsun Yueh and the Mind of Late Han China, Princeton University Press, 1980; contributor, Cambridge History of China, vol 1, Ch 15, 1985. **BUSINESS ADDRESS:** Professor, Dept of History, University of California, Santa Barbara, CA 93106-0001, (805)893-2991.

CHEN, CHIN

Educator. Chinese American. **PERSONAL:** Born Apr 15, 1927, Foochow, Fujian, China; married Concordia Chen, Jul 2, 1960; children: Marie H M, Albert C, Jennifer. **EDUCATION:** National Taiwan University, 1951; Wayne State University, MS, 1958; Boston University, PhD, 1962. **CAREER:** Taiwan Provincial Government, junior geologist, 1951-54; Wayne State University, graduate assistant, 1955-56; Chicago Field Museum, field paleontologist, 1957; Boston College, lecturer, 1961-62; Lamont-Doherty Geological Observatory of Columbia University, research scientist, 1962-68; New Paltz State College, New York, adjunct professor, 1968; Western Connecticut State University, professor, coordinator of graduate program, 1969-. **ORGANIZATIONS:** Geological Society of America, 1965-, fellow, 1974-; Geological Society of China, Taiwan, 1951-; Paleontological Society of America, 1963-78. **HONORS/AWARDS:** Sohio Petroleum Co, Sohio Scholarship, 1958. **SPECIAL ACHIEVEMENTS:** Author of numerous publications. **BIOGRAPHICAL SOURCES:** Outstanding Oversea Chinese, p239. **BUSINESS ADDRESS:** Professor, Western Connecticut State University, 181 White St, Danbury, CT 06810-6845.

CHEN, CHIN-LIN

Educator. Chinese American. **PERSONAL:** Born Mar 27, 1937, Hunan, China; son of C H Chen and C Y Wang; married Josephine C F Chen, Jun 10, 1966; children: Eugene, Christine. **EDUCATION:** National Taiwan University, BSEE, 1958; North Dakota State University, MSEE, 1961; Harvard University, PhD, 1965. **CAREER:** Harvard University, research fellow, 1965-66; Purdue University, professor, 1966-. **ORGANIZATIONS:** IEEE, senior member; URSI; Sigma Xi; Eta Kappa Nu. **BUSINESS ADDRESS:** Professor of Electrical Engineering, Purdue University, 1285 Electrical Engineering, West Lafayette, IN 47907-1285, (317)494-3525.

CHEN, CHING-CHIH

Educator, consultant, author. Chinese American. **PERSONAL:** Born Sep 3, 1937, Foochow, Fukien, China; daughter of Han-chia Liu (deceased) and May-ying Liu; married Sow-Hsin Chen, Aug 19, 1961; children: Anne, Catherine, John. **EDUCATION:** National Taiwan University, BA, 1959; University of Michigan, AMLS, 1961; Case Western Reserve University, PhD, 1974. **CAREER:** McMaster University, science library, head, 1962-64; University of Waterloo, sr science librarian, 1964-65, engineering math & science library, head, 1965-68; Massachusetts Institute of Technology, assoc science librarian, 1968-71; Simmons College, GSLIS, asst professor, 1971-75, assoc professor, asst dean, 1975-79, professor, assoc dean, 1979-. **ORGANIZATIONS:** Soros Foundation, New Information Technical Program, consultant, 1992-93; Intl Conf on New Information Technology, chief conf organizer of NIT, 1987-; USIA, consultant, speaker, 1983-; World Bank, consultant to China, 1986; UNESCO/CPI, consultant, 1981-86; World Health Org, consultant, 1981-85; American Library Assn, councilor-at-large, chair of several committees, 1981-93; American Society of Information Science, board of directors & candidate for president, 1982-84, other committee assignments, 1978-; Library & Information Technology Assn, director of the board, 1990-93; American Assn for Advancement of Science, fellow, 1985-. **HONORS/AWARDS:** Assn of Visual Communications, Cindy Award, 1983-86; US Natl Endowment for Humanities, Project Emperor-1, 1983-86; US Dept of Education, Criteria of Effectiveness of Network Delivery. . ., 1980, Regional Investigation of Citizen's Information Needs, 1978; US Natl Lib of Medicine, Publication Grant, 1977; Cutting-edge Technology Applications, numerous awards for achievement; awards from: DEC, Apple, IBM, Microtek, Sun, Emily Hollowell Fund, FID; numerous others. **SPECIAL ACHIEVEMENTS:** Author and editor of over 25 books, 1976-; founding editor-in-chief, Microcomputers for Information Management Journal, 1984-; creator of the first of Emperor of China interactive videodisc, digital CD-ROM, and multimedia products, popular version published by the Voyager Company, 1991-; electronic publishing of the first CD-ROM in library school setting, NIT-CD-ROM, 1991. **BIOGRAPHICAL SOURCES:** Directory of Online Professionals; Contemporary Authors. **BUSINESS ADDRESS:** Professor/Associate Dean, Graduate School of Library & Information Science, Simmons College, 300 The Fenway, Boston, MA 02115, (617)521-2804.

CHEN, CHONG-MAW

Educator. Taiwanese American. **PERSONAL:** Born in Taoyuan, Taiwan; son of Jen-ho Cheng and Wu-Chao Cheng; married JoAnn Chen, Dec 29, 1967; children: Sharon, Alice, Howard. **EDUCATION:** National Taiwan Normal University, BS, 1959; Kansas University, PhD, 1967; McMaster University, Ontario, Canada, postdoctorate, 1967-69; Roche Institute of Molecular Biology, research associate, 1969-71. **CAREER:** University of Wisconsin, assistant professor, 1971-73, associate professor, 1973-77, professor, 1977-. **ORGANIZATIONS:** Member of seven professional societies. **HONORS/AWARDS:** University of Wisconsin, Parkside, Excellence in Teaching Awards, 1977, 1993; University of Wisconsin System, Distinguished Professor, 1988-. **SPECIAL ACHIEVEMENTS:** Scientific publications, 90 articles, 6 book chapters. **BUSINESS ADDRESS:** Wisconsin Distinguished Professor, Biomedical Research Institute, University of Wisconsin, Parkside, Wood Rd, Kenosha, WI 53141, (414)595-2434.

CHEN, CHONG-TONG

Educator, educational administrator. Taiwanese American. **PERSONAL:** Born Dec 17, 1935, Tainan, Taiwan; son of Dan-Chiang Chen and Lai-Yen Chen; married Joyce T Chen, Jun 4, 1969; children: Gary T, Jason V. **EDUCATION:** National Chung-Hsing University, BS, 1960, MS, 1964; University of Illinois, Urban-Champaign, PhD, 1972. **CAREER:** Northeastern Illinois University, chairman & professor, 1985-. **ORGANIZATIONS:** American Accounting Association, 1980-; Institute of Management Accountants, 1984-. **HONORS/AWARDS:** American Institute of Certified Public Accountants, Certified Public Accountant, 1983; Institute of Management Accounts, certified management accountant, 1984. **BUSINESS ADDRESS:** Prof/Chmn, Dept of Acctg/Business Law/Finance, Northeastern Illinois University, 5500 N St Louis Ave, Chicago, IL 60625, (312)794-2657.

CHEN, CHUAN JU

Engineer, chemical company manager. Taiwanese American. **PERSONAL:** Born Mar 21, 1947, Tainan, Taiwan; son of Tan-Hsin Chen & Lien-Chih Chen; married Shiou-yi Chen, Aug 8, 1972; children: Roger P, Stephanie Y. **EDUCATION:** Chung Yuan University, BE (with honors), 1970; Worcester Polytechnic Institute, MS, 1974; University of Michigan, PhD, 1980. **CAREER:** Monsanto Company, sr technology engr, 1980-86, technology specialist, 1986-90, sr technology specialist, 1990-91, technology group leader, 1992-93, technology manager, 1993-. **ORGANIZATIONS:** American Chemical Society, 1978-; Society of Plastics Engineers, 1978-81. **HONORS/AWARDS:** University of Michigan, Macromolecular Research Center Fellowship, 1974-78; Sigma Xi, 1974. **MILITARY SERVICE:** Chinese Army, Taiwan, 2nd lieutenant, 1970-71. **BUSINESS ADDRESS:** Technology Manager, Monsanto Co, 730 Worcester St, Springfield, MA 01151, (413)730-2304.

CHEN, CHUNG

Educator. Chinese American. **PERSONAL:** Born Feb 21, 1953, Taipei, Taiwan; son of Yu-Da Chen & Chin-Har Lee Chen; married Ewen; children: Pamela A, Brenda R, Michael Z. **EDUCATION:** National Taiwan University, BS, 1975; University of Wisconsin, Madison, PhD, 1984. **CAREER:** University of Chicago, research associate, 1982-84; Washington State University, Pullman, assistant professor, 1984-88; Syracuse University, associate professor, 1988-. **ORGANIZATIONS:** American Statistical Association, Syracuse Chapter, president, 1991-. **HONORS/AWARDS:** Syracuse University, School of Management, Exceptional Scholarship Award, 1992. **SPECIAL ACHIEVEMENTS:** Developed theory & methods in time series analysis; Works have been published in: Technometrics, 1988; Journal of Business & Economic Statistics, 1991; Journal of American Statistical Association, 1993; developed procedures in identifying relationship between economic variables, major results published in Review of Economics & Statistics, 1991. **BUSINESS ADDRESS:** Associate Professor, Dept of Quantitative Methods, Syracuse University, School of Management, Syracuse, NY 13244-2130, (315)443-1255.

CHEN, CHUNG-HSUAN

Scientist. Taiwanese American. **PERSONAL:** Born Jan 4, 1948, Amoy, Fujian, China; son of King-Shu Chen; married Shan-Lan Chen, Jul 20, 1974;

children: Nelson, Gee-Con, Franklin Gee-Wei. EDUCATION: National Taiwan University, BS, 1969; University of Chicago, MS, chemistry, 1971, PhD, chemistry, 1974. CAREER: University of Chicago, teaching assistant, 1970; Oak Ridge National Laboratory, post doctor, 1974, research staff, 1976, group leader, 1989-. ORGANIZATIONS: American Physical Society, 1974-; American Chemical Society, 1984-; American Material Research Society, 1992-. HONORS/AWARDS: Industrial Research and Development, R & D 100 Award, 1992, 1987, 1984; Oak Ridge National Laboratory, Award for Excellent Research, 1990, Publication Award, 1989. SPECIAL ACHIEVEMENTS: 100 publications in refereed journals; US patent. HOME ADDRESS: 1812 Plumb Branch Road, Knoxville, TN 37932, (615)691-0352. BUSINESS ADDRESS: Group Leader, Photophysics Research, Oak Ridge National Laboratory, PO Box 2008, MS 6378, Bldg 5500, Oak Ridge, TN 37831-6378, (615)574-5895.

CHEN, DAVID TA-FU
Bank executive. Chinese American. PERSONAL: Born Jul 23, 1935, Nanking, China; son of Winston W T Chen & Wen Y Hu Chen; married Debbie L Chen, Dec 29, 1973; children: Winston, Wylie, Winnie. EDUCATION: National Chung Hsin University, Taipei, BA, 1959; University of Washington, BA, 1971; University of Oregon, MA, 1966. CAREER: New Castle County, Delaware, treasurer, 1974-77; City of Beaverton, Oregon, finance director, 1977-85, city councilor, council president, 1985-91; Farmers Home Administration, Oregon, director, 1985-91, associate administrator, 1992-93; American Pacific Bank, president, CEO, 1993-. HONORS/AWARDS: International Municipal Finance Officers Association, Certificates of Achievement, 1979-85; City of Kenai, AK, Proclamation, "David Chen Day," 1973. SPECIAL ACHIEVEMENTS: Publications: Municipal Government Accounting, 1972, 1977; Municipal Government Budget, 1972, 1977; proficient in Chinese; Oregon State Treasurer, candidate, 1993. BUSINESS ADDRESS: President & Chief Executive Officer, American Pacific Bank, 112 Main St, Box 350, Aumsville, OR 97325, (503)221-5801.

CHEN, DAVID TING-KAI
Educator. Taiwanese American. PERSONAL: Born Sep 6, 1935, Chang-Hwa, Taiwan; son of May Chen and Mei Yang Chen; married Paulen Wang Chen, Oct 23, 1981; children: Daniel Christoph, Benjamin Christian. EDUCATION: College of Law and Commerce, Taipei, BA, 1957; University Erlangen-Nuremberg, Germany, MS, 1962, PhD, 1973. CAREER: IBM Corp, program manager, 1963-89; Fordham University, professor, 1989-. ORGANIZATIONS: Association for Computing Machineries, 1989-; Institute of Electrical & Electronics Engineers, 1989-; New York Academy of Sciences, 1991-; Sigma Xi, 1989-; North America Taiwanese Professors' Association, 1989-; Monte Jade Science and Technology Association, 1990-; Association of Information Technology, 1991-. SPECIAL ACHIEVEMENTS: Author, "Die Volksrepublik China: Nord Und Sued In Der Entwicklung," published in Germany, 1982; "Nord- Und Suedchina: Unterschiede Der Wirtschafts- Und Sozialstruktur Afugrund Der Natuerlichen Und Kulturellen Voraussetzungen," published in Germany, 1974; more than 10 scientific papers in computer and information science areas. BUSINESS ADDRESS: Professor, Dept Computer and Info Sci, Fordham University, 441 E Fordham Rd, John Mulcahy Hall #340, Bronx, NY 10458-5148, (718)817-4483.

CHEN, DAVID W.
Librarian. Chinese American. PERSONAL: Born Jul 9, 1939, Lo-tung, Taiwan; son of Ho-tzo Chen (deceased) and Ah-ma Chen; married Mei Y Chen, Sep 16, 1967; children: Frederick Ming, Stephen Ho. EDUCATION: Taiwan Theological College, BTh, 1965; Yale University, Divinity School, BDiv, 1968; University of Pittsburgh, School of Library & Information Science, MLS, 1969. CAREER: Hartford Seminary, catalog librarian, 1969-71; Emory University, Pitts Theology Library, tech services, asst librarian, 1971-. ORGANIZATIONS: American Theological Library Assn, 1972-; Atlanta Taiwanese Presbyterian Church, clerk of session, 1989-. SPECIAL ACHIEVEMENTS: Language proficiency: English, Chinese, Taiwanese; translator: The Nestorian Church in China, Cheng, Lien-ming, 1965. HOME ADDRESS: 2127 Silversmith Lane, Stone Mountain, GA 30087-1714, (404)939-9275. BUSINESS ADDRESS: Asst Librarian, Pitts Theology Library, Emory University, 535 Kilgo Circle NE, Atlanta, GA 30322, (404)727-4166.

CHEN, DERRICK A.
Investment banker. Taiwanese American. PERSONAL: Born Jan 14, 1966, Stamford, CT; son of James Y & Vivian C Chen. EDUCATION: Harvard College, AB (magna cum laude), 1987. CAREER: Drexel Burnham Lambart,

financial analyst, 1987-89; Lazard Freres & Co, vice president, 1989-94; Goldman Sachs & Co, 1994-. ORGANIZATIONS: Asia Society, generation advisory group, 1993; A Magazine, senior editor, 1992-; Securities & Exchange Commission, registered representative, 1989-. HONORS/AWARDS: Phi Beta Kappa, 1987; Harvard College, John Harvard Scholarship, 1987. SPECIAL ACHIEVEMENTS: Mandarin Chinese, conversational French. HOME ADDRESS: 200 E 89th St, Apt 28C, New York, NY 10128.

CHEN, DI
Engineer. Chinese American. PERSONAL: Born Mar 15, 1929, Tzechi, Chekiang, China; son of H Y Chen; married Lynn Chen, Jun 14, 1958; children: Andrew A J, Daniel T Y. EDUCATION: National Chiao Tung University, Shanghai, electrical engineering, 1948-49; National Taiwan University, BS, electrical engineering, 1953; University of Minnesota, MS, electrical engineering, 1956; Stanford University, PhD, electrical engineering, 1959. CAREER: University of Minnesota, assistant professor, 1959-62; Honeywell Inc, fellow, research scientist, 1962-80; AML (CDC-Honeywell), director of engineering, 1980-82; LMSI (formerly OPL), director of technology, 1982-83; Optotech, Inc, founder and executive vp, 1984-89; Chen & Associates, president, 1989-. ORGANIZATIONS: IEEE/MAG, Twin Cities section, chairman, 1971; Optical Society of America, Optical Data Storage Conference, conference chairman, 1983-84; Applied Optics, topical editor, 1990-; SPIE, 1983-; Sigma Xi, 1954-; Eta-Kappa Nu, 1954-; Optical Society of America, 1976-. HONORS/AWARDS: IEEE, Fellow Award, 1974; Honeywell, Sweatt Scientist/Engineering Award, 1972. SPECIAL ACHIEVEMENTS: Over 100 published journal articles in the field of optical recording and laser application, 1960-; issued 17 US patents in the field of optical data storage and laser modulation/deflection, 1968-83. BUSINESS ADDRESS: President, Chen & Associates, 302 Sunbird Cliffs Ln W, Colorado Springs, CO 80919, (719)599-0093.

CHEN, DING-BOND
Engineer. Taiwanese American. PERSONAL: Born Mar 16, 1947, San Chung, Taiwan; son of Kwei-Jang Chen and A-Jau Chen; married Judy, Oct 2, 1975; children: Albert, James, Lillian. EDUCATION: National Cheng-Kung University, BSE, 1971; University of Cincinnati, MSEE, 1975. CAREER: Rotel Electronic Co, manufacturing engineer, 1972-73; Rotel of America, quality control engineer, 1975-80; Burroughs Corp, device engineer, 1980-82, senior engineer, 1982-. ORGANIZATIONS: IEEE, 1975-. HOME ADDRESS: 8950 Allenbrook Way, San Diego, CA 92129, (619)484-5286.

CHEN, DONALD S.
Educator. Taiwanese American. PERSONAL: Born Jun 21, 1940, Taipei, Taiwan; son of Su-ti & Tammui Chen; married Deborah, Aug 11, 1974; children: Stephanie Carissa, Garrett Michael. EDUCATION: Taiwan Normal University, teacher's certificate, 1960; Centenary College, bachelor of music, 1965; Union Theological Seminary, master of sacred music, 1967; The Juilliard School, master of science, 1971; University of Iowa, doctor of musical art, 1981. CAREER: Mount Holyoke College, conductor of chorus, 1971-74; Webster University, director of choral activities, 1976-82; Roosevelt University, conductor of orchestra & opera, 1982-. ORGANIZATIONS: Conductors' Guild, 1988-; North Shore Choral Society, conductor, 1983-. BUSINESS ADDRESS: Orchestra and Opera Conductor, Chicago Musical College, Roosevelt University, 430 S Michigan Ave, Chicago, IL 60605, (312)341-3729.

CHEN, EDWARD C. H.
Physician. Taiwanese American. PERSONAL: Born Aug 21, 1954, Keelung, Taiwan; son of George Chen & Lan-Chu Chen; married Shu-Wang Chen, May 20, 1983; children: Eugene B, Monica V. EDUCATION: Taipei Medical College, MD, 1980; Harvard School of Public Health, MPH, 1981. CAREER: Physician, currently. ORGANIZATIONS: American Medical Association; American College of Gastroenterology; American Gastroenterologic Association. HOME ADDRESS: 3224 Withee Court, Bethlehem, PA 18017.

CHEN, ER-PING
Research engineer. Chinese American. PERSONAL: Born May 19, 1944, Ping-Liang, Kansu, China; son of Sheng-Huang Chen and Tze-Yu C Chen; married Regina C Chen, Mar 31, 1973; children: Candice, Benjamin. EDUCATION: National Chung-Hsing University (Taiwan), BS, 1966; Lehigh University, MS, 1969, PhD, 1972. CAREER: Lehigh University, assistant professor, 1972-77, associate professor, 1977-78; Sandia National Laboratories, distinguished member of technical staff, 1978-. ORGANIZATIONS: America Society of Mechanical Engineers, 1972-, fellow, 1988-; Sigma Xi, 1972-; New Mexico Chinese Assn, 1984-, past president; Assn of Chinese-American Engi-

neers and Scientists of New Mexico, 1990-, past president; Albuquerque Sister Cities, board member, 1992-. **HONORS/AWARDS:** Sandia National Laboratories, Excellent Contribution Award, 1990, Sandia Award for Excellence, 1991. **SPECIAL ACHIEVEMENTS:** Over 90 technical papers published in technical journals, 1970-; co-author, Cracks in Composite Materials, Nijhoff, 1981. **BUSINESS ADDRESS:** Distinguished Member of Technical Staff, Sandia Natl Labs, PO Box 5800, Albuquerque, NM 87185-5800, (505)844-2033.

CHEN, FRANCIS F.
Educator. Chinese American. **PERSONAL:** Born Nov 18, 1929, Canton, Guangdong, China; son of M Conrad Chen and Evelyn S Chu; married Edna L Chen, Mar 31, 1956; children: Sheryl F, Patricia A, Robert F. **EDUCATION:** Harvard University, AB, 1950, MA, 1951, PhD, 1954. **CAREER:** Princeton Plasma Physics Lab, senior research staff, 1954-69; University of California, Los Angeles, professor, 1969-. **ORGANIZATIONS:** Amer Phys Society, fellow, Division of Plasma Physics, chairman, 1983; IEEE, fellow. **HONORS/AWARDS:** IEEE, Plasma Science and Applications Award, 1994. **BUSINESS ADDRESS:** Professor, University of California, Los Angeles, 56-125 B Engr IV, Los Angeles, CA 90024-1594, (310)825-5624.

CHEN, GEORGE CHI-MING
Business executive (retired). Chinese American. **PERSONAL:** Born Sep 21, 1923, Shanghai, China; married Nora P Chen, 1953. **EDUCATION:** Harvard College, AB, 1946. **CAREER:** George Chen & C0o, Ltd, chairman, 1950-85; Lien Chen Ltd, chairman, 1970-85; Shinung Corporation, managing director, 1970-89; Shell Pacific Development Ltd, chairman, 1984-89. **ORGANIZATIONS:** Northfield Mount Hermon School, trustee, 1988-; Golf Association of Republic of China, governor, 1970-85. **MILITARY SERVICE:** Republic of China Army, lt col.

CHEN, GONG
Educator. Chinese American. **PERSONAL:** Born Nov 26, 1953, Hai-Cheng, Liaoning, People's Republic of China; son of Ying Chen and Hui Ding; married Yuan Li, Jul 30, 1983; children: Carol T, Victor D. **EDUCATION:** Shenyang Institute of Physical Education, China, BA, 1977; Beijing Institute of Physical Education, MEd, 1981; California State Polytechnic University, post master, 1985-87; University of Arkansas, EdD, 1990. **CAREER:** Shenyang PE Institute, lecturer, 1977-78, assistant professor, 1981-84; Cal Poly University, instructor, 1985-87; TG Smith School, teacher, 1987-88; University of Arkansas, instructor, 1988-90; San Jose State University, professor, 1990-. **ORGANIZATIONS:** Center for International Sports and Human Performance, assistant director, 1992-; CAHPERD-Bay Distsrict, publication coordinator, 1992-; CAHPERD-Unit 110, vice president for health, 1992-; AAHPERD, 1989-; NAPEHE, 1992-; WCPES, 1990-; Asian Faculty Association, 1991-; Chinese-American Sports Association, consultant general, 1991-; United State Wu Shu Federation, Collegiate Division, general secretary. **HONORS/AWARDS:** San Jose State University, Outstanding Faculty Mentor, 1992-93, eight research grants, 1991-93; Shenyang PE Institute, Outstanding Teacher, 1977; Bay Area Chinese-American Athletic Games, Outstanding Professional Contributions, 1993. **SPECIAL ACHIEVEMENTS:** Two books on creativity (both in Chinese), 1986-87; sixteen articles published in US and China, 1981-93; eighteen papers presented from district to international levels, 1991-93; organized as vice president and served as chair of Arbitrary committee of Bay Area Annual Chinese-American Athletic Games, 1991-. **BIOGRAPHICAL SOURCES:** "Creative Thinking Ability of Physical Education Students," monograph series, Western College Physical Education Society, 1991. **BUSINESS ADDRESS:** Professor, Dept of Human Performance, San Jose State University, One Washington Sq, SPX Bldg #56, San Jose, CA 95192-0054, (408)924-3033.

CHEN, GUANRONG (RON)
Educator. Chinese American. **PERSONAL:** Born Jul 5, 1948, Canton, China; married Helen Q X Chen, Sep 1976; children: Julie Y, Leslie Y. **EDUCATION:** Zhongshan University, MSc, 1981; Texas A&M University, PhD, 1987. **CAREER:** Rice University, visiting assistant professor, 1987-90; University of Houston, assistant professor, 1990-. **ORGANIZATIONS:** IEEE, senior member, 1989-; AIAA, 1990-. **HONORS/AWARDS:** University of Houston, Young Faculty Research Award, 1993. **SPECIAL ACHIEVEMENTS:** 5 books published, 1987-; 50 journal papers published, 1981-; IEEE Transactions on Circuits and Systems I, associate editor, 1993-. **BIOGRAPHICAL SOURCES:** IEEE Transactions on Circuits and Systems I, vol 40, no 9, p 601, 1993; IEEE Transactions on Aerospace and Electronic Systems, vol 28, no

3, p 621, 1992. **BUSINESS ADDRESS:** Professor, Dept of Electrical Engineering, University of Houston, N313-D, Houston, TX 77204-4793, (713)743-4446.

CHEN, HAIYANG
Educator. Chinese American. **PERSONAL:** Born Oct 31, 1955, Beijing, People's Republic of China; married Yiyun Chen, 1982; children: Cheryl, Sharon. **EDUCATION:** University of International Business and Economics, BA, international trade, English, 1982; American Graduate School of International Management, MIM, international finance, 1984; Kent State University, MA, international economics, 1987, PhD, finance, 1990. **CAREER:** Youngstown University, Accounting & Finance Department, associate professor, currently. **ORGANIZATIONS:** Financial Management Association, 1987-; Chinese Economists Society, 1987-. **HONORS/AWARDS:** Youngstown State University, University Research Professor, 1992-93, 1993-94; Beta Gamma Sigma; Omicron Delta Epsilon. **SPECIAL ACHIEVEMENTS:** Co-author, refereed journal articles: "Management Ownership and Corporate Value: Some New Evidence," Managerial and Decision Economics, vol 114, no 4, pp 335-46, 1993; "Hong Kong's Investment in China and the Hong Kong's Economy," Philippine Economic Journal, forthcoming; "Country of Origin Effects of Foreign Investment in China," Journal of International Business Studies, vol 24, no 2, pp 277-90, 1993; "Foreign Ownership in Chinese Joint Ventures: A Transaction Cost Analysis," co-author, J of Bus Res, vol 26, no 2, Feb 1993, pp 149-60; "The Wealth Effect of Intl Joint Ventures: The Case of US Investment in China," co-author, Financial Mgmt, vol 20, no 4, Winter 1991, pp 31-41; refereed book chapters: "Performance of Hong Kong Foreign Subsidiaries in China," Advances in Chinese Industrial Studies, JAI Press, forthcoming; "Stock Valuation Effects International Joint Venturees: Evidence from U S Investment in Eastern European Countries," Wealth Creation in Eastern Europe: Financial Management Issues and Strategies, Haworth Press, 1992; Presentations: "Factors Explaining the Performance of Joint Venutues in China," 1992 Meeting of Western Economic Association; "Impact of US-China Joint Ventues on Stockholders' Wealth by Degree of International Involvement," PACAP Finance Conference; "A Further Inquiry into Management Ownership and Corporate Value," 1991 Meeting of Financial Management Association. **BUSINESS ADDRESS:** Professor, Accounting & Finance Dept, Youngstown State University, Youngstown, OH 44555-0002, (216)742-1883.

CHEN, HARRY W.
Company executive. Taiwanese American. **PERSONAL:** Born Jun 17, 1937, Kaohsiung, Taiwan; son of Wen-Der Chen and Su-Hua Young; married Tsai S Chen, Jun 3, 1966; children: Deborah C, Morris Y. **EDUCATION:** National Chengchi University, BA, 1960; University of Kansas, PhD, 1969. **CAREER:** Jackson Laboratory, senior staff scientist, 1970-84; DuPont, principal investigator, 1984-90, senior principal investigator, 1990-. **HONORS/AWARDS:** University of Kansas, Dr Newark's Award for Excellent Biochemical Research; University of Bern, Pathology Institute, Yamagiwa-Yoshida Award for Cancer Research. **BUSINESS ADDRESS:** Senior Principal Investigator, Du Pont Merck Pharmaceuticals, Route 141, E400/3227, Wilmington, DE 19898, (302)695-7099.

CHEN, HELEN T. W.
Business executive, author. Chinese American. **PERSONAL:** Born in Shanghai, People's Republic of China; daughter of Joyce Chen and Thomas Chen; married Keith R Ohmart, Sep 12, 1982. **EDUCATION:** Wheaton College, BA, 1968. **CAREER:** Joyce Chen Inc, president, 1983-; Keilen Ltd, president, 1991-. **ORGANIZATIONS:** Women's Culinary Guild of NE, board of directors; International Association of Culinary Professionals; the American Institute of Food and Wine. **SPECIAL ACHIEVEMENTS:** Author, Stir Fry with Helen Chen, 1988; Chinese Cooking with Helen Chen, 1992; Helen Chen's Chinese Home Cooking, William Morrow Publishers, 1994. **BUSINESS ADDRESS:** President, Joyce Chen, Inc and Keilen Ltd, 25 Industrial Way, Wilmington, MA 01887, (508)988-9088.

CHEN, HENRY
Physician. Chinese American. **PERSONAL:** Born May 23, 1941, Rangoon, Burma; son of Chin Tat Chen and Soon Tee Sio; married Cecilia, Oct 18, 1965; children: Amy, Jean, Sue, Edward. **EDUCATION:** Rangoon University, Burma, MD, 1964; Johns Hopkins University Hospital, resident anaesthesiologist, 1970-73. **CAREER:** Private practice, anaesthesiologist, 1973-. **ORGANIZATIONS:** American Society of Anaesthesiologists, 1970-; Medical Chirugical Faculty of Maryland, 1973-; Maryland DC Society of Anaesthesiol-

ogists, 1973-. **BUSINESS ADDRESS:** Physician, Harbor Hospital Center, 3001 S Hanover St, Baltimore, MD 21230.

CHEN, HENRY
Program manager. Chinese American. **PERSONAL:** Born Feb 27, 1959, Tainan, Taiwan; son of Liang-Foo Chen and Dorothy Chen; married Anne Chen, Dec 23, 1986; children: Lauren. **EDUCATION:** New York University, BA, 1982; Polytechnic University, MS, 1985. **CAREER:** IBM Corp, programmer, 1982-83, associate programmer, 1983-85, senior associate programmer, 1985-87, staff system analyst, 1987-89, advisory system analyst, 1989-91, program manager, 1991-. **ORGANIZATIONS:** Chinese Mei Society, NYU, treasurer, president, 1980-82; New York Chinese Jaycees, director, 1990-91; Univoice Chorus, director, 1990-91; Woodside Condo, bd of management, 1989-; New York Academy of Sciences, 1977-82, 1992-; Assn of Computing Machinery, 1980-82, 1992-; IEEE, 1992-. **HONORS/AWARDS:** National Honor Society, 1976l National Science Foundation, grant, 1977; IBM Corp, Outstanding Innovation Award, 1991, Informal Awards, 1989, 1992. **BUSINESS ADDRESS:** Program Manager, IBM Corp, Rockwood Road, North Tarrytown, NY 10591, (914)332-3775.

CHEN, HENRY J.
Physician. Chinese American. **PERSONAL:** Born Dec 18, 1960, Taipei, Taiwan; son of Edward and Jean Chen; married Anna Liu. **EDUCATION:** Johns Hopkins University, BA, 1983; University of Maryland, School of Medicine, MD, 1987. **CAREER:** Sequoia Hospital, cardiologist, currently. **ORGANIZATIONS:** American Medical Assn, 1987-; American College of Physicians, 1990-; American College of Cardiology, 1990-; American Society of Internal Medicine, 1987-. **BUSINESS ADDRESS:** Cardiologist, Cardiovascular Medicine and Coronary Interventions, 2940 Whipple Ave, Ste 10, Redwood City, CA 94062, (415)306-2300.

CHEN, HILO C. H.
Artist. Taiwanese American. **PERSONAL:** Born Oct 15, 1942, Yee-Lun, Taiwan; son of Yion Ho Chen & Lee Wun Chen; married Mei Wan Chen; children: Inten. **EDUCATION:** Chong Yien University, BS, architecture, 1966. **CAREER:** Artist, currently.

CHEN, HOLLIS CHING
Educator. Chinese American. **PERSONAL:** Born Nov 17, 1935, Chekiang, China; son of Yu-Chao Chen and Shui-tan Hsia; married Donna H C Liu, Sep 3, 1961 (deceased); children: Desiree R, Hollis T. **EDUCATION:** National Taiwan University, BSEE, 1957; Ohio University, MSEE, 1961; Syracuse University, PhD, 1965. **CAREER:** Syracuse University, instructor, asst prof, 1961-67; Ohio University, assistant prof, 1967-69, associate professor, 1969-75, acting dept chair, 1984-86, professor, 1975-. **ORGANIZATIONS:** Institute of Electrical & Electronics Engineers, senior member; International Union Radio Science; American Society for Engineering Education; Optical Society of America; American Geophysical Union. **HONORS/AWARDS:** National Science Foundation, grants, 1968-70; Ohio University, Faculty Excellence Award, 1990, Research Committee Grants, 1972-74. **SPECIAL ACHIEVEMENTS:** Author or co-author of more than 70 papers published in various technical journals; author, Theory of Electromagnetic Waves, McGraw-Hill, 1983; contributing author, Topics of Electromagnetic Wave, Wiley, 1981. **BUSINESS ADDRESS:** Prof, Dept of Elec & Comp Eng, Ohio University, Stocker Center 354, Athens, OH 45701, (614)593-1583.

CHEN, HONG CHYI
Educator. Taiwanese American. **PERSONAL:** Born Sep 12, 1954, Putai, Taiwan; son of Shui-Sheng Chen; married Su Jen H Chen, Oct 25, 1979; children: Leo C, Daniel E. **EDUCATION:** Fu-Jen University, Taiwan, BA, 1977; Middle Tennessee State University, MA, 1982; University of Oklahoma, PhD, 1988. **CAREER:** University of Oklahoma, graduate instructor, 1985-88; Grand Valley State University, assistant professor, 1988-. **ORGANIZATIONS:** Chinese Association of Western Michigan, president, 1993-; Chinese Language School of Grand Rapids, principal, 1993-; Psi Chi; American Psychological Association; Midwestern Psychological Association; Southwestern Psychological Association. **SPECIAL ACHIEVEMENTS:** Author and contributor: many papers and presentations on person perception, attitude and persuasion, human behavior and performance and personnel selection. **BUSINESS ADDRESS:** Professor, Psychology Dept, Grand Valley State University, 1 Campus Dr, Allendale, MI 49401-9401, (616)895-2417.

CHEN, HONGDA
Educator. Chinese American. **PERSONAL:** Born Nov 24, 1957, Xian, Shaanxi, People's Republic of China; married. **EDUCATION:** Fuzhou University, BS, 1982; University of California, Davis, MS, 1987, PhD, 1990. **CAREER:** The University of Vermont, assistant professor of food engineering, 1990-. **ORGANIZATIONS:** IFT, 1987-; ASAE, 1987-; FPE-710, vice chair, 1992-94; FPE-043, chair, 1993-95; ADSA, 1990-; SIM, 1992-; CAFS, 1985-. **HONORS/AWARDS:** University of California, Davis, G F Stewart Memorial Award, 1989, S J Leonard Memorial Award, 1986. **SPECIAL ACHIEVEMENTS:** Over 40 abstracts, publications, and presentations at professional meetings and societies. **BUSINESS ADDRESS:** Professor, Dept of Animal & Food Sciences, The University of Vermont, Terrill Hall, Burlington, VT 05405-0044, (802)656-2070.

CHEN, HOUN-GEE
Educator. Taiwanese American. **PERSONAL:** Born Jan 13, 1956, Kaohsiung, Taiwan; married Su-chan Chen, Mar 8, 1981; children: Wan-Ting, Eric. **EDUCATION:** National Tsing-Hua University, Taiwan, BS, 1978; University of Wisconsin, Madison, MS, 1985, PhD, 1988. **CAREER:** China Steel Corp, project engineer, 1980-83; University of Notre Dame, assistant professor, 1988-. **ORGANIZATIONS:** Institute of Management Science, 1987-; Society of Operations Research, 1987-; Institute of Industrial Engineer, 1986-; Decision Sciences Institute, 1989-; American Chinese Management Educators, 1990-. **HONORS/AWARDS:** University of Notre Dame, Center of Business Research, Summer Research Grants, 1989-93; ACME Conference, Best Paper Award, 1991. **SPECIAL ACHIEVEMENTS:** Author, "A Petri Net Model for Operator Scheduling," International Journal of Productions Research, 1992; "A Knowledge-Based System for Robot Scheduling," Journal of Intelligent Manufacturing, 1992; " A Study of Nested If-Then-Else Constructs," Journal of Man-Machine Studies, 1992; "An Object-Oriented DSS for Inventory Management," Computers & Industrial Engineering, 1991. **BUSINESS ADDRESS:** Assistant Professor, Dept of Management, University of Notre Dame, 201 I Hurley, Notre Dame, IN 46556, (219)631-5833.

CHEN, HSIN-PIAO PATRICK
Educator. Taiwanese American. **PERSONAL:** Born Jan 25, 1950, Taipei, Taiwan; son of Shih-Yung Chen and Mai-Ching Chen; married Hsun Hu Chen, Jan 3, 1977; children: Ingrid. **EDUCATION:** Natl Cheng-Kung University, Taiwan, Dept of Engineering Science, BS, 1972; Natl Tsing-Hua University, Taiwan, School of Power Mechanical Engineering, MS, 1976; Georgia Institute of Technology, School of Aerospace Engineering, PhD, 1983. **CAREER:** Kaohsuing Inst of Tech, Dept of Mechanical Engineering, teaching asst, 1972-74; Natl Tsing-Hua University, Dept of Power Mechanical Engineering, teaching asst, 1974-76; Chung Shan Inst of Science & Technology, asst scientific researcher, 1976-79; Georgia Inst of Technology, School of Aerospace Engineering, graduate research asst, 1979-83, postdoctoral fellow, 1984-85; Natl Cheng-Kung University, Inst of Aeronautics & Astronautics, associate professor, 1985-86; California State University, Long Beach, Dept of Aerospace Engineering, associate professor, 1986-. **ORGANIZATIONS:** California State University, Long Beach, Aerospace Engineering Dept, Graduate Studies Comm, 1988-, library rep, 1988-, Curriculum Comm, 1988-91, vice chairman, 1988-90, Comm of Recruiting, 1989-; American Institute of Aeronautics & Astronautics, 1987-, reviewer for AIAA Journal, 1991-92; Natl Science Foundation, reviewer for NSF proposal, 1991. **HONORS/AWARDS:** California State University, Long Beach, Professional Opportunities Program Award, 1988, Affirmative Action Faculty Development Program Award, 1989, Scholarly & Creative Activity Summer Stipend, 1990, CSU Award for Research, Scholarship, & Creative Activity, 1992; Phi Tau Phi Scholastic Honor Society, 1976. **SPECIAL ACHIEVEMENTS:** Co-author, "Dynamic Analysis of Delamination Growth," AIAA Journal, vol 30, no 2, pp 447-448, 1992; co-author, "Cylindrical Bending of Unsymmetric Composite Laminates," AIAA Journal, vol 30, no 5, pp 1438-1440, 1992; author, "Transverse Shear Effects on Buckling and Postbuckling of Laminated and Delaminated Plates," AIAA Journal, vol 31, no 1, pp 163-169, 1993; co-author, "Dynamic Delamination Growth in Laminated Composite Structures," Composites Science and Technology, vol 46, pp 325-333, 1993. **BUSINESS ADDRESS:** Associate Professor, Dept of Aerospace Engineering, California State University, Long Beach, 1250 Bellflower Blvd, Long Beach, CA 90840-0004, (310)985-1504.

CHEN, HUNG-LIANG (ROGER)
Educator, researcher, engineer. Taiwanese American. **PERSONAL:** Born 1959, Taipei, Taiwan; son of Jeng-Ching & Jen-Wei Chen; married Lucy Chen, 1984; children: Alan, Brian. **EDUCATION:** Taipei Institute of Technology,

diploma, 1979; Northwestern University, MS, 1985, PhD, 1988. **CAREER:** New Taiwan Foundation Construction Co, assistant engineer, 1981; National Taipei Institute of Technology, teaching assistant, 1981-83; Northwestern University, research assistant, 1983-88, research associate, 1988-89; West Virginia University, assistant professor, 1989-. **ORGANIZATIONS:** American Concrete Institute; American Society of Civil Engineers; American Society of Nondestructive Testing; ASCE, technical committee on Shock and Vibratory Effect; EMD and ASCE, Technical Committee of Dynamics. **HONORS/ AWARDS:** West Virginia University College of Engineering, Young Researcher of the Year, 1992. **SPECIAL ACHIEVEMENTS:** Language proficiency in Chinese & Taiwanese. **MILITARY SERVICE:** Army, Taiwan, 2nd lt, platoon leader, 1979-81. **HOME PHONE:** (304)598-3428. **BUSINESS ADDRESS:** Assistant Professor, Dept of Civil Engineering, West Virginia University, Engineering and Sciences Bldg, Rm 653D, Morgantown, WV 26506-6101, (304)293-3031.

CHEN, IVAN MAO-CHANG
Educator. Chinese American. **PERSONAL:** Born Oct 19, 1956, Taipei, Taiwan; married Monica J Chen, Dec 29, 1984; children: Andrew I, Kristina E, Aaron W. **EDUCATION:** Ming-Chi Institute of Technology, BS, 1977; University of Scranton, MBA, 1985; University of Missouri-Kansas City, PhD, 1991. **CAREER:** School District of Kansas City, resource teacher, 1991-. **SPECIAL ACHIEVEMENTS:** Fluent in Chinese, Mandarin and Amoyese.

CHEN, JACKSON W.
Physician. Taiwanese American. **PERSONAL:** Born Nov 13, 1941, Taiwan; son of Hoa Chen and Sue-Tze Wong Chen; married Fei-Yun Chen, Feb 12, 1969; children: Paul, Judy, Vicky. **EDUCATION:** National Taiwan University, College of Medicine, MD, 1966. **CAREER:** Rush-Presbyterian St Luke Hospital, attending physician, 1986-; Good Samaritan Hospital, attending physician, 1986-. **BUSINESS ADDRESS:** Physician, 100 E 35th St, Chicago, IL 60616, (312)225-5682.

CHEN, JAMES
Computer and software company executive. Chinese American. **CAREER:** Mitsuba Corp, president, currently. **BUSINESS ADDRESS:** President, Mitsuba Corp, 1925 Wright Ave, La Verne, CA 91750, (909)392-2000.*

CHEN, JAMES PAI-FUN
Educator, researcher. Taiwanese American. **PERSONAL:** Born May 1, 1929, Fengyuan, Taichung, Taiwan; son of Chuan Chen and Su-wuo Lin Chen; married Metis Hsiu-chun Lin Chen, Dec 19, 1964; children: Mark Hsin-tzu, Eunice Hsin-yi, Jeremy Hsin-tao. **EDUCATION:** National Taiwan University, 1949-51; Houghton College, BS, 1955; St Lawrence University, MS, 1957; Pennsylvania State University, PhD, 1962. **CAREER:** Houghton College, instructor, associate professor, 1960-64; University of Vermont College Med, res associate, 1964-65; SUNY, Buffalo School Medicine, res associate, 1965-68; University of Texas Med Branch, assistant professor, 1968-75; NASA-Johnson Space Center, sr res associate, 1975-76; University of Tennessee Mem Res Ctr, associate professor, 1976-78; University of Tennessee Coll Med, associate professor, professor, 1978-. **ORGANIZATIONS:** American Assn of Immunologists, 1975-; American Society Biochemistry & Molecular Biology, 1976-; Intl Society of Hematology, fellow, 1980-; American Heart Assn, Thrombosis Council, 1982-; Intl Society Thrombosis & Haemostasis, 1985-; Intl Fibrinogen Res Society, 1991-; American Board of Bioanalysis, Clinic Lab, director, 1991-. **HONORS/AWARDS:** Robert Welch Foundation, Research Grant, 1970-74; Ortho Research Foundation, Research Grant, 1971-75; National Institutes of Health, Research Grant, 1975-82; American Heart Association/Texas & Tennessee Affiliates, Research Grant, 1969-72, 1974-75, 1984-85, 1989-90; US Army Med Res & Development Command, Research Grant, 1988-91. **SPECIAL ACHIEVEMENTS:** Contributed over 41 articles to Thromb Haemost and other professional journals; discovered additional proteolytic fragmentation in the high temp trypsin digestion of human IgM; developed a radioimmunoassay for fragment E-neoantigen and applied it to the clinical assay of hypercoagulable state; discovered evidence of the coagulopathy in Pichinde virus-infected guinea pigs. **BUSINESS ADDRESS:** Professor of Medical Biology, University of Tennessee Medical Center, 1924 Alcoa Hwy, Knoxville, TN 37920-6999, (615)544-9468.

CHEN, JAY. *See* **CHEN, JIZENG.**

CHEN, JIANHUA
Educator. Chinese American. **PERSONAL:** Born Oct 31, 1954, Liaoyang, Liaoning, People's Republic of China; daughter of Zhi Chen & Guiquan Chen. **EDUCATION:** Jilin University, China, BS, 1982, MS, 1985, PhD, 1988. **CAREER:** Louisiana State University, assistant professor, 1988-; Beijing China Software Technique Corporation, engineer, 1988. **ORGANIZATIONS:** Association for Computing Machinery, 1989-; IEEE Computer Society, 1990-; American Association for Artificial Intelligence, 1992-. **HONORS/ AWARDS:** Jilin University, Merit Student, 1979, 1980, 1981. **SPECIAL ACHIEVEMENTS:** Research results on non-monotonic reasoning in artificial intelligence, 1991-92. **BUSINESS ADDRESS:** Assistant Professor, Computer Science Dept, Louisiana State University, Tower Dr, Coates Hall, Rm 289, Baton Rouge, LA 70803-4020, (504)388-4340.

CHEN, JIE
Educator, researcher. Chinese American. **PERSONAL:** Born May 9, 1955, Tianjin, People's Republic of China; son of Tianchi Chen and Yijun Jiang; married Su Wu, Jul 22, 1985; children: Larry Penn, Shieley Su. **EDUCATION:** Tianjin University, China, BS, 1981; Shanghai Second Medical College, China, MS, 1984; Drexel University, PhD, 1989. **CAREER:** Drexel University, postdoctoral fellow, 1989-90; Purdue University of Indianapolis, assistant professor, 1990-; Indiana University, School of Dentistry, assistant professor, 1990-. **ORGANIZATIONS:** American Society of Mechanical Engineers; International Society of Biomechanics; International Association of Dental Research. **HONORS/AWARDS:** Whitaker Foundation, The Whitaker Foundation Medical Research Award, 1992. **SPECIAL ACHIEVEMENTS:** Computer Simulation of the Human Mandible with an Endosseous Implant; Mechanical Analysis of the Human Temporomandibular Joint; The Effects of Orthodontic Forces on the Stresses in the Peridontal Ligament; Engineering Analysis of Direct Bonded Orthodontic Brackets; An Investigation on the 3-D Mechanical Characteristics of the Ankle and Subtalar Joints. **BUSINESS ADDRESS:** Assistant Professor, Dept of Mechanical Engineering, University of Indianapolis, 723 W Michigan St, SL 2150M, Indianapolis, IN 46208, (317)274-5918.

CHEN, JIZENG (JAY CHEN)
Publisher. Chinese American. **PERSONAL:** Born Sep 2, 1950, Tianjin, People's Republic of China; married YiJiang Wen, Jul 1, 1979; children: Lily. **EDUCATION:** Hebei University, China, BA, 1976; University of Hawaii, certificate, 1986; Virginia Tech, master's degree, 1988. **CAREER:** Xinhua News Agency, China, reporter, 1976-85; Voice of America, translator, 1989-91; Asian Fortune Enterprises Inc, CEO, publisher, currently. **ORGANIZATIONS:** US China People's, Friendship Association, lifetime member. **HONORS/AWARDS:** University of Hawaii, Parvin Fellowship, 1985-86. **SPECIAL ACHIEVEMENTS:** Publications, coauthor: Health Care in China, published in London, 1984; China Investment Guide, published in Hong Kong, 1984; China Yearbook, published in Hong Kong, 1984. **BUSINESS ADDRESS:** Publisher, CEO, Asian Fortune Enterprises Inc, PO Box 11256, Newport News, VA 23601, (804)596-3473.

CHEN, JOAN
Actress. Chinese American. **PERSONAL:** Born 1961, Shanghai, People's Republic of China; married Jim Lau, 1985 (divorced 1988); married Peter Hui, Jan 18, 1992. **EDUCATION:** New York State University, New Paltz, pre-med; California State University, Northridge, filmmaking. **CAREER:** Actress, films include: Youth, China; Little Flower, China; Dim Sum, 1985; Night Stalker, 1985; Tai-Pan, 1986; The Last Emperor, 1987; Blood of Heroes, 1989; The Twin Peaks Movie, 1990; Turtle Beach; Deadlock, 1991; Strangers, 1991; Golden Gate, 1993; television includes Twin Peaks series; modeling includes: Ebel, Switzerland. **HONORS/AWARDS:** Golden Rooster for Little Flower (China's top acting honors). **SPECIAL ACHIEVEMENTS:** Author, Chase, book; co-author, Mosquito Net, script; fluent in Cantonese and English; namesake fragrance, China. **BIOGRAPHICAL SOURCES:** Transpacific, July/August, 1992, p45. **BUSINESS ADDRESS:** Actress, William Morris Agency, 151 El Camino, Beverly Hills, CA 90212.*

CHEN, JOHN L. (WEN L. CHEN)
Banker. Taiwanese American. **PERSONAL:** Born Nov 11, 1934, Taipei, Taiwan; married Nancy Chen, Jan 17, 1962; children: John Jr, Christine. **EDUCATION:** University of San Francisco, MBA, 1969. **CAREER:** Bank of America, vice president, 1979-89, senior vice president, 1989-. **ORGANIZATIONS:** Taiwanese American Chamber of Commerce; Hong Kong Assn; Japan Society; Chinese Chamber of Commerce. **HONORS/AWARDS:**

Coversier, Leadership Award, 1992; Bank of America, Outstanding Performance Award, 1991, Best Achievement Award, 1992. **BIOGRAPHICAL SOURCES:** World Journal, Chinese language daily newspaper; Central Post, Chinese language weekly newspaper. **BUSINESS ADDRESS:** Senior Vice President, Bank of America NT & SA, 555 California St, San Francisco, CA 94104, (415)622-2129.

CHEN, JOHN SHAOMING
Architect, educator. Chinese American. **PERSONAL:** Born Nov 8, 1935, Tianjin, Hebei, China; son of Yu Chu Chen and Yu Xian Mai; married Hui Fang Mai Chen, Sep 11, 1963; children: Bin, Lian. **EDUCATION:** Tianjin University, China, architecture diploma, 1962; University of California, Berkeley, visiting scholar, 1982, master's degree, 1983. **CAREER:** 3rd Design Institute, China, architect in charge, 1962-80; Clement Chen Assocs, architect, 1980-82; Group Five Architects, senior designer, 1983-84; AEPA Architects, senior designer, 1984-86; Donald Coupard Assoc, senior designer, 1986-87; Howard University, assoc professor, 1987-. **ORGANIZATIONS:** American Institute of Architects; American Society of Architectural Perspectivists; Design Communicators Association, USA/Canada, charter member; Virginia, New York, Washington DC, & Maryland, licensed architect. **HONORS/ AWARDS:** Design Communication Conference, Supervising Students, 17 awards, 1990, 1991, 1992; Chinese Ministry of Railroads, 1st Award for Changsha Railroad Station Design, 1976, 3rd Prize Winner, National Competition for Small and Medium Standardized Railroad Station Design, 1980; Tianjin China Planning Commission National Competition for a 50,000 Population Residential District, 2nd Prize Winner, 1963. **SPECIAL ACHIEVEMENTS:** Author: Architecture in Pen and Ink, 1994; Master Plan for Shenzhen Bao, a Cinema City and Resort Village, China; Architectural Rendering for George Bush's Office, Washington, DC; Architectural Rendering for Ronald Reagan Library, Stanford University; Architectural Design, Barney Circle Bridge, Washington, DC. **BIOGRAPHICAL SOURCES:** Crit article: Chinese Gardens, p 44-44, 1992; Representation Article, Student Competition Winners, p 110, 112, 1990, p 54-55, 1991. **HOME ADDRESS:** 12505 Montclair Dr, Silver Spring, MD 20904. **BUSINESS ADDRESS:** Associate Professor, Howard University, School of Architecture & Planning, 2366 6th St, Architecture Bldg, Room 118, Washington, DC 20059, (202)806-7424.

CHEN, JUH WAH
Educator. Chinese American. **PERSONAL:** Born Nov 10, 1928, Shanghai, China; married Han Lin Chen; children: David, John, Jeanne. **EDUCATION:** National Cheng Kung University, BS, chemical engineering, 1953; University of Illinois, MS, chemical engineering, 1957; University of Illinois, Champaign-Urbana, PhD, chemical engineering, 1959. **CAREER:** Bucknell University, assistant professor in chemical engineering, 1959-65; Upjohn Co, consulting research engineer, 1961-65; Southern Illinois University, professor, 1965-71, chair of thermal & environmental engineering, 1971-85, associate dean of engineering, 1985-88, chair of mechanical engineering, 1986-88, professor and dean of engineering, 1988-. **ORGANIZATIONS:** AIChE; ASME; ASEE; ACS; NSPE; Tau Beta Pi; Sigma Xi. **SPECIAL ACHIEVEMENTS:** More than 40 scientific and engineering publications. **BUSINESS ADDRESS:** Professor and Dean of Engineering, College of Engineering, Southern Illinois University at Carbondale, Engineering Bldg Complex, Rm A108, Carbondale, IL 62901.

CHEN, JYH-HONG ERIC
Research scientist, educator. Taiwanese American. **PERSONAL:** Born Dec 1, 1951, Keelung, Taiwan; son of Jong and Art-Ju Lee Chen; married Lee-Yuan Liu-Chen, Aug 11, 1979; children: Justin K, Isaac E. **EDUCATION:** National Taiwan University, BS, chemical engineering, 1975; University of Connecticut, MS, materials science, 1980; Massachusetts Institute of Technology, PhD, materials science and engineering, 1982. **CAREER:** W R Grace, Construction Products Division, senior research engineer, 1982-84; MIT, summer course lecturer, 1991-93; University of Delaware, Chemical Engineering Department, adjunct professor, 1992-; E I Dupont Fibers, composites senior research engineering, 1984-93, Central Research, research associate, 1993-. **ORGANIZATIONS:** Society of Plastic Engineering, steering committee member, 1993; Materials Research Society, conference chairman, 1989; Adhesion Science and Practice Network, chairman, 1993-. **HONORS/AWARDS:** Greenwald Technical Excellence Award, 1993. **SPECIAL ACHIEVEMENTS:** Co-editor, Interfaces in Composites, 1990. **BUSINESS ADDRESS:** Research Associate, E I Dupont, Dupont Experimental Station, E304/C214, Wilmington, DE 19880-0304, (302)695-4381.

CHEN, KANGPING
Educator. Chinese American. **PERSONAL:** Born Mar 7, 1961, Daye, Hubei, People's Republic of China; son of Gui Ying Wang and Zhi Ming Chen; married Kathy P Chen, May 28, 1988; children: Andrew V. **EDUCATION:** Peking University, BS, 1982; University of Minnesota, PhD, 1990. **CAREER:** Clarkson University, assistant professor, 1990-91; Arizona State University, assistant professor, 1991-. **HONORS/AWARDS:** National Science Foundation, Presidential Young Investigator Award, 1991. **BUSINESS ADDRESS:** Assistant Professor, Arizona State University, Box 876106, Tempe, AZ 85287-6106, (602)965-0907.

CHEN, KAO
Engineer. Chinese American. **PERSONAL:** Born Mar 21, 1919, Shanghai, China; son of Chi-Son & Wei C Chen; married May Y Yoh, Nov 14, 1948; children: Jennifer C Lien, Arthur B, Carlson S. **EDUCATION:** Jiao-Tong University, China, BSEE, 1942; Harvard University, MSEE, 1948; Polytechnic University, postgraduate, EE, 1953. **CAREER:** American Gas & Electric Corp, relay specialist, 1950-52; Ebasco International, Inc, supervising engineer, 1952-56; Westinghouse Electric Corp, fellow engineer, 1956-83; North American Philips Lighting Corp, fellow engineer, 1983-86; Carlsons Consulting Engineers, president, 1987-. **ORGANIZATIONS:** IEEE, Industry Applications Society, Production & Application of Light Committee, chairman, 1983-84, IUS Department, vice chairman/chairman, 1981-84, 1985-87, delegation to visit China, 1982, New Standards Committee, 1985-86; USNC-CIE, 1983-; National Society of Professional Engineers, 1954-; Illuminating Engineering Society, Industrial Lighting & Energy Committees, 1992-; Association of Energy Engineers, 1989-; registered professional engineer, New York, New Jersey, 1954, 1963. **HONORS/AWARDS:** IEEE, Richard Harold Kaufmann Award, 1992, Centennial Medal, 1984, Life Fellow, 1986; IAS (Society of IEEE), Best Papers Awards, 1981, 1983, Award of Merit, 1985; British Industries Scholar, 1945-47; Westinghouse Engineering Achievement Award, 1971. **SPECIAL ACHIEVEMENTS:** Visiting Professor to Shanghai Fudan University, 1982; author: Industrial Power Distribution & Illuminating Systems, Marcel Dekker Inc, NY, 1990; Energy Effective Industrial Illuminating Systems, Fairmont Press/Prentice Hall Inc, NJ, 1994; seminar lecturer on "Industrial Illuminating Systems & Technology," George Washington University, 1991; IEEE Standards Seminar, "Energy Management," instructor, Sept, 1991; contributor to three engineering handbooks and six IEEE standards; published over 80 technical papers. **HOME ADDRESS:** 11816 Caminito Corriente, San Diego, CA 92128-4550. **BUSINESS ADDRESS:** President, Carlsons Consulting Engineers, Inc, PO Box 270365, San Diego, CA 92198-2365, (619)451-9854.

CHEN, KARL A.
Industrial hygiene consultant. Chinese American. **PERSONAL:** Born Sep 5, 1935, Kingston, Jamaica; son of Chip-Tseung & Moo Moy Chen; married Virginia J Chen, Apr 4, 1970; children: David A, J Christopher, Michael E. **EDUCATION:** Rensselaer Polytechnic Institute, BS, 1959; Boston College, PhD, 1993. **CAREER:** E I DuPont, chemist, analytical chemist, 1963-68, analytical chemist, research chemist, 1969-75, research chemist, laboratory supervisor, 1975-79, senior consultant, laboratory director, 1979-82, senior consultant, plant hygienist, 1983-90, Occupational Health, senior consultant, regional consultant, 1991-. **ORGANIZATIONS:** American Industrial Hygiene Assn, 1976-; American Academy of Industrial Hygiene, 1979-; Sigma Xi, 1964-; New York Academy of Science, 1965-80. **BUSINESS ADDRESS:** Senior Consultant, Occupational Health, E I DuPont DeNemours & Co, Chambers Works, CAER Bldg, Rm 208, Deepwater, NJ 08023, (609)540-3041.

CHEN, KENNY T.
Data processing supervisor. Taiwanese American/Thai American. **PERSONAL:** Born Jan 9, 1961, Jamaica, NY; son of Stephen Chen and Fong Lee. **EDUCATION:** SUNY at Buffalo; CUNY at Queens, BA, 1984. **CAREER:** FJS Systems, programmer, analyst, 1984-86; Tork Inc, EDP, supervisor, 1986-. **BUSINESS ADDRESS:** Supervisor of EDP, Tork Inc, 1 Grove St, Mount Vernon, NY 10550, (914)664-3542.

CHEN, KUANG CHUNG (K.C.)
Educator. Taiwanese American. **PERSONAL:** Born Oct 10, 1954, Tainan, Taiwan; son of Chang-Peng Chen and Chun H Yu-Chen; married Lingle Liao, Jun 25, 1990; children: Kevin, Tiffany. **EDUCATION:** National Taiwan University, BBA, 1976; Ohio State University, MBA, 1978, PhD, 1982. **CAREER:** University of Illinois, assistant professor, 1982-87, associate professor, 1988; California State University, Fresno, Theodore F Brix Professor of Fi-

nance, 1988-. **ORGANIZATIONS:** American Finance Association, 1979-; International Association of Financial Engineers, advisor, 1991-; Financial Management Association, 1979-; American Chinese Management Educators Association, director, 1991-; Western Finance Association, 1979-; The Review of Business Studies, editor, 1989-; Global Finance Journal, associate editor, 1988-; Journal of Small Business Finance, associate editor, 1989-. **HONORS/ AWARDS:** Western Decision Sciences Institute, most outstanding theoretical paper award, 1993, best paper in the finance track award, 1993; AT&T Collegiate Investment Challenge, second, educator division, 1993; California State University, Fresno, faculty research award, 1993. **SPECIAL ACHIEVEMENTS:** Author, "Pricing Contingent Value Rights: Theory & Practice," Journal of Financial Engineering, 1993; "Pricing Cross-Currency Put Warrants" Global Finance Journal, 1993; "Pricing Nikkei Put Warrants: Some Empirical Evidence," Journal of Financial Research, 1992; "Pricing the SPIN," Financial Management, 1990; fluent in Mandarin Chinese and Taiwanese. **BUSINESS ADDRESS:** Theodore F Brix Professor of Finance, School of Business, California State University, 5245 N Baker, Fresno, CA 93740-0007, (209)278-4964.

CHEN, KUANG YU
Educator, researcher. Chinese American. **PERSONAL:** Born Apr 4, 1946, Kumin, Yunnan, China; son of Yung-chien Chen and Shao-chen Tao; married Alice Y-C Liu, Aug 26, 1978; children: Andrew T, Winston T. **EDUCATION:** National Taiwan University, BS, 1967; Yale University, MPh, 1970, PhD, 1972. **CAREER:** Yale Medical School, research associate, 1975-77; Rutgers university, asst professor, 1977-82, associate professor, 1982-87, professor, 1987-, adjunct professor, 1993-. **HONORS/AWARDS:** NIH, Research Grants, 1979, 1982, 1986, 1987, 1990, 1992. **SPECIAL ACHIEVEMENTS:** Biomedical research in the areas of cancer and aging, 1975-; Archaic Chinese language, 1977-. **BUSINESS ADDRESS:** Professor, Dept of Chemistry, Rutgers University, Taylor Rd, Wright Chemistry Lab, Piscataway, NJ 08855-0939, (908)932-3739.

CHEN, KUN-MU
Educator. Taiwanese American. **PERSONAL:** Born Feb 3, 1933, Taipei, Taiwan; son of Tsa-Mo Chen & Che Wu Chen; married Shu-Shun Chen, Feb 22, 1962; children: Maggie, Kathy, Kenneth, George. **EDUCATION:** National Taiwan University, BS, 1955; Harvard University, MS, 1958, PhD, 1960. **CAREER:** University of Michigan, research associate, 1960-64; Michigan State University, associate professor, 1964-67, professor, 1967-. **HONORS/ AWARDS:** Institute of Electrical and Electronics, Engineers Fellow, 1976; Michigan State University, Distinguished Faculty Award, 1976; American Association for Advancement of Science, Fellow, 1977; Taiwanese American Foundation, Outstanding Achievement Award, 1984; Michigan State University, Withrow Distinguished Scholar Award, 1993. **SPECIAL ACHIEVEMENTS:** Published more than 200 papers in the area of electromagnetics and microwave engineering; conducted many research projects supported by federal government. **MILITARY SERVICE:** Chinese Air Force, Taiwan, lieutenant, 1955-56. **BUSINESS ADDRESS:** Professor, Dept of Electrical Engineering, Michigan State University, Room 260, Engineering Bldg, East Lansing, MI 48824, (517)355-6502.

CHEN, LE CHUN
Textile company executive. Chinese American. **PERSONAL:** Born Nov 9, 1956, Shanghai, People's Republic of China; son of Java Chen; married Maria China, Nov 2, 1987; children: Robin, Winne. **EDUCATION:** College in China, 1978. **CAREER:** Raffle America Inc, vice president, 1982-. **HOME ADDRESS:** 2 Wilfred Rd, Manalapan, NJ 07726, (908)536-5051.

CHEN, LEA DER
Educator, educational administrator. Taiwanese American. **PERSONAL:** Born Jun 1, 1952, Yuan-Lin, Taiwan; son of Der-Hwa Chen and Chuu-In W Chen; married Yuan-Yu Y Chen, Jun 16, 1977; children: Jennifer A. **EDUCATION:** National Taiwan University, BS, 1974; Pennsylvania State University, MS, 1979, PhD, 1981. **CAREER:** Pennsylvania State University, graduate assistant, 1977-80, research associate/assistant, 1980-81, assistant professor, 1981-82; University of Iowa, assistant professor, 1982-86, associate professor, 1986-91, professor, 1991-, interim chair, 1992-93, chair, 1993-. **ORGANIZATIONS:** Combustion Institute, International Symposium Program Subcommittee, 1986-, reviewer for Combustion and Flame, 1982-; American Society Mechanical Engineers, reviewer for JHT, 1981-; American Institute Aeronautics and Astronautics, reviewer for AIAAJ, JP&P, JTHT 1982-; AIAA/ASME/ SAE/ASEE, session organizer, 1990-94; APS, 1985-. **HONORS/AWARDS:**

AIAA, Aerospace Sciences Poster Merit Award, 1987; APS, Gallery of Fluid Motion, winner, 1986, 1987, 1992; University of Iowa, Old Gold Faculty Fellow, 1984; AFOSR, Summer Faculty Fellow, 1985, 1986, University Resident Research Program, Faculty Fellow, 1988-89. **SPECIAL ACHIEVEMENTS:** Published more than 30 journal articles in Combustion & Flame, AIAAJ, J Propulsion & Power, etc; published more than 50 papers in conference proceedings; pioneer research in jet diffusion flame visualization using the TiCl4 technique; pioneer research in liquid-metal wick combustion; fuels research for advanced jet engines. **HOME ADDRESS:** 2010 Rochester Ct, Iowa City, IA 52245, (319)354-1164. **BUSINESS ADDRESS:** Professor, Chair, Dept of Mechanical Engineering, University of Iowa, 2204 Engineering Bldg, Iowa City, IA 52242, (319)335-5674.

CH'EN, LENA B.
Architect. Chinese American/Vietnamese American. **PERSONAL:** Born Jun 27, 1949, Taichung, Taiwan; daughter of Ching-Ho Chen and Thi-Hoa Dang; married Jess W Speidel III, 1976; children: Chia Chen-Speidel. **EDUCATION:** Brown University, BA, architecture, 1973; Harvard Graduate School of Design, 1974-76; University of California, Berkeley, MArch, 1979. **CAREER:** Shapiro, Okino & Hom, Engineers, drafter/designer, 1977-79; Ekosea Inc, project manager, 1979-82; K Tsuruta Associates, architects, job captain, 1982-83; Marquis/Wong & Brocchini, job captain, 1983-84; JDQ Inc, architects, project architect, 1984-87; VBN Architects, project architect, 1987-88; Ch'en & Associates, owner/principal architect, 1988-. **BUSINESS ADDRESS:** Owner/Principal Architect, Chen & Associates, Architecture and Engineering, 4104 Montgomery St, Oakland, CA 94611, (510)658-5203.

CHEN, LI-FU
Educator. Taiwanese American. **PERSONAL:** Born Feb 27, 1944, Taichung, Taiwan; son of C C Chen & H C Chen; married Vineta A Chen, Jun 26, 1975; children: Stephanie C, Julie K, Andrew J. **EDUCATION:** University of Wisconsin, PhD, 1974. **CAREER:** Purdue University, associate professor, 1981-. **SPECIAL ACHIEVEMENTS:** 50 publications; language proficiency in English, Chinese, and Japanese. **BUSINESS ADDRESS:** Associate Professor, Dept of Food Sciences, Purdue University, Smith Hall, West Lafayette, IN 47907, (317)494-8263.

CH'EN, LI-LI
Educator, writer. Chinese American. **PERSONAL:** Born Apr 6, 1934, Peking, China; daughter of Shujen Ch'en and Yu-wu Kuan Ch'en. **EDUCATION:** Wilson College, BA (magna cum laude), 1957, LittD, 1980; Radcliffe College, MA, 1958; Harvard University, PhD, 1969. **CAREER:** Tufts University, prof, Chinese language and literature, 1972-. **ORGANIZATIONS:** Harvard-Yenching Inst, fellow; Ford Foundation, fellow; MacDowell Colony, fellow, 1980; Michael Karolyi Foundation, fellow, 1980; Phi Beta Kappa. **HONORS/ AWARDS:** American Council Learned Socs, grantee, 1976-77; Natl Magazine Award for Fiction, Criticism and Belles Lettres, for short story, "Peking!, Peking!," 1977; Natl Book Award for Translation, for Master Tung's Western Chamber Romance. **SPECIAL ACHIEVEMENTS:** Translator, Master Tung's Western Chamber Romance, 1977; contributor of articles to professional journals. **BUSINESS ADDRESS:** Professor, Chinese Language & Literature, Tufts University, 311 Olin Hall, Medford, MA 02155.

CHEN, LINDA
Educator. Chinese American. **PERSONAL:** Born Oct 14, 1957, Hong Kong; daughter of See Ying Chen and Lan Jan Lee Chen. **EDUCATION:** Queens College, CUNY, BA 1978; University of Massachusetts, Amherst, PhD, 1988. **CAREER:** Trinity College, graduate fellow, 1986-87; Rhodes College, Dept of Political Science, assistant professor, 1987-91; Indiana University, Dept of Political Science, assistant professor, 1991-. **ORGANIZATIONS:** American Political Science Association, 1984-; Latin American Studies Association, 1987-; Interfuture Study Abroad Program, director of studies, 1989-. **HONORS/AWARDS:** Indiana University, Summer Faculty Fellowship, 1992; Rhodes College, Faculty Development Grant, 1989; Queens College, Interfuture Study Abroad Scholarship, 1977; Interfuture Study Abroad Program, vp, 1994-. **SPECIAL ACHIEVEMENTS:** Spanish language fluency; extensive field work in Latin America. **BUSINESS ADDRESS:** Assistant Professor, Dept of Political Science, Indiana University, South Bend, 1700 Mishawaka Ave, NS 448, South Bend, IN 46634-7111, (219)237-4520.

CHEN, LINDA LI-YUEH
Educator, educational administrator. Taiwanese American. **PERSONAL:** Born Mar 22, 1937, Tokyo, Japan; daughter of Chun-mu Huang and Chiung-tien Lin;

married Boris Yuen-jien Chen, Dec 23, 1960; children: Audrey Huey-wen, Lisa Min-yi. **EDUCATION:** National Taiwan University, Taipei, Taiwan, BS, pharmacy, 1959; University of Louisville, PhD, biochemistry, 1964. **CAREER:** University of Louisville, research associate, 1964-66; University of Kentucky, assistant professor, 1967-72, associate professor, 1972-79, associate dean for research & graduate education, 1979-81, chairman, 1983-87, professor, 1979-, Multidisciplinary PhD Program in Nutritional Sciences, director, 1989-. **ORGANIZATIONS:** American Institute of Nutrition, 1974-; American Society for Clininical Nutrition, 1985-; Gerontological Society of America, 1978-. **HONORS/AWARDS:** American Home Economics Association, Borden Award for nutrition research in North America, 1990. **SPECIAL ACHIEVEMENTS:** Author, Nutrition Biochemistry-Laboratory Methods, Experiments and Exercises, 1972; editor, Nutritional Aspects of Aging, Vol I & Vol II, CRC Press, 1986; author of numerous research articles in professional journals. **BUSINESS ADDRESS:** Professor, University of Kentucky, 219 Funkhouser Building, Lexington, KY 40506-0054, (606)257-3288.

CHEN, MEANSHANG (DANIEL)
Educator. Taiwanese American. **PERSONAL:** Born Nov 15, 1953, Taipei, Taiwan; son of Chen-Juin Chen & Yeh-Li Chang; married Ming-Chu Chen, Oct 7, 1988; children: Terrie. **EDUCATION:** Taipei Institute of Technology, Diploma, 1974; South Dakota School of Mines & Technology, MS, 1979; Kansas State University, PhD, 1984. **CAREER:** Kansas State University, instructor, 1984-85; Central Michigan University, associate professor, 1985-. **ORGANIZATIONS:** American Society for Engineering Education; Society of Manufacturing Engineers. **HONORS/AWARDS:** American Society of Heating, Refrigerating, and Air-Conditioning Engineers, Homer Addams Award, 1983. **SPECIAL ACHIEVEMENTS:** Author: A Study in the USA-Guide for High School and Secondary Technical School Graduates, 1989. **BIOGRAPHICAL SOURCES:** "Taiwan's Polytechnical Educational System," Journal of Industrial Technology, vol 6, no 3, p 5, 1990. **BUSINESS ADDRESS:** Associate Professor, Central Michigan University, Mount Pleasant, MI 48859, (517)774-6441.

CHEN, MICHAEL CHIA-CHAO
Chemist. Chinese American. **PERSONAL:** Born Jan 13, 1947, Shanghai, China; son of Kuo-Chen Chen and Dorothy H F Kuo. **EDUCATION:** University of Minnesota, BS, chemistry, 1969; Massachusetts Institute of Technology, PhD, physical chemistry, 1973. **CAREER:** Massachusetts Institute of Technology, research associate, 1973-75; University of Massachusetts, research associate, 1975-76; Exxon Chemical Company, senior staff chemist, 1976-. **HONORS/AWARDS:** MIT, Sloan Research Trainee, 1972. **SPECIAL ACHIEVEMENTS:** Research and development in: polypropylene and polyethylene resins film applications; morphology, optical and mechanical properties of polymers; polymer characterization, polymer physics; structure-function correlation of nucleic acids, proteins and their model compounds, spectroscopy; proficient in Chinese, read German, French. **BUSINESS ADDRESS:** Senior Staff Chemist, Exxon Chemical Co, PO Box 5200, Baytown, TX 77522-5200, (713)425-5502.

CHEN, MICHAEL M.
Educator. Chinese American. **PERSONAL:** Born Mar 10, 1932, Hankow, Hubei, China; son of Kwang-Tzu Chen and Hwei-Chuin Deng Chen; married Ruth H Chen, Oct 15, 1961; children: Brigitte (deceased) Derek, Melinda. **EDUCATION:** National Taiwan University; University of Illinois, BS, 1955; Massachusetts Institute of Tech, SM, 1957, PhD, 1961. **CAREER:** Avco Corporation, senior staff scientist, 1960-63; Yale University, assistant professor, 1963-69; New York University, associate professor, 1969-73; University of Illinos at Urbana-Champaign, professor, 1973-91; National Science Foundation, program director, 1991-93; University of Michigan, professor, 1991-. **ORGANIZATIONS:** American Physical Society, 1969-, Committee on Heat, Transfer in Manufacturing, Chairman, 1985-90; American Society of Mechanical Engineers; American Institute of Chemical Engineers. **HONORS/AWARDS:** American Society of Mech Engineers, Heat Transfer Memorial Award, 1990. **BUSINESS ADDRESS:** Professor, University of Michigan, G G Brown, Ann Arbor, MI 48109-2125, (313)764-5241.

CHEN, MICHAEL Y. M.
Physician. Chinese American. **PERSONAL:** Born Jan 7, 1941, Shanghai, China; son of Shan Tong Chen and Kun Zhu; married Jean Y Q Hu, 1969. **EDUCATION:** Shanghai Chinese Medical School, MD, 1964. **CAREER:** Shanghai Chinese Medical Hospital, radiologist, 1964-79; Yang Poo Tumor Hospital, radiologist, 1979-83; Bowman Gray School of Medicine, fellow,

1983-87, research instructor, 1987-88, research assistant professor, 1988-93, associate professor, 1993-. **ORGANIZATIONS:** Radiological Society of North America, 1985-; Society of Gastrointestinal Radiologists, 1988-. **HONORS/AWARDS:** SMA, First Achievement Award, 1992. **SPECIAL ACHIEVEMENTS:** 1 monograph: Radiology of the Small Bowel, 1992; 112 major publications, 1979-93; 101 miscellaneous publications, 1979-93. **BUSINESS ADDRESS:** Associate Professor, Dept of Radiology, Bowman Gray School of Medicine, Medical Center Blvd, Winston-Salem, NC 27157-1088, (910)716-7260.

CHEN, MING
Educator. Chinese American. **PERSONAL:** Born Nov 2, 1955, Shanghai, People's Republic of China; daughter of Xi-Quan Chen and De-Li Whang; married Zhen-Huan Lu; children: Grace Lu. **EDUCATION:** Shanghai Arts and Crafts School, AD, 1976; Shanghai Drama Institute, BFA, 1982, MFA, 1985; University of Pittsburgh, MA, 1989. **CAREER:** Shanghai Youth Theatre, costume designer, 1982-83; Shanghai Drama Institute, instructor, 1985-86; University of Pittsburgh, graduate assistant, 1987-89; Three River Shakespeare Festival, assistant set designer, 1989; Folger Theatre, scenic artist, 1989-90; SUNY, Buffalo, assistant professor, 1990-91; Kennesaw State College, assistant professor, 1991-. **ORGANIZATIONS:** China National Theatre Design Association, 1985-; US Institution for Theatre Technology, 1991-; Association for Theatre in Higher Education, 1991-; Leadership Kennesaw State, 1992; Core Curriculum Committee, 1993. **HONORS/AWARDS:** University of Pittsburgh, scholarship, 1987-89; Prague International Stage Design Exhibition, Award: A Combination of Traditional and Contemporary Set, for the Titus Andronics set design, 1987. **SPECIAL ACHIEVEMENTS:** Five articles published in various professional magazines and newspapers; more than twenty set and costume design works staged in professional theatre productions as well as academic theatre productions; painted sets and costumes for more than thirty shows, "On Symbolic Sets," Theatre Arts, fall 1982; "Semiotic in Theatrical Design," Theatre Arts, spring 1986. **BIOGRAPHICAL SOURCES:** "'Misanthrope' More Style Than Substance," Marietta Daily Journal, May 15, 1993; Spotlight on Staff, Asides (Folger Theatre), Winter 1990; A Fury of Titans, The Ithaca Times, October 30, 1991. **BUSINESS ADDRESS:** Asst Prof, Dept of Music and Performing Arts, Kennesaw State College, PO Box 444, Marietta, GA 30061-0444, (404)423-6151.

CHEN, MING CHIH
Material process consultant. Chinese American. **PERSONAL:** Born Aug 15, 1920, Foochow, Fukien, China; married Hsiao M Chen, May 3, 1943; children: Hugo, Yvonne Lin. **EDUCATION:** SUNY, Buffalo, PhD, 1950; Purdue University, post-doctorate, 1952. **CAREER:** Sheller Globe, material process and analytical service director, 1962-89; United Technology Automotive, material process director, 1989-92, consultant, 1992-. **ORGANIZATIONS:** SPE; SAE; ACS. **HOME ADDRESS:** 22530 Benjamin, St Clair Shores, MI 48081, (313)771-4575.

CHEN, MOON SHAO-CHUANG, JR.
Editor. Chinese American. **PERSONAL:** son of Hong Moon Chen & Priscilla Chang Chen; married. **EDUCATION:** University of Michigan, BS, 1968, MS, 1974; Tulane University, MPH, 1974; Texas Woman's University, PhD, 1979. **CAREER:** US Army, captain, 1974; Texas Tech University, visiting assistant professor, 1977-79; Ohio State University, assistant/associate professor, 1979-, professor & MPH program director, 1990-. **ORGANIZATIONS:** Asian American & Pacific Islander Journal of Health, editor-in-chief, 1992-; Ohio State University, Asian American Faculty Staff Support Group, chair, 1993. **HONORS/AWARDS:** Congress on the Family, International Pathfinder Award, 1992; Ohio State University, Success Story, 1993. **SPECIAL ACHIEVEMENTS:** Founded Asian American & Pacific Islander Journal of Health, 1993. **MILITARY SERVICE:** US Army, captain, 1969-74. **BUSINESS ADDRESS:** Editor-in-Chief, Asian American & Pacific Islander Journal of Health, 5525 Corey Swirl Dr, Dublin, OH 43017, (614)766-5219.

CHEN, NAI-NI
Choreographer, dancer. Chinese American. **PERSONAL:** Born in Taipei, Taiwan; daughter of Hsing-Yin Chen and May-Yun Chen; married A Chiang. **EDUCATION:** Chinese Culture University, BA, 1982; New York University, MA, 1986. **CAREER:** Nai-Ni Chen Dance Company Inc, artistic director, 1988-. **ORGANIZATIONS:** Actor's Equity, 1986-. **HONORS/AWARDS:** New Jersey State Council on the Arts, choreography fellowship, 1992. **SPECIAL ACHIEVEMENTS:** Nai-Ni Chen Dance Company has toured 11 states in the US, and has probably developed the widest reach among Asian-American

performing arts groups, 1988-. **BIOGRAPHICAL SOURCES:** The New York Times, Sep 9, 1990; Sunday New Jersey Weekly, Mar 14, 1993; The Star Ledger, p 43, Mar 10, 1993. **BUSINESS ADDRESS:** Artistic Director, Nai-Ni Chen Dance Company, Inc, PO Box 1121, Fort Lee, NJ 07024.

CHEN, NAI Y.
Research administrator. Chinese American. **PERSONAL:** Born Jan 6, 1926, China; married 1959; children: two. **EDUCATION:** University of Shanghai, BS, 1947; LA State University, MS, 1954; Massachusetts Institute of Technology, ScD, chemical engineering, 1959. **CAREER:** Taiwan Sugar Corp, department head, 1947-52; LA State University, res assistant, 1952-54; Massachusetts Institute of Technology, res associate, 1954-60; Mobil Research and Development Corp, chemical engineer senior scientist, 1960-79, actg manager, 1979-80, manager, 1980-86, senior scientist, 1979-, res adv, 1986-. **ORGANIZATIONS:** Chinese American Chemical Society, director, 1991; Natl Academy of Engineering; American Institute of Chemical Engineers; Sigma Xi; North American Catalysis Society. **SPECIAL ACHIEVEMENTS:** Research in petroleum refining and petrochemical technologies, heterogeneous catalysis, zeolite catalysis, and global energy issues; author of more than 75 publications and 3 books; more than 120 US patents. **BUSINESS ADDRESS:** Sr Sci & Mgr-Exprty Proc Research, Mobil Research & Dev Corp, PO Box 1025, Princeton, NJ 08540, (609)737-3000.*

CHEN, PAMELA KI MAI
Attorney. Chinese American. **PERSONAL:** Born Mar 30, 1961, Chicago, IL; daughter of Homer and Phoebe Chen. **EDUCATION:** University of Michigan, BA, 1983; Georgetown University Law Center, JD, 1986. **CAREER:** Arnold & Porter, associate, 1986-89; Asbill, Junkin & Myers, associate, 1989-91; US Dept of Justice, trial attorney, 1991-. **ORGANIZATIONS:** Asian Pacific American Bar Association, 1987-, DC metropolitan area chapter, treasurer, 1992-93; National Asian Pacific American Bar Association, 1987-; District of Columbia Bar Association, 1988-; Illinois Bar Association, 1986-; Mount Pleasant Multi-Cultural Coalition, 1993-. **HONORS/AWARDS:** Dept of Justice, Special Achievement Award, Civil Rights Division, 1992, 1993. **BUSINESS ADDRESS:** Trial Attorney, US Department of Justice, Washington, DC 20534, (202)514-6261.

CHEN, PAUL KUAN YAO
Architect. Chinese American. **PERSONAL:** Born Aug 16, 1924, Shanghai, Kiangsu, China; son of K F & S Y Chen; married Rosa Lu Chen, Mar 29, 1958. **EDUCATION:** St Johns University, Shanghai, BArch, 1947; Cornell University, MArch, 1949. **CAREER:** Jose Sert, designer, draftsman, 1949-50; Ebasco Service, senior draftsman, checker, 1950-53; Kelly & Gruzen Arch, designer, project architect, 1953-58; Richard Kelly Association, partner, 1958-62; Paul K Y Chen Arch, principal, 1962-. **ORGANIZATIONS:** CIE, board member, 1965-66; AIA, visitor committee, 1968, housing committee, 1969, fee committee, 1970. **HONORS/AWARDS:** City Club of New York, Bard Award on Zum Zum Restaurant, 1970, Bard Award on Tavern on the Green, 1978; US Department of Commerce, Regional Minority Service Ind Firm of the Year, 1990; AME Church, Richard Allen Award, 1991. **SPECIAL ACHIEVEMENTS:** Works include: World's Fair, NY, Chinese Pavilon, 1964-65; Symphony Plaza Elderly Housing, Boston, 1976; Naval Aviation Museum, Pensacola, FL, 1990; Steeplechase Amusement Park, Coney Island, NY, 1995. **BUSINESS ADDRESS:** Priniipal, Paul K Y Chen Architect, 57 West 38th St, 10th Fl, New York, NY 10018, (212)869-3360.

CHEN, PING-FAN
Educator, company executive. Chinese American. **PERSONAL:** Born May 13, 1917, Kiangyin, Jiangsu, China; son of Mou-chu Chen & Lan-yin Men; married Esther Fu-Mei Chen, Dec 1, 1940; children: Jane, June, Julia. **EDUCATION:** National Central University of China, BS, 1938; University of Cincinnati, MS, 1956; Virginia Poly Institute & State University, PhD, 1959. **CAREER:** National Geological Survey of China, petroleum geologist, 1938-45; Chinese Petroleum Corporation, petroleum geologist, 1946-55; West Virginia Geological Survey & West Virginia University, petroleum geologist, professor, 1960-87; E&W United Inc, president, retired. **ORGANIZATIONS:** Geologic Society of China; Chinese Engrs Association; Chinese Association Advancement Sciences; Sigma Xi; Sigma Gamma Epsilon; West Virginia Chinese Student Association, advisor, 1962-81. **HONORS/AWARDS:** Chinese Culture University, fellow, 1976-. **SPECIAL ACHIEVEMENTS:** Publications: Mineral Resources of China, 1954; New Outlook for the Old Fields of Taiwan, 1949; Tectonic Analogies & Antitheses between Taiwan & the Appalachians, 1976;

Lower Paleozoic Stratography in the Central Appalachians, 1978. **HOME ADDRESS:** 1277 Dogwood Ave, Morgantown, WV 26505, (304)599-3229.

CHEN, ROBERT CHIA-HUA
Engineer. Chinese American. **PERSONAL:** Born Oct 26, 1946, Shanghai, Jiangsu, China; son of Kang Chen and Sylvia Chen; married I-Yu Chen, Feb 14, 1971; children: Clara An-Ru, David I-Chung. **EDUCATION:** Rensselaer Polytechnic Institute, BEE, 1966; Massachusetts Institute of Technology, SM, 1968; Carnegie Mellon University, PhD, 1974. **CAREER:** Burroughs Corp, engineer programmer, 1968-69; University of Pennsylvania, assistant professor, 1973-78; Bell Laboratories, member of technical staff, 1978-81; Digital Equipment Corp, software consultant engineer, 1981-92; Boston Technology, member of technical staff, 1992-. **ORGANIZATIONS:** Association for Computing Machinery, 1969-; Institute for Electrical & Electronics Engineers, 1966-; Usenix Association, 1991-; Tau Beta Pi, 1964; Eta Kappa Nu, 1965; Sigma Xi, associate membership, 1966; Pi Delta Epsilon, 1966. **BUSINESS ADDRESS:** Member of Technical Staff, Boston Technology, 100 Quannapowitt Pkwy, Wakefield, MA 01880, (617)246-9000.

CHEN, RONG YAW
Educator. Taiwanese American. **PERSONAL:** Born Jan 6, 1933, Taoyen, Taiwan; son of Lien Tieng Chen and Jou Cheng; married Grace Hui Mei Yang, Oct 2, 1965; children: Raymond, Reginald. **EDUCATION:** National Taiwan University, Taiwan, BSME, 1957; University of Toledo, MSME, 1963; North Carolina State University, PhD, ME, 1966. **CAREER:** Shimen Dam, Taiwan, assistant engineer, 1959-60; Barton College, assistant professor, 1965-66; New Jersey Institute of Technology, professor of mechanical engineering, 1966, associate chairman for graduate studies in mech eng, 1993-. **ORGANIZATIONS:** North America Taiwanese Professors Association, board of directors, 1982-83, New Jersey/New York Chapter, president, 1984; NJ Taiwanese Association, president, 1978; American Society of Mechanical Engineers, 1967-; Sigma Xi, 1966-. **HONORS/AWARDS:** Department of Army, research proposal, 1974; Army Research Center, research proposals, 1975-78; Thomas Betts Electric Company, research proposal, 1979. **SPECIAL ACHIEVEMENTS:** Contribute articles to professional journals on deposition of particles in tubes; Languages: Taiwanese, Japanese, Chinese; registered professional engineer in New Jersey. **MILITARY SERVICE:** Army, ROTC, Taiwan, 2nd lt, 1957-59. **HOME ADDRESS:** 67 Tanglewood Drive, East Hanover, NJ 07936-3306. **BUSINESS PHONE:** (201)596-3327.

CHEN, S. STEVE
Chemistry researcher. Taiwanese American. **PERSONAL:** Born Sep 18, 1950, Taipei, Taiwan; son of Ping-Tze and Lian-Pi Chen; married Jifang (Jenny), Aug 28, 1976. **EDUCATION:** Fu-Jen Catholic University, BS, 1974; Michigan State University, PhD, 1981. **CAREER:** University of Maryland, research associate, 1981-83; National Starch & Chemical Co, project supervisor, 1983-88, sr project supervisor, 1988-90, research associate, 1990-. **ORGANIZATIONS:** American Chemical Society, 1978-; Society for the Advancement of Material & Process Engineering, 1983-. **HONORS/AWARDS:** Phi Tau Phi, 1974. **SPECIAL ACHIEVEMENTS:** "Free Radical Ring-Opening Polymerization," proceeding, IUPAC Symposium, 1982; Journal of Macromolecular Science, 1984; "Syntheses of Organic Conductor," Heterocycles, 1984; "Free Radical Ring-Opening Polymerization & Biodegradable Polymers," 1986. **MILITARY SERVICE:** Taiwanese Army, 2nd lt, 1974-76. **BUSINESS ADDRESS:** Research Associate, National Starch & Chemical Co, 10 Finderne Ave, Bridgewater, NJ 08807, (908)685-5213.

CHEN, SAM W.
Hotel and property management executive. Chinese American/Taiwanese American/Malaysian American. **PERSONAL:** Born Dec 12, 1945, Fujian, China; married Hua Lai Chen, 1972; children: Welby, Kevin. **EDUCATION:** University of Wisconsin, MBA, hotel and restaurant management, 1972. **CAREER:** Holiday Inn, general manager, 6 years; Best Western, Landmark Hotel and Convention Center, general manager, currently; Far East Investment Company, CEO, currently. **ORGANIZATIONS:** Chamber of Commerce; Hotel and Motel Assn. **HONORS/AWARDS:** Holiday Inn Chain, Turn Around Manager of the Year. **HOME ADDRESS:** 16911 22nd Ave SE, Bothell, WA 98012, (206)481-8974.

CHEN, SHI-HAN
Educator. Chinese American. **PERSONAL:** Born Jun 29, 1936, Ping-Yang, Zhejiang, China; son of Sun-tze chen and Mu-Ling Chi; married Diana Chen, Sep 14, 1968; children: Christopher, Sandra. **EDUCATION:** Taiwan Normal

University, BS, 1959; National Taiwan University, MS, 1963; University of Texas, Austin, PhD, 1968. **CAREER:** High school teacher, 1959-61; Taiwan Normal University, instructor, 1963-64; University of Texas, research assistant, associate, 1964-69; Puget Sound Blood Center, research associate, 1969-71; University of Washington, professor, 1972-. **ORGANIZATIONS:** American Society of Human Genetics, 1966-; Association of Chinese Geneticists in America, 1986-. **HONORS/AWARDS:** March of Dimes Birth Defect Foundation, Clinical Research Grant, 1985-; National Institute of Health, Research Grant, 1973-80. **SPECIAL ACHIEVEMENTS:** Molecular biology of hemophilia B and other X-linked diseases, 1984-; genetic polymophisms in man, protein level, 1969-83. **BUSINESS ADDRESS:** Professor, Dept of Pediatrics, University of Washington, RD-20, Seattle, WA 98195, (206)527-3872.

CHEN, SHOEI-SHENG
Engineer. Taiwanese American. **PERSONAL:** Born Jan 26, 1940, Taiwan; son of Ashu Chen and Y C Chen; married Ruth C Chen, Jun 28, 1969; children: Lyrile, Lisa, Steve. **EDUCATION:** National Taiwan University, BS, 1963; Princeton University, MS, 1966, MA, 1967, PhD, 1968. **CAREER:** Argonne National Lab, assistant engr, 1968-72, mechanical engr, 1972-80, sr mechanical engr, 1980-. **ORGANIZATIONS:** ASME/PVPD, executive committee, 1990-96, honors chairman, 1990-94, chairman of Fluid-structure, technical committee, 1987-90. **HONORS/AWARDS:** University of Chicago, Distinguished Performance Award, 1986. **SPECIAL ACHIEVEMENTS:** "Flow-induced vibration of circular cylindrical structures," Hemisphere Publishing Co, 1987; about 100 papers in technical journals. **BUSINESS ADDRESS:** Sr Mechanical Engineer, Argonne National Lab, 9700 S Cass Dr, Bldg 335, Argonne, IL 60439, (708)252-6147.

CHEN, SIMON YING
Journalist. Chinese American. **PERSONAL:** Born Feb 13, 1948, Nanking City, China; son of Tao and Yapin Chen; married Yen-Ying Chen, Jan 3, 1976; children: Emily, Eric. **EDUCATION:** Far East College, BA, 1977; Columbia College, BA, 1979; Union University, MA, 1984; National University Federico Villarreal, PhD, 1990. **CAREER:** CUNY-Kingsborough, assistant to the dean, 1979-81; International Daily News, publisher, CEO, 1981-. **ORGANIZATIONS:** Associated Press Managing Editors, 1984-; Chinese-Language Press Institute, 1982-; Kiwanis Club Intl, MPK Chapter, past president, 1984-. **HONORS/AWARDS:** Oklahoma City University, Outstanding Journalist Award, 1986; Courvoisier Corp, Courvoisier Leadership Award, 1992; honorary degrees: Columbia College, LLD, 1986; Iowa Wesleyan College, DBAdm, 1991. **SPECIAL ACHIEVEMENTS:** Visiting professor, National Guangxi University, 1988-; visiting lecturer, Columbia College, 1986-. **BUSINESS ADDRESS:** Publisher/CEO, International Daily News-Chinese, 870 Monterey Pass Rd, Monterey Park, CA 91754, (213)265-1317.

CHEN, SIU LOONG
Restaurateur, realtor. Chinese American. **PERSONAL:** Born Apr 20, 1970, Fujian, People's Republic of China; daughter of Tsz Yiu Cheung and Yu Ing Cheng; married Dung King Chen, Apr 25, 1988; children: Jennifer, Cyndi. **CAREER:** China Sub Shop I, owner, president, 1988-; China Sub Shop II, owner, president, 1990-; Century 21 Ambassador Realty, associate realtor, 1992-. **ORGANIZATIONS:** Prince George's Board of Realtors, 1992-; Montgomery County Board of Realtors, 1992-. **BUSINESS ADDRESS:** Restaurateur, China Sub Shop I, 6561 Ager Rd, Hyattsville, MD 20782, (301)422-7402.

CHEN, STANFORD
Journalist. Chinese American. **PERSONAL:** Born May 15, 1947, Oakland, CA; son of Bong Yen Chen (deceased) and Chiu Shee Chen (deceased); married Beth K Erickson, May 19, 1975. **EDUCATION:** Indiana University, BA, 1969. **CAREER:** Bellingham Herald, reporter, columnist, 1969-73, sports and waterfront reporter, 1974-75, sports editor, 1975-77, photographer, 1976-77; Daily Journal of Commerce, editor, 1977-78; The Oregonian, copy editor, 1978-87, deputy forum editor, 1987-. **ORGANIZATIONS:** NW Regional China Council, board member, 1989-; Asian American Journalists Association, chapter secretary, 1987-, national secretary, 1988-90; Task Force for Minorities in Newspaper Business, executive board, 1988-. **HONORS/AWARDS:** American Association of Newspaper Publishers, Minority Fellowship, 1991. **SPECIAL ACHIEVEMENTS:** Responsible for the Sunday Forum section: received Association of Opinion Page Editors twice: Best Sunday section in US, 1991, Best Single Feature, 1992. **BUSINESS ADDRESS:** Deputy Forum Editor, The Oregonian, 1320 SW Broadway, Portland, OR 97201, (503)221-8134.

CHEN, STEPHEN C.
Software company executive. Chinese American. **PERSONAL:** Born Sep 6, 1941, Chung King, Sichuan, China; son of Han Tsing Chen and Chou Nan Shui Chen; married Bertha N Chen, Jan 9, 1971; children: Clara K, Vicki M. **EDUCATION:** Chung Yuan College of Science & Technology, BS, 1965; Tufts University, MS, 1969; Massachusetts Institute of Technology, 1973-75. **CAREER:** W R Grace & Co, engineer, 1969-72; LFE Corp, project engineer, 1972-75; Union Carbide Corp, senior engineer, 1975-79; Polaroid Corp, principal engineer, group manager, 1979-88; Automation Science Inc, president, 1988-. **ORGANIZATIONS:** Greater Boston Chinese Cultural Assn, president, 1990-91; Chinese Bible Church of Greater Boston, deacon, 1981-85; Charleston Chinese Assn, president, 1978-79. **SPECIAL ACHIEVEMENTS:** Developed a SCADA software, 1988; invented a digital recording circuit, 1974. **MILITARY SERVICE:** Taiwan Navy, ensign, 1965-66. **BUSINESS ADDRESS:** President, CEO, Automation Science Inc, 150 Buckskin Dr, Weston, MA 02193, (508)358-5747.

CHEN, STEVE S.
Computer company executive. Chinese American. **PERSONAL:** Born Feb 1, 1944, Fukien, China; married; children: three. **EDUCATION:** National Taiwan University, BS, 1966; Villanova University, MS, 1972; University of Illinois, PhD, computer science, 1975. **CAREER:** Burroughs Corp, project engineer, 1975-78; Floating Pt Systems Inc, project engineer, 1978-79; Cray Res Inc, chief designer, 1979-83, Development, vp, 1983-86, senior vp, 1986-87; Supercomputer Systems Inc, CEO, president, 1987-. **ORGANIZATIONS:** National Academy of Engineering; American Academy of Arts & Science, fellow. **BUSINESS ADDRESS:** President, Supercomputer Systs Inc, 1414 W Hamilton Ave, Eau Claire, WI 54701.*

CHEN, STUART S.
Educator, researcher. Chinese American. **PERSONAL:** Born Sep 26, 1957, Rochester, NY; son of Wilson S & Carolyn C Chen; married Pamela, Dec 1982; children: Jordan, Gabriel. **EDUCATION:** Lehigh University, BS, 1979, MS, 1984, PhD, 1988. **CAREER:** Frazier Industrial Co, design engineer, 1979-81, chief engineer of standard products, 1981-83; Lehigh University, graduate fellow, teaching and research assistant, 1983-86, ATLSS Center Scholar, 1986-88; SUNY, Buffalo, assistant professor, 1988-. **ORGANIZATIONS:** American Society of Civil Engineers, associate member, 1988-, Committee on AI & Expert Systems, 1990-, Structures Division Subcommittee on Emerging Computing Technology, 1991-; Association for Bridge Construction & Design, board of directors, 1991-; American Association for Artifical Intelligence, 1988-; Phi Beta Kappa; Tau Beta Pi; Chi Epsilon. **HONORS/AWARDS:** National Science Foundation, Presidential Young Investigator Award, 1990. **SPECIAL ACHIEVEMENTS:** Co-author: "Component-Based Building Representation for Design and Construction," Automation in Construction 1, 339-350, 1993; "An Interval-Based Matrix Analysis for Qualitative Structural Reasoning," 5th International Conf on Computing in Civil Engrg, Anaheim, CA, June 1993; "Quick-Release Behavior of Two Eastern US Highway Bridges," 9th International Bridge Conf, Pittsburgh, PA, June 1993. **BIOGRAPHICAL SOURCES:** "Smart Structures," Civil Engineering, p 68, November 1992. **BUSINESS ADDRESS:** Assistant Professor, Dept of Civil Engineering, SUNY at Buffalo, 242 Ketter Hall, Buffalo, NY 14260.

CHEN, SU-CHIUNG
Physician, educator. Taiwanese American. **PERSONAL:** Born Mar 26, 1937, Taipei, Taiwan; married. **EDUCATION:** National Taiwan University, College of Medicine, MD, 1962. **CAREER:** St Louis University, School of Medicine, professor, currently; Cardinal Glennon Children's Hospital, physician, currently. **BUSINESS ADDRESS:** Physician, Cardinal Glennon Children's Hospital, 1465 S Grand Blvd, St Louis, MO 63104.

CHEN, TA-SHEN
Educator. Taiwanese American. **PERSONAL:** Born Feb 5, 1932, Lung-Ching, Taichung, Taiwan; son of Wen Chen (deceased) and Pu Lin (deceased); married Shu-Hui Chen, Dec 23, 1964; children: Diana M, James K. **EDUCATION:** National Taiwan University, Taipei, BS, 1954; Kansas State University, Manhattan, MS, 1961; University of Minnesota, Minneapolis, PhD, 1966. **CAREER:** US Bureau of Mines, research engineer, 1961-66; University of Missouri-Rolla, assistant professor, 1967-69, associate professor, 1969-73, professor, 1973-90, Mechanical and Aerospace Engineering Department, graduate coordinator, 1986-, curators' professor, 1991-. **ORGANIZATIONS:** American Society of Mechanical Engineers, 1969-85, fellow, 1986-; American Institute of Aeronautics & Astronautics, 1986-91, associate fellow, 1992-; AIAA

Journal of Thermophysics & Heat Transfer, associate editor, 1986-; ASME K-8 Committee on Theory & Fundamentals, 1980-; Pi Tau Sigma, 1969, Sigma Xi, 1971. **HONORS/AWARDS:** University of Missouri-Rolla, Outstanding Teaching Award, 1968, Faculty Excellence Award, 1986, 1988, 1989, 1990. **SPECIAL ACHIEVEMENTS:** Researcher in the area of convective heat transfer, particularly in mixed convection, instability of flow, heat transfer in porous media and in separated flows; published over 110 technical papers in professional journals; presented over 40 papers at conferences; wrote 20 technical reports; gave numerous lectures; proficient in English, Japanese, Chinese, and Taiwanese. **BUSINESS ADDRESS:** Curators' Professor, Dept of Mechanical and Aerospace Engineering, University of Missouri-Rolla, Rolla, MO 65401-0249, (314)341-4628.

CHEN, TAI

Controller. Chinese American. **PERSONAL:** Born Aug 5, 1951, Taipei, Taiwan; son of Ping-Yuan Chen; married Li-Hui Chen, Mar 5, 1982; children: Charles, Alex. **EDUCATION:** California State University, Fullerton, BA, 1979. **CAREER:** Adohr Farm, staff accountant, 1978-80; PBS Building Systems, accounting supervisor, 1980-85; ICEE-USA, accounting manager, 1985-87; Penhall Company, controller, 1987-. **SPECIAL ACHIEVEMENTS:** Passed CPA examination, 1982; fluent in English and Chinese. **HOME ADDRESS:** 24325 Via Lenardo, Yorba Linda, CA 92687, (714)692-9408. **BUSINESS ADDRESS:** Controller, Penhall Company, 1801 Penhall Way, Anaheim, CA 92801, (714)772-6450.

CHEN, TERRY

Business executive. Hong Kong American. **PERSONAL:** Born Mar 10, 1951, Hong Kong; married Rebecca, Aug 29, 1992. **EDUCATION:** Whittier College, BA, 1974; UCLA, MBA, 1976. **CAREER:** Ernst & Young, audit supervisor, 1976-80; Cedars Sinai Medical Center, controller, 1980-85; Holy Cross Medical Center, CFO, 1985-88; Children's Hospital at Stanford, CFO, 1988-91; Allright Corp, CFO, 1991-. **ORGANIZATIONS:** AICPA, 1978-; California CPA Assn, 1978-; Texas CPA Society, 1992-. **HONORS/AWARDS:** Whittier College, Intl Students Scholarship, 1970, 1971, 1972; Ahmanson Foundation, Scholarship, 1974. **BUSINESS ADDRESS:** CFO, Allright Corporation, 1111 Fannin, Suite 1300, Houston, TX 77002, (713)222-2505.

CHEN, TERRY LI-TSENG

Restaurateur. Taiwanese American. **PERSONAL:** Born Mar 14, 1949, Taipei, Taiwan; son of Yuan Young Chen and Shu-Lin Chen; married Eunice Chen, Nov 12, 1976; children: Katie Ying, Sheney, Jordan T. **EDUCATION:** Tatong Industrial College, Taiwan. **CAREER:** China Inn Restaurant, owner, 1981-. **MILITARY SERVICE:** 2nd lt, 1972. **HOME ADDRESS:** 1825 Skyline Dr, Sherman, TX 75090, (903)893-6985.

CHEN, THOMAS K. S.

Banker. Chinese American. **CAREER:** China Trust Bank, president, currently. **BUSINESS ADDRESS:** President, China Trust Bank, Wall St Plaza, New York, NY 10005, (212)514-8000.*

CHEN, THOMAS SHIH-NIEN

Physician, educator. Chinese American. **PERSONAL:** Born Feb 28, 1936, Shanghai, China; son of Chih-Ping Chen and Tsing Ziang Liu; married Margaret W W Chang, Dec 26, 1967; children: Dehan, Dewing, Dehua, Detang. **EDUCATION:** Harvard College, AB, 1955; New York Medical College, MD, 1960. **CAREER:** New Jersey Medical School, Department of Pathology, professor, 1987-; VA Medical Center, staff pathologist, 1971-. **MILITARY SERVICE:** US Air Force, captain, 1961-63.

CHEN, TONY YOUNG

Illustrator, author, educator. Chinese American. **PERSONAL:** Born Jan 3, 1929, Kingston, Jamaica; son of Maud Marie Chen (deceased) and Arthur Chen (deceased); married Pura Chen, Mar 2, 1957; children: Richard, David. **EDUCATION:** Pratt Institute, BFA (w/honors), 1955. **CAREER:** Allied Department Store, graphic designer, illustrator, 1955-57; Pan American Broadcasting Co, graphic designer, illustrator, 1957-59; Newsweek Magazine, graphic designer, art director, 1959-70; Nassau Community College, free-lance illustrator, 1970-; art instructor, 1971-73. **ORGANIZATIONS:** Long Island Arts Council. **HONORS/AWARDS:** Society of Illustrators, Award for Excellence, 1972; The Lewis Citation, Distinguished Citation Award, Bible Art, 1983; National Science Teachers Award, Outstanding Science Book, 1980; American Institute of Graphic Arts, Certificate of Excellence, 1979; Educational Press Assn of America, Distinguished Achievement Award, 1977. **SPECIAL ACHIEVEMENTS:** Author, illustrator: Run, Zebra, Run, Lothrop Lee & Shephard, 1972; Little Koala, Holt Reinhart & Winston, 1979; Wild Animals, Random House, 1981; illustrator: Animals Showing Off, National Geographic, 1988; Illustrated Children's Bible, Doubleday, 1983, A Child's First Bible, Doubleday, 1990. **BIOGRAPHICAL SOURCES:** "The Book Illustrations of Tony Chen," American Artist Magazine, p 56-61, May 1972; The New York Times Book Review, p 31, Mar 14, 1984, p 29, Mar 31, 1991. **HOME ADDRESS:** 241 Bixley Heath, Lynbrook, NY 11563.

CHEN, TSEH AN

Educator. Chinese American. **PERSONAL:** Born Oct 26, 1928, Shanghai, China; son of L F Chen and Sun L C Chen; married Cheh-Chen Chen, Jul 4, 1954; children: Irvin, Ernest, Hope Chen Milla, Eugene. **EDUCATION:** National Taiwan University, BS, 1951; University of Wisconsin, MS, 1953; University of New Hampshire, PhD, 1962. **CAREER:** Fairleigh Dickinson University, assistant professor, 1962-69; Rutgers University, associate professor, 1969-73, professor, 1973-, chair, 1991-. **ORGANIZATIONS:** American Phytopathological Society, 1959-; American Society of Microbiology, 1972-; Society of Nematologist, 1962-; AAAS, 1970-; International Organization of Mycoplasmology, 1972-. **HONORS/AWARDS:** American Phytopath Society, fellow, 1990, Award of Merit, 1992. **SPECIAL ACHIEVEMENTS:** Over 100 publications, including articles in Science, 1970, 1975, 1982, 1985; several chapters in books on the mycoplasmas, Acad Press. **BUSINESS ADDRESS:** Prof/Chairman, Dept Plant Pathology, Rutgers University, Lipman Drive, Martin Hall, New Brunswick, NJ 08903, (908)932-9375.

CHEN, TSONG-MING (CHARLES T. M. CHEN)

Educator. Taiwanese American. **PERSONAL:** Born Nov 25, 1934, Chia-Yi, Taiwan; son of Lu Chen and Swei-Chu Hung; married Ying-Mei Chen, Dec 26, 1989; children: Kent M, David R. **EDUCATION:** National Taiwan University, BS, 1956; University of Minnesota, PhD, 1964. **CAREER:** Florida State University, assistant/associate professor, 1964-72; University of South Florida, professor, 1972-. **ORGANIZATIONS:** Institute of Electrical and Electronics Engineers, senior member; International Society for Hybrid Microelectronics; American Vacuum Society; Sigma Xi. **HONORS/AWARDS:** College of Engineering, University of South Florida, Outstanding Researcher of the Year, 1988-89; International Hybrid Microelectronics Symposium, Best Paper Award, 1982, Outstanding Educator of America, 1972; Florida State University, College of Engineering, Outstanding Professor of the Year, 1971. **SPECIAL ACHIEVEMENTS:** Over 100 publications in technical journals and conference proceedings. **BUSINESS ADDRESS:** Professor, Electrical Engineering Dept, University of South Florida, 4202 E Fowler Ave, Tampa, FL 33620, (813)974-4787.

CHEN, TUAN WU

Educator. Taiwanese American. **PERSONAL:** Born Mar 26, 1925, Chia-yi, Taiwan; son of Cheng-chong Chen and Li-yu Lin; married Laura F Chen, Jun 22, 1962; children: Christopher, Richard. **EDUCATION:** National Taiwan University, BS, 1958; National Tsing Hua Univ, MS, 1960; Syracuse University, PhD, 1966. **CAREER:** Los Alamos National Lab, visiting scientist, 1974; National Tsing-Hua University, visiting professor, 1975; California Institute of Technology, visiting research scientist, 1982; New Mexico State University, physics, assistant professor, 1968-73, associate professor, 1973-79, professor, 1979-. **ORGANIZATIONS:** American Physical Society, 1966-. **HONORS/AWARDS:** US Army, Atmospheric Science Award, 1985; American Society of Engineering Education, ASEE Award, 1993. **SPECIAL ACHIEVEMENTS:** Over sixty publications in Physical Reviews, Applied Optics, etc, 1966-93. **BUSINESS ADDRESS:** Professor, Dept of Physics, New Mexico State University, University Avenue, Las Cruces, NM 88003, (505)646-2230.

CHEN, TUNG-SHAN

Educator. Chinese American. **PERSONAL:** Born Apr 17, 1939, Chungking, China; son of Sze-Chen Lin and Mary Chen Lin; married Yolanda Chen, Dec 26, 1964; children: Andy, Lynn. **EDUCATION:** National Taiwan University, BS, 1960; University of California, Berkeley, MS, 1964, PhD, 1969. **CAREER:** California State University, Northridge, assistant professor, 1969-73, associate professor, 1973-78; professor, 1978-; Marilyn Magaram Center, California State University, director, professor, 1990-. **ORGANIZATIONS:** American Chemical Society, 1964-; American Dietetic Association, 1970-; Chinese American Engineers & Scientists Association, 1969-; Chinese American Food Society, vice president, 1974-; Institute of Food Technologists, councilor, 1964-; Southern California Institute of Food Technologists, chair of scholarship committee, 1981-. **HONORS/AWARDS:** Joseph Drown Foundation, Food Science Education Award, 1992; National Dairy Council, Research Grant Award, 1986; California State University Northridge, Meritorious Performance Award, 1985, 1988. **SPECIAL ACHIEVEMENTS:** Organizer of five international symposia on nutrition, 1990-93; published 35 research papers in professional journals; provided services to National Academy of Sciences and National Science Foundation; Assisted Chinese Universities in curriculum development. **BUSINESS ADDRESS:** Director and Professor, Marilyn Magaram Center, California State University, Northridge, 18111 Nordhoff St-FES, Northridge, CA 91330-8308, (818)885-3102.

CHEN, VICTOR JOHN
Research biochemist. Hong Kong American. **PERSONAL:** Born Sep 25, 1952, Hong Kong; son of Francis J Chen and Jui-Fang Kuang Chen; married Sau-chi Betty Yan; children: Heidi Isabel. **EDUCATION:** Grinnell College, BA, 1974; Iowa State University, PhD, 1981. **CAREER:** Eli Lilly & Co, senior biochemist, 1985-92, senior scientist, 1992-. **ORGANIZATIONS:** American Society for Biochemistry & Molecular Biology, 1987-; Protein Society, 1988-. **BUSINESS ADDRESS:** Senior Scientist, Lilly Research Laboratories, Lilly Corporate Center, Drop Code 1543, Indianapolis, IN 46285, (317)276-6698.

CHEN, VICTORIA LIU
Banker. Chinese American. **PERSONAL:** Born Jan 29, 1945, China; daughter of John H S and Kuo Liu; married Allen T H Chen, Jul 2, 1975; children: John Y, Andrew L. **EDUCATION:** National Taiwan University, BS, 1966; California State University, MBA, 1973. **CAREER:** Singer Co, accounting manager, 1973-76; Edward Walsh CPA, accountant, 1976-78; Moody National Bank of Galveston, cashier, executive vice president, 1978-. **ORGANIZATIONS:** Rotary Club of Galveston, 1993; Houston Youth, Symphony Parents Guild, president, 1991-92, treasurer, other positions, 1986-91; National Assn of Bank Women, 1980-83; Texas Society of CPA, 1985-; Houston Chapter CPA, 1985-; NASA Little League Parent Assn, 1983-88. **BUSINESS ADDRESS:** Executive Vice President, Moody National Bank of Galveston, 2302 Postoffice St, Galveston, TX 77550, (409)765-5561.

CHEN, VIRGINIA L.
Physician. Chinese American. **PERSONAL:** Born Mar 24, 1959, Rockville Centre, NY; daughter of Kelly Chen and Lihwa Yen Chen. **EDUCATION:** MIT, BS, 1978; Mount Sinai, MD, 1982. **CAREER:** Mount Sinai Medical Center, dermatology instructor, 1986-; self-employed, dermatologist, currently. **ORGANIZATIONS:** American Academy of Dermatology, fellow, 1986-; American Board of Dermatology, diplomate, 1986-; Chinese American Medical Society, board of directors, 1989-; Chinese Alumni of MIT, board of directors, 1989-92; Society of Investigative Dermatology, 1985-86. **HONORS/AWARDS:** Society of Investigative Dermatology, Honorary Certificate, 1986; New York Academy of Medicine, Second Prize, 1985; Mount Sinai Medical Center, National Institutes of Health, fellowship, 1980, 1984-85; American Medical Association, Joseph Goldberger Scholarship, 1981; Parkinson's Disease Foundation, Research Fellowship, 1979. **SPECIAL ACHIEVEMENTS:** Co-author, "Use of Nonblood Priming for Open-Heart Surgery in Dogs," American Journal of Veterinary Research, Vol 43, No 10, pp 830-832, 1982; "Anatomical Mapping of Epidermal Langerhans Cell Densities in Adults," British Journal of Dermatology, Vol 109, pp 553-558, 1983; "Hemodilution and Cardioplegia techniques for Open-Heart Surgery in Dogs," Proceedings of the Fourth Congress Federation of Asian Veterinary Associations, pp 183-87, 1984; "Immuinochemistry of Elastotic Material in Sun Damaged Skin," Journal of Investigative Dermatology, Vol 87, pp 334-337, 1986; "De Novo Synthesis of Lysozyme by Human Epidermal Cells," Journal of Investigative Dermatology, forthcoming; "Immunocompromised Patients with Recurrent Cutaneous Infections," Difficult Diagnoses in Dermatology, edited by Mark Lebwohl, MD, Churchill Livingstone, forthcoming. **BUSINESS ADDRESS:** Dermatologist, 155 E 38th Street, #2B, New York, NY 10016, (212)697-2722.

CHEN, WAI FAH
Educator. Chinese American. **PERSONAL:** Born Dec 23, 1936, Nanking, China; son of Yu-Chao Chen and Shui-Da Chen; married Lily Lin-Lin Chen, Jun 15, 1966; children: Eric, Arnold, Brian. **EDUCATION:** National Cheng-Kung University, BS, 1959; Lehigh University, MS, 1963; Brown University, PhD, 1966. **CAREER:** Lehigh University, assistant professor, 1966-71, associate professor, 1971-75, professor, 1975-76; Purdue University, professor of structural engineering, 1976, head of structural engineering, 1980-, George E Goodwin distinguished professor of civil engineering, 1992-. **ORGANIZA-**

TIONS: American Society of Civil Engineers, 1979-90; Committee on Properties of Materials, chairman, 1979-82; Structural Stability Research Council, executive committee, 1983-; American Institute of Steel Construction, Specification Committee, 1986-; American Concrete Institute. **HONORS/AWARDS:** Alexander von Humboldt Foundation, US Senior Scientist Award, 1984; American Institute of Steel Construction, T R Higgins Lectureship Award, 1985; American Society of Civil Engineers, Raymond C Reese Research Prize, 1985; Shortridge Hardesty Award, 1990; National Cheng-Kung University, Distinguished Alumnus Award, 1988. **SPECIAL ACHIEVEMENTS:** Author of 17 books, 11 edited books, 23 contributing chapters, 247 journal articles, 182 conference papers; consultantships to Exxon production; research on offshore structures, to Skidmore, Owings and Merrill on Tall Buildings, and to World Bank on the Chinese University development projects. **HOME ADDRESS:** 1021 Vine St, West Lafayette, IN 47906, (317)743-2394. **BUSINESS ADDRESS:** Professor and Head, Structural Engineering, Purdue University, School of Civil Engineering, West Lafayette, IN 47907, (317)494-2254.

CHEN, WAI JUN (PETE)
Copper mining/smelting executive. Chinese American. **PERSONAL:** Born Sep 5, 1942, Canton, Guangdong, China; son of Sak-Luen Chen and Shui-Kum Yee; married Stella Y Chen, Dec 17, 1978; children: Anthony, Bernice. **EDUCATION:** University of Arizona, BS, chemical engineering, 1970. **CAREER:** Phelps Dodge Mining Co, AJO Smelter, process engineer, acid plant foreman, 1970-74, Hidalgo Smelter, technical services dept head, asst smelter superintendent, 1974-80, director of smelter projects, Morenci Smelter, 1980-81, Morenci Branch, director of technical services & research, 1981-82, Hidalgo Smelter, smelter superintendent, 1982-89; Phelps Dodge Morenci Inc, assistant manager, 1989-92, Hidalgo Smelter and Strategic Smelting Projects, manager, 1992-. **ORGANIZATIONS:** University of Arizona Alumni Association, president, 1972-73; Rotary Club, 1981-; American Institute of Chemical Engineers, 1970-; American Institute of Mining/Metallurgical Engineers, 1970-, People to People Ambassador Program, Nonferrous Delegation to People's Republic of China, group leader, 1986, AIME-TMS, Pyromettalurgy Technical Committee, chairman, 1985-86, Copper 95 International Conference, organizing member, 1993-95; Phelps Dodge Smelter Steering Committee, chairman, 1980-85, 1992-. **HONORS/AWARDS:** Phelps Dodge Morenci, Inc, Outstanding Contributor to Safety, 1991, 1992. **SPECIAL ACHIEVEMENTS:** Contributed to an innovative process utilizing dimethylaniline to absorb sulfur dioxide gas emitted from smelting of copper concentrate; led a group of nonferrous metals delegation to the People's Republic of China for the People to People Citizen Ambassador Program, 1986; presenter, "The Role of Computer at the Hidalgo Smelter," AIME Annual Meeting, Denver, 1978; co-author, "Optimization of Flash Smelting by the Use of Oxygen," Chile, 1987; contributed to the successful start-up and operation of the first Outokumpu Flash Smelter in North America; "Modification of the Hidalgo Smelter," AIME Annual Meeting, 1985. **BIOGRAPHICAL SOURCES:** Skillings' Mining Review, p 7, July 25, 1981, p 16, July 17, 1982; Pay Dirt-Southwestern, pp 14A-15A, September 1992. **BUSINESS ADDRESS:** Manager, Hidalgo Smelter & Strategic Smelting Projects, Phelps Dodge Mining Co, PO Drawer 571, Tyrone, NM 88065, (505)538-7102.

CHEN, WAI-KAI
Educator. Chinese American. **PERSONAL:** Born Dec 23, 1936, Nanjing, China; son of You-Chao & Shui-Tan Chen; married Shirley Shiao-Ling, Sep 1, 1962; children: Jerome, Melissa. **EDUCATION:** Ohio University, BSEE, 1960, MSEE, 1961; University of Illinois, Urbana-Champaign, PhD, 1964. **CAREER:** Ohio University, assistant professor, 1964-67, associate professor, 1967-71, professor, 1971-78, distinguished professor, 1978-81; Purdue University, visiting associate professor, 1970-71; University of Hawaii, Manoa, visiting professor, 1979; University of Illinois, Chicago, professor, Department of EECS, head, professor, 1981-. **ORGANIZATIONS:** Sigma Xi; Phi Kappa Phi; Pi Mu Epsilon; Eta Kappa Nu; Institute of Electrical and Electronics Engineers, fellow; Society for Industrial and Applied Mathematics; Association for Computing Machinery; American Society for Engineering Education; American Association for the Advancement of Science, fellow; Tensor Society of Great Britain; Mathematical Association of America; National Society of Professional Engineers; Chinese Academic and Profession Association of Mid-America; Mid-America Chinese Science & Technology Association. **HONORS/AWARDS:** Alexander von Humboldt Award, Federation Republic of Germany, 1985; IEEE Circuits and Systems Society, Certificate of Appreciation, 1988; Mid-America Chinese Science and Technology Association, Outstanding Achievement Award, 1988; University of Illinois, Urbana-Champaign, Distinguished Alumnus Award, 1988; numerous honorary professorships.

SPECIAL ACHIEVEMENTS: Passive and Active Filters: Theory and Implementations, John Wiley & Sons, 1986; Broadband Matching: Theory and Implementations, World Scientific Publishing Co, 1988; Active Network Analysis, World Scientific Publishing Co, 1991; Modern Network Analysis, The People's Posts and Telecommunications Publishing Co, 1991. **BUSINESS ADDRESS:** Professor, Head, Dept of Electrical Engineering and Computer Science, University of Illinois, Chicago, 851 S Morgan St, 1120 SEO, Chicago, IL 60607-7053, (312)996-2462.

CHEN, WAYNE G.
Electrical products company executive, consultant. Taiwanese American. **PERSONAL:** Born Oct 21, 1950, Taipei, Taiwan; son of Shaw C Chen and Chia T Chen; married Jeanette Chen, Mar 19, 1988; children: Joell J. **EDUCATION:** SUNY at Stony Brook, MS, 1980, PhD, 1983. **CAREER:** ILC Data Device Corp, QA engineer, 1980-83; Intel Corp, senior reliability engineer, 1984-85; Northern Telecom Corp, senior process engineer, tech staff, senior member, 1985-89; Motorola Inc, senior technical consultant, 1989-. **ORGANIZATIONS:** American Society of Metals, 1977-80; Intl Society of Hybrid Mfr, 1980-92; IEEE, 1970-. **HONORS/AWARDS:** Northern Telecom Corp, President Award of Technical Outstanding Achievement, 1989. **SPECIAL ACHIEVEMENTS:** Thirteen publications; US patents: Thermal Fuse, 4,769,902, 1988; Laser-Acoustic Detection of SMT Assembled Joints, 4,850,225, 1989. **HOME ADDRESS:** 1704 Crested Butte Dr, Austin, TX 78746, (512)327-6625.

CHEN, WAYNE Y.
Import/export company executive. Taiwanese American. **PERSONAL:** Born Jan 14, 1942, Tainan, Taiwan; son of Ta-Shu Chen and Shu-Lan Huang; divorced; children: Thomas, Timothy. **EDUCATION:** National Cheng Kung University, BS, 1964; University of Illinois, MS, 1967; Cornell university, PhD, 1971. **CAREER:** Cornell University, post doctoral fellow, instructor, 1971-73; Purdue University, Lafayette, research associate, 1973-74, Calumet, assistant professor, 1974-78, associate professor, 1979-83; NASA, Lewis Research Ctr, summer faculty fellow, 1977-78; Argonne National Laboratory, visiting scientist, 1981-82; Modern Materials Consulting Co, president, 1983-; Sun Imports & Exports Inc, president, 1983-. **ORGANIZATIONS:** Sigma Xi, 1973-; American Society of Metals, 1971-; American Society of Engineering Education, 1974-; American Society of Mechanical Engineers 1974-; Materials Research Society, 1974-; Chinese-American Assn of Powder Metallurgy, vice pres, 1981-82; The Church in Munster, bd of trustees, president, 1991-. **HONORS/AWARDS:** Industrial Research & Devlopment Magazine, IR100 Award, 1978; Purdue University, Professor of the Year, 1975; American University, Club Award, 1964; Chinese Society of Metallurgical Engineers, Top Student Award, 1963. **SPECIAL ACHIEVEMENTS:** Publications include: "High Temperature Structural Insulating Material with Closed Cell Structure," Fine Particle Society Pacific Region Meeting, Honolulu, Hawaii, 1983; "A Closed Cell Structural Material Having High Temperature Thermal Insulating Properties," Argonne Laboratory Report, ANL-82-54, 1982; "Closed Cycle Power Systems," project summary report, FY, 1981; "Corrosion/Oxidation Behavior of Stainless Steels of Reduced Chromium Content," Review of Coatings and Corrosion, invited paper, 1979; "Anodic Polarization Behaviour of Austemitic Stainless Steel Alloys with Lower Chromium Content," 1979. **BUSINESS ADDRESS:** President, Sun Imports & Exports Inc, 910 Kennedy Ave, Schererville, IN 46375, (219)322-8866.

CHEN, WEI-YIN
Educator. Chinese American. **PERSONAL:** Born Apr 5, 1950, Taipei, Taiwan; son of Shao-Pong Chen and Fong-Hwa Tsai; married Tsuei-Ju Kao, May 18, 1987. **EDUCATION:** Tunghai University, BS, chemical engineering, 1973; State University of New York at Stony Brook, MS, applied math, 1975; Polytechnic Institute of New York, MS, chemical engineering, 1975; City College of City University of New York, PhD, chemical engineering, 1981. **CAREER:** Gulf South Research Institute, senior research engineer, 1981-85, Fuel Research, manager, 1985-87; Louisiana State University, research assistant professor, 1987-90; University of Mississippi, assistant professor, 1990-93, associate professor, 1993-. **ORGANIZATIONS:** American Institute of Chemical Engineers, 1975-; American Chemical Society, 1975-; Combustion Institute, 1986-; American Society for Engineering Education, 1990-. **HONORS/AWARDS:** Sigma Xi, 1975-; numerous research grants and contracts. **SPECIAL ACHIEVEMENTS:** Co-author, "Coal Liquefaction with Supercritical Ammonia and Amines," Supercritical Fluid Technology, JML Penninger et al, ed, Elsevier Science Publishers BV, pp 281-307, 1985; "A Practical Pulverized Coal Feeder for Bench-Scale Combustion Requiring Low Feed Rates," Rev

Sci Instrum, Vol 62(2), 480-483, 1991; "Partitioning of Nitrogenous Species in the Fuel-Rich Stage of Reburning," Energy and Fuels, vol 5(2), p 231-237, 1991; numerous papers and published reports. **BUSINESS ADDRESS:** Associate Professor, Dept of Chemical Engineering, University of Mississippi, Anderson Hall, University, MS 38677, (601)232-5651.

CHEN, WEIHANG
Educator. Chinese American. **PERSONAL:** Born Apr 29, 1940, Shanghai, China; son of Enchi Chen & Fangying Weng; married Xiaozeng Wu, Jul 14, 1970; children: Fei, Fang. **EDUCATION:** Beijing University, BS, 1962; Fudan University, Shanghai, MA, 1982. **CAREER:** Fudan University, adjunct lecturer, 1982-85; Wuhan University, associate professor, 1985-93; Queen's College, Oxford, sr researcher, 1987-88; University of Missouri-Kansas City, visiting professor, 1991-93; Hampshire College, professor, visiting scholar, 1993-. **HONORS/AWARDS:** Sino-British Friendship Scholarship, 1987; British Council, professorship, 1988; Fulbright Scholarship, 1992. **SPECIAL ACHIEVEMENTS:** Translation of Wittgenstein's Philosophical Investigations; translation of M Schlick's Philosophy of Nature; translations of British poems from Milton, Shelley, Tennyson, etc; around 20 philosophical papers and monographs. **BUSINESS ADDRESS:** Visiting Scholar, School of Communications, Hampshire College, Amherst, MA 01002, (413)582-5821.

CHEN, WEN L. *See* **CHEN, JOHN L.**

CHEN, WENXIONG
Educator. Chinese American. **PERSONAL:** Born May 30, 1952, Fuqin, Fujian, People's Republic of China; son of Zhenlin Chen and Yufeng Lin; married Guanghui Kong, Jan 16, 1984; children: Hongwei. **EDUCATION:** Minxi University, BS, 1979; Hangzhou University, Department of Mathematics, MS, 1983; Academia Sinica, Institute of Mathematics, PhD, 1986. **CAREER:** University of Pennsylvania, visiting assistant professor, 1987-90; University of Arizona, visiting assistant professor, 1990-91; Southwest Missouri State University, assistant professor, 1991-. **ORGANIZATIONS:** American Mathematical Society. **HONORS/AWARDS:** National Science Foundation, Research Grant, 1987, 1988, 1989, 1991. **SPECIAL ACHIEVEMENTS:** Published 19 papers in mathematics journals; gave presentations at annual meetings, regional meetings of American Mathematical Society, at World Congress of Nonlinear Analysis. **BUSINESS ADDRESS:** Professor, Dept of Mathematics, Southwest Missouri State University, 901 S National Ave, Springfield, MO 65804-0094, (417)836-5940.

CHEN, WILLIAM HOK-NIN
Dentist. Chinese American. **PERSONAL:** Born Jul 17, 1950, Shanghai, People's Republic of China; son of Ling Pao Chen and Shu Yung Ning Chen; married Alison P Chen, Jul 1976; children: Audrey Y, Bianca Y. **EDUCATION:** Washington University, BA, biology, 1973, School of Dental Medicine, DMD, 1976. **CAREER:** Private practice, dentist, 1976-78; Chen & Associate Ltd (Dental Professional Corp), president, 1978-; St Elizabeth Medical Center, active staff, 1981-, dental chief, 1987-. **ORGANIZATIONS:** American Equilibration Society, 1984-; American Orthodontic Society, 1987-; Tri-City Medical Society, 1981-; American Dental Assn, 1976-; Academy of General Dentistry, 1979-; Illinois Academy of General Dentistry, membership chairman, 1989-92, treasurer, 1992-; Rotary International, Granite City, 1981-; United Way, Granite City, Dental Section, chairman, 1987. **HONORS/AWARDS:** Academy of General Dentistry, Fellowship, 1985, Mastership, 1987; Academy of Continuing Education, Fellowship, 1991; Pierre Fanchard Academy, Fellowship, 1993; Academy of Dentistry International, Fellowship, 1993. **SPECIAL ACHIEVEMENTS:** Author: "Irreversible Hydrocolloid: A Clean Simple Mixing Technique," Journal of Prosthetic Dentistry, C V Mosby, Nov 1982; "Dental Health Tips," Senior News, Madison County, 1990-92. **BUSINESS ADDRESS:** President, Dentist, Chen & Associates Ltd, 4168 Nameoki Rd, Granite City, IL 62040, (618)931-2025.

CHEN, WINSTON H.
Manufacturing company executive. Taiwanese American. **PERSONAL:** Born 1941?, Taiwan. **EDUCATION:** Harvard University, MS, applied mathematics, 1967, PhD, mathematics, 1970. **CAREER:** IBM, eight years; Solectron Corporation, chairman, co-CEO, 1978-. **HONORS/AWARDS:** Malcolm Baldrige National Quality Award, 1991; United States Pan Asian American Chamber of Commerce, Excellence 2000 Award, 1992. **SPECIAL ACHIEVEMENTS:** Holds six US and international patents; five IBM invention disclosures. **BUSINESS ADDRESS:** Chairman, Co-CEO, Solectron Corporation, 777 Gibraltar Dr, Milpitas, CA 95035-6329, (408)957-8500.*

CHEN, WUN-EE CHELSEA
Attorney. Taiwanese American. **PERSONAL:** Born Feb 24, 1964, Dover, NJ; daughter of Tung-ho Chen & Mei-chih Chen. **EDUCATION:** Harvard College, BA (cum laude), 1987; Loyola Law School, JD, 1992. **CAREER:** Orrick, Herrington & Sutcliffe, legal assistant, 1987-89; Belcher Henzie & Biegenzahn, associate, 1992-. **ORGANIZATIONS:** California State Bar. **HONORS/AWARDS:** American Jurisprudence Award, for excellent achievement in civil procedure, 1990. **SPECIAL ACHIEVEMENTS:** Editor-in-Chief, Loyola of Los Angeles Entertainment Law Journal, 1991-92; author: "Pinning Opinion to the First Amendment Mat," Loyola of Los Angeles Entertainment Law Journal, 1991. **BUSINESS ADDRESS:** Attorney, Belcher, Henzie & Biegenzahn, 333 S Hope St, Ste 3650, Los Angeles, CA 90071.

CHEN, XIANGMING
Educator. Chinese American. **PERSONAL:** Born Apr 4, 1955, Beijing, People's Republic of China; son of Chunguan Chen and Shihua Xu; married Xiaoyan Hua, Dec 15, 1985; children: Kayla H, Darrel H. **EDUCATION:** Beijing Foreign Languages Institute, BA, 1982; Duke University, MA, 1984, PhD, 1988. **CAREER:** University of Illinois, Chicago, assistant professor, 1989-; University of Chicago, affiliate member, 1992-. **ORGANIZATIONS:** American Sociological Association, 1984-; North American Chinese Sociologist Association, 1988-. **HONORS/AWARDS:** Duke University, James B Duke International Fellowship, 1982; Eastern Academy of Management, Best Conceptual Paper Award, 1987; American Council of Learned Societies, Postdoctoral Fellowship, 1993. **SPECIAL ACHIEVEMENTS:** 14 publications in scholarly journals and books, 1985-. **BUSINESS ADDRESS:** Assistant Professor, Dept of Sociology, University of Illinois, Chicago, 1007 W Harrison St, 4112 Behavioral Sciences Bldg, Chicago, IL 60607-7140, (312)996-5391.

CHEN, XIANGNING
Educator. Chinese American. **PERSONAL:** Born Nov 13, 1963, Beijing, People's Republic of China; son of Ruirong Chen & Lijun Tao; married Yalei Liu, Jun 24, 1987; children: Luyao. **EDUCATION:** Beijing University, China, BSc, 1985; University of Wyoming, PhD, 1989. **CAREER:** University of North Carolina, research associate, 1989-91; Baldwin Filters, consultant, 1993-; University of Nebraska, assistant professor, 1991-. **ORGANIZATIONS:** American Chemistry Society, 1987-; Sigma Xi, 1991-; Phi Kappa Phi, 1988-. **HONORS/AWARDS:** University of Wyoming, Hans-Peter Richert Memorial Award, 1986, Superior G A Awards, 1988, 1987; American Chemical Society, Wyoming Section, Sara Jane Rhoads Award, 1989; University of North Carolina, Glaxo Fellowship, 1990; University of Nebraska, Kearney, Don Fox Professor, 1992. **SPECIAL ACHIEVEMENTS:** Co-author:"Kinetic Implications of Remote Participation During Photooxidation at Sulfur,", J Org Chem, 56, 5251-5252, 1991; "Asymmetry Synthesis and Cram's Rule," Pure & Appl Chem, 63, 1591-1598, 1991; "Chelates as Intermediates in Nucleophilic Additions to Atkoxyketones According to Cram's Rule (Cyclic Model)," Journal of American Chemical Society, vol 114, p 1778-1789, 1992. **BUSINESS ADDRESS:** Assistant Professor, Dept of Chemistry, University of Nebraska at Kearney, BHS 414, Kearney, NE 68849, (308)234-8802.

CHEN, XINFU
Educator. Chinese American. **PERSONAL:** Born Nov 6, 1964, Jiangyin, Jiangsu, People's Republic of China; son of Jianping Chen & Xingdi Ju; married Yue Zhang, Aug 12, 1986; children: Fonda. **EDUCATION:** Beijing University, BS, 1984; University of Minnesota, PhD, 1991. **CAREER:** University of Pittsburgh, assistant professor, 1991-. **ORGANIZATIONS:** AMS; SIAM. **HONORS/AWARDS:** Alfred P Sloan Foundation, Alfred P Sloan Research Fellow, 1993, Doctoral Dissertation Fellow; National Science Foundation, researcher, 1991. **SPECIAL ACHIEVEMENTS:** Author of 30 articles published in several trade jounals. **BUSINESS ADDRESS:** Professor, Dept of Mathematics & Statistics, University of Pittsburgh, 307 Thackeray Hall, Pittsburgh, PA 15260, (412)624-8362.

CHEN, YE-HWA
Educator. Chinese American. **PERSONAL:** Born Jul 8, 1956, Keelung, Taiwan; son of Shin-Gan and Ruey-Lan; married Mei-Yin Chou, Jan 20, 1984; children: Theodore Ming-Chien, Irene Yung-Shen. **EDUCATION:** National Taiwan University, BS, 1979; University of California, Berkeley, MS, 1983, PhD, 1985. **CAREER:** Syracuse University, visiting assistant professor, 1986-88; Georgia Institute of Technology, assistant professor, 1988-93, associate professor, 1993-. **ORGANIZATIONS:** American Society of Mechanical Engineers, 1986-; Institute of Electrical and Electronics Engineers, 1986-; American Society of Engineering Education, 1989-; Sigma Xi, 1989-. **HONORS/ AWARDS:** University of California, Berkeley, Department Commendation, 1983; Sigma Xi, Young Faculty Award, 1991. **SPECIAL ACHIEVEMENTS:** Author of 51 international journal papers, 1985-; author of 36 international conference papers, 1985-; editor of one conference proceeding, 1991; contributor of chapters of two research monographs, 1992, 1993; organizer and speaker, one professional workshop, 1991. **BUSINESS ADDRESS:** Professor, School of Mechanical Engineering, Georgia Institute of Technology, Atlanta, GA 30332-0405, (404)894-3210.

CHEN, YE-SHO
Educator. Taiwanese American. **PERSONAL:** Born Aug 2, 1954, Chai-ye, Taiwan; son of Jer-Chin & Ya-Jen Chen; married Rachel Y Chen, Jun 22, 1980; children: Ann. **EDUCATION:** Cheng Kung University, Taiwan, BS, 1976; Tsing Hua University, Taiwan, MS, 1979; Purdue University, School of Industrial Engineering, PhD, 1985. **CAREER:** Louisiana State University, assistant professor, 1985-90, associate professor, 1990-. **ORGANIZATIONS:** ACM; Institute of Management Science. **HONORS/AWARDS:** Louisiana State University, College of Business, The Erich Sternberg Foundation Excellence in Teaching Award, 1992. **SPECIAL ACHIEVEMENTS:** Publication of 26 technical papers in management information systems, 1985-. **BIOGRAPHICAL SOURCES:** Journal of Information Technology, vol 8, no 1, p 3-13, 1993; IEEE Transactions on Engineering Management, vol 39, no 2, p 149-157, 1992. **BUSINESS ADDRESS:** Associate Professor of Management Information Systems, Dept of Quantitative Business Analysis, Louisiana State University, Baton Rouge, LA 70803-0100, (504)388-2510.

CHEN, YEA-MOW
Educator. Taiwanese American. **PERSONAL:** Born Apr 12, 1953, Kaoshung, Taiwan; son of Shieh and Yang-Yung Chen; married Shu-Ru Chen, Aug 8, 1981; children: Elaine, Allen, Edward. **EDUCATION:** National Taiwan University, BA, 1976; Ohio State University, master's, 1980, PhD, 1984. **CAREER:** Tamkang University, finance, visiting professor, 1990-91; San Francisco State University, finance, professor, 1984-, US-China Business Institute, director, 1991-. **ORGANIZATIONS:** American Economic Association, 1984-; American Finance Association, 1984-; Asian American Bankers Association, 1991-; Taiwanese American Chamber of Commerce, 1991-; Asian Business League, San Francisco, 1988-90; Chinese American Faculty Association, 1988-, past president. **HONORS/AWARDS:** Pacific Rim Financial Market Conference, Best Research Award, 1992. **SPECIAL ACHIEVEMENTS:** "Price Limits and Stock Market Volatility in Taiwan," Pacific Rim Finance Journal, 1993; "Taiwan: Monetary and Financial System," New Palgrane Dictionary of Finance, 1992; "The Adjustment of Money Supply Expectations to Monetary Policy Regime Changes," International Journal of Economics and Finance, 1991. **BUSINESS ADDRESS:** Professor, San Francisco State University, School of Business, 1600 Holloway Avenue, San Francisco, CA 94132-1722, (415)338-2106.

CHEN, YEN-HSU
Engineering company executive. Taiwanese American. **PERSONAL:** Born May 30, 1952, Tou-Nan, Taiwan; son of Jui-Cheng Chen and Kuei-Chih Liao Chen; married Ying-Suei Weng, Feb 18, 1993. **EDUCATION:** University of Sao Paulo, BS, 1976; Colorado State University, MS, 1981. **CAREER:** Simons, Li & Associates Inc, project manager/engineer, 1981-90, vice president, 1990-. **ORGANIZATIONS:** American Society of Civil Engineers, 1982. **BUSINESS ADDRESS:** Vice President, Simons, Li & Associates Inc, 3636 Birch St, Ste 290, Newport Beach, CA 92660, (714)476-2150.

CHEN, YI-CHAO
Educator, researcher. Chinese American. **PERSONAL:** Born Aug 16, 1952, Xiamen, Fujian, People's Republic of China; son of Junmei Chen & Huina Huang; married Xiao-Qing Liu, Jan 1, 1981; children: Tanya, Jerry. **EDUCATION:** Beijing University of Aeronautics and Astronautics, 1979-80; Johns Hopkins University, MSE, 1982; University of Minnesota, PhD, 1986. **CAREER:** Cornell University, visiting professor, 1987-90; University of Houston, Department of Mechanical Engineering, assistant professor, 1990-. **ORGANIZATIONS:** American Society of Mechanical Engineers, elasticity committee, 1990-; Society for Natural Philosophy, selection committee, 1987-. **SPECIAL ACHIEVEMENTS:** Published 20 scientific papers in various journals. **BUSINESS ADDRESS:** Assistant Professor, Dept of Mechanical Engineering, University of Houston, 4800 Calhoun, Houston, TX 77204-4792, (713)743-4533.

CHEN, YI-LENG
Educator. Taiwanese American. **PERSONAL:** Born Aug 7, 1950, Tien-Chung, Taiwan; son of Yih-Hua Chen and Chin-Chun Chen; married Jane-Shen Lee, Jul 8, 1982; children: Theresa, Esther, Janice. **EDUCATION:** National Central University, BS, 1972; University of Illinois at Champaign, Urbana, MS, 1976, PhD, 1980. **CAREER:** National Center for Atmos Res, scientist I, 1980-83; Iowa State University, research associate, 1983-84; Ophir Co, atmospheric scientist, 1984; University of Hawaii, assistant professor, 1984-90, associate professor, 1990-. **ORGANIZATIONS:** American Meteorological Society, 1975-; Meteorological Society of the Republic of China, 1986-. **HONORS/ AWARDS:** Over 10 research grants from the National Science Foundation. **SPECIAL ACHIEVEMENTS:** 15 papers in international journals; 23 papers presented in professional and international conferences proceedings; research advisor, Central Weather Bureau, Taiwan, 1986; participated in four major US and international weather experiments. **BUSINESS ADDRESS:** Associate Professor, Dept of Meteorology, University of Hawaii at Manoa, Hawaii Institute of Geophysics #341, 2525 Correa Rd, Honolulu, HI 96822, (808)956-2570.

CHEN, YI-SHON
Environmental engineer. Taiwanese American. **PERSONAL:** Born Mar 31, 1939, Chia-I, Taiwan; son of Kuo Chen; married Ching-Yun Chen, Nov 25, 1967; children: Ivy, Jennifer, Lesley. **EDUCATION:** National Taiwan University, BS, civil eng, 1961, MS, civil eng, 1964; Manhattan College, ME, sanitary eng, 1967; Harvard University, MS, PhD, environmental chemistry and engineering, 1972. **CAREER:** Taiwan Institute of Environmental Sanitation, sanitary engineer, 1964-65; Manhattan College, research assistant, 1965-67; Harvard University, research assistant & associate, 1967-72; Whitman & Howard Inc, research engineer, 1972-73; Stone & Webster Engineering Corporation, environmental engineer, senior principal, 1973-. **ORGANIZATIONS:** Water Environment Federation, 1971-; American Water Work Association, 1971-; American Chemical Society, Division of Environmental Chemistry, 1974-; New England Water Environmental Association, 1971-; Sigma Xi Society, 1970-80. **HONORS/AWARDS:** Harvard University Fellowship, 1967-69; US Environmental Protection Agent, Training Fellowship, 1969-72. **SPECIAL ACHIEVEMENTS:** Principal engineer and consultant on more than 70 projects; several publications in environmental journals and society conference proceedings; professional engineer license and registration, Taiwan, 1962, Rhode Island, 1974, Massachusetts, 1986. **MILITARY SERVICE:** National Chinese Air Force, Taiwan, second lt, engineering officer, 1961-62. **BUSINESS ADDRESS:** Senior Principal Environmental Engineer, Stone & Webster Engineering Corp, 245 Summer St, Boston, MA 02210, (617)589-2733.

CHEN, YIH-WEN DAVID
Scientist. Taiwanese American. **PERSONAL:** Born Apr 10, 1948, Taichung, Taiwan; son of Fang-Long Chen and Su Chen; married Fang-Li Chen, Mar 27, 1977; children: Christine A, Deborah M. **EDUCATION:** National Tsing Hua University, BS, 1971, MS, 1974; The University of Texas, PhD, 1982. **CAREER:** Solar Energy Research Institute, postdoctoral fellow, 1982-84; Exxon Corp, research scientist, 1984-86; Warner Jenkinson Co, research chemist, 1986-87; Hilton Davis Co, senior R&D chemist, 1987-91; Brewer Science Inc, optical materials development group manager,1991-. **HONORS/ AWARDS:** Phi Kappa Phi, membership for academic achieement, 1981. **HOME ADDRESS:** Rt 4, Box 179A, Rolla, MO 65401, (314)364-2750.

CHEN, YOHCHIA
Educator. Taiwanese American. **PERSONAL:** Born Aug 25, 1956, Chung Li, Taiwan; son of Ching Tang Chen and Ping Mei Liu (deceased); married Aug 17, 1982; children: Tiffany, Albert B. **EDUCATION:** National Cheng Kung University, Taiwan, BS, 1979; University of Minnesota, MS, 1985, PhD, 1988. **CAREER:** Feng Chia University, instructor, 1979-80; Pacific Engineers & Constructors Ltd, structural engr, 1982-; Minnesota Mining and Manufacturing, structural engr, 1987-88; Howard Needle Tammen & Bergendof, bridge engr, 1987-88; Bakke Kopp Ballou & MacFarlin, bridge engr, 1988-89; Pennsylvania State University, assistant professor, 1989-. **ORGANIZATIONS:** American Society of Civil Engineers, 1986-, Steel Bridge Committee, 1991-, Technical Council on Lifeline Earthquake Engineering, 1990-; Association for Bridge Construction & Design, 1992-; American Concrete Institute, Committee 341 (Earthquake Resistant Design of Reinforced Concrete Bridges), 1993-, Committee 442 (Response of Concrete Buildings to Lateral Forces), 1993-. **HONORS/AWARDS:** University of Minnesota, Sommerfeld Fellowship, 1983-84; Engineering Foundation, Faculty Grant, 1992; Federal Emergency Management Agency, Faculty Grant, 1992; Penn State University, Outstanding

Research Award, 1993; National Research Council, Taiwan, Research Fellow, 1993; National Central University and Ministry of Education, Taiwan, Teaching Fellow, 1993. **SPECIAL ACHIEVEMENTS:** More than 30 publications, 1986-; research grants, 1989-; consultant to local industries, 1991-; paper reviewer, 1990-. **MILITARY SERVICE:** Army, First Division, lieutenant, 1975-76. **BUSINESS ADDRESS:** Assistant Professor, Pennsylvania State at Harrisburg, 777 W Harrisburg Pike, W-261, Olmstead Bldg, Middletown, PA 17057-4898, (717)948-6146.

CHEN, YU
Educator. Chinese American. **PERSONAL:** Born Jun 8, 1921, Nanking, China; married Hwei-Ju Chen; children: Margaret, Alice. **EDUCATION:** Shanghai Jiao-Tung University, BS, 1942; Harvard University, MS, 1946, ScD, 1950. **CAREER:** Ryco Engineering Inc, staff engineer, 1950-52; Burroughs Corporation, senior engineer, 1952-56; Ford Motor Engineering Research, senior engineer, 1956-59; New York University, associate professor, 1959-64; Rutgers, The State University of New Jersey, professor, 1964-91, professor emeritus, 1991-. **ORGANIZATIONS:** American Society of Mechanical Engineers, life fellow, 1954-; Sigma Xi, 1950-. **HONORS/AWARDS:** Shanghai Jiao-Tung University, Shanghai, China, Honorary Professor, 1980-. **SPECIAL ACHIEVEMENTS:** Author, Vibrations-Theoretical Methods, Addison-Wesley, 1966; author of more than 80 technical papers in applied mechanics and mechanical engineering. **BUSINESS ADDRESS:** Professor, Rutgers, The State University of New Jersey, PO Box 909, Piscataway, NJ 08855-0909, (908)932-3665.

CHEN, YU-CHARN
Educator. Taiwanese American/Chinese American. **PERSONAL:** Born Nov 3, 1954, Tainan, Taiwan; son of Chang-Shou Chen and Yu-Mei Wu; married Lih-Jiun Tsuei, Aug 3, 1986; children: Clifford L, Connie V. **EDUCATION:** National Taiwan Normal University, BEd, 1977, MEd, 1980; University of Northern Iowa, DIT, 1988. **CAREER:** Shieh-Ho Vocational High School, electrical engineering teacher, 1977-78; China Junior College of Technology, instructor, 1980-83; Ming-Chi Junior College of Technology, instructor, 1980-81; University of Northern Iowa, teaching assistant, 1984-87; Rawson Control Systems Inc, design engineer, 1986-87; San Francisco State University, professor, 1987-. **HONORS/AWARDS:** Rawson Control Systems Inc, Microcomputer Controlled System Scholarship, 1986. **SPECIAL ACHIEVEMENTS:** Published 42 dissertation abstracts and 4 articles in Taiwan; presented 2 papers to American Vocational Association, 1991. **MILITARY SERVICE:** Chinese Air Force, Taiwan, Electronics Communication Officer, second lt, 1983. **BUSINESS ADDRESS:** Professor, Dept of Design and Industry, San Francisco State University, 1600 Holloway Ave, San Francisco, CA 94132, (415)338-2211.

CHEN, YUBAO
Educator. Chinese American. **PERSONAL:** Born Apr 27, 1958, Wu, Jiangsu, People's Republic of China; son of Jinlong Chen & Falin Ma; children: Lulu. **EDUCATION:** Xian Jiaotong University, BS, 1982; University of Wisconsin, Madison, MS, 1984, PhD, 1986; University of Michigan, Ann Arbor, postdoctoral, 1987. **CAREER:** University of Wisconsin, Madison, research assistant, 1984-86; University of Michigan, Ann Arbor, postdoctoral fellow, 1987-88; University of Michigan, Dearborn, assistant professor, 1988-; City of Polytechnic of Hong Kong, visiting fellow, 1992. **ORGANIZATIONS:** American Society of Mechanical Engineers, 1987-; Society of Manufacturing Engineers, 1987-; Society of Automotive Engineers, 1989-; Institute of Industrial Engineers, 1989-; International Association of Knowledge Engineers, 1989-; American Chinese Management Educators Association, 1991-; Detroit Chinese Engineers Association, 1992-. **HONORS/AWARDS:** SME, Outstanding Young Manufacturing Engineer Award, 1990; SAE, Teetor Educational Award, 1990; Tangkakji Trust, scholarships, 1983-84; Xian Jiaotong University, Medal of Distinguished Graduate, 1982. **SPECIAL ACHIEVEMENTS:** Published more than 30 research papers; numerous presentations & seminars; received more than $500,000 in research funding from National Science Foundation, State of Michigan, industry, etc. **BIOGRAPHICAL SOURCES:** ''Kodak Helps Professor Tackle Real-word Problems,'' Report of Gining, p26-27, 1992; ''Yubao Chen Won the Outstanding Engineer Award,'' People Daily, August 15, 1990. **BUSINESS ADDRESS:** Assistant Professor, University of Michigan-Dearborn, 4901 Evergreen Rd, 114 MSEL, Dearborn, MI 48128, (313)593-5579.

CHEN, YUNG (ALICE WU CHEN)

Writer, translator. Chinese American. **PERSONAL:** Born Nov 12, 1937, Canton, China; daughter of Siu-to Wu and K K Chue; married James T T Chen, Jun 29, 1963. **EDUCATION:** Mount Holyoke College, 1960; University of Pennsylvania, PhD, 1966. **CAREER:** Author: Valentine Day, 1973; Breakers on the Sands, 1979; Travel Impressions, 1987; Twenty Moons, 1991; translator: History and Christianity, J M Montgomery, 1977; Philosophy and the Christian Faith, Colin Brown, 1980; Tyndale Commentaries: Revelations, Leon Morris, 1990; editor, translator: Kingdoms in Conflict, Charles Colson, 1992.

CHEN, ZHONG-YING

Senior scientist. Chinese American. **PERSONAL:** Born Feb 20, 1943, Shanghai, China; son of J T Chen and T Hong; married Yin Zhang, Apr 1968; children: James J. **EDUCATION:** Chinese University of Science & Technology, BS, 1965; Massachusetts Institute of Technology, SM, 1981, PhD, 1984. **CAREER:** Chinese Academy of Sciences, research scientist, 1965-79; Massachusetts Institute of Technology, research assistant, 1980-84; University of California, research chemist, 1984-87; University of Texas, Austin, research scientist, 1987-90; EOS Technologies Inc, senior scientist, 1990-92; Science Applications International, senior scientist, 1992-. **ORGANIZATIONS:** American Physical Society, 1983-; MIT Club of Washington, director, 1991-. **HONORS/AWARDS:** Chinese Academy of Sciences, Award for the Progress in Science and Technology, 1985; Robert A Welch Foundation, research fellowship, 1987-90. **SPECIAL ACHIEVEMENTS:** Numerous external publications in major journals such as Physical Review Letters, Physical Review, Journal of Chemical Physics, Journal of Physics, Physics Letters, Physica, Journal Physical Chemistry, Macromolecules and in a monograph on Jilin Meteorites. **BUSINESS ADDRESS:** Senior Scientist, Science Applications International Corp, 7600 A Leesburg Pike, Falls Church, VA 22043, (703)821-4883.

CHENG, ALEXANDER H-D.

Educator. Taiwanese American. **PERSONAL:** Born May 25, 1952, Taipei, Taiwan; son of Chia-hua Cheng and Yu-Juen Cheng; married Daisy Cheng, Nov 23, 1979; children: Jacqueline, Julia. **EDUCATION:** National Taiwan University, BS, 1974; University of Missouri, MS, 1978; Cornell University, PhD, 1981. **CAREER:** Cornell University, acting assistant professor, 1981-82; Columbia University, assistant professor, 1982-85; University of Delaware, associate professor, 1985-93, professor, 1993-. **ORGANIZATIONS:** Intl Assn Boundary Element Method, recording secretary & executive committee member, 1990-92; American Society Civil Engineers, groundwater committee, 1991-; American Geophysical Union, 1983; Society of Petroleum Engineers, 1989. **SPECIAL ACHIEVEMENTS:** Edited 3 books, 5 invited chapters in books, 39 journal papers, 40 conference proceeding papers; Editorial Board, Computational Engineering Series, Elsevier, 1991-; Associate Editor, Intl Journal for Engineering Analysis with Boundary Element, 1993-. **BUSINESS ADDRESS:** Professor, Dept of Civil Engineering, University of Delaware, Newark, DE 19716, (302)831-6787.

CHENG, AMY I.

Artist, educator. Chinese American. **PERSONAL:** Born Dec 8, 1956, Gaoshiung, Taiwan; daughter of Nai Ling Cheng and Chai-Ying Cheng. **EDUCATION:** University of Texas, Austin, BFA, 1978; Hunter College, CUNY, MFA, 1982. **CAREER:** Hunter College, lecturer, 1985-86; Princeton University, visiting assistant professor, 1989-90; Bard College, assistant professor, 1990-; artist, exhibitions include: Trabia Gallery, group, 1990; The National Museum of Women in the Arts, group, 1991; The Harrison Gallery, solo, 1991; C&A Gallery, solo, 1992. **HONORS/AWARDS:** New York Foundation for the Arts, painting fellowship, 1990; MacDowell Colony, fellowship, 1989, 1992; Yaddo Corp, Milton and Sally Avery Fellowship, 1990; Ford Foundation, painting fellowship, 1978; Arts International Travel Grant, recipient, 1994. **BIOGRAPHICAL SOURCES:** "Singular Visions," Arts Magazine, vol 62, no, 3, Nov 1987; "Romance Lives," Times-Union, Rochester, NY, Nov 30, 1989. **HOME PHONE:** (915)757-3717. **BUSINESS ADDRESS:** Assistant Professor of Studio Art, Bard College, Annandale, NY 12504.

CHENG, ANDREW F.

Physicist, laboratory supervisor. Chinese American. **PERSONAL:** Born Oct 15, 1951, Princeton, NJ; son of Sin-I Cheng and Jean Cheng; married Linda; children: Caroline, Matthew. **EDUCATION:** Princeton University, AB, 1971; Columbia University, PhD, 1977. **CAREER:** Bell Labs, post doc, 1976-78; Rutgers University, assistant professor, 1978-83; Applied Physics Lab, Phys

Section, supervisor, 1983-. **ORGANIZATIONS:** American Geophysical Union, 1979-; American Physical Society, 1978-. **HONORS/AWARDS:** American Phys Society, fellow, 1992; MD Academy of Science, Outstanding Young Scientist, 1985; NASA, Group Achievement Award, 1986, 1990. **SPECIAL ACHIEVEMENTS:** Editor, Transactions of the AGU, 1989-91; approximately 90 publications. **BUSINESS ADDRESS:** Supervisor, Physics Section, Applied Physics Lab, Johns Hopkins Road, Laurel, MD 20723, (301)953-5415.

CHENG, BENJAMIN SHUJUNG

Educator. Taiwanese American. **PERSONAL:** Born Sep 3, 1937, YunLin, Taiwan; son of Tien Cheng & A-Miao Cheng; married Amy L Cheng, Jun 18, 1967; children: Robert K, George W, Angela C, Franklin R. **EDUCATION:** Taiwan University, Taipei, BA, economics, 1960; University of California, Berkeley, MA, economics, 1966; University of Oklahoma, Norman, PhD, economics, 1971. **CAREER:** Alcorn State University, assistant professor of economics, 1971-72; Louisiana First Enterprise, secretary-treasurer, 1979-86; Southern University, Baton Rouge, assistant professor of economics, 1972-76, associate professor of economics, 1976-80, professor of economics, 1980-. **ORGANIZATIONS:** Midsouth Academy of Economics and Finance; American Economic Association; Louisiana Academy of Economists; Formosan Association for Public Affairs, board member. **HONORS/AWARDS:** Distinguished Faculty Member of the Economics Department, 1988. **SPECIAL ACHIEVEMENTS:** Published papers in: Econometrica, 1972; Journal of Economics and Statistics, 1972; Review of Economic Development; Proceedings of Midsouth Academy of Economics and Finance; language proficiency: English, Chinese, Taiwanese. **MILITARY SERVICE:** TOTC in Taiwan, 1960-61. **HOME ADDRESS:** 956 Bromley Dr, Baton Rouge, LA 70808, (504)766-3484. **BUSINESS ADDRESS:** Professor of Economics, Southern University, College of Business, Baton Rouge, LA 70813, (504)771-5641.

CHENG, BRIAN KAI-MING

Research chemist. Hong Kong American/Chinese American. **PERSONAL:** Born Jul 5, 1958, Hong Kong; son of Chuen Cheng and Wan-Chan Cheng; married Lucy Cheng, Jul 2, 1983; children: Derek. **EDUCATION:** Indiana University, BA, 1982; Washington University, MA, 1987. **CAREER:** Monsanto Co, research chemist, currently. **ORGANIZATIONS:** American Chemical Society. **HONORS/AWARDS:** Indiana State University, Summer Scholarship, 1977. **SPECIAL ACHIEVEMENTS:** Publications in numerous scientific journals including: Journal of Medicinal Chemistry, 1989-90; patent inventorships; presentations at American Chemical Society conferences.

CHENG, CARLOS

Design engineering firm executive. Chinese American. **PERSONAL:** Born Aug 3, 1946, Cavite City, Philippines; son of Lim Se and Cheng Ky; married Shirley, Jul 17, 1973; children: Carlson, Carleton. **EDUCATION:** Cleveland State University, BS, MSChE, 1972. **CAREER:** Life Science, lead process engineer, 1991; The Pleiades Group, president, currently. **ORGANIZATIONS:** American Institute of Chemical Engineers, associate member, 1982. **HOME ADDRESS:** 668 N Mayfair Ave, Daly City, CA 94015, (415)755-4479. **BUSINESS ADDRESS:** President, The Pleiades Group, 5901 Christie Ave, Ste 303, Emeryville, CA 94608, (510)653-1358.

CHENG, CHARLES CHING-AN

Educator. Chinese American. **PERSONAL:** Born Jan 18, 1948, Taipei, Taiwan; son of Teh-An Cheng and Loh-Nien Wan Cheng; married Mei T, Aug 15, 1972; children: Andrew, David. **EDUCATION:** Cheng-Kung University, Tainan, Taiwan, BS, mathematics, 1969; Rutgers University, MS, mathematics, 1973, PhD, mathematics, 1974; University of Michigan, Ann Arbor, MS, computer science, 1985. **CAREER:** Rutgers University, visiting assistant professor, 1982-83; AT&T Bell Laboratories, MTS, 1987-88; Oakland University, associate professor, 1975-. **ORGANIZATIONS:** American Math Society, 1973-86; MAA, 1976-86; SIAM, 1988-90; ACM, 1988-90. **HONORS/AWARDS:** Rutgers University, 4-year fellowship, 1970; Oakland University, summer research fellowship, 1981, 1985, research, leave for W93, 1992. **SPECIAL ACHIEVEMENTS:** "Finite Partially Ordered Sets of Cohomological Dimesnsion One," J Algebra, 1976; "Cohomological Dimension of an Abelian Monoid," Proc Amer Math Soc, 1980; "Hereditary Monoid Rings," Amer J Math, 1982; "Exact Limits," J Pure and Applied Algebra, 1983; "Separable Semigroup Algebras," J Pure and Applied Algebra, 1984; numerous others. **BUSINESS ADDRESS:** Associate Professor, Oakland University, Walton Blvd at Squirrel Rd, 300 O'Dowd Hall, Rochester, MI 48309, (313)370-3444.

CHENG, CHARMIAN S.
Librarian. Taiwanese American. **PERSONAL:** Born Jul 14, 1942, Tainan, Taiwan; married Robert C Cheng, May 6, 1967; children: Edward, Elaine. **EDUCATION:** National Taiwan University, BA, 1964; Rutgers University, MLS, 1983. **CAREER:** Chin-ch'eng Boys High School, English teacher, 1964-66; Princeton University, head, public services, Gest Oriental Library, 1983-. **ORGANIZATIONS:** AAS/CEAL, 1983-; ALA, 1984-. **BUSINESS ADDRESS:** Head, Public Services, Gest Library, Princeton University, Princeton, NJ 08544, (609)258-3259.

CHENG, CHENG-YIN
Educator. Taiwanese American. **PERSONAL:** Born Jan 29, 1930, Shinpu, Shinchu, Taiwan; son of Shu-Hsien Cheng and Hsi-Mei Chen; married Hui-Tzu Lai, Sep 16, 1972. **EDUCATION:** Berea College, BS, 1955; University of Illinois, Urbana, MS, 1956, PhD, 1960. **CAREER:** Wilson College, instructor, 1960-61; Shippensburg State College, assistant professor, 1961-63, associate professor, 1963-65; Ithaca College, associate professor, 1965-68; East Stroudsburg University, professor, 1968-. **ORGANIZATIONS:** American Chemical Society, 1959-; American Water Works Association, 1989-; Pennsylvania Academy of Science, associate editor, 1968-; Sigma Xi, 1956-; Association of Pennsylvania State College and University Faculties, 1970-. **SPECIAL ACHIEVEMENTS:** Co-author of six papers dealing with analytical chemistry and environmntal science, published in the Journal of the Pennsylvania Academy of Science, 1980, 1982, 1984, 1991, 1992. **BUSINESS ADDRESS:** Professor, Dept of Chemistry, East Stroudsburg University, East Stroudsburg, PA 18301, (717)424-3321.

CHENG, CHU-YUAN
Educator, educational administrator. Chinese American. **PERSONAL:** Born Apr 8, 1927, Shantou, Guangdong, China; son of Hung-shan & Shu-chen Cheng; married Alice Hua Liang Cheng, Aug 15, 1964; children: Anita T Cheng Lee, Andrew Y S. **EDUCATION:** National Chengchi University, Nanking, China, BA, economics, 1949; Georgetown University, MA, economics, 1962, PhD, economics, 1964. **CAREER:** Union Research Institute, Hong Kong, director of research, 1955-58; Seton Hall University, research professor, 1959-64; George Washington University, visiting research professor, 1963; University of Michigan, senior research economist, 1964-69; Lawrence University, associate professor of economics, 1970-71; Ball State University, professor of economics, Asian studies, chairman, 1972-. **ORGANIZATIONS:** Sun Yat-sen Institute in America, president, 1986-; Chinese American Society, president, 1990-92; American Association for Chinese Studies, board of directors, 1991-93; Association of Chinese Social Scientists in North America, board of directors, 1985-88, president, 1994-95; Chinese Academic and Professional Association in Mid-America, president, 1983-84; Presidential Council for National Unification, Republic of China, research member, 1992-. **HONORS/AWARDS:** Choice Magazine, Choice Outstanding Academic Book Award, 1992; Far East College, Hong Kong, Academic Medal, 1987; National Assembly, Parliament, Republic of China, medal for contributions to Sino-American Cultural Exchange, 1987; Institute of Chinese Culture, NY, Chinese Cultural Award for outstanding contributions to the promotion of Chinese culture in the US, 1984; Ball State University, Outstanding Research Award, 1976. **SPECIAL ACHIEVEMENTS:** Published 35 books on Chinese economy, including: Behind the Tiananmen Massacre: Social, Political and Economic Ferment in China, Westview Press, 1990; Sun Yat-sen's Doctrine in the Modern World, Westview Press, 1989; China's Economic Development: Growth and Structural Change, Westview Press, 1982; China's Petroleum Industry: Output Growth and Export Potential, Praeger Publishers, 1976; Scientific and Engineering Manpower in Communist China, National Science Foundation, 1965. **BUSINESS ADDRESS:** Professor, Dept of Economics, Chairman, Asian Studies Committee, Ball State University, College of Business, Muncie, IN 47306, (317)285-5366.

CHENG, CHUNG-KUAN
Educator. **PERSONAL:** married. **EDUCATION:** National Taiwan University, BS, 1976, MS, 1978; UC, Berkeley, PhD, 1984. **CAREER:** University of California, San Diego, professor, currently. **BUSINESS ADDRESS:** Professor, CSE Dept, University of California San Diego, Mail Code 0114, Gilman St, La Jolla, CA 92093-0114, (619)534-6184.

CHENG, DAVID HONG
Educator. Chinese American. **PERSONAL:** Born Apr 19, 1920, I-Shing, China; son of Tse Kuen Cheng and Tseng Sun Sheng Cheng; married Lorraine Hui-Lan Yang, Sep 4, 1949; children: Kenneth, Gloria. **EDUCATION:** Uni-

versity of Minnesota, MS, 1947, PhD; Columbia University, William Richmond Peters Jr Fellow, 1950. **CAREER:** Rutgers University, instr, 1949-50; Ammann & Whitney, structural engineer, 1950-52; M W Kellogg Co, sr engineer, 1952-55; CCNY, lecturer, 1955, asst prof, civil engineering, 1955-58, assoc prof, 1959-65, prof, 1966-86, director, grad studies & exec officer PhD programs in engineering, 1977-78, dean of engineering, 1979-86; Techtran Inc, president, 1986-; William Paterson College, trustee, 1990-. **ORGANIZATIONS:** ASCE; ASME; Chinese Inst Engineers; Sigma Xi; Tau Beta Pi; Chi Epsilon; Phi Tau Phi. **HONORS/AWARDS:** Tau Beta Pi, Outstanding Teacher Award, 1972; CCNY, 125th Anniversary Medal, 1973; Chinese Inst Engrs, Achievement Award, 1984. **SPECIAL ACHIEVEMENTS:** Author, Nuclei of Strain in the Semi-infinite Solid, 1961; Analysis of Piping Flexibility and Components, 1973. **BUSINESS ADDRESS:** Trustee, William Paterson College, Wayne, NJ 07470.

CHENG, DAVID KEUN
Educator, educational administrator. Chinese American. **PERSONAL:** Born Jan 10, 1918, Ih-Sing, Kiangsu, China; son of Han J & Ying Cheng; married Enid, Mar 27, 1948; children: Eugene. **EDUCATION:** National Chiao Tung University, China, BSEE, 1938; Harvard University, SM, 1944, ScD, 1946. **CAREER:** Central Radio Manufacturing Works, China, electrical engineer, 1938-43; USAF, Cambridge Research Labs, electronics engineer, project engineer, 1946-48; Office of Naval Research, London, liaison scientist, 1975-76; Syracuse University, assistant professor, associate professor, professor, 1948-83, centennial professor emeritus, 1984-; World Open University, acting president, 1992-. **ORGANIZATIONS:** Sigma Xi, 1944-; Eta Kappa Nu, 1949-; Institute of Electrical and Electronics Engineers, chairman and vice chairman of various boards, groups & committees, 1957-70, fellow, 1960, European distinguished lecturer, 1975-76; Phi Tau Phi, Natl Executive Council president, 1973-74; Institution of Electrical Engineers, UK, fellow and representative in USA, 1980-83; Li Institution of Science & Technology, president and chairman of board of trustees, 1992-. **HONORS/AWARDS:** John Simon Guggenheim Foundation, fellow, 1960-61; National Electronics Conference, Best Original Paper Award, 1960; Chinese Institute of Engineers, Annual Achievement Award, 1962; IEEE, Syracuse Section, Best Paper Awards: 1961, 1964-66, 1969, 1970, 1980; National Academy of Sciences, exchange scientist to Hungary, 1972, Yugoslavia, 1974, Poland and Romania, 1978; Phi Tau Phi Scholastic Honor Society, Distinguished Service Award, 1975; Syracuse University, Chancellors Citation for Exceptional Academic Achievement, 1981, Centennial Professor, 1970-; National Chiao Tung University, Honorary Doctor of Engineering Degree, 1985; honorary professor: Northwest Institute of Telecommunication Engineering, 1982; Beijing Institute of Posts & Telecommunications, 1992; Shanghai Jiao Tong University, China, 1985. **SPECIAL ACHIEVEMENTS:** Author of 3 books: Analysis of Linear Systems, 1959; Field and Wave Electromagnetics, first ed, 1983, 2nd ed, 1989; Fundamentals of Engineering Electromagnetics, 1993; author of over 130 articles in professional journals; consulting editor for Electrical Science books, Addison-Wesley Publishing Co, 1961-78; consulting editor for Electrical Engineering Monographs, Intext Educational Publishers, 1974-76; consultant to GE, IBM, TRW, Syracuse Research Corporation. **HOME ADDRESS:** 4620 N Park Ave #104E, Chevy Chase, MD 20815.

CHENG, EUGENE Y.
Educator, researcher. Chinese American. **PERSONAL:** Born May 26, 1954, Penang, Malaysia; son of George and Arlene Cheng; married Rebekah Wang-Cheng, Jul 9, 1978; children: Christopher, Andrew, Ryan. **EDUCATION:** La Sierra College, BA, 1975; Loma Linda University Medical School, MD, 1978. **CAREER:** Medical College of Wisconsin, asst professor of anesthesiology and medicine, 1985-, director of critical care medicine, anesthesiology, 1988-, associate professor of anethesiology and medicine, 1991-. **ORGANIZATIONS:** American Society of Anesthesiologists, 1983-; International Anesthesia Research Society, 1985-; American College of Physicians, 1990-; Society of Critical Care Medicine, 1985-; American Society of Critical Care Anesthesiologists, 1990. **HONORS/AWARDS:** Assn of University Anesthesiologists, 1993. **SPECIAL ACHIEVEMENTS:** Publications: Tissue Oxygenation, Lippincott, 1992; Manual of Anesthesia and Medical Illness, Lippincott, 1990; numerous articles. **BUSINESS ADDRESS:** Associate Professor of Anesthesiology and Medicine, Medical College of Wisconsin, 9200 W Wisconsin Ave, Milwaukee, WI 53226, (414)259-2715.

CHENG, FRANKLIN YIH
Educator. Chinese American. **PERSONAL:** Born Jul 1, 1936, China; married Pi-Yu C Cheng, Sep 15, 1962; children: George, Deborah. **EDUCATION:**

National Cheng-Kung University, Taiwan, BS, 1960; University of Illinois, MS, 1962; University of Wisconsin, PhD, 1966. **CAREER:** University of Missouri, Rolla, assistant professor, 1966-69, associate professor, 1969-74, professor of civil engineering, 1974-87, curators' professor of civil engineering, 1987-. **ORGANIZATIONS:** American Society of Civil Engineers, chairman, 1991-; Journal of Structural Engineering, associate editor and publications secretary, 1987-92; Chinese-American Association of Natural Disaster Mitigation Research, initiator, 1989-; Structural Stability Research Council, chairman, task group 24, 1983-92; Council on Tall Buildings and Urban Habitat, Committee 16, 1986-; International Association of Structural Safety & Reliability, structural optimization committee, 1985-; Council on Low-Rise Buildings, task group on design guidelines, 1984-88. **HONORS/AWARDS:** Taiyuan University of Technology, China, honorary professor, 1991; Xian Institute of Metallurgy and Construction Engineering, honorary professor, 1990; Harbin Institute of Architecture and Civil Engineering, honorary professor, 1981; Chi Epsilon, UMR chapter, 1988; University of Missouri, Rolla, Faculty Excellence Award, 1987; School of Engineering, UMR, Halliburton Excellence Award, 1986; University of Wisconsin, fellow, 1986; Korean Society of Civil Engineers, Plaque of Appreciation, 1986; National Taiwan Institute of Technology, Plaque of Appreciation, 1986. **SPECIAL ACHIEVEMENTS:** Author of more than 200 technical publications, 1988-93; principle investigator for more than 40 sponsored research projects during past two decades; consultant with selected companies; panelist on National Science Foundation review panels; specialist for World Bank International Advisory Panel. **BUSINESS ADDRESS:** Curators' Professor of Civil Engineering, University of Missouri, Rolla, 301A Butler-Carlton Hall, Rolla, MO 65401, (314)341-4469.

CHENG, FU-DING

Filmmaker, painter. Chinese American. **PERSONAL:** Born Feb 5, 1943, Palo Alto, CA; son of Theodore Cheng and Patricia Sung Yuan Cheng; married Linda Jacobson, May 17, 1987. **EDUCATION:** University of Southern California, School of Architecture, 1960-64; Alliance Francaise, Paris, 1965; University of California, Berkeley, BArch, 1967. **CAREER:** Self-employed, producer, writer, director, 1970-; producer/writer/director, "Zen Tales for the Urban Explorer"; other mystical adventure stories. **ORGANIZATIONS:** Independent Feature Project/West, 1983-. **HONORS/AWARDS:** Long Beach Museum of Modern Art, Open Channel Grantee, 1991; American Film Institute, Independent Filmmaker's Grant, 1977; UCLA, Research Grant, 1976; USC, Traveling Fellowship, 1964; Houston International Filmfest, Gold Prize, 1993. **SPECIAL ACHIEVEMENTS:** LA Weekly, "Video Pick of the Week," 1991; numerous film prizes at festivals, 1968-90. **BIOGRAPHICAL SOURCES:** LA Times Calendar, "Brave New Artists of Video," 1987; LA Weekly, "Pick of the Week: Zen Tales for the Urban Explorer," 1991. **HOME ADDRESS:** 209 7th Ave, Venice, CA 90291.

CHENG, H. H.

Educator. Chinese American. **PERSONAL:** Born Aug 13, 1932, Shanghai, China; son of Chi-Pao and Anna Lan Cheng; married Jo Yuan Cheng, Dec 15, 1962; children: Edwin Shih-Wen, Antony Shih-Li. **EDUCATION:** Berea College, BA, 1956; University of Illinois, MS, 1958, PhD, 1961. **CAREER:** Iowa State University, research associate, assistant professor, 1962-65; Washington State University, Dept of Agronomy and Soils, asst professor, associate professor, professor, interim chair, Program in Environmental Science and Regional Planning, chair, Graduate School, associate dean, 1965-89; University of Minnesota, Dept of Soil, Water and Climate, professor and head, 1989-. **ORGANIZATIONS:** Soil Science Society of America, div chair, 1985-86, board of directors, 1990-93; American Society of Agronomy, board of directors, 1990-93; American Chemical Society, 1961-; Society of Environmental Toxicology and Chemistry; International Society of Chemical Ecology; Council for Agricultural Science and Technology. **HONORS/AWARDS:** Fulbright Research Scholar, Belgium, 1962-63; Soil Science Society of America, Fellow, 1983-; American Society of Agronomy, Fellow, 1983-; AAAS, Fellow, 1991-; Sigma Xi; Phi Kappa Phi; Gamma Sigma Delta. **SPECIAL ACHIEVEMENTS:** Editor, Pesticides in the Soil Environment: Processes, Impacts, & Modeling, 1990; associate editor, Journal of Environmental Quality, 1983-89; consulting editor, Pedosphere, 1991-; editorial board, Botanical Bulletin of Academia Sinica, 1988. **BUSINESS ADDRESS:** Professor and Head, Dept of Soil, Water and Climate, University of Minnesota, 1991 Upper Buford Circle, Saint Paul, MN 55108, (612)625-9734.

CHENG, HERBERT S.

Educator. Chinese American. **PERSONAL:** Born Nov 15, 1929, Shanghai, China; married 1953; children: four. **EDUCATION:** University of Michigan,

BSME, 1952; Illinois Institute of Tech, MS, 1957; University of Pennsylvania, PhD, mech eng, 1961. **CAREER:** International Harvester Co, jr mechanical engineer, 1952-53; Mach Eng Co, project engineer, 1953-56; Illinois Institute of Tech, mechanical engineering instructor, 1956-57; University of Pennsylvania, mechanical engineering instructor, 1957-61; Syracuse University, assistant professor, 1961-62; Mech Tech Inc, res engineer, 1962-68; consultant for various companies and associations, including General Motors Res Lab, John Deere, National Bureau of Standards, currently; Northwestern University, Center Eng Tribology, associate professor, 1968-74, director, 1984-89, Walter P Murphy Professor of Mechanical Engineering, 1974-. **ORGANIZATIONS:** National Academy of Engineering; American Gear Mfg Association; Gear Res Institute, vp; American Society of Mech Engineers, fellow. **BUSINESS ADDRESS:** Walter P Murphy Professor of Mechanical Engineering, Northwestern University, 219 Catalysis Bldg, Evanston, IL 60208.*

CHENG, HSIANG-TAI

Educator. Taiwanese American. **PERSONAL:** Born Dec 12, 1952, Taipei, Taiwan; son of Hong-Tsai Cheng & Yu-Er Cheng; married Su-ching Cheng, Jan 30, 1980; children: Jenny, Joseph. **EDUCATION:** National Taiwan University, BS, 1980; Ohio State University, MA, 1984; Virginia Polytechnic Institute and State University, PhD, 1985. **CAREER:** University of Georgia, research coordinator, 1985-88; University of Maine, assistant professor, 1988-. **ORGANIZATIONS:** American Agricultural Economics Association, 1985-; Food Distribution Research Society, editorial board, 1988-. **BUSINESS ADDRESS:** Assistant Professor, University of Maine, 302 Winslow Hall, Orono, ME 04469, (207)581-3155.

CHENG, HSIEN K.

Educator, engineer. Chinese American. **PERSONAL:** Born Jun 13, 1923, Macao; son of Lo-Sing and Teresa Ling; married Wai Laan Cheng, May 30, 1956; children: Linda Y H. **EDUCATION:** Chiao-Tung University, Shanghai, China, BSc, 1947; Cornell University, MSc, 1950, PhD, aeronautical eng, 1952. **CAREER:** Bell Aircraft Corp, research aerodynamicist, 1952-56; Cornell Aeronatical Laboratories, research aerodynamicist, 1956-59, principal aerodynamicist 1959-61, principal engineer, 1961-63; Stanford University, special lecturer, 1963-64; University Southern California, professor, 1965-92, professor emeritus, 1992-. **ORGANIZATIONS:** American Institute Aeronautics & Astronautics, fellow, 1952-; American Physical Society, fellow, 1972-; Society of Industrial & Applied Mathematics, 1980-; Sigma Xi, 1952-. **HONORS/AWARDS:** National Academy of Engineering, elected member, 1987; Am Institute Aero Astro, fellow, 1986; Am Phy Society, Fluid Dynamics Div, fellow, 1989. **SPECIAL ACHIEVEMENTS:** Contribution to theories of subsonic, supersonic and hypersonic flows, rarefied and nonequilibrium gas dynamics, rotating and stratified fluids, flying and swimming in nature. **BUSINESS ADDRESS:** Prof Emeritus/Lecturer, Dept of Aerospace Eng, University of Southern California, University Park, RRB 211, Los Angeles, CA 90089-1191, (213)740-5365.

CHENG, HSUEH-JEN

Banker, cleric. Taiwanese American. **PERSONAL:** Born Jul 31, 1937, Ilan, Taiwan; son of Chon-Kuo Cheng and Chiu-Lan Lee Cheng; married Mang-Hsiang, Sep 4, 1967; children: Grace, David. **EDUCATION:** Princeton Theological Seminary, MTh, 1969; Fordham University, MS, 1972; St Johns University, MA, 1973; New York University, PhD candidate, 1976. **CAREER:** Golden Pacific National Bank, manager, vice pres, 1978-85; Asia Bank, manager, vice pres, 1985; Reformed Church of Newtown, pastor, 1986-89; Golden City Commercial Bank, manager, senior vice pres, 1987-; Taiwanese-American Reformed Church in Queens, pastor, 1991-94. **HOME ADDRESS:** 201-03 34th Ave, Bayside, NY 11361.

CHENG, JANE. *See* CHENG, SHEUE-YANN.

CHENG, JILL TSUI

Publishing company executive, real estate company executive. Chinese American. **PERSONAL:** Born Feb 6, 1945, Chung King, Sichuan, China; daughter of Wan Chiu Tsui & Chun-hui Chang Tsui; married Hung Cheng, Jun 7, 1968. **EDUCATION:** Radcliffe College, BA; Harvard Divinity School, master of theological studies. **CAREER:** Robert Bentley, Inc, executive vice president, 1972-75; Harrington Corner Properties, president, 1980-; Cheng & Tsui Co, Inc, president, 1975-. **ORGANIZATIONS:** Downtown Crossing Association, 1980-; Japan Society, 1983-; Organization of Chinese Americans, NE Chapter, 1984-; Asian Community Development Corp, director, 1990-; New England Women in Real Estate, 1992-; Boston Club, 1992-; Massachusetts Minority

Enterprise Investment Corp, director, 1993-. **HONORS/AWARDS:** The Massachusetts Association for Mental Health, Leadership Award, 1985; United Way of Massachusetts Bay, Allocations Leadership Award, 1985. **SPECIAL ACHIEVEMENTS:** Fluent in Chinese and Japanese. **BIOGRAPHICAL SOURCES:** Radcliffe Quarterly, p 17 & 18, Dec 1992. **BUSINESS ADDRESS:** President, Cheng & Tsui Co, Inc, 25 West St, Boston, MA 02111, (617)426-6074.

CHENG, JOE ZEN
Telecommunication company administrator. Taiwanese American. **PERSONAL:** Born Jun 26, 1958, Kaoshung, Taiwan; son of Yun-Kung Cheng and Shung-Fong Cheng; married Maotsai Wang, Apr 10, 1985; children: Jackie, Daniel. **EDUCATION:** University of Arizona, masters degree, 1984. **CAREER:** Bellcore, beginning 1984, acting director, 1991-. **BUSINESS ADDRESS:** Acting Director, Bellcore, 445 South St, MRE2J396, Morristown, NJ 07961, (201)829-3253.

CHENG, JOSEPH KWANG-CHAO
Educator. Chinese American. **PERSONAL:** Born Mar 21, 1934, Nanking, Jiangsu, China; son of Dr & Mrs Samuel Cheng (both deceased); married Kitty Yung-Mu Cheng, Dec 23, 1967; children: Daisy, Dorothy, Debbie, Dennis. **EDUCATION:** Taiwan Christian College, BS, CE, 1959; University of Massachusetts, MS, CE, 1965; University of Oklahoma, PhD, CE, 1973. **CAREER:** Andrewa & Clark Consulting, civil engineer, 1965-66; Tidwell Associated, civil engineer, 1966-67, 1970-72; Delaware Highway Department, civil engineer, 1968-70; NASA/USDA, assistant researcher, 1972-73; University of Southern Colorado, professor, 1973-. **ORGANIZATIONS:** American Society of Civil Engineers; American Society for Engineering Education; National Society of Professional Engineers; Professional Engineers of Colorado, southern chapter, vice president, 1987-88, president, 1988-89, director, 1989-90; Professional Engineers of Delaware; National Education Association; Colorado Education Association; Rocky Mountain Chinese Society of Science and Engineering, president, 1991-92. **HONORS/AWARDS:** American Society for Engineering Education, Award for Excellence in Teaching, 1978; American Biographic Institute, The Distinguished Leadership Award, 1986; University of Southern Colorado, Faculty Merit Award, 1976-77, 1980, 1982-83, Superior Achievement Award, 1988, 1991. **SPECIAL ACHIEVEMENTS:** Fortran 77 for Engineers and Scientists in Taiwan, China, with co-author Dr T Y Lee, National Tsing Hua University, 1987. **BIOGRAPHICAL SOURCES:** Engineering Education, American Society for Engineering Education, p41, October 1978; Engineering Education News, American Society for Engineering Education, p1, July 1978. **HOME ADDRESS:** 157 MacNeil Rd, Pueblo, CO 81001, (719)544-0074. **BUSINESS ADDRESS:** Professor, University of Southern Colorado, 2200 Bonforte Blvd, ASET 257, Pueblo, CO 81001, (719)549-2638.

CHENG, JOSEPHINE
TV news health reporter. Taiwanese American. **PERSONAL:** Born Dec 15, 1958, Taipei, Taiwan; daughter of H C Cheng & Anna Cheng; married Wyatt Helin. **EDUCATION:** University of California, Berkeley, BA, English, 1981; Columbia University, MS, journalism, 1982. **CAREER:** KPIX-TV, newswriter trainee, 1982-84; KVAL-TV, reporter, program host, 1984-86; KATU-TV, reporter specializing in local politics, 1986-89; KOMO-TV, general assignment reporter, 1989-93, program host, 1991-, health reporter, 1993-. **ORGANIZATIONS:** Asian American Journalists Association; National Academy of Television & Radio Artists Arts & Sciences; American Federation of Television & Radio Artists Association. **HONORS/AWARDS:** NATAS, Regional Emmy, Outstanding Reporter, 1992; Washington Press Association, Best In-Depth Reporting, 1991; Associated Press, Best Series, 1987. **BIOGRAPHICAL SOURCES:** Northwest Asian Weekly (aka Seattle Chinese Post), various. **BUSINESS ADDRESS:** Healthwatch Reporter, KOMO, News 4, 100 4th Ave N, Seattle, WA 98109.

CHENG, KUANG LU
Educator. Chinese American. **PERSONAL:** Born Sep 14, 1919, Yangchow, Kiangsu, China; son of Fung-Wu Cheng and Yi-Ming Chiang; divorced; children: Meiling C Tu, Chiling C Chien, Hans C. **EDUCATION:** Northwestern College, China, BS, 1941; University of Illinois, MS, 1949, PhD, 1951. **CAREER:** University of Illinois, postdoctoral fellow, 1951-52; Commercial Solvents Corp, microchemist, 1952-53; University of Connecticut, chemistry instructor, 1953-55; Westinghouse Electric Corp, engineer, 1955-57; Kelsey-Hayes Co, Metals Division, associate director of research, 1957-59; RCA Laboratories, member of technical staff, 1959-66; University of Missoui, Kansas City, chemistry professor, 1966-. **ORGANIZATIONS:** American Chemi-

cal Society, 1951-; American Physical Society, 1968-; American Association for Advancement of Science, fellow, 1968-; The Chemical Society, London, fellow, 1968-; Society of Applied Spectroscopy, 1970-; Sigma Xi, 1951-; American Microchemical Society, 1960-; Electrochemical Society, 1970-. **HONORS/AWARDS:** American Microchemical Society, Benedetti Pichler Memorial Award, 1989; Texas A&M University, Certificate of Recognition, 1981; RCA, Achievement Award, 1963; International Union of Pure & Applied Chemistry, titular member, 1969-79; University of Missouri, N T Veatch Award for Distinguished Research and Creative Activity, 1979. **SPECIAL ACHIEVEMENTS:** Proposed "Chemical Capacity Theory" in electrochemistry. **HOME ADDRESS:** 223-S Twin Oaks, 5050 Oak St, Kansas City, MO 64112. **BUSINESS ADDRESS:** Professor, Dept of Chemistry, University of Missouri-Kansas City, Kansas City, MO 64110.

CHENG, LANNA
Scientist. Singaporean American/Chinese American. **PERSONAL:** Born Apr 27, 1941, Singapore, Singapore; daughter of An Lun Cheng & Fu Hwang; married Ralph A Lewin, Jun 3, 1969. **EDUCATION:** University of Singapore, BSc, 1963, BSc (honors), 1964, MSc, 1966; Oxford University, Oxford, England, DPhil, 1969. **CAREER:** University of Singapore, graduate assistant, 1963-65; Oxford University, teaching assistant, 1966-67; University of Waterloo, Canada, postdoctoral fellow, 1968-69; University of California, technical translator, research associate, 1970-73, assistant research biologist, 1972-77, associate research biologist, 1977-. **ORGANIZATIONS:** Royal Entomological Society, fellow, 1966-; Western Society of Naturalists, 1970-, president, 1985; American Society of Limnology & Oceanography, 1973-; Oxford University, Malaysian-Singapore Association, president, 1967-68. **HONORS/AWARDS:** Singapore State Government, State Scholarship, 1961-64; Commonwealth Association, Commonwealth Scholarship, 1965-68; American Association of University Women, fellowship, 1970-71. **SPECIAL ACHIEVEMENTS:** Editor, Marine Insects, North-Holland Publishing Co, 1976; author of about 100 scientific papers on marine insects, etc; chief technical advisor, UNDP Project on Biotechnology in China, 1989-91; author, Chinese Cookery Made Easy, AAUW, San Diego Branch, 1974; editor, "Proc International Sym on Biotechnology of Saltponds," 1991; areas of study: applied phycology, marine entomology, and applied phycology. **BIOGRAPHICAL SOURCES:** Science Citation Index Annual, entry 17226, 1991. **BUSINESS ADDRESS:** Associate Research Biologist, University of California, San Diego, Scripps Institution of Oceanography, 9500 Gilman Dr, La Jolla, CA 92093-0202, (619)534-4836.

CHENG, LAWRENCE KAI-LEUNG
Architect. Hong Kong American. **PERSONAL:** Born Aug 5, 1954, Hong Kong; son of Cheng Tak-Yim and Chan King-Suen; divorced. **EDUCATION:** Massachusetts Institute of Technology, BSAD, 1976, M Arch, 1980; International Laboratory of Architecture & Urban Design, Urbino, Italy, 1977. **CAREER:** John Sharratt Associates, associate, 1980-87; Cambridge Seven Associates, senior architect, 1987-92; Lawrence K Cheng Associates, Inc, president, 1992-. **ORGANIZATIONS:** American Institute of Architects, 1985-; Boston Society of Architects, 1985-; Boston Urban Gardeners, board member, 1987-; First Night Inc, Boston, board member, 1992-; Chinatown Housing & Land Development Task Force, board member, 1983-. **HONORS/AWARDS:** Massachusetts Institute of Technology, Chandler Prize, 1980; Harvard University, Graduate School of Design, Loeb Fellow, 1989-90. **SPECIAL ACHIEVEMENTS:** Community activist in Boston's Chinatown; work with non-profit organizations; participating artist, Telling Circle, first night, Boston, 1992; articles in newspapers, appearance on TV. **BIOGRAPHICAL SOURCES:** Sampan Newspaper, June 1992. **BUSINESS ADDRESS:** President, Lawrence K Cheng Associates, Inc, 107 South Street, Suite 403, Boston, MA 02111, (617)728-3113.

CHENG, LOUIS TSZ-WAN
Educator. Hong Kong American/Chinese American. **PERSONAL:** Born Oct 4, 1961, Hong Kong, Hong Kong; son of Kai-Kui Cheng and Woon Cheung; married Miu-Yee Lau Cheng, Jul 18, 1986; children: Clifford Ryan, Fiona Miu. **EDUCATION:** Hong Kong Shue Yan College, diploma, 1985; Northeast Louisiana University, MBA, 1986; Louisiana Tech University, DBA, 1989. **CAREER:** Louisiana Tech University, research assistant, 1986-88, part-time instructor, 1988-89; Murray State University, assistant professor in finance, 1989-. **ORGANIZATIONS:** American Finance Association; Financial Management Association; Eastern Finance Association; Southern Financial Association. **HONORS/AWARDS:** Murray State University, Outstanding Paper Recognition Award, 1991. **SPECIAL ACHIEVEMENTS:** Published 16 arti-

cles in academic journals including the Journal of Finance and Journal of Management, 1988-93; gave seminars and lectures to students, faculty and executives in Kunming, Beijing and Guang Zhou, People's Republic of China, visiting scholar, summer 1992. **BUSINESS ADDRESS:** Asst Prof, Dept of Economics and Finance, Murray State University, College of Business and Public Affairs, Murray, KY 42071-3330, (502)762-6763.

CHENG, MEI-FANG HSIEH

Educator, educational administrator. Taiwanese American. **PERSONAL:** Born Nov 24, 1938, Kee-Long, Taiwan; daughter of Chao-Chin Hsieh & Ai Chu; married Wen-Kwei Cheng, Jun 7, 1963; children: Suzanne, Po-Yuan, Julie. **EDUCATION:** National Taiwan University, BS (summa cum laude), 1958; Bryn Mawr College, PhD, 1965. **CAREER:** University of Pennsylvania, postdoctoral/research associate, 1965-68; Rutgers University, assistant research professor, 1969-72, associate professor, 1973-78, professor, 1979-, acting director, 1989-91, Institute of Animal Behavior, director, 1991-. **ORGANIZATIONS:** NIMH Initial Review Committee on Biomedical and Neuroscience, 1979-83; NIMH Behavioral Neurobiology Subcommittee, 1991-95; Hormones and Behavior Journal, associate editor, 1986-. **HONORS/AWARDS:** Fulbright Scholar, 1959-63; NIMH, Research Scientist Award, 1974-79, 1979-84; Johnson & Johnson, Research Discovery Award, 1989; Hoechst-Celanese Pharmaceuticals Inc, Innovative Research Award, 1993. **BUSINESS ADDRESS:** Professor, Director, Institute of Animanl Behavior, Rutgers University, 101 Warren St, Smith Hall, 4th Fl, Newark, NJ 07102, (201)648-5850.

CHENG, NANCY C.

Educator. Chinese American. **PERSONAL:** Born Sep 22, 1931, Harbin, China; daughter of Dr & Mrs C Y Chen; married Ming Tzu Cheng, Jun 9, 1956; children: Andrew J, Anthony L. **EDUCATION:** Carroll College, RN, 1953, BSNE, 1955; University of Florida, MEd, 1960; Nova University, EdD, 1980. **CAREER:** St Joseph's Hospital School of Nursing, instructor/head nurse, 1954-55, St Luke's Hospital School of Nursing instructor, 1955-56; University of Florida Teaching Hospital, asst dir, 1956-60; University of Florida, instructor, 1960-64; Cerritos College, director ADN program, 1965-72; Santa Ana College, director ADN program, 1972-77; Rancho Santiago College, professor, 1977-. **ORGANIZATIONS:** Faculty Association of California Community College, 1991-; Faculty Association of Rancho Santiago College, 1977-; Christian Nurses Association of Orange County, 1988-; California Nurses Association, former member; National League of Nursing former member. **HONORS/AWARDS:** Rancho Santiago College, Faculty Achievement Award, 1988; Chinese Nurses Association, Best Visiting Professor Awards, 1986; Rancho Santiago College, Nominated for the Woman of the Year, 1988, 1989. **SPECIAL ACHIEVEMENTS:** "Pastels in Pediatrics," Nursing Outlook, 1963; "A Second Look at Nurses in Color," Hospitals, 1965; contributor to chapter in Lenburg's Career Moility in Nursing, 1973; contributor to Bullough's "Views of the Consortium Students," Nursing Outlook; proficient in Chinese. **BUSINESS ADDRESS:** Professor, Rancho Santiago College, 17th at Bristol, Santa Ana, CA 92706, (714)564-6825.

CHENG, NELLY CHING-YUN

Educator. Taiwanese American. **PERSONAL:** Born Feb 3, 1933, Tainan, Taiwan; daughter of C K Chen and K C Shih Chen; married Peter P C Cheng, Jan 20, 1962; children: Margaret Cheng Tuttle, Elizabeth N, Patricia L. **EDUCATION:** Tamkang College of Arts and Sciences, BA, 1960; Southern Illinois University, MS, 1964. **CAREER:** Nanzan University, Nagoya, Japan, visiting professor, summers 1980, 1981; University of Nebraska-Lincoln, instructor, 1972-. **ORGANIZATIONS:** Chinese Language Teachers Association, 1980-. **BUSINESS ADDRESS:** Instructor, University of Nebraska, Lincoln, NE 68588-0315, (402)472-3745.

CHENG, NORMAN ALAN

Computer systems analyst. Chinese American. **PERSONAL:** Born Aug 13, 1957, San Francisco, CA; son of Peter Cheng and Rose Marie Cheng; children: Aaron. **EDUCATION:** University of California, Berkeley, 1976-78; California State University, Hayward, BS, 1979; Golden Gate University, MBA, 1983. **CAREER:** Delmonte Corp, accountant, 1980-83; Laguna Honda Hospital, senior systems accountant, 1983-87; City of Oakland, Budget Division, senior systems analyst, 1987-. **BUSINESS ADDRESS:** Senior Systems Analyst, Budget Div, City of Oakland, 475 14th St, 9th Fl, Oakland, CA 94612, (510)238-2909.

CHENG, PING

Educator, educational administrator. Chinese American. **PERSONAL:** Born in Canton, China; married Sabrina H T, Jun 19, 1969; children: Albert H, Bonnie J. **EDUCATION:** Oklahoma State University, BS, mechanical engineering, 1958; MIT, MS, mechanical engineering, 1961; Stanford University, PhD, aero & astro, 1965. **CAREER:** New York University, research scientist of aero & astro, 1965-67; National Taiwan University, visiting professor of mech eng, 1969-70, visiting associate professor of mech eng, 1968-69; Stanford University, visiting professor of petroleum eng, 1976-77; Technical University of Munich, guest professor, 1984; University of Hawaii, professor of mech eng, 1974-, chairman of mech eng, 1989-. **ORGANIZATIONS:** AIAA, associate editor of J of Thermophysics & Heat Transfer, 1988-. **HONORS/AWARDS:** ASME, fellow, 1986; University of Hawaii Foundation, Fujio Matsuda Scholar Award, 1989. **BUSINESS ADDRESS:** Professor, Chairman, Dept of Mech Eng, University of Hawaii, 2540 Dole St, Holmes Hall, Honolulu, HI 96822, (808)956-7167.

CHENG, RICHARD TIEN-REN

Company executive. Chinese American. **PERSONAL:** Born Jun 4, 1934, Nanjing, China; son of George & Elaine Cheng; married Nancy P Cheng, Jan 24, 1960; children: James S, Raymond S. **EDUCATION:** National Taiwan Normal University, BS, 1958; University of Wisconsin, MS, 1963; University of Illinois, MSEE, 1969, PhD, 1971. **CAREER:** University of Wisconsin, asst professor, mathematics, 1971-72; Hunter College, asst professor, mathematics, 1972-73; Rochester Institute of technology, professor, chair, Computer Science, 1973-75, director, School of Computer Science & Technology, 1975-79; Old Dominion University, associate dean, College of Science, 1979-83, eminent professor & chairman, computer science dept, 1979-87; ECI Systems & Engineering, chairman and CEO, 1985-. **ORGANIZATIONS:** Virginia Beach Chamber of Commerce, board of directors, 1988-; Navy League of Hampton Roads, board of directors, 1989-; Operation Smile International, board of directors, 1992-; Norfolk State University Founders, board of directors, 1992-; Virginia Marine Science Museum, board of directors, 1991-; 2007 Steering Committee Hampton Roads, 1993-; IEEE, 1991-. **HONORS/AWARDS:** KPMG, High Tech Entrepreneur of the Year, 1992; Ernst Young-Merrill Lynch, Washington, DC Regional Entrepreneur of the Year, 1992; SBA, Natl Minority Small Business Person of the Year, 1991; Hampton Roads Chamber of Commerce, Small Business Person of the Year, 1991; Inc Magazine, Inc 500 of the Year, 1992. **SPECIAL ACHIEVEMENTS:** Presidential Mission to China with Commerce Secretary, Barbara Franklin, 1992. **MILITARY SERVICE:** Infantry, Taiwan ROTC, 2nd lt, 1958-60; Sharp Shooter, Medal for Research. **BIOGRAPHICAL SOURCES:** "$240 Million Professor" Transpacific, p 52, May 1993; "Computer Whiz," Virginia Beach Beacon, p 20, Oct 1991. **BUSINESS ADDRESS:** Chairman/CEO, ECI Systems and Engineering, 596 Lynnhaven Parkway, Virginia Beach, VA 23452, (804)498-5000.

CHENG, SHEUE-YANN (JANE CHENG)

Research scientist. Chinese American. **PERSONAL:** Born in Kaohsiung, Taiwan; daughter of Wang-lu Chang; married Ching-yao Cheng, Sep 12, 1965; children: Andrew K, Caroline K. **EDUCATION:** University of California, San Francisco Medical Center, PhD, 1966. **CAREER:** National Institutes of Health, National Cancer Institute, section chief of gene regulation section, lab of molecular biology, 1990-. **ORGANIZATIONS:** Chinese Medical and Health Association, president, 1989-90; NIH Chinese American Association, president, 1988-89; National Cancer Institute, Promotion/Tenure Review Panel, 1993-; Journal of Biomedical Science, editor, 1993-; American Thyroid Association, membership committee, 1986-89, chmn, 1989. **BUSINESS ADDRESS:** Section Chief, National Institutes of Health, 9000 Rockville Pike, Bldg 37, Rm 4B09, Bethesda, MD 20892, (301)496-4280.

CHENG, SIN I.

Educator, consultant. Chinese American. **PERSONAL:** Born Dec 28, 1921, Changchow, Jiangsu, China; son of Mou Yi Cheng and H J Hsu Cheng; married Jean J Cheng, 1943; children: Doreen, Andrew, Thomas, Irene. **EDUCATION:** Chiao-Tung University, Shanghai, China, BS, 1943; University of Michigan, Ann Arbor, MS, 1949; Princeton University, PhD, 1952. **CAREER:** Princeton University, asst professor, 1952-56, assoc professor, 1956-60, professor, 1960-. **ORGANIZATIONS:** Avco Missile System Division, consultant, 1956-68; Boeing Scientific Research Lab, consultant, 1969-73. **HONORS/AWARDS:** NorthWest Tech University, Xian, China, honorary director, Thermophysics Institute, 1986, honorary professor, 1986; National Cheng Kung University, Taiwan, Institute professor, IAA, 1989. **SPECIAL ACHIEVE-**

MENTS: Agardograph No 8, Combustion Instability in Liquid Rocket Motors, 1956; Pergamor, translated into Russian, 1958, Chinese, 1962; Computational Dynamics, lecture series in Dalker, China, 1989, edited & translated into Chinese, published by scientific publication, Beijing, 1984; over 100 journal articles & book chapters, published in various professional journals & books. **HOME ADDRESS:** 379 Prospect Avenue, Princeton, NJ 08540, (609)921-8294.

CHENG, SONGLIN
Educator. Taiwanese American. **PERSONAL:** Born Nov 22, 1949, Kaohsiung, Taiwan; son of S J Cheng and T P Cheng; married Rose Cheng, Jul 23, 1977; children: Annie, Grace. **EDUCATION:** National Cheng Kung University, BS, 1972; Wright State University, MS, 1979; University of Arizona, PhD, 1984. **CAREER:** University of Arizona, research associate, 1984-88; Hydro Geo Chemical Inc, hydrogeochemist, 1988-89; Wright State University, assistant professor, 1989-. **ORGANIZATIONS:** Geochemical Society, 1981-; American Geophysical Union, 1984-; Association of Groundwater Scientists & Engineers, 1990-. **HONORS/AWARDS:** Selco Mining Co, Canada, scholarship, 1976; National Ground Water Association, Faculty Fellowship, 1992. **SPECIAL ACHIEVEMENTS:** Published 8 papers and 13 abstracts; organized a session on Hydrogeochemistry and Isotope Hydrology of Regional Aquifer Systems, for Geological Society of America, 1992 annual meeting; "Reaction-Path Formulation of a Simple Dissolution, Model for Radiocarbon Dating Groundwater," Radiocarbon, vol 34, pp 646-653, 1992; co-author: 36 CL Studies of Water Movements Deep within Unsaturated Tuffs, 1990; co-author: Fine and Hyperfine Structure in the Spectrum of Secular Variations of Atmospheric 14 C, 1989; principal investigator and co-investigator of three external fundings during the past 3 1/2 years. **BUSINESS ADDRESS:** Asst Prof, Dept of Geological Sciences, Wright State University, Dayton, OH 45435, (513)873-3452.

CHENG, STEPHEN Z. D.
Educator. Chinese American. **PERSONAL:** Born Aug 3, 1949, Shanghai, People's Republic of China; son of Lu-Zhong Cheng and Jing-Zhi Zhang; married Susan L Z Cheng, Jun 28, 1978; children: Wendy D W. **EDUCATION:** East China Institute of Science and Technology, MS, 1981; Rensselaer Polytechnic Institute, PhD, 1985. **CAREER:** Rensselaer Polytechnic Institute, postdoctoral and research associate, 1985-87; University of Akron, assistant professor, 1987-91, associate professor, 1991-. **ORGANIZATIONS:** American Chemical Society, 1983-; American Physical Society, 1983-; North American Thermal Analysis Society, 1983-; Society for the Advancement of Materials and Process Engineering, 1986-; Material Research Society, 1990-; International Confederation for Thermal Analysis, 1984-; Society for Plastics Engineers, 1989. **HONORS/AWARDS:** NSF Presidential Young Investigator Award, 1991; University of Akron, Certificate of Appreciation of Outstanding Achievement, 1992. **SPECIAL ACHIEVEMENTS:** Over 100 publications in refereed research journals, six book chapters; advisory board, Polymer International, 1990-; editorial board, Journal of Macromolecular Science; Review of Macromolecular Chemistsry and Physics, 1992-; editorial board, Thermochemica Acta, 1992-; editorial board, Trends of Polymer Science, 1992-. **HOME ADDRESS:** 497 Tamiami Trail, Akron, OH 44303. **BUSINESS ADDRESS:** Assoc Prof, Institute & Dept of Polymer Science, University of Akron, Polymer Science Bldg 936, Akron, OH 44325-3909, (216)972-6931.

CHENG, TA-PEI
Physicist, educator. Chinese American. **PERSONAL:** Born Nov 26, 1941, Shanghai, China; son of Hok-Chow Cheng & Nancy Hsu; married Leslie Su Cheng; children: Alexander, Jeffrey, Christopher. **EDUCATION:** Dartmouth College, AB, 1964; Rockefeller University, PhD, 1969. **CAREER:** Institute for Advanced Study, 1969-71, 1977-78, 1987-88; Rockefeller University, research associate, 1971-73; Princeton University, visiting associate professor, 1977-78; University of Minnesota, visiting professor, 1979-80; Lawrence Berkeley Lab, visiting scientist, 1982-83; Chinese University of Hong Kong, honorary visiting professor, 1991-92; University of Missouri, asst professor, 1973-76, associate professor, 1976-78, professor, chairman, 1987, 1979, 1978-. **HONORS/AWARDS:** American Physical Society, fellow, 1982-. **SPECIAL ACHIEVEMENTS:** Research arcticles in: Physical Review Letters, Physical Review, Physics Letters, etc; book, Gauge Theory of Elementary Particle Physics, Oxford University Press, 1984; anthology with annotated bibliography: Gauge Invariance, AAPT, 1990. **HOME ADDRESS:** 8 Graybridge Ln, St Louis, MO 63124, (314)432-8454. **BUSINESS ADDRESS:** Professor, Physics Dept, University of Missouri, St Louis, St Louis, MO 63121, (314)553-5020.

CHENG, TU-CHEN
Chemist, biologist. Chinese American/Macanese American. **PERSONAL:** Born Oct 24, 1938, China; married Linda L Cheng; children: June. **EDUCATION:** National Taiwan University, BS, 1962, MS, 1967; Wayne State University, PhD, 1972. **CAREER:** Johns Hopkins University, post-doctorate, 1972-75, instructor, 1975-77, assistant professor, 1977-83; Public Health Institute of New York Inc, associate, 1983-85; US Army, chemist, biologist, 1985-. **BUSINESS ADDRESS:** Molecular Biologist, Chemist, US Army, ERDEC, SCBRD-RTE, E-3220, Rm 216, Aberdeen Proving Ground, MD 21010-5423, (410)671-3972.

CHENG, TUNG CHAO
Architect. Chinese American. **PERSONAL:** Born Jun 17, 1931, Chao-An, Guangdong, China; son of SeeMin Cheng and Min Yuen Cheng; married Jeanne Y Cheng, Jul 4, 1959; children: Andrew Ywan, Ann Chi Cheng Carter. **EDUCATION:** Taiwan College of Engineering, BS, arch, 1953; Virginia Polytechnic Institute & State University, MS, arch, 1957; Harvard University, Graduate School of Design, 1974. **CAREER:** Saunders & Pearson, chief designer, 1957-74; Saunders, Cheng & Appleton, Ltd, vice president, 1974-81; Henningson, Durham & Richardson, Inc, vice president, 1981-. **ORGANIZATIONS:** American Institute of Architects , 1961-; Harvard Club, 1985-. **HONORS/AWARDS:** Phi Kappa Phi, VPI & State University Chapter, 1957; Tau Sigma Delta, VPI & State University Chapter, 1957; Kaoshing, Taiwan, Nationwide Architectural Competition, Second Prize, for the President's Hall, 1953; AIA, North Virginia, Arch Award, for First Citizens National Bank Bldg; AIA, North Virginia, Arch Award, for Kings Park Library, 1973; AIA, Washington, DC, Arch Award for Northampton Golf Club House, 1980; Masonry Institute, Arch Award for Alexandria Courthouse & Office Complex, 1981; Master Plan Architect: George Mason University, 1978, King Abdulaziz University, 1982, 1992. **MILITARY SERVICE:** Chinese ROTC, 1st Lt, 1953-54. **HOME ADDRESS:** 7511 Range Rd, Alexandria, VA 22306, (703)768-7211. **BUSINESS ADDRESS:** Vice President, Henningson, Durham & Richardson, Inc, 103 Oronoco St, Alexandria, VA 22314-2096, (703)683-3400.

CHENG, YING-WAN
Educator (retired). Chinese American. **PERSONAL:** Born in London, England; daughter of Dr & Mrs F Tien-hsi Cheng. **EDUCATION:** Ginling College, 1935-36; Smith College, BA, 1943; Radcliffe College, MA, 1945, PhD, 1960. **CAREER:** Vassar College, instructor, 1954-55; Harvard University, Feinbank Research Center, research assistant, 1955-58; Hunter College, lecturer, 1958-60; Dowling College, assistant professor, associate professor, 1960-71, professor, 1971-83. **ORGANIZATIONS:** American Historical Association; Association of Asian Studies; North American Conference on British Studies. **SPECIAL ACHIEVEMENTS:** Author, Postal Communication in China & its Modernization, 1860-1896, Harvard University Press, 1970.

CHENG, YUNG-SUNG
Research scientist. Taiwanese American. **PERSONAL:** Born Apr 23, 1947, Fong-Shan, Taiwan; son of Jeng-keng Cheng and Asai Yeuh Yang; married Chui Fan Cheng, Jun 22, 1974; children: Jennifer, Vincent. **EDUCATION:** National Taiwan University, BS, chemical engineer, 1969; Syracuse University, MS, chemical engineer, 1973, PhD, chemical engineer, 1976. **CAREER:** University of Rochester, School of Medicine and Dentistry, postdoctoral, 1976-78; Inhalation Toxicology Research Institute, aerosol engineer, 1978-90, aerosol program manager, 1990-. **ORGANIZATIONS:** American Association for Aerosol Research, 1983-; American Industrial Hygiene Association, Aerosol Technology Committee, 1978-; Gesellschaft fur Aerosol for Schung, 1985-; Japanese Association for Aerosol Science & Technology, 1989-; Chinese Association for Aerosol Research, 1993. **SPECIAL ACHIEVEMENTS:** Research in: air sampling methods, inhalation toxicology, deposition of aerosol in the lung, radon measurement and aerosols. **BUSINESS ADDRESS:** Program Manager, Inhalation Toxicology Research Institute, PO Box 5890, Albuquerque, NM 87185, (505)845-1034.

CHEN-TSAI, CHARLOTTE HSIAO-YU
Material scientist, engineer & group leader. Chinese American. **PERSONAL:** Born Sep 18, 1955, Taipei, Taiwan; married Chon-Kwo Tsai, Jul 30, 1983; children: Michele Tsai, Emily Tsai. **EDUCATION:** National Tsing-Hua University, BS, industrial chemistry, 1978; University of Florida, Gainesville, ME, chem engineering, 1979; University of Massachusetts, Amherst, PhD, chem engineering, polymer sci & engr, 1984. **CAREER:** University of Massachusetts, research assistant, 1979-84, Polymer Science & Engineering, post doctoral associate, 1984-85; Alcoa, scientist, 1985-86, senior scientist, 1986-89,

staff engineer, 1989-91; technical specialist, 1991-93, technical specialist, group leader, 1993-. **ORGANIZATIONS:** Sigma Xi, 1993; Society of Plastic Engineers, voluntary speaker on plastic recycling, 1980-; American Chemical Society, 1980-; Chinese American Chemical Society, 1992-; Chinese Christian Church of Amherst, deacon, chair director, 1979-84; East Suburban Chinese Church of Pittsburgh, 1989-; Pittsburgh Chinese Church, choir director, 1985-89. **HONORS/AWARDS:** National Tsing-Hua University, Scholarships for Academic Excellence, 1975, 1977. **SPECIAL ACHIEVEMENTS:** Published and presented over 22 articles and invited lectures in the field of polymer science, engineering and material science, 1982-93; proficient in English, Mandarin Chinese, German, Japanese, Cantonese Chinese; "Biaxial Orientation of Polypropylene Under Solid State Compression," Journal of Elastomers and Plastics, 1990; "Plastics Recycling," 1992; "Mechanical, Structural and Morphological Characterization of Aluminum/Polymer Interphase: I," 1993; numerous others. **BUSINESS ADDRESS:** Technical Specialist, Group Leader, Aluminum Company of America, Alcoa Technical Center, 100 Technical Drive, Building C, Alcoa Center, PA 15069-0001, (412)337-2501.

CHEO, LI-HSIANG S.
Educator. Chinese American. **PERSONAL:** Born Jun 21, 1932, Tainan, Taiwan; daughter of Chan-Shen Shang & P C Shang; married Bernard Ru-Shao Cheo, Jun 29, 1957; children: Louise Cheo Lasota (Lin-Hsien), Lin-wen Wayne. **EDUCATION:** National Cheng-Kung University, Taiwan, BS, 1955; University of California at Berkeley, MS, 1959; New York University, PhD, 1970. **CAREER:** Bell Telephone Laboratories, member of technical staff, 1960-63; Polytechnic University, adjunct graduate professor of computer science, 1982-85; William Paterson College of NJ, assistant professor of mathematics, 1972-74, associate professor of mathematics, 1974-78, associate professor of computer science, 1978-79, professor & chairperson of computer science, 1985-93, professor of computer science, 1979-. **ORGANIZATIONS:** Association for Computing Machinery, 1974-; Organization of Chinese Americans, 1976-, NJ Chapter, executive vice president, 1992-; Association of Asian Americans, board member, 1991-; Bergen County Human Relations Commission, commissioner, 1993-; BCHRC, education committee, 1993-; Presbyterian Church of Teaneck, choir member, 1976-. **HONORS/AWARDS:** Sigma Xi, 1970-; Upsilon Pi-Epsilon, 1988-; New York University, Founders Day Award, 1971; State of New Jersey, Service Award, 15 years, 1987, 20 years, 1992; University of Chicago, Outstanding Teachers Award for Minority Education, 1985. **SPECIAL ACHIEVEMENTS:** Co-author, "The Best Test Preparation for GRE Computer Science," REA, 1991; "Management of International Information Systems/An Algorithmic Approach," ROC National Conference on Management Information Systems, 1991; author, "The Role of Technology and Liberal Arts in Management Education," Third National Conference on Management Science Education, ROC, 1991; co-author, "On The Calibration and Sensitivity Study of a Six-port Reflectometer," Los Alamos National Laboratory Technology Memorandum, 1990. **BUSINESS ADDRESS:** Professor of Computer Science, William Paterson College of New Jersey, 300 Pompton Rd, Wayne, NJ 07470, (201)595-2649.

CHEO, PETER K.
Educator, educational administrator. Chinese American. **PERSONAL:** Born Feb 2, 1930, Nanking, China; married Dorothy, Aug 18, 1957. **EDUCATION:** Aurora University, BS, 1951; Virginia Polytech Institute, MS, 1953; Ohio State University, PhD, 1963. **CAREER:** Aurora University, assistant professor, 1957-61; Bell Telephone Lab, mts, 1963-70; Aerojet General Corp, manager, 1970-71; United Technologies Res Center, prin sc, 1971-90; University of Conn, E&SE, professor and head, 1990-. **ORGANIZATIONS:** IEEE, fellow, Lasers & Electroptics, technical council, program chair, Journal of Quant Electronics, associate editor; OSA, fellow; Institute of Physics, Journal of Appl Phys, editorial board. **HONORS/AWARDS:** United Technologies Award, 1982; Aurora University, Honorary Doctor Degree, 1987. **SPECIAL ACHIEVEMENTS:** Over 50 technical papers published in prof journals; two textbooks: Fiber Optics—Systems & Comp, Fiber Optics & Optoelectronics, Prentice Hall; 12 US patents; two handbooks: Molecular Lasers, Solid-State Lasers. **BUSINESS ADDRESS:** Head, Dept of Electrical & Systems Eng, University of Connecticut, 260 Glenbrook Road, U-157, Storrs Mansfield, CT 06269-3157, (203)486-4816.

CHEONG, FIONA
Writer, educator. Singaporean American. **PERSONAL:** Born Jan 1, 1961, Singapore; daughter of Daniel Cheong & Doris Yap. **EDUCATION:** Cornell University, BA, English, 1986, MFA, fiction, 1987. **CAREER:** Cornell University, temporary lecturer in English, 1986-88; Howard University, English

teacher, 1988-. **ORGANIZATIONS:** Associated Writing Programs, 1992-. **HONORS/AWARDS:** Howard University, Faculty Research Grant, 1992, Faculty Research Grant, 1991. **SPECIAL ACHIEVEMENTS:** Novel: The Scent of the Gods, 1991; "Natives," included in anthology of Asian American literature, Charlie Chan Is Dead, ed, Jessica Hagedorn, 1993-94. **BUSINESS ADDRESS:** Professor, Dept of English, Howard University, 2400 Sixth St, NW, 250 Locke Hall, Washington, DC 20059.

CHERIAN, JOY
Consultant, former government official. Indo-American. **PERSONAL:** Born May 18, 1942, Cochin, Kerala, India; son of T Chandy and Mariam Paul Cherian; married Alice Cherian, Aug 15, 1970; children: Sheela Thomas, Saj. **EDUCATION:** University of Kerala, India, BS, 1963, BL, 1965; Catholic University, MA, 1970, PhD, 1974; George Washington University, MCL, American Practice, 1978. **CAREER:** American Council of Life Insurance, Legal Research, director, 1979-82, Law Publications, editor, 1973-79, International Insurance Law, director, 1982-87; US Equal Employment Opportunity Commission, commissioner, 1987-93; J Cherian Consultants Inc, president, currently. **ORGANIZATIONS:** American Bar Association, chairman, 1988-92, International Insurance Law, committee member, 1983-87, International Employment Law, committee member, 1987-92; Indian American Forum for Political Education, national president, founder, 1983-86; Asian American Voters Coalition, national chairman, 1983-86. **HONORS/AWARDS:** LEAP, National Community Leadership Award, 1992; National Federation of Asian Indian Organizations, Recipient Community Service, 1986; American Coalition, Service Award, 1988. **SPECIAL ACHIEVEMENTS:** Investment Contracts & Arbitration, 1975; compiled, edited, reference law manual; author of several published articles in professional periodicals & popular publications. **BUSINESS ADDRESS:** President, J Cherian Consultants Inc, 1030 15th Street NW, Suite 1030, Washington, DC 20005, (202)842-1030.

CHERYAN, MUNIR
Educator. Indo-American. **PERSONAL:** Born May 7, 1946, Cochin, Kerala, India; son of P C Cheryan and Aley Mathulla; married Leela Sundararajan, Jan 26, 1972; children: Sapna, Anura. **EDUCATION:** Indian Institute of Technology, India, BTech (honors), 1968; University of Wisconsin, Madison, MS, 1970, PhD, 1974. **CAREER:** University of Illinois, asst prof, professor, 1976-. **ORGANIZATIONS:** American Institute of Chemical Engineers, 1972-; Institute of Food Technologists, 1974-; American Chemical Society, 1976-; American Dairy Science Assn, 1976-; North American Membrane Society, 1985-. **HONORS/AWARDS:** National Corn Growers Assn, Research and Commercialization Award, 1993; American Soybean Assn, Utilization Research Team Award, 1991; Assn of Food Scientists and Technologists, India, Gardner Award, 1988; Funk Foundation, Paul Funk Award, 1987; American Oil Chemists Society, ADM Award, 1984. **SPECIAL ACHIEVEMENTS:** Author: Ultrafiltration Handbook, Technomic, 1986; editorial boards: Journal of Food Process Engineering, 1985-; International Dairy Journal, 1989-; Journal of Food Engineering, 1986-. **BUSINESS ADDRESS:** Professor, University of Illinois, Agricultural Bioprocess Laboratory, 1302 W Pennsylvania Ave, Urbana, IL 61801, (217)333-9332.

CHEUNG, CINDY SIU-WHEI
Actor. Chinese American. **PERSONAL:** Born Jan 27, 1970, Inglewood, CA; daughter of Domino K Cheung and Whei-Yuen Cheung. **EDUCATION:** University of California, Los Angeles, BS, 1992. **CAREER:** Credits include: "Company," Theatre Americana; "The Rising Tide of Color," "Into the Woods," East West Players. **SPECIAL ACHIEVEMENTS:** Proficient in Mandarin, Cantonese. **BUSINESS PHONE:** (213)994-5414.

CHEUNG, DAVID F.
Software engineer. Chinese American. **PERSONAL:** Born Jan 15, 1965, Beijing, People's Republic of China; son of Gene K H Cheung and Ling C Cheung. **EDUCATION:** MIT, BS, 1987; Tufts University, MS, 1990. **CAREER:** Papyrus Design Group, software engineer, 1989-92; Unica Technologies, vice president, senior software consultant, 1993-. **ORGANIZATIONS:** United States Table Tennis Association. **HOME ADDRESS:** 9305 Parkhill Terr, Bethesda, MD 20814. **BUSINESS PHONE:** (617)782-8888.

CHEUNG, FERNANDO C. H.
Organization executive. Chinese American/Hong Kong American/Macanese American. **PERSONAL:** Born Feb 23, 1957, Macao; son of Ho Yin Cheung; married Natalie Chan, Jan 15, 1982; children: Vincent, Vivian. **EDUCATION:** Hong Kong Baptist College, BSW, 1980; California State University, Fresno,

MSW, 1983; University of California, Berkeley, PhD, 1991. **CAREER:** Oakland Chinese Community Council, executive director, currently. **ORGANIZATIONS:** American Cancer Society, Alameda County, board member, 1992-; Alameda County Multicultural Multilingual Oversight Comm, chair, 1988-; United Way Leadership Board, Alameda County, board member, 1991-; Health & Human Service Commission, City of Oakland, commissioner, 1992-; Oakland Chinatown Lions Club, 1991-. **HONORS/AWARDS:** University of California Berkeley, Outstanding Teaching Assistant Award, 1984. **SPECIAL ACHIEVEMENTS:** Published an article on China's One Child Family Policy, in Journal of Sociology & Social Welfare, 1989. **BUSINESS ADDRESS:** Executive Director, Oakland Chinese Community Council, 168 11th St, Oakland, CA 94607, (510)839-2022.

CHEUNG, HERBERT CHIU-CHING
Scientist, educational administrator, educator. Chinese American. **PERSONAL:** Born Dec 19, 1933, Canton, China; son of K H Chang and Tak-Woo Chang; married Daisy Lee, Feb 1966; children: Sharon, Melissa. **EDUCATION:** Rutgers University, BA (with honors), 1954; Cornell University, MS, 1956; Rutgers University PhD, 1961; University of California, San Francisco, postdoctoral, 1966-69. **CAREER:** US Steel Corp, assistant scientist, 1956; Rutgers University, assistant instructor, 1958-60; FMC Corp, research chemist, 1960-63; Allied Chemical Corp, research chemist, 1963-66; University California, San Francisco, senior fellow, 1966-69; University of Alabama at Birmingham, Graduate Program in Biophysical Sciences, director, 1978-, professor of biochemistry, 1969-. **ORGANIZATIONS:** American Chemical Society; American Society for Biochemistry and Molecular Biology; Biophysical Society; Sigma Xi; National Institutes of Health, review panels, chairman, 1977-. **HONORS/AWARDS:** Corn Instustries Research Foundation, Predoctoral Fellowship, 1957; National Institute of Health, Research Career Development Award, 1972. **SPECIAL ACHIEVEMENTS:** Approximately 100 original publications in scientific journals. **BUSINESS ADDRESS:** Professor, Dept of Biochemistry and Molecular Genetics, University of Alabama at Birmingham, Birmingham, AL 35294, (205)934-2485.

CHEUNG, JOHN YAN-POON
Educator. Hong Kong American. **PERSONAL:** Born Oct 13, 1950, Hong Kong; son of Paul To-Kwon Cheung and Mei-Shin Lau; married Rose Kwan-Fun Cheung, Aug 6, 1977; children: Christina Phoebe, Jonathan Paul. **EDUCATION:** Oregon State University, BS, 1969; University of Washington, PhD, 1975. **CAREER:** Boeing Computer Services, sr engineer, 1977-78; University of Oklahoma, professor, 1978-. **ORGANIZATIONS:** IEEE, senior member, 1971-; ACM, 1980-; INNS, 1988-. **SPECIAL ACHIEVEMENTS:** Co-author, Modern Digital Systems Design, West Publishing Company, 1990; author, Solutions Manual to Modern Digital Systems Design, West Publishing Company, 1990; co-author, Knowledge-Based Systems and Neural Networks: Techniques and Applications, North-Holland Publishing Company, 1991; author, Proceedings of the Fifth Oklahoma Symposium On Artificial Intelligence, Oklahoma Center for Artificial Intelligence, 1991; also numerous book chapters, journal articles, conference papers, etc. **BUSINESS ADDRESS:** Professor, University of Oklahoma, 202 W Boyd, CEC 218, Norman, OK 73019, (405)325-4324.

CHEUNG, JOSEPH Y.
Physician, scientist. Chinese American. **PERSONAL:** Born Jun 21, 1950, Hong Kong; son of Wah Lun Cheung and Wai Ming Ho; married Barbara Miller, Jun 14, 1975. **EDUCATION:** McGill University, BSc, 1972; Pennsylvania State University, MS, 1974, PhD, 1976; Duke University School of Medicine, MD, 1978. **CAREER:** Duke University, resident in medicine, 1978-80; Harvard Med School, clinical & research fellow, 1980-83, instructor of medicine, 1983-84, assistant professor of medicine, 1984-86; Pennsylvania State University, professor of medicine, 1986-, chief, div of nephrology, currently. **ORGANIZATIONS:** Am Journal of Physiol, editorial board, 1989-; Am Heart Assn, peer review board, 1990-; Am Physiological Soc, 1981-; Am Soc Nephrology, 1983-; Am Soc Cell Biology, 1990-; Biophysical Soc, 1992-; Int Soc of Nephrology, 1981-. **HONORS/AWARDS:** McGill University, First Class Honors in biophysics, 1972; National Institutes of Health, National Research Service Award, 1981-84; Am Heart Assn, Clinician-Scientist Award, 1984-85. **BUSINESS ADDRESS:** Prof of Medicine & Physiology, Chief, Div of Nephrology and Hypertension, Pennsylvania State University, College of Medicine, M S Hershey Medical Center, Hershey, PA 17033, (717)531-8156.

CHEUNG, JULIAN F. Y.
Educator, research scientist. Chinese American. **PERSONAL:** Born Jul 15, 1956, Guangdong, People's Republic of China; son of Cheung Chun Lung and Chan Wai Ying. **EDUCATION:** Polytechnic University, BSc, electrical engineering, 1983, MSc, electrical engineering, 1984, MSc, math, 1989; PhD, electrical engineering, 1990. **CAREER:** Technical Career Institute, instructor, 1984-86; New York City Technical College, instructor, 1986-87; Polytechnic University, teaching fellow, 1987-90; Finger Matrix Corp, consultant, 1992; New York Institute of Technology, faculty researcher, 1990-, asst professor, 1990-. **ORGANIZATIONS:** Institute of Electrical & Electronics Engineers, 1984-; American Mathematical Society, 1991-; American Assn of University Professors, 1991-. **HONORS/AWARDS:** National Science Foundation, laboratory development, 1993-95; Polytechnic University, PhD Fellowship, 1987-90. **SPECIAL ACHIEVEMENTS:** Author of six technical publications. **BUSINESS PHONE:** (212)261-1640.

CHEUNG, LIM H.
Physicist, researcher. Hong Kong American. **PERSONAL:** Born Feb 18, 1953, Hong Kong, Hong Kong. **EDUCATION:** California Institute of Technology, BS, 1975; University of Maryland, PhD, 1980. **CAREER:** Harvard-Smithsonian Center for Astrophysics, research fellow, 1980-81; Gulf Oil Company, senior research geophysicist, 1981-83; Standard Oil Company, senior research geophysicist, 1983-86; Grumman Aerospace Corp, Optical Physics Laboratory, head, 1986-. **BUSINESS ADDRESS:** Head, Optical Physics Laboratory, Grumman Aerospace Corp, M/S A01-26, Bethpage, NY 11714, (516)346-6565.

CHEUNG, LUKE P.
Physician. Chinese American. **PERSONAL:** Born Aug 10, Sacramento, CA. **EDUCATION:** Harvard College, AB, 1984; Harvard Medical School, MD, 1988. **CAREER:** University of Pennsylvania, resident, 1989-93; Stanford University Medical Center, fellow, radiologist, 1993-. **ORGANIZATIONS:** Radiological Society of North America; American Roentgen Ray Society; Chinese-American Medical Society. **HOME ADDRESS:** 4779 Norm Circle, Sacramento, CA 95822.

CHEUNG, PHILIP
Educator. Chinese American. **PERSONAL:** Born Nov 20, 1958, Singapore, Singapore; son of Cheung Yat Fung & Loh Wai Chan. **EDUCATION:** University of Texas, Austin, PhD, 1990. **CAREER:** University of Minnesota, Duluth, assistant professor, 1990-. **ORGANIZATIONS:** American Physical Society, 1990-; IEEE, 1990-; Minnesota Academy of Science, 1993-. **SPECIAL ACHIEVEMENTS:** Published in Applied Physics Letter, Microwave Theory and Technique, Microwave Journal; presented academic papers at numerous conferences. **MILITARY SERVICE:** Infantry, corporal, 1977-80. **HOME ADDRESS:** 607 Kenwood Ave, #202, Duluth, MN 55811-2154, (218)728-4234. **BUSINESS ADDRESS:** Professor, Computer Engineering, University of Minnesota, Duluth, 255, MWAH, 10 University Dr, Duluth, MN 55812-2496, (218)726-6150.

CHEUNG, SHUN YAN
Educator. Chinese American. **PERSONAL:** Born 1958, Hong Kong; son of Fook Sang Cheung and Wai Ying Mo; married Stella Wai-Kwan Li, Nov 16, 1991; children: Nathanie Elim. **EDUCATION:** Delft University of Technology, The Netherlands, Ir, 1984; Georgia Institute of Technology, PhD, 1990. **CAREER:** Emory University, assistant professor, 1990-. **ORGANIZATIONS:** Institute of Electrical and Electronics Engineers, 1991. **SPECIAL ACHIEVEMENTS:** The Grid Protocol: A High Performance Scheme for Maintaining Replicated Data, IEEE Transactions on Knowledge and Data Engineering, 1992; Multi-Dimensional Voting, ACM Transactions on Computers, 1991; Optimizing Vote and Quorum Assignments for Reading and Writing Replicated Data, IEEE Transactions on Knowledge and Engineering, 1990. **BUSINESS ADDRESS:** Asst Professor, Dept of Mathematics and Computer Science, Emory University, 1300 Clifton Rd, Fishburne Rm 115A, Atlanta, GA 30322.

CHEUNG, WAI YIU
Medical research, educator. Chinese American. **PERSONAL:** Born Jul 15, 1933, Canton, Kwangtung, China; married Ling-Fai Cheung, Jun 23, 1962; children: Jane, Pauline, Sidney. **EDUCATION:** National Chung Hsing University, BS, 1956; University of Vermont, MS, 1960; Cornell University, PhD, 1964. **CAREER:** University of Pennsylvania, postdoctoral fellow, 1964-67; St Jude Children's Research Hospital, Biochemistry, assistant member, 1967-70,

associate member, 1970-71, member, 1972-; University of Tennessee, professor, 1976-. **HONORS/AWARDS:** Morrison Scholarship, 1950-52; Overseas Chinese Scholarship, 1953-56; Frank Hsu Scholarship, 1958-60; USPHS Traineeship, 1964-67; USPHS Research Career Development Award, 1971-76; Josiah Macy Jr Foundation, faculty scholar, 1979-80; Gairdner International Award, 1981; Sigma Xi, Memphis chapter, Research Excellence Award, 1983; Arthur C Corcoran Award, 1984; Harvey Lecturer, 1984; Academia Sinica, 1988. **SPECIAL ACHIEVEMENTS:** Editor, Calcium & Cell Function, vols 1-7, Academic Press, 1980-87; more than 100 scientific articles & reviews. **BUSINESS ADDRESS:** Member, St Jude Children's Research Hospital, Memphis, TN 38101-0318, (901)522-0563.

CHEW, FRANCES SZE-LING

Educator, scientist. Chinese American. **EDUCATION:** Stanford University, AB, 1970; Yale University, PhD, 1974. **CAREER:** Tufts University, assistant & associate professor, 1975-92, professor, 1992-. **BUSINESS ADDRESS:** Professor, Dept of Biology, Tufts University, Medford, MA 02155, (617)627-3195.

CHEW, KENNETH SZE-YING

Social scientist, educator. Chinese American. **PERSONAL:** Born Mar 10, 1953, Coral Gables, FL; son of Frank & Katherine Liang Chew; married Patricia Cahill, 1982; children: Kathryn, Patrick F X. **EDUCATION:** Cornell University, BA, 1974; University of California, Berkeley, MA, sociology, 1979, MA, demography, 1982, PhD, sociology, 1983. **CAREER:** University of North Carolina-Chapel Hill, postdoctoral fellow, 1983-84; University of California, Irvine, assistant to associate professor, 1985-. **ORGANIZATIONS:** American Sociological Association, 1977-; Population Association of America, 1981-; Pacific Sociological Association, 1985-. **SPECIAL ACHIEVEMENTS:** Scholarly publications in the areas of population, family studies, and suicide. **BUSINESS ADDRESS:** Associate Professor of Environmental Analysis & Design, University of California, School of Social Ecology, Irvine, CA 92717-5150, (714)856-6990.

CHEW, PAMELA CHRISTINE

Language educator. Chinese American. **PERSONAL:** Born Feb 10, 1953, Nevada, MO; daughter of Harry Chew & Dolores Trimmer Chew. **EDUCATION:** Cottey College, AA, 1973; University of Missouri, BA, 1975, MA, 1977; Universita Internazionale dell'Arte, Florence, Italy, certificate of art criticism, 1980-81. **CAREER:** Cottey College, field representative, 1976-77; Jim Halsey Company, publicist, 1977-80; University of Tulsa, archives, 1981-82; Catholic Charities, ESL instructor, 1981-88; Berlitz School of Languages, Italian instructor, 1985; University of Tulsa, French and Italian intructor, 1987-90; Tulsa Junior College, foreign language, ESL instructor, 1985-. **ORGANIZATIONS:** OFLTA, 1985-; OKTESOL, 1990-; TESOL, 1990-; SCMLA, secretary, Italian section, 1985-86; Phi Theta Kappa; Phi Sigma Iota; MENSA, 1990; AAUP, 1985-89. **HONORS/AWARDS:** Breck Corp, Breck Woman of 90's, 1989; Rotary International Scholar to Firenze, Italia, 1980-81; 1st alternate to Aix-en-Provence, 1973; MiMi Atwater Memorial Scholarship to Aix-en-Provence, France, 1973-79. **SPECIAL ACHIEVEMENTS:** Proficiency: Spanish, French, Italian, 1969-72; first place poetry award, 1979-86; Friends of Tulsa Library, children's story honorable mention, 1988. **BIOGRAPHICAL SOURCES:** Tulsa World article. **BUSINESS ADDRESS:** Instructor, Tulsa Junior College, 3727 East Apache, Tulsa, OK 74115-3151.

CHEW, RICHARD FRANKLIN

Motion picture film editor. Chinese American. **PERSONAL:** Born Jun 28, 1940, Los Angeles, CA; son of Henry F Chew & May Leong Chew; divorced; children: Jonah C, Aaron N. **EDUCATION:** University of California, Los Angeles, BA, 1964; Harvard Law School, 1964-66. **CAREER:** Independent feature film editor of productions such as The Conversation, One Flew Over the Cuckoo's Nest, My Favorite Year, Star Wars, Risky Business, Clean and Sober, Men Don't Leave, Singles, My Life. **ORGANIZATIONS:** Academy of Motion Picture Arts & Sciences, 1976-; Motion Picture & Video Tape Editors, 1976-; Directors Guild of America, 1991-. **HONORS/AWARDS:** Academy Award, Best Film Editing, 1977; British Academy Award, Best Film Editing, 1974, 1976; Academy Award nominee, Best Film Editing, 1975. **MILITARY SERVICE:** United States Navy, petty officer, third class, 1959-61. **BUSINESS ADDRESS:** Motion Picture Film Editor, c/o Sanford-Skouras-Gross & Associates Agency, 1015 Gayley Ave, Ste 301, Los Angeles, CA 90024, (310)208-2100.

CHEW, RONALD A.

Museum director. Chinese American. **PERSONAL:** Born May 17, 1953, Seattle, WA; son of Soo Hong Chew and Gam Har Chew. **EDUCATION:** University of Washington, editorial journalism, 1971-75. **CAREER:** Seattle Public Library, public information specialist, 1979; McKenzie River Gathering Foundation, Seattle office director, 1980; International Examiner, editor, 1976-79, 1981-88; Seattle Central Community Collge, multicultural programs coordinator, 1988-89; Washington Commission on Asian American Affairs, confidential secretary, 1989-91; Wing Luke Asian Museum, director, 1991-. **ORGANIZATIONS:** Asian American Journalists Association, Seattle chapter, founding member, treasurer, 1985-89; Northwest Minority Publishers Association, founding member & secretary, 1987-88; International District Improvement Association, Community Development Association, board member, 1979-92; Chinese Information and Service Center, board of directors, 1991-92; Kin On Nursing Home, publicity committee, 1987-91; Northwest Nikkei Newspaper, advisory board, 1989-91; Seattle Center Community College, publications board, 1990. **HONORS/AWARDS:** International District Economic Association, community service award, 1987; Association of King County Historical Organizations, Executive Order 9066 exhibit, Best Historical Exhibit Award, 1992; Washington Museum Association, Award of Institutional Excellence to Wing Luke Asian Museum, 1993; Washington State Historical Society, David Douglas Award, 1993. **SPECIAL ACHIEVEMENTS:** Coordinator, Shared Dreams photo exhibit on Asian Pacific Americans, 1989; Coordinator, Chinese Oral History Project of Seattle, 1990-93. **BIOGRAPHICAL SOURCES:** "Change of Emphasis Expected from Museum Director Appointee," International Examiner, Dec 19, 1990. **BUSINESS ADDRESS:** Museum Director, Wing Luke Asian Museum, 407 7th Ave S, Seattle, WA 98104, (206)623-5124.

CHEW, WELLINGTON LUM

Educator. Chinese American. **PERSONAL:** Born Sep 3, 1922, Courtland, CA; son of Chong Chew and Chung Kin Lau; divorced; children: Sharlene. **EDUCATION:** Providence College; San Francisco State University, AB, MA, 1953; University of California, Berkeley, advanced studies, 1978. **CAREER:** San Francisco Unified School District, teacher, counselor, supervisor, 1949-84; City College of San Francisco, instructor, site manager, 1982-. **ORGANIZATIONS:** Phi Delta Kappa, 1952-; San Francisco Economic Opportunity Council, exec committee, 1966; English Language Center, board of directors, 1967; Northern California Presbyterian Homes, operations committee, 1988; Services for Seniors, board of directors, 1988; Cameron House, board of directors, 1986; Chinatown Youth Center, board of directors, 1979. **HONORS/AWARDS:** Assn of Chinese Teachers, San Francisco, Outstanding Educator, 1984. **SPECIAL ACHIEVEMENTS:** First Chinese-American supervisor, San Francisco Unified School District, 1967; consultant: US Office of Education, 1973; California Dept of Education, 1970; US Civil Rights Commission, Washington, DC, 1973; Far West Laboratory, 1970; board member: Bilingual Consortium, Dallas, TX, 1969. **MILITARY SERVICE:** US Army, Office of Strategic Services, sgt, 1943-46. **BIOGRAPHICAL SOURCES:** Unimpressible Race, by Victor Low, p 162, 179; "Yellow Peril," by Tom Wolfe, Esquire Magazine, 1968. **HOME ADDRESS:** 4757 18th St, San Francisco, CA 94114-1835, (415)552-0112. **BUSINESS ADDRESS:** Site Manager, Chinatown/North Beach Campus, City College of San Francisco, 940 Filbert St, San Francisco, CA 94133, (415)561-1850.

CHEW, WENG CHO

Educator. Chinese American. **PERSONAL:** Born Jun 9, 1953, Kuantan, Pahang, Malaysia; son of F S Chew and T L Goh; married Chew-Chin Phua, Dec 21, 1977; children: Huibin Amelia, Shinen Ethan. **EDUCATION:** MIT, BSEE, 1976, MSEE, 1978, PhDEE, 1980. **CAREER:** MIT, postdoctoral associate, 1980-81; Schlumberger-Doll Research, professional staff, 1981-83, program leader, 1983-84, department manager, 1984-85; University of Illinois, associate professor, 1985-90, professor, 1980-. **ORGANIZATIONS:** IEEE-GRS, ADCOM, 1984-88, associate editor, 1984-; IEEE-APS, 1981-; Society of Exploration Geophysics, 1985-; URSI-B, 1984-; URSI-L, 1984-; IJIST, associate editor, 1987-; Radio Science, guest editor, 1986. **HONORS/AWARDS:** NSF, Presidential Young Investigator, 1986; IEEE, Senior Member, 1987, Fellow, 1993. **SPECIAL ACHIEVEMENTS:** Waves and Fields in Homogeneous Media, 1990; over 120 journal articles in refereed journals, 1980-. **HOME ADDRESS:** 2510 Stanford Dr, Champaign, IL 61820.

CHHIM, HIM S.

Non-profit organization executive. Cambodian American. **PERSONAL:** Born Apr 1, 1941, Chihe, Kompong Cham, Cambodia; son of Chheang & Sorn;

married Muyhoa, Sep 9, 1967; children: Kaneka, Viravyne. **EDUCATION:** University of Georgia, BS, agriculture, 1966, MS, agriculture, 1967; California State University, MPA, 1992. **CAREER:** National Office of Cooperatives, Cambodia, community development supervisor, marketing manager, 1967-74; World Vision International, Cambodia, administration director, 1974-75; Citroen Automobiles, France, quality control supervisor, 1977-79; Orange County Social Services, CA, social worker, employment specialist, 1980-92; Cambodian Association of American, CA, executive director, 1992-. **ORGANIZATIONS:** Cambodian Association of America, board member, chair, executive president, executive director, 1980-; Asian Service Coalition, president, 1992-; Asian Advisory Committee to the Police Department, 1992-; Asian Pacific Planning Council, 1992-; Asian Advisory Committee to the Superintendent, 1992-; Cambodian Network Council, 1992-; Long Beach Health Advisory Committee, 1992-. **SPECIAL ACHIEVEMENTS:** Introduction to Cambodian Culture, San Diego State University, 1988; fluent in Khmer, English and French. **BIOGRAPHICAL SOURCES:** "Advocate Fueled by Community Need," Long Beach Press Telegram, p B1, B2, June 8, 1992. **HOME ADDRESS:** 17325 Alfred Ave, Cerritos, CA 90701.

CHI, BO KYUNG (DAVID BOKYUNG CHI)
Engineering company manager. Korean American. **PERSONAL:** Born Jan 28, 1956, Seoul, Republic of Korea; son of Yong Tae Chi and Jung Ja Chi; married Katherine Mihee Chi, Sep 17, 1984; children: Albert Hoyoung, Lillian Soyoung. **EDUCATION:** Massachusetts Institute of Technology, Cambridge, BS, 1979; California Institute of Technology, PhD, 1986. **CAREER:** Aerojet Ordnance Co, 1986-89; Aerojet Electronic Systems, 1989-91; SPARTA, Inc, manager, 1991-. **ORGANIZATIONS:** Sigma Xi; American Defense Preparedness Association; American Institute of Chemical Engineers. **SPECIAL ACHIEVEMENTS:** Publications in technical & professional journals; presentations at international symposia, technical meetings. **HOME ADDRESS:** 1827 Calle Belleza, Rowland Heights, CA 91748. **BUSINESS PHONE:** (714)572-8929.

CHI, CHENG-CHING
Aerospace engineer. Chinese American. **PERSONAL:** Born Feb 15, 1939, Yu-Ling, Hainan, China; son of Chiang-Chien Chi and Ho-Hwa Chi; married Lan-Fang Chi, Jun 24, 1967; children: John C. **EDUCATION:** National Taiwan University, BS, 1962; Kansas State University, MS, 1965; University of California, Berkeley, PhD, 1969. **CAREER:** Garrett Corp, Airesearch Manufacturing Co, engineer, 1969-72, senior engineer, 1972-75, senior engineering specialist, 1975-79, engineering supervisor, 1979-85; Alliedsignal Aerospace Systems & Equipment, senior engineering specialist, 1985-87, engineering manager, 1987-93, senior engineering manager, 1993-. **ORGANIZATIONS:** Society of Automotive Engineers, 1990-; Society of Chinese American Aerospace Engineers, founding member, advisor, 1990-. **HONORS/AWARDS:** Phi Kappa Phi Honor Society, 1965; University of California, Anthoney Scholarship, 1968; US Department of Transportation, TTC, Certificate for World Rail/Wheel Speed Record, 1974; Airesearch Manufacturing Co, Engineering Merit Award, 1974; Republic of China Aeronautic Industrial Center, Certificate for Successful Development of IDF, 1989. **SPECIAL ACHIEVEMENTS:** Author, "A Thinner Flight Control Actuator," SAE Paper 902016, SAE Aerospace Conference, Long Beach, CA, 1990; "On Damped Nonlinear Dynamics Systems with Many Degrees of Freedom," vol 20, no 5/6, International Journal of Nonlinear Mechanics, 1985; "High-Speed Dynamics Performance of the Linear Induction Motor Research Vehicle," SAE Paper 751060, 1975; "The Solution of a Second-Order Nonlinear Differential Equation Containing Two Unknown Parameters," SIAM, 1966. **MILITARY SERVICE:** Republic of China, Military Police (ROTC), 2nd lt, 1962-63. **HOME ADDRESS:** 6454 Parklynn Dr, Rancho Palos Verdes, CA 90274. **BUSINESS PHONE:** (310)512-1581.

CHI, DAVID BOKYUNG. *See* **CHI, BO KYUNG.**

CHI, DAVID SHYH-WEI
Educator. Taiwanese American. **PERSONAL:** Born Jul 7, 1943, Tar-Char, Tai-Chung, Taiwan; son of Ching-Hsing & A-Chou Chen Chi; married Sue-Yue Lin Chi, Dec 1982; children: Michelle Tzue-E, Michael Heng-Jah. **EDUCATION:** National Chung-Hsing University, Taiwan, BS, 1965; University of Texas, Medical Branch, MA, 1974, PhD, 1977. **CAREER:** Taiwan Provincial Government, junior crop specialist, 1966-67; Taiwan Sugar Corporation, farm director, 1967-69; Chai Tai Enterprise Co, TD, assistant manager, 1969-70; New York University, postdoctoral fellow & research assistant professor, 1977-80; East Tennessee State University, associate professor, 1980-86, director,

clinical immunology lab, 1980-, Division of Biomedical Research, chief, 1981-, professor, 1986-. **ORGANIZATIONS:** Association of Medical Laboratory Immunologists, fellow, 1987; American Academy of Microbiology, fellow, 1988; Sigma Xi, 1974; The Harvey Society, 1980; American Association of Immunologists, 1981; Society for Experimental Biology & Medicine, 1981; North American Taiwanese Professors' Association, 1982; Clinical Immunology Society, 1987; American Society for Histocompatibility & Immunogenetics, 1988. **HONORS/AWARDS:** Robert A Welch Foundation, predoctoral fellowship, 1972; James W McLaughlin Fund, predoctoral fellowship, 1972-76; National Institutes of Health, PHS postdoctoral fellowship, 1977-80; National Cancer Institute, New Investigator Research Award, 1980; Harris Foundation, The Ruth R Harris Endowment, 1987. **SPECIAL ACHIEVEMENTS:** Publications: 5 book chapters, 1978, 1981, 1987, 1991; 42 journal articles, 1975-; 101 abstracts, 1973-. **BUSINESS ADDRESS:** Professor, Director, Dept of Internal Medicine, East Tennessee State University, Box 70622, Johnson City, TN 37614-0622, (615)929-6287.

CHI, JACOB
Educator, symphony director. Chinese American. **PERSONAL:** Born Dec 9, 1952, Qingdao, Shandong, People's Republic of China; son of Frank Chi and Linda Li; married Lin Chang, Jul 11, 1987. **EDUCATION:** Siena Heights College, BA (magna cum laude), 1985; University of Michigan, MMus, 1987; Michigan State University, DMA, 1994. **CAREER:** Qingdao Peking Opera, China, conductor concertmaster, composer, 1971-81; Taos Symphony, conductor, 1992-93; Pueblo Symphony Association, conductor, music director, 1991-93; University of Southern Colorado, artist-in-residence, 1991-93; Miami University, assistant professor, Miami University Symphony, conductor/music director, 1993-. **ORGANIZATIONS:** Colorado State Music, strings, director of board, 1991-; Teachers Association. **HONORS/AWARDS:** Michigan State University, graduate assistant, 1989-91. **BIOGRAPHICAL SOURCES:** US Communique, p 13-14, spring 1993. **HOME ADDRESS:** 61 Christopher Dr, Oxford, OH 45056, (513)523-1437. **BUSINESS PHONE:** (513)529-3086.

CHI, LOTTA C. J. LI
Business owner/manager. Chinese American. **PERSONAL:** Born Dec 5, 1930, New York, NY; daughter of Chen-pien Li and Han-chih Tang; married Michael Chi, Jun 15, 1957; children: Loretta Elizabeth Chi Prigal, Maxwell Michael. **EDUCATION:** Heidelberg College, BS, 1953; Rutgers University, MS, 1955. **CAREER:** National Institutes of Health, virologist, 1958-; Chi Associates, Inc, president, 1974-. **ORGANIZATIONS:** Sigma Xi, 1955-; New York Academy of Sciences, 1980-; American Society of Microbiologists, 1960-. **BUSINESS ADDRESS:** President, Chi Associates Inc, 2000 N 14th St, Ste 740, Arlington, VA 22201, (703)558-3400.

CHI, MYUNG SUN (MIKE)
Educator. Korean American. **PERSONAL:** Born Sep 28, 1940, Ik-San, Jeon Bok, Republic of Korea; son of Won Gill Chi and Soon Rae Lee; married Eun Ja, Jun 13, 1970; children: Linda, Carolyn. **EDUCATION:** Kon Kuk University, BS, 1966; Malling Agricultural College, certificate, 1967; University of Minnesota, MS, 1972, PhD, 1975. **CAREER:** University of Minnesota, research associate, 1975-77; Alcorn State University, assistant professor, 1978-81; Lincoln University, associate professor, 1981-87, professor, 1988-. **ORGANIZATIONS:** Korean United Methodist Church of Minnesota, lay leader, 1976-78; First United Methodist Church of Jefferson City, adm board, 1983-; Mid-Missouri Korean Institute, director, board of trustee, 1984-89; American Institute of Nutrition, 1981-; American Heart Association, 1982-; Int Society for the Study of Fatty Acids & Lipids, charter member, 1990-; Nutrition Research, consulting editor, 1985-. **HONORS/AWARDS:** 1890 Land Grant University Research Directors Association, Outstanding Research Paper Award, 1980, 1982; Food & Drug Administration, research grant, 1975-78; USDA/Higher Education, Capacity Building Grant, 1990-93; USDA/CSRS, research grants, 1978-81, 1983-88, 1988-93. **SPECIAL ACHIEVEMENTS:** 45 journal papers; 38 abstracts; 1 book chapter. **BUSINESS ADDRESS:** Professor, Human Nutrition Program, Lincoln University, Foster Hall Room B4, Jefferson City, MO 65102, (314)681-5381.

CHI, YINLIANG
Educator. Chinese American. **PERSONAL:** Born Sep 28, 1934, Shanghai, China; son of Sun Sun Chi and Su Chi; divorced; children: James. **EDUCATION:** Shanghai College of Finance & Economics, BA, 1954; East China Normal University, MA, 1961; Rutgers University, MA, 1993. **CAREER:** East China Normal University, associate professor, 1961-80; University of Pennsylvania, visiting professor, 1980-81; Beloit College, WI, professor, 1981-82;

Villanova University, assistant professor, 1985-. **ORGANIZATIONS:** Chinese Language Teachers Association; Fulbright Alumni Association. **HONORS/AWARDS:** US Dept of Education, Fulbright-Hays foreign curriculum consultant, 1981. **SPECIAL ACHIEVEMENTS:** Published 30 papers; selected to serve as a review reader of the International Research and Studies Program of various universities in the US, by the US Dept of Education, 1993. **HOME ADDRESS:** 151 Linwood Ave, Ardmore, PA 19003, (215)649-5836. **BUSINESS ADDRESS:** Professor, Modern Languages & Lit Dept, Villanova University, St Augustus Liberal Arts Ctr, Rm 348, Villanova, PA 19085-1672, (215)519-4702.

CHIA, DAVID
Transportation consultant. Chinese American. **PERSONAL:** Born Aug 28, 1959, New York, NY; son of Paul & Laura. **EDUCATION:** Yale University, BS, 1981; Massachusetts Institute of Technology, SM, 1983; Boston University, graduate work, 1986. **CAREER:** Ketron Inc, senior transportation planner, 1983-92; Technology and Management Systems Inc, senior transportation consultant, 1992-. **ORGANIZATIONS:** Artery Business Committee, 1989-; Yale Scientific and Engineering Association, 1981-; Sigma Xi, 1983-; Prescott Writing Group, 1992-. **SPECIAL ACHIEVEMENTS:** Accessibility Handbook for Transit Facilities, 1992. **BUSINESS ADDRESS:** Senior Transportation Consultant, Technology & Management Systems, Inc, 99 S Bedford St, Ste 211, Burlington, MA 01803, (617)272-3033.

CHIA, KAI
Educator (retired). Chinese American. **PERSONAL:** Born Oct 24, 1925, Jinan, Shandong, China; son of Chia Yung-Fu and Chia Shu-Yee; married Chia Lo shu-fang, Jul 25, 1951; children: Chia yu-kung (Paul), Chia Dee (Kirk), Chia Sun tzy-ping (Mary). **EDUCATION:** Fu-Jen Catholic University, Peking, China, BA. **CAREER:** Taipei Medical College, professor, director of library, dean of students, 1963-76; Fu-Jen Catholic University, Taiwan, History Dept, professor, chairman, 1976-88. **ORGANIZATIONS:** Association of Chinese History, ROC, director. **SPECIAL ACHIEVEMENTS:** Author: The Introduction to Chinese Historiography, 1985; The Outline of Chinese History, 1975; The Criticism of Philosophy of Sung and Ming Dynasty, 1967; The Moralist of Sung and Ming Dynasty, 1966; The Theoretician of Chinese History, 1978. **HOME ADDRESS:** 23620 99th Place W, Edmonds, WA 98020-5606.

CHIA, NING
Educator. Chinese American. **PERSONAL:** Born Dec 14, 1955, Beijing, People's Republic of China; daughter of Jia Guangshi & Sheng Fangying; married Huang Ko-Hsing, Jun 18, 1983. **EDUCATION:** Beijing Normal University, Dept of History, BA, 1982; Central Institute for Nationalities, Research Institute, 1982-83; Illinois State University, Dept of History, MA, 1985; Johns Hopkins University, Dept of History, PhD, 1991. **CAREER:** Central College, assistant professor of history, 1991-. **ORGANIZATIONS:** Association for Asian Studies; American Historical Association. **SPECIAL ACHIEVEMENTS:** "The Li-fan Yuan and the Inner Asian Rituals in the Early Qing (1644-1795)," Late Imperial China, 14:1, p60-92, June 1993; "The Manchu Collection in the Johns Hopkins University," Central and Inner Asian Studies, vol 6, p 34-43, 1992; "Chen Di and Dong-fan-ji," 1983, 1987, 1990; "History of the Aborigines of West Taiwan," Journal of the Central Institute for Nationalities, 1, p 22-28, 1987; "The Interdisciplinary Study of Anthropology and Chinese History," History and Theory (Chinese Academy of Social Sciences), 4, p 69-80, 1988; and numerous others. **BUSINESS ADDRESS:** Assistant Professor, Central College, 812 University St, Pella, IA 50219, (515)628-5323.

CHIA, ROSINA CHIH-HUNG
Educator. Chinese American. **PERSONAL:** Born Feb 24, 1939, Hong Kong; daughter of Cheng-Chien Chia & Ching-Chao Soong; divorced; children: Eugene Lao, Renee Lao. **EDUCATION:** National Taiwan University, BS, 1962; University of Michigan, MA, 1963, PhD, 1969. **CAREER:** University of Michigan, lecturer, 1968-69; National Taiwan University, visiting professor, 1984-86; East Carolina University, assistant professor to professor, 1969-, Dept of Foreign Languages, acting chair, 1991-92, Dept of Psychology, chair, 1980-85, Sasasaas China Program, 1992, Dept of Sociology, acting chair, 1993-. **ORGANIZATIONS:** APA, Accreditation Site Visit Team, 1987-, member Divs 8, 45, 35, 1969-; Asian American Psych Association, 1981-; NC Psych Association, 1969-; International Council of Psychologists, 1983-. **SPECIAL ACHIEVEMENTS:** Language proficiency: Chinese. **BUSINESS AD-**

DRESS: Professor, Dept of Psychology, East Carolina University, Rawl Bldg, Greenville, NC 27858, (919)757-6277.

CHIA, SWEE LIM
Educator. Malaysian American. **PERSONAL:** Born Jan 17, 1962, Kuala Lumpur, Malaysia; son of Kim-Chiang Chia (deceased) and Lan Lee; married May M Wong, Jan 13, 1990. **EDUCATION:** Baruch College, BA, 1987; City University of New York, PhD candidate, 1988-. **CAREER:** Baruch College, adjunct lecturer, 1989-91, instructor, 1991-92, adjunct lecturer, 1992-. **ORGANIZATIONS:** American Marketing Association, 1989-; Asian American Higher Education Council, 1993-. **SPECIAL ACHIEVEMENTS:** "Five Modern Lessons from a 55-year-Old Technological Forecast," Journal of Product Innovation Management, vol 10, p 66-74, 1993. **BUSINESS ADDRESS:** Instructor, CUNY, Bernard Baruch College, 17 Lexington Ave, New York, NY 10010, (212)447-3246.

CHIANG, ASUNTHA MARIA MING-YEE
Legislative correspondent. Thai American/Indo-American/Chinese American. **PERSONAL:** Born Jan 9, 1970, Washington, DC; daughter of Bing Chiang & Barbara Miller; children: Phillip Andrew Chiang-Smith. **EDUCATION:** The Catholic University of America, BA (cum laude), 1990. **CAREER:** The Capsule newspaper, managing editor, 1987-88; Florida Today newspaper, freelance writer, 1988; Investment Company Institute, news aide, 1990; Congressman Mineta, legislative correspondent, 1991-. **ORGANIZATIONS:** Asian American Journalists Association, 1990-; Capitol Hill Women's Political Caucus, 1992-; National Women's Political Caucus, 1992-; National League of American Pen Women, 1993; Clinton/Gore Presidential Campaign, worker, 1992; Equal Access Equal Opportunity Committee, 1987-88; Student Services at CUA, reader for blind students, 1989; Dukakis Campaign, volunteer, 1988. **HONORS/AWARDS:** Pi Gamma Mu, Honor Society, inductee, 1990; CUA, Honors Program, 1988-90; Brevard Community, Full Music Scholarship, 1987-88. **SPECIAL ACHIEVEMENTS:** Federal Asian Pacific American Council, speaker, 1993; US Judiciary Board, CUA, committee chair, 1989-90. **BIOGRAPHICAL SOURCES:** The Washingtonian, November, 1987. **BUSINESS ADDRESS:** Legislative Correspondent, Congressman Norman Y Mineta, US House of Representatives, 2221 Rayburn House Office Bldg, Washington, DC 20515, (202)225-2631.

CHIANG, BERTTRAM
Educator. Chinese American. **PERSONAL:** Born Jan 11, 1945, Chunking, Szechung, China; son of Sze-Yu Chiang & Whei-Chun Lu; married Rebecca, Feb 24, 1970; children: Timothy, Grace, Connie. **EDUCATION:** National Taiwan Normal University, BA, 1966, MA, 1971; Illinois State University, MS, 1975; University of Minnesota, PhD, 1979. **CAREER:** Jefferson School, teacher, 1975-76; University of Wisconsin, Oshkosh, assistant professor, 1979-82, associate professor, 1982-87, professor, 1987-, Department of Special Education, department chair, 1987-90, College of Education, acting associate dean, 1990. **ORGANIZATIONS:** International Council for Learning Disabilities, research committee member, 1988-; Mid-Western American Educational Research Association. **SPECIAL ACHIEVEMENTS:** Published chapters in nine different books; 21 articles in different professional journals. **BUSINESS ADDRESS:** Professor, University of Wisconsin, Oshkosh, 800 Algoma Blvd, N/E 508, COEHS, Oshkosh, WI 54901, (414)424-2246.

CHIANG, CHAO-KUO
Chemist, association executive. Taiwanese American. **PERSONAL:** Born Dec 4, 1936, Yuanlin, Taiwan; son of C M Chiang and Chien Chiang; married Judy J Chiang, Aug 15, 1964; children: Stanley F, Steven T. **EDUCATION:** Tunghai University, Taiwan, BS, 1959; University of Tennessee, PhD, 1969. **CAREER:** University of Virginia, research associate, 1969-71; University of Iowa, associate research scientist, 1972-. **ORGANIZATIONS:** Taiwanese American Foundation, president, 1992-; Taiwanese American Association, interim president, 1989; American Chemical Society, 1966-. **HOME ADDRESS:** 2014 E Court St, Iowa City, IA 52245, (319)338-9082.

CHIANG, CHIN LONG
Educator. Chinese American. **PERSONAL:** Born Nov 12, 1916, Ningpo, Zhejiang, China; son of Tze-Hsiang Chiang; married Fu Chen Chiang, Jan 21, 1945; children: William, Robert, Harriet. **EDUCATION:** Tsing Hua University, Beijing, 1936-37; South West Associated University, Kunming, China, BA, 1940; University of California, Berkeley, MA, 1948, PhD, 1953. **CAREER:** University of California, Berkeley, associate professor of biostatistics, 1962-65, professor of biostatistics, 1965-87, chairman of biostatistics program,

1975-86, chairman of division of measurement sciences, 1970-75, group of biostatistics, co-chair, 1971-86, school of public health, chairman of the faculty, 1975-76, professor emeritus, 1987-. **ORGANIZATIONS:** Biometrics, associate editor, 1972-75; Mathematical Biosciences, editorial board, 1976-87; World Health Statistics Quarterly, editorial board, 1979-88; World Health Organization, consultant, 1970-87; National Center for Health Statistics, consultant, 1973-87; Health Resources Administration, consultant, 1978; Veterans Administration, consultant, 1983; RAND Corp, consultant, 1973. **HONORS/ AWARDS:** University of California, Oriental Scholar, 1948; Fulbright Senior Lecturer to Great Britain, 1964; American Public Association, Statistics Award, 1981; University of California, The Berkeley Citation, 1987. **SPECIAL ACHIEVEMENTS:** Books published: Introduction to Stochastic Processes in Biostatistics, J Wiley, 1968; Life Table and Mortality Analysis, World Health Organization, Geneva, 1978; An Introduction to Stochastic Processes and Their Applications, R Krieger, 1980; The Life Table and Its Applications, R Krieger, 1984; Statistical Methods for Research and Analysis, Oxford University Press, 1994. **BUSINESS ADDRESS:** Professor Emeritus, University of California, Berkeley, School of Public Health, Warren Hall, Rm 140, Berkeley, CA 94720, (510)642-1593.

CHIANG, CHWAN K.
Scientist. Chinese American. **PERSONAL:** Born Jan 18, 1943, China; married 1979. **EDUCATION:** Michigan State University, PhD, physics, 1974. **CAREER:** University of Pennsylvania, research assoc, 1974-78; Natl Institute of Standards & Technology, physicist, 1978-. **ORGANIZATIONS:** American Chem Soc; American Phys Soc; Electrochem Soc. **BUSINESS ADDRESS:** Physicist, Natl Inst of Standards & Technology, Bldg 223, Rm A215, Gaithersburg, MD 20899.

CHIANG, ERICK
Government administrator, scientist. Chinese American. **PERSONAL:** Born Jun 11, 1950, Hong Kong; son of Wei Pei Chiang and Frances Mary Chiang. **EDUCATION:** Rutgers University, BA, 1972; Adelphi University, MS, 1975. **CAREER:** State University of New York, Buffalo, curator, 1975-79; National Science Foundation, field projects manager, 1979-86, special projects manager, 1986-90, Polar Operations, deputy manager, 1990-91, director, 1991-. **ORGANIZATIONS:** Standing Committee of Antarctic Logistics and Operations, 1990-; Sub-group on Alternative Energy, chmn, 1992; Sub-group on Antarctic Symposia for Technology and Operations, 1990; Sub-group for Oil Spill Contingency Planning, 1990-. **BUSINESS ADDRESS:** Director, Polar Operations, National Science Foundation, 1800 G St, NW, Rm 627, Washington, DC 20550, (202)357-7808.

CHIANG, HUAI C.
Educator, research. Chinese American. **PERSONAL:** Born in Sungkiang, Kiangsu, China; son of Wen-tze and Hsu Hsu; married Zoh Ing Chiang; children: Jeanne, Katherine, Robert. **EDUCATION:** Tsing Hua University, China, BS, 1938; University of Minnesota, MS, 1946, PhD, 1948. **CAREER:** Tsing Hua University, China, assistant, 1938-40, instructor, 1940-44; University of Minnesota, Duluth, assistant professor, 1954-57, associate professor, 1958-61; University of Minnesota, St Paul, assistant, 1945-48, research fellow, 1948-53, professor, 1961-83, professor emeritus, 1984-. **ORGANIZATIONS:** UNDP-FAO, consultant, 1970, 1972, 1975-76, 1980, 1982, 1985-88; USDA, consultant, 1975-83; Am Entom Society, scientific delegation, 1974; National Academy of Science, 1975; EPA, 1978, 1981; US Council of Environmental Quality, science panel, 1977; US Intern Communication Agency, 1979; Intern Center Insect Physiology & Ecology, 1980; Taiwan Council of Agriculture, 1979, 1984; Chinese Ministry of Agriculture, 1982. **HONORS/AWARDS:** Bowling Green State University, Honorary Doctor of Science, 1979; USDA, Certificate of Special Service, 1975; Am Institute Biol Science, Distinquished Service Award, 1979; University Minnesota, Regents Cert Merit, 1984; Ministry & Agriculture, Thailand, Distinguished Service Award, 1988; University of Minnesota, Duluth, Teacher of the Year Award, 1961; Guggenheim Foundation, Fellow, 1955; Phi Kappa Phi, National Scholar, 1983; Entomology Society America, CV Riley Award, 1983. **SPECIAL ACHIEVEMENTS:** 230 scientific publications. **BUSINESS ADDRESS:** Professor, Dept of Entomology, University of Minnesota, 1980 Folwell Avenue, 219 Hodson Hall, St Paul, MN 55108-1385, (612)624-3636.

CHIANG, JOSEPH F.
Educator. Chinese American. **PERSONAL:** Born Feb 22, 1938, Hunan, China; son of K K Chiang & W S Chiang; married Nancy Chiang, Jun 30, 1940; children: Calvin, Amy. **EDUCATION:** Tunghai University, BS, 1960; Cornell

University, MS, 1965, PhD, 1967. **CAREER:** Cornell University, NSF postdoctoral, 1967-68; State University of New York, professor, 1968-. **ORGANIZATIONS:** ACS, 1965-; APS, 1965-; CACS, 1980-; MRS, 1990-. **HONORS/ AWARDS:** NSF, fellow, 1966; NIH, fellow, 1975-76; Harvard University, visiting fellow, 1978-79; University of Chicago, visiting professor, 1984-85. **BUSINESS ADDRESS:** Professor of Chemistry and Computer Science, State University of New York, Ravine Parkway, Physical Science Building, Oneonta, NY 13820, (607)436-3181.

CHIANG, OSCAR C. K.
Journalist, writer. Chinese American. **PERSONAL:** Born Sep 18, 1932, Hubei, China; son of Chiang Fa-shen & Sun Yu-hsien; married Adelina Buhat Chiang, Mar 28, 1964; children: Carl. **EDUCATION:** National Taiwan Normal University, BA, 1957; Kansas State University of Pittsburg, MA, 1961; Columbia University, MS, 1962; St John's University, PhD, 1972. **CAREER:** China Post, English, assistant editor for foreign news, 1955-60; KSU Collegio, feature editor, 1960-61; Long Island Press, sports rewriteman, 1961-62; Time Inc, library researcher, 1962-72; Time Life Books, reporter, researcher, 1972-76; Time, magazine reporter, researcher, 1976-90, assistant, editor, Asian specialist, 1990-. **ORGANIZATIONS:** Chinese American Forum, vice president, editor, 1985-; Organization of Chinese Americans, 1990-; Association of Asian Journalists, 1990-; Association for Asian Studies, 1985-. **HONORS/ AWARDS:** Fulbright Foundation, fellow, 1960; Asian Foundation, fellow, 1961. **SPECIAL ACHIEVEMENTS:** Chinese Democracy, translator, 1992; The Successful Story of Time, in Chinese, 1993. **MILITARY SERVICE:** Chinese Army in Taiwan, 2nd lt, 1955-57. **BUSINESS ADDRESS:** Assistant Editor, Time Magazine, 1271 Avenue of the Americas, Time & Life Building, New York, NY 10020, (212)522-3574.

CHIANG, PING-WANG
Industrial company executive. Chinese American. **PERSONAL:** Born May 16, Taipei, Taiwan; son of Li-Sun Chiang and May Chen; married Theresa Chiang, Dec 12, 1965; children: Patricia, Dick, Peter. **EDUCATION:** Taiwan University, China, BSChE, 1957; University of Louisville, MSChE, 1961; University of Michigan, PhD, ChE, 1965. **CAREER:** Tecumseh Product, research fellow, 1965-68; Harris Semiconductor, asso principal engr, 1968-72; Motorola, mgr, 1972-76; Unisys, mgr, 1976-77; Amdahl, engr, mgr, 1977-92; Topometrix, consultant, 1992-; Head-Right Elec, president, chief exec officer, 1993-. **ORGANIZATIONS:** Electrochemical Society, 1965-80; American Chemical Engrs, 1965; Intl Society for Hybrid & Integrated Microelectronics, 1990-92; Taiwan University Alumnas, ChE, president, 1987; Kiwanis, 1985-86; Chinese American Citizen League, 1984-89; Vietnam Refugee Assisting League, 1980-83. **SPECIAL ACHIEVEMENTS:** Patents: 6; publications: 9; Solid State Tech, review board member, for 1 year. **HOME ADDRESS:** 115 Millrich Dr, Los Gatos, CA 95030, (408)395-2607.

CHIANG, SHIAO-HUNG
Educator. Chinese American. **PERSONAL:** Born Oct 10, 1929, Soochow, Jiangsu, China; son of Shu-Liang Chiang and Shio-Ming Lee; married Jean Jieh Lu Chiang, Jun 28, 1958; children: Grace N, Justin N, Annette N. **EDUCATION:** National Taiwan University, BS, 1952; Kansas State University, MS, 1955; Carnegie-Mellon University, PhD, 1958. **CAREER:** Linde Co, Union Carbide Corp, project eng, 1958-60; University of Pittsburgh, professor, 1960-, Ernest E Roth professor, 1988-89, Wm K Whiteford prof, 1989-. **ORGANIZATIONS:** American Chemical Society, 1958-; American Institute of Chemical Engineers, fellow, 1959-; American Society of Engineering Education, 1963-; American Mining Engineers, 1981-; American Filtration & Separation Society, board of directors, 1988-. **HONORS/AWARDS:** American Filtration & Separation Society, Frank Tiller Technical Award, 1993; Nanjing Institute of Chemical Technology, honorary professorship, 1985-. **SPECIAL ACHIEVEMENTS:** Published over 120 technical articles in scientific and technical journals and books in the fields of chemical engineering, fluid/particle separations, and fuel processing. **BUSINESS ADDRESS:** Professor, Chemical/Petroleum Engineering Dept, University of Pittsburgh, 1249 Benedum Hall, Pittsburgh, PA 15261, (412)624-9636.

CHIANG, SIE LING
Government official. Chinese American. **PERSONAL:** Born Mar 10, 1938, Tainan, Taiwan; son of Lin Tsau & Chiang Shen Wan Chiang; married Mei Lih Chiang, Aug 8, 1964; children: Andrew, Annette. **EDUCATION:** Cheng-Kung University, BSc, 1960; State University of Iowa, MSc, 1964; Pennsylvania State University, PhD, 1971. **CAREER:** Pennsylvania Department of Forests and Water, project engineer, 1964-68; Pennsylvania State University,

research assistantship, 1968-70; Pennsylvania Department of Environmental Resources, planning chief, 1970-75; US Geological Survey, Geothermal Office, Environmental & Safety Section, chief, 1975-77, Branch of Environmental Management, chief, 1977-81; US Bureau of Land Management, Branch of Technical Support, chief, 1982-88, Division of Fluid Mineral Operations, chief, 1988-91, Division of Mineral Policy Analysis & Economic Evaluation, chief, 1992-. **ORGANIZATIONS:** American Society of Civil Engineers, chairman of local chapter, 1964-83; Association of Conservation Engineers, 1973-; Geothermal Resource Council, 1985-; Commonwealth of Pennsylvania, professional engineer, 1967-; Chinese Institute of Civil and Hydraulic Engineering, 1985-; Chinese Institute of Mining & Metallurgical Engineers, 1985-. **HONORS/AWARDS:** Bureau of Land Management, DOI, Outstanding or Excellent Performance Awards, 1983-; US Geological Survey, DOI, Superior Performance Award, 1979; State University of Iowa, International Scholarship, 1963; Hsu Scholarship, Taiwan Bureau of Water Conservancy Scholarship, 1957-60. **SPECIAL ACHIEVEMENTS:** Published over 20 papers in various academic journals in English and Chinese; lectures at: Modern Technology Seminar, Taiwan, 1974; National Development Seminar, Taiwan, 1982; Taiwan Water Resource Planning Seminar, 1983; Mining & Environment Seminar, Taiwan, 1981; Oil and Gas Management, China, 1992; created a categorical exclusion review procedures to comply with the US National Environmental Policy Act; directed the water resources planning effort for the Commonwealth of Pennsylvania, 1970-75. **BIOGRAPHICAL SOURCES:** Inventory of Energy Specialists by Randa International Corp, Taipei, Taiwan; Inventory of Environmental Specialists by Taiwan EPA, Taiwan, number 41, section 1. **BUSINESS ADDRESS:** Chief, Division of Minerals Policy Analysis and Economic Evaluation, Bureau of Land Management, 1849 C St NW, WO-690, Washington, DC 20240, (202)452-0374.

CHIANG, SOONG T.
Chemical researcher. Chinese American. **PERSONAL:** Born Nov 14, 1937, Shanghai, China; married Sylvia Chiang; children: Mark, Elaine. **EDUCATION:** UCLA, BS, 1964, MS, 1966, PhD, 1970. **CAREER:** Thomas Jefferson University, research associate, 1971-73; Wyeth-Ayerst Research, senior clinical scientist, 1973-79, manager, 1979-85, associate director, 1986-88, director, 1988-90, senior director, 1990-. **ORGANIZATIONS:** American Society Clinical Pharmacology & Therapeutics, 1985-; American Association Pharmaceutical Scientists, 1992-; American College of Clinical Pharmacology, 1990-. **SPECIAL ACHIEVEMENTS:** Author of about 60 manuscripts & abstracts published in clinical pharmacology, pharmacodynamics, pharmacokinetics & pharmacometrics. **BUSINESS ADDRESS:** Senior Director, Wyeth-Ayerst Research, Radnor, PA 19087, (215)341-5712.

CHIANG, THERESA YI-CHIN TUNG
Educational administrator. Chinese American. **PERSONAL:** Born May 31, 1947, Song Yao, Jiangxi, China; daughter of Chung-Chi Tung & Chia-Yu Chao; married Tom Chiang, Jun 10, 1971; children: Alena Lynn, Alan Hal. **EDUCATION:** National Taiwan University, BA, 1969; Illinois State University, MS, 1971; University of Nevada, Las Vegas, EdD, 1992. **CAREER:** Texas A&M University, Student Union, program director, 1978-86; University of Nevada, Las Vegas, program director, student union/activities, 1986-88, dir, student union/activities & international student services, 1988-. **ORGANIZATIONS:** NAFSA: Assn of International Educators, chair of region XII, 1992-93; NACAS, multicultural committee, 1993-94; ACU-I, commission on educational programs, 1993-95; Federal Commission on Civil Rights, Nevada advisory board member, 1992-. **HONORS/AWARDS:** University of Nevada, Las Vegas, President's Most Outstanding Professional Member of the Year, 1993; Fulbright Administrator's Grant in Germany, 1994. **BUSINESS ADDRESS:** Dir of Student Union/Act & Intl Student Serv, University of Nevada, Las Vegas, 4505 Maryland Pky, MSU 111, Las Vegas, NV 89154-2008, (702)895-3221.

CHIANG, THOMAS MINGHUNG
Educator, research chemist. Taiwanese American. **PERSONAL:** Born Mar 30, 1940, Taipei, Taiwan; son of Mr and Mrs Huei Tang Chiang; married Edna Y Chiang, Mar 30, 1973; children: Elbert, Herbert. **EDUCATION:** National Chung Hsing University, BS, 1964; University of Tennessee, Memphis, PhD, 1973. **CAREER:** Military Service, 1964-65; National Chung-Hsing University, research assistant, 1965-66, teaching assistant, 1966-69; University of Tennessee, Department of Medicine, research fellow, 1973-74, research associate, 1975-76, assistant professor, 1977-84, associate professor, 1984-85, Departments of Biochemistry and Medicine, associate professor, 1985-; VA Medical Center, research chemist, 1974-. **ORGANIZATIONS:** Society of

Microbiology of Republic of China; Society of Soil and Fertilizer of Republic of China; Society of Agricultural Chemistry of Republic of China; American Association for the Advancement of Science; American Chemical Society; Sigma Xi; New York Academy of Sciences; American Society of Biochemistry and Molecular Biology; American Heart Association, Council on Basic Science, Tennessee Affiliate. **HONORS/AWARDS:** American Heart Association, Tennessee Affiliates, grants and investigator award, 1983-89; American Heart Association, Nation Center, grant, 1984-86; Department of Veterans Affair, 1984-. **SPECIAL ACHIEVEMENTS:** 52 publications including journal articles and chapters in books. **BUSINESS ADDRESS:** Research Chemist, Veterans Administration Medical Center, 1030 Jefferson Ave, SCI BE-127, Memphis, TN 38104, (901)523-8990.

CHIANG, TSUNG TING
Engineering consulting company executive. Chinese American. **PERSONAL:** Born Nov 15, 1936, Anhwei, China; son of Yuan Tien & Daisy Chiang; married Alice M F, Dec 30, 1964; children: Vincent W F, Victor W Y. **EDUCATION:** Chung-Yuan College of Sciences & Engineering, BS, 1960-; Virginia Polytechnic Inst & State University, MS, 1963, PhD, 1968. **CAREER:** Virginia Polytechnic Inst, res asst, 1964-67; Metcalf & Eddy, Inc, sr hydraulic engineer, 1967-69; Chas T Main, Inc, sr water resources engineer, 1969-71; Whitman & Howard, Inc, chief hydraulic engineer & mgr water resources, 1971-83; Northeastern University/Building design & Mgt, faculty, 1988-; H2O Engineering Consulting Associates Inc, president, 1980-. **ORGANIZATIONS:** New England Assn of Chinese Professionals, chm/board of directors, 1988-; Chinese Economic Development Council, vice chm/board of directors, 1987-; NE Monte Jade Science & Tech Assn, vice chm of board, 1992-93; Greater Boston Chinese Cultural Assn, president, 1976-77, board of directors, 1977-79; Boston South Cove & Chinatown Neigborhood Council, co-moderator, 1988-92; MA Dept of Environment Quality Engineers, water supply advisory comm, 1986-90. **SPECIAL ACHIEVEMENTS:** Many technical papers in the field of hydrology, waterworks and wastewater computer modeling. **BUSINESS ADDRESS:** President, H2O Engineering Consulting Associates, Inc, 6 Page Place, Woburn, MA 01801, (617)933-6961.

CHIANG, YI-LING F.
Educator. Chinese American. **PERSONAL:** Born May 9, 1934, Peiping, China; daughter of Yuan-Shen Fan and Guo-Yi L Fan; married Ta-kuan Chiang, Jun 23, 1962; children: Lillian W M. **EDUCATION:** Rutgers University, PhD, computer science, 1981. **CAREER:** Bell Telephone Lab, member of staff, 1960-74; University of Louisville, assistant professor, 1980-81; New Jersey Institute of Technology, assistant professor, 1981-89; William Paterson College of NJ, associate professor, 1989-90; West Virginia University, professor, 1990-92; Accutek Inc, president, 1992-. **ORGANIZATIONS:** SIAM, 1980-, Chapter of NJ, treasurer, 1983-89; ACM, 1980-; IMACS, 1981-; CACA, director, vice president, 1972-80; CPWV, 1990-. **HONORS/AWARDS:** Hellenic Woman's Club, Scholarship, 1957-58; CACA, Service Award, 1989; NASA, Faculty Fellowship, 1987. **SPECIAL ACHIEVEMENTS:** Numerous publications on scientific computation, 1960-; book, Man & Computer, 1973; essays published in newspapers and magazines, 1990-. **HOME ADDRESS:** 2021 Ices Ferry Dr, Morgantown, WV 26505, (304)594-1725.

CHIANG, YUEN-SHENG
Apparel company executive. Chinese American. **PERSONAL:** Born Feb 2, 1936, Tsingtao, China; son of Ho-Ju Chiang and Wan-Ru Chiang; married Marie Fang Chiang, Jun 24, 1967; children: Edmund, Christopher. **EDUCATION:** National Taiwan University, BSE, 1956; University of Louisville, MChE, 1960; Princeton University, PhD, 1964; Rutgers University Graduate School of Management, MBA, 1979. **CAREER:** Burroughs Laboratories, consultant, 1962-63; Princeton University, research associate, 1963; Xerox Corp, Res Labs, scientist, 1964-69, sr scientist, 1968; RCA Laboratories, member of technical staff, 1969-81; Solitron Devices Inc, corporate technical director, 1982; Jeanne Pierre Originals Inc, executive vice president, 1982-; J Breed Properties Inc, president, 1986-. **ORGANIZATIONS:** IEEE, 1980-; Sigma Xi, 1960-; Beta Gamma Sigma, 1979-. **HONORS/AWARDS:** Beta Gamma Sigma, Rutgers Chapter, Beta Gamma Sigma Key, 1979; Rutgers University, School of Business Alumni Assn Prize, 1979. **SPECIAL ACHIEVEMENTS:** Twenty-nine technical publications in various scientific journals, 1963-77. **BUSINESS ADDRESS:** Executive Vice President, Jeanne Pierre Originals, Inc, 215 Daniel St, Farmingdale, NY 11735, (516)694-9888.

CHIANG, YUNG FRANK
Educator. Taiwanese American. **PERSONAL:** Born Jan 2, 1936, Taichung, Taiwan; son of Ruey-ting Chiang & Yueg Yin Chiang; married Quay Yin Chiang, Nov 30, 1969; children: Amy, David. **EDUCATION:** Taiwan University, LLB, 1958; Northwestern University, School of Law, LLM, 1962; University of Chicago, School of Law, JD, 1965. **CAREER:** Yen & Lai, law firm, associate, 1960-61; Lawyers' Co-op Publishing Co, editor, 1965; Harvard Law School, research associate, 1965-67; University of Georgia Law School, assistant professor of law, 1967-72; Asia Bank, NA, director, vice president, 1984-86; Fordham Law School, associate professor of law, 1972-76, professor of law, 1976-. **ORGANIZATIONS:** New York State Bar Association, 1985-; Taiwan Merchant Association of New York, president, 1980-84, director, 1976-93; Formosan Association for Public Affairs, New York chapter, president, 1991-92; Law and Political Science Section, North America Taiwanese Professors'O Association, section head, 1993. **SPECIAL ACHIEVEMENTS:** Numerous published articles in commercial law and admiralty, one cited by federal courts as authority three times; language proficiency: Chinese and Japanese. **BUSINESS ADDRESS:** Professor of Law, Fordham University Law School, 140 W 62nd St, New York, NY 10023, (212)636-6835.

CHIAO, JEN WEI
Educator. Chinese American. **PERSONAL:** married Marie; children: Emmeline, Christine, Franklin. **EDUCATION:** Southwestern University, BS, 1966; University of Illinois, Chicago, MS, 1968, PhD, 1971. **CAREER:** The Rockefeller University, fellow, 1971-72; Sloan-Kettering Institute for Cancer Research, associate, 1972-82; New York Medical College, professor of medicine, 1982-, professor of immunology, 1983, professor of urology, 1984. **ORGANIZATIONS:** American Association for Immunologists, 1973-; American Association for Cancer Research, 1973-; Society for Experimental Hematology, 1973-. **HONORS/AWARDS:** National Institutes of Health, Career Development Award, 1978; Southwestern University, President's Scholarship, 1965, Brown's Scholarship, 1963, Wise Owl's Award for Art, 1965; State of Kentucky, Colonel, 1970. **BIOGRAPHICAL SOURCES:** Biological Response Modifiers and Cancer, cover, 1989.

CHIAO, LEROY
Astronaut. Chinese American. **PERSONAL:** Born Aug 28, 1960, Milwaukee, WI; son of Tsu Tao and Cherry Chiao. **EDUCATION:** University of California, Berkeley, BS, chemical engineering, 1983; University of California, Santa Barbara, MS, chemical engineering, 1985, PhD, chemical engineering, 1987. **CAREER:** University of California, Santa Barbara, postdoctorate research, 1987; Hexcel Corp, materials engineer, 1987-89; Lawrence Livermore National Lab, materials engineer, 1989-90; NASA, astronaut, 1990-. **ORGANIZATIONS:** American Institute of Aeronautics and Astronautics, 1991-; ASTM, 1989-; Society for the Advancement of Material and Process Engineers, 1987-. **SPECIAL ACHIEVEMENTS:** Invited technical seminars in China, 1988; 20 technical publications. **BUSINESS ADDRESS:** Astronaut, NASA-Johnson Space Center, Mail Code CB, Houston, TX 77058.

CHIAO, YU-CHIH
Chemist. Taiwanese American. **PERSONAL:** Born Nov 20, 1949, Hsin Chu, Taiwan; daughter of Wan-Chiu Chen and Gu-Hwa Lo Chen; married Wen B Chiao, Jun 14, 1975; children: Leo, Max. **EDUCATION:** National Tsing Hua University, BS, 1972; University of Rochester, PhD, 1976. **CAREER:** Allied Signal, research chemist, 1985-87, senior research chemist, 1987-89; Aquatech Systems, lab supervisor, 1989-. **BUSINESS ADDRESS:** Lab Supervisor, Aquatech Systems/Allied Signal Inc, 7 Powder Horn Dr, Warren, NJ 07059-5191, (908)563-2830.

CHIBA, LEE I.
Educator. Japanese American. **PERSONAL:** Born May 12, 1951, Ishikoshi, Miyagi, Japan. **EDUCATION:** University of Nebraska, BS, 1982, MS, 1984, PhD, 1989. **CAREER:** Merchant Homestead, Inc, manager, 1973-79; University of Nebraska, research and teaching assistant, 1983-89; Auburn University, assistant professor, 1990-. **ORGANIZATIONS:** American Society of Animal Science, 1984-; Gamma Sigma Delta, 1987-. **SPECIAL ACHIEVEMENTS:** Publications: Author, "Amino acids and energy interrelationships...," Journal of Animal Science, vol 69, pp 694-707, 708-718, 1991; author, "Efficacy of the urea dilution technique in...," Journal of Animal Science, vol 68 pp 372-383, 1990; contributor, "Effects of alcohol...," Journal of the Science of Food and Agriculture, vol 52, pp 193-205, 1990; author, "Use of dietary fat to reduce dust, aerial...," Transactions of the ASAE, vol 30 pp 464-468, 1987; author, "Effect of dietary fat on pig performance...," Journal of Animal Science, vol

61, pp 763-781, 1985. **BUSINESS ADDRESS:** Asst Professor, Dept of Animal & Dairy Sciences, Auburn University, 108 Animal Science Bldg, Auburn, AL 36849-5415, (205)844-1560.

CHIEN, ALAN SHUESHIH
Architect, community leader. Chinese American. **PERSONAL:** Born Oct 15, 1934, Shanghai, China; son of Sze Yee Chien & Wang Chien; children: Ava, Nina, Arthur. **EDUCATION:** Columbia University, Graduate School of Architecture and Urban Planning, MS, 1971. **CAREER:** Harrison and Abramovitz Architects, architect, 1964-71; Abacus Group of America Inc, director, 1971-85, chairman, 1985-. **ORGANIZATIONS:** Rotary Club of New York, 1977-; Community Board No 6, Borough of Manhattan, City of New York, 1988-, vice chairman, 1992-93; US/China Business Council, importers committee, chairman, 1985-91, board of directors, 1986-; US Department of Commerce, Importers Retailers Textile Advisory Committee, advisor, 1979-91; US Department of State, International Textile Program, cleared advisor, 1985-93. **SPECIAL ACHIEVEMENTS:** One of first architects who used computers in design and control of buildings' character and form; computerized-automated design of theaters; one of first Asian Americans to serve on Manhattan Community Board No 6, Borough of Manhattan. **BUSINESS ADDRESS:** Chairman, Abacus Group of America Inc, 239 East 51st St, New York, NY 10022, (212)888-6066.

CHIEN, ARNOLD JENSEN
Artificial intelligence researcher. Chinese American. **PERSONAL:** Born Sep 26, 1958, Fullerton, CA; son of Gary K L Chien and Mabel H Chien; married Margaret Connors, Mar 9, 1993. **EDUCATION:** Massachusetts Institute of Technology, BS, 1980; University of Massachusetts, PhD, 1987. **CAREER:** PRC Inc, principal systems analyst, 1987-. **ORGANIZATIONS:** Association for Computational Linguistics, 1989-; American Philosophical Association, 1992-. **HONORS/AWARDS:** University of Massachusetts, University Fellowship, 1983; Department of Philosophy, University of Massachusetts, Puryear Fellowship, 1980; Rensselaer Math & Science Medal, 1976. **SPECIAL ACHIEVEMENTS:** Presented paper at 15th International Conference on Computational Linguistics, 1992. **HOME ADDRESS:** 100 Westchester Rd, Boston, MA 02130.

CHIEN, CHIA-LING
Educator. Chinese American. **PERSONAL:** Born Nov 10, 1942, China; son of Ting Chien and An-Hsiu Wong Chien; married Christina Yueh Wong Chien, Apr 15, 1972; children: David, Doborah. **EDUCATION:** Tunghai University, BS, physics, 1965; Carnegie-Mellon University, MS, physics, 1968, PhD, physics, 1972. **CAREER:** Johns Hopkins University, research associate, 1973-74, associate research scientist, 1974-75, visiting assistant professor, 1975-76, assistant professor, 1976-79, associate professor, 1979-83, professor of physics, 1983-. **ORGANIZATIONS:** American Physical Society, fellow. **BUSINESS ADDRESS:** Professor, Dept of Physics & Astromony, Johns Hopkins University, Charles & 34th Sts, Bloomberg Center for Physics & Astronomy, Baltimore, MD 21218, (410)516-8092.

CHIEN, CHIH-YUNG
Educator, researcher. Chinese American. **PERSONAL:** Born Aug 5, 1939, Zizhong, Sichuan, China; son of Bins C Chien and Yinlow Fan Chien; married Chun-Wuei Su, Jul 6, 1963; children: Chi-Bin, Chi-Kai, Chi-An. **EDUCATION:** National Taiwan University, BS, 1960; Yale University, MA, 1963, PhD, 1966. **CAREER:** UCLA, assistant professor, 1966-69; US National Science Foundation, program director, 1986-87; Hong Kong University of Science & Technology, founding provost, 1988-92; Johns Hopkins University, professor, 1969-. **ORGANIZATIONS:** American Physical Society, 1966-; Oversea Chinese Physics Association, council member, 1990-. **HONORS/AWARDS:** Danford Foundation, Denford Fellow, 1973; US National Science Foundation, Sustained Extraordinary Achievement, 1987; Nanjing University, Honorary Professor, 1980; Chinese University of Science & Technology, Honorary Professor, 1982; Beijing Institute of Technology, Xinjiang University, Honorary Professor, 1983; Neimongju University, Hangzhou University, Zhejiang University, Yunnan University, Honorary Professor, 1984; Fuzhou University, Honorary Professor, 1993. **MILITARY SERVICE:** Artillery, 2nd lt, 1960-61. **BUSINESS ADDRESS:** Professor, Physics Dept, Johns Hopkins University, Baltimore, MD 21218, (410)516-7359.

CHIEN, GARY K.
Consultant. Chinese American. **PERSONAL:** Born Apr 1, 1928, Hankow, Hubei, China; son of M L Chien; married Mabel, Jul 4, 1953; children:

Anthony, David, Arnold, Robert. **EDUCATION:** National Central University, China, BSME, 1949; MIT, MS, 1950, ScD, 1953. **CAREER:** RCA, engineering leader, 1952-57; Beckman Instrument, chief engineer, 1957-60; Case Institute of Tech, visitig professor, 1963-64; IBM, Strategy Planning, manager, 1960-90; self employed, management consultant, 1990-. **HONORS/AWARDS:** IBM, Outstanding Contribution Awards, 1968-83. **SPECIAL ACHIEVEMENTS:** Co-author: Computer Control Systems, UCLA, 1955. **HOME ADDRESS:** 121 Sweet Briar Rd, Stamford, CT 06905, (203)322-9694.

CHIEN, SZE-FOO
Engineering research consultant. **PERSONAL:** Born Aug 1929, China; married. **EDUCATION:** National Taiwan University, BS, 1953; University of Minnesota, MS, 1956, PhD, 1961. **CAREER:** GH Tennant Co, engineering consultant, 1954-57; University of Minnesota, instructor & research fellow, 1956-61; Texaco Inc, research consultant, 1961-. **ORGANIZATIONS:** ASME, 1962-; SPE, 1991-; Sigma Xi; Professional Engr, Texas; API, Committee 13 Task Group, 1990-93. **HONORS/AWARDS:** University of Petroleum, China, Honorary Professor, 1991; United Nations, Technical Consultant, 1985; EPTD Texaco. **SPECIAL ACHIEVEMENTS:** Author and co-author of numerous publications, presentations, and patents; language proficiency: Chinese, Spanish, Japanese. **MILITARY SERVICE:** ROTC, 2nd lt, commissioned, 1953. **BUSINESS ADDRESS:** Research Consultant, EPTD Texaco Inc, PO Box 425, Bellaire, TX 77401, (713)432-3342.

CHIEN, YIE W.
Educational Administrator, educator. Taiwanese American. **PERSONAL:** Born Oct 20, 1938, Keelung, Taiwan; son of Chao-lin and Ai-wen Chien; married Chin-mei Chuang, Apr 23, 1964; children: Steven, Linda. **EDUCATION:** Kaohsiung Medical College, BPharm, 1963; Ohio State University, PhD, pharmaceutics, 1972. **CAREER:** G D Searle & Co/Searle Lab, group leader, research scientist, 1972-78; The DuPont Co/Endo Lab, section head, 1978-81; Rutgers University, College of Pharmacy, professor I, 1981-86, Controlled Drug-Delivery Research Center, dir, 1982-, Dept of Pharmaceutics, chmn, 1982-88, professor II, 1986-89, Parke-Davis Endowed Chair, 1989-. **ORGANIZATIONS:** World Health Organization, consultant, 1988-; Controlled Release Society, board of directors, 1984-87. **HONORS/AWARDS:** Rutgers University, Board of Trustees Award, 1985-86; Taiwanese American Foundation, Science-Technology Achievement Award, 1985; American Pharmaceutical Assn, Academy Fellow, 1983; American Assn of Pharmaceutical Scientists, fellow, 1986. **SPECIAL ACHIEVEMENTS:** Author: 123 research articles, 31 reviews, 67 symposium papers, 10 advanced books, 18 book chapters, 1973-; 18 US patents (with intl disclosures), 1976-. **BUSINESS ADDRESS:** Parke-Davis Endowed Chair Professor, Director, Rutgers University, Controlled Drug-Delivery Research Center, 41-D Gordon Rd, Piscataway, NJ 08854, (908)445-6180.

CHIEN, YING I.
Educator. Taiwanese American. **PERSONAL:** Born Nov 19, 1941, Taiwan; son of Chao-in Chien & Tuane Chien; married Huei Chien, Dec 6, 1979; children: Peggy, Amy. **EDUCATION:** National Taiwan University, BS, 1964; University of Manitoba, MS, 1968; University of Kentucky, PhD, 1973. **CAREER:** University of Kentucky, computer programmer, 1969-72; Morehead State University, associate professor of business administration, 1973-79; University of Scranton, associate professor of business administration, 1979-. **ORGANIZATIONS:** Decision Science Institute; American Production and Inventory Control Society. **HONORS/AWARDS:** National Science Foundation, University of Scranton, Computer Application Grant, 1980. **SPECIAL ACHIEVEMENTS:** Language proficiency in Chinese, Taiwanese; research publications in decision sciences, production and inventory management. **BUSINESS ADDRESS:** Associate Professor of Business Administration, University of Scranton, 800 Linden St, Scranton, PA 18510-2429, (717)941-7407.

CH'IH, JOHN JUWEI
Educator. Chinese American. **PERSONAL:** Born Oct 29, 1933, Tsingtao, China; son of Joachim & Anna Ch'ih; married Shirley S Sun, Dec 10, 1962; children: Michael H. **EDUCATION:** Southern Illinois University, BA, 1960; University of Delaware, MS, 1963; Thomas Jefferson University, PhD, 1968. **CAREER:** Biochemical Research Foundation, research technician, 1960-63; St Mary's Hospital, clinical chemist, 1963-66; Thomas Jefferson University, instructor, 1968-69; Hahnemann University, senior instructor, professor, 1969-. **ORGANIZATIONS:** American Society of Biochemistry & Molecular Biology, 1976-; Sigma Xi, 1968-; American Society of Cell Biology, currently;

American Association for Advancement of Science, currently; Society of Experimental Biology & Medicine, currently; American Chemical Society, 1960-92. **HONORS/AWARDS:** USPHS, predoctoral fellow, 1966-68, Senior International Fellow, 1978-79; Hahnemann University, Faculty Teaching Award, 1991, Distinguished Graduate Faculty Award, 1993. **BUSINESS ADDRESS:** Professor, Dept of Biology & Chemistry, Hahnemann University, Philadelphia, PA 19102-1192, (215)762-8144.

CHIN, ALEXANDER FOSTER
Educator. Chinese American. **PERSONAL:** Born Dec 12, 1937, Moneague, St Ann, Jamaica; son of Humphrey Chin and Betty Chin; married Barbara K Chin, Jun 9, 1946; children: Micah, Michelle. **EDUCATION:** Oklahoma State University, BSEE, 1969, MS, 1974, EdD, 1983. **CAREER:** Electronic Engineering Company of California, electronic engineer, 1970-71; Tulsa Junior College Northeast, assistant professor, 1971-. **ORGANIZATIONS:** Phi Delta Kappa, 1983-; American Technical Education Association, 1975-; Oklahoma Technical Society, life member, 1971-; Tulsa Junior College Electronics Club, faculty advisor, 1977-. **HONORS/AWARDS:** National Science Foundation, 1971; American Institute in Foreign Study, 1983. **SPECIAL ACHIEVEMENTS:** Co-author of college textbook: Electronic Instruments and Measurements, 1983; author of numerous college, technical laboratory manuals, 1972-89. **BUSINESS ADDRESS:** Assistant Professor, Tulsa Junior College Northeast, 3727 East Apache, Tulsa, OK 74115-3151, (918)631-7478.

CHIN, ALICE L.
Photographer (retired). Chinese American. **PERSONAL:** Born Mar 2, 1923, Portsmouth, NH; daughter of Henry and Louie Shee Yick (deceased); married Adam Chin, Jul 14, 1960 (deceased); children: Gregory D Jong, Cheryl E Jong, Lauri A. **CAREER:** Charlestown Navy Yard, shipfitter's helper, 1941-42; Gillette Razor Co, machine operator, 1942-45; Nuclear Metals Inc, industrial research photographer, 1956-62. **ORGANIZATIONS:** Chinese Historical Society of New England. **HONORS/AWARDS:** Day Treatment Center, volunteer service to veterans, recognition service awards, 1970-75; Photographer's Forum Magazine, Award of Excellence, photography, 1986. **SPECIAL ACHIEVEMENTS:** Photographer's Forum Magazine, Best of Photography Annual, 1986; Boston Magazine, "Boston Angels," by Anita Diamant, Dec 1987, volunteer teaching Chinese calligraphy, public schools; The Center, Bedford, MA, Northeast Market Highlights, photographs, gift and decorative accessories, 1984. **BIOGRAPHICAL SOURCES:** "Boston Angels," Boston Magazine, p180, Dec 1987. **HOME ADDRESS:** 93 Warren Ave, Boston, MA 02116, (617)266-6305.

CHIN, BEVERLY ANN
Educator. Chinese American. **PERSONAL:** Born Nov 12, 1948, Baltimore, MD; daughter of Sheung & Ruth Chin. **EDUCATION:** Florida State University, BA, 1970, MA, 1971; University of Massachusetts, Amherst, 1972-73; University of Oregon, PhD, 1975. **CAREER:** Brevard County Schools, FL, English teacher, 1971-73; University of New Orleans, assistant professor of education, 1976-77; Arizona State University, assistant professor of English, 1977-78; University of Central Florida, assistant professor of education, 1978-81; University of Montana, professor of English, director of Montana Writing project, director of composition, codirector of English teaching program, 1981-. **ORGANIZATIONS:** National Council of Teachers of English, vice president, 1993-94, president-elect, 1994-95, president, 1995-96; Montana Association of Teachers of English and Language Arts, president, 1984-85; Phi Delta Kappa, 1974; Kappa Delta Pi, 1971. **HONORS/AWARDS:** University of Montana, Distinguished Teacher Award, 1990; Burlington Northern, Faculty Achievement Award, 1985; Phi Beta Kappa, 1970. **SPECIAL ACHIEVEMENTS:** Author, On Your Own: Writing Process, 1990, On Your Own: Grammar, 1991; consultant, Writer's Choice: Composition and Grammar, 1994; contributing editor, Chinese American Literature, 1993; consultant, Tapestry: A Multicultural Anthology, 1993. **BUSINESS ADDRESS:** Professor of English, University of Montana, Missoula, MT 59812-1013, (406)243-2463.

CHIN, BRYAN ALLEN
Educator. Chinese American. **PERSONAL:** Born Jan 9, 1952, Jackson, MI; son of Wing Y Chin & Margaret Chin; married Teresa S Chin, Jun 15, 1974; children: Victor Allen, Philip Allen. **EDUCATION:** Auburn University, BS, 1973; Stanford University, MS, 1974, PhD, 1976. **CAREER:** Westinghouse Hanford Co, In-Reactor Deformation, manager, 1976-80; Department of Energy, Office of Reactor, research and development, 1980-81; Auburn University, Materials Engineering, professor, chairman, 1981-, associate vice president for research, 1992-. **ORGANIZATIONS:** National Clad/Duct Materials

Development Program, task group chairman, 1976-81; US/USSR Materials Exchange Team, 1978-; US/UK Materials Exchange Team, 1978-; US/FRG Materials Exchange Team, 1978-; Task Force to Assess FFTF Core Life, 1980; Department of Energy Materials Specialists, 1980-81; National Fusion Material Program, task group chairman, 1979-81. **HONORS/AWARDS:** University of California, Berkeley, John Dorn Memorial Award, 1977; American Welding Society, William Spraragen Award, 1984; American Council on Higher Education, Educator's Award, 1987; Auburn Civitan Club, Civitan of the Year, 1984; Civitan International, Distinguished President Award, 1986. **SPECIAL ACHIEVEMENTS:** Over 125 refereed reviews, journal and scientific publications. **BUSINESS ADDRESS:** Associate Vice President for Research, Auburn University, 202 Samford Hall, Auburn, AL 36849, (205)844-5970.

CHIN, CECILIA HUI-HSIN
Art librarian. Chinese American. **PERSONAL:** Born in Tientsin, China; daughter of Y L Chin and T Y Fan Chin. **EDUCATION:** National Taiwan University, BA, 1961; University of Illinois, MS, library science, 1963. **CAREER:** Roosevelt University, cataloger & reference librarian, 1963; Ryerson & Burnham Libraries, Art Institute of Chicago, reference librarian & indexer, 1963-70, head of reader service & indexer, 1970-75, associate librarian & head reader service, 1975-76, acting director of libraries, 1976-77, associate librarian, 1977-82; National Portrait Gallery, Smithsonian Institution, art librarian, 1982-. **ORGANIZATIONS:** Art Libraries Society of North America; DC Library Association; Washington Rare Book Group; Chinese-American Librarian Association, Greater Mid-Atlantic Chapter, president, 1993-94. **HONORS/AWARDS:** National Portrait Gallery, Smithsonian Institution, 1984, 1989. **SPECIAL ACHIEVEMENTS:** Compiler, The Art Institute of Chicago Index to Art Periodicals, 1975. **BUSINESS ADDRESS:** Librarian, National Portrait Gallery, National Museum of American Art, Smithsonian Institution, F & 8th Sts NW, #331, Washington, DC 20560, (202)357-1886.

CHIN, CHARLIE WILLIAM DAVID
Writer, musician, playwright, singer, historian. Chinese American. **PERSONAL:** Born Apr 8, 1944, New York, NY; son of David Hung Ock Chin & Mary Theresa Mon Brown Chin; married Linda Setsuko Taoka, May 11, 1984; children: David Satoru. **CAREER:** Writer, musician, playwright, singer, historian, currently. **ORGANIZATIONS:** Involved in all aspects of the political, artistic & cultural development and growth of the Asian American community, 1968-. **HOME ADDRESS:** 613 South Humboldt St, #B, San Mateo, CA 94402, (415)579-7341.

CHIN, CHEW
Wholesale seafood broker. Chinese American. **PERSONAL:** Born Jul 23, 1949, New York, NY; son of Gam Yuen Chin and See Poy Chin; married Arline, Aug 18, 1985; children: Tammie, Keith, Leila, Corey. **EDUCATION:** City College of New York, BS, 1971. **CAREER:** Self employed, wholesale seafood broker, currently. **HOME ADDRESS:** 34 E Heritage Dr, New City, NY 10956.

CHIN, CONNIE FRANCES
Government administrator. Chinese American. **PERSONAL:** Born Apr 27, 1958, New York, NY; daughter of Dan Chin and Betty Chin. **EDUCATION:** New York University, Washington Square University College, AB (cum laude), 1980; New York University, Wagner School for Public Service, MPA, 1981. **CAREER:** New York State Program, mgt intern, 1981-83; NYS Office of Mental Retardation & Developmental Disabilities, developmental disabilities program analyst, 1983-84; NYS Dept of Taxation & Finance, sr budgeting analyst, 1985-90; NYS Dept of Health, associate health planner, 1990-92; NYS Executive Chamber, asst to the governor for Asian-American affairs, 1992-. **ORGANIZATIONS:** Center for Women in Govt, advisory committee on minority women's issues, co-chair, 1991-, ACOMWI, 1986-; NYU, Washington Square University College Alumni Assn, regional director, 1990-; Chinese Community Center of the Capital District, 1992-; Chinese American Alliance of the Capital District, 1991-, secretary, 1992. **HONORS/AWARDS:** NYU Alumnae Assn, Alumnae Award, 1981; NYU, Washington Square University College, Founder's Day Award, 1980. **BUSINESS ADDRESS:** Asst to the Governor for Asian-American Affairs, New York State Executive Chamber, 2 World Trade Center 57th Fl, New York, NY 10047, (212)417-4809.

CHIN, DAVID
Company executive. Chinese American. **PERSONAL:** Born Jul 15, 1939, Kuala Lumpur, Malaysia; son of Teck Ken Chin; married Nancy Jean, Jun 6, 1968; children: Wesley David, Wendy Lee, Eric Peter. **EDUCATION:** Har-

ding University, BS, 1966. **CAREER:** Bancroft Bag, Inc, systems analysis, dp manager, 1967, MIS director, 1993, data processing, vp, 1993-. **SPECIAL ACHIEVEMENTS:** Proficient in IBM mid range systems; 27 years of programming, systems design and consulting experience. **HOME ADDRESS:** 506 Pinecrest Road, West Monroe, LA 71291, (318)396-6382. **BUSINESS ADDRESS:** VP, Data Processing, Bancroft Bag, Inc, 425 Bancroft Blvd, West Monroe, LA 71292, (318)387-2550.

CHIN, DONALD G.
Medic. Chinese American. **PERSONAL:** Born Oct 7, 1955, Seattle, WA; son of Dun Hing Chin and Myra Jean (Mar) Chin. **EDUCATION:** NSCC, CHA/EMT, 1979. **CAREER:** IDEC, lt supervisor, 1968-. **ORGANIZATIONS:** Interim, vp board, currently; IDYC, co-founder, 1971-75. **HONORS/AWARDS:** ACRS, Community Award, 1990. **BUSINESS ADDRESS:** Director/Lt Supervisor, International District Emergency Center Inc, PO Box 14103, Seattle, WA 98114, (206)623-3321.

CHIN, EDWIN, JR.
Educator. Chinese American. **PERSONAL:** Born Jun 8, 1932, Stockton, CA; son of Edwin H Chin and Mae Wah You; divorced; children: Chris, Ian. **EDUCATION:** University of California, San Francisco, Medical Center, PhD, 1963. **CAREER:** San Jose State University, Biology Department, professor of biology, 1961-. **BUSINESS ADDRESS:** Professor, Biology Dept, San Jose State University, 1 Washington Sq, DH-225, San Jose, CA 95192-0001, (408)924-4842.

CHIN, FRANK CHEW, JR.
Playwright, author. Chinese American. **PERSONAL:** Born Feb 25, 1940, Berkeley, CA; married. **EDUCATION:** University of California, Berkeley. **CAREER:** Southern Pacific Railroad, brakeman; KING-TV, Seattle, WA, writer, producer; San Francisco State University, Asian American studies, instructor; University of California at Davis, Asian American studies, instructor; playwright, works include: The Chickencoop Chinaman, The Year of the Dragon (both staged off Broadway, 1970s); author, titles include: Charlie Chan on Maui, Harper & Row, 1970s; Aiiieeeee!: An Anthology of Asian American Writers, co-editor, 1974; The Chinaman Pacific & Frisco RR Co, Coffee House Press, 1988; The Big Aiiieeeee!: An Anthology of Chinese American and Japanese American Literature, co-editor, 1991; Donald Duk, Coffee House Press, 1991. **ORGANIZATIONS:** Combined Asian American Resources Project, co-organizer; Asian American Theater Workshop, founder, 1972. **HONORS/AWARDS:** University of Iowa, Writers Workshop, Fellowship, 1961; Lannan Foundation, Fiction Fellowship, 1992. **BUSINESS ADDRESS:** Author, Donald Duk, Coffee House Books, 27 N Fourth St, Ste 400, Minneapolis, MN 55401.*

CHIN, GEORGE K. W.
Bank executive. Hong Kong American. **PERSONAL:** Born Aug 16, 1956, Hong Kong; son of Wing Dor Chin and Sau Man Chin; married Jean K Chin, Aug 8, 1988; children: Kimberly J, Calvin G. **EDUCATION:** Harvard University, AB (cum laude), 1979; New York University, Stern School of Business, MS, 1980. **CAREER:** Arthur Anderson & Company, senior accountant, 1979-81; Merrill Lynch, senior financial consultant, 1981-86, vice president, sales manager, 1988-91; Blar Stearns & Company, assistant vice president, 1986-87; Wells Fargo Bank, Asian Pacific Region, managing director, 1992-. **ORGANIZATIONS:** National Association of Asian American Professionals, co-founder, president, 1980-87; Asian American Manufacturers Association, 1992-; San Francisco Chinatown Lions Club, 1992-; Century City Rotary Club, 1990-91; Harvard Club of New York City, 1979-. **BUSINESS ADDRESS:** Managing Director, Asia Pacific Region, Wells Fargo Bank, 333 South Grand Avenue, 5th floor, Los Angeles, CA 90071, (213)253-3096.

CHIN, GRACE Y.
Architect (retired). Chinese American. **PERSONAL:** Born Nov 8, 1924, Beijing, China; daughter of K Y Yang & T L Ko; married Ming L Chin, Oct 21, 1951; children: Leslie, Lydia. **EDUCATION:** Peking University, China, BA, English literature, 1946; Oberlin College Graduate School, 1947-49; Columbia University, School of Architecture, 1954; MIT, School of Architecture, 1956-59. **CAREER:** Victor Gruen Associates Architects & Planners, planner, 1964; Skidmore Owings & Merrill Architects, senior designer, 1967-74; Stone & Webster Engineering Co, project architect, 1977-82; Lever Brothers & Co, Civil Division, project architect, 1983. **ORGANIZATIONS:** Art Students' League, 1950; MIT Women's Club, 1980; YWCA, currently. **HONORS/AWARDS:** Art Student League, NY, "Out of Town Scholarship" Award,

1950-51; Bronx Council for the Arts Award, pastel portrait, 1992, drawing, watercolor, oil painting, 1993. **SPECIAL ACHIEVEMENTS:** Senior designer; helped to create many notable public, institutional & highr-rise commercial buildings in US; designed many low-rise buildings serving industry; photographic work shown at MIT Show, IBM Little Gallery, NYC; paintings and sculpture at Vintage Art Gallery, Riverdale, NY; sterling silver jewelry designs at Elsa Mott Ives Gallery, NYC.

CHIN, HELEN
Organization administrator. Chinese American. **CAREER:** Commodore Stockton School, principal, currently. **ORGANIZATIONS:** Chinese for Affirmative Action, chair, board of trustees. **BUSINESS ADDRESS:** Chair, Board of Trustees, Chinese for Affirmative Action, 17 Walter U Lum Pl, San Francisco, CA 94108, (415)274-6750.*

CHIN, HENRY HAN
Dentist, university lecturer. Chinese American. **PERSONAL:** Born Mar 1, 1951, Guangzhou, People's Republic of China; son of Mr and Mrs Chong L Chin; married Garbo Wong Chin, Sep 4, 1988. **EDUCATION:** University of Washington, Seattle, BA, zoology, 1977, DDS, 1977, residency, 1977-78; Yeshiva University, Albert Einstein College of Medicine, certificate, general practice dental, certificate, UCP fellowship in pediatric dentistry and disabled children, 1979. **CAREER:** University of Washington, lecturer, 1980-; private practice, dentist, 1980-. **ORGANIZATIONS:** American Dental Assn, Seattle-King County and Washington State Dental Society, 1981-; American Society of Dentistry for Children, Washington State Chapter, scty, 1982, treasurer, 1983; Seattle Pankey Study Club, Dental, 1980-; Chinese Nursing Home Society, 1986-, bd mbr, exec bd mbr, vice pres, 1988; Northwest Asian American Dental Seminar, 1985-, president, 1992; L D Pankey Dental Alumni Assn, 1987-; Chinese Information & Service Center, bd mbr, 1981-85; Seattle Head Start Program, health advisory committee, co-chairperson, 1981-85. **SPECIAL ACHIEVEMENTS:** Co-author, Pedodontic Emergencies: Management of Medically Compromised Patients, 1987. **BUSINESS ADDRESS:** Dentist, Family Dentistry, 661 S Jackson St, Seattle, WA 98104, (206)621-1233.

CHIN, JOHN WAY
Pharmacist. Chinese American. **PERSONAL:** Born Feb 18, 1953, Brooklyn, NY; son of Hu Shee Chin (deceased) and Quong Hing Chin (deceased); married Rosalie Chin, Jun 24, 1973; children: Mark Anthony, Stephanie Su, Jeffrey Paul, Kimberly Ann. **EDUCATION:** New York University, 1974; Arnold and Marie Schwartz College of Pharmacy, BS, 1978, graduate studies, MS, 1982. **CAREER:** Brookdale Hospital, staff pharmacist, 1978-79, satellite clincal pharmacist, 1979-80, clinical coordinator, 1980-83; South Beach Psychiatric Center, supervising pharmacist, 1983-84; Weber's Phcy, manager, senior pharmacist, 1984-87; Brooklyn Central Phcy, owner, 1987-90; Manhattan Central Phcy Inc, d/b/a Clearfield Phcy, owner, president, 1988-. **ORGANIZATIONS:** American Pharmaceutical Assn, 1978-; Empire State Pharmaceutical Society, 1988-; American Society of Hospital Pharmacists, 1978-84; Alpha Zeta Omega Pharmaceutical Fraternity, 1977-. **HONORS/AWARDS:** Alpha Zeta Omega, Robert L Byck Award, Man of the Year, 1993. **BUSINESS ADDRESS:** President, Manhattan Central Phcy Inc, d/b/a Clearfield Pharmacy, 561 Grand St, New York, NY 10002, (212)677-0490.

CHIN, KATHERINE M.
Entertainment marketing executive. Chinese American. **PERSONAL:** Born Feb 20, 1965, Minneapolis, MN; daughter of Tony and Leeann. **EDUCATION:** Boston University, BS, 1987. **CAREER:** Clein & Feldman, jr account executive; Orion Pictures, National Promos, manager; Walt Disney, National Promos, manager; Fox Inc, Worldwide Promos, TV, vice president, currently. **ORGANIZATIONS:** Promotion Marketing Association of America, committee member; Asian Pacific Americans for Creative Quality; Coalition of Asian Pacifics in Entertainment. **BUSINESS ADDRESS:** Vice President, Worldwide Promotions, Television, 20th Century Fox Licensing & Merchandising, PO Box 900, Beverly Hills, CA 90213.

CHIN, KATHY HIRATA
Attorney. Japanese American. **PERSONAL:** Born Jul 3, 1953, Frankfurt-am-Main, Germany; daughter of Isao Hirata Jr & Mary Keeler Hirata; married Denny Chin, Jul 30, 1978; children: Paul, Christopher. **EDUCATION:** Princeton University, BA (magna cum laude), 1975; Columbia University School of Law, JD, 1980. **CAREER:** Cadwalader, Wickersham & Taft, associate, 1980-89, partner, 1990-. **ORGANIZATIONS:** Asian American Bar Association of

New York; New York County Lawyers Association; New York State Bar Association; Governor Mario M Cuomo's Judicial Screening Committee for the first Judicial Department, 1992-. **BUSINESS ADDRESS:** Partner, Cadwalader, Wickersham & Taft, 100 Maiden Ln, New York, NY 10038, (212)504-6542.

CHIN, KEN K.
Educator. Chinese American. **PERSONAL:** Born Nov 8, Shanghai, China; son of Shunpu Chin and Qunan Mei; married Rose G Chin; children: Iris Y. **EDUCATION:** Beijing Institute of Aeronautics, BS, aerodynamics, 1959; University of Georgia, MS, phys, 1982; Stanford University, PhD, appl phys, 1986. **CAREER:** University of Notre Dame, assistant research professor, 1986; New Jersey Institute of Technology, associate professor, beginning 1987, professor, 1992-. **ORGANIZATIONS:** APS, 1981; AVS, 1983. **HONORS/AWARDS:** Chinese Government, National Award for Best Popular Scientific Writing, 1981. **SPECIAL ACHIEVEMENTS:** Einstein, a Biography, China Youth Publication House, 1979; Faraday, a Biography, China Youth Publication House, 1981; M Faraday, article for Encyclopedia of China, 1982; over 40 publications in scientific journals; research areas include surface physics, semiconductor device physics, and materials science. **BUSINESS ADDRESS:** Professor, Dept of Physics, New Jersey Institute of Technology, Newark, NJ 07102, (201)596-3297.

CHIN, MARILYN MEI LING
Educator, poet. Chinese American. **PERSONAL:** Born Jan 14, 1955, Hong Kong; daughter of George & Rose Chin. **EDUCATION:** University of Massachusetts, BA, 1977; University of Iowa, MFA, 1981. **CAREER:** University of Iowa, teaching fellow, 1979, 1982, International Writing Program, translator, 1979-82; Stanford University, Stegner Fellow in Creative Writing, 1984-85; UCLA, visiting professor, 1990; University of California, San Diego, visiting professor, 1993; San Diego State University, associate professor, 1988-. **ORGANIZATIONS:** Academy of American Poets; Associated Writing Programs; PEN; Poets & Writers. **HONORS/AWARDS:** National Endowment for the Arts, poetry fellowship, 1985, 1983; Mary Roberts Rinehart Award in Poetry, 1983; Bay Area Book Reviewer's Association, award, best poetry book nomination, 1987; Yaddo, MacDowel Colony, VCCA. **SPECIAL ACHIEVEMENTS:** Author, The Phoenix Gone, The Terrace Empty, poems, 1994; Dwarf Bamboo, poems, 1987; The Selected Poems of Ai Ching, co-translations, 1985; Dissident Song: An Anthology of Asian American Literature, edited, 1992; included in the Norton Introduction to Poetry, 1991. **BIOGRAPHICAL SOURCES:** Chinese American Poetry, University of Washington Press, 1991; The Open Boat, Doubleday, 1993. **BUSINESS ADDRESS:** Associate Professor, Dept of English, San Diego State University, San Diego, CA 92182, (619)697-1941.

CHIN, MICHELLE LORRAINE
Senior legislative assistant. Chinese American. **PERSONAL:** Born Mar 4, 1969, Chicago, IL; daughter of Watson & Loan Chin. **EDUCATION:** Andrews University, BS, 1990; Southwestern Adventist College. **CAREER:** US Representative Joe Barton, senior legislative assistant, 1990-. **BUSINESS ADDRESS:** Senior Legislative Assistant, US Representative Joe Barton, 1514 Longworth House Office Bldg, Washington, DC 20515, (202)225-2002.

CHIN, MING WILLIAM
Judge. Chinese American. **PERSONAL:** Born Aug 31, 1942, Klamath Falls, OR. **EDUCATION:** University of San Francisco, BA, 1964, JD, 1967. **CAREER:** County of Alameda, dep district attorney, 1970-72; Aiken, Kramer & Cummings, partner, beginning 1972; California Court of Appeals, judge, currently. **ORGANIZATIONS:** California State Bar Association, 1970-; Alameda County Bar Association; California Trial Lawyers Association; American Trial Lawyers Association. **HONORS/AWARDS:** State Attorney General, Asian Pacific Heritage Award, 1992. **BUSINESS ADDRESS:** Judge, California Court of Appeals, 1st Dist Div 3 Marathon Plaza, South Tower, 303 Second St, Ste 600, San Francisco, CA 94107, (415)396-9780.*

CHIN, PAMELA GRACE
Attorney. Chinese American. **PERSONAL:** Born Apr 28, 1959, Malden, MA; daughter of Henry Sau Chin and Naida Lim Chin; married Marvin M Lager, Jun 9, 1989. **EDUCATION:** Harvard/Radcliffe College, BA, 1981; University of California, Los Angeles, Law School, JD, 1984. **CAREER:** Memel, Jacobs, Pierno, Gersh & Ellsworth, litigation attorney, 1984-86; Riordan & McKinzie, litigation attorney, 1986-88; Atlantic Richfield Co (ARCO), senior attorney, 1988-. **ORGANIZATIONS:** Southern California Chinese Lawyers Assn, pres-

ident, 1993-94; Legal Aid Foundation of Los Angeles, director, 1994-96; Leadership California,1993; California Women Lawyers, second vp, 1991-92; Asian Pacific American Legal Center, executive advisory board member, 1993-94. **SPECIAL ACHIEVEMENTS:** Member of mayor-elect Richard J Riordan's transition team, 1993. **BUSINESS ADDRESS:** Senior Attorney, Atlantic Richfield Co, 515 S Flower St, 46th Fl, Los Angeles, CA 90071, (213)486-3895.

CHIN, PATRICK K.

Physician. Chinese American. **PERSONAL:** Born Aug 14, 1963, Summit, NJ; son of Gilbert & Ginie Chin. **EDUCATION:** Massachusetts Institute of Technology, SB, 1985; UMD-New Jersey Medical School, MD, 1989. **CAREER:** UMDNJ-University Hospital, intern, 1989-90; Immediate Health Care Medical Center, physician, 1990-91; St Mary's Hospital, emergency room physician, 1990-92; NYU Medical Center, resident, 1991-. **ORGANIZATIONS:** American Medical Association; Association for Research in Vision and Ophthalmology; American Academy of Ophthalmology; Contact Lens Association of America; American Society for Cataract & Refractive Surgery. **SPECIAL ACHIEVEMENTS:** Numerous publications in trade journals; several presentations at ophthalmic conferences. **HOME ADDRESS:** 54 Roland Rd, Murray Hill, NJ 07974.

CHIN, RAYMOND J.

Clinical psychologist. Chinese American. **PERSONAL:** Born Jul 22, 1950, Wilmington, DE; son of Loy Chin and Annie Chin; married Mary Chin, Dec 27, 1972; children: Jason, Michael. **EDUCATION:** University of Delaware, BS, 1973; Rhode Island School of Design, MFA, 1975; Michigan State University, PhD, 1986; Harvard Medical School, fellow in psychology. **CAREER:** Rhode Island School for the Deaf, art teacher/therapist, 1977-79; Scituate Junior-Senior High School, art teacher, 1979-80; Rhode Island College, instructor, art education, 1980-81; West Central Services, Behavioral Medicine Service, coordinator, 1986-89; private practice, clinical psychologist, 1989-; Dartmouth Hitchcock Medical Center, adjunct asst professor of pediatrics & psychiatry, 1993-. **ORGANIZATIONS:** Treacher Collins Foundation, board of directors, 1992-; Asian-American Psychological Assn; American Psychological Assn, Division of Child Clinical Psychology; National Register of Health Providers in Psychology. **HONORS/AWARDS:** CIC Minorities Fellowship, 1981-85; Michigan State University, fellowship, 1981; Rhode Island School of Design, fellowship, 1973-75. **SPECIAL ACHIEVEMENTS:** Clinical psychologist specializing in pediatric behavioral medicine; co-author: "Behavioral Medicine Treatment of an Adolescent with Cystic Fibrosis: A Model of Coping with Chronic Illness," Casebook in Adolescent Behavior Therapy, Springer, 1990. **BUSINESS ADDRESS:** Adjunct Asst Professor of Pediatrics and Psychiatry, Dartmouth Hitchcock Medical Center, PO Box 31, Lyme, NH 03768, (603)643-9252.

CHIN, ROBERT ALLEN

Educator. Chinese American. **PERSONAL:** Born Oct 3, 1950, San Francisco, CA; son of Suey Hey & Stella Chin; married Susan Fleming, Jun 18, 1976. **EDUCATION:** University of Northern Colorado, BA, 1974; Ball State University, MAE, 1975; Community College of the Air Force, AAS, 1982; University of Maryland, College Park, PhD, 1986. **CAREER:** University of Northern Colorado, lab assistant, 1973-74; Ball State University, graduate teaching assistant, 1974-75; Washington Senior High School, instructor, 1975-79; University of Maryland, College Park, instructor, 1979-86; East Carolina University, assistant professor, acting chairman, 1989-90, assistant professor, 1986-92, associate professor, 1992-; US Air Force, ssg, 1968-72; South Dakota Air National Guard, ssg, 1977-79; District of Columbia Air National Guard, ssg, 1979-83, major, 1983-. **ORGANIZATIONS:** Pitt County Veterans Council, 1992-; Air Force Association, Eastern Carolina Chapter, secretary, 1988-92, president, 1992-; National Association of Industrial Technology, research committee, 1992-, journal review board, 1993-; American Society for Engineering Education, Southeastern Section, Engineering Graphics Div, chair, 1992-, journal board of review, 1988-; National Association of Industrial and Technical Teacher Educators, journal reviewer, 1987-; Council on Technology Teacher Education, Undergraduate Studies Committee, 1988-92; Iota Lambda Sigma, Nu Chapter, vp, 1984-85, president, 1985-86; Intl Technology Education Assn, 1974-. **HONORS/AWARDS:** National Association of Industrial Technology, certified senior industrial technologist, 1992; Epsilon Pi Tau; Phi Kappa Phi, laureate citation, 1981, 1991. **SPECIAL ACHIEVEMENTS:** "An Assessment of Research Activities in Engineering Design Graphics," Engineering Design Graphics Journal, 1993; "A Bibliometric Analysis of the Journal of Industrial Technology," Journal of Industrial Technology, 1992; "Profile and

Practices of Contributors to the Engineering Design Graphics Journal," Engineering Design Graphics Journal, 1991; numerous others. **MILITARY SERVICE:** Numerous honors including: Air Force Outstanding Unit Award, oak leaf clusters, 1972, 1991, 1992; National Defense Service Medal, bronze star, 1991; Armed Forces Reserve Medal, 1987; District of Columbia Community Service Ribbon, 1983; Reserve Forces, Meritorious Service Medal, 1982; National Defense Service Medal, 1968. **BUSINESS ADDRESS:** Associate Professor, Dept of Industrial Technology, East Carolina University, Flanagan Bldg, Greenville, NC 27858-4353, (919)757-4146.

CHIN, STANLEY H.

Educational administrator. Chinese American. **CAREER:** Los Medanos College, president, currently. **BUSINESS ADDRESS:** President, Los Medanos College, 2700 E Leland Rd, Pittsburg, CA 94565-5197, (510)439-2181.*

CHIN, STEVEN ALEXANDER

Journalist. Chinese American. **PERSONAL:** Born Aug 9, 1959, New York, NY; son of Leslie Chin and Ada Chin. **EDUCATION:** Duke University, BA, 1981; New York University, MA, American history, 1986. **CAREER:** San Francisco Examiner, reporter, 1988-. **ORGANIZATIONS:** Asian American Journalists Association, San Francisco Bay Area Chapter, board member, 1991, 1993-. **HONORS/AWARDS:** Asian American Journalists Association, First Place Asian American Issues, National Award, 1992; Society of Professional Journalists, N California, Outstanding Young Journalist Award, 1991. **SPECIAL ACHIEVEMENTS:** Author, When Justice Failed: The Fred Korematsu Story, children book, 1993; author, Dragon Parade: A Chinese New Year Story, children's book, 1993. **BUSINESS ADDRESS:** Reporter, San Francisco Examiner, PO Box 7260, San Francisco, CA 94120, (415)777-7889.

CHIN, STEVEN HAN-HOY

Educator. Chinese American. **PERSONAL:** Born Sep 27, 1957, Bronx, NY; son of Herbert Chin and Yiu Chin; married Jacqueline Chin, Oct 28, 1985; children: Elena, Victor. **EDUCATION:** Rutgers College of Engineering, BSEE, 1979; Johns Hopkins University, MSEE, 1982; Rutgers Graduate School, PhD, electrical engineering, 1987. **CAREER:** Westinghouse Electrical Corp, design engineer, 1979-82; American Systems Corp, technical staff, 1987-88; Catholic University, assistant professor, 1988-. **ORGANIZATIONS:** Registered Professional Engineer, 1991-; Institute of Electrical & Electronic Engineers, 1978-; International Neural Network Society, 1991-92. **HONORS/AWARDS:** Tau Beta Pi, 1978; Eta Kappa Nu, 1978. **SPECIAL ACHIEVEMENTS:** Numerous publications in the areas of communication engineering and signal processing, including, but not limited to, contributions to IEEE Globecom, Journal of The Acoustical Society of America, ASME Press Book, Elsevier Science Publishers. **BUSINESS ADDRESS:** Asst Professor, Dept of Electrical Engineering, Catholic University, Washington, DC 20064, (212)319-4784.

CHIN, TAMERA ANN (TAMMY)

Product manager. Chinese American/Taiwanese American. **PERSONAL:** Born Jul 9, 1969, Hayward, CA; daughter of Edward Chin and Marjorie Chin. **EDUCATION:** Wellesley College, 1991. **CAREER:** Mayor's Office of Consumer Affairs, investigator, 1989; City Transport, marketing manager, 1990; Colgate-Palmolive, currently. **ORGANIZATIONS:** Friends of Project One City, exec planning committee, 1992-93; Inter-Collegiate Asian Social Committee, president, 1990. **HONORS/AWARDS:** Monterey Park Mayor's Office, Outstanding Citizenship, 1990; Veterans of Foreign Wars, Speech Contest Winner, 1987; Bank of America, Social Studies Scholar, 1987. **SPECIAL ACHIEVEMENTS:** Chaired Winter Whirl on Ice, Charity Ice Skating Show, starring Asian talent, including Olympic & World Class skaters. **BUSINESS ADDRESS:** Colgate-Palmolive, 300 Park Ave, FL-9, New York, NY 10022.

CHIN, THOMAS

Business executive. Chinese American. **PERSONAL:** Born Jul 18, 1934, Boston, MA; son of Edwin K S Chin & Mary Chin; married May Y Chin, Jun 5, 1960; children: Janice E, Lawrence T. **EDUCATION:** Harvard College, AB, 1956, Graduate School of Business, MBA, 1961. **CAREER:** Raytheon Company, programs financial control manager, 1978-83, Government Accounting Policy, manager, 1983-. **ORGANIZATIONS:** Mass Board of Education, 1992-; Chinese Historical Society of NE, director, 1992-; So Cove Nursing Home, treasurer, director, 1988-; Institute of Management of Accounting, director, 1962-; National Contract Management Association, treasurer, vice president, director, 1979-; National Cont Management Association, fellow, 1987. **MILITARY SERVICE:** US Army, US Army Reserve, colonel, 1953-

86. **BUSINESS ADDRESS:** Manager, Govt Accounting Policy, Raytheon Company, 141 Spring St, Executive Offices, Lexington, MA 02173, (617)860-2421.

CHIN, WILLIAM NIGEL

Educator. Chinese American. **PERSONAL:** Born Jul 1, 1957, Minneapolis, MN; son of Leeann & Tony Chin; married Esther Beneish, Aug 5, 1991. **EDUCATION:** University of Wisconsin, PhD, 1985. **CAREER:** University of Texas, Austin, assistant professor, 1985-88; De Paul University, associate professor, 1988-. **ORGANIZATIONS:** Teaching Assistants Association, AFT #3220, executive board, 1982-85, co-president, 1984-85; American Mathematics Society, 1985-; Organization of Chinese Americans, 1993. **BUSINESS ADDRESS:** Professor, Dept of Mathematics, De Paul University, 2214 N Kenmore, Chicago, IL 60614, (312)362-5170.

CHIN, WINIFRED C.

Educator. Chinese American. **PERSONAL:** Born Apr 14, 1952, Brooklyn, NY; daughter of Tung Pok Chin (deceased) and Chin Mark Ting Fong. **EDUCATION:** Taipei Language Institute, Taiwan, 1972; Brooklyn College of CUNY, BA, 1974; Seton Hall University, Chinese-English bilingual certification, Asian studies, 1974-75; New York University, MA, 1978. **CAREER:** Simple Elegance, president, 1980-88; Ramaz Yeshiva, general studies teacher, 1986-88; St Francis College, professor of Religious Studies, 1989-. **SPECIAL ACHIEVEMENTS:** Poetry publications in various US anthologies, 1978-88; guest lecturer, Chinese studies, 1990-; proficiency in Chinese, German, Spanish; novel in progress; textbook in progress. **HOME ADDRESS:** 1345 East 4th St, #4F, Brooklyn, NY 11230. **BUSINESS ADDRESS:** Professor, St Francis College, 180 Remsen St, Room 614R, Brooklyn, NY 11201-4398, (718)522-2300.

CHIN, YEE WAH

Attorney. Chinese American. **PERSONAL:** Born Nov 23, 1952, Hong Kong; daughter of Yook Fan Chin and Sau Ling Chiu Chin. **EDUCATION:** Massachusetts Institute of Technology, SB, mathematics, 1974; Columbia University, JD, 1977. **CAREER:** Shea & Gould, associate, partner, 1977-. **ORGANIZATIONS:** Association of the Bar of the City of New York, 1991-93, Committee on International Trade, chair, 1993-, Commitee on Antitrust Trade Regulations, 1987-91, Antitrust Subcommittee of Committee on US in a Global Economy, 1992-; ABA Antitrust Section Task Force on NAFTA, 1993, 1992 Proposed NAAG Merger Guidelines, 1992, Handbook on the Premerger Process, 1993. **SPECIAL ACHIEVEMENTS:** "HSR Penalties: A Banner Year," Clayton's Commentaries, 1991; "Age of Consent: Living and Thriving with the Consent Decree," Oculus, 1990-91; "Prohibitions Against Bid Rigging and Price Fixing," Cornerstone, 1992. **BUSINESS ADDRESS:** Partner, Shea & Gould, 1251 Ave of the Americas, New York, NY 10020-1193, (212)827-3616.

CHIN, YIN-LIEN CHEN

Educator. Chinese American. **PERSONAL:** Born Jun 29, 1930, Zhoushan, Zhejiang, China; daughter of Man-sheng Chen & Lan-ying Pao; married Tsung Chin, Jan 29, 1955; children: Hsiao-lien Chin Boardman, Stephen Hsiao-tsung Chin. **EDUCATION:** Natl Taiwan Normal University, BA, Chinese literature, 1953; Georgetown University, MS, linguistics, 1972. **CAREER:** Taipei First Girls High Sch, Chinese literature teacher, 1953-55; Taiwan Normal Univ High Sch, Chinese literature teacher, 1955-63; Taipei American Sch, Chinese teacher, 1959-60; Cornell Center, Inter-Univ Prog for Chinese Lang Studies, Chinese instructor, 1960-63; Cornell Univ, visiting asst prof of Chinese, 1968, 1970; Stanford Center, Inter-Univ Prog for Chinese Lang Studies, Chinese instructor, 1963-65; Univ of Maryland, Taipei Ctr, Chinese instructor, 1965; St Albans Intl Seminars, Chinese instructor, 1966-; US State Dept Foreign Service Inst, Chinese instructor, 1966-67; Vassar Coll, asst prof of Chinese, 1967-73, assoc prof of Chinese, 1973-81, acting dir of East Asian Studies, 1978, 1981, 1985, acting dir of Asian studies, 1991, prof of Chinese, 1981-. **ORGANIZATIONS:** Calligraphy Education Group of Chinese Language Teachers Assn, associate chairperson, 1992; Assn for Students interested in Asia, advisor, 1978-; Poughkeepsie Chinese Culture Club, chairman, 1986-87, 1989, 1992; MS Society, fundraiser, 1990, 1991, 1992; Mid-Hudson Chinese Community Assn, founding member, board of directors, president, 1969-71, 1980-82, 1984-86, 1993-94. **HONORS/AWARDS:** Teachers College of Shaanxi United University, China, honorary professorship, 1992; Association of Chinese Language and Literature of the Republic of China, award, outstanding achievement in teaching Chinese, 1972. **SPECIAL ACHIEVEMENTS:** "Teaching Calligraphy at the College Level," paper at ACTFL-CLTA annual convention, Nov 1990; Stone Lion & Other Chinese Detective Stories: The Wisdom of Lord Bau, 1992; "What Makes a Calligraphy Educator," paper at ACTFL-CLTA annual convention, November 1992; chairman of panel on teaching methodology, first Intl Conference on the Teaching of Chinese as a Second Language, Taiwan, 1985; table tennis singles: Dutchess County, first place, 1993; NY State, Gold Metal, 1993; Mid-Hudson Chinese Language School, founder, 1968; Language through Literature, 1980; Dragons in the Flowery Land: An Introduction to Chinese History and Literature, 1985; Traditional Chinese Folktales, 1989; Chinese landscape paintings on display in the Hall of Asian People, American Museum of Natural History. **BIOGRAPHICAL SOURCES:** Contemporary Authors, Gale Research, Inc. **HOME PHONE:** (914)454-5518. **BUSINESS ADDRESS:** Professor of Chinese, Vassar College, Box 311, Poughkeepsie, NY 12601.

CHING, ANTHONY B.

Attorney. Chinese American. **PERSONAL:** Born Nov 18, 1935, Shanghai, China; son of William L K Ching and Christina Ching; married Nancy Ann Prigge, Apr 10, 1961; children: Anthony Jr, Alice, Alexander, Andrew, Ann, Audrey, Anastasia, Albert. **EDUCATION:** Universite Catholique de L'Ouest, 1953-54; Cambridgeshire Technical College, 1954-55; University of Cambridge, matriculated, 1955; St John's College, 1956; University of Arizona, BS, geology, 1959, JD, 1965; Harvard University, LLM, 1971. **CAREER:** Duval Sulphur, Potash and American Smelting and Refining, geologist; Marum and Marum Engineers, engineer, 1961-65; private law practice, 1965-66; Pima County Legal Aid Society, chief trial counsel, 1966-70; Harvard University, Harvard Law School, fellow in clinical legal education, 1970-71; Loyola University of Los Angeles, law professor, 1971-73, 1974-75, adjunct professor, 1982; Hawaii Legal Services, visiting director of litigation, project director, 1973-74; State of Arizona, chief counsel economic protection division, 1975-79, solicitor general, 1979-91, Civil Division, assistant attorney general, 1991-; Maricopa County, superior court judge pro tem, 1984-93; Arizona Court of Appeals, judge pro tem, 1994. **ORGANIZATIONS:** American Bar Association; State Bar of Arizona, chairman, legal services committee, 1992-93; National Legal Aid and Defender Association, treasurer, 1973-74; National Consumer Law Center, president, 1979-; Western Attorneys General Litigation Committee, chairman, 1983-86; Los Angeles Legal Aid Foundation, board member, 1971-73; Harvard Law School Association of Arizona, president, 1980-83; Young Democrats of Greater Tucson, president, 1969-70. **HONORS/AWARDS:** National Legal Aid and Defender Association, Reginald Heber Smith Award, 1969; OEO Legal Services, Runner up, Most Outstanding Attorney, 1968. **HOME ADDRESS:** 2632 S Faifield Dr, Tempe, AZ 85282.

CHING, CHEE

Educator. Chinese American. **PERSONAL:** Born Jun 23, 1961, Taiwan; daughter of Chien-Wen Ching and Ya-Chin T Ching; married Benjamin Yih-Chih Tang, Dec 5, 1988. **EDUCATION:** National Taiwan University, BS, 1983; University of South Carolina, MS, 1985; Purdue University, PhD, 1988. **CAREER:** Purdue University, visiting assistant professor, 1988-89; Arizona State University, assistant professor, 1989-. **ORGANIZATIONS:** American Chinese Management Educators' Assn, vice president, 1992-93; North America Chinese Information Systems Professors' Assn, vice president, 1991-93; Arizona State University, Asian Faculty & Staff Assn, executive board member, 1992-93. **BUSINESS ADDRESS:** Prof, Dept of Decision & Information Systems, Arizona State University, College of Business, Tempe, AZ 85287-0001, (602)965-6955.

CHING, DEBORAH F.

Non-profit agency administrator. Chinese American. **PERSONAL:** Born Nov 25, 1949, Hong Kong; daughter of George Ta-Min Ching and Tsui Lin Chan; married Mark M Mayeda, Aug 23, 1980; children: Asia, Emily, Kenyon. **EDUCATION:** University of California, Los Angeles, BA, psychology, 1971; University of Southern California, MPA, 1977. **CAREER:** Project HEAVY-West, director of Program Development, 1977-78; International Institute of LA, administrative director, 1978-80; Chinatown Service Center, deputy executive director, 1980-82, 1984-88, executive director, 1989-. **ORGANIZATIONS:** Rebuild Los Angeles, board, 1993-; Asian Pacific Planning Council, pres, 1992-, vp, 1990-92; Asian Pacific Americans for a New LA, steering comm, 1992-; Multi-Cultural Collaborative, steering comm, 1992-; Asian Pacific Health Care Venture, secretary, 1992-, pres, 1991-92, bd of dirs, 1989-; Natl Asian Pacific American Families Against Substance Abuse, bd of dirs, 1989-93; Asian Pacific Islander Advisory Comm to State of California, Dept of Alcohol & Drug Programs, chair, 1990-; Los Angeles County Alcohol & Drug Master Plan, advisory bd, 1991-; Chinese Immigrant Service Agencies Network Intl, 1984-, conference chair, 1990, executive comm & communications chair, 1991-92; LA Chinatown Mobility Action Steering Comm, 1991-; California Healthy Cities Project, Monterey Park Steering Comm, 1990-. **HONORS/AWARDS:** Volunteers of America, Community Service Award, 1991; Central City Optimist Club, Community Service Award, 1992. **BUSINESS ADDRESS:** Executive Director, Chinatown Service Center, 767 N Hill St, Ste 400, Los Angeles, CA 90012, (213)680-9956.

CHING, GALE LIN FONG
Attorney. Chinese American. **PERSONAL:** Born Nov 27, 1954, Honolulu, HI; son of Richard and Helen Ching; married Janice R Ching, Oct 4, 1986; children: Kelsey K, Jennifer G L. **EDUCATION:** University of Hawaii, BA, 1976; University of Gonzaga, School of Law, JD, 1980. **CAREER:** Honorable Ernest Kubota, law clerk, bailiff, 1980-81; Office of the Prosecuting Attorney, deputy prosecuting attorney, 1981-86; Office of Attorney General, deputy attorney general, 1986-90; Tam, O'Connor, & Henderson, attorney, 1990-. **ORGANIZATIONS:** Hawaii State Bar Association, 1980-; US Court of Appeals for Ninth Circuit, 1981-; US District Court for District of Hawaii, 1980-. **BUSINESS ADDRESS:** Attorney, Tam, O'Connor & Henderson, 220 S King St, Central Pacific Plaza, 20th Fl, Honolulu, HI 96813, (808)545-3030.

CHING, HARVEY CHO WING
Pastor, educator. Chinese American. **PERSONAL:** Born Jan 7, 1950, Honolulu, HI; son of Thomas E L & Violet A Ching; married Alanna Y Ching, Jun 29, 1975; children: Daniel J, Matthew M. **EDUCATION:** International College & Graduate School, BA, 1977, DMin, 1990; Dallas Theological Seminary, MABS, 1981. **CAREER:** International College & Graduate School, department chairman, Bible & Biblical Languages Dept, professor, 1981-; Hawaiian Puppet Moving Co, founder, director, 1985-; Kaneohe Congregational Church, senior pastor, 1981-. **ORGANIZATIONS:** Fellowship of Christian Magicians, 1990-. **MILITARY SERVICE:** Navy, airman, 1969-73. **BUSINESS ADDRESS:** Pastor, Kaneohe Congregational Church, 45-114 Waikapoki Rd, Kaneohe, HI 96744, (808)235-2764.

CHING, HUGH
Scientist, business executive. Chinese American. **EDUCATION:** Massachusetts Institute of Technology, BS, 1965, MS, 1966, ScD, 1970. **CAREER:** Courant Institute of Mathematical Sciences, associate scientist, 1970-73; National Tsing Hua University, associate professor, 1973-74; Ames Research Center, subcontractor, 1974-75; World-Wide Institute of Valuation, president, 1976-. **ORGANIZATIONS:** World-Wide Institute of Valuation, founder, 1977-; Institute of Post-Scientific Research, director, 1992-. **HONORS/AWARDS:** Watson Award, nominator; Presidential Medal of Science, nominator. **SPECIAL ACHIEVEMENTS:** Discoverer, Quantitative Theory of Value, Solution to Value, 1972; Generalized Fluid Description (Plasma Physics), 1972; World-Wide Valuation System, 1975; discoverer, Self-generating Software System, 1987. **BIOGRAPHICAL SOURCES:** World Journal, San Francisco, Dec 28, 1988, June 13, 1991, July 1, 1992; The Nineties, Hong Kong, p 86, Sept 1991. **BUSINESS ADDRESS:** President, World-Wide Institute of Valuation, PO Box 461, Berkeley, CA 94701, (510)655-7582.

CHING, JOSEPH YU NUN
Banker. Chinese American. **PERSONAL:** Born Feb 8, 1940, Yokohama, Japan; son of Ah Zai Ching and Shu Li CHing; married Audrey, Dec 25, 1979; children: Matt, Melinda; stepchildren: Cameron Sun, Serena Sun. **EDUCATION:** St Joseph College, Yokohama, Japan, 1949-60; St Mary's University, San Antonio, BA, 1964, MA, 1965. **CAREER:** Bank of America, vice pres, 1965-88; Comerica Bank-California, regional vice president, 1988-92; Commercial Bank of Fremont, pres, CEO, 1993-. **ORGANIZATIONS:** Ohlone College, Fremont, bd member, 1992-; Washington Hospital Foundation, bd member, 1991-; Rotary Club, 1991-; South Bay Self Help for the Elderly, bd member. **HOME ADDRESS:** 1440 Tarrytown St, San Mateo, CA 94402, (415)573-9314. **BUSINESS PHONE:** (510)794-7700.

CHING, MARVIN K. L.
Educator. Chinese American. **PERSONAL:** Born Aug 23, 1934, Honolulu, HI; son of Tai Lok Ching and Florence Ching; married Bertha T Ching, Aug 23, 1958; children: Bruce M, Noelani L H. **EDUCATION:** University of Hawaii, BEd, 1956, 5th year education certificate, 1957, MA, 1968; Florida State University, PhD, 1975. **CAREER:** Department of Education, State of Hawaii, teacher, language arts coordinator, 1957-72; Memphis State University, professor of English, 1974-. **ORGANIZATIONS:** Southern Conference on Linguistics, 1975-, past president, 1985; American Dialect Society, 1981-; Linguistic Society of America, 1981-. **HONORS/AWARDS:** University of Chicago,

Department of English, NEH Summer Fellowship for "Dialectology," with Raven I McDavid, Jr, 1980; University of California, Davis, Department of Rhetoric, NEH Summer Fellowship for "Ciceronian Rhetoric and Its Influence on Modern Writing," with James J Murphy, 1984; Educational Testing Service, invitation to read the Achievement Composition Test, Princeton, New Jersey, 1986, 1984, 1982, 1981. **SPECIAL ACHIEVEMENTS:** Co-translator w/Gong Zhengming, "China in the Last Decade before Tiananmen Square," Collages & Bricolages: The Journal of International Writing: 1, p. 7-53, 1993; author, "Chinese Color Terms," The SECOL (Southeastern Conference on Linguistics) Review 14, p 143-167, 1990; "Ma'am and Sir: Modes of Mitigation and Politeness in the Southern United States," Methods in Dialectology, ed, Alan R Thomas, England, Multilingual Matters, p 20-45, 1988. **BUSINESS ADDRESS:** Professor, English Dept, Memphis State University, Memphis, TN 38152-0001, (901)678-4520.

CHING, STANTON SAKAE HONG YAT
Educator. Chinese American/Japanese American. **PERSONAL:** Born Jan 8, 1962, Honolulu, HI; son of Wilbert Ching and Doris Ching. **EDUCATION:** Pomona College, BA, 1984; Northwestern University, PhD, 1988. **CAREER:** Connecticut College, assistant professor of chemistry, 1990-. **ORGANIZATIONS:** American Chemical Society, 1985-; Council on Undergraduate Research, 1991-; American Association for the Advancement of Science, 1992-. **SPECIAL ACHIEVEMENTS:** 13 published research articles in areas of inorganic chemistry and electrochemistry. **BUSINESS ADDRESS:** Assistant Professor of Chemistry, Connecticut College, 270 Mohegan Avenue, Hale Laboratory, New London, CT 06320, (203)439-2753.

CHING, THEODORA LAM
Artist, educator. Chinese American. **PERSONAL:** Born Sep 21, 1941, Honolulu, HI; daughter of Howard T F & Caroline W Lam; married Chauncey T K Ching, Jul 7, 1962; children: Donna Ching Foster, Cory David. **EDUCATION:** University of Nevada, Reno, BA, 1977; University of Hawaii, MFA, 1988. **CAREER:** Floral designer, 1962-; artist, 1982-; National Indian Council on Aging, consultant, 1992-. **ORGANIZATIONS:** Corcoran Gallery of Art, docent, 1991-; Artist in Residence, Washoe County School System, 1971-72. **SPECIAL ACHIEVEMENTS:** University of Hawaii, Commons Gallery Group Exhibition, "An Exhibition on Peace," 1988; University of Hawaii, Commons Gallery MFA thesis exhibition, "The ways I become my mother, her sister and my great-grandfather," 1988; University of Hawaii, Kennedy Theater, "Self Images," 1987; Queen Emma Gallery, "Tenth Anniversary Invitational Exhibition '77-'87," 1987; Marinda Lee Gallery, "Four by Four," 1987; Queen Emma Gallery, "Look, she still has her head in a bowl of jook!," 1986; numerous others. **HOME ADDRESS:** 2737 Devonshire Pl NW 323, Washington, DC 20008.

CHING, WAI-YIM
Educator, research scientist. Chinese American. **PERSONAL:** Born Oct 18, 1945, Shaoshing, Zhejiang, China; son of Di-Son Ching and Hung-Wong Sung; married Mon Yin Lung, Dec 27, 1975; children: Tianyu, Kunyu. **EDUCATION:** University of Hong Kong, BS, 1969; Louisiana State University, MS, 1971, PhD, 1974. **CAREER:** University of Wisconsin, research associate, lecturer, 1974-78; University of Missouri, Kansas City, assistant professor, 1978-81, associate professor, 1981-84, professor, 1984-88, curators' professor, 1988-, chairman of physics, 1990-. **ORGANIZATIONS:** American Physical Society, 1973-; American Association for Adv Science, 1978-; American Vacuum Society, 1982-; Materials Research Society, 1985-; American Ceramic Society, 1989-; Sigma Xi, 1979-. **HONORS/AWARDS:** University of Missouri, KC, NT Veatch Award for Distinguished Research, 1985; UKC-Trustees Faculty Fellowship, 1984, 1990. **SPECIAL ACHIEVEMENTS:** Research in theoretical condensed matters physics and materials sciences, study of electronic, magnetic, optical, dynamic, structural and superconducting properties of ordered and disordered solids; publications in major physics journals; grantee from US Department of Energy and Department of Navy. **BUSINESS ADDRESS:** Professor, Dept of Physics, University of Missouri-Kansas City, 4747 Troost, Room 227, Kansas City, MO 64110, (816)235-2503.

CHIN-LEE, CYNTHIA DENISE
Writer, business executive. Chinese American. **PERSONAL:** Born Oct 14, 1958, Washington, DC; daughter of William Chin-Lee and Nancy Chin-Lee; married Andrew John Pan, Apr 3, 1983; children: Vanessa Christine Pan. **EDUCATION:** National Taiwan Normal University, 1978-79; Harvard University, BA, 1980; East-West Center, 1980-81. **CAREER:** Clement Chen & Associates, assistant purchasing agent, 1981; Crocker National Bank, senior

procedures analyst, 1982-83; Storage Technology Corp, senior technical writer, 1983-84; Tandem Computers, senior technical writer, 1984-85; ESL, software technical writer, 1985-86; DeAnza College, instructor, 1985-88; Santa Clara University, adjunct lecturer, 1988-93; Precisely Write, president, 1986-; multimedia and software, consultant, 1993-. **ORGANIZATIONS:** Tandem Toastmasters, founder, 1985-; Organization of Chinese Americans, 1986-92, San Mateo Chapter, president, 1988; Asian Business League of San Francisco, 1982-84, board member, 1982; Society for Technical Communication, Silicon Valley, 1983-, vice president, 1985-88; Society of Children's Book Writers and Illustrators, 1992-. **HONORS/AWARDS:** Menlo Atherton Computer Academy, Outstanding Mentor, 1987; Organization of Chinese Americans, Outstanding Service, 1990; East-West Center, fellowship, 1980-81; White House, Presidential Scholar, 1976; Veterans of Foreign Wars, Voice of Democracy State Orator, 1976. **SPECIAL ACHIEVEMENTS:** Republican National Convention, delegate, 1980; childrens book, Almond Cookies and Dragon Well Tea, Polychrome Publishing Corp, 1993; It's Who You Know: Career Strategies for Making Effective Personal Contacts, Pfeiffer and Co, 1st printing, 1991, 2nd printing, 1993. **BUSINESS ADDRESS:** President, Precisely Write, PO Box 1276, Palo Alto, CA 94301, (415)327-2144.

CHINN, DAISY WONG

Association administrator. Chinese American. **PERSONAL:** Born Nov 8, 1908, San Francisco, CA; daughter of Walter F Wong & Annie Haw; married; children: Walter Wayne. **EDUCATION:** University of California, Berkeley. **CAREER:** Western Union Telegraph Co, teletypist, branch office, San Francisco, manager, 1930-71. **ORGANIZATIONS:** Square and Circle Chinese Women's Service Club, Inc, co-founder, 1924, president, 1973-74, 1993-94; Chinese Historical Society of America, charter, life member. **SPECIAL ACHIEVEMENTS:** Chinese Historical Society of America, first woman president, 1973-74; edits monthly newsletter "Bulletin", 1966-80; writing and editing the weekly "Chinese Digest", 1935-37, the first English language newspaper for Chinese Americans in the US.

CHINN, ROGER

Architect, city official. Chinese American. **PERSONAL:** Born May 22, 1933, Isleton, CA; son of Gee Chinn and Bessie Chinn; married Rachel H Chinn, Feb 10, 1961; children: Annette D, Robert M. **EDUCATION:** University of California, Berkeley, AB, architecture, 1957. **CAREER:** Roger Chinn Architect AIA, sole owner, principal, 1968-; Hertzka & Knowles, Architects, general partner, 1972-77; City of Foster City, councilman, 1980-, mayor, 1981, 1984, 1985, 1989 & 1991. **ORGANIZATIONS:** Lions Clubs International, district governor, 1983-84; Foster City Lions Club, president, 1972-73; Foster City Chinese Club, president, 1974-75; American Institute of Architects, corporate member, 1968-; Foster City Blood Bank, co-founder, 1968; San Francisco International Airport and Community Roundtable, chairman, 1982-93; Foster City Planning Commission, chairman, 1973-79; Community Development Agency, Foster City, president, 5 terms. **HONORS/AWARDS:** University of California, Berkeley School of Architecture, Design Prize, 1956; Lions Clubs International District, Lion of the Year, 1974; Foster City Lions Club, Lion of the Year, 1969; Lions Eye Foundation, Helen Keller Fellow, 1988. **MILITARY SERVICE:** US Army, Corps of Engineers, sp4, 1958-60. **BIOGRAPHICAL SOURCES:** Chinese American Historical Biographical Project, 1983. **HOME ADDRESS:** 833 Constitution Dr, Foster City, CA 94404, (415)345-2877. **BUSINESS ADDRESS:** Principal, Roger Chinn Architect AIA, 1485 Bayshore Blvd, Ste 305, San Francisco, CA 94124, (415)468-0787.

CHINN, THOMAS WAYNE

Typesetting company executive (retired), historian, consultant. Chinese American. **PERSONAL:** Born Jul 28, 1909, Marshfield, OR; son of Chinn Wing & Lee Shee Chinn; married Daisy Lorraine Wong Chinn, Jun 8, 1930; children: Walter Wayne. **EDUCATION:** Healds College, University of California Extension Center, San Francisco. **CAREER:** Typographer, beginning 1935; Chinese Digest, founder, editor, copublisher, 1935-37; Chinese News, founder, publisher, editor, 1940-42; US Army Quartermaster General's Office, civilian executive, 1942-49; Gollan Typography, president, 1949-80; Asian Week, consultant, currently. **ORGANIZATIONS:** American Revolution Bicentennial Administration National Advisory Committee on Racial, Ethnic and Native American Participation, 1975-76; Chinese Historical Society of America, cofounder, 1963, president, 1963-66, 1975, research papers editor, 1963-, Bulletin, editor, currently; Mayor's Citizens Committee, San Francisco's Annual Birthday, 1966-; Society of California Pioneers, 1966-; California Historical Society, 1970-; Westerners, San Francisco Chorale, 1968-; E Clampus

Vitus, Yerba Buena Chapter, 1942-. **HONORS/AWARDS:** California Historical Society, Award of Merit, 1970; Conference of California Historical Societies, Award of Merit, 1976, 1982. **SPECIAL ACHIEVEMENTS:** A History of Chinese in California, editor, 1969-; author, Bridging the Pacific—San Francisco, Chinatown, and It's People, 1989, A Historian's Reflection on Chinese-American Life in San Francisco, 1919-91, 1993. **BIOGRAPHICAL SOURCES:** Asian Week, March 26, 1993.

CHIOGIOJI, MELVIN H.

Power company executive. Japanese American. **PERSONAL:** Born Aug 21, 1939, Hiroshima, Japan; son of Yutaka Chiogioji & Harumi Chiogioji; married Eleanor N Chiogioji, Jun 4, 1961; children: Wendy A Nejame, Alan K. **EDUCATION:** Purdue University, BSEE, 1961; University of Hawaii, MBA, 1968; George Washington University, DBA, 1972. **CAREER:** Federal Energy Admin, Office of Industrial Analysis, director, 1973-75; US ERDA, Division of Building and Industry, assistant director, 1975-77; US Dept of Energy, Office of Federal Programs, director, 1977-80, State and Local Programs, deputy assistant secretary, 1980-85, Office of Transportation Systems, director, 1985-90, NPR, construction manager, deputy director, 1991-93; INTEMCO, president, 1993-. **ORGANIZATIONS:** Seabee Memorial Scholarship Association, president, 1990-93; IEEE, senior member, 1961-; Association of Science, Technology & Innovation, president, 1972-; Society of American Military Engineers, 1961-; Naval Reserve Association, 1965-; Academy of Management, 1972-; National Society of Professional Engineers, 1965-; Japanese American Citizens League, DC Chapter, president, 1970-. **HONORS/ AWARDS:** Purdue University, George A Ross Award, 1961; Chicago Tribune, Chicago Tribune Award, 1961; George Washington University, Doctoral Association Award, 1972. **SPECIAL ACHIEVEMENTS:** Author of books: Industrial Energy Conservation, Marcel Dekker Inc, 1979; Energy Conservation in Commercial & Residential Building, Marcel Dekker Inc, 1982; Evaluation of the Use of Pricing as a Tool for Conserving Water, Water Resources Research Center, Washington Technical Institute, 1973. **MILITARY SERVICE:** US Naval Reserve, rear admiral, 1961-93; 2 Legions of Merit, 3 Meritorious Service Medals, 2 Navy Commendation Medals. **HOME ADDRESS:** 15113 Middlegate Rd, Silver Spring, MD 20905.

CHIOU, MINSHON J.

Engineer. Taiwanese American. **PERSONAL:** Born Feb 1, 1951, Tainan, Taiwan; married Y C Chiou, May 1980. **EDUCATION:** National Taiwan University, BSChE, 1973; University of Delaware, PhD, ChE, 1979. **CAREER:** E I Dupont & Co, research associate, currently. **ORGANIZATIONS:** AIChE, 1976-; ACS, 1976-. **SPECIAL ACHIEVEMENTS:** Several US patents. **BUSINESS ADDRESS:** Research Associate, E I DuPont & Co, PO Box 27001, Richmond, VA 23261, (804)383-2049.

CHIOU, PAUL C. J.

Educator. Taiwanese American. **PERSONAL:** Born Nov 18, 1950, Tainan, Taiwan; son of T S Chiou & H C Chiou; married Peen-Peen Chiou, Mar 9, 1990. **EDUCATION:** National Chung Hsing University, BS, 1974; University of Texas at Arlington, MA, 1980, PhD, 1984. **CAREER:** East Texas State University, assistant professor, 1983-88; Lamar University, associate professor, 1988-. **ORGANIZATIONS:** Pi Mu Epsilon, 1979-; American Statistical Association, 1980-; Institute of Mathematical Statistics, 1986-. **HONORS/ AWARDS:** University of Texas at Arlington, Teaching Assistantship, 1978-83; Southern Methodist University, Teaching Assistantship, 1980. **SPECIAL ACHIEVEMENTS:** "Shrinkage Estimation of Scale Parameter of the Extreme-Value Distribution," IEEE Transactions on Reliability, vol 37, p 370-374, 1988; "Shrinkage Estimation of Threshold Parameter of the Exponential Distribution," IEEE Transactions on Reliability, vol 38, p 449-453, 1989; "Estimation of Scale Parameters for Two Exponential Distributions," IEEE Transactions on Reliability, vol 39, p 106-109, 1990; "Shrinkage Estimation of Reliability in the Exponential Distribution," Communications in Statistics Theory-Meth, vol 21, p 1745-1758, 1992; "Empirical Bayes Shrinkage Estimation of Reliability in the Exponential Distribution, " Communications in Statistics Theory-Meth, vol 22, p 1483-1494, 1993. **BUSINESS ADDRESS:** Associate Professor, Lamar University, East Lavaca, Lucas Bldg, Beaumont, TX 77710, (409)880-8800.

CHIOU, WEN-AN

Educator, scientist, consultant. Taiwanese American/Chinese American. **PERSONAL:** Born Jun 24, 1948, Nan-Chou, Ping-Tung, Taiwan; son of Ter-Tsai Chiou & Jane-May Liaow Chiou; married Nae-Shiang Chiou, Feb 28, 1973; children: George W, Kathy S. **EDUCATION:** Chinese Culture University, BS,

1970; National Taiwan University, postgrad study, 1971-73; University of South Florida, MS, 1976; Texas A&M University, PhD, 1981. **CAREER:** Reservoirs Inc, staff geologist to senior staff geologist, 1981-86; Accumin Analysis Inc, technical service, vice president, 1986-; University of Houston, adjunct lecturer, 1983-86; Naval Research Laboratory, Stennis Space Center, consultant research scientist, 1988-; Northwestern University, electron microscopist, TEM Facility, manager, 1986-90, associate research professor, 1991-; Marquette University, associate adjunct professor, 1990-. **ORGANIZATIONS:** Microscopy Society of America, 1980-; Japanese Society of Electron Microscopy Society, 1988-; Royal Microscopical Society, fellow, 1990-; Materials Research Society, 1988-; Minerals, Metals, and Materials Society, 1991-; Clay Minerals Society, 1975-; Mineralogical Society of America, 1984-; American Geophysical Union, 1986-. **HONORS/AWARDS:** Microscopy Society of America, Traveling Exhibit Award, 1993; Chinese Culture University, Special Honor for Outstanding Service, 1987; National Research Council, Research Associateship, 1981; Microscopy Society of America, Presidential Scholar Award, 1980; Texas A&M University, Oceanography Fellowship, 1980; Chinese Ministry of Education, Taiwan, Research Scholarship, 1972. **SPECIAL ACHIEVEMENTS:** Associate editor, Microstructure of Fine-Grained Sediments, Springer-Verlag, 1990; contributed more than 40 articles to professional and scholarly journals; presented more than 50 oral presentations to national & international universities & professional meetings. **MILITARY SERVICE:** Chinese Army, 2nd lt, 1970-71. **HOME ADDRESS:** 419 Vine St, Wilmette, IL 60091, (708)256-5879. **BUSINESS ADDRESS:** Assoc Research Professor, Dept of Materials Science & Engineering, Northwestern University, 2225 N Campus Dr, Rm 1156 MSL, Evanston, IL 60208-3108, (708)491-7807.

CHIOU, WUN C.
Company executive. Chinese American. **PERSONAL:** Born in Amoy Island Peninsula, Fukien, People's Republic of China. **EDUCATION:** Ohio State University, DPhysics, 1973. **CAREER:** US Army, civilian scientist, 1974-79; NASA, artificial intelligence expert, 1981-85; Pacific Micro, founder, president, 1987-. **BIOGRAPHICAL SOURCES:** "Chiou Bridges the Gap between IBMs and Macs," Asian Week, Feb 25, 1993, p10. **BUSINESS ADDRESS:** President, Pacific Micro, 201 San Antonio Circle, Suite C250, Mountain View, CA 94040, (415)948-6200.*

CHISHTI, ATHAR HUSAIN
Educator, research scientist. Indo-American. **PERSONAL:** Born Dec 25, 1957, Aligarh, Uttar Pradesh, India; son of M Tahir Husain Chishti and Naima Akhtar; married Yasmin Husain Chishti, Jul 25, 1987; children: Imran H. **EDUCATION:** A M University, India, BS, MS, 1980; University of Melbourne, Australia, PhD, 1984; Harvard University, post-doctoral, 1984-88. **CAREER:** Harvard University, research assoc, 1986-88; Tufts University School of Medicine, asst prof, 1988-; St Elizabeth's Hospital, assoc investigator, 1990-. **ORGANIZATIONS:** American Society of Hematology; American Society of Cell Biology; American Society of Tropical Medicine and Hygiene. **HONORS/AWARDS:** University of Melbourne, Postgraduate Award, 1981; Australia-India Governments, Commonwealth Scholarship, 1981; American Heart Assn, Postdoctoral Fellowship, 1987; Whitaker Foundation/MIT, Health Science Grant, 1990; American Cancer Society/NIH, research grants, 1991-92. **SPECIAL ACHIEVEMENTS:** Author: "Signal Transduction," Jrnl of Biological Chemistry, vol 264, p 8985-8991, 1989; "Membrane-Cytoskeleton, Cell Shape, Cancer," Nature, vol 334, p 718-721, 1988. **BIOGRAPHICAL SOURCES:** Proc National Academy of Science, USA, vol 88, p 6595-6599, 1991, 1993. **BUSINESS ADDRESS:** Assistant Professor, Tufts University Medical School, St Elizabeth's Hospital, 736 Cambridge St, ACH-4, 412 N, Boston, MA 02135, (617)789-3118.

CHITGOPEKAR, SHARAD S.
Educator. Indo-American. **PERSONAL:** Born Jan 3, 1938, Raichur, Karnataka, India; son of Shankar Rao Chitgopekar and Susheelabar Chitgopekar; married Suneeti Chitgopekar, May 26, 1969; children: Anuradha, Unmesh. **EDUCATION:** Osmania University, BA, 1957; University of Poona, MA, 1959; Florida State University, PhD, 1968. **CAREER:** Osmania University, India, lecturer in statistics, 1959-63; Florida State University, fellow, 1963-64, research assistant, 1964-68; Bell Telephone Laboratories, technical staff, 1968; Government of India, pool officer CSIR, 1969-70; Eastern Montana College, assistant professor of mathematics, 1971-72; University of Wisconsin, visiting assistant professor of statistics, 1970-71, 1972-74, 1978; University of Illinois-Chicago, assistant professor of quantitative methods, 1974-78; Illinois State University, associate professor of quantitative methods, 1978-85, professor of quantitative methods, 1985-. **HONORS/AWARDS:** Illinois State Uni-

versity, outstanding researcher, 1988; United States Educational Foundation in India, Fulbright Travel Grant, 1963; Osmania University, Sir Akbar Hydari Gold Medal, 1957. **HOME PHONE:** (309)663-1966. **BUSINESS ADDRESS:** Professor of Quantitative Methods, Illinois State University, 353 Williams Hall, Normal, IL 61761, (309)438-7993.

CHITKARA, VIJAY KUMAR
Financial manager. Indo-American. **PERSONAL:** Born Apr 10, 1949, Ludhiana, Punjab, India; son of R L Chitkara and P W Chitkara; married Monica, Jun 25, 1979; children: Vishal K, Neil K. **EDUCATION:** Kurukshetra University, India, BS, 1971; Claremont Graduate School, MBA, 1975. **CAREER:** Top Value Enterprises Inc, mgr, internal audit, 1980-86; Federated Dept Stores, sr internal auditor, 1986-88; Ponderosa Restaurants, sr auditor, 1988-89; Amcast Industrial, sr internal auditor, 1989-; Metromedia Steakhouses Company, manager, internal audit, currently. **ORGANIZATIONS:** Institute of Internal Auditors, 1980-, past exec ofcr; Ohio Society of CPA's, 1992-. **SPECIAL ACHIEVEMENTS:** Certified internal auditor; certified public accountant. **HOME ADDRESS:** 7639 Katy Dr, Dayton, OH 45459, (513)434-8694. **BUSINESS PHONE:** (513)454-2498.

CHIU, ARTHUR NANG LICK
Educator, consulting engineer. Chinese American. **PERSONAL:** Born Mar 9, 1929, Singapore; son of S J Chiu (deceased) and Y N Wong (deceased); married Katherine, Jun 12, 1952; children: Vicky L Y Chiu-Irion, Gregory L F. **EDUCATION:** Oregon State University, BA, 1952, BSCE, 1952; Massachusetts Institute of Technology, SMCE, 1953; University of Florida, PhD, 1961. **CAREER:** University of Hawaii, professor of civil engineering, 1953-. **ORGANIZATIONS:** National Research Council; Wind Engineering Research Council; American Society of Civil Engineers; American Concrete Institute; Hawaii Society of Professional Engineers; Structural Engineers Association of Hawaii; Hawaii State Earthquake Advisory Board; Chi Epsilon. **HONORS/AWARDS:** National Society of Professional Engineers, Hawaii Society of Professional Engineers, Engineer of the Year Award, 1989; Hawaii Civil Engineers, Engineer of the Month, 1959; University of Hawaii Mortar Board, One of 23 Most Inspirational Professors, 1992; numerous others. **SPECIAL ACHIEVEMENTS:** Author of: "Short-Record Based Extreme Wind Simulation," 1993; "Hurricane Iniki: Wind Induced Damage," 1993; "Computational Methods for Estimating Extreme Wind Speeds," 1992; numerous others; received numerous grants for research projects. **HOME ADDRESS:** 1654 Paul Dr, Honolulu, HI 96816-4316. **BUSINESS ADDRESS:** Professor, Dept of Civil Engineering, University of Hawaii at Manoa, 2540 Dole St, Honolulu, HI 96822, (808)956-7170.

CHIU, CHAO-LIN
Educator. Taiwanese American. **PERSONAL:** Born Nov 9, 1934, Kaohsiung, Taiwan; son of C-S Chiu and Pi-Yu Chang; married Fuh-Mei Lee, Dec 6, 1939; children: Bruce. **EDUCATION:** National Taiwan University, BS, 1957; University of Toronto, MSA, 1961; Cornell University, PhD, 1964. **CAREER:** University of Pittsburgh, assistant professor, 1964-67, associate professor, 1968-71, professor, 1972-. **ORGANIZATIONS:** American Society of Civil Engineers, 1964-; American Geophysical Union, 1964-; International Association for Hydraulic Research, 1964-; American Institute of Hydrology, 1982-. **HONORS/AWARDS:** Fulbright Senior Scholarship, 1980; Cornell Graduate School, Teaching Fellowship, 1982. **SPECIAL ACHIEVEMENTS:** Over 60 papers published in scientific/technical journals, books and proceedings of conferences. **BUSINESS ADDRESS:** Professor of Civil Engineering, University of Pittsburgh, 941 Benedum Hall of Engineering, Pittsburgh, PA 15261, (412)624-9872.

CHIU, JIM
Computer consulting company executive. Taiwanese American. **PERSONAL:** Born Feb 19, 1968, Tao Yuan, Taiwan; son of Tsau-Chi Chiu. **EDUCATION:** University of Southern California, BS, 1991. **CAREER:** Prevalence International Inc, vice pres, 1990-91; The Catalyst Group, president, consultant, 1991-; Katsai Corporation, general manager, 1992-. **BUSINESS ADDRESS:** President, The Catalyst Group, 17117 Leal Ave, Cerritos, CA 90701, (310)926-1632.

CHIU, JOHN T.
Physician. Macanese American. **PERSONAL:** Born Jan 8, 1938, Macao; son of Lan Cheong and Yau Hoon Chiu; divorced; children: Lisa, Mark, Heather. **EDUCATION:** University of Vermont, BA, 1960, MD, 1964. **CAREER:** Allergy Medical Group Inc, president, 1972-. **ORGANIZATIONS:** American

College of Chest Physicians, fellow, 1976-; American Academy of Allergy and Immunology, fellow, 1976-; American College of Allergy and Immunology, fellow, 1976-; Orange County Society of Allergy and Clinical Immunology, president, 1991-92. **HONORS/AWARDS:** American Chemical Society, Achievement Award, 1958. **SPECIAL ACHIEVEMENTS:** Orange County Medical Association, editorial board, 1993. **BUSINESS ADDRESS:** President, Allergy Medical Group Inc, 400 Newport Center Dr, Ste 401, Newport Beach, CA 92660, (714)644-1422.

CHIU, LUE-YUNG CHOW
Educator. Chinese American. **PERSONAL:** Born Sep 14, 1931, Kiang-Su, China; daughter of Hou-soo Chow and Hsing-cheng Chung Chow; married Ying-Nan Chiu, Jun 18, 1960; children: Han-Seh, Kong-Seh. **EDUCATION:** National Taiwan University, BS, 1952; Bryn Mawr College, MA, 1954; Yale University, PhD, 1957. **CAREER:** Columbia University, research associate, 1960-62; University of Chicago, research associate, 1962-64; Catholic University of America, research assistant professor, 1964-65; NASA, Goddad Space Flight Center, research associate, senior resident, 1965-68; Howard University, associate professor, 1968-72, professor, 1972-. **ORGANIZATIONS:** American Physical Society, 1958-; American Chemical Society, 1972-. **BUSINESS ADDRESS:** Professor, Depatment of Chemistry, Howard University, 525 College Street NW, Room 112, Washington, DC 20059, (202)806-6882.

CHIU, MARTHA LI
Psychologist. Chinese American. **PERSONAL:** Born Jun 14, 1953, Pasadena, CA; daughter of Ting-Yi Li and Tsun-Hwei Li; married Sheng-Yang Chiu, Jul 3, 1977; children: Christine Aiping. **EDUCATION:** Radcliffe College, BA (summa cum laude), East Asian studies, 1975; Harvard University, MA, regional studies: East Asia, 1977, PhD, history, East Asian languages, 1986; Stanford University, PhD, counseling, psychology, 1993. **CAREER:** Harvard University, East Asian studies tutor, 1979-81; Samaritans, crisis counselor, Asian community outreach worker, 1981-82; Mid-Peninsula Support Network, counselor, Asian community outreach worker, 1986-87; Stanford Counseling Institute, therapist, 1987-90; Stanford University, Counseling & Psychological Services, psychology fellow, 1989-90, School of Education, dean's assistant, 1990-91; Veterans Affairs Medical Center, Palo Alto, CA, postdoctoral fellow in neuropsychology, 1992-. **ORGANIZATIONS:** American Psychologial Association, 1993-; Asian-American Psychological Association, 1993-; National Academy of Neuropsychology, 1993-. **HONORS/AWARDS:** Phi Beta Kappa, 1974; American Psychological Association, Minority Fellowship, 1988-91; Stanford University, Matt M Goldstein Award, 1989. **SPECIAL ACHIEVEMENTS:** Specialist in assessment & treatment of neuropsychological and psychosocial problems in Asian and Asian-American populations; author of published articles on effects of Asian culture & immigration on mental health; collaborator, Chinese revision of the Luria-Nebraska Neuropsychological Battery; fluent in Mandarin Chinese; reading knowledge of literary Chinese, Japanese, French & Spanish. **BUSINESS ADDRESS:** Psychologist, Veterans Affairs Medical Center, 3801 Miranda Ave, 6B3, Palo Alto, CA 94304.

CHIU, MING S.
Physician. Taiwanese American. **PERSONAL:** Born Jul 24, 1944, Taipei, Taiwan; son of Ting-Fang Chiu & Siu-Mei Tsai; married Lois P, Mar 14, 1971; children: James, Grace. **EDUCATION:** Taipei Medical College, MD, 1969. **CAREER:** Allegheny General Hospital, resident, 1973-76; VA Hospital, Hines, senior resident, 1976-78; Virginia Cardiopulmonary Associates, private practice, 1978-. **ORGANIZATIONS:** American College of Chest Physicians, fellow, 1993; American College of Physicians, 1993; American Thoracic Society, 1993. **BUSINESS ADDRESS:** Physician, Virginia Cardiopulmonary Associates PC, 436 Clairmont Ct, Ste 102, Colonial Heights, VA 23834-1795, (804)526-0682.

CHIU, S. M.
Educator (retired). Chinese American. **PERSONAL:** Born Oct 18, 1923, Hong Kong; married Helen, Jun 27, 1970; children: Phyllis, Herman. **EDUCATION:** Indiana University, AB, 1949; University of Iowa, MA, 1950; University of Southern California, PhD, 1958. **CAREER:** Centenary College of Louisiana, asst professor, 1955-60; Princeton University, research associate, 1960-61; University of Utah, lecturer, 1962; University of Delaware, visiting associate professor, 1964, 1969; University of Southern California, visiting associate professor, 1965; Temple University, asst professor, professor, 1961-90; Beaver College, lecturer, 1990-91. **ORGANIZATIONS:** Assn for Asian Studies, 1955-; American Historical Assn, 1954-80; Asian-American Council of Greater Philadelphia, exec committee, 1970-76; US Commission on Civil

Rights, Pennsylvania State Advisory Committee, 1978-84; On Lok House of Philadelphia, bd member, 1982-. **HONORS/AWARDS:** American Philosophical Society, grant, 1967. **SPECIAL ACHIEVEMENTS:** Language proficiency: Chinese; author: 4 monographs, over 20 articles in professional journals, over 20 book reviews. **HOME ADDRESS:** 514 Cambridge Rd, Bala Cynwyd, PA 19004-2252.

CHIU, SHEAN-TSONG
Educator. Taiwanese American. **PERSONAL:** Born May 22, 1955, Hwalian, Taiwan; son of Shay-Shai Chiu and Wang-Mo Chiu; married Yuan-Yee Chiu, Oct 25, 1979; children: James, Stephanie, David. **EDUCATION:** Tsing-Hua University, Taiwan, BA, 1977; University of California, Berkeley, MA, 1981, PhD, 1984. **CAREER:** Rice University, assistant professor, 1984; Colorado State University, assistant professor, 1989, associate professor, 1993-. **ORGANIZATIONS:** Institute of Mathematical Statistics, 1982-. **SPECIAL ACHIEVEMENTS:** Publications include: 16 papers in several professional journals. **BUSINESS ADDRESS:** Associate Professor, Dept of Statistics, Colorado State University, Fort Collins, CO 80523, (303)491-6497.

CHIU, THOMAS CHEE-WANG
Structural engineer. Chinese American. **PERSONAL:** Born Sep 20, 1958, Cholon, Vietnam; son of Vinh Trieu and Phung Quach; married Julie Chiu, Oct 1, 1985; children: Christine. **EDUCATION:** Concordia University, Montreal, Canada, BSEng, 1980; University of Waterloo, Canada, MS, 1982. **CAREER:** Ertzan Associates, project engr, 1982-86; Albert C Martin Associates, sr engr, 1986-88; Dames & Moore Inc, sr engr, 1988-. **ORGANIZATIONS:** Structural Engineers of Southern California Assn, 1989-. **BUSINESS ADDRESS:** Senior Structural Engineer, Dames & Moore Inc, 911 Wilshire Blvd, Ste 700, Los Angeles, CA 90017, (213)683-1560.

CHIU, TIN-HO
Scientist. Chinese American. **PERSONAL:** Born Jun 22, 1942, Tin-Ho, Kiangsi, China; married Evelyn H Chiu; children: Christopher, Paul. **EDUCATION:** Chinese University of Hong Kong, Chung Chi College, diploma, chemistry, 1964; Center of Surface and Coating, PhD, chemistry, 1972. **CAREER:** Avco Everett Research Lab, research associate, 1971-76, principal scientist, 1976-80; Instrumentation Laboratory, program manager, 1980-86; Brown University, Division of Biology and Medicine, Biomedical Engineering, adjunct associate professor, 1985-91; Allied Signal, corporate research, research associate, 1986-89; Becton Dickinson VACUTAINERS Systems, manager of material technology, 1990-93, senior scientist, 1993-. **ORGANIZATIONS:** American Chemical Society; American Society of Artificial Internal Organs. **HONORS/AWARDS:** Allied Signal Corp, Technical Achievement Award, 1989. **HOME ADDRESS:** 754 Ridgewood Rd, Millburn, NJ 07041-1823, (201)376-1539. **BUSINESS ADDRESS:** Senior Scientist, Becton Dickinson VACUTAINERS Systems, 1 Becton Dr, Bldg II, Franklin Lakes, NJ 07417-1885, (201)847-4363.

CHIU, VICTOR
Engineer. Chinese American. **PERSONAL:** Born Nov 28, 1936, Tianjin, China; son of Kuno M Y Chiu and Vivian W Tsao; married Loretta Shih, Sep 2, 1963; children: Frederic, Cornelius. **EDUCATION:** Grantham College, Hong Kong, diploma, 1958; Kent State University, BS, 1960; Cornell University, MS, 1966, PhD, 1970. **CAREER:** Govt of Hong Kong, Education Dept, primary school master, 1956-59; College of Wooster, instr, 1966-67; Cornell University, research asst, 1967-70; University of Indianapolis, professor, physics & math, 1970-85; Structural Dynamics Research Corp, sr development engr, 1985-. **ORGANIZATIONS:** Society of Industry and Applied Math, 1986-; IEEE Computer Society, 1980-; AAUP, chapter secretary, 1976-85; US China People's Friendship Assn, charter mbr, 1972-; Sigma Xi, 1970-85; American Physics Society, 1971-85; American Assn of Physics Teachers, 1961-85. **HONORS/AWARDS:** Kent State University, Bowman Award, 1960, Pi Mu Epsilon Award, 1960; Natl Science Foundation, Research Fellowship, 1971, 1978, 1979; US Dept of Defense, Research Fellowship, 1983. **SPECIAL ACHIEVEMENTS:** Author: various publications, physics journals, 1968-85. **BUSINESS ADDRESS:** Senior Development Engineer, Structural Dynamics Research Corp, 2000 Eastman Dr, Milford, OH 45150, (513)576-2763.

CHIU, WAH
Scientist. Hong Kong American. **PERSONAL:** Born Jun 5, 1947, Hong Kong; son of Ming-Hing Chiu and Mo-Wan Tam; married Pearl Chiu, Sep 9, 1972; children: Jenifer Ann, Andreana Christiane. **EDUCATION:** University of

California, Berkeley, BA, physics, 1969, PhD, biophysics, 1975. **CAREER:** University of California, Berkeley, postdoctoral research associate, 1975-77, Lawrence Berkeley Laboratory, biophysicist, 1977-79; University of Arizona, Tucson, Dept of Cellular and Developmental Biology, asst professor, 1979-83, Dept of Biochemistry, Dept of Molecular and Cellular Biology, associate professor, 1983-88; Baylor College of Medicine, Houston, TX, Depts of Biochemistry, Molecular Virology, and Cell Biology, professor, 1988-, Dept of Molecular Physiology and Biophysics, professor, 1991-. **HONORS/ AWARDS:** Oakland City Council, Award of Merit, 1972; Electron Microscopy Society of American, Presidential Scholar, 1974; Guggenheim Fellow, 1986; Cambridge University, Clare Hall, UK, Visiting Fellow, 1986. **BUSINESS ADDRESS:** Professor, Biochemistry Dept, Baylor College of Medicine, One Baylor Plaza, Houston, TX 77030, (713)798-6985.

CHIU, YUAN-YUAN H.
Federal government official. Chinese American. **PERSONAL:** Born Mar 1, 1942, Kiangsi, China; daughter of Fa-tou Hsieh and Yun-mei Li Hsieh; married Hungdah Chiu, May 14, 1966; children: Weihsueh A. **EDUCATION:** National Cheng Kung University, BS, 1963; Wellesley College, MS, 1965; Harvard University, PhD, 1975. **CAREER:** Harvard University, teaching fellow, 1968-70, 1972-74; National Taiwan Normal University, instructor, 1971-72; Johns Hopkins University, research associate, 1975-80; Food and Drug Administration, biotechnology expert, supervisor chemist, 1980-. **ORGANIZATIONS:** American Chemical Society; American Association for the Advancement of Sciences; American Society of Testing and Materials; Sigma Xi. **HONORS/ AWARDS:** Harvard Chemistry Department, Excellence in Teaching, 1969; Food and Drug Administration, Citation in Scientific Innovation, 1985, Commendable Service Award, 1986, 1992, Award of Merit, 1991. **SPECIAL ACHIEVEMENTS:** 28 articles in the fields of chemistry, biotechnology and pharmaceutical sciences; book, Drug Biotechnology Regulations, Scientific Basis and Practices, co-editor Marcel Dekker, 1991. **BUSINESS ADDRESS:** Biotechnology Expert, Supervisory Chemist, Center for Drug Evaluation and Research, FDA, 5600 Fishers Ln, MC: HFD-510, Parklawn Bldg, Rm 14B04, Rockville, MD 20857, (301)443-3510.

CHO, ALFRED YI
Electrical engineer. Chinese American. **PERSONAL:** Born Jul 10, 1937, Beijing, China; son of Edward Cho and Mildred Chen; married Mona Willoughby, Jun 16, 1968; children: Derek Ming, Deidre Lin, Brynna Ying, Wendy Li. **EDUCATION:** University of Illinois, BS, 1960, MS, 1961, PhD, 1968. **CAREER:** Ion Physics Corp, MTS, 1961-62; TRW Space Tech Labs, MTS, 1962-65; University of Illinois, Urbana, graduate assistant, 1965-68, adjunct professor, 1978-; AT&T Bell Labs, MTS, 1968-1984, dept head, 1984-87, director, Materials Processing Research Lab, 1987-90, director, Semiconductor Research Lab, 1990-. **ORGANIZATIONS:** Molecular Beam Epitaxy Workshop, advisory board chairman, 1979-; Naval Research Opportunities in Electronic, NRC, panel of office, 1991; Air Force Studies Board, NRC, Committee on Technology, 1991; Committee on DARPA Future Technology, 1992; Office of Naval Research, board of visitors, 1992; IEEE/LEOS, Technical Committee on Materials and Processing, 1993; UCLA, regent lecturer, 1993; Academia Sinica; Third World Academy of Science; American Academy of Arts and Science; US National Academy of Engineering; US National Academy of Sciences. **HONORS/AWARDS:** American Physical Society, International Prize for New Materials; Electrochem Society, Solid State Science and Technology Medal; American Vacuum Society, Gaede-Langmuir Award; American Association for Crystal Growth, International Crystal Growth Award; National Asian American Corp, Achievement Adward, OCA, 1992; AT&T Bell Labs, Fellow Award, 1992; Chinese-American Engineers and Scientists Association of Southern California, Achievement Award, 1993; Institute of Electrical and Electronics Engineers, Medal of Honor, 1994. **SPECIAL ACHIEVEMENTS:** Published over 400 referenced journal articles; recipient of the National Medal of Science, presented by President Bill Clinton, 1993. **BUSINESS PHONE:** (908)582-2093.

CHO, ANDREW BYONG-WOO
Journalist. Korean American. **PERSONAL:** Born Feb 23, 1940, Yesan, Republic of Korea; son of Song-dong Cho and Keh-Hee Lee; married Grace, Dec 27, 1976; children: 4 boys. **EDUCATION:** Sogang University, Seoul, Korea, 1960-61; University of Hawaii, BBA (with distinction), 1976. **CAREER:** The Korea Times (Seoul, Korea), reporter, 1965-72; The Korea Times, Seattle Bureau, chief, 1977-. **ORGANIZATIONS:** American Go Assn; Seattle Korean Catholic Church, 1977-. **HONORS/AWARDS:** Beta Gamma Sigma, 1975; Phi Kappa Phi, 1975; Sogang University, Distinguished Alumni Award,

1990; Seattle Chinese Post, Man of the Year, 1990. **SPECIAL ACHIEVEMENTS:** Translated several Catholic books from English to Korean. **MILITARY SERVICE:** Korean Army, conscripted, 1961-64. **BUSINESS ADDRESS:** Publisher, The Korea Times, Northwest Edition, 430 Yale Ave N, Seattle, WA 98109, (206)622-2229.

CHO, CHIT-MYINE. *See* KHAW, BAN-AN.

CHO, CHRISTOPHER SANG KYU
Educator. Korean American. **PERSONAL:** Born Aug 13, 1950, Seoul, Republic of Korea; son of Myungchul Cho & Junguk Choi; married Jennifer J Cho, Nov 14, 1975; children: Edward I, Christine I. **EDUCATION:** Seoul National University, BS, 1973; State University of New York, MS, 1981, PhD, 1984. **CAREER:** Korean Army Ordinance School, instructor, 1973-75; Korea Atomic Energy Research Institute, research engineer, 1975-77; State University of NY, research assistant, 1978-84; Western Michigan University, mechanical engineering, assistant professor, 1984-89, associate professor, 1989-. **ORGANIZATIONS:** American Society of Mechanical Engineers, 1982-; American Institute of Chemical Engineers, 1991-; American Society of Engineering Educators, 1986-. **HONORS/AWARDS:** National Science Foundation, research grant, 1985-87; NASA, Lewis Center Summer Fellowship, 1993; Argone National Laboratory, Summer Fellowship, 1987. from Argonne National Laboratory, 1987. **SPECIAL ACHIEVEMENTS:** Over 27 publications in the mechanical engineering related field including: "Enhanced Nucleate Boiling in Structured Surface," 3rd Intersociety Conference on Thermal Phenomena in Electronic Systems, 1992; "Study on the Relationship between Spray Flow Condition and Cooling Characteristics," 1989; "Laser Flow Visualization of a Highly-Loaded Particle-Liquid Flow by Matching Refractive Indices," 1988. **MILITARY SERVICE:** Army Ordinance School, Korea, 2nd lt, 1973-75, 1st place, teaching competition in the Army School. **BUSINESS ADDRESS:** Professor, Dept of Mechanical Engineering, Western Michigan University, Kalamazoo, MI 49008, (616)387-3375.

CHO, DAVID
Health services worker. Hong Kong American/Chinese American. **PERSONAL:** Born Dec 25, 1966, Hong Kong; son of Manfield Cho & Ivy Mak. **EDUCATION:** University of California, Berkeley, BSW, 1990. **CAREER:** Asian Health Services, community health worker, 1990-92, community health specialist, 1993-, case manager, 1993-. **ORGANIZATIONS:** AIDS Community Network, board of directors, 1991-. **HONORS/AWARDS:** University of California, Berkeley, Volunteering Appreciation, 1990; Oakland Chinese Community Council, Volunteering Appreciation, 1992; Irvine Valley College, Academic Scholarship, 1987. **SPECIAL ACHIEVEMENTS:** Member of Anne Bluethenthal & Dancers, 1991-; performs with Asian American Dance Collective, 1990-; GPA Dance Co, 1991-; bilingual in Catonese & Mandarin. **BUSINESS ADDRESS:** Case Manager, AIDS Project, Asian Health Services, 310 8th St, #200, Asian Resource Center, Oakland, CA 94607, (510)444-2437.

CHO, DONG-IL DAN
Educator. Korean American. **PERSONAL:** Born Jun 15, 1958, Seoul, Republic of Korea; son of Hyo-Won Cho & On-Soon Kim; married Chi-Won Suh, May 29, 1986; children: Rebecca. **EDUCATION:** CMU, BSME, 1980; MIT, SM, 1984, PhD, 1988. **CAREER:** Princeton University, assistant professor, 1987-. **ORGANIZATIONS:** American Society of Mechanical Engineers, Council on Engineering, Emerging Technologies Committee, 1990-, Dynamics and Control Division, Micro-Mechanical Systems Panel, 1989-, Transportation Panel, 1987-, chairman, 1989-, Applied Mechanics Division, Transportation Committee, 1989-; Institute of Electrical and Electronics Engineers; Society of Automotive Engineers; Society for Industrial and Applied Mathematics; Sigma Xi; Pi Tau Sigma. **HONORS/AWARDS:** Howard Wentz Jr Class of 1952, Faculty Award, 1990; ASME, STEP Award, 1984; Korea Science and Engineering Foundation, scholarship, 1981. **SPECIAL ACHIEVEMENTS:** ASME Journal of Dynamic Systems, Measurement and Control, acting assistant technical editor, 1993-; IEEE/ASME, Journal of Microelectomechanical Systems, associate editor, 1991-; IOP Journal of Micromechanics and Microengineering, editorial board, 1991-, associate editor, 1990-91; co-editor: Micromechanical Systems, ASME Press, 1992; Micromechanical Sensors, Actuators and Systems, ASME Press, 1991; author or co-author: Micro Structures, Sensors and Actuators, ASME Press, 1990; with H K Oh, "Variable Structure Control Method for Fuel-Injecion Systems," ASME Journal of Dynamic Systems, Measurement and Control, forthcoming; "Experimental Results on Sliding Mode Control of an Electromagnetic Suspension," Journal of Mechanical Systems and Signal Processing, vol 7, forthcoming; with Y Kato

and D Spilman, "Experimental Comparison of Classical and Sliding Mode Controllers in Magnetic Levitation Systems," IEEE Control Systems Magazine, vol 13, p42-48, Feb 1993; with W N Carr, H N Yang, Electrostatic Microactuator, US patent, notice of allowability issued, 1992; Automatic Control System for IC Engine Fuel Injection, US patent, March 1993; with W N Carr, H Yu, Rotary, Vertical-Drive, Tethered Micromotor, US patent, Feb 1993. **BUSINESS ADDRESS:** Assistant Professor, Mechanical Engineering, Princeton University, Olden St, Princeton, NJ 08544.

CHO, EUN-SOOK

Physician, educator. Korean American. **PERSONAL:** Born Dec 12, 1940, Seoul, Republic of Korea; daughter of Yong-Ku Cho and Boo-Hee Kim; married Hoe-Yong Lee, Jan 21, 1969; children: Mie-Yun Lee Liu, Bryant, John. **EDUCATION:** Yonsei University, Medical College, MD; Cornell University, Medical College, residency & fellowship. **CAREER:** Sloan-Kettering Cancer Center, attending pathologist, 1973-75; University of Medicine and Denistry, New Jersey Medical School, assistant professor, 1975-77, associate professor, 1977-, University Hospital, director of neuropathology, 1975-, chief of anatomic pathology, 1993-. **ORGANIZATIONS:** American Association of Neuropathologists, 1975-; New Jersey Society of Pathologists, 1982-; American Academy of Neurology, 1977-; Se-Song School of NJ (Korean Language School), board of directors, 1977-82; World Wide Marriage Encounter, team couple, 1983-, Coordinating Team for Koreans on East coast, 1983-87; St Andrew Kim Korean Catholic Church, Sunday school coordinator, 1980-86, youth group coordinator, 1986-92. **HONORS/AWARDS:** UMD NJ Foundation, Excellence in Teaching Award, 1979; American Neurological Association, Presidential Award, 1986; Seton Hall University, honorary degree in science, 1993. **SPECIAL ACHIEVEMENTS:** Publications on neuropathology of AIDS, neurotoxicology, and demyelinating diseases.

CHO, FRANK FULAI

Consultant. Chinese American. **PERSONAL:** Born Jan 21, 1922, Beijing, China; son of Mr and Mrs H M Cho; married Joan J H Cho, 1960; children: Yee-Ping, Yee-Ann. **EDUCATION:** Harvard University, MBA, 1949. **CAREER:** Mi Chou Gallery, founder/president, 1954-60, vice president, 1960-71; Grace Tea Company Limited, co-founder/vice president, 1962-64, president, 1964-77; Associated Traders Inc, founder/president, 1968-75; Formost Tea Corporation, founder/president, 1958-77; General Tea Corporation, founder/president, 1977-88, consultant, currently. **ORGANIZATIONS:** Tea Association of the USA, board of directors, 1970s; US Board of Tea Experts, 1970s; Chinese Opera Club, NYC, co-founder, 1951-. **SPECIAL ACHIEVEMENTS:** "Reminiscences of Mi Chou: The First Chinese Gallery in America," Chinese American Forum, vol 1, no 3, May 1985. **BIOGRAPHICAL SOURCES:** "Frank Cho Celebrates 25th Anniversary in Tea Trade," Tea & Coffee Trade Journal, July 1974. **HOME ADDRESS:** 7865 E Mississipi Ave, Apt 301, Denver, CO 80231.

CHO, HYONG W.

Exporter. Korean American. **PERSONAL:** Born Jul 12, 1936, Seoul, Republic of Korea; son of Yong H Cho and Chang J Choi; married Sei I Cho, Jul 3, 1965; children: Susan, Ann. **EDUCATION:** Seoul National University, BA, 1959. **CAREER:** Oregon Hide Co, president, owner, 1974-. **ORGANIZATIONS:** American Horse Show Assn; Korean Chamber of Commerce, Oregon, bd member. **HOME ADDRESS:** 5880 Meadowcreek Ct, Lake Oswego, OR 97035-8784, (503)620-1001.

CHO, JANG YOUN

Educator. Korean American. **PERSONAL:** Born Aug 18, 1952, Choong Nam, Republic of Korea; son of Namkak Cho and Pil Soon Kim; married Kyungja Cho, Jun 10, 1979; children: Sung-jin, Hyejin. **EDUCATION:** Hankook University, Korea, BA, 1977; University of Texas at Arlington, MPA, 1983; University of Florida, PhD, 1987; State of Florida, CPA. **CAREER:** Daewoo Corporation, 1977-80; University of Florida, GTA, instructor, 1983-87; University of Nebraska, assistant prof, 1987-. **ORGANIZATIONS:** Korean Association of Lincoln, president, 1989-90; Korean School of Lincoln, chairman, 1991-. **SPECIAL ACHIEVEMENTS:** Publications: 11 articles in Contemporary Accounting Research; Journal of Accounting Literature; Accounting and Business Research, etc; presented 16 papers at AAA national conference & professional meetings. **BUSINESS ADDRESS:** Professor, College of Business, University of Nebraska at Lincoln, CBA 391, School of Accountancy, Lincoln, NE 68588-0488, (402)472-3273.

CHO, KAH-KYUNG

Educator. Korean American. **PERSONAL:** Born Jun 7, 1927, Seoul, Republic of Korea; married Sek Yen, Oct 11, 1951; children: Christine Sung Hae. **EDUCATION:** Seoul National University, BA, 1952; University of Heidelberg, PhD, 1957. **CAREER:** Seoul National University, professor, 1957-69; Yale University, visiting Fulbright Scholar, 1961-62; State University of New York, Buffalo, 1970-; University of Texas, Austin, visiting professor, 1977; University of Bochum, Germany, visiting professor, 1983; Soong Sil University, Seoul, distinguished visiting professor, 1991. **ORGANIZATIONS:** Intl Phenomenological Society, Philosophy and Phenomenological Research, editorial board, 1975-90; German Phenomenological Society, 1981-; Allgemeine Gesellschaft fur Philosophie in Deutschland, 1981-; Husserl Studies, editorial board member, 1982-; Orbis Phaenomenologicus, general editor, 1993-. **HONORS/AWARDS:** Osaka University, Japan Society for Promotion of Science, fellow, 1990; SUNY Chancellor's Award for Excellence in Teaching, 1990; Japan Society for Promotion of Science at Osaka University, fellow, 1990; Soong Sil University, Seoul, distinguished visiting professor, 1991. **SPECIAL ACHIEVEMENTS:** Books published: Philosophy of Existence, Seoul, 1961, 9th ed, 1993; Philosophy and Science in Phenomenological Perspective, 1984; Bewusstsein and Natursein, Freiburg, 1987. **HOME ADDRESS:** 189 Crestwood Lane, Williamsville, NY 14221. **BUSINESS ADDRESS:** Professor, Dept of Philosophy, SUNY, Buffalo, Baldy Hall, Buffalo, NY 14260-0001.

CHO, KANG RAE

Educator. Korean American. **PERSONAL:** Born Jun 25, 1947, Jinju, Kyungsangnam-do, Republic of Korea; son of Chang Jae Cho and Kye Pyo Hong; married Yoon Ja Cho, Oct 25, 1974; children: Hyun Woo Cho. **EDUCATION:** Korea University, BA, 1972; Utah State University, MBA, 1979; University of Washington, PhD, 1983. **CAREER:** Bank of Korea, economist, 1972-78; Pennsylvania State University, professor, 1983-90; University of Colorado, professor, 1990-. **ORGANIZATIONS:** Academy of International Business, 1982-; Academy of Management, 1983-; Korea-America Economic Association. **SPECIAL ACHIEVEMENTS:** Multinational Banks: Their Identities and Determinants, 1985; numerous articles on international business published in academic journals. **BUSINESS ADDRESS:** Professor, College of Business, Univ of Colorado-Denver, PO Box 173364, Campus Box 165, Denver, CO 80217-3364, (303)628-1280.

CHO, PECK

Educator. Korean American. **PERSONAL:** Born Nov 14, 1956, Seoul, Republic of Korea; son of Moo Joon and Jung Sook Cho; married Sung Aie Choi, Jun 24, 1984; children: Hann, Dania. **EDUCATION:** University of Wisconsin, BS, 1979; Northwestern University, MS, 1981, PhD, 1984. **CAREER:** Lawrence Berkeley Laboratory, visiting scientist, 1985-87; University of California, research engr, 1984-88; Michigan Technological University, assistant professor, 1988-92, associate professor, 1992-. **ORGANIZATIONS:** Combustion Institute, 1982-; American Society of Mechanical Engineers, 1988-; Society of Automotive Engineers, 1991-; Korean Scientists and Engineers Association, 1991-; American Institute of Aeronautics and Astronautics, 1988-89. **HONORS/AWARDS:** National Science Foundation, Research Initiation Award, 1990; Society of Automotive Engineers, Ralph R Teetor Award, 1991; Michigan Technological University, Distinguished Teaching Award, 1991, 1993; Michigan Association of Governing Board, Distinguished Faculty Award, 1992; American Society of Engineering Educators, Mikol Award, 1992. **SPECIAL ACHIEVEMENTS:** Over 20 technical publications in various journals; editor, Heat and Mass Transfer in Fire and Combustion Systems, 1992; co-author, Writing in Engineering, McGraw Hill, forthcoming. **BUSINESS ADDRESS:** Associate Professor, Mechanical Engineering, Michigan Technological University, 1400 Townsend Dr, Houghton, MI 49931, (906)487-2891.

CHO, RENEE

Literary agent. Chinese American. **PERSONAL:** Born Feb 6, 1950, New York, NY; daughter of Morley Cho and Nancy Cho; married Paul E Mesches, Jun 19, 1982; children: Tai Cho Mesches, Kim Cho Mesches. **EDUCATION:** Tufts University, BA, 1972; American Film Institute, MA, 1979. **CAREER:** WGBH-TV, associate producer, production assistant, 1975-77; Ladd Co, Lionsgate, United Artist, story analyst, 1977-82; Kings Road Productions, development executive, 1983-88; Morhaim Literary Agency, literary agent, 1989-92; McIntosh & Otis, literary agent, 1992-. **ORGANIZATIONS:** Association of Artists Reps, 1993. **HONORS/AWARDS:** Assn of Asian/Pacific American Artists, Media Award, 1986; Alfred Hitchcock Fellowship of American Film Institute, 1979. **SPECIAL ACHIEVEMENTS:** Producer/director, Jazz Is My Native Language, 1982; writer/director, The New Wife, 1981. **BUSINESS ADDRESS:** Literary Agent, McIntosh & Otis, Inc, 310 Madison Ave, New York, NY 10017, (212)687-7400.

CHO, SOUNG MOO
Engineer, educator. Korean American. **PERSONAL:** Born Oct 1, 1937, Seoul, Republic of Korea; son of Song-Nyung and Mi-Ok Cho; married Ki Sun Kim, Mar 6, 1965; children: Rose, Richard, Karen, Grace, Christopher, Andrew. **EDUCATION:** Seoul National University, Korea, BS, 1960; University of California, Berkeley, MS, 1964, PhD, 1967. **CAREER:** Korea Atomic Energy Research Institute, Seoul, researcher, 1960-61; University of California, Berkeley, research assistant, 1962-67; Garrett Corp, engineering specialist, 1967-69; Rockwell International Corp, staff consultant, 1969-73; Foster Wheeler Energy Corp, Clinton, director of engineering, 1973-; Fairleigh Dickinson University, adjunct professor, 1975-85; Stevens Institute of Technology, adjunct professor, 1975-. **ORGANIZATIONS:** American Society of Mechanical Engineers, fellow, 1968-; American Nuclear Society, 1969-; American Association for the Advancement of Science, 1973-81; National Society of Professional Engineers, 1976-79. **HONORS/AWARDS:** Government of Republic of Korea, Presidential Award, 1960; Fulbright Foundation, Fulbright Scholar, 1962. **SPECIAL ACHIEVEMENTS:** Published over 60 papers related to engineering. **BUSINESS ADDRESS:** Director of Engineering, Energy Applications Division, Foster Wheeler Energy Corp, Perryville Corporate Park, Clinton, NJ 08809.

CHO, WEOL D.
Educator. Korean American. **PERSONAL:** Born May 7, 1953, Seoul, Republic of Korea; son of Tae H Cho and Eul H Shin; married Kyung J Cho, Dec 20, 1982; children: Yoon K, Clare Y. **EDUCATION:** Hanyang University, BS, 1976; Iowa State University, MS, 1982; University of Washington, PhD, 1988. **CAREER:** University of Washington, research assistant, 1983-88; Southern Illinois University, assistant scientist, 1988-91; University of Utah, Department of Metallurgical Engineering, assistant professor, 1991-. **ORGANIZATIONS:** The Minerals Metals and Materials Society, 1985-; The Iron and Steel Society, 1987-. **BUSINESS ADDRESS:** Asst Prof, Dept of Metallurgical Engineering, University of Utah, 412 Browning Bldg, Salt Lake City, UT 84112, (801)581-6278.

CHO, WONHWA
Educator. Korean American. **PERSONAL:** Born Apr 27, 1958, Seoul, Republic of Korea; married Seungjin Cho, Dec 21, 1984; children: Brian H, Christine H. **EDUCATION:** Seoul National University, BS, 1980, MS, 1982; University of Chicago, PhD, 1988. **CAREER:** California Institute of Technology, post-doctoral research fellow, 1988-90; University of Illinois, Chicago, assistant professor, 1990-. **SPECIAL ACHIEVEMENTS:** Seven scientific publications in major journals. **BUSINESS ADDRESS:** Assistant Professor of Chemistry, University of Illinois, Chicago, 845 W Taylor St, M/C 111, Chicago, IL 60607-7061, (312)996-4883.

CHO, ZANG-HEE
Educator. Korean American. **PERSONAL:** Born Jul 15, 1936, Seoul, Republic of Korea; son of Byung-Soon Cho and Kang-Ae Cho; married Jung Sook. **EDUCATION:** Seoul National University, Korea, BSc, 1960, MSc, 1962; Uppsala University, Sweden, PhD, 1966. **CAREER:** Stockholm University, Sweden, research fellow, 1966-72, associate professor, 1972-75; Brookhaven National Lab, Wallenberg Fellow, 1971-72; University of California, Los Angeles, associate professor, 1972-78; Columbia University, professor, co-director of Imaging Research Center, 1979-85; University of California, Irvine, professor, director of NMR research, 1985-. **ORGANIZATIONS:** Institute of Electrical & Electronics Engineer, fellow, 1982; Third World Academy of Sciences, associate fellow, 1992; First International Symposium on 3-D Tomography, UCLA, chair, 1973; First International Medical Imaging Symposium, Santa Fe, chair, 1989; Special Issue on Computerized Tomography, Nuclear Science IEEE, editor, 1974, Imaging Science & Technology, editor, 1989. **HONORS/AWARDS:** American Association Medical Physicist, Sylvia Sorkin Greenfield Award, 1989; Jungjinki Foundation, Korea, Grand Science Prize, 1984; International Tomography Workshop, CA, Distinguished Scientist Award, 1982; NIH, Jacob Javitz Neuroscience Award, 1984. **SPECIAL ACHIEVEMENTS:** Development of first circular ring positron tomograph, PET, 1975; development of first convolution type 3-D image reconstruction algorithm, 1974; introduction of BGO sciatillation detector to PET field, 1976; development of first comprehensive NMR algorithm, 1982; development of first 4-um resolution NMR microscope, 1987. **BIOGRAPHICAL**

SOURCES: Physics Today, 1989; Research Light, University of California, Irvine, 1987. **BUSINESS ADDRESS:** Professor of Radiological Sciences, University of California, Irvine, Box 140B, Irvine, CA 92717-0001, (714)856-5905.

CHOE, KENNETH
Banker. Singaporean American. **PERSONAL:** Born Oct 31, 1961, Singapore; married Amy Choe-Tan, Apr 11, 1989. **EDUCATION:** University of Wisconsin-Madison, BSc, electrical engineering, computer science, 1985. **CAREER:** Citibank NA, treasury planning head, vice pres, 1986-. **HONORS/AWARDS:** Citibank, Great Performer Award, 1991. **BUSINESS ADDRESS:** Vice President, Citibank NA, 666 Fifth Ave, 6th Fl, New York, NY 10103.

CHOE, MARTHA C.
City council member. Chinese American. **PERSONAL:** Born Nov 16, 1954, New York, NY; daughter of Edward Kesoon & Yang Ja Choe. **EDUCATION:** University of Washington, BA, 1976; Seattle University, MBA, 1986. **CAREER:** Bank of California, bank officer trainee, 1982, cash mgmt marketing officer, 1982-84, corporate banking officer, 1984-86, vice president, assistant vice president, private banking, 1986-88, vice president of credit administration, 1989-90, vice president, commercial lending, 1990-91, City of Seattle, council member, 1992-. **ORGANIZATIONS:** Western Washington University, board of trustees, 1984-93, chair, 1990-92, co-chair, 1986-90; Economic Development Council, treasurer, 1992-; Washington State Trans Policy Institute, treasurer, 1993-; National League of Cities, Asian Pacific American Municipal officials, treasurer, 1992-; Big Sisters of King County, Mentorship Advisory Board, 1992; United Way of King County, board of trustees, 1987; Women and Business, president, 1987-88, board of trustees, 1984-89, 1984-92. **HONORS/AWARDS:** Seattle Chinese Post, Woman of the Year, 1990; Leadership Tomorrow, Inaugural Class, 1983-84. **BUSINESS ADDRESS:** Council Member, Seattle City Council, 600 4th Ave, 1100 Municipal Bldg, Seattle, WA 98104, (206)684-8802.

CHOE, SANG TAE
Educator. Korean American. **PERSONAL:** Born Jul 5, 1944, Kyung Puk, Republic of Korea; son of Man Hae Choe & Bongwha Sohn; married Kyung S Choe, Dec 23, 1972; children: Brian, Timothy, Hughie, Hannah. **EDUCATION:** Keimyung University, BA, 1970; American Graduate School of International Management, MIM, 1974; University of North Texas, MBA, 1977; Mississippi State University, DBA, 1984. **CAREER:** Southern Illinois University, assistant professor of marketing, 1984-85; University of Southern Indiana, professor of marketing, 1985-. **ORGANIZATIONS:** Midwest Marketing Association, director of the board, 1992-. **HONORS/AWARDS:** Army College of Korea, Performance Excellence, 1967. **SPECIAL ACHIEVEMENTS:** Established International Business Association at Southern Illinois University, 1974. **BIOGRAPHICAL SOURCES:** "Attitudinal Variations Toward Japanese Investment in the United States," SAM Advanced Management, annual, vol 54, no 3, p15-18, summer 1989; "Acculturation and Ethnic Consumer Behavior," a literature review, The Journal of Midwest Marketing, p207-213, vol 1, no 1. **HOME ADDRESS:** 608 Drexel Dr, Evansville, IN 47712. **BUSINESS PHONE:** (812)464-1822.

CHOE, SUN TOK
Martial arts instructor, educator. Korean American. **PERSONAL:** married Ki Sun Choe, Dec 25, 1975; children: Jae Young, Dae Young. **CAREER:** Florida Southern College, social science and education, adjunct professor, 1987-; World Martial Arts Federation Inc, grandmaster, owner, currently. **ORGANIZATIONS:** World Taekwon-do Association, international referee, master. **SPECIAL ACHIEVEMENTS:** 8th Degree Black Belt in Taekwon-do, grand master. **MILITARY SERVICE:** 8th Infantry Division/White Horse Division, sergeant, 1969. **BIOGRAPHICAL SOURCES:** Guinness Sports Record Book, p 131, 1989-90. **BUSINESS ADDRESS:** Grand Master, Taekwon-do School, World Martial Arts Federation Inc, 2136 E Edgewood Drive, Lakeland, FL 33803, (813)665-0488.

CHOE, TIMOTHY SONGSIK
Telecommunications company executive. Korean American. **PERSONAL:** Born Jan 20, 1963, Seoul, Republic of Korea; son of Cholwoo Choe and Hyunsoon Choe; married Soon Sil Choe, Sep 17, 1988. **EDUCATION:** DeVry Institute of Technology, EE, 3 years. **CAREER:** Intellicall, customer service manager; Servcom Ind Inc, vice pres of operations; Maxcom Communications, president, currently. **BUSINESS ADDRESS:** President, Maxcom Communications, 2115 Overview Ln, Garland, TX 75044, (214)530-4170.

CHOI, DOSOUNG PHILIP

Educator. Korean American. **PERSONAL:** Born Oct 18, 1952, Seoul, Republic of Korea; son of Eung-Sang Choi and In-Sung Kim; married Jenny S Choi, Sep 16, 1978; children: Michelle J, John S. **EDUCATION:** Seoul National University, Korea, BBA, 1974, MBA, 1976; Pennsylvania State University, PhD, 1980. **CAREER:** The Bank of Korea, Seoul, financial analyst, 1974-76; Pennsylvania State University, assistant professor of finance, 1980-81; University of Tennessee, assistant professor of finance, 1981-84, associate professor of finance, 1984-86; University of Chicago, visiting scholar, 1984-85; State University of New York, Buffalo, associate professor of finance, 1986-. **ORGANIZATIONS:** The Financial Review, associate editor, 1991-; American Finance Association, 1977-; American Economic Association, 1977-; Financial Management Association, 1977-; Korea-America Finance Association, founding board member, 1992-. **HONORS/AWARDS:** Seoul National University, Presidential Award for Highest Achievement, 1974. **SPECIAL ACHIEVEMENTS:** Numerous academic publications in financial management & economics journals, 1980-; co-author of two case books, 1985. **BUSINESS ADDRESS:** Associate Professor of Finance and Managerial Economics, State University of New York at Buffalo, School of Management, 354 Jacobs Management Ctr, Buffalo, NY 14260, (716)645-3271.

CHOI, EUNG RYONG

Physician. Korean American. **PERSONAL:** Born Mar 30, 1940, Seoul, Republic of Korea; married Youngok Lee Choi, Sep 16, 1968; children: Charles, Phil, Anne. **EDUCATION:** Catholic Medical School, Korea, MD, 1966. **CAREER:** Private practice, physician, currently. **BUSINESS ADDRESS:** Physician, 1425 E Darby Rd, Havertown, PA 19083, (215)449-2332.

CHOI, EUNHYE JENNI (JENNI)

Certified public accountant. Korean American. **PERSONAL:** Born May 24, 1963, Seoul, Republic of Korea; daughter of Kenneth and Ok Yong Park; married William Choi, Jun 6, 1987; children: Lindsay. **EDUCATION:** UC Santa Cruz, 1982-84; UC Berkeley, BA, intl business, 1986. **CAREER:** Hyundai Electronics America, marketing specialist, 1986-88; Deloitte, Haskins & Sells, sr audit accountant, 1988-90; Deloitte & Touche, sr tax consultant, 1990-92; Abbott, Stringham & Lynch, sr consultant, 1993-94; Petrinovich, Pugh & Jones, senior accountant, 1994-. **ORGANIZATIONS:** American Institute of CPA's, 1991-; California Society of CPA's, 1991-; American Society of Women Accountants, 1994-. **SPECIAL ACHIEVEMENTS:** Language proficiency: Korean; Junior Achievement, 1993. **HOME ADDRESS:** 6898 Trinidad Dr, San Jose, CA 95120. **BUSINESS PHONE:** (408)287-7911.

CHOI, FREDERICK D. S.

Educator. Korean American. **PERSONAL:** Born Sep 19, 1942, Honolulu, HI; son of Wallace P H Choi & Ethel K S Choi; married Lois S Choi, Feb 3, 1962; children: Scott A, Aaron B. **EDUCATION:** University of Hawaii, BBA, 1965, MBA, 1968; University of Washington, PhD, 1972. **CAREER:** University of Hawaii, professor, 1972-80; New York University, research professor, 1981-. **ORGANIZATIONS:** American Accounting Association, International Accounting Section, chairperson, 1993; Financial Executives Institute, 1985-; Academy of International Business, fellow, 1972-; Institute of Management Accountants, 1972-; European Accounting Association, 1981-. **HONORS/ AWARDS:** American Accounting Association, Outstanding International Accountng Educator, 1993; Citibank/New York University, Excellence in Teaching Award, 1993; American Association of Publishers, Excellence in Publishing Award, 1992; Academy of International Business, elected fellow, 1992; American Accounting Association, Wildman Gold Medal, 1986. **SPECIAL ACHIEVEMENTS:** Globalization of Financial Accounting and Reporting, Financial Executives Research Foundation, 1993; International Accounting, second edition, Prentice-Hall, Inc, 1992; Handbook of International Accounting, John Wiley & Sons, 1991; Capital Market Effects of International Accounting Diversity, Dow Jones-Irwin, 1990; Accounting and Financial Reporting in Japan, Van Nostrand Reinhold, 1987. **BIOGRAPHICAL SOURCES:** Accounting Research Monthly, Fall 1993. **BUSINESS ADDRESS:** Research Professor, NY University, Stern School of Business, 44 West 4th St, Ste 7-67, New York, NY 10012, (212)998-0420.

CHOI, HYUNGMOO

Lawyer. Korean American. **PERSONAL:** Born Apr 14, 1950, Seoul, Republic of Korea; son of Hyung Joon Choi & Tae Im Kim; married Sunny Sunhye Yoon Choi, Jun 13, 1987; children: William James. **EDUCATION:** Seoul National University, School of Law, LLB, 1976; New York University, MA, 1986; Fordham University, School of Law, foreign lawyers program, 1986-87, JD,

1993. **CAREER:** Munhwa Broadcasting Corp, reporter, 1977-81; Korea Central Daily, reporter, 1982-83; Korea Times, New York, associate city editor, 1983-84; Chosun Daily News, metropolitan editor, 1984-86; Korea Times, New York, foreign editor, 1986-90; Korea News Inc, general counsel, 1991-; private practice, attorney at law, 1993-. **ORGANIZATIONS:** American Bar Assn, 1991-; New York State Bar Assn, 1991-; New York County Lawyers' Assn, 1991-. **HONORS/AWARDS:** Admitted to the New York Bar, 1991; Tae-Neung Precint, Seoul, Award of Appreciation, 1977. **MILITARY SERVICE:** Republic of Korea Army, sergeant, 1971-74. **BUSINESS ADDRESS:** Attorney at Law, 121 W 27th St, Ste 803, New York, NY 10001, (212)645-2212.

CHOI, IN-CHAN

Educator. Korean American. **PERSONAL:** Born Nov 5, 1959, Seoul, Republic of Korea; son of Sang Jun Choi and Kyungae Chang; married Sikyung Choi, Jul 4, 1987; children: Giehae, Joonsuh. **EDUCATION:** Korea University, BS, 1982; Iowa State University, BS, 1984; Columbia University, MS, 1986, MPhil, 1988, PhD, 1990. **CAREER:** Columbia University, research, teaching assistant, 1985-90; Bell Communications Research, technical research staff, 1988; Wichita State University, assistant professor, 1990-. **ORGANIZATIONS:** Operations Research Society of America, 1984; The Institute of Management Science, 1991; Institute of Industrial Engineer, 1982; Society for Industrial and Applied Mathematics, 1989; Production and Operations Management Society, 1992. **HONORS/AWARDS:** Operations Research Society of America, Omega Rho, 1985; American Mathematics Society, Pi Mu Epsilon, 1990. **SPECIAL ACHIEVEMENTS:** Several presentations in professional conferences; articles in professional journals such as ORSA Journal on Computing, 1990, Large-Scale Numerical Optimization, 1990, Mathematical Programming, 1993, Location Science, 1993, Journal of Optimization Theory and Applications, 1994. **BUSINESS ADDRESS:** Asst Professor, Dept of Industrial Engineering, Wichita State University, 1845 Fairmount, Box 35, Wichita, KS 67208-1514.

CHOI, JAI-KEUN

Cleric. Korean American. **PERSONAL:** Born Feb 26, 1942, Hadong, Kyungnam, Republic of Korea; son of Kyung-Hwan Choi; married Seungja K Choi, May 5, 1975; children: Eileen, Kenneth. **EDUCATION:** Yonsei University, ThB, 1971, The United Graduate School of Theology, ThM, 1973; Korea Theological Seminary, 1975; University of Toronto, Emmanuel College, ThM, 1978; Yale University, Divinity School, STM, 1981, Graduate School, MA, 1983; Harvard University, Divinity School, 1984-85, Graduate School of Art and Science. **CAREER:** The Connecticut Korean Presbyterian Church, 1985-87; The Korean Presbyterian Church of Westchester, pastor, 1989-.

CHOI, JAI WON

Federal government official. Korean American. **PERSONAL:** Born Jan 1, 1937, Kumho-Up, Kyungpuk, Republic of Korea; son of Byung Zoo Choi and Kycho Kim; married Grace Park Choi, Mar 27, 1971; children: Eleanor S. **EDUCATION:** Yohsei University, BA, 1959; California Baptist College, BS (magna cum laude), 1966; University of Minnesota, MA, 1970, PhD, 1980. **CAREER:** Kyungsin High School, English teacher, 1960-63; Ohio Dept of Health, statistician, 1973-74; US Department of HHS, mathematical statistician, 1976-; Johns Hopkins University, research associate, 1985. **ORGANIZATIONS:** American Statistical Association, 1976-; Washington Statistical Society, program chairperson, 1976-89; Korean Scientists and Engineers Association, 1980-89; Biometric Society, 1981-85; Toastmaster International, club president, 1988-89. **HONORS/AWARDS:** Center for Disease Control, Best Statistical Paper Published in 1989; National Center for Health Statistics, Directors Award, 1982; California Baptist College, President's Honor Student, 1964-66. **SPECIAL ACHIEVEMENTS:** Thirty scientific papers published; 40 presentations of papers; Chi-Square Test for Goodness of Fit and Independence for Complex Data, Biometrics, p 45, 1989. **HOME ADDRESS:** 2512 Lindley Terrace, Rockville, MD 20850, (301)340-8713. **BUSINESS PHONE:** (301)436-7047.

CHOI, JAI-YOUNG

Educator. Korean American. **PERSONAL:** Born Apr 23, 1947, Seoul, Republic of Korea; son of Nam-Kyu Choi and Bong-Kyu Lee; married Kun-Woo Choi, Nov 1974; children: Mehee, Jehee. **EDUCATION:** Yonsei University, Seoul, Korea, BA, 1970; University of Kansas, Lawrence, MA, 1978; University of Oklahoma, PhD, 1982. **CAREER:** Lamar University, Economics Dept, assistant professor, 1982-86, associate professor, 1986-92, professor, 1992-. **ORGANIZATIONS:** American Economic Association; Southern Economic

Association, 1982-; Southwestern Economic Association, 1982-; Southwestern Society of Economists, 1982-; Atlantic Economic Society, 1982-; Korea-America Economic Association, 1984-. **HONORS/AWARDS:** Articles cited by other authors, 1985-; refereed numerous articles for professional economic journals such as Economica, Canadian Journal of Economics, Southern Economic Journal, etc. **SPECIAL ACHIEVEMENTS:** Three publications in Economica, 1984, 1985, 1987; Oxford Economic Papers, 1987; Canadian Journal of Economics, 1987; Southern Economic Journal (3 publications), 1984, 1987, 1991; International Economic Journal (2 publications), 1990, 1992; articles on international economics. **MILITARY SERVICE:** Korean Army, sergeant, 1970-73. **BUSINESS ADDRESS:** Professor, Dept of Economics & Finance, Lamar University, PO Box 10045, Beaumont, TX 77710, (409)880-8062.

CHOI, JIN WOOK

Educator. Korean American. **PERSONAL:** Born May 4, 1950, Chunchen, Kangwondo, Republic of Korea; son of Chang Kyung Choi & Young Ae Choi; married Hee Young Choi; children: Juliana, Jonathan. **EDUCATION:** University of Northern Iowa, BA, 1976; Iowa State University, MS, 1979, PhD, 1982. **CAREER:** Chicago Board of Trade, advisory economist, 1981-88; DePaul University, assistant professor, 1988-. **ORGANIZATIONS:** Financial Management Association; Association for Investment Management & Research; American Economics Association. **HONORS/AWARDS:** Korea Futures Trading Association, Proud Korean Futures Man, 1987. **SPECIAL ACHIEVEMENTS:** Numerous articles on futures and options markets. **MILITARY SERVICE:** Air Force, sgt, 1970-73. **BUSINESS ADDRESS:** Assistant Professor, DePaul University, 15 E Jackson Blvd, DPC 6216, Chicago, IL 60604, (312)362-8842.

CHOI, JOHN HAETAK

Research chemist. Korean American. **PERSONAL:** Born Jul 8, 1947, Kyongju, Republic of Korea; son of Hyun-Chan & Wookyung Choi; married Yeoun Choi, Oct 23, 1974; children: Hannah, David. **EDUCATION:** Seoul National University, BSc, 1973; Dartmouth College, PhD, 1980; University of Minnesota, postdoctoral fellow, 1980-84. **CAREER:** E I DuPont De Nemours & Co, research scientist, 1984-. **ORGANIZATIONS:** American Chemical Society, 1980-. **HONORS/AWARDS:** Seoul National University, Academic Honor, 1972. **SPECIAL ACHIEVEMENTS:** Publications: 10 academic research, 1980-84; 2 industrial research, 1984-92; 4 patents: printing, electronics, 1984-93. **MILITARY SERVICE:** Korean Air Force, corporal, 1968-71. **HOME ADDRESS:** 105 Joy St, Sayre, PA 18840, (717)888-3435. **BUSINESS ADDRESS:** Senior Research Chemist, Electronics R&D, EI DuPont De Nemours & Co, Patterson Blvd, Towanda, PA 18848, (717)268-3243.

CHOI, KYUNG-JU

Educator & researcher. Korean American. **PERSONAL:** Born Sep 14, 1945, Seoul, Republic of Korea; son of Soonjae & Keebun Choi; married Jung-In, Apr 11, 1976; children: Jin, Joon, Sun Grace, Young. **EDUCATION:** Youngnam University, Kyungpook, Korea, BE, 1969; Kyungpook National University, Taegu, Korea, ME, 1975; University of Tennessee, Knoxville, MS, 1980, PhD, 1983. **CAREER:** Kyungpook National University, instructor, 1975-77; University of Tennessee, Knoxville, research associate, 1983-86; Fleetguard Inc, senior staff research scientist, 1986-; Tennessee Technological University, adjunct professor, 1986-. **ORGANIZATIONS:** Fluid/Particle Separation Journal, editorial board, 1989-; Academic Solid/Fluid Separation, Relationship Committee, 1989-; Korean Scientists and Engineers in USA, president, 1990-92; Toastmaster's Club; Society of Plastics Engineers; American Filtration Society. **SPECIAL ACHIEVEMENTS:** Author of over 30 books and articles relating to polymers and filtration, including: "Pore Distribution & Permeability of Cellulosic Filtration Media," Fluid/Particle Separation Journal. **HOME ADDRESS:** 525 Laurel Park Circle, Cookeville, TN 38501, (615)526-4995. **BUSINESS ADDRESS:** Sr Staff Research Scientist, Fleetguard Inc, 1200 Fleetguard Rd, Cookeville, TN 38501, (615)528-9409.

CHOI, KYUNG KOOK

Educator. Korean American. **PERSONAL:** Born Mar 23, 1946, Seoul, Republic of Korea; son of Bong Mo Choi and Yang Keun Min; married Ho Youn Yang, Dec 30, 1976; children: Philip Yoonsung, Andrew Yoonkang. **EDUCATION:** Yon-Sei University, Korea, BS, 1970; University of Iowa, MS, 1977, PhD, 1980. **CAREER:** University of Iowa, postdoctoral fellow, 1981, assistant research scientist, 1982, assistant professor, 1984, associate professor, 1986, professor, 1990-, Center for Computer Aided Design, associate director, 1990, Center for Computer Aided Design, deputy director, 1993-. **ORGANIZA-**

TIONS: American Society of Mechanical Engineers, 1984; American Institute of Aeronautics & Astronautics, 1988; Korean Scientists and Engineers Association in America, 1989; Journal of Mechanics of Structures and Machines, associate editor, 1990; National AIAA Technical Committee on Multidisciplinary Design Optimization, 1989; CALS/CE Mechanical Tools and Technology Task Sub Group, 1989; World Congress Optimal Design of Structural Systems, advisory board, 1993; Technical Advisory Committee, NATO Science, 1993; Journal of Optimization Theory and Applications, 1993. **HONORS/AWARDS:** NIH, National Research Service Award, 1983; University of Iowa, Faculty Scholars Award, 1987-90; University of Iowa Chapter of ASME, Outstanding ME Professor Award, 1987; Phi Beta Delta, 1988. **SPECIAL ACHIEVEMENTS:** Author, Design Sensitivity Analysis of Structural Systems, Academic Press, 1986; Method of Engineering Mathematics, Prentice Hall, 1993; editor, "Special Issue on Shape Optimization," Mechanics of Structures and Machines, vol 20, no 4, 1993; 86 technical papers published. **BUSINESS ADDRESS:** Professor and Deputy Director, Dept of Mechanical Engineering, University of Iowa, 2132 Engineering Bldg, Iowa City, IA 52242, (319)335-5684.

CHOI, MICHAEL KAMWAH

Engineer, researcher. Chinese American/Hong Kong American. **PERSONAL:** Born Aug 16, 1952, Shenzhen, Quandong, People's Republic of China; son of Ying-Loi Choi and Kan-Hau Yuen Choi; married Wendy L Choi, Apr 26, 1985; children: Natalie J. **EDUCATION:** Brown University, ScB (honors, magna cum laude), 1976; Massachusetts Institute of Technology, MSME, 1978, engineer's degree, 1979. **CAREER:** Science Applications International Corporation, senior research engr, 1979-87; Fairchild Space and Defense Corp, principal thermal engr, 1987-90; National Aeronautics and Space Administration, Goddard Space Flight Center, aerospace engr, 1990-; Far Ultra-Violet Spectroscopic Explorer, thermal control subsystem mgr, 1992-. **ORGANIZATIONS:** American Society of Mechanical Engineers, 1980-; Tau Beta Pi, 1976-; Sigma Xi, 1976-; Commonwealth of Virginia Dept of Commerce, registered professional engr, 1987-; American Solar Energy Society, 1980-86; International Solar Energy Society, Solar Energy Journal reviewer, 1983-86; National Society of Professional Engineers, 1987-88; Virginia Society of Professional Engineers, 1987-88. **HONORS/AWARDS:** NASA Goddard Space Flight Center, Performance Award, 1991, 1992, Peer Award, 1991, Quality Increase Award, 1993, Special Act Group Award, 1993. **SPECIAL ACHIEVEMENTS:** Publications in American Society of Mechanical Engineers, Solar Engineering, 1984, 1986, Winter Annual Meeting, 1980; Publications in International Solar Energy Society/American Solar Energy Society annual meetings proceedings, 1980-83; reviewer: Solar Energy Journal, 1983-86; ASME Solar Engineering, 1984-87. **HOME ADDRESS:** 2237 Halter Ln, Herndon, VA 22071. **BUSINESS ADDRESS:** Aerospace Engineer, NASA Goddard Space Flight Center, Greenbelt Road, Code 724, Bldg 7, Rm 213, Greenbelt, MD 20771, (301)286-4707.

CHOI, NAMKEE GANG

Educator. Korean American. **PERSONAL:** Born Jan 26, 1955, Kyungbuk, Republic of Korea; daughter of Heedo Gang and Soon Chung; children: Yoonie Bryan. **EDUCATION:** Ewha Woman's University, Seoul, Korea, BA, 1976, MA, 1980; University of Minnesota, MSW, 1983; University of California, Berkeley, DSW, 1987. **CAREER:** University of California, Berkeley, TA/RA, 1985-87; SUNY, Buffalo, assistant professor, 1987-, associate professor, 1994-. **ORGANIZATIONS:** The Gerontological Society of America, 1988-; Council of Social Work Educators, 1988-; The Asian American Social Work Educators, 1989-. **HONORS/AWARDS:** International Rotary Foundation; International Rotary Scholar, 1981-82; Peace Education Organization; PEO Scholar, 1985-87. **SPECIAL ACHIEVEMENTS:** Articles in leading journals: "Correlates of the Elderly: Participation & Nonparticipation in SSI," 1992; "Correlates of the Economic Status of Widowed and Divorced Elderly Women," 1992; "Does Social Security Redistribute Income: A Tax-Transfer Approach," 1991; "Racial Differences in the Determinants of Living Arrangement of Widowed. . .," 1991; "Differential Life Expectancy, Socioeconomic Status, and Social Security Benefits," 1989; "Patterns & Determinants of Social Service Utilization: Comparison of the Childless Elderly, Elderly Parents Living Apart from their Children, and Elderly Parents Coresiding with their Children," 1994; others. **BUSINESS ADDRESS:** Associate Professor, School of Social Work, SUNY at Buffalo, 359 Baldy Hall, Buffalo, NY 14260-1050, (716)645-3381.

CHOI, PAUL LEE
Attorney. Korean American. **PERSONAL:** Born Sep 23, 1964, Seoul, Republic of Korea; son of Hongyung Choi and Lee K Choi; married Lisa Kim Choi, Jun 29, 1991. **EDUCATION:** Harvard College, AB (magna cum laude), 1986; Harvard Law School, JD (magna cum laude), 1989. **CAREER:** Hon Lawrence Siberman, judicial clerk, 1989-90; Sidley & Austin, associate, 1990-. **ORGANIZATIONS:** Asian American Bar Association, social committee, co-chair, 1991-; American Bar Association, 1990-; Illinois State Bar Association, 1990-; Chicago Bar Association, 1990-. **HONORS/AWARDS:** Harvard College, Phi Beta Kappa, 1985, Detur Prize, 1983, John Harvard Scholar, 1983-86; Harvard Law School, Sears Prize, 1987. **SPECIAL ACHIEVEMENTS:** Editor, Harvard Law Review, 1987-89; author, "Burdens on the Free Exercise of Religion," HLR, 1989; Harvard Law School, Legal Methods Instrutor, 1988. **BIOGRAPHICAL SOURCES:** Article in Korea Central Daily Chicago, p 3, Aug 19, 1987. **BUSINESS ADDRESS:** Associate, Sidley & Austin, One First National Plaza, Ste 4400, Chicago, IL 60603, (312)853-2145.

CHOI, PAUL W.
Bank executive. Korean American. **PERSONAL:** Born Jan 28, 1934, Taegu City, Kyung-Sang Puk Do, Republic of Korea; son of Ki Bok Choi and Kae Whan Lee; married Sook Chong Choi, Mar 5, 1960; children: Jame, William, Mary Anne. **EDUCATION:** Seton Hall University, BS, 1959; New School, Graduate Faculty, MA, 1964, PhD candidate. **CAREER:** Upsala College, adjunct professor of economics, currently; Midlantic National Bank, senior vp, currently. **ORGANIZATIONS:** American Economic Assn, 1963; American Finance Assn, 1965. **HONORS/AWARDS:** Seton Hall University, Athletic Hall of Fame, tennis. **BUSINESS ADDRESS:** Senior Vice President, Midlantic National Bank, 499 Thornall St, Edison, NJ 08818.

CHOI, RAYMOND YOONSEOK
Dentist. Korean American. **PERSONAL:** Born Jun 7, 1960, Seoul, Republic of Korea; son of Young K Choi and Jom S Choi; married Amy, Jun 18, 1988; children: Lisa M, Daniel J. **EDUCATION:** Pomona College, BA, 1983; University of Southern California, School of Dentistry, DDS, 1987. **CAREER:** USC School of Dentistry, assistant clinical professor, 1987-; self-employed dentist, currently. **ORGANIZATIONS:** American Dental Association, 1983-; California Dental Association, 1983-; Orange County Dental Society, 1991-; San Gabriel Valley Dental Society, 1993-; American Pain Society, 1991; International Association for the Study of Pain, 1991; American Association for the Study of Headache, 1993-. **HONORS/AWARDS:** American Equilibration Society, Outstanding Achievements in Studies of Occlusion and TMJ Function, 1987. **BUSINESS ADDRESS:** Dentist/Director Orofacial Pain Section, The Center for Rehabilitation and Pain Management, 474 S Raymond Ave, Ste 100, Pasadena, CA 91105, (818)564-8804.

CHOI, RICHARD YUNGHO
Broadcasting company executive. Korean American. **PERSONAL:** Born Mar 31, 1948, Seoul, Republic of Korea; son of Tae Won Choi and Bok N Choi; married Young Yun Choi, Sep 20, 1975; children: Jennifer Y, Yvonne M. **EDUCATION:** Yonsei University, Korea, MBA, 1974. **CAREER:** Southland Corporation, sales department, 1974-78; J B Mercantile Inc, vice president, 1978-88; Radio Korea, USA, executive director, 1988-. **ORGANIZATIONS:** Korean-American Chamber of Commerce, 1992-; Korean-American Broadcaster Association, 1988-. **HONORS/AWARDS:** City of Los Angeles, Outstanding Civic Service, 1992; Korean Broadcasting System, Best Radio Broadcaster of the Year, 1993. **BUSINESS ADDRESS:** Executive Director, Radio Korea USA, 2001 West Olympic Blvd, Los Angeles, CA 90006, (213)487-1300.

CHOI, SONGSU
World Bank official. Korean American. **PERSONAL:** Born Jan 23, 1950, Gwangju, Chonnam, Republic of Korea; son of Byung-Ok Choi and Gui Rye Chang; married Mihae Namkoong Choi, Jul 30, 1980; children: Wonshik Albert, Ha-Young. **EDUCATION:** Seoul National University, BE, 1972, MCP, 1974; Massachusetts Institute of Technology, PhD, 1984. **CAREER:** Government of Korea, Ministry of Construction, senior planner, 1973-76; MIT, research associate, fellow, instructor, 1979-84; Louis Berger International, senior economist, 1984-87; The World Bank, senior urban economist, 1987-. **HONORS/AWARDS:** Whitney Young Foundation, fellow, 1980; US Government, Fulbright Fellowship, 1976-80. **SPECIAL ACHIEVEMENTS:** China Housing and Social Security Systems Reform Project, Tianjin Urban and Environment Project, manager, 1992-; three finance and urban development projects financed by World Bank in India, manager, 1988-92. **BUSINESS**

ADDRESS: Senior Economist, The World Bank, 1818 H St NW, Rm F8070, Washington, DC 20433, (202)458-2945.

CHOI, SOONOK
Educator. Korean American. **PERSONAL:** Born Jan 31, 1959, Seoul, Republic of Korea; daughter of Jae-hoo Choi & Unsun Park. **EDUCATION:** Ewha Woman's University, BA, 1981, MA, 1984; University of Iowa, PhD, 1992. **CAREER:** University of Colorado at Denver, assistant professor, 1991-. **ORGANIZATIONS:** American Philosophical Association; Sierra Club. **HONORS/AWARDS:** University of Colorado at Denver, Summer Stipend Fellowship, 1992; University Of Iowa, Outstanding Teaching Assistant, 1990. **SPECIAL ACHIEVEMENTS:** Language proficiency: native Korean. **HOME PHONE:** (303)388-7328. **BUSINESS ADDRESS:** Assistant Professor, Dept of Philosophy, University of Colorado at Denver, PO Box 173364, Campus Box 179, Denver, CO 80217-3364, (303)556-8558.

CHOI, SUNG SOOK (SUNG SOOK CHANG)
Association administrator. Korean American. **PERSONAL:** Born Apr 23, 1937, Seoul, Republic of Korea; daughter of Bok Kil and Wun Hyang Chang; married Chang Kyu Choi, May 16, 1964; children: Yonhee Choi Gordon, Jeanhee, Samuel. **EDUCATION:** Ewha Women's University, BS, 1961; Clarion State University, MS, 1977. **CAREER:** Alhambra Community Hospital, medical technologist, 1967-69; Alhambra Medical Clinic, chief medical technologist, 1969-75; Clarion Community Hospital, medical technologist, 1975-80; Arlington Medical Laboratory, supervisor, 1980-85. **ORGANIZATIONS:** YWCA Metropolitan Chicago, Korean Center, director, 1991-; United Korean School of Metropolitan Chicago, vice president, board of directors, 1990-; Korean-American Senior Center, board member, 1987-, Fundraising Committee, chairman, 1992. **HONORS/AWARDS:** Ewha Women's University, four year academic scholarship, 1957-61; Ewha Women's University, president, 1960-61; International College of YWCA, president, 1959-60. **SPECIAL ACHIEVEMENTS:** Started Korean language and cultural heritage program for children, Chicago area, 1980; first to start YWCA movement in the Korean-American community in Chicago area, 1991. **HOME ADDRESS:** 545 North Hamlin, Park Ridge, IL 60068, (708)698-0332.

CHOI, TAI-SOON
Physician. Korean American. **PERSONAL:** Born Dec 29, 1935, Seoul, Republic of Korea; married Yong-ui Choi, Jun 1965; children: Susanna, Sylvia, Steven. **EDUCATION:** Seoul National University, Medical College, MD, 1961. **CAREER:** Mercy Hospital of Buffalo, director of nursery, 1973-; State University of New York, Buffalo, clinical associate professor. **BUSINESS ADDRESS:** Director of Nursery, Mercy Hospital, 565 Abbott Rd, Buffalo, NY 14220, (716)828-2572.

CHOI, TONY SUNG
Banker. Korean American. **PERSONAL:** Born May 1, 1964, Seoul, Republic of Korea; son of Kyung Wha and Wha Soon Choi. **EDUCATION:** University of California, BA (magna cum laude), 1986; Harvard University, MBA, 1988. **CAREER:** Public Development Corp, senior project mgr, 1988-90; City of New York, assistant to deputy mayor 1990-91; Sanwa Bank, assistant vice president, 1991-. **ORGANIZATIONS:** Korean-Americans in Government, 1991-. **HONORS/AWARDS:** Sloan Foundation, fellowship to Harvard, 1987; Phi Beta Kappa, 1985. **HOME ADDRESS:** 305 E 40th St, #5A, New York, NY 10016, (212)599-0959.

CHOI, YE-CHIN
Research scientist, educator. Korean American. **PERSONAL:** Born Mar 13, 1929, Yang-gu, Kangwon-Do, Republic of Korea; son of Jin-Yun Choi and Jin-Han Kim; married In-Sook Chang, Feb 8, 1949; children: Kyong-Cha, Ke-Soon, Kyoung-Hee, Won-Young, Boyoung. **EDUCATION:** University of Texas at El Paso, BS, 1971; Louisiana State University, PhD, 1976. **CAREER:** Kangwon National University, Dept of Biotechnology, visiting professor, 1991-93; New York University Medical Center, research assistant professor, 1983-91, 1993-. **ORGANIZATIONS:** American Society for Microbiology, 1972. **HOME ADDRESS:** 1631 Anderson Avenue, Fort Lee, NJ 07024, (201)944-8117. **BUSINESS PHONE:** (212)263-5599.

CHOI, YOUNG DONG
Educator. Korean American. **PERSONAL:** Born Jan 20, 1956, Seoul, Republic of Korea; son of Sang B Choi and Mi H Choi; married Sunnie S Choi, Mar 23, 1985; children: Euna, Yena. **EDUCATION:** Yonsei University, BS, 1979; Southern Illinois University, Edwardsville, MS, 1984; State University of New

York, College of Environmental Science and Forestry, PhD, 1991. **CAREER:** Yonsei University, graduate assistant, 1979-80; Southern Illinois University, graduate assistant, 1982-84; State University of New York, research assistant, 1985-89; State of New York, environmental education coordinator, 1989-90; Florida A&M University, project counselor, 1993; Purdue University, Calumet, assistant professor, 1990-. **ORGANIZATIONS:** Ecological Society of America, 1987-; Sigma Xi, associate member, 1987-; American Institute of Biological Sciences, 1987-; International Association of Ecology, 1993-; The Society for Ecological Restoration, charter member, 1989-; Natural Areas Association, 1990-. **HONORS/AWARDS:** Purdue University, Calumet, Scholarly Research Award, 1992; Edna Bailey Sussman Fund, Environmental Internship Award, 1987. **SPECIAL ACHIEVEMENTS:** Soil-vegetation Relationship in Three Razed Residential Sites in Indiana Dunes National Lakeshore, 1993; Vegetation Development on Iron Mine Tailings in Northern New York, 1991; Managing Environmental Resources, 1988; Heavy Metal Concentrations in Tower Lake Green Sunfish, Lepomis cyanellus, 1984. **BIOGRAPHICAL SOURCES:** Syracuse Post-Standard, p 12 East, Dec 14, 1989. **BUSINESS ADDRESS:** Assistant Professor, Dept of Biological Sciences, Purdue University, Calumet, Box 144, Hammond, IN 46323-2094, (219)989-2325.

CHOKSI, JAYENDRA C.
Physician. Indo-American. **PERSONAL:** Born Apr 8, 1953, Ahmedabad, Gujarat, India; son of Chamanlal M Choksi and Madhuben C Choksi; married Shaila, Nov 29, 1976; children: Rushir, Nilay. **EDUCATION:** Gujarat University, India, MBBS, 1975, MD, psychiatry, 1979; SUNY at Stony Brook, MD, psychiatry, 1984. **CAREER:** Northern Virginia Doctors Hospital, Dept of Psychiatry, medical dir, 1989-90; TGH Mental Health Services, medical dir, 1993-; private practice, psychiatrist, 1988-. **ORGANIZATIONS:** American Psychiatric Assn, 1983-; Tampa Psychiatric Society, scty, 1993; Gujarati Samaj of Tampa Bay, treasurer, 1993. **BUSINESS ADDRESS:** Physician, 4001 N Riverside Dr, Ste 205, Tampa, FL 33603, (813)238-2226.

CHOKSY, JAMSHEED KAIRSHASP
Historian, educator, researcher. Indo-American/Sri Lankan American. **PERSONAL:** Born Jan 8, 1962, Bombay, India. **EDUCATION:** Columbia University, BA, 1985; Harvard University, PhD, 1991. **CAREER:** Harvard University, junior fellow, 1988-93; Stanford University, faculty; Indiana University, assistant professor, 1993-. **ORGANIZATIONS:** Institute for Advanced Study, 1993-94. **HONORS/AWARDS:** National Endowment for the Humanities, fellowship, 1993-94; Stanford University, Andrew W Mellon Fellowship, 1991-93; North American Zoroastrian Congress, Scholar Excellence Award, 1988; numerous others. **SPECIAL ACHIEVEMENTS:** Author: Conflict & Cooperation: Muslims & Zoroastrians in Medieval Iran, Stanford University Press, 1945; Purity & Pollution in Zorastrianism: Triumph over Evil, University of Texas Press, 1989; ''Women in Early Islamic Iran,'' Women in Iran from Medieval Times to the Islamic Republic, ed, G Nashat, 1995; ''An Emissary from Akbar to Abbas I,'' Journal of the Royal Asiatic Society, 1991; ''Zoroastrianism,'' Encyclopedia of the Modern Middle East, Macmillan, 1994; ''Loan and Sales Contacts,'' Indo-Iranian Journal 31, 1988; numerous others. **BUSINESS ADDRESS:** Assistant Professor, Dept of Near Eastern Languages and Cultures, Indiana University, Bloomington, IN 47405, (812)855-4323.

CHONG, CLYDE HOK HEEN
Research chemist, consultant. Chinese American. **PERSONAL:** Born Mar 6, 1933, Honolulu, HI; son of Pang Yet Chong & Helen Say Chong; married Joy A Chong, May 23, 1964; children: John Robert, Helen Elizabeth. **EDUCATION:** Wabash College, BA, 1954; Michigan State University, PhD, chemistry, 1958. **CAREER:** Mound Laboratory, Monsanto, research chemist, 1958-1988; part-time consultant, currently. **HOME ADDRESS:** 448 Wileray Drive, Miamisburg, OH 45342.

CHONG, FRANK
Educational administrator. Chinese American. **PERSONAL:** Born Feb 3, 1957, New York, NY; son of Ning & Lin Chong. **EDUCATION:** University of California, Berkeley, BA, 1979; Harvard University, MPA, 1987. **CAREER:** Asian Manpower Services, executive director, 1979-82; Asian Community Mental Health, special services, director, 1982-86; Assembly Speaker Willie Brown, legislative assistant, 1987-91; City College of San Francisco, campus dean, 1991-93, dean of student affairs, 1993-. **ORGANIZATIONS:** Wu Yee Children Service, vice president, 1991-. **HONORS/AWARDS:** Harvard University, Class Marshal, 1987; University of California, Berkeley, President's Undergraduate Fellowship, 1979. **BUSINESS ADDRESS:** Dean of Student Affairs, City College of San Francisco, 50 Phelan Ave, #E200, San Francisco, CA 94112, (415)239-3211.

CHONG, KEN P.
Government official. Chinese American. **PERSONAL:** Born Sep 22, 1942, Linpin, Kwangtung, China; son of Chih-Hwan Chong and Sai-Chong Ho Chong; married Shuang-Ling, 1967; children: Frederic, Lillian. **EDUCATION:** Taiwan Natl Cheng Kung University, BS, 1964; University of Massachusetts, MS, 1966; Princeton University, MSE, MA, 1968, PhD, 1969. **CAREER:** University of Massachusetts, research asst, 1964-66; Princeton University, teaching fellow, 1966-69; Natl Steel Corp, R & D, sr project engineer, 1969-74; University of Wyoming, professor, 1974-84, professor & chair of structures, solid mechanics, 1984-89; Natl Science Foundation, program director, 1989-. **ORGANIZATIONS:** ASCE, Stability Committee, chairman, 1986-88, Elasticity Committee, control member, 1984-86, Materials Div, Executive Committee, board member, 1993-96, J of Engineering Mechanics, co-editor, 1986-88; Rocky Mtn Chinese Society of Science and Engineering, president, 1988-89; Natl Science Foundation of Civil Infrastructure System Working Group, chairman, 1992-93; US-Japan Program in Natural Resources, Task Committee, chairman, 1989-; Natl Research Council-Federal Construction Council, Program Committee, 1989-; Construction Metrication Council, board member, 1991-94;. **HONORS/AWARDS:** University of Hong Kong, honorary professor, 1981; American Society for Engineering Education, Dow Outstanding Young Faculty Award, 1977; Tau Beta Pi, Eminent Engineer, 1976; Halliburton Education Foundation, Outstanding Research & Teaching, 1987; Colorado Engineering Council, Professional Eminence Award, 1988; Natl Science Foundation, Special Achievement Award, 1989, 1993; Shanghai University of Technology, honorary professor. **SPECIAL ACHIEVEMENTS:** Co-chair, 5th ASCE Engineering Mechanics Conference, chair, technical programs, 1984; over 100 refereed technical papers in structures, mechanics, 1969-; author, 8 major books with ASCE, Elsevier, Prentice-Hall in structures/mechanics; editor, Intl J of Thin-Walled Structures, UK, 1987-; chair, NSF Task Committee for major US initiative on Civil Infrastructure, 1992-93; Tonji University, Tianjin University, advisory professor. **BUSINESS ADDRESS:** Research Program Director, Natl Science Foundation, 4201 Wilson Blvd, Engineering Directorate, Arlington, VA 22230.

CHONG, PEK-EAN
Data systems coordinator, contract specialist. Malaysian American/Chinese American. **PERSONAL:** Born Jan 11, 1942, Kuala Lumpur, Selangor, Malaysia; daughter of Goh Keng Swee and Ong Siew Kim; married N C Chong, Sep 13, 1973; children: Kwong Minh. **EDUCATION:** University of Malaysia, BSc (honors), 1964, dip ed, 1965, MS, agriculture, 1973. **CAREER:** Department of Public Social Services, data systems analyst II; Department of Health Services, system manager; LA Sheriff's Department, data systems coordinator, contract specialist, currently. **ORGANIZATIONS:** Don Bosco Teachers Parents Association, board member, 1992-93; Boy Scouts of America, Troop 351, communications sec, 1989-92; Huntington Memorial Library, 1992-93; KCET, 1990-93; Greater Los Angeles Zoological Association, 1992-93. **HONORS/AWARDS:** County of Los Angeles, Employee of the Month, 1989. **SPECIAL ACHIEVEMENTS:** Language proficiency: German, Russian, Spanish, Malay, Chinese, English. **BIOGRAPHICAL SOURCES:** Hike up Mount Kinabalu: Highest Mountain in SE Asia, Asian Week, 1967. **BUSINESS ADDRESS:** Data Systems Coordinator, Contract Specialist, Los Angeles Sheriff Department, 4700 Ramona Blvd, Lower Level, Monterey Park, CA 91754.

CHONG, PENG-KHUAN
Educator. Malaysian American. **PERSONAL:** Born Sep 6, 1940, Georgetown, Penang, Malaysia; married Stacey Yap, Jun 25, 1984. **EDUCATION:** Cornell University, BA, 1964; University of New Hampshire, MA, 1966. **CAREER:** Phillips Exeter Academy, 1964-66; Plymouth State College, assistant professor, 1966-. **ORGANIZATIONS:** Association for Asian Studies, 1966-; New England Political Science Association, 1966-; Centre for Asian Studies, Hong Kong, 1976-. **HONORS/AWARDS:** Plymouth State College, Distinguished Teacher of the Year, 1987. **SPECIAL ACHIEVEMENTS:** Author, Problems of Political Development: Singapore, 1971; Love in Search of Moon-Waves, 1976; My Tears Belong to Malaysia, 1979; Dimana: Love Poems, 1982. **BUSINESS ADDRESS:** Assistant Professor, Plymouth State College, Rounds Hall, Plymouth, NH 03264.

CHONG, PING
Artist. Chinese American. **PERSONAL:** Born Oct 2, 1946, Toronto, Canada. **EDUCATION:** Pratt Institute, 1964-66; School of Visual Arts, certificate,

1969. **CAREER:** Meredith Monk, House Foundation, company member, 1973-77; Ping Chong & Co, founder, artistic director, 1975-. **ORGANIZA-TIONS:** Theater Communications Group, board of directors, 1986-88; Taipai Cultural Center, NY City, board of directors, 1991-. **HONORS/AWARDS:** Village Voice, Obie Award, 1977; Theater Communications Group, USA Playwrights Award, 1988; Dance Theater Workshop, New York Dance & Performance Award, 1992; National Endowment for the Arts Fellowships: Guggenheim Fellowship, 1984 McKnight Fellowships, 1987, 1992, TCG/PEW Charitable Trust National Artist Residency Grant Recipient, 1992-95, University of Minnesota, Winton Fellow, 1993-94. **BUSINESS ADDRESS:** Artistic Director, Ping Chong and Co, 47 Great Jones St, New York, NY 10012, (212)529-1557.

CHONG, RAE DAWN
Actress. Chinese American. **PERSONAL:** Born 1960?, British Columbia; daughter of Tommy Chong; married Owen Baylis (divorced); children: Morgan. **CAREER:** Actress, films include: Quest for Fire, 1982; Commando, 1985; The Color Purple, 1985; Soul Man, 1986; The Principal, 1987; The Squeeze, 1987; Amazon, 1990; Common Bonds, 1991; Sex, Drugs, and AIDS, documentary, narrator. **ORGANIZATIONS:** Screen Actors Guild; American Federation of Television and Radio Artists. **HONORS/AWARDS:** Black Filmmakers Hall of Fame, Clarence Muse Award, 1986. **BUSINESS ADDRESS:** c/o Dipene, 261 S Robertson Blvd, Beverly Hills, CA 90211.*

CHONG, RICHARD DAVID
Architect. Chinese American. **PERSONAL:** Born Jun 1, 1946, Los Angeles, CA; son of George Chong and Mabel Dorothy Chan; married Roze Gutierrez Chong, Jul 5, 1969; children: David Gregory, Michelle Elizabeth. **EDUCATION:** University of Southern California, BArch, 1969; UCLA, MArch, 1974. **CAREER:** Pulliam, Matthews & Associates, associate, 1969-76; Community Design Center, director, 1976-77; Los Angeles Harbor Department, planning consultant, 1974-76; Southern California Institute of Architecture, assistant instructor, 1973-74; California State Polytechnic University, visiting design critic, 1975; design instructor, 1975-76; University of Utah, visiting design critic, 1976-78, adjunct assistant professor, 1980-84; Richard D Chong & Associates, principal, 1977-. **ORGANIZATIONS:** Utah Housing Coalition, Salt Lake City, board of directors, 1980-84; Salt Lake City Housing Advisory & Appeals Board, board of directors, 1976-80; Task Force for the Aged Housing Commission, Salt Lake County, 1976-77; Salt Lake City Mortgage Loan Institutions Review Committee, 1978; Neighborhood Housing Services of Federal Home Loan Bank Board, Salt Lake City, board of directors development commission, 1979-81; Water Quality Advisory Council, vice chairman, 1981-83; Public Utilities Commission, advisory board member, 1985-; Kier Management Corp, board of directors; Camp Kostopulos, board member; AIA, treasurer, 1988-89, 1991, secretary, 1992, president elect, 1993; American Planning Association, American Arbitration Association, National Panel Arbitrators. **HONORS/AWARDS:** American Inst Planning, Juror Annual Planning Award, 1984-85. **SPECIAL ACHIEVEMENTS:** Author, Design of Flexible Housing, 1974; Airmen's Dining Hall, 1st place, Military Facility Air Force Logistics Command, 1986; Oddfellows Hall, Heritage Foundation Award, 1986. **HOME ADDRESS:** 1451 Perry Ave, Salt Lake City, UT 84103-4474. **BUSINESS ADDRESS:** Principal, Richard D Chong and Associates, 248 Edison St, Salt Lake City, UT 84111-2307, (801)364-1797.

CHONG, TIMOTHY
Military officer. Chinese American/Malaysian American. **PERSONAL:** Born Nov 5, 1967, Ipoh, Malaysia; son of Samuel and Loon. **EDUCATION:** University of Michigan, BS, aero eng, 1989. **CAREER:** United States Air Force, student pilot, 1989-90, planning & analysis officer, 1990-92, crew commander, 1992, flight commander, 1992-93, Satellite Systems Engineering, deputy chief, 1993-. **ORGANIZATIONS:** Air Force Assn, 1987-; United States Naval Institute, 1989-; Scabbard & Blade, 1988-. **HONORS/AWARDS:** University of Michigan, President's Award, 1989; 1st Satellite Control Squadron, Crew of the Year, 1990; 50th Space Wing, Crew of the Quarter, 1992; US Air Force Space Operations, Crew of the Year, nominee, 1992. **MILITARY SERVICE:** US Air Force, 1st lt, 1989-92, captain, 1993-; Air Force Achievement Medal, 1992; Combat Readiness Medal, 1992. **HOME ADDRESS:** 158 Queen's Crossing, Centerville, OH 45458.

CHONG, TOMMY
Comedian, writer. Chinese American. **PERSONAL:** Born May 24, 1938, Alberta; son of Stanley and Lorna Jean Gilchrist Chong; married Shelby Chong; children: Paris, Rae Dawn. **CAREER:** Member of comedy duo Cheech and Chong, records include: Sleeping Beauty, Get Out of My Room, Los Cochinos; musical groups: The Shades, Bobby Taylor and the Vancouvers; City Works, improvisational comedy troupe, founder & performer; actor, writer, films: Up in Smoke (co-writer), 1978; Cheech and Chong's Next Movie, 1980; Cheech and Chong's Nice Dreams, 1981; Things Are Tough All Over (co-writer), 1982; Still Smokin', 1983; Yellowbeard, 1983; Corsican Brothers, 1984; After Hours, 1985; Tripwire, 1989; Far Out Man, 1990. **HONORS/AWARDS:** Grammy Award, Best Comedy Recording, for Los Cochinos, 1973. **BUSINESS ADDRESS:** Monterey Peninsula Artists, PO 7308, Carmel, CA 93921-7308.*

CHONG-GOTTINGER, IVY WOK KUONG
Guidance counselor. Chinese American/Malaysian American. **PERSONAL:** Born Sep 21, 1952, Sibu, Sarawak, Malaysia; daughter of Sia Meng Toh and Chong Chung Sing; married Rock Michael Gottinger, Aug 24, 1991. **EDUCATION:** Kentucky Wesleyan College, BEd, 1982; Western Kentucky University, MEd, 1983; University of Alabama, gifted & talented education, 1987; University of Wisconsin, Milwaukee, school counseling certification. **CAREER:** Milwaukee Public Schools, educator, 1987-92, guidance counselor, 1992-. **ORGANIZATIONS:** Council of Exceptional Children, 1983-; Wisconsin Schools Counselor's Assn, 1992-; American Counseling Assn, 1992-. **HOME ADDRESS:** 5612 W Luebbe Lane, Milwaukee, WI 53223.

CHOO, ARTHUR C. S.
Consulting structural engineer. Chinese American. **PERSONAL:** Born Oct 19, 1927, Singapore; son of Choo Siew Hong & Tham Sook Chee; married Setsuko Tamashiro Choo, 1954 (divorced); children: Arthur Jr, Victor. **EDUCATION:** University of Oregon, 1948-49; Oregon State University, BSc, engineering, 1952; Yale University, MS, struct engineering, 1954; Harvard University, MBA, 1956, doctoral research fellow. **CAREER:** Ewart & Co, Singapore, soil tester, 1947-48; Cornell, Howland, Hayes & Merryfield, draftsman, 1952-53; Cleverdon, Varney & Pike, designer, 1953-56; Linenthal and Becker, engineer, 1956-58; Hoyle, Doran & Berry, engineer, 1958-60; LeMessurier Associates, sr engr, 1960-64; Arthur Choo Associates Inc, president, 1964-. **ORGANIZATIONS:** American Society of Civil Engineers, 1965-; American Concrete Institute, 1959-; American Institute of Steel Construction, 1979-; Construction Specifications Institute; Boston Evening Medical Center, trustee, director, 1980-; YMCA South Cove Branch, director, 1985-; Arthur Choo Realty Trust, trustee; Keng Realty Trust, trustee; VAC Realty Trust, trustee. **HONORS/AWARDS:** Governor Michael Dukakis, Member of Designer Board Appreciation, 1982-84; State of Massachusetts, Chairman Designer Selection Board Appreciation, 1984-86. **SPECIAL ACHIEVEMENTS:** Various projects published by Architectural Record magazine, church organizational magazines, etc. **BIOGRAPHICAL SOURCES:** Dictionary of International Biography, p274, 1973. **HOME ADDRESS:** 294 Rock Island Rd, Quincy, MA 02169, (617)472-8599. **BUSINESS ADDRESS:** President, Arthur Choo Associates Inc, 114 South St, Boston, MA 02111, (617)451-5466.

CHOO, MARCIA
Organization administrator. Korean American. **CAREER:** Dispute Resolution Center, director, currently. **BUSINESS ADDRESS:** Director, Dispute Resolution Center, 1010 S Flower St, # 301, Los Angeles, CA 90015, (213)747-9943.*

CHOPRA, DEEPAK
Physician, association administrator, author. Indo-American. **CAREER:** Maharishi Ayurveda Health Center for Stress Management and Behavioral Medicine, medical director, endocrinologist, currently. **SPECIAL ACHIEVEMENTS:** Author: Ageless Body, Timeless Mind: The Quantum Alternative to Growing Old; Unconditional Life: Mastering the Forces that Shape Personal Reality; "Perfect health: the single women's guide to food, fitness, stess control," Mademoiselle, p 192-6, August 1990; Perfect Health: a Complete Mind/Body Guide; Quantum Healing: Exploring the Frontiers of Mind/Body Medicine; Return to the Rishi; "Are your thoughts killing you?" Nation's Business, vol 75, p 87, October 1987. **BIOGRAPHICAL SOURCES:** "Treat Whole Person, Not Just the Disease," USA Today, p 11, January 4, 1990; "Deepak Chopra," Boston Globe, p 8, June 2, 1991; "One doctor's formula for staying young," Boston Globe, p 30, August 9, 1993; "Doc of ages: Deepak Chopra offers a fountain of youth," People Weekly, p 169-70, November 15, 1993. **BUSINESS ADDRESS:** Medical Director, Maharishi Ayurvedic Health Center, PO Box 344, Lancaster, MA 01523, (508)368-1365.*

CHOPRA, DEV RAJ

Educator. Indo-American. **PERSONAL:** Born Apr 14, 1930, Jullundur City, Punjab, India; son of Jiwa Ram Chopra and Sohag Rani Chopra; married Omi Chopra, Dec 11, 1956; children: Anil Kumar. **EDUCATION:** Punjab University, MSc (with honors), 1952; University of Nebraska, MA, 1960; New Mexico State University, PhD, 1964. **CAREER:** Punjab University, lecturer, 1952-57; University of Nebraska, teaching assistant, 1958-60; New Mexico State University, research associate, 1960-64; East Texas State University, professor, 1964-. **ORGANIZATIONS:** American Physical Society, 1964; American Vacuum Society, Texas Chapter, executive committee, 1970; Sigma Xi, 1963; American Association of Physics Teachers, 1964; Texas Academy of Science, fellow, 1964; Sigma Pi Sigma, 1962. **HONORS/AWARDS:** Punjab University, Distinguished Merit Award, 1949-51; New Mexico State University, Fellowship, 1961; East Texas State University, Distinguished Faculty Award, 1979, 1990, Honors Professor of Year, 1992; NATO, Advanced Study Institute, Fellowship, 1982, 1986; Texas Assn of College Teachers, Distinguished Faculty Teaching Award, 1983; Sigma Xi, Distinguished Scientist Award, 1987, Distinguished Science Teaching Award, 1991; Mosher Institute for Defense Studies, Research Fellowship, 1988; numerous research grants, 1970-. **SPECIAL ACHIEVEMENTS:** Author: over sixty research publications in refereed journals; invited papers: NATO Advanced Study Institute on Giant Resonances in Atoms, Molecules and Solids, 1986; Scanning Microscopy International, 1987; manuscript referee, J of Vacuum Science and Technology, J of Less Common Metals, Applications of Surface Science, Rare Earth Research Conferences; invited contribution to Handbook on the Physics and Chemistry of Rare Earths, Elsevier Science Publishers, 1993; invited contribution to Encyclopedia of Analytical Chemistry, Academic Press; invited contribution to Characterization of Semiconductor Materials, Principles and Methods, Noyes Publications, 1989. **HOME ADDRESS:** 2211 Charity Road, Commerce, TX 75428, (903)886-6973. **BUSINESS ADDRESS:** Professor, Physics Dept, East Texas State University, Commerce, TX 75429, (903)886-5484.

CHOPRA, DHARAM VIR

Educator. Indo-American. **PERSONAL:** Born Oct 15, 1930, Jalandhar City, Punjab, India; son of Achhru Ram (deceased) and Vidya Wati; married Miran Devi, Jan 15, 1969; children: Sandeep Kumar. **EDUCATION:** Panjab University, India, MA, mathematics, 1953; University of Michigan, MS, statistics, 1961, MA, psychology, 1963; University of Nebraska, PhD, statistics, 1968. **CAREER:** Wichita State University, assistant professor, 1967-71, associate professor, 1971-77, professor, 1977-87, professor, 1988-; New Jersey Institute of Technology, professor, 1987-88. **ORGANIZATIONS:** Institute of Mathematical Statistics, 1968-87; American Statistical Association, 1968-87; Indian Mathematical Society, life member; Calcutta Mathematical Society, life member; V V Research Institute, life member; International Association of Survey Statisticians, 1973-; Institute of Combinatorics, 1989-. **HONORS/AWARDS:** Institute of Combinatorics, fellow, 1989. **SPECIAL ACHIEVEMENTS:** Published over 50 research papers in US and foreign journals; invited lectures at professional conferences, colleges and universities here and abroad. **BUSINESS ADDRESS:** Professor, Dept of Mathematics/Statistics, Wichita State University, Science Building, Room #352, Wichita, KS 67260-0033, (316)689-3970.

CHOPRA, INDER JIT

Physician, educator. Indo-American. **PERSONAL:** Born Dec 15, 1939, Gujranwala, India; son of Kundan Lal Chopra and Labhvati Bagga Chopra; married Usha, Oct 15, 1966; children: Sangeeta Logani, Rajesh, Madhu. **EDUCATION:** All India Institute of Medical Sciences, MBBS, 1961, MD, 1965. **CAREER:** All India Institute of Medical Sciences, New Delhi, clinical resident in medicine, 1962-65; Queens Medical Center, resident in medicine, 1966-67; Harbor-UCLA Medical Center, CA, 1967-68; UCLA School of Medicine, fellow in endocrinology, 1968-71, assistant professor of med, 1971-74, associate professor of medicine, 1974-78, professor of medicine, 1978-. **ORGANIZATIONS:** American College of Physicians, fellow; The Endocrine Society; American Society for Clinical Investigation; Association of American Physicians; American Thyroid Association. **HONORS/AWARDS:** The Endocrine Society, Ernst Oppenheimer Award, 1980; American Thyroid Association, Parke-Davis Award, 1988, Van Meter Award, 1977. **SPECIAL ACHIEVEMENTS:** US patent on Radioimmunoassay of Thyroid Hormones, published over 230 research articles in medical journals. **BUSINESS ADDRESS:** Professor, Dept of Medicine, UCLA Center for Health Sciences, 10833 Leconte Ave, Los Angeles, CA 90024, (310)825-2346.

CHOPRA, JASBIR

Banker. Indo-American. **PERSONAL:** Born Mar 21, 1951, Simla, Himachal Pradesh, India; son of Prem Rani & Dalip Rai Chopra; married Rashmi Chopra, Aug 16, 1975; children: Vilas, Vinay. **EDUCATION:** City College, BSEE, 1973; Baruch College, MBA, intl business, 1977. **CAREER:** Baruch College, adjunct lecturer, 1974-76; New York Life, field underwriter, 1975-77; National Westminster Bancorp Inc, vice president, currently. **ORGANIZATIONS:** Eta Kappa Nu; various intl chambers of commerce; various intl trade organizations. **HONORS/AWARDS:** Baruch College, Benjamin Goldman for Best Thesis, 1978, Research Award, 1973-76. **SPECIAL ACHIEVEMENTS:** "US Foreign Divestment: A 1972-1975 Updating," Columbia Journal of World Business, 1978. **BUSINESS ADDRESS:** Vice President, National Westminster Bancorp Inc, 10 Exchange Pl, Jersey City, NJ 07302.

CHOPRA, JOGINDER (JOGY)

Physician, federal medical officer. Indo-American. **PERSONAL:** Born Jun 3, 1932, Punjab, India. **EDUCATION:** Bombay University, MD, 1956; American Board of Pediatrics, FAAP, diplomate, 1961; Columbia University, MPH, MS, nutriton, 1961. **CAREER:** WHO/PAHA, Nutrition for the Caribbean, advisor, 1961-67, Maternal and Child Health for the Americas, advisor, 1967-73; Department of Health & Human Services/FDA/CFSAN, Medical Affairs, special assistant, 1973-. **ORGANIZATIONS:** American Academy of Pediatric, 1960; American Society for Clinical Nutrition, 1971; American Public Health Association, 1972; Medical Society of District of Columbia, 1973; Bristish Medical Association; Indian Medical Association. **HONORS/AWARDS:** American Academy of Pediatrics, Fellow, 1978; American College of Nutrition, Fellow, 1971; American Public Health Association, Fellow, 1971; International Year of the Child, PHS Award; FDA, Commendable Service Award, 1981. **MILITARY SERVICE:** Army Medical Corp, lt col, 1990-92. **BUSINESS ADDRESS:** Special Asst for Medical Affairs, Dept of Health and Human Services, Food & Drug Administration-CFSAN, 200 C St SW, Washington, DC 20016.

CHOPRA, RAJBIR SINGH

Physician, educator. Indo-American. **PERSONAL:** Born Nov 19, 1953, Sambhar Lake, Rajasthan, India; son of Mohinder Chopra and Ravinder Chopra; married Pamilla, Aug 4, 1980; children: Rajika, Subir, Sonika. **EDUCATION:** Medical College, Amritsar, India, MBBS, 1976; State University of New York, MD, 1982. **CAREER:** New York Institute of Technology, clinical adjunct assistant professor of medicine, 1992-; Pennisula Hospital, physician, 1987-. **HONORS/AWARDS:** Boards of Internal Medicine, Diplomate in Internal Medicine, 1984, Diplomate in Nephrology, 1986; Boards of Geriatrics, Diplomate in Geriatrics, 1992. **BUSINESS ADDRESS:** Physician, Pennisula Hospital, 5115 Beach Channel Drive, Far Rockaway, NY 11691, (718)945-7100.

CHOU, ARTHUR W. (ARTHUR W. CHOW)

Educator. Chinese American. **PERSONAL:** Born Oct 7, 1954, Taipei, Taiwan; son of Wen-Swei Chow and Lun Kwan Chow; married Te-Hui W Chou, May 26, 1984; children: Vincent, Michael. **EDUCATION:** Tunghai University, BS, 1976; State University of New York at Stony Brook, PhD, 1982. **CAREER:** Institute for Advanced Study at Princeton, 1983-84; Columbia University, visiting scientist, 1984-85; Clark University, assistant professor, 1982-90, associate professor, 1990-. **ORGANIZATIONS:** Institute for Advanced Study, 1983-84; American Math Society, 1982-91; Association for Computing Machinery, 1985-; IEEE, 1985-. **HONORS/AWARDS:** National Science Foundation, Research Grant, 1983; Clark University, Faculty Development Grant, 1986, 1992. **SPECIAL ACHIEVEMENTS:** "Dirac Operator on Singular Spaces," Transaction of AMS, no 1, vol 289, 1985; "Optimality of Krylov Information," Journal of Complexity, vol 3, 1987; "Criteria for Self-Adjointness," Proceedings of AMS, vol 106, no 4, 1989; "Two-dimensional Regions," Proceeding of STOC, 1993. **BIOGRAPHICAL SOURCES:** "Information-Based Complexity: New Questions for Mathematicians, The Mathematical Intelligences, vol 13, 1991; "Perspective on Information-Based Complexity, Bulletin of Amer Math Soc, no 2, p 34-43, vol 26, no 1, p 29-52, 1992. **BUSINESS ADDRESS:** Professor, Math Dept, Clark University, 950 Main Street, Worcester, MA 01610-1473, (508)793-7692.

CHOU, CHEN-LIN

Geologist, geochemist. Chinese American. **PERSONAL:** Born Oct 8, 1943, Jiangyin, Jiangsu, China; son of Yun-Chang Chou & Yuh-Ying Liu; married Susan S Chou, Jun 14, 1970; children: Cynthia H, Peter H. **EDUCATION:** National Taiwan University, Taipei, BS, 1965; University of Pittsburgh, PhD,

1971. **CAREER:** University of California, Los Angeles, postdoctoral scholar, 1971-72, assistant research geochemist, 1972-75; California State University at Fullerton, lecturer, 1973-74; University of Toronto, senior research associate, 1975, assistant professor, research, 1976-79; McMaster University, Ontario, postdoctoral fellow, 1979-80; Illinois State Geological Survey, assistant geologist, 1980-84, associate geologist, 1984-88, geologist, 1989-92, geochemist, 1993-; National Central University, Institute of Applied Geology, Taiwan, visiting prof, 1993-94. **ORGANIZATIONS:** Geological Society of America, 1973-; Geochemical Society, 1968-; American Geophysical Union, 1968-; Meteoritical Society, 1969-; International Association of Geochemistry and Cosmochemistry, 1970-; North American Chinese Earth Scientists Association, 1970-; Geological Society of China, Taipei, 1984-; Illinois Mining Institute, 1980-. **HONORS/AWARDS:** University of Pittsburgh, Andrew Mellon Fellow, 1967-68; Arizona State University, Nininger Award, 1971. **SPECIAL ACHIEVEMENTS:** Proficiency in Chinese; over 50 publications in geology, geochemistry, coal science and technology; co-editor, Geological Society of America Special Publication 248: Recent Advances in Coal Geochemistry, 1990; lectured in Canada, China, and Taiwan. **HOME ADDRESS:** 3007 Valley Brook Drive, Champaign, IL 61821, (217)356-9355. **BUSINESS ADDRESS:** Geochemist, Illinois State Geological Survey, 615 East Peabody Drive, Champaign, IL 61820, (217)244-2492.

CHOU, CHING-CHUNG

Educator. Taiwanese American. **PERSONAL:** Born Jun 25, 1932, Taipei, Taiwan; son of Chi-Shu Chou and Yeh Chen Chou; married Lucy Ai-Shu Chou, Nov 15, 1962; children: Jane, Belinda, Michael. **EDUCATION:** National Taiwan University, College of Medicine, MD, 1958; Northwestern University, MS, 1964; University of Oklahoma, PhD, 1966. **CAREER:** University of Oklahoma, instructor, physiology, 1964-66; Michigan State University, assistant professor, physiology & medicine, 1966-69, associate professor, 1969-73, professor, 1973-; associate chairman, dept of physiology, 1992-. **ORGANIZATIONS:** American Heart Association, fellow, 1979-; American Gastroenterological Association, 1970-; American Physiological Society, fellow, 1970-; Central Society for Clinical Research, 1971-; North American Taiwanese Professors Association; North American Taiwanese Medical Association; Splanchnic Circulation Group, president, exec secretary, 1978-83. **HONORS/AWARDS:** CAPES/Fulbright Scholar Award, 1987; Michigan State University, College Human Medicine, Distinguished Faculty Award, 1988, 1989. **SPECIAL ACHIEVEMENTS:** Textbook, Physiology of Gastrointestinal Tract, 1968; several chapters in handbooks, encyclopedias; more than 100 publications in biomedical journals. **BUSINESS ADDRESS:** Professor, Dept of Physiology, Michigan State University, East Lansing, MI 48824-1101, (517)353-3736.

CHOU, CHUNG-KWANG

Research scientist. Chinese American. **PERSONAL:** Born May 11, 1946, Chung-King, Sichuan, China; son of Gin-Chi Chou and Yu-Lien Shiao Chou; married Grace Wong, Jun 9, 1973; children: Jeffrey, Angela. **EDUCATION:** National Taiwan University, Taipei, BSEE, 1968; Washington University, St Louis, MS, electrical engineering, 1971; University of Washington, Seattle, PhD, electrical engineering, 1975. **CAREER:** University of Washington: Dept Rehabilitation Med, res associate, 1976, assistant professor, 1977-81, Center for Bioengineering, Bioelectromagnetics, Res Lab, associate director, 1981-85, res associate professor, 1981-85; City of Hope National Medical Center: Cancer Research Center, 1985-, Biomedical Eng Sec, head, Dept of Rad Res, associate director, 1985-90, director, 1991-. **ORGANIZATIONS:** Institute of Electrical & Electronics Eng, fellow, 1989-; Bioelectromagnetics Society, charter member, 1979-; American Association for the Advancement of Science, 1975-; International Microwave Power Institute, 1980-; Radiation Research Society, 1985-; North American Hyperthermia Group, charter member, 1985-; IEEE, COMAR, subcommittee chairman, 1990-, vice chairman, 1994-, SCC 28.4, working group chairman, 1992-. **HONORS/AWARDS:** International Microwave Power Institute, First Special Award for the Decade (1970-79), 1981; Journal of Microwave Power, Outstanding Paper Award, 1985; IEEE, Distinguished Lecturer, 1991-; MIT, Electromagnetics Academy, 1990-. **SPECIAL ACHIEVEMENTS:** Published 120 papers in professional journals, book chapters; appointed to several national committees; chair, speaker, technical sessions in national & international meetings; associate editor, Journal of Bioelectromagnetics, 1987-. **MILITARY SERVICE:** Army, Republic of China, second lieutenant, 1968-69. **BUSINESS ADDRESS:** Director, Research Scientist, Dept of Radiation Res, City of Hope National Medical Center, 1500 E Duarte Rd, Hawaii Building, Room #H14, Duarte, CA 91010-0269, (818)301-8355.

CHOU, DAVID YUAN-PIN

Educator. Chinese American. **PERSONAL:** Born Mar 5, 1922, Muping, Shandong, China; son of Yee-En Chou and Yu-Su Chou; married Mary Ann Chou, Sep 26, 1953; children: Timothy C-K, Stephen C-Y, Michael C-C. **EDUCATION:** Tokyo Institute of Technology, BE, 1948; University of Tokyo Graduate School, 1948-51; Ohio State University, PhD, 1954; University of Kansas, post doctoral, 1964-65. **CAREER:** St Augustine's College, associate professor/head of chemistry department, 1954-56; Lenoir-Rhyne College, professor and chairman, chemistry department, 1956-84, professor of chemistry, 1984-88, professor emeritus, 1988-. **ORGANIZATIONS:** American Chemical Society, 1956-; Kiwanis International, 1984-. **HONORS/AWARDS:** American Chemical Society, PRF Science Faculty Award, 1963; Lenoir-Rhyne College, G R Frye Professorship, 1968-88, R M Best Distinguished Professor Award, 1971. **HOME ADDRESS:** 768 8th St NE, Hickory, NC 28601, (704)327-3360.

CHOU, ERNEST YEN

Chemical distribution company executive. Chinese American. **PERSONAL:** Born Feb 6, 1948, Nanking, China; son of Eric Y S Chou & Josephine J F Chow; married Melba J Chou, Dec 7, 1976; children: Sonja L, Randal L. **EDUCATION:** Emory University, BA, psychology, 1970; Georgia State University, MBA, finance, 1974. **CAREER:** Dow Chemical Company, sales representative, 1974-81; Chou Chemical Company, president, founder, 1981-. **ORGANIZATIONS:** National Minority Business Council. **HONORS/AWARDS:** Outstanding Minority Business Award, 1992. **SPECIAL ACHIEVEMENTS:** Fluent in Cantonese and Mandarin. **BUSINESS ADDRESS:** President, Chou Chemical Company, PO Box 241025, Charlotte, NC 28224, (704)889-4000.

CHOU, HSIN-PEI

Architect, city planner. Taiwanese American. **PERSONAL:** Born Mar 2, 1952, Taipei, Taiwan; son of Chin-Yu Chou and Ai-Hun Lu Chou; married Lynn Chou, Aug 28, 1977; children: Tim, Tommy. **EDUCATION:** Tamkang University, Taiwan, BArch, 1975; Harvard University, MArch, 1979. **CAREER:** Hsin-Pein Chou, architect, president, 1983; City of San Diego, associate planner, 1990-. **HOME ADDRESS:** 14420 Meadowrun St, San Diego, CA 92129, (619)538-6253. **BUSINESS PHONE:** (619)236-6809.

CHOU, IIH-NAN

Educator. Chinese American. **PERSONAL:** Born Apr 12, 1943, Hsinchu, Taiwan; son of Ming-Ho & Hwang-Chiao Chou; married Kuo-Howere Yu Chou, Sep 8, 1968; children: Jerome, Wendy. **EDUCATION:** National Taiwan University, BS, 1966; University of Illinois, PhD, 1971. **CAREER:** Massachusetts General Hospital and Harvard Medical School, research fellow, 1972-75; Massachusetts General Hospital, assistant in biochemistry, 1975-77; Harvard Medical School, instsructor in biological chemistry, 1975-77, assistant professor, 1977-80; Boston University School of Medicine, assistant professor, 1980-82, associate professor, 1982-88, professor, 1988-. **ORGANIZATIONS:** American Society for Cell Biology, 1976-; Society for Toxicology, 1988-; American Association for the Advancement of Science; Society of Chinese Bioscientists in America, 1988-; American Chinese Toxicology Society, 1989-; National Institutes of Health Toxicology Study Section, 1991-95, ad hoc member, 1989. **HONORS/AWARDS:** National Institutes of Health, postdoctoral fellowship, 1972-74, National Research Service Award, 1974-75; American Cancer Society, Massachusetts division, Cancer Research Scholar Award, 1977-80. **SPECIAL ACHIEVEMENTS:** Published more than 50 scientific papers and 80 abstracts in international professional journals as of May 1993. **MILITARY SERVICE:** Republic of China Army, 2nd lt, 1966-67. **BUSINESS ADDRESS:** Professor, Dept of Microbiology, Boston University School of Medicine, 80 E Concord St, Boston, MA 02118, (617)638-4197.

CHOU, JAMES C. S.

Educator (retired). Chinese American. **PERSONAL:** Born Jan 13, 1920, Changzhou, Kiangsu, China; son of Zen Yi Chou & Yuan Zhen An; married Lillian T Chou, Mar 3, 1948; children: Gregory K, Thomas Q. **EDUCATION:** National Institute of Technology, BS, 1941; Georgia Institute of Technology, MSME, 1948; Oklahoma State University, PhD, 1968. **CAREER:** The Twenty-First Arsenal of China, assistant engineer, 1941-43; Chinese Air Force, maintenance engineering officer, 1943-47; Experiment Station of Georgia Technology, research assistant, 1950-51; Honolulu Iron Works, design engineer, 1951-59; Zuckerman and Chou, partner, 1959-60; University of Hawaii, faculty member, 1960-88, retired, 1988. **ORGANIZATIONS:** ASME, 1949-; ASHRAE, 1968-; Agricultural Engineering Department, review committee,

1986; Hawaii/Pacific Construction Industry Research Information Education Services, director of mechanical engineering; State Energy Plan, Governor's advisory committee; Solar Advisory Group; DPED Committee on Desalting Plant Proposal for Maui; HNEI, solar/wind coordination committee; Hawaii Energy Conservation Council, solar committee. **HONORS/AWARDS:** ASHRAE, Campbell Award of Merit in the field of Education, 1991; various grants. **SPECIAL ACHIEVEMENTS:** Numerous publications, including "Heat Recovered from Domestic Refrigerator for Water Heating," Project Report to Department of Energy, Hawaii Natural Energy Institute, 1979; assisted HNEI to prepare photovoltaic demonstration proposal, solar cooling demonstration proposal and desiccant cooling proposal to DOE; served as coordinator of mechanical engineering refresher course for practicing engineers, air conditioning seminar, and solar water heating workshop. **HOME ADDRESS:** 1105 Ala Lilikoi Place, Honolulu, HI 96818.

CHOU, KUO-CHEN

Biochemist. Chinese American. **PERSONAL:** Born Aug 14, 1938; son of Hsiu-Chi Chou & Bi-Kun Luo; married Wei-Zhu Zhong; children: James Jeiwen. **EDUCATION:** Nanking University, China, BS, physics, 1960, MS, physics, 1962; Shanghai Institute of Biochemistry, Chinese Academy of Sciences, PhD equivalent, biochemistry, 1976; Kyoto University, DSc, biological macromolecules, 1983. **CAREER:** Shanghai Institute of Biochemistry, Chinese Academy of Sciences, China, junior scientist, 1976-78, associate professor, 1978-79; Chemical Center of Lund University, Sweden and Max Planck Institute of Biophysical Chemistry, Gotigen, Germany, visiting associate professor, 1979-80; Cornell University, Department of Chemistry, visiting associate professor, 1980-84, Baker Laboratory of Chemistry, senior research scientist, 1984-85; Journal of Molecular Sciences, editor, 1983-85; University of Rochester, Department of Biophysics, Medical Center, visiting professor, 1985-86; Kodak Research Laboratories, Protein Engineering Group, senior research scientist, 1986-87; Upjohn Research Laboratories, Department of Computational Chemistry, senior scientist, currently. **ORGANIZATIONS:** AIC, fellow; New York Academy of Sciences; Sigma Xi; AAAS; ACS; Biophysical Society; American Biographical Institute, research board of advisors, 1989-. **HONORS/AWARDS:** Shanghai Municipal Award of Science and Technology, 1977; China National Award of Science and Technology, 1978; ABI, Distinguished Leadership Award, 1989, Commemorative Medal of Honor, 1991; IBC, World Leadership Award, 1990. **SPECIAL ACHIEVEMENTS:** Author of more than 100 research articles and review papers in the areas of protein folding and conformation, enzyme kinetics, graph theory, internal motion of biomacromolecules, etc. **BUSINESS ADDRESS:** Senior Scientist, Dept of Computational Chemistry, Upjohn Research Laboratories, 7247-267-1, Kalamazoo, MI 49001.

CHOU, LELAND L. C.

Educator. Chinese American. **PERSONAL:** Born Jan 25, 1925, Tientsin, China; son of L S Chou and H L Chou; married Lily Tong, Jun 22, 1968; children: Philip, Leon. **EDUCATION:** Linfield College, BA, 1951; Cincinnati Conservatory of Music, MM, 1953; School of Sacred Music, Union Theological Seminary, MSM, 1957; University of Southern California, DMA, 1975. **CAREER:** Ashland Avenue Baptist Church, minister of music, 1957-64; United Presbyterian Church USA, fraternal worker, 1964-; Silliman University, Philippines, associate professor of music, 1964-73; Soochow University, Taiwan, associate professor of music, 1973-75; Tanghai University, Taiwan, associate professor of music, 1979-80; Trinity United Methodist Church, minister of music, 1980-81; College of the Albemarle, Fine Arts Department, chairman, professor, 1981-. **ORGANIZATIONS:** Rotary Club, Philippines, 1970-73; Rotary Club, NC, 1982-, Community Service, chairperson, 1982-; Albemarle Area Family Life Council for Teenage Pregnancy Prevention, chairman, 1989-; Pasquotauk County Arts Council, 1982-; Albermarle Community Chorus, 1982-. **SPECIAL ACHIEVEMENTS:** Choral concerts every year, with orchestra: "Messiah," Handel; "Requiem," Brahms and Mozart; "Christmas Oratorio," Saint Saens; "Seven Last Words of Christ," J Hayden. **HOME ADDRESS:** 1301 Park Drive, Elizabeth City, NC 27909. **BUSINESS PHONE:** (919)335-0821.

CHOU, MEI-YIN

Physicist, educator. Chinese American. **PERSONAL:** Born Feb 17, 1958, Taipei, Taiwan; married Ye-Hwa Chen, Jan 12, 1984. **EDUCATION:** National Taiwan University, BS, 1980; University of California, Berkeley, MS, 1983, PhD, 1986. **CAREER:** Exxon Research and Engineering Company, postdoctoral fellow, 1986-88; Georgia Institute of Technology, assistant professor, 1989-93, associate professor, 1993-. **ORGANIZATIONS:** American Physical

Society; Materials Research Society. **HONORS/AWARDS:** National Science Foundation, Presidential Young Investigator Award, 1991. **BUSINESS ADDRESS:** Assoc Professor, School of Physics, Georgia Institute of Technology, Atlanta, GA 30332-0430.

CHOU, TIMOTHY C.

Computer engineer. Chinese American. **PERSONAL:** Born Jun 23, 1954, Wooster, OH; son of Mary Ann & David Chou; married Sue, Mar 4, 1989; children: Danielle Ming Ling, Alexandra Ming Yu. **EDUCATION:** NC State University, BS, 1975; University of Illinois, Urbana-Champaign, MS, 1979, PhD, 1981. **CAREER:** Tandem Computer, software designer, 1981-85, software development manager, 1985-89, competitive analysis, manager, 1989-90, future systems, product manager, 1990-91, general manager, currently. **ORGANIZATIONS:** IEEE, 1975-. **SPECIAL ACHIEVEMENTS:** Published in IEEE Transactions: SW Engineering, 1980; Computer, 1982; Reliability, 1978. **BUSINESS ADDRESS:** General Manager, Nonstop Availability Initiative, Tandem Computers, 19333 Vallco Pkwy, Cupertino, CA 94303, (408)285-7138.

CHOU, TING-CHAO (DAVID)

Educator, cancer researcher. Taiwanese American. **PERSONAL:** Born Sep 9, 1938, Hsin-Chu, Taiwan; son of Chao-Yun Chou and Sheng-Mei Chen Chou; married Dorothy Tsui-Chiu Tseng, Jun 26, 1965; children: Joseph Hsin-I, Julia Hsin-Ya. **EDUCATION:** Kaohisung Medical College, Taiwan, BS, pharmaceutical sciences, 1961; National Taiwan University, MS, pharmacology, 1965; Yale University, PhD, pharmacology, 1969; Johns Hopkins University, postdoc, pharmacology, 1970-72. **CAREER:** National Taiwan University, teaching assistant in pharmacology, 1964-65; Yale University, research assistant in pharmacology, 1969; Johns Hopkins University, fellow in pharmacology, 1970-72; Cornell University Graduate School of Medical Sciences, assistant professor, 1973-79, associate professor, 1979-88, professor, 1988-; consultant, Boehringer Ingelheim Pharmaceuticals, 1990-, Sphinx Pharmaceuticals, 1992-93, China Second Military Medical University, Shanghai, 1992-, Synaptic Pharmaceuticals, 1993-, Tungji Medical University, Wuhan, visiting professor, 1993-; Memorial Sloan-Kettering Cancer Center, Laboratory of Pharmacology, associate, 1972-79, associate member, 1979-88, member and head, 1988-. **ORGANIZATIONS:** Sigma Xi, 1968; American Assn for Advancement of Science, 1973-; American Assn for Cancer Research, 1974-; American Soc for Pharmacology & Experimental Therapeutics, 1975-; New York Academy of Science, 1976-; American Soc of Preventive Oncology, founding member, 1977-; American Soc of Biological Chemists, 1978-87; American Soc for Biochemistry & Molecular Biology, 1987-; Harvey Soc, 1992-; Society of Chinese Bioscientists in America, founding member, 1985-, president, NY-NJ-CT Tristate Chapter, 1993-94; Natl Health Research Institute, ROC, Subcommittee on Medical Biotechnology, 1992-; American Bureau for Medical Advancement in China, vp, 1994-, bd of directors, 1991-. **HONORS/AWARDS:** Research grant awards: National Cancer Institute, National Insititute of Allergy and Infectious Diseases, American Cancer Society, Elsa U Pardee Foundation, 1973-; Taiwanese Benevolent Association in America Science Award, 1988; Kaohising Medical College Outstanding Alumni Science Award, 1992; Cancer Biochemistry Biophysics, 1984-; Synaptic Pharmaceuticals, 1993-; Chinese Academy of Medical Sciences, Beijing, visiting honorary professor, 1993-. **SPECIAL ACHIEVEMENTS:** Contributor, Median-effect principle of Chou and Talalay for drug combination studies to Encyclopaedia of Medical Devices and Instrumentation, John-Wiley & Sons, NY, 1988; Encyclopaedia of Molecular Biology of Cancer, Academic Press, 1994; US patent number 5,053,401, with K A Watanabe and M Koyama, 1991; Cancer Biochemistry Physics, editorial advisory board. **MILITARY SERVICE:** Chinese Air Force, ROC, 2nd lieutenant, 1961-62. **BUSINESS ADDRESS:** Professor & Head, Laboratory of Biochemical Pharmacology/Toxicology, Memorial Sloan-Kettering Cancer Center, Cornell University Graduate School of Medical Sciences, 1275 York Ave, New York, NY 10021, (212)639-7480.

CHOU, TSU-WEI

Educator. Chinese American. **PERSONAL:** Born Jun 2, 1940, Shangai, China; son of S H Chou and M C Wu Chou; married Vivian M S L Chou, Jul 28, 1968; children: Helen H H, Vivian H C, Evan H H. **EDUCATION:** Natl Taiwan University, BS, civil engineering, 1963; Northwestern University, MS, materials science, 1966; Stanford University, PhD, materials science, 1969. **CAREER:** Argonne Natl Lab, visiting scientist, 1975-76; British Science Research Council, sr visiting research fellow, 1976; DFVLR-Germany Aerospace Research Establishment, visiting professor, 1983; US Office of Naval Research, London, liaison scientist, 1983; Tongji University, China, visiting professor, 1990; Tokyo Science University, Japan, visiting professor, 1990; University of Delaware, Jerzy L Nowinski Professor of Mechanical Engineering, 1989-. **ORGANIZATIONS:** American Soc for Mechanical Engineers; American Ceramic Soc; The Minerals, Metals and Materials Soc; ASM Intl; American Soc for Composites; Russian Soc for Composites. **HONORS/ AWARDS:** University of Delaware, Fellow, Institute for Advanced Study, 1986-87; British Science Research Council, Sr Visiting Research Fellowship, 1976; Research Corp, Frederick Gardner Cottrell Fellowship, 1970-71; Stanford University, Ford Foundation Fellowship, 1966-67; Northwestern University, Walter P Murphy Fellowship, 1964-65. **SPECIAL ACHIEVEMENTS:** Books: Structure & Properties of Composite, 1993; Microstructural Design of Fiber Composites, 1992; Use of Composite Materials in Transportation Systems, ASME, 1991; Textile Structural Composites, 1988; Composite Materials & Their Use in Structures, 1975. **BUSINESS ADDRESS:** Jerzy L Nowinski Professor of Mechanical Engineering, University of Delaware, 126 Spencer Lab, Newark, DE 19716, (302)831-2904.

CHOUDHARY, SUBODH KUMAR
Podiatrist. Indo-American. **PERSONAL:** Born Jan 4, 1963, Muzzaffarpur, Bihar, India; son of Satya Choudhary and Malti Choudhary; married Lisa, Sep 7, 1990. **EDUCATION:** State University of New York at Stony Brook, BS, 1984; California College of Podiatric Medicine, DPM, 1988, MS, 1990. **CAREER:** Private practice, podiatrist, 1991-. **ORGANIZATIONS:** American Podiatric Medical Assn, 1988-; South Carolina Podiatric Medical Assn, 1990-. **BUSINESS ADDRESS:** Podiatrist, 1208 Augusta St, Greenville, SC 29605, (803)232-3668.

CHOUDHURY, A. LATIF
Educator. Bangladeshi American. **PERSONAL:** Born Jan 1, 1933, Dhaka, Bangladesh; son of Abdur Rub & Umme Arefa Khatun Choudhury; married Jutta Kausch Choudhury, Nov 4, 1960; children: Kadjol, Marcel. **EDUCATION:** Dhaka University, Dhaka, Bangladesh, BSc (honors), 1953, MSc, 1954; Freie Universitat, Berlin, Germany, Dr rer nat, 1960. **CAREER:** Freie Universitat, Berlin, helping assistant, 1958-60; Dhaka University, senior lecturer, 1961-66, 1968, reader, 1969; Elizabeth City State University, associate professor, 1966-68, 1969-73, professor, 1973-. **ORGANIZATIONS:** American Physical Society, life member, 1969-; Bangladesh Physical Society, life member, 1978-; American Association of University Professors, 1969-; North Carolina Academy of Science, 1992-. **HONORS/AWARDS:** DAAD, German Exchange, scholarship, 1955-58; Fritz Haber Institute, Berlin, post doc fellowship, 1960; Colombo Plan, post doc at Imperial College, London, 1960-61. **SPECIAL ACHIEVEMENTS:** Over 50 research works & publications in professional journals. **HOME ADDRESS:** 605 Forest Park Rd, Elizabeth City, NC 27909-9095, (919)335-0183. **BUSINESS ADDRESS:** Professor, Elizabeth City State University, PO Box 886, Elizabeth City, NC 27909-9095, (919)335-3499.

CHOUDHURY, PINAK
Engineering manager. Indo-American. **PERSONAL:** Born Oct 1, 1947, Silchar, Assam, India; son of S Choudhury (deceased) and Mrs S Choudhury; married Hasi, Jun 20, 1992; children: Joyita, Neil, Eric. **EDUCATION:** University of North Bengal, India, BSEE, 1969; University of Louisville, MS, 1980. **CAREER:** Bechtel Petroleum Inc, project engineer, 1973-84; Raytheon Engineers & Constructors, project mgr, 1984-92; Control Systems Consultants Inc, engineering mgr, 1992-. **ORGANIZATIONS:** ISA; professional engineer, states of KY, NC; Kiwanis Club. **HOME ADDRESS:** 122 Audobon Ct, Russell, KY 41169, (606)836-2050.

CHOUDHURY, SARITA
Actress. Indo-American. **PERSONAL:** Born 1966?. **EDUCATION:** Queens University, Canada, film studies. **CAREER:** Actress, films include: Mississippi Masala, 1991; Wild West, 1994; House of Spirits, 1994; Fresh Kill, awaiting distribution; previous experience includes: editing travel guides for Italy; modeling. **BIOGRAPHICAL SOURCES:** "Wanted: Actress to Play Pakistani, Chilean or Indian," New York Times, October 31, 1993, p28H; "Choudhury Gets a Spicy First Film Role," USA Today, February 5, 1992, sec D, p5. *

CHOW, ALEXANDER WING-YAT
Insurance company branch manager. Hong Kong American. **PERSONAL:** Born Oct 1, 1955, Hong Kong; son of Ming Chung Chau and Sou Ping Chu; married Diane Yong, Jul 3, 1993; children: Timothy. **EDUCATION:** Loyola College, BComm, 1977; Life Underwriter Training Council, LUTCF, 1988;

American College, 1990-. **CAREER:** Metlife, branch manager, 1987-. **ORGANIZATIONS:** Dallas Chinese Lions Club, 1987; Dallas Cantonese Assn, vice pres, 1989-91; Asian Assn Voters Coalition, 1989-90; National Assn of Life Underwriters, 1985-93; General Agents and Management Assn, 1987-93. **HONORS/AWARDS:** Metlife, Regional Sales Office of the Year, 1987-89, Territorial Sales Office of the Year, 1989, Management Leaders Award, 1987-93; GAMA, Career Development Award, 1991-93. **SPECIAL ACHIEVEMENTS:** GAMA, Southwestern Territory Management Conference, speaker, 1989. **BIOGRAPHICAL SOURCES:** Washington Chinese News, Jun 12, 1992; numerous Metlife magazines, video. **BUSINESS ADDRESS:** Branch Manager, LUTCF, Metlife, 301 Wheaton Plaza South, Wheaton, MD 20902, (301)933-4933.

CHOW, ARTHUR W. *See* CHOU, ARTHUR W.

CHOW, BALANCE TIN-PING
Educator. Chinese American/Hong Kong American. **PERSONAL:** Born Jul 15, 1953, Sanwei, Guangdong, People's Republic of China; son of Poon Chow & Yong Lee; married Clara Yin-Ping Lam, Jun 22, 1980; children: Dawnis Mong-Lai, Athena Mong-Yau. **EDUCATION:** Chinese University of Hong Kong, BA (with honors), 1977, MPhil, 1983; University of Georgia, PhD, 1992. **CAREER:** University of Georgia, teaching assistant, 1985-90; California State University, lecturer, 1990-91; Rollins College, assistant professor, 1991-. **ORGANIZATIONS:** Phi Kappa Phi, 1990-; AAS, 1986-; MLA, 1986-; ACLA, 1986-; MELUS, 1993-; SAMLA, 1986-. **SPECIAL ACHIEVEMENTS:** Teaching Ethnic-Minority Literature & World Literature, 1990-; contributor to journals & reference books, 1989-; expert on Chinese and Chinese American literature & culture. **BUSINESS ADDRESS:** Asst Prof, Dept of English, Rollins College, Box 2651, Winter Park, FL 32789, (407)646-2216.

CHOW, BARBARA A.
Policy analyst. Chinese American. **PERSONAL:** Born Nov 25, 1955, Princeton, NJ; daughter of Wen Mou Chow & Diana Chow; married Steven Ray, Apr 6, 1985; children: Kathryn Ray, Lucas Ray. **EDUCATION:** Pomona College, BA, 1977; University of California, Berkeley, MPP, 1980. **CAREER:** Office of Management & Budget, budget examiner, 1980-1985; Senate Budget Committee, 1985-1989; Democratic Policy Committee, professional staff member, 1989-91; Price Waterhouse, sr consultant, 1991-92, manager, 1992-93; White House, special assistant to the president, 1993-. **ORGANIZATIONS:** Women in Government Relations, 1991-93; American Association of Budget and Policy Analysts, 1991-. **BUSINESS ADDRESS:** Special Assistant to the President, The White House, 1600 Pennsylvania Ave NW, Rm 107-East Wing, Washington, DC 20500.

CHOW, BOB CHING-HONG
Educator. Chinese American. **PERSONAL:** Born Jun 17, 1947, Shanghai, China; son of Fred & Patsy Chow; married Agnes S Chow, Dec 30, 1983; children: Terrence, Timothy. **EDUCATION:** San Jose State University, BS, 1973, MSc, 1976. **CAREER:** West Valley Community College, mathematics instructor, 1976-77; Grossmont Community College, mathematics instructor, 1977-. **ORGANIZATIONS:** Rancho Penasquitos Community Council, board of directors, 1992-; Crestmont Homeowners Association, president, 1990-; Citizens for Responsible Urbanization, president, 1992-; Committee on Future Urbanization Area, chair, 1992-; Casa Dorada Homeowners Association, president, board member, 1986-90; Faculty Senate, Mathematics Department, chair, Curriculum Committee, District Load Committee, Division Load Committee, 1984-88. **SPECIAL ACHIEVEMENTS:** Community activist, successfully challenged city of San Diego on land use; led and diffused a community homeowners association in crisis. **BUSINESS ADDRESS:** Instructor, Dept of Mathematics, Grossmont Community College, 8800 Grossmont College Dr, El Cajon, CA 92020, (619)465-1700.

CHOW, BRIAN GEE-YIN
Physicist. Chinese American. **PERSONAL:** Born Aug 10, 1941, Macau; son of Kai-Chuen Chow & Chi-Shiu Miao; married Pauline P Chow; children: Kira, Albert. **EDUCATION:** Case Western Reserve University, PhD, 1969; University of Michigan, MBA, 1977, PhD, 1980. **CAREER:** Pan Heuristics, Science Applications Inc, sr research specialist, 1987-79, R&D Associates, sr research specialist, 1979-89; Under Secretary of Defense for Policy, consultant, 1987-88; US President's Science Advisor, consultant, 1988-89; Office of the Chief, Naval Operations, consultant, 1989-90; Rand, sr physical scientist, 1989-. **ORGANIZATIONS:** American Institute of Strategic Cooperation, organizing

committee, 1989-. **HONORS/AWARDS:** Hong Kong Government, fellowship, 1959-63; University of Michigan, Rodkey Fellowship, 1976-77. **SPECIAL ACHIEVEMENTS:** "US Treasury Bill Futures Market: A Formulation & Interpretation," Journal of Futures Market, 1982; The Liquid Metal Fast Breeder Reactor - An Economic An Analysis, Washington, DC: American Enterprise Institute for Public Policy Research, 1975; 60 publications in professional journals, book chapters, newspapers & government reports. **BUSINESS ADDRESS:** Senior Physical Scientist, Rand, 1700 Main St, PO Box 2138, Santa Monica, CA 90407-2138, (310)393-0411.

CHOW, CHERYL
City council member. Chinese American. **CAREER:** Seattle City Council, council member, currently. **BUSINESS ADDRESS:** Member, Seattle City Council, 600 4th Ave, 11th Fl, Seattle, WA 98104-1876, (206)684-8804.*

CHOW, CHUEN-YEN
Educator. Chinese American. **PERSONAL:** Born Dec 5, 1932, Nanchang, Jiangsi, China; son of Pan-Tao Chow and Hui-Ching Yang; married Julianna Huei-Shek Chen, Jun 26, 1960; children: Chi Hui, Chi Tu, Chi An. **EDUCATION:** National Taiwan University, BSME, 1954; Purdue University, MSAE, 1958; University of Michigan, PhD, 1964. **CAREER:** University of Notre Dame, assistant professor, 1965-67, associate professor, 1967-68; University of Colorado, Boulder, associate professor, 1968-76, professor, 1976-. **ORGANIZATIONS:** American Institute of Aeronautics & Astronautics, associate fellow, 1966-; Sigma Xi, 1963-; Organization of Chinese Americans, 1981-; Rocky Mountain Chinese Society of Science and Engineering, 1982-. **HONORS/AWARDS:** US Air Force Academy, Distinguished Visiting Professor, 1979-80. **SPECIAL ACHIEVEMENTS:** Co-author, Foundation of Aerodynamics, 3rd ed, John Wiley & Sons Inc,1976, 4th ed, 1986; author, An Introduction to Computational Fluid Mechanics, John Wiley & Sons Inc, 1979. **BUSINESS ADDRESS:** Professor, Dept of Aerospace Engineering Sciences, University of Colorado, Boulder, CO 80309-0429, (303)492-7907.

CHOW, EDMUND CHUN-YING
Physician. Chinese American. **PERSONAL:** Born May 17, 1950, Hong Kong; son of Shou-Bam Chow and See-Fong Yeung Chow; married May J Chow, Aug 6, 1976; children: Alice J, Arthur L. **EDUCATION:** University of Illinois Medical Center at Chicago, College of Pharmacy, BS (with honors), pharmacy, 1976; Chicago Medical School, MD, 1983. **CAREER:** Michael Reese Hospital, registered pharmacist, 1976-79; Northwestern University, Department of Medicine, medical intern, 1983-84; University of Chicago, Department of Medicine, Section of Dermatology, resident, 1984-87, co-chief resident, 1986-87; Oak Forest Hospital, consultant, dermatologist, 1987-; Humana Michael Reese Health Plan, consultant, dermatologist, 1987-; private practice, dermatologist, 1987-. **ORGANIZATIONS:** American Academy of Dermatology, fellow, 1988-; Chicago Dermatological Society, 1988-; American Medical Assn, 1987-; Illinois State Medical Society, 1987-; Chicago Medical Society, 1987-. **HONORS/AWARDS:** Alpha Omega Alpha Medical Honor Society, Chicago Medical School Chapter, 1982; University of Illinois College of Pharmacy, Merck Award for Outstanding Senior Pharmacy Student, 1976; Phi Kappa Phi, 1975; Rho Chi Pharmacy Honor Society, 1974. **SPECIAL ACHIEVEMENTS:** American Board of Dermatology, Diplomate, 1987; National Board of Medical Examiners, Diplomate, 1984; licensed physician, surgeon, Illinois, 1984; registered pharmacist, Illinois, 1976. **BUSINESS ADDRESS:** Physician, Consultant, Suburban Heights Medical Center, 333 Dixie Hwy, Chicago Heights, IL 60411, (708)756-0100.

CHOW, IVAN S.
Architect. Chinese American/Singaporean American. **PERSONAL:** Born Jul 26, London, England; son of David Chow and Chorjee Chow; married H Miang Chow, Jun 20, 1981; children: Caroline, Jason, Wesley. **EDUCATION:** University of California, Berkeley, BA, architecture, 1979; Harvard Graduate School of Design, MArch, 1982; Gordon Conwell Theological Seminary, MA, theol studies, 1992. **CAREER:** Skidmore Owings & Merrill, designer, 1979-81; Davies & Bibbins Architects, designer, 1982-84; David Byrens Architect, designer, 1985; Architectural Dimensions, proj mgr, 1984-86; Jerry Loving Architect & Associates, architect, 1986-88; Ivan S Chow Architect, principal, 1992; Diablo Valley College, instructor, 1992; self-employed, principal architect, currently. **ORGANIZATIONS:** American Institute of Architects, 1992; National Council of Architectural Reg Boards, 1992; Singapore American Business Association, 1992. **HONORS/AWARDS:** University of California, Berkeley, department citation, 1979; Leighton Frederick Sandys Ford Fund Scholarship, National Deans List Certificate of Merit, 1989-90; Gordon

Conwell Seminary, Byington Scholarship, 1991; Gordon Conwell, Presidents Scholarship, 1991; Phi Alpha Chi, 1992; Christian Thought Div, Award for Missions, 1992. **SPECIAL ACHIEVEMENTS:** More to Be Desired Than Gold: True Stories, by J Christy Wilson, S Hamilton, 1992; art exhibition, Gordon Conwell Theological Seminary, 1992. **BUSINESS ADDRESS:** Principal, Ivan S Chow Architect, 295 Oakvue Lane, Pleasant Hill, CA 94523, (510)932-0938.

CHOW, KAO LIANG
Educator. Chinese American. **PERSONAL:** Born Apr 21, 1918, Tienjin, Hopei, China; son of Su-Tau Chow and Ta-yii Zuo; married Margaret W C Zee, Apr 2, 1964. **EDUCATION:** Yending University, China, BA, 1943; Harvard University, PhD, 1954. **CAREER:** Yerkes Laboratory of Primate Biology, research assistant, 1947-54; University of Chicago, physiology, assistant professor to associate professor, 1954-61; Stanford University Medical School, Dept of Neurology, associate professor to professor, 1961-84, professor emeritus, 1984-. **ORGANIZATIONS:** American Association for Advancement of Science, fellow, 1948-; Society of Neuroscience, 1970-; American Physiological Society, 1948-; International Brain Research Organization, 1961-. **HONORS/AWARDS:** NIH, Research Career Award, 1961-84. **BIOGRAPHICAL SOURCES:** Profiles in Excellence, by Connie Young Yu, p 51-53. **HOME ADDRESS:** 101 Alma St, Apt 805, Palo Alto, CA 94301, (415)326-2931.

CHOW, LOUISE TSI
Educator. Chinese American. **PERSONAL:** Born Sep 30, 1943, Hunan, China; daughter of David & Jane Lee Chow; married Thomas R Broker, May 26, 1974. **EDUCATION:** National Taiwan University, BS, 1965; California Institute of Technology, PhD, 1973. **CAREER:** University of California, fellow, 1973-74; Cold Spring Harbor Laboratory, staff investigator, senior staff investigator, senior scientist, 1976-84; University of Rochester, professor, 1986-92; University of Alabama, Birmingham, professor, 1993-. **ORGANIZATIONS:** American Society for Microbiology, 1975-. **HONORS/AWARDS:** NIH, US Public Health Service Awards, 1977-80, 1984-. **SPECIAL ACHIEVEMENTS:** Over 100 articles published in journals and books, 1973-. **BUSINESS ADDRESS:** Professor, Dept of Biochemistry & Molecular Genetics, University of Alabama, Birmingham, 1918 University Blvd, BHSB 510, Birmingham, AL 35294-0005, (205)975-8300.

CHOW, MICHAEL HUNG-CHUN
Orthodontist. Hong Kong American. **PERSONAL:** Born Aug 9, 1952, Hong Kong; son of Shun-Ching Chow & Tsun-Ming Chow; married Anita L Chow, Jun 11, 1976; children: Bridget E, Denise I, Ashley E. **EDUCATION:** Indiana University, Bloomington, AB, 1973; Northwestern University, Chicago, DDS, 1977; Harvard University, Cambridge, MM Sc, 1982. **CAREER:** Tufts University, associate clinical professor, 1982-92; Michael H Chow, DDS, PA, orthodontist, 1982-. **ORGANIZATIONS:** New Hampshire Academy of Pediatric Dentistry, president, 1992-93, secretary, treasurer, 1991-92; American Association of Pediatric Dentistry, 1991-93; American Association of Orthodontists, 1982-93; American Dental Association, 1987-93; NASHUA Memorial Hospital, staff, 1982-93; Lawrence General Hospital, senior staff, 1982-93; Holy Family Hospital, senior staff, 1982-93. **HONORS/AWARDS:** Harvard University/Forsyth Dental Center, Certificate of Speciality in Orthodontics, 1982; Hurley Medical Center/Mott Children's Health Center, Certified of speciality in pedodontics, 1979; Hurley Medical Center, Chief Resident, 1979, 1st Place Winner of Research Paper Award, 1979; Indiana University, Founders Day Award, 1973. **SPECIAL ACHIEVEMENTS:** Author of numerous publications. **BUSINESS ADDRESS:** President, Michael H Chow, DDS, PA, 305 Main St, Nashua, NH 03060, (603)881-8282.

CHOW, MO-YUEN
Educator. Hong Kong American. **PERSONAL:** Born Jun 26, 1960, Kowloon, Hong Kong; son of Chee-Yu Chow & Yan Wei Wong-Chow; married Sue Yee Chow, Dec 28, 1991. **EDUCATION:** University of Wisconsin-Madison, BS, 1982; Cornell University, M Eng, 1983, PhD, 1987. **CAREER:** Taiwan Power Company, consultant, 1991; J W Harley, Inc, consultant, 1992; North Carolina State University, associate professor, 1987-. **ORGANIZATIONS:** IEEE, 1987-, Industrial Electronics, associate editor, 1992-, Neural Network Council, officer, 1993; ASHRAE, 1992; ASME, 1992. **HONORS/AWARDS:** Research Projects Awarded: EPRI, Intelligent Energy Control, 1992; NSF, Incipient Fault Detection of Rotating Machines Using Artificial Neural Network, 1990; EPRC, Application of Neural Network in Power Engineering, 1991; Army, Distribution Capacitor Fault Detection, 1991; Duke Power Co, Finding Exact

Causes of Distribution Faults, 1991. **SPECIAL ACHIEVEMENTS:** Author: "On the Application and Design Consideration of Artificial Neural Network Fault Detectors," IEEE Trans on Industrial Electronics, 1993; "A Methodology Using Fuzzy Logic to Optimize Feedforward Artificial Neural Network Configuration," IEEE Trans on Systems, Man and Cybernetics, 1994; "A Novel Approach for Distribution Fault Analysis," IEEE Transaction on Power Delivery, 1993; "A Measure of Relative Robustness for Feedforward Neural Networks Subject to Small Input Perturbations," International Journal of Neural Systems, 1992; "Recognizing Animal-Caused Faults in Power Distribution System Using Artificial Neural Networks," IEEE Transactions on Power Delivery, 1993. **BUSINESS ADDRESS:** Associate Professor, Dept of Elec & Computer Eng, North Carolina State University, Box 7911, Raleigh, NC 27695-7911, (919)515-7360.

CHOW, PAUL CHUAN-JUIN
Educator. Chinese American. **PERSONAL:** Born Aug 1, 1926, Beijing, China; son of Zhou Zhong Qi & Shen Bao De; married Vera Chow, Jun 25, 1965; children: Maria, Theresa, Teh-Han. **EDUCATION:** Lingnan, 1946; San Francisco City College, AA, 1958; University of California, Berkeley, BA, 1960; Northwestern University, PhD, 1965. **CAREER:** United Nations Relief and Rehabilitation Administration, fishing boat captain, 1946-55; University of Southern California, research scientist, 1965-67; University of Texas, Austin, research scientist, 1967-68; California State University, Northridge, professor of physics, 1968-; Beijing Institute of Technology, adjunct professor, 1987-. **ORGANIZATIONS:** Los Angeles, Guangzhou Sister City Association, board of directors, chair, sci & tech committee; Science & Technology Center of Chinese Americans in Southern California, chair of bd of dirs; The China Institute, CSUN, former director, 1984-85. **SPECIAL ACHIEVEMENTS:** Consultant to World Bank, Control Data Corporation, Expert Bureau, State Council of PRC. **BUSINESS ADDRESS:** Professor, Physics, California State University, Northridge, Northridge, CA 91330.

CHOW, PETER CHI-YUAN
Educator, researcher. Taiwanese American. **PERSONAL:** Born Jan 9, 1943, Peikang, Yulin, Taiwan; son of Kim Chu Chow & Kuei Tsai Chow; married Alice Hung-Chu Chen, Jan 9, 1972; children: Isabella Pei-Ying, Philbert Chi-Hung. **EDUCATION:** National Taiwan University, BA, 1968; Southern Illinois University, MS, 1973, PhD, 1976. **CAREER:** Berry College, assistant professor of economics, 1976-81, associate professor of economics, 1981-83; Southeastern Louisiana University, associate professor of economics, 1983-86; Hoover Institution, Stanford University, visiting scholar, 1986; City College of City University of NY, professor of economics, 1986-. **ORGANIZATIONS:** American Economic Association, 1976-; Chinese Social Scientists in North America, board member, 1983-; American Association of Chinese Studies, 1981-. **HONORS/AWARDS:** Gulf Life Development Fund, grant, 1976, 1977, 1978, 1979; Asia-Pacific Educational Fund, grant, 1985, 1986, 1991; Pacific Cultural Foundation, grant, 1982, 1989, 1990, 1992; PSC-CUNY Research Award, grant, 1988, 1989, 1990, 1992; Chiang Ching-Kuo Foundation for International Scholarly Exchange, 1992. **SPECIAL ACHIEVEMENTS:** Trade—The Engine of Growth in East Asia, Oxford U Press, 1993; Review of Economics and Statistics, 1988; Journal of Development Economics, 1987, 1989; World Develoment, 1989; International Trade Journal, 1990. **BUSINESS ADDRESS:** Professor of Economics, City College of the City University of New York, Convent Ave and 138th St, New York, NY 10031, (212)650-6206.

CHOW, PHILIP YEONG-WAI
Consulting engineer. Chinese American. **PERSONAL:** Born Aug 8, 1923, Medan, Sumatra, Indonesia; son of Chee-Yee Chow and Oi-Toh Cho; married Toh-Cheen Chow, May 2, 1952; children: Yan Chiew, Chee-Chiew, Sharon Chen-yu Chow Chia, Chen-Yin, Chow Noah. **EDUCATION:** University of Arizona, BSCE (with high distinction), 1950; University of Illinois, MS, 1952; Imperial College of Science and Technology, London, Diploma of Imperial College.;1953. **CAREER:** Steen Sehested & Partners, partner, 1953-65; Santa Fe International, project engineer, 1966-71; T Y Lin Southeast Asia, managing director, 1971-76; T Y Lin International, executive vice president to chairman, 1970-. **ORGANIZATIONS:** Consulting Engineers Association of Malaysia, chairman, 1958-60; Institute of Engineers, Malaysia, board member, 1960-62; Rotary Club, Kuala Lumpur, director, district secretary, 1956-62; Federation International Beton Precontraint, London, task group chairman, 1978-86; American Concrete Institute, committee chairman, 1978-86. **HONORS/AWARDS:** Aerospace Journal, ASCE, Best Paper Award, 1990; IABSE, Most Outstanding Paper Award, 1991. **SPECIAL ACHIEVEMENTS:** Co-Author,

Handbook of Structural Concrete, Chapter 1, 1983; external lecturer, University of California, Berkeley & Stanford University, 1989-91; over 60 papers presented to engineering conferences, and published in engineering journals.

CHOW, RUSSELL W.
Computer company executive. Chinese American. **PERSONAL:** Born Mar 13, 1960, New York, NY; son of Loretta and Joseph; married Roberta, Feb 14, 1987; children: Victoria Beth. **EDUCATION:** Baruch College, 1981-83. **CAREER:** Software Systems Technology Inc, marketing/sales manager, 1986-89; Hi-Comp America Inc, vice president of sales, 1989-91; Software Systems Technology Inc, vp of marketing, 1991-. **ORGANIZATIONS:** Interex, 1987-. **SPECIAL ACHIEVEMENTS:** Language proficiency, graduated 6 years of Chinese, 1971; appeared in: television documentary, print advertising, television commercial, off-broadway production of The King & I. **BUSINESS ADDRESS:** Vice President of Marketing, Software Systems Technology, Inc, 305 Broadway, Fl 4th, New York, NY 10007, (212)964-9600.

CHOW, SHIRLEY CHIN-PING
Toy company executive. Chinese American. **PERSONAL:** Born Dec 28, 1943, Shanghai, China; daughter of T K Chang and Y Y Chang; married Shih-Chi Sheldon Chow, Jun 15, 1968; children: Pauline E, Winston P. **EDUCATION:** National Taiwan University, BA, business, 1965; University of California, Berkeley, MBA, 1968. **CAREER:** Photo & Sound Company, office manager, 1968-70, assistant controller, 1971-72; Bachmann Ind, Inc, controller, 1981-86, vice president, finance, 1986-91, senior vice president, finance-adm, 1992-; Bachmann Asia, director, currently; TCA Toys, Chief financial officer, currently. **ORGANIZATIONS:** South Jersey Chinese Community Center, founder, officer, 1979-81; National Female Executive Association, 1987-. **HONORS/AWARDS:** National Merit Association, Outstanding Youth Award, 1961. **BUSINESS ADDRESS:** Senior Vice President, Finance & Administration, Bachmann Industries Inc, 1400 E Erie Ave, Philadelphia, PA 19124, (215)533-1600.

CHOW, TSE-TSUNG
Educator, author, poet. Chinese American. **PERSONAL:** Born Jan 7, 1916, Chiyang, Hunan, China; son of P'eng-chu Chow & Ai-ku Tsou; married Nancy N H Wu; children: Lena, Genie. **EDUCATION:** National Chengchi University, Chungking, BA, 1942; University of Michigan, MA, 1950, PhD, 1955. **CAREER:** College of Public Administration, dean, 1944; President of the Republic of China, secretary to the president, 1945-47; Harvard University, research fellow, 1956-62; University of Wisconsin, Madison, Department of East Asian Languages and Literature, chairman, 1973-79, Dept of EAL, Department of History, professor, 1963-. **ORGANIZATIONS:** Chungking City Government, secretary and director, 1943-45; Chinese University of Hong Kong, visiting professor, 1981-82; Stanford University, visiting professor, 1989; National University of Singapore, visiting professor, 1987-88; Academia Sinica, visiting professor, 1991; Island Society of Singapore, honorary president, currently. **HONORS/AWARDS:** Guggenheim Foundation, fellowship, 1966-67; American Council of Learned Societies, American Academy of Sciences, Distinguished Scholar Fellowship, 1982; Ford Foundation, scholarship, 1956-57; Carnegie Foundation, scholarship, 1958-60; Chinese Government, Medal of Honor, 1946. **SPECIAL ACHIEVEMENTS:** Author: Election, Initiative, Referendum and Recall: Charter Provisions in Michigan Home Rule Cities, 1958; The May Fourth Movement: Intellectual Revolution in Modern China, 1960; Research Guide to the May Fourth Movement, 1963; Hai-yen (Stormy Petrel), collected poems, 1961; On the Chinese Couplet, 1964; A New Study of the Broken Axes in the Book of Poetry, 1969; numerous others; New Understanding Monthly, editor-in-chief, 1942-43; Rabindranath Tagore's Fireflies, 1971, 1993; Tagore's Stray Birds, 1971, 1993. **BIOGRAPHICAL SOURCES:** Wen-hsun Magazine, bimonthly, no 39, p 211-228, Taipei, Dec 1988, in Chinese. **HOME ADDRESS:** 1101 Minton Rd, Madison, WI 53711, (608)271-8666.

CHOW, WEN LUNG
Educator. Chinese American. **PERSONAL:** Born Mar 6, 1924, Hankow, Hupeh, China; son of Chi T and Sou Y; married Rhoda Y Dai Chow, Dec 27, 1952; children: Marie B, James M, Jane F Letterie, Angela M Bates, Christopher V, Gregory E. **EDUCATION:** National Central University, BSME, 1946; University of Illinois, MSME, 1950, PhD, 1953. **CAREER:** Tientsin Power Co, China, assistant engr, 1946-47; Hankow Power and Waterworks, assistant engr, 1947-49; E I Dupont & Co, development engr, 1953-55; University of Illinois, research asst prof, 1955-50, assoc prof in mech engg, 1959-63, prof of mech engg, 1963-88; Florida Atlantic University, prof of mech engg, 1988-.

ORGANIZATIONS: American Society of Mech Engrs, fellow, 1975-; American Inst of Aeronautics & Astronautics, assoc fellow, 1963-; Sigma Xi; Pi Tau Sigma. **HONORS/AWARDS:** NASA, Research Financial Award, 1959-65, 1969-79, 1986-89, 1989-; USAF, Research Financial Award, 1957-59; US Army, Research Financial Award, 1974-86; National Academy of Science, Senior Res Assoc, 1982. **SPECIAL ACHIEVEMENTS:** AIAA Jour, Jour of Aero/Space Science, 1959-93; Jour of Applied Mechs, Jour of Fluid Eng, 1964-91. **BUSINESS ADDRESS:** Professor, Dept of Mechanical Engineering, Florida Atlantic University, 500 NW 20th St, Rm 108, Bldg 36, Boca Raton, FL 33431, (407)367-2692.

CHOWDHRY, VINAY
Research and development manager. Indo-American. **PERSONAL:** Born Dec 26, 1946, Bombay, Maharashtra, India; son of Bhaskar Chowdhry and Saroj Chowdhry; married Uma Chowdhry, Jul 26, 1970. **EDUCATION:** Bombay University, BSc, 1968; Indian Institute of Technology, Bombay, MS, 1970; Harvard University, PhD, 1977. **CAREER:** DuPont, programs manager, 1986-90, business program manager, 1990-92, venture general manager, 1992-. **ORGANIZATIONS:** American Chemical Society; Institute of Food Technology. **HONORS/AWARDS:** DuPont, Corporate New Business Development, 1989; Harvard, Best Teaching Fellow, 1973; Indian Institute of Technology, Silver Medal, Top of Class MSc, 1970; AFS International Scholarship, 1963. **HOME ADDRESS:** 104 Redwood Ln, Kennett Square, PA 19348-2731, (215)444-0817.

CHOWDHURY, DIPAK KUMAR
Educator. Indo-American. **PERSONAL:** Born Nov 15, 1936, Jhargram, W. Bengal, India; son of Monoranjan Chowdhury and Hemoprova Chowdhury; married Monjusree, Jan 23, 1965; children: Sudip, Sagar. **EDUCATION:** St Xaviers College, Calcutta, India, IS, 1953; Indian Institute of Technology, Kharagpur, India, BS, 1956, MS, 1958; Texas A&M University, PhD, 1961. **CAREER:** Indian School of Mines, Dhanbad, India, assistant professor/lecturer in geophysics, 1961-67; University of British Columbia, postdoctoral fellow, 1967-69; Shell Development Co, physicist, 1969-70; Indiana University-Purdue University, Fort Wayne, asst prof, beginning 1970, assoc prof, prof, dept chair, 1974-76, 1978-91, certified geologist in IN, currently. **ORGANIZATIONS:** American Geophysical Union, Computational Seismology and Geodynamics, editor, 1992-, translation board, 1991-; Incorporated Research Institutes for Seismology, board of directors, 1990-; Seismological Society of America, 1978-; International Association of Seismology and Physics of the Earth's Interior, 1980-; American Geophysical Union, 1972-; Sigma Xi, 1961-. **HONORS/AWARDS:** Sigma Xi, IPFW, 1991 Researcher of the Year, 1991; International Association of Seismology & Physics of the Earth's Interior; IUPUFW, research and travel grants, 1971-. **SPECIAL ACHIEVEMENTS:** Over 40 research publications on seismology and geodynamics in various national and international journals, 1970-; invited speaker at a number of scientific forums, 1970-; reviewer of manuscripts for scientific journals and grant applications, 1980-. **BIOGRAPHICAL SOURCES:** Who's Who in Technology Today, 2nd ed, 1981. **HOME PHONE:** (219)485-4479. **BUSINESS ADDRESS:** Professor, Dept of Geosciences, Indiana University, Purdue University, 2101 Coliseum Blvd, Fort Wayne, IN 46805, (219)481-6250.

CHOWDHURY, NAZMUL A. (PAUL)
Company executive. Bangladeshi American. **PERSONAL:** Born Apr 1, 1958, Dhaka, Bangladesh; son of Abdur Rashid Chowdhury and Latifunnessa Chowdhury; married Edna Jo Sarabosing, Oct 24, 1987; children: Zenthor McGown, Tanweer Ahmed, Lillian Ahmed. **EDUCATION:** Mohd Government School, SSC, 1973; Adamjee Cant College, HSc, 1975; University of Dhaka, BS, math, 1978; University of Houston, 1982-84; automotive related training, 1988-93. **CAREER:** Steigenberger Restaurant, Frankfurt, Germany, 1979-80; Holiday Inn, Frankfurt, Germany, 1980; American Optical Co, Frankfurt, Germany, 1981; Steak and Ale, manager, 1983-84; CH & CA Inc, president, 1984-90; Auto Service & Collision, president, 1989-. **SPECIAL ACHIEVEMENTS:** Language proficiency: English, German, Spanish. **BUSINESS ADDRESS:** President, Auto Service & Collision, 9611 Wilcrest Drive, Houston, TX 77099, (713)498-4444.

CHOY, ANTONIO J.
Industrial engineer. Chinese American. **PERSONAL:** Born Jun 20, Lima, Peru; son of Long Fung Choy; married Lily; children: Carla, Ariana. **EDUCATION:** Universidad Nacional De Ingenieria, BSIE, 1977; San Jose State University, MSIE, 1980. **CAREER:** Cost Plus, technical services manager; Carter Hawley Hale, senior industrial engineer; C & A Building Maintenance,

senior industrial engineer, currently. **ORGANIZATIONS:** IIE. **BUSINESS ADDRESS:** Senior Industrial Engineer, C & A Building Maintenance, 3013 Leger Ct, Pleasanton, CA 94588.

CHOY, CHRISTINE
Filmmaker. Chinese American/Korean American. **PERSONAL:** Born in People's Republic of China. **EDUCATION:** Columbia University, architecture. **CAREER:** Filmmaker, films include: The Dead Earth, 1971; Nigeria, Nigeria One, 1973; Teach Our Children, 1974; From Spikes to Spindles, 1976; Permanent Wave, 1986; Haitian Corner, 1987; Who Killed Vincent Chin?, 1988; China Today, 1989; Best Hotel on Skid Row, 1989; Fortune Cookie, 1989; Cornell University, visiting professor; New York University, Tisch School of Arts, Department of TV, Radio, and Film, associate professor, currently. **ORGANIZATIONS:** Third World Newsreel. **HONORS/AWARDS:** International Black Film Festival, First Prize, for Teach Our Children; Academy Award Nomination, Best Documentary; Global Village Documentary Film Festival, Best Film Award; Hawaii International Film Festival, Best Documentary Award; International Documentary Association, Best Documentary Award; Asian CineVision, Asian American Media Award; Visual Communications, Steve Tatsukawa Memorial Fund Awards; Ann Arbor Film Festival, Best Subject Matter, 1982. **BUSINESS ADDRESS:** Instructor, Dept of Television, Radio & Film, New York University, New York, NY 10003-6607, (213)680-4462.*

CHOY, FRED KAT-CHUNG
Educator. Chinese American. **PERSONAL:** Born Jan 4, 1949, Hong Kong; son of Man-bo & Chiu-man Lee Choy; married Christina Choy, Nov 18, 1978; children: Jeremy T. **EDUCATION:** National Taiwan University, BSCE, 1971; University of Virginia, MSCE, 1973, PhD, 1977. **CAREER:** Joy Manufacturing Company, research engineer, 1977; University of Akron, assistant professor, 1983-86, associate professor, 1986-93, professor, 1993-; B&C Engineering Associates, Inc, founder and co-owner, currently. **ORGANIZATIONS:** American Society of Mech Engr, 1980; Sigma Xi, 1983. **HONORS/AWARDS:** NASA Lewis Research Center, Summer faculty fellow, 1986, 1987, 1988. **SPECIAL ACHIEVEMENTS:** Over 100 technical publications in journals and for national/international conferences; principal investigator for over $1,000,000 of federal and industrial grants. **BUSINESS ADDRESS:** Professor, Dept of Mechanical Engineering, University of Akron, Auburn Science Center 324, Akron, OH 44325, (216)972-6847.

CHOY, HERBERT Y. C.
Judge. Korean American. **PERSONAL:** Born Jan 6, 1916, Makaweli, Kauai, HI; son of Doo Wook Choy and Helen Nahm Choy; married Helen Shular Choy, Jun 16, 1945. **EDUCATION:** University of Hawaii, BA, 1938; Harvard Law School, JD, 1941. **CAREER:** City and County of Honolulu, law clerk, 1991; Fong & Miho, associate, 1946; Fong, Miho and Choy, partner, 1947-57; Hawaii Territory, attorney general, 1957-58; Fong, Miho, Choy and Robinson, partner, 1958-71; US Court of Appeals, 9th circuit judge, 1971-. **ORGANIZATIONS:** American Bar Foundation, fellow; American Bar Association; Hawaii Bar Association. **MILITARY SERVICE:** US Army, 1942-46, Reserves, lt col, retired; Order Civil Merit, Korea, 1973. **BUSINESS ADDRESS:** Senior Judge, US Circuit Judge, PO Box 50127, Honolulu, HI 96850, (808)541-1801.

CHOY, SIMON
Compensation and benefits manager. Malaysian American/Chinese American. **PERSONAL:** Born Mar 19, 1967, Kuala Lumpur, Selangor, Malaysia; son of Peter Choy and Ong Siew; married Belinda Ding, Jun 9, 1990. **EDUCATION:** Southeast Missouri State University, BSBA, finance/information systems, 1989; Florida Institute of Technology, MS, systems management, 1992. **CAREER:** Semo Computer Lab, asst lab supervisor, 1987-89; Kent Library, librarian, 1988-89; Capital Radio Service, financial operations manager, 1989-92; Manor Care Inc, senior compensation analyst, 1992-93, compensation and benefits, mgr, 1993-. **ORGANIZATIONS:** Broadcast Financial Management Assn, 1989-92; AAA, 1989-; WPA, 1993-; Central MD Compensation Assn, 1993-; American Compensation Association, 1993-; Society of Human Resources Management, 1993-; American Management Association, 1993-. **HONORS/AWARDS:** MCI Organization, Student Scholar, 1986-89. **SPECIAL ACHIEVEMENTS:** Music, Organ Technic Exam, Grade 3, 1982-84. **HOME ADDRESS:** 2100 Bowline Loop, Woodbridge, VA 22192, (703)491-3060. **BUSINESS ADDRESS:** Manager, Compensation and Benefits, Manor Care, Inc, 10750 Columbia Pike, Silver Spring, MD 20901, (301)593-9600.

CHOY, WANDA WAI YING
Physician. Chinese American. **PERSONAL:** Born May 3, 1967, New York, NY; daughter of Cheuk Ng Choy and Lai Kuen Choy. **EDUCATION:** Harvard University, BA, biochemistry, 1989; Columbia College of Physicians & Surgeons, MD, 1993. **CAREER:** University of Michigan Medical Center, medical resident, 1993-. **ORGANIZATIONS:** American Medical Association, 1989-91; New York Medical Association, Medical Student Section, 1989-. **HONORS/AWARDS:** Harvard University, Thomas T Hoopes Prize for Senior Thesis Excellence, 1989, John Harvard Scholastic Achievement Award, 1989. **SPECIAL ACHIEVEMENTS:** Research abstract presentation, Insight in Schizophrenia, American Psychiatric Association Annual Meeting, 1991; Westinghouse Science Competition, semifinalist, 1985; Otto P Burgdorf Science Competition, semifinalist, 1985. **HOME ADDRESS:** 102-48 63rd Avenue, Forest Hills, NY 11375, (718)275-5963.

CHU, ADAM
Attorney. Chinese American. **PERSONAL:** Born Apr 23, 1965, Taiwan; son of Jerry But Kwan Chu and Kit Yu (Jan) Chu. **EDUCATION:** University of Pennsylvania, BA, 1987; Northeastern University School of Law, JD, 1991. **CAREER:** Private practice, attorney, 1991-. **ORGANIZATIONS:** Quincy School Community Council, co-chair of fundraising committee, 1992-; American Bar Assn, 1992-; Massachusetts Bar Assn, 1992-; Commonwealth of Massachusetts, notary public, 1992-; United States District Court for District of Massachusetts, 1992-. **BUSINESS ADDRESS:** Attorney-at-Law, Law Office of Adam Chu, 360A Tremont St, Boston, MA 02116, (617)695-0867.

CHU, BENJAMIN
Educator. Chinese American. **PERSONAL:** Born Mar 3, 1932, Shanghai, China; son of Charles C-C & Gladys Y-C Chu; married Louisa King, Mar 30, 1959; children: Peter, Joanne Forden, Laurence. **EDUCATION:** St Norbert College, BS (magna cum laude), 1955; Cornell University, PhD, 1959. **CAREER:** Cornell University, research associate, 1958-62; University of Kansas, assistant professor of chemistry, 1962-65, associate professor of chemistry, 1965-68; State University of New York, Stony Brook, professor of chemistry, 1968-88, chairman, 1978-85, materials science and engineering, professor, 1982-, chemistry, leading professor, 1988-92. **ORGANIZATIONS:** Materials Letters, associate editor, 1986-89; Journal of Colloid and Interface Science, editorial board, 1986-89; Journal of Polymer Science Part B, Polymer Physics, editorial advisory board, 1990-95; Macromolecules, editorial advisory board, 1990-92; Review of Scientific Instruments, editorial board, 1993-95. **HONORS/AWARDS:** Japan Society for the Promotion of Science, visiting professor, 1975-76, 1992-93; Senior US Scientists, Humboldt Award, 1976-77, 1992-93; St Norbert College, Distinguished Achievement Award in Natural Science, 1981; American Institute of Chemists, fellow; American Physical Society, fellow, High Polymer Physics Prize, 1993; Chinese Academy of Sciences, honorary professor, 1992-. **SPECIAL ACHIEVEMENTS:** Author: 320 scientific papers, 5 book reviews, 6 books, 5 patents, 1 meeting report, 7 article reviews, and 16 papers in progress; consultant: Calgon Corp, Brookhaven Instruments; Universities Space Research Association, Microgravity Science & Applications Division; Eastman Kodak Co, Eastman Chemicals Division; Roche Diagnostic Systems; Bristol-Myers Squibb Co, The Squibb Institute for Medical Research; Central Research & Development Department, Polymer Products Department, DuPont, currently. **BUSINESS ADDRESS:** Distinguished Professor, Chemistry Department, SUNY, Stony Brook, Stony Brook, NY 11794-3400.

CHU, CHING-WU
Educator. Chinese American. **PERSONAL:** Born Dec 2, 1941, Hodnam, China; married 1968; children: two. **EDUCATION:** Cheng-king University, BS, 1962; Fordham University, MS, 1965; University of California, La Jolla, PhD, physics, 1968. **CAREER:** Bell Labs, AT&T, technical staff, 1968-70; Cleveland State University, assistant professor, professor, 1970-79; Argonne Natl Lab, resident research assoc, 1973; Los Alamos Sci Lab, visiting staff member, 1975-80; Magnetic Info Research Lab, director, 1984-; Space Vacuum Epitaxy Center, director, 1986-88; University of Houston, Physics Dept, professor, 1979-, Texas Center Superconductivity, director, 1987-. **ORGANIZATIONS:** American Phys Society; Natl Acad of Sci. **HONORS/AWARDS:** Honorary degrees: Fordham University, DSc, Northwestern University, Chinese University, Hong Kong, 1988; National Academy of Science, Comstock Award, 1988; New York Academy of Science, Phys & Math Award; Leroy Randle Grumman Medal. **BUSINESS ADDRESS:** Adjunct Professor, Physics, University of Houston, Houston, TX 77204.*

CHU, CHUNG KWANG (DAVID)
Educator. Korean American. **PERSONAL:** Born May 18, 1941, Seoul, Republic of Korea; married Jane Chu, May 26, 1973; children: Susan, Jackie. **EDUCATION:** Seoul National University, BS, 1964; Idaho State University, MS, 1970; SUNY, Buffalo, PhD, 1974. **CAREER:** Sloan-Kettering Institute, postdoctoral, 1974-75, res associate, 1975-80; Idaho State University, assistant professor, 1980-82; University of Georgia, assistant professor, 1982-86, associate professor, 1987-89, professor, 1990-. **ORGANIZATIONS:** American Chemical Society; American Association for Cancer Research; American Association for the Advancement of Science; American Association of College of Pharmacy; International Society for Antiviral Research; Korean Scientists and Engineering Society; Society for Biomedical Research; Nucleosides & Nucleotides, editorial board. **HONORS/AWARDS:** NIH, principal investigator; American Chemical Society, Northeast Georgia Section, Research Award; University of Georgia, Creative Research Medal. **SPECIAL ACHIEVEMENTS:** Over 100 publications in major journals; two bioactive compounds synthesized went into clinical trials; edited two books. **MILITARY SERVICE:** Korean Navy, lt, 1965-68. **BUSINESS ADDRESS:** Professor, University of Georgia, College of Pharmacy, Athens, GA 30602, (706)542-5379.

CHU, CHUNG-YU CHESTER (HING YU CHESTER HUNG)
Engineer. Chinese American. **PERSONAL:** Born Apr 30, 1950, Guang Zhou, Guangdong, People's Republic of China; son of Shao-Ji Chu and Qiao-Huan Kong; married Siu Sui Jane Chu, Jun 23, 1978; children: Vincent B, Stella S. **EDUCATION:** University of California, Berkeley, BS, 1979; California Lutheran University, currently. **CAREER:** General Motors Corp, senior engineer, 1979-92; Anheuser-Busch Inc, project engineer, 1992-. **ORGANIZATIONS:** NSPE, 1984-; CSPE, 1984-; Tau Beta Pi, 1979-. **HONORS/AWARDS:** Mercury Savings & Loans Scholarship, 1977; California Alumni Scholarship, 1977. **SPECIAL ACHIEVEMENTS:** Fluent in Chinese, Cantonese and Mandarin.

CHU, DANIEL TIM-WO
Scientist. Chinese American. **PERSONAL:** Born Aug 5, 1941, Hong Kong; son of Chu On-Tai and Tsui So; married Amy Chu; children: Dixie, Ernest. **EDUCATION:** University of Alberta, BSc, 1967; University of New Brunswick, PhD, 1971. **CAREER:** Abbott Laboratories, research chemist, group leader, 1972-85, group leader, associate research fellow, 1985-86, project leader, associate research fellow, 1986-87, project leader, research fellow, 1987-88, senior project leader, research fellow, 1988-90, senior project leader, senior research fellow, 1990-93, senior project leader, distinguished research fellow, 1993-. **ORGANIZATIONS:** American Chemical Society; Sigma Xi; American Society for Microbiology; American Institute of Chemists, fellow. **HONORS/AWARDS:** Organizations of Chinese Americans Inc, Asian-American Corporate Achievement Award, 1993; Future Trends in Chemotherapy, Hamao Umezawa International Prize, 1992; Intellectual Property Law Association of Chicago, Inventor of the Year, 1990; Abbott Laboratories, Outstanding Researcher of the Year, 1989, Chairman's/ Presidential Award, 1987, 1989, 1993. **SPECIAL ACHIEVEMENTS:** Inventor of anti-infectives: tosufloxacin, sarafloxacin, difloxacin and temafloxacin; author, co-author of 77 scientific publications; 35 United States patents and 103 international patents; 49 presentations at scientific meetings. **BUSINESS ADDRESS:** Senior Project Leader, Distinguished Research Fellow, Abbott Laboratories, One Abbott Park Road, AP9A, D-47N, Abbott Park, IL 60064, (708)937-3207.

CHU, DAVID
Fashion designer, business executive. Taiwanese American. **PERSONAL:** Born Oct 28, 1954, Taipei, Taiwan; son of Chu Cheng Heis and Chu Cheng Fan; married Gina Lin Chu, Nov 17, 1983; children: Bianca, Christie. **EDUCATION:** Fashion Institute of Technology, AS, 1977. **CAREER:** Nautica International, Inc, designer, president/CEO, 1983-. **ORGANIZATIONS:** Young President's Organization. **HONORS/AWARDS:** Crain's New York Business, "The Best 40 Under 40," 1994. **BIOGRAPHICAL SOURCES:** Forbes Magazine, Nov 25, 1991, p 152; Crain's New York Business, Jan 31-Feb 6, 1994, p 13. **BUSINESS ADDRESS:** Designer, President/CEO, Nautica International, Inc, 11 W 19th St, 11th Fl, New York, NY 10011, (212)206-7000.

CHU, DAVID S. C.
Economist. Chinese American. **PERSONAL:** Born May 28, 1944, New York, NY; son of Esther Chu and H T Chu; married Laura L Tosi. **EDUCATION:** Yale University, BA, 1964, MA, 1965, MPhil, 1967, PhD, 1972. **CAREER:** RAND, senior economist, 1970-78, senior fellow, 1993-94, Washington Re-

search Department, director, 1994-; Congressional Budget Office, assistant director for national secretary & international affairs, 1978-81; Department of Defense, Program Analysis & Evaluation, director, 1981-88, assistant secretary, 1988-93. **HONORS/AWARDS:** Department of Defense, Medal for Distinguished Public Service, 1987, 1988, 1993; National Public Academy of Administration, National Public Service Award, 1990. **SPECIAL ACHIEVEMENTS:** National Academy of Public Administration, fellow, 1990. **MILITARY SERVICE:** Army, captain, 1968-70; Army Commendation Medal, 1969; Bronze Star, 1970. **BUSINESS ADDRESS:** Senior Fellow, RAND, 2100 M St NW, Washington, DC 20037-1270, (202)296-5000.

CHU, ELIZABETH CHAN

Educator. Chinese American. **PERSONAL:** Born Dec 22, 1955, Hong Kong; daughter of Michael S L Chan and Rebecca W C Chan; married Hong C Chu, Sep 30, 1978; children: Caroline, Tiffany. **EDUCATION:** Oregon State University, BS, 1977; Peter Bent Brigham Hospital, dietetic internship, 1978; Boston University, MS, 1981. **CAREER:** St Elizabeth Hospital, clinical dietitian, 1978-80; Sherrill House Inc, consulting dietitian, 1980-82; Simmons College, instructor, 1982; Tricity Medical Center, assistant director of dietetics, 1983-88; Green Hospital of Scripps Clinic, assistant director of dietetics, 1988-90; Mesa College, assistant professor of nutrition, 1990-. **ORGANIZATIONS:** American Dietetic Association; California Dietetic Association, San Diego chapter, president, 1987-88. **HONORS/AWARDS:** American Dietetic Association, Recognized Young Dietitian of the Year, 1989. **SPECIAL ACHIEVEMENTS:** Fluent in Chinese. **BUSINESS ADDRESS:** Assistant Professor of Nutrition, Mesa College, 7250 Mesa College Dr, B 103, San Diego, CA 92111-4902, (619)627-2931.

CHU, FELIX T.

Librarian, educator. Chinese American. **PERSONAL:** Born Feb 27, 1949, Taipei, Taiwan; son of Hsin-min Chu and Hsien-hua Niu Chu; married Nancy L Chu, Aug 9, 1975; children: Jonathan. **EDUCATION:** University of Wisconsin, Madison, BA, 1972; University of Iowa, MA, 1973, MLS, 1974; Illinois State University, PhD, 1993. **CAREER:** University of Nebraska, librarian, 1975-78, data processing analyst, 1981-84; University of Iowa, librarian, 1979-80; Western Illinois University, librarian, associate professor, 1984-. **ORGANIZATIONS:** American Library Association, 1979-; Illinois Library Association, 1984-; Nebraska Library Association, 1975-78. **SPECIAL ACHIEVEMENTS:** Author: "Evaluating Systems Librarians," Encyclopedia of Library and Information Science, 49: 251-259, 1992; Explaining Staffing Needs: A Statistical Analysis, (Using Canonical Analysis and Multiple Regression), Illinois Library Association Annual Conference, Chicago, 1992; Bounded Rationality and Reference Service: Helping Students with Research, Western Teachers: Sharing Excellence Conference, Faculty Development, Western Illinois University, 1993; "Bibliographic Instruction and the Scholarship of Integration," Research Strategies, 11:66-72, 1993. **BUSINESS ADDRESS:** Librarian, Associate Professor, Western Illinois University, Library, Macomb, IL 61455, (309)298-2739.

CHU, FRANKLIN JANEN

Investment banker. Chinese American. **PERSONAL:** Born Aug 28, 1955, Taichung, Taiwan; son of Helen & Robin Chu; married Susan K Jansen; children: Jason Asuka, Hadley Holt. **EDUCATION:** Yale College, BA, 1977; Harvard Business School, MBA, 1980. **CAREER:** Drexel Burnham Lambert Inc, vice president, 1980-86; L F Rothschild & Co Inc, managing director, 1987-88; Banque Paribas, senior vice president, 1989-; Sage Capital Group Inc, president, 1993-. **ORGANIZATIONS:** Home Shopping Network Inc, director, 1985-; Sage Group Inc, director, 1987-91; The Bankers Magazine, board of advisers, columnist, 1987-; American Stock Exchange, exchange officer, 1987-90. **HONORS/AWARDS:** Council in Opportunity in Graduate Management Education, fellow, 1978-79; Yale University, Emerson Tuttle Prize, 1975-76, Mason Phelps Memorial Prize, 1974-75. **SPECIAL ACHIEVEMENTS:** Author of over 30 articles in professional journals, including: The Bankers Magazine, Journal of International Securities Markets, Journal of Business Strategy, Investment Decisions, Real Estate Finance and Appraisal Review Journal. **BUSINESS ADDRESS:** Senior Vice President, Banque Paribas, 787 Seventh Ave, New York, NY 10019, (914)698-2363.

CHU, HUNG MANH

Educator, business executive, educational administrator. Vietnamese American. **PERSONAL:** Born Oct 23, 1944, Yenthanh, Nghean, Vietnam; son of Hoa V Chu & Trieu T Dang; married Hien N Chu, Aug 19, 1972; children: Anne Marie, David, Anthony. **EDUCATION:** St Joseph's College, BS, 1967;

Northern Illinois University, MBA, 1970; Louisiana State University, PhD, 1975. **CAREER:** Louisiana State University, instructor, 1972-75; Wilkes University, professor, 1975-76; Linkust Inc, vice president, 1986-89, president & CEO, 1989-; West Chester University, professor & chairman, 1980-. **ORGANIZATIONS:** West Chester University, SBI, founder, director, 1978, SBDC, founder, 1990; Vietnamese Chamber of Commerce of Greater Philadelphia, founder, president, 1984-86. **HONORS/AWARDS:** OYM, Outstanding Young Men of America, 1979; Small Business Association of Delaware Valley, honorary member, 1983; Asian American Council of Greater Philadelphia, Special Citation, 1984; receiver of numerous grants from federal, state, local governments. **HOME ADDRESS:** 1032 Goodwin Lane, West Chester, PA 19382, (215)696-3682. **BUSINESS ADDRESS:** Professor & Chairman, Dept of Management, West Chester University, High Street & University Ave, West Chester, PA 19383, (215)436-2304.

CHU, JONATHAN MOSELEY

Educator. Chinese American. **PERSONAL:** Born Nov 4, 1945, Honolulu, HI; son of David Sung Chu and Sau Kum Wong Chu; married Maryann Elizabeth Brink, Jul 13, 1984; children: David Alexander Yian. **EDUCATION:** University of Pennsylvania, AB, 1967; University of Hawaii, MA, 1969; University of Washington, PhD, 1978; Yale Law School, MSL, 1983. **CAREER:** University of Washington, teaching associate, instructor, 1971-76; University of San Francisco, instructor, 1978; Yale Law School, graduate fellow, 1982; University of Hawaii, visiting associate professor, 1986; University of Massachusetts, Boston, assistant professor, 1978-84, associate professor, 1984-. **ORGANIZATIONS:** Organization of American Historians, 1978-; Institute of Early American History and Culture, 1972-; Society of American Legal Historians, 1983-; Essex Institute, 1974-; Society of Historians of the Early Republic, 1986-; Massachusetts Historical Society, resident member, 1992-; Colonial Society of Massachusetts, resident member, 1990-; Societe Jean Bodin, 1990-. **HONORS/AWARDS:** American Antiquarian Society, National Endowment Human Fellowship, 1988. **SPECIAL ACHIEVEMENTS:** Neighbors, Friends or Madmen: The Puritan Adjustment to Heterodoxy in 17th Century Massachusetts, Westport, CT, 1985; 4 scholarly articles; one chapter in a collection of essays; numerous book reviews. **BUSINESS ADDRESS:** Associate Professor, University of Massachusetts, Boston, 100 Morrissey Blvd, Boston, MA 02125, (617)287-6860.

CHU, JUDY M.

City official, educator. Chinese American. **PERSONAL:** Born Jul 7, 1953, Los Angeles, CA; daughter of Judson Chu and May Chu; married Michael Eng, Aug 8, 1978. **EDUCATION:** UCLA, BA, 1974; California School of Professional Psychology, MA, 1977, PhD, 1979. **CAREER:** East LA College, Asian American Studies, 1980-86, college professor, psychology, 1981-; City of Monterey Park, mayor, 1990-91, city council member, 1988-, mayor pro tem, 1993-. **ORGANIZATIONS:** Rebuild LA, board member, 1992-; Red Cross, San Gabriel Valley, vice president of board, 1987-; United Way, 1986-; San Gabriel Valley Medical Center, board member, 1992-; Asian Youth Center, board president, 1989-. **HONORS/AWARDS:** Chinese American Parent and Teachers Assn, Honoree, 1993; Alliance of Asian Pacific Labor, Public Official of the Year, 1992; UCLA Alumni of the Year for Excellence in Public Service, 1991; Sierra Madres Girl Scout Council, Georgie Award, 1991; Asian Pacific Family Center Achievement Award, 1990; Asian Pacific Legal Center's Public Service Award, 1989; United Way San Gabriel Valley, Volunteer of the Year, 1989; 59th Assembly District, Democrat of the Year, 1989; "88 for 1988," a selection by the Los Angeles Times as one of the 88 rising leaders in the LA area; Outstanding Educator for Asian Pacific Heritage Week, 1987; Humanitarian Award for Research by the LA Commission on Assaults Against Women, 1985. **SPECIAL ACHIEVEMENTS:** Author, "Asian Women in America," Ethnic Studies: Vol 1, cross cultural Asian and Afro-American Studies, ed by G Okihiro, Markus Wiener Publishers, 1989; author, "Asian American Women Studies Courses: a Look Back at Our Beginnings," Frontiers: a Journal of Women Studies, vol 8, p 96-101, 1986; "At Work," in Linking Our Lives: Chinese American Women of Los Angeles, Chinese Historical Society of Southern California, 1984. **BUSINESS ADDRESS:** Mayor Pro Tem, City of Monterey Park, 320 W Newmark Ave, Monterey Park, CA 91754, (818)307-1255.

CHU, JULIA NEE

Artist. Chinese American. **PERSONAL:** Born Dec 10, 1941, Shanghai, China; daughter of James Nee and Chou-Non Yen; married Wesley Chu, 1960; children: Milton, Christina M. **EDUCATION:** University of California, Los Angeles, BA, 1978, MFA, 1981. **CAREER:** Artist, currently. **ORGANIZA-

TIONS: Women Artists of Color, New York, 1988-; Asian American Art Center, New York, 1989-; Art Action International Group, Hong Kong, 1989-. **HONORS/AWARDS:** University of California, Los Angeles, Graduate Teaching Fellowship, 1980-81; Ford Foundation, Travel Grant, 1980; GTE, Los Angeles, Poster Award 3rd Prize, 1975. **SPECIAL ACHIEVEMENTS:** Works at: Hong Kong Museum; Sumitomo Co, Osaka, Japan; Landmark Bldg, Yokohama, Japan; Central Plaza Bldg and Grand Hyatt Hotel, Hong Kong; Fred Silverman Television Production Co, Santa Monica, CA; Solo Exhibitions: Gallery Q, Tokyo, 1993; Memorys Gallery, Nagoya, Japan, 1993; Richard Green Gallery, Santa Monica, CA, 1992; Whittier City Hall Gallery, CA, 1991; Yung-Han Gallery, Taipei, Taiwan, 1990; Gallerija Equrna, Ljubljana, Yugoslavia, 1990; Taipei Fine Arts Museum, Taipei, Taiwan, 1989; Alisan Fine Arts, Hong Kong, 1989. **BIOGRAPHICAL SOURCES:** Yesterday and Tomorrow: California Women Artists, by Kathy Zimmer, edited by Silvia Moore, Mid March Arts Press, New York, pp 179-192, photo p 191, Feb 1989. **BUSINESS ADDRESS:** Nee Chu Studio, 1520 17th St, Santa Monica, CA 90404, (310)828-5816.

CHU, KONG
Educator. Chinese American. **PERSONAL:** Born Apr 18, 1926, Shanghai, China; married Yoland C Chu, Aug 1, 1952. **EDUCATION:** National Taiwan University, BA, economics, 1952; UCLA, MA, economics, 1960; Tulane University, PhD, economics, 1964. **CAREER:** California Western University, assistant professor, 1964-66; Georgia Institute of Technology, professor, 1966-. **SPECIAL ACHIEVEMENTS:** Co-author, Computer Simulation Technique, 1966; author: Principle of Econometrics, 1968; Quantitative Methods for Business and Economic Analysis, 1972. **BUSINESS ADDRESS:** Professor of Economics, Georgia Institute of Technology, Atlanta, GA 30332, (404)894-1886.

CHU, KUANG HAN
Educator, engineer. Chinese American. **PERSONAL:** Born Nov 13, 1919, Kashan, Chekiang, China; son of Chih Hsien & Yo-Po King; married Janie, Aug 18, 1962; children: Ted Shing. **EDUCATION:** National Central University, China, BS, 1942; University of Illinois, MS, 1947, PhD, 1950. **CAREER:** Ammann & Whitney, structural designer, 1950-51; D B Steinman, structural designer, 1951-55; State University of Iowa, acting associate professor of civil engineering, 1955-56; Illinois Institute of Technology, associate professor of civil engineering, 1956-63, professor of civil engineering, 1963-84, emeritus, 1984; Shanghai Institute of Railway Technology, visiting professor, 1984-85; China Academy of Railway Sciences, visiting professor, 1985-87. **ORGANIZATIONS:** American Society of Civil Engineers, fellow; American Concrete Institute; International Association for Bridge and Structural Engineering; American Academy of Mechanics; Sigma Xi; American Society for Engineering Education. **HONORS/AWARDS:** American Society of Civil Engineers, Collingwood Prize, 1953. **SPECIAL ACHIEVEMENTS:** Approximately 70 articles published in various professional journals. **HOME ADDRESS:** 730 Washington St, Apt 101, San Francisco, CA 94108, (415)421-5089.

CHU, NHAN V.
Engineering manager. Vietnamese American. **PERSONAL:** Born Jan 16, 1951, Hanoi, Vietnam; son of Giac & Hue Chu; married Dawn; children: Eric, Mindy. **EDUCATION:** Ohio University, BS (highest honors), industrial systems engrng, 1973; Case Western Reserve University, MS, systems engrng, 1975. **CAREER:** NCR Corp, senior engr, 1975-77; ITT Telecommunications, senior engr, 1977-78; Honeywell Inc, senior engr, 1978-81; Tandem Computers Inc, software engr, 1981-87; Sun Microsystems Inc, engrng manager, 1987-. **ORGANIZATIONS:** System Performance Evaluation Cooperative, founder, vice chair, 1989-91; IEEE, 1991-. **SPECIAL ACHIEVEMENTS:** Language proficiency: Vietnamese, French. **BUSINESS ADDRESS:** Engineering Manager, Sun Microsystems Inc, 2550 Garcia Ave, MTV15-404, Mountain View, CA 94043, (415)336-4770.

CHU, NORI YAW-CHYUAN
Company manager. Taiwanese American. **PERSONAL:** Born Mar 31, 1939, Pan-Chiao, Taiwan; son of Kun-Yang Chu and Sho-Chin Chu; children: Julian J, Jennifer M. **EDUCATION:** Cheng Kung University, BS, 1961; University of Chicago, PhD, 1968. **CAREER:** American Optical Corp, principal scientist, 1973-91; AOtec Inc, director, 1991-. **ORGANIZATIONS:** American Chemical Society, Central Massachusetts Section, councilor, 1993; Chinese American Chemical Society, New England Chapter, treasurer, 1992-; Cheng Kang University alumni Association, New England Chapter, treasurer, 1993; New England Chinese Youth Camp, executive committee, 1988-90; Central Massachu-

setts Chinese School, principal, 1988. **SPECIAL ACHIEVEMENTS:** 16 patents in the field of photochromic plastic lens, laser protective devices; 15 published papers and review articles. **MILITARY SERVICE:** Signal Corp, lt, 1961-62. **BUSINESS ADDRESS:** Director of Chemical Technology, AOtec Inc, 14 Mechanic St, Southbridge, MA 01550, (508)765-2039.

CHU, PATRICIA PEI-CHANG
Educator. Chinese American. **PERSONAL:** Born in New Haven, CT; daughter of Wen Djang Chu and Helen Yu-li Chao Chu. **EDUCATION:** Yale University, BA (magna cum laude), with distinction in English lit, 1981; Cornell University, MA, English lit, 1989, PhD, English lit, 1993. **CAREER:** Random House, developmental editor, 1983-86; Cornell University, teaching assistant, 1987-91; George Washington University, English Dept, assistant professor, 1992-. **ORGANIZATIONS:** Modern Language Association, 1989-; Association for Asian American Studies, 1991-; American Studies Association, 1993-. **HONORS/AWARDS:** George Washington University, University Facilitating Fund Award, 1993; Cornell University, Mellon Dissertation Fellowship, 1991, Liu Memorial Award, 1989, English Department, Sampson Teaching Award, 1989, A D White Fellowship, 1986. **SPECIAL ACHIEVEMENTS:** ''The Invisible World the Emigrants Built: Cultural Self-Inscription and the Antiromantic Plots of the Woman Warrior,'' Diaspora: A Journal of Transnational Studies, 2:1, spring 1992. **BUSINESS ADDRESS:** Asst Professor, Dept of English, The George Washington University, Washington, DC 20052, (202)994-6180.

CHU, PAUL CHING-WU
Educational administrator. Chinese American. **PERSONAL:** Born Dec 2, 1941, Hunan, China; son of Kan-Ting & Bei-Sheir Chu; married May; children: Claire, Albert. **EDUCATION:** Cheng-Kung University, Taiwan, BS, 1962; Fordham University, MS, 1965; University of California, San Diego, PhD, 1968. **CAREER:** Fordham University, teaching assistant, 1963-65; University of California, San Diego, research assistant, 1965-68; Bell Labs, technical staff, 1968-70; Cleveland State University, assistant professor of physics, 1970-73, associate professor of physics, 1973-75, professor of physics, 1979-; National Science Foundation, Solid State Physics Program, director, 1986-87; University of Houston, Magnetic Information Research Lab, director, 1984-87, director, Space Vacuum Epitaxy Center, NASA, 1986-88, MD Anderson Chair of Physics, 1987, professor of physics, 1979-, TLL Temple Chair of Science, 1987-, Texas Center for Superconductivity, director, 1987-. **ORGANIZATIONS:** Texas Academy of Sciences, fellow, 1992; Electromagnetic Academy, 1990; American Academy of Arts and Sciences, 1989; National Academy of Sciences, 1989; Third World Academy of Sciences, 1989; Royal Society for the Encouragement of Arts, Manufacturers, and Commerce, 1989; Academia Sinica, 1988; American Physical Society, fellow, 1978; numerous national and international committees and board of directors, 1977-. **HONORS/AWARDS:** University of California, Berkeley, visiting Miller research professor, 1991; St Martin de Porres Award, 1990; Texas Instruments Founder's Prize, 1990; World Cultural Council, Medal of Scientific Merit, 1989; International Prize for the New Materials, American Physical Society, 1988; National Academy of Sciences, Comstock Award, 1988; Cheng-Kung University, Distinguished Alumnus Award, 1988; Houston Hall of Fame, 1988; National Medal of Science, 1988; numerous others; honorary doctorates and professorships: Chinese University of Science and Technology, Nankai University, Whittier College, Florida International University, SUNY at Farmingdale, Fordham University, Northwestern University, Chinese University of Hong Kong, Zhongshan University, Chinese Academy of Science, Physics Institute. **SPECIAL ACHIEVEMENTS:** Book edited: Proceedings of the 1992 TCSUH Workshop, HTS Materials, Bulk Processing and Bulk Applications, Superconductivity, 1992; High Pressure and Low Temperature Physics, 1978; articles: ''Lasers'' and ''Superconductivity,'' Funk and Wagnall's New Encyclopedia, 1982; ''High Temperature Superconductivity,'' Encyclopedia of Applied Physics, 1993; editor, ''Superconductivity,'' 4th International Conference on Modern Aspects of Superconductivity, 1992; ''Proceedings of the 1991 TCSUH Workshop, Physics and Mathematics of Anyons, 1991; over 280 refereed publications; journal editor and advisory board for 6 publications. **MILITARY SERVICE:** Nationalist Chinese Air Forces, 2nd lt, 1962-63. **BIOGRAPHICAL SOURCES:** US News and World Report, Best Researcher in the US, 1990. **BUSINESS ADDRESS:** Director, Texas Center for Superconductivity, University of Houston, Houston, TX 77204-5932, (713)743-8222.

CHU, PETER CHENG (PE-CHENG)
Educator. Chinese American. **PERSONAL:** Born Dec 1, 1944, Shanghai, China; son of Shuping & Huiqin Chu; married June Chu, Jun 30, 1976;

children: Sherry Y. **EDUCATION:** University of Nanjing, BA, 1968; University of Chicago, PhD, 1985. **CAREER:** University of Chicago, research assistant, 1980-85, research associate, 1985-86; Naval Postgraduate School, adjunct research professor, 1986-92, associate professor, 1992-. **ORGANIZATIONS:** American Geophysical Union, advisory board member, "Earth in Space," 1991-; American Meteorological Society, 1980-; The Oceanography Society, founding member, 1988-. **SPECIAL ACHIEVEMENTS:** Published nearly 30 scientific papers; editor, "Deep Convection & Deep Water Formation in Oceans," The Elsevier Oceanography, vol 57. **BUSINESS ADDRESS:** Associate Professor, Dept of Oceanography, Naval Postgraduate School, Monterey, CA 93943, (408)656-3257.

CHU, SHIRLEY S.

Educator. Chinese American. **PERSONAL:** Born Feb 16, 1929, Beijing, China; daughter of Ching Tao and Chi Chun Yu; married Ting L Chu, Sep 4, 1954; children: Dennis T, Dora T, Daniel T. **EDUCATION:** Natl Taiwan University, BS, 1951; Duquesne University, MS, 1954; University of Pittsburgh, PhD, 1961. **CAREER:** University of Pittsburgh, research associate, 1961-67; Southern Methodist University, assistant professor, 1968-73, associate professor, 1973-81, professor, 1981-88; University of South Florida, professor, 1988-92, professor emerita, 1992-. **ORGANIZATIONS:** American Crystallographic Association, Publication Committee, 1979-82; Council International Exchange of Scholars, 1986-89; National Research Council, panelist, 1982-. **HONORS/AWARDS:** Southern Methodist University, General Dynamics Award of Excellence in Teaching, 1971; University of South Florida, Outstanding Research Award, College of Engineering, 1990. **SPECIAL ACHIEVEMENTS:** Numerous articles in professional journals, 1961-93.

CHU, SUNG NEE GEORGE

Material scientist. Chinese American. **PERSONAL:** Born Sep 11, 1947, Shanghai, China; married Teresa T Chu. **EDUCATION:** National Taiwan University, BS, 1970; University of Rochester, MS, 1974, PhD, 1978. **CAREER:** Microelectronics Ltd, Hong Kong, junior physicist, 1970-71; University of Rochester, research associate, 1977-80; AT&T Bell Labs, member of technical staff, 1980-86, distinguished member of technical staff, 1986-. **ORGANIZATIONS:** Electrochemical Society, electronics division, treasurer, 1992, Young Authors Award Committee, chairman, 1992, compound semiconductor, vice chairman subcommittee, 1989-. **SPECIAL ACHIEVEMENTS:** Over 200 publications in major journals on photonics materials, III-V & II-VI compound semiconductor, laser diode reliability, etc; language proficiency: English, Chinese, Mandarin, Cantonese, Shanghainese. **BUSINESS ADDRESS:** Distinguished Member, Technical Staff, AT&T Bell Laboratories, 600 Mountain Ave, Rm 7C-221, Murray Hill, NJ 07974, (908)582-7318.

CHU, TERENCE

Attorney. Chinese American. **PERSONAL:** Born May 12, 1959, Newark, NJ; married Wendy W Chu. **EDUCATION:** University of Pennsylvania, BA, 1981; Temple University School of Law, JD, 1987. **CAREER:** Phillips, Lytle, Hitchcock, Blaine, & Huber, associate, 1987-89; Lassen, Smith, Katzenstein & Furlow, associate, 1989-91; First USA Bank, vice pres, general counsel, 1991-. **ORGANIZATIONS:** Delaware State Bar Association, 1987-; Standing Committee on Diversity, 1992-; Asian American Bar Assn of the Delaware Valley, 1987-, exec committee, 1991-; National Asian Pacific American Bar Assn, 1989-; American Corporate Counsel Assn, 1991-; American Bar Assn, 1987-. **BUSINESS ADDRESS:** Vice President & General Counsel, First USA Bank, 201 N Walnut St, Wilmington, DE 19801, (302)594-4140.

CHU, TIEN LU (ROBERT)

Educator. Chinese American. **PERSONAL:** Born Jul 29, 1934, Hsinchu, Taiwan; son of Chi Yun & Tsong Chu; married Zu Yie Chu, Dec 13, 1959; children: Ke Chi, Ke Min, Siao Mei. **EDUCATION:** National Taiwan University, BA, political science, 1957; Villanova University, MS, library science, 1964; University of Pittsburgh, Advanced Certificate, 1968. **CAREER:** Lock Haven University of Pennsylvania, associate professor, 1968-. **ORGANIZATIONS:** Association of PA State Colleges & Universities Faculty, 1972-; Lock Haven Rotary International Club, 1972-. **HONORS/AWARDS:** Rotary International Club, Paul Harris Fellow, 1988; Lock Haven Rotary Club, Rotarian of the Year Award, 1988. **SPECIAL ACHIEVEMENTS:** Published more than 40 articles in LH, APSCUF Monthly Newsgram. **MILITARY SERVICE:** Chinese Air Force, lt, 1957-59. **HOME ADDRESS:** 10 Daffodil Lane, Lock Haven, PA 17745. **BUSINESS ADDRESS:** Associate Professor, Lock Haven University of Pennsylvania, Stevenson Library, N Fairview St, Lock Haven, PA 17745, (717)893-2466.

CHU, TING L.

Educator (retired), consultant. Chinese American. **PERSONAL:** Born Dec 26, 1924, Beijing, China; married Shirley S Chu, Sep 4, 1954; children: Dennis, Dora, Daniel. **EDUCATION:** Catholic University of Peking, BS, 1945, MS, 1948; Washington University, PhD, 1952. **CAREER:** Westinghouse Research Laboratories, research scientist, fellow scientist, manager of electronic materials, 1956-67; Southern Methodist University, professor, 1967-88, Electronic Sciences Center, director, 1970-73; University of South Florida, graduate research professor of electrical engineering, 1988-91, professor emeritus, 1992-; Ting L Chu and Associatess, consultant, 1992-. **ORGANIZATIONS:** Institute of Electrical and Electronics Engineers, senior member, 1967-; Electrochemical Society, 1967-. **HONORS/AWARDS:** Southern Methodist University, Outstanding Professor, 1973; NASA, 5 Certificates of Recognition, 1973-75. **SPECIAL ACHIEVEMENTS:** Book chapters in: VLSI Handbook: Current Topics in Photovoltaics; 17 patents, semiconductors and photovoltaics; 150 papers on semiconductors and photovoltaics published in: Applied Physics Letters, Journal of Applied Physics, and numerous other professional journals. **BIOGRAPHICAL SOURCES:** American Men & Women of Science. **HOME ADDRESS:** 12 Duncannon Court, Dallas, TX 75225-1809, (214)368-2046.

CHU, TSUCHIN PHILIP

Educator. Chinese American. **PERSONAL:** Born Jun 7, 1952, Taipei, Taiwan; son of Talung Chu & Shu-Ying Chu; married Vinhhoa Katie Chu, Dec 5, 1978; children: William D. **EDUCATION:** National Cheng Kung University, Taiwan, BSE, 1974; Auburn University, MS, 1980; University of South Carolina, PhD, 1982. **CAREER:** Tatung Company, Taiwan, engineer, 1976-77; Polytechnic University, assistant professor, 1983-89; Southern Illinois University, assistant professor, 1990-. **ORGANIZATIONS:** American Society of Mechanical Engineers, associate member, 1983-; Society for Experimental Mechanics, 1983-; Chinese American Academic and Professional Society, executive committee, 1986-88. **SPECIAL ACHIEVEMENTS:** Co-author, "Application of Optical Microscopic Analysis to Composite Materials," Experimental Techniques, vol 15, no 5, p22-25, Sept/Oct, 1991; "An Application of Computer-aided Design for Modular Fixture Assembly," Proceedings of the 2nd International Conference on Automation Technology, July 4-6, 1992; "Feasibility Study for Extracting Pyrite Information from Coal Images," Proceedings of the International Conference on Coal, Energy and Environment, Oct 12-16, 1992. **MILITARY SERVICE:** ROC Army, lt, 1974-76. **BUSINESS ADDRESS:** Assistant Professor, Dept of Mechanical Engineering and Energy Processes, Southern Illinois University of Carbondale, College of Engineering, Carbondale, IL 62901, (618)453-7015.

CHU, VICTOR FU HUA

Research chemist (retired). Chinese American. **PERSONAL:** Born Jan 22, 1918, Wuhan, Hubei, China; son of Thorpe T C and Su Fang Wang Chu; married Margaret W T Tsow, May 12, 1947 (deceased); children: Franklin D Y, Daphne Y F, Jennifer P F; married You Yi Chu, Jan 31, 1987. **EDUCATION:** Central China University, BS, chemistry, 1938; Yale University, PhD, physical chemistry, 1950. **CAREER:** Guizhou Saltpeter Refinery, chemist, plant manager, 1939-43; Pei-Ye Oil Refinery, plant manager, 1943-44; Central China University, instructor of chemistry, 1944-47; E I DuPont de Nemours & Co, Imaging Systems Department, research chemist, 1950-59, senior research chemist, 1959-65, research associate, 1965-75, research fellow, 1975-82. **ORGANIZATIONS:** American Chemical Society, 1947-; Sigma Xi, 1947-. **HONORS/AWARDS:** Industrial Research Magazine, 100 Award (top 100 inventions), 1974; Photographic Society of America, Journal Award, 1954; Yale University, Loomis Fellow. **SPECIAL ACHIEVEMENTS:** Holder, 17 US patents and 63 foreign patents; co-inventor, Cromalin and Cromacheck color proofing systems. **HOME ADDRESS:** 60 N Beretania St, #2201, Honolulu, HI 96817, (808)599-1759.

CHU, VINCENT HAO-KWONG

Engineer (retired). Chinese American. **PERSONAL:** Born Oct 20, 1918, Shanghai, China; widowed; children: Jeannette L. **EDUCATION:** National Sun Yet-sen University, BS, 1943; Lehigh University, MS, 1957, PhD, 1962. **CAREER:** National Kwang-Si University, teaching assistant; Central Industrial Research Institute, Chungking, proxy engineer; Taipei Chemical Works, Taiwan Mining Corp, superintendent; Taiwan Provincial Industrial Research Institute, research fellow; Wu-Tai Chemical Company, mgr; Taiwan Camphor Bureau, consultant staff, 1943-52; R T Collier Corp, 1953-55; Bethlehem Steel Corp, engineer, 1957-83; Institute of Materials Science & Engineering, National Sun Yat-sen University, 1983-85; China Steel Corp, consultant, 1983-85;

Materials Research Laboratories, ITRI, consultant, 1986; Consarc Company of Rancoast, NJ, consultant, 1985-86; Bethleham International Engineering Corp, consultant, 1986. **ORGANIZATIONS:** Chinese Institute of Engineers, USA, president, 1981-83; Sigma Xi; SME of AIME; American Chemical Society; Chinese Institute of Engineers. **SPECIAL ACHIEVEMENTS:** Chinese patent: Method of Manufacturing Bakelite-substitute from Saw Dust; US patents: 36365694, Method of Manufacturing Manganese Oxide Pellets; 3635695, Desulfurizing with Manganese Oxide Pellets; 3715764, High Porosity Manganese Oxide Pellets; 3737301, Process for Producing Iron-Molybdenum Alloy Powder Metal; 4148692, Process for Producing Low Reactivity Calcined Coke Agglomerates.

CHU, WARREN

Engineer. Chinese American. **PERSONAL:** Born Dec 4, 1951, Shanghai, People's Republic of China; son of Johnson Chu and Hanyan Xie; married Linde Xu Chu, Apr 13, 1985; children: Jason Kai. **EDUCATION:** California State University, Northridge, BS, physics, 1977, MS, physics, 1979. **CAREER:** Ford Aerospace, associate engineer, 1978-81; Hughes Aircraft Co, member of technical staff, 1981-82; Rockwell International, member of technical staff, 1982-85; Science Applications, analyst, 1985-86; General Dynamics, senior design engineer, 1986-90. **ORGANIZATIONS:** Optical Society of America, 1992-; Society of Photo-Optical Engineers, 1992-; Institute of Electrical and Electronic Engineers, assoc member, 1992-. **SPECIAL ACHIEVEMENTS:** Novell certified NetWare engineer (CNE), 1994. **HOME ADDRESS:** 3 Via Becerra, Rancho Santa Margarita, CA 92688, (714)858-4476.

CHU, WEI-KAN

Educator. Chinese American. **PERSONAL:** Born Apr 1, 1940, Kunming, Yunnan, China; son of Mr & Mrs Din Yuan Chu; married Agnes K Chu, 1966; children: Larry. **EDUCATION:** Cheng-King University, Taiwan, BS, physics, 1962; Baylor University, MS, physics, 1965, PhD, physics 1969. **CAREER:** Baylor University, postdoctoral fellow, 1969-72; California Institute of Technology, research fellow, senior research fellow, 1972-75; IBM, advisory staff, senior engineer, 1975-81; University of North Carolina, research professor of physics, 1981-88; University of Houston, distinguished university professor of physics, 1989-; Texas Center for Superconductivity, deputy director, 1989-. **ORGANIZATIONS:** American Physical Society, fellow; Gordon Research Conf, vice chair, 1980, chairman, 1982; Materials Research Society, symposium chairperson, 1980-83, program chairperson, 1986; Nuclear Instruments & Methods (B), editorial board, 1987-88. **HONORS/AWARDS:** Baylor University, Distinguished Achievement Award, 1991; Alexander Von Humboldt-Stiftung Foundation, Senior US Scientist Award, 1989. **SPECIAL ACHIEVEMENTS:** Author, Backscattering Spectrometry, 1978; editor, HTS Materials, Bulk Processing & Bulk Applications, 1992; author, nine book chapters; author/co-author, eight patents; author/co-author, 140 journal articles; Who's Who in Technoogy, 6th ed, vol 1, p 244, 1989. **MILITARY SERVICE:** Airforce, Taiwan, 2nd lieutenant, 1962-63. **BUSINESS ADDRESS:** Professor, Deputy Director, Texas Center for Superconductivity, University of Houston, Houston Science Center, Rm 202, Houston, TX 77204-5932, (713)743-8250.

CHU, WILLIAM TONGIL

Physicist. Korean American. **PERSONAL:** Born Apr 16, 1934, Seoul, Republic of Korea; son of Yohan Chu & Sunbok Choi; married Insoo La, Jun 16, 1962; children: Joan Inyul, Jean Suyul. **EDUCATION:** Seoul National University, 1953; Carnegie Institute of Technology, BS, 1957, MS, 1959, PhD, 1963. **CAREER:** Brookhaven National Lab, postdoctoral, 1962-64; Ohio State University, assistant professor of physics, 1964-69; Loma Linda University, School of Medicine, professor, 1978-79; Lawrence Berkeley Lab, staff scientist, 1979-86, senior scientist, 1986-. **ORGANIZATIONS:** American Physical Society, 1962-; Institute of Electrical and Electronics Engineers, 1973-; Radiation Research Society, 1973-; American Association for Physicists in Medicine, 1973-; Association of Korean Physicists in America, president, 1986; Korean Scientists and Engineers in America, 1978-. **HONORS/AWARDS:** Industrial Research, IR-100, 1986; R&D Magazine, RD-100, 1992. **SPECIAL ACHIEVEMENTS:** Research in clinical use of heavy charged particles; more than 80 publications in scientific journals; author, ''Kwa Hak Eui Kil,'' Dong-A Ilbo Publishing. **HOME ADDRESS:** 3282 Ameno Drive, Lafayette, CA 94549. **BUSINESS ADDRESS:** Senior Scientist, Lawrence Berkeley Laboratory, One Cyclotron Road, 64-227, Berkeley, CA 94720, (510)486-7735.

CHUA, AMY LYNN

Attorney. Chinese American. **PERSONAL:** Born Oct 26, 1962, Champaign, IL; daughter of Leon O Chua and Diana G Chua; married Ted Rubenfeld, Oct 15, 1988; children: Sophia Chua-Rubenfeld. **EDUCATION:** Harvard-Radcliffe College, AB, 1984; Harvard Law School, JD, 1987. **CAREER:** Chief Judge Patricia M Wald, law clerk, 1987-88; Cleary, Gottlieb, Steen & Hamilton, associate, 1988-. **HONORS/AWARDS:** Phi Beta Kappa, 1984; Harvard Law Review, executive editor, 1986-87. **HOME ADDRESS:** 612 Chapel St, New Haven, CT 06511, (203)562-3119. **BUSINESS PHONE:** (212)225-2000.

CHUA, CONRAD E.

Financial planner, real estate broker. Filipino American/Chinese American. **PERSONAL:** Born Jul 23, 1951, Angeles, Pampanga, Philippines; married Evelyn Chua; children: Nelyn. **EDUCATION:** Republic College, BS, management, 1973. **CAREER:** United Financial Services, president, currently; Mortgage Insurance Co, real estate broker, currently. **ORGANIZATIONS:** California Real Estate Board; California Fire & Casualty Organization, licensed. **BUSINESS ADDRESS:** President, United Financial Services, Mortgage Insurance Company, 851 Strickroth Drive, Milpitas, CA 95035, (408)946-2905.

CHUA, LEON O.

Educator. Chinese American. **PERSONAL:** married Diana, Dec 24, 1961; children: Amy Lynn, Michelle Ann, Katrin Faye, Cynthia Mae. **EDUCATION:** Massachusetts Institute of Technology, SM, 1962; University of Illinois at Urbana, PhD, 1964. **CAREER:** Purdue University, assistant professor, 1964-67, associate professor, 1968-71; University of California, Berkeley, professor, 1972-. **HONORS/AWARDS:** IEEE, Centennial Medal, 1985; Frederick Emmons Terman Award, 1974; IEEE, Browder J Thompson Prize, 1973, W R G Baker Prize, 1974; Alexander Von Humboldt Senior US Scientist Award, 1983; Ecole Polytechnique de Lausanne, Switzerland, Doctor Honoris Causa (honorary doctorate), 1983; University of Tokushima, Japan, honorary doctorate, 1984; University of Dresden, Germany, honorary doctorate, 1992. **SPECIAL ACHIEVEMENTS:** 5 US patents; editor, Int Journal of Bifuraction of CHAOS, World Scientific Publishing Co; and numerous best paper awards. **BUSINESS ADDRESS:** Professor, Department of EECS, University of California, Berkeley, Berkeley, CA 94720, (510)642-3209.

CHU-ANDREWS, JENNIFER

Physician. Myanmar American. **PERSONAL:** Born Mar 13, 1948, Rangoon, Burma; daughter of Chu-Ah-Chway and Jane Shek; married Waverly Andrews, Jan 17, 1983; children: Justin Andrews. **EDUCATION:** Institute of Medicine, Rangoon, Burma, MD, 1971. **CAREER:** University of Pennsylvania Medical School, electrodiagnostic medicine, dir, 1977, assoc prof, 1987-. **ORGANIZATIONS:** American Medical Assn, 1977; American Academy of Physical Medicine & Rehabilitation, 1979; American Assn of Electrodiagnostic Medicine, 1980. **SPECIAL ACHIEVEMENTS:** Author: Electrodiagnosis: An Anatomical & Clinical Approach, J B Lippincott, 1986. **BUSINESS ADDRESS:** Assoc Professor, Dept of Rehabilitation Medicine, Hospital of University of Pennsylvania, 3400 Spruce St, White Bldg, Ground Fl, Philadelphia, PA 19104, (215)349-5598.

CHUANG, DE-MAW

Government official. Taiwanese American. **PERSONAL:** Born Oct 12, 1942, Tainan, Taiwan; son of Ying-Chung Chuang & Home Hsiao Chuang; married Lin-Whei Liu Chuang, Jun 8, 1968; children: Eric J, Daniel B. **EDUCATION:** National Taiwan University, Taipei, Taiwan, BS, 1966; State University of New York, Stony Brook, PhD, 1971. **CAREER:** Roche Institute of Molecular Biology, postdoctoral fellow, 1971-73; National Institute of Mental Health, section chief, 1973-. **SPECIAL ACHIEVEMENTS:** Author and co-author, 117 scientific papers published in refereed journals or books. **MILITARY SERVICE:** Marine Corp, Taiwan, lieutenant, 1966-67, retired with honor. **HOME ADDRESS:** 6909 Bright Ave, Mc Lean, VA 22101. **BUSINESS ADDRESS:** Chief, Section on Molecular Neurobiology, Biological Psychiatry Branch, National Institute of Mental Health, Bldg 10, Rm 3N 212, 9000 Rockville Pike, Bethesda, MD 20892, (301)496-4915.

CHUANG, HENRY NING

Educator, researcher. Chinese American. **PERSONAL:** Born Jul 5, 1937, Nanking, China; married Molley M Chuang, Aug 1965; children: Susan Roberts, Leah Rictor, Philip H. **EDUCATION:** National Taiwan University, BSME, 1958; University of Maryland, MSAeroE, 1962; Carnegie Institute of Technology, PhD, MEE, 1966. **CAREER:** National Taiwan University, full-time teaching assistant, 1958-59; University of Dayton, instructor, 1965-66, assistant professor, 1966-69, associate professor, 1969-78, professor, 1978-. **ORGANIZATIONS:** Ohio Board of Regents, Solar Energy Advisor Committee, 1979-81, Energy Advisory Committee, 1977-81; Montgomery County, Ohio, Energy Advisory Council, 1984-90; Republic of China National Development Council, 1992-. **HONORS/AWARDS:** Affiliated Societies Council, Dayton Area Outstanding Engineers & Scientist, 1978. **SPECIAL ACHIEVEMENTS:** Editor-in-chief of an energy education book for community colleges in Ohio, 1978; co-author, book, How Much Insulation Is Enough, 1977; active public speaker: more than 75 presentations; conducted 424 small/medium sized industry, energy audits, 1981-, sponsored by US Department of Energy. **BUSINESS ADDRESS:** Professor, MAE, University of Dayton, KL-121, Dayton, OH 45469-0210, (513)229-2997.

CHUANG, JERRY T. *See* **CHUANG, TZE-JER.**

CHUANG, STRONG C. (CHIEU-HIONG TSENG)
Engineer, scientific adviser, activist. Taiwanese American. **PERSONAL:** Born Jan 1, 1939, Tainan, Taiwan; married Chien-Mei, Jun 5, 1967; children: Rolla R, Timothy D. **EDUCATION:** National Taiwan University, BS, civil engineering, 1961; Kansas State University, MS, civil engineering, 1967; Purdue University, PhD, mechanical engineering, 1970. **CAREER:** Purdue University, research fellow, 1970-71; Procter & Gamble Co, senior engineer, 1971-89; Scott Paper Co, scientific adviser, 1989-. **ORGANIZATIONS:** Technical Association of Pulp & Paper Industry; American Society of Mechanical Engineers. **SPECIAL ACHIEVEMENTS:** Published a book on the Taiwan Independent Movement, in Taiwanese/Chinese language; numerous technical publications and patents in paper-making technology. **HOME ADDRESS:** 205 Walnut Ridge Ln, Chadds Ford, PA 19317, (215)388-6958. **BUSINESS PHONE:** (215)522-6531.

CHUANG, TZE-JER (JERRY T. CHUANG)
Physicist. Taiwanese American. **PERSONAL:** Born Jul 19, 1943, Chia-Yi, Taiwan; son of Len-Shen Chuang and Jan-Su Chuang; married Jenny H Chuang, Jun 28, 1974; children: Jonathan Y, Jessica Z. **EDUCATION:** National Cheng Kung University, BS, 1965; Duke University, MS, 1970; Brown University, PhD, 1975. **CAREER:** Taiwan Power Co, civil engineer, 1966-68; Westinghouse Electric Corp, senior engineer, 1974-80; US Department of Commerce, physicist, 1980-. **ORGANIZATIONS:** American Ceramic Society, 1980-; American Society of Mechanical Engineer, 1978-; Sigma Xi, 1974-. **HONORS/AWARDS:** PE Board of PA, PE, 1978. **SPECIAL ACHIEVEMENTS:** 50 papers published in archival journals. **MILITARY SERVICE:** Air Force, lt colonel, 1965-66. **HOME ADDRESS:** 9 Manette St, Gaithersburg, MD 20878, (301)340-0310. **BUSINESS ADDRESS:** Physicist, Ceramics Division, National Institute of Standards and Technology, Materials Bldg, Rm A329, Gaithersburg, MD 20899, (301)975-5773.

CHUANG, VINCENT P.
Physician. Taiwanese American. **PERSONAL:** Born Aug 1, 1940, Tainan, Taiwan. **EDUCATION:** College of Medicine, National Taiwan University, MD, 1965; Medical College of Virginia, Department of Radiology, 1968-72. **CAREER:** University of Michigan, Wayne County General Hospital, assistant professor, Angio Sec, chief, 1972-75; University of Kentucky, associate professor of radiology, Angiography Section, chief, 1975-78; Emory University Hospital, professor of radiology, Special Procedures Sec, chief, 1983-87; UT M D Anderson Cancer Center, professor of radiology, Special Procedures Section, chief, 1978-83, professor of radiology, 1990-. **ORGANIZATIONS:** RSNA; ARRS; SCVIR, fellow; ACR; Society of Gastrointestinal Radiology; Uroradiology Society. **HONORS/AWARDS:** Emory University Hospital-Radiology, Best Teacher, 1987. **SPECIAL ACHIEVEMENTS:** 164 published articles; 21 chapters of books; designer of Chuang catheter system for visceral angiography and abdominal cancer treatment. **BUSINESS ADDRESS:** Professor of Radiology, University of Texas M D Anderson Cancer Center, 1515 Holcombe Blvd, Box 57, Houston, TX 77030, (713)794-4855.

CHUGH, ASHOK KUMAR
Civil engineer. Indo-American. **PERSONAL:** Born Dec 9, 1942, Amritsar, Punjab, India; son of Amrita Bai Chugh & Malik Chand Chugh; married Indu Chugh, Dec 6, 1970; children: Anju, Ajay, Amita. **EDUCATION:** Punjab University, BS, 1963; University of Minnesota, MS, 1968; University of Kentucky, PhD, 1973. **CAREER:** Public Works Department, assistant engineer, 1963-67; Meyer Manufacturing Inc, structural engineer, 1968; Watkins & Associates, structural engineer, 1968-71; G R Watkins & Associates, structural engineer, 1973-74; University of Kentucky, research assistant to research

associate, 1971-76; US Bureau of Mines, research structural engineer, 1976-78; US Bureau of Reclamation, civil engineer, 1978-. **ORGANIZATIONS:** American Society of Civil Engineers, 1970-; US Committee of Large Dams, chairperson, 1985-; International Journal for Numerical and Analytical Methods in Geomechanics, editorial board, 1988-; World Bank, consulting board, 1988-; Asian Development Bank, consulting board, 1991-; United Nations Development Program, consulting board, 1992-. **HONORS/AWARDS:** Government of Japan, Research Award for Foreign Specialists, 1990; Government of India, consultant to central water commission, 1988; American Society of Civil Engineers, fellow, 1991; US Department of the Interior, Exceptional Value of Work, 1982. **SPECIAL ACHIEVEMENTS:** Over 65 papers and discussions in national and international journals; University of Colorado, lectures to graduate students; Training courses for foreign engineers; member of consulting boards. **HOME ADDRESS:** 13798 W Warren Drive, Lakewood, CO 80228, (303)986-7549. **BUSINESS ADDRESS:** Civil Engineer, Senior Technical Specialist, US Bureau of Reclamation, Mail Stop D-3620, PO Box 25007, Denver, CO 80225, (303)236-3900.

CHUGHTAI, SHAHID H.
Veterinarian. Pakistani American. **PERSONAL:** Born Dec 1, 1958, Lahore, Punjab, Pakistan; son of Razia Sultana and Abdul Hameed Chughtai; married Abida S Chughtai, Jan 7, 1984; children: Saba S, Hira S. **EDUCATION:** College of Veterinary Sciences, Lahore, Pakistan, DVM, 1981, MS, 1989. **CAREER:** Government of Punjab, Pakistan, veterinarian, 1984-91; Alta Veterinary Clinic, veterinarian, 1992-93; American Veterinary Clinic, veterinarian, 1993-. **ORGANIZATIONS:** American Veterinary Medical Assn, 1993-. **SPECIAL ACHIEVEMENTS:** Paper on oseophagotomy in dogs, 1989. **HOME PHONE:** (414)529-2210. **BUSINESS ADDRESS:** President, Chughtai Veterinary Services, American Veterinary Clinic, 7123 S 76th St, Franklin, WI 53132, (414)427-1818.

CHUI, CHARLES K.
Educator. Chinese American. **PERSONAL:** Born May 7, 1940, Macao; son of K F Chui & J Fong; married Margaret K Lee Chui, Aug 22, 1964; children: Herman, Carie. **EDUCATION:** University of Wisconsin, Madison, BS, 1962, MS, 1963, PhD, 1967. **CAREER:** State University of New York, Buffalo, assistant professor, 1967-70; Texas A&M University, associate professor, 1970-74, professor, 1974-88, distinguished professor, 1980-. **ORGANIZATIONS:** Center for Approximation Theory, director, 1987-. **HONORS/AWARDS:** Texas A&M University, Distinguished Achievement Award in Research, 1981; Ning Xia University, honorary professor, 1989. **SPECIAL ACHIEVEMENTS:** Author of: An Introduction to Wavelets, Academic Press, 1992; Multivariate Splines, SIAM, 1988; Kalman Filtering, Springer-Verlag, 1987, 2nd ed, 1991; Signal Processing and Systems Theory, Springer-Verlag, 1992; Linear Systems and Optimal Control, Springer-Verlag, 1988. **HOME ADDRESS:** PO Box 9317, College Station, TX 77842. **BUSINESS ADDRESS:** Distinguished Professor, Math Dept, Texas A & M University, College Station, TX 77843, (409)845-1269.

CHUN, AULANI
Educator. Chinese American/Pacific Islander American. **PERSONAL:** Born Aug 25, 1952, Los Angeles, CA; daughter of Robert Sung Chun Jr & Marian Lin Kim Chun; widowed; children: Michael Alexander Kalani O'pu'u Sapp-Chun. **EDUCATION:** California State University, Long Beach, BA, 1975. **CAREER:** California State University, Los Angeles, instructor, Long Beach, instructor; University of California, Irvine, instructor; San Diego Mesa College, associate professor, currently. **ORGANIZATIONS:** AFTRA; SAG; Actor's Equity Association. **SPECIAL ACHIEVEMENTS:** National touring company of The King & I; Hawaii company of A Chorus Line; special guest & principal of Kismet; TV show and movie experience; 1984 Olympics, assistant choreographer. **BUSINESS ADDRESS:** Associate Professor, San Diego Mesa College, 7250 Mesa College Dr, L101, San Diego, CA 92111.

CHUN, HON MING (VINCENT)
Research scientist, engineer. Chinese American. **PERSONAL:** Born Nov 23, 1960, Hong Kong; son of Bing Yit Chun and Lai Ping Wong; married Barbara Yu-Fong Wan, Sep 1, 1984; children: Stephanie Wing-Yee, Gregory Hae-Wor. **EDUCATION:** Illinois Institute of Technology, 1977-78; Massachusetts Institute of Technology, SB, 1981, SM, 1982, PhD, 1986. **CAREER:** NASA, engineering trainee, 1978; Draper Laboratory, Inc, Draper Fellow, intern, staff, 1979-85; Photon Research Associates, Inc, staff scientist, 1985-92, senior staff scientist, 1992-93; division technical director, 1993; Moldyn Inc, chief technical officer, 1993-. **ORGANIZATIONS:** American Institute of Aeronautics &

Astronautics, 1980-; Boston Catholic Chinese Community, treasurer, 1993-, vice president, Church Council, 1991-92; Chinese Catholic Pastoral Center, secretary, 1992-93; Boston Catholic Chinese Community, council secretary, 1986-88; Sigma Xi, 1983-. **HONORS/AWARDS:** NASA, Special Achievement Award, 1978. **SPECIAL ACHIEVEMENTS:** More than 50 publications in spacecraft dynamics, control, robotics and molecular dynamics. **HOME ADDRESS:** PO Box 397, Kendall Sq, Cambridge, MA 02142. **BUSINESS ADDRESS:** Chief Technical Officer, Moldyn Inc, 1033 Massachusetts Ave, Cambridge, MA 02138-5319, (617)354-3124.

CHUN, JOE Y. F.
Educator, educational administrator. Chinese American. **PERSONAL:** Born Jan 1, 1935, Hilo, HI; son of Chock Lin Chun and Kam Dang Chun; married Florence, Apr 1, 1967; children: Henry, Stephanie, Jennifer. **EDUCATION:** University of Hawaii, BA, MA. **CAREER:** United States Air Force, accounting supervisor; Department of Education, business teacher; Honolulu Business College, accounting instructor; University of Hawaii, Kapiolani Community College, accounting professor, currently, director of media educational services, currently. **ORGANIZATIONS:** Western Interstate Commission for Telecommunications; EDUCOM; American Educational Communications Technology. **MILITARY SERVICE:** US Army Reserve; US Air Force; 1953-58. **BUSINESS ADDRESS:** Director for Educational Media Services, Professor of Technology, Kapiolani Community College, 4303 Diamond Head Rd, Naio Educational Center, Rm 201B, Honolulu, HI 96816, (808)734-9840.

CHUN, RAYMOND W. M.
Educator. Chinese American. **PERSONAL:** Born Jan 21, 1926, Honolulu, HI; son of Yam Sing Chun and Yau Kiu Lum; married Memee K Chun, Jun 4, 1960; children: Michael R, Ruthane, Mark R. **EDUCATION:** St Joseph's University, BS, 1951; Georgetown University, School of Medicine, MD, 1955. **CAREER:** University of Wisconsin, assistant professor, 1961-92, professor emeritus, currently; Waisman Center on Mental Retardation and Human Development, medical director, 1982-92. **ORGANIZATIONS:** Child Neurology Society, president, 1982-83; Wisconsin Neurological Society, president, 1975-77; University of Wisconsin Hospital, medical staff, president, 1976-78. **SPECIAL ACHIEVEMENTS:** 60 peer-reviewed publications and 8 chapters in textbooks on child neurology subjects. **MILITARY SERVICE:** US Army, corp, 1944-47. **HOME ADDRESS:** 5058 La Crosse Ln, Madison, WI 53705.

CHUN, SHINAE
State government official. Korean American. **PERSONAL:** Born Feb 4, 1943, Osaka, Japan; daughter of Kye Yup Chun and Kee Soon Kang; married Kyong C Chun, Oct 6, 1965; children: 2. **EDUCATION:** Ewha Women's University, Seoul, Korea, BA, English literature, 1965; Northwestern University, School of Education & Social Policy, MA, 1971. **CAREER:** ESEA Midwest Resource Center, BESC Project, consultant/staff assistant, 1976-78; Midwest Indochinese Center for Material Development and Training, coordinator, 1978-79; Bilingual Education Service Center-Vocational Education, project consultant, 1979-80; Chicago Consortium of Colleges and Universities, Title IX Multiethnic Training, project director, 1980-83; State of Illinois, special assistant to the governor for Asian American affairs, 1984-89; Illinois Department of Financial Institutions, director, 1989-91; Illinois Department of Labor, director, 1991-. **ORGANIZATIONS:** Illinois Women in State Government, Women Executives in State Government, board member, 1991-; Council of 100/Northwest University; United Way, board of directors, 1986-91; Korean American Service Center, board of directors, 1986-89; Asian American Women's Network, vice president, 1983; Illinois Asian American Advisory Council to the Governor, chairperson, 1982-83; Asian American Heritage Council, co-chair, 1981-82. **HONORS/AWARDS:** Program for Senior Executives in State Government, John F Kennedy School of Government, Harvard University Fellowship, 1992; Midwest Women's Center, A Tribute to Chicago Women Award, 1990; Asian Human Services, Outstanding Leadership Award, 1990; Illinois Minority Women's Conference, Outstanding Service Award, 1985; Chinatown Chamber of Commerce, State's Outstanding Woman Award, 1984. **SPECIAL ACHIEVEMENTS:** Co-author, A Passage Through the Hermit Kingdom: Korea, book. **BUSINESS ADDRESS:** Director, Illinois Department of Labor, 160 North LaSalle St, C-1300, Chicago, IL 60601, (312)793-2800.

CHUN, SUN WOONG
Government official. Korean American. **PERSONAL:** Born Mar 30, 1934, Seoul, Republic of Korea; son of E L Chun; married Inmook, Aug 19, 1961; children: Felicia, Edward. **EDUCATION:** Ohio State University, BSChE,

1959, MS, 1959, PhD, 1964. **CAREER:** Gulf Oil Corp, 1967-75; US Department of Energy, director, 1975-. **ORGANIZATIONS:** American Institute of Chemical Engineering; American Chemical Society; American Management Association. **HONORS/AWARDS:** Ohio State University, Benjamin Lamme Award; AIChE, Diamond Jubilee Award; Pittsburgh Coal Conference, Leadership Award, Innovation Award; President Bush, Presidential Rank Award. **SPECIAL ACHIEVEMENTS:** 20 US Patents; many publications and many speeches; Pittsburgh Federal Executive Board. **HOME ADDRESS:** 3304 Hermar Dr, Murrysville, PA 15668, (412)327-0453.

CHUN, WEI FOO
Architect. Chinese American. **PERSONAL:** Born Dec 9, 1916, Canton, China; son of Mr & Mrs Chun K Chow; married Anita L Chun, Dec 26, 1948; children: Eugene L, Elaine L. **EDUCATION:** Rensselaer Polytechnic Institute, B Arch, 1942, M Arch, 1943. **CAREER:** Edward D Stone, Architect & Associates, project manager, 1958-63; Horowitz & Chun, principal, 1963-72; Office of W F Chun, architect/planner, 1972-. **ORGANIZATIONS:** American Institute of Architects; National Council of Architectural Registration Board. **HONORS/AWARDS:** Rensselaer Polytechnic Institute, undergraduate scholarship and graduate fellowship; New York State Association of Architects, Achievement Award, 1942; American Institute of Architects 20th Annual Honor Awards Program, Honor Award, 1968 for Humanities-Social Science Center, Long Island University, Brooklyn Center joint venture. **SPECIAL ACHIEVEMENTS:** Architectural design and planning licenses in the states of New York, New Jersey, Maryland, Michigan; architect for Confucius Plaza in New York City's Chinatown (affordable housing for 3000 occupants, primary school for 1200 students, community facilities, 20,000 sq ft of commercial space; dedicated March 1, 1978). **HOME ADDRESS:** 425 Riverside Dr, New York, NY 10025.

CHUNG, ANNI YUET-KUEN
Social services association administrator. Chinese American/Hong Kong American. **PERSONAL:** Born Jan 23, 1951, Hong Kong; daughter of Chung So and Chung Fung Ying-King; married Stan J Yee, Jan 7, 1990. **EDUCATION:** San Francisco State University, BA, 1973. **CAREER:** Self-Help for the Elderly, executive director, 1975-. **ORGANIZATIONS:** St Mary's Hospital & Medical Center, board of directors, 1990-; Progress Foundation, board of directors, 1991-; Consumer Action, board of directors, 1991-; Nicos Chinese Health Coalition, steering committee, 1989-; Chinatown Economic Development Group, 1992-; Senior Services Plan Task Force, 1992-. **HONORS/AWARDS:** California Legislature, Woman of the Year Award for 12th Assembly District, 1993; St Mary's Catholic Mission, Pope John XXIII Community Service Award, 1992; Martin Luther King Civic Committee, MLK Jr Community Service Award, 1992; Attorney General's Office, Asian Heritage Community Service Agency Award, 1992; United Way of the Bay Area, Seton Manning Service Award, 1983. **SPECIAL ACHIEVEMENTS:** Host and producer of weekly public affairs program on KTJF, 1987-; fluent in English, Chinese (Cantonese & Mandarin). **BUSINESS ADDRESS:** Executive Director, Self-Help for the Elderly, 407 Sansome St, Suite 300, San Francisco, CA 94111-3112, (415)982-9171.

CHUNG, CATHERINE L.
Librarian. Hong Kong American. **PERSONAL:** Born Mar 21, 1951, Hong Kong; daughter of Li Yui and Tong Shui-Ying; married Albert L Chung, May 10, 1976. **EDUCATION:** Radford College, BA, 1973; University of Maryland, MLS, 1975; Catholic University of America, post MLS, 1978. **CAREER:** Catholic University of America, librarian-cataloger, 1975-77; North Virginia Community College, librarian-cataloger, 1977-79; University of Maryland, librarian-cataloger, 1979-83; Arizona State Law Library, librarian-cataloger, 1984-86; Phoenix Public Library, librarian-cataloger, 1986-90, librarian, foreign language, 1990-. **ORGANIZATIONS:** American Library Association, 1975-; Chinese American Library Association, 1988-; Chinese American Forum, 1988-; Chinese American Citizens Association, 1991-. **HONORS/AWARDS:** Arizona State Library Association, ASLA/Horner Japanese Exchange Fellowship, 1989. **SPECIAL ACHIEVEMENTS:** Language proficiency: Chinese, English and Spanish. **BUSINESS ADDRESS:** Foreign Language Librarian, Phoenix Public Library, 12 E McDowell Rd, Phoenix, AZ 85013, (602)262-4732.

CHUNG, CHAI-SIK
Educator. Korean American. **PERSONAL:** Born Jul 14, 1930, Wonju, Kangwondo, Republic of Korea; son of Young-hun Chung and Aeduk Hahn; married Soon-ria Chung, Dec 17, 1962; children: Eugene, Warren Euwon.

EDUCATION: Yonsei University, ThM, 1957; Harvard University Divinity School, BD, 1959; Boston University, PhD, social ethics & sociology, 1964. CAREER: Emory University, Oxford College, social studies, instructor, 1962-63; Bethany College, sociology, assistant professor, 1963-64; Florida Atlantic University, sociology, assistant professor, 1965-66; Boston University, College of General Studies, soc science, assistant professor, 1966-69; Heidelberg College, associate professor to professor, 1969-80; University of California, Berkeley, Department of Sociology, Koret Visiting Professor, 1986-87; Yonsei University, professor of sociology, 1980-90; Boston University, Walter G Muelder Professor of Social Ethics, currently. ORGANIZATIONS: Association for Asian Studies, 1969-; Society for the Scientific Study of Religion, 1962-; The Society for Christian Ethics, 1990-; The American Sociological Association, 1964-90. SPECIAL ACHIEVEMENTS: Author, Consciousness and History: Korean Cultural Tradition and Social Change, 1991; co-author, Modern Science and Ethics, 1986; author, Religion and Social Change, 1982; numerous articles on religion and society in Asia, particularly Korea. BUSINESS ADDRESS: Professor of Social Ethics, Boston University, School of Theology, 745 Commonwealth Avenue, Boston, MA 02215, (617)353-6497.

CHUNG, CHEN HUA
Educator. Taiwanese American. PERSONAL: Born Oct 15, 1951, Pingtung, Taiwan; son of Piao-Man Chung and Swang-Chin Chung; married Chun Chu Chung, Dec 12, 1978; children: Eleanor L. EDUCATION: National Taiwan University, BA, commerce, 1973; Northwestern State University of Louisiana, MBA, 1977; Ohio State University, PhD, operations management, 1982. CAREER: University of Kentucky, assistant professor, 1982-87, associate professor, 1987-89, Ashland Oil research professor, 1989-92, professor of operations management, 1992-. ORGANIZATIONS: Decision Science Institute, 1980-; Institute of Management Science, 1980-; Operations Research Society of America, 1980-; American Production & Inventory Control Society, 1982-. HONORS/AWARDS: American Production & Inventory Control Society, Certified Fellow in Production & Inventory Management, 1989. SPECIAL ACHIEVEMENTS: Author, The Art of Administration, Psychology and Management; over 70 published papers. MILITARY SERVICE: Army of Taiwan, second lieutenant, 1973-75. BUSINESS ADDRESS: Professor, Dept of Decision Science & Information Systems, University of Kentucky, 425 E Business & Economics Building, Lexington, KY 40506-0034, (606)257-3258.

CHUNG, CHIN SIK (JIM)
Educator. Korean American. PERSONAL: Born May 6, 1924, Taejon, Chungnam, Republic of Korea; son of Kyung Mo & Song Ja; married Hyun Sook Chung, Aug 31, 1957; children: Raymond T, Daniel C, Joyce A. EDUCATION: Oregon State University, BS, 1951; University of Wisconsin, Madison, MS, 1953, PhD, 1957. CAREER: University of Wisconsin, research assistant, 1952-57, research associate, 1957-61; National Institutes of Health, visiting scientist, 1961-64, research biologist, 1964-65; University of Hawaii, professor of public health, 1965-, professor of genetics, 1969-. ORGANIZATIONS: American Journal of Human Genetics, associate editor; American Statistical Association; American Public Health Association; American Association for Advancement of Science; Society for the Study of Social Biology; International Society of Genetic Epidemiology; Epidemiology and Disease Control Study Section, National Institutes of Health. HONORS/AWARDS: National Institutes of Health, research grants, 1965-91, 1983-90; Centers for Disease Control, research grants, 1988-93; National Science Foundation, research grant, 1965-67. SPECIAL ACHIEVEMENTS: Genetic epidemiology: 57 articles, 5 monographs, 6 chapters, 1 review article; epidemiology and public health: 18 articles, 1 monograph. BUSINESS ADDRESS: Professor of Public Health and Genetics, University of Hawaii, 1960 East-West Rd, Biomed Bldg D104-A, Honolulu, HI 96822, (808)956-5776.

CHUNG, CONNIE (CONSTANCE YU-HWA)
Broadcast journalist. Chinese American. PERSONAL: Born Aug 20, 1946, Washington, DC; daughter of William Ling Chung and Margaret Ma Chung; married Maury Povich, Dec 2, 1984. EDUCATION: University of Maryland, BS, journalism, 1969. CAREER: CBS News, Washington, correspondent, 1971-76; KNXT-TV, Los Angeles, news anchor, 1976-83; NBC News at Sunrise, NBC Nightly News (Saturdays), NBC News Digest, anchor, 1983-86; NBC News Magazine, anchor, 1986-87; NBC News Specials, anchor, 1987-89; Saturday Night with Connie Chung, CBS, anchor, CBS Evening News (Sundays), 1989-92; CBS Evening News with Dan Rather and Connie Chung, co-anchor, 1993-. HONORS/AWARDS: Pepperdine University, Broadcast Club, honorary member, 1981-; Chinese-American Citizens Alliance, Outstanding Excellence in News Reporting, Outstanding Excellence in Public Service,

1973; Natl Academy of Television Arts and Sciences, Emmy Award, 1978, 1980, 1987; B'nai B'rith, Pacific SW Region, Portraits of Excellence Award, 1980, Anti-Defamation League, First Amendment Award, 1981; Brown University, DHL, 1987. SPECIAL ACHIEVEMENTS: Guest appearance on Murphy Brown, 1989; David Letterman's Old Fashioned Christmas, 1987; NBC News Report on America: Life in the Fat Lane, 1987; writer of television specials, including: Everybody's Doing It, 1988; Guns, Guns, Guns, 1988; Summer Showcase, 1988. BUSINESS ADDRESS: News Anchorwoman, CBS Evening News, 555 W 57th St, New York, NY 10019.*

CHUNG, DAVID YIH
Educator. Chinese American. PERSONAL: Born Nov 14, 1936, Shanghai, China; son of Chi-Yeh and Lu Way Chung; married Pay June Lin Chung, Aug 20, 1967; children: Jeffrey, Angela. EDUCATION: National Taiwan University, China, BSc, 1958; University of British Columbia, Vancouver, Canada, MSc, 1962, PhD, 1966. CAREER: National Bureau of Standards, Washington DC, research physicist, 1966-67, 1983-84, 1989-90; University of Durham, England, visiting professor, 1973-74; University of Cambridge, England, visiting professor, 1979-80; Howard University, assistant professor, 1967-71, associate professor, 1971-76, professor, 1976-. ORGANIZATIONS: American Physical Society, 1967-. HONORS/AWARDS: National Science Council, British, fellowship, 1973-74; UNESCO, Paris, consultant, 1983. SPECIAL ACHIEVEMENTS: Author of nearly 40 publication articles in natl and international journals, 1966-; presented nearly 50 seminars and talks in many international conferences, natl laboratories and universities. BUSINESS ADDRESS: Professor, Dept of Physics, Howard University, 6th St NW, Washington, DC 20059, (202)806-7903.

CHUNG, DEBORAH DUEN LING
Educator. Hong Kong American. PERSONAL: Born Sep 12, 1952, Hong Kong; daughter of Leslie Wah-Leung Chung and Rebecca Chung; married Lan Kan Wong, May 29, 1976. EDUCATION: California Institute of Technology, BS, 1973, MS, 1973; Massachusetts Institute of Technology, SM, 1975, PhD, 1977. CAREER: Carnegie Mellon University, assistant professor, 1977-82, associate professor, 1982-86; State University of New York, Buffalo, professor, 1986-, Niagara Mohawk Power Corporation Endowed Chair of Materials Research, 1991-, Dept of Mechanical & Aerospace Engineering, professor, currently. ORGANIZATIONS: Metallurgical Society of American Institute for Mining, Metallurgical and Petroleum Engineers, 1978-; ASM International, Buffalo Chapter, director, 1987-; American Carbon Society, 21st Biennial Conference on Carbon, chair, 1993. HONORS/AWARDS: American Institute for Mining, Metallurgical and Petroleum Engineering, Hardy Gold Medal, 1980; Carnegie Mellon University, Ladd Award, 1979; Society of Automotive Engineering, Teetor Educational Award, 1987; Tau Beta Pi, New York Nu Chapter, Teacher of the Year, 1992. SPECIAL ACHIEVEMENTS: Author: X-ray Diffraction at Elevated Temperatures, 1993; Carbon Fiber Composites, 1994. BUSINESS ADDRESS: Professor, Dept of Mechanical & Aerospace Engineering, State University of New York at Buffalo, Buffalo, NY 14260-4400, (716)645-2520.

CHUNG, DOUGLAS KUEI-NAN
Educator. Taiwanese American. PERSONAL: Born Jan 16, 1943, Yun-Lin, Taiwan; son of Hshang-Hso Chung and Wen-An-Mei Chung; married Ellen Chung, Sep 28, 1975; children: Hui-San, Hui-Yang. EDUCATION: Soochow University, BA, 1966; West Virginia University, School of Social Work, MSW, 1973, Ohio State University, School of Public Administration, MA, 1980; Ohio State University, College of Social Work, PhD, 1981. CAREER: Christian Children's Fund Inc, superintendent, social worker, 1967-71; Institute of Community Development, researcher, 1971-74; Fu-Jen university, lecturer, 1974-78; Mental Health Association of Franklin County, director of program evaluation and research, 1980-81; Indiana Wesleyan University, associate professor, 1981-89, director of social work education, 1986-88; Grand Valley State University, professor, 1989-. ORGANIZATIONS: Interfaith Dialogue Association, planning committee chair, 1991-; Michigan Academy of Science, Arts, and Letters, Asian Studies, chair, 1990-; The Board of Cherry Street Services Inc, Planning & Evaluation Committee, chair, 1990-91, Asian American Association, founder & president, 1984-88; Indiana Community Development Society, board member, 1985-89; Indiana association of Social Work Education, Nomination Committee, chair, Executive Committee, 1986-89; Indiana Chapter of National Association of Social Workers in America, board member, 1988-89; Council on Social Work Education, 1980-. HONORS/AWARDS: Honarary Citizen of Morgantown, W. Virginia, 1973; Institute of International Education, fellowship, 1972-; United Nations Fellowship, 1971.

SPECIAL ACHIEVEMENTS: Social work practice with Asian Americans; editor & author of two chapters, 1992; Social Probliems: Theories and Solutions, 1978; Program Design and Evaluation, 1975; Confucian Welfare Philosophy and Social Change Technology, 1993; Advocacy for a Cultural Competent Social Work Practice, 1991. **BUSINESS ADDRESS:** Professor, School of Social Work, Grand Valley State University, 25 Commerce Street, SW, Grand Rapids, MI 49503, (616)771-6559.

CHUNG, ED BAIK
Physician, educator. Korean American. **PERSONAL:** Born Mar 16, 1928, Kilchoo, Republic of Korea; son of Hi Sam Chung and Ok Bong Lee; married Ok Hyung Kang, Nov 9, 1958; children: Sophia M Holds, Jeanne M, Theodore D, Virginia M Lucci, Esther K Lee. **EDUCATION:** Severance Union Medical College, (now Yonsei University College of Medicine), MD, 1951; Georgetown University, MS, pathology, 1956, PhD, pathology, 1958. **CAREER:** Georgetown University Medical Center, resident in pathology, 1954-56, chief resident in pathology, 1956-58; Georgetown University Schools of Medicine and Dentistry, instructor in pathology, 1958-61, asst prof of pathology, 1961-63; Howard University Hospital, attending pathologist, 1964-, director of surgical pathology, 1968-; Howard University College of Medicine, assoc prof of pathology, 1964-70, prof of pathology, 1970-. **ORGANIZATIONS:** Washington Society of Pathologists, 1958-; Intl Academy of Pathology, 1959-; American Society of Clinical Pathologists, fellow, 1962-; College of American Pathologists, fellow, 1962-; New York Academy of Science, 1964-; Glen Dale Hospital, consultant in pathology, 1968-74; Coroner's Office, Washington, DC, pathology consultant, 1969-71; Washington Korean Community Service Center, board of directors, 1974-, vice chairman, 1974-81, chairman, 1981-86. **HONORS/AWARDS:** Natl Cancer Institute, Special Research Fellowship, 1971; President of Republic of Korea, Certificate of Recognition, Medal of Honor, 1985; Howard University of College of Medicine Student Council, Certificate of Recognition Award, 1986; Padua University Institute of Anatomic & Histologic Pathology, Italy, visiting professor in soft tissue pathology, 1989. **SPECIAL ACHIEVEMENTS:** Certified by American Board of Pathology in pathologic anatomy, 1959, clinical pathology, 1966; published approximately 95 articles, 60 papers & 35 abstracts in professional journals, 1960-92; "Current Classification of Soft Tissue Tumours," Pathobiology of Soft Tissue Tumours, London, Churchill Livingstone, p 43-81, 1990; co-editor, Tumor & Tumorlike Lesions of Soft Tissue, New York, Churchill Livingstone, 1991. **MILITARY SERVICE:** Republic of Korea Army Medical Corps, captain, 1952-54; Gold Star Wharang Metal of Honor, 1953. **BUSINESS ADDRESS:** Professor of Pathology, Howard University College of Medicine, 520 W St NW, Washington, DC 20059-0001, (202)806-6306.

CHUNG, EDWARD K.
Educator, physician. Korean American. **PERSONAL:** Born Mar 3, 1931, Seoul, Republic of Korea; son of Il-Chun Chung; married Lisa S Chung, May 26, 1958; children: Linda C, Christopher D. **EDUCATION:** Seoul National University, Pre-Medical School, BS, 1953, College of Medicine, MD, 1957. **CAREER:** Vanderbilt University, associate professor of medicine, 1964-68; West Virginia University, professor of medicine, 1968-73; Thomas Jefferson University, professor of medicine, 1973-. **ORGANIZATIONS:** American College of Cardiology fellow, 1967; American College of Physicians, fellow, 1971; American Medicial Association, 1958; American Heart Association, 1967; Pennsylvania Medical Society, 1973; Philadelphia Medical Society, 1973; Korea Medical Association, 1957. **HONORS/AWARDS:** Thomas Jefferson University, Distinguished Lectureship, 1990. **SPECIAL ACHIEVEMENTS:** Published 76 medical books in cardiology, 1969-; 30 books, translated 10 foreign languages, 1973-. **BIOGRAPHICAL SOURCES:** Thomas Jefferson University Bulletin, May 1990. **BUSINESS ADDRESS:** Professor of Medicine, Thomas Jefferson University, 111 South 11th St, Gibbon Bldg, Ste 5360-D, Philadelphia, PA 19107, (215)955-7303.

CHUNG, EUGENE
Professional football player. Korean American. **PERSONAL:** Born Jun 14, 1969, Prince Georges County, MD. **EDUCATION:** Virginia Tech, degree, hotel, restaurant and institutional management. **CAREER:** Played in Canadian Football League, World Football League, Arena Football League; New England Patriots, offensive tackle, 1992-. **HONORS/AWARDS:** Asian Pacific Council, Mainstream America Asian American of the Year Award, 1992. **SPECIAL ACHIEVEMENTS:** Second Korean-American to play professional football, 1994; selected by Patriots in first round of NFL draft, 1992. **BUSINESS ADDRESS:** Professional Football Player, New England Patriots, Sullivan Stadium, Rt 1, Foxboro, MA 02035.*

CHUNG, FRANK HUAN-CHEN
Chemical industry executive. Chinese American. **PERSONAL:** Born Jul 20, 1930, Pingshang, Kiangsi, China; son of Ko-Yie Chung and Chi-Ming Hsu Chung; married Chu-Feng Wen Chung, Dec 26, 1959; children: Susan Silverstein, Shirley, Sonia. **EDUCATION:** University of Minnesota, certificate; Lehigh University, certificate; Chung Cheng Institute of Technology, China, BS, 1953; Kent State University, PhD, 1968. **CAREER:** Sherwin-Williams Co, senior scientist, 1968-90; Norwestern University, invited lecturer, 1978; Marson Corp, technical dirctor, 1990, vice president, 1993-. **ORGANIZATIONS:** American Chemical Society, invited speaker; American Crystallography Association, invited speaker; Society for Applied Spectroscopy, symposium chairman; Chinese Students and Alumni Association, president, 1987-89; Chicago Society of Coatings Technology; Mid-America Chinese Science & Technology Association (MACSTA), vice president, 1986-87. **HONORS/AWARDS:** Kent State University, International Achievement Award, 1967; American Chemical Society, Irving Langmuir Award Nomines, 1977. **SPECIAL ACHIEVEMENTS:** Author of many technical papers including: "Matrix-Flushing Theory in X-ray Diffraction Analysis," Journal of Applied Crystallography, vol 7, p 519, 1974, vol 7, p 526, 1974, vol 8 p 17, 1975 series; "Unified Theory of Adhesion," Journal of Applied Polymer Science, vol 42, p 1319, 1991; United Nations, TOKTEN Consultant to China, 1985; British Crystallographic Association, Guest Speaker, 1987. **MILITARY SERVICE:** US Army, col, 1964-; Outstanding Academic Achievement Award, Commendation Letter. **BUSINESS ADDRESS:** Vice President of Research and Development, Marson Corp, 130 Crescent Ave, Automotive Division, Chelsea, MA 02150, (617)884-7760.

CHUNG, H. MICHAEL
Educator. Korean American. **EDUCATION:** UCLA, MBA, PhD. **CAREER:** Texas A&M University, Graduate School of Business, professor, currently. **ORGANIZATIONS:** The Institute for Management and Technology Studies. **BUSINESS ADDRESS:** Professor, Dept of Business Analysis and Research, Texas A&M University, Graduate School of Business, College Station, TX 77843-4217.

CHUNG, HAROLD
Banker. Chinese American. **CAREER:** American International Bank, chairman, currently. **ORGANIZATIONS:** Chinese American Business and Industry Association, president. **BUSINESS ADDRESS:** Chairman, American International Bank, 624 South Grand Ave, Los Angeles, CA 90017, (213)688-8600.*

CHUNG, HO YOUNG
Insurance company executive, city council member. Korean American. **PERSONAL:** Born Feb 11, 1934, Chung Do, Republic of Korea; son of Woo Hae Chung; married Sunny H Chung, May 20, 1961; children: Ann, Merah, Susan, Lydia. **EDUCATION:** Hankuk University of Foreign Studies, Korea, BA, 1958; Korea University, MA, 1960; James Madison University, MBA, 1977. **CAREER:** Hangang University, Korea, instructor, 1961-67; State Farm Insurance Company, agency, president, 1974-. **ORGANIZATIONS:** Orange County Human Relations Commission, 1989-93; Orange County Minority Business Council, president, 1990-91; Advisory Council on Asia, CA Commission for Economic Development, 1988-92; Federation of Korean Associations-USA, senior vice president, 1990-91; Orange County Korean American Association, president, 1990-92; Korean Chamber of Commerce of Orange County, president, 1982-83; Korean Lions Club of Orange County, charter president, 1977-78; State Farm Insurance Co, President Club, 1977; City of Garden Grove, city council memeber, mayor pro-tem, currently. **HONORS/AWARDS:** Asian Pacific Legal Center, Southern California, Legal Impact Award, 1990; Korean Christian Women Federation of USA, Comunity Service Award, 1990; Republic of Korea, President Award, 1991; Garden Grove Sister City Association, People through Peace Award, 1992; Spiritual Assembly of the Bahar's, Model of Unity Award, 1993; Coro Foundation's leadership training certificate, 1990. **MILITARY SERVICE:** Korean Military, completed. **HOME ADDRESS:** 8771 Anthony Avenue, Garden Grove, CA 92641, (714)537-5012. **BUSINESS ADDRESS:** President, Ho Chung State Farm Insurance Company, 8744 Garden Grove B1, Garden Grove, CA 92644, (714)539-2255.

CHUNG, HYUN S.
Educator. Korean American. **PERSONAL:** Born Jun 21, 1928, Seoul, Republic of Korea; daughter of Yung Kyun Shin & Bang Bum Hong; married Chin Sik Chung, Aug 31, 1957; children: Raymond T, Daniel C, Joyce A. **EDUCA-**

TION: Ewha Woman's University, BA, 1949; Skidmore College, BA, 1954; State University of New York, Albany, MA, 1955; University of Wisconsin, 1955-57. **CAREER:** Ewha Woman's University, teaching assistant, 1950-53; Education Center, instructor, 1975-76; Cannon's Business College, instructor, 1976-. **ORGANIZATIONS:** Hawaii Council of Teachers of English; Teachers of English to Speakers of Other Languages; Hawaii Association of Teachers of Japanese. **HONORS/AWARDS:** Ewha Woman's University, valedictorian. **HOME ADDRESS:** 5074 Kiai Place, Honolulu, HI 96821. **BUSINESS PHONE:** (808)955-1500.

CHUNG, JESSE Y. W.
Precious metal and chemical company executive. Hong Kong American. **PERSONAL:** Born Dec 29, 1942, Hong Kong; married Julie Chung. **EDUCATION:** Hong Kong Polytechnic, industrial chemistry, 1971, diploma, mgt studies, 1975. **CAREER:** Hong Kong Police Force, inspector, 1964-66; Jebsen and Co Ltd, Chemical Div, mgr; Degussa Canada, pigments dept, mgr, 1976-83, Degussa Corp USA, technical metal dept, mgr, Precious Metal Div, vice pres, 1984-. **ORGANIZATIONS:** New York Merchantile Exchange, metal advisory committee; British Institute of Management; British Institute of Marketing; ISA, USA; Society of Coating Technology; AMA, USA. **SPECIAL ACHIEVEMENTS:** Founder: various businesses and companies in different countries; international management exposure and experience; diversified chemical and precious metal background. **BUSINESS ADDRESS:** Vice President, Precious Metal Division, Degussa Corporation USA, 3950 S Clinton Ave, Bldg B, South Plainfield, NJ 07080, (908)668-4338.

CHUNG, JIN SOO
Educator. Korean American. **PERSONAL:** Born Jan 27, 1937, Seoul, Republic of Korea; son of Hyun Mo Chung (deceased) and Soon Mo Yu (deceased); married Yang Ja Park Chung, Aug 11, 1967; children: Claude Hunyoung, Christine Miyoung. **EDUCATION:** Seoul National University, BS, naval architecture, 1961; University of California at Berkeley, MS, naval architecture, 1964; University of Michigan, Ann Arbor, PhD, engineering mechanics, 1969. **CAREER:** Korea Electric Power Company, Korea, mechanical engineer, 1961-62; David Taylor Model Basin, research naval architect, 1964-66; Exxon Production Research Company, senior research engineer, 1969-73; Lockheed Missiles & Space Company Inc, staff engineer program manager, 1973-80; Colorado School of Mines, professor of engineering, 1980-. **ORGANIZATIONS:** International Society of Offshore and Polar Engineers, executive director, board of directors, technical editor of International Journal of Offshore and Polar Engineering; American Society of Mechanical Engineers, fellow, 1983-, technical editor, Energy Resources Technology, 1980-85, founding chairman, Offshore Mechanics & Artic Engineering Division, 1985-86, organizer and chairman of Offshore Mechanics & Artic Engineering Conferences, 1981-89. **HONORS/AWARDS:** ISOPE, Neptune Award, 1993; ASME, Eugene W Jacobson Award, best paper under Petroleum Division, 1978; Amoco Foundation, Outstanding Teaching Award, 1982-83. **SPECIAL ACHIEVEMENTS:** Area of specialization: ocean engineering and applied mechanics; founder, International Offshore Mechanics and Arctic Engineering Conference, editor of proceedings, 1981-89; founding member, Pacific/Asia Offshore Mechanics Symposium, 1990; founding member, European Offshore Mechanics Symposium; founding member, editor, International Conference on Offshore and Polar Engineering, 1991-; founding editor, International Journal of Offshore and Polar Engineering, 1991-; founding chairman, Offshore Mechanics and Arctic Engineering Division, ASME, New York, 1985. **BIOGRAPHICAL SOURCES:** Houston Chronicle, section 2, p 3, November 6, 1978; Korea Times (Korean Version, Seoul), p 9, January 20, 1990. **BUSINESS ADDRESS:** Professor of Engineering, Colorado School of Mines, 1500 Illinois St, Golden, CO 80401-1887, (303)273-3673.

CHUNG, JONG RAK PHILIP
Research scientist (retired), real estate investor. Korean American. **PERSONAL:** Born Sep 12, 1931, Chonju, Chollabuk-do, Republic of Korea; son of Jum Dong Chung and Sun Yeh Yim; married Kyung Sun Kim Chung, Jun 26, 1965; children: Hyunwoo Anthony, Hyunsuk Bernard, Hyunjin Francis, Hyunjoo Lisa. **EDUCATION:** Michigan State University, 1958-59; University of Washington, College of Fisheries, BS, fisheries, 1961, MS, fisheries, 1963, PhD, fisheries, 1968. **CAREER:** Korea Advanced Institute of Science & Technology, Seafood Processing Laboratory, head, associate professor, 1967-77; General Foods Corp, Technical Center, research specialist, 1976-79; Go 'N Joy Foods Corp, president, 1979-81; Cal-Alaska Fisheries Inc, general manager, 1983-87; Uyak Fisheries Inc, president, 1987-90. **ORGANIZATIONS:** Institute of Food Technologists, 1961-. **SPECIAL ACHIEVEMENTS:** Lan-

guage proficiency in: Korean, English, Japanese; 2 patents and 11 technical publications. **MILITARY SERVICE:** Korean Army, 1st lt, 1952-55. **HOME ADDRESS:** 1816 N 180th St, Seattle, WA 98133, (206)542-8451.

CHUNG, KING-THOM
Educator. Chinese American. **PERSONAL:** Born Apr 25, 1943, Miao Li, Taiwan; son of Aa-Yuan Chung and Yu-Ing Po Chung; married Lan-Seng Chung, Oct 27, 1973; children: Theodore, Serena. **EDUCATION:** National Taiwan University, BS, 1965; University of California, Santa Cruz, MA, 1967, Davis, PhD, 1972. **CAREER:** Frederick Cancer Research Center, scientist, 1972-77; Purdue University, visiting assistant professor, 1977-78; Tunghai University, associate professor, 1978-80; Soochow University, professor, chairman, dean, 1980-87; Roman L Hruska Meat Animal Research Center, visiting scientist, 1987-88; Memphis State University, associate professor, 1988-93, professor, 1993-. **ORGANIZATIONS:** American Society for Microbiology, 1968-; Institute of Food Technologists, 1988; Society of Environmental Toxicology and Chemistry, 1990; International Association of Milk, Food and Environmental Sanitation, 1990; Sigma Xi, 1968. **HONORS/AWARDS:** University of California, Fellowship, 1967; Memphis State University, Super Performance of University Research, 1992; American Institute for Cancer Research, Research Grant ($100,000), 1993-94. **SPECIAL ACHIEVEMENTS:** Dept of Microbiology, Soochow University, established department, first chairman, 1980; organized the International Symposium on Biogas, Micro-algae and Livestock Wastes in Taipei, Taiwan, 1980; published more than 40 refereed papers, especailly on azo dyes mutagenesis and carcinogenesis, 1973-. **BIOGRAPHICAL SOURCES:** Studio Classroom, published in Taiwan, April 1987. **HOME ADDRESS:** 8472 E Askersund Cove, Cordova, TN 38018, (901)753-4316. **BUSINESS ADDRESS:** Professor, Dept of Biology, Memphis State University, Life Science Bldg, Rm 501, Memphis, TN 38152, (901)678-4458.

CHUNG, KWONG T.
Educator. Chinese American. **PERSONAL:** Born Nov 1, 1938, Chungking, Zichuan, China; son of Ing Chung; married Sylvia S W Lee, Jun 22, 1979; children: Sarita, Sharon. **EDUCATION:** National Taiwan University, BS, 1961; SUNY, Buffalo, PhD, 1966. **CAREER:** SUNY College, Fredonia, assistant professor, 1966-68; UC, San Diego, assistant research physicist, 1968-70; North Carolina State University, assistant professor, 1970-74, associate prof, 1974-81, prof, 1981-. **ORGANIZATIONS:** American Physical Society, 1966-, fellow, 1987. **HONORS/AWARDS:** American Physics Society, Fellow, 1987. **SPECIAL ACHIEVEMENTS:** Over ninety refereed publications. **MILITARY SERVICE:** Army, 2nd lieutenant, 1961-62. **BUSINESS ADDRESS:** Professor, Dept of Physics, North Carolina State University, Raleigh, NC 27695-8202, (919)515-7074.

CHUNG, KYUNG WON
Educator. Korean American. **PERSONAL:** Born Aug 15, 1938, Seoul, Republic of Korea; son of Jin Rok & Yoon Hee Kim Chung; married Young Hee Min Chung, Aug 20, 1966; children: Harold M, John M. **EDUCATION:** Yonsei University, Seoul, BS, biology, 1964, MS, biology, 1966; St Louis University, MS, anatomy, 1969; University of Oklahoma, PhD, anatomy, 1971; Pennsylvania State University, postdoctoral, 1972. **CAREER:** Yonsei University, instructor, 1966; State University of New York, Down State Medical Center, instructor, 1972-75, assistant professor, 1975-77; University of Oklahoma College of Medicine, Department of Anatomical Sciences, assistant professor, 1977-79, associate professor, 1979-86, professor, 1986-, vice chairman, 1989-. **ORGANIZATIONS:** Asia Society of Oklahoma, Scholarship Committee, chairman, 1993-, board of directors, currently; Oklahoma Society of Korean Professors, president, 1992-93; International Foundation for the Study of Rat Genetics and Rodent Pest Control, Oklahoma City, research director, 1983-86; American Association of Anatomists, 1974-; Endocrine Society, 1979-; Research Society of Alcoholism, 1985-. **HONORS/AWARDS:** University of Oklahoma School of Medicine, David Ross Boyd Distinguished Professorship, 1993-, Stanton L Young Master Teacher Award, 1992, Edgar W Young Lifetime Achievement Award, 1990, Aesculapian Awards for Outstanding Teaching, 1979-80, 1983-84, 1986, 1988. **SPECIAL ACHIEVEMENTS:** Author, Gross Anatomy, Board Review Series, 2nd edition, Williams & Wilkins Co, Baltimore, MD, 1990; ''Alcohol and Cell Receptors In: Biochemistry and Physiology of Substance Abuse,'' CRS Press Inc, Boca Raton, FL, vol 2, chapter 8, 1990; 35 original biomedical science papers published in referred journals; presented over 50 papers at the national and international meetings. **MILITARY SERVICE:** Korean Army, cpl, 1961-63. **HOME PHONE:** (405)721-9121. **BUSINESS ADDRESS:** David Ross Professor, Vice Chair-

man, Dept of Anatomical Sciences, University of Oklahoma Health Sciences Center, 940 SL Young Blvd, Biomedical Sciences Bldg, Rm 511, Oklahoma City, OK 73104, (405)271-2377.

CHUNG, L. A. *See* **CHUNG, LISA A.**

CHUNG, LING JIA
Artist, educator. Chinese American. **PERSONAL:** Born Nov 11, 1941, Yaan, Sichuan, China; daughter of Cher Tzen Wang and Tzen Wuo Wang; married Greg D Chung, Dec 8, 1961; children: Shao Shane, Jeff Shawlon. **EDUCATION:** National Academy of Arts, Taipei, Taiwan, 1963-65; Penn Academy of Fine Arts, 1968-69; University of California, Irvine, BA, 1976; California State University, Long Beach, MFA, 1979. **CAREER:** California State University, Long Beach, lecturer, 1979-88; Art Institute of Southern California, lecturer, 1984-85; Saddleback College, lecturer, 1979-. **HONORS/AWARDS:** International Art Biennial, for Museo Hosio in Capranica-Viterbo, Italy, honorary distinction, 1984; Allied Arts Graduate Scholarship Funds, Long Beach, California, scholarship, 1978. **SPECIAL ACHIEVEMENTS:** Marknt Gallery, Langelo, Holland, one-person show, 1992; Emigrant Abstraction, Butler Gallery, Municipal Museum, Kilkenny, Ireland, 1992; International Group Show, Sata Fine Arts, Costa Mesa, California, 1991; International Art Competition & Exhibition for Museum Hosio, Capranica-Viterbo, Italy, 1984; Our Own Artists, Newport Harbor Museum, Newport, California, 1979. **BIOGRAPHICAL SOURCES:** "The Twain Shall Meet," by Lita Barrie, Vision, Summer 1991; "Ling Chung at Mills House Art Gallery," by Suvan Geer, Art Scene, June 1985. **HOME ADDRESS:** 7412 E Grovewood Ln, Orange, CA 92669.

CHUNG, LISA A. (L. A. CHUNG)
Journalist, association administrator. Chinese American. **EDUCATION:** Mills College, BA, American civilization. **CAREER:** Institute for Journalism Education, summer program; San Francisco Chronicle, reporter, 1983-93; Asian American Journalists Assn, natl executive director, 1994-. **ORGANIZATIONS:** Asian American Journalists Assn, San Francisco chapter, co-founder, 1985-, natl board of directors, 1987-. **BUSINESS ADDRESS:** Natl Executive Director, Asian American Journalists Assn, 1765 Sutter St, Ste 1000, San Francisco, CA 94115, (415)346-2051.*

CHUNG, LUKE TSUN
Computer consultant. Taiwanese American. **PERSONAL:** Born May 7, 1964, New York, NY; son of Wen-Yi Chung and Po-Ying Chung; married Beth, Aug 31, 1991. **EDUCATION:** Harvard College, AB (cum laude), 1985; Harvard University, SM, 1985. **CAREER:** Strategic Planning Associates, Inc, analyst, 1985-87; Financial Modeling Specialists, Inc, president, 1987-. **HONORS/AWARDS:** Presidential Scholar. **BUSINESS ADDRESS:** President, Financial Modeling Specialists, Inc, 8027 Leesburg Pike, Ste 410, Vienna, VA 22182, (703)356-4700.

CHUNG, PAUL MYUNGHA
Engineer, educator, administrator. Korean American. **PERSONAL:** Born Dec 1, 1929, Seoul, Republic of Korea; son of Robert Namsoo Chung and Kyung Sook Kim; married Estella Jean Judy, Mar 8, 1952; children: Maurice W, Tamara P. **EDUCATION:** University of Kentucky, BSME, 1952, MSME, 1954; University of Minnesota, PhD, 1957. **CAREER:** University of Minnesota, assistant professor, 1957-58; Ames Research Center, NASA, aeronautical research scientist, 1958-61; Aerospace Corporation, Fluid Physics Dept, head, 1961-66; University of Illinois at Chicago, Mechanical Engineering, professor, 1966-, Energy Engineering Dept, head, 1974-79, College of Engineering, dean, 1979-. **ORGANIZATIONS:** American Institute of Aeronautics & Astronautics, National Tech Committee on Plasmadynamics, 1972-74, National Tech Committee on Propellants & Combustion, 1976-80; Underwriters Laboratory, corporate member, 1983-; American Institute of Chemical Engineers, National Committee for Intl Activities, 1992-94; American Society of Engineering Education, Deans' Council, executive board, 1983-84. **HONORS/AWARDS:** American Society of Heating, Refrigeration & Air Conditioning Engineers, Addams Moulton Award, 1956; Princeton University, Baetijer Lecturer, 1976; American Institute of Aeronautics & Astronautics, fellow, 1987. **SPECIAL ACHIEVEMENTS:** Author of book, Electric Probes in Stationary and Flowing Plasmas, 1975, Russian ed, 1978; author of chapter, "Nonequilibrium Chemically Reacting Boundary Layers," Advances in Heat Transfer, 1965; "Turbulent Shear Flow of Continuum Plasma," Dynamics of Ionized Gases, 1973; over sixty research papers in nationally published technical journals. **BUSINESS ADDRESS:** Dean, College of Engineering, University of Illinois

at Chicago, 851 S Morgan Street, M/C 159, Rm 838 SEO, Chicago, IL 60607-7043, (312)996-2400.

CHUNG, ROBERT
Government official. Chinese American. **PERSONAL:** Born Sep 22, 1949, San Francisco, CA; son of Sen Chen Chung & May Wong Chung; married Kathleen Mary Rose, Sep 29, 1985; children: David Robert, Matthew Daniel. **EDUCATION:** California State College, Hayward, BS, 1971, BS, 1973; California State University Consortium, Sacramento, MA, 1984. **CAREER:** USDA Soil Conservation Service, civil engineer technician, 1972; Sacramento County, environmental technician, 1973-75; Sacramento Area Council of Governments, associate planner, 1975-86; Contra Costa County, senior planner, transportation, 1986-90; Contra Costa Transportation Authority, interim deputy director, 1988-90; California Transportation Commission, deputy director, 1990-. **ORGANIZATIONS:** American Planning Association, 1975-. **BUSINESS ADDRESS:** Deputy Director, Mass Transportation, California Transportation Commission, 1120 N St, Ste 2221, Sacramento, CA 95814, (916)653-2090.

CHUNG, RONALD ALOYSIUS
Educator. Chinese American. **PERSONAL:** Born Sep 30, 1936, Brownstown, Manchester, Jamaica; son of Henry Chung Yin Kee & Nora Young Chung; married Cecile S Lee Sue Chung, May 19, 1963; children: Paula A Mitchell, Denise, Sandra, A Musallam. **EDUCATION:** College of the Holy Cross, BS, 1959; Purdue University, MS, 1961, PhD, 1963. **CAREER:** Tuskegee University, professor, 1963-84, professor/dept head, 1984-86; University of Northern Iowa, professor/dept head, 1986-. **ORGANIZATIONS:** American Association for the Advancement of Science, fellow, 1963-; American Chemical Society, 1957-; American Home Economics Association, 1963-; Institute of Food Technologists, 1960-; American Institute of Chemists, fellow, 1986-; Sigma Xi, 1961-. **HONORS/AWARDS:** Poultry Science Association, Research Award, 1968; 1890-T I Research Directors, Morrison-Evans Outstanding Scientist, 1984; Tuskegee University, Research & Teaching Award, 1983. **SPECIAL ACHIEVEMENTS:** More than 35 publications in refereed scientific journals, 1961- on: biochemical effects of environmental pollutants, food safety assessment, effects of dietary fats and cholesterol. **BUSINESS ADDRESS:** Prof/Head, Dept of Design, Family & Consumer Scis, University of Northern Iowa, Latham 235, Cedar Falls, IA 50614-0332, (319)273-2814.

CHUNG, SIMON LAM-YING
Educator, educational administrator. Hong Kong American/Chinese American. **PERSONAL:** Born May 13, 1948, Toishan, Guangdong, China; son of Jung Kwong Chee & Chan Ping Kam; married Lucia Leung, Jul 24, 1976; children: Teresa, Stephen. **EDUCATION:** University of Illinois, Chicago, BS, 1971; Illinois Institute of Technology, MS, 1973, PhD, 1980. **CAREER:** Trinity College, Illinois, assistant professor and chairman, Department of Biology, 1977-83; Northeastern Illinois University, associate professor and chairman, Department of Biology, 1984-. **ORGANIZATIONS:** American Society of Microbiology, 1977-; American Scientific Affiliation, 1976-; American Association for the Advancement of Science, 1973-; Chinese Evangelical Free Church of Greater Chicago, chair, 1989-93; United Chinese Churches of Chicago, president, 1988-90. **SPECIAL ACHIEVEMENTS:** Research on Lake Michigan phytoplankton, ecology, 1973-. **BUSINESS ADDRESS:** Assoc Prof/Chmn, Dept of Biology, Northeasten Illinois University, 5500 N St Louis Ave, Chicago, IL 60625-4699, (312)794-2635.

CHUNG, SUE FAWN
Educator. Chinese American. **PERSONAL:** Born Mar 11, 1944, Los Angeles, CA; daughter of Walter K Chung and Jane Beverly Chan; married Alan Moss Solomon, Apr 16, 1980; children: Walter Moss Solomon, Alexander Moss Solomon. **EDUCATION:** University of California, Los Angeles, BA, 1965; Harvard University, AM, 1967; University of California, Berkeley, PhD, 1975. **CAREER:** University of California, Los Angeles, various positions, 1961-65; Harvard University, teaching fellow, 1967; San Francisco State University, lecturer, 1970-73; University of California, Berkeley, teaching assistant, 1971-73; University of Nevada, Las Vegas, assistant professor of history, 1975-78, director of international programs, 1984-87, associate professor of history, 1978-. **ORGANIZATIONS:** Nevada Humanities Committee, Asia and Nevada Project, director, 1992-94; Association for Asian Studies, 1964-; American Historial Association, 1975; Society for Qing Studies, 1975; Lied Discovery Children's Museum, consultant, various positions, 1991-; Nevada State Museum, special consultant, 1992-93; National Endowment for the Humanities, media panelist, 1992; numerous other community organizations.

HONORS/AWARDS: American Council of Learned Societies, research fellowship, 1977; National Endowment for Humanities, Nevada Humanities Committee, project grant, 1992-94; UNLV History Department, Outstanding Teacher Award nominee, 1993; UCLA, Outstanding Senior, Outstanding Junior, Outstanding Woman, 1964-65. SPECIAL ACHIEVEMENTS: Asian Nevadans: The Asian American Experience in the Silver State, traveling photo exhibit, 1993-95; Beyond Gum San: History of the Chinese in Nevada, special exhibit, state museum, 1993-95; "Chinese American Women in Nevada," forthcoming article, 1993-94; "I've Been Workin' on the Railroad," The World and I, p 420-431, August 1991; "Gue Gim Wah: A Pioneering Chinese American Woman," History and Humanities, ed F Hatigan, 1989. BUSINESS ADDRESS: Associate Professor, Dept of History, University of Nevada, Las Vegas, 4505 Maryland Pky, Las Vegas, NV 89154, (702)895-3349.

CHUNG, T. S. (TUNG SU)
Attorney. Korean American. CAREER: Kim and Andrews, attorney, currently. ORGANIZATIONS: RLA (Rebuild Los Angeles), board member; Korean American Coalition, founding president. SPECIAL ACHIEVEMENTS: Koreatown Emergency Response Task Force, organizer, 1992; LA Voices: A Discussion of Post-Unrest Relief, panel member, 1992; Mayor Tom Bradley's Task Force, co-chairman. BIOGRAPHICAL SOURCES: "T S Chung," Los Angeles Times, section M, p 3, May 24, 1992. BUSINESS ADDRESS: Attorney, Kim and Andrews, 1055 W Seventh St, Ste 20800, Los Angeles, CA 90017, (213)955-9500.*

CHUNG, TAE-SOO
Physician. Korean American. PERSONAL: Born Feb 1, 1937, Tae-Gu, Republic of Korea; son of Sang-Taik Chung and Chuwan Ha Chung; married Kwangja Park, Apr 3, 1965; children: Peter, Alexander. EDUCATION: Yonsei University, Korea, MD, 1963. CAREER: New York University Medical Center, rehab medicine, chief resident, 1967; New York Medical College, rehab medicine, fellow, 1968; Children's Rehabilitation Center, Canada, clinical director, 1969-71; New York Medical College, Children's Rehab Unit, Spinal Cord Injury Service, chief, 1971-75, clinical asst professor, 1971-80; Dover General Hospital, Physical Medicine and Rehab Dept, director, 1975-; University of Medicine and Dentistry, clinical asst professor, 1976-; Sussex County Education Commission, consultant, 1980-; Newton Memorial Hospital, Rehab Unit, director, 1981-. ORGANIZATIONS: New Jersey Society of Physical Medicine and Rehabilitation, secretary, 1979-80, president, 1983-84; American Korean Medical Society, New York Metropolitan Area, vp, 1979-80; American Medical Assn; American Academy of Physical Medicine and Rehabilitation; American Congress of Rehabilitative Medicine; New Jersey Academy of Medicine. BUSINESS ADDRESS: Clinical Asst Professor, Rehab Medicine, New Jersey Medical School, University of Medicine & Dentistry, 185 S Orange Ave, Newark, NJ 07103.

CHUNG, THOMAS D.
Research scientist. Korean American. PERSONAL: Born Mar 7, 1956, Taegu, Republic of Korea; son of Violet Y H (Chung) Ikinaga & Richard Ikinaga (stepfather) and John H Chung (deceased); married Barbara, May 28, 1988; children: Timothy William Nak Ku. EDUCATION: Massachusetts Inst of Tech, BS, 1978; Stanford University, 1978-79; University of California, Berkeley, PhD, 1986. CAREER: Exxon Research & Engineering, industrial affiliate fellow, 1979-80; SmithKline & Beecham, postdoctoral scientist, 1986-89; Merck Sharp & Dohme, research scientist I, 1989-91; Bristol-Myers Squibb, research investigator II, 1991-. ORGANIZATIONS: American Chemical Soc, 1987-; American Assn for the Advancement of Science, 1985-; Sigma Xi, assoc member, 1978-80; Alpha Chi Sigma, Zeta Chapter, founding member, 1977-80; Phi Lamda Upsilon, treasurer, 1977-78. HONORS/AWARDS: University of California, Regents' Fellowship, 1977; Natl Science Foundation, commendation, 1978; American Institute of Chemists, Student Award, 1978; Sigma Xi, Undergraduate Fellowship, 1977. SPECIAL ACHIEVEMENTS: Pharmaceutical research in virology, 1989-; research on topoisomerase isotypes, 1987-89; entymological studies on dihydrofolate reductives from Candida. HOME ADDRESS: 10 Cherry Ln, Lambertville, NJ 08530.

CHUNG, THOMAS YONGBONG
Trading company executive. Korean American. PERSONAL: Born Apr 1, 1927, Jinyoung, Republic of Korea; son of Pil Do Chung and Myung Li Hwang Chung; married Chany N Chung, Jun 16, 1980. EDUCATION: Kukmin College, BA, 1954; Cal State University, Long Beach, 1960; Southern Illinois University, MA, 1962; UCLA, 1965. CAREER: K & A Industrial Co Inc, president, 1962-72; Evergrow Industrial Co, president, 1972-; His & Her Hair

Grow Co, president, 1972-. ORGANIZATIONS: American Economic Society, 1962-. BUSINESS ADDRESS: President, His & Her Hair Goods Co, Evergrow Industrial Co, 5377 Wilshire Blvd, Los Angeles, CA 90036, (213)931-1021.

CHUNG, TZE-CHIANG (MIKE)
Educator. Taiwanese American. PERSONAL: Born Nov 28, 1953, Tainan, Taiwan; son of Shu Mu Chung & Hsiu Yueh Chung; married Ming-Yuh Chung, Nov 29, 1981; children: Bernice, Frances. EDUCATION: Chung Yuan University, BS, 1976; University of Pennsylvania, PhD, 1982. CAREER: University of California, research scientist, 1983-84; Exxon Company, research chemist, 1984-86, senior research chemist, 1986-88, staff chemist, 1987-89; The Pennsylvania State University, associate professor, 1989-93, professor, 1993-. ORGANIZATIONS: American Chemical Society, 1982-; American Institute of Chemists, 1986-; Society of Plastic Engineers, 1992-. HONORS/AWARDS: Exxon Co, Special Research Award, 1986. SPECIAL ACHIEVEMENTS: More than 90 papers published in chemistry and polymer journals; 13 US patents; chairman, symposium on new advances in polyolefins, ACS National 1992 fall meeting. MILITARY SERVICE: Navy, Taiwan, lieutenant, 1976-78. BUSINESS ADDRESS: Professor, Dept of Materials Science and Engineering, The Pennsylvania State University, Steidle Bldg, Rm 325, University Park, PA 16802, (814)863-1394.

CHUNG, Y. DAVID
Artist. Korean American. PERSONAL: Born Feb 21, 1959, Bonn, Germany; son of Kyu Sup Chung & In Sook Choi; married Tabitha Eagle Chung, May 29, 1989. EDUCATION: Corcoran School of Art, BFA, 1988; University of Virginia. CAREER: Self-employed, artist, 1977-. ORGANIZATIONS: Washington Project for the Arts, board of directors, 1988-; Afro-Asian Relaions Council, treasurer, 1988-93; Asian American Arts and Media, board of directors, 1989-91; Washington Historical society, board of managers, 1993-; US-Korea Foundation, board of advisors, 1993-. HONORS/AWARDS: DC Commission on the Arts & Humanities, GIA Fellowship, 1989-91, Outstanding Emerging Artist, 1990; Rosebud Awards, Best of Show, 1993; Mid-Atlantic Arts Foundation, artist-in-residence, 1991; Painted Bride, new forms, 1990; National Endowment for the Arts, Visual Arts Fellowship, 1993. SPECIAL ACHIEVEMENTS: Solo-exhibition, Whitney Museum of American Art, 1992; "Seoul House" Exhibition and Opera Williams College Museum of Art; solo-exhibitions, Gallery K, Washington, DC, 1987, 1989, 1990, 1993. BIOGRAPHICAL SOURCES: "The Force of Conviction. . ." New York Times, p 25, 1990; Mixed Blessings, Lucy Lippard, p 198, 1991. HOME ADDRESS: 8008-A Georgetown Pike, Mc Lean, VA 22102, (202)393-5855.

CHUNG, YIP-WAH
Educator. Chinese American. PERSONAL: Born Nov 8, 1950, Hong Kong; son of Ming & Lin-Yau; married Jar-Fee Yung, Aug 1977; children: Christina, Connie. EDUCATION: University of Hong Kong, BS, 1971, MPhil, 1973; University of California, Berkeley, PhD, 1977. CAREER: Northwestern University, Dept of Math, Science and Engineering, professor, 1977-, Center for Engineering Tribiology, director, 1988-92, Dept of Math Science and Engineering, chair, 1992-. ORGANIZATIONS: American Physical Society, life member; TMS; STLE; AVS; AAAS; Illinois Chapter, AVS, chair; World Scientific Pub Co, editor in moder tribiology. HONORS/AWARDS: University of Hong Kong, Hui Pui Hing Memorial Scholarship, 1970; University of California, Berkeley, Earl C Anthony Scholarship, 1974; Society of Automotive Engineers, Ralph A Teetor Engineering Educator Award, 1990; ASME, Best Paper Award, 1991. SPECIAL ACHIEVEMENTS: Over 90 scientific publications and 2 books in surface science, thin films, fatigue crack initiation and the science of friction, wear and lubrication. BIOGRAPHICAL SOURCES: Chemical & Engineering News, p 20, May 25, 1992; Chicago Sun-Times, p 18, Jan 28, 1993. BUSINESS ADDRESS: Professor, Northwestern University, 2225 N Campus Dr, MLSB, Rm 2036, Evanston, IL 60208, (708)491-3112.

CHUNG, YOUNG-IOB
Educator. Korean American. PERSONAL: Born Jun 21, 1928, Bi Hyon, Pyong Book, Republic of Korea; son of Moon Chul Chung and Yoon Soon Choi; married Oke Kim Chung, Jul 2, 1960; children: Jee-Won, Jeanie. EDUCATION: University of California, Los Angeles, BBA, 1952; Columbia University, MA, 1955, PhD, economics, 1965. CAREER: Moravian College, assistant professor, 1961-66; Eastern Michigan University, associate professor, 1966-70, Department of Economics, professor, head, 1970-. ORGANIZATIONS: American Economic Association, 1961-; Association for Asian Stud-

ies, 1972-. **HONORS/AWARDS:** UCLA, alumni scholarship, 1950-52; Rotary Club, scholarship, 1950-52; Phi Beta Kappa, alumni scholarship, 1952; Moravian College, Outstanding Teacher, 1964; Omicron Delta Epsilon, 1985. **SPECIAL ACHIEVEMENTS:** 25 articles published or presented on economics and Asian studies, focusing on Korea; language proficiency: Korean, Japanese, some German. **BUSINESS ADDRESS:** Professor and Dept Head, Dept of Economics, Eastern Michigan University, Ypsilanti, MI 48197-2207, (313)487-3395.

CHUONG, CHENG-MING
Educator. Taiwanese American. **PERSONAL:** Born Sep 15, 1952, Taipei, Taiwan; daughter of You-Cheng Chuong & Yu-Yn Lee Chuong; married Wei-Ping Shen, Jun 21, 1981; children: Edward. **EDUCATION:** Taiwan University, MD, 1978; The Rockefeller University, PhD, 1983. **CAREER:** The Rockefeller University, assistant professor, 1983-87; University Southern California, assistant professor, 1987-92, associate professor, 1992-. **ORGANIZATIONS:** Orange County Taiwan Physical Association, council member, 1988; Chinese Bioscientist Association, Southern California Chapter, vice president, 1993. **HONORS/AWARDS:** American Cancer Society, Junior Faculty Research Award, 1988; NIH, Adhesion Molecules in Chondrogenesis, 1988-93; NSF, Retinoid and Hox Genes in Pattern Formation, 1992-. **SPECIAL ACHIEVEMENTS:** 39 publications, 1982-; proficiency in: English, Chinese, Taiwanese. **BUSINESS ADDRESS:** Assoc Professor, Dept of Pathology, University of Southern California, HMR204, 2011 Zonal Ave, Los Angeles, CA 90033, (213)342-1296.

CHUONG, THACH. *See* CUNG, TIEN THUC.

CHYUNG, DONG HAK
Educator. Korean American. **PERSONAL:** Born Aug 5, 1937, Pyongyang, Republic of Korea; son of Bong Hyup Chyung and Choon Kyung Oh Chyung; married Kyoung Hee Lee Chyung; children: Yung Hwan, Jay Hwan. **EDUCATION:** Seoul National University, Korea, BS, 1959; University of Minnesota, MS, 1961, PhD, 1965. **CAREER:** University of Minnesota, assistant professor, 1965-66; University of South Carolina, assistant professor, 1966-68; University of Iowa, associate professor, 1968-73, professor, 1973-. **ORGANIZATIONS:** American Mathematical Society. **BUSINESS ADDRESS:** Professor, University of Iowa, Dept of Electrical & Computer Engineering, Iowa City, IA 52242, (319)335-5954.

COLLANTES, AUGURIO L.
Librarian. Filipino American. **PERSONAL:** Born Jan 21, 1928, Tanauan, Batangas, Philippines; married Lourdes Y Collantes, Oct 21, 1961; children: Andresito, Arturo. **EDUCATION:** University of the Philippines, BS, foreign serv, 1951; Rutgers University, MLS, 1967; Long Island University, MPA, 1976. **CAREER:** Hanoch, Weisman, Stern & Besser, law firm, librarian, 1972; Medgar Evers College, CUNY, coordinator, CAT, proc, 1972-79; St Peter's College, head, technical services, 1979-83; Hostos Community College, CUNY, catalog librarian, associate librarian, 1983-. **ORGANIZATIONS:** American Library Association; Asian Pacific American Librarians Association, 1980-; Library Association of the City University of NY, Cataloging Roundtable, chairperson, 1987-88; NY Technical Serv Librarians. **HONORS/AWARDS:** Federal Government, Management for Librarians, one week workshop at Clarkson College, 1978; UNDP, Transfer of Knowledge through Expatriate Nationals, 1989. **SPECIAL ACHIEVEMENTS:** Author: "Building a National Bibliographic Database in a Third World Country," Proceedings of the 6th International Conference on New Information Technology, Nov 11-13, 1993, San Juan, edited by Ching-chih Chen, MicroUse Information, p 69-74, presented Nov 11, 1993; A Multipurpose Workstation in a Cataloging Unit, 6p, 1992; "Prospects for a Local Area Network at a University Library in a Developing Country," Microcomputers for Information Management, 9:235-46, 1992; Retrospective Conversion in a Small Community College Library, New York: Hostos Community College Library, p 10, 1991; "The City University of New York, Integrated Library System," Proceedings of the 3rd International Conference on New Information Technology, November 26-28, 1990, Guadalajara, Mexico, edited by Ching-chih Chen, MicroUse Information, p 99-103, presented Nov 27, 1990. **BIOGRAPHICAL SOURCES:** The Hostos Review, p 2, December 1989; Microcomputers for Information Management, 9:68, 1992; News from CUNY Libraries, 13:1, 2, December 1989. **HOME ADDRESS:** 73 Old Farm Road, East Hills, NY 11577. **BUSINESS ADDRESS:** Catalog Librarian, Associate Professor, Hostos Community College, City University of New York, 475 Grand Concourse, 207 G, Bronx, NY 10451, (718)518-4203.

COLLANTES, LOURDES YAPCHIONGCO
Librarian. Filipino American. **PERSONAL:** Born in Manila, Philippines; daughter of Jose V Yapchiongco & Placida Hernandez; married Augurio L Collantes; children: J Andresito, Arturo. **EDUCATION:** University of the Philippines, BA, 1954; Rutgers State University, MLS, 1959, MED, 1973, PhD, 1992. **CAREER:** East Orange Public Library, library intern, 1959-60; University of the Philippines Library, junior cataloger, 1954-58, Soc Sci Division, Humanities & Reference Division, librarian in charge, 1961-67, Acquisitions Dept, head, 1968-71; University of the Philippines, instructor of library science, asst professor, 1966-70; Rutgers, Mathematical Sciences Library, asst librarian, 1972-73; SUNY College, Old Westbury, associate librarian, librarian, 1973-. **ORGANIZATIONS:** American Library Assn, Awards Committee, 1984-88, Committee on Pay Equity, 1989-91, chair, 1991-93, David Clift Scholarship, chair, 1986-87, Louise Giles Minority Scholarship, jury, 1985-88, H W Wilson Library Staff Development, jury, 1987-88; Asian Pacific American Librarians Assn, vice president, president, 1982-84, Awards Committee, chair, 1988-90; ACRL Lazerow Fellowship Committee on Research, 1988-91. **HONORS/AWARDS:** Kappa Delta Pi, 1974; People to People Library & Information Science, delegate to China, 1985; UUP Professional Development & Quality of Life Committee, librarian research, 1985, 1987-88. **SPECIAL ACHIEVEMENTS:** One of two Asian Americans & one of 8 minorities selected for ALA Committee on the Status of Women in Librarianship Oral History Project, 1989; presentation, "Agreement in Naming Objects & Concepts for Information Retrieval: a Multicultural Perspective"; conference: The American Mosaic: Mapping Curricular Revision, CUNY Queens College, 1993; moderator: ALA Annual Conference: "Are You Underpaid. . .," 1992, "Compensation Strategies. . .," 1993; editor, Asian Pacific American Librarians: A Cross-Cultural Perspective, New York, APALA, 1985, ERIC, 1986, ED 265 240. **BUSINESS ADDRESS:** Librarian, SUNY, College at Old Westbury, Box 229, 223 Store Hill Rd, Old Westbury, NY 11568, (516)876-3154.

COLLIER, IRENE DEA
Educator. Chinese American. **PERSONAL:** Born Feb 24, 1948, Canton, China; daughter of Dick Quong Dea and Won Bick Dea; married Malcolm Collier, Jun 21, 1972; children: Alina Meifong, Lora Meilin, Aram Siuvoy. **EDUCATION:** San Francisco State University, BA, 1972. **CAREER:** Wah Mei Bilingual School, director, 1978-86; San Francisco Unified School District, Chinese bilingual kindergarten teacher, 1986-. **ORGANIZATIONS:** San Francisco Unified School district, mentor teacher, 1992-, Social Studies Adoption Team, 1991, Citizen's Advisory Committee to Select the Superintendent, 1986, Bilingual Advisory Committee, chair; Mayor's Advisory Committee on Childcare; Lucinda Weeks Childcare Committee, chair; Association of Chinese Teachers, curriculum writer, 1976-77, president, 1986-88. **HONORS/AWARDS:** Association of Chinese Teachers, Outstanding Educator, 1989; Wu Yee Resource and Referral Agency, special recognition, 1989; San Francisco Board of Supervisors, Certificate of Honor, 1986; TV Channel 2: "Family to Family Moment," Outstanding Educator, 1993. **SPECIAL ACHIEVEMENTS:** Chinese Americans Past and Present, 1977; Fifteenth Anniversary Edition: TACT History, 1989, Social Studies Review, vol 31, no 3, Spring 1992. **BIOGRAPHICAL SOURCES:** Chevron Catalyst, vol 24, no 5, p 10, Fall 1985; Asian Week, front page, June 25, 1981. **BUSINESS ADDRESS:** Teacher, Spring Valley Elementary School, 1451 Jackson Street, San Francisco, CA 94109, (415)749-3535.

COMPAS, LOLITA BURGOS
Nursing educator. Filipino American. **PERSONAL:** Born Oct 11, 1946, Candelaria, Quezon, Philippines; daughter of Vicente R Compas and Luisa B Compas. **EDUCATION:** St Paul College of Manila, Philippines, BS, nursing, 1967; New York University, MA, nursing, 1977. **CAREER:** Cabrini Medical Center, registered staff nurse, 1969-71, RN team leader, medical surgical, 1972, RN team leader, ICU-CCU, 1973-76, nursing administrative coordinator, 1976-77, nursing care coordinator emergency department, 1977-81, emergency department, clinical instructor, 1981-90, critical care nursing instructor, 1990-. **ORGANIZATIONS:** Philippine Nurses Association of New York Inc, president, 1992-94; New York State Nurses Association Benefits Fund, board of trustees; NYSNA Council of Nursing Practitioners Cabrini, chairperson; American Nurses Association; American Association of Critical Care Nurses; Philippine Nurses Association of America; Asian American Federation of New York; Food for Children, Cabrini Medical Center. **HONORS/AWARDS:** New York State Nurses Association, Economic and General Welfare, 1992; New York City Council President, Asian American Role Model Award, 1993. **SPECIAL ACHIEVEMENTS:** Collective bargaining and contract negotiations, 1987,

1989, 1991, 1993; certified emergency nurse, 1981-88; certified basic cardiac life instructor, 1978-; certified advanced cardiac life instructor, 1987-; Sigma Theta Tau, 1993. **BIOGRAPHICAL SOURCES:** NYSNA Statewide, vol 10, p 4, December 1992; Philippine News, 32, no 13, p 2, December 1, 1992. **HOME ADDRESS:** 320 E 23rd St, Apt 15-G, New York, NY 10010, (212)777-6423.

CORPUZ, RAY E., JR.
City government official. Filipino American. **PERSONAL:** Born Mar 14, 1947, San Fernando, L'Union, Philippines; son of Ray E Corpuz (deceased) and Connie B Corpuz; married Lynda A Corpuz, Nov 6, 1982; children: Lynette, Dito, Christina. **EDUCATION:** Saint Martin's, BA, 1969; University of Utah, 1973-74. **CAREER:** County of Pierce, government relations director, 1989-89; City of Tacoma, various, 1972-74, comprehensive employment services director, 1974-78, intergovernmental affairs director, 1978-88, city manager, 1989-. **ORGANIZATIONS:** International City/County Management Association, 1990-, public policy committee, 1992-; American Leadership Forum, fellow, 1989-; Greater Tacoma Community Foundation, board member, 1992-; Tacoma Pierce Co Chamber of Commerce, board member, 1992-; Pierce County Alliance, board member, 1988-. **HONORS/AWARDS:** Filipino Youth Activities Inc, Filipino-American Achiever, 1979; Asian American Alliance, Outstanding Citizen's Award, 1980. **BUSINESS ADDRESS:** City Manager, City of Tacoma, 747 Market St, #1200, Tacoma, WA 98402, (206)591-5130.

CRUZ, JOSE BEJAR, JR.
Engineer, educational administrator. Filipino American. **PERSONAL:** Born Sep 17, 1932, Bacolod City, Philippines; son of Jose P Cruz and Felicidad Bejar Cruz; children (previous marriage): Fe Cruz Langdon, Ricardo A, Rene L, Sylvia C, Loretta C; married Stella E Rubia, Sep 17, 1990. **EDUCATION:** University of the Philippines, BSEE, 1953; Massachusetts Institute of Technology, SM, 1956; University of Illinois, Urbana-Champaign, PhD, 1959. **CAREER:** University of Illinois, Urbana-Champaign, assistant professor, 1959-61, associate professor, 1961-65, professor of electricial and computer engineering, 1965-86; University of California, Irvine, professor of electrical and computer engineering, 1986-92, dept chairman, 1986-90; The Ohio State University, professor of electrical engineering, dean of engineering, 1992-. **ORGANIZATIONS:** Institute of Electrical and Electronics Engineers, vice president, 1982-85, board of directors, 1980-85; Philippine American Academy of Science & Engineering, president, 1981. **HONORS/AWARDS:** National Academy of Engineering, elected member, 1980; American Society for Engineering Education, Curtis McGraw Research Award, 1973; IEEE, Emberson Award, 1989, fellow, 1965; American Association for the Advancement of Science, fellow, 1989. **SPECIAL ACHIEVEMENTS:** Author of six books. **BUSINESS ADDRESS:** Dean, College of Engineering, Ohio State University, 2070 Neil Ave, 142 Hitchcock Hall, Columbus, OH 43210-1275, (614)292-2836.

CRUZADA, RODOLFO OMEGA
Government official, attorney. Filipino American. **PERSONAL:** Born Dec 25, 1930, Tacloban, Leyte, Philippines; son of Domiciano L Cruzada and Francisca Omega; married Purita Damasen Cruzada, May 16, 1956; children: Manuel, Minvilu C Gonzales, Rommel, Joel, Angelita. **EDUCATION:** Far Eastern University, Bachelor of Laws, 1956. **CAREER:** Presidential Assistant on Community Development, Philippines, analyst, 1957-63; Commission on Elections, Philippines, election registrar, 1964-67; Department of Justice, Office of Agrarian Counsel, Philippines, trial attorney, 1968-72; Department of Public Social Services, Los Angeles County, community liaison, 1974-93. **ORGANIZATIONS:** Filipino American Press Club of Los Angeles, parliamentarian, 1978-93; Los Angeles County Filipino American Employees Association, legal adviser, board member, 1978-93; Filipino American Community of Los Angeles, Inc, board member, vice president, 1978-93; Filipino American Senior Citizen of Los Angeles, adviser & parliamentarian, 1989-93; Philippine American Networking Advocacy, Los Angeles, 1990-93; Philippine Bar, 1989-93. **HONORS/AWARDS:** Department of Public Social Services, LA County, plaque, 1993; Los Angeles County Board of Supervisors, commendation, 1990; Presidential Assistant on Community Development, certificate on community development, 1959; Rizal Memorial Colleges, most reliable student award, 1950. **SPECIAL ACHIEVEMENTS:** Man in Poetry, Literary, Philippine American Harvest Awards, 1989. **BIOGRAPHICAL SOURCES:** Anthology of Philippine Writing in America, pg. 100-101, 1989. **HOME ADDRESS:** 4839 Cutler Ave, Baldwin Park, CA 91706.

CUA, ANTONIO S.
Educator. Chinese American. **PERSONAL:** Born Jul 23, 1932, Manila, Philippines; married Shoke-Hwee Khaw, Jun 11, 1958; children: Athene. **EDUCATION:** Far Eastern University, BA, 1952; University of California, Berkeley, MA, 1954, PhD, 1958. **CAREER:** Ohio University, instructor, assistant professor, 1958-62; State University of New York, College at Oswego, professor, dept of philosophy, chairman, 1962-69; Catholic University of America, professor, 1969-. **ORGANIZATIONS:** Society for Asian & Comparative Philosophy, president, 1978-79; International Society for Chinese Philosophy, president, 1983-85. **HONORS/AWARDS:** Woodrow Wilson Center, for International Scholars, Fellow, 1982; Chiang Ching-Kuo Foundation for International Scholarly Exchange, Research Grant, 1992-93. **SPECIAL ACHIEVEMENTS:** Author: Dimensions of Moral Creativity: Paradigms, Principles, and Ideals, 1978; Reason and Virtue: A Study in the Ethics of Richard Price, 1960; The Unity of Knowledge and Action: A Study in Wang Yang-ming's Moral Psychology, 1982; Ethical Argumentation: A Study in Hsun Tzu's Moral Epistemology, 1985. **BUSINESS ADDRESS:** Professor, Catholic University of America, Washington, DC 20064, (202)319-5636.

CUAJAO, TRACY LEE
Chemical company executive. Filipino American. **PERSONAL:** Born Dec 23, 1953, San Francisco, CA; son of Baltazar Alas Cuajao and Clara Marie; children: Alexandra Katrina. **EDUCATION:** Seattle Community College, AA; Shoreline Community College, AA. **CAREER:** Evergreen State Properties, sales, 1978-80; Cuajao/Wathne Associates, partner; Berger & Co., chemical manager, 1980-85; ConAgra, chemical manager, 1985-88; Turning Point Communications, consultant, 1993; NuSource Chemical Corporation, president, CEO, 1988-. **ORGANIZATIONS:** Chief Executive Officers Club, San Francisco Chapter; Northern California Purchasing Council; Center for Entrepreneurial Management; President's Advisory Council; Drug, Chemical and Allied Trades; The International Platform Assn. **SPECIAL ACHIEVEMENTS:** Martial Arts Assn, Black Belt, 3rd Degree, Chuin Yin Wai, 1973. **BUSINESS ADDRESS:** President, CEO, NuSource Chemical Corporation, 595 Market St Ste 2170, San Francisco, CA 94105-2832, (415)495-7100.

CUETO, ALEX
Physician. Filipino American. **CAREER:** Physican, currently. **HONORS/AWARDS:** APPA, Super Active Community Leader Award, 1992. **BUSINESS ADDRESS:** Physician, 275 Haddon Ave, Collingswood, NJ 08108, (609)858-3375.*

CULP, MAE NG
Government administrator. Chinese American. **PERSONAL:** Born May 13, 1935, Elko, NV; daughter of Geo Ng and Lim Shee Ng; married Joseph G Culp, Apr 28, 1962; children: Gregory W, Jerry G. **CAREER:** NIAAA, deputy EEO officer, 1974-84; Food & Drug Administration, federal women's program manager, 1984-94; FDIC, Office of Equal Opportunity, director, 1994-. **HONORS/AWARDS:** Asian Business Association, Public Service Award, 1991; Southeastern Tribes Inc, Special Recognition Plaque, 1988; Federal Asian PAC Council, Special Recognition Plaque, 1991. **HOME ADDRESS:** 7222 S Newberry Ln, Tempe, AZ 85283.

CUNG, TIEN THUC (THACH CHUONG, DANG-HOANG)
Economist, composer. Vietnamese American. **PERSONAL:** Born Nov 27, 1938, Hanoi, Vietnam; son of Van Thuc Cung and Anh-Tuyet Dinh; married Josee N, 1964; children: Raphael Dang-Quang T. **EDUCATION:** University of New South Wales, BA, 1962; University of Cambridge, England, MA, 1972; University of East Anglia, MA, 1973. **CAREER:** Republic of Vietnam, Ministry of Planning, director-general, 1973-75; Minnesota Dept of Natural Resources, minerals economist, 1977-. **ORGANIZATIONS:** Vietnamese Cultural Association of Minnesota, president, 1989-; Minnesota Composers Forum, board member, 1992-95. **HONORS/AWARDS:** The Schubert Club of St Paul, Artist-in-Residence, 1992; The St Paul Companies, Leadership Initiatives/Art & Diversity, 1993. **SPECIAL ACHIEVEMENTS:** Languages: Vietnamese, French, speaking and writing fluency; German, Spanish, working knowledge (reading); Economic Reconstruction and Development of Post-1g75 Vietnam, Praeger Publishers; The Palace File, C & K Promotions, Inc, 1987; Paul Samuelson, Economics, Hien Dai Press, 1975. **MILITARY SERVICE:** Infantry, master sergeant, 1965-70.

D

DAGA, RAMAN LALL

Tungsten carbide industry executive. Indo-American. **PERSONAL:** Born Jan 5, 1944, Purulia, W. Bengal, India; married Shashi Daga, Nov 26, 1972; children: Amit, Riju. **EDUCATION:** BIT, BS, 1966; New Mexico Institute of Technology, MS, 1968; Case Western Reserve University, PhD, 1970. **CAREER:** GE, senior research scientist, 1970-78; GTE Product Corp, engineering manager, 1979-84; Metadyne Inc, president, CEO, 1984-. **BUSINESS ADDRESS:** President, CEO, Metadyne, Inc, 110 Home St, PO Box 242, Elmira, NY 14902.

DAI, HAI-LUNG

Educator. Chinese American. **PERSONAL:** Born Feb 25, 1954, Tauyuan, Taiwan; son of Chuan-Yen Tai and Chung-Hua Liu Tai; married Surrina Mi-Na Hu, May 23, 1992. **EDUCATION:** National Taiwan University, BS, 1974; University of California, Berkeley, PhD, 1981. **CAREER:** Massachusetts Institute of Technology, postdoctoral fellow, 1981-84; National Taiwan University, guest professor, 1991-92; National Tsing-Hua University, Taiwan, adjunct professor, 1991-92; University of Pennsylvania, assistant professor, 1984-89, associate professor, 1989-92, professor, 1992-. **ORGANIZATIONS:** University of Pennsylvania, Laboratory for Research on the Structure of Matter, executive committee, 1993-; Franklin Institute, committee on the arts and science, 1991-; American Chemical Society; Overseas Chinese Physical Society, executive council, 1990-92; Chinese American Chemical Society; Advanced Series in Physical Chemistry, associate editor, 1992-. **HONORS/AWARDS:** Morino Foundation, Japan, Morino Lectureship, 1992; The Coblentz Spectroscopy Society, Coblentz Award in Spectroscopy, 1990; Camille and Henry Dreyfus Foundation, Teacher-Scholar Award, 1989; Alfred P Sloan Foundation, fellow, 1988; American Physical Society, fellow, 1992. **SPECIAL ACHIEVEMENTS:** More than sixty publications on molecular and surface sciences; conductor, Chinese Musical Voices, choral group based in Philadelphia. **MILITARY SERVICE:** Combined Service Forces, Taiwan, 2nd lieutenant, 1974-76. **BUSINESS ADDRESS:** Professor, Dept of Chemistry, University of Pennsylvania, Philadelphia, PA 19104-6323, (215)898-5077.

DAI, LIYI

Educator. Chinese American. **PERSONAL:** Born Aug 22, 1961, Liangshan, Shandong, People's Republic of China; son of Maochai Dai and Lirong Ding; married Yun Wang, Jun 15, 1986; children: Shiqi, Matthew S. **EDUCATION:** Shandong University, China, BS, 1983; Academia Sinica, China, MSc, 1986; Harvard University, PhD, 1993. **CAREER:** Academia Sinica, assistant professor, 1986-88; Harvard University, research assistant, 1989-93; Washington Univ, asst prof, 1993-. **ORGANIZATIONS:** Institute of Electrical and Electronics Engineers, 1990-; Operations Research Society of America, 1990-. **HONORS/AWARDS:** Chinese Association of Automation, Best Paper Award, 1988. **SPECIAL ACHIEVEMENTS:** Author, Singular Control Systems, Springer-Verlag, Berlin, 1989; 25 refereed papers. **BUSINESS ADDRESS:** Dept Systems Sci & Math, Washington University, St Louis, MO 63130.

DALAL, FRAM R.

Clinical laboratorian, educator. Indo-American. **PERSONAL:** Born Jan 24, 1935, Madras, Tamil Nadu, India; son of Rustom A Dalal & Muccan R Cursetjee; married Jeroo Dalal, Jan 2, 1961; children: Niloofer Dalal. **EDUCATION:** University of Bombay, BSc, 1954, BSc, tech, 1956; University of Bombay, PhD, 1961. **CAREER:** University of Pennsylvania School of Medicine, Department of Microbiology, research associate, 1964-67; University of Bombay, reader in microbiology, 1967-69; Albert Einstein Medical Center, associate chief clinical chemistry, 1969-78; Temple University Hospital, director clinical chemistry, 1978-; Temple University School of Medicine, associate professor, 1978-. **ORGANIZATIONS:** American Association Clinical Chemistry, 1970-; National Academy Clinical Biochemistry, 1984-; Indian Alumni Clinical Chemistry, 1986-; Zordastrian Association of PA & NJ, 1985-. **HOME ADDRESS:** 7619 Mountain Ave, Elkins Park, PA 19117, (215)635-3648. **BUSINESS ADDRESS:** Director, Clinical Chemistry, Temple University Hospital, Broad & Ontario Sts, Philadelphia, PA 19170, (215)221-3441.

DALAL, SIDDHARTHA RAMANLAL (SID)

Scientist. Indo-American. **PERSONAL:** Born Oct 1, 1948, Ahmedabad, Gujarat, India; son of Ramanlal Dalal & Vasumati Dalal; married Alka, Jan 26, 1978; children: Nemil, Preeyel. **EDUCATION:** University of Bombay, BSc,

1968; University of Rochester, MBA, 1973, PhD, 1976. **CAREER:** Rutgers University, assistant professor, 1975-80; Bell Telephone Laboratory, member of technical staff, 1980-83; Bellcore, member of technical staff, 1984-89, director, 1989-. **ORGANIZATIONS:** J American Statistical Association, associate editor, 1992-; American Statistical Association, chair, marketing section, 1987-89; National Research Council, panel on software engineering, currently. **HONORS/AWARDS:** American Statistical Association, fellow, 1990, Outstanding Application Paper Prize, 1990. **SPECIAL ACHIEVEMENTS:** Numerous publications in software engineering, management, statistics and marketing journals. **BUSINESS ADDRESS:** Director, Bellcore, 445 South St, MRE ZP-392, Morristown, NJ 07960, (201)829-4292.

DALVI, RAMESH R.

Educator. Indo-American. **PERSONAL:** Born Nov 8, 1938, Talgaon, Maharashtra, India; son of Rajaram S Dalvi and Sundar R Dalvi; married Rekha R Dalvi, Jan 22, 1969; children: Rajan R, Samir R. **EDUCATION:** University of Bombay, India, BSc (honors), 1962, BSc, tech, 1964, MSc, tech, 1967; Utah State University, PhD, 1972. **CAREER:** Bhabha Atomic Research Center, Bombay, scientific officer, 1967-69; Vanderbilt University, postdoctoral fellow, 1972-74; Tuskegee University, assistant professor, 1974, professor, currently. **ORGANIZATIONS:** Society of Toxicology, 1982-; American Academy of Veterinary and Comparative Toxicology, 1975-; Tropical Veterinarian, editorial board, 1982-90; American Journal of Veterinary Research, editorial board, 1987-89; Journal of Environmental Biology, advisory board, 1988-; Journal of Maharashtra Agricultural Universities, consulting editor, 1990-; International Journal of Toxicology, Occupational and Environmental Health, ed board, 1992-; International Journal of Animal Sciences, editorial board, 1993-. **HONORS/AWARDS:** Tuskegee University, Faculty Achievement Award, 1986, Outstanding Research Award, 1990; SmithKline Beecham, Award for Research Excellence, 1991; several grants awards totaling over 2 million dollars from NIH, NSF, USDA, FDA, and other sources. **SPECIAL ACHIEVEMENTS:** American Board of Toxicology, diplomate, 1982; author or co-author of over 100 publications in scientific journals & books. **BUSINESS ADDRESS:** Professor of Toxicology, School of Veterinary Medicine, Tuskegee University, Tuskegee University, AL 36088, (205)727-8472.

DAM, QUY T. T.

State government official. Vietnamese American. **PERSONAL:** Born Jul 5, 1942, Bacninh, Vietnam; daughter of Hau Quang Dam and Nhi Thi Phan. **EDUCATION:** University of Saigon, Vietnam, BA, 1965; University of Minnesota Law School, JD, 1984. **CAREER:** LeVan Duyet High School, English Department, teacher, department chair, 1965-79; Minh Duc University, instructor, 1972-75; Vietnamese American English School, teacher, 1967-75; Minnesota Department of Human Services, contracts manager, supervisor, refugee and immigrant services section, 1985-; Minnesota State Refugee Coordinator, 1993-. **ORGANIZATIONS:** Minnesota Asian Advocacy Coalition, board member, 1984-88; BIHA Women in Action, board member, 1987; Vietnamese Buddhist Association in Minnesota, board member, 1990-; Asian Advisory Committee to the President of the University of Minnesota, 1991-; Minnesota Children's Trust Fund, committee member, 1988-90. **HONORS/AWARDS:** State of Minnesota, achievement awards, 1989, 1990. **SPECIAL ACHIEVEMENTS:** Certified Minnesota attorney, 1985. **HOME ADDRESS:** 706 Laurie Court, Maplewood, MN 55117. **BUSINESS PHONE:** (612)297-3210.

DAMRIA, MULKH RAJ

City recreation official. Indo-American. **PERSONAL:** Born Sep 14, 1942, Suva, Fiji; son of Govinda and Karmi Damria; married Kartar Raj Damria, Mar 6, 1966; children: Mukesh, Satish, Rajesh. **CAREER:** City of Livermore, golf course superntendent/manager, 1966-. **ORGANIZATIONS:** Sri Guru Ravidass Temple, chairman; Golf Course Superintendents Association of America; Golf Course Superintendents Association of Northern Calif; State of Calif, agricultural pest control adivsor; Northern Calif Golf Association; Northern Calif Turf Grass Council; CAPCA. **BUSINESS ADDRESS:** Golf Course Superintendent, City of Livermore/Las Pointas Golf Course, 1052 S Livermore Ave, Livermore, CA 94550.

DAN, PHAN QUANG

Physician (retired). Vietnamese American. **PERSONAL:** Born Nov 6, 1918, Vinh, Nghe An, Vietnam; son of Phan Huy Thinh and Phuong Xuan; married; children: Phan Quang Tue, Phan Quang Tuan (deceased), Phan Quang Dat. **EDUCATION:** Sorbonne University, Paris, France, MD (magnum cum laude), 1949; Harvard School of Public Health, DPH (cum laude), 1954.

CAREER: Emperor Bao Dai, minister of information and political counselor, 1947-49; South Vietnam's Constituent Assembly, deputy, 1966-67; Minister of State, in charge of foreign affairs, 1969; Refugees & Land Development, deputy prime minister in charge of social welfare, 1970-75; Refugee Affairs, Camp Pendleton, CA, advisor, 1975; MCH & Crippled Children, St Thomas, US Virgin Islands, physician, 1975-87; East End Family Health Center, St Thomas, US Virgin Islands, director, 1979-87. **ORGANIZATIONS:** Intl Conference on Children & Natl Development in Saigon, organizer, 1975; Interministerial Committee in charge of Repatriation and Resettlement of Vietnamese in Cambodia, chairman, 1970-73; National Political Convention, elected chairman, 1966-67; Provincial Council of Gia Dinh, elected chairman, 1965; numerous others. **SPECIAL ACHIEVEMENTS:** Fluent in Vietnamese, French & English; well versed in Chinese characters; publications: Reorganisation Sanitaire au Vietnam, Paris, 1949, Volonte Vietnamienne, Geneve, Swisse, 1951, Vietnam's Health, Boston, 1954, The War in Indochina, Boston, 1954, The Republic of Vietnam's Environment and People, Saigon, 1975. **BIOGRAPHICAL SOURCES:** The Dawn of Free Vietnam, A Biographical Sketch of Dr Phan Q Dan by Ray Fontaine. **HOME ADDRESS:** PO Box 16920, Temple Terrace, FL 33687.

DANG, HARISH C.
Investment adviser, radio host. Indo-American. **PERSONAL:** Born Jul 2, 1947, New Delhi, India; son of Shiv Lal Dang and Krishna Ahuja; married Binita Dang, May 5, 1973; children: Leena R, Amit K, Neil K. **EDUCATION:** Delhi University, School of Planning & Architecture, BArch, 1968; Harvard University, Graduate School of Design, MArch, 1972. **CAREER:** Sverdrup Corp, project architect, 1972-77; Chas T Main Inc, project architect, 1977-84; Dean Witter, Investments, vice president, 1984-87; Prudential Securities, Investments, vice president, 1987-92; First Albany Corp, Investments, vice president, 1992-. **ORGANIZATIONS:** United India Organization, director, 1990-; New England Hindu Temple Inc, executive committee, 1984-92; Sounds of India Radio Show, host, 1974-; United Way of Massachusetts, co-ordinator, 1990-92. **HONORS/AWARDS:** Indian Association of Greater Boston, Citation for Community Service, 1992; United Way of Massachusetts, Plaque for Commendable Service, 1990, 1991. **SPECIAL ACHIEVEMENTS:** Organizer of the first Indian radio show, Sounds of India in Boston Area, 1974-; sponsor of live music concerts in Boston. **BUSINESS ADDRESS:** Vice President, Investments, First Albany Corp, 53 State St, 29th Floor, Boston, MA 02109, 800-637-4003.

DANG, PHU NGOC
Electronic technician. Vietnamese American. **PERSONAL:** Born Apr 30, 1954, Saigon, Vietnam; son of Phuong Dang Ngoc and Trat Thieu Thi; married Jan 1993. **EDUCATION:** Santa Ana College, electronics certificate, 1982. **CAREER:** NH Research Inc, senior electronic technician, 1985-. **BUSINESS ADDRESS:** Technician, NH Research Inc, 16601 Hale Ave, Irvine, CA 92714, (714)474-3900.

DANG, TIM
Theater director, actor. **EDUCATION:** University of Southern California, BA, theater. **CAREER:** Barclay Theater, Irvine, "Pacific Overtures," actor; East West Players, director of: "Canton Jazz Club," "Into the Woods," Kimchee & Chitlins; East West Players, artistic director, 1993-. **HONORS/AWARDS:** Dramalogue, Best Director for "Into the Woods," 1992. **BUSINESS ADDRESS:** Artistic Director, East West Players, 4424 Santa Monica Blvd, Los Angeles, CA 90029, (213)660-0366.*

DANG-HOANG. *See* **CUNG, TIEN THUC.**

DAO, ANH HUU
Educator. Vietnamese American. **PERSONAL:** Born Jan 3, 1933, Thai-Binh, Vietnam; married Wendy, May 30, 1959. **EDUCATION:** University of Hanoi, Vietnam, BA, 1953; University of Saigon, Vietnam, MD, 1960; University of Vermont, MS, 1964. **CAREER:** University of Saigon, professor, associate dean, 1965-75; Vanderbilt University, associate professor, pathology, 1975-. **ORGANIZATIONS:** International Academy of Pathology, 1975-; American Society of Clinical Pathologists, 1965-; New York Academy of Sciences, 1978-; American Society for Microbiology, 1975-. **SPECIAL ACHIEVEMENTS:** Author of more than 30 articles published in scientific journals. **BUSINESS ADDRESS:** Associate Professor, Vanderbilt University Medical School, 21st Ave & Garland, 3221 MCN, Nashville, TN 37232, (615)322-2102.

DAO, MINH QUANG
Educator. Vietnamese American. **PERSONAL:** Born Jan 7, 1955, Hai-Phong, Vietnam; son of Thien Ngoc Dao and Kien Tam Nguyen; married Mai Thi Dao, Feb 6, 1977; children: Minh Quang Jr. **EDUCATION:** Connors State College, AS, 1976; Oklahoma State University, BS, 1978, MS, 1980; University of Illinois, Urbana-Champaign, PhD, 1987. **CAREER:** Oklahoma State University, instructor of French, 1978, 1980; Hastings College, instructor of economics, 1980-83; Eastern Illinois University, assistant professor of economics, 1987-93, associate professor of economics, 1993-. **ORGANIZATIONS:** American Economic Association, 1986-91; Western Economic Association, 1990-91; Midwest Economics Association, 1990-92; Illinois Economic Association, 1988-92. **HONORS/AWARDS:** Phi Theta Kappa, 1976; Beta Gamma Sigma, 1978; Oklahoma State University, CE Burris Scholarship, 1978; Omicron Delta Epsilon, 1979; University of Illinois, University Fellowship, 1983, 1986. **SPECIAL ACHIEVEMENTS:** "History of Land Tenure in Pre-1954 Vietnam," Journal of Contemporary Asia, Jan 1993. **HOME ADDRESS:** 932 Lynnwood Dr, Charleston, IL 61920, (217)345-1497. **BUSINESS ADDRESS:** Associate Professor of Economics, Eastern Illinois University, 600 Lincoln Ave, 208 Coleman Hall, Charleston, IL 61920-3011, (217)581-6329.

DAO, TUAN ANH
Electrical engineer. Vietnamese American. **PERSONAL:** Born Nov 29, 1966, Tan Son Hoa, Vietnam; son of Quang Dao and Duyet Dao; married Staci Sue Dao, Jun 20, 1992. **EDUCATION:** University of Washington, Seattle, BS, computer engineering, 1990, MSEE, 1991-. **CAREER:** Belshaw Brothers, electronics technician, 1985-87; Boeing Aerospace & Electronics, student engineer, 1989; Boeing Defense & Space Group, research engineer, 1990-. **ORGANIZATIONS:** Tau Beta Pi, 1987-; IEEE, 1986. **SPECIAL ACHIEVEMENTS:** Language proficiency in Vietnamese, French; published a technical paper on radiation hard VLSI Design at the Government Microcircuits Applications Conference, 1993. **HOME ADDRESS:** 11057 10th Ave SW, Seattle, WA 98146, (206)439-1128. **BUSINESS PHONE:** (206)657-9680.

DARJI, BHULESHWAR S.
Structural engineer. Indo-American. **PERSONAL:** Born Jun 11, 1939, Vadagam, Gujarat, India; son of Somabhai and Jiviben; married Sushila, May 4, 1962; children: Surendra, Premila. **EDUCATION:** SP University, India, BS, 1964; Institute of Technology, MS, 1969. **CAREER:** India-Teaching, assistant lecturer, until 1971; Babcock Wilcox, senior engineer, 1974; Gallion Corp, senior engineer, 1978; Research Cottrell, senior engineer, 1983; New Jersey Department of Transportation, principal engineer, currently. **SPECIAL ACHIEVEMENTS:** Professional engineer, NJ, PA.

DARLING, RON
Professional baseball player. **PERSONAL:** Born Aug 19, 1960, Honolulu, HI; married Toni O'Reilly, Jan 10, 1986; children: Tyler Christien. **EDUCATION:** Yale University, history; New York University. **CAREER:** Legends, co-restaurateur; pitcher: New York Mets, 1983-91; Montreal Expos, 1991; Oakland A's, 1991-. **ORGANIZATIONS:** Gov Mario Cuomo's Youth Drug Prevention Campaign, co-chairperson. **HONORS/AWARDS:** National League, Golden Glove Pitcher, 1989; Thurman Munson Awards Dinner, honoree, for charitable work, 1988. **BUSINESS ADDRESS:** Professional Baseball Player, Oakland A's, Oakland Alameda Coliseum Complex, Oakland, CA 94621.*

DARYANANI, MICHAEL
Store manager. Indo-American. **PERSONAL:** Born Nov 7, Hong Kong; married Maya Daryanani, Jul 18, 1964; children: Kavita, Meena Logan, Michael Jr. **CAREER:** Hong Kong Travel Bureau, 1963-67; Moti's Hong Kong Ltd, 1967-74; Sir Michael's Fashion, 1974-77; L Strauss Downtown, store manager, currently. **HONORS/AWARDS:** Hickey-Freeman, Top Sales Achievement; Harts-Schafner & Marx, Top Sales Achievement. **SPECIAL ACHIEVEMENTS:** Language proficiency: Indian, Chinese. **BIOGRAPHICAL SOURCES:** Business Mathematics, p 483, 1984. **HOME PHONE:** (317)845-4482. **BUSINESS ADDRESS:** Store Manager, L Strauss Downtown, 120 Monument Circle, Indianapolis, IN 46204.

DAS, KAMALENDU
Scientist. Bangladeshi American. **PERSONAL:** Born Feb 2, 1944, Sylhet, Bangladesh; son of Kailash Ch Das & Prabhasini Das; married Shyamali Chowdhury, Dec 6, 1969; children: Mrinal Kanti, Sampa. **EDUCATION:** University of Dhaka, Bangladesh, BSc (with honors), 1964, MSc, 1965; Uni-

versity of Houston, PhD, 1975. **CAREER:** Women's College/Tolaram College, Bangladesh, assistant professor, 1966-71; University of Houston, teaching assistant, research fellow, 1971-75, postdoctoral research, instructor, 1976-79; Baker Sand Control, research scientist, group leader, 1979-85; US Department of Energy, research chemist, 1985-92, physical scientist, project manager, 1992-. **ORGANIZATIONS:** American Chemical Society, 1974-; Society of Petroleum Engineers, 1981-; American Institute of Chemists; American Association for the Advancement of Science; International Union of Price and Applied Chemistry. **HONORS/AWARDS:** Bangladesh Government, talent scholarship, 1964-65; University of Houston. **SPECIAL ACHIEVEMENTS:** Contributed articles in professional journals; several reports for DOE and Baker Sand Control, some were proprietary, 1976-. **HOME ADDRESS:** 465 Lawnview Circle, Morgantown, WV 26505, (304)599-9406.

DAS, MAN SINGH
Educator. Indo-American. **PERSONAL:** Born May 6, 1932, Mainpuri, Uttar Pradesh, India; son of Bhagwan Das and Sona Bhagwan Das; married Promilla C Das, Jul 17, 1965; children: Anjali C, Sanjay A. **EDUCATION:** University of Allahabad, India, BS, 1955; Leonard Theological College, India, GTh, 1958; Serampore University, India, BD, 1958; Princeton Theological Seminary, ThM, 1960; Morehead State University, MA, education, 1961; University of Illinois, MA, sociology, 1963; Oklahoma State University, PhD, sociology, 1969. **CAREER:** United Church of North India, North India Synod, pastor & industrial evangelist, 1958-59; Morehead State University, graduate assistant, 1960-61; United Methodist Church, minister of Christian education, 1964-67; Oklahoma State University, Dept of Sociology, teaching graduate assistant, 1967-68, instructor of sociology, 1968-69; Fourth Street United Methodist Church, minister of education, 1975-76; Northern Illinois University, assistant professor of sociology, 1969-72, associate professor, 1972-80, professor, 1980-. **ORGANIZATIONS:** Numerous Natl & intl organizations including: Intl Union for the Scientific Study of Population; Intl Institute of Sociology; Intl Sociological Assn, Family Research Committee, Ethnic Committee, Race & Minority Relations, Sociology of Migration Committee; American Sociological Assn; Population Assn of America; Natl Council on Family Relations; Society for the Study of Social Problems. **HONORS/AWARDS:** Oklahoma State University, Outstanding Graduate Assistant Teacher Award, 1969. **SPECIAL ACHIEVEMENTS:** Author, Brain Drain Controversy & Intl Students, Lucknow, India, Lucknow Publishing House, p 119, 1972; editor of many works; author of chapters in books, articles, & book reviews; Intl Review of Modern Sociology, editor & founder, 1971-; Intl Journal of Sociology of the Family, editor & founder, 1971-; South Asian Witness, editor & founder, 1987-; editor of other journals. **BUSINESS ADDRESS:** Professor, Dept of Sociology, Northern Illinois University, De Kalb, IL 60115.

DAS, MOHAN N.
Company executive. **PERSONAL:** Born Jan 11, 1947, Kottayam, Kerala, India; son of G Pillai & K Amma; married Syamala Das, 1976; children: Sheena, Shilpa. **EDUCATION:** University of Kerala, India, BS, 1968, MS, 1970, PhD, 1979. **CAREER:** Long Island Jewish Medical Center, bio-medical engineer, 1980-86; NETECH Corp, president, 1986-. **ORGANIZATIONS:** AAMI; Long Island Assns. **BUSINESS ADDRESS:** President, NETECH Corp, 60 Bethpage Dr, Hicksville, NY 11801, (516)433-7400.

DAS, PHANINDRAMOHAN
Educator. Indo-American/Bangladeshi American. **PERSONAL:** Born Feb 2, 1926, Bholabo, Dacca, Bangladesh; son of Ramaniraman Das and Kusumkuntala Das; married Atri Bhoumick, Dec 9, 1955; children: Krishnakali McCotter, Krishanu, Himamauli. **EDUCATION:** Jagannath Intermediate College, inter sc, 1944; University of Dacca, BSc (w/hons), 1947, MSc, 1948; University of Chicago, PhD, 1963. **CAREER:** Radio Pakistan, technical assistant, 1948; Banaras University, India, research assistant, 1949-51, India Meteorolog Dept, assistant meteorologist, 1951-55; Indian Institute of Tech, Kharagpur, India, assistant professor, 1955-67; University of Chicago, res assistant, meteorologist, 1959-64; US Air Force, Cambridge Res Lab, res physicist, phys of atnos, 1968-70; Texas A&M University, assistant professor, 1967-68, associate professor, 1970-80, professor, 1980-. **ORGANIZATIONS:** American Meteorological Society, 1962-, fellow, 1986-; Royal Meteorological Society, fellow, 1967-; India Meteorological Society, life member, 1981-; Indian Science Congr Association. **HONORS/AWARDS:** American Meteorological Society, elected fellow, 1986. **SPECIAL ACHIEVEMENTS:** First exposition of how downdraft forms in thunderstorms, 1963; presented a new thermodynamic equation for cumulus dynamics, 1969; presented a new contributing mechanism for tornado formation, 1983; presented a new formulation

of equations of cumulus dynamics, 1979. **HOME ADDRESS:** 1005 Glade Street, College Station, TX 77840-3031, (409)696-6785.

DAS, SALIL KUMAR
Educator. Indo-American. **PERSONAL:** Born Dec 21, 1940, Rangoon, Burma; son of Santi R Das & Provabati Das; divorced; children: Shouvik. **EDUCATION:** Calcutta University, BSc (honors), 1958, MSc, 1961; Massachusetts Institute of Technology, ScD, 1966; Calcutta University, India, DSc, 1974. **CAREER:** Massachusetts Institute of Technology, research associate, 1965-66; University of Arizona, research associate, 1966-67; University of Arkansas, research associate, 1967-68; Duke University, research associate, 1968-69; Meharry Medical College, assistant professor, 1969-74, associate professor, 1974-81, professor of biochemistry, 1981-. **ORGANIZATIONS:** American Society Biochemistry & Molecular Biology, 1982-; American Institute of Nutrition, 1975-; Biochemical Society, London, 1978-; Sigma Xi, 1967-; American Oil Chemists' Society, 1973-; International Society for Pathophysiology, 1992-. **HONORS/AWARDS:** Calcutta University, MSc Exam Performance Medal, 1961; New York Academy Science, Cressy Morrison Award, 1967; recipient of numerous research grants from NIH, Army, EPA, AID, 1972. **SPECIAL ACHIEVEMENTS:** Author of over 150 research publications. **HOME PHONE:** (615)883-3196. **BUSINESS ADDRESS:** Professor of Biochemistry, Meharry Medical College, 1005 David Todd Blvd, Nashville, TN 37208, (615)327-6988.

DAS, SHOVAN
Shipping company executive. Indo-American. **PERSONAL:** Born Nov 13, 1954, Calcutta, W. Bengal, India; son of Bhabendra Nath Das and Nilima Das; married Anjana Das, Dec 17, 1988; children: Anushka. **EDUCATION:** Training Ship Dufferin, master's navigation, 1971-73; South Shields Nautical College, STCW, 1985-86; SUNY, maritime transportation, 1987. **CAREER:** Scindia Steam, navigating officer, 1978-81; Wallem Ship Management, captain, 1981-87; Ravenscroft Shipping, port captain, 1987-89; Sextant Shipping, director, operations/chartering, 1989-90; Pennant Shipping Services, founder, president, 1990-. **ORGANIZATIONS:** Louisiana Bengali Assn, vice pres. **SPECIAL ACHIEVEMENTS:** First Indian chief navigating officer, Forward Marine Steamship Line, 1984; established first US-based Office of Sextant Shipping, 1989. **BUSINESS ADDRESS:** President, Pennant Shipping Services Inc, 2 Canal St, 2840 World Trade Center, New Orleans, LA 70130, (504)581-7802.

DAS, SHYAM
Attorney, labor arbitrator. Indo-American. **PERSONAL:** Born Apr 18, 1944, Guildford, England; son of Kamleshwar Das and Jean K Das; married Eva Borsody, 1969; children: Sarah, Jason. **EDUCATION:** Harvard University, BA (magna cum laude), 1965; University of Chicago, MA, 1966; Yale Law School, LLB, 1969. **CAREER:** University of Pittsburgh, associate professor of law, 1971-78; board of arbitration for US Steel Corp and United Steelworkers of America, associate chairman, 1978-90; Bethlehem Steel Corp and United Steelworkers of America, impartial umpire, 1991-. **ORGANIZATIONS:** National Academy of Arbitrators, 1981-; US Foreign Service Grievance Board, 1983-91. **SPECIAL ACHIEVEMENTS:** Author, "Discrimination in Employment Against Aliens - the Impact of the Constitution and the Federal Civil Rights Laws," 35 University of Pittsburgh Law Review 499, 1974. **BUSINESS ADDRESS:** 225 S 15th St, Ste 1407, Philadelphia, PA 19102.

DAS DASGUPTA, SHAMITA
Association executive, psychologist. Indo-American. **PERSONAL:** Born in India; children: Sayantani Dasgupta. **CAREER:** Rutgers University, Dept of Psychology, lecturer in women's studies and psychology; Manavi, founder, president, 1985-. **SPECIAL ACHIEVEMENTS:** Formed Manavi to help combat domestic violence against Asian American women, 1985; publishes a resource directory for women in the NY-NJ-CT area. **BIOGRAPHICAL SOURCES:** "Asian, American, Feminist," The Progressive, p 16, June 1993. **BUSINESS ADDRESS:** Founder, Manavi, 7 Fletcher Dr, Montville, NJ 07045, (201)334-7356.*

DASH, SITA K.
Company executive. Indo-American. **PERSONAL:** Born Nov 15, 1942, Cuttack, Orissa, India; son of Nila Dash and Duti Dash; married Kalpana M. Dash, Jun 18, 1967; children: Rajesh, Dave. **EDUCATION:** Orissa Veterinary College, DVM, 1964; South Dakota State University, MS, 1970, PhD, 1973. **CAREER:** Government of Orissa, veterinary surgeon, 1964-67, assistant project officer, 1967-69; South Dakota State University, research assistant,

1969-73; South Dakota State Government, food & drug director, 1973-80; UAS Labs, president, 1981-. **ORGANIZATIONS:** Sigma Xi, 1970-; Council on Agricultural Science Technology, 1980-; National Nutritional Foods Association, 1981-; American Veterinary Medical Association, 1977-; American Dairy Science Association, 1970-; American Society of Animal Science, 1971-; Society of Industrial Microbiologist, 1990-; American Association of Feed Control Officials, life member, 1973-. **HONORS/AWARDS:** Lions Club, Lion of the Year, 1977; US News & World Report, Judge to Select the Best in America, 1990; NRI Institute, India, Arch of India Gold Award for Medicine, 1992. **SPECIAL ACHIEVEMENTS:** Published 25 research articles in national journals; developed DDS-Acidophilus, Keto Nutri-Acid, and Mega-D; assisted in developing patents on microbial products. **HOME ADDRESS:** 4925 Interlachen Ct, Edina, MN 55436, (612)931-9400. **BUSINESS PHONE:** (612)881-1915.

DASS, EDGAR SUSHIL
Educator. Pakistani American/Indo-American. **PERSONAL:** Born May 12, 1944, Sialkot, Punjab, Pakistan; son of Iqbal Begum and Sunder Das; married; children: four. **EDUCATION:** Punjab University, Murray College, BA, 1964, MA, 1969; Indiana University, MA, 1976, EdD, 1978. **CAREER:** Murray College, lecturer, 1966-71; University of Indianapolis, evening faculty, 1981-82; Monroe County United Ministries, executive director, 1981-83; Howard Payne University, associate professor, 1984-89, English Department, head, 1986-89; Orange County Community College, assistant professor, 189-. **ORGANIZATIONS:** Pakistani-American Christian Association, executive committee, co-chair, Pakistan-US Human Rights Commission, chair. **HONORS/AWARDS:** Second best award for college magazines in Texas. **SPECIAL ACHIEVEMENTS:** Editor, The Catalyst, Howard Payne University, Brownwood, Texas, 1987-89; proficiency in Punjabi, Urdu, Hindi; founder and editor, Impact, human rights magazine/newsletter. **HOME ADDRESS:** PO Box 548, Milford, PA 18337. **BUSINESS ADDRESS:** Assistant Professor, Orange County Community College, 115 South Street, 309 Morrison Hall, Middletown, NY 10940-6437, (914)341-4009.

DAS SARMA, BASUDEB
Educator. Indo-American. **PERSONAL:** Born Jan 1, 1923, Barisal, Bengal, India; son of Ashutosh Das Sarma (deceased) and Surabala Das Sarma (deceased); married Seba, Jun 17, 1952; children: Urmi Ghosh, Shiladitya. **EDUCATION:** B M College, Barisal, LSc, 1942, BSc, 1944; University College of Science & Technology, Calcutta, MSc, 1946, PhD, 1951. **CAREER:** Scottish Church College, professor, 1950-51; University of Calcutta, lecturer, 1951-52; University of Illinois, research associate, 1953-55; Calcutta University, lecturer in chemistry, 1955-57; Geological Survey of India, chemist-in-charge, 1957-66; West Virginia State College, professor, chairman, 1966-92, professor emeritus, 1992-. **ORGANIZATIONS:** West Virginia Academy of Science, past president, 1967; American Chemical Society, Kanawha Valley Section, secretary, 1967-; American Association of University Professors, fellow, 1967-91; Air and Waste Management Association, 1986-; American Association for the Advancement of Science, 1970-78; Lion's Club, 1970-83. **HONORS/AWARDS:** American Chemical Society, Outstanding Scientist, 1971; National Science Foundation, international travel, 1980; US EPA, research grant for air pollution, 1986; National Institute for Chemical Studies, air pollution research grant, 1987. **SPECIAL ACHIEVEMENTS:** Published over 50 papers in national and international journals on stereochemistry, analytical chemistry, geochemistry, cancer research and air pollution, 1953-. **HOME ADDRESS:** 429 25th St, Dunbar, WV 25064, (304)768-1143. **BUSINESS ADDRESS:** Emeritus Professor of Chemistry, West Virginia State College, Hamblin Hall, 325, Institute, WV 25112, (304)766-3105.

DATTA, RANAJIT KUMAR (RON)
Financial consultant. Indo-American. **PERSONAL:** Born Apr 1, 1933, Munsigunj, Dhaka, Bangladesh; son of Ramananda Datta (deceased) and Mahamaya Datta; married Bhakti Datta, Dec 12, 1964; children: Rakhi. **EDUCATION:** Calcutta University, MSc, 1958, PhD, 1963, DSc, 1975. **CAREER:** Calcutta University, researcher, 1958-63; Bengal Veterinary College, Calcutta, assistant professor, 1963-65; NY State Res Institute for Neurochem, researcher, 1965-67; College of Physicians & Surgeons, researcher, 1966-67; Beth Israel Medical Center, biophysicist, 1967-82; Mt Sinai School of Medicine, assistant professor, 1968-82; New York Life, agent, 1982-. **ORGANIZATIONS:** Cultural Association of Bengal, president, 1971-78; Associations of Indians in America, vice-president, 1979-; East Coast Durgapuja Association, president, 1972-73; American Neurochemistry Society, 1968-83; International Neurochemistry Society, 1970-82; Million Dollar Round Table, 1983-; National

Association of Life Underwriters, 1983-; Indian Brain Res Organization, jt secretary, 1962-65. **HONORS/AWARDS:** National Association Life Underwriter, National Quality Award, 1985-, Sales Achievement Award, 1985-; Cultural Association of Bengal, Distinguished Service Award, 1989; International Association of Registered Financial Planners, RFP. **SPECIAL ACHIEVEMENTS:** Editor, publisher, Cultural Association of Bengal's News-Magazine, Sangbad Bichitra, 1971-. **HOME ADDRESS:** 101 Iden Avenue, Pelham Manor, NY 10803, (914)738-5727. **BUSINESS ADDRESS:** Executive Council Agent, New York Life, 411 Theodore Fremd Avenue, Third Floor, Rye, NY 10580, (914)738-8370.

DATTA, SUBHENDU K.
Educator. Indo-American. **PERSONAL:** Born Jan 15, 1936, Howrah, W. Bengal, India; son of Srish Ch Datta & Prabhabati Ghosh; married Bishakha Datta, May 10, 1966; children: Kinshuk. **EDUCATION:** Presidency College, BSc, 1954; Calcutta University, MSc, 1956; Jadavpur University, PhD, 1962. **CAREER:** Mathematics Res Center, visiting lecturer, 1962-63; RPI, research associate, 1963-64; University of Colorado, visiting assistant professor, 1964-65; IIT/Kanpur, assistant professor, 1965-67; University of Manitoba, assistant professor, 1967-68; University of Colorado, professor, 1968-; University of Connecticut, professor/head, 1991-92. **ORGANIZATIONS:** American Society of Mechanical Engineers, fellow; American Academy of Mech, fellow; Society for Engineering Sci; Seismological Society of America; Sigma Xi. **SPECIAL ACHIEVEMENTS:** Over 100 papers in technical journals. **BUSINESS ADDRESS:** Professor, Dept of Mechanical Engineering, University of Colorado, Campus Box 427, Boulder, CO 80309-0427, (303)492-6542.

DATTA, SYAMAL K.
Physician, scientist, educator. Indo-American. **PERSONAL:** Born Sep 21, 1943, Cuttack, Orissa, India; son of Jitendra N Dutta and Kalyani Dutta; married Tapati Datta, Nov 17, 1976; children: Ronjon K. **EDUCATION:** University of Calcutta, India, Presidency College, BSc, 1960, Medical College, MBBS, 1966. **CAREER:** Tufts-New England Medical Center, instructor of medicine, 1974-76, assistant professor of medicine, 1976-79, associate professor of medicine, 1979-85, professor of medicine, 1985-93; Northwestern University Medical School, professor of medicine, 1993-, Solovy Arthritis Research Society Professor, 1993-, professor of microbiology/immunology, 1993-. **ORGANIZATIONS:** National Institutes of Health, general medicine study section, 1987-91; Sackler School-Tufts, Boston, senior faculty, graduate program immunology, 1975-93; Journal of Immunology, associate editor, 1984-93; American Association of Immunologists, 1976-; American Association for Advancement of Science, 1976-; American College of Rheumatology, 1992-; Northwestern University Medical School, steering committee, immunobiology center, 1993-. **HONORS/AWARDS:** Northwestern University Medical School, Solovy Arthritis-Research Society Professor, Endowed Chair, 1993-; National Institutes of Health, USA, Principal Investigator of Three ROI Research Grants, 1976-; American Cancer Society, Faculty Research Award, 1978-83, Cancer Research Scholar, 1975-78; American Board of Internal Medicine, Diplomate, 1972. **SPECIAL ACHIEVEMENTS:** Developed a mouse model for Human Systemic Autoimmune Disease, 1974-; defined the relation between retroviral genes and autoimmunity genes, 1976-78; cloned the T and B cells that cause autoimmune disease and defined the molecular structure of their receptors, 1979-91; identified major immunogens driving pathogenic autoimmune response, a crucial step for designing specific cures of disease, 1991-; over 100 publications in scientific journals eg Nature, Cell Journal Experimental Medicine, J Immunol, Proc National Academy Science, USA.

DATTA, VIJAY K.
Claims consultant. Indo-American. **PERSONAL:** Born Nov 11, 1939, Lahore, Punjab, India; son of Krishan Datta and Luxmi Devi; married Mina Datta, Feb 28, 1969; children: Vikram K, Angie K. **EDUCATION:** Panjab University, BScEng (with honors), 1960; Roorkee University, ME, 1961, Oxford University, PhD, 1968; New York University, diploma in building construction mgt, 1989. **CAREER:** Gibbs & Hill Inc, principal structural engr, 1970-90; Nasco Associates Inc, sr associate, 1990-91; CCS Associates Inc, sr claims consultant, 1991-. **ORGANIZATIONS:** American Concrete Institute, ACI 349 code committee, Nuclear Safety Related Concrete Structures, 1975-87; American Society of Civil Engineers, fellow, 1987; Professional Engineer (Eng); Chartered Engineer (Eng); Institution of Civil Engineers, London. **HONORS/AWARDS:** American Arbitration Assn, Construction Panelist, 1991; Rhodes Scholarship from India, 1961. **SPECIAL ACHIEVEMENTS:** Editor: Power Division Newsletter, American Society of Civil Engineers, 1973-75; published: article

on "Cogeneration," McGraw Hill Yearbook of Science and Technology, 1982-83; several papers on design of nuclear power plant structures, 1973-84. **HOME ADDRESS:** 17 Spencer Way, Kings Park, NY 11754, (516)724-4122.

DAVE, JANAK
Educator. Indo-American. **PERSONAL:** Born Mar 25, 1949, Ahmedabad, Gujarat, India; son of Ginjashanker Dave & Savitri Dave; divorced; children: Svarit. **EDUCATION:** M S University, India, BS, mechanical engineering, 1970; University of Missouri-Rolla, MS, mechanical engineering, 1973, PhD, mechanical engineering, 1976. **CAREER:** Canadian Air Compressors, chief engineer, 1978-80; Joy Manufacturing, product manager, 1981-83; University of Cincinnati, faculty member, 1983-. **ORGANIZATIONS:** ASME, 1976-; ACUG, local chairman, 1989-; ASEE, 1983-; SME, 1983-; National Science Foundation, reviewer. **HONORS/AWARDS:** ASEE Manufacturing Division, Service to Division, 1990; SME Student Section Award, Best Teacher, 1989; ASME, Region V, advisor award, 1992. **SPECIAL ACHIEVEMENTS:** Presentations in the area of CAD/CAM at ASEE, National Conference, 1985-; invited presentations in CAD at universities in Mexico & India. **BUSINESS ADDRESS:** Professor, OMI College of Applied Science, University of Cincinnati, 2220 Victory Pky, Cincinnati, OH 45206-2822, (513)556-5311.

DAVINO, CARMENCITA FERNANDEZ
Educator. Filipino American. **PERSONAL:** Born Feb 23, 1948, Gapan, Nueva Ecija, Philippines; daughter of Fernando Fernandez and Beatriz Blanco; married William A Davino, Jul 31, 1983; children: Serafin, Michael, Franz Joseph. **EDUCATION:** St Joseph's College, Philippines, AM, music, piano, 1965, BA (magna cum laude), music, piano, English and science, 1967; St Paul's College, Philippines, certificate in culinary arts, 1969; Institute of Languages, Philippines, certificate in French, 1970; Philippines School of Interior Design, certificate in interior design, 1976; University of Santo Tomas, Philippines, MA, linguistics, 1978, PhD, English, 1981; California State University, Northridge, administrative credential, 1989. **CAREER:** International Schools, teacher, 1976-81; Los Angeles Unified School District, teacher, 1982-89, categorical program advisor, 1989-91, director, A/PAEC, 1991-. **ORGANIZATIONS:** Asian American Educators Association, 1991-; Pilipino American Alliance, 1993; EDUCARE, 1983-84. **HONORS/AWARDS:** Pilipino American Women's Network, outstanding educator, 1992; LAUSD, parent recognition award, 1991. **SPECIAL ACHIEVEMENTS:** Author, column, "Stop and Think," Philippines Times, 1992-93; Valerio Street School Handbook, 1990; contributor, Asian Week, Heritage Week, 1993; Bilingual Certificate of Competence, 1985; editor, Alaala, International School Yearbook, 1980. **BIOGRAPHICAL SOURCES:** Sunday Woman, Daily News, Women's Section, p 2, May 16, 1993; Heritage Magazine, p 20, March 1993; LA Weekly, p 64, March 13, 1992; San Francisco Philippines News, p 1, March 4, 1992; TM Weekly, Cover Story, p 12, January 17, 1992, p 12; Daily News, March 1989; Special Edition Press, The World of Money, fall 1993, p 74. **BUSINESS ADDRESS:** Director, Asian Pacific American Education Commission (LAUSD), 450 N Grand Ave, Rm H-133, Los Angeles, CA 90012.

DAYAO, FIRMO SALVADOR
Stockbroker. Filipino American. **PERSONAL:** Born Aug 9, 1949, Cebu City, Philippines; son of Melchor B Dayao & Rosario Salvador; married Olivia Solis-Dayao, Jan 21, 1984. **EDUCATION:** University of Santo Tomas, MA, philosophy, 1969, MA, theology, 1973. **CAREER:** Prudential Securities, stockbroker, 1984-. **ORGANIZATIONS:** Filipino-American Community Television, president, 1993-; Oahu Visayan Council, president, 1988-; Congress of Visayan Organizations, board member, 1988-; Investment Society of Hawaii, 1984-; Honolulu Police Commission, 1992-; Honolulu Ethics Commission, 1991-92; Honolulu Mayor's Census Commission, 1990. **HOME PHONE:** (808)625-0160. **BUSINESS ADDRESS:** Stockbroker, Prudential Securities, Inc, 2 Waterfront Plaza, 500 Ala Moana Blvd, Ste 400, Honolulu, HI 96813, (808)547-5200.

DE, SURANJAN
Educator. Indo-American. **PERSONAL:** Born Mar 6, 1954, Calcutta, W. Bengal, India; son of J R De & Uma De; married Esha Niyogi De, Jun 22, 1985. **EDUCATION:** Indian Institute of Technology, BSc, 1974, MSc, 1976; Ohio State University, MS, 1980; Purdue University, PhD, 1984. **CAREER:** Purdue University, 1984-85; University of Iowa, 1985-91; Santa Clara University, professor, 1991-. **BUSINESS ADDRESS:** Professor, Decision & Information Sciences Dept, Santa Clara University, Kenna Hall, Santa Clara, CA 95053.

DEB, ARUN KUMAR
Engineering consulting executive. Indo-American. **PERSONAL:** Born May 1, 1936, Calcutta, W. Bengal, India; son of Hemanta Kumar Deb and Chapala Deb (both deceased); married Dhriti Deb, Jun 8, 1962; children: Bhaskar. **EDUCATION:** University of Calcutta, BS, 1957, PhD, 1969; University of Wisconsin, MS, 1961. **CAREER:** Chanda Engineers, India, engineer, 1957-58; Bengal Engineering College, assistant professor, 1958-71; University College, London, senior research fellow, 1971-73; University of Notre Dame, visiting professor, 1974; Roy F Weston Inc, vice president, 1974-. **ORGANIZATIONS:** American Academy of Environmental Engineers, diplomate, 1975-; ASCE, fellow, 1978-, Publications Comm, chairman, 1982-84, Sessions Programs Comm, chairman, 1984-86, Awards Comm, vice chairman, 1993-. **HONORS/AWARDS:** USAID, fellowship, 1960-61; NSF, research grants, 1977-80; Institute of Engineers, India, Publications Award, 1974. **SPECIAL ACHIEVEMENTS:** Published more than 100 technical papers on environmental engineering. **HOME ADDRESS:** 100 Trowbridge Ln, Downingtown, PA 19335. **BUSINESS ADDRESS:** Vice President, Roy F Weston Inc, One Weston Way, West Chester, PA 19380, (215)430-3175.

DEBROY, CHITRITA (CHOBI)
Scientist, educator. Indo-American. **PERSONAL:** Born Jun 1, 1946, New Delhi, India; daughter of C Guha and Usha Guha; married T Debroy, Jun 27, 1980; children: Papia, Pompa. **EDUCATION:** University of Delhi, BS, 1965, MS, 1967; Jawaharlal Nehru University, India, MPhil, 1975, PhD, 1978. **CAREER:** Boston Biomedical Research Institute, staff scientist, 1978-80; Pennsylvania State University, research associate, 1980-88, senior research associate affiliated associate professor, 1989-. **ORGANIZATIONS:** American Society for Microbiology, 1984-93; American Association for Advancement of Science, 1990-93; American Society for Microbiology, Allegheny Branch, 1990-93. **HONORS/AWARDS:** Muscular Dystrophy Association of America, post-doctoral fellowship, 1979-80. **SPECIAL ACHIEVEMENTS:** Author: "Nucleotide Sequence of Herpes Simplex Virus Type 2 Syn Gene That Causes Cell Fusion," Gene, vol 88, p 275, 1990; "Generation of Nucleic Acid Probe Molecules," Diagnostic Nucleic Acid Probe Technology, by Carl Hanser. **HOME ADDRESS:** 624 Stoneledge Rd, State College, PA 16803, (814)238-0785. **BUSINESS ADDRESS:** Sr Res Assoc, Aff Asoc Prof, Dept of Vet Sci, Pennsylvania State University, 107 Henning Bldg, University Park, PA 16802, (814)863-8280.

DEDHIA, NAVIN SHAMJI
Engineer. Indo-American. **PERSONAL:** Born Dec 25, 1940, Bombay, Maharashtra, India; son of Shamji Pancharia Dedhia & Devkaben Shamji Dedhia; married Neelam, Feb 2, 1971; children: Nivita, Neha. **EDUCATION:** University of Bombay, India, BE, electrical engineering, 1963; Tennessee Technological University, MS, electrical engineering, 1968; Golden Gate University, MBA, 1983. **CAREER:** Polychem Ltd, India, shift engineer, 1963-66; Consolidated Comstock, design engineer, 1967; IBM East Fishkill, manufacturing engineer, 1968-76; IBM San Jose, quality engineer, advisory engineer, 1976-. **ORGANIZATIONS:** American Society for Quality Control, section chair, 1987-88, chair, international chapter, 1984-, Quality World Newsletter, editor, 1982-; certification committee, CMI chair, 1986-92; Mid Husdon Valley India Association, president, 1973-74; Jain Center of Northern California, president, 1987-88; India Cultural Association, 1976-; Gujarati Cultural Association, 1991-. **HONORS/AWARDS:** American Society for Quality Control, E Jack Lancaster Award, 1992, Fellow, 1989, Testimonial Award, 1984; Mahavir Jain Vidyalaya, Gold Medal, 1960, Volunteer of the Month, 1988; Shree CVOD Jain High School, Gold Medal, 1958; Brazilian Society for Quality Control, Honorary Member, 1992. **SPECIAL ACHIEVEMENTS:** Author of: "Supplier Partnership Program," Total Quality Management Journal, 1990; "Coupled-Mode Description of Space-Charge Wave Propagation on Radially Accelerated Cylindrical Electron Beams," thesis, 1968; Quality World Newsletter, 1982; "Education and Training for Quality," ASQC Quality Progress, 1985; "Process Audit System Effectiveness," Total Quality Management, 1988. **HOME ADDRESS:** 5080 Bougainvillea Dr, San Jose, CA 95111, (408)629-1723. **BUSINESS ADDRESS:** Engineer, IBM-SSD, 791-501, 5600 Cottle Rd, San Jose, CA 95193, (408)256-4979.

DEIVANAYAGAM, SUBRAMANIAM
Educator. Indo-American. **PERSONAL:** Born Nov 15, 1941, Tirunelveli, Tamil Nadu, India; son of D Subramaniam and S Gomathy; married Ratna, Jan 17, 1971; children: Vikram, Harsha. **EDUCATION:** Annamalai University, India, BE, 1963, MSc, 1966; Texas Tech University, PhD, 1973. **CAREER:** Enfield India Ltd, graduate engineer, 1963-64; Thiagarajar College of Engi-

neering, India, lecturer, 1966-69; Texas Tech University, research assistant, 1969-72, asst professor, 1973-76; University of Texas, Arlington, professor, 1976-86; Tennessee Technological University, professor, 1986-. **ORGANIZATIONS:** Institute of Industrial Engineers; Human Factors and Ergonomics Society; Society of Manufacturing Engineers; Society of Automotive Engineers; American Society of Engineering Education. **HONORS/AWARDS:** Human Factors Society, Jerome H Ely Award, 1984. **SPECIAL ACHIEVEMENTS:** Publications in international and national journals; consulting with major organizations; invited speaker at national and international institutions; teaching and research of ergonomics, safety, industrial engineering, etc. **HOME ADDRESS:** 1135 Tanglewood Dr, Cookeville, TN 38501. **BUSINESS ADDRESS:** Professor of Industrial Engineering, Tennessee Technological University, Box 5011, Cookeville, TN 38505, (615)372-3465.

DE LA PEÑA, VIOLETA R.
Political activist. Filipino American. **CAREER:** Asian American Voters Coalition, former national chairperson; Office of Asian American Affairs, executive director. **BUSINESS ADDRESS:** Executive Director, Office of Asian Pacific American Affairs, 311 W Saratoga St Rm # 280, Baltimore, MD 21201.*

DELLA, DAVID J.
State government official. Filipino American. **PERSONAL:** Born Mar 10, 1955, Seattle, WA; son of Narciso B Della (deceased) & Inocencia A Della; married Sandra L Rowell, Jul 12, 1983; children: Jade Adrienne. **EDUCATION:** University of Washington, 1973-75; City University, Leadership Institute of Seattle, 1991-92. **CAREER:** ILWU Local 37, secretary-treasurer, 1982-84; IBU Region 37, business agent, 1984-87; Inland Boatman's Union, national representative, 1987-89; Office of the Mayor, deputy chief of staff, 1990-93; Washington State Commission on Asian American Affairs, executive director, currently. **ORGANIZATIONS:** Seattle Human Rights Commission, chairperson, 1986-89; United Way of King County, committee person, 1991-; United Nations Association, board member, 1990-; Thurston County Dispute Resolution, center director, 1993-; International District Improvement Association, board, 1992-. **HONORS/AWARDS:** Asian American Political Alliance, Brass Ring, 1993; Filipino American National Historical Society, VIP Award, 1993; United Farmworkers Union, Recognition Award, 1989. **SPECIAL ACHIEVEMENTS:** City of Seattle Mayor's Affirmative Action Task Force, chairperson, 1990-93; Governor's Diversity Initiative Task Force, 1993-; Governor's Affirmative Action Policy Committee, 1993-; Chamber of Commerce Cultural Diversity Task Force, 1992-93. **BUSINESS ADDRESS:** Executive Director, Washington State Commission on Asian American Affairs, 501 S Jackson, 301 Buty Bldg, Seattle, WA 98104, (206)464-5820.

DENG, MING-DAO
Artist, writer. Chinese American. **PERSONAL:** Born Feb 4, 1954, San Francisco, CA; son of Woodrow & Constance Ong; married Betty Gee, Jun 1, 1991. **EDUCATION:** Occidental College, 1972-74; University of California, Berkeley, BA, 1976. **CAREER:** Side by Side Studios, partner, 1987-. **ORGANIZATIONS:** International Institute of San Francisco. **HONORS/AWARDS:** Phi Beta Kappa. **SPECIAL ACHIEVEMENTS:** 365 Tao, Harper San Francisco, 1992; Scholar Warrior, Harper San Francisco, 1990; Gateway to a Vast World, Harper San Francisco, 1989; Seven Bamboo Tablets of the Cloudy Satchel, 1987; Wandering Taoist, 1983. **BUSINESS ADDRESS:** Partner, Side By Side Studios, 2424 Polk St, San Francisco, CA 94109, (415)885-6325.

DENTON, VICTORIA VILLENA-
Journalist. Filipino American. **PERSONAL:** Born Aug 23, 1959, Lucena City, Quezon, Philippines; daughter of Arsenia Tan Villena & Dominador Salazar Villena; married Frank Hardy Denton, Dec 10, 1983; children: Glen Victor, Blaine Cristopher. **EDUCATION:** University of the Philippines, AB, economics, 1979; University of California, MA, journalism, 1983. **CAREER:** Oil Daily, assistant editor, 1984-88; American Chamber of Commerce, Egypt, editor, 1988-89; Lubricants World, contributing editor, 1989-. **ORGANIZATIONS:** American Women's Club of the Philippines, editor, corresponding secretary, 1993-. **HOME ADDRESS:** MC PO Box 3006, Makati, Metro Manila 1270, Philippines.

DEOL, HARJYOT
Physician. Indo-American. **PERSONAL:** Born Jul 11, 1957, Ludhiana, Punjab, India; son of Gurucharan Deol and Rajinder Deol; married Anoop Deol, Jul 4, 1982; children: Amrit, Amrita. **EDUCATION:** Government Medical College, India, MD, 1981; Rutgers University, residency in pediatrics,

1989-92. **CAREER:** Beth Israel Hospital, Pediatric Dept, physician, 1989-92; University of Rochester, School of Medicine and Dentistry, Anesthesiology Dept, physician, 1992-. **ORGANIZATIONS:** AMA; American Academy of Pediatrics; American Society of Anesthesiology; New York Society of Anesthesiology. **HOME ADDRESS:** 1212 French Rd, Rochester, NY 14618.

DER, HENRY
Organization executive. Chinese American. **PERSONAL:** Born 1947?, San Francisco, CA. **CAREER:** Chinese for Affirmative Action, 1974-, executive director, currently. **ORGANIZATIONS:** California Postsecondary Education Commission, chairman, currently. **SPECIAL ACHIEVEMENTS:** Peace Corps volunteer, Africa, 1968-70; issued "Broken Ladder," report, Chinese for Affirmative Action, 1992. **BUSINESS ADDRESS:** Executive Director, Chinese for Affirmative Action, 17 Walter U Lum Place, San Francisco, CA 94108, (415)274-6750.*

DESAI, ASHOK GOVINDJI
Design engineer. Indo-American. **PERSONAL:** Born Mar 31, 1949, Bulsar, Gujarat, India; son of Govindji Bhikhabhai Desai and Satyavatiben Govindji Desai; married Asha, Jan 26, 1978; children: Alvina, Avita. **EDUCATION:** BSEE, 1975. **CAREER:** Electronic Comp Corp, design engr, currently. **HOME ADDRESS:** 974 Trailside Ln, Bartlett, IL 60103-5139, (708)830-9898.

DESAI, CHANDRA
Packaging engineer. Indo-American. **PERSONAL:** Born Feb 6, 1936, Mandley, Burma; son of Nathubhai G Desai; married Uma, May 20, 1966; children: Parul, Vaisu, Rahul. **EDUCATION:** Birla Institute of Technology, India, BSE, 1962; University of Akron, MSME, 1970. **CAREER:** Jessops Engineering, graduate apprentice, 1964-66; Hindustan Motors Ltd, India, tool research engr, 1966-68; White Motor Corp, process engr, 1969-70; Central States Can Co, sr engr, 1971-. **ORGANIZATIONS:** Society of Metals, 1982-88. **HOME ADDRESS:** 5306 Burlawn St NW, Canton, OH 44708, (216)478-2276.

DESAI, CHANDRAKANT S.
Educator. Indo-American. **PERSONAL:** Born Nov 24, 1936, Nadisar, Gujarat, India; son of Sankalchand P Desai and Kamala S Desai; married Patricia L Desai, 1969; children: Maya C, Sanjay C. **EDUCATION:** Bombay University, Bombay, India, BE, 1959; Rice University, MS, 1966; University of Texas, PhD, 1968. **CAREER:** Various private and govt agencies, consultant; various govt and private agencies, India, assistant engineer, 1959-64; US Waterways Expt Stn, Vicksburg, MS, research engineer, 1969-74; Virginia Polytechnic Institute and State University, professor, 1974-81; University of Arizona, Regents' Professor, 1981-. **ORGANIZATIONS:** International Association for Computer Methods and Advances in Geomechanics, president, 1991-; International J Numerical and Analytical Methods in Geomechanics, chief editor, 1977-; American Society of Civil Engineers, fellow, 1985-; Institution of Structural Engineers, London, 1965-; American Academy of Mechanics; American Society of Engineering Education; Six International Journal, editorial board; various international conferences, chair, co-chair. **HONORS/AWARDS:** US Corps of Engineers, Meritorious Civilian Service Award, 1972; Alexander von Humboldt, German Govt, Stiftung: Senior Scientist Award, 1979; International Association for Computer Methods and Advances in Geomechanics, Distinguished Contributions Medal, 1991; University of Arizona, Asian-American Faculty, Outstanding Faculty Award in Sciences, 1991; Czechoslovakian Academy of Sciences, Outstanding Contributions in Mechanics Medal, 1992. **SPECIAL ACHIEVEMENTS:** Author/editor of 17 books on computational methods and constitutive modeling; author/co-author of over 200 technical papers. **BUSINESS ADDRESS:** Regents' Professor, Dept of Civil Engineering and Engineering Mechanics, University of Arizona, Tucson, AZ 85721-0001.

DESAI, HIREN SHARAD
Plastics recycling plant manager. Indo-American. **PERSONAL:** Born May 21, 1969, Luanshya, Copperbelt, Zambia; son of Sharadchandra Nanubhai Desai and Lata Sharadchandra Desai; married Serina Hiren Desai, Jun 27, 1993. **EDUCATION:** University of Tennessee at Chattanooga, BS, economics, industrial management, 1991. **CAREER:** Hamilton Plastics Inc, recycling plant manager, 1992-. **ORGANIZATIONS:** Indo Cultural Exchange, head, committee member, 1990-91. **HONORS/AWARDS:** Omicron Delta Epsilon, Intl Honor Society for Economics, 1992. **HOME ADDRESS:** 812 La Lane, East Ridge, TN 37412, (615)855-8435.

DESAI, KANTILAL PANACHAND
Business executive. Indo-American. **PERSONAL:** Born Feb 7, 1929, Mota-Samadhiala, Gujarat, India; son of Panachand Virchand Desai and Nandakuvar P Desai; married Nilam K Desai, Nov 6, 1960; children: Jaydev K, Shubhada K, Abhilasha K. **EDUCATION:** University of Bombay, India, BSc, geology, 1952; Colorado School of Mines, geophysical engineer, 1956, MS, 1958; University of Tulsa, PhD, 1968. **CAREER:** Seismograph Service Corp, 1958-62; Sinclair Research Center, research engineer, 1962-69; Mobil Research & Development, research engineer, 1969-84; ARAMCO, PE specialist, 1985-91; KPD Petrophysical Co, owner, consultant, currently. **ORGANIZATIONS:** Society of Professional Well Log Analysts, 1965-, board member, president, 1974-75; Society of Petroleum Engineers, 1965-, reviewer of technical papers, 1969-91. **HONORS/AWARDS:** Colorado School of Mines, Graduate Fellowship, 1956-58. **SPECIAL ACHIEVEMENTS:** Received three US patents related to acoustic logging; author & co-author of a number of papers in the field of well logging. **BIOGRAPHICAL SOURCES:** Journal of Petroleum Technology, p 818, July, 1991. **HOME ADDRESS:** 7103 Schafer St, Dallas, TX 75252, (214)380-4312.

DESAI, MANISHA
Educator. Indo-American. **PERSONAL:** Born May 26, 1958, Ahmedabad, Gujarat, India; married Jeremy Geller, Oct 23, 1987; children: One. **EDUCATION:** Bombay University, BSc, 1978, MSW, 1982; Washington University, PhD, 1989. **CAREER:** Webster University, St Louis, assistant professor, 1989-90; Hobart and William Smith Colleges, assistant professor, 1990-. **ORGANIZATIONS:** American Sociology Association, 1989-; Sociologists for Women in Society, 1990-. **HONORS/AWARDS:** Washington University, Doctoral Fellowship, 1987, 1989. **SPECIAL ACHIEVEMENTS:** Book in progress on the Women's Movement in India. **BUSINESS ADDRESS:** Assistant Professor of Sociology, Hobart and William Smith Colleges, Trinity 301, Geneva, NY 14456-3397, (315)781-3445.

DESAI, SHARAD P.
Engineering manager. Indo-American. **PERSONAL:** Born Nov 5, 1946, Thordi, Gujarat, India; son of Prabhashanker V Desai and Manilaxmi P Desai; married Vandama S Joshi, Dec 16, 1980; children: Shailey S, Sharad S. **EDUCATION:** University of Bombay, India, BSME, 1970; Purdue University, MSIE, 1973. **CAREER:** Harris, project engr, 1983-85; Westinghouse Hanford Co, manager, 1985-. **ORGANIZATIONS:** Society of American Value Engineers, 1989-; Institute of Industrial Engineers, 1983-. **SPECIAL ACHIEVEMENTS:** Washington State Dept of Licensing, professional engr, 1987. **HOME ADDRESS:** 459 Mateo Ct, Richland, WA 99352.

DESAI, SUDHIR G.
Physician. Indo-American. **PERSONAL:** Born Jun 1, 1937, Hubli, Karnataka, India; son of Gurunath and Indira; married Sheela, Jun 6, 1975; children: Janhavi, Chetan. **EDUCATION:** University of Bombay, Grant Medical College, India, MBBS, 1964; American Board of Internal Medicine, internal medicine board certification, 1972; American Board of Subspecialties, pulmonary board certification, 1974. **CAREER:** Wayne County Health Department, pulmonary consultant, 1972-76; University of Michigan Medical School, instructor, 1974-76; Wayne State University Medical School, assistant professor, 1976-; VA Medical Center, staff physican, currently. **ORGANIZATIONS:** American College of Chest Physicians, FCCP, 1976-; American Thoracic Society, 1976-; Michigan Thoracic Society, 1976-; American College of Chest Physicians, Forum on Infection and Immunology, 1980-; Royal College of Physicians and Surgeons of Canada, fellow, 1973. **HONORS/AWARDS:** Deaconess Hospital, Detroit, Best Intern, 1967. **SPECIAL ACHIEVEMENTS:** Contributor, Sarcoidesis, edited by J Lieberman, 1983; various publications in medical journals, 1976-91; presentations in regional and national scientific meetings. **HOME ADDRESS:** 1501 Marie, Dearborn Heights, MI 48127. **BUSINESS ADDRESS:** Staff Physician, Pulmonary Section, VA Medical Center, Southfield and Outer Drive Rds, Allen Park, MI 48101, (313)562-6000.

DESAI, SURESH A.
Educator. Indo-American. **PERSONAL:** Born Oct 29, 1933, Ambheta, Gujarat, India; son of Ambelal Dayalji & Gajaraben A Desai; married Rambha, May 12, 1960; children: Nirjari M, Niraj S. **EDUCATION:** Gujarat University, India, BA, 1954, MA, 1956, LLB, 1957, PhD, 1960; University of California, Los Angeles, MA, 1963, PhD, 1967. **CAREER:** MTB College, assistant professor of economics, 1956-62; Hanover College, Indiana, associate professor of economics, 1967-73; Montclair State College, chair, professor of economics, 1973-81, School of Business Administration, dean, 1981-91, professor of economics and finance, 1991-. **ORGANIZATIONS:** Association of Indian Economics, program chair; American Economic Association; Eastern Economic Association; Academy of International Business; Association of Social Economics. **HONORS/AWARDS:** American Institute of Indian Studies, junior research fellow, 1965-66; National Federation of Asian Indian Organizations, Outstanding Achievement in Education, 1986. **HOME ADDRESS:** 108 Osborne St, Glen Ridge, NJ 07028-2420, (201)748-1648. **BUSINESS ADDRESS:** Professor of Economics, Finance, Montclair State College, 1 Normal Ave, 200 Morehead Hall, Upper Montclair, NJ 07043, (201)655-4370.

DESAI, SURESH A.
Manufacturing company executive. Indo-American. **PERSONAL:** Born Feb 6, 1942, Surat, Gujarat, India; son of Ambelal Desai and Deviben Desai; married Sudha Desai, Jul 19, 1964; children: Neha, Neelam. **EDUCATION:** BVM College, India, BSME, 1964; University of Missouri, MSME, 1966; University of Chicago, MBA, 1980. **CAREER:** Sherwin Williams Co, engineering manager; US Can, operations manager; Can Corp of America Inc, executive vice pres, currently. **ORGANIZATIONS:** SME; Can Manufacturers Institute. **HOME ADDRESS:** 1913 Dorset Dr, Wheaton, IL 60187. **BUSINESS PHONE:** (215)926-3044.

DESAI, UDAY
Educator, educational administrator. Indo-American. **PERSONAL:** Born Aug 23, 1943, Rajpur, Gujarat, India; son of Chhabildas Desai & Shantaben Desai; married Christina, Jun 30, 1972; children: Michael, Kavita, Neal. **EDUCATION:** SVP University, BE, 1965; City University of New York, ME, 1967; University of Pittsburgh, PhD, 1973. **CAREER:** University of Oregon, visiting assistant professor, 1972-73; Glassboro State College, assistant professor, 1973-75; Administrative Staff College of India, assistant and associate professor, 1976-78; Southern Illinois University, assistant, associate professor, 1978-90, director, MPA program, 1988-, professor, 1991-. **ORGANIZATIONS:** Policy Studies Organization; American Society for Public Administration; American Political Science Association. **HONORS/AWARDS:** American Institute of Indian Studies, Senior Research Fellow, 1982; University of Texas, visiting scholar, 1986. **SPECIAL ACHIEVEMENTS:** Co-editor-in-chief, Policy Studies Journal, 1990-. **BUSINESS ADDRESS:** Director, Professor, MPA Program, Dept of Political Science, Southern Illinois University, Faner 3141, Carbondale, IL 62901, (618)453-3177.

DESAI, VIJAY
Physician. Indo-American. **PERSONAL:** Born Sep 1, 1953, Amletha, Gujarat, India; son of Dahyabhai C Desai; married Madhu Desai, Apr 19, 1979; children: Menka, Ankit. **EDUCATION:** Government Medical College, India, MBBS, 1977. **CAREER:** Morris Hospital, emergency room physician, 1984-. **HOME ADDRESS:** 1211 Barber Ln, Joliet, IL 60435, (815)729-2102.

DESAI, VIKRAM J.
Chemical engineer, research scientist. Indo-American. **PERSONAL:** Born Sep 27, 1945, Bombay, India; son of Bindumati J and Jagannath J Desai; married Pallavi, Nov 4, 1973; children: Meghana, Rishi. **EDUCATION:** BITS, Pilani, Rajasthan, India, BSCE, 1968; MIT, SM, chemical engineering, 1969, ScD, chemical engineering, 1973. **CAREER:** Badger Co, design engineer, 1969-71; FMC Co, research engineer, 1973-77; Amoco Chemical Co, associate research engineer, 1977-. **ORGANIZATIONS:** AIChE, continuing ed committee, 1985-. **HOME ADDRESS:** 1248 Whitingham Cir, Naperville, IL 60540. **BUSINESS ADDRESS:** Associate Research Engineer, Amoco Chemical Co, PO Box 3011, Naperville, IL 60566-7011, (708)420-5459.

DESAI, VIMAL H.
Educator. Indo-American. **PERSONAL:** Born Nov 15, 1951, Baroda, India. **EDUCATION:** M S University of Baroda, BE, mechanical engineering, 1973; Clemson University, MS, bioengineering, 1979; Johns Hopkins University, PhD, materials science & engineering, 1984. **CAREER:** University of Central Florida, associate professor, 1984-. **ORGANIZATIONS:** ASM International; NACE International; TMS; ECS. **BUSINESS ADDRESS:** Associate Professor, Mech & Aerospace Eng Dept, University of Central Florida, Orlando, FL 32816-2450, (407)823-5777.

DESAIGOUDAR, CHAN
Business executive. Indo-American. **PERSONAL:** Born Dec 23, 1937. **CAREER:** California Micro Devices Corp, chairman, chief executive officer,

currently. **BIOGRAPHICAL SOURCES:** "Chan's Edge Is Communication," Industry Week, Jun 1, 1987, p54. **BUSINESS ADDRESS:** Chairman/ CEO, California Micro Devices Corp, 215 Topaz St, Milpitas, CA 95035, (408)263-3214.*

DESHPANDE, NILENDRA GANESH
Educator. Indo-American. **PERSONAL:** Born Apr 18, 1938, Karachi, Pakistan; son of Ganesh V & Myna G Deshpande; married Kanchan N Deshpande, May 15, 1960; children: Pranay, Rahul. **EDUCATION:** University of Madras, BSc (honors), 1959, MA, 1960, MSc, 1961; University of Pennsylvania, PhD, 1965. **CAREER:** Northwestern University, assistant professor, 1967-73; University of Texas, associate professor, 1973-75; University of Oregon, associate professor, 1975-83, professor, 1983-. **ORGANIZATIONS:** University of Oregon, Institute of Theoretical Science, director, 1987-92, Physics Department, head, 1992-. **HONORS/AWARDS:** Department of Energy, Outstanding Junior Investigator, 1981-86; American Physical Society, fellow, 1990. **BUSINESS ADDRESS:** Professor, Physics Dept, University of Oregon, Eugene, OR 97403, (503)346-5225.

DEV, PARVATI
Researcher, educator. Indo-American. **PERSONAL:** Born Dec 6, 1946, New Delhi, India; daughter of Velloor Vasu Dev and Meera Roy; married Kalyan Dutta, Apr 21, 1975; children: Rina Dutta, Shona Dutta. **EDUCATION:** Indian Institute of Technology, Kharagpur, BTech (honors), 1968; Stanford University, PhD, 1975. **CAREER:** Massachusetts Institute of Technology, research associate, 1975-77; Boston University, assistant professor, 1976-78; Veterans Administration Medical Center, research associate, 1979-82; CEMAX, Research & Development, vice president, 1982-89; Stanford University, School of Medicine, Summit, director, 1990-. **ORGANIZATIONS:** Many scientific organizations. **SPECIAL ACHIEVEMENTS:** Over 100 scientific publications, 1974-. **BUSINESS ADDRESS:** Director, Summit, Stanford University School of Medicine, MSOB, X329, Stanford, CA 94305, (415)723-8087.

DE VERA, FEDERICO
Gallery owner. Filipino American. **PERSONAL:** Born Mar 10, 1962, Philippines. **CAREER:** de Vera Gallery, owner, currently. **BUSINESS ADDRESS:** Owner, de Vera Gallery, 384 Hayes St, San Francisco, CA 94102.

DHALIWAL, AMRIK SINGH
Educator. Indo-American. **PERSONAL:** Born Nov 17, 1934, Ludhiana, Punjab, India; son of S Kapur S Dhaliwal and Kishan Kaur Dhaliwal; married Gurmeet K Dhaliwal, Nov 17, 1962; children: Roopinder K Grewal, Deepinder. **EDUCATION:** BS, 1954; MS, 1959; PhD, 1962. **CAREER:** Utah State University, research associate, 1962-64, assistant professor, 1964-66; Loyola University, Chicago, assistant professor, 1966-71, associate professor, 1971-75, professor, 1975-. **ORGANIZATIONS:** Illinois State Academy of Science, 1982-, councilor-at-large, 1983-, Membership Committee, chairman, 1984-, Research Grant Committee, 1984-, Microbiology, section chairman, 1985-, vp, 1989-; American Association of University Professors, 1967-; Sigma Xi, 1967-. **BUSINESS ADDRESS:** Professor, Dept of Biology, Loyola University, Chicago, 6525 N Sheridan Rd, Chicago, IL 60626.

DHARAMSI, MANOJ T.
Electronics engineer. Indo-American. **PERSONAL:** Born in Khamgam, Maharashtra, India; son of Thakarsi B Dharamsi; married Kanta M Dharamsi, May 1962; children: Neeta. **EDUCATION:** Jabalpur University, India, BE, 1959; Illinois Institute of Technology, MS, 1967; Southern Methodist University, PhD, 1972. **CAREER:** Jain Society of Metropolitan Washington, president, 1980-. **ORGANIZATIONS:** JAINA, president, 1983-85. **HOME ADDRESS:** 11820 Triple Crown Road, Reston, VA 22091, (703)620-9837.

DHILLON, JOGINDER SINGH
Attorney, military officer, educator. Indo-American. **PERSONAL:** Born Jan 29, 1961, El Centro, CA; son of Dharam Singh Dhillon & Surjit Kaur Dhillon; married Niki Dhillon, Jun 30, 1991; children: Aneil Singh. **EDUCATION:** US Air Force Academy, BS, 1982; Harvard Law School, JD, 1988. **CAREER:** Air Force Flight Test Center, B-1B/Cruise Missile Systems analyst; US Air Force Judiciary, area defense counsel; US Air Force Academy, assistant professor of law, currently. **ORGANIZATIONS:** American Bar Association; Academy Big Brothers/Big Sisters Club, assistant officer in charge. **HONORS/ AWARDS:** USAF Academy, Distinguished Graduate, 1982, Outstanding Young Attorney, 1992. **SPECIAL ACHIEVEMENTS:** B-1B Terrain Following System Technical Description, 1985. **MILITARY SERVICE:** US Air

Force, major, 1982-; Three AF Commendation Medals. **HOME ADDRESS:** 4500 C West Juniper Dr, US Air Force Academy, CO 80840. **BUSINESS PHONE:** (719)472-3680.

DHILLON, NEIL (SUNIL DHILLON)
Government official. Indo-American. **PERSONAL:** Born Apr 20, 1962, London, England; son of Ranjit Singh and Kamakjit Kaur Dhillon. **EDUCATION:** American University, BA, political science, 1984. **CAREER:** Representative Tom Luken, D-Ohio, legislative asst for health, foreign affairs, energy and commerce; Representative Robert Matsui, legislative asst, chief of staff, 1986-93; Clinton Inaugural Committee, director of corporate affairs; Congressman Norman Mineta, D-California, aide, 1993; Transportation Dept, acting asst secretary of governmental affairs; campaigning for Congress in 6th District of Maryland, currently. **HONORS/AWARDS:** Asian Americans for Clinton-Gore, Excellence Award, 1993. **BUSINESS ADDRESS:** Special Guest Lecturer, Frostberg University, 304 Bourbon St, Cumberland, MD 21502, (703)642-6235.*

DHILLON, SUNIL. *See* **DHILLON, NEIL.**

DHIR, SURENDRA KUMAR
Government official. Indo-American. **PERSONAL:** Born Aug 9, 1937, Sonekatch, Madhya Pradesh, India; son of Kislori Lal Dhir & Kaushalya Dhir; married Bina Dhir, Oct 15, 1965; children: Milan Dhir-Sandhu, Alok. **EDUCATION:** Victoria College, India, ISc, 1955; Birla Institute of Technology, India, BSME, 1960; Munich University, PhD, ME, 1964. **CAREER:** MAN, Germany, design engineer, 1964; AEG, Germany, design engineer, 1965; US Navy, branch head, 1966-86; US Department of Commerce, director, 1986-. **HONORS/AWARDS:** German Research Organization, fellowship, 1961-64; US Department of Commerce, Gold Medal Award, 1990. **SPECIAL ACHIEVEMENTS:** Published 35 papers in mechanical engineering; speak, read & write German, Hindi and English. **HOME ADDRESS:** 5808 Plainview Rd, Bethesda, MD 20817, (202)229-8392. **BUSINESS PHONE:** (202)482-5695.

DHRUV, ARVIND B.
Pharmaceutical company executive. Indo-American. **PERSONAL:** Born Oct 21, 1946, Ahmedabad, Gujarat, India; son of Babubhai K Dhruv and Taraben B Dhruv; married Rohini V Shah, Jun 22, 1974; children: Nikhil. **EDUCATION:** Gujarat University, L M College of Pharmacy, BPharm, 1968; University of Georgia, School of Pharmacy, MS, pharm, 1972; Philadelphia College of Pharmacy & Science, PhD, 1980. **CAREER:** Squibb Institute for Med Research, research investigator, 1972-82; Warner Lambert, group leader, 1982-83; Invamed Inc, vice president, owner, 1983-84; Guardian Drug Co Inc, president & CEO, 1984-. **ORGANIZATIONS:** PLMA, 1984-; AAPS, 1988-. **BUSINESS ADDRESS:** President & Chief Executive Officer, Guardian Drug Company Inc, 72 Prince Street, Trenton, NJ 08638, (609)394-5300.

DHURANDHAR, NINA R.
Physician. Indo-American. **PERSONAL:** Born Jan 6, 1937, Bombay, India; daughter of Hajimahomed Merchant and Khairunissa Merchant; married Raja W Dhurandhar, Jan 27, 1963; children: Sunita, Anjali. **EDUCATION:** University of Bombay, Bombay, India, Seth GS Medical College, MBBS, 1962. **CAREER:** GS Med College, ICEM Hospital, India, resident in pathology, 1961-63; C&A Hospital, Westpark Hospital, UK, resident, 1963-65; Tulane University Medical Center, Touro Infirmary, fellow, 1965-68, assistant professor, 1973-79, associate professor of pathology, 1979-. **ORGANIZATIONS:** College of American Pathologists, fellow, 1990-; US Canadian Academy of Pathology, 1975-; American Society of Cytology, 1979-; American Association of Physicians from India, president, 1992-93, Louisiana Chapter, life member, 1988-. **BUSINESS ADDRESS:** Associate Professor, Dept of Pathology, Tulane University Medical Center, 1430 Tulane Avenue, New Orleans, LA 70112-2699, (504)588-5224.

DIGHE, SHRIKANT VISHWANATH
Government official. Indo-American. **PERSONAL:** Born Nov 29, 1933, Murud-Janjira, Maharashtra, India; son of Vishwanath Govind Dighe & Malati V Dighe; married Judith Ginaine Dighe, Sep 12, 1964; children: Ranjit, Anand. **EDUCATION:** University of Bombay, India, BSc, 1957, MSc, 1957; University of Cincinnati, PhD, 1965; Johns Hopkins University, MAS, 1976. **CAREER:** WR Grace & Co, research chemist, 1965-71; Johns Hopkins University, School of Medicine, research associate, 1971-73; Food & Drug Administration, review scientist, 1973-78, Biopharmaceutics Review Branch,

chief, 1979-85, Division of Bioequivalence, director, 1985-. **ORGANIZA-TIONS:** American Association of Pharmaceutical Scientists, 1986-; American Chemical Society, 1961-; New York Academy of Sciences, 1965-; Institute of Chemistry, fellow, 1968-; Sigma Xi, 1964-. **HONORS/AWARDS:** FDA, PHS Special Recognition Award, 1986, Group Recognition Award, 1989, Commendable Service Award, 1978; University of Cincinnati, Petroleum Research Fund fellow, 1959-62, Laws Fellow, 1964. **SPECIAL ACHIEVEMENTS:** Co-editor, Pharmaceutical Bioequivalence, Marcel Dekker, 1991; 25 publications in scientific journals, 6 US patents, 1970-72. **HOME ADDRESS:** 9811 Wildwood Rd, Bethesda, MD 20814, (301)493-8867.

DINH, NICHOLAS NGUYEN
Insurance company manager. Vietnamese American. **PERSONAL:** Born May 28, 1941, Saigon, Vietnam; son of Sinh T Dinh and Nguyen D Luu; married Tammy H Dinh, Dec 29, 1974; children: Tino Thanh, Maurice Nam. **EDUCA-TION:** Vietnam National Military Academy, AS, sciences, 1965; Van Hanh University, BS, journalism, 1975. **CAREER:** American International Group, junior underwriter, 1975-78; Plantation, Inc, manager, 1978-80; Union National Life Insurance Group, agent, 1981-82, staff manager, 1982-83; Transamerica Life Companies, career agent, 1984-90; Mony Mutual of New York, sales manager, 1991-92; Lincoln Financial Services, unit manager, 1993-. **ORGANIZATIONS:** National Association of Life Underwriter, 1984-; General Agent and Manager Association, 1991-; The Vietnamese Military Academy Alumni Association, vice president, 1992-; Parent-Teacher Association; St Martyrs Church, president, 1990-. **HONORS/AWARDS:** National Quality Awards, 1987; National Achievement Sales Awards, 1987-88; Texas Leaders Round Table, 1989-92; numerous sales awards, 1982-89. **SPECIAL ACHIEVEMENTS:** Life Underwriter Training Council, fellow, 1989; Agency Management Training Council, graduate, 1992. **MILITARY SER-VICE:** Infantry, captain, 1963-75; numerous decorations. **BIOGRAPHICAL SOURCES:** Woburn Daily News (MA), p 1, Sept 1975. **BUSINESS AD-DRESS:** Unit Manager/Asian Marketing, Lincoln National Life Insurance Co, 24 E Greenway Plaza, Ste 609, Houston, TX 77046, (713)621-7099.

DINH, STEVEN M.
Pharmaceutical company executive. Chinese American. **PERSONAL:** Born Jul 29, 1955, Saigon, Vietnam; son of Vo Dinh and Jane Dinh; married Yuk-Ching Tse Dinh, Jun 15, 1982; children: Kate H, Alex R. **EDUCATION:** Cooper Union, BE, 1976; Cornell University, MS, 1978; MIT, ScD, 1981. **CAREER:** UCLA, assistant professor, 1981-82; DuPont, senior engineer, 1982-87; Ciba-Geigy, Basic Pharmaceutics Research, manager, 1987-. **ORGA-NIZATIONS:** American Association Pharm Sci; Controlled Relase Society; American Chem Society; AIChE; Society of Rheology; American Association Adv of Science; New York Academy of Sciences; Sigma Xi. **HONORS/AWARDS:** MIT, Industry Polymer Processing Program, Research Fellowship, 1978-81; AEMB, Outstanding Paper Award, 1977. **SPECIAL ACHIEVE-MENTS:** "Drug Delivery Systems," in Kirk-Othmer Encyclopedia of Chemical Technology, 1993; "Sorption & Transport of Ethanol & Water in Poly (ethylene-co-vinyl-acetate) Membranes," J Memb Sci, vol 69, p 223, 1992; "Treatise on Controlled Drug Delivery, Chapter I, Fundamental Concepts in Controlled-Release," Marcel-Dekker, NY, 1991; "Enhanced Transport in a Therapeutic Transdermal System," Biomaterials, vol 11, p 729, 1990; "Upper and Lower Limits of Human Skin Electrical Resistance in Iontophoresis," AIChE Journal, vol 39, p 2011, 1993. **BUSINESS ADDRESS:** Manager, Basic Pharmaceutics Research, CIBA-Geigy, 444 Saw Mill River Road, MR-2, Ardsley, NY 10502, (914)479-2853.

DINH, THUY TU BICH
Attorney, writer. Vietnamese American. **PERSONAL:** Born Jan 7, 1962, Saigon, Vietnam; daughter of Thuc Tu Dinh and Catherine Nguyen Dinh. **EDUCATION:** University of Virginia, BA, 1984, School of Law, JD, 1987. **CAREER:** Office of the Comptroller of the Currency, attorney, 1987-91; Commodity Futures Trading Commission, attorney, 1991-. **ORGANIZA-TIONS:** Pan Asian American Women, co-chair, public policy, 1993-; Mayor's Office of Asian-Pacific Islanders Affairs, advisor; Asian-Pacific Bar Association, DC chapter, 1992-; A Feel for Books, discussion leader for adult literacy program, 1993-; Pennsylvania Bar Association, 1988-. **HONORS/AWARDS:** Dynatech Corp, Essay Contest Winner on Leadership & Management, 1983. **SPECIAL ACHIEVEMENTS:** "Luggage and Shoes," UCLA Asian-American Studies Publication, 1991; "Heritage: A Current Flowing Onward," PanAsia Newsletter, May 1993; proficiency in Vietnamese & French. **HOME ADDRESS:** 1826 Harvard St, #302, Washington, DC 20009. **BUSINESS**

ADDRESS: Attorney, Commodity Futures Trading Commission, 2033 K St NW, Washington, DC 20581, (202)254-9880.

DINH, TUNG VAN
Physician, educator. Vietnamese American. **PERSONAL:** Born Aug 7, 1930, Hoian, Vietnam; son of Van Vinh Dinh (deceased) & Thi Lan Thai; married Gia Duy To, Sep 1, 1957; children: Tuan A, Tue A, Tri A, Tho A. **EDUCA-TION:** Saigon Faculty of Medicine, MD, 1958; University of Texas, Galveston, residency, pathology, 1971, residency, Ob-Gyn, 1978. **CAREER:** South Vietnam Government, Danang Hospital, director, 1965-75, Huo School of Medicine, assistant professor, 1970-75; University of Texas, Galveston, assistant professor, Ob-Gyn, 1980-83, associate professor, Ob-Gyn and pathology, 1984-88, professor Ob-Gyn and pathology, 1988-. **ORGANIZATIONS:** Society Ob-Gyn, France, 1965-; Galveston Academy Pathology, 1979-; Galveston Society Gyn Pathologists, 1981-; American College of Ob-Gyn, fellow, 1981-; American Society of Clinical Pathologists, 1983-; Association of Professors of Ob-Gyn, 1979-; Texas Medical Association, 1979-; Vietnamese American Physicians Association, USA, 1985-. **HONORS/AWARDS:** Government of South Vietnam, Medal of Health, Education, and Social Services, 1973; University of Texas, Galveston, Golden Apple Award Clinical Professor, 1984, 1987, Outstanding Faculty Member, 1986, Charpentier Award, 1986. **SPECIAL ACHIEVEMENTS:** Laser surgery of cervise in Laser Surgery Yearbook, 1989; Syllabus of Gynecologic Pathology, UT Press, 1990; Samario de Pathologia Ginecologica, La Penta Medica, 1992; Clinical Gynecologic Oncology Review, Mosby, 1993. **MILITARY SERVICE:** Military Medicine, lieutenant, 1956-57. **BIOGRAPHICAL SOURCES:** Directory of Medical Specialists. **BUSINESS ADDRESS:** Professor of Obstetrics, Gynecology and Pathology, University of Texas Medical Branch, 301 University Blvd, Galveston, TX 77555, (409)772-1555.

DINH, YUK-CHING TSE. *See* TSE DINH, YUK-CHING.

DIOKNO, ANANIAS CORNEJO
Urologist. Filipino American. **PERSONAL:** Born Aug 13, 1942, San Luis, Batangas, Philippines; son of Pedro B Diokno & Rosario Diokno; married Lourdes, Apr 29, 1967; children: Dennis A, Donna A, David H, Deana M. **EDUCATION:** University of Santo Tomas, associate arts, 1960, MD, 1965; Wayne County General Hospital, intern, resident, 1966-67; University of Michigan, resident, 1968-70. **CAREER:** University of Michigan, urology fellow, 1970-71, instructor, 1971-72, assistant, associate professor, 1976-82, professor, 1982-84, clinical professor, 1984-; William Beaumont Hospital, chief of urology, 1984-. **ORGANIZATIONS:** Philippine American Urologic Society, president, 1983-84; Michigan Urologic Society, president, 1984-85; North Central Section of American Urologic Association, secretary, 1992-95; Reed M Nesbit Urological Society, board of directors, 1988-90; International College of Surgeons, secretary elect, 1992-93; Agency for Health Care Policy & Research, chairperson, panel on incontinence, 1990-92. **HONORS/AWARDS:** Michigan Urologic Resident Essay Contest, first prize, 1970; Philippine Association of Michigan, Outstanding Man of the Year, 1976; Republic of Philippines, Outstanding Filipino Overseas, 1979; University of Michigan Medical School, Kaiser Permanente Award for Teaching Excellence, 1981; National Institutes of Health, Merit Award, 1989; University of Michigan Urology Department, Silver Cystoscope Award, 1983. **SPECIAL ACHIEVEMENTS:** Five scientific exhibits, awards; NIH grants, prinicipal investigator grants; visiting professor in USA, Europe & Asia; publications in scientific journals from 1969; 105 articles; 21 chapters in books, 1976-. **BIOGRAPHICAL SOURCES:** US Thomasian, vol 1, no 1, p 24, winter 1993; Phil Medical Bulletin, vol 26, p 12-13, June 1977. **BUSINESS ADDRESS:** Chief of Urology, William Beaumont Hospital, 13 Mile Rd, Ste 438, Medical Office Bldg, Royal Oak, MI 48073, (810)551-0387.

DIRIGE, OFELIA VILLA
Educator. Filipino American. **PERSONAL:** Born Jul 14, 1940, Manila, Philippines; daughter of Gregorio Dirige and Lourdes Dirige. **EDUCATION:** University of the Philippines, BS, 1960; University of Hawaii, MS, 1968; University of California, Los Angeles, DrPH, 1972. **CAREER:** UH Division of Nutrition, research assistant, summer 1968; UCLA School of Public Health, research, teaching assistant, 1968-72; Southwest Health Center, public health nutritionist, 1972-77; Hubert Humphrey CHC, nutrition supervisor, 1977-79; LA County Department of HS, MIC supervisor, 1979-81; University of Hawaii, SPH, assistant professor, 1982-87; SDSU, associate professor, 1987-. **ORGA-NIZATIONS:** California Nutrition Council, secretary, 1990-92; American Public Health Association, 1982-; American Dietetic Association, 1972-; Asso-

ciation of Teachers of MCH, 1987-; San Diego Dietetic Association, 1987-; Society for Nutrition Education, 1987-. **HONORS/AWARDS:** University of Philippines, College and University Scholar, 1959; East-West Center Grantee, 1966-68; Filipino Alumni Scholar, 1969. **SPECIAL ACHIEVEMENTS:** Research: Director, Project Kalusugan, a Committee Mobilization Project for Filipino Americans in San Diego County, California Department of Health Services, 1992-93; Nutrition in Day Care; presentations, Nutrition Crossroads-Foods of Many Cultures, presented at the California Food Service Association, 1992 and Asian American Nurses Association, 1992; Community Assessment of the Health Needs of Filipino Americans in San Diego County, abstract presented, 1993; Community Nutrition Strategies Toward Healthy Ethnic Families, abstract, presented at American Public Health Association 120th annual meeting, 1992. **BUSINESS ADDRESS:** Associate Professor, Division of MCH, GSPH, San Diego State University, 6505 Alvarado St, Ste 205, San Diego, CA 92120, (619)594-2795.

DIVAKARUNI, CHITRA BANERJEE
Educator. Indo-American. **PERSONAL:** Born Jul 29, 1956, Calcutta, India; daughter of R K Banerjee and Tatini Banerjee; married S Murthy Divakaruni, Jun 29, 1979; children: Anand. **EDUCATION:** Calcutta University, BA, English, 1976; Wright State University, MA, English, 1978; University of California, Berkeley, PhD, English, 1985. **CAREER:** Diablo Valley College, Department of English, Creative Writing, professor, 1987-89; Foothill College, Department of English, Creative Writing, professor, 1989-. **ORGANIZA-TIONS:** MAITRI, a help-line for South Asian women, president, 1991-; Mid-Peninsula Support Network for Battered Women, volunteer, 1990-. **HONORS/AWARDS:** Gerbode Foundation, Writing Award, 1993; Santa Clara County Arts Council, Writing Award, 1990; Barbara Deming Foundation, Memorial Award, 1989. **SPECIAL ACHIEVEMENTS:** Dark Like the River, book of poetry, 1987; The Reason for Nasturtiums, book of poetry, 1990; Black Candle, book of poetry, 1991; editor, Multitude: Cross-cultural Readings for Writers, 1993; poems & stories in over 50 magazines & journals: Ms, Chicago Review, Beloit Poetry Journal, etc. **BUSINESS ADDRESS:** Professor, Dept of Language Arts, Foothill College, 12345 El Monte Road, Los Altos, CA 94022-4504, (415)949-7557.

DIXIT, AJIT S.
Scientist. Indo-American. **PERSONAL:** Born Sep 30, 1950, Nadiad, Gujarat, India; son of Suresh C Dixit and Naren S Dixit; married Darshana A Dixit, Oct 28, 1981; children: Nilesh A. **EDUCATION:** University of Bombay, BS, 1970; Indian Institute of Technology, MS, 1973; University of Maine, MS, 1976; University of Mississippi, PhD, 1980. **CAREER:** Olin Corp, staff research chemist, 1981-85; P H Glatfelter Co, research associate, 1985-89, supervisor, 1990-. **ORGANIZATIONS:** American Chemistry Society, 1974-; Sigma Xi, 1980-; TAPPI, 1981-; American Institute of Chemistry, professional chemist, 1976-; CPPA, 1985-. **HONORS/AWARDS:** National Council for Education Research, National Science Talent Award, 1967; Rotary Club, Best Student Prize, 1970; TAPPI, Frank Ferrell Award, 1992. **SPECIAL ACHIEVEMENTS:** US Patents, 1984, 1990, 1993; published 20 journal articles, 1980-. **BIOGRAPHICAL SOURCES:** TAPPI Journal, p 223, Oct 1992. **HOME ADDRESS:** 14 Goldmine Ridge, Pisgah Forest, NC 28768, (704)884-9873. **BUSINESS ADDRESS:** Research Scientist, P H Glatfelter Co, 1 Ecusta Rd, Pisgah Forest, NC 28768-9774, (704)877-2333.

DIXIT, BALWANT N.
Educator. Indo-American. **PERSONAL:** Born Jan 7, 1933, Kerawade, Maharashtra, India; son of Narayan V Dixit and Janakibai N Dixit; married Vidya, Dec 26, 1969; children: Sunil, Sanjay. **EDUCATION:** Poona University, India, BSc, 1955, MSc, 1956; MS University of Baroda, India, MSc, 1962; University of Pittsburgh, PhD, 1965. **CAREER:** University of Pittsburgh, assistant professor, 1965-68, associate professor, 1968-74, associate dean, pharmacy, 1974-84, acting dean, pharmacy, 1976-78, chairman, pharmacology, 1974-87, assistant chairman, pharmacology, 1969-74, professor of pharmacology, 1974-. **ORGANIZATIONS:** NY Acad Sciences, 1965-; American Society Pharm & Expt Ther, 1969-; American Association Adv Science, 1965-; Society Neurosciences, 1974-; Society Xenobiotic Metab, 1969-. **HONORS/AWARDS:** International Union of Physiological Sci, international fellow, 1962; University of Pittsburgh, School of Pharmacy, Distinguished Alumnus, 1982. **BUSINESS ADDRESS:** Professor, University of Pittsburgh, 541-2 Salk Hall, Pittsburgh, PA 15261, (412)648-8582.

DIXIT, PADMAKAR KASHINATH
Educator (retired). Indo-American. **PERSONAL:** Born Aug 7, 1921, Calcutta, W. Bengal, India; married Vimal, Jan 5, 1948; children: 3. **EDUCATION:** University of Bombay, BSc, 1942, MSc, 1946, PhD, 1948. **CAREER:** University of Minnesota, professor, retired. **SPECIAL ACHIEVEMENTS:** Over 90 publications.

DIXIT, SUDHAKAR GAJANAN (BAL)
Company executive. Indo-American. **PERSONAL:** Born Mar 1, 1939, Katol Nagpur, Maharashtra, India; son of Sushila Dixit and Gajanan Dixit; married Anita Dixit, Jan 12, 1968; children: Sadhana, Sunil. **EDUCATION:** Lowell Technological Institute, MS, 1966; Rochester Institute of Technology, MBA, 1974. **CAREER:** Union Carbide Corporation, advanced technologist, 1966-68; Garlock Inc, Div of Coltec, operations manager, 1968-78; Newtex Industries Inc, founder, president, CEO, 1978-. **ORGANIZATIONS:** Greater Rochester Metro Chamber of Commerce, trustee, 1988-94, Intl Business Council, advisory board, exec vp, 1992; Rochester General Hospital, director, 1992; Compeer Inc, director, 1991; Chase Manhattan Bank, Metropolitan Advisory Board, 1986-; US Dept of Commerce, Upstate NY Dist Council Export, vice chairman, 1992-95; Finger Lakes Regional Economic Council, vice chairman, 1985-; Federal Reserve Bank of NY, advisory board, 1992. **HONORS/AWARDS:** Governor of New York State, commendation, 1989; NYS Governor's Award, 1983; Small Business Person of the Year Award, Region II, winner, 1984; Greater Rochester Metro Chamber of Commerce, Civic Award, 1991; Indian Association of Rochester, Family of the Year Award, 1992; Association of Indians of America, Genesee Valley Chapter, Civic Award, 1992; Brihan Maharashtra Mandal, Recognition Award, 1993. **SPECIAL ACHIEVEMENTS:** "Development of Asbestos Substitutes," ASTM; "Performance of Protective Clothing," ASTM. **BIOGRAPHICAL SOURCES:** Rochester Business Magazine, Dec 1992, p 28; Rochester Democrat & Chronicle, April 8, 1992. **BUSINESS ADDRESS:** President and CEO, Newtex Industries Inc, 8050 Victor-Mendon Rd, Victor, NY 14564, (716)924-9135.

DIXIT, SUDHIR SHARAN
Electrical engineer. Indo-American. **PERSONAL:** Born Jun 20, 1951, Lucknow, Uttar Pradesh, India; son of Shambhoo S Dixit & Urmila Dixit; married Asha Dixit, Feb 20, 1981; children: Sapna, Amar. **EDUCATION:** Bhopal University, India, BE, 1972; Birla Institute of Technology and Science, India, ME, 1974; University of Strathclyde, UK, PhD, 1979; Florida Institute of Technology, MBA, 1983. **CAREER:** BNR Europe Ltd, postgraduate research engineer, 1978-80; Harris Corp, associate principal engineer, 1980-83; Codex Motorola Corp, Canton, principal engineer, 1983-85; Wang Labs Inc, principal engineer, 1985-87; GTE Labs Inc, technical staff, 1987-91; NYNEX Corp, technical staff, 1991-. **ORGANIZATIONS:** Institute of Electrical & Electronics Engineers, 1980-. **HONORS/AWARDS:** GTE Corp, 3 Patent Achievement Awards, 1992; University of Strathclyde, Postgraduate Open Fellowship, 1974-78; British Council, Tuition Fee Award, 1974-75; Government of India, UGC Postgraduate Fellowship, 1972-74, Merit Certificate for Standing High in Merit, 1967. **SPECIAL ACHIEVEMENTS:** Over 20 publications, presentations in journals & international conference proceedings; 4 US patents granted, 1 patent pending. **HOME ADDRESS:** 25 Devon Rd, Norwood, MA 02062, (617)769-1107. **BUSINESS ADDRESS:** Technical Staff, NYNEX Science & Technology Inc, 38 Sidney St, Ste 180, Cambridge, MA 02139, (617)374-8061.

DJAO, ANGELA WEI
Educator, painter, writer. Chinese American. **EDUCATION:** University of Toronto, BA, 1969, MA, 1971, PhD, 1976. **CAREER:** University of Saskatchewan, assoc professor, sociology, 1978-85; University of Toronto, visiting professor, social work, 1985-86; Lingnan College, Hong Kong, sr lecturer, sociology, 1986-87; California State University, visiting professor, sociology, 1987-88; De Anza College, professor, sociology, 1989-90; University of Washington, visiting lecturer, Canadian studies, 1991-; North Seattle College, professor, Asian studies, 1993-. **ORGANIZATIONS:** Centre of Asian Studies, University of Hong Kong, visiting scholar, 1973-74; Lingnan College, Social Issues and Policy Program, coordinator, 1986-87; Asian American Committee of Community Involvement, San Jose Branch, 1989-90; Natl Child Poverty Action Assn, steering committee, 1986; Immigrant Women of Saskatchewan, vp, 1983-85; Saskatoon Self-Help, board of directors, 1984-85; Saskatoon Human Rights Assn, 1981-83; Chinese Cultural Society of Saskatchewan, president, 1979-80. **SPECIAL ACHIEVEMENTS:** Author: Choices and Chances: Sociology for Everyday Life, San Diego, Harcourt Brace Jovanovich, 1990; Inequality and Social Policy: The Sociology of Welfare, Toronto, John Wiley and Sons, 1983. **BUSINESS ADDRESS:** Professor, Social Sciences

Division, North Seattle College, 9600 College Way N, Seattle, WA 98103, (206)528-3830.

DO, TOA QUANG

Company executive, community activist. Vietnamese American. **PERSONAL:** Born Jun 28, 1950, Vietnam; son of Do Trong Thac and Nguyen Thi Huyen; married Le-Hang T Phan, Sep 1974; children: Khoi Ba, Nguyen Ba. **EDUCATION:** University of Saigon, Faculty of Letters, Vietnam, BA, English, 1971; National Institute of Administration, Saigon, MPA, 1974. **CAREER:** United Nations High Commissioner for Refugees, camp assistant, 1980; Government of Vietnam, Rach Gia City, chief of administrative service, 1975; Development Alternatives Inc, director of procurement and logistics, 1980-87; World Bank, systems consultant, 1986; Island Airline, consultant; Computer Sciences Corp, senior systems analyst, 1987-90; Amtek Systems Inc, executive vice president/owner, 1990-92; International Devlopment & Resources, senior analyst/consultant, 1992-94; Business Development Assistance Group Inc, president, 1992-. **ORGANIZATIONS:** Arlington Chamber of Commerce, board of directors, 1991-; Fairfax County School Board, Human Relations Advisory Committee, chairman, 1991-92; Arlington County Visitor's Commission, 1993-; George Mason University, Scholars Selection Committee, 1993-; Advisory Council to the African-American Indochinese Alliance, 1992-; The Vietnamese American Community of WDC-MD-VA, executive director, 1990-92; Small Business Development Program, Vietnamese, program director, 1991-93; Arlington Economic Development Commission, 1991-93; Fairfax County Community Correction Resouces Board. **HONORS/AWARDS:** Arlington Chamber of Commerce, Friends of Small Business Award, 1993; American field Service, Student Exchange Scholarship, 1967. **SPECIAL ACHIEVEMENTS:** First Asian-American ever elected to the board of directors of the Arlington Chamber of Commerce and Executive Committee, 1991; author, "Project Management Guidelines," Agency for International Development, 1987; lecturer, "Computers for Non-technical Managers," University of Pittsburgh, 1984-88, LT Associates, with Florida Atlantic University, 1988-93; chairman of the first and largest Minority Business Opportunity Fairs held in Arlington, VA, June 18, 1992, and June 23, 1993. **BIOGRAPHICAL SOURCES:** CBS News, "The World of Differneces," April 1991; The Washington Post, Feb 1991, July 1992; The Detroit News, July 1992; Arlington Journal, 1991-93; Arlington Courier, 1991-93; Voice of America, 1993. **HOME ADDRESS:** 4440 Scarborough Sq, Alexandria, VA 22309.

DOAN, PHUNG LIEN. See PHUNG, DOAN LIEN.

DODDAPANENI, NARAYAN

Scientist. Indo-American. **PERSONAL:** Born Aug 10, 1942, Khammam, Andhra Pradesh, India; son of Tirupalhamma & Pedapitchaiah Doddapaneni; married Rita, Jul 13, 1972; children: Ajay, Aruna. **EDUCATION:** Osmania University, India, BSc, 1962, MSc, 1964; Case Western Reserve University, PhD, 1972. **CAREER:** Gould Inc, staff scientist, 1977-80; Honeywell Inc, sr principal research scientist, 1980-90; Sandia Natl Laboratories, sr member of tech staff, 1990-. **ORGANIZATIONS:** American Chem Soc; Electrochem Soc. **HOME ADDRESS:** 10516 Royal Birkdale NE, Albuquerque, NM 87111, (505)293-9298.

DOI, ROY HIROSHI

Educator. Japanese American. **PERSONAL:** Born Mar 26, 1933, Sacramento, CA; son of Thomas Toshiteru Doi and Ima Doi; married Joyce N Takahashi, Aug 30, 1958 (divorced); children: Kathryn Ellen, Douglas Alan; married Joan Maria Ritchie, Feb 14, 1992. **EDUCATION:** Placer Junior College, AA, 1951; University of California, Berkeley, AB, 1953, AB, 1957; University of Wisconsin, Madison, MS, 1958, PhD, 1960. **CAREER:** Syracuse University, microbiology, assistant professor, 1963-65; University of California, biochemistry, assistant professor, 1965-66, associate professor, 1966-69, professor, 1969-; Dept of Biochem-Biophys, chair, 1974-77, Biotechnology Program, director, 1989-92. **ORGANIZATIONS:** American Society for Microbiology, 1958-; American Association for Advancement of Science, 1965-, fellow, 1988; American Society for Biochemistry & Molecular Biology, 1965-; Society of Chinese Bioscientists in America, 1988-. **HONORS/AWARDS:** National Institutes of Health, Postdoctoral Fellowship, 1960; National Science Foundation, Sr Postdoctoral Fellow, 1971; Alexander von Humboldt Foundation, Senior US Scientist Award, 1978; Naito Foundation Award, Visiting Scientist Award, 1986; American Association Advancement Science, fellow, 1988. **SPECIAL ACHIEVEMENTS:** Co-author, Outlines of Biochemistry, 1987; editor, Biology of Bacilli, 1992; over 180 publications on microbiology, molecular biology. **MILITARY SERVICE:** US Army, sp 4, 1953-55. **BUSINESS AD-**

DRESS: Professor of Biochemistry, University of California, Section of Molecular and Cellular Bology, Davis, CA 95616, (916)752-3191.

DOI, STAN SUMIO

Forestry company manager. Japanese American. **PERSONAL:** Born Feb 5, 1947, British Columbia; son of Kevichi and Sumiko; married Betty, Jul 24, 1970; children: Chad. **EDUCATION:** Selark College, 1968. **CAREER:** Triangle Pacific Corp, woodlands manager, 1968-80; Louisiana Pacific Corp, resource manager, 1981-84, general manager, 1985-. **HOME ADDRESS:** 2603 33rd Ave SE, Puyallup, WA 98374, (206)279-8014.

DOI, STANLEY T.

Business executive. Japanese American. **PERSONAL:** Born 1935, Honolulu, HI. **EDUCATION:** University of Hawaii, 1958. **CAREER:** James W Glover Ltd, president, currently. **ORGANIZATIONS:** American Society of Civil Engineers. **BUSINESS ADDRESS:** President, James W Glover Ltd, PO Box 579, Honolulu, HI 96809-0579, (808)533-1777.*

DOLOR, DEOGRACIAS ASUNCION, JR. (TONY)

Engineer. Filipino American. **PERSONAL:** Born Jun 12, 1942, Binalonan, Pangasinan, Philippines; son of Deogracias and Felipa; married Juanita Villanueva Dolor, Jan 31, 1972; children: Dinah, Marilou, Jeannette. **EDUCATION:** Mapua Institute of Technology, BSME, 1967. **CAREER:** United Drug Co, Philippines, mechanics, 1967-70; US Air Force Base, Clark Field, Philippines, civilian employee, 1970-72; Products Research & Chemical Corp, "A" mechanic, 1972-79; Southern California Edison, electrical repairman, 1979-. **ORGANIZATIONS:** Binalonan Assn of Southern California. **HONORS/AWARDS:** Various awards from Southern California Edison. **HOME ADDRESS:** 25 Viewpoint Circle, Pomona, CA 91766, (909)397-9706.

DOMINGO, CYNTHIA GARCIANO

Legislative aide. Filipino American. **PERSONAL:** Born Dec 14, 1953, Killeen, TX; daughter of Adelina and Nemesio Domingo Sr; married Garry Wade Owens, Apr 7, 1990; children: Malik Silme Domingo Owens, Jamil Nemesio Domingo Owens. **EDUCATION:** University of Washington, BA, 1976; Goddard College, MA, 1977. **CAREER:** University of California, Berkeley, program assistant, 1977-81; Committee for Justice for Domingo and Viernes, national coordinator, 1981-83; Central Area Motivation Program, program director, 1983-93; legislative aide, currently. **ORGANIZATIONS:** Northwest Labor and Employment Law Office, treasurer, 1991-; Institute for Global Security Studies, vice president, 1988-; Asia Pacific Task Force, co-chair, 1989-, Church Council of Greater Seattle, board member, secretary, 1987-92; American Friends Service Committee, Third World Coalition, 1987-1990; Union of Democratic Filipinos, national executive committee, 1976-86; Nuclear Free Pacific Network, steering committee, 1983-86. **HONORS/AWARDS:** Martin Luther King Day Organizing Committee, Annual MLK Award, 1990; Asian Pacific Women's Caucus, Woman Warrior Award in Politics, 1988; People of Color Against AIDS Network, Outstanding Community Organizer, 1990; Church Women United, Seattle Chapter, Annual Women's Award, 1991. **HOME ADDRESS:** 8025 25th Ave NW, Seattle, WA 98117, (206)789-6231.

DOMINH, THAP

Research chemist. Vietnamese American. **PERSONAL:** Born Dec 25, 1938, Tando, Hadong, Vietnam; son of Do Trong Hop and Do Thi Xang; married Lehao N Dominh, Sep 12, 1964; children: Bernard, Pauline. **EDUCATION:** University of Chicago, MS, 1962, PhD, 1966. **CAREER:** University of Alberta, research associate, 1966-69; Bell Laboratories, member of technical staff, 1969-72; Eastman Kodak, senior research chemist, 1972-78, research associate, 1978-88, technical associate, 1988-. **SPECIAL ACHIEVEMENTS:** Inventor, 15 US patents; in 1985, US patent no 4,548,987, hybrid thermal film selected as technology most likely to impact on industrial use of silver, Silver Institute, 1986; author of 24 scientific publications and 58 technical reports on reaction mechanism, photochromics, imaging sciences, photoresist and lithographic printing plates. **BUSINESS ADDRESS:** Technical Associate, Eastman Kodak Co, 9952 Eastman Park Dr, C-60, Windsor, CO 80551-1610, (303)686-4685.

DOMONDON, OSCAR

Dentist. Filipino American. **PERSONAL:** Born Jul 4, 1924, Cabu City, Philippines; son of Antero & Ursula Domondon; married Vicky G Domondon, Oct 29, 1983; children: Reinelda, Carolyn, Catherine, Oscar Jr. **EDUCATION:** Philippine Dental College, DMD, 1951; St Marys University, San Antonio

College, pre-dental, 1960; Loma Linda University, DDS, 1964; University of Washington, 1986. **CAREER:** San Bernardino County Hospital, 1960-63; dentist, 1964-; State Board of Dental Examiners, 1977-87; Cypress College, dental hygiene clinic supervisor, 1990-. **ORGANIZATIONS:** Filipino American Republicans, California state chairman, 1991-; Filipino American Chamber of Commerce of Long Beach, vp, 1993; Filipino Community Action Services, president, 1972-73; Harbor Dental Society, secretary, 1993-94; Long Beach Board of Health, 1991-93; Kavumangi Lions Club, president, 1983-94. **HONORS/AWARDS:** Academy of Continuing Education, fellowship, 1987; American College of Dentists, fellowship, 1986; International College of Dentists, fellowship, 1984; Academy of Dentistry International, fellowship, 1978; Academy of International Dental Studies, fellowship, 1982; Academy of General Dentistry, fellowship, 1971; International Institute of Community Service, fellowship, 1975. **SPECIAL ACHIEVEMENTS:** State of California, appointment to State Board of Dental Examiners, 1979. **MILITARY SERVICE:** Army, 1st sgt, 1946-49, 1954-60. **BUSINESS ADDRESS:** President, Crown Dental Supply, 3714 Atlantic Ave, Long Beach, CA 90807, (310)426-6591.

DOMOTO, DOUGLASS T.
Educator. Japanese American. **PERSONAL:** Born Sep 17, 1943, Elgin, IL; son of Toichi & Alice Domoto; married Betsy Hall Domoto, Jun 19, 1970; children: Alyson. **EDUCATION:** Stanford University, BA, 1965; Yale University, MD, 1969; St Louis University, School of Law, 1990-. **CAREER:** University of Chicago, assistant professor, 1978-82; St Louis University, associate professor, 1982-. **ORGANIZATIONS:** National Kidney Foundation, Medical Review Board, president, 1992-93; Missouri Kidney Program, advisory council, 1992-; Renal Network #12, Medical Review Board, 1988-; American Society Nephrology, 1978-; International Society for Peritoneal Dialysis, 1984-; American Society for Hypertension, 1989-. **HONORS/AWARDS:** Missouri Kidney Program, research grant, 1984-85. **MILITARY SERVICE:** Army, major, 1972-74; Joint Service Commendation Medal, 1973. **BUSINESS ADDRESS:** Associate Professor, Dept of Internal Medicine, St Louis University, 3635 Vista at Grand Blvd, PO Box 15250, St Louis, MO 63110-0250, (314)577-8765.

DON, JAMES E.
Attorney, judge. Chinese American. **PERSONAL:** Born Dec 23, 1932, Casa Grande, AZ; son of June Don & Oi Shau Don; married Nancy L Don. **EDUCATION:** Arizona State University, BS, 1956; University of Arizona Law School, JD, 1963. **CAREER:** Pinal County, Arizona, deputy county attorney, 1965, chief deputy county attorney, 1968-74, county attorney, 1974-77, Superior Court, judge, 1978-. **ORGANIZATIONS:** Arizona County Attorney's Association; Arizona Prosecuting Attorney's Advisory Council; Pinal Co Bar Association, past president; Arizona Judges Association; American Judicature Society; Phi Delta Phi, life member. **HONORS/AWARDS:** Arizona County Attorney's Association, Outstanding County Attorney of the Year, 1977. **BUSINESS ADDRESS:** Judge, Superior Court, Pinal County, Arizona, PO Box 828, Florence, AZ 85232, (602)868-6332.

DONG, ARTHUR
Filmmaker. Chinese American. **PERSONAL:** Born Oct 30, 1953, San Francisco, CA; son of Don M Dong and Zem P Dong; married Young B Gee, 1978; children: Herbie, Zippers, Velcro. **EDUCATION:** San Francisco State University, BA (summa cum laude), film, 1982; American Film Institute, Center for Advanced Film Studies, certificate of completion, Director's Fellowship Program, 1985. **CAREER:** KGO-TV, associate producer, 1981-82; KCET-TV, producer, 1991-92; Deepfocus Productions, producer, director, writer, 1982-. **ORGANIZATIONS:** Intl Documentary Assn; American Film Institute; Assn of Independent Film & Video; Film Arts Foundation; Natl Asian American Telecommunications Assn; Asian CineVision; Visual Communications, instructor; Frameline (San Francisco Lesbian & Gay Intl Film Festival), bd of advisers; Gay & Lesbian Media Coalition. **HONORS/AWARDS:** Film: Sewing Woman, Academy Award Nomination, Best Short Documentary, 1983; film: Forbidden City, USA: Hawaii Intl Film Festival, 1990, Best Documentary of the Decade, shared, 1990; Assn of Asian Pacific American Artists, "Jimmy" (James Wong Howe Media Award), 1990; American Film & Video Festival, Blue Ribbon, 1990; film: Lotus: American Film Festival, Red Ribbon, 1989; Council on Intl Non-theatrical Events, Cine Golden Eagle, 1990; other awards: Visual Communications, Steve Tatsukawa Award, 1993; California Arts Council Media Artist Fellowship, 1992; San Francisco Foundation's James D Phelan Award in Filmmaking, 1990. **SPECIAL ACHIEVEMENTS:** Producer/director/writer: Coming Out Under Fire, 1994; Tap! The Tempo Of America,

forthcoming; Forbidden City, USA, 1989; Life & Times, 10 documentaries for this series from PBS/KCET TV, Los Angeles, 1991-92; Claiming A Voice: The Visual Communications Story, director/writer, 1990; Lotus, producer/director/writer/editor, 1988. **BIOGRAPHICAL SOURCES:** Over 150 various features and reviews in national and international publications. **BUSINESS ADDRESS:** Producer, Director, Writer, Deep Focus Productions, 4506 Palmero Dr, Los Angeles, CA 90065-4237.

DONG, JOHN W.
Computer manufacturing company executive. Chinese American. **PERSONAL:** Born Jun 8, 1954, Phoenix, AZ; son of William Dong and Mary Dong; married Mimi, Aug 20, 1988. **EDUCATION:** Massachusetts Institute of Technology, BSME, 1975, MSME, 1976. **CAREER:** Hewlett-Packard Co, production engineer, 1976-77, R&D design engineer, 1978-90, production engineering manager, 1990-. **HONORS/AWARDS:** Industrial Design Magazine, Designer's Choice, 1985. **SPECIAL ACHIEVEMENTS:** Two US Patents, 1989; "A Reliable, Autoloading, Streaming 1/2 Tape Drive," Hewlett-Packard Journal, June 1988; "Streaming Tape Drive Hardware Design," Hewlett-Packard Journal, March 1985. **HOME ADDRESS:** 369 Wyndham Ave, Greeley, CO 80634, (303)330-4220.

DONG, WEI
Design educator. Chinese American. **PERSONAL:** Born Dec 3, 1959, Beijing, People's Republic of China; son of Jun-Fang Na and Jin-Lai Dong; married Xia Gu, Jun 2, 1990; children: Charles Jiayi Dong. **EDUCATION:** Central Academy of Arts & Design, BA, interior design, 1984; Virginia Commonwealth University, MFA, interior environment, 1988. **CAREER:** Beijing Institute of Architecture and Design, interior architect, 1984-86; Virginia Commonwealth University, teaching assistant, 1986-88; Marcellus Wright Cox & Smith Architects, interior designer, 1988-89; Iowa State University, assistant professor, 1989-93; University of Wisconsin, Madison, assistant professor, 1993-. **ORGANIZATIONS:** Interior Design Educators Council, Juried Exhibition Committee, corporate member, co-chair, 1989-; Design Communication Association, interior design director, 1990-; China Institute of Interior Architects, honorable member, 1992-. **HONORS/AWARDS:** College of Design, Iowa State University, Extraordinary Performance in Teaching, 1992; Interior Design Educators Council, National Juried Exhibition Winner, 1992; Iowa State University, Outstanding Instructor, selected by Kappa Sorority, 1990; China Institute of Architecture, Second Prize in Great Wall Museum Competition, 1985; Beijing Institute of Furniture Design, First Prize in Design, 1985. **SPECIAL ACHIEVEMENTS:** Panel discussion: "Global Understanding: Contributions to Interior Design Education," IOEC National Conference, 1993; paper with Mary Anne Beecher, "Harmony and Contradiction: Communication Technology as Applied Within Diverse Cultures," 10th International Conference, MIT, 1993; article, "Linkages Between Process Drawing and Theory," Representation, 1991; one person art show, Contemporary Oriental Arts, 1990. **BIOGRAPHICAL SOURCES:** "Eastern Artist Combines Cultures at VCU," Commonwealth Time, p 7, May 2, 1987; Faculty Achievements, ISU College of Design, p 4, Fall 1991. **BUSINESS ADDRESS:** Assistant Professor, Dept of Environment, Textiles and Design, University of Wisconsin, Madison, 1300 Linden Dr, Madison, WI 53706, (608)262-8805.

DONG, ZHENG-MIN
Educator. Chinese American. **PERSONAL:** Born Apr 28, 1941, Shanghai, China; son of Shang-quan Dong and Li-zhen Tang; married Wei Qian, Oct 22, 1972; children: Jun-Qing Dong. **EDUCATION:** Shanghai International Studies University, diploma, 1964, MA, 1982; University of Washington, PhD, 1990. **CAREER:** Shanghai Xin Li Middle School, Russian teacher, 1966-78; Shanghai Bei Jiao Middle School, English teacher, 1978-79; Shanghai International Studies University, lecturer, 1982-86; Washington State University, assistant professor, 1990-. **ORGANIZATIONS:** American Association of Teachers of Slavic and East European Languages, 1991-; American Association for the Advancement of Slavic Studies, 1993-; Modern Language Association, 1992-; Pacific Northwest Council on Foreign Languages, 1992-; Washington Association of Foreign Language Teachers, 1992-; China's Russian Language Teaching Association, 1982-86. **HONORS/AWARDS:** University of Washington, Recruitment Fellowship, 1986; Dissertation Scholarship, 1990; Washington State University, International Program Development Mini-Grant, 1991-92; Arts and Humanities Travel Grant, 1992-93. **SPECIAL ACHIEVEMENTS:** Books: Russian Grammar, syntax, co-translator, 1991; Schiller, co-translator, 1992; Dictionary: Government in Russian, co-author, 1987; Sentence Types in Russian, principal author, 1986; Basic Russian Textbook, principal author, 1986. **BUSINESS ADDRESS:** Asst Professor, Dept of For-

eign Languages and Literature, Washington State University, Thompson Hall, Rm 223 H, Pullman, WA 99164-2610, (509)335-4162.

DOO, JACK P., JR.
Editor, author. Chinese American. **PERSONAL:** Born Dec 12, 1953, Turlock, CA; son of Jack P Doo Sr and Mei Fun Doo; married Catherine L Doo, Jun 6, 1982; children: Brandon, Barrett. **EDUCATION:** Stanislaus State University, 1972-73; Sacramento State University, degrees, 1976. **CAREER:** The Modesto Bee, sports writer, 1977-78, business writer/columnist, 1978-90, weekend editor, 1990-. **ORGANIZATIONS:** National Automotive Journalism Association, chairman, 1989-90; Motoring Press Association, president, 1980-82; Northern California Newspaper Guild, president, 1983; North Modesto Kiwanis Club, director, 1989. **HONORS/AWARDS:** National Automotive Journalism Association, 1st place winner of six Moto awards for excellence in journalism, 1987-89. **SPECIAL ACHIEVEMENTS:** Author: Exotic Japanese Cars, Motorbooks Intl; Front-Wheel-Drive High-Performance Advantage, Motorbooks Intl; The Ultimate Owners Manual, Edmunds Publications. **BUSINESS ADDRESS:** Weekend Editor, The Modesto Bee, PO Box 3928, Modesto, CA 95352, (209)578-2340.

DOO, LEIGH-WAI
City official, attorney. Chinese American. **PERSONAL:** Born May 13, 1946, Honolulu, HI; son of Mee Chow Doo and Florence Young Doo; married Linda Carlsen Doo; children: Jamie, Adam, Britni, Tyler. **EDUCATION:** American College, Paris, France, AA, 1966; Columbia University, AB, 1968; Harvard Law School, JD, 1971. **CAREER:** Judiciary Committee, Hawaii House of Representatives, attorney, 1971-72; Counties of Kauai, Honolulu, Maui, Hawaii, chief instructor, 1972; Supreme Court, Hawaii, law clerk, 1972; University of Hawaii, Law School, founding assistant dean, 1973-77; Honolulu City Council, council member, 1983-94; Attorney in private practice, 1971-. **ORGANIZATIONS:** Chinese Chamber of Commerce Legislative and Government Affairs Commission; Pacific and Asian Affairs Council; Interfaith Ministries of Hawaii, board of directors; Japanese Chamber of Commerce; Asian Pacific Lawyers Association; National League of Cities-Asian Pacific Municipal Officers, secretary, treasurer; National Association of Counties-Chair, Subcommittee on Coastal Zone Management; American and Hawaii Bar Associations. **SPECIAL ACHIEVEMENTS:** Author, "Dispute Settlement in the Chinese-American Communities," UC Berkeley (Boalt Hall), American Journal of Comparative Law, vol 21, no 4, 1973; reprinted in Harvard Law School Studies in East Asian Law, China no 22, 1974; monograph repoduced in the Yale Law School, casebook series, and the University of Hawaii School of Law, Legal Methods Class; Malama Aina, Care for the Land, A Citizen's Guide to Land Use Planning in the City and County of Honolulu, with Roy Takemoto and Joanne Tachibana, unpublished. **HOME ADDRESS:** 3003 Waiomao Homestead Rd, Honolulu, HI 96816, (808)732-0006. **BUSINESS ADDRESS:** Council Member, City Council, City & County of Honolulu, 530 S King St, Honolulu Hale, Second Floor, Honolulu, HI 96813, (808)523-4615.

DOSHI, BIPIN N.
Gear manufacturing company executive. Indo-American. **PERSONAL:** Born Sep 12, 1939, Gujarat, India; son of Narottamdas and Pushpa; married Linda Stone, Jan 8, 1966; children: Marcus, Robert. **EDUCATION:** University of Bombay, India, BSc, chemistry, physics, 1959; University of Missouri, BSChE, 1962, MSChE, 1963. **CAREER:** Uniroyal Chemical Co Inc, new business manager, 1963-82; Uniroyal Plastics Co Inc, general manager, vice pres, 1982-88; Andert Manufacturing Inc, president, owner, 1992-; Schafer Gear Works Inc, president, owner, 1988-. **ORGANIZATIONS:** AIChE, 1963-; American Gear Mfg Assn, Small Business Council, chairman, 1992-; South Bend Symphony Orchestra, bd member, 1992-. **BUSINESS ADDRESS:** President/Owner, Schafer Gear Works, Inc, 814 S Main St, South Bend, IN 46601, (219)234-4116.

DOW, FAYE LYNN
Government administrator. Hong Kong American. **PERSONAL:** Born in Hong Kong. **CAREER:** US Department of Health and Human Services, Office of Civil Rights, equal opportunity specialist, 1992-. **SPECIAL ACHIEVEMENTS:** Language proficency: Mandarin, Cantonese, Toisanese. **BUSINESS ADDRESS:** Equal Opportunity Specialist, Office of Civil Rights, US Dept of Health & Human Services, 2201 6th Ave, Mail Stop Rx11, Seattle, WA 98121.*

DOYLE, RUTH NARITA
Religious researcher. Japanese American. **PERSONAL:** Born in London, England; daughter of Masaaki & Tami Narita; married Stephen D Doyle; children: Michael, Peter, Elizabeth. **EDUCATION:** Manhattanville College, BA, 1951; Fordham University, MA, 1955, PhD cand, 1994. **CAREER:** Executive Council of the Episcopal Church, researcher, 1969-72; Archdiocese of New York, Office of Pastoral Research & Planning, research associate, 1972-80, director, 1981-. **ORGANIZATIONS:** Religious Research Association, 1973-, board of directors, 1990-94; Conference for Pastoral Planning and Council Developments, 1973-, steering committee, 1988-91; Association for the Sociology of Religion, 1974-; Archdiocese of New York, Interreligious & Ecumenical Commission, 1988-, Intercultural Council, 1991-; Greater Chinatown Community Association, board member, 1991-. **SPECIAL ACHIEVEMENTS:** Co-editor & principal researcher for Hispanics in New York, 1st & 2nd edition, 1988; co-editors & principal researcher for One Faith, One Hope, One Baptisim, a study of the African American Community in New York; NCEA, co-editor & contributing author; A Catholic Response to the Asian Presence, 1990. **HOME ADDRESS:** 6035 Broadway, Bronx, NY 10471, (718)543-8118. **BUSINESS ADDRESS:** Director, Office of Pastoral Research & Planning, Archdiocese of New York, 1011 First Ave, New York, NY 10022-4134, (212)371-1000.

DOZONO, SHO G.
Corporate officer. Japanese American. **PERSONAL:** Born Mar 4, 1944, Okayama, Japan; son of Asao & Yoneko Dozono; married Loen Azumano Dozono, Jun 8, 1968; children: Elisa, Kristen, Alison, Stephanie, Tad. **EDUCATION:** University of Washington, BA, history, 1967; Portland State University, MEd, 1968. **CAREER:** Grant High School, history teacher, 1971-76; Dozono Enterprises, president, 1988-; ISU/Azumano Insurance, partner, 1976-; Azumano Travel Service, vice president-operations, 1980-87, president, CEO, 1987-. **ORGANIZATIONS:** Port of Portland, commissioner, 1989-93; Portland Oregon Visitors Association, board member, 1986-, past president, 1991-93; Japan America Society of Oregon, board member, 1985-; Japan America Society, president elect, 1993-95; Chamber of Commerce, board member, 1991-; Japanese Garden Society, board member, 1981-; Portland Art Museum, board member, 1990-. **HONORS/AWARDS:** Metropolitan Human Relations Commission, Distinguished Service Award, 1990. **SPECIAL ACHIEVEMENTS:** Congressional Hearing, Delta Air Lines PDX/NGO Connection, Washington, DC, 1991; World Affairs Council, "Corporate Life in the Japanese Community," 1990; Idaho Tourism Council, "Pacific Rim Tourism," 1981. **MILITARY SERVICE:** United States Army, Adjutant General Corps, 1st lieutenant, 1969-71; Distinguished Military Graduate Commission, 1969. **BUSINESS ADDRESS:** President, CEO, Azumano Travel Service, 320 SW Stark St, Ste 600, Portland, OR 97204, (503)223-6245.

D'SOUZA, HARRY J.
Educator. Indo-American. **PERSONAL:** Born Dec 24, 1955, Danambur, Karnataka, India; son of Joseph D'Souza and Lily D'Souza. **EDUCATION:** St Xavier's College, Bombay, BSc, 1976; University of Bombay, Kalina Campus, MSc, 1978; University of Notre Dame, MS, 1980, PhD, 1983. **CAREER:** University of Michigan, Flint, Dept of Math, associate professor, 1983-. **ORGANIZATIONS:** American Mathematical Society, 1978-; Mathematical Association of America, 1989-. **HONORS/AWARDS:** University of Michigan, Flint, Faculty Award for Scholarly Achievement, 1992; Michigan Association for Governors Board, Award for Scholarly Achievement, 1993; National Scholar of University Grants Commission, Bombay, 1977-78. **SPECIAL ACHIEVEMENTS:** Fluent in Hindi, Italian and 3 Indian languages; published articles in: Proceedings of AMS, 1988, Pacific J of Math, 1988, Comptes Rendues Math, Royal Society of Canada, 1989, Tohoku J of Mathematics, Japan, 1989, Math Scandinavia, Sweden, 1990. **HOME ADDRESS:** 13059 Lockmoor Drive, Grand Blanc, MI 48439-1577. **BUSINESS ADDRESS:** Associate Professor of Mathematics, University of Michigan, Flint, 303 E Kearsley St 403 MSB, Flint, MI 48502-2186, (313)762-3159.

DUBEY, SATYA DEVA
Government official. Indo-American. **PERSONAL:** Born Feb 10, 1930, Sakara Bajid, Bihar, India; son of Jagdish Narayan & Sahodra Misra Dubey; married Joyce, Jun 18, 1960; children: Jay Dev, Dean Dev, Neal Narayan. **EDUCATION:** Patna University, India, Mathematics Honors Program, BS (honors), 1951; Indian Statistical Institute, 2 year diploma, 1953; Michigan State University, PhD, statistics, 1960. **CAREER:** Procter & Gamble Co, head of statistics section, 1960-66; Ford Motor Co, principal statistician & group leader, 1966-68; NYU, associate professor, 1968-73; FDA, chief, SEB, BD,

NCBD, CDB, 1973-84, acting director, DB, 1975-76, acting director, DB, 1989-90, chief, SERB, 1984-. **ORGANIZATIONS:** American Association for the Advancement of Science, fellow; American Statistical Association, fellow; New York Academy of Sciences, fellow; Washington Academy of Sciences, fellow; Royal Statistical Society, London, fellow; International Statistical Institute; numerous others. **HONORS/AWARDS:** FDA, Commendable Service Award, 1977, Award of Merit, 1984, 1987, Equal Opportunity Achievement Award, 1986, Commissioner's Special Citation, 1987; PHS, Superior Service Award, 1988, Equal Opportunity Achievement Award, 1991; Parklawn Asian, Pacific American Community, Outstanding Achievement Award, 1989; Distinguished Leadership ABI Award, 1991; Cultural Heritage of India Honoree, 1991. **SPECIAL ACHIEVEMENTS:** Author of more than 75 res papers in various scientific journals; doctoral res dir, principal res investigator, researcher, referee, reviewer, author, editorial collaborator, organizer, chairperson, panelist, speaker, workshop/course organizer, dir, & lecturer; originator & mbr, planning comm of "Diversity within Unity Week," Office of Equal Employment Opportunity, Ctr for Drug Evaluation Research, FDA, 1993; organizer, moderator, speaker of special mtg on Global Harmonization of Good Statistical Practices in Clinical Trials at the Intl Statistical Inst Mtg in Florence, Italy, 1993; researcher on Jesus. **HOME ADDRESS:** 7712 Groton Rd, Bethesda, MD 20817, (301)469-8584. **BUSINESS ADDRESS:** Branch Chief, Statistical Evaluation and Research Branch, Food and Drug Administration, 5600 Fishers Ln, Parklawn Bldg, Rm 18B45, Rockville, MD 20857, (301)443-4594.

DUGAL, HARDEV S. (DOUG)

Company executive. Indo-American. **PERSONAL:** Born Feb 1, 1937, Bareilly, Uttar Pradesh, India; son of Baldev S Dugal and Attar K Dugal; married Mona, Feb 4, 1968; children: Rajeev, Kavita. **EDUCATION:** DAV College, India, BSc, chemistry/biology, 1955; HB Tech Institute, India, MSc, chem tech, 1958; Technische Hochschule, Germany, PhD, DrIng, 1963; LaSalle Extn University, diploma, business; Appleton, Wisconsin, postdoctoral work, 1964-66. **CAREER:** Daurala Sugar Works, India, alcohol plant, student apprentice, 1955-56; Gwaliar Rayon, India, shift chemist, 1958-59; Adam Opal, AG, Germany, student work, 1960; Shri Ram Industrial Research Institute, India, pool officer, 1966-68; Punj Sons Ltd, India, chemical technologist, 1968; Institute of Paper Chemistry, 1968-87; James River Corp, research associate, 1987-89; Integrated Paper Services Inc, president, currently. **ORGANIZATIONS:** Technical Assn of the Pulp & Paper Industry, Environment Program Committee, ex-chairman, Lake States Section, ex-chairman, board member; American Chemical Society; Cellulose Chemikar Club, Germany; Zellcheming, Germany; Indian Pulp & Paper Tech Assn; Friends of Dard Humber Museum, ex-executive secretary; Outagamic Solid Waste Adv Committee. **HONORS/AWARDS:** TAPPI, Outstanding Local Section Award, 1991; TAPPI, Fellow, 1988, Environment Division Award, 1987, Roy F Weston Prize; Shalimar Gold Medal, India. **SPECIAL ACHIEVEMENTS:** Proficient in Hindi, Urdu, English, German, Punjabe (partially); over 35 publications including article in encyclopedia; over 25 invited lectures throughout USA, Europe, India. **BUSINESS ADDRESS:** President, Integrated Paper Services, Inc, 101 W Edison Ave, Edison Bldg, Ste 250, PO Box 446, Appleton, WI 54912-0446, (414)749-3040.

DUNG, HOU CHI

Educator. Taiwanese American. **PERSONAL:** Born Mar 7, 1936, Pingtung, Taiwan; son of Sun-tu Dung & Wan-Kang Chen; married Elizabeth Izu Dunn, Jul 30, 1963; children: Y Ben Dunn, Joeming Wolfe Dunn. **EDUCATION:** National Taiwan University, BSc, 1960; University of Louisville, PhD, 1969. **CAREER:** Kaohsiung Medical College, Taiwan, teaching assistant, 1961-63; University of Louisville, research associate, 1968-70; University of Texas Health Science Center at San Antonio, associate professor, 1970-. **ORGANIZATIONS:** Taiwan Benevolent Association of America, president, 1984-85; Southern Society of Anatomists, 1967-85; Texas Society of Electron Microscopy, 1971-84; American Association of Anatomists, 1973-91; American Society of Zoologists, 1974-84; Society of Neuroscience, 1978-90; Electron Microscopy Society of America, 1979-84; International Association for the Study of Pain, 1984-90; American Pain Society, 1984-90. **HONORS/AWARDS:** Morrison Trust Foundation, Basic Science Research Award, 1974, 1975; Oversea Chinese Affairs Commission, appointed by President of Republic of China, 1981-. **SPECIAL ACHIEVEMENTS:** 21 publications in scientific medical journals; 14 abstracts in medical science meetings; 34 publications in medical journals on topic of acupuncture; teaching human gross anatomy to dental and medical students; extensive acupuncture practice with more than fourteen thousand patients to date. **MILITARY SERVICE:** Army, Republic of China,

second lt, 1960-61. **HOME ADDRESS:** 7272 Wurzbach, #203, San Antonio, TX 78240, (210)615-1331. **BUSINESS ADDRESS:** Associate Professor, Dept of Cellular and Structural Biology, University of Texas Health Science Center at San Antonio, 7703 Floyd Curl Dr, San Antonio, TX 78284-7762, (210)567-3873.

DUONG, CAMBAO DE

Educational administrator. Chinese American/Vietnamese American. **PERSONAL:** Born Jun 15, 1943, Saigon, Vietnam; son of Hon Duong and Am Luu; married Hoa Luong Duong, Jan 27, 1975; children: Sanh Phung, Nhien Yen. **EDUCATION:** University of Saigon, Faculty of Letters, BA, 1969, BEd, 1970, MA, 1973; Hunter College, BA, computer science, 1990. **CAREER:** Various high schools in Kien Tuong and Saigon, School of Language of Teacher's College, University of Saigon, teacher, principal, instructor, 1965-75; Mac Dinh Chi HS, Teachers College, teacher & instructor, 1978-80; Tuong Thanh Weaving Corporation, general manager, 1980-83; Chinatown Manpower Project Inc, Refugee Vocational Training Program, skill instructor, 1984-87, program director, 1987-, deputy director, 1989-. **ORGANIZATIONS:** The Greater NY Vietnamese-American Community Association Inc, chairperson, 1989-; Indochina Resource Action Center, board member, 1989-; Indochina Sins-American Senior Citizen Center Inc, president, 1990-; Dong Tam Vietnamese Magazine, publisher, 1991-; City of New York, Board of Education, Chancellors Asian American Advisory Council, 1991-; National Council for the Vietnamese-American Community in USA, commissioner, 1992-93; Vietnamese-American Community in the USA, advisor, 1993-; World Federation of Chinese Organizations from Vietnam, Cambodia and Laos, deputy secretary general, 1993-. **SPECIAL ACHIEVEMENTS:** Books include Tinh Trang Xa Hoi Tay Chu Qua Kinh Thi, in Chinese and Vietnamese, 1973; Tuyet Kha, in Vietnamese, 1992; Xanh Xanh Ngon Co Ben Dong, in Vietnamese, 1993. **MILITARY SERVICE:** Thu Duc, Vietnam, lieutenant, 1972-75. **BIOGRAPHICAL SOURCES:** China Times Weekly News, p8-9, Mar 14, 1992, p 8-9, Mar 21, 1992. **BUSINESS ADDRESS:** Deputy Director, Chinatown Manpower Project Inc, 70 Mulberry St, Rm 506, New York, NY 10013, (212)571-1696.

DUONG, DUC HONG

Economic developer. Vietnamese American. **PERSONAL:** Born Jun 28, 1939, Hue, Vietnam; son of Di Thieu Duong and Thuan Hoa Tran; married Tuong-Nguyen T Pham, Jan 29, 1970; children: Hai N, Dony N. **CAREER:** Vietnamese Embassy London, counselor, 1969-73; Vietnamese Government Ministry of Foreign Affairs, chief of staff, 1973-75; Washington State Government, Office of Refugee Service, director, 1975-77; Montgomery County Government, Office of Economic Development, business development rep, 1979-83, business development manager, 1983-88, assistant director, 1988-. **ORGANIZATIONS:** Maryland Vietnamese Mutual Assistance Association, founder/treasurer; Asian American Resource Development Center, co-founder; Maryland Industrial Development Association; United Way, board member; US Bureau of the Census Advisory Committee. **MILITARY SERVICE:** Vietnamese Army, Lieutenant, 1968-69. **BUSINESS ADDRESS:** Assistant Director, Montgomery County Office of Economic Development, 101 Monroe St, Ste 1500, Rockville, MD 20850, (301)217-2345.

DUONG, NGO DINH (NICK)

Engineer. Vietnamese American. **PERSONAL:** Born May 9, 1962, Quinhon, Nghiabinh, Vietnam; son of Hien D Duong and Hoa T Nguyen; married Thai M Phan, May 29, 1988; children: Michael P. **EDUCATION:** Pennsylvania State University, BSChE, 1985, MS, management, currently. **CAREER:** PA Department of Transportation, engineering intern, 1984-85; Craftlite, Inc, process/manufacturing engineer, 1985-87; Action Manufacturing Co, AMCOM Division, supervisor, process engineering, 1987-89, manager, quality engineering, 1989-92; Bulova Technologies, Inc, manager, SPC & MFG quality, 1992-. **ORGANIZATIONS:** American Society for Quality Control, 1989-; American Defense Preparedness Association, 1989-; American Institute of Chemical Engineers, 1985-; American Management Association, 1990-; American Society of Manufacturing Engineers, 1992-. **HONORS/AWARDS:** American Society for Quality Control, certification of quality engineer, 1991; PA Bureau of Professional Affairs, engineer-in-training, 1986. **HOME ADDRESS:** 1777 Southport Dr, Lancaster, PA 17603.

DURLABHJI, SUBHASH

Educator. Indo-American. **PERSONAL:** Born Feb 27, 1947, Jaipur, India; son of Girdharlal Durlabhji & Gulab Laxmi Durlabhji; married Neelam Kher Durlabhji, Jun 22, 1976; children: Raehan. **EDUCATION:** Cornell University,

BS, 1970, MBA, 1971; Michigan State University, PhD, 1981. **CAREER:** Western Michigan University, assistant professor, 1980-82; Xavier Labor Relations Institute, associate professor, 1984-87; Northwestern State University, associate professor, 1987-. **ORGANIZATIONS:** Southwestern Small Business Institute Association, president-elect, 1993-94, president, 1994-95; Association of Japanese Business Studies, 1991-. **HONORS/AWARDS:** Northwestern State University, Outstanding Research, 1992; Southwestern Small Business Institute Association, Leadership Award, 1991-93. **SPECIAL ACHIEVEMENTS:** Author of: Japanese Business, State University of NY Press, 1993; "Organization Philosophies of Japanese Companies," 1991; "Influence of Zen & Confucianism on Japanese Org," 1990. **BUSINESS ADDRESS:** Associate Professor, Northwestern State University, 105 Morrison Hall, Natchitoches, LA 71497, (318)357-5708.

DURRANI, SAJJAD HAIDAR
Electrical engineer. Pakistani American. **PERSONAL:** Born Aug 27, 1928, Jalalpur, Punjab, Pakistan; son of Inayat Ullah Khan Durrani & Hamidah Khanum Durrani; married Brita K Yasmin Portin, May 21, 1959; children: Zarina, Amina, Arif. **EDUCATION:** Government College, Lahore, Pakistan, Math, 1946; Engineering College, Lahore, BS (with honors), engineering, 1949; University of Manchester, UK, MS, elect eng, 1953; University of New Mexico, ScD, elect eng, 1962. **CAREER:** Engineering College, Lahore, Pakistan, lecturer, asst prof, 1949-51, 1953-59; University of New Mexico, research associate and instructor, 1959-62, senior engineer, 1962-64, Electrical Eng Dept, professor & chairman, 1964-65, associate professor, 1965-66; RCA Space Center, 1966-68; Comsat Labs, technical staff and branch manager, 1968-73; University of Maryland, visiting professor, 1972-73; Operations Research, Inc, senior engineer and project leader, 1973-74; National Aeronautics and Space Administration, Goddard Space Flight Center and Headquarters, 1974-92, chief scientist, Communications Division, 1979-81, system planning manager, 1981-84, research & planning manager, 1984-88; Advanced Systems, program manager, 1988-92; Network Technology Group, Computer Sciences Corp, consulting engineer, 1992-. **ORGANIZATIONS:** Institute of Electrical and Electronics Engineers Inc, board of directors, 1984-85; Aerospace & Electronic Systems Society, pres, 1982-83, Washington Section, chairman, 1981; US Activities Board, Technical Activities Board, Educational Activities Board, and Publications Board; Eascon, board of directors, National Telesystems Conference, board of directors; chairman of several committees and task forces; IEEE Spectrum, IEEE Proceedings, editorial board; Academic Press, Encyclopedia of Technology, editorial advisory board; editorial boards of other publications. **HONORS/AWARDS:** NASA, Special Achievement Award, 1977, 1978, 1990; IEEE, Citation of Honor, US Activities, 1980, Outstanding Member, Region 2, 1982, Centennial Medal, 1984, fellow, 1976. **SPECIAL ACHIEVEMENTS:** One of the earliest works on multipath effects in space communications; developed concepts for maritime communications using phased arrays; led a multibeam phased array equipment development for a potential Space Shuttle experiment; published several studies on space communications systems. **BUSINESS ADDRESS:** Consulting Engineer, Computer Sciences Corporation, 4600 Powder Mill Rd, Rm B110, Beltsville, MD 20705, (301)572-8875.

DUTT, NIKIL D.
Educator. Indo-American. **PERSONAL:** Born Nov 9, 1958, Hubli, India; son of Devdas & Ravikala Dutt; married Sujata Dutt, Dec 20, 1984; children: Shubir. **EDUCATION:** Birla Institute of Technology & Science, BE (with honors), 1981; Penn State University, MS, 1983; University of Illinois at Urbana-Champaign, PhD, 1989. **CAREER:** Penn State University, research assistant, 1981-83; University of Illinos, research assistant, 1983-89; University of California, assistant professor, 1989-. **ORGANIZATIONS:** IFIP, WG 10.2, 1991-; IEEE, HLSW92, steering committee, 1992, benchmarks chair, 1992; IEEE, HLSW94, steering committee, 1993-94, benchmarks chair, 1993-94; IFIP, CHDL, 93, program committee, 1993; IEEE APCHPLSA93, program committee, 1993. **HONORS/AWARDS:** IFIP/IEEE, Best Paper Award, CHDL89, 1989, CHDL91, 1991; NSF, Research Initiation Award, 1989. **SPECIAL ACHIEVEMENTS:** High-Level Synthesis, first textbook on topic, Kluwer, 1992; approximately 40 publications in archival journals and conferences proceedings. **BUSINESS ADDRESS:** Assistant Professor, Computer Science, University of California, Irvine, 444 CS, Irvine, CA 92717-3425, (714)856-7219.

DUTTA, MITRA
Research physicist. Indo-American. **PERSONAL:** Born Jul 3, 1953, Patna, Bihar, India; daughter of Dhiren N Dutta and Aruna Dutta; married Sudhin

Datta, Apr 26, 1993; children: Gautam Datta. **EDUCATION:** Gauhati University, BSc, 1971; Delhi University, MSc, 1973; University of Cincinnati, MS, 1978, PhD, 1981. **CAREER:** College of Arts, Science & Technology, lecturer, 1973-76; University of West Indies, lecturer, 1973-76; Purdue University, research associate, 1981-83; City College of New York, senior research associate, 1983-86; Calculon Corp, SGC Corp, research engineer, 1986-88; US Army Research Lab, research physicist, leader, optoelectronics team, 1988-. **ORGANIZATIONS:** Technical Advisory Committee for URIs at Princeton & Purdue, 1992-; Joint Defense Labs Reliance Study Photonic Subpanel, 1991-; NSF Panel on Material Science, 1992; JSEP, Technical Review Committee, 1986-; Institute of Electrical & Electronic Engineers senior member, 1991-; Optical Society of America, 1987-; American Physical Society, 1977-; Sigma Xi, 1983-. **HONORS/AWARDS:** AMC, Top Ten AMC Employee Award, 1993; ARL, Harold Jacobs Award for Scientific Achievement, 1992; US Army, R&D Achievement Award, 1992, 1990. **SPECIAL ACHIEVEMENTS:** Over 85 publications in reviewed journals. **BUSINESS ADDRESS:** Leader, Optoelectronics Team, US Army Research Lab, Electronics & Power Sources Directorate, AMSRL-EP-EF, Fort Monmouth, NJ 07703-5601, (908)544-4331.

DUTTA, PULAK
Physicist, educator. Indo-American. **PERSONAL:** Born Oct 1, 1951, Calcutta, India. **EDUCATION:** Presidency College, India, BSc (with honors), 1970; University of Delhi, MSc, 1973; University of Chicago, PhD, 1979. **CAREER:** Argonne National Lab, postdoctoral associate, 1979-81; Northwestern University, assistant professor, 1981-87, associate professor, 1987-92, professor, 1992-. **ORGANIZATIONS:** American Physical Society, 1974-; American Chemical Society, 1990-. **HONORS/AWARDS:** American Physical Society, fellow, 1992. **SPECIAL ACHIEVEMENTS:** Research in the area of condensed-matter physics studying surfaces, interfaces and thin films using synchrotron radiation. **BUSINESS ADDRESS:** Professor of Physics & Astronomy, Northwestern University, 2145 Sheridan Rd, Evanston, IL 60208-3112, (708)491-5465.

DUTTA, SHIB PRASAD
Scientist. Indo-American. **PERSONAL:** Born Nov 27, 1935, Calcutta, W. Bengal, India; son of Sadananda and Santiprova Dutta (deceased); married Bharati Dutta, May 29, 1969; children: Suparna, Reetuparna. **EDUCATION:** Calcutta University, India, BS (with honors), 1955, MS, 1958, PhD, 1968. **CAREER:** SUNY, Buffalo, research associate, 1967-69; Roswell Park Cancer Institute, cancer research scientist, 1969-. **ORGANIZATIONS:** American Chemical Society, 1971-. **BUSINESS ADDRESS:** Cancer Res Scientist, Dept of Biophysics, Roswell Park Cancer Institute, Carlton & Elm St, Crystallography Bldg, Buffalo, NY 14263, (716)845-2388.

DWIVEDI, CHANDRADHAR
Educator. Indo-American. **PERSONAL:** Born Jul 1, 1948, Jaunpur, Uttar Pradesh, India; son of Abhaya Narayan Dwivedi and Maharaji Dwivedi; married Prabha Dwivedi, Jun 21, 1966; children: Sudhanshu, Neeraja, Himanshu. **EDUCATION:** Gorakhpur University, India, BSc, 1964, MSc, 1966; Lucknow University, India, PhD, 1972. **CAREER:** T D College, India, lecturer, 1966-67; N D College, India, lecturer, 1967-69; Vanderbilt University, research associate, 1973-76; Meharry Medical College, assistant professor, 1976-82, associate professor, 1982-85; Chemical Abstracts Service, associate editor, 1986; Ohio State University, research scientist, 1986-87; South Dakota State University, associate professor, 1987-90, professor, 1990-. **ORGANIZATIONS:** American Society for Pharmacology and Experimental Therapeutics, 1983-; American Association for Cancer Research, 1992-; American Association of Pharmaceutical Scientics, 1991-; American Association of Colleges of Pharmacy, 1987-; Association of Scientists of Indian Origin in America, 1982-; Rho Chi, councilmember, 1988-; Sigma Xi, 1990-, chapter advisor, 1991-; Phi Kappa Phi, 1991-, chapter president, 1993-; American Heart Association, research policy and funding committee, 1990-93. **HONORS/AWARDS:** South Dakota State University, F O Butler Award for Excellence in Research, 1990, College of Pharmacy, Excellence in Research, 1990, Excellence in Student Services, 1993; received research grants from National Institutes of Health, National Science Foundations, March of Dimes, etc. **SPECIAL ACHIEVEMENTS:** Reviewer for archives of Environmental Contamination and Toxicology, 1980-; reviewer. Molecular and Cellular Biochemistry, 1990-; proceedings of experimental biology and medicine published about 60 research articles; about 60 presentations at scientific meetings. **BUSINESS ADDRESS:** Professor, College of Pharmacy, South Dakota State University, PO Box 2202C, Brookings, SD 57007-0197, (605)688-4247.

DWIVEDY, KESHAB K.
System engineer. Indo-American. **PERSONAL:** Born Feb 2, 1943, Cuttack, Orissa, India; son of Abhiram Dwivedy and Arnapurna Dwivedy; married Bidyut Dwivedy, Jan 16, 1969; children: Sunita, Avin S. **EDUCATION:** Indian Institute of Technology, Kharagpur, BTech (honors), 1965, MTech, 1968; State University of New York, Stony Brook, PhD, 1975. **CAREER:** Regional Engineering College, lecturer, applied mechanics, 1968-72; Nuclear Power Services, manager, analytical group, 1975-79; Burns & Roe, supervising engineer, 1979; PDC Inc, president, 1979-84; Virginia Power, system engineer, 1984-. **ORGANIZATIONS:** American Society of Mechanical Engineers, 1975-; Orissa Society of America, secretary-treasurer, life member, 1989-91; PVRC, Committee on Dynamic Analysis & Testing, 1992-. **HONORS/AWARDS:** Organization of Chinese Americans, Corporate Achievement Award, 1993; Technology Alumni Association, Best Post Graduate Allrounder, 1968; IIT-Kharagpur ANS/ASME, Best Paper describing plant safety and reliability, 1986. **SPECIAL ACHIEVEMENTS:** 15 technical Papers in ASME/ANS conferences, 1985-92. **BUSINESS ADDRESS:** System Engineer, Virginia Power, 5000 Dominion Blvd, Innsbrook Technical Center-INW, Glen Allen, VA 23060, (804)273-3098.

DWIVEDY, RAMESH CHANDRA
Utility company manager. Indo-American. **PERSONAL:** Born Mar 15, 1943, Etawah, Uttar Pradesh, India; son of Shambhoo Dayal Dubey and Parvati Devi Dubey; married Rashmi Dwivedy, Aug 2, 1967; children: Seema. **EDUCATION:** University of Allahabad, India, BE, 1963; University of Guelph, Canada, ME, 1966; University of Massachusetts, PhD, 1970. **CAREER:** University of Delaware, assistant professor, 1970-73; State of Delaware, environmental engineer, 1974-78; Delmarva Power & Light Co, Environmental Licensing & Permits, supervisor, 1978-. **ORGANIZATIONS:** Water Environment Federation, 1974-. **SPECIAL ACHIEVEMENTS:** Ten publications on aquaculture and bioenvironmental engineering. **HOME ADDRESS:** 11 Trimble Turn, Centreville, DE 19807, (302)239-6495. **BUSINESS ADDRESS:** Supervisor of Env Licensing & Permits, Delmarva Power & Light Co, 252 Chapman Road, Oxford Bldg, Newark, DE 19714, (302)452-6027.

E

EBATA, DUANE
Association administrator. Japanese American. **PERSONAL:** Born Dec 16, 1950. **CAREER:** Japanese American Cultural and Community Center, managing director, currently. **BUSINESS ADDRESS:** Managing Director, Japanese American Cultural and Community Center, 244 South San Pedro St, Ste 505, Los Angeles, CA 90012, (213)628-2725.*

EBRON, BETTY LIU
Journalist. Chinese American. **PERSONAL:** Born 1956; married. **EDUCATION:** Baruch College, BBA, 1979; Columbia University School of Journalism, MA, 1980. **CAREER:** Village Voic, promotion assistant, 1978-79; Hudson Dispatch, reporter, 1980-81; Newark Star Ledger, reporter, 1981-86; New York Daily News, reporter, 1986-88, columnist, 1988-. **ORGANIZATIONS:** Asian American Journalists Association. **BUSINESS ADDRESS:** Columnist, New York Daily News, 220 E 42nd St, 7th Fl, New York, NY 10017.

EMBREY, SUE KUNITOMI
Community activist, educator. Japanese American. **PERSONAL:** Born in Los Angeles, CA; married. **EDUCATION:** California State University, Los Angeles, BA, English; University of Southern California, MS, education. **CAREER:** Manzanar Committee, co-founder, 1972; City Commission on the Status of Women, commissioner, 10 years; Los Angeles Board of Education, Asian Pacific Education Commission, founding member; adult education teacher, English as a Second Language, currently. **ORGANIZATIONS:** Friends of Little Tokyo Branch Library, board member; Japanese American Historical Society of Southern California, board member; Natl Japanese American Historical Society; Common Cause, former board member; American Federation of Teachers. **HONORS/AWARDS:** Japanese American Historical Society of Southern California, Award for Contributions to the Japanese American Community, 1992; Asian Pacific American Labor Alliance, Honoree, 1992. **SPECIAL ACHIEVEMENTS:** Manzanar Free Press, contributor to camp newspaper, 1942; Fiftieth Year of Remembrance: Japanese American Internment, active contributor. **BUSINESS ADDRESS:** Board Member, Japanese American Historical Society of S California, 369 E 1st St, Los Angeles, CA 90012-3901, (213)662-5102.*

EMURA, CYNTHIA SANAE
Graphic designer, cleric. Japanese American. **PERSONAL:** Born Aug 4, 1944, Honolulu, HI; daughter of Herbert Masaru Iwasa & Laura Tatsue Iwasa; divorced; children: Jonathan Masaru. **EDUCATION:** University of Hawaii, BFA, 1967. **CAREER:** Self-employed, dba GrafX Inc, graphic designer, vp, 1971-; Eckankar, priest, 1979-93; Hawaii regional representative, 1986-. **HONORS/AWARDS:** University of Hawaii, Phi Kappa Phi, 1967. **SPECIAL ACHIEVEMENTS:** Author, The Onolicious Alternative, 1989. **HOME PHONE:** (808)735-8915.

ENDO, FRANK
Gymnastics judge. Japanese American. **PERSONAL:** Born Apr 20, 1923, Wilmington, CA; son of Fred Matsukichi Endo and Reiko Endo; married Mary Mieko Endo, Jul 19, 1950; children: Douglas, Richard. **CAREER:** Frank Endo Co, president, owner, 35 years; self-employed, gymnastics judge, currently. **ORGANIZATIONS:** National Gymnastics Judges Association, life member, national & international certified judge. **HONORS/AWARDS:** Japan Gymnastics Association, Hall of Fame, 1990. **SPECIAL ACHIEVEMENTS:** First American veteran of WWII in Japan to have a private act of Congress to marry and bring spouse to US, 1950. **MILITARY SERVICE:** US Army, military intelligence service, WWII.

ENDO, PAULA SAYOKO TSUKAMOTO
Photographer, educator. Japanese American. **PERSONAL:** Born Jul 2, 1938, San Francisco, CA; daughter of Joseph K Tsukamoto and Jane Y Tsukamoto; married Todd I Endo, Aug 15, 1964; children: Scott, Erik. **EDUCATION:** University of California, Berkeley; University of California, Los Angeles, BA (honors), 1961; Harvard Graduate School of Education, MAT, 1968. **CAREER:** Public school teacher, grades 4-6, Inglewood, CA and Newton, MA, 1961-67; Museum of Fine Arts, curriculum developer, 1969; US Postal (Street) Academy Program, consultant/teacher, 1971-72; Arlington Career Center, high school commercial photography teacher, 1974-90; Arlington Courier, free lance news photographer, 1990-91; American University in Cairo, free lance photographer and adjunct professor of photography, 1990, 1993-. **ORGANIZATIONS:** Natl Education Assn, until 1991; Arlington Arts Center; Society for Photographic Education; Shalem Institute for Spiritual Formation (assoc with Washington Cathedral); Bad Dog (photography) Studio. **HONORS/AWARDS:** UC Berkeley, California State Scholarship; Natl Endowment for the Arts, grant, 1980-81; Pi Lambda Theta; others. **SPECIAL ACHIEVEMENTS:** Numerous exhibitions, including: Cairo Berlin Gallery, Egypt, solo showing & conversation, 1993; Gallerie at Kei Yamagami Design, San Francisco, solo exhibition, 1993; publications include: Photos: USAID Annual Report on Education in Egypt, 1992, Canadian Medical Assn Journal, 1991-93, Washington Post, others; permanent exhibits: GR Ford Museum, Sony Gallery, others. **HOME ADDRESS:** 15 N Fenwick St, Arlington, VA 22201, (703)525-0494.

ENG, ANA MAR
Physician. Chinese American. **PERSONAL:** Born Nov 25, 1939, Manila, Philippines; daughter of Ow Yong Sai Ying and Mar Yee; married Jack Schmunk, Jul 15, 1986; children: Oliver Daniel, Tanya. **EDUCATION:** Far Eastern University, AA, 1959; University of Santo Tomas, MD, 1964. **CAREER:** De Goesbriand Memorial Hospital, internship, 1965-66; University Hospital, residency, 1966-70; University of Chicago Hospital & Clinics, residency, 1967-70, instructor, 1970-72; University of Illinois, asst prof, 1975-78, assoc prof, 1978-80; Hines VA Hospital, attending physician, 1973-; Cook County Hospital, attending physician, 1985-92; Loyola University Medical Center, clin asst prof, 1972-75, guest lecturer, 1975-80, clin assoc prof, 1981-91, clin prof, 1991-. **ORGANIZATIONS:** American Medical Assn; Illinois Medical Soc, DuPage Medical Soc; American Acad of Dermatology; Chicago Dermatological Soc, chairperson, 1979-81, treasurer, 1982-85, pres, 1985-86; American Soc of Dermatopathology; Elmhurst Garden Club; AAUW, Itasca, IL; Chicago Architectural Foundation, docent. **SPECIAL ACHIEVEMENTS:** Co-author, numerous publications, including: "Combined Congenital Icthiposiform Erythroderma and Epidermal Nevus," Intl J Derm, 30, 4:284-287, 1991; "An Unusual Presentation of Cutaneous Metastatic Malignant Melanoma," J American Acad Derm, 23:648-50, 1991; "Tranient Bullous Dermlysis of Newborns," J Cut Path, 18:328-332, 1991; "Recurrent Pyogenic Granuloma: A Form of Lobular Capillary Hemangioma," Cutis 52:101-103, 1993. **BUSINESS ADDRESS:** Dermatologist, 103 Haven, Elmhurst, IL 60126, (708)783-3222.

ENG, HENRY

Business executive. Chinese American. **PERSONAL:** Born Mar 8, 1940, Clifton, NJ; son of Yuck Wah Eng & Gam Jan Lee Eng; married Mary Eng, Jun 23, 1963; children: David, Deborah, Jeffrey. **EDUCATION:** Bloomfield College, BS, 1969. **CAREER:** AJP Scientific Inc, chief executive officer, currently. **MILITARY SERVICE:** US Air Force, airman, 1958-62. **BUSINESS ADDRESS:** President, AJP Scientific Inc, 82 Industrial East, Clifton, NJ 07012, (201)472-7200.

ENG, JAMIE PEARL

Educator. Chinese American. **PERSONAL:** Born May 9, 1951, New York, NY; daughter of Jim Eng and Juanita Eng; married John Jin Lee, Apr 30, 1983. **EDUCATION:** Mass Institute of Technology, BS, 1973; Harvard University, MS, 1975, ScD, 1977. **CAREER:** New York University, assistant professor, 1977-81; San Franciso State University, associate professor, 1981-85, professor, 1985-. **BUSINESS ADDRESS:** Professor, San Francisco State University, School of Business, 1600 Holloway Ave, San Francisco, CA 94132, (415)338-2138.

ENG, LAWRENCE FOOK

Educator. Chinese American. **PERSONAL:** Born Feb 19, 1931, Spokane, WA; son of On Kee & Hue she Eng; married Jeanne Leong, Aug 30, 1958; children: Douglas, Alice, Steven, Shirley. **EDUCATION:** Washington State University, BS, chemistry, 1952; Stanford University, MS, chemistry, 1954, PhD, chemistry, 1962. **CAREER:** VA Med Center, Laboratory Serv, chemistry sect, chief, 1961-; Stanford School of Medicine, Dept of Pathology, research associate, 1966-70, senior scientist, 1970-75, adjunct professor, 1975-82, professor, 1982-. **ORGANIZATIONS:** American Society for Neurochem, council, 1979-83, secretary, 1987-93; International Society for Neurochemistry, 1969; American Society Biochem & Molecular Biology, 1970; Society for Neuroscience, 1970; member of several editorial boards; NIH, neurol sci study section, ad hoc member, neurol b study section, ad hoc mem, 1976-79; VA Office of Regeneration Research Program, advisory board, 1985-86; VA Merit Review Board for Neurobiology, 1987-90; Natl Adv Neurol Disorders and Stroke Coun, 1991-94. **HONORS/AWARDS:** DVA William S Middleton Award, 1988; Neuroscience Investigator Award, 1987-93. **MILITARY SERVICE:** US Air Force, captain, 1952-57. **BUSINESS ADDRESS:** Chief, Chemistry Section, VA Medical Center, Pathology & Laboratory Medicine Service, 3801 Miranda Ave, #151B, Palo Alto, CA 94304.

ENG, MAMIE

Librarian. Chinese American. **PERSONAL:** Born May 21, 1954, Oceanside, NY; daughter of Yen Wah Eng & Hong Lew Eng. **EDUCATION:** Vassar College, BA, history & education, 1976; Columbia University, MS, lib science, 1977, MA, educ psych, 1979. **CAREER:** Henry Waldinger Memorial Library, adult services librarian, 1979-. **ORGANIZATIONS:** Nassau County Library Association, president, 1993, vice president/president elect, 1992, newsletter editor, 1985-88, 1989-92, ref & adult services division president, 1986-87; International Reading Association, Manhattan council, board of directors, 1985-91; New York Library Association, 1977-; Phi Delta Kappa, 1979-; American Library Association, 1977-. **SPECIAL ACHIEVEMENTS:** International Reading Association, Manhattan Council, workshop speaker, parents & reading conference, Manhattan Council, IRA, 1988-90; Urban Reading Consortium, workshop speaker, 1984-85. **BUSINESS ADDRESS:** Adult Services Librarian, Henry Waldinger Memorial Library, 60 Verona Pl, Valley Stream, NY 11582, (516)825-6422.

ENG, PATRICIA

Association administrator. **CAREER:** New York Asian Women's Center, director, currently. **BUSINESS ADDRESS:** Director, New York Asian Women's Center, 39 Bowery, Box 375, New York, NY 10002, (212)732-5230.*

ENG, WILLIAM

Educator. Chinese American. **PERSONAL:** Born Jul 30, 1950, New York, NY; son of George Eng and Sarah Eng; married Emily, Aug 13, 1973; children: Jason, Jordan, Jared, Jesse, Joshua. **EDUCATION:** City College, BS, ed, 1972, MS, ed, 1973; New York University, EdD, 1978. **CAREER:** Stuyvesant HS, physical education instructor, 1972; York College, adjunct lecturer, soccer coach, 1972-73; Baruch College, assoc professor, chairman, athletic director, 1973-. **ORGANIZATIONS:** Asian-American Higher Education Council, chair membership committee, 1993-; Baruch College, chair, SEES P & B committee, 1993-; Eastern College Athletic Conf, acting chair, award of valor

comm, 1989; Metropolitan Collegiate Athletic Directors Assn, president, 1986-88; City University of NY Athletic Conference, vice president, 1985-87. **HONORS/AWARDS:** CUNY, AC, Coach of the Year-Women's Tennis, 1985, 1988; Hudson Valley Women's Athletic Conf, Coach of the Year-Women's Tennis, 1986; Baruch College, Alumni Faculty Service Award, 1994. **BUSINESS ADDRESS:** Assoc Prof/Chm/Athletic Dir, Dept of Physical & Health Education, Baruch College, 17 Lexington Ave, New York, NY 10010-5526, (212)387-1271.

ENOMOTO, JIRO (JERRY)

Criminal justice consultant, educator. Japanese American. **PERSONAL:** Born Jan 24, 1926, San Francisco, CA; son of Naosaburo Enomoto & Kei Suzuki Enomoto; married Dorothy, Apr 20, 1982; children: Rachelli, Marcia Board, Yvonne. **EDUCATION:** University of California, Berkeley, BA, 1949, MSW, 1951. **CAREER:** California Department of Corrections, classification officer I, II, III, 1952-61, associate warden, 1961-66, chief of classification, 1966-71, deputy warden, 1971-72, warden, 1972-75, director, 1975-80; California State University, Sacramento, consultant in criminal justice/professor, 1980-. **ORGANIZATIONS:** Japanese American Citizens League-JACL, national president, 1966-70; JACL Legislative Education Committee, national chair, 1987-; Asian Pacific American Coalition-USA, regional president, 1986-; Commission on Accreditation for Corrections, commissioner, 1972-80; South Sacramento Mental Health Clinic, board member, 1988-; College Horizons, board member, 1989-93; Friends Outside National Organization, board president, 1990-. **HONORS/AWARDS:** JACL, JACLer of the Biennium, 1956, Distinguished Achievement Award, 1976; Sacramento Human Rights & Fair Housing Commission, Human Rights Award, 1988; California Federation of Business & Professional Womens Clubs, Top Hat Award, 1976; North California Asian Peace Officers Association, Asian Pioneer in Law Enforcement, 1987. **SPECIAL ACHIEVEMENTS:** Sacramento County Grand Jury, foreman, 1992-93. **MILITARY SERVICE:** US Army, private, 1945-46. **HOME ADDRESS:** 7751 Sleepy River Way, Sacramento, CA 95831.

ERRAMILLI, SHYAMSUNDER

Educator. Indo-American. **PERSONAL:** Born Feb 18, 1957, Poona, Maharashtra, India; son of Venkata Chelam Erramilli and Satyavati Mylavarapu. **EDUCATION:** Fergusson College, Poona, BSc, 1977; IIT, Bombay, MSc, 1979; University of Illinois, Urbana, PhD, 1986. **CAREER:** University of Illinois, research assistant, 1979-86; Princeton University, assistant professor, 1986-. **ORGANIZATIONS:** American Physical Society, 1984-; American Association for the Advancement of Science, 1992-; Biophysical Society, 1985-. **SPECIAL ACHIEVEMENTS:** Author of 25 research papers. **BUSINESS ADDRESS:** Assistant Professor, Princeton University, PO Box 708, Princeton, NJ 08544, (609)258-3158.

ESCLAMADO, ALEJANDRO A.

Publisher. Filipino American. **PERSONAL:** Born Apr 2, 1929; married. **CAREER:** Philippine News, publisher, editor-in-chief, currently. **HONORS/AWARDS:** Ellis Island Medal of Honor, first Filipino winner; President Aquino, Filipino Legion of Honor, 1988-89. **BUSINESS ADDRESS:** Publisher/Editor-in-Chief, Philippine News, 156 S Spruce #207, South San Francisco, CA 94080, (415)872-3000.*

ESGUERRA, ARTURO SAZON (ARTHUR SEITZ ESQUIRE)

Marketing officer. Filipino American. **PERSONAL:** Born Sep 17, 1941, Quezon City, Rizal Province, Philippines; son of Gorgonio Guevara Esguerra and Gregoria Roxas Sazon; married Ana Marie Aure Esguerra, Dec 16, 1972; children: Aristotle, Adrian, Anne Therese. **EDUCATION:** University of Santo Tomas, Manila, Philippines, BSC, 1962; The College of Insurance, New York City, MBA, 1973; Adelphi University, CFP, 1984. **CAREER:** NCR Corp, computer sales rep, 1962-65; Philamlife Insurance Co, unit supervisor, 1965-67; Travelers Insurance Co, agency trainee, 1968-70; Union Central Life Insurance Co, unit manager, 1970-71; New York Life Insurance Co, general manager, 1971-88; American Business & Professional Program Inc, vice president, 1989-; Financial Control Associates, Inc, national financial manager, 1992-. **ORGANIZATIONS:** Brooklyn General Agents & Managers Association, president, 1981-83; Brooklyn Association of Life Underwriters, president, 1986-87; The College of Insurance, adjunct professor, 1985-86; Knights of Columbus Council 2310, Grand Knight, 1987-88; Saint Mary's Pastoral Council, 1985-88; Saint Mary's Church, lector, 1981-; New York City Association of Life Underwriters, director, 1986-87; MBA Society of the College of Insurance, vice president, 1981-82. **HONORS/AWARDS:** New York State Jaycees

Speak-Up Champion, 1970-71. **HOME ADDRESS:** 101 Willow St, Roslyn Heights, NY 11577, (516)621-0489. **BUSINESS PHONE:** (516)627-3900.

ESQUIRE, ARTHUR SEITZ. *See* **ESGUERRA, ARTURO SAZON.**

EU, MARCH FONG
State official. Chinese American. **PERSONAL:** Born Mar 29, 1923, Oakdale, CA; daughter of Yuen Kong and Shiu Kong; married Henry Eu. **EDUCATION:** University of California, Berkeley, BS; Mills College, MEd; Stanford University, EdD; Columbia University; California State College, Hayward. **CAREER:** University of California Medical Center, Division of Dental Hygiene, chairman; Oakland Public Schools, dental hygienist; Alameda County Schools, supervisor of dental health education; Mills College, lecturer; Bureau of Intergroup Relations, California State Department of Education, special consultant; Sausalito Public Schools, Santa Clara County Office of Education, Santa Clara High School, Santa Clara Elementary School District, Live Oak Union High School District, educational and legislative consultant; State of California, secretary of state, 1974-; ambassador designate to Micrononesia, currently. **ORGANIZATIONS:** Alameda County Board of Education, president; Alameda County School Boards Assn, president; Chinese Young Ladies Society of Oakland, chapter president; Oakland YMCA, board of directors; Council of Social Planning, Citizens Committee on Housing; March of Dimes, Alameda County Mothers March, chairman; American Dental Hygienists' Assn, president; California Literacy Advisory Board, charter member; Asian Library Campaign of Friends of the Asian Library, honorary chair; Assembly Environmental Quality Committee, chairman; California State World Trade Commission, chair, 1983-87, ex officio member, 1987-. **HONORS/AWARDS:** Golden Gate Chapter of the Business and Professional Women's Club, Woman of Achievement Award; California Assn of Adult Education Administrators, Citation of Merit; Club Filipino Award of Honor, 1988; Natl Assn of Chinese American Bankers, Special Appreciation, 1990. **SPECIAL ACHIEVEMENTS:** Implementation of voter registration by mail; reduction of the cost of complying with the federally-mandated Voting Rights Act; elimination of notary public abuse of powers; streamlining and automation of filing requirements and procedures in the corporate, uniform commercial code and political reform divisions; fair implementation of the Political Reform Act of 1974 at a minimum cost to taxpayers; launched a traveling exhibit program, 1979; legislative approval and funding for a new archives building, 1988. **BUSINESS ADDRESS:** Secretary of State, State of California, 1230 J St, Ste 209, Sacramento, CA 95814, (916)445-6371.

EVANGELISTA, STELLA
Pediatrician, association administrator. Filipino American. **PERSONAL:** Born 1945, Cebu, Philippines; married Jose Evangelista; children: six. **CAREER:** Self-employed, pediatrician, currently. **ORGANIZATIONS:** Philippine Medical Association; Philippine-American Community Council; State of Michigan, Asian Advisory Council; American Citizens for Justice. **BUSINESS ADDRESS:** Pediatrician, 10475 Farmington Rd, Livonia, MI 48150.*

F

FA, ANGIE
Educational administrator. Chinese American. **EDUCATION:** Brown University, undergraduate and graduate degrees; University of California, Berkeley, PhD candidate, ethnic studies, currently. **CAREER:** City College of San Francisco, Asian American Studies Dept, chair, instructor, currently. **ORGANIZATIONS:** San Francisco Unified School District, board member, 1992-; Harvey Milk Democratic Club, president, 1992; Chinese American Democratic Club, board of directors; Palo Alto Tri-School Advisory Committee. **BUSINESS ADDRESS:** Board Member, Board of Education Office, San Francisco Unified School District, 135 Van Ness, Rm 120, San Francisco, CA 94102, (415)241-6000.*

FAJARDO, BEN
City government official. Filipino American. **PERSONAL:** married Adeline; children: B J, Julie, Tony, Melissa. **CAREER:** Dean Witter Financial Services Corp, computer systems consultant, currently; Village of Glendale Heights, village trustee, currently. **ORGANIZATIONS:** Community Organization Reaching Everyone; West Suburban Civic Group; Baranggay Lions Club; Filipino American Basketball League. **BUSINESS ADDRESS:** Village Trustee, District 6, Village of Glendale Heights, 300 Fullerton, Glendale Heights, IL 60139, (708)260-6000.*

FAJARDO, PETER
City government official. Filipino American. **CAREER:** Carson City Council, mayor pro tem, 1993, councilman, currently. **BUSINESS ADDRESS:** Mayor Pro Tem, Councilman, Carson City Council, 701 E Carson St, Carson, CA 90745, (310)830-7600.*

FALANIKO, FRANK, JR.
Landscape construction executive. Pacific Islander American. **PERSONAL:** Born Mar 30, 1956, American Samoa; son of Seli & Vui Falaniko; married Rosemarie Falaniko, Nov 2, 1985; children: Anthony, Andrew, Anmarie. **EDUCATION:** Seattle University, BA, public administration, 1979. **CAREER:** Green City Inc, president, currently. **BUSINESS ADDRESS:** President, Green City Inc, 14231 SE Allen Rd, Bellevue, WA 98006.

FALEOMAVAEGA, ENI FAAUAA HUNKIN, JR.
Government official. Pacific Islander American. **PERSONAL:** Born Aug 15, 1943, Vailoatai, American Samoa; son of Eni F and Taualai Manu; married A Hinanui Bambridge Cave; children: Temanuata, Taualai, Nifae, Vaimoana, Leonne. **EDUCATION:** Church College of Hawaii, AA, 1964; Brigham Young University, Provo, BA, 1966; University of Houston Law School, JD, 1972; University of California, Berkeley, Boalt Hall Law School, LLM, 1973. **CAREER:** American Samoa delegation to Washington, administrative asst to delegate, 1973-75; American Samoa Government, deputy attorney general, 1981-84, lieutenant governor, 1985-89; US House of Representatives, Committee on Interior Affairs, asst counsel, 1975-81, delegate for American Samoa, 1989-. **ORGANIZATIONS:** US House of Representatives, Committee on Foreign Affairs, 1989-, Committee on Natural Resources, 1989-, Committee on Education and Labor, 1992-; US Supreme Court Bar, 1978-. **MILITARY SERVICE:** US Army, captain, 1966-69; USAR, advocate general corp, judge. **BUSINESS ADDRESS:** 109 Cannon House Office Bldg, Washington, DC 20515-5201.

FAN, ADA MEI
Educator, advisor, writer. Chinese American. **PERSONAL:** Born Apr 5, 1953, Princeton, NJ; daughter of Chung Teh Fan and Mook-Lan Mui Fan; married Peter Warsaw, Sep 7, 1975; children: Arianna Solange Warsaw-Fan, Marina Cybele Warsaw-Fan. **EDUCATION:** Harvard University, AB (cum laude), folklore & mythology, 1975; Boston University, School of Public Communication, MS, film, 1979; University of Rochester, MA, English lit, 1981, PhD, English lit, 1988. **CAREER:** City Rochester Weekly, photographer, 1979-80, arts critic, 1980-81, contributing writer, 1981-84; University of Rochester, Department of English, assistant lecturer, 1981-82, assistant to director of expository writing, 1982-83, assistant director, composition and computation, 1983; Phillips Academy, advisor to Asian and Asian-American students, 1992-, instructor of English, 1983-. **ORGANIZATIONS:** MLA, 1980-; Asian American Resource Workshop, 1992-. **HONORS/AWARDS:** Phillips Academy, Francisc C Robertson Bicentennial Instructorship, 1993; PA William R Kenan Charitable Trust, Kenan Grant, 1991, 1989, 1984; New York State Press Association, 1st Place, best feature, div 2, 1982; University of Rochester, Rush Rhees & University Fellowships, 1979-82; IBM, Thomas Watson Memorial Scholarship, National Merit, 1971. **SPECIAL ACHIEVEMENTS:** White Snake, Black Ghost, novel in progress; "In Defense of Film: Teaching Film and Writing," A Very Good Place To Start, Boynton-Cook/Heinemann, 1990; contributor, Dictionary of American Book Publishing, 1986; David Raymond, sculptor, Art New England, July/August 1986. **BIOGRAPHICAL SOURCES:** Encyclopedia of Walt Disney's Animated Characters, Harper & Row, p 241-242, 1987. **BUSINESS ADDRESS:** Instructor of English, Advisor to Asian and Asian-American Students, Phillips Academy, Andover, MA 01810, (508)749-4185.

FAN, CAROL C.
Educator. Chinese American. **PERSONAL:** Born in China; daughter of Kie and Shao-yi Huang Fan; married Pow-foong Fan, Jan 30, 1965; children: Evelyn, Laura, Samuel. **EDUCATION:** University of California, Los Angeles, PhD, 1965. **CAREER:** University of Hawaii, Honolulu Community College, lecturer of history, 1975-80; University of Hawaii, Department of History, lecturer, 1981-89, Women's Studies Program, assistant professor, 1989-, Office For Women's Research, director, associate specialist, 1990-. **ORGANIZATIONS:** Association for Asian Studies; Asian American Studies; Western Association of Women Historians; National Organization for Women. **SPECIAL ACHIEVEMENTS:** Fluent in Chinese, reading knowledge of Japanese and French; author, "Asian American Women," "People's Republic of China," "Chinese Women in Hawaii: Migration, Work and Status," "Mod-

ernization, Christianity, and Higher Education: Ginling Women's College," "Geographic Distribution of Leadership in China, 1875-1937". **BUSINESS ADDRESS:** Professor, Women's Studies, University of Hawaii, 2424 Maile Way, Porteus 722, Honolulu, HI 96822, (808)956-8579.

FAN, CHANG-YUN
Educator (retired). Chinese American. **PERSONAL:** Born Jan 7, 1918, Nantong, Jiangsu, China; son of Li-Zhuan and Sze-Shue Chen; married Tsung-Ying Teng Fan, Sep 29, 1950; children: Paula, Anna, Michael. **EDUCATION:** Central University, China, BA, 1941; University of Chicago, PhD, 1952. **CAREER:** University of Chicago, research associate, 1952-57; University of Arkansas, assistant professor, 1957-58; University of Chicago, senior physicist, research associate, professor, 1958-67; University of Arizona, professor, 1967-88, professor emeritus, 1988-. **ORGANIZATIONS:** American Physical Society, fellow; American Geophysical Union. **SPECIAL ACHIEVEMENTS:** Discovery of 33p nuclide, new 02 band in auroral emission, high energy electrons near the earth's bow shock, H and He isotopes in primary cosmic radiation, partially stripped ions in solar cosmic rays, and Li and B isotopes in cosmic dust particles; measured Lamb shift in 6 $Li++$ and $1607+$ ions. **HOME ADDRESS:** 1760 N Potter Place, Tucson, AZ 85719, (602)325-4252. **BUSINESS ADDRESS:** Professor, Dept of Physics, University of Arizona, Tucson, AZ 85721, (602)621-2778.

FAN, CHIEN
Engineer. Chinese American. **PERSONAL:** Born Apr 1, 1930, Hai-men, Jiangsu, Taiwan; son of Chin-Meng Fan and Shi-Mei Fan; married Ning-Sun Fan, May 3, 1958; children: Albert, May, Marie. **EDUCATION:** National Taiwan University, BS, 1954; University of Illinois, MS, 1958, PhD, 1964. **CAREER:** Florida State University, assistant professor, 1961-65; Lockheed Missiles & Space Company, group engineer, 1987-89, project engineer, 1989-91, sr staff engineer, 1991-. **ORGANIZATIONS:** ASME, 1961-75; AIAA, 1961-75; New York Academy of Sciences, 1972-82; Pi Mu Epsilon, 1962-; Sigma Xi, 1962-. **HONORS/AWARDS:** Lockheed, President's Award, 1984; NASA, Head-Quarter's Award, 1986; National Science Foundation, Visiting Scientist to Republic of China, 1970. **SPECIAL ACHIEVEMENTS:** Published numerous papers and research reports in the areas of heat transfer, fluid mechanics, rarefied gas, dynamics and applied mathematics, 1964-; languages: Chinese, English, French, German. **BUSINESS ADDRESS:** Senior Staff Engineer, Lockheed Missiles & Space Co, 1111 Lockheed Way, PO Box 504, Sunnyvale, CA 94086.

FAN, LIANG-SHIH
Educator. Taiwanese American. **PERSONAL:** Born Dec 15, 1947, Taiwan; married. **EDUCATION:** Natl Taiwan University, BSChE, 1970; West Virginia University, MSChE, 1973, PhD, ChE, 1975; Kansas State University, MS, statistics, 1978. **CAREER:** Taiwan Sugar Corp, 1968; Taiwan Cyanamide Co, pharmaceutical technician, 1968; West Virginia University, graduate research asst, 1971-75; postdoctoral research associate, 1975; Mebtex Co, process engineer, 1974-75; Kansas State University, postdoctoral research associate, 1975-76; visiting asst professor, 1976-78; University of Tokyo, visiting asst professor, 1978; Ohio State University, asst professor, 1978-81, associate professor, 1981-85, professor, 1985-; Amoco Oil Co, research engineer, 1979; Argonne Natl Lab, research associate, 1980; Pittsburgh Energy Technology Center, research fellow, 1982; US Dept of Energy, research fellow, 1983; Japan Society for the Promotion of Science, visiting professor, 1991. **ORGANIZATIONS:** AIChE; Sigma Xi; Society of Chemical Engineering of Japan; Fine Particle Society; ACS; ASEE; American Filtration Society. **HONORS/AWARDS:** Battelle Memorial Inst, Res Award, 1980; Ohio State University, Sr Res Award, 1982, 1985, 1989, Lumley Res Award, 1993, Distinguished Res/Scholar Award, 1983, Stanley E Harrison Faculty Award for Excellence in Engg Educ, 1987, Charles E Macquigg Award for Outstanding Teaching, 1989, Intl Outstanding Faculty Award, 1992; Sigma Xi, Res Award, 1983; AIChE, Innovation in Chemical Engg Award, 1985; ·University of Cambridge, Fulbright-Hays Scholar, 1991; 1994 American Institute of Chemical Engineers Fluid-Particle Systems Plenary Lectureship Award, 1992; Alexander von Humbolt Foundation, US Distinguished Sr Scientist Award, Germany, 1993.

FANG, CHENG-SHEN
Educator. Taiwanese American. **PERSONAL:** Born Mar 29, 1936, Taipei, Taiwan; son of Ho-Chin Fang and Lai-Mei P Fang; married Fei-Ying Fang, Oct 5, 1972. **EDUCATION:** National Taiwan University, BS, 1958; University of Houston, MS, 1965, PhD, 1968. **CAREER:** Taiwan Fertilizer Co, Factory No 6, shift-supervisor, 1960-62; University of Houston, postdoctoral fellow, 1968-

69; University of Southwestern Louisiana, professor, 1969-. **ORGANIZATIONS:** American Institute of Chemical Engineers, 1969-; Society of Petroleum Engineers, 1980-. **HONORS/AWARDS:** University of Southwestern Louisiana, Elori Girard Professorship in Engineering, 1987-93. **SPECIAL ACHIEVEMENTS:** 15 papers in refereed journals; 27 presentations in national professional society meetings; 2 computer software packages marketed by Gulf Publishing Co, Houston TX. **BUSINESS ADDRESS:** Professor, Dept of Chemical Engineering, University of Southwestern Louisiana, PO Box 44130, Lafayette, LA 70504, (318)231-5350.

FANG, FABIAN TIEN-HWA
Educator. Chinese American. **PERSONAL:** Born Oct 14, 1929, Nanjing, Jiangsu, China; son of Thome H Fang and Lillian Y Kao; married Mei-Ling Fang, Dec 9, 1978; children: Grace L, Linda S. **EDUCATION:** National Central University, China, BS, 1949; University of Illinos, Urbana-Champaign, MS, 1952, PhD, 1954. **CAREER:** Rohm & Haas Company, senior research chemist, 1957-64; University of Wisconsin, Milwaukee, assistant professor of chemistry, 1964-69; California State University, Bakersfield, associate professor of chemistry, 1970-72, Department of Chemistry, chair, 1970-74, professor of chemistry, 1972-, Center of International Education, director, 1988-. **BUSINESS ADDRESS:** Director, Center of Intl Education, California State University, Bakersfield, 9001 Stockdale Highway, Bakersfield, CA 93311-1099.

FANG, FLORENCE
Newspaper executive. Chinese American. **CAREER:** Asian Week, owner, currently. **ORGANIZATIONS:** Asian Americans for Bush/Quayle 92, rally co-chair, 1992; Mayor Frank Jordan's Transition Team for Economic Development, chair, 1992. **BUSINESS ADDRESS:** Owner, Asian Week, 809 Sacramento, San Francisco, CA 94108.*

FANG, FLORENCE S.
Scientist. **CAREER:** Department of Health and Human Services, Chemistry II Division, branch chief, currently. **BUSINESS ADDRESS:** Branch Chief-Chemistry II Division, Dept of Health and Human Services, Office of Generic Drugs, 5600 Fishers Ln, Rockville, MD 20857, (301)295-8305.*

FANG, FRANK F.
Physicist, researcher. Chinese American. **PERSONAL:** Born Sep 11, 1930, Peiping, China; married 1957; children: four. **EDUCATION:** Natl University, Taiwan, BS, 1951; University of Notre Dame, MS, 1954; University of Illinois, PhD, electrical engineering, 1959. **CAREER:** University of Illinois, associate, physics and electronics, 1957-59; Boeing Airplane Co, research engineer, 1959-60; IBM Corp, T J Watson Research Center, research staff member, 1960-. **ORGANIZATIONS:** IEEE; American Physics Society; Franklin Institute; Sigma Xi; Natl Academy of Engineering. **HONORS/AWARDS:** IEEE, David Sarnoff Award, 19817; American Physics Society, Oliver E Buckley Prize, 1988; Humboldt Award, 1990; Natl Chiaotung University, honorary DSc, 1989. **BUSINESS ADDRESS:** Research Staff Member, Thomas J Watson Research Center, IBM Corp, PO Box 218, Yorktown Heights, NY 10598.*

FANG, JAMES
City government official. Chinese American. **CAREER:** Office of Economic Planning & Development, director of commerce & trade, currently. **BUSINESS ADDRESS:** Director of Commerce & Trade, Office of Economic Planning & Development, Rm 156, City Hall, San Francisco, CA 94102, (415)554-6477.*

FANG, JIN BAO
Mechanical engineer. Taiwanese American. **PERSONAL:** Born Sep 20, 1934, Tainan, Taiwan; married Jenny Chin-Fong Huang, Dec 23, 1964; children: Vickie, Kenneth. **EDUCATION:** National Taiwan University, BSc, chemical eng, 1957; University of New Brunswick, MSc, chemical eng, 1966, PhD, chemical eng, 1969. **CAREER:** US Department of Commerce, National Institute of Standards and Technology, chemical engineer, 1969-81, mechanical engineer, 1981-. **ORGANIZATIONS:** American Institute of Chemical Engineers; North American Taiwanese Professors Association. **SPECIAL ACHIEVEMENTS:** "Field Measurement of the Thermal Resistance of Office Buildings," Thermal Insulation: Material and Systems, F J Powell and S L Matthews, American Society for Testing and Materials, Philadelphia, 1987, p 107-123; over 30 other publications. **MILITARY SERVICE:** Taiwanese Army, 2nd lieutenant, 1958-59. **HOME ADDRESS:** 16412 Montecrest Lane, Gaithersburg, MD 20878, (301)869-3539. **BUSINESS ADDRESS:** Mechanical/Chemical Engineer, US Department of Commerce, National Insti-

tute of Standards and Technology, Building and Fire Res Lab, Room A313, Gaithersburg, MD 20899, (301)975-6417.

FANG, JOHN TA-CHUAN. *See* Obituaries.

FANG, LOUIS LI-YEH
Aerospace engineer. Taiwanese American. **PERSONAL:** Born Jul 14, 1963, Taipei, Taiwan; son of James C Fang and Judy L Fang. **EDUCATION:** Cerritos Community College, 1981-83; California State Polytechnic University, Pomona, BSc, 1986; California State University, Long Beach, 1986-87; University of Colorado, Boulder, MEng, 1993. **CAREER:** Martin Marietta, inertia upper stage independent verification and validation guidance and navigation engr, 1987-90; Titan IV flight control software and validation engr, 1990-. **ORGANIZATIONS:** Sigma Gamma Tau, 1985. **BUSINESS ADDRESS:** Engineer, Martin Marietta, Astronautics Group, PO Box 179, MSL-5420, Denver, CO 80201, (303)971-3165.

FANG, MING M. *See* Obituaries.

FANG, PEN JENG
Consulting engineering company executive. Taiwanese American. **PERSONAL:** Born Jul 13, 1931, Taiwan; son of Den Chuan Fang and Wu Tian Su Fang; married Elizabeth M Fang; children: Kenneth Z, Terry C, Shona C. **EDUCATION:** National Taiwan University, BS, 1955; Oklahoma State University, MS, 1960; Cornell University, PhD, civil engineering, 1966. **CAREER:** Inar C Hillman & Associates, section leader, 1960-62; US Steel Corporation, senior research engineer, 1965-68; Sir George Williams University, assistant professor, 1968-70; University of Rhode Island, associate professor, 1970-82; Federal University of Rio de Janeiro, University of Sao Paulo, visiting professor, 1977-79; ITT-Grinnell Corporation, engineering analysis manager, 1982-85; Roger Williams College, coordinator of engineering, professor, 1987-90; Engitek Incorporated, president, 1985-. **ORGANIZATIONS:** American Society of Civil Engineers, 1963-; American Water Works Association, 1991-; Association of Energy Engineers, senior member, 1988-; National Fire Protection Association, 1990-; Rotary Club, 1989-; Rhode Island Police Chiefs Association, associate member, 1989-; Rhode Island Fire Safety Board, 1988-; Zoning Board of Review, N Kingston, Rhode Island, 1990-. **HONORS/ AWARDS:** American Society of Civil Engineers, Collingwood Prize, 1967. **SPECIAL ACHIEVEMENTS:** 25 technical papers in civil, structural and mechanical engineering journals, proceedings, 1966-84; language proficiency in Chinese, Japanese and Portugese; designed numerous structures for multistory buildings, power stations, chemical plants, piping networks, 1960-. **BUSINESS ADDRESS:** President, Engitek, Incorporation, 1370 Plainfield St, Cranston, RI 02919-6891.

FARHATAZIZ
Physician. Pakistani American/Indo-American. **PERSONAL:** Born Dec 19, 1932, Amritsar, Punjab, India; son of Abdul Haq and Khurshaid Begum; married Nasra Farhataziz, Aug 29, 1970; children: Shaneela, Nabeel, Ebram. **EDUCATION:** Panjab University, BSc, BSc (honors), 1951, 1953, MSc (honors), 1954; Cambridge University, PhD, 1959; University of Texas Health Science Center, MD, 1988. **CAREER:** Panjab University, lecturer, 1954-56, 1959-60; Pakistan Atomic Energy Commission, principal scientific officer, 1960-70; University of Notre Dame, officer, post doctoral fellow, 1970-77; Texas Woman's University, research faculty associate professor, 1977-84; St Paul Medical Center, resident, 1988-90; University of Texas Health Science Center, resident, 1990-93; Daisy Marquis Jones Radiation Oncology Center, physician, currently. **ORGANIZATIONS:** American Society for Therapeutic Radiology and Oncology, 1990-; American Medical Association, 1988-; Texas Medical Association, 1988-; Bexar County Medical Association, 1992-. **HONORS/AWARDS:** Panjab University, Oman Prize, Gold Medal, 1953, 1956; Govt College, Academic Role of Honor, 1954; The Royal Commission for Scholarship for PhD, 1956-59; The Exhibition of 1851, Pakistan Atomic Energy Commission, Honoraria, 1963, 1970. **SPECIAL ACHIEVEMENTS:** Published more than 60 research publications, reports, books in radiation chemistry and physical chemistry. **BUSINESS ADDRESS:** Physician, Daisy Marquis Jones Radiation Oncolgy Center, Highland Hospital, 1000 South Ave, Rochester, NY 14620.

FAROOQUI, MOHAMMED Y. H.
Educator. Indo-American. **PERSONAL:** Born Aug 12, 1947, Hyderabad, Andhra Pradesh, India; son of Mohammed Z H Farooqui and Izzat Fatima; married Ather Vaseema Farooqui, Jun 23, 1978; children: Mohammed Z H,

Seema Y, Mohammed A R. **EDUCATION:** Andhra Pradesh Agricultural University, BS, 1968, MS, 1970; University of Illinois, MS, 1975, PhD, 1979. **CAREER:** University of Illinois, teaching assistant, 1977-79; University of Texas, Galveston, post doc research assoc, 1979-84, assistant professor, 1984-88; University of Texas, Pan American, Edinburg, associate professor, 1988-94, professor, 1994-. **ORGANIZATIONS:** Intl Soc for the Study of Xenobiotics, 1990-; Soc of Toxicology, 1987-; Gulf Coast Soc of Toxicology, 1985-; Entomological Soc of America, 1980-; American Chemical Soc, Pesticide Div, 1984-; University of Texas Radiation Safety Officers Group, 1990-; Natl Career Institute, advisory board, 1991-92. **HONORS/AWARDS:** NIGMS, Minority Biomedical Research Support Award, 1990-94; NIH, Academic Research Enhancement Award, 1990-93, Minority Biomedical Research Support Award, 1986-90; University of Texas Pan American, Outstanding Faculty Award, 1989, Research Awards, 1984-87. **SPECIAL ACHIEVEMENTS:** Established a toxicology laboratory, developed Radiation Safety Program, University of Texas Pan American; co-author: "Toxicokinetics of Allylnitrile in Rats," Drug Metab Dispos, vol 21, p 460-66, 1993; "Metabolism of Allylnitrile to Cyanide: In vitro Studies," Res Commun Chem Pathol Pharmacol, vol 81, p 355-68, 1993. **BUSINESS ADDRESS:** Professor of Biology, University of Texas Pan American, 1201 W University Dr, Science Bldg, Rm 0235, Edinburg, TX 78539-2999, (210)381-3537.

FAROUK, BAKHTIER
Educator. Bangladeshi American. **PERSONAL:** Born Dec 5, 1951, Dhaka, Bangladesh; son of Abdullah & Sophia Farouk; married Nadira, Aug 22, 1982; children: Samira. **EDUCATION:** Bangladesh University of Engineering & Technology, BS, 1975; University of Delaware, MS, 1979, PhD, 1981. **CAREER:** Bangladesh University, Engineering & Technology, lecturer; University of Houston, research assistant, 1976-77; University of Delaware, research/ teaching assistant, 1977-81; Drexel University, assistant professor, 1981-86, associate professor, 1986-89, professor of mechanical engineering, 1989-. **ORGANIZATIONS:** American Society of Mechanical Engineer, 1981-; Combustion Institute, 1982-; American Institute of Astronautics, 1986-. **HONORS/AWARDS:** Society of Automotive Engineers, Teetor Award, 1986; American Society of Metals, Henry Marion Howe Medal, 1988; Drexel University, Research Achievement Award, 1993. **SPECIAL ACHIEVEMENTS:** Development of computational models for complex industrial flow problems; modeling of turbulent and non-reactive and reactive flows; modeling of multiphase flows for plasma deposition; CVD and chemical reactors. **HOME ADDRESS:** 16 Tunbridge Rd, Cherry Hill, NJ 08003, (609)751-2935. **BUSINESS ADDRESS:** Professor, Dept of Mechanical Engineering & Mechanics, Drexel University, 32 & Chestnut Streets, Philadelphia, PA 19104, (215)895-2287.

FASANG, PATRICK PAD
Semiconductor company executive. Thai American. **PERSONAL:** Born Nov 14, 1941, Bangkok, Thailand; son of Wah Sung Tang & Yok Sim Huang; married Kazuko Kay Shinoda, Jun 16, 1972; children: Mary Sim, Naomi Mitz, Patricia Hazel. **EDUCATION:** California State University, Fresno, BSEE, 1965, San Jose, MSEE, 1968; Oregon State University, PhD, elec engineering, 1974. **CAREER:** Sprague Electric, electronic design engr, 1967-69; University of Portland, associate professor, 1972-78; Bonneville Power Administration, cons engineer, 1975-78; RCA Corp, administrator, 1978-79; Siemens Corp, group leader, 1980-83; Gen Electric Co, mgr, 1983-86; Spectrum Semiconductor Inc, director, beginning 1987; Hitachi America, manager, currently. **ORGANIZATIONS:** Computer Society, chmn, Portland chpt; IEEE, fellow, Industrial Electronics Society, vp, tech activities, 1981-83, publs, 1984-85, board of directors, 1986-; Electronics Group Club, chairman, 1975-76. **HONORS/AWARDS:** Centennial Medal, 1984; Anthony J Hornfeck Service Award, 1987; Spain, Master of Gold Award, 1986. **HOME ADDRESS:** 19915 Wellington Ct, Saratoga, CA 95070. **BUSINESS PHONE:** (415)244-7271.

FEN, ALLAN MING
Investment company executive. Chinese American. **PERSONAL:** Born Jan 20, 1957, Durham, NC; son of Sing-Nan Fen and Sylvia Fen; married May Zhang Fen, Aug 19, 1989; children: Cameron. **EDUCATION:** University of Nebraska, BS (high distinction), math, economics, 1979. **CAREER:** Northwestern National Life, asst vice pres, 1979-83; John Hancock Financial Services, associate actuary, 1983-87; Fidelity Investments, senior vice pres, 1987-. **ORGANIZATIONS:** Society of Actuaries, fellow, 1979-; American Academy of Actuaries, 1981-; Boston Actuaries Club, 1983-, president, 1993-. **HONORS/AWARDS:** Phi Beta Kappa, 1979. **SPECIAL ACHIEVEMENTS:** Articles: "Using Interest Rate Futures in the Financial Management

of GIC's,'' Transactions of the Society of Actuaries Journal, 1985; ''Performances Measurement for GIC,'' Pensions and Investments Magazine. **BUSINESS ADDRESS:** Senior Vice President, Fidelity Investments, 82 Devonshire St, L10B, Boston, MA 02109-3614, (617)570-5651.

FENG, GUOFU JEFF (G. F.)
Semiconductor engineer. Chinese American. **PERSONAL:** Born Oct 10, 1957, Ningbo, Zhejiang, People's Republic of China; son of Deming Feng and Juhua Zhang; married Qinghua Jenny Cai, Feb 17, 1986; children: Sandra C, Lynna C. **EDUCATION:** Peking University, BS, 1982; Chinese Academy of Science, Institute of Physics, 1982-83; Virginia Polytechnic Institute & State University, PhD, 1989. **CAREER:** Virginia Tech, graduate research asst, 1983-89; University of Illinois, research associate, 1989-92, sr research engr, 1992; Applied Materials, sr process engr, 1992-. **ORGANIZATIONS:** American Physical Society, 1983-; Materials Research Society, 1990-. **SPECIAL ACHIEVEMENTS:** Published: 18 research articles in scientific journals including Physical Review, Applied Physics Letter; made over ten presentations in national and international conferences; co-invented three pending US patents. **BUSINESS ADDRESS:** Senior Process Engineer, Applied Materials, 3050 Bowers Ave, Santa Clara, CA 95054, (408)235-6901.

FENG, JONATHAN LEE
Researcher. Chinese American. **PERSONAL:** Born Mar 6, 1967, Ann Arbor, MI; son of Lydia Lee Feng and William Feng. **EDUCATION:** Harvard University, BA, 1988; Cambridge University, Trinity College, MA, 1990; Stanford University, PhD candidate, 1990-. **CAREER:** Stanford Linear Accelerator Center, researcher, currently. **ORGANIZATIONS:** Phi Beta Kappa, 1987-; American Physical Society, 1987-; Harvard-Radcliffe Orchestra, 1984-88. **HONORS/AWARDS:** Marshall Scholar, 1988; National Science Foundation, Graduate Fellowship, 1989; Time Magazine Inc, College Achievement Award, 1987; Presidential Scholar, 1984. **SPECIAL ACHIEVEMENTS:** Stanford University, Concerto Competition Award Winner, trumpet, 1991, Levine Excellence in Teaching Award, 1993. **BUSINESS ADDRESS:** Researcher, Stanford Linear Accelerator Center, Bin 81, PO Box 4349, Stanford, CA 94309, (415)926-4410.

FENG, THEO-DRIC
Behavioral analyst, broadcast producer/host. Chinese American. **PERSONAL:** Born Jun 16, 1953, Springfield, VT; son of Tsun-Ying Feng and Rohran Tung. **EDUCATION:** UCLA, BA, 1975; SFSU, MS, 1979. **CAREER:** Census Bureau, personnel management specialist, 1979-82; Army Research Institute, research psychologist, 1982-92; Army Research Laboratory, behavioral analyst, 1992-; WPFW, Gold Mountain Radio Show, host/producer, 1979-. **ORGANIZATIONS:** Asian American Arts & Media, Inc; Asian American Journalists Association; National AA Telecommunications Association, 1980-82; Asian Pacific Personnel Association, 1979-82; Association of AA Studies. **SPECIAL ACHIEVEMENTS:** Author: Measures of Effectiveness Compendium for Army Systems, 1991; ''Earrradiation: Gold Mountain Radio,'' Moving the Image: Independent Asian Pacific Amer Media Arts, UCLA Asian Amer Studies Ctr & Visual Communications, 1991; presenter, ''Asian American Music,'' Asian Amer studies conference, 1992; judge, Corp for Public Broadcasting Public Radio Awards, 1990; judge, American Psychological Assn, Award for Radio Coverage, judge, 1993. **BIOGRAPHICAL SOURCES:** ''The Voice of Asian Americans,'' by Valerie Chow Bush, Washington Post, Style section, Sep 10, 1990. **BUSINESS ADDRESS:** Host/Producer, Gold Mountain Radio Show, WPFW, 702 H St NW, Washington, DC 20001.

FENG, TSE-YUN
Educator. Chinese American. **PERSONAL:** Born in Hangzhou, Zhejiang, China; son of Shih-ching Feng & Lin Shao; married Elaine Feng; children: Wuchun, Wu-chi, Wu-che, Wu-chang. **EDUCATION:** National Taiwan University, BS; Oklahoma State University, MS; University of Michigan, PhD. **CAREER:** Syracuse University, assistant professor, 1967-71, associate professor, 1971-75; Wayne State University, professor, 1975-79; Wright State University, professor, chairman, 1979-80; Ohio State University, professor, 1980-84; Pennsylvania State University, Computer Engineering Program, director, 1984-88, Binder professor of computer engineering, 1984-. **ORGANIZATIONS:** IEEE Computer Society, IEEE Transactions Parallel and Distributed Systems, editor-in-chief, 1989-, Computer Standards History Committee, chairman, 1989-92, Distinguished Visitors Program, chairman, 1987-91; Computer Science Accreditation Commission, program evaluator, 1986-92; The Computer Museum, founder, 1983-. **HONORS/AWARDS:** IEEE Computer

Society, Technical Achievement Award, 1991, Outstanding Contribution Award, 1991; Pennsylvania State Engineering Society, Outstanding Research Award, 1989; IEEE Computer Society, Meritorious Service Award, 1987, Richard E Merwin Distinguished Services Award, 1985; IEEE Computer Society, Special Award, distinguished service as president of IEEE Computer Society during the years 1979-80, 1981. **SPECIAL ACHIEVEMENTS:** Co-guest editor, Proceedings of the IEEE, December 1989; ''A New Fault-Tolerant Network Architecture,'' Workshop on the Future Trends of Distributed Computing Systems, September 1993; ''Parallel Processors,'' The Electrical Engineering Handbook, Richard C Dorf, CRC Press, Boca Raton, pp89.1-8, January 1993; Y M Yeh, ''On a Class of Rearrangeable Networks,'' IEEE Trans on Computers, pp1361-1379, November 1992; patent, Associative Memory System with Reduced Redundancy of Stored Information, patent 3,618,017, November 1971. **BIOGRAPHICAL SOURCES:** A Century of Honors, IEEE, 1984.

FENG, XIN
Educator. Chinese American. **PERSONAL:** Born Jul 1, 1951, Beijing, People's Republic of China; son of Jie-chen Lin & Zheng Feng; married Ling Tian, Aug 25, 1977; children: Justin S, Jing. **EDUCATION:** Beijing Institute of Technology, BS, 1975, MEng, 1981; Washington University, St Louis, MS, 1984, PhD, 1987. **CAREER:** Washington University, St Louis, research assistant, 1982-87; Marquette University, assistant professor, 1987-. **ORGANIZATIONS:** Institute of Electrical and Electronics Engineers, 1986-; Association of Computing Machinery, 1988-; American Association for Artificial Intelligence, 1989-; American Society for Engineering Education, 1987-. **HONORS/AWARDS:** Tau Beta Pi, 1986-; Sigma Xi, 1988-90. **SPECIAL ACHIEVEMENTS:** Distinguished scholar in the area of Optimization Theory and Applications, Artificial Intelligence, Neural Networks, and Expert Systems; published more than 30 papers in journals and conferences. **BUSINESS ADDRESS:** Ast Professor, Dept of Electrical and Computer Engrg, Marquette University, 1515 W Wisconsin Ave, Milwaukee, WI 53233-2295, (414)288-3504.

FINUCANE, MATTHEW H.
Labor official. Japanese American. **PERSONAL:** Born Apr 2, 1952, Washington, DC; son of James Finucane & Kiyoko Nishiyama; married Alexandra Finucane, Apr 1, 1979; children: Brendan, Adrienne. **EDUCATION:** Carleton College, BS, 1974; Georgetown University Law School, JD, 1978, LLM, labor law, 1988. **CAREER:** Center for Auto Safety, attorney, 1979-80; Aviation Consumer Action Project, director, 1980-84; Association of Flight Attendants, AFL-CIO, safety & health director, 1984-92; Asian Pacific American Labor Alliance, AFL-CIO, executive director, currently. **ORGANIZATIONS:** Japanese American Citizens League; National Asian Pacific American Bar Association. **BUSINESS ADDRESS:** Executive Director, Asian Pacific Amer Labor Alliance, AFL-CIO, 1444 Eye St NW, Ste 702, Washington, DC 20006, (202)842-1263.

FISCHER, TAKAYO
Actress. Japanese American. **PERSONAL:** Born Nov 25, Hardwick, CA; daughter of Chukuro & Kinko Tsubouchi; married Sy Fischer, Nov 29, 1980; children: Toya Gabeler, John Howland Doran, Juliet Doran. **EDUCATION:** Rollins College, 1951-53. **CAREER:** Actress, currently; theatre experience includes: Sayonara, Alex Theatre; Mothers, Crossroads Theatre Co; Into the Woods, East West Players; Tea, Syracuse Stage, numerous other stages; Canton Jazz Club, East West Players; To Sir With Love, Musical Workshop;Radio Shows, LA Theatre Works; Oyakoshinju, LA Theatre Works; Mothers, LA Theatre Works; motion pictures include: Bloodrunner; The Dangerous; Showdown in Little Tokyo; Pacific Heights; Dad; The Wash; When Time Ran Out; Rollercoaster; telvision movies include: Stolen Hearts; Based on an Untrue Story; Internal Affairs; American Geisha; Flight of the Enola Gay; Father Damien-The Leper Priest; The Franken Project; numerous episodic telvision appearances. **HONORS/AWARDS:** Dramalogue Award, ensemble performance of Tea, Old Globe Theatre performance in San Diego, 1988; Miss Misei Queen, Chicago. **SPECIAL ACHIEVEMENTS:** Into the Woods, 1992. **HOME ADDRESS:** 10590 Wilshire Blvd, #1601, Los Angeles, CA 90024, (310)475-5801.

FITZPATRICK, EILEEN TABATA
Fashion industry executive. Japanese American. **PERSONAL:** Born Apr 19, 1944, Rivers, AZ; daughter of Masanobu & Suyeko Tabata; married Robert Fitzpatrick, Oct 11, 1975. **EDUCATION:** San Jose State University, BS, 1967. **CAREER:** TMI Corporation, executive vice president, 1971-88; Kanojo USA,

co-founder, principal, 1990-. **ORGANIZATIONS:** National Association Women Business Owners, currently; Japanese American National Museum, currently; Japanese American Citizens League, Selanoco Chapter; National Japanese American Historical Society. **SPECIAL ACHIEVEMENTS:** Designs inducted into Smithsonian Institution, Washington, DC, 1993. **BUSINESS ADDRESS:** Co-Founder, Principal, Kanojo USA, 18003 Sky Park Circle, Ste G, Irvine, CA 92714, (714)955-2250.

FLEMMING, STANLEY LALIT KUMAR
State official, physician. Indo-American. **PERSONAL:** Born Mar 30, 1953, Rosebud, SD; son of Homer W Flemming & Evelyn C Misra Flemming; married Martha S Flemming, Jul 2, 1977; children: Emily, Drew, Claire. **EDUCATION:** Pierce College, AAS, 1973; University of Washington, BS, 1976; Pacific Lutheran University, MA, 1979; College of Osteopathic Medicine of the Pacific, DO, 1985. **CAREER:** Community Health Care Delivery System, medical director, 1990-; Washington House of Representatives, representative, 1993-. **ORGANIZATIONS:** American Osteopathic Association; American Medical Association; American Academy of Family Practice; American College of General Practice; Society of Adolescent Medicine; Association of Military Surgeons of the United States; Rotary International; Washington Osteopathic Medical Association; Washington State Medical Association. **HONORS/AWARDS:** College of Osteopathic Medicine of the Pacific Alumni, Outstanding Service Award, 1992; Washington Osteopathic Medical Association, Physician of the Year, 1993; Long Beach Medical Services Association, Resident of the Year, 1988; Pacific Hospital of Long Beach, Intern of the Year, 1986, Outstanding Teacher Award, 1988; College of Osteopathic Medicine of Pacific, Pauline Pumerantz-Weiss Award, Role Model Physician, 1985. **MILITARY SERVICE:** US Army, lt col, 1974-; The Bronze Star, 1991; Meritorious Service Medal, 1981; Army Commendation Medal, 1986, 1988; Reserve Commendation Medal, 1985, 1989; Army Reserve Medal, 1984; National Defense Medal, 1991; Southwest Asia Medal, 1991; Kuwait Liberation Medal, 1991; Combat Medical Badge, 1991; Flight Surgeon Wings, 1985. **BUSINESS ADDRESS:** Representative, Washington House of Representatives, John L O'Brien Bldg, Rm 428, State Capital Campus, Olympia, WA 98504, (206)786-7958.

FLORENTINO, LEILA SAN JOSE
Actress, singer. Filipino American. **PERSONAL:** Born Aug 12, Quezon City, Manila, Philippines; daughter of Alberto Florentino and Eva Florentino. **EDUCATION:** University of the Philippines, 1981-84. **CAREER:** Solo cabaret show, New York City, producer, director, performer, until 1992; Miss Saigon, Broadway, plays lead role of Kim, 1992-.

FLORES, SUSAN GUMABAO
Physician. Filipino American. **PERSONAL:** married Toribio (Roy) Flores; children: Michael, Jennifer. **EDUCATION:** University of Santo Tomas, Manila, graduate of medicine, 1973; Cleveland Institute of Music, piano. **CAREER:** Elizabeth General Hospital, intern, 1976-77; Lutheran Medical Center, internal medicine residency, 1977-80, chief resident, 1979-80; St Alexis Hospital, internist, 1990-. **ORGANIZATIONS:** Association of Philippine Physicians; Philippine American Society; Broadway School of Music and the Arts. **HONORS/AWARDS:** St Alexis Women's Health Champion, 1992. **BUSINESS ADDRESS:** Internist, St Alexis Women's Center, 5163 Broadway Ave, Cleveland, OH 44127, (216)429-8443. *

FOK, AGNES KWAN
Educator. Chinese American. **PERSONAL:** Born Dec 11, 1940, Hong Kong; daughter of Sun Kwan and You Ng Kwan; married Yu-Si Fok, Jun 8, 1965; children: Licie E, Edna C. **EDUCATION:** College of Great Falls, BA, 1965; Utah State University, MS, 1966; University of Texas, PhD, 1971. **CAREER:** University of Hawaii, asst research professor, pathology dept, 1973-74, Ford Foundation Postdoctoral Fellow, anatomy dept, 1975, associate research professor, biology program, 1985, graduate faculty, microbiology dept, 1977-; Pacific Biomedical Research Center, University of Hawaii, asst research professor, 1975-82, associate research professor, 1982-88, research professor, 1988-. **ORGANIZATIONS:** Sigma Xi, treasurer of local chapter, 1979-; American Society for Cell Biology, 1977-; Society for Protozoologist, 1977-. **HONORS/AWARDS:** University of Hawaii, Ford Foundation Postdoctoral Fellow, 1975. **SPECIAL ACHIEVEMENTS:** Numerous scientific publications in refereed journals. **BUSINESS ADDRESS:** Research Professor, University of Hawaii, 2538 The Mall, Snyder Hall, Room 306, Honolulu, HI 96822, (808)956-8029.

FOK, SAMUEL SHIU-MING
Engineer (retired), consultant. Chinese American. **PERSONAL:** Born Feb 15, 1926, Macau, Kwangtung Province, China; son of Yan Nung Fok and Bick Lan Cheong Fok; married Ruth Sing-Lan Sung Fok, Aug 16, 1952; children: William David Z C, John Peter Z Y, James Andrew Z M. **EDUCATION:** Lingnan University, 1945-47; Ohio State University, BChE, 1949; Case Institute of Technology, MSChE, 1951, PhD, chemical engineering, 1955. **CAREER:** Industrial Rayon Corporation, research engineer, 1954-56; Shockley Transistor Corporation, senior staff engineer, 1956-60; Fairchild R&D Lab, technical staff, 1960-70; Siliconix Inc, mask tech manager, 1971-74; FCT Brothers Company Ltd, Bangkok, Thailand, deputy director, 1975-77; Perkin-Elmer EBT Division, principal engineer, 1977-90; E-Bean Lithography, consultant, president, 1990-. **ORGANIZATIONS:** American Vacuum Society; Soc Photographic Instrument Engineers; Semiconductor Mfg Engineers Institute, micropatterning committee; Stanford Area Chinese Club, past president, chartered member, 1965-; Palo Alto Chinese Language School, principal, 1962-66; Pacific Art League of Palo Alto; Chinese Institute of Engineers, permanent member; American Soc Testing Materials, F-1 committee. **HONORS/AWARDS:** Sigma Xi, Cleveland Chapter, 1951; Tau Beta Pi, Columbus, Ohio Chapter, 1949. **SPECIAL ACHIEVEMENTS:** Over 60 published technical articles in submicron lithography field; troubleshooting in material and processes for various customers worldwide; amature Chinese brush painter; language proficiency in: Mandarin and Cantonese Chinese. **BIOGRAPHICAL SOURCES:** Leading Consultants in Technology, 2 edit, vol 1, p 54. **BUSINESS PHONE:** (415)493-0262.

FOK, YU-SI
Educator. Chinese American. **PERSONAL:** Born Jan 15, 1932, Canton, China; son of Chun Ching Fok and Mong So T Fok; married Agnes, Jun 5, 1965; children: Licie C, Edna C. **EDUCATION:** National Taiwan University, BS, 1955; Utah State University, MS, 1959, PhD, 1964. **CAREER:** Utah State University, assistant research engineer, 1963-66; Illinois State Water Survey, hydrologist, 1966-68; Texas Water Rights Commission, section head, 1968-70; University of Hawaii, Manoa, associate professor, 1970-77, professor, 1977-. **ORGANIZATIONS:** American Society of Civil Engineers, fellow, 1963-; American Geological Union, 1968-; International Water Resources Association, fellow, 1970-; Sigma Xi, 1964-; International Rainwater Catchment Systems Association, president, life member, 1989-. **HONORS/AWARDS:** Chinese Hydraulic Engineers Association, Annual First Paper Award, 1966; Chinese Society of Agricultural Engineers, Annual Paper Award, 1972. **SPECIAL ACHIEVEMENTS:** Published over 80 papers in professional societies journals, proceedings, etc; editor, Infiltration Development and Application and Infiltration Principles and Practices; general chairman, Proceedings of Rain Water Cistern Systems, 1st conference; presented more than 20 papers at professional societies conferences; registered professional civil engineer, Illinois, 1967-, Hawaii, 1972-; patent award #5,229,005 classified in 210-652,000 474 Utility, "Ocean Depth Reverse Osmosis Fresh Water Factory.''. **BUSINESS ADDRESS:** Professor, Dept of Civil Engineering, University of Hawaii, Manoa, 2540 Dole St, Holmse Hall 380, Honolulu, HI 96822, (808)956-6561.

FONG, APRIL ANN
Educator. Chinese American. **PERSONAL:** Born in San Francisco, CA. **EDUCATION:** University of California, Berkeley, BA, biology, psychology, 1984; University of California, Davis, MS, entomology, 1992. **CAREER:** Los Angeles Unified School District, interpretative naturalist, 1985; University of California, Davis, teaching assistant, research assistant, 1986-90; American River College, biology instructor, 1989-93; Portland Community College, biology instructor, 1993-. **HONORS/AWARDS:** Humboldt City Office of Education and Humboldt State University, Leadership Institute for Environmental Education, fellow, 1993-94; University of Georgia and the Department of Energy, undergraduate ecology intern. **BUSINESS ADDRESS:** Biology Instructor, Science & Physical Education Division, Portland Community College, PO Box 19000, Portland, OR 97280-0990, (503)244-6111.

FONG, BERNARD WAH DOUNG
Physician. Chinese American. **PERSONAL:** Born May 18, 1926, Honolulu, HI; son of Leonard K & Frances Chang Fong; married Roberta Wat Fong, Aug 14, 1950; children: Phyllis, Jeffrey, Camille, Allison. **EDUCATION:** Bucknell University, BS, 1948; Jefferson Medical College, MD, 1952. **CAREER:** Bernard W D Fong MD Inc, president, 1956-93; John Burns School of Med, University of Hawaii, clinical professor of medicine, 1982-; Aetna Insurance Co, Medicare part B for Hawaii and Guam, medical director, 1988-. **ORGANIZATIONS:** Hawaii Heart Association, president, 1963-64; Chung Shan Asso-

ciation, Hawaii, president, 1970-71; United Chinese Society of Hawaii, president, 1973-74; American College of Physicians, governor, 1972-76; American College of Cardiology, governor, 1992-; Wong Leong Doo Benevolent Society, vice president, 1972-; Ocean View Cemetery, vice president, 1984-; National Heart, Lung and Blood Institute, advisory council, 1976-80; Hawaii Society of Internal Medicine, president, 1982-84; Third Conference on Cardiovascular Risk Factors in Minorities, chairperson, 1985. **HONORS/AWARDS:** American College of Physicians, Hawaii chapter, Inaugural Awardee, Outstanding Internist, 1988; Society Internal Medicine, Hawaii Chapter, Outstanding Internist, 1989. **MILITARY SERVICE:** USNR, phm3/c, 1944-46. **BUSINESS ADDRESS:** Physician, 1380 Lusitana St, Suite 706, Honolulu, HI 96813, (808)538-1168.

FONG, CHARLEN
Newspaper marketing administrator. Chinese American. **CAREER:** San Jose Mercury News, community marketing manager, currently. **BUSINESS ADDRESS:** Community Marketing Manager, San Jose Mercury News, 750 Ridder Park Dr, San Jose, CA 95190, (408)920-5380.

FONG, DEWEY
Law enforcement official. Chinese American. **PERSONAL:** Born in People's Republic of China; married. **EDUCATION:** State University of New York, BS. **CAREER:** New York City Housing Police Dept, inspector, currently. **ORGANIZATIONS:** New York City Police Asian Jade Society. **BUSINESS ADDRESS:** Inspector, Headquarters, New York City Housing Police Dept, 216 E 99th St, New York, NY 10029, (212)410-8500.

FONG, EVA CHOW
Consultant. Chinese American. **PERSONAL:** Born Nov 8, 1939, Sacramento, CA; daughter of Chow Chew and Wong Yit Ying; married Lester Fong, Jul 23, 1961; children: Tiffany Allison Fong Garcia, David William. **EDUCATION:** Sacramento City College, AA, 1960; CSU, Sacramento, BA, 1962; LaVerne University, MA, 1977; University of the Pacific, EdD, 1984. **CAREER:** Sacramento Unified School Dist, handicapped, resource specialist, training specialist, 1962-80; teacher, pre-school, K-6, special education, 1962-80, advisor, human relations & affirmative action office, 1980-83, coordinator, elementary education, 1983-85; California Dept of Education, consultant/community liaison, external affairs office, Asian/Pacific Islanders affairs, 1985-88, director, ethnic advisory councils office, 1989-92, consultant, history-social science office, 1992-. **ORGANIZATIONS:** Asian Pacific State Employees Association, vice president, 1988, chair, Heritage Month, 1989-91; Chinese American Council of Sacramento, board of directors, chair, issues & concerns committee, editorial staff newspaper, 1989-90; Sacramento Asian/Pacific Women's Network, treasurer, 1984-85; American Cancer Society, special populations committee, 1986; Association of California School Administrators, Affirmative Action Committee, 1983-84; Sacramento Asian Educators, founding member, 1983; California Office of Tourism, ethnic tourism marketing committee, 1990; California School Leadership Academy, under-represented groups task force, 1991-90. **HONORS/AWARDS:** Sacramento Council for International Visitors, Appreciation, 1990; KCRA TV-3, Appreciation, Judge for Ewing C Kelly Scholarship, 1992; University of the Pacific, fellowship recipient, bilingual, 1981; CSU, Sacramento, fellowship recipient, bilingual, 1975; Educational Institute for Overseas Koreans, fellowship, Korean Staff Development Program, 1986. **SPECIAL ACHIEVEMENTS:** Prepared CDE documents: "Our Parents Care, Too," 1991, "Superintendent's Response to His Advisory Council on Asian/Pacific Islanders Affairs," 1986, "California's Gold Teacher's Guide," 300 and 400 series, 1992, 1993; thesis: "Barriers to Leadership Aspirations as Perceived by California Women Administrators," 1984. **HOME ADDRESS:** 24 Reef Ct, Sacramento, CA 95831. **BUSINESS PHONE:** (916)657-2917.

FONG, GLENN RANDALL
Educator. Chinese American. **PERSONAL:** Born Aug 26, 1955, Berkeley, CA; son of Sidney S Fong & Esther L Fong; divorced. **EDUCATION:** University of California, Berkeley, BA (with honors), 1977; Cornell University, MA, 1980, PhD, 1982. **CAREER:** Harvard University Graduate School of Business Administration, postdoctoral research fellow, 1982-84; University of Illinois, Chicago, assistant professor of political science, 1984-92; American Graduate School of International Management, assistant professor of international studies, 1992-. **ORGANIZATIONS:** American Political Science Association, 1982-; International Studies Association, 1982-. **HONORS/AWARDS:** University of Illinois Institute of Government & Public Affairs, Ameritech Research Fellowship, 1990; Social Science Research Council, Grant

for Advanced International Research, 1988; Cornell University, Peace Studies Research Fellowship, 1977; University of California, Berkeley, Distinct in General Scholarship, 1977. **SPECIAL ACHIEVEMENTS:** The Future of Pentagon-Industry Collaboration in Technology Development, 1991; State Strength Industrial Structure & Industrial Policy: American & Japanese Experiences in Microelectronics, 1990; The Potential for Industrial Policy: Lessons from the Very High Speed Integrated Circuit Program, 1986. **BUSINESS ADDRESS:** Professor, Dept of International Studies, American Graduate School of International Management, 15249 N 59th Ave, Glendale, AZ 85306-6011, (602)978-7181.

FONG, HAROLD MICHAEL
Judge. Chinese American. **PERSONAL:** Born Apr 28, 1938, Honolulu, HI; married Judith Tom, 1966; children: Harold Michael, Terrence Matthew. **EDUCATION:** University of Southern California, AB (cum laude), 1960; University of Michigan, JD, 1964. **CAREER:** City and County of Honolulu, deputy prosecuting attorney, 1965-68; Mizuha and Kim, associate, 1968-69; District of Hawaii, assistant US attorney, 1969-73; US attorney, 1973-78; Fong and Miho, partner, 1978-82; US District Court of Hawaii, judge, 1982-84, chief judge, 1984-. **BUSINESS ADDRESS:** District Judge, US District Court of Hawaii, PO Box 50128, Honolulu, HI 96850, (808)541-1807.*

FONG, HARRY H. S.
Educator. Chinese American. **PERSONAL:** Born Jun 30, 1935, Guangdong, China; son of William Fong and Susan Fong; married Jane C Y Fong, Dec 19, 1964; children: Terrence, Tamara, Timothy. **EDUCATION:** University of Pittsburgh, BS, 1959, MS, 1961; Ohio State University, PhD, 1965. **CAREER:** University of Pittsburgh, teaching assistant, 1959-61, pharmacist, 1959-61; assistant/associate professor of pharmacognosy, 1965-70; Ohio State University, research assistant, 1961-65; University of Illinois, Chicago, professor of pharmacognosy, 1970-, Department of Medical Chemistry and Pharmacognosy, assistant head, 1991-. **ORGANIZATIONS:** American Society of Pharmacognosy, 1959-, president, 1978-79; Society for Economic Botany, 1970-, president, 1981-82. **HONORS/AWARDS:** Chinese University of Hong Kong, Honorary Visiting Research Fellow, 1977; World Health Organization, consultant, 1977; Guangzhou College of Traditional Chinese Medicine, visiting professor, 1993-95. **SPECIAL ACHIEVEMENTS:** More than 100 research papers on chemistry and biological activity of medicinal plant constituents, 1962-93; Journal Natural Products, associate editor, 1993-. **BUSINESS ADDRESS:** Professor, College of Pharmacy, University of Illinois, Chicago, 833 S Wood St, 310 Pharmacy (M/C 877), Chicago, IL 60612, (312)996-5972.

FONG, HERBERT S.
Engineer. Chinese American. **PERSONAL:** Born Oct 6, 1939, Sacramento, CA; son of James Fong; married Bella Wu Fong, Sep 13, 1986; children: Deidra, Ted. **EDUCATION:** University of California, Berkeley, BS, 1962, MS, 1963; University of Southern California, PhD, 1972. **CAREER:** Rockwell Corp, research engineer, 1963-65; Booz-Allen Applied, research senior scientist, 1965-67; Hughes Aircraft Co, senior scientist, 1967-. **ORGANIZATIONS:** Institute of Electrical & Electronics Engineers; American Institute of Aeronautics. **HONORS/AWARDS:** Hughes Aircraft, Group Invention, Award of the Year, 1990, Group High Achiever of the Year, 1991. **SPECIAL ACHIEVEMENTS:** US Patent Office, No 5067673, 1991. **BUSINESS ADDRESS:** Senior Scientist, Hughes Aircraft Co, PO Box 92919, S50/x346, Los Angeles, CA 90009, (310)416-3369.

FONG, HIRAM LEONG
Federal official (retired), financial services company executive. Chinese American. **PERSONAL:** Born Oct 15, 1906, Honolulu, HI; son of Sau How Fong & Chai Har Lum Fong; married Ellyn Sai Ngun Lo, Jun 25, 1938; children: Hiram Leong Jr, Rodney Leong, Merie-Ellen Fong Gushi, Marvin Allan Leong. **EDUCATION:** University of Hawaii, AB (with honors), 1930, LLD, 1953; Harvard University, JD, 1935. **CAREER:** City and County of Hawaii, deputy attorney, 1935-38; Hawaii Legislature, 1938-54, speaker, 1948-54; Fong, Miho, Choy and Robinson, founder, partner, until 1959; US Senate, 1959-77; Finance Factors, Grand Pacific Life Insurance Co, founder, board chair emeritus; Ocean View Cemetery Ltd, president; Senator Fong's Plantation and Gardens, owner, operator; Finance Investment Co, Market City Ltd, Finance Enterprises Ltd, Finance Factors Foundation, founder, board chair, currently. **ORGANIZATIONS:** Market City Foundation, founder, president, chairman of the board; Commission on Revision, Federal Court Appellate System, 1975-; Hiram and Ellyn Fong Foundation, founder; US Military Academy, board of visitors, 1971-; American Legion; VFW. **HONORS/AWARDS:** Republic of

China, Order of Brilliant Star; Republic of Korea, Gwanghwan Medal; Phi Beta Kappa; China Airlines, honorary consultant; University of Hawaii Alumni Association, Distinguished Alumnus Award, 1991; LLD: Tufts University, 1960; Lafayette College, 1960; Lynchburg College, 1970; California Western School of Law, 1976; Lincoln University, 1971; Soochow University, 1978; China Academy, 1978; numerous others. **SPECIAL ACHIEVEMENTS:** Delegate, Republican National Conventions, 1952, 1956, 1964, 1968, 1972; delegate, US-Canadian Interparliamentary Union Conference, 1961, 1965, 1967, 1968; delegate, Mexico-US Interparliamentary Conference, 1968. **MILITARY SERVICE:** US Air Force, major, 1942-44; US Air Force Reserves, ret colonel. **HOME ADDRESS:** 1102 Alewa Dr, Honolulu, HI 96817-1507, (808)595-4518.

FONG, J CRAIG
Organization executive. Chinese American. **PERSONAL:** Born Jul 4, 1955, Fairfield-Suisun, CA; son of Ralph Fong and Mai Fong. **EDUCATION:** Yale University, BA, 1978; University of Pennsylvania Law School, JD, 1981; University of Madrid, certificate, 1984. **CAREER:** Pillsbury, Madison & Sutro, associate, 1980-82; Chapman and Cutler, associate attorney, 1983-85; Security Pacific Corp, attorney, 1985-86; Asian Pacific American Legal Center, Immigration Project, director, 1987-91; Los Angeles County Bar Association, Immigration Project, assistant director, 1991-92; Lambda Legal Defense & Education Fund, Western Regional Office, director, 1992-. **ORGANIZATIONS:** AIDS Healthcare Foundation, community advisory board, 1992-; AIDS Clinical Trials Group, community constituency group, 1990-92; Lawyers for Human Rights, 1992-; Tom Hohmann Law Association, 1993-; National lesbian and Gay Law Association, 1992-; State Bar of California, 1982-; Illinois State Bar, 1982-; Gay Asian Pacific Support Network, 1992-; Gay Asian Pacific Alliance, 1993-. **SPECIAL ACHIEVEMENTS:** HIV and the Legalization Applicant, 1989; Asian Pacifics and US Immigration Policy, 1988. **HOME ADDRESS:** 7027 Lanewood Ave, Apt 404, Los Angeles, CA 90028-7075. **BUSINESS ADDRESS:** Director, Western Regional Office, Lambda Legal Defense and Education Fund Inc, 6030 Wilshire Blvd, Ste 200, Los Angeles, CA 90036-3617, (213)937-2728.

FONG, JACK SUN-CHIK
Pediatrician, educator. Chinese American. **PERSONAL:** Born Jan 6, 1941, Hong Kong; son of Bik-Chee Fong and Ngan-Ching Li Fong; married Margaret Z L Chen, Jun 1, 1968; children: Jay, Derek, Christopher. **EDUCATION:** McGill University, Montreal, BSc, 1964, MSc, MD, CM, 1968. **CAREER:** McGill University, assistant professor of pediatrics, 1974-77, associate professor of pediatrics, 1977-85; Yale University, clinical associate professor of pediatrics, 1985-; Hahnemann University, clinical assistant professor of pediatrics, 1988-; Danbury Hospital, chairman of pediatrics, 1985-. **ORGANIZATIONS:** Canadian Paediatrics Society, fellow, 1978-; American Academy of Pediatrics, fellow, 1980-; Clinical Immunology Society, 1986-; American Association Immunologists, 1971-; Conn State Medical Society, CME Committee, chairman, 1992-; Royal College of Physicians & Surgeons of Canada, fellow, 1976-. **HONORS/AWARDS:** McGill University, Fraser Scholarship, 1974-81; Medical Research Council of Canada, fellowship, 1986-72; Kidney Foundation of Canada, research grant, 1978-82; Montreal Children's Hospital, Research Scientist Award, 1978-81; McGill University, University Scholarship, 1962-65. **SPECIAL ACHIEVEMENTS:** Isolation of Glomeruli for Metabolic Studies, 1968; A Plate Method of Hemolytic Complement Assay, 1978; Platelet Function in Hemolytic Uremic Syndrome, 1982; Kidney Glomeruli in "Methods in Enzymology," p 653, 1974; Hemolyic Uremic Syndrome in "Ped Clin N Amer," p 835, 1982. **BUSINESS ADDRESS:** Chairman, Dept of Pediatrics, Danbury Hospital, 24 Hospital Avenue, Danbury, CT 06810-6099, (203)797-7940.

FONG, JOSHUA
Optometrist, banking executive. Chinese American. **PERSONAL:** Born Apr 17, 1924, Centerville, CA; son of Fong So Yick and Annie Low; married Lena C Fong, Oct 17, 1954; children: Neal, Jill Au, Heidi J Young, Charlotte, Polly. **EDUCATION:** University of California, Berkeley, AA, 1949; Los Angeles College of Optometry, OD, 1952; Southern California College of Optometry, doctor of optometry, 1970. **CAREER:** Self-employed, doctor of optometry, 1952-87; San Leandro Optometry Group, 1987-93; Bay Bank of Commerce, director, 1981-, chairman of board, 1984-93; Bay Commercial Services, chairman, 1993-. **ORGANIZATIONS:** Kiwanis Club of East Oakland, 1954-77, charter member, president, 1958; Wa Sung Service Club, 1953-, president, 1956; San Leandro Chamber, director, 1974-83; Doctors Hospital of San Leandro, board of trustees, 1976-80; Humana Hospital of San Leandro, board

of trustees, 1980-84; Chinese Presbyterian Church of Oakland, trustee, 1960-62; Newlife Christian Fellowship, founding member, 1991-; City of San Leandro, Personel Relations Board, commissioner. **HONORS/AWARDS:** City of Oakland, Citizen of Day, 1959; Kiwanis Club of East Oakland, Citizen of the Year, 1959; Wa Sung Service Club, Man of the Year, 1958. **MILITARY SERVICE:** US Navy, 1943-45. **BUSINESS ADDRESS:** Chairman of the Board, Bay Commercial Services, 1495 E 14th St, San Leandro, CA 94577.

FONG, KAI MENG
Sports administrator. Chinese American. **PERSONAL:** Born Feb 12, 1960, Kuala Lumpur, Malaysia; son of Ying Hong Fong and Mee Sim Cheong; married Judy Ann Hansmann-Fong, Jun 20, 1985; children: Yuen Mei, Yuen Kim. **EDUCATION:** New Mexico Military Institute, 1979; Arizona Western College, 1980; University of Idaho, BS, secondary physical eduation, 1983, MS, sports & recreation management, 1985. **CAREER:** John Gardiners Tennis Ranch, tennis professional, 1980, 1984; University of Idaho, teaching assistant, PE, 1984-85; Robertson Wilson & Jamil, sales representative, 1987; Institute Technology of Malaysia, PE instructor, 1987; Raintree Club, tennis professional, 1987-88; Lewis-Clark State College, tennis coach, facility coordinator, 1988-. **ORGANIZATIONS:** United States Tennis Association, lifetime member; Intercollegiate Tennis Association, 1989-. **HONORS/AWARDS:** Intercollegiate Tennis Assoication, Academic All American, 1982, 1983; University of Idaho, Alumni Award for Seniors, 1983, Scholar Athlete, 1980-83; NAIA District I, Coach of the Year, 1990, 1992. **BUSINESS ADDRESS:** Tennis Coach/Facility Coordinator, LCSC Tennis Center, Lewis-Clark State College, 500 8th Avenue, Lewiston, ID 83501, (208)799-2309.

FONG, KEVIN MURRAY
Attorney. Chinese American. **PERSONAL:** Born Jan 25, 1955, San Francisco, CA; son of William W Fong & Lillian Fong; married Rosalia Han-Ming Ting, Mar 22, 1980; children: Elliot. **EDUCATION:** Harvard College, AB, 1976; Harvard Law School, JD, 1979. **CAREER:** US District Judge Constance Baker Motley, law clerk, 1979-80; Pillsbury Madison & Sutro, partner, 1980-. **ORGANIZATIONS:** Asian Pacific Bar of California, president, 1989-90; Asian American Bar Association of the Greater Bay Area, president, 1990-91; Bar Association of San Francisco, board of directors, 1990-92; Harvard Civil Rights-Civil Liberties Law Review, editor-in-chief, 1978-79. **BUSINESS ADDRESS:** Partner, Pillsbury Madison & Sutro, PO Box 7880, San Francisco, CA 94120, (415)983-1270.

FONG, MARY HELENA
Art historian. Chinese American. **PERSONAL:** Born Mar 20, 1924, Helena, MT; daughter of Yuen Fong (deceased) & Soo Hoo Shee (deceased). **EDUCATION:** St John's University, BA, 1965; Hunter Graduate School, MA, 1967; New York University, PhD, 1972. **CAREER:** Elementary School, Kwangtung, teacher, 1944-45; Catholic Center, Hong Kong, secretary, 1946-48; Mater Amabilis, Surabay, E Java, acting principal, 1955-61; Occidental College, assistant professor of art history, 1972-76; University of California, Davis, professor of art history, 1976-. **ORGANIZATIONS:** Association for Asian Studies, 1971-; College Art Association, 1971-. **HONORS/AWARDS:** University of California, Davis, Faculty Research Grants, 1978-92, Faculty Summer Planning Award, 1991, Faculty Development Award, 1979, Regent's Faculty Fellowship in Humanities, 1978; JDR III Fund Travel Research Grant, Europe & Asia, 1970; New York University Fellowships, 1968-71. **SPECIAL ACHIEVEMENTS:** Numerous articles on Chinese art in art journals: Artibus Asiae, Archives in Asian Art, Oriental Art, Ars Orientalis, Orientations, etc; "Antecedents of Sui-Tang Burial Practices in North China," Artibus Asiae, Li, p 147-98, 1991; "Chuanshen," Pre-Tang Human Figure Painting, as Evidenced in Archeological Findings, Oriental Art, ns, XXXVIV 1, p 4-21, spring 1993. **BUSINESS ADDRESS:** Director, Program in Art History, Professor of Chinese Art History, University of California, Davis, Davis, CA 95616, (916)752-0105.

FONG, MATTHEW K.
Government official. Chinese American. **PERSONAL:** Born Nov 20, 1953, Oakland, CA; son of March Fong Eu and Chester Fong; married Paula; children: Matthew II, Christina. **EDUCATION:** USAF Academy, BS, 1975; Pepperdine University, MBA, 1982; Southwestern University, School of Law, JD, 1985. **CAREER:** USAF Academy, minority recruiter, pilot trainer, data processing mgr, acting comptroller, systems integrator, 1975-80; self-employed, 1981-84; Sheppard Mullin Richter & Hampton, attorney, 1985-90; Board of Equalization, vice chair, 1991-. **ORGANIZATIONS:** Pepperdine University, regent, 1993; Children's Hospital of LA, regent, 1993; LA County

Museum of National History, trustee and governor, 1988-; Young Executives of America, director, 1991-; Council of Asian Republican Elected Officials, president, 1991-. **HONORS/AWARDS:** Pepperdine University, School of Management, Outstanding Alumnus, 1992; California Republican Party, Rising Star Award, 1991. **SPECIAL ACHIEVEMENTS:** Republican nominee for California state controller, 1990. **MILITARY SERVICE:** US Air Force Reserves, major, 1981-; Meritorious Service Medal. **BUSINESS ADDRESS:** Vice Chair, California State Board of Equalization, 13200 Crossroads Pky North, Ste 450, Industry, CA 91746-3497, (310)908-0524.

FONG, NELSON C.
Educator. Chinese American. **PERSONAL:** Born Dec 17, 1944, Hong Kong; son of Mr & Mrs C S Fong; married Janeta Prior, Jun 7, 1970; children: Shun-Szu, Shun-Lee, Shun-Yenn, Shun-Bok, Shun-Luoi, Shun-Ching, Shun-Sho. **EDUCATION:** Harding University, BS, 1967; Memphis State University, MS, 1969; University of Nebraska, PhD, 1974. **CAREER:** York College, assistant professor, 1969-75; Metro Tech College, assistant professor, 1975-76; University of Maine, assistant professor, associate professor, professor, 1976-81; Seattle Pacific University, associate professor, 1981-82; University of Nebraska, Kearney, associate professor, 1982-84; Creighton University, associate professor, 1984-. **ORGANIZATIONS:** American Statistical Association, 1985-89; American Scientific Affiliation, 1971-75; Operations Research Society of America, 1984-85. **BUSINESS ADDRESS:** Professor, Dept of Mathematics, Creighton University, 24th St and California Ave, Omaha, NE 68178-0001, (402)280-2430.

FONG, RAYMOND
Ophthalmologist. Chinese American. **PERSONAL:** Born Jul 19, 1955, Hong Kong; son of Wing Kwong Fong and Wai Yee Chan Fong; married Winnie Moy Fong, Oct 10, 1992. **EDUCATION:** Harvard College, AB, 1976; Cornell Medical School MD, 1981. **CAREER:** Beth Israel Hospital, internship, 1981-82; Manhattan Eye, Ear & Throat Hospital, residency, 1982-85; New York Eye Center, ophthalmologist/owner, 1985-. **ORGANIZATIONS:** Chinese American Medical Society, secretary; Chinatown Health Clinic, advisory board; Chinese American Businessman's Assn, honorary medical consultant. **BIOGRAPHICAL SOURCES:** Tai Pan, cover story, Feb 1992, p 16. **BUSINESS ADDRESS:** Owner, New York Eye Center, 109 Lafayette St, 4th Fl, New York, NY 10013, (212)274-1900.

FONG, THOMAS Y. K.
Federal judge. Chinese American. **PERSONAL:** Born Nov 14, 1949, Honolulu, HI; son of Clarence K B Fong and Thelma D T Fong; married Sharon Ann Wroten, Jul 1, 1972; children: Daniel, Traci, Michael. **EDUCATION:** Brigham Young University, College of Business, BS, 1972, J Reuben Clark Law School, JD (cum laude), 1977. **CAREER:** City and County of Honolulu, Dept of the Corporation Counsel, law clerk, 1976; US Dept of Justice, USINS, LA, trial attorney, 1977-82; Arlington, VA, acting appellate trial attorney, 1982, LA, chief district counsel, 1982-84; US Immigration Court, Los Angeles, Central District of California, judge, 1984-, presiding judge, 1990-. **ORGANIZATIONS:** National Assn of Immigration Judges, 1984-; Boy Scouts of America, scouter and merit badge counselor, 1979-; J Reuben Clark Law Society, 1977-; Hawaii State Bar Assn, 1977-; BYU College of Business Alumni Assn, 1972-; California Judges Association, 1991-. **HONORS/AWARDS:** J Reuben Clark Law Society, Outstanding Young Lawyer, 1993; Centennial Alumni Gallery, Kamehameha HS, 1 of 100 Outstanding Graduates, 1987; US Attorney General, Exceptional Attorney Performance Award, 1981-84; US Attorney, under the attorney general's Honor Law Program, 1977. **MILITARY SERVICE:** US Army, 1st lieutenant, 1972-74. **BUSINESS ADDRESS:** Presiding Judge, US Immigration Court, Los Angeles, Central District of CA, 300 N Los Angeles St, Federal Bldg, Suite 2001, Los Angeles, CA 90012.

FONG-TORRES, BEN
Journalist, broadcaster. Chinese American. **PERSONAL:** Born Jan 7, 1945, Alameda, CA; son of Ricardo Torres and Connie Fong-Torres; married Dianne, May 1, 1976; children: Buster. **EDUCATION:** San Francisco State University, BA, 1966. **CAREER:** KFOG-FM, announcer, writer, 1967-68; Pacific Telephone, magazine editor, 1968-69; KSAN-FM, weekend announcer, 1970-79; Rolling Stone, senior editor, writer, 1969-80; GQ Magazine, columnist, 1984-87; San Francisco Chronicle, feature writer, columnist, 1983-92. **ORGANIZATIONS:** Asian-American Journalists Assn; National Asian-American Telecommunications Assn; Media Alliance. **HONORS/AWARDS:** Billboard Magazine, Award for Broadcast Excellence, 1976; ASCAP, Deems Taylor

Award for Magazine Writing, 1974; Radio-TV Guild, San Francisco State, Broadcast Preceptor Award, 1966; San Francisco State, Outstanding Journalist, 1966; Northern California NARAS, Emmy, Steve Martin interview, 1977. **SPECIAL ACHIEVEMENTS:** The Rice Room (memoirs), Hyperion, New York, 1994; Hickory Wind: The Life & Times of Gram Parsons, Pocket Books, 1991; The Motown Album, St Martin's Press, NY, 1990; articles anthologized in numerous books; TV documentary, Cycling Through China, 1982. **BIOGRAPHICAL SOURCES:** The Ben Fong-Torres Interview, Big O Magazine, Oct 1991, p 74-75; Playing Hard, Dying Young, Washington Post, Bookworld, June 30, 1991, p 1.

FONG-TORRES, SHIRLEY
Tour operator, Asian food expert. Chinese American. **PERSONAL:** Born Nov 16, 1946, Oakland, CA; daughter of Richard & Connie Fong-Torres; married Bernard Cawer, Aug 8, 1988; children: Kristina Carrie Dong. **EDUCATION:** University of California, Berkeley, BA, 1970. **CAREER:** Levi Strauss, operations manager, 1977-84; self-employed, president, owner, 1986-. **ORGANIZATIONS:** Rotary Club of San Francisco, 1993-; San Francisco Convention & Visitors Bureau, board of directors, 1990-92, 1993-; Chinese Culture Center, 1990-; Chinese Historical Society, 1990-; Professional Food Society, 1991-; American Institute of Wine & Food, 1991-. **HONORS/AWARDS:** California Senate, Dedication to Community, 1992; City of San Francisco, Shirley Fong-Torres Day, 1991; University of California, Berkeley, Miss Spring Informal Contest, 1967. **SPECIAL ACHIEVEMENTS:** In the Chinese Kitchen, 1993; San Francisco Chinatown: A Walking Tour, 1991; Wok Wiz Cookbook, 1988; perform on TV: informercials, Cooking & Travel Show; proficient in English, Chinese, some Spanish. **BUSINESS ADDRESS:** President, Wok Wiz Chinatown Tours & Cooking Co, 750 Kearny St, Ste 800, San Francisco, CA 94108, (415)355-9657.

FOO, CHARLES. *See* **WONG, CHARLES FOO, JR.**

FOONG, NICOLAI YEIN
Obstetrician, gynecologist. Chinese American. **PERSONAL:** Born Apr 11, 1960, London, England; son of Weng Cheong Foong and Gek Huah Miki Lim. **EDUCATION:** Stanford University, BA, 1981; UCLA School of Medicine, MD, 1985. **CAREER:** Cedars-Sinai Medical Center, resident physician, 1985-89; self-employed, private practice, ob/gyn, 1989-. **ORGANIZATIONS:** Los Angeles Chinatown Service Center, medical director, 1990-. **BUSINESS ADDRESS:** Obstetrician/Gynecologist, 500 N Garfield Ave, No. 310, Monterey Park, CA 91754, (818)288-3015.

FOSHEE, THUONG NGUYEN (CUC)
Landscaping company executive. Vietnamese American. **PERSONAL:** Born Apr 16, 1948, Son Tay, Vietnam; daughter of Toa D Nguyen and Ty T Nguyen; married Edgar E Foshee, Apr 19, 1970; children: Elizabeth. **EDUCATION:** College graduate, business, 1969. **CAREER:** Foshee Brothers Inc, president, 1975-84; T N Grassing, president/owner, 1985-. **ORGANIZATIONS:** Pine Castle Garden Club, 1984-93; Heritage Asian of Central Florida, 1988-90; Vietnam Vet Association, 1980-93; Seventh Day Adventist Church, 1991. **HONORS/AWARDS:** Central Florida Vietnam Vet Association, Officer of the Year, 1990. **BUSINESS ADDRESS:** President/Owner, T N Grassing, 5448 Hoffner Ave, #306, Orlando, FL 32812, (407)277-0484.

FRANCIA, LUIS H. F.
Writer/critic. Filipino American. **PERSONAL:** Born Jan 20, 1945, Manila, Philippines. **EDUCATION:** Ateneo de Manila University, BA (cum laude), humanities, 1965. **CAREER:** Village Voice, assistant editor, currently. **ORGANIZATIONS:** Asian American Journalists Assn, 1989-; Asian CineVision, 1981-; Natl Writers' Union, 1983-. **HONORS/AWARDS:** Edna St Vincent Millay Colony for the Arts, Writing Fellowship, 1992; Asian CineVision, Writer-in-Residence, 1988; Columbia University, Writer-in-Residence, 1986; New York State Council of the Arts, translation grant, 1985; Palanca Memorial Awards, Manila, First Prize, Poetry, 1978. **SPECIAL ACHIEVEMENTS:** Publications: The Arctic Archipelago & Other Poems, 1992; Her Beauty Likes Me Well (with David Friedman), 1979; "Asian Cinema & Asian-American Cinema: Separated by a Common Language?," Raising the Image, 1991; "Days in the Country," The Best of Caracoa, 1991; "A Fever in February," Versus: Philippine Protest Poetry, 1986; editor, Brown River, White Ocean: An Anthology of Twentieth-Century Philippine Literature in English, 1993; film, writer, director, narrator: Flip's Adventures in Wonderland, 1990. **HOME ADDRESS:** PO Box 1696, New York, NY 10013-0870. **BUSINESS PHONE:** (212)475-3333.

FRANCISCO, EMILIANO ALONZO
Publisher, writer, editor. Filipino American. **PERSONAL:** Born 1908?, Laogag, Ilocos Nortre, Philippines; married Angelina Reyes; children: Pamela. **EDUCATION:** University of Washington, Seattle; University of Idaho. **CAREER:** Workers' & Farm Laborers Union #18275, organizer; Boeing, inventory acquisitions expeditor; Filipino-American Herald (was Filipino American Tribune), founder, publisher, editor, 1933-. **ORGANIZATIONS:** Free Masons, Grand Master. **HONORS/AWARDS:** Filipino Community of Seattle Inc, Filipino American Man of the Year, 1992; International Examiner, Asian Pacific American Community Voice Award, 1993. **MILITARY SERVICE:** US Army, corporal, 1942. **BUSINESS ADDRESS:** Publisher, Editor, Filipino-American Herald, 508 Maynard Ave South, PO Box 14240, Seattle, WA 98114, (206)725-6606. *

FREY, FRANCESCA
Attorney. Chinese American. **CAREER:** Los Angeles County, deputy district attorney, Sexual Crimes Division, district attorney, currently. **ORGANIZATIONS:** Southern California Chinese Lawyers Association, Board of Governors, board member, 1993. **BUSINESS ADDRESS:** District Attorney, Sexual Crimes Division, Hall of Records, 320 W Temple, Rm 772, Los Angeles, CA 90012, (213)974-5927.*

FU, JYUN-HORNG (ALEX)
Educator. Taiwanese American. **PERSONAL:** Born Jun 5, 1959, Taipei, Taiwan; son of Hsin-Fa & Mei-Yu Lee Fu; married Mou-Mei Fu, Jan 10, 1984; children: Josephine T. **EDUCATION:** National Chiao-Tung University, Hsin-Chu, Taiwan, BS, 1981; University of Maryland, College Park, Department of Electrical Engineering, MS, 1985, PhD, 1988. **CAREER:** University of Maryland, College Park, Department of Electrical Engineering, teaching assistant, 1984, research assistant, 1984-86, Systems Research Center, fellow, 1986-88; Wright State University, Department of Mathematics and Statistics, assistant professor, 1988-. **ORGANIZATIONS:** Institute of Electrical and Electronic Engineering, 1984-; Society of Industrial and Applied Mathematics, 1987-. **SPECIAL ACHIEVEMENTS:** Author of numerous articles relating to applied mathematics. **MILITARY SERVICE:** Chinese Marine Corp, 2nd lt, 1981-83. **BUSINESS ADDRESS:** Professor, Dept of Mathematics, Wright State University, 3640 Colonel Glenn Hwy, Dayton, OH 45435, (513)873-2512.

FU, KAREN K.
Educator. Chinese American. **PERSONAL:** Born Oct 15, 1940; daughter of Ping-Sen Fu and Lien-Sun Ho. **EDUCATION:** Columbia University, AB (cum laude), 1963, MD, 1967. **CAREER:** University of California, San Francisco, clinical instructor, 1972-73, assistant professor, 1973-76, associate professor, 1976-82, professor, 1982-. **ORGANIZATIONS:** Society of Chinese Bioscientists in America, 1988-; American College of Radiology, representative, 1988-96; Northern California Oncology Group, chairperson, executive committee, 1983-, radiosensitizer sub com, chair, 1985-; Radiation Therapy Oncology Group, chairperson, 1987-; Rush Cancer Center, external advisory board, 1987-; San Francisco Head & Neck Surg Found, medical advisory board, 1985-. **HONORS/AWARDS:** Columbia University, Mabel Mead Scholarship, 1963-67; Abbott Student Fellowship, 1966; American Cancer Society Jr Faculty, fellowship, 1976-79. **SPECIAL ACHIEVEMENTS:** Numerous publications, including: co-author, "Recurrent Locally Advanced Nasopharyngeal Carcinoma Treated with Heavy Charged Particle Irradiation," Intl J Radiat Oncol Biol Phys, vol 23, p 881-884, 1992; "Interactions of Chemotherapeutic Agents with Radiotherapy," Frontiers in Radiation Therapy and Oncology, vol 26, p 16-30, 1992. **BUSINESS ADDRESS:** Professor, University of California San Francisco, 505 Parnassus Ave, Rm L-08, San Francisco, CA 94143-0226, (415)476-4815.

FU, KUAN-CHEN
Educator. Chinese American. **PERSONAL:** Born Feb 2, 1933, Nanking, Taiwan; son of Kwan-Lyn Fu; married Ching-Chi Liu Fu, Apr 27, 1963; children: Karen, Kelvin. **EDUCATION:** National Cheng-Kung University of Taiwan, The Republic of China, BS, 1958; University of Notre Dame, MS, 1959, PhD, 1967. **CAREER:** Charles Cole Consulting Engrs, bridge designer, 1959-64; University of Toledo, civil engineering, professor, 1967-. **ORGANIZATIONS:** American Society of Civil Engineers, fellow, 1967-; American Society of Eng Education; Sigma Xi; Chi Epsilon. **HONORS/AWARDS:** United Nations, International Lecture Tours, 1990; NASA, Research Grant on Stress Analysis, 1982-88; NSF, Research Grant on Structural Optimization, 1969-71; State of Indiana, Professinal Engineer in Structures, 1962-. **SPE-**

CIAL ACHIEVEMENTS: "The Effect of Initial Curvature on the Natural Frequency of a Thin Plate," ASCE Journal of Mech Engineering, 1993; "A 3-D Morphometrical Study of Distal Human Femur," Journal of Eng in Medicine, 1992; "Optimization of Axially Loaded Column," Journal of Structures & Computers, 1990; "Analysis of Optimum Design of Spherical Shell," ASCE Journal of Eng Mech, 1990; "The Develoment of Integral Equation Method," ASCE Journal of Eng Mech, 1990. **BUSINESS ADDRESS:** Professor of Civil Engineering, University of Toledo, Toledo, OH 43606, (419)537-2522.

FU, LIMIN
Educator. Taiwanese American. **PERSONAL:** Born Dec 8, 1953, Taipei, Taiwan; son of Tsai-Yi Fu & Jen-Yui Huang-Fu; married Lienfen Yueh-Fu, May 22, 1989; children: Katherine. **EDUCATION:** National Taiwan University, BM, MD (summa cum laude), 1978; Stanford University, MS, 1982, PhD, 1985. **CAREER:** National Taiwan University, associate professor, 1985-87; Allied Signal Inc, research scientist, 1987-88; University of Wisconsin, assistant professor, 1988-90; University of Florida, associate professor, 1990-. **ORGANIZATIONS:** IEEE, 1985-; AAAI, 1985-; Sigma Xi, 1989-; Computer & Medicine Association, vice president, 1993; New York Academy of Sciences. **HONORS/AWARDS:** National Science Foundation USA, research awards, 1992-95; National Taiwan University, Academic Achievement Awards, 1971-78; Medical Society ROC, T M Du Award, 1978; National Taiwan University Hospital, Best Intern, 1978; National Science Council ROC, Research Performance Award, 1987. **SPECIAL ACHIEVEMENTS:** Book: Neural Networks in Computer Intelligence, McGraw Hill, 1994; monograph, "Pattern Learning and Discovery," Library Congress, 1992; software, 3 pieces, RL, Ejaundice, Knowledgetron, 1984-93; technical papers, more than 50, 1984-93; languages: Chinese, English; patent holder. **BUSINESS ADDRESS:** Professor, Dept of Computer and Information Science, University of Florida, 301 CSE, Gainesville, FL 32611-2002, (904)392-1485.

FU, MICHAEL CHUNG-SHU
Educator. Chinese American. **PERSONAL:** Born Feb 24, 1962, Lafayette, IN; married Fan Chen Fu. **EDUCATION:** Massachusetts Institute of Technology, SM, SB, 1985; Harvard University, MS, 1986, PhD, 1989. **CAREER:** University of Maryland at College Park, assistant professor of management science & statistics, 1989-. **ORGANIZATIONS:** IEEE, 1987-; ORSA, 1988-; Tau Beta Pi, elected 1983; Eta Kappa Nu, elected 1983. **HONORS/AWARDS:** National Science Foundation, Graduate Fellowship, 1985-88; Mitre Corporation, scholarship, one annual award for McLean High School, 1980. **BUSINESS ADDRESS:** University of Maryland at College Park, Van Munching Hall, College Park, MD 20742.

FU, PAUL CHUNG, JR.
Physician, consultant. Chinese American. **PERSONAL:** Born Jul 7, 1969, Torrance, CA; son of Paul and Joan. **EDUCATION:** Boston University, College of Liberal Arts, BA, 1993, School of Medicine, MD, 1993. **CAREER:** Microsoft Corporation, systems engineer, 1989-91; Laurier Assciates, senior consultant, 1990-; Harbor-UCLA Medical Center, clinical resident in pediatrics, 1993-. **ORGANIZATIONS:** American Academy of Pediatrics, 1993-; American Medical Association, 1989-; Massachusetts Medical Society, 1989-; Christian Medical and Dental Society, 1989-; Association for Computing Machinery, 1988-. **SPECIAL ACHIEVEMENTS:** Editor, Literary Magazine of Boston University Medical Center, 1990-92. **BUSINESS ADDRESS:** Clinical Resident, Dept of Pediatrics, Harbor-UCLA Medical Center, 1000 W Carson Street, Torrance, CA 90509.

FU, PAUL S.
Law librarian. Chinese American. **PERSONAL:** Born Sep 7, 1932, Shen-Young City, Liaoning, China; son of Mu-Shien Fu and Shieh-Wei Chang Fu; married Doris S Fu; children: Eugene Y, Vincent Y. **EDUCATION:** Soochow University, China, School of Law, LLB, 1960; University of Illinois, MCL, 1962; Villanova University, MSLS, 1968. **CAREER:** Detroit College of Law, assistant librarian and lecturer in law, 1968-69; Ohio Northern University College of Law, law librarian and associate professor of law, 1962-72; Supreme Court of Ohio, law librarian, 1972-. **ORGANIZATIONS:** American Society of International Law, 1969-74; American Library Association, 1973-; American Association of Law Libraries, 1968-, chair of comms, secretary, 1989-93. **HONORS/AWARDS:** University of Illinois, University Fellowship, 1961-62. **SPECIAL ACHIEVEMENTS:** Author, Law Library Handbook of the Supreme Court of Ohio, 1974; Handling Water Damage in a Law Library, 79 Law Library Journal 667, 1987; The Legal and Judicial System of the People's Republic of China, 2 Ohio Lawyer, No 4, 19, 1988; New Hampshire State Law

Library, consultant, 1987; Supreme Court of Illinois Law Library, consultant, 1988. **HOME ADDRESS:** 940 Evening Street, Worthington, OH 43085. **BUSINESS ADDRESS:** Law Librarian, Supreme Court of Ohio Law Library, 30 East Broad Street, Columbus, OH 43266-0419, (614)466-2044.

FU, PETER K.
Electrical engineer. Hong Kong American. **PERSONAL:** Born Sep 4, 1959, Hong Kong; son of Shek K Fu and Kum Kwun Fu; married Melinda Fu, 1984; children: Enrico. **EDUCATION:** University of California, Santa Barbara, BSEE, 1983. **CAREER:** Boeing Co, electrical design engr, senior engr, currently. **BUSINESS ADDRESS:** Senior Electrical Engineer, Boeing Co, 499 Boeing Blvd, M/S JR-54, PO Box 240002, Huntsville, AL 35824, (205)461-5233.

FU, SHOU-CHENG JOSEPH
Educator. Chinese American. **PERSONAL:** Born Mar 19, 1924, Peking, China; son of W C Joseph Fu and W C Tsai Fu; married Susan B Guthrie, Jun 21, 1951; children: Robert W G, Joseph H G, James B G. **EDUCATION:** Catholic University, Peking, BS, MS, 1944; Johns Hopkins University, PhD, 1949. **CAREER:** Natl Institutes of Health, Natl Cancer Institute, postdoctoral fellow, 1949-51, scientist, 1951-55; University College, London, Gustav Bissing Fellow Johns Hopkins University, 1955-56; Children's Cancer Research Foundation, Enzyme & Bioorganic Chemistry Lab, chief, 1956-57; Chinese University, Hong Kong, univ prof, chm bd chemistry, 1967-70, dean science faculty, 1967-69; Columbia University, College Physicians & Surgeons, visiting prof, 1970-71; University of Medicine & Dentistry, prof biochemistry and molecular biology, 1971-, asst dean, 1975-77, Grad Sch Biomed Scis, acting dean, 1977-78, professor of ophthalmology, joint appointment, 1989-. **ORGANIZATIONS:** US Public Health Service Reserves, 1959-, captain; Sigma Xi, sec, 1974-76, 1981-82, chapter pres, 1976-80; Royal Hong Kong Jockey. **HONORS/AWARDS:** AAAS, fellow; Royal Soc Chemistry, London, fellow; Gustav Bissing Fellow. **SPECIAL ACHIEVEMENTS:** Numerous articles in professional journals. **BUSINESS ADDRESS:** Prof, Dept of Biochem & Molecular Biol, New Jersey Med School, University of Medicine & Dentistry, 185 S Orange Ave, Newark, NJ 07103.

FU, TINA C.
Library services director. Chinese American. **PERSONAL:** Born Nov 25, 1939, Nanchang, Giansi, China; daughter of Dayi Cheng and Maria Giwu Cheng; married Sherwin S S Fu, Sep 2, 1965; children: Shelley L. **EDUCATION:** National Taiwan Normal University, BA, 1962; Marquette University, MA, 1965; University of Wisconsin, Madison, MALS, (with distinction), 1968, PhD, 1988. **CAREER:** Western Carolina State College, lecturer, 1965-66; University of Wisconsin-Oshkosh, assistant director, 1969-93; Eastern Connecticut State University, director of library services, 1993-. **ORGANIZATIONS:** American Library Association, comm member, 1976-; Association of College & Research Libraries, 1984-; Wisconsin Library Association, committee chair, 1969-; Wisconsin Association of Academic Libraries, committee chair, 1969-; Delta Kappa Gamma, comm member, 1985-; Beta Phi Mu, 1988-. **HONORS/AWARDS:** Delta Kappa Gamma, Hazel Duling Scholarship, 1987; US Government, HEA Title V Scholarship, 1966-68; Marquette University, university scholarship, 1963-65. **SPECIAL ACHIEVEMENTS:** Directory of Library and Information Professionals Women's Groups, editor, 1983; numerous professional presentations in conferences proceedings; columnist for China Times, numerous articles, 1971-76; some essays collected into anthologies; special lecture series at Zhongshan University, Guang-zhou, China, 1989-90. **BUSINESS ADDRESS:** Director of Library Serivces, Eastern Connecticut State University, 83 Windham Street, J Eugene Smith Library, Willimantic, CT 06226, (203)456-5425.

FUGH, JOHN L.
Lawyer, retired army general officer. Chinese American. **PERSONAL:** Born Sep 12, 1934, Beijing, Hopei, China; son of Philip and Sarah Fugh; married June C Fugh, Jul 30, 1960; children: Justina C, Jarrett L. **EDUCATION:** Georgetown University, School of Foreign Svc, BS, 1957; George Washington University Law School, JD, 1960; Harvard University, Sch of Govt, SDM, 1984. **CAREER:** US Army, 1961-93, attained rank of major general; brigadier general, 1984; asst judge advocate general for civil law, 1984-90, asst judge advocate general, 1990-91, judge advocate general, 1991-93; McGuire, Woods, Battle & Boothe, partner, 1994-. **ORGANIZATIONS:** Committee of 100; Organization of Chinese Americans; Rho Psi; Atlantic Council of the US, councillor; Natl Conference of Christians & Jews, board of directors. **HONORS/AWARDS:** Chinese American Planning Council (NY), Honoree of

the Year, 1994; Asian Pacific American Heritage Council, Outstanding Asian Pacific American Award, 1992; Federal Asian Pacific American Council, Exemplary Leadership & Dedicated Service to US Govt, 1989. **SPECIAL ACHIEVEMENTS:** First Chinese American to attain general officer status in US Army, 1984. **MILITARY SERVICE:** US Army, major general, 1961-93; Defense Superior Service Medal; Legion of Merit; Meritorious Service Medal; Air Medal; Joint Service Commendation Medal; Army Commendation Medal; Distinguished Service Medal, 1993. **BUSINESS ADDRESS:** Attorney, McGuire, Woods, Battle & Boothe, Army & Navy Club Bldg, 1627 Eye St NW #1000, Washington, DC 20006, (202)857-1700.

FUGITA, STEPHEN SUSUMU
Educator. Japanese American. **PERSONAL:** Born Apr 6, 1943, Jerome, AR; son of Tom and Toshiye Fugita; married Karen Fugita, Aug 16, 1969; children: Stephanie S. **EDUCATION:** Ohio State University, BS, 1965; University of California, Riverside, MA, 1968, PhD, 1969. **CAREER:** University of Akron, assistant to associate professor, 1971-87; University of Illinois at Chicago, associate to acting director of the Pacific/Asian American Mental Health Research Center, 1987-90; Santa Clara University, director of ethnic studies, associate to full professor, 1990-. **ORGANIZATIONS:** American Psychological Association, 1969-; American Sociological Association, Section on Asian & Asian America Council, 1990-; Association for Asian American Studies, 1980-, past vice president; Asian Americans for Community Involvement, board member, 1990-91; Japanese American National library, sec, board of directors, 1991-; Japanese American Resource Center, 1990-, past director; Japanese American National Museum, scholarly advisory board, 1990-. **HONORS/AWARDS:** Association for Asian American Studies, National Book Award in Social Science, 1992. **SPECIAL ACHIEVEMENTS:** With D J O'Brien, Japanese American Ethnicity: The Persistence of Community, Seattle: University of Washington Press, 1991; The Japanese American Experience, Bloomington: University of Indiana Press, 1991. **MILITARY SERVICE:** US Army, colonel, active, 1969-71, reserves, 1974-; Army Commendation Medal, 1988; Army Reserve components Achievement Medal, 1988; National Defense Service Medal, 1969. **BIOGRAPHICAL SOURCES:** Santa Clara Magazine, pg 7, winter 1992. **BUSINESS ADDRESS:** Professor of Psychology, Director of Ethnic Studies Program, Santa Clara University, Santa Clara, CA 95053, (408)554-6880.

FUJII, JACK KOJI
Educator, educational administrator. Japanese American. **PERSONAL:** Born Jun 9, 1940, Phoenix, AZ; son of Richard Masuo Fujii and Chiye Fujii; married Gail M Fujii, Jul 17, 1967; children: Scott K, Todd M, Jeff Y. **EDUCATION:** University of California, Berkeley, BS, 1963; University of Hawaii, Manoa, MS, 1968, PhD, 1975. **CAREER:** University of Hawaii, Hilo, College of Agriculture, dean, professor of entomology, currently. **BUSINESS ADDRESS:** Dean of College of Agriculture, University of Hawaii, Hilo, Hilo, HI 96720-4091, (808)933-3393.

FUJIKAWA, DENSON GEN
Neurologist, educator, research scientist. Japanese American. **PERSONAL:** Born Oct 23, 1942, Denson, AR; son of Yoshihiko Fred Fujikawa (deceased) and Alice M Fujikawa; divorced. **EDUCATION:** Harvard University, AB (magna cum laude), 1964; University of Southern California School of Medicine, MD, 1969; Columbia-Presbyterian Medical Center, post graduate certificate, 1971; UCLA Center for the Health Sciences, post-graduate certificate, 1973; Harbor-UCLA Medical Center, post-graduate certificate, 1981. **CAREER:** Columbia-Presbyterian Medical Center, general surgery resident, 1969-71; UCLA Medical Center, neurosurgery resident, 1971-73; County of Los Angeles, dispensary physician, 1975-76; City of Los Angeles, examining physician, 1976-78; Harbor-UCLA Medical Center, neurology resident, 1978-81; Olive View Medical Center, EEG fellow, 1981-83; Sepulveda VA Medical Center, staff neurologist, 1983-; UCLA School of Medicine, Dept of Neurology, clinical instructor, 1981-83, assistant adjunct professor, 1983-90, associate adjunct professor, 1990-. **ORGANIZATIONS:** American Academy of Neurology, 1979-; Society for Neuroscience, 1984-; International Society of Cerebral Blood Flow & Metabolism, 1987-; American Society for Neurochemistry, 1990-; American Epilepsy Society; American Electroencephalographic Society; American Association for the Advancement of Science, 1982-; Los Angeles Society of Neurological Sciences, 1979-. **HONORS/AWARDS:** USC School of Medicine, research fellowship in physiology, 1966, 1967. **SPECIAL ACHIEVEMENTS:** Author of more than 70 research articles, book chapters and abstracts, 1983-. **BUSINESS ADDRESS:** Staff Neurologist, VA Medical Center, 16111 Plummer St, Sepulveda, CA 91343, (818)895-9473.

FUJIKI, MARJORIE

Attorney. Japanese American. **PERSONAL:** Born Jul 28, 1954, San Mateo, CA; daughter of Kiyoko Fujiki and Jack Fujiki; married Akira Tana, Sep 1987; children: Kyle Tana, Ryan Tana. **EDUCATION:** University of San Francisco School of Law; University of California, Santa Cruz. **CAREER:** Legal Aid Society, Criminal Defense Division, staff attorney, 1982-85; Equal Rights Advocates, staff attorney, 1985-86; New York Attorney General, Civil Rights Bureau, deputy bureau chief, 1987-. **ORGANIZATIONS:** Asian American Legal Defense & Education Fund, board member, 1987-; Committee Against Anti-Asian Violence, board member, 1991-. **BUSINESS ADDRESS:** Deputy Bureau Chief, New York State Dept of Law Civil Rights Bureau, 120 Broadway, 23rd Fl, Rm 160, New York, NY 10271, (212)416-8245.

FUJIMATSU, TADAO

Airline executive, writer. Japanese American. **PERSONAL:** Born Apr 5, 1935, Kamakura, Kanagawa, Japan; married Atsuko Fujimatsu. **EDUCATION:** Tokyo University, law, 1959. **CAREER:** Japan Air Lines Intl Service, chairman, currently. **ORGANIZATIONS:** Midori Foundation, vice president; Japanese American Social Srvice Inc, director. **BUSINESS ADDRESS:** Chairman, JAL Intl Service, 3 Park Ave, 28th Fl, New York, NY 10016, (212)679-7924.

FUJIMOTO, ISAO

Educator, community organizer. Japanese American. **PERSONAL:** Born Sep 28, 1933, Wapato, WA; son of Taichi & Ayako Fujimoto; married Christine Fry; children: Caedmon, Basho, Esumi Gaia. **EDUCATION:** University of California, Berkeley, BA, 1955; Stanford University, MA, 1960; Cornell University, PhD, 1967. **CAREER:** University of California, Davis, lecturer, 1967-76; National Center for Appropriate Technology, associate director, 1977-78; University of California, Davis, senior lecturer, chair, graduate program in community development, Asian American program, director, currently. **ORGANIZATIONS:** Rural America, board of directors, vice president, 1979-87; American Friends Service Committee, Northern California, executive comm, 1985-89; Data Center, board of directors; California Institute for Rural Studies, chairman of board, 1992-. **HONORS/AWARDS:** City of Davis, California, Human Relations Award, 1986; University of California, Davis, Outstanding Adviser Award, 1987; Rural Sociological Society, Excellence in Instruction Award, 1993. **SPECIAL ACHIEVEMENTS:** Co-Author, Change in Rural America, "The One Village, One Product Movement in Japan," Community Development Journal, p 10-20, 1992. **MILITARY SERVICE:** US Army, correspondent, Korea, 1956-58. **BIOGRAPHICAL SOURCES:** Communties: "Conversation with Isao Fujimoto," Winds of Change 1, p 3, 4, 8, Feb 1981; "A House That's More than a Home," San Jose Mercury, p 1-2D, 1985; "How A Networker Networks," Workers Collectives in California, in Japanese, p 127-137, 1987. **HOME ADDRESS:** 870 Linden Ln, Davis, CA 95616, (916)753-3148. **BUSINESS ADDRESS:** Sr Lecturer/Chair, Dept of Applied Behavioral Sciences, University of California, Davis, 1331 Hart Hall, Davis, CA 95616, (916)752-1805.

FUJIMOTO, JACK

Educational administrator. Japanese American. **CAREER:** Los Angeles Mission College, president, currently. **SPECIAL ACHIEVEMENTS:** Los Angeles Mission College was first college to launch a Quality Workforce Development Training Program, 1993. **BUSINESS ADDRESS:** President, Los Angeles Mission College, 13356 Eldridge Ave, Sylmar, CA 91342-3200, (818)364-7600.*

FUJIMOTO, JAMES G.

Educator, scientist. Japanese American. **PERSONAL:** Born Sep 28, 1957, Chicago, IL; son of Harold H Fujimoto and Jane S Fujimoto; married Carla H Fujimoto. **EDUCATION:** MIT, SB, 1979, SM, EE, 1981, PhD, 1984. **CAREER:** Harvard Med School, visiting lecturer, 1987-91; MIT Lincoln Labs, consultant, 1985-, assistant professor, 1985-88, associate professor, 1988-. **ORGANIZATIONS:** IEEE, senior member; Optical Society of America, fellow; America Physical Society; American Association for the Advancement of Science; New York Academy of Science. **HONORS/AWARDS:** National Science Foundation, Presidential Young Investigator, 1986; NAS, William Baker Award, 1990; IEEE, LEOS Travelling Lecturer, 1990. **SPECIAL ACHIEVEMENTS:** Research in lasers and optics, ultrafast phenomena, and laser medicine. **BUSINESS ADDRESS:** Associate Professor, Massachusetts Institute of Technology, 77 Massachusetts Ave, Building 36-345, Cambridge, MA 02139.

FUJIMOTO, JAMES RANDALL

Judge. Japanese American. **PERSONAL:** Born Dec 1, 1954, Chicago, IL; son of Ralph & Margaret Fujimoto; married Carol R Fujimoto, Nov 18, 1989; children: Keith Harris (stepson). **EDUCATION:** University of Chicago, AB, 1976; DePaul University College of Law, JD, 1979. **CAREER:** Masuda, Funai, Eifert & Mitchell, associate, 1978-81; Alexander, Fennerty & Fujimoto, partner, 1981-90; Department of Justice, Executive Office for Immigration Review, US immigration judge, 1990-. **ORGANIZATIONS:** Japanese American Citizens League, board of directors, 1986-90, Chicago Chapter, president, 1990. **SPECIAL ACHIEVEMENTS:** Various legal publications, 1981-90. **BUSINESS ADDRESS:** Immigration Judge, Executive Office for Immigration Review, 536 S Clark St, Ste 646, Chicago, IL 60605, (312)353-7313.

FUJIMOTO, ROBERT I.

Engineering consulting company executive. Japanese American. **CAREER:** US Bureau of Reclamation, design engineer; Boeing Co, safety engineer; Mine Safety and Health Administration, branch chief; Goodson & Associates, Inc, president/principal; Foothill Engineering Consultants, Inc, president/owner, currently. **ORGANIZATIONS:** Consulting Engineers Council; American Society of Civil Engineers; International Commission on Large Dams; professional engineer, California, #0354; National Society of Professional Engineers; Colorado Center of Environmental Management, steering committee; Asian Chamber of Commerce; Denver Central Optimists. **HONORS/AWARDS:** Denver Chamber and Denver Post, Minority Business of the Year Finalist, 1993; US Army Corps of Engineers, Certificate of Recognition, 1993; US SBA, Small Business Person of the Year Award, 1992, Prime Contractor of the Year, Region VIII, 1982; USGS, Department of Interior's Minority Entrepreneur of the Year, nominee 1991-92. **SPECIAL ACHIEVEMENTS:** Development of Systematic Waste Disposal Plans for Metal & Nonmetal Mines, 1982; Department of Interior's Task Force, Buffalo Creek Disaster, 1972; assisted writing federal regulations on disposal of coal waste refuse, 1974. **MILITARY SERVICE:** US Navy, lt, 1961-64, active, 1967, reserves; Communications "C" and Operations "E", 1964. **BIOGRAPHICAL SOURCES:** "Firms Cut Own Paths to Success," The Denver Post, p 1H, April 25, 1993. **BUSINESS ADDRESS:** President, Owner, Foothill Engineering Consultants, Inc, 350 Indiana St, Ste 415, Golden, CO 80401, (303)278-0622.

FUJIMOTO, WILFRED YORIO

Educator. Japanese American. **PERSONAL:** Born Jul 15, 1940, Hilo, HI; son of Shigeki and Kikue Fujimoto; married Jean Setsu Fujimoto, May 22, 1971; children: Pamela Naomi, Michael Ken. **EDUCATION:** Johns Hopkins University, BA, 1962, MD, 1965; Columbia Presbyterian Medical Center, residency, 1965-67; University of Washington, School of Medicine, residency and fellowship, 1969-71. **CAREER:** University of Washington, instructor, 1970-71, assistant professor of medicine, 1971-76, associate professor of medicine, 1976-83, professor of medicine, 1983-. **ORGANIZATIONS:** American Federation for Clinical Research, 1971-; American Diabetes Association, 1972-; Epidemiology Council, secretary-treasurer, 1991-93, vice chair, 1993-; Endocrine Society, 1972-; King County Medical Society, 1979-; American College of Physician, fellow, 1976-; Western Association of Physician, 1989-. **HONORS/AWARDS:** National Institutes of Health, Research Career Development Award, 1971-76; Japan Society for Promotion of Science, fellow, 1979-80; Johns Hopkins University, Phi Beta Kappa, 1962, Alpha Omega Alpha, 1965. **SPECIAL ACHIEVEMENTS:** Multiple publications on diabetes, both laboratory and clincial, with focus on diabetes in Asian Americans, 1972-. **MILITARY SERVICE:** Public Health Service, surgeon, 1967-69. **BUSINESS ADDRESS:** Professor of Internal Medicine, University of Washington, Health Sciences Building, RG-26, Seattle, WA 98195, (206)543-3470.

FUJIMURA, ROBERT KANJI

Biochemist. Japanese American. **PERSONAL:** Born Jul 28, 1933, Seattle, WA; son of Tamiko Ruth Fujimura and Tatsuo Fujimura; married Shigeko I Fujimura, Dec 1, 1962; children: Dan, Tomi, Kei. **EDUCATION:** University of Washington, BS, 1956; University of Wisconsin, Madison, MS, 1959, PhD, 1961. **CAREER:** Oak Ridge National Laboratory, senior research staff I, 1963-90; University of Tennessee, Knoxville, adjunct professor, 1970-92; consultant, Japanese biotechnology, 1986-; self-employed, 1990-; Food and Drug Administration, senior resident research associate, 1992-. **ORGANIZATIONS:** Department of Commerce & American Embassy, Tokyo, foreign commercial service (biotechnology), 1985-86; General Board of Church & Soc, United Methodist Church Genetic Science Task Force, 1989-91; American Soc Biochemistry & Molec Biology, 1970-; Sigma Xi, 1959-. **HONORS/AWARDS:** US National Institutes of Health, postdoctoral fellow, Osaka University, Japan,

1961; Japan Soc Promotion of Science, fellow, 1981; National Research Council, senior fellow, 1992. **SPECIAL ACHIEVEMENTS:** Publications of original research in refereed professional journals, 1962-; reports on Japanese biotechnology through National Tech Information Service, 1988, 1989, 1992; organized and chaired Intl Symposim on DNA Transcription, Replication & Repair, 1981; co-organizer of Symposium on Societal Impact of Human Genetic Engineering, 1991. **BUSINESS ADDRESS:** Senior Resident Research Associate, Center for Devices & Radiological Health, Food & Drug Administration, 12709 Twinbrook Pky, Rm 12, HFZ 113, Rockville, MD 20852, (301)443-6510.

FUJIMURA, ROBERT KIYOSHI
Association executive. Japanese American. **PERSONAL:** Born Mar 13, 1959, Rochester, NY; married Anne Marie Fujimura; children: Kathryn, Jillian, Emylianne. **EDUCATION:** Liberty University; Monroe Community College; Wharton School, University of Pennsylvania. **CAREER:** Fujimura Taekwondo School Inc, CEO, 1984-; United States Taekwondo Union, executive director, 1988-. **ORGANIZATIONS:** Japanese American Citzens League, Cincinnati Chapter, board member, 1991; United States Taekwondo Union, life member, 1983-; Pan American Taekwondo Union, Pan American referee, 1987-; World Taekwondo Federation, international referee, 1989-, Kukkiwon, fourth degree black belt, 1990; 11th US Junior Olympic Taekwondo Championship, advisory chairman, 1991; International Martial Arts Federation, vice president, 1988-91; Annalori Corporation, vice president, 1993-. **HONORS/AWARDS:** World Taekwondo Federation, Letter of Commedation, 1989, Letter of Appreciation, 1992; Virginia State Taekwondo Association, Letter of Commendation, 1988. **SPECIAL ACHIEVEMENTS:** US Taekwondo Journal, editorial assistant, 1985; Taekwondo USA, editor, 1989-92; 1992 Pan American Taekwondo Championship, tournament director, 1992; 1992 US Olympic Taekwondo Team Trials, tournament director, 1992; US Olympic Committee, alternate, board of directors, 1990-91; US Taekwondo Team Trials Director; 11th World Taekwondo Championships, advisory committee; 1994 Goodwill Games, national governing body representative for taekwondo. **BIOGRAPHICAL SOURCES:** 1992 Taekwondo Fact Book: Capture the Dream, p 10, 1992. **BUSINESS ADDRESS:** Executive Director, United States Taekwondo Union, One Olympic Plaza, Suite 405, Colorado Springs, CO 80909, (719)578-4632.

FUJIOKA, TAKASHI
Chemical plant manager. Japanese American. **PERSONAL:** Born Oct 17, 1946, Futsukaichi, Fukuoka, Japan; son of Koki Fujioka and Kuniko Fujioka; married Rebecca Heeter Fujioka, Jun 9, 1973; children: Ruth Megumi, Chie Theresa. **EDUCATION:** Kyushu Institute of Technology, BS, 1969; Carnegie-Mellon University, MS, 1971, PhD, 1978. **CAREER:** Alcoa, engr, senior engr, 1977-81, Moralco, production manager, 1981-87, senior process engr, 1987-89, area supervisor, 1988-91, works manager, 1991-. **ORGANIZATIONS:** American Ceramic Society, 1987-; Sigma Xi, 1977-. **SPECIAL ACHIEVEMENTS:** Publication: "Morphological Stability of Disc Crystals," Journal of Crystal Growth 24/25, p 84-93, proceedings of the 4th Intl Conference of Crystal Growth, 1974. **BUSINESS ADDRESS:** Works Manager, Aluminum Company of America, PO Box 896, Fort Meade, FL 33841, (813)285-8101.

FUJIWARA, THERESA
Counseling service administrator. Japanese American. **CAREER:** Asian Counseling and Referral Service, beginning 1981, executive director, beginning 1986; City of Seattle, Office of Inter-Governmental Relations, regional coordinator, 1993-. **ORGANIZATIONS:** United Nations Association, Human Rights Day Award. **BUSINESS ADDRESS:** Regional Coordinator, Office of Inter-Govermental Relations, City of Seattle, 618 2nd Ave, Seattle, WA 98104, (206)684-0500. *

FUKAI, MASANI (MAS)
City council member. Japanese American. **PERSONAL:** Born Jan 2, 1927, Gardena, CA; married Lillie; children: Rick, Janice. **EDUCATION:** Los Angeles Trade-Tech College; California School of Insurance, 1963. **CAREER:** Automotive repair business, self-employed, 13 years; Wada, Asato Insurance Agency, 1963-73; Los Angeles County, Narcotics and Dangerous Drugs Commission, 1968; Los Angeles County Supervisor Kenneth Hahn, deputy, 1975, chief deputy, 1987-92; Southern California Rapid Transit District, Los Angeles County Transportation Commission, retired 1992; Gardena Municipal Mutual Insurance Co, founder, 1993; Gardena City Council, city councilman, 1974-. **ORGANIZATIONS:** Gardena Friends of Richard Junior Sports Association, founder; Kiwanis; YMCA; VFW; Japanese American Citi-

zens League; Million Dollar Conference, life member. **HONORS/AWARDS:** Black Business Assn, Special Recognition Award; Boy Scouts of America, Man of the Year Award; Japanese Cultural Institute, Man of the Year Award; US Congress, resolution of commendation; California State Legislature, resolution of commendation; Franklin Million Dollar Conference, Franklin Life's Leading Nisei, 1965-73; Center for Pacific-Asian Family, Recognition Award, 1992; Hawaiian Inter-Club Council, Ho'olaule'a festival, grand marshal, 1992. **MILITARY SERVICE:** US Army, corporal, 1945-47. **BUSINESS ADDRESS:** City Councilman, City of Gardena, 1700 West 162nd St, Gardena, CA 90247, (310)217-9500.

FUKUHARA, HENRY
Artist, educator. Japanese American. **PERSONAL:** Born Apr 25, 1913, Los Angeles, CA; son of Ichisuke Fukuhara & Ume Sakamoto; married Fujiko Yasutake, Aug 18, 1938; children: Joyce Fukuhara Bowensox, Grace Fukuhara Niwa, Rackham, Helen. **CAREER:** Las Palmas Nurseries, partner, 1935-41; Fukuhara Green House, Inc, president, 1946-77; self-employed artist, 1972-. **ORGANIZATIONS:** Japanese American Citizens League, Bay District Chapter, president, 1941-42; Aquaelle Club; Pittsburgh Watercolor Society; Watercolor Society of Alabama; National Watercolor Society. **HONORS/AWARDS:** Nassau Community College, Purchase Award, 1976; Elise Brown Memorial, 1978; Best in Show Watercolor, 1979; numerous others. **SPECIAL ACHIEVEMENTS:** Permanent collection: Heckshen Museum, NY; Nassau Community College; Abilene Museum Fine Art; Los Angeles County Museum, numerous others. **BIOGRAPHICAL SOURCES:** Watercolor Energies, NY Times, Frank Webb, Feb 17, 1980, p 112-113; Nancy Dostim Wall Moore; Vibrant Portrait of a Watercolor, Los Angeles Times, May 2, 1992; Janice Lovoos, American Artist, May 1993; others. **HOME ADDRESS:** 1214 Marine St, Santa Monica, CA 90405.

FUKUNAGA, KEINOSUKE
Educator. Japanese American. **PERSONAL:** Born Jul 23, 1930, Himeji-Shi, Hyogo-Ken, Japan; son of Choji & Tama Fukunaga; married Reiko, Mar 25, 1957; children: Gen, Nina. **EDUCATION:** Kyoto University, BSEE, 1953, PhD, 1962; University of Pennsylvania, MSEE, 1959. **CAREER:** Mistubishi Electric Co, section head, 1953-66; Purdue University, professor, 1966-. **HONORS/AWARDS:** Institute of Electrical & Electronics Engineers, fellow, 1979. **BUSINESS ADDRESS:** Professor, Electrical Engineering, Purdue University, West Lafayette, IN 47907-1285, (317)494-3479.

FUKURAI, HIROSHI
Educator. Japanese American. **PERSONAL:** Born Oct 22, 1954, Sendai-city, Miyagi-ken, Japan; son of Yoshikichi Fukurai and Michie Fukurai; married Chikako Fukurai, Jan 17, 1960; children: Yuuki. **EDUCATION:** California State Fullerton, BA, 1979; University of California at Riverside, MA, 1982, PhD, 1985. **CAREER:** University of California, Riverside, junior programmer, 1984-85, visiting assistant professor of sociology, 1986-87; Texas A&M University, assistant professor of sociology, 1988-90; University of California, Santa Cruz, assistant professor of sociology, 1990-. **ORGANIZATIONS:** American Sociological Association; Society for the Study of Social Biology; American Society of Crminology; Society for Applied Sociology; Pacific Sociological Association; Society for the Study of Social Problems. **HONORS/AWARDS:** University of California, Riverside, Postdoctoral Fellowship, 1985, Graduate Student Fellowship, 1983; Miyagi Technical College, Japan, Ikuei Scholarship, 1975; University of California System, with Richard Appelbaum, David Smith, Edgar W Butler, Allen Scott, and Soohyun Chon, The Pacific Rim Research Program Fellowship, 1991, 1992. **SPECIAL ACHIEVEMENTS:** Publication of 3 books: Race & the Jury: Racial Disenfranchisement & The Search for Justice, Plenum Press, 1993; Common Destiny: Japan and the United States in the Global Age, McFarland, 1990; Anatomy of a Jury: The McMartin Child Molestation Trial, Rutgers University Press, 1994. **BUSINESS ADDRESS:** Assistant Professor of Sociology, University of California, Santa Cruz, Adlai E Stevenson College, Santa Cruz, CA 95064, (408)459-2971.

FUKUSHIMA, EIICHI
Scientist. Japanese American. **PERSONAL:** Born Jun 3, 1936, Tokyo, Japan; son of Shintaro Fukushima and Chiyo Maeyama Fukushima; married Pamelia S Fukushima, Dec 22, 1963; children: Craig Chiharu, Noelle Hoshiko. **EDUCATION:** University of Chicago, AB, SB, 1957; Dartmouth College, MA, 1959; University of Washington, PhD, 1967. **CAREER:** Los Alamos National Laboratory, staff member, 1967-85; Lovelace Medical Foundation, scientist, senior scientist, 1985-. **SPECIAL ACHIEVEMENTS:** Area of specialization: basic

and applied research in flows by magnetic resonance. **BUSINESS ADDRESS:** Senior Scientist, Lovelace Medical Foundation, 2425 Ridgecrest Dr SE, Albuquerque, NM 87108, (505)262-7155.

FUKUYAMA, FRANCIS
Author. Japanese American. **EDUCATION:** Cornell University, classics; Yale University, comparative literature. **CAREER:** Rand Corp, resident consultant, currently. **SPECIAL ACHIEVEMENTS:** Author, publications include: "Immigrants and Family Values," Commentary, vol 95, May 1993; The End of History and the Last Man, Free Press. **BUSINESS ADDRESS:** Resident Consultant, Rand Corp, PO Box 2138, Santa Monica, CA 90407, (310)393-0411.*

FULBECK, KIP
Artist, educator. Chinese American. **PERSONAL:** Born Apr 30, 1965, Fontana, CA; son of John Fulbeck & Seckyue Fung Fulbeck. **EDUCATION:** UCSD, MFA, 1992. **CAREER:** University of California, Santa Barbara, Asian American Studies Program, lecturer, 1992, Art Studio Dept, assistant professor, 1992-. **ORGANIZATIONS:** Association of Independent Video & Filmmakers; Film Arts Foundation; Association of Asian American Studies. **HONORS/AWARDS:** Red River International Film & Video Festival, 1st Place, 1991; Santa Barbara International Film Festival, Best Local Filmmaker, 1993. **SPECIAL ACHIEVEMENTS:** Banana Split, video, 1991; Game of Death, video, 1991; A Day at the Fair, video, 1990; Just Stand Still, video, 1990; white rice/mixed blood, performance, 1993. **BIOGRAPHICAL SOURCES:** "Kip Fulbeck: Split, Half-Baked, Half-Bred, Mixed, Half-and-Half, Hapa. . ." Asian New Yorker, 5, no 3, p 2, June, 1993; "Where From, Mac?" The Village Voice XXXVIII, no 19 p 60-1. **BUSINESS PHONE:** (805)893-3138.

FUNABIKI, JON
Journalist, educator. Japanese American. **PERSONAL:** Born Jun 21, 1949, San Jose, CA; son of Mason and Grace Funabiki; married Amy, 1969; children: Marge. **EDUCATION:** San Francisco State University, BA, 1971. **CAREER:** San Diego Tribune, journalist, 1972-73; San Diego Union, journalist, 1973-90; San Francisco State University, Center for Integration & Improvement of Journalism, director, 1990. **ORGANIZATIONS:** Asian American Journalists Association; Society of Professional Journalists; World Affairs Council. **HONORS/AWARDS:** University of California, Santa Barbara, National Endowment for the Humanities, Professional Summer fellowship, 1981; Stanford University, John S Knight Professional Journalism Fellowship, 1985; East-West Center, Jefferson Fellowship for Journalists, 1989. **SPECIAL ACHIEVEMENTS:** Specialty in Asian economics and politics and US-Asia affairs; director of Project Zinger, an annual report/critique of news media coverage and portrayals of Asian Americans. **BUSINESS ADDRESS:** Director, Center for Integration and Improvement of Journalism, San Francisco State University, 1600 Holloway, HSS 205, San Francisco, CA 94132, (415)338-7434.

FUNG, BING M.
Educator. Chinese American. **PERSONAL:** Born Aug 15, 1939, Hong Kong; son of Hon-Wah Fung and Fung-Ngor Lam; married Mildred Wei-Yum Mah, Aug 26, 1967; children: Archon. **EDUCATION:** Chung Chi College, (now Chinese University of Hong Kong), diploma, 1963; California Institute of Technology, PhD, 1967. **CAREER:** Union Carbide, research scientist, 1967; Tufts University, assistant professor, 1966-72; University of Oklahoma, associate professor, 1972-76, professor, 1976-. **ORGANIZATIONS:** American Chemical Society, 1965-; American Association for the Advancement of Science, 1976-; Chinese American Chemical Society, 1987-. **HONORS/AWARDS:** Sigma Xi, Faculty Research Award, 1974; NIH, Research Career Development Award, 1975-80; University of Oklahoma, Distinguished Lecturer, 1984-85, 1988-89, Regents' Award for Superior Research, 1985; American Chemical Society, Oklahoma Chemist of the Year, 1993. **BUSINESS ADDRESS:** Professor, Dept of Chemistry, University of Oklahoma, 620 Parrington Oval, Norman, OK 73072-0370, (405)325-3092.

FUNG, DANIEL YEE CHAK
Educator. Chinese American. **PERSONAL:** Born May 15, 1942, Hong Kong; son of Francis K K Fung (deceased) and Beatrice Wong (deceased); married Catherine Lee Fung, Feb 17, 1968; children: Francis Y C. **EDUCATION:** International Christian University, BA, 1965; University of North Carolina, Chapel Hill, MSPH, 1967; Iowa State University, PhD, 1969. **CAREER:** Pennsylvania State University, assistant professor, assistant director, 1969-78;

Kansas State University, assistant professor, 1978-81, associate professor, 1981-85, Food Science Graduate Program, chair, 1979-87, professor, 1985-. **ORGANIZATIONS:** American Society for Microbiology, Group III representative, 1992-94, Food Microbiology Division, chair, 1990-91; Institute of Food Technologists, International Relations Committee, chair, 1993-94, International Division, chair, 1993-94; Chinese American Food Society, president, 1988-89; Gamma Sigma Delta, Eta Chapter, president, 1989; Sigma Xi, KSU Chapter, president, 1987. **HONORS/AWARDS:** Intl Gamma Sigma Delta, Distinguished Service to Agriculture Award, highest award, 1993; Sigma Xi, Outstanding Scientist Award, 1993; Gamma Sigma Delta, Distinguished Faculty Award, 1993; numerous others. **SPECIAL ACHIEVEMENTS:** Journal of Food Protection, editorial board, 1976-; Journal Environmental Health, editorial board, 1981-; Journal of Rapid Methods and Automation in Microbiology, editor, 1992-; more than 350 publications in journals, books; co-editor, Handbook in Anaerobic Fermentation, Marcel Dekker, Inc, 1988; Instrumental Methods for Quality Assurance in Foods, Marcel Dekker, Inc, 1991. **BUSINESS ADDRESS:** Professor of Food Science, Kansas State University, 225 Call Hall, Manhattan, KS 66506-1600, (913)532-5654.

FUNG, DENNIS LUNG
Educator, physician. Chinese American. **PERSONAL:** Born Feb 7, 1940, Sacramento, CA; son of Lung Fung and Ruby M Yuke Fung; married Sylvia Wong Fung, Jun 19, 1966; children: Maxwell, Shelly, Melinda. **EDUCATION:** Stanford University, BS (with distinction), 1962; University of California San Francisco, MD, 1966. **CAREER:** Sacramento County Hospital, intern, 1966-67; Stanford University Hospital, resident & fellow, 1967-70; University of California Davis, asst professor, beginning 1972, professor, currently. **ORGANIZATIONS:** Association University Anesthesiologists, 1989-; American Medical Association, 1967-; American Society Anesthesiologists, 1970-; American Society for Regional Anesthesia; International Anesthesia Research Association; Society for Education in Anesthesia. **SPECIAL ACHIEVEMENTS:** Anesthesia-related articles and book chapters. **MILITARY SERVICE:** Air Force, major, 1970-72. **BUSINESS ADDRESS:** Professor, Dept of Anesthesiology, University of California, Davis, 2315 Stockton Blvd, Room 2304, Sacramento, CA 95817, (916)734-5171.

FUNG, GORDON L.
Physician, educator. Chinese American. **PERSONAL:** Born Jul 24, 1951, San Francisco, CA; son of Paul Francis Fung and Victoria Toy Fung; married Peggy Toy Fung, May 4, 1980; children: Kelly Ann, Everett Paul, Jana Marie. **EDUCATION:** UCSF School of Medicine, MD, 1979; UC Berkeley School of Public Health, MPH, 1979. **CAREER:** Laguna Honda Hospital, San Francisco, cardiology consultant; Consulting Cardiology Associates, partner, 1988-89; private practice, cardiovascular disease consultant, 1985-; UCSF School of Medicine, assistant clinical prof of medicine, 1987-. **ORGANIZATIONS:** American Heart Association, San Francisco Chapter, board of directors president, 1992-93, vp, development, 1988-91; Friends, founding member, 1989-; California Affiliate, AHA, director at large, 1993-; AHA, Chinese Community Cardiac Council, steering committee chairperson, 1993-; Ding Sum, Inc, president, 1993-; Friends, non-profit organization founding member, music director, 1989-; Book Bank, USA, board member, 1986, vp, 1989-. **HONORS/AWARDS:** AHA, SF Chapter, Community Programs Award, 1988; Fund Development Award, 1989; California Pacific Medical Center, Teacher of the Year Award, 1987. **SPECIAL ACHIEVEMENTS:** Fluent in Cantonese. **BUSINESS ADDRESS:** Gordon L Fung, MD, MPH, Inc, 789 Vallejo St, San Francisco, CA 94133-3834, (415)982-6691.

FUNG, HENRY C.
Educator, educational administrator. Chinese American. **PERSONAL:** Born Feb 5, 1939, San Francisco, CA; son of Mr and Mrs Henry G Fung; married Janet Y Fung, Jun 18, 1961; children: Brian, Bruce, Brent. **EDUCATION:** University of California, Berkeley, BA, 1959, San Francisco, MT certificate, 1960; San Francisco State University, MA, 1962; Washington State University, PhD, 1966. **CAREER:** San Francisco State University, technical asst, 1960-62; Washington State University, teaching asst, 1962-64, research asst, 1964-66; California State University-Long Beach, asst prof, microbiology, 1966-70, assoc prof, microbiology, 1970-75, professor, microbiology, 1975-, acting assoc dean, 1991-. **ORGANIZATIONS:** American Society of Microbiology, Committee on Undergraduate & Graduate Education, chair, 1981-90, Board of Education and Training, 1981-90, Southern California Branch, secty, 1976-78, pres-elect, 1979-81, president, 1981-83; American Public Health Assn, AAM Board for Med Microbiology, rep, 1987-92; California Public Health Directors Assn, Training Committee, 1991-; WSU, College of Sciences, Board of Visi-

tors, 1993-. **HONORS/AWARDS:** California Polytechnic University-Pomona, External Reviewer in Microbiology, 1990; University of Wisconsin-LaCrosse, External Reviewer in Microbiology, 1988; CSULB Disabled Students Comm, Recognition, 1989, Associated Student Body, Professor of the Year Award, 1976; Long Beach Unified School Dist, Senior High Dist Curriculum Comm, 1984-86. **SPECIAL ACHIEVEMENTS:** Author: "Elevated Levels of Serum Immunoglobulins in Asymptomatic Carriers of Clostridium difficile," 1993; "Microbiology," The College Board Guide to 150 Popular College Majors, 1992. **BUSINESS ADDRESS:** Professor, Associate Dean, California State University, College of Natural Sciences and Mathematics, 1250 Bellflower Blvd, Faculty Office Bldg 5, Rm 104, Long Beach, CA 90840-0004, (310)985-7898.

FUNG, HO-LEUNG
Educator, scientist. Chinese American. **PERSONAL:** Born Nov 17, 1943, Hong Kong; son of Kan-Lim Fung and Lai-Kum Lui; married Sun-Mi Oh, Sep 5, 1970; children: Eric K, Vicki C. **EDUCATION:** Victorian College of Pharmacy, Australia, certificate pharm, 1967; University of Kansas, PhD, 1970. **CAREER:** SUNY, Buffalo, assistant professor of pharmaceutics, 1970-75, associate professor of pharmaceutics, 1975-80, professor/chair of pharmaceutics, 1980-. **ORGANIZATIONS:** National Institutes of Health, pharmacology study section, 1986-90. **HONORS/AWARDS:** American Association Advancement of Science, fellow, 1990; American Association Pharmaceutical Scientists, fellow, 1987; Academy of Pharmaceutical Sciences, fellow, 1982; American Association Pharmaceutical Scientists, Research Achievement Award, 1988; American Pharmaceutical Association, Research Achievement Award, 1992. **SPECIAL ACHIEVEMENTS:** Published over 160 scientific papers, most in the areas of pharmacology and therapeutics of nitrovasodilators. **BUSINESS ADDRESS:** Professor & Chair, Dept of Pharmaceutics, SUNY at Buffalo, 513 Hochstetter Hall, Buffalo, NY 14260-0001, (716)645-2842.

FUNG, HUNG-GAY
Educator. Chinese American. **PERSONAL:** Born Oct 20, 1955, Canton, Kwangtung, People's Republic of China; son of Lai-Hing Fung and Luk-Mei Lee; married Linda Dan Zou, Jun 21, 1986; children: Anna. **EDUCATION:** Chinese University of Hong Kong, BBA (with honors), 1978; Georgia State University, PhD, 1984. **CAREER:** North Dakota State University, assistant professor, 1984-87; University of Rhode Island, assistant professor, 1987-88; University of Baltimore, assistant professor, 1989-91, associate professor, 1992-. **ORGANIZATIONS:** Southern Business & Economic Journal, editorial board, 1993-; International Association of Business Forecasting, board of directors, 1990-93; Financial Management Association, International Finance Program Track Committee, 1992. **HONORS/AWARDS:** Black and Decker Corp, Research Award, 1992; Financial Management Association, Presentation Award, 1986. **SPECIAL ACHIEVEMENTS:** Research in international finance; research in options, futures and derivative instruments. **BIOGRAPHICAL SOURCES:** Managerial Finance, Vol 16, number 3, front page, 1990. **BUSINESS ADDRESS:** Associate Professor, Dept of Economics and Finance, University of Baltimore, 1420 N Charles St, Baltimore, MD 21201, (410)837-4956.

FUNG, KEE-YING
Educator, educational administrator. Chinese American. **PERSONAL:** Born Dec 20, 1948, Hunan, China; son of Nan-Hing & Yuk-Kwong Fung; married Ivy W Fung, Mar 15, 1987; children: Elysia, E-Dean. **EDUCATION:** National Taiwan University, BS, 1972; Cornell University, PhD, 1976. **CAREER:** University of Arizona, research associate, 1975-78, research assistant professor, 1978-79, assistant professor, 1979-85, associate professor, 1985-; University of Miami, professor, director of aerospace program, 1993-. **ORGANIZATIONS:** DFVLR, W Germany, visiting scientist, 1981; ICASE, NASA Langley, visiting scientist, 1985; National Cheng-Kung University, visiting professor, 1986-87; NASA-Ames Research Center, visiting scientist, 1987; Asian American Faculty & Staff Association, president, 1989-90. **HONORS/AWARDS:** Alexander von Humboldt Foundation, fellow, 1981. **SPECIAL ACHIEVEMENTS:** Numerous scientific articles on aerodynamics; fluid mechanics and computational methods in journals and book volumes. **BUSINESS ADDRESS:** Professor, University of Miami, Coral Gables, FL 33124, (305)284-3287.

FUNG, SHUN C.
Research scientist. Chinese American. **PERSONAL:** Born Jan 28, 1943, Kwong Tung, China; son of Shum Fung & F Ping Fung; married Juliana S Y Fung, Oct 22, 1972; children: Carina, Allen. **EDUCATION:** University of

California, Berkeley, BS, 1965; University of Illinois, Urbana, MS, 1967, PhD, 1969. **CAREER:** Exxon Research & Engineering Company, engineering associate, 1969-. **ORGANIZATIONS:** ACS; Catalysis Society of Metropolitan New York; North American Catalysis Society. **SPECIAL ACHIEVEMENTS:** Author, "Strong Metal-Support Interactions: Occurence among the binary oxides of groups IIA-VB," J Catalysis, vol 55, p29-35, 1978; expert in redispensing agglomerated noble metals on high surface oxide supports. **BUSINESS ADDRESS:** Engineering Associate, Exxon Research and Engineering Company, Rte 22 East, LD-280, Clinton Township, Annandale, NJ 08801, (908)730-2590.

FUNG, SUI AN
Space scientist. Chinese American. **PERSONAL:** Born Dec 18, 1922, Shanghai, Chekiang, China; married; children: Joan C, Jean C, John J, Peter J, Jim J. **EDUCATION:** Natl Cent University, NanKing, BS, 1948; University of Rochester, MS, 1956; Cornell University, PhD, 1965. **CAREER:** Signal Equip Co, mech engineer/supervisor & manager, 1948-52; University of Evansville, asst prof, mech engg, 1956-59; Texas Tech University, assoc prof, 1959-62; Rockwell Intl, Space Div, mem staff, beginning 1965; South Bay University, prof, beginning 1979. **ORGANIZATIONS:** American Inst of Aeronautics & Astronautics; AAAS; American Soc of Mech Engineers; American Soc Engineering Educ. **HONORS/AWARDS:** NSF scholar, 1966. **BUSINESS ADDRESS:** Rockwell Intl Corp, PO Box 146, Beverly Hills, CA 90212.

FUNG, SUN-YIU
Educator. Chinese American. **PERSONAL:** Born Dec 27, 1932, Hong Kong; son of Lok-Chi Fung & Lai-Lan Tong Fung; married Helen W Fung, Feb 9, 1964; children: Eric T, Linette M. **EDUCATION:** University of San Francisco, BS, 1957; University of California, Berkeley, PhD, 1963. **CAREER:** Lawrence Berkeley Lab, research associate, 1964; Rutgers-The State University, research associate, 1964-66; University of California, Riverside, Physics Dept, asst professor, 1966-70, associate professor, 1970-76, chairman, 1979-85, 1990-91, professor, 1976-. **ORGANIZATIONS:** American Physical Society, 1962-; American Association of Physics Teachers, 1976-; Chinese American Faculty Association, 1972-, president, 1990-91; Overseas Chinese Physicist Association, 1991-, regional coordinators, 1991-93; Riverside Chinese Memorial Pavilian Committee, chairman, 1985-87. **BUSINESS ADDRESS:** Professor, Physics Dept, University of California, Riverside, Riverside, CA 92521-0001, (909)787-5636.

FUNG, YUAN-CHENG BERTRAM
Bioengineering educator, author. Chinese American. **PERSONAL:** Born Sep 15, 1919, Yuhong, Changchow, Kiangsu, China; son of Chung-Kwang and Lien Hu Fung; married Luna Hsien-Shih Yu, Dec 22, 1949; children: Conrad Antung, Brenda Pingsi. **EDUCATION:** National Central University, China, BS, 1941, MS, 1943; California Institute Tech, PhD, 1948. **CAREER:** Bur Aero Research China, research fellow, 1943-45; California Institute Tech, research assistant, research fellow, 1946-51, faculty, 1951-66, aerospace, professor, 1959-66; University of California, San Diego, bioengineering & applied mechanics, professor, 1966-; aerospace industrial firms, consultant, 1949-. **ORGANIZATIONS:** Natl Acad of Sci; Natl Acad of Eng; Institute of Medicine; Society of Engineering Science; Microcirculatory Society; American Physiol Society; Natl Heart Assn; Basic Science Coun; Sigma Xi. **HONORS/AWARDS:** Chinese Institute Engineers, Achievement Award, 1965, 1968; Microcirculatory Society, Landis Award, 1975; Intl Society of Biorheology, Poiseville Medal, 1986; San Diego Engineering Society, Engineer of the Year, 1986; ASCE, von Karman Medal, 1976; Biomedical Engineering Society, ALZA Award, 1989; ASME, fellow, Lissner Award, 1978, Centennial Medal, 1978, Worcester Reed Warner Medal, 1984, Timoshenko Medal, 1991; American Society of Biomechanics, Borelli Award; Guggenheim fellow; AIAA, fellow. **SPECIAL ACHIEVEMENTS:** Author: Theory of Aeroelasticity, 1985, 1993; Foundations of Solid Mechanics, 1965; A First Course in Continuum Mechanics, 1969, 1977, 1992; Biomechanics, 1972; Biomechanics: Mechanical Properties of Living Tissues, 1980, 1992; Biodynamics: Circulation, 1984; Biomechanics: Motion, Flow, Stress and Growth, 1990; editor: Journal Biorheology, Journal Biomechanical Engineering. **BUSINESS ADDRESS:** Prof, Dept of Applied Mechanics/Bioengineering, University of California-San Diego, 9500 Gilman Dr, La Jolla, CA 92093-0412. *

FURUKAWA, FRED M.
Educator. Japanese American. **PERSONAL:** Born Mar 3, 1932, Hana, Maui, HI; son of Thelma N. Furukawa; married Patricia Tilli-Furukawa, Jun 13, 1981; children: Karen Furukawa-Schlerth, Carolee, Glenn, Michael Norton, Eric

Norton. **EDUCATION:** University of Hawaii, BS, 1955, MEd, 1964; University of Southern California, EdD, 1969. **CAREER:** University of Hawaii, instructor, 1957-65; Los Angeles Unified School District, teacher, 1965-68; California State University, Northridge, assistant professor, 1968-69; California State University, Sacramento, professor, 1969-. **ORGANIZATIONS:** Phi Beta Delta, Omicron Chapter, 1993-; Western College of Phy Educ, 1975-89, president, 1983; California HHG, Physical Educ, recreations & dance association, athletics, vice pres, 1970-80; AAHPER, 1969-75. **HONORS/AWARDS:** CSUS, visiting scholar to Shanghai Institute, 1989. **SPECIAL ACHIEVEMENTS:** Chief evaluator for National Youth Sports Program, 1981-. **MILITARY SERVICE:** US Medical Services Corp, 1st lieutenant, 1955-57. **HOME ADDRESS:** 1251 Vanderbilt Wy, Sacramento, CA 95825, (916)925-5520. **BUSINESS ADDRESS:** Professor, California St University, Sacramento, 6000 Jay St, c/o HPE, SLN Hall, Rm 4042, Sacramento, CA 95819-2605, (916)278-6004.

FURUKAWA, LARRY KIYOSHI
Educator. Japanese American. **PERSONAL:** Born Feb 10, 1952, Los Angeles, CA; son of Hesami Furukawa and Fumiko Furukawa; married Cecelia, May 6, 1976; children: Bryan, Christy. **EDUCATION:** UCLA, BA, 1975. **CAREER:** Los Angeles Unified Schools, teacher, science, 1983-. **ORGANIZATIONS:** LAEP Target Science, 1990-. **BUSINESS ADDRESS:** Science Teacher, Bravo Medical Magnet High School, 1200 N Cornwell St, Rm 115, Los Angeles, CA 90033.

FURUKAWA, THEODORE PAUL
Social worker. Japanese American. **PERSONAL:** Born Feb 28, 1944, Honolulu, HI; son of Theodore Masao & Chiyo A Monobe Furukawa; married Kathleen M Laughlin Furukawa, Aug 31, 1968. **EDUCATION:** University of California, Berkeley, BA, 1965; West Virginia University, MSW, 1969; University of Denver, PhD, 1981. **CAREER:** State of Florida, Volunteers in Service to America, 1965-66; State of West Virginia, Volunteers in Service to America, 1966-67; Family Services of Harrison and Marion Counties, social work counselor, 1969; Walter Reed Army Medical Center, social work service, assistant chief, 1970-72, Race Relations Training Office, assistant chief, 1972-73, director of human resources, 1982-84; US Army Hospital, Iran, chief, Social Work and Community Mental Health Activity, 1974-76; US Army Academy of Health Sciences, social work researcher, 1978-82; Walter Reed Army Institute of Research, senior principal investigator, 1984-87; US Army Community and Family Support Center, Research and Evaluation Division, chief, 1988-90; University of Hawaii, associate professor of social work, 1990-93; Hina Mauka, executive director, 1993-. **ORGANIZATIONS:** Council on Social Education, board of directors, 1992-94; National Association of Social Workers, National Committee on Inquiry, 1991-93; CSWE Annual Program Meeting Coorsponding Committee, 1992-93, 1993-94; American Evaluation Association, 1987-; Inter-University Seminar on Armed Forces and Society, 1987-; Society of Hospital Social Work Directors, 1971-76, 1990-; National Asian Pacific American Families Against Substance Abuse, 1991-; Association for the Advancement of Social Work with Groups, 1992-. **HONORS/AWARDS:** Clinical Social Work, board certified diplomate, 1987-. **SPECIAL ACHIEVEMENTS:** Planner, committee to devise state-wide strategy for prevention of alcohol and other drug abuse in Hawaii, 1991-93. **MILITARY SERVICE:** US Army Medical Department, lt col, 1970-90, Legion of Merit, 1990; Meritorious Service Medal, 1973, 1976, 1982, 1984, 1988. **HOME ADDRESS:** 44-133 Hako St, #1205, Kaneohe, HI 96744.

FURUTA, HARRY
Television executive. Japanese American. **CAREER:** JTV Satellite Broadcasting, president, currently. **BUSINESS ADDRESS:** President, JTV Satellite Broadcasting, PO Box 1066, Downey, CA 90240, (310)862-9264.*

FURUTA, KARIN L.
Orchestra administrator. Japanese American. **PERSONAL:** Born Oct 17, 1963, Los Angeles, CA; daughter of Stanley Furuta and Jean Furuta. **EDUCATION:** California State University, Northridge, BA, journalism, 1986. **CAREER:** The Enterprise Simi Valley, 1986-88; Daily News of Los Angeles, 1989; The NIKKEI, editorial assistant, 1989-91; Niigata Board of Education, assistant English teacher, 1991-92; Los Angeles Philharmonic, community programming coordinator, currently. **HONORS/AWARDS:** Dow Jones Newspaper Fund, scholarship, internship, 1986. **BUSINESS ADDRESS:** Community Programming Assistant, Los Angeles Philharmonic, 135 N Grand Avenue, Los Angeles, CA 90012, (213)972-0705.

FURUTA, OTTO K.
Chemical company executive. Japanese American. **PERSONAL:** Born Mar 4, 1943, Rivers, AZ; son of Mr and Mrs Joe Kasamatsu; married Patricia Ann, Jun 30, 1972; children: Ryan. **EDUCATION:** University of California, Berkeley, BS, 1965; University of Colorado, PhD, 1968. **CAREER:** Monsanto, senior research chemist, 1968-74; Diamond Shamrock, R&D, group leader, 1974-79; UOP Inc, manager, technology, 1979-80; Great Lakes Chemical Corp, director of corporate purchasing, currently. **ORGANIZATIONS:** American Chemical Society, 1965-; Japanese-American Citizens League, vice pres, 1972-74. **SPECIAL ACHIEVEMENTS:** Language proficiency: Japanese. **BUSINESS ADDRESS:** Director, Corporate Purchasing, Great Lakes Chemical Corp, 1801 Highway 52 W, West Lafayette, IN 47906.

FURUTA, RICHARD K.
Educator. Japanese American. **PERSONAL:** Born Jan 14, 1953, Auburn, AL; son of Tokuji Furuta and Emi Kuzuhara Furuta; married. **EDUCATION:** Reed College, BA, 1974; University of Oregon, MS, 1978; University of Washington, PhD, 1986. **CAREER:** University of Maryland, asst professor, 1985-93; Texas A&M University, associate professor, 1993-. **ORGANIZATIONS:** TeX Users Group, steering committee, 1982-88, vice president, 1988-91; Association for Computing Machinery SIGLINK Special Interest Group, chair, 1993-. **SPECIAL ACHIEVEMENTS:** US editor, Electronic Publishing: Origination, Dissemination & Design, 1990-; Electronic Publishing, editorial board, 1987-90, Hypermedia, 1992-; program chair: ACM Hypertext, 1993; Principles of Document Processing Workshop, 1992; Annual Symposium of the DC area chapter of the ACM, 1991; Intl Conf on Electronic Publishing, EP90, 1990; Co-author, Structured Documents, 1989; Electronic Publishing, 1990. **BUSINESS ADDRESS:** Associate Professor, Dept of Computer Science, Texas A&M University, College Station, TX 77843-3112.

FURUTA, SOICHI
Poet, educator, art consultant. Japanese American. **PERSONAL:** Born Jul 1, 1927, Los Angeles, CA; son of Junzo Furuta and Yae Kitahara; married Misao Furuta, Nov 2, 1958; children: Yoshiya. **EDUCATION:** University of California at Los Angeles, BA (cum laude), 1954. **CAREER:** Triad Inc Design Co, partner, 1957-59; Francis Blod Design Associates, senior design director, 1959-64; Stuart, Gunn & Furuta Inc, president, 1964-85; H Lehman College/CUNY, adjunct associate professor of art, 1968-78; Urban Art Research Center, curatorial director, 1986-87; St Andrews Presbyterian College, adjunct professor of literature, 1988-. **ORGANIZATIONS:** Haiku Society of New York, president, 1980-82; Asian-American Arts Center, advisory board, 1988-. **HONORS/AWARDS:** Graphic Design Awards from PDC, AIGA, ID, Idea, Graphis etc, 1957-85; New York Haiku Society, Hakobune Award, 1980; St Andrews College, Editor's Choice Poetry Award, 1985. **SPECIAL ACHIEVEMENTS:** "Montefeltro the Hawk Nose," nominated for the Pulitzer Poetry Prize, 1989; "To Breathe," poems, 1980; "Chieko's Sky," English translation of Takamura Kotaro's Poems, 1978; "Cape Jasmine & Pomegranates," English trans of Japanese Haiku, 1974; wrote English poems that were translated (published) in German, Italian, Czech, and Japanese. **MILITARY SERVICE:** US Army, Engineering Corp, 4/A, 1955-56. **BIOGRAPHICAL SOURCES:** "Soichi Furuta," The World Mainstreet, Asahi Shimbun Newspaper, June 17, eve, 1988; "Like Father, Like Son," Essay Magazine, Jinbutsu-O-Rai-Ki, vol 1, US Japan Publication, NY Inc, April 11, 1992. **HOME ADDRESS:** 28 Goodwin Ave, White Plains, NY 10607, (914)592-6229.

FURUTANI, WARREN
City official. **CAREER:** Los Angeles City Board of Education, past president, board member, currently. **ORGANIZATIONS:** Manzanar Committee, co-founder, 1972; RLA (Rebuild Los Angeles) Board. **HONORS/AWARDS:** Asian Pacific American Legal Center of Southern California, Public Service Award, 1992. **BUSINESS ADDRESS:** Board Member, Los Angeles Board of Education, 450 North Grand Ave, Rm A201, Los Angeles, CA 90012, (213)625-6388. *

FURUTO, SHARLENE BERNICE CHOY LIN
Educator. Japanese American/Chinese American. **PERSONAL:** Born Sep 29, 1947, Honolulu, HI; daughter of Harry Tadao & Bernice Kam Lan Maeda; married David Masaru Furuto, Apr 1, 1977; children: Linda, Matthew, Michael, Daniel. **EDUCATION:** Brigham Young University, BS, 1969, EdD, 1981; University of Hawaii, MSW, 1972. **CAREER:** Hawaii State Social Services Department, social worker, 1969-70; Hawaii State Health Dept, social worker, 1970-71; Nanaikapono Elem & Preschool, school social worker, 1972-73; LDS Church, volunteer missionary, 1973-74; Maile Community Services

Center, director, 1974-75; Brigham Young University Hawaii, professor of social work, 1975-. **ORGANIZATIONS:** Council on Social Work Education, 1978-; National Association of Social Workers, 1978-; Asian American Social Work Educators, 1985-. **HONORS/AWARDS:** American Business Women's Association, Koolauloa Chapter, Woman of the Year, 1984. **SPECIAL ACHIEVEMENTS:** Editor, author, Social Work Practice with Asian Americans, 1991; selected David O McKay Lecturer, 1993. **BUSINESS ADDRESS:** Professor, Social Science Division, Brigham Young University - Hawaii, 55-220 Kulanui St, Laie, HI 96762, (808)293-3838.

G

GAJENDAR, NANDIGAM
Educator. Indo-American. **PERSONAL:** Born Nov 29, 1940, Nellore, Andhra Pradesh, India; son of N Subbarayulu (deceased) and N Neelaveni Amma (deceased); married Shobha, Jul 28, 1974; children: Uday. **EDUCATION:** Sri Venkateswara University, BA, 1959, MSc, 1961; Indian Institute of Technology, Kharagpur, PhD, 1965. **CAREER:** IIT, Kharagpur, lecturer, 1965-70; Grambling College, assistant professor, 1970-74; Grambling State University, associate professor, 1974-80, professor/systems analyst, 1980-. **ORGANIZATIONS:** Association for Computing Machinery, 1970-; IEEE-Computer Society, 1980-; Intl Journal of Information, Science & Technology, adv editorial board, 1991-.

GAJJAR, JAGDISH TRIKAMJI
Educator. Indo-American. **PERSONAL:** Born May 23, 1940, Bombay, Maharashtra, India; son of Trikamji Kanji Gajjar and Ramabai Trikamji Gajjar; married Chandrika, Aug 28, 1966; children: Neha, Arish. **EDUCATION:** Bombay University, India, BSEE, 1960, BSME, 1961; University of Oklahoma, MSEE, 1963; University of Houston, PhD, 1970. **CAREER:** Oklahoma University Research Institute, research fellow, 1962-63; Fishbach and Moore Systems Inc, project engineer, 1963-64; University of Oklahoma, special instructor, 1964-66; University of Tulsa, instructor, 1966-67; University of Houston, teaching fellow, 1967-70; GE Corp Research & Development, consultant, 1977-86; US Army, Watervliet Arsenal, consultant, 1990-; Union College, professor of EE/CS, 1970-. **ORGANIZATIONS:** IEEE Schenectady Section, section chairman, 1981-82; IEEE Region I, student activities chairman, 1975-78. **HONORS/AWARDS:** Indian Telecom Training Center, honorary fellow, 1990. **SPECIAL ACHIEVEMENTS:** Fulbright Exchange Fellow, 1985-86; Nine US Patents. **HOME ADDRESS:** 8 Twinbrook Ct, Clifton Park, NY 12065, (518)371-5606. **BUSINESS ADDRESS:** Professor, EE/CS Dept, Union College, Steinmetz Hall, Schenectady, NY 12308, (518)388-6014.

GAM, PAUL JONATHAN
Business executive. Chinese American. **PERSONAL:** Born Jul 9, 1959, Hong Kong; son of S Mcadow Gam and Mae L Gam; married Queenie K Gam, Jul 8, 1981; children: Ashley B, Kevin M. **EDUCATION:** American Institute of Certified Public Accountants, CPA certificate, 1988; University of MN, Carlson School of Management, BS, 1984; Queen's College, Hong Kong, certificate of education, 1980; University of Pennsylvania, Wharton School, certificate, M&A, 1990. **CAREER:** Equitable Financial Companies, registered representative, 1982-83; Ernst Young, CPA, auditor, 1983-84; Grant Thornton International, audit supervisor, 1984-88; Donahue Enterprises, corporate controller, 1988; US Communications, vice president, finance, 1988-91; US Directives Corp, senior vice president, CFO, 1991-. **ORGANIZATIONS:** Minnesota World Trade Center Corp, director, 1992-94, executive committee, chair, 1993-94; Organization of Chinese Americans of Minnesota, president, 1992-94; Minnesota Society of CPAs, professional ethics committee, 1990-94; University of Minnesota, Carlson School of Management, undergraduate advisory board, 1990-94; Summit Brewing Company, board of directors, 1989-94; Richway Acquisition Corporation, board of directors, 1991-92; Minneapolis/Hennepin County, international trade advisory board, 1993. **HONORS/AWARDS:** Minneapolis International Citizen Award, 1993; Council on Asian-Pacific Minnesotans, Leadership Award, 1993; U S Communications Corporation, Beyond the Call Award, 1990; Office of the Governor of Minnesota, commendation for community service, 1993; President Ronald Reagan, Presidential Sports Award, 1982; Equitable Life Assurance Society of the US, Production Club Award, 1982. **SPECIAL ACHIEVEMENTS:** Japanese karate, black belt; proficient in Chinese. **BIOGRAPHICAL SOURCES:** Minnesota Management Review, p 9, Summer, 1991; Asian Business & Community Directory, p 25, 1992. **BUSINESS ADDRESS:** Senior Vice President

& CFO, U S Directives Corporation, 300 Clifton Ave, Minneapolis, MN 55403, (612)874-1000.

GAMBLIN, NORIKO
Museum curator. Japanese American. **PERSONAL:** Born Oct 27, 1956, Kobe, Japan; daughter of Arthur E Gamblin and Haruko Ohno Gamblin. **EDUCATION:** College of William & Mary, BA, Asian studies, 1978; University of Delaware, MA, art history, 1989. **CAREER:** J Paul Getty Museum, dept of photographs, graduate intern, 1987-88; Museum of Contemporary Art, Los Angeles, NEA curatorial intern, 1989; Long Beach Museum of Art, curator, 1990-. **HONORS/AWARDS:** Smithsonian Institution and the Office of Museum Programs, Museum Leadership Award, 1991. **SPECIAL ACHIEVEMENTS:** Publications: Art in the Age of the Plague: The Work of Stephanie Wilde, 1993, co-author, Sugar 'n' Spice, 1993, Virgin Territories, 1993, Relocations & Revisions: The Japanese-American Internment Reconsidered, 1992, Elegies: The Paintings of Darren Waterston, 1992, Nancy Haynes: The Lacuna of Certainty, 1991, Terry Braunstein: Stations, 1991, Landed Images: Selections form the Permanent Collection, 1990, John McLaughlin Paintings, 1990 (all published by Long Beach Museum of Art); "Jay McCafferty," 75 Works, 75 Years: Collecting the Art of California, Laguna Art Museum, 1993; "Changing Role of Art Museums," Artweek, December 1991; co-author, Guide to the Galleries, Constructing a History: A Focus on MOCA's Permanent Collection, 1989, Guide to the Galleries, Rita & Taft Schreiber Collection, 1989, Guide to the Galleries, Garry Winogrand, 1989 (all published by Museum of Contemporary Art, Los Angeles); "Garry Winogrand," Contemporary, vol 6, 1989; lecturer, "Contemporary Artists/Contemporary Art Museums," Long Beach Museum of Art for University of California, Irvine, 1993; "Art Museum's Place in the Community," Long Beach, 1992; guest curator for the Public Corp for the Arts, "Primitive Leanings," Long Beach, 1992; Love in the Ruins: Art and the Inspiration of LA, 1994. **BUSINESS ADDRESS:** Curator, Long Beach Museum of Art, 2300 East Ocean Blvd, Long Beach, CA 90803, (310)439-2119.

GAN, JOSÉ C.
Educator. Filipino American. **PERSONAL:** Born Nov 30, 1933, Pavia, Iloilo, Philippines; son of Timoteo & Genoveva Gan; married Norma, Sep 24, 1960; children: Yvonne Gan Bennett, Karen. **EDUCATION:** University of Wisconsin, BS, pharmacy, 1957; State University of Iowa, MS, hospital pharmacy, 1959; University of Illinois, Med Center, PhD, biochemistry, 1964. **CAREER:** University of California, San Francisco, postdoctoral, 1964-66, Berkeley, postdoctoral, 1966-68; University of Texas Med Br, Dept Human Biol, Chem and Genetics, professor, 1968-. **ORGANIZATIONS:** American Society for Biochem and Molecular Biol, 1972-; American Chemical Society, 1968-. **HONORS/AWARDS:** Alameda County Heart Association Postdoctoral Fellow, 1964-66; San Francisco Heart Association, postdoctoral fellow, 1966-67. **SPECIAL ACHIEVEMENTS:** 44 publications refereed in various biochemical journals, 1966-. **BUSINESS ADDRESS:** Professor, Dept of Human Biology, Chemistry and Genetics, University of Texas Medical Branch, Galveston, TX 77550, (409)772-2774.

GANDHI, ARUN MANILAL
Educator. Indo-American. **PERSONAL:** Born Apr 14, 1934, Durban, Republic of South Africa; son of Manilal Gandhi and Sushila Gandhi; married Sunanda, Jun 10, 1958; children: Archana Prasad, Tushar. **CAREER:** Times of India, assistant editor, 1957-80; Imprint, magazine editor, 1980-83, columnist, 1983-87, book research, 1987-91; M K Gandhi Institute, director, professor, 1991-. **ORGANIZATIONS:** George Mason University, Institute of Conflict Analysis and Resolution, advisory board. **HONORS/AWARDS:** Lincoln Memorial University, Hon Doct (Humane Letters), 1990; Gwynedd-Mercy College, Hon Doct (Humane Letters), 1993; The Peace Abbey, Courage of Conscience Award, 1992; Memphis City Council, Humanitarian Award, 1993; several keys to US cities. **SPECIAL ACHIEVEMENTS:** A Patch of White, South African Racism, 1969; Voices of Poverty, 1979; Kasturba Gandhi, Biography, 1982; Morarji Papers, Rise and Fall of Janata Party, 1985; articles in numerous US newspapers. **BUSINESS ADDRESS:** Director, M K Gandhi Institute for Nonviolence, 650 E Parkway S, Memphis, TN 38104, (901)725-0815.

GANDHI, HOMI D.
Stock exchange manager. Indo-American. **PERSONAL:** Born in Bharuch, Gujarat, India; son of Dosabhai N Gandhi & Dhunmai D Gandhi; married Villy Gandhi, Apr 29, 1971; children: Hanoz, Navroz. **EDUCATION:** Sydenham College, Bombay University, BCom, (with honors), 1961; University of London, England, BSc, economics, 1964; Institute of Chartered Accountants in

England & Wales, FCA, 1967. **CAREER:** Touche, Ross, Bailey & Smart, UK, US, and Canada, senior auditor, 1964-69; A F Ferguson & Co, Bombay, India, principal, 1970-79; Spicer & Oppenheim, Nigeria, manager, 1980-81; Oppenheim, Appel, Dixon & Co, manager, 1981-82; Stephen P Radics & Co, manager, 1982-83; New York Stock Exchange, manager, 1984-. **ORGANIZATIONS:** The Institute of Chartered Accountants in England & Wales, member/fellow, 1967-; The Institute of Chartered Accounts of India, member/fellow, 1970-; The Institute of Chartered Accounts of Nigeria, 1980-; The Zoroastrian Associate of Greater New York, treasurer, 1987-; Darbe Meher Zoroastrian Temple, trustee/treasurer, 1993. **HONORS/AWARDS:** Institute of Chartered Accountants, England and Wales, honors rank, 1965; J N Tata Endowments, selected as a scholar for further studies in the UK, 1961-64. **HOME ADDRESS:** 704 Harristown Rd, Glen Rock, NJ 07452, (201)445-3917.

GANDHI, MUKESH P.
Electrical engineer. Indo-American. **PERSONAL:** Born Jun 16, 1964, Navsari, Gujarat, India; son of Parbhubhai G Gandhi and Savita P Gandhi; married Falguni Gandhi, Jul 7, 1990; children: Sonia. **EDUCATION:** University of Illinois, BSEE, 1986. **CAREER:** The Bergen Record, megnetics engineer, 1986-90; Chicago Tribune, electrical engineer, project manager, 1990-. **HOME ADDRESS:** 8883 Grand, Niles, IL 60714. **BUSINESS PHONE:** (312)222-2649.

GANDHI, NATWAR MOHAN
Government official. Indo-American. **PERSONAL:** Born Oct 4, 1940, Savarkundla, Gujarat, India; son of Mohanlal Gandhi and Shantaben Gandhi; married Nalini, May 7, 1962; children: Apoorva, Sonal. **EDUCATION:** University of Bombay, BCom, 1961, LLB, 1964; Atlanta University, MBA, 1967; Louisiana State University, PhD, 1974. **CAREER:** University of Pittsburgh, instructor, 1973, assistant professor of accounting, 1974-75, Dept of Accounting, coordinator, 1975-76; US General Accounting Office, senior evaluator, 1976-83, assistant director, 1983-92, associate director, 1992-; State of New Jersey, special assistant to governor, 1991. **ORGANIZATIONS:** National Tax Association, 1990; American Accounting Association, 1969; Gujarati Literary Academy of North America, secretary, 1981-84. **HONORS/AWARDS:** US General Accounting Office, Distinguished Service Award, 1986, Meritorious Service Award, 1983, Certificates of Merit, 1981, 1982, 1986; Louisiana State University, Haskins & Sells Fellowship, 1972; American Accounting Association, doctoral fellow, 1971. **SPECIAL ACHIEVEMENTS:** Professional papers published in learned journals: Accounting, Organizations & Society, 1976; Policy Sciences, 1977; International Journal of Accounting, 1974; Monograph on Indian-Americans in USA in Gujarati Language, 1978; proficient in Gujarati and Hindi. **BIOGRAPHICAL SOURCES:** India Today, p 52c, 52d, Sept 30, 1992; Society Monthly, Dec 1986; India Abroad, Oct 17, 1986, Jan 3, 1992, p 18, May 1, 1992. **HOME PHONE:** (301)384-6252. **BUSINESS ADDRESS:** Associate Director of Tax Policy, United States General Accounting Office, 1440 New York Ave NW, Suite 400, Washington, DC 20548, (202)272-3320.

GANDHI, PRASHANT P.
Educator. Indo-American. **PERSONAL:** Born Mar 15, 1965, Ahmedabad, Gujarat, India; son of Pradyumna R & Pramila P Gandhi; married Monisha P Gandhi, Dec 29, 1991. **EDUCATION:** University of Maryland, BSEE, 1984; University of Pennsylvania, MSEE, 1986, PhD, elect eng, 1990. **CAREER:** Villanova University, assistant professor, 1990-. **ORGANIZATIONS:** Institute of Electrical and Electroics Engineering, 1986-; Sigma Xi, 1991-; American Association of University Professors, 1992-; Society of Indian Academics in America, 1993-. **HONORS/AWARDS:** Burroughs, Inc, graduate fellowship, 1985-86; Villanova University, Faculty Research Grant, 1992; Navy, ASEE, Summer Research Fellowship, 1993. **SPECIAL ACHIEVEMENTS:** "Analysis of CFAR Processors in Nonhomogeneous Background," IEEE AES Trans, 1988; "Nonlinear Smoothing Filters," IEEE ASSP Transactions, 1989; "Design and Performance of C-Filters," IEEE ASSP Trans, 1991; "A Variably Trimmed Mean CFAR Radar Detector," IEEE AES Trans, 1992. **HOME ADDRESS:** 4 Redwood Ave, Cherry Hill, NJ 08002. **BUSINESS PHONE:** (610)519-4974.

GANDHI, VIKRAM H.
Orthopedic surgeon, educator. Indo-American. **PERSONAL:** Born Mar 19, 1945, Gujarat, India; married. **EDUCATION:** MS University, Baroda, India, MBBS, 1968, MS, 1973; American Board of Orthopedic Surgeons, 1979-. **CAREER:** Chicago Medical School, asst professor of orthopedic surgery, currently; Vikram Gandhi MDSC, president, 1981-. **SPECIAL ACHIEVEMENTS:** Involvement with Eye Camps in Rajpipla. **BIOGRAPHICAL**

SOURCES: Times of India, newspaper. **BUSINESS ADDRESS:** President, Vikram Ghandi MDSC, 7101 W Higgins Ave, Chicago, IL 60656, (312)792-1444.

GANDHI, VIKRAM IJATRAI
Systems analyst. Indo-American. **PERSONAL:** Born Dec 5, 1960, Bhavnagar, Gujarat, India; son of Ijatrai Damodardas Gandhi and Malini Ijatrai Gandhi; married Pragna Vikram Gandhi, Jun 17, 1989; children: Nirav Vikram. **EDUCATION:** Maharaja Sayajirao University, Baroda, BE, 1984; University of North Carolina, Charlotte, MS, 1986-88; Stevens Institute of Technology, MIS, 1988-89. **CAREER:** Royal Industrial Corp, sales engineer, 1984-86; Panasonic Techniques, programmer, 1988-89; Fluor Daniel, systems analyst, 1989-. **ORGANIZATIONS:** IAAA; India Association; Greenville Geetmala, producer. **HOME ADDRESS:** 5155 Maplewood Dr, Greenville, SC 29615. **BUSINESS PHONE:** (803)281-4949.

GANGAL, SHIVA SHANKER
Engineering company executive. Indo-American. **PERSONAL:** Born May 7, 1934, Khair, Uttar Pradesh, India; son of Piarey Lal Gupta and Kastoori Devi; married Sheh Lata, Feb 17, 1959. **EDUCATION:** Indian Institute of Science, Bangalore, MSEE, 1957. **CAREER:** Hindustan Steel, design engineer, 1957-67; Phoenix Steel, superintendent maint/senior elec engineer, 1967-73; General Electric Co, facilities manager, 1973-77; Reliance Electric, plant engineering manager, 1977-79; Lever Brothers, project engineering manager, 1979-81; Consolidated Aluminum Co, engineering manager, 1981-83; Tri State Engineering, CEO/president, 1983-. **ORGANIZATIONS:** Professional Engineers, Delaware, 1970-. **HONORS/AWARDS:** West Virginia State, Minority Business Person of the Year, 1991. **BUSINESS ADDRESS:** CEO and President, Tri State Engineering & Management Consultants, Inc, 237 E Thistle Ct, New Martinsville, WV 26155, (304)455-6264.

GANGOPADHYAY, CHITTA R.
Educator, consultant. Indo-American. **PERSONAL:** Born Sep 5, 1934, Calcutta, W. Bengal, India; son of Bishnupada Gangopadhyay & Hashi Gangopadhyay; married Monjusha, Jun 11, 1968; children: Chirantan, Jay. **EDUCATION:** Indian Institute of Technology, Kharagpur, India, BTech (with honors), 1956, MTech, structural engineering, 1957; University of Illinois, Urbana-Champaign, MS, geotech, 1959, PhD, geotech, 1962. **CAREER:** Soil & Materials Engineering, chief soil engineer, project engineer, senior engineer, 1974-77, principal & chief engineer, 1978-80; STS Consultants, principal, chief engineer & director, 1977-78; Wayne State University, associate professor, 1980-85; University of Detroit-Mercy, civil & environmental engineering, chairman & professor, 1985-. **ORGANIZATIONS:** American Society of Civil Engineers, 1960-, fellow, 1984; American Society of Engineering Education, 1985-; National Society of Professional Engineers, 1975-; Michigan Society of Professional Engineers, 1975-; International Society of Soil Mech & Foundation Engineering, 1960-; American Society of Indian Engineers, 1986-; Indian League of America, 1981-; Chi Epsilon, 1980-. **HONORS/AWARDS:** Wayne State University, Civil Engineering Students Group, Best Teacher, 1980, 1981; National Science Foundation, Instructional Equipment Award, 1982. **SPECIAL ACHIEVEMENTS:** Thirty publications in refereed journals and conferences in the area of geotechnical engineering; overseer for the foundation engineering of most of the tall structures built for the renaissance of downtown Detroit.

GANGULEE, AMITAVA
Consultant. Indo-American. **PERSONAL:** Born Apr 26, 1941, Rajshahi, Bengal, India; son of Hiren C Gangulee (deceased) and Maya Gangulee (deceased); married Suzanne G Lorant, 1989. **EDUCATION:** Harvard University, 1962; Brown University, ScM, 1964; Massachusetts Institute of Technology, ScD, 1967; Pace University, MBA, 1989. **CAREER:** Metal Engineering & Treatment Co, partner, 1962-67; Massachusetts Institute of Technology, research staff, 1965-67; IBM Corp, senior staff scientist, 1967-86; Logic, Science & Innovations, president, 1989-. **ORGANIZATIONS:** The Institute of Management Science, 1988-; American Physical Society, 1967-; American Institute of Metallurgical Engineering, 1964-; American Crystallographic Association, 1967-; American Vacuum Society, 1969-; American Association for Advancement of Science, fellow, 1964-. **HONORS/AWARDS:** IBM Corp, Invention Achievement Award, 1970, 1973, 1978, 1982; International Society for Hybrid Microelectronics, Plaque of Honor, 1983. **SPECIAL ACHIEVEMENTS:** Over 100 scientific and technical publications; 6 US patents; 3 European patents. **BUSINESS ADDRESS:** President, Logic, Science and Innovations, 12 Hayden Ln, Bedford, MA 01730, (617)275-8791.

GANGULY, JIBAMITRA
Education. Indo-American. **PERSONAL:** Born Oct 24, 1938, Calcutta, W. Bengal, India; son of Santosh & Bivaranee Ganguly; married Sucheta, Dec 14, 1966; children: Rajib, Sujoy. **EDUCATION:** Calcutta University, BSc, 1958; Jadavpur University, India, MSc, 1960; University of Chicago, PhD, 1967. **CAREER:** Yale University, postdoctoral fellow, 1967-69; Birla Institute of Science & Technology, India, assistant professor of chemistry, 1971; University of California, Los Angeles, research geophysicist, 1972-75; University of Arizona, assistant professor, 1975-81, associate professor, 1981-86, professor of geosciences, 1986-. **SPECIAL ACHIEVEMENTS:** Co-author, Mixtures and Mineral Reactions, Springer-Verlag, 1987; editor, Diffusion, Atomic Ordering and Mass Transport, Springer-Verlag, 1991. **BUSINESS ADDRESS:** Professor, Dept of Geosciences, University of Arizona, Gowd-Simpson Bldg, Tucson, AZ 85721.

GANGULY, SUMAN
Scientist. Indo-American. **PERSONAL:** Born Feb 9, 1942, Dacca, India; son of Satish ch Ganguly (deceased) and Rani Ganguly. **EDUCATION:** Calcutta University, BSc, 1960, MSc, 1962, PhD, 1970. **CAREER:** Delhi University, senior fellow, 1970-72; Institute of Radio Physics, senior fellow, 1972-74; Lancaster University, Leverhulme Fellow of Royal Society, 1974-76; Arecibo Observatory, senior scientist, 1976-79; Rice University, senior scientist, 1979-85; Center for Remote Sensing, scientist, CEO, 1985-. **ORGANIZATIONS:** American Geophysical Union; IEEE; SPIE. **SPECIAL ACHIEVEMENTS:** Published over 100 journal articles in various refereed journals; edited COSPAR journals. **BUSINESS ADDRESS:** CEO, Center for Remote Sensing, 8260 Greensboro Dr, Ste 328, PO Box 9244, McLean, VA 22102, (703)848-0800.

GANGWAL, RAKESH
Airline executive. Indo-American. **PERSONAL:** Born Jul 25, 1953, Calcutta, W. Bengal, India; son of K P and C D Gangwal; married Shobha Agarwal, Mar 16, 1983; children: one daughter. **EDUCATION:** Indian Institute of Technology, BS, mechanical engineering, 1975; University of Pennsylvania, Wharton School of Business, MBA, 1979. **CAREER:** Philips India Ltd, Calcutta, 1975-77; Ford Motor Co, Michigan, financial analyst, 1979-80; Booz, Allen & Hamilton, Chicago, 1980-84; United Airlines, Chicago, strategic planning manager, director, 1985-86, flight administration vp, 1986-87, revenue management vice president, 1987, senior vp, currently. **BUSINESS ADDRESS:** Senior VP, United Airlines Headquarters, PO Box 66100, Chicago, IL 60666, 800-722-5243. *

GAO, JIALI
Educator. Chinese American. **PERSONAL:** Born Jan 4, 1962, Jixi, Heilongjiang, People's Republic of China; son of Fanfu Gao & DuanXiang Zhang. **EDUCATION:** Beijing University, China, BS, 1982; Purdue University, PhD, 1987. **CAREER:** Harvard University, postdoctoral fellow, 1987-90; State University of New York, assistant professor of chemistry, 1990-. **ORGANIZATIONS:** American Chemical Society, 1983-. **SPECIAL ACHIEVEMENTS:** Published 35 research articles in chemical journals, 1983-. **BUSINESS ADDRESS:** Professor, Dept of Chemistry, State University of New York at Buffalo, Buffalo, NY 14214, (716)829-2090.

GARG, ARUN
Educator. Indo-American. **PERSONAL:** Born Aug 9, 1947, Kanpur, Uttar Pradesh, India; married Anu; children: Anjali. **EDUCATION:** IIT Kanpur, BS, 1969; Villanova University, MS, 1971; University of Michigan, IOE, 1973, PhD, 1976. **CAREER:** University of Michigan, management systems coordinator, 1973-76; University of Miami, assistant prof, 1976-1977; University of Wisconsin, assistant prof, 1977-81, associate prof, 1981-88, prof, 1988-; Medical College of Wisconsin, clinical prof, 1991-. **ORGANIZATIONS:** Human Factors Society; American Industrial Hygiene Assn; IIE; International Industrial Ergonomics & Safety; Tau Beta Pi. **HONORS/AWARDS:** University of Wisconsin-Milwaukee, Outstanding Research Award, 1988; Plant Engineering, Editorial Excellence Award, 1983. **SPECIAL ACHIEVEMENTS:** Published over 80 journal articles; served as consultant to NIOSH, OSHA, EEOC, and several private industries; chief consultant to NIOSH for "Revised NIOSH Guide for Manual Lifting"; board certified ergonomist. **BUSINESS ADDRESS:** Professor, Industrial & Systems Engineering, University of Wisconsin-Milwaukee, PO Box 784, Milwaukee, WI 53201, (414)229-6240.

GARG, DEVENDRA
Financial executive. Indo-American. **PERSONAL:** Born Feb 14, 1948, Mathura, Uttar Pradesh, India; son of Lalta Prasad Garg and Sushila Elhence; married Manju Gupta, May 8, 1973; children: Sumeet, Preeti. **EDUCATION:** II Science, Bangalor, India, BEEE, 1970, MEEE, 1972; University of Pennsylvania, graduate studies, computers, 1972-74; RPI, MBA, 1977. **CAREER:** Univac, systems engr, 1973-75; Comten, systems/market analyst, 1975-77; Xerox Corp, manager, region audit, 1977-85, manager, planning/analysis, reprographics, 1987-89, manager, business analysis, 1989-90, manager, financial planning/systems, 1990-92, controller, worldwide manufacturing, 1992-. **ORGANIZATIONS:** Roch School District, budget steering committee, 1990-91; Pittsford School District, academically talented program, 1990-91. **SPECIAL ACHIEVEMENTS:** Adjunct faculty, St John Fisher College, 1988-91. **BUSINESS ADDRESS:** Controller, Worldwide Manufacturing, Xerox Corp, 800 Phillips Rd, 212-06S, Webster, NY 14580-9791, (716)422-5880.

GARG, PREM
Government official. Indo-American. **PERSONAL:** Born May 14, 1944, Raman Mandi, Punjab, India; son of Chanan Ram and Parsini Devi Garg; married Sunita Garg, May 5, 1973; children: Sherry S, Salil. **EDUCATION:** Punjab University-Chandigarh, BSCE, 1967; University of Cincinnati, MS, 1974. **CAREER:** City of Cincinnati, supervising engineer, 1985-89, acting city stormwater engineer, 1989-90, city stormwater engineer, 1990-92, acting superintendent, sanitation, 1992-93, deputy director of public works, 1993-, city engineer, 1993-. **ORGANIZATIONS:** American Public Works Assn, appointed to Institute of Water Resources, 1991; National Flood Plain Management Association, technical advisory group; Engineers and Scientists of Cincinnati, board of directors. **SPECIAL ACHIEVEMENTS:** Published paper on stormwater management in Cincinnati; technical paper on National Pollution Discharge Elimination System Permit Requirements. **HOME PHONE:** (513)232-5333. **BUSINESS ADDRESS:** City Engineer, City of Cincinnati, 801 Plum St, City Hall, Rm 440, Cincinnati, OH 45202, (512)352-3720.

GARG, RAJINDER P.
Federal government official. Indo-American. **PERSONAL:** Born Oct 14, 1942, Kalayat, Haryana, India; son of Raghbir Chand Garg and Krishna Wati Garg; married Kiran Garg, Jan 14, 1969; children: Rajat, Rishi. **EDUCATION:** Thapar Polytechnic, diploma in mechanical engineering, 1962; Howard University, BS, mechanical, 1966; Catholic University of America, MS, mechanical engineering, 1968. **CAREER:** Dalton, Dalton, Little, Newport, project engineer, 1972-75; Dept of Veteran Affairs, operations & energy, management division, chief, 1975-. **ORGANIZATIONS:** National Society of Professional Engineers; American Society of Heating, Refridgating & Air Conditioning Engineers. **BUSINESS ADDRESS:** Chief, Operations & Energy Management Division, Department of Veterans Affairs, 810 Vermont Ave NW, Lafayette Bldg, Room 436, Washington, DC 20420, (202)233-2869.

GARG, RAMESH CHANDRA
Educator. Indo-American. **PERSONAL:** Born Dec 5, 1943, Mhow, Madhya Pradesh, India; married Rita Garg; children: Manish, Aashish, Monika. **EDUCATION:** Vikram University, India, BComm, 1964; Kent State University, MBA, 1967, DBA, 1974. **CAREER:** Western Michigan University, assistant professor of finance, 1971-73; Marist College, assistant professor of finance, 1973-77; Philadelphia College of Textile & Science, associate professor of finance, 1977-78; Eastern Michigan University, professor of finance, 1978-. **ORGANIZATIONS:** International Trade and Finance Association, 1991-; Business Association of Latin American Students, 1985-. **HONORS/AWARDS:** University of Virginia, AACSB Fellowship Award, 1983; Eastern Michigan University, Faculty Achievement Award, 1980-81. **SPECIAL ACHIEVEMENTS:** Financial Administration Theory and Practice, textbook, 1989, 1991; Finance Principles, textbook, 1985; several journal articles. **HOME PHONE:** (313)995-2212. **BUSINESS ADDRESS:** Professor, Dept of Finance & CIS, Eastern Michigan University, Ypsilanti, MI 48197, (313)487-2454.

GARG, UMESH
Educator. Indo-American. **PERSONAL:** Born Mar 29, 1953, Bikaner, Rajasthan, India; son of Shiv Nandan Garg and Shakuntala Garg; married Anita P Garg, Dec 28, 1980; children: Noopur N, Neehar N. **EDUCATION:** Birla Institute of Technology & Science, Pilani, India, BS, 1972, MS, 1974; State University of New York, Stony Brook, MA, 1975, PhD, 1978. **CAREER:** State University of New York, Stony Brook, graduate assistant, 1974-78; Texas A & M University, research associate, 1978-82; University of Notre Dame,

assistant professor, 1982-87, associate professor, 1987-. **ORGANIZATIONS:** American Physical Society, 1978-; American Chemical Society, associate member, 1985-; American Chapter of Indian Physics Association, president, 1986, chairman, nominating committee, 1992-. **SPECIAL ACHIEVEMENTS:** More than 100 publications in scholarly journals and books. **HOME ADDRESS:** 18254 Westover Dr, South Bend, IN 46637. **BUSINESS ADDRESS:** Professor, Physics Dept, University of Notre Dame, 211 NSH, Notre Dame, IN 46556, (219)631-7352.

GARG, VIJAY KUMAR
Educator. Indo-American. **PERSONAL:** Born Oct 25, 1963, Agra, India; married. **EDUCATION:** University of California, Berkeley, PhD, 1988; IIT, Kanpur, India, BTech, 1989. **CAREER:** Patni Computer Systsems, Bombay, software engineer, 1984; University of California, Berkeley, EECS dept, teaching asst, 1984, electronics research lab, research assistant, 1984-86, postgraduate researcher, 1986-88; University of Texas, Austin, assistant professor, 1989-. **ORGANIZATIONS:** First International Conference on System Integration, program committee, 1990; Second International Conference on System Integration, program committee, 1992; 11th International Conference on Distributed Computing Systems, program committee, 1991; 30th Conference on Decision and Control, awards panel, 1992; IEEE, Computer Society, Central Texas chapter, secretary, 1991-92; IEEE Computer Society; Control Society; Association for Computing Machinery; ACM Special Interest Group on Operating Systems, Special Interest Group on Theory; Society of Industrial and Applied Mathematicians. **HONORS/AWARDS:** TRW Faculty Assistantship award, 1992-95; General Motors Foundation, Centennial Teaching Fellowship, electrical engineering, 1993; National Science Foundation, Research Initiation Award, 1991-93; University of California, non-resident tuition scholarship, 1984-87; IIT, Merit Scholarship and Achievement Award, 1980-84; India, National Talent Scholarship, 1979-84; TRW, Foundation, Faculty Assistantship Award, co-recipient, 1992-95. **SPECIAL ACHIEVEMENTS:** Supervised a PhD dissertation nominated by the Electrical and Computer Engineering Department for the best dissertation in the University; University of Texas, Austin Bureau of Engineering Research, Algebraic characterization of Petri Nets, Principal Investigator, 1989-90; University of Texas, Austin, University Research Institute, High Level Communication Abstraction Mechanisms, Principal Investigator, 1989, Decentralized Control of Discrete Event Systems, Principal Investigator, 1990; National Science Foundation Research Initiation Program, A Debugging System for Distributed Programs, Principal Investigator, 1991-93; International Business Machines, Research in distributed computing, Computer and Vision Research Center member, 1991-92; Office of Naval Research, Distributed Simulation, Principal Investigator, 1992-93. **BUSINESS ADDRESS:** Professor, Electrical Computer & Engineering Dept, University of Texas, Austin, TX 78712, (512)471-9424.

GATDULA, FRANCISCO RIC
Communications technician. Filipino American. **PERSONAL:** Born Oct 29, 1958, Cebu City, Cebu, Philippines; son of Santiago Roxas (deceased) and Cirila Gatdula Barrientos; married Salome B Gatdula, Jan 14, 1984; children: Sahlee Mae, Francis James. **EDUCATION:** Cebu Velez College, 1976; San Joaquin Delta College, AA, 1985; University of San Francisco, BS, 1994. **CAREER:** Prudential Insurance, life & disability agent, 1983; Avantek Inc, lead technician, 1983-91; Hewlett Packard, product & process technician, 1992-. **ORGANIZATIONS:** Stockton Delta Amateur Radio Club, president, 1991, 1992; American Radio Relay League, 1990-; Boy Scouts of America, asst den leader, 1993; Filipino-American Chamber of Commerce, 1991-. **SPECIAL ACHIEVEMENTS:** First Filipino to be president of the Stockton Delta ARC, founded 1931, 1991, 1992. **MILITARY SERVICE:** US Air Force, sgt, 1978-82; US Air Force Commendation Award, 1982. **HOME ADDRESS:** 2915 Angel Drive, Stockton, CA 95209, (209)473-4419.

GAVANDE, SAMPAT A.
Engineer, consultant. Indo-American. **PERSONAL:** Born Mar 1, 1936, Nasik, Maharashtra, India; son of A B Gavande; married Shaila S Gavande, Feb 25, 1968; children: Neil, Vikram. **EDUCATION:** Poona University, India, agr sciences, 1958; Kansas State University, agr engineering, 1962; Utah State University, soil physics irrigation and drainage, 1966. **CAREER:** FAO of United Nations, tech officer, 1966-73, chief tech advisor, 1975-77, chief tech advisor, 1987-89; Radian Corp, senior scientist, 1977-83; TWC/Texas Dept Health, senior engr, 1983-87; United Nations in India, Indonesia, Iran, Chile, Mexico, Peru, Kenya, consultant, 1984-91; Texas Natural Resources Conservation Commission, senior engineer, team leader, 1989-. **ORGANIZATIONS:** American Society Agronomy, 1965-; American Society Soil Science, 1965-;

Soil Science Society of America, 1965-; American Society Agr Engineers, 1981-; ASTM, 1978-. **HONORS/AWARDS:** Texas Board of Registered Professional Engineers, PE, 1984; ASA/SSSA, certified prof, 1978, soil scientist, agronomist, 1978. **HOME ADDRESS:** 4501 Upvalley Court, Austin, TX 78731-3666, (512)451-1400. **BUSINESS PHONE:** (512)239-6734.

GAWANDE, ATUL A.
Government official. Indo-American. **PERSONAL:** Born Nov 5, 1965, Brooklyn, NY; son of Atmaram Gawande and Sushila Gawande; married Kathleen Hobson, Nov 28, 1992. **EDUCATION:** Stanford University, BA, BS, 1987; Balliol College, Oxford University, MA, 1989; Harvard Medical School, 1990-. **CAREER:** Harvard University, teaching assistant, 1991, research assistant, 1991-92; Boston University, teacher, 1991-92; Clinton-Gore Campaign, health and social policy adviser, 1992; Clinton's Presidential Transition Team, deputy director for health policy, 1992-93; US Department of Health and Human Services, senior adviser to assistant secretary, 1993-. **HONORS/AWARDS:** Oxford University, Rhodes Scholar, 1987-89. **BIOGRAPHICAL SOURCES:** "A Diverse Team Aids Clinton on Health Care," Washington Post, Oct 27, 1992; "Clinton's Young Staff," Associated Press, April 14, 1993. **BUSINESS ADDRESS:** Sr Adviser to Asst Sec for Planning & Evaluation, Office of Secretary, US Dept of Health and Human Services, 200 Independence Ave SW, Hubert H Humphrey Bldg, Rm 424-E, Washington, DC 20201.

GEAGA, JAIME V.
Association executive. Filipino American. **PERSONAL:** Born Apr 20, 1953, Baguio, Philippines; son of Mr & Mrs Jose V Geaga. **EDUCATION:** Stanford University Medical Center, PA-C, 1984; San Francisco State University, BA, biology, 1986; UC, Berkeley, MPH, 1993. **CAREER:** California Pacific Medical Center, physician assistant, 1985-91; Filipino Task Force on AIDS, executive director, 1990-. **ORGANIZATIONS:** San Francisco HIV Planning Council, 1990-; AHCPR Guideline Panel on HIV, 1991-; National Minority AIDS Council, executive committee, 1991-. **BUSINESS ADDRESS:** Executive Director, Filipino Task Force on AIDS, 1540 Market St, Ste 325, San Francisco, CA 94102, (415)703-9880.

GEE, ARTHUR
Eduator, consultant, engineer. Chinese American. **PERSONAL:** Born Apr 12, 1937, Hoi Ping, Canton, China; son of Kwong Li Gee and Ma Chi Yu; married Betty Gee, Aug 18, 1962; children: Clinton, Darrin, Evette. **EDUCATION:** Polytechnic University of New York, BSEE, 1962, MSEE, 1963. **CAREER:** IBM Corp, engineer, 1959-63; RCA Corp, engineer, 1963-65; RCA Institute of Technology, dean of instruction, 1965-71; CUNY-CCNY, assistant professor, 1971-77; Lockheed Missle & Space Corp, consulting engineer, 1981; Hewlett-Packard Corp, consulting engineer, 1983; California State University, professor electrical engineering, 1977-. **ORGANIZATIONS:** California Faculty Association, California State University, vice president, 1987-88, assemblyman, 1987, Political Action Committee, 1989-, Faculty of Color Mentor Program, chairman, 1990-. **HONORS/AWARDS:** California State University, MPPP-Performance Awards, 1987, 1989; California Faculty Association, Best Service Award, 1986; RCA Corp, Best Service Award, 1968. **SPECIAL ACHIEVEMENTS:** New York Licensing Dept, professional engineer, 1972-; textbook, Principles of Feedback Control Systems, 1976; high-tech lecture tour conducted for Taiwan, Hong Kong, Singapore, Malaysia, Manila, Bangkok, 1989. **MILITARY SERVICE:** Armour-Tank Commander Crew, pfc, 1959; Best Soldier of the Class, 1959. **BUSINESS ADDRESS:** Professor, EE Dept, California State University, Warner St, Zip 888, Chico, CA 95929, (916)898-5816.

GEE, DOLLY M.
Lawyer. Chinese American. **PERSONAL:** Born Jul 1, 1959, Hawthorne, CA; daughter of Jimwah & Helen Gee. **EDUCATION:** UCLA, BA, 1981, JD, 1984. **CAREER:** Hon Milton L Schwartz, US District Court, eastern district of California, law clerk, 1984-86; Schwartz, Steinsapir, Dohrmann & Sommers, partner/lawyer, 1986-. **ORGANIZATIONS:** Asian Pacific Americans for a New Los Angeles, co-chair, 1993-94; Southern California Chinese Lawyers Association, president, 1992-93; LA County Bar Association, board of trustees, 1993-95; Western Center on Law & Poverty, board of directors, 1993-2000; Southern California Civil Rights Coalition, co-chair, 1990-93; Asian Pacific American Labor Alliance, 1990-; Asian Pacific American Legal Center of Southern California, executive advisory board, 1992-93. **HONORS/AWARDS:** UCLA, Phi Beta Kappa, 1981; State Bar of California, Wiley Manuel Pro Bono Services Award, 1991, 1992; Coalition of Women from Asia & Middle East, Civil Rights Award, 1991. **BUSINESS ADDRESS:** Partner,

Schwartz, Steinsapir, Dohrmann and Sommers, 3580 Wilshire Blvd, Ste 1820, Los Angeles, CA 90010, (213)487-5700.

GEE, MONTGOMERY M.
Mechanical engineer. Chinese American. **PERSONAL:** Born Aug 2, 1948, Canton, China; son of Bing H Gee and Sue S Gee; married Wah L Gee, Feb 16, 1978; children: Benjamin M, Stephen M. **EDUCATION:** California Polytech State University, BS, 1976; California Western University, MS, 1983. **CA-REER:** Long Beach Naval Shipyard, mechanical engr, 1976-81; Metrology Engineering Center, mechanical engr, 1981-88; Naval Warfare Assessment Center, mechanical engr, 1988-. **ORGANIZATIONS:** American Society of Mechanical Engineers, 1986-88, research committee on fluid meters; National Conference of Standard Laboratories, 1988, national measurement requirement committee for flow, fluid property and particle size metrology, chairman; Measurement Science Directorate, 1993-, calibration engr support committee. **MILITARY SERVICE:** US Army, e-4, 1968-70; Bronze Star, Good Conduct, Army Commendation, 1969-70, Vietnam Campaign, Vietnam Services. **BIO-GRAPHICAL SOURCES:** The Characterization of a Piston Displacement-Type Flowmeter Calibration Facility and the Calibration and Use of Pulsed Output-Type Flowmeter, vol 97, num 5, p 30, Sep/Oct 1992. **HOME AD-DRESS:** 3030 Deolinda Dr, Hacienda Heights, CA 91745-5309. **BUSINESS PHONE:** (909)273-5423.

GEE, NORMAN F.
Educator. Chinese American. **PERSONAL:** Born Jul 25, 1940, San Francisco, CA; son of Vincent S & Mae L Gee; married Helen K Gee, Jun 27, 1965; children: Mikka, Brian. **EDUCATION:** California College of Arts and Crafts, BFA, 1965, MFA, 1967. **CAREER:** University of Kansas, professor of art, 1969-. **ORGANIZATIONS:** Lawrence Task Force on Racism and Discrimination, 1991-92; Lawrence Alliance, advisory board, 1993. **HONORS/AWARDS:** Pacific Cultural Foundation, travel grant, 1979-80. **SPECIAL ACHIEVEMENTS:** East Meets West in Lawrence, KS, Wichita Art Museum, 1992-93; Chinese American Painters, Hearst Center for the Arts, Cedar Falls, IA, 1991-92; Norman Gee Recent Works, John B Davis Gallery, Pocatello, ID, 1988; Painting: An Asian Perception, University of Nevada, Las Vegas, Barrick Museum of Natural History, the Nevada Art Museum, Reno, Nevada, 1994. **BUSINESS ADDRESS:** Professor, Dept of Art, University of Kansas, 300 Art and Design, Lawrence, KS 66045-0501, (913)864-4401.

GEE, ROBERT W.
Public utility commission member. Chinese American. **CAREER:** Public Utility Commission of Texas, chairman, currently. **BUSINESS ADDRESS:** Chairman, Public Utility Commission of Texas, 7800 Shoal Creek Blvd, Austin, TX 78757, (512)458-0295. *

GEE, VIRGINIA CATHERINE
City government official. Chinese American. **PERSONAL:** Born May 19, 1941, San Francisco, CA; daughter of Ng Jeong Sue & Hom Chew Wing; married Herbert H Gee, May 12, 1962; children: Christopher Lawrence. **EDU-CATION:** University of San Francisco, BS, business, public administration, 1961; Coro Foundation, Public Policy Program, fellow, 1986; University of California, MA (candidate), 1988. **CAREER:** Pacific Bell, operations manager, 1964-74; Stanford University, recruitment administrator, 1974-84; State of California, Department of Industrial Relations, executive assistant, 1984-93; San Francisco Public Library Commission, first vice president, 1993-. **ORGA-NIZATIONS:** California Apprenticeship Council, chair, 1974-84; San Francisco Private Industry Council, vice president, 1981; Stanford Federal Credit Union, board member, 1976-78; Asian Pacific Personnel Association, founding president, 1981-82; Chinese American Citizens Alliance, San Francisco Lodge, president, 1991-92, National Grand Board, 1992-; League of Women Voters, San Francisco, board member, 1993-; San Francisco Conservation Corps, board member, 1989-; California Community College Placement Association, vice president, 1982; Coro Foundation, board member, 1987-91; Coro National, board of governors, 1987-91; Bay Area American Red Cross, board member, 1994-; Mayor's Office of Children, Youth and Their Families, Allocation Committee, 1994-; San Francisco General Hospital, Citizens Advisory Committee to the Executive Administrator, 1993-. **HONORS/AWARDS:** University of California, San Francisco, Outstanding Service, Chancellors Award, 1989; California State University, Hayward, Equity Award, 1984; City & County of San Francisco, Board of Supervisors and Mayor's Outstanding Leadership Award, 1993; California State Assembly, Outstanding Service Award, 1992; California State Senate, Outstanding Service Award, 1992; Governor of Kentucky, Honorary Colonel, 1979. **SPECIAL ACHIEVE-**

MENTS: First woman chair in the 50-year history of the California Apprenticeship Council; first woman president of the Chinese American Citizens Alliance in its 80 year history, 1991. **BUSINESS ADDRESS:** Commissioner, First Vice President, San Francisco Public Library Commission, Civic Center, San Francisco, CA 94102, (415)557-4233.

GEE, ZAND F.
Photographer, graphic designer. **PERSONAL:** Born May 6, 1955, Oroville, CA; daughter of Sun Gee & Mae Gee; married Brian Fessenden, Oct 9, 1988. **EDUCATION:** University of California at Davis, BFA, 1977; San Francisco Art Institute, MFA, 1981. **CAREER:** Fantasy Records, graphic designer, 1977-80; self-employed, graphic designer, 1980-86; Aspen Records, art director, 1986-87; Blue Peter, exhibition-graphic designer, 1987-90; Farallon Films, associate producer, 1990-. **ORGANIZATIONS:** Kearny St Workshop, executive director, 1983-. **SPECIAL ACHIEVEMENTS:** Publication, "Pursuing Wild Bamboo," photo book, group, 1993; publication, "Texas Long Grain," photo book, group, 1983.

GENG, SHU
Educator. Chinese American. **PERSONAL:** Born Sep 3, 1942, ChungChing, Sichuan, China; son of Mei-Chang Geng and Shi-Qua Geng; married Hai Yen Carolyn Geng, Jun 30, 1968; children: Eluin Hsing, Joy Jai. **EDUCATION:** National Taiwan University, BS, 1964; Kansas State University, MS, 1969, PhD, 1972. **CAREER:** The UpJohn Co, statistician, 1972-76; University of California, Davis, assistant professor to associate professor, 1976-84, associate dean, 1988-91, professor, 1984-. **ORGANIZATIONS:** International Development, Education Agriculture and Life Sciences Inc, board of directors, 1990-; American Association for the Advancement of Science, 1977-; American Society Agronomy, 1977-; Biometrics, 1977-. **SPECIAL ACHIEVE-MENTS:** Published 2 books and more than 80 technical papers in scientific journals. **BUSINESS ADDRESS:** Professor, Dept of Agronomy and Range Science, University of California, Davis, CA 95616-8515, (916)752-6939.

GEORGE, K. P.
Educator. Indo-American. **PERSONAL:** Born Jun 13, 1933, Kadayiruppu, Kerala, India; son of K V Pily and Sara Pily; married Mary M George, Oct 19, 1988; children: Sarah, Anil. **EDUCATION:** National Institute of Engr, BE, 1956; Iowa State University, MS, 1961; Iowa State University, PhD, 1963. **CAREER:** Kerala Public Works, 1956-59; Iowa State University, res assoc, 1959-63; The University of Mississippi, assistant professor, beginning 1963, assoc professor, professor, currently. **ORGANIZATIONS:** Transportation Research Board, committee member, 1963-; American Society of Civil Engineers, 1966-; Registered Professional Engineer, Mississippi. **SPECIAL ACHIEVE-MENTS:** More that 70 technical publications; author of chapter in Civil Engineering Practices, edited by P N Chenemisinott, N D Chenmisinott, and S C Cheng. **BUSINESS ADDRESS:** Professor, Civil Engineering Dept, University of Mississippi, University, MS 38677, (601)232-5365.

GHANDHI, SORAB K.
Educator. Indo-American. **PERSONAL:** Born Jan 1, 1928, Allahabad, Uttar Pradesh, India; son of Khushro S Ghandhi and Dina K Ghandhi; married Cecilia, Oct 20, 1981; children: Khushro, Rustom, Behram. **EDUCATION:** Benares Hindu University, BS, electrical and mechanical engineering, 1947; University of Illinois, MS, 1948, PHD, 1951. **CAREER:** General Electric Co, engineer, 1951-60; Philco Corp, Components Group, manager, 1960-63; Rensselaer Polytechnic, professor, 1963-. **ORGANIZATIONS:** MCT Conference, chairman, 1992; MCT Program Committee, 1986-91; American Standards Association, 1958-85; IEEE Press, editorial board, 1984-89; Solid State Electronics, associate editor, 1993-. **HONORS/AWARDS:** IEEE, Fellow, 1965; RPI, Distinguished Teaching Award, 1977, Distinguished Faculty Award, 1991. **SPECIAL ACHIEVEMENTS:** Co-author, Principles of Transistor Circuits, 1953; Transistor Circuit Engineering, 1957; author, Theory and Practice of Microelectronics, 1967; Semiconductor Power Devices, 1977; VLSI Fabrication Principles: Si & GaAS, 1983. **BUSINESS ADDRESS:** Professor, Rensselaer Polytechnic Institute, 6022 JEC, Troy, NY 12180, (518)276-6085.

GHIM, THAD T.
Educator. Korean American. **PERSONAL:** Born Jan 25, 1939, Seoul, Republic of Korea; married Heather, Jun 20, 1970; children: Michael. **EDUCA-TION:** Seoul National University, MD, 1963. **CAREER:** Henrietta Egleston Children's Hospital, chief of hematology/ancology section, 1991-93; Emory University School of Medicine, acting director, Division of Pediatric Hematol-

ogy/Oncology, 1991-93, assoc prof, currently. **ORGANIZATIONS:** American Academy of Pediatrics, 1974-; American Society of Clinical Oncology, 1982-; American Society of Hematology, 1982-; American Society of Pediatric Hematology, Oncology, 1982-. **HONORS/AWARDS:** Georgia Human Relations Commission, 1991-. **SPECIAL ACHIEVEMENTS:** Author, Aniridia-Wilms Tumor in Diseases Affecting the Eye and the Kidney, The Kargen, Basel, p 23-28, 1993. **BUSINESS ADDRESS:** Assoc Professor, Dept of Pediatrics, Emory University School of Med, 2040 Ridgewood Dr NE, Atlanta, GA 30322, (404)727-4451.

GHOSH, AMAL K.

Physicist (retired). Indo-American. **PERSONAL:** Born Jun 21, 1931, Thato, Myanmar; son of Satyendro Mohon Ghosh & Jiban Prova Ghosh; married Gita Ghosh, Jun 21, 1961; children: Ajoy, Anita, Rita. **EDUCATION:** University of Calcutta, India, PhD, 1961. **CAREER:** Argonne National Lab, physicist, 1960-65; Itek Corp, scientific staff member, 1965-70; Exxon Research & Engineering Co, senior associate, 1971-86. **ORGANIZATIONS:** American Physical Society, fellow. **SPECIAL ACHIEVEMENTS:** Author of over 75 publications in various scientific journals. **HOME ADDRESS:** 75 Twin Oaks Rd, Bridgewater, NJ 08807, (908)722-3955.

GHOSH, AMITAVA

Research engineer. Indo-American. **PERSONAL:** Born Oct 20, 1957, Calcutta, W. Bengal, India; son of Nirmal Kumar Ghosh and Siuli Ghosh; married Shampa Ghosh, Jan 1, 1987. **EDUCATION:** Indian Institute of Technology, India, BTech, 1978; University of Arizona, MS, 1983, PhD, 1990. **CAREER:** IDL Chemicals Ltd, India, technical services engineer, 1978-81; University of Arizona, graduate assistant, associate, 1982-90; University of Nevada, Reno, post doctoral research fellow, 1990-92; Southwest Research Institute, research engineer, 1992-. **ORGANIZATIONS:** International Society for Rock Mechanics, 1990-; International Association for Mathematical Geology, 1990-; American Geophysical Union, 1993-. **HONORS/AWARDS:** International Society for Rock Mechanics, Rocha Medal Award, 1992; SME, Graduate Division, Outstanding Student Paper Contest, 1989; University of Arizona, Sulzer Memorial Scholarship, 1984; Indian Institute of Technology, Kharagpur, Silver Medal, 1978; Mining, Metallurgical, and Geological Institute of India, Chandrakala Medal, 1978. **SPECIAL ACHIEVEMENTS:** Co-author, Fractal Characteristics of Rock Discontinuities, 1993; The Frictional Component of the Indentation Size Effect in Low Load Microhardness Testing, 1993; Fractal-Based Approach to Determine the Effect of Discontinuities on Blast Fragmentation, 1990; Validation of Exponential Decay Blast Vibration Predictor with Case Studies, 1991; An Expert System Approach to Geomechanics Design Problems, 1987; also 20 other publications. **BUSINESS ADDRESS:** Research Engineer, Center for Nuclear Waste Regulatory Analyses, Southwest Research Institute, 6220 Culebra Road, San Antonio, TX 78238, (210)522-3314.

GHOSH, BHASKAR KUMAR

Educator. Indo-American. **PERSONAL:** Born Feb 10, 1936, Dibrugarh, India; married. **EDUCATION:** University of Calcutta, BSc, 1955; University of London, PhD, 1959. **CAREER:** Atomic Power, London, statistician, 1959-60; University of London, assistant professor, 1960-61; Lehigh University, assistant professor, beginning 1961, associate professor, professor, currently. **ORGANIZATIONS:** Royal Statistical Society, London, fellow, 1960-; Institute of Math Statistics, fellow, 1961-. **HONORS/AWARDS:** Alexander von Humboldt Senior US Scientist, 1986-87. **SPECIAL ACHIEVEMENTS:** Author of books and journal articles, 1961-. **BUSINESS ADDRESS:** Professor of Mathematics, Lehigh University, Xmas-Saucon Hall 14, Bethlehem, PA 18015, (215)758-3722.

GHOSH, BIVAS KANTI

Financial/commercial analyst. Indo-American. **PERSONAL:** Born Mar 7, 1954, Mugkalyan, Howrah, W. Bengal, India; son of Krishnadhan Ghosh (deceased) and Sushilabala Ghosh (deceased); married Sukla Ghosh, Apr 24, 1980; children: Bitan K, Salon R. **EDUCATION:** Shaw University, BA (magna cum laude), liberal arts, 1977; NC State University, BS (honors) pulp & paper, 1977; Iona College, MBA (honors), 1987. **CAREER:** Champion Papers, process engineer, 1977-79; Clupak Inc, service engineer, 1979-88; Westvaco Corp, commercial analyst, 1988-; Fax-Tastic Products, founder, 1993. **ORGANIZATIONS:** Tech Association of Pulp & Paper Ind, 1982-, Cultural Association of Bengal, exec secretary, 1984-86;. **HONORS/AWARDS:** Shaw University, Scholastic Achievement Award, 1976. **HOME ADDRESS:** 4511 Wellingborough Lane, Paducah, KY 42003, (502)554-7815.

GHOSH, CHINMOY (GORA)

Educator. Indo-American. **PERSONAL:** Born May 7, 1953, Calcutta, W. Bengal, India; son of Nitya Gopal Ghosh & Ranu Ghosh; married Bedabati Jumi Ghosh, Jun 19, 1976; children: Debraj, Dipayan. **EDUCATION:** Presidency College, BSc, 1974; Indian Institute of Management, MBA, 1976; Pennsylvania State University, PhD, 1986. **CAREER:** CESC Ltd, commercial officer, 1977-81; Pennsylvania State University, lecturer, 1984-86; University of Connecticut, associate professor, 1986-. **ORGANIZATIONS:** Financial Management Association, 1984-; American Finance Association, 1984-. **SPECIAL ACHIEVEMENTS:** Author, "An Analysis of Exchangeable Debt Offers," Journal of Financial Economics, 1990; "Wealth Effects of Regulatory Reform: The Case of California's Proposition 103," Journal of Financial Economics, 1990. **BUSINESS ADDRESS:** Associate Professor, Dept of Finance, University of Connecticut, School of Business Administration, Storrs, CT 06268, (203)486-4431.

GHOSH, KALYAN K.

Educational administrator. Indo-American. **PERSONAL:** Born Feb 28, 1938, Calcutta, India; married 1965; children: two. **EDUCATION:** University of Calcutta, BSc, 1958, MSc, 1961, PhD, polymer chemistry, 1965. **CAREER:** University of Calcutta, lecturer of applied chemistry, 1965-66; Shaw University, assistant professor, associate professor, 1967-76, chairman of natural and physical science, 1969-74, vice president of academic affairs, beginning 1974, professor of chemistry, beginning 1976; Worcester State College, president, currently. **ORGANIZATIONS:** American Chemical Society; AAAS; NY Academy of Science. **HONORS/AWARDS:** University of Wisconsin, chemistry fellow, 1966-67; Fulbright Travel Award, 1966. **SPECIAL ACHIEVEMENTS:** Research projects: solution properties of polymers; cellulose chemistry; graft polymerization; carbohydrate reactions; biomedical polymers. **BUSINESS ADDRESS:** President, Worcester State College, 486 Chandler St, Worcester, MA 01602-2597, (508)793-8000. *

GHOSH, NIMAI KUMAR

Executive. Indo-American. **PERSONAL:** Born Jan 6, 1943, Calcutta, W. Bengal, India; son of Abanish Chandra Ghosh (deceased); married Jayasri Ghosedastidar, May 7, 1990; children: Rakhi, Abhimanyu. **EDUCATION:** University of Calcutta, BS (honors), 1963, MS, geology, 1965; NYU, 1976. **CAREER:** Textile Alliance, traffic manager, 1976-81; APC, 1982-90; J F Braun & Sons/Conaga, traffic manager, currently. **ORGANIZATIONS:** Association of Food Industries; Traffic Club, NY. **HOME ADDRESS:** 6411 99th St #611, Flushing, NY 11374-2642. **BUSINESS ADDRESS:** Traffic Manager, J F Braun & Sons, A Division of Conagra, 265 Post Avenue, Westbury, NY 11590, (516)997-2200.

GHOSH, SUBHAS

Educator. Indo-American. **PERSONAL:** Born Jul 2, 1944, Calcutta, W. Bengal, India; son of P C Ghosh & S Ghosh; married Indrani Ghosh, Nov 22, 1972; children: Palula, Roopa. **EDUCATION:** University of Calcutta, India, BS, tech; University of Manchester, England, MS, PhD. **CAREER:** National Spinning Co, Quality Control, director; Institute of Textile Technology, research, professor/director, currently. **ORGANIZATIONS:** Textile Institute, England; Council of Near Infrared Spectroscopy; Textile Quality Control Association of America. **HONORS/AWARDS:** Textile Fraternity of America, honorary member. **SPECIAL ACHIEVEMENTS:** Developed application of near infrared spectroscopy in textiles; developed new method of measuring cotton maturity, now being used in various countries; published approximately 45 papers in Textile Science; presented research papers in America, Europe, & Asia; author, "A Practical Method of Yarn Evaluation Using the Continuous Thread Tester," Melliand Textilberichte, 1993; "Yarn Texturing at ITMA '91," America's Textile Intl, 1992; "Effects of Various Package Building Parameters on Unwinding Performance of Textured Yarn," Melliand Textilberichte, 1991; "Rapid Identification of Heatset Carpet Yarns by Near Infrared Reflectance Analysis," Melliand Textilberichte, 1988; numerous others. **BUSINESS ADDRESS:** Professor, Institute of Textile Technology, PO Box 391, Route 250 West By-Pass, Charlottesville, VA 22902, (804)296-5511.

GHOSH, SUJAN

Chemical company executive. Indo-American. **PERSONAL:** Born Nov 1, 1946, Calcutta, W. Bengal, India; son of Sudhir Chandra Ghosh and Manisha Ghosh (deceased); married Esha Ghosh, Dec 9, 1973. **EDUCATION:** Indian Institute of Technology, KGP, India, BSChE, 1969; West Virginia College of Graduate Studies, MSE, 1977. **CAREER:** Shriram Chemical Industries, India, graduate engr, 1970-71; Fike Chemicals Inc, pilot plant supervisor, 1972-74;

FMC Corporation, chem engr, supervisor, 1974-80, technical manager, 1980-86, technology manager, 1987-. **ORGANIZATIONS:** AIChE, local chapter, 1976-74. **HOME ADDRESS:** 1542 Clark Dr, Yardley, PA 19067. **BUSINESS PHONE:** (215)299-6727.

GHOSH, SWAPAN KUMAR
Educator. Indo-American. **PERSONAL:** Born Jan 1, 1942, Calcutta, W. Bengal, India; son of Nihar R Ghosh and Chhaya Ghosh; married Rita Ghosh, Feb 21, 1970; children: Tista S, Pritha T. **EDUCATION:** Calcutta University, IS, 1959, BS, 1962, MS, 1964, PhD, 1969. **CAREER:** R G Kar Medical College, Calcutta, lecturer, 1967-69, North Bengal University, W Bengal, Ind, lecturer, 1969-71; University of Illinois Med Center, Chicago, USPHS Fellow, 1971-72; State University of NY, Buffalo, sen res associate, 1972-76; Roswell Park Mem Inst, cancer scientist, 1976-89; Indiana State University, professor, 1989-. **ORGANIZATIONS:** ISU Animal Care & Use Committee, chair, 1991-; American Association of Immunologists, 1985-; Sigma Xi, 1991-; Ind Acad Sciences, 1989-. **HONORS/AWARDS:** Calcutta University, scholarship, 1964-68; USPHS Fellowship/NIH, 1971-72; NIH, Individual Post-Doct Fellowship, 1976-78, Grant RO1, 1985-88; American Cancer Society, grant, 1985-86. **SPECIAL ACHIEVEMENTS:** Published papers in research. **BUSINESS ADDRESS:** Professor of Immunology, Indiana State University, Science Bldg, S204, Terre Haute, IN 47809, (812)237-2416.

GIAM, CHOO SENG
Educator. Singaporean American. **PERSONAL:** Born Apr 2, 1931, Singapore, Singapore; son of Mr & Mrs C H Giam; married Mun-Yung; children: Benny, Patrick, Michael. **EDUCATION:** University of Singapore, BSc, 1954, BSc (honors), 1955; University of Sask, Canada, MSc, 1961, PhD, 1963. **CAREER:** University of Pittsburgh, professor of health sciences and chemistry, 1983-87; Texas A&M University, professor of chemistry, 1966-82, professor, CZL director, 1988-. **ORGANIZATIONS:** American Chemical Society, 1965-. **HONORS/AWARDS:** Texas A&M University, Distinguished Faculty Research, 1978; NIH, USA, Special Research Fellow, 1971. **SPECIAL ACHIEVEMENTS:** More than 170 refereed publications in chemistry, environmental science, 1959-. **BUSINESS ADDRESS:** Professor, Texas A&M University, 5007 Ave U, Costal Zone Lab, Galveston, TX 77551.

GIDDA, JASWANT SINGH
Researcher, educator. Indo-American. **PERSONAL:** Born Oct 1, 1946, Hoshiarpur, Punjab, India; son of Ram Rattan Singh and Shakuntla Devi; married Raj K Gidda, Dec 16, 1975; children: Vipul J, Archanta R. **EDUCATION:** Panjab University, Chandigarh, India, BSc, 1965, BSc (with honors), 1967, MSc (with honors), 1968, PhD, 1973. **CAREER:** University of Texas at Dallas, research asst, 1973-76, University of Texas Health Science Ctr, Dallas, instructor, 1976-78, San Antonio, instructor, 1978-81; Harvard Medical School, Boston, instructor, 1981-84; Bristol-Myers Co, sr res sci, 1984-87; Eli Lilly Research Labs, group leader, 1987-; Indiana University Med Ctr, adjunct assoc prof of med, 1988-. **ORGANIZATIONS:** American Gastroenterological Association, 1984; American Physiological Society, 1985; American Motility Society, 1984. **HONORS/AWARDS:** CSIR, India, Junior Res Fellowship, 1968. **BUSINESS ADDRESS:** Group Leader, Eli Lilly & Co, Lilly Corporate Ctr 0815, Indianapolis, IN 46285, (317)276-4055.

GIL, LIBIA SOCORRO
Educational administrator. Chinese American. **PERSONAL:** Born Jan 18, 1947, Hong Kong; daughter of Jose Gil Jaubert & Phoebe Cecilia Gil Ling; married Richard Hanks, Apr 16, 1977; children: Leilani Gil Neville, Anica Gil Hanks, Solana Gil Hanks, Kolina Gil Hanks. **EDUCATION:** California State University, Los Angeles, BA, 1970, MA, 1972; University of Washington, PhD, 1989. **CAREER:** Los Angeles Unified School District, Los Angeles, teacher, 1970-72; ABC Unified School District, Cerritos, teacher, 1972-78, Chinese bilingual teacher, 1978-79, bilingual/ESL resource specialist, 1980-81, special projects coord/ESAA director, 1981-82, elementary school principal, 1982-86; Seattle Public Schools, area director, zone administrator, 1986-89, director of instructional support, staff development, 1989-90, director of summit/levy implementation, 1990-91, assistant superintendent for curriculum & instruction, 1991-93; Chula Vista Elementary School District, superintendent, 1993-. **ORGANIZATIONS:** American Association of School Administrators, 1993-94; Association of California School Administrators, 1993-94; Association for Supervision and Curriculum Development, 1986-94; California Association for Supervision and Curriculum Development, 1993-94; American Educational Research Association, 1979-94; California Association for Bilingual Education, 1993-94; California School Boards Association, 1993-94;

Coalition of Asian Pacific Directors, until 1994; National Staff Development Council, 1993-94; Chula Vista Human Services Council, 1993-94; Chula Vista Rotary Club, 1993-94; Junior Achievement of San Diego County, board of directors, 1993-94; South Bay Family YMCA, board of management, 1993-94. **HONORS/AWARDS:** Seattle Chinese Post, Chinese Woman of the Year, 1993; University of Washington, Title VII Fellow, 1979. **SPECIAL ACHIEVEMENTS:** With J Lepley & A Ng, The Asian American Story: Teaching It through the Seattle Chinese Post, Decade of Challenge, 1992. **BUSINESS ADDRESS:** Superintendent, Chula Vista Elementary School District, 84 East J St, Chula Vista, CA 91910, (619)425-9600.

GIN, JERRY B.
Pharmaceutical company executive. Chinese American. **PERSONAL:** Born Jun 29, 1943, Tucson, AZ; son of Gin Shue & Lee S Fong; married M Peggy Gin, Jul 31, 1965; children: Rodney, Brian. **EDUCATION:** University of Arizona, BS, 1964; University of California, Berkeley, PhD, 1968; Loyola College, MBA, 1978. **CAREER:** Bio Science Labs, (Smith Kline/Beedram Labs), director, 1970-78; Dow Chemical, Business Operations, manager, 1978-80; Dow Diagnostics, International Marketing, director, 1980-83; Syva, Strategic Planning/New Business Development, director, 1983-88; Visionex, president, 1986-93; ChemTrak, executive vice president, founder, 1988-93; Oculex Pharmaceuticals, president, founder, 1993-. **ORGANIZATIONS:** Chinese American Ophthalmological Society, 1988-93; American Association for Clinical Chemistry, fellow, 1974-93; American Society of Clinical Pathologists, specialist in chemistry, 1974-93; American Chemical Society, 1968-83. **HONORS/AWARDS:** Phi Beta Kappa, 1964; Phi Beta Phi, 1964; Phi Lambda Upsilon, 1964; US Public Health Service, Fellowship, 1964-68. **SPECIAL ACHIEVEMENTS:** Founder of ChemTrak; 1st over-the-counter home cholesterol test, 1988-93; new drug release technology to treat diseases, 1989-93. **MILITARY SERVICE:** Public Health Service, captain (scientist), 1968-70. **BIOGRAPHICAL SOURCES:** "Chinese American Brings Cholesterol Testing Home", Asian Week, p 1, April 2, 1993; "ChemTrak Heads Home" in Winhovers In Vivo, p 37, July/Aug 1993; "Profiles of Excellence," ABC-TV, aired July 4, 1993. **BUSINESS ADDRESS:** President & CEO, Oculex Pharmaceuticals, 3180 Porter Dr, Bldg 1, Palo Alto, CA 94304, (415)813-1031.

GIRI, JAGANNATH
Aerospace company executive. Indo-American. **PERSONAL:** Born Jan 16, 1933, Bharahopur, Bihar, India; son of Deo Dutta Giri and Jagadipa; married Radha Giri, Jun 10, 1958; children: Punam, Madhu, Uma, Bala Krishna. **EDUCATION:** Bihar Institute of Technology, Sindri, Bihar, India, BSME (with distinction), 1957; University of Maine, MSME, 1972; Georgia Institute of Technology, PhD, 1976. **CAREER:** The Indian Tube Company Ltd, Jamshedpur, Bihar, India, foreman, production planning, 1958-62; Regional Institute of Technology, Jamshedpur, Bihar, India, lecturer, 1962-66, asst professor, 1966-70; University of Maine, graduate assistant, 1970-72; Georgia Institute of Technology, graduate assistant, 1972-76, senior research engr, 1976-79; Cessna Aircraft Company, senior engr, 1979-82; Beech Aircraft Corporation, senior group engr, 1982-88, staff engr, 1988-92, senior tech specialist, 1992-. **ORGANIZATIONS:** AIAA, 1981-; Professional Engineers, 1977-; ASME, 1978-91; Beechmasters, Toastmasters, 1990-91, educational vice pres, 1990, president, 1991; Boy Scouts of America, Troop 526, advancement chairman, 1983-84; University of Maine, Intl Students Organization, secretary, 1971-72; Students Hostel, Rit, Jamshedpur, warden, 1966-70. **HONORS/AWARDS:** Young's Farmers Club, Bit, Sindri, chairman, 1956; director of public instruction, Bihar, scholarship, 1955-57. **SPECIAL ACHIEVEMENTS:** Published: 6 technical reports; 18 technical papers in professional technical intl journals; presented: 16 papers at professional meetings. **HOME ADDRESS:** 2524 N Fox Run Ct, Wichita, KS 67226, (316)634-2537.

GN, THYE-WEE
Publishing company administrator. Chinese American. **PERSONAL:** Born May 10, 1962, Singapore; son of Gn Yong Swee and Choo Mei Leng; married Jitpin Lim, May 17, 1989. **EDUCATION:** University of Oregon, finance, 1986. **CAREER:** Oregon Ballet Theatre, controller, 1986-92; The Desktop Publishing Studio, principal, currently. **SPECIAL ACHIEVEMENTS:** Language proficiency: English, Mandarin. **BUSINESS ADDRESS:** Principal, The Desktop Publishing Studio, 816 SW Tenth Ave, Portland, OR 97205, (503)241-9710.

GNANADESIKAN, RAMANATHAN (RAM)
Educator. Indo-American. **PERSONAL:** Born Nov 2, 1932, Madras, Tamil Nadu, India; son of Ambalavanan Ramanathan & Jegathambal; married Mrudulla Gnanadesikan, Feb 18, 1965; children: Anand, Mukund. **EDUCATION:** Madras University, BSc (with honors), 1952, MA, 1953; University of North Carolina, PhD, 1957. **CAREER:** Procter & Gamble Co, senior research statistician, 1957-59; Bell Telephone Labs, member of technical staff, 1959-60, supervisor, 1960-68, department head, 1968-83; Bellcore, division manager, 1983-86, assistant vice president, 1986-91; Rutgers University, professor, 1991-. **ORGANIZATIONS:** Institute of Mathematical Statistics, president, 1988-89; International Association for Statistical Computing, president, 1981-83; American Association for Advancement of Science, chairman of section U, 1987-88; American Statistical Association, board of directors, 1983-85; US Census Bureau, advisory committee, 1967-69; Math Sciences Education Bd of the National Academy of Sciences, 1989-92; National Institute of Statistical Science, bd of governors, 1990-; NJ State Coalition for Math Education, bd of governors, 1991-. **HONORS/AWARDS:** Association of Indians in America, Annual Honoree, 1989; State of New Jersey Senate, Citation Certificate, 1989; University of North Carolina, Order of the Golden Fleece, 1957. **SPECIAL ACHIEVEMENTS:** Author of over 75 publications in scholarly research journals; 3 books.

GO, DANIEL Y.
Dentist. Chinese American. **PERSONAL:** Born Mar 10, 1958, Seattle, WA; son of Jack D L Go and Nancy Go; married Cindy S Go, Apr 9, 1982; children: Tiffany Ann, Samantha Christi. **EDUCATION:** University of Washington School of Dentistry, DDS, 1986. **CAREER:** Private practice, dentist, 1986-; Renton Technical College, dentistry instructor, 1990-92. **ORGANIZATIONS:** American Dental Assn, 1986-; Washington Dental Service, 1986-; Washington State Dental Assn, 1986-; Seattle/King County Dental Society, 1986-; Renton Technical College, advisory committee, 1990-; Northwest Asian-American Dental Seminar, 1990-; Summit Dental Seminar, 1990-; Seattle Chinese Athletic Assn, 1973-. **HONORS/AWARDS:** Phi Beta Kappa, 1976. **SPECIAL ACHIEVEMENTS:** Dental restorative, 1985; periodontics, 1986. **BUSINESS ADDRESS:** Dentist, 333 Rainier Ave N, Suite 201, Renton, WA 98055, (206)226-1990.

GO, HOWARD T.
Consulting firm executive. Chinese American. **PERSONAL:** Born Nov 15, 1933, Solo, Java, Indonesia; son of Joe Gwan Go and Oei Erkien; married Mary Go, Jun 22, 1960; children: Joan M, Brian M. **EDUCATION:** University of Technology, Delft, Netherlands, IR, 1958; California Western University, PhD, 1979. **CAREER:** Philips Lamp, Eindhoven, development engineer, 1957-60; Transitron Electronics, Reliability & Quality Assurance, director, 1960-63; Westinghouse Space & Defense, fellow engineer & program manager, 1963-66; Fairchild Electronic & Space, Reliability, Maintainable & Quality Assurance, director, 1966-68; Interscience Management Corp, president, 1968-71; UMAB, School of Medicine, associate professor, 1974-84; Management Advisory Service Inc, ceo, 1971-; Johns Hopkins, faculty, 1972-. **ORGANIZATIONS:** Baltimore Temporaries Inc, board member, 1990-92; Leland Temporaries Inc, board member, 1990-92. **HONORS/AWARDS:** Deventer-Maas, Scholar, 1956, 1957, 1958; Eastman Kodak, United Kingdom, R&D Award, 1988. **SPECIAL ACHIEVEMENTS:** Co-author, Integrated Electronic System Handbook, 1970; co-author, American Management Handbook, 1970; PEST Forecasting Method, 1976; POS Process Control Method, 1989. **BUSINESS ADDRESS:** CEO, Management Advisory Services, Inc, 5501 Twin Knolls Professional Center, Ste 104, Columbia, MD 21045, (410)730-5128.

GO, MATEO LIAN POA
Educator (retired). Chinese American. **PERSONAL:** Born Sep 17, 1918, Amoy, Fujian, China; son of Ramon Go Occo; married Jean Cheng Go, May 18, 1946; children: Genevieve, Mateo Jr, Marilyn Dolan. **EDUCATION:** Cornell University, BCE, 1942; MIT, SMCE, 1943; Cornell University, PhD, 1946. **CAREER:** Mateo L P Go Const Co, Cebu, Philippines, president, 1947-53; Go Occo & Co, Manila, Philippines, technical consultant, 1949-54, branch manager, 1954-56; Syracuse University, assistant professor, 1957-59; University of Hawaii, associate professor, 1959-63, professor, 1963-81, Department of Civil Engineering, chairman, 1969-72, 1979-81. **ORGANIZATIONS:** Waikiki Rotary Club, 1969-; Engineering Associates, Hawaii, vice president, president, 1974-; American Concrete Institute; American Society of Civil Engineering; American Society of Engineering Education; Hawaii Academy of Science; Rho Psi, president; Sigma Xi; Phi Kappa Phi; Tau Beta Pi; Chi Epsilon. **HONORS/AWARDS:** Cornell University, Chi Epsilon Freshman

Scholarship Award, 1938-39, MacMillan Scholarship, 1939-42, McGraw Fellowship, 1943-46; MIT, scholarship, 1942-43; National AIA, Award of Merit, 1970. **SPECIAL ACHIEVEMENTS:** Author, "Natural Frequencies & Mode Shapes of Beams by Sonic Method," 1943; "Air Transportation & Airport Problems," 1946; "Limit Design of Unsymmetrical Grid Frameworks," 1966. **HOME ADDRESS:** 2415 Ferdinand Ave, Honolulu, HI 96822, (808)949-1404.

GODHANIA, LAXMAN P.
Civil engineer. Indo-American. **PERSONAL:** Born Jun 24, 1945, Khambhodar, Gujarat, India; son of Parbat H Godhania; married Geeta L Godhania, Nov 21, 1973; children: Vaidehi L. **EDUCATION:** Gujarat University, BS, civil engineering, 1968; Oklahoma University, MS, civil engineering, 1972. **CAREER:** KCG & Associates, vice president, 1978-81; MGR Inc, president, 1981-. **ORGANIZATIONS:** Rotary Club of Edmond, Central, treasurer, 1989-90; India Cultural Foundation, chairman, 1989-91; American Society of Civil Engineers, 1980-; American Concrete Institute, 1980-; National Society of Professional Engineers, 1980-; American Public Works Authority, 1980-; American Consulting Engineering Council, 1980-. **HONORS/AWARDS:** Rotary Club District #575, Service Above Self, 1989; India Association of Oklahoma, Community Service, 1992; Rotary International, Paul Harris Fellow, 1984. **SPECIAL ACHIEVEMENTS:** Co-author, City of Edmond Drainage Ordinance, 1973-74; professional engineer in the states of Oklahoma, Colorado, Arizona, Kansas, Georgia, Mississippi and Arkansas. **BUSINESS ADDRESS:** President, MGR Inc, 1224 S Kelly Ave, Edmond, OK 73003-5862, (405)341-1698.

GODSAY, MADHU P.
Company research and development manager. Indo-American. **PERSONAL:** Born Jul 16, 1932, Bombay, India; son of PN Godsay; married Sunita, May 4, 1955; children: Sumitra Chaphekar, Milind. **EDUCATION:** University of Bombay, India, BSc, 1955; University of Manchester, UK, DTC, 1958; Queen's University, Kingston, Canada, MSc, 1959; Polytechnic University, NY, PhD, 1985. **CAREER:** Madhusudan Mills, Bombay, India, shift supervisor, 1955-57; Courtaulds Ltd, Canada, manager of research & development & technical services, 1959-67; International Paper, manager R&D, 1967-. **ORGANIZATIONS:** Technical Association of Pulp & Paper, 1970-; American Chemical Society, 1970-; TRI-Princeton, research advisory, 1980-; Syracuse University, Environmental Science & Forestry, research advisory, 1991-; Empire State Pulp & Paper, fiber physics, 1991-; Research Association, committee chairman. **SPECIAL ACHIEVEMENTS:** Various scientific publications & patents; publications in Marathi on philosophy. **HOME ADDRESS:** PO Box 38, Southfields, NY 10975, (914)783-3376. **BUSINESS ADDRESS:** Manager, Fiber Sciences, International Paper, Long Meadow Rd, Tuxedo, NY 10987, (914)577-7319.

GOEL, SUBHASH CHAND
Product manager. Indo-American. **PERSONAL:** Born Oct 3, 1957, Neemchana, Uttar Pradesh, India; son of Sagar Mal and Fool Wati Devi (deceased); married Anita Goel, Nov 7, 1986; children: Anish Raja, Avnish Samraat. **EDUCATION:** Indian Institute of Technology, New Delhi, MS, 1982; George Washington University, MS, 1986. **CAREER:** LCC, LLC, product manager, 1986-. **ORGANIZATIONS:** IEEE, 1991-. **HOME ADDRESS:** 12706 Roark Court, Herndon, VA 22071, (703)471-8430.

GOELA, JITENDRA SINGH
Research scientist. Indo-American. **PERSONAL:** Born Apr 20, 1951, Delhi, Delhi, India; son of Umrao Singh Goela (deceased) & Sushila Devi Goela; married Geeta Goela, Mar 4, 1979; children: Naveen, Vikas. **EDUCATION:** Indian Institute of Technology, India, BTech, mech eng, 1972; Brown University, MSc, engineering, 1974, PhD, engineering, 1976; Northeastern University, MBA, 1991. **CAREER:** Physical Sciences Inc, principal scientist, 1976-78; Indian Institute of Technology, lecturer/assistant professor, 1978-84; Sanders Associates, consultant, 1985-86; Efficient Systems Inc, president, 1987-89; Morton International/CVD Inc, principal scientist, 1984-. **ORGANIZATIONS:** New York Academy of Sciences, 1988-; American Society of Mechanical Engineers, 1980-; American Physical Society, 1984-; American Ceramic Society, 1989-; Optical Society of America, 1985-. **HONORS/AWARDS:** Optical Society of America, Engineering Excellence Award, 1991; Indian National Science Academy, India, Young Scientist Medal, 1982; American Society of Mechanical Engineers, Arthur L Williston Medal, 1978. **SPECIAL ACHIEVEMENTS:** Published over 50 technical articles in reputed international journals, shared four patents: Method to Prevent Backside Growth

on Substrates in Vapor Dep, US Patent 4,963,393, 1990; Selective Area Growth in a Vap Dep System, US Patent 4,990,374, 1991; Fab of Lightweight Ceramic Mirror by Means of a CVD Process, US Patent 5,071,596, 1991; Method of Fabricating Lightweight Honeycomb Type Structures, US Patent 5,150,507, 1992. **BIOGRAPHICAL SOURCES:** In Search of a Much Higher Source of Energy, Yankee, p 69, March 1979. **HOME ADDRESS:** 12 Messina Drive, Andover, MA 01810. **BUSINESS ADDRESS:** Principal Scientist, Morton Advanced Materials, 185 New Boston Street, Woburn, MA 01801, (617)937-9116.

GOH, BEN K.
Educational administrator. Chinese American/Malaysian American. **PERSONAL:** Born Oct 6, 1961, Klang, Selangor, Malaysia; son of Kim-Hock Goh. **EDUCATION:** Tunku Abdul Rahman College, ACA, 1982; Texas Tech University, BS, 1986, MBA, 1988. **CAREER:** Malayan United Bank, loan officer, 1982-83; Texas Tech University, instructor, 1988-90, assistant director hotel program, 1990-91, assistant chairperson, 1991-. **ORGANIZATIONS:** American Hospitality Financial Management Society, 1989-93; Beta Gamma Sigma; Phi Beta Delta, 1988-93; Eta Sigma Delta, 1986-93; Council of Hotel, Restaurant & Institutional Management, 1988-93; Texas Tech University, College of Human Sciences, Computer User Committee; Texas Tech University, Chi Omega, faculty adviser, 1991-93; University Computer Usage-Accreditation Self Study, committee member. **HONORS/AWARDS:** Texas Tech University, Extra-Miles Award, 1992. **SPECIAL ACHIEVEMENTS:** Hospitality Cost Control I Manual; Hospitality Cost Control II Manual; Read and write Chinese, Malay, Indonesian. **BUSINESS ADDRESS:** Assistant Chairperson - ENRHM Dept, Texas Tech University, Broadway and University Ave, Human Sciences Bldg., Rm. 601, Lubbock, TX 79409, (806)742-3068.

GOH, DAVID S.
Educator. Chinese American. **PERSONAL:** Born Jul 9, 1941, Jiangsu, China; son of Y H and Pei Shu Goh; married Jane C Goh. **EDUCATION:** National Taiwan Chung Kung University, BA; Illinois State University, MS; University of Wisconsin-Madison, PhD, 1973. **CAREER:** University of Wisconsin, psychology, assistant professor, 1973-75; Central Michigan University, psychology, associate professor, 1975-80; Southern Illinois University, Carbondale, school psychology, professor, 1980-88; City University of New York, school psychology, professor, 1988-. **ORGANIZATIONS:** Asian American Psychological Association, president, 1990-91, Division of School Psychology, vice president, 1990-92, Committee on Psychological Tests and Assessment, 1992-94; National School Psychology Certification Board, 1990-93;. **HONORS/AWARDS:** American Psychological Assn, fellow; American Psychological Society, fellow; American Assn of Applied Preventive Psychology, fellow; National Assn of School Psychologists, Outstanding Leadership & Service Award, 1993. **SPECIAL ACHIEVEMENTS:** Psychological Tests and Assessment, 1987, 2nd ed, 1992; numerous articles on psychology in professional journals; language proficiency in Chinese (Mandarin), Taiwanese. **BUSINESS ADDRESS:** Professor, Graduate Program in School Psychology, City University of New York, Queens College, PH 049 G, Flushing, NY 11367-0904, (718)997-5236.

GOISHI, DEAN M.
Association administrator. Japanese American. **PERSONAL:** Born Jan 1, 1943, Posten, AZ; son of Shizuko and Kazuto. **EDUCATION:** University of California, Berkeley, BS, 1966. **CAREER:** Asian Pacific Health Care Venture, Asian Pacific AIDS Education Project, project director, 1989-93; Special Service for Groups, Asian Pacific AIDS Intervention Team, director, currently. **ORGANIZATIONS:** Asian Pacific Planning Council, HIV Committee, 1989-; Los Angeles County HIV Health Services Planning Council, 1990-; City of Los Angeles AIDS Panel, 1991-; California State Office of AIDS, Multicultural Liaison Board, 1992-; National Minority AIDS Council, advisory board member, 1992-; Los Angeles Unified School District AIDS Advisory Board, 1990-; Asian Pacific Lesbians & Gays Inc, AIDS Intervention Team, chair, 1987-93; US Conference of Mayors, Community Advisory Board, member, 1992-; National Asian Pacific American Families Against Substance Abuse, 1991-. **MILITARY SERVICE:** US Army, captain, 1967-71, Army Commendation Medal. **BUSINESS ADDRESS:** Director, Asian Pacific AIDS Intervention Team, Special Service for Groups, 1313 W 8th St, Ste 201, Los Angeles, CA 90017, (213)484-0380.

GOLLAHALLI, SUBRAMANYAM RAMAPPA
Educator. Indo-American. **PERSONAL:** Born Nov 26, 1942, Sadali, Karnataka, India; son of B Ramappa and Nagalakshamma; married Rangamani

Gollahalli, Dec 25, 1968; children: Suma, Anil. **EDUCATION:** University of Mysore, India, BE, mech eng, 1963; Indian Institute of Science, Bangalore, India, ME, mech eng, 1965; University of Waterloo, MA Sc, mech eng, 1970, PhD, mech eng, 1973. **CAREER:** Indian Institute of Science, lecturer, 1965-68; University of Waterloo, assistant professor, 1973-76; University of Oklahoma, asst professor, 1976-80, associate professor, 1980-84, professor, 1984-92, Lesch Centennial professor, 1992-. **ORGANIZATIONS:** American Society of Mech Engrs, Emerging Energy Committee, chair, 1990-93; American Inst of Aeronautics and Astronautics, Tech Committee, 1983-86; Combustion Institute, tech comm, 1980-; Society of Automotive Engrs, 1965-88; Sigma Xi, honorary member, 1978-; Oklahoma Academy of Sciences, 1978-85; American Society of Engineering Educator, 1978-86. **HONORS/AWARDS:** American Society of Mech Engrs, Ralph James Award, 1993, Sam Collier Award, 1993, fellow, 1992; Canadian Society of Mech Engrs, Robert Angus Medal, 1978; Society of Automotive Engrs, Ralph Teetor Award, 1978. **SPECIAL ACHIEVEMENTS:** Published over 70 articles on combustion science; conducted sponsored research for several federal agencies and industries. **BUSINESS ADDRESS:** Lesch Centennial Professor, University of Oklahoma, School of Aerospace & Mechanical Engineering, 865 Asp Ave, Felgar Hall, Rm 212, Norman, OK 73019, (405)325-5011.

GONG, GINNY
Educator, administrator. Chinese American. **PERSONAL:** Born Mar 15, 1948, Canton, China; daughter of Bing Eng & Oy Jee Eng; married; children: Jennifer Lai, Brian Michael, David Alan. **EDUCATION:** State University of New York, Cortland, BS, 1971; Queens College, NY, masters, 1973. **CAREER:** Clifton Heights Public Schools, PA, 1975-77; Port Washington Public Schools, NY, mathematics teacher, 1971-75, 1979-82; Herricks Public Schools, NY, mathematics teacher, 1985-92; Montgomery County Public Schools, Recruitment & Retention, personnel specialist, 1993-. **ORGANIZATIONS:** Organization of Chinese Americas Inc, national president, 1993-, national vice president for chapter development, 1992, national treasurer, 1990, 1991; OCA-LI, local chapter president on Long Island, 1989; Asian Pacific American Heritage Council, board member, coordinator of annual citywide festival, 1992; Montgomery County Community Service Partnership, board member, 1992; Herricks Community Coalition, faculty rep on council, 1991. **HONORS/AWARDS:** OCA, Distinguished Service Award, 1991; Maryland Governor Schaeffer's Office, Distinguished Community Service Award, 1993; Office of Governor Schaeffer, Governor's Asian Advisory committee of Distinguished Asian Americans, appointed member. **BIOGRAPHICAL SOURCES:** The World Journal, front page, May 1993. **HOME ADDRESS:** 12601 Maidens Bower Dr, Potomac, MD 20854. **BUSINESS PHONE:** (202)223-5500.

GONG, JIN KANG
Educator. Chinese American. **PERSONAL:** Born Jul 7, 1957, Shanghai, People's Republic of China; son of Qi Chen Gong and Xuelian Yin; married Xuexing Deng, Oct 14, 1984; children: Lucy, Kevin. **EDUCATION:** East China Normal University, BA, English language, 1978, BS, chemistry, 1982; Purdue University, PhD, inorganic chemistry, 1990. **CAREER:** Southeast Missouri State University, asst professor, 1990-. **ORGANIZATIONS:** American Chemical Society; Inorganic Chemistry Division; Organometallic Chemistry Division; Missouri Academy of Science. **HONORS/AWARDS:** Research Corporation, Cottrell College Science Award, 1992; NASA Joint Venture Research Program, research fellow, 1993; Faculty Research Achievement Award, SEMO, College of Sci & Tech, 1992-93. **SPECIAL ACHIEVEMENTS:** Ten publications in the field of chemistry; recent research interests: photovoltaic materials and the homogeneous catalysis of carbon dioxide into organic molecules and dioxygen molecules. **BIOGRAPHICAL SOURCES:** Southeast Missourian, p 13A, Dec 13, 1992, p 1A, Apr 16, 1993, p 11A, Oct 17, 1993. **BUSINESS ADDRESS:** Professor, Dept of Chemistry, Southeast Missouri State University, Cape Girardeau, MO 63701, (314)651-2371.

GONZALEZ-PARDO, LILLIAN
Educator, pediatric neurologist. Filipino American. **PERSONAL:** Born Feb 5, 1939, Manila, Philippines; daughter of Eduardo Legaspi and Lumen Vida Penaflorida Gonzalez; married Manuel Pardo, Jun 20, 1964; children: Manuel, Lillian, Patrick. **EDUCATION:** University of the Philippines, AA, 1957, MD, 1962; University of Kansas Medical Center, postgrad study. **CAREER:** Philippine General Hospital, intern, 1962-63; Children's Mercy Hospital, resident in pediatric neurology, 1967-68; practice in Manila, 1969-71; University of Kansas Medical Center, neurology resident, 1963-66, pediatrics resident, 1974, Children's Rehabilitation Unit, medical director, beginning 1975, Dept of Pediatrics and Neurology, asst professor, beginning 1975, clinical professor,

currently. **ORGANIZATIONS:** American Medical Women's Assn, Kansas City Chapter, president, 1981, national president, 1992; American Academy of Mental Deficiency; Kansas City Neurological Society. **HONORS/AWARDS:** US Pan Asian American Chamber of Commerce, Excellence 2000, 1993; American Academy of Pediatrics, Fellow; American Board of Psychiatry and Neurology, Diplomate. **SPECIAL ACHIEVEMENTS:** First Asian American to head the American Medical Women's Assn; author of numerous articles in professional journals in the field of developmental disabilities, child abuse, etc. **BUSINESS ADDRESS:** Clinical Professor, Dept of Pediatrics & Neurology, University of Kansas Medical Center, 3901 Rainbow Blvd, Kansas City, KS 66160, (913)588-5000.∗

GOO, EDWARD KWOCK WAI
Educator. Chinese American. **PERSONAL:** Born Nov 25, 1956, Honolulu, HI; son of See Hong & Rose Goo; married Grace, Dec 20, 1986; children: William, Elizabeth, James. **EDUCATION:** Cornell University, BS, 1978; University of California, Berkeley, MS, 1981; Stanford University, PhD, 1985. **CAREER:** Lawrence Berkeley Laboratory, staff scientist, 1984-85; University of Southern California, associate professor, 1985-. **HONORS/AWARDS:** American Society of Metals, Robert Lansing Hardy Gold Medal, 1986; National Science Foundation, Presidential Young Investigator, 1988; University of Southern California, Northrop Junior Faculty Award, 1989; Office of Naval Research, Young Investigator Award, 1990. **BUSINESS ADDRESS:** Associate Professor, Dept of Materials Science & Engineering, University of Southern California, 712 Vivian Hall of Engineering, Los Angeles, CA 90089, (213)740-4426.

GOPALAKRISHNA, K. V.
Physician. Indo-American. **PERSONAL:** Born Jan 11, 1944, Mysore, Karnataka, India; son of K Vasudeva Rao & K V Padmavathi; married Kimberly, Jun 6, 1992; children: Sheela, Arun, Veena, Rajesh, David, Edward. **EDUCATION:** Mysore Medical School, MBBS, 1965. **CAREER:** Case Western Reserve University, Medical School, associate clinical professor of medicine; VA Hospital, chief, general medicine, 1972-73, chief, infectious diseases, 1973-77; Fairview General Hospital, chief, infectious diseases, 1977-. **ORGANIZATIONS:** American College of Physicians, fellow; Infectious Diseases Society, fellow; American Society for Microbiology; American Medical Association. **HONORS/AWARDS:** Health Cleveland Internal Medicine Residency Program, Teacher of the Year, 1992. **SPECIAL ACHIEVEMENTS:** Many publications in medical magazines. **BUSINESS ADDRESS:** Chief of Infectious Diseases, Fairview General Hospital, 18101 Lorain Ave, Cleveland, OH 44111, (216)476-7106.

GOPIKANTH, M. L.
Technology manager. Indo-American. **PERSONAL:** Born Aug 9, 1954, Mysore, India; son of M K Laxmikanth & M K S Laxmikanth. **EDUCATION:** University of Mysore, India, BS, 1972; Birla Institute of Tech & Science, India, MS, 1974; Indian Institute of Science, India, PhD, 1978; Northeastern University, MBA, 1986. **CAREER:** Cardiac Pacemakers Inc, sr staff scientist, 1980-82; Duracell Inc, sr staff scientist, 1982-86; Life Systems Inc, principal engineer, 1986-87; Chemtech Systems Inc, president, 1986-91; Ultralife Batteries Inc, director, technology, 1991-. **ORGANIZATIONS:** American Chemical Society, 1979-; American Electrochemical Society, 1979-; AAMBA, 1984-; Sigma Xi, 1980-. **SPECIAL ACHIEVEMENTS:** Author of several scientific publications, 1976-; 6 US patents. **HOME ADDRESS:** PO Box 1067, Burlington, MA 01803, (617)273-4170. **BUSINESS PHONE:** (315)332-7194.

GORLA, RAMA S. R.
Educator. Indo-American. **PERSONAL:** Born Jul 1, 1941, Palagiri, Andhra Pradesh, India; son of Subba Reddy Gorla & Tirupelamma Gorla; married Vijaya Lakshmi, Oct 15, 1965; children: Madhu Sudan Reddy, Sudhakar Reddy. **EDUCATION:** SV University, BS, 1963; Indian Institute of Technology, MS, 1965; University of Toledo, PhD, 1972. **CAREER:** Teledyne CAE, research engineer, 1972-73; Chrysler Corporation, research engineer, 1973-74; Gannon University, assistant professor, 1974-77; Cleveland State University, professor, 1977-. **ORGANIZATIONS:** ASME, 1972-; ASEE, 1972-; AIAA, 1972-; AAUP, 1992-. **HONORS/AWARDS:** ASME, Man of the Year, 1975; University of Toledo, Outstanding Graduate Student of the Year, 1971. **SPECIAL ACHIEVEMENTS:** Published over 200 technical papers in journals of international recognition. **HOME ADDRESS:** 8041 Oxford Drive, Strongsville, OH 44136, (216)243-1180. **BUSINESS ADDRESS:** Professor of Mechanical Engineering, Cleveland State University, Cleveland, OH 44115, (216)523-7276.

GOSWAMI, PANKAJ P.
Plant manager. Indo-American. **PERSONAL:** Born Jun 27, 1947, Baroda, Gujarat, India; son of Prabhatkumar H Goswami and Savitaben P Goswami; married Elizabeth, Jul 24, 1976; children: Nicole, Neal. **EDUCATION:** MS University, Baroda, India, BSChE, 1969; University of Missouri at Rolla, MSChE, 1971; SUNY at Buffalo, MBA, 1974. **CAREER:** Sherwin Williams Co, process engr; Mobil Chemical Co, process engr; Steinerfilm Inc, plant manager, currently. **ORGANIZATIONS:** AIChE.

GOTANDA, PHILIP KAN
Playwright. Japanese American. **PERSONAL:** Born Dec 17, 1949, Stockton, CA. **EDUCATION:** University of California, Santa Barbara, BA, Asian studies; Hastings College of Law, JD. **CAREER:** Playwright: The Advocado Kid; Song for a Nisei Fisherman, 1981; The Wash, 1986; Yankee Dawg You Die; Fish Head Soup; Day Standing on Its Head, 1993; Bullet Headed Birds; Zero; director, Uncle Tadao, 1991; film director, The Kiss, 1991; screenplay: Mona Lisa, Mon Amour, forthcoming; Taper, associate artist. **ORGANIZATIONS:** New Dramatists; Asian American Musicians Organization, co-founder. **HONORS/AWARDS:** Guggenheim Fellow, 1990; NEA, Playwriting Fellow; TCG/NEA, Playwriting Fellow; 3 Rockefeller Playwriting Awards; Stanford University, Okada House, artist-in-residence. **SPECIAL ACHIEVEMENTS:** The Wash was made into a feature film, shown on PBS. **BUSINESS ADDRESS:** Playwright, Mark Taper Forum, 135 North Grand, Los Angeles, CA 90012.∗

GOTERA, VICENTE FERRER (VINCE)
Poet, educator. Filipino American. **PERSONAL:** Born Jun 20, 1952, San Francisco, CA; son of Martin A Gotera and Candida Fajardo Gotera; married Mary Ann Blue Gotera, Nov 24, 1984; children: Martin Adan, Amanda Blue, Amelia Blue, Melina Blue. **EDUCATION:** City College of San Francisco, AA, 1977; Stanford University, BA, 1979; San Francisco State University, MA, 1981; Indiana University, MFA, 1989, PhD, 1991. **CAREER:** Federal Civil Service, military pay clerk, supervisor, 1975-78; Saint Rose High School, teacher, 1979-80; US Army Corps of Engineers, writer, editor, graphic artist, 1980-81; Indiana University, associate instructor, 1982-89; Humboldt State University, assistant professor, 1989-. **ORGANIZATIONS:** American Culture Association, 1988-; Popular Culture Association, area chair, Vietnam War, 1992-; Modern Language Association, 1988-, Executive Committee of Asian American Literature Discussion Group, 1992-; Association for Asian American Studies, 1990-; Academy of American Poets, 1990-. **HONORS/AWARDS:** National Endowment for the Arts, Creative Writing Fellowship, 1993; University of Wisconsin, Madison, Felix Pollak Prize in Poetry, 1988; George Mason University, Mary Roberts Rinehart Award in Poetry, 1988; Academy of American Poets, Academy of American Poets Prize, 1988. **SPECIAL ACHIEVEMENTS:** Radical Visions: Poetry by Vietnam Veterans, University of Georgia Press, 1994; Madarika: Homeless Wanderer, book chapter of poems, Burning Cities Press, 1994; Pacific Crossing, a book of poems; numerous poems in such journals as Ploughshares, Amerasia, and anthologies, such as: Open Boat Poems from Asian America; poetry editor, Asian America: A Journal of Culture and the Arts. **MILITARY SERVICE:** US Army, specialist five, 1972-75. **BUSINESS ADDRESS:** Assistant Professor, English Dept, Humboldt State University, Arcata, CA 95521-8299, (707)826-5939.

GOTO, GEORGE
Educational administrator, athletic director (retired). Japanese American. **PERSONAL:** Born Mar 3, 1926, Penryn, CA; son of Kazumasa Goto (deceased) and Sada Goto (deceased); married Susan T Goto, Aug 13, 1955; children: Leslie Goto-Pineschi, Eric K. **EDUCATION:** Placer Junior College, AA, 1952; California State University, Sacramento, BA, 1954, teacher credential, 1955, MA, 1960. **CAREER:** Roseville High School District, teacher, coach, physical education department chair; 1955-62; Sierra College District, teacher, coach, 1962-86, associate dean of physical education division, 1983-86. **ORGANIZATIONS:** California Teachers Association, 1955-83; California Junior College Coaches Association, 1963-70; Moose Lodge, 1986-93; Elks Lodge 2248, 1981-86; City of Roseville Park & Recreation Department, 1991-; Association of California Community College Administrators, 1983-86. **HONORS/AWARDS:** California Junior College State, MVP Basketball, 1950; Golden Valley Conference, Coach of the Year-Basketball, 1967, Coach of the Year-Golf, 1977; Northern California All Sports Hall of Fame, inducted, 1993; California State University, Sacramento, Athlete of the Year, 1954; Nichei Bei Times, San Francisco, Athlete of the Year, twice; Tulelake Relocation Center, Baseball All Star, 1944, 1945; Placer, Nevada County, Baseball All Star, 1953.

MILITARY SERVICE: Army, cpl, 1946-49. **HOME ADDRESS:** 230 Diamond Oaks Rd, Roseville, CA 95678, (916)783-4053.

GOTO, JOSEPH N.
Artist. Japanese American. **PERSONAL:** Born Jan 7, 1916, Kaiwiki, Hilo, HI; son of Naoki Goto and Tsuru Goto; married June Cushing; children: Kai Thomas, Joji Margret. **EDUCATION:** Roosevelt University, painting and drawing; School of the Art Institute of Chicago. **CAREER:** Brandeis University, Shirley and Maurice Salzman Professor of Sculpture, lecturer; Carnegie-Mellon University, Andrew Mellon Professor of Sculpture, lecturer; University of Illinois, Chicago, lecturer; Rhode Island School of Design, assistant professor of art; University of Michigan, College of Architecture and Design, assistant professor of art; Richmond Professional Institute, assistant professor of art; painter, sculptor, artist, currently. **HONORS/AWARDS:** Fellowships: John Hay Whitney Foundation; Graham Foundation for Advanced Studies in the Fine Arts; National Council on the Arts; John Simon Guggenheim; College Women's Association of Japan Scholarship, Tokyo, grant to study in Japan; The Art Institute of Chicago, The Linde Award; Detroit Institute of Arts, Detroit Prize for Drawing; Museum of Art, Providence, RI, Governor's Award. **SPECIAL ACHIEVEMENTS:** Museum of Modern Art, New York City; Whitney Museum of American Art; The Art Institute of Chicago; Smithsonian Institution; numerous others.

GOTO, LEO K.
Restaurateur. Japanese American. **PERSONAL:** Born Jun 2, 1936, Sacramento, CA; son of Harvey and Tokie Goto; married Linda Goto, May 1, 1992; children: Timothy, Leilani. **EDUCATION:** University of Denver, BSBA, MBA. **CAREER:** Westin Intl Hotels, food & beverage manager, beginning 1954; Trader Vics, manager, until 1969; Leo's Place, owner, 1969-80; Wellshire Inn, owner, 1976-. **ORGANIZATIONS:** University of Denver, trustee; Colorado Tourism Board, Board member; Mile High United Way, director; Colorado Restaurant Assn, director; AIWF, director; US Commission on Civil Rights, advisory committee; Art Reach, director; Variety Club, director. **HONORS/AWARDS:** Rky Mtn Chefs de Cuisine, Chef of the Year, 1969; KUSA-TV, 9 Who Care Award, 1979; American Institute for Public Service, Outstanding Citizens Award, 1980; Colorado Restaurant Assn, Hall of Fame Award, 1980. **MILITARY SERVICE:** US Air Force, airman 1st class, 1960-66. **BUSINESS ADDRESS:** Owner, Wellshire Inn, 3333 S Colorado Blvd, Denver, CO 80222, (303)759-3333.

GOTO, MIDORI. *See* MIDORI.

GOTO, UNOJI
Physician. Japanese American. **PERSONAL:** Born Jun 24, 1918, Kealakekua, Kona, HI; son of Unokichi Goto and Yana Goto; married Florence Kiyeko Goto, Feb 28, 1948; children: Linda K Hirai, Wayne K, Steven J, Paul R, Mark A. **EDUCATION:** University of Hawaii, 1939-41; University of Cincinnati, BS, 1944, MD, 1948. **CAREER:** University of Cincinnati, instructor in internal medicine, 1955-57; The Honolulu Medical Group, physician, 1957-; University of Hawaii, John A Burns Medical School, associate clinical professor of medicine, 1965-. **ORGANIZATIONS:** Hawaii Heart Association, president, 1964-65; American Heart Association, board of directors, 1966-70; Queens Medical Center, chief of staff, 1970-72; Regional Medical Program, Heart, Cancer & Stroke Comm, 1957-, board of directors, 1967-72; American College of Physicians, 1968-; Physicians Comm of Aloha United Fund, chairman, 1968. **HONORS/AWARDS:** American College of Physicians, fellow, 1968; American Heart Association, Distinguished Service, 1968. **SPECIAL ACHIEVEMENTS:** Started first cardiac catheterization in Hawaii, 1957; made first heart lung machine in Hawaii, 1957-59; cardiologist on first open heart surgery team in Hawaii, 1959; introduced training coronary care, cardiopolmonary resuscitation program in all hospitals in Hawaii, 1968-72; member of first committee of Aloha United Fund, 1964; one of 20 health care people who had an impact on health care delivery in Hawaii; 20th year of statehood for Hawaii, Star Bulletin, Februrary 20, 1979. **MILITARY SERVICE:** US Navy, lt, sg, 1952-54. **BUSINESS ADDRESS:** Physician, The Honolulu Medical Group, 550 S Beretania St, Honolulu, HI 96813, (808)537-2211.

GOTO, YUKIHIRO
Educator, actor, performing arts director. Japanese American. **PERSONAL:** Born Apr 9, 1954, Omachi, Fukuoka, Japan; son of Tadashi Goto and Haruko Goo; married Tomoko Goto, Jun 15, 1990. **EDUCATION:** Waseda University, Tokyo, Japan, 1974-75; University of Wisconsin, Superior, BFA, 1978; University of Minnesota, MFA, 1981; University of Hawaii, Manoa, PhD, 1988. **CAREER:** Stage, TV, films, actor, director, 1978-; University of Hawaii at Manoa, graduate assistant, 1981-84, lecturer, 1984-88; State University of New York, Stony Brook, assistant professor, 1988-90; San Francisco State University, associate professor, 1990-. **ORGANIZATIONS:** Theatre of Yugen, board of directors, 1993-; Theatre Forte, board of directors, 1992-; Theatre Bay Area, 1990-; Association for Theatre in Higher Education, 1988-; Association for Asian Performance, 1988-; Association for Asian Studies, 1990-. **HONORS/AWARDS:** SUNY, Stony Brook, Lilly Endowment Teaching Fellowship, 1989-90; Japan Foundation, Japan Foundation Fellowship, 1986-87; US Department of Education, National Graduate Fellowship in Humanities and Sciences, 1986-88; American College Theatre Festival, Meritorious Achievement Award, 1989-90; California State University, Research, Scholarship, or Creative Activity Award, 1990-91. **SPECIAL ACHIEVEMENTS:** Director of Western classics in a Japanese-theatre style, including: Hamlet, 1994, The Trojan Women, 1993, Shogun Macbeth, 1992, Clytemnestra, 1991, Rashomon, 1989; author, "Theatrical Fusion of Suzuki Tadashi," Asian Theatre Journal, 6.2, 1989, translation, Terasaki Hironori, "Trends in Japanese Theatrical World," Asian Theatre Journal, 1.1, 1984. **BIOGRAPHICAL SOURCES:** Directory of Japan Specialists and Japanese Studies Institutions in the United States and Canada, Japan Foundation, p 139, 1989; Newsday, New York, "Greek Classics, Japanese Spin," March 21, 1990; Leisure, "Japanese Director Teaches Theater, Learns Appreciation," 1989; Asian Week, San Francisco, "S.F. State Learns: Just Say Noh," 1991. **BUSINESS ADDRESS:** Associate Professor, Dept of Theatre Arts, San Francisco State University, 1600 Holloway Ave, San Francisco, CA 94132-1722, (415)338-7780.

GOUW, CYNTHIA GIE-KIOK
Anchor, reporter. Chinese American. **PERSONAL:** Born May 30, 1963, San Pablo, CA; daughter of Tan Hok Gouw & Norma B Gouw. **EDUCATION:** UCLA, BA, 1985, School of Law, JD, 1991. **CAREER:** KABC-TV, "Eye on LA," co-host, 1987-88; E! Entertainment, host, 1991-92; KPFK-FM, reporter, 1992; KTVU-TV, "On the Money," co-anchor, reporter, 1992; KERO-TV, "23 News," reporter, 1992; KDFW-TV, "News 4 Texas," anchor, reporter, 1993-. **ORGANIZATIONS:** Asian American Journalist's Association, 1991-; Asian Pacific American Women's Network, 1991-. **HONORS/AWARDS:** Distinctions: First Asian American television news anchor in Dallas/Fort Worth area; Star Search, grand champion. **SPECIAL ACHIEVEMENTS:** Star Trek V, The Final Frontier, co-star. **BUSINESS ADDRESS:** c/o The Flavoral Company, PO Box 773, El Cerrito, CA 94530, (214)720-3258.

GOVIL, NARENDRA KUMAR
Educator. Indo-American. **PERSONAL:** Born Jan 5, 1940, Aligarh, Uttar Pradesh, India; son of Panna Lal Govil (deceased) & Kamla Devi Govil; married Urmila Govil, Feb 1, 1964; children: Sanjay, Sandeep. **EDUCATION:** Agra University, India, BSc, 1957; Aligarh Muslim University, India, MSc, 1959; University of Montreal, PhD, 1968. **CAREER:** Concordia University, lecturer/assistant professor, 1967-70; Indian Institute of Technology, assistant/associate professor, 1970-80, professor, 1980-85; University of Alberta, visiting professor, 1981; Auburn University, visiting professor, 1983-85, associate professor, 1985-86, professor, 1986-. **ORGANIZATIONS:** American Mathematical Society, 1988-; Indian Mathematical Society; National Academy of Sciences, India; Mathematical Reviews, reviewer, 1985-; Forum for Interdisciplinary Mathematics, executive committee, 1989-91; India Cultural Association of East Alabama, president, 1991. **HONORS/AWARDS:** National Academy of Sciences, India, elected fellow, 1979; Sigma Xi, 1987. **SPECIAL ACHIEVEMENTS:** Published about 40 research papers in international mathematical journals. **HOME ADDRESS:** 523 Owens Rd, Auburn, AL 36830, (205)887-5418. **BUSINESS ADDRESS:** Professor, Dept of Mathematics, Auburn University, 218 Parker Hall, Auburn, AL 36849, (205)844-4290.

GOVINDARAJULU, ZAKKULA
Educator. Indo-American. **PERSONAL:** Born May 15, 1933, Armakur, Andhra Pradesh, India; married Gayatri; children: Sushma Magnuson, Sadhna, Usha. **EDUCATION:** University of Madras, BA (honors), 1952, MA, 1953; University of Minnesota, PhD, 1961. **CAREER:** University of Minnesota, instructor, 1960-61; Case Institute of Technology, Dept of Math, asst professor, 1961-64, associate professor, 1964-67; University of California, Berkeley, visiting associate professor, 1964-65; Stanford University, visiting professor, 1983-84; Columbia University, visiting professor, 1988-89; University of Kentucky, professor of statistics, 1968-. **ORGANIZATIONS:** Institute of Math Statistics, fellow, 1974-; American Statistical Assn, fellow, 1965; Royal Statistical Society, England, fellow, 1969; American Assn for the Adm Sci, fellow, 1965; International Statistical Institute, elected member, 1969; Indian Statisti-

cal Institute, life member, 1969; Natl Academy of Science, India, life member, 1987; Indian Society of Probability and Statistics, life member. **HONORS/ AWARDS:** Honorable Order of Kentucky Colonels; Natl Academy of Science, India; Sigma Xi. **SPECIAL ACHIEVEMENTS:** Author of 128 published papers; Statistical Techniques in Bioassary, S Karger, A G Publishers, Switzerland, 1988; Sequential Analysis of Hypothesis Testing, Estimation and Decision Theory, American Science Press, 1987; J of Statistical Plannings and Inference, guest editor, vol 9, no 3, 1984; American J of Math and Management Sciences, guest editor, vol 10, 1991. **BIOGRAPHICAL SOURCES:** Who's Who in Technology Today; Personalities in the South. **HOME ADDRESS:** 425 Texas St, San Francisco, CA 94107-2932, (606)223-9661. **BUSINESS ADDRESS:** Professor, Dept of Statistics, University of Kentucky, S Lime Stone St, 817 POT, Lexington, KY 40506-0027, (606)257-4950.

GOVINDJEE
Educator. Indo-American. **PERSONAL:** Born Oct 24, 1933, Allahabad, Uttar Pradesh, India; son of Vishveshwar Prasad and Savitri Devi; married Rajni Varma, Oct 24, 1957; children: Anita, Sanjay. **EDUCATION:** Allahabad University, India, BSc, 1952, MSc, 1954; University of Illinois, Urbana-Champaign, PhD, 1960. **CAREER:** Allahabad University, lecturer in botany, 1954-56; University of Illinois, graduate fellow and assistant, 1956-60, USPHS postdoctoral fellow, 1960-61, assistant professor, 1961-65, associate professor, 1961-69, professor, 1969-. **ORGANIZATIONS:** American Society for Photobiology, 1972-, council member, 1975-77, finance committee member, 1976-77, president, 1981; USDA-India Program, cooperating scientist, 1983-90; Sigma Xi, 1961-; American Society of Plant Physiologists, 1961-; Biophysical Society of America, 1965-. **HONORS/AWARDS:** American Assn for the Advancement of Science, fellow, 1976; University of Illinois, Distinguished Lecturer of Life Sciences, 1978; National Academy of Sciences, India, fellow, life member, 1979; 6th Intl Photosynthesis Congress, plenary speaker, 1983; University of Illinois, Center for Advanced Study, associate, 1989. **SPECIAL ACHIEVEMENTS:** Co-author, ''Photosynthesis,'' John Wiley and Sons, 1969; editor, ''Bioenergetics of Photosynthesis,'' Academic Press, 1975; editor, ''Photosynthesis,'' 2 volumes, Academic Press, 1982; co-editor, ''Light Emission by Plants and Bacteria,'' Academic Press, 1986; co-editor, ''Molecular Biology of Photosynthesis,'' Kluwer Academic, 1988; ''Photosynthesis Research,'' editor in chief, 1985-88, editor, Historical Corner, 1988-, Kluwer Academic. **HOME ADDRESS:** 2401 S Boudreau, Urbana, IL 61801-6655, (217)337-0627. **BUSINESS ADDRESS:** Professor of Plant Bio & Biophysics, University of Illinois at Urbana-Champaign, 505 S Goodwin Ave, 265 Morrill Hall, Urbana, IL 61801-3707, (217)333-1794.

GOW, HAVEN BRADFORD
Columnist. Chinese American. **PERSONAL:** Born Jul 5, 1950, Fall River, MA; son of Joseph W Gow & Elizabeth Hall Gow. **EDUCATION:** Southeastern Massachusetts University, BA, English, 1972; Boston College, MA, American studies, 1975. **CAREER:** National Journalism Center, intern, 1980; International Life Times, staff writer, 1980-82; Wilbur Foundation, literary fellow, 1983; American Federation of Police, associate editor, 1983-91; Catholic League for Religious & Civil Rights, editor, 1989-92; Foundation for Economic Education, intern, 1992; Christian News, columnist, 1978-. **HONORS/ AWARDS:** National Association of Chiefs of Police, honored for writing on behalf of missing and exploited children; Young Americans for Freedom, Freedoms Foundation, honored for writing. **SPECIAL ACHIEVEMENTS:** Published more than 1,000 articles and reviews in 100 magazines and newspapers such as Mademoiselle, New York City Tribune, Baltimore Evening Sun, Indianapolis Star, Manchester (NH) Union Leader, Human Events, Chicago Sun-Times, etc; guest speaker on television and radio across the country to discuss a variety of current topics, including: drug abuse, sex crimes, education, sexuality issues, First Amendment, criminal justice system, religious freedom. **BIOGRAPHICAL SOURCES:** ''Gow Peels Potatoes between Editorial Replies,'' Home Times, page 10, September 1992. **BUSINESS ADDRESS:** Columnist, Christian News, RR 1, Box 309A, New Haven, MO 63068.

GOYAL, MEGH R.
Educator. Indo-American. **PERSONAL:** Born Aug 1, 1949, Sangrur, Punjab, India; son of Babu Ram & Daya Wanti; married Subhadra D Goyal, Feb 14, 1970; children: Vijay, Vinay, Neena. **EDUCATION:** Punjab Agricultural University, India, BSc, 1971; Ohio State University, MSc, 1977, PhD, 1979. **CAREER:** Hisar Agricultural University, research assistant, 1972-75; Ohio State University, research assistant, 1975-79; University of Puerto Rico, professor, 1979-. **ORGANIZATIONS:** American Society Agricultural Engineers, 1979-. **HONORS/AWARDS:** ASAE, Blue Ribbon Award, 1990, 1991, 1992,

ASAE Research Paper, 1983, Young Scientist, 1987, Puerto Rico Chapter, Engineer of Year, 1991. **HOME PHONE:** (809)265-4702. **BUSINESS ADDRESS:** Professor, University of Puerto Rico, Box 5984, College Station, Mayaguez, PR 00681-5984.

GOYAL, SURESH
Research engineer, scientist. Indo-American. **PERSONAL:** Born Dec 6, 1960, Bhatinda, Punjab, India; son of Babu Ram Goyal and Parsinni Goyal; married Shefali Goyal, 1990. **EDUCATION:** IIT Kharagpur, India, BTech, mechanical engineering, 1982; University of Iowa, MS, 1984; Cornell University, PhD, mechanical engineering, 1988. **CAREER:** University of Kentucky, research, teaching assistant, 1982-83; University of Iowa, research, teaching assistant, 1983-84; Cornell University, research, teaching assistant, 1984-88, computer science, post doctoral, 1988-89; AT&T Bell Labs, MTS, 1989-. **ORGANIZATIONS:** IEEE, 1988-; ASME, 1990-. **SPECIAL ACHIEVEMENTS:** Research papers on: simulation, modeling of mechanical systems; dynamics; geometric description of friction, dynamics, spinal biomechanics. **HOME ADDRESS:** 420 River Rd, #K10, Chatham, NJ 07928. **BUSINESS ADDRESS:** MTS, AT&T Bell Labs, 600 Mountain Ave, Rm 1B-212, Murray Hill, NJ 07974-0636, (908)582-5959.

GRAMM, WENDY LEE
Former commodities trading commissioner. Korean American. **PERSONAL:** Born 1945?, Hawaii; daughter of Joshua Lee and Angeline AnChin Lee; married Phil Gramm, Nov 2, 1970; children: Marshall Kenneth, Jefferson Philip. **EDUCATION:** Wellesley College, BA, economics, 1966; Northwestern University, PhD, economics, 1971. **CAREER:** University of Illinois, Dept Quantitative Methods, staff, 1969; Texas A&M University, assistant professor, 1970-74, Dept Economics, associate professor, 1975-79; Institute of Def Analyses, research staff, 1979-82; Federal Trade Commission, Bureau of Economics, assistant director, 1982-83, director, 1983-85; Office of Management & Budget, Office Information and Regulatory Affairs, administrator, 1985-87; Commodity Futures Trading Commission, chairperson, 1988-93. **SPECIAL ACHIEVEMENTS:** Author of numerous articles in professional journals. **HOME ADDRESS:** PO Box 39134, Washington, DC 20016.*

GREEN, YOSHIKO OKADA
Educator. Japanese American. **PERSONAL:** Born in Tokyo, Japan; daughter of Tomio Okada and Kimiko Okada; married Bruce E Green, Dec 15, 1969; children: Eddy, Tom, Natalie. **EDUCATION:** Western Michigan University, BS, 1991; Indiana University, MS, currently. **CAREER:** Southwestern College, instructor; Indiana University at South Bend, continued education instructor; Indiana University at South Bend, Japanese instructor, currently. **SPECIAL ACHIEVEMENTS:** Japanese dance teaching certificate, Natori. **HOME ADDRESS:** 62000 Lewis Lake Rd, Vandalia, MI 49095.

GREENBERG, ASHA SAUND
City government official. Indo-American. **PERSONAL:** Born May 6, 1952, Delhi, India; daughter of Amrik Singh Saund & Kamla Saund; married Maxwell E Greenberg; children: David J, Jonathan A. **EDUCATION:** Delhi University, BA, 1971; Whittier College School of Law, JD (magna cum laude), 1982. **CAREER:** Coast Federal Savings, operations officer, 1978-83; Ross, Fields & Zax, civil litigator, 1983; City of Los Angeles, deputy city attorney, 1983-; City of Santa Monica, council member, 1992-. **ORGANIZATIONS:** League of Women Prosecutors, vice president; Indian Lawyers Association of America, director; Asian Indian Womens' Network, advisory board; B'Nai B'rith Women, life member; National Women's Political Caucus; Womens Alliance for Israel. **HONORS/AWARDS:** Whittier College, American Jurisprudence Awards, 1981-82; President George Bush, Point of Light Award, for narcotics abatement program. **SPECIAL ACHIEVEMENTS:** Publications: ''Case Note: In Re-Marriage of Lucas,'' Whittier Law Review, vol 3, no 4, p617, 1981; ''Income Property: The Immigrant's Dream or Nightmare?,'' India West; Forum Firing Line, weekly column, Santa Monica Life. **BIOGRAPHICAL SOURCES:** The Outlook, Nov 5, Nov 6, 1992; Los Angeles Times, p J7, Nov 5, 1992. **BUSINESS ADDRESS:** Deputy City Attorney, Los Angeles Attorney's Office, 1645 Corinth Ave, Rm 203, Los Angeles, CA 90025, (310)575-8412.

GREWAL, PERMINDER SINGH
Physician. Indo-American. **PERSONAL:** Born Apr 12, 1956, New Delhi, India; son of Sampuran Singh Grewal and Herchint Kaur Grewal; married Neena Bhatia, Apr 6, 1980; children: Subir, Simryn Sahil. **EDUCATION:** Government College, Ludhiana, India, pre-medical, 1973; Christian Medical

College, Ludhiana, India, MBBS, 1980. **CAREER:** Bronx-Lebanon Hospital, resident, internal medicine, 1981-84; Lincoln Hospital, fellow, cardiology, 1984-86; New York Medical College, asst professor, Lincoln Hospital, Cardiology Dept, 1986-87; private practice, physician, currently. **ORGANIZATIONS:** American College of Cardiology, fellow, 1987; American Board of Internal Medicine, diplomate, 1985; American College of Chest Physicians, fellow, 1992. **HOME ADDRESS:** 12 Fieldstone Ct, New City, NY 10956. **BUSINESS PHONE:** (914)942-1001.

GUEN, AMY CHIN
Social worker (retired). Chinese American. **PERSONAL:** Born Jan 1, 1924, Boston, MA; daughter of Mr & Mrs Wah Chin; married Edward James Guen, Aug 23, 1952; children: Leo, Michael, Timothy, Theresa Guen-Murray. **EDUCATION:** Regis College, BA, 1950; Boston College Graduate School of Social Work, MSW, 1952. **CAREER:** VAH, med social worker, 1952-53; Boston City Hospital, med social worker, 1954-55; Youville Hospital and Rehabilition Center, 1967-88, director of SS, 1970-88. **ORGANIZATIONS:** National Association of Social Workers, 1970-, Mass chapter, 1979-81, nominating committee, 1977-79; American Hospital Association; Society for Hospital Social Work Directors, 1970-89, board member, 1979-80; The Commonwealth of Mass, board of registration of social workers, 1982-87; New England Medical Center Hospital, board of trustees, 1973, board of governors, 1980-93. **HONORS/AWARDS:** National NASW Life Achievement Award, 1992; Mass Chapter Life Achievement Award, 1992; Boston YWCA, 120th Anniversary Award, 1986; Big Sister Association, Boston, award, 1987; Asian Community Development Corporation, Boston, Community Services Award, 1993; The National Conference of Christians & Jews Inc, Good Neighbor Award, 1987. **SPECIAL ACHIEVEMENTS:** Language proficiency, Chinese; annual newsletter of South Cove Manor Nursing Home, Boston, editor. **HOME ADDRESS:** 1499 Great Plain Ave, Needham, MA 02192, (617)449-1849.

GUILLERMO, TESSIE
Association administrator. Filipino American. **PERSONAL:** Born May 17, 1957. **CAREER:** Asian American Health Forum, executive director, currently. **BUSINESS ADDRESS:** Executive Director, Asian American Health Forum, 116 New Montgomery St, Ste 531, San Francisco, CA 94105, (415)541-0866.*

GUINGONA, MICHAEL PATRICK
Attorney, city councilman. Filipino American. **PERSONAL:** Born Mar 17, 1962, San Francisco, CA; son of Concepcion Limjap & Jose Guingona. **EDUCATION:** Skyline College, AA, 1983; University of California, Los Angeles, BA, 1985; University of San Francisco, JD, 1989. **CAREER:** Office of Public Defender SF, attorney, 1990-; City of Daly City, city councilmember, 1993-. **ORGANIZATIONS:** Asian American Recovery Service, board chair, 1991-; San Mateo County Delinquency Prevention & Juvenile Justice Commissioner, 1993-; Daly City Filipino Organizing Project, vice president, 1993; Filipino Bar Association of Northern California, vice president, 1992. **BUSINESS ADDRESS:** City Councilman, City of Daly City, 333 90th St, City Hall, Daly City, CA 94015, (415)991-8008.

GULATI, ADARSH KUMAR
Educator, researcher. Indo-American. **PERSONAL:** Born Jul 1, 1956, Karnal, India; son of Harbans and Kailash Gulati; married Nidhi K. Gulati, May 23, 1987; children: Priya, Akash. **EDUCATION:** Delhi University, India, BS, 1975; West Virginia University, PhD, 1979. **CAREER:** National Institutes of Health, research associate, 1979-84; Medical College of Georgia, associate professor, 1984-. **ORGANIZATIONS:** Hindu Temple Society, president, 1991-92. **HONORS/AWARDS:** Medical College of Georgia, outstanding young faculty, 1988; National Insitutes of Health, visiting fellowship, 1979-82. **SPECIAL ACHIEVEMENTS:** Over thirty publications in refereed journals, 1980-93; book chapters, Extracellular Matrix Structure and Function, 1985. **BUSINESS ADDRESS:** Assoc Professor, Dept of Cellular Biology and Anatomy, Medical College of Georgia, Augusta, GA 30912-2000, (706)721-2061.

GULOY, POMPEYO B., JR.
Association administrator. **CAREER:** United Asian Coalition, chairman, currently. **BUSINESS ADDRESS:** Chairman, United Asian Coalition, Washington State Reformatory, PO Box 777, Monroe, WA 98272.*

GULRAJANI, ROBERT B.
Certified public accountant. Indo-American. **PERSONAL:** Born Jul 24, 1953, Bombay, Maharashtra, India; son of Bhagwan K Gulrajani and Sheila B Gulrajani; divorced; children: Alyssa, Andria, Amber. **EDUCATION:** University of Washington, BA, 1975. **CAREER:** KRSP Radio, controller, 1976-79; Robison Hill & Co, staff accountant, 1979-80; Smith Olson & Hill, senior accountant, 1980-82; Gulrajani & Co, CPA, 1982-88; Berkman Burgher & Purdy, CPA, 1988-90; SCS Compute Inc, tax analyst, 1990-93. **ORGANIZATIONS:** American Institute of CPAs, 1982-; Utah Association of CPAs, 1982-; Washington Society of CPAs, 1989-; Rotary International, 1987-90; Toastmasters International, 1990-. **HONORS/AWARDS:** Rotary International, Group Study Exchange Fellowship to India, 1985; Toastmasters International, Competent Toastmaster, 1992. **SPECIAL ACHIEVEMENTS:** "Accounting in India," Journal of Accountancy, 1987. **BIOGRAPHICAL SOURCES:** Practical Accountant, "Vanilla Bob Puts Rap on Tax Season," p 9, April 1993. **HOME ADDRESS:** Box 6544, Bellevue, WA 98008, (206)957-0191.

GUNARATNE, DHAVALASRI SHELTON ABEYWICKREME
Educator. Sri Lankan American. **PERSONAL:** Born Jan 22, 1940, Weligama, Southern, Sri Lanka; son of Don William Abeywickreme Gunaratne (deceased) and Keliduwa Widanagamage Ariyawathie Gunaratne; married Yoke-Sim Gunaratne, Sep 11, 1976; children: Junius Asela Abeywickreme, Carmel Maya Abeywickreme. **EDUCATION:** University of Ceylon, BA, 1962; University of Oregon, MA, 1968; University of Minnesota, PhD, 1972. **CAREER:** Associated Newspapers of Ceylon Ltd, reporter, 1962-67; University of Minnesota, research assistant/fellow, 1969-71; Central Missouri State University, assistant professor, 1972-73; University of Florida, assistant professor, 1973; Universiti Sains Malaysia, lecturer, 1974-76; University of Central Queensland, lecturer I, 1976-85; Moorhead State University, associate professor, beginning 1985, professor, currently. **ORGANIZATIONS:** Moorhead Central Lions Club, president, 1992-93; Intl Communication Assn; Assn for Education in Journalism and Mass Communication; Society of Professional Journalists; World Assn for Christian Communication; North Dakota Professional Communicators; Assn for Asian Studies. **HONORS/AWARDS:** World Press Institute, permanent fellow, 1967; University of Minnesota, Macmillan Fellowship, 1971; Kappa Tau Alpha, honorary member, 1968. **SPECIAL ACHIEVEMENTS:** Publications: Modernization and Knowledge: A Study of Four Ceylonese Villages, AMIC, Singapore, 1976; The Taming of the Press in Sri Lanka, AEJMC, Lexington, KY, 1975; Global Communication and Dependency: Links Between NIEO and NWICO Demands and Withdrawals from UNESCO, Moorhead State University, MN, 1988. **HOME ADDRESS:** 3215 Village Green Drive, Moorhead, MN 56560, (218)233-0453. **BUSINESS ADDRESS:** Professor, Moorhead State University, 1104 Seventh Ave S, MacLean 267B, Moorhead, MN 56563, (218)236-4035.

GUO, DAVID
Journalist. Chinese American. **PERSONAL:** Born Jun 12, 1952, Philadelphia, PA; son of James and Lois; married Tamara Shenberger. **EDUCATION:** Temple University, BA, 1975; University of Pittsburgh, MBA, 1984. **CAREER:** Pittsburgh Post Gazette, reporter, editor, projects, 1974-. **HOME ADDRESS:** 6503 Lilac Street, Pittsburgh, PA 15217, (412)521-5213. **BUSINESS PHONE:** (412)263-1601.

GUO, HUA
Educator. Chinese American. **PERSONAL:** Born Aug 20, Chong Qin, Sichuan, People's Republic of China; married Qian-yun Zhang, Sep 10, 1985; children: Mindy. **EDUCATION:** Chengdu Institute of Electric Eng, China, BS, 1982; Sichuan University, China, MS, 1985; Sussex University, UK, PhD, 1988. **CAREER:** Northwestern University, research associate, 1988-90; University of Toledo, assistant professor, 1990-. **ORGANIZATIONS:** American Physical Society, 1990-; American Chemical Society, 1990-; Sigma Xi, 1990-. **SPECIAL ACHIEVEMENTS:** 25 published papers, 1988-93. **BUSINESS ADDRESS:** Professor, Chemistry Dept, University of Toledo, Toledo, OH 43606, (419)537-0485.

GUPTA, AJAY
Air quality engineer. Indo-American. **PERSONAL:** Born Jun 17, 1959, Agra, Uttar Pradesh, India; son of Devi Saran Gupta and Prem Lata Gupta. **EDUCATION:** Harcourt Butler Technological Institute, BTech, 1979; University of North Dakota, MS, 1986; Louisiana State University, PhD, 1991. **CAREER:** Bhabha Atomic Research Center, India, scientific officer, 1979-84; Jacobs Engineering, process engr, 1991; Woodward-Clyde Consultants, asst project engr, 1991-93; Coastal Refining and Marketing, sr air quality engineer, 1993-. **ORGANIZATIONS:** Air and Waste Management Assn, 1992-; AIChE, 1993; American Chemical Society, 1991. **SPECIAL ACHIEVEMENTS:** Registered professional engineer, Louisiana State Board, 1993; six publications in

renowned national and international journals, 1985-91. **HOME ADDRESS:** 6350 Meadow Vista Dr, #1521, Corpus Christi, TX 78414, (512)992-4241.

GUPTA, AJAY KUMAR
Educator. Indo-American. **PERSONAL:** Born Jul 13, 1961, Udaipur, Rajasthan, India; son of Jagdish Pd Gupta and Aruna Devi Gupta; married Geeta Gupta, Jan 23, 1988; children: Akash. **EDUCATION:** Birla Institute of Technology & Science, Pilani, India, BE (honors), 1982; University of Cincinnati, MS, math, 1984; Purdue University, MS, computer science, 1986, PhD, computer science, 1989. **CAREER:** National Thermal Power Corp, India, electronics engineer, 1981; SRG Data Center, Jaipur, India, system analyst, 1982; University of Cincinnati, teaching assistant, 1982-84; Purdue University, research assistant, 1984-89; Western Michigan University, assistant professor, 1989-. **ORGANIZATIONS:** Association of Computing Machinery, 1986-; Institute of Electrical & Electronics Engineers, 1989-. **HONORS/AWARDS:** National Science Foundation, undergraduate research lab, 1990; IBM, Formal Specifications for Ade Rendezvous, 1991, Simulators for Formal Specifications Languages, 1991; Western Michigan University, Engineering Design Institute, 1992. **SPECIAL ACHIEVEMENTS:** "Optimal 3-dimensional Layouts of Complete Binary Trees," IPL, 1987; "Load Balanced Tree Embeddings," Parallel Computing, 1992; "Compress Tree Machines," IPPS, 1992; "Multiple Network Embeddings into Hypercubes," JPDC, 1993; "Incomplete Hypercubes: Algorithms & Embeddings," TJS, 1993. **BUSINESS ADDRESS:** Assistant Professor, Computer Science Dept, Western Michigan University, 3090 Friedman Hall, Kalamazoo, MI 49008, (616)387-5645.

GUPTA, AMIT
Educator. Indo-American. **PERSONAL:** Born Aug 19, 1962, Delhi, India; son of Badri Prasad Gupta and Santosh Gupta; married P Kanchan Gupta, Jul 2, 1987; children: Nishi. **EDUCATION:** IIT, Kanpur, BTech, 1984; Indiana University, MBA, 1985, PhD, 1989. **CAREER:** University of Wisconsin-Madison, asst prof, 1989-. **ORGANIZATIONS:** ORSA, 1987; TIMS, 1987; DSI, 1987; ACM, 1992. **SPECIAL ACHIEVEMENTS:** Author: "A Multi-Echelon Queueing Model with Dynamic Priority," EJOR; "Steady-State Approximations of a Multi-Echelon Multi-Indentured Repairable-Item Inventory System with a Single Repair Facility," NRL, 1993; "Approximate Solution of a Single Base Multi-Indentured Repairable-Item Inventory System," JORS, 1993. **BUSINESS ADDRESS:** Professor, University of Wisconsin-Madison, School of Business, Grainger Hall, 975 University Ave, Madison, WI 53706-1323, (608)262-2714.

GUPTA, ANIL K.
Educator. Indo-American. **PERSONAL:** Born Feb 5, 1949, Ambala Cantt, Haryana, India; son of Des Raj Gupta and Pushpa Wati Jain; married Leah Savion, Oct 21, 1983 (divorced); children: Daniel. **EDUCATION:** University of London, U.K., BSc (honors), 1969; University of Pittsburgh, MA, 1973, PhD, 1977. **CAREER:** McGill University, assistant professor, 1975-79, associate professor, 1980-82; University of Illinois, Chicago, associate professor, 1982-89; Indiana University, professor, 1989-. **ORGANIZATIONS:** Journal of Philosophical Logic, editor, 1991-; Association for Symbolic Logic, executive committee, 1991-; Journal of Indian Council for Philosophical Research, editorial board, 1991-; American Philosophical Association, 1975-. **HONORS/AWARDS:** University of Pittsburgh, Andrew Mellon Fellowship, 1970-71, 1973-74; University of Illinois at Chicago Institute for Humanities Fellowship, 1985-87; National Endowment for the Humanities Fellowship for University Teachers, 1988-89. **SPECIAL ACHIEVEMENTS:** The Logic of Common Nouns, New Haven and London, Yale University Press, 1980; "Truth & Paradox," Journal of Philosophical Logic, 1982; "Remarks on Definitions and the Concept of Truth," Aristotelian Society, 1989; The Revision Theory of Truth, co-author with Nuel Belnap, MIT Press, 1993. **BUSINESS ADDRESS:** Professor, Philosophy Dept, Indiana University, Sycamore Hall 026, Bloomington, IN 47405-1101.

GUPTA, ANIL S.
Company executive. Indo-American. **PERSONAL:** Born Jan 28, 1961, Bombay, Maharashtra, India; son of Shankarlal Gupta and Premlata Gupta. **EDUCATION:** Bombay University, BCom, LLB. **CAREER:** Kris Gem International, Inc, president, currently. **HOME ADDRESS:** 43-23 Colden St, Apt 12D, Flushing, NY 11355, (718)460-8610.

GUPTA, ARJUN K.
Educator, consultant. Indo-American. **PERSONAL:** Born Jul 10, 1938, Purkazi, Uttar Pradesh, India; son of Amar Nath & Leela Gupta; married

Meera, Dec 25, 1967; children: Alka, Mita, Nisha. **EDUCATION:** Benaras Hindu University, BS (honors), 1957; Poona University, BSc (with honors), 1958, MSc, 1959; Purdue University, PhD, 1968. **CAREER:** Benaras Hindu University, assistant professor, 1962-63; University of Arizona, assistant professor, 1968-71; University of Michigan, assistant professor, 1971-76; Bowling Green State University, associate professor, 1976-78, professor, dept of math & statistics, chair, 1978-. **ORGANIZATIONS:** American Statistical Association, fellow; Institute of Statisticans, fellow; International Statistical Institute; Royal Statistical Society, fellow. **HONORS/AWARDS:** Olscamp Research Award, 1990. **SPECIAL ACHIEVEMENTS:** Author, Elliptically Contoured Models in Statistics; editor, Advances in Multivariate Statistical Analysis; editor, Multivariate Statistical Modeling and DATA Analysis; editor, The Analysis of Categorical Data Analysis. **BUSINESS ADDRESS:** Professor of Mathematics and Statistics, Bowling Green State University, Mathematical Sciences Building 416, Bowling Green, OH 43403, (419)372-2636.

GUPTA, ARUN PREMCHAND
Educator. Indo-American. **PERSONAL:** Born Oct 14, 1958, Poona, Maharashtra, India; son of Premchand Gupta and Shobha Gupta; married Anshu J Gupta, May 23, 1985; children: Ankit, Avni. **EDUCATION:** Indian Inst of Tech, India, B Tech, 1982; University of Texas, Arlington, M Eng, 1986, PhD, 1990. **CAREER:** University of Texas, Arlington, chem dept, grad teaching assistant, 1982-83, SLC, grad teaching assistant, 1983-86, CSE dept, grad teaching assistant, 1986-90; GSW College, CAS dept, assistant professor, 1990-. **ORGANIZATIONS:** Tau Beta Pi, 1987-; Upsilon Pi Epsilon, 1986-. **HONORS/AWARDS:** Darpa, research funding, 1992. **SPECIAL ACHIEVEMENTS:** Onion: A Development Method for Data-Dominant Systems, 1990; Incremental Software Delivery Using ADT & Requirement Clustering, 1992. **HOME ADDRESS:** 103-D Knollwood Drive, Americus, GA 31709, (912)928-9408.

GUPTA, ASHOK K.
Educator, educational administrator. Indo-American. **PERSONAL:** Born Nov 1, 1950, Merrut, Uttar Pradesh, India; son of Amba Shankar Gupta (deceased) and Shiv Kumari Gupta; married Sudha Agrawal, Jun 22, 1978; children: Aniruddha, Anurag. **EDUCATION:** Indian Institute of Technology, Kanpur, India, BTech, 1972; Xavier Labor Relations Institute, Jamshedpur, India, PGDBM, 1978; Syracuse University, MBA, 1982, PhD, 1984. **CAREER:** TELCO, Jamshedpur, India, engineer, 1973-78; NTPC, New Delhi, India, sr finance officer, 1978-80; Ohio University, professor, chairman of marketing dept, 1984-. **ORGANIZATIONS:** American Marketing Association, 1985-; Product Development Management Association, founder, president, Ohio chapter, 1986-. **HONORS/AWARDS:** Government of India, National Scholarship for Studies Abroad, 1980; Lehigh University, Research Award, 1989; Marketing Science Institute, Industrial Research Institute, honorable mention in research competition, 1990; Council for International Exchange of Scholars, Fulbright Scholar, 1993-94. **SPECIAL ACHIEVEMENTS:** Book: Managing R&D, Marketing Interface in Telecom Industry, 1991; published about 20 articles in scholarly journals on technology and innovation management. **HOME ADDRESS:** 129 Lamar Drive, Athens, OH 45701, (614)593-5137. **BUSINESS ADDRESS:** Professor and Chairman, Marketing Dept, Ohio University, College of Business Administration, Hanning Hall, Athens, OH 45701, (614)593-2030.

GUPTA, ASHWANI KUMAR
Educator. Indo-American. **PERSONAL:** Born Oct 23, 1948, Jagraon, Punjab, India; son of Ram Nath Gupta. **EDUCATION:** Panjab University, BSc, 1966; Southampton University, UK, MSc, 1970; Sheffield University, UK, PhD, 1973. **CAREER:** Intl Combustion Ltd, England, research engineer, 1967-71; Sheffield University, research assistant, 1971-73, research fellow, independent research worker, 1973-76; MIT, research staff, 1977-82; University of Maryland, professor, 1983-. **ORGANIZATIONS:** AIAA, propellants & combustion tech committee, chairman, 1988-90; terrestrial energy tech committee, chairman, 1991-; ASME, 1991-; Combustion Institute, 1973-. **HONORS/AWARDS:** Sheffield University, DSc, 1986; AIAA, fellow, 1992, Best Paper Awards & Energy Systems Award, 1987, 1989, 1990, 1991; Institute of Energy, fellow, 1987; ASME, Best Paper Award, 1991. **SPECIAL ACHIEVEMENTS:** Author of two books-Swirl Flows, 1984; Flowfield Modeling & Diagnostics, 1985; editor of nine books in Energy & Engineering Science series, 1984-; author/co-author of over 150 technical publications. **BUSINESS ADDRESS:** Professor, Dept of Mechanical Eng, University of Maryland, College Park, MD 20742, (301)405-5276.

GUPTA, BHAGWANDAS

Anesthesiologist. Indo-American. **PERSONAL:** Born Jan 13, 1946, Hyderabad, Andhra Pradesh, India; son of Sriram & Badamibai Gupta; married Bhagirathi Gupta, Jul 10, 1970; children: Rashmi, Rohit, Ruchi. **EDUCA-TION:** Osmania University, Gandhi Medical College, MBBS, 1970, Osmania Medical College, MD, 1976. **CAREER:** Osmania Medical College, post-graduate, internal medicine, 1972-75; New York University Medical Center, resident, anesthesiology, 1976-79, instructor, 1979-81; Ohio State University Hospital, assistant professor, associate professor, 1981-. **ORGANIZATIONS:** American Society of Anesthesiologists, 1976-; Ohio Society of Anesthesiologists, 1981-; Columbus Society of Anesthesiologists, 1981-; AAPI, central Ohio, president, 1991-93. **HONORS/AWARDS:** Ohio State University, Department of Anesthesiology, Teacher of the Year, 1990. **SPECIAL ACHIEVEMENTS:** Anesthesiological Considerations for Spine Surgery, forthcoming; "Induced Hypotension," chapter, 1980; extensive presentations on fiberoptic methods, difficult airway, neuroanesthesic, etc. **BUSINESS ADDRESS:** Associate Professor, Clinical, Ohio State University, College of Med, 410 West 10th Ave, Doan Hall, Rm N-429, Columbus, OH 43210, (614)293-8487.

GUPTA, BHUPENDER S.

Educator, researcher. Indo-American. **PERSONAL:** Born Mar 29, 1937, Delhi, India; son of Om Parkash Gupta and Lila Vati Gupta; married Vasudha G Gupta, Jan 31, 1967; children: Sumedha, Apurve, Anoopum. **EDUCA-TION:** Punjab University, BS, 1958; Manchester University, PhD, 1963. **CAREER:** Modi Textile Mills, India, supervisor, 1959-60; North Carolina State University, exchange scientist, 1963-66, asst/assoc professor, 1966-79, professor, 1979-, assistant head, 1983-. **ORGANIZATIONS:** Textile Institute, fellow, 1962-; Fiber Society, 1966-; American Assn of Textile Technology, faculty adviser, 1980-; American Chemical Society, 1980-90; Technical Assn of Pulp & Paper Ind, steering committee, 1989-. **HONORS/AWARDS:** The Textile Institute, Fellow, 1977; Society of Cosmetic Chemists, Best Paper, 1984; Fulbright Foundation, Fulbright Fellow, 1985. **SPECIAL ACHIEVE-MENTS:** Over 80 research papers in various areas of fiber and textile physical and mechanical properties, structural mechanics, and biomedical applications. **HOME ADDRESS:** 5005 Lakemont Drive, Raleigh, NC 27609, (919)782-2633. **BUSINESS ADDRESS:** Professor, College of Textiles, North Carolina State University, 2401 Research Drive, Room 3250, Raleigh, NC 27695, (919)515-6559.

GUPTA, BRIJ MOHANLAL

State government official. Indo-American. **PERSONAL:** Born Aug 25, 1932, Khanna, Punjab, India; son of Mukandilal and Devki; married Nirmal, Jun 5, 1957; children: Adarsh, Jayshree Aggarwal, Anand. **EDUCATION:** University of Punjab, BCom, 1953. **CAREER:** State of Tennessee, auditor, 1986-. **ORGANIZATIONS:** Association of Government Accountants, 1986-. **HOME ADDRESS:** 427 Belle Pinte Dr, Nashville, TN 37221-3464, (615)646-0220.

GUPTA, CHITRANJAN J.

Company executive. Indo-American. **PERSONAL:** Born Nov 2, 1941, Lahore, Punjab, India; son of J R Gupta (deceased) and Sheela D Gupta; married Kamlesh Gupta, Feb 8, 1968; children: Minoo, Anu. **EDUCATION:** Panjab Engineering College, India, BSME, 1963; Wayne State University, MSME, 1969. **CAREER:** Holcroft, sales manager, 1975-84; Atmosphere Furnace Co, sales engr, 1969-75, vice pres, marketing & technology, 1984-. **ORGANIZATIONS:** American Society of Metal, 1973-; American Vacuum Society, 1982-. **BUSINESS ADDRESS:** Vice President, Atmosphere Furnance Company, 49630 Pontiac Trail, PO Box 317, Wixom, MI 48393-0317, (810)624-8191.

GUPTA, DHARAM V.

Research scientist. Indo-American. **PERSONAL:** Born Sep 4, 1945, New Delhi, India; son of Hari Charan Das Gupta & Kala Vati Gupta; married Shobha Gupta, Feb 10, 1981; children: Mona, Tina, Neil. **EDUCATION:** Worcester Polytechnic Institute, PhD, 1975. **CAREER:** American Cyanamid Co, senior research engineer, 1974, group leader, technical director, 1993-. **ORGANIZATIONS:** American Institute of Chemical Engineers; American Management Association; American Catalysis Society. **HOME PHONE:** (203)625-0221. **BUSINESS ADDRESS:** Research Scientist, American Cyanamid Co, 1937 W Main St, No 275, Stamford, CT 06904-0060.

GUPTA, GIAN CHAND

Educator. Indo-American. **PERSONAL:** Born Oct 10, 1939, Delhi, India; son of Bhagat Ram and Shanti Gupta; married Hirdesh Bindu Gupta, Apr 18, 1972; children: Tarra, Suneal. **EDUCATION:** Panjab University, BS, 1959, B Teach, 1960; Vikaram University, India, MS, 1962; Roorkee University, India, PhD, 1966. **CAREER:** University of Maryland, Eastern Shore, asst prof, 1977-83, assoc prof, 1983-90, professor, 1990-. **ORGANIZATIONS:** American Chemical Society, 1972-; American Society of Agronomy, 1972-; National Environmental Health Assn, 1972-. **HONORS/AWARDS:** NSF/CSIR, Visiting Scientist to India Award, 1992. **SPECIAL ACHIEVEMENTS:** More than 55 research publications in scientific journals in the area of soil, water, & air pollution. **HOME ADDRESS:** Scotland Parkway, #27110, Salisbury, MD 21801, (410)742-8413. **BUSINESS ADDRESS:** Professor & Acting Chairman, DNS, University of Maryland, Eastern Shore, Backbone Road, Carver Hall #1101, Princess Anne, MD 21853, (410)651-6013.

GUPTA, JATINDER NATH DASS

Management educator. Indo-American. **PERSONAL:** Born Sep 27, 1942, Moga, Punjab, India; son of Babu Ram and Soshila Aggarwal Gupta; married Harsh Sahney, Oct 22, 1983. **EDUCATION:** University of Delhi, India, BS, mechanical engineering, 1964; Indian Institute Tech, India, MS, industrial engineering, & ops research, 1967; Texas Tech University, PhD, industrial engineering, 1969. **CAREER:** Swastika Engineering Works, India, apprentice mech engr, 1964; Natl Projects Construction Corp, New Delhi, asst executive engr, 1964-65; Texas Tech University, instr, res asst, 1967-69; University of Alabama, Huntsville, asst prof engineering, 1969-71; Alabama A&M University, associate prof business admin, 1971; Sangamon State University, asst prof admin, coordinator business admin, 1971-73; US Postal Service, Washington, statis systems requirements div, 1973-77, gen mgr info tech div, 1977-80; George Washington University, adjunct prof, 1974-84; Energy Info Admin, Washington, director applied scis div, 1980-81, ops res analyst, 1981-83, computer systems analyst, 1985; University of Baltimore, prof info & quantitative sciences, 1982-85; Ball State University, prof chmn, dept of mgmt, 1985-, prof info & communication sciences, 1986-, prof industry & technology, 1987-. **ORGANIZATIONS:** Sigma Xi; American Production & Inventory Count Soc. **HONORS/AWARDS:** Ball State University, Outstanding Research Award, 1988. **SPECIAL ACHIEVEMENTS:** University Twenty, Enschede, The Netherlands, visiting professor, 1990; University of Southampton, visiting research scholar, 1991, 1992, 1993; University of Lyon, France, visiting professor, 1993; Intl Journal Management & Systems, associate editor, 1984-; Computers and Ops Research, editorial adv bd, 1974-; Operational Research, fellow, 1984; co-author, textbook; contributed articles to prof jours. **BUSINESS ADDRESS:** Professor/Chairman, Dept of Management, Ball State University, Rm WB 205, Muncie, IN 47306.

GUPTA, JIWAN D.

Educator. Indo-American. **PERSONAL:** Born Feb 1, 1940, Ashti, Maharashtra, India; son of Shaligram and Janki Devi Gupta; married Meena Gupta, Dec 6, 1969; children: Geetika, Ruchika. **EDUCATION:** University of Waterloo, PhD, 1978. **CAREER:** University of Toledo, professor, 1981-, Creativity Center, director, currently. **ORGANIZATIONS:** Institute of Transportation Engineers; Transportation Research Board; ASCE; ASEE, annual conference, general chairman, 1992; OAS; India Association of Toledo, president, 1988; Hindu Temple of Toledo, chairman building committee, 1984-88. **SPECIAL ACHIEVEMENTS:** Author of numerous research papers. **BUSINESS ADDRESS:** Professor, Dept of Civil Engineering, Director, Creativity Center, University of Toledo, 2801 W Bancroft St, Toledo, OH 43606-3390, (419)537-2361.

GUPTA, KAMLA P.

Technology training company executive. Indo-American. **PERSONAL:** Born Oct 15, 1947, Bulandshahr, Uttar Pradesh, India; son of Kishan Lal Gupta and Prem Vati Gupta; married Sandhya, Dec 11, 1975; children: Vidooshi, Vikas. **EDUCATION:** Milwaukee School of Engineering, MS, eng mgt, 1982. **CAREER:** Bharat Heavy Electricals Ltd, India, supervisor, 1966-73; Allis Chalmers Corp, engr, 1974-80; Harley Davidson Motor Co, engr, 1980-82; Eaton Corp, project mgr, 1982-85; Admiral Tool & Mfg, mgr, plant mgr, 1985-89; Tru-Die Inc, vice pres, mfg, 1989-90; Continuous Improvement Technology, president, 1991-. **ORGANIZATIONS:** American Society for Quality Control, senior member, 1974-, Section 1212, chairman, 1988, education & training director, 1992; FMA International, 1989-. **HONORS/AWARDS:** American Society for Quality Control, Section 1212, Distinguished Service Award, 1990; Board of Examiners, Malcolm Baldrige National Quality Award, 1988. **SPE-**

CIAL ACHIEVEMENTS: Language proficiency: Russian, Hindi. BUSI-NESS ADDRESS: President, Continuous Improvement Technology, 113 McHenry Rd, Ste 211, Buffalo Grove, IL 60089, (708)634-6207.

GUPTA, KRISHAN L.
Educator. Indo-American. PERSONAL: Born May 21, 1946, Bhiwani, Haryana, India; son of Sat Narain Gupta (deceased) & Chameli Devi Gupta; married Veena Gupta, Dec 2, 1972; children: Shalini & Sheila. EDUCATION: Panjab University, India, MBBS, 1970; Royal College of Physicians, England, MRCP, 1976; American College of Physicians, FACP, 1992. CAREER: Herts and Essex General Hospital, England, resident, 1976-77; Basildon and Orsett Hospital, General Medicine, registar, 1977-78; Manor Hospital, registrar, 1978-79; The London Hospital, senior registrar, 1979-84; St George Hospital, consultant physician, 1984-85; Coler Memorial Hospital, consultant, 1985-89; Franklin Delano Roosevelt Veteran's Hospital, consultant, 1985-; Ruth Taylor Geriatric and Rehabilitation Institute, medical director, associate chief of medical services, currently; University Hospital, Westchester County Medical Center, attending physician, currently; New York Medical College, associate professor of medicine, 1985-91, pro of clinical medicine, currently. ORGANIZATIONS: American Geriatrics Society, 1986-; Gerontological Society of America, fellow, 1991-; American College of Physicians, fellow, 1992; New York Academy of Medicine, fellow, 1987-; VA Medical Center, consultant, 1985-; numerous others. SPECIAL ACHIEVEMENTS: Author/co-author/editor of 15 books/book chapters, published in several countries, including: "Age, Sexuality and Sexual Function in Men," 1989; "Managing Chronic Constipation," 1990; "Ease Fear, Build Staff in Nursing Homes," 1991; "Metabolic Profile of the Elderly Upon Entry to the Nursing Home," 1992. BUSINESS ADDRESS: Professor of Clinical Medicine, New York Medical College, Grassland Rd, Munger Pavilion, Valhalla, NY 10595-1600, (914)285-7729.

GUPTA, MADHU SUDAN
Company executive. Indo-American. PERSONAL: Born Jun 13, 1945, Lucknow, Uttar Pradesh, India; son of Manohar Lal Gupta and Premvati Gupta; married Manorama Gupta, May 29, 1985; children: Jay Mohan, Vineet Mohan. EDUCATION: Lucknow University, India, BS, 1963; Allahabad University, India, MS, 1966; Florida State University, MS, 1967; University of Michigan, MA, 1968, PhD, 1972. CAREER: Queen's University, Canada, assistant professor of elec eng, 1972-73; Massachusetts Institute of Technology, assistant professor of elec engineering, 1973-78; associate professor of elec engineering, 1978-79; University of Illinois at Chicago, associate professor of elec engineering, 1979-84; University of California, Santa Barbara, visiting professor, 1985-86; University of Illinois, professor of electrical engineering, 1984-87; Hughes Aircraft Co, senior staff engineer and program manager, 1987-. ORGANIZATIONS: Institute of Electrical and Electronics Engineers, fellow, 1989-; IEEE Microwave Theory and Techniques Society, Chicago Chapter, chairman, 1986-87, Boston Chapter, chairman, 1977-78. SPECIAL ACHIEVEMENTS: Editor, Electrical Noise: Fundamentals and Sources, IEEE Press, 1977; editor, Teaching Engineering: A Beginner's Guide, IEEE Press, 1986; editor, Noise in Circuits and Systems, IEEE Press, 1987; approximately 100 published papers in professional journals. BUSINESS ADDRESS: Senior Staff Engineer, Hughes Aircraft Co, 2000 E Imperial Highway, Mail Stop RE/ROI/B512, El Segundo, CA 90245, (310)334-7257.

GUPTA, MANJULA K.
Clinical immunochemist. Indo-American. PERSONAL: Born Aug 17, 1942, Sambhal, Uttar Pradesh, India; daughter of Jitendra Vir and Chandra Vati; married Satyendra, Jan 26, 1968; children: Seema, Neera. EDUCATION: Agra University, India, BS, 1959, MS, 1961, PhD, 1966. CAREER: Agra University, asst professor, 1965-68; Cleveland State University, assistant clinical professor, 1977-91, adjunct clinical professor, 1992-; Cleveland Clinic Foundation, Immunopathology Dept, associate staff, 1974-75, Clinical Pathology Dept, staff member, 1975-, Endocrinology Dept, secondary appt, 1985-. ORGANIZATIONS: American Assn of Immunologists; Endocrine Society; American Thyroid Assn, membership committee; American Assn for Cancer Research; AAAS; American Society of Clinical Pathologists; American Society for Clinical Chemistry; National Academy of Clinical Biochemistry. SPECIAL ACHIEVEMENTS: Areas of study: hormone and breast cancer research, 1977-, thyroid autoimmunity, 1980-, myelin basic protein in multiple sclerosis, 1984-88. BUSINESS ADDRESS: Staff Member, Dept of Clinical Pathology, Cleveland Clinic Foundation, 9500 Euclid Ave, Laboratory Medicine L12, Cleveland, OH 44195.

GUPTA, NAIM C.
Educator (retired). Indo-American. PERSONAL: Born Aug 25, 1933, Nagina, Haryana, India; married Shailla Gupta, Jul 14, 1959; children: Himanee, Nisha Gupta-Verwiebe, Anju. EDUCATION: Agra University, MSc, 1955; Panjab University, BEd, 1956; Delhi University, MEd, 1961; University of Iowa, PhD, 1965. CAREER: KM Training College, lecturer, 1957-61; Educational Research Council of Greater Cleveland, research associate, 1965-66; Ball State University, assistant professor, 1966-71, associate professor, 1971-77, professor, 1977-93. ORGANIZATIONS: American Educational Research Association, 1965-91; Midwestern Educational Research Association, 1985-92; Indian Academy of Applied Psychology, life member; Kiwanis Club of Muncie, 1992-. SPECIAL ACHIEVEMENTS: Author: "Comparison of Anxiety among American and Indian College Students," Journal of Indian Academy of Applied Psychology, vol 16, pp18-20, 1990; "Cross-Cultural Comparison of Self-Concept among American and Indian College Students," DEI Research Journal, vol 7, pp5-7, 1989. HOME ADDRESS: 3901 N Redding Rd, Muncie, IN 47304, (317)289-3747.

GUPTA, OM PRAKASH
Educator, periodontist. Indo-American. PERSONAL: Born Feb 8, 1926, Rupar, Punjab, India; son of Harish Chandra & Poornima Devi Gupta; married Yamuna Gupta, Dec 17, 1957; children: Pradee K, Praveen, Sareeta Viadero. EDUCATION: Bombay University, India, BDS, 1950; Harvard University, School of Public Health, MS, 1954, DrPH, 1956; New York University, College of Dentistry, MSD, 1958; University of Pittsburgh, School of Dental Medicine, DMD, 1967. CAREER: Harvard University School of Dental Medicine, post doctoral reseach fellow, 1953-56; New York University, research associate, 1956-58; University of Illinois, assistant professor, 1958-60; Government Dental College, India, director, dean, 1960-63; University of Pittsburgh, professor and head, 1963-73, professor, 1965-73; Howard University, professor and chairman, 1973-. ORGANIZATIONS: International Association for Dental Research, life member, 1955-; American Association of Dental Research, life member; American Public Health Association, 1963-73; American Academy of Periodontology, life member, 1958-; Federation International Dentaire, 1968-73; American Dental Association, 1967-; Indian Dental Association, 1960-63. HONORS/AWARDS: International College of Dentists, fellow, 1958; American College of Dentists, fellow, 1973; American Association for the Advancement of Science, fellow, 1959. SPECIAL ACHIEVEMENTS: Author, consultant, researcher on periodontal disease and methods. HOME PHONE: (301)299-6859. BUSINESS ADDRESS: Professor, Chairman, Dept of Periodontics, Howard University, College of Dentistry, 600 W St NW, Russell Dixon Bldg, Washington, DC 20059, (202)806-0424.

GUPTA, OMPRAKASH K.
Educator. Indo-American. PERSONAL: Born Dec 1, 1950, Ahmedabad, Gujarat, India; son of Kalyanprasad and Triveni; married Savitri, May 22, 1973; children: Kavita, Kriti, Kovid. EDUCATION: Gujarat University, BS, 1971, MS, 1973; Purdue University, MS, 1975, PhD, 1980. CAREER: Indian Institute of Management, assistant professor, 1982-85, associate professor, 1986-89; CMC Ltd, education & training manager, 1985-86; Ball State University, associate professor, 1989-90; Indiana University, associate professor, 1990-. ORGANIZATIONS: The Institute of Management Science; Operations Research Society of America; Operational Research Society of India; Production & Operations Management Society; International Society of Inventory Research. SPECIAL ACHIEVEMENTS: Editorial board, The International Journal of Management & Systems; published numerous articles in national & international journals; editor, conference proceedings; presented papers in many national and international meetings. BUSINESS ADDRESS: Associate Professor, Division of Business and Economics, Indiana University, Northwest, 3400 Broadway, Gary, IN 46408-1197, (219)980-6901.

GUPTA, PARDEEP K.
Educator. Indo-American. PERSONAL: Born Nov 22, 1958, Ludhiana, Punjab, India; son of Om Parkash & Sheela Gupta; married Rekha Gupta, Jan 17, 1988. EDUCATION: Panjab University, BPharm, 1979, MPharm, 1981; Philadelphia College of Pharmacy & Science, MS, 1984; University of Wisconsin, PhD, 1990. CAREER: Philadelphia College of Pharmacy & Science, assistant professor, 1990-. ORGANIZATIONS: American Association of Pharmaceutical Scientists, 1986-; Sigma Xi; Rho Chi; ACS; AAAS. HONORS/AWARDS: Commission of India, Panjab University, grants, Senior Research Fellowship, 1980-82. SPECIAL ACHIEVEMENTS: 7 publications in refereed journals, 1984-; 3 chapters in books, 1987-. BIOGRAPHICAL

SOURCES: Treatise on Controlled Drug Delivery, 1991; Biradhesive Drug Delivery Systems, 1989. **HOME ADDRESS:** 240 Oxford Road, West Chester, PA 19380, (215)344-0994. **BUSINESS ADDRESS:** Assistant Professor, Philadelphia College of Pharmacy & Science, 600 South 43rd Street, McNeil 103, Philadelphia, PA 19104, (215)895-1141.

GUPTA, PARVEEN P.
Educator. Indo-American. **PERSONAL:** Born Apr 26, 1957, New Delhi, India; son of Netar Prakash & Bimla Gupta; married Parveen Taruna Gupta, Jul 27, 1980; children: Jatin Prakash, Mukul Mohan. **EDUCATION:** University of Delhi, India, BCom (with honors), 1976, LLB, 1980; University of Connecticut, MBA, 1983; Pennsylvania State University, PhD, 1987. **CAREER:** Jay Engineering Works Ltd, financial accountant, 1977-80; Dalmia Diary Industries, senior administrative officer, 1980; University of Connecticut, research assistant, 1980-83; Pennsylvania State University, teaching assistant, 1984-86; Lehigh University, assistant professor, 1987-. **ORGANIZATIONS:** American Accounting Association; Academy of International Business; The Institute of Management Studies; The Institute of Internal Auditors; Academy of Management; Beta Alpha Psi. **HONORS/AWARDS:** Grants: Lehigh University, Department of Accounting Summer Research Grant, 1990; Penn State University, Center for Interdisciplinary Research, 1991; Institute of Internal Auditors Research Foundation, Monograph Grant, 1991, numerous others; AAA's Behavioral Accounting Section, Best Dissertation Award, nominatee, 1987; AAA's Non-Profit and Governmental Accounting Section, Best Dissertation Award, nominatee, 1987; Beta Gamma Sigma, 1987; Association of Chartered Accountants, Outstanding Paper Award, 1990. **SPECIAL ACHIEVEMENTS:** "Spiraling Upward," Internal Auditor, June 1991; "Towards the Development of Accounting Heterogeneity Measures: Potential Uses in International Business Research," Accounting Enquiries: A Research Journal, August 1991; "International Reciprocity," Journal of Accountancy, January 1992; "The Changing Roles of the Internal Auditor," Managerial Auditing Journal, January 1992; "Implementing Activity Based Costing," Internal Auditor, December 1992; "Managing Internal Audit Teams," Managerial Auditing Journal, January 1993; numerous others. **HOME ADDRESS:** 900 Mickley Rd, W1-3, Whitehall, PA 18052, (215)821-7910. **BUSINESS ADDRESS:** Professor of Accounting, Lehigh University, 621 Taylor St, Rauch Business Center, #37, Bethlehem, PA 18015, (215)758-3443.

GUPTA, PRADEEP KUMAR
Scientist. Indo-American. **PERSONAL:** Born Jul 9, 1944, Bandikui, Rajasthan, India; son of Mr. and Mrs. Maya Ram Gupta; married Shelly Gupta, Nov 21, 1977; children: Neha, Priya. **EDUCATION:** Birla Institute of Science & Technology, BE (with honors), 1966; Massacusetts Institute of Technology, MS, 1968, mechanical engineer, 1969, DSc, 1970. **CAREER:** Massachusetts Institute of Technology, research assistant, 1966-70; Mechanical Technology Inc, senior scientist, 1971-82; PKG Inc, president, 1983-. **ORGANIZATIONS:** American Society of Mechanical Engineers, 1967-; Society of Tribologists and Lubrication Engineers, 1985-; Sigma Xi, 1968-. **HONORS/AWARDS:** Birla International, Institute Gold Medal, 1966; American Society of Mechanical Engineers, Burt L. Newkirk Award, 1978; National Academy of Sciences, Research Fellowship, 1982. **SPECIAL ACHIEVEMENTS:** Advanced Dynamics of Rolling Elements, book, Springer-Verlag; Adore (Rolling Bearing Dynamics Computer Program), world wide distribution. **BUSINESS ADDRESS:** President, Chief Scientist, PKG Inc, 117 Southbury Rd, Clifton Park, NY 12065-7714, (518)383-1167.

GUPTA, RAJ KUMAR
US government civil rights attorney. Indo-American. **PERSONAL:** Born Feb 13, 1943, Delhi, India; son of Gopal Narain Gupta and Mem Vati Gupta; married Madeline Gupta, Jun 7, 1970; children: Sanjay, Anjeli. **EDUCATION:** Delhi University, BCom, 1962, LLB, 1964, LLM, 1966; Columbia University, MCL, 1967; New York University, LLM, 1968. **CAREER:** NYU Medical Center, attorney, managed NIMH-funded study in law and psychiatry, 1969-71; Prentice-Hall Inc, editor, tax services, 1971-72; University of Delhi, law lecturer, 1972-73; Dalmia Cement (Bharat) Ltd, general counsel, 1973; Chadbourne, Park, Whiteside & Wolff, attorney, 1974-76; US EEOC, Office of General Counsel, appellate attorney, 1976-79, Office of Policy Implementation, supervisory attorney, 1979-82, Office of Policy Implementation, acting director of Research and Hearings Group, 1981-82, EEOC Commissioner William A Webb, executive assistant-attorney advisor, 1982-86, Office of Review and Appeals, special assistant to director, 1986, EEOC Vice Chairman R Gaull Silberman, special assistant, 1986-87, EEOC General Counsel Charles A Shanor, special assistant, 1987, EEOC Commissioner Joy Cherian, executive

assistant-senior attorney advisor, 1987-93; US Senate Office of Fair Employment Practices, on detail from EEOC as legal advisor, 1993-. **ORGANIZATIONS:** New Mark Commons Homes Association Inc, board of directors, 1987-90, architectural control committee, 1989-90; Trust for Education to Promote Progress, board of trustees, 1972-84, secretary, 1972-74; Delhi University Law Review, 1972-73; Bharat Darshan, board of editors, 1969-70; Radio Bharat Darshan, founding director, 1968-69; India Club of New York University, founding member & secretary, 1968-69; The International House, New York City, chairman, 1968, president's advisory council, 1967-68, steering committee, 1968. **HONORS/AWARDS:** Federal Asian Pacific American Council, Award for Outstanding EEO Committment, 1991; Bellcore Asian Americans for Affirmative Action, Special Dedication Award, 1992; AT&T Asian Americans for Affirmative Action, Distinguished Speaker Award, 1992; US National Archives, US EEOC Oral History Project, 1993. **SPECIAL ACHIEVEMENTS:** Directly supervised EEOC Guidelines on National Origin Discrimination, 45 Fed Reg 85632, 1980; co-author: Federal Equal Opportunity 1992 Desk Book, Federal Equal Opportunity 1993 Desk Book; author of numerous law journal articles on EEO and other subjects; only civil rights attorney in EEOC to serve as a legal advisor to four presidential appointees (2 commissioners, vice chair, & general counsel) spanning over a decade. **BIOGRAPHICAL SOURCES:** "Raj Gupta-India's Proud Scholar," EEOC Mission, Vol 10, No 2, 1982 pg 22. **BUSINESS ADDRESS:** Advisor, Office of Senate Fair Employment Practices, US Senate, 103 Senate Hart Office Bldg, Washington, DC 20510, (202)224-6666.

GUPTA, RAJAT KUMAR
Director, consultant. Indo-American. **PERSONAL:** Born Dec 2, 1948, New Dehli, India; son of Ashwini Kumar Gupta & Pran Kumari Mehra; married Anita Mattoo Gupta, Aug 5, 1973; children: Geetanjali, Megha, Aditi, Deepali. **EDUCATION:** India Institute of Technology, BTech, 1971; Harvard, MBA, 1973. **CAREER:** McKinsey & Company Inc, 1973-. **ORGANIZATIONS:** Kellogg School of Management, advisory board, 1993. **BUSINESS ADDRESS:** Managing Director, McKinsey & Company, Inc, One First National Plaza, Ste 2900, Chicago, IL 60603, (312)551-3500.

GUPTA, RAJESHWAR KUMAR
Educator. Indo-American. **PERSONAL:** Born Sep 19, 1931, Lahore, Punjab, India; son of Lakshmi Chand Gupta and Bhagirathi Devi Gupta; married Nirmal, Nov 23, 1957; children: Lily Agrawal, Rakesh Kamal. **EDUCATION:** Dyal Singh College, FSc, 1948; City & Guilds of London Institute, final diploma, 1950; Delhi Polytechnic, BSE, 1951; University of Michigan, MSE, 1952, PhD, 1956. **CAREER:** University of Michigan, research associate, teaching assistant, 1952-56; Caltex Oil Refining, India, process engineer, 1956-57; DCM Ltd, India, senior manager, chief designer, 1957-86; GMI Engineering & Management Institute, adjunct faculty, lecturer, 1986-87; University of Michigan, Flint, associate professor, director co-op in engineering science, 1987-. **ORGANIZATIONS:** Indian Institute of Chemical Engineers, 1960-, chairman, 1980-85; American Institute of Chemical Engineers, 1985-; ASM International, 1988-; American Society for Engineering Education, 1988-; Engineering Society of Detroit, co chair, 1991, 1988-; Society of Manufacturing Engineers, 1989-; Society of Automobile Engineers, 1991-; Chemical Society, UK, heat transfer activity, 1988-, fellow, 1978-80. **HONORS/AWARDS:** University of Michigan, Flint, Faculty Development Award, 1988, 1989, 1990, 1991; ASM International, ASM-IIM Visiting Lecturer, 1989; Japan Electrochemical Society, Plenary Lecturer at Annual Meet, 1980; Chemicals, Pharmaceuticals & Cosmetics Export Promotion Council, Delegation Leader to Africa, 1979; India Chemical Manufacturer's Association, Chlorine Technology Development, 1981. **SPECIAL ACHIEVEMENTS:** Author: Materials selection for Corrosion Control, 1993. **HOME ADDRESS:** 5370 Tulip Tree Ct, Flint, MI 48532, (313)733-7841.

GUPTA, RAJIV
Educator. Indo-American. **PERSONAL:** Born Feb 23, 1961, Patiala, Punjab, India; son of Prem Sagar and Raj Rani. **EDUCATION:** Indian Institute of Technology, New Delhi, India, BTech, electrical engineering, 1982; University of Pittsburgh, MS, computer science, 1984, PhD, computer science, 1987. **CAREER:** Philips Laboratories, senior member, research staff, 1987-90; University of Pittsburgh, assistant professor of computer science, 1990-. **ORGANIZATIONS:** Association of Computing Machinery; Special Interest Group on Programming Languages; Special Interest Group on Computer Architecture. **HONORS/AWARDS:** National Science Foundation, Presidential Young Investigator, 1991; Philips Laboratories, Making A Difference Award, 1988; University of Pittsburgh, Andrew Mellon Predoctoral Fellowship, 1985. **SPE-**

CIAL ACHIEVEMENTS: Published over 65 technical papers in the area of computer science; associate editor, Journal of Parallel Computing. HOME ADDRESS: 1206 Macon Avenue, Pittsburgh, PA 15218, (412)243-2478. BUSINESS ADDRESS: Assistant Professor, University of Pittsburgh, University Drive, 211 Mineral Industries Building, Pittsburgh, PA 15260, (412)624-8421.

GUPTA, RAJIV KUMAR
Computer consultant. Indo-American. PERSONAL: Born Oct 9, 1964, Bulandshahr, Uttar Pradesh, India; son of Anand Swaroop Gupta and Sheela Gupta. EDUCATION: University of Roorkee, India, BEE, 1985, MS, computer science, 1987. CAREER: TCS, India, computer consultant, 1987-90; AGS Information Services, computer consultant, 1990-. HOME ADDRESS: 6252 Twin Oaks Dr #2245, Colorado Springs, CO 80918, (719)548-9576.

GUPTA, RAKESH KUMAR
Fiber company executive. Indo-American. PERSONAL: Born Jan 15, 1947, Delhi, India; son of Desh Raj Gupta and Chandravati Devi Gupta; married Rama Rani Gupta, Nov 17, 1970; children: Rohit, Ruchi. EDUCATION: Indian Institute of Technology, Delhi, B Tech, 1968; NC State University, MS, 1970, PhD, 1974. CAREER: American Cyanamid Co, scientist, 1970-71; Hercules Incorporated, director, functional fibers, 1974-. ORGANIZATIONS: The Fiber Society. BUSINESS ADDRESS: Director, Functional Fibers, Hercules Inc, 7101 Alcovy Road, Covington, GA 30209, (404)786-7011.

GUPTA, RAM BIHARI
Laboratory administrator. Indo-American. PERSONAL: Born Sep 25, 1954, Dholpur, Rajasthan, India; son of Shiv Prasad Gupta and Vimla Devi Gupta; divorced; children: Anita, Vinita, Sunita, Divya. EDUCATION: MD, 1984. CAREER: InterScience Diagnostic Laboratories Inc, administrative director, currently. HOME ADDRESS: 61-15 98th St, #10G, Rego Park, NY 11374, (718)271-2886.

GUPTA, RAMESH K.
Engineering executive, educator. Indo-American. PERSONAL: Born Nov 13, 1953, Dhuri, Punjab, India; son of Hans R Gupta and Parsini D Gupta; married Nitu Gupta, Jan 10, 1982; children: Raman, Nikhil. EDUCATION: Punjab University, India, BSc, engineering, 1974; University of Alberta, MSc, 1976, PhD, 1980; University of Pennsylvania, MBA, 1989. CAREER: Comsat Labs, technical staff, 1980-85, staff scientist, 1985-87, associate manager, 1987-89, senior scientist, 1989-90; adjunct associate professor, University of Maryland, University College, 1991-92; Comsat Corporation, manager, 1990-. ORGANIZATIONS: Institute of Electrical & Electronics Engineers, student member, 1978-80, member, 1980-86, senior member, 1986-; Comsat Technical Review, editorial board, 1989-93. HONORS/AWARDS: Dav College, Punjab University, India, Roll of Honor, 1970; Punjab University, Merit Scholarships, 1970-74; Alberta Govt Telephones, fellowship, 1976-79; University of Alberta, fellowship, 1979-80; International Conf on Digital Satellite Comm, Best Paper Award, 1992. SPECIAL ACHIEVEMENTS: Granted two patents; Microwave Digitally Controlled Solid-State Alternators, 1990; Multiple Spot Beam Systems for Satellite Communications, 1989; published more than 50 articles in leading journals and conferences; BUSINESS ADDRESS: Manager, Comsat Laboratories, 22300 Comsat Dr, Clarksburg, MD 20871, (301)428-4141.

GUPTA, RATANLAL N.
Educator. Indo-American. PERSONAL: Born Oct 10, 1931, Gulabganj, Madhya Pradesh, India; divorced; children: Nira Gupta-Casae, Nilima Chitgopekar, Reshamon, Scarborough Asima, Ashish. EDUCATION: University of Bombay, BA (honors), 1954, MA, ad politics; Howard University, MA, govt, PhD, 1964. CAREER: Fort Valley State College, associate professor, currently. ORGANIZATIONS: Georgia Political Science Association, executive committee, 1967-68; India Cultural Association of Middle Georgia, secretary. HONORS/AWARDS: Fort Valley State College, Most Congenial Professor of the Year, 1973. SPECIAL ACHIEVEMENTS: UK Krishna Menon: An Appraisal of the Man & His Rhetoric, 1973. HOME PHONE: (912)987-0596. BUSINESS ADDRESS: Professor, Fort Valley State College, College St, Fort Valley, GA 31030, (912)825-6230.

GUPTA, RON SINGH
Engineering executive. Indo-American. PERSONAL: Born Apr 1, 1949, Gohana, Haryana, India; son of Ram Narain Gupta and Kapoori Devi Gupta;

married Chitra Gupta, Jun 10, 1975; children: Avni, Neil. EDUCATION: Indian Institute of Technology, Kharagpur, India, BArch, 1971; Carnegie-Mellon University, MArch program, 1971-73. CAREER: University of Miami, visiting professor, 1975-78; Connell Metcalf & Eddy, project manager, 1973-80; Wolfberg Alvarez & Associates, associate, 1980-82; Gupta Associates Inc, president, 1982-; GAI, chief engineer, 1991-. ORGANIZATIONS: Western Berks Refuse Authority, Berks County, PA, board member of municipal authority, 1993-; Wyomissing Area School District, PA, ad-hoc committee, 1992-; American Institute of Architects, 1980-; registered architect: Florida, Pennsylvania, New York; licensed real estate broker: Florida, Pennsylvania. HONORS/AWARDS: American Institute of Architecture, Reynolds Alum Prize for Arch, 1972, 1973, Biscayne West Housing Competition, 1976; Indian Institute of Technology, Silver Medal for First Rank, 1971. SPECIAL ACHIEVEMENTS: Chief planner, Downtown Government Center, Miami, FL, 1975; chief designer, numerous projects for the department of defense, Washington, DC. HOME ADDRESS: 7 Wickford Ct, Wyomissing, PA 19610.

GUPTA, SAMIR
Entrepreneur. Indo-American. PERSONAL: Born Dec 24, 1965, Digboi, Assam, India; son of Kirti and Reeta Gupta. EDUCATION: Texas Tech; University of Houston Baptist; University of Houston, BSc, 1987; University of Texas Medical Center. CAREER: Harris County, TX, paramedic, administrator; Car Jacker Inc, president, chief exec officer, currently. SPECIAL ACHIEVEMENTS: Inventor: anti-carjacking device, 1991. BIOGRAPHICAL SOURCES: Dallas Morning News, Apr 18, 1993. HOME PHONE: (713)464-6848. BUSINESS ADDRESS: President/CEO, Car Jacker, Inc, 11811 North Freeway, 5th Fl, #518, Houston, TX 77060, (713)227-5225.

GUPTA, SANJAY
Educator. Indo-American. PERSONAL: Born Feb 27, 1957, Agra, Uttar Pradesh, India; son of S D Gupta and Malti R Gupta; married Kiran Gupta; children: Priyanka, Neha. EDUCATION: Bombay University, India, BCom, 1977; Calcutta University, India, LLB, 1981; Bowling Green State University, MAcc, 1982; Michigan State University, PhD, 1990. CAREER: Singh & Verma, junior, 1978-80; University of Toledo, adjunct faculty instructor, 1982-84; Andray & Associates CPAs, consultant, 1982-84; Michigan State University, grad asst, 1984-87; Arizona State University, asst professor, 1990-. ORGANIZATIONS: American Accounting Association, 1985-; American Taxation Association, 1985-; National Tax Association, 1985-; professional certifications: Ohio Society of CPAs, certified public accountant, 1984-; Institute of Company Secretaries of India, associate member, 1981-. HONORS/AWARDS: Beta Gamma Sigma; Price Waterhouse & Co, CPAs, Fellowship in Taxation, 1993; Ernst & Young, CPAs, Tax Research Grant, 1991; Arizona State University, Faculty Grant-In-Aid Awards, 1990, 1992, 1993; American Taxation Association, Student Tax Manuscript Award, 1989; Michigan State University, Outstanding Doctoral Instructor, 1987-88. SPECIAL ACHIEVEMENTS: "Determinants of Tax Preparer Usage," National Tax Journal, Dec 1993; "Corporate Average Effective Tax Rates after Tax Reform Act of 1986," Tax Notes, May 4, 1992; "New Evidence on Secondary Evasion," Journal of American Taxation Association, Spring 1993; ranked #1 Eastern Region of Final Exam of Institute of Company Secretaries of India, awarded several gold medals and awards, 1980. BUSINESS ADDRESS: Professor, Arizona State University, School of Accountancy, Tempe, AZ 85287-3606, (602)965-6618.

GUPTA, SANJEEV
Physician, scientist, educator. Indo-American. PERSONAL: Born Apr 23, 1954, Jaipur, Rajasthan, India; son of Krishan Dayal Gupta and Kusum Lata Gupta; married Neena M Gupta, Jan 26, 1984; children: Sanchit, Sonika. EDUCATION: University of Rajasthan, Sardar Patel Medical College, MBBS, 1976; Postgraduate Institute of Medical Education & Research, Chandigarh, India, MD, 1980; Royal Physicians of London, MRCP, UK, 1982. CAREER: Hammersmith Hospital, UK, registrar, 1983-85; University of Southern California, instructor, 1985-87; Albert Einstein College of Medicine, senior fellow, 1987-89, assistant professor of medicine, 1989-. ORGANIZATIONS: Association of Physicians of India, 1981-; British Society of Gastroenterology, 1990-; American Association for Studies of Liver Diseases, 1989-; American Federation of Clinical Research, 1991-; American Gastroenterological Association, 1986-. HONORS/AWARDS: University of Rajasthan, Sawai Mansingh Gold Medal, 1977; Pfizer Incorporated, Pfizer Gold Medal, 1980; Postgraduate Institute of Medical Education & Research, First Order of Merit Medal, 1980; American Liver Foundation, Fellowship Award,

1988; NIH, Clinical Investigator Award, 1989. **SPECIAL ACHIEVE-MENTS:** Approx 150 scientific publications, 1977-. **BUSINESS ADDRESS:** Assistant Professor of Medicine, Albert Einstein College of Medicine, 1300 Morris Park Ave, Ullman 625, Bronx, NY 10461, (718)430-2098.

GUPTA, SANTOSH
Researcher. Indo-American. **PERSONAL:** Born Aug 12, 1940, Karnal, India; daughter of Rameshwar Goyal; married Virendra K Gupta, Dec 10, 1961; children: Mayank, Varun. **EDUCATION:** University of Rajasthan, India, BSc, 1960, MSc, 1962; University of Delhi, India, PhD, 1980. **CAREER:** University of Delhi, research assistant, research associate, 1975-80, PL 480 Project, honorary research associate, 1965-75; American Entomological Institute, research associate, 1980-90; University of Florida, adjunct assistant professor of entomology, 1982-. **ORGANIZATIONS:** Association for the Study of Oriental Insects, 1967-92; Florida Entomological Society, 1982-91. **SPECIAL ACHIEVEMENTS:** Research on the taxonomy of Oriental insects of the family Ichneumonidae; published a monograph on the taxonomy of Gabuniini, 1983; author, book on the bibliography of the Ichneumonidae, 1991; author of 10 research papers on the Oriental and American Ichneumonidae, 1978-93. **BUSINESS ADDRESS:** Adjunct Assistant Professor, Dept of Entomology, University of Florida, Bldg 970, Hull Rd, Gainesville, FL 32611-0620, (904)391-1901.

GUPTA, SAROJ LATA
Librarian. Indo-American. **PERSONAL:** Born Apr 6, 1948, Rajouri, Jammu and Kashmir, India; daughter of Behari Lal Gupta and Shakuntala Devi; married Surendra K Gupta, Jan 16, 1971; children: Salil, Shilpi. **EDUCATION:** BEd, BPolSc; MPolSc; 1970; MLS, 1988. **CAREER:** Bryant Library, reference librarian, 1988-. **ORGANIZATIONS:** Nassau County Library Assn; Assn of Indians in America; Long Island Assn of Indians. **HOME ADDRESS:** 1 Hemlock Lane, Roslyn Heights, NY 11577.

GUPTA, SUNIL
Educator. Indo-American. **PERSONAL:** Born Sep 21, 1958, Jind, Haryana, India; son of Sohan Lal Gupta & Kamlesh Gupta; married Kamal Gupta, Feb 11, 1983; children: Tarun M. **EDUCATION:** Indian Institute of Technology, BTech, 1979; Indian Institute of Management, PGDM, 1981; Columbia University, PhD, 1986. **CAREER:** HMM Ltd, product executive, 1981-83; University of California, Los Angeles, assistant professor, 1986-90; Columbia University, associate professor, 1990-. **ORGANIZATIONS:** Institute of Management Science, 1984-; Marketing Modelers Group, steering committee, 1991-; Journal of Marketing Research, editorial board, 1992-; Marketing Letters, editorial board, 1989-. **HONORS/AWARDS:** Marketing Science Institute, Winner of Doctoral Proposal Award, 1985; American Marketing Association, Doctoral Consortium Fellow, 1985; Education Board, India, National Certificate of Merit, 1974; National Science Talent Institute, India, Scholar, 1973; William F O'Dell Award, for outstanding research article, 1993. **SPECIAL ACHIEVEMENTS:** Several publications in scholarly journals including Marketing Science, Journal of Marketing Research, Applied Psychological Measurement, Journal of Consumer Research, 1987-92; television interviews with CNN & NTV, German TV, 1992-93; consulting & seminars at several US companies, 1990-92; invited speaker at several universities & conferences in US & Europe, 1986-92. **BUSINESS ADDRESS:** Associate Professor, Graduate School of Business, Columbia University, 116th St & Broadway, Rm 508, New York, NY 10027-6940, (212)854-3467.

GUPTA, SURENDRA K.
Chemical company executive. Indo-American. **PERSONAL:** Born Apr 5, 1938, Delhi, India; son of Bishan Chand Gupta and Devki Gupta; married Karen P Gupta, Oct 12, 1968; children: Jay, Amanda. **EDUCATION:** Delhi University, India, BSc (w/honors), 1959, MSc, 1961; IIT, Bombay, India, MTech, 1963; Wayne State University, PhD, 1968. **CAREER:** Western Michigan University, research associate, 1968-73; New England Nuclear, group leader, 1974-81; Pathfinder Labs, group leader, 1981-83; American Radiolabeled Chemicals Inc, founder, president, 1983-. **ORGANIZATIONS:** American Chemical Society, 1967-, Kalamazoo Section, public relations chairman, 1968-73; Sigma Xi, 1966. **SPECIAL ACHIEVEMENTS:** Over 70 publications in all aspects of chemistry in various national and international journals. **BUSINESS ADDRESS:** President, American Radiolabeled Chemicals, Inc, 11624 Bowling Green Dr, St Louis, MO 63146, (314)991-4545.

GUPTA, SURENDRA KUMAR
Physician. Indo-American. **PERSONAL:** Born Sep 23, 1944, Jammu, Jammu and Kashmir, India; son of Girdhari Lal Gupta and Shanti Devi; married Saroj L Gupta, Jan 16, 1971; children: Salil, Shilpi. **EDUCATION:** Catholic Medical Center, residency program; fellowship in nephrology; India, MD, 1967. **CAREER:** Queens Associates, nephrologist, 1972-. **ORGANIZATIONS:** Queens Medical Society; International Kidney Foundation; National Kidney Society; International Kidney Association; Long Island Association of India; AIA, India Association of America; UPI; Association of Physicians in America. **HOME ADDRESS:** 1 Hemlock Ln, Roslyn Heights, NY 11577.

GUPTA, TAPAN K.
Educator. Indo-American. **PERSONAL:** Born Sep 5, 1941, Calcutta, W. Bengal, India; son of Gopeswar Gupta & Kanaklata Gupta; married Arundhati Gupta, Mar 7, 1976; children: Atreyee. **EDUCATION:** Indian Institute of Technology, MS, 1982; Boston College, PhD, 1986. **CAREER:** Lehigh University, postdoctoral fellow, 1986-87; Tufts University, analog devices career development professor, 1987-. **ORGANIZATIONS:** IEEE; American Physical Society; International Society for Hybrid Microelectronics; Eta Kappa Nu. **HONORS/AWARDS:** Rotary International, Rotary International Foundation Scholarship, 1975-76; Boston College, Teaching Excellency Award, 1985. **SPECIAL ACHIEVEMENTS:** Books on thick and thin film hybrid circuits, microelectronics fabrication. **BUSINESS ADDRESS:** Professor, Tufts University, 161 College Ave, Halligan Hall, Medford, MA 02155.

GUPTA, TEJ R.
Educator. Indo-American. **PERSONAL:** Born Mar 3, 1942, Katra, Jammu and Kashmir, India; son of Chuni Lal Gupta (deceased) and Chanan Devi; married Sanjokta Gupta, May 6, 1968; children: Amit, Ritu, Amol. **EDUCATION:** Jammu & Kashmir University, BS, 1962; University of Roorkee, MS, 1966, PhD, applied math, 1970; Virginia Polytechnic Institute & State University, PhD, engineering mechanics, 1977. **CAREER:** University of Roorkee, research asst, 1967-70, postdoctoral fellow/pool officer, 1972-74; G B University of Agriculture and Technology, instructor, 1970-72; Virginia Polytechnic Inst & State University, instructor, 1975-77, asst prof, 1978-79; Embry Riddle Aeronautical University, assoc prof, 1797-84, prof, 1984-. **ORGANIZATIONS:** American Institute of Aeronautics & Astronautics, 1975-84, assoc fellow, 1984-; American Academy of Mechanics; American Soc of Engineering Education. **HONORS/AWARDS:** Graduating class of Dec 1992, Outstanding Faculty Member, 1992; Embry Riddle Aeronautical University, finalist for Outstanding Teaching Award, 1991-92; numerous awards from university organizations. **SPECIAL ACHIEVEMENTS:** Has published numerous papers in various journals of professional interest. **BIOGRAPHICAL SOURCES:** Beyond the Horizon, ERAU Newsletter, Jan-Feb 1983; Avion, ERAU Newspaper, Jan 31, 1990. **BUSINESS ADDRESS:** Professor, Dept of Aerospace Engineering, Embry Riddle Aeronautical University, 600 S Clyde Morris Blvd, Daytona Beach, FL 32114-3900, (904)226-6756.

GUPTA, UDAYAN
Journalist. Indo-American. **PERSONAL:** Born Jan 15, 1950, Patna, Bihar, India; son of Umapati Gupta and Asoka Gupta; married Kathleen Gupta, Feb 19, 1978; children: Arun. **EDUCATION:** Harvard College, AB, 1971; Boston University, MS, 1976. **CAREER:** Freelance journalist; Black Enterprise, contributing editor; Venture, Electronic Media, 1978-85; Wall Street Journal, senior special writer, 1985-. **ORGANIZATIONS:** Asian-American Journalists Assn, 1990-. **HONORS/AWARDS:** Columbia University, Bagehot Fellowship, 1981-82; American Assn of Mesbics, Outstanding Journalistic Contribution, 1987. **BIOGRAPHICAL SOURCES:** Media Guide, 1993. **HOME ADDRESS:** 395 Southend Ave, 10-N, New York, NY 10280. **BUSINESS PHONE:** (212)416-3188.

GUPTA, VENU GOPAL
Educator. Indo-American. **PERSONAL:** Born Apr 3, 1934, Hoshiarpur, Punjab, India; son of L Ram Dass and Ram Piari; married Sunita Gupta, Nov 29, 1961; children: Sunil, Sanjiv. **EDUCATION:** Punjab University, BA, 1953, MA, 1955; Delhi University, BEd, 1958; Punjab University, MEd, 1959; Georgia State University, PhD, 1974. **CAREER:** Colleges of Punjab and Kurukshetra Universities, lecturer, 1955-63; University of Alberta, teaching and research fellow, 1963-66; University of Wisconsin, Stevens Point, assistant professor, 1966-68; Eastern Kentucky University, assistant professor, 1968-72; Georgia State University, teaching and research fellow, 1972-74; Kutztown University of Pennsylvania, professor, 1974-. **ORGANIZATIONS:** American Psychological Association; American Educational Research Association;

American Personnel and Guidance Association; American Association for Counseling and Development; American Association for Counselor Education and Supervision; American Mental Health Counselors Association; American Association for the Advancement of Science; American Association of University Professors; Phi Delta Kappa; International Council of Psychologists; International Association of Applied Psychology; International Association for Cross-cultural Psychology; International Council on Education for Teaching. **SPECIAL ACHIEVEMENTS:** Proficiency in several Indian languages: Hindi, Punjabi, Urdu and Sanskrit; Research Studies: Intercorrelations of WISC Subtest-Scores of Seventy Children, Tested two years Apart; Self-actualization—East and West, Students' Perception of College Instructors Based on Faculty-Evaluation ratings; Piaget: A Human Learning Theory, Effects of Different Instructions on Student Ratings of University Faculty. **HOME ADDRESS:** 744 Highland Ave, Kutztown, PA 19530, (610)683-6545. **BUSINESS ADDRESS:** Professor of Psychology, Kutztown University of Pennsylvania, Kutztown, PA 19530, (610)683-1367.

GUPTA, VIJAY
Educator. Indo-American. **PERSONAL:** Born Dec 30, 1962, New Delhi, India; son of Jagdish Prasad Gupta and Uma Gupta; married Deepti Gupta, May 10, 1992. **EDUCATION:** Indian Institute of Technology, Bombay, BS, technology civil engineering, 1985; Massachusetts Institute of Technology, MS, civil engineering, 1987, PhD, mechanical engineering, 1989. **CAREER:** Thayer School of Engineering, Dartmouth College, professor, 1990-. **ORGANIZATIONS:** American Society of Mechanical Engineers, associate member, 1990-; Metallurgical Society of AIME, associate member, 1991-; Materials Research Society, 1987-; American Ceramic Society, 1992-; American Society for Composites; Dartmouth College, committee on graduate programs, 1992-. **HONORS/AWARDS:** JN Tata Endowment, JN Tata Award for Outstanding Engineering Graduates of India, 1985; Indian Institute of Technology, Bombay, Institute's Silver Medal for Best Scholastic Performance Class of 1985 Civil Engineering; Tau Beta Pi Engineering Society, Honorary Membership, 1988; International Union of Materials Research Societies, Outstanding Young Investigator Award, 1993. **SPECIAL ACHIEVEMENTS:** Published 60 articles, 35 in refereed international journals; two book chapters; over 100 invited presentations at various universities, companies, and international conferences; three patent disclosures; three major invited presentations in Department of Defense-sponsored workshops on future of composite materials, 1990-1993; research in mechanics, materials science, composites, ice mechanics and thin film; developed a new technique to measure the strength of thin film interfaces used in the composites, multi-layer device and thin film industries. **BIOGRAPHICAL SOURCES:** Materials Research Society Bulletin, vol XVI-4, p 29, 1991. **HOME ADDRESS:** 3 Chandler Dr, Hanover, NH 03755, (603)643-5121. **BUSINESS ADDRESS:** Professor, Thayer School of Engineering, Darthmouth College, Cummings Hall, Hanover, NH 03755-1739, (603)646-3863.

GUPTA, VIRENDRA K.
Educator. Indo-American. **PERSONAL:** Born Mar 14, 1932, Delhi, India; son of Sri Narain Gupta; married Santosh, Dec 10, 1961; children: Mayank, Varun. **EDUCATION:** University of Delhi, India, BSc (honors), 1952, MSc, 1954; University of Michigan, ScD, 1961. **CAREER:** University of Delhi, lecturer, reader, professor, 1961-80; American Entomology Institute, director, 1980-82; University of Florida, professor, 1982-. **ORGANIZATIONS:** Entomology Society of India, fellow; Association for the Study of Oriental Insects, founder. **HONORS/AWARDS:** British Council, visiting fellowships to UK, 1967, 1975. **SPECIAL ACHIEVEMENTS:** Project leader, PL-480, projects on insects, 1965-75; published over 125 papers, including 10 books on Oriental and American insects. **BUSINESS ADDRESS:** Professor of Entomology, University of Florida, Bldg 970 Hull Rd, Gainesville, FL 32611-0620, (904)392-1901.

GUPTA, YOGENDRA MOHAN
Educator. Indo-American. **PERSONAL:** Born Jul 24, 1949, New Delhi, India; son of Brij Mohan and Prabha Gupta; married Barbara Mackay Gupta, Jun 21, 1975; children: Anjuli Monica, Sonia Michelle. **EDUCATION:** Birla Institute of Tech & Science, Pilani, India, BSc, 1966, MSc, physics, 1968; Washington State University, PhD, physics, 1973. **CAREER:** Brown University, postdoctoral research associate, 1974; Stanford Research Institute, physicist, sr physicist, assistant director, 1975-81; Washington State University, post-doctoral research associate, 1973-74, associate professor, beginning 1981, professor, 1984-. **ORGANIZATIONS:** American Physical Society, 1971-, fellow, 1991; Topical Group on Shock Compression of Condensed Matter, vice-

chairman, 1994, chairman, 1995; American Academy of Mechanics, 1988-. **HONORS/AWARDS:** Phi Kappa Phi, Scholastic Honor, 1973. **SPECIAL ACHIEVEMENTS:** Editor, Shock Waves in Condensed Matter, Plenum Press, 1986; over 100 publications; over 140 invited and contributed presentations; supervised the work of over 30 graduate students and research associates. **BUSINESS ADDRESS:** Professor of Physics, Director, Shock Dynamics Center, Washington State University, Physical Sciences, 948, Pullman, WA 99164-2814, (509)335-7217.

H

HA, CHONG W.
State government official. Korean American. **PERSONAL:** Born Oct 25, 1938, Jinju, Kyung-Nam, Republic of Korea; son of Kyung Sik Ha and Gyung Nam Park; married Hye-Ja Ha, Aug 19, 1968; children: Jean F, Julie A. **EDUCATION:** UCLA, BA, 1970; Claremont Graduate School, MA, 1985. **CAREER:** First Interstate Bank, data processing manager, 1978-85; Ticor Title Insurance Co, vice president, MIS, 1985-91; MCA/Universal Studios, associate director, 1991; State of California, Stephen P Teale Data Center, director, currently. **ORGANIZATIONS:** Asian Pacific American Legal Center, advisory board member, 1986-; Korean Youth Center, board member, 1989-92; Asian Pacific Alumni of UCLA, advisory board, 1988-; Government Technology Conference, advisory board member, 1992; Society of Information Management, 1990-. **SPECIAL ACHIEVEMENTS:** Reserve police officer, Monterey Park Police Department, 1982-84. **BUSINESS ADDRESS:** Director, Stephen P Teale Data Center, State of California, 2005 Evergreen St, PO Box 13436, Sacramento, CA 95813-4436, (912)263-1816.

HA, JOSEPH MAN-KYUNG
Educator. Korean American. **PERSONAL:** Born Dec 26, 1936, Republic of Korea; married Kay; children: Karen C. **EDUCATION:** University of Washington, BA, political science; Columbia University, certificate from Russian Institute, PhD, international politics. **CAREER:** Columbia University, 1962-67; New York Institute of Technology, 1968-69; Kings College, 1969-70; Institute of Diplomacy and National Security, Ministry of Foreign Affairs, ROK, visiting professor, 1977-78; Institute of USA & Canada Studies, Russian Academy of Sciences, professor of international politics, 1992-; Lewis & Clark College, International Affairs Dept, professor and chair, 1971-; K-Tel Global Inc, chair, 1991-. **ORGANIZATIONS:** American Political Science Assn; International Studies Assn; American Assn for the Advancement of Slavic Studies; Faculty NW Regional Seminar on China; American Professors for Peace in the Middle East; Korean Institute of International Affairs, Seoul, research associate; Korean Observer, editorial board; Asian Perspective, editorial board. **HONORS/AWARDS:** Kyoto University of Foreign Studies, Honorary Professor, 1992; Institute of USA & Canada Studies, Russian Academy of Sciences, Honorary Doctor, 1992; Korea Unification Board, chaired by president of ROK, chair, 1988-; Lewis & Clark College, faculty research grants, 1974-; Danforth Foundation, grants, 1966-67. **SPECIAL ACHIEVEMENTS:** Author: more than seven books on foreign policy, including several on Korean American relations; consultant and advisor on issues from international affairs to education. **BUSINESS ADDRESS:** Chairman, Professor of International Affairs, Lewis and Clark College, 0615 SW Palatine Hill Road, Portland, OR 97219, (503)768-7635.

HAGEDORN, JESSICA TARAHATA
Author. Filipino American. **PERSONAL:** Born 1949, Philippines; children: one daughter. **CAREER:** Performance artist, late 1970s; author, publications include: Dangerous Music, 1975; Pet Food and Tropical Apparitions, 1981; Dogeaters, 1989; Danger and Beauty, 1993; "Mango Tango," multimedia piece; contributor: Four Young Women: Poems, McGraw, 1973; Between Worlds: Contemporary Asian-American Plays, Theatre Communications Group, 1989. **HONORS/AWARDS:** National Book Award Nomination, for Dogeaters, 1990; Before Columbus Foundation Book Award. **SPECIAL ACHIEVEMENTS:** Language proficiency: English, Spanish, Tagalog; bandleader, The Gangster Choir. *

HAGIWARA, KOKICHI
Steel company executive. Japanese American. **PERSONAL:** Born 1924, Tokyo, Japan. **EDUCATION:** Tokyo University, graduate, 1947. **CAREER:** National Steel Corp, former president, former COO, chairman, CEO, board of directors, currently. **BUSINESS ADDRESS:** Chairman/CEO, National Steel Corp, 4100 Edison Lakes Pky, Mishawaka, IN 46545, (219)273-7000. *

HAHN, BESSIE KING

Librarian. Chinese American. **PERSONAL:** Born May 14, 1939, Shanghai, China; daughter of Jen Fong and Wei Lok King; married Roger Carl Hahn, 1962 (divorced 1983); children: Angela, Michael, Belinda; married David Ware Duhme, 1989. **EDUCATION:** Mt Marty College, BA, 1961; Syracuse University, MSLS, 1972. **CAREER:** Librarian Carrier Corp, 1972; Syracuse University Libraries, life science bibliographer, 1973-75, head science and tech, 1975-78; Johns Hopkins University Library, assistant director reader services, 1978-81; Brandeis University, director libraries, 1981-. **ORGANIZATIONS:** Abraham Lincoln Brigade Archives, board of governors, 1989-; New England Associations of Schools and Colleges Inc, 1991-; ALA, Chinese-American Librarians Association, 1982-83; Brandeis University, Natl Women's Committee, honorary benefactor, 1986, honorary life member, 1990-. **HONORS/AWARDS:** Shanghai Jiao Tong University Library, cons, 1983-, honorary professor, 1984; Johns Hopkins University, Golden Cup Award, 1980. **SPECIAL ACHIEVEMENTS:** Journal Educational Media and Library Sciences, editor, 1983-; contributor to articles in professional journals. **BUSINESS ADDRESS:** University Librarian, Brandeis University, Main Library, 400 South St, Waltham, MA 02254-9110, (617)736-4710. *

HAHN, HWA SUK (HOWARD)

Educator (retired). Korean American. **PERSONAL:** Born Nov 1, 1924, Pusan, Republic of Korea; son of Heong-Kyo Hahn; married Y Jean, Oct 31, 1949; children: Sonia Patrick. **EDUCATION:** Seoul National University, BS, 1949; University of Oregon, MS, 1957; University of Illinois, PhD, 1961. **CAREER:** Pusan National University, Korea, instructor and assistant professor, 1949-55; PA St University, assistant professor, 1961-67, West Georgia College, associate professor & professor, 1967-92. **ORGANIZATIONS:** Math Association of American, 1957-91. **SPECIAL ACHIEVEMENTS:** On The Relative Growth of Differences of Partition Function, Pacific Journal of Math, vol 14, no 1, pp 93-106, 1964; A Counting Function of Integral n-Tuples, Fibonacci Quarterly, vol 10, no 6, pp 609-628, Dec 1972. **HOME ADDRESS:** 108 Dunwoody Drive, Carrollton, GA 30117.

HAHN, LIANG-SHIN

Mathematician. Taiwanese American. **PERSONAL:** Born Sep 20, 1932, Tainan, Taiwan; son of Shyr-Chyuan Hahn and Shiu-Luan Tsung Hahn; married Hwei-Shien Lee Hahn, Sep 14, 1958; children: Shin-Yi (Samuel), Shin-Jen (James), Shin-Hong (Paul). **EDUCATION:** National Taiwan University, BS, 1956; Stanford University, PhD, 1966. **CAREER:** Johns Hopkins University, 1966-68; University of New Mexico, mathematician 1968-; University of Washington, visiting scholar, 1974-76; National Taiwan University, visiting scholar, 1979-80; University of Tokyo, visiting scholar, 1981-, 1985-87; International Christian University, visiting scholar, 1986-87; Sophia University, 1987. **SPECIAL ACHIEVEMENTS:** "Complex Numbers and Geometry," Mathematical Association of America, 1993; Lectures on Classical Complex Analysis, 1994. **BUSINESS ADDRESS:** Mathematician, Dept of Mathematics & Statistics, University of New Mexico, Central Ave NE, Rm 451, Humanity Bldg, Albuquerque, NM 87131-1141, (505)277-2234.

HAHN, YOUNGJA CHOI

Association administrator. Korean American. **PERSONAL:** Born Jan 8, 1918, Kang-Neung, Kangwondo, Republic of Korea; daughter of Sung-Kyu Choi and Kyung-Ok Lee; married Kyung-Suk Hahn, Jun 18, 1939 (deceased); children: Alice Kim, Chang-Ho, Julie Chung, Chang-Joo. **EDUCATION:** Kook-Je College, BA, 1964. **CAREER:** Garfinkel, sales, 9 years; National YWCA-Korea, social worker, 18 years; Elementary school teacher, 16 years. **ORGANIZATIONS:** Korean Family Counseling & Research Center, board, 1983-; Korean-American Senior Citizens Association, board, 1980-. **HONORS/AWARDS:** K-F-C, Korea, 1986; K-F-C, Wash Branch, 1987; Korean-American, Senior Center, 1989. **SPECIAL ACHIEVEMENTS:** Mrs Washingtonian, in Korean, 8 peoples essays, 1991; The Second Mrs Washingtonian, 12 people essays, 1993. **HOME ADDRESS:** 101 Odendhal Ave #805, Gaithersburg, MD 20877, (301)869-6756.

HAHN, YUKAP

Educator. Korean American. **PERSONAL:** Born Jul 28, 1932, Seoul, Republic of Korea; son of Chi Chin Hahn; married Byung Chai Chang, May 1956; children: Chisong, Chiwon, Chihoe. **EDUCATION:** University of Southern California, BA, 1956; Yale University, MS, 1958, PhD, 1962. **CAREER:** New York University, research scientist, 1961-65; University of Connecticut, professor, 1965-. **ORGANIZATIONS:** American Physical Society, fellow.

BUSINESS ADDRESS: Professor, Physics Dept, University of Connecticut, Storrs, CT 06268, (203)486-4469.

HAJELA, PRABHAT

Educator. Indo-American. **PERSONAL:** Born Dec 25, 1956, Kanpur, Uttar Pradesh, India; son of K P Hajela and Rajeshwari Hajela; married Aparna Mehrotra, May 15, 1991; children: Animesh Mehrotra-Hajela. **EDUCATION:** Indian Institute of Technology, Kanpur, BS, 1977; Iowa State University, MS, aerospace engineering, 1978; Stanford University, MS, mechanical engineering, 1981, PhD, aeronautics, 1982. **CAREER:** Stanford University, research assistant, 1979-82; University of California, Los Angeles, research fellow, 1982-83; University of Florida, Gainesville, assistant & associate professor, 1983-90; Rensselaer Polytechnic Institute, associate & professor, 1990-. **ORGANIZATIONS:** American Institute of Aeronautics & Astronautics, associate fellow, 1976-, technical committee on Multidisciplinary Design Oplimization, chair of education subcommittee, education committee, professional member; American Society of Engineering Education, 1985-; American Association for Artificial Intelligence, 1987-; Society of Automotive Engineers, 1987-91; AIAA Journal, associate editor, 1989-93, editorial board of 3 intl journals, 1992-, American Helicopter Society, 1993-. **HONORS/AWARDS:** University of Florida, Teacher of the Year Award, 1989; Rensselaer Polytechnic Institute, L T Assini Teaching & Counseling Award, 1992; Society of Automotive Engineers, Ralph R Teetor Award, 1987; American Institute of Aeronautics & Astronautics, Faculty Adviser Award, 1988. **SPECIAL ACHIEVEMENTS:** Published over 100 technical papers, 1980-; edited and co-edited two books, 1987, 1989; proficiency in Hindi and English; working knowledge of Spanish. **BIOGRAPHICAL SOURCES:** The Economist, Science Section, Nov 9-16, 1990. **BUSINESS ADDRESS:** Professor, Rensselaer Polytechnic Institute, 5020 JEC, RPI, Troy, NY 12180.

HAJIYANI, MEHDI HUSSAIN

Educator. Indo-American. **PERSONAL:** Born Oct 8, 1939, Chital, Saurashtra, India; son of Alibhai V Hajiyani and Sakina P Hajiyani; married Dolat M Hajiyani, Jan 30, 1960; children: Shirin. **EDUCATION:** Osmania University, Hyderabad, India, BSc, 1960; University of Southern California, PhD, 1970. **CAREER:** University of Southern California, teaching/research assistant, 1960-69; Calbio Chem, Catatomic Division, senior radio chemist, 1967-68; California State College, Dominguez Hills, instructor, 1968-69; University of the District of Columbia, associate professor, 1971-. **ORGANIZATIONS:** American Chemical Society, 1962-; Washington, DC, Chemical Society, currently; The Planetary Society, currently; The National Geographic Society, 1970-. **HOME ADDRESS:** 1420 Gerard St, Rockville, MD 20850, (301)424-7051.-

HALDAR, DIPAK

Educator. Indo-American. **PERSONAL:** Born Dec 8, 1937, Bankura, W. Bengal, India; son of Bholanath Haldar and Renuka Haldar; married Jaya Haldar, Jul 3, 1963; children: Joydeep, Deeya. **EDUCATION:** University of Calcutta, BS (with honors), 1956, MS, 1958, DPhil, 1963; University of London, PhD, 1966. **CAREER:** St Jude Children's Res Hospital, assistant member, 1969-71; University of Calcutta, biochemistry, lecturer, 1971-73; Public Health Res Institute of the City of New York, visiting investigator, 1974-75; St John's University, assistant professor, 1975-78, associate professor, 1979-82, bio sci, professor, 1983-. **ORGANIZATIONS:** American Society for Biochemist & Molec Biol, 1982-; AAAS, 1969-; American Society for Cell Biology, 1978-. **HONORS/AWARDS:** Royal Commission for the Exhibition of 1851, Overseas Science Research Scholarship, 1963-66; Postdoctoral Fellowship of MRC, Canada, 1966-67; grants from National Science Foundation, National Institutes of Health, 1982, 1984, 1986-95. **SPECIAL ACHIEVEMENTS:** Over 40 articles in various scientific journals. **BUSINESS ADDRESS:** Professor of Biological Sciences, St John's University, 8000 Utopia Parkway, Jamaica, NY 11439, (718)990-1697.

HALEMANE, THIRUMALA RAYA

Physicist, educator, software engineer. Indo-American. **PERSONAL:** Born May 27, 1953, Ednad Village, Kasaragod, India; son of H Shama Bhat and Thirumaleshwari Ambikana; married Usha Kumari Kailar, Aug 30, 1976; children: Kaviraj Shama Bhat, Shilpi Shankara Bhat. **EDUCATION:** St Joseph's College, Bangalore, BSc (honors), 1972; Indian Institute of Technology, MSc, 1974; University of Rochester, MA, math, 1980, PhD, physics, 1980. **CAREER:** Rutgers University, research associate, 1979-81; State University College, Fredonia, assistant professor, 1981-85; Physical Research Laboratory, India, visiting scientist, 1983; Pennsylvania State University, visiting assistant professor, 1984; Monmouth College, New Jersey, adjunct faculty, 1988-91; AT&T Bell Labs, New Jersey, 1985-92. **ORGANIZATIONS:** Hindu American Temple and Cultural Center, Inc, founder/president, 1988-89, chairman, 1988-90; Optical Society of America, education council, 1989-91. **HONORS/ AWARDS:** University of Rochester, Rush Rhees Fellowship, 1976; Bangalore University, S Nijahingappa Gold Medal, 1972. **SPECIAL ACHIEVE-MENTS:** 4 patents on optical memory and optical amplifier, 1989-91; articles on physics, lightwave communications, nuclear disarmament and social issues in professional journals and newspapers. **HOME ADDRESS:** 62 Yellowstone Ln E, Howell, NJ 07731, (908)938-3039.

HALEY, MARIA LUISA MABILANGAN
Government official. Filipino American. **PERSONAL:** Born in Philippines; married John Haley. **EDUCATION:** Villa de L'Assumption, Paris; Universidad Central de Madrid, French and Spanish languages and civilizations. **CAREER:** Manila Hilton, director of marketing; Arkansas Industrial Development Commission, director of marketing, 1981-90, director of communications, 1991-92; President Bill Clinton's Transition's Office, deputy assistant director for political affairs, 1992; The White House, special assistant to the president, associate director of presidential personnel for economics, commerce and trade, currently. **ORGANIZATIONS:** Filipino Youth Scholarship Foundation, cofounder. **SPECIAL ACHIEVEMENTS:** Cofounder, the Karilagan School, the first finishing school in the Far East; only female and only Asian American deputy to the assistant director for political affairs, David Wilhelm, 1992. **BUSINESS ADDRESS:** Associate Director, Presidential Personnel, 1120 Vermont NW, Washington, DC 20270, (501)682-7678. ∗

HAMAMOTO, DARRELL YOSHITO
Author. Japanese American/Pacific Islander American. **PERSONAL:** Born Feb 18, 1953, Honolulu, HI; son of Joel Koichi Hamamoto and Joan Kimiko Kakazu Hamamoto; married June Fujiko Kurata, Mar 1979; children: Gena Sayoko. **EDUCATION:** California State University, Long Beach, BA, 1975; Bowling Green State University, MA, 1976; University of California, Irvine, PhD, 1982. **CAREER:** University of California, Los Angeles, visiting professor, 1991-92; University of California, Irvine, lecture, 1989-; nonfiction writer, currently. **ORGANIZATIONS:** Speech Communication Association, 1988-93; Society for Cinema Studies, 1991-93; Association for Asian American Studies, 1991-93; American Sociological Association, 1990; Popular Culture Association, 1991. **HONORS/AWARDS:** Fulbright, lectureship to Japan, 1993; Rockefeller Foundation, research fellowship to UCLA, 1990. **SPECIAL ACHIEVEMENTS:** Monitored Peril: Asian Americans and the Politics of TV Representation, Minnesota, 1994; Nervous Laughter: Television Situation Comedy and Liberal Democratic Ideology, Praeger, 1989. **HOME ADDRESS:** PO Box 51471, Irvine, CA 92619-1471, (714)551-0977.

HAMASAKI, LES
Energy company executive. Japanese American. **PERSONAL:** Born 1939?, Hawaii; married Miwa, 1960; children: two. **EDUCATION:** University of California, Los Angeles; California Polytechnic State University, Pomona, BA, landscape architecture. **CAREER:** City of Los Angeles, urban planner, 1965-81; Amerasia Group, Inc, president, currently; Sun Utlity Network, president, currently. **ORGANIZATIONS:** Los Angeles Airport Commission, appointed commissioner, 1993; Little Tokyo Arts, founder, 1978-; Los Angeles Festival; California Solar Energy Assn, board member; Japanese American Cultural & Community Center, board member, 1980-; Los Angeles City Employees Asian American Assn, founder. **BUSINESS ADDRESS:** President, AmerAsia Group, 626 Wilshire Blvd, Ste 711,Los Angeles, CA 90017, (213)623-9935.∗

HAN, ANNA M.
Educator. Chinese American. **PERSONAL:** Born Apr 18, 1956, Taipei, Taiwan; married Daniel B Klein; children: Dana Han-Klein, Devon Han-Klein. **EDUCATION:** University of California, Berkeley, BA (honors), 1978; Hastings College of the Law, JD, 1981. **CAREER:** Heller, Ehrman, White & McAuliffe, associate, 1981-83; McCutchen, Doyle, Brown, Enersen, partner, Shanghai, 1983-89; Santa Clara University, associate professor, 1989-. **ORGANIZATIONS:** American Bar Association, 1981-; California Bar Association, 1981-; San Francisco Bar Association, 1981-; China Law Committee, chair, 1991-; Asian American Bar Association, 1983-; International Bar Association, 1985-91; Journal of International Franchising and Distribution Law, associate editor, 1988-. **SPECIAL ACHIEVEMENTS:** Fluency in Chinese, four dialects. **BUSINESS ADDRESS:** Professor, School of Law, Santa Clara University, Bergan 204, Santa Clara, CA 95053, (408)554-4711.

HAN, BYUNG JOON
Engineer. Korean American. **PERSONAL:** Born Aug 15, 1959, Seoul, Republic of Korea; married SungAe Moon Han; children: Young Michael, Sun Murray. **EDUCATION:** Han Yang University, BE, 1982; Tennessee Technological University, MS, 1985; Columbia University, MPh, 1988, PhD, 1988. **CAREER:** IBM T J Watson Res Ctr, research assoc, 1986-88; AT&T Bell Labs, member of technical staff, 1988-. **ORGANIZATIONS:** Korean Scientists & Engineers Association Inc, chapter president, 1985-; Sigma Xi, 1984-; Material Research Society, 1986-; Society Plastics Engr. **HONORS/ AWARDS:** Exxon, Exxon Scholarship Award, 1986. **SPECIAL ACHIEVEMENTS:** More than 30 technical publications. **BUSINESS ADDRESS:** Member of Technical Staff, AT&T Bell Laboratories, 600 Mountain Ave, Rm IE302, Murray Hill, NJ 07974, (908)582-3753.

HAN, CHIEN-PAI
Educator. Chinese American. **PERSONAL:** Born Dec 17, 1936, Hunan, China; son of C S Han and P W Liu; married Maria L Han, Aug 28, 1965; children: Richard, Julie. **EDUCATION:** National Taiwan University, BA, 1958; University of Minnesota, MA, 1962; Harvard University, PhD, 1967. **CAREER:** Museum of New Mexico, statistical consultant, 1965; Iowa State University, assistant professor, 1967-69, associate professor, 1970-75, professor, 1975-82; Harvard University, visiting assistant professor, 1970; University of Texas, Arlington, professor, 1982-. **ORGANIZATIONS:** American Statistical Association; Institute of Mathematical Statistics; International Statistical Institute; International Chinese Statistical Association, director, 1987-92; Sigma Xi; Mu Sigma Rho. **HONORS/AWARDS:** Communications in Statistics, editorial board, 1975-92, associate editor, 1993-. **SPECIAL ACHIEVEMENTS:** Over 70 papers published in scientific journals; co-author with T A Bancroft, Statistical Theory and Inference in Research, 1981. **BUSINESS ADDRESS:** Professor, Dept of Mathematics, University of Texas at Arlington, Box 19408, Arlington, TX 76019, (817)273-3798.

HAN, CHINGPING JIM
Educator. Chinese American. **PERSONAL:** Born Aug 24, 1957, Shanghai, People's Republic of China; son of Bao-San Zhang & Xiao-xian Han; married Manxia Maria Zhang, Feb 22, 1982; children: George Han. **EDUCATION:** Dalian Institute of Technology, BSME, 1982; Pennsylvania State University, MS, industrial engineering, 1985, PhD, industrial engineering, 1988. **CAREER:** National Forge Co, PA, project coordinator, 1988; Florida Atlantic University, assistant professor, 1988-93, associate professor, 1993-. **ORGANIZATIONS:** Society of Manufacturing Engineering; North American Manufacturing Research Institute; Institute of Industrial Engineers; The Institute of Management Sciences. **HONORS/AWARDS:** National Science Foundation, grantee, 1990-95; Florida Atlantic University, Outstanding Faculty Award, 1990. **SPECIAL ACHIEVEMENTS:** 14 journal and refereed publications; 29 published conference papers; 18 research reports in public domain. **BUSINESS ADDRESS:** Assoc Prof, Dept of Mech Eng, Florida Atlantic University, 500 NW 20th St, Boca Raton, FL 33431, (407)367-2691.

HAN, GRACE YANG
Educator. Taiwanese American. **PERSONAL:** Born Jul 17, 1941, Tzihuh, Changhwa, Taiwan; daughter of C M & Y E Yang; married Peter F Han, Mar 28, 1967; children: Joan Christine. **EDUCATION:** Tamkiang University, BS, 1963; University of Massachusetts, Amherst, MS, 1967, PhD, 1969. **CAREER:** Tamkiang University, teaching assistant, 1963-64; University of Massachusetts, Amherst, teaching assistant, 1965-67, research assistant, 1967-69, postdoctor, NIH fellow, 1969-72; Morehouse College, NSF research fellow, 1973-75, assistant professor, 1976-82, associate professor, 1982-87, professor of chemistry, 1987-. **ORGANIZATIONS:** American Chemical Society, 1965-. **HONORS/AWARDS:** Morehouse College Health Careers Society, Best Teacher Award, 1987. **SPECIAL ACHIEVEMENTS:** Author and lecturer of several publications and symposia. **HOME ADDRESS:** 2696 Cosmos Dr, Atlanta, GA 30345-1355.

HAN, IN-SOP
Government official, broadcaster. Korean American. **PERSONAL:** Born Dec 15, 1936, Seoul, Republic of Korea; son of Keun Shik Han and Jung Sun Park Han; married Hee Ja Kim Han; children: David, Jenny. **EDUCATION:** Seoul National University, BA, political science, 1959; George Washington University, 1973-76. **CAREER:** American Embassy, media specialist, 1965-71; Voice of America, international radio broadcaster, 1971-85, chief, Korean service, 1985-. **ORGANIZATIONS:** Retired Korean Air Force Officers' Association of USA, president, 1983-84; Maryland Council of Korean Americans,

board of directors, 1983-91; Korean Association of Greater Washington, board of directors, 1983-84; League of Korean Americans, executive director, 1984-85; Association of Korean American Schools, board of directors, 1986-87; Korean-American Association of Greater Washington, board of advisors, Council of Compilation of History, 1993-94. **HONORS/AWARDS:** Voice of America, cash performance award, 1980; US Information Agency, superior honor award, 1989; Montgomery, department of police, volunteer service award, 1991; Voice of America, special commendation, 1983. **SPECIAL ACHIEVEMENTS:** Author, "Is Spring Coming to the Tumen River?" Hankook Weekly Magazine, Korea, June 21, 1992; one of the first Asian-born Americans to become a Service Chief of Voice of America, 1985. **MILITARY SERVICE:** Republic of Korea Air Force, public info officer, 1st lt, 1959-63. **BIOGRAPHICAL SOURCES:** "This Man-the First Korea-Born Service Chief in VOA's 43-year History," Chosun Weekly Magazine, p 64, November 24, 1985. **BUSINESS ADDRESS:** Chief, Korean Service, Voice of America, US Information Agency, 330 Independence Ave SW, Cohen Bldg, Rm 2709, Washington, DC 20547, (202)619-3694.

HAN, JAOK
Cardiologist, medical educator. Korean American. **PERSONAL:** Born Jul 16, 1930, Chinnampo, Republic of Korea; son of Choon Hun Han & Chung Ryo Kim; married Yangsook Chun Han, Jan 21, 1961; children: Sylvia, Julia, Andrew. **EDUCATION:** Kyung-Puk University College of Medicine, MD, 1951; State University of NY Upstate Medical Center, PhD, 1962. **CAREER:** Jersey City Medical Center, resident in medicine, 1955-57; State University of NY upstate Medical Center, research fellow in physiology, 1957-60; Masonic Med Research Laboratory, research associate, 1960-66; University of Rochester Medical Center, fellow in cardiology, 1966-67; Albany Medical College, associate professor of medicine, 1968-73, professor of medicine, 1973-; Albany Medical Center Hospital, attending cardiologist, 1968-, director of electrocardiography, 1968-. **ORGANIZATIONS:** New York Academy of Science, 1970-; American Physiological Society, 1964-; American Heart Association, fellow, 1970-; American College of Cardiology, fellow, 1968-; American Heart Association, NY State Affiliate, research committee, 1976-79; American Heart Association, Northeastern NY chapter, vice president, 1978-80, president, 1980-82; National Institute of Health, Workshop on Clinical Pharmacology, co-chairman, 1982; National Heart, Lung and Blood Institute, cardiology advisory committee, 1981-85, special project review committee, 1974-. **HONORS/AWARDS:** International Society of Cardiology Foundation, fellowship, 1960-61; Masonic Foundation for Medical Research, fellowship, 1961-63; NY State Heart Assembly, research grant awards, 1963-68; National Institute of Health, research grant awards, 1969-85; American Heart Association, research grant awards, 1978-90. **SPECIAL ACHIEVEMENTS:** Author, Cardiac Arrhythmias, 1972; 100 research and clinical papers on cardiac electrophysiology and arrhythmias published in various physiological and cardiological journals, 1972-; editorial board member, Journal of Electrocardiology, 1984-. **BUSINESS ADDRESS:** Professor, Albany Medical College, 47 New Scotland Ave, Albany, NY 12208, (518)262-5263.

HAN, JE-CHIN
Educator. Taiwanese American. **PERSONAL:** Born Sep 15, 1946, Kaohsiung, Taiwan; son of Swin and Yeh-Yen; married Su-Huei, Aug 3, 1973; children: George, Jean. **EDUCATION:** National Taiwan University, BS, 1970; Lehigh University, MS, 1973; MIT, ScD, 1976. **CAREER:** Ex-Cell-O Corp, process development engineer, 1976-77; National Tsing Hua University, visiting associate professor of power mechanical engineering, 1977-78; Ex-Cell-O Corp, senior research engineer, 1978-80; Texas A&M University, assistant professor of mechanical engineering, 1980-84, associate professor of mechanical engineering, 1984-89, professor of mechanical engineering, 1989-93, endowed HTRI professor of mechanical engineering, 1993-. **ORGANIZATIONS:** American Society of Mechanical Engineers, 1980-91, fellow, 1991-; American Society of Engineering Education, 1982-; American Institute of Aeronautics and Astronautics, 1985-; Pacific Center of Thermal-Fluids Engineering, advisory board member, 1985-; North American Taiwanese Professors Association, 1985-; The Honor Society of Phi Kappa Phi, 1990-; ASME K-14 Gas Turbine Heat Transfer Committee, 1983-. **HONORS/AWARDS:** Texas A&M University, Halliburton Professorship, 1991-92; ASME, Fellow, 1991, Texas Engineering Experiment Station, Senior Fellow, 1988-, Fellow, 1987-88, Young Fellow, 1984-85. **SPECIAL ACHIEVEMENTS:** More than 100 technical publications in the field of gas turbine heat transfer and cooling technology. **BUSINESS ADDRESS:** Professor, Mechanical Engineering Dept, Texas A&M University, College Station, TX 77843, (409)845-3738.

HAN, JINCHEN
Architect, acoustician. Chinese American. **PERSONAL:** Born Feb 21, 1938, Peking, China; son of Wenyo Han and Jingru Cao; divorced; children: Cong. **EDUCATION:** Tsinghua University, Peking, China, master's degree, 1982; SUNY at Buffalo, master's degree, 1989. **CAREER:** Peeking Institute of Arch and Civil Eng, associate professor, 1982-88; SUNY at Buffalo, visiting associate professor, 1988-90; FRE Architects and Engineers, NYC, designer, 1990-92; Spector/Jao Architects, NYC, designer, 1992-. **ORGANIZATIONS:** Health in Housing, World Health Organization, fellow, 1989-90. **HONORS/AWARDS:** SUNY, Graduate Fellowship, 1988. **SPECIAL ACHIEVEMENTS:** Publications: On Methodology of Architectural Design, China, 1987; Stage Sound Reflectors in Hangzhou Theater, England, 1988; A Manual of Architectural-Acoustical Design, China, 1987; Acoustical Effects of Stage Reflectors and Their Design, Hong Kong, 1985; Chinese translation: Science and Technology in World Development, Robin Clarke, 1987. **BIOGRAPHICAL SOURCES:** A Decade of Health in Housing 1982-92, p 6, 138, 1992. **HOME ADDRESS:** 144-12 28th Ave, Flushing, NY 11354, (718)460-0159.

HAN, KENNETH N.
Educator. Korean American. **PERSONAL:** Born Jul 3, 1938, Seoul, Republic of Korea; son of Chiy-Kyong Han and Tack-soon Sim; married Helen Hyi-Won, Sep 1, 1967; children: Iris, Vincent, Alison. **EDUCATION:** Seoul Natl University, BS, 1961, MS, 1963; University of Illinois, Urbana, MS, 1967; University of California, Berkeley, PhD, 1971. **CAREER:** Seoul Natl University, res asst/assoc, 1961-65; University of Illinois, res asst, 1965-67; University of California, Berkeley, visiting prof, 1974-79; Monash University, Australia, lecturer/sr lecturer, 1971-80; South Dakota School of Mines & Technology, prof, 1981-, dept head, 1987-, director for EPSLOR, 1989-93, director of Institute for Min & Met, 1988-. **ORGANIZATIONS:** Australian Inst Mining & Met Soc, 1971-81; American Inst of Mining & Met Pet, 1981-; AIME, 1985-; SME/AIME/Min & Met Proc, secretary/treasurer, 1992-; Met Proc Fund/AIME/SME, chairman, 1992-93. **SPECIAL ACHIEVEMENTS:** Over 80 papers in refereed journals; over 50 paper presentations with abstract at natl & intl conferences; 5 monographs; Min Proc & Ext Met Review, editor-in-chief, 1984; editorial: Met Transactions (AIME), 1985-; Min & Met Processing (AIME), 1986-; Intl Journal of Min Proc, 1988-. **BUSINESS ADDRESS:** Prof & Head, Dept of Metallurgical Engineering, South Dakota School of Mines & Technology, 501 E St Joseph St, MI Bldg, Rm 108, Rapid City, SD 57701-3995, (605)394-2342.

HAN, MOO-YOUNG
Educator, physicist. Korean American. **PERSONAL:** Born Nov 30, 1934, Seoul, Republic of Korea; son of Sung-Hoon Han (deceased) and Kie-Jer Kim (deceased); married Chang-Ki Hong Han, Aug 29, 1959; children: Grace Wolf, Chris, Anthony. **EDUCATION:** Seoul National University, College of Engineering, 1952-54; Carroll College, BS, 1957; University of Rochester, PhD, 1964. **CAREER:** Boston University, research asst prof, 1963-64; Syracuse University, research associate, 1964-65; University of Pittsburgh, visiting asst prof, 1965-67; Duke University, asst professor, associate professor, professor, 1967-; Tsukuba National Lab, visiting professor, 1974; Kyoto University, visiting professor, 1974; KAIST, visiting professor, 1982. **ORGANIZATIONS:** Assn of Korean Physicists in America, president, 1985-86; Korean Scientists and Engineers Assn, president, 1991-92; Pan-World Assn of Korean Scientists and Engineers, vice president, 1992. **HONORS/AWARDS:** Duke University, Outstanding Professor Award, 1971; Duke University Alumni, Distinguished Undergraduate Teaching Award, 1972. **SPECIAL ACHIEVEMENTS:** Co-discoverer of the color charges of quarks, 1965; author, The Secret Life of Quanta, McGraw-Hill, 1990; author, The Probable Universe, McGraw-Hill, 1992. **BIOGRAPHICAL SOURCES:** The Timetables of Science, Simon and Schuster, p 547. **HOME ADDRESS:** 615 Duluth St, Durham, NC 27705-1824. **BUSINESS ADDRESS:** Professor, Dept of Physics, Duke University, Durham, NC 27708-0305, (919)660-2575.

HAN, SHERMAN HSIAO-MIN
Educator. Taiwanese American. **PERSONAL:** Born Oct 13, 1948, Taipei, Taiwan; son of Chi-lian Han & Eng Chang Han; married Meei-huey Han, Jun 25, 1976; children: Anne, Andrew. **EDUCATION:** Tamkang University, BA, 1973; Central Missouri State University, MA, 1974; Brigham Young University, Provo, PhD, 1980. **CAREER:** Brigham Young University, Hawaii, professor of English, 1980-. **ORGANIZATIONS:** Rocky Mountain Modern Language Association, committee chair for ethnic studies, 1981, 1986; Hawaii Chinese Scholars Association, 1980-. **HONORS/AWARDS:** National Endowment for Humanities, fellowship, 1981, 1985. **SPECIAL ACHIEVEMENTS:**

Root & Buds: The Literature of the Chinese-Americans; essays on Journey to the West. **BUSINESS ADDRESS:** Professor, Brigham Young University of Hawaii, 55-220 Kulanui St, Box 1894, Laie, HI 96762.

HAN, SUSAN S.
Educator. Taiwanese American. **PERSONAL:** Born Dec 24, 1957, Manila, Philippines; daughter of Chen-Shiun Han and Yan Yan Soo; married You-Pan Tzeng, Jul 7, 1984; children: Jesse C. **EDUCATION:** National Taiwan University, BS, 1980; University of Missouri, Columbia, MS, 1984; University of California, Davis, PhD, 1988. **CAREER:** National Taiwan University, research technician, 1980-82; University of Massachusetts, asst professor, 1989-. **ORGANIZATIONS:** American Society for Horticultural Science, 1989-. **SPECIAL ACHIEVEMENTS:** Role of Sugars in Bud Development and Vase Life of Cut Liatris Spicata, 1992; The Role of Ethylene and Pollination in Petal Senescence and Ovary Growth of Brodiaea, 1991; Postharvest Handling of Brodiaea Flowers, 1991; Enhancement of Growth and Flowering of Triteleia Laxa by Ethylene, 1990; Flowering and Corm Yield of Brodiaea in Response to Temperature, Photoperiod, Comsize and Planting Depth, 1990. **BUSINESS ADDRESS:** Professor, Dept of Plant & Soil Sciences, University of Massachusetts, French Hall, Rm 204B, Amherst, MA 01003, (413)545-5228.

HAN, XIANMING LANCE
Physicist, educator. Chinese American. **PERSONAL:** Born May 3, 1963, Xinfeng, Jiangxi, People's Republic of China; son of Xipei Han and Fumei Liu; married Hong Zeng, Jun 26, 1988; children: Andromeda Zeng. **EDUCATION:** University of Science and Technology of China, Hefei, BS, 1982; University of Colorado, Boulder, MS, 1986, PhD, 199. **CAREER:** University of Colorado, Boulder, Joint Institute for Laboratory Astrophysics, research assistant, 1983-89; University of Idaho, Moscow, Department of Physics, visiting assistant professor, 1989-91; Butler University, Department of Physics, assistant professor, 1991-. **ORGANIZATIONS:** American Physical Society, 1985-. **HONORS/AWARDS:** University of Colorado, Doctoral Fellowship, 1984-87. **SPECIAL ACHIEVEMENTS:** Discovery of alignment to orientation conversions in atomic sodium, 1991; polarization effects in superfluorences in calcium atomic vapor, 1991; first measurement of backward electron-atom scattering cross sections, 1990; development of a novel laser spectroscopic method to study electron-atom collisions, 1988; development of an accurate theory for optogalvanic effects, 1993. **BUSINESS ADDRESS:** Asst Prof, Dept of Physics, Butler University, 4600 Sunset Ave, Indianapolis, IN 46208-3443, (317)283-9873.

HANAFUSA, HIDESABURO
Educator, virologist. Japanese American. **PERSONAL:** Born Dec 1, 1929, Nishinomiya, Japan; son of Kamehachi and Tomi Hanafusa; married Teruko Inoue, May 11, 1958; children: Kei. **EDUCATION:** Osaka University, Japan, BS, 1953, PhD, 1960. **CAREER:** Osaka University, Research Institute for Microbial Diseases, research associate, 1958-61; University of California, Berkeley, Virus Lab, postdoctoral fellow, 1961-64; College de France, Paris, visiting scientist, 1964-66; City of New York Inc, Public Health Research Institute, Department of Viral Oncology, chief, associate member, 1966-68, member, 1968-73; Rockefeller University, professor, 1973-, Leon Hess professor, 1986-. **ORGANIZATIONS:** American Society of Microbiology; American Society of Virology; AAAS; New York Academy of Science; American Soc of Biol Chemistry; American Association Cancer Research; National Academy of Science. **HONORS/AWARDS:** Howard Taylor Ricketts Award, 1981; Albert Lasker Basic Med Research Award, 1982; Asahi Press Prize, 1984; Clowes Memorial Award, 1986; Culture Merit Award, Japan, 1991; National Cancer Institute, grantee, 1966-. **SPECIAL ACHIEVEMENTS:** Editorial board: Journal of Virology, 1975-, Molecular Cell Biology, 1984-; contributes articles to professional journals. **BUSINESS ADDRESS:** Leon Hess Professor, Rockefeller University, 1230 York Ave, New York, NY 10021.*

HANAMI, CLEMENT S.
Educator, museum administrator. Japanese American. **PERSONAL:** Born Nov 30, 1961, Los Angeles, CA; son of Tomeo Hanami and Yasuko Hanami Moriwaki; married Guadalupe Hanami, Jul 4, 1983; children: Dylan Rebecca. **EDUCATION:** East Los Angeles College, AA, 1985; UCLA, BA, 1988, MFA, 1992. **CAREER:** UCLA, teachers associate, 1989-93; Palms Jr High, education aide III, 1990-92; Museum of Contemporary Art, outreach educator, 1991-92; Windward High School, art teacher, 1992; Cypress College, art instructor, 1993-; Japanese American National Museum, Legacy Center, manager, 1992-. **ORGANIZATIONS:** API Visions, 1988-; College Art Association, 1993. **HONORS/AWARDS:** Rockefeller, Rockefeller Travel Grant,

1993; Cultural Affairs LA, Arts Recovery Fund, 1992; UCLA Art Council, 1992. **SPECIAL ACHIEVEMENTS:** World Record, oral history project, 1993; Westworld, Long Beach Museum of Art, 1992; Family Values, Santa Monica Museum of Art, 1992; Panopticon, UCLA Wight Art Gallery, 1992; VU's from the Pacific Rim, curator for video screening at Society for Photographic Education, 1992. **BIOGRAPHICAL SOURCES:** Then and Now, LA Times Calendar, p 85, May 23, 1993; "Behind the Scenes," JANM Bulletin, p 8, V8, N1, winter 1993. **BUSINESS ADDRESS:** Manager, Legacy Center, Japanese American National Museum, 369 East First Street, Los Angeles, CA 90012, (213)625-0414.

HANG, TRU
Machine operator. Laotian American/Chinese American. **PERSONAL:** Born Sep 14, 1945, Lao People's Democratic Republic; son of Youa Ya Hang & La Chang Hang; married Lee Nong Hang, Jan 15, 1965; children: Yee Leng, Lao Lu, Yee Chang, Fu Pang Kau, Pang Wour, Kong Chee, Tou Ger. **EDUCATION:** Technical Military School, 1966; Okinawa Military Academy, intelligence course, 1973. **CAREER:** General Motors, machine operator, 1987-. **ORGANIZATIONS:** Tri-City Lao-Hmong Association, president, 1980-82, 1984-86, board member, 1989-91; Hang Association, president, 1990-92, board member, 1984-90; UAW, 1981-; Hmong Federation of America, 1982-; Lao-Hmong Organization of Michigan, president, 1977-78; Refugee Service of Saginaw, Child Human Development, 1983-84. **HONORS/AWARDS:** Tri-City Lao-Hmong Association, Community Leadership, 1990. **SPECIAL ACHIEVEMENTS:** CIA operative in Laos, 1961-75. **HOME ADDRESS:** 3304 S Van Buren, Richville, MI 48758, (517)868-3444.

HAQUE, M. SHAMSUL
Educator, certified public accountant. Bangladeshi American. **PERSONAL:** Born Feb 2, 1934, Bahari, Chandpur, Bangladesh; son of Md Abdul Qadir Master (deceased); married Abeda Haque, Aug 22, 1962; children: Nabilah A, Mustafa A, Karima S. **EDUCATION:** Govt College of Commerce, Bangladesh, B Com, 1953; Dhaka University, Bangladesh, M Com, 1955; American University, MBA, 1961; American University, PhD, bus admin, 1967. **CAREER:** Habiganj College, Sylhet, Bangladesh, professor of commerce, 1955-56; Qaidi Azam College, Dhaka, professor of commerce, 1956-58; Akbar G Mechart & Co, chartered accountant, senior accountant, 1957-58; Pakistan Embassy, chief accountant, 1959-65; Dyke College, assistant professor, 1965-70; University of District of Columbia, associate professor, 1970-71; Howard University, professor of accounting, 1971-. **ORGANIZATIONS:** AICPA; AAA; AMS; CCA; MACPA. **HONORS/AWARDS:** Fulbright Scholarship, 1958-59; American University, Hall of Nations Award, 1961-62; IBSCUG, Best Award for Scholarly Presentation, 1989. **SPECIAL ACHIEVEMENTS:** Certified public accountant, 1967-; author of Lotus 1-2-3 Made Easy, 1984; Lotus Symphony Book, 1987; Holy Qur'an, Pt 30; Arabic Qaidah; Surah Baqarah, Holy Onic Pt 1-2-3; Life of Prophet Muhammed-Final Messenger; Practice in Commercial Mathematics; World Islamic Service Mission, Inc., president. **HOME PHONE:** (301)622-4744. **BUSINESS ADDRESS:** Professor of Accounting, Howard University, School of Business, Rm 318, Washington, DC 20059-0002, (202)806-1587.

HAQUE, ZAHUR U.
Educator. Bangladeshi American. **PERSONAL:** Born Mar 3, 1950, Comilla, Bangladesh; son of Abdul & Rowshan Ara Haque; married Jasmine Haque, Sep 1974; children: Nadia, Rezwan, Monica. **EDUCATION:** Dhaka University, Bangladesh, BS (honors), 1974, nutrition diploma, 1977, MS, 1976; United Nations University, Japan, certificate food tech, 1980; Kyoto University, Japan, PhD, 1984; Cornell University, postdoctorate, 1984. **CAREER:** Dhaka University, assistant professor, 1980; Cornell University, research associate II, 1986; Mississippi State University, associate professor, 1988, professor, 1993-. **ORGANIZATIONS:** Sigma Xi, 1989-; Phi Tau Sigma, 1988-; IFT, 1987-; ADSA, 1987-; ABC, Japan, 1993-. **SPECIAL ACHIEVEMENTS:** More than 160 articles, abstracts and book chapters in refereed journals; numerous patents; proficiency in 4 languages.

HARA, LLOYD
Federal government official. Japanese American. **PERSONAL:** Born 1940?. **CAREER:** King County, WA, auditor, nine years; City of Seattle, treasurer, 1979-92; Federal Emergency Management Agency, Region X, director, 1994-. **SPECIAL ACHIEVEMENTS:** Member of Washington state Asian-American Clinton-Gore presidential transition team. **BUSINESS ADDRESS:** Director, Region X, Federal Emergency Management Agency, Federal Regional Center, 130-228th St SW, Bothell, WA 98021, (206)487-4604.*

HARA, SABURO
Physician, educator. Japanese American. **PERSONAL:** Born Feb 16, 1928, Yamanashiken, Japan; son of Taneyoshi and Taki Ogawa; married Marjorie E Hara, Dec 21, 1958; children: Mary K Hara Binkley. **EDUCATION:** Tokyo Medical College, MD, 1952. **CAREER:** Meharry Medical College, professor, chairman, 1989-. **ORGANIZATIONS:** American Academy of Pediatrics; Alpha Omega Alpha; Ambulatory Pediatrics Association. **HONORS/AWARDS:** Nashville Memorial Hospital, Southern Society for Pediatric Research, founder, 1965. **SPECIAL ACHIEVEMENTS:** Published 69 scientific papers in peer-reviewrd journals in area of medicine. **BUSINESS ADDRESS:** Professor, Chairman, Meharry Medical College, 1005 D B Todd Blvd, Nashville, TN 37208-3501, (615)327-6332.

HARAMAKI, CHIKO
Educator. Japanese American. **PERSONAL:** Born Oct 3, 1925, Hayward, CA; son of Saburo Haramaki and Mite (Sato) Haramaki. **EDUCATION:** University of California, Berkeley; University of Minnesota; Oregon State University, BS, 1952; University of Illinois, MS, 1953; Ohio State University, PhD, 1957. **CAREER:** University of California, Riverside, expt stat associate, 1970-71; Pennsylvania State University, asst professor, 1957-68, associate professor, 1968-77, professor, 1977-86, professor emeritus, 1986-. **ORGANIZATIONS:** New York Academy of Sciences; American Assn for the Advancement of Science, 1957-; American Soc for Horticultural Science, 1957-; Intl Plant Propagators Soc, 1958;-; Northeastern Weed Science Soc, 1959-; Natl Ski Patrol System, patrol leader, section chief, 1958-86; Intl Soc for Arboriculture, 1958-86; Intl Soc for Horticultural Science. **HONORS/AWARDS:** NE Weed Science Society, Distinguished Service Award, 1985; Pi Alpha Xi, natl vp & natl president, 1979-80; Sigma Xi; Alpha Zeta; Gamma Sigma Delta; Phi Epsilon Phi; Natl Ski Patrol System, Natl Ski Patrolman #2648, 1963. **SPECIAL ACHIEVEMENTS:** Over 100 published professional and technical articles and chapters in books. **MILITARY SERVICE:** US Army Air Force, Sgt, 1946-49. **HOME ADDRESS:** 7012 7th Ave Blvd NW, Bradenton, FL 34209-1547, (813)795-2762. **BUSINESS ADDRESS:** Professor Emeritus, Dept of Horticulture, Pennsylvania State University, 101 Tyson Bldg, University Park, PA 16802.

HARA-NIELSEN, SYLVIA ANN
State official. Japanese American. **PERSONAL:** Born Nov 8, 1948, Hilo, HI; daughter of Elsie & Harry H Hara; married Kenneth Nielsen, Nov 1975; children: Chelsey Aiko. **EDUCATION:** San Jose State University, BA, tchg cred, 1970; University of Hawaii, MEd, 1975, MPA, 1994. **CAREER:** Office of the Governor, State of Hawaii, services coordinator, 1971-80; State Department of Labor & Industrial Relations, assistant director, 1980-83, program director, 1983-87, administrator, 1987-. **ORGANIZATIONS:** Governor's Office of Children & Youth Advisory Council, vice pres, 1987-93; Hawaii State Coordinating Commission on Deafness, 1987-91; International Association of Personnel Security Employees, president, 1986-89; Hawaii Personnel and Guidance Association, 1968-91; American Vocational Association, 1988-91. **HONORS/AWARDS:** US Department of Labor, Youth 2000 Award, Grant, 1989. **SPECIAL ACHIEVEMENTS:** Evaluation Team, Alternative Sentencing Program, Public Defenders Office, 1992-93. **BIOGRAPHICAL SOURCES:** Kona Echo, Biographical Account of Grandfather, 1990. **BUSINESS ADDRESS:** Administrator, Office of Special Programs, State Dept of Labor and Industrial Relations, 830 Punchbowl St, Honolulu, HI 96813.

HARANO, ROSS MASAO
Association executive. Japanese American. **PERSONAL:** Born Sep 17, 1942, Fresno, CA; son of Masashi Harano and Takeko Mayewaki Harano; divorced; children: Michelle Akiko Kolak, Michael Abe, Mark Aiji. **EDUCATION:** University of Illinois, BS, finance, 1965; DePaul University, 1965-67. **CAREER:** Continental Assurance Co, actuarial analyst, 1965-66; New England Mutual Life Insurance Co, agent, 1966-74; Power-Ski Corp, vice president, 1974-76; Panagraphic Corp, president, 1976-80; Bank of Chicago, vice president, 1978-80; Community Bank of Edgewater, vice president, 1980-81; Landmark Enterprises of Illinois, president, 1981-84; Medport, executive vice president, 1984-87; Marble Supply International, chief financial officer, 1987-88; Office of the Attorney General, EEO officer, 1988-91, director of advisory councils, 1989-91, crime victims division, chief, 1990-93; World Trade Center, Chicago, president, 1993-. **ORGANIZATIONS:** Japanese American Citizens League, Chicago chapter chairperson, 1969-70, 1993-94, national legislative committee chairperson, 1970-72, Midwest district council, governor, 1971-74; Illinois Special Events Commission, 1977-79; Illinois Ethnic Coalition, chairperson, 1993-94; Uprtown Chicago Commission, president, 1976-77; Asian

American Advisory Councils, to governor, 1982-88, to Senator Alan Dixon, 1985-92, to Senator Paul Simon, 1985-90; City of Chicago, Commission on Asian American Affairs, 1984-94, chair, 1984-86; numerous others. **HONORS/AWARDS:** Japanese American Citizens League, Silver Pin, 1970, Sapphire Pin, 1973; Chicago Jr Chamber of Commerce, Ten Outstanding Young Citizens Award, 1976; Illinois Department of Human Rights Award, 1984; Chicago Commission on Human Relations Award, 1985; Illinois Ethnic Consultation American Pluralism Award, 1989. **HOME ADDRESS:** 1349 W Winnemac Ave, Chicago, IL 60640, (312)275-4988. **BUSINESS ADDRESS:** President, World Trade Center Chicago Association, 929 The Merchandise Mart, Chicago, IL 60654, (312)467-0550.

HASAN, SYED E.
Educator. Indo-American. **PERSONAL:** Born Apr 15, 1939, Patna, Bihar, India; son of Syed & Hayat Hasan; married Farrukh Hasan, Jan 26, 1968; children: Danish, Zeenat, Zeba. **EDUCATION:** Patna University, BS, 1960; Roorkee University, MS, 1963; Purdue University, PhD, 1978. **CAREER:** Geological Survey of India, junior geologist, 1965-70, senior engineering geologist, 1970-73; Houghton Technological University, visiting assistant professor, 1978; University of Arizona, visiting assistant professor, 1978-79; University of Missouri, Geology, assistant professor, 1979-84, associate professor, 1984-. **ORGANIZATIONS:** Association of Engineering Geologist, KC-O Section, chair, 1989-91; Association of Engineering Geologist, tunneling committee, 1985-. **SPECIAL ACHIEVEMENTS:** Several papers in the fields of engineering and environmental geology, 1981-; language proficiency: Urdu, Hindi. **BUSINESS ADDRESS:** Associate Professor, Dept of Geosciences, University of Missouri, 300 GP, Kansas City, MO 64110-2499, (816)235-2976.

HASEGAWA, JACK KOICHI
Educational administrator. Japanese American. **PERSONAL:** Born Jun 11, 1944, Greeley, CO; son of Peter Kaoru Hasegawa and Yoshino Tajiri Hasegawa; married Nancy Polk; children: Mira Lee, Ken, Peter. **EDUCATION:** University of the Pacific, AB, 1965; Harvard University, MTS, 1968. **CAREER:** United Methodist Board of Missions , missionary, 1968-72; Friends World College, executive vp, 1972-80; Yale University, Dwight Hall, general secy, 1980-93; State of Connecticut, Dept of Education, Quality Integrated Education, education consultant, 1993-. **ORGANIZATIONS:** Governor's Council on Voluntary Service, 1985-86; Columbus House Shelter, chairman of the board, 1981-84; Campus Outreach Opportunity League, chairman of the board, 1982-87; Kiyosato Educational Experimental Program Board, 1986-90; Kyoto International School, chairman of the board, 1974-77; Interfaith Housing Research Council of Western Japan, director, 1970-74; Asian American Student Association, advisor, 1980-84; Asian Community Services, chairman of the board, 1984-88; Yale College, Minority Affairs Council, 1983-85. **HONORS/AWARDS:** City of New Haven, Citation for Outstanding Service, 1992; Congressional Citation for Community Service, 1983; University of the Pacific, Outstanding Graduate Senior, Bishop Tippett Award, 1965; New Haven School Volunteers, Volunteer Leadership Award, 1992; Trumbull College at Yale, fellow, 1981-. **SPECIAL ACHIEVEMENTS:** Fluent in Japanese; founder, Campus Outreach Opportunities League; founder, Columbus House Shelter; founder, Community Action by Students Together; advisor to National Commission on Community Service. **BIOGRAPHICAL SOURCES:** Special Report, p 19, Nov 11, 1992; New York Times, ct section, Oct 7, 1990; Foundation News, Yale Alumini Mag, p 38, March 1989, p 16, Nov 1985. **HOME ADDRESS:** 1932 Litchfield Turnpike, Woodbridge, CT 06525, (203)397-2799.

HASHIMOTO, AKIRA
Carbon and graphite machine shop executive. Japanese American. **PERSONAL:** Born Mar 8, 1949, Gifu, Japan; son of Shugo Hashimoto and Hatsuko Hashimoto; married Miyuki Hashimoto, Mar 8, 1973; children: Miho. **EDUCATION:** Keio University, graduated, 1971. **CAREER:** Ibiden Co Ltd, Ceramic Division, sales & marketing mgr; Micro Mech Inc, president, currently. **BUSINESS ADDRESS:** President, Micro Mech, Inc, 33 Newburyport Turnpike, Ipswich, MA 01938, (508)356-2966.

HASHIMOTO, EIJI
Educator, performing artist. Japanese American. **PERSONAL:** Born Aug 7, 1931, Tokyo, Japan; son of Tokusaburo and Haruko Hashimoto; married Ruth Laves Hashimoto, Jun 8, 1963; children: Christine Hashimoto Merritt, Ken Laves, Erica Joan. **EDUCATION:** Tokyo University of Fine Arts & Music, BMusic, 1954; University of Chicago, MA, 1959; Yale University, School of Music, MMus, 1962. **CAREER:** Toho Gakuen School of Music, lecturer,

1966; University of Cincinnati, College-Conservatory of Music, assistant professor, 1968-72, associate professor, 1972-77, professor, 1977-, artist-in-residence, 1968-. **HONORS/AWARDS:** Japanese Ministry of Cultural Affairs, Prize of Excellence, 1978, 1981; University of Cincinnati, Rieveschl Award for Excellence, 1984. **SPECIAL ACHIEVEMENTS:** Concerts as a solo harpsichordist throughout the USA and in 23 countries, 1962-; LP/CDs from recording companies in US and Japan; publications from US, England, France, and Japan. **BUSINESS ADDRESS:** Professor of Harpsichord, Artist-in-Residence, University of Cincinnati, College-Conservatory of Music, Cincinnati, OH 45221-0003, (513)556-9558.

HASHIMOTO, KEN
Physician, educator, educational administrator. Japanese American. **PERSONAL:** Born Jun 19, 1931, Niigata, Niigata, Japan; son of Takashi and Kiku Hashimoto; married Noriko, Oct 23, 1961; children: Naomi, Martha, Eugene, Amy. **EDUCATION:** Niigata University School of Medicine, MD, 1955. **CAREER:** Tufts University, assistant professor, 1963-68; University of Tennessee, professor, 1968-76; Wright State University, professor, director, 1977-80; Wayne State University, professor, chairman, 1980-. **ORGANIZATIONS:** NIH Study Section, 1974-; National Board of Medical Examiners, 1989-92; American Society of Dermatopathology, president, 1986-87; Society for Investigative Dermatolgy, vice president, 1980-81. **HONORS/AWARDS:** Fulbright Scholarship, 1956-59; Veterans Administration, Medical Investigatorship, 1969-78; Japanese Dermatological Association, honorary member, 1991. **SPECIAL ACHIEVEMENTS:** Author, six books; over 300 scientific publications in refereed journals; thirty-three book chapters. **HOME ADDRESS:** 7000 Warren Road, Ann Arbor, MI 48105. **BUSINESS PHONE:** (313)577-5061.

HASHIMOTO, RENTARO
Educator. Japanese American. **PERSONAL:** Born Jul 2, 1930, Oakland, CA; son of Kinnosuke Hashimoto and Setsu Yoshida; married Ayae Hashimoto, Dec 28, 1968; children: Mari. **EDUCATION:** City College of New York, BA, 1952; University of Mexico, MA, 1953; Fordham University, PhD, 1963. **CAREER:** Vanguard Recording Society, coordinator, 1957-60; Saint Francis College, adjunct lecturer, 1961-62; Fordham University, adjunct lecturer, 1961-62; Manhattan College, associate professor of philosophy, 1962-. **ORGANIZATIONS:** American Association of University Professors, 1965-. **HONORS/AWARDS:** Phi Beta Kappa, 1952. **MILITARY SERVICE:** US Army, spc 2nd class, 1954-56. **BUSINESS ADDRESS:** Associate Professor of Philosophy, Manhattan College, Riverdale, NY 10471, (718)920-0326.

HASHIMOTO, STEVEN GEORGE
Musician, composer. Japanese American. **PERSONAL:** Born Feb 20, 1953, Chicago, IL; son of George Hiroshi Hashimoto and Alice Asako Maeda. **CAREER:** Steve Hashimoto Music, president, currently. **HONORS/AWARDS:** Chicago Office of Fine Arts, assistant grant, 1987-90. **SPECIAL ACHIEVEMENTS:** Appeared at Chicago Jazz Festival, leading own band, Mothra, 1991; compositons featured on jazz album by Fireworks Jazz, 1991, 1992; released albums of compositions: Sansei, 1991; In Dreams Begin Responsibilities, 1989; Farewell to Manzanar, 1987. **BIOGRAPHICAL SOURCES:** Chicago Tribune, Aug 2, 1992, Feb 4, 1993, section 1, back page, Feb 19, 1993; Jam Sessions, p 4, Nov 1988; Chicago Sun-Times, Dec 10, 1987; Asian Week, Jul 1, 1988; Illinois Entertainer, Jun 1990, Nov 1991. **HOME PHONE:** (312)342-2043. **BUSINESS ADDRESS:** President, Steven Hashimoto Music, PO Box 47470, Chicago, IL 60647.

HASHMI, MOHAMMED ZAFAR
Business executive. Pakistani American. **PERSONAL:** Born May 7, 1956, Karachi, Pakistan; son of Mohammed Qamar Hashmi; married Abida Hashmi, Oct 16, 1982; children: Shariq, Tariq, Sarah. **EDUCATION:** West Coast University, BSEE, 1976; UCLA, MBA, 1979. **CAREER:** Eaton, project mgr, 1981-83; Varian, marketing mgr, 1983-91; Goodyear, chief excutive officer, 1992-. **ORGANIZATIONS:** Gilroy Chamber of Commerce, economic committee. **BUSINESS ADDRESS:** Owner, Goodyear, 7634 Monterey St, PO Box A, Gilroy, CA 95020, (408)842-2520.

HASHMI, SAYED A.
Engineer, government official. Indo-American. **PERSONAL:** Born Sep 15, 1942, Budaun, Uttar Pradesh, India; son of Sayed Alay Nabi (deceased) and Hanifa Bano (deceased); married Shahrukh Hashmi, Aug 26, 1973; children: Maaria, Afifa. **EDUCATION:** Aligarh Muslim University, India, MS, 1969. **CAREER:** Empire Soils Inc, junior engr, 1974-76; MCA Engineering Corp, engineering geologist, 1975-76; City of Baltimore, pollution control analyst III,

1976-. **HONORS/AWARDS:** Aligarh Alumni Association, Washington DC, president, 1984, 1989. **HOME ADDRESS:** 6210 Craigmont Rd, Baltimore, MD 21228, (410)744-3318. **BUSINESS ADDRESS:** Pollution Control Analyst III, City of Baltimore, 200 E Lexington St, A W Wolman Municipal Bldg, Rm 407, Baltimore, MD 21202, (410)396-4840.

HATA, DAVID M.
Educator, educational administrator. Japanese American. **PERSONAL:** Born Jun 24, 1947, Yakima, WA; son of Yoshio & Carmen Hata; married Susan, Jun 20, 1970; children: Jonathan, Aaron, Abigail. **EDUCATION:** Washington State University, BS, electrical engineering, 1969; University of Washington, MS, electrical engineering, 1971. **CAREER:** Portland Community College, Department of Microelectronics Technology, professor, chair, 1971-. **ORGANIZATIONS:** Institute of Electrical & Electronics Engineers, TAC/ABET accreditation visitor, 1982-93; American Society for Engineering Education, 1982-93; Association for Computing Machinery, two-year college task force, 1988-93. **HONORS/AWARDS:** ASEE, Chester F. Carlson Award, 1992; IEEE, Education Society, Innovation in Engineering Education, 1991; Portland Community College, Faculty Execellence Award, 1988; IEEE Computer Society, Meritorious Service Award, 1983. **SPECIAL ACHIEVEMENTS:** Co-author, Circuits: Principles, Analysis, and Simulation, Saunders Publishing Company, 1992. **BIOGRAPHICAL SOURCES:** ASEE Prism Magazine, June 1993. **BUSINESS ADDRESS:** Professor, Portland Community College, 12000 SW 49th Ave, PO Box 19000, Portland, OR 97280-0990, (503)244-6111.

HATA, DONALD TERUO, JR.
Educator. Japanese American. **PERSONAL:** Born Mar 4, 1939, Los Angeles, CA; son of Teruo Hata and Yachiyo Hata; married Nadine Ishitani Hata, Dec 24, 1966. **EDUCATION:** University of Southern California, BA, 1962, MA, 1964, PhD, 1970. **CAREER:** Occidental College, visiting instructor, 1967-68; California State University, Dominguez Hills, assistant professor, 1970-80; California State University, Sacramento, director of development and executive assistant to the president, 1982-83; California State University, Dominguez Hills, professor of history, 1983-. **ORGANIZATIONS:** California Historical Society, vice president, 1988-89, board of trustees, 1979-89; Historical Society of Southern California, board of directors, 1978-80; Mid-Cities Credit Union, board of directors, 1986-89; City of Gardena, California, city council, 1971-76; planning commission, 1971-73; Western Law Center for the Handicapped, board of directors, 1978-80; American Historical Association, 1966-; Organization of American Historians, 1970-. **HONORS/AWARDS:** California Historical Society, Award of Merit, 1980; California State University, Dominguez Hills, Lyle Gibson Distinguished Teaching Professor Award, 1977; California State University, Board of Trustees, Outstanding Professor Award of the 20-Campus system, 1990; US National Defense Act, Graduate Fellow in Chinese and Japanese, 1962-65. **SPECIAL ACHIEVEMENTS:** Book: Undesirables, Early Immigrants and the Anti-Japanese Movement in San Francisco, 1892-93, Prelude to Exclusion, Arno Press, 1978; co-author, "George Shima: The Potato King of California," Journal of the West, Jan 1986; "California Asians," A Guide to the History of California, 1989; "Asian and Pacific Angelenos: Model Minorities and Indispensable Scapegoats," 20th Century Los Angeles: Power, Promotion and Social Conflict, 1990; Japanese Americans and World War II, Forum, 1974, 5th printing 1980. **HOME PHONE:** (310)316-4894. **BUSINESS ADDRESS:** Professor of History, California State University, Dominguez Hills, 1000 E Victoria St, Carson, CA 90747, (310)516-3448.

HATA, HIROAKI
Educator. Japanese American. **PERSONAL:** Born Nov 9, 1940, Hiroshima, Hiroshima, Japan; son of Juro & Suneno Hata; married Mette Andersson Hata, Jun 8, 1989. **EDUCATION:** Ochanomizu Academy of Fine Arts, 1962-63; Reitaku University, AB, 1963; Washington University, MArch, 1969; Harvard University, MArch in Urban Design, 1978. **CAREER:** Sert, Jackson and Associates, senior project designer, 1971-73; Pietro Belluschi and Jung, Brannen, Assoc, senior project designer, 1973-74; Anselevicius, Rupe, Assoc, senior project designer, 1970-71, 1974-75; Boston Architectural Center, instructor, 1972-79; Harvard University, instructor, 1978-79; School of Architecture, Aarhus, Denmark, visiting associate professor, 1985-86; SUNY, Buffalo, assistant professor of architecture, 1979-85, associate professor of architecture, 1985-. **ORGANIZATIONS:** American Institute of Architects, 1983-; Institute for Urban Design, 1980-. **HONORS/AWARDS:** International Biographical Center, Men of Achievement Award, 1986; Graham Foundation, Graham Scholar, Travelling Fellowship, 1968; Washington University, Frederick Widman Prize, 1968; Buffalo Urban Retail Core International Design Competi-

tion, third prize, 1986. **SPECIAL ACHIEVEMENTS:** Published monograph, Harbor Cove Waterfront Plan, Gloucester, MA, 1981; published articles on Josep Lluis Sert's work in architecture & urbanism, 1975, 1977; exhibited own and architecture studio work in Buffalo, Cambridge, MA; master plans for downtowns, waterfront and neighborhoods in western New York, 1982-. **BUSINESS ADDRESS:** Associate Professor, Dept of Architecture, SUNY, Buffalo, School of Architecture and Planning, South Campus, Hayes Hall, Buffalo, NY 14214-3087, (716)829-3483.

HATA, NADINE ISHITANI

Educator. Japanese American. **PERSONAL:** Born Mar 15, 1941, Honolulu, HI; daughter of Ichiro and Sumako Ishitani; married Donald Teruo Hata Jr, Dec 1966. **EDUCATION:** University of Hawaii, BA (w/honors), history, 1963; University of Michigan, MA, far eastern studies, 1965; University of Southern California, PhD, history, 1983. **CAREER:** California State University, Long Beach, asst professor, 1967-68; California State College, Dominguez Hills, lecturer in history, 1969-70; Los Angeles County Probation Dept, Staff Training Office, visiting instructor in Asian American history, 1972-73; El Camino College, Div of Behavioral and Social Sciences, dean, 1984-92, professor of history, 1970-, vp of instruction, asst superintendent, 1992-. **ORGANIZATIONS:** California State Advisory Committee to the US Commission on Civil Rights, 1973-85, vice chair, 1974-81; California State Historical Resources Commission, 1976-84, chair, 1979-81, 1982-83; California State Heritage Task Force, 1982-84; American Historical Association, Teaching Div, 1983-85; California Preservation Foundation, board of trustees, 1985-88; Los Angeles Conservancy, board of directors, 1991-93; Japanese American Natl Museum, Scholarly Advisory Council, 1989-; Medici Foundation, Renaissance TV Series, Princeton University, board of education advisors, 1983-. **HONORS/AWARDS:** Soroptimist Intl, Women's Achievement Award, 1980; City of Gardena, Resolution of Commendation for Public Service, 1980; Mayor of Los Angeles, Commendation for Public Service, 1980; California State Legislature, Joint Rules Committee, Resolution of Commendation for Service on State Heritage Task Force, 1984; California Historical Society, Award of Merit, 1980. **SPECIAL ACHIEVEMENTS:** Publications: The Historic Preservation Movement in California, 1940-76, Sacramento, State Dept of Parks and Recreation, 1992; Japanese Americans and World War II, Forum Press, 5th printing, 1980; numerous articles and chapters on Asian American history. **HOME PHONE:** (310)316-4894. **BUSINESS ADDRESS:** Academic Affairs VP, Assistant Superintendent, El Camino Community College District, 16007 Crenshaw Blvd, Torrance, CA 90506, (310)715-3119.

HATAYAMA, RODNEY KEN

Veterinarian. Japanese American. **PERSONAL:** Born Jul 16, 1950, Fowler, CA; son of Aiko Hatayama and Narumi Hatayama; married Patti, Oct 13, 1984; children: Stephanie, Clinton. **EDUCATION:** California State University, Fresno, BA, zoology, 1973; University of California, Davis, DVM, 1979. **CAREER:** South County Veterinary Hospital, veterinarian, currently. **ORGANIZATIONS:** American Veterinary Assn, 1979-; California Veterinary Assn, 1992-; California Aquaculture Assn, 1985-; California Farm Bureau. **BUSINESS ADDRESS:** Veterinarian, South County Veterinary Hospital, 1811 Whitson, Selma, CA 93662, (209)896-8616.

HATTORI, JAMES

Journalist. Japanese American. **CAREER:** CBS News, foreign news correspondent, Tokyo, currently. **ORGANIZATIONS:** San Francisco State University, Center for Integration & Improvement of Journalism/Asian American Journalists Assn, Project Zinger Advisory Board, 1992. **SPECIAL ACHIEVEMENTS:** Covered 1994 Winter Olympics in Lillehammer, Norway. **BUSINESS ADDRESS:** Journalist, CBS News, 51 West 52nd St, New York, NY 10019-6165. ∗

HAUH, PAUL-THOMAS B.

Association consultant. Korean American. **PERSONAL:** Born Jun 19, 1963, Seoul, Republic of Korea; son of Joseph and Maria. **EDUCATION:** University of California, BA, 1986; Harvard University, EdM, 1988, 1989-. **CAREER:** Korean Martyrs Youth Assn, executive director, 1983-87; Collegiate Dynamics, executive director, 1988; Diocese of Orange, consultant, 1989-90; Harvard University, teaching fellow, 1990; The Boston Foundation, project staff, 1990-91; Public Education Fund Network, field director, consultant, 1991-92; Nouveau Collections, chief financial officer, 1993-; Hauh & Associates, consultant, currently. **ORGANIZATIONS:** Harvard Alumni Assn, 1988-; Maryknoll Fathers & Brothers Society, lay member, 1986-; University of California Alumni, 1986-; Phi Delta Kappa Honor Society, 1988-; Harvard University, Dean's

Advisory Council, chair, 1987-, Human Development Dept, advisor, 1989, School of Education, faculty search committee, 1990. **HONORS/AWARDS:** Harvard University, Doctoral Entering Award, 1989; Korean American Professional, Presenters Award, 1988; Phi Delta Kappa, honors, 1988. **SPECIAL ACHIEVEMENTS:** California Catholic Institute, catechist teacher, 1984-87; Korean American College Conference, counselor, 1989; Harvard University, research fellow/student, 1987-92; Korean American Family Symposium, lecturer, 1989. **BIOGRAPHICAL SOURCES:** "Upcoming Professional," Korea Times, Los Angeles, Aug 19, 1988; US-Korea Catholic News, p 1-2, Mar 26, 1989. **HOME ADDRESS:** PO Box 111021, Santa Barbara, CA 93107.

HAYAKAWA, NOBORU (ARNIE)

Sewing machine manufacturing company executive. Japanese American. **PERSONAL:** Born Nov 21, 1938, Yokosuka, Kanagawa, Japan; son of Ryuzo Hayakawa and Tomiko Hayakawa; married Yoko Hayakawa, May 28, 1967; children: Gen, Shuhei. **EDUCATION:** Japan National Defence Academy, graduated, 1961. **CAREER:** Nissan Motor Co, Japan, mgr, export dept, 1975-76, 1980-84, Industrial Division, deputy general mgr, 1985; Nissan Cooperation Office, Saudi Arabia, mgr, service, 1978-80; Nissan Industrial Equipment Co, vice pres, technical, 1986-88; Barrett Industrial Truck Inc, senior adviser, 1988-90; Union Special Corp, senior vp, TQM Worldwide, 1991-. **BUSINESS ADDRESS:** Senior Vice President, TQM Worldwide, Union Special Corp., One Union Special Plaza, Huntley, IL 60142, (708)669-4378.

HAYAKAWA, S. I. *See* Obituaries.

HAYAKAWA, SIDNEY AKIRA

Criminal investigator. Japanese American. **PERSONAL:** Born Dec 22, 1948, Honolulu, HI; son of Haruo Hayakawa and Tsueno Hayakawa; married Marsha Leimomi Hayakawa, Mar 16, 1974; children: Tracy Kehaulani. **CAREER:** Honolulu Police Department, police officer, 1968-72; Drug Enforcement Agency, criminal investigator, executive secretary to career board, 1972-. **SPECIAL ACHIEVEMENTS:** First Asian American to attain the rank of GM-15 agent within DEA. **BUSINESS ADDRESS:** Executive Secretary to the Career Board, Drug Enforcement Administration, 700 Army-Navy Drive, West Building, Arlington, VA 22202, (202)307-7349.

HAYASE, JOSHUA YOSHIO

Electrical engineer. Japanese American. **PERSONAL:** Born Aug 9, 1925, Seattle, WA; son of Ryoichi Henry Hayase and Satoko Matsuoka Hayase; married Viola I Hayase, Sep 12, 1950; children: David Alan. **EDUCATION:** Tokyo Rika Daigaku, 1944-45; Massachusetts Inst of Tech, SB, 1952, SM, 1957, degree of electrical engineer, 1957. **CAREER:** Department of Air Force, civilian employee, assistant bldg commandant, 1945-49; Massachusetts Inst of Tech, research & teaching assistant, 1952-57; Sylvania Electric Prod, advanced research engineer, 1952-57; General Electric, engineer, 1957-63; IBM, senior engineer, 1963-91; Information Systems International, organizer, president, 1991-. **ORGANIZATIONS:** Sigma Xi, 1957-62; Research Engineering Society of America, 1958-63; IBM Golden Circle, 1987; IBM Marketing Conference, 1989. **HONORS/AWARDS:** IBM, Outstanding Contribution Award, 1987, Quarter Century Club, 1988, Outstanding Contribution Award, 1989, informal awards, 1980, 1984. **SPECIAL ACHIEVEMENTS:** Coinventor: US Patents, 3,497,627, (1970), 3,534,264, (1970), 3,700,820, (1972); US patent on file: 07/912,702, (1992); papers presented: American Institutes of Aeronautics and Astronautics, 1966; National Electronics Conf, 1966, IEEE Electronics & Aerospace Systems Conv, 1970; IBM Creativity Publication, Sept 1990, March 1991. **HOME ADDRESS:** 9903 Carnegie Terrace, Bethesda, MD 20817, (301)530-8698.

HAYASHI, DENNIS WAYNE

Federal government official. Japanese American. **PERSONAL:** Born May 31, 1952, Los Angeles, CA; son of George and Yukiko Hayashi. **EDUCATION:** Occidental College, BA, 1974; Hastings College of Law, JD, 1978. **CAREER:** Asian Law Caucus, attorney, 1979-91; Japanese American Citizens' League, national director, 1991-93; US Department of Health and Human Services, Office for Civil Rights, director, 1993-. **ORGANIZATIONS:** California Bar Association, 1979-; National Asian American Bar Association, 1989-93; Asian American Bar Association, 1972-85. **SPECIAL ACHIEVEMENTS:** "Legal Reforms in the Garment Industry," Yale Law School, Journal of International Law, 1992; "Wards Cove: A Case Study of Stymied Justice," Asian American Policy Review, Kennedy School of Government, Harvard University, Spring 1993; op-ed pieces published in the Washington Post, Los Angeles Times, San Francisco Chronicle, and others. **BUSINESS ADDRESS:** Director, Office for

Civil Rights, US Dept of Health and Human Services, 330 Independence Ave SW, Cohen Bldg, Rm 5400, Washington, DC 20201, (202)619-0403.

HAYASHI, ELMER KINJI
Educator. Japanese American. **PERSONAL:** Born Oct 9, 1938, Sacramento, CA; son of James Juichi Hayashi & Tsugiko Handa Hayashi; married Betty Misaye Akiyama Hayashi, Jul 24, 1965; children: Janet Kimiko, Judith Tamiko Hayashi Edwards. **EDUCATION:** University of California at Davis, AB, 1960; San Diego State College, MS, 1968; University of Illinois, Champaign-Urbana, PhD, 1973. **CAREER:** Santa Clara High School, teacher, 1961-67; Wake Forest University, asst professor, 1973-79, assoc professor, 1979-88, professor, 1988-. **ORGANIZATIONS:** Mathematical Association of America, 1970-; American Mathematical Society, 1973-; Association for Computing Machinery, 1986-; North Carolina Council of Teachers of Mathematics, 1989-; Fibonacci Society, 1990-. **HONORS/AWARDS:** Phi Kappa Phi, 1968; University of Illinois, fellowship, 1972; Wake Forest University, Excellence in Teaching Award, 1980; National Science Foundation, Young Scholars in Computer Science Grant, 1989. **SPECIAL ACHIEVEMENTS:** Author: "An Elementary Method for Estimating Error Terms in Addictive Number Theory," Proc American Math Society, 1975; "Factoring Integers Whose Digits Are All Ones," Math Mag, 1976; "Omega Theorems for the Iterated Additive Convolution of a Nonnegative Arithmetic Function," Journal of Number Theory, 1981; "Fibronacci Numbers, Recursion, Complexity, and Induction Proofs," College Math Journal, 1992. **BUSINESS ADDRESS:** Professor of Mathematics and Computer Science, Wake Forest University, PO Box 7388, 314 Babcock Hall, Winston Salem, NC 27109, (910)759-5353.

HAYASHI, FUMIHIKO
Government official, biochemist. Japanese American. **PERSONAL:** Born Mar 28, 1930, Tokyo, Meguro-ku, Japan; son of Ryokichi Hayashi and Reiko Hayashi; married Noriko Hayashi, Oct 16, 1990. **EDUCATION:** University of Kagoshima, Dept of Agricultural Chemistry, BS, 1955; University of California, Davis, Dept of Vegetable Crops, fellow, 1960; University of Tokyo, Dept of Agricultural Chemistry, PhD, 1965; Michigan State University, Dept of Biochemistry, postdoc, 1966. **CAREER:** University of Tokyo, research assistant, 1957; University of California, Davis, research associate, 1960; Michigan State University, research associate, 1968; Woodard Research Corporation, sr biochemist, 1970; US Environmental Protection Agency, pesticide program, 1972, toxic substance, sr biochemist, 1980-. **ORGANIZATIONS:** American Society of Plant Physiologists, 1960-; Weed Science Society of America, 1960; American Society for Horticulturists, 1960-; New York Academy of Science, 1960-; American Chemical Society, 1960-; Sigma Xi, 1960-. **HONORS/AWARDS:** National Institutes of Health, grant, 1960-63; Japanese National Education Grant, 1950-54; Herman Frash Foundation, 1966-68. **SPECIAL ACHIEVEMENTS:** 26 publications in scientific journals; 2 governmental prints; administrative and regulatory position for pesticide and industrial toxic chemicals in the US government (EPA), review work for research related to regulation guidelines; international ecological work with the UNESCO. **BUSINESS ADDRESS:** Sr Biochemist, Office of Toxic Substance (TS-796), US Environmental Protection Agency, 401 M Street, SW, 431 G East Tower, Waterside Mall, Washington, DC 20460, (202)260-1278.

HAYASHI, JAMES AKIRA
Educator. Japanese American. **PERSONAL:** Born Dec 18, 1926, Alameda, CA; son of Hisaki Hayashi and Chitose Hayashi; married Carrie C Hayashi, Apr 13, 1955 (divorced); children: William H, Karl K, Vivian C. **EDUCATION:** Northern Illinois State Teachers College, BS, 1948; University of Wisconsin, Madison, MS, 1954, PhD, 1955. **CAREER:** University of Illinois Coll of Med, research associate, 1955-57, assistant professor, 1957-64, associate professor, 1964-68, professor, 1968-91; Rush Med Coll, Presbyterian St Luke's Hospital, professor, 1971-. **ORGANIZATIONS:** Sigma Xi, 1955-; American Society for Biochemistry and Molecular Biology, 1963-. **SPECIAL ACHIEVEMENTS:** Various publications on structure and function of bacteria; textbooks: Basic Biochemistry, 3rd ed, Rafelson, Binkley, Hayashi; Basic Biochemistry, 4th ed, Rafelson, Hayashi, Bezkorovainy. **MILITARY SERVICE:** Army of the United States, sergeant, 1945-46. **BUSINESS ADDRESS:** Professor, Rush Medical College, 600 S Paulina St, Chicago, IL 60612-3832, (312)942-2715.

HAYASHI, MASATO
Educator. Japanese American. **PERSONAL:** Born Nov 1938, Los Angeles, CA; son of Yoshio & Shigeko Hayashi. **CAREER:** Irvine Valley College, professor, currently. **ORGANIZATIONS:** Mathematical Association of

America; CMC3. **SPECIAL ACHIEVEMENTS:** Published textbook on basic programming. **MILITARY SERVICE:** US Air Force. **BUSINESS ADDRESS:** Professor, Irvine Valley College, 5500 Irvine Center Dr, B-268, Irvine, CA 92714, (714)559-3317.

HAYASHI, MASUMI
Artist, educator. Japanese American. **PERSONAL:** Born Sep 3, 1945, Gila Rivers Relocation Camp, AZ; daughter of Sakae & Tomio Hayashi; divorced; children: Dean Akira Keesey. **EDUCATION:** Florida State University, Tallahassee, Florida, BA, visual arts, 1975, MFA, visual arts, 1977; Sheridan College, Oakville, Ontario, Canada, post college certificate, computer graphics, 1985. **CAREER:** University of Central Florida, adjunct professor, 1980-82; Cleveland State University, associate professor, 1982-; Loyola Marymount College, adjunct professor, 1993. **ORGANIZATIONS:** Society for Photographic Education; Spaces Art Gallery, board member, 1990-; Ohio Arts Council, panel member. **HONORS/AWARDS:** Arts Midwest Fellowship, artist fellowship, 1989; Ohio Arts Council, artist fellowship, 1988; Headlands Center for the Arts, artist in resident, 1989-90; Koehler Art Center, artist in resident, 1985; Florida Arts Council, artist fellowship, 1980. **SPECIAL ACHIEVEMENTS:** One-person exhibits: "EPA Superfund Sites," by Barbara Tanenbaum & Wendy Kendall-Hess, Akron Art Museum, Ohio, 1992; "Ohio Steel Mills: A Post Industrial Perspective," Butler Institute of American Art, Youngstown, Ohio, 1990; "Masumi Hayashi," Art Gallery, Edinburgh College of Art, Lauriston Place, Edinburgh, Scotland, traveling 3-D photography show to Dundee and Glasco, 1985; group exhibitions: "War Works," 10 women photographers curated by Victoria Albert Art Museum, London, England, 1994; "The Country Between Us," curated by Barbara Boswick and Laura McFee, Massachusetts College of Art, Boston, exhibit of women landscape photographers, 1992; "Taking Liberties," New York Museum of Art, Albany, 1986, traveling 2 other NY sites. **BIOGRAPHICAL SOURCES:** Re Framings: New Women Photographers, an anthology edited by Diane Newmyer; "Undertone: Nine Unacculturated Women Photographers," by Lucy Lippard, 1993; The Invitational: Artists of Northeast Ohio, exhibition catalogue curated by Tom Hinson, The Cleveland Museum of Art, Cleveland, Ohio, 1991. **HOME ADDRESS:** 1401 West 75th St, Ste G, Cleveland, OH 44102, (216)961-0026.

HAYASHI, MIDORI
Civil servant. Japanese American. **PERSONAL:** widowed. **EDUCATION:** Sophia University, International Division, Tokyo, Japan, BA; Harvard Graduate School, Oriental Department, MA; Drexel University, Library Science Department, MS. **CAREER:** Intellectual Interchange & International House, Japan committee; Japan Society, NY; Du Pont de Nemours & Co; University of Pennsylvania; City of Philadelphia, Mayor's Office, Labor Standards Unit, deputy of labor, currently. **ORGANIZATIONS:** Japan Society, NY; Intellectual Interchange & International House, Japan committee. **HONORS/AWARDS:** University of Pennsylvania, Teaching Fellowship; Institute for Far Eastern Librarianship, Full Scholarship; Pendle Hill, Full Scholarship; Sophia University, Scholarship (partial). **HOME ADDRESS:** 4247 Locust St, Fairfax Apartments, Apt 112, Philadelphia, PA 19104, (215)387-6164.

HAYASHI, MIE MAY
Physician, educator. Japanese American. **PERSONAL:** Born Apr 15, 1962, New York, NY; daughter of Hiroyuki Hayashi and Satoko Hayashi. **EDUCATION:** Harvard-Radcliffe, BA, 1984; SUNY, Stony Brook Medical School, MD, 1988. **CAREER:** Montefiore Medical Center, intern & resident, 1988-91; Mount Sinai Medical School and Hospital, instructor, 1991-. **ORGANIZATIONS:** American College of Physicians, associate member, 1989-; Japanese Medical Society of America, 1991-. **SPECIAL ACHIEVEMENTS:** Proficient in Japanese and Spanish. **BUSINESS ADDRESS:** Instructor in General Internal Medicine, Mount Sinai Medical School & Hospital, 5 E 98th St, 11th Fl, Box 1088, New York, NY 10029, (212)241-9411.

HAYASHI, ROBERT H.
Physician, health services administrator. Japanese American. **PERSONAL:** Born Mar 29, 1938, Sacramento, CA; son of Akio Hayashi and Alice Hayashi; married Toni, May 19, 1979; children: Robert Akio, Richard Jinosuko, Suzanne Miszo, Magen, Matthew Hideki. **EDUCATION:** University of California, Berkeley, 1956-59; Temple University, MD, 1963; University of Michigan, residency, Ob/Gyn, 1970. **CAREER:** University of Pittsburgh, fellowship, 1970-72; University of Texas Health Science Center, San Antonio, faculty, 1972-83; Harbor/UCLA Medical Center, professor, chief of obstetrics, 1983-85; University of Michigan, professor, director of maternal fetal medicine,

1985-. **ORGANIZATIONS:** Society of Perinatal Obstetricians, 1976-, president, 1983; Society of Gynecologic Investigation, 1981-; American College of Obstetricians and Gynecologists, 1974-; American Medical Association, 1976-. **HONORS/AWARDS:** University of Michigan, J Robert Willson Professorship, 1990; Temple University School of Medicine, Alumni Achievement Award, 1993; NIH, University of Pittsburgh, Training Fellowship, 1977. **SPECIAL ACHIEVEMENTS:** Grants Review Committee, Maternal Child Health Bureau, DHHS, 1991-95. **MILITARY SERVICE:** US Army, captain, 1964-66. **HOME ADDRESS:** 1012 Spruce, Ann Arbor, MI 48104, (313)971-1052. **BUSINESS ADDRESS:** J. Robert Willson Professor of Obstetrics, Director of Maternal-Fetal Medicine Div, University of Michigan Medical Center, 1500 E Medical Ctr, Womens Hospital L-3228, Ann Arbor, MI 48109-0264, (313)764-1406.

HAYASHI, SEIGO
Vocational rehabilitation company owner. Japanese American. **PERSONAL:** Born Nov 3, 1943, Gila, AZ; son of Tomio and Sakaye Hayashi; married Sachi Mochizuki Hayashi, Sep 11, 1980; children: Stacy Junko, Sandy Keiko. **EDUCATION:** UCLA, BA, psychology, 1969; Cal State University, LA, MS, rehabilitation counseling, 1971. **CAREER:** Oriental Svc Ctr, rehab counselor, 1971-72; California State Dept of Rehab, rehab counselor, 1972-74; Asian American Drug Abuse Prog, director of treatment, 1974-75; Asian Rehabilitation Svcs, director of svcs, 1975-78; Portals House, director of svcs, 1979-80; Vocation Inc, owner, 1980-87; Hayashi & Associate, owner, 1988-. **ORGANIZATIONS:** Asian Rehab Svcs, LA, board member, 1981-91, chairman of the board, 1991-94; National Rehab Assn, 1971, So Cal, board member, 1978; National Fed of Concerned Drug Abuse Workers, board member, 1974-75; GIDRA magazine, organizer, editor, writer, 1969-70; Project Access California, advisory committee, 1978; California Regional Conference on Handicapped, delegate, 1976; White House Conf on Handicapped, alternate delegate, 1977. **HONORS/AWARDS:** State Dept of Rehab, Los Angeles, Award of Merit, 1975; National Distinguished Service Registry, Medical and Vocational Rehabilitation, 1987, 1989. **SPECIAL ACHIEVEMENTS:** Co-founder, Asian Rehabilitation Svcs, 1972; first treatment director, Asian American Drug Abuse Program, 1974; numerous presentations on working with Asian American disabled. **MILITARY SERVICE:** Army, 1966-68. **BUSINESS ADDRESS:** President, Hayashi & Associates, PO Box 3905, Glendale, CA 91221, (818)244-8912.

HAYASHI, TETSUMARO
Educator, association executive. Japanese American. **PERSONAL:** Born Mar 22, 1929, Sakaide, Kagawa, Japan; son of Tetsuro Hayashi and Shieko H Hayashi; married Akiko S Hayashi, Apr 14, 1960; children: Richard H. **EDUCATION:** Okayama University, Japan, BA, 1953; University of Florida, Gainesville, MA, 1957; Kent State University, MALS, 1959, PhD, 1968. **CAREER:** Culver-Stockton College, college library, assistant professor, associate director, 1959-63; Kent State University, instructor of English, 1965-68; Ball State University, assistant professor of English, 1968-72, associate professor of English, 1972-77, professor of English, 1977-93; Kwassui Women's University, Nagasaki, Japan, visiting professor, 1993-. **ORGANIZATIONS:** John Steinbeck Society of America, co-founder, director, 1966-81, president, 1981-83; International Steinbeck Society, president, 1983-95; Modern Language Association of America, 1967-; Shakespeare Society of Japan, 1965-. **HONORS/AWARDS:** Ball State University, Outstanding Research Award, 1981-82; John Steinbeck Center Foundation, Outstanding Service Award, 1984, 1992; Steinbeck Society of Japan, Outstanding Service Award, 1988, Outstanding Lifelong Achievement Award, 1991; Ball State University, Graduate Programs in English, Outstanding Service Award, 1992. **SPECIAL ACHIEVEMENTS:** Steinbeck Quarterly and Steinbeck Monograph Series, editor-in-chief, founder, 1968-93; author, editor of 31 books, 20 monographs on British American Literature, 1970-91; more than 100 lectures on Steinbeck in US, Canada, Great Britian and Japan. **BUSINESS ADDRESS:** Visiting Professor, English Dept, Kwassui Women's College, 1-50 Higashi-Yamate-Machi, Nagasaki-shi 850, Japan.

HAYASHI, WILLIAM YASUO
Educator, educational administrator. Japanese American. **PERSONAL:** Born Dec 2, 1941, Santa Rosa, CA; son of Tanio & Shizue Hayashi; married Kiyomi Hayashi, Nov 17, 1991; children: Kiyoshi. **EDUCATION:** Stanford University, BA, 1964; University of Chicago, MA, 1965, PhD, 1976. **CAREER:** University of Iowa, instructor, 1967-68; Roosevelt University, instructor, 1968-74; YMCA Community College, instructor, 1974-80; Columbia College, professor, coordinator of humanities, 1980-. **ORGANIZATIONS:** SYDA Foun-

dation, teacher of meditation, 1980-; Focusing Institute, teacher, 1978-. **HONORS/AWARDS:** Phi Beta Kappa; Woodrow Wilson Fellow; NED Scholar. **SPECIAL ACHIEVEMENTS:** Workshops in self-recognition training, Japan, currently; workshops in creativity, meditation, experiential focusing, currently; various articles on Japanese film and culture. **HOME ADDRESS:** 806 S Ridgeland Ave, #1N, Oak Park, IL 60304. **BUSINESS ADDRESS:** Coordinator/Prof of Humanities, Dept of Liberal Educ, Columbia College, 600 S Michigan Avenue, Chicago, IL 60605-2418, (312)663-1600.

HAYASHIDA, CHARLEY TAKETOSHI. *See* Obituaries.

HAYASHIDA, FRANK
Educator, educational administrator. Japanese American. **PERSONAL:** Born Feb 9, 1933, Artesia, CA; son of Tamehachi Hayashida and Chiya Furuta Hayashida. **EDUCATION:** Wilson Community College, AAS, 1955; Chicago State University, B Ed (honors), 1958; Indiana State University, MA, 1960; Indiana University, 1960-62; University of Illinois, Chicago, 1989. **CAREER:** Wilson/Kennedy-King College, faculty, 1962-; Wilson College, director, Student Activities, 1962-69; Kennedy-King College, admin asst, 1969-73, dean, planning & development, 1973-81, Broadcasting Dept, chairman, 1991-93. **ORGANIZATIONS:** Japanese American Citizens League, 1981-; Shawnee Theatre, board of directors, 1967-89, secretary, 1967-77, secretary-treasurer, 1977-81; WKKC-FM, exec board member, 1983-85; Young People's Network, treasurer, 1984-; Knights of Peter Claver, Grand Knight, 1985-; volunteer: Pegasus Players, Chicago Foundation for Education, WVON, MASCA, NAACP, JACL, 1981-. **HONORS/AWARDS:** John Hay Whitney, Scholarship, 1959; Lucille Gafford, Scholarship, 1960; Theta Alpha Phi, Karl Malden Award, 1958; Shawnee Theatre, Board Plaque, 1985. **SPECIAL ACHIEVEMENTS:** Communication Through Speaking, college text, 1983; Shawnee Theatre, technical director, 1960-81, associate producer, 1967-81, producer director, 1981-87; Chicago Access Corp, producer, cable television, 1988-91. **MILITARY SERVICE:** US Army, sgt, 1953-55. **HOME ADDRESS:** 6904 S Harvard Avenue, Chicago, IL 60621, (312)873-6327. **BUSINESS ADDRESS:** Chairman, Dept of Speech, Theatre & Broadcasting, Kennedy-King College, 6800 S Wentworth Ave, Chicago, IL 60621, (312)602-5530.

HAYASHIDA, RONALD HIDEO
Educator. Japanese American. **PERSONAL:** Born Jul 8, 1942, Paia, Maui, HI; son of Hideyuki & Hatsuyo Hayashida; married Susan M Hayashida, May 28, 1982; children: Alix Hideko. **EDUCATION:** Columbia University, PhD, 1973. **CAREER:** Jersey City State College, adjunct professor, 1973-74; Ramapo College of New Jersey, associate professor of comparative politics, 1974-. **ORGANIZATIONS:** American Association for the Advancement of Slavic Studies; Association of Asian Studies; American Political Science Association. **HONORS/AWARDS:** IREX, award for exchange to USSR, 1970; several jr college awards. **SPECIAL ACHIEVEMENTS:** Articles on Russian history. **BUSINESS ADDRESS:** Assoc Professor of Comparative Politics, Ramapo College of New Jersey, 505 Ramapo Valley Rd, Mahwah, NJ 07430-1623, (201)524-7422.

HAYASHIKAWA, DORIS S.
Librarian. Japanese American. **PERSONAL:** Born Aug 4, 1943, Heart Mount, WY; daughter of Yasuo & Teruko Ige; married William C Bryant. **EDUCATION:** University of Hawaii at Manoa, BA, chemistry, 1965; University of Texas at Austin, MLS, 1971; University of Pittsburgh, PhD, library science, 1983. **CAREER:** Shell Oil Co, information technologist, 1971-71; Texas A&M University, monographs cataloger, 1972-83; University of Hawaii, sci-tech reference librarian, 1976-83, sci-tech reference, head, 1983-87, monographs, assistant head, 1987-89; University of Pittsburgh, ULS, copy cataloging, head, 1989-, catalog dept, head, 1991-. **ORGANIZATIONS:** American Library Association, 1980-; Friends of the Carnegie Library of Pittsburgh, 1990-. **HONORS/AWARDS:** Phi Beta Kappa, 1965. **BUSINESS ADDRESS:** Head, Catalog Dept, University of Pittsburgh, University Library System, G49A Hillman Library, Pittsburgh, PA 15260.

HAYSLIP, LE LY
Writer, foundation administrator. Vietnamese American. **PERSONAL:** Born May 10, 1950, Ky La Village, Vietnam; daughter of Phung Van Trong & Tran Thi Huyen; widowed; children: James, Thomas, Alan. **CAREER:** Self-employed, author, currently; East Meets West, director, currently. **SPECIAL ACHIEVEMENTS:** Books include: When Heaven and Earth Change Places, 1989; Child of War, Woman of Peace, 1993; Village of Hope, a Displaced Children's Center in Vietnam, 1993; Peace Village Medical Center, 1991;

Compassion School for Children in Grades 2-5, 1992; Mobile Medical Unit Serving 200-500 Patients Each Week in Outlying Villages, 1992. **BIOGRAPHICAL SOURCES:** LA Times Magazine, p 6-13, Feb 5, 1989; NY Times Book Review, p 1, June 25, 1989; film: Heaven and Earth, directed by Oliver Stone, Warner Bros, Dec 1993. **BUSINESS ADDRESS:** Director, East Meets West Foundation, 725 Washington St, Ste 310, Oakland, CA 94607, (510)834-0301.

HAZAMA, CHUCK
City government official. Japanese American. **CAREER:** City of Rochester, MN, mayor, 1979-. **ORGANIZATIONS:** Citizens's Committee on Traffic; Energy Awareness Committee; Task Force on Hunger; Greater Rochester Area University Committee; Rochester Airport Commission; League of Minnesota Cities, board of directors, 1983, 1985, membership chair, 1984, board of directors, vp, 1986, board of directors, president, 1987; National League of Cities, Election '88 Committee, 1987, APAMO, president, 1990, board of directors, 1992; US Conference of Mayors, Energy and Environment Committee, 1982, 1985, Resource and Recovery Committee, chairman, 1989; Minnesota Mayors Association, vice president, 1990, president-elect, 1991. **HONORS/AWARDS:** University of Northern Iowa, Alumni Service Award, 1987; Taekwondo Federation, Honorary Blackbelt, 1989; Mayo Clinic Fellows Association, honorary member, 1990; Rochester Racquetball Hall of Fame, inductee, 1991; League of Minnesota Cities, C C Ludwig Award for Distinguished Municipal Service, 1992. **SPECIAL ACHIEVEMENTS:** Under Hazama's administration: City of Rochester averaged $127 million in development and growth per year for the past ten years; Rochester maintained Triple-A bond rating from Moody, Standard and Poors for 15 consecutive years; established Mayor's Advisory Committee on Alcohol and Drug Abuse; established Historic Preservation Committee; established International Affairs Committee; established Annual Rochesterfest Celebration; initiated and established Rochester Area Economic Development Inc; established Mayor's Medal of Honor. **BUSINESS ADDRESS:** Mayor, City of Rochester, Rm 200, City Hall, Rochester, MN 55902.

HEE, EDWARD K. Y.
Program manager. Chinese American. **PERSONAL:** Born Apr 2, 1933, Honolulu, HI; son of Tai Tong Hee and Wong Yee Hee; married C Jane, Oct 8, 1988; children: Leslie Wong, Darren, Lynelle. **EDUCATION:** Stanford University, BSEE, 1963; University of Southern California, MBA, 1972. **CAREER:** US Air Force, Systems Effectiveness, chief, 1972-76; C F Braun, project program control, 1976-79; General Atomic Company, Ft Vrain Scheduling, mgr, 1979-80; Princeton Plasma Physics Lab, technical staff, 1980-82; Engineered Magnetics Inc, program mgr, 1982-. **ORGANIZATIONS:** Mesa Pines Homeowners Assn, president, 1979-80. **MILITARY SERVICE:** US Air Force, lt colonel, 1954-76; Silver Star, 1971. **BUSINESS ADDRESS:** Program Manager, Engineered Magnetics, Inc, 18435 Susana Rd, Rancho Dominguez, CA 90221, (310)635-9555.

HEMRAJANI, RAMESH RELUMAL
Chemical engineer. Indo-American. **PERSONAL:** Born Dec 12, 1943, Sukkar, Pakistan; son of Relumal Hemrajani and Savitri Hemrajani; married Veena Hemrajani, Jul 11, 1975; children: Milan, Mumal. **EDUCATION:** University of Bombay, India, ISc, 1963, BChE, 1967; Northwestern University, MS, 1969, PhD, 1972. **CAREER:** McMaster University, postdoctoral fellow, 1972-74; Alcoa, research engr, 1974-77; Exxon Research & Engineering Co, engineering associate, 1977-. **ORGANIZATIONS:** AIChE; NAMF, communications committee, head. **HONORS/AWARDS:** Northwestern University, Murphy Fellowship, 1967-72. **SPECIAL ACHIEVEMENTS:** Several publications and conference presentations in mixing and reactor engineering, 1975-; workshops on mixing, 1989, 1993; 3 patents. **HOME ADDRESS:** 238 Skyline Dr, Millington, NJ 07946, (908)647-4108. **BUSINESS ADDRESS:** Engineering Associate, Exxon Research and Engineering Co., PO Box 101, Florham Park, NJ 07932, (201)765-6478.

HENNESSY, SUMIKO TANAKA
Association administrator. **CAREER:** Asian Pacific Development Center, executive director, currently. **BUSINESS ADDRESS:** Executive Director, Asian Pacific Development Center, 1818 Gaylord, Denver, CO 80206, (303)355-0710.*

HER, CHOU
Counselor. Laotian American. **PERSONAL:** Born Nov 2, 1960, Ban Nam Tuang, Lao People's Democratic Republic; son of Kiapao Her & Chia Vang; married Maiyia Vue, Oct 17, 1988; children: Joshua Chao Herr, Mary Shoua Herr. **EDUCATION:** Indian Hills Community College, AA, 1982; University of Northern Iowa, BT, 1984. **CAREER:** Garn Inc, draftsman & quality control; TSP, draftsman; Mayo Clinic, interpreter; Vermeer Manufacturing, draftsman; Intercultural Mutual Assistance Association, family counselor, currently. **HOME PHONE:** (507)281-2423.

HIGA, KUNIHIKO
Educator. Japanese American. **PERSONAL:** Born Feb 2, 1956, Naha, Okinawa, Japan; son of Saburoh Higa and Mariko Higa; married Miki Higa, May 28, 1978; children: Kento. **EDUCATION:** University of Arizona, BSBA (with distinction), 1984, PhD, 1988. **CAREER:** Oki Electric Industry, computer programmer, 1974-77; Yoshinoya Co, assistant computor service manager, 1978-80; University of Arizona, adjunct lecturer, 1988-89; Georgia Institute of Technology, assistant professor, 1989-. **ORGANIZATIONS:** Association for Computing Machinery, 1987-; IEEE Computer Society, 1989-; The Institute of Management Science, 1989-; ACM Special Interest Group of Business Information Technology, 1989-; Journal of Database Management, editorial review, 1992-. **HONORS/AWARDS:** University of Arizona, Academic Scholarship, 1982-84, Research Associateship, 1987-89; Decision Science Institute, Best Paper Award finalist, 1991. **SPECIAL ACHIEVEMENTS:** Six journal articles, 1988-; eleven conference proceedings and presentations, 1988-; one book article in Expert System and Advanced Data Processing, 1991; MIS session chair for the International Conference of Simulation and Gaming, 1991; Japanese language. **BUSINESS ADDRESS:** Assistant Professor, School of Management, Georgia Institute of Technology, Atlanta, GA 30332-0001, (404)894-4365.

HIGA, LESLIE HIDEYASU
Educator. Japanese American. **PERSONAL:** Born Oct 8, 1925, Hawi, HI; son of Shuko & Kame Higa; married Lila H Higa, Sep 23, 1961; children: Mark, Elliott, Elizabeth. **EDUCATION:** Grinnell College, BA, 1953; University of Missouri, Kansas City, DDS, 1960; University of Chicago, MS, 1965. **CAREER:** University of Chicago, postdoctoral fellow, 1960-65; University of Iowa, professor of dentistry, 1965-93, Department of Oral Surgery, professor, currently. **ORGANIZATIONS:** American Academy of Oral Pathology, 1963-; Diplomate American Board of Oral Pathology, 1972-; American Dental Association, 1965-; International Association of Dental Research, 1966-. **HONORS/AWARDS:** University of Iowa, Instructor/Teacher of the Year, six times; Iowa Dental Association, Educator of the Year, 1984. **SPECIAL ACHIEVEMENTS:** Mouth Disorders, Conn's Current Therapy, 1985; ''Role of Protein Malnutrition in the Pathogenesis of Ulcerative Lazarine Leprosy,'' International Journal of Leprosy, 1973. **MILITARY SERVICE:** Army, T/4, 1944-46. **BUSINESS ADDRESS:** Professor, Dept of Oral Surgery, University of Iowa, Dental Science Bldg, Rm S457, Iowa City, IA 52246, (319)335-7460.

HIGA, ROSS RIKIO
Educator. Japanese American. **PERSONAL:** Born Jan 31, 1959, Honolulu, HI; son of Thomas Tokusei Higa and Chieko Higa; married Carol Lai Hoong Higa, Jun 25, 1983; children: Brandon Takeshi. **EDUCATION:** University of Hawaii, Manoa, BBA, finance, 1981. **CAREER:** Bank of Hawaii, management trainee, loan assistant, regional credit assistant; Kauai Hilton, tennis professional; Leeward Community College, assistant professor, currently. **ORGANIZATIONS:** Kauai Jaycees, community development vice president, treasurer. **BUSINESS ADDRESS:** Assistant Professor, Leeward Community College, 96-045 Ala Ike St, BE-223, Pearl City, HI 96782-3366, (808)455-0618.

HIGA, WALTER HIROICHI
Physicist (retired). Japanese American. **PERSONAL:** Born Sep 21, 1919, Maui, HI; son of Gizen Higa & Kama Higa; married May Ota Higa, Aug 3, 1946; children: Lani Higa Reinhart, Walter Noel, Craig Marshall. **EDUCATION:** Tri-State College, BSEE, 1942; University of Cincinnati, MS, physics, 1947, PhD, physics, 1949. **CAREER:** Seattle University, physics, instructor, 1949-50; North American Aviation, research engineer, 1950-54; Jet Propulsion Laboratory, research physicist, 1955-80. **ORGANIZATIONS:** American Physical Society, 1955-; American Association Physics Teachers, 1955-; Institute of Electrical and Electronics Engineers, senior member, 1955-. **HONORS/AWARDS:** Institute for Advancement of Engineering, fellow, 1977. **SPECIAL ACHIEVEMENTS:** Developed low-noise receivers (MASERS) for NASA's deep space communications network; developed cryogenic systems for the MASERS; published in technical books and journals. **MILITARY SERVICE:** US Army, Pvt, 1945-46, Army Specialized Training Program, Ohio State University, 1945. **BIOGRAPHICAL SOURCES:** ''An Interplane-

tary Feat," Pacific Citizen, p5, July 25, 1986. **HOME ADDRESS:** 600 Tamarac Dr, Pasadena, CA 91105, (213)255-3314.

HIGASHI, KERWIN MASUTO
Food service administrator. Japanese American. **PERSONAL:** Born Feb 20, 1961, Honolulu, HI; son of Harold & Joan Higashi; married Allyn T Higashi, Dec 14, 1986. **EDUCATION:** Seattle University, BBA, 1983. **CAREER:** Marriott Corporation, food service director, 1983-. **ORGANIZATIONS:** Hawaii Island Chamber of Commerce, 1991-; Hilo Bay Rotary Club, 1992-. **HOME ADDRESS:** 518 A Hinano Street, Hilo, HI 96720, (808)935-3651. **BUSINESS ADDRESS:** Food Service Director, Marriott Corporation, 200 West Kawili Street, Hilo, HI 96720, (808)933-3303.

HIGUCHI, CLAYTON T.
Company executive. Japanese American. **PERSONAL:** Born Jun 17, 1948, Lihue, HI; son of Juro & Sadalco Higuchi; married Kathryn O Higuchi, Jan 9, 1972; children: Kimberly, Todd. **EDUCATION:** Idaho State University, BBA, 1970. **CAREER:** Ameron Inc, Ready Mix Division, manager, 1981-83, Concrete Products Division, manager, 1983-85; Pre-Mixed Concrete Co, transportation manager, 1985-86; H G Fenton Material Co, operations manager, 1986-88, assistant general manager, 1988-90; Pre-Mixed Concrete Co, vice president/general manager, 1990-92; H G Fenton Material Co, vice president/general manager, 1992-. **ORGANIZATIONS:** Rancho Penasquitos Planning Group, 1991-; San Diego Rock Producers Association, director, 1991. **BUSINESS ADDRESS:** Vice President & General Manager, H G Fenton Material Company, 7220 Trade St, Ste 300, San Diego, CA 92121, (619)566-2000.

HIHARA, LLOYD HIROMI
Educator, engineer. Japanese American. **PERSONAL:** Born Oct 29, 1961, Honolulu, HI; son of Matsuhisa Hihara and Toshie Hihara. **EDUCATION:** University of Hawaii, Manoa, BS, 1983; Massachusetts Institute of Technology, SM, 1985, PhD, 1989. **CAREER:** Massachusetts Institute of Technology, teaching assistant, 1985-86, research assistant, 1987-89; University of Hawaii at Manoa, assistant professor, 1989-. **ORGANIZATIONS:** The Electrochemical Society; The National Association of Corrosion Engineers; The Metallurgical Society of AIME, ASM International; The American Society of Mechanical Engineers; The American Water Works Association; Sigma Xi. **HONORS/AWARDS:** Boeing Company, Boeing Faculty Award, 1993; National Science Foundation, Presidential Young Investigator Award, 1990; Greater Boston Section of the National Association of Corrosion Eng, Student H H Uhlig Award, in Corrosion, 1988; ARCS Foundation, Achievement Rewards for College Scientists Award, 1981. **SPECIAL ACHIEVEMENTS:** Co-author with RM Latanision, "Supressing Galvanic Corrosion in Graphite/Aluminum: Metal-Matrix Composites," Corrosion Science, 1993; "Galvanic-Corrosion of Aluminum Matrix Composites," Corrosion, 1992; "Localized Corrosion Induced in Graphite/Aluminum MMCs by Residual Microstructural Chloride," Corrosion, 1991; "Residual Microstructural Chloride in Graphite/Aluminum MMCs," Materials Science and Eng A, 1990; "Cathodic Overprotection of SIC/6061 and Graphite/Aluminum Alloy MMC," in Scripta Metallurgica, 1988. **BIOGRAPHICAL SOURCES:** "Award is Big Opportunity for UH Engineering Prof," Honolulu Star-Bulletin, p A-5, May 28, 1990. **BUSINESS ADDRESS:** Assistant Professor, Dept of Mechanical Engineering, University of Hawaii at Manoa, 2540 Dole St, Holmes Hall 302, Honolulu, HI 96822, (808)956-2365.

HIKIDA, ROBERT SEIICHI
Educator. Japanese American. **PERSONAL:** Born Jun 3, 1941, Long Beach, CA; son of Fred Hikida and Shizuye Hikida; married Geraldine Oki Hikida, Jun 14, 1964; children: Stephen Michael. **EDUCATION:** University of Illinois, Champaign, BS, 1963, MS, 1965, PhD, 1967; Columbia University, postdoctoral research, 1967-69. **CAREER:** Columbia University, research associate, 1967-69, visiting professor of biology, 1970; Ohio University, assistant professor of zoology, 1969-73, associate professor of zoology, 1973-76, professor of biological sciences, 1976-, College of Osteopathic Medicine, professor of microanatomy, 1991-. **ORGANIZATIONS:** American Society of Zoologists, 1964-; American Association of Anatomists, 1971-; American Society for Cell Biology, 1975-. **HONORS/AWARDS:** Ohio University, College of Osteopathic Medicine, Outstanding Faculty, First Year Class, 1992, 1993, College of Arts & Sciences, Grasselli Outstanding Teaching Award, 1992, Graduate Student Union, Outstanding Graduate Faculty, 1976. **SPECIAL ACHIEVEMENTS:** Associate editor, Anatomical Record, Wiley-Liss, 1981-; 50 research publications in scientific and medical journals. **BUSINESS ADDRESS:**

Professor of Anatomy, Dept of Biological Sciences, Ohio University, Irvine Hall, Room 211, Athens, OH 45701, (614)593-2323.

HILL, AMY
Comedienne. Japanese American. **PERSONAL:** Born 1953?. **CAREER:** Comedienne, writer, performer, one woman shows include: Tokyo Bound, Mrs Hill and Mudd, Beside Myself; acting experience includes: Dim Sum, Scrooged, Ghostdad, Circuitry Man, Rising Sun; television appearances include: Beverly Hills 90210, The Tracey Ullman Show, Night Court, Perfect Strangers; Asian American Theater Co, 8 years; The Eureka Theater; Mark Taper Forum; Los Angeles Theater Center; Cold Tofu, performer. **BIOGRAPHICAL SOURCES:** "Amy Hill and Her Looking Glass," Los Angeles Times, Section F, p 1, July 20, 1992. **BUSINESS ADDRESS:** Comedienne, Tokyo Bound Productions, 642 Maltman Ave, Los Angeles, CA 90026. *

HING, BILL ONG
Educator, lawyer. Chinese American. **CAREER:** Stanford University School of Law, associate professor, currently. **SPECIAL ACHIEVEMENTS:** Author, Making and Remaking Asian America through Immigration Policy, 1850-1990, Stanford University Press. **BUSINESS ADDRESS:** Associate Professor, Stanford University School of Law, Crown Quad, Stanford, CA 94305-8610.*

HINGORANI, BHAGWAN V.
Engineer. Indo-American. **PERSONAL:** Born Nov 11, 1936, Lemri, Baluchistan, India; son of Shamibai and Virumal A Hingorani; married Shanti B Hingorani, Jan 26, 1963; children: Helen K Ramchandani, Vinita J Schroeder. **EDUCATION:** University of Oklahoma, ME, 1965. **CAREER:** Oklahoma State Dept of Hwys, engr I-IV, 1965-73; MW Kellogg, senior engr, 1973-77; Eagleton Engineering Co, project mgr, 1977-. **ORGANIZATIONS:** Registered professional engr in the states of Texas and Oklahoma. **HOME ADDRESS:** 10522 Kiber Dr, Houston, TX 77031, (713)779-4106.

HINGORANI, NARAIN G.
Research institute executive. Pakistani American. **PERSONAL:** Born Jun 15, 1931, Tatta, Pakistan; son of Ghuriomal Khatansingh and Rukumani Hingorani; married Joyce Hingorani; children: Naren, Devi. **EDUCATION:** Baroda University, India, BE, 1953; Manchester University, England, MS, 1957, PhD, 1960. **CAREER:** Inst Sci & Technology, University of Manchester, research fellow, 1957-61; Loughborough University, England, Electrical Engineering, lecturer, 1961-63; University of Salford, England, sr lecturer, 1963-68; Bonneville Power Administration, consultant, 1968-74; Electric Power Research Institute, program manager, 1974-85, board of directors, vp, 1985-88, Electrical Systems, vp, 1988-. **ORGANIZATIONS:** Natl Acad of Eng. **HONORS/AWARDS:** IEEE Power Engineering Society, prize winning paper award, 1980; Uno Lamm Award, 1985; American Society for Metals, Materials Achievement Award, 1987; Manchester University, Fellow, 1960; IEEE, Fellow. **SPECIAL ACHIEVEMENTS:** Co-author: HVDC Power Transmission, 1958; author of over 150 articles; inventor in field. **BUSINESS ADDRESS:** VP, Electrical Systems, Electric Power Research Institute, Inc, 3412 Hillview Ave, Palo Alto, CA 94304. *

HINOKI, GEORGE
Attorney, county official. Japanese American. **PERSONAL:** Born Feb 23, 1927, Colusa, CA; son of Frank S Hinoki (deceased) and Miyako Hinoki (deceased); married Patricia Naomi Hinoki, Nov 1983. **EDUCATION:** Hastings College of Law, LLB, JD, 1957. **CAREER:** Morozumi & Hinoki Law Offices, attorney, 1958-61; Nakahara & Hinoki Inc, attorney, 1962-. **ORGANIZATIONS:** State of California Bar Association, 1958-; American Bar Association, 1958-; Santa Clara County Planning Commission, 1975-86; Santa Clara County Parks & Recreation Commission, 1986-94. **MILITARY SERVICE:** US Army, 1945-46. **BUSINESS ADDRESS:** Vice President, Nakahara & Hinoki Inc, Law Corp, 90 E Taylor St, San Jose, CA 95112, (408)297-3707.

HIRABAYASHI, GORDON
Educator. Japanese American. **PERSONAL:** Born Apr 23, 1918, Seattle, WA; son of Shungo & Mitsu Hirabayashi; married Susan Carnahan, Apr 25, 1986; children: Sharon Mitsu Yuen, Marion Setsu Oldenburg, Jay. **EDUCATION:** University of Washington, BA, 1946, MA, 1949, PhD, 1952. **CAREER:** University of Washington, instructor, 1951-52; American University of Beirut, Lebanon, assistant to associate professor, 1952-55; American University in Cairo, Egypt, Social Research Center, associate professor, assistant director, 1955-59; University of Alberta, associate professor, 1959-64, professor, 1964-83, professor emeritus, 1983-. **HONORS/AWARDS:** Western Oregon State

College, Distinguished Service Award, 1993; Michigan State University, Honorary Doctor of Humanities, 1991; Haverford College, Honorary Doctor of Laws, 1984; Hamline University, Honorary Doctor of Humane Letters, 1984; N California Foundation, ACLU, Earl Warren Civil Liberties Award, 1983; Asian American Legal Defense & Education Fund, NYC, Justice in Action Award, 1992. **SPECIAL ACHIEVEMENTS:** "Growing Up American in Washington," in Washington Comes of Age, WSU Press, 1992; co-editor, Visible Minorities: Asians in Canada, Butterworth, Toronto, 1981; "Why Revive the Japanese American Wartime Cases?," Toronto, Aug 1985; "After 50 Years: Where Do We Go From Here?," The Friends Journal, Nov 1992. **BIOGRAPHICAL SOURCES:** A Personal Matter: Gordon Hirabayashi v The United States, The Constitution Project, Portland, Oregon, PBS Documentary, 28 minutes; "Am I An American," with author Peter Lyons, The Courage of Their Convictions, NY Free Press, 1988; a chapter, "The Idealist," in Justice At War, Peter Irons, Oxford University Press, 1983. **HOME ADDRESS:** 11645-91st Avenue, Edmonton, AB, Canada T6G 1A8, (403)433-5058.

HIRABAYASHI, LANE RYO
Anthropologist, educator. Japanese American. **PERSONAL:** Born in Seattle, WA; son of James & Joanne Hirabayashi. **EDUCATION:** California State University, Sonoma, The Hutchins School of Liberal Studies, BA (with distinction), 1974; University of California at Berkeley, MA, anthropology, 1976; University of California at Berkeley, PhD, anthropology, 1981. **CAREER:** San Francisco State University, associate professor, 1984-88, professor, 1988-91; University of Colorado, associate professor, coordinator of Asian American studies, 1991-. **ORGANIZATIONS:** Association for Asian American Studies, 1985-; Society for Latin American Anthropology, 1992-; Society for Urban Anthropology, 1985-; American Anthropological Association, 1985-; California Historical Society, California History Journal, editorial board, 1987-; Center for Japanese American Studies, 1975-; Japanese American National Museum, 1987-. **HONORS/AWARDS:** InterAmerican Foundation, doctoral fellowship, 1977-79; UCLA, Institute of American Cultures, post-doctoral fellowship, 1981-82; National Science Foundation, grant, 1990-92. **SPECIAL ACHIEVEMENTS:** Author, Cultural Capital: Mountain Zapotec Migrant Associations in Mexico City, Tucson, Arizona: University of Arizona Press, 1993; co-editor, Migrants, Regional Cultures and Latin American Cities, 1994; co-author, "The Issei Community in Moneta and the Gardena Valley," Southern California Quarterly, 1988; co-author, "The Credible Witness," Views From Within, 1989; author, "The Impact of Incarceration on Nisei Schoolchildren," Japanese Americans, 1981. **BUSINESS ADDRESS:** Associate Professor of Anthropology, Center for Studies of Ethnicity and Race in America, University of Colorado at Boulder, Ketchum 30, Campus Box 339, Boulder, CO 80309-0339, (303)492-0419.

HIRAMOTO, JONI T.
Attorney. Japanese American. **PERSONAL:** Born Feb 28, 1961, Berkeley, CA; daughter of John J Hiramoto and Ruby S Hiramoto; married Douglass C MacMaster, Jul 1, 1989; children: Jitsutaro Brennan MacMaster. **EDUCATION:** Harvard University, Radcliffe College, AB (magna cum laude), 1983; Kyoto University, International Law Dept, 1984; University of California, Berkeley, School of Law, JD, 1987. **CAREER:** McCutchen Doyle Brown & Enersen, associate, 1987-92; Securities & Exchange Commission, enforcement attorney, 1992-. **ORGANIZATIONS:** Asian American Bar Association of the Greater Bay Area, co-chair, employment committee, 1989, board of directors, 1990-92, treasurer, 1993; San Francisco Women Lawyers Alliance, board of directors, 1992, vice president, 1993, co-chair, bias committee, 1992-93. **HONORS/AWARDS:** Rotary Club, International Graduate Fellowship, 1982. **BUSINESS ADDRESS:** Enforcement Attorney, Securities & Exchange Commission, 44 Montgomery St, 11th Fl, San Francisco, CA 94104, (415)744-3229.

HIRANO, ASAO
Physician. Japanese American. **PERSONAL:** Born Nov 26, 1926, Tomioka, Gunma, Japan; son of Yoshiro & Miyoe Hirano; married Keiko Hirano, May 23, 1959; children: Michio, Ikuo, Yoko, Shigeo. **EDUCATION:** Kyoto University, MD, 1952. **CAREER:** Montefiore Medical Center, Division of Neuropathology, head, 1965-; Albert Einstein College of Medicine, professor of pathology, 1971-, professor of neuroscience, 1974-. **ORGANIZATIONS:** American Association of Neuropathologists, 1965-; American Neurological Association, 1977-; International Society of Neuropathology, 1974-; Association for Research in Nervous & Mental Dis Inc, 1975-; Japanese Neuropathological Association, 1984-; Australian & New Zealand Society for Neuropathology, honorary member, 1986-; Japanese Society of Neurology, honorary

member, 1988-; The Japan Neurosurgical Society, senior member, 1992-. **HONORS/AWARDS:** AMA, Billings Silver Medal, 1959; American Association of Neuropathologists, Weil Award, 1961; Montefiore Medical Center, Henry Moses Research Award, 1968; Osaka, Japan, Key to Osaka City, 1977; US House of Representatives, Hon Ben Blaz, Comm Award, 1992. **SPECIAL ACHIEVEMENTS:** Author of: A Guide to Neuropathology, 1981; Metastatic Tumors of the Nervous System, 1982; Color Atlas of Neuropathology, 1988; editor, Neuropsychiatric Disorders in the Elderly, 1983; Pathology of the Myelinated Axon, 1985. **BUSINESS ADDRESS:** Physician, Montefiore Medical Center, Neuropathology Division, 111 E 210 St, Central 213, Bronx, NY 10467, (718)920-4447.

HIRANO, IRENE YASUTAKE
Museum administrator. Japanese American. **PERSONAL:** Born 1948?; children: 1 daughter. **EDUCATION:** University of Southern California, Masters, health adminstration. **CAREER:** Asian Women's Center; THE Clinic for Women, executive director, 1975-88; Japanese American National Museum, executive director, president, 1988-. **ORGANIZATIONS:** Asian Pacific Women's Network Los Angeles, president, currently; Leadership Education for Asian Pacifics, co-founder, 1983, vp, 1986-91; Los Angeles Women's Foundation; Trusteeship/Intl Women's Forum; Coalition of 100; Los Angeles Regional Family Planning Cuncil, board of directors, 1985-88; Natl Network of Asian & Pacific Women, chairperson/founding member, 1982-84; Asian Pacific American Focus Project, 1986-88. **HONORS/AWARDS:** NEA, National Outstanding Asian/Pacific Islander Award, 1983; Business & Professional Women, Achievement Award, 1983; Natl Institute for Women of Color, Outstanding Service Award, 1984; Natl Women's Political Caucus, Outstanding Service Award, 1986; Liberty Hill Foundation, Outstanding Community Service Award, 1986. **SPECIAL ACHIEVEMENTS:** Appointed to Commission on the Future of the Smithsonian Institution, 1994; California Commission on the Status of Women, chair, 1976. **BUSINESS ADDRESS:** President, Executive Director, Japanese American National Museum, 369 E 1st St, Los Angeles, CA 90012-3901, (213)625-0414.*

HIRANO, KYOKO
Administrator, educator. Japanese American. **PERSONAL:** Born Jun 15, 1952, Tokyo, Japan; daughter of Itsuro Hirano and Tazu Hirano; divorced. **EDUCATION:** Waseda University, BA, 1975; University of Tokyo, MA, 1978, certificate in journalism, 1979; New York University, PhD, 1988. **CAREER:** New York University, lecturer of cinema studies, 1983,1990-92; Japan Society, film program, coordinator, 1986-88, film center, director, 1989-. **ORGANIZATIONS:** Association for Asian Studies, 1983-; Society for Cinema Studies, 1985-; Asian Cinema Studies Society, executive council member, 1988-92; Inamor: Foundation, Kyoto Prize selecting committee, 1983, 1986, 1991; New York State Council for Humanities, film grants selection committee, 1993. **HONORS/AWARDS:** Japan Foundation, Publication Assistance Award, 1992; New York University, Jay Lydon Memorial Award for Academic Achievement, 1988; Toyota Foundation, Humanities Grant, 1985-86; Fulbright Award for postgraduate study, 1979-82; Yugoslav Government, award for postgraduate study in Yugoslavia, 1976-77. **SPECIAL ACHIEVEMENTS:** Author, "Mr Smith Goes to Tokyo: Japanese Cinema Under the American Occupation, 1945-52," Smithsonian Institution Press, 1992; articles in Japanese, 1976-, English, 1984-. **BUSINESS ADDRESS:** Director, Film Center, Japan Society, 333 East 47th St, New York, NY 10017, (212)832-1155.

HIRANO-NAKANISHI, MARSHA JOYCE
Educator, educational administrator. Japanese American. **PERSONAL:** Born Oct 10, 1949, Chicago, IL; daughter of Ben and Alice Hirano; married Don Nakanishi, 1974; children: Tom. **EDUCATION:** Stanford University, BS, mathematics, 1971; Harvard University, EdD, social policy, 1981. **CAREER:** National Center for Bilingual Research, research manager, 1981-84; CSU, Los Angeles, analytic studies, associate director, 1984-86; CSU, Northridge, analytic studies, director, 1986-89; CSU System, analytic studies, director, 1989-. **ORGANIZATIONS:** Los Angeles City Commission on the Status of Women, 1991-93; State Bar of California, Judicial Nominees Evaluation Commission, 1992-, Committee of Bar Examinees, various subcommittees, chair, 1988-92; American Educational Research Association, Ad Hoc Committee on Minority Doctoral Fellowships, chair, Division J, Postsecondary Education, annual program, chair, Division J, Affirmative Action Committee, chair, Division J, Postsecondary Education Evaluation Committee, chair, Division G, Dissertation Awards Committee, 1974-; Association of Institutional Research, Forum Advisory Committee, 1984-. **BUSINESS ADDRESS:** Director, Analytic Stud-

ies, The California State University System, 400 Golden Shore, Long Beach, CA 90802, (310)985-2528.

HIRAOKA, LESLIE SATOSHI
Educator, educational administrator. Japanese American. **PERSONAL:** Born Jun 18, 1941, Honolulu, HI; son of George Y Hiraoka and Ellen F Hiraoka. **EDUCATION:** University of Hawaii, 1959-61; University of Washington, BS, 1963; Columbia University, MS, 1964, ScD, engineering, 1969; Rutgers University, MBA, 1971. **CAREER:** Esso Research & Engineering Co, engineer, 1968-71; US Department of Commerce, program analyst, 1977-78; Kean College of New Jersey, Department of Management Science, chairman, 1975-77, professor of management science, 1971-. **ORGANIZATIONS:** Engineering Management Journal, American Society for Engineering Management, associate editor, 1989-; National Advisory Committee on Rice, US Department of Agriculture, 1975-79. **HONORS/AWARDS:** Utah State University, Shigeo Shingo Prize for Manufacturing Excellence, faculty competition, 1989; American Assembly of Collegiate Schools of Business, Sears Roebuck, Federal Government, faculty fellowship, 1977-78. **SPECIAL ACHIEVEMENTS:** Management Science Program, founder, 1972; paper presentations at the 6th & 8th World Productivity Congress, Montreal, 1988, Stockholm, 1993; congressional testimony before US House & Senate subcommittees on agriculture policy, 1974-75. **BIOGRAPHICAL SOURCES:** Acknowledgement by the Hon Bill Alexander, Congressional Record, p E6837, Dec 19, 1975. **BUSINESS ADDRESS:** Professor of Management Science, Kean College of New Jersey, 1000 Morris Ave, Willis 403B, Union, NJ 07083-7131.

HIRASAKI, GEORGE JIRO
Educator. Japanese American. **PERSONAL:** Born Sep 26, 1939, Beaumont, TX; son of Tokuzo Hirasaki and Toki Hirasaki; married Darlene Hirasaki, Jul 10, 1993. **EDUCATION:** Lamar University, BS, 1963; Rice University, PhD, 1967. **CAREER:** Shell Development Company, 1967-93; Rice University, professor, 1977-. **ORGANIZATIONS:** National Academy of Engineers, 1991-; Society of Petroleum Engineers; American Institute of Chemical Engineers; American Chemical Society; Society of Core Analysts; Society of Industrial Applied Mathematics. **HONORS/AWARDS:** National Academy of Engineers, 1991; Society of Petroleum Eng, Lester Uren Award, 1990. **SPECIAL ACHIEVEMENTS:** Author of 27 publications. **MILITARY SERVICE:** US Marine Corps Reserves, Sgt, 1957-62. **BUSINESS ADDRESS:** Professor, Chemical Engineering, Rice University, PO Box 1892, Houston, TX 77251, (713)285-5416.

HIRASUNA, ALAN RYO
Engineer. Japanese American. **PERSONAL:** Born Sep 27, 1939, Fresno, CA; son of Fred & Setsuko Hirasuma; married Teresa, Feb 22, 1986; children: Brian Kirk. **EDUCATION:** UC Berkeley, BS, 1962; USC, MS, 1969. **CAREER:** Chevron, refinery engineer, 1962-64; Ford Aeronutronic, prog engineer, 1964-71; L'Garde Inc, vice president, board of directors, 1971-. **ORGANIZATIONS:** AASRC, director, 1984-; Tustin Chamber of Commerce, ambassador, 1988-; ASME; ACS-Rubber Division; ADPA; Cal Engineering Alumni Association; MENSA; JACL. **HONORS/AWARDS:** Geothermal Resources Council, Best Paper, 1980. **SPECIAL ACHIEVEMENTS:** 3 US patents, 1981-86; over 35 papers published in technical journals and reports, 1974-. **HOME PHONE:** (714)759-0898.

HIRATA, HENRY MINORU
Public works administrator. Japanese American. **PERSONAL:** Born Mar 29, 1937, Stockton, CA; son of Roy Hirata (deceased) & Toshiye Hirata; married Alice Hirata, Jun 23, 1962; children: Lori, Karen. **EDUCATION:** Stockton Junior College, AA, 1961; University of Pacific, BSCE, 1964. **CAREER:** State of California, junior civil engineer, 1964; San Joaquin County, assistant civil engineer, 1964-74, associate civil engineer, 1974-76, senior civil, 1976-78, principal civil engineer, 1978; deputy director, 1978-83, director, 1983-. **ORGANIZATIONS:** County Engineers Association California, secretary, vice president, president; American Society Civil Engineers, Central Branch, vice president, president, Sacramento Section, director; University of Pacific School of Engineering Alumni Association, vice president, president; San Joaquin Valley Road Commission and County Engineering, vice president, president; California Central Valley Flood Control Association, director; United Way, public employee campaign chairman; Stockton Sunrise Rotary. **HONORS/AWARDS:** University of Pacific, Alumni Fellow, 1983; San Joaquin Engineering Council, Engineer of Year, 1985; Stockton Buddhist Church, Parent of the Year, 1980; United Way, Hall of Fame Volunteer, 1992. **SPECIAL ACHIEVEMENTS:** Appointed County Road Advisor for Region 9 by Federal Hwy Administration, 1991-; staff responsible for formulating & directing vertical control network control program and road inventory, ten year plan each receiving the National Association Counties County Achievement Award. **MILITARY SERVICE:** US Army, sp4/c, 1956-57; Good Conduct Medal/ Sharp Shooter. **BIOGRAPHICAL SOURCES:** Profile, Stockton Record Newspaper, Jan 4, 1992. **HOME ADDRESS:** 5247 Shippee Ln, Stockton, CA 95212, (209)931-1279.

HIRATA, HOSEA
Educator. Japanese American. **PERSONAL:** Born Jul 22, 1952, Yokosuka, Kanagawa, Japan; son of Masao Hirata and Kei Hirata; married Catherine Costello Hirata, Aug 31, 1985; children: Sean. **EDUCATION:** McGill University, BA, 1979; University of British Columbia, MFA, 1981, PhD, 1987. **CAREER:** Pomona College, assistant professor, 1987-90; Princeton University, assistant professor, 1990-. **ORGANIZATIONS:** Association for Asian Studies; Association of Teachers of Japanese; American Comparative Literature Association; International Association of Philosophy and Literature. **HONORS/AWARDS:** Princeton University, Charles Osgood Preceptorship, 1992-95; American Council Learned Societies, fellowship, 1992-93; Pomona College, Yale Griffith Summer Fellowship, 1988; Izaak Walton Killam Memorial Pre-Doctoral Fellowship, 1984-86. **SPECIAL ACHIEVEMENTS:** Author: The Poetry and Poetics of Nishiwaki Junzaburo, Princeton UP, 1993; "Violation of the Mother Tongue," Comparative Literature, vol 45, no 1, 1993; "To Slit the Beautiful Body/Text," LIT, vol 2, no 2, 1990; "Pure Poetry and Differance," Journal of the ATJ, vol 26, no 1, 1992; "Return or Noreturn," Literary History, Narrative and Culture, 1989. **BUSINESS ADDRESS:** Assistant Professor, East Asian Studies, Princeton University, 211 Jones Hall, Princeton, NJ 08544, (609)258-4284.

HIRONAKA, STEVE
Government official. Japanese American. **PERSONAL:** Born May 24, 1943, Honolulu, HI; son of Seiichi Hironaka and Sumiko Hironaka; married Carol R Hironaka, Apr 18, 1970; children: Chad S, Coleen S. **EDUCATION:** Chaminade College of Honolulu, BA, 1968. **CAREER:** Internal Revenue Service, Honolulu, HI, revenue agent, 1972, special agent, 1972-81, San Diego, group manager, CID, 1981-83, Washington DC, section chief, 1983-85, Houston, assistant chief, CID, 1985-87, Seattle, chief, CID, 1987-91, San Francisco, executive assistant, ARC CI, 1991-. **MILITARY SERVICE:** US Army, specialist e-4, 1962-65. **HOME ADDRESS:** 503 Burns Circle, San Ramon, CA 94583, (510)828-0986. **BUSINESS ADDRESS:** Executive Assistant to Asst Regional Commissioner, Criminal Investigation, Internal Revenue Service, 1650 Mission St, Rm 508, San Francisco, CA 94103, (415)556-0584.

HIROSHIGE, ERNIE
Judge. Japanese American. **CAREER:** Los Angeles County Superior Court, judge, currently. **HONORS/AWARDS:** Commendation for work on UCLA's commemoration of 50th anniversary of Executive Order 9066, 1993. **BUSINESS ADDRESS:** Judge, Los Angeles County Superior Court, Central/Civil West, 600 Commonwealth, Dept 324, Los Angeles, CA 90005, (213)351-8508.*

HISATOMI, JOHN A.
Insurance company executive. Japanese American. **PERSONAL:** Born Nov 12, 1945, Pendleton, OR; son of Kay Hisatomi & Keiko Hisatomi; divorced; children: James, Jennifer, Carrie, Mary. **EDUCATION:** Oregon State University, BS, civil engineer, 1967; Southern Illinois University, MBA, 1972. **CAREER:** American Benefits, owner, currently. **ORGANIZATIONS:** Rotary; Oregon Executives. **HONORS/AWARDS:** American College of Life Underwriters, Chartered Life Underwriter, 1993. **MILITARY SERVICE:** US Air Force, captain, 1968-73; Air Medal (Viet Nam). **HOME ADDRESS:** 1707 NW Caxton Ct, Portland, OR 97229. **BUSINESS ADDRESS:** Owner, American Benefits, 6441 SW Canyon Ct, #280, Portland, OR 97221, (503)292-0369.

HIURA, ALAN
Dentist. Japanese American. **PERSONAL:** Born 1951?; married Jean; children: Jaclyn, Julie. **EDUCATION:** University of California, Berkeley; University of the Pacific Dental School, endodontics; Temple University. **CAREER:** Endodontics Associates, dentist, currently. **ORGANIZATIONS:** Almaden Country Club, board, 1990-93, president, 1993. **BUSINESS ADDRESS:** Endodontist, Endodontics Associates, 841 Blossom Hill Rd, Ste 202, San Jose, CA 95123, (408)224-8266. *

HO, ALEXANDER KITMAN (A. KITMAN HO)
Film producer. Hong Kong American. **PERSONAL:** Born Jan 15, 1950, Hong Kong; son of Poon and Ruby Chin Ho. **EDUCATION:** Goddard College, 1972; New York University, 1974. **CAREER:** Film producer: The Loveless, 1983; Born on the Fourth of July, 1989; The Doors, 1991; JFK, 1991; co-producer: Platoon, 1986; Wall Street, 1987; Talk Radio, 1988; associate producer: Too Scared to Scream, 1985; Offbeat, 1986; At Mother's Request, 1987; film production manager: Out of the Darkness, 1985; Year of the Dragon, 1985; Heartland, 1979; Fame, 1980; Reds, 1981; My Favorite Year, 1982; Romantic Comedy, 1983; The Hunger, 1983; Svengali, 1983; Today's FBI, 1984; Chiefs, 1986; unit manager: To Kill a Cop, 1978; King of the Gypsies, 1978; The Warriors, 1979; One Trick Pony, 1980; First Deadly Sin, 1980. **BUSINESS ADDRESS:** Film Producer, Warner Brothers, 4000 Warner Blvd, Burbank, CA 91522, (818)954-6000. *

HO, ANDREW KONG-SUN
Educator. Hong Kong American. **PERSONAL:** Born Apr 22, 1939, Hong Kong; son of Kaak-Yan Ho and Han Li; married Susan J Ho; children: Shirley Ann-Fun, Allan An-Li. **EDUCATION:** University of Melbourne, BSc, 1963, MSc, 1965; Monash University, PhD, 1968. **CAREER:** New York University Medical Center, post doctoral fellow-NIMH, 1968-70; University of California, San Francisco, research associate, 1970-72; Wayne State University, assistant professor, 1972-74, associate professor, 1974-75; University of Illinois, College of Medicine, associate professor, 1975-85, professor, 1985-. **ORGANIZATIONS:** American Society of Pharmacology, experimental therapeutics, 1977-; International Society for Biomedical Research on Alcoholism, 1981-; Association of Medical Education & Research in Substance Abuse, charter member; Career Teachers in Substance Abuse, alumni member; Research Society on Alcoholism; Anatomical Society of Australia & New Zealand, 1966-70; Sigma Xi, Rho Chi; Proctor Community Hospital, community advisory board in chemical dependence, 1978-83. **HONORS/AWARDS:** National Institutes of Health, grant; National Institute on Drug Abuse, Career Teacher Award, 1975-78; American Heart Association, Illinois, grant; Alberta Heritage Foundation for Medical Research, visiting scientist, 1983; Pharmaceutical Manufacturers Association, award, 1968-70. **SPECIAL ACHIEVEMENTS:** Research publications in scientific journals, in areas of pharmacology, biochemistry, behavior, alcoholism and substance abuse, anatomy-cell biology; US Patent No 560,018; alcohol aversion process by enzyme inhibitions. **BUSINESS ADDRESS:** Professor of Pharmacology, College of Medicine, University of Illinois, One Illini Dr, Peoria, IL 61605, (309)671-8533.

HO, BENSON P.
Engineering and technology director. Chinese American. **PERSONAL:** Born Nov 9, 1947, Shanghai, China; son of Lincoln Ho and Jean Hsu; married Venna Lee, Oct 5, 1973; children: Vennette W, Vanessa P. **EDUCATION:** MIT, BS, 1970; Cornell University, MS, 1972. **CAREER:** Cornell University, microwave instructor, 1970-73; Sperry Gyroscope, engineer, 1973-75; Norden System, senior engineer, 1975-76, project engineer, 1978-81; China Steel Works, Hong Kong, manager, 1976-78; Raytheon, director, project engineering, 1981-88; Lockheed Sanders, director of engineering & technology, 1988-. **ORGANIZATIONS:** IEEE, 1973-; American Management, 1973-75. **HONORS/AWARDS:** Eta Kappa Nu, Academic Honor Society, 1972. **HOME ADDRESS:** 2 Breckenridge Rd, North Andover, MA 01845, (508)686-9380. **BUSINESS PHONE:** (603)885-5905.

HO, BIRONG A.
Librarian. Taiwanese American. **PERSONAL:** Born Sep 3, 1958, Hsinchu, Taiwan; daughter of Shin-Chia Ho and Chiu-Hsia Ho; married Yihfang Jeng, Jun 10, 1985; children: Winnie Jeng, Alvin Jeng. **EDUCATION:** University of Wisconsin, Madison, MA, English, 1985, MA, libraries and information science, 1986. **CAREER:** Wayne State University Libraries, librarian, 1986-. **ORGANIZATIONS:** American Libraries Association, retrospective conversion, chair, 1990-. **SPECIAL ACHIEVEMENTS:** Author, "Using OCLC Passport, Biblio-Links and Pro-cite to Create a Bibliography," OCLC Micro, v 8, n 5, pp 28-32, October 1992; "A Technical Service Librarian's Desktop," OCLC Micro, v 8, n 2, pp 29-30, April 1992. **BUSINESS ADDRESS:** Librarian, Wayne State University Libraries, 5048 Gullen Mall, Detroit, MI 48202, (313)577-4005.

HO, CHI-TANG
Educator. Chinese American. **PERSONAL:** Born Dec 26, 1944, Fuzhou, Fujian, China; son of Chia-jue Ho and Siu Lin; married Mary S Ho, Jun 29, 1974; children: Gregory, Joseph. **EDUCATION:** National Taiwan University,

BS, 1968; Washington University, MA, 1971, PhD, 1974. **CAREER:** Rutgers University, postdoctoral research associate, 1975-76, assistant professor, 1976-83, associate professor, 1983-87, professor, 1987-. **ORGANIZATIONS:** American Chemical Society, division of agricultural and food chemistry, vice chairman, 1993-, subdivision of flavor, secretary, vice chairman, chairman, 1980-92, fellow, 1988-; Institute of Food Technologists, 1978-; American Oil Chemists' Society, 1977-; Chinese Americans at Rutgers, president, 1992; Chinese American Food Society, executive committee, 1989-91. **HONORS/AWARDS:** Wuxi Institute of Light Industry, China, Honorary Professor, 1988; Beijing Agricultural Engineering University, honorary, 1988. **SPECIAL ACHIEVEMENTS:** Co-editor, "Food Extension Science and Technology," 1992; "Phenolic Compounds in Food and Their Effects on Health," vol I &II, 1992, "Thermal Generation of Aromas," 1988; "Flavor Measurement," 1992; author and co-author of over 180 publications in refereed journals. **BIOGRAPHICAL SOURCES:** Community Leaders of America, p 151, 1981. **BUSINESS ADDRESS:** Professor, Dept of Food Science, Rutgers University, Cook College, New Brunswick, NJ 08903, (908)932-9672.

HO, CHIEN
Educator. Chinese American. **PERSONAL:** Born Oct 23, 1934, Shanghai, China; son of Ping Yin and Chin Chiu Hwa; married Nancy Tseng, Dec 21, 1963; children: Jeanette, Carolyn. **EDUCATION:** Williams College, BA, 1957; Yale University, PhD, 1961; Massachusetts Institute of Technology, postdoctoral, 1962-64. **CAREER:** Union Carbide Corporation, research chemist, 1960-61; Massachusetts Institute of Technology, postdoctoral research associate, 1961-64; University of Pittsburgh, assistant, associate professor of biophysics, microbiology, 1964-70, professor of molecular biology, 1971-79; Princeton University, Stanford University, John Simon Guggenheim Fellow, 1970-71; Carnegie Mellon University, professor of biological sciences, 1979-, alumni professor of biological sciences, 1985-. **ORGANIZATIONS:** NIH, biophysics and biophysical chemical B study section, 1974-78; Stanford Magnetic Resonance Lab, Stanford University, advisory committee, chairman, 1975-82; NIH, Division of Research Resources, biotechnology resources review committee, chairman, 1979-83; National Science Foundation, molecular biology advisory panel, 1980-84; University of Wisconsin, Madison, National Advisory Committee for the National Biomedical NMR Resource, chairman, 1985-90; NIH, National Institute of General Medical Sciences, cellular and molecular basis of disease review committee, 1987-90; Council on the International Conference on Magnetic Resonance Biological Systems, 1988-; Academia Sinica, Institute of Molecular Biology, Taipei, Taiwan, director, 1990. **HONORS/AWARDS:** Academia Sinica, Taiwan, 1980; National Heart, Lung & Blood Institute, merit award, 1986. **SPECIAL ACHIEVEMENTS:** Published over 170 scientific papers. **BUSINESS ADDRESS:** Professor, Dept of Biological Sciences, Carnegie Mellon University, 4400 Fifth Avenue, Pittsburgh, PA 15213-2683, (412)268-3395.

HO, CHIH-MING
Educator, educational administrator. Chinese American. **PERSONAL:** Born Aug 16, 1945, Chung King, China; son of Shao-nan & I-chu Ho; married Shirley T S Ho, Mar 4, 1972; children: Dean. **EDUCATION:** National Taiwan University, BS, 1967; The Johns Hopkins University, PhD, 1974. **CAREER:** Johns Hopkins University, associate research scientist, 1974-75; USC, assistant, associate, professor, 1976-91; UCLA, professor, 1991-, Center for Micro Systems, director, 1993-. **ORGANIZATIONS:** American Physical Society, 1976-; American Institute of Aeronautics & Astronautics, 1984-; American Mechanical Engineering Society, 1990-. **HONORS/AWARDS:** American Physical Society, fellow, 1989; American Institute of A&A, fellow, 1993; Nanking Aeronautical Institute, honorary professor, 1985. **SPECIAL ACHIEVEMENTS:** 90 papers in professional journals, 1968-; 2 American patents. **BUSINESS ADDRESS:** Professor, Director of Center for Micro Systems, University of California, Los Angeles, 405 Hilgard Ave, Engr IV 38-137J, Los Angeles, CA 90024, (310)825-9993.

HO, CHIN CHIH
Financial analyst. Taiwanese American. **PERSONAL:** Born Jun 12, 1961, Chia-I, Taiwan; son of Rong-Mei Hou and Even Hwang; married Yu-I Yang, Jul 29, 1989; children: Kelvin, Wesley. **EDUCATION:** National Taiwan University, BS, 1983; University of Illinois Urbana-Champaign, MBA, finance, 1988. **CAREER:** Tokai Bank of California, financial analyst, 1988-93; Uwin Investment Inc, vice president, finance, currently. **HOME ADDRESS:** 1017 Paloma Dr, Arcadia, CA 91007, (818)574-8254.

HO, CHRWAN-JYH (DAVID HO)

Educator. Taiwanese American. **PERSONAL:** Born Mar 25, 1954, Taipei, Taiwan; son of Dau-Shih Ho and Shu-Luan Lin Ho; married Ting-Ing Ho, Dec 28, 1976; children: Eric, Lesley. **EDUCATION:** National Chiao-Tung University, BS, 1976; University of Georgia, MBA, 1978; Michigan State University, PhD, 1986. **CAREER:** Oklahoma State University, assistant professor, 1983-87, associate professor, 1987-92; Chinese University of Hong Kong, visiting scholar, 1991-92; Oklahoma State University, profesor, 1992-. **ORGANIZATIONS:** Decision Sciences Institute, 1983-91; The Institute of Management Science, 1983-91; American Production and Inventory Control Society, 1981-86. **HONORS/AWARDS:** American Production and Inventory, Control Society, Certified Production and Inventory Management, 1982. **SPECIAL ACHIEVEMENTS:** Published more than 25 articles in academic journals and conference proceedings. **BIOGRAPHICAL SOURCES:** Journal of Business Logistics, vol 13, no 2, p 152, 1992; Management Science, p 1750, Dec 1992. **BUSINESS ADDRESS:** Professor, Oklahoma State University, 342 BUS, Stillwater, OK 74074, (405)744-8634.

HO, CHUNG-WU

Educator. Chinese American. **PERSONAL:** Born May 29, 1938, Hankow, Taiwan; son of Shih-Lun Ho and Cheng-hsien Wu Ho; married Yin-hsin Hsieh, Jun 20, 1965; children: Minnie, Ronald. **EDUCATION:** University of Washington, BS, math, physics (cum laude), 1964, MA, mathematics, 1965; Massachusetts Institute of Technology, PhD, mathematics, 1970. **CAREER:** Taiwan Railroad Administration, assistant engineer, 1959-60; MIT, teaching assistant, 1965-70; Northeastern University, lecturer, 1969-70; University of Texas, Austin, visiting professor, 1980; Washington University, visiting professor, 1984-85; University of Science and Technology of China, overseas consultant to the gifted program, 1985-; Southern Illinois University, professor, chairman, 1970-. **ORGANIZATIONS:** Mathematical Association of America, 1963-, Visiting Lecturers Program, panel, 1993-97; American Mathematical Society, 1968; New York Academy of Sciences, 1973; Sigma Xi, 1974. **HONORS/AWARDS:** Hangzhou Teachers College, Honorary Professorship, 1992; Hefei Educational Institute, Honorary Professorship, 1985; Southern Illinois University, Edwardsville, Teaching Excellence Award, 1973, 1983, Research Scholar Award, 1981-82; Sigma Xi of Southern Illinois University, Award for Outstanding Research, 1979. **SPECIAL ACHIEVEMENTS:** Twenty five research articles, 50 reviews in Zentralblatt fur Mathematik; publications include: co-author, "Sizes of Elements in the Complement of a Submonoid of Integers," Fibonacci Numbers and Their Applications, 4, p 139-144, 1991; "A Fast Algorithm for the Chinese Remainder Theorem," Fibonacci Numbers and Their Applications, 4, p 241-246, 1991. **BUSINESS ADDRESS:** Prof & Chairman, Dept of Mathematics & Statistics, Southern Illinois University at Edwardsville, SL1314, Edwardsville, IL 62026-1118, (618)692-2385.

HO, DANIEL F.

Educator. Chinese American. **PERSONAL:** Born Jun 12, 1956, Hong Kong; son of Chia-hua Ho and Siu Fong Yung; married Ginny Ho, Dec 31, 1991; children: Roy C, Charlene Y. **EDUCATION:** Fu Jen Catholic University, Taiwan, BA, 1978; University of Texas, MS, 1986; George Mason University, PhD candidate. **CAREER:** Center for Strategic & International Studies, manager, 1987-89; Southeastern University, chairman, 1988-92, professor, dean, 1992-. **ORGANIZATIONS:** American Chinese Management Educators, president, 1993, president elect, 1992-, vice president, 1991-92. **HONORS/AWARDS:** Southeastern University, Distinguished Professor Award, 1990. **BUSINESS ADDRESS:** Professor, Dean of Information Studies, Southeastern University, 501 Eye St SW, Washington, DC 20024-2788, (202)488-8162.

HO, DAVID. *See* HO, CHRWAN-JYH.

HO, DAVID D.

Health facility administrator. Chinese American. **PERSONAL:** Born Nov 3, 1952, Taiwan; son of Paul Ho and Sonia Ho; married Susan, Aug 8, 1976; children: Jaclyn, Jonathan, Kathryn. **EDUCATION:** Massachusetts Institute of Technology, 1970-71; California Institute of Technology, BS, 1974; Harvard Medical School, MD, 1978. **CAREER:** Cedars-Sinai Medical Center, Div of Infectious Diseases, Dept of Medicine, physician, research scientist, 1986-90; UCLA School of Medicine, asst professor of medicine in residence, 1986-89, associate professor of medicine in residence, 1989-90; NYU School of Medicine, Center for AIDS Research, co-director, 1990-, professor oof medicine and microbiology, 1990-; Aaron Diamond AIDS Research Center, scientific director, chief executive officer, 1990-. **ORGANIZATIONS:** 10th Intl Conference on AIDS, chairman, organizing committee, 1993-94; Interscience Conference

on Antimicrobial Agents and Chemotherapy, organizing committee, 1993-; NIH HIV Vaccine Working Group, subcommittee chairman, 1992-; American Bureau for Medical Advancement in China, board member, 1992-; Busines/Medical Coordinating Committee on AIDS, 1990-92; Chinese American Leadership Organization, committee of 100, 1990-; American Foundation for AIDS Research, scientific advisory board, 1990-; NIH, Study Section on AIDS Immunology, 1988-93. **SPECIAL ACHIEVEMENTS:** Author of over 100 scientific publications. **BUSINESS ADDRESS:** Director, Aaron Diamond AIDS Research Center, 455 First Ave, 7th Fl, New York, NY 10016.

HO, DENNIS

Government official. Chinese American. **PERSONAL:** Born Feb 16, 1945, Keichow, China; son of Ho Yee Ju and Irene Hwang Ho; married Susan Ho, Jul 1, 1976; children: Stephanie, Dion. **EDUCATION:** VPI, BSCE, 1968. **CAREER:** Delaware DOT, rd design engineer, 1980-87, assistant district eng, 1987-91, district engineer, 1991-. **ORGANIZATIONS:** ASCE; DAPE; Dover Little League, board of directors; Kent County Tourism, board of directors; Elks. **BUSINESS ADDRESS:** District Engineer, Delaware DOT, PO Box 778, Dover, DE 19903, (302)739-4219.

HO, EDWIN SOON HEE

Computer programming supervisor. Chinese American. **PERSONAL:** Born May 4, 1959, Santa Monica, CA; son of Ernie Ho and Loretta Ho; married Mona Kim Sakata-Ho, Nov 13, 1983; children: Chelsea Kim Akemi. **EDUCATION:** Kapiolani Community College, AS, 1985. **CAREER:** Pioneer Federal Savings Bank, 1987; Kaiser Permanente, supervisor, programmer/analyst, currently. **HOME ADDRESS:** 1043 B Ilima Dr, Honolulu, HI 96817, (808)595-8273.

HO, FRED WEI-HAN (FRED WEI-HAN HOUN)

Musician, composer, band leader. Chinese American. **PERSONAL:** Born Aug 10, 1957, Palo Alto, CA; son of Franklin Wu Houn and Frances Lu. **EDUCATION:** Harvard University, BA, sociology, 1979. **CAREER:** Afro-Asian Music Ensemble, director, leader, 1982-. **ORGANIZATIONS:** Meet the Composer, board of directors, 1993-; ASCAP, 1985-. **HONORS/AWARDS:** Chinese for Affirmative Action, Honoree, 1990; Black Musicians Conference, Duke Ellington Distinguished Artist, 1988; National Endowment for the Arts, Music Composition Fellowship, 1993; Harvard University, Peter Ivers Fellow, 1987. **SPECIAL ACHIEVEMENTS:** Recording: "Tomorrow Is Now!" Soul Note Records, 1986; "Bamboo That Snaps Back," Finnadar, Atlantic Records, 1987; "A Song for Manong," Asian/Improv Records, 1988; "We Refuse to Be Used and Abused," Soul Note Records, 1988; "The Underground Railroad to My Heart," Soul Note Records, 1994. **BUSINESS ADDRESS:** Musician, American International Artists, 515 E 89th St, Suite 6B, New York, NY 10128, (212)996-6131.

HO, HON HING

Educator. Chinese American. **PERSONAL:** Born May 3, 1939, Hong Kong; son of Wa-Ching Ho and Yin-Hing Kong; married Lucinda C Chui, Jun 28, 1968; children: Cynthia M, Nancy M. **EDUCATION:** University of Hong Kong, BSc, 1962, 1963; University of Western Ontario, PhD, 1966. **CAREER:** University of Western Ontario, postdoctoral fellow, 1966-67; Ohio Wesleyan University, assistant professor, 1967-68; State University of New York, assistant professor, 1968-70, associate professor, 1971-78, professor, 1979-. **ORGANIZATIONS:** Mycological Society of America, 1968-; American Phytopathological Society, 1964-. **HONORS/AWARDS:** Canadian Government, Commonwealth Scholarship, 1963; State University of New York, exchange scholar, 1991; Education Commission of China, 2nd prize in scientific achievements, 1992. **SPECIAL ACHIEVEMENTS:** Over 60 published papers in scientific journals, 1966-93; Academia Sinica, Taipei, visiting professor, 1989-92; Nanjing Agricultural University, visiting professor, 1982, 1992-93; proficient in Cantonese and Mandarin. **HOME ADDRESS:** 11 Bonticouview Dr, New Paltz, NY 12561, (914)255-6512. **BUSINESS ADDRESS:** Professor and Chairman, Dept of Biology, State University of New York, New Paltz, NY 12561-2407, (914)257-3780.

HO, JOHN TING-SUM

Physicist, educator. Chinese American. **PERSONAL:** Born Jul 5, 1942, Hong Kong; son of Sui-Ming Ho & Ping-Chun Yang; married Martha C Leung, Aug 8, 1970. **EDUCATION:** University of Hong Kong, BSc, general, 1964, BSc, special, 1965; Massachusetts Institute of Technology, PhD, 1969. **CAREER:** University of Pennsylvania, assistant professor of physics, 1969-74; University of Houston, associate professor of physics, 1974-75; State University of New

York at Buffalo, associate professor of physics, 1975-83, Natural Sciences & Mathematics, interim dean, 1984-85, professor of physics, 1983-, Natural Sciences & Mathematics, associate dean, 1983-. **ORGANIZATIONS:** American Physical Society, 1969-, New York State Section, executive committee, 1983-87, 1993-97. **HONORS/AWARDS:** EI DuPont De Nemours & Co, DuPont Young Faculty Award, 1970-74; American Physical Society, fellow, 1990; Guggenheim Memorial Foundation, fellow, 1990-91. **SPECIAL ACHIEVEMENTS:** Over 60 scientific publications in professional journals, 1969-. **BUSINESS ADDRESS:** SUNY at Buffalo, Faculty of Natural Sciences & Mathematics, 411 Capen Hall, Buffalo, NY 14260, (716)645-2531.

HO, JU-SHEY
Educator, researcher. Taiwanese American. **PERSONAL:** Born Dec 20, 1935, Taipei, Taiwan; son of Kai-sheng Ho & Keh-Cheng; married Pao-Hsi Ho, Aug 28, 1965; children: Min-Min, Phi-Lip. **EDUCATION:** National Taiwan University, BS, 1958; Boston University, MS, 1965, PhD, 1969. **CAREER:** National Taiwan University, teaching assistant, 1960-62; Boston University, teaching fellow, 1962-64, research assistant, 1964-68, research associate, 1968-70; California State University, Long Beach, assistant professor, 1970-74, associate professor, 1974-79, professor, 1979-. **ORGANIZATIONS:** World Association of Copepodologists, vice president, 1993-96, executive council, 1987-93; The Crustacean Society, founding member, 1980-; North America Taiwanese Professors' Association, founding member, 1980-, board of governors, 1985-87; The Japan Research Group of Fish Pathology, 1973-; American Association for the Advancement Science, 1972-; Sigma Xi, 1964-. **HONORS/AWARDS:** Taiwan Fishermen's Association, Scholarship in Fishery Biology, 1955-58; California State University, Distinguished Faculty Scholarly and Creative Achievement Award, 1986, Meritorious Performance and Professional Promise Award, 1988. **SPECIAL ACHIEVEMENTS:** Laboratory/Field Worksheets for Marine Natural History, 1993; Laboratory Manual for Invertebrate Zoology, 1978; over 130 scientific papers and monographs on copepod parasites of marine animals, 1961-; fluent in Taiwanese, Mandarin, Japanese. **MILITARY SERVICE:** Chinese Army, 2nd lieutenant, 1958-60. **BUSINESS ADDRESS:** Professor, Dept of Biological Sciences, California State University, 1250 Bellflower Blvd, Long Beach, CA 90840-3702, (310)985-4812.

HO, KHANG-CHENG
Pathologist, neuropathologist, educator. Taiwanese American. **PERSONAL:** Born Mar 22, 1940, Ping-Tung, Taiwan. **EDUCATION:** Kaohsiung Medical College, MD, 1965; DC General Hospital, internship, mixed medical, 1966-67, residency & fellowship, internal medicine, 1967-68; Upstate Medical Center, neurology, 1968-69; Northwestern University Medical School, neurology, 1969-71; Case Western Reserve University, neuropathology, fellowship, 1971-73, pathology, anatomic, 1973-75, PhD, anatomy, 1975. **CAREER:** Zablock VA Medical Center, physician, 1979-; Children's Hospital of Wisconsin, consultant in neuropathology, 1980-; Milwaukee County Medical Examiner's Office, consultant in neuropathology, 1988-; Waukesha County Medical Examiner's Office, consultant in neuropathology, 1991-; Froedtert Memorial Lutheran Hospital, staff pathologist & senior attending medical staff, 1981-; Milwaukee County Medical Complex, staff pathologist & senior attending medical staff, 1981-; Medical College of Wisconsin, assistant professor, pathology, 1975-81, neurology, secondary, 1980-81, associate professor, pathology, 1981-, neurology, 1981-. **ORGANIZATIONS:** American Medical Association, 1977-; State Medical Society of Wisconsin, 1977-; The Medical Society of Milwaukee County, 1977-; The American Academy of Neurology, 1978-; American Association of Neuropathologists Inc, 1985-; International Academy of Pathology, 1989-. **SPECIAL ACHIEVEMENTS:** 66 publications; 60 abstracts; 7 video cassettes; 7 computer programs; 1 book; research: Alzheimer's disease, development of brain. **MILITARY SERVICE:** Air Force, Taiwan, 2nd lt, 1965-66. **BUSINESS ADDRESS:** Associate Professor, Dept of Pathology, Medical College of Wisconsin, Box 152, 8700 W Wisconsin Ave, Milwaukee County Medical Complex, Milwaukee, WI 53226, (414)257-6210.

HO, LOP-HING
Educator. Chinese American. **PERSONAL:** Born Jul 3, 1957, Hong Kong; son of Wai-Ying Lee and Yat-Kwong Ho; married Manyee D Ho, Aug 22, 1982; children: Sharon, Tiffany. **EDUCATION:** Chinese University of Hong Kong, BSc, 1979; Princeton University, PhD, 1983. **CAREER:** Rutgers University, asst prof, 1983-84; Hong Kong Polytechnic, lecturer, 1984-89; Wichita State University, asst prof, 1989-. **SPECIAL ACHIEVEMENTS:** Author: "Exact Subelliptic Estimates for n-1 Forms," 1992; "J-problem on Weakly g-Convex Domains," 1991; "An Inequality with Applications to the Subellipticity of J-

Neumann Problem," 1991; "Subelliptic Estimates for the J-Neumann Problem for n-1 Forms," 1991; "Subellipticity of the J-Neumann Problem on Non-Pseudo Convex Domains," 1991. **BUSINESS ADDRESS:** Assistant Professor, Math Dept, The Wichita State University, Wichita, KS 67260, (316)689-3944.

HO, MICHAEL SHIUKEUNG
Librarian. Hong Kong American. **PERSONAL:** Born Dec 25, 1935, Hong Kong; son of Leung Shang Ho and Wah Fong Leung; married Rebecca Ho, Jul 13, 1962; children: Winston. **EDUCATION:** Taiwan Normal University, BA, 1961; University of North Texas, MLS, 1970. **CAREER:** Wong Shui Chi High School, teacher, 1963-68; East Texas State University, librarian, 1970-. **ORGANIZATIONS:** Texas Assn of College Teachers, 1970-. **HONORS/AWARDS:** Minority Students Assn, ETSU, Certificate of Appreciation, 1988. **HOME ADDRESS:** 2505 Park St, Commerce, TX 75428, (903)886-8673.

HO, PETER PECK KOH
Attorney, scientist. Chinese American. **PERSONAL:** Born Sep 12, 1937, Fukien, China; son of Jiann-Chaur Ho; married Jessica Shen-Ho, Jun 17, 1962; children: Michael J, Angelin J. **EDUCATION:** Chung Chi College, Hong Kong, BSc, 1958; University of Washington, PhD, 1963; Indiana University, JD (summa cum laude), 1984. **CAREER:** University of California, Berkeley, post-doctoral fellow, 1963-64; Eli Lilly & Company, research advisor, 1964-93; US Patent and Trademark Office, patent examiner, 1993; Norris, Choplin & Schroeder, attorney, 1994-. **ORGANIZATIONS:** American Chemical Society, 1964-; American Society of Biochemistry & Molecular Biology, 1972-; Council on Arterioscelersis, 1990-; State Bar of Indiana, 1985-; State Bar of California, 1985-; American Bar Association, 1985-; Indiana State Bar Association, 1985-; US patent and Trademark Office, 1986-. **HONORS/AWARDS:** Indiana University, Woodard Fellow, 1983. **SPECIAL ACHIEVEMENTS:** 54 publications in scientific journals. **BUSINESS ADDRESS:** Attorney, Norris, Choplin & Schroeder, 101 West Ohio Street, Indianapolis, IN 46204, (317)269-9330.

HO, PING PEI
Educator. Chinese American. **PERSONAL:** Born May 19, 1949, Kaoh siung, Taiwan; son of H T Ho and C F Ho; married Ann Ho, Oct 8, 1988; children: Benjamin, Derek, Daniel, David. **EDUCATION:** Tsing-Hua University, BS, 1970; City College of New York, MA, 1974; City University of New York, PhD, 1978; Kent State University, MBA, 1983. **CAREER:** NCR Corp, senior engineer, 1979-83; City of New York, professor, electrical engineering, 1983-. **ORGANIZATIONS:** Optical Society of America, 1993-; Review of Scientific Instrument, editor board, 1992-. **SPECIAL ACHIEVEMENTS:** Over 100 publications in technical journals; seven patents awarded. **BUSINESS ADDRESS:** Professor of Elec Engrg, City College of New York, 138th St & Convent Ave, Rm J201, New York, NY 10031-9101.

HO, REGINALD C. S.
Physician. Chinese American. **PERSONAL:** Born Mar 30, 1932, Hong Kong; son of Chow Ho and Elizabeth Wong Ho; married Sharilyn Dang Ho, Nov 14, 1964; children: Mark, Reginald, Gianna Masca, Timothy. **EDUCATION:** St Louis University, School of Arts and Sciences, 1951-54, School of Medicine, MD, 1959; University of Cincinnati Hospitals, residency, 1959-62; Washington University, Barnes Hospital, oncology fellowship, 1962-63. **CAREER:** Straub Clinic and Hospital, vice president, 1972-73, president, 1973-76, dept chief of oncology and hematology, 1963-; University of Hawaii School of Medicine, clinical professor of medicine, 1977-; Cancer Research Center of Hawaii, clinical science adjunct professor, 1989-. **ORGANIZATIONS:** American Cancer Society, national president, 1992-93, vice president, 1991-92. **HONORS/AWARDS:** American Cancer Society, national division award, 1979, Hawaii division, honorary life member, 1989; St Louis University School of Medicine, Alpha Omega Alpha, 1958. **BIOGRAPHICAL SOURCES:** Asian American and Pacific Islander Journal of Health, pp 111-13, 1993; World Journal West, pp1, 4, September 12, 1993. **BUSINESS ADDRESS:** Chief of Department, Oncology and Hematology, Straub Clinic and Hospital, 888 S King St, Honolulu, HI 96813, (808)522-4333.

HO, RICHARD H.
Government official. Chinese American. **PERSONAL:** Born Dec 2, 1943, Shensi, China; married Cora C Ho; children: Bryan, Justin. **EDUCATION:** National Taiwan University, BA, 1965; University of Denver, MSW, 1968; Smith College School of Social Work, DSW, 1973. **CAREER:** Tufts University Medical School, psychiatry, instructor, 1974-76; Brookline Mental Health

Center, consultant, 1975-85; Boston University Medical School, psychiatry, instructor, 1978-85, chief social worker, 1978-81; Solomon Carter Fuller Mental Health Center, clinical director, 1981-85; Simmons College School of Social Work, adjunct assistant professor, 1982-86; Smith College School for Social Work, lecturer, 1983-85; Commonwealth of Massachusetts, Department of Social Service, assistant area director, 1985-88, area director, 1988-90, director of foster care services, 1990-91, assistant commissioner, 1991-. **ORGANIZATIONS:** South Cove Health Center, board of directors, 1987-89; Greater Boston Chinese Cultural Association, board of directors, 1985-87; Chinese Economic Development Council, board of directors, 1985-87; NASW. **HOME ADDRESS:** 25 Larch Rd, Wellesley, MA 02181, (617)237-9544. **BUSINESS PHONE:** (617)727-0900.

HO, THIERRY
Financial services company executive. Chinese American. **PERSONAL:** Born Nov 9, 1957, Paris, France; son of Nounsan Ho and Sayman Ho. **EDUCATION:** Harvard College, BA (magna cum laude), 1979; University of Pennsylvania, MBA, 1981. **CAREER:** American Express Company, director, business analysis, 1981-87; Goldman, Sachs & Co, vice president, operations administration, 1987-. **ORGANIZATIONS:** New York Society of Security Analysts, 1992-; International Society of Financial Analysts, 1993-; Association for Investment Management & Research, 1992-. **HONORS/AWARDS:** Association for Investment Management and Research, chartered financial analyst, 1992; Association of Management Accounting, certified management accounting, 1985. **BUSINESS ADDRESS:** VP, Operation & Technology Division, Goldman, Sachs & Co, 85 Broad St, 10th Floor, New York, NY 10004, (212)902-8837.

HO, THOMAS TONG-YUN
Petroleum geologist. Taiwanese American. **PERSONAL:** Born Jul 2, 1931, Taichung, Taiwan; son of Ching-Tui Ho & Wan Shi Hsieh; married Yvonne Ya-Ching Lai, Jun 2, 1964; children: Anthony, Victor. **EDUCATION:** National Taiwan University, Taipei, BS, 1955; University of Kansas, MS, 1961, PhD, 1964. **CAREER:** University of Arizona, research associate, 1964-67; UCLA, visiting scientist, 1967; Exxon Production Research Co, sr research scientist, 1967-75; Conoco, director, 1975-79, senior research associate, 1979-85, researcher, Du Pont Fellow, 1985-. **ORGANIZATIONS:** Geological Society of America, fellow, 1963-; Geochemical Society, 1975-; American Association of Petroleum Geologists, 1974-, offshore technology committee, 1978; Taiwanese Association of North America, Houston Chapter, president, 1973, Oklahoma Chapter, board member, 1992. **HONORS/AWARDS:** Technical advisor to United Nations, 1980; American Association of Petroleum Geologists, Best Paper Award, 1991. **SPECIAL ACHIEVEMENTS:** Contributor to scientific journals: Sciences, Bulletin of Geological Society of America, Bulletin of American Association of Petroleum Geologists, Norway Petroleum Society; developed computer model that led to the discovery of giant oil field Heidrun in Norway, 1985. **MILITARY SERVICE:** Chinese Army, Taiwan, lt, 1955-56. **HOME PHONE:** (405)762-4470. **BUSINESS ADDRESS:** DuPont Fellow, Conoco, 1000 S Pine, 6451 Geosciences Reservoir Research & Development Center, Ponca City, OK 74601, (405)767-3094.

HO, TING
Educator. Chinese American. **PERSONAL:** Born in Chungking, China; married. **EDUCATION:** Bucknell University, BA, 1967; Kent State University, MA, 1970; Eastman School of Music, PhD, 1974. **CAREER:** Montclair State College, professor, currently. **ORGANIZATIONS:** Society of Composers Inc, executive committee, 1987-; Broadcast Music Inc, BMI. **HONORS/AWARDS:** New Jersey Council on the Arts, Distinguished Artist Award, 1987; National Endowment for the Arts, Composer Fellowship. **SPECIAL ACHIEVEMENTS:** Voice of America Broadcast to the Orient. **BUSINESS ADDRESS:** Professor, Music Dept, Montclair State College, 1 Normal Ave, Montclair, NJ 07043-1624, (201)893-7212.

HO, VERNON S. C.
Business consultant. Chinese American. **PERSONAL:** Born in Honolulu, HI. **EDUCATION:** Willamette University, BA, 1966. **CAREER:** Ho & Associates, president, currently. **ORGANIZATIONS:** City of Eugene, Planning Commission; Asian Council, Eugene, Springfield; Pacific NW Organization Development Network; NW Regional China Council. **HONORS/AWARDS:** Association for Quality & Participation, award, 1993. **BUSINESS ADDRESS:** President, Ho & Associates, 1800 Valley River Drive, Suite 250, Eugene, OR 97401, (503)344-3096.

HO, XUAN MICHAEL
Educator, educational administrator. Vietnamese American. **PERSONAL:** Born Sep 30, 1951, Saigon, Vietnam; son of Danh C Ho and Bong T Vo; married Mai; children: Troy, Hien, Noelle. **EDUCATION:** Columbia Pacific University, MS, 1991; Fielding Institute, PhD, currently. **CAREER:** Santa Rosa Memorial Hospital, radiology supervisor, 1980-89; Santa Rosa Junior College, instructor, program director, 1986-. **ORGANIZATIONS:** American Society of Radiologic Technologists, 1993; American Registry of Radiologic Technologist, 1993; California Society of Radiologic Technologists, 1993; Association of Educators in Radiologic Technology, 1993; Round Table Business Exchange, 1993. **BUSINESS ADDRESS:** Professor, Program Director, Health Sciences, Santa Rosa Junior College, 1501 Mendocino Ave, Santa Rosa, CA 95401, (707)527-4346.

HO, YU-CHI
Educator, company executive. Chinese American. **PERSONAL:** Born Mar 1, 1934, China; son of Chin-Woo Ho and Ching-Yi Pan; married Sophia, Oct 10, 1959; children: Adrian, Christine Kim, Lara. **EDUCATION:** MIT, SBEE, 1954; Harvard University, PhD, 1961. **CAREER:** Harvard University, T Jefferson Coolidge Professor of Applied Math, 1962-. **ORGANIZATIONS:** Network Dynamics Inc, chairman of the board, 1984-. **HONORS/AWARDS:** National Academy of Engineering, 1987; IEEE, Control Science and Engineering Award, 1989, Best Paper Award, 1974; SCI, Most Cited Book Award, 1978; Chiang Technology Achievement Award, 1993. **SPECIAL ACHIEVEMENTS:** Over 100 papers & 3 books published. **BUSINESS ADDRESS:** Professor, Harvard University, Pierce Hall, Cambridge, MA 02138, (617)495-3992.

HO, YUH JYUE AGNES WANG
Librarian. Chinese American. **PERSONAL:** Born Aug 27, 1946, Taiwan; daughter of Griffith & K P Mau Wang; married Chung Fah Howard Ho, Feb 11, 1973; children: Vicki, Jason. **EDUCATION:** Fu Jen Catholic University, Taiwan, BA, 1968; Syracuse University, MSLS, 1970. **CAREER:** Utica Public Library, reference librarian, 1970-73; Lenoir Community College, cataloger, 1973; Neuse Regional Library, associate director, 1973-. **ORGANIZATIONS:** Grainger-Hill Performing Arts Center, board member, 1991-; American Library Association, 1970-; North Carolina Library Association, 1973-, Roundtable on Ethnic Minority Concerns, secretary, 1990. **HONORS/AWARDS:** North Carolina Public Library Directors Association, Outstanding Staff Development Program Award, 1988. **SPECIAL ACHIEVEMENTS:** Publisher of The Public Image, an International Public Relations Quarterly, 1991-. **BUSINESS ADDRESS:** Associate Director, Neuse Regional Library, 510 N Queen St, Kinston, NC 28501, (919)527-7066.

HO, YUI TIM
Educator. Hong Kong American. **PERSONAL:** Born Jan 14, 1945, Hong Kong; son of Chak-Lam & Lin-Ho Ho; married Wooping Pattie Ho, Aug 9, 1973; children: Sylvia, Melody. **EDUCATION:** Chinese University of Hong Kong, BS, 1967; University of Minnesota, MS, 1969, PhD, 1973. **CAREER:** University of Wisconsin, Eau Claire, lecturer, 1972-73, assistant professor, 1973-81, associate professor, 1981-89, professor, 1989-. **HONORS/AWARDS:** University of Wisconsin, Eau Claire, Schools of Arts & Sciences, Effective Teaching Recognition Award, 1988. **SPECIAL ACHIEVEMENTS:** Interacting Lobo transposous in an inbred strain and interaction regulation in hybrids Drosophila melanopaslin, 1993. **BUSINESS ADDRESS:** Professor, Biology Dept, University of Wisconsin, Eau Claire, Park & Garfield, Phillips 337, Eau Claire, WI 54701, (715)836-3020.

HOANG, FRANK H.
Steel company executive. Vietnamese American. **PERSONAL:** Born Aug 14, 1950, Vietnam; married Chi Hoang. **EDUCATION:** San Diego State University, BA; University of BC, MBA. **CAREER:** Georgetown Wire Co, K-Lath Division, vice president, general manager, currently. **ORGANIZATIONS:** ICBO; WLBCA. **HOME PHONE:** (714)998-7271. **BUSINESS ADDRESS:** Vice President, General Manager, K-Lath Division, Georgetown Wire Co, 13470 Philadelphia Ave, Fontana, CA 92335, (909)360-8288.

HOANG, GIAO
Organization executive. Vietnamese American. **PERSONAL:** Born May 15, 1934, Hue, Vietnam; married. **EDUCATION:** School of Law, 1956; University of Public Administration, BA, 1957; University of NSW, MA, economics, 1970. **CAREER:** Department of Planning, Vietnam, director, 1963-67; Ministry of Economy, Vietnam, director, 1968-70; Ministry of Education, Vietnam,

director, 1970-72. **ORGANIZATIONS:** Vietnamese Chamber of Commerce, vice president, 1980-91; Economic and Employment Development Center, director, 1985-; Mutual Assistance Association Coalition, board of directors, 1989-; Asian Pacific Planning Council, board of directors, 1990-; Asian Pacific Health Care Venture, board of directors, 1990-; Indochinese Senior Citizens Association, secretary, 1988-. **SPECIAL ACHIEVEMENTS:** Publications: Land Reform in Vietnam, 1968; How to Invest in the United States, 1982; Economic Glossary, English-Vietnamese, 1990. **BUSINESS ADDRESS:** Executive Director, Economic & Employment Development Center, 2323 Beverly Blvd, Ste 208, Los Angeles, CA 90057, (213)413-4859.

HO-GONZÁLEZ, WILLIAM
Government official. Chinese American. **PERSONAL:** Born Mar 27, 1957, New York, NY; son of Jack Ho and Iluminada Gonzalez; married Elizabeth Perez, Jun 8, 1985. **EDUCATION:** Columbia College, BA, 1979; Harvard Law School, JD, 1982. **CAREER:** Department of Transportation, aeronautics attorney, 1983-87; Department of Justice, assistant US attorney, 1987-92, special counsel for immigration-related unfair, employment practices, 1992-. **HONORS/AWARDS:** Council for Legal Educational Opportunity, CLEO Fellowship, 1979; Department of Transportation, Special Achievement Award, 1986; Department of Justice, Special Achievement Award, 1991. **SPECIAL ACHIEVEMENTS:** Fully proficient in Spanish; "Worry about the Nannies," New York Newsday, Feb 25, 1993. **BIOGRAPHICAL SOURCES:** National Journal, p 1945, Aug 3, 1991; Interpreter Releases, p 940, July 24, 1991. **BUSINESS ADDRESS:** Special Counsel for Immigration-Related Unfair Employment Practices, US Department of Justice, 1425 New York Ave, NW, Ste 900, Washington, DC 20005.

HOKAMA, YOSHITSUGI
Educator, researcher. Japanese American/Pacific Islander American. **PERSONAL:** Born Oct 25, 1926, Nuilii, HI; son of Royei & Kamado Matsudo Hokama; married Haruko Yoshimoto Hokama, Feb 3, 1951; children: Jon-Keith Yoshimoto, Julie Lynne Rosemary Hokama Shirai. **EDUCATION:** University of California, Los Angeles, BA, 1951, MA, 1953, PhD, 1957. **CAREER:** UCLA, research associate, 1952-57, assistant researcher, 1957-66; California State University, associate professor, 1964-66; University of Hawaii, associate professor of pathology, 1966-68, professor of pathology, 1968-, CRCH, laboratory director, 1980-84; SmithKline Lab, laboratory director, consultant, 1974-. **ORGANIZATIONS:** American Society Micro, 1957-; NY Academy Society, 1957-; American Association CA Res, 1966-; American Society Invest Path, 1968-; American Association Immunol, 1974-; Leukoyte Biol Society, 1970-; International Society Toxinol, 1984-. **HONORS/AWARDS:** NIH, C-reactive protein catalase studies, 1968, C-reactive protein studies, 1971; FDA, Ciguatera Testing, 1978; NMFS, Ciguatera Studies, 1990; State of Hawaii, Ciguatera Studies, 1980. **SPECIAL ACHIEVEMENTS:** Co-author, textbook: Immunol & Immunopath, Little, Brown & Co, 1989; patent no 4,816,392, March 28, 1989; Stick Test for Ciguatera Detection; published: 270 manuscripts and abstracts, in various scientific journals and monograph chapters. **MILITARY SERVICE:** Army, sgt 1st class, 1945-48, Good Conduct Medal. **BUSINESS ADDRESS:** Professor, Dept of Pathology, University of Hawaii, School of Medicine, 1960 East-West Rd, Biomedical Bldg, Rm T512, Honolulu, HI 96822, (808)956-8682.

HOKOYAMA, J. D.
Association administrator. Japanese American. **PERSONAL:** Born Nov 25, 1945. **CAREER:** Leadership Education for Asian Pacifics, executive director, president, currently. **BUSINESS ADDRESS:** President, Leadership Education for Asian Pacifics, 327 E Second St, Ste 226, Los Angeles, CA 90012, (213)485-1422. *

HOLL, JULIE KAWAHARA
Public health services administrator. Japanese American. **PERSONAL:** Born Aug 1, 1960, Chicago, IL; daughter of Sakie Takehara Kawahara & James Tasuku Kawahara; married Nelson Jang Holl, Jul 11, 1987; children: Cameron James. **EDUCATION:** University of Illinois, Champaign-Urbana, BS, 1985. **CAREER:** Asian American Recovery Services, prevention coordinator, 1985-88; SF Dept of Public Health, planner/program administrator, 1989-93, associate director, 1993-. **ORGANIZATIONS:** Asian Pacific Advocacy & Resource Council, 1992-; Asian Women's Shelter, Chair-Event Committee, board member, 1988-92; Japanese Mental Health Task Force, 1987-89; National Asian Pacific American Families against Substance Abuse, 1989-; Asian American Recovery Services, volunteer, 1988-90. **HONORS/AWARDS:** Boston University, Join Together, Leadership Institute Fellow, 1992. **SPECIAL**

ACHIEVEMENTS: San Francisco master plan to reduce problems caused by drug & alcohol use, 1993; San Francisco problem assessment of health indicator data, 1992. **BUSINESS ADDRESS:** Associate Director of Planning & Personnel, San Francisco Department of Public Health-Substance Abuse, 1380 Howard St, 4th Floor, San Francisco, CA 94103, (415)255-3528.

HOM, HARRY LEE, JR.
Educator. Chinese American. **PERSONAL:** Born Dec 10, 1942, Helena, MT; son of Harry & May Hom; married Susan, May 26, 1973; children: Brian, Andrew. **EDUCATION:** Lewis & Clark College, BS, 1965; University of Montana, MA, 1969, PhD, 1971. **CAREER:** Huron College, assistant professor, department chair, 1971-72; SW Missouri State University, professor, 1972-. **ORGANIZATIONS:** American Psychological Society; North American Society for the Psychology of Sport & Physical Activity; Sigma Xi; Society for Research in Child Development; American Psychological Association; Motivation in Education. **HONORS/AWARDS:** Southwest Missouri State University, Excellence in Research Award, 1987. **SPECIAL ACHIEVEMENTS:** Author, Mood Induction Effects Upon Goal Setting Performance in Young Children, Motivation & Emotion, vol 12, p 113-122, 1988; Correlates of Goal Orientations Among Young Athletes, Pediatric Exercise Science, vol 5, p 168-176, 1993. **BIOGRAPHICAL SOURCES:** A Theory of Goal Setting & Task Performance, p 122, 1990. **BUSINESS ADDRESS:** Professor, Psychology Department, Southwest Missouri State University, 901 S National, Springfield, MO 65804, (417)836-4790.

HOM, KATHLEEN B.
Government official. Chinese American. **PERSONAL:** Born Mar 11, 1947, San Diego, CA; daughter of Rose Jung Hom and Miles Hom; married David C Williams, Aug 3, 1974; children: Melinda Rose (Mei-Yin) Hom-Williams, Terri Lynn Garman, John David Williams, Sheryl Anne Lindsay. **EDUCATION:** San Diego City College, AA, liberal arts, 1969; San Diego State University, BA, political science, 1970, MPA, 1972. **CAREER:** City of Phoenix, legislative asst to city manager, 1972-74; US Conference of Mayors, Urban Affairs, program assoc, 1974-76; Hom-Williams Inc, co-owner, principal, 1976-78; Dept of Transportation, chief management analyst, 1978; K B Hom & Associates, owner & president, 1979-89; CACI, manager, publications team, 1989-1991; Office of Asian Affairs, director, 1992-. **ORGANIZATIONS:** Chinese Community Church, board, chair of audit comm, 1992-93; Asian Community Liaison, Democratic natl comm, 1990-; Intl City Management Assn; American Assn of Retired Persons & Univ of Dist of Columbia, Women's Financial Information Prog, comm & task force member, 1992-; Organization of Chinese American Women, 1988-; Smithsonian, Experimental Gallery, community bridge member, 1992. **HONORS/AWARDS:** Korean Amercian Assn, Service Paaque, 1993; Japan-America Student Fdn, Certificate of Honor, 1992; Chinese Community Church, Certificate of Honor, Summer Chinese Program, 1989; Multi-Cultural Center Inc, Program Work Award, 1990; American Society for Public Administration, Intergovt Prog Work Award, 1979; American Assn of Retired Persons & University of DC, Honor for Participation in WFIP, 1992. **SPECIAL ACHIEVEMENTS:** Publications include: ICMA-How to Assess Local Services, DHUD, Section 8 Programs for Cities, DOE-Community Impacts of Oil Shale Development, VA-Entrepreneurship and Veterans; invited to tour People's Republic of China & lecture on impacts of energy projects at Beijing Normal University. **BIOGRAPHICAL SOURCES:** Washington Post, Feb 1, 1992, p A-10; Asian Weekly, April 8, 1993; "Envoy in the Aftermath of Violence," Washington Post, Oct 29, 1993, p A-1. **BUSINESS ADDRESS:** Mayor's Special Asst for Asian Affairs, Executive Office of the Mayor, 1 Judiciary Sq, 441 4th St NW, Ste 1130, Washington, DC 20001, (202)727-3120.

HOM, MEI-LING
Artist, educator. Chinese American. **PERSONAL:** Born Aug 2, 1951, New Haven, CT; daughter of You Dong Hom & Grace Chin Hom; married. **EDUCATION:** Kirkland College, NY, BA, 1973; New York State College of Ceramics at Alfred University, MFA, 1987. **CAREER:** Community College of Philadelphia, art, adjunct instructor, 1979-83, assistant professor, 1983-. **HONORS/AWARDS:** Lila Wallace-Reader's Digest Fund, Arts International Residency, Thailand, 1992; Delaware Art Museum, Biennial '91, Juror's Award, 1991; Pennsylvania Council on the Arts, Fellowship in Visual Arts, 1991; Cite Internationale Des Arts, Residency Award, Paris, France, 1989, 1993; Beaver College Art Gallery, Mildred Bougher Award, 1991. **SPECIAL ACHIEVEMENTS:** Picturing Asian America, community collaboration and site installation, San Francisco, 1993; Thai Space, site installation, Bangkok, 1993; Grave Sweeping, site installation, Philadelphia, 1992; Feeding Ancestral

Ghosts, site installation, Philadelphia, 1991; China Wedge, commissioned installation, Philadelphia Convention Center, 1994. **BIOGRAPHICAL SOURCES:** Artists Choose Artists, Institute of Contemporary Art, p 79, 115, 1991; Contemporary Philadelphia Artists, Philadelphia Museum of Art, p 26, 142, 1990. **HOME ADDRESS:** 2306 Fitzwater St, Philadelphia, PA 19146. **BUSINESS ADDRESS:** Assistant Professor of Art, Community College of Philadelphia, 1700 Spring Garden St, M2-22, Philadelphia, PA 19130, (215)751-8302.

HOM, PETER WAH
Educator. Chinese American. **PERSONAL:** Born Apr 25, 1951, San Francisco, CA; son of Ting Hom and Nguey Kun Wong Hom. **EDUCATION:** New York University, BA, 1972; University of California, Berkeley, MA, 1974; University of Illinois, PhD, 1979. **CAREER:** Kent State University, assistant/associate professor, 1978-84; Arizona State University, associate professor, 1984-. **ORGANIZATIONS:** American Psychological Association, 1978-; Society for Industrial/Organizational Psychologists, 1980-; Academy of Management, 1978-. **HONORS/AWARDS:** Arizona State University, Distinguished Faculty Research Award, 1986; Academy of Management, Best Paper Award, 1987. **SPECIAL ACHIEVEMENTS:** With F Caranikis-Walker, Prussia, & R Griffith, "A Met-analytical Structural Equations Analysis of a Model of Employee Turnover," Journal of Applied Psychology, 1992; with R Griffeth, "Structural Equations Modeling Test of a Turnover Theory: Cross-sectional and Longitudinal Analyses," Journal of Applied Psychology, 1991. **HOME ADDRESS:** 1390 N Ellis St, Chandler, AZ 85224. **BUSINESS ADDRESS:** Associate Professor, Dept of Management, Arizona State University, College of Business, Tempe, AZ 85287, (602)965-3431.

HOM, ROSE
Judge. Chinese American. **PERSONAL:** Born 1949?, Gangzhou, People's Republic of China; married; children: two. **EDUCATION:** University of Southern California, BA (magna cum laude), English, master's degree, public education, JD. **CAREER:** Public Defender's Office, until 1985; Municipal Court, Trial Court, judge, 1985-88; Los Angeles Superior Court, Pasadena Juvenile Court, supervising judge, beginning 1988, Compton Juvenile Court, supervising judge, currently. **SPECIAL ACHIEVEMENTS:** President's Commission on Model State Drug Laws, appointee, 1992. **BUSINESS ADDRESS:** Judge, Los Angeles Superior Court, Compton Courthouse, 200 W Compton Blvd, Dept C, Compton, CA 90220, (310)603-7000.*

HON, ANDREW
Engineer, auditor. Chinese American. **PERSONAL:** Born Mar 12, 1953. **EDUCATION:** Columbia University, BS, 1976. **CAREER:** C F Braun & Co, computer system analyst, 1976-77; US Nuclear Regulatory Commission, reactor safety research engineer, 1977-83, resident inspector, 1984-92; US Department of Energy, nuclear safety engineer/lead auditor, 1992-. **ORGANIZATIONS:** American Society of Mechanical Engineers, 1987-; American Nuclear Society, 1975-. **HONORS/AWARDS:** US Nuclear Regulatory Commission, Special Achievement Award, 1986, 1991; US Department of Energy, Special Act Award, 1992. **SPECIAL ACHIEVEMENTS:** Registered Professional Engineer, State of Maryland, 1984. **HOME ADDRESS:** 6713 W 9th Place, Kennewick, WA 99336. **BUSINESS PHONE:** (509)376-7127.

HON, DAVID NYOK-SAI
Educator. Malaysian American. **PERSONAL:** Born Jun 19, 1974, Kluang, Johor, Malaysia; son of Tai Sun & Chai Pong Hon; married Michelle Hon, Oct 10, 1972; children: Hong-Yi, Gordon. **EDUCATION:** Tokyo University, BS, 1972; Gunma University, MS, 1974; Virginia Technology, PhD, 1977. **CAREER:** Virginia Technology, assistant professor, 1977-82, associate professor, 1982-83; Clemson University, professor, director, 1984-. **ORGANIZATIONS:** American Chemical Society, 1976-; Technology Association for Pulp and Paper, 1976-; Forest Products Research Society, 1977-; Society of Plastic Engineering, 1989-. **HONORS/AWARDS:** Lee Foundation, Research Award, 1974-76; Ministry of Trade, Japan, Japanese Government Research Award, 1982-83; TAPPI Todd Domm Memorial Awards, 1986; Clemson University, Alumni Award for Distinguished Research, 1990. **SPECIAL ACHIEVEMENTS:** Book: Graft Copolymerization of Lignocellulosic Materials, 1982; book: Wood and Cellulosic Chemistry, 1991; 90 technical papers; languages: Chinese (Mandarin, Hakka, Cantonese, Hokken, Malay), Japanese, Spanish. **BUSINESS ADDRESS:** Professor, Director, Clemson University, 128 Lehotsky Hall, Clemson, SC 29634-1003.

HONDA, ALLEN SHIGERU
Educator. Japanese American. **PERSONAL:** Born Jun 17, 1947, Berkeley, CA; son of Robert Tatsuo Honda and Akiko Honda; married Barbara, Oct 8, 1977; children: Karin Otey. **EDUCATION:** Chabot College, AA, 1967; California State University at Hayward, BA, 1970, MS, 1988. **CAREER:** California State University at Hayward, field work supervisor, 1989-91; Castro Valley Unified School District, teacher, 1971-79, educational specialist, 1979-80, Canyon Junior High School, asst principal, 1980-81, Castro Valley High School, asst principal, 1981-86, Procter Elementary, principal, 1986-92, Canyon Middle School, principal, 1992-. **ORGANIZATIONS:** Castro Valley School Administrators Assn, president, 1985; National Assn of Secondary School Principals, 1992; Assn of California School Administrators, 1980; Assn of Asian-American Administrators, 1990. **HONORS/AWARDS:** Castro Valley School Administrators Assn, Administrator of the Year, 1992; PTA, Honorary Service Award, 1987, Continuing Service Award, 1988. **BUSINESS ADDRESS:** Principal, Canyon Middle School, 19600 Cull Canyon Rd, Castro Valley, CA 94552, (510)538-8833.

HONDA, MAYA
Educator. Japanese American. **PERSONAL:** Born Dec 8, 1955, San Diego, CA; daughter of Masami Honda & Yaeko Ruth Honda. **EDUCATION:** Brandeis University, AB (magna cum laude), 1977; Harvard University, EDM, 1979. **CAREER:** UC San Diego, teaching assistant, psychology, 1979-80; Salk Institute, research assistant, 1979-80; MIT, research assistant, linguistics, 1980-82, research assistant, psychology, 1983-84; Shandong University, China, instructor, English, 1982-83; Harvard University, research assistant, education, 1984-88; Wheelock College, instructor, psychology & education, 1990-. **ORGANIZATIONS:** American Association for the Advancement of Science, 1988-; Association for Asian American Studies, 1993-; Linguistics Society of America, 1985-; Massachusetts Asian American Educators Association, 1992-; National Association for Asian & Pacific American Education, 1992-; Asian American Resource Workshop, 1980-; Asian Women's Task Force Against Domestic Violence, 1992-; National Organization for Women, 1985-. **SPECIAL ACHIEVEMENTS:** Co-founder, co-coordinator of linguists for Nicaragua, 1985-91. **HOME ADDRESS:** 31 Bourneside St, Dorchester, MA 02124. **BUSINESS ADDRESS:** Instructor, Wheelock College, 200 The Riverway, Boston, MA 02215-4176, (617)734-5200.

HONDA, MICHAEL M.
County government official. Japanese American. **PERSONAL:** Born Jun 27, 1941. **CAREER:** Santa Clara County Board of Supervisors, District 1, supervisor, currently. **BUSINESS ADDRESS:** Supervisor, District 1, Santa Clara County Board of Supervisors, Government Ctr, East Wing, 10th Fl, 70 W Hedding St, San Jose, CA 95110, (408)299-2323. *

HONDA, SHIGERU IRWIN
Educator. Japanese American. **PERSONAL:** Born Nov 16, 1927, Seattle, WA; son of Masaru & Shieu Honda; divorced. **EDUCATION:** California Institute of Technology, BS, 1950; University of Wisconsin, MS, 1952, PhD, 1954. **CAREER:** Commonwealth Scientific & Industrial Research Organization, Australia, research officer, 1953-56; US Department of Agriculture, chemist, 1956-61; UCLA, associate research plant physiologist, 1960-67, visiting plant physiologist, 1971, CSIRO Div of Horticulture, visiting plant physiologist, 1985-86; Wright State University, professor, 1967-. **HONORS/AWARDS:** US Ed Exchange Grant, Fulbright Award, Australia, 1953; US Public Health Service, UCLA, special research fellow, 1961; NIH, General Medicine, UCLA, Research Career Development Award, 1963-66, research grant, 1963-66; Botanical Society of America, Travel Grant, Xth International Botanical Congress, 1964; New Zealand Science Congress, Diploma of Merit, 1966; NASA-ASEE, Johnson Space Center, fellow, 1973, 1974. **BUSINESS ADDRESS:** Professor of Biology, Wright State University, Dayton, OH 45435, (513)873-2306.

HONG, CARL
Association administrator. Chinese American. **CAREER:** Chinese American Association of Commerce, president, currently. **BUSINESS ADDRESS:** President, Chinese American Association of Commerce, 838 Grant Ave, Ste 301, San Francisco, CA 94108, (415)362-4306.*

HONG, DANIEL CHONGHAN
Educator. Korean American. **PERSONAL:** Born Mar 3, 1956, Seoul, Republic of Korea; son of Ki-Cheorl Hong and Bong Ju Gu Hong; married Susy S Hong, Aug 15, 1981; children: Susan H, Annie H, Daniel H. **EDUCATION:** Seoul

National University, BS, 1979, MS, 1981; Boston University, PhD, 1985. **CAREER:** Korea Military Academy, lecturer, 1981; Institute for Theoretical Physics, postdoctoral fellow, 1985-87; Emory University, visiting scientist, 1987-88; Lehigh University, assistant professor, 1988-. **ORGANIZATIONS:** American Physical Society, 1987-; Materials Research Society, 1988-; Sigma Xi, 1992-. **HONORS/AWARDS:** Korean Government, National Faculty Fellowship, 1979-81. **SPECIAL ACHIEVEMENTS:** 41 publications in professional journals, 1983-. **HOME PHONE:** (610)867-0234. **BUSINESS ADDRESS:** Asst Professor, Lehigh University, Physics Bldg 16, Bethlehem, PA 18015-3044, (610)758-3904.

HONG, FRANCES

Government official. Chinese American. **PERSONAL:** Born Nov 20, 1933, Marysville, CA; daughter of Wong Dung Kay & Gong She Wong; married Shew Gong Hong, Jun 1954; children: David B. **CAREER:** City of Stockton, California, city clerk, 1954-. **BUSINESS ADDRESS:** City Clerk, City of Stockton, 425 N El Dorado St, Stockton, CA 95202, (209)937-8458.

HONG, GEORGE K.

Educator. Hong Kong American. **EDUCATION:** Chinese University of Hong Kong, BSS, 1974; University of North Carolina, Chapel Hill, MA, 1978; Hofstra University, MA, 1979, PhD, 1982. **CAREER:** South Cove Community Health Center, Boston, psychologist, 1982-90; private practice, clinical psychologist, 1990-; California State University, Los Angeles, associate professor, 1990-. **ORGANIZATIONS:** American Psychological Association, 1983-; American Counseling Association, 1990-; Asian American Psychological Association, 1983-; Western Psychological Association, 1990-. **SPECIAL ACHIEVEMENTS:** Author or co-author of many professional papers, a book, numerous presentations and talks at professional conferences and groups; fluent in Chinese; licensed psychologist in California, Massachusetts, New York. **BUSINESS ADDRESS:** Associate Professor, Div of Administration & Counseling, California State University, Los Angeles, Los Angeles, CA 90032.

HONG, GLENN THOMAS

Scientist. Chinese American. **PERSONAL:** Born Mar 28, 1954, East Meadow, NY; son of Leon Hong and Margaret Riker Hong; married Karen Sullivan Hong, Jul 31, 1977; children: Andrew, Elizabeth, Jessica. **EDUCATION:** State University of New York at Albany, BS, 1976; Massachusetts Institute of Technology, ScD, 1981. **CAREER:** Nera, associate, 1983-85; Modar Inc, program manager, 1981-83; principal scientist, 1985-93, vice president, 1994-. **ORGANIZATIONS:** American Institute of Chemical Engineers, 1981-; Sigma Xi, 1981-. **HOME ADDRESS:** 332 Lancaster Dr, Tewksbury, MA 01876, (508)851-8417. **BUSINESS ADDRESS:** Vice President, Modar Inc, 14 Tech Cir, Natick, MA 01760, (617)237-7071.

HONG, GONG-SOOG

Educator. Korean American. **PERSONAL:** Born Mar 28, 1950, Jeonju, Jeonbug, Republic of Korea; daughter of Jin-Ok Kang and Soon Kwon; married Sung Young Hong, Jun 2, 1978; children: Bryan, Erick. **EDUCATION:** Ewha Women's University, Korea, BS, 1972, MS, 1975; Utah State University, MS, 1985; Cornell University, PhD, 1990. **CAREER:** Utah State University, research assistant, 1984-85; Cornell University, research assistant, 1985-88; Oklahoma State University, assistant professor, 1989-92; Purdue University, assistant professor, 1992-. **ORGANIZATIONS:** American Council on Consumer Interest, 1985-; American Home Economics Association, 1990-; International Federation for Home Economics, 1992-; National Council on Family Relations, 1992-; Phi Upsilon Omicron Honor Society, 1984-. **HONORS/AWARDS:** Consumer Sciences and Retailing, Outstanding Achievement Award, 1993. **SPECIAL ACHIEVEMENTS:** Program co-chair of 39th Annual Conference of American Council on Consumer Interest, 1993; program co-chair of 13th Mid-American Consumer Conference, 1990; Publications include: Gong-Soog Hong & Pat Wellen, "Welfare Use: Implications for Teenage Mother's Education," in Home Economics Research Journal; Gong-Soog Hong & Shelley White-Means, "Do Working Mothers Have Healthy Children?" Journal of Family and Economic Issues; Gong-Soog Hong and Lori Worthington, "Divorce and Remarriage," in Journal of Home Economics; numerous presentations made at various conferences as a researcher, panelist, or presider. **BUSINESS ADDRESS:** Assistant Professor, Consumer Sciences and Retailing, Purdue University, 226 Matthews Hall, West Lafayette, IN 47907-1262, (317)494-8302.

HONG, IL SIK

Landscaping firm owner. Korean American. **PERSONAL:** Born Apr 15, 1948, Pohang, Kyungbok, Republic of Korea; son of Sun Chool Hong and Bok Ran Hong; married Deborah K Hong, Aug 25, 1975; children: Dail Sung, Theodore Sung, Jewell Kay. **EDUCATION:** Missouri State University, North Carolina State University: worked with the Korean 4-H Foundation, horticulture, 1973-75; Kansas State University, correspondence course, landscape design, 1977. **CAREER:** Sunnyside Nursery, apprentice-salesman, 1974-75, salesman, 1976; City of Wichita, Park Board, garden II, 1976-78; Commercial Builders of Kansas, personal gardener, 1978-79; Hong's Landscape, owner, 1979-. **ORGANIZATIONS:** Wichita Lawn Flower & Garden Show, bd mbr, 1985-; Wichita Chamber of Commerce, 1987-; Botanica, The Wichita Garden, charter mbr, 1987-; Western Nurserymen's Assn, 1988-; Kansas Nurserymen's Assn, 1992-; Wichita Nurserymen's Assn, 1985-92; Wichita Korean Assn, past president, 1985, current member. **HONORS/AWARDS:** Lawn, Flower & Garden Show, Best of Show, Center Garden Display, 1985, Best Incorporation of Theme, Service Firm, 1986, Best Display of Product, Green Goods, 1987, Excellence in Green Goods Class I, 1988, Judges Choice Center Garden Award, 1992. **MILITARY SERVICE:** KATUSA (Korean Army to USA Army), sgt, 1969-72. **BUSINESS ADDRESS:** Owner, Hong's Landscape, 8825 East 31st St S, Wichita, KS 67210, (316)687-3492.

HONG, ILYOO BARRY

Educator. Korean American. **PERSONAL:** Born May 16, 1957, Seoul, Republic of Korea; son of Joong-Hoo Hong & Eun-Hee Choi Hong; married Hae Ok Naomi Kim Hong, Jun 16, 1985; children: Matthew, Isaac. **EDUCATION:** Indiana University, BA, 1982; University of Illinois, MS, 1983; University of Arizona, PhD, 1989. **CAREER:** Western Kentucky University, assistant professor, 1989-. **SPECIAL ACHIEVEMENTS:** Journal article in Decision Sciences, vol 22, no 1, winter 1991; journal article in International Journal of Info Management, spring 1993. **BUSINESS ADDRESS:** Assistant Professor, Western Kentucky University, Grise Hall, Rm 322, Bowling Green, KY 42101, (502)745-4120.

HONG, JIN SUNG

Researcher. Korean American. **PERSONAL:** Born Aug 29, 1958, Seoul, Republic of Korea; son of Chun Sik Hong and Kyu Rae Hong; married Eunice Sookhui Hong, Apr 1, 1989. **EDUCATION:** Han Yang University, BS, 1984; University of Illinois at Chicago, MS, 1988, PhD, 1991. **CAREER:** Gold-Star Electronics Co, researcher, 1984-85; Sae-saak Korean School, chief of school affairs, 1991-; Chicago Honors School, chief of school affairs, 1991-; University of Illinois at Chicago, teaching assistant, research assistant, 1986-91, research associate, 1992-. **ORGANIZATIONS:** ASME, AIAA, SAE, KSEA: associate member, 1986-. **HONORS/AWARDS:** UIC, assistantship, scholarship, 1986-91, postdoctoral fellowship, 1991-; Han Yang University, Honor Award, two semesters, 1983; Gold-Star Electronics Co, fellowship, 1983. **SPECIAL ACHIEVEMENTS:** 12 publications including: "Experimental Heat Transfer," Hemisphere, vol 3, April 1990; ICHMT, vol 17, num 4, Pergamon Press PLC, 1990; AIAA-90-1727, AIAA/ASME 5th Joint Conference, Seattle, WA, 1990; AIAA Journal of Thermophysics and Heat Transfer, vol 5, No. 3, July-Sep 1991; Int Conference, sponsored by PIThE, Waikiki, HI, March 1992; ASME National Conference, Atlanta, GA, Aug 1993. **BIOGRAPHICAL SOURCES:** "Experimental Study of Melting Phenomena with and without Influence of Ultrasonic Vibrations," UIC, May 1988; "Dynamics and Thermal Behaviors of Droplets Impinging Upon a Rotary Disk," UIC, Sep 1991. **BUSINESS ADDRESS:** Research Professor, Dept of MEM, Drexel University, 32nd & Chestnut St., Philadelphia, PA 19104, (215)895-1218.

HONG, JOHN SONG YOOK

Attorney. Korean American. **PERSONAL:** Born Feb 7, 1944, Seoul, Republic of Korea; son of Kil Soo Hong; married Myungok Hong, Jul 6, 1976; children: Lily, Brian. **EDUCATION:** Korea University, College of Law, LLB, 1971; Dickinson School of Law, MCL, 1974; University of Michigan Law School, LLM, 1975; Harvard Law School, SJD, 1980. **CAREER:** Korea University, assistant professor of law, 1980-82; Law offices of Harold Kingsley, associate, 1982-84; Law offices of Song Yook Hong, owner, sole proprietor, 1984-. **ORGANIZATIONS:** American Bar Association, 1990-; New York State Bar Association, 1984-; Asian American Advisory Committee for Governor of the State of New York, 1990-; Korean Lawyers Association of New York, president, 1992-. **SPECIAL ACHIEVEMENTS:** Discertation: An Analysis of the Exclusive Economic Zone Doctrine: from the Dispute Settlement Perspective, Harvard Law School, June 1980. **MILITARY SERVICE:** Korean Army, sgt,

1966-69. **BUSINESS ADDRESS:** Owner, Law Offices of Song Yook Hong, 1261 Broadway, Ste 201, New York, NY 10001, (212)532-1770.

HONG, KENNETH
Communications specialist. Korean American. **PERSONAL:** Born Feb 6, 1967, Seoul, Republic of Korea. **EDUCATION:** Pennsylvania State University, BA, 1989. **CAREER:** Beach Advertising, public relations associate, 1989-91; Big Brothers/Big Sisters of America, public relations coordinator, 1991-93; LaSalle University, assistant director of communications, 1993-. **ORGANIZATIONS:** Pi Kappa Phi, former secretary, 1987; Order of Omega, 1991-; Skull & Bones, 1988-; Ad 2 Philadelphia, vice president emeritus, 1991-92; Philadelphia Hat & Tie Society, public relations chair, 1992-. **HOME ADDRESS:** PO Box 358, Ambler, PA 19002-0358, (215)646-7628. **BUSINESS ADDRESS:** Assistant Director of Communications, LaSalle University, 1900 W Olney Ave, Philadelphia, PA 19141-1199, (215)951-1085.

HONG, LILY TOY
Illustrater, designer, writer. Chinese American. **PERSONAL:** Born May 3, 1958, Salt Lake City, UT; daughter of Raymond Hee Hong & Heng Tsoi Hong; married Kellan Hatch, Sep 8, 1990; children: Evan Leung Hatch. **EDUCATION:** University of Utah, 1976-77; Utah Technical College, AAS, 1981; Utah State University, BFA (magna cum laude), 1983. **CAREER:** Hallmark Cards Inc, production artist, 1983-84, artist/designer, 1984-86; self-employed, freelance designer, illustrator, writer, 1988-. **ORGANIZATIONS:** Phi Kappa Phi, 1983-; Society of Childrens Book Writers and Illustrators, 1988-. **HONORS/AWARDS:** For How the Oxstar Fell from Heaven: Parents' Choice, Picture Book Honor, 1991, Parenting Magazine, Year's Ten Best Books, 1991; SCBWI, Don Freeman Memorial Grant-in-Aid, honorable mention, 1989. **SPECIAL ACHIEVEMENTS:** Books: Two of Everything, author, illustrator, 1993; How the Oxstar Fell from Heaven, author, illustrator, 1991. **BIOGRAPHICAL SOURCES:** BYU Children's Book Review, Nov/Dec, 1993; Junior Library Guild, new books, p7, April 1993-Sep 1993; Something about the Author, vol 76, 1994. **BUSINESS ADDRESS:** c/o Albert Whitman & Co, 6340 Oakton St, Morton Grove, IL 60053.

HONG, RYANG H.
Mold making company executive. Korean American. **PERSONAL:** Born Aug 2, 1933, Wonju, Republic of Korea; son of Wan-sik Hong; married Susan, Dec 27, 1960; children: Kiepok, Kiemi, Kiesou. **EDUCATION:** Kyung-Hee University, Seoul, BA, 1959. **CAREER:** Apex Mold & Engineering Inc, president/CEO, currently. **ORGANIZATIONS:** Society of Plastics Engineers; Association of Korean Professionals in the American Automotive Industries; Michigan Minority Business Development Council. **MILITARY SERVICE:** Korean Army Air-Corp, captain, 3 medals. **BUSINESS ADDRESS:** President & CEO, Apex Mold & Engineering Inc, 42345 Yzarego Drive, Sterling Heights, MI 48314, (313)739-0333.

HONG, S. K.
Association executive. Korean American. **CAREER:** Korean American Heritage Foundation, chairman, currently. **BUSINESS ADDRESS:** Chairman, Korean American Heritage Foundation, c/o Korean Center, 1362 Post St, San Francisco, CA 94109, (415)441-1881.∗

HONG, S. THEODORE
Educator (retired). Korean American. **PERSONAL:** Born Aug 3, 1930, Pyung Yang, Republic of Korea; son of Chong Oh Hong (deceased) and Look Yob Lee (deceased); married Lillian Hong, Jun 6, 1959; children: Thomas C, Mira Hong Mariano. **EDUCATION:** Han Kuk University, Korea, BA, 1953; New York University, MBA, 1958, PhD, 1972. **CAREER:** Hofstra University, instructor, 1961-67; Bentley College, associate professor, 1970-75; Price Waterhouse, certified public accountant, 1967-70; SUNY, Plattsburgh, associate professor, 1975-78; Clarion University, professor, 1978-86; West Chester University, professor, 1986-92. **ORGANIZATIONS:** American Institute of CPAs, 1972-92; American Association of University Professors, 1961-92; Association of Penn State College & University Professors, 1978-92; Association of Penn State Coll & University Retired Professors, 1992-. **HONORS/AWARDS:** New York University, Founder's Day Award, 1973. **SPECIAL ACHIEVEMENTS:** Certified Public Accountant, New York, 1972, Massachusetts, 1975; Author, Accounting Education: An Innovative Approach, Vantage, 1975. **MILITARY SERVICE:** Army, The Republic of Korea, 1st Lt, 1950-53. **HOME ADDRESS:** 1314 Edwards Drive, Downingtown, PA 19335, (610)269-3414.

HONG, SHUGUANG
Educator. Chinese American. **PERSONAL:** Born Oct 3, 1954, Qianxi, Guizhou, People's Republic of China; son of Yunshan Hong and Cuixian Ma; married Mingjia Li, Jul 26, 1982; children: En. **EDUCATION:** Chongqing University, BS, 1982; Worcester Polytechnic Institute, 1983-84; University of Connecticut, MS, 1985, PhD, 1989. **CAREER:** Chongqing University, lecturer, 1982; Worcester Polytechnic Institute, adjunct assistant professor, 1989-; Ontologic Inc, senior software engineer, 1989-90; Georgia State University, assistant professor, 1990-. **ORGANIZATIONS:** Association for Computing Machinery, voting member, 1984-; Computer Society, IEEE, 1985-. **HONORS/AWARDS:** Phi Kappa Phi National Honor Society, 1987; Upsilon Espilon National Computer Science Honor Society, 1988; University Connecticut R&D Corp, High Technology Fellowships, 1988. **SPECIAL ACHIEVEMENTS:** "Representation of Object-Oriented Data Models," Information Sciences, Dec, 1990; "Generating Object-Oriented Database Systems with the Data Model Complier," in On Object-Oriented Database Systems, Springer-Verlag, 1991; as author or co-author, published more than a dozen papers, various international conferences. **BUSINESS ADDRESS:** Asst Prof, Dept of Computer Information Systems, Georgia State University, PO Box 4015, Atlanta, GA 30302-4015, (404)651-3880.

HONG, SUK KI
Educator. Korean American. **PERSONAL:** Born Oct 16, 1928, Kyonggi Do, Republic of Korea; son of Sung Cho Hong and K R You Hong; married Kay Hong, Jun 27, 1959; children: Robert, Peggy. **EDUCATION:** University of Rochester, PhD, 1956. **CAREER:** Yonsei University, Korea, assistant, associate professor, 1959-66, professor, chairman of physiology, 1966-68; University of Hawaii, professor, chairman of physiology, 1968-75; SUNY, Buffalo, professor of physiology, 1975-. **ORGANIZATIONS:** American Physiological Society, 1969-; Undersea and Hyperbaric Medical Society, 1969-; AAAS, 1969-; American Society of Nephrology, 1969-. **HONORS/AWARDS:** Samil Foundation, Samil, Cultural Prize, 1963; Undersea Medical Society, Stover-Link Award, 1983; SUNY, Buffalo, Stockton Kimball Award, 1987; Kyungpook National University, Korea, Honor DSc, 1983. **BUSINESS ADDRESS:** Professor, State University of New York at Buffalo, School of Medicine, 124 Sherman Hall, Buffalo, NY 14214-3002, (716)829-3531.

HONG, SUNG OK
Educational administrator. **PERSONAL:** Born Sep 26, 1931. **CAREER:** Chicago Board of Education, assistant superintendent, currently. **BUSINESS ADDRESS:** Assistant Superintendent, Chicago Board of Education, 1819 W Pershing Rd, Chicago, IL 60609.∗

HONG, WEIHU
Educator. Chinese American. **PERSONAL:** Born Jun 4, 1956, Jiande, Zhejiang, People's Republic of China; son of Jiale Hong & Xiao-Jiao Huang; married Wenqing Wu, Oct 3, 1983; children: Peter, Alice. **EDUCATION:** Nan-Kai University, Tianjin, China, BS, 1982; Montana State University, MS, 1986; University of South Carolina, PhD, 1991. **CAREER:** Hangzhou College of Electronic Engineering, instructor, 1982-85; University of South Carolina, graduate teaching assistant, 1986-91; Mars Hill College, assistant professor, 1991-. **ORGANIZATIONS:** Mathematical Association of America, 1991-; American Mathematical Society, 1987-; North Carolina Council of Teachers of Math, 1991-. **HONORS/AWARDS:** University of South Carolina, teaching assistantship, 1980-91. **SPECIAL ACHIEVEMENTS:** Short talk: Interpolation of Sobolev Spaces, Joint Meeting of AMS & MAA, 1991; Collequium: The Real Method of Interpolation of Operators, Western Carolina University, February 14, 1992. **BUSINESS ADDRESS:** Assistant Professor, Dept of Mathematics, Mars Hill College, Mars Hill, NC 28754, (740)689-1195.

HONG, YOOPYO
Mathematician. Korean American. **PERSONAL:** Born Dec 19, 1949, Wonju, Kangwon, Republic of Korea; son of Soonchul Hong & Byung Soon Yoo; married Suklim Hong, Apr 17, 1976; children: Andrea, Sara, Michael. **EDUCATION:** University of Maryland, BS, 1974; University of Rhode Island, MS, 1980; The Johns Hopkins University, PhD, 1984, MSE, 1984. **CAREER:** University of Maryland at Baltimore County, assistant professor, 1984; Northern Illinois University, associate professor, 1993-. **ORGANIZATIONS:** SIAM, 1983-; SIAG, 1983-. **SPECIAL ACHIEVEMENTS:** Published papers in Linear Algebra and Applications, SIAM Journal, Linear and Multilinear Algebra, AMS Journal, Linear Algebra and Numerical Linear Algebra, and numerous others. **HOME ADDRESS:** 230 Fairmont Dr, De Kalb, IL 60115, (815)756-8672.

HONGO, GARRETT KAORU
Educator, poet. Japanese American. **PERSONAL:** Born May 30, 1951, Volcano, HI; married Cynthia Anne Thiessen, 1982; children: two. **EDUCATION:** Pomona College, BA (honors), 1973; University of Michigan, Ann Arbor, 1974-75; University of California, Irvine, MFA, English, 1980, additional studies, 1980-82. **CAREER:** Asian Exclusion Act, director, 1976-78; Seattle Arts Commission, poet-in-residence, 1977-78; University of California, Irvine, teaching assistant, 1980-82, visiting instructor, 1983-84; University of Southern California, visiting assistant professor, 1982-83; University of Missouri, assistant professor, 1984-89; University of Houston, visiting associate professor, 1988; University of Oregon, associate professor, director of creative writing, beginning 1989, full professor, currently. **ORGANIZATIONS:** Pacific Northwest Asian American Writers Conference, co-coordinator. **HONORS/AWARDS:** National Endowment for Arts, fellowship, 1982, 1988; Guggenheim fellowship, 1990; Academy of American Poets, Lamont Poetry Selection, 1987; finalist, Pulitzer Prize, 1989; Thomas J Watson Fellowship; Hopwood Prize; Nation/Discovery Award. **SPECIAL ACHIEVEMENTS:** Work has appeared in the New Yorker, Antaeus, The Nation, Poetry Northwest, Honolulu Star-Bulletin; The Buddha Bandits Down Highway 99, 1978; Yellow Light, 1982; The River of Heaven, 1988; Nisei Bar and Grill, play, 1976; The Open Boat, editor, 1993; Heart Mountain, 1988; Missouri Review, poetry editor, 1984-89. **BUSINESS ADDRESS:** Professor, Dept of Creative Writing, University of Oregon, 118 PLC, Eugene, OR 97403, (503)346-3944. *

HONMA, SHIGEMI
Educator (retired). Japanese American. **PERSONAL:** Born Feb 14, 1920, Hawaii; married Isao, Oct 1945; children: Valerie Edith Kennedy, Alan Kern. **EDUCATION:** Cornell University, BA, 1949; University of Minnesota, PhD, 1953. **CAREER:** University of Minnesota, research assistant, 1950-52; University of Nebraska, assistant horitculturist, 1953-55; Michigan State University, professor, 1955 until retirement. **ORGANIZATIONS:** American Society for Horticultural Science; American Genetics Association. **HONORS/AWARDS:** Bean Improv Coop, Meritorious Service Award; American Society of Horticulture Science, fellow, 1975; University of Minnesota, Department of Horticulture Science, Distinguished Alumni Lecturer, 1981. **SPECIAL ACHIEVEMENTS:** Plant genetics & breeder (vegetables). **MILITARY SERVICE:** US Army, 442nd Regimental Combat Team, corporal; Purple Heart, bronze star, unit citation. **BUSINESS ADDRESS:** Professor Emeritus, Horticulture Dept, Michigan State University, East Lansing, MI 48823.

HOO, JOE-JIE
Educator. Chinese American/Indonesian American. **PERSONAL:** Born Jul 7, 1944, Malang, East-Java, Indonesia; son of Heng-Seng Hoo & Ru-Ing Oei; married Lanlan Hoo, Jan 12, 1973. **EDUCATION:** Philipps University of Marburg, Germany, MD, 1972. **CAREER:** University of Hamburg, Germany, research fellow, 1979-81; University of Giessen, Germany, geneticist, 1981-82; University of Calgary, Canada, geneticist, assistant professor, 1982-85; University of Illinois, Chicago, Cytogenetics Lab, director, associate professor, 1985-90; Rush-Presbyterian-St Luke's Medical Center, geneticist, 1990-93; SUNY Health Science Center, Syracuse, Division of Genetics, head, professor, 1993-. **ORGANIZATIONS:** American Academy of Pediatrics, fellow, Section of Genetics, charter member, 1981-; American Society of Human Genetics, 1976-; American College of Medical Genetics, founding fellow, 1992-; American Medical Association, 1988-. **HONORS/AWARDS:** Medical Research Council of New Zealand, Fellowship Award, 1978-79; Volkswagen Foundation, research grant, 1979-81; Alberta Heritage Foundation for Medical Research, Major Equipment Grant, 1983-85; Baxter Inc, Assays Development Grant, 1991-93. **SPECIAL ACHIEVEMENTS:** More than 80 publications in peer-reviewed journals, 1971-; 5 book chapters, 1971-; proficient in Chinese, Malay, German and English. **BUSINESS ADDRESS:** Professor of Pediatrics, Head, Division of Genetics, SUNY Health Science Center, 750 E Adams St, Syracuse, NY 13210, (315)464-7610.

HOQUE, ENAMUL
Civil engineer. Bangladeshi American. **PERSONAL:** Born Jun 26, 1951, Shapmara, Bangladesh; son of Fazlul Hoque and Rahima Hoque; married Mahmuda Houque, Nov 21, 1980; children: Sharif M, Nadim M. **EDUCATION:** Bangladesh Engineering University, BS, 1974; Arizona State University, MS, 1985, PhD candidate, 1986-. **CAREER:** Bangladesh Public Health Engineering, engr, 1974-75; Bangladesh Water Dev Board, design engr, 1975-78; Municipality of Brak, Libya, engr, 1978-80; Arizona State University, teaching assistant, 1981-87; Western Technology, geotech engr, 1987-89; Law Engineering, senior geotech engr, 1989-92; SCS Engineers, project manager,

1992-. **ORGANIZATIONS:** American Society of Civil Engineers, 1985-; Geological Society of America, 1990-; American Society of Civil Engineers, Geotech Division, publication committee member; Arizona Geological Society; New Mexico Geological Society; Structural Engineers Assn of Arizona, education committee, editorial board, chairman, 1991-93. **HONORS/AWARDS:** Tau Beta Pi, Chi Epsilon Chapter. **HOME ADDRESS:** 4662 W Earhart, Chandler, AZ 85226-4662, (602)940-1207. **BUSINESS PHONE:** (602)840-2596.

HORI, TOM NICHI
Engineering and computer consulting firm executive. Japanese American. **PERSONAL:** Born Dec 3, 1940, Ogden, UT; son of Fusakichi & Tsuneyo Hori; married Marion H Hori, Jul 28, 1962; children: Lance S, Jaclyn S, Crystalyn S. **EDUCATION:** Weber State University, BS, bus mngt, 1968. **CAREER:** Small Business Adminstration, loan officer, 1968-75; Sander Exploration Ltd, vice president, finance, 1975-77; REDCON Inc, president, CEO, 1977-. **ORGANIZATIONS:** Intermountain Minority Contractors & Business Association, pres, board member, 1990-; Wasatch Front, No JACL Chapter, past president, 1979-82; Kaysville Chamber of Commerce, past president, 1976-77; US Civil Rights Commission, 1970-72; US Small Business Admin, advisory council, 1991-; University of Utah, division of continuing ed, advisory board, 1992-; National Federation of Independent Business, 1981-; Greater Salt Lake Area and Bountiful Area C of C, 1989-. **HONORS/AWARDS:** Utah Suppliers Development Council, Minority Business of the Year, 1992; US Small Business Administration, Minority Business of the Year, 1990, Minority Advocate of the Year, 1990; Society of Logistics Engineers, Logistic Management Achievement, 1990; Dept of Air Force-Hill Air Force Base, Minority Contractor of the Year, 1989. **SPECIAL ACHIEVEMENTS:** Chairman for Public Service Comm on Governor Mike Leavitt Transition Team, 1992; completed leadership Utah course through Salt Lake C of C, 1992; completed MBE Program, Amos Tuck School of Business at Dartmouth College, 1991; testified before US Commission on Minority Business Development, 1990. **MILITARY SERVICE:** US Army Reserve, spec-5, 1959-62. **BUSINESS ADDRESS:** President/CEO, REDCON, Inc, 655 E Medical Drive, Suite 150, Bountiful, UT 84010, (801)298-2401.

HORI, YUTORIO CLAUDE (TERRY)
Publishing executive. Japanese American. **PERSONAL:** Born Jul 11, 1945, Newell, CA; son of Kiyoshi Hori & Grace Chiaki Hori; married Pamela Anne Carpenter, Mar 31, 1973; children: Lance I. **EDUCATION:** University of California, Los Angeles, BA (magna cum laude), 1967; University of Illinois, Urbana-Champaign, MA, 1969, PhD, 1972. **CAREER:** Encyclopaedia Britannica, assistant production editor, 1972-73; World Book Inc, associate editor, 1973-81; Encyclopaedia Britannica, senior editor, 1981-91, managing editor, 1991-. **ORGANIZATIONS:** UCLA Alumni Association, 1967-. **HONORS/AWARDS:** Phi Beta Kappa, 1967-; University of Illinois, Phi Kappa Phi, 1972. **BUSINESS ADDRESS:** Managing Editor, Encyclopaedia Britannica Inc, 310 South Michigan Ave, Britannica Centre, 3rd Fl, Chicago, IL 60604-4293, (312)347-7412.

HORIUCHI, CHIKAMASA PAUL (PAUL HORIUCHI)
Artist. Japanese American. **PERSONAL:** Born Apr 12, 1906, Yamanashiken, Japan; son of Daisaku & Yasu Horiuchi; married Bernadette, Jun 11, 1935; children: Paul, Jon, Vincent. **CAREER:** Artist, currently. **HONORS/AWARDS:** Mead Corporation, Purchase Award; Tupperware National Competition, 1955; Ford Foundation, Purchase Award, 1960; One from Each State, Burpee Award, 1970; Emperor of Japan, 4th Class Treasure, 1988; Artist of the Year, Governor Award, 1970; honorary degrees: Saint Martins College, doctor of fine arts, 1979; University of Puget Sound, doctor of humanities, 1968; Seattle University, doctor of humanities, 1988. **SPECIAL ACHIEVEMENTS:** Mosaic, mural, Seattle Center, 1963; mosaic, Venice, Italy.

HORIUCHI, GLENN
Pianist. Japanese American. **EDUCATION:** University of California, Riverside, classical piano, 1974-77. **CAREER:** Jazz pianist, composer, musical director, currently; works include: "Poston Sonata," AsianImprov Records, 1992; "Oxnard Beet," 1993; "About Love," docu-drama, Asian Pacific Women's Network, Los Angeles City Attorney's Office, 1992. **BUSINESS ADDRESS:** Pianist, AsianImprov Records, 1433 Grant St, Berkeley, CA 94703-1109. *

HORIUCHI, PAUL. *See* **HORIUCHI, CHIKAMASA PAUL.**

HORN, JENNIE A.
Educator, educational administrator. Chinese American. **PERSONAL:** Born Mar 25, 1945, Canonsburg, PA; daughter of Fred Fong Horn and Yee Shee Horn. **EDUCATION:** San Francisco State College, BA, 1967; San Francisco State University, MA, 1976, 1982-84. **CAREER:** San Francisco Unified School District, Roosevelt Junior HS, teacher, 1968-71, George Washington HS, teacher, 1971-78, program resource/department head, 1978-84; J Eugene McAteer HS, assistant principal, 1984-90, Woodrow Wilson HS, assistant principal, 1990-91, principal, 1991-93; San Francisco Unified School District, Educational Placement Center, supervisor, 1993-. **ORGANIZATIONS:** United Administrators of San Francisco, 1984-; Association for Supervision & Curriculum Development, 1984-94; Association for Chinese American Administrators, 1984-94; The Association of Chinese Teachers, 1969-94; Teachers of English to Speakers of Other Languages, 1975-94; California Teachers of English to Speakers of Other Languages, 1975-94; California Association for Asian-Pacific Bilingual Education, 1987-94; Chinese for Affirmative Action, 1970-94. **HOME ADDRESS:** 4517-19th St, San Francisco, CA 94114-2332.

HORNG, JOHN JANG-JI
Engineer. Taiwanese American. **PERSONAL:** Born Oct 28, 1950, Keelung, Taiwan; son of King-Chang Horng and Wu-Tsai-Phone Horng; married Karin W Horng, Dec 25, 1978; children: Katie, Steven. **EDUCATION:** Tatung Institute of Technology, Taiwan, BSME, 1974; Stevens Institute of Technology, MSE, 1980. **CAREER:** Diamond Aerosol Corp, senior engr, 1980-84; Nashua Corporation, chief engr, 1984-86; Weldotron Corporation, project engr, 1986-87; Somerset Tech Inc, chief engr, 1987-92; Prosystem USA Inc, vice pres, engineering, 1992-. **BUSINESS ADDRESS:** Vice President, Engineering, Prosystem USA, Inc, 12F Worlds Fair Dr, Somerset, NJ 08873.

HOSHI, MINEO (JOHN)
Accounting manager. Japanese American. **PERSONAL:** Born Feb 16, 1950, Fukushima, Japan; son of Sakae Hoshi and Haruno Hoshi; married Setsuko Hoshi, Dec 6, 1992; children: Arnold T, Ethel H. **EDUCATION:** Yamano Beauty College, cosmetology license, 1973; Woodbury University, BS, 1976. **CAREER:** TEC America Inc, asst accounting mgr, 1978-86; Rikuo Corp, accounting mgr, 1986-89; Kintetsu Intermodel-USA Inc, accounting division, mgr, 1989-92; Hitachi Transport Systems-America LTD, accounting mgr, 1993-. **ORGANIZATIONS:** Soka Gakkaz Intl, 1972-; Fukashima Kenjinkai, 1991; Los Angeles Superior Court Probate Volunteer Alliance, 1992; notary public: California, 1989; Board of Barbering and Cosmetologists, licensed cosmetologist, 1973; PFS Investment Inc, registered representative, 1991; California Real Estate Board, license, 1988. **HONORS/AWARDS:** California State Polytechnic, Certificate of Achievement, 1981; TEC, Personal Contribution Award, 1981; Los Angeles Superior Court Probate Volunteer Alliance, Certificate of Appreciation, 1992. **SPECIAL ACHIEVEMENTS:** Participant: Bicentennial Convention, held American flag along with 10,000 others, Washington, DC, 1976. **BIOGRAPHICAL SOURCES:** "Kai Gai Chu Zai," Interworld, p 73, May 1988. **HOME PHONE:** (310)327-9733. **BUSINESS ADDRESS:** Accounting Manager, Hitachi Transport Systems-America, Ltd, 2459 W 208th St, Torrance, CA 90501, (310)782-2003.

HOSHIKO, MICHAEL
Educator. Japanese American. **PERSONAL:** Born in British Columbia; son of Tsunehachi & Toshie Kuroda Hoshiko; married Rose Dege Hoshiko, Apr 7, 1955; children: Ceciley Mitsie Hoshiko Sample, Sumi Lynne Hoshiko Ozer, Lance Tisdale Isamu, Hoshiko. **EDUCATION:** Heidelberg College, BA, 1948; Bowling Green State University, MA, 1949; Purdue University, PhD, 1957; Johns Hopkins School of Medicine, post-doctoral, 1966. **CAREER:** University of Kansas, instructor, 1949-50; Illinois State University, psychologist, 1950-51; University of Toronto Medical School, psychologist, 1952-55; Purdue University, research fellow, 1955-57; McMaster University Medical School, visiting professor, 1981; Southern Illinois University, professor, 1957-91. **ORGANIZATIONS:** American Psychological Association, 1952-; American Speech Language Hearing Association, fellow, 1956-, multiculture board member, 1990-92; Biofeedback Association, 1974-90; American Radio Relay League, life member 1975-; Japanese American Amateur Radio Association, 1989-; Japanese American Citizens League, St Louis, board member, 1987-95. **HONORS/AWARDS:** National Institutes of Health, Fellowship, 1966-67; Research Grants, 1961-68; American Cancer Society, Research Grant, 1967-68; State of Illinois, Department of Mental Health, Research Grant, 1967-69. **SPECIAL ACHIEVEMENTS:** Contributor, New Canadian Newspaper, 1939-; Certificate of Competence, speech/language, 1960; Certificate of Competence, biofeedback, 1975; Certificate in Voiceprint Identification, 1975; extra class in amateur radio, W9CJW, 1981, VE7SIU, 1993-; licensed speech/language pathologist, State of Illinois, 1989-. **HOME PHONE:** (618)549-5129. **BUSINESS ADDRESS:** Professor, Dept of Communication Disorders & Sciences, Southern Illinois University, Carbondale, IL 62901, (618)453-4301.

HOSMANE, RAMACHANDRA S.
Educator. Indo-American. **PERSONAL:** Born Dec 12, 1944, Gokarn, Karnataka, India; son of Sadashiv & Lalitha; married Raji, Aug 13, 1975; children: Mala. **EDUCATION:** Dr Baliga College of Arts & Science, BS, 1966; Karnataka University, India, MSc, 1968; University of South Florida, MS, 1976, PhD, 1978. **CAREER:** University of Illinois, post-doctoral research associate, 1978-82; University of Maryland, assistant professor, 1982-86, associate professor, 1986-93, professor, 1993-. **ORGANIZATIONS:** American Chemical Society, 1976-; Chemical Society, London, 1976-; Sigma Xi, 1977-; International Society of Heterocyclic Chemistry, 1977-; American Association for the Advancement of Science, 1985-. **HONORS/AWARDS:** Grants include: National Institutes of Health, NHLBI, 1993-96, NIGMS, 1985-88, 1992-95; Maryland Industrial Partnerships, 1992-95, 1991-94; National Institutes of Health, NCI, 1984-91; E I du Pont de Nemours & Co, 1986-; Eli Lilly (Dow-Elanco) Co, 1986-; Monsanto Agricultural Company, 1989-; Behringer Mannheim Corporation, 1991-; Rhone-Poulenc Agricultural Company, 1991-; Martin-Marietta Corporation, 1993-; Project SEED, 1983-. **SPECIAL ACHIEVEMENTS:** Research in anti-AIDS nucleosides, blood substitutes, and anti-tumor compounds, 1982-. **BUSINESS ADDRESS:** Professor of Chemistry & Medicinal Chemistry, University of Maryland, Baltimore County Campus, 5401 Wilkens Ave, Chemistry/Physics Rm 520, Baltimore, MD 21228, (410)455-2520.

HOSOKAWA, FUMIKO
Educator, therapist. Japanese American. **PERSONAL:** Born May 2, 1947, Long Beach, CA; daughter of Frank Isamu Hosokawa and Teruko Kawamoto Hosokawa. **EDUCATION:** California State University, Long Beach, BA, 1969; UCLA, MA, 1971, PhD, 1973; California State University, Dominguez Hills, MS, 1984. **CAREER:** UCLA, teaching assistant, lecturer, 1971-72; East Los Angeles City College, instructor, 1975; Los Alamitos Couns Ctr, intern & family therapist, 1982-89; Interval House, consultant, 1982-90; Calif State University, Dominguez Hills, professor, 1972-; Helpnet, Inc, case manager, 1988-; private practice, marriage and family therapist, 1989-. **ORGANIZATIONS:** American Association Marriage, Family Therapists; American Society on Aging; Pacific Sociological Association; American Sociological Association; Calif Association of Marriage, Family Therapists; Calif Council on Family Relations; Calif Sociological Association; World Fed Mental Health. **HONORS/AWARDS:** HEW Office of Education, Grant, 1979; Cal State Dominguez Hills, Professional Development Project Award, 1982, Affirmative Action Faculty Dev Project Award, 1982, 1983, Educational Equity Award, 1987, Meritorious Performance & Professorial Promise Award, 1990. **SPECIAL ACHIEVEMENTS:** Publication: The Sansei-Social Interaction & Ethnic Identif Among Third-Generation Japanese, 1978; "A Functional Theory of Ethnic Stereotypes," 1980; Stages in the Development of Individual Ethnic Ident, 1981; Directory of Ethnic Community Agencies & Training Manual, 1980. **BUSINESS ADDRESS:** Professor, Dept of Sociology, California State University, Dominguez Hills, 1000 E Victoria St, Carson, CA 90747-0001, (310)516-3482.

HOSOKAWA, WILLIAM K.
Journalist (retired), author. Japanese American. **PERSONAL:** Born Jan 30, 1915, Seattle, WA; son of Setsugo and Kimiyo Omura Hosokawa; married Alice Tokuko Miyake, Aug 28, 1938; children: Michael, Susan Hosokawa Boatright, Peter, Christie Hosokawa Harveson. **EDUCATION:** University of Washington, BA, 1937. **CAREER:** Singapore Herald, managing editor, 1939-40; Far Eastern Rev, Shanghai, writer, 1940-41; Heart Mountain Sentinel, WY, editor, 1942-43; Des Moines Register, copy editor, 1943-46; Denver Post, 1946-83, war correspondent, 1950; Empire Magazine, editor, 1950-57, executive news editor, 1957-58, asst mng ed, 1958-60, Sunday ed, 1960-62, assoc ed, 1963-77, editorial pg ed, 1977-83, columnist, 1983-84; Rocky Mountain News, columnist, 1985-92; Pulitzer prize journalism juror, 1969-70, 1975-76, 1981; University of Northern Colorado, lecturer, 1973-75; University of Colorado, lecturer, journalism, 1974, 1976; University of Wyoming, lecturer, journalism, 1985. **ORGANIZATIONS:** Colorado Freedom of Info Council, president, 1988-91; Iliff Sch of Theology, bd of directors, 1985-91. **HONORS/AWARDS:** Japanese Order of the Rising Sun, 1987; Japanese Am Citizens League, Distinguished Achievement Award, 1952; University of Colo, Out-

standing Journalist Award, 1967; Colo Soc Prof Journalists, Outstanding Journalist Award, 1976, Lowell Thomas Award, 1990; Denver Press Club, Outstanding Colorado Communicator Award, 1985; Institute for Intl Educ, World Citizen Award, 1991. **SPECIAL ACHIEVEMENTS:** Author, Nisei: The Quiet Americans, 1969, The Two Worlds of Jim Yoshida, 1972, Thunder in the Rockies, 1976, 35 Years in the Frying Pan, 1978; co-author, East to America, 1980, JACL in Quest of Justice, 1982, They Call Me Moses Masaoka, 1987; delegate: Japanese-American Assembly, 1972, Japanese-American Bilateral Meeting, International Press Institute, 1972-73, 1975, 1979, 1981; Japan for Colorado, honorary consul-general, 1975-.

HOTELLING, KATSUKO TSURUKAWA
Librarian. Japanese American. **PERSONAL:** Born Jul 11, Isahaya, Nagasaki-ken, Japan; widowed; children: Harold Alfred. **EDUCATION:** University of North Carolina, Chapel Hill, BA, 1983, MLS, 1985; University of Oregon, MA, 1990. **CAREER:** Arizona State University, Hayden Library, Japanese studies librarian, currently. **BUSINESS ADDRESS:** Librarian, Arizona State University, Hayden Library, Tempe, AZ 85287-9169, (602)965-7199.

HOTTA, GINA H.
Radio producer, administrator. Japanese American. **EDUCATION:** University of California, Berkeley, BA, 1975. **CAREER:** Japan Pacific Resource Network, freelance radio producer, administrator, currently. **ORGANIZATIONS:** KPFA Radio, "Inside/Eastside," co-producer, 1989-. **HONORS/AWARDS:** National Federation of Community Broadcasters, First Place Golden Reel Radio Award, 1992, 1993; Asian American Journalist Association, First Place Award, radio documentary. **BIOGRAPHICAL SOURCES:** "Local Producer Wins Award," Hokubei Mainichi Newspaper, p 1, April 21, 1993. **BUSINESS ADDRESS:** Administrator, Japan Pacific Resource Network, 310-8th St, #305B, Oakland, CA 94607, (510)891-9045.

HOU, WILLIAM CHEN-NAN
Attorney. Chinese American. **PERSONAL:** Born Sep 5, 1955, Geneva, NY; son of Chi-ming and Irene Hou. **EDUCATION:** Vassar College, BA, 1977; Duke University Institute for Public Policy Sciences, MA, 1981, Duke University Law School, JD, 1981. **CAREER:** WJS Intl Inc, account manager, 1982-85; Surrey & Morse, associate, 1985-87; Hamel & Park, associate, 1987-89; Hopkins & Sutter, partner, 1989-92; self-employed, principal, 1992-. **ORGANIZATIONS:** Organization of Chinese Americans Inc, national general counsel, 1988-89, North Virginia chapter, counsel, 1990-; ABA; National Asian Pacific American Bar Association, Legislative Committee, chair, 1991, president, 1993-; numerous others. **SPECIAL ACHIEVEMENTS:** New York Bar, 1982; Washington DC Bar, 1985. **BUSINESS ADDRESS:** Attorney, Law Offices of William C Hou, 888 16th St NW, Ste 400, Washington, DC 20006, (202)416-0653. *

HOUN, FRED WEI-HAN. *See* **HO, FRED WEI-HAN.**

HOUSTON, JEANNE WAKATSUKI
Writer. Japanese American. **PERSONAL:** Born Sep 26, 1934, Inglewood, CA; daughter of George Ko Wakatsuki & Riku Sugai Wakatsuki; married James D Houston, Mar 27, 1957; children: Corinne Riku Traugott, Joshua Dudley Ko, Gabrielle Alice Toyo. **EDUCATION:** San Jose State University, BA, 1956; Sorbonne, France, certificate, French civilization, 1959. **CAREER:** Hillcrest Juvenile Hall, group supervisor, 1954-56; University of California, Santa Cruz, student activities coordinator, 1964-67; writer, currently. **ORGANIZATIONS:** Pacific Rim Film Festival, coordinator, 1992; Santa Cruz Cultural Council, 1988-91; Children's Programming, Humanities Prize, board of trustees, 1985-; El Teatro Campesino, advisory board, 1979-85; Tandy Beal Dance Co, advisory board, 1985-; Writers Guild of America, West, 1974-; Hawaii International Film Festival, advisory board, 1988-90. **HONORS/AWARDS:** Human Family Education and Cultural Institute, Humanitas Prize, 1976; Christopher Foundation, Christopher Award, 1976; National Women's Political Caucus, Woman of Achievement Award, 1979; Arts America, travel grant to Asia, 1984; Wonder Woman Foundation, Wonder Woman Award, 1984; NEA, US Japan Friendship Society, fellowship, 1991. **SPECIAL ACHIEVEMENTS:** With James D Houston, Farewell to Manzanar; with Paul Hensler, Don't Cry, It's Only Thunder; Beyond Manzanar, Views of Asian American Womanhood; Barrio, film project with James D Houston. **BIOGRAPHICAL SOURCES:** Contemporary Authors, Autobiography Series, vol 16, p 171-186, 1992. **HOME ADDRESS:** 2-1130 East Cliff Dr, Santa Cruz, CA 95062. **BUSINESS PHONE:** (408)475-2050.

HOUSTON, VELINA HASU
Playwright, screenwriter, educator. Japanese American. **PERSONAL:** Born May 5, 1957, Fort Riley, KS; daughter of Setsuko Takechi & Lemo Houston; children: Kiyoshi Sean Shannen. **EDUCATION:** Kansas State University, BA, journalism, mass communications, theatre, 1979; UCLA, MFA, playwriting, screenwriting, 1981. **CAREER:** Playwright, screenwriter, essayist & poet, 1981-; USC School of Theatre, Playwriting Program, head, 1989-. **ORGANIZATIONS:** The Amerasian League, president, 1981-; Japanese American Citizens League, Scan Chapter, board of directors, 1986-; Multiracial Americans of Southern California, 1990-; Phi Beta Kappa, 1979-. **HONORS/AWARDS:** Phi Beta Delta, International Honor Society, 1993; University of Southern California, James Zumberge Research and Innovation Fellow, 1991; The Women's Building, VESTA Award, 1991; Rockefeller Foundation, playwriting fellow, 1984, 1987; American Multicultural Playwrights' Festival for "Tea," National First Prize, 1986; Phi Beta Kappa, 1979; numerous others. **SPECIAL ACHIEVEMENTS:** Publications: "Green Tea Girl in Orange Pekoe Country," Caffeine, 1993; "Multiculturalism and the American Theatre: Out of the Hysteria and into the Realities," The Dramatists Guild Newsletter, 1993; editor, The Politics of Life: Four Plays by Asian American Women, Temple University Press, 1993; plays include: Tea, Plays in Process, 1989; Necessities; American Dreams; Thirst; Albatross; Kokoro; Unbroken Thread; numerous other plays, screen plays and television scripts. **BIOGRAPHICAL SOURCES:** The Politics of Life, Temple University Press, 1993; Unbroken Thread, University of Massachusetts Press, 1993. **HOME ADDRESS:** 2210 Wilshire Blvd, Ste 331, Santa Monica, CA 90403-5784.

HSI, BARTHOLOMEW P.
Educator, educational administrator. Chinese American. **PERSONAL:** Born Dec 10, 1925, Shanghai, China; son of Chien T Hsi and Chu C K Hsi; married On Tsui Hsi, Jul 18, 1964; children: Benjamin, Julia Morris. **EDUCATION:** University of Minnesota, MA, 1962, PhD, 1964. **CAREER:** University of Minnesota, Statistical Laboratory, supervisor statistician; Case Western University, Medical School, assistant professor; University of Texas, Houston, School of Public Health, professor, dept head, currently. **ORGANIZATIONS:** Military Experience Directed into Health Careers, project, director; Journal of Clinical Pharmacology and Therapeutics, editorial board; Veterans Administration Hospitals Cooperative Studies, operations committee. **HOME ADDRESS:** 5650 Indigo, Houston, TX 77096-1125. **BUSINESS ADDRESS:** Professor, Dept Head, University of Texas, School of Public Health, 1200 Herman Pressler, Rm 729, Houston, TX 77030-3900.

HSI, DAVID C.
Association executive, educator. Chinese American. **PERSONAL:** Born May 17, 1928, Shanghai, China; son of Yulin Hsi (deceased) and Sue Jean Jing Hsi (deceased); married Kathy C Hsi, Jun 19, 1952; children: Andrew C, Steven D. **EDUCATION:** St John's University, Shanghai, BSA, 1948; University of Georgia, MSA, 1949; University of Minnesota, PhD, 1951. **CAREER:** New Mexico State University, plant pathologist, professor, 1952-92; US Cotton Field Station, postdoctoral fellow, 1951-52; University of Minnesota, graduate teaching assistant, 1950; University of New Mexico, biologist, adjunct professor, 1986-. **ORGANIZATIONS:** National Association of Academies of Science, president, 1993-94; New Mexico Academy of Science, president, 1981, 1983, treasurer, 1984-92; American Peanut Research & Education Society, president, 1982-83; New Mexico Chinese Association, president, 1984, 92; Kiwanis International, Clovis Club, president, 1972; Albuquerque Sister Cities Board, president, 1986-89; Albuquerque Board of Education, vice president, 1985. **HONORS/AWARDS:** American Association for the Advancement of Science, fellow, 1969; New Mexico Academy of Science, Distinguished Scientist, 1984; NMSU College of Agriculture, Distinguished Service, 1985, Distinguished Research, 1971; Sigma Xi, 1949. **SPECIAL ACHIEVEMENTS:** From Sun Daggers to Space Exploration, p 434, 1986. **HOME ADDRESS:** 1611 Ridgecrest Drive SE, Albuquerque, NM 87108.

HSIA, JUDITH ANN
Physician, educator. Chinese American. **PERSONAL:** Born Jan 29, 1954, Boston, MA; daughter of David Yi-yung Hsia & Hsio Hsuan Shih Hsia; married Ernest Jay Isenstadt, Jan 28, 1982; children: Jill Hsia Isenstadt, Ruth Hsia Isenstadt. **EDUCATION:** Harvard College, AB, 1974; University of Illinois School of Medicine, MD, 1978. **CAREER:** Tufts-New England Medical Center, intern/resident, 1978-81; National Heart Lung and Blood Institute, research associate, 1981-84; George Washington University, cardiology fellow, 1984-87, assistant professor, 1987-93, associate professor, 1993-. **ORGANIZATIONS:** Alpha Omega Alpha, 1978-; American College of Cardiology,

fellow, 1990-. **HONORS/AWARDS:** Pfizer Pharmaceuticals, Pfizer Scholar's Award for New Faculty, 1987; American Heart Association, Nation's Capital Affiliate Mamie Doud Eisenhower Fellowship Award, 1986.

HSIA, JUDO JEOUDAO
International management company executive. Chinese American. **PERSONAL:** Born Apr 22, 1947, Taipei, Taiwan; son of Dar-Ming Hsia and Ing Wei; married Diane Wong, Aug 17, 1980. **EDUCATION:** National Cheng Chi University of Taiwan, LLB, 1968; Howard Payne University of Texas, business, 1974; Central State University of Oklahoma, MBA (summa cum laude), 1975. **CAREER:** Orient Overseas Container Line, traffic rep, 1969-72; Tamsui Olford College of Taiwan, asst professor, 1975-78; Chinese Culture University of Taiwan, associate professor, 1975-78; Han Te Intl Corp, managing dir, 1978-80; Transworld Business Inc, vice pres, gen mgr, 1981-. **ORGANIZATIONS:** Chinese Friend's Assn, dir, 1982-, chmn, 1986-87; MBA Assn, 1975-78. **HONORS/AWARDS:** Texas State Government, Honorable Citizen, 1992; Chinese Friend's Assn, Best Service, 1989. **MILITARY SERVICE:** Chinese Army, lt, 1968-69. **BUSINESS ADDRESS:** General Manager, Transworld Business Inc, 1178 Folsom St, San Francisco, CA 94103, (415)626-8180.

HSIA, LISA
Film director, television and film producer. Chinese American. **PERSONAL:** Born Feb 16, 1958, Evanston, IL; daughter of David Yi-Yung Hsia and Hsio Hsuan Hsia. **EDUCATION:** Harvard University, BA (magna cum laude), 1980; Beijing University, 1981; Stanford University, 1993. **CAREER:** Orion Classics, "Old Enough," feature film, associate producer, 1984, "A Great Wall," feature film, line producer, 1985; Made in China, director/producer, 1985; PBS "Adam Smith's Money World," producer, 1985-87; "The Emperor's Eye: Art and Power in Imperial China," director/producer, 1989; ABC News "Prime Time Live," producer, 1989-. **ORGANIZATIONS:** Asian American Journalists Association; International Film Seminars, board member; New York Women in Film; Women Make Movies, board member. **HONORS/AWARDS:** 4 National Emmy Awards for News & Documentary, 1990, 1991, 1992; Investigative Editors & Reporters Award, Headliners Award, 1990; Easter Seal Society, EDI Award, 1992; 3 CINE, Golden Eagle Awards; National Educational Film Festival, 2 First Prizes; Knight Foundation, Journalism Fellowship, Stanford University, 1993. **HOME ADDRESS:** 15 W 84th St, New York, NY 10024.

HSIA, YUCHUEK
City planner. Chinese American. **PERSONAL:** Born Sep 19, 1944, China; son of Wei-Lin Hsia and Wai-Fong Hsia; married Lynne Kastel Hsia, Jul 28, 1984; children: Rebecca Kastel. **EDUCATION:** City College of San Francisco, AA, 1965; University of California, Berkeley, BArch, 1969; Kansas State University, Manhattan, MCRP, 1975. **CAREER:** State of Wisconsin, community devel specialist, 1974-78; County of Klamath, OR, sr planner, 1978-79; Monterey County Planning Dept, CA, principal planner, 1979-83; City of Scotts Valley, CA, dir of community devel, 1983-86; City of Saratoga, CA, planning dir, 1986-88; California State University, chief of planning, 1988-90; City of Ontario, code enforcement manager, 1990-. **ORGANIZATIONS:** American Planning Assn, 1969-; Community Development Society of America, 1974-. **SPECIAL ACHIEVEMENTS:** Comprehensive Plan, Sugar Creek, MO, 1971; Happiness Is a Green Place: Park and Recreation Plan, Kansas City Metropolitan Region, 1972; General Plans: Monterey County, CA, 1983; Scotts Valley, CA, 1985; Saratoga City, CA, 1987. **HOME ADDRESS:** 1505 Gemwood Dr, Whittier, CA 90601, (818)330-8986.

HSIA, YUKUN
Engineering management/investment executive. Chinese American. **PERSONAL:** Born Feb 21, 1941, Kunming, Yunnan, China; son of Wei Lin Hsia; married Helen L, Aug 15, 1965; children: Eric, Curtis. **EDUCATION:** UC Berkeley, BS, 1961; UCLA, MS, 1964, PhD, 1969. **CAREER:** NCR, section chief, design engineering, 1961-66; North American Aviations, MTS, 1967; Litton Industries, principal investigator, 1968-74; McDonnell Douglas, microelectronics, branch chief, 1974-82; University of Southern California, graduate lecturer, 1976-82; Fairchild Semiconductor, divisional engineering manager, 1982-87; Santa Clara University, graduate lecturer, 1982-87; Northrop, engineering manager/director, 1987-. **ORGANIZATIONS:** YHL, consulting partner, 1980-; IEEE, senior member, 1961-. **HONORS/AWARDS:** Tau Beta Pi, 1969; Phi Eta Sigma, 1958; Electronics Products Magazine, Product of the Year, 1977. **SPECIAL ACHIEVEMENTS:** 39 published technical papers; 10 US patents; various DOD contract awards on research and development pro-

grams and projects. **HOME ADDRESS:** 1821 Park Skyline Rd, Santa Ana, CA 92705, (714)838-4146. **BUSINESS PHONE:** (213)600-4567.

HSIAO, BENJAMIN S.
Research scientist. Chinese American. **PERSONAL:** Born Aug 12, 1958, Taipei, Taiwan; son of Fu Hsiao and Kuei-Min Hsiao; married Caroline M S Hsiao, Oct 7, 1987; children: Stefan, Athan. **EDUCATION:** National Taiwan University, BS, 1980; University of Connecticut, PhD, 1987. **CAREER:** University of Massachusetts, post-doctoral fellow, 1987-89; DuPont CR&D, research scientist, 1989-. **ORGANIZATIONS:** American Chem Soc, 1985; American Phys Soc, 1985; Materials Research Soc, 1986; Society of Plastic Eng, 1984. **HONORS/AWARDS:** University of Conn, Doctoral Research Fellowship, 1985; SPE, best papers, 1991. **SPECIAL ACHIEVEMENTS:** 40 + reviewed journal publications, 1993; 30 + conference proceedings, 1993. **BUSINESS ADDRESS:** Research Scientist, DuPont Co, PO Box 80302, Exp Station, Wilmington, DE 19880-0302, (302)695-4668.

HSIAO, FENG (FRED SHAW)
Construction company executive. Chinese American. **PERSONAL:** Born May 20, 1919, Ta Chao, Shansi, China; son of Heng Chien Hsiao and Chiao Shih Hsiao; married Jennie Hsiao, Jun 7, 1958; children: Howell, Hoyt, Holden. **EDUCATION:** National Wu-Han University, China, BS, civil engineering, 1942; Massachusetts Institute of Technology, MS, civil engineering, 1946; University of Minnesota, Institute of Technology, post-graduate studies in hydraulic engineering, 1951. **CAREER:** Shensi Province Govt, China, dept of food management, associate engineer, 1942-43; Dept of National Highways, Chungking, China, associate engineer, 1943-44; Orville E Madsen & Son Inc, estimator, 1949-54, vice president, board of directors, 1954-74; Shaw-Lundquist Associates Inc, president, treasurer, chairman of the board, 1974-. **ORGANIZATIONS:** Chinese Christian Fellowship, Twin Cities, elder, 1967, chairman & executive officer, 1957-65, founder, 1950; Chinese Senior Citizen Society, advisory board, chairman, 1982-; National Association of Minority Contractors, vice president, 1988-89, 1991, treasurer, 1987-88, secretary, 1987-; Associated General Contractors of Minnesota, 1974-; Chapter of the Organization of Chinese Americans, advisory council, 1984-; Minnesota Higher Education Facilities Authority, board member, 1991-. **HONORS/AWARDS:** Chinese American Association of Minnestoa, Award of Recognition, 1971; Minnesota Purchasing Council, Minority Supplier of the Year, 1984; Minnesota Chapter of the National Association of Minority Contractors, Outstanding Service Award, 1987; NAMC, Outstanding Service Award, 1992; State of Minnesota, Governor's Office, Certificate of Commendation for Success ande Leadership in Business Community, 1993. **BUSINESS ADDRESS:** President, Shaw-Lundquist Associates, Inc, 2805 Dodd Rd, St Paul, MN 55121, (612)454-0670.

HSIAO, JOAN HSI-MIN
Banking/finance company associate. Chinese American. **PERSONAL:** Born Aug 10, 1965, Seattle, WA; daughter of David Ching-Hsi Hsiao and Martha Yuen Tsao Hsiao; married Jim Bromley, Jun 23, 1990. **EDUCATION:** Harvard College, AB (cum laude), 1986; National University of Singapore, political science, 1989; Yale University, School of Organization & Mgmt, MPPM, 1992. **CAREER:** First Boston, analyst, 1986-88; City of New York, senior analyst, 1990; Lehman Brothers, associate, 1992-. **ORGANIZATIONS:** Harvard Crimson, graduate board, 1986-. **HONORS/AWARDS:** Rotary Foundation, Rotary Scholar, 1988.

HSIAO, JULIA
Association administrator. Chinese American. **CAREER:** Asian Business League of San Francisco, executive director, currently. **BUSINESS ADDRESS:** Executive Director, Asian Business League, 233 Sansome St, Ste 1102, San Francisco, CA 94104, (415)788-4664. *

HSIAO, MARGARET SHENG-MEI
Chemical engineer. Chinese American/Taiwanese American. **PERSONAL:** Born Jan 5, 1956, Taipei, Taiwan; daughter of Victor Hsiao and Manna Chien; married Dennis Wayne Peters, Oct 8, 1982. **EDUCATION:** Cooper Union, BChE, 1977; University of Notre Dame, MBA, 1993. **CAREER:** Procter & Gamble, engr, 1977-78; American Cyanamid, engr, 1978-83; Wacker Chemie, engr, 1983-85; Union Carbide, group leader, 1985-86; Perrigo Co, mgr, purchasing, business development, 1986-. **ORGANIZATIONS:** American Institute of Chemical Engineers; Society of Women Engineers; American Assn of Pharmaceutical Scientists; American Chemical Society. **SPECIAL ACHIEVEMENTS:** Language proficiency: Chinese (Mandarin), French, Ital-

ian, German. **HOME ADDRESS:** 10749 West M Ave, Kalamazoo, MI 49009. **BUSINESS ADDRESS:** Manager, Purchasing/Business Development, Perrigo Company, 117 Water St, Allegan, MI 49010.

HSIAO, SIDNEY C. *See* Obituaries.

HSIAO, TONY AN-JEN
Architect. Chinese American. **PERSONAL:** Born Mar 7, 1958, Ann Arbor, MI; son of Sun Chien Hsiao & Betty Ye-May Hsiao; married Karen Fung, Jun 19, 1993. **EDUCATION:** University of Michigan, BS, 1980; Harvard Graduate School of Design, MArch, 1984. **CAREER:** Ullstrut Corporation, draftsman, 1979; Hardy Hazman Pfeiffer, jr designer, 1980-81; Graham Gund Associates, designer, 1981-83; Finegad Alexander & Associates Inc, associate, 1984-. **ORGANIZATIONS:** American Institute of Architects, 1986-; Boston Society of Architects, 1986-; Art Deco Society of Boston, 1990-.

HSIAO, TYZEN
Composer, pianist. Taiwanese American. **PERSONAL:** Born Jan 1, 1938, Kaohsiung, Taiwan; son of Zui-An Shaw and Hsue-Yun L Shaw; married Jenchu Kao Hsiao, Feb 7, 1963; children: Rosemary, Jeff, Stephen, Joseph. **EDUCATION:** National Taiwan Normal University, BA, 1963; Musashino Music Academy, 1965-67; California State University, Los Angeles, MA, 1987. **CAREER:** Wun-Chau Technological Academy, instructor, 1967-68; Tainan Technological Academy, associate professor, 1970-76; National Taiwan Normal University, instructor, 1973-76; Taiwan Theological College, instructor, 1975. **ORGANIZATIONS:** Music Teachers Association of California, 1980-; Pacific Contemporary Music Center, 1987-; Taiwanese Music Society of Southern California, chairman, 1982-; Great Performers from Taiwan, board of directors, 1992-; Taiwanese American Citizen League, 1985-; Taiwanese American Professor's Association, 1986-; North America Taiwanese Writers/Artist Association, president, 1984, Chamber Orchestra, conductor, 1982-89. **HONORS/AWARDS:** President C K Yun, Special Interview and Recognition, 1975; Taiwanese-American Professor's Association, Compositions "Psalms of the Taiwanese," special recognition, 1987; Taiwanese-American Foundation, Science of Humanities Award, 1989; California Music Teacher's Association, State Winner of Composition Contest, 1990. **SPECIAL ACHIEVEMENTS:** World Premiere of the Cello Concerto in Taipei, 1992; World Premiere of the Violin Concerto by world famous violinist Cho-liang Lin and the San Diego Symphony Orchestra, 1992; World Premiere of the Piano Concerto OP53 by pianist Jonathan Tang and the Vancouver Symphone Orchestra in Vancouver, BC, 1994. **MILITARY SERVICE:** Taiwanese Military Service. **BIOGRAPHICAL SOURCES:** The Dream of the Taiwanese Culture, Taiwan Publishing Co, p 265, 307-317. **HOME ADDRESS:** 14952 Novak St, Hacienda Heights, CA 91745, (818)961-6543.

HSIAO, WILLIAM C.
Health care economist, educator. Chinese American. **PERSONAL:** Born Jan 17, 1936, Beijing, China; son of Chu Hsiao; married Ruth Yu Hsiao; children: Roderick, Douglas. **EDUCATION:** Ohio Wesleyan University, BA, mathematics & physics, 1959; Harvard University, MPA, public administration, 1972, MA, economics, 1974, PhD, economics, 1982. **CAREER:** Connecticut General Life Insurance, actuary & financial director, 1959-68; US Social Security Admin, deputy chief actuary, 1968-71; Harvard Business School, member of faculty, 1974-77; Harvard University, associate professor economics health policy & mgt, 1974-84, professor economics & health policy, 1985-. **ORGANIZATIONS:** World Bank, consultant on health & social welfare systems, 1983-; Intl Labor Organization, consult on social insurance, 1991-; World Health Organization, consult on health care finance, 1989-; US Senate, consul to comm on finance & medicare/medicaid, 1974-, consult to comm on aging & regulation of fees, 1983-; Soc of Actuaries, bd mbr-elect, 1991-; United Methodist Bd of Pensions, bd mbr-elect, 1991-93; Council on Economic Planning, Taiwan, chief adviser to lead task force, 1989-90; US Natl Academy of Science, Institute of Medicine, 1992; Natl Academy of Social Insurance, founding mbr, 1992. **HONORS/AWARDS:** Beijing Medical University, honorary professor, 1985; Shanghai Medical University, honorary professor, 1985. **SPECIAL ACHIEVEMENTS:** Numerous publications, including: coauthor: "An Overview of the Development & Refinement of the RBRVS, Foundation for Reform of US Physician Payment," Medical Care, Nov 1992; "Results & Impacts of the Resource-Based Relative Value Scale," Medical Care, Nov 1992; author, "Comparing Health Care Systems: What Lessons Nations Can Learn from Others," Journal of Health Policy, Politics, & Law, Jan 1993. **BUSINESS ADDRESS:** Program in Health Care Finance, Harvard School of Public Health, Holyoke Center 726, 1350 Massachusetts Avenue, Cambridge, MA 02138, (617)496-8820.

HSIE, ABRAHAM WUHSIUNG
Educator. Taiwanese American. **PERSONAL:** Born Mar 3, 1940, Hsinwu, Taiwan; son of Yuantsai & Lanmai Drung Hsie; married Mayphoon H Hsie, Jun 15, 1963; children: Marvin Suchin, Dora Yuchin. **EDUCATION:** National Taiwan University, BS, 1962; Indiana University, MA, 1965, PhD, 1968; University of Colorado Medical Center & Eleanor Roosevelt Institute for Cancer Research, postdoctoral fellow, 1969-71. **CAREER:** University of Tennessee-Oak Ridge Graduate School of Biomedical Sciences; Oak Ridge National Laboratory, lecturer, 1972-76, group leader of mammalian somatic cell genetics and biochemistry, 1972-77, mammalian cell genetic toxicology, 1977-84, biodosimetry, 1984-86, professor, 1972-86; University of Texas Medical Branch, Galveston, Departments of Preventive Medicine & Community Health, Human Biological Chemistry and Radiation Therapy, professor, 1986-, Center for Molecular Science, senior scientist, 1991-. **ORGANIZATIONS:** American Association for Cancer Research; American Society for Biological Chemists and Molecular Biologists; Environmental Mutagen Society; Radiation Research Society; Society of Toxicology; US Environmental Mutagen Society, Publication Policy Committee; Education Committee, 1991-93; Chinese Society for Agricultural Chemistry, life member; Society of Chinese Bioscientists in America, life member; Houston Hakka Chinese Association, first vice president, 1993-; The University of Texas Medical Branch, Chinese Students and Scholars Association, faculty advisor, 1991-. **HONORS/AWARDS:** Indiana University, Distinguished Alumni Service Award, 1980; US EPA, Washington, DC, Distinguished Visiting Scientist, 1985-88; Florida International University, Distinguished Visiting Lecturer, 1990; Japan Society for the Promotion of Science, fellow, 1977. **SPECIAL ACHIEVEMENTS:** Pioneered a study on the role of cyclic nucleotide in carcinogenesis: a reversal of cancerous behavior of hamster cells to the normal state by treating cells with cyclic adenosine 3', 5'-monophosphate; pioneered the development of cellular and molecular assays for the determination of the mutagenic activity of physical or chemical agents either singly or in combination in the environment and for studies of mechanisms of mammalian mutagenesis. **MILITARY SERVICE:** Republic of China Air Force, 2nd lt, 1962-63. **BUSINESS ADDRESS:** Professor, Associate Director, Division of Environmental Toxicology, University of Texas Medical Branch, 700 Strand, 2-102 Ewing Hall, J-10, Galveston, TX 77555-1010, (409)772-1803.

HSIEH, BRIAN (TSUNG-PEI)
Machinery company executive. Chinese American/Taiwanese American. **PERSONAL:** Born Oct 9, 1964, Chiayi, Taiwan; son of Horng-Bin Hsieh and Hui-Ing Chiang Hsieh; married Isabel Lai, Jul 22, 1989. **EDUCATION:** National Taiwan University, BS, 1986; UCLA, School of Engineering, MS, 1991; UCLA, Business School, MBA, currently. **CAREER:** UCLA, research assistant, 1989-90; Helisys, Inc, research engineer, 1990-92, manager, manufacturing operations, 1992-93, vice president of operations, 1993-. **ORGANIZATIONS:** Pacific MBA Association, director, 1993-; Society of Manufacturing Engineers, 1988-; American Society of Mechanical Engineers, 1989-. **BUSINESS ADDRESS:** Vice President of Operations, Helisys, Inc, 2750 Oregon Ct, Bldg M-10, Torrance, CA 90503, (310)782-1949.

HSIEH, CARL CHIA-FONG
Educator. Taiwanese American. **PERSONAL:** Born Jan 5, 1939, Peikang, Taiwan; son of Chun-Yen Hsieh and Hsu Hsieh; married Shu-Mei Hsieh, Nov 10, 1962; children: Janet, Louis, Helen, Christine. **EDUCATION:** National Taiwan University, BSCE, 1961; South Dakota School of Mines & Technology, MSCE, 1964; Northwestern University, PhD, 1968. **CAREER:** Taiwan Public Works Bureau, structural engr, 1962-64; Chrysler Corp, body research engr, 1968-70; Bechtel Corp, engineering specialist, 1977; California Polytechnic State University, professor, 1970-. **ORGANIZATIONS:** American Society of Civil Engineers, branch vp, branch secretary/treasurer, 1971-; American Society for Engineering Education, 1974-; Chinese Professsional Society, Cal Poly, founding vp, president, 1979-; National Society of Professional Engineers, 1973-76; California Faculty Assn, 1983-; California State Employee's Assn, 1979-82; United Professors of California, 1982-83; California Society of Professional Engineers, chapter treasurer, 1973-76. **HONORS/AWARDS:** California Polytechnic State University, Meritorious Performance & Professional Promise Award, 1988; NASA-ASEE, Summer Faculty Research Fellowships, 1975, 1979, 1985; Northwestern University, ARPA Research Assistantship, 1965-68. **SPECIAL ACHIEVEMENTS:** Referee, Journal of Computing in Civil Engineering, ASCE, 1986-; reviewer, the journal, Building

and Environment; 9 technical publications; registered professional engineer in California. **MILITARY SERVICE:** Nationalist Chinese Air Force (ROTC), 2nd lieutenant, engineering officer, 1961-62. **HOME ADDRESS:** 1730 Jalisco Ct, San Luis Obispo, CA 93405. **BUSINESS PHONE:** (805)756-2755.

HSIEH, CHUNG-CHENG
Educator. Taiwanese American. **PERSONAL:** Born Sep 27, 1954, Taichung, Taiwan; son of Miao-chang Hsieh and Pao-Ai Hsieh Chang; married Fei-Fang Hsu, Jul 3, 1991. **EDUCATION:** National Taiwan University, BS, 1976, MPH, 1978; Harvard University, MS, 1980, ScD, 1985. **CAREER:** Harvard University School of Public Health, assistant professor of epidemiology, 1985-91, associate professor of epidemiology, 1991-. **ORGANIZATIONS:** Society for Epidemiologic Research, 1979-; Biometric Society, 1982-. **HONORS/AWARDS:** Ministry of Education, Taiwan, Scholarship, 1978; Project HOPE, Stomatology Fellow, 1987, Cancer Fellow, 1991; Intl Agency for Research on Cancer, Visiting Scientist Award, 1988. **SPECIAL ACHIEVEMENTS:** Published more than 90 peer-reviewed scientific papers on cancers of the breast, stomach, and pancreas, and on methods in epidemiology; language proficiencies: English, Chinese (Mandarin), Taiwanese, and Hukka. **BUSINESS ADDRESS:** Assoc Professor, Dept of Epidemiology, Harvard University School of Public Health, 677 Huntington Ave, Boston, MA 02115, (617)432-4564.

HSIEH, CYNTHIA C.
Educator, librarian, company executive, writer. Taiwanese American. **PERSONAL:** Born Sep 1, 1961, Taipei, Taiwan; married Wenje Lai, 1986; children: Whitney. **EDUCATION:** National Taiwan University, BA, 1984; University of Wisconsin, Madison, MLS, 1985. **CAREER:** University of Wisconsin, resident librarian, 1985; Graceland College, assistant librarian, 1986; Columbia College, technical services librarian, 1987-; MITT Professional Group, Inc, vice president, 1992-; Chinese American News, reporter, 1988-; Pacific Journal, contract writer, 1992-. **ORGANIZATIONS:** American Library Association, new member roundtable, chair of midwinter meeting committee, 1989; Chinese American Librarians Association, membership committee, chair, 1990, midwest chapter president, 1991; Chinese Academic and Professional Association in Mid-America, newsletter; Asian American Journalists Association, Chicago Chapter, member editor, 1991; Taiwanese American Association, Greater Chicago Chapter, 1991-; LIBRAS Group, Serials Interest Group, chair, 1992-93. **HONORS/AWARDS:** National Taiwan University, Book Coupon Awards, 1981; Chinese Academic and Professional Association, Service Awards, 1991. **SPECIAL ACHIEVEMENTS:** Advocator of getting Chinese Americans appointed to local governments; co-editor, The Midwest Science News, 1992-; editor, CAPAMA Newsletters, 1991-92; author of many articles regarding Chinese Americans in Chinese American News, Pacific Journal and World Journal; project leader of the Midwest Area Chinese American Resources Guide. **BUSINESS ADDRESS:** Technical Services Librarian, Columbia College, 600 S Michigan Ave, Chicago, IL 60605.

HSIEH, DANIEL SEBASTIAN
Management consultant. Chinese American. **PERSONAL:** Born Jun 23, 1964, Pasadena, CA; son of Din-Yu & Lily Hsieh. **EDUCATION:** Harvard University, SB, 1985; University of Chicago, MBA, 1989. **CAREER:** Strategic Planning Associates, research analyst, 1985-87; William Kent International, principal, 1989-. **ORGANIZATIONS:** Children's Hospital Young Perspectives Council, executive committee, 1992-. **HONORS/AWARDS:** Office of the President, Presidential Scholar, 1981; Institute of Nuclear Power Operations, scholar, 1985; Beta Gamma Sigma, 1989. **SPECIAL ACHIEVEMENTS:** Fluency in Mandarin.

HSIEH, DEAN SHUI-TIEN
Pharmaceutical company executive. Taiwanese American. **PERSONAL:** Born Feb 10, 1948, Tainan, Taiwan; son of Wen Hsieh and Dom-Mei Hsieh; married Phyllis W Hsieh, Nov 20, 1982; children: Esther, Matthew, Joseph. **EDUCATION:** National Taiwan University, Taipei, Taiwan, BS, 1970; Massachusetts Institute of Technology, MS, 1974, PhD, 1978. **CAREER:** Massachusetts Institute of Technology, research assistant, 1972-78, research affiliate, 1978-82; Boston Children's Hospital, research associate, 1978-1980; Harvard Medical School, instructor, 1980-82; Rutgers University, NJ, assistant professor, 1982-85; Conrex Pharmaceutical Corp, chairman, CEO, founder, 1985-. **ORGANIZATIONS:** Mt Jade Science & Technology Assn/Greater Phila, president, 1993; Controlled Release Society, 1979-; American Assn of Pharmaceutical Scientists, 1985-; American Assn for Advancement of Science, 1990; Journal of Pharmaceutical Science, reviewer, 1984-85; Biomaterials, reviewer,

1983-85; NIH Special Study Section, reviewer, 1991-93. **HONORS/AWARDS:** Juvenile Diabetes Foundation, Postdoctoral Fellowship, 1980-82; Pharmaceutical Manufacturers Association Foundation, Research Starter Grant, 1981-82; American Diabetes Association, Feasibility Grant, 1983-85; National Institutes of Health, SBIR Grant; Ben Franklin Partnerships, Seed Grant, Challenge Grant, Center for Excellence Grant, 1987-93. **SPECIAL ACHIEVEMENTS:** Author, Controlled Release Systems: Fabrication Technology, vol I and II, CRC Press, 1988; Drug Permeation Enhancement: Theory & Applications, Marcel Dekker Inc, 1993; Patents: Transdermal & Transmembrane Delivery of Drugs, US Pat #5023252, June 1991; Methods of Making Prolonged Release Body, US Pat #4357312, 1982; Methods of Making Soybean Milk Beverage, US Pat #4119733, 1978. **BIOGRAPHICAL SOURCES:** Controlled Release Systems: Fabrication Technology, vol I, II, CRC Press, Inc, 1988. **BUSINESS ADDRESS:** Chairman of the Board, CEO, Conrex Pharmaceutical Corp, 300 Kinberton Rd, Phoenixville, PA 19460, (215)935-6940.

HSIEH, DURWYNNE
Educator, composer, cellist. Chinese American. **PERSONAL:** Born May 15, 1963, Hartford, CT; son of Hazel Tseng & Hsueh Ying Hsieh. **EDUCATION:** MIT, SB, 1985; University of California, Berkeley, PhD, 1990. **CAREER:** Los Medanos College, instructor, 1990-93. **SPECIAL ACHIEVEMENTS:** Incidental Music for MacBeth, 1991. **BUSINESS ADDRESS:** Instructor, Los Medanos College, 2700 E Leland Rd, Pittsburg, CA 94565-5197, (510)439-2181.

HSIEH, FRANKLIN
Engineer. Chinese American. **PERSONAL:** Born Oct 5, 1947, Manila, Philippines; son of William Hsieh; married. **EDUCATION:** Taiwan University of Marine & Oceanic Technology, BS, 1972; Sinclair College, continuing education, 1992. **CAREER:** Hitachi Zozen Robin Dockyard, asst dept chief, 1974-77; Niedermeyer-Martin, sales rep, 1977-81; Day Star Shipping, Tokyo, Japan, owner rep, 1981-84; United Dockyard Ltd, Hong Kong, sr sales exec, 1984-85; UDI Limited, mgr, 1985-87; Carey Group, contract administrator, vice pres, 1987-89; Ikeda Interior Systems Inc, QC asst mgr, engr, 1991-. **ORGANIZATIONS:** American Society of Quality Control, 1991-; Society of Naval Architect & Marine Engineering, 1975-85. **BUSINESS ADDRESS:** Quality Control Asst Manager/Engineer, Ikeda Interior Systems Inc, 1630 Ferguson Court, Sidney, OH 45365.

HSIEH, HSIN-NENG
Educator. Taiwanese American. **PERSONAL:** Born Jun 25, 1947, Hunan, China; married. **EDUCATION:** Cheng-Kung University, BS, 1970; University of Iowa, MS, 1973; University of Pittsburgh, PhD, 1983. **CAREER:** China Engineering Consultants Inc, environmental engineer, 1973-75; Moh & Associates Inc, project engineer, 1976-79; New Jersey Institute of Technology, assistant professor, 1983-89, associate professor, 1989-. **ORGANIZATIONS:** American Society of Civil Engineers; Water Environment Federation; American Water Works Association. **HONORS/AWARDS:** University of Pittsburgh, University Scholar, 1983; New Jersey Institute of Technology, Outstanding in Teaching, 1989, 1991, 1992. **SPECIAL ACHIEVEMENTS:** Over 40 publication in the areas of water and wastewater treatment, sludge treatment, hazardous waste treatment. **BUSINESS ADDRESS:** Associate Professor, Dept of Civil & Environmental Engineering, New Jersey Institute of Technology, University Heights, Newark, NJ 07102, (201)596-5859.

HSIEH, JEANETTE L.
Educator. Chinese American. **PERSONAL:** Born May 22, 1943, Oakland, CA; daughter of Herbert and Anne Lowe; married Theodore Hsieh, Aug 20, 1966; children: Matthew, Benjamin. **EDUCATION:** Westmont College, BA, 1964, MA, 1966, Northern Illinois University, EdD, 1988. **CAREER:** Deerfield Public Schools, 5th, 6th grade teacher, 1966-69; School District U46, middle school teacher, 1969-72; Judson College, professor, dir of teacher education, 1972-90; Wheaton College, assoc prof of educ, coordinator of MAT program, chair of educ dept, 1990-. **ORGANIZATIONS:** Illinois Association of Colleges for Teacher Education, president-elect, 1991-, publications committee, chairperson; Illinois Association for Teacher Education in Private Colleges, pres-elect, pres, past president, 1986-92; Illinois Association for Supervision and Curriculum Development, 1990-, Private College Higher Education Representative, board member; Ecker Mental Health Center, 2nd vice president, secretary, board member, 1989-. **SPECIAL ACHIEVEMENTS:** Team member of Illinois State Board of Eduacation Review Teams, 1982-; various educational presentations at professional organizations. **BUSINESS AD-**

DRESS: Assoc Professor, Coordinator of MAT Program, Wheaton College, Wheaton, IL 60187, (708)752-5763.

HSIEH, LI-PING (LIU CHERE)
Musician. Chinese American. **PERSONAL:** Born 1941, Nanking, China; daughter of Yu-tsai Hsieh and Yvonne Ho; married Hsien-Tung Liu, 1964; children: Benjamin Liu, Lisa Liu. **EDUCATION:** Conservatorio di Musica Giuseppe Verdi, 1962; Juilliard School, 1963-65; Duquesne University Music School, BM, 1977, MM, 1979. **CAREER:** La Roche College, lecturer of music, 1978-80; Point Park College, lecturer of music, 1983-86; Albert Kay Associates, Inc, concert artist, 1981-. **ORGANIZATIONS:** San Francisco Opera-Merola Opera, soprano, 1966-; Pittsburgh Opera, soprano, 1969-; various orchestras, soprano. **HONORS/AWARDS:** Concert Artists Guild, NY, First place, annual audition, 1971; Natl Arts Club, First place, Music Competition, 1971; San Francisco Opera, Stipend, 1966; Sacramento Opera Guild, winnner of audition, 1966; N Ohio Opera Assn, M A Ireland Award; W Matthews Sullivan Musical Foundation, Grant. **SPECIAL ACHIEVE-MENTS:** Leading roles and solos with opera companies and symphony orchestras; concerts in Italy, Germany, Austria, US, and the Far East. **HOME ADDRESS:** 2205 Bentley Dr, Bloomsburg, PA 17815.

HSIEH, PHILIP PO-FANG
Educator. Taiwanese American. **PERSONAL:** Born Jul 10, 1934, Tainan, Taiwan; son of Chai-Seng & Tsai-Ping Hsieh; married Emmy Hui-Mei Hsieh, Jul 8, 1991; children: Paul Sek-Bin, Timothy In-Chhu. **EDUCATION:** National Taiwan University, BSc, 1957; University of Minnesota, MSc, 1961, PhD, 1964. **CAREER:** University of Wisconsin, visiting associate professor, 1968; UCLA, visiting associate professor, 1969; US Naval Research Laboratory, research mathematician, 1970-71; Western Michigan University, assistant professor, 1964-67, associate professor, 1967-73, professor, 1973-. **ORGANIZATIONS:** American Mathematical Society, 1964-; Mathematical Association of America, 1964-; Society of Industrial and Applied Mathematics, 1965-; Mathematical Society of Japan, 1967-. **HONORS/AWARDS:** US Naval Research Lab, Research Publication Award, 1972. **SPECIAL ACHIEVE-MENTS:** Published several mathematical articles in professional journals; "Analytic Theory of Differential Equations," co-editor, Lecture Notes in Math, no 183, 1971; co-editor, Trends and Developments in Ordinary Differential Equations, World Scientific Publishing Co, 1994. **BUSINESS ADDRESS:** Prof, Dept of Math & Statistics, Western Michigan University, Kalamazoo, MI 49008-5152, (616)387-4545.

HSIEH, TOM
City government official, architect. Chinese American. **CAREER:** Thomas Hsieh AIA Architects; San Francisco Board of Supervisors, supervisor, 1986-, Budget Committee, chair, 1993-. **ORGANIZATIONS:** San Francisco Arts Commission, 1970; Democratic National Committee, currently. **SPECIAL ACHIEVEMENTS:** Author, San Francisco ballot measure that called for the creation of a $350 million fund to assist in retrofitting buildings to meet seismic standards, 1992; mayoral candidate, San Francisco, 1992; first Asian on SF Board of Supervisors. **BUSINESS ADDRESS:** Supervisor, City of San Francisco, City Hall, Rm 235, San Francisco, CA 94102, (415)554-5015. *

HSIEH, WEN-JEN
Educator. Taiwanese American. **PERSONAL:** Born Feb 2, 1955, Chung Hua, Taiwan; daughter of Yen-tai Hsieh & Chin-ying Huang; married Eric H Hsu; children: Alan Y. **EDUCATION:** Fu-Jen Catholic University, Taiwan, BA, 1977; National Taiwan University, MA, 1979; Columbia University, PhD, 1985. **CAREER:** Columbia University, preceptor, 1981-84; Academia Sinica, Taiwan, assistant research fellow, 1983; Brown University, post-doctoral fellow, 1985-87; University of Cincinnati, assistant professor of economics, 1987-. **ORGANIZATIONS:** American Economic Association, 1984-; University of Cincinnati, Asian Studies Committee, 1987-, Women Studies Committee, 1988-91; Chinese Economic Association in North America, 1986-; Ohio Association of Economists & Political Scientists, 1991-; Chinese Economists Society, 1991-; Committee on the Status of Women in the Economics Profession, 1988-. **HONORS/AWARDS:** University of Cincinnati, Taft Grants for research travel, 1992, 1989, 1988, Summer Faculty Research Fellowship, 1989; Delta Tau Kappa, 1988; Brown University, Joukowsky Post-doctoral Fellowship, 1985-87; Columbia University, President Fellow, 1979-80. **SPECIAL ACHIEVEMENTS:** "Increasing Sensitivity of Public College Enrollment to Changes in Tuition," Atlantic Economic Journal, Vol 21, No 1, March 1993; "Technology Transfer to China: A Path to Growth Different from Japan's," International Review of Economics & Business, forthcoming; "Test of Nonlin-

ear Consumption Functions: The Case of Korea, Taiwan, Thailand & India," with Yu Hsing, International Economic Journal, forthcoming; "Impact of Deregulation on Returns to Scale in Telecommunications," with Yu Hsing, Atlantic Econ J, forthcoming. **HOME ADDRESS:** 1503 Eisner Ave Apt 1B, Sheboygan, WI 53083-2962.

HSIEH, WINSTON WEN-SUN
Historian, writer, educator. Chinese American. **PERSONAL:** Born Mar 28, 1935, Shanghai, China; son of M Y Hsieh and H P Sheu; married Frances M Y Hsieh, Apr 2, 1965; children: Alan. **EDUCATION:** Natl Taiwan University, BA, 1957; Harvard University, MA, 1962, PhD, 1970. **CAREER:** Institute of Modern History, Academia Sinica, Taipei, Oral History Project, on 20th-century China, co-founder, interviewer, 1959; Social Science Research Council, Chinese Society Bibliography Project, assoc director & co-editor, 1966-72; University of Washington, History & Far Eastern Studies, visiting asst prof, 1969-72; University of Hong Kong, Intl Seminar on Canton Delta, director, 1973; University of Chicago, visiting research prof of modern China seminar, 1979; University of Missouri, St Louis, history, asst prof, 1972-75, assoc prof, 1975-. **ORGANIZATIONS:** Midwest Conference on Asian Affairs, pres-elect, 1992-93; Assn for Asian Studies, 1964-; Intl Conference on Rural Changes & Population Structure, cosponsored by Chinese Academy of Social Sciences & United Nation Population Fund, co-pres, 1989; American Historical Assn, 1975-; Natl Trust for Historic Preservation, 1979-; American Society for Economic & Business History, 1992-. **HONORS/AWARDS:** American Assn of University Presses, annual book award; co-editor, Modern Chinese Society: An Analytic Bibliography, vol II, Stanford University Press, 1974; Golden-Bell Publication Award Committee, annual award for book; Chien-hsia Li Po, Taipei, vol 1, 1979. **SPECIAL ACHIEVEMENTS:** Essays in: Saint Louis Post-Dispatch; Literary Page, China Times; United Daily News, Taiwan; book reviews for American Historical Review, Journal of Asian Studies, and other scholary journals; biographies on republican Chinese leaders for Oral-History Project of Academia Simica, Institute of Modern History; Chinese Historiography on 1911 Revolution; Hoover Institution, 1975; co-editor, Modern Chinese Society: An Analytic Bibliography, Mulit-lingual, vol 2, Stanford University Press, 1973; Chien-hsia Li Po, vol I, Taipei, 1979. **BIOGRAPHICAL SOURCES:** Dictionary of International Biography, vol 13, p 39, Cambridge, 1977; John Israel's "Preface," Chinese Historiography on the 1911 Revolution, Hoover Institution, 1975. **HOME ADDRESS:** 14 Washington Terrace, Saint Louis, MO 63112, (314)367-1861.

HSIEH, YOU-LO
Educator. Chinese American. **PERSONAL:** Born Feb 14, 1953, Taipei, Taiwan; daughter of Men-Che Hsieh and Tze-Hue Hsiao; married A Bruce Playle, May 11, 1980; children: Arlo J, Alma H. **EDUCATION:** Fu-Jen University, Taiwan, BS, 1975; Auburn University, MS, 1977; University of Maryland, College Park, PhD, 1981. **CAREER:** University of Maryland, CP, grad research & teaching assistant, 1977-81; University of California, Davis, assistant professor, 1981-88; associate professor, 1988-. **ORGANIZATIONS:** American Chemical Society; American Physical Society; Fiber Society; American Association of Textile Chemists & Colorists; Sigma Xi. **HONORS/AWARDS:** German Academic Exchange Services, Deutscher Akademischer Anstansh Dienst Research Award, 1987; National Science Foundation, Research Grant, 1993; Camille & Henry Dreyfuss Foundation, Education Program Grant, 1993. **SPECIAL ACHIEVEMENTS:** Coauthor, Relationship of substratum wettability measurements and initial Staphylococcus aureus adhesion on films and fabrics, Journal of Colloid and Interface Science, vol 123, no 1, p 275-86, 1988; Oxidation on mechanical and physical properties of ultrahigh modulus and molecular weight polyethylene (UHMWPE) fibers, Polymer vol 33, no 3, p 536-45, 1992; and numerous other articles. **BUSINESS ADDRESS:** Associate Professor, Division of Textiles, University of California, Davis, CA 95616-8722, (916)752-0843.

HSIN, CHEN-CHUNG
Engineer. Chinese American. **PERSONAL:** Born Jul 26, 1947, Shanghai, China; son of Charles C L Shin and Eugenia H Shin; married Anna Y Hsin, Feb 27, 1971; children: Yu-Chieh Ernest, Yu-Lun Lawrence. **EDUCATION:** National Taiwan University, BS, 1969; University of Virginia, MS, 1972; MIT, PhD, 1976. **CAREER:** Tracor, consultant, 1976; MITRE Corp, technical staff, 1976-81, group leader, 1981-83, group/site leader, 1983-88, associate department head, 1988-92, department head, 1992; ARINC Research Corp, senior director, 1992-. **ORGANIZATIONS:** AIAA, senior member, 1971-, Air Transportation Technical Committee, 1981-85. **HONORS/AWARDS:** RTCA, William Jackson Memorial Award, 1977; AIAA, Graduate Student Technical

Competition, First Place, 1972. **BUSINESS ADDRESS:** Senior Director, ATM Systems Integration, ARINC Research Corporation, 2551 Riva Road, 3-103, Annapolis, MD 21401-7465, (410)266-4465.

HSIN, LIANG YIH
Forest geneticist. Taiwanese American. **PERSONAL:** Born Feb 20, 1939, Taipei, Taiwan; son of Chien Fu Hsin and Chen Yu Hsin; married Sue Jen Hsin, Nov 2, 1971; children: Jay Sung. **EDUCATION:** National Taiwan University, BS, 1963; University of Idaho, MF, 1968, PhD, 1972. **CAREER:** National Taiwan University, Forestry Dept, teaching assistant, 1964-65; Weyerhaeuser Co, research scientist, 1972-78; USDI, Bureau of Land Management, forest geneticist, program manager, 1978-. **ORGANIZATIONS:** Western Forest Genetics Assn, 1972-; Pacific Northwest Tree Improvement Research Coop, technical committee, 1983-; Northwest Tree Improvement Coop, steering committee, 1984-; Northwest Seed Orchard Manager's Assn, 1980-; Northwest Forest Tree Seed Certifiers Assn, 1980-; Western Forestry and Range Seed Council, 1980-. **HONORS/AWARDS:** USDI Bureau of Land Management, Superior Performance, 1990, Special Achievement, 1988; Taiwan Ministry of Education, Certified Agricultural Engr, 1963; Taiwan Ministry of Agriculture, Certified Civil Service Qualification, 1963. **SPECIAL ACHIEVEMENTS:** Co-author, "Girdling: An Effective and Practical Treatment for Enhancing Seed Yields in Douglas-fir Seed Orchards," Can Jrnl Forst Research, 15, p. 505-518, 1985; thesis: Karyotype Analysis in the Genus Abies, 1972; guest speaker for the Taiwan Tree Improvement Workshop and Symposium, 1980, 1988. **HOME ADDRESS:** 306 Khyber Court SE, Salem, OR 97306-1873, (503)588-1163.

HSING, RODNEY W.
Company sales executive. Chinese American. **PERSONAL:** Born Mar 17, 1962, Washington, DC; son of Po You Hsing and Thauai Hsing. **EDUCATION:** University of Maryland, College Park, BA, economics, 1985. **CAREER:** Cir-Q-Tel Inc, purchasing agent, 1984-85, sales manager, 1985; Andersen Laboratories, southern regional manager, 1985-88; MACOM ANZAC Division, southern regional manager, 1988-90; Litton Industries Hyletronics Group, director of sales, 1990-93; Penstock Inc, field sales engineer, 1993-. **ORGANIZATIONS:** Association of Old Crows, 1986-; Chinese Culture Club 1980-85. **BUSINESS ADDRESS:** Field Sales Engineer, Penstock Inc, 60 Mall Rd, Ste 310, Burlington, MA 01803, (617)229-9100.

HSIUNG, GUEH DJEN (EDITH)
Educator, researcher. Chinese American. **PERSONAL:** Born Sep 16, 1918, Hubei, China; daughter of Chu-yun Hsiung (deceased) and Bao-yu Wu (deceased). **EDUCATION:** Ginling College, BS, 1942; Michigan State University, MS, 1948; Michigan State University, PhD, 1951. **CAREER:** Yale University, assistant professor of epidemiology, 1962-65; New York University School of Medicine, associate professor of medicine, 1965-67; Veterans Administration Hospital, chief, virology laboratory, 1967-88; Yale University School of Medicine, dept of laboratory med, associate professor, 1969-74, professor, 1974-89, professor emeritus, 1989-. **HONORS/AWARDS:** Federal Executive Association of New Haven, CT, Woman of the Year, 1975; American Society for Microbiology, Becton-Dickinson Award in Clinical Micro 1983; Hubai Medical College, Honorary Professor of Virology, 1984; China National Center for Preventive Medicine, 1985; Pan American Group for Rapid Viral Diagnosis, Burroughs Wellcome Diagnostic Award for Achievement in Viral Diagnosis, 1988; Michigan State University, Doctor of Science, honorary degree, 1989. **SPECIAL ACHIEVEMENTS:** Author, Diagnostic Virology, Yale University Press, 1st edition, 1964, 2nd-1973, 3rd-1982, 4th-1994; CRC Handbook in Clinical Laboratory Science, Section H, Virology & Rickettsiology, 1978. **BUSINESS ADDRESS:** Professor Emeritus, Yale University Medical School-VA Medical Center, 950 Compbell Avenue, Building 5, Room 248, West Haven, CT 06516, (203)937-3441.

HSU, ALBERT YUTIEN
Educator, consultant. Chinese American/Taiwanese American. **PERSONAL:** Born Sep 27, 1922, Liaoyang, Liaoning, China; son of Kwang-Yuan Hsu and Ya-Chuang Bai; married Alice Hsu, 1958; children: Teresa C C, Wesley C Y. **EDUCATION:** Yenching University, China, BA, 1947; International Marketing Institute, certificate, 1968; Chinese Culture University, Taiwan, MA, 1965; Harvard University, MPA, 1972. **CAREER:** China Productivity Center, Taiwan, trade promotion & information, director, 1961-72; CETDC, Taiwan, market intelligence, founder & director, 1970-80; Taiwanese commercial delegation to Australia, chief delegate of trade, 1980-85; Fu Jen University, Export Market Development, professor, 1985-. **ORGANIZATIONS:** Export Market-

ing Association, Taiwan, founder & director, 1976-; American Marketing Association, 1968-80; Academy of International Economics, Australia, 1981-85; Economics Association, Taiwan, 1970-; Association of Management Advancement, Taiwan, committee head, 1962-87; National Association of Chinese Library Science, Taiwan, committee head, 1961-83. **HONORS/AWARDS:** Harvard University and Ford Foundation, Scholarship for Development Study, 1971-72; Yenching University, Fu Sing Scholarship for International Trade Research, 1975-77. **SPECIAL ACHIEVEMENTS:** During service as an export marketing and trade information expert with the China Producitivity Center (Taiwan), consulted with approximately 750 export manufacturers, to improve their export management & strategies, 1961-72; as chief of trade delegation to Australia, successfully raised the value of Taiwanese exports from 13th position of total Australian imports to 6th position, following up 5 industrialized and one OPEC countries, 1980-85. **MILITARY SERVICE:** Combined Service Force, Taiwan, lt col, 1951-54, Distinguished Service Award in Foreign Liaison, Defense Department, 1953. **BIOGRAPHICAL SOURCES:** Model of International Trade Information Networks Designed for Developing Countries, An Effective Approach for Export Expansion, 120 p, 1973; Policy Tools for Solving Taiwanese Power Shortage Problems, 100 p, 1975. **HOME ADDRESS:** 213 Woodbridge Circle, San Mateo, CA 94403.

HSU, CATHY H. C.
Educator. Taiwanese American/Chinese American. **PERSONAL:** Born Jun 1, 1962, Taipei, Taiwan; daughter of Yue-Wu Shu and Chun-Yun Yen; married Thomas S. C. Sun, Mar 12, 1988. **EDUCATION:** Fu-Jen University, Taiwan, BS, 1984; Iowa State University, MS, 1986, PhD, 1989. **CAREER:** McDonald's Corporation, management trainee, 1984; Memorial Union, Iowa State University, food service assistant, 1985-87; Dept of Residence Food Service, assistant manager, 1987-89; Dept of Hotel, Restaurant, and Institution Management, Iowa State University, assistant professor, 1989-. **ORGANIZATIONS:** Council on Hotel, Restaurant, and Institutional Education, 1991-, Committee on Computer Users Special Interest Section, 1991-, Committee on Quality and Ethics, 1991-; Midwest Assn of Hospitality Educators, newsletter editor, 1992-; Hospitality Sales and Marketing Assn Intl, 1991-; The Society of Travel and Tourism Educators, 1991-; Kappa Omicron Nu National Home Economics Honor Society, 1987-; Phi Kappa Phi, 1989-. **HONORS/AWARDS:** IBM Corp, Coursework Development, 1993. **SPECIAL ACHIEVEMENTS:** "Restaurant Managers' Learning Styles and Their Implications," Intl Journal of Hospitality Management, 1991; "Training and Development Needs of University Residence Hall Food Service Manager," NACUFS Journal, 1990-91; "Competencies Needed and Demonstrated by Hospitality Management Graduates: Perceptions of Employers," NACUFS Jouranal, 1992; "Alumni Perspectives of an Undergraduate Hospitality Curriculm," Hospitality and Tourism Educator, 1993. **BUSINESS ADDRESS:** Asst Prof, Dept of Hotel Restaurant & Institution Management, Iowa State University, 11 Mackay Hall, Ames, IA 50011, (515)294-9945.

HSU, CHARLES FU-JEN
Research chemist. Chinese American. **PERSONAL:** Born May 9, 1920, Kiang-Tu, Kiang-Su, China; married Irene W Hsu, Jan 15, 1947; children: Phyllis H Shaw, Andrew A, Kenneth K, Rosa Hsu Huie. **EDUCATION:** National Chung Cheng University, BS, 1946; DePaul University, MS, 1962; University of Illinois, PhD, 1964. **CAREER:** N-E Cement Plant, assistant chemical engineer, 1946-48; Taiwan Ga-yi Industrial School, Taiwan, head teacher, 1948-52; National Chung-Hsin University, Taichung, associate professor, 1952-59; Ivy Cancer Research Foundation, research associate, 1961-63; GD Searle & Co, research chemist, 1964-85. **HONORS/AWARDS:** Chicago Metro Citizenship Council, Outstanding New Citizen Award, 1969; Taiwan Government Colleges, Best Chemistry Professor Award, 1955; Taiwan Government, NIT Awardee, 1958. **SPECIAL ACHIEVEMENTS:** Publications & patents in microbiology transformation of prostaglandins & steroids for anti-hypertension & anti-peptic ulcer agents; pre-control human embryo's sex before fetal formation. **HOME ADDRESS:** 4953 Elm St, Skokie, IL 60077, (708)676-3584.

HSU, CHARLES JUI-CHENG
Manufacturing company executive. Taiwanese American. **PERSONAL:** Born Mar 17, 1930, Taipei, Taiwan; son of Neng-Tsai Hsu & Kao Yun Hsu. **EDUCATION:** Taiwan Provincial College of Law and Commerce, BA, 1958; Baylor University, MA, 1965. **CAREER:** Charles Michelson Inc, export manager, 1965-67; Retawmatic Corporation, president, 1967-. **ORGANIZATIONS:** Taiwan Mchts Association; International Biographical Association,

fellow. **HONORS/AWARDS:** US Patent #5146778, oil and/or water detection apparatus, 1992; US Patent 890485, mechanism which reacts to the presence of oil and/or water, 1990; US Patent #448027, US Patent #4419236; US Patents #4160465, 3951812, 3745659, 3562731, 3280549 & other foreign patents; 3 US patents pending. **BUSINESS ADDRESS:** President, Retawmatic Corporation, 521 Fifty Ave, Box 460 Grand Central Station, New York, NY 10175, (212)687-0890.

HSU, CHEN-CHI

Educator. Chinese American. **PERSONAL:** Born Sep 20, 1935, Pen-Fuh, Taiwan; married Pi-Yung Wang Hsu, Jun 15, 1963; children: Sandra, Michael, Daniel. **EDUCATION:** National Taiwan University, BS, 1957; University of Michigan, MS, 1961, PhD, 1965. **CAREER:** South Dakota State University, assistant professor of mechnical engineering, 1966-68; Colorado State University, assistant professor of mechanical engineering, 1971-73; University of Michigan, visiting assistant professor of applied mechanics, 1973-75; Amoco Production Co, Offshore Engineering, senior research engineer, 1975-78; University of Florida, associate professor, graduate coordinator, 1978-81, professor of aerospace engineering, mechanics and engineering science, 1981-. **HONORS/AWARDS:** National Research Council, Office of Aerospace Research, Postdoctoral Resident Research Associateship at Wright-Patterson Air Force Base, 1968-70. **SPECIAL ACHIEVEMENTS:** Research on boundary-layer flows, transonic turbulent flow simulation, vortical flow simulation, and high velocity impact dynamics simulation. **MILITARY SERVICE:** Chinese Air Force, reserved officer, second lieutenant, 1957-59. **BUSINESS ADDRESS:** Professor, University of Florida, 231 Aerospace Building, Gainesville, FL 32611-6250, (904)392-9823.

HSU, CHIEH-SU

Educator. Chinese American. **PERSONAL:** Born May 27, 1922, Suzhou, Jiangsu, China; son of Chung-Yu Hsu & Yong-Feng Wu; married Helen Yung-Feng Tse, Mar 28, 1953; children: Raymond Hwa-Chi, Katherine Hwa-Ling. **EDUCATION:** National Institute of Technology, Chungking, China, graduate, 1945; Stanford University, MS, 1948, PhD, 1950. **CAREER:** Shanghai Naval Dockyard and Engineering Works, engineer, 1946-47; Stanford University, research assistant, 1948-51; IBM Corp, engineer, 1951-55; University of Toledo, Ohio, associate professor, 1955-58; University of California, Berkeley, associate professor, 1958-64, chairman, Division of Applied Mechanics, 1969-70, professor, 1964-. **ORGANIZATIONS:** Sigma Xi, 1948-; American Institute of Aeronautics and Astronautics, 1949-; American Society of Mechanical Engineers, 1965-; Western Committee of Applied Mechanics, 1966-71; Western Applied Mechanics Conference, secretary of the committee, 1969-70, chairman of the committee, 1970-71, general chairman, 1971; Society of Industrial and Applied Mathematics, 1967-90; American Academy of Mechanics, 1977-, fellow, 1980-. **HONORS/AWARDS:** John Simon Guggenheim Fellowship, 1964-65; University of California, Berkeley, Miller Research Professorship, 1973-74; Fellow of the American Society of Mechanical Engineers, 1980-; Fellow of the American Academy of Mechanics, 1980-; American Society of Mechanical Engineers Centennial Award, 1980; Alexander von Humboldt Senior US Scientist Award, 1986; National Academy of Engineering, USA, elected member, 1988; Academia Sinica, Republic of China, elected member, 1990. **SPECIAL ACHIEVEMENTS:** Chief-editorship, technical editor, Journal of Applied Mechanics, 1976-82; associate editor, 9 scholarly journals; author, Cell-To-Cell Mappping, Springer Verlag, 1987; contributing author to 2 books; 98 technical papers. **BUSINESS ADDRESS:** Professor, Dept of Mechanical Engineering, University of California, Berkeley, Berkeley, CA 94720, (510)642-3087.

HSU, DONALD K.

Educational administrator. Chinese American. **PERSONAL:** Born Apr 17, 1947, Shanghai, China; son of Kuo Chung Hsu and Ching Hwa Hsu (deceased); married Salome Hsu, Mar 18, 1972; children: Douglas. **EDUCATION:** National Cheng Kung University, Taiwan, BS, 1969; Fordham University, New York City, PhD, 1975. **CAREER:** TCK Industries, vice president, business operations, 1977-80; New Jersey Institute of Technology, special lecturer, 1977-78; St Peter's College, assistant professor, 1978-83; Felician College, coordinator of computer science education, 1983-88; Dun & Bradstreet, technical instructor, 1988; Otsubo International, marketing consultant, 1989-, Dominican College, division business administration, director, 1988-. **ORGANIZATIONS:** Chinese American Scholars Association, vice president of special projects, 1992-93; American Association University Professors, 1979-; Association Computing Machinery, 1981-; Institute of Electrical Electronics Engineers, 1985-; National Association of Realtors, 1984-; New York Academy of Science, 1983-; United Societies of Engineering & Science of New Jersey, president, 1991-93; World League Freedom & Democracy, NY Chapter, president, 1992-93. **HONORS/AWARDS:** State of New Jersey, Department of Higher Education, Felician College, 4 computer grants, 1985-88; National Science Foundations, St Peter's College, CAUSE grant in computer assisted institutions, 1982-83, post doctoral fellowship, 1976; National Aeronautics Space Administrators, postdoctoral fellowship, 1975. **SPECIAL ACHIEVEMENTS:** "Micro-Mainframe Link," Network Applications, Meckler Publishing, pp 120-124, Dec 1991; "Teaching Artificial Intelligence," Journal Computing Small Colleges, vol 5, no 2, p 30-33, 1989; "Computer and the Chinese," For World Peace, Freedom & Justice, Adams Press, 2nd edition, April 1988; two books, 26 papers, 145 invited seminars in laser, computer, business, 1970-. **BIOGRAPHICAL SOURCES:** Member activity of "Donald K Hsu," CASA Newsletter, vol 4, no 1, Sept 1992. **BUSINESS ADDRESS:** Director, Division of Business Administration, Dominican College, Western Hwy, Casey Hall, Orangeburg, NY 10962-1299, (914)359-7800.

HSU, EVELYN

Editor. Hong Kong American. **PERSONAL:** Born 1953?, Hong Kong; married; children: two. **EDUCATION:** University of California, Berkeley. **CAREER:** San Francisco Chronicle, city hall beat writer, 1979-86; Washington Post, metropolitan staff member, 1986-92, Weekly Section, writer, editor, 1992-. **ORGANIZATIONS:** Asian American Journalists Association, president, 1992-. **BUSINESS ADDRESS:** Editor, Local Weekly Section, Washington Post, 1150 15th St NW, Washington, DC 20071-0001, (202)334-6000.*

HSU, FRANK H.

Educator. Chinese American. **PERSONAL:** Born Dec 26, 1935, Nanjing, China; son of Tseng-Pen and Cheng-Ing Hsu; married Paula W Hsu, Sep 15, 1965; children: Gene J. **EDUCATION:** National Taiwan University, BS, physics, 1959; Columbia University, MS, physics, 1964, PhD, physics, 1967. **CAREER:** Columbia University, teaching asst, 1961-64, Pegram Nuclear Physics Labs, graduate research assistant, 1964-67, post doctoral research scientist, 1967-69; Georgia State University, asst professor, 1969-72, associate professor, 1972-82; National Taiwan University, visiting professor, 1977-78; Georgia State University, professor, 1982-. **ORGANIZATIONS:** American Physical Society; American Physical Society, Southeastern Section; American Assn of Physics Teachers; Materials Research Society; Sigma Pi Sigma; Assn of Chinese Scholars in Southeastern US; Natl Academy of Sciences, intl consultant; Intl Centre for Theoretical Physics, Trieste, Italy, advisor; Chinese Community Center, Atlanta, president, 1981-91, Chinese School, principal, 1993. **HONORS/AWARDS:** Grants awarded by Research Corp, Natl Science Foundation, Natl Academy of Sciences, Air Force Astronautics Lab, GSU Research Fund. **SPECIAL ACHIEVEMENTS:** "Positron Annihilation Studies of Age-Induced Changes in Animal Lenses," Physics Stat Sol, vol A, 102, p 571, 1987, Werningerode, G D R, vol 1, part 2, SL 22, 1987; "Positron Annihilation Studies of Electronic Effect of Derivation of Porphin," Positron Annihilation Studies of Fluids, S C Sharma, World Scientific Publishing Co Pte Ltd, Singapore, p 150-55, 1988; "Positron Annihilation Lifetime Studies of Filled Polymers," Positron and Positronium Chemistry, Y C Jean, World Scientific Publishing Co Pte Ltd, Singapore, p 47-53, 1990. **BUSINESS ADDRESS:** Professor, Dept of Physics and Astronomy, Georgia State University, Atlanta, GA 30303, (404)651-3221.

HSU, GEORGE CHI-YUNG

Chemical company executive. Taiwanese American. **PERSONAL:** Born Feb 24, 1945, Chang-Hwa, Taiwan; son of Chin-Ann Hsu and Doh-Yeh Hsu; married Mercedes Hsu, Apr 11, 1970; children: Joyce C, Kenneth T. **EDUCATION:** Tohoku University, Sendai, Japan, BSChE, 1970; USC, Los Angeles, MSChE, 1973. **CAREER:** United Foam Corp, technical mgr, 1978-79; Polymer Chemicals Corp, vice pres, 1980-81; Universal Polymer Corp of California, president, CEO, 1982-; Aster Capital Corp, president, 1986-. **BUSINESS ADDRESS:** President, Universal Polymer Corporation of California, 14989 S Sierra Bonita Lane, Chino, CA 91710, (909)597-7716.

HSU, HSIU-SHENG

Educator. Chinese American. **PERSONAL:** Born Oct 26, 1931, Guangzhou, China; son of Dr & Mrs Kang-liang Hsu (deceased); married Barbara Chew, 1958; children: 4. **EDUCATION:** McGill University, Canada, BSc, 1955; University of Pennsylvania, MS, 1956, PhD, 1959, postdoctoral, 1959-62; Johns Hopkins Medical School, postdoctoral, 1963-64. **CAREER:** Sir William Dunn School of Pathology, University of Oxford, visiting fellow, 1973; Medical College of Virginia, instructor, 1964-65, assistant professor, 1965-69, associate professor, 1969-. **ORGANIZATIONS:** American Society for Microbiology; New York Academy of Science; Reticuloendothelial Society; Sigma Xi. **HONORS/AWARDS:** American Thoracic Society, research grant, 1965-68; National Institute of Allergy & Infectious Diseases, research grants, 1965-73, 1984-90. **SPECIAL ACHIEVEMENTS:** "Pathogenesis and Immunity in Marine Salmonellosis," 1989; "Pathogenesis of Typhoid Fever: An Experimental Model," 1992; "Is Salmonella an Intracellular Pathogen?," 1993. **BUSINESS ADDRESS:** Associate Professor, Dept of Microbiology & Immunology, Medical College of Virginia, VCU, Richmond, VA 23298-0678, (804)786-9728.

HSU, IMMANUEL C. Y.
Educator. Chinese American. **PERSONAL:** Born May 6, 1923, Shanghai, China; son of Thomas Hsu & Mary Loh; married Dolores Menstell Hsu, Apr 14, 1962; children: Vadim M. **EDUCATION:** Yenching University, BA, 1946; University of Minnesota, MA, 1950; Harvard University, PhD, 1954. **CAREER:** Fletcher School of Law and Diplomacy, lecturer, 1953; University of California, Berkeley, visiting assistant professor of history, 1958-59; Harvard University, postdoctoral research fellow, 1955-58, Harvard University, summer school, visiting associate professor, 1961, 1964, visiting professor, 1968, 1975; Hamburg University, visiting professor, 1973; University of Leningrad, visiting professor, 1990-91; Stockholm University, 1990; University of California, Santa Barbara, assistant professor, 1959-60, associate professor, 1960-65, professor, 1965-. **HONORS/AWARDS:** Harvard-Yenching Fellowship, 1950-54; Guggenheim Fellowship, 1962-63; University of California, Santa Barbara, Faculty Research Lecturer, 1971; Commonwealth Literary Prize of California, 1971; Fulbright Award, 1973; National Academy of Sciences, Distinguished Scholar to China, 1983. **SPECIAL ACHIEVEMENTS:** The Rise of Modern China, Oxford, 1990; China Without Mao: The Search for a New Order, Oxford, 1990; The Ili Crisis: A Study of Sino-Russian Diplomacy, 1871-1881, Oxford, 1965; numerous others. **BUSINESS ADDRESS:** Professor, History Dept, University of California, Santa Barbara, Santa Barbara, CA 93106.

HSU, JOHN TSENG-HSIU
Educator, musician. Chinese American. **PERSONAL:** Born Apr 21, 1931, Swatow, Kwangtung, China; son of Benjamin and Lucy Zi Hsu; married Martha Russell, Jul 31, 1968. **EDUCATION:** New England Conservatory of Music, BMus, 1953, MMus, 1955. **CAREER:** Cornell University, instructor of music, 1955-58, assistant professor of music, 1958-62, associate professor of music, 1962-67, Department of Music, chairman, 1966-71, professor of music, 1967-76, Old Dominion Foundation prof of humanities and music, 1976-. **HONORS/AWARDS:** Ramapo College of New Jersey, Honorary Doctor of Arts, 1986; New England Conservatory of Music, Doctor of Music, 1971. **SPECIAL ACHIEVEMENTS:** Author, A Handbook of French Baroque Viola Technique, 1981; editor, "Instrumental Works of Marin Marais," 1980-; music director and conductor, Apollo Ensemble, 1990-; player of viola da gamba, baryton and cello, concertized throughout USA and Europe, 1955-; artistic director, Aston Magua Foundation for Music and the Humanities, 1984-90. **HOME ADDRESS:** 601 Highland Road, Ithaca, NY 14850, (607)257-7622.

HSU, JOHN Y.
Educator. Chinese American. **PERSONAL:** Born Mar 17, 1938, Nanking, China; married Sheryl, Dec 18, 1965; children: Mary, David. **EDUCATION:** Natl Taiwan University, BSEE, 1959; University of California, Berkeley, MSEE, 1964, PhD, 1969. **CAREER:** Consultant: Federal Electric/ITT, 1971-79; Institute for Information Industry in Taiwan, 1980; Control Data Corp, 1981; IBM, 1987-89; California Polytech State University, San Luis Obispo, professor, computer sci, 1970-. **ORGANIZATIONS:** IEEE; Assn Comput Mach.

HSU, JONG-PING
Scientist, educator. Taiwanese American. **PERSONAL:** Born Feb 17, 1939, Potz, Taiwan; son of Mau-Yuan Hsu and Yu-Tz Huang; married Bonnie (Mei-chu) Hsu, Aug 17, 1968; children: Leonardo, Leslie. **EDUCATION:** National Taiwan University, bachelors, 1962; National Tsing-Hua University, masters, 1965; University of Rochester, PhD, 1969. **CAREER:** National Research Council, sr research assoc, 1978; MIT, visiting scientist, 1985; National Taiwan University, visiting prof, 1993; University of Massachusetts-Dartmouth, asst prof, 1978-83, assoc prof, 1983-87, professor, 1987-. **SPECIAL ACHIEVEMENTS:** Author: "Four-Dimensional Symmetry from a Broad Viewpoint," vols I through XI, Nuovo Cimento, 74B, 67, 1983; 78B, 85 1983; 80B, 183, 1984; 80B, 201, 1984; 81B, 153, 1984; 88B, 140, 1985; 88B, 156, 1985; 89B,

14, 1985; 89B, 30, 1985; 89B, 209, 1985; 91B, 100, 1986; Nature, editorial, 303, p 129, May 12, 1983. **BUSINESS ADDRESS:** Professor, Dept of Physics, University of Massachusetts, Dartmouth, Old Westport Rd, North Dartmouth, MA 02747-2300, (508)999-8363.

HSU, JONG-PYNG
Environmental chemistry administrator. Taiwanese American. **PERSONAL:** Born May 21, 1951, Pington, Taiwan; son of Dao Ming Hsu and Chii-Fen Ho Hsu; married Ying-Ju Hsu, Apr 25, 1976; children: E-Kai, J-Kai, Wha-Yin. **EDUCATION:** Fu-Jen University, Taipei, Taiwan, BS, 1973; Washington University, PhD, 1981. **CAREER:** Sverdup Technology Inc, organic analyst, 1981-83; NUS Corp, organic lab, manager, 1983-85; Southwest Research Institute, environmental chemistry, director, 1985-. **SPECIAL ACHIEVEMENTS:** Author (with others): "Analytical Methods for Detection of Nonoccupational Exposure to Pesticides," Journal of Chromatographic Science, vol 26, No 4, p 181-189, 1988; "Analytical Method for Determination of Trace Organics in Gas Samples Collected by Canister," Journal of Chromatographic Science, vol 29, No 2, p 83-88, 1991; "Fast Turnaround Multiresidue Screen for Pesticides in Produce," Journal of the Assn of Analytical Chemistry, vol 74, No 5, p 886-892, 1991. **HOME ADDRESS:** 9210 Chaddsford, San Antonio, TX 78250. **BUSINESS PHONE:** (210)522-2228.

HSU, KENNETH HSUEHCHIA
Engineer. Taiwanese American. **PERSONAL:** Born Aug 21, 1950, Taipei, Taiwan; married Carole Y; children: Irene, Stephen. **EDUCATION:** Kansas State University, BS, 1972, MS, 1974, PhD, 1978. **CAREER:** Durkee Foods Co, senior research chemist; Iowa State University, associate professor, assistant professor; Nabisco, principal engineer, supv engineer, currently. **ORGANIZATIONS:** AACC; AIChE, IFT. **BUSINESS ADDRESS:** Principal Engineer, Nabisco Foods Group, 200 DeForest Ave, East Hanover, NJ 07936, (201)503-3784.

HSU, KONRAD CHANG
Educator, scientist. Chinese American. **PERSONAL:** Born Aug 28, 1901, Taichow, Kiangsu, China; son of George C & Wu Yu Hsu; married Kit Yuk Ng, Aug 17, 1984. **EDUCATION:** St John's University, Shanghai, China, BS, 1921; Columbia University, MA, 1923, PhD, 1924. **CAREER:** Great China University, Shanghai, China, professor, 1924-26; Chinese Government, military service, 1926-28; Chan Hwa & Co, China, general manager, 1928-41, New York, president, 1941-46; Sino-Hawaii Corp, New York, vice president, 1946-54; Columbia University, assistant professor, associate professor, professor, professor emeritus, 1954-. **ORGANIZATIONS:** Free & Accepted Masons, post master, 1957-58; Royal Arch Masons, high priest, 1956-57; Adorium Council, master, 1965-; Knight Templar, past commander, 1958-; Masonic Veterans, past commander, 1966-; Knight York Cross of Honor, past prior, 1971-; American Institute of Immunologist, life member; Federation of American Society of Experimental Biologist, life member. **HONORS/AWARDS:** National Institute of Health, Bethesda, MD, Research in kidney disease, 1960-70. **MILITARY SERVICE:** Northwest Frontier Defense, China, colonel 28. **BIOGRAPHICAL SOURCES:** About 150 papers published in US & European immunological journals & text books. **HOME ADDRESS:** 41-40 Union St, Apt 12-R, Flushing, NY 11355, (718)461-6889.

HSU, LAURA LING
Educational administrator. Chinese American. **PERSONAL:** Born Aug 22, 1939, Kwei-yan, Kwei-chow, China; daughter of Shao-Wen Ling and Jeanette Chiang Ling; married Thomas T C Hsu, Jul 20, 1963; children: Lynne Ling, Mia Ming Hsu Burton. **EDUCATION:** Acadia University, Canada, BSc (cum laude), 1961; Cornell University, MS, 1964; University of Miami, PhD, 1974. **CAREER:** Evanston Hospital, Parasitology & Mycology Labs, supervisor, 1964-67; St Francis School of Nursing, instructor, 1967-68; Northwestern University, medical technology, lecturer, 167; University of Miami, research asst professor, 1974-79; Natl Taiwan University, visiting assoc professor, 1978-79; Rice University, instructor of biology, 1980-84, director of programs, 1984-, asst dean, 1991-. **ORGANIZATIONS:** American Soc of Clinical Pathologists, Registrant M(ASCP), 1964-; Assn of Community Service & Continuing Education, 1984-; Natl University Continuing Education Assn, 1986-; Assn of Women in Science, USA, 1980-; Intl Soc of the Study of the Origin of Life, 1974-; Sigma Xi, 1974-; Chinese Professional Club, Scholarship Committee, 1988; Chinese Community Ctr, Houston, Advisor Bd, 1990. **HONORS/AWARDS:** Acadian University, Clara Marshall Scholar, 1961; Rice University, Teaching Development Award, 1982; City of Houston, Mayor's Transition Committee on Education, 1993, Mayoral Asian Appointee,

1993. **SPECIAL ACHIEVEMENTS:** First Asian American woman appointed into Dean's ranking at Rice University; publications: chapter in book, Molecular Evolution-Pre & Biological, 1972; chapter in book, Molecular Evolution & Protobiology, 1984; chapter in volume, Intl Review of Cytology, 1988; media appearances include: Chinese TV Houston, Mrs Shen's Hour: "How to Select a College," Oct 30, 1990; Channel 26 Fox News, with Fran Fawcette on Cultural Diversity in Houston, Feb 16, 1993; fluent in English and 4 Chinese dialects; knowledgeable in French and Thai. **BIOGRAPHICAL SOURCES:** World Journal, Weekly (Chinese Daily News, N American edition), April 11, 1993, p 9. **BUSINESS ADDRESS:** Asst Dean, School of Continuing Studies, Rice University, PO Box 1892, Houston, TX 77251, (713)520-6022.

HSU, LIANG-CHI
Educator. Taiwanese American/Chinese American. **PERSONAL:** Born Sep 1, 1931, Yunlin, Taiwan; son of Hai-Hsi Hsu and Tung Lin Hsu; married Shu-Huei Tsai Hsu, Apr 24, 1960; children: Celia Bishop, Felix, Grace Woo, Rick. **EDUCATION:** National Taiwan University, BS (with honors), geology, 1956, MS, geology, 1961; University of California, Los Angeles, PhD, geology, 1966. **CAREER:** National Taiwan University, instructor, 1961-63; University of California, Los Angeles, teaching & research assistant, 1963-66; Pennsylvania State University, research associate, 1966-68; University of Nevada, Reno, assistant professor, mineralogist, 1969-72, associate professor, mineralogist, 1972-78, professor, mineralogist, 1978-. **ORGANIZATIONS:** Geological Society of America, fellow, 1971-; Mineralogical Society of America, fellow, 1980-; American Geophysical Union, 1962-; Geochemcial Society, 1970-; Society of Economic Geologists, 1974-; International Association of Geochemistry and Cosmochemistry, 1978-; Mineralogical Association of Canada, 1976-. **HONORS/AWARDS:** Ministry of Economic Affairs, fellowship, 1954-56; Li Foundation, fellowship, 1958-60. **SPECIAL ACHIEVEMENTS:** Published scores of scientific papers in professional journal; edited special publication in professional journal; contributed to sections of a book; promoted understanding in petrogenesis and ore genesis; language proficiency in Chinese, Japanese, German. **BUSINESS ADDRESS:** Professor, Dept of Geological Sciences & Nevada Bureau of Mines/Geology, University of Nevada, Reno, NV 89557, (702)784-6691.

HSU, MARGARETHA
Educator. Chinese American. **PERSONAL:** Born in Taipei, Taiwan; married Tai Chi Yu; children: Kevin Yu, Rita Yu. **EDUCATION:** Fu-Jen Catholic University, BA, 1968; Oakland University, MA, 1971; VPI & SU, PhD, 1978. **CAREER:** Shippensburg University, professor, 1979-. **ORGANIZATIONS:** American Statistical Association, 1979-. **HONORS/AWARDS:** Shippensburg University, Business Scholar, 1991. **SPECIAL ACHIEVEMENTS:** Several publications and presenting papers in the area of applied statistics at the conferences of professional organizations. **BUSINESS ADDRESS:** Professor, FAMSIS Dept, Shippensburg University, Shippensburg, PA 17257, (717)532-1422.

HSU, MEI-LING
Educator. Chinese American. **PERSONAL:** Born 1932, Tientsin, Tianjin, Taiwan; daughter of H C Hsu. **EDUCATION:** National Normal University, Taiwan, BA, 1954; Southern Illinois University, MA, 1956; University of Wisconsin, Madison, MA, 1959, PhD, 1966. **CAREER:** National Taiwan University, visiting professor, 1969; University of Washington, visiting professor, 1973; Chinese University of Hong Kong, visiting professor, 1978; University of Hawaii, visiting professor, 1978; University of Minnesota, Cartographic Research Lab, director, 1962-65, East Asian Studies, chair, 1974-76, 1979-80, China Center, director, 1980-85, professor, 1972-. **ORGANIZATIONS:** Assn of American Geographers, National Nominating Committee, annual meeting chairs, organizers; Assn for Asian Studies, annual meeting organizers, chairs; American Cartographic Assn, chair of steering committee, nominating committee, annual meeting chairs, organizers. **HONORS/AWARDS:** National Science Foundation, Research Grant, 1984-86, 1990-93; National Academy of Sciences, CSCPRC Fellowship, American Scholar, 1992-93. **SPECIAL ACHIEVEMENTS:** First researcher using quantitative methods to analyze Map Error, wrote PhD dissertation and published The Fidelity of Isopleth Maps, University of Minnesota Press; published first medium scale map on Population of Taiwan, with extensive notes on growth and urbanization; several articles on Chinese history of Cartography in Imago Mund, and the Annals of the Association of American Geographers; articles on demographic, economic and urban development of the People's Republic of China. **BUSINESS AD-** DRESS: Professor, Dept of Geography, University of Minnesota, 414 Social Science Bldg, 267 19th Ave S, Minneapolis, MN 55455-0499, (612)625-6080.

HSU, MERLIN
Architect. Taiwanese American. **PERSONAL:** Born Mar 11, 1954, Taipei, Taiwan; son of In-Quen Hsu and Wao-Show Yang Hsu; married Sandra Lo, Apr 16, 1988; children: Winston. **EDUCATION:** Chung Yuan College, Taiwan, BArch, 1977; Harvard Graduate School of Design, MArch, 1981. **CAREER:** Skidmore, Owings, & Merrill, designer, 1981-83; The Neenan Co, designer, 1983-84; A Epstein and Sons, Inc, assistant project manager, 1985; Kohn Pedersen Fox Conway, architect, 1986-87; The RBA Group, architect, 1987-88; Haines Lundberg Waehler, project architect, 1988-90; The Architectural Group, project manager, 1990-92; architect, currently. **ORGANIZATIONS:** American Institute of Architects, New Jersey Central Chapter, 1986. **SPECIAL ACHIEVEMENTS:** NCARB Certification. **MILITARY SERVICE:** Chinese Military Police, cpl, 1977-79; MP Honorary Medal, 1979. **HOME ADDRESS:** 424 W County Dr, Branchburg, NJ 08876. **BUSINESS PHONE:** (908)722-9687.

HSU, NAI-CHAO
Mathematician, educator. Taiwanese American. **PERSONAL:** Born Nov 27, 1927, Changhua, Taiwan; son of Chia-chung Hsu & Ti-yun Hsu; married Yu-chiao Hsu, Oct 28, 1958; children: Stephen, Susan, Saunders. **EDUCATION:** National Taiwan University, BSc, 1950; Washington University, PhD, 1960. **CAREER:** International Business Machines, staff member, 1960-63; State University of New York, professor, 1963-66; Eastern Illinois University, professor, 1966-. **HOME ADDRESS:** 1030 Colony Ln, Charleston, IL 61920, (217)345-4997.

HSU, PAUL (PO-SIU)
Educator. Taiwanese American. **PERSONAL:** Born Oct 1, 1949, Taipei, Taiwan; son of Chi-Wan Hsu & Pau-chu Wang; married Betsy Boehm, Jun 27, 1982; children: Jenny T, Brook H. **EDUCATION:** National Taiwan University, BS, 1972; Cornell University, MLA, 1982; University of Maine, 1989-. **CAREER:** Kingswood Landscape Consultants, principal, 1982-85; Washington State University, assistant professor, 1984-85; Computer Graphic Design, general manager, 1985-88; University of Idaho, assistant professor, 1988-89; Oklahoma State University, assistant professor, 1990-. **ORGANIZATIONS:** American Society of Landscape Architects, 1990-; Sigma Xi, 1991-; International Society of Certified Electronic Technican, 1985-; Council of Education in Landscape Architecture, 1990-; Urban Regional Information System Association, 1990-. **HONORS/AWARDS:** ASLA & ALCA Student Club, OSU Chapter, Outstanding Teacher Award, 1992, 1993; Okalahoma Fall Arts Institute, scholarship, 1992, 1993; Alpha Beta Kappa Honor Society, Devotion to Science Honor, 1985; Coop Extension, NY, Outstanding Contribution in Community Development, 1982; National Student Design Competition by NSA, instructor, Third Place, 1992, ASLA, Special Commendation, 1992. **SPECIAL ACHIEVEMENTS:** Book: An Introduction to Taiwan Landscape, Harvest Association, 1980. **BUSINESS ADDRESS:** Assistant Professor, Oklahoma State University, Hort & LA, 360 Ag Hall, Stillwater, OK 74078-0511, (405)744-5421.

HSU, PING
Educator. Chinese American. **PERSONAL:** Born Nov 18, 1957, Taiwan; son of Shu-Sen Hsu and Pei-Fan Chang; married Naiyi Hsueh, May 21, 1981; children: Justin, Esther, Emily. **EDUCATION:** Southern Methodist University, MS, 1979; University of California, Berkeley, PhD, 1988. **CAREER:** University of Illinois, Urbana-Champaign, assistant professor, 1989-90; San Jose State University, associate professor, 1990-. **ORGANIZATIONS:** IEEE Santa Clara Valley Section, Control System Society Chapter, secretary, 1992-. **HONORS/AWARDS:** National Science Foundation, Research Initiation Award, 1989. **SPECIAL ACHIEVEMENTS:** Co-author: "Adaptive Control of Mechanical Manipulators," Intl Journal of Robotics Research, 6:2, p3-15, 1987; "Grasping & Manipulation of an Object by a Multifingered Robot Hand," Intl Journal of Robotics Research, July 1989; "On the Stability of Second-Order Multidimensional Linear Time-Varying Systems," AIAA Journal of Guidance, Control & Dynamics, p1040-1045, Sep 1991; "Dynamic Control of Sliding by Robot Hands for Regrasping," IEEE Transactions on Robotics & Automation, 8:1, p42-51, Feb 1992; author: "Dynamics & Control Design Project Offers Taste of Real World," IEEE Control Systems Mag, 12:3, p31-38, Jun 1992. **BUSINESS ADDRESS:** Professor, Electrical Engineering Dept, San Jose State University, One Washington Square, San Jose, CA 95192, (408)924-3838.

HSU, ROBERT YING

Educator. Chinese American. **PERSONAL:** Born Oct 10, 1926, Beijing, China; son of Ching-Tze & Ta-feng Wang Hsu; married Gretchen C Hsu, Apr 7, 1962; children: David Robert, Hanson Kelvin. **EDUCATION:** University of Wisconsin, PhD, 1961. **CAREER:** Armour Pharmaceutical Co, scientist, 1961-62; Rutgers, The State University, assistant professor, 1966-68; State University of New York Health Science Center, Syracuse, assistant professor, 1968-70, associate professor, 1970-77, professor, 1977-. **ORGANIZATIONS:** NIH Physiological Chemistry Study Section; NSF Adhoc committee for reviewing grants. **HONORS/AWARDS:** NIH, research grant for the last 26 years; British Royal Society, Oxford University, visiting scholar, 1982; British Science Council, Bristol University, visiting professor, 1990. **SPECIAL ACHIEVEMENTS:** Reviewer for Journal of Biological Chemistry, Biochemistry, Biochemical et Biophysical Acta, and other journals; published 45 original articles in journals including a number of book chapters. **HOME ADDRESS:** 3225 Hidden Creek Ave, Thousand Oaks, CA 91360, (805)493-8311. **BUSINESS ADDRESS:** Professor, Dept of Biochemistry and Molecular Biology, State University of New York Health Science Center, Syracuse, 776 Irving Ave, Weiskotten Hall, Rm 4327B, Syracuse, NY 13210, (315)464-8713.

HSU, SAMUEL

Educator. Chinese American. **PERSONAL:** Born Jun 20, 1947, Shanghai, China; son of John and Dorothy Hsu. **EDUCATION:** Philadelphia College of Bible, BS, Bible, BMus, 1969; University of California, Santa Barbara, PhD, 1972; The Juilliard School, 1972-75. **CAREER:** Westmont College, instructor in piano, 1971-72; Philadelphia College of Bible, professor of music, 1972-; CSEHY Summer School of Music, chairman of piano department, 1974-. **ORGANIZATIONS:** Philadelphia Music Teachers Association, board of directors, 1976-; CSEHY Summer School of Music, board of directors, 1982-. **HOME ADDRESS:** PO Box 2340, Philadelphia, PA 19103. **BUSINESS ADDRESS:** Professor of Music, Philadelphia College of Bible, 200 Manor Ave, Langhorne, PA 19047, (215)752-5800.

HSU, SHAW LING

Educator. Chinese American. **PERSONAL:** Born Jul 14, 1948, Shanghai, China; married Lilian, Aug 15, 1970; children: David, Jennifer. **EDUCATION:** Rutgers University, BS, 1970; University of Michigan, MS, 1972, PhD, 1975. **CAREER:** University of Massachusetts, materials lab, director, 1984-91; Allied Signal, research scientist, 1976-78; University of Freiburg, visiting professor, 1984; Cal Tech, visiting professor, 1988; UC Berkeley, visiting professor, 1987, University of Massachusetts, adjunct professor, chemistry, 1986-, professor, 1978-. **ORGANIZATIONS:** American Physical Society, fellow, 1975-; American Chemical Society, 1980-. **HONORS/AWARDS:** Danforth Foundation, fellowship, 1971; National Science Foundation, Creativity Award, 1987; Phi Beta Kappa, 1970. **SPECIAL ACHIEVEMENTS:** Over 125 publications in the area of polymer science, polymer physics. **BUSINESS ADDRESS:** Professor, Polymer Science and Engineering Dept, University of Massachusetts, Graduate Research Tower, Amherst, MA 01003, (413)545-0433.

HSU, STEPHEN CHARLES

Engineer. Taiwanese American. **PERSONAL:** Born Nov 13, 1960, North Tarrytown, NY; son of Nai-chao Hsu & Yu-chiao Hsu. **EDUCATION:** California Institute of Technology, BSc, 1982; Massachusetts Institute of Technology, PhD, 1988. **CAREER:** David Sarnoff Research Center, staff member, 1988-. **BUSINESS ADDRESS:** Staff Member, David Sarnoff Research Center, Princeton, NJ 08543, (609)734-2417.

HSU, STEPHEN M.

Research scientist, administrator. Chinese American. **PERSONAL:** Born Nov 20, 1943, Shanghai, China; married Stella, 1968; children: Stephanie, Vivian. **EDUCATION:** Virginia Tech, BS, chemical engineering, 1968; Pennsylvania State University, MS, chemical engineering, MS, 1972, PhD, chemical engineering, 1974. **CAREER:** Amoco Chemicals, research engr, 1974-78; National Bureau of Standards, research engr, 1978-79; NBS, group leader, 1979-84, division chief, 1985-91; Pennsylvania State University, visiting professor, 1991-92; NIST, group leader/sr scientist, 1992-. **ORGANIZATIONS:** ASME, Research Committee on Tribology, 1984-; Society of Tribologists & Lubrication Engineers Society, board of directors, 1987-; ASTM, chairman D-2, P, 1981-84; American Ceramic Board on Phase Diagrams, 1989-92; SAE, organization representative, Washington chapter, 1980-; National Academy of Science, National Materials Advisory Board Committee on Ceramic Tribology, 1985-87; COMAT Subcommittee on Ceramic; Government Steering Committee, Tribology Information System, 1984-92. **HONORS/AWARDS:** Phi Kappa Phi, Phi Lambda Upsilon, Sigma Xi, 1970-74; STLE, Capt Alfred E Memorial Medal, 1980, STLE, Al Sonntag Award, 1991; Department of Commerce, Bronze Medal, 1983, Silver Medal, 1990; Asian Pacific Council, Senior Executive Award, 1989. **SPECIAL ACHIEVEMENTS:** Developed & executed the technical program on recycled oil under congressional mandate, 1978-83; developed the ceramic program for NIST, & champion of congressional budget initiative, 1984-85; set up the Tribology Program for NIST, & established a world-class facility, 1979-85; set up the ceramic surface properties group, 1991-; managed the ceramic division, & made the division nationally known, 1985-91. **BUSINESS ADDRESS:** Sr Scientist/Group Leader, National Institute of Standards and Technology, Bldg 223, Rm A256, Gaithersburg, MD 20899, (301)975-6119.

HSU, TIMOTHY

Executive, physician. Chinese American. **PERSONAL:** Born Dec 26, 1952, New York, NY; son of John J Hsu and Elizabeth C Hsu; married Beth M Hsu, Jun 15, 1985; children: Claire E, John M. **EDUCATION:** Harvard University, AB, 1974; Michigan State University, MD, 1978. **CAREER:** Mayo Clinic, resident, 1979-88; University of Michigan, lecturer, 1988-91; Catherine McAuley Health System, program director, 1989-; Clinical Systems Inc, chairman, CEO, 1991-. **ORGANIZATIONS:** American Medical Association, 1975-; American Psychiatric Association, 1985-; American Sleep Disorders Association, 1992-. **BUSINESS ADDRESS:** Chairman, CEO, Clinical Systems, Inc, 3055 Plymouth Rd, Ste 201, Ann Arbor, MI 48105, (313)741-0883.

HSU, TSE-CHI

Educator. Taiwanese American/Chinese American. **PERSONAL:** Born Sep 19, 1936, Yunlin, Taiwan; son of Nan-Ying & May; married Chun-Chin, Oct 5, 1965; children: John, Howard. **EDUCATION:** National Taiwan Normal University, BA, 1958; University of Tennessee, MA, 1964; University of Iowa, PhD, 1968. **CAREER:** Yeshiua University, director of evaluation, 1968-69; University of Pittsburgh, professor, assoc professor, assist prof, 1969-93. **ORGANIZATIONS:** American Educational Research Association, 1968-; National Council on Measurement in Education, 1976-; Psychometric Society, 1969-; American Statistical Association, 1971-; The Comparative and International Education Society, 1993-; Chinese American Educational Research and Development Association, steering committee, 1992-. **HONORS/AWARDS:** American Educational Research Association, The Palmer O Johnson Award, 1970; Institute of International Education, Fulbright-Hays Grant, 1979. **SPECIAL ACHIEVEMENTS:** Coauthor with Michelle Liou, Introduction ot Item Response Theory, Chinese Behavioral Sciences, 1993; coauthor with S F Sadock, Computer-Assisted Test Construction: The State of the Art, ERIC/TME Report No 88, Educational Testing Service, 1986. **BUSINESS ADDRESS:** Professor, University of Pittsburgh, 5A28 Forbes Quad, Pittsburgh, PA 15260, (412)624-7236.

HSU, YU CHU (DAVE)

Educator. Chinese American. **PERSONAL:** Born Oct 3, 1930, Djakata, Indonesia; son of Yin Po & Fu Yin Hsu; married Tzy Lan Hsu, 1965; children: Phillips K K, Victoria K H. **EDUCATION:** National Chung Hsing University, BS, 1954, MS, 1960; Cornell University, PhD, 1965. **CAREER:** University of Malaya, lecturer of agricultural economics, 1965-69; National Cheng Chi University, 1969-78, chairman of economics dept & dean of Graduate Institute of Economics, 1972-78; Colgate University, Picker Professor of Economics, 1978; Southern Connecticut State University, chairman of dept of economics, 1983-85, professor of economics, 1978-. **ORGANIZATIONS:** Intl roster of candidates for the UN Technical Co-operation Program, 1990-; senior adviser, Intl Venture Capital Investment Corp, Taiwan, 1989-91; senior economist, National Center for Finance & Econ Information, Ministry of Finance & National Economy, Kingdom of Saudi Arabia, 1985-86; economic adviser, Economic Development & Planning Council, Taiwan, 1973-78; economic adviser, Ministry of Economic Affairs, Taiwan, 1970-78; consultant & chief of first section, Commission Taxation Refrom, Taiwan, 1969-70. **HONORS/AWARDS:** Chai-Yin University, China, Honorable Professor, 1988; Zhong-Kai Agricultural College, China, Honorable Professor, 1986; Council for International Exchange of Scholars, Exchange Scholar, 1978; Argricultural Development Council, Fellowship, 1962-65. **SPECIAL ACHIEVEMENTS:** Economics of Rural Development (book), Hunan Chung Yuan Farmers Publishing Co, 1989; Theory and Practice of Development Economics (book), Beijing Chinese Enterprise Management Association, 1982; "Measurement of Potential Labor Reserve in Taiwan," Economic Development & Cultural Change, Chicago University, 1982; Comparative Value-Added Tax System (book),

Taipei, Ministry of Finance, 1971. **HOME ADDRESS:** 1687 Hartford Turnpike, North Haven, CT 06473, (203)239-4552. **BUSINESS ADDRESS:** Professor of Economics, Southern Connecticut State University, 501 Crescent St, Seabury Hall, New Haven, CT 06515, (203)397-4465.

HSU, YUAN-HSI
Educator. Chinese American. **PERSONAL:** Born Jan 10, 1945, Hunan, China; son of Kou Hsu and Farn J Hsu; married Ling-chih Hsu, Jun 1976; children: Sarah M, Stephen J. **EDUCATION:** National Taiwan University, BA, 1967; Northern Illinois University, MBA, 1970; Louisiana State University, PhD, 1977. **CAREER:** Alabama A&M University, assistant professor; East Carolina University, associate professor, currently. **BUSINESS ADDRESS:** Associate Professor, East Carolina University, Greenville, NC 27858, (919)757-6572.

HSUEH, CHUN-TU
Foundation executive. Chinese American. **PERSONAL:** Born in Canton, China; married Cordelia Huang, Dec 1952. **EDUCATION:** The China School of Journalism, Hong Kong, certificate, 1939; Chaoyang University Law College, China, LLB, 1946; Raffles College, Singapore, 1946-49; Columbia University, MA, 1953, PhD, 1958. **CAREER:** University of Hong Kong, lecturer in history, 1962-64; University of Maryland, College Park, professor, 1965-92; Columbia University, professor of political science, 1969, 1989; Free University of Berlin, visiting professor, acting director of China and East Asian Politics, research office, 1970; Harvard University, professor, summer, 1979, 1984; Hebrew University of Jerusalem; Australian National University, Canberra, visiting fellow, 1984-85; The Huang Hsing Foundation, USA, president, currently. **ORGANIZATIONS:** Asian Political Scientists Group in the USA, executive director, 1975-; Washington and Southeast Regional Seminar of China, chairman, 1974-79; National Bicentennial Ethnic-Racial Council, 1975-76; Maryland Bicentennial Commission, advisory committee, 1975-76; Committee on Scholars of Asian Descent, chairman, 1981-85; Jinan University, Guangzhou, China, board of trustees, 1991-; St Anthony's College, Oxford University, senior associate member, 1969; American Committee on US-Soviet Relations, 1990-92. **HONORS/AWARDS:** Universidad San Martin de Porres, Lima, Peru, Doctor Honoris Causa, 1984; Zhongshan, Wuhan, Peking Universities, Distinguished Visiting Professor, honorary lifetime appointment, 1983, 1990, 1984-; Hong Kong University, honorary professor, 1991-; People's University of China, honorary professor, 1993-; Fundan University, Shanghai, advisory professor, 1985-. **SPECIAL ACHIEVEMENTS:** To date, the only Asian American political scientist ever nominated to the Council of the American Political Science Association, 1975; author, editor or translator, eight books in English, Oxford University Press and other publishers; Huang Hsing and the Chinese Revolution, Stanford University Press; The Chinese Revolution of 1911: New Perspectives, Hong Kong, Joint Publishing Co, 1986. **BUSINESS ADDRESS:** President, The Huang Hsing Foundation, 14017 Wagon Way, Silver Spring, MD 20906, (301)460-6733.

HSUEH, YI-FUN
Attorney. Chinese American. **PERSONAL:** Born May 27, 1964, Taipei, Taiwan. **EDUCATION:** Harvard College, AB (cum laude), 1987; University of Oxford, MSt, 1988; Harvard Law School, JD, 1991. **CAREER:** Hale and Dorr, Litigation Department, associate, 1991-93; Warner & Stackpole, Litigation Department, associate, 1993-. **ORGANIZATIONS:** American Bar Association, 1991-; Asian-American Lawyers Association of Massachusetts, 1992-; Boston Bar Association, 1991-; Harvard-Radcliffe Schools and Scholarships Committee, 1990-; Radcliffe College Alumnae Association Board of Management, 1992-. **HONORS/AWARDS:** Harvard University, Newbold Rhinelander Landon Memorial Scholarship, 1987. **SPECIAL ACHIEVEMENTS:** Fluency in Taiwanese. **BUSINESS ADDRESS:** Associate, Warner & Stackpole, 75 State St, Boston, MA 02109, (617)951-9000.

HSUI, ALBERT TONG-KWAN
Educator. Chinese American. **PERSONAL:** Born Mar 19, 1945, Canton, China; married Loretta Y Hsui, Jun 19, 1971; children: Emily F, Jennifer F. **EDUCATION:** University of Massachusetts at Lowell, BS, 1968; Cornell University, ME, 1969, PhD, 1972. **CAREER:** NASA, Ames Research Center, research associate, 1972-73; Bell Telephone Laboratory, member of technical staff, 1973-75; Massachusetts Institute of Technology, research associate, 1975-79; University of Illinois, professor, 1980-. **ORGANIZATIONS:** American Geophysical Union, 1972-; Society of Explorational Geophysicists, 1989-. **BUSINESS ADDRESS:** Professor, Dept of Geological Sciences, University of Illinois, 245 NHB, 1301 W Green Street, Urbana, IL 61801, (217)333-7732.

HU, ALBERT KE-JENG
Educator. Chinese American. **PERSONAL:** Born Oct 13, 1961, Zuasua, Taiwan; son of Tsun-Hu Hu and Tsing-Fong Liang; married Jessie Hsiaomei Liu, Jan 5, 1987. **EDUCATION:** National Taiwan University, BS, 1985; Massachusetts Institute of Technology, MS, 1988, PhD, 1993. **CAREER:** MIT, research assistant, 1987-92; AT&T Bell Labs, summer member of technical staff, summer, 1991; San Jose University, assistant professor, 1992-. **ORGANIZATIONS:** IEEE; ASME; International Semiconductor Manufacturing Science Symposium, steering committee, 1993. **HONORS/AWARDS:** AT&T Bell Labs, UR Program for Outstanding Student and Faculty, 1991; NSF, Young Investigator Award, nominee, 1994. **SPECIAL ACHIEVEMENTS:** Author of more than 20 technical papers; invited speaker at AT&T and DEC technical seminars; invited speaker at MIT and U of M EECS depts; speaker at intl microelectronics mfg conferences. **BUSINESS ADDRESS:** Professor, San Jose State University Mechanical Engineering Dept, One Washington Square, Room E310C, San Jose, CA 95192-0087, (408)924-3988.

HU, BAMBI
Educator. Chinese American. **PERSONAL:** Born Jun 4, 1945, Chongqing, Sichuan, China; son of I-Ping Hu & Pie Wang; married Betty K Y Hu, Dec 12, 1975; children: Chu-Mei, Chu-Ching, Chu-Ying. **EDUCATION:** University of California at Berkeley, BA, 1967; Cornell University, MS, 1970, PhD, 1974. **CAREER:** Cornell University, instructor, research associate, 1973-74; Centre d'Etudes Nucleaires de Saclay, France, research associate, 1974-75; Ecole Polytechnique, France, research associate, 1975-77; Brown University, research associate, 1977-78; University of Houston, assistant professor, 1978-83, associate professor, 1983-87, professor, 1987-; Shandong University, adjunct professor, 1985-; Shandong Normal University, adjunct professor, 1988-; Beijing Normal University, adjunct professor, 1988-. **ORGANIZATIONS:** Overseas Chinese Physics Association, divisional coordinator, 1991-93; Academia Sinica, Taiwan, academic advisory council, 1991-93. **HONORS/AWARDS:** Phi Beta Kappa, 1967. **SPECIAL ACHIEVEMENTS:** 70 publications in theoretical physics, including nonlinear dynamics, critical phenomena, and quantum field theory. **BUSINESS ADDRESS:** Professor, Dept of Physics, University of Houston, 4800 Calhoun, Houston, TX 77204-5506, (713)743-3532.

HU, BEI-LOK BERNARD
Educator. Chinese American. **PERSONAL:** Born Oct 4, 1947, Chungking, China; son of I-Ping Hu & Pie Wang; married Chun-Chu Yee, Jun 24, 1972; children: Tung-Hui, Tung-Fei. **EDUCATION:** University of California, Berkeley, AB, 1967; Princeton University, MA, 1969, PhD, 1972. **CAREER:** Institute for Advanced Study, Princeton, 1972-73; Stanford University, research associate, 1973-74; University of California, Berkeley and Santa Barbara, research mathematician and physicist, 1975-79; Cornell University, visiting professor, 1989; University of Maryland, assistant professor, associate professor, 1980-88, professor, 1988-. **ORGANIZATIONS:** American Physical Society; Intl Society for General Relativity and Gravitation; New York Academy of Sciences; Assn of Members of the Inst for Adv Study, trustee, 1984-90; Chinese Society on Grav Physics and Relativistic Astrophysics, council, 1979-85; Intl Advisory Comm for the Third Marcel Grossmann Mtg on General Relativity, Shanghai, China, 1982; International Conference on Gravitation and Cosmology, Goa, India, 1987; 1st, 2nd, & 3rd International Workshop on Thermal Field Theories, 1988, 1990, 1993. **HONORS/AWARDS:** Princeton University, Princeton National Fellow, 1967; University of Maryland, General Research Board Award, 1994; Harvard University, honorary research fellow, 1979. **SPECIAL ACHIEVEMENTS:** Research in general relativity, quantum field theory, statistical mechanics, cosmology. **BUSINESS ADDRESS:** Professor, Dept of Physics, University of Maryland, College Park, MD 20742, (301)405-6029.

HU, CAN BEVEN
Technical engineer. Chinese American. **PERSONAL:** Born Oct 31, 1949, Taipei, Taiwan; son of Te Chang Hu and Chi Shen Hu; married Li-Wen Yu, Nov 24, 1982; children: Alexander H, Irene H. **EDUCATION:** National Taiwan University, BS, 1972; University of Kentucky, MS, 1976; Massachusetts Institute of Technology, PhD, 1980. **CAREER:** Thoratec Labs Corp, manager, materials development, 1980-83; Procter & Gamble Co, staff scientist, 1983-84; Becton Dickinson Polymer Research, senior scientist, 1984-88; Baxter Healthcare Corp, project engineer, 1988-. **ORGANIZATIONS:** American Chemical Society, polymer chemistry, PMSE division, 1979; Society of Plastic Engineering; Sigma Xi. **HONORS/AWARDS:** MIT, Whitaker Health Sciences Fellowship, 1978-80; National Taiwan University, Shu-Chuan Schol-

arship, 1969-70. **SPECIAL ACHIEVEMENTS:** 30 publications in polymer, biomaterial related journals; 9 US patents & several other related Japan & European patents regarding the biomaterials research. **BUSINESS ADDRESS:** Project Engineer, Edwards CVS Division, Baxter Healthcare Corp, 17221 Red Hill Ave, MS 22, Irvine, CA 92714, (714)588-2722.

HU, CHAO HSIUNG
Government official. Taiwanese American. **PERSONAL:** Born Apr 1, 1939, Tainan, Taiwan; son of Lao Tu Hu and Sue Jeng Chen Hu; married Karen O Hu, Aug 3, 1964; children: Julie C, Edward P. **EDUCATION:** National Cheng Kung University, BS, 1961; Duke University, MS, 1968, PhD, 1970. **CAREER:** National Cheng Kung University, teaching assistant, 1962-65; Duke University, teaching/research assistant, 1965-70; Delaware Dept of Transportation, civil engineer, 1970-84, state bridge engineer, 1984-91, assistant highway director, design, 1991-. **ORGANIZATIONS:** AASHTO Subcommittee on Bridges and Structures, 1984-; Delaware Society of Professional Engineers, 1972-. **SPECIAL ACHIEVEMENTS:** "Fire Damage to the Christina River Bridge," with Brett Hestdaien, Del DOT & FHWA, 1992; "Prestressed Concrete Bridge Durability in Delaware," with Charles Dolan, ACI Concrete International, 1991; "Peak Rates of Runoff for Small Watersheds in Delaware," Del DOT, 1972; "Flexural Microcracking in Unreinforced Concrete Beans," with P W Abeles, ACI Journal, 1970. **BUSINESS ADDRESS:** Assistant Highway Director, Design, Delaware Dept of Transportation, PO Box 778, Dover, DE 19903, (302)739-4355.

HU, CHENMING
Engineer, educator. Chinese American. **PERSONAL:** Born Jul 12, 1947, Beijing, China; son of Chang-chi Hu and Su-Hung Hu; married Margaret, Feb 14, 1972; children: Raymond, Jason. **EDUCATION:** National Taiwan University, BS, 1968; University of California, Berkeley, MS, 1970, PhD, 1973. **CAREER:** Massachusetts Institute of Technology, assistant professor, 1973-76, electronics industry, consultant, 1973-; University of California, Berkeley, professor, 1976-. **ORGANIZATIONS:** Institute of Electrical and Electronic Engineers, fellow, 1974-; Chinese Institute of Engineers, life member, 1984-; Chinese American Political Association, life member, 1986-. **HONORS/AWARDS:** Beijing University, Honorary Professor, 1989; Tsinghua University, Honorary Professor, 1991; Chinese Academy of Science, Honorary Professor, 1991; Design News, Excellence in Design Award, 1991; Semiconductor Research Council, Technical Excellence Award, 1991; Outstanding Inventor Award, 1993. **SPECIAL ACHIEVEMENTS:** Solar Cells, McGraw Hill, 1983; Nonvolatile Semiconductor Memory, IEEE, 1991; over 300 articles on semiconductor devices and technology from 1976 to 1993; eight patents in the field of semiconductor devices. **BUSINESS ADDRESS:** Professor, Dept of Electrical Engineering & Computer Sciences, University of California, Berkeley, CA 94720, (510)642-3393.

HU, CHI YU
Educator. Chinese American. **PERSONAL:** Born Feb 12, 1933, Szchwan, China; daughter of C T Hu & P S Yang; divorced; children: Marcia Hu Yee, Mark, Albert, Han Chin. **EDUCATION:** National Taiwan University, BS, 1955; MIT, PhD, 1962. **CAREER:** California State University, Long Beach, assistant professor, 1963, associate professor, 1968, professor, 1972. **ORGANIZATIONS:** American Physical Society, 1963-. **HONORS/AWARDS:** US National Science Foundation, visiting professorship, 1988-90; DOE, research grants, 1986-88; NSF, research grants, 1986-88, 1990-92, 1992-. **SPECIAL ACHIEVEMENTS:** Author, publication in quantum few body theory; muon catalyzed fusion; fadder scattering theory.

HU, CHIA-REN
Educator. Chinese American. **PERSONAL:** Born May 25, 1939, Shanghai, China; son of Chuan-Hou Hu & Ing-Mei Chu Hu; married Lorinda Shi-ging Cheng, Jun 17, 1967. **EDUCATION:** National Taiwan University, BSc, 1962; University of Maryland, PhD, 1968. **CAREER:** University of Illinois, research associate, 1968-69; University of Southern California, assistant professor, 1969-76; Texas A&M University, visiting associate professor, 1976-78, associate professor, 1978-84, professor, 1984-. **ORGANIZATIONS:** American Physical Society, 1968-. **BUSINESS ADDRESS:** Professor, Dept of Physics, Texas A&M University, En/Ph 522, College Station, TX 77843-4242, (409)845-3531.

HU, DANIEL CHING
Electronics company executive. Chinese American. **PERSONAL:** Born Apr 27, 1944, Kukong, Kwongtung, China; son of Che-Wu Hu and Mo-Ching

Tong; married Alice T Hu, Apr 12, 1969; children: Grace, Ying, Janie, Eric. **EDUCATION:** University of Illinois, BSEE, 1967; University of California, Los Angeles, MSEE, 1968; University of Santa Clara, MBA Program, 1970. **CAREER:** Intel Corp, Die Production Dev, dept manager, 1976-78; Natl Semiconductor Inc, director, Asic Business Operations, 1978-85; Exel Microelectronics Inc, Operations & Engineering, vp, 1985-86; Advanced Micro Devices Inc, California Operations, vp, 1987-89; Lattice Semiconductor Corp, vp of operations, 1989-91; Elite Microelectronics Inc, president & COO, 1991-92; Superconductor Technologies Inc, president & CEO, 1992-. **ORGANIZATIONS:** Asian American Manufacturers Assn, board director, 1987-89; Moute Jade Technology Assn, board director, 1992-; Chinese Institute of Engineers, 1979-; Signapore National Science & Technology Board, intl advisor, 1991-; Singapore Institute of Microelectronics, intl advisory panel punch, 1991-; Electronic Research & Services Organization, Taiwan, intl advisory board, 1976-85. **SPECIAL ACHIEVEMENTS:** Seven Mask Isoplanar Silicon Gate CMOS Process, 1972; Self-aligned Advanced Bipole Structure, 1980; Programmable Semiconductor Antifuse and Method of Fabrication, filed, 1991. **BUSINESS ADDRESS:** President and CEO, Superconductor Technologies Inc, 460 Ward Drive, Suite F, Santa Barbara, CA 93111-2310, (805)683-7646.

HU, JANE H.
Health scientist administrator. Chinese American. **PERSONAL:** Born Mar 6, 1940, Chekiang, China; daughter of Wei-fan Hu & Shih Ching Hu; married Wen-jin Woan, Jan 4, 1970; children: John, Diane. **EDUCATION:** New York University, Washington Square College, BA, 1963; Columbia University, College of Physicians & Surgeons, PhD, 1968. **CAREER:** Columbia University, instructor, 1966-67; University of Illinois, research associate, 1967-70; Naval Medical Research Institute, physiologist, 1971-73; Howard University Cancer Center, associate director, 1974-78; National Institutes of Health, health scientist administrator, 1978-. **ORGANIZATIONS:** Asian American Fund, chairperson, 1984-; Asian American Voters Coalition, founder, 1983-; NIH Asian Pacific Islanders, advisory committee, 1991-92; Defense Advisory Committee on Women in the Services, 1991-94; Phi Beta Kappa; Sigma Xi; International Society of Poets. **HONORS/AWARDS:** International Society of Poets, The International Poet of Merit Award; World of Poetry, Golden Poet Award. **SPECIAL ACHIEVEMENTS:** Numerous scientific publications; English poems published by the American Poetry Anthology, 1990; Selected Works of World's Best Poets, 1991; The Sound of Poetry, 1992; National Library of Poetry, 1993; The Best Poems of '90s, 1992; Foot Print On the Sand of Time, Road Publisher, 1993. **HOME ADDRESS:** 9216 Falls Chapel Way, Potomac, MD 20854, (301)340-2065.

HU, JIMMY
Corporate executive. Chinese American. **PERSONAL:** Born in Shanghai, China; son of Lee Sung Hu and Chow-Tze Hu. **EDUCATION:** Dai-Dong University, China, BSEE, 1955; Columbia University, MBA, 1967. **CAREER:** Marine Works Inc, president, 1966-71; UNI Enterprises Inc, president, 1971-; Humaco Realty Corp, president, 1973-79; Kahu Mgmt Corp, president, 1973-80; Hu-Kron Realty Corp, president, 1973-78; Hujim Realty Corp, president, 1974-; Giant Trading Corp, president, 1974-; KHCK Realty Corp, president, 1974-; La Concha Catering & Restaurant Corp, president, 1982-; J M Limousine Service Corp, president, 1983-. **ORGANIZATIONS:** Society of Naval Architects & Marine Engineers. **BUSINESS ADDRESS:** President, UNI Enterprises Inc, 437-439 3rd Ave, Brooklyn, NY 11215.

HU, JOHN NAN-HAI
Chemical engineer. Chinese American. **PERSONAL:** Born Aug 14, 1936, Kaifeng, Honan, China; son of Po-han & Ti-fei Hu; married Frances, May 31, 1964; children: Patrick, Michelle. **EDUCATION:** Taiwan University, BS, 1958; University of Notre Dame, PhD, 1965. **CAREER:** Ethyl Corp, 1964-, R&D advisor, currently. **ORGANIZATIONS:** Mayor's Office, international relations commission, 1990-93. **SPECIAL ACHIEVEMENTS:** Language proficiency: Chinese. **MILITARY SERVICE:** Chinese Air force-Taiwan (ROTC), lieutenant, 1958-60. **BUSINESS ADDRESS:** R & D Advisor, Ethyl Corp, 8000 GSRI Ave, Baton Rouge, LA 70820, (504)768-5667.

HU, JOSEPH KAI MING
Insurance agency executive. Chinese American. **PERSONAL:** Born Oct 3, 1953, Hong Kong; son of Hon Wai Hu and Kwan Yee Hu; married Donna T Aihara, Mar 31, 1984; children: Jennifer C. **EDUCATION:** University of Hawaii, BBA, marketing, 1980; The American Institute for Property and Liability Underwriters Inc, CPCU, 1986. **CAREER:** Bankers Life Nebraska, sales representative, 1980-82; Royal Insurance Agency Inc, commercial lines

manager, 1982-86; Frank B Hall of Hawaii Inc, account executive, 1986-87; Jardine Insurance Brokers Inc, account executive, 1987-88; American Insurance Agency Inc, senior vice pres, 1988-. **ORGANIZATIONS:** Chartered Property and Casualty Underwriters, Hawaii Chapter, 1986-, president, 1990-91; Professional Insurance Agents, Hawaii Chapter, president, 1993-94, director, 1988-; Waikiki Rotary, 1988-, treasurer, 1991-92; Chinese Chamber of Hawaii, 1990-; Intl Insurance Society, 1991-. **HOME ADDRESS:** 5333 Likini St, #1010, Honolulu, HI 96818, (808)839-0123. **BUSINESS PHONE:** (808)521-5323.

HU, PAUL Y.
Engineer. Chinese American. **PERSONAL:** Born Nov 6, 1938, Shanghai, China; son of Ming Yu Hu; married Lucia L Hu, Sep 19, 1965; children: Charlene, Caroline, Evaleen. **EDUCATION:** University of Maryland, BS, 1961; California Institute of Technology, MS, 1962, PhD, 1966. **CAREER:** University of Arizona, adjunct professor, 1986; IBM, senior engr, 1977-. **ORGANIZATIONS:** IEEE, senior member, 1966-; ASME, 1966-. **HONORS/AWARDS:** IBM: Outstanding Achievement Awards, 1975; Outstanding Invention Award, 1976; Outstanding Contribution Award, 1989; 9 Invention Achievement Awards. **SPECIAL ACHIEVEMENTS:** 25 technical publications; 36 US patents; 101 inventions. **BUSINESS ADDRESS:** Senior Engineer, IBM, 75H/071, Tucson, AZ 85744, (602)799-2137.

HU, SHIU-LOK
Biotechnology executive. Chinese American. **PERSONAL:** Born Nov 10, 1949, Hong Kong, China; son of I-Ping Hu & Pie Wang Hu; married Gail Hu, Dec 20, 1984; children: Emily, Alice. **EDUCATION:** University of California, Berkeley, BA (with great distinction), 1971; University of Wisconsin, Madison, PhD, 1978; Cold Spring Harbor Laboratory, postdoctoral training, 1978-81. **CAREER:** Cold Spring Harbor Laboratory, postdoctoral fellow, 1978-81; Molecular Genetics Inc, senior scientist, 1981-83, director of molecular biology, 1983-84; Oncogen, senior scientist, 1985-86; Bristol-Myers Squibb PRI, virology, lab director, 1986-90, executive director, 1990-; University of Washington, research associate professor of microbiology, 1988-. **ORGANIZATIONS:** NIAID, NIH, AIDS Research Review Committee, 1990-93; Society of Chinese Biochemists in America; American Society for Microbiology; American Society for Virology; International AIDS Society. **HONORS/AWARDS:** National Institutes of Health, postdoctoral fellowship, 1980-81; Damon Runyon-Walter Winchell, Cancer Research Fellowship, 1978-80; University of California, Regents Scholar, 1969-71; Miriam Merck Memorial Scholarship, 1968. **SPECIAL ACHIEVEMENTS:** Author of 71 scientific papers which have appeared in various journals. **BUSINESS ADDRESS:** Executive Director, Bristol-Myers Squibb Pharmaceutical Research Institute, 3005 First Ave, Seattle, WA 98121, (206)727-3680.

HU, STEVE SENG-CHIU
Business executive, educational administrator. Chinese American. **PERSONAL:** Born Mar 16, 1922, Yang-Chou, Jiangsu, China; son of Yu-Bin Hu and Shu-Chang Lee Hu; married Lily Li-Wan Liu Hu, Oct 2, 1977; children: April Swan-Do, Yen-Do, Victor Wee-Do. **EDUCATION:** Chiao-Tung University, Shanghai, BS, 1939; Rensselaer Polytechnic Institute, MS, 1940; Massachusetts Institute of Technology, ScD, 1942; University of California, Los Angeles, certificate degree, 1966. **CAREER:** Douglas Aircraft Corp, China Aircraft/China Motor Inc, president, 1943-49; RCA, Arizonia Div, meteorology research director, 1955-58; Jet Propulsion Lab, Cal Tech Institute, research scientist, 1957-60; Northrop Corp, Huntsville Div, managing technical director, 1961-71; University of Alabama & Auburn University, professor, 1961-67; American Technical College, president, 1980-90; University of America United Research Institute, president, 1971-; University America Foundation, USA & Taiwan, president, 1977-; Century Research Inc, president & research director, 1971-. **ORGANIZATIONS:** American Astronautical Society, executive vice president, director, 1961-72; National Association of Technical Colleges, 1980-90; American Institute of Aeronautics & Astronautics, 1943-60; Overseas Association of Shanghai Industrial Shan-Yi Associates, honorary chairman of board, 1991-. **HONORS/AWARDS:** Tien-Tsu Education Foundation, cash award & certificate, 1939; Lien-Tsai Foundation, cash award & certificate, 1941; Salisbury Prize Foundation, cash award & certificate, 1941; Sloan Automotive Foundation, cash award & certificate, 1941; Rensselaer Institute, cash award & certificate, 1940; Air Force, Republic of China, cash award & certificate of merit, 1944; RCA Corp, Meterology Sec, cash award & certificate of merit, 1957; Northrop Corp Space Lab, cash award & certificate of merit, 1965. **SPECIAL ACHIEVEMENTS:** Author, Supersonic Gas Flow Dynamics of Automotive & Jet Exhaust, AIAA, 1943; Optimal

Space Flight Path by Variable Calculus, AIAA, 1967; Conic Nozzle Flow Dynamics of Jet Propulsion, Aeroject General Series, 1957; Direct Mathematics of Optimal Guidance Function, AIAA, 1966; Principles of Navigation, Guidance, Delivery & Optimization of Space Vehicles, University of Alabama, 1969; chief editor, co-author, Yearbook of Saturn V/Apollo & Moon Landing, AAS, 1967. **BUSINESS ADDRESS:** President, Century Research, Inc, 16935 South Vermont Avenue, Office Section, Suite-B, Gardena, CA 90247.

HU, WAYNE
Real estate analyst. Chinese American. **PERSONAL:** Born Dec 12, 1944. **CAREER:** Kensington Investment Ltd, real estate broker, currently. **ORGANIZATIONS:** City Planning Commission, City of San Francisco, past president. **SPECIAL ACHIEVEMENTS:** Chinese New Year Parade, chair; consultant to community non-profit housing organization. **BUSINESS ADDRESS:** Real Estate Analyst, Kensington Investment Ltd, 809 Montgomery St, 2nd Fl, San Francisco, CA 94133, (415)986-1370.*

HUANG, ALICE SHIH-HOU
Educator. Chinese American. **PERSONAL:** Born Mar 22, 1939, Nanchang, Kiangsi, China; daughter of Quentin K Y and Grace Betty Soong Huang; married David Baltimore, 1968; children: one. **EDUCATION:** Wellesley College, 1957-79; Johns Hopkins University, BA, 1961, MA, microbiology, 1963, PhD, microbiology, 1966. **CAREER:** Taiwan, asst professor of zoology, 1966; Salk Institute for Biological Studies, fellow, 1967; Massachusetts Institute of Technology, fellow, 1968-69, research associate, 1969-70; Harvard University School of Medicine, microbiology & molecular genetics, asst professor, 1971-73, assoc professor, 1973-78, prof, 1979-91; Harvard-MIT Program, professor, 1979-91; New York University, dean for science, professor of biology, 1991-; Children's Hospital Medical Center, director, 1979-. **ORGANIZATIONS:** AAAS; American Society of Biological Chemists; American Society of Microbiologists, president, 1988-89; Infectious Diseases Society of America; Intervirology, editorial board, 1973-; NIH, virology study section, 1973-77; Sigma Xi. **HONORS/AWARDS:** USPHS Award, 1972-77; San Francisco Chinese Hospital Award, 1989; Natl Cathedral School, Alumni Citation, 1978; John Hay Whitney Foundation, fellow, 1960-61; Buroughs Wellcome Travelling Fellowship, 1979; Eli Lilly Award in Microbiology & Immunology, 1977; honorary degrees: Wheaton College, DSc, 1971; Mt Holyoke College, 1987; Harvard University, 1980; Medical College, 1991; visiting professor at several universities. **BUSINESS ADDRESS:** Dean for Science, Professor of Biology, New York University, Box 500 1230 York Ave, New York, NY 10021-6399.*

HUANG, ARNOLD
Banking executive. Chinese American. **CAREER:** Washington First International Bank, chairman, currently. **BUSINESS ADDRESS:** Chairman, Washington First International Bank, 9709 Third Ave NE, Seattle, WA 98115, (206)525-8118.*

HUANG, BARNEY KUO-YEN
Educator, consulting company executive. Taiwanese American/Chinese American. **PERSONAL:** Born Jan 27, 1931, Taipei, Taiwan; son of S K & S H Chen Huang; married Lindy Wang Huang, Dec 25, 1964; children: Lucas K, Rosa M, Ulric K. **EDUCATION:** Natl Taiwan University, BS (high distinction), agric engg, 1954; University of Illinois, MS, agric engg, 1960; Purdue University, PhD, agric engg, 1963; Stevens Institute of Technology, advanced studies: system analysis & control, 1964; Wayne State University, experimental stress analysis, 1966; Princeton University, computer & processing systems, 1967, system synthesis & computation, 1968; Polytechnic Institute of Brooklyn, research instrumentation, 1969; Pennsylvania State University, advanced hybrid computation, 1969; University of Wisconsin, physics of differential equations, 1970; University of Santa Clara, nonlinear systems, 1970; Syracuse University, mechanics & aerodynamics, 1971, noise control in engg design, 1973; Oklahoma State University, engg design of machine mechanisms, 1973. **CAREER:** Natl Taiwan University, asst instructor, 1954-58; University of Illinois, graduate asst, 1958-60; Purdue University, graduate asst, 1960-62; consultant: Harrington Manufacturing Co, 1973-76; Joint Commission on Rural Reconstruction, 1974-75; Taiwan Tobacco & Wine Monopoly Bureau, 1976; Bud Antle Inc, 1976; Research Triangle Inst, 1976-77; Union Carbide Corp, 1977-79; Sugano Farm Machinery Co, 1979-81; NC Dept of Transportation, 1979-81; United Nations, 1980-81; Southwest Research Inst, 1981-82; Valmont Industries Inc, 1983-84; AT&T Technologies, Inc, 1987-88; North Carolina Agricultural & Technical State University, 1988; National Academy of Sciences, international advisory panel, 1991; Shiijazhuang Agricultural

Machinery Plant, 1992; Jilin University of Technology, 1992; Harbin Farm Machinery Plant, 1992; lectureships: Tehran University, 1975; Japan Society of the Promotion of Science, 1979-80; Natl Taiwan University, 1979-80; Korea Tobacco Research Inst, 1980; Jilin University of Tech, 1983, 1987; Shenyang Agricultural University, 1988; NC State University, asst prof, 1963-67, assoc prof, 1967-73, prof, 1973-; Innovative Ideas Tech Inc, pres, currently. **ORGANIZATIONS:** Amer Soc of Agricultural Engineers, NC section, vp, 1966-67, Tractor & Implement Hydraulic Comm, sec, 1967-68, Plant Dynamics Sub-Comm, chm, 1968-69, Publications Review Comm, chm, 1975-76, Textbook Comm, advisor, Nursery & Greenhouse Mechanization Comm, Aquaculture Engineering Comm; Amer Soc for Engineering Education; Amer Assn for the Advancement of Science; NC Acoustical Soc of America; NC Solar Energy Assn; Natl Geographic Soc; Journal of Grey System, editorial bd. **HONORS/ AWARDS:** Sigma Xi; Tau Beta Pi; Gamma Sigma Delta; Alpha Epsilon, Lin's Fellowship, 1960-61; ASAE, Paper Award, 1965, 1971, 1974, Honorable Mention Award, 1976; Korea Tobacco Research Institute, Excellence Award, 1980; Honorary Professorships: Shenyang Agricultural Univ, 1987, Jilin Univ of Tech, 1992, Henan Agricultural Univ, 1992; ABI, Distinguished Leadership Award, 1988; Golden Academy Award for Lifetime Achievement, 1992. **SPECIAL ACHIEVEMENTS:** Author, co-author of over 100 technical and research articles and books; patentee of over 25 US, Canadian, European, Chinese and Japanese patents. **HOME ADDRESS:** 3332 Manor Ridge Dr, Raleigh, NC 27603-4845, (919)772-8446.

HUANG, C.-T. JAMES
Educator. Taiwanese American/Chinese American. **PERSONAL:** Born Jun 4, 1948, Hualien, Taiwan; son of Ching-Fa Huang and Hsiu-O Chen-Huang; married H Y Emily Huang, Nov 30, 1977; children: Yi-Ching D, David J. **EDUCATION:** National Taiwan Normal University, BA, 1972, MA, 1974; Massachusetts Institute of Technology, PhD, 1982. **CAREER:** University of Hawaii, assistant professor, 1982-83; National Tsing Hua University, assistant professor, 1983-85; Cornell University, assistant/associate professor, 1985-90; University of California, Irvine, professor, 1990-. **ORGANIZATIONS:** Linguistic Society of America, 1973-, program committee, 1993-; International Association of Chinese Linguistics, executive secretary, 1992-; Summer Institute of Chinese Linguistics, director, 1991; Journal of East Asian Linguistics, editor, 1992-; Linguistic Inquiry, associate editor, 1987-. **HONORS/ AWARDS:** John Simon Guggenheim Foundation, fellowship, 1989; Center for Advanced Studies in the Behavioral Sciences, Stanford, fellowship, 1993. **SPECIAL ACHIEVEMENTS:** Hanyu Shengcheng Yufa, Chinese Generative Grammar, 1983; "On the Distribution and Reference of Empty Pronouns," 1984; "Modularity and Chinese A-not-A Questions," 1991; "Reconstruction and the Structure of VP," 1993. **BIOGRAPHICAL SOURCES:** Move Alpha, MIT Press, Cambridge, MA, 1992; Word Order and Constituency in Mandarin Chinese, Kluwer, Holland, 1990. **BUSINESS ADDRESS:** Professor, University of California, Irvine, School of Social Sciences, Irvine, CA 92717, (714)856-7525.

HUANG, CHAOFU
Engineer. Chinese American. **PERSONAL:** Born Apr 3, 1959, Taipei, Taiwan. **EDUCATION:** University of California, Santa Barbara, MS, 1986. **CAREER:** West Coast Research Corp, consultant, 1986-88; Electro-Optek Corp, senior engineer, 1988-93. **ORGANIZATIONS:** America-China Association for Science and Technology Exchange, board of directors, 1992-. **HONORS/ AWARDS:** Phi Tau Phi Scholar Society, 1985. **SPECIAL ACHIEVEMENTS:** Developed a long-wavelength infrared detector process using InAs5B/InSb epitaxy, 1992; developed a high-efficiency amorphous silicon solar cell, 1985; co-invented a high-efficiency knudsen cell for molecular beam epitaxy. **HOME ADDRESS:** 22818 Broadwell Ave, Torrance, CA 90502, (310)534-8608.

HUANG, CHARLES (CHIANG-LIANG)
Design and manufacturing engineering company executive. Taiwanese American. **PERSONAL:** Born Jul 24, 1947, Yuan-Lin, Taiwan; married; children: Gregory, Joshua. **EDUCATION:** National Taiwan University, Taipei, Taiwan, BSEE, 1969; University of Alabama, Tuscaloosa, MSEE, 1971; University of California, Berkeley, PhD, EE, 1975. **CAREER:** University of California, research assistant, 1971-75; Hewlett Packard Co, project manager, 1975-80; Avantek, Inc, general manager, 1980-84; Anadigics, Inc, vice president, engineering, 1985-86, executive vice president, 1985-. **ORGANIZATIONS:** IEEE, Advisory Board for the Committee on Design and Manufacturing Engineering, 1991-, MIT-IMS Technical Program Committee, 1991-, MTT Manufacturing Technology Committee, conference chairman, 1990-; NJIT/New

Jersey RF/Microwave Industries Association, executive committee, 1991-. **HONORS/AWARDS:** IEEE, fellow, 1994. **BUSINESS ADDRESS:** Executive Vice President, Anadigics, Inc, 35 Technology Dr, Warren, NJ 07059, (908)668-5000.

HUANG, CHAU-TING
Biochemist. Taiwanese American/Chinese American. **PERSONAL:** Born Mar 28, 1939, Kaohsiung, Taiwan; son of Tan-Sung Huang and Ta-Fung Chen Huang; married Su-Yueh Huang, Jul 1, 1970; children: Judy Ann, Thomas. **EDUCATION:** National Taiwan University, BS, 1961; University of Alberta, MS, 1967, PhD, 1970. **CAREER:** Procter & Gamble Pharmaceuticals, scientist, 1987, senior scientist, 1993-. **ORGANIZATIONS:** American Physiological Society, 1986-. **BUSINESS ADDRESS:** Senior Scientist, Procter & Gamble Pharmaceuticals, PO Box 191, Woods Corners Facilities, Norwich, NY 13815, (607)335-2651.

HUANG, CHENG-CHER
Educator. Taiwanese American. **PERSONAL:** Born May 25, 1947, Taipei, Taiwan; son of Yuang-Lang Huang & Sue Chu Huang; married Tsuey-chung Huang; children: Andrew, Benjamin. **EDUCATION:** National Taiwan University, BS, 1969; University of Pennsylvania, PhD, 1975. **CAREER:** Chalmers University of Technology, visiting professor, 1984; AT&T Bell Laboratory, visiting scientist, 1985; University of Minnesota, assistant professor, 1977-82, associate professor, 1982-87; professor, 1987-; 3M Central Research Lab, consultant, 1990-92; Nation Sun Yat-Sen University, Taiwan, visiting professor, 1992. **ORGANIZATIONS:** American Physical Society, 1974-. **HONORS/AWARDS:** University of Minnesota, Faculty Summer Research Award, 1978, Single Quarter Leave Award, 1982, 1985, 1990; University/ Student Alumni Association Award, 1987; American Physical Society, fellow, 1993. **SPECIAL ACHIEVEMENTS:** "Liquid-lexatic phase transitions in single molecular layers of liquid-crystal films," Nature, vol 355, p 152, 1992; "Simultaneous measurements of heat capacity and in-plane density of thin liquid-crystal free-standing films," Phys Rev Lett, vol 68, p 2944, 1992. **BUSINESS ADDRESS:** Professor, Dept of Physics, University of Minnesota, 116 Church St SE, Minneapolis, MN 55455, (612)624-0861.

HUANG, CHENG-CHI
Educator. Taiwanese American. **PERSONAL:** Born Jul 11, 1941, Tainan, Taiwan; son of Chung-Yi Huang & Yang Hong-Kan Huang; married Seng-In Hsiao, Dec 24, 1988; children: An-Huey. **EDUCATION:** National Taiwan Normal University, BS, 1964; Auburn University, MS, 1969; Iowa State University, PhD, 1977. **CAREER:** Taipei Second Girls' High, math, teacher, 1965-67; Iowa State University, math, instructor, 1972-76; University of Minnesota, Morris, math, assistant professor, 1976-77; Marshall University, math, associate professor, 1977-84; Auburn University, Montgomery, math, associate professor, 1984-. **HONORS/AWARDS:** Tainan city government, scholarship, 1955, 1956, 1961. **SPECIAL ACHIEVEMENTS:** Author of several publications regarding mathematical principles. **BUSINESS ADDRESS:** Associate Professor, Auburn University, Montgomery, 7300 University Dr, Montgomery, AL 36117-3596, (205)244-3320.

HUANG, CHI-CHIANG
Educator. Chinese American. **PERSONAL:** Born Jun 10, 1949, Taoyuan, Taiwan; son of Ching-yu Huang & Feng-ying Tseng; married Ten-yun Huang, Oct 4, 1976; children: Sharon, Catherine. **EDUCATION:** National Chengchi University, 1968; National Taiwan University, BA, 1973, MA, 1976; University of Arizona, PhD, 1986. **CAREER:** University of Arizona, teaching associate, 1984-86; Amherst College, visiting assistant professor, 1986-87; Mount Holyoke College, assistant professor, 1986-87; Hobart & Wm Smith Colleges, assistant professor, 1987-92, associate professor, 1992-. **ORGANIZATIONS:** Cornell University, East Asia Program, associate-in-research, 1988-; AAS. **HONORS/AWARDS:** NEH, Summer Institute Award, 1989; ROC, Ministry of Education, Conference Grant, 1992; Center for Chinese Studies, Taipei, Summer Research Grant, 1990; Council for Cultural Planning and Development, Conference Grant, 1989; Chinese Cultural Foundation, Taipei, Conference Grant, 1987; Xibei University, International Tang Dynasty Culture Research Center, honorary research fellow. **SPECIAL ACHIEVEMENTS:** Author: "Growing up as a Loyalist's Son: Li Yeh-ssu (1622-1680), Ming Studies, vol 30, 1991; "Buddhist Historian Hui-hung and His View on the. . ., Ta-lu tsa-chih, vol 80, nos 4 & 5, 1991; "Eleventh-Century Korean Monk Uichon and His Pilgrimage to the Sung China," New History, vol 3 no 1, 1991; several others. **BUSINESS ADDRESS:** Associate Professor, Dept of Modern

Languages, Hobart & Wm Smith Colleges, PO Box F-97, Geneva, NY 14456-3397, (315)781-3553.

HUANG, CHI-LUNG DOMINIC
Educator. Chinese American. **PERSONAL:** Born Oct 10, 1930, Chian-chow, Fukien, China; son of T C Huang & C Kane Huang; married Li-Fang Claire Huang, Aug 20, 1960; children: Agnes S, Dennis F, Donald J, Thomas J. **EDUCATION:** National Taiwan University, BS, 1954; University of Illinois, MS, 1960; Yale University, PhD, 1964. **CAREER:** Taiwan Power Co, engineer, designer, 1955-58; University of Illinois, research assistant, 1958-60; Ammann & Whitney, engineer, designer, 1960-61; Yale University, research assistant, 1961-64; Kansas State University, assistant professor, 1964-68, assistant professor, 1968-74, professor, 1974-. **ORGANIZATIONS:** Society of Engineering Science, 1964-; American Institute of Aeronautics & Astronautics, 1968-; American Academy of Mechanics, 1968-; American Society of Mechanical Engineers, 1975-; American Society of Engineering Education, 1972-; 16th Midwestern Mechanics Conference, co-chairman, 1978. **HONORS/AWARDS:** Kansas State University, Phi Kappa Phi Faculty Scholar Award, 1991; International Bio Ctr of Cambridge, England, Man of Achievement, 1984. **SPECIAL ACHIEVEMENTS:** 162 archival publications, 1964-. **MILITARY SERVICE:** Engineering Corps, lieutenant, 1955. **BIOGRAPHICAL SOURCES:** Directory of World Researchers, Tokyo, Japan, 1979. **BUSINESS ADDRESS:** Professor, Dept of Mechanical Engineering, Kansas State University, Durland Hall 322, Manhattan, KS 66506-5106, (913)532-5610.

HUANG, CHIN-PAO
Educator. Taiwanese American. **PERSONAL:** Born Oct 4, 1941, Changhua, Taiwan; son of Wang-Chi Huang and You Liang-Huang; married Yu-chu Huang, Apr 1, 1971; children: Catherine K, Calvin K. **EDUCATION:** National Taiwan University, BS, 1961; Harvard University, MS, 1967, PhD, 1971. **CAREER:** Wayne State University, assistant professor, 1971-74; University of Delaware, assistant professor, 1974-80, associate professor, 1980-84, professor, 1984-92, distinguished professor, 1992-. **ORGANIZATIONS:** America Society of Civil Engineers, 1984-; American Chemical Society; International Association of Water Quality, 1989-. **HONORS/AWARDS:** Overseas Chinese Environmental Engineers and Scientists Association, Outstanding Research Award, 1991, Outstanding Service Award, 1993. **SPECIAL ACHIEVEMENTS:** Over 140 scientific publications in refereed journals, technical reports, proceedings and books chapters. **BUSINESS ADDRESS:** Distinguished Professor of Environmental Engineering, University of Delaware, 352 DuPont Hall, Newark, DE 19716, (302)831-8428.

HUANG, DENIS K.
Chemical engineering consultant. Chinese American. **PERSONAL:** Born May 14, 1925, Quongzhou, Quongtong, China; son of Shui-Fu Wong and Wei Men Lo; married Betty J, 1956; children: Lloyd K. **EDUCATION:** St John's University, BS, math, 1944; University of California, BS, chem eng, 1950; University of Maine, MS, chem eng, 1951; Polytechnic Institute of Brooklyn, PhD, chem eng, 1958. **CAREER:** International Paper Co, head chemist, 1958-62; Simonie Research Div, senior chemist, 1962-65; Westvaco Corp, senior research engr, 1965-78; Federal Paper, proc engr consultant, 1978-90; Technical Consultants International, associate consultant, 1990-. **ORGANIZATIONS:** Unido, technical expert to India, 1970-71; Organizations of Amer States, consultant, Argentina, 1972; UNDP, consultant to China, 1983. **HONORS/AWARDS:** Phi Lambda Upsilon, 1956; Sigma Xi, 1956. **SPECIAL ACHIEVEMENTS:** Encyclopedia of Material Science and Engineering, 1986; Tappi Monograph, Mol Structures & Binder Perf; Tappi Casting Seminar, Blade Scratch Problem, 1988; over 60 US & foreign patents. **HOME ADDRESS:** 3641 Nassau Dr, Augusta, GA 30909, (706)738-8902.

HUANG, EUGENE YUCHING
Civil engineer, educator. Chinese American. **PERSONAL:** Born Nov 28, 1917, Changsha, Hunan, China; son of Sam Huang and Yi Yun Chao Huang; married Hele Woo Huang, Aug 20, 1955; children: Martha, Pearl, William, Mary, Priscilla, Stephen. **EDUCATION:** University of Utah, MS, 1950; University of Michigan, ScD, 1954. **CAREER:** Chinese National Highway Administration, assistant engineer, 1941-45, associate engineer, 1945-48; University of Michigan Engineering Research Institute, research assistant, 1953-54; University of Illinois, Civil Engineering, research assistant professor, 1954-58, associate professor, 1958-63; Michigan Technological University, Transportation Engineering, professor, 1963-84, professor emeritus, 1984-. **ORGANIZATIONS:** American Society of Civil Engineers, fellow, 1949-; American Society for Engineering Education, 1955-; American Society for Testing and

Materials, 1962-; American Railway Engineering Association, 1963-; Association of Asphalt Paving Technologists, 1964-; The Institute of Management Science, 1965-; Highway Research Board/Transportation Research Board, university representative, 1955-85; American Association for the Advancement of Science, 1959-85. **HONORS/AWARDS:** Michigan Technological University, faculty research award, 1967; Tau Beta Pi, 1964; Chi Epsilon, 1964; Sigma Xi, 1954; Phi Tau Phi, 1965-. **SPECIAL ACHIEVEMENTS:** Author, Manual of Current Practice for the Design, Construction, and Maintenance of Soil-Aggregate Roads; An Overview of the American Transportation System; also numerous articles in technical journals. **HOME ADDRESS:** 400 Garnet St, Houghton, MI 49931. **BUSINESS ADDRESS:** Professor Emeritus, Dept of Civil and Environmental Engineering, Michigan Tech University, 1400 Townsend Drive, Houghton, MI 49931.

HUANG, FENG HOU
Educator. Taiwanese American. **PERSONAL:** Born Sep 23, 1930, Taiwan; married Su-Yuan Huang. **EDUCATION:** Chung Hsing University, BS, 1954; Colorado State University, MS, 1967; West Virginia University, PhD, 1972. **CAREER:** West Virginia University, research associate, 1972-74; Beckman Institute, chemist, 1974-79; University of Arkansas, professor, 1979-. **ORGANIZATIONS:** Tissue Culture Association, 1979-. **HONORS/AWARDS:** Sigma Xi, 1980; Phi Beta Delta, Beta Eta member, 1991. **SPECIAL ACHIEVEMENTS:** Author, numerous publications on agro-forest-biotechnology, 1979-. **HOME ADDRESS:** 3175 Loxley Ave, Fayetteville, AR 72703, (501)521-1482. **BUSINESS ADDRESS:** Professor, Dept of Horticulture & Forestry, University of Arkansas, Maple St, 316 Plant Science Bldg, Fayetteville, AR 72701, (501)575-2603.

HUANG, GARNG MORTON
Educator. Chinese American. **PERSONAL:** Born Oct 22, 1951, Taipei, Taiwan; son of Merge Huang and Tzih-Yih Huang; married Limei Huang, Dec 25, 1978; children: Felix, Gilbert. **EDUCATION:** National Chiao Tung University, BSEE, 1975, MSEE, 1977; Washington University, St Louis, DSc, 1980. **CAREER:** Washington University, St Louis, assistant professor, 1980-84; Texas A&M University, assistant professor, 1984-87, associate professor, 1987-92, professor, 1993-. **ORGANIZATIONS:** IEEE Trans on Automatic Control, energy system committee chairman, 1992-. **HONORS/AWARDS:** AT&T, Educational Award, 1984; IEEE, senior member, 1984. **SPECIAL ACHIEVEMENTS:** Published more than one hundred papers and reports in the area of large system theory and its applications to power systems, data network, and flexible structures. **BIOGRAPHICAL SOURCES:** IEEE Trans on Computers, vol 41, no 6, p 724, 1992; IEEE Proceedings of the 18th Power Industry Computer Application, p 81, 1993. **BUSINESS ADDRESS:** Professor, Dept of Electrical Eng, Texas A&M University, Zachry 216Q, College Station, TX 77843-3128, (409)845-7476.

HUANG, GEORGE WENHONG
Educator. Taiwanese American. **PERSONAL:** Born Apr 20, 1936, Miao-li, Taiwan; son of A-chun and Jun-keng; married Linda, Dec 10, 1961; children: John, Joseph. **EDUCATION:** Taiwan Normal University, BA, 1959; Vanderbilt University, MLS, 1963; New Mexico Highlands University, MEd, 1967; University of Idaho, PhD, 1969. **CAREER:** National Central Library, Taiwan, librarian, 1959-60; Provincial Hsin Chu High School, Taiwan, librarian, 1961-62; Taipei American School, librarian, 1962; New Mexico Highlands University, librarian, 1963-67; University of Idaho, teaching fellow, 1967-69; California State University, Chico, professor of education, 1969-, coordinator of Asian studies, 1979-88; University of Malaya, Malaysia, coordinator & Fulbright Professor, 1988-89. **ORGANIZATIONS:** American Library Association, 1963-; California Media & Library Educator's Association, 1969-; Phi Delta Kappa, 1969-; Chinese Librarians Association, president, 1979; Chinese American Librarians Association, California chapter, president, 1983; Association for Asian Studies, 1979-; American Library Association, LITA education committee, 1985-87; American Library Association, university press books for secondary school libraries committee, 1981-85. **HONORS/AWARDS:** Asian Foundation, Grant for American Library Association Annual Conference, 1963; US Department of Education, Fulbright Summer Seminar in Korean Studies, 1987; California State University, Chico, Meritorious Performance Award, 1988, 1990; Council for International Exchange of Scholars, Fulbright Scholar Award, 1988-89. **SPECIAL ACHIEVEMENTS:** Author of 26 articles published in professional journals. **BUSINESS ADDRESS:** Professor of Education, California State University-Chico, Chico, CA 95929-0222, (916)898-6421.

HUANG, H. T. (HSING TSUNG)
Science administrator (retired). Chinese American. **PERSONAL:** married Rita Q Huang, Dec 17, 1949; children: Pamela C, Terence M. **EDUCATION:** Hong Kong University, BS, 1941; Oxford University, England, DPhil, 1947. **CAREER:** Rohm, Haas Co, research biochemist, 1951-55; Pfizer Inc, research supervisor, 1955-64; International Minerals & Chem, Biological Science, director, 1964-73; Baxter Lab, Wallenstein Division, Tech Service, director, 1973-75; National Science Fdn, program director, 1975-90; Needham Research Institute, Cambridge, England, deputy director, 1990-. **ORGANIZATIONS:** American Chemical Society; American Society Biochem & Mol Biol; Society for Invertebrate Biol; Association for the Advancement of Industrial Crops; History of Science Society. **HONORS/AWARDS:** AAIC, Guayule Special Recognition Award, 1988. **SPECIAL ACHIEVEMENTS:** Author of publications in chemistry, biochemistry and history of science; 18 US patents. **HOME ADDRESS:** 309 Yoakum Pkwy, #403, Alexandria, VA 22304, (703)751-1216.

HUANG, HUEY-WEN
Educator. Taiwanese American. **PERSONAL:** Born Feb 22, 1940, Tainan, Taiwan; son of Chin-Chiang Huang and Lin Shin Huang; married Yu-Ru Y Huang, Jul 1, 1989; children: Emily Pei-Hsin, Patrick Pei-Yuen. **EDUCATION:** National Taiwan University, BS, 1962; Cornell University, PhD, 1967. **CAREER:** Columbia University, research associate, 1967-69; Yale University, lecturer, 1969-71; Southern Illinois University, assistant professor, 1971-73; Yale University, visiting professor of biophysics, 1987-88; Rice University, assistant professor, 1973-77, associate professor, 1977-82, professor of physics, 1982-. **ORGANIZATIONS:** American Physical Society, 1971-; American Association for the Advancement of Science, 1984-; Biophysical Society, 1976-. **HONORS/AWARDS:** American Physical Society, fellow. **SPECIAL ACHIEVEMENTS:** Publications in professional journals on statistical physics and membrane biophysics. **MILITARY SERVICE:** Taiwan Air Force, 2nd lt, 1962-63. **BUSINESS ADDRESS:** Professor of Physics, Rice University, PO Box 1892, Houston, TX 77251-1892, (713)527-4899.

HUANG, I-NING
Educator. Chinese American. **PERSONAL:** Born Dec 11, 1939, Hangchou, China; son of Chi-tsy & Woo-chin Huang; married Joyce L Huang, Aug 11, 1985; children: Kuang-Yu, Kuang-Hao, Kuang-Hung. **EDUCATION:** National Taiwan University, BS, 1961; New Mexico State University, MA, 1964; University of Texas, Austin, PhD, 1968. **CAREER:** National Taiwan University, visiting associate professor, 1970-71; University of Wisconsin, Whitewater, assistant professor, 1968-73, associate professor, 1973-76, professor, 1976-. **ORGANIZATIONS:** Midwestern Psychological Association, 1968-; American Psychological Society, 1991-. **HONORS/AWARDS:** University of Wisconsin, State Research Grants, 1968-88. **SPECIAL ACHIEVEMENTS:** 23 publications/papers on learning & conditioning & human memory, 1968-. **BUSINESS ADDRESS:** Professor, Dept of Psychology, University of Wisconsin-Whitewater, Whitewater, WI 53190, (414)475-5417.

HUANG, IAN
Company executive. Chinese American. **PERSONAL:** Born in Hong Kong; married Louise; children: Denise, Monique, Ianna. **EDUCATION:** Carnegie-Mellon University, BSEE, MS; University of Portland, MSEE. **CAREER:** Digital Equipment, group manager, FDDI program, 1986-87; Hughes Lan Systems, engineering, vice president, 1991-. **ORGANIZATIONS:** Asian Business League, board member, 1991-; Advanced Computing Committee, Association for Computer Machinery, chairman, 1981; Asian Management Institute, co-chairperson, 1992. **HONORS/AWARDS:** Electronic Engineering Times, Logic Analyser Application, 1976. **BUSINESS ADDRESS:** President, CEO, XNET Technology Inc, 426 S Hillview Dr, Milpitas, CA 95035, (408)263-6888.

HUANG, JACK J. T.
Attorney. Taiwanese American. **PERSONAL:** Born Oct 11, 1952, Taipei, Taiwan; son of Ping-Hwei Huang and Ching-Chu Lee Huang; married Shelly Y S Huang, Oct 2, 1977; children: Andrew C C, Angela C W. **EDUCATION:** National Taiwan University, LLB, 1975; Northwestern University, LLM, 1979; Harvard University, SJD, 1983. **CAREER:** Lee and Li, Taipei, associate, 1977-78; Coudert Brothers, Hong Kong, associate, 1979-80, New York, associate, 1983-86; Jones, Day, Reavis & Pogue, New York, associate, 1986-89, Taipei partner-in-charge, 1990-. **ORGANIZATIONS:** New York City Bar Association, 1983-; Taipei Bar Association, 1977-; Taipei American School, board director, 1992-; Moral Re-Armament Association of ROC, advisor,

1990-. **SPECIAL ACHIEVEMENTS:** Frequent contributor of articles to various legal journals; proficient in English and Mandarin and Taiwanese Chinese. **BIOGRAPHICAL SOURCES:** "Meeting for the Future of Taiwan," Global Views Magazine, p 74-75, Nov 15, 1991. **BUSINESS ADDRESS:** Partner-in-charge, Taipei Office, Jones Day Reavis & Pogue, Tun Hwa South Road, 7th Floor, No 2, Sec 2, Taipei 10022, Taiwan, 886-2-7046808.

HUANG, JACOB WEN-KUANG
Educator, physicist. Chinese American. **PERSONAL:** Born Nov 7, 1935, Canton, Kwangtung, China; married Caroline K E Huang, Dec 2, 1967; children: Brian, Alicia. **EDUCATION:** National Taiwan University, BS, 1958; Virginia Poly Tech, 1961; Johns Hopkins University, PhD, 1968. **CAREER:** Towson State University, assistant professor, 1967-71, associate professor, 1971-78, professor, 1978-, Physics Department, chair, 1991-. **ORGANIZATIONS:** Optical Society of America, 1975-; American Association of Physics Teachers, 1967-; American Physical Society, 1967-78; Sigma Xi, 1978-; Physics Student Honor Society, 1961-. **HONORS/AWARDS:** Johns Hopkins University, President Fund Fellowship, 1962-65; NSF summer research participation, Texas Instrument Central Research Lab, 1976, Brown University, 1968; ASEE summer research participation, GSFC/NASA, 1984, 1985. **BUSINESS ADDRESS:** Professor and Chair, Physics Dept, Towson State University, Towson, MD 21204, (410)830-3009.

HUANG, JAMIN
Chemist. Taiwanese American. **PERSONAL:** Born Aug 1, 1951, Taipei, Taiwan; son of Lung-Gi Huang & Yu-Yen Kao Huang; married Gloria Wen-Wah Huang, Aug 25, 1979; children: Diana W, Bernice K. **EDUCATION:** Chung-Hsing University, Taiwan, BS, 1973; Cornell University, MS, 1978, PhD, 1980. **CAREER:** Union Carbide Ag Prod Co, senior chemist, 1980-83, project scientist, 1984-86; Rhone-Poulenc Ag Co, France, research scientist, 1987-91, research scientist, 1989-90 (France), senior research scientist, 1991-. **ORGANIZATIONS:** American Chemical Society, 1978-. **HONORS/AWARDS:** Rhone-Poulenc SA, Prix de la Research Award, 1992. **SPECIAL ACHIEVEMENTS:** 11 publications in the areas of organic synthesis & natural product isolation; 10 US patent applications, several issued; one French patent; patents related to novel insecticides or fungicides; languages; Chinese, French, German (reading). **MILITARY SERVICE:** Air Force, Taiwan, second lieutenant, 1973-75. **HOME ADDRESS:** 233 Old Forest Creek, Chapel Hill, NC 27514, (919)968-1516. **BUSINESS ADDRESS:** Senior Research Scientist, Rhone-Poulenc Ag Co, PO Box 12014, 2 TW Alexander Drive, Research Triangle Park, NC 27709, (919)549-2634.

HUANG, JENNMING STEPHEN
Chemical engineer. Taiwanese American/Chinese American. **PERSONAL:** Born Jul 30, 1947, Changhua, Taiwan; son of Ho-Yian & Chung-Mei H Huang; married Yuhua S Huang, Dec 25, 1968; children: Raymond J, Rayleen S. **EDUCATION:** National Taiwan University, BS, chemical engineering, 1969; Syracuse University, MS, chemical engineering, 1972, PhD, chemical engineering, 1975. **CAREER:** International Flavors & Fragrances Inc, senior engineer, 1976; research engineer, 1976-77, senior research engineer, 1977-78, project engineer, 1978-80, Corp Engineering Technology, manager, 1980-82, director, 1982-91, USA vice president, 1992-. **ORGANIZATIONS:** AIChE, 1975-. **HONORS/AWARDS:** Syracuse University, fellowship, 1973-75; National Taiwan University, Merit Fellowship, 1965-69. **SPECIAL ACHIEVEMENTS:** Publications in AIChE Journal; delivered papers at Bath Process Automation Conferences; established joint venture in China for aroma chemical manufacture. **BUSINESS ADDRESS:** Vice President, International Flavors & Fragrances Inc, 1515 Highway 36, Union Beach, NJ 07735, (908)888-2529.

HUANG, JIANN-SHIUN
Educator. Chinese American. **PERSONAL:** Born Apr 19, 1954, Taipei, Taiwan; son of Suei-Sen Huang and Chao-Tze Huang; married Arnfong Huang, Nov 26, 1980; children: Ming-Ern, Katherine. **EDUCATION:** Tunghai University, Taiwan, BS, 1976; Virginia Polytechnic Institute & State University, MS, 1984, MS, 1985, PhD, 1991. **CAREER:** Cornell Dubilier Electronics, Taiwan, process engineer, 1978-83; Virginia Tech (VPI&SU), graduate teaching assistant, 1983-991; Columbia College, visiting assistant professor, 1991-. **ORGANIZATIONS:** Society of Actuaries, associate, 1993-; Mathematical Association of America, 1991-; International Chinese Statistical Association, 1989-. **HONORS/AWARDS:** Middle Atlantic Actuarial Club, Student Awards, 1990; VPI&SU Department of Statistics, Boyd Harshbarger Award,

1984; Tunghai University, Service Award, 1976. **HOME PHONE:** (314)446-0155. **BUSINESS ADDRESS:** Visiting Assistant Professor, Columbia College, 1001 Rogers St, 224 St Clair Hall, Columbia, MO 65216, (314)875-7583.

HUANG, JIN

Educator. Chinese American. **PERSONAL:** Born Nov 8, 1946, Chongqing, Sichuan, China; son of Jinyuan Huang and Xumu Zhou; married Guoqing Zhan, Mar 5, 1972; children: Cen Michael. **EDUCATION:** University of Science and Technology of China, BS, 1970; Montana State University, MS, 1983, PhD, 1987. **CAREER:** High School, China, teacher, 1972-78; University of Science & Technology of China, teaching assistant, 1978-81; University of Oregon, postdoctoral research associate, 1987-89; University of Wisconsin, Eau Claire, assistant professor, 1989-. **ORGANIZATIONS:** American Physics Society. **HONORS/AWARDS:** Montana State University, Outstanding Teaching Assistant, 1984. **SPECIAL ACHIEVEMENTS:** "Use of Phase-Noisy Laser Fields in the Storage of Optical Puse Shapes in Inhomogenously Broadened Absorbers," Optical Letter, vol 16, No 2, p 103, 1991; "On the Shifting of Optical Transition Frequencies," Journal Lumin, vol 75, p 392, 1990; "Excess Dephasing in Photon Echo Experiments," Physicians Review Letter, vol 63, p 78, 1989; "Rsesonant Enhancement of Direct Two-Photon Absorption," Physician Review, B39, 1989. **BUSINESS ADDRESS:** Professor, Dept of Physics and Astronomy, University of Wisconsin, Eau Claire, Eau Claire, WI 54702, (715)836-2272.

HUANG, JOHN SHIAO-SHIH

Physicist. Chinese American. **PERSONAL:** Born Feb 22, 1940, Chung-King, China; son of T S Huang and Joy Huang; married Helen W Huang, Sep 2, 1967; children: Enoch, Christopher, Karen. **EDUCATION:** National Taiwan University, BS, physics, 1962; Cornell University, MS, physics, 1966, PhD, physics, 1969. **CAREER:** Rutgers University, assistant professor of physics, 1969-73; University of Pittsburgh, visiting faculty, 1973-76; Exxon Research & Engineering, staff physicist, 1976-88, science area leader, 1988-89, section head, 1989-. **ORGANIZATIONS:** NASA, Fundimental Processes Working Group, 1987-93; DOE, Panel on Neutron Source, 1992; American Physical Society, industrial associate advisory board, 1989-93; Lehigh University, industrial advisory council, 1991-93; NATO Advanced Institute of Study, co-organizer, 1991-; Ambassadors for Christ, board member, 1977-. **HONORS/AWARDS:** Max Planck Gesellshaft, Max Planck Research Award, 1990; American Physical Society, fellow, 1990. **BUSINESS ADDRESS:** Section Head, Exxon Research & Engineering Co, Rt 22E, Room LA-352, Annandale, NJ 08801, (908)730-2865.

HUANG, JOSEPH CHI KAN

Scientist, research program manager. Chinese American. **PERSONAL:** Born May 21, 1938, Hangzhou, Zhejiang, China; son of Frank Ho Huang; married Nancy W Huang, Jul 1, 1967; children: Pearl Syng, Jade Syng, Cara Syng. **EDUCATION:** Naval Academy, BS, 1959; University of Michigan, MS, 1965, PhD, 1969; Scripps Institute of Oceanography, University of California, San Diego, postdoctoral, 1970. **CAREER:** Scripps Institute of Oceanography, University of California, San Diego, res professor, 1970-81; University of Michigan, Great Lakes Environmental Research Lab, NOAA, adj professor, 1976-81; National Oceanic & Atmospheric Administration, US Dept of Commerce, sr scientist, 1981-. **ORGANIZATIONS:** American Association for the Advancement of Science, 1970-; American Geophysical Union, 1970-; Oceanography Society, 1990-; American Meteorology Society. 1970-. **HONORS/AWARDS:** Sigma Xi, 1967; Rackham School of Graduate Studies, University of Michigan, Full Fellowship, 1964, 1965; University of Michigan, Outstanding Research Award, 1969; NOAA, Distinguished Achievement Awards, 1983, 1985, 1987, 1988. **SPECIAL ACHIEVEMENTS:** Published more than 50 papers in reviewed journals and publications. **MILITARY SERVICE:** Chinese Navy, lt. **HOME ADDRESS:** 9813 Korman Ct, Potomac, MD 20854, (301)983-1798. **BUSINESS PHONE:** (301)713-2797.

HUANG, JOSEPH T.

Educator. Taiwanese American/Chinese American. **PERSONAL:** Born May 29, 1962, Taipei, Taiwan; son of Shean Huang and Anna Lu Huang; married Silvana Gauassa Huang, Dec 27, 1988; children: Katherine Alyssa. **EDUCATION:** University of British Columbia, BSc, 1985; Louisiana Tech University, MS, 1987. **CAREER:** Howard Comm College, Computer Science/Networking, assoc prof, 1987-; APG Inc, MIS, manager, 1990-93. **BUSINESS ADDRESS:** Associate Professor of Comp Science/Networking, Howard Community College, 10901 Little Patuxent Pkwy, Business/CS Divsion, Columbia, MD 21044, (410)992-4874.

HUANG, JOYCE L.

Librarian. Chinese American. **PERSONAL:** Born Jan 28, 1943, Si-Ying, Kwangtung, China; daughter of Choke-Nam Leung and Kun-Bing Lee; married I-Ning Huang. **EDUCATION:** University of Hong Kong, BA, 1966; University of Maryland, MLS, 1970; Northeastern University, MA, 1978. **CAREER:** Good Hope School, teacher, 1966-68; Bridgewater State College, reference department, head, 1970-85; University of Wisconsin, Whitewater, reference librarian, 1985-90, collection mgt, head, 1990-92, technical processing service, head, 1992-. **ORGANIZATIONS:** American Library Association, 1970-; American Association of University Women, 1972-92; New England Library Association, 1970-85; Wisconsin Library Association, 1985-; WAAL Edu & Librarian Use Com, chair, 1988, 89; College & Research Librarians, 1970-; Beta Phi Mu. **HONORS/AWARDS:** University of Wisconsin System, grant, 1992-93; Bridgewater State College, Distinguished Service Award, 1978-79, 1984-85. **SPECIAL ACHIEVEMENTS:** "Minimum Library Users Skills Survey," ERIC, ED, 297-758, 1988. **BUSINESS ADDRESS:** Head, Technical Processing Service, University of Wisconsin, Whitewater, Andersen Library, 800 Main Street, Whitewater, WI 53190, (414)472-5516.

HUANG, JU-CHANG (HOWARD)

Educator. Taiwanese American. **PERSONAL:** Born Jan 3, 1941, Kaohsiung, Taiwan; son of Ti & Bih Lin Huang; married Jolynn C Huang, Nov 26, 1986; children: Alina, Nancy, Jacqueline. **EDUCATION:** National Taiwan University, BS, 1963; University of Texas, Austin, MS, 1966, PhD, 1967. **CAREER:** Austin, Smith & Associates, Inc, chief env engineer, 1972-73; University of Missouri, Rolla, assistant professor of civil engineering, 1967-70, associate professor of civil engineering, 1970-75, professor, director, environment research center, 1975-92; Hong Kong University of Science and Technology, professor of civil engineering, 1993-. **ORGANIZATIONS:** American Society of Civil Engineers, 1967-86, fellow, 1986-; Water Pollution Control Federation, 1967-. **HONORS/AWARDS:** American Society of Civil Engineers, Walter L Huber Civil Engineering Research Award, 1979; Missouri Society of Professional Engineers, Young Engineer of the Year, 1976; American Society for Engineering Education, ASEE-Ford Foundation Resident Fellow Award, 1972. **SPECIAL ACHIEVEMENTS:** Published over 100 technical articles in various journals and professional confernece proceedings, 1967-. **HOME ADDRESS:** 1405 Highland Drive, Rolla, MO 65401. **BUSINESS ADDRESS:** Professor of Civil Engineering, Hong Kong University of Science and Technology, Clearwater Bay, Kowloon, Hong Kong, 852-358-7165.

HUANG, JUNG-CHANG

Educator, educational administrator. Taiwanese American. **PERSONAL:** Born Apr 7, 1935, Taoyuan, Taiwan; son of Mr & Mrs You-kun Huang; married Shih-wen Huang; children: Frederick, Joyce, Warren. **EDUCATION:** Kansas State University, MS, 1962; University of Pennsylvania, PhD, 1969. **CAREER:** Western Electric Company, design engineer, 1962-66; University of Pennsylvania, teaching, research fellow, 1967-69; University of Houston, assistant professor, 1969-73, associate professor, 1973-80, professor, 1980-, department of computer science, chairman, 1992-. **ORGANIZATIONS:** Association of Computing Machinery, 1966-; Institute of Electrical and Electronics Engineers, senior member, 1962-. **BUSINESS ADDRESS:** Professor and Chairman, Dept of Computer Science, University of Houston, 4800 Calhoun, Houston, TX 77204-3475, (713)743-3350.

HUANG, KEE CHANG

Educator. Chinese American. **PERSONAL:** Born Jul 22, 1917, Canton, Kwangtung, China; married Shou-shan Chang Huang, Feb 16, 1947; children: Kou Chu, Anna K Huang Shrader, Karen T Huang Soo. **EDUCATION:** Dr Sun Yet-san University, Medical College, MD, 1940; Columbia University, P & S, PhD, 1953. **CAREER:** National Health Institute of China, research fellow, 1940-46; Shanghai Medical College, Shanghai, China, instructor, 1946-49; University of Louisville, Medical Science Center, research associate, 1953-56, assistant professor, 1956-59, associate professor, 1959-63, professor, 1963-. **HONORS/AWARDS:** University of Louisville, Distinguished Professor Award, 1982, Medical School, Outstanding Teacher Award, 9 years. **SPECIAL ACHIEVEMENTS:** Author, Pharmacology of Chinese Herbs, CRC Press, 1992; Outline of Pharmacology, 1974, Drug Absorption, Excretion and Elimination, 1972, author and co-authors of more than 60 research publications. **BUSINESS ADDRESS:** Professor, University of Louisville, Medical Science Center, MDR Bldg, Rm 428, Louisville, KY 40292, (502)852-5347.

HUANG, KEN SHEN
Educator. Taiwanese American. **PERSONAL:** Born Mar 19, 1937, Taipei, Taiwan; married Chris Huang, Nov 1969; children: Everest W. **EDUCATION:** Taiwan Normal University, BA, 1961; University of Iowa, MA, 1972, MFA, 1973. **CAREER:** Memphis State University, instructor, 1973, assistant professor, 1978, associate professor of art, 1982-. **ORGANIZATIONS:** Formosan Association for Human Rights; College Art Association; National Conference of Christians and Jews, Memphis region. **HONORS/AWARDS:** National Conference of Christians and Jews, Memphis region, Community Service Award. **SPECIAL ACHIEVEMENTS:** Art works in the permanent collections of: The White House, Tennessee State Museum, Masur Museum of Art, University Gallery, Morehead State University, Kentucky; cash & purchase awards from national juried shows: National Painting Show, Southeast State University, Minnesota, Monroe National Show, Monroe, Louisiana. **HOME PHONE:** (901)680-0618. **BUSINESS ADDRESS:** Associate Professor of Art, Memphis State University, Central & Patterson, 101 Art Bldg, Memphis, TN 38152, (901)678-2359.

HUANG, KO-HSING
Educator. Chinese American. **PERSONAL:** Born Apr 22, 1953, Shanghai, People's Republic of China; son of Huang Yan and Yang Xining; married Chia Ning, Jun 18, 1983. **EDUCATION:** Beijing Normal University, BA, 1982; Illinois State University, MA, 1985; Johns Hopkins University, PhD, 1993. **CAREER:** Loyola College, adjunct professor, 1991-92; Central College, adjunct professor, 1992-. **BUSINESS ADDRESS:** Professor, Political Science Dept, Central College, Pella, IA 50219.

HUANG, LIANG HSIUNG
Microbiologist. Taiwanese American. **PERSONAL:** Born Jul 16, 1939, I-Lan, Taiwan; son of Kin Shi and A Chaw; married Jane Huang, Jul 23, 1970; children: Grace, Amy. **EDUCATION:** National Taiwan University, BS, 1962; The University of Wisconsin, Madison, MS, 1965, PhD, 1971. **CAREER:** Ohio State University, postdoc res fellow, 1972-73; The University of Georgia, postdoctoral res fellow, 1973-75; Pfizer Inc, Central Res, research scientist, 1975-78, senior research scientist, 1978-83, senior research investigator, 1983-91, principal research investigator, 1991-. **ORGANIZATIONS:** Mycological Society of America, 1967-; US Federation for Culture Collections, 1975-; American Society for Microbiology, 1975-; Selection Committee of J R Porter Award, 1988-91; Society for Industrial Microbiology, 1975-; New York Academy of Sciences, 1982-; Amer Assoc for the Advt of Sci, 1992-; US Fed for Culture Collections, newsletter editor, 1987-88, vp, 1988-90, president, 1990-92. **HONORS/AWARDS:** American Type Culture Collection, Adv Com of Mycology Dept, 1989-92. **SPECIAL ACHIEVEMENTS:** Published 37 scientific papers; 10 US patents; discovered new development type of ascocarp centrum, new polycyclic ether antiobiotics, ansamycin antibiotics; discovered new genus of actinomycetes and new species of Nocardia, Actinomadura, Nocardiopsis, Aspergillus, Eleutherascus, Gliocephalotrichum, Neurospora, Triangularia, and Zopfiella; Antimicrobial Agts, and Chemotherapy, editorial board, 1977-82; Journal Antibiotics, editorial board, 1990-. **HOME ADDRESS:** 23 Sunrise Trail, East Lyme, CT 06333, (203)739-0493. **BUSINESS ADDRESS:** Principal Research Investigator, Central Research, Pfizer Inc, Eastern Point Road, Bldg. 118, Rm 345, Groton, CT 06340, (203)441-3569.

HUANG, MING-HUI
Educator. Taiwanese American. **PERSONAL:** Born Nov 3, 1951, Taipei, Taiwan; son of Danny Huaqng and Amy Huang; married Christina Huang, Dec 12, 1976; children: Connie, Sylvia. **EDUCATION:** Tunghai University, BS, physics, 1973; Ohio University, PhD, physics, 1981; Iona College, MS, computer science, 1987. **CAREER:** Hocking Technical College, instructor, 1979-80; Shawnee State College, assistant professor, 1980-83; Iona College, assistant professor, 1983-89, associate professor, 1989-, chairman, 1990-. **ORGANIZATIONS:** APS; AAPT. **SPECIAL ACHIEVEMENTS:** Author, "Computer Simulation of Dice Game," Pittsburgh Conference on Modeling & Simulation, 1988; "Computerization of Titration Analysis Using ASYST," 1988; "Computerization of Titration Analysis," Scientific Computing & Automation, 1989; "Interface Microcomputer to Spectrophotometer Using ASYST," 1989; "Business Forecasting beyond Spread Sheet," 1990. **MILITARY SERVICE:** Artillery Battalion, Taiwan Army, 2nd lt, 1973-75. **BUSINESS ADDRESS:** Chairman, Physics Dept, Iona College, 715 North Ave, New Rochelle, NY 10801-1890, (914)633-2236.

HUANG, NAI-CHIEN
Educator. Chinese American. **PERSONAL:** Born Jul 8, 1932, Nantong, Jiangsu, China; son of Mr & Mrs Chi-Tseng Huang; married Geraldine S M Huang, Jul 29, 1963; children: Sheila Huang Humpheries, Nathan. **EDUCATION:** National Taiwan University, BS, 1953; Brown University, MS, 1958; Harvard University, PhD, 1963. **CAREER:** Stanford University, research associate, 1963-65; University of California, San Diego, assistant professor, 1965-69; University of Notre Dame, professor, 1969-. **SPECIAL ACHIEVEMENTS:** Author, Fundamental Aspects of Solid Propellent Rockets, 1969; 80 technical papers, 1969-. **HOME PHONE:** (219)234-0393. **BUSINESS ADDRESS:** Professor, Dept of Aerospace & Mechanical Engineering, University of Notre Dame, Notre Dame, IN 46556, (219)631-6403.

HUANG, PEI
Educator. Chinese American. **PERSONAL:** Born 1928, Haimen County, Kiangsu, China; married Hetty H H Huang, 1965; children: two sons. **EDUCATION:** National Taiwan University, BA, 1956, MA, 1959; Indiana University, PhD, 1963. **CAREER:** University of Iowa, visiting assistant professor, history, 1965-66; University of Wisconsin, River Falls, assistant professor, history, 1966-69; Youngstown State University, associate professor to professor, 1969-. **ORGANIZATIONS:** American Historical Association; American Association for Chinese Studies; Association for Asian Studies; Historical Society of 20th Century China in North America International Southern Society; National Education Association. **HONORS/AWARDS:** State of Wisconsin, Board of Regents, research grant, 1969; National Endowment for the Humanities, research grant, 1976; Youngstown State University, research professorship, 1988, 1992. **SPECIAL ACHIEVEMENTS:** Autocracy at Work, Indiana University Press, 1974; editor, The Early Ch'ing Dynasty: State and Society, 2 vols, Chinese Studies in History, summer and fall-winter, 1981-82; "The Grand Council of the Ch'ing Dynasty," Bulletin of the School of Oriental and African Studies, 48, 3:502-15, 1985; "New Light on the Origins of the Manchus," Harvard Journal of Asiatic Studies, 501:239-282, 1990; editor, Modern China: Reform, Protest, Protest and Revolution, 2 vols, Chiese Studies in History, spring and summer, 1992. **BUSINESS ADDRESS:** Professor, Dept of History, Youngstown State University, Youngstown, OH 44555-3452, (216)742-3452.

HUANG, SAMUEL T.
Research librarian. Chinese American. **PERSONAL:** Born Jun 23, 1939, Amoy, Fukien, China; son of Yen Hui Haung & Wa-Tan Chen; married Corinna K Huang, Sep 9, 1971; children: Leslie, Jonathan. **EDUCATION:** Tamkang University, BA, 1962; Northern Illinois University, MALS, 1967, MS, 1977. **CAREER:** Northern Illinois University, Interlibrary Loans Department, head, 1973-78, General Education Library, assistant head, 1978-80, Library Services for the Physically Impaired, coordinator, 1980-85, Computer Reference Services, coordinator, 1985-87, senior reference librarian, 1987-89, Rare Books & Special Collections, head, 1989-. **ORGANIZATIONS:** American Library Association, 1980-; Illinois Library Association, 1972-. **HONORS/AWARDS:** Prince University of Songkhla, Thailand, USIS Research Grant, 1991; Northern Illinois University, Director's Research Support Program Award, 1988; Faculty Career Enhancement Grant, 1992; DeKalb Handicapped Advisory Commission, Outstanding Service to the Disabled Individuals in the DeKalb Community, 1986. **SPECIAL ACHIEVEMENTS:** Presentations, "Will CD-ROM Databases Replace Online searching in Libraries?" Mexico, 1993; "CD-ROM LANS: A New Challenge for Reference Librarians," National Online Meeting, New York, 1992; "The Changing Role of Reference Librarians in Modern Academic Libraries," Illinois Library Association Annual Conference, 1989; editor, Modern Library Technology and Reference Services, Haworth Press, Inc, 1993; author, "Library Resources on the Employment of People with Disabilities," Library Services for Career Planning, Job Searching and Employment Opportunities, edited by Byron Anderson, Haworth Press, Inc, 1992; "Communications and Speech" and "Disabilities," Magazines for Libraries, seventh edition, ed by Bill Katz, R R Bowker, pp 292-296, 344-353, 1992; Library Journal, book reviewer. **BIOGRAPHICAL SOURCES:** Directory of Library and Information Professionals, p 568, 1988; The Directory of Ethnic Professionals in LIS, p 103, 1991. **BUSINESS ADDRESS:** Professor, Head, Rare Books & Special Collections, Northern Illinois University, The University Libraries, FML 403, Normal Road, De Kalb, IL 60115, (815)753-0255.

HUANG, SHAN-JEN CHEN
Educator. Taiwanese American/Chinese American. **PERSONAL:** Born Oct 22, 1951, Tainan, Taiwan; daughter of L T Chen & Chung-Siang Wu; married

T J Huang, Jul 8, 1977; children: Mike Tze-Wei, Daniel Tze-Young. **EDUCATION:** Chun-Yuan University, BS, 1973, MS, 1976; University of Pittsburgh, PhD, 1989. **CAREER:** Chun-Yuan University, instructor, 1977-78; Fu-Jen University, instructor, 1978-83; University of Pittsburgh, teaching fellow, 1983-88; Morgan State University, instructor, 1991-. **SPECIAL ACHIEVEMENTS:** Theoretical study in physical chemistry. **HOME ADDRESS:** 9818 Hickoryhurst Dr, Baltimore, MD 21236, (410)529-7331.

HUANG, SHIH-WEN
Physician, educator. Taiwanese American. **PERSONAL:** Born Sep 25, 1936, Tainan, Taiwan; son of Chin-Chiang Huang and Lin Shing Huang; married Sophie Shih-Huey Huang, Dec 17, 1966; children: Daniel, Paul, Benjamin. **EDUCATION:** National Taiwan University, MD. **CAREER:** University of Wisconsin, fellow, instructor, 1970-73; University of Maryland, assistant professor, chief allergy, immunology, 1973-76, associate professor, chief allergy, immunology, 1976-84, professor, chief allergy, immunology, 1984-85; University of Florida, professor, chief allergy division, 1985-. **ORGANIZATIONS:** American Academy of Pediatrics, fellow, 1972; American Academy of Allergy & Immunology, fellow, 1976; Society of Pediatric Research; American Pediatric Society; Clinical Immunology Society; American Association of Immunology. **HONORS/AWARDS:** Allergy Foundation of America, fellow, 1972; American Lung Association, citation, distinguished service, 1985. **SPECIAL ACHIEVEMENTS:** Established autoimmunity as the cause of Type 1 diabetes, 1976; secretory component of IgA is produced by epithelial cells, 1978; platelet activation in allergy, 1987; language proficiency: Mandarin, Taiwanese, Japanese. **MILITARY SERVICE:** Chinese Navy, compulsory, Ensign, 1962-63. **BUSINESS ADDRESS:** Prof, Div of Allergy/Immunology, Dept of Pediatrics, University of Florida College of Medicine, JHMHC, Gainesville, FL 32610, (904)392-9397.

HUANG, THOMAS TAO-SHING
Educator, educational administrator. Chinese American. **PERSONAL:** Born Jul 3, 1939, Chungking, China; son of Te-Hsin Huang & Shao-Mei Chen; married M Janice F Huang, Jun 12, 1965; children: Margaret L, Steven H. **EDUCATION:** National Taiwan University, BS, 1961; East Tennessee State University, MA, 1964; University of Illinois, Urbana, PhD, 1969. **CAREER:** University of Illinois, post-doctural research associate, 1968-69; University of Kentucky, assistant professor, 1969-71; East Tennessee State University, assistant professor, 1971-78, associate professor, 1978-83, professor & chair of chemistry, 1979-. **ORGANIZATIONS:** American Chemical Society, 1968-; ACS, Regional Meeting SE, general chair, 1993; Northeast Tennessee Section, president, 1976; Phi Kappa Phi, ETSU Chapter, president, 1987-90; Sigma Xi; Phi Kappa Phi. **HONORS/AWARDS:** ETSU, Outstanding Faculty Award, 1988; ACS, NE Tennessee, Speaker of the Year, 1975; AEC Fellow, 1967-69. **SPECIAL ACHIEVEMENTS:** Published many papers in professional journals; two laboratory manuals; taught in China as visiting professor, summers of 1980, 1981, 1985, 1988, 1990, 1992; presented seminars at numerous universities in US and abroad. **MILITARY SERVICE:** Chinese Taiwan Armored Corp, second lieutenant, 1961-62. **BUSINESS ADDRESS:** Professor & Chair, Dept of Chemistry, East Tennessee State University, Johnson City, TN 37614-0695, (615)929-4367.

HUANG, THOMAS W.
Attorney. Chinese American. **PERSONAL:** Born Feb 1, 1941, Taipei, Taiwan; son of Lienteng Huang and Helen Yen; children: Charlotte. **EDUCATION:** Taiwan University, BA, law, 1964; Indiana University Law School, JD, 1970; Harvard Law School, LLM, SJD, 1970-75. **CAREER:** Reiser & Rosenberg, 1982-87; Law Offices of Thomas W Huang & Associates, principal, 1987-88; Hale, Sanderson, Byrnes & Morton, member, 1988-. **ORGANIZATIONS:** National Association of Chinese Americans, legal counsel, 1979-80; Chinese Economic Development Council, board of directors, 1978-80; Massachusetts Governor's Advisory Council on Guangdong, 1984-87; Minority Business Task Force, Senator Kerry's Office, 1988-; Asian American Bank & Trust, director/clerk, 1992-; National Association of Chinese Americans, Boston Chapter, president/vice president, 1984-88; Boston Bar Association, International Law Sec, steering committee, 1979-90. **SPECIAL ACHIEVEMENTS:** Author, ''The Critique of Law in Social Theories'' (in Chinese), China Times Press, 1991; ''Reflections on Law & the Economy in the People's Republic of China,'' 14 Harv Int'l LJ, 261, 1973; ''The Protection of American Copyrights under Nationalist Chinese Law,'' 12 Harv Int'l LJ, 90, 1971. **MILITARY SERVICE:** Army, Taiwan, lt, 1964-65. **BUSINESS ADDRESS:** Attorney at Law, Hale, Sanderson, Byrnes & Morton, One Center Plaza, Boston, MA 02108, (617)227-2070.

HUANG, TSENG
Educator. Chinese American. **PERSONAL:** Born Dec 9, 1925, Jiangsu, China; son of Mo-Hsing Huang and Yu-Lan Shih; married Yoemin Liu Huang, Jun 12, 1960; children: Lawrence Peter, Austin Lancelot, Minnie Victoria. **EDUCATION:** Chiao Tung University, BSCE, 1947; University of Oklahoma, MCE, 1955; University of Illinois, PhD, 1960. **CAREER:** Keelung Harbor Bureau, Taiwan, civil engineer, 1947-54; Silo Bridge Office, Taiwan, civil engineer, 1952; Oklahoma Highway Department, bridge designer, 1955-56; University of Illinois, research assistant, associate, assistant professor, 1957-61; University of Texas at Arlington, associate professor, 1961-63, professor, 1963-. **ORGANIZATIONS:** American Society of Civil Engineers; American Society of Mechanical Engineers; Structural Stability Research Council; Phi Kappa Phi; Sigma Xi; Chi Epsilon; Tau Beta Pi; International Society of Offshore and Polar Engineers. **HONORS/AWARDS:** University of Oklahoma, scholarship, 1954; University of Illinois, fellowship, 1956; ASME Petroleum Division, Eugene W Jacobson Award, 1980; University of Texas at Arlington, Distinguished Research Award, 1980; ASME OMAE Division, Achievement Award, 1988; Intl Society of Offshore and Polar Engineers, ISOPE Award, 1993. **BUSINESS ADDRESS:** Professor, Dept of Civil Engineering, University of Texas at Arlington, Box 19308, Arlington, TX 76019-0308, (817)273-3665.

HUANG, VICTOR TSANGMIN
Food researcher. Taiwanese American. **PERSONAL:** Born Dec 12, 1951, Pu-Hsin Hsiang Chang-Hua Huien, Taiwan; son of Shen-Tang Huang & Lai Ye-Gee Huang; married Jean Huang, Aug 9, 1978; children: Hank, Andrea. **EDUCATION:** Tsing-Hua University, BS, chemistry, 1973; University of Chicago, MS, chemistry, 1977; Ohio State University, PhD, food science, 1981. **CAREER:** Pillsbury Co, scientist, 1981-85, senior scientist, 1985-88, research scientist, 1988-90, senior research scientist, 1990-92, research fellow, 1992-. **ORGANIZATIONS:** American Chemical Society, 1989; American Association of Cereal Chemists, 1981; American Dairy Science Association, 1977; Institute of Food Technologists, 1977. **SPECIAL ACHIEVEMENTS:** 10 patents on food formulation/processing, 1981-93, both US & abroad; 15 published articles in food science/technology journals, 1981-93; 30 presentations, both in US and abroad, 1979-83. **MILITARY SERVICE:** Taiwanese Army, 2nd lt, 1973-75. **BUSINESS ADDRESS:** Research Fellow, Pillsbury Co, 330 University Ave, SE, Minneapolis, MN 55414.

HUANG, WEI-CHIAO
Educator. Taiwanese American. **PERSONAL:** Born Nov 13, 1955, Takia, Taiwan; son of Tony Huang and Ya-Chung Huang; married Wei-Jang Huang, Jul 8, 1978; children: Charissa, Jasmine, Alexander. **EDUCATION:** National Taiwan University, BA, 1977; University of California, Santa Barbara, MA, 1979, PhD, 1984. **CAREER:** University of California, Santa Barbara, lecturer, 1983-84; University of Connecticut, visiting assistant professor, 1984-85; Western Michigan University, assistant professor, 1985-90, associate professor, 1990-. **ORGANIZATIONS:** Chinese Association of Greater Kalamazoo, membership committee chairperson, 1987-90, board of directors, 1991-93; Kalamazoo Chinese Christian Fellowship, executive committee member, 1985-; Hope Reformed Church, deacon, 1988-90; Eastern Economic Association, area representative of Michigan, 1988-. **HONORS/AWARDS:** Western Michigan University, Faculty Research & Creative Activities Award, 1986, 1993. **SPECIAL ACHIEVEMENTS:** Editor, ''Organized Labor at the Crossroads,'' 1989; published numerous articles in professional economics journals, 1986-. **BUSINESS ADDRESS:** Professor, Dept of Economics, Western Michigan University, Kalamazoo, MI 49008-5001, (616)387-5547.

HUANG, WEI-SUNG WILSON
Educator. Taiwanese American. **PERSONAL:** Born Nov 26, 1956, Taipei, Taiwan; son of Chen-Hsia Huang and Chiu-Shen Yen Huang; married Yuei-Er Serena Chang, Dec 28, 1984; children: Joanna Jai-Jai, Jonathan Tin-Hsing. **EDUCATION:** Central Police College, Taiwan, LLB, 1979; Arizona State University, MS, 1984; University of Maryland, College Park, PhD, 1990. **CAREER:** Georgia Statistical Analysis Bureau, research associate, 1990-; Georgia State University, Dept of Criminal Justice, assistant professor, 1990-. **ORGANIZATIONS:** American Society of Criminology, membership committee, 1993-94; American Sociological Association, 1989-; American Criminal Justice Science, 1991-; Arizona State University, Chinese Student Association, president, 1983. **SPECIAL ACHIEVEMENTS:** Publication in International Journal of Comparative and Applied Criminal Justice, 1993; publications in Criminal Justice Policy Review, 1989, 1992; Research Directory, published by the National Institute of Justice, 1990; other publications in Criminal Justice Review, 1993 and International Criminal Justice Review,

1991. **BUSINESS ADDRESS:** Asst Professor, Dept of Criminal Justice, Georgia State University, College of Public and Urban Affairs, Atlanta, GA 30302-4018, (404)651-3515.

HUANG, WEIFENG (CHRIS)
Educator. Chinese American. **PERSONAL:** Born Jan 23, 1930, Shanghai, China; married Dinah C Huang. **EDUCATION:** University of Michigan, BS, 1958, MS, 1959; University of Virginia, PhD, 1963. **CAREER:** University of Virginia, research scientist, 1962-63; University of Louisville, Dept of Physics, professor, 1963-. **ORGANIZATIONS:** American Physical Society, 1962-. **SPECIAL ACHIEVEMENTS:** Material research, catalysts, 1990-; positron annihilation, 1963-. **BUSINESS ADDRESS:** Professor of Physics, University of Louisville, Belknap Campus, Natural Science Bldg, Louisville, KY 40292, (502)588-6787.

HUANG, WILLIAM H.
General contractor. Taiwanese American. **PERSONAL:** Born Sep 1, 1947, Taiwan; son of Shih-Lin Huang and Su-Len Liu Huang; married Alice K Huang, Aug 14, 1977; children: Frank Y, May Y, Sunny Y. **EDUCATION:** Feng Chia University, Taiwan, BS, 1971; University of Florida, master's degree, 1980. **CAREER:** C K Chen & Associates, Architects & Engineers, Taiwan, 1973-77; Baxter Construction Co, 1981-85; Ruby Builders Inc, chief estimator, 1986-88; Great Wall Constructors Inc, president, 1988-. **ORGANIZATIONS:** NHBA. **HOME ADDRESS:** 3123 Raven Rd, Orlando, FL 32803, (407)895-0869. **BUSINESS PHONE:** (407)898-0480.

HUANG, WUU-LIANG
Researcher. Taiwanese American. **PERSONAL:** Born Feb 28, 1944, Taipei, Taiwan; son of Shen Huang and Chin Lee Huang; married Shwu-Yong Huang, Jul 29, 1973; children: Bert. **EDUCATION:** National Taiwan University, BS, 1968; University of Chicago, MS, 1971, PhD, 1973. **CAREER:** National Taiwan University, associate professor, 1975-78; Academia Sinica, adjunct researcher, 1976-79; National Taiwan University, professor, 1978-80; Lunar and Planetary Institute, Houston, visiting scientist, 1979-80; Exxon Production Research Company, sr research geophysist, 1980-82, sr research specialist, 1982-86, sr research staff, 1986-. **ORGANIZATIONS:** North American Chinese Earth Scientist Association, president, 1984-85; Chinese American Petroleum Association, president, 1988; Organization of Chinese Americans, 1990-; American Association Petroleum Geologists, 1984-; American Geophysical Union, 1972-; Mineralogical Society of America, 1973-; Clay Minerals Society, 1985-. **HONORS/AWARDS:** Company President Award, 1986; Chinese American Petroleum Association, Outstanding Service Award, 1988. **SPECIAL ACHIEVEMENTS:** More than 40 scientific papers published in refereed journals; more than 20 presentations at national & international conferences; several invited paper presentations at conferences; service on organization committees at several conferences. **MILITARY SERVICE:** Engineering Army, 2nd lieutenant, 1968-69. **HOME PHONE:** (713)493-9524. **BUSINESS ADDRESS:** Senior Research Staff Member, Exxon Prod Research Company, PO Box 2189, Houston, TX 77252-2189, (713)965-7948.

HUANG, XUN-CHENG
Mathematics educator, researcher. Chinese American. **PERSONAL:** Born Aug 18, 1946, Shanghai, China; son of Chang-Zhong Huang & Han-Ying Ruei; married Fu-Fu Xie, Feb 6, 1977; children: Jia-Chun Huang. **EDUCATION:** East China Normal University, Shanghai, BS, 1969; Shanghai Jiaotong University, MS, 1982; Marquette University, MS, 1987, PhD, 1988. **CAREER:** Yiyang Serpentine Mining Institute, lecturer, 1973-78; Shanghai Institute of Computer Technology, research lecturer, 1982-84; Shanghai Science Industry Co, president, 1983-84; Marquette University, research fellow, 1986-88; Infront Institute of Human Living Environment, professor, president, 1993-; New Jersey Institute of Technology, associate professor, 1988-. **ORGANIZATIONS:** American Mathematics Society, 1984-, Mathematical Association of America, 1984-; Chinese Society of Mathematics, 1982-; Sigma Xi, 1986-. **HONORS/AWARDS:** Mathematical Association of America, Carl B Allendoerfer Award, 1993; New Jersey Institute of Technology, Mathematics Professor of the Year, 1990-91, Outstanding Faculty Award, 1991, Excellence in Teaching Award, 1992, Mathematics Teacher of the Year, 1988-89; Arthur J Schmitt Foundation, Schmitt Research Fellowship, 1986-88. **SPECIAL ACHIEVEMENTS:** More than 130 articles to professional journals, 1982-; author, Concepts of Computer Science, 1987; translator, The Inverse Scattering Transformations and the Theory of Solitons, 1984; translator, An Introduction to Applied Optimal Control, 1985. **BUSINESS ADDRESS:** Associate Profes-

sor, Dept of Mathematics, New Jersey Institute of Technology, 323 Dr M L King Jr Blvd, Cullimore Hall 610, Newark, NJ 07102, (201)596-3489.

HUANG, YASHENG
Educator. Chinese American. **PERSONAL:** Born Mar 3, 1960, Beijing, People's Republic of China; son of Huang Kang and Tan Jiakun. **EDUCATION:** Harvard College, BA, 1985; Harvard University, PhD, 1991. **CAREER:** World Bank, consultant, 1988-89; University of Michigan, assistant professor, 1991-; Suzhon Municipal Government, Jiangsu Province, China, consultant, 1994-. **ORGANIZATIONS:** American Political Science Association, 1991-; Center for Chinese Studies, University of Michigan, faculty associate, 1991-; Fairbanks Center at Harvard University, 1993-94. **HONORS/AWARDS:** American Council of Learned Society, Chiang-Ching Kuo Post-doctoral Fellowship, 1993-94; University of Michigan, Faculty Recognition Award, 1993-95, Faculty Development Fund, 1992-94. **SPECIAL ACHIEVEMENTS:** Author, "China's Economic Development," Adelphi Paper, p 275, 1993; "The Origins of China's Pro-democracy Movement," Fletcher Forum, 1990; "Webs of Interests and Patterns of Behavior," China Quarterly, 1990; "World Bank and China," Harvard Development Forum, 1990; "Information, Bureaucracy and Economic Reforms in China and the Former Soviet Union," World Politics, Oct 1994. **BUSINESS ADDRESS:** Professor, University of Michigan, 204 S State St, CCS, Lane Hall, Ann Arbor, MI 48109-1290, (313)998-7560.

HUANG, ZHEN
Educator. Chinese American. **PERSONAL:** Born Dec 21, 1951, Shanghai, People's Republic of China; son of Xi-yuan Huang and Yunqiu Huang. **EDUCATION:** East China Normal University, BA, 1976, MA, 1982; Hofstra University, PhD, 1991. **CAREER:** East China Normal University, lecturer of English, 1976-86; Hofstra University, adjunct instructor of reading, 1988-90; Suffolk Community College, assistant professor of reading, 1990-. **SPECIAL ACHIEVEMENTS:** Co-author of Step By Step, A Listening Comprehension Course, 1984-86. **BUSINESS ADDRESS:** Assistant Professor of Reading, Suffolk Community College, Selden, NY 11784-0745, (516)451-4364.

HUANG, ZHEN-FEN
Musical conductor. Chinese American. **PERSONAL:** Born Oct 2, 1956, People's Republic of China. **CAREER:** Washington Chinese Youth Orchestra, conductor, currently; Seattle Chinese Orchestra, conductor, currently. **ORGANIZATIONS:** Chinese Art and Music Association, president. **HONORS/AWARDS:** Governor of Virginia, Outstanding Performance Award. **SPECIAL ACHIEVEMENTS:** Performed at Smithsonian Institution; appeared on The Tonight Show with Johnny Carson. **BUSINESS ADDRESS:** Conductor, Seattle Chinese Orchestra, c/o Warren Chang, Music Director, 3613 13th Ave South, Seattle, WA 98144, (206)433-4301.*

HUEY, JOLENE W.
Human resources professional. Chinese American. **PERSONAL:** Born in San Francisco, CA; married Wei Tueng Huey; children: Daniel. **EDUCATION:** San Francisco State University, BA, health sciences, MA, labor economics/employment studies. **CAREER:** Lockheed Missiles and Space Co, senior programs plans analyst, 1981-90; SRI International, compensation analyst, 1990-91; Finnigan Corp, compensation analyst, 1990; Blue Shield, compensation analyst, 1992-93; Hitachi Data Systems, compensation consultant, 1993-; Pac Tel Corp, human resources consultant; Ellington Group, director of human resources, currently. **ORGANIZATIONS:** Asian Business League, San Francisco, leadership committee, co-chair, 1992-, career development committee, co-chair, 1989-91, board member, 1990-91; Northern California Human Resources Council, vice president of external affairs, 1993-94; NCHRC, first Asian female board member, 1990-; American Compensation Association, 1989-; Commonwealth Club, 1989-; Asian Pacific Personnel Association, 1980-. **HONORS/AWARDS:** Asian Business League, Distinguished Board Member, 1992; San Jose Mercury Human Resources Symposium, Steering Committee, 1992; Society of Human Resources Management, PHR certification. **SPECIAL ACHIEVEMENTS:** NCHRC, planned, conducted & organized major symposiums & workshops on human resources, leadership, and communications, 1988-; as director of communications, developed and re-engineered communications function, 1992-; ABL-APPA, started cross-cultural diversity workshops, 1989, involved with employment skills, resume banks, job fairs, assisted in the transition from social service, non-profit institutions to government to private sectors. **BIOGRAPHICAL SOURCES:** NCHRC Quarterly, 1992-; ABL Business Link, 1989-; AAMA News, 1994. **BUSINESS ADDRESS:** Director of Human Resources, The Ellington Group,

The Stock Exchange Tower, 155 Sansome St, Ste 800, San Francisco, CA 94104, (415)989-3039.

HUH, BILLY K.
Medical resident. Korean American. **PERSONAL:** Born Jan 3, 1958, Pusan, Republic of Korea; son of Dr & Mrs Yeon Huh; married Sabina M Lee, Jun 28, 1986; children: Albert S, Eric J. **EDUCATION:** Georgia Institute of Technology, BS, 1980, MS, 1982, PhD, 1985; University of Alabama, School of Medicine, MD, 1993. **CAREER:** Georgia Institute of Technology, teaching and research assistant, 1980-85; Mobil Research and Development Co, senior staff engineer, 1985-88; ARCO Chemical Co, principal engineer, 1988-89; University of North Carolina Hospitals, medical resident, currently. **ORGANIZATIONS:** American Medical Association, 1992-; American Chemical Society, 1983-88; American Institute of Chemical Engineering, 1980-89; Korean Scientists and Engineers in America, 1979-89. **HONORS/AWARDS:** Georgia Institute of Technology, Dean's List, 1976-80, Phi Kappa Phi, 1979, Tau Beta Pi, 1978. **SPECIAL ACHIEVEMENTS:** Fluent in Korean; US patent 4,828,680, Catalytic Cracking of Hydrocarbons, 1989; US Patent 4,871,444, Distillate Fuel Quality of Cycle Oils, 1990; US Patent 4,982,033, Process for Converting Light Aliphates to Aromatics, 1991. **HOME ADDRESS:** 215 Robert Hunt Dr, Carrboro, NC 27510.

HUI, SEK WEN
Research scientist, educator. Chinese American. **PERSONAL:** Born Jul 15, 1935, Kunming, Yunnan, China; son of Shun-kai and Sui Fun Hui; married Hildagardis Hui; children: Jennifer, Peter. **EDUCATION:** University of Western Australia, BS, 1964; Monash University, PhD, 1968. **CAREER:** Flinders University of South Australia, lecturer, 1968-69; Carnegie-Mellon University, research scientist, 1969-72; State University of New York, Buffalo, research professor, 1975-; Roswell Park Cancer Institute, cancer research scientist VI, 1972-. **ORGANIZATIONS:** National Institutes of Health Study Section, 1986-90; Electron Microscopy of America, director, 1985-87; Biophysical Society, 1972-; American Physical Society, 1968-; American Society for Cell Biology, 1982-; editorial board, Biophysical Journal, 1992-. **HONORS/AWARDS:** National Institutes of Health, Career Development Award, 1975, Special Fellow, 1972. **SPECIAL ACHIEVEMENTS:** Over 100 articles in scientific journals; edited and contributed to 24 books. **BUSINESS ADDRESS:** Research Scientist, Roswell Park Cancer Institute, Elm and Carlton Streets, Buffalo, NY 14263.

HUIE, CARMEN WAH-KIT
Educator. Chinese American/Hong Kong American. **PERSONAL:** Born Aug 7, 1959, Hong Kong; son of Shui and May-Kuen Lee. **EDUCATION:** University of Wisconsin, BS (summa cum laude), chemistry, BS (magna cum laude), math, 1980; Iowa State University, PhD, chemistry, 1986. **CAREER:** Environmental Protection Agency, research assistant, 1978; University of Wisconsin, teaching assistant, 1977-80; Iowa State University, teaching assistant, 1980-81; Department of Energy, research assistant, 1981-85; State University of New York-Binghamton, visiting assistant professor, 1986-89, assistant professor, 1989-. **ORGANIZATIONS:** American Chemical Society, 1985-; Sigma Xi, 1988-. **HONORS/AWARDS:** Applied Spectroscopy Society, Lester Strock Award Citations, 1990. **SPECIAL ACHIEVEMENTS:** More that 30 research papers published in the area of analytical chemistry; book chapter, "Exploitation of Lasers, Surfactants and Chemiluminescence in Analytical Chemistry," in Trends in Applied Spectroscopy, 1993; invited lecturer, XXVII Colloquim Spectroscopium Internationale, Lofthus, Norway, 1991. **HOME ADDRESS:** 201 Evergreen St Apt 3-3C, Vestal, NY 13850. **BUSINESS ADDRESS:** Asst Professor of Chemistry, State University of New York at Binghamton, Vestal Parkway East, PO Box 6000, Binghamton, NY 13902-6000, (607)777-4605.

HUMAYUN, M. ZAFRI
Educator. Indo-American. **PERSONAL:** Born Feb 11, 1949, India. **EDUCATION:** Andhra University, India, BSc, 1967; Madras University, India, MSc, 1970; Indian Institute of Science, PhD, 1975. **CAREER:** Harvard University, postdoctoral fellow, 1974-76; New York University Medical Center, assistant research scientist, 1976-79; UMDNJ-New Jersey Medical School, assistant professor, 1979-83, associate professor, 1983-89, professor, 1989-. **HONORS/AWARDS:** Research grants: National Institutes of Health, American Cancer Society, 1980-; NIH Research Cancer Development Award, 1984-89. **SPECIAL ACHIEVEMENTS:** 36 publications in peer-reviewed scientific journals, 1973-. **BUSINESS ADDRESS:** Professor, Microbiology & Molecular Genetics, UMDNJ-New Jersey Medical School, 185 S Orange Ave, MSBF607, Newark, NJ 07103-2714, (201)982-5217.

HUNG, CHAO-SHUN
Educator, educational administrator. Taiwanese American. **PERSONAL:** Born Jan 20, 1942, Taiwan; son of You-mei Hung; married Jane Anne Hung, May 14, 1984. **EDUCATION:** National Taiwan Normal University, BA, 1964; Saint Louis University, MBA, 1972; Texas A&M University, PhD, 1982. **CAREER:** Florida Atlantic University, associate professor of economics and chairperson, 1982-. **ORGANIZATIONS:** American Economic Association, 1982-; Atlantic Economic Society, 1985, 1991-; Western Economic Association, 1989; Chinese Economic Association in North America, 1990; Chinese American Scholars Association of Florida, 1992-. **HONORS/AWARDS:** Florida Atlantic University, College Awards for Excellence in Undergraduate Teaching, 1990, University Research Award, 1993. **SPECIAL ACHIEVEMENTS:** The Economics of Imperfect Competition: A Spatial Approach, Cambridge University Press, co-author, 1987; The Savings and Loan Crisis, Kendall-Hunt, co-author, 1992. **HOME ADDRESS:** 4931 Acorn Drive, Boca Raton, FL 33431, (407)241-5672. **BUSINESS ADDRESS:** Professor, Chairperson, Dept of Economics, Florida Atlantic University, 500 NW 20th Street, Boca Raton, FL 33431-6498, (407)367-3222.

HUNG, CHIH-CHENG
Computer scientist. Taiwanese American. **PERSONAL:** Born Sep 20, 1954, Ping-Tong, Taiwan; son of Lau-Chin Hung & Chen-Dou Hung; married Ming-Huei Lu, Jul 25, 1983; children: Avery, David. **EDUCATION:** Soochow University, Taipei, Taiwan, BS, 1978; University of Alabama in Huntsville, MS, 1986, PhD, 1990. **CAREER:** Cathay Insurance Company, programmer/system analyst, 1980-83; University of Alabama in Huntsville, graduate research and teaching assistant, 1984-90; Intergraph Corporation, senior software analyst, 1990-93; Alabama A&M University, adjunct faculty, 1990-93, assistant professor, 1993-. **ORGANIZATIONS:** IEEE Computer Society, 1990-; Pattern Recognition Society, 1991-; Classification Society of North America, 1992-; Chinese Academy and Professional Association in Mid-America, 1993-; Upsilon Pi Epsilon, 1990. **SPECIAL ACHIEVEMENTS:** Author, "An Image Classification Algorithm Based on Contextual Information," 1993; coauthor, "Certain and Correlated Neighboring Pixels in Multispectral Image Classification," Proceedings of Canadian Conference on Electrical & Computer Engineering, Vancouver, Canada, September 14-17, 1993; "A Neural Network Training Based Image Classification System for Multispectral Data Analysis," in proceedings of the 2nd International Conference on Systems Science and Systems Engineering, Beijing, PR China, Aug 24-27, 1993. **BUSINESS ADDRESS:** Assistant Professor, Department of Computer and Information Science, Alabama A&M University, Normal, AL 35762, (205)851-5570.

HUNG, JAMES CHEN
Educator. Chinese American. **PERSONAL:** Born Feb 18, 1929, Fuzhou, Fukien, China; son of David S Hung & Pearl C Hung; married Sufenne H Hung, Apr 3, 1958; children: John Y, Samuel M, Stephen T. **EDUCATION:** National Taiwan University, BS, EE, 1953; New York University, MEE, 1956, DEngSc, 1961. **CAREER:** New York University, instructor, 1956-61; University of Tennessee, assistant professor, 1961-62, associate professor, 1962-65, professor, 1965-. **ORGANIZATIONS:** IEEE, fellow, 1984-, general chair, international symposium on industrial electronics, 1992, track chairman, IECON, 1988, 1989, 1990. **HONORS/AWARDS:** University of Tennessee, Distinguished Professor, 1984; NASA, Technology Award, 1969, Certificate of Contribution, 1970; US Army, Letter of Commendation, 1981; University of Tennessee, Brooks Distinguished Engineering Professor Award, 1973; Nanjing Aeronautical Institute, honorary professor, 1989; Sigma Xi; Tau Beta Pi; Eta Kappa Nu; Phi Kappa Phi. **SPECIAL ACHIEVEMENTS:** Published more than 180 technical articles, 1956-; IEEE, editor-in-chief, IEEE Transactions on Industrial Electronics, 1991-. **HOME ADDRESS:** 9537 Gulf Park Dr, Knoxville, TN 37923, (615)693-2736.

HUNG, KEN
Educator. Chinese American. **PERSONAL:** Born Jul 14, 1947, Taipei, Taiwan; son of An-Chou Hung and Ah-Shiu Yen Hung; married Shu-Ping Fang Hung, Mar 8, 1975; children: Shine-May, Harrison Eugene. **EDUCATION:** National Taiwan University, Taipei, BS, 1971; Virginia Polytechnic Institute & State University, MBA, 1982; University of Maryland, PhD, 1986. **CAREER:** Western Washington University, professor of decision sciences, 1990-. **ORGANIZATIONS:** Decision Sciences Institute, 1985-; International Institute of Forecasters, 1986-; The Institute of Management Science, 1988-; American Society of Quality Control, 1992-; American Statistical Association, 1990-. **HONORS/AWARDS:** Beta Gamma Sigma, 1987; Phi Beta Phi, 1986; Omega

Rho, 1984. **SPECIAL ACHIEVEMENTS:** Author, Chapter 18, "Time Series Analysis," Handbook of Statistical Methods for Engineers and Scientists, edited by Harrison M Wadsworth, 18.1 - 18.36, with Frank B Alt and Lap-Ming Wun, 1990; "Simulation Study on Variance of Forecast Error for Vector Arima Models," Communications in Statistics: Simulation and Computation, B19, 1, 125-144, 1990; "Interrelations Among Various Definitions of Bivariate Positive Dependence," Topics in Statistical Dependence, vol 16, Institute of Mathematical Statistics Lecture Notes Monograph Series, pp 333-349, with S Kotz and Q Wang, 1991. **BUSINESS ADDRESS:** Professor, Dept of Decision Sciences, Western Washington University, College of Business and Economics, Bellingham, WA 98225-9077, (206)650-3488.

HUNG, KUEN-SHAN
Educator. Taiwanese American. **PERSONAL:** Born Jan 13, 1938, Chia-Yi, Chia-Yi, Taiwan; son of Tien-Won Hung & Guam T Hung; married Shirley H Hung, Nov 30, 1968; children: Irene, Melissa. **EDUCATION:** National Taiwan University, BS, 1960; University of Kansas Medical Center, PhD, 1969. **CAREER:** University of South Dakota, assistant professor of anatomy, 1969-71; University of Southern California, assistant professor of anat & pathol, 1971-74; University of Kansas, assistant professor & associate professor of anat, 1974-83, professor of anat & cell biol, 1983-. **ORGANIZATIONS:** Microscopy Soc of America, 1968-; Sigma Xi, 1970-; American Association of Anatomists, 1973-. **HONORS/AWARDS:** American Lung Association, research grant, 1974-76; NIH, research grant, 1976-81; American Heart Association, Kansas affiliate, resarch grant, 1981-87, 1991-93. **SPECIAL ACHIEVEMENTS:** 30 research publications: journal articles and book chapters; 38 abstracts; focus of research work: lung cell biology. **MILITARY SERVICE:** Infantry, Taiwan, second lieutenant, 1960. **BUSINESS ADDRESS:** Professor, Dept of Anatomy & Cell Biology, University of Kansas Medical Center, 3901 Rainbow, Kansas City, KS 66160, (913)588-2728.

HUNG, PAUL P.
Drug company executive, educator. Taiwanese American. **PERSONAL:** Born Sep 30, 1933, Taipei, Taiwan; son of Yau-Hsun Hung and Shiu-Chin Hung; married Nancy Clark Hung, May 5, 1956; children: Pauline Sandquist, Eileen Lambo, Clark. **EDUCATION:** Millikin University, BS, 1956; Purdue University, PhD, 1960. **CAREER:** Abbott Labs, Molecular Virology and Biology, head, 1960-81; Northwestern University Medical School, adjunct professor, 1976-86; Bethesda Research Labs, general manager, 1981; Wyeth-Ayert Labs, asst vice president, 1982-. **ORGANIZATIONS:** US Dept of Health and Human Services, National Vaccine Advisory Committee, 1991-; United Nations Industrial Development Organization, consultant, 1982; American Society of Microbiology; American Society of Biochemistry and Molecular Biology; American Association for Cancer Research; American Chemical Society; American Institute of Chemists. **HONORS/AWARDS:** Purdue University, Distinguished Alumnus, 1994. **SPECIAL ACHIEVEMENTS:** Over two hundred seventy publications, book chapters on genetic engineering, molecular biology, biochemistry, cell biology and immunology, tissue plasminogery activators, viruses, vaccines, antibiotics. **HOME PHONE:** (215)525-8887. **BUSINESS ADDRESS:** Asst Vice President, Wyeth-Ayerst Labs, PO Box 8299, Philadelphia, PA 19101, (215)341-2420.

HUNG, RU J.
Educator. Taiwanese American. **PERSONAL:** Born Jun 17, 1934, Hsin Chu, Taiwan; son of Hsiao Feng Hung and Lan Chang Hung; married Nancy Hung, Sep 24, 1966; children: Elmer, Christine. **EDUCATION:** National Taiwan University, BS, 1957; The University of Osaka, MS, 1966; University of Michigan, PhD, 1970. **CAREER:** Advanced Technical Institute, design engineer, 1957-64; University of Osaka, Ministry of Education, foreign scholar, 1964-66; University of Michigan, research associate, 1966-69, postdoctoral fellow, 1969-70; NASA/Ames Research Center, research associate, 1970-72; University of Alabama in Huntsville, professor, 1972-. **ORGANIZATIONS:** Sigma Xi, 1970-; Pi Tau Sigma, 1973-; Phi Kappa Phi, 1992-; Royal Meterological Society, Fellow, 1987-; American Institute of Aeronautics and Astronautics, Associate Fellow, 1975-; American Geophysical Union, 1973-; American Meteorological Society, 1975-; National Society of Professional Engineers, 1980-. **HONORS/AWARDS:** Ministry of Education, Japan, Foreign Scholar Fellowship, 1964; National Academy of Sciences, Research Fellowship, 1971; American Institute of Aeronautics and Astronautics, Research Awards, 1989; National Aeronautics and Space Administration, Research Awards, 1990; Sigma Xi, Outstanding Research Awards, 1992. **SPECIAL ACHIEVEMENTS:** Principal investigator of more than 30 research projects sponsored by the US Government, including NASA, National Science Founda-

tion, US Army, etc; published more than 120 technical papers in international scientific and technical journals; presented more than 150 papers in international scientific and technical conferences. **HOME ADDRESS:** 2610 Guenevere Ave, Huntsville, AL 35803, (205)883-2346. **BUSINESS ADDRESS:** Professor, University of Alabama in Huntsville, Huntsville, AL 35899, (205)895-6077.

HUNG, STEPHEN CHIFENG
Engineer. Taiwanese American. **PERSONAL:** Born Jun 15, 1941, Kaohsiung, Taiwan; son of Kunhwa Hung and Hsueh-Ying Hung; married Therese C Hung, Dec 28, 1969; children: Richard B, Helen B. **EDUCATION:** National Cheng Kung University, Taiwan, BS, 1964; University of Cincinnati, MS, 1968. **CAREER:** St Lawrence Seaway Corp, director of operations & maintenance, 1990-, director of engineering & planning, 1984-90, chief of special projects planning, 1977-1984; US Army Corps of Engineers, civil engineer, 1976-77; Dodson Lindblom Assocs, civil engineering, 1968-75. **ORGANIZATIONS:** American Society of Civil Engineers, 1970-; US Dept of Transportation, Navigation Working Group. **HONORS/AWARDS:** State of Ohio, Registered Professional Engineer; State of New York, Registered Professional Engineer; Commonwealth of Virginia, Registered Professional Engineer; DOT, Secretary's Award for Meritorious Achievement, 1993. **SPECIAL ACHIEVEMENTS:** ASCE, "Hydrologic Applications for Electronic Spreadsheets," 1982; "Seaway Emergency Response Plan," International Oil Spill Conference, 1991; proficient in Chinese. **BUSINESS ADDRESS:** Director of Operations & Maintenance, St Lawrence Seaway Development Corporation, PO Box 520, Massena, NY 13662, (315)764-3265.

HUNG, TIN-KAN
Educator. Chinese American. **PERSONAL:** Born Jun 12, 1936, Nanking, China; son of Mao-Hsiang and Yu-Hwa Cheng Hung; married Shu-Nan Cho, Feb 14, 1971; children: Chee-Hahn, Chee-Ming, Chee-Yuen. **EDUCATION:** National Cheng-Kung University, BS, 1959; University of Illinois, MS, 1962; University of Iowa, PhD, 1966. **CAREER:** Iowa Institute of Hydraulic Research, research engineer and instructor, 1966-67; University of Illinois at Chicago Circle, visiting associate professor, summer, 1972; Carnegie-Mellon University, assistant professor, 1967-70, associate professor, 1970-75; University of Pittsburgh, research professor of civil and biomedical engineering and neurosurgery, 1975-89, professor of civil engineering, research professor of neurosurgery, 1989-. **ORGANIZATIONS:** ASCE, Fluids Committee, chairman, 1976-78, Bioengineering Committee, chairman, 1978-80, Task Committee on Bioengineering & Human Factors, chairman, 1972-76, J of Engineering Mechanics, editorial board, 1974-80, 1981-82; J of Hydraulic Research, editorial board, 1980-; US National Committee on Biomechanics, 1982-84. **HONORS/AWARDS:** ASCE, W L Huber Civil Engineering Research Prize, 1978; American Institute for Medical and Biological Engineering, founding fellow, 1993. **SPECIAL ACHIEVEMENTS:** Published over 90 papers in computational fluid mechanics, membrane blood oxgenation, spinal cord injury, and earthquake hydrodynamics, 1966-93. **BIOGRAPHICAL SOURCES:** Hydraulics in the United States 1776-1976, pp 208-209, 1978. **BUSINESS ADDRESS:** Prof of Civil Eng, Dept of Civil Eng, Res Prof of Neurosurgery, University of Pittsburgh, Pittsburgh, PA 15261, (412)624-9896.

HUNG, YEN-WAN
Educator. Chinese American. **PERSONAL:** Born Jan 8, 1944, Taipei, Taiwan; daughter of Chin-Ho Hung and Chun-Mei Hung. **EDUCATION:** National Cheng-Kung University, BS, 1967; Marquette University, MS, 1972; Northeastern University, PhD, 1976. **CAREER:** Clarkson College of Technology, post-doctoral fellow, 1976-77; University of Maryland, Eastern Shore, lecturer, 1977-84; Livingstone College, associate professor, 1984-91, professor and department head, 1991-. **ORGANIZATIONS:** American Chemical Society, 1976-. **HONORS/AWARDS:** EPA Faculty Fellows Program, Summer Faculty Fellow, 1990; DOE Faculty Summer Research Participation, Research Fellow, 1985-88; NASA, Research Grants, 1980-82; NOAA Research Grant, University of Maryland Sea Grant Program, 1979; Research Corporation, Fellowship, 1974; US Dept of Education, Minority Science Improvement Program, Grant, 1992-94. **SPECIAL ACHIEVEMENTS:** Y-90 Labeled Monoclonal Antibodies for Cancer Therapy, 1986; Effects of Temperature and Chelating Agents on Cadmium Uptake in Oyster, 1982; The Studies of Labile Carbonato Cobalt III Complexes, 1976; The Studies of Carbonato Cobalt III Complexes, 1976; Separation of Acetylacetonate Chelates by TLC, 1975; The TLC Separation of Some Metal Acetylacetonate Complexes and Some Optically Active Inorganic Complexes, 1972. **BUSINESS ADDRESS:** Professor and Chairper-

son, Dept of Life & Physical Sciences, Livingstone College, 701 W Monroe St, Salisbury, NC 28144, (704)638-5618.

HUR, JOHN CHONGHWAN
State government administrator. Korean American. **PERSONAL:** Born Jun 13, 1931, Japan; son of Ok Hur and Por Sun Hur; married Jewel Okhui Hur, Jun 9, 1958; children: Mike, Susan Kim, Charles, Barbara. **EDUCATION:** Seoul National University, Korea, BBA, 1955. **CAREER:** Irvine Business Group, general manager; State of California, Employment Development Department, Disability Insurance Field Office, program manager, currently. **BUSINESS ADDRESS:** Program Manager, Employment Development Dept, State of California, Disability Insurance Field Office, PO Box 3096, Los Angeles, CA 90051, (213)744-2059.

HUSAIN, MUSTAFA MAHMOOD
Educator, physician. Pakistani American. **PERSONAL:** Born Jul 19, 1956, Karachi, Pakistan; son of Hamid Husain and Khursheed Hamid; married Subuhi N Husain; children: Saira, Zamin. **EDUCATION:** Adamji Science College, Pakistan, HSc; Dow Medical College, Pakistan, MD. **CAREER:** Duke University Medical Center, Dept of Psychiatry, NIMH Fellow, Geriatric Psychiatry, 1989-91; ECT Fellow, 1990-91; Parkland Memorial Hospital, Inpatient Psychiatry, asst dir, 1991-; University of Texas Southwestern Medical School, Geriatric Psychiatry Training Program, dir, 1991-, Medical Center, asst prof, 1991-. **ORGANIZATIONS:** American Assn for Geriatric Psychiatry; American Psychiatric Assn; Texas Medical Assn; Dallas County Medical Society; American Board of Psychiatry & Neurology Inc, examiner. **SPECIAL ACHIEVEMENTS:** Author: "Maintenance ECT for Refractory OCD: A Case Report," American Jrnl of Psych, 1993; "Maintenance ECT for Treatment of Recurrent Mania: A Case Report," American Jrnl of Psych, 1993; "MRI Detection of Abnormality in the Corpus Callosum & Late-Onset Depression," Depression, 1993; "Does Gender Affect Brain Aging and Cognition?," New England Jrnl of Medicine, under review, 1992; "Subcortical Brain Anatomy in Anorexia and Bulimia," Biol Psych, Apr 1992. **HOME ADDRESS:** 1208 St Tropez, Carrollton, TX 75006.

HUSSAIN, FAZLE
Educator. Bangladeshi American. **PERSONAL:** Born Jan 20, 1943, Dhaka, Bangladesh; son of Mohammed Tarik Ullah and Begum Farhtunnessa; married Rehana Hussain, Nov 10, 1968; children: Shama. **EDUCATION:** Dhaka College, int sci, 1959; Bangladesh University of Engineering & Technology, BSME, 1963; Stanford University, MS, 1966, PhD, 1969. **CAREER:** The Johns Hopkins University, visiting assistant professor, 1969-71; University of Houston, assistant professor, 1971-73, associate professor, 1973-76, professor, 1976-, Distinguished University professor, 1985-89, Cullen Distinguished Professor, 1989-. **HONORS/AWARDS:** Stanford University, Eckert Prize for Outstanding PhD, 1971; University of Houston, Engineering College Research Award, 1978, Senior Research Excellence Award, 1985; ASME, Freeman Scholar, 1984; APS, fellow; ASME, fellow. **SPECIAL ACHIEVEMENTS:** Published over 250 scientific papers, 1971-; presented over 70 invited lectures, obtained over 70 competitive federal research grants, 1971-; editorial bd of different conferences; assoc editor, The Physics of Fluids, 1981-84. **BUSINESS ADDRESS:** Professor, Dept of Mechanical Engineering, University of Houston, 4800 Calhoun St, Houston, TX 77204-4792, (713)743-4545.

HUSSAIN, RIAZ
Educator. Pakistani American. **PERSONAL:** Born Jan 18, 1937, Gujranwala, Pakistan; son of Noor Hussain and Barkat Bibi Hussain; married Atiya Hussain, Jun 23, 1978; children: Altaf. **EDUCATION:** Forman College, Lahore, Pakistan, BSc, 1954; University of Punjab, Lahore, Pakistan, MSc, 1956; Johns Hopkins University, PhD, 1973; University of Scranton, MBA, 1980; Lehigh University, PhD, 1993. **CAREER:** Forman College, lecturer, 1956-60; Boston University, research assistant, 1960-61; Johns Hopkins University, research assistant, 1961-67; University of Scranton, instructor, 1967-, associate professor, currently. **ORGANIZATIONS:** American Finance Association; Association for Investment Management and Research. **HONORS/AWARDS:** US Govt, Fulbright Fellowship, 1960. **HOME ADDRESS:** 540 N Webster Avenue, Scranton, PA 18510, (717)347-8077. **BUSINESS ADDRESS:** Professor, School of Management, University of Scranton, Scranton, PA 18510, (717)941-7497.

HUYNH, BOI-HANH (VINCENT)
Educator. Chinese American. **PERSONAL:** Born Nov 13, 1946, Saigon, Vietnam; son of Tich Huynh Huynh & Uyen Van Luc. **EDUCATION:** Na-

tional Taiwan University, Taipei, BS, 1969; Columbia University, MA, 1971, PhD, 1974. **CAREER:** Harvard University, postdocotral fellow, 1974-77; University of Minnesota, research specialist, 1977-80; Emory University, assistant professor, 1981-85, associate professor, 1985-90, professor, 1990-93; Samuel Candler Dobbs professorship, 1993-. **ORGANIZATIONS:** American Physical Society, 1982-; American Physics Teacher, 1982-; Federation of American Society for Experimental Biology, 1986-. **HONORS/AWARDS:** Over-sea Chinese Committee, Excellent Over-sea Undergraduate Scholarship, 1966-69; National Institutes of Health, Research Career Development Award, 1983-88. **SPECIAL ACHIEVEMENTS:** Published over 70 refereed research articles and 5 book chapters on spectroscopic studies of metalloproteins, which include heme proteins, iron-sulfur proteins and ribonucleotide reductase. **BUSINESS ADDRESS:** Professor, Emory University, 1510 Clifton Rd, Rollins Research Center, Rm 1021, Atlanta, GA 30322, (404)727-4295.

HUYNH, DUNG THIET
Educator. Vietnamese American/Chinese American. **PERSONAL:** Born Sep 27, 1953, Minhhai, Vietnam; son of Vinh Huynh. **EDUCATION:** University of Saarland, Germany, MS, 1977, PhD, 1978. **CAREER:** University of Saarland, postdoctate research associate, 1978-82; University of Chicago, visiting assistant professor, 1982-83; Iowa State University, assistant professor, 1983-86; University of Texas, Dallas, associate professor, 1986-91, professor, 1991-. **ORGANIZATIONS:** Association of Computing Machinery, 1983-; IEEE Computer Society; European Association for Theoretical Computer Science. **SPECIAL ACHIEVEMENTS:** Over 30 articles in theoretical computer science journals, 1980-. **BIOGRAPHICAL SOURCES:** "Computational Complexity," Wagner & Wechsung, p 271, 1986; "Data Structures & Algorithms 2," Mehlhorn, p 235, 1984. **BUSINESS ADDRESS:** Professor, Computer Science Program, University of Texas-Dallas, PO Box 830688, Richardson, TX 75083-0688, (214)690-2169.

HUYNH, EMMANUELLE
Legal office support assistant. Vietnamese American. **PERSONAL:** Born Nov 2, 1947, Hanoi, Vietnam; daughter of Quy Tuoc Bui & Quy Hien Thi Nguyen; married Qui Van Huynh, Jun 4, 1967; children: Nathalie, Frederic. **CAREER:** Los Angeles County District Attorney, legal office support assistant, 1979-. **HONORS/AWARDS:** Los Angeles County District Attorney, Frank & Jane Jemison Award, 1990; Los Angeles County, Employee of the Month, 1992. **SPECIAL ACHIEVEMENTS:** Fluent in Vietnamese, French, and English. **BIOGRAPHICAL SOURCES:** County of Los Angeles, County Digest, August, 31, 1992. **BUSINESS ADDRESS:** Legal Office Support Assistant, District Attorney Office, Los Angeles County, 300 East Walnut, Rm 103, Pasadena, CA 91101, (818)356-5620.

HWA, JESSE CHIA-HSI
Consultant, business executive. Chinese American. **PERSONAL:** Born Jul 12, 1924, Wuhan, Hupei, China; son of Hwa Tso-Shu & Chen Sho-May; married Dolores Lowe, Jun 9, 1949; children: Nancee, David John, Nadine Carol Ungless. **EDUCATION:** St John's University, Shanghai, China, BS, (with honors), 1945; University, of Illinois, MS, 1947, PhD, 1949. **CAREER:** Rohm & Haas Co, research chemist, group leader, 1949-63; Stauffer Chemical Co, Eastern Research Center, Polymer Research Department, manager, 1963-72, Research Department Administration, director of development, 1972-82, corporate headquarters, corporate project director, 1982-85; HWA International, Inc, president, 1985-. **ORGANIZATIONS:** American Chemical Society, Division of Polymer Chemistry, chairman, 1973, councilor, 1975-86, historian, 1988-; Macromolecular Secretariat, 1972-76, international activities committee, 1976-84, Division Councilors Caucus, chairman, 1976-82, volunteer career consultant, 1990-; Chinese American Chemical Society, founder, president, 1981-85, board member, 1989-, chairman, Tristate Chapter, 1990-92; Chinese American Forum, advisor to board, 1987-88, board member, 1989-. **HONORS/AWARDS:** American Chemical Society, Division of Polymer Chemistry Service Award, 1987, Special Service Award, 1991; Chinese American Chemical Society, Distinguished Service Award, 1991. **SPECIAL ACHIEVEMENTS:** 20 technical articles, 13 non-technical articles, 47 US patents; senior consultant to the Ministry of Light Industry, China, 1985. **BUSINESS ADDRESS:** President, HWA International, Inc, 54 Westhill Circle, Stamford, CT 06902, (203)323-8114.

HWANG, ANGE
Executive director. Chinese American/Taiwanese American. **PERSONAL:** Born Dec 19, 1961, Taipei, Taiwan; daughter of Sin-Ling Hwang & S K Mak; married Stephen J Lu, Aug 4, 1989. **EDUCATION:** Chung-Hsing University,

BS, 1983; University of Iowa, MA, 1986; Metropolitan State University, MMA, 1992. **CAREER:** Chinese Culture University, drama & cinema department, lecturer, 1986-87; Cultural & Society Production, executive producer, 1987-92; Metro State University, media foundation, faculty, 1990-; Asian Media Access, executive director, 1992-. **ORGANIZATIONS:** Asian Media Access, founder, steering committee, head, 1992-; Asian Benefit Committee, 1993; Resources and Counseling for the Arts, board member, 1993-; Asian American Journalists Association, 1991-; Cable Access St Paul, development committee, 1990-; Ethnics Day, planning committee, 1990. **HONORS/ AWARDS:** Minnesota Television Committee, MN Community TV Awards, 1993; St Paul Companies, Leadership Initiatives in Neighborhoods Award, 1992. **SPECIAL ACHIEVEMENTS:** Minnesota State Arts Board, arts board advisor, 1993; Judge for Minnesota Community Television Awards, Music/ Arts Category, 1991, 1992; Judge for Hometown Video Contest, International Category, 1989; author: When Considering a Cable Network in Taiwan: Strategies & Practices, 1993; ''Behind the Scenes of 'East Meets West,''' Asian American Press, 1990; weekly cable series, ''East Meets West,'' Asian American variety comedy show color-aberration; over 60 completed video and film works; language proficiency: Mandarin, Cantonese. **HOME ADDRESS:** 3028 Oregon Ave S, Minneapolis, MN 55426. **BUSINESS ADDRESS:** Executive Director, Asian Media Access, 262 E Fourth St, St. Paul, MN 55101, (612)223-5493.

HWANG, CHARLES C.

Educator. Chinese American. **PERSONAL:** Born Apr 7, 1930, Taiwan; married Sandra S Hwang; children: Margaret, Elizabeth. **EDUCATION:** Harvard University, PhD, 1968. **CAREER:** University of Pittsburgh, associate professor, currently. **ORGANIZATIONS:** ASME; The Combustion Institute, assistant treasurer. **HONORS/AWARDS:** NASA-ASEE, Summer Faculty Fellow, 1971; ASME Advanced System Divsion, Outstanding Paper Award, 1989. **SPECIAL ACHIEVEMENTS:** Fluent in Chinese and Japanese. **BUSINESS ADDRESS:** Assoc Professor, Dept of Mechanical Engineering, University of Pittsburgh, Pittsburgh, PA 15261, (412)624-9604.

HWANG, CHERNG-JIA

Physicist. Taiwanese American. **PERSONAL:** Born Oct 1, 1937, Changhua, Taiwan; son of Shieu-Kai Hwang & Po-Yeh Hwang; married Elizabeth Y Hwang, Jul 2, 1965; children: Karen C, Dennis C. **EDUCATION:** National Taiwan University, BSEE, 1960; University of Washington, Seattle, MSEE, 1964, PhD, 1966. **CAREER:** Bell Telephone Laboratories, technical staff member, 1966-73; Hewlett Packard Laboratories, group leader, 1973-77; General Optronics Corp, president, 1977-88; Laser Diode Inc, vice president, 1988-90; Photon Imaging Corp, president, 1990-91; Applied Optronics Corp, president, CEO, 1991-93; Telecommunication Laboratories, Ministry of Transportation and Communications, Taiwan, ROC, chief advisor, 1994-. **ORGANIZATIONS:** US Department of Commerce, Telecommunications Equipment Technical Advisory Committee, 1986-90; American Physical Society, 1969-; Optical Society of America, 1985-; Society of Photo-Optical Instrumentation Engineers, 1990-. **HONORS/AWARDS:** Telecommunications Bureau of Taiwan, scholarship, 1959-60; National Science Foundation, fellowship, 1962-66; UNESCO, visiting specialist to Telebras, Brazil, 1974-77. **SPECIAL ACHIEVEMENTS:** First Asian American to start a high-tech optoelectronics company, 1977; first to introduce laser printers using semiconductor lasers, 1979; first to introduce cw semiconductor laser to market, 1977. **HOME ADDRESS:** 170 Hill Hollow Rd, Watchung, NJ 07060. **BUSINESS PHONE:** 886-3-424-4423.

HWANG, CHING-LAI

Educator. Taiwanese American. **PERSONAL:** Born Jan 22, 1929, Tainan, Taiwan; son of Kuang-Min Hwang & Uen-chu Hwang; married Meilang Liu Hwang, Jan 22, 1954; children: Grace Y, Frank P, Jean G. **EDUCATION:** National Taiwan University, BS, 1953; Kansas State University, MS, 1959, PhD, 1962. **CAREER:** Tatung Institute of Technology, instructor, 1953-58; Washburn University, Topeka, asst professor, 1962-64; Technical University of Denmark, guest professor, 1974-75; National Defense Academy, Japan, guest professor, 1986; Kansas State University, asst prof, beginning 1965, assoc prof, professor, currently. **ORGANIZATIONS:** North America Taiwanese Professors Association, board of directors, 1982-84; ASME; Japan Association of Automatic Control Engr; Phi Kappa Phi, 1960, Sigma Xi, 1962. **SPECIAL ACHIEVEMENTS:** Publications: 124 journal articles primarily in operations research, decision theory, systems engineering, environmental quality control, 1962-; books: Multiple Objective Decision Making, 1979; Multiple Attribute Decision Making, 1981; Group Decision Making under Multiple Criteria,

1987; Fuzzy Multiple Attribute Decision Making, 1992; Fuzzy Mathematical Programming, 1993; Optimization of Systems Reliability, 1980; Fuzzy Multiple Objective Decision Making, 1994. **HOME ADDRESS:** 1604 Virginia Dr, Manhattan, KS 66502.

HWANG, CHONG F. (ANNA)

Restaurateur. Korean American. **PERSONAL:** Born Feb 13, 1958, Seoul, Republic of Korea; daughter of U Son Kum; divorced; children: Two. **CAREER:** Oyster Restaurant, owner, currently. **BUSINESS ADDRESS:** Owner, Oyster Restaurant, 116 Main St, Huntington Beach, CA 92648, (714)960-9476.

HWANG, DAVID HENRY

Playwright, screenwriter. Chinese American. **PERSONAL:** Born Aug 11, 1957, Los Angeles, CA; son of Henry Yuan & Dorothy Yu Hwang. **EDUCATION:** Stanford University, BA, 1979; Yale School of Drama, 1980-81. **CAREER:** Playwright, screenwriter; plays include: FOB, 1980; The Dance and the Railroad, 1981; Family Devotions, 1981; The House of Sleeping Beauties & the Sound of a Voice, 1983; Rich Relations, 1986; 1000 Airplanes on the Roof, 1988; M Butterfly, 1988; Bondage, 1992; The Voyage, 1992; Face Value, 1993; films, screenwriter: Golden Gate, 1993; M Butterfly, 1993. **ORGANIZATIONS:** Asian Pacific Americans for Clinton/Gore, honorary co-chair, 1992; Pitzer College, CA, board of trustees. **HONORS/AWARDS:** Guggenheim, Rockefeller, NYSCA, National Endowment for the Arts Fellowships; Tony, Drama Desk, John Gassher, Outer Critics Circle Awards, for M Butterfly, 1980; Drama-Logue Award, for The House of Sleeping Beauties and the Sound of a Voice, 1985; Drama Desk nomination for Family Devotions, 1982; Drama Desk nomination, CINE Golden Eagle Award, for The Dance and the Railroad, 1981; OBIE, Best Play, Drama-Logue Award, for FOB, 1980. **SPECIAL ACHIEVEMENTS:** Publications: Broken Promises, 1983; M Butterfly, 1989; FOB & Other Plays, 1990. **BUSINESS ADDRESS:** Author, c/o William Craver, Writers and Artists Agency, 19 West 44th St, Ste 1000, New York, NY 10036, (212)391-1112.

HWANG, DENNIS B. K.

Educator, educational administrator. Taiwanese American. **PERSONAL:** Born Apr 15, 1949, Hsinchu, Taiwan; son of Yeong Shan Hwang and Mang-Mei Hwang; married Min Li Hwang, Jan 10, 1974; children: Louisa, Diana. **EDUCATION:** Cheng Chi University, Taipei, BA, 1971; University of Oklahoma, MA, 1984, PhD, 1984. **CAREER:** RCA Corp, Taiwan, production controller, 1973; Central Bank of China, section chief, 1973-78; College of St Scholastica, associate professor, 1984-89; Bloomsburg University, associate professor of accounting, 1989-, Institute of Comparative and International Management Studies, director, 1993-. **ORGANIZATIONS:** Institute of Management Accountants, 1987-, Director of Educational Programs, Susquehana Chapter, 1993-; American Accounting Assn, 1988-; Eastern Economic Assn, 1990-; Intl Lions Club, lion tamer, 1989-92; American Chinese Management Educators Assn, 1992-93; American Chinese Accounting Professors Assn, 1992-; Chinese Student Assn, University of Oklahoma, president, 1980. **HONORS/ AWARDS:** IMA, CMA, 1987; Minnesota State Board of Accountancy, CPA, 1988; Bloomsburg University, 5 grants and awards for research; College of St Scholastica, Outstanding Service Award, 1988; University of Oklahoma, Outstanding International Student Award, 1983. **SPECIAL ACHIEVEMENTS:** Published more than 18 articles in professional journals and conference proceedings, such as Journal of Energy and Development, Accountng Research Monthly, Energy Economics, Journal of Macro-Economics, Monthly Journal of Taipei City Bank, Journal of Bank of Taiwan, Indian Journal of Economics; language proficiency: Mandarin, English, Taiwanese and Hakka; literature published in Shell Magazine and The Free Youth, Taipei. **MILITARY SERVICE:** Chinese Air Force, 2nd lt, 1971-72. **BIOGRAPHICAL SOURCES:** The Causal Relationship Between Energy and GNP: The Case of Taiwan, The Journal of Energy and Development, vol XVI, No 2, p 219, spring 1991. **BUSINESS ADDRESS:** Director of ICIMS, Assoc Prof of Accounting, Bloomsburg University, Bloomsburg, PA 17815-1301, (717)389-4817.

HWANG, ENOCH OI-KEE

Educator. Chinese American. **PERSONAL:** Born Sep 3, 1959, Hong Kong; son of Milton & Lillian Hwang; married Windy, Dec 25, 1988. **EDUCATION:** University of British Columbia, BS (with honors), 1982; Simon Fraser University, MS, 1985. **CAREER:** Park Plaza Country Club, Vancouver, system analyst programmer, 1983-85; Hong Kong Adventist College, system analyst, programmer, teacher, 1985-87; La Sierra University, CA, associate director of academic computing, 1988-90, director of academic computing, 1991-. **ORGANIZATIONS:** DECUS, 1988-. **HONORS/AWARDS:** La Sierra University, service award, 1993. **SPECIAL ACHIEVEMENTS:** Thesis, Experimental Analysis of Broadcasting Algorithms to Perform Set Operations, 1985; book, Computer Questions & Answer Notes for the HKCEE, Hung Fung Book Co, Ltd, 1989; Royal School of Music Examinations, London, 1973. **HOME ADDRESS:** 11531 Norwood Ave, Riverside, CA 92505, (909)688-4873. **BUSINESS ADDRESS:** Director of Academic Computing, La Sierra University, 4700 Pierce St, Ambs Hall, Rm 115, Riverside, CA 92515, (909)785-2554.

HWANG, GUANN-JIUN
Educator. Chinese American. **PERSONAL:** Born Jul 7, 1951, Taipei City, Taiwan; son of Yu Hwang & Shie-Fong Ho; married Cindy C Hwang, May 19, 1979; children: Jennifer, Julie. **EDUCATION:** Taiwan Provincial College of Marine & Oceanic Technology, BS, 1973; Asian Institute of Technology, ME, 1984; Clarkston University, PhD, 1990. **CAREER:** Taichung Harbor Bureau, assistant engineer, beginning 1976; Keelung Harbor Bureau, engineer, beginning 1981; New England College, assistant professor, beginning 1989; Dames and Moore, project engineer, currently. **ORGANIZATIONS:** American Society of Civil Engineers; American Geophysical Union. **HONORS/AWARDS:** Republic of China Government, scholarship, 1983. **SPECIAL ACHIEVEMENTS:** Publications: journal papers, reports, conference papers, etc. **BUSINESS ADDRESS:** Project Engineer, Dames and Moore, 9665 Chesapeake Dr, Ste 201, San Diego, CA 92123, (619)541-0890.

HWANG, HENRY Y.
Banker. Chinese American. **PERSONAL:** Born Nov 28, 1929, Shanghai, China; son of S K Hwang and I C Hwang; married Dorothy Hwang, Jun 11, 1955; children: David H, Margery A, Grace E. **EDUCATION:** University of Shanghai, China; National Taiwan University, Taipei, BA, political science, 1950; Linfield College, OR, BS, international relations, 1951, LLD, 1988; USC, Grad School, 1951-55. **CAREER:** Hwang Accountancy Corporation, CPA's, president, 1960-78; Far East National Bank, chairman, president, chief executive officer, 1974-. **ORGANIZATIONS:** Claremont University Center & Graduate School, Board of Fellows, vice chairperson; National Association of Chinese American Bankers, president; YMCA -Los Angeles Metropolitan, board of directors; Catholic Charities, board of directors, 1993; Huntington Memorial Hospital, board of directors; California Bankers Insurance Services Inc, board of directors; American Bankers Association, Government Relations Council. **HONORS/AWARDS:** US Small Business Admin, Financial Advocate of the Year, 1986; Executive Magazine, Executive of the Year, 1987; Asian Business League, Businessman of the Year, 1987; Merrill Lynch/Ernst & Young, Entrepreneur of the Year, 1991. **SPECIAL ACHIEVEMENTS:** Proficient in Chinese. **BUSINESS ADDRESS:** Chairman, President & CEO, Far East National Bank, 123 South Figueroa Street, Los Angeles, CA 90012, (213)253-0500.

HWANG, HI SOOK
Educator. Korean American. **PERSONAL:** Born Dec 5, 1929, Seoul, Republic of Korea. **EDUCATION:** Seoul National University, Liberal Arts and Science College, BA, 1952; University of Tampa, BA, 1957; Emory University, MAT, 1959; SUNY at Buffalo, PhD, 1971. **CAREER:** SUNY at Fredonia, instructor, 1962-69; Moorhead State University, asst prof, French, 1969-76, assoc prof, French, 1976-88, professor, French and Japanese, 1988-. **ORGANIZATIONS:** AATF; AMLA; AAS; AATJ. **HONORS/AWARDS:** Moorhead State University, Summer Faculty Research Grant, 1976, Summer Faculty Improvement Grant, 1985, 1989; NEH Summer Institute on Curricular Models for Japanese Lit and Criticism, 1981; French Government Scholarship for Intl Students, 1960-61. **SPECIAL ACHIEVEMENTS:** Author: "Jules Valles et l'enseignement," Etudes Francaise, University of Montreal, Winter 1989; "La Vision du peuple chez Jules Valles," Modern Language Studies, Fall 1985; book reviewer: Lumiere sur la Coree, Korean Studies, vol VIII, 1985; Christianity in Modern Korea, Korean Studies, vol XI, 1987; 1971: La Commune de Paris, Nineteenth Century French Studies, vol XIII, 1985. **BUSINESS ADDRESS:** Professor of French and Japanese, Moorhead State University, Moorhead, MN 56560, (218)236-4059.

HWANG, HSIN-GINN
Educator. Taiwanese American. **PERSONAL:** Born Feb 15, 1953, Hsin-Chu, Taiwan; son of Tze-Ching Hwang & Ferng-Chio Tseng. **EDUCATION:** National Chiao Tung University, BS, 1978; University of Detroit, MBA, 1984; University of Texas, Arlington, PhD, 1989. **CAREER:** Chu-Chang Rubber Co, manager, 1980-82; Computer Communications of America, systems programmer, 1983-84; University of Texas, Arlington, assistant instructor, 1986-89; Northeast Louisiana University, assistant professor, 1989-. **HONORS/**

AWARDS: International Business School; Computer Users Group, 18th Annual Conference, Best Theory Paper Award, 1990; University of Texas, Arlington, Outstanding International Leadership Award, 1989. **SPECIAL ACHIEVEMENTS:** Author, Establishing an Ergonomic Multimedial Environment to Support Information Systems Instruction: A Case Study, 1993; A New Approach to Cutting Tool Selection Using the Taguchi Method and Expert Systems, 1992; Computer-Aided Decision Making in Large Groups, 1992. **MILITARY SERVICE:** Taiwan Army, 2nd lt, 1978-80. **BUSINESS ADDRESS:** Assistant Professor, Dept of COIS, Northeast Louisiana University, 700 University Dr, Administration Bldg, Monroe, LA 71209-0120, (318)342-1137.

HWANG, IVY
Attorney. Singaporean American. **PERSONAL:** Born Apr 8, 1957, Singapore; daughter of Wong Sheuan Ching & Lin Hui Yu; married Kenneth Stoner Kail, Apr 18, 1986. **EDUCATION:** University of Singapore, LLB, 1980; Harvard Law School, LLM, 1982. **CAREER:** Simpson, Thacher & Bartlett, associate, 1982-83; Cleary, Gottlieb, Steen & Hamilton, associate, 1983-87; Citicorp Securities Markets Inc, senior securities counsel, 1987-. **ORGANIZATIONS:** American Bar Association; Association of the Bar of the City of New York. **HONORS/AWARDS:** Winner of the Philip C Jessup International Moot Court, 1980. **BUSINESS ADDRESS:** General Counsel, Citicorp Securities Markets Inc, 399 Park Avenue, 6th Floor, Zone 9, New York, NY 10043.

HWANG, JOHN C.
Educator. Chinese American. **PERSONAL:** Born Jun 6, 1940, Kwangtung, China; son of Doo-Sheng & Bing Hwang; married Becky Hwang, Dec 26, 1989; children: Shirley, Margaret. **EDUCATION:** Taiwan University, BA, 1966; University of Oregon, MA, 1968, PhD, 1971. **CAREER:** Broadcasting Corp of China, newscaster, 1963-66; University of Oregon, TV production coordinator, 1968-71; Hawaii Public Television, research specialist, 1971-72; California State University, Sacramento, professor of communication, 1972-, director, Asian American studies, 1991-. **ORGANIZATIONS:** Foster Grandparents of Sacramento, board member, 1976-78; Chinese Community Service Center, Sacramento, board member, 1986-88; Asian Pacific Community Counseling, board member, 1991-. **SPECIAL ACHIEVEMENTS:** Viewing of Public Television on Oahu, 1972; Oral Communication: Theory and Practice of Public Speaking, 1993; fluent in Chinese. **BUSINESS ADDRESS:** Professor of Communication Studies, California State University, 6000 J St, Sacramento, CA 95819-2605, (916)278-6688.

HWANG, MARK I.
Educator. Taiwanese American. **PERSONAL:** Born Nov 3, 1956, Taichung, Taiwan; married Yihjy Evelyn Wang, Dec 20, 1986. **EDUCATION:** National Chengchi University, BC, 1978; Lamar University, MBA, 1985; University of North Texas, PhD, 1990. **CAREER:** University of North Texas, visiting assistant professor, 1990-91; University of Texas-Pan American, assistant professor, 1991-. **SPECIAL ACHIEVEMENTS:** Published research papers in Data Base, Journal of Computer Information Systems, and Journal of Information Technology Management. **BUSINESS ADDRESS:** Assistant Professor, School of Business, University of Texas-Pan American, Edinburg, TX 78539-2999, (210)381-3558.

HWANG, NEN-CHEN RICHARD
Educator. **PERSONAL:** Born Aug 3, 1957, Taipei, Taiwan; married Hsiu-Hui Hwang, Jul 30, 1983; children: Cathy, Angela. **EDUCATION:** National Cheng-Kung University, BBA, 1980; University of Missouri-Kansas City, MS, 1985; St Louis University, PhD, 1990. **CAREER:** Union Group Corporation, 1982-83; Peat Marwick & Main, auditor, 1985-87; St Louis University, instructor, 1987-91; California State University, assistant professor, 1991-. **ORGANIZATIONS:** AICPA, 1991-; Institute of Management Accountant, 1991-; California Society of CPAs, 1991-. **HONORS/AWARDS:** California State University, Faculty Merit Award, 1993; St Louis University, Outstanding International Student Award, 1990. **BUSINESS ADDRESS:** Assistant Professor of Accounting, California State University, San Marcos, San Marcos, CA 92069-0001, (619)752-4211.

HWANG, ROLAND
Attorney, state official. Chinese American. **PERSONAL:** Born May 17, 1949, Detroit, MI; son of David Nien-Tzu Hwang and Hung Ping Wong Hwang; married Christina Grace Shieh, Aug 29, 1983. **EDUCATION:** University of Michigan, BSME, (ME), 1971, MBA, 1976; Wayne State University, JD, 1980, LLM, 1984. **CAREER:** Livonia Public Schools, substitute teacher, 1971-72;

Ford Motor Company, Customer Service Division, customer service representative, 1971, Car Engineering, product engineer, 1972-81, Office of General Counsel, staff attorney, 1981-88; Madonna College, Labor Law & Employment Discrimination course, instructor, 1983; Michigan Dept of Attorney General, assistant attorney general, 1988-. **ORGANIZATIONS:** American Citizens For Justice, 1983-, president, 1992-93, secretary, 1985-86, treasurer, 1984; International Institute of Metropolitan Detroit, 1986-, member's council, 1987-90, board of directors, 1990-, vice president, scholarship, 1992-93; Economic Club of Detroit, 1986-; Asian American Bar Association of Michigan, 1986-, president, 1987; Association of Chinese Americans, 1982-, president, 1982-83; State Bar of Michigan, 1981-, Civil Liberties committee, 1987-90, underrepresented groups in the law committee, 1985-86. **HONORS/AWARDS:** Greater Detroit Chamber of Commerce, participant, Leadership Detroit XIV, 1993; American Citizens for Justice, Justice Award, 1989; Association of Chinese Americans, Service Award, 1986; University of Michigan, Office of Minority Student Services, Service Award, 1993. **SPECIAL ACHIEVEMENTS:** Credited with acknowledgment in Intro to Readings & Cases in Labor Relations and Collective Bargaining, by J Martin, Addison-Wesley, 1985; acknowledgment in Land Use Permitting, chapter 5, Michigan Environmental Law, ICLE Publication, 1982; co-author, "Case-Michigan Demolition & Salvage," Entrepreneurial Function, by L Hosmer, Prentice-Hall, 1977. **HOME ADDRESS:** 17914 Maple Hill Drive, Northville, MI 48167-3224, (810)347-1663. **BUSINESS ADDRESS:** Asst Attorney General, Natural Resources Div, Michigan Department of the Attorney General, PO Box 30028, 530 W Allegan St, 8th Floor, Lansing, MI 48909, (517)373-7540.

HWANG, SHIN JA JOO
Educator. Korean American. **PERSONAL:** Born May 24, 1943, Nanam, Ham Kyung, Republic of Korea; daughter of Byung Im Joo & Dong Joo Wol Cho; married Myung Kyu Hwang, Dec 16, 1967; children: Harold, Grace, Lisa. **EDUCATION:** Ewha Women's University, Seoul, Korea, BA, English, 1965; University of Oklahoma, MLS, 1968; University of Texas at Arlington, MA, 1974, PhD, linguistics, 1981. **CAREER:** University of Southern California Library, librarian, 1968-71; Summer Institute of Linguistics and University of Texas at Arlington, adjunct associate professor, 1982-. **ORGANIZATIONS:** Linguistic Society of America, 1980-; Linguistic Association of Canada & the US, 1986-; Linguistic Association of the Southwest, 1985-; Internation Circle of Korean Linguistics, 1990-. **SPECIAL ACHIEVEMENTS:** Editor, book, Language in Context: Essays for Robert E Longacre, 1992; author, books: Discourse Features of Korean Narration, 1987, Korean Clause Structure, 1975; articles in linguistic journals and books. **BUSINESS ADDRESS:** Adjunct Associate Professor, Summer Institute of Linguistics, University of Texas at Arlington, 7500 W Camp Wisdom Rd, Dallas, TX 75236, (214)709-2400.

HWANG, SHOI YEAN
Educator. Chinese American. **PERSONAL:** Born Nov 22, 1931, Fuchow, Fukien, China; son of Daw Kwei Hwang and Ching King Kuo; married Mary Show-Ping Hwang, Sep 2, 1961; children: Irving, Vivian. **EDUCATION:** National Cheng Kung University, Taiwan, BS, 1954; Colorado State University, MS, 1958; Rensselaer Polytechnic Institute, PhD, 1968. **CAREER:** Taiwan Power Co, junior civil engineer, 1955-56; McCormick-Taylor Associates, consulting engineers, senior civil engineers, 1958-64; South Carolina State University, associate professor of civil engineering technology, 1969-76, professor of civil engineering technology, 1976-91, School of Engineering Technology, professor/dean, 1991-. **ORGANIZATIONS:** American Society of Civil Engineers, 1958-; American Society for Engineering Education, 1970-; American Concrete Institute, 1972-; National Society of Professional Engineers, 1992-; State Board for Engineering and Land Surveying, Registered Professional Engineer, NY, 1970-. **HONORS/AWARDS:** Transportation Systems Center, Certificate of Recognition for Faculty Summer Research, 1980, 1981; NASA/ASEE, Certificate of Recognition for Faculty Summer Research, 1987, 1988. **SPECIAL ACHIEVEMENTS:** Author, "Discharge Formula," ASCE Transaction, vol 126, 1961; author, "Free Surface Instability of Rotating Liquid Film," Rheology Acta 17, p 471, 1978; articles appearing in Journal of Mechanics, Physics of Solids, vol 8, p 52-65, Pergamon Press, London, 1960; Journal of Hydraulics Division, Proceedings of ASCE, paper no. 2260, p 65-97, 1959; NASA Technical paper 2421, 1984; NASA Technical Memorandum 86913, 1985, 87213, 1986. **BUSINESS ADDRESS:** Professor/Dean, School of Engineering Technology, South Carolina State University, Box 7504, Orangeburg, SC 29117-0002, (803)536-7132.

HWANG, SHYSHUNG (STEVE)
Project manager. Taiwanese American. **PERSONAL:** Born Oct 28, 1938, Taichung, Taiwan; son of Ching-pao Hwang and Shang Chang Hwang; married Cecilia C Hwang, Nov 25, 1972; children: Katherine, Jennifer, Victoria. **EDUCATION:** National Taiwan University, BS, 1962; University of Rochester, MS, 1965, PhD, 1967. **CAREER:** Xerox, associate scientist, 1967-70, scientist/project manager, 1970-74, senior scientist/project manager, 1974-78, member research staff/project manager, 1978-82, senior technical specialist/project manager, 1982-84, senior member research staff/project manager, 1984-. **ORGANIZATIONS:** Sigma Xi, 1967-; ASME, 1976-; Imaging Science & Technology, 1987-; American Physical Society, 1972-84. **HONORS/AWARDS:** National Taiwan University, top 5 percent award, 1960; Taiwan Machinery Company, scholarship, 1960-62; Xerox, special merit award, 1982, 1984. **SPECIAL ACHIEVEMENTS:** Over 75 publications, 1962-; proficiency in Chinese and Taiwanese; patents. **MILITARY SERVICE:** Chinese Air Force (Taiwan), 2nd lieutenant, 1962-63. **BUSINESS ADDRESS:** Project Manager, Xerox, 800 Phillips Road, 0114-22D, Webster, NY 14580.

HWANG, SUEIN LIM
Reporter. Korean American. **PERSONAL:** Born Dec 21, 1968, Hilo, HI; daughter of Suk Hwang and Yangsoo Hwang. **EDUCATION:** Princeton University, AB, 1990. **CAREER:** Dow Jones & Company, Wall Street Journal, reporter, 1990-. **BUSINESS ADDRESS:** Staff Reporter, Wall Street Journal, 200 Liberty St, New York, NY 10281, (212)416-3139.

HWANG, TE-LONG
Physician, educator. Chinese American. **PERSONAL:** Born Nov 4, 1943, Hualien, Taiwan; son of Ten-Fu Hwang and Tien Liu; married Ai-Yu Hwang; children: Tang-Hau Jimmy, Tang-Chieh George. **EDUCATION:** National Defense Medical Center, MD, 1970; University of Texas Medical School at Houston, neurology residency, 1979-82; University of Texas, M D Anderson Cancer Center, Neuro-Oncology Fellowship, 1983-85. **CAREER:** VA Medical Center, Topeka, SC, attending neurologist, 1986-87; Dorns VA Medical Center, attending neurologist, 1987-; University of South Carolina School of Medicine, associate professor in neurology, 1987-. **ORGANIZATIONS:** American Academy of Neurology; American Medical Association; Southern Medical Association; South Carolina Medical Association; American Heart Association, Stroke Council. **HONORS/AWARDS:** South Carolina Cancer Research and Treatment Center, Research Award, 1993. **SPECIAL ACHIEVEMENTS:** Special interest and research areas: metastatic brain tumors, stroke and SPECT scan for neurologic disorders; teaching neurology for medical students and residents. **BUSINESS ADDRESS:** Associate Professor, School of Medicine, University of South Carolina, 3555 Harden St Extension, Ste 104B, Columbia, SC 29203, (803)434-4260.

HWANG, WEI-YUAN
Research manager. Chinese American. **PERSONAL:** Born Oct 31, 1949, Taichung, Taiwan; married Shauley Hwang, Jun 7, 1981. **EDUCATION:** National Taiwan University, BS, mechanical engineering, 1972; MIT, SM, ocean engineering, 1976, ocean engineer, 1978, PhD ocean engin, 1980. **CAREER:** National Central University, associate professor, 1980-81; National Taiwan University, associate professor, 1981-83; Ship Analytics, project manager/hydrodynamicist, 1983-87; Marine Safety Int, prin research engr, 1987-92, research mgr, 1993; Simship, vp, 1993-. **ORGANIZATIONS:** SNAME, panelist of ship control; Society for Computer Simulation. **HONORS/AWARDS:** Chinese American Academic & Professional Society, Outstanding Service Team Award, 1990. **BUSINESS ADDRESS:** Vice President, Simship, 260 Main St, Northport, NY 11768, (516)757-5306.

HWANG, WILLIAM GAONG
Engineer. Chinese American. **PERSONAL:** Born Jun 17, 1949, Shanghai, China; son of John Ding and Sylvia Hwang; married Stella T Hwang, 1978; children: 2 boys. **EDUCATION:** California Institute of Technology, BS, physics, 1971; Cornell University, MS, applied math, 1974, PhD, EE, applied math, 1978. **CAREER:** The BDM Corp, associate manager, 1978-82; M/A-COM Linkabit, director, 1982-88; Science Applications International Corp, vice president, 1988-. **ORGANIZATIONS:** IEEE, 1975-; Society of Industrial and Applied Mathematics, 1975-; Armed Forces Communication Electronics Association, 1982-; AIAA, 1990-. **SPECIAL ACHIEVEMENTS:** Publication in IEEE Transaction on Automatic Control, Best Paper Award Honorable Mention, 1979. **MILITARY SERVICE:** Army, captain, 1973-81. **BUSINESS ADDRESS:** Vice President, Science Applications International Corp, 1710 Goodridge Drive, McLeau, VA 22102, (703)448-6405.

HWANG, XOCHITL
Publisher. Korean American. **PERSONAL:** Born Oct 19, 1956, Seoul, Republic of Korea; daughter of Sun Kyung Hwang and Duk Sung Kim. **EDUCATION:** EWHA Women's University, Seoul, Korea; San Francisco Art Institute. **CAREER:** Enfoque, ASA Intl, president, currently. **BUSINESS ADDRESS:** President, Enfoque, ASA International, 607 S Park View St, Executive Ste, Los Angeles, CA 90057, (213)736-0001.

HWU, PETER S.
Attorney. Taiwanese American. **PERSONAL:** Born Feb 6, 1966, Taipei, Taiwan; son of Chin-Lian Hwu and Chi-Yu Shih Hwu. **EDUCATION:** University of Florida, BS, 1986; University of California, Davis, JD, 1989. **CAREER:** Cummins & White, associate attorney, 1989-90; Crosby, Heafey, Roach & May, PC, associate attorney, 1990-92; Law Offices of Peter S Hwu, partner, currently. **ORGANIZATIONS:** Southern California Chinese Lawyers Association, board of governors, 1991-. **SPECIAL ACHIEVEMENTS:** Article: "Alien Labor Certification: A 'Shell Game' for United States Workers?," Suffolk Transnational Law Journal, spring, 1991. **BUSINESS ADDRESS:** Partner, Law Offices of Peter S Hwu, 17800 Castleton Street, Suite 190, City of Industry, CA 91748, (818)854-2112.

HYUN, BONG HAK
Educator. Korean American. **PERSONAL:** Born Jun 23, 1922, Hamhung, Republic of Korea; son of Won Kook Hyun and Ai Kyun Shin; married Sun Sook, Oct 20, 1951; children: Marian Kyunghi Hyun Harris, Esther Kyungsun, Helen Kyungeun Hyun Bowlin, Philip Jungju. **EDUCATION:** Yonsei University Medical School, Korea, MD, 1944; University of Pennsylvania, Graduate School of Medicine, DSc, med, 1959. **CAREER:** Medical College of Virginia, assoc prof of pathology, 1960-61; Muhlenberg Regional Medical Center, Dept of Pathology, chairman, 1962-88; Columbia University College of Physicians & Surgeons, asst prof of pathology, 1964-70; Yonsei University College of Medicine, visiting prof of pathology, 1966-72; UMDNJ-Robert Wood Johnson Medical School, prof of pathology, 1966-88; Yanbian Medical College, prof emeritus, 1987-; Thomas Jefferson University Hospital, prof of pathology/director of hematology, 1988-. **ORGANIZATIONS:** Korean Medical Assn of America, pres, 1977-87, Education & Scientific Comm, chairman, 1974, 1982-83, exec vp, 1993-; American Soc of Clinical Pathologists, chair, 1981-82, member, 1976-81; College of American Pathologists, Hematology Resource Comm, 1981-, Intl Relations Comm, 1986-90; Korean-American Pathologists Assn, pres, 1991-; United Board for Christian Higher Education in Asia, trustee, 1974-84, counselor, 1984-; Harvard-Yenching Institute, trustee, 1982-85; Intl Soc for Korean Studies in the Americas, pres, 1991-. **HONORS/AWARDS:** Muhlenberg Regional Medical Center, William Augustas Muhlenberg Award, 1980; American Society of Clinical Pathologists, Israel Davidsohn Distinguished Service Award, 1992; Yonsei University, Korea, Honorary Dr of Science Degree, 1991; Muhlenberg Regional Medical Center named the newly renovated computerized laboratories, "The Bong Hak Hyun, MD Clinical Laboratories," 1988. **SPECIAL ACHIEVEMENTS:** Co-author: Koreans in China, 1984; Practical Hematology, W B Saunders Co, 1975; Color Atlas of Hematology, Igaku-Shoin, Tokyo, 1985; Editor, Bone Marrow Examination, Clinics of North America, Saunders, 1988; Hematopathology, W B Saunders Co, 1975. **MILITARY SERVICE:** Korean Marine Corps, Civilian Adviser, beginning 1951; US Army, X Corps, civil affairs adviser to the commanding general, 1950-51. **BIOGRAPHICAL SOURCES:** In Mortal Combat: Korea, 1950-53, by John Toland, Wm Morrow & Co, pp 369-370, 1991; Korea-USA Centennial 1882-1982, by Yonhap News Agency, Seoul, Korea, p 106, 1982. **BUSINESS ADDRESS:** Professor of Pathology and Director of Hematology, Thomas Jefferson University Hospital, 125 S 11th St, Pavilion Bldg, Rm 301, Philadelphia, PA 19107.

HYUN, KUN SUP
Scientist. Korean American. **PERSONAL:** Born Feb 25, 1937, Seoul, Republic of Korea; son of Yong Han Hyun and Samsoon Ahn Hyun; married Sung Za Lee Hyun, Aug 5, 1963; children: Eileen Hyun Kim, Phillip Joonsuk, Paul Joonki. **EDUCATION:** Seoul National University, BSChE, 1959; University of Missouri-Columbia, MSChE, 1962, PhD, chemical engineering, 1966. **CAREER:** The Dow Chemical Company, sr research engr, 1966-69, research specialist, 1969-73, research specialist II, 1973-79, research assoc, 1979-85, assoc scientist, 1985-89, sr associate scientist, 1989-. **ORGANIZATIONS:** Korean Scientists and Engineers Assn in America, president, 1992-93, vice pres, 1981-82; Society of Plastics Engineers, Extrusion Div Board, dir, 1991-, Fellows Committee, chmn, 1992-, Technical Review Committee, 1989-; Global Korean Scientists and Engineers Council, vice pres, 1992-93.

HONORS/AWARDS: Dow Chemical Co, General Managers Quality Award, 1989, Michigan R&D Scientists Award, 1983; Society of Plastics Engineers, Extrusion Divison, Best Paper Award, 1992. **SPECIAL ACHIEVEMENTS:** Early Korean Saints: An Anthology of Personal Histories, 1992. **MILITARY SERVICE:** Republic of Korea Air Force, 2nd lt, 1958-60; ROK Air Force Chief of Staff Award for Top Cadet Officer. **HOME ADDRESS:** 613 Nakoma Dr, Midland, MI 48640, (517)631-4091. **BUSINESS ADDRESS:** Senior Associate Scientist, Polymer Processing Technology, Dow Chemical Co, 433 Bldg, Midland, MI 48667, (517)636-0288.

I

ICHIYE, TAKASHI
Educator, researcher. Japanese American. **PERSONAL:** Born Oct 1, 1921, Kobe, Hyogo, Japan; son of Mankichi & Toyo Ichiye; married Chiyoko Ichiye, Oct 10, 1952; children: Toshiko Ichiye-Pate, Keiko. **EDUCATION:** Geophysics Institute, University of Tokyo, BS, 1944, DS, 1953. **CAREER:** Kobe Marine Observatory, oceanographer, 1946-57; Japan Meteorological Agency, associate to section head, 1953-57; Woods Hole Oceanographical Institution, visiting scientist, 1957; Florida State University, research associate, assistant professor, 1958-63; Lamont Geological Observatory, Columbia University, senior research scientist, 1963-68; Texas A&M University, professor, 1968-92. **ORGANIZATIONS:** American Geophysical Union, 1957-; American Meteorological Society, 1959-; Oceanographical Society of Japan, overseas correspondent, 1951-; French-Japanese Oceanographical Society, overseas editor, 1978-. **HONORS/AWARDS:** Chinese Academy of Science, 3-month visiting lecturership, 1985; Japanese Society for Promotion of Sciences, research fellowship, 1987; Seoul National University, Japan & East China Sea Study Program, 1989; Japan Meteorological Agency, Award for Excellence in Research, 1952. **SPECIAL ACHIEVEMENTS:** Coordinator, Japan & East China Sea Study Program, 1981-91; convener, Japan & East China Sea Study Workshop, 1981, 1983, 1985, 1987, 1989, 1991; author: Oceanography of Japan & East China Seas, Elsevier, 1984; Graphical Oceanography, Tokyo, Tosho, 1952. **MILITARY SERVICE:** Japanese Navy, lt jg, 1944-45. **HOME ADDRESS:** NE 855 D St, Pullman, WA 99163, (509)332-1967.

IDNANI, KAMAL M.
Business executive. Indo-American. **PERSONAL:** Born Jul 15, 1948, Indore, Madhya Pradesh, India; son of Motiram A Idnani and Putli M Idnani; married Maya K Idnani, Feb 16, 1973; children: Varkha K, Aneela K. **EDUCATION:** University of Indore, Seksaria Institute of Technology, EE, 1970; Indian Institute of Management, Calcutta, MBA, 1972; CUNY, Baruch College, post graduate, 1981. **CAREER:** Diversified Impex Corp, asst manager, 1975-77; Romanoff Intl, export operations manager, 1977-78; Drake America Corp, asst division manager, 1978-85; Singer Products Co, marketing manager, 1985-86; John Prior Inc, marketing manager, 1986-92; Sunroc Corp, manager, international sales, 1992-. **SPECIAL ACHIEVEMENTS:** Author: "Understanding and Managing the EMC-Manufacturer Relationship," Middle East Executive Digest, 1989; adjunct professor: Long Island University, Brooklyn & C W Post campuses; chairman, various seminars, World Trade Institute, NY; invited seminar speaker, SBA, World Trade Center, numerous others. **BUSINESS ADDRESS:** Manager, International Sales, Sunroc Corporation, 300 S Pennell Rd, Media, PA 19063, (516)367-6288.

IGASAKI, PAUL
Attorney. Japanese American. **PERSONAL:** Born Jul 25, 1955. **CAREER:** Asian Law Caucus, executive director, currently. **BUSINESS ADDRESS:** Executive Director, Asian Law Caucus, 468 Bush, 3rd Fl, San Francisco, CA 94108, (415)391-1655.∗

IH, CHARLES CHUNG-SEN
Educator. Chinese American. **PERSONAL:** Born May 15, 1933, Hankow, Hubei, China; son of Y H Ih and Moon-Hua Lee Ih; married Donna M Ih, Sep 15, 1959; children: Ronald, Bennet. **EDUCATION:** National Taiwan University, BS, EE, 1956; Lehigh University, MS, EE, 1959; University of Pennsylvania, PhD, physics, 1966. **CAREER:** Sperry Rand Unival, (now Unisys), engineer, 1959-63; University of Pennsylvania, research associate, 1966-67; RCA Laboratories, member of technical staff, 1967-71; CBS Laboratories, director, Dennis Gabor lab, senior physicist, 1971-75; University of Delaware, electrical engineering, professor, 1975-. **ORGANIZATIONS:** OSA, 1975-, Technical Program, chair, several times; IEEE, 1983-; APS, 1970-. **HONORS/AWARDS:** RCA Labs, Special Award, 1969. **SPECIAL ACHIEVE-**

MENTS: Inventor of holographic color image preservation, 1979; inventor of holographic scanner, 1983; more then 60 technical publications, 1975-. BIOGRAPHICAL SOURCES: Scientific Australia, p 22, Feb 1979; "Preserve Color Film," The New York Times, P A12, March 16, 1978; The Philadelphia Inquirer, p B1, April 2, 1978. BUSINESS ADDRESS: Professor, Dept of Electrical Engineering, University of Delaware, Newark, DE 19716, (302)831-8173.

IHM, TYSUN
Attorney. Korean American. PERSONAL: Born Oct 10, 1957, Seoul, Republic of Korea; son of Kyong An Nam; married Alice Park Ihm, Jan 5, 1985; children: Austin, Terence. EDUCATION: Yale University, BA, 1980; Harvard Law School, JD, 1983. CAREER: Peabody, Lambert and Meyers, associate, 1983-84; Swidler and Berlin, counsel, 1985-87; United Enterprise Inc, director, president, 1988-90; Ihm and Associates, attorney, 1991-. ORGANIZATIONS: Board of Trade, Greater Washington Area, international committee, 1993-; American Bar Association, 1983-; Korean American Scholarship Foundation, Eastern Regional Chapter, legal advisor, 1994-. BUSINESS ADDRESS: Attorney, Ihm and Associates, 1155 Connecticut Ave NW, Ste 300, Washington, DC 20036, (202)429-6556.

IIYAMA, CHIZU
Educator (retired). Japanese American. PERSONAL: Born Nov 14, 1921, San Francisco, CA; daughter of Motoji Kitano and Kou Yuki; married Ernest, Jul 27, 1943; children: Patricia Iiyama Freiwirth, Mark, Laura. EDUCATION: UC, Berkeley, BA, psychology, 1942; University of Chicago, MA, human development and education, 1952. CAREER: Psychology Corp, researcher, 1943-44; Richmond Unified School District, 1958-65; Chicago Resettlers Committee, 1950-52; Parkway Community Center, 1948-50; Contra Costa College District, 1965-87. ORGANIZATIONS: Early Childhood Mental Health Board, 1980-; National JA Historical Society, vice president, 1990-; El Cerrito Human Relations Committee, past president, past vice president, 1988-; Japanese American Citizens League, North California District, women's caucus, rotating chair, 1990-. HONORS/AWARDS: JCCC, JA Community Award, 1990; CCC, Contra Costa Children's Council, 1986; Japanese American Citizens League, sapphire pin, 1987; Bahai, Woman of the Year, 1990. SPECIAL ACHIEVEMENTS: Co-chair, exhibit, Strength and Diversity, History of Japanese American Women; chair, SF Curriculum Committee on Japanese Americans in WW2, publication of curriculum guides; chair, Oral History Project, NJAHS, oral history guide. BUSINESS ADDRESS: Vice President, National Japanese American Historical Society, 1855 Folsom, San Francisco, CA 94103.

IJAZ, LUBNA RAZIA
Business executive, educator (retired). Pakistani American. PERSONAL: Born Mar 27, 1940, Lahore, Pakistan; daughter of Mirza Nazir Hussain & Amtul Aziz Moughal (deceased); married Mujaddid A Ijaz, Jun 18, 1960 (deceased); children: M Mansoor, Farouk A, Atif J, Mujeeb I, Neelam R. EDUCATION: Peshawar University, BSc, 1957; Punjab University, MS, 1960; Virginia Polytechnic Institute and State University, PhD, 1975. CAREER: Virginia Polytechnic Institute & State University, assistant professor of physics, 1975-79, adj professor electrical engr, 1979-83; King Faisal University, associate professor of physics, 1979-81, professor of physics, 1981-83; Solar Energy Education and Res Corp, president, 1980-83; International Summer College on Physics and Contemporary Needs, Nathia Gali, Pakistan, visiting solar scientist & lecturer; International Solar & Electronic Indus, chair, CEO, 1983-. ORGANIZATIONS: AAAS, 1983-; NSTA, 1975-; New York Academy of Sciences, 1993-; American Association of Physics Teachers, 1975-; Phi Delta Kappa, 1975-. HONORS/AWARDS: Montgomery County, Woman of the Year in Education, 1976; Blacksburg-Christiansburg, Woman of the Year in Physics Education, 1976; International Women's Committee; National Science Teacher Association, innovative college science teaching, 1977; Virginia Educational Research Association, certificate of recognition for distinguished research in education, 1975, 1976, 1977, 1978; Department of Energy & Honeywell, solar energy heating and cooling systems, 1978. SPECIAL ACHIEVEMENTS: US Patent, thin film solar cells, 1983. HOME ADDRESS: 2236 Archer Rd, Shawsville, VA 24162, (703)382-5528.

IKEDA, ELIZABETH RAE
Educator. Japanese American. PERSONAL: Born Mar 18, 1955, Great Falls, MT; daughter of Tsugio Ikeda and Cecelia Fuji Koga Densley; married Dan E Sieckman, Jun 20, 1993. EDUCATION: University of Montana, BS, 1979; Mayo School of Allied Health Professions, certification, physical therapy,

1981; Institute of Graduate Health Professions, certification, manual therapy, 1987; Massachusetts General Hospital Institute of Health Professions, MS, 1989. CAREER: Deaconess Hospital, staff physical therapist, 1981-84; Missoula General Hospital, director of physical therapy, 1984-87; Missoula Community Hospital, staff physical therapy, 1987-88; Boston Beth Israel Hospital, staff physical therapist, 1988-89; University of Montana, assistant professor, 1990-. ORGANIZATIONS: Montana Chapter, American Physical Therapy Association, 1984-; American Physical Therapy Association, 1979-; MAPTA, research committe chair, 1985-88, nominating committee, 1991-, nominating committee chair, 1992-; Montana Gerontology Society, 1990-. HONORS/AWARDS: MGH Institute of Health Professions, Marjorie Ionta Outstanding Graduate Student Award, 1989; Missoula General Hospital, Employee of the Year, 1986. SPECIAL ACHIEVEMENTS: Board certification in specialty of orthopedic physical therapy, 1992; publication: Journal of American Physical Therapy Assn, 1991. BUSINESS ADDRESS: Asst Professor, Physical Therapy Dept, University of Montana, 026 McGill Hall, Missoula, MT 59812, (406)243-4753.

IKEDA, KAZUO
Neurophysiologist. Japanese American. EDUCATION: University of Tokyo, PhD. CAREER: City of Hope's Beckman Research Institute, Neuroscience Dept, head of neurophysiology, 1967-. HONORS/AWARDS: Received fellowships from: University of Minnesota, University of Connecticut, Cal Tech, Pasadena; National Institutes of Health, Jacob Javits Neuroscience Investigator Award, 1985, 1993. SPECIAL ACHIEVEMENTS: Author/co-author of over 100 articles and abstracts. BUSINESS ADDRESS: Head of Neurophysiology, Neuroscience Dept, City of Hope's Beckman Research Institute, 1450 E Duarte, Duarte, CA 91010, (818)359-8111.*

IKEDA, NAOMI RUTH
Librarian. Japanese American/Pacific Islander American. PERSONAL: Born Oct 11, 1963, Oberlin, OH; daughter of Kiyoshi Ikeda and Jane Saeko Ikeda. EDUCATION: Carleton College, BA, 1986; University of Michigan, School of Information and Library Studies, MILS, 1989. CAREER: University of Michigan, Taubman Medical Library, library associate, 1987-89; Yale University, Cushing/Whitney Medical Library, reference librarian, 1989-94, collection development and management librarian, 1994-. ORGANIZATIONS: Medical Library Association, 1988-; American Library Association, 1988-; Literacy Volunteers, volunteer tutor, 1992-; Phi Beta Mu, 1989. SPECIAL ACHIEVEMENTS: Author, Bulletin of the Medical Library Association, vol 80(2), p 124-30, 1992. BUSINESS ADDRESS: Collection Development and Management Librarian, Yale University, Cushing/Whitney Medical Library, 333 Cedar St, PO Box 208014, New Haven, CT 06520-8014, (203)737-2961.

IKEDA, SHIGEMASA
Physician. Japanese American. PERSONAL: Born Aug 7, 1937, Okayama, Japan; son of Tamakichi & Kimika Ikeda; married Kazuko Ikeda, Aug 16, 1968; children: Megumi, Ken Kiyoshi, Hiroshi Daniel. EDUCATION: Okayama University, MD, 1965, PhD, 1972. CAREER: University of Vermont, associate, 1969-72; State University of New York, assistant instructor, 1973-75; St Louis University, assistant professor, 1975-85, associate professor, 1985-91, professor of anesthesiology, 1991-. ORGANIZATIONS: American Society of Anesthesiologists; International Anesthesia Research Society; Society of Cardiovascular Anesthesiologists. HONORS/AWARDS: American Board of Anesthesiology, diplomate; American College of Anesthesiologists, fellow. SPECIAL ACHIEVEMENTS: Numerous publications to anesthesiology journals: Anesthesia and Analgesia, Anesthesiology, Canadian Journal of Anesthesia, Journal of Clinical Anesthesia, etc. BUSINESS ADDRESS: Professor of Anesthesiology, St Louis University, 3635 Vista Avenue at S Grand Blvd, PO Box 1250, St Louis, MO 63110-0250, (314)577-8750.

IKEDA, TSUGUO (IKE)
Management consultant. Japanese American. PERSONAL: Born Aug 15, 1924, Portland, OR; son of Tom Minoru Ikeda and Tomoe Ikeda; married Sumiko Ikeda, Sep 2, 1951; children: Wanda Chandler, Helen Mari, Julie Oshiro, Patricia Matsumiya. EDUCATION: Lewis and Clark College, BA, 1949; University of Washington, School of Social Work, MSW, 1951. CAREER: Univ of Washington, resident advisor, 1950-51; Neighborhood House, social worker, 1951-53; Atlantic Street Center, exec director, 1953-86; Asian American Alliance, interim exec director, 1987; Mt Baker Youth Service Bureau, interim executive, 1987; Urban Partnership, president, 1986-88; Tsuguo "Ike" Ikeda & Associates, president, 1988. ORGANIZATIONS: Secretary of Health Ed Welfare, citizen advisor, 1976; Nat Conf on Social

Welfare, 3rd vice president, 1977-79; Asian American Social Workers of Washington, chairperson, 1978; Nat Assn of Social Workers, Nat Comm on Minority Affairs, 1980-82; Seattle Central Comm College, Asian American Task Force, chancellor, chair, 1983; Gov Commission on Vocation Education, chair, 1986-87; Dept of Social & Health Services, regional ad comm, chair, 1991-92; State Comm on Ethics in Govt/Campaign Practices, 1993-94. **HONORS/AWARDS:** Seattle Central Community College, Asian Reality Award, 1984; Pacific Northwest Conf, United Methodist Church, Bishop's Award, 1985; Seattle Rotary's Community Service Award, 1985; Municipal League Seattle/King County, Citizen of the Year, 1986. **SPECIAL ACHIEVEMENTS:** First Asian American social worker in US, exec dir, 1953; Princ Invest Effectiveness of Social Work with Acting-out Youth, 1962-72; Prog Mg Develop State Plan on Del Prev, 1969-72; initiated Minority Exec Dir Coalition of King Co, 1980; established first minority inmate coalition in the US, 1985. **MILITARY SERVICE:** Army, Military Intelligence Language School, private, 1945-46; Good Conduct Medal. **BIOGRAPHICAL SOURCES:** Book, Research/Huyman Services, Guide to Collaboration, 1970; Ike's Principles, Japanese American Perspectives, 30 p, 1987. **HOME ADDRESS:** 2629 South Angeline, Seattle, WA 98108, (206)721-0303.

IKEGAWA, SHIRO

Artist, educator. Japanese American. **PERSONAL:** Born Jul 15, 1933, Tokyo, Japan; son of Sumie Ikegawa; divorced; children: Jima. **EDUCATION:** Tokyo University of Arts; Otis Art Institute of Los Angeles, MFA, 1961. **CAREER:** Pasadena City College, assistant professor of art, 1961-67; California State University, LA, assistant professor of art, 1967-76; Otis Art Institute of Parsons School of Design, chair of printmaking dept, 1979-85; Claremont Graduate School, visiting professor, 1987; University of California, Davis, visiting professor, 1989. **HONORS/AWARDS:** Ford Foundation Faculty Enrichment Grant, 1977, 1980; National Endowment for the Arts, Fellowship for Conceptual Art and Performance Art, 1981, Fellowship for Printmaking, 1974; Westside Jewish Community Center, Merchandise Award for Print, 1970. **SPECIAL ACHIEVEMENTS:** Numerous art exhibitions, including: Shinno Gallery, Los Angeles, 1984; Northern Arizona University, Flagstaff, 1985; Soker-Kaseman Gallery, San Francisco, 1985; Monterey Bay Gallery, 1987; Southern Oregon College, Ashland, 1987. **BIOGRAPHICAL SOURCES:** "Focus on Art: Twelve Major Printmakers of the USA," Sceptre Magazine, 1966; "Interview," monograph, Asian American Studies Center, University of California, Los Angeles, 1973.

IKO, MOMOKO MARLENE

Writer. Japanese American. **PERSONAL:** Born Mar 30, 1940, Wapato, WA; daughter of Kyokuo and Natsuko. **EDUCATION:** University of Illinois, 1961; University of Iowa Writer's Workshop, 1965. **CAREER:** Writer, currently; plays include: Gold Watch, 1972; When We Were Young, 1974; Second City Flat, 1978; Hollywood Mirrors, 1978; Flowers and Household Gods, 1981; Boutique Living and Disposable Icons, 1988. **ORGANIZATIONS:** Pacific Asian American Women Writers West, chair of board, 1978-; Writers Guild of America, 1975-85. **HONORS/AWARDS:** Two Rockefeller Playwright-In-Residence Grants, 1974, 1978; Rockefeller Individual Grant in Playwrighting, 1977; National Endowment for the Arts Individual Grant, 1976; Zellenbach Grant, 1978; California Arts Council Playwright-in-Residence Grant, 1983; Brody Arts Fund Artist Fellowship, 1987; California Arts Council Artist Fellowship, 1990-91. **SPECIAL ACHIEVEMENTS:** Gold Watch, directed by Lloyd Richards, was produced for television on the PBS American plays series Visions, and was one of two American entries, along with Roots, invited by the Monte Carlo International Television Festival, 1977, published in Unbroken Thread, an anthology of plays by Asian American women playwrights, U Mass, Amherst, 1993; Boutique Living and Disposable Icons, produced by Pan Asian Repertory in the summer of 1988 for the First New York International Festival of the Arts; plays have been produced in New York, Los Angeles, San Francisco, Seattle, and Palo Alto. **BUSINESS ADDRESS:** PO Box 172, Los Angeles, CA 90078.

IKUHARA, AKIHIRO. *See* Obituaries.

IM, JIN-HYOUK

Educator. Korean American. **PERSONAL:** Born Feb 15, 1952, Kyung-Joo, Kyungsangbuk-do, Republic of Korea; son of Dong-Sik Im and Sil-Kun Kim; married Young-Ok Lee Im, Dec 18, 1976; children: Sung-Kyun (Michael), Ko-Un (Linda), Paul. **EDUCATION:** Seoul National University, BBA, 1975; University of Hawaii, MBA, 1983; University of Nebraska, PhD, 1986. **CAREER:** Korea Long Term Credit Bank, assistant mgr, 1974-81; University of

Nebraska-Lincoln, teaching/research assistant, 1983-86; University of New Orleans, assistant professor, 1986-90, associate professor, 1990-. **ORGANIZATIONS:** Journal of Operations Management, editorial review board, 1990-92; Decision Sciences Institute, 1983-; Data Processing Management Association, 1992-; Pan-Pacific Business Association, 1986-. **HONORS/AWARDS:** University of Nebraska, Maude H Fling Fellowship, 1985. **SPECIAL ACHIEVEMENTS:** How Do Just-in Time Systems Affect Human Resource Management?, 1993; Software Piracy and Software Security Measures in Business Schools, 1992; Manufacturing Environments in South Korea, Japan and the USA, 1992; Rethinking of the Issue Whether IS People are Different from non-IS People, 1990; How Does Kanban Work in American Companies?, 1989. **BIOGRAPHICAL SOURCES:** "Software Piracy and Software Security Measures in Business Schools," Information and Management, vol 23, p 193, 1992. **HOME ADDRESS:** 36 Spanish Fort Blvd, New Orleans, LA 70124, (504)288-5954. **BUSINESS ADDRESS:** Associate Professor, Dept of Management, University of New Orleans, Lake Front, New Orleans, LA 70148, (504)286-6481.

IM, YOUNG-AI

Educator. Korean American. **PERSONAL:** Born Feb 28, 1962, Seoul, Republic of Korea; daughter of Hong-Jae Im & Kija-Im. **EDUCATION:** Ewha Women's University, BS, 1984; Texas Woman's University, MS, 1987, PhD, 1991. **CAREER:** Russell-Newman Mfg Co, CAD/CAM operator, 1989-90; University of Southwestern Louisiana, A-CIM Center, CAD/CAM operator, 1990-, assistant professor, 1990-. **ORGANIZATIONS:** International Textile & Apparel Association, 1987-; American Home Economics Association, 1992-; American Collegiate Retailing Association, 1991-; University Women's Club, 1991-. **HONORS/AWARDS:** State of Louisiana, LEQSF Enhancement Grant, ($246,000), 1992; University of Southwestern Louisiana, Frem Boustany Sr Professorship, pending. **SPECIAL ACHIEVEMENTS:** Bilingual, Korean & English; publications in various proceedings, eg, ITAA Proceedings, 1991, 1992; AHEA Proceedings, 1992; ACRA Proceedings, 1992; presentations in various national conferences, 1991, 1992. **BIOGRAPHICAL SOURCES:** "USL Apparel Center Saves Time, Dollars," The Daily Advertiser, D-5, July 15, 1992. **BUSINESS ADDRESS:** Assistant Professor, University of Southwestern Louisiana, 610 McKinley Street, Hamilton Hall #319, Lafayette, LA 70504, (318)231-6132.

IMAI, DOUGLAS SCOTT

Television editor, photographer. Japanese American. **PERSONAL:** Born Dec 10, 1961, Anaheim, CA; son of Tetsuo and Grace Imai; married Julie Imai, Nov 3, 1991. **EDUCATION:** Fullerton College, AA, 1982; California State Fullerton, BA, 1985. **CAREER:** KBAK-TV, eng photographer, 1988; KCBS-TV, eng photographer, currently. **ORGANIZATIONS:** American Asian Journalist Association, currently. **HONORS/AWARDS:** Radio, TV, News Association of Southern California, Golden Mike, 1991. **BUSINESS ADDRESS:** Eng Photographer, Editor, KCBS-TV, 6121 Sunset Blvd, Los Angeles, CA 90028, (213)460-3316.

IMAMURA, LAWRENCE JUNJI

Office furniture and supply company executive. Japanese American. **PERSONAL:** Born Dec 29, 1946, Seattle, WA; married Marcia; children: Devin, Alissa. **EDUCATION:** Olympic College, AA, 1968; Washington State University, BA, 1970. **CAREER:** Discount Office Furniture Mart, manager, 1971-73; Officemporium Inc, president, 1973-. **ORGANIZATIONS:** Northwest Minority Supplier Development Council, advisory board; Natl Advisory Board for Small Business-US West; Natl Minority Supplier Development Cuncil, area vice chairman; Intl District Economic Assn, treasurer/vp; Office of Minority and Women Business Enterprises Advisory Committee, 1985-87; Puget Sound Minority Supplier Development Council, 1985; Asian Men's Basketball League, founder. **HONORS/AWARDS:** Golden Thunderbird Award, 1992; Intl District Economic Assn, commendation. **SPECIAL ACHIEVEMENTS:** Company has received numerous awards & honors, including: Boeing Co, Chairman's Award, 1988; Puget Sound Minority Supplier Development Council, Business of the Year, 1988, Category III, Business of the Year, 1993; Natl Supplier Development Council, Natl Business Supplier of the Year, 1989. **MILITARY SERVICE:** US Army, 5th, 1970-76. **BIOGRAPHICAL SOURCES:** "Success Story," Small Business News, April 15-28, 1992, p1; Your Business, Winter, 1992, p36. **BUSINESS ADDRESS:** President/CEO, Officemporium, Inc, 1715 E Olive Way, Seattle, WA 98102, (206)720-4000.

INABA, JEFFREY NORIHISA
Educator, architect. Japanese American. **PERSONAL:** Born Sep 17, 1962, Northridge, CA; son of Kaname & Kuriyo Inaba. **EDUCATION:** University of California, Berkeley, BA, 1985; Harvard University, MA, design studies, 1989, MArch, 1990. **CAREER:** Rhode Island School of Design, faculty, 1990-91; Rice University, adjunct professor of architecture, 1993; Arizona State University, assistant professor of architecture, 1991-. **HONORS/AWARDS:** Rockefeller Foundation, Urban Forum Fellow, 1992; Harvard University, John B Thayer Scholarship, 1990, Julia Amory Appleton Fellowship, 1990, John Templeton Kelly Prize, 1990. **BUSINESS ADDRESS:** Assistant Professor, School of Architecture, Arizona State University, Tempe, AZ 85287-1605, (602)965-3536.

INADA, LAWSON FUSAO
Poet. Japanese American. **PERSONAL:** Born May 26, 1938, Fresno, CA; son of Fusaji Inada and Masako Saito Inada; married Janet Francis, Feb 19, 1962; children: Miles Fusao, Lowell Masao. **EDUCATION:** University of California, Berkeley, 1956-57; Fresno State College, BA, 1959; University of Iowa, grad study, 1960-62; University of Oregon, MFA, 1966. **CAREER:** Southern Oregon State College, Ashland, Dept of English, associate professor, 1966-77, professor, 1977-, Students of Other Cultures Project, director, 1970-72, Combined Asian American Resources Project, director, beginning 1971; poet, works include: Three Northwest Poets: Drake, Inada, Lawder, Quixote Press, 1970; Before the War: Poems as They Happen, Morrow, 1971; co-editor, Aiiieeeee!: An Anthology of Asian-American Writers, Howard University Press, 1974; The Buddha Bandits on the Tokaido 99: Hongo, Inada, Lau; co-editor, The Big Aiiieeeee!: An Anthology of Chinese American and Japanese American Literature, 1991; Legends from Camp, Coffeehouse Press, 1992. **ORGANIZATIONS:** Japanese American Citizens League. **HONORS/ AWARDS:** American Book Award, 1988; Natl Endowment for the Arts; Oregon State Poet of the Year, 1991. **BUSINESS ADDRESS:** Professor, English Dept, Southern Oregon State College, 1250 Siskiyou Blvd, Ashland, OR 97520-2268, (503)552-6639. *

INAGAMI, TADASHI
Educator. Japanese American. **PERSONAL:** Born Feb 20, 1931, Kobe, Japan; son of Yoshio Inagami and Yoshi Inagami; married Masako Inagami, Nov 12, 1961; children: Sanae, Mari. **EDUCATION:** Kyoto University, BS, 1953, DSc, 1963; Yale University, MS, 1955, PhD, 1958. **CAREER:** Nagoya City University, instructor of biochemistry, 1962; Yale University, research associate in molecular biophysics, 1962-66; Vanderbilt University, asst professor of biochemistry, 1966-69, associate professor of biochemistry, 1970-75, professor of biochemistry, 1975-92, professor of medicine (secondary), 1991-, Stanford Moore Professor of Biochemistry, 1992-. **ORGANIZATIONS:** Am Society Biological Chemistry and Molecular Biology; Endocrine Society; American Heart Assn, High Blood Pressure Research Council, councilor; American Society of Physiology; American Society of Hypertension; Japanese Biochemical Society; Japanese Society of Endocrinology. **HONORS/AWARDS:** American Heart Association, CIBA Award for Excellence in Hypertension Research, 1985; Belgian National Research Funds, SPA Award for Scientific Research, 1986; Fumbolt Awards for Senior US Scientist, 1981; Vanderbilt University, Sutherland Prize, 1991; Japanese Society of Endocrinolgy, honorary membership, 1991-. **SPECIAL ACHIEVEMENTS:** Numerous important contributions on hypertensive and vasoactive substances: Purification of Renin, 1975; Purification and Cloning of Atrial Natriuretic Factor, 1984; Cloning of Angiotensin Receptor, 1991; Identification of a Candidate Gene for Hypertension, 1991. **BUSINESS ADDRESS:** Professor of Biochemistry, Vanderbilt University School of Medicine, 23rd Ave at S Pierce, Rm 663 Light Hall, Nashville, TN 37232, (615)322-4347.

INATOME, JOSEPH T.
Computer company executive (retired). Japanese American. **PERSONAL:** Born Jun 3, 1925, San Francisco, CA; married A Nan Inatome; children: Rick. **EDUCATION:** Wayne State University, BS, mechanical engineering. **CAREER:** CEC Michigan, mechanical engineering director; Inacomp Computer Centers Inc, co-founder, president, chairman of the board, beginning 1976, retired. **ORGANIZATIONS:** CSI, Detroit chapter, board of directors; ASHRAE; NSPE; International Solar Engineering Society; ACEC; Cons Engineers Council of Metro Detroit, past president. **SPECIAL ACHIEVEMENTS:** Business proposition with Isiah Thomas to purchase majority share of American Speedy Printing, 1992. **BUSINESS ADDRESS:** Retired Co-founder, Inacomp Computer Centers, 1800 W Maple Rd, Troy, MI 48084-7104, (810)637-2100. *

INATOME, RICK
Computer resale company executive. Japanese American. **PERSONAL:** Born Jul 27, 1953, Detroit, MI; son of Joseph T Inatome and A Nan Inatome; married Joyce, Aug 18, 1979; children: Dania, Evan, Blake, Jaron. **EDUCATION:** Michigan State University, bachelor's degree, economics, 1976. **CAREER:** Inacomp Computer Centers, president, chairman, 1976-91; InaCom Corp, chairman of the board, currently. **ORGANIZATIONS:** Henry Ford Medical Center Northeast, chairman, 1992-; Liberty BIDCO, chairman, 1992-; MSU Citizens Advisory Board, director, 1991-; Eton Academy, director, 1993-; Cranbrook Institute of Science, governor, 1985-; University of Michigan, Dearborn, citizen advisor, director, 1992-; Greater Detroit Chamber of Commerce, director, 1990-; Oakland Bar Association, advisory committee, 1991-. **HONORS/AWARDS:** Computer Reseller News, Most Influential Executives, 1983-91; Inc Magazine, Entrepreneur of the Year, retail, 1991; Harvard University Business Club of Detroit, Entrepreneur of the Year, 1985; Michigan Jaycees, Outstanding Young Man, 1983; MSU Graduate School of Business, Financial Leadership Award, 1985; The Detroit News, Michiganian of the Year, 1984. **BUSINESS ADDRESS:** Chairman of the Board, InaCom Corp, 1800 W Maple Rd, Troy, MI 48084, (313)649-5580.

ING, LAWRENCE N. C.
Judge. **PERSONAL:** Born Aug 4, 1941, Honolulu, HI. **EDUCATION:** University of Hawaii, BA, 1963; University of California, JD, 1966. **CAREER:** City and County of Honolulu, deputy corporate counsel, 1966-67; law practice, attorney, 1967; Maui, deputy county attorney, 1967-68; Ueoka, Vail, Luna and Ing, partner, 1969-72; law practice, attorney, beginning 1972; Maui Community College, Dept of Education, instructor, beginning 1974; US District Court, asst magistrate judge, 12 years; Ing, Ige and Horikawa, partner, currently. **ORGANIZATIONS:** Big Brothers of Maui Inc, board of directors; Maui Assn to Help Retarded Citizens, board of directors; Maui County Board of Realtors; Maui County Bar Assn, past president; Maui Chamber of Commerce; Maui Jaycees, past president. **BUSINESS ADDRESS:** Partner, Ing, Ige & Horikawa, 2145 Wells St, Ste 204, Wailuku, HI 96793, (808)242-4555. *

ING, MALCOLM ROSS
Eye surgeon, educator. Chinese American. **PERSONAL:** Born Oct 31, 1934, Honolulu, HI; son of Edmund Ing; married Audrey, Dec 22, 1955; children: Karen, Debra, Sandra. **EDUCATION:** Harvard University, 1952-55; Yale University School of Medicine, MD, 1959, residency ophthalmology, 1960-63; Children's Hospital District of Columbia, fellowship, pediatric ophthalmology, 1963-64. **CAREER:** Queen's Medical Center, chief of ophthalmology, 1970-73, 1983-85, 1987-88; University of Hawaii School of Medicine, professor, chief of ophthalmology, 1983-; Kapiolani Medical Center, chief of ophthalmology, 1988-. **ORGANIZATIONS:** Hawaii Medical Association Investigative Committee, Public Relations Committee, 1992-93; Honolulu County Medical Society, Medical Practice Committee, chairman, 1968-; Hawaii Ophthalmological Society, president, 1983-85; American Ophthalmological Society, 1981-; American Academy of Ophthalmology, 1966-. **HONORS/AWARDS:** Havard Book Prize for Outstanding Scholarship, 1953. **SPECIAL ACHIEVEMENTS:** Numerous publications on pediatric ophthalmology; most often cited publication: "Early Surgical Alignment for Congenital Esotropia," accepted as thesis, published by Transactions, American Ophthalmological Society, 1981. **MILITARY SERVICE:** US Army, captain, 1966-68. **BUSINESS ADDRESS:** Professor, Chief of Ophthalmology, University of Hawaii, School of Medicine, 1319 Punahou Street, Ste 110, Honolulu, HI 96826, (808)955-5951.

INOKUTI, MITIO
Researcher. Japanese American. **PERSONAL:** Born Jul 6, 1933, Tokyo, Japan; son of Haruhisa Inokuti and Takako Kure Inokuti; married Makiko Omori Inokuti, Mar 10, 1960; children: Mika Inokuti Cusick. **EDUCATION:** University of Tokyo, BS, history and philosophy of science, 1956, MS, applied physics, 1958, PhD, applied physics, 1962. **CAREER:** University of Tokyo, instructor in mathematical physics, 1961-64; Northwestern University, research associate, 1962-63; Argonne National Laboratory, research associate, 1963-65, associate physicist, 1965-73, senior physicist, 1973-. **ORGANIZATIONS:** American Physical Society, fellow, 1969-; The Institute of Physics, London, fellow, 1965-; Physical Society of Japan, 1956-; Radiation Research Society, 1968-; International Commission on Radiation Units and Measurements, 1985-; International House of Japan, 1960-. **HONORS/AWARDS:** University of Chicago, Medal for Distinguished Performance, 1990. **SPECIAL ACHIEVEMENTS:** Inelastic Collisions of Fast-Charged Particles with Atoms and Molecules—The Bethe Theory Revisited; Reviews of Modern Physics 43, 297-347 (1971); 160 original papers in professional scientific journals.

HOME ADDRESS: 6481 Blackhawk Trail, La Grange, IL 60525, (708)246-4058. **BUSINESS ADDRESS:** Senior Physicist, Argonne National Lab, 9700 S Cass Ave, Bldg 203, Argonne, IL 60439, (708)252-4186.

INOUE, MICHAEL SHIGERU
Engineering company executive. Japanese American. **PERSONAL:** Born Jun 27, 1936, Tokyo, Japan; son of Takajiro Inoue and Kazuko Inoue (deceased); married Mary L Inoue, Sep 23, 1965; children: Stephen Minoru, Rosanne Emi, Marcus Satoru, Joanne Kimi, Suzanne Tami. **EDUCATION:** University of Dayton, BSEE (magna cum laude), 1959; Johns Hopkins University, 1963; Oregon State University, PhD, MSIE, 1966. **CAREER:** Black and Decker Mfg Co, Applied Res Lab, sr research engineer, 1961-63; Johns Hopkins University, McCoy College, instructor, 1960-62; Oregon State University, professor of industrial engineering, 1963-82; Kyocera Northwest Inc, vice president of administration, 1985-86; Kyocera International Inc, consumer products manager, 1982-85, vice president, 1986-. **ORGANIZATIONS:** Tau Beta Pi, 1958-; Sigma Xi; Alpha Pi Mu; IIE, sr member; Decision Science Institute; Management Science Institute; American Ceramic Society. **HONORS/AWARDS:** American Institute of Industrial Engineers, IBM Graduate Research Award, second place, 1964; IIE Portland Chapter, IE of the Year, 1977; State of Oregon, registered professional engineer, 1977; State of California, registered professional engineer, 1980; ICCP, certified data processor, 1978. **SPECIAL ACHIEVEMENTS:** Author and co-author of many publications, including: Introduction to Operations Research and Management Science, McGraw Hill Book Co, 1975; Circlos de Calidad, Editorial Tecnologica de Costa Rica, 1984; visiting professor, Monterey Institute of Technology (Mexico), Kyoto University (Japan), Costa Rica Institute of Technology (Costa Rica), Latvia Academy of Science (Latvia). **HOME ADDRESS:** 5154 Via Playa Los Santos, San Diego, CA 92124-1555, (619)576-6866.

INOUYE, CHARLES SHIRŌ
Educator. Japanese American. **PERSONAL:** Born Jun 11, 1954, Richfield, UT; son of Charles Ichirō Inouye & Bessie Shizuko Murakami; married Sibyl Johnston Inouye, May 26, 1984; children: Mie, Leif. **EDUCATION:** Stanford University, AB, 1978; Kobe University, MA, 1982; Harvard University, PhD, 1988. **CAREER:** Harvard University, teaching assistant; Wesleyan University, assistant professor of Japanese; Tufts University, assistant professor of Japanese, currently. **ORGANIZATIONS:** Association for Asian Studies, 1988-; Modern Languages Association, 1992-; Reischauer Institute, research associate, 1988-; Kyoka Kenkyu Kai (Kyoka Research Circle), 1987-. **HONORS/AWARDS:** Fulbright-Hays, Social Science Research Council Dissertation Grant, 1986; Reischauer Institute, Post-Doctoral Grant, 1990; Japan Foundation, Research Grant, 1993; Mellon Faculty Research Grant, 1994; American Council of Learned Societies, 1991. **SPECIAL ACHIEVEMENTS:** Author: Three Tales of Mystery and Imagination: Japanese Gothic by Izumi Kyoka, 1992; "Pictocentrism," Yearbook of Comparative and General Literature, 1993; "Water Imagery in the Work of Izumi Kyoka," Monumenta Nipponica, vol 46, no 1, 1991; "Toward a Theory of Pictocentrism," Proceedings of the Tokyo Conference of International Comparative Literature Association, 1993. **HOME ADDRESS:** 1590 Cambridge St, Cambridge, MA 02138. **BUSINESS ADDRESS:** Asst Prof, Dept of German, Russian & Asian Languages & Literatures, Tufts University, Olin Center 306, Medford, MA 02155, (617)628-5000.

INOUYE, DANIEL K.
US senator. Japanese American. **PERSONAL:** Born Sep 7, 1924, Honolulu, HI; son of Hyotaro & Kame; married Margaret, Jun 12, 1949; children: Daniel K Jr. **EDUCATION:** University of Hawaii, BA, 1950; George Washington University Law School, JD, 1952. **CAREER:** Honolulu Deputy City Prosecutor, deputy prosecutor, 1953-54; Territorial House, representative, 1954-58; Territorial Senate, senator, 1958-59; United States House of Representatives, congressman, 1959-62; United States Senate, senator, 1963-. **ORGANIZATIONS:** Senate Committee on Indian Affairs, chairman; Senate Committee on Communications, chairman; Senate Committee on Defense Appropriations, chairman. **HONORS/AWARDS:** Aloha Council Boy Scouts of America, Distinguished Citizen of the Year, 1988; Statue of Liberty-Ellis Island Foundation/New York Statue of Liberty Centennial Commission, Ellis Island Medal of Honor, 1986; Veterans of Foreign Wars of the US, Congressional Award, 1986; Central Intelligence Agency, Agency Seal Medallion, 1986. **SPECIAL ACHIEVEMENTS:** Senate Watergate Committee, 1973-74; first chairman, Senate Select Committee on Intelligence, 1976-77; chairman, Iran-Contra Committee. **MILITARY SERVICE:** US Army, capt, 1943-47; Distinguished Service Cross, Bronze Star; Purple Heart with clusters; others. **BIOGRAPHI-**

CAL SOURCES: Journey to Washington, autobiography, 1967. **BUSINESS ADDRESS:** Senator, US Senate, 722 Hart Senate Office Bldg, Washington, DC 20510, (202)224-3934.

INOUYE, RICHARD SABURO
Educator. Japanese American. **PERSONAL:** Born Aug 18, 1953, Philadelphia, PA; son of William Yoshio Inouye and Eleanor Ward Inouye; married Nancy Huntly, May 20, 1980; children: Aaron Christoper, Martha Catherine. **EDUCATION:** Reed College, BA, 1976; University of Arizona, PhD, 1982. **CAREER:** Earlham College, assistant professor of biology, 1981-82; University of Minnesota, post-doctoral research, 1982-86; Idaho State University, associate professor of ecology, 1988-, Center for Ecological Research and Education, director, currently. **ORGANIZATIONS:** Ecological Society of America; American Naturalist Society; British Ecological Society; American Society for the Study of Evolution. **HONORS/AWARDS:** Grants from: National Science Foundation, Environmental Protection Agency, Department of Energy. **SPECIAL ACHIEVEMENTS:** Numerous scientific articles in refereed journals. **BUSINESS ADDRESS:** Associate Professor of Ecology, Director of Center for Ecological Research and Education, Idaho State University, Campus Box 8007, Pocatello, ID 83209-8007, (208)236-2933.

IQBAL, S. MOHAMMED
Psychologist. Pakistani American. **PERSONAL:** Born Jul 9, 1932, Udaipur, India; son of Dr. Fazluddin and Fatima Fazluddin; married Maryam F Iqbal, Aug 4, 1963; children: Azeem. **EDUCATION:** University of Karachi, BA, 1965, MA, 1969; Pepperdine University, MA, 1970; USIU, San Diego, California, PhD, 1975. **CAREER:** Self-employed consulting psychologist in DE, PA, MD; Delaware State Hospital, forensic psychologist, 1974-. **ORGANIZATIONS:** American Psychological Association, 1972; Eastern Psychological Association, 1975; Maryland Psychological Association, fellow, 1991. **HONORS/AWARDS:** American Board of Professional Disability Consultants, certified diplomate, 1992; American Board of Medical Psychotherapy, diplomate, 1991. **HOME ADDRESS:** 109 Dutton Dr, New Castle, DE 19720, (302)322-2689.

IQBAL, ZAFAR
Educator, research scientist. Indo-American. **PERSONAL:** Born Jul 12, 1946, Lucknow, Uttar Pradesh, India; son of Shujaat Ali and Saleha Begum; children: Jameel Z, Shareen A. **EDUCATION:** Lucknow University, BS, 1961, MS, 1963, French, 1965; All-India Institute of Medical Sciences, PhD, 1971. **CAREER:** All-India Institute of Medical Sciences, New Dehli, asst research officer, 1968-72; Indiana University Medical School, Indianapolis, asst professor, 1972-82; University of Health Science, associate professor, 1985-88; Northwestern University Medical School, asst professor, 1982-85, associate professor, 1988-. **ORGANIZATIONS:** American Physiological Society; Intl Brain Research Organization; Intl Society for Neurochemistry; Society for Neuroscience; American Society for Neurochemistry; Society for Experimental Biology & Medicine; Assn of Scientists of Indian Origin in America, councilor, 1987-90; Sigma Xi; life member of the following: Indian Academy of Neuroscience; Neuroscience Society of India; Society of Biological Chemists, India; Indian Science Congress Association; Lucknow University Biochemistry Society; Oxygen Society of America; Neurochemical Research, editorial board member. **HONORS/AWARDS:** Council of Scientific and Industrial Research, United Nation's Development Program, TOKTEN Expert Award, 1987, 1993; NATO International Award, 1990; National Science Foundation, International Exchange of Scientists Award, 1984, 1985; grant recipient from the following organizations: NIH, 1973-77; Muscular Dystrophy Association of America, 1975-77; American Cancer Society, 1979-80; NSF, 1981, 1984; Juvenile Diabetes Foundation, 1981; American Diabetes Association, 1980; NSF Foundation, International Travel Award, 1984; Fidia Research Foundation Award, 1987; UN Development Program, International Expert Award, 1987. **SPECIAL ACHIEVEMENTS:** Invited lecturer at various symposia and workshops; contributing author, publications include: Macromolecules in Storage and Transfer of Biological Information, 1969; Macromolecules and Behavior, 1972; Growth and Development of the Brain, 1975; Mechanism, Regulation and Special Function of Protein Synthesis in the Brain, 1977; Neuropathies, 1978; Neurochemistry and Clinical Neurology, 1980; Calcium-Binding Proteins, 1980; Axoplasmic Transport, 1981, editor, 1986; Recent Progress in Polyamine Research, 1986; Immunology: Perspective in Reproduction and Human Biology, 1992; contributor of more than 50 articles to journals. **BUSINESS ADDRESS:** Associate Professor, Neurology, Northwestern University Medical School, 303 E Chicago Ave, Mail Code T-235, Tarry 13-724, Chicago, IL 60611, (312)503-2446.

ISAKI, CARY T.
Government researcher. Japanese American. **PERSONAL:** Born Aug 28, 1944, Honolulu, HI; son of Raymond T Isaki and Edith Y Isaki; married Leslie S Shigemitsu, Jun 15, 1968; children: Bianca K, Reid K. **EDUCATION:** University of Hawaii-Manoa, BA, 1966; Iowa State University, MS, 1968, PhD, 1970. **CAREER:** Bureau of the Census, Statistical Research Division, principal researcher, 1970-. **ORGANIZATIONS:** American Statistical Assn, 1968-; Boy Scouts of America, 1988-92; Journal of Official Statistics, area representative, 1985-. **HONORS/AWARDS:** Phi Beta Kappa, University of Hawaii Chapter, 1966; Phi Kappa Phi, 1970, Mu Sigma Rho, 1970, Iowa State University Chapters; US Dept of Commerce, Bronze Medal, 1981, Silver Medal, 1987. **SPECIAL ACHIEVEMENTS:** Published 13 papers in refereed journals and book chapters; associate editor: Journal of the American Statistical Assn, 1992-. **BUSINESS ADDRESS:** Principal Researcher, Statistical Research Division, Bureau of the Census, Room 3132-4, Washington, DC 20233, (301)763-5437.

ISAKI, PAUL
Professional baseball executive. Japanese American. **PERSONAL:** Born Jun 6, 1944, Utah; married Lucy. **EDUCATION:** University of California, Berkeley, business degree. **CAREER:** Anti-poverty programs, various real estate and management jobs, until 1985; State of Washington, Governor Booth Gardner, adviser, 1985-90, Trade and Economic Development, director, 1990-92; Seattle Mariners, Business Development, vice president, 1993-. **SPECIAL ACHIEVEMENTS:** As adviser to Gov Gardner, aided in development of Everett Navy Homeport and State Convention & Trade Center projects. **BUSINESS ADDRESS:** Vice President, Business Development, Seattle Mariners, PO Box 4100, Seattle, WA 98104, (206)628-3555.*

ISHAQ, ASHFAQ M.
Company executive, educator. Pakistani American. **PERSONAL:** Born Jan 20, 1953, Lahore, Punjab, Pakistan; son of Muhammed Ishaq and Sitara Begum; married Katayoun Guerami, Dec 1992. **EDUCATION:** Government College, Lahore, BA, 1973; University of Punjab, Lahore, MPA, 1975; George Washington University, MPhil, 1979, PhD, 1984. **CAREER:** The World Bank, consultant, 1979-87; George Washington University, assistant professor, 1983-87, adjunct professor, economics, 1990-; USA International, president, 1987-. **ORGANIZATIONS:** Florida International Alliance, advisor, 1985-88; Pakistan Committee of Asia Society, chairman, 1979-82; US-Africa Chamber of Commerce, advisory board, currently. **SPECIAL ACHIEVEMENTS:** Co-author, "Success in Small- and Medium-Scale Enterprises: Evidence from Colombia," Oxford University Press, 1987; co-author, "Military Burden, Security Needs and Economic Growth in the Middle East," Journal of Conflict Resolution, 1987; author, "Private Sector Infrastructure Projects," USA International report, 1993; articles on international private power have appeared in Institutional Investor and Infrastructure Finance; chaired a session on private power in developing countries at the 56th annual American Power Conference, 1994; appeared as an expert discussant on a Worldnet tv program in Central Asia, broadcast by US Information Service; has acted as a principal investigator, Federal Emergency Management Agency. **BUSINESS ADDRESS:** President, USA International, 1120 19th St, NW, Ste 750, Washington, DC 20036, (202)872-1800.

ISHI, TOMOJI
Researcher. Japanese American. **PERSONAL:** married. **EDUCATION:** UCLA, Asian American Studies Program, MA, 1983; University of California, Berkeley, PhD candidacy, 1988. **CAREER:** San Jose State University, instructor; University of California, Berkeley, instructor; Japan Pacific Resource Network, executive director, 1986-93, senior researcher, 1993-. **ORGANIZATIONS:** Japanese American National Museum, scholarly advisory council; Nobiru Kai, advisory board. **HONORS/AWARDS:** Gerbode Foundation and University of California, Berkeley, Gerbode Fellowship, 1992; Center for Third World Organizing, George Wiley Award. **SPECIAL ACHIEVEMENTS:** Multicultural America, Akashi Shoteu, Tokyo, 1990. **BIOGRAPHICAL SOURCES:** "Journeyman's Heart in San Francisco," Japan Times, Kobe Shimbun, 1992. **BUSINESS ADDRESS:** Senior Researcher, Japan Pacific Resource Network, 310 8th St, Oakland, CA 94607.

ISHIDA, ANDREW
Researcher, educator. Japanese American. **PERSONAL:** Born 1951, Los Angeles, CA; married. **EDUCATION:** University of California, Los Angeles, PhD, 1981. **CAREER:** University of California, associate professor, currently. **ORGANIZATIONS:** Society for Neuroscience, 1988-; International Brain Research Organization, 1988-. **HONORS/AWARDS:** National Institutes of Health, Independent Research Grant Award, 1988-. **SPECIAL ACHIEVEMENTS:** Research publications in: Progress in Brain Research, 1992; Proceedings of the National Academy of Sciences, USA, 1991; Journal of Neurophysiology, 1991. **BUSINESS ADDRESS:** Assoc Prof, Sect of Neurobiology, Physiology, & Behavior, University of California, Briggs Hall, Davis, CA 95616.

ISHIDA, DIANNE N.
Educator. Japanese American. **PERSONAL:** Born May 18, 1946, Honolulu, HI; daughter of Edward Y Yasui & Katherine Yasui; married Howard Ishida, Oct 21, 1972; children: Renee, John, Katherine. **EDUCATION:** University of Hawaii, BS, 1968; University of California, San Francisco, MS, 1969; University of Hawaii, Manoa, MA, 1991, doctoral candidate, anthropology, currently. **CAREER:** Saint Francis Hospital, nurse clinician, 1969-76; University of Hawaii, instructor, assistant professor, 1976-. **ORGANIZATIONS:** Sigma Theta Tau, treasurer, counselor, eligibility committee, 1980-; American Nurses' Association, 1968-; Hawaii Nurses Association, chair, cabinet on professional nurses education, cabinet nursing research; The Council of Nursing and Anthropology, 1980-; Hawaii Anthropological Society, 1982-; Asian American Pacific Islanders Nurses' Association, 1992-; National Education Association; American Diabetes Association, Hawaii Affiliate, patient education committee, 1985-87. **HONORS/AWARDS:** Sigma Theta Tau, Gamma Psi Chapter, Research Award, 1979, 1982, 1991; American Nurses' Association, Minority Research Fellowship, 1982-87; National Institutes of Health, nurse traineeship, 1968-69; Univ of Hawaii, School of Nursing, Nurse Educator Award, 1993. **SPECIAL ACHIEVEMENTS:** Publications: "Japanese American," Transcultural Nursing, in press; "Learning Among Ethnically Diverse Nursing Students & Faculty," Nurse Educator; "Multimodal Teaching Strategies—A Student-Friendly Approach," Journal of Nursing Education; "The Elderly Samoan," Public Health Nursing; "A Comparison of Role Conceptions and Role Deprivations of Baccalaureate Students in Nursing Participating in a Preceptorship or a Traditional Clinical Program," Journal of Nursing Education. **BUSINESS ADDRESS:** Assistant Professor, University of Hawaii, School of Nursing, Honolulu, HI 96822, (808)587-3325.

ISHIDA, TAKANOBU
Educator, researcher. Japanese American. **PERSONAL:** Born Mar 22, 1931, Kyoto, Japan; son of Takakiyo Ishida and Tsuneko Ishida; married Michiko Ishida, Jan 18, 1964; children: Nobuyuki, Emi. **EDUCATION:** Kyoto University, BS, 1953, MS, 1955; New York University, MS, 1958; Massachusetts Institute of Technology, PhD, 1964. **CAREER:** Brooklyn College, professor, 1968-79; State University of NY at Stony Brook, professor, 1979-. **ORGANIZATIONS:** American Chemical Society; American Physical Society. **HOME ADDRESS:** 28 Hilltop Ln, Setauket, NY 11733, (516)689-9693.

ISHII, ROBERT FRANK
Real estate company executive. Japanese American. **PERSONAL:** Born Aug 26, 1956, Albuquerque, NM; son of Edward F Ishii and Rose K Ishii; married Donna Marie Ishii, Aug 15, 1981; children: Taylor C, Spenser M, Chase M, Larson C. **EDUCATION:** University of Nebraska, BSBA, 1982. **CAREER:** Avco Corp, Avco Financial Services, auditor, manager, 1978-83; Cathedral Mortgage Company, asst director, 1983-84; Centennial Community Developers Inc, Centennial Properties Inc, Centennial Capital Inc, Centennial Estates Inc, vice pres, treasurer, 1984-; The Centennial Group Inc, exec vice pres, chief operating officer, 1984-. **BUSINESS ADDRESS:** Executive Vice President/COO, The Centennial Group, Inc, 282 S Anita Dr, Orange, CA 92668, (714)634-9200.

ISHII, THOMAS KORYU
Educator. Japanese American. **PERSONAL:** Born Mar 18, 1927, Tokyo, Japan; son of Yoshitada Ishii and Taka Furukawa; married Elko Bernadette Ishida, Nov 29, 1958; children: Mutsumi Michael, Naomi Bernadette, Megumi Margaret Wiersma, Mayumi Mary. **EDUCATION:** Nihon University, Tokyo, BS, 1950; University of Wisconsin, Madison, MS, 1957, PhD, 1959; Nihon University, Tokyo, DEng, 1961. **CAREER:** Nihon University, instructor, 1950-56; University of Wisconsin, research assistant, 1956-59; Marquette University, assistant professor, 1959-60, associate professor, 1960-64, professor, 1964-. **ORGANIZATIONS:** Institute of Electrical and Electronics Engineers, life senior member, 1955; American Society of Engineering Education, 1962; National Society of Professional Engineers, 1965; American Assn of University Professors, 1965; Wisconsin Society of Professional Engineers, 1965; Sigma Xi, Marquette Chapter, president, 1957; Eta Kappa Nu Assn, 1960; Tau

Beta Pi Assn, 1962. **HONORS/AWARDS:** Milwaukee Section, IEEE, Memorial Award, 1969; IEEE, Centennial Medal Award, 1984; Engineers and Scientists of Milwaukee, Engineer of the Year Award, 1988; Marquette University, L G Haggerty Awards of Teaching Excellence, 1989, Sigma Xi Chapter, Research Achievement Awards, 1989. **SPECIAL ACHIEVEMENTS:** Microwave Engineering, 1966, 2nd ed, 1989; Masers and Laser Engineering, 1980; Practical Microwave Electron Devices, 1990. **HOME ADDRESS:** 6601 W Carolann Drive, Brown Deer, WI 53223, (414)354-5933. **BUSINESS PHONE:** (414)288-6998.

ISHIKAWA, ISHI (SHINICHI)
Educator. Japanese American. **PERSONAL:** Born Jun 12, 1934, Urasoe, Okinawa, Japan; son of Saburo Ishikawa & Kana Ishikawa; married Myrna Ellen Ishikawa, Dec 28, 1972; children: John Mark, Sharon Rose. **EDUCATION:** Ryukyu University, Okinawa, Japan, BS, 1958; Emporia State University, MS, 1962; State University of Iowa; University of Western Ontario. **CAREER:** Evangel College, instructor, 1963-67; Greenville Christian College, Southwest Baptist College, 1970-73; Okinawa Information Processing Center, se, 1973-75; General Council of Assemblies of God, applications programmer, 1975-77; University of Idaho, applications programmer, 1977-79; Southern Arkansas University Tech, associate professor, 1979-. **ORGANIZATIONS:** IEEE, currently; National Computer Educators Institute, currently; Computer Users of South Arkansas, co-chairman, currently. **HONORS/AWARDS:** NISOD, Teaching Excellence Award, 1993. **SPECIAL ACHIEVEMENTS:** Compiled Insurance Client Tracking System, written in dBase III Plus & Clipper. **BUSINESS ADDRESS:** Associate Professor, Southern Arkansas University Tech, SAU Tech Station, Camden, AR 71701-1902, (501)574-4587.

ISHIKAWA-WOLF, ANA YOSHIKO
Illustrator, educator. Japanese American. **PERSONAL:** Born May 16, 1931, Sacramento, CA; daughter of Taneo Harry Ishikawa & Taka Ohira Ishikawa-Yoshioka; married Bernard Wolf, Apr 1969; children: Michael S C Wolf. **EDUCATION:** NYU, BS, MA; Parson's School of Design, certificate, 1953; Chicago Art Institute, Chicago Academy of Art. **CAREER:** Vogue Pattern Mag, staff artist; freelance: Conde Nast Publications, Vogue Pattern Mag, Glamour Mag, Vogue Mag, Vogue Promotions, NY Times, Herald Tribune Mag, Henri Bendels, Bonwit Teller; Fashion Institute of Technology, professor, currently. **BUSINESS ADDRESS:** Professor, Fashion Institute of Technology, 227 W 27th St, D Bldg 309, New York, NY 10001.

ISHIMARU, AKIRA
Educator. Japanese American. **PERSONAL:** Born Mar 16, 1928, Fukuoka, Japan; son of Shigezo Ishimaru & Yumi Ishimaru; married Yuko Ishimaru, Nov 21, 1956; children: John, Jane Riley, James, Joyce Walborn. **EDUCATION:** University of Tokyo, BS, 1951; University of Washington, PhD, 1958. **CAREER:** University of Washington, assistant professor, 1958-61, associate professor, 1961-65, professor, 1965-. **ORGANIZATIONS:** URSI-USNC, Commission B; AGU, editor, Radio Science; IOP, editor-in-chief, "Waves in Random Media"; IEEE; OSA. **HONORS/AWARDS:** University of Washington, Boeing Martin Professorship, 1993; University of Washington, Faculty Achievement Award in Outstanding Research, 1990; IEEE, Centennial Medal, 1984; IEEE, fellow, 1973; OSA, fellow, 1982. **SPECIAL ACHIEVEMENTS:** Wave Propagation and Scattering in Random Media, Academic Press, 1978; Electromagnetic Wave Propagation, Radiation and Scattering, Prentice Hall, 1991. **BUSINESS ADDRESS:** Professor, Electrical Engineering Dept, University of Washington, FT-10, Seattle, WA 98195, (206)543-2169.

ISLAM, NURUL
Government official. Bangladeshi American. **PERSONAL:** Born Dec 13, 1939, Bogra, Bangladesh; son of Jasimuddin and Aysha Khatun; married Jahanara Islam, Jul 15, 1971; children: Samrina, Shakil, Sharmina. **EDUCATION:** Dhaka University, Bangladesh, BS, 1962; Tuskegee Institute, MS, 1965; West Virginia University, PhD, 1968. **CAREER:** Dept of Natural Resources, chief, planning, 1969-80; REA/USDA, env protection specialist, 1981-. **SPECIAL ACHIEVEMENTS:** Twenty publications in biological and natural resources areas. **HOME ADDRESS:** 357 Copperfield Lane, Herndon, VA 22070, (703)742-9756.

ISMAIL, AMIN RASHID
Educator. Indo-American. **PERSONAL:** Born Mar 18, 1958, Bombay, Maharashtra, India; son of Rashid Ismail & Salma Ismail; married Rhonda Copley, Sep 9, 1991. **EDUCATION:** University of Dayton, AT, 1977, BSc,

1978, MsC, 1981. **CAREER:** Milmar Century Corp, consultant, 1989-; University of Dayton, associate professor, 1980-. **ORGANIZATIONS:** IEEE, 1976-; ASEE, 1985-; ACM, 1980-. **HONORS/AWARDS:** University of Dayton, Duke Golden Award, 1979, EDT Award for Teaching, 1982. **SPECIAL ACHIEVEMENTS:** Textbooks published: Microprocessors and Microcomputers, MacMillan, 1984; Microprocessor Hardware & Software Concepts, MacMillan, 1987; Digital Concepts & Applications, Saunders, 1990, 2nd ed, 1993. **BIOGRAPHICAL SOURCES:** The Registry of Dayton, p 83, 1987-88. **HOME ADDRESS:** 5640 Waterloo Road, Dayton, OH 45459. **BUSINESS PHONE:** (513)229-3614.

ISOKAWA, NED
Attorney, association administrator. Japanese American. **CAREER:** Crosby, Heafey, Roach & May, litigation partner, 1976-. **ORGANIZATIONS:** Asian American Bar Association, Greater Bay Area, president, 1993-. **BUSINESS ADDRESS:** Partner, Crosby, Heafey, Roach & May, 1999 Harrison St, 21st Fl, Oakland, CA 94612-3572, (510)763-2000. *

ITAKURA, KEIICHI
Scientific research administrator. Japanese American. **PERSONAL:** Born Feb 18, 1942, Tokyo, Japan; married 1970; children: two. **EDUCATION:** Tokyo College of Pharm, BS, 1965, PhD, pharm sci, 1970. **CAREER:** Natl Research Council of Canada, Chem, fellow, 1971-74, visiting scientist, 1974-75; California Institute of Technology, senior scientist, 1974-76; City of Hope Natl Medical Center, associate research scientist, 1976-78, Dept of Molecular Genetics Laboratory, senior research scientist of biology, director, 1978-. **ORGANIZATIONS:** AAAS; ACS. **HONORS/AWARDS:** Genentech, Inc, co-principal investigator, 1976-; California Institute of Technology, principal investigator, 1977-, visiting associate, 1978-; NIH, principal investigator, 1978-81. **BUSINESS ADDRESS:** Director, Dept of Molecular Genetics, City of Hope Natl Med Ctr, 1500 E Duarte Rd, Duarte, CA 91010. *

ITO, CARYL
Organization administrator. Japanese American. **CAREER:** Social worker, 17 years; currently employed in educational toy market; Commission on the Status of Women, currently, chaired the Committee on Domestic Violence. **ORGANIZATIONS:** Pacific Asian American Women Bay Area Coalition, board member, currently. **BUSINESS ADDRESS:** Chairperson, Commission on the Status of Women, 25 Van Ness Ave, Rm 130, San Francisco, CA 94102, (415)252-2570. *

ITO, HENRY M.
Homecare industry executive. Japanese American. **PERSONAL:** Born Nov 3, 1941, Gardena, CA; son of Shigeru Sam Ito and Mario Mary Ito; married Arlene, Apr 4, 1964; children: Eric Minoru, Brandon Shigeru. **EDUCATION:** Woodbury University, BBA, 1966. **CAREER:** Abbey Medical, operations mgr, 1966-84; Primedica, regional vice pres, 1984-92; Health Team Management Services, president, 1992-. **ORGANIZATIONS:** VFM Youth Group, chmn, 1973-82; CA Assn of Medical Products, board member, 1987-89. **MILITARY SERVICE:** US Marine Corps Reserve, corporal, 1960-66. **BUSINESS ADDRESS:** President, Health Team Management Services, Inc, 1202 Olympic Blvd, Santa Monica, CA 90404, (310)452-3535.

ITO, LANCE A.
Judge. Japanese American. **PERSONAL:** Born in Los Angeles, CA. **CAREER:** Los Angeles Superior Court, judge, currently. **SPECIAL ACHIEVEMENTS:** Ruled that Charles Keating, of the Lincoln Savings & Loan, did not break the law as was stated in the case against him, 1991. **BUSINESS ADDRESS:** Judge, Los Angeles Superior Court, 210 W Temple, Dept 100, Los Angeles, CA 90012, (213)974-5411. *

ITO, MARK MITSUO
Educator. Japanese American. **PERSONAL:** Born Jan 6, 1959, San Francisco, CA; son of Takashi J Ito and Marian T Ito. **EDUCATION:** University of California, Berkeley, BA, 1980; Cornell University, MS, 1983, PhD, 1986. **CAREER:** Brookhaven National Lab, assistant physicist, 1986-89; Princeton University, assistant professor, 1989-. **ORGANIZATIONS:** American Physical Society, 1983-. **BUSINESS ADDRESS:** Professor, Dept of Physics, Princeton University, Jadwin Hall, Princeton, NJ 08544-1099, (609)258-5592.

ITO, MICHAEL SHUJI
Psychologist. Japanese American. **PERSONAL:** Born Nov 6, 1955, Los Angeles, CA; son of Shuichi Ito and Aiko Ito; married Cindy L Kissel-Ito, Mar 3,

1984; children: Owen Katsuyuki, Emma Tamayo. **EDUCATION:** University of Southern California, AB, 1977; Baylor University, PsyD, 1981. **CAREER:** Middle Peninsula-Northern Neck Counseling Center, regional coordinator, 1983-85; Department of Youth & Family Services, supervising psychologist, 1987-90; Eastern State Hospital, supervising psychologist, 1985-87, director of psychology, research and forensic services, currently. **HONORS/AWARDS:** Jaycees, Outstanding Young Men of America, 1981; University of Southern California, Skull & Dagger Society, 1977; Commonwealth of Virginia, State Board of Psychology, appointed by Gov. L D Wilder, 1990, 1993. **HOME ADDRESS:** 8040 Deer Run Road, New Kent, VA 23124, (804)966-5475. **BUSINESS ADDRESS:** Director of Psychology, Research & Forensic Services, Eastern State Hospital, PO Box 8791, Williamsburg, VA 23187-8791, (804)253-5282.

ITO, NORIAKI
Cleric. Japanese American. **PERSONAL:** Born Sep 8, 1948, Kumamoto, Japan; son of Horyu & Kazuko Ito; married Janet G Ito, May 12, 1979; children: Mika, Gaku, Kisa. **EDUCATION:** Occidental College, BA, 1971; Otani University, Kyoto, Japan, MA, 1975. **CAREER:** Higashi Honganji Buddhist Temple, minister, 1975-87; West Covina Buddhist Temple, minister, 1988-93; Higashi Honganji Buddhist Temple, Rinban-head minister, 1993-. **SPECIAL ACHIEVEMENTS:** Fluency in Japanese. **HOME ADDRESS:** 1210 N Glendora Ave, Covina, CA 91724. **BUSINESS PHONE:** (213)626-4200.

ITO, PHILIP JITSUO
Educator, horticulturist, consultant. Japanese American. **PERSONAL:** Born Mar 11, 1932, Kauai, HI; son of Minoru Ito and Kikuyo Ito; married Carole Keiko Ito, Jun 27, 1959; children: Bryan, Caryn, Ann. **CAREER:** University of Hawaii, professor, 1964-. **ORGANIZATIONS:** International Society for Horticultural Science; American Society of Horticultural Science; Tropical Region Horticultural Science. **HONORS/AWARDS:** US Government, Fulbright Grant. **SPECIAL ACHIEVEMENTS:** Publications on tropical fruits and nuts. **MILITARY SERVICE:** Army Engineers, sp-4, 1953-56. **BUSINESS ADDRESS:** Professor, Beaumont Research Laboratory, University of Hawaii, 461 W Lanikaula St, Hilo, HI 96720, (808)935-2885.

ITO, SATOSHI
Educator. Japanese American. **PERSONAL:** Born Mar 25, 1937, Gardena, CA; son of Sam Shigeru & Mary Mario Ito; married Carolyn True, Jun 27, 1987; children: Sarah L True, Loren Abbott, Betsey B True, Todd T. **EDUCATION:** El Camino College, AA, 1957; California State University, Long Beach, BA, sociology, 1960; University of North Carolina, Chapel Hill, MA, sociology, 1963, PhD, sociology, 1969. **CAREER:** College of William and Mary, associate professor, 1965-. **ORGANIZATIONS:** American Sociological Association, 1960-; Southern Sociological Society, 1960-; Eastern Sociological Society, 1991-92; Southern Poverty Law Center, 1978-; Eastern State Hospital, VA, patients rights committee, chair, 1983-89; American Association of University Professors, 1965-; American Civil Liberties Union, 1965-; National Urban League, 1982-. **SPECIAL ACHIEVEMENTS:** Selected as a participant in a faculty development seminar entitled Japan's Role in the New World Order, Tokyo, Japan, International Educational Exchange, 1993. **BUSINESS ADDRESS:** Associate Professor, College of William and Mary, Williamsburg, VA 23187-8795, (804)221-2594.

ITO, THOMAS HIROSHI
Writer. Japanese American. **PERSONAL:** Born Apr 13, 1949, Los Angeles, CA; son of Thomas Kiyoshi Ito and Kayoko Nomura Ito. **EDUCATION:** Los Angeles City College. **CAREER:** Soul of the Sword Publishers, president, founder, 1988-91; Lucent Books, Publishing Co, author, 1992-. **ORGANIZATIONS:** Free Arts for Abused Children, 1990-. **HONORS/AWARDS:** Women's American ORT, named as one of the country's prestigious authors, 1993. **SPECIAL ACHIEVEMENTS:** Author, Conversations with Michael Landon, 1992, The Importance of John Steinbeck, 1993, The Importance of John Muir, 1994; publisher and editor, Yesteryears magazine, 1988-89; Overview Series: Child Abuse, Lucent Books, forthcoming. **BIOGRAPHICAL SOURCES:** "Personalities: Conversations with Michael Landon," article, Los Angeles Japanese Daily News, Nov 7, 1992.

ITO, YOICHIRO
Government scientist. Japanese American. **PERSONAL:** Born Dec 22, 1928, Osaka, Japan; son of Taichi Ito and Ai Kubota Ito; married Ryoko Tanioka Ito, Dec 23, 1963; children: Koichi, Shin. **EDUCATION:** Osaka City University

Medical School, MD, 1958. **CAREER:** US Yokosuka Naval Hospital, rotating intern, 1958-59; Cleveland Metropolitan General Hospital, pathology resident, 1959-61; Michael Reese Hospital, pathology resident, 1961-63; Osaka City University Medical School, Osaka, instructor, physiology, 1963-68; National Institutes of Health, visiting scientist, 1968-78, medical officer, 1978-. **HONORS/AWARDS:** Fulbright, Exchange Scholarship in Medicine, 1959-63; Cleveland Metropolitan General Hospital, First Award in Sci Res Meeting, 1960; World Health Organization, Research Travel Fund, 1968. **SPECIAL ACHIEVEMENTS:** Inventor: Coil Planet Centrifuge, 1963; Rotary-Seal-Free Blood Centrifuge, 1975; initiator and developer: Countercurrent Chromatography, 1963-. **HOME ADDRESS:** 6003 Melvern Dr, Bethesda, MD 20817, (301)530-8746.

IWAHASHI, SATOSHI
Landscape contractor, arborist. Japanese American. **PERSONAL:** Born Jun 30, 1949; son of Mr & Mrs Calvin Iwahashi; married Elsie Lum, Jun 4, 1984; children: Miyuki, Gregory, Nicole. **EDUCATION:** Diablo Valley College, AA, 1969; UC Berkeley, BS, 1971. **CAREER:** Harry's Nursery, supervisor, 1975; SC Iwahashi Landscape & Associates, owner, currently. **ORGANIZATIONS:** Bonsai Society of East Bay, 1976; East Bay Gardner Association, secretary, 1977; Asian American Foundation, co-founder, 1972. **BIOGRAPHICAL SOURCES:** Sunset Magazine. **BUSINESS ADDRESS:** Owner, SC Iwahashi Landscape & Associates, 111 Homewood Dr, Concord, CA 94518, (510)930-7499.

IWAMOTO, SATORI
Physician. Japanese American. **PERSONAL:** Born Apr 9, 1958, Tokyo, Japan; son of Takeo Iwamoto and Masako Iwamoto; married Carole Lengyel, Oct 30, 1988; children: Alexander Taro, Nicholas Kenji. **EDUCATION:** Harvard College, AB, 1980; Rockefeller University, PhD, 1986; Harvard Medical School, MD, 1989. **CAREER:** University of Washington, School of Medicine, physician, currently. **ORGANIZATIONS:** Mass Medical Society; American Psychiatric Association, 1993-. **HONORS/AWARDS:** Dista Society of Biol Psych Award, 1993. **SPECIAL ACHIEVEMENTS:** Iwamoto and Hsu, Nature, 1993; Iwamoto et al, J Virol, 1986. **BUSINESS ADDRESS:** Physician, Div of Dermatology, University of Washington School of Medicine, Seattle, WA 98195-0007.

IWANAGA-PENROSE, MARGARET
Association administrator. **CAREER:** State of California Department of Alcohol and Drugs, Asian/Pacific American Committee, team member, currently; San Diego County, Union of Pan Asian Communities, executive director, currently. **ORGANIZATIONS:** National Asian and Pacific Islander Families Against Abuse, national board; State of California Asian and Pacific Islander Alcohol and Drug Services Committee; Asian Affirmative Action, advisory board. **SPECIAL ACHIEVEMENTS:** Advocate for substance abuse research programs for San Diego County such as Pan-Asian High-Risk Youth and Pilipino Juvenile Delinquency. **BUSINESS ADDRESS:** Executive Director, Union of Pan Asian Communities, 1031 25th St, San Diego, CA 92102, (619)232-6454. *

IWASAKI, IWAO
Educator. Japanese American. **PERSONAL:** Born Feb 6, 1929, Tokyo, Japan; son of Kuramatsu and Ichi Iwasaki; married Junko Ikegami, Aug 31, 1972; children: Eiji, Yoko, Miwa. **EDUCATION:** University of Tokyo, 1948-50; University of Minnesota, BS, 1951, MS, 1953; Massachusetts Institute of Technology, ScD, 1957. **CAREER:** University of Minnesota, assistant professor, 1957-59; Nippon Steel Corp, Tokyo, research engineer, 1959-63; University of Minnesota, associate professor, 1963-66, professor of metallurgical engineering, 1966-; Mitsubishi Material Corp, Central Research Institute, Tokyo, technical councilor, 1991-. **ORGANIZATIONS:** American Institute of Mining, Metallurgical and Petroleum Engineers, 1951-; Mining and Material Procssing Institute of Japan, 1948-; Research Society of Resources Processing, Japan, 1992-. **HONORS/AWARDS:** Tohoku University, Doctor of Engineering, 1961; AIME, A M Gaudin Award, 1981, A F Taggart Award, 1982, R H Richards Award, 1986. **SPECIAL ACHIEVEMENTS:** Frequent contributor to professional journals. **BUSINESS ADDRESS:** Professor of Metallurgical Engineering, University of Minnesota, 500 Pillsbury Drive, SE, Minneapolis, MN 55455.

IWASAKI, RONALD SEIJI
Insurance claims manager. Japanese American. **PERSONAL:** Born Dec 10, 1947, Los Angeles, CA; son of Joe Sotowo and Helen Tomiko Iwasaki; married

Elaine Ida Iwasaki, Jan 4, 1982. **EDUCATION:** CSU Long Beach, BA, 1970; Insurance Institute of America, certificate in general insurance, 1986; associate in claims, 1990; American Educational Institute, legal principles, 1990. **CAREER:** Goodyear Tire & Rubber, manager, retail sales, 1972-73, store manager, 1973-76; Farmers Insurance, claims representative, 1976-77, senior claims representative, 1977-80, branch claims supervisor, 1980-82, branch claims manager, 1982-, special branch claims manager, 1991-. **ORGANIZATIONS:** Community Leaders of America, 1991; Farmers Employees, agents political action committee, 1991, 1992, 1993; Japanese American National Museum, 1993. **HONORS/AWARDS:** Farmers Insurance, graduate in claims administration, 1990, Award for Management Excellence, 1990, Top Subrogation Collections Award, 1986, Service and Efficiency Award, 1985; Goodyear Tire & Rubber, Sales Achievement Awards, 1973-75. **BIOGRAPHICAL SOURCES:** International Directory of Distinguished Leadership, 1990, 1991, 1992. **BUSINESS ADDRESS:** Special Branch Claims Manager, Farmers Insurance, 4300 E Pacific Coast Hwy, PO Box 4748, Long Beach, CA 90804.

IWASE, RANDALL Y.
State senator. Japanese American. **PERSONAL:** Born Dec 1, 1947, Honolulu, HI; son of Bruce Hamada and Ruby Hamada; married Jan, Jan 8, 1977; children: Justin, Jarand, Jordan. **EDUCATION:** University of San Francisco; University of Florida; University of Hawaii. **CAREER:** State of Hawaii, deputy attorney general, 1974-85; City Council Honolulu, city councilman, 1985-88; Aloha Tower Department, executive director, 1989-90; State Senate of Hawaii, state senator, 1990-. **ORGANIZATIONS:** Hawaii State Bar Association, 1974-; Japanese American Citizens League (JACL), 1988-; YMCA, board of directors, 1990-. **HONORS/AWARDS:** PHi Kappa Phi, 1971; Phi Beta Kappa, 1971. **BUSINESS ADDRESS:** State Senator, State of Hawaii, State Office Tower, Rm 409, Honolulu, HI 96813, (808)586-6740.

IWATA, BRIAN A.
Psychologist. Japanese American. **PERSONAL:** Born Aug 20, 1948, Scotch Plains, NJ; son of Harry and Margaret Iwata; married Margaret Moore, May 30, 1970; children: Christina, Mary. **EDUCATION:** Loyola College, BA, 1970; Florida State University, MS, 1972, PhD, 1974. **CAREER:** Western Michigan University, assistant professor, 1974-78; Johns Hopkins Univ School of Medicine, associate professor, 1978-86; University of Florida, professor, 1986-; Florida Center on Self-Injury, director, 1988. **ORGANIZATIONS:** American Psychological Association, Division 33, president, 1993; Florida Association for Behavior Analysis, president, 1993; Society for the Advancement of Behavior Analysis, president, 1989; Society for the Experimental Analysis of Behavior, vice president, 1987; Association for Behavior Analysis, president, 1988. **HONORS/AWARDS:** American Association on Mental Retardation, Richard S Dillon Award for Excellence in Research, 1992. **SPECIAL ACHIEVEMENTS:** Over 150 scientific publications. **HOME ADDRESS:** 4312 NW 12th Place, Gainesville, FL 32605, (904)377-6045. **BUSINESS ADDRESS:** Professor, Psychology Dept, University of Florida, Gainesville, FL 32611, (904)392-4895.

IWATA, JERRY T.
Government official. Japanese American. **PERSONAL:** Born Oct 30, 1937, Ewa Beach, HI; son of Goichi & Kikuno Iwata; married Susan T Iwata, Apr 14, 1987; children: Harrison H. **EDUCATION:** University of Hawaii, BBA, accounting, 1961, public adm certificate, 1987. **CAREER:** City and County of Honolulu, Dept of Finance, real estate appraiser, 1978-86; State of Hawaii, Dept of Trans, right-of-way branch manager, 1986-. **ORGANIZATIONS:** Toastmasters International, past president, 1987-. **MILITARY SERVICE:** US Coast Guard Reserve, seaman 1st class, 1961-66. **BUSINESS ADDRESS:** Right-of-Way Branch Manager, Highways Division, Hawaii Department of Transportation, 888 Mililani Street, Suite 502, Honolulu, HI 96813, (808)587-2019.

IWATA, PAUL YOSHIO
General contracting company executive, civil engineer. Japanese American. **PERSONAL:** Born Jul 25, 1951, Honolulu, HI; son of Harry Iwata and Helen Iwata; married Carol N Iwata, Apr 16, 1977; children: Dawn, Cheryl, Garret. **EDUCATION:** University of Hawaii, BSCE, 1974. **CAREER:** Koga Engr & Constr Inc, exec vice pres, 1974-84; KECI Colorado Inc, pres, owner, 1984-. **ORGANIZATIONS:** CCA, affirm action comm, chairman, 1992-; CDOT, advisory comm, chairman, 1992-, constr concerns comm, chairman, 1990-. **HONORS/AWARDS:** FHWA, MBE Contractor of the Year, 1993. **BUSINESS ADDRESS:** President, Owner, KECI Colorado, Inc, 5750 W Airport Rd, Sedalia, CO 80135, (303)791-3759.

IWATAKI, DAVID MICHAEL
Musician, composer, publisher. Japanese American. **PERSONAL:** Born May 13, 1954, Los Angeles, CA; son of Kuwashi E Iwataki & Sadae N Iwataki; married Lourdes Tomelden-Iwataki, Oct 3, 1981; children: Ana Aiko, Ian Akira. **EDUCATION:** West LA Junior College, AA, 1973; California State University, Northridge, 1973-74; UCLA Ext, songwriting, film scoring. **CAREER:** Hiroshima, composer, keyboards/synth programmer, 1975-79; Willie Bobo, keyboards/synthesizer programmer, 1980; Jon Lucien, keyboards/synthesizer programmer, 1981; Alphonse Mouzon, keyboards/synthesizer programmer, 1982; Tom Scott, keyboards/synthesizer programmer, 1982; Olivia Newton-John, keyboards/synthesizer programmer, 1982; Paul Anka Productions, keyboards/synthesizer programmer, 1983-93; musician, composer, publisher, currently. **HONORS/AWARDS:** LA Arts Recovery Program, grant, for "The Healing Drums.". **SPECIAL ACHIEVEMENTS:** "The Healing Drums," musical project; David Iwataki & Friends, concert sponsored by Japanese American Cultural and Community Center; musical director, 10th Annual Day of Remembrance; music director, 1993 Asian-American All-Star Band, Asian-American Drug Abuse Program Fundraiser; assistant music director, original Mark Taper production of Zoot Suit. **BUSINESS PHONE:** (213)936-1758.

IWATAKI, MIYA
Health services administrator. Japanese American. **PERSONAL:** Born May 22, 1944, Little Rock, AR; daughter of Sadae Marion Nomura & Kuwashi Edward Iwataki; divorced. **EDUCATION:** CORO-Leadership Southern California, 1992; CSULA, BA, 1993. **CAREER:** Japanese American Community Services, administrator, 1969-72; Association Womens Center, exec dir, 1972-74; KCET-TV Public Broadcasting, story analyst, 1974-76; Asian Womens Health Project, founding director, 1977-80; KPFK-FM Pacifica Radio, development director, 1981-84; Congressman Mervyn M Dymally, press director, 1984-88; LA County Health Services Administration, Office of Community Relations, manager, 1989-. **ORGANIZATIONS:** LA County Commission on the Status of Women, 1981-89; LA Unified School District Commission on Sex Equity, 1988-, co-chair, 1989-91; KCET-TV, community advisory board, 1987-, board president, 1989-91; National Coalition for Redress/Reparations, national legislative director, 1980-; Liberty Hill Foundation, community funding board, 1990-; Asian Pacific Community Fund, board of directors, 1991-; East West Players Theatre, board of directors, 1992-; Asian Pacific Legal Defense & Education Fund, board of directors, 1990-. **HONORS/AWARDS:** Little Tokyo Service Center, Annual Community Service Award, 1991; Westside Optimist Club, Women of the Year, 1992; Department of Justice, Community Service Plaque/Recognition, 1989; LA County Commission for Women, Annual Service to Women Award, 1989; LA County Board of Supervisors for co-chairing 1990 National Commissions for Women Convention. **SPECIAL ACHIEVEMENTS:** Executive producer/host, "East Wind" weekly radio series on Asian Pacific issues, politics, art, 1982; US representative, International Conference on Wartime Reparations in Osaka, Japan, 1992; UN Decade for Women Convention in Nairobi, Kenya, one of 37 women sponsored by UN-NGO office, 1985; coordinated delegation of 140 to Washington DC making 101 Congressional visits for passage of Redress, 1987; Womens Healthcare Delegation to Peoples Republic of China, 1980. **BIOGRAPHICAL SOURCES:** Various articles in Rafu Shimpo Newspaper, Tozai Times; poetry published in East Wind Magazine, unrelated to radio program. **HOME ADDRESS:** 619 El Centro St, South Pasadena, CA 91030. **BUSINESS ADDRESS:** Manager, Office of Community Relations, LA County Department of Health Services, 313 N Figueroa St, Rm 1012, Los Angeles, CA 90012, (213)240-8287.

IYENGAR, DORESWAMY RAGHAVACHAR
Scientist, educator. Indo-American. **PERSONAL:** Born Jul 3, 1930, Nanjangud, Karnataka, India; son of Shallammal and Raghavachar; married Kowsalya, May 27, 1966; children: Veena, Pramod. **EDUCATION:** University of Mysore, India, BSc (with honors), 1951; University of Madras, India, MSc, 1954; University of Miami, PhD, 1963; Lehigh University, Dupont Postdoctoral Fellowship, 1962-64. **CAREER:** US Army, physical scientist, 1964-66; Lehigh University, Center for Surf & Coatings, associate professor, 1966-70; Sherwin-Williams Company, senior staff scientist, 1970-75; BASF America, senior research associate, 1975-86; Flint Ink Corp, Research Center, technical manager, principal scientist, 1986-90; Science and Technology Consultants, currently. **ORGANIZATIONS:** Royal Society for Chemistry, London, fellow, 1969-; Oil & Color Chemistry Association, London, fellow; American Institute of Chemists, fellow; Sigma Xi. **HONORS/AWARDS:** United States Educational Foundation, New Delhi, Fulbright Award, 1959; US

Army, Frankford Arsenal, Commendation for Research, 1964; Government of India, Ministry of Education, junior fellowship, 1956-58. **SPECIAL ACHIEVEMENTS:** Editor, book, Semiconductor Surface Phenomena and Adsorption & Catalysis on Semiconducting Materials, North Holland Company, 1969; published 50 scientific articles in professional journals; 12 US and German patents; co-author, 3 book chapters. **HOME ADDRESS:** 1474 Hidden Creek S, Saline, MI 48176.

IYER, ANANTH. V.
Educator. Indo-American. **PERSONAL:** Born Aug 7, 1960, Trivandrum, Kerala, India; son of V A Venkatraman and T P Bhagavathy; married Vidhya Iyer, Dec 13, 1990. **EDUCATION:** Indian Institute of Technology, BTech, 1982; Syracuse University, MS, 1983; Georgia Institute of Technology, PhD, 1987. **CAREER:** University of Chicago, asst prof, 1987-91, assoc prof, 1991-. **ORGANIZATIONS:** Operations Research Society of America; The Institute of Management Sciences. **SPECIAL ACHIEVEMENTS:** Author of numerous academic papers in various journals. **BUSINESS ADDRESS:** Associate Professor, University of Chicago, 1101 E 58th St, Chicago, IL 60637, (312)702-4514.

IYER, EASWAR S.
Educator. Indo-American. **PERSONAL:** Born Nov 5, 1949, Madras, India; married Nalini Easwar; children: Karthik, Kapil. **EDUCATION:** Indian Institute of Technology, BTech, 1971; Indian Institute of Management, MBA, 1973; University of Pittsburgh, PhD, 1984. **CAREER:** Toshniwal Industries, consultant, 1970-71; Godrej & Boyce Corp Ltd, consultant, 1972; Asian Paints, marketing executive, 1973-75; Garware Paints Inc, executive asst to CEO, export manager, 1975-78; Pullman-Swindell Inc, consultant, 1981; Holyoke Center of Aging, consultant, 1986; Greenfield Community College, consultant, 1986; Indian Institute of Management, Calcutta, India, tutor, 1971-73; Bangalore, India, visiting prof, 1990; University of Pittsburgh, teaching asst, 1981, instructor in marketing, 1982-83; St Petersburg State University, Russia, visiting faculty, 1992; University of Massachusetts, Amherst, MA, asst prof of marketing, 1984-90, assoc prof of marketing, 1990-. **ORGANIZATIONS:** American Marketing Assn; Assn for Consumer Research; Academy of Marketing Science; American Academy of Advertising. **HONORS/AWARDS:** Academy of Marketing Science Conference, award winning paper, 1989; University of Massachusetts, Marketing Professor of the Year, 1985; University of Pittsburgh, Heinz (USA) Fellowship, 1983, Graduate School of Business Fellow, 1982-83, AMA Doctoral Consortium Fellow, 1981. **SPECIAL ACHIEVEMENTS:** Co-author, "Origin of Rumor & Tone of Message in Rumor Quelling Strategies," Psychology & Marketing, 8 (3), p 161-75, 1991; author, "Anatomy of Green Advertising," Advances in Consumer Research, vol 20, Association for Consumer Research, 1992; "Marketing in the 90's: Lessons for the Public Sector Undertakings," presented at conference of Directors of Public Sector, August, 1990; "Expertise in New Product Introductions: A Protocol Analysis," Conference on Managerial Thought & Cognition, Washington, DC, Aug, 1989. **HOME ADDRESS:** 32 Goldenrod Circle, Amherst, MA 01002, (413)549-2644. **BUSINESS ADDRESS:** Associate Professor of Marketing, University of Massachusetts, School of Management, Amherst, MA 01003, (413)545-5667.

IYER, HARIHARAIYER MAHADEVA
Government official, scientist. Indo-American. **PERSONAL:** Born Jun 21, 1931, Attingal, Kerala, India; son of Harihara Iyer and Parvathy Iyer; married Krishnaveni, Oct 20, 1972; children: Swarna Parvathy Mahadeva, Anuradha Mahadeva. **EDUCATION:** Kerala University, Trivandrum, India BSc, 1951, MSc, 1953; London University, London, PhD, 1959. **CAREER:** Naval Physical and Oceanographic Lab, Cochin, India, 1953-60; IGPP University of California, San Diego, LaJolla, Seismology, fellow, 1960-61; British Meteorological Office, Bracknell, England, Seismology, fellow, 1961-63; Bhabha Atomic Research Centre, Bombay, India, scientific officer, 1963-67; US Geological Survey, geophysicist, 1967-. **ORGANIZATIONS:** American Geophysical Union; Seismological Society of America; Association of Exploration Geophysicists, fellow. **HONORS/AWARDS:** Indian Geophysical Union, Gold Medal, 1967. **SPECIAL ACHIEVEMENTS:** About 100 scientific publications in seismology including editor, "Seismic Tomography"; chapters in books; proficient in three Indian languages; consultant and expert to many US and foreign organizations; presented numerous invited talks at scientific meetings. **BUSINESS ADDRESS:** Geophysicist, Asst Branch Chief, US Geological Survey, MS977, 345 Middlefield Rd, Menlo Park, CA 94025, (415)329-4756.

IYER, PREM SHANKAR
Educator. Indo-American. **PERSONAL:** Born Apr 16, 1936, Hyderabad, Andhra Pradesh, India; son of S Sundaram Iyer & Meenakshi Iyer; married Brinda Iyer, Feb 2, 1966; children: Sudha, Shailaja. **EDUCATION:** Maharaja's College, Jaipur, ISc, 1953, BSc, 1956; Birla College, Pilani, MSc, 1958; Birla Engineering College, Pilani, MTech, 1960. **CAREER:** Indian Iron & Steel Co Ltd, officer trainee, 1960-62, FSA, assistant manager, 1962-80, dy manager, 1980-84; Augusta Technical Institute, instructor, 1985-92, chairperson, 1992-93, professor, currently. **ORGANIZATIONS:** Institute of Engineers, India, associate member, 1970-84; IEEE, associate member, 1985-93. **HOME ADDRESS:** 131 Shawns Way, Martinez, GA 30907. **BUSINESS PHONE:** (706)771-4144.

IYER, RAM RAMASWAMY
Engineer. Indo-American. **PERSONAL:** Born Apr 17, 1953, Pallavaram, Tamil Nadu, India; son of Mythili & Narayan Swamy; married Rupa Iyer, Sep 5, 1982; children: Amrit, Tara. **EDUCATION:** Bangalore University, BCE, 1974; Indian Institute of Science, ME 1976; Brooklyn Polytechnic, DE, 1978; Drexel University, MBA, 1986. **CAREER:** Sun Tech, Inc, design engineer, 1978-82; Sun Refining & Marketing Co, senior staff engineer, 1983-87, senior project engineer, 1987-89, manager f&d purchases, 1987-89; Sun Co, manager contracts, marketing, 1989-91, technical specialist, 1991-92, manager, equipment engineering, 1992-. **ORGANIZATIONS:** American Society of Mechanical Engineers, 1986-, chairman, Piping, Pressure Vessels & Materials Subcommittee, Delaware Valley, 1985-90; American Society of Civil Engineers, 1980; American Concrete Institute, 1991-. **HONORS/AWARDS:** National Science Foundation, Fellowship, 1977. **SPECIAL ACHIEVEMENTS:** Earthquake Resistant Design of Concrete Structures, 1977; "Confined Concrete," masters thesis, 1976; Registered Professional Engineer, Commonwealth of Pennsylvania, 1981-. **HOME ADDRESS:** 7 Bon Air Dr, Marlton, NJ 08053-1858, (609)596-9307. **BUSINESS ADDRESS:** Manager, Equipment Engineering, Sun Co, 1501 Blueball Ave, Linwood, PA 19061, (215)497-6271.

IYER, RAVISHANKAR KRISHNAN
Educator. Indo-American. **PERSONAL:** Born Dec 4, 1949, New Delhi, India; son of Krishna Venkateshwara Iyer & Janaky Narayana Iyer; married Marie Pamela Carpenter, Aug 19, 1982; children: Priya, Marika. **EDUCATION:** University of Queensland, Australia, BE, 1973, PhD, 1977. **CAREER:** University of Trondheim, Norway, Norwegian Institute of Technology, research fellow, 1978-79; Stanford University, visiting scholar, 1979-80, acting assistant professor & research associate, 1980-83; IBM Research Lab, Zurich, visiting scientist, 1987; LAAS-CNRS, Toulouse, France, visiting professor, 1987; NASA ICLASS, co-director, 1985-; Center for Reliable & High-Performance Computing, director, 1989-; University of Illinois, research assistant professor, 1983-85, Elec & Computer Engineering, assistant to senior research professor, 1985-. **ORGANIZATIONS:** Transactions on Computers, special issue, guest editor, 1994; Dependability Working Group, founding member, 1989-; IEEE, fellow, 1990-, distinguished visitor, 1989-; Transactions on Parallel & Dist Computer, special issue, guest editor, 1991, Transactions on Software Engineering, guest editor, 1990; AIAA, senior member; ACM; IFIP, technical committee; FTCS, program committee, 1983-; Computer Science Accreditation Board, program evaluator, 1988-; Accreditation Board for Engineering & Technology, program evaluator, 1988-; Intl Journal of Real-Time Systems, editorial board; Intl Journal of Electronic Testing Theory Applications, editorial board; Sigma Xi. **HONORS/AWARDS:** AIAA, Information Systems Award, 1993; Senior Humboldt Award, 1991; FTCS-19, Outstanding Contribution Award, 1989; International Computer Foundation, Japan, Distinguished International Lecturer, 1987; Commonwealth Scientific & Industrial Research Organization, Australia Postdoctoral Research Award, 1978. **SPECIAL ACHIEVEMENTS:** Keynote address, International Conference on Computing Systems & Information Technology, 1989; numerous consulting positions; numerous publications including, Computer Reliability and System Activity: Measurement-Based Analysis, Dependable Computing and Fault-Tolerant Systems, Springer-Verlag, NY. **HOME ADDRESS:** 608 S Highland Ave, Champaign, IL 61821-3911. **BUSINESS ADDRESS:** Prof of Electrical & Computer Engg, Computer Sci Coordinated Sci Lab, University of Illinois, 1308 W Main St, 255 Computer & Systems Research Lab, Urbana, IL 61801, (217)333-9732.

IYER, SIDDHARTH PICO
Writer. Indo-American. **PERSONAL:** Born Feb 11, 1957, Oxford, England; son of Raghavan Iyer and Nandini (Mehta) Iyer. **EDUCATION:** Oxford University, BA, 1978, MA, 1982; Harvard University, AM, 1980. **CAREER:** Time Magazine, essayist, 1982-; Conde Nast Traveler, contributing editor,

1988-. **SPECIAL ACHIEVEMENTS:** Author: Falling off the Map, 1993; The Lady and the Monk, 1991; Video Night in Kathmandu, 1988. **BUSINESS ADDRESS:** Contributor, c/o Tosca Laboy, Time Magazine, Rockefeller Center, New York, NY 10020.

IZUMIGAWA, WALLACE MINORU

Research administrator. Pacific Islander American/Japanese American. **PERSONAL:** Born Sep 5, 1953, Honolulu, HI; son of Noboru Izumigawa and Grace Tsuruyo Izumigawa; married Sheila Mae Izumigawa, Aug 27, 1977; children: Kyle Noboru, Summer Yoshiko, Heather Tsuruko. **EDUCATION:** University of Hawaii at Manoa, BBA, 1975; Chaminade University of Honolulu, MBA, 1985. **CAREER:** East-West Center, East-West Communication Institute, fiscal assistant, 1973-76; University of Hawaii, Sea Grant College Program, cost-benefit analyst/budget coordinator, 1976-77; Research Corporation of University of Hawaii, Cancer Research Center of Hawaii, administrative officer II, 1977-80; Pacific Health Research Institute, administrator, 1980-. **ORGANIZATIONS:** Society of Research Administrators, 1989-; Delta Mu Delta, 1985-; Leeward Oahu JayCees, 1979. **BUSINESS ADDRESS:** Administrator, Pacific Health Research Institute, 846 S Hotel St, Ste 303, Honolulu, HI 96813, (808)524-4411.

J

JACOBSEN, OLIVIA VILLA-REAL. *See* VILLA-REAL, OLIVIA CANCHELA.

JAGADEESH, G.

Governmental official, pharamacologist. Indo-American. **PERSONAL:** Born Sep 18, 1949, Tumkur, Karnataka, India; son of G Honnagangappa & T C Bramarambha; married Gurudevi Jaya Jagadeesh, Jun 28, 1978; children: Shilpa, Neetal. **EDUCATION:** Bangalore University, India, BPharm, 1970; All-India Institute of Medical Sciences, New Delhi, MS, 1973; Banaras Hindu University, India, PhD, 1980. **CAREER:** Inst Medicine & Medical Research, India, research officer, 1975; Canadian Heart Foundation, Ottawa, research fellow, 1982-85; Banaras Hindu University, India, assistant professor pharmacology, associate professor pharmacology, 1975-86; Northeastern University College Pharmacy, staff scientist, 1986-90; US Food & Drug Administration, pharmacologist, 1990-. **ORGANIZATIONS:** Indian Pharmacological Society, 1972-. **HONORS/AWARDS:** Canadian Heart Foundation, research fellowship, 1982-85; Council of Scientific & Industrial Research, India, research fellowship, 1972-74. **SPECIAL ACHIEVEMENTS:** Published 21 original research articles in peer reviewed scientific & professional journals, 2 review articles; contributed 4 articles in books; presented 31 research findings in various scientific meetings. **BIOGRAPHICAL SOURCES:** Pharmacology and Pharmacologists, An International Directory, Oxford University Press. **HOME ADDRESS:** 8700 Cathedral Way, Gaithersburg, MD 20879-1789, (301)963-7593. **BUSINESS ADDRESS:** Pharmacologist, Center for Drug Evaluation & Research, Food & Drug Asministration, Div of Cardio-Renal Drug Products, Parklawn Bldg, Rm 16B-19, Rockville, MD 20857, (301)443-0316.

JAGLAN, PREM S.

Research scientist. Indo-American. **PERSONAL:** Born Sep 17, 1929, Naultha, Haryana, India; son of Giani Ram and Chhoto Devi; married Mohinder, May 29, 1951; children: Vikramjit S, Samarjit S, Amarjit S. **EDUCATION:** Delhi University, India, BS (honors), 1951; Punjab Agriculture University, India, MS (honors), 1965; University of California, Riverside, PhD, 1969. **CAREER:** Department of Agriculture, Punjab, India, extension officer, 1952-65; University of California, Riverside, teaching assistant, 1965-68; Upjohn Co, scientist, 1969-. **ORGANIZATIONS:** American Chem Society, 1970-; International Soc of Xenobitics, charter member, 1979-. **HONORS/AWARDS:** University of California, Riverside, Distinguished Scholar, 1969; Upjohn Company, Distinguished Scientist, 1990. **SPECIAL ACHIEVEMENTS:** Drug Metabolism, 1965-; Residue Method Development, 1965-. **BUSINESS ADDRESS:** Senior Research Scientist IV, Upjohn Co, 2000 Portage St, 209-518, Kalamazoo, MI 49001, (616)385-7821.

JAIN, ARUN K.

Engineering manager. Indo-American. **PERSONAL:** Born Feb 12, 1952, Delhi, India; son of Raj K Jain and Shakuntla Jain; married Sangita Jain, Dec 20, 1978; children: Neha, Nisha, Sonia. **EDUCATION:** Delhi College of Engineering, BSEE, 1973. **CAREER:** SRPR, trainee, 1973; BHEL, India,

senior engineer, 1974-78; Nagarjuna Steels, India, manager, 1979-84; Siemens, engineering manager, 1984-. **ORGANIZATIONS:** IEEE, 1992-. **HOME ADDRESS:** 3268 Mountain Hollow Dr, Marietta, GA 30062.

JAIN, ASHIT

Physician. Indo-American. **PERSONAL:** Born Jan 29, 1960, Jhansi, India; son of Saroj Kumar and Saroj Jain; married Monisha Jain, Jan 12, 1984; children: Nikhil, Megha. **EDUCATION:** Delhi University, BSc, 1977, MD, 1981. **CAREER:** Georgetown University, resident, 1975-88; Michael Reese Hospital, cardiology fellow, 1988-90; Oschner Hospital, cardiology fellow, 1990-92; California Cardiovascular, consultant, private physician, 1992-. **ORGANIZATIONS:** American College of Cardiology, 1987-; American College of Angiology, 1991-; American Heat Association, 1987-; ACCMA, 1993-; AAPIO, 1993-. **HONORS/AWARDS:** Georgetown University, Best Intern of the Year, 1986. **SPECIAL ACHIEVEMENTS:** Author of several papers, abstracts, and directed studies in the field of cardiovascular medicine, including submissions to American Heart Journal and the Journal of the American Society of Echocardiography. **HOME ADDRESS:** 45449 Little Foot Place, Fremont, CA 94539. **BUSINESS ADDRESS:** Consultant, California Cardiovascular, 1900 Mowry Ave, Ste 309, Fremont, CA 94538, (510)796-0222.

JAIN, BIMLA AGARWAL

Educator. Indo-American. **PERSONAL:** Born Jun 23, 1933, Ranipur, United Provinces, India; daughter of Dau Dayal & Champa Agarwal; married Prakash Chandra Jain, Jul 12, 1956; children: Ritu, Ratna Jain Stroumza, Swapna. **EDUCATION:** University of Lucknow, India, BS, 1954, MS, 1956; California State University, Sacramento, teaching credential, 1970; various postgraduate studies and fellowships. **CAREER:** Fiji School of Medicine, senior lecturer, 1957-67; Hiram Johnson High School, science teacher, 1970-. **ORGANIZATIONS:** NEA, SCTA, 1970-; SCTA, teachers representative, one year; Jain Association of Northern California, coordinator, 1974-; Cultural Association of India, president, 1979; Sacramento Multicultural Park, coordinator, 1986-; Multicultural Park Foundation, Organizational Policy, board advisor, 1993; SCATS, improving & enhancing science educators steering committee, 1987. **HONORS/AWARDS:** Charles Merrill, Reviewer & Editor "Focus on Physical Science," text, 1987; Sacramento City School District, commendation letter, 1985. **HOME ADDRESS:** 4255 North River Way, Sacramento, CA 95864, (916)488-3530.

JAIN, HIMANSHU

Educator. Indo-American. **PERSONAL:** Born Jan 20, 1955, Mainpuri, Uttar Pradesh, India; son of Chandra K Jain and Kusuma D Jain; married Sweety Jain, Feb 14, 1990; children: Isha H. **EDUCATION:** Kanpur University, India, BS, 1970; Banaras University, India, MS, 1972; Indian Institute of Technology, India, MTech, 1974; Columbia University, EngScD, 1979. **CAREER:** Argonne National Lab, postdoctoral appointee, 1980-82; Brookhaven National Lab, assoc scientist, 1982-85; Lehigh University, asst prof, assoc prof, professor, 1985-. **ORGANIZATIONS:** American Ceramic Society, 1977-, Lehigh Valley Chapter, chairperson, 1990; Materials, Minerals and Metals Society. **HONORS/AWARDS:** Alexander von Humboldt Foundation, Germany, Humboldt Fellow, 1991-92; Columbia University, Campbell Fellow, 1974. **SPECIAL ACHIEVEMENTS:** Author: Over 75 publications in national and international journals, 1975-; 2 US patents: electro-optic polymers, 1992; Discovery of Anomalous Isotope Mass Effect in a Glass, 1982. **BUSINESS ADDRESS:** Professor, Dept of Matl Science & Engineering, Lehigh University, 5 E Packer Ave, Whitaker Lab #5, Bethlehem, PA 18015-3195, (215)758-4217.

JAIN, JITENDER K.

Physician. Indo-American. **PERSONAL:** Born Jul 5, 1947, Morena, Madhya Pradesh, India; son of Savita Ben and Mohan Lal; married Bhavna, Dec 29, 1978; children: Jagruti, Sangeeta, Nimish. **EDUCATION:** Medical School, MD, 1970; post graduate training, MD, 1977. **CAREER:** Saratoga Community Hospital, Medical Staff, president; Community Clinical Oncology Program, clinical investigator; private practice, clinical medicine and medical oncology, 1977-. **ORGANIZATIONS:** American College of Physicians; American Medical Association; American Society of Clinical Oncologists; Michigan Society of Hematology and Oncology; Wayne County Medical Society; Michigan Association of Physicians from India, board member, 1984-86, president, 1987; Council of Organization of Asian Indians in Michigan, founding member and first president, 1987, chairman, advisory borad, 1991; National Federation of Asian Indian Organization in America, joint secretary, 1987-88, regional vice president, 1989-90. **HONORS/AWARDS:** COAIM, Outstanding Community

Services Award, 1991; American Citizens for Justice, Recognition Award, 1992; NRI Institute, Arch of India International Golden Award, 1992. **HOME ADDRESS:** 2912 Homewood Dr, Troy, MI 48098, (313)641-9777. **BUSINESS PHONE:** (313)774-9010.

JAIN, MAHENDRA K.
Educator. Indo-American. **PERSONAL:** Born Oct 12, 1938, Ujjain, Madhya Pradesh, India; son of Hira Lal Shastri; divorced; children: Dipti, Vyom, Seema, Preeti. **EDUCATION:** Weizman Institute, Israel, PhD, 1967. **CAREER:** University of Delaware, professor, 1973-. **SPECIAL ACHIEVEMENTS:** More than 150 publications, 4 books. **BUSINESS ADDRESS:** Professor, Dept of Chemistry & Biochemistry, University of Delaware, Brown Laboratory, Newark, DE 19716, (302)831-2968.

JAIN, NARESH C.
Educator, toxicology laboratory administrator. Indo-American. **PERSONAL:** Born Dec 30, 1932, Meerut, Uttar Pradesh, India; son of Dalip Singh and Makhmali Devi Jain; married Gerda Jain, Nov 27, 1987. **EDUCATION:** Lucknow University, India, BS, 1951, MS, 1954; University of California, Berkeley, PhD, 1965. **CAREER:** County of LA, chief of toxicology, 1971-92; USC Med School, professor, 1971-; Natl Toxicology Labs, director, 1987-. **ORGANIZATIONS:** American Academy of Forensic Sciences, fellow, 1966-; Society of Forensic Toxicologists, 1978-; Calif Assn of Toxicologists, 1973-; Society of Toxicology, 1968-; Intl Assn of Forensic Toxicologists, 1962-. **HONORS/AWARDS:** University of Ghent, Belgium, American Board of Forensic Toxicology, Diplomate. **SPECIAL ACHIEVEMENTS:** Author of numerous publications in toxicology; expert in: medico-legal work; driving under the influence of alcohol/drugs; environmental toxicology, etc. **BUSINESS ADDRESS:** Professor, USC Medical School, 5451 Rockledge Dr, Buena Park, CA 90621, (714)521-1891.

JAIN, PIYARE LAL
Educator. Indo-American. **PERSONAL:** Born Dec 11, 1921, Hoshiarpur, Punjab, India; son of Labh Chand Jain and Maya Devi Jain; married Sulakshna Kumari Jain, Feb 15, 1966; children: Navin Kumar, Atul. **EDUCATION:** SD College, Punjab, BA, 1944, MA, 1948; Michigan State University, PhD, 1954. **CAREER:** University of Minnesota, Chemistry Department, research associate, 1953-54; Lawrence Berkeley Laboratory, visiting scientist, 1959-60; University of Chicago, visiting scientist, 1958-59; Bristol University, visiting professor, 1961-62; SUNY, Buffalo, assistant professor, 1954-61, associate professor, 1961-67, professor of physics, 1967-. **HONORS/AWARDS:** Fulbright Offices, Fulbright Professor, 1965-66; US Embassy, India (AID), science adviser, 1966-; American Physical Society, fellow, 1966; SUNY at Buffalo, Distinguished Service Professor, 1991. **SPECIAL ACHIEVEMENTS:** Has written more than 150 research papers in journals. **HOME ADDRESS:** 223 Surrey Run, Williamsville, NY 14221, (716)632-3716. **BUSINESS ADDRESS:** Professor, Physics Dept, State University of New York at Buffalo, Maple Rd, 339 Fronczak Hall, Buffalo, NY 14260, (716)645-2538.

JAIN, RAJEEV K.
Physician. Indo-American. **PERSONAL:** Born Nov 4, 1957, Muzaffarnagar, Uttar Pradesh, India; son of Kanta Jain and Nem Chand Jain; married Seema Jain, Jul 9, 1983; children: Deeptee, Namita. **EDUCATION:** All India Institute of Medical Sciences, MBBS, 1979, MD, 1982; American Board of Internal Medicine, diplomate, 1987; American Board of Endocrinology & Metabolism, diplomate, 1989. **CAREER:** Georgetown University, Dept of Medicine, DC General Hospital, Washington, DC, 1984-87; New York University Medical Center, Division of Endocrinology, 1987-89; Milwaukee Medical Clinic, 1989-. **HOME ADDRESS:** 4626 W Deer Run Dr, #103, Brown Deer, WI 53223. **BUSINESS ADDRESS:** Physician, Milwaukee Medical Clinic, 3003 W Good Hope Rd, Milwaukee, WI 53217, (414)352-3100.

JAIN, RAKESH
Research scientist. Indo-American. **PERSONAL:** Born Mar 5, 1956, Khekra, Uttar Pradesh, India; son of Pawan Kumar Jain and Pushpa Jain; married Indu Jain, Nov 29, 1987; children: Vibhor Kumar. **EDUCATION:** University of Delhi, India, BS, 1976; Himachal Pradesh Agricultural University, India, MS, 1979; University of Alberta, Canada, MSc, 1983; Virginia Polytechnic Institute & State University, PhD, 1987. **CAREER:** University of Florida, research associate, 1987-89; Sandoz Argo Inc, senior scientist, 1989-. **ORGANIZATIONS:** Expert Committee on Weeds, Western Canada, 1980-84; Weed Science Society of America, 1983-; International Weed Science Society, 1983-; Southern Weed Science Society, 1984-; Soil Science Society of America,

1989-; Sigma Xi, 1986-; Phi Kappa Phi, 1986-. **HONORS/AWARDS:** Himachal Pradesh University, India, University Merit Scholarship, 1977; Northeastern Weed Science Society, 1st Place Graduate Student, 1986; Dep Plant Path, Phys & Weed Sci, VPI & SU, Arthur J Weber Award, 1987; Sandoz Argo Inc, Presidential Award, 1992, 1993. **SPECIAL ACHIEVEMENTS:** Author: "Recent Approaches in the Chemical Control of Broomrape, Orobanche SPP," 1989; "Effects of a Synthetic Polymer on Adsorption and Leaching of Herbicides in Soil," 1992. **HOME ADDRESS:** 18023 Hillwood Lane, Morgan Hill, CA 95037-3525, (408)778-6904. **BUSINESS PHONE:** (408)848-1474.

JAIN, SAVITRI
Physician. Indo-American. **PERSONAL:** Born Dec 4, 1930, New Delhi, Delhi, India; married Satyenra Kumar Jain, Dec 14, 1960; children: Sanjay, Monica, Neena. **CAREER:** Private practice, physician, currently; Cardiovascular Associates Inc, president, currently. **HONORS/AWARDS:** American College of Physicians, fellow, 1970; American College of Cardiology, fellow, 1974; American Heart Association, Clinical Council on Cardiology, fellow, 1980. **BUSINESS ADDRESS:** President, Cardiovascular Associates Inc, 533 Couch Ave, Ste 186, St Louis, MO 63122.

JAIN, SULEKH CHAND
Engineering research company executive. Indo-American. **PERSONAL:** Born Mar 5, 1937, Delhi, India; son of Chater Sain Jain and Parmeshwari Devi Jain; married Ravi Jain, Jul 15, 1961; children: Anudeep, Vandana. **EDUCATION:** Punjab University, Chandigarh, India, BS, 1960; Indian Institute of Technology, Kharagpur, India, MTech, 1962; Birmingham University, PhD, 1969; Clark University, MBA, 1977. **CAREER:** Wyman-Gordon Co, research group leader, 1969-80; Combustion Engineering, technical director, 1980-83; GE Aircraft Engines, senior staff engr, 1984-. **ORGANIZATIONS:** Federation of Jain Associations in North America, president, 1989-93; ASME, 1971-; ASM International; TMS; SME. **HONORS/AWARDS:** ASME, Centennial Medal, 1980; GE Aircraft Engines, Professional Societies Activities Award, 1991; Federation of Jaina, Leadership Award, 1993. **SPECIAL ACHIEVEMENTS:** Eight US patents on technology; approx 40 publications & technical papers; delivered lectures at many universities & conferences; proficiency in several Indian languages. **HOME ADDRESS:** 9831 Tall Timber Drive, Cincinnati, OH 45241, (513)777-1554.

JAIN, SURENDER K.
Educator. Indo-American. **PERSONAL:** Born Nov 16, 1938, Amritsar, Punjab, India; son of Roshan Lal Jain and Parkash V Jain; married Parvesh Jain, Dec 8, 1965; children: Nisha Jain Bhatt, Steve. **EDUCATION:** Panjab University, India, BA (with honors), 1957, MA, 1959; University of Delhi, PhD, 1963. **CAREER:** University of California, research math, visiting lecturer, 1963-65; University of Delhi, India, reader in math, 1965-70; Ohio University, professor, 1970-. **ORGANIZATIONS:** American Math Society; Society Industrial & Applied Math; Indian Math Society. **HONORS/AWARDS:** German Government, DAAD Award; Fulbright Award. **SPECIAL ACHIEVEMENTS:** Published more than 65 research articles in professional journals such as: Transactions American Math Society, Proceedings AMS, Pacific J Math, Journal of Algebra, SIAM J Discrete Math, SIAM J Matrix Analysis, Archiver der Math, Zeitschrift Math, Encyclopedia of Physical Science; co-author & co-editor, book, Basic Abstract Algebra, Cambridge University Press; co-editor, Non Commulative Rings, Lecture Notes in Math, Springer Verlag, Heidelberg, Berlin; co-editor, Ring Theory: Proc OSU-Denison Conference, World Scientific Press. **BUSINESS ADDRESS:** Professor of Math, Ohio University, Athens, OH 45701.

JAIN, SUSHIL C.
Engineer. Indo-American. **PERSONAL:** Born Jun 14, 1939, Lucknow, Uttar Pradesh, India; son of Ishwar Dayal Jain and Mohini Jain; married Usha Jain, Nov 20, 1969; children: Rachna, Mohit. **EDUCATION:** Saint John's College, Agra, India, BSc, 1957; Indian Institute of Technology, India, BSEE, 1961; Purdue University, MSIE, 1964. **CAREER:** Safran Printing, industrial engineer, 1966-68; Edwards Brothers, senior industrial engineer, 1971-78; Alco-Gravure, staff engineer, 1973-78; Rayne Industries, manufacturing director, 1978-79; Unified Data Products, industrial engineer, manager,1979-81; Universal Folding Box, industrial engineering director, 1981-89; Sealed Air Corp, process engineer, 1990-92; Jain Consulting, president, currently. **ORGANIZATIONS:** Institute of Industrial Engineers, senior member, 1965-; American Society of Quality Control, 1992-. **HONORS/AWARDS:** ASQC, Professional

Engineer, 1976; Certified Quality Engineer, 1993. **HOME ADDRESS:** 60 Winthrop Rd, Hillsdale, NJ 07642, (201)664-5838.

JAISINGHANI, RAJAN A.
Company executive, consultant. Indo-American. **PERSONAL:** Born Jan 21, 1945, Karachi, Sind, Pakistan; son of Amrit H Jaisinghani & Kirpa A Jaisinghani; married Christina, Mar 28, 1993; children: Nikhil, Priya. **EDUCATION:** Banaras Hindu University, BS, 1969; University of Wisconsin, MS, 1973. **CAREER:** United Film Makers, writer, 1970; Fiebing Chemical Co, plant engineer, 1971-73; Nelson Industries, manager, R&D, 1973-82; American Filtrona, director, R&D, 1982-90; PDA Inc, president, 1990-. **ORGANIZATIONS:** AICLE, 1970-; AAAR, 1985-; Filtration Society, 1973-90; SAE, 1973-90; Fine Particle Society, 1982-91; APCA, 1983-90; ACS, 1983-91. **SPECIAL ACHIEVEMENTS:** Over 20 scientific & technical publications; author, chapters in Handbook of Multiphase Systems, McGraw Hill, 1982; Physical Separations, Engg Foundation, 1977. **BUSINESS ADDRESS:** Research & Development Executive, Product Development Assistance Inc, 13511 East Boundary Rd, Ste D & E, Midlothian, VA 23112, (804)744-0604.

JAISWAL, GOPALJEE
Attorney, certified public accountant. Indo-American. **PERSONAL:** Born Nov 22, 1937, Dumraon, Bihar, India; son of Bhagwati P Jaiswal (deceased); married Kamala, Jun 10, 1954; children: Arun, Barun, Meena. **EDUCATION:** Ranchi University, LLB, 1967; Banaras Hindu University, India, BCom, 1955; Calcutta University, India, MCom, 1957; New York University, LLM, 1977. **CAREER:** CPA firms, 1970-71; Health & Hospital Corporation, accountant, 1971-72; City of New York, Dept of Health, sr accountant, 1972-73; City University of New York, budget director, 1973-74; attorney-at-law, certified public accountant, currently. **ORGANIZATIONS:** Nassau County Bar Assn, numerous committees. **HONORS/AWARDS:** Banaras Hindu University, Rank II, 1953. **HOME PHONE:** (516)338-5529. **BUSINESS ADDRESS:** Attorney at Law, CPA, 50 Clinton St, Ste 510, Hempstead, NY 11550, (516)538-8400.

JALIL, MAZHAR
Public health scientist. Indo-American. **PERSONAL:** Born Nov 2, 1938, Ballia, Uttar Pradesh, India; son of Mohammed Ahmed Jalil and Safia Jalil; married Betty Jalil, Feb 28, 1970; children: Tariq, Khalid, Aisha. **EDUCATION:** University of Nottingham, England, MS, 1963; University of Waterloo, Canada, PhD, 1967; University of Kentucky, postdoctoral trainee, 1967-69. **CAREER:** University of Nottingham, England, instructor, 1962-64; University of Waterloo, Canada, instructor, 1964-67; University of Kentucky, research associate, 1967-69; United Nations Development Program, consultant, 1980-81; Ohio Department of Health, entomologist/microbiologist, 1969-. **ORGANIZATIONS:** Islamic Foundation of Central Ohio, president, 1984-88, director of community relations, 1989-, chairman, board of trustees, 1990-92; Islamic Council of Ohio, chairman, 1991-; Columbus Commission on Ethics & Values, 1989-91; A World of Difference Campaign, chairman, Religion Committee, 1991-92; Science Advisory Committee, City Hall, Columbus, chairman, 1991-92. **HONORS/AWARDS:** Columbus Dispatch, Community Service Award (individual category), 1991, Community Service Award (group category), 1993; Mayor's Voluntary Service Award, 1993; University of Nottingham, England, Lord Belper Post-graduate Scholarship, 1961-63; University of Waterloo, Canada, Ontario Graduate & Teaching Fellowship, 1964-67; University of Kentucky, Postdoctoral Fellowship, 1967-69;. **SPECIAL ACHIEVEMENTS:** Published dozens of scientific papers in Canada, England, Holland & USA, 1964-74; attended conferences in Canada, England, India, Pakistan, Saudi Arabia & USA, 1963-80; established a surveillance program in arbovirus nationwide in Pakistan, 1980-81; advised the Columbus City Hall on scientific matters, 1991-92; promotes friendly relations between Muslims, Christians and Jewish communities in Columbus through conferences and dialogues, 1985-. **HOME ADDRESS:** 2769 Heston Ct, Columbus, OH 43235, (614)457-2518. **BUSINESS ADDRESS:** Entomologist/Microbiologist, Ohio Dept of Health, PO Box 2568, Columbus, OH 43216-2568, (614)644-4672.

JALURIA, YOGESH
Educator. Indo-American. **PERSONAL:** Born Sep 8, 1949, Nabha, Punjab, India; son of Jagdishwar & Maya Jaluria; married Anuradha Jaluria, Sep 9, 1975; children: Pratik, Aseem, Ankur. **EDUCATION:** Indian Institute of Technology, Delhi, BS, 1970; Cornell University, MS, 1972, PhD, 1974. **CAREER:** Bell Labs, member of the technical staff, 1974-76; Indian Institute of Technology, Kanpur, assistant professor, 1974-80, visiting professor, 1988-

89; Rutgers University, assistant professor, 1980-82, associate professor, 1982-85, professor, 1985-90, professor II, distinguished professor, 1990-. **ORGANIZATIONS:** American Society Mechanical Engineers, National Heat Transfer Conference, chairman, 1991-92, Conference Coordination Committee, chairman, 1992, program chairman, 1990, General Papers, chairman, 1986-88, K-17 Committee, 1982-92; American Physical Society, 1980-; Combustion Institute, advisory committee for international conference, 1984-. **HONORS/AWARDS:** American Society Mechanical Engineers, fellow, 1991; National Institute Standards, Certificate of Recognition, 1982; National Science Academy, India, Young Scientist Award, 1979; IIT, Delhi, Silver Medal, 1970; National Council of Education Research, India, Science Talent Award, 1965. **SPECIAL ACHIEVEMENTS:** Four books: Natural Convection Heat & Mass Transfer, Perganon, 1980; Computational Heat Transfer, Hemisphere, 1986; Buoyancy Induced Flows, Hemisphere, 1988; Computer Methods for Engineering, Prentice-Hall, 1988; over 200 papers, many chapters in books, review articles, keynote lecturers; proficient in Hindi, Punjabi, English. **BUSINESS ADDRESS:** Professor, Rutgers University, Engineering Bldg, Busch Campus, Piscataway, NJ 08855-0909, (908)832-3652.

JAMERO, PETER M.
Health/human services executive. Filipino American. **PERSONAL:** Born Aug 27, 1930, Oakdale, CA; son of Ceferino Jamero & Apolonia Madelo Jamero; married Teresa Romero, Oct 3, 1953; children: Karen Armada, Cheryl Organo, Peter Jr, Julie Hada, Jacqueline Berganio, Jeanine Silverio. **EDUCATION:** San Jose State University, BA, 1955; UCLA, MSW, 1957; Stanford University, certificate public affairs, 1970. **CAREER:** US Dept of HEW, regional representative, 1970-72; Washington State Div of Voc Rehab, director, 1972-79; University of Washington, assistant professor of rehab med, 1979-83; King County Dept of Human Resources, director, 1983-86; Seattle/King County United Way, vice president, 1986-89; SF Human Rights Commission, executive director, 1989-91; Asian American Recovery Services, executive director, 1991-. **ORGANIZATIONS:** Filipino American National Historical Society, vice pres, founding member, 1984-; YMCA Embarcadero, board of governors, 1991-; United Way of Bay Area, board of directors, 1990-92; SF Leadership Council, United Way, vice chair, 1989-; SF Filipino American Democratic Club, 1989-; Seattle/King County Area Agency on Aging, sponsor, 1983-88; Human Resources Coalition, 1983-88; Council of St Administrators for Voc Rehab, exec com, 1976-79. **HONORS/AWARDS:** Eye Publishers, Role Model Award, 1991; Filipino Youth Activities (SEA), Achievers Award, 1985; International Examiner (SEA), Outstanding Asian American, 1982, 1984; City of Tacoma, Mayor's Commendation, 1981; State of Washington, Outstanding Filipino in Government, 1976. **SPECIAL ACHIEVEMENTS:** Publications: "Independent Living Evaluation," Journal of Rehab Admin, 1983; "Three Common Neuromuscular Diseases," Journal of Rehabilitation, 1982; "Org Configurations. . ." Rehab, Administration, & Supervision, 1981; "Preparing Rehab Social Workers," Rehab and the Soc Work Role, 1980; "Handicapped in the Changing Workforce," Journal of Contemporary Bus, 1979. **MILITARY SERVICE:** US Navy, yn2, 1948-52. **BUSINESS ADDRESS:** Executive Director, Asian American Recovery Services, 300 4th St, Rm 200, San Francisco, CA 94107, (415)541-9285.

JAMMALAMADAKA, SREENIVASA RAO
Educator, educational administrator. Indo-American. **PERSONAL:** Born Dec 7, 1944, Munipalle, Andhra Pradesh, India; son of Rama Murty and Seetha Ramamma; married Vijaya, Jul 1, 1972; children: Arvind, Aruna. **EDUCATION:** Indian Statistical Institute, Calcutta, BStat, 1964, MStat, 1965, PhD, 1969. **CAREER:** Visiting professorships at the following: University of Wisconsin, Madison, University of Leeds, UK, Upsala University, Goteborg University, Sweden, Indian Statistical Institute, Calcutta, Indian Institute of Technology, Bombay; Indiana University, visiting assistant professor, 1969-76; University of California, Santa Barbara, assistant, associate professor, 1976-83, professor, 1983-. **ORGANIZATIONS:** ASA, Southern California Chapter, president, 1988-90, vice president, 1987-88, Comm of International Relations, 1991-93; Visiting Lecturer Program, Comm of Presidents of Stat Societies, lecturer, 1990-. **HONORS/AWARDS:** International Statistical Institute, elected member, 1977; Institute of Mathematical Stats, elected fellow, 1990; Institute of Combinatories and Applications, elected fellow, 1990; American Statistical Association, elected fellow, 1993. **SPECIAL ACHIEVEMENTS:** Involved in extensive consulting activities in statistics; published over 75 research articles in international journals. **HOME ADDRESS:** 1304 Ferrelo Road, Santa Barbara, CA 93103-2122, (805)963-2622. **BUSINESS ADDRESS:** Professor, Chairman, Dept of Statistics, University of California, Santa Barbara, CA 93106, (805)893-3119.

JAN, HAN S.
Electronic company executive. Chinese American. **PERSONAL:** Born Sep 23, 1936, Canton, China; son of Wah Jan; married Josephine P C Jan, Dec 28, 1974; children: Roly R, Rosario R, Johnny R, Theresa, Christine, Kenneth. **EDUCATION:** Benjamin Franklin University, 1959-61; Capital Radio Engineering Institute, 1962-66. **CAREER:** Bamboo Palace Rest, president, 1964-68; CTL Communications, president, 1969-. **ORGANIZATIONS:** Chew Lun Family Association, eastern US, co-chairman. **MILITARY SERVICE:** USAF, airman, 2nd class, 1953-57. **HOME PHONE:** (301)299-2334. **BUSINESS ADDRESS:** President, Communications Televideo Limited, 9301 Georgia Ave, Silver Spring, MD 20910, (301)585-6311.

JAN, KUNG-MING
Physician. Chinese American. **PERSONAL:** Born Jan 14, 1943, Hsin-Chu, Taiwan; son of Yuan-chu Jan and Yu-tsai Huang; married Connie Jan, Aug 10, 1975; children: Rex, Stephen, Thomas. **EDUCATION:** National Taiwan University, MD, 1967; Columbia University, PhD, 1971. **CAREER:** Columbia University, instructor of physiology, 1971-73, assistant professor of physiology, 1974-80, assistant professor of physiology and medicine, 1980-85, associate professor of physiology and medicine, 1985-89, associate professor of clinical medicine, 1989-. **ORGANIZATIONS:** Presbyterian Hospital, clinical fellow in cardiology, 1979-80, assistant attending physician, 1980-85, associate attending physician, 1985; National Taiwan University, visiting professor, 1981-83; Academia Sinica, visiting research professor, 1987-88; ABMAC, vice president, 1989-. **HONORS/AWARDS:** Columbia University, University Fellowship, 1968; New York Heart Association, postdoctoral fellowship, 1971; National Institutes of Health, Research Career Development Award, 1975. **SPECIAL ACHIEVEMENTS:** Research in cardiovascular physiology, 1971-; clinical cardiology, 1980-. **BUSINESS ADDRESS:** Physician, Columbia Presbyterian Riverdale Medical Pavilion, 3765 Riverdale Avenue, Suite 5, Riverdale, NY 10463, (718)601-8724.

JANG, DENNIS
Banker. Chinese American. **PERSONAL:** Born Jan 22, 1963, Oakland, CA; son of Bruce O Jang and Elsie C Jang; married Susan Minami. **EDUCATION:** University of California, Berkeley, School of Business, BS, 1984, CPA, 1986. **CAREER:** KPMG Peat Marwick, auditor, 1984-88; Trans-Pacific National Bank, asst vice president, 1988-. **ORGANIZATIONS:** Chinatown Resource Center, San Francisco, treasurer, 1992-; Progress Foundation, San Francisco, board, 1992-; Chinatown YMCA, San Francisco, board, 1984-87. **BUSINESS ADDRESS:** Assistant Vice President, Trans-Pacific National Bank, 44 Second St, San Francisco, CA 94105, (415)543-3377.

JANG, JON
Composer, pianist, lecturer. Chinese American. **PERSONAL:** Born Mar 11, 1954, Los Angeles, CA; son of James J Jang & Etta Jang; married Joyce Nakamura, Sep 8, 1990. **EDUCATION:** Oberlin Conservatory of Music, BMus, 1978. **CAREER:** Compositions and recordings include: "Never Give Up!," 1990; "Self-Defense!," 1992; "The Color of Reality," 1992; "Tiananmen!," 1993; "Concerto for Jazz Ensemble and Taiko"; University of California, Berkeley, visiting lecturer, 1992-. **ORGANIZATIONS:** Asian Improv aRts, co-founder, 1988-; Asian Improv Records, co-founder, 1987-. **HONORS/AWARDS:** NEA Inter-Arts, jazz emsemble, 1990, 1993; Berkeley Repertory Theatre, commission, 1993; Rockefeller, multi-arts commission 1992; CAL Performances, commission, 1993; California Arts Council, touring roster/innovative programming, 1990-96; Asian Business League of San Francisco, Distinguished Asian Leadership Award, 1992. **SPECIAL ACHIEVEMENTS:** Commissioned by Festival 2000 to compose "Sense Us-Rainbow Anthems," a collaboration featuring Max Roach, Sonia Sanchez, Genny Lim, John Santos and Victor Hernandez Cruz, world premier at Davies Symphony Hall, 1990; Toured Europe, Canada. **BUSINESS ADDRESS:** Composer, Jon Jang Performances, PO Box 640897, San Francisco, CA 94164-0897, (415)931-8815.

JAO, RADMAR AGANA
Actor. Filipino American/Chinese American. **PERSONAL:** Born Nov 7, 1966, Gary, IN; son of Rodolfo Labay Jao & Maria Teresa Agana Jao. **EDUCATION:** Indiana University, BA, 1988. **CAREER:** United Consumers Club, industrial video producer/director, 1988-89; Warner Bros, "China Beach," assistant to exec producer, 1989-90; Warner Bros, "Undercover," assistant to producer, 1990-91; actor, "Dragonwings," Berkeley, New York, Seattle, Atlanta, 1991-93; various theater projects in Los Angeles. **ORGANIZATIONS:** Screen Actor's Guild, 1992-; Actor's Equity Association, 1992-; East West Players; East West Players Actors Network, founding member; West Coast Ensemble. **SPECIAL ACHIEVEMENTS:** "Dragonwings," originated role of Moonshadow; The Yellow Pages, jazz group, founder. **BIOGRAPHICAL SOURCES:** Ang Northwest Pilipino (The Northwest Filipino), p 8, April 1993; American Theatre ("Dragonwings," featured in photos), featured playscript, Sept 1992. **HOME ADDRESS:** 4866 1/2 Tujunga Ave, North Hollywood, CA 91601.

JAPRA, ROMESH K.
Hospital administrator. Indo-American. **PERSONAL:** Born Jan 3, 1950. **CAREER:** Washington Hospital, medical chief of staff, 1993-. **ORGANIZATIONS:** Federation of Indo-American Associations of Northern California, former president. **BUSINESS ADDRESS:** Medical Chief of Staff, Washington Hospital, 1900 Mowry Ave, Ste 201, Fremont, CA 94538, (510)790-2202.∗

JARIWALA, SHARAD LALLUBHAI
Pharmaceutical company executive. Indo-American. **PERSONAL:** Born Oct 15, 1940, Patan, Gujarat, India; son of Lallubhai C Jariwala and Savitaben L Jariwala; married Adelfa F Jariwala, Mar 22, 1969; children: Ravi Sharad, Nisha Adelfa. **EDUCATION:** University of Bombay, India, BS, chem engg, 1962; Johns Hopkins University, PhD, chem engg, 1966. **CAREER:** Tenneco, res engr, 1966-70; The Upjohn Co, vice president, 1970-. **HOME ADDRESS:** 512 Barberry, Portage, MI 49002, (616)323-1892. **BUSINESS ADDRESS:** Vice President, Fermentation Operations, The Upjohn Co, 7000 Portage Rd, 1800-91-2, Kalamazoo, MI 49001, (616)323-5364.

JAVED, MOHD S.
Import company executive. Indo-American. **PERSONAL:** Born Jul 16, 1952, Mehbooba, Uttar Pradesh, India; son of M Shahid and Membooba Khatoon; married Firoza, Aug 16, 1973; children: Shiraz, Maryam, Yusuf. **EDUCATION:** KGK College, BA, 1972. **CAREER:** Global Creations Ltd, president, 1973-80; Variety Universal Imports Inc, president, 1982-. **ORGANIZATIONS:** Islamic Centre of Long Island. **HONORS/AWARDS:** Salesman of the Year in India, in Export Trade, 1982. **BUSINESS ADDRESS:** President, Variety Universal Imports, Inc, 49-16 28th Ave, Woodside, NY 11377, (718)545-1000.

JAYACHANDRAN, TOKE
Educational administrator. Indo-American. **EDUCATION:** University of Wyoming, MS, 1962; Case Institute of Technology, PhD, 1967. **CAREER:** Naval Postgraduate School, dean of computer & information services, currently. **BUSINESS ADDRESS:** Dean of Computer & Information Services, Naval Postgraduate School, Code 05, Monterey, CA 93943.

JAYARAM, MYSORE
Editor. Indo-American. **PERSONAL:** Born Dec 15, 1926, Mysore, Karnataka, India; son of T R Krishna Rau and M Rukminamma; married Shyamala Jayaram, Oct 25, 1957; children: Mohanram, Sriram. **EDUCATION:** Maharaja's College, Mysore, India, BA (with honors), 1947, MA, 1948; Ohio State University, MA, 1954. **CAREER:** USIA, exhibit designer, 1950-54, exhibits chief, 1956-83; Ohio State University, graduate assistant, 1954-56; Sakow Associates, special assistant, 1986-89; The Rafu Shimpo, business editor, 1989-. **HONORS/AWARDS:** Smithsonian Institution, commendation for acting as curator, Small Sculpture Exhibit Tour of India, 1986. **HOME PHONE:** (818)810-4347. **BUSINESS ADDRESS:** Business Editor, The Rafu Shimpo, 259 S Los Angeles St, Los Angeles, CA 90012, (213)629-2231.

JAYASWAL, RAOHESHYAM K.
Educator. Indo-American. **PERSONAL:** Born Jul 6, 1949, Ramganj, Uttar Pradesh, India; son of Kantilal R Jayaswal and Kaushilya Jayaswal; married Premlata, Oct 26, 1977; children: Vikas, Kavita. **EDUCATION:** University of Bombay, India, BSc, 1973, MSc, 1980; Purdue University, PhD, 1985. **CAREER:** TIFR Bombay, India, scientific assistant, 1974-80; Purdue University, research assistant, 1980-85, research associate, 1985-88; Illinois State University, assistant professor, 1988-. **ORGANIZATIONS:** American Society of Microbiology; American Society Plant Pathology; Sigma Xi; Phi Sigma. **HONORS/AWARDS:** University of Bombay, Merit Scholarship, 1969-73; Illinois State University, Research Initiative Award, 1990; NIH, Academic Enhancement Award, 1990-95; American Heart Association, Grant In Aid, 1991-95. **SPECIAL ACHIEVEMENTS:** Published 25 research papers in professional journals. **HOME ADDRESS:** 1418 Godfrey Dr, Normal, IL 61761, (309)454-2463. **BUSINESS ADDRESS:** Asst Professor, Dept of Bio-

logical Sciences, Illinois State University, Felmley Hall, Normal, IL 61761-4120, (309)438-5128.

JEEVANANDAM, MALAYAPPA
Research scientist. Indo-American. **PERSONAL:** Born Jun 14, 1931, Tirumangalan, Tamil Nadu, India; son of K S M K Malayappa; married Chellam, Jul 12, 1959; children: Valluvan, Geetha J Damodaran. **EDUCATION:** Presidency College, Madras University, India, MA, 1959; Columbia University, MA, 1961, PhD, 1965. **CAREER:** Columbia University, P&S, research associate, 1971-81; Sloane-Kettering Cancer Center, associate lab member, 1981-86; St. Joseph's Hospital, research director, 1986-. **ORGANIZATIONS:** American Institute of Nutrition, 1980-; American Society of Clinical Nutrition, 1980-; Am Soc Parenteral and Enteral Nutrition, 1982-; New York Academy of Sciences, 1983-; Sigma Xi, 1980-; Am Association for the Advancement of Science, 1986-. **HONORS/AWARDS:** Japan Soc for Promotion of Science, visiting professor, 1974. **SPECIAL ACHIEVEMENTS:** Published more than 100 articles in peer-reviewed, reputed, scientific journals; published 114 abstracts and presented papers at scientific societies and international meetings in Australia, Hungary, Italy, Austria, Greece; contributed chapters to books on clinical nutrition. **HOME ADDRESS:** 8725 E San Esteban Dr, Scottsdale, AZ 85258, (602)483-6625. **BUSINESS ADDRESS:** Research Director, Trauma Center, St Joseph's Hospital & Medical Center, 350 W Thomas Rd, Phoenix, AZ 85013, (602)285-3092.

JEN, CHIH KUNG
Educator (retired), researcher. Chinese American. **PERSONAL:** Born Aug 15, 1906, Qin, Shanxi, China; son of Xiang-Tin Jen and Xiang-Mei Jen; married Paocheng Tao, Jul 27, 1937; children: May Koo, Linda Jacobson, Phyllis, Erica. **EDUCATION:** Tsing Hua College, 1926; Mass Institute of Technology, BS, 1928; University of Pennsylvania, MS, 1929; Harvard University, PhD, 1931. **CAREER:** Tsing Hua University, professor of physics and electrical engineering, 1934-37, director, Institute of Electronics, 1938-45; National South-West University, professor of physics and electrical engineering, 1938-45; Harvard University, research fellow of electronics, 1946-50; Johns Hopkins University, associate director of Research Center Applied Physics Laboratory, 1958-74, William Parsons Professor of Chemical Physics, 1966-67. **ORGANIZATIONS:** American Physical Society, fellow, 1959-. **HONORS/AWARDS:** Academia Sinica, Taiwan, Academician, 1962; Tsing Hua University, China, Honorary Professor; Chengdua University, China, Honorary Professor; University of Science and Technology, China, Honorary Professor; University of Technology of Shanghai, China, Honorary Professor; Shanxi University, Honorary Professor. **SPECIAL ACHIEVEMENTS:** Published more than fifty papers in Physics in World Standard Journals, 1929-81; Microwave Quantum Physics, Science Publishing Co, 1980; Zeeman and Stark Effect, Encyclopedia of Physics, 1981. **BIOGRAPHICAL SOURCES:** Recollections of a Chinese Physicist, Signition Co, 1990, translation, 1992. **HOME ADDRESS:** 10203 Lariston Lane, Silver Spring, MD 20903, (301)439-9440.

JEN, GISH. *See* JEN, LILLIAN C.

JEN, HORATIO H. (HSIAO HSIEN)
Educator. Chinese American. **PERSONAL:** Born Oct 20, 1936, Shanghai, China; married Rosa Y Jen, Dec 21, 1965; children: Ming M, Ching C. **EDUCATION:** National Taiwan University, BA, 1958; Peabody College, Vanderbilt University, MA, 1960; Florida Southern College, BS, 1966; Middle Tennessee State University, MST, 1969; University of South Carolina, PhD, 1975. **CAREER:** Westmoreland County Community College, professor of math, 1976-. **ORGANIZATIONS:** NEA; PSEA; AMATC. **HOME ADDRESS:** 40 Windsor St, Indiana, PA 15701. **BUSINESS PHONE:** (412)925-4184.

JEN, JAMES A.
Business executive. Chinese American. **PERSONAL:** Born Jan 28, 1944, Yuan Ling, Hunan, China; son of H C Jen and Lucia Jen; married Lucy Jen, Dec 20, 1969; children: Jennifer, Natalie. **EDUCATION:** Tunghai University, Taiwan, FS, industial engineering, 1968; Stevens Inst of Technology, MS, management science, 1971; Rutgers University, MS, computer science, 1983. **CAREER:** Mercer County College, asst professor, 1982; American Bell Inc, consultant, 1982-83; GE Consultant Co, sr software consultant, 1985-86; Digital Equipment Corp, VAX/VIA team lead, 1983-85, database administrator, 1986-87, architect of FAB4 automation, 1987-89, architect of Boeing SMARTS program, 1989-92, director of Asia sales programs, 1992-. **ORGANIZATIONS:** IEEE, 1983; Aircraft Owner & Pilot Assn, 1979. **HONORS/AWARDS:** Digital Equipment Corp, TOPS Award, 1990; US Air Force, Certificate of Merit (for B1B project), 1985. **SPECIAL ACHIEVEMENTS:** Work Cell Strategy, 1986. **MILITARY SERVICE:** Taiwan Army, second lieutenant, 1967-68. **HOME ADDRESS:** 107 Cherry St, Shrewsbury, MA 01545, (508)842-7254.

JEN, JOSEPH JWU-SHAN
Educator, educational administrator. Chinese American. **PERSONAL:** Born May 8, 1939, Chung King, China; son of H C Jen & Lucia C Jen; married Salina Fond, Sep 4, 1965; children: Joanne Paulina Jen Ryan, Jeffrey Jay. **EDUCATION:** National Taiwan University, BS, 1960; Washington State University, MS, 1964; University of California, Berkeley, PhD, 1969; Southern Illinois University, MBA, 1986. **CAREER:** US Department of Agriculture, research food technologist; Clemson University, assistant, associate professor; Michigan State University, professor; Campbell Soup Company, director of research; University of Georgia, division chairman; California Polytechnic State University, College of Agriculture, dean, currently. **ORGANIZATIONS:** Institute of Food Technologists, Div of Fruit & Vegetable, chairman, 1987; Chinese American Food Society, president, 1978; United Nations Development Program, consultant, 1985, 1988. **HONORS/AWARDS:** Institute of Food Technologists, fellow, 1992; Ministry of Agriculture, Republic of China, Merit of Appreciation, 1988; Ministry of Economic Affairs, Merit of Appreciation, 1982; many other university & industry minor awards. **SPECIAL ACHIEVEMENTS:** Author, Chemistry and Function of Pectin, 1986; Quality Factors of Fruits and Vegetables, 1989; over 150 book chapters, professional journal articles and proceedings, 1968-93. **BUSINESS ADDRESS:** Dean, College of Agriculture, California Polytechnic State University, San Luis Obispo, CA 93407, (805)756-2161.

JEN, LILLIAN C. (GISH JEN)
Writer. Chinese American. **PERSONAL:** Born Aug 12, 1955, New York, NY; married. **EDUCATION:** Harvard University, BA, 1977; University of Iowa, Writer's Workshop, MFA, 1983. **CAREER:** Writer, currently. **HONORS/AWARDS:** Guggenheim Foundation, fellowship; National Endowment for the Arts, fellowship; Massachusetts Artists Foundation, fellowship; Bunting Institute, fellowship; shortlisted for National Book Critics' Circle Award. **SPECIAL ACHIEVEMENTS:** Typical American, novel, 1991. **HOME ADDRESS:** 18 Bates St, Cambridge, MA 02140.

JEN, PHILIP HUNGSUN
Educator. Chinese American. **PERSONAL:** Born Jan 11, 1944, Hunan, China; son of Shou-shon Jen & Yu in Kou Jen; married Betty Y Jen, Feb 20, 1971. **EDUCATION:** Tunghai University, Taiwan, BS, 1967; Washington University, MA, 1971, PhD, 1974. **CAREER:** Washington University, research associate, 1974; University of Missouri, Division of Biological Sciences, assistant professor, 1975-80, associate professor, 1981-83, professor, 1984-. **ORGANIZATIONS:** Society for Neurosciences, 1974-; American Association for the Advancement of Science, 1978-; International Society for Neuroethology, 1984-; Acoustic Society of America, 1974-; Association for Research in Otolaryngology, 1987-; Society of Chinese Bioscientists in America, 1987-; Chinese Physiology Society, 1984-; New York Academy of Science, 1980-. **HONORS/AWARDS:** National Institutes of Health Research Career Award, 1980-85; University of Missouri, Byler Distinguished Professor Award, 1988; Mid-America State University Association, honorary lecturer, 1981. **SPECIAL ACHIEVEMENTS:** 60 papers in scientific journals, 1973-. **MILITARY SERVICE:** Chinese Air Force, second lieutenant, 1967-68; Best Instruction Award, 1967. **HOME ADDRESS:** 6200 S Riverhills Road, Columbia, MO 65203. **BUSINESS ADDRESS:** Professor, Div of Biological Sciences, University of Missouri, 208 Lefevre Hall, Columbia, MO 65211, (314)882-7479.

JEN, SERENA
Business executive. Taiwanese American. **PERSONAL:** Born in Taiwan; daughter of Shou-Ting Cheng and Ming-Hsiang Lou Cheng; married Frank Jen; children: James, Henry. **EDUCATION:** National Chen-Chi University, bachelor's degree. **CAREER:** Pandick Enterprise Corp, president, currently. **BUSINESS ADDRESS:** President, Pandick Enterprise Corp, Expressway Plaza 4, Roslyn Heights, NY 11577, (516)484-6090.

JENA, PURUSOTTAM
Educator. Indo-American. **PERSONAL:** Born Feb 5, 1943, Mukhura, Orissa, India; son of Binod B Jena and Taramani Jena; married Tripti B Jena, Dec 12, 1969; children: Anupam. **EDUCATION:** Utkal University, India, BSc (hon-

ors), 1964, MSc, 1966; University of California, Riverside, PhD, 1970. **CAREER:** Dalhousie University, post-doctoral fellow, 1971-73; University of British Columbia, research associate, 1973-75; Northwestern University, visiting assistant professor, 1975-77; Argonne National Lab, visiting scientist, 1977-78; Michigan Technological University, associate professor, 1978-80; National Science Foundation, program director, 1986-87; Virginia Commonwealth University, professor, 1980-. **ORGANIZATIONS:** American Physical Society; Sigma Pi Sigma; Phi Kappa Phi; Indian Physical Society. **HONORS/ AWARDS:** Virginia Commonwealth University, University Award of Excellence, 1993, Distinguished Scholar Award, 1987. **SPECIAL ACHIEVEMENTS:** Work activities include: electronic, magnetic, and optical properties of metal clusters; electronic structure of defects in metals, semiconductors, and insulators; liquid and amorphous metals. **BIOGRAPHICAL SOURCES:** Science News, p 197, Sept 26, 1992. **BUSINESS ADDRESS:** Professor of Physics, Virginia Commonwealth University, 1020 W Main St, Box 2000, Richmond, VA 23284-2000, (804)367-8991.

JEONG, WALLACE DUN
Architect. Chinese American. **PERSONAL:** Born Jul 22, 1929, Kaiping, Canton, China; son of Jimmy Jeong; married Margaret Jeong, Aug 5, 1961; children: William, Monica. **EDUCATION:** University of California, Berkeley, BA, architecture, 1956; University of Southern California, MPA, planning, 1969. **CAREER:** Eugene Choy, AIA architectural draftsman, 1956-57; William H Harrison, FAIA architectural draftsman, 1957-58; Allison & Rible, FAIA architectural draftsman, 1958-59; Los Angeles City Department of Airports, airport architect, 1959-. **ORGANIZATIONS:** American Institute of Architects, 1965-82; Society of American Registered Architects, 1989-. **MILITARY SERVICE:** US Army Corps Engineers, intelligence analyst, 1952-54; Meritorious Service Medal and Citation. **HOME ADDRESS:** 6121 Andy St, Lakewood, CA 90713, (310)925-8994.

JETHANANDANI, ASHOK
Publisher. Indo-American. **PERSONAL:** Born Jan 29, 1958, Naya Nangal, Punjab, India; son of Hemraj Jethanandani and Savitri Jethanandani. **EDUCATION:** Indian Institute of Technology, Bombay, India, BS, 1979; Stanford University, MS, 1983. **CAREER:** Tata Engineering, engineer, 1979-82; Perkin Elmer, engineer, 1984-85; Ultratech Stepper, engineer, 1985-91; India Currents, publisher, 1991-. **HONORS/AWARDS:** Inlaks Foundation, London, Inlaks Scholarship, 1983; Government of India, Merit Scholarship, 1973. **SPECIAL ACHIEVEMENTS:** Shabari River Valley Expedition, 1977; Bharata Natya Arangetram, 1991. **BIOGRAPHICAL SOURCES:** India West, p 66, Aug 30, 1991. **BUSINESS ADDRESS:** Publisher, India Currents, PO Box 21285, San Jose, CA 95151.

JHA, MAHESH CHANDRA
Mining company manager. Indo-American. **PERSONAL:** Born Mar 13, 1945, Darbhanga, Bihar, India; son of Rameshwar Jha and Baccha Devi Jha; married Subhadra, Jun 4, 1964; children: Amitabh, Arunabh. **EDUCATION:** Bihar Institute of Technology, Ranchi University, Sindri, India, BSc, metallurgical engineering, 1965; Michigan Technological University, MS, 1970; Iowa State University, PhD, 1973. **CAREER:** BIT, Sindni, India, lecturer, metallurgical engineering, 1965-66; University of Roorkee, India, lecturer, 1966-69; Michigan Technological University, research assistant, 1969-70; Iowa State University, research assistant, 1970-73; Amax R&D Center, research metallurgist, group leader, 1973-76, section supervisor, 1977-85, manager, 1986-. **ORGANIZATIONS:** The Mineral, Metals and Materials Society, 1973-; American Institute of Chemical Engineers, 1976-. **HONORS/AWARDS:** TMS-AIME, Extractive Metallurgy Technology Award, 1986. **SPECIAL ACHIEVEMENTS:** 40 published papers; 13 patents; editor of 1 book. **BUSINESS ADDRESS:** Manager, Energy R&D, Amax Research & Development Center, 5950 McIntyre St, Golden, CO 80403-7499, (303)273-7200.

JHAVERI, ARUNKUMAR GANPATLAL
Energy technologies engineer/manager, city official. Indo-American. **PERSONAL:** Born Jun 14, 1938, Bombay, India; son of Ganpatlal Maganlal Jhaveri (deceased) and Nirmala Ganpatlal Jhaveri (deceased); married Valerie Norcross Jhaveri, Jun 5, 1965; children: Varun Marron, Vanashree Norcross. **EDUCATION:** University of Bombay, BSc, general science, 1958; University of Washington, BS, engineering physics, 1961, technology management & mechanical engineering, 1976-; University of Massachusetts, MS, physics, 1964. **CAREER:** Boeing Co, commercial airplane div, research engineer, 1967-71; AGM Inc, acoustech, director of research & product development, 1971-79; City of Seattle, mayor's office, science/technology advisor, 1977-79;

John Graham Co, energy management specialist, 1979-82; US Army Corps of Engineers, engineering project manager, 1982-91; City of Burien, mayor, currently; US Department of Energy, energy program, project manager, 1991-92, energy technologies engineer/manager, 1992-. **ORGANIZATIONS:** Acoustical Society of America, NW Chapter, pres, 1968-71; American Society of Testing & Materials, national member, 1970-72; Institute of Noise Control Engineering, international member, 1970-76; Society of American Military Engineers, treasurer, 1985-91; Assn of Energy Engineers, charter member, 1989-; Natl League of Cities, Transportation & Communications Committee, 1993-; Assn of Washington Cities, New City (Burien), 1993-; Assn of Professional Energy Managers, bd member, 1993-94; Foundation for International Understanding through Students, pres, bd of directors, 1982; EEO/HRM Committee, Seattle District Corps of Engineers, chr, 1989-90; Burien Area Support Incorporation Committee, chr, 1989-92. **HONORS/AWARDS:** US delegation to UNCSTD, Vienna, Austria, 1979; graduate of Leadership Tomorrow, Seattle, Washington, 1991. **SPECIAL ACHIEVEMENTS:** Master of science thesis in physics: Ion/Atomic Collisions Below 2 Kev, 1964; Role of Sister Cities in Science & Technology for Urban Development/UNCSTD, 1979; Energy-Efficient Design of New Madigan Army Medical Center, Fort Lewis, Washington, AEE, 1988; Aircraft/Airport Noise Control for Community Relief, Institute of Noise Control, Engineering Conference, Japan, 1971; Role of Local Governments in Sustainable Community Development, International Conference, 1993. **BIOGRAPHICAL SOURCES:** Seattle Times, South Bureau/Special Edition, Mayor of Burien, March, 1993; Asian News Weekly, December '92 Annual Dinner Meeting Recognition, Mayor, City of Burien, December, 1992. **HOME ADDRESS:** 1250 SW 152nd St, Burien, WA 98166, (206)243-2102. **BUSINESS PHONE:** (206)553-2152.

JHON, MYUNG S.
Educator. Korean American. **PERSONAL:** Born Dec 3, 1944, Chinju, Republic of Korea; son of Young Sook & Sun Nam; married Young Shim Jhon, Jun 25, 1973; children: Peter, Mark. **EDUCATION:** Seoul National University, BS, 1967; University of Chicago, PhD, 1974. **CAREER:** University of Minnesota, research specialist, 1976-80; Carnegie Mellon University, assistant professor, 1980-84, associate professor, 1984-88, professor, 1988-; Almaden Research Center, IBM Division, visiting scientist, 1988-; University of California, Berkeley, visiting professor, 1989-; US Department of Energy, visiting professor, 1992-. **ORGANIZATIONS:** American Institute of Chemical Engineers; American Physical Society; American Chemical Society; American Society of Mechanical Engineers; Sigma Xi; Korean Magnetic Society; The Korean Scientists and Engineers Association in America, auditor. **HONORS/ AWARDS:** Carnegie Mellon University, George Tallman Ladd Award, 1981, William S & Frances F Ryan Teaching Award, 1984, Benjamin Richard Teare Award for Excellence in Teaching, 1984; United Nations, expert consultant, 1986. **SPECIAL ACHIEVEMENTS:** Co-author, Advance Chemical Phys, vol 46, p 279-362, 1981; co-author, Proc National Academy Science, vol 83, p 4973-77, 1986; co-author, Advance Chemical Phys, vol 66, p 153-211, 1987; Colloids and Surfaces, vol 80, no 1, guest editor; Wear, 168, 59-76, coauthor, 1993. **BUSINESS ADDRESS:** Professor of Chemical Engineering, Carnegie Mellon University, 500 Forbes Ave, Pittsburgh, PA 15213-3890, (412)268-2233.

JI, CHUENG RYONG
Physicist, educator. Korean American. **PERSONAL:** Born Jan 7, 1954, Seoul, Republic of Korea; son of Jong Goo Ji and Young Hye Lee; married Mikyoung, Jan 18, 1983; children: Stephen Jongseok, Lisa Seungyun, David Youngseok. **EDUCATION:** Seoul National University, BS, 1976; Korea Advanced Institute of Science and Technology, MS, 1978, PhD, 1982. **CAREER:** Stanford Linear Accelerator Center, long term visiting scientist, 1982-84; Stanford University, postdoctoral research affiliate, 1984-86; Brooklyn College of the City, University of New York, research associate, 1986-87; North Carolina State University, assistant professor, 1987-92, associate professor, 1992-. **ORGANIZATIONS:** American Physical Society, 1989; Association of Korean Physicists in America, regional representative, 1990; Korean Scientists and Engineers Association in America, North Carolina, chapter president, 1992; Sigma Xi, 1990. **HONORS/AWARDS:** Department of Energy, Grants Award, 1989-; North Carolina State University, Faculty Research and Professional Development Fund Award, 1990; Conference on Intersections between Particle and Nuclear Physics, Dirac Scholarship, 1990. **SPECIAL ACHIEVEMENTS:** Publisher of the North Carolina KSEA Newsletter, 1992-; organizing conferences for Korean Scientists and Engineers in America, 1989-. **BUSINESS ADDRESS:** Dept of Physics, North Carolina State University, Box 8202, Bureau of Mines, Rm 217A, Raleigh, NC 27695-8202, (919)515-3478.

JI, INHAE
Educator. Korean American. **PERSONAL:** Born May 17, 1938, Seoul, Republic of Korea; married Tae H Ji. **EDUCATION:** Seoul National University, BS, 1961; University of Wyoming, PhD, 1977. **CAREER:** Harvard Medical School, postdoctoral fellow, 1977-78; University of Wyoming, postdoctoral research associate, 1978-91, research professor, 1991-. **ORGANIZATIONS:** American Society of Cell Biologists, 1985-; Endocrine Society, 1981-. **SPECIAL ACHIEVEMENTS:** Gonadotropin Receptors in Reproductive Endocrinology, 1993. **BUSINESS ADDRESS:** Research Professor, Dept of Molecular Biology, University of Wyoming, Laramie, WY 82071-3944, (307)766-3126.

JI, TAEHWA
Educator. Korean American. **PERSONAL:** Born Apr 7, 1941, Seoul, Republic of Korea; married Inhae Ji, May 15, 1965. **EDUCATION:** Seoul National University, BS, 1964; University of California, San Diego, PhD, 1968. **CAREER:** University of Minnesota, postdoctoral fellow, 1969-70; University of Wyoming, assistant professor, 1970-74, associate professor, 1974-77; Harvard University, visiting professor, 1977-78; University of Wyoming, professor of molecular biology, 1977-. **ORGANIZATIONS:** Endocrine Society, 1981-; American Society of Biochemistry and Molecular Biology, 1976-; Protein Society, 1990-; Society for Studies on Reproduction, 1985-. **HONORS/AWARDS:** American Cancer Society, Scholar in Cancer Research, 1977; American Cancer Society, Senior Faculty Award, 1981-86; Burlington Northern, Burlington Northern Award, 1989; University of California, Regent Fellow, 1964. **SPECIAL ACHIEVEMENTS:** Gonadotropin Receptors, 1993; Gonadotropin Receptor Genes, 1993. **BUSINESS ADDRESS:** Professor, Dept of Molecular Biology, University of Wyoming, Laramie, WY 82071-3944, (307)766-6272.

JIANG, NAI-SIANG
Educator, consultant. Chinese American. **PERSONAL:** Born Jun 6, 1931, Nanking, Jiangsu, China; married Helen H Jiang, Aug 19, 1958; children: Grace W Jiang Goggin, David I. **EDUCATION:** National Taiwan University, Taiwan, BS, 1955; Emory University, MS, 1959, PhD, 1962. **CAREER:** Emory University, instructor in biochemistry, 1962-66; Mayo Clinic and Foundation, consultant, 1966-68, assistant professor, consultant, 1968-75, associate professor, consultant, 1975-80, head of clinical chemistry, 1983-90, professor, consultant, 1980-. **BUSINESS ADDRESS:** Professor, Mayo Clinic & Foundation, 200 First Street, Room 730A, Hilton Building, Rochester, MN 55905, (507)284-3670.

JIANG, WILLIAM YUYING
Educator. Chinese American. **PERSONAL:** Born Jan 18, 1955, Hengyang City, Hunan, People's Republic of China; son of Hongkang Lei and Rongguang Jiang; married Leslie Rongqui Yi, Sep 5, 1988; children: Cosmo Y, Cordelia Y. **EDUCATION:** Hunan Normal University, China, BA, English, 1981; University of Illinois, Urbana-Champaign, MA, comparative literature, 1985, MS, library & information science, 1986; Columbia University, Graduate School of Business, MPhil, management, 1990, PhD, management, 1991. **CAREER:** Xiamen University, instructor, 1982-84; University of Illinois, Urbana-Champaign, instructor, 1984-86; Columbia University, instructor, 1987-91; San Jose State University, assistant professor, 1991-93, associate professor, 1993-. **ORGANIZATIONS:** Academy of Management, program committee, 1988-; Association of Management, Human Resource Group, chair, 1991-; Industrial Relations Research Association, 1987-; American Economic Association, 1988-; Western Academy of Management, program committee, 1991-; Monte Jade Science & Technology Association, 1993-. **HONORS/AWARDS:** Beta Gamma Sigma, 1990-; Columbia University Presidential Fellowship, 1987; Columbia University, Marjorie Hope Nicolson Fellowship, 1986-90; Xiamen University, China, Outstanding Instructor Award, 1983. **SPECIAL ACHIEVEMENTS:** Published over ten articles in professional journals or conference proceedings; presented over ten papers at different professional conferences; published over thirty literary articles, essays as part of creative writing hobby; published over twenty translations of English, American, and French stories in Chinese; published two translated novels in Chinese: To Kill A Mockingbird, by Harper Lee; The Egoist, by George Meredith. **BUSINESS ADDRESS:** Associate Professor, Dept of Organization & Management, San Jose State University, College of Business, One Washington Square, Business Tower, Room 662, San Jose, CA 95192-0070, (408)924-3572.

JIANG, XIXIANG
Educator. Chinese American. **PERSONAL:** Born Jan 18, 1957, Shanghai, People's Republic of China; son of Linhai Jiang and Jindi Wu; married Linda Liu, Feb 24, 1986; children: Cecilia. **EDUCATION:** Shanghai International Studies University, BA, 1979; The American University, MA, 1986, PhD, 1994. **CAREER:** American University, lecturer, 1986-; Washington Center for China Studies, director of program development, 1990-; Center for Applied Linguistics, program director, 1989-. **ORGANIZATIONS:** Chinese Language Teachers Assn, 1989-; American Council for the Teaching of Foreign Languages, 1989-; Foreign Language Annals, reviewer, 1990-. **HONORS/AWARDS:** United Nations, UNDP Fellowship, 1985; American University, Hall of Nations Fellowship, 1986. **SPECIAL ACHIEVEMENTS:** Teacher training in language instruction, foreign language teaching & testing, cross-cultural communications; voluntary work for Chinese weekend schools. **HOME ADDRESS:** 7826 Muirfield Ct, Potomac, MD 20854. **BUSINESS ADDRESS:** Program Director, Center for Applied Linguistics, 1118 22nd St NW, Washington, DC 20037, (202)429-9292.

JIANG, ZHENYING
Educator. Chinese American. **PERSONAL:** Born Nov 13, 1949, Zhenjiang, Jiangsu, People's Republic of China; son of Yuan Jiang & Bowen Qu; married Chaohua Fang, Jan 6, 1986; children: Fonda. **EDUCATION:** East China Normal University, Diploma, 1974; Shanghai Foreign Language Institute, Diploma, 1983; University of Utah, MS, 1987, PhD, 1991. **CAREER:** Shanghai Farm, director of corrections office, 1968-72; Chinese Medical College, Shanghai, faculty & head, coach, 1974-83; University of Utah, College of Health, Instructing Computing Lab, instructor, 1983-91; Barstow College, Division of Math, Science and Health, Lifetime Fitness Lab, faculty, 1991-. **ORGANIZATIONS:** Barstow College Council, Faculty Senate, 1993-94; National Education Association, 1991-; California Teachers Association, 1991-; American Alliance for Health, PE, Recreation & Dance, 1987-; USA Alliance for Health Education, 1987-; American Red Cross, certified first aid/CPR/WSI instructor, 1989-; American Heart Association, CPR instructor, 1991-; American Coaching Effectiveness Program, coaches' coach, 1989-. **HONORS/AWARDS:** Barstow College, Achievement of Lifetime Fitness Lab, 1991; University of Utah, Teaching Assistantship, 1984-88, Teaching Fellowship, 1989-91. **SPECIAL ACHIEVEMENTS:** "The Effects of Breathing Medication on Post-workout Anxiety and Heart Rate Recovery of High School Athletes," AAHPERD (SW), 1992; "The Study of Technique, Principle and Characteristics of One Arm Giant Swing Backward," Technique, vol 9, #3, 1989; "Dinosaur," Tai Chi Performance, TV Channel 5, Salt Lake City, UT, 1988. **BIOGRAPHICAL SOURCES:** Relax! Meditation Might be the Missing Component, The Salt Lake Tribune, May 19, 1990. **BUSINESS ADDRESS:** Faculty member, Barstow College, 2700 Barstow Rd, T7, T8, or T10, Barstow, CA 92311, (619)252-2411.

JIMENEZ, CHRISTINA LEE
Travel industry consultant. Chinese American. **PERSONAL:** Born Jan 6, 1958, Tai-Chung, Taiwan; daughter of Joseph & Helena Jimenez. **EDUCATION:** Northern Virginia Community College, AS, 1980; George Washington University, BS, 1982. **CAREER:** Advanced Technology, cost analyst, 1982-84; BDM, operations research analyst, 1984-86; TASC, technical staff member, 1986-92, consultant, 1992-; ABC Travel Service, president/owner, 1992-. **BUSINESS ADDRESS:** President, ABC Travel Service, 8027 Leesburg Pike St, Ste 408, Vienna, VA 22182, (703)847-0330.

JIMENEZ, JOSEPHINE SANTOS
Portfolio manager. Filipino American. **PERSONAL:** Born Jun 6, 1954, Lucena, Quezon, Philippines; daughter of Jose Hirang Jimenez and Virginia Villapando Santos Jimenez. **EDUCATION:** New York University, BS, 1979; MIT, MS, 1981; Institute of Chartered Financial Analysts, CFA, 1989. **CAREER:** Massachusetts Mutual, analyst, 1982-83; Shawmut Corp, analyst, 1984-88; Emerging Markets Investors Corp, senior portfolio manager, 1988-91; Montgomery Asset Management, managing director, 1991-. **ORGANIZATIONS:** AIMR, 1989-. **SPECIAL ACHIEVEMENTS:** Languages: Tagalog, Spanish, Portuguese. **BIOGRAPHICAL SOURCES:** Wall Street Journal, Business Week, Wall Street Week, with Louis Rukeyser, Feb 1993. **BUSINESS ADDRESS:** Managing Director, Partner, Montgomery Asset Management, 600 Montgomery St, San Francisco, CA 94111, (415)627-2478.

JIN, MORGAN
Sales representative. Chinese American. **PERSONAL:** Born Mar 25, 1925, Chicago, IL; son of Jin Leung Po; married Mary, Aug 15, 1950; children:

Patricia Ann, David Morgan. **EDUCATION:** NY Institute of Dietetics, certificate; SUNY, Morrisville, associate. **CAREER:** The NY World-Telegram & Sun, 1952-66; The World-Journal Tribune, 1966-67; The New York Times, sales representative, 1967-. **ORGANIZATIONS:** Newspaper Guild of NY, unit vice chairman at NY Times, chairman, City Wide Human Rights Committee. **HONORS/AWARDS:** Asian American Journalists Association, Lifetime Achievment Award, 1992; Asian American Pacific Alliance, Lifetime Achievment Award, 1992. **SPECIAL ACHIEVEMENTS:** New York Times, Publisher's Award, 1979, 1980, 1983, 1985, 1986, 1991, 1992. **MILITARY SERVICE:** US Army Air Corps, Air Cadet, 1941-45. **HOME ADDRESS:** 58 Country Club Lane, Pomona, NY 10970, (914)354-5298. **BUSINESS ADDRESS:** Sales Representative, New York Times, 229 W 43rd St, New York, NY 10036, (212)556-1134.

JINDAL, OM P.
Pharmacist. Indo-American. **PERSONAL:** Born in Kamas Pur, Haryana, India; married Madhu Jindal, Jan 19, 1983. **EDUCATION:** Delhi University, College of Pharmacy, BS, pharmacy, 1976; Panjab University, Dept of Pharmaceutical Sciences, MS, pharmacy, 1978. **CAREER:** Walgreens, staff pharmacist, currently. **ORGANIZATIONS:** Assn of Indian Pharmacists in America, life member, 1991-. **HOME ADDRESS:** 1952 Slippery Rock Rd, Naperville, IL 60565, (708)983-8363.

JOE, ALEXANDER H.
Accountant. Chinese American. **PERSONAL:** Born Jun 30, 1947, Fall River, MA; son of Arthur K Joe and Diana M Joe; married Patricia, Jun 3, 1972; children: Matthew A, Stephan P. **EDUCATION:** Northeastern University, BA, 1970; Roger Williams University, BS (magna cum laude), 1990. **CAREER:** US Army/Army National Guard, officer, 1970-; H&R Block Inc, franchise owner, 1978-; Naval Audit Service, auditor, 1979-90; Naval Education and Training Center, command evaluation officer, 1991-. **ORGANIZATIONS:** Association of Certified Fraud Examiners, 1990-; American Legion, 1989-; National Guard Association, 1976-. **HONORS/AWARDS:** National Association of Certified Fraud Examiners, CFE, 1990. **SPECIAL ACHIEVEMENTS:** Graduate of Command and General Staff College, USA, 1988; Rhode Island Artillery Hall of Fame, 1992. **MILITARY SERVICE:** Army National Guard, Major, 1970-92; Humanitarian Service, Vietnam Cross of Gallantry, Distinguish Service Medal, Bronze Star, Army Commendation, Air Medal. **HOME ADDRESS:** PO Box 5109, Newport, RI 02841. **BUSINESS ADDRESS:** Forensic Accountant/Owner, H&R Block, 711 Metacom Ave, Bristol, RI 02809, (401)253-1179.

JOE, CLARENCE
Physician. Chinese American. **PERSONAL:** Born Dec 21, 1950, Augusta, GA; son of Mr & Mrs David Joe. **EDUCATION:** Medical College of Georgia, School of Dentistry, DMD, 1973, School of Medicine, MD, 1977, radiology residency, 1980-83; US Public Health Service Hospital, internship, 1977-78. **CAREER:** US Public Health Service, medical director, 1978-80; Medical College of Georgia, assistant professor of radiology, 1980-. **ORGANIZATIONS:** Radiological Society of North America; American Roentgen Ray Society; Medical Association of Georgia; American Medical Association; Richmond County Medical Society; Central Savannah River Girl Scout Council, board of directors, chair of the nominating committee; Medical College of Georgia, School of Medicine, chairman, curriculum committee, 1991-94. **HONORS/AWARDS:** Alpha Omega Alpha, National Medical Honor Society, 1991. **SPECIAL ACHIEVEMENTS:** Perform and teach musculoskeletal procedures, diagnoses, and radiology. **MILITARY SERVICE:** US Public Health Service, Lt Cmd, 1977-80. **BUSINESS ADDRESS:** Assistant Professor of Radiology and Surgery, Medical College of Georgia, 1120 Fifteenth St, BA-N252, Augusta, GA 30912-3910.

JOE, KAREN ANN
Educator. Chinese American. **PERSONAL:** Born Jun 3, 1959, San Francisco, CA; daughter of William and Dorothy Joe. **EDUCATION:** University of California Davis, BA, 1981, MA, 1986, PhD, 1991. **CAREER:** National Council on Crime and Delinquency, research associate, 1982-87; California Attorney General's Office, research fellow, 1987-88; Evaluation, Management and Training, research associate, 1989-90; Institute for Scientific Analysis, research, 1990-; University of Hawaii, assistant professor, sociology, 1991-. **ORGANIZATIONS:** Academy of Criminal Justice Sciences; American Society of Criminology, committee on grants and contracts; American Sociological Association; Society for the Study of Social Problems; Women and Criminal Justice, journal reviewer; The Gang Journal, review editor; Chinese Commu-

nity Action Coalition, board member. **HONORS/AWARDS:** The Gang Journal, Frederick Thrasher Research Award, 1993; University of California, Davis, dissertation fellowship, 1990-91; American Sociological Association, minority research fellow, 1985-88; Phi Beta Kappa, 1981. **SPECIAL ACHIEVEMENTS:** Author: "Getting into the Gang: Methodological Issues in Studying Ethnic Gangs," NIDA monograph, 1993; Chinese Gangs and Tongs: An Exploratory Look at Connection on West Coast, American Criminology Meeting, 1992; "Incarceration of Minority Youth," Crime & Delinquency Journal, 1987; Asian Runaways in San Francisco, forum speaker, Organization of Chinese Americans, 1992. **BUSINESS ADDRESS:** Assistant Professor, Dept of Sociology, University of Hawaii, 2424 Maile Way, 247 Porteus Hall, Honolulu, HI 96822, (808)956-8090.

JOHNSTON, GEORGE TOSHIO
Journalist. Japanese American. **PERSONAL:** Born Nov 19, 1961, Tachikawa Airbase, Japan; son of James & Toshiko Johnston. **EDUCATION:** University of Colorado, Boulder, BA, journalism, 1986. **CAREER:** Pasadena Star-News, copy editor, currently. **BUSINESS ADDRESS:** Vice President, Media Action Network for Asian Americans, PO Box 1881, Santa Monica, CA 90406-1881.

JONG, MARK M. T.
Educator, educational administrator. Taiwanese American. **PERSONAL:** Born Oct 20, 1937, Er-Lun Hsiang, Yun-Lin, Taiwan; married Michelle M Jong, Aug 25, 1963; children: Carol N, Andrew K. **EDUCATION:** National Taiwan University, BSEE, 1960; South Dakota School of Mines & Technology, MSEE, 1965; University of Missouri-Columbia, PhD, 1967. **CAREER:** National Taiwan University, teaching assistant, 1961-63; University of Missouri-Columbia, research assistant, assistant instructor, 1965-67; Wichita State University, assistant professor, 1967-71, associate professor, 1971-79, associate professor, graduate coordinator, 1979-80, professor, graduate coordinator, 1980-90, associate dean, professor, 1990-. **ORGANIZATIONS:** Institute of Electrical and Electronics Engineers, senior member, 1980-, Computer/Control Systems Chapter, chairman, 1983-88, Region V 1984 Conference, program chair, 1985, Wichita Section Meeting, program chair, 1990; American Society Engr Educ, 1975; Mid-America Engr Guidance Council, 1990-. **HONORS/AWARDS:** Eta Kappa Nu; Phi Kappa Phi. **SPECIAL ACHIEVEMENTS:** Methods of Discrete Signal and System Analysis, McGraw-Hill Book Co, 1982; over 30 articles in technical journals. **BUSINESS ADDRESS:** Professor, Associate Dean of Engineering, Wichita State University, 1845 Fairmount, Campus Box 44, Wichita, KS 67260-0044, (316)689-3408.

JOSHI, BHAIRAV D.
Educator. Indo-American. **PERSONAL:** Born Mar 5, 1939, Dungrakot, Uttar Pradesh, India; son of Leeladhar and Jayanti Joshi; married Barbara Ravenell, Jan 14, 1967. **EDUCATION:** University of Delhi, BS (w/honors), 1959, MS, 1961; University of Chicago, MS, 1963, PhD, 1964. **CAREER:** University of Chicago, post doc, 1964-66; Indian Institute of Tech, Kampur, India, asst professor, 1966-67; University of Delhi, India, reader, 1967-69; SUNY, Stony Brook, research associate, 1969-70; SUNY, College at Geneseo, asst professor, 1970-78, associate professor, 1978-85, professor, 1985-. **ORGANIZATIONS:** American Chemical Society, 1969-; Sigma Xi, 1976-; Association for the Advancement of Computing in Education, 1981-. **SPECIAL ACHIEVEMENTS:** "Electronic Reports and...," J Comp Math & Sc Teaching, vol 10, p37, 1990; "Spreadsheet Template for...," J Comp Small Colleges, 9:2, p 174-185, 1993; "Equilibrium Calculations...," J Comp Math & Science Teaching, 12:3/4, p 261-276, 1993. **BUSINESS ADDRESS:** Professor, Chem Dept, State University of New York, College at Geneseo, 1 College Circle, Greene 327, Geneseo, NY 14454-1494.

JOSHI, JAGMOHAN
Educator. Indo-American. **PERSONAL:** Born Mar 20, 1933, Dhanoa, Punjab, India; son of Pandit Gian Chand Joshi and Savitri Devi Joshi; married Santosh Joshi, Feb 19, 1961; children: Shallin, Shushen, Shailesh. **EDUCATION:** Panjab Agricultural College, BS, 1953; Panjab University, MS, 1960; Ohio State University, PhD, 1972. **CAREER:** Extension Training Center, HP India, lecturer, 1956-61; Coffee Research Station, Ruiru, Kenya, assistant agriculture officer, 1961-66; Ohio State University, research associate, 1966-73; University of Maryland Eastern Shore, research associate, 1973-77, research assistant professor, 1977-85, dir, soybean research institute, 1976-, research associate professor, 1985-. **ORGANIZATIONS:** American Society of Agronomy, 1972-; Crop Science Society of America, 1972-; American Soybean Association, 1973-; Delmarva Soybean Association, 1973-; Mid-Atlantic Soybean Association, 1973-. **SPECIAL ACHIEVEMENTS:** More than 70 research

articles in the area of host plant resistance and cultural control of insect pests of soybean. **BIOGRAPHICAL SOURCES:** USDA News Release, 4 pages, April 30, 1975; Agriculture Yearbook, p 230, 1975.

JOSHI, MUKUND SHANKAR
Scientist. Indo-American. **PERSONAL:** Born Jun 11, 1947, Mahad, Maharashtra, India; son of Shankar K Joshi; married Geeta M Joshi; children: Mandar, Mahesh. **EDUCATION:** VJT Institute, LTC, 1969; University of Maryland, MS, 1973, PhD, 1976. **CAREER:** Asian Paints, India, 1969-71; Upjohn Co, senior research scientist, chemical process research & development, 1976-88, associate director, bioprocess research & development, 1988-. **ORGANIZATIONS:** AIChE; ACS. **HONORS/AWARDS:** Government of Denmark, fellowship, 1975-76. **BUSINESS ADDRESS:** Associate Director, Bioprocess Research & Development, Upjohn Co, Portage Rd, 1400-89-1, Kalamazoo, MI 49001, (616)329-3516.

JOSHI, SADA D.
Engineering corporation executive. Indo-American. **PERSONAL:** Born Mar 15, 1950, Maharashtra, India; son of Dattatray Joshi & Sumati Karulkar; married Claudette, Dec 22, 1979; children: Monical, Jay, Anita. **EDUCATION:** Walchad Coo, Sangli, India, BS, 1972; India Institute Technology, Bombay, MS, 1974; Iowa State University, PhD, 1978. **CAREER:** Phillips Petroleum Co, 1980-88; JTI, president, 1988-. **ORGANIZATIONS:** SPE, 1982-; AAPG, 1990; ASME; Tulsa Chamber of Commerce. **SPECIAL ACHIEVEMENTS:** Author, "Horizontal Well Technology," PennWell Pub; founder, Joshi Technologies International Inc. **BUSINESS ADDRESS:** President, Joshi Technologies Inc, 5801 E 41st St, Ste 603, Tulsa, OK 74135, (918)665-6419.

JOSHI, SEWA RAM
Federal government official. Indo-American. **PERSONAL:** Born Oct 15, 1933, Baluana, Punjab, India; son of Hari Ram Joshi and Maya Devi Khindria; married Surinder Rani Joshi, Aug 1954; children: Ashok Kumar. **EDUCATION:** Punjab University, Punjab Veterinary College, India, B Vet Science, 1954; Cornell University, MS, animal physiology, 1963, PhD, animal physiology, 1965. **CAREER:** Civil Veterinary Dept, Punjab, state veterinarian, 1954-55; Indian Veterinary Research Institute, research associate, 1955-61; Harvard Medical School, Cancer Research Foundation, Path & Toxicol, research associate, 1965-71; National Cancer Institute, National Institutes of Health, senior staff fellow, 1971-76; FDA, Center for Drug Evaluation & Research, physiologist, toxicologist, 1976-. **ORGANIZATIONS:** Society of Toxicology; Teratology Society; Society for the Study of Reproduction; Environ Mutagen Society; NY Academy Sciences; Sigma Xi. **HONORS/AWARDS:** US Public Health Service Career Award, 1982. **SPECIAL ACHIEVEMENTS:** Scientific publications; more than 40; author of a book chapter. **HOME ADDRESS:** 9905 Sunset Drive, Rockville, MD 20850-3658, (301)738-9184.

JOSHI, SURESH MEGHASHYAM
Research engineer. Indo-American. **PERSONAL:** Born Jul 10, 1946, Poona, Maharashtra, India; son of M C Joshi and S M Joshi; married Shyamala, Jun 16, 1974; children: Sucharit, Sujay. **EDUCATION:** Banaras University, India, BS, electrical engineering, 1967; Indian Institute of Technology, Kanpar, India, MTech, electrical engineering, 1969; Rensselaer Polytechnic Institute, PhD, electrical engineering, 1973. **CAREER:** Stone and Webster Engineering Corp, Boston, specialist engineer, 1972-73; National Research Council-NASA, postdoctoral fellow, 1973-75; Old Dominion University, Norfolk, VA, research professor, 1975-83; NASA-Langley Research Center, senior research scientist, 1983-; University of Virginia, visiting professor, 1991-93. **ORGANIZATIONS:** Institute of Electrical and Electronics Engrs, fellow, board of governors, 1969-; American Institute of Aeronautics and Astronautics, journal editor, committee member, fellow, 1984-; American Society of Mechanical Engrs, chair of aerospace technical panel, 1988-. **HONORS/AWARDS:** Rensselaer Polytechnic Institute, Allen B DuMont Prize, 1973; NASA-Langley Research Center, many outstanding performance awards, 1975-93; Thompson Fellow Award, 1992; IEEE, Fellow Award, 1993; AIAA, Fellow Award. **SPECIAL ACHIEVEMENTS:** Author, Control of Large Flexible Space Structures, Springer-Verlag, 1989; also 120 technical articles and reports. **BUSINESS ADDRESS:** Senior Research Scientist, NASA-Langley Research Center, Mail Stop 230, Hampton, VA 23681.

JOTWANI, CHANDRU
Business executive. Indo-American. **PERSONAL:** Born Feb 10, 1945, Hyderabad, Pakistan; son of T S Jotwani and T T Jotwani; married Asha Chandru Jotwani, Dec 27, 1971; children: Manish Kiran, Seema Chandru. **EDUCATION:** BA. **CAREER:** Crystal World Tours & Travel LTD, president, currently. **ORGANIZATIONS:** SANJ, vice pres; LISA, mbr-at-large; Diwane-Khas, president; Sindhu Sangam; Sadhu Vaswani Center, member. **HONORS/AWARDS:** AT&T, Decision Maker of the Year. **HOME ADDRESS:** PO Box 42, Demarest, NJ 07627, (201)767-9493. **BUSINESS ADDRESS:** President, Crystal World Tours & Travel Ltd, India Bldg, 146 W 29th St, 11th Fl, New York, NY 10001, (212)629-3060.

JU, FREDERICK D.
Educator. Chinese American. **PERSONAL:** Born Sep 21, 1929, Shanghai, China; married Ruby K Y, Jan 29, 1956; children: Wilfred T Y, Manfred T S, Winifred C T. **EDUCATION:** National Taiwan University, 1951-52; University of Houston, BSME, 1953; University of Illinois, Urbana, MS, 1956, PhD, 1958. **CAREER:** University of New Mexico, assistant professor, 1958-62, associate professor, 1962-67, chair, 1973-76, 1989-92, professor, 1967-. **ORGANIZATIONS:** ASME, fellow, 1986, Technical Comm on Vibration & Sound, chair, 1992-94. **HONORS/AWARDS:** University of New Mexico, Presidential Professor, 1985, Halliburton Professor, 1991-94, College of Engg, Outstanding Researcher, 1985, Outstanding Teacher, 1988; American Society of Mech Engrs, fellow, 1986; Society TAM & Society Mat Sci, ROC Achievement Award, 1986. **SPECIAL ACHIEVEMENTS:** Fracture Damage Diagnosis in Structures, 1981-90; Reliability Assessment of Damaged Structures, 1981-90; Damage Through "Heat Checking" in Seals, 1981-85; High Speed Frictional Damage in Coated Media, 1984-92; Reliability and Life of Wear Media, 1987-. **BUSINESS ADDRESS:** Professor, Mechanical Engineering Dept, University of New Mexico, Albuquerque, NM 87131-1361, (505)277-6280.

JUANITAS, CYRIL E. B., JR.
City government administrator. Filipino American. **PERSONAL:** Born 1961, Dallas, TX; married; children: 2 sons. **EDUCATION:** University of California, Davis, BA, English literature; Georgetown University Law Center, JD. **CAREER:** Teacher of high school physics, chemistry, anatomy and English; Private Industry Council, public relations officer; Foundry Housing Corp, counselor; Seattle Councilmember Dolores Sibonga's staff, council assistant, 1988; City of Seattle, Office of Intergovernmental Relations, federal relations coordinator, until 1993; Mayor Norm Rice, deputy chief of staff, 1993-. **BUSINESS ADDRESS:** Deputy Chief of Staff, Office of Mayor Norm Rice, Municipal Bldg, 12th Fl, 600 Fourth Ave, Seattle, WA 98104-1873, (206)684-4000.*

JUE, FRANCIS
Actor. Chinese American. **PERSONAL:** Born Sep 29, 1963, San Francisco, CA; son of Frank & Jennie Jue. **EDUCATION:** Yale University, BA, 1986. **CAREER:** Actor: M Butterfly, Broadway and National Tours; Pacific Overtures, Off-Broadway; Arizona Theatre Co; TheatreWorks, CA; Intiman Theatre, WA; Cidermill Playhouse, NY; Hippodrome State Theatre, FL; Lorraine Hansberry Theatre Co, CA; Asian American Theatre Co, CA; San Francisco AIDS Foundation, executive secretary, 1987-89. **ORGANIZATIONS:** Actors' Equity Association, 1984-. **HONORS/AWARDS:** Bay Area Critics Circle Award, Best Featured Actor, 1989. **SPECIAL ACHIEVEMENTS:** Theatrical appearances include: M Butterfly, Song Liling; Cabaret, emcee; Peter Pan, Peter Pan; Pacific Overtures, Manjiro, lion dancer, boy in the tree, Dutch admiral; A Song for a Nisei Fisherman, Jeffrey. **BIOGRAPHICAL SOURCES:** LA Times, Arts Calendar, first page, December 31, 1991. **HOME ADDRESS:** 2649 Alma St, Palo Alto, CA 94306. **BUSINESS PHONE:** (212)391-4545.

JUN, HUNG WON
Educator. Korean American. **PERSONAL:** Born Aug 2, 1939, Daegu, Kyungbuk, Republic of Korea; son of Yong-Bum Jun and Du-Yun Kim; married Jung-Ja Yoo, Nov 3, 1964; children: Sandy, Albert, Jason. **EDUCATION:** Yungnam University, Korea, BS, 1962; University of Alberta, PhD, 1970. **CAREER:** University of Georgia, research associate, 1970-71; University of Georgia, assistant professor, associate professor, professor, 1972-. **ORGANIZATIONS:** American Association College of Pharmacy; American Association of Pharmaceutical Scientists; Korean Scientists & Engineers Association; The Honor Society of International Scholars; The Society of Korean American Pharmaceutical Scientists. **MILITARY SERVICE:** The

Korean Air Force, 1st lt, pharmacy officer, 1962-65. **HOME ADDRESS:** 330 Millstone Circle, Athens, GA 30605, (706)549-7609. **BUSINESS ADDRESS:** Prof, Dept of Pharmaceutics, Univ of Georgia, Coll of Pharmacy, Athens, GA 30602, (706)542-5759.

JUN, JONG S.
Educator, educational administrator. Korean American. **PERSONAL:** Born Jul 26, 1936, Sunsan, Kyungbook, Republic of Korea; son of Myung-Duck Jun & Jumson Pai; married Soon Y Jun, Sep 16, 1964; children: Eugene, Amy. **EDUCATION:** Young Nam University, LLB, 1960; University of Oregon, MA, 1964; University of Southern California, PhD, 1969. **CAREER:** Hosei University, Tokyo, Japan, visiting professor, 1992-93; Institute for Governmental Research and Training, director, 1993-; California State University, Hayward, professor, 1968-. **ORGANIZATIONS:** International Association of Schools and Institutes of Administration, managing board, 1992-; National Association of Schools of Public Affairs and Administration, executive council, 1991-; National Academy of Public Administration, associated member of the federal system panel, 1992-; member of the editorial board of several professional journals, 1990-. **HONORS/AWARDS:** San Francisco, Santa Clara Chapters of the American Society for Public Administration, Outstanding Academic Achievement Award, 1982; Social Science Research Council, New York, research grant, 1978; National Association of Schools of Public Affairs and Administration and the US Civil Service Commission, faculty fellowship, 1972-73. **SPECIAL ACHIEVEMENTS:** Published several books, including: Development in the Asia Pacific, Walter de Gruyter, 1993; Public Administration: Design and Problem Solving, Macmillan, 1986. **HOME PHONE:** (510)538-2318. **BUSINESS ADDRESS:** Professor, California State University, Hayward, 25800 Carlos Bee Bvd, Hayward, CA 94542-3000, (510)881-3282.

JUN, JOOSUNG
Educator. Korean American. **PERSONAL:** Born Mar 14, 1957, Republic of Korea; married Youngah Jun; children: Hankyung, Yunsok. **EDUCATION:** Seoul National University, BA, 1978; Harvard University, MA, 1985, PhD, 1988. **CAREER:** Yale University, assistant professor, 1988-.

JUNG, AUDREY MOO HING
Educator, performer, choreographer. Chinese American. **PERSONAL:** Born Jun 13, 1945, Honolulu, HI; daughter of Amy Y M Char and Albert K W Jung; married Kenneth M Stepman, Jul 25, 1982. **EDUCATION:** University of California, Long Beach Summer School of Dance, 1969, 1971, 1973, 1974; University of Hawaii, Manoa, BA, 1972; University of Illinois, Urbana, MA, 1974; Laban/Bartenieff Institute of Movement Studies, CMA, 1979. **CAREER:** Katherine Litz Dance Co, Hawaii Dance Theatre, Alfred Durano Filipino Dance Co, Asian American Dance Theatre, Chinese Dance Co of NY, Morita Dance Co, San Francisco Chinese Folk Dance Co, performer; Actors/Directors Lab, NY, dance faculty, 1978-81, acting dance director, 1981; Wells College, assistant professor, director dance program, 1981-82; University of Wisconsin, Milwaukee, assistant professor, 1982-86; Virginia Commonwealth University, Department of Dance & Choreography, chairperson, 1986-91, professor, 1986-; VCU Cultural Heritage Dance Series, "The African-American Dance Experience," creator, producer, 1989, "Stepping, Tapping and Hoofing," creator, producer, 1990; "Elements of Three," choreographer, 1992. **ORGANIZATIONS:** American College Dance Festival, board member, 1988-, secretary, 1988-90; National Association of Schools of Dance, 1988-91; Virginia Fine Arts Museum, multicultural advisory panel member, 1990-; Virginia Commission for the Arts, advisory panel member, 1990; US China Peoples Friendship Association, Richmond Chapter, board member, 1990-, president, 1993-; National Society of Arts and Letters, Richmond, dance committee chairperson, 1989-92, honorary member, 1992-; Independent Performing Artists Alliance of Wisconsin, board member, 1983-86, acting chair, 1985-86. **HONORS/AWARDS:** National Endowment for the Arts, Presenter Grant, 1989; Mid-Atlantic Arts Foundation, Presenter Grant, 1990; Virginia Commission for the Arts, Dance Initiative, 1988-90; Virginia Commonwealth University, Faculty-Grant-in-Aid, 1992; Artist-in-the-Schools, NYC, 1981, Hawaii, 1973; Hawaii State Community Grant for Dance, 1972; Soong Foundation Cultural Award, 1964. **BUSINESS ADDRESS:** Professor, Dept of Dance & Choreography, Virginia Commonwealth University, 1315 Floyd Ave, Richmond, VA 23284-3007, (804)367-1711.

JUNG, BYUNG IL
Educator. Korean American. **PERSONAL:** Born Oct 13, 1942, Jeonnam, Republic of Korea; son of Jea Goo Jung and Jung Duk Kim; married Young Ja

Jung, Dec 19, 1970; children: Dorian C, Nina Y. **EDUCATION:** Wongkwang University, BA, 1964; University of Oklahoma, MA, 1978, PhD, 1984. **CAREER:** City of Texarkana, Texas, city planner, 1978-80; Ace Consultants, Inc, planner, 1984-88; University of Central Oklahoma, professor, 1989-. **ORGANIZATIONS:** Western Pacific Institute, director, 1990-; American Association of Geographers, 1980-; American Planning Association, 1976-. **SPECIAL ACHIEVEMENTS:** Organized Japan-US Symposium, 1992; Organized China, Hong Kong-US Symposium, 1993; author, Koreans In China, in Korean, 1989; author, The History of Nation Building: Korea, forthcoming; author, Living Essays, in Korean, forthcoming. **MILITARY SERVICE:** South Korean Army, capt, 1964-72. **BUSINESS ADDRESS:** Professor, University of Central Oklahoma, 100 N University Dr, Edmond, OK 73034-5224.

JUNG, EMMA
Journalist (retired), community activist. Chinese American. **PERSONAL:** Born Feb 25, 1915, Oakland, CA; daughter of Wong Low Gut & Moy Lee; married Ben Kam, Jan 10, 1934 (deceased); children: Walter Kam, Camille Wong, Jo Ann Jung Mo; married Joseph Jung, Jul 28, 1946. **CAREER:** Hertz, licensee counter, manager, 1967-77; Mid-Valley News, writer, 1965-. **ORGANIZATIONS:** El Monte Women's Club, El Monte Republican Women's Club, past president; Friend O'Garden Club El Monte; Sister City commissioner; El Monte High School PTA, president; PTA Council, corresponding secretary; El Monte Coordinating Council. **HONORS/AWARDS:** El Monte Coordinating Council, Distinguished Citizen; El Monte Women's Club, Woman of the Year Award; PTA, honorary award. **SPECIAL ACHIEVEMENTS:** Actress and singer.

JUNG, JOHN R.
Educator. Chinese American. **PERSONAL:** Born Apr 2, 1937, Macon, GA; son of Frank Jung and Grace Jung; married Phyllis, Jun 4, 1968; children: Jeffrey, Tomy. **EDUCATION:** University of California, Berkeley, BA, 1959; Northwestern University, MS, 1960, PhD, 1962. **CAREER:** California State College, assistant professor of psychology, 1962-65; York University, Canada, associate professor of psychology, 1965-68; California State University, professor of psychology, 1968-. **ORGANIZATIONS:** American Psychological Society, 1989-; Society of Behavioral Medicine, 1993-. **SPECIAL ACHIEVEMENTS:** Under the Influence: Alcohol and Human Behavior, Brooks/Cole Publishing Co, 1993; program director, Minority Access to Research Careers (MARC) Program funded by the National Institute of Mental Health, 1981-; four other books and over 30 journal articles. **BUSINESS ADDRESS:** Professor of Psychology, California State University, 1250 Bellflower Blvd, Psychology Bldg 429, Long Beach, CA 90840, (310)985-5046.

JUNG, KWAN YEE
Artist. Chinese American. **PERSONAL:** Born Nov 25, 1932, Toisun, Guangdong, China; son of Fred Jung and Shun-Tong Lee; married Yee Wah Jung; children: Jeanne, Kathy Lee, Laura Lisa. **EDUCATION:** New Asia College, BA, 1961; San Diego State University, post-grad, 1968-69. **CAREER:** Self employed, artist, 1963-. **ORGANIZATIONS:** Asiatic Art Guild, San Diego, CA, president, 1992-; Watercolor West, CA, 1973-; National Watercolor Society, CA, 1973-; American Watercolor Society, NY, 1974-; National Academy of Design, 1993-. **HONORS/AWARDS:** San Diego Watercolor Society 10th Annual, first place, 1973; Springville Museum of Art, 50th Annual, April Art, Purchase Award, 1974; American Watercolor Society, 106th Annual, Clare Stout Award, 1973; Sumi-E Society of America, 15th Annual, Best of Show, 1979; National Academy of Design, 167th Annual, Merit Award, 1992. **BIOGRAPHICAL SOURCES:** "Special Focus on California," Kwan Y Jung, San Diego, Art Voices, p 41, Jan/Feb 1982; "Environmental Escape," Kwan Y Jung & Yeewah Jung, Southwest Art, p 68, Jan 1983; "America's Best Contemporary Watercolors, Splash I," Art of California Magazine, p 10D, Nov 1991; "Watercolor Breakthroughs, Splash II," Art of California Magazine, p 72, 1992; "The Art of Kwan Jung and Yee Wah Jung," Art of California Magazine, p 57, Nov 1992. **HOME ADDRESS:** 5468 Bloch St, San Diego, CA 92122, (619)453-5380.

JUNG, LAWRENCE KWOK LEUNG
Educator, scientist, physician. Chinese American. **PERSONAL:** Born Aug 5, 1950, Canton, People's Republic of China; son of Joe Jung and Helen Jung; married L Dianne, Aug 5, 1977; children: Tamara Wynn-Mun, Ross Ian Hunn. **EDUCATION:** University of Sasketchewan, College of Arts & Sciences, BSc, 1972, College of Medicine, MD, 1975. **CAREER:** Hospital for Sick Children, Toronto, pediatric resident, 1975-77; McMaster University Medical Center, researcher, pediatric fellow, 1977-80; Memorial Sloan-Kettering Cancer Cen-

ter, research fellow, 1980-82; University of Oklahoma Medical School, post-doctoral fellow, 1982-84, asst prof, 1984-89; University of Mass Medical School, asst prof, 1989-. **ORGANIZATIONS:** American Assn of Immunologists, 1986; Clinical Immunology Society, 1987; American Assn for Advancement of Science, 1981; New York Academy of Science, 1981. **HONORS/AWARDS:** NIH, Public Health Service Grant, 1989-, New Investigator Award, 1986-89. **SPECIAL ACHIEVEMENTS:** Author, immunology and clinical immunology: 30 publications, 1980-. **BUSINESS ADDRESS:** Asst Professor, Dept of Pediatrics, University of Massachusetts Medical Center, 55 Lake Ave N, Worcester, MA 01655, (508)856-6282.

JUNG, LOUISE REBECCA
Attorney. Chinese American. **PERSONAL:** Born 1949, Baltimore, MD; daughter of Jennie & Simon Jung; married Lewis Morris, 1983; children: Samuel Morris, Michelle Morris. **EDUCATION:** University of Maryland, BA, 1971; University of Michigan Law School, JD, 1975. **CAREER:** Federal Trade Commission, special assistant for enforcement, currently. **BUSINESS ADDRESS:** Special Assistant for Enforcement, Federal Trade Commission, 6th St & Pennsylvania Ave NW, 601 Bldg, Rm 4604, Washington, DC 20580.

JUNG, MANKIL
Organic chemist, educator. Korean American. **PERSONAL:** Born Oct 27, 1950, Ongjin, Hwanghaedo, Republic of Korea; son of Hyung Sam Jung & Yoosoon Kim; married Soonboon Park Jung, May 22, 1983; children: Diana Euncho, Albert Jiwoong. **EDUCATION:** Yonsei University, Seoul, BS, chemistry, 1974; Massachusetts Institute of Technology, MS, organic chemistry, 1978; Oxford University, England, PhD, chemistry, 1981. **CAREER:** Harvard University, research fellow, 1981-82; University of Notre Dame, postdoctoral associate, 1983-84; University of Mississippi, assistant professor, 1984-91, associate professor, 1991-. **ORGANIZATIONS:** American Chemical Society, 1977-; Alpha Chi Sigma, 1978-; American Society of Pharmacognosy, 1988-; The Oxford Society, Mississippi, honorary branch secretary, 1988-. **SPECIAL ACHIEVEMENTS:** US Patent, 4920147, 1990; US Patent 5023353, 1991; American Chemical Society, Reviewer of Journal of Organic Chemistry, 1990-; Reviewer of Journal of Medicinal Chemistry, 1989-; World Health Organization, Reviewer of Malaria Grant, 1993-; Current Medicinal Chemistry, editorial board, 1993-; US patent 5,225,562. **HOME ADDRESS:** 81 Jeff St, Oxford, MS 38655. **BUSINESS ADDRESS:** Associate Professor, School of Pharmacy, University of Mississippi, University, MS 38677, (601)232-5931.

JUNG, SOON J.
Librarian. Korean American. **PERSONAL:** Born Jan 1, 1941, Seoul, Republic of Korea; daughter of Hyun-Bae & Chung-Sook Kim; married John Jonghyun Jung, May 22, 1971; children: Ina, Dale, Jayne. **EDUCATION:** Ewha Woman's University, Seoul, Korea, BA, (summa cum laude), lib sci, 1964; Drexel University, MLS, 1968. **CAREER:** Haverhill Public Lib, head of technical services, 1969-71; Encyclopedia Britannica, Lib Resources Inc, cataloger, 1971-73; Occidental Petroleum Corp, Research Center, indexer, 1981; Newport Beach Public Library, Cataloging, supervisor, 1983-. **ORGANIZATIONS:** Public Library Association; California Lib Association, council member, 1990-93, Tech Service Chapter; State of California Library Networking Task Force, planning committee, 1989-91; Korean-American Libns Association, vice president, president, 1988-90; Korean American Research & Education Project, County of Los Angeles Pub Lib, coalition task force; American Library Association, Asian-Pacific American Librarians Association, membership committee, 1991-92. **BUSINESS ADDRESS:** Head Cataloger, Newport Beach Public Library, 856 San Clemente Drive, Newport Beach, CA 92660, (714)644-3185.

JUNG, YEE WAH
Artist. Chinese American. **PERSONAL:** Born Sep 4, 1936, Canton, Guangdong, China; daughter of Ying-Chun Yip and Shiu-Fong Poon; married Kwan Y Jung, Sep 10, 1962; children: Jeanne, Kathy Lee, Laura Lisa. **EDUCATION:** Chung Nam Art School, Hupei, China, 1954-58; Tak Ming College, Hong Kong, BA, 1963; New Asia College, Hong Kong, BS, 1962. **CAREER:** Self-employed, artist, 1963-. **ORGANIZATIONS:** Asiatic Art Guild, 1992-; Watercolor West, 1973-; National Watercolor Society, 1973-; Watercolor USA Honor Society, 1973-. **HONORS/AWARDS:** Southern California Expo Art, Del Mar, CA, First Prize, 1971; National Watercolor Society, 53rd Annual, CA, Watercolor USA Award, 1973; Watercolor USA Annual, MI, Society Cash Award, 1973; 25th Art Festival, San Diego, CA, First Place, 1988; 7th Annual Advent Art, San Diego, CA, Three Kings Award, 1989. **BIOGRAPHICAL SOURCES:** "Environmental Escape," *Southwest Art*, p 68, Jan 1983;

"America's Best Contemporary Watercolors, Splash 1," p 138, Nov 1991; "The Art of Kwan Jung and Yee Wah Jung," *Art of California*, p 57, Nov 1992. **HOME ADDRESS:** 5468 Bloch St, San Diego, CA 92122, (619)453-5380.

JUNGALWALA, FIROZE BAMANSHAW
Scientist. Indo-American. **PERSONAL:** Born Aug 28, 1936, Surat, Gujarat, India; son of Bamanshaw Dadabhai Jungalwala and Tehmina Ratanshaw Chiniwala; married Khorshed Dhunjishaw Wadira, Mar 17, 1968; children: Ferzin, Jehangir. **EDUCATION:** Gujarat University, Ahmedabad, India, BS, 1956, MS, 1958; Indian Institute of Science, Bangalore, India, PhD, 1963. **CAREER:** Cambridge University, England, research fellow, 1968-70; E K Shriver Center, associate biochemist, 1971-79; Massachusetts General Hospital, assistant and associate biochemist, 1972-84; Harvard University Medical School, principal research associate, 1975-89; E K Shriver Center, senior biochemist, 1979-93, biomedical sciences, chairman, 1994-; Hospital, biochemist, 1985-; Harvard Medical School, associate professor of neuroscience, 1989-. **ORGANIZATIONS:** American Society for Neurochemistry, 1972-; International Society for Neurochemistry, 1975-; American Society for Biochemistry and Molecular Biology, 1972-; Association of American Advancement of Science, 1978-; Journal of Lipid Research, editorial board, associate editor, 1980-86; National Institutes of Health, advisory committee, 1985-; Journal of Neurochemistry, editorial board, 1994-. **HONORS/AWARDS:** National Multiple Sclerosis Society, New York, Fellow, 1968-70; National Institutes of Health, Research Career Development Award, 1975-80; National Institutes of Health, Principal Investigator, 1972-. **SPECIAL ACHIEVEMENTS:** Over 100 scientific publications in areas of nutrition, medicine, and neuroscience, 1962-. **BUSINESS ADDRESS:** Chairman, Biomedical Sciences, E Kennedy Shriver Center, 200 Trapelo Rd, Waltham, MA 02254.

K

KABADI, BALACHANDRA NARAYAN
Chemist (retired), association executive. Indo-American. **PERSONAL:** Born Jul 15, 1933, Gadag-Betgeri, Karnataka, India; son of Narayanaia R Kabadi; married Kamala, Apr 27, 1950; children: Mohan, Ashok, Dileep, Nirmala. **EDUCATION:** Karnatak University, India, BS (honors), chemistry; University Department of Technology, Bombay, India, BS, technical pharmacy; University of Washington, MS, pharmacy, 1963, PhD, pharmacy, 1965. **CAREER:** University of South Carolina, Department of Chemistry, research associate, 1965; University of Michigan, Ann Arbor, School of Pharmacy, research associate, 1966; Florida Agricultural & Mechanical University, School of Pharmacy, associate professor of pharmacy, 1967; Bristol Meyers Squibb, senior research scientist, 1968-90. **ORGANIZATIONS:** American Pharmaceutical Association, associate, 1962-91; American Chemical Associations, associate, 1963-; SSKNA, religious Hindu organization, president, 1990-; Sigma Xi, 1965; Rho Chi, 1965. **SPECIAL ACHIEVEMENTS:** Published over 10 papers in leading American pharmaceutical journals, 1963-90; presented 2 papers at American Pharmaceutical Science Academy meetings, 1972-83; patented a syringe filler, US patent 4,335,760, 1982.

KABIR, ABULFAZAL M. FAZLE
Educator. Bangladeshi American. **PERSONAL:** Born in Dhaka, Bangladesh; son of Mr & Mrs M Eunus. **EDUCATION:** Indiana University, PhD, 1982, MA, education, 1987. **CAREER:** University of Dhaka, assistant professor, 1965-73; Indiana University, adjunct faculty, 1979-80; Clark-Atlanta University, assistant professor, 1987-93, associate professor, 1993-. **ORGANIZATIONS:** ALA, personal member, 1987-; Association for Library and Information Studies Education, 1987-; Bangladesh Library Association, life member. **HONORS/AWARDS:** Indiana University, Fee Scholarship, 1986-87; The Asia Foundation, Grant for Master's Program in US, 1963, Grant for Doctoral Program in US, 1973. **SPECIAL ACHIEVEMENTS:** Libraries of Bengal, 1700-1947, 1987; Libraries of Bengal: Story of Bengali Renaissance, 1700-1947, Indian ed, 1989; "Ranganathan: The Educator and His Influence in the Western World," in Ranganathan and the West, ed R N Sharma, New Delhi, Sterling Publishers, 1992; CD-ROM Sources in the Reference Collection: Issues of Access and Maintenance, 1990; several book reviews: Library Times International, Jan-Sept 1993. **BUSINESS ADDRESS:** Associate Professor, School of Library & Information Science, Clark-Atlanta University, 223 James Brawley Dr SW, Atlanta, GA 30314, (404)880-8701.

KACHRU, BRAJ B.

Educator. Indo-American. **PERSONAL:** Born May 15, 1932, Srinagar, Kashmir, India; son of Shyamlal & Tulsidevi; married Yamuna, Jan 22, 1965; children: Amita, Shamit. **EDUCATION:** Jammu & Kashmir University, BA, 1952; Allahabad University, MA, 1955; University of Edinburgh, Dip App Ling, 1959; University of Edinburgh, PhD, 1962. **CAREER:** Lucknow University, assistant professor, 1962-63; University of Illinois, Jubilee Professor of Liberal Arts and Sciences, professor in the Center for Advanced Study, and professor of linguistics, 1963-. **ORGANIZATIONS:** Linguistics Society of America, 1963-; Linguistic Society of India, life member; American Association for Applied Linguistics, 1979-; Teachers of English to Speakers of Other Languages. **HONORS/AWARDS:** Honoured by the Association of Indians in America, 1992; Hyderabad University, India, first occupant of the Radhakrishnan Chair, 1990; Duke of Edinburgh, English Language Book Competition, Joint First Prize, 1987; The East-West Center, Fellow; Ford Foundation Grant; Arnold O Beckman Research Award. **SPECIAL ACHIEVEMENTS:** Editor and contributor, The Other Tongue: English Across Cultures, 1992; co-editor, Language and Identity, Journal of Asian Pacific Communication, 1993; "World Englishes and Applied Linguistics," 1990; "World Englishes and Applied Linguistics," 1991; editor, "Introduction: The Other Side of English and the 1990s," The Other Tongue: English Across Cultures, University of Illinois Press, 1992. **BIOGRAPHICAL SOURCES:** Contemporary Authors, 1961-64. **HOME PHONE:** (217)328-2885. **BUSINESS ADDRESS:** Professor of Liberal Arts & Sciences, University of Illinois, 707 S Mathews Ave, Urbana, IL 61801, (217)333-3563.

KACKER, RAGHU NATH

Government official. Indo-American. **PERSONAL:** Born Jun 24, 1951, Faridabad, Haryana, India; married Sanita Kacker, Dec 12, 1979. **EDUCATION:** University of Delhi, India, BS, 1971; Agra University, India, MStat, 1973; University of Guelph, Canada, MS, 1975; Iowa State University, PhD, 1979. **CAREER:** AT&T Bell Laboratories, distinguished MTS, 1980-88; Natl Institute of Standards & Technology, mathematical statistician, 1988-. **SPECIAL ACHIEVEMENTS:** Proficient in Japanese. **BUSINESS ADDRESS:** Mathematical Statistician, National Institute of Standards and Technology, Bldg 101 Rm A337, Gaithersburg, MD 20899, (301)975-2109.

KADABA, PRASANNA VENKATARAMA

Educator, mechanical engineer. Indo-American. **PERSONAL:** Born Jul 4, 1931, Gundlupet, Karnataka, India; son of Venkatarama Iyengar Kadaba (deceased) and Venkatarama Sharadamma Kadaba (deceased); married Usha Rani Rajgopal, Nov 14, 1966; children: Vaibhav P. **EDUCATION:** University of Mysore, India, BE, mech, 1952, BE, elec, 1954; University of Kentucky, MS, mech, 1956; Illinois Institute of Technology, PhD, mech, 1964. **CAREER:** Borg-Warner R&D, senior research engineer, 1963-67; Westinghouse Elec Corp, senior research scientist, 1967-69; Georgia Institute of Technology, associate professor, 1969-; University of Carabobo, Venezuela, visiting professor, 1973, 1975; University of Cincinnati, visiting professor, 1988-90. **ORGANIZATIONS:** ASHRAE, technology comm, 1974-; ASME, 1966-; AIChE, 1987-; ASEE, 1975-; Sigma Xi, 1956-; Tau Beta Pi, 1963-; Pi Tau Sigma, 1980-; Society of Indian Academics in America, 1993-. **HONORS/AWARDS:** ASHRAE, fellow, 1993, Atlanta chapter, Engineer of Year in Education, 1977, 1980, Appreciation Award, 1984-85; Georgia Society of Professional Engineers, Energy Action Comm Award, 1984-85. **SPECIAL ACHIEVEMENTS:** Publications in the fields of heat transfer, fluidized beds, availability analysis, solar energy, heat pumps, cryogenics and productivity effectiveness; keynote speaker: invited guest of Malaysian Government to their International Energy Conference, 1991, and Forum on Energy Research and Development, January 1992. **HOME ADDRESS:** 1071 Parkland Run, Smyrna, GA 30082, (404)433-1885. **BUSINESS ADDRESS:** Associate Professor, Mechanical Engineering, Georgia Institute of Technology, Atlanta, GA 30332-0405, (404)894-3291.

KADOHATA, CYNTHIA LYNN

Novelist. Japanese American. **PERSONAL:** Born Jul 2, 1956, Chicago, IL; daughter of June Akiko Kaita and Toshiro Kadohata; married Mark Metcalf, Aug 30, 1992. **CAREER:** Novels, In the Heart of the Valley of Love, Viking, 1992; The Floating World, Viking, 1989. **ORGANIZATIONS:** Authors Guild; PEN. **HONORS/AWARDS:** Mrs Giles Whiting Foundation, Whiting Writers' Award, 1991; National Endowment for the Arts, writing fellowship/grant, 1991. **BIOGRAPHICAL SOURCES:** Interview, Publishers Weekly, August 3, 1992, p48; interview, Elle, July/August, 1989; Asian Week, September 4, 1992, p27. **BUSINESS ADDRESS:** Novelist, Wylie, Aitken & Stone, c/o Deborah Karl, 250 W 57th St, Ste 2114, New York, NY 10107, (212)246-0069.

KADOMOTO, THOMAS

Controller (retired). Japanese American. **PERSONAL:** Born Aug 24, 1917, Phoenix, AZ; son of Shosaku Kadomoto & Kio Kadomoto; married Kiyomi K, Mar 24, 1942; children: Eileen Fukunaga, Nancy Matsui, Dan, Larry. **EDUCATION:** Lamson Business College, 1947, 1948; Licensed Public Accountant, licensed, 1953. **CAREER:** Public Accounting Business, self-employed, 1953-72; Arizona Automotive Institute, controller, 1972-76; Phoenix Technical Institute, controller, 1976-90; retired October 1980-November 1983; Mtn States Tech Institute, controller, 1983-91;. **ORGANIZATIONS:** Pacific Rim Advisory Council, City of Phoenix, 1990-; National Conference of Christians and Jews, life member; Japanese American Citizens League, past president, 1952; Dawnbuster Toastmaster Club, Glendale, past president, 1961; PTA Glendale Elementary School Unit IV, past president, 1962; United Fund, Glendale Area, past campaign chairman, 1963; Glendale Board of Realtor, past president, 1964; Glendale Elementary School Board, past president, 1969. **HONORS/AWARDS:** His Majesty the Emperor of Japan, Kunsho Award for Promoting US-Japan goodwill; Phoenix Civic Club, Good Citizenship Award for helping over 100 Japanese Obtain US citizenship; Glendale Chamber of Commerce, Outstanding Civic Service Award, 1963; Glendale United Fund, Top Worker Award, 1963; ASU Centennial Merit Award, 1985; Japanese Government Award, 11 day paid visit to Japan, 1985. **MILITARY SERVICE:** US Army, 2nd lt, 1941-46; Bronze Star Medal. **BIOGRAPHICAL SOURCES:** The Arizona Republic, December 4, 1992, June 2, 1969, December 14, 1974; Phoenix Gazette, May 2, 1992; Wall Street Journal, January 13, 1975; Glendale News-Herald, June 4, 1969. **HOME ADDRESS:** 7635 N 46 Ave, Glendale, AZ 85301. **BUSINESS PHONE:** (602)272-2112.

KADOWAKI, JOE GEORGE

Optical manufacturing/supply company executive. Japanese American. **PERSONAL:** Born Jul 19, 1919, Santa Ana, CA; son of Katsu and Tsune Kadowaki; married Toshi, Jul 27, 1940; children: Janet Kadowaki Green, Kathyrn Kadowaki Tashima. **EDUCATION:** Western Reserve University, Cleveland College, BBS, 1953. **CAREER:** W A Jones Optical Co, mgr, 1950-65; Harlequin Corp, designer, sales mgr, 1965-68; Toledo Optical Laboratory Inc, exec vice pres, 1968-72, president, treasurer, 1972-90, chairman of the board, 1990-. **ORGANIZATIONS:** Optical Laboratories Assn, board of directors, 1978-86; Ohio Valley Optical Wholesalers Assn, secretary, board of directors, 1974-78; Cleveland Nationalities Services Center, board of directors, 1955-60; Japanese-American Citizens League, Cleveland Chapter, president, 1956-57, Midwest District, chmn, 1958-59, national board of directors, 1960-64. **HONORS/AWARDS:** Japanese-American Citizens League, JACLer of the Biennium, 1960; Japanese Government, Citation for Bettering Relations between the US and Japan. **SPECIAL ACHIEVEMENTS:** Chaired, initiated: JACL Hawaii Disaster Fund, Hawaii Tidal Wave Relief Fund, 1959. **MILITARY SERVICE:** 442nd Regimental Combat Team, Military Intelligence, 1st sgt, 1943-46; Bronze Star. **BIOGRAPHICAL SOURCES:** Cleveland Press, Feature Page, Bob Seltzer, Apr 6, 1964. **BUSINESS ADDRESS:** Chairman of the Board, Toledo Optical Laboratory, Inc, 1201 Jefferson St, Toledo, OH 43624, (419)248-3384.

KAGETSU, TADASHI JACK

Consultant. Japanese American. **PERSONAL:** Born Apr 22, 1931, British Columbia; son of Eikichi Kagetsu and Toyo Nakamoto; married Kanaye Kay (Tsuchida) Kagetsu, Jul 20, 1957; children: Nolan Jack, Naomi Jayne Bukowski. **EDUCATION:** University of Toronto, BASc, 1954, MASc, 1955, PhD, 1957. **CAREER:** UCC Nuclear Div, assoc engineer, 1961-64; UCC Mining & Metals Div, project engineer, 1964-67, staff engineer, 1967-75; UCC Metals Div, manager process engineering, 1975-77, manager design engineering, 1977-78; Union Carbide Copr, Metals Div, asst dir technology, 1978-86; consultant, 1986-. **ORGANIZATIONS:** American Institute Chemical Engineers, 1957-87; American Institute Mining Metallurgical & Petroleum Eng, 1964-87; Electrochemical Soc, 1958-64; Y's Men's Club, pres, 1960-61; Mended Hearts, Chapter #203, pres, 1992-95. **HONORS/AWARDS:** Intl Nickel Co of Canada Ltd, fellowship, 1954-57. **SPECIAL ACHIEVEMENTS:** With others: US Patent 4,207,295, Processing of Chromium Ore, 1980; US Patent 4,230,677, Recovery of Chromium from a Chromium Bearing Solution, 1980; publication: "Rates of Dissolution of 95/5 Brass in Sulfuric Acid Solutions," Journal of the Electrochemical Soc, 1963. **HOME ADDRESS:** 435 Dutton Dr, Lewiston, NY 14092, (716)754-4710.

KAGIWADA, GEORGE
Educator (retired). Japanese American. **PERSONAL:** Born 1931, Hollywood, CA; married Nina Graham Kagiwada (deceased); children: Cindy, Jennifer, Paul. **EDUCATION:** Undergraduate and graduate work, sociology, ethnic and race relations; University of California, Los Angeles, PhD, 1958. **CAREER:** Educator at numerous colleges and universities in California and Canada; University of California, Davis, Dept of Applied Behavorial Sciences, Asian American Studies Program, 1970-89, College of Letters and Science, Asian American Studies Program, 1989-93. **ORGANIZATIONS:** Sacramento Asian Community Resources/Asian Legal Services Outreach, board member; Davis Asians for Racial Equality. **SPECIAL ACHIEVEMENTS:** UCD, Asian American Studies Program, developer. *

KAGIWADA, HARRIET H. NATSUYAMA
Educator. Japanese American. **PERSONAL:** Born Sep 2, 1937, Honolulu, HI; daughter of Kenjiro Natsuyama & Yakue Natsuyama; children: Julia, Conan. **EDUCATION:** University of Hawaii, BA, 1959, MS, 1960; Kyoto University, PhD, 1965. **CAREER:** Rand Corporation, mathematician, 1961-77; University of Southern California, adjunct assoc professor, 1972-79; Hughes Aircraft Company, senior scientist, 1979-87; Infotec Development Inc, chief engineer, 1987-89; California State University, Rockwell International professor, 1990-. **ORGANIZATIONS:** Graduate Women in Science, president, 1990-91, past president, 1991-92, director, 1992-; Institute of Electrical and Electronics Engineers; Society of Women Engineers. **HONORS/AWARDS:** University of Hawaii, Distinguished Alumna of the Year, 1991; Phi Beta Kappa, 1954; Phi Kappa Phi, 1954. **SPECIAL ACHIEVEMENTS:** Author of five books; over 150 papers in mathematics, computing, science, & engineering. **BUSINESS ADDRESS:** Rockwell Int Prof of Systems Engineering, California State University, Fullerton, CA 92634, (714)773-3192.

KAGY, TOM
Publisher. **CAREER:** Transpacific Media, publisher, currently; periodicals include: Transpacific, Face. **BUSINESS ADDRESS:** Publisher, Transpacific Media, 23715 W Malibu Rd, No 390, Malibu, CA 90265, (310)399-6908.*

KAI, ROBERT T.
Insurance company executive. Japanese American. **PERSONAL:** Born Jun 24, 1944, Newell, CA; son of Kimi and Shizuo; married Sheila, Sep 26, 1969 (divorced 1993); children: Kelley, Courtney. **EDUCATION:** Gonzaga University, BA, 1966; Gonzaga University School of Law, 1972. **CAREER:** Unigard Insurance Group, district underwriting mgr, 1967-78; Transamerica Insurance Group, exec vice pres, 1978-93; Houston General Insurance Group, sr sales vp, 1993-. **ORGANIZATIONS:** Knights of Columbus, 1979-; Ballet Guild of Mission Viejo, president, 1983-87; Idaho Rating & Surveying Bureau, president, 1985-86; Santa Margarita High School Parents Board, director, 1990-92; Santa Margarita Pep Squad Booster, president, 1991-92; Big Brothers of Washington, 1976-78. **BUSINESS ADDRESS:** Senior Vice President, Houston General Insurance Group, 4055 Internal Plaza, Fort Worth, TX 76109, (817)377-6020.

KAITA, ROBERT
Physicist. Japanese American. **PERSONAL:** Born Sep 2, 1952, Tokyo, Japan; son of Reiichi Kaita and Midori Kokita Kaita; married Chiu-Tze Lin, Apr 19, 1980; children: Courtney Lin. **EDUCATION:** State University of New York at Stony Brook, BSc, 1973; Rutgers University, PhD, 1978. **CAREER:** Princeton University, research associate, 1978-80, research staff physicist, 1980-84, research physicist, 1984-90, principal research physicist, 1990-. **ORGANIZATIONS:** American Physical Society, 1973; American Association for the Advancement of Science, 1975; Sigma Xi, 1976. **HOME ADDRESS:** 27 LeValley Drive, Manalapan, NJ 07726. **BUSINESS ADDRESS:** Principal Research Physicist, Princeton University Plasma Physics Laboratory, PO Box 451, Princeton, NJ 08543.

KAJI, AKIRA
Educator. Japanese American. **PERSONAL:** Born Jan 13, 1930, Tokyo, Japan; son of Chiyo Hanai & Kiichi Kaji; married Hideko, Aug 22, 1958; children: Kenneth, Eugene, Naomi, Amy. **EDUCATION:** University of Tokyo, Faculty of Pharmaceutical Sciences, BS, 1953; Johns Hopkins University, McCollum Pratt Institute, PhD, 1958. **CAREER:** Imperial Cancer Research Fund Labs, London, John Simon Guggenheim scholar, 1972-73; Tokyo University, professor, chairman, 1972-73; Kyoto University, visiting professor, Fogarty International Senior Fellow, 1985; University of Pennsylvania School of Medicine, assistant professor, 1964-67, associate professor, 1967-72, professor, 1972-.

ORGANIZATIONS: Sigma Xi; American Society for Microbiology; British Society of Biological Chemists; American Society of Biological Chemists; Japanese Society of Biological Chemists; American Society of Chemistry; American Society of Cell Biology. **HONORS/AWARDS:** John Simon Guggenheim Memorial Foundation, fellowship, 1972; University of Pennsylvania, Helen Hay Whitney Established Investigator, 1964-69; Vanderbilt University, Helen Hay Whitney Foundation Fellowship, 1959-62; Japan Society, Japan Society Fellowship, 1957. **SPECIAL ACHIEVEMENTS:** 170 journal publications and 95 meeting presentations, 1957-. **BUSINESS ADDRESS:** Professor of Microbiology, University of Pennsylvania School of Medicine, Philadelphia, PA 19104-6076, (215)898-8828.

KAJI, BRUCE
Association administrator. Japanese American. **CAREER:** Japanese American National Museum, founder, board of trustees, various other committees, currently. **BUSINESS ADDRESS:** Founder, Japanese American Natl Museum, 369 E 1st St, Los Angeles, CA 90012-3901, (213)625-0414.*

KAJI, JONATHAN T.
Real estate investor. Japanese American. **PERSONAL:** Born Oct 2, 1955, Los Angeles, CA; son of Bruce & Frances Kaji. **EDUCATION:** University of Southern California, Los Angeles, BA (cum laude), history and East Asian Studies, 1976; Waseda University, Tokyo, Japan, 1974-75; Loyola University School of Law, 1976-77; University of California, Los Angeles, 1980-. **CAREER:** Yamamoto, Takeda & Associates, legal intern, 1977; City of Los Angeles, Community Develoment Department, labor market analyst, 1977-79; Merit Savings Bank, vice president, 1979-82; Trans-Continental Investment Co, Ltd, senior vice president, 1982-84; J T Kaji, Inc, president, 1984-; Japanese American Minority Ent, Inc, DBA Gourmet West, Ltd, president, 1987-; Director for Asia CA Office of Trade and Investment, 1993-. **ORGANIZATIONS:** Los Angeles Baptist City Mission Society, president, 1992; Japanese American Citizens League, secretary/treasurer, 1992-94; President's Export Council, 1990-; Japan America Society of Los Angeles; Japanese American Citizens League; Japanese American Republicans; Japanese American Cultural & Community Center; Japanese American National Museum; Asian American Journalist Association; Gardena Valley Baptist Church; Gardena/Carson Family YMCA; Republican National Committe; numerous others. **SPECIAL ACHIEVEMENTS:** Alternate delegate, Republican National Convention, 1992. **BUSINESS ADDRESS:** President, Kaji and Associates, 18527 S Western Ave, Ste 15, Gardena, CA 90248.

KAJIOKA, JUNE J.
Interior designer. Japanese American. **PERSONAL:** Born Jan 12, 1938, San Francisco, CA; daughter of Hisako Miho Kajioka and Albert Juzo Kajioka. **EDUCATION:** Drexel University, BS, 1959. **CAREER:** Marvin I Bornfriend, AIA, interior designer, 1960-62; James Irvine, junior interior designer, 1962-64; Levitt & Sons Inc, Interior Design Dept, mgr, 1964-72; W & J Sloane, senior interior designer, 1971-72; self-employed, interior designer, 1972-. **ORGANIZATIONS:** American Society of Interior Designers, past chair, admissions, co-chair, directory, Design Center Tours, co-chair. **BUSINESS ADDRESS:** Interior Designer, Kajioka Design Associates, 2614 Ross Rd, Chevy Chase, MD 20815, (301)565-3535.

KAJIWARA, KENNETH KYO
Architect. Japanese American. **PERSONAL:** Born Mar 10, 1953, Tokyo, Japan; son of Etsue E Kajiwara and Martha H Kajiwara; married Leila Kajiwara, Jul 1, 1988. **EDUCATION:** University of Maryland, BAr, 1976. **CAREER:** University of Maryland, teaching assistant, 1975-76; TCB/Morris International, draftsman, 1976-77; Dewberry, Nealon & Davis, draftsman, 1977-78; Roger Lewis & Associates, designer, 1978; Metcalf & Associates, project architect, 1979-84; Wimberly, Allison, Tong and Goo, project manager, 1984-89; Ken Kajiwara Architects, principal, 1989-. **ORGANIZATIONS:** American Institute of Architects, 1989-; International Council of Building Officials, 1992-. **BUSINESS ADDRESS:** Principal, Ken Kajiwara Architects, 2534 Akepa St, Pearl City, HI 96782, (808)456-0929.

KAK, SUBHASH CHANDRA
Educator. Indo-American. **PERSONAL:** Born Mar 26, 1947, Srinagar, Kashmir, India; son of Ram Nath Kak and Sarojani Kak; married Navnidhi Kak, Jan 21, 1979; children: Abhinav Gautam, Arushi. **EDUCATION:** Kashmir University, India, BE, 1967; Indian Institute of Technology at Delhi, India, PhD, 1970. **CAREER:** Indian Institute of Technology at Delhi, India, lecturer, 1971-74, asst prof, 1974-79; UNESCO, consultant, 1986, 1989-90;

Information Science, assoc editor, 1993-; Louisiana State University, assoc prof, 1979-83, professor, 1983-. **ORGANIZATIONS:** IEEE Computer, guest editor, 1981-82; Information Science, guest editor, 1991-93; Circuits, Systems, Signal Processing, guest editor, 1992-93; UNESCO, consultant, 1986, 1989-90. **HONORS/AWARDS:** Indian National Science Academy, Science Academy Medal, 1977; Kothari Institute, Kothari Award, 1977. **SPECIAL ACHIEVEMENTS:** Author, physics, computers and history of science: 10 books, 150 research articles, numerous papers; partially deciphered the Indus-Sarasvati (writings of 3rd millennium BC); discovered the Rigvedic astronomical code. **BIOGRAPHICAL SOURCES:** Science Reporter, 1978. **BUSINESS ADDRESS:** Professor, Electrical & Computer Engineering, Louisiana State University, Baton Rouge, LA 70803-5901, (504)388-5552.

KAKKAR, RITA
Health services manager. Indo-American. **PERSONAL:** Born Aug 9, 1948, Gwalior, Madhya Pradesh, India; daughter of Shivlal & Sarla Goswami; married Subhash Kakkar, Jul 29, 1973; children: Rahul, Nitin. **EDUCATION:** Bangalor, India, BS, home science; Genessee Hospital, internship in dietetics, 1973. **CAREER:** Genessee Hospital, therapeutic dietitian; Minuteman Home Care, case mgr in nutrition, currently. **HOME ADDRESS:** 15 Tanglewood Ln, Winchester, MA 01890, (617)721-2360.

KAKKAR, SUBASH
Steel company executive. Indo-American. **PERSONAL:** Born Nov 27, 1938, Peshawer, Punjab, India; son of Vishwa Mittar Kakkar and Kaushalya Kakkar; married Rita Kakkar, Jul 29, 1973; children: Rahul, Nitin. **EDUCATION:** Dehli Polytechnic, pre-engineering, 1960; VJTI, Bombay, India, BE, electrical, (w/honors), 1965; Deutsches Elektronen Synch, Germany, research, 1966-75. **CAREER:** North Shore Steel Co Inc, president, CEO, 1976-. **BUSINESS ADDRESS:** President & CEO, North Shore Steel Co Inc, 16 Oakville St, PO Box 330, Lynn, MA 01905, (617)598-1645.

KAKU, MICHIO
Educator. Japanese American. **PERSONAL:** Born Jan 24, 1947, San Jose, CA; son of Hideko Maruyama and Toshio Kaku. **EDUCATION:** Harvard, BA, 1968; University of California, Berkeley, PhD, 1972. **CAREER:** Princeton University, research associate, 1972-73; New York University, visiting professor, 1988-89; Institute for Advanced Study at Princeton, visiting professor, 1991; City University of New York, professor, 1973-. **ORGANIZATIONS:** American Physical Society, fellow, 1975-; Asian-Americans for Equality, board of directors, 1991-; National SANE/Freeze, board of directors, 1990-; Institute for Security and Co-operation in Outer Space, board of directors, 1983-. **HONORS/AWARDS:** America Physical Society, fellow. **SPECIAL ACHIEVEMENTS:** Published 70 articles in physics journals; author, 8 books: Beyond Einstein, Bantam; To Win A Nuclear War, South End Press; Quantum Field Theory, Oxford; Quarks, Symmetries & Strings, World Scientific Pubs; Introduction to Superstrings, Springer; Strings, Conformal Fields, and Topology, Springer; Nuclear Power: Both Sides, W W Norton; Hyperspace, Oxford. **BUSINESS ADDRESS:** Professor, Dept of Physics, City University of New York, 138th Street at Convent Avenue, New York, NY 10031, (212)650-8448.

KAKUTANI, MICHIKO
Book reviewer. Japanese American. **CAREER:** New York Times Book Review, book critic, culture reporter, currently. **BUSINESS ADDRESS:** Book Critic, Culture Desk, New York Times, 229 W 43rd St, New York, NY 10036, (212)556-1466. *

KALE, JAYANT R.
Educator. Indo-American. **PERSONAL:** Born Aug 8, 1955, Poona, Maharashtra, India; son of Raghunath B Kale and Kusumavati R Kale (deceased); married Alka J Kale, Sep 30, 1979; children: Sameer J. **EDUCATION:** Birla Institute of Technology & Science, BSc (with honors), 1975; Indian Institute of Management, PGDM, 1979; University of Texas, Dallas, 1981-83; The University of Texas, Austin, PhD, 1987. **CAREER:** Ballarpur Industries Ltd, executive assistant, purchase, 1979-81; University of Texas, Austin, assistant instructor, 1983-86; Georgia State University, assistant professor of finance, 1986-91, associate professor of finance, 1991-. **ORGANIZATIONS:** American Finance Association, 1985-; Financial Management Association, 1985-; Western Finance Association, 1985-; Eastern Finance Association, 1986-; Southern Finance Association, 1986-; Phi Kappa Phi, 1985-90. **HONORS/AWARDS:** Financial Management Assn, Best Paper in Corporate Finance, 1989, Best Paper in Investments, 1988; Eastern Finance Assn, Outstanding Paper in Corporate Finance, 1992, 1988, Outstanding Paper

in Investments, 1988, Outstanding Paper in Options/Futures, 1991; Southern Finance Assn, Best Paper in Corporate Finance, 1989; Georgia State University, Faculty Recognition Award for Research, 1990. **SPECIAL ACHIEVEMENTS:** Several publications in: Journal of Finance, Journal of Financial Economics, Financial Management, Journal of Financial Research, Rand Journal of Economics, Economics Letters, Journal of Risk and Insurance, International Review of Economics and Finance, Quarterly Review of Economics and Finance. **BUSINESS ADDRESS:** Associate Professor, Dept of Finance, Georgia State University, College of Business Administration, Atlanta, GA 30303, (404)651-2798.

KALIMI, MOHAMMED YAHYA
Educator. Indo-American. **PERSONAL:** Born Nov 3, 1939, Surat, Gujarat, India; son of Yahya Kalimi & Safiya Kalimi; married Robina Kalimi, Aug 24, 1985; children: Omar. **EDUCATION:** Bombay University, India, BS, 1961, MS, 1964, PhD, 1970. **CAREER:** Columbia University, research trainee, 1972-74; Baylor College of Medicine, Houston, research associate, 1974-75; Albert Einstein College of Medicine, research assistant professor, 1975-79; Medical College of Virginia, assistant professor, 1979-81, associate professor, 1981-89, professor, 1989-. **ORGANIZATIONS:** Endocrine Society, 1980-; American Physiological Association, 1980-; American Association for Advancement of Science, 1980-. **HONORS/AWARDS:** NIH, Research Career Development Award, 1980-85. **SPECIAL ACHIEVEMENTS:** Author of over 60 manuscripts; 3 review articles; editor, Peptide Hormone Receptors; editor, The Biologic Role of Dehydro-epi androsterone. **BUSINESS ADDRESS:** Professor, Medical College of Virginia, Sanger Hall, Rm 3036, Box 551, Richmond, VA 23298-0551, (804)786-9500.

KALRA, BHUPINDER SINGH
Librarian. Indo-American. **PERSONAL:** Born Jun 15, 1936, Gujranwala, Punjab, India; son of Ishar Singh Kalra and Kartar Kaur; married Satnam Kaur, Jan 5, 1960; children: Punitinder, Pavneet, Upinder. **EDUCATION:** Panjab University, BA, 1957, BT, 1958, MA, 1965; University of Western Ontario, MLS, 1970. **CAREER:** Khalsa High School, Eng & Soc Studies Dept, head, 1958-62; Central School, India, History Dept, head, 1962-67; City of Ontario, Dept of Education, principal, elementary schools, 1967-69; Niles Library District, asst librarian, 1970-73, head branch librarian, 1973-86, reference librarian, 1987-. **ORGANIZATIONS:** ALA, PLA & RASD Divisions, 1977-, sections: MLS, PLSS, SMLS, IIS, MARS, round table: EMIERT; Sikh Religious Society, religious scty, 1982, exec scty, 1983, financial scty, 1984. **SPECIAL ACHIEVEMENTS:** Proficient in Hindi, Urdu & Panjabi; conservation & preservation of library materials; holding summer camps; teaching religious & cultural values to community children. **HOME ADDRESS:** 1156 S Glenn Trail, Elk Grove Village, IL 60007, (708)529-8607. **BUSINESS ADDRESS:** Reference Librarian, Niles Public Library District, 6960 Oakton St, Niles, IL 60714, (708)967-8554.

KALRA, RAJIV
Educator. Indo-American. **PERSONAL:** Born Jun 15, 1952, Bareilly, India; son of Satya Pal Kalra and Tara Kalra; married Seema R Kalra, Mar 17, 1979; children: Nidhi R, Anita R. **EDUCATION:** Agra University, MSc, 1972; Delhi University, LLB, 1975; Loyola University, Chicago, MBA, 1986; University of Cincinnati, PhD, 1989; Institute of Chartered Financial Analysts, Virginia, chartered financial analysts, 1993. **CAREER:** K D R Wool Products Pvt Ltd, commercial manager, 1977-83; Cargill Inc, research chemist, 1984-86; University of Cincinnati, graduate assistant, 1987-89; Moorhead State University, associate professor, 1989-. **ORGANIZATIONS:** Financial Management Association, 1989-; American Finance Association, 1989-; Eastern Finance Association, 1989-; Mid-West Finance Association, 1989-; Southern Finance Association, 1989-; Southwestern Finance Association, 1989-; Investment Management Institute, 1989-. **HONORS/AWARDS:** Moorhead State University, research fellowship, 1989-93; faculty improvement grant, 1990-92, research release time, 1990-91, cash merit award, 1989-90; University of Cincinnati, Val E Boeh Outstanding Graduate Student, 1988. **SPECIAL ACHIEVEMENTS:** "The Chernobyl Nuclear Accident & Electric Utility Share Prices," QJBE, September, 1993; "In Defense of Plant Closings," Jl App Bus Rsch, September 1992; "Common-Time Disaster Studies: A Case Example Using the Bhopal...," 1992; "A Note on Plant Closing Decisions," Financial Management, forthcoming; "Federal National Mortgage Association...," Great Events from History II, 1994. **BUSINESS ADDRESS:** Associate Professor of Finance, Dept of Business Administration, Moorhead State University, 260A Bridges, Moorhead, MN 56563-0001, (218)236-4655.

KAM, JAMES T.-K.
Engineer. Chinese American. **PERSONAL:** Born Jul 29, 1945, Hong Kong; son of Nai-Fai Kam and Big-Chun Au; married Winna M Kam, Jun 9, 1974; children: Kelvin K, Theresa P. **EDUCATION:** University of Manitoba, Canada, BS, 1970; U of C, Berkeley, PhD, 1974. **CAREER:** UC, Berkeley, research assistant, 1970-74; UC, Davis, research/teaching associate, 1974-75; International Engineering Company, associate engineer, 1975-79; Science Application Inc, senior engineer, 1979-81; Davy Mckee, chief engineer, 1981-85; Morrison Knudsen, principal engineer, 1985-. **ORGANIZATIONS:** American Society of Civil Engineers, 1979-; National Association of Groundwater; Scientists and Engineers, 1987-; Sigma Xi, 1974-75; Lions Club, director, 1983-85. **HONORS/AWARDS:** U of C, Berkeley, Carolyn Meek Graduate Fellowship, 1973-74. **SPECIAL ACHIEVEMENTS:** Book, "Computer Methods for the 80's in the Mineral Industry," Society of Mining Engineers of the American Institue of Mining, Metallurogical and Petroleum Engineer New York, 1979. **HOME ADDRESS:** 2430 35th Ave, San Francisco, CA 94116. **BUSINESS PHONE:** (415)442-7549.

KAM, LIT-YAN
Engineer. Chinese American. **PERSONAL:** Born Aug 25, 1939, Canton, Kwong Tung, China; son of Kum-Chuen and Wah Kwok Kam; married Sau-Wai Kam, Apr 22, 1973; children: Kerwin K W, Clarence K L, Clement K M. **EDUCATION:** National Taiwan University, BSME, 1962; Georgia Institute of Technology, MSME, 1970. **CAREER:** Giffels Associates LTD, mech engr, 1965; Canadian Marconi Co, mech design engr, 1965-68; Modine Mfg Co, design devel engr, 1970-72; Emerson Elec Co, In-Sink-Erator Div, project engr, 1972-77; Shick Inc, advance devel engr, 1977-78; AMP Inc, proj mgr, devel engr, 1978-86; AT&T-Bell Labs, mbr of tech staff, 1986-. **ORGANIZATIONS:** American Society of Mechanical Engineers, 1971-; State of Wisconsin, professional engr, 1972-; Province of Ontario, Canada, professional engr, 1965-88; Jersey Shore Chinese School, bd mbr, treasurer, 1988-; AT&T-Bell Labs Asian Americans for Affirmative Action Committee, 1988-91; The United Chinese Americans of Monmouth, 1987-; Chinese-American Culture Assn, 1989-. **HONORS/AWARDS:** US government patent awards: Terminal for Connection to a Flat Conductor, 1982, Socket for a Bubble Memory Package, 1982, Socket for a Ceramic Chip Carrier, 1983, Flat Cable to Planar Circuit Connector, 1983, Multi-Contact Connectors for Closely-Spaced Conductors, 1984. **SPECIAL ACHIEVEMENTS:** Author: The Finite Element Method for Stress and Deformation Analysis, master's thesis, Georgia Institute of Technology, 1970; teacher: Jersey Shore Chinese School, 1988-. **BUSINESS ADDRESS:** Technical Staff Member, AT&T Bell Laboratories, 101 Crawfords Corner Rd, Rm 3D602, PO Box 3030, Holmdel, NJ 07733-3030, (908)949-2652.

KAM, MEI-KI F. P.
Artist. Chinese American. **PERSONAL:** Born Aug 8, 1938, Zhu Hai, Guangdong, China; daughter of Yuk-Tung Cheung & Chi-Sand Young; married Raymond Y W Chow, Oct 9, 1963; children: Vanki Chow, Dominic C Chow. **EDUCATION:** New York University, cert interior decor, 1967; Art Student League, 1977-78; Edgar Whitney Workshop, 1979-82. **CAREER:** Salmagundi Club, watercolor instructor, 1982-85; Pastel Society of America, pastel instsructor, 1987-88; Jackson Height Art Club, watercolor instsructor, 1985-86. **ORGANIZATIONS:** Salmagundi Club; Pastel Society of America; Hudson Valley Art Association; Knickerbocker Artists; Audubon Artists; US Coast Guard Artists; Pen & Brush; American Artist Professional League. **HONORS/AWARDS:** Salmagundi Club, awards, 1982-93; Hudson Valley Art Association, Charles Davies Memorial Award of Excellence in Water Colors, 1985; Pastel Society of America, Morilla Canson Talens Award, 1987-88; Pastel Society of America, Sidney Kalikow Award, 1992; Pen & Brush, solo watercolor exhibition, 1990, solo pastel exhibition, 1991. **SPECIAL ACHIEVEMENTS:** Drawing with Pastel by Ron Lister, Prentice Hall, 1982; Reader Pictures Exhibited, The Artist, England, Aug 1981. **BIOGRAPHICAL SOURCES:** Art Speak, NY, Solos Place An Artist At Risk, p 18, April 1992, Can Representational Painting be New Art, p 21, May 1991. **HOME ADDRESS:** 45-23 Union St, Flushing, NY 11355, (718)539-1642.

KAM, THOMAS K. Y.
Educator. Chinese American. **PERSONAL:** Born Nov 12, 1955, Honolulu, HI; son of William K Y & Mae S M Kam; married Sally B H Kam, Jul 9, 1983; children: Tiffany L M, Stephen C M. **EDUCATION:** University of Hawaii, BBA, 1975, MBA, 1978. **CAREER:** Coopers & Lybrand, intern, 1975-76; Beckers CPA Review Course, instructor, 1982-83; Hawaiian Electric Co, Inc, statistical assistant, 1976-78, associate budget analyst, 1978-86; West Oahu College, lecturer, 1986; State of Hawaii, adult education teacher, 1977-; Hawaii Pacific University, assistant professor, 1984-. **ORGANIZATIONS:** Toastmasters, 1977-; Hawaii Adult Education Association, 1977-; Hawaii Business Educators Association, 1981-; Institute of Management Accountants, 1977-; American Institute of CPA's, 1977-; Friends of the Library of Hawaii; Kam's Society, 1983-; Junio Achievement, 1970-84; Kams' Society, 1983-; numerous others. **HONORS/AWARDS:** Phi Eta Sigma; Hawaii Adult Education Association, Co-Adult Education Teacher of the Year, 1988; Institute of Management Accountants, CMA Certificate, 1987; State of Hawaii, CPA Certificate, 1977. **BUSINESS ADDRESS:** Assistant Professor of Accounting & Finance, Hawaii Pacific University, 1060 Bishop St, Rm 402, Honolulu, HI 96813.

KAM, VERNON T.
Educator. Chinese American. **PERSONAL:** Born Sep 2, 1933, Honolulu, HI; son of Henry Kam and Maizie Kam; married Alice, Aug 15, 1965; children: Carolyn, Garret. **EDUCATION:** University of Hawaii, BA, 1955; University of California, Berkeley, MBA, 1959, PhD, 1968. **CAREER:** Los Angeles County, auditor, 1959-60; University of Illinois, Chicago, assistant professor, 1965-69; California State University, Hayward, professor, 1969-87, Department of Accounting & CIS, chair, 1987-. **ORGANIZATIONS:** American Accounting Association, 1965-; American Institute of CPAs, 1969-. **SPECIAL ACHIEVEMENTS:** Author, Accounting Theory, John Wiley, 1986, 1990; Survey: Consolidation of Financial Statements, McGraw-Hill, 1992. **MILITARY SERVICE:** US Army, 1st lt, 1955-57. **BUSINESS ADDRESS:** Professor, California State University, Hayward, School of Business and Economics, Hayward, CA 94542-3000, (510)881-3336.

KAM, WILLIAM
Structural engineer. Chinese American. **PERSONAL:** Born Sep 9, 1923, Canton, China; son of Yu Tong Kam and Wai Shi; married Sue Lee Kam, Aug 29, 1955; children: Christopher, Christina. **EDUCATION:** University of Tennessee, BSCE, 1950, MSCE, 1952; Columbia University, attended 1952-54. **CAREER:** Singstad and Kehart, sr structural engineer, 1949; Howard Needles Tammen & Bergendorf, sr structural engineer, 1949-52; Hardesty & Hanover, sr structural engineer, 1952-56; Stone & Webster, sr structural engineer, 1956; Ebasco Services Inc, sr structural engineer, 1957-58; Ammann & Whitney, sr structural engineer, 1958-62; Parsons, Brinckerhoff, lead structural engineer, 1962-. **ORGANIZATIONS:** State of New York, Licensed Professional Engineer. **SPECIAL ACHIEVEMENTS:** Principal structural designer for the Aqueduct Station, proposed John F Kennedy International Airport Connection; participated in the design of the Delair Bridge, the world's third-longest-span vertical lift bridge; participated in the design of the Gateway Arch, St Louis; participated in the design of the Pittsburgh Amphitheater; principal structural engineer for major and prestigious immersed tube tunnels throughout the US, Denmark and Hong Kong. **BUSINESS ADDRESS:** Lead Structural Engineer, Parsons, Brinckerhoff Quade & Douglas Inc, One Penn Plaza, New York, NY 10119, (212)465-5195.

KAMIYAMA, OSAMU
Organization/sports administrator. Japanese American. **PERSONAL:** Born Oct 24, 1947, Tokyo, Japan; son of Jiro and Fumiko; married Tsuneko, Nov 1, 1982; children: Kento, Go. **EDUCATION:** Nihon University, BA, 1970; Ithaca College, MS, 1976; Springfield College, PhD candidate, 1980. **CAREER:** Japanese School of NY, physical ed dir, 1976-80; Tokyo-NY YMCA Partnership, program dir, 1982-86; Staten Island YMCA, sr program dir, 1986-90; Ridgewood YMCA, US-Japan Relationship, program development, dir, 1990-. **ORGANIZATIONS:** Professional Directors Assn, 1982-. **HONORS/AWARDS:** New York YMCA, Excellence Achievement Award, 1989. **SPECIAL ACHIEVEMENTS:** Fluent in Japanese; article published in Perspective, the professional directors magazine, 1993; organized, directed: first Senior Olympics, New York, 1989-90. **BUSINESS ADDRESS:** Director, US-Japan Relationship, Program Development, YMCA, 112 Oak St, Ridgewood, NJ 07450, (201)444-5600.

KAMO, YOSHINORI
Educator. Japanese American. **PERSONAL:** Born Jun 20, 1958, Ashikaga, Tochigi, Japan; son of Yutaka and Tamae Kamo; married Akiko Kamo, Mar 21, 1982; children: Shota Jason, Kenta Sean. **EDUCATION:** Tokyo University, BA, 1982; University of Washington, MA, 1985, PhD, 1989. **CAREER:** University of Washington, research assistant, 1985-89; Louisiana State University, asst professor, 1989-. **ORGANIZATIONS:** American Sociological Assn, 1987-; Intl Institute of Sociology, 1986-; National Council of Family Relations,

1988-; Southern Sociological Society, 1990-; Research on Aging, editorial board, 1988-. **SPECIAL ACHIEVEMENTS:** 20 publications on sociology; volunteer interpreter for Mr and Mrs Hattori, whose son was shot and killed in Baton Rouge. **BUSINESS ADDRESS:** Assistant Professor, Sociology, Louisiana State University, Baton Rouge, LA 70803, (504)388-5352.

KAN, DIANA
Painter, lecturer. Chinese American. **PERSONAL:** Born Mar 3, 1926, Hong Kong; daughter of Kar Kam Shek & Sing Ying (both deceased); married Paul Schwartz, May 24, 1952 (deceased); children: Sing-Si Schwartz. **EDUCATION:** The Arts Students League, 1949; Beaux-Arts; Grande Chaumiere, Paris, 1952. **CAREER:** Self-employed painter, currently; Art Students League of New York, instructor, Smithsonian Institution's Resident Association Program, instructor. **ORGANIZATIONS:** National Academy of Design, associate member; Royal Society of Arts, fellow. American Watercolor Society, board of directors; Allied Artists of America, corresponding secretary; Audubon Artists, vice president; The Pen and Brush, board of directors; Catherine Lorillard Wolfe Art Club; The Art Students League of New York; The National Arts Club, exhibition committee; The Overseas Press Club of America, art committee, co-chairman; The National League of American Pen Women; Washington Square Business and Professional Women's Club, art chairman; The Lotos Club; The Salmagundi Club; Knickerbocker Artists. **HONORS/ AWARDS:** The National Arts Club, Popular Prize Award, 1986; Catherine Lorillard Wolfe Art Club 90th Annual, Dorothy Barber's Award, 1986; Knickerbocker Artists, New York, The Silver Medal of Honor, 1988; Allied Artists of America, The Mary Lou Fitzgerald Memorial Award, 1988, Gold Medal Honor, 1991; The National Arts Club Artist Members Exhibition, Special Award, 1989; The Pen and Brush, Margaret Sussman Memorial Award, 1989, Margaret Sussman Award, 1987; The Allied Artists of America 73rd Annual, National Arts Club Award, 1986; Catherine Lorillard Wolfe Art Club 91st Annual, Grand Central Art Galleries Award, 1987, Gold Medal of Honor, 1990; Knickerbocker Artists NY, Gold Medal of Honor, 1990; National Academy of Design Certificate of Merit, 1991, 1992; Audubon Artists, Gold Medal of Honor, 1991; Honorable Raymond L Flynn, mayor of Boston, ploclamation, Diana Kan Appreciation Day, 1991. **SPECIAL ACHIEVEMENTS:** "White Cloud," Commercial Press, Shanghai, China, 1938; "The How and Why of Chinese Painting," Van Nostrand Reinhold Co, 1986, Simon and Schuster Inc, 1990; several exhibitions, 1935-; Eastern Spirit, Western World, film, acquired by BBC and broadcast throughout Great Britain, broadcast on "Western World: A Profile of Diana Kan," US, 126 stations, 1992. **BUSINESS ADDRESS:** Artist, The National Arts Club, 15 Grammercy Park S, New York, NY 10003, (212)420-8632.

KAN, KIT-KEUNG
Physicist. Chinese American. **PERSONAL:** Born Dec 7, 1943, Canton, China; son of Ho-Ming Kan and Ngan-Chok Hon Kan; married Yuen-Han Kam Kan, Sep 2, 1969; children: Min-Yen, Min-Ying. **EDUCATION:** Chinese University of Hong Kong, BSc, 1966; University of Maryland, PhD, 1975. **CAREER:** University of Texas, research associate, 1975-78; University of Maryland, research associate, 1978-81; JAYCOR, principal scientist, 1981-. **ORGANIZATIONS:** American Physical Society, 1973-. **HONORS/AWARDS:** Chatham Gallery, Hong Kong, 1st place award, watercolor, First Open Competition, 1964; Greater Reston Art Center, Reston, VA, Audrey Lyle Memorial Award, 1982. **SPECIAL ACHIEVEMENTS:** Published in Nuclear Physics, Physical Review, Review of Modern Physics, 1975-83; art work exhibited in Hong Kong, Taipei, New York and Washington DC, 1968-. **BIOGRAPHICAL SOURCES:** Hsiung Shih Art Monthly 242, p 152, 1991, 214, p 115, 1988; Artists of Chinese Origin in North American Directory, 1st ed, p 95, 1993. **HOME ADDRESS:** 6809 Tammy Ct, Bethesda, MD 20817.

KAN, MICHAEL
Museum administrator. Chinese American. **PERSONAL:** Born Jul 17, 1933, Shanghai, China; married Mimi Kan; children: Gregory. **EDUCATION:** Columbia University, BA, art history, anthropology, 1953, MA, art history, 1969, MPhil, art history, 1973; SUNY, MFA, ceramics, 1957. **CAREER:** University of California, Berkeley, Dept of Environmental Design, lecturer, 1964-66; Finch College, Dept of Art History, lecturer, 1966-67; Brooklyn Museum, Dept of African, Oceanic and New World Cultures, curator, 1968-75; Detroit Institute of Arts, beginning 1976, Art Dept, executive asst director, currently. **ORGANIZATIONS:** Los Angeles County Museum, guest curator, 1970; American Assn of Museums; Institute of Andean Studies. **SPECIAL ACHIEVEMENTS:** Author of numerous exhibition catalogues. **MILITARY SERVICE:** US Army, 1957-59. **BUSINESS ADDRESS:** Executive Asst

Director, Arts Dept, Detroit Institute of Arts, 5200 Woodward Ave, Detroit, MI 48202, (313)833-4003.*

KAN, VICTOR
Computer service company executive. Chinese American. **PERSONAL:** Born Sep 30, 1946, Shanghai, China; son of Shek Nung Kan and Lily Kan; married Lucy Kan, Aug 17, 1974; children: Erik, Christopher, Jennifer. **EDUCATION:** University of Illinois, Chicago, BS, 1971. **CAREER:** Systems Architects, vice president, 1971-84; ViaTech Systems, president, 1984-. **ORGANIZATIONS:** Fairfax County Public School Education Foundation, trustee, 1993-; George Mason University Century Club. **HONORS/AWARDS:** Government Computer News, Industry Information Technology Award, 1991-93. **SPECIAL ACHIEVEMENTS:** Washington Technology, Fastest Growing Co in Mid Atlantic, 1988-92. **BUSINESS ADDRESS:** President, ViaTech Systems, Inc, 510 W Annandale Rd, Falls Church, VA 22046, (703)237-6864.

KAN, YUE-SAI (YU-XI JIN)
Television executive, cosmetics executive. Chinese American. **PERSONAL:** Born Oct 6, 1947, Guilin, China; daughter of Kan Wing-Lin & Lee Wai-Kun; married James R McManus, Feb 1989. **EDUCATION:** BYU, Hawaii, BA, 1969. **CAREER:** "One World," television show, producer, host, 1987-90; Yue-Sai Kan Inc, president, 1969-; Yue-Sai Kan Cosmetics Ltd, president, 1990-. **ORGANIZATIONS:** Tianjin University, China, professor; Women's Forum; Heilongjiang Tourism Bureau, China, advisor, vice chairman; Guangzhou Province Overseas Chinese Association, advisor. **HONORS/ AWARDS:** Better World Society, Global Communications Award, 1988; entered into Congressional Record, 3 times, 1987-89; Massachusetts State College, honorary doctorate degree in humanities, 1990. **SPECIAL ACHIEVEMENTS:** Author: Yue-Sai's Guide to Asian Beauty, San Lian Publishing, Shanghai, 1993; produced video cassette: Guide to Asian Beauty, China Video. **BIOGRAPHICAL SOURCES:** "Queen of the Middle Kingdom," Time Magazine, December 19, 1988; "Empire of Day & Night Creams," New York Times, August 16, 1992; People Magazine, May 18, 1987. **HOME ADDRESS:** 6 Sutton Square, New York, NY 10022, (212)223-0278.

KAN, YUET WAI
Educator. Hong Kong American. **PERSONAL:** Born Jun 11, 1936, Hong Kong; son of Tong Po Kan and Lai Wan Li; married Alvera Lorraine Limauro, May 10, 1964; children: Susan Jennifer, Deborah Ann. **EDUCATION:** University of Hong Kong, BS, MB, 1958, DSc, 1980. **CAREER:** Harvard Medical School, asst professor of pediatrics, 1970-72; University of California, SF, assoc prof of med & lab med, 1972-77, prof of med & lab med, 1977-, Louis K Diamond prof of hematology, 1983-; San Francisco Gen Hosp, hematology service chief, 1972-1979; Howard Hughes Med Inst, investigator, 1976-; University of Hong Kong, director, institute of molecular biology, 1990-. **ORGANIZATIONS:** National Academy of Sciences, chairman, section 41; American Society of Hematology, fmr president; American Society of Human Genetics; Association of American Physicians; Royal Society, fellow; Assn of Chinese Geneticists in America, fmr president; Society of Chinese Bioscientists in America, fmr sec-treasurer; Amer Academy of Arts & Sciences, fellow. **HONORS/AWARDS:** US Pan Asian America Chamber of Commerce, Excellence 2000 Award, 1993; NIH Christopher Columbus Award, 1992; Lasker Foundation, Albert Lasker Clinical Medical Research Award, 1991; Warren Alpert Fdn, Fdn Prize, 1989; Sanremo International Award for Genetic Research, 1989; honorary degrees: University of Cagliari, Sardinia, Italy, MD, 1981; Chinese University of Hong Kong, DSc, 1981; University of Hong Kong, DSc, 1987. **SPECIAL ACHIEVEMENTS:** Author, "On a Slow Boat from China," Clin Res, vol 32: pp 487-490, 1984. **BUSINESS ADDRESS:** Louis K Diamond Professor of Hematology, University of California, San Francisco, Third & Parnassus Avenues, Rm U426, San Francisco, CA 94122, (415)476-5841.

KANAYA, BARBARA J.
Retail company executive. Japanese American. **PERSONAL:** Born Jul 9, 1946, Ontario, OR; daughter of Tadao Inouye and Susan Inouye; married Doug, May 30, 1970; children: Melissa, Craig. **EDUCATION:** University of Washington, BA, business, 1968. **CAREER:** Nordstrom, vice president, corp merchandise manager, women's accessories, 1974-. **HOME ADDRESS:** 16757 154 Ave SE, Renton, WA 98058, (206)226-3018.

KANEDA, HIROMITSU
Educator. Japanese American. **PERSONAL:** Born Jun 5, 1934, Osaka, Japan; married Noriko; children: David H, Stephen A, Kyoko L. **EDUCATION:**

Doshisha University, BA, 1957; Amherst College, BA, 1959; Stanford University, MA, 1961, PhD, 1964. **CAREER:** University of California, Davis, assistant professor, 1963-68; Yale University, visiting economist, 1966-67; University of California, associate professor, 1968-73; Pakistan Institute of Development Economics, research advisor, 1968-69; World Bank, senior economist, 1975-76; University of California, professor, 1973-. **ORGANIZATIONS:** Applied Economics Research Center, University of Karachi, Pakistan, international board of editors, 1982-; American Economic Association, 1964-. **BUSINESS ADDRESS:** Professor, Dept of Economics, University of California, Davis, CA 95616, (916)752-1581.

KANEGAI, TOY
Community center administrator. Japanese American. **CAREER:** West Los Angeles Japanese American Community Center, president, 1993-.∗

KANEKO, RYOJI LLOYD
Personal computer trainer/systems analyst. Japanese American. **PERSONAL:** Born Apr 11, 1951, Los Angeles, CA; son of Hayao Kaneko and Yoshiko Kawaguchi Kaneko; married Marie A Kaneko, Jun 29, 1985; children: Laura Shigemi. **EDUCATION:** East Los Angeles College, 1969-71; California State University, Long Beach, BA, creative writing, 1974; University of California, Los Angeles, professional designation, training & human resource development, 1985. **CAREER:** Disneyland, character, toy soldier, 1972-75; Teledyne-Geotronics, International Training, supervisor, 1975-80; Hughes Aircraft Company, production control, administrator, 1980-87; Great Western Bank, PC trainer, systems analyst III, 1987-. **ORGANIZATIONS:** Chorale Bel Canto, bass singer, program editor, 1992-; American Society for Training and Development, Los Angeles interchange editor, 1982-85; Trainers Association of Southern California, 1992-; Southern California Judges Association, associate chief judge, director of training, 1973-. **HONORS/AWARDS:** California State University, Long Beach, Athletic Letter-Rowing, 1974, Gold Press Card, 1972; International Association of Quality Circles, Los Angeles, guest speaker, 1985, Orlando, Florida, guest speaker, 1986. **SPECIAL ACHIEVEMENTS:** CSU, Long Beach, Prospector Yearbook, academics editor, 1972; ''Building Teamwork and Productivity through Individual Development,'' IAQC, 1985; ''Quality Circles Turnover,'' IAQC, 1986; Drum Corps News, Boston, Mass, senior staff writer, 1973-75; Bellflower First Christian Church, soloist/choir member, 1980-92. **HOME ADDRESS:** 11139 Loch Avon Drive, Whittier, CA 90606-1641. **BUSINESS PHONE:** (818)775-8870.

KANEKO, WILLIAM MASAMI
Association executive. Japanese American. **PERSONAL:** Born Nov 22, 1960, Honolulu, HI; son of Tadashi & Sadako Kaneko; married Reyna A Kaneko, Jul 5, 1992. **EDUCATION:** University of Puget Sound, BA, 1983. **CAREER:** Amdahl Corp, staff accountant, 1983-85; American Medical Intl, sr intl accountant, 1985-87; CORO Foundation, fellow in public affairs, 1987-88; Office of the Governor, Hawaii, policy analyst, 1988-93. **ORGANIZATIONS:** Japanese American Citizens League, national vp, Public Affairs, 1990-, Honolulu Chapter, president, 1990-93; State of Hawaii, board of public accountancy, 1990-93; US Dept of Justice, office of redress admin, Citizens Adv Bd, 1991; University of Puget Sound, national alumni bd member, 1991-; American Planning Association, bd member, 1989-91; East West Players, bd member, 1986-87. **HONORS/AWARDS:** US Dept of Justice, Attorney General's Award for Public Service, 1992; ACLU of Hawaii, Allan Saunders Award for Civil Liberties, 1993; JACL of Hawaii, Distinguished Service Award, 1993; State of Hawaii House & Senate, Commendation for Public Service, 1993. **HOME ADDRESS:** 8500 16th St #423, Silver Spring, MD 20910, (310)589-5452. **BUSINESS ADDRESS:** National Vice President, Public Affairs, Japanese American Citizens League, 1765 Sutter St, San Francisco, CA 94115, (415)921-4225.

KANEMITSU, MATSUMI. *See* Obituaries.

KANESHIGE, HARRY MASATO
Educator. **PERSONAL:** Born Jul 11, 1929, Aiea, HI; son of Jiro and Tsurue Kaneshige; married Sally, Aug 22, 1963 (died 1975); children: Loren, Michael; married Susan, Aug 29, 1981. **EDUCATION:** University of Wisconsin, Madison, BSCE, 1951, MSCE, 1952, PhD, 1959. **CAREER:** University of Wisconsin, Madison, instructor/project associate, 1954-58; Ohio University, asst professor, beginning 1958, professor, currently. **ORGANIZATIONS:** Ohio Environmental Protection Agency, advisory board of examiners, 1967-; Ohio Department of Natural Resources, Ohio Water Advisory Council, 1991-; City of Athens Planning Commission, 1990-. **HOME ADDRESS:** 179 Longview

Heights, Athens, OH 45701-3341, (614)593-5285. **BUSINESS ADDRESS:** Professor, Dept of Civil Engineering, Ohio University, Stocker Ctr, Athens, OH 45701-2979, (614)593-1472.

KANG, BYUNG I.
Librarian. Korean American. **PERSONAL:** Born Aug 31, 1943, Seoul, Republic of Korea; daughter of Young Lee and Jai Song; married Dae Ki Kang, Dec 6, 1969; children: Eric C, Anne C. **EDUCATION:** Ewha Womans University, Korea, BA, 1965; University of Oregon, MLS, 1969. **CAREER:** Palomar College, Library/Media Center, cataloging librarian, 1990-. **ORGANIZATIONS:** California Library Association, 1990-; Technical Processing Group of Southern California, 1990-; Korean American Library Association, 1990-. **SPECIAL ACHIEVEMENTS:** Language proficiency: Korean. **BUSINESS ADDRESS:** Cataloging Librarian, Palomar College, Library/Media Center, 1140 W Mission Road, San Marcos, CA 92069, (619)744-1150.

KANG, CHANG-YUIL
Immunologist. Korean American. **PERSONAL:** Born Nov 28, 1954, Pusan, Republic of Korea; son of Hee-Kyong Kang & Yang-Hee Oh Kang; married Young-Youn Kang, Jan 27, 1984; children: Stephen D, Catherine. **EDUCATION:** Seoul National University, BSc, 1977, MS, 1981; State University of New York at Buffalo, PhD, 1987. **CAREER:** Seoul National University, department assistant, 1981-82; Roswell Park Cancer Institute, research affiliate, 1983-86, postdoctoral research fellow, 1986-87; IDEC Pharmaceutical, scientist I, 1987-89, scientist II, 1989-92, scientist III, 1992-. **ORGANIZATIONS:** American Association of Immunologists, 1989-. **HONORS/AWARDS:** National Institutes of Health, Small Business Innovation Grant, 1990-94. **SPECIAL ACHIEVEMENTS:** Over 40 articles in scientific publications, 1977-93; invention of AIDS therapeutic vaccine, 1993. **HOME ADDRESS:** 1736 Buttercup Rd, Encinitas, CA 92024, (619)436-6518. **BUSINESS ADDRESS:** Scientist III, IDEC Pharmaceutical Corp, 11011 Torreyana Rd, San Diego, CA 92121, (619)550-8664.

KANG, EUN CHUL
Educator. Korean American. **PERSONAL:** Born May 24, 1953, Seoul, Republic of Korea; son of Sun Kook Kang and Kum Ye Kim; married Esther Ruth Kang, Oct 15, 1981; children: Elizabeth, Samuel. **EDUCATION:** Sung Kyun Kwan University, BL, 1977; Seoul National University Graduate School, 1977-79; University of Michigan, MBA, 1985; University of Pennsylvania, PHD, 1991. **CAREER:** University of Pennsylvania, teaching assistant, 1986-91; California State University, San Marcos, assistant professor, 1991. **ORGANIZATIONS:** American Finance Association, 1988-; Western Finance Association, 1992-; The Society for Financial Studies, 1992-; Financial Management Association, 1993-. **MILITARY SERVICE:** Korean Navy, lieutenant junior, 1979-82. **BUSINESS ADDRESS:** Assistant Professor, California State University, 333 Twin Oaks Valley Rd, San Marcos, CA 92096-0001, (619)752-4223.

KANG, HEESOOK SOPHIA
Government official. Korean American. **PERSONAL:** Born Mar 29, 1958, Seoul, Republic of Korea; daughter of Seong Ho Kang and Hae Soon Kang. **EDUCATION:** Ewha Womens University, 1977-78; Maryland Institute College of Art, BFA, 1982; Pratt Institute Graduate School, MFA, 1984. **CAREER:** Metropolitan Museum of Art, assistant coordinator, 1985-87; The City of New York, deputy director of the Mayor's Office for Asian Affairs, 1987-. **ORGANIZATIONS:** Asia Society, Korea Advisory Committee, 1992-; Korea Society, Young Professionals Committee, 1992-; Coalition of Asian/Pacific Americans, Steering Committee, 1989-; Asian American Arts Alliance, Inc, Advisory Committee, 1989-; Korean American Crime Prevention Committee, advisor, 1991-; Korean YMCA, youth advisor, 1991-. **HONORS/AWARDS:** Korean American Small Business Serv Ctr of NY, Certificate of Merit, 1989; Korean Apparel Contractors Association of NY, Certificate of Merit, 1991; Korean American Students Conference V, Certificate of Appreciation, 1991; Korean Association of New York, Certificate of Merit, 1991; Korean Construction Association of New York, Certificate of Merit, 1992; Korean American Community Service Center of New York, Certificate of Merit, 1993. **SPECIAL ACHIEVEMENTS:** Asian Community Relations, liaison between the mayor and Asian community; coordination with other city agencies; assist visiting Asian delegation. **BIOGRAPHICAL SOURCES:** The Korea Times, interview, p1, December 15, 1988; The Korea Central Daily, close-up, p2, August 19, 1988; The Sae Gae Times, interview, p2, August 31, 1988; Channel 31, WNYC, TBC Studio, 1989; The Korea Times, English Edition, interview, August 17, 1990; Open, Monthly Magazine, Korea, Korean Woman Power, pp

182-185, March, 1991; Channel 25, WNYE, Korean Town, April 5, 1991; The Korea Times (LA), "Korean American in The Mainstream," March 7, 1992. **BUSINESS ADDRESS:** Deputy Director, The Mayor's Office for Asian Affairs, 52 Chambers St, #317, New York, NY 10007, (212)788-2694.

KANG, HYUNGWON
Photojournalist. Korean American. **PERSONAL:** Born Mar 7, 1963, Kochang, Cholla Bukdo, Republic of Korea; son of Dae-Yang Kang & Kum-Rae Kang; married Daisy Kang, Apr 19, 1992. **EDUCATION:** UCLA, BA, political science, 1987. **CAREER:** Time Magazine, freelance photographer, 1987-; Los Angeles Times, staff photographer, 1990-. **ORGANIZATIONS:** Asian American Journalists Association; Korean American Journalists Association; National Press Photographers Association. **HONORS/AWARDS:** LA Times coverage of LA Riots, Pulitzer Prize, 1992. **SPECIAL ACHIEVEMENTS:** From the Streets to the Olympics, book, 1989.

KANG, JAMES JYH-HUEI
Consulting engineer. Taiwanese American. **PERSONAL:** Born Jul 2, 1955, Taitung, Taiwan; son of Young-Kun Kang and Shiao-Lien Kang; married Jung C Kang, Jun 12, 1982; children: Stacey C, Christine A. **EDUCATION:** National Tsing Hua University, BSCE, 1978; National Taiwan University, MSCE, 1980; Auburn University, PhD, chemical engineering, 1986. **CAREER:** Auburn University, research associate, 1986-88; Post, Buckley, Schuh & Jernigan Inc, sr chemical engr, 1988-90; Dames & Moore, sr chemical engr, 1990-93, mgr, associate, 1993-. **ORGANIZATIONS:** National Waterwell Assn, 1993-; Hazardous Research Control Inst, 1989-; Instrumentation Society Assn, 1992-. **SPECIAL ACHIEVEMENTS:** Several publications in the areas of soil/groundwater remediation and coal-based asphalt research. **BUSINESS ADDRESS:** Manager, Design and Construction Services Group, Dames & Moore, 6 Hutton Centre Dr, Ste 700, Santa Ana, CA 92707, (714)433-2000.

KANG, JOONHEE
Scientist. Korean American. **PERSONAL:** Born Feb 5, 1955, Seoul, Republic of Korea; son of Il-Hyung Kang and Jeom-Hee Jeon; married Mee Hye Kang, Aug 23, 1979; children: Angela S, Clara S. **EDUCATION:** Seoul National University, BS, 1977; Korea Advanced Science and Technology, MS, 1979; University of Minnesota, PhD, 1987. **CAREER:** Ulsan Institute of Technology, full-time instructor, 1979-82; University of Minnesota, research assistant, 1983-87; Argonne National Lab, research associate, 1987-89; Westinghouse Science & Technology Center, senior scientist, 1989-. **ORGANIZATIONS:** American Physical Society, 1986-. **HONORS/AWARDS:** Seoul National University, Presidential Award, 1977; Argonne National Lab, Pacesetter Award, 1988, Director's Award, 1989; Westinghouse, George Westinghouse Signature Award, 1990. **BUSINESS ADDRESS:** Senior Scientist, Westinghouse Science & Technology Center, 1310 Beulah Rd, 401-3X9B, Pittsburgh, PA 15235, (412)256-1472.

KANG, JUN-KOO
Educator. Korean American. **PERSONAL:** Born Mar 28, 1957, Munkyung, Kyung Sang Bukdo, Republic of Korea; son of Soo-suk Kang; married Myung-Sook Kang, Nov 20, 1982. **EDUCATION:** Korea University, BBA, 1982; Iowa State University, MS, 1986; Ohio State University, PhD, 1991. **CAREER:** Bank of Korea (central bank), junior economist, 1982-84; University of Rhode Island, assistant professor, 1991-. **ORGANIZATIONS:** American Finance Association, 1991-; Financial Management Association, 1991-; Western Finance Association, 1993-. **HONORS/AWARDS:** Korea University, Outstanding Academic Performance, 1975-78. **SPECIAL ACHIEVEMENTS:** "The International Market for Corporate Control: Mergers and Acquisitions of US Firms by Japanese Firms," Journal of Financial Economics, 1993; proficient in Korean, German. **BUSINESS ADDRESS:** Assistant Professor, Dept of Finance, University of Rhode Island, College of Business Administration, Ballentine Hall, #357, Kingston, RI 02881-0802, (401)792-5970.

KANG, KEEBOM
Educator. Korean American. **PERSONAL:** Born Jun 27, 1953, Seoul, Republic of Korea; son of Dr & Mrs Pong-shik Kang; married Reenah Choy, Dec 30, 1978; children: Janet, Hannah. **EDUCATION:** Seoul National University, Korea, BS, 1976; University of Texas, Austin, MS, 1979; Purdue University, PhD, 1984. **CAREER:** University of Miami, assistant professor, 1983-88; US Naval Postgraduate School, associate professor, 1988-. **ORGANIZATIONS:** Operations Research Society of America, 1978-; Institute of Industrial Engineers, 1980-; Institute of Management Science, 1980-; Society for Computer Simulations, 1980-; Sigma Xi, 1984-. **HONORS/AWARDS:** Naval Postgrad-

uate School, Faculty Performance Award, 1992, 1993; Purdue University, David Ross Fellowship, 1979. **SPECIAL ACHIEVEMENTS:** More than 30 technical articles and presentations published in professional journals and conference proceedings; language proficiency: Korean. **BUSINESS ADDRESS:** Professor, Dept of Systems Management, Naval Postgraduate School, Code AS/KK, Monterey, CA 93943, (408)656-3106.

KANG, SHIN T.
Educational administrator. **CAREER:** Kaes College, president, chancellor, currently. **BUSINESS ADDRESS:** President/Chancellor, Kaes College, 5909 N Rogers Ave, Chicago, IL 60646-5963, (312)725-1925.*

KANG, SUGWON
Educator. Korean American. **PERSONAL:** Born Oct 5, 1936, Seoul, Republic of Korea; son of Mr and Mrs Dae Gon Kang (both deceased); married Diana Staley Kang, Jul 1, 1972; children: Jonathan Logan, Caroline Evans. **EDUCATION:** Washburn University, BA, 1960; University of Kansas, MA, 1962; Columbia University, PhD, 1972. **CAREER:** Brooklyn College, CUNY, lecturer, instructor, 1964-67; New York University, instructor, assistant professor, 1967-73; Hartwick College, associate professor, professor, 1973-. **ORGANIZATIONS:** American Political Science Association, 1973-. **HONORS/AWARDS:** Columbia University, East Asian Institute Fellowship, 1962-64; American Philosophical Society, Research Grant, 1980; National Endowment for the Humanities, Fellowship, 1980-81. **SPECIAL ACHIEVEMENTS:** Publications in several areas of competence. **HOME PHONE:** (607)432-6916. **BUSINESS ADDRESS:** Professor, Hartwick College, Oneonta, NY 13820, (607)431-4930.

KANG, WENG POO
Educator. Chinese American. **PERSONAL:** Born Apr 6, 1953, Penang, Malaysia; son of Gek Meng Kang and Cheng Nai Lim; married Cen Li, Nov 27, 1991. **EDUCATION:** University of Texas, BSEE, 1981; Rutgers University, MSEE, 1983, PhD, 1988. **CAREER:** Rutgers University, teaching assistant, 1981-88; Vanderbilt University, assistant professor, 1988-. **ORGANIZATIONS:** IEEE, 1983-; International Meeting on Chemical Sensors, session chairperson, 1992. **HONORS/AWARDS:** Eta Kappa Nu, 1980; Tau Beta Pi, 1980. **SPECIAL ACHIEVEMENTS:** "Pd-SnOx MIS Capacitor as a New Type of Oxygen Sensor," IEEE Electron Device Letters, 1987; "Sensing Behavior of Pd-SnOx MIS Structure for Oxygen Detection," Sensor and Actuators, 1987; "Catalyst-Adsorptive Oxide-Semiconductor MIS Gaseous Detectors," Sensor and Actuators, 1993; "Novel Platinum-Tin Oxide-Silicon Nitride-Silicon Dioxide-Silicon Gas Sensing Device at Low Temperature," Applied Phys Lett, 1993; "Gas Sensitivities of Silicon MIS Capacitors Incorporated with Catalyst and Oxide Layers", J Electro Chem, 1993. **BUSINESS ADDRESS:** Assistant Professor, Vanderbilt University, Box 1661, Station B, Nashville, TN 37235, (615)322-0952.

KANG, WI JO
Educator, cleric. Korean American. **PERSONAL:** Born Mar 10, 1930, Jinju, Kyungnam, Republic of Korea; married Chong-Ja Nam. **EDUCATION:** Concordia Theological Seminary, MDiv, 1960; University of Chicago, PhD, 1967. **CAREER:** Columbia University, 1964-66; Valparaiso University, 1966-68; Concordia Seminary, 1968-74; Christ Seminary, Seminex, 1974-78; Yonsei University, Seoul, Korea, 1978-79; Wartburg Theological Seminary, world religions and mission, Wilhelm Loehe Professor, 1980-. **ORGANIZATIONS:** International Association of Mission Studies, executive committee, 1964-66; Association of Professors of Mission, president, 1989-90. **HONORS/AWARDS:** John Behnken Post Doctoral Fellowship, 1975; Lutheran Brotherhood Fellowship, 1985, 1987, 1991. **MILITARY SERVICE:** US Army, 7th US Army Division, 1950-53. **BUSINESS ADDRESS:** Wilhelm Loehe Professor of World Religions and Mission, Wartburg Theological Seminary, 333 Wartburg Place, Fritschel Hall, Dubuque, IA 52003.

KANG, YUNG C.
Dentist, educator. Korean American. **PERSONAL:** Born Aug 2, 1955, Seoul, Republic of Korea; married Wha-In Kang, Aug 2, 1982; children: Paul, Stephen. **EDUCATION:** Boston University, DMD, 1986; NYU, certificate, 1989. **CAREER:** Private practice, dentist, currently; NYU Dental School, asst professor, currently. **BUSINESS ADDRESS:** Dentist, 44 Sylvan Ave, #2E, Englewood Cliffs, NJ 07632, (201)944-0990.

KAN-MITCHELL, JUNE
Educator. Hong Kong American. **PERSONAL:** Born Jun 3, 1949, Hong Kong; daughter of Sewan Kaan & Kathleen Yueng; married Malcolm Stuart Mitchell, Aug 14, 1978; children: Ian Douglas Mitchell. **EDUCATION:** Smith College, BA, 1971; Yale University, PhD, 1977. **CAREER:** Yale University, postdoctoral fellow, 1977-78; University of Southern California School of Medicine, asst professor, 1982-91, assoc professor, 1991-. **ORGANIZATIONS:** Journal of Clinical Laboratory Analysis, assoc editor, 1985-; Human Antibodies and Hybridonas, assoc editor, 1989-; Vaccine Research, assoc editor, 1990-; Cancer Immunology Immunotherapy, assoc editor, 1993-97; Assoc Research Vision and Ophthalmology, committee, 1992-94; American Assn for Cancer Research, State legislative. **BIOGRAPHICAL SOURCES:** Cancer Immunol Immunotherapy, 1993; Investigative Ophthalmology Visual Science, 1993. **BUSINESS ADDRESS:** Assoc Professor, Pathology, University of Southern California, School of Medicine, 2025 Zonal Ave, Los Angeles, CA 90033, (213)224-6545.

KANO, SACHIO
Organization administrator. Japanese American. **CAREER:** Asian Rehabilitation Services, cofounder, 1972, board member, currently. **BUSINESS ADDRESS:** Board Member, Asian Rehabilitation Services, 601 S San Pedro St, Los Angeles, CA 90012, (213)623-2313.*

KANOJIA, RAMESH MAGANLAL
Research scientist. Indo-American. **PERSONAL:** Born Feb 15, 1933, Mangrol, Saurashtra, India; son of Maganlal H Kanojia and Maniben M Kanojia; married Neela, Dec 22, 1967; children: Preeti, Amee. **EDUCATION:** University of Bombay, Siddharth College, BS (honors) 1954, Dept of Chemical Technology, BS tech, 1956, MS, tech, 1961; University of Wisconsin, School of Pharmacy, PhD, 1966. **CAREER:** University of Bombay, Govt of India, sr research fellow, 1956-58, instructor, lecturer, 1958-60, Chaugule & Co, sr research chemist, 1960-61; University of Wisconsin, NIH Research Fellow, 1961-66; Ortho Pharmaceutical Corp, associate scientist, beginning 1965, scientist, until 1975, sr scientist, beginning 1976, principal scientist, until 1987; R W Johnson Pharmaceutical Research Institute, sr research scientist, 1987-. **ORGANIZATIONS:** University of Wisconsin, Indian Students Association, president, 1964-65. **HONORS/AWARDS:** University of Bombay, Mrs S D Masters Scholarship Award, 1956, Government of India, Senior Research Scholarship, 1956-58; University of Wisconsin, NIH Research Fellowship, 1961-66; Ortho Pharmaceutical Corporation, Philip B Hoffman Research Scientist Award, 1977, Discovery Awards (two), 1990. **SPECIAL ACHIEVEMENTS:** A total of about fifty publications and patents combined, 1966-; area of research: drug discovery. **HOME ADDRESS:** 18 Jeffrey Court, Somerville, NJ 08876-3611, (908)526-1328. **BUSINESS ADDRESS:** Senior Research Scientist, R W Johnson Pharmaceutical Research Institute, Route 202 South, PO Box 300, Raritan, NJ 08869, (908)704-4414.

KAO, KUNG-YING TANG
Biochemist (retired). Chinese American. **PERSONAL:** Born May 8, 1917, Nanjing, Kiangsu, China; daughter of Ti-Chi Tang & Nan-Fun C Tang; married Ching-Tai Byron Kao, Jul 26, 1943; children: Chien-Song Kao Shan, Daniel T, Donald T, David Byron. **EDUCATION:** National Kiangsu Medical College, MD, 1940; Purdue University, MS, 1950; University of Maryland, PhD, 1953. **CAREER:** Veterans Administration Center, chief, Geriatrics Research Laboratory, 1957-78. **ORGANIZATIONS:** American Institute of Nutrition, 1960-; American Chemical Society, 1950-; American Association for the Advancement of Science, 1957-. **BIOGRAPHICAL SOURCES:** Handbook of Geriatric Nutrition, edited by Jeng M Hsu & David, Robert L, p 56-57, Noyes Publications, 1981. **HOME ADDRESS:** 5 Gum Spring Rd, Brunswick, MD 21716, (301)834-8451.

KAO, RACE L.
Educator. Chinese American. **PERSONAL:** Born Dec 1, 1943, Chungking, China; son of Yu-Ho Kao and Tsing Tsou Kao; married Lidia Kao, Aug 18, 1969; children: Elizabeth, Grace. **EDUCATION:** National Taiwan University, BS, 1965; University of Illinois, MS, 1971, PhD, 1972. **CAREER:** M S Hershey Med Ctr, asst professor, 1976-77; University of Texas Med Branch, Galveston, asst professor, 1977-82; Washington University, associate professor, Dept of Surg, 1982-83; Allegheny-Singer Res Inst, director of surg res, 1983-92; Med Col of PA, professor of surgery (cardiothoracic), 1988-92; East Tennessee State University, Dept of Physiology, adjunct professor, 1992-, Dept of Surgery, prof & Carroll H Long Chair of Excellence for Surgical Research, 1992-. **ORGANIZATIONS:** Veterans Affairs, reviewer, 1988-; National Institutes of Health, reviewer and consultant, 1984-92; American Heart Assn (PA

Affiliate), res peer review, 1984-92, Animal Res Task Force, 1990-92; ASRI, editorial board, 1990-91, Scientific Report, 1990, Cardiovas/Pulmonary Standing Committee, 1989-92, Biological Committee, 1989-92. **SPECIAL ACHIEVEMENTS:** The Role of Adenosine in Cardioplegia, 1993; Cell Transplantation for Myocardial Repair: an Experimental Approach, 1992; Correlation of Electrophysiological Activation Patterns to Tension Generation, 1992; Right Latissimus Dorsi Cardiomyoplasty for Left Ventricular Failure, 1992; A Model of Left Ventricular Dysfunction Caused by Intracoronary Adriamycin, 1992. **BUSINESS ADDRESS:** Professor, Dept of Surgery, Carroll H Long Chair of Excellence for Surgical Research, East Tennessee State University, James H Quillen College of Medicine, Box 70, 575, Johnson City, TN 37614-0575, (615)461-7449.

KAO, TAI-WU
Educator. Chinese American. **PERSONAL:** Born Feb 8, 1934, ChenWu, Shantung, China; married Sun-yun Kao, Oct 25, 1959; children: Susan, Nancy, Cindy, John, James. **EDUCATION:** National Taiwan University, BSEE, 1958; National Chiaotung University, MSEE, 1961; University of Utah, PhD, 1965. **CAREER:** Loyola Marymount University, professor, 1965-; TRW Inc, senior system engineer, 1977-92. **ORGANIZATIONS:** IEEE, 1963-. **BUSINESS ADDRESS:** Professor, Loyola Marymount University, Loyola Blvd & W 80th St, Los Angeles, CA 90045-2699, (310)338-2824.

KAO, TIMOTHY TIEH-HSIUNG
Mental health service executive. Taiwanese American/Chinese American. **PERSONAL:** Born Feb 13, 1932, Taipei, Taiwan; son of Ming-Sue Kao and Yeh-Ho Lin-Kao; married Setsuko Kao, Jan 2, 1958; children: James, David. **EDUCATION:** University of California, Berkeley, 1954-55; University of Oregon, BS, 1958; Portland State University, MBA, 1960. **CAREER:** Oregon Primate Research Center, superintendent, 1960-65; University of Oregon Medical School, research associate, 1958-64; Microlaboratory, Inc, CFO/treasurer, 1967-70; Western Washington University, controller, 1970-76; University of Redland, vice president of finance, 1976-78; Waverly Children's Home, associate director, 1980-. **ORGANIZATIONS:** United Way Agency Association, treasurer/member of executive committee, 1992-. **SPECIAL ACHIEVEMENTS:** Oriental language interpreter for Mayor of Bellingham, Washington, 1972-76. **BUSINESS ADDRESS:** Associate Director/CFO, Waverly Children's Home, 3550 SE Woodward St, Portland, OR 97202, (503)234-7532.

KAO, YASUKO W.
Library administrator. Japanese American. **PERSONAL:** Born Mar 30, 1930, Tokyo, Japan; daughter of Kichiji and Sato Tanaka Watanabe; married Shih-Kung Kao, Apr 1, 1959 (deceased); children: John Sterling, Stephanie Margaret. **EDUCATION:** Tsuda University, BA, 1950; Waseda University, BA, 1955; University of Southern California, MSLS, 1960. **CAREER:** Takinogawa High School, teacher, 1950-57; University of Utah, catalog librarian, 1960-67, Catalog Division, head, 1975-90; Teikyo Loretto Heights University, library director, 1991-. **ORGANIZATIONS:** American Library Association, 1960-; ALA Resources and Technical Services Division, 1960-; ALA Asian Pacific Librarians Association, 1979-; Colorado Library Association, 1991-; Utah Library Association, 1975-90; Utah College Council, 1975-90, Asian Association of Utah, volunteer, 1984-90; Utah Chinese Community School, volunteer, 1974-80; American Lib Association, Beta Phi Mu Library Science Honorary Society, 1960-. **HONORS/AWARDS:** Waseda University, graduate fellowship, 1955-57. **SPECIAL ACHIEVEMENTS:** Contributor of articles to professional journals; directed major microform sets cataloging projects funded by US Dept of Education, 1981-83, 1985-86, 1987-89; project director for grant proposals to Japan Foundation and awarded library support fundings, 1983, 1985, 1987-89. **BUSINESS ADDRESS:** Library Director, Teikyo Loretto Heights University, 3001 S Federal Blvd, May Bonfils Stanton Library, Room 202, Denver, CO 80236, (303)937-4249.

KAPADIA, BHARAT S.
Business owner. Indo-American. **PERSONAL:** Born May 20, 1954, Valsad, Gujarat, India; son of Sakarlal C Kapadia; married Bhavna B Kapadia, Mar 2, 1979; children: Hetal B, Nirali B. **EDUCATION:** South Gujarat University, Surat, BCOM, 1976. **CAREER:** Howland, accounts payabel, 1977-84; D&B Computing Co, staff a/c, 1984-86; General Data Com Engineering, staff a/c, 1986-88; Interstate Beverage Store, owner, 1988-. **BUSINESS ADDRESS:** President, H&N Interstate Package Store, 1625 Hardeman Ave, Macon, GA 31201, (912)746-1620.

KAPADIA, H. VIREN

Company finance executive. Indo-American. **PERSONAL:** Born Sep 17, 1960, Bombay, India; son of Viren and Hansa; divorced. **EDUCATION:** Bombay International School, ICSE, 1976; Atlantic Community College, AS, 1983; Drexel University, BS, 1986. **CAREER:** Robert Morris Associates, financial analyst trainee, 1984-85; Sun Co, federal tax trainee, 1985-86; Kapadia & Co Inc, owner, 1986-; Sovereign Bank, AVP, 1990-; LSI Technologies, CFO, owner, 1986-. **HONORS/AWARDS:** Sovereign Bank, President's Club, 1991, President's Club & CEO Club, 1992, CEO & Director's Club, 1993. **BUSINESS ADDRESS:** CFO, LSI Technologies Inc, 600 Lower Landing Rd, Blackwood, NJ 08012, (609)228-9300.

KAPOOR, HARISH K.

High tech company executive. Indo-American. **PERSONAL:** Born Mar 2, 1957, Mandi, Himachal Pradesh, India; son of K P Kapoor and Kusum Kapoor. **EDUCATION:** Jiwaji University, BSEE, 1978; IIT, senior research fellow, 1978-81; University of Miami, MS, bio-med engineering, 1986; Florida Atlantic University, 1989-90. **CAREER:** IIT Delhi, 1978-81; University of Miami, Jackson Memorial Hospital, research assistant, 1981-82; Mount Sinai Medical Center, research assistant, 1982-84; DME Corp, project engineer, 1984-86; Computer Aided Logistics Engineering, president/founder, 1986-. **ORGANIZATIONS:** Greater Miami Chamber of Commerce, Bio-Med Exchange. **HONORS/AWARDS:** IEEE, India, Student Chapter, joint secretary, 1976; first prize for tech model, 1978. **SPECIAL ACHIEVEMENTS:** Dedicated some time working with the blind and children suffering with cerebral palsy; fluent in Hindi, English, Punjabi, Spanish, German. **BIOGRAPHICAL SOURCES:** The News, business section, Dec 25, 1991. **BUSINESS ADDRESS:** President, Computer Aided Logistics Engineering Inc, 555 SW 12th Ave, Ste 106, Pompano Beach, FL 33069, (305)785-5433.

KAPOOR, JAGMOHAN

Educator. Indo-American. **PERSONAL:** Born Aug 11, 1940, Ambaler, Punjab, India; son of Shadi Ram Kapoor and Lajwarti Kapoor; married Shuchi Kapoor, Jan 16, 1966; children: Supereena K Brown, Tricia, Eric Jag. **EDUCATION:** Delhi University, BS (honors), 1960, MS, 1962; University of British Columbia, PhD, 1970. **CAREER:** Delhi University, lecturer, 1962-66; University of British Columbia, teaching assistant, fellowship, 1966-70, postdoctoral fellowship, 1970-71; University of Maryland, adjunct professor, 1973-; Anne Arundel Community College, professor, 1971-. **HONORS/AWARDS:** Delhi University, Best Undergrad Student Award, 1960, Best Graduate Student Award, 1962; AACC, nominee, Teacher of the Year Award, 1991. **SPECIAL ACHIEVEMENTS:** Publications in: Journal of Linear Algebra, 1972, 1973; Math Education, 1975; MATYC Journal, Problem Solution, 1975-80; electronic lectures on calculus, Atlanta University, 1993; Dr Kapoor's Problem Solving Cards, Calculus I, under print. **HOME ADDRESS:** 463 Highfield Ct, Severna Park, MD 21146, (410)647-2530.

KAPOOR, SANJIV

Computer system analyst. Indo-American. **PERSONAL:** Born Aug 23, 1961, Iringa, United Republic of Tanzania; married Geeli Kapoor, 1985; children: Ishaan, Kannov. **EDUCATION:** Rutgers, Thomas Edison State College, BSc, 1985. **CAREER:** Sealed Air Corporation, system analyst, currently. **HOME ADDRESS:** 6 Black Ct, Bridgewater, NJ 08807.

KAPOOR, SHIV G.

Educator. Indo-American. **PERSONAL:** Born Jun 3, 1948, Laharpur, Uttar Pradesh, India; son of Jagmohan Lal & Chunni Devi Kapoor; married Rashmi, Jun 15, 1980; children: Anchit, Shuchi. **EDUCATION:** IT Bhu, India, BSc, engineering, 1969; IIT Kanpur, India, MTech, 1971; University of Wisconsin, Madison, PhD, 1977. **CAREER:** University of Wisconsin, research assistant, 1974-77, research associate, 1977-79; University of Illinois, assistant professor, 1979, associate professor, 1985, professor, 1990-. **ORGANIZATIONS:** ASME, Production Engineering Division, chair, 1992-95, Journal of Engineering for Industry, technical editor, 1991-96; NAMRI/SME, scientific committee, 1990-; SME, education committee, 1986; Alpha Pi Mu, faculty advisor, 1984-. **HONORS/AWARDS:** ASME, Blackall M/c Tool Gage Award, 1992; University of Illinois, Everit Award for Best Teaching, 1984, Department of Mechanical & Industrial Engineering, Two-Year Effective Teaching, 1986; University of Wisconsin, Madison, Graduate Resident Fellowship, 1975. **SPECIAL ACHIEVEMENTS:** Author of more than 80 research articles. **HOME ADDRESS:** 2214 Scottsdale Dr, Champaign, IL 61821. **BUSINESS ADDRESS:** Professor, University of Illinois at Urbana-Champaign, 1206 W Green St, Rm 140, MEB, Urbana, IL 61801, (217)333-3432.

KAPOOR, TARUN

Educator, consultant. Indo-American. **PERSONAL:** Born May 23, 1955, Bangalore, Andhra Pradesh, India; son of O P Kapoor; married Sandy, Aug 21, 1983. **EDUCATION:** Institute of Hotel Management, New Delhi, India, 3-yr diploma, 1975; University of Wisconsin-Stout, BS, hotel mgt, 1977; Michigan State University, MBA, 1978; The Educational Institute of the American Hotel & Motel Assn, Certified Hotel Administrator, 1989. **CAREER:** Minneapolis Athletic Club, maitre d', 1976-78; Gapor's at Ravinia, general mgr, 1979-82; Hyatt Regency, Delhi, hotel mgr, 1983; Kapoor & Kapoor, managing partner, 1988-; Kebabi Inc, owner, president, 1984-92; California State Polytechnic University, professor & director, 1988-. **ORGANIZATIONS:** Council of Hotel, Restaurant & Institutional Educators, co-chair, strategic planning, 1991-; American Institute of Wine & Food, LA, board of directors, 1991-; TGI Fridays, Human Resource Advisory Council, 1992-. **HONORS/AWARDS:** Southwest State University, Minnesota, Award of Merit, 1982; National Restaurant Association, NRA/NIF Work Study Grant, 1981; Bush Foundation, The Bush Grant, 1981; Statler Foundation, Statler Grant, 1978. **SPECIAL ACHIEVEMENTS:** Big Brothers of Los Angeles, 1989-; Author: "Ethically Empowering Others to Win in the 90's," 1992; A New Look at Ethics, 1991; Developing & Implementing & Adhering to a Code of Ethics, 1992; Ethics and the Hotel/Motel Manager, 1990. **BUSINESS ADDRESS:** Director, Professional Development Institute, California State Polytechnic University, 3801 W Temple Ave, Pomona, CA 91768, (909)869-4285.

KAPUR, KAMAL K.

Educator, writer. Indo-American. **PERSONAL:** Born Jul 27, 1948, Panjab, India; married Donald Powell, Jul 20, 1991. **EDUCATION:** Kent State University, MA, 1972. **CAREER:** Grossmont College, educator, currently. **HONORS/AWARDS:** Sultan Padamsee Awards, for playwriting. **SPECIAL ACHIEVEMENTS:** Radha, a book of poems, 1987; several plays have been produced in India. **BUSINESS ADDRESS:** Educator, Grossmont College, 8800 Grossmont College, El Cajon, CA 92020-1765, (619)465-1700.

KARIYA, PAUL

Professional hockey player. Japanese American. **PERSONAL:** Born in Vancouver, Canada; son of Tetsuhiko Kariya. **EDUCATION:** University of Maine, currently. **CAREER:** Drafted by the Mighty Ducks, Natl Hockey League, 1993. **HONORS/AWARDS:** Decathlon Athletic Club, Hobey Baker Memorial Award. **BIOGRAPHICAL SOURCES:** "Maine Attraction," Boston Globe, March 26, 1993, p 51; "Is the Next Gretzky in Orono?," Boston Globe, Nov 1 1992, p 75. **BUSINESS ADDRESS:** Anaheim Mighty Ducks Hockey Club, 2695 Katella Ave, PO Box 61077, Anaheim, CA 92803-6177, (714)704-2700. *

KARTHA, MUKUND K.

Medical physicist. Indo-American. **PERSONAL:** Born Jul 31, 1936, Vayalar, Kerala, India; son of Krishnan Namboodiri and Ammalu Kunjamma; married Mally Kartha, Jan 31, 1963; children: Vyas, Neela. **EDUCATION:** Kerala University, India, BSc, 1958; Sagar University, India, MSc, 1961; University of Western Ontario, Canada, PhD, 1967. **CAREER:** Bhabha Atomic Res Center, scientific officer, 1961-63; Ontario Cancer Foundation, research fellow, 1963-66, jr physicist, 1966-68; Ohio State University, professor of radiology, 1968-83; Medical Physics Incorporated, consultant, president, 1983-. **ORGANIZATIONS:** American Association Phys Med, 1969-; American College of Med Phys, diplomate, 1989-; American College of Radiology, diplomate, 1979-; Rad Society North American, 1970-90; American Soc Ther Rad & Onc, 1982-90; Rad Res Society, 1971-90. **HONORS/AWARDS:** National Cancer Institute, brain tumor study grant, 1973, rad ther outreach study grant, 1973. **SPECIAL ACHIEVEMENTS:** 31 publications, including: "Dosimetry Disparities Resulting from Two Accepted Methods of Calibration of Cobalt-60 Teletherapy Machines," R P Nair, N S Menon, Revista Interamericana de Radiologia, 11:17, 1981; "Optimization of External Beam Radiation Therapy," C Sekar, S Vasan and T Broadwater, Proceedings of 1985 Mevatron Users Conference, Hilton Head, SC, p 225-249, 1985. **HOME ADDRESS:** 5003 Eleventh Avenue, Vienna, WV 26105-3152.

KASHIWA, HANK CHARLES

Ski company executive, professional sports commentator, former athlete. Japanese American. **PERSONAL:** Born May 26, 1949, Old Forge, NY; son of Henry and Miriam Kashiwa; married Anne D Kashiwa, Oct 8; children: Hennie D. **EDUCATION:** University of Colorado, AA, liberal arts, 1971. **CAREER:** US Olympic Ski Team, 1967-72; World Pro Tour, 1972-81; self-employed, endorser/representative, skiing industry, 1982-90; "GGP Ski Magazine," television show host, currently; The Volant Ski Corporation, president, 1990-. **ORGANIZATIONS:** American Federation of Television and Radio Announcers, 1972-. **HONORS/AWARDS:** US Ski Assn, National Champion, 1969; Professional Ski Racers Assn, World Pro Champion, 1975. **SPECIAL ACHIEVEMENTS:** Raced in Sapporo Olympics, Alpine Skiing, 1972; television announcer: ABC, CBS, GGP, ESPN, 1978-. **MILITARY SERVICE:** US Army, sp-4, 1967-69. **BIOGRAPHICAL SOURCES:** Numerous articles in magazines, including: Ski; Skiing; People; Sports Illustrated; Newsweek; Wall Street Jouranl. **BUSINESS ADDRESS:** President, Volant Incorporated, 3280 Pearl St, Boulder, CO 80301, (303)443-3378.

KASHIWAGI, BRIAN RIO
Engineer. Japanese American. **PERSONAL:** Born Jan 16, 1942, Seattle, WA; son of John Mitsuo Kashiwagi & Kiyo Esther Kashiwagi; married Marilyn Jean Plett, Dec 27, 1983; children: Marc Alain. **EDUCATION:** Massachusetts Institute of Technology, SB, 1964; Stanford University, MS, 1966. **CAREER:** Exxon Chemical Co, engineer, 1966-71; Esso Research & Engineering Co, project engineer, 1971-73; Exxon Chemical Co, staff engineer, 1974-81, sr staff engineer, 1981-89, engineering associate, 1989-. **ORGANIZATIONS:** American Institute of Chemical Engineers, 1967-; Japanese American Citizens League, 1971-. **HONORS/AWARDS:** Tau Beta Pi, 1963; Phi Lambda Upsilon, 1964. **HOME ADDRESS:** 14307 Sun Harbor Dr, Houston, TX 77062.

KASHIWAGI, SOJI CHARLES
Playwright, writer. Japanese American. **PERSONAL:** Born Sep 10, 1962, Oakland, CA; son of Hiroshi & Sadako Kashiwagi. **EDUCATION:** San Francisco State University, BA, 1985. **CAREER:** KNBR Radio, intern, 1985-86; PM Magazine TV Show, researcher, 1986; Asian American Drug Abuse Program, communications coordinator, 1987-. **ORGANIZATIONS:** Young Buddhist Association, San Francisco, president, 1985; San Francisco Buddhist Church Dharma School, assistant superintendent, 1986. **HONORS/AWARDS:** Young-Buddhist Association, Bussei Recognition Award, 1986; Asian American Journalists Association, Scholarship Award, 1984. **SPECIAL ACHIEVEMENTS:** The Grapevine, first play produced at Los Angeles Theatre Center, 1993; writer and director, short dramatic film, Honorable Mention, 1988. **BUSINESS ADDRESS:** Communications Coordinator, Asian American Drug Abuse Program, 5318 S Crenshaw Blvd, Los Angeles, CA 90043, (213)293-6284.

KASHYAP, MOTI LAL
Physician, scientist. Indo-American/Singaporean American. **PERSONAL:** Born Feb 19, 1939, Singapore; son of Ram Nath & Vidya Vati Kashyap; married Suman, Dec 8, 1970; children: Keshini, Vikram, Ishaan. **EDUCATION:** University of Singapore, MB, BS, 1964; McGill University, MS, 1967; Royal College of Physicians of Canada, FRCP, 1969; University of California, San Francisco, Cardiovascular Research Institute, senior fellow, 1971. **CAREER:** Royal Victoria Hospital, Canada, int med resident, endocrin fellow, McGill University, lecturer, 1969-70; University of California, San Francisco, senior fellow, 1970-71; University of Singapore, senior lecturer, 1971-74; University of Cincinnati, OH, professor of medicine, Lipid Research Clinic, (NIH supported) associate director, Coronary Primary Prevention Trial, director, 1974-86; University of California, Irvine, professor of medicine, 1986-; Department of Veterans Affairs, Long Beach, CA, gerontology, chief, cholesterol center, director, 1986-. **ORGANIZATIONS:** Endocrine & Metabolism Society of Singapore, former secretary, vice president, 1971-73; Central Society for Clinical Investigation, former member, 1974-86; Canadian Society of Endocrinology & Metabolism, 1974-; International Society & Federation of Cardiology, 1974-; American Federation of Clinical Research, senior member, 1974-; Academy of Medicine of Singapore, fellow, 1974-; Arteriosclerosis Council, AHA, fellow, 1978-; American College of Physicians, fellow, 1978-. **HONORS/AWARDS:** University of Singapore, Gold Medal, Biochemistry, Silver Medal, Basic Medical Sciences, Senior Scholarship, 1960-64; American Heart Association, Senior Research Fellowship, 1970-71; International Society of Cardiology, International Fellowship, 1972; International Society of Angiology, Distinguished Lecturer, 1983; Indian Medical Association, Distinguished Physician Award, 1992. **SPECIAL ACHIEVEMENTS:** "Clinical Utility and Methods for Assessing Triglyceride-Rich Lipoprotein Metabolism," 1991; "Ethanol Stimulates Apolipoprotein A-1 Secretion in Human Hepatocytes: Implications for Atherosclerosis Protection, 1992; Diet and Drug Controversies in the Management of Dyslipoproteinemia in the Elderly," 1993; numerous research grants and publications on lipoprotein metabolism. **BUSINESS ADDRESS:** Professor of Medicine, Dir, Cholesterol Ctr/Chief of Ge-rontology, University of California, Irvine, VA Medical Center, 111GE, 5901 E Seventh St, Long Beach, CA 90822, (310)494-5953.

KASHYAP, PANKAJ KUMAR
Physician. Indo-American. **PERSONAL:** Born Oct 31, 1962, Bombay, India; son of Raj Kashyap and Neelam Kashyap; married Vandna Kashyap, Dec 2, 1990; children: Nisha. **EDUCATION:** University of California, Berkeley, AB (with honors and distinction), biochemistry, 1984; University of California, Los Angeles, MD, 1988; Harbor-UCLA Medical Center, internship, 1988-89, gastroenterology fellowship, 1992-94. **CAREER:** Transamerica Relocation, Inc, accounting, 1981; University of California, Berkeley, English tutor, 1982; Diablo International Resource Center for Peace and National Security, lecturer, 1983; Communication & Information Services, word processor, 1983; Ecumene & Associates, preparation of environmental impact reports, 1984; UCLA Medical Center, physician, currently. **ORGANIZATIONS:** American Medical Association; American College of Physicians; California Medical Association; Los Angeles County Medical Association; National Board of Medical Examiners, diplomate; American Gastroenterological Association; American Society for Gastrointestinal Endoscopy; Research and Education Institute, Harbor-UCLA. **HONORS/AWARDS:** Dean Mellinkoff Honor Society, 1984-88; Lazarus Medical Scholarship, 1984-87; Kirshner Medical Scholarship, 1985-87; Levin Medical Scholarship, 1985-86; MacKenzie Scholarship, 1986-88; Guthman Medical Scholarship, 1987-88; Distinguished Research Award (WSMRC), 1986; Research Presentation Award (MFMRF), 1987; Solomon Scholars Outstanding Research Award, 1991; Distinguished Author's Award, 1991; McNeil Pharmaceutical Outstanding Merit Award, 1986. **SPECIAL ACHIEVEMENTS:** Publications, with S P Bhat, "In Vitro Synthesis of Ocular Lens Proteins," 1986; with J C Puffer, "The Pre-Participation Examination: A Comparison of Multistation vs. Single Examiner Methods in Detecting Abnormalities," 1987; Pressure Ulcers in the Elderly, textbook, Geriatric Dermatology: Clinical Diagnosis and Practical Therapy, 1988; with K A Narahara, I Mena, "Correlation of Thallium-201 SPECT Determination of Perfusion Defects with Cardiac Catheterization," 1989; licensed in California, 1989-; with C Dilorenzo, P Hyman, "Children and Adults Non-Ulcer Dyspepsia; Do They Have The Same Disease?" submitted to the Scandinavian Journal of Digestion, 1991; research projects: with Dr William Snape, Pathophysiology of Upper Gastrointestinal Motility Disorders, Harbor-UCLA Medical Center, 1991; with Drs S Targan, P Choi, A Randomized Double-Blind, Placebo-Controlled Study of Human Recombinant Interleukin-1 Receptor Antagonist in Patients with Ulcerative Colitis, Cedars-Sinai Medical Center, 1993. **HOME ADDRESS:** 4927 Indian Wood #472, Culver City, CA 90230.

KATAGIRI, GEORGE
Educator, state official (retired). Japanese American. **PERSONAL:** Born Sep 22, 1926, Portland, OR; son of Chiharu Katagiri and Teruye Katagiri; married Helen H, Jul 26, 1948 (deceased); children: Douglas G, David A, Stephen J. **EDUCATION:** University of Minnesota, BS, 1950; Oregon State University, MEd, 1954. **CAREER:** Portland Public Schools, elementary teacher,1950-56, high school science teacher, 1956-59; Oregon Department of Education, science specialist, instructional television instructor, director of information dissemination, director of instructional technology, 1959-84, coordinator of ECIA, ch 2 (part-time), 1985-92. **ORGANIZATIONS:** Council for Elementary Science International, board of directors, 1964-67; Council of State Science Supervisors, president, 1966; National Science Supervisors Association, member-at-large, 1965-66; Oregon Museum of Science and Industry, board of trustees, 1961-69; Portland Zoological Society, board of trustees, 1969-73; Comprehensive Options for Drug Addicts, advisory board, 1979-82; Japanese American Citizens League, Portland, advisory board, 1989-93. **HONORS/AWARDS:** Oregon Museum of Science and Industry, Outstanding Science Educator, 1963; State of Oregon, Oregon State Employee of the Year, 1969; National Institute of Education, Service Award, 1977; Oregon Science Teachers Association, Service Award, 1970; Comprehensive Options for Drug Addicts, Board Member of the Year, 1982. **SPECIAL ACHIEVEMENTS:** Author, Self-Paced Investigations for Elementary Science, Silver Burdett, 1976; writer, Learning in Science Labs, Science Research Associates, Chicago, 1960-62; teaching film writer and teacher, "A Technique for Classroom Investigations," 1963; developed state curriclm documents in science and environmental education, 1970, 1965; coordinated development of museum exhibit on "Issei Pioneers of Oregon," 1993. **MILITARY SERVICE:** US Army, Military Language Intelligence Service, 1945-46. **HOME ADDRESS:** 3228 SW 13th Ave, Portland, OR 97201-3029, (503)227-7079.

KATO, DEAN M.
Attorney. Japanese American. **PERSONAL:** Born May 27, 1965, Los Angeles, CA; son of Kenji Allen Kato and Yukiko Kato. **EDUCATION:** Oxford University, 1985-86; Columbia University, BA, 1987; Harvard Law School, 1990-91; University of California, Berkeley, JD, 1991; Tokyo University Faculty of Law, visiting researcher, Fulbright Scholar, 1991-92. **CAREER:** O'Melveny & Myers, associate, currently. **HONORS/AWARDS:** Fulbright Foundation, Fulbright Scholarship, 1991-92. **BUSINESS ADDRESS:** Associate, O'Melveny & Myers, 400 S Hope Street, Los Angeles, CA 90071, (213)669-6000.

KATO, GORO
Educator. Japanese American. **PERSONAL:** Born Jun 9, 1948, Kariya, Aichi, Japan; son of Takeo Kato and Misao Kato; married Christine Willis, Aug 14, 1974; children: Alexander Benkei Kato-Willis. **EDUCATION:** Shizuoka University, Japan, BS, 1972; West Virginia University, MA, 1974; University of Rochester, PhD, 1979. **CAREER:** Institute for Advanced Study, visiting member, 1986, 1989, 1990; West Virginia University, visiting asst professor, 1979-80; East Carolina University, visiting asst professor, 1980-81; University of Calabria, Italy, professore contrato, 1989; Cal Poly St Univ, professor, 1981-. **ORGANIZATIONS:** Mediterranean Press USA, editor, 1989-; Math Association of Japan, 1982-. **HONORS/AWARDS:** Rotary International Fellowship, 1972-73. **SPECIAL ACHIEVEMENTS:** "A p-Adic Cohomological Method for the Weierstrass Family and Its Zeta Invariants," in p-Adic Methods in Number Theory and Algebraic Geometry, Contemporary Mathematics, AMS, vol 133, 1992; Theory of Algebraic Functions, translation of the book Daisu Kansuron, by K Iwasawa, AMS Translations of Mathematical Monographs, vol 118, 1993; "Cohomology and D-Modules," Seminars and Conferences, Editel, forthcoming; Fundamentals of Microlocal Analysis and D-Modules, Monographs and Textbooks in Pure and Applied Mathematics, Marcel Dekker forthcoming. **HOME PHONE:** (805)543-1606. **BUSINESS ADDRESS:** Professor, Mathematics Dept, California Polytechnic State University, San Luis Obispo, CA 93407.

KATO, MASATOSHI
Manufacturing company manager. Japanese American. **PERSONAL:** Born Apr 13, 1945, Hourai-chyo, Aichi, Japan; son of Eizo Kato and Toshi Kato; married Sumiko Kato, Apr 21, 1974; children: Takenao, Naomi. **EDUCATION:** Nagoya University, bachelor's degree, 1970. **CAREER:** Nippon Koukan Co, manager, 1991; Natl Steel Corp, Granite City Div, manager, currently. **ORGANIZATIONS:** Japanese Language School, president, 1992. **BUSINESS ADDRESS:** Manager, Granite City Division, National Steel Corp, 20th & State Sts, Granite City, IL 62040, (618)451-4653.

KATO, THEODORE TOSHIHIKO
Financial executive. Japanese American. **PERSONAL:** Born Jan 20, 1936, Kobe, Hyogo Prefecture, Japan; married Claudette L Kato, Nov 3, 1962; children: Denise Lynn, Yvonne M. **EDUCATION:** Roosevelt University, BSBA; University of Illinois, CPA, 1973. **CAREER:** Rescar Inc, manager of financial services, 1991-, controller, 1980-90; self employed, public accountant, 1974-79; Klemp Corporation, controller, 1972-74. **ORGANIZATIONS:** Addison School Dist #4, school board member, 1973-, president 1975-77, 1991-; Japanese Mutual Aid Society, auditor, 1988-; Japanese Chamber of Commerce and Industry of Chicago, 1991-93; Japanese American Association of Chicago, 1991-93; Illinois CPA Association, 1973-; American Institute of CPA, 1980-. **HONORS/AWARDS:** Illinois Association of School Administrators, Outstanding Board Member, 1993. **HOME ADDRESS:** 900 N Lincoln, Addison, IL 60101.

KATO, TOSIO
Educator. Japanese American. **PERSONAL:** Born Aug 25, 1917, Kanuma, Japan; married 1944. **EDUCATION:** University of Tokyo, BS, 1941, DSc, physics, 1951. **CAREER:** University of Tokyo, assistant professor, professor of physics, 1943-62; University of California, Berkeley, professor of math, 1962-. **ORGANIZATIONS:** American Math Society; Math Society of Japan. **HONORS/AWARDS:** Asahi Award, 1961; Norbert Wiemer Prize, 1980. **BUSINESS ADDRESS:** Professor of Math, University of California, Berkeley, Berkeley, CA 94720.*

KATO, WALTER Y.
Physicist. Japanese American. **PERSONAL:** Born Aug 19, 1924, Chicago, IL; son of Naotaro Kato and Hideko Kato; married Anna K Kato, Jun 26, 1953; children: Norman S, Cathryn J, Barbara J. **EDUCATION:** Haverford College,

BS, 1946; University of Illinois, MS, 1949; Pennsylvania State University, PhD, 1954. **CAREER:** Argonne National Laboratory, senior physicist, 1953-75; University of Michigan, visiting professor, department of nuclear energy, 1974-75; Brookhaven National Laboratory, dept of nuclear energy, associate chairman, 1975-80, deputy chairman, 1980-88, chairman, 1988-91, senior scientist, currently. **ORGANIZATIONS:** American Nuclear Society, fellow, board of directors, 1990-; American Physical Society; AAAS; Sigma Xi; Japan Society of New York; International House of Japan. **HONORS/AWARDS:** Japanese Government, Order of Sacred Treasure, Third Class, 1992; Argonne University Association, Distinguished Appointment Award, 1973; Fulbright Commission, Fulbright Research Professor, 1958. **MILITARY SERVICE:** Army Ordnance, Tech 4, 1946-47. **HOME ADDRESS:** 3 Chips Court, Port Jefferson, NY 11777, (516)473-3295. **BUSINESS ADDRESS:** Senior Scientist, Brookhaven National Laboratory, Bldg 197C, Upton, NY 11973, (516)282-2444.

KATTAKUZHY, GEORGE CHACKO
Statistician. Indo-American. **PERSONAL:** Born Dec 30, 1944, Kottayam, Kerala, India; son of Varkey Chacko Kattakuzhy and Aleyanna Chacko Kattakuzhy; married Regini Titus Kattakuzhy, Aug 26, 1974; children: Sandhya Elizabeth, Anita Martha, Sarah Mariam. **EDUCATION:** Kerala University, India, BS, 1966, MS, 1969; Temple University, MA, 1973, PhD, 1975. **CAREER:** Temple University, instructor, math, 1973-75, lecterer in stat, 1973-78; Pahlavi University, assistant professor of stat, 1975-76; Phila College of Phar & Sci, assistant professor of math, 1976-78; US Dept of Health & Human Services/HCFA, statistician, 1978-. **ORGANIZATIONS:** Syrian Orthodox Church, managing editor, magazine, 1990-, National Council, 1987-; St Thomas Church, treasurer/secretary, 1982-; Am Stat Association, MD chapter, treasurer, 1986-90. **HONORS/AWARDS:** HCFA, Administrator Citation, 1982, 1991. **HOME ADDRESS:** 3611 Morningview Court, Ellicott City, MD 21042. **BUSINESS ADDRESS:** Health Statistician, HHS/HCFA/HSQB, 6325 Security Blvd, 2D2 ME, Baltimore, MD 21207, (410)966-7200.

KATTI, SHRINIWAS K.
Educator. Indo-American. **PERSONAL:** Born Jun 20, 1936, Bijapur, Karnataka, India; son of Keshav N Katti & Yamuna K Katti; married Pramila, Sep 24, 1960; children: Romney, Anita. **EDUCATION:** University of Delhi, India, BS, 1956; Iowa State University, MA, 1958, PhD, 1960. **CAREER:** Florida State University, assistant professor, associate professor, 1960-69; University of Missouri, professor, 1969-. **ORGANIZATIONS:** American Statistical Association, patron member, 1975-; Biometric Society, 1963-; Institute of Mathematical Statistics, 1963-; American Mathematical Society, 1968-; Mathematical Association of America, 1968-. **HONORS/AWARDS:** American Biographical Society, Intellectual of the Year, 1993, Man of the Year, 1991, Most Admired Man of the Year, 1992; American Statistical Association, fellow, 1970. **SPECIAL ACHIEVEMENTS:** Author of over 80 publications in refereed journals, 1960; guided over 15 doctoral students.

KAUL, BALKRISHENA
Toxicologist. Indo-American. **PERSONAL:** Born Aug 13, 1940, Srinagar, Jammu and Kashmir, India; son of Damodar & Dhanvati Kaul; divorced; children: Asheesh. **EDUCATION:** University of Jammu & Kashmir, India, BS, 1957; University of Lucknow, India, MS, 1959; University of Nebraska, MS, 1966, PhD, 1969. **CAREER:** New Jersey Medial/Dental School, postdoctoral fellow, clinical pharmacologist, 1969-70, instructor of pharmacology, 1971-72; State of New Jersey, principal forensic toxicologist, 1972-73; City of New York, Department of Health, clinical & environmental toxicology labs, director, 1974-89, LIP special chemistry, director, 1986-89; Kaulson Laboratories Inc, president, ceo, research & development, director, 1989-. **ORGANIZATIONS:** College of Clinical Pharmacology, fellow, 1970-; American Pharmaceutical Association, 1975-; American Association Clinical Chemistry, 1975-; American Academy Clinical Toxicology, 1976-; Sigma Xi, 1966-; Rho Chi, 1966-. **SPECIAL ACHIEVEMENTS:** Author of nearly 50 papers in the area of drug abuse, occupational & environmental lead poisoning, clinical pharmacology and related fields; holds three patents: on first medicinal plant tissue culture (production of precursor - diosgenin - for cortisone and contraceptive agents), development of radioimmunoassay for cocaine abuse detection and polyvalent simultaneous multiple drug immunoassays; invited by the United Nations to serve as a consultant to the Peoples Republic of China in the field of occupational health sponsored by WHO. **BUSINESS ADDRESS:** President, Director, Research and Development, Kaulson Laboratories Inc, 687-693 Bloomfield Ave, West Caldwell, NJ 07006, (201)226-9494.

KAUL, MAHARAJ KRISHEN
Engineer. Indo-American. **PERSONAL:** Born Nov 11, 1940, Srinagar, India; son of Kashi Nath and Shobhawati Kaul; married Girja Kaul, Apr 26, 1969; children: Aparna. **EDUCATION:** Punjab University, India, BS, 1962; State University of New York, Stony Brook, MS, 1967; University of California, Berkeley, PhD, 1972. **CAREER:** Impell Corporation/EDS Nuclear Inc, senior engineer, 1972-77; Quadrex Corporation, consultant engineer, 1977-79; Engineering Mechanics Research Inc, senior staff engineer, 1980-93; General Electric Nuclear Energy, principal engineer, 1993-. **ORGANIZATIONS:** American Society of Civil Engineers, 1980-87, Committee on Probabilistic Methods, Journal of Engineering Mechanics Division, 1980-82; American Nuclear Society, 1982-83. **SPECIAL ACHIEVEMENTS:** Author of a dozen technical papers, 1972-80; co-author of book, 1976. **HOME ADDRESS:** 43670 Vista Del Mar, Fremont, CA 94539.

KAUL, PRADAMAN
Aircraft company executive. Indo-American. **CAREER:** Hughes Network Systems, president, currently. **BUSINESS ADDRESS:** President, Hughes Network Systems, 11717 Exploration Ln, Germantown, MD 20876. *

KAUL, SANJIV
Cardiologist. Indo-American. **PERSONAL:** Born Aug 18, 1951, Srinagar, Kashmir, India; son of Amarendra Kaul and Leela Kaul; married Cindy Tucker Kaul, Jun 18, 1981; children: Nisha Leela. **EDUCATION:** University of Delhi, India, pre-med, 1969, MB, BS, 1975. **CAREER:** Chicago Medical School, PGY 1 Medicine, 1977-78; University of Vermont, PGY 2 & 3 Medicine, 1978-80; UCLA, PGY 4 & 5 Cardiology, 1980-82; Mass Genl Hospital, Harvard, Cardiology, clinical & research fellow, 1982-84; University of Virginia, assistant professor of med, Non-Invasive Lab, associate director, 1984-85, Cardiac Computer Center, assistant professor of med, director, 1985-88, associate professor of med, dir of CCC, Non-Invasive Imaging, co-dir, 1988-. **ORGANIZATIONS:** American Society of Nuclear Cardiology, founding member, 1993-; American Society of Clinical Investigation, 1993-; American Society of Echo, Publications, 1991-94; American Heart Association-VA affiliated, president, 1992-93; American Journal of Nuclear Medicine, editorial board, 1993; International Cardiac Doppler Society, board of directors, 1992; Diagnostic & Therapeutic Tech, assessment program panelist, 1992; University of VA, rep to American Federation of Clinical Research, 1990-92. **HONORS/AWARDS:** National Institutes of Health, research grant, 1992-97; American Heart Association, National Center, Established Inv Award, 1992-97, Grant-in-Aid, 1992-95, sponsor, training grant, 1992-94; Mallinckrodt Corporation, sponsor, fellowship training grant, 1992-94. **SPECIAL ACHIEVEMENTS:** Invited faculty and chair at over 75 national and international meetings, 1985-; visiting professor to over 30 academic institutions, 1985-; over 75 publications, 1983-. **BUSINESS ADDRESS:** Professor of Med, Dept of Internal Med, Division of Cardiology, University of Virginia, Box 158, Charlottesville, VA 22908, (804)924-5928.

KAUNG, ROSE TAN. *See* TAN, SINFOROSA G.

KAWAFUCHI, GLENN MISAKI
Management trainer. Japanese American. **PERSONAL:** Born Mar 11, 1951, Los Angeles, CA; son of Kazumi Kawafuchi and Kimi Kawafuchi; married Carolyn Motokane, Oct 6, 1986; children: Kai Yoshio, Emily Kimiko. **EDUCATION:** University of California, Los Angeles, BA, sociology, 1973; California State University, Long Beach, California community college counselor life credential, 1978; California State University, Dominguez Hills, MA, applied behavioral science, 1989. **CAREER:** Gardena Valley Japanese Cultural Institute, youth coordinator, 1976-78; California State University, Dominguez Hills, placement coordinator, 1978; Rancho Santiago Community College District, counselor, instructor, job developer, 1978-85; Hughes Aircraft Co, career development specialist, 1985-88; Chapman University, instructor, 1991-; The Aerospace Corp, manager, educational programs, management development, 1988-. **ORGANIZATIONS:** Leadership Education for Asian Pacifics, Leadership Management Institute, board member, vice chair, 1985-; United Way Kellogg Training Center, board member, 1991-; American Society for Training and Development, 1985-; National Society for Performance & Instruction, 1993-. **HONORS/AWARDS:** The Aerospace Corp, Asian Pacific American of the Year, 1993; American Society for Training & Development, Recognition for Excellence, 1991; California State University, Long Beach Dean's List, William H McCreary Scholarship in Pupil Personnel, 1976. **BUSINESS ADDRESS:** Manager, Management Development/Educational Programs, The Aerospace Corp, PO Box 92957, M3/435, Los Angeles, CA 90009, (310)336-5077.

KAWAGUCHI, STANLEY KENJI
Consulting engineer. Japanese American. **PERSONAL:** Born Jan 26, 1940, Honolulu, HI; son of Edwin Masao Kawaguchi and Lillian Ichiko Kawaguchi; married Carol Kaoru Shirakata, Dec 17, 1966; children: Maya Kazue, Grant Kazuaki. **EDUCATION:** University of Hawaii, BS, 1963; Massachusetts Institute of Technology, MS, 1964. **CAREER:** Parsons Brinckerhoff Quade & Douglas, Inc, vice president & regional manager, 1968-. **ORGANIZATIONS:** American Consulting Engineers Council, vice president, 1993-; Hawaii Construction Industry Legislative Organization, director, 1987-; Hawaii Section - American Soc of Civil Engineers, president, 1981; Consulting Engineers Council of Hawaii, president, 1987, national director, 1988. **HONORS/AWARDS:** Chi Epsilon, University of Hawaii Chapter, Honor Member, 1991. **MILITARY SERVICE:** US Army, Corps of Engineers, Captain, 1965-68. **BIOGRAPHICAL SOURCES:** Parsons Brinckerhoff-The First 100 Years, Benson Bobrick, Van Nostrand Reinhold Co Inc, p 200, [1985]. **HOME ADDRESS:** 98-839 Leihulu Place, Aiea, HI 96701. **BUSINESS ADDRESS:** Vice President, Parsons Brinckerhoff Quade & Douglas Inc, Two Waterfront Plaza, Suite 220, 500 Ala Moana Boulevard, Honolulu, HI 96813, (808)531-7094.

KAWAHARA, LINDON KEN
Oral surgeon. Japanese American. **PERSONAL:** Born Sep 7, 1955, Los Angeles, CA; son of Lindbergh S & Yone Kawahara; married Debra, Jun 13, 1981; children: Nicole, Justin. **EDUCATION:** UCLA, BA, 1977; Harvard, School of Dental Medicine, DMD, 1981; Harvard Medical School, MD, 1983. **CAREER:** Massachusetts General Hospital, oral & maxillofacial surgery residency, 1986; University of Southern California, Los Angeles, Aesthetic maxillofacial surgery, 1991; Blair G Ora, MD, DDS Inc, surgeon, officer, 1987-93; UCLA, School of Dentistry, adjunct assistant professor, 1993. **ORGANIZATIONS:** Southern California Society of Oral and Maxillofacial Surgeons, 1989; California Dental Association, 1989; California Medical Association, 1987; Los Angeles County Medical Association, 1987. **HONORS/AWARDS:** American Board of Oral and Maxillofacial Surgeons, diplomate, 1990. **BUSINESS ADDRESS:** 1600 Redondo Beach Blvd, Ste 406, Gardena, CA 90247, (310)515-0579.

KAWAHARA, WILLIAM T.
Industrial designer. Japanese American. **PERSONAL:** Born Jun 11, 1937, Seattle, WA; son of Makie Kawahara and Catherine Kawahara; married Beth K Kawahara, Jul 24, 1966; children: Brent F. **EDUCATION:** University of Washington, BA, 1966. **CAREER:** Container Corp of America, design manager, 1966-73; Packaging Northwest Inc, CEO, president, 1973-. **ORGANIZATIONS:** Rokka Ski School, director, 1963-93; Professional Ski Institute of America, 1960-. **MILITARY SERVICE:** US Army, LCpl, 1956-59. **BUSINESS ADDRESS:** President, CEO, Packaging Northwest, Inc, 2217 15th Ave W, Seattle, WA 98119, (206)284-1700.

KAWAICHI, KEN M.
Judge. Japanese American. **PERSONAL:** Born Oct 23, 1941, Los Angeles, CA; son of George Kawaichi and Margaret Kawaichi; married Susan J Tamura, Feb 4, 1973; children: Kathryn Tamura, Ken Christopher. **EDUCATION:** Pomona College, AB, 1963; University of California, JD, 1966. **CAREER:** Yonemura & Yasaki, associate, 1967-68; Yonemura, Yasaki & Kawaichi, partner, 1969-75; University of California, asst professor, 1970-72; Oakland-Piedmont-Emeryville Municipal Court, judge, 1975-80; Alameda Superior Court, judge, 1980-. **ORGANIZATIONS:** Allied Fellowship Service, president and board, 1972-75; California Asian Judges Association, president, 1980-81; Chancellor's Community Advisory Committee, 1990-; Alameda-Contra Costa Health Systems Agency, chair, 1977-81; Judicial Council Advisory Committee, Civil, 1993-; Judicial Council Advisory Committee, Race & Ethnic Bias Subcomm, chair, 1991-; Piedmont Asian American Club, president, board, 1989-92; Task Force on University Admissions, co-chair, 1986-90. **HONORS/AWARDS:** Alameda-Contra Costa Trial Lawyers Association, Trial Judge of the Year, 1989. **SPECIAL ACHIEVEMENTS:** Editorial board, Effective Introduction of Evidence, CEB. **BUSINESS ADDRESS:** Judge, Dept 14, Alameda Superior Court, 1225 Fallon St, Oakland, CA 94612, (510)272-6119.

KAWAJA, KALEEM U.
Government official. Indo-American. **PERSONAL:** Born Mar 5, 1941, Kanpur, India; son of Mr & Mrs Hakeem Kawaja; married Tahoora Kawaja,

Feb 8, 1975; children: Mona Kaleem, Omar Kaleem. **EDUCATION:** Indian Institute of Technology, India, BS, 1963; Brooklyn Polytechnic Institute, MS, 1973. **CAREER:** Ebasco Services Inc, project engineer, 1969-73; Stone & Webster Inc, project manager, 1973-77; Brown & Root Inc, engineering project manager, 1977-80; Bechtel Corp, engineering supervisor, 1980-85; Bendix Corp, engineering manager, 1985-89; NASA, engineering manager, 1989-. **ORGANIZATIONS:** American Society of Mechanical Engineers, 1970-80; The Organization for Universal Communal Harmony, president, 1992-94; The Association of Indian Muslims of America, president, 1987-; Indian Cultural Coordination Committee, executive board member, 1987-. **HONORS/ AWARDS:** NASA, NASA Honor Award for Group Achievement, 1992, Performance Management & Recognition Award, 1991, 1992, 1993; Non Resident Indians Welfare Society, New Delhi, Jewel of India Award, 1991. **SPECIAL ACHIEVEMENTS:** Published several articles & columns in various newspapers and magazines in the US and India, 1987-. **HOME ADDRESS:** 11649 Masters Run, Ellicott City, MD 21042, (410)730-5456.

KAWAMOTO, BRIAN MICHIO
Insurance broker, consultant. Japanese American. **PERSONAL:** Born Oct 28, 1953, Berkeley, CA; son of Mr and Mrs Yukio Kawamoto; married Robin Jean; children: Kenneth, Nicholas, Jewel, Brooke. **EDUCATION:** University of Virginia, BA, 1976; Institute of Property-Liability Underwriters, CPCU, 1981; George Washington University, MBA, 1986. **CAREER:** Willis Corroon, executive vice pres, managing director, 1981-. **ORGANIZATIONS:** Japan Studies Institute, San Diego State University, bd member, 1990-91; Japan American Society; Society of CPCU, 1981-; Inc Magazine, insurance advisory committee, 1990. **BUSINESS ADDRESS:** Executive Vice President, Managing Director, Willis Corroon, Advanced Risk Management Services, 26 Century Blvd, Nashville, TN 37214, (615)872-3200.

KAWANO, ARNOLD H.
Business executive, attorney. Japanese American. **PERSONAL:** Born Mar 27, 1948, Philadelphia, PA; son of James Tadao Kawano and Shigeko Sakamoto Kawano; married Sandra K Lee, Jul 1, 1970; children: Thomas Lee, Mark Lee. **EDUCATION:** Columbia University, BS (magna cum laude), 1975; Columbia Law School, JD, 1977. **CAREER:** Reid & Priest, associate, 1977-80; Weil, Gotshal & Manges, associate, 1980-81; Sumitomo Corp of America, counsel, 1981-84; Law Office of Arnold H Kawano, attorney, 1984-86; J P Morgan, vice president, 1987-91; Inouye & Ogden, partner, 1991-93; ORIX USA Corp, vice president, 1993-. **ORGANIZATIONS:** Asian American Bar Assn of New York, board member; Asian American Legal Defense & Education Fund, Inc, board member, 1977-88; Assn of the Bar of The City of New York, committee on real property law, landmark subcommittee, chair, 1990-93; newsletter subcommittee, chair, 1991-93; New York Civil Liberties Union, board member; American and New York State Bar Assns; District of Columbia Bar; Japanese American Citizens League; NAACP. **HONORS/AWARDS:** Columbia Law School, Harlan Fiske Stone Scholar, 1976; Phi Beta Kappa, 1975. **SPECIAL ACHIEVEMENTS:** Co-editor-in-chief, Metes & Bounds, newsletter of the Committee on Real Property of the Association of the Bar of the City of New York, 1991-93; associate editor, Foreign Investment in US Real Estate, Chicago: American Bar Association, 1990. **HOME ADDRESS:** 176 Overlook Ave, Great Neck, NY 11021, (516)482-1494. **BUSINESS ADDRESS:** Vice President, ORIX USA Corp, 780 Third Ave, 48th Fl, New York, NY 10017-7088, (212)418-8355.

KAWASAKI, LILLIAN Y.
Municipal government official. Japanese American. **PERSONAL:** Born Sep 17, 1950, Denver, CO. **EDUCATION:** California State University, Los Angeles, BS, zoology, 1974, MS, biology, 1980. **CAREER:** Los Angeles City Harbor Department, director of environmental management, 1988-90; University of California, Los Angeles, part-time faculty, 1990-; Los Angeles City Environmental Affairs Department, general manager, 1990-. **ORGANIZATIONS:** US EPA National Advisory Council for Environmental Policy and Technology, 1991-; Southern California Academy of Sciences, board of directors, 1992-; California State University, 1993-; Los Angeles City Mayor's Council on International and Sister Cities, environment chairperson, 1993-; American Lung Association, Los Angeles Chapter, board of directors. **HONORS/AWARDS:** California State University, Los Angeles, Distinguished Alumna Award, 1992; Asian-American Architects/Engineers, President's Award, 1992. **BUSINESS ADDRESS:** General Manager, Environmental Affairs Dept, City of Los Angeles, 200 N Spring St, Rm 1500, Mail Stop 177, Los Angeles, CA 90012, (213)237-0352.

KAWASHIMA, EDITH T.
Graphic arts company executive. Japanese American. **PERSONAL:** Born Nov 16, 1932, Honolulu, HI; daughter of Tsunesaburo and Masa Nii; married Toshio (Jeff), Nov 19, 1955; children: William M, Tyrus T. **EDUCATION:** Honolulu Business College, 1952. **CAREER:** Hawaii Blueprint & Supply, clerk, 1950-52; Blue Print Co, office manager, 1952-63; Honolulu Graphic Arts, secretary to the president, beginning 1964-, president, currently. **ORGANIZATIONS:** Pacific Printing Industries, board of directors, 1987-93, Hawaii Division, secretary of the board, 1992-93; Sales & Marketing Executives, 1990-; Hawaii Publishers Assn, 1991-; Printing Industries of America, board of directors, 1993-. **HONORS/AWARDS:** Advertising Assn of Hawaii, Lifetime Achievement, 1990. **BUSINESS ADDRESS:** President, Honolulu Graphic Arts, Inc, 849 Halekauwila St, Honolulu, HI 96813, (808)591-8228.

KAWATA, PAUL AKIO
Association administrator. Japanese American. **PERSONAL:** Born Jul 24, Salt Lake City, UT; son of William & Miyeko Kawata. **EDUCATION:** University of the Pacific, BA; Antioch, MA. **CAREER:** Mayor's Staff, aide, 1982-85; National AIDS Network, executive director, 1985-89; National Minority AIDS Council, executive director, 1989-. **ORGANIZATIONS:** Management Assistant Group, board; International Committee of AIDS Service Org, board. **HONORS/AWARDS:** City of New Orleans, Honorary Citizen. **BUSINESS ADDRESS:** Executive Director, Natl Minority AIDS Council, 300 I St NE, Ste 400, Washington, DC 20002, (202)544-1076.

KAY, HELEN
Museum administrator. Chinese American. **CAREER:** Wing Luke Asian Museum Board, co-president, currently. **BUSINESS ADDRESS:** Co-President, Wing Luke Asian Museum Board, 407 Seventh Ave S, Seattle, WA 98104, (206)623-5124. *

KAYA, DOUGLAS HIFUTO, JR.
Educator. Japanese American. **PERSONAL:** Born Dec 13, 1939, Honolulu, HI; son of Ellen T Gushiken Kaya and Douglas H Kaya. **EDUCATION:** University of Hawaii, BA, 1961, MFA, 1964. **CAREER:** Honolulu Theatre for Youth, director, 1968-69; University of Hawaii, assistant professor, 1968-70; Leeward Community College, professor, 1970-. **ORGANIZATIONS:** Hawaii State Theatre Council, vice president, 1991-92, secretary, 1990-91, 1992-93; State Board on Speech Pathology and Audiology, 1988-92; Pacificare, advisory committee, 1990-91; State Foundation on Culture and the Arts, advisory panel, 1988, 1991, 1993; State Board of Osteopathic Examiners, board member, 1985-88; Hawaii Recreation and Park Association, president, 1974-75; State Commission on Children and Youth, 1976-77; Honolulu Theatre for Youth, board of directors, 1962-64. **SPECIAL ACHIEVEMENTS:** Stage performances include: Flower Drum Song, 1989; Damn Yankees, 1989; Mardi Gras Follies, 1991, 1992, 1993; public speaker. **HOME ADDRESS:** 98-1770 D Kaahumanu St, Pearl City, HI 96782, (808)456-4494. **BUSINESS ADDRESS:** Professor, Language Arts, Leeward Community College, 96-045 Ala Ike, Pearl City, HI 96782-3366, (808)455-0330.

KE, GANG
Educator, association executive. Chinese American. **PERSONAL:** Born Oct 30, 1950, Tai Yuan City, Shaanxi, People's Republic of China; son of Cheng Ke & Xianlu Li; married Meng Zhang, Jan 31, 1984; children: Jessica Judith. **EDUCATION:** Jilin University, BA, 1982; University of Toledo, MA, 1987; University of Maryland, MA, 1991, PhD, 1993. **CAREER:** Chinese Academy of Social Sciences, researcher, 1981-84; University of Toledo, teaching assistant, 1985-87; University of Colorado, teaching assistant, 1987-88; Virginia Technology Institute, research assistant, 1988-89; University of Maryland, instructor, 1989-93. **ORGANIZATIONS:** Washington Chinese Entrepreneurs Association, president, 1993-; Chinese Student Entrepreneurs Association in America, vice president, 1993-; Orient Exchange Inc, president, 1990-; Committee of Chinese Correspondence, president, 1989-. **HONORS/AWARDS:** Sun Yat-Sen Culture Education Foundation, Sun Yat-Sen Overseas Scholarship Award, 1992; Li Yujie Academic Foundation, Scholarship Incentive Award, 1990; University of Maryland, dean's fellowship, 1989; University of Colorado, dean's fellowship, 1987. **SPECIAL ACHIEVEMENTS:** Book: Reflections on the Grand Failure of Communist Political Economy, 1994; articles: ''A Doomed Model of Institutional Design,'' International Social Science Journal, Aug 1994; ''A Comparative Study between Liberalism and Socialism,'' Philosophy of Social Sciences, March 1990. **HOME ADDRESS:** 8131 Heatherton Ln, Apt 304, Vienna, VA 22180, (703)560-8001.

KEDIA, ULLAS V.
Administrative services director. Indo-American. **PERSONAL:** Born Nov 3, 1946, Patna, Bihar, India; son of Bajrang Lal Kedia and Parbati Debi Kedia; married Anita Kedia, Mar 13, 1970; children: Shalini, Jeanie, Jay V. **EDUCATION:** Banaras Hindu University, India, BCom (honors in accounting), 1968, MBA, 1970. **CAREER:** Ocotillo Plastics, office manager, controller, 1971-74; Vardhan Brothers, self-employed, 1974-80; Teledyne Economic Development, director, administrative services, 1980-. **ORGANIZATIONS:** Institute of Management Accountants, 1982-. **HOME ADDRESS:** 13422 S 38th St, Phoenix, AZ 85044. **BUSINESS PHONE:** (602)254-5921.

KEE, WILLIE
Photographer, writer. Chinese American. **PERSONAL:** Born Nov 19, 1936, Oakland, CA; son of William and Alice Louie Kee; married Jeanne Young Kee, Nov 8, 1970. **CAREER:** KTVU News, video photographer, 1970-; San Leandro Times, food writer, restaurant reviewer, 1991-. **ORGANIZATIONS:** California Press Photographer Association, board of directors, 1976-84; San Francisco Bay Area Press Photographers Association, president, 1981-82; National Academy TV Arts & Sciences, Northern California Chapter, board of governors, 1976-; Oakland High School Visual Arts Magnet Program, advisory board, 1991-. **HONORS/AWARDS:** National Academy of TV Arts & Sciences, Northern California Chapter, 12 Emmy awards for photography, producing and writing, 1976-88; Marcus Foster Educational Award, Distinguished Alumnus, 1984; San Francisco Bay Area Press Photographers, Photographer of the Year, 1979, 1981; California Press Photo Association, Photographer of the Year, 1977. **SPECIAL ACHIEVEMENTS:** 1100 illustrative photographs in Chinese Techniques, chef Ken Hom's first cookbook, Simon and Schuster, 1981; co-host, television special, Chinese New Year parade in San Francisco by KTVU, 1988, 1989. **MILITARY SERVICE:** US Marine Corps, sergeant, 1955-58, active duty. **BIOGRAPHICAL SOURCES:** Hayward Daily Review, p 45, February 17, 1989; Asian Week, p 54, February 26, 1988. **HOME ADDRESS:** 32979 Lake Wawasee St, Fremont, CA 94555, (510)471-3045.

KELLY, DARLENE OKAMOTO
Property manager. Japanese American. **PERSONAL:** Born Dec 6, 1944, Denver, CO; daughter of Ricky Rikio Yamamura & Minnie Misao Okada Yamamura; married Ronald William Kelly, Oct 29, 1983; children: Jeffrey Shiro Okamoto, Sean Kelly. **EDUCATION:** Saint Mary's College, BA, 1983. **CAREER:** Multi Financial Corp, office manager, 1972-75; Dealey, Renton & Associates, vice president, 1975-84; Levine Financial Group, associate, 1984-85; Storek & Storek, administrative manager, 1985-91; Bramalea Pacific, property manager, 1991-. **ORGANIZATIONS:** Asian Community Mental Health Services, director, 1986-; Last Monday Club, convener, 1983-; Donner Lake Prop Owner's Association, director, 1988-; A Central Place, advisory board, 1985-. **HOME ADDRESS:** 4001 Midvale Ave, Oakland, CA 94602, (510)482-3122. **BUSINESS ADDRESS:** Property Manager, Bramalea Pacific, 484 Ninth St, Oakland, CA 94607, (510)238-1630.

KENNARD, JOYCE L.
Judge. Indonesian American/Chinese American. **CAREER:** California Supreme Court, associate justice, currently. **BUSINESS ADDRESS:** Associate Justice, California Supreme Court, 303 Second St, South Tower, 9th Fl, San Francisco, CA 94107.

KERKAR, AWDHOOT VASANT
Research engineer. Indo-American. **PERSONAL:** Born Sep 20, 1963, Bombay, Maharashtra, India; son of Vasant B Kerkar & Sunita V Kerkar; married Sharmila A Kerkar, Sep 8, 1990. **EDUCATION:** University of Bombay, B chem eng, 1984; University of Pittsburgh, MS, 1986; Case Western Reserve University, PhD, 1990. **CAREER:** WR Grace & Co, research engineer, 1990-. **ORGANIZATIONS:** AIChE; American Ceramic Society, program chair, 1987-. **SPECIAL ACHIEVEMENTS:** US Patent no 5,194,129, Manufacture of Optical Ferrules, 1993; author, "Mechanical Characterization of Unidirectional Carbon/Carbon Compsiles," Ceram Eng Sci Proc 770, 1992; Ceram Eng Sci Proc, 12 (9-10), 1933 (1991); J Am Ceram Soc 73 (10), 2879-2889, 1990; US Patent no 5,279,994, Aqueous Tape Casting; European Patent no 93250250.3, Manufacture of Conical Pore Ceramics by Electrophoretic Desposition. **BUSINESS ADDRESS:** Senior Research Engineer, W R Grace & Co, 7379 Rte 32, Columbia, MD 21044, (410)531-4693.

KESHAVAN, KRISHNASWAMIENGAR
Educator. **PERSONAL:** Born Jun 5, 1929, Hassan, Karnataka, India; son of K R Krishnaswamiengar (deceased) and K Padmamma (deceased); married Sita Keshavan, Nov 13, 1957; children: Rangaswamy, Padma, Leela. **EDUCATION:** University of Mysore, India, BS, 1950, BE, 1955; University of Iowa, MS, 1960; Cornell University, PhD, 1963. **CAREER:** Govt of India, section officer, 1955-58; University of Maine, associate professor, 1963-67; Worcester Polytechnic Inst, head of civil eng, 1976-86, prof, 1967; UNESCO, senior advisor, 1975-76. **ORGANIZATIONS:** ASCE, 1965-; Chi Epsilon, 1971-; Sigma Xi, 1964-. **HONORS/AWARDS:** University of Iowa, International Scholarship, 1958-59. **SPECIAL ACHIEVEMENTS:** 25 technical publications, several reports: UNESCO, UNDF, UNDP, UNEP. **BUSINESS ADDRESS:** Professor of Civil Engineering, Worcester Polytechnic Inst, 100 Institute Rd, Kaven Hall, Worcester, MA 01609, (508)831-5142.

KHAN, MAHBUB R.
Industrial researcher, executive. Bangladeshi American. **PERSONAL:** Born Sep 11, 1949, Dhaka, Bangladesh; son of Ebarat Ali Khan and Zahura Khatun; married Reena Yasmeen Khan, Sep 10, 1976; children: Madhury, Kamal, Jamal, Monika. **EDUCATION:** Dhaka University, Bangladesh, BSc (honors), 1969, MSc, 1970; Boston College, PhD, 1979. **CAREER:** University of Nebraska, research associate, 1979-80; Argonne National Lab, post-doc, 1981-83; Control Data Corp/MPI, senior scientist, 1983-85; Stolle Corp/AlCOA, senior scientist, 1985-86; Seagate Magnetics, manager, 1986-. **ORGANIZATIONS:** American Physical Society, life member, 1980-; IEEE, 1989-; IEEE Magnetics Society, 1985-. **HONORS/AWARDS:** Secondary Education Board, gold medal, 1964. **SPECIAL ACHIEVEMENTS:** Over 35 publications in reputed journals on the subjects of thin films, magnetic properties and materials. **BUSINESS ADDRESS:** Manager, Thin Film Dev, Technology Dept, Seagate Magnetics, 47010 Kato Road, Fremont, CA 94538, (510)490-3222.

KHAN, MOHAMMAD ASAD
Educator, geophysicist. Pakistani American. **PERSONAL:** Born Aug 13, 1940, Aima, Lahore, Pakistan; son of Ghulam Qadir and Hijira Khan; married Tahera Pathan, Jan 4, 1974; children: Shehzi Samira. **EDUCATION:** University of Punjab, BS, 1957, MS, 1963; Harvard University, 1964-65; University of Hawaii, PhD, 1967. **CAREER:** University of Punjab, lecturer, geophysics, 1963-64; University of Hawaii, asst prof, geophysics/geodesy, 1967-71, assoc prof, 1971-74, prof, 1974-; NASA, Goddard Space Flight Ctr, sr visiting scientist, 1972-74; Computer Scis Corp, sr scientist, 1974-76, sr consultant, 1976-77; Govt of Pakistan, minister of petroleum & natural resources, 1983-86, senator, 1984-86, intl advisers, chairman, 1987-. **ORGANIZATIONS:** Hawaii Environ Council, 1979-83; American Geophys Union; Pakistan Assn for the Advancement of Science; American Geological Inst. **HONORS/AWARDS:** East West Center Alumni Assn, Distinguished Alumnus Award, 1984; Pakistan Assn Minorities, Gold Medal, 1984, 1985. **BUSINESS ADDRESS:** Professor, University of Hawaii, Hawaii Institute of Geophysics, 2525 Correa Rd, Honolulu, HI 96822.

KHAN, MOHAMMED ABDUL QUDDUS
Educator. Pakistani American. **PERSONAL:** Born Mar 15, 1939, Kaimgunj, Uttar Pradesh, India; son of Mohammed & Maryam Hanif Khan; married Anwarun N Khan, Jul 14, 1974; children: Sara, Samreen, Yaseen. **EDUCATION:** University of Karachi, Pakistan, BSc, 1957, MSc, 1959; University of Western Ontario, Canada, PhD, 1964; Universidad Autonoma de Ciudad Juarez, Mexico, MD, 1984. **CAREER:** University of Western Ontario, research assistant, 1961-65; North Carolina State University, research associate, 1965-67; Oregon State University, research associate, 1967-68; Rutgers, The State University of New Jersey, research associate, 1968-69; University of Illinois, associate professor of biological sciences, 1969-74, professor of biological sciences, 1974-. **ORGANIZATIONS:** American Association Advancement of Science; Society of Toxicology; Society of Environmental Toxicology and Chemistry, charter member; International Society Study of Xenobiotics; Sigma Xi. **HONORS/AWARDS:** Fulbright, CIES, Senior Fulbright Fellowship, 1992-93; University of Wageningen, The Netherlands, Faculty Fellowship, 1982-83; Lady Davis Fellowship, Faculty Fellowship, 1992-93; National Institutes of Health, visiting scientist, 1975, Research Award, 1972-80. **SPECIAL ACHIEVEMENTS:** Books edited and co-edited: Survival in Toxic Environments, Academy Press, 1974; Pesticides in Aquatic Environments, Plenum, 1976; Pesticide & Xenobiotic Metabolism in Aquatic Organisms, American Chemistry Society, 1975; Toxicology of Halogenated Hydrocarbons, Pergamon, 1980; founding editor, Journal of Biochemical Toxicology. **BUSINESS ADDRESS:** Professor of Biological Sciences, University of Illinois, Chicago, PO Box 4348, 3364 SES, Chicago, IL 60680, (312)996-5449.

KHAN, SHAKIL AHMAD

Industrial company manager. Pakistani American. **PERSONAL:** Born Mar 1, 1947, Bareilly, India; son of Shafi and Namat Khan; married Kristine A Khan, Apr 7, 1974; children: Julianna Marie, Nicholas Evan, Rachel Olivia. **EDUCATION:** University of Karachi, Pakistan, MS, 1968; University of Islamabad, Pakistan, MS, 1969; Northwestern University, PhD, 1974. **CAREER:** Miles Inc, manager, 1977-. **ORGANIZATIONS:** American Chemical Society, 1977-. **HONORS/AWARDS:** UNESCO, merit scholarship for four years, 1970. **SPECIAL ACHIEVEMENTS:** Author, "Laboratory Automation Using Personal Computers," 38th Pittsburgh Conference & Exposition, 1987; "Chromatographic Data Acquisition and Data Analysis System-Part I," Instruments & Computers, Jan/Feb, 12, 1986; "A Chromatographic Data Acquisition and Processing System Using Personal Computer and IEEE-488 Interface Bus," 36th Pittsburgh Conference & Exposition, 1986. **BUSINESS ADDRESS:** Manager, Miles Inc, Mobay Road, Building 8, Pittsburgh, PA 15205, (412)777-4753.

KHAN, WALAYET A.

Educator. Pakistani American. **PERSONAL:** Born Aug 16, 1953, Faisalabad, Punjab, Pakistan; son of Musahib-Ud Din Khan & Wazir Begum; married Bushra Khan, Dec 31, 1986; children: Zeryab A, Zonair A. **EDUCATION:** University of Punjab, BA, 1974; RCD International School of Insurance, BS, 1979; University of Arkansas, MBA, 1985, PhD, 1990. **CAREER:** National Insurance Co, aviation insurance expert, 1977-79; University of Evansville, assistant professor of finance, 1989-. **ORGANIZATIONS:** FMA, 1989-; SFA, 1989-; EFA, 1989-; MWA, 1989-. **SPECIAL ACHIEVEMENTS:** Publications: "Dual Domestic Listing, Market Structure and Shareholder Wealth," Finance Review, vol 28, p 371-383, Aug 1993, summary of article, Bowne: Review for CFO's & Investment Bankers, vol 5, p 4-5, Nov 1993; "Unlisted Trading Privileges, Liquidity, and Stock Returns," Journal of Financial Research, vol 16, p 221-235, fall 1993; "Management Motives for Dual Listings: A Survey," Midwestern Journal of Business & Economics, vol 7, p 1-11, Winter 1993; presented numerous research papers in regional and national financial conventions. **HOME ADDRESS:** 132 Kimber Ln, Evansville, IN 47715, (812)473-3951. **BUSINESS ADDRESS:** Assistant Professor of Finance, School of Business Administration, University of Evansville, 1800 Lincoln Ave, Evansville, IN 47722, (812)479-2869.

KHANNA, NAVEEN

Educator. Indo-American. **PERSONAL:** Born Dec 17, 1951, Simla, Himachal Pradesh, India; son of Janki Nath Khanna (deceased) and Krishna Khanna; married Havovi Khanna, Sep 1, 1982; children: Jahan, Sharuk. **EDUCATION:** Northwestern University, PhD, finance, 1986. **CAREER:** University of Michigan, asst prof, finance, 1985-. **ORGANIZATIONS:** Western Finance Assn, 1986-; American Finance Assn, 1986-. **SPECIAL ACHIEVEMENTS:** Author: numerous publications in leading academic journals, 1989-92. **BUSINESS ADDRESS:** Professor, School of Business, University of Michigan, Tappan St, Ann Arbor, MI 48109-1234, (313)763-2170.

KHANNA, RAJIVE KUMAR

Educator. Indo-American. **PERSONAL:** Born Oct 28, 1954, Meerut, Uttar Pradesh, India; son of J K Khanna and Rama Khanna; married Dipti Vajpayee, Jul 20, 1990; children: Pooja. **EDUCATION:** University of Cambridge, Indian School Certificate, 1970; University of Delhi, BS, 1974; Indian Institute of Technology, Delhi, MS, 1976; Indian Institute of Technology, Kanpur, Phd, 1983. **CAREER:** Iowa State University, postdoctoral fellow, 1983-85; Georgia Institute of Technology, postdoctoral fellow, 1986-88; University of Southern Mississippi, assistant professor, 1988-. **ORGANIZATIONS:** American Chemical Society, 1987-; Mississippi Academy of Sciences, 1989-; International Union of Pure and Applied Chemistry, associate member, 1988-. **HONORS/AWARDS:** Indian Institute of Technology, Delhi, Merit Award, 1974, 1976; Council of Scientific and Industrial Research, Junior Research Fellow, 1977. **SPECIAL ACHIEVEMENTS:** 28 research publications, 1983-; 7 invited lectures/seminars, 1989-; 36 research presentations at scientific meetings, 1982-; invited to deliver a plenary lecture at the Gordon Research Conference on free radical reactions, 1993. **BIOGRAPHICAL SOURCES:** American Chemical Society Directory of Graduate Research, p 711, 1991; Chemical Sciences Graduate School Finders, p 439, 1992. **HOME PHONE:** (601)268-8834. **BUSINESS ADDRESS:** Assistant Professor, University of Southern Mississippi, Southern Station Box 5043, Hattiesburg, MS 39406-5043, (601)266-5527.

KHANNA, RAMESH

Physician, educator, researcher. Indo-American. **PERSONAL:** Born Sep 27, 1942, Udipi, Karnataka, India; son of Milkhiram Khanna & Champa Khanna; married Pushpa Khanna, Sep 9, 1970; children: Prema, Ashish. **EDUCATION:** University of Bombay, Jai Hind College, interscience, 1961, Seth GS Medical College, MB, BS, 1967, MD, 1971; Cleveland Clinic Foundation, postdoctoral subspecialty, hypertension & nephrology, 1982. **CAREER:** KEM Hospital, India, Internal Medicine, medical registrar, 1967-69, senior medical registrar, 1969-70; Cleveland Clinic Foundation, hypertension & nephrology fellow, 1972-75; Tirath Ram Shah Hospital & St Stephens Hospital, staff nephrologist, 1975-79; Toronto Western Hospital, research associate, lecturer in medicine, 1979-83; University of Missouri & Harry S Truman VA Hospital, associate professor of medicine, director of peritoneal dialysis, 1983-89; University of Missouri, School of Medicine, professor of medicine, 1989-. **ORGANIZATIONS:** International Society of Nephrology; American Society of Nephrology; American Society for Artificial Organs; Indian Society of Nephrology; European Dialysis and Transplantation Association; Boone County Medical Association; Missouri State Medical Association; American College of Physicians, fellow, 1987. **HONORS/AWARDS:** Cleveland Clinic Foundation, William E Lower Clinical Award, 1975; KEM Hospital Research Society, Dr M D Motashaw Oration, 1984; Sigma Xi, 1985; Association of Physicians from India, Illinois Chapter, Distinguished Physician of the Year, 1988; recipient of 16 research grants, 1979-89. **SPECIAL ACHIEVEMENTS:** Patent obtained for original invention, Missouri Swan-neck catheter, 1987; associate editor of Peritoneal Dialysis International, 1987-; contributed chapters to 59 medical texts, 1981-; delivered 295 scientific presentations/speeches internationally, 1974-. **BUSINESS ADDRESS:** Professor, University of Missouri, One Hospital Dr, MA436 Health Sciences Center, Columbia, MO 65212, (314)882-7991.

KHANNA, SHIV NARAIN

Educator. Indo-American. **PERSONAL:** Born Aug 3, 1950, Delhi, India; son of K N Khanna and C R Khanna; married Sarup Rani Khanna, Oct 4, 1978; children: Payal, Eera. **EDUCATION:** University of Delhi, BS, 1970, MS, 1972, PhD, 1976. **CAREER:** Swiss Federal Institute of Technology, scientific collaborator, 1980; Northeastern University, Boston, visiting associate professor, 1983; Virginia Commonwealth University, assistant professor, 1984-89, associate professor, 1989-93, professor, 1993-. **ORGANIZATIONS:** American Physical Society; Hindu Center of Virginia, publicity director, editor. **HONORS/AWARDS:** Swiss Federal Institute of Technology and CNRS, Grenoble, France, visiting professorships, summers of 1987-92. **SPECIAL ACHIEVEMENTS:** More than 110 research publications in: Physical Review Letters, Physical Review, Chemical Physical Letters. **BIOGRAPHICAL SOURCES:** Physics and Chemistry of Small Clusters, Plenum Press, 1987; Physics and Chemistry of Finite Systems: From Clusters to Crystals, Kluwer, 1993. **BUSINESS ADDRESS:** Professor, Physics Dept, Virginia Commonwealth University, Richmond, VA 23284-2000, (804)367-7076.

KHARE, BISHUN NARAIN

Scientist. Indo-American. **PERSONAL:** Born Jun 27, 1933, Varanasi, Uttar Pradesh, India; son of Dwarka Nath Srivastava & Ram Pyari; married Jyoti Rani Khare, Dec 7, 1962; children: Reena, Archana. **EDUCATION:** Banaras Hindu University, India, BSc, 1953, MSc, 1955; Syracuse University, PhD, physics, 1961. **CAREER:** Syracuse University, graduate research assistant, 1956-61; University of Toronto, postdoctoral research associate, 1961-62; State University of New York, Stony Brook, postdoctoral research associate, 1962-64; Ontario Research Foundation, associate research scientist, 1964-66; Smithsonian Astrophysical Observatory, physicist, 1966-68; Harvard University, associate, 1966-68; Cornell University, senior research physicist, currently. **ORGANIZATIONS:** American Physical Society; American Association for Advancement of Science; American Astronomical Society; American Chemical Society; International Astronomical Union; International Society for the Study of the Origin of Life; Astronomical Society of India, life member; Sigma Xi; Planetary Society. **HONORS/AWARDS:** National Science Foundation, travel grant, 1990, 1991, 1992; International Astronomical Union, travel grant, 1990. **SPECIAL ACHIEVEMENTS:** Production of amino acids from gaseous mixtures using ultraviolet light, US patent 3756934, 1973; Reflectance Spectra of Dark Materials: Implications for the Outer Solar System, 1992; Titan's Organic Chemistry: Results of simulation experiments, 1991; "First Foods," Discover, p 18, Feb 1991; numerous others. **BUSINESS ADDRESS:** Senior Research Physicist, Cornell University, 306 Space Science, Ithaca, NY 14853, (607)255-3934.

KHARE, MOHAN
Company executive. Indo-American. **PERSONAL:** Born May 15, 1942, Varamasi, Uttar Pradesh, India; son of DN Srivastava & RP Devi; married Meena Khare, Nov 20, 1973; children: Rohit. **EDUCATION:** Banaras Hindu University, BSc, 1961, MSc, 1963, PhD, 1967; University of Maryland, postdoctoral, 1967-69. **CAREER:** University of Maryland, Oregon State University, postdoctoral research associate, 1967-70; Cornell University, senior research associate, 1970-78; Hydroscience, Subsidiary of Dow Chemical Co, senior scientist, technologist, 1978-81; University of Nevada, USEPA Cooperative Aggrement Research Professor, manager, 1981-83; Rockwell, International, manager, organic lab, 1983-84; EA Engineering Science & Technology, director, chemistry lab, 1985-88; Recra Environmental, Inc, senior vice president, 1988-89; Envirosystems Inc, president, CEO, 1989-. **ORGANIZATIONS:** American Chemical Society, 1967-; American Associate for Advancement of Science, 1978-; American Mass Spectrometry Society, 1983-87; American Waterworks Association, 1992-. **HONORS/AWARDS:** Council of Scientific & Industrial Research, Government of India Research Fellowship, 1964-67. **SPECIAL ACHIEVEMENTS:** Wrote more than 35 research publications and scientific presentations; several in-house reports, standard operating procedures, and OAIOC manuals. **BUSINESS ADDRESS:** President, CEO, Envirosystems, Inc, 9200 Rumsey Rd, Ste B102, Columbia, MD 21045, (410)964-0330.

KHATWANI, MAHESH
Executive. Indo-American. **PERSONAL:** Born Nov 17, 1954, Bombay, Maharashtra, India; son of Kanayalal Khatwani; married Kalpana, Feb 15, 1989; children: Rachna. **EDUCATION:** College in India, bachelor's, 1981. **CAREER:** Main Computer Systems Inc, CEO, currently; Express Computer Rentals, vice president, currently. **BUSINESS ADDRESS:** CEO, Main Computer Systems Inc, 409 S Spuce Ave, South San Francisco, CA 94080, (415)615-0101.

KHAW, BAN-AN (CHIT-MYINE CHO)
Educator. **PERSONAL:** Born Jul 25, 1947, Bassein, Burma; son of Kon Saing Khaw and Shu Khin Ong; married Sharon Khaw, Aug 21, 1976; children: Julia, Larah, Alexander, Adam-Ridgely. **EDUCATION:** State University of New York, Oswego, BA, 1969; Boston College, MS, 1970, PhD, 1974. **CAREER:** Massachusetts General Hospital, fellow to associate professor, 1973-; Northeastern University, professor, 1991-. **ORGANIZATIONS:** Society of Nuclear Medicine, 1984-; Chinese American Society Nuclear Medicine, 1986-, president, 1990-92; American Heart Association, 1985-; American Chem Society, 1993; American Soc Nuclear Cardiology, 1993. **HONORS/AWARDS:** Society Nuclear Medicine, Berson-Yalow Award, 1991; 20th Intl Symposium on Controlled Release of Bioactive Materials, Outstanding Pharmaceutical Paper, 1993. **SPECIAL ACHIEVEMENTS:** Over 140 scientific publications and chapters; one book. **BUSINESS ADDRESS:** George D Behrakis Professor of Pharm Sciences, Bouve College of Pharmacy & Health Sciences, Northeastern University, Mugar Bldg, Rm 205, Boston, MA 02115, (617)377-4203.

KHIM, JAY WOOK
Business executive. Korean American. **PERSONAL:** Born Oct 22, 1940, Teagu, Republic of Korea; married Millie M Khim; children: Katheryn Khim Zupan, Anthony. **EDUCATION:** Kyungpook National University, BS, agricultural economics, 1963, MA, agricultural economics, 1966; University of Maryland, PhD program in economics, 1965-69. **CAREER:** Brookings Institution, research staff; NAB, senior economist, 1967-69; Department of Labor, 1969-72; Planning Research Corporation, associate, 1972-74; JWK International Corporation, CEO, chairman, 1973-; Virginia 11th Congressional District, US congressional candidate, 1992. **ORGANIZATIONS:** George Mason Institute, George Mason University, board of directors, 1983-; World President's Org, 1992-; Fairfax Hospital, board of trustees, 1986-. **HONORS/AWARDS:** Fulbright Scholar, 1965, 1966; Randolph-Macon College, Honorary LLD, 1988; Kyungook National University, Korea, Honorary PhD, 1990. **BUSINESS ADDRESS:** Chairman, CEO, JWK International Corporation, 7617 Little River Turnpike, Ste 1040, Annandale, VA 22003, (703)750-0500.

KHORANA, HAR GOBIND
Educator, chemist. Indo-American. **PERSONAL:** Born Jan 9, 1922, Raipur, India; son of Shri Ganpat Rai and Shrimati Devi Krishna Khorana; married Esther E Sibler, 1952; children: Julia, Emilie, Dave Roy. **EDUCATION:** Punjab University, India, BS, 1943, MS, 1945; Liverpool University, UK, PhD, 1948; University of Chicago, DSc, 1967. **CAREER:** Rockefeller Institute, visiting professor, 1958-; University of Wisconsin, Institute of Enzyme Re-

search, co-director, 1960-70, Dept of Biochemistry, professor, 1962-70, Conrad A Elvehjem Professor of Life Sciences, 1964-70; Massachusetts Institute of Technology, Alfred P Sloan Professor of Biology and Chemistry, 1970-. **ORGANIZATIONS:** Natl Academy of Science; American Academy of Arts and Sciences, fellow; Churchill College, Overseas Fellow, 1967; Journal of the American Chemical Society, editorial board, 1963-. **HONORS/AWARDS:** German Democratic Republic, Dannie-Heinneman Preiz, 1967; Johns Hopkins University, Remsen Award, 1968; American Chemical Society, Louisa Gross Horwitz Prize, 1968; Nobel Prize in Medicine, 1968. **SPECIAL ACHIEVEMENTS:** Deutsche Akademie der Naturforscher Leopoldina HalleSaale, elected member, 1968; contributor of numerous articles to professional journals in the fields of medicine and chemistry. **BUSINESS ADDRESS:** Alfred P Sloan Professor, Dept of Biology & Chemistry, Massachusetts Institute of Technology, Room 180511, Cambridge, MA 02139.*

KHORASANEE, BARKER M.
City government official. Myanmar American. **PERSONAL:** Born Jan 1, 1943, Rangoon, Myanmar; son of Mohamed J Khorasanee and Daw Mya May; married Mari Khorasanee, Sep 17, 1978; children: Adrienne, Jacqueline. **EDUCATION:** Institute of Economics, Rangoon, BComm, 1966. **CAREER:** City of Los Angeles, director of financial management, 1972-. **ORGANIZATIONS:** GFOA, 1988-; City of Los Angeles Foundation, treasurer, 1985-; Small Business Loans, Loan Committee, member; City of Los Angeles Municipal Accountants and Auditors Association, past president. **BUSINESS ADDRESS:** Director of Financial Management, Community Development Dept, City of Los Angeles, 215 W Sixth Streeet, Suite 500, Los Angeles, CA 90014, (213)485-7258.

KHOSLA, MAHESH CHANDRA
Chemist. Indo-American. **PERSONAL:** Born Jul 6, 1925, Rajoya, Hazara, India; son of Jai R Khosla and Dewki Khosla; married Santosh Bhandari, May 30, 1957; children: Renu, Rajan, Rajesh. **EDUCATION:** Panjab University, India, BS, 1950, MS, 1952, PhD, 1957. **CAREER:** Cen Drug Research Institute, sr science officer, India, 1963-69; Cleveland Clinic Foundation, assoc staff, 1971, staff, 1972-. **ORGANIZATIONS:** American Chem Soc; American Soc Biol Chemists; Intl Soc Hypertension; American Soc Hypertension. **HONORS/AWARDS:** NIH, grants, 1978-; Council High Blood Pressure Research, fellow. **SPECIAL ACHIEVEMENTS:** Patents in field of hypertension; contributor of articles to professional journals. **BUSINESS ADDRESS:** Cleveland Clinic Foundation, Health Sci Ctr REBV/NC3-147, 9500 Euclid Ave, Cleveland, OH 44195-5286.

KHURANA, KRISHAN KUMAR
Researcher. Indo-American. **PERSONAL:** Born Jun 1, 1955, New Delhi, India; son of T C Khurana & L W Khurana; married Amber, 1981. **EDUCATION:** University of Delhi, BSc, 1974; Osmania University, Hyderabad, India, MSc, geophysics, 1977, PhD, geophysics, 1981; Durham University, UK, PhD, geophysics, 1984. **CAREER:** IGPP, UCLA, research geophysicist, 1985-. **ORGANIZATIONS:** American Geophysical Union, 1986-; American Astronomical Society, associate member, 1990-; American Institute of Physics, associate member, 1986-. **HONORS/AWARDS:** Commonwealth, Commonwealth Scholarship, 1981. **SPECIAL ACHIEVEMENTS:** More then 15 research publications in space physics and geophysics, 1981-93. **BUSINESS ADDRESS:** Researcher, Institute of Geophysics & Planetary Physics, UCLA, Slichter Hall, Los Angeles, CA 90024, (310)825-8240.

KIANG, CLYDE Y.
Educator. Taiwanese American. **PERSONAL:** Born Dec 4, 1936, Chichi, Japan; son of Ching-Ding & Yuen-Mei Chieu Kiang; married May Guo, Dec 28, 1978; children: Justin, Kylene. **EDUCATION:** National Taiwan University, BA, 1960; Western Michigan University, MA, 1964; Michigan State University, MA, 1971. **CAREER:** Minot State University, cataloger, head librarian, 1964-69; Gale Research Co, editorial associate, 1969-71; California University of Pennsylvania, chief cataloger, professor, 1972-. **ORGANIZATIONS:** Association of Pennsylvania State College & University Faculties, 1976-; North American Taiwanese Professors' Association, 1985-; American Association of University Professors, 1979-; Taiwan Hakka Association for Public Affairs in North America, 1990-. **HONORS/AWARDS:** Taiwan Foundation, Professor Ong Research Grant, 1992. **SPECIAL ACHIEVEMENTS:** Author, The Hakka Odyssey & Their Taiwan Homeland, 1992; The Hakka Search for a Homeland, 1991. **MILITARY SERVICE:** Taiwan Army, captain, 1960-61. **BIOGRAPHICAL SOURCES:** "The Hakka Odyssey," by Mike Sajna, Pittsburgh Tribune-Review, Focus, p4, May 16, 1993. **BUSINESS**

ADDRESS: Chief Cataloger & Associate Professor, Louis L Manderino Library, California University of Pennsylvania, California, PA 15419-1394, (412)938-5763.

KIANG, PETER NIEN-CHU
Educator. Chinese American. **PERSONAL:** Born Nov 20, 1958, Boston, MA; son of Nelson Yuan-sheng Kiang and Madlyn J Rowe; married Vivian Wai-fun Lee, Aug 11, 1989. **EDUCATION:** Harvard College, BA, 1980; Harvard Graduate School of Education, EdM, 1986, EdD, 1991. **CAREER:** Asian American Resource Workshop, program director, 1980-86; Boston University, lecturer, 1987; Yale University, lecturer, 1988; University of Massachusetts, Boston, lecturer & research associate, 1987-91, assistant professor, 1991-. **ORGANIZATIONS:** Association for Asian American Studies, 1984-, east coast rep, 1989-91; Chinese Historical Society of New England, founding board member, 1992-; Massachusetts Asian American Educators Association, board member, 1991-93; American Friends Service Committee, national community relations committee, 1986-; Teens as Community Resources, board member, 1988-93; New England American Studies Association, board member, 1992-93. **HONORS/AWARDS:** Massachusetts Teachers Association, Human & Civil Rights Award, 1991; NAACP, Human Rights Award, 1990; Massachusetts Association for Bilingual Education, first prize, monograph competition, 1990; Community Change, Drylongso Award, 1989; Anti-Defamation League, World of Difference Award, 1988; Boston Foundation, Showing the Way Award, 1993. **SPECIAL ACHIEVEMENTS:** Asian American Studies Curriculum Resource Guide, 1992; many journal articles, monographs, grants in the areas of Asian American Studies, multicultural education, and community development; "Southeast Asian Parent Empowerment," monograph, 1990; videos: "Asian Americans in Cambridge," 1988; "Boston Chinatown History," 1983; films: Tao Te Ching, 1979; Cahoon Hollow, 1979, shown in festivals in Boston, Chicago, NY, San Francisco, Hong Kong. **BUSINESS ADDRESS:** Asst Professor, Grad College of Education, University of Massachusetts, Boston, 100 Morrisey Blvd, Boston, MA 02125-3393, (617)287-7614.

KIANG, ROBERT L.
Engineer. Chinese American. **PERSONAL:** Born Nov 30, 1939, Chungking, China; son of Johnson Kiang and C C Kiang; married Ming D Kiang, Apr 12, 1986; children: Jennifer D. **EDUCATION:** National Taiwan University, BS, 1961; Stanford University, MS, 1964, PhD, 1969. **CAREER:** SRI International, research engineer, 1964-87; Naval Surf Warfare Ctr, mechanical engineer, 1987-. **ORGANIZATIONS:** ASME. **BUSINESS ADDRESS:** Mechanical Engineer, Naval Surface Warfare Center, Carderock Division, Annapolis Detachment, 3A Leggett Circle, Annapolis, MD 21402, (410)267-3836.

KIKUCHI, CARL H.
Government employee. Japanese American. **PERSONAL:** Born Jun 23, 1950, Lansing, MI; son of Chihiro Kikuchi and Grace Kikuchi; married Janice D Kikuchi, Jul 1981; children: Colin P. **EDUCATION:** Harvard University, AB, 1972; University of Iowa, MFA, 1975. **CAREER:** Control Data Corporation, branch manager, 1975-1984; US Dept of Justice, Office of Litigation Support, branch chief, 1984-. **SPECIAL ACHIEVEMENTS:** Published poet. **HOME ADDRESS:** 218 W Greenway Blvd, Falls Church, VA 22046.

KIKUCHI, GEORGE SUSUMU
Postmaster. Japanese American. **PERSONAL:** Born in Seattle, WA; son of Isamu and Marian Kikuchi. **EDUCATION:** University of Washington, graduate, finance. **CAREER:** United States Postal Service: various postions, including acting postmaster of Palm Springs, 1985; Western Regional Headquarters, San Francisco, beginning 1972, San Bruno, regional manager for budget, until 1992; City of San Francisco, postmaster, 1992-. **SPECIAL ACHIEVEMENTS:** Fourth highest-ranking Japanese American in United States Postal Service, 1992. **BUSINESS ADDRESS:** Postmaster, US Post Office, Box 885046, San Francisco, CA 94188-5046, (415)550-5001.*

KIKUCHI, SHINYA
Educator. Japanese American. **PERSONAL:** Born May 12, 1943, Kobe, Japan; son of Saburo and Hideko Kikuchi; married Laura, Dec 17, 1975. **EDUCATION:** Hokkaido University, Japan, BS, 1967, MS, 1969; University of Pennsylvania, PhD, 1974. **CAREER:** Transportation Development Associates, associate, 1974-77; General Motors Corporation, sr project engineer, 1977-82; University of Delaware, assistant professor, 1982-87, associate professor, 1987-93, professor, 1993-. **ORGANIZATIONS:** American Society of Civil

Engineers; Institute of Transporation Engineers; Society of Logistics Engineers; Transportation Research Board, university representative. **HONORS/ AWARDS:** International Road Union, Best Paper Award, 1992. **SPECIAL ACHIEVEMENTS:** Many papers on transportation planning and engineering. **BUSINESS ADDRESS:** Professor, Civil Engineering, University of Delaware, Newark, DE 19716, (302)831-2657.

KIKUCHI, WILLIAM KENJI
Educator, archaeologist. Japanese American. **PERSONAL:** Born Jun 27, 1935, Honolulu, HI; son of Edward Goro & Gladys Kikue Kikuchi; married Delores Lorene Kikuchi, Dec 28, 1968; children: Kristina P, Kathleen K, Michelei K. **EDUCATION:** University of Washington, 1955-57; University of Hawaii, BA, 1960, MA, 1963; University of Arizona, PhD, 1973. **CAREER:** Boeing Airplane Company, draftsman, 1955-57; Bernice P Bishop Museum, asst archaeologist, 1964-67, research associate, archaeology, 1986-95; Kauai Community College, full professor, anthropology, 1972-. **ORGANIZATIONS:** Native Hawaiian Culture & Arts Program, trustee, 1987-93; Kauai County Historic Pres Rev Comm, archaeologist, 1981-83, 1987-95; Hawaii Historic Places Rev Board, archaeologist, 1971-86; Society for Hawaiian Archaeology, 1986-; Polynesian Society, 1960s-; New Zealand Archaeological Assn, 1970s-; Sigma Xi, 1960-; Society for American Archaeology, 1970-. **HONORS/ AWARDS:** University of Texas, Medallion, 1985; University of Hawaii, Excellence in Teaching, 1981; Kauai Comm College, Merit Award, 1981; State of Hawaii, ten year service award, 1982, twenty year service award, 1992. **SPECIAL ACHIEVEMENTS:** Founder/editor, Archaeology on Kauai, 1972-; author, The Fireball in Hawaiian Folklore: Essays in Honor of Katherine Luomala, 1975; "Prehistoric Hawaiian Fishponds," Science, vol 153, pp 235-239, 1966; "Petroglyphs in American Samoa," Journal of Polynesian Soc, vol 73, no 2, pp 163-166, 1964; "Additional Petroglyphs from American Samoa," Journal of Polynesian Soc, vol 76, no 3, pp 372-373, 1967. **MILITARY SERVICE:** US Air Fore, a3c, 1957. **BUSINESS ADDRESS:** Professor, Kauai Community College, 3-1901 Kaumualii Hwy, Lihue, HI 96766-9591.

KIKUMURA, AKEMI
Anthropologist, writer, museum administrator. Japanese American. **PERSONAL:** married Gary K Yano, Jun 9, 1979; children: Remi Manning, Gregory Yano. **EDUCATION:** University of California, Los Angeles, PhD, 1979. **CAREER:** University of Southern California, assistant professor, 1978-80; University of California, Los Angeles, postdoctoral fellow, lecturer, 1981-83; Japanese American National Museum, director of program development, 1989-. **ORGANIZATIONS:** Visual Communications, board of directors, 1978-; Screen Actors Guild, 1973-92. **HONORS/AWARDS:** Little Tokyo Service Center, Community Involvement Award, 1987; Ruby Yoshino Schaar Playwright Award, 1986; UCLA Alumni Association, Award for Academic Distinction, 1978. **SPECIAL ACHIEVEMENTS:** National Endowment for the Humanities, project director, The Nisei Years exhibit, 1993-; Meyer Memorial Trust, project director, The Oregon Issei Pioneers exhibit, 1992; Issei Pioneers: Hawaii and the Mainland, 1885-1924, Japanese American National Museum, 1992; Promises Kept, Chandler & Sharp, 1991; Through Harsh Winters, 9th printing, Chandler & Sharp, 1981; Issei Pioneer: Hawaii & the Mainland, inaugural exhibit, 1992-; In This Great Land of Freedom: The Japanese Pioneers of Oregon, 1993-. **BIOGRAPHICAL SOURCES:** Rafu Shimpo, Holiday Edition, December, 1992; Humanities, Jan/Feb 1994, vol 15, no 1, p 25. **BUSINESS ADDRESS:** Director of Program Development, Japanese American National Museum, 369 E First St, Los Angeles, CA 90012, (213)625-0414.

KIM, ALAN HYUN-OAK
Educator. Korean American. **PERSONAL:** Born Sep 6, 1932, Nishiwaki, Hyogo Prefecture, Japan; divorced; children: Elaine, Mirena, Frances (Serena). **EDUCATION:** Seoul National University, Korea, MA; San Jose State University, MA, linguistics; University of Southern CA, PhD, linguistics, 1985. **CAREER:** Korean Air Force Academy, instructor, 1958-62; California State University, lecturer, 1979-80; Harvard University, Linguistics Department, visiting scholar, 1980-82; UCLA, Asian American Studies Center, postdoc fellow, 1985-86; Portland State University, assistant professor of Japanese & Korean, 1986-88; Southern Illinois University, Carbondale, associate professor of Japanese & linguistics, 1988-, East Asian Studies Program, head, 1993-. **ORGANIZATIONS:** Linguistic Society of America; Linguistic Society of Korea; International Circle of Korean Language & Linguistics; Association for Asian Studies; Association for Teachers of Japanese; Association for Asian Philosophy. **HOME PHONE:** (618)529-4120. **BUSINESS ADDRESS:**

Professor, Dept of Foreign Languages & Literatures, Southern Illinois University, Carbondale, IL 62901-4521, (618)536-5571.

KIM, ANNA CHARR

Educator, counselor. Korean American. **PERSONAL:** Born in Chicago, IL; daughter of Easurk Charr and Evelyn Charr; married Andrew S Kim, Feb 22, 1958; children: Mickey, Jenny, Ben. **EDUCATION:** Park College, BA, biology, 1952; Oberlin College, MA, zoology, 1954; National-Louis University, certificate advance studies, special education, 1982. **CAREER:** Chicago Public School, substitute, 1964-65; University of Chicago, editor, 1965-66; University of Wisconsin, editor, 1966-67; Summit School, LD teacher, 1974-79; SD 214, LD teacher, 1979-82; National-Louis University, evaluator, 1982-88, assistant professor, 1988-. **ORGANIZATIONS:** Midwest College Learning Center Association, 1988-; National Association Developmental Education, 1988-; International Reading Association, 1991-93. **HONORS/AWARDS:** NLU, Teacher of the Year, 1991. **SPECIAL ACHIEVEMENTS:** Set up & coordinate College LD Program, 1991-; student of Russian language, St Petersburg University, Russia, summer, 1991, summer 1992. **BIOGRAPHICAL SOURCES:** Golden Mountain, father's autobiography, to be re-issued by University of Illinois, Chicago, p301. **HOME ADDRESS:** 170 W King Ln, Des Plaines, IL 60016, (708)296-2579. **BUSINESS ADDRESS:** Assistant Professor, National-Louis University, 2840 Sheridan Rd, Bldg 6, Evanston, IL 60201, (708)475-1100.

KIM, AUGUSTINE H.

Attorney. Korean American. **PERSONAL:** Born Jun 14, 1965, Seoul, Republic of Korea; son of Simon T Kim & Julie Anne H Kim. **EDUCATION:** Harvard University, AB, 1988; New York University School of Law, JD, 1991. **CAREER:** Thacher Proffitt & Wood, associate, 1991-92; O'Sullivan Graev & Karabell, associate, 1992-. **ORGANIZATIONS:** American Bar Association, 1991-. **BUSINESS ADDRESS:** Associate, O'Sullivan Graev & Karabell, 30 Rockefeller Plaza, New York, NY 10112, (212)408-2465.

KIM, BANG JA (B. J.)

Educator. Korean American. **PERSONAL:** Born Sep 2, 1940, Pusan, Republic of Korea; married Han J Kim, May 21, 1966; children: Amy, Alice. **EDUCATION:** Ewha University, BA, 1962; University of Oregon, MA, 1965; Oregon State University, 1966-67. **CAREER:** University of Oregon, instructor/librarian, 1965-66; South Dakota State University, instructor/assistant reference librarian, 1967-70, assistant professor/assistant reference librarian, 1972-83, Documents Department, associate professor/head, 1980-84, Catalog Department, professor/head 1985-. **ORGANIZATIONS:** American Library Association, 1988-; ALA Association of College and Research Libraries, 1988-; ALA Library and Information Technology Association, 1988-; Mountain Plains Library Association, 1990-; South Dakota Library Association, 1972-; South Dakota Library Network Tech Contacts, 1988-; US Civil Rights Commission, South Dakota Advisory Council, 1992-. **HONORS/AWARDS:** South Dakota Librarian of the Year, 1981. **SPECIAL ACHIEVEMENTS:** Sioux Falls Argus Leader Index, 1979-; SDSU Collegian Index, 1980-; Keyword Index to the SDSU Agricultural Experiment and Extension Service Publication, 1976, 1986; The Sioux Falls Argus-Leader, 1982-92, 1993. **BUSINESS ADDRESS:** Professor/Head, Catalog Dept, H M Briggs Library, South Dakota State University, Brookings, SD 57007, (605)688-5560.

KIM, BONG HWAN

Association administrator. Korean American. **CAREER:** Korean Youth Center, executive director, currently. **ORGANIZATIONS:** Black Korean Alliance, co-chair. **HONORS/AWARDS:** American Thai Institute, Certificate of Appreciation, 1992. **BUSINESS ADDRESS:** Executive Director, Korean Youth Center, 3470 Wilshire Blvd, Ste 1110, Los Angeles, CA 90010, (213)365-7400. *

KIM, BONG YOHL

Business executive. Korean American. **PERSONAL:** Born Mar 16, 1932, Hung Nam, Hamgyung Do, Republic of Korea; son of Sam Bok Kim (deceased) and Bok Nam Kim (deceased); married Josephine F Kim, Jul 27, 1961; children: Paul B, Debra R Kim-Bieda. **EDUCATION:** Indiana University, business management, 1976. **CAREER:** Union Tank Car Co, senior buyer, currently. **ORGANIZATIONS:** Lakeside Federal Credit Union, Credit Committee, chairman. **MILITARY SERVICE:** Republic of Korea Army, staff sgt, 1958-61. **HOME ADDRESS:** 8558 Liable Rd, Highland, IN 46322. **BUSINESS PHONE:** (219)392-6211.

KIM, BONN-OH (BONG-OH)

Educator. Korean American. **PERSONAL:** Born Nov 16, 1956, Seoul, Republic of Korea; married Jeeyoung Kim; children: Allen, Eumie. **EDUCATION:** Seoul National University, BA, 1978; University of Washington, MBA, 1984; University of Minnesota, PhD, 1991. **CAREER:** Korea Development Bank, economist, 1981-82; University of Minnesota, teaching assistant, 1984-89; University of Nebraska, professor, 1989-. **ORGANIZATIONS:** American Association of Artificial Intelligence, 1984-; Association of Computing Machinery, 1984-. **BUSINESS ADDRESS:** Professor, Management Dept, University of Nebraska, College of Business Administration, Lincoln, NE 68588-0491, (402)472-2317.

KIM, BYONG-KON

Educator. Korean American. **PERSONAL:** Born May 28, 1929, Taegu, Republic of Korea; married Setsuko K Kim, Feb 19, 1966; children: Adrienne, Vivienne, Janette. **EDUCATION:** Indiana University, Bloomington, M Music, 1964, D Music, 1968. **CAREER:** Villa Maria Institute of Music, head of theory program, 1966-68; California State University, Los Angeles, professor of music, 1968-. **ORGANIZATIONS:** Pacific Contemporary Music Center, director, 1986-. **HONORS/AWARDS:** California State University, Los Angeles, Outstanding Professor Award, 1991. **BIOGRAPHICAL SOURCES:** Baker's Biographical Dictionary of Musicians, p 915, 1992. **HOME ADDRESS:** 30458 Via Victoria, Rancho Palos Verdes, CA 90274, (310)377-6637.

KIM, BYUNG GUK

Educator. Korean American. **PERSONAL:** Born Mar 7, 1953, Seoul, Republic of Korea; son of Chang-Soo Kim and Yong-Kyun Lee; married Yoo Kyung Kim, Dec 30, 1980; children: Lida, Clara. **EDUCATION:** Seoul National University, BS, 1975; University of Massachusetts, Amherst, MS, 1978, PhD, 1980. **CAREER:** Wright State University, assistant professor, 1980-84; University of Massachusetts, Lowell, assistant/associate professor, 1984-. **ORGANIZATIONS:** Institute of Electrical & Electronics Engineers, 1979-; Korean Scientists & Engineers Association, general secretary, staff member, 1984-. **SPECIAL ACHIEVEMENTS:** Author, "Discrete-time Models for Telecommunications including ATM," Kluwer Publishing Co, 1992; approximately 20 other publications in technical conferences/journals. **MILITARY SERVICE:** Korean military. **BUSINESS ADDRESS:** Associate Professor, Computer Science Dept, University of Massachusetts, Lowell, Lowell, MA 01854-2881, (508)934-3617.

KIM, BYUNG SUK

Educator. Korean American. **PERSONAL:** Born Mar 20, 1942, Republic of Korea; son of Yong Taik Kim; married Oak Kim, Apr 9, 1967; children: Peggy, Charles. **EDUCATION:** Seoul National University, BS, 1967; Virginia State University, MS, 1969; University of Illinois, PhD, 1973. **CAREER:** Columbia University, senior staff associate, 1973-74; University of Chicago, research assistant professor, 1974-76; Northwestern University, assistant professor, 1976-81, associate professor, 1981-91, professor, 1991-. **ORGANIZATIONS:** American Association of Immunologists, 1976-; Korean Scientists and Engineers Association, 1976-; Chicago Association of Immunologists, 1978-; NIH, Study Section, 1985-89. **HONORS/AWARDS:** California Institute Technology, visiting professor, 1984. **SPECIAL ACHIEVEMENTS:** Author of more than 60 articles in scientific journals. **MILITARY SERVICE:** Korean Army, 18th Regieme, corp, 1963-65. **BUSINESS ADDRESS:** Professor, Northwestern University Medical School, 303 E Chicago Ave, 6-711 Tarry Bldg, Chicago, IL 60611, (312)503-8693.

KIM, CHAESIK

Researcher. Korean American. **PERSONAL:** Born Jun 18, 1949, Seoul, Republic of Korea; son of Won Bae Kim and Soon Duk Kim; married Young Soon Kim, Dec 25, 1976; children: Peter Heetae, Paul Heetak. **EDUCATION:** Hanyang University, BSEE, 1970. **CAREER:** Wayne State University, Kresge Eye Institute, researcher, currently. **HOME ADDRESS:** 6770 White Pine Dr, Bloomfield Hills, MI 48301, (313)932-0649.

KIM, CHAN-HIE

Educator, cleric. Korean American. **PERSONAL:** Born Jun 7, 1935, Hoeryung, Republic of Korea; son of Chong Jin Kim and Kansung Moon Kim; married Sook-Chung Kim, Sep 9, 1962; children: Alexis Hangin. **EDUCATION:** Yonsei University, Korea, BA, 1958; University of Heidelberg, Germany, 1960-61; Vanderbilt University, BD, 1964, PhD, 1970. **CAREER:** Yonsei University, asst prof of religion, 1971-72; University of Montana, visiting asst professor, 1972-74; United Methodist Church, Bd of Discipleship, staff, 1974-77; Center for Asian-American Ministries, director, 1977-87; Claremont Graduate School, professor of religion, 1978-, School of Theology at Claremont, professor of New Testament, 1987-. **ORGANIZATIONS:** United Methodist Church, ordained elder, 1965-; Society of Biblical Literature, 1968-; American Academy of Religion, 1968-. **SPECIAL ACHIEVEMENTS:** Author, Form and Structure of Familiar Greek Letter of Recommendation, 1971; language proficiency: Korean, Japanese, Hellenistic Greek, Hebrew, classical Chinese, French, German. **MILITARY SERVICE:** Korean Air Force, 1st lt, 1958-60. **BUSINESS ADDRESS:** Professor, School of Theology at Claremont, 1325 N College Ave, Claremont, CA 91711, (909)626-3521.

KIM, CHAN-WUNG
Educator. Korean American. **PERSONAL:** Born Jun 8, 1958, Pusan, Republic of Korea; son of Sung-Do Kim and Soon-Jo Chung Kim; married Hyun-Sook Kim, Jun 22, 1986; children: Jee-Yeon, Dong-Woo. **EDUCATION:** Sung Kyun Kwan University, Korea, BBA, 1981; Seoul National University, MBA, 1983; University of Iowa, MA, 1989, PhD, 1991. **CAREER:** Kiet, researcher, 1983-85; University of Iowa, research assistant, 1985-87, instructor, 1987-91; University of Massachusetts, Boston, assistant professor, 1991-. **ORGANIZATIONS:** Financial Management Association, 1985-; American Finance Association, 1985-. **HONORS/AWARDS:** University of Massachusetts, Boston, Summer Research Grant, 1992; University of Iowa, Ponder Fellowship, 1986-90; Seoul National University, University Award, 1981-83; Sung Kyun Kwan University, Alumni Fellowship, 1979-84. **SPECIAL ACHIEVEMENTS:** Publications in the Journal of Futures Markets, 1988, Pacific-Basin Capital Markets Research, 1992. **BUSINESS ADDRESS:** Professor, Accounting and Finance Dept, University of Massachusetts, Boston, College of Management, 100 Morrissey Blvd, Boston, MA 02125, (617)287-7672.

KIM, CHANG KYU
Association executive. Korean American. **PERSONAL:** Born May 19, 1949, Onyang, Chungnam, Republic of Korea; son of Byung Sung Kim and Soon Ryea Kim; married Sung-Hee Kim, Aug 29, 1986; children: Ronald. **EDUCATION:** Yonsei University, BS, economics, 1972; Seoul National University, MA, journalism, 1974; Western Illinois University, MBA, marketing, 1977. **CAREER:** Shinjin Corp, assistant manager, 1974; Southland Corp, management trainee, 1977-78; Rotary International, correspondent, 1978-79, area supervisor for southeast Asia, 1979-87, Korea branch office manager, 1987-92, Asia & Pacific department manager, 1990-. **ORGANIZATIONS:** Rotary Club of Wilmette, 1986-87, 1991-; Rotary Club of Seoul, 1988-90; Society of 300 Free Thinkers in Korea, 1989-; District 3650 of Rotary International, Rotary Information Committee, chairman, 1988-90; Sharon United Methodist Church, founding member, 1980-90. **HONORS/AWARDS:** Rotary Foundation, Paul Harris Fellow, 1991; Secretary of State, Arkansas, Certificate of Appreciation, 1990; District 3300 of Rotary International, Certificate of Appreciation, 1980; Rotary Club of Navotas South in the Philippines, Certificate of Appreciation, 1982; District 3650 of Rotary International, Plaque of Appreciation/Achievement, 1991. **BUSINESS ADDRESS:** Manager, Asia & Pacific Dept, Rotary International, 1560 Sherman Ave, 16th Fl, Evanston, IL 60201, (708)866-3254.

KIM, CHANGWOOK
Educator. Korean American. **PERSONAL:** Born Jan 18, 1953, Taegu, Republic of Korea; married. **EDUCATION:** Seoul National University, BS, 1975; Pennsylvania State University, MS, 1982; Northwestern University, PhD, 1986. **CAREER:** University of Oklahoma, assistant professor, 1986-92, associate professor, 1992-. **ORGANIZATIONS:** Association for Computing Machinery, 1981-; European Association for Theoretical Computer Science, 1982-; Institute of Electrical and Electronics Engineers, 1986-. **BUSINESS ADDRESS:** Associate Professor, University of Oklahoma, School of Computer Science, EL 114A, Norman, OK 73019-0470, (405)325-4281.

KIM, CHANGYUP DANIEL
Educator, clergy. Korean American. **PERSONAL:** Born Aug 10, 1921, Jung-Joo, North Korea; son of Kwang-Ok and Shin-Ok Kim; married Suksoon Elizabeth Kim, Mar 7, 1942; children: Won-Ok, John S, Sungae Esther, Sungha Paul. **EDUCATION:** Young Nam University, Korea, BA, 1952; Presbyterian General Assembly Theological Seminary, Korea, BD, 1955; New York Theological Seminary, STM, 1960; Dallas Theological Seminary, ThD, 1963. **CAREER:** Evangelical Covenant Church, Missoula, MT, pastor, 1963-66; Central Baptist Theological Seminary, professor, 1966-78; The Korean Church of Twin Cities, pastor, 1967-78; The Korean First Baptist Church of Minnesota, founder, emeritus pastor, 1978-; Liberty Baptist Theological Seminary, professor, 1978-; The Korean Baptist Church of Roanoke, VA, founder, emeritus

pastor, 1980-; The Korean Baptist Church of Blacksburg, VA, founder, emeritus pastor, 1981-. **ORGANIZATIONS:** Evangelical Theological Society, 1978-. **HONORS/AWARDS:** The Korean First Baptist Church of Minnesota, Honor for Service, 1978, 1984, 1993; The Korean Baptist Church of Blacksburg, Honor for Service, 1989. **SPECIAL ACHIEVEMENTS:** Author, Salvation, Sanctification & Service, 1988; trained in Chinese, German, Greek, Hebrew; proficient in Korean, Japanese, and English. **HOME PHONE:** (804)239-9562. **BUSINESS ADDRESS:** Professor, Liberty Baptist Theological Seminary, PO Box 20000, Lynchburg, VA 24506.

KIM, CHIN
Educator. Korean American. **PERSONAL:** Born Dec 19, 1926, Pusan, Kyungsang, S Province, Republic of Korea; son of Woo Yung Kim; married Bok Lim C Kim, Sep 20, 1956; children: Mary Ann Y, Stanley Y. **EDUCATION:** Korea University, LLB, 1951; Florida Southern College, AB (cum laude), 1954; George Washington University, master of comparative law, 1955; Yale University, master of laws, 1956, Law School, doctor of juridical science, 1958; Columbia University, MS, 1967. **CAREER:** Seoul National University, professor of law, 1958-68; University of Illinois, professor of law and library adm, 1968-78; California Western School of Law, professor of law, 1978-. **ORGANIZATIONS:** American Society of Comparative Law, editorial board, 1980-. **HONORS/AWARDS:** French Ministry of Foreign Affairs, Post Doctorate Fellow, 1960-61; American Political Science Association, Congressional Fellow, 1964-65. **SPECIAL ACHIEVEMENTS:** Selected writings on: Asian law, 1982; Chinese Criminal Code, 1982; Chinese Criminal Procedure Code, 1985; Korean Law Study Guide, 1987. **BUSINESS ADDRESS:** Professor, California Western School of Law, 350 Cedar St, San Diego, CA 92101, (619)525-1429.

KIM, CHIN HUI
Educator. Korean American. **PERSONAL:** Born Sep 2, 1956, Seoul, Republic of Korea; daughter of Ki Hwan Kim and Ok Soon Lee-Kim; married Sterling Delone, Feb 10, 1993; children: Tahirah Kim Felton, Brandon T Felton. **EDUCATION:** California State University, Los Angeles, MA, 1987. **CAREER:** Los Angeles Unified School Dist, coordinator, 1980-; Loyola Marymount University, lecturer, 1992-. **ORGANIZATIONS:** Korean American Educators Association, past president, executive board member, 1986-. **HONORS/AWARDS:** US Dept of Education, Title VII Grant, 1992. **SPECIAL ACHIEVEMENTS:** Bilingual Certificate of Competence in Korean, 1980; Language Development Specialist Certificate, 1986; published an article in the Bilingual Education Outreach, 1993. **BIOGRAPHICAL SOURCES:** The Pacific Rim Newsletter of the UCLA Center for Pacific Rim Studies; Korean Two-Way Bilingual Education Program in Los Angeles Schools, p1, 10, 11, spring/summer, 1993; Building Unity and Valuing Diversity, Bilingual Education Office Outreach, Cal State Dept, p 33, 1993. **BUSINESS ADDRESS:** Coordinator, Los Angeles Unified School District, 450 N Grand Avenue, G-290, Los Angeles, CA 90012, (213)625-6106.

KIM, CHONG LIM
Educator. Korean American. **PERSONAL:** Born Jul 17, 1937, Seoul, Republic of Korea; son of Soo Myung Kim and Chung Hwa Kim; married Eun Hwa Kim, Aug 21, 1963; children: Bohm S, Lahn S, Lynn S. **EDUCATION:** Seoul National University, BA, 1960; University of Oregon, MA (honors), 1964, PhD, 1968. **CAREER:** University of Tokyo, visiting assistant professor, 1969; University of Iowa, assistant professor, 1968-70, associate professor, 1971-75, professor 1975-. **ORGANIZATIONS:** Comparative Legislative Research Center, director, 1982-92; American Political Science Association, 1966-; Midwest Political Science Association, 1967-. **SPECIAL ACHIEVEMENTS:** Books: Legislative Connection: The Politics of Representation, 1984; Legislative Process in Korea, 1981; Political Participation in Korea, 1980; Legislative Systems in Developing Countries, 1975; Patterns of Recruitment, 1974. **BUSINESS ADDRESS:** Professor, Dept of Political Science, University of Iowa, Schaeffer Hall, 315SH, Iowa City, IA 52242, (319)335-2344.

KIM, CHOONG SOON
Educator. Korean American. **PERSONAL:** Born May 28, 1938, Seoul, Republic of Korea; son of Byong Kern Kim & Hukyung Kang; married Sang Boon Kim, Jun 25, 1965; children: JOhn J, Andrew H. **EDUCATION:** Yonsei University, Seoul, Korea, Law School, BA, 1961, Graduate School, MA, 1963; Emory University, MA, 1968; University of Georgia, PhD, 1971. **CAREER:** University of Tennessee at Martin, professor of anthropology, 1971-. **ORGANIZATIONS:** Anthropologists for Korean Studies, president, 1981-; American Anthropological Association, fellow; Society for Applied Anthropology,

fellow; Current Anthropology, associate; American Ethnological Society, fellow; Association of Asian Studies. **HONORS/AWARDS:** Fulbright, Research Award, 1988-89, lecture, research, 1993-94; Rockefeller Foundation, Scholar-in-Residence at Bellagio Center, 1993. **SPECIAL ACHIEVEMENTS:** An Asian Anthropologist in the South, University of Tennessee Press, 1977, 1984, 1991; Faithful Endurance, University of Arizona Press, 1988; The Culture of Korean Industry, University of Arizona Press, 1992. **BUSINESS ADDRESS:** Professor, Dept of Sociology & Anthropology, University of Tennessee at Martin, Sociology Building, Martin, TN 38238-1000, (901)587-7517.

KIM, CHULWAN

Educator. Korean American. **PERSONAL:** Born Sep 2, 1954, Seoul, Republic of Korea; son of Yong Sul & Kyeng Poon Kim; married Mihae Kim, Jan 13, 1982; children: Vena V, Vienn V. **EDUCATION:** Seoul National University, 1973-75; Sung Kyun Kwan University, BA, 1980; Stevens Institute of Technology, MMS, 1982; The Wharton School, University of Pennsylvania, PhD, 1989. **CAREER:** Dong Chun Enterprise, president, 1977-80; Korea Economic Research Institute, researcher, 1979-80, 1982-83; The Wharton School, University of Pennsylvania, teaching assistant, 1984-89; Chulwan Investments Inc, president, 1992-; Georgia Institute of Technology, assistant professor of marketing, 1989-. **ORGANIZATIONS:** American Marketing Association, 1984-; The Institute of Management Science, 1981-; Operations Research Society of America, 1982-. **SPECIAL ACHIEVEMENTS:** Exercises in Marketing Research, Malhotra/Kim, 1992; book review on Robuet Estimation, JMR, November, 1991. **BUSINESS ADDRESS:** Assistant Professor, Georgia Institute of Technology, Sch of Management, Ivan Allen College, Atlanta, GA 30332-0520, (404)894-4361.

KIM, CHUNG-SOOK CHARLOTTE

Library administrator, librarian. Korean American. **PERSONAL:** Born Apr 15, 1940, Seoul, Republic of Korea; daughter of Soon-Kyung Hong & Un-Yun Kim; married Ben H Kim, Nov 17, 1985; children: Patricia Jean, Claudia Suk-Jin Kang. **EDUCATION:** Yonsei University, Seoul, Korea, BA; Duquesne University, MEd, 1967; University of Pittsburgh, MLS, 1968. **CAREER:** Whitehall Public Library, branch librarian, children's librarian, 1965-76; Carnegie Library of Pittsburgh, children's librarian, 1968-71, branch head, 1971-76, division head, 1976-85; Chicago Public Library, branch head, 1986-88, district chief, 1989-90, assistant commissioner, 1990-. **ORGANIZATIONS:** American Library Association, councilor, 1993-97, Ethnic Materials and Information Exchange Round Table, board of directors, 1992-94, Advisory Group for President Hardy Franklin, 1992-94; Chicago Library System, board of directors, 1991-95; Asian/Pacific American Librarians Association, president, 1991-92; Public Library Association, International Relations Comm, 1992-94; Korean American Scholarship Foundation, Midwest Chapter, board of directors, 1993-; Korean American Community Services, board of directors; Korean American Senior Center, board of directors, 1990-. **HONORS/AWARDS:** Asian Human Services of Chicago, Distinguished Services Award, 1992; Korean Central Daily of Chicago, Man of the Year Award, 1988; Friends of Chicago Public Library, Outstanding Public Service Award, 1987; Illinois delegation to the White House Conference on Library and Information Serivces, 1991-. **SPECIAL ACHIEVEMENTS:** "Thriving on Challenges," speech at the Midwest Chapter, Chinese American Librarians Association Conference, 1993; "Cultural Diversity," speech at the Indian Prairie Public Library Workshop District, 1992; "Farewell to the Melting Pot: Public Libraries in a Multicultural Society," Public Libraries, vol 31, no 41; "Reaching Out to Asian Minorities in Your Community," speech, Public Library, 1992; "Between the Ages: Intergenerational Programs in Libraries," speech, American Library Association Conference, 1992. **BUSINESS ADDRESS:** Assistant Commissioner of Neighborhood Services, The Chicago Public Library, 400 S State St, Chicago, IL 60605, (312)747-4212.

KIM, CHUNG WOOK

Educator. Korean American. **PERSONAL:** Born Jan 8, 1934, Kure, Hiroshima, Japan; son of Chan-Soo Kim and Yoon-Soon Rho; married Young Ja Kang Kim, Jul 25, 1960; children: Janet H Cahill. **EDUCATION:** Seoul National University, BS, 1958; Indiana University, PhD, 1963. **CAREER:** University of Pennsylvania, research associate, 1963-66; Johns Hopkins University, assistant professor, 1966-69, associate professor, 1969-73, professor, 1973-. **ORGANIZATIONS:** American Physical Society, fellow, 1963-. **HONORS/AWARDS:** Seoul National University, Seung Man Rhee Prize, 1958. **SPECIAL ACHIEVEMENTS:** 150 publications in professional journals; 2 books published. **BUSINESS ADDRESS:** Professor, Dept of Physics

and Astronomy, Johns Hopkins University, 3400 N Charles St, Baltimore, MD 21218, (410)516-7373.

KIM, DAVID DOYUNG

Journalist, writer, editor. Korean American. **PERSONAL:** Born Aug 11, 1966, Ann Arbor, MI; son of Chong Bin Kim and Kyung Soon Kim. **EDUCATION:** Brown University, BA, 1989. **CAREER:** Village Voice, editorial assistant, 1989, associate editor, 1990-92, senior editor, 1993-. **ORGANIZATIONS:** Asian American Journalists Association, New York Chapter, vice president, 1990. **SPECIAL ACHIEVEMENTS:** Guest editor of Voices Stirring: An Anthology of Korean American Writing, 1992; panelist for Chinese American Fiction Forum at China Institute, 1993; guest editor for The Nation, 1993. **BUSINESS ADDRESS:** Senior Editor, Village Voice, 36 Cooper Square, New York, NY 10003, (212)475-3300.

KIM, DAVID HO-SIK

Educator, cleric. Korean American. **PERSONAL:** Born Jul 20, 1935, Yeasan, Chung Nam, Republic of Korea; married Grace Un Chung, Feb 24, 1963; children: Amelia, Annabelle, Adrienne, Chung Il. **EDUCATION:** Dallas Theological Seminary, ThD, 1970; Florida International University, BA, 1974; New School for Social Research, MA, 1976; Washington College of Law, American University, JD, 1981. **CAREER:** Korean Bible College, professor of theology, 1970-72; Baptist University of America, professor of theology, 1972-74; Baptist College and Seminary, professor of theology, 1974-78; Baptist College & Seminary, Washington, president, professor of theology, 1982-. **SPECIAL ACHIEVEMENTS:** Christian Literature Crusade, "Spiritual Life," 1984, "Biblical Eschatology," 1984; numerous articles in various periodicals. **MILITARY SERVICE:** Korean Army, sgt, 1955-59. **BUSINESS ADDRESS:** President, Baptist College and Seminary of Washington, 103 W Columbia St, Falls Church, VA 22046.

KIM, DAVID SANG CHUL

Educational administrator. Korean American. **PERSONAL:** Born Nov 9, 1915, Seoul, Republic of Korea; married Eui Hong Kang, Jan 6, 1942; children: Sook Hee, Sung Soo, Hyun Soo, Young Soo, Joon Soo. **EDUCATION:** Chosen Christian College, Korea, BA, 1939; University of Wales, postgrad, 1954-55; Western Conservative Baptist Seminary, 1959-61; University of Oregon, MA, 1965; Pacific School Religion, California, 1965-66; Columbia Pacific University, PhD, 1988. **CAREER:** Chosen Rubber Industry Association, Korea, 1939-45; US Military, Korea, financial assistant, 1945-48; Ministry of Foreign Affairs Government of Republic of Korea, Ministry of Social Affairs and Health, Ministry of Finance, govt official, 1948-59; Unification Church, Korea, charter member, 1954, missionary, evangelist, 1959-70; Clearfield Job Corps Center, Utah, counseling supervisor, 1966-70; Rose of Sharon Press (was Cornerstone Press), founder, president, 1978; Unification Theological Seminary, president, 1975-. **ORGANIZATIONS:** World Relief Friendship Foundation Inc (now International Relief Friendship Foundation Inc), 1974-; International One World Crusade Inc, 1975-; International Religious Foundation Inc, charter member, 1982-; numerous others. **SPECIAL ACHIEVEMENTS:** Author of numerous publications, including: Individual Preparation for His Coming Kingdom: Interpretation of the Principle, 1964; Victory Over Communism and the Role of Religion, 1972. **BUSINESS ADDRESS:** President, Unification Theological Seminary, 10 Dock Rd, Barrytown, NY 12507-5000, (914)758-6881. *

KIM, DAVID U.

Educator. Korean American. **PERSONAL:** Born May 29, 1932, Chunchon, Republic of Korea; son of Mr & Mrs Jong Shiek Kim; married Helen K Kim; children: Douglas. **EDUCATION:** Villanova University, MSLS, 1966; Indiana University, PhD, 1980. **CAREER:** Indiana State University, acquisitions librarian, 1969-78; University of Lowell, head of library technical services, 1978-81; Sam Houston State University, assistant director of library, 1981-90; Salve Regina University, director of library, 1990-. **ORGANIZATIONS:** American Library Association; Association of College and Research Libraries, publications committee, Library Information and Technology Association; Catholic Library Association, New England Chapter, chair, academic libraries section. **SPECIAL ACHIEVEMENTS:** "Online Searching with a Microcomputer, a High-Speed Modem, and a Local Printer," Library Journal, v. 111, May 1986, LC16-18, between pages 88-89; Policies of Educational Software Publishers: A Guide for Authors, Woodlands, Texas: New Technology Press, 1991; "CDS 224 Autodial Modem and PC-Talk III," OCLC Micro, v. 3, April 1987, 28-29. **BIOGRAPHICAL SOURCES:** Contemporay Authors. **BUSI-**

NESS ADDRESS: Director of Library, Associate Professor, Salve Regina University, McKillop Library, Newport, RI 02840.

KIM, DONALD CHANG WON
Engineering company executive. Korean American. **PERSONAL:** Born Dec 14, 1928, Seoul, Republic of Korea; son of Yu Ho Kim and Sook Kyung Lee Kim; married Iris Kyong Ok Yoo Kim, Dec 29, 1962; children: Rex Kee Chul, Dean Sang Kee. **EDUCATION:** University of Hawaii, College of Engineering, BS, 1958. **CAREER:** Kilohana Corp, president, director, 1982-; Amkor Architects & Engineers Inc, chairman of the board, 1982-; Keahole Associates Inc, chairman of the board, 1988-; R M Towill Corp, vice president, 1971-72, executive vice president, 1972-78, president, 1978-, chairman & CEO, 1982-. **ORGANIZATIONS:** University of Hawaii Foundation, trustee, founders club, president's club, 1980-; University of Hawaii Alumni Association, life member, president, 1994; Hawaii Pacific University, Business Administration Advisory Council, 1988-; Korean University Club, president, 1958-; Friends of the Center for Korean Studies, director, 1985-; Rotary Club of Honolulu, 1976-; Bishop Museum, director, 1989-; Navy League of the US & Association of the US Army, life member, 1979-. **HONORS/AWARDS:** University of Hawaii, Distinguished Alumni, 1982, Alumni Association, Overall Distinguished Alumnus, 1990, Engineering College, Noblesse Oblige to the College, 1990; Republic of Korea, Presidential Outstanding Community Service, 1991; Chi Epsilon, honorary member, 1993. **SPECIAL ACHIEVEMENTS:** Korean Pacific Weekly, editor, 1956-70; language proficiency: Korean, Japanese. **BUSINESS ADDRESS:** Chairman and CEO, R M Towill Corp, 420 Waiakamilo Rd, Ste 411, Honolulu, HI 96817, (808)842-1133.

KIM, DONGCHEOL
Educator. Korean American. **PERSONAL:** Born Jul 17, 1955, Gochang, Jeonbook, Republic of Korea; married Kyungsook Kim, Apr 22, 1984; children: Deborah, Benjamin, Jessica. **EDUCATION:** Seoul National University, BSE, 1979; Korea Advanced Institute of Science & Technology, MS, 1981; University of Michigan, MA, 1988, PhD, 1989. **CAREER:** Rutgers University, assistant professor, 1989-. **BUSINESS ADDRESS:** Assistant Professor, Dept of Finance, Rutgers University, School of Business, Rockefeller Rd., New Brunswick, NJ 08903, (908)932-4195.

KIM, DONNA MERCADO
City government official. Korean American/Filipino American. **PERSONAL:** Born Jul 31. **CAREER:** City Council of Honolulu, council member, currently, City Zoning Committee, chair, currently. **BUSINESS ADDRESS:** Council Member, Honolulu City Council, 530 S King St, 2nd Fl, Honolulu, HI 96813, (808)523-4978.*

KIM, EDWARD IK HWAN
Cleric. Korean American. **PERSONAL:** Born Jan 29, 1919, Anju, Pyong Nam, Republic of Korea; son of Dong Jum Kim and Chong Sook Kim; married Yun Ae Kim, Mar 4, 1944; children: In Ja Hwang, Choong Ryong, Jane, Richard, Insih Chang. **EDUCATION:** Azusa Pacific University, BA, 1967; Southern California Theological Seminary, master of ministry, 1986, doctor of ministry, 1987. **CAREER:** Soong Sil High School, Pusan, Korea, teacher, 1952-53; Ontario Monclair School District, 1968-69; Korean Alliance Church, senior pastor, 1968-88; San Antonio Community Hospital, ground supervisor, 1971-79; Korean Alliance Bethel Church, interim senior pastor, 1989-90; Southern California Korean Minister's Association, vice president, 1987-; Southern California Eastern Region Korean Minister's Association, president, 1988; Southern California Alliance Seminary, professor & president, 1989; Christian and Missionary Alliance Korean District, president, 1992-. **ORGANIZATIONS:** Christian and Missionary Western Region, president, 1986-; True Light Christian Service Center, president, 1988-89. **HONORS/AWARDS:** US Air Force, Superior Performance, 1964; Worldwide Broadcasting Network Inc, Appreciation Award, 1979; Korea School of Pomona Valley, A Testimonial of Appreciation, 1981; Bethel Korean Church in Orange County, Appreciation Award, 1990; Korean Alliance Church of Pomona Valley, Appreciation Award, 1993; Korea Central Daily News, superior achievement award for "My Immigration Journey.". **SPECIAL ACHIEVEMENTS:** Management Course for Air Force Working Leaders, mgt 2, May 12, 1964; Supervisor's Safety Course, 6316th Air Base Group, APO 970, 1963; Industrial Safety Supervisors Training Course, Tokyo, Japan, 1962. **MILITARY SERVICE:** Korean Air Force, 5th air force 314 air division, safety advisor, 1954-65. **BIOGRAPHICAL SOURCES:** Publication of Safety Beacon, 934 Air Division, 10 pages, 1955-65; Victorious Life, Korean Church of Pomona, p 8-9, May 1993. **HOME ADDRESS:** 1317 W Ralstone St, Ontario, CA 91762, (909)984-3443. **BUSI-**

NESS ADDRESS: President, Christian and Missionary Alliance Korean District, 904 East D St, Ontario, CA 91764, (909)983-0994.

KIM, EDWARD J.
Consultant. Korean American. **PERSONAL:** Born May 13, 1934, Republic of Korea; son of Jaehyuk Kim (deceased) and Jum Park; married Angela Kim; children: Jason, Jaewon. **EDUCATION:** Korea University, Seoul, BA, 1959; Northern State University, South Dakota, MS, 1968; Century University, 1992. **CAREER:** Sejong University, Seoul, professor, 1969-79, department of education, director, 1970-73, graduate studies, professor, 1974-79; Mobil Gas Station, owner/manager, 1981-83; Defense Language Institute, language professor, 1981-83; University of California, Los Angeles, 1988; Walden University, Minneapolis, 1990; Century University, 1992; Far East Realty and Investment Co, owner, consultant, 1984-93. **ORGANIZATIONS:** Northern State University Alumni, Southern California; San Fernando Valley Board of Realtors, Los Angeles, realtor. **SPECIAL ACHIEVEMENTS:** Introduction to Education (Korean Language), 1975; Guidance and Learning, Korean Language, 1977. **HOME ADDRESS:** 3903 Southhampton Rd, Moorpark, CA 93021, (805)523-7246.

KIM, EUN MEE
Educator. Korean American. **PERSONAL:** Born Sep 10, 1958, Taegu, Kyungsang-buk-do, Republic of Korea; daughter of Hogwon Kim and Kyung Ae Kang. **EDUCATION:** Ewha Woman's university, Seoul, Korea, BA (honors), 1981; Brown University, MA, 1983, PhD, 1987. **CAREER:** Korean Education Development Institute, researcher, 1984; Brown University, lecturer, 1986; Temple University, assistant professor, 1990-91; University of Southern California, asst professor, 1991-93, associate professor, 1993-. **ORGANIZATIONS:** American Sociological Association, 1985-; Association for Asian Studies, Executive Committee on Korean Studies, 1993-; American Political Science Association, 1989-; Korean American National Museum, board of directors, 1991-; Asia Society, Advisory Committee for Festival of Korea, 1993-94. **HONORS/AWARDS:** Social Science Research Council, International Doctoral Research Fellowship, 1986; International Cultural Society of Korea, Research Fellowship, 1989; University of Southern California, Faculty Research and Innovation Fund, 1988; Brown University, University Fellowships, 1981-82. **SPECIAL ACHIEVEMENTS:** Book: Big Business, Strong State: Collusion and Conflict in South Korean Development, University of California Press, 1994; "Contradictions and Limits of a Developmental State: With Illustrations from the South Korean Case," Social Problems, May, 1993; "Foreign Capital in Korea's Economic Development, 1960-85," Studies in Comparative International Development, 1989; "From Dominance to Symbiosis: State and Chaebol in Korea, "Pacific Focus, 1988; conference chair, "Korea: Past to Present," University of Southern California, Los Angeles Unified School District, Los Angeles County Office of Education, 1988. **BUSINESS ADDRESS:** Associate Professor, Dept of Sociology, University of Southern California, Los Angeles, CA 90089-2539, (213)740-3537.

KIM, HAEWON CHANG
Physician, educator. Korean American. **PERSONAL:** Born May 16, 1943, Seoul, Republic of Korea; married. **EDUCATION:** Ewha Woman's University, School of Medicine, MD, 1968. **CAREER:** Children's Hospital of Philadelphia, senior physician, 1988-; University of Pennsylvania, School of Medicine, associate professor of pediatrics, 1987-. **ORGANIZATIONS:** American Federation for Clinical Research, 1979-; American Society of Hematology, 1980-; American Association of Blood Banks, inspector, 1979-; American Society of Pediatric Hematology/Oncology, 1981-; American Society for Apheresis, 1988-; International Society of Blood Transfusion, 1990-; Philadelphia Hematology Society, 1979-. **HONORS/AWARDS:** Children's Hospital of Philadelphia, Ethel Brown Foerderer Fund for Excellence, 1985. **SPECIAL ACHIEVEMENTS:** Differentiation of Bone and Bone Marrow Infarcts from Osteomyelitis in SS Disorders, Clinical Nuclear Med, 14:249-254, 1989; variants of Sickle Cell Disease (Chapter 9) in Hemoglobinopathies in Children, 1980; Blood Component Therapy in the Neonate (Chapter 8) in Developmental & Neonatal Hem, 1988; Separation of Hemoglobins (Chapter A8) in Hematology, 4th ed, 1990; Use of Blood and Blood Products, Pract Problems in Pediatric Oncology and Current Treatment Methods, 1992. **BUSINESS ADDRESS:** Medical Director, Transfusion/Apheresis Service, The Children's Hospital of Philadelphia, 34th St & Civic Ctr Blvd, Main Bldg, Rm 5112A, Philadelphia, PA 19104, (215)590-2260.

KIM, HAKLIN
Educator. Korean American. **PERSONAL:** Born Feb 11, 1956, Dajon, Choong-Nahm, Republic of Korea; son of Chang-Shik Kimm & Eui-Soon Lee; married Hyo S Kim, Dec 6, 1980; children: Soun, Jiun, Hanki. **EDUCATION:** Korea University, BE, industrial engineering, 1979; University of Oklahoma, MS, computer science, 1984, PhD, computer science, 1988. **CAREER:** Korea Computer Center, programmer, 1980-81; University of Oklahoma, research assistant, 1983-85, research associate, 1985-86, programmer analyst, 1986-87, systems analyst, 1987-89, professor, 1989-. **ORGANIZATIONS:** ACM; IEEE Computer Society. **HONORS/AWARDS:** Oak Ridge National Lab, research participation, 1992-93. **SPECIAL ACHIEVEMENTS:** Author: "Finding a Maximum Independent Set in a Permutation Graph," Information Processing Letters, 36 (1990) 19-23; "Economical Predictive Testing in Manufacturing Electronic Circuits," Economics of Design and Test for Electronic Circuits, Ellis Horwood, England, July, 1992. **BUSINESS ADDRESS:** Professor, Math and Computer Science, University of Tennessee, Martin, TN 38238-1000, (901)587-7360.

KIM, HAN-SEOB
Pathologist, educator. Korean American. **PERSONAL:** Born Sep 5, 1934, Seoul, Republic of Korea. **EDUCATION:** Seoul National University, College of Medicine, MD, 1959, Graduate School, MS, 1962, Graduate School, PhD, 1968. **CAREER:** Seoul National University, College of Medicine, assistant professor, 1969; Baylor College of Medicine, instructor, professor, 1971-. **ORGANIZATIONS:** American Association of Investigative Pathology, 1978-; US and Canadian Academy of Pathology, 1972-; College of American Pathologists, 1974-92; American Association of Neuropathologists, 1977-; American Society of Cytology, 1992-; Society for Cardiovasculer Pathology, 1988-. **BUSINESS ADDRESS:** Professor, Dept of Pathology, Baylor College of Medicine, One Baylor Plaza, Houston, TX 77030.

KIM, HEE-JIN
Educator. Korean American. **PERSONAL:** Born Apr 8, 1927, Masan, South Kyongsang-do, Republic of Korea; son of Young-Ho Kim & Eum-Jun Kim; married Jung-Sun Kim, Feb 7, 1965; children: Sun-Chul, Hae-Sil, Yeong-Jue. **EDUCATION:** University of California, Berkeley, BA, 1957, MA, 1958; Claremont Graduate School, PhD, 1966. **CAREER:** University of Vermont, philos & religion, assistant professor, 1965-67; Wright State University, religion, assistant professor, 1967-70; Claremont Graduate School, religion, visiting assistant professor, 1970-72; University of Oregon, religious studies, assistant/associate professor, 1973-83, professor, 1983-91, professor emeritus, 1991-. **ORGANIZATIONS:** Association for Asian Studies; Society for Asian and Comparative Philosophy; American Academy of Religion; International Association of Buddhist Studies; Tibet Society; Society for the Study of Chinese Religions; Society for the Study of Japanese Religions; Society for Tantric Studies. **HONORS/AWARDS:** Blaisdell Institute for Advanced Study in World Cultures and Religions, research fellowship, 1970-72. **SPECIAL ACHIEVEMENTS:** Author, Dogen Kigen-Mystical Realist, Association for Asian Studies Monograph Series, no 29, 1975, 1987; Flowers of Emptiness: Selections from Dogen's Shobogenzo, Edwin Mellen Press, 1985. **HOME ADDRESS:** 570 Ful Vue Dr, Eugene, OR 97405, (503)344-9578. **BUSINESS ADDRESS:** Professor Emeritus, Dept of Religious Studies, University of Oregon, Eugene, OR 97403, (503)346-4971.

KIM, HEEMIN
Educator. Korean American. **PERSONAL:** Born Jun 24, 1958, Seoul, Republic of Korea; son of Young Dong Kim and Gyeong Deuk Lee Kim; married Yun Gyeong Kim, Jun 16, 1981; children: Sujin, Sungshik Patrick. **EDUCATION:** Hankuk University of Foreign Studies, Seoul, Korea; University of Minnesota, BA, 1983, MA, 1984; Washington University, St Louis, PhD, 1990. **CAREER:** HongSung Publishing Co, Seoul, Korea, editorial staff, 1980-81; Washington University, St Louis, research assistant, 1985-87, teaching assistant, 1985-86, 1988; Florida State University, assistant professor, 1989-. **ORGANIZATIONS:** American Political Science Association, 1985-; Midwest Political Science Association, 1986-; Association of Korean Political Studies in North America, 1986-; International Society for Korean Studies, 1992-. **HONORS/AWARDS:** American Political Science Association, Annual Meeting Travel Grant Award, 1985; Washington University, Graduate Fellowships, 1984-87, Graduate School of Arts and Sciences Dissertation Fellowship, 1988-89; Pi Sigma Alpha, 1988-; Florida State University, The Council on Research and Creativity Assistant Professor, summer research grant, 1992. **SPECIAL ACHIEVEMENTS:** "A Theory of Government-Driven Democratization: The Case of Korea," World Affairs, 1994; "Political Parties as Rational Agents and

the Elite Behavior," Theories of Party System, 1994; "The Strongly Stable Core in Weighted Voting Games," Public Choice, 1994; Rationality in the Korean Peninsular, 1994; 11 professional research article presentations, 1988-93. **BUSINESS ADDRESS:** Asst Prof, Dept of Political Science, Florida State University, Tallahassee, FL 32306-2049, (904)644-7319.

KIM, HELEN
Scientist. Korean American. **PERSONAL:** Born Feb 10, 1948, Seoul, Republic of Korea; daughter of Charles Kim & Mary Kim; married Lester I Binder, Jun 19, 1976; children: Sabrina Kim Binder, Shannon Marie Binder. **EDUCATION:** Mary Washington College of the University of Virginia, BS, 1970; Yale University School of Forestry & Environmental Studies, MFS, 1972; University of Virginia, PhD, 1983. **CAREER:** University of Alabama, Birmingham, assistant professor, 1985-93; Molecular Geriatrics, group leader, 1993-. **ORGANIZATIONS:** American Society Cell Biology, 1983-. **HONORS/AWARDS:** NIH, research grant, ROI, 1991-94; National Sci Foundation, research grant, 1990-94; Leukemia Society, fellow award, 1983-85. **HOME ADDRESS:** 533 Kelly Avenue, Grayslake, IL 60030-3613, (708)548-4237. **BUSINESS ADDRESS:** Group Leader, Molecular Geriatrics Corporation, 101 Waukegan Road, Suite 970, Lake Bluff, IL 60044, (708)234-5711.

KIM, HESOOK SUZIE
Educator. Korean American. **PERSONAL:** Born Apr 3, 1939, Kaesung, Republic of Korea; daughter of Sung Jin Kim and Ok Kyung Lee; married Hyung Gul Park, Dec 6, 1982; children: Peter H Kang, Michael H Kang. **EDUCATION:** Indiana University, BS, 1962, MS, 1963; Brown University, MA, 1972, PhD, 1977. **CAREER:** Roger Williams General Hospital, School of Nursing, director, 1964-72; University of Rhode Island, associate professor, 1973-77, professor, 1977-82, College of Nursing, dean, 1982-88, professor, 1988-. **ORGANIZATIONS:** American Nurses' Association, 1964-, Council of Nurse Researchers, 1973-; American Public Health Association, 1972-; National Advisory Council on Nursing Research, 1990-94. **HONORS/AWARDS:** International Institute of Rhode Island, Distinguished Citizen Award, 1985; Indiana University School of Nursing Alumni Association, Distinguished Alumna Award, 1990; Sigma Theta Tau, Delta Upsilon Chapter, Louisa White Award, 1986. **SPECIAL ACHIEVEMENTS:** The Nature of Theoretical Thinking in Nursing, Appleton-Century Crofts, 1983. **BUSINESS ADDRESS:** Professor, College of Nursing, University of Rhode Island, White Hall #234, Kingston, RI 02881-0814, (401)792-2766.

KIM, HONG NACK
Educator. Korean American. **PERSONAL:** Born Aug 20, 1933, Youngchun, Kyoungbuk, Republic of Korea; son of Sang-Do Kim and Nam-Jo Seong; married Boohi Seo Kim, Mar 26, 1967; children: Michael Kihyun, Jeffrey Jaehyun, Brian Yuhyun. **EDUCATION:** Seoul National University, BA, 1956; Georgetown University, MA, 1960, PhD, 1965. **CAREER:** Georgetown University, lecturer, 1965-66; North Texas State University, assistant professor, 1966-67; Keio University, visiting professor, 1979, 1982; Seoul National University, visiting professor, 1990-91; West Virginia University, assistant professor, 1967-72, associate professor, 1972-77, professor, 1977-. **ORGANIZATIONS:** Association of Korean Political Scientists in North America, president, 1983-85; Association of Asian Studies, Mid Atlantic Region, advisory board, 1992-. **HONORS/AWARDS:** US Dept of Education, Fulbright Research Grant, 1979, 1982; Council on Exchange of Scholars, Fulbright Lectureship & Research Grant, 1990; West Virginia University, College of Arts & Sciences, Outstanding Researcher, 1985. **SPECIAL ACHIEVEMENTS:** Co-editor, Korean Reunification: New Perspectives & Approaches, Seoul, Kyungnam University Press, 1984; co-editor, Korea & Major Powers after the Seoul Olympics, 1989; author, Scholars' Guide to East Asian Studies, Smithsonian Institution Press, 1979; co-editor, Essays in Political Science, Kendall & Hunt, 1972; "Deradicalization of the Japanese Communist Party," World Politics, January 1976. **BUSINESS ADDRESS:** Professor, Political Science, West Virginia University, 316 Woodburn Hall, Morgantown, WV 26505, (304)293-3811.

KIM, HONG YUNG (HY)
Educator. Korean American. **PERSONAL:** Born Sep 18, 1939, Republic of Korea; son of Jae-bong Kim and Soon-nam Chang; married Sung-hei Kim, Apr 5, 1967; children: Sung, John. **EDUCATION:** Sung-Kyn-Kwan University, BA, 1961-65; Seoul National University, EdM, 1967-69; Ball State University, EdD, 1971-74; University of Maryland, post doc, 1979-80. **CAREER:** Youngstown State University, professor; Pittsburg State University, associate professor; University of Maryland, Eastern Shore, instructor; Arlington Public

School, bilingual specialist; Illinois Benedictine College, assistant professor. **ORGANIZATIONS:** NCTM; NSTA; NEA. **HONORS/AWARDS:** Youngstown State University, Distinquished Professor in Teaching, 1992, Research Professor, 1991-92. **SPECIAL ACHIEVEMENTS:** "Showy Science Demonstrations," Good Year Book, Scott Foreman, 1994; "Mathematics Instruction in Elementary and Middle School," Youngstown State University; many articles in journals of math and science education. **BUSINESS ADDRESS:** Professor, College of Education, Youngstown St University, 410 Wick Ave, Youngstown, OH 44555-0002, (216)742-3253.

KIM, HYONG SOK
Educator. Korean American. **PERSONAL:** Born Apr 13, 1962, Seoul, Republic of Korea; son of Hung Min Kim & Kwang Soon Kim; married Sang-Weon Gang, Jul 7, 1990; children: Justine S, Jeremie S. **EDUCATION:** McGill University, BEng, 1984; University of Toronto, MA Sc, 1987, PhD, 1990. **CAREER:** Northern Telecom, lecturer, 1989; Bell-Northern Research, research consultant, 1992; Carnegie Mellon University, assistant professor, 1990-. **ORGANIZATIONS:** IEEE, 1983-; ACM, 1991-; Sigma Xi, 1992-. **HONORS/AWARDS:** NSERC, NSERC Fellowship, 1987-94; University of Toronto, Mary Beatty Fellowship, 1989. **SPECIAL ACHIEVEMENTS:** Over 30 publications in international journals & conferences; one pending patent. **BUSINESS ADDRESS:** Asst Professor, Dept of Electrical & Computer Engineering, Carnegie Mellon University, 5000 Forbes Ave, Pittsburgh, PA 15213-3890, (412)268-6491.

KIM, HYUN KAP
Educator. Korean American. **PERSONAL:** Born Nov 17, 1934, Republic of Korea; married Maria H Kim, Feb 26, 1968; children: Peter, Maxine, Eugene. **EDUCATION:** Seoul National University, LLB, 1959; Southern Illinois University, MA, 1973, PhD, 1975. **CAREER:** Hapdong News Agency, South Korea, reporter, editor, 1959-69; Southern Illinois Univ, faculty research associate, 1975; Univ of Wisconsin-Stevens Point, assistant professor, 1975-80, associate professor, 1981-91, Division of Communication, professor, 1992-. **ORGANIZATIONS:** Association for Education in Journalism and Mass Communication; Wisconsin Communication Association; Korean American Communication Association, president, 1985-87; Korean American University Professors Association, head, Social Science Division. **HONORS/AWARDS:** Poynter Institute, teaching fellowship, 1988; Southern Illinois University, fellowship, 1974; Institute of International Education, Fulbright Scholarship, 1970-71. **SPECIAL ACHIEVEMENTS:** Published and presented numerous research articles on mass communication and communication competence. **BUSINESS ADDRESS:** Professor, Division of Communication, University of Wisconsin-Stevens Point, Stevens Point, WI 54481, (715)346-3240.

KIM, HYUN WANG
Educator. Korean American. **PERSONAL:** Born Feb 23, 1945, Chulsan, Republic of Korea; son of Chong M and Sook R Kim; married Heasoon, Nov 13, 1971; children: Anthony. **EDUCATION:** Seoul National University, BS, 1968; University of Michigan, MS, 1975; University of Toledo, PhD, 1980. **CAREER:** Korea Naval Shipyard, engineer, 1968-71; Korea Institute of Science & Tech, engineer, 1971-73; R A Stearns Inc, engineer, 1974; Rochester Institute of Technology, professor, 1980-83; Youngstown State University, professor, 1983-. **ORGANIZATIONS:** American Society of Mechanical Engineers, 1978-; American Society of Engineering Education, 1993-; Sigma Xi, 1980-; Phi Kappa Phi, 1980-; Pi Tau Sigma, 1979-; Korean Scientists and Engineers of American, 1974-80. **HONORS/AWARDS:** Korea Naval Shipyard, Outstanding Engineer Award, 1971. **SPECIAL ACHIEVEMENTS:** "Momentum an Heat Transfer in Power-Law Fluids," Int J Heat & Mass Transfer, 1983; "Convective Heat Transfer Near Separation Point," Proc Heat Transfer Conf, HTD 96, 1988; "Forced Convection of Power-Law Fluids," HTD V-174, ASME, 1991; "Forced Convection over Rotating Bodies," J of Thermophysics and Heat Transfer, 1993; Convective Heat Transfer from Moving Surfaces, proc 9th ICMCM Conf, 1993. **MILITARY SERVICE:** Korean Navy, lieutenant, j g, 1968-71. **BUSINESS ADDRESS:** Associate Professor, Mechanical Engineering Dept, Youngstown State University, Youngstown, OH 44555-0002, (216)742-1730.

KIM, HYUNG J.
Insurance company manager. Korean American. **PERSONAL:** Born Mar 10, 1943, Republic of Korea; son of Eum S Kim and Sook J Kim; married Lydia Y Kim, Oct 25, 1992; children: Edward, David. **EDUCATION:** Yonsei University, BA, 1962; State University, Long Beach, BS, 1972. **CAREER:** The Equitable Life, 1973-, agency mgr, 1980-83, 1993-, vice president, 1988-93.

ORGANIZATIONS: United Korea Foundation, president, 1990-, secretary, 1976-.

KIM, IL-WOON
Educator. Korean American. **PERSONAL:** Born Sep 30, 1949, Seoul, Republic of Korea; son of Joonhwang Kim & Sookil Park; married Jinwon Kim, Mar 11, 1978; children: Andrew, Daniel, David. **EDUCATION:** Yonsei University, Korea, BBA, 1976; Arizona State University, MBA, 1980; University of Nebraska, PhD, 1985. **CAREER:** Doosan Corporation, Korea, accountant, 1975-78; University of Akron, professor, 1986-. **ORGANIZATIONS:** Institute of Management Accountants, Akron chapter, board member; American Accounting Association; Decision Science Institute; Southern Finance Association. **HONORS/AWARDS:** Yonsei University, graduated with honors, 1976; National Association of Accountants, Member of the Year, 1989, certificate of merit, 1990; International Business Association, University of Akron, Award of Gratitude, 1992; Institute of Management Accountants, University of Akron, certificate of appreciation, 1993. **SPECIAL ACHIEVEMENTS:** An Investors Guide to the Korean Capital Market, Quorum Books, 1992; Making Effective Investment Decisions on Advanced Manufacturing Technology, Korean Chamber of Commerce Industry, 1990; published numerous articles in accounting and finance journals. **BUSINESS ADDRESS:** Professor, School of Accountancy, University of Akron, 302 Buchtel Common, Akron, OH 44325, (216)972-7461.

KIM, IL YOUNG
Physician. Korean American. **PERSONAL:** Born Feb 13, 1947, Republic of Korea; married Myeong, Apr 5, 1972; children: Eugenia, Diana, Richard, Angela. **EDUCATION:** Seoul Natl University, MD, 1971. **CAREER:** Physician, currently. **ORGANIZATIONS:** American College of Cardiology, fellow; American College of Chest Physicians, fellow; AMA; LACMA. **BUSINESS ADDRESS:** 3919 Beverly Blvd, Los Angeles, CA 90004-3432, (213)662-1175.

KIM, ILPYONG J.
Educator. Korean American. **PERSONAL:** Born Aug 15, 1931, Yongwol, Kangwon-Do, Republic of Korea; son of Suk Dae Kim & Ui Bong Lim; married Hyunyong Chung Kim, Jun 26, 1963; children: Irene, Katherene. **EDUCATION:** Asbury College, BA, 1953-57; Columbia University, Russian Institute, certificate, 1962, MA, 1962, PhD, 1968. **CAREER:** East-West Center, research associate, 1963-65; Indiana University, assistant professor, 1965-70; University of Connecticut, associate professor, 1970-76; University of Tokyo, Fulbright Professor, 1976-77; Columbia University, visiting professor, 1985; Seoul National University, Fulbright Professor, 1991-92; University of Connecticut, Department of Political Science, professor, 1976-. **ORGANIZATIONS:** New England Association of Asian Studies, president, 1978-79, vice-president, 1977-78; Association of Asian Studies, 1965-; American Political Science Association, 1961-; Korean-American Scholarship Foundation, board member, 1989-; Korean-American Society of Connecticut, board member, 1985-93. **HONORS/AWARDS:** US Department of Army, US Bronze Star Medal, 1953; National Defense Education Act, fellowship, 1961-63; Social Science Research Council, fellowship, 1969; US Department of State, Fulbright Fellowship, 1976-77, Fulbright Lectureship, 1991-92. **SPECIAL ACHIEVEMENTS:** Author, The Politics of Chinese Communism: Kiangsi Under the Soviets, 1973; Communist Politics in North Korea, 1975; Development and Cultural Change, 1986; The Strategic Triangle: China, the Soviet Union and the US, 1987; Korean Challenges and American Policy; 12 books and 39 articles published. **MILITARY SERVICE:** The ROK Army, capt, 1950-53; US Bronze Star Medal. **BUSINESS ADDRESS:** Professor, Dept of Political Science, University of Connecticut, 341 Mansfield Rd, Box U-24, Rm 137, Storrs, CT 06269-1024.

KIM, JAE HOON (JAY)
Principal scientist. Korean American. **PERSONAL:** Born Jan 8, 1952, Seoul, Republic of Korea. **EDUCATION:** Seoul National University, Korea, BS, 1976, MS, 1978; University of Florida, Gainesville, PhD, 1986. **CAREER:** Naval Academy, instructor, 1978-81; NASA Jet Propulsion Lab, member technical staff, 1987-89, task manager, 1989-91; Boeing High Technology Center, principal scientist, 1991-93; Boeing Defense & Space Research & Engineering Center, principal scientist, 1993-. **ORGANIZATIONS:** IEEE, 1976-; American Physical Society, 1986-93; SPIE, 1988-94; KSEA, 1986-. **HONORS/AWARDS:** Naval Academy, Outstanding Faculty Award, 1981; NASA, seven Technology Innovation Awards, 1987-91, three New Technology Patent Awards, 1987-91. **SPECIAL ACHIEVEMENTS:** About 40 publi-

cations in professional journals, such as IEEE Photonics Technology Letter, APS Applied Physics Letter, IEE Electronics Letter, etc, 1986-93; about 25 technical conference presentation and 7 NASA publications, 1986-93. **MILITARY SERVICE:** Naval Academy, lieutenant, 1978-81, Naval Academy superintendent, Outstanding Faculty Award. **BIOGRAPHICAL SOURCES:** KSEA Lett, vol 19, no 6, p29, 1991. **BUSINESS ADDRESS:** Principal Scientist, Boeing Defense & Space Group, PO Box 3999, MS/3W-51, Seattle, WA 98124-2499, (206)657-7685.

KIM, JAE WON
Educator. Korean American. **PERSONAL:** Born Jan 17, 1947, Chon-Nam, Republic of Korea; son of Kwang-Hee and Geum-Duck; married Chae Soon, Jan 7, 1971; children: Lisa, Jane, Beatrice. **EDUCATION:** Seoul National University, B Commerce, 1969; Andrews University, MBA, 1983; Mississippi State University, DBA, 1988. **CAREER:** Bank of Korea, department chief, 1969-80; University of Texas, Pan American, asst professor, 1988-89; Walla Walla College, asst professor, 1989-. **ORGANIZATIONS:** Decision Sciences Institute, 1988-; TIMS, 1988-. **HOME ADDRESS:** 27 NE Ash, College Place, WA 99324, (509)522-2178.

KIM, JAMES JOO-JIN
Electronics company executive. Korean American. **PERSONAL:** Born Jan 8, 1936, Seoul, Republic of Korea; son of Hyang-Soo Kim and Seung-Ye Oh; married Agnes Chung-Sook Kil, Dec 30, 1961; children: Susan, David, John. **EDUCATION:** University of Pennsylvania, Wharton School, BS, economics, 1959; University of Pennsylvania, MS, economics, 1961, 1961-63. **CAREER:** Villanova University, asst professor, economics, 1964-70; Amkor Electronics Inc, chmn, chief exec officer, 1968-. **ORGANIZATIONS:** Villanova University Development Council, 1984-; University of PA Board of Overseers, School of Arts & Sciences, 1989-; Korean Assn of Greater Philadelphia, former chmn. **HONORS/AWARDS:** Republic of Korea, President Park, Presidential Commendation for Contribution to Advancing the Nation's Electronics Industry, 1979, President Chun, Presidential Order of Industrial Service Merits in Export Promotion, 1983, President Roh, Presidential Tin-Tower Order of Industrial Service Merits in Export Promotion, 1990; Honorary Degree: Villanova University, Doctor of Commercial Science, 1990. **SPECIAL ACHIEVEMENTS:** Founder, chairman, chief exec officer: Amkor Electronics Inc, 1968, The Electronics Boutique Inc, 1977, Forte Systems Inc, 1989. **BUSINESS ADDRESS:** Chairman, CEO, Amkor Electronics, Inc, 1345 Enterprise Dr, West Chester, PA 19380.

KIM, JASON JUNGSUN
Educator. Korean American. **PERSONAL:** Born Jan 25, 1947, Seoul, Republic of Korea; son of Kwang J Kim; married Soonrae C Kim, Oct 20, 1973; children: Olivia, Edward. **EDUCATION:** Seoul National University, BS, 1970, MBA, 1974; University of Tennessee, MS, 1976, PhD, 1985. **CAREER:** TVA, industrial engineer, 1970-79; CRA, co-project director, 1979-84; University of Tennessee, research associate, instructor, 1985-87; Northeastern University, assistant professor, 1987-. **ORGANIZATIONS:** Korean Scientist and Engineers Association, New England Chapter, president, 1990-91; KSEA-Tennessee chapter, president, 1986-87; Boston Korean School, principal, 1987-; Korean Church of Boston, elder, 1987-. **HONORS/AWARDS:** American Society for Engineering Education, Scholarship for Faculty Development, 1990; Tau Beta Pi. **SPECIAL ACHIEVEMENTS:** Co-author, Economic and Financial Justification of Advanced Manufacturing Tech, Elsevier Science Pub, 1992. **BIOGRAPHICAL SOURCES:** International Journal of Engineering Education, February, 1993. **BUSINESS ADDRESS:** Assistant Professor, Northeastern University, 360 Huntington Ave, 323 Snell Engr Center, Boston, MA 02115-5096, (617)373-3630.

KIM, JAY C. (CHANG JOON)
Congressman. Korean American. **PERSONAL:** Born 1939, Republic of Korea; married June, 1961; children: Richard, Kathy, Eugene. **EDUCATION:** Chaffey College; University of Southern California, BS, MCE; California State University, MPA. **CAREER:** City of Diamond Bar, city council member, 1990, mayor, 1991; JayKim Engineers Inc, founder, president; State of California, 103rd Congress, 41st District, congressman, 1993-. **HONORS/AWARDS:** Outstanding Achievement in Business and Community Development Award; Engineer of the Year Award; Caballero de Distinction Award; Engineer Business of the Year Award; various others. **BUSINESS ADDRESS:** Congressman, US House of Representatives, 2433 Rayburn House Office Bldg, Washington, DC 20515-0541, (202)225-3201. *

KIM, JAY CHUL
Information technology manager. Korean American. **PERSONAL:** Born Jan 29, 1936, Pusan, Republic of Korea; son of Yuhwan Kim; married Sylvia Kim, Jul 22, 1963; children: Jennifer, Sandra, Steven. **EDUCATION:** Naval Academy, Korea, BA, electrical engineering, 1958; US Naval Post Graduate School, MA, physics, 1964; Cal State University, Los Angeles, 1982-84. **CAREER:** IBM, systems analyst, 1966-68; Los Angeles Water & Power, MIS, systems & programming, mgr, 1968-. **ORGANIZATIONS:** American Management Society; American Image Info Systems Society; American Computer Graphics Society. **MILITARY SERVICE:** Korean Navy, lt, 1958-64. **HOME ADDRESS:** 1373 Warner Ave, Los Angeles, CA 90024.

KIM, JAY S. (JONG-SUNG KIM)
Educator. Korean American. **PERSONAL:** Born Jan 2, 1958, Seoul, Republic of Korea; son of Man Jai Kim and Chang Moon Lee; married Jeong H Kim, Oct 27, 1982; children: Jane, Leslie. **EDUCATION:** Seoul National University, BA, 1980; Bowling Green State University, MBA, 1985; Ohio State University, PhD, 1989. **CAREER:** Bowling Green State University, instructor, 1985-86; Ohio State University, teaching/research associate, 1986-89; Boston University, assistant professor, 1989-. **SPECIAL ACHIEVEMENTS:** Manufacturing Strategies of US Firms, 1992. **MILITARY SERVICE:** Korean Navy, officer, 1980-83. **BUSINESS ADDRESS:** Assistant Professor, School of Management, Boston University, 621 Commonwealth Ave, Boston, MA 02215-1609, (617)353-9749.

KIM, JINCHOON
Scientist. Korean American. **PERSONAL:** Born Mar 5, 1943, Republic of Korea; son of Kyu-Koo Kim; married Yoonchung Kim, 1970; children: Nina, Margaret, Angela. **EDUCATION:** Seoul National University, BS, 1965; University of California, Berkeley, MS, 1968, PhD, 1971. **CAREER:** The Cyclotron Corp, physicist, 1971-74; Oak Ridge National Lab, research staff, 1974-80; General Atomics, principal scientist, 1980-. **ORGANIZATIONS:** American Phys Society, 1969-; Korean Nuclear Society, permanent member. **SPECIAL ACHIEVEMENTS:** Published over 130 papers; three US patents. **BUSINESS ADDRESS:** Principal Scientist, General Atomics, 3550 General Atomics Ct, San Diego, CA 92121-1194, (619)455-3138.

KIM, JOANNE YOUNG
Librarian, educator. Korean American. **PERSONAL:** Born Jan 22, 1940, Seoul, Republic of Korea; daughter of Hung Kyum Ko and Bok-chung Lee; married Myron Myung-whan Kim, Mar 22, 1967; children: Brian, Jason. **EDUCATION:** Ewha Woman's University, BA, MA, 1963; University of Colorado, MA, 1966; Indiana University, 1966-69; University of South Carolina, ML, 1975. **CAREER:** Ewha Woman's University, English instructor, 1964; Allen University, librarian, 1971-75; Modesto Junior College, English instructor & librarian, 1976-81; Pasadena City College, English instructor & librarian, 1981-84, assistant dean for library services, 1984-90, associate professor & librarian II, 1990-. **ORGANIZATIONS:** Community College Lib Chapter, California Lib Association, president, 1991-92, Academic Section, steering committee, 1991-; American Library Association, 1985-92; California Library Networking Taskforce, steering committee, 1990-92; Korean American Librarians Association, president, 1987-89; Asian Pacific American Librarians Association, 1991-; California Teachers Association, 1976-. **BUSINESS ADDRESS:** Associate Professor of Library Services, Acquisitions Librarian, Pasadena City College, 1570 E Colorado Blvd, Shatford Library, Pasadena, CA 91106-2003, (818)585-7837.

KIM, JONATHAN JANG-HO
Missionary priest, company manager (retired). Korean American. **PERSONAL:** Born Jun 11, 1932, Gwang Ju, Chollanamdo, Republic of Korea; son of Jae Ie Kim & Sun-Sam Cho; married Kunai Chu Kim, Oct 27, 1958; children: David J. **EDUCATION:** Seoul National University, BSc, 1955; Carnegie-Mellon University, MS, 1961; University of Oklahoma, PhD, 1966; University of Toronto, Trinity College, diploma in theology, 1993. **CAREER:** Scientific Research Institute, Department of National Defense, metallurgical engineer, 1955-59; Lummus Co, Combustion Engineering Inc, process design engineer, 1955-57; Kennecott Copper Corp, Ledgement Lab, staff scientist, 1967-80; Carorundum Co, Process Technology, manager, 1980-91; Episcopal Diocese of Western New York, missionary priest, 1993. **SPECIAL ACHIEVEMENTS:** 22 US patents issued, numerous foreign patents, 1970-93; proficient in: Japanese, German, Korean; technical publication papers in journals of the Metallurgical Society and American Ceramic Society. **MILI-**

TARY SERVICE: Air Force, Republic of Korea, 1st lt, 1957-59. **HOME ADDRESS:** 79 Brandywine Dr, Williamsville, NY 14221, (716)688-1819.

KIM, JONG H.
Educator. Korean American. **PERSONAL:** Born Jun 6, 1952, Pusan, Republic of Korea; son of Yak Kim and Jeong Kim; married Young Kim; children: Chris, Peter. **EDUCATION:** University of Toledo, MBA, 1984; University of Missouri, PhD, 1988. **CAREER:** University of Missouri, instructor; California State University, professor, currently. **ORGANIZATIONS:** Sierra Lions Club, secretary, currently. **HOME ADDRESS:** 9084 Approach Ct, Fair Oaks, CA 95628. **BUSINESS ADDRESS:** Associate Professor, California State University, 6000 J St, 2059 Business Administration Bldg, Sacramento, CA 95819-6088, (916)278-7396.

KIM, JONG-JIN
Educator. Korean American. **PERSONAL:** Born Jan 22, 1952, Seoul, Republic of Korea; son of Un-Bae Kim & Ki-Bun Rho; married Jinrae Kim, Feb 27, 1978; children: Wontae, Brian. **EDUCATION:** Seoul University, BS, 1975; University of Texas, Austin, MArch, 1981; University of California, Berkeley, PhD, 1987. **CAREER:** Lawrence Berkeley Lab, research scientist, 1985-88; Arizona State University, assistant professor, 1988-91; University of Michigan, assistant professor, 1991-. **ORGANIZATIONS:** American Solar Energy Society, 1988-; Society of Building Science Educator, 1988-; Intelligent Building Institute, 1993-; American Society of Heating Refrigerating and Air-Conditioning Engineers, 1990-; Illuminating Engineering Society, 1989-. **HONORS/AWARDS:** Progressive Architecture, research citation, 1981; University of Michigan, Research Grant Award, 1992. **SPECIAL ACHIEVEMENTS:** ACSA Technology Conference, chair, 1994; 20 papers published in various journals & publications. **BUSINESS ADDRESS:** Assistant Professor, College of Architecture, University of Michigan, 2000 Bonisteel Blvd, Ann Arbor, MI 48109-1189, (313)763-3518.

KIM, JONG KOO
Physician. Korean American. **PERSONAL:** Born Dec 19, 1933, Taegu, Kyungpook, Republic of Korea; son of Jee Kyung Kim and Shin Kyung Sunu; married Hyo Soon Lee, Mar 19, 1960; children: Min, Won, David. **EDUCATION:** Kyungpook National University, School of Medicine, MD, 1958, MS, 1962, MScD, 1966. **CAREER:** Chicago Medical School, clinical asst prof, 1977-87; Edgewater Hospital, co-dir, intensive care, 1976-, medical staff, vice pres, 1993; Edgewater Ambulatory Care Center, medical director, 1985-. **ORGANIZATIONS:** Korean Medical Assn of America, vice pres, 1977, president, 1994; Korean Medical Assn of Chicago, president, 1977; Kyungpook National University, School of Medicine Alumni Assn of North America, president, 1983. **HONORS/AWARDS:** American Board of Internal Medicine, 1977, Advanced Achievement, 1987; American Board of Quality Assurance, 1990; American College of Physicians, Fellow, 1991. **SPECIAL ACHIEVEMENTS:** Author, 6 articles including: "Studies on the Variation of Degrees Resistance in INH-Resistant Tubercle Bacilli," 1962-66. **MILITARY SERVICE:** Republic of Korean Army, major, 1958-66. **BUSINESS ADDRESS:** Medical Director, Ambulatory Care Center, Edgewater Medical Center, 5700 N Ashland, Chicago, IL 60660.

KIM, JONG-SUNG. *See* **KIM, JAY S.**

KIM, JOOCHUL
Educator. Korean American. **PERSONAL:** Born Jun 21, 1948, Republic of Korea; son of Koobong Kim & Kumsoon Song; married Shinja R Kim, Sep 16, 1969; children: Matthew H. **EDUCATION:** University of California, Berkeley, BA, 1973; University of Michigan, MUP, 1977, PhD, 1979. **CAREER:** Raytheon Service Co, senior research analyst, 1977-80; Boston University, lecturer, 1977-80; Regis College, lecturer, 1978; Arizona State University, assistant, associate professor, 1980-, management intern, 1990, special assignment to the office of the president, 1990-92, loaned executive to the city of Phoenix, 1992-. **ORGANIZATIONS:** American Association of University Professors, currently; Association for Asian Studies, currently; American Planning Association, International Division, currently; Planners Network, steering committee, currently; Korean Urban and Regional Planning Association, currently; Journal of Planning Education and Research, editorial board, currently; City of Tempe, Task Force member for Vision Tempe, 1990-91. **HONORS/AWARDS:** Fulbright Scholarship, 1986-87. **SPECIAL ACHIEVEMENTS:** Book, reports, professional journal articles, and popular articles, 1977-; invited speaker at many universities and professional meetings, 1977-; invited speaker to universities in China and Korea, 1985-. **HOME ADDRESS:** PO Box 24072,

Tempe, AZ 85285, (602)921-3668. **BUSINESS ADDRESS:** Associate Professor, Arizona State University, Tempe, AZ 85287, (602)965-2768.

KIM, JOSEPH K.
Attorney. Korean American. **PERSONAL:** Born Nov 26, 1959, Seoul, Republic of Korea; married. **EDUCATION:** University of California, Berkeley, BA, 1981; Harvard Law School, JD, 1986; Harvard Business School, MBA (magna cum laude), 1986. **CAREER:** McKinsey & Co, research analyst, 1982-83; O'Melveny & Myers, attorney, 1986-. **ORGANIZATIONS:** Harvard Law Review, editor, 1984-86. **HONORS/AWARDS:** University of California, Berkeley, Highest Distinction, 1981; Phi Beta Kappa, 1981. **BUSINESS ADDRESS:** Attorney, O'Melveny & Myers, 400 S Hope St, Los Angeles, CA 90071, (213)669-6660.

KIM, JUNG HWAN
Educator. Korean American. **PERSONAL:** Born Feb 20, 1955, Pusan, Republic of Korea; son of Sung Hyun Kim and Namee Oh; married Insook Kim, May 1, 1980. **EDUCATION:** Seoul National University, BS, 1979; University of Iowa, MS, 1982, PhD, 1987. **CAREER:** University of Iowa, research assistant, 1982-87; University of Southwestern Louisiana, assistant professor, 1988-. **ORGANIZATIONS:** Institute of Electrical and Electronic Engineers, senior member. **HONORS/AWARDS:** Louisiana State Board of Regents, research award, 1992. **SPECIAL ACHIEVEMENTS:** Publication: IEEE Transactions on Computers, 1989. **BIOGRAPHICAL SOURCES:** The Daily Advertiser, June 1993. **BUSINESS ADDRESS:** Assistant Professor, University of Southwestern Louisiana, 2 Rex Street, Conference Center, Room 448, Lafayette, LA 70504-4330, (318)231-6732.

KIM, JUNGNAM EGO
Dentist. Korean American. **PERSONAL:** Born Feb 15, 1943, Hwanghaedo, Republic of Korea; son of Saepoong Kim & Haksil Choi; married Myung Hee Kim, Mar 28, 1976; children: Sharon Eunyoung, Daniel Jinwoo. **EDUCATION:** Brooklyn College, NY, BS, 1975; Harvard School of Dental Medicine, DMD, 1979. **CAREER:** Private dental office, owner, dentist, currently. **ORGANIZATIONS:** Cleveland Korean American Association, board of trustees. **BUSINESS ADDRESS:** Owner, Jungnam E Kim D M D Dental Office, 7543 Broadview Rd, #2, Seven Hills, OH 44131, (216)642-1313.

KIM, JUNGUK LAWRENCE
Educator. Korean American. **PERSONAL:** Born Sep 9, 1955, Seoul, Republic of Korea; son of Duk-Jun Kim and Sin-Jung Kim. **EDUCATION:** Sung Kyun Kwan University, BS, 1978; University of Illinois, Urbana-Champaign, MS, 1984, PhD, 1987. **CAREER:** McDonnell Douglas Corp, engineer/scientist, 1979-82; Construction Engineering Research Lab, operations research analyst, 1982-83; Texas A&M, University, assistant professor, 1987-. **ORGANIZATIONS:** IEEE, 1988-; ACM, 1988-. **SPECIAL ACHIEVEMENTS:** Contributor: IEEE Journal; Journal of Data and Knowledge Engineering; Information Processing Letters. **BUSINESS ADDRESS:** Asst Professor, Dept of Computer Science, Texas A&M University, 301 H R Bright Bldg, College Station, TX 77843-3112, (409)845-8872.

KIM, JWA KEUN
Educator. Korean American. **PERSONAL:** Born May 13, 1952, Taegu, Republic of Korea; son of Hacksoo and Pilsun Kim; married Weon Hee Kim, Oct 1, 1981; children: Young, John, Jin. **EDUCATION:** Kyungpook National University, BEd, 1980, MEd, 1982; University of Oklahoma, PhD, 1989. **CAREER:** Middle Tennessee State University, associate professor, 1989-. **ORGANIZATIONS:** Psychometric Society, 1989-; Southeastern Psychological Association, 1990-; Mid-South Educational Research Association, 1990-, editorial board, 1993-, publication, communication committee, 1993-, program committee, 1993-; Tennessee Academy of Science, 1989-. **HONORS/AWARDS:** Middle Tennessee State University, faculty research grants, 1990-93. **SPECIAL ACHIEVEMENTS:** Publications: "Ability Estimation for Conventional Tests," Psychometrika, 1993; "Intellectual Structure of Decision Support System," Decision Support System, 1993; "The Prevalence and Contributing Factor of Sexual Misconduct Among Southern Baptist Pastors in Six Southern States," The Journal of Pastoral Care, 1993. **BUSINESS ADDRESS:** Assistant Professor, Dept of Psychology, Middle Tenn State University, 1500 Greenland Drive, Murfreesboro, TN 37132-0002, (615)898-2002.

KIM, KARL EUJUNG
Educator. Korean American. **PERSONAL:** Born Sep 5, 1957, Junction City, KS; son of Yee S Kim and Young S Lee Kim; married Shilla K H Yoon, Apr

25, 1989; children: Kelly Hosue, Kenneth Taysoo. **EDUCATION:** Brown University, AB, 1979; Massachusetts Institute of Technology, PhD, 1987. **CAREER:** MIT, research assistant, 1979-84; University of Hawaii, assistant professor, 1987-92, associate professor, 1992-. **ORGANIZATIONS:** State of Hawaii, Rental Housing Trust Fund, commissioner, 1992; Makiki Neighborhood Board, elected board member, 1988; Oahu Metropolitan Planning Organization, committee member, 1988; University of Hawaii, faculty senate, elected, 1992, Honors Council, 1991, Faculty Executive Committee, 1988, Center for Korean Studies, elected, 1987. **HONORS/AWARDS:** Fulbright Research Award, Korea, 1991; Western Governors Association, Scholar in Residence, 1990; International Cultural Society of Korea, scholar, 1988. **SPECIAL ACHIEVEMENTS:** Publication of numerous articles and papers on urban planning, traffic safety, and environmental management in the US and Asia, 1987-. **BUSINESS ADDRESS:** Associate Professor, Dept of Urban and Regional Planning, University of Hawaii, 2424 Maile Way, Porteus Hall 107, Honolulu, HI 96822, (808)956-7381.

KIM, KATHLEEN M.
Physician, educator. Korean American. **PERSONAL:** Born Jan 23, 1958, Baltimore, MD; daughter of Martin & Christine Kim; married Zachary Rattner, Dec 15, 1992. **EDUCATION:** Brown University, BA, 1979, MD, 1983; Harvard School of Public Health, MPH, 1983. **CAREER:** Yale University School of Medicine, asst professor, 1989-; Yale-New Haven Hospital, director of psychiatric ambulatory services, currently. **ORGANIZATIONS:** APA, general member, 1984-. **HONORS/AWARDS:** MEAD Johnson, fellowship, 1985. **BUSINESS ADDRESS:** Director of Psychiatric Ambulatory Services, Yale-New Haven Hospital, 425 George St, New Haven, CT 06511, (203)785-3182.

KIM, KEN I.
Educator. Korean American. **PERSONAL:** Born Mar 3, 1941, Hoeyang-Kun, Kangwon-Do, Republic of Korea; son of Byung Hak Kim and Young Sook Kim; married Hazel K Kim, Oct 25, 1978; children: Young W, Gene W. **EDUCATION:** Seoul National University, Korea, bachelor of economics, 1964; Indiana University, Bloomington, MBA, 1976, DBA, 1979. **CAREER:** Kolon Industries Inc, Korea, deputy manager, 1964-73; Tennessee State University, assistant professor, 1978-80; Bowling Green State University, assistant professor, 1980-85; University of Toledo, professor, 1985-. **ORGANIZATIONS:** Academy of Management, 1978; Academy of Interntional Business, 1978; Decision Sciences Institute, 1993. **HONORS/AWARDS:** Beta Gamma Sigma, 1978; Sigma Iota Epsilon, 1978. **SPECIAL ACHIEVEMENTS:** Academy of Management Journal, article, 1990; Journal of International Business Studies, article, 1986; Management International Review, several articles, 1989-. **MILITARY SERVICE:** Korean Army (compulsory service), corporal, 1961-63. **BIOGRAPHICAL SOURCES:** The Blade, Toledo, OH, p 21-22, June 7, 1993. **BUSINESS ADDRESS:** Professor, College of Business Administrtion, University of Toledo, W Bancroft St, Toledo, OH 43606-3390, (419)537-2264.

KIM, KI HANG
Educator. Korean American. **PERSONAL:** Born Aug 5, 1936, Mundok, Pyong-nam, Korea (North); son of Jin Gyong Kim and Mi Ran Hong; married Myong Ja Hwang Kim, Jul 31, 1963; children: John Churl, Linda Youngmi. **EDUCATION:** University of Southern Mississippi, BS, 1960; George Washington University, PhD, 1971; MIT, postdoc, 1970-71. **CAREER:** University of Hartford, instructor of mathematics, 1961-66; George Washington University, lecturer of math, 1966-70; Saint Mary's College of Maryland, associate professor of math, 1968-70; Pembroke State University, associate professor of mathematics, 1970-74; Alabama State University, Distinguished Professor of Mathematics, 1974-. **ORGANIZATIONS:** Comm for the Preservation of Sci Inf Resources, co-chair, 1993-; Americans for Change Presidential Task Force, charter member, 1993-; Mathematical Social Sciences, editor in chief, 1980-; Future Generations Computer Systems, editorial board, 1985-; Pure Mathematics and Applications, editorial board, 1991-. **HONORS/AWARDS:** National Science Foundation, research grant, 1981-; US Army Research Office, research grant, 1973-80. **SPECIAL ACHIEVEMENTS:** Conducted research in boolean matrices, algebraic varieties, elliptic curves, mathematical social sciences, symbolic dynamics, and Diophantine equations, 1971-; author and coauthor of 7 books and more than 100 articles in the above mentioned areas. **MILITARY SERVICE:** US Army infantry, sp/4, 1954-57; Outstanding UN soldiers in Korea, 1957. **HOME ADDRESS:** 416 Arrowhead Drive, Montgomery, AL 36117, (205)277-0436. **BUSINESS ADDRESS:** Distinguished Professor of Mathematics, Alabama State University, 915 South Jackson Street, Room 310C, Science Building, Montgomery, AL 36101-0271, (205)293-4484.

KIM, KI HOON
Educator. Korean American. **PERSONAL:** Born Jan 23, 1933, Taegu, Kyungbuk, Republic of Korea; son of Yoon Sung Kim and Ha Hyang Kwon; married Soo Wha Kim, Jun 6, 1964; children: Albert Sung-Chan, Noel Mi-Hye. **EDUCATION:** College of Commerce, Seoul National University, BA, 1956; New York Theological Seminary, MRE, 1960; Clark University, MA, 1962; University of Connecticut, PhD, 1968. **CAREER:** The Bank of Korea, clerk, 1956-57; The University of Connecticut, graduate asst, 1963-67; Central Connecticut St University, assistant professor of economics, 1967-72, associate professor of economics, 1972-81, professor of economics, 1981-. **ORGANIZATIONS:** American Economic Association, 1967-; American Association of University Professors, 1975-; Omicron Delta Epsilon, 1975-; The Korean-American University Professors, 1988-; The Korean-America Economic Association, 1989-. **HONORS/AWARDS:** Institute of International Education, Development Fellowship Award, 1965-67; Yale University, Fellowship Award, 1982-83; Connecticut World Trade Association, Special Award, 1987; Han Nam University, Plaque of Appreciation, 1988; Central Connecticut State University, established the Ki Hoon Kim Scholarship Fund, 1993. **SPECIAL ACHIEVEMENTS:** Director of The Connecticut Institute for Asian and American Studies, 1990-; "The Brain Drain: Causes and Remedies," won first prize, The 15th Essay Contest, sponsored by The Asian Student, 1967; "The Economics of the Brain Drain: Pros, Cons, and Remedies," J of Econ Development, pp 55-80, 1976; "The Role of the US in the Economic Development of Korea," Chap 8, Forty Years of Korea-US Relations 1948-88, pp 137-169, 1990. **MILITARY SERVICE:** The Republic of Korea Air Force, private first class, 1956-57. **BIOGRAPHICAL SOURCES:** Forty Years of Korea-US Relations, 1948-88 (Eds T H Kwak et al), p xii, 1990. **HOME ADDRESS:** 497 Commonwealth Avenue, New Britain, CT 06050. **BUSINESS ADDRESS:** Professor of Economics, Central Connecticut State University, 1615 Stanley St, Room 115A, Marcus White Hall, New Britain, CT 06050, (203)827-7408.

KIM, KI HWAN
Research scientist. Korean American. **PERSONAL:** Born May 12, 1946, Pyung Yang, Republic of Korea; son of Tae Bok Kim and Hak Chan Chung; married Kyung Hee Kim, Oct 24, 1970; children: Daniel Hyun-Ho, Angela Hye-Ran, Jane Hye-Rim. **EDUCATION:** Yonsei University, Seoul, Korea, BS, 1969, MS, 1971; University of Kansas, MS, 1976, PhD, 1981. **CAREER:** Pomona College, research assistant, 1971-73; research associate, 1976-80; Abbott Labs, research investigator, 1980-. **ORGANIZATIONS:** American Chemical Society, currently; International QSAR Society, currently; International Group for Correlation Analysis, currently; Korean-American Science & Engineering Profession Society, currently. **HONORS/AWARDS:** Yonsei University, Chemistry Department Scholar, 1965-66, 1969-71, Chancellor Scholar, 1966-68; University of Kansas, Medicinal Chemistry Department Research Fellow, 1973-76. **SPECIAL ACHIEVEMENTS:** Author or co-author of over 60 publications in the fields of medical chemistry and drug development. **BUSINESS ADDRESS:** Research Investigator, Abbott Laboratories, Biomolecular Computational Chemistry, D46Y, AP9A, Abbott Park, IL 60064, (708)937-5797.

KIM, KITAI
Physician, educator. Korean American. **PERSONAL:** Born Jun 5, 1933, Sangjoo, Kyungbook, Republic of Korea; son of Byung-Ok Kim and Soon-Ak Park; married Chung-Ok Roh Kim, Apr 3, 1960; children: Steve H, David H. **EDUCATION:** Seoul National University, pre medical course, 1954, College of Medicine, MD, 1958; Case Western Reserve University, Institute of Pathology, residency & fellow, 1968-72. **CAREER:** Medical College of Ohio, professor of pathology, Surgical Pathology & Cytology, director, 1972-. **ORGANIZATIONS:** College of American Pathologists, fellow, 1972-; Intl Academy of Pathology, fellow, 1972-; Intl Academy of Cytology, fellow, 1972-; American Society of Cytology, 1972-; American Association for the Advancement of Science, 1980-; Eastern Cooperative Oncology Group, 1980-. **SPECIAL ACHIEVEMENTS:** Textbooks include: Practical Guide to Surgical Pathology with Cytologic Correlation, Springer-Verlag, 1991; Gastrointestinal Cancer, ed R Dobelbower, contributed to chapter 3, "Gastrointestinal Pathology;" sixty five publications in refereed journals and abstracts. **MILITARY SERVICE:** Army Medical Corp, ROKA, captain, mc, 1958-64. **BUSINESS ADDRESS:** Professor of Pathology, Director of Surgical Pathology and Cytology, Medical College of Ohio, 3000 Arlington Avenue, PO Box 10008, Toledo, OH 43699-0008, (419)381-3482.

KIM, KUNSOO

Educator. Korean American. **PERSONAL:** Born Jul 11, 1943, Seoul, Republic of Korea; son of Keun-Shik Kim and Sung-June Lee; married Haeily Kim, Jun 20, 1970; children: Phil Y. **EDUCATION:** Seoul National University, BS, 1967; University of Minnesota, MS, 1972; University of Wisconsin, Madison, PhD, 1976. **CAREER:** University of Minnesota, research assistant, 1970-72; University of Wisconsin, research assistant, 1972-75; Michigan Technological University, associate professor, assistant professor, 1975-80; Rockwell International, principal engineer, group manager, 1980-86; Westinghouse, fellow scientist, 1986-88; Battelle Memorial Institute, staff scientist, 1988-89; Columbia University, associate professor, 1990-. **ORGANIZATIONS:** International Society for Rock Mechanics, commission member, 1972-; American Geophysical Union, 1975-; American Institute for Mining, Metallurgical & Petroleum Engineers; Society of Mining Engineers, 1972-; Society of Petroleum Engineers, 1992-; Sigma Xi, 1975-. **HONORS/AWARDS:** USDOE, Office of Geologic Disposal, Certificate of Appreciation, 1986. **SPECIAL ACHIEVEMENTS:** Editor, Environmental Issues and Waste Management in Energy & Minerals Production; design, execution and analysis of a large scale in site thermomechanical test for siting high level nuclear waste repository, 1993. **MILITARY SERVICE:** Korean Army, enlisted man, 1964-66. **BUSINESS ADDRESS:** Associate Professor, Columbia University, 809 Seeley W Mudd, New York, NY 10027-6940, (212)854-8337.

KIM, KWAN HEE

Molecular biologist, educator. Korean American. **PERSONAL:** Born Feb 19, 1952, Seoul, Republic of Korea; daughter of Young Choo Kim & Kwang Ok Yoon; married Cornelius F Ivory, Oct 13, 1979; children: Danielle Ivory. **EDUCATION:** Wheaton College, BA, 1974; Princeton University, PhD, 1982. **CAREER:** University of Chicago, postdoctoral research associate, 1981-87; Washington State University, research assistant professor, 1987-89, assistant professor, 1989-. **ORGANIZATIONS:** American Society of Cell Biology; American Association for the Advancement of Science; New York Academy of Science; Endocrine Society; Society for the Study of Reproduction. **HONORS/AWARDS:** Phi Beta Kappa. **BUSINESS ADDRESS:** Assistant Professor, Dept of Genetics & Cell Biology, Washington State University, Pullman, WA 99164-4234, (509)335-7022.

KIM, KWANG-SHIN

Educator. Korean American. **PERSONAL:** Born Nov 15, 1937, Seoul, Republic of Korea; son of Dae-Woo & Sung-Duk Kim; married Bu-Choon Chung Kim, Sep 10, 1965; children: Edwin C M, Andrew K M. **EDUCATION:** National Seoul University, BS, 1959; Rutgers State University, MS, 1963, PhD, 1967. **CAREER:** New York University Medical Center, associate research scientist in microbiology, 1968-71; New York University Medical Center and School of Medicine, assistant professor, 1971-76, associate professor, 1976-. **HONORS/AWARDS:** Merck Co Foundation, Grant for Faculty Development, 1974; Andrew W Mellon Foundation Fund, 1973-76. **SPECIAL ACHIEVEMENTS:** Mycobacterium Bacteriological Reviews, 1977; American Society for Microbiology, Propionicbacterium, Corymebacterium, Mycobacterium and Lepra Bacilli, ACTA Leprologica, vol II, p 153-174, 1984; Bacterial Structure in Medical Microbiology, Samuel Baron, editor, 1991. **HOME ADDRESS:** 462 Barbara Ave, Wyckoff, NJ 07481, (201)848-8097. **BUSINESS ADDRESS:** Professor, Dept of Microbiology, New York University Medical Center and School of Medicine, 550 First Ave, New York, NY 10016, (212)263-5154.

KIM, KYOO HONG

Educator. Korean American. **PERSONAL:** Born Apr 10, 1948, Seoul, Republic of Korea; son of Doo Young Kim & Jung Shik Shin; married YoungHee Kim, Aug 19, 1972; children: Irene, Michael. **EDUCATION:** Seoul National University, BS, 1971; University of Wisconsin, Madison, MS, 1975, PhD, 1978. **CAREER:** Bowling Green State University, professor of economics, currently. **BUSINESS ADDRESS:** Professor of Economics, Bowling Green State University, College of Business Administration, Bowling Green, OH 43403, (419)372-2735.

KIM, LEO

Company executive. Korean American. **PERSONAL:** Born Oct 3, 1942, California; married; children: Two. **EDUCATION:** Reedley College, AA, chemistry, 1962; Fresno State College, BS, chemistry, 1964; University of Kansas, PhD, organic chemistry, 1967; Massachusetts Institute of Technology, postdoctoral studies, 1967-68. **CAREER:** Massachusetts Institute of Technology, research associate, 1967-68; Shell Development Co, Emeryville Research Ctr, research chemist, 1968; Westhollow Research Ctr & Bellaire Research Ctr, staff research chemist, group leader, 1974-78; Shell Biological Laboratories, Shell Intl Research, special exchange assignment, 1978-79; Shell Development Co, Line/Staff Assignment to President of Shell Development, special assignment, 1979; Biological Sciences Research Ctr, Special Assignment in Biotechnology, Organic Chemistry, dept head, 1980, Biological Chemistry, manager, 1980-81; Shell Oil Co, Interferon, research and development director, 1982-83; Shell Oil Co, Biomedical Ventures, research and development director, 1982-83; Shell Development Co, principal scientist, 1983-86; Mycogen Corp, research, vp, 1986-89, executive vp, chief technical officer, 1989-. **ORGANIZATIONS:** American Institute of Chemists; Phi Lambda Epsilon; Sigma Xi; American Chemical Society; New York Academy of Science; American Association for the Advancement of Science. **SPECIAL ACHIEVEMENTS:** Structured Mycogen/Kubota, Mycogen/Japan Tabacco, and Mycogen/Royal Dutch Shell relationships which were unique in technology transfer relationships and in US Japanese joint ventures, relationships and income totaling $29,000,000; design and implementation of a worldwide agricultural biopesticide research strategy involving five laboratories, four companies, three countries, and involving nearly two hundred researchers; interactions with over 80 Japanese companies and institutions. **BUSINESS ADDRESS:** Executive VP, Research/Chief Technical Officer, Mycogen Corp, 4980 Carroll Canyon Rd, San Diego, CA 92121, (619)453-8030.

KIM, MICHAEL KYONG-IL

Architect, educator. Korean American. **PERSONAL:** Born Mar 5, 1940, Seoul, Republic of Korea; son of Sang-Hoo & Hwa-Soon Chong Kim; married Samyoung Kim, Apr 4, 1964; children: Alexander Dojun, Andrew Dohyung, Susan Kyonghee. **EDUCATION:** Seoul National University, Korea, BS, architecture, 1964; Ohio State University, MArch, 1972; University of California, Berkeley, PhD, architecture, 1980. **CAREER:** William Dorsky Associates, architectural designer, 1968-69; Ohio State University, research associate, 1970-72; TAET Architects & Planners, project architect, 1972-74; University of California, Berkeley, associate, 1974-77; Harvard University, associate professor, 1977-84; Michael K Kim, PhD, AIA Consulting Architect, principal, 1981-; University of Illinois, professor, 1984-, Architectural Practice and Technology Division, chairman, currently. **ORGANIZATIONS:** American Institute of Architects, 1974-; Boston Society of Architects, 1989-; American Society of Heating, Refrigeration & Air Conditioning Engineer, 1993-; CIB World Congress Organizing Committee, 1986. **HONORS/AWARDS:** Harvard University, Presidential Award for Innovative Teaching, 1981; NASA, faculty fellowship, 1976. **SPECIAL ACHIEVEMENTS:** Author, The Logic of Designing Buildings as Facility & Process Complementary Systems; Development of Machine Intelligence for Inference of Design Intent Implicit in Design Specifications; Countermodeling as a Strategy for Decision-Making: Epistemological Problems in Design; Decomposition of Multi-cell Complexes Using "Multi-Terminal Maximal Flow Theorem;" representative architectural projects: Centennial High School and Blue Cross/Blue Shield of Central Ohio, Columbus. **BUSINESS ADDRESS:** Chairman, Arch Practice & Tech Div, Professor of Architecture, University of Illinois, 608 E Lorado Taft Dr, 404 Architecture Bldg, Champaign, IL 61820-6969, (217)244-8012.

KIM, MICHAEL WOOYUNG

Educator. Korean American. **PERSONAL:** Born Aug 15, 1958, Seoul, Republic of Korea; son of Yong Sun & Myung Sook Hwang Kim; married Moon Sook Kim, Oct 10, 1982; children: John H, Michelle H. **EDUCATION:** University of California, Santa Barbara, BA; Stanford University, MS, 1985, PhD, 1991. **CAREER:** Mission Insurance Group, actuary, 1983-84; Stanford University, research assistant, 1985-89, teaching fellow, 1989-90; University of California, Riverside, assistant professor, 1990-. **ORGANIZATIONS:** Operations Research Society, member, 1987-; Institute of Management Science, 1988-. **HONORS/AWARDS:** Korean Government, Presidential Scholarship, 1986; University of California, Santa Barbara, Phi Beta Kappa, 1983. **BUSINESS ADDRESS:** Assistant Professor, Graduate School of Management, University of California, Riverside, CA 92521, (909)787-4557.

KIM, MICHAEL YONG

Interior designer. Korean American. **PERSONAL:** Born Mar 2, 1962, Seoul, Republic of Korea; son of Helen Kim; married Sunsin Kim, Jul 14, 1990. **EDUCATION:** Fashion Institute of Design & Merchandising, AA, 1988. **CAREER:** Pace Art & Graphic Co, technical artist, 1984; Life Construction Co, interior designer, 1989; Oxford Interior Co, vice president, 1990; Western Design Center, interior designer, 1992; Michael Kim Interior, president, currently. **SPECIAL ACHIEVEMENTS:** Ramada Hotel Interior Design, San

Bernardino, 1990; Rosalia Home Fashion Store Design, 1992. **BUSINESS ADDRESS:** President, Michael Kim Interior, 4201 Wilshire Blvd, #622, Los Angeles, CA 90010, (213)938-9998.

KIM, MOON G.
Educator. Korean American. **PERSONAL:** Born Jan 23, 1941, Poun Chung-buk, Republic of Korea; son of Mr & Mrs Bok S Kim; married Reina Lyou, Aug 4, 1964; children: Susan Eunkyung, James Jin-Seong. **EDUCATION:** Kyung Hee University, Korea, BS, 1964; Kansas State University, PhD, 1973. **CAREER:** Korea Institute of Science and Technology, 1968; Weyerhaeuser Co, senior scientist, 1974-84; Georgia-Pacific Corp, senior chemist, 1984-88; Mississippi State University, associate professor, 1988-. **ORGANIZATIONS:** American Chemcial Society, 1968-; Forest Products Society, 1988-. **SPECIAL ACHIEVEMENTS:** Publications in the field of polymer chemistry and wood products. **MILITARY SERVICE:** Korean Army, 2nd lt, 1964-66. **BUSINESS ADDRESS:** Professor, Dept of Wood Products, Mississippi State University, 100 Blackjack Rd, Starkville, MS 39759.

KIM, MOON H.
Educator, physician. Korean American. **PERSONAL:** Born Nov 30, 1934, Seoul, Republic of Korea; son of Jae-Hang & Kum-Joo Choi Kim; married Yong Cha Pak-Kim, Jun 20, 1964; children: Peter, Edward. **EDUCATION:** Yonsei University, College of Medicine, MD, 1960. **CAREER:** Cleveland Metropolitan General Hospital, resident in obstetrics & gynecology, 1962-66; University of Washington, research fellow, 1966-67; University of Toronto, research fellow, 1968-70; University of Chicago, assistant professor, director of division of reproductive endocrinology, 1970-74; Ohio State University, director, division of reproductive endocrinology, 1975-91, professor, vice chairman, obstetrics & gynecology, 1980-, Richard L Meiling Chair, Professor in Obstetrics & Gynecology, 1988-. **ORGANIZATIONS:** American Journal of Obstet/Gynecol, associate editor, 1991-; American College of Ob/Gyn, fellow, 1971-; Society for Gynecologic Investigation, 1974-; Endocrine Society, 1974-; American Gynecological Obstetric Society, fellow, 1986-; American Fertility Society, 1974-; Association of Professors of Obstet/Gynecol, 1975-; American Board of Obstet & Gynecol, examiner, 1978-; Central Association Obstet & Gynecol, life member, 1976-. **HONORS/AWARDS:** University of Chicago, McClintock Award for Outstanding Teaching, 1976; Ohio State University, Professor of the Year, 1977, Clinical Teaching Award, 1980; Korean Association Obstet & Gynecol, honorary member. **SPECIAL ACHIEVEMENTS:** 96 publications. **BUSINESS ADDRESS:** Professor, Ohio State University, College of Medicine, 1654 Upham Dr, Means Hall 535, Columbus, OH 43210-1238.

KIM, MOON KYU
Educator. Korean American. **PERSONAL:** Born Oct 25, 1943, Republic of Korea; married Jung C Kim; children: Peter, Geoffrey. **EDUCATION:** Seoul National University, BS, 1968; University of Illinois, MBA, 1971, PhD, 1974. **CAREER:** University of Illinois, visiting assistant professor, 1974-75; Syracuse University, assistant professor, 1975-79, associate professor, 1979-86, professor of finance, 1986-. **ORGANIZATIONS:** American Finance Association, 1973-; American Economic Association, 1983-; Financial Management Association, 1972-; Western Finance Association, 1973-. **SPECIAL ACHIEVEMENTS:** "Inflationary Effects in Capital Investment Process," Journal of Finance, 1979; with K Zummwalt, "An Analysis of Risk in Bull and Bear Markets," Journal of Financial and Quantitative Analysis, 1979; with B Ismail, "On the Association of Cash Flows with Market Risk," Accounting Review, 1989; with C Wu, "Macro-Economic Factors and Stock Returns," Journal of Finance Research, 1987. **MILITARY SERVICE:** Korean Air Force, sergeant, 1963-66. **BUSINESS ADDRESS:** Professor, School of Management, Syracuse University, Syracuse, NY 13244, (315)443-2963.

KIM, MYUNG-HYE
Educator. Korean American. **PERSONAL:** Born Oct 22, 1953, Seoul, Republic of Korea; daughter of Bok-Kil Kim and Soon-Ok Min; married Robert Thomas Huesca, Jan 3, 1988; children: Gabi Kim Huesca. **EDUCATION:** Seoul National University, BA, 1977; University of Georgia, Athens, MA, 1982; University of Texas, Austin, PhD, 1987. **CAREER:** IBM Korea Inc, systems engineer, 1977-79; Ohio State University, assistant professor, 1988-. **ORGANIZATIONS:** American Anthropological Assn, fellow; Korean Society for Cultural Anthropology, Seoul, 1973-; Anthropologists for Korean Studies, 1980-; American Ethnological Society, 1985-; Assn for Asian Studies, 1988-; Society for Korean Studies, 1988-; Committee on Women in Asian Studies, 1989-; Society for Urban Anthropology, 1990-; numerous university-

related committees, organizations, academic unts. **HONORS/AWARDS:** Seoul National University, Korea, University Fellowship, 1974-75; Ohio State University, nominated for Multicultural Teaching and Success Stories Award, 1992; US Department of Education, National Resource Center Grant ($5,544), for development of course titled Women in East Asia, 1990; Ohio State University, university seed grant ($16,000), Gender and Family Structure in Urban Korea; Korea Foundation, fellowship for Korean studies ($9,500), Women and the Family in South Korea: The Challenge of Political/Economic Perspective, 1993. **SPECIAL ACHIEVEMENTS:** "Late-Industrialization & Women's Work in Urban South Korea," City & Society, 6(2):156-173, 1992; "Transformation of Family Ideology in Upper-Middle Class Families in Urban South Korea," Ethnology, 32(1):69-85, 1993; book reviews published in refereed journals: Over the Mountain Are Mountains, by Clark W Sorensen, American Ethnologist, 18(3):628-629, 1991; Faithful Endurance, by Choong Soon Kim, American Ethnologist, 18(3):629, 1991; language proficiency: Korean, Spanish. **BUSINESS ADDRESS:** Assistant Professor, Dept of Anthropology, Ohio State University, 124 W 17th Ave, 216 Lord Hall, Columbus, OH 43210, (614)292-1054.

KIM, MYUNG MI
Educator. Korean American. **PERSONAL:** Born Dec 6, 1957, Seoul, Republic of Korea; daughter of Yong Ok Kim and Soo Bok Kim; married Kevin Magee, Jun 18, 1988; children: Malcolm Song-ok. **EDUCATION:** Oberlin College, BA, 1979; Johns Hopkins University, MA, 1981; University of Iowa, MFA, 1986. **CAREER:** Chinatown Manpower Project, NYC, ESL teacher, 1981-82; Stuyvesant High School, NYC, English teacher, 1983-84; University of Iowa, teaching-writing fellow, 1984-86; Luther College, Student Support Services, director, 1987-91; San Francisco State University, Creative Writing, assistant professor, 1991-. **HONORS/AWARDS:** San Francisco State University, Faculty Affirmative Action Award, 1992, 1993; Djerassi Resident Artists Program, Residency, 1993. **SPECIAL ACHIEVEMENTS:** Poems: Under Flag, 1991; anthologies: Forbidden Stitch: An Asian American Women's Anthology, 1989; The Greenfield Review, Anthology of Asian American Writing, 1994; publications in literary journals: Antioch Review, Ironwood, How(ever), Hambone, Avec, O-blek, Notus, Zyzzyva, Sulfur, Conjunctions, numerous others; numerous poetry readings. **BUSINESS ADDRESS:** Assistant Professor, Creative Writing, San Francisco State University, 1600 Holloway Ave, School of Humanities, San Francisco, CA 94132-1722.

KIM, NEUNG JIP
Educator. Korean American. **PERSONAL:** Born Feb 22, 1952, Seoul, Republic of Korea; son of Yoonki Kim and Seungdoo Park; married Sook Ja Kim, Dec 11, 1978; children: Deborah, Elizabeth, Michael. **EDUCATION:** Seoul National University, BS, 1975; Temple University, PhD, 1988. **CAREER:** KIST, researcher, 1975-79; St Joseph University, assistant professor, 1987-88; CSU, LA, associate professor, 1988-. **ORGANIZATIONS:** American Accounting Association, 1988-. **HONORS/AWARDS:** CSU, LA, Grant-in-Aid, 1991, Excellence in Advising, 1993. **SPECIAL ACHIEVEMENTS:** "Do Long-term Incentive Plans Matter?" business forum, 1990; "Predicting Financial Condition of an Industry," Journal of Business Forecasting, 1992. **BUSINESS ADDRESS:** Professor, California State University, 5151 State University Dr, School of Business and Economics, Los Angeles, CA 90032, (213)343-2830.

KIM, PAUL MYUNGCHYUN
Law enforcement official. Korean American. **PERSONAL:** Born Jul 23, 1951, Seoul, Republic of Korea; son of John Young & Soo Bok Kim; married Jane, Jun 19, 1982; children: Amanda. **EDUCATION:** Pepperdine University, BS, 1973, MPA, 1978; FBI National Academy, certificate, 1993. **CAREER:** La Habra Police Department, officer, 1975-77; Los Angeles City College, instructor, 1979-; Los Angeles Police Department, lieutenant, 1977-. **ORGANIZATIONS:** Koreatown Rotary, charter secretary, 1990; California Police Officers Association; California Narcotics Officers Association; State of California, Community College System, board of governors. **HONORS/AWARDS:** President of Korea, Community Service Award, 1984; Mayor of Los Angeles, Police Officer of the Year, 1992. **MILITARY SERVICE:** US Marine Corps, captain, 1972-75. **HOME ADDRESS:** 12227 Leayn Ct, North Hollywood, CA 91605, (818)765-1022. **BUSINESS PHONE:** (213)237-0080.

KIM, PILKYU
Educator. Korean American. **PERSONAL:** Born Apr 28, 1940, Seoul, Republic of Korea; son of Mr and Mrs Youngkwon Kim; married Bocksoon C Kim, Apr 30, 1970; children: Bonnie Sue. **EDUCATION:** Hankuk University of

Foreign Studies, Seoul, BA, 1964; Kansai University of Foreign Studies, Japan, Asian studies certificate, 1974; East Carolina University, MA, 1975; University of Arizona, PhD, 1985. **CAREER:** University of Arizona, teaching associate, 1979-84; American Graduate School of International Management, visiting professor, 1985; University of Maryland, overseas program, lecturer, 1986-87; Hope College, professor, 1987-. **ORGANIZATIONS:** UN-USA Michigan Division, board of directors, 1989-; American Society of International Law, 1978-; United Nations Association of the USA, 1985-; International Studies Association, 1987-; American Political Science Association, 1985-; Association of Asian Studies, 1987-; Arizona Court of Interpreters Association, 1985-86. **HONORS/AWARDS:** The Advisory Council of Peaceful Unification, Chicago, Outstanding Contribution, 1991, 1993; Korean Association of Southern Arizona, Outstanding Contribution, 1981; Associated Students of University of Arizona, Excellence in Teaching, 1978-79, 1982-83. **SPECIAL ACHIEVEMENTS:** Proficient in Korean, Japanese, Chinese and German; National Endowment for the Humanities, grant for study of human rights, SUNY, Buffalo, 1992; Hope College Faculty Development Grant, travel to China, visiting professor, Yanbian University, 1992-93. **MILITARY SERVICE:** Air Force, capt, 1964-68. **BUSINESS ADDRESS:** Professor, Dept of Political Science, Hope College, 126 10th St, Lubbers Hall, Rm 209, Holland, MI 49423.

KIM, PO HYUN. *See* **KIM, POE.**

KIM, POE (PO HYUN KIM)
Artist. Korean American. **PERSONAL:** Born in Changnyung, Kyungnam, Republic of Korea; son of Jae-Ho Kim & Sun Yoo Kim; married Sylvia Wald. **EDUCATION:** University of Illinois, MFA, 1957. **CAREER:** New York University, instructor; Chosun University, professor & chairman of arts. **SPECIAL ACHIEVEMENTS:** Collection of Solomon R Guggenheim Museum, Chicago Art Institute; many public and private, one-man and group shows.

KIM, QUEE-YOUNG
Educator, sociologist. Korean American. **PERSONAL:** Born Sep 12, 1940, Seoul, Republic of Korea; son of Chong-chol Kim & In-Soon Lee; married Eun-Kyung Kim; children: Michael B, Benjamin Y. **EDUCATION:** Seoul National University, BA, 1966; University of Houston, MA, 1968; Harvard University, PhD, 1975. **CAREER:** Harvard University, teaching asst, 1970-75; Oberlin College, asst professor, 1975-78; University of Wyoming, assoc professor, 1978-. **HOME ADDRESS:** 1714 Symons St, Laramie, WY 82070, (307)721-8883. **BUSINESS ADDRESS:** Professor, University of Wyoming, 410 Ross Hall, Laramie, WY 82071, (307)766-5230.

KIM, RHYN H.
Educator, engineer. Korean American. **PERSONAL:** Born Feb 4, 1936, Republic of Korea; son of Wonsik Kim and Yushim Chung; married Songhae, Sep 24, 1966 (deceased); children: Julia, Allis, Steven. **EDUCATION:** Seoul National University, BSME, 1958; Michigan State University, MSME, 1961, PhD, mechanical engineering, 1965. **CAREER:** Michigan State University, assistant instructor, 1962-65; US Environmental Protection Agency, Research Triangle Park, staff engineer, 1976-78; University of North Carolina, Charlotte, assistant professor, 1965-71, associate professor, 1971-83, professor, 1983-. **ORGANIZATIONS:** American Society of Mechanical Engineers, 1967-, Piedmont Carolina Section, vice president, 1974-75, secretary, 1973-74; American Society of Heating, Refrigerating, Air-Conditioning Engineers, 1978-; Instrument Society of America, 1985-; North Carolina State Board of Plumbing, Heating and Sprinklers Contractors, 1988-91. **HONORS/AWARDS:** National Aeronautics and Space Administration, Langley Research Center, Summer Research Faculty Fellow, 1974, Lewis Research Center, Summer Research Faculty Fellow, 1985, 1986, 1987, Goddard Space Flight Center, Summer Research Faculty Fellow, 1990. **SPECIAL ACHIEVEMENTS:** Contributor, International Journal of Heat Mass Transfer, International Communications of Heat Mass Transfer, Journal of Fuel, London, Proceedings of National Heat Transfer Conference of AME. **BUSINESS ADDRESS:** Professor of Mechanical Engineering, University of North Carolina at Charlotte, University City Blvd, Smith Bldg, Rm 238, Charlotte, NC 28223-0001, (704)567-4160.

KIM, RICHARD E.
Author. Korean American. **PERSONAL:** Born Mar 13, 1932, Hamheung, Hamkyung, Republic of Korea; son of Chan Doh Kim and Okhyun Kim; married Penelope Groll Kim; children: David, Melissa. **EDUCATION:** Middlebury College, 1955-59; Johns Hopkins University, MA, 1960; University of

Iowa, MFA, 1962; Harvard University, MA, 1963. **CAREER:** Long Beach State College, instructor, 1963-64; University of Massachusetts, associate professor, 1964-69; Syracuse University, visiting professor, 1970; San Diego State University, visiting professor, 1977-79; writer, currently. **ORGANIZATIONS:** US-Korea Society, board of directors, 1990-. **HONORS/AWARDS:** National Endowment for the Arts, 1978; Fulbright Fellow, 1981-83; Guggenheim Foundation, Guggenheim Fellow, 1965-66; Ford Foundation, Ford Foundation Fellow, 1962-63; University of Iowa, Writing Fellowship, 1960-62; Johns Hopkins University, Graduate Fellow, 1959-60. **SPECIAL ACHIEVEMENTS:** "Trans-Siberian Railway," tv documentary, 1989; "Koreans in Russia," tv documentary, 1988; "Koreans in China & Russia," photo essays, 1990; "Lost Names," novel, 1970; "The Innocent," novel, 1968; "The Martyred," novel, 1964. **MILITARY SERVICE:** Republic of Korea Army, infantry, first lieutenant, 1951-54. **HOME ADDRESS:** 59 Leverett Road, Shutesbury, MA 01072, (413)259-1326.

KIM, ROBERT
Physician. Korean American. **PERSONAL:** Born Jul 28, 1930, Waialua, HI; son of Won Do Kim and Elsie Yang; married Martha-May Chai, Sep 1957; children: Deborah Louise, Cynthia Lynn Moffatt. **EDUCATION:** University of Oregon, BA, 1952, MD, 1955; University of Minnesota, MS, 1962; Mayo Clinic, dermatology fellowship, 1958-62. **CAREER:** University of Hawaii, Burns Medical School, associate professor of medicine; Straub Clinic and Hospital, chief of dermatology, 1967-87. **ORGANIZATIONS:** American Academy of Dermatology; American Society of Dermatopathology; Pacific Dermatological Association; Hawaii Medical Association; Hawaii Dermatologic Society. **HONORS/AWARDS:** Alpha Omega Alpha, Medical Honor Society, 1955. **MILITARY SERVICE:** USAF, capt, 1955-58. **BUSINESS ADDRESS:** Straub Clinic & Hospital, 888 S King Street, Honolulu, HI 96813.

KIM, ROBERT HYUNG-CHAN
Educator. Korean American. **PERSONAL:** Born Nov 4, 1938, Seoul, Republic of Korea; son of Yong-bin Kim and Keum-son Huh; married Corrine Kwang oak Kim, Sep 6, 1980; children: Jerome, Justin. **EDUCATION:** Hankuk University of Foreign Studies, Seoul, Korea, BA, 1961; George Peabody College, Vanderbilt University, BA, 1964, MA, 1965, EdD, 1969. **CAREER:** Kimpo Middle School, principal, 1960-62; Columbia Community College, part-time instructor, 1966-68; George Peabody College, foreign student advisor, 1967-68; Auburn University, assistant professor, 1968-71; Western Washington University, professor, 1971-. **ORGANIZATIONS:** Association of Asian and Pacific American Studies, founding member, 1984-; Association of Asian Studies; Educational Studies Association; Comparative and International Education Society. **SPECIAL ACHIEVEMENTS:** Asian Americans and the Supreme Court, 1992; Asian American Studies: A Research Guide, 1990; Dictionary of Asian American History, 1986; Education in North Korea, 1990-; The Korean Diaspora, 1976. **BIOGRAPHICAL SOURCES:** Leaders in Education, p 590, 1974; Contemporary Authors, vol 57-60, p 318, 1976. **HOME ADDRESS:** 530 Briar Road, Bellingham, WA 98225. **BUSINESS ADDRESS:** Professor of Education and Asian American Studies, College of Education, Western Washington University, Bellingham, WA 98225, (206)650-3867.

KIM, SAEJA OH
Educator. Korean American. **PERSONAL:** Born Aug 10, 1953, Onyang, Chungnam, Republic of Korea; daughter of Baik-Whan Oh & Jin-Kee Sung; married Kyung-Suk Kim, Apr 10, 1976; children: Irence, Clare, Eunice. **EDUCATION:** Seoul National University, BS (magna cum laude), 1975; Brown University, MS, 1985; University of Illinois, Urbana-Champaign, PhD, 1988. **CAREER:** University of Illinois, Urbana-Champaign, teaching and research assistant, 1985-87; Harvard University, post doctoral fellow in mathematics, 1988; Wolfram Research Institute, consultant, 1988-89; University of Illinois, Urbana-Champaign, visiting scholar in mathematics, 1988-89; University of Massachusetts, Dartmouth, full-time visiting lecturer, 1990-93, assistant professor, 1993-. **ORGANIZATIONS:** American Mathematical Society, 1982-; Mathematical Association of America, 1991-; Association for Women in Mathematics, 1990-. **HONORS/AWARDS:** NSF & ONR, AWM postdoctoal workshop, 1992; Korean Government, honor scholarship, 1983, 1984. **SPECIAL ACHIEVEMENTS:** "Repairing Noncommutative Diagrams," Journal of Algebra. **BUSINESS ADDRESS:** Professor, Dept of Mathematics, University of Massachusetts at Dartmouth, North Dartmouth, MA 02747, (508)999-8316.

KIM, SANG PHILL
Educator. Korean American. **PERSONAL:** Born Jul 16, 1954, Pusan, Republic of Korea; son of Young Ki Kim and Chul Ja Yoon; married Eun Sung Kim, Aug 21, 1989. **EDUCATION:** Yon-Sei University, BA, 1976; Santa Clara University, MBA, 1980; Ohio State University, PhD, 1984. **CAREER:** Seoul Securities Company, research associate, 1975-77; Ohio State University, teaching associate, 1980-84; Syracuse University, assistant professor, 1984-88; Bentley College, assistant professor, 1988-. **ORGANIZATIONS:** Financial Management Association; Korean American Economic Association; Southern Financial Association; Eastern Financial Association; Pan-Pacific Financial Association. **HONORS/AWARDS:** Government of Korea, Madam Park Scholarship, 1978-80; Syracuse University, Institutional Research Grant, 1986-87; Bentley College, research grant, fellowship, 1989-90. **SPECIAL ACHIEVEMENTS:** Author of: ''Imperfect Capital Market and Cap M,'' Journal of Portfolio Management, 1986; ''Korean Housing Market,'' International Economic Journal, 1987; ''Wealth Effect of Formation of Captive Insurance Company,'' Journal of Risk and Insurance, 1988; ''Informational Effect on International Investment,'' DSI, 1993. **HOME ADDRESS:** 23 Longmeadow Road, Weston, MA 02193, (617)891-4714.

KIM, SOON JIN (JIM)
Educator. Korean American. **PERSONAL:** Born Oct 24, 1927, Kopyong, Pyong An Nam-do, Republic of Korea; son of Soo Nam Kim (deceased) & Sung Mun Lee; married Aie Kyung (Yoon) Kim, Oct 14, 1960; children: Sori Azalea Meredith, Mari Echo Karpe, Kari Brown, Yuri Crystal Bernstein, Jessica. **EDUCATION:** Kagoshima (Japan) College, Sci Assoc, 1946; Korea Univ of Foreign Studies, BA, Spanish, 1960; Univ of Missouri Sch of Journalism, MA, 1970; San Carlos Univ of Guatemala, licenciado, history/journalism, 1972; Univ of Maryland, PhD, humanities, 1982. **CAREER:** Korean Republic, city reporter, 1959-61, Latin American correspondent, 1961-68; Pan American World Airways, Guatemala, corp relations, 1961-68; Columbia Missourian, asst editor & staff writer, 1968-69; Univ of Missouri, Spanish Dept, asst instr, 1969-70, journalism instr, 1970-72, Sch of Journalism, Central Amer Graduate Reporting Prog, director, 1970-72; La Nacion, Guatemala, founding foreign news editor, 1970; Japan Air Lines, Guatemala, regional rep, 1970-74; Univ of El Salvador, visiting journalism prof, 1970-74; Acontecer, Radio Continental, El Salvador, news editor, 1970-74; Noticia de Leon, Channel 3 TV, El Salvador, news adviser, 1970-74 Towson State Univ, journalism prof, 1975-; Complutense Univ, Madrid, visiting journalism prof, 1985; Sung Kyung Kwan Univ, Seoul, visiting journalism prof, 1989; People's Univ of China, Beijing, visiting prof, 1992; XINHUA News Agency, Beijing, Spanish copy-polisher, 1992. **ORGANIZATIONS:** Intl Org of Journalists, 1984-; Union of Democratic Communications, 1984-; Intl Assn for Mass Comm Research, 1984-; Assn for Educ in Journalism & Mass Comm, 1970-; Amer Civil Liberties Union, 1970-; Soc of Professional Journalists, 1975-; Assn for Asian Studies, 1979-; Asian-Amer Journalists Assn, 1990-; Japan Assn for Chinese Studies, 1992-. **HONORS/AWARDS:** Omicron Delta Kappa, 1986. **SPECIAL ACHIEVEMENTS:** US State Dept Grants: $153,791 to exchange 20+ Chinese & US journalists, 1993-94; $69,860 to exchange 20+ Chinese & US profs, 1991-94; Tinker Foundation Grant, $20,000 to research & write a book; conference, Sophia Univ Journalism, Tokyo, 1991. **HOME ADDRESS:** 16 Wandsworth Bridge Way, Timonium, MD 21093, (410)321-4286. **BUSINESS PHONE:** (410)830-2889.

KIM, SOON-KYU
Educator. Korean American. **PERSONAL:** Born in Hadong, Republic of Korea; son of Hyungjo and Ul-soon Kim; married Kang-Un Seong Kim, Apr 14, 1959; children: Jin-Chul, Jin-kyung, Jin-Wook. **EDUCATION:** Seoul National University, Korea, BS, 1957, MS, 1959; University of Michigan, Ann Arbor, PhD, 1967. **CAREER:** Kunkook University, Korea, instr, 1959-62; Seoul National University, Korea, lecturer, 1960-62; University of Illinois at Urbana, instr, 1966-69; University of Connecticut, Dept of Mathematics, asst prof, 1969-73, assoc prof, 1973-83, prof, 1983-, dept head, 1988-. **ORGANIZATIONS:** American Mathematical Society; Korean Mathematical Society; Korean Scientists & Engineers Assn Inc, vice pres, pres, council mbr, regional chapter pres, various committees. **HONORS/AWARDS:** Yanbian University, Jilin, ROC, Honorary Professor, 1992. **SPECIAL ACHIEVEMENTS:** Research in mathematics; author of over 20 articles, 1967-. **BUSINESS ADDRESS:** Professor, Dept Head, Dept of Mathematics, University of Connecticut, U-9, Storrs, CT 06268, (203)486-1290.

KIM, SUNG BOK
Educator. Korean American. **PERSONAL:** Born Sep 11, 1932, Pusan, Republic of Korea; son of Ki-Woon Kim and Sa Nyu Kang; married Leda D Kim, Jan 8, 1965; children: Briana D, Cortland R, Blakeley E. **EDUCATION:** Seoul National University, College of Arts and Sciences, BA, history, 1956; University of Wisconsin, MS, history, 1962; Michigan State University, PhD, history, 1966. **CAREER:** Kyung Pook National University, history instructor, 1956-60; American International College, assistant professor, 1964-68; College of William and Mary, assistant professor, 1968-71; University of Illinois at Urbana, asst professor, 1971-73; State University of New York at Albany, asst professor to professor of history, 1973-, dean of undergraduate studies, associate vice president for academic affairs, 1987-. **ORGANIZATIONS:** Institute of Early American History and Culture, VA, associate, 1975-; Albany County Historical Association, trustee, 1989-; New York State Archives, visiting committee, 1989-. **HONORS/AWARDS:** Harvard University, Charles Warren Fellow, 1980-81; Society of Colonial Wars, Best Book Citation, 1979; State University of New York at Albany, Collins Award for Distinguished Service, 1993. **SPECIAL ACHIEVEMENTS:** Author, translator, The Federalist Papers, in Korean, 1960; author, Landlord and Tenant in Colonial New York: Manorial Society, 1665-1775, 1978; numerous articles in scholarly journals and books, 1958-. **BUSINESS ADDRESS:** Prof of History, Dean of Undergraduate Studies, State University of New York at Albany, 1400 Washington Ave, Administration 214, Albany, NY 12222.

KIM, SUNG WAN
Educator. Korean American. **PERSONAL:** Born Aug 21, 1940, Pusan, Republic of Korea; married Hee K Kim, Sep 3, 1966; children: Alex Sukwon, Kara Soyon. **EDUCATION:** Seoul National University, BS, 1963, MS, 1965; University of Utah, PhD, 1969. **CAREER:** University of Utah, Dept of Pharmaceutics, asst professor, 1973-76, associate professor, 1976-80, professor, 1980-, Center for Controlled Chemical Delivery, director, 1986-. **ORGANIZATIONS:** TheraTech Inc, board of directors, 1986-; AIMBE, fellow, 1992-; NIH, Surgery and Bioengineering Study Section, 1986-89, editorial board, Artificial Organs, 1990-, editorial board, J Controlled Release, 1984-; Utah Governor's Biomedical Advisory Board, 1989-; American Assn Pharm Sci, fellow, 1988-. **HONORS/AWARDS:** Biomaterials Society, Clemson Basic Research Award, 1988; Governor of Utah, Governor's Medal for Science, 1989; University of Utah, Distinguished Faculty Research Award, 1987; US NIH, NIH Research Development Award, 1977. **SPECIAL ACHIEVEMENTS:** Author, subjects of polymers, biomaterials, pharmaceutics: 300 publications in scientific journals; 6 edited books. **BIOGRAPHICAL SOURCES:** New York Times, p 1, Nov 25, 1992. **BUSINESS ADDRESS:** Professor, Dept of Pharmaceutics and Pharmaceutical Chemistry, Director, Center for Controlled Chemical Delivery, University of Utah, 421 Wakara Way #321, Salt Lake City, UT 84108, (801)581-6801.

KIM, SUZY LINDA
Physician. Korean American. **PERSONAL:** Born May 17, 1961, Seoul, Republic of Korea. **EDUCATION:** Brown University, BA, 1983; University of PA, MD, 1987; University Hospital, residency, 1987-90; Emory University School of Medicine, fellowship in GI, 1990-92. **CAREER:** Emory University School of Medicine, junior attending physician, gastroenterology, 1992-93, Digestive Disease Division, asst professor of medicine, 1993-. **ORGANIZATIONS:** American College of Gastroenterology, 1992-; American Gastroenterological Assn, 1990-; American College of Physicians, 1989-. **SPECIAL ACHIEVEMENTS:** Co-author, works include: ''Sarcoidosis with Multiple Hepatic and Splenic Nodules on Dynamic Computed Tomography,'' Annals of Internal Medicine, vol 117, num 5, p 399-400, 1992; ''Detection by Scanning Electron Microscopy of a Distinctive Esophageal Surface Cell at the Junction of Squamous and Barrett's Epithelium,'' Digestive Diseases and Sciences, vol 38, num 1, p 97-108, 1993; book chapter: ''Inflammatory Bowel Disease,'' Medical Management of the Surgical Patient, 3rd edition, Lippincott Co, 1994. **BUSINESS ADDRESS:** Assistant Professor, Digestive Disease Division, Emory University School of Medicine, P.O. Drawer AL, Woodruff Memorial Bldg, Atlanta, GA 30322.

KIM, THOMAS KUNHYUK
Educational administrator. Chinese American. **PERSONAL:** Born Feb 18, 1929, Shanghai, China; son of Hong Suh and Chong (Kim) Kim; married Martha Alice Zoellers, Jun 4, 1958; children: Lawrence Thomas, Catherine Ann. **EDUCATION:** Berea College, BA, 1952; Indiana University, MBA, 1954; Tulane University, PhD, 1961. **CAREER:** University of Akron, assistant professor of economics, 1961-62; Baker University, associate professor, 1962-

65; Texas Tech University, professor, 1965-70; McMurry University, president, 1970-. **ORGANIZATIONS:** Phi Kappa Phi; Omicron Delta Epsilon. **HONORS/AWARDS:** Southwestern University, LHD, 1973. **SPECIAL ACHIEVEMENTS:** Author, Introductory Mathematics for Economic Analysis, 1971. **BUSINESS ADDRESS:** President, McMurry University, McMurry Station South, 14th & Sayles Blvd, Abilene, TX 79697-0001.*

KIM, UICHOL
Educator. Korean American. **PERSONAL:** Born Oct 13, 1958, Seoul, Republic of Korea; son of Ukill Kim and Hyon Chol Kim; married Jungyeon L Kim, Mar 7, 1987; children: Young-Jin David. **EDUCATION:** University of Toronto, BSc, 1982; Queen's University, MA, 1984, PhD, 1988. **CAREER:** University of Hawaii, assistant professor, 1988-. **ORGANIZATIONS:** Journal of Cross Cultural Psychology, consulting editor, 1992-. **SPECIAL ACHIEVEMENTS:** Indigenous Psychologies: Research and Experience in Cultural Context, Sage, 1993. **BUSINESS ADDRESS:** Assistant Professor, Dept of Psychology, University of Hawaii, 2430 Campus Rd, Gartley Hall 101D, Honolulu, HI 96822-2294, (808)956-7343.

KIM, VIVIAN C.
Small business program manager, procurement analyst. Korean American. **PERSONAL:** Born Nov 15, 1941, Seoul, Republic of Korea; daughter of Hyun Chea Yang & Young Aae Yim; divorced; children: John, Susanna. **EDUCATION:** University of the District of Columbia, MA, 1983. **CAREER:** Department of Health & Human Services, Public Health Service, procurement analyst & Asian Program manager, currently. **ORGANIZATIONS:** National Association of Professional Asian American Women, chair, founder, 1987-; Federal Asian Pacific American Council, past chair, 1989-90; Asian American Resources Development & Employment Center, board of directors, 1991-93. **HONORS/AWARDS:** National Business Council of Women Business Owners, Outstanding Achievement, 1989; Federal Asian Pacific American Council, Outstanding Leadership, 1990; Department of Health & Human Services, Administrator's Award, 1984, Public Health Service, Special Recognition, 1991; The Filipino American Women's Network, Outstanding Leadership, 1991. **SPECIAL ACHIEVEMENTS:** National Training Conference, sponsored by the National Association of Professional Asian American Women, 1987-, planning, 1994. **BIOGRAPHICAL SOURCES:** Patriots, Asian American Heritage Month issue, p 98, 1992, p 63, 1990. **BUSINESS ADDRESS:** Chairperson, National Association of Professional Asian American Women, PO Box 494, Washington Grove, MD 20880, (301)530-3651.

KIM, WENDELL KEALOHOPAULOE
Professional baseball coach. Korean American/Pacific Islander American. **PERSONAL:** Born 1950?, Honolulu, HI; married Natasha; children: Donald. **EDUCATION:** California Polytechnic State University, Pomona. **CAREER:** San Francisco Giants, minor league, player, 1978, minor league, farm teams manager, 1981-88, major league, third base coach, 1993-. **HONORS/AWARDS:** San Francisco Giants, Minor League Manager of the Year. **BUSINESS ADDRESS:** Coach, San Francisco Giants, Candlestick Park, San Francisco, CA 94124.*

KIM, WUN JUNG
Physician, educator. Korean American. **PERSONAL:** Born Aug 8, 1950, Seoul, Republic of Korea; son of C K Kim and J S Shin; married Yongjin Kang, Jul 10, 1980; children: Jamie, Jennifer, Alex. **EDUCATION:** Seoul National University, MD, 1975; Johns Hopkins University, post-graduate training, 1981; University of Michigan, MPH, 1985. **CAREER:** Johns Hopkins University, fellow, 1978-81, instructor, director, 1981-82; Medical College of Ohio, associate professor, assistant training director, 1982-. **ORGANIZATIONS:** American Psychiatric Association, committee of Asian-American psychiatrists, 1991-; American Academy of Child Adolescent Psych, committee of ethnic & cultural issues, 1991-; Association of Korean-American Psychiatrists, secretary, vice president, president elect, 1991-; Korean Association of Greater Toledo, president, 1991-. **SPECIAL ACHIEVEMENTS:** 17 publications on child psychiatric and cross-cultural issues in journals, textbooks; numerous presentations at national and international meetings. **BUSINESS ADDRESS:** Associate Professor, Medical College of Ohio, 3000 Arlington Street, Capri, Toledo, OH 43699, (419)381-3815.

KIM, YEE S.
Educator. Korean American. **PERSONAL:** Born Apr 15, 1928, Seoul, Republic of Korea; son of Ikyong Kim and Ohmin Oh; married Young S Lee Kim; children: Karl, Ruth, Grace, Elizabeth. **EDUCATION:** Seoul National Univer-

sity, BS, 1950; Kansas State University, BS, MS, 1960; St Louis University, PhD, 1965. **CAREER:** Miles Laboratory, consultant, 1964-71, research chemist, 1960-63; St Louis University, asst prof, beginning 1966, prof, currently. **ORGANIZATIONS:** ASPET, 1967-; ACS, 1967-; AIC, fellow, 1970-80; AAUP, 1970-; NYAS, 1967-65. **HONORS/AWARDS:** NIH, fellow, 1965-66, research grants, 1967-82; American Diabetes Association, grants, 1979-82; Cancer Inst, grants, 1967-70. **SPECIAL ACHIEVEMENTS:** Research work on glucocorticoid steroid: publications in JBCPNAS, US, Mol Pharm; research work on diabetic pregnancy: publications in Diabetologia AJ Obst; research work on Vitamin D: publications in Endocr, JASBMR. **MILITARY SERVICE:** Republic of Korea Navy, lt, 1951-54. **BUSINESS ADDRESS:** Professor, Dept Pharm/Physiol, St Louis University School of Medicine, 1402 South Grand, St Louis, MO 63104, (314)577-8558.

KIM, YONG BOK
Video engineer. Korean American. **PERSONAL:** Born May 10, 1940, Namwon, Chunbuk, Republic of Korea; son of Chern Ki Kim & Oak Soon Kim; married Wun Sook Kim, Sep 30, 1973; children: Andrew H, Deborah Y. **EDUCATION:** Chunnam University, Engineering College, BSEE, 1962. **CAREER:** Electro Brand Inc, head technician; Pars Electronic Engineering Co, owner; All Technical Service Co, owner; Rank Video Service America, Video Maintenance Engineering and Blank Video Tape Loading Dept, technician, team leader, currently. **ORGANIZATIONS:** Korean Bethel Church of Chicago, PCA, elder. **HOME ADDRESS:** 8443 N Menard Ave, Morton Grove, IL 60053-3317, (708)965-0208.

KIM, YONG CHOON
Educator. Korean American. **PERSONAL:** Born Jan 1, 1935, Kyongju, Kyongsang Bukdo, Republic of Korea; son of Chang Ho Kim & Chung Ja Choi; married Joyce C Kim, Dec 18, 1965; children: Grace. **EDUCATION:** Belhaven College, BA, 1960; Westminster Theological Seminary, M Div, 1963, ThM, 1964; Temple University, PhD, 1969. **CAREER:** York College of Pennsylvania, assistant professor of Asian studies, 1969-70; Cleveland State University, assistant professor of philosophy & religion, 1970-71; University of Rhode Island, assistant professor of philosophy, 1971-74, associate professor of philosophy, 1974-79, professor of philosophy, 1979-. **ORGANIZATIONS:** Assn for Asian Studies; American Academy of Religion; Society for Asian and Comparative Philosophy; Assn for American University Professors; Korean-American University Professors Assn: chair, Law and Ethics Committee. **HONORS/AWARDS:** Academy of Korean Studies, fellowship, 1982; University of Rhode Island, Summer Faculty fellowship, 1988; Korea Foundation, Fellowship, 1992; National Endowment for Humanities, Summer Seminar Grant, 1993. **SPECIAL ACHIEVEMENTS:** Author: Oriental Thought, 1973, 1987; The Ch'ondogyo Concept of Man: An Essence of Korean Thought, 1978; fluent in Korean; read Chinese. **HOME ADDRESS:** 134 Parkwood Dr, Kingston, RI 02881, (401)789-8940. **BUSINESS ADDRESS:** Professor, Dept of Philosophy, University of Rhode Island, Kingston, RI 02881, (401)792-2208.

KIM, YONG-GWAN
Educator. Korean American. **PERSONAL:** Born Aug 4, 1957, Kwangju, Republic of Korea; son of Chun-Soo Kim and Yang-Soon Choi; married Sukhyang Lee-Kim, Jun 30, 1985; children: Grace Juyun. **EDUCATION:** Seoul National University, Korea, BA, 1981; Yonsei University, Korea, MA, 1983; University of California, San Diego, PhD, 1990. **CAREER:** Seoul City University, instructor of economics, 1984-85; University of California, San Diego, teaching assistant, research assistant, 1985-90; University of Iowa, assistant professor of economics, 1990-. **ORGANIZATIONS:** American Economic Association, 1987-; Econometric Society, 1987-. **SPECIAL ACHIEVEMENTS:** "Evolutionary Stability in Games of Communication," Games and Economic Behavior, 1993 (with A Blume & J Sobel); "Evolutionary Stability in the Asymmetric War on Attrition," Journal of Theoretical Biology, 1993. **BUSINESS ADDRESS:** Asst Professor of Economics, University of Iowa, 511 Phillips Hall, Iowa City, IA 52242, (319)335-3810.

KIM, YONG IK
Writer, educator (retired). Korean American. **PERSONAL:** Born May 15, Chong Moo, Kyong-Nam, Republic of Korea; son of Choe O Kim & Jung Ok; married Im Bok Kim; children: Lee. **EDUCATION:** Florida Southern College, BA; University of Kentucky, MA; University of Iowa, Writers Workshop; Aoyama Gakuin College, Tokyo, English literature. **CAREER:** Korea University, professor; Western Illinois University, assistant professor; Lockhaven State College, associate professor; University of California, Berkeley, visiting lecturer; Duquesne University, professor; freelance writer, currently.

HONORS/AWARDS: 1st Korean Overseas Lit Association Prize, 1990; Asian Pacific Council, Mainstream American Award in Excellence for Literature, 1991; NEA, Fellowship in Fiction, 1985; Pennsylvania Council on Arts, Fellowship, 1993. **SPECIAL ACHIEVEMENTS:** Moons of Korea published by Tae Han Kong Ron Sa, Seoul, Korea; The Happy Days, novel, Little Brown; The Diving Gourd, novel, Alfred A Knopf; Blue in the Seed, novel, Little, Brown; Love in Winter, short stories, Double Day; The Shoes from Yang San Valley, novella, Double Day. **HOME ADDRESS:** 1030 Macon Ave, Pittsburgh, PA 15218. **BUSINESS PHONE:** (412)243-9495.

KIM, YONG K.
Company executive. Korean American. **PERSONAL:** Born Oct 7, 1947, Seoul, Republic of Korea; son of Yoon H Kim and Sook J Kim; married Meranda, Dec 4, 1974; children: Kandis, Thad, Anisha. **EDUCATION:** KIT, Korea, BS, electronic engineering, 1970; American University, MS, technology of management, 1980; Nova University, doctoral studies, 1983; Harvard University, Owner/President Management Program, 1992-94. **CAREER:** Korea Support Command, US Army Pacific, senior systems analyst, 1966-72; Computer Sciences Corp, senior scientific programmer, 1972-73; Coopers & Lybrand, senior programmer, systems analyst, 1973; Advanced Computer Techniques, project manager, contract manager, 1973-74; VSE Corporation, technical director, 1975-85; User Technology Associates Inc, president, CEO, 1985-. **ORGANIZATIONS:** Minority Business Association of Northern Virginia, International Committee, chairman, 1992-93; Washington Technology Past 50 Council, president, 1994; US Congressional Advisory Board, special advisor, 1985; Washington Technology Fast 50 Council, 1990-93; American Management Association, President's Association, 1992-93; Arlington Chamber of Commerce, 1985-93; Institute of Electrical & Electronic Engineers, 1980; Heath/Zenith Users Group, 1980. **HONORS/AWARDS:** KPMG, Peat Marwick, High Tech Entrepreneur Award, 1993; Ernst & Young, Inc Magazine, Merrill Lynch, Entrepreneur of the Year, 1992; Inc Magazine, Inc 500, #49, 1992, #209, 1993; Washington Technology, Fast 50, #1 for 1991, #8 for 1992, #22 for 1993, #4 for 1994; US Army, SBIS Quality Award, 1992. **SPECIAL ACHIEVEMENTS:** Department of Commerce Trade Delegation to Mexico City, 1993; Minority Business Development Trade Mission to Persian Gulf, 1992; Canadian Embassy Partnership Program, 1992, 1993; host, Virginia Trade Delegation, Nigerian Government, 1992. **BIOGRAPHICAL SOURCES:** Fairfax County: A Contemporary Portrait, 156, 1992; CBS TV: Success Stories, Television Biography, Sept 1991, June 1992. **BUSINESS ADDRESS:** President, Chief Executive Officer, User Technology Associates Inc, 4301 N Fairfax Dr, Ste 400, Arlington, VA 22203, (703)522-5132.

KIM, YONG-KI
Physicist. Korean American. **PERSONAL:** Born Feb 20, 1932, Seoul, Republic of Korea; married Younghee Kim, Dec 15, 1963; children: Edward, Charlotte. **EDUCATION:** Seoul National University, BS, 1957; University of Delaware, MS, 1961; University of Chicago, PhD, 1966. **CAREER:** Argonne National Lab, asst physicist, physicist, sr physicist, 1966-83; National Institute Standards & Tech, physicist, supervisory physicist, 1983-. **ORGANIZATIONS:** American Physical Society, fellow, 1964-; Radiation Research Society, 1974-; Korean Scientists & Engineers in America, councillor, regional chapter president, 1973-. **HONORS/AWARDS:** US Dept of Commerce, Silver Medal, 1989. **SPECIAL ACHIEVEMENTS:** Over 70 articles in professional journals. **BUSINESS ADDRESS:** Supervisory Physicist, National Institute of Standards and Technology, Bldg 221, Rm A267, Gaithersburg, MD 20899, (301)975-3203.

KIM, YONGSHIK
Methodist minister (retired), educator (retired), business executive. Korean American. **PERSONAL:** Born Jul 27, 1925, Soon Chon, Pyong Nam, Republic of Korea; son of Yang Pil Kim and Shin Doh Park; married Sa Eun Kim, Jun 25, 1960; children: Sue, Young Lei. **EDUCATION:** Methodist Seminary, Seoul, Korea, diploma, 1948; International College, Seoul, Korea, BA, 1956; Boston University, STM, 1961; Brigham Young University, PhD, 1972. **CAREER:** ROK Army, chaplain, 1950-58; Boston University Student Church, pastor, 1959-60; Wahiawa Korean Christian Church, pastor, 1962-68; Pahala Naalehu United Methodist Church, pastor, 1969-72; Leeward Community College, lecturer, 1972-78; Aiea Korean United Methodist Church, pastor, 1975-88; KAYASA Enterprises, owner, president, 1989-. **ORGANIZATIONS:** American Academy of Comparative Religion, 1972-80; Korean Council of Christian Churches in Hawaii, president, 1978-80; United Methodist Church, Board of Global Ministries, 1987-89, retired clergy member, 1989-; Suzanah Wesley Center, board member, 1985-87. **HONORS/AWARDS:**

United Methodist Churches in the USA, Crusade Scholarship, 1959-61; Republic of Korea, Presidential Award for the Service to the Korean Community in Hawaii, 1980. **SPECIAL ACHIEVEMENTS:** Establishment of Aiea Korean United Methodist Church, 1978; development of weekly Hawaii Korean TV program: "The Living Wisdom," as a spiritual/moral guidance program, 1980-86; development of Korean Immigrant Service in Hawaii, 1978-80; wrote, edited, translated manuals and educational materials for ROK Army chaplains, 1953-58. **MILITARY SERVICE:** Republic of Korean Army, captain, 1950-58; Outstanding Service Award, 1955, 1958. **BUSINESS ADDRESS:** Owner, President, KAYASA Enterprises, 2878 Stoneridge Dr, Garland, TX 75044.

KIM, YOONCHUNG PARK (Y. C.)
Educator, artist. Korean American. **PERSONAL:** Born Sep 5, 1944, Seoul, Republic of Korea; daughter of Nam Chul Park and Yang Sook Lee; married Jinchoon Kim, Apr 11, 1970; children: Nina, Margaret, Angela. **EDUCATION:** Seoul National University, BFA, 1966, MFA, 1968; University of California, Berkeley, MA, 1969. **CAREER:** Roane State College, Fine Arts, instructor; San Diego Mesa College, Fine Arts, instructor; San Diego State University, Fine Arts, instructor; Mira Costa College, Fine Arts, instructor; Grossmont College, Fine Arts, instructor; San Diego City College, Fine Arts, assistant professor, currently. **ORGANIZATIONS:** Allied Clattsmen; San Diego Artist Guild; Employee Training Institute, San Diego City College, board member. **HONORS/AWARDS:** Second Korean Design Exhibition, Prime Minister's Award; Korean National Fine Arts Exhibition, Merit Award; Third Korean Design Exhibition, Merit Award; Regents of University of California, regent fellowship; California State Fair, second prize. **SPECIAL ACHIEVEMENTS:** Co-curator of Korean Contemporary Ceramics Exhibition during 27th National Council on Education for Ceramic Arts-NCECA; panel moderator: "Tradition Versus Diversity," 27th NCECA; selected for Young American '69 with "Come on Patrick," sculpture; invited to Ceramic 70 Plus, Everson Museum, Syracuse, NY. **BIOGRAPHICAL SOURCES:** "Yoonchung Park Kim," review by Elain Levin, American Ceramics, Oct 3, 1993; "San Diego Sixteen," by Gerry Williams, Studio Potter, Dec 1992. **BUSINESS ADDRESS:** Assistant Professor, San Diego City College, 1313 12th Ave, Fine Arts, San Diego, CA 92101-4712, (619)230-2600.

KIM, YOUN-SUK
Educator. Korean American. **PERSONAL:** Born Sep 15, 1934, Kwangju, Republic of Korea; son of Jaekyu Kim and Youngun Chung; married Yongho H Kim, Apr 23, 1966; children: Y Herb, Y Nancy, John Y. **EDUCATION:** Seoul National University, BA, 1958; New School for Social Research, MA, 1967, PhD, 1973. **CAREER:** American Photo Corporation, statistician, 1964-66; Caudeub, Heissch & Associates, statistician, 1967-68; Fairleigh Dickinson University, adjunct professor, 1968-73; Kean College of New Jersey, professor, 1974-. **ORGANIZATIONS:** American Economic Association, 1968-; American Statistical Association, 1967-; Atlantic Economic Association, 1974-; Eastern Economic Association, 1975-; Korea-America Economic Association, 1985-, president, 1993. **HONORS/AWARDS:** Northeast Asian Economic Council, grant, 1978-79; faculty research grants, 1980, 1983, 1988, 1990, 1993; Fulbright-Hays Travel Grant, Japan, 1990; Korea Economic Research Grant, 1988. **SPECIAL ACHIEVEMENTS:** 3 books on economics; over 60 articles published on economic development, Korean economics, and on East-Asia economics. **HOME ADDRESS:** 102 E Madison Avenue, Cresskill, NJ 07626, (201)568-5399. **BUSINESS ADDRESS:** Professor, School of Business, Government and Technology, Kean College of New Jersey, Morris Avenue, Union, NJ 07083, (908)527-2489.

KIM, YOUNG-BAE
Educator. Korean American. **PERSONAL:** Born Apr 5, 1936, Republic of Korea; married Sook-Hyun Kim, 1960; children: William, Grace. **EDUCATION:** Yonsei University, BA, 1960; Indiana University, MA, 1965; University of Kansas, PhD, 1973. **CAREER:** Graceland College, assistant professor, 1969-75, associate professor, 1975-79; Maryville College, professor, 1979-. **ORGANIZATIONS:** Association for Asian Studies, 1969-. **HOME ADDRESS:** 10248 Tan Rara Dr, Knoxville, TN 37922, (615)966-4574. **BUSINESS ADDRESS:** Professor, Dept of Political Science, Maryville College, Maryville, TN 37801, (615)981-8260.

KIM, YOUNG CHAN
Educator, physician. Korean American. **PERSONAL:** Born Aug 23, 1956, Pusan, Republic of Korea; son of Kun Hum Kim and Jin Sook Hong; married Eunjung Park, Jan 5, 1986; children: Insun, Insue. **EDUCATION:** Yonsei University Medical College, MD, 1982, PhD, 1991. **CAREER:** Duke Univer-

sity Medical Center, fellow, urology, 1992; University of North Carolina Hospital at Chapel Hill, research asst professor, 1993-. **ORGANIZATIONS:** American Urological Assn, 1992; American Andrologica Assn, 1992. **SPECIAL ACHIEVEMENTS:** Author: "Clinical Value of Scrotopenogram for Evaluation Varicocele and Erectile Dysfunction," Urology, vol 34, p 150-156, 1992. **MILITARY SERVICE:** General Armed Forces Hospital, Korea, captain. **BUSINESS ADDRESS:** Research Assistant Professor, University of North Carolina Hospital at Chapel Hill, 427 Bumett, Womack Building, CB 7235, Chapel Hill, NC 27599-7235, (919)966-2571.

KIM, YOUNG-GURL
Educator. Korean American. **PERSONAL:** Born May 11, 1956, Sangdong, Kang Won, Republic of Korea; son of Byung Kim (deceased) & Nomie Kim; married Joung-Min, Apr 23, 1983; children: Yoon Jesse, Min-Young Andrew, Enae Mary. **EDUCATION:** Hanyang University, Korea, BS, 1983; University of Wyoming, MS, 1985; Princeton University, MA, PhD, 1990. **CAREER:** University of Wyoming, graduate assistant, 1983-85; Princeton University, research assistant, 1985-90; John Brown University, assistant professor, 1990-. **ORGANIZATIONS:** ASME, associate member, 1991-. **SPECIAL ACHIEVEMENTS:** "Modern Technology and Christian Response," 1993; "Finite Element Analysis of Stress Wave Propagation in Circular Plates. . .," 1993; "Electromagnetic Radiation from Doubly Rotated Crystal Quartz. . .," 1990; "Electro-Elastic Interactions in Defectors & Conductors," PhD Thesis, 1990; "Elect of Boron on the Structure-Property Relations on . . .," MS thesis, 1985. **MILITARY SERVICE:** ROK Army, South Korean, sergeant, 1977-80. **HOME ADDRESS:** 1205 Hennegar Drive, Siloam Springs, AR 72761, (501)524-9833. **BUSINESS ADDRESS:** Professor, John Brown University, 2000 W University Street, Siloam Springs, AR 72761, (501)524-7206.

KIM, YOUNG-JIN
Educator. Korean American. **PERSONAL:** Born Jan 4, 1932, Soonchon, Chullanamdo, Republic of Korea; son of Sook-Joo Kim and Jum-Rye Choi; married Soon-Kyu Song, Jan 18, 1966; children: Kathrene D, Helen S. **EDUCATION:** University of Minnesota, Duluth, BA, 1959; University of Minnesota, Twin Cities, MA, 1963; University of Oklahoma, PhD, 1975. **CAREER:** Chung-Ang University, Seoul, Korea, visiting professor, 1990-91; University of Wisconsin, River Falls, professor of management, 1964-. **ORGANIZATIONS:** Assn of Productivity of Korea, 1990-; Wisconsin World Trade Center, education committee, 1988; American Assn of Management, 1987; Assn of Asian Studies, 1989. **HONORS/AWARDS:** Association of Productivity of Korea, Outstanding Paper, 1991; Chung-Ang University, Korea, Distinguished Professor of the Year, 1991. **SPECIAL ACHIEVEMENTS:** Author, The Economy of South Korea and Labor Productivity, 1991; A Study of US and South Korea Trade Relations and the Age. . ., 1991; Productivity Improvement through Participative Management, 1991; An Analysis of the Trade Policy of South Korea, 1990. **BIOGRAPHICAL SOURCES:** Labor Productivity and Economy in South Korea, Monthly Business Management, #410, June 1992, pp 113-19; Economy and Productivity of South Korea, Productivity Review, Korea Productivity Assn, vol 6, March 1992, pp 11-22. **BUSINESS ADDRESS:** Professor of Management, University of Wisconsin-River Falls, Cascade, North Hall 315, River Falls, WI 54022, (715)425-3335.

KIM, YOUNGSOO RICHARD
Educator, civil engineer. Korean American. **PERSONAL:** Born Jan 31, 1958, Seoul, Republic of Korea; son of Jeongwhan Kim and Kisook Kim; married JeeHye Kim, Dec 22, 1986; children: Frances Y, Daniel S. **EDUCATION:** Seoul National University, BS, 1980; Texas A & M University, MS, 1985, PhD, 1988. **CAREER:** Dong-Ah Const Ind Co Ltd, engineer, 1979-81, chief engineer, 1981-82; Texas Transporation Institute, research assistant, 1983-88, engineering research associate, 1989; Texas A & M University, teaching assistant, 1988; North Carolina State University, assistant professor, 1989-. **ORGANIZATIONS:** Tau Beta Pi; American Society of Civil Engineers; Association of Asphalt Paving Technologists; Transportation Research Board; Korean Scientists & Engineers Association; Korean-American Transport Association. **HONORS/AWARDS:** Korean Government, Presidential Korean Honor Scholarship, 1986; NCSU, Civil Engr Dept, Kimley-Horn Faculty Award, 1993. **SPECIAL ACHIEVEMENTS:** ASCE, Engineering Mechanics Division, Properties of Materials Committee, nominee for a medal, 1990. **BUSINESS ADDRESS:** Professor, Civil Eng Dept, North Carolina State University, Box 7908, Raleigh, NC 27695-7908, (919)515-7758.

KIM, YOUNGSUK
Educator. Korean American. **PERSONAL:** Born Feb 12, 1954, Pusan, Republic of Korea; son of Kiyoon Kim and Dong-Kee Lee; married Kyungsook Cho, Mar 1982; children: Francis, Soo-In. **EDUCATION:** Seoul Natl University, BM, 1978; New England Conservatory of Music, MM, 1983; University of Miami, DM, 1987. **CAREER:** Mansfield University, assoc prof, 1988-. **ORGANIZATIONS:** Natl Assn of Teachers of Singing, 1988-; College Music Soc, 1988-. **HONORS/AWARDS:** Pi Kappa Lambda, 1988; American Biographical Assn, Service to Performing Profession, 1989. **SPECIAL ACHIEVEMENTS:** Music director and conductor: Sweeney Todd; Into the Woods; Mikado; Big River; The Music Man; Gallantry; Telephone; Joseph and the Amazing Technicolor Dreamcoat; Nunsense, 1989-; tenor soloist: Messiah; Jesus on the Mt Olive. **HOME PHONE:** (717)537-2060. **BUSINESS ADDRESS:** Professor, Dept of Music, Mansfield University, Butler Ctr, Mansfield, PA 16933, (717)662-4724.

KIM, YUN
Educator, educational administrator. Korean American. **PERSONAL:** Born Jul 28, 1934, Changnyung, Kyungnam, Republic of Korea; son of Tai Shik Kim & Cha Kyee Lee Kim; married Wendy Y Kim, Feb 16, 1963; children: Harold Young, Donald Young, Gloria Young. **EDUCATION:** Seoul National University, Korea, BA, 1958; Princeton University, cert, 1962; University of Pennsylvania, MA, 1963; Australian National University, PhD, 1967. **CAREER:** Economic Planning Board, assistant statistician, 1957-61; United Nations, UN expert, 1972-73, Development Programme, senior advisor, 1976-77, 1981-83; USAID, Islamabad, Pakistan, resident advisor, 1987-89; Utah State University, assistant professor, associate professor, 1966-72, Department of Sociology, professor, head, 1972-81, professor of sociology, associate dean, 1973,1988-89, Center for International Studies, director, currently. **ORGANIZATIONS:** International Union for the Scientific Study of Population; Population Association of America; American Sociological Association; International Studies Association; Korean-American University Professors Association in North America. **HONORS/AWARDS:** Government of Pakistan, Meritorious Service, 1989; Government of the Philippines, Outstanding Service, 1977, 1973; Australian National University, research scholarship, 1963-66; Population Council Fellowship, 1961-63; United Nations Fellowship, 1959-60. **SPECIAL ACHIEVEMENTS:** "Some Demographic Measurements for Korea Based on Quasi-Stable Populaton Theory," Demography, Vol II, August 1965; 46 other books, reports, & articles; consultant and adviser to Philippines, Pakistan, Korea, UNESCO Office in Asian Bangkok, Thailand, Trust Territory of the Pacific Islands, Commonwealth of the Northern Mariana Islands, United Nations, UNDP, UNOTC; languages: Korean, Japanese, Chinese. **HOME ADDRESS:** 968 Green Oaks Drive, Bountiful, UT 84010, (801)295-5006. **BUSINESS ADDRESS:** Professor of Sociology, Director, Center for Intl Studies, Utah State University, Logan, UT 84322-0700, (801)750-1231.

KIM, YUNG MO
Educator, attorney. Korean American. **PERSONAL:** Born Jul 30, 1939, Seoul, Republic of Korea; son of Won Tae Kim; married Boin Cho Kim, Feb 24, 1968; children: Sandra J, Richard W. **EDUCATION:** Syracuse University, MPA, 1962; Clark University, AM, 1965; SUNY/Buffalo PhD, 1971, JD, 1983. **CAREER:** SUNY, College at Buffalo, instructor, 1968-69, assistant professor, 1969-74, associate professor, 1974-85, professor, 1985-; self-employed attorney at law, 1989-. **ORGANIZATIONS:** Korean Language School of Western New York, chairman/founder, 1978-80; Western New York Korean Association, president, 1970-72; Dae Han Foundation of Western New York, board of trustees, 1980-83, legal counselor, 1992-; tax & legal adviser to various profit & nonprofit organizations, 1983-. **HOME ADDRESS:** 22 Carriage Hill Ct, Williamsville, NY 14221, (716)688-5657. **BUSINESS ADDRESS:** Professor of Economics & Finance, State University of New York College at Buffalo, 1300 Elmwood Ave, Buffalo, NY 14222, (716)878-6930.

KIM, YUNGHI
Photojournalist. Korean American. **PERSONAL:** Born Jan 25, 1962, Taegue, Republic of Korea; daughter of Ouk Lee; married Jason Seiken. **EDUCATION:** Boston University, BA. **CAREER:** The Patriot Ledger, staff photographer; Boston Globe, staff photographer, currently. **ORGANIZATIONS:** National Press Photographers Association; Boston Press Photographers Association. **HONORS/AWARDS:** Finalist in photography category for Pulitzer Prize for Somalia Coverage, 1993; received awards in Picture of the Year Competition, National Press Photographers Association. **BUSINESS ADDRESS:** Staff Photographer, Photo Dept, The Boston Globe, 135 Morrissey Blvd, Boston, MA 02107, (617)929-2650.

KIMURA, BRIAN

Educator. Japanese American. **PERSONAL:** Born Jul 6, 1949, San Jose, CA; son of Phil K & Faye T Kimura; married Meixiang Mika Kimura, Dec 24, 1990; children: Jade Wu. **EDUCATION:** San Jose State University, BA, 1971; Stanford University, MFA, 1981. **CAREER:** Various San Francisco architectural firms, designer, 1971-77; Hellmuth, Obata, & Kassabaum, designer, 1977-79; Skidmore, Owings, & Merrill, designer, 1979-82; San Jose State University, professor, 1982-. **ORGANIZATIONS:** Stanford University Alumni Association, 1981-; Industrial Designers Society of America, educator, consultant, 1983-. **SPECIAL ACHIEVEMENTS:** Office environment furniture designer & consultant to major office furniture manufacturers in the United States & Japan. **BUSINESS ADDRESS:** Professor, San Jose St University, 1 Washington Sq, School of Art & Design, San Jose, CA 95192-0089, (408)924-4392.

KIMURA, DONNA JUNKO

Newspaper reporter. Japanese American. **PERSONAL:** Born Aug 12, 1964, Concord, CA; daughter of Toshi Kimura and Yoshiko Kimura. **EDUCATION:** University of California at Santa Cruz, 1982-84; San Francisco State University, BA (magna cum laude), journalism, 1986. **CAREER:** Albuquerque Tribune, intern, 1986; Yuba-Sutter Appeal Democrat, reporter/staff writer, 1986-89; Santa Cruz Sentinel, reporter/staff writer, 1989-. **ORGANIZATIONS:** Amnesty International; Golden Key National Honor Society, 1986-; Asian American Journalists Association, 1993. **HONORS/AWARDS:** California Newspaper Publishers Award, 2nd Place Best Writing, 1990. **HOME ADDRESS:** 710-A Nobel Drive, Santa Cruz, CA 95060. **BUSINESS ADDRESS:** Newspaper Reporter, Santa Cruz Sentinel, 207 Church Street, Santa Cruz, CA 95060, (408)423-4242.

KIMURA, GWEN C.

Instructor. Japanese American. **PERSONAL:** Born Sep 25, 1955, Hilo, HI; daughter of Setsuyo Tanabe; married Guy Kimura, Aug 23, 1986. **EDUCATION:** University of Hawaii, Manoa, BEd, 1977, MEd, 1980. **CAREER:** Hawaii Community College, assistant professor in reading, 1987-. **ORGANIZATIONS:** Governor's Council for Literacy, representative, 1987-; Phi Lambda Theta, 1988; Phi Theta Kappa, advisor, 1993; College Reading Learning Assistance (CRLA), Hawaii, state director, 1993. **HONORS/AWARDS:** Hawaii Community College, Board of Regents Excellence in Teaching Award, 1993. **BUSINESS ADDRESS:** Assistant Professor in Reading, Hawaii Community College, 200 West Kawili St, General Education Division, Hilo, HI 96720-4091, (808)933-3503.

KIMURA, KOLIN M.

Manufacturing company executive. Japanese American. **PERSONAL:** Born Nov 6, 1950, Tokyo, Japan; son of Makoto & Seiko Kimura; divorced. **EDUCATION:** Loyola University, BA, 1973. **CAREER:** Sears, assistant store manager, 1976-87; Genmark Inc, national sales manager, 1987-88; King O'Lawn Inc, national sales manager, 1988-90, executive vice president, 1990; McLane Mfg, national sales manager, 1990-91, vice president, 1991-92, president, 1992-. **BUSINESS ADDRESS:** President, McLane Manufacturing Inc, 7110 E Rosecrans Ave, Paramount, CA 90723, (310)633-8158.

KIMURA, KONGO

Educator (retired). Japanese American. **PERSONAL:** Born Jul 21, 1919, Kona, HI; married Sueko Kimura, Apr 17, 1942; children: Laraine Yasui, Karen, Bruce, Christine. **EDUCATION:** University of Hawaii, BS, 1941, 5th year teachers certificate, 1948. **CAREER:** Pahoa High & Elementary School, teacher, 1942-74. **ORGANIZATIONS:** Hilo Teacher's Association, president, 1942-74; Hawaii State Teachers Association, 1942-74; National Education Association, 1942-74. **HONORS/AWARDS:** Future Farmers of America, Honorary American Farmer, 1974; Hawaii Visitors Bureau, Mahalo Award, 1983. **HOME ADDRESS:** 165 Kupaa St, Hilo, HI 96720, (808)959-5687.

KIMURA, LILLIAN C.

Management consultant. Japanese American. **PERSONAL:** Born Apr 7, 1929, Glendale, CA; daughter of Homer Hisaichi Kimura and Hisa Muraki Kimura. **EDUCATION:** University of Illinois, BA, 1951; University of Illinois School of Social Work, MSW, 1954. **CAREER:** Olivet Community Center, program director, 1954-68, director, 1968-71; YWCA of the USA, program consultant, 1971-78, Mid State Regional Office, director, 1978-80, Field Services, executive, 1980-84, asst natl executive director, 1984-87, associate natl executive director, 1987-92; Kimura Associates, consultant, currently. **ORGANIZATIONS:** Japanese American Citizens League, natl president, 1992-, New York Chapter, president, 1986-92, Midwest District Council, governor, 1973-79; Japanese American Service Committee, president, 1973-79; Nonprofit Management Assn, natl board/secretary, 1985-91; Assn for the Advancement of Social Work with Groups, natl board, 1988-92; Cause Effective, advisory committee, 1992-. **HONORS/AWARDS:** Government of Japan, Order of the Precious Crown, Wisteria, 1993; YWCA of the USA, First Ambassador Award, 1993, Racial Justice Award, 1988; Japanese American Citizens League, Sapphire Pin, c1977. **SPECIAL ACHIEVEMENTS:** Columnist for Pacific Citizen, natl JACL weekly newspaper, 1992-. **HOME ADDRESS:** 75 Grove St, Bloomfield, NJ 07003.

KIMURA, MINEO

Physicist, educator. Japanese American. **PERSONAL:** Born Nov 15, 1946, Tokyo, Japan; son of Shoichi & Tsugiko Kimura; married Keiko Kimura, Dec 2, 1973; children: Kana, Mari, Nao. **EDUCATION:** Waseda University, Japan, BSc, 1970; University of Tokyo, Japan, MSc, 1972; University of Alberta, Canada, PhD, 1984. **CAREER:** University of Missouri, assistant professor of physics, 1981-83; Joint Institute for Laboratroy Astrophysics, scientist, 1983-86; Rice University, adjunct professor of physics, 1988-; Argonne National Laboratory, physicist, 1986-. **ORGANIZATIONS:** American Physical Society; International Atomic Energy Agency, consultant; US Department of Energy, review committee. **HONORS/AWARDS:** Harvard University, research scholarship, 1993; RIKEN, Japan, Visiting Scientist Scholarship, 1993; Harvard-Smithsonian Fellowship, 1992; US/Yugoslavia Research Program, NSF, research grant, 1989-92; US/Japan Research Program, NSF, research grant, 1987-93. **BUSINESS ADDRESS:** Physicist, Argonne National Laboratory, 9700 S Cass Ave, Bldg 203, Argonne, IL 60439, (708)252-6766.

KIMURA, RISABURO

Painter, printmaker. Japanese American. **PERSONAL:** Born Oct 13, 1924, Yokosuka, Kanagawa, Japan; son of Tokuzo & Kathu Kimura; divorced. **EDUCATION:** Yokohama University, graduate, education, 1947; Hosei University, graduate, philosophy, 1954. **CAREER:** Painter, printmaker, currently. **HONORS/AWARDS:** International Biennial of Prints, Tokyo, Japan; National Print Exhibition, The Brooklyn Museum, NY; National Exhibition, Oklahoma Art Center. **SPECIAL ACHIEVEMENTS:** USA Pavillion of the Expo '70, Osaka, Japan; Japan Art Festival, Guggenheim Museum, NY; Japan Art Festival, Brazil, Italy, Paris, Brussels, Mexico; Gimpel Gallery, NY; National Museum of Modern Art, Tokyo, Japan. **BIOGRAPHICAL SOURCES:** Modern Japanese Print Artists, Gaston Petit; Introduction to Contemporary Art, Sumio Kuwabara.

KINAGA, PATRICIA ANNE

Attorney. Japanese American. **PERSONAL:** Born Nov 28, 1953, Santa Monica, CA; daughter of Rose and Thomas Kinaga. **EDUCATION:** University of California, Los Angeles, BA (cum laude), 1975; University of California, Berkeley, MA, 1977; Georgetown University, JD, 1984. **CAREER:** Los Angeles City Attorney, attorney, 1986-. **ORGANIZATIONS:** Asian Pacific Dispute Resolution Center, Board of Directors, chair, 1990-; Asian Pacific Women's Network, president, 1988-89; Planned Parenthood, Los Angeles, board member, 1989-; City Hearts, Board of Directors, chair, currently; Asian Pacific Americans for New Los Angeles, Steering Committee, 1992-; Big Sister, Los Angeles, Personnel Committee, 1991-; Japanese American Bar Association, 1987-; Women Lawyers Association of Los Angeles, 1987-; Womens Leadership Council, 1988-89. **HONORS/AWARDS:** Los Angeles Mayor's Asian Pacific Heritage Committee, Award of Achievement, 1993; Academy of Television Arts & Sciences, Emmy nomination, for production, 1993; City of Los Angeles, Certificate of Commendation in Domestic Violence, 1992; Asian Pacific American Legal Center, Pro Bono Award, 1991; Los Angeles County Domestic Council, Award of Excellence, 1992; Women for Community Service Award, 1990. **SPECIAL ACHIEVEMENTS:** Wrote, produced, co-directed the nationally distributed educational drama on domestic violence, "About Love"; helped organize Asian Pacific Islanders for Choice, first A-P pro-choice organization in Los Angeles:; helped organize APANLA, only A-P response to 1992 civil unrest in Los Angeles; helped organize first A-P project for Big Sisters, and first A-P domestic violence council. **BIOGRAPHICAL SOURCES:** Los Angeles Times, 1992. **HOME ADDRESS:** 832 Magnolia Avenue #17, Pasadena, CA 91106, (818)577-5345.

KINGMAN, DONG (MOY SHU)

Educator, artist. Chinese American. **PERSONAL:** Born Mar 31, 1911, Oakland, CA; son of Chuan-Fee Dong and Lew She Dong; married Wong Shee, Sep 1929 (died 1954); children: Eddie, Dong Jr; married Helena Kuo, Sep 1956. **EDUCATION:** Lingnan, Hong Kong, 1924-26; Fox and Morgan Art

School. **CAREER:** Works Progress Administration, project artist, 1936-41; Academy of Advertising Art, lecturer, 1938; San Diego Art Gallery, teacher, 1941-43; visiting lecturer: University of Wyoming, 1944, Mills College, 1945, 1952; Columbia University, art instructor, 1946-58; Hunter College, instructor, watercolor, history of Chinese art, 1948-53; Famous Artists School, beginning 1954; Living Artist Production, treasurer, beginning 1954; Hewitt Travelling Painting Workshops, faculty, beginning 1957; US Dept of State, International Cultural Exchange Program, lecturer, 1954. **ORGANIZATIONS:** American Watercolor Society; National Academy of Design; West Coast Watercolor Society; Audubon Society; Dutch Treat Club. **HONORS/AWARDS:** Guggenheim fellow, 1942-43; American Watercolor Society Award, 1956, 1960, 1962-65, 1967, 1972; Dolphin Medal Award, 1987; Key to the City of Cincinnati, 1980; San Diego Watercolor Society, prize, 1984; Chinatown Planning Council, New York City, Man of the Year, 1981; Oakland, CA, Chinese Community Council, Man of the Year, 1991; Rotary Club, Man of the Year, 1991; Chinese Affirmative Action, Man of the Year, 1991; numerous others. **SPECIAL ACHIEVEMENTS:** Works represented in numerous collections, including Whitney Museum of Art, American Academy of Arts and Letters, Metropolitan Museum of Art, Chicago Art Institute; murals at R H Macy & Co, Lincoln Savings Bank, other sites; illustrator, coauthor, with Helena Kuo Kingman, spouse, Dong Kingman's Watercolors, 1980; illustrator: Paint the Yellow Tiger, 1991; The Bamboo Gate, 1946; others; art work has appeared in motion pictures, including Fifty-Five Days at Peking, 1963; Sand Pebbles, 1966; Lost Horizon, 1973. **MILITARY SERVICE:** US Army, 1945-46. **BUSINESS ADDRESS:** c/o Conacher Gallery, 134 Maiden Lane, San Francisco, CA 94108.*

KINGSTON, MAXINE HONG

Author. Chinese American. **PERSONAL:** Born Oct 27, 1940, Stockton, CA; daughter of Tom Hong and Ying Lan Chew Hong; married Earll Kingston, Nov 23, 1962; children: Joseph Lawrence. **EDUCATION:** University of California, Berkeley, BA, 1962. **CAREER:** English teacher: Sunset High School, Hayward, CA, 1965-66, Kahuku High School, HI, 1967, Kahaluu Drop-In School, HI, 1968, Kailua High School, HI, 1969, Honolulu Business College, 1969, Mid-Pacific Inst, Honolulu, 1970-77; University of Hawaii, prof English, visiting writer, 1977; Eastern Michigan University, Thelma McCandless Distinguished Professor, 1986; University of California, Berkeley, Chancellor's Distinguished Professor, 1990-. **HONORS/AWARDS:** The Woman Warrior, 1976: Natl Book Critics Circle Award for Non-fiction, cited by Time, New York Times Book Review, and Asian Mail as one of the best books of the year and decade; Mademoiselle award, 1977; Anisfield Wolf Book Award, 1978; named Living Treasure of Hawaii, 1980; Asian-Pacific Women's Network, Woman of the Year, 1981; China Men, 1981: Natl Book Award, runner-up for Pulitzer Prize, Natl Book Critics Circle Award Nominee, 1988; California Arts Commission Award, 1981; Hawaii Award for Literature, 1982; Tripmaster Monkey-His Fake Book, 1989: PEN West Award in Fiction; Governor's Award for Arts, 1989; Brandeis University, Natl Women's Com, Major Book Collection Award, 1990; American Acad and Inst of Arts and Letters, award in literature, 1990; Lila Wallace Readers Digest Writing Award, 1992; inducted into American Acad of Arts and Sciences, 1992; honorary doctoral degrees: Eastern Michigan University, 1988, Colby College, 1990, Brandeis University, 1991, University of Massachusetts, 1991, Starr King School for the Ministry, 1992. **SPECIAL ACHIEVEMENTS:** Author: The Woman Warrior: Memoirs of a Girlhood among Ghosts, 1976; China Men, 1981; Hawai'i One Summer, 1987; Tripmaster Money-His Fake Book, 1989; Through the Black Curtain, 1988; numerous short stories, article and poems in periodicals, including: American Heritage, Hungry Mind Rev, Iowa Rev, Los Angeles Times, Michigan Quarterly, Mother Jones, Ms, New York Times, New Yorker, Redbook, Caliban.

KINOSHITA, JIN H.

Medical researcher, educator. Japanese American. **PERSONAL:** Born Jul 21, 1922, San Francisco, CA; married Kay. **EDUCATION:** Columbia University, Bard College, AB, 1944; Harvard University, PhD, 1952. **CAREER:** Harvard Medical School, Biochemistry & Ophthalmology, professor, 1952-72; National Eye Institute, NIH, scientific director, 1972-90; University of California, Davis, clinical research professor, 1990-; Shojin Research Associate, president, CEO, 1991-. **ORGANIZATIONS:** National Foundation for Eye Research, Scientific Advisory Committee, chairman, 1985-; Research to Prevent Blindness, Scientific Advisory Committee, 1992-. **HONORS/AWARDS:** Bard College, DSc (honorary), 1969; Oakland University, DSc (honorary), 1989; Association Research in Ophthalmology, Friedenwald Award, 1965, Proctor Award, 1974; US Government, Presidential Award for Meritorious Service, 1988. **SPECIAL**

ACHIEVEMENTS: Over 250 research articles published. **BIOGRAPHICAL SOURCES:** Jin H Kinoshita International Symposium in Experimental Eye Research, vol 50, p 567-819, 1990; Congressional Record, "Salute to Dr Kinoshita," by Hon Norman Mineta, Sept 21, 1989. **HOME PHONE:** (916)753-7766.

KINOSHITA, TOICHIRO

Educator. Japanese American. **PERSONAL:** Born Jan 23, 1925, Tokyo, Japan; son of Tsutomu Kinoshita & Fumi Ueda; married Masako Kinoshita, Oct 14, 1951; children: Kay, June, Ray. **EDUCATION:** Tokyo University, BS, 1947, PhD, 1952. **CAREER:** Institute for Advanced Study, member, 1952-54; Columbia University, postdoctoral fellow, 1954-55; Cornell University, research associate, 1955-58, assistant professor of physics, 1958-60, associate professor of physics, 1960-63, professor of physics, 1963-92, Goldwyn Smith professor of physics, 1992-. **ORGANIZATIONS:** National Academy of Sciences, 1991; American Association for Advancement of Sciences, fellow, 1989-; American Physical Society, fellow, 1971-. **HONORS/AWARDS:** Guggenheim Foundation, J S Guggenheim Memorial Fellow, 1973-74; American Physical Society, J J Sakurai Prize, 1990. **SPECIAL ACHIEVEMENTS:** Author of a book and over 100 articles in professional journals; Technical Advisory Panel, Department of Energy, 1982-83; Committee on Fundamental Constants, National Research Council, 1984-86. **BUSINESS ADDRESS:** Goldwin Smith Professor of Physics, Cornell University, 310 Newman Laboratory, Ithaca, NY 14853.

KINRA, VIKRAM KUMAR

Educator, scientist. Indo-American. **PERSONAL:** Born Apr 3, 1946, Lyallpur, India; son of Chaudhary Gurmukh Chand & Gianvati Kinra; married Vishal; children: Anushka, Rajeev. **EDUCATION:** Indian Institute of Technology, Kanpur, India, BTech, 1967; Utah State University, MS, 1968; Brown University, PhD, 1975. **CAREER:** University of Colorado, assistant professor, 1975-82; Texas A&M University, professor, associate director, 1982-. **ORGANIZATIONS:** Society for Experimental Mechanics, 1974-; American Society of Mechanical Engineers, fellow, 1979-; Acoustical Society of America, 1989-; American Society for Testing and Materials, 1989; American Society for Engineering Education, 1979-; American Academy of Mechanics, 1976-; American Society for Metals, 1985-; The American Society for Nondestructive Testing, 1988; American Institute of Aeronautics and Astronautics, senior member, associate fellow, 1992-; Pi Tau Sigma, 1980-; Sigma Xi, 1983-. **HONORS/AWARDS:** American Society for Engineering Education, Dow Outstanding Young Faculty Award, 1980; Society of Automotive Engineers, Ralph R Teetor Educational Award, 1982; Texas A&M University, Halliburton Professorship, 1986; Society for Experimental Mechanics, Hetenyi Award, 1991, 1994; Texas A&M University, Outstanding Aerospace Professor, 1992-93; Texas Engineering Experiment Station, research fellow, 1991, 1992, senior research fellow, 1993; American Society of Mechanical Engineers, fellow, 1993. **SPECIAL ACHIEVEMENTS:** Author of one book; 55 journal publications; 50 publications in conference proceedings; 3 chapters in books. **HOME ADDRESS:** 1106 Deacon Dr, College Station, TX 77845, (409)764-8494. **BUSINESS ADDRESS:** Professor, Associate Director, Dept of Aerospace Engineering, Texas A&M University, College Station, TX 77843-3141, (409)845-1667.

KIRCHNER, BHARTI

Author. Indo-American. **PERSONAL:** Born in Calcutta, India; daughter of Anima Nandi and Amiya Nandi; married Tom Kirchner, Jul 13, 1976. **EDUCATION:** Calcutta University, BS, MS. **CAREER:** Bank of America, systems manager, 1980-84; IBM, advisory systems engineer, 1984-89. **ORGANIZATIONS:** National Writer's Club, 1987-; International Association of Culinary Professionals, 1993-. **HONORS/AWARDS:** Campbell Soup, Souped-up-Soup Recipe Contest, 1990; Philadelphia Writer's Conference, first place nonfiction book proposal, 1992. **SPECIAL ACHIEVEMENTS:** Cookbooks: The Healthy Cuisine of India, 1992; Indian Inspired, 1993. **HOME ADDRESS:** 5217 Keystone Place N, Seattle, WA 98103-6233, (206)547-8027.

KIRIYAMA, IKU

Association administrator. Japanese American. **CAREER:** Japanese American Historical Society of Southern California, founder, co-chair, 1986-. **SPECIAL ACHIEVEMENTS:** The Future of the Japanese American Community, conference, Los Angeles, co-chair, 1992. **BUSINESS ADDRESS:** Founder, Co-Chair, Japanese American Historical Society of Southern California, PO Box 3164, Torrance, CA 90510-3164, (310)326-0608.*

KIRON, RAVI (RAVI KIRON MINHA ANANTHA)
Senior research scientist. Indo-American. **PERSONAL:** Born Mar 4, 1959, Shimoga, Karnataka, India; son of M G Anantha Padmanabha Setty & M A Lalitha Setty; married Dheena Kiron, Aug 21, 1989. **EDUCATION:** Bombay University, India, BS, 1979, MS, 1981; Indian Institute of Science, Bangalore, India, PhD, 1986. **CAREER:** Cornell University, Medical College, research associate, 1986-89, assistant professor, 1989-91; Pfizer Inc, senior research scientist, 1991-. **ORGANIZATIONS:** American Association for Advancement of Science, 1989-; American Society for Biochemistry & Molecular Biology, 1993-; Harvey Society, 1988-91; Eastern Hypertension Society, 1988-91; American Society for Hypertension, 1989-92; New York Academy of Sciences, 1990-93. **HONORS/AWARDS:** Eastern Hypertension Society, Boehringer Ingelheim Young Investigator Award, 1988; American Biograph Institute, Distinguished Young Leadership Award, 1986; Indian Institute of Science, senior research fellowship, 1985-86; US Department of Agriculture, senior research fellowship, 1982-85. **SPECIAL ACHIEVEMENTS:** At Pfizer, involved in development of drugs to treat hypertension; rsch: characterization of receptors for angiotensin at Cornell University Medical College, New York. **HOME ADDRESS:** 15 Obed Heights Rd, Old Saybrook, CT 06475, (203)388-0853. **BUSINESS ADDRESS:** Senior Research Scientist, Pfizer Inc, Eastern Point Rd, Groton, CT 06340, (203)441-6098.

KISHIMOTO, RICHARD NORIYUKI
Publishing company executive. Japanese American. **PERSONAL:** Born Feb 5, 1939, Hilo, HI; son of Richard Hozo Kishimoto and Ruth Miyoko Kishimoto; married Wendy Yee Kishimoto, Mar 20, 1992; children: Kevin Kenji, Kimberly Lum Perreira, Cindy Ichiko Chidester. **EDUCATION:** University of Hawaii, 1958-59; Clark College, AA, 1961; Washington Military Academy, commissioned officer, 2nd LT, 1966; City College, BS, 1980. **CAREER:** Xerox, senior sales rep, 1961-69; Massachusetts Mutual Life Insurance Co, agent, 1969-70; San Francisco Advertiser, general manager, editor, 1970; Xerox, field service manager, 1971-86; The Advertiser, vice president of operations, currently. **ORGANIZATIONS:** Lions Club Dist, 4C4, zone 2 chairman, 1992-93; National Japanese American Hictorical Society, treasurer, 1993-; Japanese American Citizens League, secretary, 1990-91; Portland Urban League, chairman, 1984-85; Southwest Washington Hospitals, board of trustees, 1978-81; State of Washington, state legislator, 1973-74; Nikkei Lions Club, president, 1991-92; Bentham Lions Club, president, 1967-68. **HONORS/AWARDS:** Japanese American Citizens League, Outstanding Political Achievement & Leadership, 1974. **SPECIAL ACHIEVEMENTS:** 4SPA Performed in "Mickie Finn Show," Reno, Nevada, 1968; Forest Grove, Oregon, first prize, Babershop Contest, 1969; Region Competition, Barbershop Quartet, Spokane, Washington, Fourth Prize, 1969; sang the National Anthem, Giants baseball games, Candlestick Park, 1988-90. **MILITARY SERVICE:** US Army Reserves, 1st LT, Sgt Major, 1956-93; Meritorious Service Medal, 1990, 1993; MSM, 1991; Army Commendation Medal, 1989; Hitchcock Award, 1966; Army Achievement Medal, 1985, 1986. **BUSINESS ADDRESS:** Vice President of Operations, The Advertiser, 130 Tenth St, San Francisco, CA 94103, (415)861-8370.

KISHIMOTO, YASUO
Researcher. Japanese American. **PERSONAL:** Born Apr 11, 1925, Osaka, Japan; son of Yasuichi and Chiyono Kishimoto; married Miyoko Kishimoto, May 12, 1949; children: Tsutomu, Yoriko, Takashi (Kei), Momoko Anne. **EDUCATION:** Kyoto University, Japan, BS, 1948, PhD, 1956. **CAREER:** University of Michigan, Mental Health Research Institute, asst biochemist, 1962-67; G D Searle & Co, sr investigator, 1967-69; Eunice Kennedy Shriver Center, sr investigator, 1969-76; Massachusetts General Hospital, assoc biochemist, 1969-76; Kennedy Institute, biochem research, dir, 1976-88; Johns Hopkins University Medical School, professor, 1976-88; University of California-San Diego, adj prof, 1988-. **ORGANIZATIONS:** American Society of Biological Chemistry and Molecular Biology, 1965-; American Society of Neurochemistry, 1970-; Intl Society of Neurochemistry, 1977-; Society for Complex Carbohydrate, 1981-. **HONORS/AWARDS:** National Institutes of Health, research grants, 1969-; National Science Foundation, research grants, 1978-84; Japanese Assn for Promotion of Science, visiting professorship, 1977; Tokyo Metropolitan Institute of Medical Science, visiting professorship, 1987. **SPECIAL ACHIEVEMENTS:** Determined fine structures of Cerebrosides (the major component of brain myelin), 1957-87; discovered and characterized fatty acid Alpha-Hydroxylation enzyme and its relation to brain development, 1969-87; discovery of cause of adrenoleukodystrophy (a peroxisomal disorder), 1975-87; discovery and characterization of saposin proteins (sphingolipid activator proteins), 1987-. **BUSINESS ADDRESS:** Adjunct Professor, University of California, San Diego, Center for Molecular Genetics, 9500 Gilman Dr, Rm 107, La Jolla, CA 92093-0634.

KISHIMOTO, YORIKO
US-Japan business consultant, author. Japanese American. **PERSONAL:** Born Sep 8, 1955, Shizuoka, Japan; married Leland D Collins; children: two. **EDUCATION:** Wesleyan University, BA, 1977; Stanford University, MBA, 1981. **CAREER:** Nomura Research Institute, fellow, 1979-80; Japan Pacific Associates, president, 1982-. **ORGANIZATIONS:** Coalition for the Presidio Pacific Center, organizing committee, 1992-, planning director; Comprehensive Plan Advisory Committee, City of Palo Alto, California, 1993-. **HONORS/AWARDS:** University of San Francisco, Fourth Annual Osamu Yamada Distinguished Lecture, 1993. **SPECIAL ACHIEVEMENTS:** Co-author, Third Century: America's Resurgence in the Asian Era, Crown Publishers, 1988; editor, Biotechnology in Japan: The Reference Source, 1984; author, "Theory F," April 1986; "Let's Quit Whining and Get to Work!," The Washington Post Sunday Outlook, Jan 17, 1988; "Venture Capital a la Japonaise," Venture Japan, spring 1988; many others. **BUSINESS ADDRESS:** President, Japan Pacific Associates, 467 Hamilton Ave, Ste 2, Palo Alto, CA 94301, (415)322-8441.

KITA, SADAO
Association executive. Japanese American. **EDUCATION:** Kobe University, Japan, BS, intl economics, 1956. **CAREER:** Pioneer Electronics Corp, Japan and US, various positions; Alpine Electronics Manufacturing of America Inc, vp of administration; Japan Business Assn of Southern California, executive director, currently. **BUSINESS ADDRESS:** Executive Director, Japan Business Assn of Southern California, 345 S Figueroa, Ste 206, Los Angeles, CA 90071, (213)485-0160.✳

KITAGAWA, JOSEPH MITSUO. *See* Obituaries.

KITAHARA, DAVID JAMES
Dentist. Japanese American. **PERSONAL:** Born Oct 25, 1951, Washington, DC; son of James Hajime Kitahara and Evelyn Toshiye Kitahara; married Arlene Marie Kitahara, Jul 6, 1974; children: Bryan Jason. **EDUCATION:** University of Maryland, College Park, BS, 1973; University of Maryland School of Dentistry, Baltimore College of Dental Surgery, DDS (magna cum laude), 1978. **CAREER:** Veterans Administration Medical Center, general practice resident, 1978-79; Dr Franklin Frush DDS, associate dentist, 1979-82; Dr Walter Ganes DDS, PA, associate dentist, 1979-84; Dr Walter Ganes, DDS & Dr David Kitahara, DDS, PA, partner, owner, dentist, 1984-87; Dr Camps & Casper, Childrens Dental Office, associate dentist, 1982-88; private practice, owner, dentist, 1987-. **ORGANIZATIONS:** American Dental Assn; Maryland State Dental Assn; Southern Maryland Dental Assn; Academy of General Dentistry; Academy of GP Orthodontics; Chinese Dental Study Club, secretary; Laurel Lakes Executive Park Condo Assn, board of directors, director; Omicron Kappa Upsilon Honorary Dental Society. **HONORS/AWARDS:** University of Maryland School of Dentistry, Baltimore College of Dental Surgery, Harry B Schwartz Award, 1978. **BUSINESS ADDRESS:** Dentist, 8339 Cherry Lane, Laurel, MD 20707, (301)498-0545.

KITAHATA, STACY DEE
Global educator, administrator. Japanese American. **PERSONAL:** Born Mar 8, 1961, Los Angeles, CA; daughter of Shiuzo M Kitahata & Naoye Umekubo Kitahata; married Frank Granquist Steinhauer, Jun 6, 1992. **EDUCATION:** University of California, Los Angeles, BA, psychology, 1984; Lutheran School of Theology, Chicago, currently enrolled. **CAREER:** UCLA Business Forecast, administrative assistant, 1982-84; Lutheran Social Services of Southern California, emergency assistance, employment developer, 1984-86; Hunger Program, South Pacific District, American Lutheran Church, director, 1986-88; ELCA Division for Global Mission, Global Mission Education, associate director, 1988-. **ORGANIZATIONS:** Center for Responsible Travel, bd member, 1989-; Bread for the World, 1986-; Amnesty International, 1989-; Girl Scouts USA, 1968-; Office on Global Education, NCCUSA, bd member, 1990-; UCLA Alumni Association, lifetime member; ELCA Asian Association, 1989-; Japanese American National Museum, charter member. **SPECIAL ACHIEVEMENTS:** Writer, editor, Having an Excellent Adventure: A Handbook for Responsible Travel, 1992; Missionary Sponsorship Handbook, 1994; contributor: Lutheran Woman Today, 1989, 1993; Lutheran Human Relations Vanguard, 1992; Lutheran Standard, 1987; multiple denominational resources including Open Hearts diversity curriculum; Global Education Handbook, in progress. **BIOGRAPHICAL SOURCES:** Lutheran Woman Today, 1988;

bulletin insert-ELCA Hunger Program, 1987. **BUSINESS ADDRESS:** Associate Director, Global Mission Education, Evangelical Lutheran Church in America, Division for Global Mission, 8765 W Higgins Rd, Chicago, IL 60631, (312)380-2651.

KO, ADA
Attorney. Chinese American. **PERSONAL:** Born Dec 9, 1956, Seattle, WA; daughter of Perry & Sue Wah Ko. **EDUCATION:** University of Washington, BA, public relations and dance (cum laude), 1975, MBA candidate, business administration, finance, 1976; University of Puget Sound School of Law, JD, 1983. **CAREER:** Della Femina Travisano & Partners, Kraft Smith Advertising, media buyer, 1974-78; StarMaster, Inc, marketing manager, 1977-78; IBM Co, systems engineer, 1978-84; Cable, Barrett, Langenbach & McInerney, intern/assoc, 1982-84; American Institute of Banking-Washington Bankers Association, instructor, 1984-; Rainier National Bank, financial counsel, 1984-86; Hatch & Leslie, bankruptcy assoc, 1986-87; University of Puget Sound School of Law, adjunct prof of law, 1987-88, 1991-92; O'Shea, Straight, Barnard & Martin, litigation assoc, 1987-90; King County Superior Court, judge & commissioner pro tem, Mandatory Arbitration Program, arbitrator; City of Seattle, director of Civil Enforcement Section, asst city attorney, 1990-. **ORGANIZATIONS:** Washington State Bar Assn, 1983; Seattle King County Bar Assn; Asian Bar Assn of Washington; Natl Asian Pacific American Bar Assn; Washington Women Lawyers; Washington State Minority & Justice Commission; WSBA, SKCBA & ABAW Law School Mentorship Program, 1987-; SKCBA Ethnic Diversity in the Legal Profession Committee, 1991-; Washington State Minority & Justice Commission, technical support staff member, 1991-; APEC Leaders Host Committee, human resources coordinator; Chinese Information & Service Center, board of directors; South China Restaurant, board of directors. **SPECIAL ACHIEVEMENTS:** Directed, participated, and/or catered fundraising activities for: Keiro Nursing Home, Kin On Nursing Home, CISC, Asian Counseling and Referral Service, Seattle Chinese Athletic Assn, Wing Luke Asian Museum, Asian Bar Assn. **BUSINESS ADDRESS:** Director, Civil Enforcement, Seattle City Attorney's Office, 600 4th Ave, 10th Fl, Municipal Building, Seattle, WA 98104, (206)684-8746.

KO, BING H.
Physician, executive. Chinese American. **PERSONAL:** Born Jun 28, 1955, Hong Kong; married. **EDUCATION:** Cal Tech, BS, 1978; MIT, ScD, 1984; Harvard Medical School, MD, 1986. **CAREER:** Mystic Valley Medical Associates, vice president, currently. **ORGANIZATIONS:** Chinese American Medical Society, Boston Chapter, president, 1991-93; American College of Physicians, 1992-; Tau Beta Pi Engineering Society, 1976-; Audoborn Society, 1991-; Physicians for Human Rights, 1992-. **HONORS/AWARDS:** AIChE, Excellence in Undergraduate Chemical Engineering, 1976. **SPECIAL ACHIEVEMENTS:** Publications in American Journal of Emergency Medicine, Nov 1987. **BIOGRAPHICAL SOURCES:** Medford Daily Mercury, front page, July 31, 1989. **BUSINESS ADDRESS:** Vice President, Mystic Valley Medical Associates, 101 Main St, Ste 110, Medford, MA 02155, (617)396-4514.

KO, CHENG CHIA CHARLES
Physician, obstetrician/gynecologist (retired). Taiwanese American. **PERSONAL:** Born Jun 18, 1929, Shin Tsu, Taiwan; son of Su Yen Ko and Wu Yu Ko; married Hsiu Hua (Margaret) Ko, Jun 1961; children: William, Judy, Stephen. **EDUCATION:** National Taiwan University, School of Medicine, MD, 1956; National Taiwan University Hospital, OB-GYN Department, residency, 1958-62; Woman's Hospital, Detroit, Michigan, internship, 1964-65; Wayne State University, OB-GYN Dept, residency, 1969-73. **CAREER:** Planned Parenthood League Inc, attending physician, 1972-74; Lakeside Medical Center, attending physician, 1974-76; California Medical Group, attending physician, 1977-78; Cheng C Ko MD, A Prof Corp, physician, owner, 1978-92. **ORGANIZATIONS:** American College of Obstetricians and Gynecologists, fellow, 1976-; Los Angeles County Medical Assn, 1981-; Garfield Medical Center, Dept of OB-GYN, chmn, 1985, 1989, chief of staff elect, 1990, chief of staff, 1991. **HONORS/AWARDS:** American College of Obstetricians and Gynecologists, Fellowship, 1976. **SPECIAL ACHIEVEMENTS:** American Bd of Obstetrics and Gynecology, certification, 1975. **HOME ADDRESS:** 2695 Wallingford Rd, San Marino, CA 91108, (818)577-0779.

KO, EDMOND INQ-MING
Educator. Hong Kong American. **PERSONAL:** Born Jul 8, 1952, Hong Kong; son of Peter Ko and Sau-Yung Cheung. **EDUCATION:** University of Wisconsin, Madison, BS, 1974; Stanford University, MS, 1975, PhD, 1980. **CA-**

REER: Exxon Research & Engineering Co, research fellow, 1975-76; University of California, Berkeley, visiting assoc prof, 1987-88; Carnegie-Mellon University, Dept of Chemical Engineering, asst prof, 1980-84, assoc prof, 1984-88, prof, 1988-. **ORGANIZATIONS:** American Assn for the Advancement of Science, 1974-; American Chemical Society, 1976-; AIChE, 1976-; American Society for Engineering Education, 1992-; American Assn for Higher Education, 1993-; Materials Research Society, 1991-; North American Catalysis Society, 1980-. **HONORS/AWARDS:** Carnegie-Mellon University, Ryan Teaching Award, 1986; Pittsburgh-Cleveland Catalysis Society, Award in Catalysis, 1992; Chemical Mfgs Assn, National Catalyst Award, 1992. **SPECIAL ACHIEVEMENTS:** Author: over 60 articles, professional journals; editor: Catalytic Conversion with Niobium Materials, 1990. **BUSINESS ADDRESS:** Professor, Dept of Chemical Engineering, Carnegie-Mellon University, 5000 Forbes Ave, Pittsburgh, PA 15213-3890, (412)268-3857.

KO, ELAINE IKOMA
Business owner, government official. Chinese American/Japanese American. **PERSONAL:** Born Dec 28, 1952, Seattle, WA; daughter of Raymond Ko & Kazuko Ikoma; married John Foz, Nov 21, 1981; children: Renato Sadahiko Foz, Kimiko Ko Foz. **EDUCATION:** University of Washington, BA (magna cum laude), communications; City University, Seattle, MBA candidate. **CAREER:** International District Improvement Association, assistant director, 1975-80; International District Housing Alliance, executive director, 1980-84; King County Women's Program, coordinator, 1985-90; City of Seattle, Office for Women's Rights, director, 1990-93; Financial Services Business, owner, 1993-. **ORGANIZATIONS:** Asian Pacific Women's Caucus, 1985-90; International Examiner Newspaper, 1991-93;. **HONORS/AWARDS:** University of Washington, Phi Beta Kappa, 1975, Women's Alumni Fund scholarships, 1971-75; Washington State Women's Political Caucus Award, 1993. **SPECIAL ACHIEVEMENTS:** Seattle Chamber of Commerce, Leadership Tomorrow Program, Graduate, 1988. **BUSINESS ADDRESS:** 6111-23rd Avenue S, Seattle, WA 98108.

KO, HON-CHUNG
Chemist. Chinese American. **PERSONAL:** Born Jun 27, 1937, Canton, China; married Erh-Mei Ko, Jul 6, 1968; children: Benjamin Y. **EDUCATION:** Chung Chi College, Hong Kong, BS, 1959; University of Virginia, MS, 1962; Carnegie Institute of Technology, PhD, 1964. **CAREER:** Rocket Power Inc, research chemist, 1963-67; Space Sciences Inc, research chemist, 1967-68; University of Chicago, postdoctoral research chemist, 1969-70; University of Pittsburgh, postdoctoral research chemist, 1970-72; University of Lethbridge, postdoctoral research chemist, 1972-74; US Bureau of Mines, research chemist, 1974-. **ORGANIZATIONS:** American Chemical Society, 1961-; Sigma Xi, 1961-80. **HONORS/AWARDS:** Frank Hsu Scholarships, 1957-59. **SPECIAL ACHIEVEMENTS:** Areas of study: thermochemistry, thermodynamics, phase equilibria, solution chemistry, analytical chemistry, spectroscopy; 35 journal publications. **BUSINESS ADDRESS:** Research Chemist, Albany Research Center, US Bureau of Mines, 1450 Queen SW, Albany, OR 97321.

KO, KATHLEEN LIM
Health administrator. Chinese American. **PERSONAL:** Born Apr 26, 1958, Shaker Heights, OH; daughter of Wen Hsiung & Christina Chen Ko; married Maurice Lim Miller, Mar 29, 1986; children: Alicia Berta Lim, Nicholas Hilario Lim. **EDUCATION:** London School of Economics, 1978; Fudan University, 1980; Stanford University, BA, 1980; Harvard School of Public Health, MS, 1984. **CAREER:** Planned Parenthood, clinic assistant, 1981-82; Institute for Health Policy Studies, policy intern, 1981-82; San Francisco General Hospital, administrative analyst, 1983; Asian Health Services, operations director, 1984-88, program, planning & development officer, 1989-92, associate director, 1993-. **ORGANIZATIONS:** Asian Women's Shelter, president, board of directors, 1988-93; Bay Area Asian Health Alliance, president, 1990-, board of directors, 1981-; Californians United, board of directors, 1987-88; American Public Health Association, 1985-. **HONORS/AWARDS:** Stanford Asian Pacific Alumni Club, Distinguised Service Award, 1993. **SPECIAL ACHIEVEMENTS:** Contributor, Bay Area Neonatal Mortality, Institute for Health Policy Studies, University of California, San Francisco, vol 1, no 1, Feb 1983; Chen, Lew, Thai, Ko, Okahara, et al, Behavioral Risk Factor Survey of Chinese-California 1991, Morbidity and Mortality Weekly Report, vol 41, p 266-270, April 1992; co-author, Cigarette Smoking Among Chinese, Vietnamese and Hispanics-California 1989-91, Morbidity and Mortality Weekly Report, vol 41, no 20, p 362-368, May 22, 1992; co-producer, "Impossible Choices," video about Asian American women, 1993-94. **BUSINESS AD-**

DRESS: Associate Director, Asian Health Services, 310-8th St, Ste 200, Oakland, CA 94607, (510)465-3271.

KO, KEI-YU
Research scientist, engineer. Hong Kong American/Chinese American. **PERSONAL:** Born in Hong Kong. **EDUCATION:** University of Illinois, MS, 1983; Massachusetts Institute of Technology, PhD, 1987. **CAREER:** Eastman Kodak Co, senior research scientist, currently. **BUSINESS ADDRESS:** Senior Research Scientist, Eastman Kodak Co, Kodak Research Labs, Bldg 81, MC 02023, Rochester, NY 14650, (716)722-9192.

KO, STEVEN W.
Accountant, auditor. Chinese American. **PERSONAL:** Born Jan 9, 1967, Chicago, IL; son of Hugh K Ko and Pearl L Ko. **EDUCATION:** Aquinas College, BSBA, 1989. **CAREER:** Prangley, Marks & Co, staff accountant, 1989-90; Hochfelder, Birkenstein, Benjamin & Weber, Ltd, senior accountant, 1992-. **ORGANIZATIONS:** Chinese American Service League, volunteer, 1990-; National Association of Asian American Professionals, 1991-. **HOME ADDRESS:** 2546 S Wentworth Ave, Chicago, IL 60616, (312)842-2051.

KO, WEN HSIUNG
Educator. Chinese American. **PERSONAL:** Born Apr 12, 1923, Shang-Hong, Fujian, China; son of Sing-Ming Ko and Shu-yu Kao; married Christina Ko, Oct 12, 1957; children: Kathleen, Janet, Linda, Alexander. **EDUCATION:** National Amoy University, Fukien, China, BSEE, 1946; Case Institute of Technology, MSEE, 1956, PhD EE, 1959. **CAREER:** Taiwan Telecommunication Admin, engineer and senior engineer, 1946-54; Case Western Reserve University/CIT, asst professor of surgery, asst professor, associate professor, electrical engineering, 1962-70; CWRU, Biomedical Electronics Resource, director, Microelectronics Lab for Biomedical Sciences, director, 1967-84, Electronics Design Center/Engineering Design Center, director, 1970-83, Otolaryngology Dept, professor, 1990-, Electrical Engineering and Biomedical Engineering, professor, 1967-93, Electrical Engineering, professor emeritus, 1993-. **ORGANIZATIONS:** IEEE, AIMBE, fellow, 1987, 1991; Sigma Xi, Eta Kappa Nu, 1956; Chinese Inst of Engineers in the US, 1974; National Amoy University, Fukien, China, Tan-Ka-Kee Fellowship, 1944-46; ISHM, 1987-. **HONORS/AWARDS:** Chinese Inst of Engineers in the US, Achievement Award, 1977; Chinese Assn of Greater Cleveland, Distinguished Service Award, 1979; 4th Intl Meeting on Chemical Sensors, Outstanding Research Award, 1992. **SPECIAL ACHIEVEMENTS:** Stanford University School of Medicine, NIH Postdoctoral Fellowship, Post PhD, 1967-68; published 113 journal papers and chapters in books, 173 conference papers; International Conference in Solid State Sensors and Actuators, chairman, 1985; International Steering Committee on Solid State Sensors and Actuators Conferences, chairman, 1983-87; Steering Committee of International Meeting on Chemical Sensors, chairman, 1989-92. **BUSINESS ADDRESS:** Professor, Electronics Design Center, Case Western Reserve University, 10900 Euclid Ave, Cleveland, OH 44106.

KO, WEN-HSIUNG
Educator. Taiwanese American. **PERSONAL:** Born May 14, 1939, Chao Chow, Taiwan; son of Ming-Jee Ko and Wang Huang Ko; married Sachi Su Ko, Jan 12, 1968; children: Subo, Supin. **EDUCATION:** National Taiwan University, BS, 1962; Michigan State University, PhD, 1966. **CAREER:** Michigan State University, postdoctoral res assoc, 1966-69; University of Hawaii, Manoa, assistant professor, 1969-72, associate professor, 1972-76, professor, 1976-. **ORGANIZATIONS:** Phytopathology, associate editor, 1980-82; Plant Disease, associate editor, 1988-90; Botanical Bulletin of Academic Sinica, editorial board member, 1988-; American Phytopathological Society, 1963-; Mycological Society of America, 1970-; Phytopathological Society of Japan, 1980-. **HONORS/AWARDS:** American Phytopathological Society, Ruth Allen Award, 1984, Fellow Award, 1990. **SPECIAL ACHIEVEMENTS:** Publication of more than 150 papers in various scientific journals. **BUSINESS ADDRESS:** Professor, Dept of Plant Pathology, University of Hawaii at Manoa, 461 W Lanikaula Street, Hilo, HI 96720, (808)935-2885.

KO, WILLIAM WENG-PING
Ophthalmologist. Taiwanese American. **PERSONAL:** Born Sep 13, 1962, Taiwan; son of Cheng Chia Ko and Hsiu Hua Ko; married Margaret Huang, May 1989; children: Stephanie. **EDUCATION:** Harvard College, AB (magna cum laude), biochemical sciences, 1984; Boston University School of Medicine, MD, 1988; University of Southern California Medical Center, Los Ange-

les, internship, 1988-89; Boston University, residency fellowship, 1989-92; University of California, San Diego, 1992-93. **CAREER:** Ophthalmologist, currently. **ORGANIZATIONS:** American Academy of Ophthalmology; California Association of Ophthalmology; American Medical Association. **HONORS/AWARDS:** Harvard College, Harvard College Scholarship, 1982-83; Westinghouse Corp, Westinghouse Science Talent Search, 1981. **HOME ADDRESS:** 2218 S 5th Ave, Arcadia, CA 91006.

KO, WINSTON T.
Educator. Chinese American. **PERSONAL:** Born Apr 5, 1943, Shanghai, China; married Katy C M S Ko, Sep 14, 1989; children: Hao, Joy. **EDUCATION:** Carnegie-Mellon University, BS, 1965; University of Pennsylvania, PhD, 1971. **CAREER:** University of California, Davis, assistant research physicist, 1970-72, assistant professor of physics, 1972-76, associate professor of physics, 1976-82, professor of physics, 1982-. **HONORS/AWARDS:** Fulbright Senior Scholar, 1992-93. **SPECIAL ACHIEVEMENTS:** Over eighty journal articles on high energy physics. **BUSINESS ADDRESS:** Professor of Physics, University of California, Davis, Davis, CA 95616, (916)752-1283.

KOBASHIGAWA, BEN
Educator. Japanese American. **PERSONAL:** Born Apr 23, 1944, Aberdeen, ID; son of Dick Jiro Kobashigawa and Sumiye Kobashigawa; married Barbara F Bates, Jul 26, 1975; children: Lorin, Jun Dai Bates. **EDUCATION:** UCLA, BA, 1967; University of Michigan, MA, 1973; University of Edinburgh, PhD, 1983. **ORGANIZATIONS:** Japanese American National Library, treasurer, 1992-; Japan Pacific Resource Network, board member, 1992-; Northern California Okinawa Kenjinkai, 1986-; Hokubei Okinawa Kenjinkai, 1983-. **HONORS/AWARDS:** Phi Beta Kappa, 1967. **SPECIAL ACHIEVEMENTS:** Translator, editor, History of Okinawans in North America, UCLA, 1988. **BUSINESS ADDRESS:** Associate Professor, Asian American Studies Dept, School of Ethnic Studies, San Francisco State University, 1600 Holloway Avenue, San Francisco, CA 94132, (415)338-7585.

KOBAYASHI, ALBERT SATOCHI
Educator. Japanese American. **PERSONAL:** Born Dec 9, 1924, Chicago, IL; son of Toshiuki Taka Kobayashi; married Elizabeth M Kobayashi, Sep 24, 1953; children: Dori Kobayashi Ogami, Tina, Laura. **EDUCATION:** University of Tokyo, BS, 1947; University of Washington, MSME, 1952; Illinois Institute of Technology, PhD, 1958. **CAREER:** Konishiroku Photo Industry, Japan, tool engineer, 1947-50; Illinois Tool Works, design engineer, 1953-55; Armour Research Foundation, Illinois Institute of Tech, res engr, 1955-58; University of Washington, assistant professor, associate professor, professor, 1958-. **ORGANIZATIONS:** Society for Experimental Mechanics, fellow, 1956-; American Society of Mechanical Engineers, fellow, 1953-; American Ceramic Society, 1984-; American Society for Testing Materials, 1992-; Japan Society of Mechanical Engineers, 1991-; National Academy of Engineering, 1986-. **HONORS/AWARDS:** Burlington Resources Foundation, Faculty Achievement Award for Outstanding Research, 1991-92; Japan Society of Mechanical Engineers, Mechnical & Materials Award, 1991; International Conference on Dynamic Fracture Mechanics, Honoree, 1984; Society for Experimental Stress Analysis, William Murray Medal, 1983. **SPECIAL ACHIEVEMENTS:** General chairman, 12th US National Congress of Applied Mechanics, 1994; editor, Handbook of Experimental Mechanics, first and second editions, 1987, 1993; over 380 publications in the area of experimental mechanics, structure mechanics, biomechanics and fracture mechanics. **BUSINESS ADDRESS:** Boeing Pennell Professor in Structural Mechanics, Dept of Mechanical Engineering, FU-10, University of Washington, MEB 314, Seattle, WA 98195, (206)543-5488.

KOBAYASHI, BERT NOBUO
Educator. Japanese American. **PERSONAL:** Born May 30, 1933, Kahului, Maui, HI; son of Torao & Takayo; divorced; children: Kim Elliott, Marsi, Paul. **EDUCATION:** Indiana University, BA, 1955, MA, 1959; Scripps Institution of Oceanography, PhD, 1972. **CAREER:** University of California, San Diego, supervisor of physical education, 1969-, lecturer in marine biology, 1976-; Sea Camp, director of academic affairs, 1987-. **ORGANIZATIONS:** Scuba Schools International Inc, College & University SCUBA Programs, consultant, 1989-, course manuals, consultant, 1989-; La Jolla Underwater Park Committee, 1983-, chair, 1992; Seal Rock Reserve Committee, 1993; Professional Association of Diving Instructors; San Diego County Coroner's Committee on SCUBA Fatalities; San Diego Diving Instructors Association. **HONORS/**

AWARDS: Students and Alumni of the UCSD SCUBA Program, Stephen Birch/Scripps Aquarium California Spiny Lobster Tank Commemoration, 1988; Scuba Schools International, Diving Equipment Manufacturers Association Trade Show, Certificate of Appreciation & Recognition, 1990-92; Diving Equipment Manufacturers Association Trade Show, Platinum Pro 5000 Diver Award, February, 1993. **SPECIAL ACHIEVEMENTS:** Contributor, Dive Control Specialist Manual, Scuba Schools Intl Inc, 1992; field and technical editor, Open Water Instructor Manual, Scuba Schools Intl Inc, 1992-; guest speaker and consultant, SCUBAPRO Save Our Seas Program, presented in conjunction with The Nature Company, 1993; "The Aquatic Environment," chapter 9 in SSI Dive Control Specialist Manual, published by Concept Systems, Jan 1993; "Marine Biology," chapter in Seacamp Manual, April 1993. **MILITARY SERVICE:** US Army, Infantry, captain, 1955-56; reserves. **HOME ADDRESS:** 3074 West Fox Run Way, San Diego, CA 92111, (619)576-9599.

KOBAYASHI, BERTRAND
State senator. Japanese American. **PERSONAL:** Born Jun 19, 1944, Honolulu, HI; married; children: one. **EDUCATION:** University of Hawaii, BA; Michigan State University, MA, PhD. **CAREER:** State of Hawaii, District 9, state representative, 1978-82, Red Tape Committee, chairman, 1983, Transportation Committee, chairman, 1984, Health Committee, chairman, 1985-88, District 13, state senator, 1982-. **ORGANIZATIONS:** Kaimuki-Waialae YMCA; Kaimuki Business & Professional Association; Waikiki Residents Association. **BUSINESS ADDRESS:** State Senator, Hawaii Legislature, State Capitol, Honolulu, HI 96813, (808)586-6860. *

KOBAYASHI, DEANNA HASUYE
Librarian (retired). Japanese American. **PERSONAL:** Born Mar 9, 1941, Hoodriver, OR; daughter of Yutaka Yabitsu and Yoshiye Yabitsu; married Donald Kobayashi, Jan 30, 1965; children: Michael Ken, Janell Kimiko. **EDUCATION:** California State University, Fresno, BA, 1963; University of California, Berkeley, MLS, 1964. **CAREER:** San Francisco Public Lib, children's libn, libn I, 1964-66; Harlandale School Dist, San Antonio, TX, librarian, 1966; Burlington Co Library, NJ, children's libn, libn I, 1966-67; Fresno County Library, extra help children's librarian, libn II, 1968-75; Merced County Library, reference librarian, libn I, 1978-80, head of reference, libn II, 1980-92, library division chief, public services, 1982-94. **ORGANIZATIONS:** American Association of University Women, vp-membership, 1993-94; California Libr Assn, 1982, scholarship com for minority students, 1986-89, chair, 1989, counselor, 1989-91, finance comm, 1990-91, reference service press fellowship committee chair, 1992-93; Japanese American Citizens League, 1990-; American Library Assn, 1982-. **SPECIAL ACHIEVEMENTS:** Wrote and administered Calif Arts Council Grant for arts in libraries, 1988; wrote and administered LSCA grant, Library Services for New Americans, 1988-90; presented workshops on library services to Hmong community, 1989-92; rated foreign language material grants for US Dept of Education library programs, 1992. **HOME ADDRESS:** 1453 Oregon Drive, Merced, CA 95340. **BUSINESS ADDRESS:** Librarian Division Chief, Merced County Library, 2100 O Street, Merced, CA 95340, (209)385-7484.

KOBAYASHI, FRANCIS MASAO
Educator. **PERSONAL:** Born Nov 19, 1925, Seattle, WA; son of Michael Masuichi Kobayashi & Mary Kumayo Kobayashi; married Monique Hai-Yen Kobayashi, Jun 8, 1963; children: John Francis, Yvonne, Monique, Robert Francis. **EDUCATION:** Loras College, 1945; University of Notre Dame, BS, 1947, MS, 1948, ScD, 1953. **CAREER:** National Science Foundation, assistant program director, engineering science, 1959-60; University of Notre Dame, teaching assistant-professor, 1948-, assistant vice president, research, 1968-. **HONORS/AWARDS:** University of Notre Dame, Service Award for Professors from Student Government, 1958, Presidential Award, 1972. **BUSINESS ADDRESS:** Assistant Vice President for Research, Professor of Aerospace and Mechanical Engineering, University of Notre Dame, Main Bldg, Rm 312, Notre Dame, IN 46556, (219)631-7378.

KOBAYASHI, HIDEAKI
Educator. Japanese American. **PERSONAL:** Born Jun 27, 1950, Tokyo, Japan; son of Masao Kobayashi and Takako Kobayashi; married Atsuko Kobayashi, Dec 25, 1980; children: Naoki, Anna, Rina. **EDUCATION:** Waseda University, BS, 1973, MS, 1975, PhD, 1979. **CAREER:** University of South Carolina, visiting asst prof, 1980-81, asst prof, 1981-85, assoc prof, 1985-; National Technological University, instr, 1985-. **ORGANIZATIONS:** VLSI Design Journal, regional ed, USA, 1988-93; Knowledge Based Silicon Corp, chmn,

1985-. **HONORS/AWARDS:** National Science Foundation, Engineering Research Initiation Grant, 1982. **SPECIAL ACHIEVEMENTS:** Author: numerous articles, professional journals; International Journal of Computer-Aided VLSI Design, guest editorial, 1989. **BUSINESS ADDRESS:** Associate Professor, Dept of Electrical & Computer Engineering, University of South Carolina, Swearingen Engineering Center, Columbia, SC 29208, (803)777-4195.

KOBAYASHI, JERRY T.
Packaging company executive. Japanese American. **PERSONAL:** Born Nov 28, 1952, Gilroy, CA; son of Hideo Kobayashi and Emiko Kobayashi. **EDUCATION:** Los Angeles Valley College, AA, 1976; California State University, Northridge, BS, 1978. **CAREER:** Carnation Co, territory manager sales, 1978-80; Gillette Co, Papermate Division, district manager sales, 1980-82; Sugar Foods Corp, vice president, general manager, 1982-. **SPECIAL ACHIEVEMENTS:** San Fernando Valley Japanese Language School, 1970. **MILITARY SERVICE:** US Army, spec 4, 1972-74.

KOBAYASHI, JOHN M.
Epidemiologist. Japanese American. **PERSONAL:** Born Jun 23, 1948, Texas. **EDUCATION:** Stanford University Medical School; Harvard University, School of Public Health. **CAREER:** Centers for Disease Control, trainee, 1980; State of Washington, chief epidemiologist, infectious diseases, 1982-. **SPECIAL ACHIEVEMENTS:** Investigated the illness of 28 scientists working near the Mt St Helens eruption; headed the investigation into the 18,000 hepatitis cases in Washington, 1985-90; investigator in the E coli poisoning resulting from tainted meat in Walla Walla, 1986; investigator in the E coli poisoning resulting from tainted meat at Jack in the Box restaurants, 1993; worked to make Washington the first State to require that illnesses be reported to the county health departments. **BUSINESS ADDRESS:** State Epidemiologist, Washington State Dept of Health, 1610 NE 150th St, Seattle, WA 98155, (206)361-2831. *

KOBAYASHI, KEY K. *See* Obituaries.

KOBAYASHI, KOICHI
Landscape architect. Japanese American. **PERSONAL:** Born Jun 4, 1945, Osaka, Japan; son of Yoshiro Kobayashi and Nobuko Kobayashi; married Fukuko Kobayashi, Jul 4, 1970; children: Eureka. **EDUCATION:** Kyoto University, BS, 1969; University of California, Berkeley, MSLA, 1972. **CAREER:** Ohio State University, Landscape Architecture, assistant professor; Cummings & Schlatter, landscape architect; City of Bellevue, WA, landscape architect; Sugio-Kobayashi-Ullman, president; Kobayashi & Associates, president, currently. **ORGANIZATIONS:** American Society of Landscape Architects; Japanese Institute of Landscape Architects; American Planning Association. **HONORS/AWARDS:** University of California, Berkeley, Ferand Award. **SPECIAL ACHIEVEMENTS:** Translation: Garret Eckbo, Landscape Architecture; translation; Michael Lowry, Landscape Architecture. **BUSINESS ADDRESS:** President, Kobayashi & Associates, Inc, 675 S Lane St, #400, Seattle, WA 98104, (206)682-3730.

KOBAYASHI, NOBUHISA
Educator, educational administrator. Japanese American. **PERSONAL:** Born May 4, 1950, Osaka, Japan; son of Shigeko Kobayashi and Kazunobu Kobayashi; married Sharon Fisher Kobayashi, Aug 13, 1983; children: Sachi C, Orion A. **EDUCATION:** Kyoto University, Japan, BCE, 1974, MCE, 1976; Massachusetts Institute of Technology, PhD, 1979. **CAREER:** Brian Watt Associates Inc, senior consulting engineer, 1979-81; University of Delaware, assistant professor, 1981-86, associate professor, 1986-91, professor, 1991-. **ORGANIZATIONS:** American Society of Civil Engineers, 1979-; American Geophysical Union, 1981-; International Association for Hydraulic Research, 1983-; Japan Society of Civil Engineers, 1978-. **SPECIAL ACHIEVEMENTS:** Center for Applied Coastal Research, associate director, 1989-; Journal of Waterway, Port, Coastal and Ocean Engineering, American Society of Civil Engineers, editor, 1992-; Journal of Coastal Research, editorial board, co-editor of special issue. **BUSINESS ADDRESS:** Professor and Associate Director, University of Delaware, Center for Applied Coastal Research, Ocean Engineering Laboratory, Newark, DE 19716, (302)831-8044.

KOBAYASHI, WILLIAM N., JR.
Management consultant. Japanese American. **PERSONAL:** Born Oct 1, 1946, Olney, MD; married Betty, Aug 30, 1969; children: Jennifer, Stephani, Kristin. **EDUCATION:** Contra Costa College, AA, 1965; San Jose State University, BS, 1967. **CAREER:** Bullocks Dept Stores, buyer, divisional mdse mgr, 1967-

83; William Forrest, owner, chief exec officer, 1983-88; Designer Collections Intl, president, 1988-92; Cosmo Electronics Inc, president, 1992-93; G A Wright, Inc, consultant, 1993-. **ORGANIZATIONS:** Pasadena Tournament of Roses, 1984-; Pasadena Tournament of Roses Foundation, board of directors, treasurer; La Canada Booster Club, director, vice pres, 1983-; Crescenta Junior Chamber of Commerce, vice pres, 1976-83; La Canada Jr Baseball Assn, vice pres, mgr, 1980-; American Management Assn, 1970-79. **HONORS/ AWARDS:** Jaycee, Jr Chamber, Jaycee of the Year, 1977-78. **HOME ADDRESS:** 5203 Crown Ave, La Canada, CA 91011.

KOBAYASHI, YOSHIKO (SHI SHI)
Japan consultant, educator. Japanese American. **PERSONAL:** Born Oct 9, 1937, Miyazaki-shi, Miyazaki-ken, Japan; daughter of Atsuro Kobayashi & Machiko Kobayashi; children: Sasha K Diedrich. **EDUCATION:** Doshisha University, BA, literature, 1960; The Claremont Graduate School, MA, education, 1962; San Diego State University, communication arts, 1968-70; San Francisco State University, humanities, 1981-82. **CAREER:** San Diego State University, lecturer, classical & Oriental languages, comparative literature, 1969-71; California Institute of Asian Studies, assistant professor, Japanese studies, 1974-76; College of Marin, lecturer for Japanese culture, literature & languages, 1974-86; City College of San Francisco, instructor, foreign languages, 1985-91; San Francisco State University, lecturer, foreign languages & literatures, humanities, 1976-92; Dominican College, lecturer, foreign languages, 1992-; University of San Francisco, lecturer, modern & classical languages, 1992-. **ORGANIZATIONS:** Northern California Teachers' Association; Asian Art Museum & De Young Memorial Museum of San Francisco, Museum Society. **HONORS/AWARDS:** San Francisco State University, Meritorious Performance and Professional Promise Award. **SPECIAL ACHIEVEMENTS:** Produced a public television program, "Ikebana wit Shi Shi," and acted as a personality in the series which were shown on NET; published an article in the International Journal of Philosophy, "The Functions and Effects of Nature on the Japanese Mind, Language and Culture," Psychology and Spirituality, vol 2, no 2, 1993. **HOME ADDRESS:** 915 E Blithedale Ave, #12, Mill Valley, CA 94941, (415)381-5871. **BUSINESS ADDRESS:** Lecturer, Dept of Modern & Classical Languages, University of San Francisco, 2130 Fulton St, San Francisco, CA 94117-1080.

KOBAYASHI, YUTAKA
Biochemistry company executive. Japanese American. **PERSONAL:** Born Mar 11, 1924, San Francisco, CA; son of Harutoyo Kobayashi and Haru Murata; married Martha Kitaoka, Aug 21, 1954 (died 1979); children: Andrew Yutaka, David Hatuo, Thomas Sachio; married E Maureen Byrne, Dec 29, 1982. **EDUCATION:** Iowa State College, BS, chemical technology, 1946, MS, bio-organic chemistry, 1950; State University of Iowa, PhD, biochemistry, 1953. **CAREER:** Northwestern Medical School, Rheumatic Fever Research Institute, USPHS postdoctoral fellow, 1953-55, research fellow, 1955-57; Worcester Foundation for Experimental Biology, scientist, senior scientist, 1958-74; New England Nuclear, applications laboratory manager, 1974-80; DuPont, applications laboratory manager, 1980-85; Ko-By Associates, president, currently. **ORGANIZATIONS:** American Chemical Society, 1946-; American Society for Biochemistry and Molecular Biology; American Society for Pharmacology and Experimental Therapeutics; Sigma Xi; American National Standards Institute, sub committee N14; Biochemcial Pharmacology, editorial advisory board member. **SPECIAL ACHIEVEMENTS:** Book: Biochemical Applications of Liquid Scintillation Counting, co-author, 1974; over 150 scientific papers & publications.

KOCHHAR, DEVENDRA M.
Biomedical scientist. Indo-American. **PERSONAL:** Born Mar 10, 1938, Sialkot, Punjab, India; son of Trilok Nath Kochhar and Savitri D Abbi Kochhar; married Omila Sagar, Sep 14, 1962 (died 1993); children: Vineet Sagar, Romeen. **EDUCATION:** Panjab University, India, BS (honors), 1958, MS, 1959; University of Florida, PhD, 1964. **CAREER:** Karolinska Inst, Stockholm, post doctoral trainee, 1965-66; Strangeway Research Lab, Cambridge, England, visiting scientist, 1966-67; Rockefeller University, guest investigator, 1967-68; University of Iowa, assoc prof, 1968-71; University of Virginia, prof, 1971-76; Thomas Jefferson University, prof, 1976-. **ORGANIZATIONS:** Editorial boards: Life Scis, 1979-89, Reproductive Toxicology, 1987-, Pergamon Press; Teratology Soc, Warkany lecturer, 1990, pres, 1982-83. **HONORS/ AWARDS:** Panjab University, Medal, 1958; Helen Hay Whitney Fellowship, 1965-68; NIH Merit Award, 1988. **SPECIAL ACHIEVEMENTS:** Co-editor, Handbook of Exp Pharmacology, 1983; In Vitro Techniques in Developmental Toxicology, 1990; first identification of the teratogenic activity of a metabolite

of vitamin A. **BUSINESS ADDRESS:** Professor, Dept of Anatomy and Develop Biol, Thomas Jefferson University, 1020 Locust St, Philadelphia, PA 19107.

KOCHHAR, MAN MOHAN
Pharmacologist. Indo-American. **PERSONAL:** Born Sep 14, 1932, Lahore, Punjab, India; son of B D Kochhar & Vidya Kochhar; married Satya Kochhar, Dec 3, 1954; children: Abha, Anjali Milano, Anita Reynolds. **EDUCATION:** Punjab University, BS, pharmacy, 1953; University of Texas, Austin, MS, pharmacy, 1961, PhD, pharmacy, 1964. **CAREER:** Auburn University, professor of toxicology, 1964-79; EPA, consultant, 1977-79; NIH, visiting scientist, 1977-; Medical Diagnostics, director and consultant, 1979-83; Food & Drug Administration, pharmacologist, 1983-. **HONORS/AWARDS:** NIDA, grant, 1973-77; State of Alabama, grant, 1975-77. **SPECIAL ACHIEVEMENTS:** Published many papers in scientific journals, 1963-85; associate of the Staff College, CDER, FDA, 1992. **HOME ADDRESS:** 9458 Macomber Lane, Columbia, MD 21045. **BUSINESS ADDRESS:** Pharmacologist, Div of Bio-equivalence, Food & Drug Administration, 7500 Standish Place, Room 279, Rockville, MD 20855, (301)295-8345.

KOCHIYAMA, WILLIAM. *See* Obituaries.

KOGA, MARY H.
Artist, photographer. Japanese American. **PERSONAL:** Born Aug 10, 1920, Sacramento, CA; daughter of Hisakichi Ishii and Tsugime Ishii; married Albert M Koga, Jun 28, 1947. **EDUCATION:** University of California, Berkeley, BA, 1942; University of Chicago, MA, 1947; School of the Art Institute of Chicago, MFA, 1973. **CAREER:** United Charities, Chicago, caseworker, 1947-52; Northwestern University Medical School, chief psychiatric soc wker/ associate, 1952-58; University of Chicago, Sch Soc Serv Admin, assistant professor, 1959-69; Columbia College, Photography Dept, instructor, 1973-80; self-employed, artist/photographer, 1973-. **ORGANIZATIONS:** Japan America Society of Chicago, bd mem, 1970-, vp & chm pub comm, 1981-90; Society for Photographic Education, 1973-; Chicago Artists Coalition, 1980-; National Association for Social Work, 1947-; Japanese American Service Committee Member, former bd member, 1947-. **HONORS/AWARDS:** Chicago Dept of Cultural Affairs, Fellowship Grants, 1990, 1989, 1988; Illinois Arts Council, Fellowship Grants, 1984, 1979; National Endowment for the Arts, Wash, DC, Fellowship Grants, 1982; City of Chicago, Senior Citizen's Hall of Fame, 1990. **SPECIAL ACHIEVEMENTS:** Numerous photographic exhibitions: over 70 one-person and group, invitational, juried, national and international exhibitions; numerous photographs in public museums, corporate and private individual collections; represented in many publications. **BIOGRAPHICAL SOURCES:** Chicago Tribune; Corpus Christi; Caller Times; Evening Observer, Dunkirk-Fredonia, NY 1990; Women Artists, Rutgers U, 1988; Human Condition, The City and Its Artists, 1945-78. **HOME ADDRESS:** 1254 Elmdale Ave, Chicago, IL 60660, (312)274-6479.

KOGA, ROKUTARO
Research physicist. Japanese American. **PERSONAL:** Born Aug 18, 1942, Nagoya, Japan; son of Toyoki Koga & Emiko Koga; married Cordula Koga, May 5, 1981; children: Evan A, Nicole A. **EDUCATION:** University of California, Berkeley, BA, 1966; University of California, Riverside, PhD, 1974. **CAREER:** Case Western Reserve University, research associate, 1974-78, assistant professor, physics, 1979-80; The Aerospace Corp, research physicist, 1980-. **ORGANIZATIONS:** American Physical Society, 1970-; American Geophysical Union, 1981-; Institute of Electrical and Electronics Engineering, 1980-. **SPECIAL ACHIEVEMENTS:** Over 80 publications in professional journals, 1975-. **BUSINESS ADDRESS:** Research Physicist, The Aerospace Corporation, PO Box 92957, YM2-259, Space Science Lab, Los Angeles, CA 90009.

KOGA, TOYOKI
Physicist (retired). Japanese American. **PERSONAL:** Born Apr 1, 1912, Hanaishi, Hokkaido, Japan; son of Tamejiro Koga and Kiku Koga; divorced; children: Rokutaro, Akiya. **EDUCATION:** Tokyo University, BS, 1937, DSc, 1948. **CAREER:** Tokyo University, research fellow, 1937-40; Nagoya University, assistant & professor, 1940-59; California Institute of Technology, senior research fellow, 1955-56; University of California, Berkeley, visiting professor, 1956-57; University of Southern California, research scientist, 1959-63; North Carolina State University, professor, 1963-64; Polytechnic Institute, visiting professor, 1964-67. **ORGANIZATIONS:** Japan Physical Society, 1937-59; American Physical Society, 1958-. **HONORS/AWARDS:** US Gov-

ernment, Fulbright Scholar, 1955. **SPECIAL ACHIEVEMENTS:** Books: Introduction to Kinetic Theory, 1970; Foundtions of Quantum Physics, 1981; Inquiries into Foundations of Quantum Physics, 1983; Memoranda of Modern Physics, 1989; The Need for Quantum Kinetics, 1993. **HOME ADDRESS:** 3061 Ewing Ave, Altadena, CA 91001, (818)794-6186.

KOGA, YOSHI TANJI
Educator. Japanese American. **PERSONAL:** Born Sep 10, 1924, Puunene, Maui, HI; daughter of Tsuto S Tanji & Kiyo S Tanji; married Kenneth Kenji Koga, Jul 10, 1954 (deceased); children: Brian Toshiaki & John Tanji. **EDUCATION:** University of Hawaii, BEd, 1951, 5th year certificate, 1952; Columbia University, MA, 1953. **CAREER:** University of Hawaii, Manoa, instructor, head of dental hygiene, 1953-60, department of dental hygiene, instructor, chairman, 1961-63, assistant professor, chairman, 1964-73, associate professor, chairman, 1973-90, emeritus associate professor of dental hygiene, 1991-. **ORGANIZATIONS:** American Association of Dental Schools, 1969-90; American Dental Hygienists Association, 1951-90; Hawaii Dental Hygientists Association, 1951-90; American Association of University Professors, 1954-85; National Education Association, 1953-90; Hawaii Education Association, 1953-90; Hawaii Fluoridation Council, 1961-90; University of Hawaii Alumni Association, 1953-90. **HONORS/AWARDS:** Hawaii Dental Association, honorary member, 1990; University of Hawaii Founder's Alumni Association, Lifetime Achievement Award, 1989; University of Hawaii School of Nursing, Distinguished Alumnus Award, 1984; University of Hawaii, Merit Awards, 1965, 1970, 1976, 1981. **SPECIAL ACHIEVEMENTS:** Consultant, speaker on dental hygiene education to various dental & dental hygiene schools in Japan & Honolulu, 1980-. **BUSINESS ADDRESS:** Associate Professor Emeritus, Dept of Dental Hygiene, University of Hawaii at Manoa, 2445 Campus Rd, Hemenway Hall, Rm 200B, Honolulu, HI 96822.

KOH, KILSAN
Surgeon. Korean American. **PERSONAL:** Born Jul 10, 1950, Wando, Chollanam-Do, Republic of Korea; son of Hyung Jeon Koh; married Patricia P Koh, May 29, 1977; children: Linda, Isaac. **EDUCATION:** Seoul National University, BS, 1973; University of Texas, San Antonio, 1977-79; Loma Linda University School of Medicine, MD, 1983. **CAREER:** Private practice, surgeon, 1989-. **ORGANIZATIONS:** American Medical Assn, 1983-; American College of Surgeons, fellow, 1993. **BUSINESS ADDRESS:** Surgeon, 1136 Alpine St, Ste 220, Boulder, CO 80304, (303)449-1634.

KOH, KWANG K.
Business executive. Korean American. **CAREER:** Chrysan Industries, Inc, CEO, 1977-. **BUSINESS ADDRESS:** CEO, Chrysan Industries, Inc, 14707 Keel St, Plymouth, MI 48170, (313)451-5411.∗

KOHARA, DAVID NOBORU
Horticultural company administrator. Japanese American. **PERSONAL:** Born Oct 6, 1950, Hilo, HI; son of Masatoshi and Harue Kohara; married Donna Verne S Kohara, Jul 20, 1974. **EDUCATION:** University of Hawaii, BS, 1972. **CAREER:** State of Hawaii, U of H, resident mgr, 1973-76; Dole Pineapple, research coordinator, 1976-80; Ka'u Agribusiness, horticulturist, 1980-90; Golden Touch, owner, 1991-; HGP Inc, branch mgr, 1991-. **ORGANIZATIONS:** Hawaii State PSTA, fourth vice pres, 1987-92, first vice pres, 1992-94; Hawaii Lions Clubs, zone chair, 1989-90; Naalehu Hongwanji, second vice pres, scty, auditor, 1992-94; Ka'u Federal FCU, vice pres, 1989-94; Naalehu School PTA, president, 1981-84; Hawaii Farm Bureau, 1991-93; Hawaii Turfgrass Assn, 1991-93. **HONORS/AWARDS:** National PTA, National Honorary Life Membership, 1992. **BUSINESS ADDRESS:** Branch Manager, HGP Inc, 761 Kanoelehua Ave, Hilo, HI 96720, (808)935-9304.

KOHASHI, ETHEL TSUKIKO. *See* Obituaries.

KOIDE, FRANK TAKAYUKI
Educator. Japanese American. **PERSONAL:** Born Dec 25, 1935, Honolulu, HI; son of Sukeichi Koide & Hideko Koide; divorced; children: Julie, Cheryl. **EDUCATION:** Illinois Institute of Technology, 1955-56; University of Illinois, BSEE, 1958; Clarkson University, master's degree, 1961; University of Iowa, PhD, 1966. **CAREER:** Iowa State University, assistant professor of electrical engineering, physiology, pharmacology, and biomedical engineering, 1966-68; Technology Inc, principal biomedical engineer, 1968-69; University of Hawaii, associate professor of electrical engineering, 1969-72, associate professor of electrical engineering & physiology, 1972-74, professor of electrical engineering & physiology, 1974-. **ORGANIZATIONS:** Institute of Elec-

trical & Electronic Engineers. **HONORS/AWARDS:** University of Notre Dame, Microcomputer-based Instrumentation Grantee, 1988; NASA Spacecraft Center, Space Systems Design Fellow, 1967; NIH, predoctoral fellow, 1962-66. **SPECIAL ACHIEVEMENTS:** Papers on operational amplifiers, galvanotropism, mechanical impedance, bioelectricity, membrane ionics, biolelectricty of nerve, smooth muscle conduction, ionospheric propogation and electromagnetics. **BUSINESS ADDRESS:** Professor, University of Hawaii, 2540 Dole St, Honolulu, HI 96822, (808)956-7406.

KOIDE, SAMUEL SABURO
Scientist. Japanese American. **PERSONAL:** Born Oct 6, 1923, Honolulu, HI; son of Sukeichi Koide and Hideko Koide; married Sumi M Mitsudo, Nov 26, 1960; children: Mark K, Eric A. **EDUCATION:** University of Hawaii, BS, 1945; Northwestern University Med School, MD, 1953; Northwestern University, MS, 1955, PhD, 1960. **CAREER:** Memorial Sloan-Kettering Cancer Center, associate, 1960-65; Rockefeller University, The Population Council, senior scientist, 1965-. **ORGANIZATIONS:** Archives of Andrology, editorial board, 1987-93; Biological Bulletin, editorial board, 1983-85. **HONORS/AWARDS:** Institute of Medicine, Chicago, Joseph A Capps Prize for Medical Research, 1955; NIAMD, NIH, Career Development Award, 1963-65. **MILITARY SERVICE:** Infantry & Military Intelligence, 1st lieutenant, 1945-47. **BUSINESS ADDRESS:** Senior Scientist, Rockefeller University, The Population Council, 1230 York Ave, Tower 522, New York, NY 10021, (212)327-8751.

KOKAN, GHIASUDDIN (ASIM)
Plant manager. Indo-American. **PERSONAL:** Born May 27, 1945, Madras, India; son of Mohammad Jalaluddin Kokan and Ayesha Begum; married Tayyeba Sughra Kokan, Dec 30, 1973; children: Aamir Ahmed, Sameer Ahmed. **EDUCATION:** Government Arts College, Madras, India, BS, 1965; Government Law College, Madras, India, LLB, 1967; Illinois Institute of Technology, MS, 1980. **CAREER:** Westinghouse Electric Corp, IL, quality assurance mgr, 1977-83, NC, technical services mgr, 1984-88, NY, plant mgr, 1988-93; Eaton Cutler-Hammer Inc, plant manager, 1994-. **ORGANIZATIONS:** New York Export Council, 1992-94; Chemung County Chamber of Commerce, bd mbr, 1991-94, first vice pres, 1993-; Chemung County United Way, major corp fund-raising committee, chmn, 1991; Finger Lakes Islamic Assn, vice pres, 1992, president, 1993; South Eastern North Carolina Indian Assn, vice pres, 1987-88. **HOME ADDRESS:** 1639 Pinehurst Ct, Pittsburgh, PA 15237.

KOKATNUR, MOHAN GUNDO
Educator, research scientist, clinical chemist. Indo-American. **PERSONAL:** Born Mar 19, 1930, Belgaum, Karnataka, India; son of Gundo Ramachandra Kokatnur & Shanta Kumthekar; married Saroj Saraf, Aug 4, 1963; children: Sharmila, Vinita. **EDUCATION:** Poona University, Fergusson College, India, BSc, 1951; Nagpur University, Laxminarayan Institute of Technology, BSc, tech, 1953; University of Illinois, PhD, 1959. **CAREER:** University of Illinois, research associate, 1959-61; Central Food Tech Res Institute, fellowship CSIR-Pool, 1961-63; University of Illinois, research associate, 1963-66; LSU Medical Center, assistant professor, 1966-71, associate professor, 1971-93, professor, 1993-. **ORGANIZATIONS:** American Association of Indian Professionals, founder board member, 1984-; American Institute of Nutrition, 1968-; American Society for Clinical Nutrition, 1972-; American Association for Clinical Chemistry, 1974-; Society for Exp Biol & Medicine, 1988-. **BUSINESS ADDRESS:** Professor, Louisiana State University Medical Center, Medical Education Bldg, 1901 Perdido St, New Orleans, LA 70112, (504)568-6046.

KOMAI, MICHAEL MIKIO
Publisher. Japanese American. **PERSONAL:** son of Akira Komai. **CAREER:** Rafu Shimpo, president, 1983-. **BUSINESS ADDRESS:** President, Rafu Shimpo, 259 S Los Angeles St, Los Angeles, CA 90012, (213)629-2231. ∗

KOMPALA, DHINAKAR S.
Educator. Indo-American. **PERSONAL:** Born Nov 20, 1958, Madras, Tamil Nadu, India; son of Sathyanaltran & Sulochana S Kompala; married Sushila D Kompala, Nov 18, 1983; children: Tejaswi D, Chytanaya R. **EDUCATION:** Indian Institute of Technology, Madras, BTech, 1979; Purdue University, MS, 1982, PhD, 1984. **CAREER:** University of Colorado, assistant professor, 1985-91, associate professor, 1991-. **ORGANIZATIONS:** American Chemcial Society, Division of Biochemical Technology, program chairman, spring 1993. **HONORS/AWARDS:** National Science Foundation, Presidential

Young Investigator's Award, 1988-93. **SPECIAL ACHIEVEMENTS:** Editor, Cell Separation Science & Technology, 1991. **BUSINESS ADDRESS:** Associate Professor, Dept of Chemical Engineering, University of Colorado, Campus Box 424, Boulder, CO 80309.

KONDO, C. KIMI
Municipal court judge. Indo-American. **CAREER:** Seattle Municipal Court, judge, currently. **BUSINESS ADDRESS:** Judge, Seattle Municipal Court, 600 3rd Ave, Seattle, WA 98104, (206)684-8709. *

KONG, ANA C.
Educator. Chinese American. **PERSONAL:** Born Aug 9, 1940, Manila, Philippines; married Pedro Lee Kong; children: Avery, Peter, Pia. **EDUCATION:** Far Eastern University, Philippines, BS, 1964; University of Illinois at Champaign-Urbana, MS, 1969, PhD, 1973. **CAREER:** University of Illinois, research assoc, 1970-72; Governors State University, professor, communication studies, 1972-. **HONORS/AWARDS:** East-West Center, Mass Media Seminar participant, 1977, TV & Socialization Project, 1979-80, Summer Fellow, 1981. **SPECIAL ACHIEVEMENTS:** Author: Legibility and Labeling Studies, Pesticides Communications, 1970-73; Cross-Cultural Study of Television and Socialization, 1979-81. **BUSINESS ADDRESS:** Professor, Governors State University, University Park, IL 60466, (708)534-4083.

KONG, CHHEAN
Community services counselor. Cambodian American. **PERSONAL:** Born Sep 5, 1945, Kompong Cham, Cambodia; son of Oung Mao and Srun Sorn. **EDUCATION:** Buddhist University, Cambodia, BA, 1968; Bihar University, India, MA, 1972; Banaras Hindu University, India, PhD, 1975; Pepperdine University, MA, 1976; American Commonwealth University, PhD, 1989. **CAREER:** Long Beach Asian Pacific Mental Health Program, Department of Mental Health, Los Angeles County, community services counselor, community services coordinator I, currently. **ORGANIZATIONS:** Cambodian Buddhist Temple, executive director. **HONORS/AWARDS:** Los Angeles County, Commendation; Long Beach Police Department, Chief's Chaplaincy Advisory. **SPECIAL ACHIEVEMENTS:** Assisted in rebuilding Cambodian Buddhist Temple in Long Beach; American-Cambodian Senior Citizen Committee on Aging; A Study of Buddhist Political Thought; Cambodian Folk Stories; The Khmer Concept of Mental Health. **HOME ADDRESS:** 2100 W Willow St, Long Beach, CA 90810, (310)595-0566.

KONG, CORITA SHUK SINN
Educator. Chinese American. **EDUCATION:** Chaminade University, Honolulu, BA, 1963; St John's University of New York, MA, 1965, PhD, 1974. **CAREER:** Suffolk Community College, professor of history, 1967-. **ORGANIZATIONS:** American Historical Association; Association of Asian Studies. **BUSINESS ADDRESS:** Professor of History, Suffolk Community College, 533 College Rd, Southampton Bldg, Rm 123, Selden, NY 11784, (516)451-4344.

KONG, DONGSUNG
Educator. Korean American. **PERSONAL:** Born Jul 18, 1957, Republic of Korea. **EDUCATION:** Seoul National University, MS, public admin, 1983; Arizona State University, DPA, 1990. **CAREER:** San Jose State University, professor, currently. **ORGANIZATIONS:** Korea Americans for Political Empowerment, committee chair. **BUSINESS ADDRESS:** Professor, San Jose State University, 1 Washington Sq, BT 465, San Jose, CA 95192, (408)924-5343.

KONG, ERIC SIU-WAI
Research scientist. Chinese American. **PERSONAL:** Born Jan 14, 1953, Hong Kong; son of Woon-Man & Chau-Mui Mo Kong. **EDUCATION:** University of California, Berkeley, BA, 1974; Rensselaer Polytechnic Institute, MSc, 1976, PhD, 1978. **CAREER:** NASA Ames Research Center, research scientist, 1979-83; Sandia National Laboratories, member of technical staff, 1983-84; Hewlett Packard Laboratories, member of technical staff, 1984-86; University of California, San Francisco, faculty of science & pharmacology, 1986-89; Materials Science & Technology Institute, research director, 1989-91; Materials Science and Technology Institute, research director, 1992-. **ORGANIZATIONS:** American Institute of Chemists, fellow, 1983-; New York Academy of Science, fellow, 1983-. **HONORS/AWARDS:** Japan Society for the Promotion of Science, fellowship and grant, 1983; NASA, grant, 1979-83. **SPECIAL ACHIEVEMENTS:** Over 50 scientific publications, 1978-. **HOME ADDRESS:** 936 Bluebonnet Dr, Sunnyvale, CA 94086. **BUSINESS ADDRESS:** Research Director, Materials Science and Technology Institute, 923A La Mesa Terrace, Sunnyvale, CA 94086, (415)739-8239.

KONG, RONALD A.
Educational administrator. Chinese American. **PERSONAL:** Born Aug 23, 1937. **CAREER:** San Jose City College, chancellor, currently. **BUSINESS ADDRESS:** Chancellor, San Jose City College, 4750 San Felipe Rd, San Jose, CA 95135-1510, (408)298-2181. *

KONG, STANLEY YOUNG
Designer, educator. Chinese American. **PERSONAL:** Born Nov 25, 1957, Pasadena, CA; son of Susie Young and David Young. **EDUCATION:** Pasadena City College, 1976-79; Art Center College of Design, BS, 1983; UCLA, Adult Education, 1989-90. **CAREER:** Vemco Corporation, designer, 1982-86; Art Center College of Design, instructor, 1985-; Pasadena City College, instructor/head of design area, 1987-; Stan Kong Design, design consultant, 1981-. **ORGANIZATIONS:** Pasadena City College, head of design area, 1988-, design advisory board, chairperson, 1987-, artist in residency committee, 1987-, art gallery director, 1987-88; Pasadena Visual Arts and Design Academy, member of steering committee, member of curriculum development and articulation committee, 1991-. **HONORS/AWARDS:** Art Directors Club of Los Angeles, Award for Excellence in Design, 1985; Vemco/US Patent Office, US Design Patents, 1985; Porsche Motor Cars, Honorable Mention-Concept Development, 1983; Ford Motor Company, Academic Scholarship, 1981-83. **SPECIAL ACHIEVEMENTS:** ADLA (publication), Xenoworks Corporate Identity Program, 1986. **BUSINESS ADDRESS:** Professor, Art Center College of Design, 1700 Lida St, Pasadena, CA 91105, (818)396-2200.

KONG, WILLIAM T.
Journalist. Chinese American. **PERSONAL:** Born Apr 1, 1929, Hilo, HI; son of Sing Loy and Samang Kong; divorced; children: Randall, Roberta Melton, Ann, David. **EDUCATION:** University of Missouri, bachelor of journalism, 1950. **CAREER:** Mexico (MO) Ledger, sports editor, city editor, 1950-55; Des Moines Tribune, reporter, assistant city editor, 1955-80; San Francisco Examiner, copy editor, makeup editor, 1980-. **ORGANIZATIONS:** Society of Professional Journalists, regional director, 1967-74, Mid-Missouri Chapter, secretary, 1954-55, Des Moines Chapter, president, 1956-59, San Francisco Chapter, president, 1986-88. **HONORS/AWARDS:** Society of Professional Journalists, Wells Key, 1974. **MILITARY SERVICE:** US Marine Corps, sgt, 1951-53. **HOME ADDRESS:** 315 Roosevelt Way, #6, San Francisco, CA 94114, (415)626-6935.

KONISHI, MASAKAZU
Educator, biologist. Japanese American. **PERSONAL:** Born Feb 17, 1933, Kyoto, Japan. **EDUCATION:** Hokkaido University, Japan, BS, 1956, MS, 1958; University of California, Berkeley, PhD, zoology, 1963. **CAREER:** University of Wisconsin, asst professor of zoology, 1965-66; Princeton University, Biology Dept, asst professor to associate professor, 1970-75; California Institute of Technology, Dept of Biology, professor, 1975-79, Bing Professor of Behavioral Biology, 1979-. **ORGANIZATIONS:** Salk Institute, 1991-; Journal of Neuroscience, associate editor, 1980-89, section editor, 1990-; Journal of Comparative Physiology, editorial advisory board; Natl Academy of Science. **HONORS/AWARDS:** American Ornithologists Union, Elliot Coues Award, 1983; Japan Society for the Promotion of Science, Intl Prize for Biology, 1990; University of Ala, David Sparks Award in Integrative Neurophysiology, 1992, Charles A Dana Award for Pioneering Achievements in Health and Education, 1992; Alexander von Humboldt Fellow, 1963-64; Hokkaido University, honorary LLD, 1991. **BUSINESS ADDRESS:** Bing Professor of Behavioral Biology, California Institute of Technology, 1201 E California Blvd, Div Biol 216-76, Pasadena, CA 91125, (818)395-6816. *

KONO, HIDETO
Educational administrator. Japanese American. **PERSONAL:** Born May 11, 1922, Kaumana, HI; son of Hidekichi Kono and Tsugi Kono; married Fannie Kono, Jan 14, 1951; children: Dwight H, Laurel Lei Hamaya, Dayne O, Daryn D. **EDUCATION:** University of Hawaii, BA, 1949, MA, 1952. **CAREER:** US Govt, US Army Pacific Headquarters, management analyst, 1952-57; Dole Co, Honolulu, asst to president, asst to vp, finance budget analyst, 1957-64; Jintan-Dole Co, Ltd, Osaka, Japan, vp, director, 1965-74; Dole-Itochu Food Co, Ltd, Tokyo, Japan, vp, director, 1965-74; Castle & Cooke East Asia, Ltd, Honolulu, HI and Tokyo, Japan, president, director, 1965-74; Hawaii State Govt, Governor's Cabinet, Hawaii State Planning & Economic Development, director, 1974-83, Hawaii State Tax Review Commission, chairman, 1983-84,

Hawaii State Public Utilities Commission, member, 1985, chairman, 1986-88; Japan-America Institute of Management Science, president, 1988-. **ORGANIZATIONS:** Japan-Hawaii Economic Council, 1989-, advisor, 1975-80; University of Hawaii, Advisory Council for Center for Intl Bus Education, 1989-; Governor's Congress on Intl Opportunities for Hawaii, committee member, 1988-89; Hawaii State Telework Center, advisory committee, 1988-92; numerous others. **HONORS/AWARDS:** US National Governors' Association, Award for Outstanding State Planning, 1982; US Dept of Commerce, Certificate of Appreciation, 1982; Japanese Government, Ministry of Foreign Affairs, Certificate of Appreciation, 1985, Imperial Award, The Order of the Rising Sun, Gold Rays with Rosette, 1992. **SPECIAL ACHIEVEMENTS:** Language proficiency: Japanese. **MILITARY SERVICE:** US Army, Tech 4, 1943-45. **BIOGRAPHICAL SOURCES:** Life story in series of 10 articles, East-West Journal (Honolulu), January 1 - April 15, 1993 (in Japanese). **BUSINESS ADDRESS:** President, Japan-America Institute of Management Science, 6660 Hawaii Kai Dr, Honolulu, HI 96825, (808)395-2314.

KONO, TETSURO
Researcher (retired), educator. Japanese American. **PERSONAL:** Born May 17, 1925, Tokyo, Japan; son of Ichiro & Hiroko Sasaki; married Seiko Kanda, Dec 18, 1961; children: Michiko, Masahiro, Kenji. **EDUCATION:** University of Tokyo, BA, 1947, PhD, 1958. **CAREER:** Johns Hopkins University, research associate, 1958-59; University of Tokyo, instructor, 1960-63; Vanderbilt University, research associate, 1959-60, faculty, 1963-, professor physiology, 1974-85, professor, molecular physiology & biophysics, 1958-92, professor emeritus, molecular physiology and biophysics, 1992-. **ORGANIZATIONS:** Sigma Xi, 1960-; American Society Biological Chemists, 1970-; American Diabetes Association, 1984-92; American Journal Diabetes, editorial board, 1986-88; NIH Study Sections, adjunct hoc member, 1983-91. **HONORS/AWARDS:** NIH, research grants, 1961-92. **SPECIAL ACHIEVEMENTS:** Studies of mechanisms of insulin actions, 1958-92. **BUSINESS ADDRESS:** Professor Emeritus, Dept of Molecular Physiology and Biophysics, Vanderbilt University Sch Med, 1313 21st Ave South, Oxford House, Rm 212, Nashville, TN 37232-4245, (615)936-0715.

KONOSHIMA, JOJI
Company executive. Japanese American. **PERSONAL:** Born Jan 24, 1920, Tokyo, Japan; son of Kisaburo & Yoshi Konoshima. **EDUCATION:** New School for Social Research, graduate faculty, 1945-47; University of California, Berkeley, AB, 1953; Columbia University, MA, 1958; New York University, education degree, 1959-60. **CAREER:** New York University, associate professor, 1961-73; American Federation of Teachers, assistant to president, 1974-75; Jimmy Carter Presidential Campaign, labor liaison, 1976; Democratic National Committee, Asian/Pacific American Unit, national director, 1977-81; US-Asia Institute, president, co-founder, 1979-93. **ORGANIZATIONS:** US Department of State, East Asia/Pacific Bureau, advisory committee, 1979-80; Immigration-Naturalization Service, national advisory board, 1977-80; Presidential Commission on executive exchange, 1980-81; Japan Hispanic Institute, board of directors, 1990-. **HONORS/AWARDS:** Member of Presidential Delegation to Prime Minister Ohira Funeral Ceremony, 1980. **SPECIAL ACHIEVEMENTS:** Organizing Educational & Cultural Exchange Programs for Senior Congressional Staffers to Peoples Republic of China, Japan, Singapore, Malaysia, Indonesia, 1979-93. **BUSINESS ADDRESS:** President, CEO, US-Asia Institute, 232 East Capitol St NE, Washington, DC 20003, (202)544-3181.

KOO, ANTHONY YING CHANG
Educator. Chinese American. **PERSONAL:** Born Nov 22, 1918, Shanghai, China; son of Vee Sing Koo and May Ling So; married Delia Z F Wei Koo, Jun 6, 1943; children: Victoria M, Margery E, Emily D. **EDUCATION:** St John's University, China, BA, 1940; University of Illinois, Urbana, MS, 1941; Harvard University, AM, 1943, PhD, 1946. **CAREER:** Chinese Delegation to the Far Eastern Commission, counselor, 1945-50; University of Michigan, professor of economics, 1964-67; Michigan State University, assistant professor, associate professor, 1950-64, professor of economics, 1967-. **ORGANIZATIONS:** Academia Sinica, 1968-. **HONORS/AWARDS:** Michigan State University, Distinguished Teacher Award, 1956, Distinguished Faculty Award, 1976. **SPECIAL ACHIEVEMENTS:** Author, Land Reform and Economic Development A Case Study of Taiwan; author, Environmental Repercussions on Trade and Investment; author, Land Market Distortion & Tenure Reform; editor, selected essays of Gottfried Hoberler, Liberal Economic Order-Selected Essays of Gottfried Hoberler, vols I and II. **BIOGRAPHICAL SOURCES:** China Yearbook, Republic of China. **HOME PHONE:** (517)332-1443. **BUSI-**

NESS ADDRESS: Professor, Dept of Economics, Michigan State University, East Lansing, MI 48824.

KOO, BENJAMIN HAI-CHANG
Educator, engineer. Chinese American. **PERSONAL:** Born Apr 4, 1920, Shanghai, China; son of Ve-Sing Koo; married Gretchen Koo, Aug 1955 (deceased). **EDUCATION:** St John's University, BS, 1941; Cornell University, MS, 1942, PhD, 1946. **CAREER:** Corbett & Tingnir Engineers, engineer, 1950-54; Tippets-Abbett-McCarthy-Stratton Consultants, engineer, 1954-56; W H Treadwell Engineers, engineer, 1956-61; ACF Industries, development engineer, 1961-64; University of Toledo, professor, 1965-90, professor emeritus, 1990-. **ORGANIZATIONS:** American Concrete Institute; American Society of Civil Engineers, fellow, life member; American Society of Engineering Education. **HONORS/AWARDS:** Sigma-Xi, 1973; Phi-Kappa-Phi, 1973; Tau-Beta-Pi, 1979; Pi-Mu-Epsilon, Outstanding Teacher Award, 1974. **BUSINESS ADDRESS:** Professor, Civil Engineering Dept, University of Toledo, 2801 W Bancroft Street, Engineering Building, Toledo, OH 43606, (419)537-2642.

KOO, DELIA
Educator. Chinese American. **PERSONAL:** Born May 14, 1921, Wuhan, China; daughter of W H T Wei & S L Wei; married Anthony Koo, Jun 6, 1943; children: Victoria Hitchins, Margery Bussey, Emily. **EDUCATION:** St John's University, China, BA, 1941; Radcliffe College, AM, 1942, PhD, 1947; Michigan State University, MA, 1954. **CAREER:** Eastern Michigan University, professor of mathematics, 1978-85, professor emerita, 1985-. **ORGANIZATIONS:** Phi Kappa Phi; Pi Mu Epsilon; Phi Tau Phi; Phi Beta Kappa; Sigma Xi; Mathematical Association of America, Michigan Section, governor, 1979-81, chair, 1979-78, vice chair, 1976-77, secretary, treasurer, 1974-76. **HONORS/AWARDS:** Mathematical Association of America, Meritorious Service Award, 1992; MAA, Michigan Section, Distinguished Service Award, 1988; Radcliffe College, Ann Radcliffe Fellow, 1945-46, Evans Fellow, 1942-43. **SPECIAL ACHIEVEMENTS:** Books: First Course in Modern Algebra, Frederick Ungar, 1963; Elements of Optimation, Springer Verlag, 1977; author of journal papers; organizer and coordinator of volunteer teaching of English language to international graduate students at Michigan State University and at Florida State University. **BIOGRAPHICAL SOURCES:** Science Citation Index, Institute for Scientific Information, p 40509, 147759, 1986.

KOO, GEORGE P.
Management consultant. Chinese American. **PERSONAL:** Born Jun 4, 1938, Changting, Fujian, China; son of Ted Swei Yen Koo and Pei Fen Yang; married May Jen Koo, May 5, 1962; children: Denise, Douglas, Alyssa. **EDUCATION:** Massachusetts Institute of Technology, SB, 1960, SM, 1962; Stevens Institute of Technology, ScD, 1969; Santa Clara University, MBA, 1975. **CAREER:** SRI International, Chemical Industries, associate director, 1972-78; Chase Pacific Trade Advisors, vice president, 1978-79; Bear Stearns China Trade Advisors, managing director, 1979-83; Microelectronic Business International, president, 1983-85; Tiara Computer Systems, vice president, finance & admin, director, 1985-86; H&Q Technology Partners, principal, international, 1987; International Strategic Alliances, managing director & CEO, 1988-. **ORGANIZATIONS:** Asian American Manufacturers Association, Executive Committee, 1990-; Mountain View Tennis Club, Executive Committee, 1991-; Monte Jade Science & Tech Association, 1990-. **HONORS/AWARDS:** Atomic Energy Commission, fellow, 1960; Plastics Institute of America, fellow, 1966. **SPECIAL ACHIEVEMENTS:** Chairman, Annual Conference on Asian Financing & Alliances with American Companies, 1990-. **BUSINESS ADDRESS:** Managing Director & CEO, International Strategic Alliances Inc, 1265 Montecito Avenue, Suite 109, Mountain View, CA 94043, (415)969-1671.

KOO, JA HUNG
Educator. Korean American. **PERSONAL:** Born Apr 20, 1938, Seoul, Republic of Korea; son of Young Koo and Kisook Whang; married Mi Jong Koo, Dec 26, 1969; children: Ben, Eunice. **EDUCATION:** Seoul National University, BA, 1961; University of Oregon, BS, 1966; University of Nevada, Reno, MA, 1972. **CAREER:** Seoul Girls High School, teacher, 1961-64; Oriental Daily News, reporter, 1974-76; Korean School of Southern California, principal, 1980-82; Belmont High School, teacher, 1977-; West LA Korean School, principal, 1992-. **ORGANIZATIONS:** The Korean Church of Jesus Christ, elder, 1980-. **HONORS/AWARDS:** Ministry of Edu, Republic of Korea, Korean Educator Abroad Award, 1982. **SPECIAL ACHIEVEMENTS:** Author: American News Coverage of Asian Countries, MA thesis, University of

Nevada, Reno, 1972. **HOME ADDRESS:** 3420 Bentley Ave, Los Angeles, CA 90034.

KOO, MICHELLE E. M.

Landscape architect. Korean American. **PERSONAL:** Born Aug 26, 1956, Seoul, Republic of Korea; daughter of Hi-Yong and Bon-Seung Koo. **EDUCA-TION:** City College of San Francisco, architecture; UC Berkeley, BA, landscape architecture, 1981. **CAREER:** MPA Design, designer, 1982-85; Amphion Environmental Inc, sr designer, 1985-86; PBA Planning and Design, sr designer, 1986-88; Michelle, the Cater for Business, owner, 1988; Thompson & Merrill, associate partner, 1989; Edaw Inc, sr designer, 1990-92; Michelle Koo Design, Landscape Architecture, owner, 1991-. **HONORS/AWARDS:** UC Berkeley, Landscape Architecture Dept, The H Leland Vaughan Award, 1981. **SPECIAL ACHIEVEMENTS:** Guest design critic: UC Davis, UC Berkeley; landscape architect-in-residence: LEAP Program, Cabrillo Elementary School. **BUSINESS ADDRESS:** Owner, Michelle Koo Design, Landscape Architecture, 18 Bartol St, San Francisco, CA 94133.

KORTEN, GERALDINE B.

Travel agency owner. Filipino American. **PERSONAL:** Born Dec 10, 1946, Laoag City, Philippines; daughter of Santiago & Floy Barangan; married Klaus, Feb 1970; children: Carlos Wilhelm, Santiago Ernst. **EDUCATION:** University of the Philippines, BSN, 1967; Boston University, MS, nursing administration, 1981. **CAREER:** Rochester Hospital, intensive unit nurse, 1969-71; Norden Krankenhaus, intensive unit nurse, 1971-72; Medical Pool, intensive unit nurse, 1978-80; Massachusetts General Hospital, nurse supervisor, 1981-82; East West Travel Inc, president, 1983-. **ORGANIZATIONS:** Rotary Club of Charles River, president, 1992-93; American Society of Travel Agents, 1983-93; Metrowest Chamber of Commerce, Small Business Committee, 1986-88; Meadowbrook School Fund Raising Committee, co-chairman, 1984-85; Milton Academy, board for middle school, 1987-88; Society of Incentive Travel Executives, 1992-; International Society of Meeting Planners, 1991-; National Contract Management, 1993. **HONORS/AWARDS:** Sigma Theta Tau, Nursing's Honor Society, inductee, 1981. **SPECIAL ACHIEVE-MENTS:** Working on a novel, Golden Showers, pending publication; speaks German, Spanish, Tagalog, Ilocano, English; paints watercolors; writes on travel for publication. **BIOGRAPHICAL SOURCES:** The Road Less Traveled, NewsWest, 1986; Gerri Korten, From Bedside to Business Travel, May 1987; Planning Around the Globe, Metrowest Business Review, p 54, June 1987; "Profit Time—Helping Addicts Make The Grade," Travel Weekly, p 27, 29, Jan 4, 1990; "Agency Holds Career Training Seminars," Tour & Travel, p 12, 1989. **HOME ADDRESS:** 4 Ernest Dr, Natick, MA 01760. **BUSINESS PHONE:** (508)655-5900.

KOTANI, SHIGETO (TONY)

Company executive. Japanese American. **PERSONAL:** Born Mar 1, 1945, Kyoto, Kyoto, Japan; son of Shigeo and Chieko Kotani; married Masako Kotani, May 7, 1972; children: Junko, Keisuke. **EDUCATION:** Kyoto University, BS, 1961, MS, 1971. **CAREER:** Kobe Steel, Ltd, application engr, compressor, 1971-81, eng mgr, 1982-85, personnel mgr, 1985-88; Kobelco Compressors, vice pres, 1988-92, president, 1993-. **ORGANIZATIONS:** Japan Society of Mechanical Engineers, 1966-88. **SPECIAL ACHIEVE-MENTS:** Developer: high-speed compressors, 1983, smallest dry-screw compressors, 1985; author: Wear, engineering paperwork, 1972. **BUSINESS ADDRESS:** President, Kobelco Compressors (America), Inc, 3000 Hammond Ave, Elkhart, IN 46516, (219)295-3145.

KOTHARI, AJAY P.

Engineering company executive, actor. Indo-American. **PERSONAL:** Born Nov 22, 1954, Dhanera, Gujarat, India; son of Prasannajit S Kothari and Pushpa P Kothari. **EDUCATION:** Bombay University, BSc; University of Maryland, MS, PhD. **CAREER:** Bell Aerospace Textron, senior development engineer, 1979-81; University of Maryland, assistant research professor, 1981-87; Astrox Corp, president, CEO, 1987-. **ORGANIZATIONS:** University of Maryland, Indian Students Association, faculty advisor, 1986-88; AIAA; Screen Actors Guild. **HONORS/AWARDS:** Government of India, National Merit Scholar, 1966. **BIOGRAPHICAL SOURCES:** India Abroad, p 18, Feb 19, 1993; News India, p 43, Feb 19, 1993; Span Magazine, December 1992. **BUSINESS ADDRESS:** President, CEO, Astrox Corp, 15825 Shady Grove Rd, Ste 50, Rockville, MD 20850, (301)948-4646.

KOUL, HIRA LAL

Educator, researcher. Indo-American. **PERSONAL:** Born May 27, 1943, Srinagar, Kashmir, India; son of Radha Krihen (Gassi) Koul & Prabhawati (Dhar) Koul (both deceased); married Shyam Pyari Fotedar, Nov 7, 1969; children: Amitav, Ajeet. **EDUCATION:** Jammu and Kashmir University, BA, 1962; Poona University, MA, 1964; University of California, Berkeley, PhD, 1967. **CAREER:** University of California, Berkeley, teaching and research assistant, 1965-67; La Trobe University, Australia, visiting fellow, 1975-76; Poona University, ISI, India, visiting professor, 1982-83; Justus Liebig University, Germany, guest professor, 1988; University of Wisconsin, visiting professor, 1989; Center for Stochastic Processes, visiting scholar, 1990; Mathematical Science Research Institute, visiting research professor, 1991; Michigan State University, assistant professor, 1968-72, associate professor, 1972-77, professor, 1977-. **HONORS/AWARDS:** Indian Mathematical Golden Jubilee Prize, First in MA in Statistics; Institute of Mathematical Statistics, fellow. **SPECIAL ACHIEVEMENTS:** Over 57 publications; numerous speaking engagements; International Statistical Institute, elected member. **HOME AD-DRESS:** 1739 Ann St, East Lansing, MI 48823. **BUSINESS ADDRESS:** Professor of Statistics, Michigan State University, A435 Wells Hall, East Lansing, MI 48823-1027, (517)353-7170.

KRIPALANI, KISHIN J.

Scientist. Indo-American. **PERSONAL:** Born Oct 3, 1937, Karachi, Sind, Pakistan; son of Jethanand Tilumal and Mulibai; married Shanu; children: Anjali, Renu. **EDUCATION:** University of Bombay, India, BSc (honors), 1957, BSc, tech, 1959; University of California, PhD, 1966. **CAREER:** Worcester Foundation, staff scientist, 1967-68, NJH fellow, 1968-69; E R Squibb & Sons, research investigator, 1969-76, senior research investigator, 1976-78, research group leader, 1978-89; Bristol-Myers Squibb, associate director, 1989-. **ORGANIZATIONS:** American Chemical Society, 1968-; American Association of Pharmaceutical Scientists, 1988-; International Society for Study Xenobiotics, 1980-; American Society for Pharmacology & Experimental Therapeutics, 1975-; New York Academy of Sciences, 1970-75. **HONORS/AWARDS:** University of Bombay, Merit Scholarship, 1957-58. **SPECIAL ACHIEVEMENTS:** Over 70 scientific publications; Drug Metabolism and Disposition Journal, editorial advisory board, 1987-90; invited speaker at Gordon Research Conference, 1975. **BUSINESS ADDRESS:** Associate Director, Bristol-Myers Squibb, PO Box 4000, Fl 3414A, Princeton, NJ 08543-4000, (609)252-4508.

KRISHEN, KUMAR

Technologist/scientist. Indo-American. **PERSONAL:** Born Jun 22, 1939, Srinagar, Jammu and Kashmir, India; son of Sri Kanth Bhat and Dhanwati Bhat; married Vijay L Krishen, Aug 6, 1961; children: Lovely K Fotedar, Sweetie, Anjala Kachroo. **EDUCATION:** Jammu & Kashmir University, BA, physics/math, 1959; Calcutta University, BTech, 1962, MTech, 1963; Kansas State University, MS, 1966, PhD, 1969. **CAREER:** Kansas State University, asst prof, elec engg, 1968-69; Lockheed Electronics Co, staff scientist and engineer, 1969-76; NASA, Johnson Space Ctr, mgr, microwave program, 1976-78, mgr, advanced microwave programs, 1978-81, coordinator, advanced programs expt systems div, 1981, mgr, advanced programs tracking & communications, 1981-88, chief technologist, NIO, 1990-; Mission Support Directorate, asst for tech & advanced programs, 1988-89; Rice University, adj prof, 1986-. **ORGANIZATIONS:** Krishen Trio Performers, coordinator, 1969-; Krishen Foundation for Arts and Sciences, founder, 1983-; Hindu Worship Soc, cofounder, pres, 1970-72, 1974, 1979-80, 1983; ICC-CL, president, 1987; NASA/JSC, Asian American Committee, chairman, 1989; Sigma Xi; Phi Kappa Phi; Eta Kappa Nu. **HONORS/AWARDS:** Calcutta University, Gold Medalist, 1963; NASA/JSC, Certificate of Commendation, 1987; Govt of India Merit Scholar, 1959-61. **SPECIAL ACHIEVEMENTS:** Articles on radar tech, robotic vision, sensing, communications, culture, and human development. **HOME ADDRESS:** 4127 Long Grove Dr, Seabrook, TX 77586, (713)326-2282.

KRISHNA, DARSHAN

Educator. Indo-American/Pakistani American. **PERSONAL:** Born May 25, 1935, Jhang, Pakistan; daughter of P D Singh and Devki Bai; married Raj Krishna, Feb 9, 1961; children: Astra, Reitu, Anamika. **EDUCATION:** University of Delhi, India, BA (honors), 1955, MA, 1957. **CAREER:** Indra Prastha College, lecturer, 1957-58; University of Delhi, tutorial fellow, 1958-60; Lady Shri Ram College, lecturer, 1960-62; Australian National University, research assistant, 1963-65, School of General Studies, lecturer, 1963; India School Inc, director, 1973-; MC School, Department Human Relations, teaching, 1990-91; India School Inc, director, 1973-; Intl Center for Language Studies and World Bank, Diplomatic Language Institute, teacher, 1989-. **ORGANIZATIONS:** Asian American Advisory, Committee of Social Studies Curriculum, Montgomery County, currently. **HONORS/AWARDS:** Association of Indians in America, award for work in education, 1980; Montgomery County, Certificate for Outstanding Service to Community, 1980; Mayor of Baltimore, Citizen Citation, 1987; DC Office of Human Rights, cultural contribution, 1988. **SPECIAL ACHIEVEMENTS:** Editor, Highlights: A Magazine of News, Views and Articles on Arts of India, 1986-; contributing editor, Calcutta Heritage, 1991; educated numerous students in languages and culture of India, 1973-; organized cultural programs in the Washington metropolitan area. **BUSINESS ADDRESS:** Director, India School, Inc, PO Box 30275, Bethesda, MD 20824, (301)654-6915.

KRISHNA, GOPAL T. K.

Engineering executive. Indo-American. **PERSONAL:** Born Feb 16, 1947, Hyderabad, Andhra Pradesh, India; son of Srinivasachariar and Rajammal; married Rajakumari Krishna, Jul 1, 1974; children: Alvin S, Dean V, Golden G. **EDUCATION:** Osmania University, India, BE, elec engineering, 1968; University of Kansas, MS, elec engineering, 1970; Drake University, MBA, 1973; Iowa State University, MS, sanitary engineering, 1982. **CAREER:** Veenstra & Kimm, design engineer, 1970-80; Krishna Engineering Consultants, Inc, president, 1980-; Simpson College, instructor, 1987-90, 1992. **ORGANIZATIONS:** Iowa Engg Soc, Central Iowa Chap, sec, 1980-81, vp, 1981-82, pres-elect, 1982-83, pres, 1983-85; Water Pollution Control Fed; Natl Soc of Professional Engineers; Iowa Water Pollution Control Assn; Assn of MBA Executives; Natl Fire Protection Assn; American Water Works Assn; Assn of Energy Engineers; American Inst of Parliamentarians; Indo-American Assn of Iowa, pres, 1993; Asian American Council of Iowa, pres, 1992-94; Republican Senatorial Trust, 1993; Republican Senatorial Inner Circle; Asian Americans for Bush-Quayle, natl vice chp; State Central Comm, Republican Party of Iowa, 1990-94; Indigent Defense Advisory Commn, chair, 1992-96. **SPECIAL ACHIEVEMENTS:** Contributor, "Writing Electrical Specifications," Electrical Construction & Maintenance, 1976; author, "Sequencing Batch Reactors for Activated Sludge Treatment," 1981; "Non-Sanitary Engineering Features Can Help Ensure a Plant's Success," Water Engineering & Management, 1987. **HOME ADDRESS:** 3901 Stonebridge Road, West Des Moines, IA 50265, (515)225-1320. **BUSINESS ADDRESS:** President, Krishna Engineering Consultants Inc, 1454 30th St, 204 W Winds, West Des Moines, IA 50266, (515)224-6300.

KRISHNA, N. RAMA

Scientist. Indo-American. **PERSONAL:** Born in Masulipatam, India. **EDUCATION:** Andhra University, India, BSc (honors), 1965, MSc, 1966; Indian Institute of Technology, Kanpur, PhD, 1972. **CAREER:** University of Alabama, Birmingham, Dept of Biochemistry, assistant professor, 1979-85, NMR Core Facility, Cancer Center, director, 1984-, Comprehensive Cancer Center, scientist, 1985-, Dept of Biochemistry, associate professor, 1985-92, professor, 1992-. **ORGANIZATIONS:** Biophysical Society, 1989-; FASEB, 1985-. **HONORS/AWARDS:** Leukemia Society of America, Scholar Award, 1982-87. **SPECIAL ACHIEVEMENTS:** Published numerous articles in peer reviewed journals on research dealing with the application of nuclear magnetic resonance to biological systems. **BUSINESS ADDRESS:** Professor, Dept of Biochemistry, University of Alabama at Birmingham, 933 South 19th Street, CH19-B31, NMR Core Facility, Birmingham, AL 35294, (205)934-5695.

KRISHNAMOORTHY, GOVINDARAJALU

Educator. Indo-American. **PERSONAL:** Born Jan 1, 1931, Thanjavur, Tamil Nadu, India; son of Krishnaswamy Govindarajalu & Sathia Bama Ammal; married Kousalya, Oct 16, 1956; children: Rama, Praba. **EDUCATION:** Illinos Institute of Technology, MS, civil engr, 1961; PhD, civil engr, 1965. **CAREER:** Illinois Institute of Technology, instructor, 1961-65, professor of civil engr, 1965-68; San Diego State University, professor of civil engr, 1968-. **ORGANIZATIONS:** ASCE, 1960-. **HONORS/AWARDS:** Chi Epsilon, 1963; Tau Beta Pi, 1964; Sigma Xi. **SPECIAL ACHIEVEMENTS:** Earthquake engineering, masonry structures, 1982-88; computer graphics, 1989-93; Computer Aided Design, 1991-94. **BUSINESS ADDRESS:** Professor of Civil Engineering, San Diego State University, San Diego, CA 92182, (619)594-6291.

KRISHNAMURTHY, GERBAIL T.

Nuclear medicine physician. Indo-American. **PERSONAL:** Born Aug 3, 1937, N R Pura, Chickmagalore Dt, Karnataka, India; son of Gerbail Thimme Gowda

and Manjamma Thimme Gowda; married Shakuntala Krishnamurthy, Dec 26, 1969; children: Anil Raj, Kalpana. **EDUCATION:** Mysore Medical College, MBBS, 1964; University of California, Los Angeles, MS, 1971. **CAREER:** Wadsworth VA Medical Center, Nuclear Medicine, staff physician, 1971-77; UCLA School of Medicine, assistant professor of medicine, 1971-77, associate professor of medicine, 1977; Oregon Health Sciences University, director of nuclear medicine, 1977-, adjunct professor of medicine, 1984-, professor of radiology, 1987-; VA Medical Center, Nuclear Medicine Service, chief, 1977-92, staff physician, 1992-. **ORGANIZATIONS:** Indo-American Society of Nuclear Medicine, president, 1985-86; UCLA Club of Oregon, president, 1992-93, VA Task Force for PET, chairman, 1990-91. **HONORS/AWARDS:** American College of Physicians, Fellowship, 1973; Nuclear Medicine Communication, London, advisory editor, 1980-87. **SPECIAL ACHIEVEMENTS:** Published 100 papers and 90 abstracts on nuclear medicine in peer reviewed journals; more than 50 presentations on nuclear medicine to national and international organizations; author of 7 book chapters. **BUSINESS ADDRESS:** Professor of Radiology, Nuclear Medicine Service (115P), VA Medical Center, PO Box 1034, Portland, OR 97207.

KRISHNAMURTI, T. N.

Educator. Indo-American. **PERSONAL:** Born Oct 1, 1942, Madras, India; son of TJ & Meena Natarajan; married Ruby Krishnamutri, Sep 23, 1969. **EDUCATION:** University of Chicago, PhD, 1960. **CAREER:** University of Chicago, research associate, 1960; University of California, Los Angeles, assistant professor, 1961-65; Florida State University, professor, 1965-. **ORGANIZATIONS:** American Meteorological Society, fellow, 1975; Royal Meteorological Society, fellow, 1963. **HONORS/AWARDS:** AMS, Rossby Medal, Highest Award, 1985, Charney Award, 2nd Highest Award, 1974. **SPECIAL ACHIEVEMENTS:** First mapping of global subtropical jet, 1961; first to propose semi-La grangian advection, 1962; first to map East-West circulations, 1971; first to define physical intialization, 1985. **BIOGRAPHICAL SOURCES:** Monsoon Meterology, Cambridge University Press, 1987; Tropical Meteorology, WMO, 1979. **BUSINESS ADDRESS:** Professor, Dept of Meteorology, Florida State University, 423 Love Bldg, Tallahassee, FL 32306, (904)644-2210.

KRISHNAN, CHIRAKKAL

Educational administrator. Indo-American. **PERSONAL:** Born 1937?, Kerala, India; children: two. **EDUCATION:** MS; PhD; SUNY at Stony Brook, post-doctoral research, 1967. **CAREER:** State University of New York at Stony Brook, Chemistry Department, professor, researcher, currently. **HONORS/AWARDS:** Disney's American Teacher Awards, American Teacher of the Year in Science, 1992; US Presidential Science Award, for teaching, 1984; Toyota Motor Sales, USA Tapestry Award. **SPECIAL ACHIEVEMENTS:** Bombay's Nuclear Research Center, among the first group of trainees; conducts summer program, providing hands-on chemistry and physics activities for 5-12 year-olds; has conducted over 200 "Magic with Chemistry" demonstrations; Special Preparations in Science and Engineering, hands-on demonstrator; Liberty Partnership, hands-on demonstrator. **BUSINESS ADDRESS:** Professor, Chemistry Dept, SUNY at Stony Brook, Stony Brook, NY 11794, (516)632-6000. *

KRISHNAN, GOPAL (P. V. GOPALAKRISHNAN)

Laboratory administrator. Indo-American. **PERSONAL:** Born Mar 15, 1935, Kancheepuram, Tamil Nadu, India; son of P V Srinivasa Raghavachari and P V Kalyani; married Prema Krishnan, Aug 30, 1967; children: Madahavan, Deepa. **EDUCATION:** Annamalai University, India, MA, 1955, MSc, 1956; University of Madras, India, PhD, 1965. **CAREER:** Jefferson Medical College, assistant professor, biochem research instructor (medicine), 1974-76; St Vincent Hospital, NY, immunologist, 1977-82; Mercy Catholic Medical Center, PA, immunology research director, 1982-92; Our Lady of Lourdes Medical Center, director, tissue-typing lab & research division, 1984-. **ORGANIZATIONS:** Mercy Catholic Medical Center, institutional review board, 1984-89; American Society of Transplant Physicians, 1986-; American Association of Histocompatibility and Immunogenetics. **HONORS/AWARDS:** American Association of Immunologists, merit travel award, 1977; WHO and St Vincent Medical Award, Italy, nominee, 1982. **SPECIAL ACHIEVEMENTS:** 36 publications on immunology, immunochemistry, cancer and transplantation, 1967-; first to propose a thesis about the involvement of B cells in graft rejection, 1989; first to propose the existence of a common tumor specific cytokine, 1983; Methods in Enzymology series, invited contributor, 1976. **BUSINESS ADDRESS:** Director of Tissue-Typing Laboratory and Research

Div, Our Lady of Lourdes Medical Center, 1565 Haddon Ave, Camden, NJ 08103, (609)757-3209.

KRISHNAN, KALLIANA R.

Engineer, general contractor. Indo-American. **PERSONAL:** Born Jun 23, 1944, Trichur, Kerala, India; son of Krishnaswamy (deceased) & Rughmaniammal (deceased); married Carol Linda, Mar 13, 1970; children: Shree Jay, Dev A. **EDUCATION:** Nagpur & Bombay University, BEE, 1966; Nova Scotia Technical College, MSEE, 1970; Golden Gate University, graduate studies, business. **CAREER:** India Institute of Technology, sr technical asst, 1966-68; Fraser Company, project engineer, 1970-72; Sandwell International Inc, electrical engineer, 1973; Crown Zellerbach, electrical project engineer/estimator, 1974-81; Kaiser Engineers, chief estimator, 1982-87; Kal Krishnan Consulting Services Inc, president/CEO, 1987-. **ORGANIZATIONS:** Institute of Electrical & Electronic Engineers; SAVE; Association of Professional Estimators. **HONORS/AWARDS:** USSBA, Minority Small Business Advocate of the Year, 1991. **SPECIAL ACHIEVEMENTS:** Author of more than 20 technical papers and articles on estimating, value engineering, and electrical engineering including: "Applying VE to Design/Build Project," Value World, Dec, 1986; "Estimating Installation of Transformers," Cost Engineering; "Optimum By-Product Power Generation Can Reduce Costs-Can We Optimize?", Pulp and Paper, Mar, 1982; "VE at Metro Rail-A Case Study," paper presented at the SAVE conference, May, 1987; conducted and participated in several seminars. **BUSINESS ADDRESS:** President/CEO, Kal Krishnan Consulting Services Inc, 334 19th St, Oakland, CA 94612, (510)465-9800.

KRISHNAN, RADHA

Educator. Indo-American. **PERSONAL:** Born Apr 12, 1959, Delhi, India; daughter of Chudamani and Krishnan; married Balaji Raghanachari, Feb 26, 1984. **EDUCATION:** Indian Institute of Technology, India, BTech, 1984; Pennsylvania State University, MS, 1989, PhD, 1992. **CAREER:** University of Maryland, assistant professor, 1992-. **ORGANIZATIONS:** IEEE/Computer, 1992-; ASME, 1992-; SPIE, 1991-. **BUSINESS ADDRESS:** Professor, Mechanical Engineering Dept, University of Maryland, Baltimore County, 5401 Wilkens Ave, 318 ECS, Catonsville, MD 21228, (410)455-3314.

KRISHNAN, SUNDARAM

Chemical engineer. Indo-American. **PERSONAL:** Born Nov 19, 1941, Bombay, India; son of Rajam Sundaram and Subbiah Sundaram; married Gita Krishnan, May 18, 1972; children: Shiva, Ram. **EDUCATION:** Boston University, PhD, 1970. **CAREER:** Raffi & Swanson, assistant director of research, 1969-. **ORGANIZATIONS:** American Chemical Society; American Rubber Group; Plastics Engineering Society. **SPECIAL ACHIEVEMENTS:** Several patents. **HOME ADDRESS:** 5 Brookbridge Rd, Stoneham, MA 02180-1345.

KRISHNASWAMY, RUKMINI

Educator (retired), health food manufacturer. Indo-American. **PERSONAL:** Born Apr 13, 1922, Tinnevelly, Madras, India; daughter of P Ramaseshan and Mary; married R Krishnaswamy, Jun 8, 1950 (deceased); children: Ramachandran, Premachandran Krish. **EDUCATION:** Madras University, India, BA, 1942, MA, 1945; Iowa State University, MA, 1949, PhD, 1950. **CAREER:** Federal Govt of India, Bureau of Textbook Research & Curriculum, director, 1960-64; Bombay Intl School, principal, 1965-66; Birlatrust, Girls' School, Bombay, India, principal, 1967-70; Warren, Ohio, County Children's Home, social case worker, 1971-72; Kent State University, assistant professor, psychology, 1971-72; Madras Specialties, president, 1986-. **ORGANIZATIONS:** Phi Beta Lambda. **SPECIAL ACHIEVEMENTS:** Started Chanda Mama, the most widely-circulated children's magazine, 1946; wrote school & college textbooks for Madras State, India, 1945-47; as curriculum director, produced the curriculum for schools in Free India, curriculum now in use in India, 1962. **HOME ADDRESS:** 845 Archwood Place, Altadena, CA 91001, (818)794-8619.

KRIST, ELIZABETH CHENG

Photography editor. Chinese American. **PERSONAL:** Born Jan 26, 1957, St Louis, MO; daughter of William Cheng and Chuan-Huan Cheng; married Gary Krist, Oct 2, 1983; children: Anna Chang-yi. **EDUCATION:** Princeton University, AB (cum laude), 1979. **CAREER:** Visual Education Corp, associate producer, 1979; Harper & Row, production assistant, 1980; The Asia Society, photo editor, 1980-82; Fortune, assistant picture editor, 1982-. **ORGANIZATIONS:** Asian American Journalists Association, 1988-; In Touch Networks, reader, 1988-91; Phelps Hospice, volunteer, 1994-. **HONORS/AWARDS:**

Princeton University, National Merit Scholar, 1975; White House Presidential Scholar, 1975. **SPECIAL ACHIEVEMENTS:** Images edited, American Photography Annual, 1993. **BUSINESS ADDRESS:** Assistant Picture Editor, Fortune Magazine, 1271 Sixth Ave, Rockefeller Center, Time & Life Bldg, 16th Fl, New York, NY 10020, (212)522-3506.

KSHIRSAGAR, ANANT M.

Educator. Indo-American. **PERSONAL:** Born Aug 16, 1931, Satara, Maharashtra, India; son of Madhav K & Satyabhama Kshirsagar; married Achala, Jul 5, 1957; children: Rahul, Amit. **EDUCATION:** University of Bombay, India, BSc, 1948, MSc, 1951; University of Manchester, England, PhD, 1961, DSc, 1972. **CAREER:** Bombay University, assistant professor, 1951-63; Government of India, Defence Ministry, senior scientific officer, 1963-68; Southern Methodist University, associate professor, 1968-71; Texas A&M University, professor, 1971-77; University of Michigan, professor, 1977-. **ORGANIZATIONS:** American Statistical Association, fellow; Institute of Math Statistics, fellow; Indian Statistical Association, life member; International Statistics Association. **SPECIAL ACHIEVEMENTS:** Author, Multivariate Analysis; A Course in Linear Models; approximately 85 research publications in reputed statistical journals; associate editor of Communications in Statistics, Journal of Indian Statistical Association, American Statistician, Letters in Probability and Statistics. **HOME ADDRESS:** 1125 Morehead, Ann Arbor, MI 48103, (313)995-1711. **BUSINESS ADDRESS:** Professor, Biostatistics Dept, University of Michigan (SPH-II), 109 S Observatory, Ann Arbor, MI 48109-2029, (313)936-1008.

KU, DAVID NELSON

Educator, physician. Chinese American. **PERSONAL:** Born Mar 15, 1956, St Louis, MO; son of N T Nelson Ku and P T Patricia Ku; married. **EDUCATION:** Harvard University, AB, 1978; Emory School of Medicine, MS, 1984; Georgia Institute of Technology, PhD, 1983. **CAREER:** University of Chicago, surgical resident, 1984-86; Georgia Institute of Technology, professor of mechanical engineering, 1986-; Emory University, professor of surgery, 1986-. **ORGANIZATIONS:** American Society of Mechanical Engineers, 1986-; American College of Angiology, fellow, 1987-; American Medical Association, 1984-. **HONORS/AWARDS:** American Society Mechanical Engineers, Y C Fung Award, 1959; National Science Foundation, Presidential Young Investigator Award, 1987; Fulbright Fellow, Germany, 1985. **SPECIAL ACHIEVEMENTS:** Over 50 publications in the area of hemodynamics and atherosclerosis. **BIOGRAPHICAL SOURCES:** Newton Magazine; American Heart Association. **BUSINESS ADDRESS:** Professor, Georgia Institute of Technology, School of Mechanical Engineering, SST 313A, Atlanta, GA 30332-0405, (404)894-6827.

KU, MEI-CHIN HSIAO

Educator. Taiwanese American. **PERSONAL:** Born Nov 1, 1937, Taiwan; daughter of Chi-Chung Hsiao and Chow-Men Hsiao; married Hsu-Tung Ku, Jun 1964; children: Li-Ru, Wen-Cheng. **EDUCATION:** National Taiwan Normal University, BS, 1961; Syracuse University, MS, 1964; Tulane University, PhD, 1967. **CAREER:** University of Massachusetts, assistant professor, 1970-76, associate professor, 1976-82, professor, 1982-. **ORGANIZATIONS:** The Mathematical Association of America, 1967-. **HONORS/AWARDS:** NSF Grant, 1971. **SPECIAL ACHIEVEMENTS:** 40 articles have been published in various journals, 1967-92; Lecture Notes in Mathematical Sciences, by Hsu-Tung Ku & Mei-Chin Ku; Vector Bundles, Connections, Minimal Submanifolds & Gauge Theory, 76 pages, 1986. **BUSINESS ADDRESS:** Professor, Dept of Mathematics & Statistics, University of Massachusetts, Amherst, MA 01003, (413)545-2857.

KU, PETER

Educational administrator. Taiwanese American. **PERSONAL:** Born Apr 8, 1938. **EDUCATION:** Chung-Hsing University, Taiwan, bachelor's degree, law, 1960; East Carolina University, MA, educational administration; University of Minnesota, MLS; Duke University, PhD, educational administration, 1972. **CAREER:** Howard Community College, vice president and dean of instruction, 1974-90; North Seattle Community College, president, 1990-. **ORGANIZATIONS:** Seattle Community College District, vice chancellor, 1992-; Chinese American Assn of Professionals, board; Chong Wah Benevolent Assn, board; American Assn of Community and Junior Colleges; Fred Hutchinson Cancer Research Center, elected to board of trustees, 1992-. **SPECIAL ACHIEVEMENTS:** First Asian American president of a community college in Washington state. **BUSINESS ADDRESS:** President, North

Seattle Community College, 9600 College Way North, Seattle, WA 98103, (206)527-3600. *

KU, WEN-CHI
Engineer. Chinese American. **PERSONAL:** Born May 18, 1942, Hunan, China; son of S K Ku and L F Ku; married Gloria Ku, Aug 2, 1969. **EDUCATION:** National Cheng Kung University, Taiwan, BS, 1964; Harvard University, MS, 1967; University of Massachusetts, Amherst, PhD, 1975. **CAREER:** Whitman & Howard, Boston, sanitary engineer, 1967-69; Dufresne-Henry Engineering Corporation, department head, 1974-78; Indiana University-Purdue University at Indianapolis, adjunct faculty, 1989-92; HNTB Corporation, senior project manager, 1978-. **ORGANIZATIONS:** Indianapolis Association of Chinese-Americans, president, 1986, 1988; Overseas Chinese Environmental Engineers and Scientists Association, president, 1987-88; Nationalities Council of Indiana Inc, president, 1992; Indiana Chinese Professionals Association, president, 1993; Water Pollution Control Federation, research committee, 1974-75; Water Environment Federation, 1968-; American Academy of Environmental Engineers, diplomate, 1988-. **HONORS/AWARDS:** Overseas Chinese Environmental Engineers & Scientists Association, Outstanding Environmental Service Award, 1990. **SPECIAL ACHIEVEMENTS:** Author, Handbook for Sewer System Evaluation and Rehabilitation, a technical manual prepared for the US Environmental Protection Agency, 1975; over ten technical papers published in the Journal of Water Pollution Control Federation and Water Research or presented to annual conferences of the Water Pollution Control Federation and the Indiana Water Pollution Control Association. **HOME ADDRESS:** 3768 Canterbury Court, Carmel, IN 46033, (317)846-0136.

KU, WILLIAM H.
Bank executive. Taiwanese American. **PERSONAL:** Born Sep 9, 1950, Taiwan; son of Yun C Ku and Sau C Ku; married Miriam, Jun 11, 1988; children: David, Stephanie. **EDUCATION:** Massachusetts Institute of Technology, SB, 1972, SM, 1972; Columbia University, MPhil, 1974, PhD, 1976. **CAREER:** Columbia University, assistant professor of physics, senior research, 1976-87; Citicorp Mortgage, vice president, 1987-. **HOME ADDRESS:** 2208 Joyceridge Ct, Chesterfield, MO 63017.

KUAN, DAVID A. (AH-SENG)
Librarian. Malaysian American/Chinese American. **PERSONAL:** Born Aug 22, 1940, Kuching, Sarawak, Malaysia; son of Ping Hua Kuan and Suat Boi Lo; married Mary N Kuan; children: Caroline L, Dana O. **EDUCATION:** National Cheng Chi University, BA, 1968; Atlanta University, MLS, 1971. **CAREER:** Morgan State University, head cataloger, 1972-. **ORGANIZATIONS:** American Library Association; Library Resources & Technical Services; Maryland Library Association. **HOME ADDRESS:** 504 Goucher Blvd, Baltimore, MD 21286, (410)825-2716. **BUSINESS PHONE:** (410)319-3457.

KUAN, JENNY W.
Librarian. Chinese American. **PERSONAL:** Born Mar 29, 1944, Shao-Yung, Hunan, China; daughter of Ping-Fan Mo and Mu-Ping Wu; married Hu Kuan, Mar 27, 1971; children: Christine, Debora. **EDUCATION:** Soochow University, Taiwan, BA, 1965; Brigham Young University, MLS, 1968. **CAREER:** Utah Tech College, asst libn, 1968-71; Columbus Public Library, cataloger, 1971-74; Day & Zimmermann Engineering Firm, ref libn, 1981-83; Cherry Hill Free Public Library, ref libn, 1983-. **ORGANIZATIONS:** South Jersey Chinese Community Center, president, 1993; Document Assn of New Jersey, 1989-93; New Jersey Librarian Assn, 1983-; American Library Assn, 1983-. **SPECIAL ACHIEVEMENTS:** Translator; freelance writer. **BUSINESS ADDRESS:** Reference Librarian, Cherry Hill Free Public Library, 1100 Kings Hwy N, Cherry Hill, NJ 08034, (609)429-5049.

KUAN, KAH-JIN (JEFFREY)
Educator. Chinese American. **PERSONAL:** Born Dec 7, 1957, Ipoh, Perak, Malaysia; son of Choon-Hock Kuan & Geok-Luen Ong; married Poh-Gaik Toh, May 16, 1981; children: Valene Min-Lin. **EDUCATION:** Trinity Theological College, Singapore, BTh, 1980; Southern Methodist University, MTS, 1986; Emory University, PhD, 1993. **CAREER:** The Methodist Church in Malaysia, assistant minister, 1980-83; Candler School of Theology, part-time instructor, 1989-91; Pacific School of Religion, assistant professor, 1991-. **ORGANIZATIONS:** Society of Biblical Literature, 1986-; American Schools of Oriental Research, 1988-; American Academy of Religion, 1989-91; Biblical Archaeology Studies Group of Greater Atlanta, 1988-90. **HONORS/AWARDS:** Luce Foundation, Luce Faculty Grant in Asian Studies, 1992;

ASOR Southeast Region, Joseph A Callaway Award in Biblical Archaeology, 1991; Emory University, George W Woodruff Graduate Fellowship, 1986-89; Perkins School of Theology, Charles C Selecman Award in New Testament Greek, 1986, Dr and Mrs JP Bray Award in Hebrew, 1985. **SPECIAL ACHIEVEMENTS:** Co-editor, History and Interpretation: Essays in Honor of John H Hayes, 1993; author, "Was Omri a Phoenician," History and Interpretation, 1993; "Hosea 9:13 and Josephus's Antiquities IX, 277-287," PEQ, vol 123, p 103-108, 1991; with John H Hayes, "The Final Years of Samaria (730-720BC)," Biblica, vol 72, p 153-81, 1991; "Third Kingdoms 5:1 and Israelite-Tyrian Relations during the Reign of Solomon," JSOT, vol 46, p 131-46, 1990. **BUSINESS ADDRESS:** Professor, Pacific School of Religion, 1798 Scenic Ave, Berkeley, CA 94709-1323, (510)848-0528.

KUAN, SHIA SHIONG
Government official. Chinese American. **PERSONAL:** Born Oct 18, 1933, Canton, Gwongdong, China; son of Chung Liu Kuan and Gung Lin Kuan; married Juichang W Kuan; children: Nolan. **EDUCATION:** Natl Chung Hsing University, BS, 1953; West Virginia University, PhD, 1968. **CAREER:** Taiwan Sugar Crop, research leader, 1954-63; West Virginia University, research asst, 1964-86; Louisiana State University, postdoctoral fellow, 1968-70; University of New Orleans, sr research associate, 1970-80, adjunct full professor of chemistry, 1981-; Food & Drug Administration, director of research ctr, 1980-. **ORGANIZATIONS:** American Chemical Soc, 1969-; American Assn for the Advancement of Science, 1972-; Sigma Xi, 1967-; NY Academy of Science, 1973-89; AOAC, 1981-; American Ceramic Soc, 1988-; Intl Assn Milk, Food & Environmental Sanitation, 1988-; American Soc of Pharmacognosy, 1989-. **HONORS/AWARDS:** West China University of Medical Sciences, Honor Professorship, 1992. **SPECIAL ACHIEVEMENTS:** Has published 9 book chapters and 78 scientific papers in refereed journals. **HOME ADDRESS:** 3020 Transcontinental Dr, Metairie, LA 70006.

KUAN, WEI EIHN
Educator. Chinese American. **PERSONAL:** Born Mar 18, 1933, Rutong, Jiangsu, China; son of Teh-Kou Kuan & Chin-Lang Wang; married Hea ja Kim, Jul 27, 1989; children: Lisa, Jenny, Amy Juen. **EDUCATION:** National Taiwan University, BS, 1956; Marquette University, MS, 1960; University of California, PhD, 1966. **CAREER:** Michigan State University, director, professor, 1966-. **ORGANIZATIONS:** American Mathematical Society, 1965-. **BUSINESS ADDRESS:** Professor, Michigan State University, D307 Wells Hall, East Lansing, MI 48824, (517)353-8497.

KUBOTA, CAROLE ANN
Educator. Japanese American. **PERSONAL:** Born May 26, 1946, Minneapolis, MN; daughter of Noboru & Mary Koura; married Kay Kubota, Aug 4, 1968; children: Travis, Curtis. **EDUCATION:** University of Washington, BA, 1968, MEd, 1977, PhD, 1985. **CAREER:** Pacific Science Center, teacher, 1968-70, supervisor, 1970-75, field center director, 1973-75; Western Washington State University, part-time instructor, 1985; Seattle Pacific University, part-time lecturer, 1985, assistant director, Washington Jr Science and Humanities Symposium, 1985-87; Seattle University, part-time lecturer, 1985-88; University of Washington, part-time lecturer, 1985-88, Elementary Science Institute, co-director, 1987, research assistant professor, director of the Science/Mathematics Project, 1988-. **ORGANIZATIONS:** National Science Teachers Association: 1968-, local arrangements chair, 1967 regional conference in Seattle; college representative, 1989 national conference in Seattle; program chair, 1991 regional conference in Vancouver, Canada; multi-cultural science education committee, 1993; National Association for Research in Science Teaching: 1982-; Washington Science Teachers Association, 1968-; secretary, 1974; president, 1976; higher education representative, 1992; Phi Delta Kappa: 1985-; Association for the Education of Teachers of Science: 1985-. **HONORS/AWARDS:** Outstanding College Science Educator, 1993; University of Washington, fellowships, 1977, 1984; Gubernatorial Appointment to the Education Commission of the States, 1977-81. **SPECIAL ACHIEVEMENTS:** Education-Business Partnerships: Scientific Work Experience Programs, 1993; Effects of Novelty-Reducing Preparation on Exploratory Behavior and Cognitive Learning in a Science Museum Setting, Journal of Research in Science Teaching, 1989; When You're Home Alone, Pugent Power & Light Company, 1987; Puzzles and Thinking Games, Educational Insights, 1987; Effects of Novelty-Reducing Preparation on Exploratory Behavior and Cognitive Learning in a Science Museum Setting, Dissertation, 1985; Asian Activities in Science and Mathematics, 1977; Tangrams: A Conceptual Skills Development Kit, 1976; also numerous conference presentations; educational consultant to various groups & educational facilities. **BUSINESS ADDRESS:** Research Assistant

Professor, University of Washington, 122 Miller Hall DQ-12, Seattle, WA 98195-0001, (206)543-6636.

KUBOTA, GERALD K. (JERRY)
Postal service administrator. Japanese American. **CAREER:** United States Postal Service, Denver, western area manager, currently. **SPECIAL ACHIEVEMENTS:** One of the three highest-ranking Japanese Americans in the US Postal Service. **BUSINESS ADDRESS:** Western Area Manager, Processing & Dist, United States Postal Service, 1745 Stout St, Ste 1000, Denver, CO 80299-5000, (303)296-2920.*

KUBOTA, KENNETH R.
Architect. Japanese American. **PERSONAL:** Born Oct 17, 1952, Seattle, WA; son of Ted & Betty Kubota; married P Grace Kubota, Feb 16, 1986; children: Keilene Alia, Miles Douglas. **EDUCATION:** University of Washington, BA, environmental design, 1974; University of California, Berkeley, MArch, 1976. **CAREER:** Arai/Jackson, associate, 1978-88; Architects Kubota/Kato Inc PS, president, 1988-. **ORGANIZATIONS:** International Special Review District Board, vice-chair, 1992-; Wing Luke Asian Museum Board, building committee, 1982-85; Japanese Chamber of Commerce, 1992-. **SPECIAL ACHIEVEMENTS:** Project architect, Seattle Keiro Nursing Home, 1985; project architect, Nikkei Concerns Assisted Housing, 1993. **BUSINESS ADDRESS:** President, Architects Kubota/Kato Inc PS, 307 Sixth Ave S, Ste B, Seattle, WA 98104-2713, (206)623-9169.

KUBOTA, MITSURU
Educator. Japanese American. **PERSONAL:** Born Sep 25, 1932, Eleele, HI; son of Giichi Kubota and Kyono Nakashima Kubota; married Jane K Taketa, Jun 30, 1956; children: Lynne Kazue, Keith Noboru. **EDUCATION:** University of Hawaii, Manoa, BA, 1954; University of Illinois, Urbana, MS, 1957, PhD, 1960. **CAREER:** Harvey Mudd College, professor of chemistry, 1959-. **ORGANIZATIONS:** American Chemical Society, 1958-; American Association for the Advancement of Science, 1963-; Royal Society of Chemistry, fellow, 1968-; Sigma Xi, 1959-. **HONORS/AWARDS:** American Chemical Society, Research at an Undergraduate Institution, 1992; Fulbright, Advanced Research Fellow, 1973; National Science Foundation, Science Faculty Fellow, 1966, Professional Development Award, 1982; National Institutes of Health, Special Fellow, 1974. **SPECIAL ACHIEVEMENTS:** Over 45 papers in: Journal American Chemistry Society, Inorganic Chemistry, Organometallics, Journal Chemical Society, Dalton Transitions, etc. **MILITARY SERVICE:** Infantry-Army, 1st lt, 1954-56. **HOME ADDRESS:** 1033 Maryhurst Dr, Claremont, CA 91711. **BUSINESS ADDRESS:** Professor, Harvey Mudd College, 12th and Columbia, Claremont, CA 91711, (909)621-8092.

KUDO, EIGO H.
Certified public accountant. Japanese American. **PERSONAL:** Born Sep 4, 1933, Lima, Peru; son of Rokuichi Kudo and Yoshiko Kudo; married Elsa Higashide Kudo, Aug 8, 1959; children: Eimi Kudo Murata, Tami Kudo Harnish. **EDUCATION:** University of Illinois, BS, accountancy, 1961. **CAREER:** Arthur Andersen & Co, staff, manager, 1961-71; The Marmon Group, director, intl operations, 1971-74; Deloitte & Touche, manager, partner, 1975-. **ORGANIZATIONS:** Honolulu Japanese Chamber of Commerce, 1975-, board of directors, past chairman; Chamber of Commerce of Hawaii, director, 1981-, past vice chairman; Japan-America Society of Hawaii, bd of trustees, 1977-; Hawaii Economic Research Assn, board of directors, 1977-; Japan Cultural Center of Hawaii, bd of governors, 1989-; Mayor's Oahu Traffic Safety Council, 1984-85; Better Business Bureau, board of directors, 1987-88; Hawaii Society of CPA's, 1975-, standards committee, past chairman; American Institute of CPA's, 1962-. **MILITARY SERVICE:** US Army, sp-3, 1954-56; American Defense, Good Conduct, 1956. **BUSINESS ADDRESS:** Partner, Deloitte & Touche, 1132 Bishop St, Suite 1200, Honolulu, HI 96813, (808)543-0700.

KUH, ERNEST SHIU-JEN
Educator. Chinese American. **PERSONAL:** Born Oct 2, 1928, Beijing, China; son of Z Keh and T Chu; married Bettine Kuh, Aug 4, 1957; children: Anthony, Theodore. **EDUCATION:** Shanghai Jiao Tong University, 1945-47; University of Michigan, BS, elect engineering, 1949; Massachusetts Institute of Technology, SM, elect engineering, 1950; Stanford University, PhD, elect engineering, 1952. **CAREER:** Bell Telephone Laboratories, member technical staff, 1952-56; Newark College of Eng, lecturer, 1955-56; University of California, Department of EE, associate professor, 1956-62, Dept of Electrical

Engineering & CS, chair, 1968-72, College of Engineering, dean, 1973-80, professor, 1962-92, William S Floyd Jr Professor in Engineering, 1991-92, William S Floyd Jr Professor Emeritus in Engineering, 1993-. **ORGANIZATIONS:** Institute of Electrical & Electronic Engineers, fellow; American Association for the Advancement of Science, fellow; National Academy of Engineering; Academia Sinica. **HONORS/AWARDS:** University of California, Berkeley, Citation, 1993; Society of Hong Kong Scholars, 1990; IEEE, Circuits and Systems Society Award, 1988, Centennial Medal, 1984; Japan Society for Promotion of Science Award, 1981. **SPECIAL ACHIEVEMENTS:** Linear & Nonlinear Circuits, with L Chua & C Desoer, McGraw Hill, 1987; Basic Circuit Theory, with c Desoer, McGraw Hill, 1969; Theory of Linear Active Networks, with R Rohrer, Holden-Day, 1967; Principles of Circuit Synthesis, with D Pederson, McGraw Hill, 1959; over 150 papers in comuter-aided design of integrated circuits. **BUSINESS ADDRESS:** William S Floyd Jr Professor Emeritus, Dept of Electrical Engineering & Computer Sciences, University of California, Berkeley, CA 94720, (510)642-2689.

KULKARNI, ANAND K.
Educator. Indo-American. **PERSONAL:** Born Oct 18, 1946, Gokak, Karnataka, India; son of Krishnarao and Ramabai; married Vasu, Nov 23, 1971; children: Deepak. **EDUCATION:** Karnatak University, BSc, 1967, MSc, 1970; Iowa State University, MS, 1975; University of Nebraska, Lincoln, PhD, 1979. **CAREER:** Symptronics, Pune, India, assistant engineer, 1971; Alisda, Bangalore, India, junior scientific assistant, 1971-72; Iowa State University, research and teaching assistant, 1973-75; University of Nebraska-Lincoln, research assistant, 1976-78; Michigan Technological University, assistant, associate professor, 1978-. **ORGANIZATIONS:** American Vacuum Society, 1978-; IEEE, 1979-92; ISHM, 1990-92; ASM; SAE; Sigma Xi. **HONORS/AWARDS:** Society of Automotive Engineers, Ralph R Teetor Educational Award, 1986. **SPECIAL ACHIEVEMENTS:** More than 50 articles published in a variety of journals. **HOME ADDRESS:** 105 W Houghton Ave, Houghton, MI 49931, (906)482-7483. **BUSINESS ADDRESS:** Professor, Dept of Electrical Engineering, Michigan Technological University, 1400 Townsend St, Houghton, MI 49931-1295.

KULKARNI, ARUN DIGAMBAR
Educator. Indo-American. **PERSONAL:** Born Dec 14, 1947, Poona, India; son of Digambar Kulkarni and Sumati Kulkarni; married Vasanti A Kulkarni, Oct 15, 1978; children: Himani, Prathit, Shradha. **EDUCATION:** University of Poona, BE, 1969; Indian Institute of Technology, Bombay, MTech, 1973, PhD, 1978. **CAREER:** National Remote Sensing Agency, senior scientist, 1976-84; VPI & Su, research associate, 1984-85; University of Southern Mississippi, visiting professor, 1985-86; University of Texas, Tyler, assistant professor, 1986-91, associate professor, 1991-. **ORGANIZATIONS:** Association of Computer Machinery, 1986-; International Society of Neural Networks, 1991-; IEEE, 1989-. **HONORS/AWARDS:** Fulbright Fellowship Award for Postdoctoral Study, 1984. **SPECIAL ACHIEVEMENTS:** Author, Neural Networks for Image Understanding, Van Nostrand Publishing Co, New York, 1994; two chapters in books; numerous papers in journals and proceedings. **BUSINESS ADDRESS:** Associate Professor, Computer Science Dept, University of Texas at Tyler, 3900 University Blvd, Tyler, TX 75701, (903)566-7402.

KULKARNI, ARUN P.
Educator. Indo-American. **PERSONAL:** Born Dec 7, 1941, Karad, Maharashtra, India; son of P D Kulkarmi and S P Kulkarmi; married K A Kulkarmi, Jun 30, 1971; children: Arvind A, Aparna A. **EDUCATION:** University of Poona, India, BSc, 1962, MSc, 1965; Indian Agric Res Inst, India, PhD, 1969. **CAREER:** North Carolina State University, res associate, 1969-80; University of Michigan, assistant professor, 1980-87; University of South Florida, professor, 1987-, Toxicology Program, director, 1988-, Florida Toxicology Res Center, director, 1988-, environmental health sciences, coordinator, 1992-, College of Medicine, professor of neurology, 1992-, assistant dean for research, 1993-. **ORGANIZATIONS:** Society of Toxicology, 1976-; Teratology Society, US, 1989-; Entomology Society of India, 1964-. **HONORS/AWARDS:** USF, S C Johnson Distinguished Professor, 1991; COPH, USF, Outstanding Research Award, 1992, Outstanding Professor of the Year, 1991; Lindbergh Foundation, Charles A Lindbergh Research Award, 1985; Gurprasad, Gold Medal. **SPECIAL ACHIEVEMENTS:** 18 book chapters reviews; 110 peer reviewed publications; 90 abstracts; area of specialization: biochemical toxicology. **BUSINESS ADDRESS:** Assistant Dean for Research, Professor of Toxicology, College of Public Health, University of South Florida, 13201 Bruce B Downs Blvd, 1118 CPH, MDC-56, Tampa, FL 33612, (813)974-6637.

KULKARNI, DILIP
Investment banker. Indo-American. **PERSONAL:** Born Apr 19, 1950, Bombay, India; married. **EDUCATION:** BITS, India, BE, (honors), 1971; University of Wisconsin, Madison, MS, 1972, MBA, 1973. **CAREER:** Unisys, project leader, 1974-77; Touche Ross, consultant, 1977-79; Booz Allen, associate, 1979-83; Smith Barney, vice president, 1983-87; Bank of Boston, director, 1987-90, Weston Group, managing director, currently. **BUSINESS ADDRESS:** Managing Director, Weston Group, 5 Legion Rd, Weston, MA 02193, (617)899-3938.

KULKARNI, GOPAL S.
Educator. Indo-American. **PERSONAL:** Born Jun 22, 1927, Yamkanmardi, Karnataka, India; son of S R Kulkarni & R S Kulkarni; married May 25, 1951; children: Sunita Pandit, Nitin, Rajiv. **EDUCATION:** Karnataka University, BSc, 1950; Banares Hindu University, MSc, 1952; University of Pittsburgh, PhD, 1965. **CAREER:** Nowrosjee Wadia College, India, 1956-62; University of Pittsburgh, teaching fellow, 1962-64; Indiana State College, 1964-65; Gokhale Institute, India, 1966-68; Indiana University of Pennsylvania, professor, 1969-91. **ORGANIZATIONS:** Association of American Geographers, 1969-; Association for Asian Studies, 1972-; National Association of Geographers, India, 1980-; Indian Cartographic Association, 1980-. **HONORS/ AWARDS:** Fulbright Travel Award, 1962-65; IUP, Teaching Excellence, 1974, Faculty Research, 1987; AAG/Asian Specialty Group, Recognition, 1992. **SPECIAL ACHIEVEMENTS:** Teacher training seminars on India for US school/college teachers, funded by the US Department of Education, 1972, 1974, 1977, 1985, 1992. **BUSINESS ADDRESS:** Professor, Dept of Geography & Regional Planning, Indiana University of Pennsylvania, Leonard Hall, Indiana, PA 15701, (412)349-2250.

KULKARNI, KISHORE G.
Educator. Indo-American. **PERSONAL:** Born Oct 31, 1953, Pune, Maharashtra, India; son of Sindhu Dhekane & Ganesh Y Dhekane; married Jayashree, Aug 17, 1980; children: Lina, Aditi. **EDUCATION:** University of Poona, India, BA (with honors), 1974, MA, 1976; University of Pittsburgh, MA, 1978, PhD, 1982. **CAREER:** University of Pittsburgh, Johnstown, 1980-82; University of Central Arkansas, 1982-86; Northeast Louisiana University, 1986-89; University of Colorado, visiting professor, 1990-; University of Denver, GSIS, adjunct professor, 1992-; Metropolitan State College of Denver, 1989-. **ORGANIZATIONS:** American Economic Association, 1989-; Southern Economic Association, 1984-; Association of Indian Economic Studies, life member. **HONORS/AWARDS:** Forum of Free Enterprise, Bombay, first prize in essay competition, 1975; University of Poona, India, SK Shinde Prize, 1976; Metropolitan State College of Denver, Golden Key Honor Society, finalist in Outstanding Teaching Award, 1992; University of Pittsburgh, professor at Semester at Sea, spring 1994. **SPECIAL ACHIEVEMENTS:** Author of 2 books, 4 monographs, and 30 journal articles. **HOME PHONE:** (303)423-7235. **BUSINESS ADDRESS:** Professor, Dept of Economics, Metropolitan State College of Denver, PO Box 173362, Campus Box 77, Denver, CO 80217-3362, (303)556-2675.

KULKARNI, KRISHNAJI HANAMANT
Educator. Indo-American. **PERSONAL:** Born Jun 1, 1948, Hunkunti, Karnataka, India; son of Hanamant S Kulkarni and Shantabai H Kulkarni; married Usha Krishnaji Kulkarni, Jun 15, 1983; children: Nitin K, Sachin K. **EDUCATION:** Karnatak University, India, BSc, 1969, MSc, 1971, PhD, 1977; University of Alabama, Birmingham, MS, 1991. **CAREER:** Victoria Jubilee Tech Institute, India, College of Health Sciences, Bahrain, lecturer, 1978-81, senior lecturer, 1981-88; Rust College, assistant professor, 1990-. **HONORS/AWARDS:** Karnatak University, research studentship, 1972-75; University of Alabama, Birmingham, Graduate Research Assistantship, 1989-90. **SPECIAL ACHIEVEMENTS:** Transitive digraphs and topologies on a set, 1973; minimally locally 1-connected graphs, 1978; sufficient conditions for edge-locally connected and n-connected graphs, 1981; optimal parallel algorithms for finding cut vertices and bridges of interval graphs, 1992. **BUSINESS ADDRESS:** Assistant Professor, Rust College, 150 Rust Avenue, Holly Springs, MS 38635.

KULKARNI, RAVI S.
Educator. Indo-American. **PERSONAL:** Born May 22, 1942, Solapur, Maharashtra, India; widowed. **EDUCATION:** Poona University, BA, 1962; Harvard University, PhD, 1967. **CAREER:** Johns Hopkins University, assistant professor of math, 1968-73; Columbia University, assistant professor of math, 1973-76; Rutgers University, associate professor of math, 1976-77;

Indiana University, professor of math, 1977-87; CUNY, Queens College, professor of math, 1986-, Graduate School and University Center, professor of math and computer science, 1986. **ORGANIZATIONS:** American Math Society, 1965-; Math Association of America, 1970-; Maharashtra Foundation, vp, 1988-89; Society of Indian Academics in America, 1987-; Foundation for the Advancement of Arts and Sciences from India Inc, president, 1993; Institute for Advanced Study, Princeton, 1971-73, 1976, 1994; Max Planck Institut, Germany, 1970-71, 1984-86; Mittag Leffier Institut, Sweden, 1989; Intl Center for Theoretical Physics, Italy, 1993. **HONORS/AWARDS:** Guggenheim Fellowship, 1981-82; National Science Foundation Grants, 1968-, International Program Grants, 1976, 1985, 1989; PSC-CUNY, grants. **SPECIAL ACHIEVEMENTS:** Moderate proficiency in French and German; proficiency in English, Hindi, Marathi; 2 books and over 70 publications, 2 books forthcoming. **BUSINESS ADDRESS:** Professor, City University of New York, Graduate Center, 33 W 42nd St, New York, NY 10036, (212)642-2578.

KULKARNI, UDAY RAVINDRA
Educator. Indo-American. **PERSONAL:** Born May 24, 1954, Bombay, Maharashtra, India; son of Ravindra & Gulab; married Sarita, Aug 24, 1980; children: Anshula, Sanasi, Suvan. **EDUCATION:** Indian Institute of Technology, Bombay, BTech, 1977; Indian Institute of Management, Calcutta, MBA, 1979; University of Wisconsin, Milwaukee, PhD, 1989. **CAREER:** Crompton Greaves Ltd, India, finance officer, 1979-81; Asian Paints Ltd, India, finance executive, 1981-84; Arizona State University, assistant professor, 1988-. **ORGANIZATIONS:** ACM, 1987-; IEEE, 1987-. **BUSINESS ADDRESS:** Assistant Professor, DIS Dept, Arizona State University, Tempe, AZ 85287-4206, (602)965-6191.

KUMAI, MOTOI
Research physicist (retired). Japanese American. **PERSONAL:** Born Mar 22, 1920, Nagano, Nagano-ken, Japan; son of Matsunosuke Kumai and Chika Kinebuchi; married Mutsuko Yamanouchi, Oct 8, 1948; children: Keiko Ihara, Etsuko Kumai Azar. **EDUCATION:** Science University of Tokyo, BS, 1941; Hokkaido University, Japan, PhD, physics, 1957. **CAREER:** Hokkaido University, research associate, 1942-55, lecturer, 1955-58; University of Chicago, research associate, 1958-61; US Army Cold Regions Research and Engineering Laboratory, research physicist, 1961-89. **ORGANIZATIONS:** American Meteorological Society, 1953-; Sigma Xi, 1965-; Japanese Society of Snow and Ice, 1955-; International Glaciological Society, 1967-; Clay Minerals Society, 1987-. **HONORS/AWARDS:** Cold Regions Research & Engineering Laboratory, Special Act Award, 1965, 1966, 1967. **SPECIAL ACHIEVEMENTS:** Discovery of snow crystal nuclei by electron microscopy, 1951; formation and limitation of ice fog, 1969; transmission on infrared radiation in ice fog, 1973; acidity of snow and its reduction by alkaline aerosols, 1984; scanning electron microscopy of aerosol particles in Greenland deep ice cores, 1988.

KUMAR, ARVIND
Editor. Indo-American. **PERSONAL:** Born Jan 1, 1956, Varanasi, Uttar Pradesh, India; son of Mahendra Prasad & Leela Verma; married Ashok Jethanandani. **EDUCATION:** Indian Institute of Technology, Kanpur, BTech, 1979; University of Rochester, MBA, 1982. **CAREER:** Hewlett Packard, software engineer, 1982-87; India Currents, editor, 1987-. **ORGANIZATIONS:** Trikone, president, 1986-. **HONORS/AWARDS:** Federation of Indo-American Associations, Cultural Awareness through Journalism, 1991. **BIOGRAPHICAL SOURCES:** San Jose Metro, p 14, Dec 24-30, 1993; San Jose Mercury News, p 18A, Dec 31, 1993; Grand Folks Herald, ND, Focus Section, Nov 22, 1992. **BUSINESS ADDRESS:** Editor, India Currents, PO Box 21285, San Jose, CA 95151, (408)274-6966.

KUMAR, ASHIR
Physician, educator. Indo-American. **PERSONAL:** Born Mar 11, 1945, Fatehpur, Uttar Pradesh, India; son of Birj Behari Lal and Shobha Saxena; married Kusum, May 27, 1972; children: Sanjay. **EDUCATION:** All India Institute of Medical Sciences, New Delhi, MB, BS, 1966, MD, pediatrics, 1972. **CAREER:** Saint Luke's Hospital, Pediatric Infectious Disease, director, 1977-83; Case Western Reserve University, Pediatrics, assistant professor, 1977-83; Michigan State University, assistant professor of pediatrics and human development, 1983-86, associate professor of pediatrics & human development, 1986-92, professor of pediatrics and human development, 1992-. **ORGANIZATIONS:** American Society for Microbiology, 1977-; Pediatric Infectious Disease Society, 1983-; Infectious Disease Society of American, 1984-91, fellow, 1991-; American Academy of Pediatrics, fellow, 1986; Michigan Association of Physicians from India, life member, 1988-; American Association of

Physicians from India, patron member, 1989; Aiimsonians of America, life member, 1991-. **HONORS/AWARDS:** Pediatric Residency, University Teaching Award of Excellence, 1992; MSU, College of Human Medicine, Faculty Teaching Award Class of 1989; American Academy of Family Physicians, Recognition for Teaching Award, 1988; Graduate Medical Education Inc, Pediatric Residency Teaching Award, 1986; Saint Luke's Hospital, Award for Excellence in Education & Dedication to Teaching, 1983. **SPECIAL ACHIEVEMENTS:** Published several scientific articles; several clinical safety and efficacy studies with new antibiotics. **BUSINESS ADDRESS:** Professor of Pediatrics & Human Development, Michigan State University, B240 Life Sciences, East Lansing, MI 48824-1317, (517)353-3529.

KUMAR, ASHOK
Educator. Indo-American. **PERSONAL:** Born Nov 11, 1949, Delhi, India; son of Behari Lal Sharma & Shanti Sharma; married Sunita Kumar, Feb 4, 1976; children: Amita, Anupam. **EDUCATION:** University of Delhi, BS, mathematics, 1969, MS, mathematics, 1971, PhD, mathematics, 1979; Ball State University, MS, computers, 1983. **CAREER:** Delhi University, assistant professor, 1973-81; Ball State University, assistant professor, 1982-83; University of Scranton, assistant professor, 1983-89; Allentown College, assistant professor, 1989-. **ORGANIZATIONS:** SIGCSE; ACM; SCSCCC; Indian Mathematics Society; Indian Science Congress; Upsilon Pi Upsilon, 1985. **SPECIAL ACHIEVEMENTS:** Fixed Point Theory, 1972-82; Programming Languages, 1988. **HOME ADDRESS:** 4329 Schaller Dr, Allentown, PA 18104. **BUSINESS ADDRESS:** Assistant Professor, Allentown College of Saint Francis Desales, 2755 Station Ave, Center Valley, PA 18034-9565, (215)282-1100.

KUMAR, ASHOK
Educator. Indo-American. **PERSONAL:** Born Aug 28, 1949, Aligarh, Uttar Pradesh, India; son of C B Agarwal and Uma Vati; married Meera Agarwal; children: Vikas Agarwal. **EDUCATION:** Aligarh Muslim University, India, BSc (with honors), eng, 1970; University of Ottawa, Canada, MS, 1972; University of Waterloo, Canada, PhD, 1977. **CAREER:** University of Calgary, assistant analyst, 1973-74; Syncrude Canada Ltd, atmospheric physicist, 1977-80; University of Toledo, professor, 1980-. **ORGANIZATIONS:** Air and Waste Management Association, Higher Education Division, chairman, 1993-; Journal of Hazardous Material, editorial board, 1992-; Environmental Progress, AIChE, software reviews, editor, 1988-. **HONORS/AWARDS:** Professional Engineer, Alberta; DEE, American Academy of Environmental Engineers. **BUSINESS ADDRESS:** Professor, Dept of Civil Engineering, University of Toledo, Toledo, OH 43606-3390, (419)537-2312.

KUMAR, ATUL
Educator, educational administrator. Indo-American. **PERSONAL:** Born Jun 1, 1962, Muzaffarnagar, Uttar Pradesh, India; son of Virendra Singhal and Mridul Singhal (deceased); married Maya Nair, May 17, 1993. **EDUCATION:** Meerut University, India, BS, 1981, MS, 1985; North Central College, MS, 1988; Tulane University, pursuing PhD, currently. **CAREER:** Regional Rural Bank, India, officer, manager, 1985-86; Xavier University, instructor, computer science, 1988-90, chairperson, instructor, computer science, 1990-. **ORGANIZATIONS:** Association of Computing Machinery, 1989-. **BUSINESS ADDRESS:** Chair, Computer Science Dept, Xavier University of Louisiana, 7325 Palmetto St, New Orleans, LA 70125-1056, (504)483-7456.

KUMAR, DEVENDRA
Educator, researcher. Indo-American. **PERSONAL:** Born Sep 14, 1944, Delhi, India; son of Badri Narayan Singh (deceased) and Janki Devi; married Usha Srivastava, Nov 20, 1969; children: Ajay Kumar. **EDUCATION:** University of Delhi, India, physics, BS (honors), 1963, MS, 1965, PhD, 1976. **CAREER:** Kirori Mal College, University of Delhi, assistant lecturer, physics, 1965-68, lecturer, physics, 1968-78; Louisiana State University, postdoctoral research associate, 1978-85, assistant professor-research, chemistry, 1986-91, associate professor-research, chemistry, 1991-. **ORGANIZATIONS:** Institute of Electrical and Electronics Engineers, senior member; Optical Society of America; American Chemical Society. **HONORS/AWARDS:** Department of Energy Research Grantee, 1985. **SPECIAL ACHIEVEMENTS:** Published 30 research papers on laser optogalvanic, photoacoustic and microwave spectroscopy; US patent on analysis of radiofrequency discharges in plasma. **BUSINESS ADDRESS:** Assoc Professor, Dept of Chemistry, Louisiana State University, Baton Rouge, LA 70803, (504)388-2945.

KUMAR, JATINDER
Energy consultant. Indo-American. **PERSONAL:** Born Dec 10, 1940, Rawaldindi, Punjab, Pakistan; son of Makhan Lal & Sushila Devi; married Vijaya Kumar, Jul 24, 1970; children: Varun, Ruchi. **EDUCATION:** Indian School of Mines, BS, BTech, 1963; French Petroleum Institute, MS, 1966; University of California, Berkeley, MS, 1967. **CAREER:** Oil & Natural Gas Commission, senior technical assistant, 1963; Oil India Ltd, engineer, 1964; Indian Standards Institute, extra assistant director, 1964-65; Standard Oil of California, engineer, 1967-69; Pacific Gas & Electric Co, project engineer, 1969-72; Associated Regulatory Consultants Inc, vice president, 1972-80; Economic & Technical Consultants, president, 1981-. **ORGANIZATIONS:** Society of Petroleum Engineers, senior member; American Society of Mechanical Engineers, senior member; National Association of Accountants; Friends of India Society International, president; Vishwa Hindu Parishad, executive committee; India Development Relief Fund, founding member. **HONORS/AWARDS:** French Petroleum Institute, fellowship, 1965-66. **SPECIAL ACHIEVEMENTS:** Testified as expert witness in about 200 cases involving public utilities and energy companies before 24 jurisdictions and courts around the country. **BUSINESS ADDRESS:** President, Economic & Technical Consultants Inc, 6241 Executive Blvd, Rockville, MD 20852, (301)984-7050.

KUMAR, JOTHI V.
Educator. Indo-American. **PERSONAL:** Born in Kattumannar Koil, Tamil Nadu, India; daughter of Mrs & Mr S V Ramasamy; married Vijaya Kumar, May 26, 1978; children: Madhu S. **EDUCATION:** Annamalai University, BS, 1968; Kansas State University, PhD, 1975. **CAREER:** US EPA, contractor, 1990, senior environ specialist, 1988-89, faculty fellow, 1987; US Dept of Energy, faculty intern, 1986; North Carolina A&T State University, professor, 1975-. **ORGANIZATIONS:** American Institute of Chemists, fellow, 1987-; Phi Lambda Upsilon, 1973-; NC Institute of Chemists, president-elect, 1993-95; NC Academy of Science, 1980-, vice president, 1991; International Lioness Club, 1981-; Guilford County Environmental Coaliton, 1992-; League of Women Voters, 1988-; Guilford County Local Emergency Planning Board, 1987-. **HONORS/AWARDS:** CIES, Fulbright Fellow, 1991-92; AIC, Certified Professional Chemist, 1987-; Govt of India, National Merit Scholarship, 1965-66; NC A&T State University, Outstanding Faculty, 1991-92; Chemistry Graduate Committee, Advisor of the Year, 1979. **SPECIAL ACHIEVEMENTS:** Fulbright lecture tour to India, 1991-92; Bioconversion of Food Wastes to Alcohol, 1989-90; Waste Management through Alcohol Production, 1991-92; Biopolymers from Food Wastes, 1992-93; Sampling and Analysis of Air Toxics, 1989-90. **BUSINESS ADDRESS:** Professor, North Carolina A&T State University, 1601 E Market St, Hines Hall, Greensboro, NC 27411, (919)334-7601.

KUMAR, KAMALESH
Educator. Indo-American. **PERSONAL:** Born Jul 18, 1957, Muzafarpore, Bihar, India; son of R B Mishra & Sharda Mishra; married Chitra Kumar, Nov 28, 1979; children: Rishtee Shekhar. **EDUCATION:** Patna College, India, BA, English honors, 1977; Missouri So St College, BS, 1985; University of North Texas, MBA, 1987, PhD, 1990. **CAREER:** Steel Authority of India, assistant personnel manager, 1979-84; University of North Texas, lecturer, 1989; Arkansas State University, assistant professor, 1990-93; University of Michigan, Dearborn, associate professor, 1993-. **ORGANIZATIONS:** Academy of Management, 1988-93; Southern Management Association, 1988-92; International Academy of Business Disciplines, 1991-93. **HONORS/AWARDS:** Richard D Irwin & Southern Management Association, Best Research Award, 1992; Arkansas State University, Outstanding Scholar, 1992. **SPECIAL ACHIEVEMENTS:** 35 papers presented in national and international conferences; 10 research articles in journals including: Academy of Management Journal, Journal of Applied Psychology. **BIOGRAPHICAL SOURCES:** Academy of Management Journal, June 1993; Journal of Applied Psychology, December 1991. **HOME ADDRESS:** 15602 Middlebury Dr, Dearborn, MI 48120, (313)240-6217. **BUSINESS ADDRESS:** Associate Professor of Management, School of Management, University of Michigan-Dearborn, 4901 Evergreen, Dearborn, MI 48128, (313)593-5214.

KUMAR, KUSUM
Physician. Indo-American. **PERSONAL:** Born Aug 27, 1949, India; married Ashir Kumar; children: Sanjay. **EDUCATION:** All India Institute of Medical Sciences, MBBS, 1971. **CAREER:** Michigan State University, professor, currently. **ORGANIZATIONS:** Member of several professional and community organizations. **HONORS/AWARDS:** AIIMSONIANS of America, Distinguished Alumnus Award, 1992; NIH Award, for research work on Brain

Ischemia, 5 years; several teaching awards. **SPECIAL ACHIEVEMENTS:** Several publications in the following areas: neuroscience; pathology education, especially computer assisted medical education. **HOME ADDRESS:** 3885 Highwood Place, Okemos, MI 48864.

KUMAR, KUSUM VERMA
Educator. Indo-American. **PERSONAL:** Born Nov 18, 1930, Chhindwara, Madhya Pradesh, India; daughter of R N Verma and Raj Pyari Verma; married Gobind Jay Kumar, Jun 13, 1966; children: Arvind. **EDUCATION:** Science College, Nagpur, India, BSc, 1950, MSc, 1952; Vikram University, India, PhD, 1963. **CAREER:** Kamla Raja Girls' College, assistant professor, biology department, head, 1954-63; University of Iowa, postdoctoral fellow, 1963-66; Tennessee Technological University, instructor, 1966-69; Vanderbilt University, research associate, 1969-76; Meharry Medical College, assistant professor, 1976-. **HONORS/AWARDS:** IIE, Fulbright travel grant, 1963. **SPECIAL ACHIEVEMENTS:** 14 papers published; two articles in Vishva International Hindi Magazine; In "Cyclic Nucleotides," Dowden, Huntingson, Ross, 1976; "Initiation of DNA Synthesis," Nature, 239:90, pp 74-76, 1972; "Regional Differences in Skin Gland Differentiation," Journ Morph Phil, 117, 1965; Notes on the Anatomy of Indian Tree Shrew, Mammalia, Paris, 29-3, 1965; "The Hybrid Region of Ind Hedgehogs," Ann Mag Nat Hist, London, 13:1, 1958. **HOME ADDRESS:** 930 Downey Drive, Nashville, TN 37205.

KUMAR, MEERA
Educator. **PERSONAL:** Born Dec 12, Fatehpur, Uttar Pradesh, India; daughter of R N Bakshi and Suniti Bakshi; married Vinod Kumar, Jan 24; children: Vishesh, Viraaj. **EDUCATION:** Convent of Jesus & Mary, ISC; Delhi University, BA (honors), MA; Meerut University, PhD. **CAREER:** University of Delhi, lecturer; San Diego Community District College, assistant professor, currently. **BUSINESS ADDRESS:** Asst Professor, English, San Diego Mesa College, 7250 Mesa College Dr, San Diego, CA 92111-4902.

KUMAR, MYTHILI
Dance company executive. Indo-American. **PERSONAL:** Born Apr 10, 1954. **CAREER:** Abhinaya Dance Company, Dussera dance presentation, director, "Festival of Dussehra," artistic director. **ORGANIZATIONS:** Served on arts councils for the state of California. **HONORS/AWARDS:** National Endowment of Arts, fellowship, 1989-94; City of Cupertino's Distinguished Artist Award, 1993; Rockefeller Foundation Award, 1991. **BUSINESS ADDRESS:** Artistic Director, Abhinaya Dance Co, 476 Park Ave, San Jose, CA 95110, (408)993-9231.*

KUMAR, NARINDER M.
Association executive. Indo-American. **CAREER:** Endocrinologist, currently. **ORGANIZATIONS:** Association of Indians in America, president, currently. **BUSINESS ADDRESS:** Physician, 68-15 Central Ave, Glendale, NY 11385, (718)497-0060. *

KUMAR, PANGANAMALA RAMANA
Educator. Indo-American. **PERSONAL:** Born Apr 21, 1952, Nagpur, India; son of Panganamala Bhavanarayana Murthy and Panganamala Kamala Murthy; married Panganamala Jayashree Kumar, Jan 22, 1982; children: Panganamala Ashwin, Shilpa Panganamala. **EDUCATION:** Indian Institute of Technology, BTech, 1973; Washington University, MS, 1975, DSc, 1977. **CAREER:** University of Illinois, professor of electrical & computer engineering, 1987-. **HONORS/AWARDS:** Institute of Electrical and Electronics Engineers, fellow, 1988; American Automatic Control Council, Donald P Eckman Award, 1985. **SPECIAL ACHIEVEMENTS:** Published book, several research articles in journals, numerous book chapters, 1977-. **BUSINESS ADDRESS:** Professor, Coordinated Science Lab, University of Illinois, 1308 W Main St, Urbana, IL 61801, (217)333-7476.

KUMAR, PRASANNA K.
Educator, physician. Indo-American. **PERSONAL:** Born Oct 23, 1937, Bangalore, India; son of V S Krishna Murthy and Nagarathna Krishna Murthy; married Savitri Kumar, Aug 22, 1971; children: Mona, Pratima. **EDUCATION:** Mysore University, Bangalore, India, BS (honors), 1958, MSc, 1959; Temple University, Philadelphia, PA, MA, 1967, PhD, 1973. **CAREER:** University of Pennsylvania, research fellow, Med Physics, 1980-82, assistant professor of Physics, 1982-86; William Beaumont Hospital, director of clinical physics, 1986-90; Flower Memorial Hospital, dir of med physics, director, 1990-92; Temple University Hospital, chief of physics, 1992-. **SPECIAL ACHIEVEMENTS:** Publications in physics journals, 1969-88. **BUSINESS**

ADDRESS: Chief of Physics, Dept of Radiation Oncology, Temple University Hospital, 3401 N Broad St, Philadelphia, PA 19140, (215)221-2085.

KUMAR, PREM
Writer, editor. Indo-American. **PERSONAL:** Born Jan 3, 1945, Amritsar, Punjab, India; son of Harbans Lal Sharma and Raj Rani Sharma; married Swarn Kumar, Jul 6, 1970; children: Rashmi. **EDUCATION:** Panjab University, India, BA, 1966, MA, 1968; University of Idaho, Moscow, MAT, 1973; Washington State University, WA, PhD, 1978. **CAREER:** Washington State University, assistant professor, 1978-81; University of Miami, assistant professor, 1982-83; Colorado State University, visiting assistant professor, 1983-84; The Boeing Co, author, editor, 1986-. **ORGANIZATIONS:** Society for Technical Communications, senior member, 1992-; India Association of Western Washington, vp, 1993-94, president, 1994-. **HONORS/AWARDS:** Boeing Computer Services, Outstanding Performance, 1989. **SPECIAL ACHIEVEMENTS:** Published two collections of poems; articles in literary journals; poems, stories, translations in English.

KUMAR, RAJ
Educator. Indo-American. **PERSONAL:** Born Jun 30, 1932, Bijnor, Uttar Pradesh, India; son of Bishan Kumar & Shivrani; married Priti Kumar, Nov 17, 1959; children: Anuradha. **EDUCATION:** Agra University, India, MS, 1953; Government Central Pedagogical Institute, India, MEd, 1955; Kent State University, MA, 1971; Ohio University, PhD, 1989. **CAREER:** All India Radio, program executive, 1958-69; Boise State University, assistant professor, 1973-74; Weber State University, assistant professor, 1972-73, associate professor, 1974-. **ORGANIZATIONS:** Broadcast Education Association, chairman, 1991-92; Phi Kappa Phi, Chapter 119, International Div, president, 1989-90. **HONORS/AWARDS:** Weber State University, Hemingway Research Grant, Europe, 1990, research grant, China, 1992. **SPECIAL ACHIEVEMENTS:** Proficiency in Hindi & Urdu languages; publication in Phi Kappa Phi Newsletter, 1992. **HOME ADDRESS:** 812 Cassie Drive, Ogden, UT 84405, (801)479-4146.

KUMAR, RAM SAKTHI
Marketing and sales executive. Indo-American. **PERSONAL:** Born Jun 29, 1959, Madras, India; son of Sinnathamby Ramaswamy and Pavammal Ramaswamy; married Tamilarasi Kumar, Jul 6, 1987; children: Karthik Ashwin. **EDUCATION:** University of Madras, BSEE, 1981; Marquette University, MSEE, 1985; University of San Diego, MBA, 1990. **CAREER:** IBM Corp, associate engr, 1983-86, sr associate engr, 1986-88, account marketing rep, 1988-91, advisory marketing rep, 1991-. **ORGANIZATIONS:** United Way, corporate volunteer, 1984, 1988. **HONORS/AWARDS:** Beta Gamma Sigma, 1991. **SPECIAL ACHIEVEMENTS:** Designer, developer: marketing control book, 1992. **BUSINESS ADDRESS:** Advisory Marketing Specialist, IBM Corp, 8845 University Center Ln, San Diego, CA 92122, (619)587-5327.

KUMAR, RAMESH
Educator, educational administrator. Indo-American. **PERSONAL:** Born Jun 19, 1949, Moga, Punjab, India; married Kusam, 1975; children: Anjuli, Ajay, Sunjay. **EDUCATION:** Punjab Agricultural University, Ludhiana, India, BSc, 1970; University of California, Davis, MS, 1975, PhD, 1978. **CAREER:** Punjab Agricultural University, India, research assistant, 1970-73; University of California, Davis, research engineer, 1973-79; California State Polytechnic University, Pomona, professor & chair, 1980-. **ORGANIZATIONS:** American Society of Agricultural Engineers, 1974-; American Society of Engineering Education, 1978-; Sigma Xi, 1977-. **SPECIAL ACHIEVEMENTS:** Published a number of various technical papers; language proficiency, Hindi, Punjab, and Urdu. **BUSINESS ADDRESS:** Professor and Chair, Agricultural Engineering, California State Poly University, 3801 W Temple Ave, Pomona, CA 91768-2557, (909)869-2085.

KUMAR, RANGANATHAN
Educator. Indo-American. **PERSONAL:** Born Jul 17, 1954, Kumbakonam, India; son of V Ranganathan and Ambuja Ranganathan; married Geeta, Dec 14, 1980; children: Nikhil. **EDUCATION:** University of Madras, BS, 1973; Madras Institute of Technology, BTech, 1976; Georgia Institute of Technology, MS, 1978; University of Illinois at Urbana-Champaign, PhD, 1983. **CAREER:** Clemson University, assistant professor, 1983-91, associate professor, 1991-. **HONORS/AWARDS:** Clemson University, Byars' Prize for Teaching Excellence, 1985. **SPECIAL ACHIEVEMENTS:** Numerous technical articles in journals such as Heat Transfer. **BUSINESS ADDRESS:** Assoc Prof, Dept of

Mechanical Engineering, Clemson University, 321 A Riggs Hall, Clemson, SC 29631.

KUMAR, ROMESH
Chemical engineer. Indo-American. **PERSONAL:** Born Oct 18, 1944, Rajpura, Punjab, India; son of Sh Kundan Lal and Smt Pushpa Wati; married Kumkum Kumar, Feb 22, 1976; children: Rahul, Ritu. **EDUCATION:** Panjab University, Chandigarh, India, BS, 1965; University of California, Berkeley, MS, 1968, PhD, 1972. **CAREER:** Argonne National Laboratory, group leader, 1972. **ORGANIZATIONS:** American Institute of Chemical Engineers, 1974. **HONORS/AWARDS:** Panjab University, Silver Medal, 1965. **SPECIAL ACHIEVEMENTS:** Author or co-author of about 80 publications, 1968-; 6 patents and 25 technical presentations. **HOME ADDRESS:** 1549 Ceals Ct, Naperville, IL 60565, (708)355-5107. **BUSINESS ADDRESS:** Group Leader, Argonne National Laboratory, Chemical Technology Division, 9700 South Cass Ave, Bldg 205, Argonne, IL 60439-4837, (708)252-4342.

KUMAR, SARAN KANDAKURI
Scientist. Indo-American. **PERSONAL:** Born Jun 13, 1953, Hyderabad, Andhra Pradesh, India; son of L Venkatratnam and V Sarojini Ratnam; married Indira, Sep 12, 1979; children: Navin, Sonia. **EDUCATION:** BITS, Pilani, India, BS, pharmacy, 1975; Pharmaceutical Sciences, UK, Wales, MS, 1977; Industrial Pharmacy, St John's, NY, PhD, 1986. **CAREER:** Ahmadu Bello University, Nigeria, lecturer, 1977-82; St John's University, NY, teaching fellow, 1982-86; Hoffmann-La Roche Inc, research investigator, 1986-. **ORGANIZATIONS:** AAAS, 1986-; AAPS, 1985-; Controlled Rel Society, 1987-. **HONORS/AWARDS:** Rho Chi. **SPECIAL ACHIEVEMENTS:** Several scientific publications. **HOME ADDRESS:** 720 Mill St, G-5, Belleville, NJ 07109, (201)450-0870.

KUMAR, SATYENDRA
Educator. Indo-American. **PERSONAL:** Born Oct 22, 1954, Rasoolpur, Uttar Pradesh, India; son of Asharam Numberdar and Khazani Devi; married Sadhna Kumar, Jan 12, 1986; children: Paurav. **EDUCATION:** Panjab University, BS, 1973, (honors school), MS, Physics, 1974; University of Nebraska, MS, 1975; University of Illinois, PhD, 1981. **CAREER:** Massachusetts Institute of Technology, research associate, 1981-84; Tektronix Incorporated, senior physicist, 1984-87; Kent State University, associate professor of physics, 1987-. **ORGANIZATIONS:** American Physical Society; India Physics Association. **SPECIAL ACHIEVEMENTS:** Author of numerous research publications; World Scientific Publications Inc, editorial board. **BUSINESS ADDRESS:** Associate Professor, Dept of Physics, Kent State University, Kent, OH 44242, (216)672-2566.

KUMAR, SUDHIR (SUD)
Educator, engineer. Indo-American. **PERSONAL:** Born Oct 31, 1933, Saharanpur, Uttar Pradesh, India; son of D Raj & Raj Dulari; married Jyotsna K Kumar, Dec 18, 1960; children: Nisha R, S Raj, Anita R. **EDUCATION:** Agra University, BS, 1950, MA, 1952; Indian Institute of Science, MS, 1955; Pennsylvania State University, PhD, 1958. **CAREER:** Duke University, adjunct lecturer through associate professor, 1958-71; US Army Research Office, chief to associate director, engineering, 1958-71; Illinois Institute of Technology, professor, chairman MAE department, 1971-79, professor, director railroad engineering lab, 1979-90, professor, director academy of railroad engineering and transportation management, 1990-. **ORGANIZATIONS:** India League of America Foundation, board member, 1980-; India League of America, board member, 1972-80; Westerbn Society of Engineers, chairman, education, 1975-78; American Institute of Aeronautics & Astronautics, chairman, Carolina section, 1967-68; Tranergy & Astronautics Corp, chairman of the board, 1986-. **HONORS/AWARDS:** Western Society of Engineers, Octave Chamute Medal, 1986. **SPECIAL ACHIEVEMENTS:** Indian Railways, organized & conducted advanced railroad officer training, 1986-90; Tanzania Zambia Railways, 1991; promotion of trade in railways between 8 African countries and the US, 1992-93. **HOME ADDRESS:** 1903 Darien Circle Dr, Darien, IL 60561, (708)968-3793. **BUSINESS ADDRESS:** Professor, Illinois Institute of Technology, 10 W 32nd St, Rm 250, Chicago, IL 60616-3732, (312)567-3211.

KUMAR, SURENDRA MOHAN
Physician. **PERSONAL:** Born Jan 25, 1956, Allahabad, Uttar Pradesh, India; son of Tek Chand Chugh and Raj Rani Chugh; married Aruna Kumar, May 9, 1986; children: Sunayna, Alpana. **EDUCATION:** Medical College, MBBS, 1979. **CAREER:** Southern Maryland Hospital Center, chief of pediatrics,

1986-87; Johns Hopkins Health Plan, pediatrician, 1987-89; private practice, physician, director, 1989-. **ORGANIZATIONS:** American Academy of Pediatrics, 1985-. **HOME ADDRESS:** 2602 Arden Forest Lane, Bowie, MD 20716, (301)390-7435.

KUMAR, SURESH A.
Glass company executive. Indo-American. **PERSONAL:** Born Apr 20, 1953, Madras, Tamil Nadu, India; son of A V Anandakumar and Visalam Anandakumar; married Joyce M Kumar, Jun 29, 1984; children: Jacqueline V, Justin A. **EDUCATION:** Indian Institute of Technology, Madras, India, BSIE, 1974; Southern Illinois University, Carbondale, MBA, 1975. **CAREER:** E F Johnson Co, cost analyst, 1976-78; G D Searle, manager, financial analysis, 1978-80; Beatrice Foods, manager, planning, 1980-87; American Brands, Business Planning, director, 1987-89; VVP America Inc, Business Development, vice president, 1989-. **ORGANIZATIONS:** Planning Forum. **HOME ADDRESS:** 2059 Northbridge Drive, Germantown, TN 38139, (901)754-2459. **BUSINESS PHONE:** (901)767-7111.

KUMAR, SUSHIL
Educator. Indo-American. **PERSONAL:** Born Dec 28, 1939, New Delhi, India; son of Dropati and Bhagwant Rai; married Indu, Feb 20, 1965; children: Anjali Gupta, Manish. **EDUCATION:** Roorkee University, MS, 1973; Washington State University, PhD, 1979. **CAREER:** Wade, Trim & Assoc, hydraulic engineer, 1979-81; Tri-State University, assistant professor, 1981-83, associate professor, 1983-91, professor of civil engineering, 1991-. **ORGANIZATIONS:** American Society of Civil Engineers; Sigma Xi. **HONORS/AWARDS:** Tri-State University, McKetta-Smith Excellence-In-Teaching Award, 1990-91. **SPECIAL ACHIEVEMENTS:** Several publications in the area of rough pipe flow; contributed a paper to the book Channel Flow Resistance, 1991. **BUSINESS ADDRESS:** Professor of Civil Engineering, Tri-State University, Angola, IN 46703, (219)665-4218.

KUMAR, V.
Educator, consultant. Indo-American. **PERSONAL:** Born Jun 4, 1957, Madras, Tamil Nadu, India; son of S Viswanathan and Patta Viswanathan; married Meena Kumar, Jun 6, 1979; children: Anita, Prita. **EDUCATION:** Indian Institute of Technology, Kharagpur, BTech (honors), 1979; Indian Institute of Technology, Madras, MTech (with distinction), 1981; University of Texas at Austin, PhD, 1985. **CAREER:** University of Iowa, professor, 1985-87; University of Houston, professor, 1987-. **ORGANIZATIONS:** American Marketing Assn, 1983-, Education Div Council, 1993-; Institute of Management Science 1985-; Research Round Table, Houston, 1987-; Intl Institute of Forecasters, 1988-; Who's Who Worldwide, 1992-. **HONORS/AWARDS:** University of Houston, teaching excellence award, 1989, 1990, 1991, 1992, 1993, research excellence award, 1989; IIT, Madras, gold medalist, 1981; University of Texas at Austin, presidential scholarship, 1984-85. **SPECIAL ACHIEVEMENTS:** Numerous research publications; currently working on 3 textbooks. **BUSINESS ADDRESS:** Professor, University of Houston, College of Business, Marketing, 4800 Calhoun Blvd, Ste 375H, Houston, TX 77204-6283, (713)743-4569.

KUMAR, VIJAY A.
Steel foundry executive. Indo-American. **PERSONAL:** Born Jun 16, 1940, Chintamani, Karnataka, India; son of M Aswathnarayan Rao and Kausalyamma; married Vasanthy V Kumar, Oct 21, 1973; children: Chetan M, Chitra M. **EDUCATION:** University of Mysore, Bangalore, India, BScEng, 1961; Indian Institute of Science, Bangalore, India, MScEng, 1963. **CAREER:** Heavy Engg Corp, India, superintendent, tech, 1963-73; Sivanandha Steels, Madras, India, tech director, 1974; Heavy Electricals, India, manager, MET, 1975-80; Monett Steels, plant manager, 1980-84; Ancast, vice pres, 1985-. **ORGANIZATIONS:** American Foundryman Society, 1985-93; Steel Founder Society of America, 1990-92. **SPECIAL ACHIEVEMENTS:** Language proficiency, read, write, and speak: Czech; technical paper in Steel Founder's Society of America. **HOME ADDRESS:** 50877 Sturdy Oak Ct, Granger, IN 46530, (219)272-4865. **BUSINESS ADDRESS:** Vice President, Ancast, Inc, 3194 Townline Rd, Sodus, MI 49126, (616)927-1985.

KUMAR, VIPIN
Educator. Indo-American. **PERSONAL:** Born Oct 21, 1956, Muzaffarnager, Uttar Pradesh, India; married Renu G Kumar. **EDUCATION:** University of Roorkee, India, BE, electronics & communication engineering, 1977; Philips International Institute, Netherlands, ME, electronics engineering, 1979; University of Maryland, College Park, PhD, computer science, 1982. **CAREER:**

University of Texas, Austin, Department of Computer Science, assistant professor, 1983-89; University of Minnesota, Department of Computer Science, associate professor, 1989-. **ORGANIZATIONS:** IEEE, senior member; ACM. **HONORS/AWARDS:** Association of Computing Machinery, Samuel Alexander Fellowship Award, 1981; Sigma Xi, Maryland Chapter, Graduate Student Research Excellence Award, 1982; Gordon Bell competition for practical parallel processing research, honorable mention, 1989. **SPECIAL ACHIEVEMENTS:** Author of numerous publications; recipient of numerous research grants. **BUSINESS ADDRESS:** Associate Professor, Dept of Computer Science, University of Minnesota, 200 Union Street SE, EE/CSci 4-192, Minneapolis, MN 55455, (612)624-8023.

KUMARAN, A. KRISHNA
Educator. Indo-American. **PERSONAL:** Born Jul 17, 1932, Govada, Andhra Pradesh, India; son of Alapati Venkata Krishnaiah and Alapati Saranu Seethamma; married Jyoti, May 4, 1956; children: Nanda K Alapati. **EDUCATION:** Madras University, Pachaiyappa's College, BSc, 1950, Presidency College, BSc (honors), 1952, MSc, 1955, PhD, 1959. **CAREER:** SV University, demonstrator, 1956-57, lecturer in zoology, 1957-62; Western Reserve University, visiting assistant professor, biology, 1965; Osmania University, reader in zoology, 1965-68; Case Western Reserve, research associate, 1968-69; Marquette University, associate professor of biology, 1969-73, professor of biology, 1973-. **ORGANIZATIONS:** Soc Dev Biology America, 1965-; Sigma Xi, 1965-; American Association Adv Sci, fellow, 1982-; American Soc Cell Biol, 1970-; Ent Soc Amer, 1974-; American Soc Zool, 1970-. **HONORS/AWARDS:** Outstanding Educators America, Distinguished Educator, 1974; National Academy of Science, visiting scientist to China, 1989, visiting scientist to Czechoslovakia, 1978. **SPECIAL ACHIEVEMENTS:** Author or co-author of over 80 research papers in developmental biology of insects; co-author, textbook, Biology, Prentice Hall, 1985; executive editor, Arch Ins Bioch Physiol, American Ent Soc, John Wiley, 1993-. **HOME PHONE:** (414)542-0504. **BUSINESS ADDRESS:** Wehr Professor of Biology, Dept of Biology, Marquette University, 530 North 15th St, Milwaukee, WI 53233, (414)288-1478.

KUMAROO, K.
Life scientist. Indo-American. **PERSONAL:** Born Apr 6, 1931, Pathanamthitta, Kerala, India; son of Krishnan & Velumpi; married Vatsala, Jul 31, 1978; children: Vinod, Manoj. **EDUCATION:** Kerala University, India, BS, 1955; University of North Carolina, Chapel Hill, PhD, 1968. **CAREER:** AB High School, Kerala, physical sciences, head, 1953-54; Capsulation services Ltd, Bombay, junior chemist, 1954-55; Grand Medical College, Bombay, biotechnologist, 1955-57; Kuwait Oil Co, petroleum chemist, 1957-63; University of North Carolina, Chapel Hill, graduate student, 1963-68, professor of biochemistry, 1971-79; University of Michigan Medical Center, research trainee, 1969-71; Naval Medical Research Institute, research biochemist, 1979-. **ORGANIZATIONS:** American Association for the Advancement of Science, 1969-73; Council for Exceptional Children, 1969-; American Society for Biochemistsry and Molecular Biology, 1984-; Undersea Medical Society, 1984-; Planetary Society, 19987-; Oxygen Society, 1987-; Sigma Xi, 1967-. **HONORS/AWARDS:** Kerala University, Merit Award, 1950-53; Kerala Dewaswam Scholarship, 1949-53; NIH, Postdoctoral Fellowship, 1968-71, Career Award, 1973-78; University of North Carolina, Special Grant for Cataract Research, 1979. **SPECIAL ACHIEVEMENTS:** Author: "Alcaligenes Eutrophys as a Source of Hydrogenase," 1990; "Superoxide Anions Inhibit the Activity of Adenylate Cyclase Enzyme Complex in Platelets," 1988; "Platelet Activiting Factor Receptor Blockade Enhances Recovery after Multifocal Brain Ischemia," 1987; numerous others. **HOME ADDRESS:** 2614 Urbana Dr, Wheaton, MD 20906, (301)949-7713. **BUSINESS ADDRESS:** Research Biochemist, Department of Hyperbaric Medicine, Naval Med Res Institute, Bldg 53, Bethesda, MD 20889, (301)295-2451.

KUMATA, GERALD HIROSHI
Principal architect. Japanese American. **PERSONAL:** Born Apr 13, 1943, Hunt, ID; son of Isamu Kumata and Tazuko Kumata; married Agnes Yue; children: Michelle, Julie, Allison, Benjamin. **EDUCATION:** University of Washington, BArch, 1971. **CAREER:** Gerald H Kumata & Associates Architects, principal, 1971-. **BUSINESS ADDRESS:** Principal, Gerald H Kumata & Associates, Architects, 2002 Ninth Avenue, Seattle, WA 98121, (206)467-8227.

KUNDU, BEJOY B.
Physician. Indo-American. **PERSONAL:** Born Mar 6, 1938, Parerhat, Bangladesh; son of Nanda Lal Kundu (deceased) and Suvashini Kunda (deceased); married Aparna Kundu, Dec 12, 1991; children: Renita, Bijit. **EDUCATION:** Calcutta University, India, BS, 1957; Darra Medical College, Bangladesh, MD, 1963; Royal College of Physician & Surgeon, London, UK, DTM & H, 1966. **CAREER:** State of New Hampshire, senior physician, 1974-93; New Hampshire Technical Institute, adjunct professor, 1988; New Hampshire Rehabilitation Hospital, consultant staff, 1993; CMC Hospital, courtesy medical staff, 1975-; PNHS at New Hampshire, medical director, currently. **ORGANIZATIONS:** New Hampshire Medical Society, 1975; Merrimack County Medical Society, 1975; General Medical Council, London, UK, 1964; New Hampshire Asian Indian Society, board of directors, 1990. **HOME ADDRESS:** 8 Longview Drive, Bow, NH 03304-4808. **BUSINESS ADDRESS:** Medical Director for PNHS, New Hampshire Hospital, 105 Pleasant St, Thayer Bldg, Concord, NH 03301.

KUNDU, MUKUL RANJAN
Educator. Indo-American. **PERSONAL:** Born Feb 10, 1930, Calcutta, India; son of Makhan Lal Kundu (deceased) and Monoroma Kundu; married Ranu Kundu, Sep 9, 1958; children: Krishna, Rina, Sanjit. **EDUCATION:** Calcutta University, BS (first class honors), 1949, MS, 1951; University of Paris, DSc, 1957. **CAREER:** National Physical Laboratory, India, research fellow, 1958-59; University of Michigan, associate research scientist, 1959-62; Cornell University, associate professor, 1962-65; Tata Institute of Fundamental Research, India, associate professor, 1965-68; University of Maryland, director of astronomy, 1978-85, professor of astronomy, 1968-. **ORGANIZATIONS:** American Astronomical Society, 1961-; Royal Astronomical Society, fellow, 1960-; American Physical Society, fellow, 1989-; Astronomical Society of India, life member, 1967-; Sigma Xi, 1960-; Institute Electrical & Electronic Engineers, 1960-; American Geophysical Union, 1986-. **HONORS/AWARDS:** Calcutta University, Krishna Lal De Gold Medal, 1949, University Medal, 1951; Humboldt Foundation, US Senior Scientist Award, 1978; Japan Society for Promotion of Science, Fellowship, 1986. **SPECIAL ACHIEVEMENTS:** Over 300 publications on astronomical research in refereed journals; author of 1 book, editor of 3 books; organized 4 International Astron Union symposia; National Academy NRC fellowship panels, chairman. **HOME ADDRESS:** 14303 Notley Road, Silver Spring, MD 20904. **BUSINESS ADDRESS:** Professor, Dept of Astronomy, University of Maryland, College Park Campus, Computer-Space Sciences Bldg., College Park, MD 20742, (301)405-1524.

KUNG, ALICE HOW KUEN
High technology company executive. Chinese American/Hong Kong American. **PERSONAL:** Born Nov 26, 1956, Hong Kong; daughter of Yam Sang Kung & Yuet Shoung Kung. **EDUCATION:** Stanford University, BA, economics, 1978; Harvard Business School, MBA, 1983. **CAREER:** Arthur Andersen & Company, consultant, 1978-81; Arthur D Little, consultant, intern, 1982; Gould AMI, customer marketing manager, 1983-84; IBM/Rolm Systems, Voice Messaging Products, product manager, 1985-86, market & business development manager, Asia & Latin America, 1987-89; Minx Software, international sales director, 1989-92; SuperMac Technology, Far East/Pacific, director, 1992-94, general manager Asia/Pacific, 1994-. **ORGANIZATIONS:** Harvard Business School Community Partners, volunteer for community work, 1993; Asian American Manufacturers' Association, 1986-; Sources 91, organizing committee, 1991; Asian Biz League/Silicon Valley, 1987-; International Biz Club, officer, 1981-83; Chinese Students Association, Stanford, 1975-78. **HONORS/AWARDS:** Minx Software, Eagle Club Winner, 1990, 1991; IBM/Rolm Systems, President Club, 1988, Division Achievemnent Award, 1986; Harvard, scholarship, 1982, 1983; Phi Beta Kappa, 1978. **SPECIAL ACHIEVEMENTS:** Fluent in speaking & writing Cantonese & Mandarin; State of California, certified public accountant, 1981; author, "Macro Cell Fulfills Speech Synthesis Requirements," Mid Con Westcon, Sept 1984, Nov 1984; "Semicustom ICs Simplify Electronic Speech Synthesis in Automobiles," Audio Systems Conference, 1985. **BUSINESS ADDRESS:** Director, Far East/Pacific, SuperMac Technology, 215 Moffert Park Dr, Sunnyvale, CA 94089-1374, (408)541-5493.

KUNG, FRANK F. C.
Biopharmaceutical company executive. Chinese American. **PERSONAL:** Born in China; married Viola; children: Audrey, Stephanie, Tiffany. **EDUCATION:** University of California, Berkeley, MBA, PhD, molecular biology. **CAREER:** Cetus Immune Corp, director; Genelabs Technologies Inc, presi-

dent, chief exec officer, 1984-. **ORGANIZATIONS:** Biotechnology Industry Organization, board of directors; University of North Carolina School of Pharmacy, board of visitors; NIH, natl biotechnology policy board. **HONORS/ AWARDS:** Governor of State of California, Best Use of Innovative Technology; Asian Business League, Outstanding Entrepreneurship Award; Arthur Young & Inc, Entrepreneur of the Year, 1989. **BUSINESS ADDRESS:** President, CEO, Genelabs Technologies Inc, 505 Penobscot Dr, Redwood City, CA 94063, (415)369-9500.

KUNG, H. T.
Educator. Chinese American. **PERSONAL:** Born Nov 9, 1945, Shanghai, China. **EDUCATION:** National Tsing Hua University, Taiwan, BS, math, 1968; University of New Mexico, MA, applied math, 1970; Carnegie Mellon University, PhD, math & computer science, 1974. **CAREER:** Carnegie Mellon University, computer science, assistant professor, 1974-78, associate professor, 1978-82, professor, 1982-92; Harvard University, Gordon McKay Professor of Electrical Engineering and Computer Science, 1992-. **ORGANIZATIONS:** Computing Research Association, board of directors, 1992-93; National Research Council, Committee to Study Academic Careers for Experimental Computer Scientists, 1992-93; NSF Advisory Committee for the Division of Microelectronic Information Processing Systems, chairman, 1987-90; Scientific and Industrial Advisory Committee, Telecommunications Research Institute of Ontario, Canada, chairman, 1989; Office of Science and Technology Policy and National Research Council Panel on Computer Architecture, panelist, 1984; National Research Council to Survey International Developments in Computer Science, panelist, 1981. **HONORS/AWARDS:** Guggenheim Fellowship, 1983; Shell Distinguished Chair in Computer Science, 1985-90; Pittsburgh Intellectual Property Law Association, Inventor of the Year Award, 1991; elected to Academia Sinica, Taiwan, 1990; elected to National Academy of Engineering, 1993. **SPECIAL ACHIEVEMENTS:** Author or co-author of 120 publications; holds two patents; editorial service to several publications, including: Journal of Computer Science and Technology, Journal of VLSI Signal Processing, Computers and Artificial Intelligence, Journal of Complexity. **BUSINESS ADDRESS:** Gordan McKay Professor of Elec Eng & Comp Science, Division of Applied Sciences, Harvard University, 29 Oxford St, 110 Pierce Hall, Cambridge, MA 02138, (617)496-6211.

KUNG, HAROLD H.
Educator. Chinese American. **PERSONAL:** Born Oct 12, 1949, Hong Kong; son of Shien Cho Kung; married Mayfair, Jul 21, 1971; children: Alexander, Benjamin. **EDUCATION:** University of Wisconsin, BS, chemical engineering, 1971; Northwestern University, PhD, chemistry, 1974. **CAREER:** E I du Pont de Nemours & Co, research scientist, Central Research & Development Dept, 1974-76; Northwestern University, postdoctoral fellow, 1974, asst professor, chemical engineering, 1976, asst professor, chemical engineering & chemistry, 1977, associate professor, chemical engineering & chemistry, 1981, professor, chemical engineering & chemistry, 1985-, chairman, chemical engineering, 1986-92, Center for Catalysis & Surface Science, director, 1993-. **ORGANIZATIONS:** American Chemical Society; American Institute of Chemical Engineers; Phi Lambda Epsilon; Catalysis Society; Chicago Catalysis Club, program chair, 1992, president, 1993. **HONORS/AWARDS:** Catalysis Society, Paul H Emmett Award, 1991. **SPECIAL ACHIEVEMENTS:** Industrial consulting: Union Camp Corp, 1986; Amoco Chemical Co, 1988, 1991-92; Catalytica Inc, 1990; DuPont Co, 1993; author, Transition Metal Oxides, Surface Chemistry and Catalysis, 1989; co-author, Catalyst Modification-Selective Oxidation Processes, Catalytica Study, 1991; patents: Photolysis of Water Using Rhodate Semiconductive Electrodes, Oxidative Dehydrogenation of Alkanes to Unsaturated Hydrocarbons, 1988; over 90 scientific publications. **BUSINESS ADDRESS:** Professor, Dept of Chemical Engineering, Northwestern University, Evanston, IL 60208, (708)491-7492.

KUNG, JEFFREY
Electronic engineering manager. Chinese American. **PERSONAL:** Born Nov 12, 1939, Chungking, Sichuan, China; son of Henry and Jessic Kung; married Lily Kung, Mar 3, 1963; children: Lisa, Lucy. **EDUCATION:** National Chengchi University, Taipei, Taiwan, LLB, 1961; City College of New York, BEE, 1970, MEE, 1972; C W Post College, LIU, Greenvale, NY, MS, engineering management, 1978. **CAREER:** General Precision Lab, technician, 1966-67; Del Electronics Inc, engineer, 1967; Alphanumerics Inc, engineer, 1967-70; RCA Institutes, instructor, 1970-72; Harris Corp, project engineer, section head, dept manager, 1972-. **ORGANIZATIONS:** Organization of Chinese Americans, Long Island, NY, Chapter, president, national vp of chapter development, national board director, 1981-91; Tri-State Coalition of Chinese Amer-

icans of NY, NJ & Connecticut, vp of community coalition, board director, 1983-89; Buddha's Light International Assn, Florida Chapter, president, 1993. **HONORS/AWARDS:** Organization of Chinese Americans, Service Awards (3), 1985-89; Tri-State Coalition of Chinese Americans, Service Award, 1989. **SPECIAL ACHIEVEMENTS:** Numerous articles about Chinese Americans, voter's registrations, civil rights movement, English only movement, in Chinese newspapers, magazines published in the US, 1978-89; professional engineering articles, 1979. **MILITARY SERVICE:** Nationalist Chinese Army, ROTC, 2nd lt, 1961-63. **BUSINESS ADDRESS:** Engineering Manager, Harris Corporation, PO Box 94000, MS 100-4894, Melbourne, FL 32902-9400, (407)384-1922.

KUNG, PATRICK CHUNG-SHU
Biotechnology company executive. Chinese American. **PERSONAL:** Born Jul 10, 1947, Nanjing, China; son of Tao Kung & Yu-ing Li Kung; married Rita Wu, Feb 11, 1980; children: Julia, Calvin. **EDUCATION:** Fu Jen Catholic University, Taiwan, BS, 1968; University of California, Berkeley, PhD, 1974. **CAREER:** EI duPont, staff scientist, 1977-78; Ortho Pharmaceutical, senior research fellow, 1978-81; Centocor, director, human immunology research, 1981-82, vice president of research, 1982-84; T Cell Sciences, chief scientific officer & founder, 1984-92, vice chairman of the board, 1992-; Asian American Bank and Trust, executive board, 1993-. **ORGANIZATIONS:** Park School, Brookline, trustee, 1992-; Organization of Chinese Americans, 1989-; American Association of Immunologists, 1987-; Society of Chinese Bioscientists in America, 1991-. **HONORS/AWARDS:** American Pharmaceutical Manufacturers Association, Discoverers Award, 1991; Research & Development Council of New Jersey, Thomas Alva Edison Patent Award, 1991; Chinese Institute of Engineers, Annual Achievement Award, 1988; Johnson & Johnson Co, Philip B Hoffman Award, 1979. **SPECIAL ACHIEVEMENTS:** Co-inventor of the drug OKT3, used to treat organ transplant rejection; co-inventor of tests (CD4 t-cell count) to monitor disease progress in in AIDS patients. **BUSINESS ADDRESS:** Vice Chairman of the Board, T Cell Sciences Inc, 38 Sidney St, Cambridge, MA 02139, (617)621-1400.

KUNG, SHAIN-DOW
Educator, educational administrator. Chinese American. **PERSONAL:** Born Mar 14, 1934, Shandong, China; son of Zhao-zeng Kung (deceased) and Zhu-shi Kung; married Helen C C Kung, Sep 6, 1964; children: Grace, David, Andrew. **EDUCATION:** University of Chung-Hsing, Taichung, Taiwan, BSc, 1958; University of Guelph, Ontario, Canada, MSc, 1965; University of Toronto, Canada, PhD, 1968. **CAREER:** University of Maryland, Dept of Biological Sciences, acting chairman, 1982-84, arts & sciences, associate dean, 1985-87, College Park, College of Life Sciences, Dept of Botany, professor, 1986-93, Centre for Agricultural Biotechnology, director, 1988-93; Maryland Biotechnology Institute, acting provost, 1989-91; Hong Kong University of Science & Technology, dean of science, 1991-92, pro-vice-chancellor for academic affairs, professor, 1992-. **ORGANIZATIONS:** NIH, Biological Sciences Study Section, 1993-; National Natural Science Foundation of China, science advisor, 1991-94; Butterworths Publishing Co, editorial board, Biotechnology Series, 1990-; US Department of Agriculture's Agricultural Biotechnology Research Advisory Committee, 1988-90; Society of Plant Physiology, 1973; Society of Chinese Bioscientists in America, 1986-; American Association for the Advancement of Science, 1971-. **HONORS/AWARDS:** Chung Hsing University, Taiwan, Outstanding Alumni, 1993, Department of Horticulture, Outstanding Alumni, 1992; Fudan University, Shanghai, Honorary Professor, 1986; Fulbright Award, 1983; Award for Distinguished Achievement in Tobacco Science, 1979; Honorary Citizenship of Baltimore, 1974. **SPECIAL ACHIEVEMENTS:** Publications: "Tobacco Fraction 1 Protein-a Unique Genetic Market," Science, 191:429-434, 1976; "Expression of Chloroplast Genomes in Higher Plants," Ann Rev Plant Physiol, 28:401-437, 1977; with C J Arntzen, ed, Plant Biotechnology, Butterworths Publishing Co, 1989; with D Bills, Biotechnology & Food Nutrition, Butterworths Publishing Co, 1991; with R Wu, ed, Transgenic Plants, vols I and II, Academic Press, 1993. **BIOGRAPHICAL SOURCES:** Global Views Monthly, Taiwan, p 144-145, 9/15/1992. **BUSINESS ADDRESS:** Pro-Vice-Chancellor for Academic Affairs, Professor, Hong Kong University of Science and Technology, Clear Water Bay, Academic Building, Room 6331, Kowloon, Hong Kong, 852 358 6122.

KUO, ALBERT YI-SHUONG
Educator, educational administrator. Taiwanese American. **PERSONAL:** Born Nov 4, 1939, Taoyuan, Taiwan; son of Hsu-Fang and Chow-mei Kuo; married Shiow-chyn Kuo, Nov 1965; children: Catherine, Nancy. **EDUCATION:**

National Taiwan University, BS, 1962; University of Iowa, MS, 1965; The Johns Hopkins University, PhD, 1970. **CAREER:** College of William and Mary, professor and chair, 1970-. **ORGANIZATIONS:** ASCE; Estuarine Research Federation; VA Academy of Science. **BUSINESS ADDRESS:** Professor, School of Marine Science, Virginia Institute of Marine Science, College of William and Mary, Gloucester Point, VA 23062, (804)642-7212.

KUO, CHAO YING
Educator. Chinese American/Taiwanese American. **PERSONAL:** Born Apr 27, 1940, Miaoli, Taiwan; son of Shih-An Kuo and Lily-Fan Kuo; married Grace Lo Kuo, Sep 17, 1967; children: Alice Ann, Bobby Feung. **EDUCATION:** National Taiwan Normal University, Taipei, BS, 1964; Indiana State University, MA, 1970; University of Iowa, PhD, 1974. **CAREER:** University of Iowa, assistant research scientist, 1974-79; University of Tennessee, Memphis, instructor, 1980-81, assistant professor, 1981-84, assistant professor, 1991-. **SPECIAL ACHIEVEMENTS:** Cooperative Binding of a Complement Component to Antigen-Antibody Complexes, 1976; A New Allergen from the Perienteric Fluid of Ascaris Suum, 1977; Formation of "Pseudo Islets" from Human Pancreatic Cultures, 1992; Histological Structure of Hybrid Islet Organoid, 1992; Reversal of Hyperglycemia by Islet Transplantation into Subcutaneous Hybrid Organoid, 1993. **BUSINESS ADDRESS:** Assistant Professor, Dept of Pediatrics, University of Tennessee, College of Medicine, 956 Court Ave, Coleman Bldg, Rm B-310, Memphis, TN 38163, (901)528-5942.

KUO, CHARLES CHANG-YUN
Microelectronics company director. Chinese American. **PERSONAL:** Born Dec 13, 1923, Chiang-Ling, Hubei, China; son of Hui-Ting Kuo and Chin-Yin Wang; married Deborah Tze-Te Liu, Dec 12, 1948; children: Sze-Ping, Sze-Wen, Scot, Stanley. **EDUCATION:** College of Ordnance Engineering, China, BS, 1945; Lehigh University, MS, 1957, PhD, 1961. **CAREER:** College of Ordnance Engineering, assistant professor, 1949-55; Lehigh University, research fellow, 1955-61; AT&T Bell Labs, member of technical staff, 1961-67; GTE Labs, engineering specialist, 1967-69; Columbia Components Corp, director of research and development, 1969-70; Engelhard Ind, department head, 1970-77; CTS Corp, technical director, 1977-. **ORGANIZATIONS:** Society of Functional Materials, special editor, 1990-; American Ceramic Society, 1974; International Society Microelectronics, 1967; American Chemical Society, 1958; Sigma Xi, 1957. **HONORS/AWARDS:** International Society for Hybrid Microelectronics, ISHM, John Wagnon Technical Achievement Award, 1987, Best Paper Award, 1981; International Symposium in Microelectronics, Best Paper Award, 1993. **SPECIAL ACHIEVEMENTS:** Author: Engineered Materials Handbook, vol 4, 1991; chapters in books; more than 80 technical papers; holder of 34 patents in microelectronics; derived 3 generalized equations, one of which was named Kuo Constant. **HOME ADDRESS:** 7 Swanson Manor, Elkhart, IN 46516. **BUSINESS PHONE:** (219)293-7511.

KUO, CHUNG-CHIEH JAY
Educator. Taiwanese American. **PERSONAL:** Born Dec 6, 1957, Hsinchu, Taiwan; son of King-Fa Kuo and King-Au Wu. **EDUCATION:** National Taiwan University, BS, 1980, MIT, SM, 1985, PhD, 1987. **CAREER:** UCLA, research assistant professor, 1987-88; University of Southern California, assistant professor, 1989-. **ORGANIZATIONS:** IEEE; SIAM; ACM; SPIE. **HONORS/AWARDS:** NSF, Research Initiation Award, 1990, Young Investigator Award, 1992, Presidential Faculty Fellow Award, 1993. **BUSINESS ADDRESS:** Professor, University of Southern California, 3740 McClintock Ave, EEB 440, Los Angeles, CA 90089-2564, (213)740-4658.

KUO, CHUNG MING
Research chemist. Chinese American. **PERSONAL:** Born Aug 6, 1935, Chang-Hwa, Taiwan; married Freda Lai Kuo, Jun 12, 1966; children: Michael, Susan. **EDUCATION:** Chung-Hsing University, Taiwan, BS, 1958; Syracuse University, MS, 1964, PhD, 1968. **CAREER:** Eastman Chemical Co, research chemist, 1968-71, senior research chemist, 1971-81, research associate, 1981-. **ORGANIZATIONS:** American Chemical Society. **BUSINESS ADDRESS:** Research Associate, Eastman Chemical Co, Eastman Kodak, Research Laboratories, Bldg 150B, Kingsport, TN 37662, (615)229-6053.

KUO, FENG YANG KUO
Educator. Taiwanese American. **PERSONAL:** Born Jun 8, 1956, Chiayi, Taiwan; son of Wen-Tung Kuo and Jin-Yu Kuo; married Hsueh-Ching Kuo, Dec 20, 1981. **EDUCATION:** National Chiao-Tung University, BS, 1978; Clarkson College, MS, 1981; University of Arizona, PhD, 1985. **CAREER:**

University of Arizona, research assistant, 1981-85; University of Colorado, assistant professor, 1985-92, associate professor, 1992-. **ORGANIZATIONS:** Association of Computing Machinery, 1981-. **HONORS/AWARDS:** University of Colorado, Junior Faculty Award, 1989; MIS Interrupt, One of the Most Prolific Researchers, 1991, 1992. **SPECIAL ACHIEVEMENTS:** "Understanding Human Computer Interactions for Information Systems Design," MIS Quarterly, vol 15, no 4, 1991; "An Approach to the Recursive Retrieval Problem in Relational Database," Committee of the ACM, vol 32, no 2, 1989; "Dialogue Management-Support for Dialogue Independence," MIS Quarterly, vol 12, no 3, 1988; "User Interface Design from a Real-time Perspective," Committee of the ACM, vol 31, no 12, 1988; "A Cognitive Engineering Approach to Designing Hypermedia Systems," forthcoming in Information & Management, 1993. **HOME ADDRESS:** 10467 E Weaver Circle, Englewood, CO 80111. **BUSINESS PHONE:** (303)628-2351.

KUO, JAMES K. Y.
Educator. Chinese American. **PERSONAL:** Born Dec 25, 1920, Soochow, China; son of C Z Kuo and B C Dan; married Agnes Kan-ping Kuo, Jul 8, 1950; children: Anna, Nina, Donna. **EDUCATION:** Soochow Art Institute, China, 1939; University of Missouri, Columbia, BA, art, 1947, MFA, 1949. **CAREER:** Mount Mary College, assistant professor of art, 1949; Rosary Hill College, professor of art, 1955; Daemen College, art department chairperson, 1989, professor of art, 1992-. **ORGANIZATIONS:** Buffalo Fine Arts Academy, Albright-Knox Art Gallery, 1989; Americn Crafts Council, artist, 1984; Buffalo Craftsmen, artist, 1975; Patteran Artistis Society, board of directors, 1970. **HONORS/AWARDS:** Daemen College, Professor Emeritus Award, 1992, Outstanding Personal Achievement Award, 1986; Chautauqua Institution, Katherine Hipple Baker Award, 1962, 8th Chautauqua National Exhibition Award, 1986; Marine Trust Company, Niagara Art Exhibit, first prize award, 1965. **SPECIAL ACHIEVEMENTS:** "Reflections #1," painting, Albright-Knox Art Gallery Collection, 1980; "Growth Series #1," painting, Burchfield Art Center Collection, 1992; "Composition," wood cuts, Buffalo State College Collection, 1982; one man show, Elliott Museum, Florida, 1991; "Spring Vista," painting, Graphic Controls Corporation Collection Show, 1980. **BIOGRAPHICAL SOURCES:** Albright-Knox Art Gallery, The Painting & Sculpture Acquisitions, 1972-, p 197, 1987; "Prize Winning Art," Watercolor, p 22, 1966. **HOME ADDRESS:** 235 Wellingwood Dr, East Amherst, NY 14051, (716)688-1165.

KUO, JOSEPH C. (JOSEPH YAN-HUA)
Educator, educational administrator. Chinese American. **PERSONAL:** Born Feb 2, 1922, Beijing, Hebei, China; son of Chuan-fa Kuo and Mary C Kuo; married Mary H Y Kuo, Sep 17, 1948; children: John L S, Rose, Simon, David. **EDUCATION:** China University, LLB, 1946. **CAREER:** Chung Ying School, Hong Kong, director, 1953-56; American Consulate Gen Hong Kong, instructor, 1956-59; Yale University, instructor, 1959-65; Washington University of St Louis, instructor, 1965-67; Loyola Academy, instructor, 1967-68; University of Kansas, assistant and associate professor, 1968-92, associate professor emeritus, 1992-, academic program coordinator, advisor, currently. **ORGANIZATIONS:** Kansas Foreign Language Association, 1979-91; Association for Asian Studies, 1976-; Chinese Language Teachers Association, 1962-; International Society for Chinese Language Teaching, 1987-; American Association of University Professors, 1970-90; American Council on the Teaching of Foreign Languages, 1969-77; American Association of Teachers of Chinese Language and Culture, 1962-72; Chinese Students & Scholars Association, KU, faculty advisor, 1975, 1979, 1987-92. **HONORS/AWARDS:** Phi Beta Delta, Honor Society for International Scholars, 1992. **SPECIAL ACHIEVEMENTS:** Co-author, Chinese Reader, Center for East Asian Studies University of Kansas, 1990; Radio Broadcasts from China-23 series in 9 volumes, EAS Center, University of Kansas, 1982-89; co-author, Speak Mandarin-Student's Workbook, Yale Linguistic Series, Yale University Press, 1967; co-author, Speak Mandarin-Teacher's Manual, Yale Linguistic Series, Yale University Press, 1967; Languages: Chinese/Mandarin, Cantonese, Shanghai dialect and English. **HOME ADDRESS:** 409 Utah St, Lawrence, KS 66046-4845, (913)843-1757. **BUSINESS ADDRESS:** Professor, Dept of East Asian Languages & Cultures, University of Kansas, 2118 Wescoe Hall, Lawrence, KS 66045-2143, (913)863-3100.

KUO, KEN NAN
Surgeon, educator. Taiwanese American. **PERSONAL:** Born Dec 20, 1940, Taipei, Taiwan; son of Chien Yuan Kuo and Yu Hua Hsu Kuo; married Angela S M Kuo, Nov 9; children: Eugene, Joya, Christina. **EDUCATION:** National Taiwan University Medical College, MD, 1966. **CAREER:** University Ortho-

pedics, senior partner, 1978-93; Rush Medical College, professor of orthopedic surgery, 1988-. **ORGANIZATIONS:** Illinois Orthopedic Society, president, 1992. **HONORS/AWARDS:** Shriner Foundation, grant, 1977; Orthopedic Research and Education Foundation, grant, 1977. **SPECIAL ACHIEVEMENTS:** Many written medical publications, 1972-93. **BUSINESS ADDRESS:** Professor, Orthopedic Surgery, Rush Prebyterian-St Luke's Medical Center, 1725 West Harrison, Chicago, IL 60612, (312)243-4244.

KUO, MING-MING SHEN
Academic librarian, educator. Chinese American. **PERSONAL:** Born Nov 17, 1937, Shanghai, China; daughter of Zah Dah Sung Shen and Fung-Cheung Hung Sung Shen; married You-yuh Kuo, Jun 10, 1967; children: Sheau-wu Sherwood, Sheau-ming Serena. **EDUCATION:** Tunghai University, Taichung, Taiwan, BA, English, 1960; Mount Holyoke College, MA, English, 1962; Columbia University, MS, library service, 1964; Ball State University, MA, executive development, 1985. **CAREER:** The H W Wilson Co, cataloger & indexer, 1964-65; St. John's University Library, assistant librarian, 1965-67; Bloomsburg State College Library, assistant catalog librarian & assistant professor, 1967-69; Ball State University Libraries, collections development librarian & associate professor, 1971-. **ORGANIZATIONS:** Chinese American Librarians Association, 1982-, board member, 1990-93, cultural studies task force, 1992-93, chair of task force on guidelines of conference planning & cooperation, 1991-92, board member & president, Midwest chapter, 1987-88; American Library Association, 1964-65, 1983-; American Association of University Professors, 1967-69. **HONORS/AWARDS:** Ball State University, Library Faculty Achievement Awards, 1983-93; Friends of Alexander M Bracken Library Research Grant, 1992, Friends of Alexander M Bracken Library Faculty Development Grants, 1983, 1985, 1987, 1991; Mount Holyoke College, fellowships, 1960-62; Tunghai University, scholarships, 1956-60. **SPECIAL ACHIEVEMENTS:** A Guide to Selected Microform Collection in the Ball State Univ Libraries, 1990; Indiana Chinese American Resources Directory, 1992; "The Impact of Planned Organizational Change on an Academic Library," Resources in Education, July 1991; reviews in Journal of Library Information Science, 1987-, International Journal of Reviews in Library and Information Science, 1985-88. **HOME ADDRESS:** 5204 N Leicester Dr, Muncie, IN 47304. **BUSINESS ADDRESS:** Collections Development Librarian, Associate Professor of Library Service, University Libraries, Ball State University, BL 32 Bracken Library, Muncie, IN 47306-0160, (317)285-5307.

KUO, MING-SHANG
Pharmaceutical scientist. Taiwanese American. **PERSONAL:** Born Oct 11, 1949, Kaohsiung, Taiwan; son of Tseng-Yu & Yee-Rong Kuo; married Hwa-Mei Kuo, Jan 1, 1974; children: Alexander, Michelle. **EDUCATION:** National Tsing-Hua University, Taiwan, BS, 1971; Michigan State University, PhD, 1979. **CAREER:** The Upjohn Company, senior research scientist, 1979-. **ORGANIZATIONS:** American Society of Chemistry, 1979-; American Society of Industrial Microbiology, 1988-, Education Committee, 1991-; American Society of Pharmacognosy, 1988-. **BUSINESS ADDRESS:** Senior Research Scientist, The Upjohn Company, 7000 Portage Rd, 7295-25-6, Portage, MI 49002, (616)385-7802.

KUO, NINA L.
Artist, photographer. Chinese American. **PERSONAL:** Born in Milwaukee, WI; daughter of James Kuo. **EDUCATION:** SUCB at Buffalo, BS, art education, 1975; International Center of Photography, color photography, 1980-82. **CAREER:** Asian American Art Center, 1988-89; Chinatown History Museum, artist-in-residence, 1991-92, photographer, 1993; St Francis Residence, art instructor, 1992-94; artist, photographer, currently. **ORGANIZATIONS:** Asian American Arts Alliance, advisory board; Godzilla Visual Arts Organization. **HONORS/AWARDS:** Arts International, NEA, Travel Grant to China, 1993; New York Foundation for the Arts, grant, 1993; Art Matters Grant, 1992, 1990; New York State Arts Council Grant, 1991; Artist Space Grant, 1990. **SPECIAL ACHIEVEMENTS:** Artmakers, artist for a subway station mural, 1990; permanent collections: Library of Congress, Washington, DC; Brooklyn Museum, NY; Blblioteque Nationale, Paris, France; Chicago Art Institute Library, IL. **BIOGRAPHICAL SOURCES:** "Mixed Blessings," by Lucy Lippard, Pantheon Press, 1991; "Ikon, Asian American Issue," 1992. **HOME ADDRESS:** 233 E 88th St, Apt 3W, New York, NY 10128-3367, (212)348-6589.

KUO, SHIOU-SAN
Educator. Taiwanese American. **PERSONAL:** Born Aug 17, 1939, Ping-Tung, Taiwan; son of Ching-Shiang Kuo and Chu-Su Kuo; married Pao-Yu Kuo, Jun

20, 1971; children: Eric, Clifton, Amy. **EDUCATION:** National Cheng-Kung University, Taiwan, BS, 1963; Mississippi State University, MS, 1967; Michigan State University, PhD, 1972. **CAREER:** Tung-Ta High Schoool, math teacher, 1964-65; Michigan Deprtment of Transportation, senior transportation engineer, 1967-81; University of Central Florida, professor of engineering, 1981-. **ORGANIZATIONS:** American Society of Civil Engineers, 1967-; National Society of Professional Engineers, 1975-; Flordia Engineering Society, 1981-; Transportation Research Board, 1990-; US University Council on Geotech Engineering Research, 1985-; The International Association of Foundation Drilling, 1987-. **HONORS/AWARDS:** Depart of Civil & Env Engineering, Outstanding Researcher of the Year, 1989; UCF College of Engineering, Research of the Year, 1989; Dept of Civil & Env Engineering, Excellence in Advising Award, 1990; UCF College of Engineering, Excellence in Advising Award, 1990, Research Achievement Award, 1992. **SPECIAL ACHIEVEMENTS:** Written testimony on reducing environmental costs for US Congressional Subcommittee on Science, Space and Technology, 1992; "New Innovative Technology on Computer Automated Inspection," 1992, "Testing of Bridge Expansion Joints by Large Scale Testing Apparatus," 1993, TRB Journal papers; over 30 journal proceedings and reports. **MILITARY SERVICE:** No 6 Army Training Corp, Taiwan, second lieutenant, 1963-64. **HOME ADDRESS:** 419 Mallard Circle, Winter Park, FL 32789, (407)645-5461. **BUSINESS ADDRESS:** Professor, Dept of Civil Engineering, University of Central Florida, Orlando, FL 32816-2450, (407)823-2280.

KUO, WAY
Educator. Taiwanese American. **PERSONAL:** Born Jan 5, 1951, Taipei, Taiwan; son of Raysen Kuo and Hua Lee; married Suzanne Lee, Aug 24, 1977; children: Wenpei, Wensing. **EDUCATION:** National Tsing-Hua University, Taiwan, BS, 1972; Kansas State University, MS, 1977, PhD, 1980. **CAREER:** Oak Ridge National Lab, visiting scientist, 1981; Bell Labs, technical staff, 1981-84; Iowa State University, assistant professor, 1984-88, professor, associate professor, professor 1984-88, chairman and professor, 1989-93; Texas A&M University, professor, head, 1993-. **ORGANIZATIONS:** Institute of Industrial Engineers, director of qc & re, 1988-90; Institute of Electrical and Electronic Engineers, associate editor, IEEE Trans Reliability, 1990-. **HONORS/AWARDS:** Institute of Industrial Engineers, fellow, 1990; Institute of Electrical and Electronics Engineers, fellow, 1991; American Society for Quality Control, fellow, 1993. **SPECIAL ACHIEVEMENTS:** Author or co-author of 6 books and more than 75 articles, 1978-93. **MILITARY SERVICE:** Twaiwan Marines, lleutenant, 1972-74; Distinguished Service Award by Secretary of Navy. **BIOGRAPHICAL SOURCES:** IEEE Transactions on Reliability, 1993 Optimization of Systems Reliability, back page 1985. **BUSINESS ADDRESS:** Professor and Head, Dept of Industrial Engineering, Texas A&M University, Zachry Engineering Center, College Station, TX 77843-3131, (409)845-5535.

KUO, WAYNE WEN-LONG
Engineer. Taiwanese American. **PERSONAL:** Born Apr 25, 1964, Taiwan, People's Republic of China; son of Kuo Chung Yung and Tsi Ben Ching. **EDUCATION:** Chung Yung University, Taiwan, civil engineering; Azusa Pacific University, MA, 1991. **CAREER:** Ova Technology Inc, design engineer, 1991-. **HOME ADDRESS:** 960 S Sunnyhill Place, Diamond Bar, CA 91765, (714)860-7857.

KUO, WEN HSIUNG
Educator. Taiwanese American. **PERSONAL:** Born May 2, 1940, Yenshui, Taiwan; married Hao Mei Kuo, Dec 21, 1968; children: Benjamin Fei, Thomas Yin. **EDUCATION:** Tunghai University, sociology, 1962; State University of New York, Buffalo, sociology, 1968; Johns Hopkins University, social relations, 1971. **CAREER:** Tunghai University, department of sociology, assistant, 1963-66; Columbia University, department of sociology, assistant professor, 1971-72; University of Utah, department of sociology, assistant professor to professor, 1972-. **ORGANIZATIONS:** American Sociological Association, 1972-; Pacific Sociological Association, 1990-; International Sociological Association, 1988-; US Department of Health & Human Services, advisory committees, 1985-93. **HONORS/AWARDS:** Institute of Mental Health, research grants, 1982-85, 1991-96; Ford Foundation, research grant, 1972; East-West Center, visiting fellow, 1987; US Information Services, Beijing University, Fulbright Award, visiting professor, 1985-86. **SPECIAL ACHIEVEMENTS:** Author, Urban Sociology, Modern Urban Society, and many journal articles in the area of political sociology, race relations, Asian Americans, mental health, Chinese Americans, and China & Taiwan development issues.

BUSINESS ADDRESS: Professor, Dept of Sociology, University of Utah, Salt Lake City, UT 84112, (801)581-6153.

KUO, YIH-WEN

Educator. Taiwanese American/Chinese American. **PERSONAL:** Born Feb 7, 1959, Hsin-Chu, Taiwan; married Song-In Wang. **EDUCATION:** Southern Illinois University, MFA, 1988. **CAREER:** Northern Illinois University, assistant professor, 1990-. **ORGANIZATIONS:** NCECA, 1986-. **HONORS/AWARDS:** Illinois Art Council, fellowship, 1993; Pennsylvania Art Council, fellowship, 1990. **BUSINESS ADDRESS:** Assistant Professor, School of Art, Northern Illinois University, De Kalb, IL 60115, (815)753-4702.

KURAMITSU, HOWARD K.

Microbiologist, educator. Japanese American. **PERSONAL:** Born Oct 18, 1936, Los Angeles, CA; son of Richard Kuramitsu and Shirley Kuramitsu; married LeKim Kuramitsu, Jul 17, 1970; children: Kristine C, Tracy L. **EDUCATION:** UCLA, BS, 1957, PhD, 1962. **CAREER:** Northwestern University Medical School, assistant professor, 1967-73, associate professor, 1973-79, professor of microbiology, 1979-89; University of Texas Health Science Center, professor of pediatric dentistry, 1989-93; SUNY, Buffalo, professor of oral biology, 1993-. **ORGANIZATIONS:** American Society of Microbiology, 1966-; American Society for Molecular Biology and Biochemistry, 1972-; International Association Dental Research, micro/imm group, president, 1975-; American Association Adv Science, 1972-. **HONORS/AWARDS:** National Institutes of Health, merit award, 1985. **BUSINESS ADDRESS:** Professor of Oral Biology, State University of New York, 3435 Main St, Foster Hall 304, Buffalo, NY 14214-3092, (716)829-2068.

KURODA, EMILY

Actress. Japanese American. **PERSONAL:** Born Oct 30, 1952, Fresno, CA; daughter of Kay & William Kuroda; married Alberto Isaac, Jul 2, 1984. **EDUCATION:** Fresno State University, MA, 1978. **CAREER:** Actress, movies include: Pad, Broken Words, About Love, Late for Dinner; TV appearances include: ''LA Law,'' ''Doogie Howser''; theatre: East West Players, Mark Taper Forum, Berkeley Rep. **ORGANIZATIONS:** Screen Actors Guild, 1979-; Actors Equity Association, 1982-; Asian Pacific American Artists' Association, 1978-; American Federation of Television, Radio Artists, 1980-. **HONORS/AWARDS:** City of LA, Commendation, 1993; Dramalogue Award, Outstanding Actor, 1987, 1989, 1992. **HOME PHONE:** (213)250-4864.

KURODA, KOSON

Educator, physician. Japanese American. **PERSONAL:** Born Jul 18, 1929, Long Beach, CA; son of Mumekichi & Tokuyo Yoshihara Kuroda; married Karen Lee White, Dec 23, 1966; children: Greg Koson, Alexandra Mariko. **EDUCATION:** University of California, Berkeley, BA, 1954; Northwestern University Medical School, MD, 1960; Philadelphia General Hospital, internship resident, radiology, 1960-61, 1961-64; Graduate Hospital of the University of Pennsylvania, fellow, cardiovascular radiology, 1964-65. **CAREER:** Graduate Hospital of the University of Pennsylvania, instructor, associate in radiology, 1965-68; Thomas Jefferson University Hospital, associate professor, clinical professor of radiology, section of cardiovascular interventional radiology, head, 1968-77; Cooper Hospital/University Medical Center, department of diagnostic radiology and nuclear medicine, chief, 1977-90. **ORGANIZATIONS:** Japanese American Citizens League, Phila Chapter member, 1974-, newsletter editor, 1978-80, board of governors, 1974-78, chairman, 1976; Cooper Hospital, University Medical Center, chief department radiology, 1977-90, medical staff attending, 1977-, educ comm, 1980-90, institutional review comm, 1978-90, executive committee, 1977-90; Robert Wood Johnson Medical School, Camden Campus, executive faculty, 1980-90, curriculum committee, 1980-84, clinical professor & chief, department radiology, 1980-90; Radiological Society of New Jersey, 1978-, executive committee, 1980-90; Association of University Radiologists, 1971-; Radiological Society of North America, 1988-; American Heart Association, radiology council member, 1973-; Camden County Medical Society, 1977-; New Jersey Medical Society, 1977-; American Medical Association, 1977-; Philadelphia County Medical Society, 1971-77; Pennsylvania Medical Society, 1971-77; Philadelphia Roeutgen Ray Society, 1970-; Society of Cardiovascular Interventional Radiology, 1987-; Philadelphia Angiography-Interventional Society, 1966-; American College of Radiology, 1971-; Pennsylvania Radiological Society, 1971-77; Pan America Medical Association, 1971-90. **HONORS/AWARDS:** American College of Radiology, fellowship, 1990; American Board of Radiology, certification, 1966. **SPECIAL ACHIEVEMENTS:** Co-author or author of many

articles in medical journals. **MILITARY SERVICE:** Army, sp-4, 1954-56. **BUSINESS ADDRESS:** Clinical Prof of Radiology, Dept of Diagnostic Radiology & Nuclear Med, Robert Wood-Johnson Medical School, Cooper Hospital, University Medical Center, 1 Cooper Plaza, Camden, NJ 08103, (609)342-2383.

KURODA, TERUHISA (TERRY)

Financial software firm executive. Japanese American. **PERSONAL:** Born Sep 9, 1936, Washington, DC; son of Otoshiro Kuroda & Meiko Yamada Kuroda; married Deanna I Kuroda; children: Christopher, Melissa, Andreia. **EDUCATION:** MIT, BS, 1959; University of Pennsylvania, 1960. **CAREER:** McKinsey & Company, associate, 1969-72; Citibank, operations head, 1972-76; Salomon Brothers, vice president, 1976-81; Merrill Lynch & Company, group vice president, 1981-84; Securities Industry Automation Corp, senior vice president, 1984-88; Kuroda & Company Inc, president, founder, 1988-. **MILITARY SERVICE:** US Naval Reserves, 1954-62. **BUSINESS ADDRESS:** President, Kuroda & Company Inc, One Evertrust Plaza, Jersey City, NJ 07302, (201)915-0200.

KURODA, YASUMASA

Political scientist. Japanese American. **PERSONAL:** Born Apr 28, 1931, Tokyo, Japan; son of Shohei & Jake Kuroda; married Alice, Mar 23, 1961; children: Kamilla Kassis McClelland, Kamil Kassis. **EDUCATION:** Waseda University, 1951; University of Oregon, BA, sociology, 1956, PhD, political science, 1961; Princeton University, post doctorate, 1961. **CAREER:** University of Oregon, graduate assistant, 1957-60; Montana State University, instructor, assistant professor of government, 1960-64; USC, assistant professor of political science, 1964-66; UCLA, visiting assistant professor of political science, 1965-66; University of Hawaii, associate professor, 1966-72, professor of political science, 1972-. **ORGANIZATIONS:** Japanese Cultural Center of Hawaii, board of governors and program committee, 1988-; Japanese American Citizen's League, board of directors, Honolulu chapter, 1982-92; International Political Science Association, Research Committee on Comparative Study of Local Government & Politics, vice chair, 1970-76; Hawaii Federation of College Teachers, secretary, 1971-72, Manoa chapter, chair, 1976-77; Japan Study Group, University of Hawaii, chair, 1972-75; The Journal of Arab Affairs, editorial board, 1981-; Center for Japanese Studies, executive committee, 1989-92. **HONORS/AWARDS:** State University of New York, Distinguished Visiting Lecturer, 1994; Hebrew University of Jerusalem's Peace Institute, fellowship, 1992; Toyota Foundation, research grant, 1984-85, 1986-90; Social Science Research Council, research grant, 1966-67; Rockefeller Foundation, research grant, 1963-64. **SPECIAL ACHIEVEMENTS:** Reed Town, Japan, Honolulu, The University Press of Hawaii, 1974; Chihotoshi no Kenryokukozo Tokyo, Keisoshobo, 1976; Palestinians without Palestine, Wash DC, The University Press of America, 1978; Studies in Political Socialization in the Arab States, Lynne Reinner Publ, 1987; A Study of Japanese Americans in Honolulu, Tokyo, The Institute of Statistical Math, 1972; Japan in a New World Order: Contributing to the Arab-Israeli Peace Process, Nova Science Publishers, 1994. **BUSINESS ADDRESS:** Professor of Political Science, University of Hawaii at Manoa, Portens 640, 2424 Maile Way, Honolulu, HI 96822, (808)956-8694.

KUROIWA, GEORGE MASAHARU

Company executive. Japanese American. **PERSONAL:** Born Jul 27, 1918, Seattle, WA; son of Masako & Manji; married Haru, Apr 18, 1946; children: Paul, Katherine Scarcliff. **EDUCATION:** University of Washington, BA, 1941. **CAREER:** Dry Cleaners & Laundry, owner, 1944-92; TAK Petroleum, president, 1993-. **ORGANIZATIONS:** North Spokane Rotary Club, 1949-, president, 1974. **SPECIAL ACHIEVEMENTS:** SBA Advisory Council, 1980-85; Office of Minority and Womens Business Enterprises Advisory Council for State of Washington, 1986-91. **BUSINESS ADDRESS:** President, Tak Petroleum Inc, E 59 Queen Ave, Ste 104, Spokane, WA 99207, (509)483-1005.

KUROSE, RUTHANN

State official, association executive. Japanese American. **PERSONAL:** Born Aug 2, 1951. **EDUCATION:** University of Washington, BA, political science. **CAREER:** US Office of Education, Seattle, resource specialist, 1974-77; US Community Services Administration, project director, 1977-79; Office of Congressman Mike Lowry, senior community representative, 1979-81, legislative assistant, 1981-84; City of Seattle, international trade and tourism director, 1984-86; City of Tacoma, international affairs manager, 1986-88; Governor Mike Lowry, Citizens Cabinet member, currently. **ORGANIZATIONS:**

Bellevue Community College, trustee; Seattle Center, board member. **SPE-CIAL ACHIEVEMENTS:** NW Asian Weekly, Top Ten Contributor for 1992; served as member of Governor-elect Lowry's transition team; first Asian American congressional aide in Washington state, 1979; first Asian American hired in international affairs positions for cities of Seattle and Tacoma, 1980s; completed numerous education and training programs at such institutions as the UN, International Leadership Development Institute, and International Fellows Program; national delegate to USSR-US Adult Leadership Program. **BIO-GRAPHICAL SOURCES:** NW Asian Weekly, p 10, Dec 26, 1992, Mar 14, 1993. **BUSINESS ADDRESS:** Advisory Commission, Seattle Center, 305 Harrison St, Seattle, WA 98109, (206)684-7200. *

KURUP, SHISHIR RAVINDRAN
Actor, writer, director, educator. Indo-American. **PERSONAL:** Born Nov 2, 1961, Bombay, Maharashtra, India; son of Ravi Kurup and Bhavani Mathews. **EDUCATION:** University of Florida, BFA, 1984; University of California, San Diego, MFA, 1987. **CAREER:** Los Angeles County Museum of Art, audio/visual tech, 1988-91; LATC, Asia American Theatre Project, director, 1990-91; LATC & Mark Taper Forum, faculty, Young Conservatory, 1990-92; Great Leap, performer, Slice of Rice, 1992-; UC, Irvine, drama faculty, 1992-; UCLA, Asian Studies, co-faculty, 1993; Paramount, Actor, Coneheads: The Movie, 1993. **ORGANIZATIONS:** The Artists' Collective, associate director, 1992-; South Coast Repertory, advisory committee, Nexus program, 1993-; Audrey Skirball Kenis Theatre, playwrights advisory committee, 1992-; Museum of Contemporary Art, Asian access advisory committee, 1992-; Young Conservatory, Mark Taper forum, founding faculty, 1990-92; Asian American Theatre Project, director, 1990-91; The Raven Group, co-director, 1991-. **HONORS/AWARDS:** Princess Grace Award, 1993; Flintridge Foundation, 1991, 1992; Grant from Highways for "Exile...," for "Driving Solo" series, 1992; Grant from Japan America, friendship committee to study with Tadashi Suzuki, 1986. **SPECIAL ACHIEVEMENTS:** Assimilation, solo performance at Mark Taper Forum & Public Theatre, 1992; Exile: Ruminations on a Reluctant Martyr, solo performance at Highways, 1992; co-writer/actor: Life & Death: The Vaudeville Show, performed in Santiago, Cuba, 1993; playwright/director: "Ghurba," LA Festival, Cornerstone Theatre Company, created within the Arab-American community. **HOME ADDRESS:** 12480 Greene Ave, Los Angeles, CA 90066, (310)305-7456.

KUSHIDA, TOSHIMOTO
Educator. Japanese American. **PERSONAL:** Born Feb 13, 1920, Tokyo, Japan; son of Toshio Kushida and Fumi Kushida; married Mieko Kushida, Jan 15, 1946; children: Hiroko Barnes, Makiko Pirscher, Yayoi. **EDUCATION:** Hiroshima University, Japan, ScB, 1944, ScD, 1956; Harvard University, ScM, 1956. **CAREER:** Hiroshima University, Japan, professor, physics, 1961; Ford Motor Co, Scientific Lab, principal scientist, 1961-88; Wayne State University, research professor of research, 1988-. **ORGANIZATIONS:** American Physical Society, fellow, 1965-; IEEE, 1965-. **HONORS/AWARDS:** American Physical Society, fellow. **SPECIAL ACHIEVEMENTS:** Experimental Physics Series, part, 1988. **BUSINESS ADDRESS:** Professor, Wayne State University, 666 W Hancock, Physics Building, Detroit, MI 48201, (313)577-2757.

KUSUMOTO, SADAHEI
Photo and business equipment company executive. Japanese American. **PERSONAL:** Born Apr 15, 1928, Seoul, Republic of Korea; son of Enichiro Kusumoto; married Kuniko, 1960; children: Eriko Kusumoto Gottner, Mariko Kusumoto Sanger. **EDUCATION:** Keio University, Japan, BEc, 1951. **CAREER:** Minolta Camera Co Ltd, director of export, 1960; Minolta Corporation, president, 1969, chairman, 1992-. **ORGANIZATIONS:** Japanese Chamber of Commerce & Industry, executive vice president; United-Way of Bergen County, director. **HONORS/AWARDS:** Photo Marketing Association, Hall of Fame, 1986; Japanese Government, Foreign Minister Award, 1993. **SPECIAL ACHIEVEMENTS:** My Bridge to America, autobiography, E P Duton, 1990, Japanese Style Success, autobiography, Kodansha, 1991. **HOME ADDRESS:** 1 Horizon Rd, #624, Fort Lee, NJ 07024, (201)224-2851.

KUTTAN, APPU
Educator, entrepreneur, investment adviser, tennis innovator, futurist. Indo-American. **PERSONAL:** Born Jul 28, 1941, Quilon, Kerala, India; son of Narayanan Palpu & Narayani Lakshmi; married Claudia, Jul 23, 1967; children: Roger, Maya. **EDUCATION:** University of Kerala, India, BS, electrical engineering, 1963; Washington University, St Louis, MS, industrial engineering, 1966; University of Wisconsin, Madison, PhD, industrial engineering & management, 1968. **CAREER:** University of Puerto Rico, professor, 1968-71;

Government of Venezuela, adviser, 1976-78; Government of India, adviser, 1983; Nick Bollettieri Tennis Academy, chairman, 1985-87; Appu Kuttan and Associates, president, 1969-; National Education Foundation, chairman, 1990-. **ORGANIZATIONS:** American Institute of Industrial Engineers, 1968-76; Institute of Electrical & Electronic Engineers, 1968-; World Hunger Program, adviser, 1986; Refugees International, founder, 1990; American Diet Foundation, founder, 1989; McDonald's National Junior Tennis Tournament, chairman, 1986. **HONORS/AWARDS:** University of Kerala, Athletic Champion & Soccer Captain, 1963; All-India Tata Endowment, Tata Scholar, 1964; University of Puerto Rico, Best Professor Award, 1969; Puerto Rico Safety Council, Distinguished Traffic Safety, 1971; Venezuela Chamber of Commerce, Distinguished Natl Service, 1978; US Tennis Foundation, Distinguished Service, 1988; Natl Education Foundation, Innovative Educator, 1993. **SPECIAL ACHIEVEMENTS:** Author of MBS (Management By Systems); co-author, Kuttan Momentum Investment Model; author, Kuttan Learning System, set up USA 2100 Program; author, Total Tennis Program, helped develop top pros, including Jim Courier, Andre Agassi, and Monica Seles; fluent in Spanish. **BIOGRAPHICAL SOURCES:** "Dr Appu Kuttan: Systems Management Entrepreneur," Gulfshore Life, p 19, Aug 1984; "Appu Kuttan-Wizard in Venezuela's Social Security," Zeta, Natl Weekly, May 1, 1977; "Kuttan, President Clinton's Friend," Malayala Manorama, India's largest daily, p 1, Jan 26, 1993. **BUSINESS ADDRESS:** Chairman, National Education Foundation, 8027 Leesburg Pike, Vienna, VA 22182, (703)821-2100.

KUTTAN, ROGER
Investment adviser. Indo-American. **PERSONAL:** Born Dec 23, 1973, Madison, WI; son of Appu Kuttan & Claudia Kuttan. **EDUCATION:** Duke University, 1987; Simons Rock of Bard College, MA, 1987-88; Johns Hopkins University, 1990; Stanford University, 1988; American University, BABS (summa cum laude), finance, 1992. **CAREER:** US Congress, congressional aide, 1992; Kuttan and Associates, president, 1992-; National Education Foundation, vice president, 1992-. **ORGANIZATIONS:** Financial Management Association, 1992-; Beta Gamma Sigma, 1992-; National Dean's List, 1992; Phi Kappa Phi, 1992-; Sigma Phi Omega, 1992-; Alpha Lambda Delta, 1992-. **HONORS/AWARDS:** US Presidential Inaugural, President Clinton's Face of Hope, the only Asian American, 1993; American University, Top Business Senior, Valedictorian, 1992; Volvo Tennis All-American, scholar-athlete, 1992. **SPECIAL ACHIEVEMENTS:** Author, Kuttan Stock Momentum Investment Model, 1992; author, Kuttan Commodity Momentum Investment Model, 1993; at age 19, youngest & one of the most successful money managers in Wall Street, 1993; at age 18, youngest business graduate in the US, 1992; at age 18, youngest to graduate from American University, 1992. **BIOGRAPHICAL SOURCES:** "Roger Kuttan Is Honored by President Clinton," Bradenton Herald, p 3, Jan 26, 1993; "This Roger's No Rabbit," The Week, India's largest weekly, cover, p 14-18, Feb 21, 1993; "Tennis Whiz Takes Stock," USA Today, p C-1, May 20, 1992. **BUSINESS ADDRESS:** President, Kuttan and Associates, 1120 Marion Ave, Mc Lean, VA 22101, (703)821-0001.

KUWAHARA, FRANK
City government official, association executive. Japanese American. **CAREER:** Floriculturist, retired; City of Los Angeles, Community Redevelopment Agency, vice chairman, 1984-93; Southern California Flowers Growers Assn, president, currently. **BUSINESS ADDRESS:** President, Southern California Flower Growers, 755 Wall St, Los Angeles, CA 90014, (213)627-2482. *

KUWAHARA, STEVEN SADAO
Biochemist, pharmacologist, manager. Japanese American. **PERSONAL:** Born Jul 20, 1940, Lahaina, Maui, HI; son of Toshio Kuwahara and Hideko Sasaki Kuwahara; married Rene Mikie Miyajima Kuwahara, Jun 24, 1973; children: Daniel Toshiro, Sara Sadae. **EDUCATION:** Cornell University, BS, 1962; University of Wisconsin, Madison, MS, 1965, PhD, 1967. **CAREER:** University of Wisconsin, research assistant, 1962-66; University of Washington, research associate, 1966-67; California State University, Long Beach, assistant professor, 1967-71; University of California, Irvine, assistant research biologist, 1971-73; Michigan Dept of Public Health, section chief, 1973-82; Baxter Healthcare, manager, 1982-. **ORGANIZATIONS:** Boy Scouts of America, scoutmaster, troop 402, 1987-93; West Covina Buddhist Temple, member of the board, 1984-; Society for Experimental Medicine and Biology, 1980-; American Federation for Clinical Research, 1979-; American Society for Microbiology, 1971-; American Chemical Society, 1964-; American Association for the Advancement of Science, 1962-; Wilderness Medicine Society, 1992-. **HONORS/AWARDS:** Long Beach Heart Association, merit award,

1969; National Institute of General Medical Sciences, special research fellowship, 1971; BSA-National Eagle Scout Association, Scoutmaster Award of Merit, 1992. **SPECIAL ACHIEVEMENTS:** 27 publications in the fields of analytical biochemistry, microbiology, and thrombosis-hemostasis, 1969-88; 15 meetings and other presentations, 1969-85. **HOME ADDRESS:** 975 W Amador Street, Claremont, CA 91711. **BUSINESS ADDRESS:** Manager of Validations, Quality Assurance Dept, Baxter Healthcare Immunotherapy Div, 1720 Flower St, Duarte, CA 91010, (818)305-6051.

KUWAYAMA, GEORGE
Curator. Japanese American. **PERSONAL:** Born Feb 25, 1925, New York, NY; son of Senzo Kuwayama and Fumiko Kuwayama; married Lillian Y, Dec 5, 1961; children: Holly A, Mark K, Jeremy S. **EDUCATION:** Williams College, BA, 1948; Institute of Fine Arts, New York University; University of Michigan, MA, 1956. **CAREER:** Cooper Union Museum, keeper's assistant, 1954; Los Angeles County Museum, curator of Oriental art, 1959-69; Los Angeles County Museum of Art, senior curator for Far Eastern art, 1969-. **ORGANIZATIONS:** Association for Asian Studies; College Art Association; American Oriental Society; International House of Japan; Japan Seminar; China Colloquium; Korea Society; Asia Society. **HONORS/AWARDS:** University of Michigan, Freer Scholar, 1955-56; American Oriental Society, Hackney Fellow, 1956-57; Inter-University Fellow, 1957-58; NEA, research grantee; Asian Cultural Council, research grantee. **SPECIAL ACHIEVEMENTS:** Author, Art Treasures of Japan, 1965; The Bizarre Imagery of Yoshitoshi, 1980; Far Eastern Lacquer, 1982; Shippo-The Art of Enameling in Japan, 1987; The Quest for Eternity, 1987. **MILITARY SERVICE:** US Army, parachute infantry, pfc, 1944-46. **HOME ADDRESS:** 1417 Comstock Ave, Los Angeles, CA 90024, (310)277-2306. **BUSINESS ADDRESS:** Senior Curator, Los Angeles County Museum of Art, 5905 Wilshire Blvd, Los Angeles, CA 90036, (213)857-6029.

KWAK, NO KYOON
Educator. Korean American. **PERSONAL:** Born Nov 24, 1932, Seoul, Republic of Korea; son of Hee Young Kwak and Boo Soon Maeng; married Renee L Kwak, Nov 10, 1962; children: Eunice, Amy, Alvin. **EDUCATION:** Seoul National University, BS, 1955; United States International University, BA, 1956; University of California, Berkeley, MA, 1958; University of Southern California, PhD, 1964. **CAREER:** Eastern New Mexico University, assistant professor of economics, 1964-65; Clemson University, assistant professor of industrial management, 1965-68; Texas A&M University, visiting professor of business research, 1982; St Louis University, associate professor of management sciences, 1968-71, professor of decision sciences, 1971-. **ORGANIZATIONS:** American Economic Association, 1964-; Decision Sciences Institute, 1978-; Operations Research Society of America, 1972-; The Institute of Management Sciences, 1968-. **HONORS/AWARDS:** Hays Foundation, fellowship, 1961-62; Helms Foundation, fellowship, 1962-64; J E Sirrine Foundation, Faculty Research Grant, 1967-68; St Louis University, Outstanding Teacher Award, 1987, Outstanding Research Scholar Award, 1993; Council for International Exchange of Scholars, Fulbright Senior Scholar Award. **SPECIAL ACHIEVEMENTS:** Author: Mathematical Programming with Business Applications, 1973; Quantitative Decision Theory for Management, 1979; Quantitative Models for Business Decisions, 1980; Managerial Applications of Operations Research, 1982; Introduction to Mathematical Programming, 1987. **BUSINESS ADDRESS:** Professor of Decision Sciences, St Louis University, School of Business Administration, 3674 Lindell Blvd, Davis-Shaughnessy Hall, St Louis, MO 63108, (314)658-3867.

KWAK, WIKIL
Educator. Korean American. **PERSONAL:** Born Apr 2, 1956, Youngcheun, Republic of Korea; son of Guha Kwak and Okche Yun Kwak; married Eunhee Kwak, May 10, 1981; children: Gene, Annie, Kevin. **EDUCATION:** Kyungbuk National University, Korea, BA, 1980; Iowa State University, MS, 1985; University of Nebraska, Lincoln, PhD, 1990. **CAREER:** University of Nebraska-Lincoln, teaching assistant, 1986-89; University of Nebraska-Omaha, assistant professor, 1990-. **ORGANIZATIONS:** American Accounting Assopciation, 1990-; Institute of Management Accountant, 1987-; AAA: International Accounting Section, 1990-; Management Accounting Section, 1990-, Auditing Section, 1990-. **BUSINESS ADDRESS:** Assistant Professor, University of Nebraska at Omaha, College of Business Administration, 60th & Dodge, 408K Professional Acctg, Omaha, NE 68182-0048, (402)554-2821.

KWAN, CATHERINE NING
Educator. Chinese American. **PERSONAL:** Born Mar 8, 1938, Hankow, China; daughter of En Cheng Ning & Chien Sheng Ning; married Benjamin Kwan, Aug 29, 1964; children: San San, David. **EDUCATION:** National Taiwan University, BS, 1959; State University of South Dakota, MA, 1960; University of Maryland, PhD, 1965. **CAREER:** Washington University, postdoctoral fellow, 1965-67, research associate, 1973-76; Texas Christian University, assistant professor, 1969-70; UCLA, lecturer of microbiology, 1976-78; Mt St Mary's College, professor of biology, 1978-. **ORGANIZATIONS:** Chinese American Engineers & Scientists Association of Southern California, president, 1992-93; Alumni Association of National Taiwan University, president, 1991-92; Alumni Association of Taipei 1st Girls School, president, 1987-88; American Society of Microbiologist, 1965-; Sigma Xi; AAUP. **HONORS/AWARDS:** Chinese America Engineers & Scientists Association of Southern California, Service Award, 1988; Joint Alumni of Taiwan Universities, Achievement Award, 1992. **BUSINESS ADDRESS:** Professor of Biology, Mt St Mary's College, 12001 Chalon Rd, Los Angeles, CA 90049-1526, (310)440-3278.

KWAN, FRANCO CHANG-HONG
Episcopal priest. Chinese American. **PERSONAL:** Born Sep 24, 1950, Kwangchow, Kwangtung, People's Republic of China; son of Lok Ping Kwan and Kwok Ming Kwan; married Mei Bak Kwan, Jul 4, 1976; children: Grace, William, Calvin. **EDUCATION:** University of Chinese Culture, Taiwan, LLB, 1976; Chinese University of Hong Kong, BD, 1979; Hunter College, School of Social Work, MSW, 1989; New York Theological Seminary, DMin, 1993. **CAREER:** All Saints' Middle School, director of general affairs, 1971-72; Church of Advent, rector, 1979-83; St John's & St Mary's Technology Institute, Counseling Center, director, 1979-83, lecturer, 1979-83; Church of Our Savior, priest-in-charge, 1983-87; St George's Parish, vicar, 1987-. **ORGANIZATIONS:** Episcopal Diocese of Long Island, Diocesen Council, 1992-; Racial Justice Commission, commissioner, 1991-; Asian American Ministry, DIL, chair, 1992-; Ecumenical Working Group of Asian & Pacific Americans, Episcopal delegate, 1989-; Queens Community Board #7, board member, 1990-; Asian Committee on Aging, chair, 1985-; Hamilton-Madison House, advisory board, 1985-. **HONORS/AWARDS:** President George Bush, Proclamation, 1990; Manhattan Borough President David Dinkins, Proclamation, 1988; Census '90, Certificate of Appreciation, 1990. **SPECIAL ACHIEVEMENTS:** Author: Needs of the Chinese Elderly—Who Should Care for Them, 1987; "Cultural Responses to Issues of Death & Dying - A Chinese Viewpoint," Pride Institute Journal; founder of Asian Committee on Aging, 1986. **BUSINESS ADDRESS:** Vicar, St. George's Parish, 135-32 38th Avenue, Flushing, NY 11354, (718)359-1171.

KWAN, KIAN M.
Educator. Chinese American. **PERSONAL:** Born Jun 15, 1929, Hoiping, Guangdong, China; son of Jose C Kwan and Tak Quon Mar; married Grace L Kwan, Dec 30, 1961; children: Joseph H, Gregory L, Christie F. **EDUCATION:** Far Eastern University, BA (magna cum laude), 1952; University of California, Berkeley, MA, 1954, PhD, 1958. **CAREER:** Ohio University, instructor to assistant professor, 1958-65, chairperson, dept of sociology, 1963-65; University of Hawaii, visiting professor, 1972-73; California State University, associate to professor, 1965-, chairman, dept of sociology, 1969-71. **ORGANIZATIONS:** American Sociological Association, 1964-; California Alumni Association, 1958-. **HONORS/AWARDS:** California State University, Northridge, faculty research grant, 1985; John Randolph Haynes & Dora Haynes Foundation, research fellow, 1957-58; University of California, Berkeley, University fellow, 1955-57. **SPECIAL ACHIEVEMENTS:** T Shibutani & Kian M Kwan, Ethnic Stratification, Macmillan, 1965; T Shibutani, Kian M Kwan & Charles Nam, "The Transformation of Minorities," in Helen MacGill Hughes, ed., Racial & Ethnic Relations, Allyn & Bacon, 1970. **BUSINESS ADDRESS:** Professor, Dept of Sociology, California State University, Northridge, 18111 Nordhoff St, Northridge, CA 91330, (818)885-3591.

KWAN, NANCY KASHEN
Actress. Hong Kong American. **PERSONAL:** Born May 19, 1939, Hong Kong; children: Bernie. **EDUCATION:** Royal Ballet School, England. **CAREER:** Actress, films include: The World of Susie Wong, 1960; Flower Drum Song, 1961; The Main Attraction, 1962; The Girl Who Knew Too Much, 1969; The Last Ninja; Noble House; Dragon: Life of Bruce Lee, 1993; numerous others; television series include: Wonder Woman, 1973; Hawaii Five-O; Fantasy Island; Kung Fu; numerous others; Oriental Pearl Cream, spokeswoman; "Arthur and Leila," San Francisco, play, 1993. **ORGANIZATIONS:** Associ-

ation of Asian Pacific American Artists, panelist, 1993. **HONORS/AWARDS:** Hollywood Foreign Press, International Star of Tomorrow, 1960. **SPECIAL ACHIEVEMENTS:** "T'ai Chi Ch'uan Touching the Clouds," instructional videotape; author, "Loose Woman with No Face," screenplay. **BIOGRAPHICAL SOURCES:** Contemporary Theatre, Film, and Television, volume 7, 1989; AsianWeek, pg 4, Oct 22, 1993. *

KWAN, SIMON HING-MAN
Educator. Hong Kong American/Chinese American. **PERSONAL:** Born Jun 11, 1961, Hong Kong; son of Kam Oi Seto and Wing Shue Kwan; married Krammie Chan, May 5, 1990; children: James C. **EDUCATION:** University of North Texas, BBA, 1983, MBA, 1986; University of North Carolina, PhD, 1990. **CAREER:** University of Arizona, professor of finance, 1990-. **ORGANIZATIONS:** American Finance Association, 1989-; Financial Management Assn, 1989-. **SPECIAL ACHIEVEMENTS:** Risk Taking Behavior of Banking Firms, Federal Reserve Bank of Chicago, 1991; "Re-examination of Commercial Bank Stock Returns," Journal of Financial Services Research, 1991; "Beta in the Oil & Gas Industry," Journal of Petroleum Accounting, 1987. **BUSINESS ADDRESS:** Professor, Dept of Finance, University of Arizona, College of Business Administration, Tucson, AZ 85721, (602)621-5589.

KWAN, YUEN-YIN KATHY
Librarian. Chinese American. **PERSONAL:** Born Nov 19, 1959, Hong Kong. **EDUCATION:** University of Hong Kong, BSS, 1982; State University of New York, MLS, 1988; City University of New York, MA, computer science, 1993. **CAREER:** Millard Fillmore Hospital, assistant librarian, 1987-88; Winthrop University Hospital, systems librarian, 1988-. **ORGANIZATIONS:** New York/New Jersey Chapter of Medical Library Association, Microcomputer Users Group, chair, 1990-; Metropolitan New York Chapter of American Society for Information Science, program committee, 1992; Medical Library Association, 1988-; American Library Association, 1987-; Library & Information Technology Association, 1990-; American Society for Information Science, 1991-. **HONORS/AWARDS:** Hospital Library Section, Medical Library Association, Professional Recognition Certificate, 1992. **SPECIAL ACHIEVEMENTS:** Y Kathy Kwan, "Teaching miniMEDLINE with HyperCard Stacks," FLIS Project News, vol 2, #3, pg 3, 1991; Medical Library Association Annual Conference, presentation of a poster: "Teaching End-User searching with HyperCard," 1991. **BUSINESS ADDRESS:** Systems Librarian, Winthrop University Hospital, Hollis Health Sciences Library, 259 First St, Mineola, NY 11501, (516)663-2783.

KWAN-GETT, MEI LIN
Lawyer. Chinese American. **PERSONAL:** Born May 2, 1967, Cleveland, OH; daughter of Clifford S Kwan-Gett and Joo Een Kwan-Gett. **EDUCATION:** Harvard/Radcliffe University, AB, 1989; Yale Law School, JD, 1992. **CAREER:** Honorable George C Pratt, judicial clerk, 1993-. **ORGANIZATIONS:** California Bar Association, 1993-. **HONORS/AWARDS:** US Congressional Presidential Scholar, 1985. **SPECIAL ACHIEVEMENTS:** Editor-in-Chief, The Yale Law Journal, vol 101, 1991-92.

KWEI, TI-KANG
Educator. Chinese American. **PERSONAL:** Born Mar 19, 1929, Shanghai, China; married. **EDUCATION:** National Chiao-Tung University, China, BS, 1949; University of Toronto, MS, 1954; Polytechnic Institute of Brooklyn, PhD, 1959. **CAREER:** Standard Oil Co of Indiana, research chemist, 1958-59; Interchemical Corp, group leader, 1959-65; Bell Telephone Laboratories, supervisor, 1965-81; Industrial Tech Research Institute, Taiwan, vice president, 1981-84; Polytechnic University, professor, 1984-. **ORGANIZATIONS:** Chinese American Chemical Society, board member, 1989-92; American Chemical Society, 1959-; Sigma Xi, 1959-; Chinese Institute of Engineers USA, life member, 1974-, board member, 1976-79. **HONORS/AWARDS:** Sigma Xi, outstanding research award, 1990; Society of Materials Science, Taiwan, achievement award, 1984; Chinese Institute of Engineers USA, achievement award, 1978. **SPECIAL ACHIEVEMENTS:** About 150 scientific publications on polymer science, 1954-. **BUSINESS ADDRESS:** Professor, Polytechnic University, 6 Metrotech Center, Brooklyn, NY 11201.

KWOH, STEWART
Attorney. Chinese American. **PERSONAL:** Born Sep 16, 1948, Nanking, China; son of Edwin and Beulah (Quo) Kwoh; married Patricia Lee Kwoh; children: two. **EDUCATION:** University of Los Angeles, BA, 1970, JD, 1974. **CAREER:** Asian Law Collective, 1975-78; Law Office of Stewart Kwoh, 1978-83; Asian Pacific American Legal Center of Southern California, execu-

tive director, 1983-; University of California at Los Angeles, Asian Americans and the Law, instructor, 1984-. **ORGANIZATIONS:** Rebuild Los Angeles, board of directors, 1992-; UCLA Asian Pacific Alumni Association, president, 1991-92; Southern California Chinese Lawyers Association, president, 1988; National Asian Pacific American Legal Consortium, co-founding board member, 1992-; Los Angeles Methodist Urban Foundation, secretary of board, 1988-; California Consumer Protection Foundation, trustee, 1991-; California Tomorrow, board member, 1988-; Leadership Education for Asian Pacifics, board member, 1988-; Los Angeles City Human Relations Commission, president, 1990. **HONORS/AWARDS:** Public Counsel, individual award, 1991; Mayor's Asian Pacific Heritage Month, individual award, 1993; American Civil Liberties Union, Southern California, individual award, 1993; CORO Foundation, individual award, 1993; Martin Luther King Jr Birthday Dinner, President's Award, 1994. **BUSINESS ADDRESS:** Executive Director , President, Asian Pacific American Legal Center of S California, 1010 S Flower St, Rm 302, Los Angeles, CA 90015, (213)748-2022.

KWOK, CHUCK CHUN-YAU
Educator. Hong Kong American. **PERSONAL:** Born Sep 2, 1956, Hong Kong; married Shirley Wai-Ying. **EDUCATION:** Chinese University of Hong Kong, BS, 1979, MPh, sociology 1981; University of Texas at Austin, PhD, international business, 1984. **CAREER:** University of South Carolina, International Business, assistant professor, 1984-90, associate professor, 1990-. **ORGANIZATIONS:** Academy of International Business; American Finance Association; Financial Management Association. **HONORS/AWARDS:** University of South Carolina, MIBS, Outstanding Professor Award, 1993, Alfred Smith Teaching Award, 1991. **SPECIAL ACHIEVEMENTS:** Numerous articles including: Co-author, "What Are International Business Centers?," International Executive, 1992; "An Empirical Examination of Foreign Exchange Market Efficiency: Applying the Filter Rule Strategy to Intra-Daily DM/$ Exchange Rates," Journal of International Financial Management and Accounting, Spring 1992; "An Examination of the Distribution of Intra-Daily Exchange Rate Changes," Global Finance Journal, vol 3, no 2, 1992; editorial board, Journal of International Business Studies, 1989-92; ranked among the top 10 contributors to the Journal of International Business Studies for the ten-year period of 1980-89. **BUSINESS ADDRESS:** Professor, University of SC, College of Business Administration, Columbia, SC 29208, (803)777-3606.

KWOK, DANIEL W. Y.
Educator. Chinese American. **PERSONAL:** Born Sep 3, 1932, Shanghai, China; son of Tak-Wa Kwok (deceased) and Grace W Kwok (deceased); married Nancy C Kwok, Sep 15, 1954; children: Theodore J, Alison G. **EDUCATION:** Brown University, BA, 1954; Yale University, MA, 1956, PhD, 1959. **CAREER:** Yale University, lecturer, 1957-59; Knox College, assistant professor, 1959-61; University of Hawaii, professor, 1961-. **ORGANIZATIONS:** American Historical Association, 1956-, nominating committee, 1979-82; Association for Asian Studies, 1956-, development committee, 1979-80; World History Association, 1988-; National Committee on US-China Relations, 1979-. **HONORS/AWARDS:** University of Hawaii, Presidential Citation for Excellence in Teaching, 1988; Social Science Research Council, fellow, 1975-76; East-West Center, senior fellow, 1968-69; Hong Kong University, Research Professorships, 1975-76, 1982-83. **SPECIAL ACHIEVEMENTS:** Scientism in Chinese Thought 1990-1950, Yale University Press, 1965, Chinese Translation, Jiangsu Ren Min, 1989; Cosmology, Ontology, Human Efficacy: Essays in Chinese Thought, University of Hawaii Press, 1993. **BUSINESS ADDRESS:** Professor, Dept of History, University of Hawaii, 2530 Dole St, Honolulu, HI 96822, (808)956-7733.

KWOK, DAPHNE
Organization administrator. Chinese American. **EDUCATION:** Wesleyan University, East Asian studies, music; CUNY, Baruch College, MPA. **CAREER:** US Department of Education, staff member, voter's registration, seminar coordinator; Office of Asian and Pacific Islander Affairs, staff assistant; Organization of Chinese Americans, executive director, currently. **ORGANIZATIONS:** Wesleyan Asian Interest Group, founder; Wesleyan Asian Alumni Council, founder; Wesleyan, elected trustee, currently. **SPECIAL ACHIEVEMENTS:** Worked within a coalition to pass the Voting Rights Improvement Act of 1992. **BIOGRAPHICAL SOURCES:** "Community Profile," Asian Week, Oct 16, 1992, p15. **BUSINESS ADDRESS:** Executive Director, Organization of Chinese Americans, 1001 Connecticut Ave NW, Ste 707, Washington, DC 20036, (202)223-5500. *

KWOK, HOI-SING
Educator. Chinese American. **PERSONAL:** Born Mar 1, 1951, Hong Kong; married Ying-Hong Tung; children: Theresa, Janet, Eric. **EDUCATION:** Northwestern University, BSEE, 1973; Harvard University, MS, 1974, PhD, 1978. **CAREER:** Lawrence Berkeley Lab, Berkeley, CA, research associate, 1978-80; State University of New York at Buffalo, assistant professor, 1980-83, associate professor, 1983-85, professor, 1985-. **ORGANIZATIONS:** Institute of Electrical and Electronic Engineers; Optical Society of America; American Physical Society; Tau Beta Phi & Eta Kappa Nu. **HONORS/AWARDS:** Presidential Young Investigator Award, 1984; Science News Most Cited Paper, 1988; New York State/UUP Excellence Award, 1991. **SPECIAL ACHIEVEMENTS:** Over 170 journal publications; 28 invited conference presentations, 21 invited lectures; over 120 conference presentations. **BUSINESS ADDRESS:** Professor, Dept of Electrical and Computer Engineering, State University of New York at Buffalo, 214 Bonner Hall, Amherst, NY 14260, (716)645-3119.

KWOK, JOSEPH
Banker. Chinese American. **PERSONAL:** married Sharon; children: Steven, Jason. **CAREER:** San Francisco Thrift & Loan, executive officer, chairman, currently. **ORGANIZATIONS:** United Way of the United Bay Area, Chinese Advisory Board, co-chairman; International Lion's District, regional chairman; Shanghai Children's Medical Center, vice-chairman. **BUSINESS ADDRESS:** Chairman/Executive Officer, San Francisco Thrift & Loan, 2501 Clement St, San Francisco, CA 94121-1817, (415)668-8288. *

KWOK, REGINALD YIN-WANG
Educator. Chinese American. **PERSONAL:** Born Jan 24, 1937, Hong Kong; son of Kwok On & Poon Yee Fong; married Annette, Aug 29, 1964; children: Zoe Song-Yi. **EDUCATION:** The Polytechnic, London, diploma, architecture, 1963; Architectural Association, London, diploma, tropical studies, 1967; Columbia University, MSUP, MS, arch, 1969, PhD, urban planning, 1973. **CAREER:** Chamberlin Powell & Bon, London, assistant architect, 1960-61; Palmer & Turner, Hong Kong, architect, 1964-65; Denys Lasdun & Partners, London, architect, 1963-64, 1965-66; Columbia University, urban planning, assistant professor, 1974-76, associate professor, 1976-80; University of Hong Kong, urban studies & urban planning, director/professor, 1980-89; University of Hawaii at Manoa, Asian studies/urban & regional planning, professor, 1989-. **ORGANIZATIONS:** Eastern Regional Organizatin for Planning & Housing, honorary president, 1986-; Architectural Society of China, honorary council member, 1983-; Hong Kong Institute of Planners, honorary member, 1985-; Hong Kong Institute of Architects, associate member, 1981-; Royal Institute of British Arch, associate member, 1985-; Hong Kong Housing Authority, appointed member, 1982-89; Town Planning Board, Hong Kong, appointed member, 1987-89; Shenzhen City Planning Committee, appointed member, 1986-. **HONORS/AWARDS:** Eu Tong Sen Endowment, study grant, 1992-93; University of Hawaii/East-West Center, research grant, 1991-93; Hawaii Committee of the Humanities, grant for conference organization, 1990; Ministere Des Affaires Etrangeres, France, study visit, 1988. **SPECIAL ACHIEVEMENTS:** Numerous publications, including: author, Chengshi Guihua Gailun (General Theories of Urban Planning), 1992; Shek Kip Mei Syndrome: Economic Development & Public Housing in Hong Kong & Singapore, 1990; Chinese Urban Reforms: What Model Now?, 1990; Planning in Asia: Present & Future, 1984; languages: English, Chinese (Mandarin, Cantonese). **BUSINESS ADDRESS:** Professor, University of Hawaii at Manoa, School of Hawaiian, Asian and Pacific Studies, Moore Hall 316, Honolulu, HI 96822, (808)956-9196.

KWOK, WO KONG
Chemical company researcher. Chinese American. **PERSONAL:** Born Jan 13, 1936, Hong Kong; married Tzu Wen Kwok. **EDUCATION:** National Taiwan University, BS, 1958; East Tennessee State University, MS, 1963; Illinois Institute of Technology, PhD, 1966. **CAREER:** DuPont Company, senior research associate, 1966-. **ORGANIZATIONS:** American Chemical Society, 1966-. **HONORS/AWARDS:** IITRI, Research Fellowship, 1965-66. **SPECIAL ACHIEVEMENTS:** Published more than 30 papers, 1964-91; 4 patents. **HOME ADDRESS:** 11 McCormick Drive, Hockessin, DE 19707. **BUSINESS PHONE:** (302)999-2918.

KWON, JEFFREY YOUNG
Pharmacy administrator. Korean American. **PERSONAL:** Born Oct 2, 1956, Los Angeles, CA; son of Youngman Kwon and Carrie Kwon; married Allyson Kwon, Mar 1, 1986; children: Garrett Nabeshima. **EDUCATION:** UCLA,

biology, 1978-82; USC, School of Pharmacy, DPharm, 1982. **CAREER:** Beverly Hills Medical Center, clinical coordinator, 1986-87, director of pharmacy, 1987-89; Norrell Health Care, director of pharmacy, 1989-90; Critical Care America, director of pharmacy, 1990-93; Life Care Solutions, director of pharmacy, 1993-. **ORGANIZATIONS:** American Cancer Society, pharmacists, nurses committee chairman, 1991; California Society of Hospital Pharmacists, South Bay Chapter, secretary, 1991. **SPECIAL ACHIEVEMENTS:** Author: "The Hospital Formularity as a Tool for Quality Assurance," Topics in Hospital Pharmacy Management, 1989. **HOME ADDRESS:** 3384 McLaughlin Ave, Los Angeles, CA 90066, (310)398-1751. **BUSINESS ADDRESS:** Director of Pharmacy, Life Care Solutions, 381 Van Ness Way, Ste 1514, Torrance, CA 90501, (310)781-2061.

KWON, MYOUNG-JA L.
Librarian, educational administrator. Korean American. **PERSONAL:** Born Feb 21, 1943, Seoul, Republic of Korea; daughter of Hong-jik Yi and Kyongnam Suh; married; children: William L. **EDUCATION:** Seoul National University, Seoul, Korea, BA, history, 1965; Brigham Young University, MLS, 1968; University of Nevada, Las Vegas, MA, history, 1980, history, currently. **CAREER:** University of Nevada, Las Vegas, assistant cataloger, 1968-79, nonbook librarian, 1979-83, systems librarian, 1983-89, systems & budget, associate university librarian, 1989-92, interim dean of libraries, 1992, associate dean of libraries, 1992-. **ORGANIZATIONS:** American Library Association, 1974-; Library Information Technology Association, 1976-; Association of College and Research Libraries, 1985-; Library Administration and Management Association, 1988-. **HONORS/AWARDS:** University of Nevada, Las Vegas, Phi Kappa Phi, 1980, Phi Alpha Theta, History, 1980, Bright Light Award, 1993. **SPECIAL ACHIEVEMENTS:** Co-author, "INNOPAC Online Catalog at the University of Nevada," The Online Catalog Book, Walt Crawford, editor, distributed by LITA, pp XV 1-XV 33, 1992; co-author, "The Management of Change: Minimizing the Negative Impact on Staff and Patrons," Library Systems Migration: Changing Automated Systems in Libraries & Information Centers, Gary Atkin, editor, Meckler, 1991; author, "Koreans in Nevada," Nevada Public Affairs Review, no 2, p 52-55, 1987. **HOME ADDRESS:** 3023 Paintedhills Ave, Las Vegas, NV 89120. **BUSINESS ADDRESS:** Associate Dean of Libraries, University of Nevada, Las Vegas, 4505 Maryland Pkwy, James R Dickinson Library, Las Vegas, NV 89154, (702)895-3286.

KWON, RONALD CHI-OH
Physician. Japanese American/Korean American. **PERSONAL:** Born Jan 14, 1947, Wailuku, HI; son of John Heong-Sik Kwon and Mitsugi Hamada Kwon; married Carolyn Sue, Oct 30, 1982; children: Mark, Elizabeth, Allison, Carolyn, David. **EDUCATION:** Harvard University, BA (cum laude), 1969; University of Colorado Medical School, MD, 1974; Tufts-New England Medical Center, intership, residency, internal medicine, 1974-79. **CAREER:** Private practice, physician, 1979-. **ORGANIZATIONS:** American College of Physicians, 1979-; Mass Medical Society, 1979-; Hawaii Medical Assn, 1985-; American Medical Assn, 1989-; American Society for Microbiology, 1985-; Hale Makua Health Services, bd of trustees, 1987-; Hale Makua Foundation, vice pres, 1992-. **HONORS/AWARDS:** University of Colorado Medical School, Alpha Omega Alpha, 1973. **BUSINESS ADDRESS:** Physician, 99 S Market St, Wailuku, HI 96793, (808)244-4887.

KWON, YOUNG HA
Physician. Korean American. **PERSONAL:** Born Feb 20, 1962, Seoul, Republic of Korea; son of Tae Sung Kwon & Hae Hong Kwon; married Laurie Lee Collier, Dec 22, 1991; children: Ogi Kwon. **EDUCATION:** Massachusetts Institute of Technology, BS, 1984; Yale University School of Medicine, MD, 1991; Massachusetts Institute of Technology, PhD, 1991. **CAREER:** Mount Auburn Hospital, Internal Medicine, intern, 1991-92; Massachusetts Eye & Ear Infirmary, resident in ophthalmology, 1992-. **ORGANIZATIONS:** American Academy of Ophthalmology, 1992-; The Association for Research in Vision and Ophthalmology, 1992-; American Medical Association, 1991-92. **HONORS/AWARDS:** Massachusetts Institute of Technology, Asinari Award for Excellence in Research, 1983. **SPECIAL ACHIEVEMENTS:** 5 publications of original scientific research articles, 8 research abstracts presented at meetings, 1984-. **HOME ADDRESS:** 2456 Massachusetts Ave, Ste 401, Cambridge, MA 02140.

KWON, YOUNG WUK
Educator. Korean American. **PERSONAL:** Born Apr 20, 1959, Chunju, Republic of Korea; son of Jung Ho Kwon and Hee Jong Lee; married Soon Ja

Kwon, Aug 23, 1981; children: Aric, Elliot. **EDUCATION:** Seoul National University, BS (magna cum laude), 1981; Oklahoma State University, MS, 1983; Rice University, PhD, 1985. **CAREER:** Oil Technology Services, Inc, senior engineer, 1985-86; University of Missouri, Rolla, assistant professor, 1987-90; Naval Postgraduate School, associate professor, 1990-. **ORGANIZATIONS:** American Society of Mechanical Engineers, 1984-; Society of Petroleum Engineers, 1985-. **HONORS/AWARDS:** Society of Petroleum Engineers, Cedric Ferguson Medal, 1989; Naval Postgraduate School, Outstanding Research Award, 1992; United States National Dean's List, 1983; Naval Postgraduate School, Outstanding Teaching Award, 1993. **SPECIAL ACHIEVEMENTS:** Over sixty technical publications published in professional journals. **BUSINESS ADDRESS:** Associate Professor, Dept of Mechanical Engineering, Naval Postgraduate School, 699 Dyer Rd, Monterey, CA 93943-5000, (408)656-3385.

KWON-CHUNG, KYUNG JOO
Researcher, government official. Korean American. **PERSONAL:** Born Oct 5, 1933, Seoul, Republic of Korea; daughter of C T Kwon and S I Cho; married Young M Chung, Apr 7, 1957; children: Jay, John, Mia. **EDUCATION:** Ewha Womans University, Korea, BS, 1956, MS, 1958; University of Wisconsin-Madison, MS, 1963, PhD, 1965. **CAREER:** Euha Womans University, research assistant, 1956-58, assistant professor, 1958-61; University of Wisconsin, Madison, research assistant, 1961-65; National Institutes of Health, post-doctoral fellow, 1966-68, senior investigator, 1968-. **ORGANIZATIONS:** American Society for Microbiology, 1965-; Medical Mycological Society, 1968-; Mycological Society of America, 1968-; International Society of Human and Animal Mycology, 1968-, associate editor, 1983-. **HONORS/AWARDS:** US State Dept, Fulbright Exchange Professorship, 1961-62; NIH, NIH Director's Award, 1976; International Society of Human & Animal Mycology, ISHAM Award, 1982, Lucill George Award, 1982. **SPECIAL ACHIEVEMENTS:** 150 scientific articles published in scientific journals; published Medical Mycology, text book, 1992. **BUSINESS ADDRESS:** Senior Investigator, National Institutes of Health, 900 Rockville Pike, Bldg 10, 11C304, Bethesda, MD 20817, (301)496-1602.

KWONG, BILL WAI LAM
Educator. Chinese American. **PERSONAL:** Born Dec 29, 1958, Hong Kong; son of Glenn and Margaret Kwong; married Joy Joy Ma. **EDUCATION:** Cornell University, BS, 1981; New York University, MS, 1991. **CAREER:** Dalton School, math teacher, 1984-91; Chinatown Planning Council, ave director, 1983; Crystal Springs Uplands School, math teacher, 1991-. **ORGANIZATIONS:** NAIS; CAIS. **HONORS/AWARDS:** Dalton School, Excellence Award in Teaching, 1989. **SPECIAL ACHIEVEMENTS:** China Exchange Coordinator, educational exchange, 1986-. **BUSINESS ADDRESS:** Math Teacher, Crystal Springs Uplands School, 400 Uplands Drive, Hillsborough, CA 94010, (415)342-4175.

KWONG, EVA
Artist, educator. Hong Kong American. **PERSONAL:** Born Feb 9, 1954, Hong Kong; daughter of Tony Kwong and Ivory Kwong; married Kirk Mangus, 1976; children: Una Mangus, Jasper Mangus. **EDUCATION:** Rhode Island School of Design, BFA, 1975; Tyler School of Art, Temple University, MFA, 1977. **CAREER:** Cleveland Institute of Art, visiting faculty, 1982-83, summer faculty, 1991; Penland School of Crafts, summer faculty, 1989-90; Miami University, summer faculty, 1990; Kent State University, part-time faculty, 1990-94; Summer Art Academy, Slippery Rock State University, summer faculty, 1991-92; Ohio University, summer faculty, 1992; artist, currently. **ORGANIZATIONS:** American Craft Council, 1980-; NCECA, 1986-. **HONORS/AWARDS:** National Endowment for the Arts, Visual Arts Fellowship, 1988-89; Ohio Arts Council, Individual Artist Fellowship, 1988; Arts Midwest, Visual Arts Fellowship, 1987; Pennsylvania Council on the Arts, Crafts Fellowship, 1985, 1981; Mid-Atlantic States Arts Consortium, Scholarship Grant, 1981. **SPECIAL ACHIEVEMENTS:** Eva Kwong—Opposites Attract Series, South Bend Museum of Art, South Bend, IN, 1993; Ohio Perspectives—5 Sculptors, Akron Art Museum, Akron, OH, 1993; Clay National 1993 NCECA Conference, San Diego Museum of Art, CA, 1993; Fiction, Function and Figuration-The 29th Ceramic National, Everson Museum of Art, Syracuse, NY, 1993; The Legacy of Archie Bray Foundation, Archie Bray Foundation, Helena, NT, and Bellevue Art Museum, WA, 1993; Eva Kwong/Kirk Mangusie, Joan Farrell Collection, Washington, DC, 1993. **BIOGRAPHICAL SOURCES:** Included in the following magazines: American Ceramics, American Craft, Ceramics Monthly, Studio Potter, Dialogue, New Art Examiner, Monthly Crafts Magazine, NCECA Journal, Star Date; Ohio

Perspectives 5 Sculptors, by Barbara Tannelbaum, Akron Art Museum, Ohio, p 4-5, 1993; Porcelain—Traditions and Art Visions, by Jan Axel, and Karen McCready, Watson and Guptill, p 184-185, 1981. **HOME PHONE:** (216)678-3766. **BUSINESS ADDRESS:** 320 Rellim Dr, Kent, OH 44240, (216)672-3360.

L

LABASAN, ALEJANDRO B.
Entrepreneur. Filipino American/Pacific Islander American. **PERSONAL:** Born May 3, 1935, Bacarra, Ilocos Norte, Philippines; son of Mr and Mrs Liborio Labasan (both deceased); married Laetitia V Labasan, Dec 16, 1967. **EDUCATION:** University of Hawaii, 2 years; Cal-Poly University, BS, agricultural services & insp, 1960, BS, agricultural science, 1963, graduate business management courses. **CAREER:** Di Giorgio Fruit Co, inspector, 1960; Pavich Ranch, inspector, foreman; Tradewinds, manager, 1970's; Alex's Rattan & Wicker Shop, owner, 1975-; Alex's Rattan, Cane & Hawaiian Shop, owner, currently. **ORGANIZATIONS:** Optimist Club, 1960; San Gabriel Kiwanis Club, president, 1988-89, treasurer, 1989-90, board of directors, 6 years; San Gabriel Chamber of Commerce; San Gabriel Tennis Club; Almansor Golf Men's Club. **HONORS/AWARDS:** San Gabriel Kiwanis Club, Man of the Year Award, 1985, 1986. **HOME ADDRESS:** 930 Ramona St, San Gabriel, CA 91776.

LACHICA, EDWARD ANTHONY
Neuroscientist. Filipino American. **PERSONAL:** Born Mar 21, 1960, Pasay City, Luzon, Philippines; son of Edward John and Marianita Roxas; married Sandra Lee, May 23, 1986; children: Evan Mychal. **EDUCATION:** University of California-Riverside, BA, physiol psych, 1982; Vanderbilt University, PhD, neuroscience, 1990; University of Washington, developmental neurobiology. **CAREER:** University of California-Riverside, Dept of Entomology, research technician, 1982-85; Vanderbilt School of Medicine, Dept of Cell Biology, graduate research assistant, 1985-90; Virginia Merill Bloedel Hearing Research Institute, research fellow, 1990-92; University of Washington Medical Ctr, Dept of Otolaryngology-Head & Neck Surgery, research assistant professor, currently. **ORGANIZATIONS:** Society for Neuroscience; J B Johnson Club for Comparative Neuroanatomy; Assn for Research in Otolaryngology; Assn for Research in Vision and Ophthalmology. **HONORS/AWARDS:** Deafness Research Foundation, grants in aid of research, 1992; National Institutes of Health, National Institute of Deafness and Communicative Disorders, postdoctoral fellowship, 1990-93; National Institutes of Health, National Institute of Mental Health, predoctoral fellowship, 1987-90; National Science Foundation, predoctoral fellowship, 1985. **SPECIAL ACHIEVEMENTS:** Co-author, 30 publications, including: ''Intrinsic Connections of Layer III of Striate Cortex in Squirrel Monkey and Bush Baby,'' Journal of Comparative Neurology, p 163-187, 1993; ''Evidence that the Superior Olivary Nucleus in the Chicken forms Connections with Nucleus Magnocellularis and Nucleus Laminaris,'' Assn for Research in Otolaryngology, Abstract, p 125, 1993. **BUSINESS ADDRESS:** Research Asst Professor, Dept of Otolaryngology, Head & Neck Surgery, University of Washington Medical Center, Seattle, WA 98195, (206)543-5230.

LACUESTA, LLOYD R.
Broadcast journalist. Filipino American. **PERSONAL:** Born May 20, 1947, Honolulu, HI; son of Pedro & Angelita Runes LaCuesta; children: Angelisa, Elena. **EDUCATION:** San Jose State University, BA, journalism, 1969; UCLA, master's, journalism, 1973. **CAREER:** KMPC Radio, news writer, 1968-69; KNX Radio, news producer, 1969-72; KABC Radio, news producer/writer, 1972-73; KABC TV, news producer/ writer, 1973-75; KGO TV, news producer/writer, 1975-76; KTVU TV, South Bay bureau chief, 1976-. **ORGANIZATIONS:** Asian American Journalists Association, national president, 1987-90; Unity '94, national president, 1990-91, national board member, 1991-; Society of Professional Journalists. **HONORS/AWARDS:** National Academy of TV, Arts & Science, Emmy nominations, 1982; Associated Press, Best Documentary, California/Arizona, 1986; Peninsula Press Club, Best News Story, 1985, 1988, 1989. **MILITARY SERVICE:** US Army, ssgt, 1969-71. **BUSINESS ADDRESS:** South Bay Bureau Chief, KTVU-TV, 1735 Technology Dr, Ste 320, San Jose, CA 95110, (408)441-8842.

LACUESTA, WESLEY RAY, SR.
Law enforcement administrator. Filipino American. **PERSONAL:** Born Sep 14, 1942, Honolulu, Oahu, HI; son of Pedro D LaCuesta and Angelita R LaCuesta; married Nelda L LaCuesta, Sep 18, 1983; children: Wesley Jr, Kim

Martinez, Damon; stepchildren: Angela Thompson, Cameron Thompson. **EDUCATION:** Los Angeles Harbor College; Compton College; El Camino College; Cal State, Los Angeles, BA, sociology, 1969; University of Texas, BS, criminal justice, 1974. **CAREER:** State of California, various law enforcement agencies, 1962-70; State of New Mexico, Farmington Police, Espanola Police, Santa Fe Sheriff's Dept, Springer Police, police ofcr, deputy sheriff, lieutenant, 1970-78; State of Texas, Quanah, chief of police, Hardeman & Denton Counties, deputy sheriff, Dallas County Police, police investigator, Seagoville Police, chief investigator, until 1984; Arizona Dept of Corrections, correctional srvc ofcr, correctional prgm ofcr, 1987; Veterans Administration, US Dept of Veterans Affairs Police, VA Medical Ctr, Long Beach, CA, police ofcr, corporal, watch cmndr, sgt, Jackson, MS, chief of police, Durham, NC, asst chief of police, currently. **ORGANIZATIONS:** Intl Assn of Chiefs of Police; Natl Assn of Chiefs of Police; Texas Narcotics Officers Assn; Intl Narcotics Officers Assn; California Law Enforcement Officers Assn; Mississippi Assn of Police Chiefs; Fraternal Order of Police; Intelligence Officers Assn; Order of the Blue Knight, Order of St Michael the Arch Angel/patron of Law Enforcement; Civil Air Patrol, former squadron commander/major; numerous others. **HONORS/ AWARDS:** Arizona Rangers, Company Commander (Pima County), 1986. **SPECIAL ACHIEVEMENTS:** Author, 5 published works including: "Every Cop a Super Salesman," Law and Order Magazine, 1976; has participated in all jurisdictions of law enforcement: city, county, state, and currently federal. **MILITARY SERVICE:** US Air Force; Reserves; State Guard (US Army), star grade. **BIOGRAPHICAL SOURCES:** The New Mexican, several issues, 1972-75; Phil-American News, Hawaii edition, 1978; The Daily Territorial, Tucson, AZ, front pg, Jul 21, Jul 24, 1986. **HOME ADDRESS:** 3614 Sunningdale Way, Durham, NC 27707. **BUSINESS ADDRESS:** Assistant Chief of Police, US Dept of Veterans Affairs Police, 508 Fulton, Durham, NC 27705.

LAGURA, FRANKLIN SASUTANA
Visual artist. Filipino American. **PERSONAL:** Born Aug 11, 1937, Stockton, CA; son of Emiliano and Frances Lagura; married Annette, Jan 28, 1960; children: Benjamin, Jennifer, Jessica. **EDUCATION:** California State University, Sacramento, BFA, 1961. **CAREER:** Visual artist; Mobil, art director, 1963-. **HONORS/AWARDS:** Mobil, Outstanding Achievement in Graphic Co-ordinations, 1982; Perfect Client Award, 1989. **SPECIAL ACHIEVEMENTS:** Exhibited painting, NFA Institute, Boston, MA, 1993. **MILITARY SERVICE:** US Air Force, airman 1st class, 1954-59. **BIOGRAPHICAL SOURCES:** Encyclopedia of Living Artists, 8th edition, 1993. **HOME ADDRESS:** PO Box 924, Davis, CA 95617.

LAI, ALBERT WENBEN
Educator. Taiwanese American. **PERSONAL:** Born Jun 15, 1952, Taipei, Taiwan; married Sofia Hsiouhuei Lai, Oct 20, 1983; children: Joseph P, Alice P. **EDUCATION:** Taiwan University, BA, 1980; National Sun Yat-sen University, MBA, 1982; Northwestern University, MS, 1986; University of Wisconsin-Madison, currently. **CAREER:** National Sun Yat-sen University, lecturer, 1986-. **ORGANIZATIONS:** American Marketing Assn, 1992-; Assn for Consumer Research, 1992-. **HONORS/AWARDS:** Institute of International Education, Fulbright Scholar to USA, 1984. **HOME ADDRESS:** 606-A Eagle Heights, Madison, WI 53705, (608)238-0278.

LAI, AMY
Physician. Taiwanese American/Chinese American. **PERSONAL:** Born May 23, 1966, Taipei, Taiwan; married. **EDUCATION:** Harvard and Radcliffe Colleges, AB (magna cum laude), 1988; Harvard Medical School, MD, 1993. **CAREER:** Massachusetts General Hospital, staff intern, 1993-94. **ORGANIZATIONS:** PBK, 1988-. **HONORS/AWARDS:** Johnson and Johnson, Research Award, 1990-91; Howard Hughes Medical Institute, Research Award, 1991-92.

LAI, CHING-SAN
Educator. Taiwanese American. **PERSONAL:** Born Nov 27, 1946, Keelung, Taiwan; son of Dong-Chong Lai and Sheue Wu Lai; married Shan-Lan Liu Lai, Sep 9, 1972; children: Jennifer Y, Shawn S. **EDUCATION:** National Taiwan Normal University, BS, 1970; University of Hawaii, PhD, 1978. **CAREER:** Medical College of Wisconsin, assistant professor, 1981-85, associate professor, 1986-90, professor, 1991-. **ORGANIZATIONS:** Medical College of Wisconsin, Biophysics Graduate Program, co-chairman and program director, 1986-88, vice section head/biophysics, 1989-91; Biophysical Society, 1979-; Society of Magnetic Resonance in Medicine, 1987-; American Association for the Advancement of Science, 1987-; International EPR Society, 1989-. **HONORS/AWARDS:** National Institutes of Health, Research Grants, 1982-.

SPECIAL ACHIEVEMENTS: Major research interests: biomedical application of electron spin resonance spectroscopy, structure and function of cell adhesive glycoproteins. **HOME ADDRESS:** 17765 Bolter Lane, Brookfield, WI 53045, (414)796-0057. **BUSINESS ADDRESS:** Professor, Medical College of Wisconsin, 8701 Watertown Plank Road, Milwaukee, WI 53226, (414)266-4051.

LAI, DENNIS FU-HSIUNG
Engineer. Chinese American. **PERSONAL:** Born Dec 13, 1939, Taiwan; son of Chin-Chih Lai and Fang-Chu Lai; married Margaret H Lai, Sep 14, 1969; children: Theodore, Winston. **EDUCATION:** National Taiwan University, BS, 1963; Syracuse University, MS, 1966; Massachusetts Institute of Technology, PhD, 1970. **CAREER:** Ebasco Services, principal engineer, 1970-73; Dames and Moore, senior engineer, 1973-75; Clinton Bogert Associates, associate, 1975-. **ORGANIZATIONS:** Water Environment Federation, CSO Pollution Manual of Practice, reviewer, 1990; USEPA, CSO Research Grant, extramural reviewer, 1985-90; Association of Chinese Schools, president, 1989-90; Chinese American Cultural Association, president, 1984-86, director, 1980-; Mid-Jersey Chinese School, principal, 1979-80; Alumni Association of National Taiwan University, Greater New York, president, 1993-95. **HONORS/AWARDS:** Tiananmen Memorial Foundation, Education Award, 1989. **HOME ADDRESS:** 18 Manton Ave, East Brunswick, NJ 08816, (908)247-3539.

LAI, JAI-LUE LEON
Aircraft engine company manager. Taiwanese American/Chinese American. **PERSONAL:** Born Dec 9, 1940, Taipei, Taiwan; married Winifred Y Lai; children: Emory K, Valerie K. **EDUCATION:** National Taiwan University, BSE, 1962; Polytechnic University of New York, MSE, 1966; Princeton University, PhD, 1969. **CAREER:** BF Goodrich, associate R&D fellow, 1968-87; Gen Corp Automotive, Advanced Projects, director, 1987-92; Pratt & Whitney, Manufacturing Technology, manager, 1992-. **ORGANIZATIONS:** ASME; AIAA; SAE; SAMPE. **HOME ADDRESS:** 106 Barrington Way, Glastonbury, CT 06033-4343, (203)659-4347. **BUSINESS ADDRESS:** Manager, Manfacturing Technology, Pratt & Whitney/United Technologies Corp, 400 Main St, M/S 114-37, East Hartford, CT 06108, (203)565-3154.

LAI, KAI SUN
Engineer. Chinese American. **PERSONAL:** Born Dec 11, 1937, Kowloon, Hong Kong; son of Chaak Tin Lai and Bessie M Lai; married Elizabeth Copley Lai, Aug 12, 1967; children: Kristine W, Scott W. **EDUCATION:** Pennsylvania State University, BS, 1959. **CAREER:** Aerojet General Corporation, engineer, 1959-62; Atlantic Research Corp, senior engineer, 1962-68; Teledyne McCormick Selph, senior scientist, 1968-84; United Technologies Corp, Design, group head, 1984-. **ORGANIZATIONS:** Gilroy Planning Commission, commissioner, chair, 1992-; Santa Clara County Justice Advisory Board, 1990-; Santa Clara County Committee on School District Organization, chair, 1984-; Gilroy Unified School District, Board of Education, president, 1981-90; Asian/Pacific Islander School Board Members Asssociation, vice president, 1988-90; Santa Clara County School Board Members Association, executive board, 1988-90; American Institute of Aeronautics & Astronautics, 1964-. **HONORS/AWARDS:** Santa Clara County Supervisors, Resolution of Commendation, 1990. **SPECIAL ACHIEVEMENTS:** Various classified papers on rocket propulsion technologies, to professional organizations 1964-. **BIOGRAPHICAL SOURCES:** Asian/Pacific American Elected/Appointed Officials Directory, p 42, 1990. **HOME ADDRESS:** 855 West Eighth Street, Gilroy, CA 95020, (408)842-7355.

LAI, KUO-YANN
Industrial research and development manager. Chinese American. **PERSONAL:** Born Sep 13, 1946, Miao-Li, Taiwan; married Mei-Chen Lai. **EDUCATION:** National Cheng Kung University, Taiwan, BS, chemical engineering, 1969; University of Texas, El Paso, MS, chemistry, 1974; Clarkson University, Potsdam, NY, PhD, chemistry, 1977. **CAREER:** Colgate-Palmolive Co, Chemical Research, research chemist, 1977-80, senior research chemist, 1980-83, research associate, 1983; Basic Research, section head & senior section head, 1983-87, Oral Product Development, manager, 1987-93, Household Surface Care Product Development, associate director, currently. **ORGANIZATIONS:** American Chemical Society. **HONORS/AWARDS:** Organization of Chinese Americans, Asian American Corporate Achievement Award, 1992; Colgate-Palmolive Co, The Chairman's You Can Make a Difference Award, 1992, President's Award for Technical Excellence, 1984; National Science Foundation, Research Fellowship, 1974-77; Robert A Welch Founda-

tion, Predoctoral Fellowship, 1972-74. **SPECIAL ACHIEVEMENTS:** Patent holder for Palmolive Sensitive Skin Diswashing Liquid; 7 US patents; author of the book, Material and Energy Balances, vol I & II, 1971. **MILITARY SERVICE:** Chinese Artillery, second lt, 1969-70. **BUSINESS ADDRESS:** Associate Director, Research and Development, Technology Center, Colgate-Palmolive Co, 909 River Rd, Piscataway, NJ 08855-1343, (908)878-7835.

LAI, MICHAEL MING-CHIAO
Educator. Taiwanese American. **PERSONAL:** Born Sep 8, 1942, Tainan, Taiwan; son of Tsai-Sen Lai and Tsan-Hwa Shih; married Cathy Hwei-ying Wung, Jul 28, 1972; children: Cindy, Jennifer. **EDUCATION:** National Taiwan University, College of Medicine, MD, (BM), 1968; University of California, Berkeley, PhD, 1973. **CAREER:** University of Southern California, assistant professor, 1973-78, associate professor, 1978-83, professor, 1983-; Howard Hughes Medical Institute, investigator, 1990-. **ORGANIZATIONS:** Academia Sinica, 1992-; Federation of American Societies for Experimental Biology, 1984-; American Society for Virology, 1982-; American Society for Microbiology, 1978-, RNA Virus Division, chairman, 1992-93; Society of Chinese Bioscientists in America, 1985-, president, 1991-92. **HONORS/AWARDS:** University of SC, Burlington Northern Foundation Award for Outstanding Scholar, 1989; Society of Chinese Bioscientists in America, Cathay Foundation Award, 1990. **SPECIAL ACHIEVEMENTS:** Scientific publications in Science Nature Proceedings of National Academy of Sciences, Journal of Virology, Virology, EMBO Journal, numerous others; 147 publications to date. **BUSINESS ADDRESS:** Professor of Microbiology, University of Southern California, School of Medicine, 2011 Zonal Avenue, HMR-503, Los Angeles, CA 90033, (213)342-1748.

LAI, MING-YEE
Telecommunication company executive. Taiwanese American. **PERSONAL:** Born Aug 1, 1952, Taichung, Taiwan; son of Yin-Shu Lai and Shou-Shin Lai; married Yuan-Fen Lai, May 12, 1981; children: Stephanie, Christine. **EDUCATION:** National Taiwan University, BSEE, 1974; Harvard University, MS, computer science, 1979, PhD, computer science, 1982. **CAREER:** Rand Corporation, research consultant, 1979; Anathon Corp, lead consultant, 1980; Bell Labs, Advanced Database System Exploratory, MTS, 1982-84; Bellcore, Computer Science Research, MTS, 1984-87, XIS Service Architecture, district manager, 1987-90, Information Networking Architecture, district manager, 1990-91, Software Technology Analysis, director, 1991-. **ORGANIZATIONS:** IEEE, senior member, 1979-. **MILITARY SERVICE:** Army, Signal Corps, second lieutenant, 1974-76. **BIOGRAPHICAL SOURCES:** IEEE Selected Areas in Communications, p 322, April 1989; IEEE Network, p 6, November 1990. **BUSINESS ADDRESS:** Director, Bellcore, 331 Newman Springs Rd, NVC 2X165, Red Bank, NJ 07701, (908)758-4160.

LAI, PATRICK KINGLUN
Educator. Chinese American. **PERSONAL:** Born Oct 10, 1944, Hong Kong; son of Cho-Kwai Lai & Siu-Man Cheung; married Priscilla Ting Ping; children: Lee James Robert Allum, Chay Antony Paul Allum. **EDUCATION:** University of Western Australia, BS, 1970, PhD, 1978; Royal College of Pathologists, London, associate, 1980. **CAREER:** University of Ottawa, research associate, 1978-80; University of London, research fellow, 1980-83, senior res officer, 1983-84; University of Nebraska Med Ctr, assistant professor, 1984-87; Tampa Bay Research Institute, assistant member, 1987-90, member, 1990-; Salem-Teikyo University, associate professor, 1993-. **ORGANIZATIONS:** American Association for Immunologists, 1976-; New York Academy of Sciences; American Association for the Advancement of Sciences. **HONORS/AWARDS:** European Molecular Biology Organization, fellowship, 1981; Imperial Cancer Research Fund, England, research fellowship, 1980-83; World Health Organization, research fellowship, 1976-77; International Agency for Res on Cancer, fellowship, 1975. **SPECIAL ACHIEVEMENTS:** More than 40 publications in scientific and medical journals and books, 1973-; two biotechnology patents pending, 1991-. **BUSINESS ADDRESS:** Associate Professor, Salem Teikyo University, 10900 Roosevelt Blvd, Saint Petersburg, FL 33716, (813)576-6675.

LAI, RALPH WEI-MEEN
Federal government official. Taiwanese American. **PERSONAL:** Born Dec 17, 1936, Tou-Lu, Taiwan; son of Chung-Ten Lai and Kaku Lai; married Cindy S Lai; children: Naline L, Melisa W. **EDUCATION:** Cheng-Kung University, BSc, 1959; S D School of Mines & Technology, MS, 1964; University of California, Berkeley, PhD, 1970. **CAREER:** Cyprus Industrial Minerals Corp, research engr, 1969-73; Anglo-American Clays Corp, sr engr, 1973-74; Ken-

necott Copper Corp, sr scientist, 1974-83; US Dept of Energy, project mgr, 1985-. **ORGANIZATIONS:** American Chemical Society; Society of Mining, Metallurgy and Exploration Engineers; Japan Institute of Mining and Metallurgy. **SPECIAL ACHIEVEMENTS:** Author: The Overlooked Law of Nature, 1990; over 30 professional journal papers. **BUSINESS ADDRESS:** Project Manager, US Dept of Energy-PETC, Cochran Mill Run Road, PO Box 10940, Pittsburgh, PA 15236, (412)892-4649.

LAI, RICHARD THOMAS
Educator, attorney, CPA. Chinese American. **PERSONAL:** Born Aug 12, 1953, New York, NY; son of Ging Gee Lai and Ng Fung San Lai. **EDUCATION:** Hunter College, BS, accounting, 1975; Boston College Law School, JD, 1978; New York University School of Law, LLM, taxation, 1983. **CAREER:** KPMG Peat Marwick, tax specialist, 1978-81; Richard T Lai, tax attorney/CPA 1983-; Iona College, Department of Accounting & Business Law, assistant professor, 1985-87; St John's University, Department of Accounting & Taxation, associate professor, 1984-85, 1987-. **ORGANIZATIONS:** American Institute of CPAs, 1985-; American Association of Attorney-CPAs, 1987-90; American Accounting Association, 1988-90; Asian American Bar Association of New York, 1991-. **SPECIAL ACHIEVEMENTS:** Author: "Self-Employment Taxes, Other Technical Issues," The Practical Accountant, June 1992; "Reducing Net Earning of Self-Employment Activities," Taxes-The Tax Magazine, June 1991; "Tax Saving Tips for Parents," The Practical Accountant, June 1990; "Compensating S Corporation Officers," Taxes-The Tax Magazine, March 1989; "Planning for L/T Medical Care & Tax Consequences of Lifetime Transfers," Tax Ideas, June 1991. **HOME ADDRESS:** 1053 Morris Park Avenue, Bronx, NY 10461, (718)409-9383.

LAI, RICHARD TSENG-YU
Educator. Chinese American. **PERSONAL:** Born Jan 14, 1937, Beijing, China; son of Shih Chen Lai and Hsiao-hsin Chang Lai; married Barbara E Lai, Dec 26, 1975; children: Valdrian J Hsiao-su, Alexander C Hsiao-chen. **EDUCATION:** Princeton University, AB, architecture, 1958, MFA, architecture, 1960; University of Pennsylvania, PhD, city planning, 1975. **CAREER:** Arizona State University, Department of Planning, professor, 1973-. **ORGANIZATIONS:** American Institute of Architects; American Institute of Certified Planners. **SPECIAL ACHIEVEMENTS:** Law in Urban Design and Planning: The Invisible Web, 1988. **BUSINESS ADDRESS:** Professor, Dept of Planning, Arizona State University, Tempe, AZ 85287-2005, (602)965-7167.

LAI, TSONG-YUE
Educator. **PERSONAL:** Born Mar 8, 1947, Tainan, Taiwan; married Shu-Yuan Lai, Apr 7, 1975; children: Sharon, Irving. **EDUCATION:** National Taiwan University, BS, math, 1971; SUNY Buffalo, MBA, 1980; Yale University, MA, 1982, PhD, 1983. **CAREER:** Artillery Military School, lt lecturer, 1971-72; Academia Sinica, Institute of Mathematics, asst researcher, 1972-75; Natl Taiwan University, math lecturer, 1973-75; Florida State University, assistant professor, 1984-88; Kansas State University, associate professor, 1988-91; California State University, Fullerton, professor, 1991-. **SPECIAL ACHIEVEMENTS:** Publications: "An Examination of the Relationship Between the Forward Exchange Risk Premium and Spot Rate Volatility," International Journal of Finance, 1993; "An Alternative Method for Obtaining the Implied Standard Deviation," The Journal of Financial Engineering, 1992; "Deriving Option Pricing Model: A Synthesis," Advances in Investment Analysis and Portfolio Management 1, 1991; numerous others. **MILITARY SERVICE:** Lieutenant, 1971-72. **BUSINESS ADDRESS:** Professor, Dept of Finance, California State University-Fullerton, Fullerton, CA 92634, (714)773-3855.

LAI, TZE LEUNG
Educator. Chinese American. **PERSONAL:** Born Jun 28, 1945, Hong Kong; son of Chi Yau Lai & Wai Chun Cheng; married Letitia C Lai, Jun 23, 1975; children: Peter, David. **EDUCATION:** University of Hong Kong, BA, 1967; Columbia University, MA, 1970, PhD, 1971. **CAREER:** University of Hong Kong, demonstrator of mathematics, 1967-68; Columbia University, assistant professor, 1971-74, associate professor, 1974-77, professor, 1977-86, Higgins Professor of mathematical statistics, 1986-87; Universitat Heidelberg, visiting professor, 1979; Stanford University, professor, 1987-. **ORGANIZATIONS:** Stanford University, Center for AIDS Research, research statistician, 1989-; Columbia University, Pediatric Pulmonary Division, consulting statistican, 1977-87; Brookhaven National Laboratory, research collaborator, 1977-81; Chinese University of Hong Kong, external assessor, 1991-; National Univer-

sity of Singapore, external examiner, 1989-93; World Scientific Publishing Company, editorial consultant, 1991-; Academia Sinica, Taipei, advisory committee, 1991-; International Chinese Statistical Association, council member, 1992-. **HONORS/AWARDS:** Committee of Presidents of Statistical Societies, COPSS Award, 1983; John Simon Guggenheim Foundation, Guggenheim Fellowship, 1983-84; Institute of Mathematical Statistics, special invited paper, 1980; University of Hong Kong, Y C Wong Special Lectures, 1989, Chan Kai Ming Prize & Walter Brown Prize, 1967. **SPECIAL ACHIEVEMENTS:** "Rank Regression Methods for Left Truncated and Right Censored Data," Annals of Statistics, 1991; "Weak Convergence of Time-Sequential Censored Rank Statistics with Applications to Sequential Testing in Clinical Trials," in Annals of Statistics, 1991; "Bootstrap Confidence Bounds for Spectra and Cross-Spectra," IEEE Trans Signal Processing, 1992; "Open Bandit Processes and Optimal Scheduling of Queueing Networks," Advances of Applied Probability, 1988; "Asymptotically Efficient Adaptive Allocation Rules," Advances of Applied Mathematics, 1985. **BUSINESS ADDRESS:** Professor, Dept of Statistics, Stanford University, Sequoia Hall, Stanford, CA 94305, (415)723-2622.

LAI, WAIHANG
Educator. Chinese American. **PERSONAL:** Born Jan 7, 1939, Hong Kong; son of Lai Sing; married Celia, 1966; children: Cynthia. **EDUCATION:** Chinese University of Hong Kong, BA, 1964; Claremont Graduate School, MA, 1967. **CAREER:** Arizona State University, visiting professor of art, 1967; Mauna Olu College, assistant professor of art, 1968-70; Kauai Community College, associate professor of art, 1970-. **ORGANIZATIONS:** American Watercolor Society; Philadelphia Water Color Club; Kauai Watercolor Society, president, 1974-; Kauai Oriental Art Society, president, 1981-. **HONORS/AWARDS:** University of Hawaii Board of Regents, Excellence in Teaching Award, 1992; NISOD, Excellence Award, 1993; International Directory of Distinguished Leadership, Distinguished Leadership Award, 1993. **SPECIAL ACHIEVEMENTS:** Author: The Chinese Landscape Painting of Waihang Lai, 1966; The Watercolors of Waihang Lai, 1967; books illustrated: The Tao of Practice Success, 1991; Advertisements for Acupuncturists, 1992; one man shows: Watercolor Painting Exhibition, Kauai Museum, 1993; Computer Painting Exhibition, Kauai Museum, 1992; Chinese Painting Exhibition, Kauai Museum, 1989. **HOME ADDRESS:** PO Box 363, Lihue, HI 96766. **BUSINESS ADDRESS:** Associate Professor of Art, Kauai Community College, Fine Arts 102, Lihue, HI 96766, (808)245-8315.

LAI, YING-SAN
Safety & hydraulic valve & gas spring company executive. Taiwanese American. **PERSONAL:** Born Sep 9, 1937, Chutung, Taiwan; son of June-Lai Lai and Ching-Mei Lai; married Nancy P Lai, Feb 26, 1966; children: Nolan, Ormond, Lynna. **EDUCATION:** National Taiwan University, BSME, 1960; University of Iowa, MSME, 1963; Northwestern University, PhD, 1973. **CAREER:** CBI Industries, design engineer, 1963-69; Dresser Valve Division, chief engineer, 1973-92; Teledyne Farris Engineering, engineering vice president, 1992-93; Teledyne Fluid Systems, engineering vice president, 1993-. **ORGANIZATIONS:** ASME, technical committee, 1969-; API, technical committee, 1984-; ISA, 1991-. **SPECIAL ACHIEVEMENTS:** Published more than two dozen technical papers; contributed to Lyon's Valve Designer's Handbook, 1982; awared two patents; fluent in Chinese. **BUSINESS ADDRESS:** Vice President of Engineering, Teledyne Fluid Systems, 10367 Brecksville Rd, Brecksville, OH 44141, (216)526-5900.

LAIGO, VALERIANO EMERCIANO MONTANTE. *See* Obituaries.

LAKKARAJU, HARINARAYANA SARMA
Educator. Indo-American. **PERSONAL:** Born Sep 20, 1946, Bapatla, Andhra Pradesh, India; married. **EDUCATION:** Andhra University, Waltair, AP India, BSc, 1964, MSc, 1967; Fairleigh Dickinson University, Teaneck, NJ, MS, 1973; State University of New York, Buffalo, PhD, 1979. **CAREER:** National Physical Laboratory, senior scientific assistant, 1970-71; Texas A & M University, visiting assistant professor, 1979-81; San Jose State University, professor, 1981-. **ORGANIZATIONS:** American Physical Society, currently; Optical Society of America, currently; SPIE (International Optical Engineering Society), currently; SPIE, Northern California, vice president, 1991-92, president, 1992-93; Optical Society of Northern California, board of directors, 1983-88. **HONORS/AWARDS:** Andhra University, Waltair, India, Metcalffe Gold Medal, 1967. **SPECIAL ACHIEVEMENTS:** Several publications in scientific journals covering lasers, spectroscopy, nonlinear optics, and plasma phys-

ics. **BUSINESS ADDRESS:** Professor, Physics, San Jose State University, One Washington Sq, San Jose, CA 95192-0106, (408)924-5268.

LAKSHMAN, GOVIND
Manufacturing company executive. Indo-American. **PERSONAL:** Born May 6, 1948, Bangalore, Karnataka, India; son of Govindappa and Chennamma; married Malini Lakshman, Aug 13, 1975; children: Archana, Ajay. **EDUCATION:** Bangalore University, BSME, 1971; West Virginia Institute of Technology, BS, 1973. **CAREER:** Polyurethane Products Co, president, 1978-. **BUSINESS ADDRESS:** President, Polyurethane Products Corporation, 100 Interstate Road, Addison, IL 60101, (708)543-6700.

LAKSHMANAN, CHITHRA
Educator, educational administrator. Indo-American. **PERSONAL:** Born Oct 19, 1933, Davis, CA; daughter of Balagopal & Sathya Mulyil; married C Lakshmanan, Feb 5, 1967; children: Rayan, Hari. **EDUCATION:** Queen Mary's College, India, BA, economics, 1954; London University, MA, sociology, 1960. **CAREER:** Walter Thompson, Ltd, India, copy writer, advertising, 1964-64, advertising executive, 1964-67; Jack & Jill Pre-School, owner, director, currently. **ORGANIZATIONS:** International Friendship Group, University of California, Davis, founder, member; India Association of Davis, founder, 1987; Natya Shree Academy of Northern California; Dance Academy founder, owner, 1990; Indo-American Political Assn, founder, board member, chair, 1992; Malayalee Assn of Northern California, founder; City of Davis, Social Services Commission, commissioner, 1992. **HONORS/AWARDS:** Child Care Commission, Yolo County Agency, Davis Branch, pre-school, Best Teacher Award; Federation of Indo-American Associations, Outstanding Community Service and Participation, 1992. **SPECIAL ACHIEVEMENTS:** Serial author, Absorbent Mind series, Child Care Bulletin; producer, Natya Shree Academy, Northern California. **HOME ADDRESS:** 4400 El Macero Dr, Davis, CA 95616, (916)756-0416.

LAL, DHYAN
Educator, educational administrator. Pacific Islander American. **PERSONAL:** Born Mar 29, 1948, Suva, Fiji; son of Uttam Lal and Phul Kuar Lal; married Shirley Lal; children: Dhyan Decaux, Amrit Uttam, Roshni Devi. **EDUCATION:** California State University, Los Angeles, BA, 1970, MA, 1974; California Lutheran University, MS, 1979; Nova University, EdD, 1985. **CAREER:** Los Angeles Unified School District, teacher, 1973-77, resource specialist, 1977-80, dean of students, 1980-82, administrative dean, 1983-86, assistant principal, 1986-88, principal, 1988-. **ORGANIZATIONS:** Association of Pacific Island Educators, president, 1988-; Alliance of Asian Pacific Administrators, 1989-; Council of Mexican American Administrators, 1983-; Associated Administrators of Los Angeles, 1983-; Filipino American Alliance, 1993-; Samoan Parents Association, 1989-. **HONORS/AWARDS:** City of Los Angeles, Asian Pacific American Heritage Leader, 1993; Democratic National Committee, Outstanding Citizen, 1992; City of Carson, Service Honor, 1992; Association of Pacific Island Educators, Leadership Award, 1990; Tenth District PTA, Los Angeles, Service to Youth Award, 1986. **SPECIAL ACHIEVEMENTS:** Book, Controlling Gangs on School Campuses, 1993; papers presented: Proactive Approach to Education, 1992; Nova University, Education in a Diverse Society, 1991; KCET TV Show, "No Man Is An Island," 1992. **BIOGRAPHICAL SOURCES:** "The Guy In The Skirt," LA Times, May 13, 1992. **HOME ADDRESS:** 30420 Calle De Suenos, Rancho Palos Verdes, CA 90274. **BUSINESS PHONE:** (310)835-0181.

LAL, RATTAN
Educator. Indo-American. **PERSONAL:** Born Sep 15, 1944, Karyal, Punjab, India; son of Jagan Nath & Krishna Nath; married Sukhvarsha S Lal, Dec 12, 1971; children: Priya, Pratibha, Abhishek, Vivek. **EDUCATION:** Punjab Agricultural University, India, BSc, 1963; Indian Agricultural Research Institute, India, MSc, 1965; Ohio State University, PhD, 1968. **CAREER:** The Rockefeller Foundation, India, res asst, 1963-65; Ohio Agric Res & Dev Center, res associate, 1966-68; Univ of Sydney, Australia, sr res fellow, 1968-69; International Institute of Tropical Agric, Nigeria, soil physicist, 1970-87; Ohio State Univ, professor, 1987-. **ORGANIZATIONS:** World Assn of Soil & Water Conservation, president, 1988-91; International Soil Tillage Research Organization, president, 1988-91. **HONORS/AWARDS:** Soil Science Soc America, fellow, 1986, International Soil Sci Award, 1988, Soil Sci Applied Res Award, 1992; American Society of Agronomy, fellow, 1985; Third World Academy of Science, fellow, 1992. **SPECIAL ACHIEVEMENTS:** Tropical Ecology & Physical Edaphology, J Wiley & Sons, UK, 1987; Soil Erosion in the Tropics, Principles & Mgmt, McGraw Hill, 1990; editor & co-editor of 15

other books; author & co-author of 500 scientific articles. **BUSINESS ADDRESS:** Prof, Dept of Agronomy, Ohio State University, 2021 Coffey Rd, 202 Kottman Hall, Columbus, OH 43210.

LALY, AMY
Television producer. Indo-American. **PERSONAL:** Born May 19, 1947, Bombay, India. **CAREER:** Tapestry Productions, producer, director, currently; works include: Street Players, documentary, 1992; Windows, documentary; "Audacious Women," talk show, 1993; Ballad of the Causeway, documentary; Torch the Pyre, documentary. **SPECIAL ACHIEVEMENTS:** Street Players, played at Intl Festival of Films by Women Directors, Seattle, 1992. **BUSINESS ADDRESS:** Producer, Tapestry Productions, 1015 W Nickerson, Ste 116, Seattle, WA 98119, (206)657-3101.∗

LAM, ALEX W.
Educator. Hong Kong American/Chinese American. **PERSONAL:** Born in Hong Kong; married. **EDUCATION:** University of Illinois, PhD, 1987. **CAREER:** University of Massachusetts, assistant professor, 1987-90; Naval Postgraduate School, associate professor, 1990-. **SPECIAL ACHIEVEMENTS:** Spread spectrum communications papers published in IEEE transactions on communications. **HOME ADDRESS:** 2219 Best Ct, San Jose, CA 95131. **BUSINESS ADDRESS:** Professor, EC/LA Naval Postgraduate School, Monterey, CA 93943, (408)656-3044.

LAM, AN NGOC
Computer programmer. Vietnamese American. **PERSONAL:** Born Dec 7, 1964, Saigon, Vietnam; son of Su Van Lam and Quy Thi Nguyen. **EDUCATION:** California State Polytechnic University, BS (honors), comp sci, 1988; Santa Clara University, MS, comp eng, 1992. **CAREER:** IBM Corp, sr associate programmer, 1988-; Phi Kappa Phi National Academic Honor Society. **ORGANIZATIONS:** Aid to Refugee Children Without Parents, board of directors, 1988-; Young Vietnamese-Americans for Tomorrow, treasurer, 1992-. **HONORS/AWARDS:** IBM, Teamwork Award, 1992. **SPECIAL ACHIEVEMENTS:** Author: Poems and short stories published in Vietnamese magazines, including: Goplua, Lua Viet, Van Lang. **BUSINESS ADDRESS:** Senior Associate Programmer, IBM, 5600 Cottle Rd, Bldg 50, Dept M36, San Jose, CA 95193.

LAM, CHOW-SHING
Educator. Chinese American. **PERSONAL:** Born Nov 18, 1947, Hong Kong; married Irene Lam, Dec 19, 1975; children: Jonathan, Christopher. **EDUCATION:** University of Wisconsin, Whitewater, BS, 1974, MEd, 1976; University of Wisconsin, Madison, MS, 1984, PhD, 1985. **CAREER:** Illinois Institute of Technology, associate professor, director, Rehabilitation Psychology, 1985-. **ORGANIZATIONS:** American Psychological Association, 1985-; American Counseling Association, 1980-; American Rehabilitation Counseling Association, council chair, 1980-; National Rehabilitation Association, 1980-; National Rehabilitation Counseling Association, 1980-; National Council on Rehabilitation Education, board of directors, 1980-. **HONORS/AWARDS:** World Rehabilitation Fund, Fellow, 1990-91; National Council on Rehabilitation Education, Young Educator of the Year, 1993; American Rehabilitation Counseling Association, Research Awards, 1985, 1989. **SPECIAL ACHIEVEMENTS:** Published 40 articles, 7 book chapters and monographs, 23 presentations. **BUSINESS ADDRESS:** Associate Professor, Dept of Psychology, Illinois Institute of Technology, 3101 S Dearborn St, LS, Room 236, Chicago, IL 60616, (312)567-3515.

LAM, CHUN H.
Educator. Hong Kong American/Chinese American. **PERSONAL:** Born in Hong Kong; son of Wing Cheong Lam & Choi Chu Chan; married Edith Lam, Jun 14, 1975; children: Jon, Jay, Rick. **EDUCATION:** Duke University, BSE, 1971, MBA, 1974, PhD, 1977; Princeton University, MSE, 1972. **CAREER:** Corning International Corp, business analyst, 1974; Duke University, instructor, 1976-77; Tulane University, assistant professor of finance, 1977-81; Southern Methodist University, department of finance, chairman, 1988-91, associate professor of finance, 1981-. **ORGANIZATIONS:** Pacific Southwest Bank, FSB, director, 1990-; First International Bank, director, 1992-; North Texas Mesbic, Inc, director, 1990-93; Trinity Christian Academy, advisory board, 1992-; Willow Bend National Bank, associate director, 1987-89. **HONORS/AWARDS:** Tulane University, Howard Wissner Teaching Award, 1981; Prochnow Foundation, research award, 1987; Duke University, Phi Beta Kappa, Tau Beta Pi, Eta Kappa Nu, 1971, George Sherrerd III Memorial Award, 1971, James B Duke Fellow, 1976. **SPECIAL ACHIEVEMENTS:**

Author, Microcomputer Applications in Banking, Quorum Books, 1986; numerous papers on finance, banking, and economics. **BUSINESS ADDRESS:** Associate Professor, Edwin L Cox School of Business, Southern Methodist University, Dallas, TX 75275-0001, (214)768-2240.

LAM, DICK
Investment adviser. Hong Kong American. **PERSONAL:** Born Mar 27, 1939, Hong Kong; son of Choy Lam and Pui Lim Lam; married Virginia Lam, Jan 1, 1980; children: Justin, Julian. **EDUCATION:** University of San Francisco, BS, 1968. **CAREER:** Davis Skaggs & Company Inc, general partner & vp, 1970-83; Shearson Lehman American Express, vice president, 1983-89; Lam Securities Investment, CEO, sole owner, currently. **ORGANIZATIONS:** SEC; NASD; MSRB. **HONORS/AWARDS:** San Francisco Chronicle and Examiner, Man of the Year, one of six, 1991. **SPECIAL ACHIEVEMENTS:** Pioneered the first minority broker/dealer firm certified by the city and county of San Francisco. **HOME PHONE:** (415)752-0102. **BUSINESS ADDRESS:** CEO, Lam Securities Investments, 235 Montgomery, Suite 630A, San Francisco, CA 94104, (415)398-6181.

LAM, EPPIE C. F.
Realtor, developer, property manager. Chinese American. **PERSONAL:** Born Feb 12, 1941, Kowloon, Hong Kong; daughter of Chung Yuk Hing & Tien Kwei Yuen; married David Lam, Aug 1, 1967; children: David Jekit, Jesun. **EDUCATION:** University of Toronto, BA, 1967; Northeastern University, Medical Records Administration Certificate, 1969; Devonshire Oaks Convalescent Hospital, Nursing Home Administration Apprenticeship, Certificate, 1983. **CAREER:** Carney Hospital, medical records department, director, 1969-72; numerous convalescent hospitals in San Francisco Bay area, consultant, 1973-84; Del Investment, developer, property manager, 1980-; Cornish & Carey, realtor, 1992-. **ORGANIZATIONS:** Self Help for the Elderly, Santa Clara, Advisory Council, chairperson, 1993-, South Bay, founding president, 1989-92; Chinese Historical & Cultural Project, board of directors, 1988-90, chair/co-chair, fundraising events, co-chair, Ground Breaking Committee, co-chair, 1988-89; Lucille Packard Children's Hospital, Woodside-Atherton Auxillary, Stanford, 1988-. **HONORS/AWARDS:** Self Help for the Elderly, San Francisco, Outstanding Service Award, 1991, 1992. **HOME PHONE:** (415)949-3319. **BUSINESS ADDRESS:** Realtor, Cornish & Carey, PO Box 1407, Los Altos, CA 94022.

LAM, FAT C.
Educator. Chinese American. **PERSONAL:** Born Jul 17, 1946, Canton, China; married Kay H Lam, 1975. **EDUCATION:** Gallaudet University, BA, 1971; George Washington University, MA, 1974; University of Montana, PhD, 1987. **CAREER:** IBM Thomas J Watson Research Center, 1979; Defense Mapping Agency, faculty fellow, 1993; Gallaudet University, associate professor of math, 1981-. **ORGANIZATIONS:** London Mathematical Society; Mathematical Association of America; Sigma Xi. **SPECIAL ACHIEVEMENTS:** First deaf person of Chinese ancestry to have received a PhD degree. **BIOGRAPHICAL SOURCES:** Ming Pao, Hong Kong, March, 1993; Washington Chinese News, April, 1993. **BUSINESS ADDRESS:** Professor, Dept of Math & CS, Gallaudet University, 800 Florida Ave NE, Washington, DC 20002.

LAM, GILBERT NIM-CAR
Pharmaceutical company executive. Chinese American. **PERSONAL:** Born Nov 10, 1951, Shanghai, People's Republic of China; married May Y Lam; children: Tracey W. **EDUCATION:** Vincennes University, AS, chemistry, 1974; SUNY at Buffalo, BS, pharmacy, 1976; University of Illinois, PhD, pharmacokimetics, 1981. **CAREER:** El DuPont de Nemours & Co, research biochemist, senior research biochemist, research supervisor, 1981-91; Dupont Merck Pharmaceutical Co, associate director, 1991-. **ORGANIZATIONS:** American Association of Pharmaceutical Scientists , 1985-; International Society for the Study of Xenobiotics, 1989-; Rho Chi Society, 1976-; Chinese American Community Center Inc, chairman, 1991-93. **HOME ADDRESS:** 20 Coach Hill Ct, Newark, DE 19711, (302)453-1426.

LAM, LEO KONGSUI
Physicist. Hong Kong American. **PERSONAL:** Born Sep 12, 1946, Hong Kong; son of K K Lam and S B Kong; married Florence W Lam, Nov 26, 1984; children: Stephen C, Jonathan C. **EDUCATION:** Hong Kong University, BSc, 1968; Columbia University, MA, 1970, PhD, 1975. **CAREER:** National Bureau of Standards, research associate, 1975-77; University of Missouri-Rolla, research assistant professor, 1977-79; USC, research assistant professor, 1979-81; Litton Guidance & Control Systems, senior technical staff member, 1981-.

ORGANIZATIONS: Optical Society of America, 1981-. **BUSINESS ADDRESS:** Senior Member, Technical Staff, Litton Guidance & Control Systems, 5500 Canoga Ave, MS 12, Woodland Hills, CA 91367, (818)715-4272.

LAM, LUI
Physicist. Chinese American. **PERSONAL:** Born Nov 17, 1944, Lianxian, Guangdong, China; son of Lap-Chung Lam and Lai-Jane Wong; married Heung-Mee Lee, Jul 1, 1972; children: Charlene. **EDUCATION:** University of Hong Kong, BS, 1965; University of British Columbia, MS, 1968; Columbia University, MA, 1969, PhD, 1973. **CAREER:** City College, CUNY, research associate, 1972-75; University Instelling Antwerpen, Belgium, research scientist, 1975-76; University Saarlandes, Federal Republic of Germany, research scientist, 1976-77; Institute of Physics, Academia Sinica, China, associate research professor, 1978-83, adjunct professor, 1984-; City College, Queensborough Community College, CUNY, professor, 1984-87; San Jose State University, professor, 1987-. **ORGANIZATIONS:** International Liquid Crystal Society, founder, board of directors, chairman of conference committee, 1990-; American Physical Society, 1984-. **HONORS/AWARDS:** Nordita, fellow, 1976; Columbia University, Eugene Higgin Fellow, 1966-67; University of Hong Kong, Li Po Kwai Scholar, 1963-65. **SPECIAL ACHIEVEMENTS:** Co-editor of books: Liquid Crystalline & Mesomorphic Polymers, 1994; Modeling Complex Phenomena, 1992; Solitons in Liquid Crystals, 1992; Nonlinear Structures in Physical Systems, 1990; Wave Phenomena, 1989; founder & editor, Partially Ordered Systems, book series; Woodward Conference, book series. **BUSINESS ADDRESS:** Professor, Physics Dept, San Jose State University, San Jose, CA 95192-0106, (408)924-5261.

LAM, NELSON JEN-WEI
Banker. Chinese American. **PERSONAL:** Born Jul 16, 1960, Princeton, NJ; son of Sau-Hai Lam and Patsy C Lam. **EDUCATION:** High School, Tufts University, BSME, 1982; University of Pennsylvania, Wharton School, MBA, finance, 1987. **CAREER:** J P Morgan, assistant treasurer, 1982-85; Merrill Lynch Capital Markets, assistant vice president, 1987-90; UBS Securities, vice president, 1990-.

LAM, SAU-HAI (HARVEY)
Educator, educational administrator. Chinese American. **PERSONAL:** Born Dec 18, 1930, Macao; son of Ngai-Pak Lam & Wen-Hing Au Lam; married Patsy C Lam, Jun 6, 1959; children: Nelson, Karen, Philip. **EDUCATION:** Rensselaer Polytechnic Institute, BAE, 1954; Princeton University, MA, 1956, PhD, 1958. **CAREER:** Cornell University, assistant professor, 1959-60; Princeton University, research associate, 1958-59, assistant professor, 1960-63, associate professor, 1963-67, associate dean of engineering, 1980-81, Dept of Mechanical/Aerospace Engineering, chair, 1983-89, professor, 1967-. **ORGANIZATIONS:** American Physical Society. **HONORS/AWARDS:** National Science Foundation, Senior Post-Doctoral Fellow, 1976-77. **SPECIAL ACHIEVEMENTS:** Li & Lam, Principles of Fluid Mechanics, Addison-Wesley, 1964. **BUSINESS ADDRESS:** Professor, Princeton University, Olden Street, Engineering Quad, Princeton, NJ 08544, (609)258-5133.

LAM, SIMON SHIN-SING
Educator, educational administrator. Chinese American. **PERSONAL:** Born Jul 31, 1947, Macao; son of Chak Han Lam & Kit Ying Tang; married Amy Leung Lam, Mar 29, 1971; children: Eric Leung. **EDUCATION:** Washington State University, BSEE, 1969; University of California, Los Angeles, MS, 1970, PhD, 1974. **CAREER:** University of California, Los Angeles, ARPANET Measurement Center, postgraduate research engineer, 1971-74; IBM Watson Research Center, research staff member, 1974-77; University of Texas, Austin, assistant professor, 1977-79, associate professor, 1979-83, professor, 1983-, endowed professorship, 1985-, Department of Computer Science, chairman, 1992-. **ORGANIZATIONS:** IEEE/ACM Transactions on Networking, editorial board, 1992-; IEEE Transactions on Software Engineering, editorial board, 1990-; Performance Evaluation, editorial board, 1981-93; IEEE Transactions on Communications, editorial board, 1984-90; Proceedings of the IEEE, editorial board, 1985-89; National Science Foundation Division of Networking, advisory panel, 1992; Institute of Electrical & Electronics Engineers, fellow, 1985-; Association for Computing Machinery, 1972-. **HONORS/AWARDS:** IEEE Communications Society, Leonard G Abraham Award, 1975. **SPECIAL ACHIEVEMENTS:** Principal investigator/project director of 5 research grants from the National Science Foundation, 1978-; principal investigator/project director of 5 other research grants from the Department of Defense and the Texas Coordinating Board, 1988-; editor, Principles of Communication and Networking Protocols, IEEE Computer Society

Press, 1984; author of more than 80 published research articles. **BUSINESS ADDRESS:** Professor, Chair, Dept of Computer Science, University of Texas at Austin, Taylor 2.124, Austin, TX 78712, (512)471-9590.

LAM, THOMAS MANPAN
Architect. Chinese American. **PERSONAL:** Born Dec 14, 1957, Hong Kong; son of Irene and Yuen Lam; married Lisa S Lam, Nov 19, 1983. **EDUCATION:** Iowa State University, BArch (with honors), 1980; Harvard University Graduate School of Design, MArch, 1983. **CAREER:** Skidmore Owings & Merrill, designer, 1984-85; The Architects Collaborative, project designer, 1985-89; Ellenzweig Associates, architect, 1989-92; TRO (The Ritchie Organization), project architect, 1992-. **ORGANIZATIONS:** American Institute of Architects, 1986-; National Council of Architectural Registration Board, 1989-; Trinity Congregational Church, chairman, missions committee, 1993-94. **HONORS/AWARDS:** Iowa State University, Pace Award, 1980-81; Leo Daly Architects, Leo Daly Award, 1980-81. **SPECIAL ACHIEVEMENTS:** Student projects published in Iowa Architect, Spring 1979, 1980. **HOME ADDRESS:** 12 Harrison St, Maynard, MA 01754. **BUSINESS ADDRESS:** Project Architect, TRO/The Ritchie Organization, 80 Bridge St, Newton, MA 02158.

LAM, TOAN HOANG
Pediatrician. Vietnamese American. **PERSONAL:** Born Jun 11, 1951, Saigon, Vietnam; son of Lam Tuong and Anh Huynh; married Debbie Lam, Apr 7, 1990; children: Andrew. **EDUCATION:** University of Hawaii, School of Medicine, MD, 1980, pediatric residency, 1983, board certification, 1989. **CAREER:** University of Hawaii, assistant clinical professor, 1983-85; University of Utah, assistant clinical professor, 1985-, Physician Asst Program, instructor in pediatrics, 1986-; FHP, Dept of Pediatrics, dept head, 1988-90, pediatrician, currently. **ORGANIZATIONS:** American Academy of Pediatrics, fellow, 1989-; Utah Medical Assn, 1985-; Intermountain Pediatric Society, 1985-. **BUSINESS ADDRESS:** Pediatrician, FHP, 7495 South State Street, Midvale, UT 84047, (801)561-2231.

LAM, TONY
Businessman, city official. Vietnamese American. **PERSONAL:** Born Oct 4, 1936, Vietnam; son of Cat Lam; married; children: six. **CAREER:** Previous positions: shipping company supervisor, insurance salesman, immigration consultant, advertising executive; three Vietnamese restaurants, owner, currently; Westminster City Council, council member, 1992-. **ORGANIZATIONS:** Republican Party. **SPECIAL ACHIEVEMENTS:** First Vietnamese American ever elected to public office, 1992. **BIOGRAPHICAL SOURCES:** "A Vietnamese American Becomes a Political First," New York Times, Nov 16, 1992, sec A p11. **BUSINESS ADDRESS:** Council Member, Westminster City Council, 8200 Westminster Blvd, Westminster, CA 92683, (714)898-3311.∗

LAN, CHUAN-TAU EDWARD
Educator. Chinese American. **PERSONAL:** Born Apr 21, 1935, Kaohsiung, Taiwan; son of Tu-sen Lan & Tsai Mei Lan; married Sumy C Lan, Feb 12, 1961; children: Susan Lan Woolsey, Justin, Austin. **EDUCATION:** National Taiwan University, BS, engineering, 1958; University of Minnesota, MS, 1963; New York University, PhD, 1968. **CAREER:** New York City Board of Water Supply, assistant engineer, 1963-65; University of Kansas, assistant professor, 1968-74, associate professor, 1974-78, professor, 1978-92, Bellows Distinguished Professor, 1992-. **ORGANIZATIONS:** American Institute of Aeronautics, associate fellow, 1980-; Sigma Gamma Tau, 1967-; Tau Beta Pi. **HONORS/AWARDS:** NASA, Certificate of Recognition, 1978, 1980, 1982, 1986; University of Kansas Aero Engineering, Outstanding Aerospace Engineering Educator, 1991. **SPECIAL ACHIEVEMENTS:** Author of textbooks: Airplane Aerodynamics and Performance, 1981; Applied Airfoil and Wing Theory, 1988; articles in steady and unsteady aerodynamics and flight dynamics; numerous NASA reports in aerodynamics. **BUSINESS ADDRESS:** Professor, Dept of Aerospace Engineering, University of Kansas, Learned Hall, Rm 2004, Lawrence, KS 66045, (913)864-3596.

LAN, DONG PING
Engineer. Chinese American. **PERSONAL:** Born Feb 2, 1947, Guang Xi, China; married Huixian Tang, Feb 1, 1973; children: Jie, Qing. **EDUCATION:** Wuhan University, BS, 1969; Rutgers University, MS, 1989. **CAREER:** Intertek Labs Inc, electronics engineer, 1986-89; Vankel Indus Inc, senior engineer, 1989-. **HOME ADDRESS:** 147 Matis St, South Plainfield, NJ 07080. **BUSINESS PHONE:** (908)548-3616.

LAND, MING HUEY
Educational administrator. Taiwanese American. **PERSONAL:** Born Jul 10, 1940, Hsinchu, Taiwan; son of Jin-Tu Land & Jen Huang Land; married Wheiing Yang Land, Jul 30, 1970; children: Judy, Michael. **EDUCATION:** National Taiwan Normal University, BS, 1963; Northern Illinois University, MS, 1968; Utah State University, EdD, 1970. **CAREER:** Hsinchu, Taiwan, high school teacher, 1963-66; Eastern Illinois University, assistant professor, technology, 1970-71; Miami University, Industrial Ed & Architecture, professor, 1971-83; Appalachian State University, Dept of Technology, chair, 1983-89, College of Fine & Applied Arts, dean, 1989-. **ORGANIZATIONS:** International Council of Fine Arts Deans, 1990-; American Society for Engineering Education, 1975-; International Technology Education Association, 1967-; American Vocational Association, 1969-; National Association of Industrial Technology, 1985-; Epsilon Pi Tau, 1967-; Phi Kappa Phi, 1990-; North American Taiwanese Professors Association, 1983-. **HONORS/AWARDS:** International Technology Education Association, Special Recognition Award, 1990; Epsilon Pi Tau, Laureate Citation, 1987; Northeast University, China, Honorary Professor, 1986; Chungnam National University, Korea, Fulbright Scholar, 1981. **SPECIAL ACHIEVEMENTS:** Over 50 publications in Engineering Design Graphics Journal, School Shop/Tech Directions, Engineering Graphics, The Technology Teacher, Industrial Education, Taiwan Journal of Educational Supervision, Korean Journal of Manpower, Korean Journal of Industrial Education, etc. **HOME PHONE:** (704)264-0740. **BUSINESS ADDRESS:** Dean, College of Fine and Applied Arts, Appalachian State University, Wey Hall, Boone, NC 28608.

LANDERO, REYNALDO RIVERA, II
Physician. Filipino American. **PERSONAL:** Born Oct 3, 1941, Manila, Philippines; son of Frisco Cabal Landero and Maria Rivera Landero; married Lydia B Landero, May 5, 1960; children: Rey Raleigh III, Lorelei Landero-Garin, Rosanna Landero-Diwa, Rey Rainier IV, Rey Randall V. **EDUCATION:** University of the East, Manila, BS, pre-med, 1962; Manila Central University, MD, 1967; Case Western Reserve-St Thomas Hospital of Akron, Ohio, internship, 1969; University of California, Irvine-Long Beach VA, Training program, int medicine residency, 1971; UCLA-Wadsworth VA Medical Center, pulmonology program, fellowship, 1973. **CAREER:** LA Emergency Medical Group, co-director; Long Beach Doctors Hospital & Bellflower City Hospital, Respiratory Dept, medical director; internist & chest disease consultant, various hospitals; White Memorial Medical Ctr, attending staff, 1973-; University of California, clinical instructor in medicine, 1974-, Los Angeles County Medical Ctr, attending staff, 1974-; Imperial Hospital, chief, cardio-pulmonary Lab, 1978-79; Long Beach Hospital & Norwalk Community Hospital, in-service teachings, 1985; Landero Medical Ctr, physician, owner, currently. **ORGANIZATIONS:** California Medical Assn; California: Soc of Internal Medicine; LA County Medical Assn; American Medical Assn; American Soc of Internal Medician; American Thoracic Soc; Philippine College of Physicians, fellow; MCU Medical Alumni Assn in American, Southern California Chapter, pres, 1993-; Cultural Heritage Commission, City of Los Angeles, vp, 1993-. **HONORS/AWARDS:** Fil-Am Image Publication, 20 Outstanding Filipino Americnas in the US, 1992-93; Fil-Am Community of La, Distinguished Achievers & Pillars of the Community Award, 1993. **SPECIAL ACHIEVEMENTS:** Lecture, "Common Medical Problems in the Community," to Los Angeles Downtown Optimists Club, 1992, to Philippine Women's Club, 1993. **BUSINESS ADDRESS:** Physician & Owner, Landero Medical Clinic, 23251 S Main St, Carson, CA 90745, (310)830-4561.

LANEWALA, MOHAMMED ALI
Consultant, business executive. Indo-American. **PERSONAL:** Born in Dohad, Gujarat, India; son of Jafarbhai & Rani Lanewala; married Jean, Aug 10, 1968; children: Rani, Shirin. **EDUCATION:** Calcutta University, BSc (with honors), 1956, MSc, tech, 1959; University of Toronto, MASc, 1961; New York University, PHD, 1967. **CAREER:** Union Carbide Corp, project engineer, 1964-68, senior staff engineer, 1968-77, computer tech coordinator, 1977-83, consultant, 1983-87; UOP, consultant, 1987-92; Research Systems, owner, 1992-. **ORGANIZATIONS:** International Management Council, president, 1989-90; MENSA, president, 1983-85; India Association of Mobile, president, 1981, 1988; United Way of Mobile, loaned executive, 1983, 1984. **HONORS/AWARDS:** St Xavier's College, Sir P C Ray Gold Medal in Chemistry, 1956; New York University, J Henry Mason Award, 1963, Founders Day Award, 1967. **SPECIAL ACHIEVEMENTS:** Author or co-author of 11 technical papers, 1965-70; inventor or co-inventor of 2 US patents, 1966-69; copyright author of software package, 1992. **HOME ADDRESS:** 5909 Ole Mill Rd,

Mobile, AL 36609, (205)661-5793. **BUSINESS ADDRESS:** Owner, Research Systems, 5909 Ole Mill Rd, Mobile, AL 36609, (205)666-1155.

LANG, DAVID C.
Political consultant. Chinese American. **PERSONAL:** Born Feb 3, 1956, Hong Kong. **EDUCATION:** London School of Economics & Political Science, MSc, 1980. **CAREER:** Lieutenant Governor Leo McCarthy of California, assistant chief of staff, 1988-89; Dianne Feinstein for California Governor Campaign, fundraising consultant, 1990; Congressman Bob Matsui for US Senate Campaign, fundraising consultant, 1990-91; LA Councilman Mike Woo, senior deputy, 1990-92, Mike Woo for Mayor Campaign, finance director, 1992-93. **ORGANIZATIONS:** Organization of Chinese-Americans, LA chapter, advisory board; Chinese American Entrepreneurs Association, advisor. **HONORS/AWARDS:** University of Hawaii, East-West Center, fellowship, 1982-83. **HOME ADDRESS:** 17837 Calle Los Arboles, Rowland Heights, CA 91748, (818)965-6926.

LANGIT, RALPH P., JR.
Business executive. Filipino American. **PERSONAL:** Born Dec 6, 1936, New York, NY; son of Ralph C Langit and Francesca Langit; married Barbara, Jun 7, 1958; children: Ralph III, Nadine Sienko, Michael, Vincent. **EDUCATION:** St John's University. **CAREER:** Capital Records, office manager; Ebasco Services, planning engineer, 1969; Braun of Rutherford, sales rep, 1975; Biber Bros, sales rep, 1980; ASD Office Systems, sales rep, 1985; Langit & Associates, president, currently. **ORGANIZATIONS:** Rotary Middletown, board of directors; Institute for Industry, Government & Business; Boces. **BUSINESS ADDRESS:** President, Langit & Associates, 5 Conning Ave, Middletown, NY 10940, (914)692-6446.

LANGRANA, NOSHIR A.
Educator. Indo-American. **PERSONAL:** Born Oct 1, 1946, Bombay, India; son of Ardesher J Langrana & Ratamai A Langrana; married Dinaz, Jan 1, 1972; children: Anita, Shereen. **EDUCATION:** University of Bombay, BE (with honors), 1968; Cornell University, MS, mechanical engineering, 1971, PhD, mechanical engineering, 1975. **CAREER:** UMDNJ, Dept of Orthopaedic Surgery, adjunct associate professor; Rutgers University, Graduate School Program MAE, biomedical engineering, asst professor, 1976-82, associate professor, 1982-87, College of Engineering CAD Lab, director, 1984-, professor, 1987-, Mechanical & Aerospace Engineering Program, executive officer, 1990-. **ORGANIZATIONS:** American Society of Mechanical Engineers; Sigma Xi; Orthopaedic Research Society; International Society for the Study of the Lumbar Spine; North American Spine Society. **HONORS/AWARDS:** Society of Automotive Engineers, Ralph R Teetor Award, 1977; American Society of Mechanical Engineers, fellow, 1992. **SPECIAL ACHIEVEMENTS:** SPINE, associate editor, 1993-; State of New Jersey, professional engineer; patents issued: with others, Functional & Biocompatible Intervertebral Disc Spacer, US patent, 1990; Functional and Biocompatible Intervertebral Disc Spacer Containing Elastomeric Material of Varying Hardness, US patent, 1992; editor, book, 1993 Bioengineering Conference; Biomechanical Analyses of Loads on the Lumbar Spine, in Lumbar Spine, 2nd ed, 1994; refereed articles in journals: "Rule Based Design of a Material Processing Components," Journal of Engineering with Computers, 1993. **BUSINESS ADDRESS:** Professor, Dept of Mechanical & Aerospace Engineering, Rutgers-The State University of New Jersey, PO Box 909, Piscataway, NJ 08855-0909, (908)932-3628.

LAO, BINNEG Y.
Wireless and microwave engineering company executive. Chinese American. **PERSONAL:** Born Feb 25, 1945, China; son of Kan Lao and Yenpu Lao; married Jennifer, Jul 11, 1970; children: Catherine Yunghui, Richard Yungchih. **EDUCATION:** UCLA, BS (summa cum laude), 1967; Princeton University, MA, 1969, PhD, 1971. **CAREER:** Dow Chemical, principal physicist, 1974-76; Bendix, principal scientist, 1976-80; Magnavox, manager, 1980-86; Rand Corporation, consultant, 1986-87; Sierra Monolithics, CEO, 1988-. **ORGANIZATIONS:** American Physical Society, 1970-; Institute of Electric & Electronic Engineers, 1986-. **HONORS/AWARDS:** Magnavox, Management Award, 1985; Ford Foundation, Woodrow Wilson Fellow, 1967; UCLA, E. Lee Kinsey Award, 1967; Phi Beta Kappa, 1967. **SPECIAL ACHIEVEMENTS:** 30 technical publications on physics and electronics; 8 patents. **BUSINESS ADDRESS:** CEO, Sierra Monolithics, Inc, 103 W Torrance Blvd, Ste 102, Redondo Beach, CA 90277, (310)379-2007.

LAO, CHANG S.
Mathematical statistican, federal official. Chinese American. **PERSONAL:** Born Dec 10, 1935, Shanghai, China; son of K J Lao and M T Lao; married Ching C Lao, Nov 20, 1966; children: Allen, Lawrence, Cathy. **EDUCATION:** National Taiwan University, BA, 1960; University of Massachusetts, MS, 1966; Yale University, PhD, 1973. **CAREER:** E I du Pont DeNemours & Co, statistician, 1966-68; Pennsylvania Dept of Health, medical research scientist, 1973-74; Food & Drug Administration, mathematical statistician, 1974-. **ORGANIZATIONS:** American Statistical Association, 1966-; Biometric Society, 1975-; Association of Analytical Chemists, consultant, 1975-88. **HONORS/ AWARDS:** National Taiwan University, scholarship, 1955-60; US Public Health Service, traineeship, 1968-73; FDA Outstanding Employee Awards, 1982, 1985, 1992. **SPECIAL ACHIEVEMENTS:** Statistical Principles for Clinical Investigations in Support of a Premarket Approval Application, 1982; Projecting Mortality on the Effect of Radiation in Beagle Dogs, 1987; The FDA Report on Intraocular Lenses, 1983. **HOME ADDRESS:** 15429 Narcissus Way, Rockville, MD 20853. **BUSINESS PHONE:** (301)594-0630.

LASKAR, DEVI SEN
Journalist. Indo-American. **PERSONAL:** Born Oct 22, 1966, Chapel Hill, NC; daughter of Pranab K Sen and Gauri D Sen; married Joy Laskar, Jun 30, 1990. **EDUCATION:** University of North Carolina, Chapel Hill, BA, 1988; University of Illinois, Urbana, MA, 1992. **CAREER:** Atlanta Journal-Consititution, intern, 1988; News-Press, Florida, reporter, 1988-89; Commercial News, Illinois, reporter, 1989-90; Honolulu Star-Bulletin, reporter, 1992-. **ORGANIZATIONS:** AAJA Hawaii Chapter, 1993-. **HONORS/AWARDS:** University of Illinois, MA program in Asian studies, fellowship. **BUSINESS ADDRESS:** Journalist, Honolulu Star-Bulletin, 605 S Kapiolani Blvd, Honolulu, HI 96813, (808)525-8621.

LATEEF, ABDUL BARI
Educator. Pakistani American. **PERSONAL:** Born Apr 4, 1939, Faisalabap, Punjab, Pakistan; son of Mohammad Abdul Lateef & Fatima Lateef; married Kauser Lateef, Jan 10, 1970; children: Babur, Omar. **EDUCATION:** Punjab University, Pakistan, BS, 1959, MS, 1961; Newcastle University, England, PhD, 1966. **CAREER:** Youngstown State University, Criminal Justice Dept, chairman, 1969-; Tri-State Labs, CEO, 1981-. **ORGANIZATIONS:** American Academy of Forensic Sciences; Academy of Criminal Justice Sciences; Sigma Xi. **HOME ADDRESS:** 165 Mayflower Dr, Youngstown, OH 44512, (216)758-7818. **BUSINESS PHONE:** (216)797-8844.

LAU, ALBERT KAI-FAY
Educational administrator. Chinese American. **PERSONAL:** Born Nov 8, 1949, Canton, People's Republic of China; son of William Lau and Sun Young Lee. **EDUCATION:** MIT, BS, 1972. **CAREER:** Boston Public Schools, director of MIS, 1992-. **ORGANIZATIONS:** Asian American Resource Workshop, founder, 1975-. **BUSINESS ADDRESS:** Director, Office of Information Systems, Boston Public Schools, 26 Court St, Boston, MA 02108, (617)635-9199.

LAU, BENNETT M. K.
Physician. Chinese American. **PERSONAL:** Born May 28, 1930, Honolulu, HI; son of Luck Yee Lau and Juliette K Lau; married Yvonne, Apr 21, 1960; children: DeeAnne K. **EDUCATION:** Loma Linda University, MD, 1955; La Sierra University, BA, 1951. **CAREER:** US Army, hospital commander, 1961-62, chief, general surgery, 1962-1966, chief, plastic surgery, TAMC, HI, 1968-77; Micronesia, consultant, plastic surgery, 1972-77; University of Hawaii John Burns Medical School, associate clinical professor of surgery, 1970-; private practice, 1977-. **ORGANIZATIONS:** American Society of Plastic and Reconstruction Surgery, 1972-; American College of Surgery, 1963-; Pan Pacific Surgical Society, 1970-; Hawaii Plastic Surgery Society, 1980-. **MILITARY SERVICE:** US Army, colonel, 1956-77. **BUSINESS ADDRESS:** Physician, 1380 Lusitana, Suite 702, POBI, Honolulu, HI 96813, (808)524-1551.

LAU, CHERYL ANN
State government official. Chinese American. **PERSONAL:** Born Dec 7, 1944, Hilo, HI; daughter of Ralph K Y Lau and Beatrice Loo Lau. **EDUCATION:** Indiana University, BME, 1966; Smith College, MAT, 1968; University of Oregon, DMA, 1971; University of San Francisco, JD, 1981. **CAREER:** State of California, professor of music, CSUS, 1975-87; State of Nevada, deputy attorney general, 1987-91, secretary of state, 1991-. **ORGANIZATIONS:** Project Democracy, chairman, 1993-; Nevada Women's Commission, chairman, 1992-93; Nevada Tahoe Regional Planning Agency, chairman, 1991-93;

Western Nevada Community College Fund, 1991-; National Association of Secretaries of State, 1991-; Republican National Platform Committee, vice chair, 1992-. **HONORS/AWARDS:** Indiana University, Foundation Award, Service Award, Metz Scholar, 1966; University of Oregon, Research Fellowship, 1970; California State University, Sacramento, Faculty Research Grant, 1977, Affirmative Action Faculty Development Program Grant, 1979; Hilo Chinese Association, Education Grant, 1977-80. **SPECIAL ACHIEVEMENTS:** Co-author, "Talking About the Cheng and Seh," 1972, "An Investigation of the Chinese Fiddle and Itu Music," 1972; composition entitled Aculturation, performed by Indianapolis Symphony percussion section, 1976. **BUSINESS ADDRESS:** Secretary of State, Secretary of State's Office, Capitol Complex, Carson City, NV 89710, (702)687-6926.

LAU, DAVID T.
Board of education executive. Hong Kong American/Chinese American. **PERSONAL:** Born Apr 26, 1939, Hong Kong; son of George Y Lau (deceased) & Nancy T Lau; married Cecilia L Lau, Jan 28, 1967; children: Michael D, Michelle W. **EDUCATION:** Idaho State University, BS, 1965; Pace University, MBA, 1968. **CAREER:** Monterey Park City, Park & Recreation Commission, commissioner, 1985-91, president, 1990-91; Los Angeles County Human Relations, vice president, commissioner, 1992-; Garvey School District, vice president, board of education, 1993-; Kaiser Permanente Medical Care Program, senior human relations rep, 1985-. **ORGANIZATIONS:** Asian Youth Center, vice president, board of directors, 1990-; Asian Pacific Advocates, United Way, vice president, 1993-; Asian Pacific Family Center, secretary, advisory council, 1992-; Family Counseling Services, board of directors, 1992-. **HONORS/AWARDS:** Organizations of Chinese Americans, Asian American Achievement Award, 1985; SER, Jobs for Progress, Amigos De Ser Award, 1979. **SPECIAL ACHIEVEMENTS:** Chairperson, co-editor, Reflections-A History Book 1916-1991, City of Monterey Park-75th Anniversary. **BIOGRAPHICAL SOURCES:** Asian Week, p 11, May 22, 1992; Asian Pacific Community Line, p 2, Oct 1993. **HOME ADDRESS:** PO Box 451, Monterey Park, CA 91754.

LAU, EDWARD C. Y.
Attorney. Chinese American. **PERSONAL:** Born Nov 10, 1942, Los Angeles, CA; son of Arthur G W Lau and Marietta Lau; married Shirley Chuang, Jun 15, 1965; children: Steven, Elaine. **EDUCATION:** University of California, Berkeley, AB, 1965; Golden Gate University, JD, 1973. **CAREER:** Ed Lau Insurance Agency, owner, 1965-73; Law Offices of Edward C Y Lau, proprietor, 1973-. **ORGANIZATIONS:** American Trial Lawyers Association, sustaining member, standing committee, 1988-, Minority Committee, 1992; National College of Advocacy, faculty, 1992-; Congressional Advisory Committee, 12th disrict, committeeman, 1988-; Asian American Bar Association, sustaining member, 1980-; California Trial Lawyers Association, 1978-; American Immigration Lawyers Association, lecturer, author, 1976-; World Affairs Council, lecturer, 1992-; Silicon Valley for Democracy in China, founder, chairman, 1989-. **HONORS/AWARDS:** National College of Advocacy, diplomate in trial advocacy, 1993; Free China Relief, Human Rights Advocacy Award, 1984; Bar Association of San Francisco, Pro Bono Volunteer of the Month, 1992. **SPECIAL ACHIEVEMENTS:** Active in pro bono work involving civil rights, Asian community Chinese asylum; mentor attorney working with newer attorneys for Bar Association, Immigration Legal Resources, Chinese for Affirmative Action; General Counsel for Consul General of the Republic of China, frequent lecturer. **BUSINESS ADDRESS:** Attorney, Law Offices of Edward C Y Lau, 555 Montgomery St, #500, San Francisco, CA 94111-2555, (415)956-1111.

LAU, ESTELLE PAU ON
Educator. Chinese American. **PERSONAL:** Born in Honolulu, HI; daughter of Kam Tomy Lau and Wong Shee Lau; divorced; children: Bradford Clark Gaffney, Ann Gaffney Shores, Stuart Morgan Gaffney. **EDUCATION:** University of California, Berkeley, BA; University of Chicago, MA; Marquette University, PhD, 1976. **CAREER:** University of California, Berkeley, teaching assistant; University of Minnesota, teaching asst; Moorhead State University, Social Sciences Division, instructor; Alverno College, Department of History, chair, associate professor; University of the Pacific, social foundations and multicultural education, professor, women's studies, professor, currently. **ORGANIZATIONS:** Comparative and International Education Society, racial/ethnic issues committee appointee, gender and education committee; Association of Asian American Studies; Association of Asian Studies. **HONORS/AWARDS:** University of the Pacific, Research Grant, 1990; Pacific Telesis, Research Grant, 1990; University of the Pacific, Teaching Incentive Awards,

1984, 1985, 1988. **SPECIAL ACHIEVEMENTS:** Co-author, "Value Differences as Reflected in Interactions in a Cambodian and an American First Grade Class," Anthology, Washington University Press, in press; author, "Multicultural Education: A Means for Integrating Non-Western Perspectives in the Curriculum," Intl Review of History and Political Science, vol 4, Spring, 1989. **HOME PHONE:** (209)957-0719. **BUSINESS ADDRESS:** Professor, University of the Pacific, Pacific at Stadium, 100 D Education Building, Stockton, CA 95211, (209)946-2168.

LAU, FRED H.
Law enforcement official, educator. Chinese American. **PERSONAL:** Born Jun 26, 1949, San Francisco, CA; married Barbara Chinn Lau. **EDUCATION:** City College of San Francisco, alumnus; San Francisco State University, alumnus; San Francisco Police Department, police academy graduate. **CAREER:** San Francisco State University, adjunct professor, currently; San Francisco Police Department, Central Station, patrol, 1971, 1976, Community Relations, Asian community liaison, 1972, Intelligence, Gang Task Force, 1977, assistant inspector Q-35, 1980, sergeant, inspector Q-50, 1980, Police Academy, staff, instructional assignments, 1979-82, Ingleside Station, patrol sergeant, 1982, temporary Q-60 lieutenant, 1983, Richmond Station, lieutenant, 1984, temporary Q-80 captain, 1986, Golden Gate Division, captain, 1986-87, Metro Division, captain, 1987, Tactical Co, captain, 1987-88, captain, 1989, Patrol Bureau, commander of patrol, 1988-90, Field Operations, deputy chief of police, 1990, 1992, Administration, deputy chief of police, 1992-93, chief of inspectors, 1993-. **HONORS/AWARDS:** Bronze Medal of Valor; three Meritorious Conduct Awards; two Police Commission Commendations; numerous Captain's Complimentaries. **SPECIAL ACHIEVEMENTS:** First Chinese-American lieutenant, captain, commander, deputy chief in the San Francisco Police Department. **BUSINESS ADDRESS:** Chief of Inspectors, San Francisco Police Department, 850 Bryant St, San Francisco, CA 94103.

LAU, FREDERICK C.
Educator, musician, conductor. Hong Kong American. **PERSONAL:** Born Feb 18, 1957, Hong Kong; son of Chak-Kwong Lau and Kwan-Ying Lau; married Inui Choi, Jun 15, 1991. **EDUCATION:** Chinese University of Hong Kong, BA; Guildhall School of Music & Drama, London, post-graduate diploma, 1982; University of Illinois at Urbana-Champaign, MA, 1984, DMA, 1991. **CAREER:** Illinois Summer Youth Music, lecturer, 1987-91; University of Illinois at Urbana-Champaign, teaching assistant, 1984-91; Millikin University, visiting adjunct assistant professor, 1988-89; University of Wisconsin at Eau Claire, visiting assistant professor, 1990; California Polytechnic State University, assistant professor, 1991-. **ORGANIZATIONS:** Society for Ethnomusicology, 1987-; Society for Asian Music, 1987-; Assn for Asian Studies, 1988-; Intl Consul for Traditional Music, 1990-. **HONORS/AWARDS:** CSCPRC, National Academy of Sciences, Dissertation Research, 1986; Affirmative Action Office, Faculty Development Grant, 1992; Graduate College, University of Illinois, Dissertation Research, 1986; Royal Hong Kong Jockey Club, Music Scholarship, 1981; DAAD, Germany, Summer Study Grant, 1979. **SPECIAL ACHIEVEMENTS:** Contributor to the Garland Encyclopedia of World Music, 1993; solo flute recitals, annually 1987-, chamber music; principal flutist, Decatur Symphony Orchestra, 1989-90; conductor, SLO County Youth Symphony Orchestra, 1991-, Cal Poly Chamber Orchestra, 1991-; Contemporary Music Ensemble, 1991-. **BUSINESS ADDRESS:** Assistant Professor, Music Dept, California Polytechnic State University, San Luis Obispo, CA 93407, (805)756-7464.

LAU, GILBERT MINJUN
Business owner (retired). Chinese American. **PERSONAL:** Born Aug 25, 1927, Honolulu, HI; son of Ah Chew Lau and Yuk Kno Wong; married Joan Carol Rothenay, Sep 15, 1962; children: Melissa Ann, Gabriel Tobias, Lucius Bernard, Jason Dominic. **EDUCATION:** Washington State College, 1945-46, 1948-49; Stanford University, BA, economics, 1951; Stanford Grad School of Business, MBA, 1956. **CAREER:** Collins Radco, manager, engineering, 1957-60; North American Aviation, supervisor, management information systems, 1960-65, contracts, general office, 1965-68; North American Rockwell, administrative manager, engineer, 1968-69; Green Genie Nursery, owner, general manager, 1969-90. **ORGANIZATIONS:** California Laubach Literacy, Valley Center Chapter, co-director, 1990-91; St Stephen's Catholic Church, Valley Center, founding president, council of ministries, 1982-83; Valley Center Union School District, president, board of trustees, 1979-81; California State Board of Education, Book Review Committee, 1978-79; Valley Center 4-H, community leader, 1977-79; Valley Center Pop Warner, head coach, 1977-79. **HONORS/AWARDS:** Washington State College, Bacteriology, Sigma Alpha

Omicron, 1948; California Legislature, Bicentenniel Farm Family, 1976. **MILITARY SERVICE:** US Army, t/5, 1946-48; Good Service, 1948. **HOME ADDRESS:** 10161 Circle R Dr, Valley Center, CA 92082, (619)749-0973.

LAU, GLORIA J.
Bank executive. Chinese American. **PERSONAL:** Born Apr 4, 1954, Kearny, NJ; daughter of Richard Lau and Eleanor Lau; married Robert Burkhead, May 26, 1985; children: Matthew Burkhead, Jake Burkhead. **EDUCATION:** Sarah Lawrence College, BA, 1976; Harvard Business School, MBA, 1978. **CAREER:** General Foods, associate product manager, 1978-80; Del Monte R J Reynolds, product manager, 1980-83; Activision, group marketing manager, 1983-85; Citibank, marketing manager, assets, CA, 1985-87, director of marketing, CA, 1987-92, vice president, marketing, western region, 1992-. **ORGANIZATIONS:** Harvard Business School Association, 1978-. **HONORS/AWARDS:** Harvard Business School, Li Ming Fellowship, 1976.

LAU, HON-SHIANG
Educator. Singaporean American. **PERSONAL:** Born Dec 18, 1947, Singapore; son of Pichau Lau & Swee-Yong Chee; married Amy Hing-Ling Lau, Aug 20, 1971; children: Wunji, Wendy. **EDUCATION:** University of Singapore, BEng, 1969; University of North Carolina, Chapel Hill, PhD, 1973. **CAREER:** Oklahoma State University, Regents professor of management, 1983-. **BUSINESS ADDRESS:** Regents Professor, Dept of Management, Oklahoma State University, Stillwater, OK 74078-0001, (405)744-5105.

LAU, JARK C.
Engineer, researcher. Chinese American. **PERSONAL:** Born Oct 18, 1935, Singapore, Singapore; son of Choh Poh Lau; widowed; children: Yung R, Ming S Ligman. **EDUCATION:** Royal Melbourne Institute of Technology, Australia, FRMIT, 1956; California Institute of Technology, AE, 1964; ISVR University of Southampton, England, PhD, 1971. **CAREER:** Singapore Polytechnic, senior lecturer, 1958-71; University of Singapore, associate professor, 1971-75; Lockheed-Georgia Co, technical consultant, 1975-80; Kimberly-Clark Corp, senior research fellow, principal research fellow, 1980-. **ORGANIZATIONS:** American Institute of Aeronautics & Astronautics, associate fellow, 1976-. **SPECIAL ACHIEVEMENTS:** Many technical papers in international journals; patents, US and other. **HOME ADDRESS:** 2525 Powder Ridge Dr, Roswell, GA 30076, (404)998-2419. **BUSINESS ADDRESS:** Principal Research Fellow, Kimberly-Clark Corp, 1400 Holcomb Bridge Rd, Roswell, GA 30076, (404)587-8563.

LAU, JENNI MEILI
Writer, photographer. Chinese American. **PERSONAL:** Born Jul 26, 1966, Honolulu, HI; daughter of Eugene W I Lau & Dierdre F Lau. **EDUCATION:** New York University, BA, English, photography, 1989. **CAREER:** West Side Spirit, staff photographer, 1986-89; Live Wire News Service, staff photographer, 1987-89; Archtype Magazine, contributing photographer/writer, 1987-88; Courier Newspaper, contributing photographer/writer, 1987-89; Larry Busacca Studio, photographic assistant, 1988-89; 7 Days Magazine, contributing photographer, 1989; Ear Magazine, editorial assistant/contributing writer, 1989; Metropolis Magazine, contributing writer, 1993-; W Magazine, a Fairchild Publication, associate editor, 1989-93; freelance writer, currently. **ORGANIZATIONS:** Museum of Modern Art, New York, 1989-92; National Origami Society, 1991. **HONORS/AWARDS:** United Nations/International Council of Photography, Photojournalism Award, 1989; NYU, Founder's Day Award for Academic Achievement, 1989. **SPECIAL ACHIEVEMENTS:** Series of Portrait Paintings of Grandparents, 1992-93; Roundabout: Evolving piano composition, 1990-93; Detritus: series of mixed media canvas compositions, 1993; Faces, series of pen line-drawing portraits, 1993; series of female nude torsos painted on wood, 1993. **HOME ADDRESS:** 3079 La Pietra Circle, Honolulu, HI 96815.

LAU, JOSEPH T. Y.
Research scientist. Hong Kong American. **PERSONAL:** Born Mar 21, 1953, Hong Kong; married Karen, Sep 3, 1989. **EDUCATION:** University of Washington, BS, 1975; Purdue University, PhD, 1980; Johns Hopkins School of Medicine, postdoctorate, 1985. **CAREER:** Johns Hopkins School of Medicine, research assoc, 1983-85; Roswell Park Cancer Institute, cancer research scientist, 1985-. **ORGANIZATIONS:** Society for Complex Carbohydrate; AAAS; ASBMB. **BUSINESS ADDRESS:** Cancer Research Scientist, Roswell Park Cancer Institute, Elm & Carlton Sts, C & V Rm 337, Buffalo, NY 14263, (716)845-8914.

LAU, LAWRENCE JUEN-YEE
Educator, consultant. Chinese American. **PERSONAL:** Born Dec 12, 1944, Guizhou, China; son of Shai-Tat Liu and Chi-Hing Yu Liu; married Tamara Jablonski Lau, Jun 23, 1984; children: Alexander M. **EDUCATION:** Stanford University, BS (with great distinction), 1964; University of California, Berkeley, MA, 1966, PhD, 1969. **CAREER:** Stanford University, acting assistant professor of economics, 1966-67, assistant professor of economics, 1967-73, associate professor of economics, 1973-76, professor of economics, 1976-, Kwoh-Ting Li Professor of Economic Development, 1992-, Asia/Pacific Research Center, co-director, 1992-. **ORGANIZATIONS:** Self-help for the Elderly, advice board, 1982-; Chiang Ching-Kuo Foundation for International Scholarly Exchange, board of directors, 1989-; Governor's Council of Economic Policy Advisers, State of California, 1993. **HONORS/AWARDS:** John Simon Guggenheim Memorial Fellow, 1973; Center for Advanced Study in Behavioral Sciences, fellow, 1982; Cambridge University, Overseas Fellow, Churchill College, 1984. **SPECIAL ACHIEVEMENTS:** Farmer Education and Farm Efficiency, with D T Jamison, Johns Hopkins University Press, 1982; Models of Development: A Comparative Study of Economic Growth in S Korea & Taiwan, ICS Press, 1986, revised edition, 1990. **BUSINESS ADDRESS:** Professor, Dept of Economics, Stanford University, Stanford, CA 94305-6072, (415)723-3708.

LAU, LESLIE
Anesthesiologist (retired). Chinese American. **PERSONAL:** Born Jan 7, 1926, Port-of-Spain, Trinidad and Tobago; son of Verna Emelda Huggins & George Lionel Francis Lau; divorced; children: Patrick Bernard, Verna Marie Domzalski, Paul Edward. **EDUCATION:** Harvard College, AB, biology, 1948; National University of Ireland, Medical School, 1953. **CAREER:** Queen Mary's Hospital for the East End of London, resident, 1954-55; Connaught Hospital, resident, 1955; University College, Dublin, demonstrator in anatomy, 1955-56; Saint Andrews Hospital, registrar, 1956-57; Royal Free Hospital & Medical School, instructor in dental anesthetia, 1958; Eastman Dental Hospital, Institute of Dental Surgery, senior registrar, 1958-59, lecturer in dental anesthetics, 1958-59; General Hospital, Port-of-Spain, consultant anesthesiologist, senior consultant, 1959-64; Antoni Clinic, group practice, 1964-67; Providence Medical Center, staff anesthesiologist, 1968-85. **ORGANIZATIONS:** Inter-Plast, anesthesiologist volunteer, 1987. **HONORS/AWARDS:** Rockefellar Foundation, Inter Caribbean Travel Grant, 1962; Mayo Clinic, fellow, 1959; University of Oregon Health Science Center, fellow, 1967-68. **SPECIAL ACHIEVEMENTS:** Author, "General Anesthesia with the EMO Inhaler Using Air," West Indian Medical Journal, 1964; first degreed anesthesiologist in Trinidad; helped to set up the anesthesia department in Port-of-Spain. **HOME ADDRESS:** 4926 SW Corbett Ave, Ste 307, Portland, OR 97201, (503)241-2905.

LAU, NGAR-CHEUNG
Research scientist, educator. Hong Kong American/Chinese American. **PERSONAL:** Born Jul 21, 1953, Hong Kong; son of Sheung Lau and Woon-Kam Lee; married Chih-Ping Flossie Hsu, Dec 15, 1979; children: Michelle. **EDUCATION:** Chinese University of Hong Kong, BSc, 1974; University of Washington, PhD, 1978. **CAREER:** University of Washington, research asst, 1974-78; Princeton University, research scientist, 1978-84, associate professor, currently; GFDL, NOAA, US Dept of Commerce, research scientist, sr research scientist, 1984-. **ORGANIZATIONS:** American Meteorological Society, fellow, 1974-; American Geophysical Union, 1993-; Hong Kong Meteorological Society, corresponding mbr, 1990-; NOAA/Equatorial Pacific Ocean Climate Studies, council mbr, 1985-; Dynamics of Atmospheres and Oceans, journal editor, 1988-; Climate Variations Committee, 1990-93; World Meteorological Organization, conference committee, 1982; USA/China Monsoon Workshop, US delegate, 1987. **HONORS/AWARDS:** American Meteorological Society, Clarence Leroy Messinger Award, 1990, Rank of Fellow, 1991; US Dept of Commerce, Unusually Outstanding Performance Award, 1991; National Research Council, Taiwan, Lectureship Award, 1992; US Climate Research Committee, invited keynote speaker, 1993; Chinese University of Hong Kong, C N Yang Visiting Fellow, 1993. **SPECIAL ACHIEVEMENTS:** Author: over 50 scholarly articles in journals and monographs, 1977-; extensive data atlas of atmospheric circulation statistics, 1979, 1984; coordination of research groups in studies of climate variability, 1990-; editor: Proceedings for Intl Conference on East Asia Meteorology and Climate, 1992; US Delegate to intl conferences: Leningrad, Paris, and Tokyo. **BIOGRAPHICAL SOURCES:** Bulletin of the American Meteorological Society, vol 71, no 6, p 924, Jun 1990. **BUSINESS ADDRESS:** Senior Research Scientist, Geophysical Fluid Dynamics Laboratory-NOAA, Princeton University, PO Box 308, Princeton, NJ 08542.

LAU, PETER MAN-YIU
Physician, educator. Chinese American. **PERSONAL:** Born May 15, 1932, Canton, Kwong Tung, China; son of Kam-King Lau & Shuk-Han Y Lau (both deceased); married May-Dor; children: Stephan, Christopher. **EDUCATION:** University of Santo Tomas, MD, 1963. **CAREER:** University of Pennsylvania, assistant professor, pathology/medicine, 1973-75; Medical College of Ohio, professor, pathology/medicine, 1975-. **ORGANIZATIONS:** American Society of Hematology, 1972; American Association of Blood Banks, 1974; Ohio Association of Blood Banks, board of directors, 1975. **BUSINESS ADDRESS:** Professor, Pathology/Medicine, Medical College of Ohio, C S 10008, Toledo, OH 43699, (419)381-5250.

LAU, REGINA
Association administrator. Hong Kong American. **CAREER:** Asian American Manufacturers Association, executive director, currently. **SPECIAL ACHIEVEMENTS:** Association co-hosted Sources 1992, a conference on roads to liquidity, 1992. **BUSINESS ADDRESS:** Executive Director, Asian American Manufacturers Assn, 770 Menlo Ave, Ste 227, Menlo Park, CA 94025, (415)321-2262.∗

LAU, SHUK-FONG
Librarian. Hong Kong American. **PERSONAL:** Born Jun 25, Hong Kong; daughter of Chok-hi Lau and Yun-yung Hung; married Kwok-hung Chan, Dec 28, 1984. **EDUCATION:** Chinese University of Hong Kong, bachelor's of social science, 1983; University of Western Ontario, MLS, 1986; Memphis State University, MBA, international business, 1992. **CAREER:** Chinese University of Hong Kong, teaching assistant, 1983-84; Vocational Training Council of Hong Kong, assistant librarian, 1987-89; Memphis State University, reference/information retrieval librarian, 1989-. **ORGANIZATIONS:** American Library Association, 1989-; Tennessee Library Association, 1990-, Reference Round Table, chair, 1992-93, vice chair, 1991-92. **HONORS/AWARDS:** Chinese University of Hong Kong, New Asia College, Cheng Ming Award, 1983-84, Readers Digest Scholarship, 1982-83. **SPECIAL ACHIEVEMENTS:** Contributed article, "Chinese Personal Names and Titles: Issues in Cataloging and Retrieval," to Encyclopedia of Library and Information Science, 1993; "Chinese Personal Names and Titles: Problems in Cataloging and Retrieval," Cataloging & Classification Quarterly, 1991. **HOME ADDRESS:** 1485 Wood Trail Circle, Cordova, TN 38018. **BUSINESS ADDRESS:** Reference/Information Retrieval Librarian, Reference Dept, Memphis State University Libraries, Memphis, TN 38152, (901)678-2208.

LAU, TIN MAN
Educator. Hong Kong American. **PERSONAL:** Born Sep 27, 1958, Hong Kong; son of Chi San Liu and Shiu Fong Yau; married Tsai Miao Lau, Nov 21, 1987; children: Jeekin, Mojen. **EDUCATION:** National Cheng Kung University, Taiwan, BS, 1983; Ohio State University, MA, 1986. **CAREER:** Taiwan Kolin Co Ltd, assistant engineer, 1983-84; College of Arts Computer Lab, Instruction and Research Computer Center, programmer, 1985-86; Auburn University, Department of Industrial Design, assistant professor, 1986-91, associate professor, 1991-. **ORGANIZATIONS:** Industrial Designers Society of America, 1986-; Chinese Association of Industrial Design, 1992-; Mid-South Education Research Association, 1991-; Society of Computer Simmulation, 1987-; Auburn University Senate, senator, 1991-; Phi Beta Delta Honor Society for International Scholars, 1992-. **HONORS/AWARDS:** Student Government Association of Auburn University, Outstanding Faculty Award, 1990; China External Trade Development Council, Collegiate Product & Packaging Design Exhibition Design Award, 1983. **SPECIAL ACHIEVEMENTS:** An Approach of Establishing a Perspicuous Archetype for a Product, University of Michigan, Ann Arbor, MI, 1990; Computer Aided Design: A Computer Generated 3-D Anthropometric Human Figure Data-Base for Design Professions, IDG China, 1992. **BUSINESS ADDRESS:** Associate Professor, Dept of Industrial Design, Auburn University, OD Smith Hall, Auburn, AL 36849, (205)844-2373.

LAU, YUEN-SUM (VINCENT)
Educator. Chinese American. **PERSONAL:** Born Dec 24, 1950, Shanghai, People's Republic of China; son of Sau-Ching Lau and Wei-Chu Tao Lau; married Janine Li-Jing Wong, Dec 10, 1981; children: Clara, Hubert. **EDUCATION:** University of Hawaii, BS, 1973, MS, 1977, PhD, 1978. **CAREER:** University of Michigan, postdoctoral scholar, 1978-80; Creighton University, assistant professor, 1980-86, associate professor, 1985-90, professor, 1986-. **ORGANIZATIONS:** American Society for Pharmacology and Experimental Therapeutics, 1984-; Society for Neuroscience, 1983-; Society of Chinese

Bioscientists in America, committee representative, 1985-. **HONORS/ AWARDS:** Creighton University, Outstanding Young Investigator Award, 1985, James M Keck Faculty Development Award, 1985, co-founder, Parkinson's Disease Research Program, 1986. **SPECIAL ACHIEVEMENTS:** NINDS/Experimental Therapeutic Branch, Bethesda, MD, visiting research scientist, 1990-91; 71 research publications and abstracts; Language proficiency: English, Chinese (Mandarin, Shanghai, Canton dialects). **BUSINESS ADDRESS:** Professor of Pharmacology, Creighton University Medical School, 2500 California Plaza, Omaha, NE 68178, (402)280-3184.

LAU, YVONNE M.
Educational administrator. Chinese American. **CAREER:** Loyola University, assistant dean of multicultural affairs, 1989-. **HONORS/AWARDS:** National Association of Asian American Professionals, Recognition Award, 1992. **BUSINESS ADDRESS:** Assistant Dean of Multicultural Affairs, Loyola University of Chicago, 6525 N Sheridan Rd, Chicago, IL 60626, (312)508-3334.*

LAW, H. DAVID
Business executive. Hong Kong American/Chinese American. **PERSONAL:** Born Feb 12, 1949, Hong Kong; son of Wan-Hei Lo and Yee-Hwui Lin Lo; married Ruby H Law, Jun 16, 1973; children: Jeremy, George. **EDUCATION:** University of Washington, BSEE, 1972; Cornell University, MSEE, 1975, PhD, 1977. **CAREER:** Rockwell Science Center, member of technical staff, 1977-80; TRW Inc, optoelectronics lab manager, 1980-84; PCO Inc, vice president, 1984-91; HDL Inc, president, 1991-93; ArterNet Corp, president, 1993-. **ORGANIZATIONS:** IEEE, senior member, 1977-; American Physical Society, 1977-; American Society of Quality Control, 1991-. **HONORS/ AWARDS:** Tau Beta Pi. **SPECIAL ACHIEVEMENTS:** Over 35 published scientific papers and chapters in books. **BUSINESS ADDRESS:** President, ArterNet Corp, 22543 Ventura Blvd, Ste 215, Woodland Hills, CA 91364, (818)222-0748.

LAZO, DOUGLAS T.
Educational administrator. Filipino American. **PERSONAL:** Born Apr 29, 1942. **EDUCATION:** San Jose State University, MA, education administration, MS, administration of justice, MS. **CAREER:** Santa Clara Juvenile Probation Center, group counselor, 1973-78; San Jose State University, assistant professor, 1974-77; Chicago School Board, Dept of Facilities, currently. **ORGANIZATIONS:** Hispanic Institute of Law Enforcement; FEMA. **MILITARY SERVICE:** National Defense Exec Reservist. **BUSINESS ADDRESS:** Dept of Facilities, Chicago School Board, 1819 W Pershing Rd, Chicago, IL 60609, (312)535-8000.

LE, BINH P.
Librarian. Vietnamese American. **PERSONAL:** Born May 19, 1959, Da Nang, Vietnam; son of Toan Le & Chin Phan; married Christine Ann Le, Apr 25, 1980; children: Lida Ann. **EDUCATION:** Eastern Michigan University, BA, 1981; Western Michigan University, MA, 1984; Indiana University, MLS, 1987. **CAREER:** Purdue University, assistant reference and instruction librarian, 1987-; The Pennsylvania State University, senior assistant librarian, 1988-. **ORGANIZATIONS:** American Library Association, 1987-, Student Membership Task Force Committee, 1989-91, Bibliographic Planning Committee, 1990-92; American Political Science Association, 1989-; MidAtlantic Region/ Association for Asian Studies, 1990-. **HONORS/AWARDS:** Pi Sigma Alpha, 1982. **SPECIAL ACHIEVEMENTS:** Contributor, American Reference Books Annual, 1990-; contributor, Encyclopedia of Library History, 1993. **BUSINESS ADDRESS:** Senior Assistant Librarian, The Pennsylvania State University, Ogontz Campus, 1600 Woodland Rd, Abington, PA 19001, (215)881-7426.

LE, CHRISTINE DUNG
Social services administrator. Vietnamese American. **PERSONAL:** Born Jul 18, 1958, Saigon, Vietnam; daughter of Linh The Le & Hien Minh Le; married Phong Dang Nguyen, Jul 6, 1984; children: Nathan Dang Khoa Nguyen. **EDUCATION:** Reegina Mundi-Couvent Des Diseaux, baccalaureat II, 1977; Calvin College, BA, French & sociology, 1984; Aquinas College, MM, marketing, 1992. **CAREER:** Amway of Canada, marketing rep/personnel distributor, 1984-85; P5 Video Rentals, assistant manager, sales, 1984-85; Bethany Christian Services, licensing coordinator, 1985-. **ORGANIZATIONS:** American Management Association, 1993; National Association of Female Executives, 1992-92; United Way-Project Blue Print, steering committee member, 1991-92; American Red Cross, volunteer for Language Bank, 1981-84; La Societe De La Croix Rouge Canadienne (Canadian Red Cross), blood donor clinic/

tracing department, 1984-85. **SPECIAL ACHIEVEMENTS:** Proficient in French & Vietnamese. **BUSINESS ADDRESS:** Licensing Coordinator, Bethany Christian Services, 3206 Eastern SE, Refugee Services Program, Grand Rapids, MI 49508, (616)245-7100.

LÊ, HY XUÂN
Researcher. Vietnamese American. **PERSONAL:** Born Feb 25, 1957, Saigon, Vietnam; son of Le Dinh Ty and Nguyen Thi Lieu; married Tran Thi Hoa, Aug 1992; children: An Hoa. **EDUCATION:** Alice Lloyd College, AA, 1976; St Louis University, BS (summa cum laude), psychology, BA (summa cum laude), philosophy, 1982; Washington University, MA, PhD, 1982-85; Harvard University, predoc, 1985-86; George Washington University, postdoc, currently. **CAREER:** Washington University, instructor, 1983-85; Rockhurst College, assistant professor, 1986-88; Washington University, assistant professor, 1988-90; USGAO, Program Evaluation & Methodology Division, analyst, 1990-. **ORGANIZATIONS:** American Psychological Association, 1986-; Asian American Psychological Association, 1992-. **HONORS/AWARDS:** Society for Personality Assessment, Samuel Beck Award, 1989; American Psychological Association Minority Fellowship Program, Fellow, 1983-86. **BUSINESS ADDRESS:** Analyst, USGAO, Program Evaluation & Methodology Division, 441 G St NW, 5844, Washington, DC 20548.

LE, TIENG QUANG
Educator. Vietnamese American. **PERSONAL:** Born Apr 2, 1944, Mytho, Vietnam; son of Le Van Dleu and Nguyen Thi Tha; married Kimanh Thi Le, Dec 1969; children: Linh-U, Mai-U. **EDUCATION:** University of Saigon, BA, 1966; University of California, Los Angeles, MA, 1969; University of Southern California, PhD, 1974. **CAREER:** Northrop University, associate professor, 1980-91; Pasadena City College, instructor, 1982-; Glendale Community College, instructor, 1989-; American College, associate professor, 1991-; Citrus College, instructor, 1992-. **SPECIAL ACHIEVEMENTS:** Chief of the working group in an Indonesian refugee camp to help the United Nations High Commission on Rufugees, to resettle the refugees in various courtries, 1979-80. **HOME ADDRESS:** 3305 E Orange Grove, Pasadena, CA 91107.

LE, VY PHUONG
Oil and gas company executive. Vietnamese American. **PERSONAL:** Born Nov 13, 1960, Saigon, Vietnam; son of Mr and Mrs Lea Bierbraugh. **EDUCATION:** Texas Tech University, BS, petroleum engineering, 1983. **CAREER:** Pennzoil Company, petroleum engineer, 1983-84; WMT Operating Company, petroleum engineer, 1984-86; Vanguard Production Company, president, CEO, 1986-. **ORGANIZATIONS:** Independent Petroleum of America, 1989-; Society of Petroleum Engineers, 1986-; Texas Chamber of Commerce, 1990-; Lubbock Asian Assn, president, 1989-; Permian Basin Organization. **SPECIAL ACHIEVEMENTS:** United Way, organizer, 1990-91; Food Banks, organizer, 1989-91. **BIOGRAPHICAL SOURCES:** Engineering Today, Texas Tech University, p 38, Winter 1993. **HOME PHONE:** (806)796-0376. **BUSINESS ADDRESS:** President, CEO, Vanguard Production Company, 2503 74th St, Ste 201, Lubbock, TX 79423, (806)745-4180.

LE, XUAN KHOA
Association administrator. Vietnamese American. **CAREER:** Indo China Resource Action Center, director, 1982-. **BUSINESS ADDRESS:** Director, Indo China Resource Action Center, 1628 16th St NW 3rd Fl, Washington, DC 20009, (202)667-4690.*

LEE, ALBERT W.
Environmental equipment manufacturing executive. Chinese American. **EDUCATION:** University of Detroit, BCE, 1962; Northwestern University, MSCE, 1963; Illinois Institute of Technology, PhD, 1968. **CAREER:** Tenco Hydro Inc, president, 1969-. **ORGANIZATIONS:** Water Environment Federation, 1970-; American Society of Civil Engineers, 1962-. **HONORS/AWARDS:** Tau Beta Pi, 1961-; Chi Epsilon, Outstanding Civil Engineer Graduate, 1962. **BUSINESS ADDRESS:** President, Tenco Hydro Inc, 4620 Forest Ave, Brookfield, IL 60513, (708)387-0700.

LEE, ANG
Film director. Chinese American. **PERSONAL:** Born 1955?, Taiwan; married Jane Lin; children: two sons. **EDUCATION:** University of Illinois, theater, 1978; New York University, film, 1984. **CAREER:** Filmmaker, films include: Fine Line, 1985; Pushing Hands, 1991; Wedding Banquet, 1993; Eat Drink Man Woman. **HONORS/AWARDS:** 16th Asian American Intl Film Festival,

Asian American Media Award, for Wedding Banquet, 1993; Berlin Film Festival, Golden Bear Award, for Wedding Banquet, 1993; Asian Pacific Film Festival, Best Film Honors, for Pushing Hands, 1992; Pushing Hands nominated for Golden Horse Award in Taiwan, received a Special Jury Prize. **BIOGRAPHICAL SOURCES:** "A Director's Trip from Salad Days to a 'Banquet'," New York Times, section 2, p 25, August 1, 1993. **BUSINESS ADDRESS:** Filmmaker, c/o Good Machine, 526 W 25th St, New York, NY 10001, (310)552-2255.*

LEE, ANGEL WAI-MUN
Educator. Hong Kong American. **PERSONAL:** Born Aug 17, 1952, Hong Kong; daughter of Diana Ching-Hsien Hsieh & Che Wah Lee; married David States, Sep 1, 1979. **EDUCATION:** Wellesley College, BA, 1975; Harvard Medical School, MD, 1984; Harvard University, PhD, 1984. **CAREER:** University of California, San Diego, intern, 1984-85, resident, 1985-86; National Institutes of Health, medical staff fellow, 1986-89, senior staff fellow, 1989-92; Washington University School of Medicine, assistant professor, 1992-. **ORGANIZATIONS:** Sigma Xi, 1975-; Phi Beta Kappa, 1974-; American Society of Microbiology, 1992-; American Society for Biochemistry & Molecular Biology, 1993-. **HONORS/AWARDS:** American Cancer Society, Institutional Review Grant, 1992; American Heart Association, Missouri-affiliate Grant-in-aid, 1993; National Science Foundation, Research Planning Grant, 1993. **SPECIAL ACHIEVEMENTS:** Co-author: "Functional Dissection of Structural Domains in the Receptor for Colony-Stimulating Factor 1," J Biol Chem, vol 267, p 16472-83, 1992; "Structure-Specific Modeling in Hemoglobin," Proc National Acad Sci USA, vol 80, p 7055-7059; "Mechanism of Kinase Activation in the Receptor for Colony-stimulating Factor-1," Proc National Acad Sci USA, vol 87, p 7270-7274; "Signal Transduction by the Colony-stimulating Factor-1 Receptor; a comparison to other Receptor Tyrosine Kinases," Current Topics in Cellular Regulation, vol 32, p 73-181; numerous others. **BUSINESS ADDRESS:** Asst Prof, Dept of Biochem & Molecular Biophys, Washington University School of Medicine, 660 S Euclid Ave, Box 8231, North Bldg, Rm 3814, St Louis, MO 63110, (314)362-4466.

LEE, ARTHUR RICHARD
Engineer, federal official. Chinese American. **PERSONAL:** Born Sep 17, 1955, Baltimore, MD; son of Fong Wing Lee and Annie Ding Gim Lee; married Po Chu Lee, Jul 19, 1981; children: Beverly J, Lauren J. **EDUCATION:** BS, civil engineering, 1978; MS, environmental engineering, 1981. **CAREER:** US Army Corps of Engs, Baltimore District, civil engineer, 1978-80; Naval Fac Eng Command, Chesapeake Division, environmental engineer, 1980-83, general engineer, 1983-85; USAF/Air National Guard, environmental engineer, 1985-87; NASA Headquarters, Facilities Planning & Programming, program manager, 1987-90, Space Tech, special assistant to director, 1990-91, Space Flight Programs Division, program manager, 1991-93, safety and mission assurance, program manager, 1994-. **ORGANIZATIONS:** American Society for Civil Eng; Air National Guard Civil Eng Association; Professional Housing Management Association. **HONORS/AWARDS:** NASA, Quality Step Increased Award, 1989. **SPECIAL ACHIEVEMENTS:** Navy Instruction for Coal Conversion Projects, 1982; NASA Management Instruction for Enviromental Policies, 1989; Licensed Professional Engineer, Maryland. **BUSINESS ADDRESS:** Program Manager, Safety and Risk Management, NASA Headquarters, Office of Safety and Mission Assurance, 300 E St SW, Washington, DC 20546, (202)358-4670.

LEE, BING
Artist, educator. Chinese American. **PERSONAL:** Born Sep 15, 1948, Canton, China; son of Lee Wing Tak; married Laura Lee, Jul 25, 1981; children: TyAnn. **EDUCATION:** Columbus College of Art & Design, BFA, 1977; Syracuse University, College of Visual & Performing Arts, graduate program, 1977-79. **CAREER:** Asian American Arts Centre, prgm dir, 1986-90; School of Visual Arts, Chinese Art Students Program, directory, 1990-. **ORGANIZATIONS:** Godzilla, Asian American Art Network, founding mbr, 1990-; EPOXY Art Group, NY, founding mbr, 1983-89; Visual Art Society, Hong Kong, founding mbr, 1973-. **HONORS/AWARDS:** National Endowments for the Arts, fellowship, 1991; New York Foundation for the Arts, G. Millard fellowship, 1993; Chinese American Pioneers in the Artws, Honor of Merit, 1993. **SPECIAL ACHIEVEMENTS:** Commissioned works include: "Canal Street Station," New York Public Art, Metropolitan Transportation Authority, 1993; "Townsend Harris High School," New York Public Art, Public Art for Public Schools, 1991; "AIDS," television public service annoucement, Public Art Fund, New York, 1991; "P.S. 88 Queens," Site for Students, Public Art for Public Schools, 1993. **BIOGRAPHICAL SOURCES:** Mixed Blessings, Lucy

Lippard, p 36, 102, 230, 1990; New York Newsday, close-up section, Dec 1, 1992. **BUSINESS ADDRESS:** Chinese Art Students Program Director, School of Visual Arts, 209 E 23rd St, New York, NY 10010-3994, (212)592-2313.

LEE, BRADFORD YOUNG
Cardiac surgeon. Chinese American. **PERSONAL:** Born Mar 21, 1944, Oakland, CA; son of George & Esther Lee; married Sally Lynum Lee, Jan 23, 1993; children: Janine Sherri, Steven Kenneth. **EDUCATION:** Stanford University, BA, 1964; University of California, Medical School, MD, 1968; Cleveland Clinic Foundation, general surgery, 1976; University of Miami, Jackson Memorial Hospital, cardiac surgery, 1980. **CAREER:** Cardiac surgeon, currently. **MILITARY SERVICE:** US Army, major, 1970-72. **BUSINESS ADDRESS:** Cardiac Surgeon, 2211 Moorpark Ave, Ste 290, San Jose, CA 95128, (408)298-1003.

LEE, BRANDON. *See* Obituaries.

LEE, BYUNG-JOO
Educator. Korean American. **PERSONAL:** Born Apr 13, 1954, Busan, Republic of Korea; son of Hwa-chae Lee and Dang-Yon Kim; married Myung-Wook Lee; children: Susie, Cecile. **EDUCATION:** Seoul National University, BA, 1982; Pennsylvania State University, MA, 1984; University of Wisconsin-Madison, PhD, 1988. **CAREER:** University of Wisconsin, graduate student, 1984-88; University of Colorado, assistant professor, 1988-. **ORGANIZATIONS:** American Economic Association, 1984-; Econometric Society, 1986-; Korea America Economic Association, 1986-. **HONORS/AWARDS:** University of Colorado, Junior Faculty Development Award, 1989; University of Wisconsin, Distinguished Teaching Assistant Award, 1986; Pennsylvania State University, Charles V Donohoe Memorial Award, 1983. **SPECIAL ACHIEVEMENTS:** Econometric papers published in Econometrica, The Review of Economics and Statistics, etc, 1992-. **HOME ADDRESS:** 317 Grouse Court, Louisville, CO 80027, (303)666-8316. **BUSINESS ADDRESS:** Professor, Dept of Economics, University of Colorado, Boulder, CO 80309-0256, (303)492-2108.

LEE, BYUNG-MOON (MOON LEE)
Business executive. Korean American. **PERSONAL:** Born Nov 1, 1933, Seoul, Republic of Korea; son of Choo-Sang Lee and Su-Im Lee (both deceased); married Ok-Sook Shin Lee, Nov 4, 1961; children: Ken Kyung-Hoon, Ju-Wan. **EDUCATION:** Korean Naval Academy, Chin Hae, Korea, BS, 1956; United States Marine Corps Officer's School, Quantico, VA, 1957; Kook Min College, Seoul, bachelor's degree, politics, 1962; National Defense College, Korea, military attache course, 1968. **CAREER:** Korean Marine Corps School, instructor, 1957-59; Korean Navy Headquarters, aide to chief of naval operations, 1959-62; Ministry of National Defense, Korea protocol officer, 1967-68; Korean Embassy, Saigon, assistant armed forces attache, 1968-70, Tokyo, Japan, assistant defense attache, 1970-71; Moon Creations Inc, president, currently. **ORGANIZATIONS:** Assistant Armed Forces Attache Corps, Tokyo, president, 1971; Korean-American Businessmen & Professional Association, Central Florida, founder & president, 1979-81; Korean-American Golf Club of Central Florida, founder & president, 1983-84; Asian American Advisory Committee to Orlando Mayor, 1990-92; Asian American Social Service, Inc, chairman, board of directors, 1990-91; Asian Chamber of Commerce of Greater Orlando, director, 1991-92. **HONORS/AWARDS:** Korean American Businessmen & Professional Association, appreciation, 1982, 1983; Korean American Golf Club of Central Florida, appreciation, 1988. **MILITARY SERVICE:** Korean Marine Corps, lieutenant colonel, 1956-71; Naval Academy Award, 1956; Korean Navy Award, 1962; Korean Marine Corps Award, 1971. **BUSINESS ADDRESS:** President, Moon Creations Inc, 5840 S Orange Ave, Orlando, FL 32809, (407)851-3210.

LEE, CHE-FU
Educator. Chinese American. **PERSONAL:** Born Dec 5, 1941, Chiayi, Taiwan; son of Lien-teng Lee and Yin-seng Lee; married Ling W Lee, Jun 4, 1966; children: Conn Lee Martin, Tien F. **EDUCATION:** National Taiwan University, BS, 1963; Oklahoma State University, MA, 1967; University of North Carolina, PhD, 1970. **CAREER:** United Nations, senior advisor, 1975-76; The Catholic University of America, professor, 1970-, director, Life Cycle Institute, 1985-88, chair, department of sociology, 1992-; Sociometrics, Inc, senior associate, 1988-. **ORGANIZATIONS:** Nankai University, PRC, visiting professor, 1981-82; US Academy of Sciences, consultant, 1978-79; Hwazhong Science and Technology University, PRC, honorary professor, 1985-86; China Board of 1982 Census, editorial advisor, 1987. **HONORS/AWARDS:** US

Public Health Services, Research Grants, 1971, 1976; The Asian Society, Research Grant, 1972; Alpha Delta Kappa Honorary Sociological Society, Emory Borgardus Award, 1981. **SPECIAL ACHIEVEMENTS:** "Respite Service to Family Caregivers by the Senior Companion Program: An Urban-rural Comparison," Journal of Applied Gerontology, Dec 1992; "A Demographic Profile of American Hispanics," in Strangers and Aliens No Longer, 1992; "New Demographics and Old Designs: The Chinese Family and Induced Population Transition," Social Science Quarterly, 1988; Method of Social Survey and Statistical Analysis, Beijing: People's Publishers, 1989. **BUSINESS ADDRESS:** Professor and Chair, Dept of Sociology, The Catholic University of America, 620 Michigan Ave NE, Marist Hall, Washington, DC 20064, (202)319-5445.

LEE, CHEN HUI
Educator. Taiwanese American. **PERSONAL:** Born Dec 2, 1929, Taipei, Taiwan; son of Su-Chen Lee; married Shu-Fang Lee; children: San San Lee Kletzien, Eric T. **EDUCATION:** Michigan State University, PhD, 1966. **CAREER:** University of Wisconsin-Stevens Point, asst prof, 1966-71, assoc prof, 1971-77, professor, 1977-. **ORGANIZATIONS:** Society of American Foresters, 1966-; Intl Assn of Wood Anatomist, 1987-. **HONORS/AWARDS:** University of Wisconsin-Stevens Point, University Scholar, 1990. **SPECIAL ACHIEVEMENTS:** Author of 30 technical papers about forest genetics and tree improvements, 1967-. **BUSINESS ADDRESS:** Professor, University of Wisconsin-Stevens Point, College of Natural Resources, Stevens Point, WI 54481, (715)346-4186.

LEE, CHEN LOK
Educator, artist. Chinese American. **PERSONAL:** Born May 18, 1937, Beijing, China; son of Roy Hui Lee and He Yin; married Linda Sue Heinle, Jan 1972; children: Romana, Raymond. **EDUCATION:** Canton China Public Art College, BA, 1958; Hong Kong University, 1958-59; Art Student League, New York, NY, 1959-62; Temple University, Tyler School of Art, Philadelphia, MFA, 1971. **CAREER:** Moore College of Art & Design, professor, 1980-; private classes in Chinese painting & calligraphy, 1983-. **ORGANIZATIONS:** NEA, Brandywine Workshop, Philadelphia, visiting artist, 1990. **HONORS/ AWARDS:** Ford Foundation Fellowship, Tamarind Lithographics, 1972-73. **SPECIAL ACHIEVEMENTS:** City University of NY, graduate school, participated in forum with artists & scholars from China & America, 1986; Mayor's Commission for Cultural Exchange: Philadelphia/Tienjin, 1986-87; University of Michigan, assistant curator, NEA funded, 1990; Her Majesty's Service, travelling art exhibition, Hong Kong, 1982. **BIOGRAPHICAL SOURCES:** The Print World Dictionary, Print World Co, 1983-84. **HOME ADDRESS:** 149 Fernbrook Ave, Wyncote, PA 19095, (215)886-5288. **BUSINESS ADDRESS:** Professor, Moore College of Art & Design, 1920 Race St, Philadelphia, PA 19103-1178, (215)568-4515.

LEE, CHENG-CHUN
Research scientist. Chinese American. **PERSONAL:** Born May 24, 1922, Jiangdu, Jiangsu, China; married Janice W, Feb 9, 1959; children: James P, Ray W. **EDUCATION:** Natl Central University, Chungking, BS, veterinary medicine, 1945, Nanjing, MS, veterinary medicine, 1948; Michigan State University, MS, pharmacology, 1950, PhD, physiology, 1952. **CAREER:** Lilly Research Labs, Eli Lilly & Co, Indianapolis, IN, pharmacologist, 1952-58, sr pharmacologist, 1958-63; Midwest Research Institute, Pharmacology and Toxicology, sr pharmacologist, 1963-66, principal pharmacologist, 1966-67, head, 1967-76, Biological Sciences Div, assistant director, 1976-77, associate director, 1977-78, deputy director, 1977-78; US EPA, sr science advisor, 1979-; University of Missouri, lecturer, 1964-70; Kansas University Medical School, lecturer, 1966-79; World Health Organization, consultant, 1980, 1982, 1989, 1993; George Washington Medical School, professorial lecturer, 1981-92. **ORGANIZATIONS:** Chinese Animal Husbandry & Veterinary Medical Assn, 1945; AAAS, 1953; American Physiological Society, 1956; American Society for Pharmacology and Experimental Therapeutics, 1957; American Societies for Experimental Biology & Medicine, 1957; New York Academy of Sciences, 1958; Society of Toxicology, 1966; American College of Toxicology, 1980. **HONORS/AWARDS:** Midwest Research Institute, Principal Advisor Award, 1979; EPA, Bronze Medal, 1980, Special Achievement & Contributions, 1981, Special Achievement, 1989. **SPECIAL ACHIEVEMENTS:** Contributor to over 125 publications and presentations in American and intl scientific journals on pharmacology and toxicology of therapeutic agents (chemotherapeutic, antimicrobial, antimalarial, and anticancer drugs), toxicology of environmental chemicals, disposition and metabolism of drugs, developmental

toxicity and carcinogenecity of chemicals. **HOME ADDRESS:** 1351 Snow Meadow Ln, Mc Lean, VA 22102-2529, (703)790-9333.

LEE, CHEW-LEAN
Educator. Chinese American/Malaysian American. **PERSONAL:** Born Feb 2, 1948, Kulim, Kedah, Malaysia; daughter of Liam-Keng Lee and Siew-Har Ho; married Ker-Fong Lee, Jun 19, 1977; children: Maxwell Hwaming. **EDUCATION:** Vassar College, AB, physics and chemistry, 1972; Florida State University, PhD, 1979. **CAREER:** Florida State University, research associate in theoretical nuclear physics, 1980; Florida A & M University, assistant professor of physics, 1979-83; Florida Community College at Jacksonville, professor of physics, 1983-. **ORGANIZATIONS:** Northeast Florida Chinese American Association, 1987-; Society of Physics, Students Chapter at Florida Community College at Jacksonville, faculty adviser, 1988-. **HONORS/AWARDS:** Vassar College, Physics Prize for majors, 1972; Outstanding Young Women of America Association, Outstanding Young Woman of America, 1982. **BUSINESS ADDRESS:** Professor of Physics, Florida Community College at Jacksonville, Jacksonville, FL 32202-3056, (904)633-8459.

LEE, CHI-HANG
Research director. Chinese American. **PERSONAL:** Born Jan 1, 1939, Vinh Long, Vietnam; married Sep 19, 1964. **EDUCATION:** Southern Illinois University, BA, 1960; Rutgers University, PhD, 1966. **CAREER:** General Foods Corporation, various positions, 1967-78; Del Monte Corporation, various positions, beginning 1978, director of analytical services, currently. **ORGANIZATIONS:** American Chemical Society, 1961-; American Scientific Affiliation, 1960-, executive council, 1979-84, president, 1982. **HONORS/AWARDS:** Ministry of Economic Affairs, Taiwan, Republic of China, Taiwan Food Research & Development Advisory Committee, 1979-89; General Foods Corporation, Chairman's Award, 1977. **SPECIAL ACHIEVEMENTS:** About 50 articles and one book published in the last 25 years; proficient in French and several Chinese dialects. **BUSINESS ADDRESS:** Director of Analytical Services, Del Monte Corporation, 205 N Wiget Ln, PO Box 9004, Walnut Creek, CA 94598, (510)944-7273.

LEE, CHI-JEN
Government official. Taiwanese American. **PERSONAL:** Born Feb 8, 1936, Yi-Lan, Taiwan; son of Chao-Huei Lee and Sian-Sim Chung Lee; married Sue-Yuan Lee, Oct 10, 1960; children: Johns, Lucia, Benjamin. **EDUCATION:** National Taiwan University, School of Pharmacy, College of Medicine, BS, pharmacy, 1957; Johns Hopkins University, ScD, biochemistry, 1966. **CAREER:** China Chemical & Pharmaceutical Plant, pharmacist, 1959-62; Johns Hopkins University, Dept Biochemistry, research associate, 1966-67; Rockefeller University, research associate, 1967-68, assistant professor, 1968-73; National Institute Child Health & Human Dev, NIH, senior staff fellow, 1973-74; National Cheng Kung University, College of Medicine, Dept Biochem, visiting professor, 1984; Center for Biologics Evaluation and Research, FDA, supervisory research chemist, 1974-. **ORGANIZATIONS:** Polysaccharide Vaccine Committee, chairman, 1974-; American Society for Biochemistry and Mol Biology; American Association of Immunologists; American Society for Microbiology; New York Academy of Sciences; American Association for the Advancement of Science; George Washington University, Medical Center, Department Microbiol, thesis director for PhD candidate, 1988-91. **HONORS/ AWARDS:** FDA Award of Merit, 1991; National Taiwan University Alumni Association in N America, Distinguished Achievement Award in Government Service, 1988; FDA, Commendable Service Award, 1988, 1978, Award of Merit, 1986. **SPECIAL ACHIEVEMENTS:** Publications: more than 55 papers in professional journals; more than 20 lectures, national and international scientific meetings and research institutes; author of book: Development and Evaluation of Drugs: From Laboratory, Licensure, to Market, CRC Press Inc, 1993; language proficiency: English, Chinese, Japanese. **HOME PHONE:** (301)897-5641. **BUSINESS ADDRESS:** Supervisory Research Chemist, Center for Biologics Evaluation and Research, FDA, 8800 Rockville Pike, Room 405, NIH Building 29, Bethesda, MD 20892.

LEE, CHIHO (KEIKO)
Pharmacologist. Taiwanese American. **PERSONAL:** Born Jul 2, 1941, Taitung, Taiwan; son of Ching Lee and Shih Lee; married Chin-Chin Lee, Dec 1972; children: Roger. **EDUCATION:** Kaohsiong Medical College, Taiwan, BS, 1967; University of Tokyo, Japan, MS, 1972; Cornell University Medical College, PhD, 1976. **CAREER:** Syntex Research, staff researcher, 1978-. **ORGANIZATIONS:** Western Pharmacology Society; International Society for Heart Research; American Society of Hypertension; American Heart Asso-

ciation, Hypertension Council. **SPECIAL ACHIEVEMENTS:** Various pharmacology publications; language proficiency in: Taiwanese, Chinese, & Japanese. **HOME ADDRESS:** 3758 La Donna Avenue, Palo Alto, CA 94306, (415)493-0721. **BUSINESS ADDRESS:** Staff Researcher, Syntex Research, 3401 Hillview Avenue, R2-101, Palo Alto, CA 94304.

LEE, CHIN-CHUAN
Educator. Chinese American. **PERSONAL:** Born Sep 20, 1946, Taiwan; married Chia-Chih Yen Lee, Sep 9, 1972; children: Chu-An, Chu-Min. **EDUCATION:** National Chengchi University, Taiwan, BA, 1969; University of Hawaii, MA, 1973; University of Michigan, PhD, 1978. **CAREER:** Chinese University of Hong Kong, lecturer, 1978-82; University of Minnesota, associate professor, professor, 1982-. **ORGANIZATIONS:** International Communication Association, 1982-; Chinese Communication Association, president, 1990-; Association for Education in Journalism & Mass Communication, 1978-. **SPECIAL ACHIEVEMENTS:** Published books: Media Imperialism Reconsidered, 1980; Voices of China: The Interplay of Politics and Journalism, 1990; Mass Media and Political Transition: The Hong Kong Press in China's Orbit, 1991; Sparking a Fire: The Press and the Ferment of Democratic Change in Taiwan, 1993; China's Media, Media's China, 1994. **HOME ADDRESS:** 516 Montrose Ln, Saint Paul, MN 55116, (612)699-3350. **BUSINESS ADDRESS:** Prof/Dir, China Times Ctr for Media & Social Studies, Univ of Minnesota, School of Journalism & Mass Comm, 206 Church St SE, 210 Murphy Hall, Minneapolis, MN 55455-0488, (612)626-7446.

LEE, CHONG SUNG
Educator. Korean American. **PERSONAL:** Born Sep 4, 1939, Seoul, Republic of Korea; married Jacqueline Vaughan Lee, Aug 12, 1972; children: Christopher, Jennifer. **EDUCATION:** Seoul National University, BS, 1964; California Institute of Technology, PhD, 1970. **CAREER:** California Institute of Technology, graduate teaching & research assistant, 1964-69, postdoctoral research fellow, 1969-70; Harvard Medical School, postdoctoral research fellow, 1970-72, visiting associate professor, 1982-83; University of Texas, assistant professor, 1972-78, associate professor, 1978-. **ORGANIZATIONS:** Am Soc Biochem Mol Biol; Gen Soc Am; Am Soc Cell Biol; Am Association Adv Sci; Korean Chem Soc; Korean Sci Eng Association in Am. **SPECIAL ACHIEVEMENTS:** Research and teaching in the area of molecular genetics and molecular evolution; 30 plus publications in professional journals. **BUSINESS ADDRESS:** Professor, Dept of Zoology, University of Texas, Patterson Room 424, Austin, TX 78712.

LEE, CHOONG YANG
Educator. Korean American. **PERSONAL:** Born Oct 1, 1954, Pusan, Republic of Korea; son of Sung Pyo Lee & Soonae P Lee; married Janet K Lee, Jan 3, 1982; children: David H, Jennifer Y. **EDUCATION:** Seoul National University, BS, 1977; University of Iowa, MS, 1982, PhD, 1988. **CAREER:** Daewoo Engineering Co, Korea, project engineer, 1978-80; University of Iowa, instructor, 1988-89; Pittsburg State University, Kansas, assistant professor, 1989-. **ORGANIZATIONS:** Beta Gamma Sigma, 1989-; Pan-Pacific Business Association, charter member, 1989-; Operations Research Society of America, 1985-; The Institute of Management Science, 1985-; Decision Science Institute, 1985-; Production and Operations Management Society, 1990-; American Production and Inventory Control Society, 1990-; Institute of Industrial Engineers, 1990-. **HONORS/AWARDS:** Pittsburg State University, Excellence in Research Award, 1992. **SPECIAL ACHIEVEMENTS:** More than 20 research papers and articles published or forthcoming in professional journals. **BUSINESS ADDRESS:** Asst Professor, Dept of Management & Marketing, Pittsburg State University, Kelce School of Business, Pittsburg, KS 66762.

LEE, CHRISTOPHER
Motion pictures executive. Chinese American. **PERSONAL:** Born Oct 30, 1956. **CAREER:** ABC, Good Morning America, producer; Wayne Wang film, Dim Sum, first assistant director, assistant editor; Tri-Star, Sony Pictures Entertainment Inc, Motion Picture Production, senior vice president, currently. **HONORS/AWARDS:** Asian Business League, Business Person of the Year Award, 1992. **BUSINESS ADDRESS:** Senior Vice Pres, Motion Picture Prod, Tri Star - Sony Pictures Entertainment, Inc, 10202 W Washington Blvd, Culver City, CA 90232-3195, (310)280-8000. ∗

LEE, CHUNG
Scientist. Chinese American. **PERSONAL:** Born Sep 18, 1936, Shanghai, China; son of H C Lee & H C Pao-Lee; married Daphne, Sep 21, 1965; children: Michael, Traci. **EDUCATION:** National Taiwan University, BS,

1959; West Virginia University, MS, 1966, PhD, 1969; Albany Medical College, postdoctoral fellow, 1971. **CAREER:** Cook County Graduate School of Medicine, lecturer, 1977-80; Northwestern University, Medical School, associate, 1971-73, assistant professor, 1974-78, associate professor, 1979-84, director, urology research labs, 1974-, professor, department of urology, 1985-, professor, department cell, molecular, structure biology, 1987-, John T Grayhack Professor of Urological Research, 1992-. **ORGANIZATIONS:** American Cancer Society, Cancer Prevention Committee, Illinois Division, 1988-; Society for Basic Urologic Research, treasurer, chairman, finance committee, 1988-90; American Urological Association, consultant on prostate cancer research, American Urological Association program committee, 1991-92, basic scientist consultant to research committee, 1991-93; The Population Council, research consultant, 1992-97; Society for the Study of Reproduction, membership committee, 1992-; Society for Basic Urologic Research, vice president, 1993-94; American Society of Andrology, education policy committee, 1993-. **SPECIAL ACHIEVEMENTS:** Over 100 publications. **BUSINESS ADDRESS:** Professor, Director of Urology Research labs, Northwestern University Medical School, 303 E Chicago Ave, Tarry Bldg, Rm 11-715, Chicago, IL 60611-3008, (312)908-2916.

LEE, CHUNG
Educator. Korean American. **PERSONAL:** Born Jul 12, 1943, Seoul, Republic of Korea; son of Joe Young Lee and Kap Sung Kim-Lee; married In Ja; children: Gina, Mia. **EDUCATION:** Seoul National University, BS, 1965, MS, 1967; Michigan State University, PhD, 1970. **CAREER:** San Fernando Health Center, programmer/MIS, 1973-78; California State Polytechnic University, chancellor's office, programmer, 1978-82, associate professor, 1982-87, professor, 1987-. **ORGANIZATIONS:** ACM, 1980-; IEEE, 1988-; Amer Statistical Assn, 1970-; Biometrics Soc, 1967-80. **HONORS/AWARDS:** National Institutes of Health, scholarship, 1971-72. **SPECIAL ACHIEVEMENTS:** Twenty-five publications, 1978-; 12 program manuals, 1978-. **BUSINESS ADDRESS:** Professor, Dept of Computer Science, California State Polytechnic University, 3801 W Temple Ave, Pomona, CA 91768, (909)869-3449.

LEE, CHUNG-YEE
Educator. Taiwanese American. **PERSONAL:** Born Nov 27, 1949, Tainan, Taiwan; son of Tern Fa & Hon Tau Liu Lee; married Chiou Kuey-Lan Lee, Oct 6, 1974; children: Michael Yueh-Tai, Daniel Yuo-Tai. **EDUCATION:** National Chiao-Tung University, Taiwan, BS, 1972, MS, 1976; Northwestern University, MS, 1980; Yale University, PhD, 1984. **CAREER:** Li-Chuan Sporting Equipment Manufacturing Co, manager, 1976-77; National Taiwan Institute of Technology, lecturer, 1977-78; Ming Chwan Business College, lecturer, 1977-79; Intl Business Consulting Co, manager, 1977-79; University of Florida, assistant professor, 1984-89, associate professor, 1989-. **ORGANIZATIONS:** Operations Research Society of America; The Institute of Management Sciences; Institute of Industrial Engineers; American Chinese Management Educator Association; Tau Beta Pi, 1988. **HONORS/AWARDS:** University of Florida, Outstanding Faculty Award, 1985, 1988; College of Engineering Teacher of the Year. **SPECIAL ACHIEVEMENTS:** Published over 40 articles in refereed journals, including: Mathematics of Operations Research, 1986; Discrete Applied Mathematics, 1991; Transportation Science, 1991; Operations REsearch, 1992; Management Science, 1993. **MILITARY SERVICE:** Marine Corps, Taiwan, 2nd lt, 1972-74. **BUSINESS ADDRESS:** Associate Professor, Dept of Industrial and Systems Engineering, University of Florida, 303 Weil Hall, Gainesville, FL 32611-2002, (904)392-3426.

LEE, CLARENCE KIM MUN
Graphic designer. Chinese American. **PERSONAL:** Born Feb 1, 1935, Honolulu, HI; son of Young Fai Lee & Helen Chong Lee; married Elsa C Lee, Sep 6, 1983; children: Catherine Lee Mosteller, Douglas C, Emily Carl. **EDUCATION:** Pomona College, 1953-55; Yale University, BFA, 1958. **CAREER:** Lester Beall Design Group, designer, 1959-61; IBM, project designer, 1962-65; Clarence Lee Design and Associates, president, 1966-. **ORGANIZATIONS:** Hawaii Art Directors' Club, president, 1966-86; American Institute of Graphic Arts, chairman, 1987-93. **HONORS/AWARDS:** Deco Press, Top Symbol & Trademarks of the World, 1974; Hawaii Jaycees, Outstanding Young Man in Hawaii, 1967; American Advertising Federation, Silver Medal Award, 1987; Aloha United Way, Outstanding Communications Volunteer, 1990; Honolulu Academy of Arts, Artist of Hawaii, 1992. **SPECIAL ACHIEVEMENTS:** Design of symbol commemorating Chinese in Hawaii Bicentennial, 1990; "Six Overseas Chinese Designers," Design Exchange Magazine, 1990; design of US postage stamps, Happy New Year, 29 cents, 1992, Year of the Dog, 29 cents, 1993; design of first USA-China joint-issue stamp, 1994. **MILITARY**

SERVICE: Signal Corps, 1st lt, 1958-59. **BIOGRAPHICAL SOURCES:** Pacific Rim Designers, Quon editions, p 81-94, 1991; CA Magazine, Palo Alto, CA, p 44-53, Jan/Feb, 1981. **BUSINESS ADDRESS:** President, Clarence Lee Design and Associates, 2333 Kapiolani Blvd, Ground Floor, Honolulu, HI 96826, (808)941-5021.

LEE, CONRAD
City council member. Chinese American. **PERSONAL:** Born 1939?, China; married Winnie; children: 1 daughter, 1 son. **EDUCATION:** University of Michigan, BS, engineering; University of Washington, MBA. **CAREER:** Solid waste planner; project manager; Bellevue City Council, council member, 1993-. **ORGANIZATIONS:** Washington State Games, past chairman; Bellevue Transportation Commission, chair; Factoria Subarea Citizen Advisory Committee, chair; City-In-A-Park Committee, vice-chair; United Way, volunteer. **SPECIAL ACHIEVEMENTS:** Bellevue Ethnic Chinese New Year Festival, chair, 1993; first Asian American elected to Bellevue city council. **BUSINESS ADDRESS:** City Council Member, Bellevue City Council, 11511 Main St, PO Box 90012, Bellevue, WA 98009-9012, (206)453-2979. *

LEE, DAE SUNG
Educator, educational administrator. Korean American. **PERSONAL:** Born Nov 16, 1938, Seoul, Republic of Korea; son of Ho Kyung Lee; married Chung Ja Lee, Aug 15, 1969; children: Katherine, David. **EDUCATION:** Yon Sei University, BA, 1960; University of Massachusetts, MA, 1966, PhD, 1970. **CAREER:** Kentucky State University, assistant professor, 1969, associate professor, 1974, professor, 1978, dean, 1987-. **ORGANIZATIONS:** American Econ Association, 1968; American Agr Econ Association, 1972; Midwest Econ Association, 1980; Eastern Econ Association, 1982; Kentucky Econ & Business Association, 1980. **HONORS/AWARDS:** Kentucky State University, Distinguished Professor Award, 1989. **SPECIAL ACHIEVEMENTS:** Over 40 articles and presentations, various professional journals and organizations. **HOME ADDRESS:** 1015 Silver Lake Blvd, Frankfort, KY 40601. **BUSINESS ADDRESS:** Dean, School of Business, Kentucky State University, East Main Street, Bradford Hall #105, Frankfort, KY 40601, (502)227-6714.

LEE, DAEYONG
Educator. Korean American. **PERSONAL:** Born Jun 16, 1933, Ham Nam, Republic of Korea; married Youngja Kang; children: Chungho Jaime, Sohie Joyce, Jinho Davin. **EDUCATION:** Ripon College, BA, 1958; MIT, BS, 1958, MS, 1961, ScD, 1965. **CAREER:** Ladish Co, mechanical engineer, 1958; GE CRD, staff, 1966; Rensselaer Polytechnic Institute, professor of mechanical engineering, 1985-, CMP, director, 1992-. **ORGANIZATIONS:** ASME; ASM; Society Plastic Engineers; AIME; ADDRG. **HONORS/AWARDS:** ASME, Best Paper Award, 1982. **SPECIAL ACHIEVEMENTS:** Published over 120 technical papers; 12 patents. **BUSINESS ADDRESS:** Director, Professor, Center for Manufacturing Productivity, Rensselaer Polytechnic Institute, CII 9015, Troy, NY 12180-3590, (518)276-6021.

LEE, DAH-YINN
Educator. Chinese American. **PERSONAL:** Born Jun 4, 1934, Tsingtao, Shandong, China; son of D T & T M Lee; divorced; children: John, Kevin. **EDUCATION:** Cheng Kung National University, Taiwan, BS, 1958; Iowa State University, PhD, 1964. **CAREER:** Federal Highway Administration, Dwight D Eisenhower Faculty Fellow, 1992-93; Iowa State University, research assistant, 1960-64, professor, 1964-. **ORGANIZATIONS:** American Society Civil Engineers, chair, 1992, Materials Division, executive committee, 1989-93, Materials Engineering Division, chair, executive committee, 1990-92; ASTM, American Society Testing & Materials, committees C-9, D-4, 1965-; Association Asphalt Paving Technologists, 1965-; American Concrete Institute, committees 221, 548, 1975-; Transportation Research Board, 1968-. **HONORS/AWARDS:** International Surfacing Seals Association, service, 1978, 1984. **SPECIAL ACHIEVEMENTS:** Co-author, "Hot Mix Asphalt: Materials, Mixture Design & Construction," 1991; co-editor, "New Horizons: Construction Materials," 1988; more than 60 technical papers. **BUSINESS ADDRESS:** Professor, Dept of Civil & Construction Engineering, Iowa State University, 476 Town Engineering Bldg, Ames, IA 50011, (515)294-7439.

LEE, DAVID C.
Attorney. Chinese American. **PERSONAL:** Born Mar 13, 1963, Hong Kong; son of Jam Lee & Pui Ching Lee. **EDUCATION:** University of California, Berkeley, BA, 1987; Stanford Law School, JD, 1990. **CAREER:** Pillsbury, Madison & Sutho, attorney, 1991-92; Wilson, Sonsini, Goodrich & Rosati, attorney 1992-93; Venture Law Group, attorney, 1993-. **ORGANIZATIONS:** California State Bar Association, 1991-; Asian American Bar Association, 1992-; Asian Community Immigration Clinic, staff attorney, 1990-; Asian Manufacturers' Association, 1992-. **HONORS/AWARDS:** Phi Beta Kappa, 1987. **BUSINESS ADDRESS:** Attorney, Venture Law Group, 2800 Sand Hill Road, Menlo Park, CA 94025, (415)854-4488.

LEE, DAVID OI
Engineer. Chinese American. **PERSONAL:** Born Feb 5, 1940, Hong Kong; son of Quay Fong & Hun Yung Lee; children: Andrea Lee Wolf. **EDUCATION:** Texas A&M University, BS, ME, 1962, MS, ME, 1964; Northwestern University, 1964-67. **CAREER:** Sandia National Labs, member technical staff, 1967-. **ORGANIZATIONS:** Society of Mechanical Engineers, 1991-; Society of Petroleum Engineers, 1982-; American Society of Quality Control, 1990-; Sigma Xi, associate member, 1966-; ASME Committee on Nuclear Quality Assurance, Subcommittee on Programatic Activities-Working Group member on R&D QA, 1993; ASQC Energy and Environmental Quality Division, vice chairman, subcommittee on environmental R&D, 1993-. **SPECIAL ACHIEVEMENTS:** Author and inventor of several publications and patents. **HOME ADDRESS:** 6409 Quemado NE, Albuquerque, NM 87109.

LEE, DAVID SEN-LIN
Communications company executive. Chinese American. **PERSONAL:** Born Jun 23, 1937, Pei Ping, China; son of Wen-Chi Lee and Li-Ping Wong Lee; married Chi-Ming Wan, Jan 8, 1966; children: Eric, Gloria, Randy. **EDUCATION:** Montana State University, BSME, 1960; North Dakota State University, MSME, 1962. **CAREER:** NCR, engineer, 1962-64; Singer, manager, 1964-69; Diablo Systems, manager, 1969-73; QUME Corporation, executive vice president, 1973-81, president, chairman, director, 1981-. **ORGANIZATIONS:** Chinese Institute of Engineers, member, currently, vice president, 1981, president, 1982; Asian Business League; Tau Beta Pi; Pi Tau Sigma; American Electronics Assn. **SPECIAL ACHIEVEMENTS:** Inventor of the daisy-wheel printer, 1971. **BUSINESS ADDRESS:** President, QUME Corporation, 500 Yosemite Dr, Milpitas, CA 95035-8010, (408)942-4000. *

LEE, DER-TSAI
Educator. Taiwanese American. **PERSONAL:** Born Apr 5, 1949, Taipei, Taiwan; married. **EDUCATION:** National Taiwan University, BS, 1971; University of Illinois at Urbana-Champaign, MS, 1976, PhD, 1978. **CAREER:** National Taiwan University, teaching assistant, 1973-74; University of Illinois at Urbana-Champaign, research assistant, 1974-78; National Science Foundation, program director, 1989-90; Northwestern University, assistant professor, 1978-81, associate professor, 1981-86, professor, 1986-. **ORGANIZATIONS:** IEEE, fellow, 1992-; SIAM, 1983-; ACM, 1978-. **SPECIAL ACHIEVEMENTS:** Over 100 technical papers published in various computer science journals. **BIOGRAPHICAL SOURCES:** Algorithmic Aspects of VLSI, World Scientific Publishing Co, 1993. **BUSINESS ADDRESS:** Professor, Dept of Electrical Engineering/Computer Science, Northwestern University, 2145 Sheridan Road, Tech 3848, Evanston, IL 60208, (708)491-5007.

LEE, DIANA MANG
Biomedical researcher. Chinese American. **PERSONAL:** Born Oct 10, 1932, Mukden, China; daughter of Chenying Chung & Lian Lin; married Fu Chu Lee, Jan 30, 1960; children: Amy J Munro. **EDUCATION:** National Taiwan University, BS, 1955; Utah State University, MS, 1960; University of Chicago, PhD program, 1960-61; University of Oklahoma, PhD, 1967. **CAREER:** Yung-Kang Cement Corp, Pu-Sin, Taiwan, chemist, 1955-57; Utah State University, Logan, university asst, 1957-59; University of Chicago, university asst, 1960-61; Presbyterian-St Luke's Hospital, supervisor, clinical lab, 1961-64; University of Oklahoma, School of Medicine, research assoc, 1968-71, asst professor, 1972-76, assoc professor, 1976-; Oklahoma Medical Research Foundation, trainee, 1964-67, sr investigator, 1967-71, asst member, 1971-75, assoc member, 1975-. **ORGANIZATIONS:** American Chemical Society, 1965-; Sigma Xi, 1967-; American Assn for the Advancement of Science, 1969-; Council on Arteriosclerosis of the American Heart Assn, fellow, 1971-; American Oil Chemists Society, 1979-; New York Academy of Sciences, 1981-; American Society of Biochemistry & Molecular Biology, 1982-; Society of Chinese Biochemists in America, 1988-. **HONORS/AWARDS:** National Heart, Lung & Blood Institute, NIH Member of the Arteriosclerosis, Hypertension & Lipid Metabolism Advisory Committee, 1992-96; Biochimica et Biophysica Acta, editor, 1984-87; Progress in Lipid Research, guest editor, 1990-91; American Heart Assn, Credentials Committee, council on Arteriosclerosis, 1973-75; Artery, assoc editor, 1975-. **SPECIAL ACHIEVEMENTS:** Author of 6 chapters in 6 books on lipoproteins, atherosclerosis and

related areas, 1986-93; author of 38 papers published in scientific journals, 1970-93, 64 abstracts &/or presentations in natl &/or intl scientific conferences, 1965-93; 15 invited lectures at universities, natl or intl meetings, 1978-92; editor, Chemistry & Metabolism of Lipoprotein Particles, 1991. **BUSINESS ADDRESS:** Associate Member, Oklahoma Medical Research Foundation, 825 NE 13th St, Oklahoma City, OK 73104, (405)271-7500.

LEE, DO IK
Research scientist. Korean American. **PERSONAL:** Born Mar 6, 1937, Chinnampo, Pyungan-Namdo, Republic of Korea; son of Hyun Joo Lee and Sang Duk Suh; married Ilhae Kim Lee, Jul 25, 1970; children: Albert Kimin. **EDUCATION:** Seoul National University, BS, Chem Eng, 1959; Columbia University, MS, Chem Eng, 1964, DES, 1967. **CAREER:** Columbia University, research assistant, 1962-67; The Dow Chemical Company, research scientist, 1967-. **ORGANIZATIONS:** American Chemical Society, 1967-; American Institute of Chemical Engineers, 1969-; AAAS, 1980-; Technical Association of Paper & Pulp Industry, fellow, 1972-; TAPPI-Korea, 1985-; Korean Scientsits and Engineers in America, council member, 1982-85 chapter president, 1979, vice president, 1986; auditor, 1991-94; Sigma Xi; Polymer Society of Korea, 1982-, editorial advisor, 1993. **HONORS/AWARDS:** TAPPI, Coating & Graphic Arts Division Award and Chales W Engelhard Medallion, 1986, fellow; ACS, Midland Section Award, 1989; Saginaw Valley Patent Law Association, Fire of Genius Award, 1992. **SPECIAL ACHIEVEMENTS:** More than 30 technical papers published in various technical journals; 25 US patents and more than 120 international patents obtained. **MILITARY SERVICE:** Korea Air Force, 1st lt, 1958-61. **HOME PHONE:** (517)631-6127. **BUSINESS ADDRESS:** Research Scientist, The Dow Chemical Company, Designed Latex Research Laboratory, 1604 Bldg, Midland, MI 48674, (517)636-2460.

LEE, E. STANLEY
Educator. Chinese American. **PERSONAL:** Born Sep 7, 1930, Hopei, China; married Mayanne Lee, Dec 21, 1957 (died 1980); children: Linda Julia, Margaret Helen; married Yuan C Lee, Mar 8, 1983; children: Lynn Hua, Jin Hua, Ming Hua. **EDUCATION:** Chung Cheng Institute of Technology, Taiwan, BS, 1953; North Carolina State University, MS, 1957; Princeton University, PhD, 1962. **CAREER:** Phillips Petroleum Co, research engineer, 1960-66; University of Southern California, professor, 1973-76; Kansas State University, assistant professor, beginning 1966, associate professor, professor, until 1973, professor, 1976-. **ORGANIZATIONS:** Operations Research Society of America; North American Fuzzy Information Processing Society; International Neural Network Society. **SPECIAL ACHIEVEMENTS:** Published over 100 refereed journal articles; Quasilinearization and Invariant Imbedding with Applications to Chemical Engineering and Adaptive Control, Academic Press Inc, New York, 1968; coeditor, Energy Conversion Engineering, by RC Baille, Addison-Wesley, 1978; coeditor, Coal Conversion Technology, Addison-Wesley, 1980; coeditor, Coal Iquefaction, by Shah, Addison-Wesley, 1981; Operations Research II, Dynamic Programming, Markov Process and Queueing Theory, forthcoming; coauthor, Fuzzy Sets, Factor Space and Set-Value Statistics: An Introduction with Applications, forthcoming; editor or associate of various technology journals, including: Journal of Mathematical Analysis and Applications; Computers and Mathematics with Applications; Journal of Chemistry and Metallurgy; Journal of Nonlinear Differential Equations. **BUSINESS ADDRESS:** Professor, Dept of Industrial Engineering, Kansas State University, Durland Hall, Manhattan, KS 66506, (913)532-5606.

LEE, GUS CHIEN-SUN
Attorney, author, lecturer. Chinese American. **PERSONAL:** Born in San Francisco, CA; son of Tsung-Chi Lee & Da-Tsien Tsu; married Diane; children: Jena, Eric. **EDUCATION:** USMA West Point; University of California, Davis, BA, 1969, JD, 1976. **CAREER:** University of California, Davis, assistant dean, 1969-74; US Army, command judge advocate, 1977-80; Sacramento, California, Office of the DA, deputy DA, 1980-85; California District Attorneys Association, deputy director, 1985-89; State Bar of California, senior executive, legal education, 1989-; author, currently. **ORGANIZATIONS:** Boys & Girls Club, board member, 1991-; Main Library Campaign, literary luminary, 1991-; West Point Association of Graduates, 1984-; UCD Alumni Association, 1977-; Asian Pacific American Alumni Association, UCD, 1993. **HONORS/AWARDS:** University of California, Davis, Alumni Citation for Excellence, 1991; New York Times, Best 100 Book List, 1991; California District Attorneys Association, Service/Top Instructor, 1988, 1989; Office of the DA, Sacramento, Order of the Silk Purse, 1984; State Bar of California, service, 1993. **SPECIAL ACHIEVEMENTS:** Author of: China Boy, 1991;

Honor & Duty, 1994; one-page article on California, Time, November 18, 1991, p99; SBC Instructors Manual, 1993; SBC Videos: Law & Mr Finnegan, 1990-93. **MILITARY SERVICE:** US Army, cpt, 1964-68, 1977-80, Parachutist Wings; Meritorious Service Medal w/oak leaf cluster, ARCOM; AAM. **BIOGRAPHICAL SOURCES:** New York Times, Washington Post, SF Chronicle/Examiner, Denver Post, San Diego Times, Chicago Times, CNN, Good Morning America, etc. **BUSINESS ADDRESS:** PO Box 791, Colorado Springs, CO 80901.

LEE, GUY. *See* Obituaries.

LEE, HAK-KWON
Cleric, educator. Korean American. **PERSONAL:** Born Sep 5, 1954, Dae-Goo, Kyeongbuk, Republic of Korea; son of Seok-Kyu Lee and Chai Ok Kim; married Son N Lee, Jul 4, 1983; children: Benjamin J, Elliot D, Daniel C. **EDUCATION:** New York University, BA, 1984; Princeton Theological Seminary, M Div, 1987; Harvard University, ThM, 1988; Teacher's College, Columbia University, currently. **CAREER:** Han Sung Presbyterian Church, director of education, 1984-88; The Korean-American Christian College Student's Association, director, 1988-90; New Jersey Bible Institute, professor, 1988-; The New Church of New York, pastor, 1991-. **ORGANIZATIONS:** Korean American Inter-Collegiate, advisor, 1988-; New York City Presbytery Candidate Preparation Committee, 1993-, Racial-Ethnic Force, 1993-; The Korean American Church Council, Committee of Education, chair, 1992-. **HONORS/AWARDS:** The Korean-American Christian Woman's association, Seminarian of the Year, 1984; Lion's Club of New York City, Community Service Honor, 1989. **SPECIAL ACHIEVEMENTS:** Numerous seminars on Korean American identity on many campuses including Harvard, MIT, Columbia, SUNY, etc. **HOME ADDRESS:** 143-57 37th Ave, Flushing, NY 11354, (718)463-7524.

LEE, HARVEY SHUI-HONG
Mechanical engineer. Chinese American. **PERSONAL:** Born Feb 7, 1949, People's Republic of China; son of Tung Yee Lee and May Ngook Lee. **EDUCATION:** Newark College of Engineering, BS, Mechanical Engineering, 1972; Ohio State University, MS, 1974. **CAREER:** US Department of Transportation, mechanical engr, 1975-. **ORGANIZATIONS:** ASME, 1974-. **SPECIAL ACHIEVEMENTS:** Influence of Axle Load, Track Gage, and Wheel Profile on Rail-Vehicle Hunting, 1977. **BUSINESS ADDRESS:** Mechanical Engineer, US Department of Transportation, Volpe National Transportation Systems Center, Kendall Square, Cambridge, MA 02142.

LEE, HEAKYUNG
Educator. Korean American. **PERSONAL:** Born Jul 2, 1955, Seoul, Republic of Korea. **EDUCATION:** Sogang University, Seoul, BS, 1978; University of Wisconsin, Milwaukee, master's, 1984, PhD, 1986. **CAREER:** Bongchun High School, Seoul, 1978-80; University of Wisconsin, Milwaukee, teaching assistant, 1980-86, instructor, 1986-87; Winthrop University, assistant professor, 1987-. **ORGANIZATIONS:** American Math Society, 1980-. **SPECIAL ACHIEVEMENTS:** Research papers on rings, branch of math, 1988-92. **HOME ADDRESS:** 524 Woodberry Rd, Rock Hill, SC 29732, (803)329-4314. **BUSINESS ADDRESS:** Assistant Professor, Dept of Mathematics, Winthrop University, Rock Hill, SC 29732, (803)323-4603.

LEE, HENRY JOUNG (HEE)
Educator. Korean American. **PERSONAL:** Born Nov 17, 1941, Seoul, Republic of Korea; son of Hun Sang Lee and Chung Ok Kim; married Hyoja Lee, Jul 11, 1969; children: Lois, Angie, Jenny. **EDUCATION:** Seoul National University, BS, 1964, MS, 1966; Oklahoma State University, PhD, 1971. **CAREER:** Mt Sinai School of Medicine, postdoctoral trainee, 1971-73; Rockefeller University, visiting professor, 1979; University of Geneva, visiting professor, 1986; Center for Drug Discovery, director, 1990-; Florida A&M University, assistant professor, 1973-79, associate professor, 1979-82, professor, 1982-. **ORGANIZATIONS:** Interscience World Conference on Inflammation, board member, 1990-; Association of Minority Health Profession School, Drug Res, director, 1990-; International Youth Education of Florida, vice president, 1989-; Sigma Xi, 1969-; American Chemical Society, 1969-; American Society of Biological Chemistry, 1975-; American Association of College of Pharmacy, 1980-. **HONORS/AWARDS:** The White House, Science & Tech, Outstanding Achievement Award, 1990; Florida A&M University, Pestle and Mortar Award, 1989, Centennial Medallion, 1988, Rattler's Pride Award, 1987; NAFEO, Research Achievement Award, 1987. **SPECIAL ACHIEVEMENTS:** US patents: No 4,588,530: "Anti-inflammatory Prednisolone Ste-

roids," 1986, no 4,762,919: "Anti-inflammatory Carboxy Pregnans Steroids," 1988, no 4,840,624: "Female Condom Device," 1989, No 5,200,518: "Anti-inflammatory Carboxycyclic," 1993; "Anti-inflammatory Steroids without P-A Suppression," Science, 215, 989, 1982. **MILITARY SERVICE:** Korean Army, private, 1961-62. **BUSINESS ADDRESS:** Professor of Medicinal Chemistry, Florida A&M University, College of Pharmacy, Clifford Dyson Building, Room 227, Tallahassee, FL 32307, (904)599-3308.

LEE, HEUNGSOON FELIX
Educator. Korean American. **PERSONAL:** Born Dec 18, 1959, Seoul, Republic of Korea; son of Sukho Lee & Soobok Wee; married Guim Kwon, Jul 31, 1989. **EDUCATION:** Hanyang University, Seoul, BSIE, 1982; Oklahoma State University, Stillwater, MSIE, 1984; University of Michigan, PhDIE, 1989. **CAREER:** Oklahoma State University, teaching assistant, 1983-84; University of Michigan, teaching assistant, 1985-88, research assistant, 1986-87; Southern Illinois University, Edwardsville, assistant professor, 1989-. **ORGANIZATIONS:** Institute of Industrial Eng, 1983-; ORSA/TIMS, 1986-; American Society of Engineering Education, 1989-92. **HONORS/AWARDS:** Hanyang University, Study-abroad Scholarship, 1982-84; University of Michigan, Johnson Fellowship, 1989; Southern Illinois University, Teacher of the Year, 1989-90, Outstanding Student Advisor, 1991-92. **SPECIAL ACHIEVEMENTS:** Received NSF research grant on an FMS design-aid tool with K Stecke, 1992; Author: "A line balancing strategy for designing flexible assembly systems," IJFMS, vol 3, p 91-120, 1991; "Design and scheduling of flexible assembly systems. . .," J of Manuf Sys, vol 10, p 54-66, 1991; "Characteristics of optimal workload allocation. . .," Perf Eval, vol 13, p 255-268, 1991; "Optimal Configuration and workload allocation. . .," IJFMS, vol 3, p 213-230, 1991. **BUSINESS ADDRESS:** Asst Professor, Dept of Industrial Engineering, Southern Illinois University at Edwardsville, Box 1802, Edwardsville, IL 62026-1802, (618)692-3389.

LEE, HWA-WEI
Library administrator, educator. Chinese American. **PERSONAL:** Born Dec 7, 1933, Guangzhou, Guangdong, China; son of Luther Kan-Chun Lee & Mary Hsiao-Wei Wang; married Mary Frances Kratochvil, Mar 14, 1959; children: Shirley Kennedy, James, Pamela, Edward, Charles, Robert. **EDUCATION:** National Taiwan Normal University, BEd, 1954; University of Pittsburgh, MEd, 1959; Carnegie Mellon University, MLS, 1961; University of Pittsburgh, PhD, 1964. **CAREER:** National Taiwan Normal University, teaching assistant, 1955-57; University of Pittsburgh Library, assistant librarian, 1959-62; Duquesne University Library, head of technical serv, 1962-65; Edinboro University of Penna, chief librarian, associate professor, 1965-68; Asian Institute of Tech, director of lib, 1968-75; Colorado State University, assoc director of library, professor, 1975-78; Ohio University, dean of lib & professor, 1978-. **ORGANIZATIONS:** American Library Association, councilor, 1988-92, 1993-; Ohio Library Association, director, 1989-92; American Society for Information Science, 1966-; Association of College & Research Libs, 1959-; Athens Rotary Club, director, chair, 1980-; Chinese Academic & Prof Association, Ohio, founding president, 1985-. **HONORS/AWARDS:** American Library Association, Humphry/OCLC Award for Significant Contributions to International Librarianship, 1991; Asian Pacific American Libns Association, Distinguished Serv Award, 1991; Chinese Acad & Prof Association in Mid-Am, Distinguished Serv Award, 1990; Library Association of China, Taiwan, Distinguished Serv Award, 1989; Ohio Library Association, Ohio Librarian of the Year, 1987; Chinese American Librarians Association, Distinguished Service Award, 1983. **SPECIAL ACHIEVEMENTS:** Delegate to the 1991 White House Conference on Library & Information Services; two books published: Librarianship in World Perspective: Selected Writings, 1963-89; over 60 published journal articles, conference papers, and consultant reports; co-executive editor: Journal of Educational Media and Library Science; frequent international library consultant and lecturer; Fundraising for the 1990s: The Challenge Ahead. **MILITARY SERVICE:** ROTC, Chinese Army, lieutenant, 1954-55. **BUSINESS ADDRESS:** Dean of University Libraries, Professor, Ohio University, Park Place, Alden Library 512, Athens, OH 45701, (614)593-2705.

LEE, HYUNG MO
Physician. Korean American. **PERSONAL:** Born Oct 27, 1926, Tanchon, Republic of Korea; son of Yoon Shik Lee and Ae Soon Lee; married Kyung C Ok Lee, Feb 7, 1959; children: Margaret Mikung, Bennett Byung Hun. **EDUCATION:** Keijo Imperial University, BS, 1945; Seoul National University Medical School, MD, 1949; Medical College of Virginia, residency, 1959-63. **CAREER:** Medical College of Virginia, VCU, instructor of surgery, 1963-64,

assistant professor of surgery, 1964-66, associate professor of surgery, 1966-70, professor of surgery, 1970-, Division of Vascular and Transplant Surgery, chairman, 1973-. **ORGANIZATIONS:** American College of Surgeons, fellow, 1967-; American Society of Transplant Surgeons, 1976-, secretary, 1981-82, president, 1984-85; International Cardiovascular Surgical Society, 1986-; Asian American Health Forum, chairman, board of directors, 1985-; Seoul National University College of Medical Alumni Association, board of directors, 1988-89; Southen Association for Vascular Surgery, 1978-; Transplantation Society, 1966-; American Association of University Professors; Medical Association of America, president, 1984-85. **HONORS/AWARDS:** Alpha Omega Alpha Honorary Society, 1978; Virginia Commonwealth University, University Award of Excellence, 1990; Medical College of Virginia ALumni Assn, Distinguished Faculty Award, 1990. **SPECIAL ACHIEVEMENTS:** "Complications of Renal Transplantation," Complications in Surgery and Trauma, 1984; "Surgical Techniques of Renal Transplantation," Kidney Transplantation Principles and Practice, 1987; author or co-author of over 200 publications. **BUSINESS ADDRESS:** Professor and Chairman, Division of Vascular and Transplant Surgery, Medical College of Virginia, Virginia Commonwealth University, 1200 E Broad St, Box 57, Nelson Clinic, 401 N 11th St, Rm 407, Richmond, VA 23298.

LEE, JAE-WON
Educator. Korean American. **PERSONAL:** Born Jan 30, 1940, Chinju, Kyongsang-namdo, Republic of Korea; son of Song-yol Lee; married Jin-won K Lee, Nov 6, 1966; children: Eric Suhyon, Gina Sujin. **EDUCATION:** Seoul National University, BA, 1963, MA, 1966; Marquette University, MA, 1969; University of Iowa, PhD, 1972. **CAREER:** The Korea Times, reporter, 1963-67; University of Iowa, research teaching assistant, 1969-72; Illinois State University, assistant professor, 1972-73; Cleveland State University, professor, 1973-. **ORGANIZATIONS:** Association for Education in Journalism and Mass Communication, 1972-; Society of Professional Journalists, Cleveland Professional Chapter, board member, 1993-; Kappa Tau Alpha, 1971-; International Association for Mass Communication Research, 1982-; International Political Science Association, 1986-; Fulbright Association, 1988-; International Services Center of Cleveland, board member, 1982-87; Korean American Communication Association, former president, 1978-80, 1990-92. **HONORS/AWARDS:** Fulbright Scholarship, 1967; Fulbright Professorship, 1988; Poynter Institute, National Teaching Award for Journalism, 1987; Government of Korea, Olympic Service Medal, 1989; American Press Institute, fellow, 1993. **SPECIAL ACHIEVEMENTS:** Editor, book, Seoul Olympics and the Global Community, 1992; co-author, book, Modernization vs Revolution, 1993. **HOME ADDRESS:** 6180 Coldstream Rd, Highland Heights, OH 44143, (216)461-9508. **BUSINESS ADDRESS:** Professor, Dept of Communication, Cleveland State University, Music & Communication Center, Cleveland, OH 44115, (216)687-4632.

LEE, JAI HYON
Educator, journalist. Korean American. **PERSONAL:** Born May 29, 1926, Yongdong, Chungchong-Pukto, Republic of Korea; son of Kyusok & Sosun; married Myongja May Choi, Dec 25, 1951; children: Nancy Ellerman, Eugene, Giny Lozano, Anna Nykaza. **EDUCATION:** Syracuse University, New York, PhD, 1965. **CAREER:** Republic of Korea Government, press secretary to the President, 1960; Korean National Reconstruction Agency, deputy director for research, 1960-61; Korean Ministry of Culture and Information, director of public information, 1961-63; Radio Voice of Free Korea, director-general, 1963-65; Korean Embassy in Paris, director of information service, delegate to UNESCO, 1965-69; Korean Embassy in Washington, director of Korean information office, 1970-73; Western Illinois University, professor, director of journalism, 1974-. **ORGANIZATIONS:** Society of Professional Journalists, 1965-; Association for Education in Journalism and Mass Communication, 1973-; The Journal of Developing Areas, editorial board, 1979-; Korean American Communication Association, charter member, 1977-; North American Coalition for Human Rights in Korea, advisory council, 1973-91. **HONORS/AWARDS:** Korean Government, Hongjo Medal of Honor for Distinguished Civil Service, 1970; Western Illinois University, Faculty Lecturer, 1980; Korea Church Coalition for Peace, Justice, and Reunification (NCCCUSA), Korea Peace and Reunification Award, 1991. **SPECIAL ACHIEVEMENTS:** Author, Korea and the UN (in Korean), 1953; Korean Lore, 1953; Korean Perspective, 1954; A Handbook of Korea, 1956; fluent in Korean, French and Japanese. **BIOGRAPHICAL SOURCES:** The Washinton Post, p A1, col 5, June 1973; Gifts of Deceit, by Robert Boettcher, p 1-8, 131, 207, 250, 265. **HOME ADDRESS:** 90 N Yorktown Rd, Macomb, IL 61455, (309)837-3861. **BUSINESS ADDRESS:** Professor, Director of Jour-

nalism, Western Illinois University, W Adams St, Simpkins Hall 226, Macomb, IL 61455, (309)298-1424.

LEE, JANG YUN
Medical science research fellow. Korean American. **PERSONAL:** Born Jan 3, 1944, Taegu, Republic of Korea; son of Jae Hak Lee & Hee Lim Park; married Moon Hi Chae Lee, Dec 26, 1970; children: Christine, Julie, David. **EDUCATION:** Yeungnam University, School of Pharmacy, BS, 1967; University of Georgia, MS, 1974, PhD, 1977. **CAREER:** Chong Kun Dang Pharmacy Co, Korea, pharmacist, 1967-70; Smith Kleine & French Labs, predoctoral research fellow, 1974-76; G D Searle Co, research investigator, 1977-81, research scientist, 1981-85; Abbott Laboratories, senior research scientist, 1985-88, research investigator, 1988-93, associate research fellow, 1993-. **ORGANIZATIONS:** American Society for Pharmacology & Experimental Therapeutics, 1985-, Great Lakes Chapter, 1988-; Society for Experimental Biology and Medicine, 1984-; American Heart Association, Basic Science Council, 1990-; American Society of Hypertension, 1988-; Korean Scientists and Engineers in America, 1977-; Korean Pharmacist Association, 1967; Society of Korean American Biologists, 1990; Korean American Community Services, Chicago, board of directors, 1992-. **HONORS/AWARDS:** Abbott Labs, Outstanding Achievements Award, 1992, Volwiler Society membership, 1993, Outstanding Research Award, 1992; Smith Kleine & French Labs, predoctoral fellowship, 1974-76; Yeungnam University, School of Pharmacy, First Honored Graduate Award, 1967; The May 16th Educational Foundation, Korea, 4 year scholarship, 1963-67. **SPECIAL ACHIEVEMENTS:** Major contributions for research of new therapeutic agents, Abbott Labs, 1985-, GD Searle, 1977-85; more than 40 publications and 80 abstracts in professional journals of pharmacology and related areas. **BUSINESS ADDRESS:** Associate Research Fellow, Abbott Laboratories, 1 Abbott Park Rd, Dept 47V, Bldg AP9, Abbott Park, IL 60064-3500, (708)937-2240.

LEE, JASON SCOTT
Actor. Chinese American/Pacific Islander American. **PERSONAL:** Born Nov 19, 1966?, Los Angeles, CA; son of Sylvia and Robert Lee. **EDUCATION:** Fullerton College. **CAREER:** Friends and Artists Theater Ensemble, member; actor, television appearances include: Vestige of Honor, CBS-TV movie; American Eyes, after-school special; films include: Marat/Sade; Balm in Gilead; Born in East LA; Back to the Future, Part II; Map of the Human Heart, 1993; Dragon, 1993. **BUSINESS ADDRESS:** Actor, UTA, c/o Jim Burkas, 9560 Wilshire Blvd, Ste 500, Beverly Hills, CA 90212.*

LEE, JEFF S.
Landscape architect, planner. Korean American. **PERSONAL:** Born Sep 21, 1955, Seoul, Republic of Korea; son of In Sung Lee & Sook Hwan Kim. **EDUCATION:** University of Virginia, School of Architecture, BS, landscape architecture. **CAREER:** Hyundai Engineering & Construction Co Ltd, 1978-81; The Architects Collaborative Ltd, 1981-83; EDAW Inc, associate, 1983-86; Lee & Liu Associates Inc, president, founding principal, 1987-. **ORGANIZATIONS:** DC Habitat for Humanity, board of directors, 1992-; Community Design Services, steering committee, 1991-; Urban Forestry Council, chairman of technical committee, 1992-; American Society of Landscape Architects, 1984-; National Capital Greenway Allience, founding member, 1989-; Northern Virginia Community Appearance Alliance, board member, 1993. **HONORS/AWARDS:** State of Virginia, Council of Higher Education Scholar to Study Architecture, 1977. **SPECIAL ACHIEVEMENTS:** Notable projects: Ciragan Palace Kempenski Hotel, Istanbul, Turkey, 1991; Finnish Chancery, Washington, DC; principal in charge, IRS National Headquarters Project, currently; tourism master plan for Mediterranean fishing village, Kalkan, Turkey, 1991; publications: "Legacy of Open Space Planning in the Nation's Capital," ASLA annual meeting, 1992; "How Small Firms Can Market Effectively Overseas," SMPS National Newsletter, 1993. **BUSINESS ADDRESS:** President, Principal, Lee & Liu Associates Inc, 1001 Connecticut Ave NW, Ste 825, Washington, DC 20036, (202)466-6666.

LEE, JEN-SHIH
Educator, educational administrator. Chinese American. **PERSONAL:** Born Aug 22, 1940, Canton, China; son of R Z & Y Z Lee; married Lian-Pin, Jun 11, 1966; children: Lionel, Grace, Albert. **EDUCATION:** National Taiwan University, BS, 1961; California Institute of Technology, MS, 1963, PhD, 1966. **CAREER:** California Institute of Technology, research fellow, 1966; University of California, research engineer, 1966-69; University of Virginia, assistant professor, 1969-74; Johns Hopkins University, visiting associate professor, 1979-80; University of Virginia, associate professor of biomedical engineering,

1974-83, professor of biomedical engineering, 1983-, chair of Dept of Biomedical Engineering, 1988-. **ORGANIZATIONS:** Biomedical Engineering Society, president-elect, 1993-94, chair of program comm, 1991-93, board of directors, 1990-93; American Society of Mechanical Engineers, fellow, 1993; American Institute of Medical and Biological Engineers, fellow, 1992; American Association for Advancement of Sciences, 1966; Chinese Biomedical Engineering Society, 1983; American Physiological Society, 1972. **HONORS/AWARDS:** American Society of Mechanical Engineers, fellow, 1993; American Institute of Medical and Biological Engineers, fellow, 1992; Chong-Qing University, Honorary Professor, 1983; National Institutes of Health, Research Career Develoment Award, 1974-79; California Institute of Technology, Anthony Scholar, 1964-66. **SPECIAL ACHIEVEMENTS:** 62 refereed journal publications and book chapters; edited one book, Microvascular Mechanics; contribution to basic understanding of cardiovascular mechanics and microvascular function. **MILITARY SERVICE:** Army, lieutenant, 1961-62. **BUSINESS ADDRESS:** Professor, Chair, Dept of Biomedical Engineering, University of Virginia, Box 377, Health Sciences Center, Stacey Hall, Charlottesville, VA 22903.

LEE, JOHN CHUNG
Educator. Chinese American. **PERSONAL:** Born Mar 2, 1936, Shanghai, China; son of W D K Lee; married June M Lee, Jun 15, 1963; children: Andrew J, Nathan E. **EDUCATION:** Purdue University, PhD, 1966. **CAREER:** Taylor University, visiting lecturer, 1966-67; Massachusetts Institute of Technology, instructor, 1967-68; University of Texas Health Science Center, assistant professor, beginning 1969, professor, currently. **ORGANIZATIONS:** American Society of Biological Chemistry & Molecular Biology, 1972-; American Chemical Society, 1966-; American Association for the Advancement of Science, 1987-. **HONORS/AWARDS:** Alexander von Humboldt Foundation (Germany), Research Fellowship, 1976. **BUSINESS ADDRESS:** Professor, Dept of Biochemistry, University of Texas Health Science Center, 7730 Floyd Curl Dr, Rm 427B, San Antonio, TX 78284-7760, (210)567-3777.

LEE, JOHN JONGJIN
Librarian. Korean American. **PERSONAL:** Born Jun 7, 1933, Seoul, Republic of Korea; son of Donkyu Lee and Sun Young Woo Lee; married Wol Sue Chun, Mar 19, 1965; children: Carol, Christopher. **EDUCATION:** Kon-Kuk University, Seoul, MA, intl rels, 1962; Tufts University, MA, political sci, 1968; George Peabody College for Teachers, MLS, 1969. **CAREER:** Encyclopedia Britannica, regional rep, 1963-65; New York Public Library, reference librarian, 1968-70; SUNY Maritime College, Bronx, library readers' services, 1971-. **ORGANIZATIONS:** Maritima, editor, 1971-; SUNY, Albany, Chancellor's Advisory Committee for Excellence in Librarianship, 1984-87; United University Professions, academic delegate, Maritime chapter, 1975-; New York State Librs Assn; numerous others. **HONORS/AWARDS:** United University Professions, research grantee, 1985-86, 1987-88; SUNY, Albany, Chancellor's Award, 1983. **SPECIAL ACHIEVEMENTS:** Author, An Annotated List of Currently Published Maritime Periodicals. **MILITARY SERVICE:** US Army Civilian Personnel Training Office, Seoul, training officer, 1960-62. **BUSINESS ADDRESS:** Associate Librarian, SUNY, Maritime College, Bronx, NY 10465, (718)409-7230. *

LEE, JONG SEH
Educator, researcher. Korean American. **PERSONAL:** Born Oct 31, 1954, Namwon, Chunbook, Republic of Korea; son of Kyo-Whan & Hyo-Nam Yu Lee; married Kyoung Sook Lee, Jan 7, 1985; children: Suemin J, Brian S. **EDUCATION:** Yonsei University, Seoul, BS, 1981; University of Pennsylvania, MS, 1983; Princeton University, PhD, 1989. **CAREER:** University of Pennsylvania, research assistant, 1981-83; Princeton University, research and teaching assistant, 1983-88; Clarkson University, instructor, 1988, assistant professor, 1989-. **ORGANIZATIONS:** ASCE, 1987-, EMD: elasticity committee, 1992-, experimental analysis & instrumentation committee, 1991-; ASME, 1988-, AMD-MD joint committee on constitutive equations, 1992-; IEEE; AAM; ASEE; IASMIRT; IACAM; SES; KSEA. **HONORS/AWARDS:** Institute of International Education, ITT International Fellow, 1981; NSF, Engineering Research Initiation Award, 1990. **SPECIAL ACHIEVEMENTS:** 43 technical publications, 1988-; 33 seminars, presentations, 1988-; 1 book edited, 1993; principal organizer "Symposium on Electro-Magneto-Elastic Materials & Structures," 1993. **BUSINESS ADDRESS:** Professor, CEE Dept, Clarkson University, Box 5710, Camp Bldg 202, Potsdam, NY 13699-5710, (315)268-3851.

LEE, JOOH
Educator. Korean American. **PERSONAL:** Born Apr 28, 1948, Jungup, Junbuk, Republic of Korea; son of Jae-Kun and Ki-Soon; married Rebecca Cho, Aug 15, 1985; children: David Hyuk. **EDUCATION:** Kook-Min University, BBA (summa cum laude), 1975; Colorado State University, MS, management, 1981; University of Mississippi, PhD, business, 1987. **CAREER:** Rowan College of New Jersey, associate professor, 1988-. **ORGANIZATIONS:** Ssangyong Corporation, deputy manager, 1974-79. **HONORS/ AWARDS:** Phi Kappa Phi, National Honor Society, 1987; Beta Gamma Sigma, National Honor Society, 1988; National Academy of Business, Best Interdisciplinary Paper Award, 1992; Jung-up Agricultural High School, Provincial Education Superintendent's Prize, 1967. **SPECIAL ACHIEVEMENTS:** 30 papers, presentations, and proceedings published in academic journals and publications of National Academic Conference; "Profitability and Sales Growth in Industrialized vs Newly Industrializing Countries," 1990; "A Comparative Study of the Relationship between Strategy and Business Performance," UMI, 1988; "A Cross National Comparison of the Relationship between Corporate Strategy and Financial Performance," Asian-Pacific Journal, 1993; "Determinants of Firm Performance in Newly Industrializing Countries: The Korean Cases," The Review of Business and Economics, 1994; others. **MILITARY SERVICE:** Korean Army General Financial Corps, noncommissioned officer, 1971-73; President's Prize, top honor graduate. **BUSINESS ADDRESS:** Associate Professor, Rowan College of New Jersey, School of Business, Glassboro, NJ 08028-1701.

LEE, JU-CHEON
Doctor of Oriental Medicine. Korean American. **PERSONAL:** Born Feb 10, 1929, Kum-Cheon, Whang-Hae-Do, Republic of Korea; son of Wha-Won Lee & Cha-Neu Lim; married Jung-Hee Lee, Apr 26, 1959; children: Seon Huan, David H, Tae Huan. **EDUCATION:** Kyung-Hee University, Oriental Medical School, BOM, Graduate School of Oriental Medicine, MOM. **CAREER:** Oriental Medical Clinic, Sam-Ju, Seoul, director, 1950-71; Kyong Hee University Hospital, clinical professor, 1972-73; Acupuncture Center of Korea, owner, 1975-. **ORGANIZATIONS:** Nevada Oriental Medical Association, 1974-; Nevada Oriental Medicine Advisory Committee; OM Association, Montana, California, New York Chapters. **SPECIAL ACHIEVEMENTS:** Effect of Kam-Du-Decoction on the Obstacle of the Metabolism due to the Thioacetamide Intoxication, dissertation, 1971; Effect of Three Kinds of Oriental Prescribed Medicine on the Damaged Liver of Mice due to the Thioacetamide Intoxication, 1971. **HOME ADDRESS:** 6301 Tara Ave, Las Vegas, NV 89102.

LEE, JUNE KEY
Educator. **PERSONAL:** Born Aug 9, 1943, Seoul, Republic of Korea; son of Chan Sae Lee; married Yoon Kyung Lee, Jan 2, 1971; children: Jane Soyung, Judy Boyung, Julie Meyung. **EDUCATION:** Hanyang University, BS, 1965; Tennessee Technological University, MS, 1970; University of Texas, PhD, 1976. **CAREER:** UAH Research Institute, research associate, 1970-73; University of Texas, Austin, research assistant & instructor, 1973-76; Drexel University, assistant professor, 1976-77; Ohio State University, assistant professor, 1977-81, associate professor, 1981-86, professor, 1986-. **ORGANIZATIONS:** ASME; KSEA; AAM. **SPECIAL ACHIEVEMENTS:** Published over 100 scientific research articles; supervised over 20 PhD dissertations. **HOME ADDRESS:** 2227 Picket Post Lane, Upper Arlington, OH 43220, (614)457-3916. **BUSINESS ADDRESS:** Professor of Engineering Mechanics, Ohio State University, 155 W Woodruff Ave, Columbus, OH 43210, (614)292-7371.

LEE, JUNG YOUNG
Educator, clergy member. Korean American. **PERSONAL:** Born Aug 20, 1935, Sunchun, Pyungnam, Republic of Korea; son of Dong-hi Lee & In-duk Cho; married Gy Whang Lee, Jun 6, 1965; children: Sue I, Jonathan J. **EDUCATION:** University of Findlay, BS, 1957; Garrett-Evangelical Theological Seminary, BD, 1961; Case Western University, MS, 1962; Boston University, ThD, 1968. **CAREER:** Ohloff Memorial Methodist Church, pastor, 1961-63; Ohmer Park United Methodist Church, associate pastor, 1964-65; Otterbein College, assistant professor of religion, 1968-72; University of North Dakota, assistant professor of religious studies, 1972-74, associate professor of religious studies, 1974-79, professor of religious studies, 1979-89; Drew University, professor of systematic theology, 1989-. **ORGANIZATIONS:** American Academy of Religion, Korean Religions Group, chair, 1984-90; Korean Society for Religious Studies in North America, president, 1977-92; Foundation for Continuing Education of Korean Ministers, president, founder, 1964-85; North

Central Jurisdiction of Asian-American United Methodists, president, 1986-88; Association for Korean Christian Scholars, board member, 1991-; Korea Journal, UNESCO, contributing editor, 1976-; Journal of Dharma, board member, 1982-; Multi-Ethnic Support Association and Community Housing Resources, board member, 1987-89. **HONORS/AWARDS:** US Government, Senior Fulbright-Hays Scholar, 1977-78, Outstanding Educator of America, 1971. **SPECIAL ACHIEVEMENTS:** Author: The I, 1971, The Principle of Change, 1971; The I Ching and Modern Man, 1975; Cosmic Religion, 1973, 1978; God Suffers for Us, 1974, Death and Beyond Eastern Perspective, 1976; Patterns of Inner Process, 1976; The Theology of Change, 1979; Death Overcome, 1993; Ancestor Worship and Christianity in Korea, 1984; Sermons to the Twelve, 1988; Emerging Theology in World Perspective, 1988; Korean Shamanistic Rituals, 1981. **BUSINESS ADDRESS:** Professor, Drew University Theological School, Seminary Hall, Room 104, Madison, NJ 07940, (201)408-3979.

LEE, JUWAN
Management consultant. Korean American. **PERSONAL:** Born Oct 11, 1966, Seoul, Republic of Korea; son of Byung Moon Lee & Ok Sook Lee. **EDUCATION:** University of California, Berkeley, BS, industsrial engineering and operations research, 1989. **CAREER:** Bank of America NT & SA, management consultant, 1989-93, project analyst, 1988-89; Osprey Global Advisors, associate, 1990-; Montgomery Asset Management, analyst, 1993-. **ORGANIZATIONS:** The Korean American Professional Society, co-founder, 1992-, president, 1992, board member, 1992-; Institute of Industrial Engineers, program coordinator, 1987-89; Theta Chi Fraternity, project coordinator, 1986. **SPECIAL ACHIEVEMENTS:** Co-author, Tole with a Oriental Touch, 1984; Fluent in Korean and English; conducted speech during the aftermath of the Los Angeles Riots of 1992 at Japan Town; co-founded and set up the Korean American Professional Society, 1992. **HOME ADDRESS:** 6363 Christie Ave, #1721, Emeryville, CA 94608. **BUSINESS PHONE:** (415)627-2239.

LEE, K. J.
Physician. Chinese American. **PERSONAL:** Born Sep 7, 1940, Penang, Malaysia; son of C T Lee; married Linda Ho, Aug 20, 1966; children: Kenneth, Lloyd, Mark. **EDUCATION:** Harvard University, AB (with honors), 1962; Columbia University, MD, 1965; Harvard Medical School, residency, 1970. **CAREER:** Harvard Medical School, teaching fellow, 1969-70; University of Washington, clinical instructor, 1970-72; Yale University, clinical instructor, 1972-76, assistant clinical professor, 1976-91, associate clinical professor, 1991-; Hospital of St Raphael, public educational committee, chairman, president of medical staff, 1983, chairman of medical board, 1983, chief of otolaryngology; HSR Laser Surgery Center, director, currently; K J Lee, MD, PC, president, currently. **ORGANIZATIONS:** American Board of Otolaryngology, certified, 1991; American Board of Laser Surgery, certified, 1985; American College of Surgeons, fellow; American Academy of Ophthalmology and Otolaryngology, fellow, faculty, 1973-; Centurion Club of the Deafness Research Foundation, life member; Deafness Research Foundation, state co-chairman; American Society for Head and Neck Surgery, fellow; The Triological Society, fellow; Association of Harvard Chemists; Connecticut State Medical Society; New England Otolaryngological Society; Medcom Educational Products, faculty; Ear Research and Educational Center, director; American Academy of Otoloaryngologic Allergy. **HONORS/AWARDS:** Presidential Citation for Otolaryngology-Head and Neck Surgery, Washington, DC, Sept 13, 1992. **SPECIAL ACHIEVEMENTS:** Author of numerous books, including: Textbook of Otolaryngology: Head and Neck Surgery, Elsevier Science Publishing Co Inc, 1989; Essential Otolaryngology, Elsevier Science Publishing Co Inc, 5th ed, 1991; Ear Nose Throat Journal, editorial board; lecturer, "Medical Marketing," "Investment Strategy," "CPT Coding, HMO's, Insurance Claims Processing and Medicare Rules and Regulations," presented at AAO, 1990. **BUSINESS ADDRESS:** President, K J Lee, MD, FACS, PC, 98 York St, University Towers, New Haven, CT 06511, (203)777-4005.

LEE, K. W. *See* **LEE, KYUNG WON.**

LEE, KAI-FONG
Educator. Chinese American. **PERSONAL:** Born Jul 17, 1939, Kwangchow, Kwangtung, China; son of Chiu-Yan Lee and Shui-Man Mark; married Shiow-Lie, Dec 23, 1971; children: Walter, Steven, Amy. **EDUCATION:** Queen's University, Canada, BSc, 1961, MSc, 1963; Cornell University, PhD, 1966. **CAREER:** National Center for Atmospheric Research, visiting scientist, 1968-69; Catholic University of America, assistant professor, 1967-69, associate

professor, 1969-72; National Oceanic and Atmospheric Administration, senior resident research associate, 1972-73; Chinese University of Hong Kong, lecturer, senior lecturer, reader, 1973-84; City Polytechnic of Hong Kong, Department of Electronic Engineering, head, 1984-85; University of Akron, professor of electrical engineering, 1985-88; University of Toledo, chairman, professor of electrical engineering, 1988-. **ORGANIZATIONS:** IEEE, senior member, 1975-; IEEE, London, fellow, 1985-; MIT Electromagnetics Academy, 1990-; ASEE, 1992-; American Physical Society, 1966-92. **HONORS/AWARDS:** ASEE, Summer Faculty Fellowship, 1986-87; National Science Foundation, research grants, 1970-72; NASA, research grants, 1987-94. **SPECIAL ACHIEVEMENTS:** Author: Principles of Antenna Theory, John Wiley and Sons, 1984; book chapter, Handbook of Microstrip Antennas, Peter Peregrinus Ltd, 1989; over 160 articles on antennas and plasmas in professional journals and conference proceedings, 1966-. **HOME ADDRESS:** 7147 Finchley Court, Toledo, OH 43617. **BUSINESS PHONE:** (419)537-2580.

LEE, KANG IN
Polymer scientist. Korean American. **PERSONAL:** Born Nov 2, 1946, Seoul, Republic of Korea; son of Ki Chong Lee and Myong Soon Lee; married Miryoung Lee, Jan 10, 1975; children: Grace, Albert. **EDUCATION:** Murray State University, BA, 1970; State University of New York, Buffalo, MA, 1972; Polytechnic Institute of Brooklyn, PhD, 1975. **CAREER:** University of Akron, research associate, 1975-76; Firestone Tire & Rubber Company, research scientist, 1976-80; GTE Labs, scientist, 1980-84; Monsanto Company, scientist, 1984-. **ORGANIZATIONS:** American Chemical Society, 1970. **HONORS/AWARDS:** Polytechnic Institute of Brooklyn, Shapiro L Seymour Award, 1974. **SPECIAL ACHIEVEMENTS:** 12 US patents; 30 publications on polymer synthesis. **BUSINESS ADDRESS:** Scientist, Monsanto Co, 730 Worcester St, Bldg 123, Springfield, MA 01151, (413)730-2967.

LEE, KANGOH
Educator. Korean American. **PERSONAL:** Born Apr 4, 1955, Seoul, Republic of Korea; son of Ki-Se Lee and Hyangran Kim; married Jungnyeon Lee, May 30, 1984; children: Ann Jungyun, Jay Eric. **EDUCATION:** Seoul National University, Korea, BA, economics, 1979, MA, public administration, 1982; University of Illinois, Urbana-Champaign, PhD, economics, 1990. **CAREER:** Economic Planning Board, Seoul, Korea, assistant chief, 1980-84; University of Illinois, Urbana-Champaign, lecturer, 1988-90; Towson State University, assistant professor, 1990-. **ORGANIZATIONS:** American Economic Association, 1990-; Western Economic Association International, 1993-. **HONORS/AWARDS:** Seoul National University, graduated first place in the department, 1979; Ministry of General Affairs, graduated with excellence in the government's officers training program, 1980; Seoul National University, graduated first place in the School of Public Administration, 1982. **SPECIAL ACHIEVEMENTS:** "Bureaucrats and Tax Limitation," 1993; "Equilibrium Pricing of Congested Public Goods with Imperfect Information," 1991; "Moral Hazard, Insurance and Public Loss Prevention," 1992; "Economies of Scope and Multiproduct Clubs," 1991; "Club Theory with a Peer-Group Effect," 1989. **BUSINESS ADDRESS:** Asst Professor, Dept of Economics, Towson St University, Towson, MD 21204, (410)830-3551.

LEE, KAREN
Journalist. Chinese American. **PERSONAL:** Born Feb 14, 1959, Hong Kong; daughter of Betty & Danny Lee. **EDUCATION:** University of Southern California, BS, 1981. **CAREER:** KNX News Radio, intern writer, 1979-80; KNBC-TV, writer, production assistant, 1982-84; KTXS-TV, anchor, reporter, 1984-1986; KFSN-TV, reporter, 1986-. **ORGANIZATIONS:** Asian American Journalists Association, 1982-; Tree Fresno, board member, 1990-; Central California Asian Pacific Women, 1989-91. **HONORS/AWARDS:** RTNDA, Best Live Coverage, 1991; APTRA, Best Live Coverage, 1991. **BUSINESS ADDRESS:** News Reporter, KFSN-TV, 1777 G St, Fresno, CA 93706, (209)485-0930.

LEE, KER-FONG
Educator. Chinese American/Malaysian American. **PERSONAL:** Born Jan 27, 1948, George Town, Penang, Malaysia; son of Yit-Ken Lee and Khim-Yin Leong; married Chew-Lean Lee, Jun 19, 1977; children: Maxwell Hwaming. **EDUCATION:** Denison University, BS, physics & chemistry, 1972; Florida State University, PhD, 1981. **CAREER:** Florida State University, postdoctoral associate in theoretical chemical physics, 1981; Florida Community College at Jacksonville, professor of chemistry and physics, 1982-. **ORGANIZATIONS:** Jacksonville Chinese School of Florida, principal, 1991-94; Northeast Florida Chinese American Association, board of directors, 1990-94; Society of Physics

Students, Chapter at Florida Community College at Jacksonville, faculty advisor, 1988-; International Students Association at Florida State University, president, 1974-75; International Students Association at Denison University, president, 1970-72. **HONORS/AWARDS:** Foreign Ministry of the Republic of China, Outstanding Service & Leadership to Overseas Chinese, 1992; American Association of Community & Junior Colleges, nominee of Florida Community College at Jacksonville, for Academic Excellence Award in liberal arts teaching, 1986; Phi Kappa Phi, 1978; Sigma Xi, 1977; Sigma Pi Sigma, 1971; Omicron Delta Kappa, 1971; Denison University, Lubrizol Foundation, Lubrizol Chemistry Prizes, 1969-72. **BUSINESS ADDRESS:** Professor of Chemistry & Physics, Florida Community College at Jacksonville, Jacksonville, FL 32202-3056, (904)633-8141.

LEE, KIMYEONG
Educator. Korean American. **PERSONAL:** Born May 27, 1959, Jangheung, Junnam, Republic of Korea; married Chan E Chi Lee, May 6, 1988; children: William Dongil. **EDUCATION:** Seoul National University, BS, 1981; Columbia University, PhD, 1987, MS, 1993. **CAREER:** Fermi National Accelerator Lab, research assoc, 1986-88; Boston University, research assoc, 1988-90; Institute for Advanced Studies, 1993; Columbia University, asst prof, 1990-. **ORGANIZATIONS:** American Physics Society, 1986-. **HONORS/AWARDS:** National Science Foundation, Presidential Young Investigator, 1990; Sloan Foundation, fellow, 1990; Usan Foundation, fellow, 1981. **SPECIAL ACHIEVEMENTS:** Author: over 30 research papers published in major peer-reviewed journals, 1984-. **BUSINESS ADDRESS:** Assistant Professor, Dept of Physics, Columbia University, 2960 Columbia University, New York, NY 10027-6940.

LEE, KING Y.
Physician. Chinese American. **PERSONAL:** Born Jan 15, 1936, Dermott, AR; son of Mr & Mrs Eugene H Lee; married Ping; children: Brenda Stacey, Michael King. **EDUCATION:** University of Arkansas, BS, 1958; University of Missouri, ophthalmology resident, 1966; Retina Service, Massachusetts Eye and Ear Infirmary, Harvard Medical School, fellowship, 1968-70. **CAREER:** Midwest Eye Consultants, ophthalmologist, 1970-93; educator, currently; self-employed, ophthalmologist, 1993-. **ORGANIZATIONS:** Chinese-American Ophthalmological Society, president, 1990-92; American Medical Association; Missouri Ophthalmological Society, 1963-93, past president; American College of Surgeons; Retina Society; Eye Foundation of Kansas City, board. **HONORS/AWARDS:** Heart of American Chapter of American Diabetes Association, Educator of the Year; Menorah Medical Center, Outstanding Intern of the Year, 1962-63; American Academy of Ophth, Second Place, Scientific Exhibit Award, 1984, Honor Award for Educational Service and Contributions to our Profession, 1985. **SPECIAL ACHIEVEMENTS:** Co-editor, "Combined Iodine-125 Plaque Irradiation and Laser Photocoagulation in the Treatment of Choroidal Malignant Melanoma," Kugler Publications, p 441-447, September 1989; papers presented: The Trabeculo-Suprachoroidal Shunt for Treating Recalcitrant and Neovascular Glaucoma, The Retina Society Meeting, New York City, September 1992; Evaluation and Treatment of Retinal Disease with Indicyanine Green Angiography, Has Its Time Come?, The Retina Society Meeting, September 1992. **MILITARY SERVICE:** US Army, captain, 1966-68. **HOME ADDRESS:** 5825 Pembroke Court, Mission Hills, KS 66208, (913)677-5825. **BUSINESS ADDRESS:** Physician, 8901 West 74th St, Georgetown Medical Bldg, Ste 385, Shawnee Mission, KS 66204-2240, (913)362-7800.

LEE, KOK-MENG
Educator. Singaporean American. **PERSONAL:** Born Aug 20, 1952, Singapore; son of Joo-Seng Lee & Ah-Luan Choo Lee; married Hwer-Eng Lee, Jul 4, 1982; children: Kerry Lee. **EDUCATION:** State University of New York, Buffalo, BS, 1980; Massachusetts Institute of Technology, SM, 1982, PhD, 1985. **CAREER:** BP Refinery, Singapore Pte, Ltd, vocational training, 1976; Development Resources, Singapore Pte, Ltd, technical officer, 1977-78; Heat Transfer Laboratory, SUNY-Buffalo, undergraduate research, 1979-80; Fluid Power Control Lab, MIT, research assistant, 1980-85; Massachusetts Institute of Tech, postdoctoral research associate, 1985; Georgia Institute of Technology, assistant professor, 1985-90, associate professor, 1990-. **ORGANIZATIONS:** American Society of Mechanical Engineering; Institute of Electrical and Electronic Engineers; Society of Manufacturing Engineers; American Society of Engineering Education; Instrument Society of America; Sigma Xi; IEEE International Conference on Robotics and Automation, local arrangements chair, 1993. **HONORS/AWARDS:** National Science Foundation, Presidential Young Investigator, 1989; Sigma Xi, Junior Faculty Research, 1989;

Invention Clubs of America, New Technology Award, 1992. **SPECIAL ACHIEVEMENTS:** Three Degrees-of-Freedom Variable-Reluctance Spherical Motors, 1987-93; research in flexible part-feeding for automated assembly, 1988-91; flexible integrated vision system research, 1990-93. **BIOGRAPHICAL SOURCES:** World Journal, in Chinese, p 16, May 9, 1989; The Atlanta Journal/Atlanta Constitution, p F2, November 28, 1991. **HOME ADDRESS:** 5595 Covena Court, Norcross, GA 30092, (404)449-9953. **BUSINESS ADDRESS:** Associate Professor, Georgia Institute of Technology, George W Woodruff School of Mechanical Engineering, Atlanta, GA 30332-0405, (404)894-7402.

LEE, KUO-HSIUNG
Educator. Taiwanese American. **PERSONAL:** Born Jan 4, 1940, Kaohsiung, Taiwan; son of Ching-Tsung Lee and Chin-Yeh Yang; married Lan-Huei Chen, Jul 1968; children: Thomas Tung-Ying, Catherine Tung-Ling. **EDUCATION:** Kaohsiung Medical College, Kaohsiung, Taiwan, BS, 1961; Kyoto University, Kyoto, Japan, MS, 1965; University of Minnesota, Minneapolis, PhD, 1968; University of California, Los Angeles, postdoctoral scholar, 1968-70. **CAREER:** University of North Carolina at Chapel Hill, assistant professor of medicinal chemistry, 1970-74, associate professor of medicinal chemistry, 1974-77, professor of medicinal chemistry, 1977-91, director, natural products laboratory, school of pharmacy, 1983-, Kenan Professor of Medicinal Chemistry, 1992-. **ORGANIZATIONS:** American Chemical Society, 1970-; American Society of Pharmacognosy, 1970-; The Chemical Society, London, fellow, 1971-; American Association of Pharmaceutical Scientists, 1985-; American Association for the Advancement of Science, 1989-; The Society of Synthetic Organic Chemistry, Japan, 1986-; The Phytochemical Society of North America, 1992-. **HONORS/AWARDS:** The Lifu Academic Award for Chinese Medicine, 1994; Genelabs Achievement Award, 1993; Kaohsiung Medical College, Taiwan, Distinguished Alumni Award, 1992; University of North Carolina at Chapel Hill, Dean's Special Research Award, Kenan Professor, an Endowed Chair Professor, 1992; University of Minnesota, Taito O Soine Memorial Award, 1990; American Association of Pharmaceutical Scientists, fellow, 1986; Academy of Pharmaceutical Sciences, American Pharm Assn Academy Fellow, 1978. **SPECIAL ACHIEVEMENTS:** Over 280 research articles published in refereed journals; discovered more than 200 novel potent bioactive natural products and their analogs as antitumor, anti-HIV, anti-malarial, antifungal and anti-arthritis agents; served as a member of the editorial advisory board of nine journals relating to research on natural products and Chinese medicine; served as a member of numerous NIH study sections in the areas of cancer as well as bioorganic & natural products chemistry; supervised approximately 100 PhDs for research work dealing with medicinal chemistry of the bioactive natural products. **BUSINESS ADDRESS:** Kenan Professor, University of North Carolina, School of Pharmacy, CB# 7360, Beard Hall, Chapel Hill, NC 27599-7360, (919)962-0066.

LEE, KWANG K.
Educator. Chinese American/Taiwanese American. **PERSONAL:** married Nancy S Lee; children: Elaine, Daniel, Victoria. **EDUCATION:** National Taiwan University, BS, 1963; Duke University, MS, 1966; Cornell University, PhD, 1969. **CAREER:** University of Wisconsin, Water Resources and Environmental Engineering, professor, 1970-. **ORGANIZATIONS:** American Society of Civil Engineers; American Geophysical Union; International Water Resources Association. **SPECIAL ACHIEVEMENTS:** Author of over 50 publications on water resources and environmental engineering. **BUSINESS ADDRESS:** Professor of Water Resources and Environmental Engineering, University of Wisconsin, Milwaukee, 3200 N Cramer St, Engineering and Mathematical Sciences Bldg, Milwaukee, WI 53217, (414)229-4377.

LEE, KYO RAK
Radiologist, educator. Korean American. **PERSONAL:** Born Aug 3, 1933, Seoul, Republic of Korea; son of Ke Chong Lee and Ok Hi Um; married Ke Sook Lee, Jun 27, 1964; children: Charles Andrew, John Stewart. **EDUCATION:** Seoul National University, Korea, liberal arts & sciences, 1955, College of Medicine, MD, 1959; Seoul National University Hospital, resident, radiology, 1963; University of Missouri, Columbia, MO, Resident-Radiology, 1968. **CAREER:** University of Missouri-Columbia, instructor, 1968-69, assistant professor, 1969-71; University of Kansas School of Medicine, assistant professor, 1971-76, associate professor, 1976-81, professor, 1981-. **ORGANIZATIONS:** American College of Radiology, fellow, 1980; American Medical Association; Radiological Society of North America; Society of Cardiovascular and Interventional Radiology; Kansas Radiological Society, chairman, membership committee, 1987-; Kansas, Wyandotte County and Greater Kansas City

Medical Societies; Association of University Radiologists; Korean Radiological Society of N America, sec, 1980-82, vice pres, 1983-85, pres, 1985-88. **HONORS/AWARDS:** American College of Gastroenterology, Best Radiological Paper, 1975; American College of Radiology, Fellow, 1980; Radiological Society of North America, Certificate of Merit, 1982, Cum Laude Award, 1983. **SPECIAL ACHIEVEMENTS:** Over 100 scientific publications in medical books and journals; over 50 scientific exhibits at medical meetings. **MILITARY SERVICE:** Republic of Korea Army, private. **HOME ADDRESS:** 9800 Glenwood, Overland Park, KS 66212. **BUSINESS ADDRESS:** Professor of Diagnostic Radiology, University of Kansas Medical Center, 3901 Rainbow Blvd, Kansas City, KS 66160-7234.

LEE, KYUNG WON (K. W. LEE)
Journalist. Korean American. **PERSONAL:** Born Jun 1, 1928, Kaesong, Republic of Korea; son of Hyung-Soon Lee and Soon-Bok Kim; married Peggy N Lee, Nov 1, 1959; children: Shne, Sonia, Diana. **EDUCATION:** West Virginia University, BSJ, 1953; University of Illinois, MSJ, 1955; University of North Carolina, postgraduate work, 1968. **CAREER:** Kingsport Times-News, 1955-58; Charleston Gazette, staff reporter, 1958-70; Sacramento Union, investigative reporter, 1970-89; Korea Times, English weekly edition, editor, 1989-93; Sacramento Union, investigative reporter, intern program coordinator, 1994. **ORGANIZATIONS:** Korean American Journalists Association, founder, president. **HONORS/AWARDS:** University of North Carolina, Mark Ethridge Fellow, 1968; LA County Human Rights Commission, John Anson Award, print media, 1992; Asian American Journalists Association, Award of Excellence, first AAJA convention, 1987; National Headliners Club, National Headliners Award, 1974, 1983; Columbia University Graduate School, Paul Tobenkin Memorial Award, Special Citation, 1979. **SPECIAL ACHIEVEMENTS:** "Fair Elections in West Virginia," Appalachia: Its People, Heritage and Problems, Frank S Riddel, ed, Kendell/Hunt Publishing Co, 1974; "Fair Elections in West Virginia," Appalachia in the Sixties, David S Walls, ed, University Press of Kentucky, 1972; "Catalyst of the Black Lung Movement," Appalachia in the Sixties, University Press of Kentucky, 1972.

LEE, LEE HWANG
Educator. Chinese American. **PERSONAL:** Born in Taiwan; daughter of S L Hwang & C J Hwang; married Yun-shen Lee; children: Jason, Kenneth. **EDUCATION:** National Taiwan University, BS, plant pathology and entomology, 1972; Hunter College, SUNY, MS, biology, 1977; City University of NY, PhD, biology, 1980. **CAREER:** Brooklyn College, City University of New York, assistant professor, 1981-82; Montclair State College, assistant professor, 1982-89, associate professor, 1989-92, full professor, 1994-. **ORGANIZATIONS:** American Association of Microbiology; Phi Kappa Phi, vp; Sigma Xi; American Association for the Advancement of Science; Council on Undergraduate Research. **HONORS/AWARDS:** National Science Foundation, grant; Association of Chinese Schools, Outstanding Teachers Award. **SPECIAL ACHIEVEMENTS:** Published 16 papers, some on the molecular study of ASI-/Anacyscts nidulans infective system, some on the heavy metal containment use of anacyscts as an environmental pollution indication; co-author, "Production of Antibacterial Substances by Macroalgae of the New York/New Jersey Coast, USA," Bull Environ Contam Toxicol, vol 49, p743-749, 1992; "Effect of Copper on the Growth of Anacystis Nidualns," Bull Environ Contam Toxicol, 1993; "Effect of Zinc on Cyanobacteria Anacystis nidulans," Sigma Xi Student Conference, p2.4, 1992. **BUSINESS ADDRESS:** Professor, Biology Dept, Montclair State College, Upper Montclair, NJ 07043, (201)655-7164.

LEE, LESTER HSIN-PEI
Business executive, educational administrator. Chinese American. **PERSONAL:** Born in China; married Helen; children: four. **EDUCATION:** University of Illinois, BS, 1952, MS, mechanical engineering, 1953; MIT, graduate study, 1964; Stanford University, PhD, mechanical engineering, 1965. **CAREER:** Link Aviation and Curtiss-Wright Corp, flight simulator designer; Ampex Corp, research manager; Lear Jet Corp, chief scientist; Recortec Inc, founder, president, chairman of the board, 1969-. **ORGANIZATIONS:** ASME; IEEE; SMPTE; Chinese Institute of Engineers, president, 1983-84; Asian American Manufacturing Association, president, 1987, chairman, 1988, political action committee, founder; Monte Jade Technology Assn, founder, chairman, 1992-93. **SPECIAL ACHIEVEMENTS:** University of CAL, appointed as regent, March 1993, first Chinese American to serve on the governing body of the UC system. **BUSINESS ADDRESS:** Recortec Inc, 1290 Lawrence Station Rd, Sunnyvale, CA 94089-2220, (408)734-1290.

LEE, LIHSYNG STANFORD

Biotechnology company research manager. Chinese American. **PERSONAL:** Born Oct 28, 1945, China; son of Honping Lee and Kuorung Shea; married Alice S F Lee, Sep 8, 1974; children: Jenny, Oriana. **EDUCATION:** National Taiwan University, BS, 1968; Yale University, MPh, 1971, MS, 1972, PhD, 1974. **CAREER:** Roswell Park Cancer Hospital, postdocotoral fellow, 1974-76; Columbia University, staff associate, 19786-79; GE Research Center, staff, 1979-84; Cytogen Corp, principal research scientist, 1984-88; Enzo Biochem, investigator, 1988-90; Enzon, group leader, 1990-. **ORGANIZATIONS:** American Society for Pharmacology and Experimental Therepeutics, 1980-; American Association for Cancer Research, 1979-; American Association for the Advancement of Sciences, 1979-. **HONORS/AWARDS:** National Taiwan University, Yen Yu Tan Award, 1965; Yale University, Yale University Fellowship, 1972; Sigma Xi, honorary member, 1985. **SPECIAL ACHIEVEMENTS:** Publication of 50 papers in biochemistry, molecular biology, hybridoma genetic engineering and biotechnology in past 15 years; 2 patents on protein drugs that treat genetic disease. **HOME ADDRESS:** 22 Van Wyck Drive, Princeton Junction, NJ 08550, (609)275-1069.

LEE, MARIE GRACE

Writer. Korean American. **PERSONAL:** Born Apr 25, 1964, Hibbing, MN; daughter of William Chae-sik Lee and Grace Koom-soon Lee. **EDUCATION:** Brown University, BA, economics, 1986. **CAREER:** Data Resources Standard & Poor's, consultant, 1986-88; Goldman Sachs & Co, editor, equity research, 1988-90; writer, currently. **ORGANIZATIONS:** Asian American Writers' Workshop, vice president, board of directors, 1991-; Asian American Arts Alliance, 1991-; Women's National Book Association, 1992-; Authors' Guild, 1993-; Society of Children's Book Writers and Illustrators, 1990-. **HONORS/AWARDS:** Friends of American Writers, Best Book Award, 1993; American Library Association, Best Book for the Reluctant Y A Reader, 1992; New York Public Library, Best Book for the Teen Age, 1983. **SPECIAL ACHIEVEMENTS:** Author, Saying Goodbye, Houghton Mifflin, 1994, If It Hadn't Been for Yoon Jun, Houghton Mifflin, 1993; Finding My Voice, Houghton Mifflin Company, 1992; "We Koreans Need an Al Sharpton," The New York Times, December 12, 1991; New Worlds of Literature, anthologized, Norton, 1994; Matters of Fact, anthologized, Prentice-Hall, 1991. **BIOGRAPHICAL SOURCES:** Rosey Grier's All-American Heroes: Multicultural Success Stories, Master Media, 134, 1993; Lives of Famous Asian Americans: Literature, Chelsea House. **BUSINESS ADDRESS:** Writer, Harold Ober Associates, c/o Wendy Schmaltz, 425 Madison Avenue, New York, NY 10017, (212)759-8600.

LEE, MARIETTA Y. W. T.

Educator. Chinese American. **PERSONAL:** Born Mar 3, 1943, Canton, China; daughter of Michael C H Tsang and Marion Lo Tsang; married Ernest Lee, Nov 1, 1969; children: Patrick. **EDUCATION:** Nazareth College, BS, 1965; New York University, MS, 1968; University of Miami, PhD, 1973. **CAREER:** IBM Watson Lab, staff member, 1968-69; Howard Hughes Med Institute, fellow, 1978-80; University of Miami, assistant professor, beginning 1978, professor, currently. **ORGANIZATIONS:** American Society for Biochemistry and Molecular Biology, Committee on Equal Opportunity for Women, 1988-91; American Heart Association Scientific Careers Committee, 1986-90; NIH Biochemistry Study Section, 1990-94. **HONORS/AWARDS:** American Heat Association, established investigator, 1984-89; NIH, GM31973, 1983-, AI29158, 1989-; State of Florida, High Technology and Industry Council, 1990-. **SPECIAL ACHIEVEMENTS:** "Characterization of Human DNA Polymerase Delta," J Biol Chem, 266, 2423-2429, 1991; "Induction of DNA Polymerase Activities in Regenerating River," Bichemistry 30, 7534, 1991; "Molecular Cloning of Human Polymerase Delta," Nucleic Research, 20, 735, 1992; "Chromosomal Localization of Human Polymerase Delta," Genomics, 14 205, 1992; "Structal and Functional Relationships of Human DNA Polymerase," Chromosome 102, 1992. **BUSINESS ADDRESS:** Professor, University of Miami, 1600 NW 10th Avenue, Room 7014, RMSB, PO Box 016960, R57, Miami, FL 33101, (305)547-6338.

LEE, MIKO

Actor. Chinese American. **PERSONAL:** Born Aug 18, 1965, Greenbrae, CA; daughter of Robert Lee and May Lee. **EDUCATION:** San Francisco State University, BA, 1987. **CAREER:** Theatre of Yugen, associate artist, currently; Red Ladder Theatre Co, San Jose Repertory, artistic director, currently; Kai Sheng Productions, artistic director, currently. **ORGANIZATIONS:** Actor's Equity Association; American Federation on Television & Radio Artists; Theatre Bay Area, Theatre Services Committee. **SPECIAL ACHIEVE-**

MENTS: Performed with San Francisco Shakespeare Festival, Marin Shakespeare Festival, the California Shakespeare Festival, Berkeley Repertory Theatre, San Francisco Mime Troupe, San Jose Repertory, Antenna Theatre Co; choreographed at American Conservatory Theatre and the Cowell Theatre. **BIOGRAPHICAL SOURCES:** Noh News, vol 3, issue 3, p 2, May 1992; Asian Week, 9/21/1990. **BUSINESS ADDRESS:** Artistic Director, Theatre of Yugen, 2840 Mariposa St, San Francisco, CA 94110, (415)621-0507.

LEE, MIN-SHIU

Research and development manager. Chinese American. **PERSONAL:** Born Jun 30, 1940, Taipei, Taiwan; son of Thoan-Chip and Ping Hsuey Lee; married Yen-Mei Lee, Apr 16, 1966; children: Terri Sue, David Marshall. **EDUCATION:** National Taiwan University, BS, chem engr, 1962; New Mexico Highlands University, MS, physical chem, 1966; Case Western Reserve University, PhD, polymer science engr, 1969. **CAREER:** FMC, senior research scientist; Jelco, Johnson & Johnson, manager, materials research, 1976-80; CRITIKON, Johnson & Johnson, manager, material & process, 1980-86; Becton Dickinson Vascular Access, R&D manager, 1986-. **ORGANIZATIONS:** Amer Chem Soc, Dayton Investment Committee, chairman, 1989-92; Dayton Taiwanese Association, president, 1990-92; Suncoast Assn Chinese Americans, board member, 1983-86. **HONORS/AWARDS:** Case Institute Tech, Case Chemisty Fellowship, 1966-67; New Mexico Highlands University, Institute of Scientific Research, 1964-66; Becton Dickinson Vascular Access, New Production Introduction Award, 1992-93, New Process Improvement Award, 1992-93. **SPECIAL ACHIEVEMENTS:** Medical Grade Tubing, Criteria for Catheter Application, Montreal, Canada, SPE, ANTEC, 1991; Evaluation of Medical Grade Catheter Tubing, Mid-Am-Chinese Professional Meetings, Chicago, 1981; US Patent, 4,990,357: Hydrophilic Lubricious Coating; US Patent 5,030,665, 5,35,964: UV Curable Polyurethene Films; US Patent 5,116,323: arterial catheters; US Patent 5,226,899: Catheter Tubing of Controlled in vivo softening. **MILITARY SERVICE:** ROC, Ordnance, 2nd lt; Cash Award from National Defense Ministry, 1962. **BUSINESS ADDRESS:** R&D Manager, Becton Dickinson Vascular Access, 9450 South State St, Sandy, UT 84070, (801)565-2783.

LEE, MING T.

Water resources engineer. Taiwanese American. **PERSONAL:** Born Aug 15, 1940, Taipei, Taiwan; son of Mu-Ho Lee and Young-chin Lee; married Catherine A Lee, Jan 23, 1970; children: Daniel E, David Y. **EDUCATION:** National Taiwan University, BS, 1963, MS, 1966; University of Cincinnati, MS, 1968; Purdue University, PhD, 1972. **CAREER:** Water Resources Planning Commission, engineer, 1966-67; University of Illinois, research associate, 1972-75; Illinois State Water Survey, professional scientist, 1975-93; Greiner Inc, water resources engineer, 1993-. **ORGANIZATIONS:** American Society of Civil Engineers, 1973-; American Geophysical Union, 1969-; Soil and Water Conservation Society of America, 1975-. **HONORS/AWARDS:** Soil and Water Conservation Society of America, President Citation, 1985, Illinois Chapter Award, 1986. **SPECIAL ACHIEVEMENTS:** Languages: Chinese, Taiwanese & Japanese; NATO Water Resources Fellowship, 1988; "A Variable Source Area Model of Rainfall-Runoff Process Based on Watershed Stream Networks," Water Resources Research, vol 2B, pp 1029-1036; "A Procedure for Estimating Off Site Sediment Damage," Water Resources Bulletin, vol 12(3), pp 561-576. **HOME ADDRESS:** 1852 Union Street, Clearwater, FL 34623. **BUSINESS PHONE:** (813)286-1711.

LEE, MING-TUNG (MIKE)

Educator. Chinese American. **PERSONAL:** Born Jul 28, 1961, Taitung, Taiwan; son of Chung-Shan Lee and A-Shun Chang; married Wan-Fei Yang, May 30, 1984; children: E-Ting, Oscar. **EDUCATION:** Tunghai University, BA, 1983; University of Kentucky, MA, 1986, PhD, 1990. **CAREER:** California State University, professor of marketing, 1990-. **ORGANIZATIONS:** Jinan-Sacramento Sister City Association, treasurer, 1992; DL Pacific Group, president, 1993. **SPECIAL ACHIEVEMENTS:** Director, Sales Management Development Program, CSUS, 1991-92. **BUSINESS ADDRESS:** Professor, Dept of Management, California State University, Sacramento, CA 95819-6088, (916)278-6003.

LEE, MOON. *See* LEE, BYUNG-MOON.

LEE, MYUNG-SOO

Educator. Korean American. **PERSONAL:** Born Mar 17, 1958, Seoul, Republic of Korea; son of Dong-Ho Lee and Boon-Ye Lee; married Miae Lee, Jan 8, 1984; children: Michael J, Margaret S. **EDUCATION:** Chung Ang University,

Seoul, BBA, 1983; SUNY, Albany, MBA, 1985; SUNY, Buffalo, PhD, 1992. **CAREER:** State University College at Buffalo, instructor, 1988-89; Baruch College, CUNY, instructor, 1990-92, assistant professor, 1992-. **ORGANIZATIONS:** OBUSTY Local Development Corp, board member, 1992-; American Marketing Association, 1989-; Association for Consumer Research, 1988-; Institute of Management Science, 1989-. **HONORS/AWARDS:** SUNY, Buffalo, Excellence in Teaching Award, 1990; Baruch College, CUNY, Excellence in Teaching Award, 1993. **HOME ADDRESS:** 1320 E 92nd St, Brooklyn, NY 11236, (718)531-7278. **BUSINESS ADDRESS:** Assistant Professor, Baruch College, City University of New York, 17 Lexington Ave, Box 508, New York, NY 10010, (212)447-3106.

LEE, NAN-NAN

Educator. Chinese American. **PERSONAL:** Born Aug 21, 1955, Hwa-Lien, Taiwan; married. **EDUCATION:** National Taiwan University, BA, 1977; Southern Illinois University, MA, 1980, PhD, 1993. **CAREER:** Furman University, 1985-87; Chicago State University, 1988; St Xavier University, professor, 1988-. **ORGANIZATIONS:** American Philosophical Association, 1980-; Amnesty International USA, 1992-. **BUSINESS ADDRESS:** Professor, Philosophy Dept, St Xavier University, 3700 W 103rd St, Chicago, IL 60655, (312)298-3457.

LEE, OCKSOO KIM

Educator. Korean American. **PERSONAL:** Born Sep 3, 1941, Seoul, Republic of Korea; daughter of Young Chul Kim; married Chang Y Lee, Jan 27, 1968; children: Janette J, Christina J. **EDUCATION:** Ewha Women's University, BA, 1963; Wayne State University, MA, 1966; Wayne State University, MSLS, 1968. **CAREER:** Finger Lakes Library System, conversion staff, 1981-83; Cornell University, Mann Library, data editor, 1985-87, Hotel Library, reference librarian, 1987-88, Olin Library, cataloger, 1989-93, Dept of ML & L, lecturer, 1990-. **ORGANIZATIONS:** ALA, 1987-. **HOME ADDRESS:** 50 Highgate Circle, Ithaca, NY 14850, (607)257-6238. **BUSINESS ADDRESS:** Lecturer, Dept of Modern Languages & Linguistics, Cornell University, 405 Morrill Hall, Ithaca, NY 14853, (607)255-8447.

LEE, PAMELA TAU

Educator. Chinese American. **PERSONAL:** Born Feb 16, 1948, San Francisco, CA; daughter of John C Tau and Mignon Tau; married Ben Lee, Sep 18, 1977; children: Dennis. **EDUCATION:** San Francisco City College, AA, 1968; California State University-Hayward, BS, 1970, Teachers Corps, 1970-72. **CAREER:** Chinese Progressive Assn, dir, 1977-85; various San Francisco hotels, waitress, bartender, union steward, 1981-85; Hotel Employees Restaurant Employees Union, Local #2, field rep, 1985-90; University of California-Berkeley, Labor Occupational Health Prgm, labor health educator, 1990-. **ORGANIZATIONS:** Asian Pacific Environmental Network, Steering Committee; Lawyer's Committee for Civil Rights Under Law, Environmental Justice Project; People of Color Leadership Summit, occupational health facilitator; Asian Pacific American Labor Alliance; American Public Health Assn; University and College Labor Education Assn. **HONORS/AWARDS:** Charles Bannerman Memorial Fellowship. **SPECIAL ACHIEVEMENTS:** Presentations: "Workers of Color and Environmental Justice," first people of color environmental leadership summit; "Asians and the Environment," US Congress, May 1993; articles include: "Asian Workers in the US: A Challenge for Labor," Ameriasia Journal, 1992. **BUSINESS ADDRESS:** Labor Health Educator, University of California-Berkeley, Labor Occupational Health Program, 2515 Channing Way, 2nd Fl, Berkeley, CA 94720-0001, (510)643-7594.

LEE, PAUL WAH

Attorney. Chinese American. **PERSONAL:** Born Oct 16, 1950, Boston, MA; son of Richard T N Lee and Chou B K Lee; married Mary Chin, Dec 28, 1980; children: Gregory J, Samantha B. **CAREER:** Donovan, Leisure, Newton & Irvine, associate, 1976-81; Goodwin, Procter & Hoar, associate, 1981-84, partner, 1984-. **ORGANIZATIONS:** United Way of Massachusetts Bay, Nominating Committee, 1989-92; South Cove Community Health Center, board of directors, 1982-87; Asian American Lawyers Association of Massachusetts, founder, 1983, president, 1983-86, board of directors, 1983-; Asian Community Development Corp, board of directors, 1988-; National Asian Pacific American Bar Association, secretary, 1992-93, board of governors, 1993-94. **BUSINESS ADDRESS:** Partner, Goodwin, Procter & Hoar, Exchange Place, Boston, MA 02109, (617)570-1590.

LEE, PETER WANKYOON

Research scientist. Korean American. **PERSONAL:** Born May 30, 1939, Seoul, Republic of Korea; son of Byung-Jae Lee and Joonsun Chang; married Lucy Honghy-Park Lee, Jun 10, 1967; children: Eugene Taejin, David Kyungjin. **EDUCATION:** Seoul National University, BSCE, 1961; Marquette University, BSME, 1966, MS, 1968; Drexel University, PhD, 1972. **CAREER:** The Timken Company, research metallurgist, 1968-69, research specialist, 1972-77, sr research specialist, 1977-86, research scientist, 1986-. **ORGANIZATIONS:** ASM International, National Shaping Tech Div, chairman, Powder Metallurgy Comm, chairman, Technical Division Board; Society for Mfg Engineers; American Powder Metallurgy Institute; Boy Scouts of America, Troop 122 Committee, chairman; St Michael Catholic Church, mens' club president, parish council. **HONORS/AWARDS:** ASM International, fellow, 1988; Tau Beta Pi, 1965; NASA, Certificate of Recognition for Tech Innovation, 1989. **SPECIAL ACHIEVEMENTS:** Chapter on "Powder Metallurgy-Consolidation of Metal Powders," ASM Metals Handbook, vol 7, 9th ed; "Powder Metallurgy," ASM Metals Handbook, desk edition, 1984; chapter on "Cold Upset Testing" on Workability Testing Techniques, ASM, 1983; 3 US patents; several technical publications in metal forming and powder metallurgy. **BUSINESS ADDRESS:** Research Scientist, The Timken Company, 1835 Dueber Avenue SW, Res-20, Canton, OH 44706, (216)471-2082.

LEE, RICHARD FAYAO

Educator. Chinese American. **PERSONAL:** Born Jul 13, 1941, Shanghai, China; son of Peter Awah Lee and Elizabeth Lee; married Josephine Lee, Jun 19, 1970; children: Elizabeth, Lori. **EDUCATION:** San Diego State University, BA, 1964, MA, 1966; University of California, San Diego, PhD, 1970. **CAREER:** Pennsylvania State University, research associate, 1971-72; Skidaway Institute of Oceanography, professor, 1973-. **ORGANIZATIONS:** American Chemical Society, 1964-; American Society Limnol Oceanography, 1967-; Sigma Xi, 1970-; Inner City Night Shelter, vice president of board, 1988-. **SPECIAL ACHIEVEMENTS:** Author, "Lipoproteins of the Hemolymph and Eggs of Marine Invertebrates," Advances in Comparative and Environmental Physiology, vol 7, p 187-207, 1991; co-author with L M Haddad, "Toxic Marine Life," p 600-612; Clinical Management of Poisoning and Drug Overdose, W B Saunders; over 200 scientific papers. **BUSINESS ADDRESS:** Professor, Skidaway Institute of Oceanography, 10 Ocean Science Circle, Savannah, GA 31411, (912)598-2494.

LEE, ROBERT

Publisher, author, corporate executive, educator (retired). Chinese American. **PERSONAL:** Born Apr 28, 1929, San Francisco, CA; son of Frank Lee; married May Gong Lee, Feb 4, 1951; children: Mellanie, Marcus, Matthew, Wendy, Miko. **EDUCATION:** University of California, Berkeley, BA, 1951; Pacific School of Religion, MA, 1953; Union Theological Seminary, DD, 1955; Columbia University, PhD, 1958. **CAREER:** San Francisco Theological Seminary, Margaret Dollar Professor of Social Ethics, director, Institute of Ethics & Society, 1961-83; Alaska Pacific University, vp, academic affairs, 1983-86; Enfield Resources, president, 1985-87; Heald College Institute of Technology, international student studies, dean, 1987-88; United Way of Bay Area, vp, 1989-91; Pathway Press, president, currently. **ORGANIZATIONS:** Chinese for Affirmative Action, board of directors, 1978-93; Dominican College, president's council, 1993-; Peace Corps, coordinator of community relations, 1991-; Marin Chinese Culture Group, 1990-; Foundation for Theological Education in South East Asia, London, 1980; East West Center, Hawaii, senior fellow, 1972-73. **HONORS/AWARDS:** University of California, Berkeley, Chinese Alumni Association, Outstanding Graduate, Class of 1951; White House, Washington, DC, book, Social Sources of Church Unity, selected for the White House Library, 1961; Martin Luther King, Jr. Humanitarian Award, 1993. **SPECIAL ACHIEVEMENTS:** Author of 15 books including Faith and the Prospects of Economic Collapse, 1981; Guide to Chinese American Philanthropy and Charitable Giving Patterns, 1990; editor, The Church and The Exploding Metropolis, 1965; Action/Reaction: Pacific Theological Review; contributor to professional journals. **HOME ADDRESS:** 717 Montecillo Rd, San Rafael, CA 94903-3135, (415)492-9637.

LEE, ROBERT TERRY

Actor. Chinese American. **PERSONAL:** Born Nov 18, 1957, San Francisco, CA; son of Robert L & Barbara A Lee. **EDUCATION:** University of San Francisco, BA, 1980; Menlo Academy of Dance; Dancers Theatre Studio. **CAREER:** Film: After the Shock, To Sleep with Anger, Empire of the Sun, Surf Nazis Must Die, Pulling It Off, Healer, Surf Ninjas; television: Knots Landing, Moonlighting, Cagney and Lacey, Out On A Limb, Columbo, Incredagirl; stage: Gotta Sing, Gotta Dance, 7 Brides for 7 Brothers, The Wiz, Oklahoma, Westside Story, Alice in Wonderland, 'Twas the Night Before, It's Showtime; several commercials. **ORGANIZATIONS:** Salvation Army, volunteer, 1975-; Hind Factory Race Team, inline professional skater. **SPECIAL ACHIEVEMENTS:** US Acrobatic Team, 6th place, "World Championships," Poland, 1980; Hayward Acrobatics Club, 1st Place Nationals, 1977-80; dialects: Chinese, Vietnamese, Japanese. **HOME ADDRESS:** 1916 Stoner Ave, Los Angeles, CA 90025.

LEE, SANG MOON
Educator. Korean American. **PERSONAL:** Born Apr 1, 1939, Seoul, Republic of Korea; son of Chang Woo Lee and Duck Soon Lee; married Joyce A Lee, Mar 16, 1991; children: Tosca Phillips, Amy. **EDUCATION:** Seoul National University, BA, 1961; Miami University, Ohio, MBA, 1963; University of Georgia, PhD, 1968. **CAREER:** Virginia Polytech University, professor, management science, 1968-76; University of Nebraska, University Eminent Scholar, chair, management department, 1976-. **ORGANIZATIONS:** Decision Sciences Institute, fellow, 1968-, president, 1983-84; Academy of Management, fellow, 1970-; Pan-Pacific Business Association, president, 1984-. **HONORS/AWARDS:** Valley Forge Freedoms Foundation, Leavey Award, 1993; Decision Sciences Institute, Distinguished Service Award, 1981; University of Nebraska, Regents Distinguished Professor, 1980. **SPECIAL ACHIEVEMENTS:** Author of 36 books on goal programming, management science, etc; 150 journal articles published; over $3 million in grants. **BUSINESS ADDRESS:** Chair, Management Dept, University of Nebraska, 210 CBA, Lincoln, NE 68588-0491, (402)472-3915.

LEE, SHENG YEN
Chemist (retired), magazine publisher. Chinese American. **PERSONAL:** Born Dec 28, 1924, Xinyang, Henan, China; son of Yi-San Lee and Qin-Yuan Gan; married Winnie Cho Lee, Aug 25, 1949; children: Yin May. **EDUCATION:** National Northeastern University, China, BS, chemistry, 1946; University of Colorado, PhD, chemistry, 1964. **CAREER:** Agricultural Inspection Bureau, Taiwan, chemist inspector, 1948-51; Chinese Army, Taiwan, language interpreter, 1951-53; Agricultural Chemical Works, Taiwan, chemical engineer, 1953-59; Polymer Corporation Ltd, Sarnia, Canada, chemist, 1965-68; Harry Diamond Labs, US Army, supervisory chemist, 1969-79; Goddard Space Flight Center, NASA, chemist, 1979-91; Chinese American Forum, Inc, founder, president & editor, 1982-. **ORGANIZATIONS:** American Chemical Society; Society for the Advancement of Materials and Processing Engineering; Association for Promoting Democracy in China, Washington, DC Area; Organization of Chinese Americans. **HONORS/AWARDS:** Xinyang Teachers College, honorary professor, 1991; NASA, Goddard Space Flight Center, Inventor of the Year, 1990. **SPECIAL ACHIEVEMENTS:** 6 US patents, 1975-90; author, science & technology papers, 14 journal papers, 1966-90. **HOME ADDRESS:** 606 Brantford Ave, Silver Spring, MD 20904, (301)622-3053. **BUSINESS ADDRESS:** President, Chinese American Forum, Inc, 606 Brantford Ave, Silver Spring, MD 20904, (301)622-3053.

LEE, SHIH YING
Educator, engineer. Chinese American. **PERSONAL:** Born Apr 30, 1918, Peking, China; son of Tse-Kung and Pei-Jour Tao Lee; married Lena Yin, Aug 18, 1973; children: Carol Sana, David, Linda Grace, Eileen M. **EDUCATION:** MIT, ScD, 1945. **CAREER:** Government of China, bridge design engineer, 1940-41, hydraulic power research engineer, 1941-42; Cram and Ferguson, design engineer, 1945-47; MIT, research engineer, 1947-52, faculty, 1952-74, mechanical engineering professor, 1966-; Setra Systems Inc, president, CEO, currently. **ORGANIZATIONS:** National Academy of Engineering. **BUSINESS ADDRESS:** President, Setra Systems, 45 Nagog Pk, Acton, MA 01720-3421, (508)263-1400.*

LEE, SHUISHIH SAGE
Physician. Chinese American. **PERSONAL:** Born Jan 5, 1948, Soochow, Kiang Su, China; daughter of Wilson Wei Ping Chang & Min Chen Sun Chang; married Chung Seng Lee, Mar 31, 1973; children: Yvonne Claire, Michael Chung. **EDUCATION:** National Taiwan University, MD, 1972; University of Rochester, PhD, 1976. **CAREER:** Allied Hospital Pathologist PC, pathologist, currently.

LEE, SHYU-TU
State government administrator. Taiwanese American. **PERSONAL:** Born Jul 1, 1940, Taipei, Taiwan; son of Cheung-Chih and Jean-yeh Lee; married Margaret Jyu-jy Lee, Sep 14, 1969; children: Anton, Adabel. **EDUCATION:**

Chung-Yuan College of Engineering & Science, BS, civil engineering, 1963; Waseda University, Japan, ME, 1967; University of Michigan, MSE, 1977; Western Michigan University, MPA, 1979, DPA, 1985. **CAREER:** Michigan Department of Transportation, highway design engineer, 1969-75, engineering systems analyst, 1975-79, supervising engineer, 1979-87, systems development manager, 1987-89, data center administrator, 1989-92, assistant chief information officer, 1992-94, executive of management assessment, 1994-. **ORGANIZATIONS:** American Society for Public Administration; Mid-Michigan Asian Pacific American Association, board of directors; Urban and Regional Information Systems Association. **HONORS/AWARDS:** US Department of Transportation, Highway Transportation Research and Education Fellowship Award, 1976. **SPECIAL ACHIEVEMENTS:** Registered professional engineer in the State of Michigan, 1978; one of the ten finalists for doctoral dissertation award in the field of public administration, 1986; language proficiency: English, Chinese, Taiwanese and Japanese. **HOME ADDRESS:** 6479 Island Lake Drive, East Lansing, MI 48823. **BUSINESS PHONE:** (517)335-2400.

LEE, SI YOUNG
Research engineer. Korean American. **PERSONAL:** Born Mar 20, 1951, Daegu, Kyungsangbuk-Do, Republic of Korea; son of Joan Lee; married Haejin Lee, Jan 13, 1980; children: Alexander, Misha. **EDUCATION:** Seoul National University, BS (with honors), 1979; Massachusetts Institute of Technology, MS, 1984; University of California, Berkeley, PhD, 1989. **CAREER:** Korea Electric Power Co, nuclear engineer, 1978-80; Westinghouse Savannah River Co, research engineer, 1989-. **ORGANIZATIONS:** American Society of Mechanical Engineers, 1991-; American Nuclear Society, 1991-. **HONORS/AWARDS:** ASME, Best Paper Award, Heat Transfer Div, 1991. **SPECIAL ACHIEVEMENTS:** Development of Two-phase Thermal-hydraulics Code, 1993. **MILITARY SERVICE:** Anti-aircraft Hawk Missiles Div, private, 1973-76; Service Excellence Award, 1974. **HOME ADDRESS:** 1019 Kismet Dr, Aiken, SC 29803. **BUSINESS PHONE:** (803)725-2328.

LEE, SIANI
Broadcast journalist. Korean American. **PERSONAL:** Born Oct 8, 1962, Seoul, Republic of Korea; daughter of Lillian Englett. **EDUCATION:** Hampton University, BA, mass media communication & journalism. **CAREER:** WCHV-AM, radio reporter, anchor, 1987-88; WTKR-TV, TV news producer, 1986-89; WTOC-TV, tv news, anchor, reporter, producer, 1989-90; WMAR-TV, tv news anchor, reporter, 1990-91; Channel 8 News, tv anchor, reporter, 1991-. **ORGANIZATIONS:** Asian American Journalists Association, Washington DC Chapter, vice president, 1991-92; National Association of Professional Asian Women, advisory board, 1992-93; Asian Pacific American Heritage Council, 1992-93. **HONORS/AWARDS:** Society of Professional Journalists, Dateline Award, 1993; National Association of Professional Asian Women, Distinguished Service, 1993. **SPECIAL ACHIEVEMENTS:** Virginia Association of Broadcasters Scholarship, 1986. **BIOGRAPHICAL SOURCES:** Korean American Life Magazine, p 4, Sep 1992. **BUSINESS ADDRESS:** TV News Anchor/Reporter, News Channel 8, 7600-D Boston Blvd, Springfield, VA 22153, (703)912-5357.

LEE, SIU-LAM
Educator. Chinese American. **PERSONAL:** Born Oct 3, 1941, Macao; son of Ying-Lam Lee & Stella Lee; married Felicia T Lee, Jun 20, 1982; children: Terence, Timothy, Serena. **EDUCATION:** Chinese University of Hong Kong, Chung Chi College, BSc, 1962; Oberlin College, MA, 1963; Cornell University, PhD, 1967. **CAREER:** University of Massachusetts, Lowell, associate professor, 1967-. **ORGANIZATIONS:** Entomological Society of America, ex-officio, 1967-; Sigma Xi, 1963-; International Bee Research Association, 1967-; National Geographic Society, 1968-; Asian Holocaust Resource Group, treasurer, 1991-; American Contract Bridge League, life master, 1978-; World Health Organization, Hong Kong Chapter, president, 1960-62. **HONORS/AWARDS:** NSF, Academic Extension Research Grant, 1969-72, research grant, 1969; University of Massachusetts, research grant, 1984-88; Allied Chemical Co, research grant, 1963-67; Mayor Flynn, Boston, Community Service Award, 1985. **SPECIAL ACHIEVEMENTS:** Coauthor, Laboratory Manual for Life Sciences I & II, 1985, 1988; coauthor, Principles, Processes and Organisms, 1971, 1974; coauthor, Bilingual English, vol 1-5, 1981, 1984; coauthor, A Guide to the Flora of the Lowell-Dracut Forest, 1978; consultant; reviewer; keynote speaker; panelist; judge; 1969-. **BUSINESS ADDRESS:** Associate Professor, Dept of Biology, University of Massachusetts, Lowell, 1 University Ave, Olsen Bldg, Lowell, MA 01854-2881, (508)934-2873.

LEE, SOO SEE
Clinical pharmacist, educator. Malaysian American. **PERSONAL:** Born Mar 13, 1966, Kuala Lumpar, Malaysia. **EDUCATION:** University of Illinois, College of Pharmacy, PharmD, 1990. **CAREER:** Wm S Middleton VAH, pharmacy resident, 1990-91; Saint Louis Veterans Administration Medical Center, John Cochran, 1991-; Saint Louis College of Pharmacy, pharmacy practice, assistant professor, 1991-. **ORGANIZATIONS:** American College of Clinical Pharmacists, 1993; American Society of Hospital Pharmacists, 1989-; American Diabetes Association, 1992-; Arthritis Foundation, professional education committee, 1991-. **BUSINESS ADDRESS:** Assistant Professor of Pharmacy Practice, Saint Louis College of Pharmacy, 4588 Parkview Pl, St Louis, MO 63110, (314)652-4100.

LEE, SOO-YOUNG
Educator. Korean American. **PERSONAL:** Born Jul 25, 1955, Seoul, Republic of Korea; son of Hong-Koo Lee and Ock-Nyu Kim; married Seong-Hee Kim, Jan 9, 1987; children: Albert Hyunjick, Bryan Hyunje. **EDUCATION:** Seoul National University, BS (magna cum laude), 1978; Korea Advanced Institute of Science, MS, 1980; University of Texas, Austin, PhD, 1987. **CAREER:** Kyung-Pook National University, instructor, 1980-83; Cornell University, assistant professor, 1987-. **ORGANIZATIONS:** Institute of Electrical & Electronics Engineers, 1987-. **SPECIAL ACHIEVEMENTS:** Research work on parallel processing: algorithms, mapping, communication, etc; development of proximity effect correction scheme for electron beam lithography. **BUSINESS ADDRESS:** Professor, Electrical Engineering, Cornell University, Engineering & Theory Center 336, Ithaca, NY 14853, (607)255-8810.

LEE, SOONCHA A.
Librarian. Korean American. **PERSONAL:** Born in Seoul, Republic of Korea. **EDUCATION:** Columbia University, School of Library Services, MLS, 1963. **CAREER:** Public Library of Cincinnati, Hamilton County, Serials Department, head, 1978-. **ORGANIZATIONS:** American Library Association, 1980-. **BUSINESS ADDRESS:** Head, Serials Dept, Public Library of Cincinnati and Hamilton County, 800 Vine Street, Cincinnati, OH 45215, (513)369-6083.

LEE, SUE YING
Educator. Chinese American. **PERSONAL:** Born Jan 11, 1940, Schenectady, NY; daughter of Wong Sing Lee and Suey Lon Lee; married Archie S Mossman, Jul 28, 1973; children: Mathew. **EDUCATION:** SUNY, Albany, BS, 1961, MS, 1963; University of Illinois, PhD, 1968. **CAREER:** University of Illinois-Chicago Circle, instructor, 1967-69; Humboldt State University, professor, 1969-. **ORGANIZATIONS:** American Cancer Society, CanSupport & Reach to Recovery volunteer; American Association of Anatomists; American Association for Advancement of Science; American Institute of Biological Sciences; American Society of Mammalogists, Comm on Women and Minorities Issues, member; Sigma Delta Epsilon, Graduate Women in Science, undergraduate programs chair and fellowships comm member; Society of Vertebrate Paleontology; Western Society of Naturalists; California Faculty Association; America Society of Zoologists. **HONORS/AWARDS:** Humboldt State University Foundation, Small Grant Awards, 1987-92. **SPECIAL ACHIEVEMENTS:** Co-author: "Host-finding reactions of some siphonaptera," Proc XII Int Cong Ent, 1964; "A histochemical study of twitch and tonus fibers," J Morph, p 133, 253-272, 1971; "Wildlife utilization and game ranching," IUCN Occassional Paper, No 17, pp 98, 1976; "Ultrastructure of the placenta and fetal membranes of the dog, vol II, the yolk sac," Am J Anat, Vol 166, p 313-328, 1983; others. **BUSINESS ADDRESS:** Professor, Dept of Biological Sciences, Humboldt State University, Arcata, CA 95521, (707)826-5553.

LEE, SUK HUN
Educator. Korean American. **PERSONAL:** Born Oct 28, 1957, Pusan, Republic of Korea; son of Myung Kwan Lee and Ae Sin Lee; married Joan Keum-Joo Lee, May 31, 1986; children: Daniel Jeong-Hwan, Ruth So-Young. **EDUCATION:** Florida Institute of Technology, BS, 1980; Florida State University, MBA, 1981; University of Southern California, PhD, 1988. **CAREER:** University of Southern California, teaching asst, research asst, instr, 1983-88; Loyola University of Chicago, asst prof, 1988-. **ORGANIZATIONS:** Good Shepherd-Sangdong United Methodist Church, young adult couple chrpn, 1993-. **HONORS/AWARDS:** Florida State University, Beta Gamma Sigma, 1981. **SPECIAL ACHIEVEMENTS:** Language proficiency: Spanish; author: "Using terms of Rescheduling as Proxy for Partial Reneging on LDCs Debt in a Test of Willingness-to-Pay Model," Journal of Intl Money and Finance, 10, 1991; "Are the Credit Ratings Assigned by Bankers Based on the Willingness-of-Borrower to Repay?," Journal of Development Economics, 40, 1993; "Significance of Political Instability and Economic Variables on Perceived Country Creditworthiness," Journal of Intl Business Studies, 1993. **BUSINESS ADDRESS:** Assistant Professor, Loyola University of Chicago, Lewis Tower, 820 N Michigan Ave, Chicago, IL 60611, (312)915-7071.

LEE, SUN-YOUNG WON
Art educator, artist. Korean American. **PERSONAL:** Born Sep 17, 1943, Seoul, Republic of Korea; daughter of Myoung-Soo Won and Ki-Seung Song; married Tae-Ahn Thomas Lee, Sep 4, 1971; children: Christine Ko-Eun, Jacque Ji-Eun. **EDUCATION:** Ewha Woman's University, Seoul, Korea, BA, western paintings, 1965, MA, western paintings, 1967; Pratt Institute, Brooklyn, MFA, painting & graphic arts, 1970; Ohio State University, PhD, art education, 1988. **CAREER:** Saint Henry School, art teacher, 1974-75; Lima Art Assoc, printmaking instructor, 1978-80; Wapakoneta Public Schools, art teacher, 1980-81; Bowling Green State University, lecturer, 1987-89; Ohio State University, Lima, Saturday art class & summer art camp director, 1984, assistant professor of art education, 1989-. **ORGANIZATIONS:** National Art Education Association, active member, 1984-; Ohio State Art Education Association, active member, 1988-; Ohio State University, Lima, cultural affairs committee, 1989-; Bowling Green University, School of Art, Medici Circle patron, 1988-; Lima Art Association, board of directors, exhibition committee, patron, 1979-; Annual National Art Exhibition, Seoul, Korea, jury-free artist, 1967-. **HONORS/AWARDS:** Lima Art Association, The Best of Show Award for Annual Spring Show, 1983; Annual National Exhibition, Seoul, Korea, The Ministry of Education, Jury-free Artist Award, 1967, special prizes for 4 consecutive years, 1963-66. **SPECIAL ACHIEVEMENTS:** Publications: "Professional Criticism in the Secondary Classroom: Opposing Judgments of Contemporary Art Enhance the Teaching of Art Criticism," Art Educ, Journal of the Natl Art Educ Assn, 46(3), pp 42-51, May 1993; "Critical Writings of Lawrence Alloway," Studies in Art Educ, Natl Art Educ Assn, A Journal of Issues & Research, 32(3), pp 171-177, Spring 1991; exhibitions: Contemporary Korean Artists in America, invitational show, Korean Cultural Service, Los Angeles, Jan 15-Feb 5, 1986; Korean Artist Abroad, invitational show, Natl Museum of Art, Seoul, Korea, April 1982; Toledo Area Artists' Annual Exhibition, Toledo Museum of Art, Ohio, 1984, 1985, 1992. **BIOGRAPHICAL SOURCES:** "Lima Woman Wins Art Association Show," The Lima News, page B7, Sunday, April 24, 1983. **BUSINESS ADDRESS:** Assistant Professor of Art Education, Ohio State University at Lima, 4240 Campus Drive, Galvin Hall, Lima, OH 45804-3504, (419)221-1641.

LEE, SUNG MOOK
Educator, educational administrator. Korean American. **PERSONAL:** Born Mar 2, 1933, Seoul, Republic of Korea; son of Byung Taik Lee and Keh Ho Cho; married Incha Kim, Dec 21, 1958; children: Peter, Patricia Gray, Janet. **EDUCATION:** Yonsei University, BS, 1955; Ohio State University, MS, 1959, PhD, 1965. **CAREER:** Denison University, assistant professor, 1961-65; Michigan Tech University, assistant, associate and professor, 1965-, Keweenaw Research Center, professor & director, 1976-92, vice provost, dean, 1988-. **ORGANIZATIONS:** American Physical Society, currently; Intl Glaciological Society, 1986-; Army Science Board, 1991-; Arctic Research Consortium of the United States, board member, 1990-92; National Research Council, Transportation Board, 1986-90. **HONORS/AWARDS:** Michigan Tech University, Faculty Research Award, 1972; NATO, Senior Fellow, 1974; National Science Foundation and US Navy, Antarctica Service Medal, 1987. **BUSINESS ADDRESS:** Vice Provost for Research, Dean of the Graduate School, Michigan Technological University, 1400 Townsend Drive, Houghton, MI 49931-1295, (906)487-2327.

LEE, SUNGGYU
Educator. Korean American. **PERSONAL:** Born Mar 11, 1952, Kangjin-kun, Chun-nam, Republic of Korea; son of Seung Hyun Lee and Jom-nim Yim Lee; married Kyung P Lee, Aug 8, 1980; children: Tracy Yoonjin, Jo Jo Yoonjo, Leroy Jonghoo. **EDUCATION:** Seoul National University, BS, 1974, MS, 1976; Case Western Reserve University, PhD, 1980. **CAREER:** Seoul National University, Computer Center, manager, 1977; Case Western Reserve University, graduate assistant, 1977-80; University of Akron, assistant professor, 1980-85, associate professor, 1985-87, director, Process Research Center, 1988-, R Iredell Professor & head, 1988-. **ORGANIZATIONS:** American Inst of Chem Engineers, 1977-, Fuels & Petrochemicals Div, vice chair, 1993-, Alternate Energy & Solid Fuels, program committee chair, 1989-; American Chemical Society, 1980-; Tau Beta Pi; Sigma Xi, 1980-, president, Akron Chapter, 1987-88; Kaufa, 1992-. **HONORS/AWARDS:** University of Akron,

Outstanding Teacher Award, 1987, Outstanding Researcher Award, 1993, Louis A Hill Award, 1987; Marcel Dekker, Best Paper of the Year Award, 1991; American Institute of Chemical Engineers, Akron Chemical Engineer of the Year, 1993. **SPECIAL ACHIEVEMENTS:** Methanol Synthesis Technology, CRC Press, 1990; Oil Shale Technology, CRC Press, 1991; Chemical Modifications of Polymers, Technomic Publishing Co, in press; over 200 publications; over 200 published technical reports; 12 patents. **BUSINESS ADDRESS:** R Iredell Professor & Head, Chemical Engineering, University of Akron, 302 E Buchtel Ave, Whitby Hall, 103, Akron, OH 44325-3906, (216)972-7283.

LEE, SUSAN H.
Physician. Chinese American. **PERSONAL:** Born in Taiwan; daughter of Y W Chou & C K Lee. **EDUCATION:** National University of Buenos Aires, School of Medicine, MD, 1982; Harvard University, School of Public Health, MPH, 1984. **CAREER:** Saint Vincent's Hospital & Medical Center, 1984-87; New York Hospital-Cornell Medical Center, 1987-89; Centers for Disease Control, 1989-. **ORGANIZATIONS:** American Medical Association; American Public Health Association; American Pediatric Association. **SPECIAL ACHIEVEMENTS:** JAMA, vol 267, p 2616-20, 1992; AIDS, vol 12, p 1301-2, 1990; MMWR, vol 39, no 25, June 29, 1990; Pediatric Research, vol 25, p 1651, abs, 1989; Am Journal of Trop Med Hyg, vol 48, no 2, p 178-185, 1993; Clinics in Gastroenterology, vol 10, no 2, p 475-77, 1981; fluent in Spanish and Chinese. **HOME ADDRESS:** 3728-1 Peachtree Rd, Atlanta, GA 30319.

LEE, TAEHEE
Educator. Korean American. **PERSONAL:** Born Apr 24, 1952, Taejun, Chungnam, Republic of Korea; son of Sang-kuk Lee and Soon-nam Oh Lee; married Jihee Lee, Apr 14, 1958; children: Clara, Christina. **EDUCATION:** Ulsan University, BS, 1975; Korea University, ME, 1978; North Carolina State University, MS, 1982; Cleveland State University, PhD, 1988. **CAREER:** Korea Information Computing Co, system programmer, 1975-77; Telecommunication Research Institute, researcher, 1977-80; Chonmam National University, instructor, 1980-81; Case Western Reserve University, research assistant, 1984-85; Cleveland State University, research associate, 1985-87; Wilkes University, assistant professor, 1987-. **ORGANIZATIONS:** IIE, 1983-; ORSA, 1991-; SCS. **HONORS/AWARDS:** Wilkes University, Outstanding Teaching Award, 1989; CSU, Alpha Phi Mu, 1987; Ulsan University, British Ambassador to Korea Award, 1975. **SPECIAL ACHIEVEMENTS:** "Expert System for the Integration of CIM Systems," International Journal of Computers and Industrial Engineering, 19:1, p202, 1991; "New Jobs Regeneration Methods for CIM," Simulators, Society for Computer Simulation Intl, 22:2, p 202, 1991; "Batch Sizing Effect on Machine Utilization, Duedates, and WIP," 20th Pittsburgh Conferences on Modelling and Simulation, 20:2, p513, 1987. **HOME PHONE:** (717)822-7595. **BUSINESS ADDRESS:** Assistant Professor, Wilkes University, 160 S Franklin St, Stark Learning Center, Wilkes-Barre, PA 18766, (717)831-4888.

LEE, TIEN-CHANG
Educator. Taiwanese American. **PERSONAL:** Born Jul 1, 1943, Nantou, Taiwan; son of Chen Chou Lee; married Zora M Lee, Dec 22, 1969; children: Cin-Ty, Cin-Young. **EDUCATION:** National Taiwan University, BS, 1965; University of Idaho, MS, 1969; University of Southern California, PhD, 1974. **CAREER:** Woods Hole Oceanographic Institution, post-doctoral; University of California, professor of geophysics, 1974-. **ORGANIZATIONS:** American Geophysical Union, 1970-; Society of Exploration Geophysicists, 1974-. **SPECIAL ACHIEVEMENTS:** Registered geologist, California, currently; registered geophysicist, California, currently. **BUSINESS ADDRESS:** Professor, Dept of Earth Science, University of California, Riverside, CA 92521-0412, (909)787-4506.

LEE, TONY J. F.
Educator. Taiwanese American. **PERSONAL:** Born Nov 10, 1942, Hualien, Taiwan; son of Huo-Yen Lee and Wan Lee; children: Cheryl, Jonathan. **EDUCATION:** Taipei Medical College, BS, 1967; West Virginia University, PhD, 1973. **CAREER:** Southern Illinois University, asst professor, 1975-81, associate professor, 1981-87, professor, 1987-. **ORGANIZATIONS:** American Society for Pharmacology and Exp Ther, 1981; American Society for the Advancement of Science; Society of Neuroscience. **HONORS/AWARDS:** Natl Institutes of Health, research, 1992, 1994; AHA, research, 1992. **SPECIAL ACHIEVEMENTS:** Numerous publications. **BUSINESS ADDRESS:** Prof, Southern Illinois University School of Medicine, PO Box 19230, Springfield, IL 62794-9230, (217)785-2197.

LEE, TSAIFENG MAZIE
Educator. Chinese American. **PERSONAL:** Born Nov 10, 1936, Old China; daughter of Harold & Pearl Hong lee. **EDUCATION:** University of Hawaii, Honolulu, MA, applied linguistics, 1972. **CAREER:** Peking University, English teacher, 1981-82; Brigham Young University, assistant professor, 1975, Chinese Section, Department of Asian and Near Eastern Languages, head, 1976-79, 1982-84, instructor, Department of Foreign Languages, 1965-, professor emeritus, 1992, research associate, 1992-. **ORGANIZATIONS:** American Council on the Teaching of Foreign Languages; Chinese Language Teachers Association; Association for Asian Studies. **HONORS/AWARDS:** Professional Associate Award, East-West Center, Honolulu, HI, 1983; University of Michigan, fellow, 1967; University of Washington, fellow, 1966. **SPECIAL ACHIEVEMENTS:** "Contrastive Analysis of Chinese and American Cultures," 1991; Books, Events and People that Changed the Chinese Life in the Last Hundred Years, 1990; numerous others. **BUSINESS ADDRESS:** Research Associate, Professor Emeritus, Brigham Young University, 231 HRCB, Provo, UT 84602.

LEE, TSOUNG-CHAO
Educator. Chinese American. **PERSONAL:** Born Oct 25, 1935, Taipei, Taiwan; son of Chiou-Chin Lee and Yu-Ing Chen; married Chung-lien Lee, Jan 25, 1964; children: Tony, Jean. **EDUCATION:** National Taiwan University, Taipei, BS, 1958; University of Illinois, Champaign-Urbana, MS, 1965, PhD, 1967. **CAREER:** National Taiwan University, Taipei, teaching assistant, 1960-63, visiting professor, 1989; University of Illinois, Champaign-Urbana, research assistant, 1963-65; University of Georgia, visiting professor, 1977-78; University of Connecticut, assistant professor, 1967-71, associate professor, 1971-75, professor, 1975-. **HONORS/AWARDS:** The National Reference Institute, Outstanding Educators of America, 1975; Gamma Sigma Delta, Award Certificate, 1972; University of Illinois, Wright Fellowship, 1965-67; The American Farm Economics Association, Master's Thesis Award, 1965; Agricultural Development Council, NY, travel fellowship, 1963-67. **SPECIAL ACHIEVEMENTS:** Books: Estimating the Parameters of the Markov Probability Model from Aggregate Time Series Data, North-Holland, Amsterdam, 1970, 1977; The Theory and Practice of Econometrics, Wiley, 1980, 1985; Introduction to the Theory and Practice of Econometrics, Wiley, 1982, 1988. **MILITARY SERVICE:** Army, Taiwan, second lt, 1958-60. **BUSINESS ADDRESS:** Professor, University of Connecticut, 1376 Storrs Road, U-21, Storrs Mansfield, CT 06269-4021, (203)486-2741.

LEE, TSUNG-DAO
Educator, physicist. Chinese American. **PERSONAL:** Born Nov 25, 1926, Shanghai, China; son of Tsing-Kong L and Ming-Chang Chang; married Jeannette Chin, Jun 3, 1950; children: James, Stephen. **EDUCATION:** National Chekiang University, Kweichow, China, 1943-44; National SW Assoc University, Kunming, China, 1945-46; University of Chicago, PhD, 1950. **CAREER:** University of Chicago, research associate in astronomy, 1950; University of California, Berkeley, research associate, physics lecturer, 1950-51; Harvard University, Loeb Lecturer, 1957, 1964; Institute for Advanced Study, Princeton University, physics professor, 1960-63; Columbia University, assistant professor, 1953-55, associate professor, 1955-56, professor, 1956-60, 1963-, adjunct professor, 1960-62, Enrico Fermi Professor of Physics, 1964-. **ORGANIZATIONS:** Institute for Advanced Study, Princeton University, 1951-53; Academia Sinica; NAS; American Academy of Arts and Sciences; American Philosophical Society; Acad Nazionale dei Lincei. **HONORS/AWARDS:** With Chen Ning Yang, Nobel Prize in physics, for disproving principle of conservation of parity, 1957; Yeshiva University, Albert Einstein Science Award, 1957; Princeton University, DSc, 1958; Chinese University, Hong Kong, LLD, 1969; CCNY, DSc, 1978; Italian Republic, Order of Merit, Grande Ufficiale, 1986. **SPECIAL ACHIEVEMENTS:** Weak Interactions and High Energy Neutrino Physics, editor, 1966; Particle Physics and Introduction to Field Theory, editor, 1981. **BUSINESS ADDRESS:** Enrico Fermi Professor of Physics, Dept of Physics, Columbia University, New York, NY 10027, (212)854-1754.∗

LEE, TUNG-KWANG
Physician. Chinese American. **PERSONAL:** Born Oct 6, 1934, Shanghai, China; son of Chie-Tsai Lee and Chong-Wen Ding; married You-An Sun Lee, Jan 30, 1974; children: Hao. **EDUCATION:** Shanghai First Medical College, MD, 1955. **CAREER:** Bowman Gray School of Medicine, research associate, 1980-85; East Carolina University, School of Medicine, research instructor, 1985-88, research assistant professor, 1988-. **ORGANIZATIONS:** International Academy of Cytology, 1984-; American Association for Cancer Re-

search, 1990-; Eastern Carolina Multicultural Center, board of directors, 1992-. **SPECIAL ACHIEVEMENTS:** Publications: 45 articles (24 in English); 17 abstracts; 3 book chapters (one in English). **HOME ADDRESS:** 1403 Evergreen Dr, Greenville, NC 27858, (919)756-3393. **BUSINESS ADDRESS:** Professor, Dept of Radiation Oncology, Leo Jenkins Cancer Center, East Carolina State University, Greenville, NC 27834, (919)816-2900.

LEE, TZESAN DAVID
Educator. Chinese American. **PERSONAL:** Born Jul 1947, Amoy, Fukien, China; married Tingting Teresa Lee, Apr 1974. **EDUCATION:** National Chung-Hsing University, BS, 1970; State University of New York at Stony Brook, PhD, 1976. **CAREER:** National Chung-Hsing University, 1976-77; Michigan State University, instructor, 1978-80; Western Illinois University, associate professor, 1980-. **ORGANIZATIONS:** American Statistical Association, 1980-; International Chinese Statistical Association, 1987-. **HONORS/AWARDS:** NASA-Johnson Space Center, Summer Faculty Research Fellowship, 1992. **SPECIAL ACHIEVEMENTS:** "Mortality among Workers in a Thorium-Processing Plant: A Second Follow-Up," Scandinavian J of Work Environmental Health, 18, 162-168, 1992. **BUSINESS ADDRESS:** Associate Professor, Western Illinois University, 900 W Adams St, 484 Morgan Hall, Macomb, IL 61455, (309)298-1485.

LEE, VIC LING
Television correspondent. Chinese American. **PERSONAL:** Born Sep 29, 1946, Shanghai, China; son of Chia & Topaz Lee; married Suzanne; children: Natalie. **EDUCATION:** San Jose State University, CA, 1964-69. **CAREER:** New York Times, intern, 1966; UPI, correspondent, 1970-72; KRON TV correspondent, 1972-. **ORGANIZATIONS:** Asian American Journalists Association, vice pres San Francisco chapter, 1993. **HONORS/AWARDS:** George Polk Journalism Award, 1986; Emmy Awards for: Best Writing, Best News Story, Best Series, Best Specialized Reporting, Best Religious & History Reporting, Best Spot News; UPI Award, Best Spot News; AP, Best Live Coverage; Cine Golden Eagle Award, Best Documentary; New York Film Festival, Gold Medal, Best Documentary. **SPECIAL ACHIEVEMENTS:** Fluent in Japanese and Mandarin Chinese. **BUSINESS ADDRESS:** Correspondent, KRON-TV, 1001 Van Ness Ave, San Francisco, CA 94109, (415)561-8952.

LEE, YING J.
Research management, educator. Chinese American. **PERSONAL:** Born Jul 28, 1951, Columbus, OH; son of Chee & June Lee; married May D Lee, Aug 14, 1974; children: Adrianne J, Derric J. **EDUCATION:** Ohio State University, BA, 1971; University of Illinois, MS, 1973, PhD, 1975. **CAREER:** American Cyanamid, Princeton, NJ, summer research chemist, 1970-71; American Cyanamid, Pearl River, NY, principal scientist, 1977-80, project leader, 1980-81, group leader, 1981-87, senior research group leader, 1987-89, head, department of chemistry, 1989-. **ORGANIZATIONS:** American Chemical Society, NY section, director at large, 1993-95; International Society of Heterocyclic Chemistry, organizing committee, 1992-; National Institutes of Health Medicinal Chemistry Study Section, 1989-93; American Chemical Society, 1967-; American Society of Microbiology; American Association for Advancement of Science. **HONORS/AWARDS:** UpJohn Fellow, 1974-75; National Institutes of Health, postdoctoral fellow, 1975-77; Scientific Achievement Award for American Cyanamid, 1981. **HOME PHONE:** (914)357-5303. **BUSINESS ADDRESS:** Head, Dept of Chemistry for Infectious Diseases, Lederle Lab, American Cyanamid Co, N Middletown Rd, 65A-302A, Pearl River, NY 10965, (914)732-2501.

LEE, VIVIAN WAI-FUN
Association administrator. Chinese American. **PERSONAL:** Born Oct 10, 1959, Hong Kong; daughter of Chui Pan Lee & Lai Wah Wong; married Peter Kiang, Aug 11, 1989. **EDUCATION:** Harvard-Radcliffe College, BA, 1984; University of Massachusetts, MA, 1995. **CAREER:** Boston Children's Service Association, head teacher, 1980-82; Massachusetts Dept of Social Services, respite care area coordinator, 1985; Boston Public Schools, JQ Quincy School, senior staff assistant, 1984-85, district zone specialist, 1985-88, chapter 636 coordinator, 1988-91; National Coalition of Advocates for Students, project director, 1991-94. **ORGANIZATIONS:** Massachusetts Asian American Educators Association, chair, 1991-; Chinese Progressive Association, steering committee, 1986-; Asian American Resource Workshop, board chair, 1984-86, steering committee, 1980-86; ESL, volunteer, citizenship teacher, 1982-; Asian American Civic Association, Literacy Initiative Advisory Board, 1992-. **HONORS/AWARDS:** Asian American Resource Workshop, Distinguished

Service Award, 1985. **SPECIAL ACHIEVEMENTS:** Co-wrote, "Exclusion or Contribution? Education K-12 Policy," in The State of Asia Pacific America; featured on cable TV, 1993; production host, Dragon Gate Radio, Chinese community program, WUMB FM, 1988-91; also many presentations on education, the immigrant experience, Chinatown community. **HOME ADDRESS:** 40 Seaverns Ave, Jamaica Plain, MA 02130-2865, (617)524-0560.

LEE, WEA HWA
Publisher. Chinese American. **PERSONAL:** Born Mar 29, 1948, Long Ling, Yunnan, China; married Catherine C Lee, 1973; children: Howard, Margaret. **EDUCATION:** National Cheng-Chi University, Taiwan, BL, 1969; Lamar University, MA, 1974. **CAREER:** China Broadcasting Corporation, editor, 1966-69; Southern Chinese Journal, editor, 1975-77; LC Paper Company, president, 1979-; USA Printing, president, 1979-; Texas Chinese Television, president, 1979-; Dallas Chinese Times, publisher, 1979-; Chicago Chinese Times, publisher, 1979-; Washington Chinese News, publisher, 1979-; Southern Chinese Daily News, publisher, 1979-. **ORGANIZATIONS:** National Republican Asian Assembly, vice-chairman, 1992; Asian Houstonians for Bush/Quayle 92, co-chairman, 1992; Asian Gala, GOP Convention 92, co-chairman, 1992; Asian American Republican National Federation, vice-chairman, 1992. **HONORS/AWARDS:** Advisor to Republic of China Overseas Affairs Commission, 1976; Outstanding Overseas Chinese Young Man of the Year, 1976; Pi Sigma Alpha, Outstanding Member, 1974; City of Houston, Certificate of Appreciation, 1990; Houston Cable TV Company, board member, 1992. **BIOGRAPHICAL SOURCES:** Houston Business Journal. **BUSINESS ADDRESS:** President, Southern Chinese Newspaper Publishing Company, 12129 Bellaire Blvd, Houston, TX 77072, (713)498-4310.

LEE, WEI-CHIN
Educator. Taiwanese American. **PERSONAL:** Born Nov 1, 1956, Su-Ao, I-Lan, Taiwan; son of Han-lin lee and A-hsi Lee-Liu; married Chin-wen Cristina Yu, Jul 7, 1983; children: Rae-yao. **EDUCATION:** National Taiwan University, BA, political science, 1978; University of Oregon, MA, political science, 1983, PhD, political science, 1986. **CAREER:** University of Oregon, teaching assistant, 1983-86, instructor, 1985, 1986; Wake Forest University, assistant professor, 1987-93, associate professor, 1993-. **ORGANIZATIONS:** Journal of Asian and African Studies, book review editor, 1993-; American Political Science Association, 1985-; Association for Asian Studies, 1986-; International Studies Association, 1988-. **HONORS/AWARDS:** Pew Foundation, grant, 1989; Carnegie Council, fellowship, 1990; Institute on Global Conflict and Cooperation, fellowship, 1990; Wake Forest University, Archie Grant and Research Grant, 1992-94; Japan Daiichi Kangyo, bank scholarship, 1978. **SPECIAL ACHIEVEMENTS:** Publications include: "Taiwan's Foreign Aid Policy," Asian Affairs: An American Review, 1993; "Crimes of the Heart: Political Loyalty in Socialist China," Studies in Comparative Communism, 1992; "Read My Lips or Watch My Feet: The State and Chinese Dissident Intellectuals," Issues and Studies, 1992; "Heaven Can Wait? Rethinking the Chinese Notion of Human Rights," Asian Thought and Society, 1991; "Iron and Nail: Civil-military Relations in the People's Republic of China," Journal of Asian and African Studies, 26 (1-2), 1991, 132-148; Taiwan, Oxford, Clio, 1990. **BIOGRAPHICAL SOURCES:** Access Asian: A Guide to Specialists and Current Research, p 171, 1993. **BUSINESS ADDRESS:** Associate Professor of Politics, Wake Forest University, Reynolda Station, Box 7568, Winston-Salem, NC 27109, (910)759-5455.

LEE, WEI-KUO
Chemical engineer. Chinese American. **PERSONAL:** Born Mar 25, 1943, Hopei, China; son of Shyue-Hai & Yu-Chin Sha Lee; married Shuh-Hui Goh, Jun 30, 1990; children: Jane Jin-En Lee. **EDUCATION:** National Taiwan University, BSChE, 1965; University of Houston, PhD, 1972; University of Delaware, postdoctoral, 1973. **CAREER:** Celanese Research Company, research engineer, 1973-77; New Jersey Institute of Technology, adjunct professor, 1975-81; Exxon Research & Engineering Co, staff engineer, 1977-87; Shell Development Co, senior research engineer, 1987-88; Union Carbide Chemicals & Plastics Co, senior research engineer, 1988-. **ORGANIZATIONS:** American Institute of Chemical Engineers, 1971-; Society of Rheology, 1971-; Society of Plastics Engineers, 1987-; Chinese Institute of Engineers, USA, 1984-. **HONORS/AWARDS:** Sigma Xi; Phi Kappa Phi; Phi Tau Phi; American Institute of Chemical Engineers, Best Fundamental Publication Award, 1981. **SPECIAL ACHIEVEMENTS:** Author of several publications; "A Review of the Rheology of Magnetically Stabilized Fluidized Beds," Powder Technology, vol 64, p69-80, 1991; "The Rheology of Magnetically Stabilized Fluidized Solids," AIChE Symp Ser 222, vol 79, p87-96, 1983; "A

Slit Die Design for Sable Film Extrusion," Adv in Rheology, vol 4, p473-481, 1984. **MILITARY SERVICE:** First Armored Division, Republic of China, 2nd lt, 1965-66. **BUSINESS ADDRESS:** Union Carbide Chemicals & Plastics Co, Weston Canal Center, 1 Riverview Dr, Somerset, NJ 08873.

LEE, WEI-NA
Educator. Taiwanese American. **PERSONAL:** Born Sep 9, 1957, Taipei, Taiwan; daughter of Ying-Hsiang Lee and Ying-Hwa H Lee; married Hao Ling, Dec 21, 1984; children: Chloe Ling. **EDUCATION:** Tamkang University, Taiwan, BA, 1980; University of Wisconsin, Madison, MA, 1982; University of Illinois, Urbana-Champaign, MS, 1984, PhD, 1988. **CAREER:** University of Texas, assistant professor, 1988-. **ORGANIZATIONS:** Association for Consumer Research, 1986-; American Academy of Advertising, 1986-; Society of Consumer Psychology, 1988-; Association for Education in Journalism and Mass Communication, 1988-. **HONORS/AWARDS:** American Academy of Advertising, research fellowship, 1992; Association for Education in Journalism and Mass Communication, African, Hispanic, Asian and Native American Research Award, 1991. **SPECIAL ACHIEVEMENTS:** Co-Author, refereed journals: "Changing Media Consumption in a New Home: Acculturation Patterns among Hong Kong Immigrants to Canada," Journal of Advertising, "A Content Analysis of Animation and Animated Spokes-Characters in Television Commercials," Journal of Advertising; "Removing Negative Country Images: Effects of Decomposition, Branding and Product Experience," Journal of International Marketing; author, "Acculturation and Advertising Communication Strategies: A Cross-Cultural Comparison of Chinese and Americans," Psychology and Marketing, vol 10, no 5, forthcoming; "The Potential of Advertising on Pre-recorded Videocassettes in the 1990s: A Survey Among Top US Advertising Agencies," Journal of Media Planning, vol 7, no 1, pp 25-35, 1991. **BUSINESS ADDRESS:** Assistant Professor, Dept of Advertising, University of Texas, CMA 7.142, Austin, TX 78712, (512)471-8149.

LEE, WEI-PING ANDREW
Physician. Chinese American. **PERSONAL:** Born Jun 7, 1957, Taiwan; son of Hsueh-Yen Lee and Nora Tsu-ching Lee; married Teresa C Lee, Aug 10, 1980; children: Jonathan K, Jacqueline K, Joshua K. **EDUCATION:** Harvard University, BA, 1979; Johns Hopkins University School of Medicine, MD, 1983. **CAREER:** Massachusetts General Hospital, attending surgeon in plastic surgery, 1991-. **HONORS/AWARDS:** American Academy Orthopaedic Surgeons, Kappa Delta Young Investigator Award, 1991; Plastic Surgery Educational Foundation, Scholarship Essay Contest, 1989, 1990; Northeastern Society Plastic Surgeons, Scientific Presentation, 1989, 1991. **SPECIAL ACHIEVEMENTS:** Published in Plastic and Reconstructive Surgery, for research on vascularized limb tissue allografts, 1991, 1994. **BUSINESS ADDRESS:** Massachusetts General Hospital, Ambulatory Care Center 453, Boston, MA 02114, (617)724-0400.

LEE, WILLIAM WAI-LIM
Scientist. Chinese American. **PERSONAL:** Born Aug 6, 1948, Shanghai, China; son of Frank H Lee & Jean H L. **EDUCATION:** Tulane University, BSE, 1969; University of Michigan, MSE, 1970; Massachusetts Institute of Technology, SMCE, 1976, ScD, 1977. **CAREER:** Los Angeles County Sanitation Districts, project engineer, 1970-72; Woodward-Clyde Consultants, staff scientist, 1977-79; University of Pennsylvania, assistant professor, 1979-82; R F Weston Inc, project director, 1982-85; Lawrence Berkeley Lab, University of California, staff scientist, 1985-92; Environmental Evaluation Group, senior scientist, 1992-. **ORGANIZATIONS:** San Francisco Bay Area Engineering Council, president, 1992, vice president, 1991, secretary, 1989-90; American Society of Civil Engineers, various committees; American Nuclear Society, public policy committee, 1992-94; American Geophysical Union, public policy committee, 1989-90. **SPECIAL ACHIEVEMENTS:** Author of 3 books, 100 papers, and 32 technical reports. **HOME PHONE:** (505)821-5148. **BUSINESS ADDRESS:** Senior Scientist, Environmental Evaluation Group, 7007 Wyoming Blvd NE, Ste F-2, Albuquerque, NM 87109, (505)828-1003.

LEE, WOL SUE
Librarian. Korean American. **PERSONAL:** Born Jan 11, 1938, Seoul, Republic of Korea; daughter of Si Woo Chun and Iee Nyo Choi; married Jong Jin, Mar 19, 1965; children: Carol, Christopher. **EDUCATION:** Ewha University, BA; Boston University, EdM; George Peabody Library School, MLS. **CAREER:** Boston University Education Library, student aid, 1965-66; Somerville Public Library, ref librarian, 1966-68; New York Public Library, supervising librarian, 1969-88, principal librarian, 1988-91, senior coordinator, 1992-, dept

head, currently. **ORGANIZATIONS:** American Library Association, Ethnic Materials/Information committee; Korean American Library Association; Ewha Womens Alumni Association, past president; New York Library Association, RASS, EMIRT. **SPECIAL ACHIEVEMENTS:** Regular contributor for: Booklist, ALA. **BUSINESS ADDRESS:** Dept Head, Senior Coordinator, General Reference & Advisory Services, Mid-Manhattan Library, New York Public Library, 455 5th Avenue, 2nd Floor, New York, NY 10016-0122, (212)340-0861.

LEE, WONYONG
Educator. Korean American. **PERSONAL:** Born Dec 29, 1930, Hamhung, Republic of Korea; son of Zae Taek Lee and Ho Soon Kim; married Soo Fong, Jun 1991; children: Adrian Tae-Jin. **EDUCATION:** California Institute of Technology, BS, 1957; University of California-Berkeley, PhD, 1961. **CAREER:** University of California-Berkeley, research assoc, 1961-62; Columbia University, Dept of Physics, professor, physics, 1962-. **ORGANIZATIONS:** American Physical Society, fellow, 1958-; Nevis Laboratory, dir, 1980, 1985-90. **HONORS/AWARDS:** Alfred P Sloan Foundation, Fellow, 1965-67; John Simon Guggenheim Foundation, Fellow, 1979. **BUSINESS ADDRESS:** Professor of Physics, Columbia University, 538 W 120th St, New York, NY 10027, (212)854-3352.

LEE, WOOYOUNG
Chemical company executive. Korean American. **PERSONAL:** Born Jan 2, 1938, Pusan, Republic of Korea; son of Jong-soon Lee; married June Ja Moon, Jun 24, 1966; children: Marjorie, Christina. **EDUCATION:** Seoul National University, BS, chem engineering, 1961; University of Wisconsin, MS, chem engineering, 1964, PhD, chem engineering, 1966; Wharton School, University of Pennsylvania, ABA, business admin, 1981. **CAREER:** Mobil Research & Development Corp, research engineer, 1966-78, Reforming & Special Processes, manager, 1978-84; Mobil Chemical Co, Princeton Laboratory, manager, 1984-85, Polyolefins Process, manager, 1985-86; Edison Res, manager, 1986-. **ORGANIZATIONS:** American Chemical Society; American Institute of Chemical Engineers; Society of Plastics Engineering; Rutgers University, Chemical Engineering Department, advisory board; NJ Institute of Technology, Chemical Engineering Dept, advisory board; Korean Scientist & Engineers Association; Jaisohn Memorial Foundation, Philadelphia, board chairman. **SPECIAL ACHIEVEMENTS:** 13 US patents; numerous lectures & technical publications in chemical engineering. **BUSINESS ADDRESS:** Manager, Edison Research Laboratory, Mobil Chemical Company, PO Box 3029, Rte 27 & Vinyard Rd, Edison, NJ 08818, (908)321-6200.

LEE, YEU-TSU MARGARET
Surgeon, educator. Chinese American. **PERSONAL:** Born Mar 18, 1936, Xian, Shensi, China; daughter of Kiang-Piao Nee; divorced; children: Maxwell Ming-Dao. **EDUCATION:** University of South Dakota, AB, 1957; Harvard Medical School, MD, 1961. **CAREER:** Tripler Army Medical Center, chief, surgical oncology, 1983-; Uniformed Services University of the Health Sciences, clinical associate professor, 1986-; University of Hawaii, School of Medicine, clinical professor of surgery, 1993-. **ORGANIZATIONS:** American College of Surgeons; Society of Surgical Oncology; Hawaii Surgical Society; American Society of Clinical Oncology; Association of Women Surgeons. **HONORS/AWARDS:** United Chinese-American League, Service to Humanity, 1975; Asian-Pacific Women's Network, Science-Medicine Woman Warrior, 1983; Chinese-American Engineers & Scientists Association of Southern California, Achievement in Medical Science, 1987. **SPECIAL ACHIEVEMENTS:** Published one medical book; 15 chapters in reference books; over 150 papers in scientific journals, 1965-93; cancer specialist. **MILITARY SERVICE:** Army, Medical Corps, Col (06), 1983-; Army Commendation Medal, 1991, Army Meritorious Medal, 1992. **HOME ADDRESS:** PO Box 618H, Honolulu, HI 96818. **BUSINESS PHONE:** (808)433-5312.

LEE, YING K.
Chemist, research leader. Chinese American. **PERSONAL:** Born Dec 14, 1932, Shanghai, China; son of D T Lee and S Y Lee; married Theresa Lee; children: Arthur C, Annette, Angela. **EDUCATION:** Taitung University, China, BS, 1951; University of Leeds, England; University of Cincinnati, PhD, 1961. **CAREER:** E I du Pont de Nemours & Co Inc, research chemist, 1965-68, staff chemist, 1968-72, research associate, 1972-78, research fellow, 1978-85, senior research fellow, 1985-88, Dupont fellow, 1988-. **ORGANIZATIONS:** American Chem Society. **SPECIAL ACHIEVEMENTS:** Inventors of Lucite Dispersion Lacquer for cars; developmental team leader, Pyralin polyimide coating for microelectronics. **BUSINESS ADDRESS:** Dupont Fel-

low, E I du Pont de Nemours & Co Inc, 35th Grays Ferry Avenue, Philadelphia, PA 19146, (215)339-6344.

LEE, YOW-MIN R.
Educator. Chinese American. **PERSONAL:** Born Nov 18, 1924, Kirin, China; married Grace Ning Lee, Jun 29, 1973; children: Marcia. **EDUCATION:** Hitotsubashi University, Tokyo, MA, management accounting, 1956; Miami University, Ohio, MBA, 1959; University of Illinois, Urbana, MS, mathematics, 1961; University of Missouri, PhD, accountancy, 1973. **CAREER:** Country Life Insurance Company, actuarial cost analyst, 1962-65; San Fernando Valley State College, assistant professor, 1965-70; California State University, Northridge, associate professor, 1973-78, professor, 1978-. **ORGANIZATIONS:** China Institute, CSUN, director, treasurer, executive committee, 1980-92; San Fernando Valley Chinese Cultural Association, treasurer, director, 1982-85; National Association of Accountants, San Fernando Chapter, director, 1976-78, vice president, 1979-80; American Institute of Certified Public Accounts, 1974-; National Association of Realtors, 1979-; Institute of Management Accounting, 1974-. **HONORS/AWARDS:** Ford Foundation Grant, 1964-65; University of Illinois, scholarship, 1960-61; University of Missouri, scholarship, 1971-73. **SPECIAL ACHIEVEMENTS:** Author: "Introduction to Matrix Operations in Accounting," Management Accounting, 1985; "The Integration of Quantitative Methods in Management," American Accounting Association, Annual Western Meeting, Fullerton, CA, 1982; "A Survey of Current Practice in Overhead Costing Analysis," AAA Western Meeting Proceeding, San Diego, CA, 1980. **HOME PHONE:** (818)882-0964. **BUSINESS ADDRESS:** Professor, Dept of Accounting & MIS, California State University, Northridge, 18111 Nordhoff Street, Northridge, CA 91328-1280, (818)885-2439.

LEE, YUAN TSEH
Educator, scientist. Chinese American. **PERSONAL:** Born Nov 29, 1936, Hsinchu, Taiwan; son of Pei Tasi and Tsefan Lee; married Bernice Wu, Jun 28, 1963; children: Ted, Sidney, Charlotte. **EDUCATION:** National Taiwan University, BS, 1959; National Tsinghua University, Taiwan, MS, 1961; University of California, Berkeley, PhD, 1965. **CAREER:** University of Chicago, assistant professor to professor, 1968-74; University of California, Berkeley, Lawrence Berkeley Lab, principal investigator, professor, 1974-. **ORGANIZATIONS:** Camille and Henry Dreyfus Foundation Tchr, scholar, 1971-74; NAS; American Assn for the Advancement of Sci; American Chemical Society. **HONORS/AWARDS:** Nobel Prize in Chemistry, 1986; Dept of Energy, Ernest O Lawrence Award, 1981; Natl Medal of Science, 1986; Peter Debye Award, for Phys Chemistry, 1986; Alfred P Sloan Fellow, 1969-71; American Physical Society Fellow; John Simon Guggenheim Fellow, 1976-77. **SPECIAL ACHIEVEMENTS:** Contributor of numerous articles on chemical physics to professional journals. **BUSINESS ADDRESS:** Professor of Chemistry, Principal Investigator, Lawrence Berkeley Laboratory, University of California at Berkeley, Berkeley, CA 94720-0001. *

LEE, YUE-WEI
Research chemist. Chinese American. **PERSONAL:** Born Mar 9, 1946, San-Tong, China; son of Lee Shu-Yun and Lee S Jane; married Tina S Lee, Jul 4, 1972; children: Vickie Y, Grace, Edward. **EDUCATION:** Columbia University, PhD, 1978. **CAREER:** Research Triangle Institute, sr research chemist, 1978-. **ORGANIZATIONS:** American Chemical Society, 1976. **HONORS/AWARDS:** Research Triangle Institute, PDA Award, 1985. **BUSINESS ADDRESS:** Sr Research Chemist, Research Triangle Institute, PO Box 12194, MCB-176, Research Triangle Park, NC 27709, (919)541-6694.

LEE, YUL W.
Educator. Korean American. **PERSONAL:** Born Mar 8, 1951, Republic of Korea; son of Pyo Y Lee & Jae J Kim; married Maria K Lee, Dec 19, 1981; children: Catherine, Christopher. **EDUCATION:** Yonsei University, BA, economics, 1974; University of Texas, Austin, MA, math, 1986, PhD, finance, 1986. **CAREER:** The Bank of Korea, junior economist, 1974-80; University of Missouri, assistant professor, 1986-92; University of Rhode Island, LA associate professor, 1992-. **ORGANIZATIONS:** American Finance Association, 1984-; American Economic Association, 1986-. **HONORS/AWARDS:** Southwestern Finance Association, Best Paper Award, 1992; Midwest Finance Association, Distinguished Paper Award, 1992. **BUSINESS ADDRESS:** Professor, Dept of Finance, University of Rhode Island, College of Business Administration, Kingston, RI 02881-0802, (401)792-4360.

LEE, YUR-BOK
Educator. Korean American. **PERSONAL:** Born Nov 15, 1934, Seoul, Republic of Korea; son of Won-Koo and Ka-soon Lee; married Ae-Hyung Lee, Jun 15, 1966; children: Grace, Edward. **EDUCATION:** LaGrange College, BA, 1958; University of Georgia, MA, 1960, PhD, 1965. **CAREER:** University of Georgia, graduate assistant, 1960-65; Virginia Polytechnic Institute, assistant professor, 1965-66; University of Arkansas, Little Rock, assistant professor, 1966-67; North Dakota State University, assoc professor, 1967-73, professor, 1973-. **ORGANIZATIONS:** Association for Asian Studies; American Historical Association; Canadian Asian Studies Association; Association Internationale d'Etudes Coreennes et Comparees; Association for Korean Studies in Europe; New Zealand Asian Studies Society; Asian Studies Association of Australia; British Association for Korean Studies. **HONORS/AWARDS:** National Science Foundation Fellowship, 1970. **SPECIAL ACHIEVEMENTS:** Diplomatic Relations between US and Korea, Humanities Press, 1970; Establishment of a Korean Legation in US, University of Illinois, 1983; One Hundred Years of Korean-American Relations, University of Alabama Press, 1986; West Goes East, University of Hawaii Press, 1988; language proficiency: Korean, Japanese, Chinese, German, and French; "Cultural Dissonance in the American-Japanese Trade Realtionship," Journal of Social Sciences and Humanities, no 71, June 1993; "Paul Georg von Mullendorff and the Anglo-Russian Conflict over Korea in the mid-1880s," Russia and the Pacific, June 1993; "Li Hung-chang and Robert Hart in China's Control of Korean Customs Service, 1885-1895," Korean Studies in Canada, vol 1, 1993. **BUSINESS ADDRESS:** Professor, Dept of History, North Dakota State University, University Station, Minard Hall, Fargo, ND 58105, (701)237-8825.

LEI, SHAU-PING
Biochemist. Taiwanese American. **PERSONAL:** Born Oct 7, 1953, Taipei, Taiwan; daughter of Yu Lei and Pei-Chi Hu; married Hun-Chi Lin, Jul 6, 1980; children: Victoria Lin, Benita Lin. **EDUCATION:** National Taiwan University, BS, 1976, MS, 1980; UCLA, PhD, 1985. **CAREER:** INGENE, project director, 1985-89; TRIGEN, project director, 1989-90; XOMA, director, 1990-. **HONORS/AWARDS:** UCLA, Rittenberg Award, 1984. **BUSINESS ADDRESS:** Director, XOMA, 1545 17th Street, Santa Monica, CA 90404.

LEIGHTON, VERONICA V.
Publisher, television producer. Filipino American. **PERSONAL:** Born May 31, 1940, Navotas, Rizal, Philippines; daughter of Cipriano & Adoracion Bacatan; married Robert A Leighton, May 29, 1971; children: Robert E. **EDUCATION:** University of the Philippines, BS, foreign service, 1961. **CAREER:** VIA Times, Video Philippines, publisher, currently. **ORGANIZATIONS:** Asian American Journalists Association, Chicago Chapter, chapter secretary, 1989-91; Chicago Philippine Press Club, vice president, 1990-; Chicago Women in Publishing, currently. **HONORS/AWARDS:** Asian American Coalition, Most Outstanding Asian, 1986; Asian Human Services, Most Outstanding Asian in Journalism, 1986; Mason Lodge No 937, Community Builders Award, 1987; Caribe Association of America, Most Outstanding Filipino in Humanities, 1989; Minority Enterprise Development, City of Chicago, Publisher of the Year, 1989; City of Chicago, Women's Hall of Fame, 1991. **HOME ADDRESS:** 5855 N Sheridan Rd, Chicago, IL 60660.

LEM, KWOK WAI
Research scientist. Chinese American. **PERSONAL:** Born Jul 14, 1952, Kaiping, Guangdong, People's Republic of China; son of Man Oi Lem & Lau Yuet Wong Lem; married Margaret Yun-Ming Hsieh Lem, Mar 22, 1986; children: Paul C, Richard C. **EDUCATION:** University of Toronto, BASc, eng sci, 1976; Polytechnic Institute of New York, MS, poly sci eng, 1980, PhD, poly sci eng. 1983. **CAREER:** Canadian Hanson, chemical specialist, 1976-77; Schenectady Chemical, polymer chemist, 1977-78; Allied Signal, research engineer, 1983-87, senior research engineer, 1987-93, research scientist, 1993-; Polytechnic University, adjunct professor, 1991-. **ORGANIZATIONS:** Sigma Xi, 1982-; Tau Beta Pi, 1982-. **HONORS/AWARDS:** Ontario Scholar, 1972; Melvin M Gerson Award, 1981, 1982; AlliedSignal R & T Team Development Award, 1991. **HOME ADDRESS:** 11 Old Coach Rd, Randolph, NJ 07869, (201)895-4836.

LEONG, JACK Y. H.
Wholesale distributor, company executive. Chinese American. **PERSONAL:** Born Apr 1, 1925, Honolulu, HI; son of Beu Leong and Chang Tai Leong; married Edith Leong, Apr 1, 1944; children: Diane Bishop, James, Robert, David. **CAREER:** Dave's Ice Cream, Inc, chairman/CEO; JRD Enterprises, Inc, chairman/CEO; Mutual Envelope & Label, Inc, president/CEO; Process

Equipment Pacific, Inc, president/CEO; Mutual Distributors, Ltd, president/CEO, currently. **BUSINESS ADDRESS:** President, CEO, Mutual Distributors, Ltd, 320-C Waiakamilo Rd, Honolulu, HI 96817, (808)847-5941.

LEONG, ROBIN YEE
Student. Chinese American. **PERSONAL:** Born Jul 21, 1971, Seattle, WA; son of John S S Leong & Kar Ling Chiang. **EDUCATION:** University of Washington, speech communications, 1989-94. **CAREER:** Boy Wonders, owner, manager, 1987; Seattle Maritial Arts, instructor, 1988-; Blier & Associates, assistant manager, 1990; L&L Investments, real estate management, 1992-; Four Seasons Investments, property management, 1992-; King County Public Defenders Office, investigative intern, 1993. **ORGANIZATIONS:** Chinese Student Association, 1991-, president, 1992-93; Association for Student Journalists of Color, anchor, 1992; Flilpino Student Association, 1992; Asian Student Commission, organizer, 1992; Hong Kong Student Association, 1992-. **HONORS/AWARDS:** Seattle CAN/AM Martial Arts Championships, 1st Place, Fighting, 1987; Seattle Metro League, 1st Team All-Metro Baseball, 1989; Jinan China World Championships, 1st Place, Forms Competition, 1991. **SPECIAL ACHIEVEMENTS:** 1993 Asian Women's Calendar, organizer & developer, 1992, 1993; movie actor, Hong Kong, 2 feature films, 1991, 1992, 1993; master of ceremonies of the 1st Shaolin Kung Fu Monks Exhibition, Seattle, Washington, 1992. **BIOGRAPHICAL SOURCES:** Northwest Asian Weekly, p 12, June 13, 1992. **HOME ADDRESS:** 1936 7th Ave West, Seattle, WA 98119, (206)284-9906.

LEONG, RUSSELL C.
Editor, writer. Chinese American. **PERSONAL:** Born Sep 7, 1950, San Francisco, CA; son of Charles L Leong & Mollie Joe Leong. **EDUCATION:** San Francisco State College, BA, 1978; UCLA, MFA, 1990. **CAREER:** UCLA Asian American Studies Center, Amerasia Journal, editor, 1977-; resource development and publications, publications head, senior editor, currently. **SPECIAL ACHIEVEMENTS:** Numerous publications and issues, including: The Country of Dreams and Dust, poetry collection, West End Press, New Mexico, 1993; "The Painted Branch," New England Review, Summer, 1993; "Geography One," in Charlie Chan is Dead: An Anthology of Contemporary Asian American Fiction, edited by Jessica Hagedorn, Viking Penguin Books, 1993; "Unfolding Flowers, Matchless Flames," in Tricycle: The Buddhist Review, Spring 1993. **BUSINESS ADDRESS:** Senior Editor, UCLA Asian American Studies Center, 405 Hilgard Ave, 3230 Campbell Hall, Los Angeles, CA 90024, (310)825-2974.

LEU, DENNIS THOMAS
Chemical company executive. Chinese American. **PERSONAL:** Born Feb 7, 1953, Chicago, IL; son of Guie K Leu and Soo W Leu; married Louise A Wood; children: Emily, Daniel, Robert. **EDUCATION:** Northern Illinois University, BS, 1974; Northwestern University, MS, management, 1983. **CAREER:** Velsicol Chemical Co, Chemical Group, vice president, 1983-. **ORGANIZATIONS:** Chicago Drug and Chemical; AMA; RFCI. **BUSINESS ADDRESS:** Vice President, Chemical Group, Velsicol Chemical Company, 10400 Higgins Rd, Rosemont, IL 60018, (708)635-3488.

LEU, MING C.
Educator. Taiwanese American. **PERSONAL:** Born Apr 27, 1951, Taoyuan, Taiwan; son of Der-Young Leu and Tao Huang Leu; married Sophie, Jul 16, 1978; children: Paul, John, Karen. **EDUCATION:** National Taiwan University, BS, 1972; Pennsylvania State University, MS, 1977; University of California, Berkeley, PhD, 1981. **CAREER:** University of California, Berkeley, research assistant, 1977-81; Cornell University, assistant professor, 1981-87; New Jersey Institute of Technology, professor, 1987-. **ORGANIZATIONS:** ASME, 1975-, prod engineer division, secretary, 1986-87, program chairman, 1987-88, vice chairman, 1988-89, chairman, 1989-90; IEEE, 1981-; Japan-USA Symposium on Flex Auto, program chairman, 1992. **HONORS/AWARDS:** Forest Product Research Society, Wood Award, 1981; NSF, Presidential Young Investigator, 1985; Society of Manuf Engineering, Ralph R Teetor Award, 1985. **SPECIAL ACHIEVEMENTS:** About 100 publications in journals and conference proceedings; one US patent; received over 2 million dollars in research grants from NSF, ONR, and industry; seminars at universities, research labs and conferences in the US, Canada, Italy, France, Japan & Taiwan. **BUSINESS ADDRESS:** Professor, New Jersey Institute Technology, 323 King Blvd, Room 311, MEC, Newark, NJ 07102-1824, (201)596-3335.

LEU, RONG-JIN
Consultant. Taiwanese American. **PERSONAL:** Born Mar 6, 1956, Chia-I, Taiwan; son of Hsi-Pei Leu and Huang Tsui-hsia Leu; married Chwei-Ching Chang, Sep 22, 1987; children: Christie, Alex. **EDUCATION:** National Tsing-Hua University, BS, chemical engineering, 1979; University of Missouri, Columbia, MS, chemical engineering, 1983; Pennsylvania State University, MS, environmental engineering, 1985, PhD, environmental engineering, 1990. **CAREER:** University of Missouri-Columbia, research assistant, 1983-84; Pennsylvania State University, research assistant/coordinator, 1984-90; Gannett Fleming, Inc, project manager/project engineer, 1990-. **ORGANIZATIONS:** Overseas Chinese Environmental Engineers and Scientists Association, 1991-; Pennsylvania State Alumni Association, 1990-; American Water Works Association, 1986-90; Water Pollution Control Federation, 1986-90; Phi Lambda Upsilon Honorary Chemical Society, 1983. **HONORS/AWARDS:** Chromatography Forum of Delaware Valley, Student Award Symposium, 1988. **SPECIAL ACHIEVEMENTS:** Proceedings of the Environmental Engineering Sessions at Water Forum '92, ASCE, 1992; Journal of Environmental Engineering, ASCE, 1991; Journal of Chromatography, 1990; AIChE Journal, 1988; Journal of American Water Works Association, 1988. **MILITARY SERVICE:** Artillery, Chinese Army, 2nd lt, 1979-81. **HOME ADDRESS:** 10706 Westcastle Pl T-1, Cockeysville, MD 21030, (410)667-4829. **BUSINESS ADDRESS:** Project Manager, Gannett Fleming Inc, 200 E Quad, The Village of Cross Keys, Baltimore, MD 21210, (410)433-8832.

LEUNG, BENJAMIN SHUET-KIN (BENJAMIN XERJEN LIANG)
Educator, educational administrator. Chinese American. **PERSONAL:** Born Jun 30, 1938, Hong Kong; son of Frank Yun Pei Leung and Kan-Yan Leung; married Helen T Hsu Leung, Oct 19, 1964; children: Kay, Titus, Steven. **EDUCATION:** Hong Kong Baptist College, Hong Kong, chemistry & zoology, 1960-61; Seattle Pacific College, BS, chemistry, 1963; Colorado State University, PhD, biochemistry, 1969; Vanderbilt University, postdoctoral fellow, 1969-71. **CAREER:** Pacific Northwest Research Foundation, research assistant, 1964-66; Vanderbilt University, Department of Ob/Gyn, postdoctoral fellow, 1969-71; Oregon Health Sciences Center, Dept of Surgery, assistant to associate professor, Clinical Research Center Lab, director, 1971-76; Cedars-Sinai Medical Center, senior research scientist, 1976-78; University of Minnesota, Department of Ob/Gyn and Animal Sci, associate professor, director of res, 1978-84, Div Cell Biology, director, professor, 1984-, dir of grad studies, 1990-. **ORGANIZATIONS:** American Association for the Advancement of Science; American Association for Cancer Research Inc; American Society of Biological Chemists; Endocrine Society; Society of Chinese Bioscientists in America, lifetime member; New York Academy of Science; Society for Gynecologic Investigation. **HONORS/AWARDS:** Minnesota Ob/Gyn Society, honorary membership; National Institutes of Health, Predoctoral Fellowship, 1966-70; Ford Foundation, Postdoctoral Fellowship, 1970-71; NIH, NCI, American Cancer Society & other private foundations, 33 grant awards, 1971-; Fed Am Soc Exptl Bio, visiting professor program, 1982, 1990. **SPECIAL ACHIEVEMENTS:** Over 83 publications in scientific journals in the field of breast and gynecologic cancer, 1991-93; editor, 2 Vol, Hormonal Reg of Mammary Tumors, Eden Press, 1982; ad hoc editor for many scientific journals, 1972-; ad hoc member of study sections for NIH, NCI, and other grant funding agencies. **BUSINESS ADDRESS:** Professor & Director, Div of Cell Biology, Dept of Obstetric & Gynecology, University of Minnesota, 420 Delaware St SE, Box 395 UMHC, Minneapolis, MN 55455-0374, (612)626-3967.

LEUNG, CHARLES CHEUNG-WAN
Semiconductor company executive. Hong Kong American. **PERSONAL:** Born Jun 27, 1946, Hong Kong; son of Leung Mo-Fan and Tam Lai-Ping; married Jessica Lee, Sep 1, 1971; children: Jennifer, Cheryl, Albert. **EDUCATION:** University of Hong Kong, BSc (honors), 1969; University of Chicago, MS, 1971, PhD, 1975. **CAREER:** Corning, senior member of technical staff, 1975-79; Motorola, senior member of technical staff, 1979-81; Avantek Inc, engineering manager, 1981-88; Bipolarics Inc, chairman, president, founder, 1988-. **ORGANIZATIONS:** Asian American Manufacturers Association, 1988-; IEEE, 1979-; American Physical Society, 1972-; American Vacuum Society, 1972-. **HONORS/AWARDS:** Canada, British Commonwealth Scholarship, 1968. **SPECIAL ACHIEVEMENTS:** US patent 4,672,023; 20 publications in scientific journals. **BUSINESS ADDRESS:** President, Bipolarics Inc, 108 Albright Way, Los Gatos, CA 95030, (408)379-4543.

LEUNG, CHI KIN
Educator. Chinese American. **PERSONAL:** Born Nov 13, 1958; married. **EDUCATION:** Chinese University of Hong Kong, BSSc, 1981; University of Sydney, MTCP, 1983; University of Hawaii at Manoa, PhD, 1989. **CAREER:** State Government of New South Wales, data and systems consultant, 1983; University of Hawaii at Manoa, teaching/research assistant, 1984-87; East-West Center, research assistant, 1988; California State University, Fresno, assistant professor, 1989-. **ORGANIZATIONS:** Association of American Geographers, 1982-; American Society of Photogrammetry and Remote Sensing, 1989-; Institute of British Geographers, 1992-. **SPECIAL ACHIEVEMENTS:** "Personal Contacts, Subcontracting Linkages, and Development in the Hong Kong-Zhujiang Delta Region," Annals of the Assn of American Geographers, 83(2): 272-302, 1993; with C T Wu, Research and Development among Hong Kong Manufacturers, a Report to the Hong Kong University of Science and Technology, 1992; "Shanxi Energy Base: Planning Principles and Regional Development Implications," G Veeck, ed, The Uneven Landscape: Geographical Studies in Post-Reform China, pp 125-49, 1991; "Locational Characteristics of Foreign Equity Joint Venture Investment in China, 1979-85," The Professional Geographer, 42(4):403-21, 1990; language proficiency: Chinese, English. **BUSINESS ADDRESS:** Assistant Professor, Dept of Geography, California State University, Fresno, 2555 East San Ramon Avenue, Fresno, CA 93740-0069, (209)278-2845.

LEUNG, CHRISTOPHER CHUNG-KIT
Educator, scientist. Chinese American. **PERSONAL:** Born Jan 3, 1939, Hong Kong; son of Nai Kuen Leung and Sau Wah Chan; married Stella M Tang, Apr 11, 1970; children: Jacquelyn W Y, Therese S Y. **EDUCATION:** Jefferson Medical College, PhD, 1969. **CAREER:** Jefferson Medical College, from assistant professor to associate professor, 1969-75; University of Kansas School of Medicine, assistant professor, 1975-79; Louisiana State University School of Medicine, associate professor, 1979-85; New Jersey Medical School, associate professor, 1985-. **ORGANIZATIONS:** American Association of Immunologists, 1971-; American Association of Anatomists, 1969-; American Society of Cell Biology, 1975-; Teratology Society, 1969-. **HONORS/AWARDS:** National Institutes of Health, research grants, 1978-89; New Jersey Medical School, Exceptional Merit Award, 1986, Golden Apple Award for Best Teaching, 1993; Louisiana State University School of Medicine, Dean's Research Achievement Award, 1984. **SPECIAL ACHIEVEMENTS:** Published 23 research articles in research journals, 1969-93. **BUSINESS ADDRESS:** Associate Professor, New Jersey Medical School, 185 S Orange Ave, Medical Science Bldg G-683, Newark, NJ 07103, (201)982-4330.

LEUNG, CHUNG-NGOC
Physicist. Chinese American. **PERSONAL:** Born May 12, 1956, Macao; son of Shu Fan Leung and Jung Fung Nee; married Lily Leung. **EDUCATION:** University of Minnesota, BS, 1977, PhD, 1983. **CAREER:** Fermi National Accelerator Laboratory, research associate, 1983-85; Max-Planck-Institut fur Physik und Astrophysik, Munich, Germany, research sciencist, 1986-87; Purdue University, research associate, 1985-89; University of Delaware, assistant professor, 1989-. **ORGANIZATIONS:** American Physical Society. **BUSINESS ADDRESS:** Asst Prof, Dept of Physics and Astronomy, University of Delaware, Newark, DE 19716.

LEUNG, DENNIS B.
Import/export company executive. Chinese American. **PERSONAL:** Born Sep 1, 1945, Hong Kong; son of Martin Leung; married Tess Leung, 1967; children: Christina. **EDUCATION:** Hong Kong University, BA, 1964; California Coast University, BA, 1976, MBA, 1980. **CAREER:** Levi Strauss & Co, chief accountant, 1979-81; Monsac Ltd, president, 1982-88; Johnson Controls Intl Inc, financial controller, 1989-91; US Worldwide Sourcing Inc, president, 1992-. **HOME ADDRESS:** 367 Live Oak Dr, Danville, CA 94506. **BUSINESS PHONE:** (415)543-4848.

LEUNG, EDWIN PAK-WAH
Educator. Hong Kong American/Chinese American. **PERSONAL:** Born Aug 2, 1950, Hong Kong; son of Leung Liu and Lee Shui; married Vera, Aug 21, 1977; children: Immanuel. **EDUCATION:** Chinese University of Hong Kong, BA, 1972; University of California, MA, 1974, PhD, 1978. **CAREER:** Seton Hall University, assistant professor, 1978-84, associate professor, 1984-82, professor, 1992-; Wuhan University, visiting professor, 1983, 1989, 1993; Princeton University, visiting fellow, 1986; Columbia University, visiting university faculty, NEH scholar, 1986; University of Hong Kong, visiting fellow, 1992-93. **ORGANIZATIONS:** Asia Center, Seton Hall University,

senior fellow, 1990-; Hong Kong Club of New Jersey, vice president, 1992-; Livingston Chinese School, board director, 1991-. **HONORS/AWARDS:** Choice, Outstanding Academic Book, 1992; Chinese Student Association of Seton Hall University, Outstanding Service Award, 1992; Livingston Chinese School, Outstanding Service Award, 1993. **SPECIAL ACHIEVEMENTS:** Author, Historical Dictionary of Revolutionary China, 1992; Modern Changes in Chinese Diplomacy, 1990; China & the West, 1988; Ethnic Compartmentalization and Regional Autonomy in the People's Republic of China, 1982. **BUSINESS ADDRESS:** Professor, Dept of Asian Studies, Seton Hall University, South Orange Ave, South Orange, NJ 07079-2697, (201)761-9000.

LEUNG, IDA M.
Financial planner. Chinese American. **PERSONAL:** Born Dec 29, 1951, Oakland, CA; daughter of Moy Yook Moon and Fook Leung; married Francis LeB Montgomery, Jan 4, 1982; children: Sarah Montgomery. **EDUCATION:** Barnard College, BA. **CAREER:** Manufacturers Hanover Trust Co, asst vice pres, 1977-87; IDS Financial Services, financial planner, 1987-. **ORGANIZATIONS:** IBCFP, 1987-; Clinton Library Board, trustee, 1992-; Natl Women's Political Caucus, 1988-. **BUSINESS ADDRESS:** Financial Planner, IDS Financial Services, PO Box 127, Clinton Corners, NY 12514, (914)266-8399.

LEUNG, JOSEPH YUK-TONG
Educator, educational administrator. Hong Kong American. **PERSONAL:** Born Jun 25, 1950, Hong Kong; son of Kun Leung and Fung Leung; married Maria Leung, Jan 1983; children: Jonathan. **EDUCATION:** Southern Illinois University, BS, 1972; Pennsylvania State University, PhD, 1977. **CAREER:** Virginia Technology, assistant professor, 1976-77; Northwestern University, associate professor, 1977-85; University of Texas, Dallas, professor, 1985-90; University of Nebraska-Lincoln, professor and chairman, 1990-. **ORGANIZATIONS:** IEEE, senior member, 1978-; ACM, 1974-. **SPECIAL ACHIEVEMENTS:** Published many technical papers. **BUSINESS ADDRESS:** Prof & Chmn, Dept of Computer Science & Eng, University of Nebraska-Lincoln, 115 Ferguson Hall, Lincoln, NE 68588-0115, (402)472-3200.

LEUNG, KA-WING
Television journalist. Chinese American. **PERSONAL:** Born Dec 19, 1952, Hong Kong; son of Ip-Lam Leung and Sau-Ying Chau; married Rebecca Leung, Jul 8, 1988; children: Jianjia, Qin. **EDUCATION:** Hong Kong Baptist College, diploma in communication, w/honors, 1975. **CAREER:** HK-TVB, managing editor/anchor, 1977-91; KTSF, managing editor/anchor, 1991-. **BUSINESS ADDRESS:** Managing Editor, KTSF-TV, Channel 26, 100 Valley Dr, Brisbane, CA 94005, (415)468-2626.

LEUNG, KAI-CHEONG
Educator. Hong Kong American. **PERSONAL:** Born Jun 19, 1936, Hong Kong; son of S K Leung; married Alice Tse Leung; children: Christopher, Cynthia. **EDUCATION:** University of Hong Kong, BA (honors), Dip Ed, MA, 1963; University of Leeds, PDES, 1966; University of California, Berkeley, PhD, 1974. **CAREER:** Queen Elizabeth College, 1960-61; Hong Kong Government, Education Department, 1961-64; Grantham College of Education, 1964-69; San Jose State Univ, assistant prof/professor, 1974-. **ORGANIZATIONS:** Chinese Language Teachers Assn of California, chair, 1978-80, 1989-; California State Dept of Education, Advisory Committee on the Teaching of Chinese, 1989-92; Foreign Language Assn of Northern California, executive council, 1979-81; Asian Studies Center, San Jose State Univ, board of directors, 1989-; Assn of Bay Area Chinese Schools, executive board, 1979-81; Bay Area Bilingual Education League, University Representative, Bilingual Education Certification Panel, 1979-81; Canadian Research Council for Social Sciences & Humanities, assessor, 1988-90. **HONORS/AWARDS:** Kong University Bursary, 1956-60; British Commonwealth University Bursary to study at Leeds, 1965-66; San Jose State University, Merit Award, 1988, Deans Grants, 1993, 1988, 1990, Research Grant. **SPECIAL ACHIEVEMENTS:** Hsu Wei as Drama Critic, University of Oregon, 1988; "Visions of Cathay," Tsing Hua Journal of Chinese Studies, Dec 1979; "Ten Ming Songs," A Brotherhood in Song, ed S C Soong, Hong Kong, 1985; "Literature in the Service of Politics," World Literature Today, Winter 1981; numerous articles and reviews, poetry readings, 1983. **BUSINESS ADDRESS:** Professor, Dept of Foreign Languages, San Jose State Univ, San Jose, CA 95192, (408)924-4623.

LEUNG, KENNETH CH'UAN-K'AI
Financial analyst. Chinese American. **PERSONAL:** Born Jul 5, 1944, Washington, DC; son of Frank B Leung and Jean Yang; married Margaret Monsor

Leung, Aug 20, 1983; children: Darien Gabriel, Catherine Allen. **EDUCATION:** Fordham University, BA, 1967; Columbia University, MBA, 1970. **CAREER:** Chase Manhattan, credit analyst, 1967-68; Chemical Bank, assistant treasurer, 1968-69, 1970-74; Eberstadt, vice president, 1974-77; Smith Barney Shearson, manager director, 1977-. **ORGANIZATIONS:** Brooklyn Botanic Garden, trustee, 1991-. **BUSINESS ADDRESS:** Managing Director, Smith Barney Shearson, 1345 Avenue of Americas, 28th Fl, New York, NY 10105, (212)698-6258.

LEUNG, KOK MING
Educator. Chinese American. **PERSONAL:** Born Feb 17, 1951, Hong Kong; son of Sang Leung and Seon-Wan Chang; married Li-Hwa Hung, Oct 3, 1988; children: Alan, Stephanie. **EDUCATION:** University of Missouri, Kansas City, BS, 1972, Columbia, MS, 1973; University of Wisconsin, PhD, 1979. **CAREER:** University of Missouri-Columbia, teaching assistant, 1972-73; University of Wisconsin, teaching assistant, 1973-76, research assistant, 1976-79, University of California, Santa Barbara, postdoctoral fellow, 1979-82; Polytechnic University, assistant professor of physics, 1982-88, associate professor of physics, 1988-90, professor of physics, 1990-. **ORGANIZATIONS:** American Physical Association, 1975-; Optical Society of America, 1985-; Electromagnetics Academy, 1989-; Overseas Chinese Physics Association, lifetime member, 1989-; Chinese Student Association at Polytechnic University, faculty advisor, 1992-. **HONORS/AWARDS:** Sigma Pi Sigma, 1971-; Electromagnetics Academy, 1989. **SPECIAL ACHIEVEMENTS:** Over 60 research publications in science journals, 1975-; co-organizer of Microparticle Photophysics Seminar/Workshop, 1984; National Science Foundation Workshop on Future Directions in Electromagnetics Research, panel member, 1989; Office of Naval Technology, National Institute of Standards and Technology Postdoctoral Fellowship Program, review panel, 1990; Army Research Office Workshop on the Development and Application of Photonic Band Gap Structures, panel member, 1992. **HOME ADDRESS:** 1045 Kingsland Lane, Fort Lee, NJ 07024, (201)224-3706. **BUSINESS ADDRESS:** Professor, Physics Dept, Polytech University, 333 Jay St, Nichols 212, Brooklyn, NY 11201-2990, (718)260-3380.

LEUNG, LOUIS W.
Educator. Chinese American. **PERSONAL:** Born Oct 19, 1954, Hong Kong; son of Lam Lai Ping & Leung Mei Chuen. **EDUCATION:** University of Texas, Austin, BS, 1980, MA, 1984, PhD, 1989. **CAREER:** University of Texas, Austin, lecturer & computer coordinator, 1988-91; University of Hawaii, assistant professor, 1991-. **ORGANIZATIONS:** International Communication Association, 1991; Association for Education in Journalism & Mass Communication, 1991; Society of Advanced Learning Technology, 1991. **SPECIAL ACHIEVEMENTS:** Author: "The Information Economy," Sage Publications, 1988; "The Adoption of Multimedia Instructional Technology," Pacific Telecommunication Proceedings, 1993. **BUSINESS ADDRESS:** Assistant Professor, Dept of Communication, University of Hawaii, Honolulu, HI 96822, (808)956-3347.

LEUNG, MARGARET W.
Certified public accountant. Hong Kong American. **PERSONAL:** Born Jul 21, 1964, Kowloon, Hong Kong. **EDUCATION:** Loyola Marymount University, BA, finance, marketing, 1983; UCLA, certificate, advertising management, 1985. **CAREER:** Ogilvy & Mather, media assistant; Automatic Data Processing, sr account executive; Tech Power Inc, branch general mgr; Coopers & Lybrand, associate consultant, currently. **ORGANIZATIONS:** Delta Sigma Pi. **HONORS/AWARDS:** US Small Business Administration. **BUSINESS ADDRESS:** Associate Consultant, Coopers & Lybrand, 350 S Grand Ave, Los Angeles, CA 90071, (213)356-6000.

LEUNG, PAK SANG
Scientist. Chinese American. **PERSONAL:** Born Jun 8, 1935, Shanghai, China; son of Yat Wing Leung and Kin Fong Chan; married Priscilla Han Heung Chan, Dec 7, 1965; children: Kent H, Ross H. **EDUCATION:** National Taiwan University, BSc, 1957; Columbia University, MA, 1962, PhD, 1967. **CAREER:** Hong Kong Baptist College, demonstrator, 1959-61; Brookhaven National Laboratory, research scientist, 1966-67; Union Carbide Corporation, senior research scientist, 1967-93; Orange County College, lecturer, 1993-. **ORGANIZATIONS:** American Chemical Society, colloid division, 1967; Sigma Xi, 1967; Orange County Chinese Association, president, 1990-92. **SPECIAL ACHIEVEMENTS:** 35 published in scientific journals; 11 U S patents. **HOME ADDRESS:** 15 Woodland Rd, Highland Mills, NY 10930, (914)928-6838.

LEUNG, PETER
Toxicologist. Chinese American. **PERSONAL:** Born Apr 12, 1955, New York, NY; son of Richard Leung and Yim C Leung. **EDUCATION:** Johns Hopkins University, BA, 1977; State University of NY, Health Science Center at Brooklyn, PhD, 1983. **CAREER:** State University of New York, teaching assistant, 1978-83; Texas A & M University, postdoctoral fellow, 1983-86; Schering-Plough Corp, senior scientist, 1986-89; State of California, EPA, staff toxicologist, 1989-. **ORGANIZATIONS:** Society of Toxicology, 1988-; American Society for Pharmacology & Experimental Therapeutics, 1989-; American College of Toxicology, 1989-. **HONORS/AWARDS:** US Public Health Service, predoctoral fellowship, 1978-83; National Institutes of Health, postdoctoral fellowship, 1983-86; American Society for Pharmacology & Experimental Therapeutics, travel award, 1984. **SPECIAL ACHIEVEMENTS:** Certification: Diplomate of the American Board of Toxicology, 1987; doctoral dissertation: "Modulation of Murine Fetal Liver Erythroid Colony Formation by Glucocorticoids," 1983. **BUSINESS ADDRESS:** Staff Toxicologist, Dept of Pesticide Regulation, CA/EPA, Medical Toxicology Branch, 1020 N St, Sacramento, CA 95814, (916)324-3470.

LEUNG, PINGSUN
Educator. Hong Kong American. **PERSONAL:** Born Mar 27, 1952, Hong Kong; son of Chuen Leung and Sui Ha Kam; married Mildred Lai Yew Leung, Jun 4, 1978; children: Shelton Siu Wah, Lorina Mei Ling. **EDUCATION:** University of Hawaii, BBA, business economics & statistics, 1973, MS, information & computer sciences, 1975, MS, agricultural & resource economics, 1977, PhD, agricultural systems analysis, 1977. **CAREER:** State of Hawaii, econometrician, 1978-81; University of Hawaii, lecturer of decision sciences, 1978-81; Japan-American Institute of Management Science, lecturer, 1980-81; East-West Center, research fellow, 1986, 1990; Jilin University, Fulbright professor of management science, 1987-88; University of Hawaii, graduate chair of agricultural & resource economics, 1989-91, professor of agricultural & resource economics, 1981-. **ORGANIZATIONS:** American Agricultural Economics Association, 1981-; World Aquaculture Society, 1988-; International Society on Multiple Criteria Decision Making, 1989-; International Institute of Fisheries Economics & Trade, 1990-; Fulbright Association, 1988-90. **HONORS/AWARDS:** Fulbright Award, 1987-88; Gamma Sigma Delta, Outstanding Researcher, 1989; University of Hawaii, Presidential Citation for Meritorious Teaching, 1990; Jilin University, honorary guest professor, 1992; National Taiwan Ocean University, honorary guest professor, 1992. **SPECIAL ACHIEVEMENTS:** Recent publications: "Optimal Harvest Age for Giant Clam Tridacna Derasa: An Economic Analysis," Journal of Applied Aquaculture, 1993; "Minimum Cost Palatable Diet: A Pilot Study," Agricultural Systems, 1992; Bioeconomic Modeling of Shrimp and Prawn: A Methodological Comparison, 1993; Soviet-Asian Minerals Trade: Past Performance and Future Outlook, 1993; Intensive Grazing Management: Forage, Animals, Men, Profits, 1986; author and co-author of over 80 journal articles, books, and research reports. **BUSINESS ADDRESS:** Professor, Agricultural & Resource Economics Dept, University of Hawaii, 3050 Maile Way, Gilmore Hall 115, Honolulu, HI 96822, (808)956-8562.

LEUNG, PUI-TAK (PETER)
Educator, research scientist. Hong Kong American/Chinese American. **PERSONAL:** Born Aug 23, 1953, Macau, People's Republic of China; son of Chin-Pang Leung & Hon-Yin Luk; married Pei-Yi Feng, Apr 19, 1985; children: Jonathan Li-Chung, Rosalyn Roh-Shi. **EDUCATION:** Chinese University of Hong Kong, BSc, 1976; State University of New York, Buffalo, MEd, 1979, MA, 1979, PhD, 1982. **CAREER:** Tamkang University, Taiwan, associate professor of physics, 1982-83; State University of New York, Buffalo, research associate, 1985-88; Portland State University, assistant professor of physics, 1988-91; Amersham International PLC, England, consultant, biosensor research, 1989-92; IBM Almaden Research Center, visiting scientist, 1991-92; Portland State University, associate professor of physics, 1991-. **ORGANIZATIONS:** American Physical Society, 1992-. **HONORS/AWARDS:** Portland State University, Outstanding Junior Faculty Award, 1992; IBM, Visiting Scientist Fellowship, 1991. **SPECIAL ACHIEVEMENTS:** Consultant, Amersham International plc in England on Biosensor Research, 1989-92; 46 publications in refereed professional journals, including, with others, "Transient Optical Transmission Measurement in Excimer-Laser Irradiation of Amorphous Silicon Films," Journal of Heat Transfer, 115, p178-183, 1993; "Nonlocal Electrodynamic Modeling of Frequency Shifts of Molecules at Rough Metal Surfaces," Journal of Chemical Phys, 98, p5019-5022, 1993; invited visitor, Pollards Wood Laboratories in England, 1989; invited speaker, Society of Photo-Optical Instrumentation Engineers Conference, 1989. **HOME**

ADDRESS: 3342 NW Brandt Place, Portland, OR 97229, (503)645-4513. BUSINESS ADDRESS: Associate Professor of Physics, Portland State University, PO Box 751, Portland, OR 97207-0751, (503)725-3818.

LEUNG, SOM-LOK
Management consultant. Hong Kong American. PERSONAL: Born Dec 5, 1965, Hong Kong; son of Yee and Yuet-wah. EDUCATION: Harvard University, BA, psychology (summa cum laude), 1988. CAREER: Oliver Wyman & Co, associate, 1988-. ORGANIZATIONS: Harvard Club of New York, 1988-. BUSINESS ADDRESS: Associate, Oliver Wyman & Co, 666 Fifth Ave, 16th Fl, New York, NY 10103, (212)541-8100.

LEUNG, WING HAI
Educator. Hong Kong American. PERSONAL: Born Jul 29, 1937, Hong Kong; son of Ju-Dug and Ping-Fan; married Lai-Yin, Aug 12, 1965; children: Kar-Woo (Billy), Kar-Hong (Michael), Kiar-Peck (Patrick). EDUCATION: Hong Kong University, BSc (honors), 1963; University of Miami, MS, 1970, PhD, 1974. CAREER: State University of New York, Buffalo, research associate, 1974-76; GAF, senior chemist, 1976-77; Clinton Cora Corp, research scientist, 1977-78; Hampton Institute, assistant professor, 1978-82; Hampton University, associate professor, 1982-. ORGANIZATIONS: American Chemical Society, 1971-; American Geophysical Union, 1976-; Sigma Xi, 1970-. HONORS/AWARDS: NASA, research grant, 1982. SPECIAL ACHIEVEMENTS: Contributed articles to professional journals. BUSINESS ADDRESS: Associate Professor, Hampton University, E Queen St, Turner Hall, Hampton, VA 23668.

LEUNG, WOON-FONG (WALLACE)
Scientist. Chinese American. PERSONAL: Born Jan 25, 1954, Hong Kong; son of Lam Leung and So-Wan Cheung; married Stella P Leung, Jun 25, 1978; children: Jessica W Y, Jeffrey K W. EDUCATION: Cornell University, BSc, mech & aerospace eng, 1977; MIT, SM, mech eng, 1978, ScD, 1981. CAREER: Gulf Research & Development Company, research engineer, 1981-84; Schlumberger Technology, project leader, 1984-86; Bird Machine Company, senior reserach scientist, 1986-. ORGANIZATIONS: American Filtration & Separation Society, 1988-92; director, 1993; American Society of Mechanical Engineers, 1981-; Society of Petroleum Engineers, 1981-; American Institute of Aeronautics & Astronautics, 1981-88; Society of Rheology, 1990-93. HONORS/AWARDS: American Filtration & Separation Society, Engineering Merit Award, 1991; Baker Hughes, Technical Achievement Award, 1992; Society of Petroleum Engineers, Cedric Ferguson Award, 1987; Cornell University, Sibiley Award, 1977. SPECIAL ACHIEVEMENTS: 5 pending patents holder; 13 published articles; editor of Adv Sep Technology, 700 pages; 300+ in-house technical reports; author, Perry and Chilton's 7th edition, Chemical Engineers' Handbook on Centrifuges, 1994; organizer & chairman of largest technical AFS meeting on separation technology, with 176 oral presentations, 1993; organizer of Chinese musical instrumental concert at MIT, 1991, 800 attendees. BIOGRAPHICAL SOURCES: Chemical Index. BUSINESS ADDRESS: Sr Research Scientist, Bird Machine Co, 100 Neponset St, South Walpole, MA 02071.

LEUNG, YUEN-SANG (PHILIP)
Educator. Hong Kong American. PERSONAL: Born Oct 29, 1949, Hong Kong; son of S T Leung; married Hau-Ming Yu, Feb 28, 1976; children: Hans, Nathan, Barbara. EDUCATION: BA, 1972; MPhil, 1974; PhD, 1980. CAREER: National University of Singapore, lecturer, senior lecturer, 1980-87; California State University, Los Angeles, associate professor, 1986-. ORGANIZATIONS: Chinese American Faculty Association, Southern California, president, 1993-94; Society for Confucian Studies, president, 1991-92; Chinese American Professional Association, 1987-93. HONORS/AWARDS: CSLA, Outstanding Professor Award, 1989. SPECIAL ACHIEVEMENTS: The Shanghai Taotai: Linkage Man in a Changing Society, 1843-90, Singapore University Press, Hawaii University Press, 1990; Young J Allen in China (in Chinese), Chinese University Press, 1978. BUSINESS ADDRESS: Professor, History Dept, California State University, Los Angeles, 5151 State University Dr, Los Angeles, CA 90032, (213)343-2044.

LEW, ALAN AUGUST
Educator. Chinese American. PERSONAL: Born Apr 13, 1955, Sacramento, CA; son of Gimpock P Lew and Inger Ida Lew; married Mable Wong Lew, Dec 26, 1987; children: Lauren, Skylan, Chynna. EDUCATION: University of Hawaii, Hilo, BA, 1981; University of Oregon, MA, 1983, MUP, 1983, PhD, 1986. CAREER: University of Tubingen, Germany, visiting professor, 1989;

Northern Arizona University, associate professor, 1986-. ORGANIZATIONS: Association of Pacific Coast Geographers, secretary, treasurer, 1993-; Arizona Geographic Information Council, board member, 1990-; Tourism Recreation Research Journal, resource editor, 1993-; Arizona Planning Association, academic liaison, 1989-90. HONORS/AWARDS: American Institute of Certified Planners, certification, 1991. SPECIAL ACHIEVEMENTS: Articles in: Annuals of Tourism Research, Journal of Geography, Journal of Cultural Geography, Journal of Travel Research, Journal of the Urban and Regional Information Systems Association, The Professional Geographer, etc. BUSINESS ADDRESS: Professor, Dept of Geo & Public Planning, Northern Arizona University, Box 15016, Flagstaff, AZ 86011-5016, (602)523-6567.

LEW, EUGENE
Architect. Chinese American. PERSONAL: Born Feb 22, 1937, White Plains, NY; son of Frank Lew and Hong Gay Lew; married Ellen J-L Chang, Sep 18, 1960; children: Stefanie Ellen. EDUCATION: Harvard College, AB, MD, 1958; Harvard Graduate School of Design, BArch, 1961, MArch, 1970; University of California, MArch, 1962. CAREER: Sert, Jackson & Gourley, designer, 1961; DeMars & Reay, designer, 1963-66; Roger Lee & Associates, associate, 1966-69; EPR, partner, 1969-73; Eugene Lew & Associates, president, 1973-. ORGANIZATIONS: American Institute of Architects, corp member, 1966-, Housing Committee, past chair; Institute of Business Designers, 1970-; Junior Achievement, director, 1983-87; Enterprise for High School Students, director, 1981-86; Harvard Club of San Francisco, director, 1989-92. HONORS/AWARDS: Phi Beta Kappa, 1958; Institute of International Education, Fulbright Fellowship, 1962; AIA, Honolulu Chapter, Honor Award, 1966; University of California Art Museum Design Competition, Second Place, 1966; City of Miami, Biscayne West Competition, hon mention, 1976. SPECIAL ACHIEVEMENTS: Paxson Apts, House & Home, 1966; Architect's Office, Japan Architect, 1976; UC Art Center Design, Art Forum, 1966; thesis, Architectural Forum, 1961. BUSINESS ADDRESS: President, Eugene Lew & Associates, 222 Kearny St, Suite 300, San Francisco, CA 94108, (415)433-4204.

LEW, GLORIA MARIA
Educator. Chinese American. PERSONAL: Born Mar 7, 1934, Kingston, Jamaica; daughter of Mr & Mrs George Lew. EDUCATION: Mt St Vincent College, BA, biology & Latin, 1956; Boston College, MS, biology, 1958; University of California, Berkeley, PhD, zoology, 1972. CAREER: University of California, Berkeley, research assistant; Michigan State University, professor of anatomy, currently. ORGANIZATIONS: American Society of Neuroscience, 1980-; American Society of Neurochemistry, 1991-; American Association of Anatomists, 1972-; American Society of Zoologists, 1972-. HONORS/AWARDS: American Association of University Women, fellowship, 1971; Margaret McGee Award for Scholarship, 1956. HOME PHONE: (517)351-3117. BUSINESS ADDRESS: Professor of Anatomy, Michigan State University, Grand River Ave, Giltner Hall, East Lansing, MI 48824.

LEW, RONALD S. W.
Judge. Chinese American. PERSONAL: Born Sep 19, 1941, Los Angeles, CA; married Mamie Gee Lew; children: Leslie, Leila, Lorelei, David. EDUCATION: Loyola University, Los Angeles, BA, political science, 1964; Southwestern University School of Law, JD, 1971. CAREER: Los Angeles City Attorney's Office, deputy city attorney, 1972-74; Avans and Lew, partner, 1974-82; City of Los Angeles, fire and police pension, commissioner, 1976-82; County of Los Angeles, municipal court judge, 1982-84; superior court judge, 1984-87; US District Court, Central District, judge, 1987-. ORGANIZATIONS: California State Bar; American Judicature Society, 1983-; California Judges Assn, 1982-; California Asian Judges Assn, 1982-; Southern California Chinese Lawyers Assn, 1976-; California Assembly Los Angeles Court Improvement Commission; Minority Bar Assn of Southern California, 1977-82; Los Angeles County Municipal Court Judges Assn, 1982-84; Los Angeles County Bar Assn, 1972-; Judicial Education & Research Assn. HONORS/AWARDS: United Way of Los Angeles, Volunteer Award, 1979; Los Angeles Human Relations Commission, Certificate of Merit, 1977, 1982. MILITARY SERVICE: US Army, 1st lt, 1967-69. BUSINESS ADDRESS: US District Judge, US District Court, Central District of California, 312 North Spring St, Los Angeles, CA 90012, (213)894-3508.

LEW, SUSIE Q.
Physician. Chinese American. PERSONAL: Born Oct 28, 1954, New York, NY; married. EDUCATION: Brooklyn College, BS, 1976; SUNY Downstate Medical Center, MD, 1979. CAREER: George Washington University, physi-

cian, assistant professor, 1985-. **ORGANIZATIONS:** American College of Physicians, fellow, 1985; American Society of Nephrology, 1985; International Society of Nephrology, 1985; American Society of Artifical Organs; Chinese Medical & Health Association. **BUSINESS ADDRESS:** Assistant Professor, George Washington University, 2150 Pennsylvania Avenue NW, Room 4-425, Washington, DC 20037, (202)994-4244.

LEW, WILLIAM W.
Educator. Chinese American. **PERSONAL:** Born May 7, 1941, Seattle, WA; son of Mr and Mrs Geat Song Lew; married Aimee Toyoko Lew, Feb 21, 1966; children: David, Kristen, Damon. **EDUCATION:** Central Washington State College, BA, 1964; University of Oregon, MFA, 1966; Ohio University, PhD, 1976. **CAREER:** University of Kansas Museum of Art, registrar, 1971-73; Washburn University of Topeka, assistant professor of art, 1973-77; Murray State University, assistant professor of art, 1977-82; Weber State College, assistant professor of art, curator of art gallery, 1982-85; University of Northern Iowa, Dept of Art, professor and head, 1985-. **ORGANIZATIONS:** College Art Association of America; National Association of Schools of Art and Design; National Council of Art Administrators. **HONORS/AWARDS:** Rockefeller Foundation, speaker/chair travel grant, 1993; National Endowment for Humanities, Summer Institute, 1991; Iowa Arts Council, mini-grant, 1989; Iowa Humanities Board, Small Grants Award, 1987, 1988. **SPECIAL ACHIEVEMENTS:** Return of the Yellow Peril: The Works of Roger Shimomura, exhibition catalog, 1993; Chinese American Painters: Cheng, Choy, Gee & Yehp, exhibition catalog, 1992; Dennis Gould Retrospective Exhibition 1967-87, exhibition catalog, 1987, "Journey to Minidoka: The Paintings of Roger Shimomura," 1984; Unbuilt Utah An Exhibition of Architectural Models, exhibition catalog, 1984. **BUSINESS ADDRESS:** Head, Dept of Art, University of Northern Iowa, Cedar Falls, IA 50614, (319)273-2077.

LEWIS, LOIDA NICOLAS
Foods company executive, attorney. Filipino American. **PERSONAL:** married Reginald Lewis (died 1993). **CAREER:** Immigration and Naturalization Services, immigration attorney, until 1990; TLC Beatrice International Holdings Inc, board of directors, 1993-, chair, 1994-. **SPECIAL ACHIEVEMENTS:** Coauthor, How to Get a Green Card: Legal Ways To Stay in the USA, 1993. **BUSINESS ADDRESS:** Chair, TLC Beatrice International Holdings Inc, 9 W 57th St, 48th fl, New York, NY 10019. *

LI, BICHUAN
Educator, musician. Chinese American. **PERSONAL:** Born Oct 30, 1951, Shanghai, People's Republic of China; daughter of Pei Pei Lin and Xiao Da Li; divorced. **EDUCATION:** Shanghai Teachers University, BA, 1982; University of Hawaii, MM, 1985. **CAREER:** University of Hawaii, lecturer, 1986-. **ORGANIZATIONS:** Honolulu Piano Teachers' Association, president, 1989-91, 1992-93; Hawaii Music Teachers' Association, 1988-; Musicians' Association of Hawaii, 1985-. **HONORS/AWARDS:** Shanghai Teachers' University, honorary associate professor, 1991-. **SPECIAL ACHIEVEMENTS:** Chinese Piano Music, 1989-. **HOME PHONE:** (808)944-2977. **BUSINESS ADDRESS:** Lecturer, University of Hawaii, 2411 Dole Street, Honolulu, HI 96822-2398, (808)956-7756.

LI, BING AN
Educator. Chinese American. **PERSONAL:** Born May 24, 1941, Pingdu, Shandong, China; son of Mao-en Li & Yu-hua Pan; married Mei-man Zhang, May 28, 1968; children: Hao Xin Zhang, Jian Sheng. **EDUCATION:** University of Science & Technology of China, 1964; Institute of High Energy Physics, graduate study, PhD equivalent, 1968. **CAREER:** Institute of High Energy Physics of China, professor, 1985-88; Graduate School, Academia Sinica of China, professor, 1988; University of Kentucky, associate professor, 1988-90, professor, 1990-. **HONORS/AWARDS:** Academia Sinica of China, First Prize of Progress in Science and Technology, 1986. **SPECIAL ACHIEVEMENTS:** More than 80 papers have been published; research field: theoretical particle physics. **BUSINESS ADDRESS:** Professor, Dept of Physics & Astronomy, University of Kentucky, Rose Street, Chemistry/Physics Building, Room 377, Lexington, KY 40506, (606)257-1486.

LI, BOB CHENG-LIANG
Banking executive. Taiwanese American. **PERSONAL:** Born Sep 14, 1936, Taiwan; son of Su-Tu Li; married Betty H Li, Oct 30, 1960; children: John, Ivy. **EDUCATION:** National Taiwan University, BA, 1959; University of Oregon, MS, 1963; Stanford University, MS, 1967; University of Wisconsin, Madison, PhD, 1971. **CAREER:** University of Wisconsin, Madison, faculty, 1968-72;

The World Bank, division chief, 1972-. **ORGANIZATIONS:** Asian Economics Association, director of the board, 1988-. **BIOGRAPHICAL SOURCES:** Independent Evening Daily, edition 2, March 25, 1993; The Journalist, Taipei, p 18-20, March 28, 1993. **HOME ADDRESS:** 12 Baughman Ct, Silver Spring, MD 20906, (301)598-6223.

LI, C. C. (CHING CHUN)
Educator. Chinese American. **PERSONAL:** Born Oct 27, 1912, Tientsin, China; son of Li Jui & Li-Liu; married Clara Lem, Sep 20, 1941; children: Carol S, Steven M. **EDUCATION:** University of Nanking, Agricultural College, Nanking, China, BS, 1936; Cornell University, PhD, 1940; Columbia University, postdoctoral, 1940-41; University of Chicago, summer session, 1940. **CAREER:** Yenching University, agriculture experiment station, 1936-37; Agric College, Kwanghsi University, associate professor, 1943; University of Nanking, Chengdu, professor, 1943-46; Peking University, Department of Agronomy, professor and chairman, 1946-50; University of Pittsburgh, professor, 1951-69, Department of Biostatistics, chairman, 1969-75, retired 1982. **ORGANIZATIONS:** American Society of Human Genetics, president, 1960-61. **HONORS/AWARDS:** American Statistical Association, Pittsburgh Chapter, Statistician of the Year. **SPECIAL ACHIEVEMENTS:** Author of 8 books; translated 2 books from English to Chinese: Introduction to Experimental Statistics, McGraw-Hill; First Course in Population Genetics, Boxwood, CA; Path Analysis, A Primer, Boxwood Press, CA. **BIOGRAPHICAL SOURCES:** Ching Chun Li, Courageous Scholar of Population Genetics, Human Genetics, and Biostatistics, A Living History Essay, by Eliot B Spiess, American Journal of Medical Genetics, vol 16, p 603-630, 1983. **BUSINESS ADDRESS:** Professor, Dept of Human Genetics, Graduate School of Public Health, University of Pittsburgh, Pittsburgh, PA 15261, (412)624-5393.

LI, CHARLES N.
Educator, educational administrator. Chinese American. **PERSONAL:** Born Feb 6, 1940, Shanghai, China; son of Sheng-wu Li & Edith H Lee; married Katherine Saltzman Li, Apr 9, 1983; children: Rachel A, Gabriel E. **EDUCATION:** Bowdoin College, BA, 1963; Stanford University, 1963-66; University of California, Berkeley, PhD, 1971. **CAREER:** Linguistic Society of America, visiting assistant professor, 1976; UC, Santa Barbara, associate professor of linguistics, 1976-80, professor of linguistics, 1980-, professor of anthropology, 1984-, dean, graduate divison, 1989-. **ORGANIZATIONS:** Linguistic Society of America, 1967-; European Linguistic Society, 1984-; Society for the Study of Indigenous Languages of America, 1988-; AAAS, 1970-. **HONORS/ AWARDS:** Phi Beta Kappa, 1963; National Science Foundation, various research grants; National Endowment for Humanities, various research grants; American Council of Learned Societies, fellowship, 1975. **SPECIAL ACHIEVEMENTS:** Subject and Topic, ed, 1976; Mechanisms of Syntactic Change, ed, 1978; Word Order & Word Order Change, ed, 1975; Mandarin Chinese: A Functional Reference Grammar, 1981, 1989. **BUSINESS ADDRESS:** Dean, Graduate Division, University of California, Cheadle Hall, Santa Barbara, CA 93106, (805)893-2013.

LI, CHE-YU
Educator. Chinese American. **PERSONAL:** Born Nov 15, 1934, Hunan, China; son of Hsien-Wen & Elaine Li; married Myung Han, Jun 24, 1989; children: Michelle Kuehn, Mark, Jason. **EDUCATION:** Taiwan College of Engineering, BSE, 1954; Cornell University, PhD, 1960. **CAREER:** US Steel Research Center, Ford Foundation resident, 1965-66; Argonne National Labs, group leader, section chief, 1969-71; Cornell University, MSE, research associate, 1969-62, assistant professor, 1962-66, associate professor, 1966-72, professor, 1972-, Electronic Packaging Program, director, 1990-. **ORGANIZATIONS:** IEEE, Trans for Adv Packaging, editor, 1993-; APS; ASTM; ASM; AIME-TMS. **BUSINESS ADDRESS:** Professor, MSE, Director, Electronic Packaging Program, Cornell University, Bard Hall, Ithaca, NY 14853-1501, (607)255-4349.

LI, CHENG
Educator. Chinese American. **PERSONAL:** Born Oct 20, 1956, Shanghai, People's Republic of China; son of Yonggui Li and Zengjing Yao. **EDUCATION:** East China Normal University, BA, 1985; University of California, MA, 1987; Princeton University, MA, 1989, PhD, 1992. **CAREER:** University of California, Berkeley, visiting research associate, 1990; Hamilton College, assistant professor, 1991-. **ORGANIZATIONS:** Institute of Current World Affairs, fellow, 1993-; Association of Asian Studies, 1993-. **HONORS/ AWARDS:** Institute of Current World Affairs, Fellowship, 1993; Hamilton College, The Excellence in Teaching Award, 1993; Princeton University, Char-

lotte E Proctor Honorific Fellowship, 1990-91. **SPECIAL ACHIEVE-MENTS:** The Rise of Technocracy: Elite Transformation & Ideological Change in Post-Mao China, 1992; "China's Technocratic Movement & the World Economic Herald," Modern China, 1991; "Localism, Elitism, and Immobilism," World Politics, 1989; "Elite Transformation & Modern Change in Mainland China & Taiwan," China Quarterly, 1990; "From Mobilizers to Managers," Asian Survey, 1988. **BIOGRAPHICAL SOURCES:** "Hamilton Teacher Wins Class of 1963 Award," Observer-Dispatch p 3E, May 23, 1993; "California Dreaming," Asiaweek, pp34-49, December 4, 1987. **HOME ADDRESS:** 198 College Hill Rd, Clinton, NY 13323, (315)853-1903. **BUSINESS ADDRESS:** Professor, Dept of Government, Hamilton College, 198 College Hill Rd, Clinton, NY 13323.

LI, CHIA-CHUAN
Aerospace company manager. Taiwanese American. **PERSONAL:** Born Dec 29, 1946, Taipei, Taiwan; son of Weitong Li & San Huang Li; married Clemencia V Li, Nov 26, 1983; children: Angie, Andrew. **EDUCATION:** National Taiwan University, BS, 1969; Rutgers University, MS, 1974; University of Michigan, PhD, 1977; Pepperdine University, MBA, 1986. **CAREER:** General Atomic Co, senior engineer, 1977-84; Hughes Aircraft Co, systems engineer, 1984-85; Rockwell International, program manager, 1985-. **ORGANIZATIONS:** Alpha Sigma Mu, lifetime member; Sigma Xi; American Society for Metals. **SPECIAL ACHIEVEMENTS:** Over 20 technical journal publications. **HOME ADDRESS:** 11 Meadow Wood Dr, Trabuco Canyon, CA 92679, (714)858-8586. **BUSINESS PHONE:** (714)762-2561.

LI, CHIA-YU
Educator, educational administrator. Chinese American. **PERSONAL:** Born May 5, 1941, Shanghai, China; son of Mr and Mrs M S Li; married You-riu Chu Li, Jun 1969; children: Jonathan, Jeffrey, Jennifer. **EDUCATION:** Taiwan Normal University, Taipei, BS, chemistry, 1963; University of Louisville, MS, chemistry, 1967; Wayne State University, PhD, chemistry, 1972. **CAREER:** East Carolina University, Chemistry Dept, assistant professor, 1973-78, associate professor, 1978-84, professor, 1984-, chairman, 1988-. **ORGANIZATIONS:** American Chemical Society, 1968-; Sigma Xi, 1973-; Society of Electroanalytical Chemistry, 1984-. **HONORS/AWARDS:** ECU Chapter, Sigma Xi, Research Award, 1988; ECU, Teaching Award, semifinalist, 1986-91. **SPECIAL ACHIEVEMENTS:** Publications include scholarly papers on electroanalytical chemistry, 1972-. **BUSINESS ADDRESS:** Professor and Chairman, Chemistry Dept, East Carolina University, Flanagan Bldg, Greenville, NC 27858, (919)757-6711.

LI, CHING-CHUNG
Educator. Chinese American. **PERSONAL:** Born Mar 30, 1932, Changshu, Kiangsu, China; son of Lung-Han Li and Lien-Tseng Hwa Li; married Hanna Wu, Jun 10, 1961; children: William Wei-Lin, Vincent Wei-Tsin. **EDUCATION:** National Taiwan University, Taipei, BSEE, 1954; Northwestern University, MSEE, 1956, PhD, 1961. **CAREER:** Westinghouse Electric Corp, Analytical Dept, jr engineer, 1957; Northwestern University, Dept of Electrical Engineering, institute fellow, 1957-59; University of California, Berkeley, visiting associate professor of electrical engineering, 1964; Alza Corp, Biodynamics Lab, visiting principal scientist, 1970; MIT, Lab for Information and Decision Systems, 1988-; University of Pittsburgh, assistant professor of electrical engineering, 1959-62, associate professor of electrical engineering, 1962-67, professor of electrical engineering, 1967-; professor of computer sciences, 1977-. **ORGANIZATIONS:** Institute of Electrical and Electronics Engineers, fellow, 1978-, various technical committees, committee chairman, 1967-; Society of Pattern Recognition, associate editor of Journal of Pattern Recognition, 1985-; Biomedical Engineering Society, charter member; American Association for the Advancement of Science; New York Academy of Sciences; Sigma Xi. **HONORS/AWARDS:** Radiological Society of North America, co-recipient, Certificate of Merit, 1979. **SPECIAL ACHIEVEMENTS:** Published over 150 papers in professional journals and major conference proceedings in the field of biomedical pattern recognition and images processing, computer vision, industrial applications of pattern recognition, and biocybernetics. **BUSINESS ADDRESS:** Professor of Electrical Engineering, University of Pittsburgh, Pittsburgh, PA 15261, (412)624-9679.

LI, CHING JAMES
Educator. Taiwanese American. **PERSONAL:** Born Nov 11, 1957, Tainan, Taiwan; son of Ruenn-Tsun Li and Mei-Hui Liu; married Yuh-ling Li, Jul 9, 1983; children: Jonathan, Daniel. **EDUCATION:** National Taiwan University, BS, 1980; University of Wisconsin-Madison, PhD, 1987. **CAREER:** Colum-

bia University, assistant professor, 1987-92, associate professor, 1993-; Rensselaer Polytechnic Institute, associate professor, 1993-. **ORGANIZATIONS:** American Society of Mechanical Engineers, associate member, 1988-93. **HONORS/AWARDS:** Recipient of more than 10 research grants, which total $1M. **SPECIAL ACHIEVEMENTS:** Author of more than 30 technical papers on control, signal processing, mechanical diagnostics and neural networks; referee for National Science Foundation, Israel Science Foundation and a number of technical journals. **BUSINESS ADDRESS:** Assoc Prof, Dept of Mech Eng, Aeron Eng & Mechanics, Rensselaer Polytechnic Institute, Troy, NY 12180-3590, (518)276-6192.

LI, CHU-TSING
Educator. Chinese American. **PERSONAL:** Born May 1920, Canton, Kwangtong, China; son of Li Wu-tzu and Hsieh Ren-lan; married Yao-wen Kwang Li; children: B Ulysses, Amy Li Lee. **EDUCATION:** University of Nanking, BA, 1943; University of Iowa, MA, 1949, PhD, 1955. **CAREER:** Oberlin College, acting assistant professor, 1955-56; University of Iowa, instructor to professor, 1954-66; University of Kansas, art history, professor, 1966-72, professor and chairman, 1972-78, J H Murphy Professor of Art History, 1978-90, J H Murphy Professor of Art History, emeritus, 1990-. **ORGANIZATIONS:** College Art Association, 1953-; Association for Asian Studies, 1960-. **HONORS/AWARDS:** University of Nanking, Phi Tau Phi Society, 1943; University of Kansas, Phi Beta Kappa, honorary member, 1983. **SPECIAL ACHIEVEMENTS:** Author: Autumn Colors on the Ch'iao and Hua Mountains, Ascona, Switzerland, 1965; A Thousand Peaks and Myriad Ravines, Ascona, Switzerland, 1974; Trends in Modern Chinese Painting, Ascona, Switzerland, 1979; mnay other titles and articles in various journals. **HOME ADDRESS:** 1108 Avalon Road, Lawrence, KS 66044, (913)842-1446. **BUSINESS ADDRESS:** J H Murphy Professor of Art History, Emeritus, University of Kansas, 209 Spencer Museum of Art, Lawrence, KS 66045-0501, (913)864-4713.

LI, CONAN K. N.
Financial services company executive. Chinese American. **PERSONAL:** Born Feb 17, 1951, Seattle, WA; son of James C M Li & Lily Y C Li; married Jenny; children: Jason, Stephanie. **EDUCATION:** Massachusetts Institute of Technology, SB, 1972; Harvard University, PhD, 1978. **CAREER:** Ortho Diagnostics, scientist, 1980-86; University of Utah, visiting associate professor, 1983; Ilex Corp, Immunosensor R&D, director, 1986-87; Abbott Laboratories, R&D, manager, 1987-93; Cambridge Financial Group Inc, president, CEO, 1993-. **ORGANIZATIONS:** Organization of Chinese Professionals, co-founder, 1983, president, 1983-94; Great Lakes Construction, president, 1991-; Electrochemical Society Sensors Committee, chairman, 1986. **SPECIAL ACHIEVEMENTS:** Numerous scientific publications, 1975-86; patents in the biophysical sciences, 1985-90; editor, Electrochemical Sensors, 1986. **HOME ADDRESS:** PO Box 855, Libertyville, IL 60048, (708)680-6727.

LI, DENING
Educator. Chinese American. **PERSONAL:** Born Mar 24, 1947, Nanjing, Jiangsu, China; son of Qihua Li and Zhaoxian Zhang; married Mingzhu Zhang, Jan 8, 1977; children: Jennifer Xinge. **EDUCATION:** Fudan University, Shanghai, MSc, 1981, PhD, 1985. **CAREER:** Nanjing Aeronautical Institute, lecturer, 1981-82; Southeast University, China, assistant professor, 1985-86; University of British Columbia, postdoctoral work, 1986-87; University of Colorado, Boulder, visiting assistant professor, 1987-88; West Virginia University, assistant/associate professor, 1988-. **BUSINESS ADDRESS:** Professor, Math Dept, West Virginia University, 423 Armstrong Hall, Morgantown, WV 26506-6310, (304)293-2011.

LI, DIANE DAI (DIANE)
Librarian. Chinese American. **PERSONAL:** Born Feb 16, 1962, Beijing, People's Republic of China; daughter of Xin Li. **EDUCATION:** Peking University, First Branch, BA, library science, 1986; Clarion University, Pennsylvania, MLS, 1991. **CAREER:** Library of Research Institute of Petrochemical Processing, librarian, 1986-90; US Department of Agriculture, National Agricultural Library, intern, 1991; Russell Memorial Library, City of Chesapeake Public Library System, assistant branch manager, 1992-. **ORGANIZATIONS:** American Library Association, 1991; Social Responsibility Round Table, 1991; Virginia Library Association, Continuing Education Committee, 1993. **HONORS/AWARDS:** National Agricultural Library, Rural Information Center, Certificate of Appreciation, 1991; City of Chesapeake Star Performance awardr, 1992; Friends of the Chesapeake Public Library Scholarship to VLA Ann Mtg, 1993. **BUSINESS ADDRESS:** Librarian, Chesapeake City Public

Library System, Russell Memorial Library, 2808 Taylor Road, Chesapeake, VA 23321, (804)465-0369.

LI, GEORGE S.
Scientist. Chinese American. **PERSONAL:** Born Oct 24, 1943, Chung King, Sichuan, China; son of Shih-Chang Li & I-La Ma; married Tung Chia Li, Feb 6, 1971; children: Kenneth C. **EDUCATION:** Cheng King University, BS, chemistry, 1965; Purdue University, PhD, chemistry, 1971. **CAREER:** Purdue University, research associate, 1971-73; Standard Oil, Ohio, research associate, 1974-85; British Petroleum Chemicals Research, research scientist II, 1985-. **ORGANIZATIONS:** American Chemical Society, 1966-. **HONORS/AWARDS:** BP America, Inventor Hall of Fame, 50 patents, 1988; Sohio, Inventor Hall of Fame, 25 patents, 1980. **SPECIAL ACHIEVEMENTS:** Involved in the discovery and development of new polymers, 56 US patents; areas of study: process optimization and scale-up, barrier packaging polymers, membrane separations. **BIOGRAPHICAL SOURCES:** Who's Who in Technology Today, 4th ed, 1982. **BUSINESS ADDRESS:** Research Scientist II, BP Chemicals Research, 4440 Warrensville Center Road, Cleveland, OH 44128, (216)581-6707.

LI, GUODONG
Actuary. Chinese American. **PERSONAL:** Born Jul 20, 1958, Man Zhou Li, Neimenggu, People's Republic of China; son of Zhen Qi Li and Guiqin Xu; married Quan Yi, Jul 1, 1986; children: Angela Lee, Hillary Lee. **EDUCATION:** Harbin Institute of Technology, BS, MS; Ohio State university, MS. **CAREER:** W F Corroon, actuarial analyst, 1990-. **ORGANIZATIONS:** Society of Actuaries, 1991-; Mathematics Society. **HONORS/AWARDS:** Society of Actuaries, 1991. **HOME ADDRESS:** 1014 E Rue De La Banque, Creve Coeur, MO 63141, (314)993-8553.

LI, HANNA WU
Educator, educational administrator. Chinese American. **PERSONAL:** Born Mar 28, 1934, Canton, China; daughter of Yat Chih Wu and Wei Ying Lo Wu; married Ching-Chung Li, Jun 10, 1961; children: William Wei-Lin, Vincent Wei-Tsin. **EDUCATION:** National Taiwan Normal University, BA, piano, 1956; Northwestern University, MMus, piano, 1961. **CAREER:** Soloist, accompanist, chamber music, 1954-58; National Taiwan Normal University, Dept of Music, instructor of piano, 1956-58; Carnegie Mellon University, Preparatory School, Dept of Music, instructor of piano, 1969-84, director of piano, 1984-, Dept of Music, instructor of piano, 1974-78, artist lecturer in piano, 1979-88, associate professor of music, director of program in piano pedagogy, 1988-. **ORGANIZATIONS:** American Music Scholarship Association, Eastern Region, chairman, 1975-; Pittsburgh Concert Society, board of directors, 1984-; Pi Kappa Lamda; Music Teachers National Association; Young Keyboard Artist Association, Ann Arbor, Michigan, adjudicator, international piano competitions, 1985; judge, young musicians auditions, Wheeling, West Virginia, 1979, 1992. **SPECIAL ACHIEVEMENTS:** Developed distinctive pedagogy program for children; invited to conduct master classes & give lectures at Guang Zhou Conservatory, China, & Central Conservatory of Music, Beijing, 1986; invited by Chinese Musicians National Association to give 5-day lectures on piano pedagogy at Shanghai, 1993; her students have: won numerous first prize and grand prize awards in AMSA World Piano Competitions in Cincinnati, Ohio; been presented as soloists in piano concerto with Pittsburgh Symphony Orchestra in Young People's Concerts, and as young artists in Pittsburgh Concert Society's Annual Young Artist Concerts. **BUSINESS ADDRESS:** Associate Professor, Dept of Music, Carnegie Mellon University, College of Fine Arts, Pittsburgh, PA 15213, (412)268-2376.

LI, IVAN C.
Banking executive. Hong Kong American. **PERSONAL:** Born Feb 15, 1955, Hong Kong; son of Ngong Li and Hipyee Chu Li; married Psyche T Li, Jul 4, 1957; children: Michael, Janice. **CAREER:** Wo Kee Hong Ltd, 1975-77; DHL Group, 1977-82; Hong Kong and Shanghai Bank, vice pres, sr vice pres, 1982-. **ORGANIZATIONS:** Hong Kong Computer Society, vice pres, BBS, SIG, 1987-88; Wahchai District Bd, area subcommittee. **BUSINESS ADDRESS:** Senior Vice President, The Hong Kong and Shanghai Banking Corp, 254 Canal St, 4th Fl, New York, NY 10013, (212)925-8880.

LI, JAMES C. M.
Educator. Chinese American. **PERSONAL:** Born Apr 12, 1925, Nanking, Jiangsu, China; son of Vei-Shao Li & In-Shey Mai Li; married Lily Y C Wang, Aug 5, 1950; children: Conan K N, May K M Li Yu, Edward K H. **EDUCATION:** National Central University, Nanking, China, BS, 1947; University of

Washington, MS, 1951, PhD, 1953. **CAREER:** University of Washington, Med School, chemist, 1951-53; University of California, Berkeley, research associate, 1953-55; Carnegie Inst of Technology, supervisor, 1955-56; Westinghouse, chemist, 1956-57; US Steel Corp, senior scientist, 1957-69; Allied Chemical, manager, 1969-71; University of Rochester, Hopeman Professor, 1971-. **ORGANIZATIONS:** American Phys Society, fellow; American Chem Society; American Academy of Mechanics; ASM International, fellow, chair, Met Sci Division; Minerals, Metals & Materials Society, fellow; Materials Research Society. **HONORS/AWARDS:** The Metallurgical Society, Champion Mathewson Gold Medal, 1972, Robert F Mehl Medal, 1978; University of Rochester, Graduate Teaching Award, 1993; Chinese Society Met Sci, Lu Tse-Hon Medal, 1988; ASM International, Acta Metallurgical Gold Medal, 1990. **SPECIAL ACHIEVEMENTS:** Helped Allied Chemical develop a new industry in making Metglas (TM) by rapid quenching, initiated research & development, 1971; developed the thermodynamics of stressed solids, 1966; developed the concept of thermokinetic potential, 1962. **BUSINESS ADDRESS:** Hopeman Professor, Dept of Mechanical Engineering, University of Rochester, Rochester, NY 14627.

LI, JENNIFER L. H.
City government official. Chinese American. **PERSONAL:** Born Nov 10, 1954, Tainan, Taiwan; daughter of Chung-Yao Li and Shiao-pai Hung; married David Wu; children: Emma Wu. **EDUCATION:** Fu Jen Catholic University, BS, economics, 1977; Texas Woman's University, MBA, 1982. **CAREER:** American International Rent-A-Car Corp, programmer, 1982-83; City of Dallas, Budget and Research Department, budget analyst, 1983-85, project administrator, 1985-86, assistant director, 1986-92, Court Service Department, assistant director, 1992-93, Budget and Research Department, director, 1993-. **ORGANIZATIONS:** Government Finance Officers Association, 1987-; Organization of Chinese Americans, Inc, 1991-. **HONORS/AWARDS:** City of Dallas, Standard of Excellence Award, 1984, Commitment to Excellence Award, 1985, Excellence in Service Award, 1990. **SPECIAL ACHIEVEMENTS:** Foreign Investment Opportunities in Taiwan, 1982; completion of Dale Carnegie Effective Speaking and Human Relations Course, 1990. **BIOGRAPHICAL SOURCES:** Texas Woman's University Alumnae Directory, p 252, 1989. **BUSINESS ADDRESS:** Director, Budget and Research Dept, City of Dallas, 1500 Marilla Street, City Hall, 4F North, Dallas, TX 75201, (214)670-3659.

LI, JIA
Educator. Chinese American. **PERSONAL:** Born Jul 15, 1945, Guangnan, Yunnan, China; married Suxin Feng, May 1, 1974; children: Sherri Li. **EDUCATION:** Hanan University, mathematics, 1966; Huazong University of Science & Technology, MS, mathematics, 1981; University of Tennessee, PhD, mathematics, 1987. **CAREER:** University of Tennessee, Knoxville, department of mathematics, postdoctoral research associate and visiting assistant professor, 1987-88; University of Arizona, department of mathematics, visiting assistant professor, 1988-89; Los Alamos National Laboratory, Center for Nonlinear Studies and Theoretical Division, postdoctoral fellow, consultant, 1989-91, consultant, 1992-93; Cornell University, Biometrics, Center for Applied Mathematics, visiting assistant professor, 1993, Mathematical Science Institute, visiting scientist, 1993; University of Alabama, Huntsville, department of mathematical sciences, assistant professor, 1990-. **ORGANIZATIONS:** American Mathematical Society; Society of Mathematical Biology; International Association of Nonlinear Analysts. **HONORS/AWARDS:** UTK and ORNL Science Alliance, fellowship, 1984-87; UTK, dept of mathematics, Academic Achievement Award, 1987; Los Alamos National Laboratory, postdoctoral fellowship, 1989-91. **SPECIAL ACHIEVEMENTS:** Author, Effects of Risk Behavior Change on the Spread of AIDS Epidemic, Mathl Comput Modelling, vol 16, 103-111, 1992; presenter, "Thresholds on Structured AIDS models," Conference on Population Structure, University of California, Davis, September, 1989; "Exclusion or Coexistence of Viral Strains in an S-I-S STD model," Society for Mathematical Biology Annual Meeting, Cornell University, 1993; many others. **HOME PHONE:** (205)880-6914. **BUSINESS ADDRESS:** Professor, Dept of Mathematics, University of Alabama in Huntsville, 4701 University Dr, Huntsville, AL 35899.

LI, KAI
Educator. Chinese American. **PERSONAL:** Born Jun 9, 1954, Changchun, Jilin, People's Republic of China; son of Chujie Li and Daohui Cai; married Haishu Wang, Jan 5, 1988. **EDUCATION:** Jilin University, BS, 1977; University of Science & Tech of China, MS, 1981; Yale University, PhD, 1986. **CAREER:** Princeton University, assistant professor, 1986-92, associate pro-

fessor, 1992-; Digital Equipment Co, consultant, 1987-; INTEL Supercomputer Systems Division, consultant, 1987-; Matsushita Info Tech Lab, consultant, 1992. **SPECIAL ACHIEVEMENTS:** Research and teaching in parallel computer architecture and systems.

LI, KE WEN
Manufacturing company adminstrator. Taiwanese American. **PERSONAL:** Born Sep 28, 1933, Tainan, Taiwan; son of Ten-Chu Lee and Chuan Wang Lee; married Louise Li; children: John, Linda. **EDUCATION:** Cheng Kung University, Taiwan, BS, 1957; Purdue University, MS, 1963, PhD, 1969. **CAREER:** Cheng-Kung University, instructor, 1963-66; Lummus Co, process design manager, 1981-88; M W Kellogg Co, senior process development manager, 1988-. **ORGANIZATIONS:** American Institute of Chemical Engineers, 1981-. **SPECIAL ACHIEVEMENTS:** 20 years of experience in: chemical engineering, reaction engineering; chemical plant design. **BUSINESS ADDRESS:** Senior Process Development Manager, The M W Kellogg Co, 601 Jefferson Ave, PO Box 4557, Houston, TX 77210, (713)753-2589.

LI, KUIYUAN
Educator. Chinese American. **PERSONAL:** Born Nov 11, 1955, Henan, Henan, People's Republic of China; son of Xuren Zhang and Peilan Li; married Xiuqing Wang, Feb 18, 1982; children: Lei, Kay. **EDUCATION:** Taiyuan University of Technology, BS, 1981; Michigan State University, PhD, 1991. **CAREER:** Taiyuan University of Technology, instructor, 1982; Michigan State University, teaching assistant, 1986; University of West Florida, assistant professor, 1991-. **ORGANIZATIONS:** Mathematical Association of America, 1991; International Linear Algebra Society, 1991. **HONORS/AWARDS:** University of West Florida, Summer Research Award, 1992; Michigan State University, An Award for Excellence in Teaching, 1990. **SPECIAL ACHIEVEMENTS:** Author, A Homotopy Algorithm for a Symmetric Generalized Eigenproblem, 1993; An Algorithm for Symmetric Tridiagonal Eigenproblem, 1993; Homotopy Method for Sinular Symmetric Tridiagonal Eigenproblem, 1993; Some Criteria for the Symmetric Method for Tridiagonal Eigenproblem, 1993; A Fully Parallel Method for Symmetric Eigenproblem, 1993. **BUSINESS ADDRESS:** Professor, Dept of Mathematics & Statistics, University of West Florida, University Pkwy 11000, Pensacola, FL 32514-5732, (904)474-2287.

LI, LILLIAN M.
Educator. Chinese American. **EDUCATION:** Harvard University, PhD, 1975. **CAREER:** Swarthmore College, professor of history, currently. **ORGANIZATIONS:** Association for Asian Studies. **HONORS/AWARDS:** Woodrow Wilson International Center, fellow, 1993-94. **SPECIAL ACHIEVEMENTS:** Author, China's Silk Trade: Traditional Industry in the Modern World, 1981; co-editor, Chinese History in Economic Perspective, 1992. **BUSINESS ADDRESS:** Professor of History, Swarthmore College, 500 College Ave, Swarthmore, PA 19081.

LI, LILY ELIZABETH
Financial services company administrator. Chinese American. **PERSONAL:** Born Aug 22, 1962, New York, NY; daughter of Richard Li and Dorothy Li. **EDUCATION:** University of Chicago, BS, 1984, MBA, 1987. **CAREER:** Merrill Lynch, associate, 1987-89; Wood Gondy/CEF Securities, mgr, 1989-91; UBS Securities, vice pres, 1991-93; MeesPierson Securities, managing director, 1993-. **HOME ADDRESS:** 135 E 54th St, Apt 11H, New York, NY 10022, (212)751-1389. **BUSINESS ADDRESS:** Managing Director, MeesPierson Securities, 3 E 54th St, 12th Fl, New York, NY 10022, (212)308-6834.

LI, LING-FONG
Educator. Chinese American. **PERSONAL:** Born Apr 17, 1944, Sha, Fukien, China; son of Tin-Shun and Lansing Li; married Chi-Chuang Liang, Jan 3, 1977; children: Victor Wei-chi, Herman Wei-min. **EDUCATION:** National Taiwan University, BS, 1965; University of Pennsylvania, MS, 1967, PhD, 1970. **CAREER:** Rockefeller University, research associate, 1970-72; Stanford Linear Accelerator Center, research associate, 1972-74; Carnegie-Mellon University, assistant professor of physics, 1974-79, associate professor of physics, 1979-83, professor of physics, 1983-. **ORGANIZATIONS:** American Physical Society, 1977-; Oversea Chinese Physicist Association, 1989-. **HONORS/AWARDS:** Alfred P Sloan Foundation, Alfred P Sloan Research Fellow, 1979; American Physical Society, fellow, 1985. **SPECIAL ACHIEVEMENTS:** Book, "Gauge Theory of Elementary Particle Physics,"

1984. **BUSINESS ADDRESS:** Professor, Dept of Physics, Carnegie-Mellon University, 5000 Forbes Ave, Pittsburgh, PA 15213, (412)268-2758.

LI, MARJORIE H.
Librarian, association executive. Chinese American. **PERSONAL:** Born Jul 27, 1942, Fujian, China; daughter of Kai-an Hsu and Sou-fen Chen; married Peter Li, Sep 21, 1968; children: Jennifer, Caroline. **EDUCATION:** National Taiwan University, BA, 1964; University of Chicago, MA, 1968. **CAREER:** Northwestern University, serial cataloger, 1968-69; Center for Research Libraries, monographs cataloger, 1969-72; Rutgers University, beginning 1973, special collections archivist, 1981-86, RECON Project, coordinator, 1986-89, acting East Asian librarian, 1989-90, RLIN CJK liaison in charge of East Asian materials, 1990-. **ORGANIZATIONS:** American Library Association, 1968-; Association of Asian Studies, 1989-; Chinese American Librarians Association, 1979-; Asian Pacific American Librarians Association, 1980-, president, 1992-; Chinese American Cultural Association, president, 1993-94. **HONORS/AWARDS:** Rockefeller Foundation, fellowship, 1966-67; ALA Sarah Bogel Foundation, travelling grant, 1985; Chinese American Librarians Association, research grant, 1985-86; Rutgers University, President's Coordinating Council on International Programs, 1989-90; State Council on the Arts, Middlesex County Cultural & Heritage Commission, 1990-94. **SPECIAL ACHIEVEMENTS:** Book edited, Understanding Asian Americans, 1990; Culture and Politics in China: An Anatomy of Tiananmen, 1991. **BUSINESS ADDRESS:** President, Asian Pacific American Librarians Association, c/o TAS, Rutgers University Libraries, Busch Campus, New Brunswick, NJ 08903, (908)932-5904.

LI, MING
Educator. Chinese American. **PERSONAL:** Born Apr 1, 1959, Guangzhou, Guangdong, People's Republic of China; married Wan Chen Li; children: Huihui. **EDUCATION:** Guangzhou Institute of Physical Culture, BEd, 1983; Hangzhou University, PR China, MEd, 1986; University of Kansas, EdD, 1991. **CAREER:** Guangzhou Institute of Physical Culture, lecturer, 1986-88; University of Kansas, graduate teaching assistant, 1988-91; Georgia Southern University, assistant professor, 1991-. **ORGANIZATIONS:** American Alliance for Health, Physical Education, Recreation & Dance, 1991-; North American Society for Sport Management, 1991-; Georgia Association for Health, Physical Education, Recreation & Dance, 1992-93. **BUSINESS ADDRESS:** Assistant Professor, Dept of Sport Science and Physical Education, Georgia Southern University, Landrum Box 8076, Statesboro, GA 30460, (912)681-5267.

LI, NORMAN N.
Chemical company executive. Chinese American. **PERSONAL:** Born Jan 14, 1933, Shanghai, China; son of Lieh-wen Li and Amy H Li; married Jane C Li, Aug 17, 1963; children: Rebecca H, David H. **EDUCATION:** Natl Taiwan University, BSCE, 1955; Wayne State University, MS, 1957; Stevens Institute of Technology, PhD, 1963. **CAREER:** Exxon Research and Engineering Co, sr scientist, 1963-81; UOP, Separation Science and Technology, director, 1981-88; Allied-Signal Inc, Engineered Products and Process Technology, director, 1988-. **ORGANIZATIONS:** NRC, 1985-89; AIChE, lecturer, 1975-86, fellow; NAE; American Chemical Society; North American Membrane Society, president, 1992-. **HONORS/AWARDS:** AIChE, Alpha Chi Sigma Research Award, 1988; American Chemical Society, Separation Science and Technology Award, 1988. **SPECIAL ACHIEVEMENTS:** Editor of thirteen books about separation science and technology; contributor of articles to professional journals; patent holder. **BUSINESS ADDRESS:** Director, Engineered Products, Allied-Signal Research Center, PO Box 5016, Des Plaines, IL 60017-5016.*

LI, PETER TA
Publisher. Chinese American. **PERSONAL:** Born Jul 9, 1938, Hong Kong; son of Norman C Li & Hazel Chow; divorced; children: Lisa Ann, Susan Ann. **EDUCATION:** Duquesne University, BA, 1961. **CAREER:** Sewickley Herald, advertising manager, 1959-61; Pittsburgh Courier, advertising director, 1961-63; Geo A Pflaum, publisher, publishing director, 1963-71; Peter Li Education Group, chairman, CEO, 1971-. **ORGANIZATIONS:** NSSEA, treasurer, 1992-; NCEE, executive director, 1987-; ICIA, chairman, religious council/exhibition committee, 1972-88; AAP; NCEA; CPA; Ed Press, regional director; SPA, 1993. **HONORS/AWARDS:** Archdiocese of Brooklyn, Distinguished Service to Catholic Education, 1990; NCEE, Distinguished Service to Catholic Education, 1993; ICIA, Distinguished Service Award, 1988; NSSEA, Distinguished Service Award, 1985, 1988, 1990. **SPECIAL ACHIEVEMENTS:** Publisher of: Catechist, Today's Catholic Teacher, Technology and

Learning, School and College, Early Childhood News, Visions, Venture, Good News, Promise, Quest. **BUSINESS ADDRESS:** Chairman, CEO, Peter Li Education Group, 330 Progress Rd, Dayton, OH 45449, (513)847-5900.

LI, PETER WAI-KWONG
Educator. Chinese American. **PERSONAL:** Born Apr 18, 1952, Hong Kong; son of Chun Tat Li and Lai Mui Sum; married Glenna Li, Oct 30, 1982; children: Tiana, Natasha, Talia. **EDUCATION:** California State University, Fresno, BA, 1974; University of California, Berkeley, MA, 1977, PhD, 1979. **CAREER:** Institute for Advanced Study, research member, 1979-80; Stanford University, assistant professor, 1980-83; Purdue University, associate professor, 1983-85; University of Utah, professor, 1985-89; University of Arizona, professor, 1989-91; University of California, Irvine, professor, 1991-, chair, 1993-. **ORGANIZATIONS:** American Mathematical Society, 1993-. **HONORS/AWARDS:** Alfred P Sloan Foundation, Sloan Fellowship, 1982; John Simon Guggenheim Foundation, fellowship, 1989. **SPECIAL ACHIEVEMENTS:** Lecture Notes on Geometric Analysis, Lecture Notes #6, Korea, 1993; The Theory of Harmonic Functions and Its Relation to Geometry, Proc Symp Pure Math, 54, p 307-315, 1993. **BUSINESS ADDRESS:** Chair & Professor, Dept of Mathematics, University of California, Irvine, Irvine, CA 92717-3875, (714)856-7049.

LI, QIANG
Educator. Chinese American. **PERSONAL:** Born Mar 5, 1953, Xian, Shanxi, People's Republic of China; son of Xinpei Li and Xuemei Lu; divorced. **EDUCATION:** Xian Jiaotong University, BS, 1982; Florida International University, MS, 1984, PhD, 1989. **CAREER:** Xian Radio Technology Company, China, technician, 1973-77; Southeast Regional Data Center, system software specialist, 1983-89; Florida International University, visiting assistant professor, 1989-90; Santa Clara University, assistant professor, 1990-. **ORGANIZATIONS:** IEEE Computer Society; ACM; Silicon Valley Parallel Processing Connections, member of the board. **BUSINESS ADDRESS:** Asst Prof, Dept of Computer Engineering, Santa Clara University, Santa Clara, CA 95053-0001, (408)554-2730.

LI, SAN-PAO
Educator. Chinese American. **PERSONAL:** Born Sep 21, 1942, Sichuan, China; son of Chaoying Li and Chuanying Li (both deceased); married Shu-chuen Li, Jun 9, 1969; children: Michelle, Jennifer. **EDUCATION:** Tunghai University, BA, 1966; Harvard University, MA, 1970; University of California, Davis, PhD, 1978. **CAREER:** Harvard University, teaching fellow, 1969-70; University of California, Berkeley, teaching assistant, 1970-71; University of California, Davis, lecturer, 1971-76; Tunghai University, Taiwan, chair, political science department, director, Institute of Political Science, 1991-92; California State University, Long Beach, full professor, 1976-, chair, dept of Asian and Asian American studies, 1984-91. **ORGANIZATIONS:** Association for Asian Studies, 1969-; Society for Ch'ing Studies, 1970-; American Association for Chinese Studies, 1968-, local chair, 1979, board of directors, 1980-82; Chinese American Professional Society, 1979-, board of directors, humanities and social science division, chairman, 1992-; Historical and Cultural Foundation of Orange County, 1982-, executive board, 1986, Chinese-American Council, chairman, 1986; Chinese Language Teachers Association, 1987-; Chinese American Faculty Association, 1978-, president, 1994-95. **HONORS/AWARDS:** University of California, Davis, Inter-Campus Research Awards, 1972-75; California State University, Long Beach, New Faculty Research Award, 1976, Faculty Research Award & University Research Committee Award, 1980, Outstanding Professor Award, 1984-85, Meritorious Performance Award, 1985-89; Center for Chinese Studies, Taiwan, research fellowship, 1990-91. **SPECIAL ACHIEVEMENTS:** More than twelve major scholastic articles published in juried professional journals; received recognition for calligraphic work; calligraphic works used on many book covers and brochures. **BUSINESS ADDRESS:** Professor, California State University, Long Beach, 1250 Bellflower Blvd, Long Beach, CA 90840, (310)985-5493.

LI, SHENG S.
Educator. Taiwanese American. **PERSONAL:** Born Dec 10, 1938, Hsinchu, Taiwan; son of Swei-Hsing Li and Ku-Se Li; married Bih-Jean Li, Apr 19, 1964; children: Jim, Grace, Jeanette. **EDUCATION:** National Cheng-Kung University, Taiwan, BSEE, 1962; Rice University, MSEE, 1966, PhD, 1968. **CAREER:** China Electric Company, Taiwan, engineer, 1963-64; Rice University, teaching assistant, 1964-67; National Bureau of Standards, electronic engineer, 1975-76; University of Florida, professor, 1968-. **ORGANIZATIONS:** Institute of Electrical & Electronic Engineers, senior member, 1986-;

American Physical Society, 1972-. **HONORS/AWARDS:** University of Florida, top 100 researchers, 1989, 1990, Outstanding Faculty Research Paper, 1992; National Cheng-Kung University, top ranked in his graduating class, 1962. **SPECIAL ACHIEVEMENTS:** "Semiconductor Physical Electronics," Plenum Publishing Company, 1993. **MILITARY SERVICE:** Army, Taiwan, 2nd lt, 1962-63. **BUSINESS ADDRESS:** Professor, University of Florida, 231 Benton Hall, Build 720, Gainesville, FL 32611, (904)392-4937.

LI, SHIN-HWA
Researcher. Taiwanese American. **PERSONAL:** Born Apr 8, 1958, Taipei, Taiwan; son of Vivian Li & Yuan Mo Li; married Yina Gan Li, Jul 10, 1983; children: Crystal Gan. **EDUCATION:** National Central University, BS, 1980; University of Southwestern Louisiana, MS, 1985; University of Utah, PhD, 1991. **CAREER:** Ko-Sheng Enterprises, Taiwan, process engineer, 1982-83; University of Southwestern Louisiana, research assistant, 1983-85; University of Utah, research assistant, 1985-91; University of Michigan, research scientist, 1991-. **ORGANIZATIONS:** Institute of Electrical & Electronic Engineers, 1990-; Minerals, Metals, Materials Society, 1989-. **HONORS/AWARDS:** Minerals, Metals, Materials Society, Best Student Paper, 1991. **SPECIAL ACHIEVEMENTS:** Over 30 scientific papers in various journals, books, 1988-93; over 12 presentations in various international conferences, 1988-93. **MILITARY SERVICE:** 651st Regiment, 2nd lt, 1980-82; Distinguished Reserved Officer. **BUSINESS ADDRESS:** Research Scientist, University of Michigan, 1301 Beal Avenue, 1124 EECS Building, Ann Arbor, MI 48109-2122, (313)936-2966.

LI, SHING TED (PETER)
Electronics engineer. Chinese American. **PERSONAL:** Born Aug 15, 1938, Chin-Chiang, Fujian, China; son of Ming Fa Li and Feng Yu Chang; married Florence Lengpo Lee, Dec 30, 1966. **EDUCATION:** Taipe Institute of Technology, Taiwan, diploma, electrical engineering, 1958; University of Tennessee, MSEE, 1965; Georgia Institute of Technology, PhD, electrical engineering, 1974. **CAREER:** Taiwan Power Co, assistant engr, 1958-59, 1961-64; Simons Eastern Engineering Co, design engr, 1965-69; Georgia Institute of Technology, graduate teaching/research asst, 1969-74; NCCOSC, RDT&E Div, DP IV engr, project mgr, 1974-. **ORGANIZATIONS:** IEEE, 1969-, Intl Symposium on EMC, section chmn, 1985; Pi Mu Epsilon, 1974-; Sigma Xi, 1974-; ACES, committee chmn, 1985-; NARTE, certified EMC engr, sr member, 1989-; State of Georgia, resistered professional engr, 1968-; Republic of China, registered professional engr, 1960-72. **HONORS/AWARDS:** NOSC, Sustained Superior Performance Award, 1978, Quality Salary Increase Award, 1980. **SPECIAL ACHIEVEMENTS:** Co-author: two technical books, 1983, 1988; author, co-author: over 70 technical papers and reports, 1965-. **MILITARY SERVICE:** Nationalist Chinese Army, second lt, 1959-61. **BUSINESS ADDRESS:** Electronics Engineer, Naval Command, Control and Ocean Surveillance Center, RDT&E Div Code 822, 53225 Millimeter St, Rm 110, San Diego, CA 92152-7304, (619)553-5089.

LI, SHUHE
Economist, educator. Chinese American. **PERSONAL:** Born Aug 17, 1961, Zizhou, Shaanxi, People's Republic of China; married Lifang Sun, Jul 19, 1989. **EDUCATION:** Northwestern University, PRC, BS, 1983, MA, 1987; University of Minnesota, PhD, 1993. **CAREER:** Northwestern University, PRC, lecturer, 1983-85; Economic Reform Research Institute of China, research fellow, 1986-88; University of Minnesota, instructor, 1989-. **ORGANIZATIONS:** Chinese Economists Society, 1989-. **HONORS/AWARDS:** Northwestern University, PRC, Outstanding Student, 1983; Shannxi Province, PRC, Outstanding Paper, 1987; University of Minnesota, fellowship, 1989. **SPECIAL ACHIEVEMENTS:** "Stability of Voting Games," Social Choice & Welfare, 1993; "Far Sighted Equilibrium & Oligopoly," Economic Letters, 1993; "Nash Implementation of Pareto. . .," Journal of Comparative Econ, 1982; The Growth & Fluctuations of China's Economy, Shanghai Normal University Press, 1987; proficient in Chinese and English. **HOME ADDRESS:** 2033 Knapp Ave, #W-1, St Paul, MN 55108, (612)646-3564. **BUSINESS ADDRESS:** Instructor, Dept of Economics, University of Minnesota, 271 19th Avenue S, 1035 Mgmt/Econ, Minneapolis, MN 55455, (612)626-9248.

LI, STEVEN SHOEI-LUNG
Research scientist, educator. Taiwanese American. **PERSONAL:** Born Oct 20, 1938, Taiwan; married Pearl Li, Jul 25, 1967; children: Michael, Nancy. **EDUCATION:** National Taiwan University, BS, 1961, MS, 1963; University of Missouri, Columbia, PhD, 1968. **CAREER:** University of Texas, Austin, postdoctoral fellow, 1968-70; Stanford University, research associate, 1970-74;

Mt Sinai School of Med, associate professor, 1974-77; NIEHS, NIH, research geneticist, 1977-; University of North Carolina, CH, adjunct professor, 1977-. **ORGANIZATIONS:** American Society for Biochemistry and Molecular Biology; American Society for Microbiology; AAAS; Genetics Society of America; Biochemical Society of United Kingdom; Chinese Society of Genetics (Taiwan); Chinese Society of Agriculture (Taiwan). **HONORS/AWARDS:** National Institute of Health, grants, 1975-77; NIEHS, Outstanding Performance Award, 1986, 1989. **SPECIAL ACHIEVEMENTS:** More than 100 research publications on genetics, molecular biology, biochemistry. **BUSINESS ADDRESS:** Research Scientist, National Institute of Environmental Health Sciences/NIH, 111 T W Alexander Drive, Laboratory of Genetics, Research Triangle Park, NC 27709, (919)541-4253.

LI, TIEN-YIEN
Educator. Chinese American. **PERSONAL:** Born Jun 28, 1945, Fujian, China; children: Teddy. **EDUCATION:** National Tsing Hua University, Taiwan, BS, 1968; University of Maryland, PhD, 1974. **CAREER:** University of Utah, instructor, 1974-76; University of Wisconsin, Mathematics Research Center, visiting associate professor, 1977-78; Kyoto University, Research Institute for Mathematical Sciences, Japan, special visiting professor, 1987-88; Michigan State University, assistant professor, 1976-78, associate professor, 1979-83, professor, 1983-. **ORGANIZATIONS:** American Mathematical Society; Society for Industrial and Applied Mathmatics. **HONORS/AWARDS:** Tsing Hua University, Jilin University, People's Republic of China, Honorary Professor. **BUSINESS ADDRESS:** Professor, Dept of Mathematics, Michigan State University, East Lansing, MI 48824-1027, (517)353-3836.

LI, TINGYE
Electrical engineer. Chinese American. **PERSONAL:** Born Jul 7, 1931, Nanking, China; son of Chao Li and Lily Wei-ping Sie Li; married Edith Hsiuhwei, Jun 9, 1956; children: Deborah Chunroh, Kathryn Dairoh. **EDUCATION:** University of Witwatersrand, South Africa, BS, elec eng, 1953; Northwestern University, MS, 1955, PhD, 1958. **CAREER:** AT&T Bell Labs, technical staff, 1957-67, Bell Labs, Repeater Techniques Research Dept, head, 1967-76, Lightwave Media Research Dept, 1976-84, Lightwave Systems Research Dept, 1984-. **ORGANIZATIONS:** AAAS; Photonics Society Chinese-Americans; Optical Society of America, Optical Communications Technology Group, chair, 1979-80, board of directors, 1985-87, International Activities Committee, chair, 1988-90, Photonics Division, chair, 1991-92, vice president, 1993-; Sigma Xi; National Academy of Engineering; numerous others. **HONORS/AWARDS:** Northwestern University, Alumni Merit Award, 1981; IEEE, fellow, W R G Baker Prize, 1975, David Sarnoff Award, 1979; Chinese Institute Engineers, USA, Achievement Award, 1978; numerous others. **SPECIAL ACHIEVEMENTS:** Author and contributor of numerous articles in professional journals and book chapters; Optics Letters, associate editor, 1977-78, topical editor, 1989-91; Journal of Lightwave Technology, associate editor, 1983-86; numerous others. **BUSINESS ADDRESS:** Electrical Engineer, AT&T Bell Labs, P O Box 400, Holmdel, NJ 07733-0400.✳

LI, VICTOR C.
Educator. Hong Kong American. **PERSONAL:** Born Jan 15, 1954, Hong Kong; son of Li Yu-Sang and Siu Yin-Fong; married Stella Pang; children: Dustin J. **EDUCATION:** Brown University, BA (magna cum laude), economics, 1977, BSE, 1977, MSME, 1978, PhD, solids and structures, 1981. **CAREER:** Massachusetts Institute of Technology, asst prof, 1981-85, assoc prof, 1985-90; University of Michigan, Ann Arbor, assoc prof, 1990-93, professor, 1993-. **ORGANIZATIONS:** American Concrete Institute, chief editor, STP-81, 1989; American Society of Civil Engineers, Delegation on Western European CE Tech, 1993; Intl Sym Brittle Matrix Composites BMC4, Warsaw, Poland, conference co-chmn, 1994; National Science Foundation, chartered panelist, 1991, 1992; American Society for Mechanical Engineers, guest editor, 1992. **HONORS/AWARDS:** Tech University, Denmark, guest professor, 1992; Brown University, University Fellow, 1977; MIT, Edgerton Chair, 1983-85; University of Mich, Faculty-Student Partnership Award, 1992; Tau Beta Pi, 1981-; Sigma Xi, 1981-; CEE Research Excellence Award, 1993. **SPECIAL ACHIEVEMENTS:** Author: over 80 publications in professional journals of fracture mechanics and composites, 1981-. **BUSINESS ADDRESS:** Professor, Dept of Civil and Env Engineering, University of Michigan, 2326 G G Brown Bldg, Ann Arbor, MI 48109-2125.

LI, VICTOR ON-KWOK
Educator. Hong Kong American. **PERSONAL:** Born Oct 11, 1954, Hong Kong; son of Chia-Nan Li and Wai-Ying Chan; married Regina Wai, Aug 14,

1977; children: Ronald, Nathan. **EDUCATION:** Massachusetts Institute of Technology, EE &CS: SB, 1977, SM, 1979, ScD, 1981. **CAREER:** University of Southern California, electrical engineering, asst prof, 1981-87, assoc prof, 1987-92, prof, 1992-, director, Communication Sciences Institute, 1993-. **ORGANIZATIONS:** Intl Conference on Computer Commun & Networks, steering comm chair, 1992-, general chair, 1992; IEEE Communications Soc, tech comm on computer commun chair, 1987-89; IEEE Information Theory Group, Los Angeles Chapter, chair, 1983-85; IEEE Tencon, intl advisory comm, 1990, 1994; IEEE Sicon, intl advisory bd, 1991, 1993; IEEE Iscom, intl advisory bd, 1991; IEEE Infocom, tech prog comm, member, 1986-94, vice chair, 1995. **HONORS/AWARDS:** IEEE, Fellow, 1992; Institute for the Advancement of Engineering, Fellow, 1984; Natl Science Council, Taiwan, Distinguished Lecturer, 1993; California Polytechnic Institute, Distinguished Lecturer, 1990; NSF Research Inititation Award, 1982; New York City Urban Fellow, 1975. **SPECIAL ACHIEVEMENTS:** Over 130 articles in intl journals & conference proceedings, 1981-93; consults & lectures extensively around the world. **BUSINESS ADDRESS:** Professor, Dept of Electrical Engineering, University of Southern California, EEB 500, Los Angeles, CA 90089-2565, (213)740-4665.

LI, VIVIEN
Non-profit organization executive. Chinese American. **PERSONAL:** Born Feb 23, 1954, New York, NY; daughter of Tsiang Kwang Li and Dora Mei Li; married Robert E Holland, Mar 24, 1984; children: Caroline Li Holland, Andrea Li Holland. **EDUCATION:** Barnard College, Columbia University, BA, 1975; Princeton University, master's, public administration, 1983. **CAREER:** Massachusetts Public Health Commissioner, executive asst, 1983-87; Governor Michael Dukakis, senior staff, 1988-91; Boston Harbor Assn, executive director, currently. **ORGANIZATIONS:** Sierra Club, board of directors, 1986-92, asst treasurer, 1986-92; Princeton University Woodrow Wilson School, class fundraising chair, 1991-; Women's Educational & Industrial Union, board of directors, 1989-. **HONORS/AWARDS:** Presidential Environmental Award, 1976; New Jersey Sierra Club Chapter Award, 1983. **SPECIAL ACHIEVEMENTS:** Publications on women and workplace issues and on environmental issues; fluent in Cantonese and French. **BIOGRAPHICAL SOURCES:** Boston Business Journal, Feb 19-25, 1993, p10. **HOME ADDRESS:** 222 Marlborough St, Boston, MA 02116. **BUSINESS PHONE:** (617)482-1722.

LI, WEN-HSIUNG
Educator (retired). Chinese American. **PERSONAL:** Born Nov 5, 1918, Sin-Hui, Guangdong, China; son of Li Sung and Lai Yup-Hing; married Kuan-Ming Ling Li, Sep 16, 1950; children: Charlene C, Li Harris. **EDUCATION:** Jiao Tong University, Shanghai, China, BS, 1941; University of Manchester, England, PhD, 1947. **CAREER:** Chinese government, engineer, 1942-45; Johns Hopkins University, fellow, assistant professor, associate professor, 1948-59; Syracuse University, professor, 1959-82, professor emeritus, 1982-. **ORGANIZATIONS:** International Association for Hydraulic Research, 1953-85; American Society of Civil Engineers, 1950-. **HONORS/AWARDS:** Federation of Sewage & Industrial Wates Associations, The Harrison Prescott Eddy Medal for Noteworthy Research, 1952-. **SPECIAL ACHIEVEMENTS:** 4 textbooks: Engineering Analysis, Prentice-Hall, 1960; co-author, Principles of Fluid Mechanics, Addison Wesley, 1964; Differential Equations of Hydraulic Transients, Dispersion and Groundwater Flow, Prentice-Hall, 1972; Fluid Mechanics in Water Resources Engineering, Allyn & Bacon, 1983; about 40 research papers in journals. **BUSINESS ADDRESS:** Professor Emeritus, Syracuse University, College of Engineering, Syracuse, NY 13210.

LI, WILLIAM WEI-LIN
Physician. Chinese American. **PERSONAL:** Born Jul 1, 1962, Pittsburgh, PA; son of Ching-chung Li and Hanna Wu Li. **EDUCATION:** Harvard College, AB, 1984; University of Pittsburgh, School of Medicine, MD, 1991. **CAREER:** Children's Hospital, Harvard Medical School, research fellow, 1987-89; Massachusetts General Hospital, medical intern, 1991-92, clinicl fellow, 1992-. **HONORS/AWARDS:** National Institutes of Health, Research Award, 1992; Harvard Medical School, Andrus Fellowship in Surgical Research, 1987; University of Pittsburgh School of Medicine, Mirsky Award, 1991; Alpha Omega Alpha, Research Fellowship Award, 1987. **SPECIAL ACHIEVEMENTS:** Medical research in angiogenesis; publications in Science, 1989, Investigative Ophthalmology and Visual Sciences, 1991, Annals of Surgery, 1991; Enymine Graphics, founder & president, 1983; language proficiency: Chinese, Mandarin, French, Italian. **HOME ADDRESS:** 2130 Garrick Dr, Pittsburgh, PA 15235.

LI, WU
Educator. Chinese American. **PERSONAL:** Born Nov 8, 1958, Wenzhou, Zhejiang, People's Republic of China; son of Chang-Feng Li and Chun-Fang Li; married Wan Hu, Dec 11, 1985; children: M Maryann, Victoria M. **EDUCATION:** Zhejiang Normal University, BMath, 1982; Hangzhou University, MMath, 1984; Pennsylvania State University, MCS, 1990, PhD, mathematics, 1990. **CAREER:** Hangzhou University, lecturer, 1984-86; Old Dominion University, assistant professor, 1990-. **ORGANIZATIONS:** SIAM; ORSA. **HONORS/AWARDS:** Pennsylvania State University, graduate school fellowship, 1988, The Homeyer Graduate Fellowship, 1988. **SPECIAL ACHIEVEMENTS:** Monograph: Continous Selections for Metric Projections and Interpolating Subspaces, 1991; numerous articles published in the following journals: Trans Amer Math Soc, SIAM Journal on Optimization, SIAM J Math Analysis, SIAM J Control Option, J Math Analysis Appl, J Optim Theory Appl, J Approx Theory, Linear Alg Appl, Scientia Sinica, Acta Mathematica Sinica, 1987-93. **BIOGRAPHICAL SOURCES:** Mathematical Reviews, Mathematics Abstracts. **BUSINESS ADDRESS:** Assistant Professor, Dept of Mathematics and Statistics, Old Dominion University, Hampton Boulevard, Norfolk, VA 23529-0001, (804)683-3918.

LI, XIAO-BING
Educator. Chinese American. **PERSONAL:** Born Feb 5, 1954, Beijing, People's Republic of China; son of Wei-Ying Li and Xiao-Yi Zhang; married Tran Lai Li, Jul 23, 1988; children: Kevin Jiajing. **EDUCATION:** Nankai University, BA, 1982; Carnegie Mellon University, MA, 1984, PhD, 1991. **CAREER:** Chinese Academy of Social Science, assistant research fellow, 1982-83; University of Pittsburgh, teaching assistant, 1984; Carnegie Mellon University, research assistant, 1988, teaching assistant, 1989-91; Phillips University, assistant professor, 1991-93; University of Central Oklahoma, assistant professor, 1993-; Western Pacific Institute, associate director, currently. **ORGANIZATIONS:** Chinese Historians in the US, board of directors, 1991-94, editor of the CHUS Newsletter, 1991-94; Association for Asian Studies, 1990-; American Historical Association, 1990-; Oklahoma Association of Professional Historians, 1992-; China Confucius Society, Liaison Department, deputy director, 1991-. **HONORS/AWARDS:** Luce Foundation, Luce Teaching Scholarship for China Teaching, 1991; Carnegie Mellon Foundation, Graduate Study Fellowship, 1984-86, 88-89; Mellon Fellowship, Richard King Mellon Fellowship, 1983-84; Chinese Academy of Social Sciences, Prize for Outstanding Research Papers, 1983. **SPECIAL ACHIEVEMENTS:** Book: Diplomacy through Militancy: Crisis Politics and Sino-American Relations in the 1950's, 1993. **HOME ADDRESS:** 3346 NW 29th St, Oklahoma City, OK 73107, (405)946-3107. **BUSINESS ADDRESS:** Assistant Professor, History Dept, University of Central Oklahoma, 100 N University Ave, Edmond, OK 73034, (405)341-2980.

LI, YA
Educator. Chinese American. **PERSONAL:** Born May 12, 1960, Anhui, People's Republic of China; daughter of Yin Li and Aidong Wu; married Zhongming Fang, Apr 1985; children: Andrew Fang, Katherine Fang. **EDUCATION:** University of Science and Technology of China, 1982; University of Utah, PhD, 1990. **CAREER:** Utah Valley Community College, instructor, 1990-92; Teikyo Westmar University, assistant professor, 1992-. **ORGANIZATIONS:** American Mathematical Society, 1982-. **BUSINESS ADDRESS:** Assistant Professor, Teikyo Westmar University, 1002 3rd Avenue SE, Le Mars, IA 51031, (712)546-2507.

LI, YAO TZU
Engineer. Chinese American. **PERSONAL:** Born Feb 1, 1914, Beijing, China. **EDUCATION:** Massachusetts Institute of Technology, ScD, 1939. **CAREER:** Setra Systems Inc, chairman, treasurer, 1968-; MIT, professor, control and guidance, 1970-79, Innovation Center, director, 1972-79. **ORGANIZATIONS:** Natl Academy of Engineering, Fellow. **BUSINESS ADDRESS:** Chairman, Setra Systems Inc, 45 Nagog Pk, Acton,MA 01720, (508)263-1400.*

LI, YONGJI
Educator, health administrator. Chinese American. **PERSONAL:** Born Sep 5, 1933, Beijing, China; son of Zhi-Ping Lee and Zhi-Zhang Chen Lee; married Zhihua Y Li, Jun 30, 1956; children: Zidan, Lisa. **EDUCATION:** Beijing University, BS, 1955; State University of New York at Buffalo, PhD, 1985. **CAREER:** Jilin University, China, lecturer, instructor of physics, 1955-81; SUNY, Buffalo, research assistant/teaching assistant, 1981-85; University of New Orleans, postdoctoral research associate, 1985-89; University of Puerto Rico, associate professor of chemistry, 1989-, x-ray laboratory, director, cur-

rently. **ORGANIZATIONS:** American Chemical Society, 1984-; American Crystallographic Association, 1985-. **HONORS/AWARDS:** NSF, grant, 1992; High Education Ministry, China, competition winner of high pressure physics grants among universities, 1979. **SPECIAL ACHIEVEMENTS:** Constructed the first Chinese ultra-high pressure mini-generator: diamond anvil cell, (300kb without a gasket), 1978; X-ray crystal structure determination of inorganic and/or biologically active compounds; accurate measurements of electron density distribution; 28 publications.

LI, YU-KU (HUZO)
Educator, certified public accountant. Chinese American. **PERSONAL:** Born Oct 7, 1939, Kuoshi, Hunan, China; son of Kuo-Kan Li & Yu-May Chen Li; married Christine Li, Jun 9, 1972; children: Darren. **EDUCATION:** National Taiwan University, BA, 1961; University of California, Berkeley, MBA, 1965, PhD, 1968. **CAREER:** Ohio State University, assistant professor, 1967-73; State University of New York, Oswego, associate professor, 1973-77; Yu-ku Li, CPA's, owner, 1983-; State University of New York, Brockport, professor, 1977-. **ORGANIZATIONS:** American Institute of CPA's, 1986-89. **HONORS/AWARDS:** Ford Foundation, Doctoral Student Award, 1965-68. **HOME PHONE:** (716)225-9521. **BUSINESS ADDRESS:** Professor, Dept of Business Administration, State University College, Brockport, Brockport, NY 14420.

LI, YUZHUO
Educator. Chinese American. **PERSONAL:** Born Feb 28, 1958, Tianjin, People's Republic of China; son of Xiuqin Li and Xuehui Zhu; married Ning Gao, Jan 8, 1986. **EDUCATION:** Nankai University, BS, 1982; University of Illinois, Urbana, PhD, 1988. **CAREER:** SUNY, Potsdam, assistant professor, 1989-90; Clarkson University, assistant professor, 1990-. **ORGANIZATIONS:** American Chemical Society, Northern-New York Section, chairman; Sigma Xi; Inter-American Photochemical Society. **HONORS/AWARDS:** University of Illinois, R C Fuson Research Award, 1988; Clarkson University, Outstanding New Teacher Award, 1993. **SPECIAL ACHIEVEMENTS:** Published several articles in scientific journals including Journal of Organic Chemistry, Journal of the American Chemical Society, and Journal of Chem Phys. **BUSINESS ADDRESS:** Professor, Chemistry Dept, Clarkson University, Box 5810, Potsdam, NY 13699-5810, (315)268-2355.

LIAN, ERIC CHUN-YET
Physician, educator. Chinese American. **PERSONAL:** Born Nov 11, 1938, Tainan Hsien, Taiwan; son of Z T Lian and T O Chiu-Lian; married Maria, 1972; children: Elizabeth, Alexander. **EDUCATION:** National Taiwan University, MD, 1964. **CAREER:** University of Miami, assistant professor, 1973-78, associate professor, 1978-87, director hematosis lab, 1976-, director, comprehensive hemophilia & thrombosis ctr, 1976-, professor, 1987-; VA Medical Center, staff physician, 1973-. **ORGANIZATIONS:** AFCR, 1973-; ACP, 1974-; American Society of Hematology, 1975-; International Society on Thrombosis & Hemostasis, 1983-; American Society Biochem Molecular Biology, 1989-. **HONORS/AWARDS:** VA, Factor VIII, 1976, role of plasma factor in TTP, 1979-; NIH, platelet agglutination thrombotic microangiopathy, 1981-. **SPECIAL ACHIEVEMENTS:** 64 published papers on hematology, hemostasis and thrombosis; language proficiency: Taiwanese, Mandarin. **MILITARY SERVICE:** Army of Republic of China, surgeon, 1964-65. **BUSINESS ADDRESS:** Professor, VA Medical Center, University of Miami, 1201 NW 16th St, Miami, FL 33125, (305)326-8041.

LIAN, MARIA Z. N.
Educational administrator. Chinese American. **PERSONAL:** Born Apr 5, 1939, Shanghai, China; daughter of T L Tsong and Z L Pei; married Eric Lian; children: Elizabeth, Alexander. **EDUCATION:** Wesleyan College, AB, 1961; University of Chicago, MS, 1964; MIT, MS, 1970; University of Miami, MS, 1982. **CAREER:** Beth Israel Hospital, research associate; University of Miami, database analyst; Bacardi, consultant; Cargill, consultant; University of Miami, special projects director, currently. **HOME ADDRESS:** 1037 Castile Ave, Coral Gables, FL 33134, (305)445-0064. **BUSINESS ADDRESS:** Special Projects Director, University of Miami, 800 Brunson Dr, Allen Hall Rm 118, Coral Gables, FL 33146, (305)284-3049.

LIANG, BRUCE T.
Physician. Chinese American. **PERSONAL:** Born Mar 11, 1956; married. **EDUCATION:** Harvard College, BA, 1978, Medical School, MD, 1982. **CAREER:** University of Pennsylvania Hospital, professor of medicine, currently.

LIANG, CHANG-SENG
Educator, researcher, cardiologist. Chinese American. **PERSONAL:** Born Jan 6, 1941, Chang-chow, Fukien, China; son of You-Rang Liang and Mu-lan Cheng Liang; married Betty, Jul 29, 1967; children: Marilyn, Marybeth, Michelle. **EDUCATION:** National Taiwan University, MD, 1965; Boston University, PhD, 1972. **CAREER:** Boston University, assistant professor to associate professor, 1973-82; University of Rochester, associate professor of medicine, 1982-86, professor of medicine, 1986-. **ORGANIZATIONS:** American Heart Association; American Physiological Society; American Society for Clinical Investigation; American Society for Pharmacology & Experimental Therapeutics; American Chinese Medical Society. **HONORS/AWARDS:** National Institutes of Health, research grants; American Heart Association, research grants. **SPECIAL ACHIEVEMENTS:** Scientific publications in many peer-reviewed journals. **BUSINESS ADDRESS:** Professor of Medicine, University of Rochester Medical Center, 601 Elmwood Ave, Cardiology Unit, Box 679, Rochester, NY 14642, (716)275-2348.

LIANG, DIANA F.
Librarian. Chinese American. **PERSONAL:** Born in Shanghai, China; daughter of C C Fang and Feng Mei Fang; married Joseph J Liang, Jun 10, 1965; children: Patrick C, Michael N. **EDUCATION:** National Taiwan University, BA, 1960; Vanderbilt University, MA, 1964. **CAREER:** Fairfield County District Library, acting librarian, 1964-66; Chemical Abstract Services, assistant editor, 1967-69; University of South Florida, university librarian, 1972-. **ORGANIZATIONS:** American Library Association, 1978-; Suncoast Association of Chinese Americans, board member, 1983-; University of South Florida Botanical Garden, 1991-. **HONORS/AWARDS:** University of South Florida, President Council, Grant, 1985-86. **SPECIAL ACHIEVEMENTS:** "Mathematical Journals: An Annotated Guide," Scarecrow Press, 1992; search committee member, President of University of South Florida position. **BIOGRAPHICAL SOURCES:** Choice, Feb 1993, p 942; Wilson Library Bulletin, Jan 1993, p 111. **BUSINESS ADDRESS:** University Librarian, University of South Florida, 4202 E Fowler Avenue, LIB 020, Tampa, FL 33620, (813)974-4293.

LIANG, EDISON PARK-TAK
Educator. Chinese American/Hong Kong American. **PERSONAL:** Born Jul 22, 1947, Canton, China; son of Chi-Sen Liang & Siu-Fong Law; married Lily, Aug 7, 1971; children: Olivia, James, Justin. **EDUCATION:** University of California, Berkeley, BA, 1967, PhD, 1971. **CAREER:** University of Texas, Austin, research associate, 1971-73; University of Utah, research associate, 1973-75; Michigan State University, professor, 1975-76; Stanford University, professor, 1976-80; Lawrence Livermore National Lab, physicist, associate division leader, 1980-91; Rice University, professor, 1991-. **ORGANIZATIONS:** American Physical Society, Astrophysics Division Executive Committee, fellow; American Astronomical Society; International Astronomical Union; Sigma Xi; Phi Beta Kappa. **HONORS/AWARDS:** University of California, Science Fellow, 1967-69, Anthony Scholar, 1967-69; Organization of American States, visiting professorship, 1973; Science Research Council of UK, Senior Fellowhsip, 1974. **SPECIAL ACHIEVEMENTS:** Over 100 scientific publications on astrophysics and cosmology. **BUSINESS ADDRESS:** Professor of Space Physics & Astronomy, Rice University, 6100 Main St, Space Science Building, PO Box 1892, Houston, TX 77251-1892, (713)527-8101.

LIANG, GEORGE HSUEH-LEE
Educator. Chinese American. **PERSONAL:** Born Oct 1, 1934, Peking, Hebei, China; son of Chieh-Cheng Liang and Wen-Chiang Y Liang; married Yun-Teh S Liang, Jun 8, 1963; children: J May, Roy C. **EDUCATION:** Chung-Hsing University, Taichung, Taiwan, BS, 1956; University of Wyoming, MS, 1961; University of Wisconsin, PhD, 1965. **CAREER:** University of Wyoming, graduate research assistant, 1960-61; University of Wisconsin, graduate research assistant, 1961-64; Kansas State University, assistant professor, 1964-69, associate professor, 1969-76, professor, 1976-, chairman, genetics program, 1982-. **ORGANIZATIONS:** The American Genetic Association; American Society of Agronomy; Genetics Society of Canada. **HONORS/AWARDS:** Phi Kappa Phi, 1983; Alpha Zeta, 1960; Sigma Xi, 1961; Gamma Sigma Delta, 1961; Chinese Academy, Distinguished Research Professorship, 1987. **SPECIAL ACHIEVEMENTS:** Author: Plant Genetics, 1st edition, 1982, 2nd edition, 1991; "Wheat Breeding: Novel Approaches to Wheat Improvement," book chapter, 1987; "A Direct Generation System for Wheat Haploid Production," book chapter, 1990; "Regeneration of Plants from Alfa Protoplasts by Direct Embryogenesis," book chapter, 1993. **MILITARY SERVICE:** Army

artillery, second lt, Taiwan, 1956-58. **BUSINESS ADDRESS:** Professor, Dept of Agronomy, Kansas State University, Throckmorton Hall, Rm 349, Manhattan, KS 66506-5501, (913)532-7225.

LIANG, MATTHEW H.
Physician. Chinese American. **PERSONAL:** Born May 24, 1944, Santa Monica, CA; son of Ping Yee Liang and Alice Kao Liang; married Irmhild Prowe Liang, Jun 1, 1969; children: Peter Yen, Ursula Shih, Stefanie Hsien. **EDUCATION:** Johns Hopkins University, AB, 1965; Dartmouth Medical School, DMS, 1967; Harvard Medical School, MD, 1969; Harvard School of Public Health, MPH. **CAREER:** Robert B Brigham Multipurpose Arthritis Center, director, 1980-; Harvard Medical School, associate professor of medicine, 1986-; Brigham & Women's Hospital, physician, currently. **ORGANIZATIONS:** Arthritis Foundation; American College of Rheumatology; Wellmark, Medical Foundation, board of directors. **HONORS/AWARDS:** Medical Foundation, Fellow, 1979; American College of Physicians, Teaching & Research Scholar, 1980. **MILITARY SERVICE:** US Army, major, 1973-75; Certificate of Achievement for Outstanding Service, 1975; Army Commendation Medal, 1975. **BIOGRAPHICAL SOURCES:** Harvard Medical Unit at Boston City Hospital, Finland, M, Castle, WB, editors, Boston, Commonwealth Fund, p 1391-93, 1983. **BUSINESS ADDRESS:** Brigham & Women's Hospital, 75 Francis St, Boston, MA 02115, (617)732-5356.

LIANG, STEVEN YUEHSAN
Educator. Taiwanese American. **PERSONAL:** Born Nov 18, 1958, Kaohsiung, Taiwan; son of Chu-Hung and Ling-Ling Liang; married Charng Jen Liang, Mar 28, 1986; children: Vincent Yaw. **EDUCATION:** National Cheng-Kung University, Taiwan, BS, 1980; Michigan State University, MS, 1984; University of California at Berkeley, PhD, 1987. **CAREER:** Michigan State University, graduate assistant, 1982-84; University of California at Berkeley, graduate assistant, 1984-87; Oklahoma State University, academic faculty member, 1987-89; Georgia Institute of Technology, academic faculty member, 1990-. **ORGANIZATIONS:** Monte Jade Science & Tech Association at Southeastern US, president, 1994-95; Chinese-American Academic Professional Association, board of directors, 1993-94; American Society of Mechanical Engineers, executive committee, 1991-93; North American Manufacturing Research Institute, editorial board member, 1993-95; Winter Annual Meeting of ASME, symposium organizer, 1990-94; Society of Manufacturing Engineers, senior member, 1988-; ASME, 1984-; Chinese Institute of Engineers, Cheng Kung University Chapter, president, 1977-78. **HONORS/AWARDS:** Society of Manufacturing Engineers, Robert B Douglas Outstanding Young Manufacturing Engineer Award, 1991; Sigma Xi, 1991; Ministry of Education, Republic of China, Outstanding Student Society Leadership Award, 1979. **SPECIAL ACHIEVEMENTS:** Over 40 publications in archival journals and professional conference proceedings; 10 invited speeches at academic institutions and industries in 5 different countries; provided engineering consulting service to over 10 manufacturing companies. **MILITARY SERVICE:** Chinese Army Ordnance, 2nd lt, 1980-82. **BIOGRAPHICAL SOURCES:** World Journal Weekly, p 9, Nov 25, 1990; People's Daily, p 5, Nov 30, 1990. **HOME ADDRESS:** 3249 Hunterdon Way, Marietta, GA 30067, (404)916-1632. **BUSINESS ADDRESS:** Academic Faculty Member, School of Mechanical Engineering, Georgia Institute of Technology, Atlanta, GA 30332-0405, (404)894-8164.

LIANG, TEHMING
Dermatologist, biochemist, educator. Taiwanese American. **PERSONAL:** Born Apr 14, 1945, Tainan, Taiwan; married. **EDUCATION:** National Taiwan University, Taipei, BS, 1968; University of Chicago, PhD, biochem, 1973; University of Miami, MD, 1987. **CAREER:** University of Chicago, research associate, 1973-76, research assistant professor, 1976-77; Merck Sharp and Dohme Research Lab, senior research biochemist, 1977-81, research fellow, 1981-85; Robert Wood Johnson University Hospital, resident in internal medicine, 1987-88; University of Chicago, resident in dermatology, 1989-91; Wright State University, School of Medicine, Dept of Dermatology, associate professor, 1992-. **ORGANIZATIONS:** American Society for Biochemistry & Molecular Biology; The Endocrine Society; Society for Neuroscience; Society for Investigative Dermatology; New York Academy of Sciences; American Medical Association; Ohio State Medical Association; Montgomery County Medical Association. **BUSINESS ADDRESS:** Associate Professor, Dept of Dermatology, School of Medicine, Wright State University, PO Box 927, Dayton, OH 45401-0927, (513)262-0214.

LIAO, MEI-JUNE
Biochemical researcher. Taiwanese American. **PERSONAL:** Born Mar 20, 1951, Taipei, Taiwan; married David B Viscio, May 16, 1984; children: Michael. **EDUCATION:** National Tsing-Hua University, Taiwan, BS, 1973; Yale University, MPh, 1977, PhD, 1980. **CAREER:** MIT, postdoctoral associate, 1980-83; Interferon Sciences Inc, group leader, 1983-84, director of cell biology, 1985-86, director of research & development, 1987-. **ORGANIZATIONS:** American Society for Biochemistry & Molecular Biology, currently; International Society for Interferon Research, currently; Society for Chinese Bioscientists in America, currently. **SPECIAL ACHIEVEMENTS:** Author: Approx 55 publications in scientific journals, 1973-; about 5 US patent applications pending. **BUSINESS ADDRESS:** Director, Research & Development, Interferon Sciences Inc, 783 Jersey Ave, New Brunswick, NJ 08901, (908)249-3232.

LIAO, MING
Educator. Chinese American. **PERSONAL:** Born Nov 11, 1950, Hong Kong; son of Guoying Liao and Huijuan Zhou; married Junwei Xue, Jan 25, 1978; children: Xiaojuan. **EDUCATION:** Shandong Tai'an Teachers College, China, 1978; Institute of Mathematics, Academi Sinica, 1978-80; Stanford University, PhD, 1985. **CAREER:** Nankai University, China, lecturer, 1985-86, associate professor, 1986-87, professor, 1988-90; University of Florida, visiting professor, 1987-88; University of Michigan, visiting professor, 1990; Auburn University, assistant professor, 1990-92, associate professor, 1992-. **ORGANIZATIONS:** Chinese Probability and Statistics Association, member of board of directors. **HONORS/AWARDS:** Tianjin City, China, Young Scientist Award, 1990; Hou Ying Dong Education Foundation, Grant Award, 1990. **SPECIAL ACHIEVEMENTS:** Published 17 articles in internationally recognized mathematical journals. **BIOGRAPHICAL SOURCES:** Contemporary Mathematics, vol 73, p 152, 267, 268, 1988; Diffusion Processes and Related Problems in Analysis, vol II, p 9, 1992. **BUSINESS ADDRESS:** Professor, Department of Mathematics, Auburn University, Auburn, AL 36849-3501, (205)844-6568.

LIAO, PAUL FOO-HUNG
Research executive. Chinese American. **PERSONAL:** Born Nov 10, 1944, Philadelphia, PA; son of Tseng Wu Liao & Tung Mei Liao; married Karen A Liao, Aug 31, 1968; children: Teresa S, Joanna S. **EDUCATION:** MIT, BS, physics, 1966; Columbia University, PhD, physics, 1973. **CAREER:** Bell Laboratories, department head, 1980-83; Bellcore, division manager, 1984-89, general manager, 1989-. **ORGANIZATIONS:** IEEE Lasers & Electro-Optics Society, president, 1987; Joint Council on Quantum Electronics, president, 1985-87; Christ Church United Methodist, Administrative Council, chairman, 1988; Conference on Lasers and Electro-Optics, chairman, 1989. **HONORS/AWARDS:** Optical Society of America, fellow; American Physical Society, fellow; Institute of Electrical and Electronic Engineers, fellow. **SPECIAL ACHIEVEMENTS:** Published over 80 papers in technical journals; editor, Journal of Optical Society of America, 1988-; editor, Academic Press Series on Quantum Electronics. **BUSINESS ADDRESS:** General Manager, Bellcore, 331 Newman Springs Road, Red Bank, NJ 07701.

LIAO, SHUN-KWUNG
Physician. Taiwanese American/Chinese American. **PERSONAL:** Born Feb 25, 1937, Miaoli, Taiwan; son of Run-sen Liao and Fa-Mei Hsu; married Judy Jui-chun Liao, Apr 13, 1965; children: Margaret, David. **EDUCATION:** Kaohsiung Medical College, MD, 1962; University of Tokyo, DMS, 1968. **CAREER:** Kaohsiung Medical College Hospital, internship, 1961-62; University of Tokyo Hospital, residency, 1964-68; Toranomon Hospital, Tokyo, 1965-66; Bronx-Lebanon Hospital, 1968-69; University of Hawaii, integrated surgical residency program, 1969-73; University of Hawaii, John A Burns School of Medicine, assistant professor of surgery, 1973; private practice, physician, currently. **ORGANIZATIONS:** American Society for Gastrointestinal Endoscopy, 1980-; Pan Pacific Surgical Association; Hawaii Medical Association, Takung Mandarine School, board of directors. **HONORS/AWARDS:** American College of Surgeons, fellow, 1975. **BUSINESS ADDRESS:** President, Shun-Kwung Liao, MD, Inc, 1380 Lusitana St, Honolulu, HI 96822, (808)524-5940.

LIAO, SHUTSUNG
Educator. Taiwanese American. **PERSONAL:** Born Jan 1, 1931, Tainan, Taiwan; son of Chi-Chun Liao & Chin-Shen Lin; married Shuching Liao, Mar 19, 1960; children: Jane, Tzufen, Tzuming, May. **EDUCATION:** National Taiwan University, BS, 1953, MS, 1956; University of Chicago, PhD, 1961.

CAREER: University of Chicago, instructor, 1963-64, assistant professor, 1964-69, associate professor, 1969-71, professor, 1972-. **ORGANIZATIONS:** American Society Biochemistry & Molecular Biology; American Association Cancer Research, associate editor, 1982-89; Endocrine Society; North American Taiwanese Professors' Association, president, 1980-81, executive director, 1981-; J Steroid Biochemistry & Molecular Biology, editorial board member, currently; Receptors, editorial board member, currently. **HONORS/AWARDS:** Clinical Research Institute of Montreal, Pfizer Travelling Fellow Award, 1972; Taiwanese-American Foundation, Science and Technology Achievement Award, 1983; Worcester Foundation, Gregory Pincus Medal and Award, 1992; Farmosan Medical Assn, Tu, C. M. Award, 1993. **SPECIAL ACHIEVEMENTS:** Molecular basis of androgen action; discovery of androgen and other nuclear receptors; structure and mutation of androgen receptor genes; Therapeutic Agents for Androgen-Dependent Diseases. **BUSINESS ADDRESS:** Professor, Ben May Institute, University of Chicago, 5841 S Maryland, Box MC 6027, Rm N-460B, Chicago, IL 60637, (312)702-6999.

LIAO, T. WARREN
Educator. Taiwanese American. **PERSONAL:** Born Mar 19, 1957, Huwei, Yunlin, Taiwan; son of Shuh-min Liao and Moon-Dan Lian; married Chi-Fen Ting, Feb 23, 1989; children: Allen. **EDUCATION:** Lehigh University, MSIE, 1986, PhD, 1990. **CAREER:** Lehigh University, teaching assistant, 1986-90; Louisiana State University, assistant professor, 1990-. **ORGANIZATIONS:** Society of Manufacturing Engineers, 1989-; IEEE, 1992-; IIE, 1984-; ASME, 1992-. **HONORS/AWARDS:** Board of Regents of Louisiana State, LEQSF Award, 1993. **SPECIAL ACHIEVEMENTS:** Design of Line Type Cellular Manufacturing Systems, 1993; An Evaluation of ART1 Neural Models for Part Family and Machine Cell Forming, 1993; Integration of a Feature Based CAD System and an ART1 Neural Model for GT Coding and Part Family Forming, 1993; A Shielded Metal Arc Welding Expert System, 1993; On the Study of Creep Feed Grinding of Alumina, 1993. **MILITARY SERVICE:** Army Tank Division, second lieutenant, 1977-79. **BUSINESS ADDRESS:** Asst Prof, IE Dept, Louisiana State University, 3128 CEBA, Baton Rouge, LA 70803-6409, (504)388-5365.

LIAO, WOODY M.
Educator. Taiwanese American. **PERSONAL:** Born Jul 14, 1942, Chia-Yi, Taiwan; son of Mr & Mrs Deh-li Liao; married Marie Liao. **EDUCATION:** National Chengchi University, BS, 1966; Illinois State University, MS, 1970; University of Florida, PhD, 1974. **CAREER:** Bank of Communications, staff clerk, 1967-69; Virginia Polytechnic Institute & State University, assistant professor of accounting, 1974-78; University of Houston, professor of accounting, 1978-91; University of California, professor of accounting, 1991-. **ORGANIZATIONS:** American Accounting Association; Institute of Certified Management Accountants; Institute of Decision Sciences. **HONORS/AWARDS:** Deloitte, Haskins & Sells, PhD Research Grant, 1974; Peat, Marwick, Mitchell & Co, research grant, 1982; University of Houston, Halliburton Research & Service Award, 1990. **SPECIAL ACHIEVEMENTS:** CPA; CMA. **BUSINESS ADDRESS:** Professor, University of California, Riverside, Graduate School of Management, Riverside, CA 92521, (909)787-6451.

LIDDELL, GENE CANQUE
Educator, state government official. Filipino American. **PERSONAL:** Born Jun 10, 1942, Kahuku, HI; daughter of Antonio and Sally Nuez Canque; married John A Liddell, Oct 31, 1964; children: Keone Anthony, Kimo Adrian. **EDUCATION:** Washington State University, BS, 1964; University of Oregon, MS, 1978; St Martin's College, psych; University of Washington, PE. **CAREER:** Olympia Schools, junior high teacher, 1966-75; Office of Superintendent of Public Instruction, supervisor, 1975-87; City of Lacey, council member, 1987-93, mayor, 1991-93; State of Washington, curriculum director, 1987-92, Dept of community development, 1993-94, director, Governor's Council on School-to-Work Opportunity System, executive director, 1994-. **ORGANIZATIONS:** JACL, vice president, 1985-87; APAMO, president, 1991-92; National Asian Pacific American Elected Officials. **HONORS/AWARDS:** Northwest Women's Law Center, Leadership Award, 1985; Washington Education Association, Leadership Award, 1985. **BUSINESS ADDRESS:** Executive Director, Governor's Council on School-to-Work Opportunity System, 605 Woodland Sq, Lacey, WA 98503, (206)438-4659.

LIEM, KAREL FREDERIK
Educator, educational administrator. Indonesian American/Chinese American. **PERSONAL:** Born Nov 24, 1935, Java, Indonesia; married Hetty Liem, Sep 4, 1965; children: Karel F Jr, Erika E. **EDUCATION:** University of Indonesia,

Java, BS, biology, 1957, MS (cum laude), 1958; University of Illinois, Urbana, PhD, zoology, 1961. **CAREER:** University of Leiden, The Netherlands, asst prof of zoology, 1962-64; University of Illinois, College of Medicine, asst prof of anatomy, 1964-67, assoc prof of anatomy, 1967-72; Field Museum of Natural History, assoc curator of vertebrate anatomy, 1968-72; University of Chicago, lecturer in evolutionary biology, 1967-72; Harvard University, Master of Dunster House, 1989-, Henry Bryant Bigelow Professor of Ichthyology, curator of Ichthyology, prof of biology, 1972-. **ORGANIZATIONS:** American Soc of Zoologists, president, 1989; American Soc of Ichthyologists and Herpetologists, board of governors, 1987; Sigma Xi, Harvard, Radcliffe Chapter, president, 1990, 1991; Journal of Experimental Morphology, executive editor, 1987-; Evolution, associate editor, 1987-91; Zoological Soc of London, scientific fellow, 1963; American Assn for the Advancement of Sciences, 1967-; Environmental Biology of Fishes, editor, 1979-. **HONORS/AWARDS:** Guggenheim Foundation, Fellowship, 1970-71, 1979-80; Linnean Society of London, fellow, 1971; University of Illinois Medical Center, Golden Apple Award, 1967, 1969; Phi Beta Kappa, teaching award, 1987; Hoopes Prize for Excellence in Teaching, 1985, 1987. **SPECIAL ACHIEVEMENTS:** "Tetrapod Parallelisms & other Features in the Functional Morphology of the Blood Vascular System of Fluta Alba (Pisces, Teleostei)" Journal of Morphology, vol 108, p 131-144, 1961; "Evolutionary Strategies & Morphological Innovations: Cichlid Pharyngeal Jaws," Systematic Zoology, vol 22, no 4, p 425-441, 1974; co-author, Life: An Introduction to Biology, Harper Collins, 3rd ed, 1991; "Aquatic Versus Terrestrial Feeding Modes: Possible Impacts on the Trophic Ecology of Vertebrates," American Zoology, vol 30 p 209-211, 1990; "Speciation & Adaptive Radiation in Groundfishes: The Origin of New Taxa," American Society of Zoologists, Plenary Abstract, 1990. **BIOGRAPHICAL SOURCES:** "Animals: Form and Function—An Interview with Karl Liem," Biology, 3rd ed, Campbell, pp 778-781, 1993. **BUSINESS ADDRESS:** Henry Bryant Bigelow Professor, Curator of Ichthyology, Professor of Biology, Master of Dunster House, Harvard University, Museum of Comparative Zoology, 26 Oxford St, Labs 112, Cambridge, MA 02138.

LIEM, RONALD KIAN HONG
Educator. Chinese American/Indonesian American. **PERSONAL:** Born Feb 8, 1946, Praya, Lombok, Indonesia. **EDUCATION:** Amherst College, BA, 1967; Cornell University, PhD, 1973. **CAREER:** New York University School of Medicine, assistant/associate professor, 1978-87; Columbia University, professor, 1987-. **BUSINESS ADDRESS:** Professor of Pathology and Anatomy & Cell Biology, Columbia University, College of Physicians & Surgeons, 630 W 168th St, P&S Bldg 15-421, New York, NY 10038, (212)305-4078.

LIEU, GEORGE Y.
Educator. Korean American. **PERSONAL:** Born Feb 3, 1947, Republic of Korea; son of Hee J Lieu and Duck H Lieu; married Karen K Lieu, Apr 8, 1978; children: James, Jennifer. **EDUCATION:** Korea University, BA, 1972; University of Wisconsin, Madison, MA, 1975; Oklahoma State University, PhD, 1986. **CAREER:** Korea Development Institute, research associate, 1972-78; King Sejong University, assistant professor, 1979-81; Samsung Group, manager, 1978; Oklahoma State University, instructor, 1985-86; Paul Quinn College, assistant professor, 1986-88; Tuskegee University, assistant professor, 1988-92, associate professor, 1992-. **ORGANIZATIONS:** American Economic Association, 1985; Southern Economic Association, 1985; International Assistant Project of Alabama Inc, advisory board, 1992; Beta Gamma Sigma, 1984; Phi Kappa Phi, 1986. **HONORS/AWARDS:** Tuskegee University, Outstanding Faculty Research, 1992, Outstanding Faculty Teaching, 1993. **SPECIAL ACHIEVEMENTS:** Author: "Economic Progress of Black Males in the South, 1970-1980," Business and Economic Review, fall, 1992; "Economic Progress in the Black South: The Case of High School and College Graduates, 1970-1980," Southern Ohio Business Review, spring, 1991; other publications. **HOME ADDRESS:** 2020 Woodmere Loop, Montgomery, AL 36117, (205)270-0646. **BUSINESS ADDRESS:** Professor, School of Business, Tuskegee University, School of Business, Tuskegee, AL 36088, (205)727-8733.

LIEU, HOU-SHUN
Economist, educator. Chinese American. **PERSONAL:** Born May 13, 1921, Peking, China; son of D K Lieu & Helen Yungtsing King; married Lucy Hsu, Feb 14, 1957; children: Diane Te-Lan Dobbs, Vincent Te-Feng, Helena Te-Yun Cooney. **EDUCATION:** National Chungking University, BA, 1944; New York University, Graduate School of Business Administration, MBA, 1948. **CAREER:** US Department of War, civilian expert, 1945-46; Bank of China, economist, 1946-67; Suffolk County Public Employment Relations Board,

chairman, 1968-; SUNY College of Technology, professor of economics, 1967-. **ORGANIZATIONS:** The Foreign Trade Monthly, Taipei, editorial board, 1956-60; Journal Lit and Social Studies, editorial adviser, 1971-; American Economic Association; NY Social Security Analysts; AAAS; Econometrics Soc; Chinese American Academy and Prof Association; numerous others. **HONORS/AWARDS:** US Presidential Medal of Freedom, 1945; Omicron Delta Epsilon, 1962; Linguistics Society of China, Medal of Merit, 1973; Society of Arts and Letters, ROC, elected fellow, 1993; numerous others. **SPECIAL ACHIEVEMENTS:** Author: A Draft Plan for an Asian Payments Union and an Asian Development Bank, 1959; The Concept of Economic Homeostasis, 1956; International and Interregional Economics, 1960; Notes from Ipanchu, 1972; Essays on Linguistics, 1974, 1980; A General Study of the Multinational Enterprise, 1975, 4th edition, 1987; Learning Languages by Playing Games, 1979, 1981; The Pleasure of Reading and Writing, 1979; Genesis of Criminology, 1988; Words and Legends, 1988; A Tiny Room with Boundless Spacetime, 1990. **MILITARY SERVICE:** Military Intelligence, maj, 1944-45. **HOME ADDRESS:** 28 Marshmallow Dr, Commack, NY 11725-1023.

LI-LAN
Artist. Chinese American. **PERSONAL:** Born Jan 28, 1943, New York, NY; daughter of Yun Gee and Helen Wimmer; divorced. **CAREER:** Artist; public collections: Virginia Museum of Fine Arts; Parrish Art Museum; Guild Hall Museum; William Benton Museum of Art; Heckscher Museum; Seibu Museum of Art, Tokyo; Ohara Museum of Art, Kurashiki, Japan; Modern Art Museum, Toyama, Japan; Sydney and Frances Lewis Foundation Collection; solo exhibitions: Nantenshi Gallery, Tokyo, 1971, 1974, 1977, 1980, 1985; Robert Miller Gallery, 1978; Asher/Faure Gallery, 1980; O K Harris Gallery, 1983, 1985, 1987; Franz Bader Gallery, 1989; William Benton Museum of Art, 1990; New Arts Program, Kutztown, PA, 1991; Lung Men Art Gallery, 1993; group exhibitions: Guild Hall Museum, 1978, 1983; Phoenix Art Museum, 1979; Pensacola Museum of Art, 1979; Mississippi Museum of Art, 1980; Ft Lauderdale Museum of Art, 1980; Worcester Art Museum, 1982; American Acad and Inst of Arts & Letters, 1983, 1987; Sydney & Frances Lewis Foundation Collection, 1985; Arno Maris Gallery, 1991; Parrish Art Museum, 1988, 1993; Intl Travelling Exhibition, 1989-90; Nahan Contemporary, 1990; PS 1 Museum, 1992; Hecksher Museum, 1992. **ORGANIZATIONS:** East Hampton Ctr for Contemporary Art, Artists Advisory Board, 1989-90; Parrish Art Museum, Regional Council, 1984-87. **HONORS/AWARDS:** Artists Space, Artists Grant, 1988, 1990. **SPECIAL ACHIEVEMENTS:** Autobiography: Canvas with an Unpainted Part, Asahi Shimbun, Tokyo, 1976; catalogs: Lung Men Art Gallery, Taipei, Taiwan, 1993; William Benton Museum of Art, Nov 1990; Nantenshi Gallery, Tokyo, May 1977, Nov 1980. **BIOGRAPHICAL SOURCES:** Numerous articles in periodicals. **HOME ADDRESS:** PO Box 1194, East Hampton, NY 11937.

LIM, ANTONIO LAO
Construction company estimator. Filipino American/Chinese American. **PERSONAL:** Born Dec 7, 1935, Bato, Leyte, Philippines; son of Pacito Lim and Eufronia L Lim; married Elsie Cerilles-Lim, Jun 10, 1967; children: Eugene E. **EDUCATION:** University of San Carlos, Cebu City, Philippines, BSCE, 1961. **CAREER:** Houdaille Inc, design engr, 1972-74; Paramount Industries Inc, scheduling mgr, 1974-78; Claremont Contruction Group, estimator, 1979-84, chief estimator, 1985-. **BUSINESS ADDRESS:** Chief Estimator, Claremont Construction Group, Milltown Rd, #460, Bridgewater, NJ 08807, (908)772-5600.

LIM, BILLY LEE
Educator. Malaysian American/Chinese American. **PERSONAL:** Born Aug 23, 1962, Georgetown, Penang, Malaysia; son of Yew Khoon Lim and Siew Lee Tan; married Lee L Lim, Mar 8, 1992. **EDUCATION:** University of Toronto, BS, 1984; University of Southwestern Louisiana, MS, 1985, PhD, 1992. **CAREER:** Jackson State University, assistant professor, 1985-90; Lawrence Berkeley Laboratory, computer scientist, 1986, 1987; State Farm Insurance Companies, faculty intern, 1993; Illinois State University, assistant professor, 1990-. **ORGANIZATIONS:** Association for Computing Machinery, 1984-; IEEE Computer Society, 1984-; SIGMOD, 1988-. **HONORS/AWARDS:** National Security Agency, Human Factors Prototyping Capability Grant, 1988; Illinois State University, Cast Research and Instructional Travel Grant, 1991-93, University Teaching Improvement Program, 1993, Cast Multimedia Mentorship Grant, 1993. **SPECIAL ACHIEVEMENTS:** Nominee, National Science Foundation, Presidential Faculty Fellow Award, 1992; Midwest Computer Conference, program chair, 1994; "Object-Centered Con-

straints,'' Proc 7th International Conference on Data; "Constraint Analysis of Object-Centered Constraints: A Logical Framework for Database Semantic,'' Journal of Expert System, June 1993; "DB Tool: A Graphical Database Design Tool for an Undergraduate Course,'' ACM SIGCSE, 23:1, 1992. **BUSINESS ADDRESS:** Asst Prof, Applied Computer Science Dept, Illinois State University, 5150, Normal, IL 61761-5150, (309)438-7589.

LIM, CHHORN E.
Government scientist. Cambodian American. **PERSONAL:** Born Apr 12, 1945, Takeo, Cambodia; son of Say Yek Ear and Leang Ke Lim; married Brenda G Lim. **EDUCATION:** University of Agronomic Sciences, Ing, 1971; Auburn University, MS, 1975, PhD, 1977. **CAREER:** Auburn University, graduate research assistant, 1973-76, postdoctoral fellow, 1985-87; Aquaculture Dept, Southeast Asian Fisheries Development Center, researcher and head, nutrition section, 1977-79, station head, 1979-81, research director, researcher, 1981-82; Resource Management International, fish nutrition expert, 1983-85; USDA-ARS, research leader, research biologist, 1988-. **ORGANIZATIONS:** Asian Fisheries Society, 1988-; American Fisheries Society, 1989-; World Aquaculture Society, 1988-; American Chemists' Society, 1991-; American Oil Chemists' Society, 1991-; Journal of Applied Aquaculture, editorial board, 1989-; Sigma Xi, associate member, 1977-; International Academy of Fisheries Scientists, 1976-. **HONORS/AWARDS:** USDA-ARS, certificate of merit, 1990, 1992; Gamma Sigma Delta, Outstanding Achievement, 1974; received 7 certificates of appreciation from various private and government institutions in Indonesia and the Philippines. **SPECIAL ACHIEVEMENTS:** Responsible for planning, budgeting, supervising and implementation of research in aquaculture and fish nutrition, performed several short and long-term consultancies; about 60 publications in scientific journals and book chapters; languages: Cambodian, English, French, Indonesian. **BUSINESS ADDRESS:** Research Leader, US Department of Agriculture, Agricultural Research Sevice, Tropical Aquaculture Research Unit, H1MB, PO Box 1346, Kaneohe, HI 96744.

LIM, CHONG C.
Art work company executive. Korean American. **PERSONAL:** Born Nov 17, 1946, Seoul, Republic of Korea; son of Young Son Lim and Jung Sup Lim; married Judith, Feb 22, 1969; children: Jennifer. **EDUCATION:** Concordia Academy, diploma, 1968; Minneapolis College of Art & Design, BFA, 1971. **CAREER:** Island Designs, owner, currently. **ORGANIZATIONS:** Island Artisans, advertising committee, 1983-; Ohio Designer Craftsmen, 1986-; Michigan Guild of Artists & Artisans, block captain, 1986-; Directions of Maine, 1982-. **HONORS/AWARDS:** Pennsylvania Horticultural Society, Honorable Mention Trade Award, 1993; Maine Organic Farmers & Gardeners, Trade Award, 1991; Massachusetts Horticultural Society, Trade Award, 1984; Rising Paper Co, Award for Excellence, 1985. **BUSINESS ADDRESS:** Owner, Island Desgins, 25 Cleftston Rd, Bar Harbor, ME 04609, (207)288-4250.

LIM, DANIEL V.
Educator. Chinese American. **PERSONAL:** Born Apr 15, 1948, Houston, TX; son of Lucy Toy Lim and Don H Lim; married Carol, Sep 3, 1973. **EDUCATION:** Rice University, BA, biology, 1970; Texas A&M University, PhD, microbiology, 1973; Baylor College of Medicine, post-doctorate, 1973-76. **CAREER:** University of South Florida, assistant professor, associate professor, professor, 1976-, chairman of biology, 1983-85, Institute for Biomolecular Science, director, 1988-93. **ORGANIZATIONS:** American Society for Microbiology, 1973-, Southeastern Branch, 1976-, president, 1990-91; American Academy of Microbiology, fellow, 1983-; Inter-American Society for Chemotherapy, vice president, 1983-89; American Association for the Advancement of Science, 1973-; Sigma Xi, 1976-; Suncoast Association of Chinese Americans, past treasurer. **HONORS/AWARDS:** Phi Sigma, Graduate Research Award for Outstanding Dissertation, 1974; American College of Obstet & Gynecology, Searle/Donald Richardson Memorial Award, co-recipient, 1987; Florida Governor's Office, Governor's Award for Outstanding Contribution in Science & Technology, 1990; American Society for Microbiology, Southeastern Branch, Margaret Green Outstanding Teacher Award, 1989; University of South Florida, Outstanding Undergraduate Teaching Award, 1991. **SPECIAL ACHIEVEMENTS:** Author, Microbiology, college textbook, West Publishing Company, 1989; co-author, Introduction to Microbiology Laboratory Manual, Contemporary Publishing Company, 1993; inventor, Lim Group B Strep Broth, bacteriological medium, 1985; author/co-author of 26 scientific publications and 62 published scientific abstracts. **BUSINESS ADDRESS:** Professor,

Dept of Biology, University of South Florida, 4202 E Fowler Avenue, LIF 136, Tampa, FL 33620-5150, (813)974-1618.

LIM, DAVID J.
Government official, researcher. Korean American. **PERSONAL:** Born Nov 27, 1935, Seoul, Republic of Korea; son of Yang Sup Lim and Cha Nang Yoo; married Young Sook Lim, May 14, 1966; children: Michael, Robert. **EDUCATION:** Yonsei University, AB, 1953-55, College of Medicine, MD, 1955-60; National Medical Center, Seoul, residency certificate, 1961-64; Mass Eye and Ear Infirmary, Research Fellowship, certificate, 1965-66. **CAREER:** Ohio State University, Otolaryngology, research associate, 1966-67, assistant professor, 1967-71, associate professor, 1971-76, Neurobiol Anatomy, Cell Biology, professor, 1977-91, Otolaryngology, professor, 1976-91, professor emeritus, 1992-; National Institute on Deafness and Other Communication Disorders, scientific director, 1992-. **ORGANIZATIONS:** American Academy of Otolaryngology & HNS, scientific fellow, 1991-; Association for Research Otolaryngology, editor, historian, 1980-93, president, 1975-76; Society of University Otolaryngologists, honorary member, 1986-; Deafness Research Foundation, board, 1980-; Collegium Oto-rhino-laryngologicum Amicitiae Sacrum, 1976-; US Delegation of XI US-USSR Joint Working Group on Space Biology, 1980-. **HONORS/AWARDS:** Association for Research Otolaryngology, Award of Merit, 1993; Collegium Otolaryngologicum Amicitiae Sacrum, Shambaugh Prize, 1992; NIDCD-NIH, Claude Pepper Award, 1989, Javits Award, 1986; Ohio State University, Distinguished Scholar Award, 1985. **SPECIAL ACHIEVEMENTS:** Over one hundred ninety scientific publications & ten book chapters, 1960-93; organized and edited twelve proceedings of International Symposium & Research Conferences, 1970-93; received thirty eight research grants, ten research contracts, 1969-91; invited speaker, 63rd Nobel symposium on Cellular Mechanisims in Hearing, 1985. **BUSINESS ADDRESS:** Director, Div of Intramural Research, National Institute on Deafness & Communication Disorders, 5 Research Court, Rockville, MD 20850, (301)402-2829.

LIM, EDWARD HONG
Painter, illustrator, real estate development manager. Chinese American. **PERSONAL:** Born Sep 1, 1956, Shanghai, People's Republic of China; son of David D P and Linda Q D Lim; married Shelley Xiang Lim, Aug 5, 1989; children: Monica Lisa. **EDUCATION:** City College of San Francisco, ABA, 1982; Academy of Arts College, 1982-84. **CAREER:** Art Work, art director, 1983-84; outside contractor, fine illustration, 1984-, clients include: J Walter Thompson, Young & Rubincam, McKen & Ericson, Gray Advertising, Sarchi & Sarchi, Hal & Rhiney; H K Company Ltd, vice pres, currently. **ORGANIZATIONS:** San Francisco Society of Illustrators, 1983-. **HONORS/AWARDS:** Academy of Arts College of San Francisco, full scholarship, 1982; American Air Force Museum, works selected for collection, 1985. **SPECIAL ACHIEVEMENTS:** Artist, illustrator, solo shows: City College of San Francisco, 1982; Redwood Bank of San Francisco, 1983; College of Marin, 1989; group shows: American Air Force Museum, 1984; Art in Chicago, 1992; Shanghai Exhibition of Fine Arts, 1978; corporate collectors include: Chevron, Exxon Corp, Twentieth Century Fox, Pacific Telesis Group, Mexicana Airlines, and Quantas Airways; numerous private collectors in Asia. **BIOGRAPHICAL SOURCES:** Artists of Chinese Origin in North America, p 21, 1993; Rong Bao Zhai Hong Kong Auction Book, p 21, 1992. **HOME PHONE:** (415)664-0709. **BUSINESS PHONE:** 2 8913342.

LIM, JOHN K. (YONG KEUN LIM)
State senator, manufacturing company executive. Korean American. **PERSONAL:** Born Dec 23, 1935, Yoju, Kyunggido, Republic of Korea; son of Eun Kyu Lim and Seu Nyu Chung; married Grace Y Lim, Dec 9, 1963; children: Peter, Billy, Gloria. **EDUCATION:** Seoul Theological College, BA, religion, 1964; Western Evangelical Seminary, MDiv, 1970. **CAREER:** American Royal Jelly Co, chmn, currently; State of Oregon, state senator, 1993-. **ORGANIZATIONS:** Asian American Voters Coalitions, chmn, 1989-90; Federation of Korean-American Assns USA, natl president, 1988-89; Federation of Korean Chambers of Commerce USA, natl president, 1989-90. **SPECIAL ACHIEVEMENTS:** Publications: World Korean Directory, 1989; World Korean Chamber Directory, 1990; GOP gubernatorial candidate: State of Oregon, 1990; John Lin Scholarship, 1990-; Governor's Task Force on DUII, 1993-. **HOME ADDRESS:** 740 SE 25th St, Gresham, OR 97080. **BUSINESS PHONE:** (503)238-9719.

LIM, JOO KUN
Architect. Chinese American. **PERSONAL:** Born Aug 17, 1956, Hutan Melintang, Perak, Malaysia. **EDUCATION:** Massachusetts Institute of Technology, BS, art & design, 1980, BSCE, civ eng, 1980, MArch, 1984. **CAREER:** Twinspine Architects, principal, 1991-. **BIOGRAPHICAL SOURCES:** Boston Globe, Real Estate, front page, Jan 3, 1993. **HOME PHONE:** (617)783-9207. **BUSINESS ADDRESS:** Principal, Twinspine Architects, 35 Medford St, Somerville, MA 02143, (617)629-0059.

LIM, JOSEFINA PAJE
Librarian. Filipino American/Chinese American. **PERSONAL:** Born Mar 19, 1941, Floridablanca, Pampanga, Philippines; daughter of Maria Paje & Benito Lim Chee. **EDUCATION:** University of the East, Manila, BS, education, 1963; Pratt Institute, MLS, 1972. **CAREER:** Cornell University Medical College, assistant cataloger, 1969-71, associate librarian, 1978-87; Mt Sinai School of Medicine, instructor, assistant cataloger, 1971-76; Georgetown University Medical Center, technical services librarian, 1976-78; Montefiore Medical Center, library director, 1987-. **ORGANIZATIONS:** Medical Library Association, 1971-, NY/NJ Chapter, 1971-, chairperson, governmental relations, 1991, chairperson, continuing education committee, 1983, executive committee, 1983-85, secretary, 1983-85; Asian Pacific Librarians Association, 1985-; National Association of Suggestion Systems, NY Chapter, 1989-. **HONORS/AWARDS:** Academy of Health Information Professionals, 1991. **SPECIAL ACHIEVEMENTS:** Co-principal investigator, National Library of Medicine Grant, 1985-87, "Partnering in the 1990's: the Montefiore Medical Center and the Albert Einstein College of Medicine Collaborate on Library Automation," High-Performance Medical Libraries: Advances in Information Manager for the Virtual Era, NC Broering, editor, Westport, CT, Meckler, 1993. **HOME ADDRESS:** 1385 York Ave, #6D, New York, NY 10021. **BUSINESS ADDRESS:** Director, Health Sciences Library, Montefiore Medical Center, Tishman Learning Center, 111 E 210th St, Bronx, NY 10467, (718)920-4666.

LIM, KAM MING
Educator. Malaysian American. **PERSONAL:** Born Apr 1, 1964, Penang, Malaysia. **EDUCATION:** Eastern Michigan University, BS, 1986, MS, 1988; Miami University, PhD, 1992. **CAREER:** Eastern Michigan University, graduate assistant, 1986, resource coordinator, 1986-88, teaching assistant, 1987-88; Miami University, graduate assistant, 1988-89, teaching associate, 1989-92, visiting assistant professor, 1992-; Northern Kentucky University, adjunct assistant professor, 1993. **ORGANIZATIONS:** American Psychological Association, 1993-; American Psychological Society, 1993-; Midwestern Psychological Association, 1990-; Psi Chi, 1987-; Sigma Xi, 1992-; Society for Personality & Social Psychology, 1990-. **HONORS/AWARDS:** American Psychological Association, Dissertation Research Award, 1992; Eastern Michigan University, Barton Scholarship, 1986; Psi Chi, National Service Award, 1987. **SPECIAL ACHIEVEMENTS:** Co-author, "Determinants of Spatial Priming in Environmental Memory," Memory & Cognition, 19, 283-292, 1991; co-author of 5 posters presented at the American Psychological Society annual conventions, 1990-93; co-author of a paper presented at the Michigan Academy of Science, Arts, and Letters annual convention, 1986. **BUSINESS ADDRESS:** Visiting Assistant Professor, Dept of Psychology, Miami University, Benton Hall, Oxford, OH 45056, (513)529-2454.

LIM, KAP CHUL
Educator. Korean American. **PERSONAL:** Born Apr 4, 1947, Kyong Ki-Do, Republic of Korea; son of Wol Rae Lim; married Jung Ok Lim, Oct 1, 1972; children: Il. **EDUCATION:** University of Sciences in America, PhD, 1992. **CAREER:** Weber State University, professor, currently. **HOME ADDRESS:** 888 E Hwy 193, Layton, UT 84040, (801)771-8673.

LIM, KWEE-ENG LYN
Educator. Chinese American/Malaysian American. **PERSONAL:** Born Nov 17, 1945, Johor Bahru, Johor, Malaysia; daughter of Hock Joo Lim & Sai Peng Yeo; married Wah-See Ho, Aug 8, 1971; children: Alvin H Ho, Adelene V Ho. **EDUCATION:** Malaysian Teacher College, teaching diploma, 1967; University of the Ozarks, BA, English (magna cum laude), 1983; Oklahoma State University, MA, 1985, EdD, 1992 . **CAREER:** Malaysian Public Schools, teacher, 1967-81; Langston University, assistant professor, 1990-92, assistant professor, reading lab, director, 1992-. **ORGANIZATIONS:** Oklahoma Multicultural Institute Conference, planning committee, 1992-93; State Department of Education, textbook selection committee, 1992-93; National Reading Conference, presenter, 1991-; OK Reading Council, 1992; OK TESOL, presenter, 1983-; TESOL, 1991-; National Multicultural Urban Conference, 1990.

HONORS/AWARDS: Saint John's Ambulance Brigade, Volunteer Nursing Service Award, 1979; Langston University, Outstanding in Scholarly Presentations, 1993. **SPECIAL ACHIEVEMENTS:** Read and write English and Malay; speak 5 Chinese dialects including Mandarin. **BUSINESS ADDRESS:** Professor, Langston University, Jones Hall, Rm 100, Langston, OK 73050, (405)466-3440.

LIM, NANCY WONG
Educator. Chinese American. **PERSONAL:** Born Sep 6, 1948, Bakersfield, CA; daughter of W Wong; married William F Lim, Dec 8, 1979; children: Christina, Ryan. **EDUCATION:** BA, education; MEd, Univ of Arizona, doctoral program, currently. **CAREER:** Tucson Unified School District, teacher, 1970-. **ORGANIZATIONS:** Phi Delta Kappa, 1992-; Pi Lambda Theta, 1989-; Junior League, 1993; American Heart Association, Heart Ball fundraising, 1993. **HONORS/AWARDS:** William F Fulbright, 1974-75. **HOME ADDRESS:** 8831 E Palisade Circle, Tucson, AZ 85749.

LIM, PAUL STEPHEN
Educator, writer. Chinese American/Filipino American. **PERSONAL:** Born Jan 5, 1944, Manila, Philippines; son of Teh Ngo Lay and Lim Lian Hong. **EDUCATION:** University of Kansas, BA, 1970, MA, 1974. **CAREER:** University of Kansas, lecturer, 1976-88, associate professor, 1989-. **ORGANIZATIONS:** English Alternative Theatre, artistic director, 1989-; Dramatists Guild, 1976-; Authors League of America, 1976-. **HONORS/AWARDS:** American College Theatre Festival, Best Original Play, 1976; Palanca Memorial Awards, Best Short Story, 1976; Kansas Arts Commission Fellowship, 1989; Phi Beta Kappa Society, 1979-. **SPECIAL ACHIEVEMENTS:** Conpersonas, 1977; Some Arrivals, But Mostly Departures, 1982; plays: Flesh, Flash and Frank Harris, Woeman, Homerica, Mother Tongue, Figures in Clay. **BUSINESS ADDRESS:** Professor, English Dept, University of Kansas, Wescoe Hall, Lawrence, KS 66045-0501.

LIM, PAULINO MARQUEZ, JR.
Educator, novelist. Filipino American. **PERSONAL:** Born Aug 23, 1935, Camalig, Albay, Philippines; son of Paulino Lim Sr & Emerenciana Marquez Lim; married Barbara, Oct 23, 1960; children: Claire-Dee. **EDUCATION:** University of Santo Tomas, Manila, BSE, 1956, MA, 1959; University of California, Los Angeles, PhD, 1967. **CAREER:** San Beda College, Manila, instructor, 1959-63; California State University, professor of English, 1967-. **ORGANIZATIONS:** Modern Language Association, 1967-; PEN West, 1990-; Association for Asian Studies, 1992-. **HONORS/AWARDS:** Fulbright Lecturer, Taiwan, 1986-87. **SPECIAL ACHIEVEMENTS:** Author, The Style of Lord Byron's Plays, scholarly monograph, 1973; Passion Summer and Other Stories, fiction, 1988; Tiger Orchids on Mount Mayon, first novel of trilogy, 1990; Sparrows Don't Sing in the Philippines, second novel of trilogy, 1993; Requiem for a Rebel Priest, third novel of trilogy, forthcoming. **BIOGRAPHICAL SOURCES:** Return of a Native Son, Asiaweek, p 56, January 1986; Overseas Filipino Goes Home Again, Advertising Supplement, Los Angeles Times, p 11, November 1989. **BUSINESS ADDRESS:** Professor of English, California State University, 1250 Bellflower Blvd, McIntosh Humanities Bldg, 303, Long Beach, CA 90840-2403, (310)985-4214.

LIM, POH C.
Software engineer. Malaysian American. **PERSONAL:** Born Feb 27, 1957, Taiping, Perak, Malaysia; married. **EDUCATION:** Massachusetts Institute of Technology, SB, electrical, 1980, SB, computer, 1980, MS, 1982, EE, 1984. **CAREER:** Pilot Software Inc, principal software engineer, 1986-; Infocom Inc, principal software engineer, 1984-. **ORGANIZATIONS:** IEEE, 1976-; ACM, 1976-; Sigma Xi, associate member, 1980-; Eta Kappa Nu, 1980; Tau Beta Pi, 1980. **HONORS/AWARDS:** Eta Kappa Nu; Tau Beta Pi. **BUSINESS ADDRESS:** Principal Software Engineer, Pilot Software Inc, 40 Broad St, Ste 300, Boston, MA 02109.

LIM, RALPH WEI HSIONG
Educator. Chinese American. **PERSONAL:** Born Oct 3, 1953, New York, NY; son of Yuen and Huan Lim. **EDUCATION:** Princeton University, BSE, 1975; University of Pennsylvania, Wharton Graduate School, MBA, 1977. **CAREER:** International Paper Company, financial executive, 1977-82, consultant, 1982-; Sacred Heart University, professor, 1984-. **ORGANIZATIONS:** Civil Air Patrol, major, 1978-; Darien Town Legislature, representative, 1988-89; Darien Housing Authority, commissioner, 1991-; Association for Investment Management & Research, 1992-. **HONORS/AWARDS:** Yale University, visiting faculty fellow, 1988. **SPECIAL ACHIEVEMENTS:** Chartered financial

analyst, 1992; pilot; actor in several movies & industrial films. **HOME ADDRESS:** PO Box 938, Darien, CT 06820.

LIM, RAMON KHE-SIONG
Medical scientist, educator, physician. Filipino American/Chinese American. **PERSONAL:** Born Feb 5, 1933, Cebu City, Philippines; son of Eng-Lian Lim and Su Yu Lim; married Victoria K Sy, Jun 21, 1961; children: Jennifer Lim-Dunham, Wendell, Caroline Starbird. **EDUCATION:** University of Santo Tomas, Manila, AB, 1953, MD (cum laude), 1958; University of Pennsylvania, PhD, biochemistry, 1966. **CAREER:** University of Michigan, research neurochemist, 1966-69; University of Chicago, assistant professor/associate professor, 1969-81; University of Iowa, professor of neurology, 1981-, Div Neurochem & Neurobiology, director, 1981-. **ORGANIZATIONS:** Am Soc Biochem and Molecular Biology, 1974-; International Society Neurochemistry, 1969-; Am Society Neurochemistry, 1969-; Society Neuroscience, 1972-; Am Society Cell Biology, 1974-; International Society Develop Neurosci, membership committee, 1980-; Am Academy of Neurology, 1987-; International Journal Develop Neurosci, editorial board, 1984-91. **HONORS/AWARDS:** Art Assoc of the Phillipines, 3rd prize, abstract painting, 1957; Taipei, Taiwan, Outstanding Overseas Young Chinese Award, 1961; University of Pennsylvania, Harrison Scholarship, 1960-62; National Inst Mental Health, special fellowship, 1968-69; US Dept Veterans Affairs, Career Investigatorship, 1983-86. **SPECIAL ACHIEVEMENTS:** Contributed numerous literary works (short stories and poetry) to Chinese literary publications in the Phillipines, Hong Kong, Taiwan, and mainland China; contributed numerous scientific articles to world leading scientific journals and books. **BUSINESS ADDRESS:** Professor of Neurology, College of Medicine, University of Iowa, Iowa City, IA 52242, (319)356-3524.

LIM, RICHARD
Educator. Chinese American. **PERSONAL:** Born Sep 8, 1963, Hong Kong; son of Collin Lim and Mary Rose Lim. **EDUCATION:** University of California, Berkeley, AB, 1985; Princeton University, MA, 1988, PhD, 1991. **CAREER:** Princeton University, preceptor, 1986; Smith College, instructor, 1990-91, assistant professor, 1992-. **ORGANIZATIONS:** American Philological Association, 1991-; International Association for Manichaean Studies, 1991-. **HONORS/AWARDS:** University of California, Berkeley, Phi Beta Kappa, 1985; Whiting Fellowship in the Humanities, 1989-90; Harvard University, Dumbarton Oaks Byzantine Studies Summer Fellowship, 1992; National Endowment for the Humanities, summer grant, 1993, fellowship, 1994-95. **SPECIAL ACHIEVEMENTS:** Public Disputation, Power and Social Order in Late Antiquity, forthcoming book from University of California Press, 1995; articles in Revue des Etudes Augustiniennes, Vigiliae Christianae, Journal of Hellenic Studies, Recherches Augustiniennes, Historia. **BUSINESS ADDRESS:** Assistant Professor, Dept of History, Smith College, Dewey 8, Northampton, MA 01063-0048, (413)585-3717.

LIM, RODNEY GENE
Educator. Chinese American. **PERSONAL:** Born Sep 26, 1963, San Francisco, CA; son of Richard Lim and Janet Lim. **EDUCATION:** University of California, Berkeley, BA, 1985; University of Illinois, MA, 1988, PhD, 1990. **CAREER:** Tulane University, assistant professor of organizational behavior, 1990-. **ORGANIZATIONS:** Academy of Management, 1990-; American Psychological Association, 1990-; International Association of Conflict Management, 1990-; Society for Industrial Organizational Psychology, 1988-; Society for Judgment and Decision Making, 1989-. **HONORS/AWARDS:** Tulane University, AB Freeman School of Business, Outstanding Young Researcher Award, 1992; American Psychological Association, Dissertation Research Award, 1990; Phi Beta Kappa, 1985. **SPECIAL ACHIEVEMENTS:** Coauthor, "Contingencies in the Mediation of Disputes," Journal of Personality and Social Psychology, 1990; "An Evaluation of Two Methods for Estimating Item Response Theory Parameters when Assessing Differential Item Functioning," Journal of Applied Psychology, 1990. **BUSINESS ADDRESS:** Professor, Tulane University, A. B. Freeman School of Business, New Orleans, LA 70118, (504)865-5665.

LIM, SHIRLEY GEOK-LIN
Educator. Malaysian American/Chinese American. **PERSONAL:** Born Dec 27, 1944, Malacca, Malaysia; daughter of Lim Chin Som and Ang Chye Neo; married Charles Bazerman, Nov 1972; children: Gershom Kean Bazerman. **EDUCATION:** University of Malaya, BA (first class honors), 1967; Brandeis University, MA, 1971, PhD, 1973. **CAREER:** City University of New York, assistant professor, 1973-76; State University of New York, associate profes-

sor, 1976-90; University of California, professor, 1990-. **ORGANIZATIONS:** Modern Language Association, Division on Ethnic Literature, executive committee, 1993-98, Committee on Languages & Literatures of the United States, 1993-98; American Studies Association, minorities committee, 1993-96; Feminist Studies, editorial board, 1992-; Melus, editorial board, 1993-97; Ariel, editorial board, 1993-97; Calyx, advisory editorial board, 1989-; Belles Lettres, advisory editorial board, 1989-. **HONORS/AWARDS:** Before Columbus, American Book Award, 1990; State University of New York, Chancellor's Award for Excellence in Teaching, 1980; Asiaweek, Short Story Competition Prize, 1982; Commonwealth Institute, Commonwealth Poetry Prize, 1980; Brandeis University, Wien International Award, 1969; Fulbright, Fulbright Fellowship, 1969. **SPECIAL ACHIEVEMENTS:** Many books, articles, essays & presentations including: Nationalism and Literature: English Language Writing from the Philippines and Singapore, New Day Publishers, 1993; One World of Literature, 6th ed; The Forbidden Stitch; Reading the Literatures of Asian America, Houghton Mifflin, 1992; Moving Her Self: A Woman in the Shadow of Empire, Feminist Press, forthcoming; What the Fortune Teller Didn't Say, forthcoming; three books of poetry: Crossing the Peninsula; No Man's Grove; Modern Secrets; one collection of short stories: Another Country. **BIOGRAPHICAL SOURCES:** Oxford Companion to Twentieth Century Poetry in English, 1992; Bloomsbury Guide to Women's Literature, London, 1992. **BUSINESS ADDRESS:** Professor, English & Women's Studies, University of California, Santa Barbara, CA 93106-0001, (805)893-3441.

LIM, SOON-SIK
Educator. Korean American. **PERSONAL:** Born Mar 2, 1944, Kaesung, Republic of Korea; married Jae Yeon, Apr 21, 1973; children: Steve, Anna. **EDUCATION:** Yonsei University, Korea, BS, 1971; Wayne State University, MS, 1975, PhD, 1981. **CAREER:** Wayne State University, research assistant, 1975-81; Youngstown State University, professor, 1981-. **ORGANIZATIONS:** American Institute of Chemical Engineers; Sigma Xi; American Chemical Society. **BUSINESS ADDRESS:** Professor, Chemical Engineering Dept, Youngstown State University, 410 Wick Ave, Youngstown, OH 44555, (216)742-3022.

LIM, TECK-KAH
Educator. Malaysian American/Chinese American. **PERSONAL:** Born Dec 1, 1942, Malacca, Malaysia; son of Chin-Toh Lim and Siew-Leng Sim Lim; married Nyok-Kheng Liew, Jan 28, 1966; children: Kian-Tat, Ai-Li. **EDUCATION:** University of Adelaide, Australia, BSc (honors), 1965, PhD, 1968. **CAREER:** University of Malaya, lecturer, 1968; Florida State University, research associate, 1968-70; Drexel University, assistant professor, 1970-75, associate professor, 1975-82, professor, 1982-. **ORGANIZATIONS:** American Physical Society, secretary/treasurer, 1987-93, Topical Group on Few-Body Systems; Philadelphia Academy of Science, founder, consultant, 1978-; Ministry of Education, Guangxi, PRC, consultant, 1985-; United Nations Development Program, consultant, 1985. **HONORS/AWARDS:** American Physical Society, Fellowship, 1988; Humboldt Foundation, Fellowship, 1980; Chapel of Four Chaplains, Legion of Honor, 1978. **SPECIAL ACHIEVEMENTS:** Over 90 papers in various journals; organizing committee member of number of international conferences. **BUSINESS ADDRESS:** Professor of Physics, Drexel University, 32nd & Chestnut Streets, Philadelphia, PA 19104, (215)895-2717.

LIM, YONG KEUN. See **LIM, JOHN K.**

LIMB, BEN QUINCY
Attorney, association administrator. Korean American. **PERSONAL:** Born Nov 28, 1936, Taejon, Republic of Korea; son of San-jong Lee and Tong-shik Limb; married Mary Shinkawa, Feb 4, 1968; children: Amy, Lisa. **EDUCATION:** Korea Univ, BA, 1961; Seton Hall University, MA, 1969; New York Law School, JD, 1984; St John's University, PhD, 1979. **CAREER:** Korea Institute for Human Rights, human rights advocate, 1983-; private practice, attorney, 1985-. **ORGANIZATIONS:** Korean Institute for Human Rights, Washington, president, 1989-; Overseas Koreans for Natl Re-unification, NYC, co-chair, 1988-; ABA; Federal Bar Assn; New York State Bar Assn; NY County Lawyers Assn, Committee on Minorities & the Law, 1989-; Korean-American Lawyers Assn of New York; Intl Assn of Korean Lawyers, vp, 1988-; NY Law School Alumni Assn, board of directors, 1987-; American Immigration Lawyers Assn; Korea Bar Assn; Mayor Dinkin's Fact Finding Committee on Racial Conflicts in Brooklyn, 1990; Democratic Natl Committee, Asian Pacific American Advisory Committee, 1992. **HONORS/AWARDS:** Association of Korean Christian Scholars in North America, LA,

Appreciation Award, 1988. **SPECIAL ACHIEVEMENTS:** Bar admissions: NY, 1985; US Court of Appeals, federal circuit, 1988; US Court of Intl Trade, 1988; US Supreme Court, 1991; speaker, nationality law and human rights, The Law of the World Conference, 1987; Station KBC-Radio Legal Education Program, lecturer, 1990; Han Nam Univ, Taejon, Republic of Korea, anniversary lecturer, 1991. **BUSINESS ADDRESS:** 350 Fifth Ave, Ste 4805, Empire State Bldg, New York, NY 10118, (202)863-8000.∗

LIN, BINSHAN
Educator. Taiwanese American. **PERSONAL:** Born Jun 23, 1953, Chia-Yi, Taiwan; son of Min-Kwei Lin and Yu-Jen Hwang; married Eileen Lin, Mar 31, 1991. **EDUCATION:** National Chengchi University, BS, 1976; Louisiana State University, MA, applied statistics, 1985, PhD, 1988. **CAREER:** Louisiana State University, Shreveport, associate professor, 1988-. **ORGANIZATIONS:** Industrial Management and Data Systems, North American editor, 1992-; Quarterly Journal of Ideology, associate editor, 1991-; Journal of International Information Management, editorial review board, 1991-; Journal of Small Business Strategy, editorial advisory board, 1990-; Journal of Applied Business Research, editorial review board, 1990-; Louisiana State University, Shreveport, awards and recognition committee, 1992-. **HONORS/AWARDS:** Louisiana State University, Shreveport, Outstanding Faculty Award, 1991-92, 1989-90; Small Business Institute Directors Association, Distinguished Paper Award, 1990; Beta Gamma Sigma, 1993. **SPECIAL ACHIEVEMENTS:** Published 29 articles in refereed journals, 1988-93; published 3 articles in refereed books, 1990-91; published 27 articles in refereed proceedings, 1988-93; presented 21 papers in national conference, 1988-93; presented 22 papers in regional conferences, 1988-93. **HOME ADDRESS:** 10013 Commander Drive, Shreveport, LA 71106, (318)797-5880. **BUSINESS ADDRESS:** Associate Professor, Dept of Management & Marketing, Louisiana State University, Shreveport, 1 University Pl, Shreveport, LA 71115-2301, (318)797-5186.

LIN, CEN-TSONG
Educator. Chinese American/Taiwanese American. **PERSONAL:** Born Jul 31, 1952, Taichung, Taiwan; married Yu-Ling Lin; children: Michael, Jason. **EDUCATION:** Texas Tech University, PhD, 1986. **CAREER:** Central Washington University, mathematics associate professor, 1986-. **BUSINESS ADDRESS:** Associate Professor of Mathematics, Central Washington University, Bouillon Hall, Ellensburg, WA 98926, (509)963-2842.

LIN, CHAOTE
Educator. Taiwanese American. **PERSONAL:** Born Dec 9, 1930, Taiwan; married Ginny, Sep 1, 1962; children: Kenneth, Anna. **EDUCATION:** University of Oregon, BA, 1956, MA, 1958; University of Michigan, PhD, 1966. **CAREER:** San Jose State University, Dept of Foreign Languages, professor, 1966-. **HOME ADDRESS:** 401 Ariel Dr, San Jose, CA 95123, (408)225-8902.

LIN, CHARLES FLEY-FUNG
Investment company executive. Taiwanese American. **PERSONAL:** Born May 23, 1942, Taiwan; son of Chin-Chee Lin and Han-Shao Liu; married Diana Bi-Shier Lien, Apr 2, 1969; children: Angy In-Shio, Frank Chan-Chin. **EDUCATION:** University of Missouri, Columbia, master's degree, 1983; Michigan State University, PhD, 1988. **CAREER:** Nestle Los Angeles, sr flavor scientist, 1990; Seven Candle Sticks Inc, owner, chief exec officer, currently. **ORGANIZATIONS:** Industry Food Technologists, 1987; American Chemist Assn, 1992. **HONORS/AWARDS:** Taiwan Sugar Co, The Best Performance Group Leader, 1981. **BUSINESS ADDRESS:** Owner & CEO, Seven Candle Sticks, Inc, 4601 Genefield Rd, St Joseph, MO 64506, (816)364-0753.

LIN, CHENGMIN MICHAEL
Manufacturing company sales administrator. Taiwanese American. **PERSONAL:** Born Oct 1955, Taiwan; son of C S Lin; married Feb 1982 (divorced); children: C Lin. **EDUCATION:** National Chung-Hsing University, Taipei, Taiwan, 1977; University of Hawaii Graduate School, MA, 1982. **CAREER:** Associated System Inc, consultant, 1983; J-M Mfg Inc, marketing coordinator, 1985, staff mgr, marketing, 1986, quotation mgr, marketing, 1990, product mgr, sales, 1991-. **BUSINESS ADDRESS:** Product Manager, J-M Manufacturing Inc (Formosa USA Group), 9 Peach Tree Hill Rd, Livingston, NJ 07039, (201)535-1633.

LIN, CHHIU-TSU
Educator. Chinese American. **PERSONAL:** Born Jan 9, 1943, Yensui, Taiwan; son of Chuwan-Wen Lin and Kao-Chi Lin; married Mara Gurgel Valente

Lin, Mar 29, 1974; children: Monique Gurgel, Cristiane Gurgel. **EDUCATION:** Tamkang University, Taiwan, BS, 1966; Brock University, Canada, MS, 1970; University of California, Los Angeles, PhD, 1974; State University of Campinas, Brazil, Livre-Docencia, 1983. **CAREER:** State University of Campinas, Brazil, assistant professor, 1974-75; associate professor 1976-78, professor, 1978-86; University of Southern California, UNESCO visiting scientist, 1980-81; Thomas J Watson Research Center, IBM World Trade Visiting Scientist, 1981-82; National University of Singapore, senior teaching fellow, 1983; Tamkang University, Taiwan, special-invited lecturer, 1983; University of California, Los Angeles, visiting professor, 1984-85; Northern Illinois University, associate professor, 1985-89, professor, 1989-. **ORGANIZATIONS:** Sigma Xi, 1972; American Chemical Society, 1986; Material Research Society, 1989; American Association for Advancement of Science, 1989; Chinese American Chemical Society, 1990; American Society for Photobiology, 1989. **HONORS/AWARDS:** University of California, Los Angeles, Departmental Outstanding Teaching Assistant Prize, 1972, Bronze Medallion, for outstanding academic achievement in physical sciences from UCLA Alumni Association, 1974. **SPECIAL ACHIEVEMENTS:** Lasers and Applications, Springer series on Optical Sciences, Vol. 26, 1981; production of PT/PZT/PLZT thin films, powders and laser 'direct write' patterns, US patent 5,188,902, 1993; "Chemistry of Single-Step Phosphate/Paint System," Ind Eng Chem Res, 31, 424, 1992. **BUSINESS ADDRESS:** Professor, Dept of Chemistry, Northern Illinois University, De Kalb, IL 60115-2862, (815)753-6861.

LIN, CHI YUNG (FOREST LIN)
Educator. Taiwanese American. **PERSONAL:** Born Sep 8, 1938, Meinung, Taiwan; son of Chin-mei Lin & Feng-chuen Lin; married Vicki Lin, Mar 20, 1968; children: Tony, Norman. **EDUCATION:** Tunghai University, Taiwan, BA, 1961; Kansas State University, MA, 1966; Southern Illinois University, PhD, 1969. **CAREER:** Tulsa Junior College, professor, currently. **SPECIAL ACHIEVEMENTS:** Published 10 books on DOS, 1-2-3, and WordPerfect. **BUSINESS ADDRESS:** Professor, Tulsa Junior College, 909 S Boston St, Tulsa, OK 74119-2095, (918)631-7131.

LIN, CHIA CHIAO
Mathematician. Chinese American. **PERSONAL:** Born Jul 7, 1916, Fukien, China; son of Kai and Y T Lin; married Shou-Ying Liang, 1946; children: one daughter. **EDUCATION:** Natl Tsing Hua University, China, BS, 1937; University of Toronto, MA, 1941; California Institute of Technology, PhD, aeronautics, 1944. **CAREER:** Tsing Hua University, China, asst, 1937-39; California Institute of Tech, from asst to res engineer, 1943-45; Brown University, asst prof, 1945-46, assoc prof, appl math, 1946-47; Massachusetts Institute of Technology, assoc prof, 1947-53, prof, 1953-66, Inst Prof, 1966-87, Emeritus Inst Prof of Math, 1987-. **ORGANIZATIONS:** Natl Academy of Sci; American Astron Soc; Soc for Industrial & Applied Maths, pres, 1973; American Math Soc; American Acad Arts & Sci, fellow; American Philos Soc; American Phys Soc; Inst Aerospace Sci, fellow. **HONORS/AWARDS:** Chinese University Hong Kong, LLD, 1973; Guggenheim Fellow, 1954-55, 1960; Soc for Industrial & Applied Maths, John von Neumann Lecturer, 1967; Natl Acad of Sci, Appl Math & Numerical Analysis Award, 1977. **SPECIAL ACHIEVEMENTS:** Theory of Hydrodynamic Stability, 1955; Turbulent Flow, Theoretical Aspects, 1963. **BUSINESS ADDRESS:** Emeritus Inst Prof, Dept of Mathematics, Massachusetts Institute of Technology, Cambridge, MA 02139.

LIN, CHIEN-CHANG
Project manager. Taiwanese American. **PERSONAL:** Born Feb 28, 1937, Hsinchu, Taiwan; son of F L Lin & C P Lin; married Jing J Lin, Aug 19, 1967; children: Kelly M, Arthur M, Eunice M. **EDUCATION:** Tunghai University, Taiwan, BS, 1959; University of New Mexico, Albuquerque, PhD, 1968; Washington University, St louis, postdoctoral fellow, 1967-70. **CAREER:** General Electric Co, principal engineer, project manager, 1971-. **ORGANIZATIONS:** American Chemistry Society; American Nuclear Society. **HONORS/AWARDS:** Sigma Xi; Phi Kappa Phi. **SPECIAL ACHIEVEMENTS:** More than 100 published articles in technical journals and monograph reports. **BUSINESS ADDRESS:** Project Manager, General Electric Co, Vallecitos Nuclear Center, PO Box 460, Pleasanton, CA 94566, (510)862-4566.

LIN, CHIN-CHU
Physician, educator, researcher. Taiwanese American. **PERSONAL:** Born Oct 24, 1935, Taichung, Taiwan; son of Kun-Yen Lin & Nung Chiang; married Sue S Hsu, Oct 24, 1964; children: Jim, John, Juliet T. **EDUCATION:** National Taiwan University, BS, 1956, MD, 1961; Columbia University School of Medicine, resident, Ob/Gyn, 1971-74. **CAREER:** Albert Einstein College of

Medicine, fellow of maternal-fetal medicine, 1974-76; University of Chicago, Ob/Gyn Department, assistant professor, 1976-80, associate professor, 1980-87, professor, 1987-. **ORGANIZATIONS:** North America Taiwanese Professors' Association, board of directors, 1988-91, vice president, 1988-89, president, 1989-90; North American Taiwanese Medical Association, board of directors, 1991-93; Taiwanese United Fund, Chicago TUF, president, 1984-85; American College of Obstetricians & Gynecologists, fellow, 1978-; Association of Professors of Ob/Gyn, 1978-; Society of Perinatal Obstetricians, 1979-; Central Association of Obstetricians & Gynecologists, 1981-; Chicago Gynecological Society, 1980-. **HONORS/AWARDS:** American College of Ob/Gyn, Purdue Frederick Award, 1978; Formosan Medical Association, Distinguished Scholar Award, 1981; Kinki Ob/Gyn Society, Osaka, Japan, Scientific Award, 1984; North American Taiwanese Professors Association, 10th annual conference chairman, 1990; Natl Taiwan University, College of Medicine, selected candidate for dean, 1993. **SPECIAL ACHIEVEMENTS:** Author: Intrauterine Growth Retardation, McGraw Hill, 1984; The High Risk Fetus, Springer-Verlag, 1993; editor in chief: series of medical issues, Taiwan Tribune, 1986-88; author of over 60 scientific research papers in peer review journals; journal reviewer: Am J Ob/Gyn; Ob-Gyn; J of Perinatal Med; Journal of Maternal-Fetal Med. **BUSINESS ADDRESS:** Professor of Obstetrics & Gynecology, University of Chicago, 5841 South Maryland Avenue, Chicago Lying-In Hospital, MC 2050, Chicago, IL 60637, (312)702-6590.

LIN, CHINLON
Optoelectronics engineer. Taiwanese American/Chinese American. **PERSONAL:** Born Jan 19, 1945, Chia-Yi, Taiwan; son of Bing-Chaun Lin and Shiao-Che Lin; married Helen Chou Lin, Aug 10, 1969; children: Thomas Y, Daniel Y. **EDUCATION:** National Taiwan University, Taiwan, BSEE, 1967; University of Illinois at Champaign-Urbana, MS, 1970; University of California at Berkeley, PhD, 1973. **CAREER:** Technical University of Denmark, guest professor, optoelectronics, 1984; AT&T Bell Labs, Laser Sciences Research Dept, MTS, 1974-85; BELLCORE, Broadband Lightwave Systems Research, dir, 1986-. **ORGANIZATIONS:** IEEE, fellow, 1974-; OSA, fellow, 1974-; Photonics Society of Chinese Americans, president, 1994. **HONORS/AWARDS:** IEEE, Fellow Award, 1991; OSA, Fellow Award, 1985; IEE, Electronics Letters Premium, 1980. **SPECIAL ACHIEVEMENTS:** 10 patents in optical fiber communications, 1974-; first proposal and demonstration of dispersion-shifted single-mode fibers for high-speed long-distance optical fiber communication, 1979. **BUSINESS ADDRESS:** Director, BELLCORE, 331 Newman Springs Rd, NVC 3X249, Red Bank, NJ 07701, (908)758-3020.

LIN, CHIU-HONG
Scientist. Taiwanese American. **PERSONAL:** Born Nov 25, 1934, Pingtung, Taiwan; son of Chang Lin and Yao-Mei Lin; married Alice, Jul 3, 1965; children: Emily, Janet. **EDUCATION:** National Taiwan University, BS, 1957, MS, 1960; The University of Chicago, PhD, 1968. **CAREER:** University of Chicago, Ben May Lab for Cancer Research, research associate, 1968-72, research associate, assistant professor, 1972-73; Upjohn Co, senior research scientist, 1973-92, medical chemistry research, senior scientist, 1992-. **ORGANIZATIONS:** American Chemical Society, 1963-; American Association for Advancement of Science, 1985-. **SPECIAL ACHIEVEMENTS:** Many scientific publications in chemistry journals such as Journal of the American Chemistry Society, Journal of Organic Chemistry, Journal of Medical Chemistry; research work in the area of Prostaglandin, Prostacyclin, Serotonin, and Dopamine related compounds. **BUSINESS ADDRESS:** Senior Scientist, The Upjohn Co, Henrietta St, 7246-209-6, Kalamazoo, MI 49001, (616)385-7992.

LIN, DENNIS KON-JIN
Educator. Taiwanese American/Chinese American. **PERSONAL:** Born Nov 2, 1959, I-Lan, Taiwan; son of Wei-Hsin Lin & Su-Chin Lin; married Mei-Fen Lin, Feb 8, 1983; children: Vincent, Janice. **EDUCATION:** National Tsing Hua University, BA, 1981; University of Wisconsin-Madison, PhD, 1988. **CAREER:** University of Toronto, research fellow, 1989; IBM, visiting scientist, 1993-94; University of Tennessee, professor, 1989-. **ORGANIZATIONS:** American Statistical Association, 1987-; Institute of Mathematical Statistics, 1987-; Royal Statistical Society, fellow, 1989-; International Chinese Statistical Association, 1987-; American Society of Quality Control, 1994-. **HONORS/AWARDS:** American Statistical Association, SPES Section, Most Outstanding Presentation Award, 1993; University of Tennessee, Alma & Hal Reagan Scholars Award, 1992, Allen H Keally Outstanding Teaching Award, 1992. **SPECIAL ACHIEVEMENTS:** More than 30 publications in professional journals; area of specialization: quality engineering. **HOME PHONE:** (615)675-1742. **BUSINESS ADDRESS:** Professor of Statistics, University of Tennessee, 331 Stokely Management Center, Knoxville, TN 37996-0532, (615)974-2556.

LIN, DIANE CHANG
Scientist. Chinese American. **PERSONAL:** Born Aug 6, 1944, Shi-An, Shen-Shi, China; daughter of Raymond & Shirley Chang; married Shin Lin, Jun 21, 1969; children: Howe, Payton. **EDUCATION:** National Taiwan University, BS, 1966; University of California, Los Angeles, PhD, 1971. **CAREER:** University of California, San Franciso, research scientist, 1971-74; Johns Hopkins University, research scientist, 1974-. **BUSINESS ADDRESS:** Research Scientist, Dept of Biophysics, Johns Hopkins University, 3400 N Charles St, Jenkins 404, Baltimore, MD 21218, (410)516-7693.

LIN, ELIZABETH
Mental health researcher. Chinese American. **PERSONAL:** Born Mar 18, 1950, New York, NY; daughter of Paul Jen-su Lin & San-su Chen Lin; married Thomas Allen Foard, May 29, 1983. **EDUCATION:** Radcliffe College, BA, 1971; University of Louisville, MS, 1981, PhD, 1988. **CAREER:** University Psychiatric Services, research scientist, 1985-88; University of Louisville, assistant professor, dept of psychiatry, 1988-89; Clarke Institute, research scientist, 1989-. **ORGANIZATIONS:** American Evaluation Association, 1990-; International Society for the Systems Sciences, 1990-. **BUSINESS ADDRESS:** Research Scientist, The Clarke Institute of Psychiatry, 250 College St, Toronto, ON, Canada M5T 1R8.

LIN, EVA I.
Physician. Taiwanese American. **PERSONAL:** Born Jul 14, 1964, Taipei, Taiwan; daughter of Juiyuan W Lin and Meihui S Lin; married Yuan-Chi Lin, Jun 15, 1991; children: Katerina V. **EDUCATION:** Harvard University, BA (summa cum laude), 1986, MA, 1986, Harvard Medical School, MD, 1990. **CAREER:** Evanston Hospital, physician, 1990-91; University of California, San Francisco, physician, 1991-. **ORGANIZATIONS:** American Roentgen Ray Society; Radiological Society of North America; American Medical Association; Phi Beta Kappa, undergraduate marshal. **HONORS/AWARDS:** Harvard University, Detur Prize, 1983, Sophia Freund Prize, 1986, National Merit Scholar, 1982. **BUSINESS ADDRESS:** Resident, Dept of Radiology, University of California, San Francisco, 505 Parnassus Ave, San Francisco, CA 94122, (415)476-8358.

LIN, FELIX
Product marketing manager. Taiwanese American/Chinese American. **PERSONAL:** Born Dec 6, 1963, Newark, NJ; son of Alfred C K Lin and Elizabeth Lin. **EDUCATION:** Massachusetts Institute of Technology, BS, electrical engineering, 1985, MS, computer science, 1986, MS, management, 1988. **CAREER:** Oracle Corp, associate consultant, 1988-89, staff consultant, 1989, senior consultant, 1989-90, principal consultant, 1990-91, project manager, 1991; Cadre Technologies, technical marketing management, 1991-93; NEXT Inc, product manager, 1993-. **ORGANIZATIONS:** Sigma Xi, 1986-. **HONORS/AWARDS:** Society for Information Management, scholarship, 1988; Oracle Consulting Group, MVP, 1989. **HOME ADDRESS:** 1139 Blythe St, Foster City, CA 94404, (415)570-7505.

LIN, FENG-BAO
Educator. Taiwanese American. **PERSONAL:** Born Sep 16, 1954, Nantou, Taiwan; son of Yi-Hsiung Lin & Shu-Ju Lin; married Jenny Lin, 1983; children: James, Megan. **EDUCATION:** National Taiwan University, BS, civil engineering, 1976, MS, structural engineering, 1982; Northwestern University, PhD, structural mechanics, 1987. **CAREER:** C C Yan & Associates, Architects & Engineers, assistant engineer, 1976-78; Taiwan Development & Trust Corporation, associate engineer, 1978-80; Van Nung Institute of Technology, instructor, 1982-83; Northwestern University, research assistant, 1983-87; Argonne National Laboratory, resident student associate, 1985; Polytechnic University, associate professor, 1987-. **ORGANIZATIONS:** ASCE/ACI Joint Committee 447 on Finite Element Method of RC Strutures; ACI Committee on Fracture Mechanics of RC Structures; ASCE EMD Committee on Properties of Materials; American Society of Civil Engineering; American Concrete Institute; International Society for Boundary Elements; American Academy of Mechanics; Sigma Xi. **HONORS/AWARDS:** Polytechnic University, 1991 Teacher of the Year Award, 1991; National Taiwan University, Sinotech Engineering Fellowship, 1980-82. **SPECIAL ACHIEVEMENTS:** "Fracture Energy Release and Size Effect in Borehole Breakout," 1993; "Stability Against Localization of Softening in Ellipsoids and Bands," 1989; "Nonlocal Smeared Cracking Model for Concrete Fracture," 1988; "Nonlocal Yield

Limit Degradation," 1988; "Concrete Model with Normality and Sequential Identification," 1987. **BUSINESS ADDRESS:** Associate Professor, Dept of Civil Engineering, Polytech University, 6 Metrotech Center, Brooklyn, NY 11201, (718)260-3676.

LIN, FOREST. *See* **LIN, CHI YUNG.**

LIN, FRED REGGIE
Volleyball coach, sports consultant. Taiwanese American. **PERSONAL:** Born Aug 10, 1965, Taipei, Taiwan; son of Chung Kuan Lin and Fea Tsu Lin. **EDUCATION:** University of Michigan. **CAREER:** Burns Computer Services, consultant, 1988-91; Clinton High School, volleyball/track coach, 1989-93; Sports Consulting Services, consultant, owner, 1991-; Hillsdale College, volleyball coach, 1993-. **SPECIAL ACHIEVEMENTS:** Regional Coach of the Year, 1990. **HOME ADDRESS:** 3642-5 Partridge Path, Ann Arbor, MI 48108, (313)973-0972.

LIN, GEORGE H. Y.
Scientist. Chinese American. **PERSONAL:** Born Mar 9, 1938, Yantai, Shantung, China; son of Tung W Lin and Yu Y Lin; married Margaret Y Lin, Jun 14, 1969; children: Benjamin. **EDUCATION:** Tunghai University, Taiwan, BS, 1960; University of Nevada, MS, 1965; University of California, Davis, PhD, 1969. **CAREER:** University of Wisconsin, Madison, research associate; University of California, research associate; Xerox Corp, senior scientist, principal scientist, currently. **ORGANIZATIONS:** Society of Toxicology; Environmental Mutagen Society. **HONORS/AWARDS:** American Board of Toxicology, Diplomate, 1982, 1987, 1992. **SPECIAL ACHIEVEMENTS:** 39 scientific publications, 1969-93. **HOME ADDRESS:** 770 Daventry Circle, Webster, NY 14580, (716)671-3438. **BUSINESS ADDRESS:** Principal Scientist, Xerox Corp, 800 Salt Rd, Bldg 843, Webster, NY 14580, (716)422-2081.

LIN, HSIU-SAN
Physician, educator. Taiwanese American. **PERSONAL:** Born Mar 15, 1935, Nagoya, Japan; son of Mao-Sung Lin & Tao Tsuang Lin; married Su-Chiung Chen Lin, Sep 22, 1962; children: Kenneth, Bertha, Michael. **EDUCATION:** National Taiwan University Medical School, MD, 1960; University of Chicago, PhD, 1968. **CAREER:** University of Oxford, visiting scientist, 1977-78; Harvard University Medical School, visiting scholar, 1993; Washington University, assistant professor of radiology, 1971-76, associate professor of radiology, 1976-84, associate professor of molecular microbiologist, 1985-, professor of radiology, 1984-. **ORGANIZATIONS:** Organization of Chinese Americans, St Louis Chapter, board of directors, 1983-86; Taiwanese American Citizen's League, St Louis Chapter, board of directors, 1991-93, vice president, 1992; St Louis Radiological Society, Radiation Oncology, head, 1991-92; American Society of Therapeutic Radiology and Oncology, 1983-; American Association of Cancer Research, 1970-; Taiwanese Association of St Louis, president, 1984. **HONORS/AWARDS:** National Cancer Institute, Research Career Development Award, 1974-79. **SPECIAL ACHIEVEMENTS:** Published over 70 articles in peer-reviewed journals; obtained several research grants from National Cancer Institute, National Heart, Lung and Blood Institute, National Institute of Infectious Diseases, as principal investigator, 1976-90. **BUSINESS ADDRESS:** Professor of Radiology, Washington University Medical School, 510 S Kings Hwy, St Louis, MO 63110, (314)362-7030.

LIN, HUNG CHANG (JAMES)
Educator. Chinese American. **PERSONAL:** Born Aug 8, 1919, Shanghai, China; son of Dau-Yang Lin & Ying-Mei Chen; married Anchen Wang, Nov 26, 1949; children: Robert Y, Daniel H. **EDUCATION:** Chiao Tung University, China, BSEE, 1941; University of Michigan, MSE, 1948; Polytechnic Institute of Brooklyn, DEE, 1956. **CAREER:** Central Radio Works, China, engineer, 1941-43; Central Broadcasting Station, China, engineer, 1944-47; RCA Labs, 1948-56; CBS Semiconductor Operations, 1956-59; Westinghouse, 1959-69; University of Maryland, professor, 1969-. **ORGANIZATIONS:** Institute of Electrical & Electronic Engineers, student member, 1948, fellow, 1969; J Solid State Circuits, senior editor; Solid State Circuits Conference, program committee; Intl Electron Device Mtg, senior chairman. **HONORS/AWARDS:** IEEE Electron Device Society, Efers Award, 1978; University of Maryland, Innovation Hall of Fame, 1992. **SPECIAL ACHIEVEMENTS:** 50 US patents issued, including: the quasi-complementary transistor amplifier, lateral PNP transistor, current mirror; over 150 published articles; author of 1 book, co-author of 4 others. **BUSINESS ADDRESS:** Professor, Electrical

Engineering Dept, University of Maryland, College Park, MD 20742, (301)405-3653.

LIN, ILAN S.
Artist. Chinese American. **PERSONAL:** Born Apr 13, 1949, I-Lan, Taiwan; daughter of Fan Su & Yai Shen Chang; married Kwok Liang Lin, Jul 12, 1972; children: Frank. **CAREER:** Artist, currently. **ORGANIZATIONS:** Lanting Chinese Artist Association, art consultant, 1989-90; Chinese Artist Association of Southern America; Houston Women's Caucus for Art; Association Pour La Promotion Du Patrimoine Artistique Francois; The International Association for Contemporary Art. **HONORS/AWARDS:** Wilson Business Products Co Art Show winner; Pasadena Art League Show, first prize. **SPECIAL ACHIEVEMENTS:** Group shows: Houston Chinese Artists Show; Houston Art League Show; Contemporary Art, France-USA; Houston Westchase Library Show. **HOME ADDRESS:** 903 Bayou Parkway, Houston, TX 77077, (713)558-2766.

LIN, JAMES C.
Educator. Chinese American. **PERSONAL:** Born Aug 12, 1932, Macao; son of Zee Ping Lin (deceased) and Ren Sen Wu; married Hsiao-yu Lin, Aug 1967 (deceased); children: David, Gilbert, Bruce. **EDUCATION:** Taiwan Normal University, BS, 1955; Rice University, MA, 1960; North Carolina State University, PhD, 1965. **CAREER:** National Taiwan University, instructor, 1955-57; Methodist Hospital, research assistant, 1959-60; Northwestern State University, assistant professor, 1965-70, associate professor, 1970-75, professor, 1975-; University of Texas, M D Anderson Hospital and Tumor Institute, visiting professor, 1980-81. **ORGANIZATIONS:** Tissue Culture Association, 1982-86; Louisiana Academy of Science, 1969-90; Genetic Society of America, 1963-80; Sigma Xi, 1959-92; Biological Association of National Taiwan Normal University, 1951-86. **HONORS/AWARDS:** Northwestern State University, Research Fellowship, 1986, 1992. **SPECIAL ACHIEVEMENTS:** The Distribution of Ni-63 in Habrobracon Radiation research, 25(1):24, 1965; Expression and Regional Assignment of Chinese Hamster ESD and RNA Genes, Cell Genet, 38:(132-137). **BUSINESS ADDRESS:** Professor, Northwestern State University, College Ave, Natchitoches, LA 71497, (318)357-5329.

LIN, JAMES CHIH-I
Educator, educational administrator. Chinese American. **PERSONAL:** Born Dec 29, 1942; married Mei Fei Lin, Mar 21, 1970; children: Janet Y, Theodore L, Erik L. **EDUCATION:** Whitworth College, Spokane, WA, 1962-64; University of Washington, Seattle, BS, 1966, MS, 1968, PhD, 1971. **CAREER:** University of Washington, Seattle, assistant professor of rehabilitation medicine, 1971-74; Wayne State University, professor of electrical and computer engineering, 1974-80; University of Illinois, Chicago, director, Robotic Automation Lab, 1982-89, head, Bioengineering Dept, 1980-92, professor of bioengineering, electrical engineering, physiology, 1980-, director of special projects, 1992-. **ORGANIZATIONS:** Chinese American Academic and Professional Convention, chair of steering committee, 1993; International Union of Radio Science, US Commission K, chairman, 1990-; IEEE Committee on Man and Radiation, chairman, 1990-91; National Council on Radiation Protection an Measurement, SC 89 member, 1992-96; National Institutes of Health, Special Study Section, chairman, 1986-90, Diagnostic Radiology Study Section, 1981-85; IEEE Engineering in Medicine and Biology Society, administrative committee, 1986-88; Bioelectromagnetics Society, 1986-89, board of directors, 1980-81, president, 1994-95. **HONORS/AWARDS:** American Association for the Advancement of Science, fellow, 1989; American Institute for Medical and Biological Engineering, founding fellow, 1992; Institute of Electrical and Electronic Engineers, fellow, 1986; IEEE Transactions in Electromagnetic Compatibility, Best Paper, 1975; Chinese American Professional and Academic Association, Distinguished Service, 1989; University of Illinois, Chicago, Best Engineering Advisor. **SPECIAL ACHIEVEMENTS:** US President's Committee for the National Medal of Science, 1992-93; author, Microwave Auditory Effects and Applications; Biological Effects and Health Implications of Radiofrequency Radiation; Electromagnetic Interactions with Biological Systems; 100 scientific and engineering journal papers; visiting professor to universities in China, Italy and Taiwan, 1981, 1984, 1988. **BUSINESS ADDRESS:** Professor, Director, University of Illinois, Chicago, 851 S Morgan St, 1030 SEO, MC 154, Chicago, IL 60607-7053, (312)413-1052.

LIN, JAMES CHOW
Consulting company executive. Chinese American. **PERSONAL:** Born Mar 28, 1954, Taipei, Taiwan; son of Ho-Ting Lin and Tsung-Mei C Lin; married

Josephine Lau, May 1, 1993. **EDUCATION:** National Tsing-Hua University, BS, 1976; University of California, Los Angeles, MS, 1980. **CAREER:** PLG Inc, consultant, 1980-87, lead consultant, 1987-89, manager engineering services, 1989-92, partner, 1992-. **ORGANIZATIONS:** American Nuclear Society, 1978-88, finance chairman for ANS winter meeting, 1987, registration chairman for ANS Thermal Reactor Safety Conference, 1986; American Society for Quality Control, 1982-88. **HONORS/AWARDS:** California Board of Registration for Professional Engineers and Land Surveyors, Professional Engineer, Nuclear, 1983; American Society for Quality Control, Certified Reliability Engineer, 1982. **SPECIAL ACHIEVEMENTS:** Risk Management of the Japanese Experiment Module on Space Station Freedom, to be presented at the Intl Conference on Process Safety Assessment & Management; Human Reliability Analysis for Surry Midloop Operations, to be presented at the Intl Conference on PSAM, 1994; Space Station Freedom Quantitative Risk Assessment Program, PSAM, 1991; Future Development in Probabilistic Safety Assessment, CSNI Workshop on Applications & Limitations of Probabilistic Safety Assessment, 1990; PRA Modularization & Application of the Plant Model for Management Decision Making, Intl Conference on Structural Mechanics in Reaction Technology, 1989; numerous others. **MILITARY SERVICE:** Combined Service Forces, Republic of China, 2nd lt, 1976-78; Instructor at Combined Service Forces Ordnance Technical School, Mechanical Engineering Officer, 1978. **BUSINESS ADDRESS:** Partner, PLG, Inc, 4590 MacArthur Blvd, Ste 400, Newport Beach, CA 92660, (714)833-2020.

LIN, JAMES P.
Electrical engineer (retired). Chinese American. **PERSONAL:** Born Mar 17, 1917, Foochow, China; son of Ching Po Lin (deceased) and Bik-chun Wong (deceased); married Lydia Miao-chun Lin, May 6, 1966; children: David T Chen (step-son). **EDUCATION:** New York City Community College (now New York City Technical College), AS, applied science, 1968. **CAREER:** New York City Department of General Service, electrical engineering draftsman, 1962-71, assistant electrical engineer, 1971-85, supervisor of elec installation, 1985-89. **ORGANIZATIONS:** Institute of Electrical and Electronics Engineers, 1968-. **HOME ADDRESS:** 333 Pearl St, Apt 6C, New York, NY 10038.

LIN, JAMES PEICHENG
Educator. Chinese American. **PERSONAL:** Born Sep 30, 1949, New York, NY; son of Tung Hua Lin and Susan Lin; married Julie Lin, Jun 24, 1990; children: Kelly Keiko. **EDUCATION:** UC, Berkeley, BS, 1970; Princeton University, PhD, 1974. **CAREER:** Hebrew University, Israel, visiting professor, 1981-82; Neuchatel, Switzerland, visiting professor, 1984; MIT, visiting professor, 1983-84; Math Science Research Institute, visiting professor, 1989-90; UCSD, assistant professor, 1974-78, associate professor, 1978-81, professor, 1981-. **ORGANIZATIONS:** Asians in Higher Education, board of directors, 1988-90; National Research Council, Panel on Equity/Diversity, math science education board panel, chair, 1992-; Chinese American Faculty Association, 1988-90; Asian Educators, founding member, 1986. **HONORS/AWARDS:** Union of Pan Asian Communities, Commitment to Education Award, 1986; Chancellor's Association, Award for Excellence in Teaching, 1981; Phi Beta Kappa, 1974-. **SPECIAL ACHIEVEMENTS:** Initiated Asian American Studies Program at UCSD, 1986; helped create Ethnic Studies dept at UCSD, 1990. **BUSINESS ADDRESS:** Professor, Dept of Math, Unv of California, San Diego, 7157 APM, La Jolla, CA 92093, (619)534-2646.

LIN, JAMES Y.
Consultant. Taiwanese American. **PERSONAL:** Born Aug 25, 1958, Taipei, Taiwan; son of Pei Hua Lin and Linda C Lin; married Jean S Lee, Mar 8, 1988; children: Krystal S, Kristopher J. **EDUCATION:** University of California, Los Angeles, BSEE, 1980. **CAREER:** TRW Inc, mts, 1979-85; Hughes Aircraft Inc, section head, 1985-88; Occidental Capital Management, vice president, 1988-90; Portfolio Advisory Services, director of research, 1990-91; JJK Capital Inc, managing director, 1991-. **SPECIAL ACHIEVEMENTS:** US Investing Champion Open, 1992; US Investing Champion 50+, 1991. **HOME ADDRESS:** 4259 Vista Largo, Torrance, CA 90505, (310)325-2111. **BUSINESS PHONE:** (310)325-6827.

LIN, JASON JIA-YUAN
Educator. Taiwanese American. **PERSONAL:** Born May 24, 1955, Chiayi, Taiwan; son of Yaw-chuan Lin & Shiow-Mei Lieu Lin; married Jane Chein-Hsing Sung, Jun 20, 1982; children: Kirk, Grace. **EDUCATION:** National Taiwan University, BS, 1978; Wayne State University, MA, 1981, PhD, 1985. **CAREER:** Chinese Army, lieutenant, 1978-80; Wayne State University, grad-

uate assistant, 1980-84, instructor, 1984-85; Tiffin University, assistant professor, 1985-86; Northeast Missouri State University, assistant professor, 1986-91, associate professor, 1991-. **ORGANIZATIONS:** American Finance Association; American Economic Association; Western Economic Association; Midwest Economic Association. **HONORS/AWARDS:** Chia-Hsin Co, Chia-Hsin College Merit Award, 1977; Wayne State University, Mendleson Research Grant, 1984; Northeast Missouri State University, Faculty Research Grant, 1987, 1988, 1990. **SPECIAL ACHIEVEMENTS:** Published 8 articles in the Central Daily News, 1990-91. **BUSINESS ADDRESS:** Associate Professor, Div of Business & Accounting, Northeast Missouri State University, Kirksville, MO 63501, (816)785-4349.

LIN, JENNIFER JEN-HUEY
Architect. Taiwanese American. **PERSONAL:** Born Dec 19, 1964, Taipei, Taiwan; daughter of Chin-Ying & Cheng-Te Lin. **EDUCATION:** MIT, BSAD, 1987; Case Westrn Reserve University, Medical School, 1989; MIT, MArch, 1992. **CAREER:** Woo & Williams architect intern, 1985; Tsomides Associate, architect, 1990; Williams Associate, architect, 1992; Richard Larson Architects, architect, 1992; KMD, architect, 1992-. **ORGANIZATIONS:** Bay Area Young Architects; Philanthrophy by Design; MIT Alumni. **HONORS/AWARDS:** MIT Architect Department, scholarship, 1987; MIT Council for the Arts, grant, 1986; CWRU, research fellowship, 1988. **SPECIAL ACHIEVEMENTS:** Home at Work, Work at Home, thesis, 1992; Attitudes and Awareness of AIDS in Japan, research fellowship, 1988; A Detour through MIT, art exhibit, 1986; Technology Talk, 1986. **HOME ADDRESS:** 5424 Cerro Sur, El Sobrante, CA 94803. **BUSINESS ADDRESS:** Architect, Kaplan, McLaughlin, Diaz, 222 Vallejo St, San Francisco, CA 94111, (415)399-4917.

LIN, JIAN
Scientist. Chinese American. **EDUCATION:** University of Science & Technology of China, BS, 1982; Brown University, MS, 1984, PhD, 1988. **CAREER:** Brown University, research, teaching assistant, 1982-88; US Geological Survey, visiting research associate, 1987-88; Southern California Earthquake Center, visiting fellow, 1991; Woods Hole Oceanographic Institution, assistant scientist, 1988-92, associate scientist, 1992-. **ORGANIZATIONS:** American Geophysical Union, Tectonophysics Program, Spring National Meeting Committee, chair, 1992-93; Journal of Geophysical Research, associate editor, 1992-94; American Geophysical Union, 1982-; Geological Society of America, 1992-; Sigma Xi, 1988-; Ocean Drilling Program, Tectonic Advisory Board, 1994-96; US Geological Survey, External Research Funding, advisory panel member, 1993; American Association for the Advancement of Science, 1994-. **HONORS/AWARDS:** University of Sci-Tech of China, Guo-Muo Ruo Medal for Exceptional Achievement, 1982; Woods Hole Oceanographic Institution, Culpepper Foundation, Culpepper Young Scientist Award, 1988, Mellon Independent Research Award, 1990, 1992; National Science Foundation, Southern California Earthquake Center, visiting fellow, 1991. **SPECIAL ACHIEVEMENTS:** More than 20 publications in Nature, Science, Journal of Geophysical Research, Marine Geophysical Research, Geophysical Research Letters, Bulletin of Seismological Society of America, Oceanus, others; co-author: "Evidence from Gravity Data for Focused Magmatic Accretion along the Mid-Atlantic Ridge," Nature, 344, 627-632, 1990; co-author: "Changes in Failure Stress on the Southern San Andreas Fault System Caused by the 1992 M=7.4 Landers Earthquake," Science, 256, 1928-1932, 1992. **BIOGRAPHICAL SOURCES:** "American Scientists Make a New Prediction: California's Big One(s) Getting Closer," Wood Hole Currents, vol 2, no 1, p 1 & 10, winter 1993. **BUSINESS ADDRESS:** Assoc Scientist, Dept of Geology & Geophysics, Woods Hole Oceanographic Institution, Woods Hole, MA 02543.

LIN, JIANN-TSYH
Chemist. Taiwanese American. **PERSONAL:** Born Jan 15, 1940, Taoyuan, Taiwan; son of Yuan-I Lin and Mu-Mien Lin; married Cheng-Ling Lin, Jun 24, 1989; children: Robert Chen-Yu, Jeffrey Chen-Chuen. **EDUCATION:** Chung-Hsing University, BS, 1963; University of Mississippi, MS, 1967; Drexel University, PhD, 1971. **CAREER:** University of Tennessee, research associate, 1971-72; University of Minnesota, research associate, 1972-76; University of Washington, research associate, 1976-77; US Department of Agriculture, research chemist, 1978-. **ORGANIZATIONS:** American Chemical Society, 1971-; American Society of Plant Physiologists, 1985-; Plant Growth Regulator Society of America, 1987-; Japan Society for Bioscience, Biotechnology and Agrochemistry, 1990-; North America Taiwanese Professors' Association, 1982-. **HONORS/AWARDS:** Northern California Formosan Federation, Outstanding Contribution, 1993. **SPECIAL ACHIEVEMENTS:**

Scientific papers about plant hormones, steroids and lipids published in journals, 1971-; language proficiency in Taiwanese and Chinese. **BUSINESS ADDRESS:** Research Chemist, US Department of Agriculture, 800 Buchanan Street, Room 1106, Albany, CA 94710, (510)559-5764.

LIN, JOSEPH PEN-TZE
Neuroradiologist. Chinese American. **PERSONAL:** Born Nov 25, 1932, Fuzhou, Fujien, China; son of Da-Sui and Chin-sien Lin; married Lillian Yu-Feng, Dec 23, 1959; children: James, Carol, Julia. **EDUCATION:** National Taiwan University, MD, 1957. **CAREER:** Robert B Green Mem Hospital, rotating intern, 1959-60; Santa Rosa Med Center, resident, radiology, 1960-61; Bellevue Hospital Center, resident, radiology, 1961-63; New York University Med Center, neuroradiology fellow, 1963-65, assistant professor in radiology, 1965-69, associate professor in radiology, 1969-74, professor in radiology, 1974-. **ORGANIZATIONS:** Am Society of Neuroradiology, 1965-; American College of Radiology, fellow, 1978-; Association of University Radiology, 1978-; Radiology Society of North America, 1965-; America Chinese Medical Society, president, 1978. **SPECIAL ACHIEVEMENTS:** Publications on neuroradiology and chapters in related books; books in radiography of the spine. **BUSINESS ADDRESS:** Professor, Dept of Radiology, New York University Medical Center, 550 First Ave, New York, NY 10016-6402, (212)263-5218.

LIN, JUIYUAN WILLIAM
Certified public accountant. Taiwanese American. **PERSONAL:** Born Jul 8, 1937, Chia-Yi, Taiwan; son of Pi Lin and Chuan Sing Lin; married Meihui Su Lin, May 27, 1963; children: Eva, Karen Lin. **EDUCATION:** National Chuang Hsing University, Taiwan, BA, 1960; Illinois State University, MBA, business administration, 1970. **CAREER:** Chia-yi Business School, accounting teacher, 1961-62; Bank of Communications, Taiwan, China, chief accountant, 1962-69; Computer Service Inc, controller, 1970-75; Teng & Associates, Inc, senior associate/controller, 1975-90; New Asia Bank, board of directors, 1989-; Executive Building Corp, president, 1990-; Lin & Lincoln CPA's, Ltd, president, 1990-. **ORGANIZATIONS:** American Institute of Certified Public Accountants, 1980-; Illinois CPA Society, tax committee, 1980-; Monte Jade Association for Technology & Enterprise, board of directors, 1991-; US-China Economic and Trade Council, treasurer, 1992-; Taiwanese American Chamber of Commerce, board of directors, 1990-92; Wilmette Family Service Center, board of directors, 1989-91; Taiwanese American CPA Association, 1992-; Presidential Task Force, life member, 1980-. **HONORS/AWARDS:** Presidential Task Force, Medal for Merit, 1985. **SPECIAL ACHIEVEMENTS:** Economic Advisor Committee for Republic of China, 1988; passed CPA examiniation in USA, 1980; passed CPA examiniation in Taiwan, Republic of China, 1961. **BUSINESS ADDRESS:** President, Lin & Lincoln CPA's Ltd, 1132 Waukegan Rd, Ste 101, Glenview, IL 60025-3060, (708)998-8888.

LIN, JULIA C.
Educator. Chinese American. **PERSONAL:** Born May 4, 1928, Shanghai, China; daughter of Dr & Mrs F S Tsang; married Henry H Lin, Dec 28, 1951 (deceased); children: Tan A, Maya Y. **EDUCATION:** Smith College, BA, 1951; University of Washington, MA, 1952, PhD, 1965. **CAREER:** Ohio University, professor of English, full-time, until 1993, part-time, 1993-. **ORGANIZATIONS:** Association of Asian Studies, 1965-; American Literary Translation Association, 1989-. **HONORS/AWARDS:** American Council of Learned Societies & Social Science Research, research grant, 1968-69; NEH, National Endowment for Youngest Humanist Award, 1975-76. **SPECIAL ACHIEVEMENTS:** Modern Chinese Poetry: An Introduction, University of Washington Press, 1972; Essays on Contemporary Chinese Poetry, Ohio University, 1985; Women on the Red Plains An Anthology of Contemporary Chinese Women's Poetry, Penguin Press, 1993. **HOME PHONE:** (614)593-7359. **BUSINESS ADDRESS:** Professor, English Dept, Ohio University, Athens, OH 45701-2979.

LIN, KAI-CHING
Educator. Taiwanese American. **PERSONAL:** Born Oct 21, 1955, Kaohsiung, Taiwan; son of Wei-Chih Lin & Mei-Ying Wu Lin. **EDUCATION:** National Taiwan University, BS, 1977; University of California, PhD, 1984. **CAREER:** University of Chicago, Dickson Instructor, 1984-86; University of Wisconsin, Madison, Van Vleck Assistant Professor, 1986-90; Mathematical Science Research Institute, postdoctorate, 1987-88; University of Alabama, associate professor, currently. **BUSINESS ADDRESS:** Associate Professor, Dept of Mathematics, University of Alabama, Tuscaloosa, AL 35487, (205)348-1975.

LIN, KUAN-PIN
Educator. Taiwanese American/Chinese American. **PERSONAL:** Born Mar 1, 1948, Taiwan; son of Ching-Nan Lin; married Chaling Lin, Oct 15, 1978; children: Jamie, Candice. **EDUCATION:** National Chengchi University, Taipei, Taiwan, BL, 1970; State University of New York at Stony Brook, MA, 1973, PhD, 1977; Harvard University, post-doctoral, 1979. **CAREER:** Chung-Hua Institution for Economic Research, visiting fellow, 1981; Reed College, visiting associate professor, 1982-83; Bonneville Power Administration, industry economist, 1984-85; Portland State University, Economics, assistant professor, 1979-82, associate professor, 1982-86, professor, 1986-. **ORGANIZATIONS:** American Economic Association, 1979-; Econometric Society, 1979-; Society of Computational Economics, 1989-. **HONORS/AWARDS:** Fulbright Hays Research Scholar, 1985-86. **SPECIAL ACHIEVEMENTS:** Author, "Qualitative Economic Reasoning," Journal of Economics Dynamics & Control, 1990; eDATA: A General Purpose Economic Database and Retrieval Program, 1986-; Stability of the Short-Run Money Demand in the United States, Journal of Finance, 1984. **MILITARY SERVICE:** Taiwan, 1978-79. **BUSINESS ADDRESS:** Professor, Dept of Economics, Portland State University, PO Box 751, Portland, OR 97207-0751, (503)725-3931.

LIN, L. YU
Educator. Taiwanese American. **PERSONAL:** Born Aug 21, 1957, Taipei, Taiwan; son of Chung-Kong Lin; married Shin-Yun Tsao, Jul 1993. **EDUCATION:** Feng-chia University, BSE, 1981; University of Cincinnati, MS, 1986; University of Central Florida, PhD, 1990. **CAREER:** University of Central Florida, teaching assistant, instructor, 1986-90; Christian Brothers University, assistant professor, 1990-. **ORGANIZATIONS:** American Society of Civil Engineers; American Society of Engineering Education. **HONORS/AWARDS:** Department of Professional Board, Florida, Professional Engineer, 1992. **BUSINESS ADDRESS:** Asst Professor, Engineering School, Christian Brothers University, 650 E Parkway S, N130, Memphis, TN 38104-5519, (901)722-0403.

LIN, LAWRENCE I-KUEI
Statistician. Chinese American. **PERSONAL:** Born May 21, 1948, Fujou, Fujian, China; son of Ching Chong Lin & Pi-Chin Cheh Lin; married Sha-Li Yen Lin, Aug 14, 1971; children: Juintow, Buortau, Shintau. **EDUCATION:** National Chen-Chi University, Taipei, BS, 1970; University of Iowa, MS, 1973, PhD, 1979. **CAREER:** Institute of Agricultural Medicine, University of Iowa, statistician, 1973-79; Baxter Healthcare Co, senior statistician, research statistician, senior research statistician, 1979-. **ORGANIZATIONS:** Performing Arts Club of Chinese Americans in Greater Chicago, president, 1992-; Mont Jade Technology & Enterprises Association, board member, 1993-; Hai-Wha Club, vice president, 1992-; Northern Illinois Chapter of American Statistical Association, president, 1994-; Biometrics Society, 1975-; American Statistical Association, 1973-. **HONORS/AWARDS:** Baxter Healthcare Co, Technical Operation Support, 1986. **SPECIAL ACHIEVEMENTS:** University Contest on English Speech, 3rd place, 1968; published 20 peer reviewed articles in various professional journals; proficient in Chinese & English. **MILITARY SERVICE:** Army of Republic of China, 2nd lt, 1970-71. **BUSINESS ADDRESS:** Senior Research Statistician, Baxter Healthcare Co, Rte 120 & Wilson, WG2-3S, Round Lake, IL 60073, (708)270-5394.

LIN, LIANG-SHIOU
Government official. Taiwanese American/Chinese American. **PERSONAL:** Born Nov 30, 1953, Sin-Ying, Taiwan; son of Chin-Long Lin & Gee Shen Lin; married Jih-Jing Lin, Jun 4, 1978; children: Emery, Joyce. **EDUCATION:** National Taiwan University, BS, 1976; University of Illinois, Urbana-Champaign, MS, 1980, PhD, 1987. **CAREER:** Washington University, postdoctoral fellow, 1987-90; US Dept of Agriculture, program director, 1990-. **ORGANIZATIONS:** American Institute of Biological Sciences, 1979-; Botanical Society of America, 1991-; American Society of Plant Physiologists, 1983-; Asian Pacific American Network in Agriculture, 1990-. **HONORS/AWARDS:** Phi Kappa Phi, 1981. **SPECIAL ACHIEVEMENTS:** Proficient in English, Mandarin Chinese, and Taiwanese/Fukienese; 14 publications in scientific journals; books. **MILITARY SERVICE:** Army, Taiwan, 2nd lt, 1976-78. **BUSINESS ADDRESS:** Program Director, USDA/CSRS/NRIGEP, Rm 323 Aerospace Bldg, 901 D St SW, Washington, DC 20250-2241, (202)401-5042.

LIN, MAYA YING
Architect, designer. Chinese American. **EDUCATION:** Yale University, BA, 1981, MArch, 1986; Harvard University. **CAREER:** Cooper-Lecky Partnership, design consultant, 1981-82; Peter Forbes & Associates, Boston, archit

designer, 1983, New York, design associate, 1986-87; Batey & Mack, archit designer, 1984; Fumihiko Maki & Associates, Japan, architect apprentice, 1985; Maya Lin Studio, owner, 1987-. **ORGANIZATIONS:** Commission on the Future of the Smithsonian Institution, one of 26 named to committee, 1994. **HONORS/AWARDS:** AIA, Henry Bacon Memorial Award, 1984; NEA, grant, 1988; Metropolitan Home, Elements of Style, Design 100, 1990. **SPECIAL ACHIEVEMENTS:** Exhibitions include: 60's-80's Sculpture Parallels, Sidney Janis Gallery, 1988; Jane Voorhees Zimmerli Art Museum, Rutgers State University, 1985; group exhibition: Rosa Esman Gallery, New York, 1990; works include: Vietnam Veterans War Memorial, Washington, DC, designer, 1981; Southern Poverty Law Center, Montgomery, Alabama, memorial designer, 1988; Museum for African Art, New York City, co-designer with David Hotson, 1993. **BUSINESS ADDRESS:** Sculptor, Architect, c/o Sidney Janis Gallery, 110 W 57th St, New York, NY 10019. *

LIN, MING-CHANG
Educator. Taiwanese American. **PERSONAL:** Born Oct 24, 1936, Hsinchu, Taiwan; son of Fushin Lin & T May Hsu; married Juh-Huey Chern, Jun 26, 1965; children: Karen, Linus H, Ellena J. **EDUCATION:** Taiwan Normal University, Taipei, Taiwan, BSc, 1959; University of Ottawa, Ontario, Canada, PhD, 1966. **CAREER:** University of Ottawa, postdoctoral fellow, 1965-67; Cornell University, postdoctoral associate, 1967-69; Naval Research Lab, research chemist, 1970-74, supervisory research chemist, 1974-82, senior scientist for chem kinetics, 1982-88; Emory University, Robert W Woodruff professor of chemistry, 1988-. **ORGANIZATIONS:** American Chemical Society, 1970-; American Vacuum Society, 1989-; The Combustion Institute, 1985-; Materials Research Society, 1989-; Sigma Xi, 1974-; North-American Taiwanese Professors Association, chp president, 1982-; Formosan Association for Public Affairs, central committee member, 1983-. **HONORS/AWARDS:** Chemical Society of Washington, Hillebrand Prize, 1975; Washington Academy of Sciences, Physical Science Award, 1976; US Navy, Navy Meritorious Civilian Award, 1979; Guggenheim Foundation, Guggenheim Fellow, 1982-83; Humboldt Foundation, Alexander von Humboldt Award, 1982; Taiwanese-American Foundation, TAF Award for Science and Technology, 1989. **SPECIAL ACHIEVEMENTS:** Author/co-author of over 250 technical papers in the areas of chemical kinetics, chemical lasers and the applications of lasers to study homogeneous and heterogeneous chemical processes relevant to combustion, propulsion and microelectronic fabrication reactions. **MILITARY SERVICE:** ROTC, Taiwan, 2nd lt, 1959-61.

LIN, NINA S. F.
Cosmetics company sales administrator. Chinese American. **PERSONAL:** Born Sep 8, 1946, Hunan, China; daughter of Heng-Ling and Mu-Lan Hsiung; married Shing-Shyong Lin, Aug 2, 1971; children: M Mei-I, V Sun-Kai. **EDUCATION:** National Taiwan University, Taipei, Taiwan, BLib, 1966; University of Washington, Seattle, MLS, 1971. **CAREER:** Seattle Public School, teacher's aide, librarian, 1971-74; Mary Kay Cosmetics, sr sales director, 1978-. **ORGANIZATIONS:** Seattle Chinese Women's Club, officer, 1990-. **HONORS/AWARDS:** Mary Kay Cosmetics, Circle of Achievement, (Top Sales in the Nation), 1982, 1988-92, (Top Sales to Lead the Unit), 1982-, Queen's Court in Personal Sales, Nationwide, 1987-88, 1990, Cadillac Winner Honor, 1982-. **BIOGRAPHICAL SOURCES:** Seattle Chinese Post, Feb & Mar 1991, Oct 1987, Oct & Dec 1988; Ladies, Chinese magazine, p 131, Oct 1991; Central Daily News, May 1992; Seattle Times, p D4, Jan 13, 1992; World Journal, p 229, Mar 19, 1991. **BUSINESS ADDRESS:** Senior Sales Director, Mary Kay Cosmetics, 6164 NE 192nd St, Seattle, WA 98155, (206)486-9744.

LIN, PATRICIA YU
Educator. Taiwanese American. **PERSONAL:** Born Nov 11, 1969, Arlington, MA; daughter of Siu-Shyong Lin and Pei-Hui Lin. **EDUCATION:** Princeton University, BA (magna cum laude), history, 1991; University of California, Berkeley, MA, history, 1993, pursuing PhD, currently. **CAREER:** Dow Chemical USA, computer programmer, 1985; Opus Telecom Inc, computer programmer, 1986; Raytheon Co, computer progammer/analyst, 1987; Lotus Development Corp, product marketing research associate, 1988, marketing programs associate, 1989; University of California, Berkeley, teaching assistant, 1993; Professor Thomas W Laqueur, research assistant, 1991-. **ORGANIZATIONS:** Bay Area War, Society and Culture Group, founder and convener, 1993-; Bay Area Eighteenth Century Studies Group, steering committee, co-convener, 1992-; American Historical Association, 1992-; Berkeley-Stanford British Studies Reading Group, coordinator, 1991-93; Bay Area History of Medicine and Culture Group, coordinator, 1991-93. **HONORS/AWARDS:** University

of California, Berkeley, Mellon Foundation Dissertation Prospectus Fellowship, 1993; Rock Island Arsenal, Illinois, Richard C Maguire Scholarship, 1992; University of California, Berkeley, Non-Resident Tuition Scholarship, 1991; 1990: Citibank Summer Research Grant, Princeton University Department of History Grant, Princeton University Office of the Dean of the College Grant; grants from the Princeton University classes of 1934, 1939, 1942 and 1955; University of California, Berkeley, Mentored Research Award, 1993-94. **SPECIAL ACHIEVEMENTS:** Review of publication: Bromley House: Four Essays Celebrating the 175th Anniversary of the Foundation of Nottingham Subscription Library 1816-1991, Libraries and Culture, 28, p 223-224, spring 1993; established "Patricia Y Lin Collection of Overseas Evacuee Records," Imperial War Museum, London, 1991. **BUSINESS ADDRESS:** Research Assistant, Dept of History, University of California, Berkeley, 3310 Dwinelle Hall, Berkeley, CA 94720, (510)642-2034.

LIN, PAUL KUANG-HSIEN
Educator. Taiwanese American. **PERSONAL:** Born Nov 12, 1946, Tung-Shih, Taiwan; son of Jen-Hsang Lin and Yei-Mei Lin; married Catherine Kai-Lin Jen, Aug 5, 1978; children: Elizabeth, John. **EDUCATION:** Fu-Jen University, Taiwan, BS, 1970; Brigham Young University, MS, 1975; Wayne State University, PhD, 1980. **CAREER:** Oakland University, assistant professor, 1980-82; Western Michigan University, assistant professor, 1982-84; The University of Michigan, Dearborn, associate professor, 1984-. **ORGANIZATIONS:** American Society for Quality Control, 1990-; American Statistical Association, 1981-; Institute of Mathematical Statistics, 1978-; The Taiwan Benevolent Association of Michigan, president, 1992-; Sigma Xi, 1980-. **HONORS/AWARDS:** State of Michigan, Research Excellence and Economic Development Fund, 1988, 1989; The University of Michigan, Dearborn, Educational Enhancement Award, 1985, 1986, Equipment and Research Incentive Award, 1986. **SPECIAL ACHIEVEMENTS:** "Using Taguchi Methods in Quality Engineering," Quality Progress, 1990; "A Simple Method for Constructing Confounded Designs for Mixed Factorial Experiments," Communications in Statistics, 1987; "Using Chinese Remainder Theorem in Constructing Confounded Designs for Mixed Factorial Experiments," Communications in Statistics, 1986. **BUSINESS ADDRESS:** Associate Professor of Statistics, The University of Michigan, Dearborn, 4901 Evergreen Rd, University Mall, Rm 1174, Dearborn, MI 48128, (313)593-5414.

LIN, PEN-MIN
Educator. Chinese American. **PERSONAL:** Born Oct 17, 1928, Mukden, Liaoning, China; married Louise Lee, Dec 29, 1962; children: Marian, Margaret, Janice. **EDUCATION:** National Taiwan University, BSEE, 1950; North Carolina State University, MSEE, 1956; Purdue University, PhD, 1960. **CAREER:** Bell Telephone Labs, technical staff, 1960-61; Purdue University, assistant professor, 1961-66, associate professor, 1966-74, professor, 1974-. **ORGANIZATIONS:** IEEE, fellow, 1981-. **SPECIAL ACHIEVEMENTS:** Co-author, Computer-Aided Analysis of Electronic Circuits, Prentice-Hall, 1975; author, Symbolic Network Analysis, Elsevier, 1991. **HOME ADDRESS:** 3029 Covington St, West Lafayette, IN 47906-1107, (317)463-2426.

LIN, PI-ERH
Educator. Chinese American. **PERSONAL:** Born Jan 8, 1938, Taichung, Taiwan; son of Yuan-Fu Lin; married Mei-Hua L Lin, Jan 17, 1963; children: Chen-Tan, Michelle, Christine. **EDUCATION:** Taiwan Normal University, BS, 1961; Columbia University, PhD, 1968. **CAREER:** Florida State University, assistant professor, 1969-75, associate professor, 1975-81, professor, 1981-. **ORGANIZATIONS:** American Statistics Association, 1970-; Institute of Math Statistics, 1973-; International Chinese Statistics Association, 1987-; Annals of Statistics, associate editor, 1975-76; Communications in Statistics, associate editor, 1983-; Math Reviews, reviewer, 1976-86; International Statistics Institute, 1989-. **HONORS/AWARDS:** Florida State University, Advising Award, 1991. **SPECIAL ACHIEVEMENTS:** "Non Parametric Estimation of a Vector-Valued Bivariate Failure Rate," Annals of Stat, 5, 1027-1038, 1977; "Non Parametric Est of a Regression Function," Z Wahrs Verw Gebiete 57, 222-233, 1981; "Measures of Association between Vectors," Communications in Stat, A16 (2), 321-338, 1987. **MILITARY SERVICE:** Chinese Armored Artillery, second lieut, 1961-62. **BUSINESS ADDRESS:** Professor, Dept of Statistics, Florida State University, West Tennessee St, B-167, Tallahassee, FL 32306-3033, (904)644-6697.

LIN, PING-WHA
Educator. Chinese American. **PERSONAL:** Born Jul 11, 1925, Canton, China; son of Li-Yu and Shutz Lin (deceased); married Sylvia Lin, Feb 14, 1960;

children: Karl, Karen. **EDUCATION:** Chiao-Tung University, China, BS, 1947; Purdue University, MS, 1950, PhD, 1951. **CAREER:** Ammon & Whitney, J G White Corporation, Lockwood Greene Engineers, Inc, engineer, 1951-61; World Health Organization, project manager/consultant/environmental engineer, 1962-66, 1979-81, 1984; Lin Technologies, Inc, president, 1989-; Tri-State University, Dresser Chair Professor, 1966-79, 1981-. **ORGANIZATIONS:** American Society of Civil Engineers, fellow, 1968-; American Chemical Society; National Society of Professional Engineers; American Waterworks Association, life member; Sigma Xi; Chi Epsilon. **HONORS/AWARDS:** The United Inventors & Scientists of America, Achievement Award, 1974; Dept of Energy, Grantee, 1983-84. **SPECIAL ACHIEVEMENTS:** More than forty papers published in professional magazines; holder of thirteen American patents in the field of air pollution control construction materials, materials for water & wastewater treatment, soil and foundation stabilization, energy development, etc. **BIOGRAPHICAL SOURCES:** "Prof's Discovery Lets Acid Rain Take a Powder," The Journal-Gazette, October 28, 1984; "Lin Addresses International Audience," To-Day, Spring, 1993. **HOME ADDRESS:** 506 S Darling St, Angola, IN 46703, (219)665-5425.

LIN, POPING
Educator, librarian. Chinese American. **PERSONAL:** Born Mar 21, 1954, Beijing, People's Republic of China; daughter of Tongqi Lin & Shulan Ye. **EDUCATION:** Saint Mary College, BA, history, 1985; Simmons College, Graduate School of Lib & Inf Sci, MLS, 1987. **CAREER:** Boston College, assistant librarian, cataloging dept, 1987, reference librarian, 1987-88; Northeastern University, reference librarian, 1987-89, bibliographic services librarian, 1989-90; Purdue University, assistant professor of lib sci, assistant reference & instruction librarian, 1991-. **ORGANIZATIONS:** American Library Association, 1989-; American College & Research Libraries, 1989-, BI for Diverse Populations Committee, 1992-95; Library & Information Technology Association, various committees, 1989-. **HONORS/AWARDS:** Beta Phi Mu, 1987-. **SPECIAL ACHIEVEMENTS:** "A Built-in Teaching Function for the End User/Machine Interface," paper presented in 3rd National Conference of Library and Inforamtion Technology, 1992; "Exploring Collection Development Guidelines for American Studies in China: An Integration of Academic & Pragmatic Approaches," American Studies International, Vol XXX, no 2, p 35-52, Oct 1992; numerous others. **BUSINESS ADDRESS:** Assistant Professor of Library Science, Librarian, Purdue University, Stewart Center, West Lafayette, IN 47907-1531, (317)494-6735.

LIN, ROBERT PEICHUNG
Educator, researcher. Chinese American. **PERSONAL:** Born Jan 24, 1942, Kwangsi, China; son of Tung Hua Lin and Zu Yee; married Lily, Aug 14, 1983; children: Linus. **EDUCATION:** California Institute of Technology, BS, 1962; University of California, Berkeley, PhD, 1967. **CAREER:** University of California, Berkeley, assistant research physicist, 1967-74, associate research physicist, 1974-79, research physicist, 1979-91, senior fellow, 1980-88, adj professor astronomy, 1988-91, professor of physics, 1991-, Space Science Lab, associate director, 1992-. **ORGANIZATIONS:** American Geophysical Union, 1965; American Astronomical Society, 1975-. **HONORS/AWARDS:** NASA, special recognition for service as a principal investigator; NASA, Goddard Space Flight Center, ISEE-C Project, recognition for outstanding contribution. **SPECIAL ACHIEVEMENTS:** Over 200 publications on solar and interplanetary physics, lunar and planetary studies, high energy astrophysics, and physics of Earth's magnetosphere, 1965-93. **BUSINESS ADDRESS:** Professor, Space Sciences Lab, University of California, Berkeley, Berkeley, CA 94720, (510)642-1149.

LIN, ROXANNE VERONICA
Educator. Taiwanese American. **PERSONAL:** Born Nov 4, 1957, Taipei, Taiwan; daughter of Bengee (deceased) & Verna B Lin; divorced; children: Benjamin Lucas Klein. **EDUCATION:** University of California, San Diego, BA, 1982, PhD, 1988. **CAREER:** San Diego State University, lecturer in women's studies, 1988-89; University of Vermont, assistant professor of English, 1989-. **BUSINESS ADDRESS:** Assistant Professor, English Dept, University of Vermont, 315 Old Mill, Burlington, VT 05405-0114, (802)656-3056.

LIN, SHIELD B.
Educator. Taiwanese American. **PERSONAL:** Born Jun 16, 1953, Gia-Yi, Taiwan; married Liu C Lin. **EDUCATION:** Texas A&M University, PhD, 1986. **CAREER:** Prairie View A&M University, Mechanical Engineering Dept, department head, 1988-. **ORGANIZATIONS:** Sigma Xi, Prairie View

Club, president, 1988-89, vice president, 1987-88; ASME; SME; Pi Tau Sigma; Tau Beta Pi. **BUSINESS ADDRESS:** Dept Head, Mechanical Engineering Dept, Prairie View A&M University, PO Box 397, Prairie View, TX 77446, (409)857-4023.

LIN, SHIN
Educator, educational administrator. Hong Kong American. **PERSONAL:** Born Feb 14, 1945, Hong Kong; son of Wilhoit Y M Lin and Mary Lew Lin; married Diane C Lin, Jun 21, 1969; children: Howe, Payton. **EDUCATION:** Foothill College, chemistry, 1961-63; University of California at Davis, BS, chemistry, 1965; San Diego State University, MS, chemistry, 1967; UCLA, PhD, biological chemistry, 1971. **CAREER:** University of California at San Francisco, postdoctoral fellow of biochemistry & biophysics, 1971-74; Johns Hopkins University, assistant professor of biophysics, 1974-79, associate professor of biophysics, 1979-82, professor of biophysics & biology, 1982-, chairman of biophysics, 1983-, School of Arts & Sciences, associate dean for research & graduate studies, 1992-. **ORGANIZATIONS:** Am Association for Advancement of Science, fellow, 1982-; American Society for Cell Biology; American Society of Biological Chemists & Molecular biologists; Biophysical Society. **HONORS/AWARDS:** National Institutes of Health, Research Career Development Award, 1976-81; San Francisco Bay Area Heart Association, Outstanding Research Fellow Award, 1974. **SPECIAL ACHIEVEMENTS:** Author of numerous scientific arcticles & books, 1970-; consulting editor in Biophysics, McGraw Hill Encyclopedia of Science & Technology, 1991-; National Institutes of Health's Study Section on Cell Biology, public advisory commitee, 1980-83; American Heart Association Research Committee, 1986; Journal of Receptor Research, editorial board, 1980-84. **BUSINESS ADDRESS:** Professor, Johns Hopkins University, 3400 N Charles St, 400 Jenkins Hall, Baltimore, MD 21218, (410)516-7248.

LIN, SIN-SHONG
Researcher. Taiwanese American/Chinese American. **PERSONAL:** Born Oct 24, 1933, Kao-Hsiung, Taiwan; son of Tu-Sen Lin and Chi-yuan Liu; married Juey-Shin Lin, Aug 8, 1964; children: I-Mei, I-Ann, I-Jong. **EDUCATION:** National Taiwan University, BS, 1956; National Tsing Hua University, Taiwan, MS, 1958; University of Kansas, PhD, 1966. **CAREER:** US Army Research Laboratory, senior research chemist, 1966-. **ORGANIZATIONS:** American Chemical Society, 1964-; American Vacuum Society, 1970-; Material Research Society, 1986-; Electrochemical Society, 1975-; Tsinq Hua Alumni Association Boston, president, 1990. **SPECIAL ACHIEVEMENTS:** Numerous awards in the Army's laboratory & several citations, publications exceeding 75 papers; proficiency in Chinese, Japanese. **BIOGRAPHICAL SOURCES:** SAMPE Journal, Vol 28, No 4, p9, 1992. **BUSINESS ADDRESS:** Research Chemist, Army Research Laboratory, Materials Directorate, Arsenal St, B292, ATTN: AMSRL-MA-PB-292, Watertown, MA 02172-0001, (617)923-5390.

LIN, STEPHEN YAW-RUI
Researcher. Chinese American. **PERSONAL:** Born Apr 23, 1939, Taiwan; son of Lun-yun and Sun-mei Lin; married Ilona Klara Szabo, Dec 23, 1972; children: Stephen San, Eva Mae. **EDUCATION:** National Taiwan University, BS, 1962; University of Washington, MS, 1967; North Carolina State University, PhD, 1970. **CAREER:** Masonite Corp, research techologist, 1967-68; Swedish Forest Products Research Lab, visiting scientist, 1970-71; North Carolina State University, research fellow, 1971-72; Westvaco Corp, senior research chemist, 1972-79; American Can Co, senior research supervisor, 1979-81; Reed Lignin/Daishowa Chemicals Inc, research manager, 1981-90; LignoTech USA Inc, research manager, 1990-. **ORGANIZATIONS:** TAPPI, wood chemistry committee, chair, 1984-86; AWPA, 1991-; International Symposium on Wood and Pulping Chemistry, committee, 1989-93. **HONORS/AWARDS:** American Paper Institute, George Olmsted Award, 1972; American Can Company, Highest Achievement Award, 1981. **SPECIAL ACHIEVEMENTS:** Editor, Method in Lignin Chemistry, Springer-Verlag, 1992; author, "Lignin," in Ullmann's Encyclopedia of Industrial Chemistry, 1985; inventor, over 20 US patents. **BUSINESS ADDRESS:** Research Manager, Lignotech USA Inc, 100 Hwy 51 S, Rothschild, WI 54474, (715)355-3615.

LIN, SU-CHEN JONATHON
Educator. Taiwanese American. **PERSONAL:** Born Oct 8, 1953, Kauoshung, Taiwan; son of Kim-Hua Lin and Mon-Lian Lin; married Hui-Chung Lin, May 25, 1980; children: Andrew, Carol. **EDUCATION:** National Taiwan Normal University, MEd, 1978; Iowa State University, MS, 1985, PhD, 1985, PhD,

1987. **CAREER:** Moorhead State University, asst prof, 1986-88; Eastern Michigan University, assoc prof, prof, 1988-. **ORGANIZATIONS:** American Society of Mechanical Engineers, tech exec committee, publication editor, paper reviewer, conference section chmn, 1987-; National Assn of Industrial Technology. **HONORS/AWARDS:** Eastern Michigan University, College of Technology, Outstanding Professor Award, 1993; Teaching Excellence Award, 1993. **SPECIAL ACHIEVEMENTS:** Author: over 50 articles and papers, various journals and magazines, 1985-; 2 publications, CNC and fluid power; CNC textbook for colleges and universities, 1993;. **BUSINESS ADDRESS:** Professor, Dept of Industrial Technology, Eastern Michigan University, SILL 118, Ypsilanti, MI 48197.

LIN, SUNG P.
Educator. Chinese American. **PERSONAL:** Born Apr 18, 1937, Taipei, Taiwan; son of Lin Zuyang and Sieh Shejiau; married Charlotte A Lin, Apr 9, 1966; children: Anna L, Martin T. **EDUCATION:** Taiwan University, BS, 1958; University of Utah, MS, 1961; University of Michigan, PhD, 1965. **CAREER:** University of Michigan, research asst, 1961-65, lecturer, 1965-66; Clarkson University, asst prof, 1966-69, assoc prof, 1969-74, professor, 1974-. **ORGANIZATIONS:** American Physical Society, fellow, 1973-; American Society of Mechanical Engineers, 1986-; American Institute of Aeronautics & Aerospace, associate fellow, 1987-. **HONORS/AWARDS:** University of Michigan, Rackham Fellow, 1963; APS, Fellow, 1992. **SPECIAL ACHIEVEMENTS:** Author: over 80 pulications, 1965-; editorial board, Intl Journal of Eng Fluid Mech, 1986-; editor, selected work of C S Yih, 1991; Proceedings of IOTAM Symposium: Nonlinear Instability of Nonparallel Flows. **BUSINESS ADDRESS:** Professor, Dept of Mech & Aero Engineering, Clarkson University, Old Main, Rm 306, Potsdam, NY 13699-5725, (315)268-6584.

LIN, TING-TING YAO
Educator. Chinese American. **PERSONAL:** Born Jun 19, 1958, Taipei, Taiwan; daughter of Ko-Min Yao and Yeou-Chi Chang; married Yeou-Lin Lin, Jun 25, 1983; children: Cheryl Chang, Calvin Yao. **EDUCATION:** National Chiao Tung University, BS, 1980; Philips International Institute, ME, 1983; Carnegie Mellon University, PhD, 1988. **CAREER:** National Chiao-Tung University, lecturer, 1980-81; IBM/System Technology Development Corporation, ce consultant, 1986-88; University of California, San Diego, assistant professor, 1988-. **ORGANIZATIONS:** IEEE, 1984-; Sigma Xi, 1989-. **HONORS/AWARDS:** NCR Stakeholders Award, 1991; IEEE/ACM, Best Paper Award, nominee, 1991; Philips, scholarship, 1982. **SPECIAL ACHIEVEMENTS:** Published in IEEE Transactions on Reliability, 1990, 1992; IEEE Design and Test of Computers, 1993; published in conference proceedings: ICCD, 1986; FTCS-18, 1988; OSA, 1991-92; Software Reliability, 1991, 1992; ASIC 1991, 1992; ICCAD, 1992, IPPS, 1993; ICCAD graphics, 1993. **HOME ADDRESS:** 13175 Janetta Place, San Diego, CA 92130, (619)792-4524. **BUSINESS ADDRESS:** Prof, Dept of Electrical & Computer Engineering, University of California, San Diego, 9500 Gilman Dr, Mail Code 0407, La Jolla, CA 92093-0407, (619)534-4738.

LIN, TUNG YEN
Civil engineer, educator. Chinese American. **PERSONAL:** Born Nov 14, 1911, Foochow, China; son of Ting Chang and Feng Yi Kuo Lin; married Margaret Kao, Jul 20, 1941; children: Paul, Verna. **EDUCATION:** Chiaotung University, BS, civil engineering, 1931; University of California, Berkeley, MS, 1933. **CAREER:** Chinese Government, chief bridge engineer, chief design engineer, 1933-46; University of California, assistant professor, associate professor, 1946-55, professor, 1955-76, structural engineering division, chairman, 1960-63; T Y Lin International, chairman of the board, 1953-87, honorary chairman of the board, 1987-92; Inter-Continental Peace Bridge Inc, president, 1968-. **ORGANIZATIONS:** World Conference, Prestressed Concrete, chairman, 1957; Western Conference, Prestressed Concrete Buildings, chairman, 1960; ASCE; National Academy of Engineering; American Concrete Institute. **HONORS/AWARDS:** Chinese University, LLD, 1972; Golden Gate University, LLD, 1982; Tongji University, honorary prof, 1984, LLD, 1987; Chiaotung University, honorary prof, 1982, LLD, 1987; Berkley Citation Award, 1976; Quarter Century Award, 1977; AIA, honor award, 1984; President's Natl Medal of Science, 1986; American Construction Engineers, Merit Award, 1987; John A Roebling Medal, 1990; American Segmental Bridge Institute, Leadership Award, 1992; University of California, Engineering Alumni Association, Outstanding Alumni of the Year, 1984, fellow; Shanghai Chiaotung University, honorary prof, 1985; ASCE, Wellington Award, Howard Medal; Prestressed Concrete Institute, Medal of Honor. **SPECIAL**

ACHIEVEMENTS: Author, Design of Prestressed Concrete Structures, 1955, 3rd edition, 1981; co-author, Design of Steel Structures, revised ed, 1968; co-author, Structural Concepts and Systems, 1981, 2nd ed, 1988; contributed articles to professional journals. **BUSINESS ADDRESS:** T Y Lin International, 315 Bay St, San Francisco, CA 94133. ∗

LIN, WEN CHUN
Educator. Chinese American. **PERSONAL:** Born Feb 22, 1926, Kutien, Fukien, China; son of B C Lin & S D Lin; married Shung-Ling Lin, Jun 6, 1956; children: Carole, Grace, Wendy. **EDUCATION:** National Taiwan University, Taiwan, BSEE, 1950; Purdue University, MSEE, 1956, PhD, 1965. **CAREER:** Taiwan Power Co, engineer, 1950-54; General Electric Co, engineer, 1956-59; Computer Div, Honeywell, senior engineer, 1959-61; Purdue University, instructor, 1961-65; Case Western Reserve University, professor, 1965-78; University of California, professor, 1978-. **ORGANIZATIONS:** IEEE, senior member, 1969-. **SPECIAL ACHIEVEMENTS:** Author of 3 books on computer/digital systems; editor of 1 book on microcomputers; published over 70 articles on computers, biomedical and signal processing. **BUSINESS ADDRESS:** Professor, Dept of Electrical & Computer Engineering, University of California, Davis, CA 95616.

LIN, WUNAN
Physicist. Taiwanese American. **PERSONAL:** Born Aug 1, 1942, Tainan, Taiwan; son of Shui-Ynen Lin and Mao-Yang Hong; married Doris S Lin, Apr 23, 1947. **EDUCATION:** Cheng-Kung University, Taiwan, BS, 1964; University of California, Berkeley, MS, 1970, PhD, 1977. **CAREER:** Cheng-Kung University, professor's assistant, 1965-67; University of California, Berkeley, research assistant, 1970-76; Lawrence Livermore National Laboratory, physicist/task leader, 1977-. **ORGANIZATIONS:** American Geophysical Union, 1970-; IEEE; International Rock Mechanics Society; North America Taiwanese Professors Association, 1983-, president, 1990-91; Union of Concerned Scientists, 1991-. **HONORS/AWARDS:** Chou Kai-chi Foundation, fellowship, 1962-64; Jane Lewis Foundation, fellowship, 1968-70. **SPECIAL ACHIEVEMENTS:** Determination of the P-Wave Velocity of the California Coastal Range Rocks at high pressure and high temperature, 1977; transport properties of rocks at high pressure and high temperature, 1984-88; Study of fracture heading in tuffaceous rocks, 1984-91; In Situ testing of the near-field environment of a nucleus waste repository, 1991; patent pending: In Situ Ultrasonic remedation of pollited aguifer, 1992. **MILITARY SERVICE:** Air force, Republic of China, 2nd lt, 1964-66. **BUSINESS ADDRESS:** Task Leader, Lawrence Livermore National Lab, University of California, 7000 East Ave, L-201, PO Box 808, Livermore, CA 94550, (510)422-7162.

LIN, XIAO-SONG
Educator, mathematician. Chinese American. **PERSONAL:** Born Jul 27, 1957, Suzhou, Jiangsu, People's Republic of China; son of Rui-Zhang Lin and Jing-Jun Pu; married Jian-Pin He, Jan 18, 1984; children: Hai-Jian, Hai-Bing. **EDUCATION:** Nanjing Institute of Posts and Telecommunications, China, BS, 1982; Peking University, China, MS, 1984; University of California-San Diego, PhD, 1988. **CAREER:** Institute for Advanced Study, Princeton University, 1987-88; Columbia University, asst prof, 1988-92, assoc prof, 1992-. **ORGANIZATIONS:** American Mathematical Society, 1984-. **HONORS/AWARDS:** A P Sloan Foundation, Sloan Research Fellow, 1992-94. **SPECIAL ACHIEVEMENTS:** Author: "The Classification of Links Up to Link-Homotopy," Journal of American Mathematical Society, 1990; "A Knot Invariant Via Representation Spaces," Journal of Differential Geometry, 1992; "Knot Polynomials and Vassiliev's Invariants," Inventiones Mathematicae, 1993. **BIOGRAPHICAL SOURCES:** "Knotty Views," Ivars Peterson, Science News, p 186, Mar 21, 1992. **BUSINESS ADDRESS:** Associate Professor, Dept of Mathematics, Columbia University, Broadway & W 116th St, New York, NY 10027.

LIN, YEONG-JER
Educator. Taiwanese American. **PERSONAL:** Born Nov 11, 1936, Taipei, Taiwan; son of Yu-Chin Lin (deceased); married Chiung-Chen Wang Lin, Jun 8, 1966; children: Kathleen, Diana. **EDUCATION:** National Taiwan University, BS, 1959; University of Wisconsin-Madison, MS, 1964; New York University, PhD, 1969. **CAREER:** St Louis University, assistant professor, 1969-72, associate professor, 1972-76, professor, 1976-. **ORGANIZATIONS:** American Meterologial Society, 1970; American Geophysical Union, 1970; Sigma Xi, 1972. **HONORS/AWARDS:** St Louis University, Senior Grantman, 1981, Outstanding Teacher of the Year, 1987; St Louis University, Burlington Northern Foundation, Outstanding Research Award, 1992. **SPECIAL**

ACHIEVEMENTS: Published more than 40 articles in the Journal of Atmospheric Sciences, Monthly Weather Review, Tellus, Boundary-Layer Meteorology, and papers in Meteorological Research, Terrestrial, Oceanic and Atmospheric Sciences, etc. **BUSINESS ADDRESS:** Professor of Meteorology, Dept of Earth and Atmospheric Sciences, St Louis University, 221 N Grand Blvd, MW 305, St Louis, MO 63103, (314)658-3122.

LIN, YOU-AN ROBERT
Educator. Chinese American. **PERSONAL:** Born Aug 12, 1950, Taipei, Taiwan; son of Pao-shan Lin and Ruby Hou; married Aileen, Dec 9, 1978; children: Ellie, Eva. **EDUCATION:** National Central University, BS, 1973; Embry-Riddle University, MBA, 1981; Florida State University, Master, 1983; UCLA, PhD, 1989. **CAREER:** Certified management accountant, 1983-; University of California, Los Angeles, teaching fellow, 1983-88; California State University, Hayward, associate professor, 1989-. **ORGANIZATIONS:** American Accounting Association; Institute of Management Accountants, director of manuscript. **SPECIAL ACHIEVEMENTS:** Managerial Accounting: A Planning-Operating-Control Framework, 1989. **BUSINESS ADDRESS:** Assoc Prof, Dept of Accounting & CIS, California State University, Hayward, 25800 Calos Bee Blvd, Hayward, CA 94542-3000, (510)881-3002.

LIN, YU-CHONG
Educator. Taiwanese American. **PERSONAL:** Born Apr 24, 1935, Taiwan; son of Shing-Chern Lin and Shern Lin; married Dora, Apr 27, 1960; children: Mimi, Betty. **EDUCATION:** University of New Mexico, MS, 1964; Rutgers-The State University, PhD, 1968. **CAREER:** University of California at Santa Barbara, research associate, 1968-69; University of Hawaii, assistant professor, 1969-74, associate professor, 1974-76, professor, 1976-. **ORGANIZATIONS:** American Physiological Society; Undersea and Hyberbaric Medical Society. **SPECIAL ACHIEVEMENTS:** Author: Hyperbaric Medicine and Physiology, Best Publising Co, 1988; Man in the Sea, Vol I and II, Best Publishing Co, 1989; published more than 120 scientific papers. **BUSINESS ADDRESS:** Professor of Physiology, John A Burns School of Medicine, Unv of Hawaii, Biomedical Bldg T-608, Honolulu, HI 96822, (808)956-8640.

LIN, YÜ-SHENG
Educator. Chinese American. **PERSONAL:** Born Aug 7, 1934, Shenyang, China; married; children: two. **EDUCATION:** Natl Taiwan University, BA, history, 1958; University of Chicago, PhD, social thought, 1970. **CAREER:** Yale University, instructor, 1962; University of Virginia, visiting asst prof, 1966-67, acting asst prof, 1967-68; University of Oregon, Institute of Intl Studies, research assoc at the East Asian Research Ctr, Harvard University, 1968, acting asst prof, 1968-69; Harvard University, East Asian Research Ctr, post-doctoral res fellow, 1969-70; University of Wisconsin-Madison, asst prof, 1970-72, asst to assoc prof, 1972-81, prof, 1981-; Academia Sinica, Taipei, adj res prof, 1983-; Institute of East Asian Philosophies, Singapore, sr res fellow, 1988-90. **ORGANIZATIONS:** American Historical Assn; Assn for Asian Studies; American Soc of China Scholars. **HONORS/AWARDS:** University of Wisconsin-Madison, Research Fellowship, Inst for Research in the Humanities, 1986-87; Inst of East Asian Philosophies, research grants, 1990-. **SPECIAL ACHIEVEMENTS:** Numerous publications, including: The Crisis of Chinese Consciousness: Radical Antitraditionalism in the May Fourth Era, 1979; Essays in Social Thought and Chinese Intellectual History, 1993. **BUSINESS ADDRESS:** Professor, Dept of History, University of Wisconsin-Madison, 3211 Humanities Bldg, Madison, WI 53706.

LIN, YUET-CHANG JOSEPH
Educator. Hong Kong American. **PERSONAL:** Born Aug 18, 1951, Hong Kong; son of Shik Lin and Pui-Hong Lin; married Yin Ada Lee, Aug 5, 1975; children: Chit-Kwan Siufu. **EDUCATION:** Carleton College, BA (magna cum laude), 1972; University of Minnesota, PhD, 1986. **CAREER:** Louisiana State University, professor, economics, 1985-87; Tulane University, professor, economics, 1987-89; University of California, professor, management & economics, 1989-. **ORGANIZATIONS:** American Economic Association, 1983-; European Economic Association, 1991-; Economic Society, 1983-. **HONORS/AWARDS:** Pi Mu Epsilon, 1971; Phi Beta Kappa, 1972; Sloan Foundation, fellowship, 1983-85. **SPECIAL ACHIEVEMENTS:** Author of publications appearing in: American Economic Review, 1988; Southern Economic Journal, 1988; Journal of Industrial Economics, 1990; Mathematical Social Sciences, 1992. **BUSINESS ADDRESS:** Professor of Management & Economics, University of California, Graduate School of Management, Riverside, CA 92521-0001.

LIN, YUH-LANG
Educator. Taiwanese American. **PERSONAL:** Born Aug 27, 1949, Fang-Liao, Ping-Tong, Taiwan; son of Tan Lin & Yueh Cheng Lin; married Emily Fu-Ying Lin, Oct 25, 1975; children: Michelle H, Jessica S. **EDUCATION:** Fu-Jen University, Taiwan, BS, 1976; Fordham University, MA, 1978; Yale University, PhD, 1984. **CAREER:** Yale University, postdoctoral associate, 1983-84; Drexel University, Drexel fellow, 1984-87; North Carolina State University, assistant professor, 1987-93, associate professor, 1993-. **ORGANIZATIONS:** American Meteorological Society, 1979-; Taiwanese Association of American, 1980-; North America Taiwanese Professors Association, 1990-; Sigma Xi, 1984-. **SPECIAL ACHIEVEMENTS:** Published more than 20 articles in international journals, such as Journal of Atmospheric Science, Monthly Weather Review, etc; chaired national and international scientific conferences. **BUSINESS ADDRESS:** Professor, Dept of Marine, Earth & Atmospheric Sciences, North Carolina State University, Raleigh, NC 27695-8208, (919)515-7977.

LIN, YUYI
Educator. Chinese American. **PERSONAL:** Born 1952, Fujian, People's Republic of China; son of Yongchang Lin & Runzhen L Lin; married Donghua Lin, Jan 1980; children: Qi, Helen Yao. **EDUCATION:** Fuzhou University, Fujian, China, BS, equivalent, 1978; University of California, Los Angeles, MS, 1984; University of California, Berkeley, PhD, 1989, postdoctoral, 1989-90. **CAREER:** Fuzhou University, instructor, 1978-82; University of California, Los Angeles, research assistant, 1984; University of California, Berkeley, research assistant, 1985-89, visiting assistant research engineer, 1989-90; University of Missouri, assistant professor, 1990-. **ORGANIZATIONS:** Society of Automotive Engineers, 1993-; Society of Manufacturing Engineers, senior member, 1992-; American Society of Mechanical Engineers, associate member, 1987-. **HONORS/AWARDS:** National Science Foundation, research initiation, 1992; University of Missouri Alumni Association, Faculty Course Development, 1992. **SPECIAL ACHIEVEMENTS:** Fluent in Chinese, reading comprehension of French; research papers in Journal of Applied Mechanics and Journal of Mechanical Design; professional engineer. **BUSINESS ADDRESS:** Asst Professor, Dept of Mechanical & Aerospace Eng, University of Missouri, Columbia, E2412 Engineering Bldg East, Columbia, MO 65211, (314)882-7505.

LING, ALEXANDER
Neurological surgeon. Chinese American. **PERSONAL:** Born Jun 24, 1922, Tientsin, Hubei, China; son of Ping Ling and Clara Soo-Hoo; married Flora Lee Silver, Apr 1, 1946; children: Alexander Jr, Cynthia Cheng. **EDUCATION:** St John's University, Shanghai, BS, 1941; Washington University, St Louis, MD, 1944. **CAREER:** Northeast Ohio Neurosurgical Associates, senior partner, starting 1952. **ORGANIZATIONS:** American Medical Association, 1952-; American Association of Neurological Surgery, 1956-; Congress of Neurological Surgery, 1957-; American College of Surgery, 1958. **MILITARY SERVICE:** US Army, captain, 1945-47. **HOME ADDRESS:** PO Box 40240, Bay Village, OH 44140-0240.

LING, AMY
Educator. Chinese American. **PERSONAL:** Born May 28, 1939, Beijing, China; daughter of Theodore Ling and Leah Traub Ling; married Gelston Hinds Jr, Feb 17, 1979; children: Arthur Ling Hinds, Catherine Ling Hinds. **EDUCATION:** CUNY, Queens College, BA (cum laude), 1959; University of California, Davis, MA, 1962; New York University, PhD, 1979. **CAREER:** City College of New York, SEEK Program, lecturer, 1966-69; Brooklyn College, SEEK Program, instructor, 1969-72; Rutgers University, assistant professor, English, 1972-88; Georgetown University, adjunct instructor, English, 1989-89; Harvard University, visiting associate professor, English, 1991; Trinity College, visiting associate professor, English, 1991; University of Wisconsin, English Department, associate professor, director of Asian studies program, 1991-. **ORGANIZATIONS:** MELUS, secretary, 1992-, editorial advisory board, 1982-, chairperson, 1979-81; Modern Language Association, Division on Women's Studies in Languages and Literature, executive committee, 1987-92, Asian American Lit Discussion Group, executive committee, 1985-89, Commission on Lits and Languages of America, 1983-85. **HONORS/AWARDS:** Phi Beta Kappa, 1958; Queens College, Rockefeller Fellowship, 1989-90; ACLA, travel grant, 1983. **SPECIAL ACHIEVEMENTS:** Author: Between Worlds: Women Writers of Chinese Ancestry, 1990; Chinamerican Reflections, a chapbook of poems and paintings, 1984; Editor, Reading the Literatures of Asian America, with Shirley Lim, 1992; Visions of America: Personal Narratives from the Promised Land, with Wesley Brown, 1992;

Imagining America: Stories from the Promised Land, 1991; The Heath Anthology of American Literature, 1990. **BUSINESS ADDRESS:** Director, Asian American Studies Program, University of Wisconsin, 600 North Park, 7185 Helen C White, Madison, WI 53706, (608)263-3785.

LING, CHRISTINE N.
Public health educator/administrator (retired). Chinese American. **PERSONAL:** Born Dec 24, 1926, Honolulu, HI; daughter of Alim Ling & Elizabeth Mark. **EDUCATION:** University of Hawaii, BE, 1950; University of Michigan, MPH, 1954. **CAREER:** California State Health Department, aide, Health Education, 1954; Oregon State Health Department, health education consultant, 1955-60; Hawaii State Health Department, assistant chief, 1960-70, chief, health promotion & education, 1970-90; University of Hawaii, adjunct professor, 1990-. **ORGANIZATIONS:** Asian American Health Forum, board member, 1988-; Organization of Chinese American Women-Hawaii, president, 1990-; American Chinese University Women-Hawaii, president, 1966-; American Public Health Association, executive board, 1980-84; US Consumer Product Safety Commission, advisory council, 1977-79. **HONORS/AWARDS:** Conference of State & Territorial Directors of Public Health & Education, leadership award, 1986; University of Hawaii, School of Public Health, outstanding professional award, 1988; Radio Station KGU, outstanding citizen award, 1980. **HOME ADDRESS:** 91-335 A Ewa Beach Road, Ewa Beach, HI 96706.

LING, HAO
Educator. Taiwanese American/Chinese American. **PERSONAL:** Born Sep 26, 1959, Taichung, Taiwan; son of Kuo-Chang Ling and Sing-Ming Ling; married Wei-Na Lee, Dec 21, 1984; children: Chloe. **EDUCATION:** Massachusetts Institute of Technology, BS, 1982; University of Illinois, Urbana-Champaign, MS, 1983, PhD, 1986. **CAREER:** University of Texas, Austin, Dept of Electrical and Computer Engineering, asst professor, 1986-90, associate professor, 1990-. **ORGANIZATIONS:** Institute of Electrical and Electronic Engineers, senior member, 1983-; International Union of Radio Science, associate member, 1987-. **HONORS/AWARDS:** National Science Foundation, Presidential Young Investigator Award, 1987; National Aeronautics and Space Administration, certificate of recognition, 1991; University of Texas, Gulf Oil Foundation centennial fellowship in engineering, 1990, Archie Straiton Junior Faculty Teaching Execellence Award, 1993. **BUSINESS ADDRESS:** Associate Professor, Dept of Electrical and Computer Engineering, University of Texas, Austin, TX 78712-1084, (512)471-1710.

LING, HSIN YI
Educator. Taiwanese American. **PERSONAL:** Born Dec 5, 1930, Taichung, Taiwan; son of Kuei-Tuang Ling and Yung-Yu Ho Ling; married Su Yu Lee Ling, Jul 17, 1958; children: Dorothy Huei Lin, Richard Kuang-Che. **EDUCATION:** National Taiwan University, BS, 1954; Tohoku University, Japan, MS, 1958; Washington University, PhD, 1963. **CAREER:** Pan American Petroleum Corp, Research Center, research engineer, 1960-63; University of Washington, Department of Oceanography, research instructor, 1963-64, research assistant professor, 1964-69, research associate professor, 1969-74, research professor, 1974-78; Northern Illinois University, Department of Geology, professor, 1978-. **ORGANIZATIONS:** American Association for the Advancement of Science, fellow, 1981-; Paleontological Society of America, 1963-; Geological Society of Japan, 1960-; Paleontological Society of Japan, 1963-. **HONORS/AWARDS:** Northern Illinois University, Presidential Research Professorship, 1989-93; National Science Foundation, numerous grants; North Atlantic Treaty Organization, grant, 1991-93; Smithsonian Institution, grant, 1987-92. **SPECIAL ACHIEVEMENTS:** Over 115 publications in scientific books, journals and proceedings. **BUSINESS ADDRESS:** Professor, Dept of Geology, Northern Illinois University, De Kalb, IL 60115-2853, (815)753-7951.

LING, HUBERT
Educator. Chinese American. **PERSONAL:** Born Apr 28, 1942, Ch'ungch'ing, Szechwan, China; son of Theodore & Leah Ling; married Mildred, Dec 10, 1967; children: Jonathan, Matthew. **EDUCATION:** Queens College, BS, 1963; Brown University, MS, 1966; Wayne State University, PhD, 1969. **CAREER:** University of Delaware, assistant professor, associate professor, 1969-77; E I du Pont, research microbiologist, 1977-80; Ethicon (J&J), sterilization scientist, 1980-81; Samsen Nursery, plant scientist, 1981; County College of Morris, associate professor, 1983-. **ORGANIZATIONS:** NJ Native Plant Society, plant propagator, board member, 1986-; Rave & Endangered Native Plant Exchange, coordinator, 1984-85; Torrey Botanical Club, 1992-;

American Orchid Society, 1981-; American Botanical Society, 1962-88; Mycological Society of America, 1962-84; Trinity Evangelical Free Church, deacon, 1985. **HONORS/AWARDS:** University of Delaware Research Foundation, grant, 1977; US Public Health Service, grant, 1972; Research Corporation, grant, 1970; Wayne State University, fellowship, 1968, 1969; NASA, research fellowship, 1965. **SPECIAL ACHIEVEMENTS:** "Mating Types in the Myxomycete Didymium," A J Bot 51:315, 1964; "Light and Fruiting," Didymium, Mycol, 60:966, 1968; "Ultrastructure of Cytoplasmic Incompatibility," L J Ex Bot, 1976; "Somatic Cell Incompatibility," A J Bot 68:1191, 1981; "Propagation of Cypriepedium Acaule," Brandwine Cons, 1989. **HOME ADDRESS:** 1030 Rector Rd, Bridgewater, NJ 08807, (908)231-9115. **BUSINESS ADDRESS:** Professor, Biology/Chemistry Dept, County College of Morris, 214 Center Grove Rd, Randolph, NJ 07869, (201)328-5371.

LING, HUNG CHI
Scientist. Chinese American. **PERSONAL:** Born Apr 22, 1950, Wenchen, Zhechiang, People's Republic of China; son of Chi Ming Ling & Fung Ying Ng; married Gigi Hsu, Jun 17, 1979; children: Maya, Alicia, Byron. **EDUCATION:** MIT, BS, 1972, ScD, 1978; State University of New York, Stony Brook, MA, 1974. **CAREER:** MIT, research associate, 1978-81; AT&T Bell Laboratories, technical manager, distinguished member of technical staff, 1981-. **ORGANIZATIONS:** American Ceramic Society, Electronics Division, program chair, 1992, vice chair, 1993, chair, 1994; IEEE, senior member, 1991-; Optical Society of America; Materials Research Society. **HONORS/AWARDS:** American Ceramic Society, fellow, 1991. **SPECIAL ACHIEVEMENTS:** 7 patents; 70 publications; several book chapters; editor of 2 books. **BUSINESS ADDRESS:** Technical Manager, AT&T Bell Laboratories, PO Box 900, Princeton, NJ 08542-0900, (609)639-2538.

LING, JACK CHIEH-SHENG
Educator. Chinese American. **PERSONAL:** Born Sep 24, 1930, Shanghai, China; son of C W Ling (deceased) & Aline Ling; married Christine Yuan Ling, Jan 28, 1956; children: Genevieve Ling-Tom, Laurence. **EDUCATION:** Saint John's University, China, 1946-49; Syracuse University, BA, 1954; Stanford University, MA, 1955; Columbia University, Teachers College, doctoral program, 1988. **CAREER:** Kong Sheung Daily, Hong Kong Standard, reporter, 1945-51; Pan-Asia Newspaper Alliance, war correspondent, 1951; UNICEF, regional information officer, 1956-62, Division of Information and Communication, director, 1962-82; World Health Organization, Division of Public Information and Education for Health, director, 1982-86; University of Southwestern Louisiana, visiting professor of communication, 1986-87; Columbia University Teachers College, adjunct associate professor, 1987-88; UNDP/UNICEF/WHO, communication advisor, consultant, 1988; Tulane University, International Communication Enhancement Center, director, 1989-. **ORGANIZATIONS:** WHO, Expert Advisory Committee on Information, Education and Communication, 1991-, Expert Advisory Committee on Cancer, 1986-90; Intl Council for the Control of Iodine Deficiency Disorders, 1992-; Louisiana State Disability Prevention Advisory Council, 1990-; Intl Technical Panel of Pari, Educational Development Center, 1993-; Intl Public Relations Assn, editorial board, 1989-91; Assn for Education of Journalism and Mass Communication, 1970-; American Public Health Assn, 1990-. **HONORS/AWARDS:** Stanford University, Jacoby Fellowship, 1954, 1955, visiting scholar, 1981; Syracuse University, university scholar, 1953-54; Syracuse-in-Asia, Executive Award, 1954; Delta Omega, 1990. **SPECIAL ACHIEVEMENTS:** Co-author, Two Brothers of Peru, picture book for children, Simon Schuster, 1968; co-author, Shager of Afghanistan, Simon Schuster, 1968; Far Eastern Economic Review, guest columnist on health communications, Oct 1984; Annual Review of Public Health, chapter on social marketing, 1992; general editor, Action-Oriented School Health Curriculum, vol 1-6, WHO/UNICEF, 1988; St John's Dial, editor, university's bi-lingual paper, 1949;. **HOME ADDRESS:** 1550 2nd St, Apt 7B, New Orleans, LA 70130, (504)891-7271. **BUSINESS ADDRESS:** Director, Intl Communication Enhancement Ctr, Tulane University, School of Public Health & Tropical Med, 1501 Canal St, Ste 1300, New Orleans, LA 70112, (504)584-3542.

LING, MATTHEW S.
Manufacturing company executive. Malaysian American. **PERSONAL:** Born May 3, 1963, Sibu, Sarawak, Malaysia; son of Ling Yung Sie; married Mooi Em Lim. **EDUCATION:** Tunku Abdul Rahman, diploma, electrical engineer, 1984; Oklahoma University, BS, (w/honors), 1986, CPA, MBA, (w/honors), 1988. **CAREER:** Ginseng Up Corp, CFO, 1988-. **ORGANIZATIONS:** AMA, speaker, 1988-; Henry Davis Association, consultant, director, 1988-;

AICPA, 1988-. **BUSINESS ADDRESS:** Executive Officer/CFO, Ginseng Up Corp, 401-B 5th Ave, New York, NY 10016, (212)696-0130.

LING, PAUL
Engineer. Chinese American. **PERSONAL:** Born Aug 4, 1949; married. **EDUCATION:** National Cheng-Kung University, Rep of China, BS, 1972; Virginia Polytechnic Institute and State University, MS, 1976; University of Michigan, MS, 1986. **CAREER:** Ford Motor Co, materials engr, product materials formability engr, 1985-87, DDD engr, 1987-91, draw die development specialist, 1991-. **ORGANIZATIONS:** Chinese Christian Fellowship, elder; Detroit Chinese Singers, conductor. **SPECIAL ACHIEVEMENTS:** Several papers on Finite Element Analysis of Draw Forming Process. **BUSINESS ADDRESS:** Manufacturing Specialist, Ford Motor Company, PO Box 2053, BCE, Rm 2065A, Dearborn, MI 48123.

LING, PAUL KIMBERLEY
Clinical psychologist. Chinese American. **PERSONAL:** Born Jul 12, 1953, Oceanside, NY; son of Sun-hong (Frank) Ling and Annette A Larned; married Theslee J DePiero, Aug 26, 1976; children: Alexandra E. **EDUCATION:** Harvard College, AB, (cum laude), social relations, 1975; Harvard Grad School of Education, EdM, 1975; Boston University, PhD, clinical psych, 1981. **CAREER:** South Shore Counsel Association, staff psychologist, 1978-82; self-employed, private practice in clinical psychology, 1982-; Boston University School of Medicine, instructor in psychology. **ORGANIZATIONS:** American Psychology Association; Massachusetts Psychology Association. **BUSINESS ADDRESS:** Clinical Psychologist, 59 Coddington St, Ste 201, Quincy, MA 02169, (617)472-3125.

LING, TA-YUNG
Educator. Chinese American. **PERSONAL:** Born Feb 2, 1943, Shanghai, China; son of Yuan-Kai Ling & Hsieh-Pu Ling; married Marjorie C H Ling, Jun 27, 1945; children: Benjamin, Alan, Theresa. **EDUCATION:** Tunghai University, Taiwan, BS, 1964; University of Waterloo, MS, 1966; University of Wisconsin, Madison, PhD, 1971. **CAREER:** University of Wisconsin, research associate, 1971-72; University of Pennsylvania, research associate, 1972-75, assistant professor, 1975-77; Ohio State University, assistant professor, 1977-79, associate professor, 1979-83, professor, 1983-. **ORGANIZATIONS:** American Physical Society, 1977-. **HONORS/AWARDS:** US Dept of Energy, Outstanding Junior Investigator, 1977-79; Ohio State University, Distinguished Research Award, 1979. **MILITARY SERVICE:** Navy, Republic of China, 1st lieutenant, 1964-65. **BUSINESS ADDRESS:** Professor, Dept of Physics, Ohio State University, 174 W 18th Ave, Smith Laboratory, Columbus, OH 43210, (614)292-7537.

LING, YU-LONG
Educator, educational administrator. Chinese American. **PERSONAL:** Born Nov 5, 1938, Chungking, China; son of Mr and Mrs Shou-tzu Ling; married Yuriko Ling, Feb 19, 1971; children: Tony. **EDUCATION:** Soochow University, LLB, 1963; Indiana University, MA, 1973, LLM, 1979, PhD, 1980. **CAREER:** National Taiwan University, Fulbright Professor, 1979-80; Franklin College, Political Science Dept, chairperson, 1975-90, professor, 1985-, The Williams Chair in Law and Public Service, 1991-. **ORGANIZATIONS:** Chinese Academic and Professional Association in Mid-America, president, 1983-84; Chinese Academic and Professional Association in Indiana, president, 1991-92; Franklin College Faculty, Steering Committee, chair, 1989-90; Promotion Committee, chair, 1987-88; American Association for Pre-law Advisors. **HONORS/AWARDS:** Franklin College, Faculty Distinguished Service Award, 1982, Clifford and Paula Dietz Award for Faculty Excellence, 1987; Rotary Foundation of Rotary International, Pail Harris Fellow, 1992. **SPECIAL ACHIEVEMENTS:** Books: Southeast Asian Nationalism and the Overseas Chinese, Franklin College Press, 1985; Sun Yat-sen's Doctrine of Democracy and Human Rights, Westview Press, 1989; "Functional Compared to Traditional Privileges and Immunities," Washington and Lee Law Review, winter 1976. **BUSINESS ADDRESS:** The Williams Chair in Law and Public Service, Franklin College, Franklin, IN 46131, (317)738-8265.

LING, ZHI-KUI
Educator. Chinese American. **PERSONAL:** Born Oct 18, 1961, Shanghai, People's Republic of China; son of Chong-Yu Ling and Sen-He Yuan. **EDUCATION:** Northeastern University, BS, 1983, MS, 1985; University of Minnesota, PhD, 1990. **CAREER:** Michigan Technological University, assistant professor, 1989-. **ORGANIZATIONS:** ASME, 1984-; Tau Beta Pi, 1982-; Sigma Xi, 1991-. **BUSINESS ADDRESS:** Asst Prof, Mechanical Engineering & Eng Mechanics Dept, Michigan Technological University, 1400 Townsend Dr, Houghton, MI 49931-1295, (906)487-2620.

LINGAPPA, BANADAKOPPA THIMMAPPA
Educator. Indo-American. **PERSONAL:** Born Mar 19, 1927, Hulimane, Sagara/Shimoga, Karnataka, India; son of Patel Thimmappa and Laxmamma; married Yamuna Lingappa, Mar 23, 1953; children: Vishwanath Rao, Jaisri Rao, Jairam Rao. **EDUCATION:** Banaras Hindu University, Banaras, UP, India, BS, 1950, MS, 1952; Purdue University, PhD, 1957. **CAREER:** University of Michigan, Bio Dept, 1957-59; Michigan State University, 1959-60; Madras University Madras, India, 1960-61; Holy Cross College, professor, 1962-. **ORGANIZATIONS:** Sigma Xi; American Society for Microbiology; Mycological Society of America; American Phytopathological Society; National Association of Biology Teachers; American Association for the Advancement of Science. **HONORS/AWARDS:** Sigma Xi, Recognition of Service, 1982; National Science Foundation, Research Grants, 1963, 1967, Teaching Grant, 1972, 1988; National Institutes of Health, Research Grants, 1966, 1968. **SPECIAL ACHIEVEMENTS:** Published scientific papers in various scientific journals, 1953-; produced a movie on Glomerella Fungus, EDC, Newton, MA, 1970; developed a methane generator, US patent, 4349355, 1982; co-author, Wholesome Nutrition. . ., Ecobiology Foundation International, 1992. **HOME ADDRESS:** 4 McGill Street, Worcester, MA 01607. **BUSINESS ADDRESS:** Professor, The College of the Holy Cross, 1 College Street, Worcester, MA 01610, (508)793-3417.

LINGAPPA, YAMUNA
Research scientist, foundation administrator. Indo-American. **PERSONAL:** Born Dec 6, 1929, Nanjangud, Mysore, India; daughter of Kamala & Laxminarayana Rao; married Banadakoppa Lingappa, Mar 23, 1953; children: Vishu, Jaisri, Jairam. **EDUCATION:** Mysore University, India, BSc, 1950; Madras University, India, BT, 1952; Purdue University, PhD, biological sciences, 1958. **CAREER:** Mysore, India, teacher, 1950; Banaras Hindu University, demonstrator, 1952-53; Purdue University, research assistant, 1953-58; University of Michigan, research associate, 1958-59; Michigan State University, research associate, 1959-60; Madras University, India, pool officer, 1961; Annapurna Inc, president, 1976-93; Ecobiology Foundation International, president, currently. **ORGANIZATIONS:** American Institute for Biological Sciences, currently; American Women in Science, currently. **HONORS/AWARDS:** Governor's Commission on Women, commissioner, 1972. **SPECIAL ACHIEVEMENTS:** Research in biology and human nutrition; book, Wholesome Nutrition. . ., 1992; published original research papers in scientific journals regarding microbiology. **BUSINESS ADDRESS:** President, Ecobiology Foundation International, 4 McGill St, Worcester, MA 01607.

LIOU, FUE-WEN (FRANK)
Educator. Taiwanese American. **PERSONAL:** Born Sep 24, 1957, Taichung, Taiwan; son of Feng-Nien Liou and Jai-Yu Lai; married Min-Yu Liou, Aug 14, 1987; children: Jonathan. **EDUCATION:** National Cheng-Kung University, Taiwan, BS, 1980; North Carolina State University, MS, 1984; University of Minnesota, Minneapolis, PhD, 1987. **CAREER:** University of Minnesota, teaching assistant, 1984-85, research assistant, 1985-87, University of Missouri-Rolla, assistant professor, 1987-92, associate professor, 1993-. **ORGANIZATIONS:** Society of Manufacturing Engineers, 1990-; Society of Automotive Engineers, 1989-; American Society of Mechanical Engineers, associate member, 1987-. **HONORS/AWARDS:** McDonnell Douglas Faculty Excellence Award, 1993-94; University of Missouri-Rolla, Outstanding Teacher Award, 1992-93; Society of Automotive Engineers, Ralph R Teetor Educational Award, 1990; National Science Foundation, Research Initiation Award, 1992; National Cheng-Kung University, Outstanding Youth, 1979. **SPECIAL ACHIEVEMENTS:** Publications: "Analysis of High-Speed Flexible Four-bar Linkage," ASME Journal of Vib, 1989; "Dynamic Analysis of Motor-Gear-Mechanism System," Mech and Machine Theory, 1991; "Experimental Vibration Analysis of Mechanisms," Shock and Vibration Digest, 1992; "Development of Feature-based Fixture Planning for Flexible Assembly," Journal of Manufacturing Systems, No 2, Vol 11, p 102-113, 1992. **BUSINESS ADDRESS:** Associate Professor, University of Missouri at Rolla, 121 ME Annex, UMR, Rolla, MO 65401, (314)341-4603.

LIOU, K. T.
Educator. Taiwanese American. **PERSONAL:** Born Jan 5, 1956, Taipei, Taiwan; married Susan Liou. **EDUCATION:** University of Oklahoma, masters, 1984, doctorate, 1987. **CAREER:** Drake University, visiting assistant professor, 1989-90; Florida Atlantic University, assistant professor, 1990-.

ORGANIZATIONS: American Society for Public Administration, 1987-; Policy Studies Organization, 1991-. **BUSINESS ADDRESS:** Assistant Professor, Florida Atlantic University, University Tower, 220 SE 2nd Avenue, Fort Lauderdale, FL 33301, (305)760-5667.

LIOU, KUO-NAN
Educator. Taiwanese American/Chinese American. **PERSONAL:** Born Nov 16, 1943, Taipei, Taiwan; married Agnes L Y Liou, Aug 3, 1968; children: Julia, Clifford. **EDUCATION:** National Taiwan University, BS, 1965; New York University, MS, 1968, PhD, 1970. **CAREER:** Goddard Institute for Space Studies, research associate, 1970-72; University of Washington, assistant professor, 1972-74; University of Utah, associate professor, 1975-80, professor, 1980-, Center for Atmosphere and Remote Sensing Studies, University of Utah, director, 1987-. **ORGANIZATIONS:** American Meteorological Society, 1969-, chairman, atmospheric radiation committee, 1982-84; Optical Society of America, 1970-; American Geophysical Union, 1969-; American Association for the Advancement of Science; Meteorology and Atmospheric Physics, Springer-Verlag, editor, 1985-; Theoretical and Applied Climatology, Springer-Verlag, editor, 1985-. **HONORS/AWARDS:** New York University, Founders Day Award, 1971; University of Utah, David P. Gardner Fellow, 1978; Optical Society of America, Fellow, 1983; American Meteorological Society, Fellow, 1987. **SPECIAL ACHIEVEMENTS:** Over 100 publications, author, An Introduction to Atmospheric Radiation, Academic Press, 1980; author, Radiation and Cloud Processes in the Atmosphere, Oxford University Press, 1991. **BUSINESS ADDRESS:** Professor and Director, Dept of Meteorology, CARSS, University of Utah, 809 William Browning, Salt Lake City, UT 84112, (801)581-3336.

LIOU, MING JAW
Electronics company executive. Taiwanese American. **PERSONAL:** Born May 12, 1956, Taiwan; married Chi Lon Liou; children: Alan Y. **EDUCATION:** Massachusetts Institute of Technology, MS, 1984, PhD, 1987. **CAREER:** Ohio State University, assistant professor, 1987-92; Beta Electronics Inc, president, currently. **BUSINESS ADDRESS:** President, Beta Electronics, Inc, 2209 Cloverdale Court, Columbus, OH 43235, (614)792-1181.

LIOU, SHY-SHENG P.
Educator. Chinese American. **PERSONAL:** Born Sep 28, 1959, Tainan, Taiwan; son of Mao-Shun Liou and Pei-Hwa Chen; married Feng Ying, Dec 31, 1983; children: Emily. **EDUCATION:** National Taiwan University, BSEE, 1981; University of Texas at Austin, MSEE, 1985, PhD, 1989. **CAREER:** University of Texas at Austin, research engineer, 1989-91; San Francisco State University, assistant professor, 1991-. **ORGANIZATIONS:** IEEE, 1985-; CAFA, 1991-. **HONORS/AWARDS:** National Taiwan University, Book Coupon Award, 1977-81. **SPECIAL ACHIEVEMENTS:** Five technical papers on IEEE PES transactions, 1988-91; seven conference papers, 1987-93. **MILITARY SERVICE:** Chinese Air Force, 2nd lt, 1981-83. **BUSINESS ADDRESS:** Assistant Professor, San Francisco State University, Division of Engineering, 1600 Holloway Ave, SCI-120, San Francisco, CA 94132-1722, (415)338-7733.

LIOU, SY-HWANG
Educator. Taiwanese American. **PERSONAL:** Born Mar 13, 1951, Keelung, Taiwan; son of Ding-Chiang Liu and Chiu-Yun Hsu; married Mei-Lan Lin, Dec 4, 1977; children: Jenny. **EDUCATION:** Soochow University, BS, 1974; Florida Institute of Technology, MS, 1979; Johns Hopkins University, MA, 1981, PhD, 1985. **CAREER:** Soochow University, instructor, 1976-77; Johns Hopkins University, postdoctoral fellow, 1985-86; AT&T Bell Laboratories, postdoctoral member of technical staff, 1986-88; University of Nebraska, assistant professor, 1988-93, associate professor, 1993-. **ORGANIZATIONS:** Applied Physics Communication, co-editor, 1990-; American Physical Society, 1981-. **SPECIAL ACHIEVEMENTS:** 96 publications, 94 presentations, 22 invited presentations, 1 patent. **BUSINESS ADDRESS:** Associate Professor, University of Nebraska, 10th, 367 Behlen, Lincoln, NE 68588-0111.

LIOU, YIHWA IRENE
Educator. Taiwanese American. **PERSONAL:** Born Nov 8, 1958, Taipei, Taiwan; daughter of Cheng-i Liu and Kuei-chao Hsu Liu; married Minder Chen, Feb 22, 1985; children: Justin G Chen. **EDUCATION:** National Taiwan University, BA, 1981; University of Southern Mississippi, MLS, 1985; University of Arizona, MS, 1987, PhD, 1989. **CAREER:** University of Arizona, teaching associate, 1985-89; University of Baltimore, asst professor, 1981-. **ORGANIZATIONS:** IEEE, 1989-; ACM, 1989-; AAAI, 1989-; DSI, 1991-;

TIMS, 1989-. **HONORS/AWARDS:** Black and Decker, Black and Decker Research Award, 1993. **SPECIAL ACHIEVEMENTS:** An Investigation into Knowledge Acquisition Using a Group Decision Support System, Information and Management, Vol 24, 121-132, 1993; An Assessment of an Electronic Meeting Center, Journal of Information Technology Management, Vol 3, 1992; Developing Intelligent Organizations: A Context-Based Approach to Individual and Organizational Effectiveness, Journal of Organizational Computing, Vol 2, No 2, 181-202, 1992; Collaborative Knowledge Acquisition, Expert Systems with Applications: An International Journal, Vol 5, 1-13, No 1, 1992; Knowledge Acquisition: Issues, Techniques and Methodology, Data Base, Vol 23, No 1, 59-64, Winter 1992. **BIOGRAPHICAL SOURCES:** Information and Management, Vol 24, 1993, p 121-132.

LIU, ALAN FONG-CHING
Engineer. Chinese American. **PERSONAL:** Born Mar 25, 1933, Canton, China; son of Gee Call Liu and Shuk Hing Chen Liu; married Iris P Chan, Sep 2, 1962; children: Kent, Willy, Henry. **EDUCATION:** University of Chiba, Japan, BSME, 1958; University of Bridgeport, MSME, 1965. **CAREER:** Lockheed-California Co, senior structures engineer, 1968-73; Rockwell International Space Division, senior engineering specialist/project manager, 1973-76; Northrop Corp, North American Aircraft Division, senior engineering specialist/project manager, 1976-88; Rockwell International, North American Aircraft, senior engineering specialist/project manager, 1988-. **ORGANIZATIONS:** American Institute of Aeronautics and Astronautics, associate fellow; ASM International; American Society for Testing and Materials. **SPECIAL ACHIEVEMENTS:** Published extensively in the technical journals and proceedings of national and international symposiums of the AIAA, ASM, ASTM, and the American Society of Mechanical Engineers on the subject of fracture mechanics, and durability and damage tolerance of aircraft structures. **BUSINESS ADDRESS:** Senior Engineering Specialist, Rockwell International, North American Aircraft, PO Box 92098, Mail Code GC15, Los Angeles, CA 90009.

LIU, ALFRED H.
Architect, business developer. Chinese American. **PERSONAL:** Born Dec 30, 1942, China; married Dwan Tai, Nov 11, 1976; children: Amerasia. **EDUCATION:** Aquinas College, BS, physics, math, 1965; Columbia University, MA, physics, 1967, Graduate School of Architectere, BArch, 1971. **CAREER:** International Institute of Interior Design, engineering instructor; Columbia University, engineering instructor; AEPA Architects Engineers, PC, president, 1976-. **ORGANIZATIONS:** American Institute of Architects; American Association for Laboratory Animal Sciences; National Republican Asian Assembly, national chairman, 1991-95; USA-ROC Economic Council, 1990; DC Building Industry Association; Chinese Consolidated Benevolent Association; DC Downtown Partnership, 1984-; DC Commission on Arts & Humanities, steering committee, 1990. **HONORS/AWARDS:** DC Government, Theodore R Hagans Jr Memorial Achievement Award, for Outstanding Business Person of the Year, 1987; DC Housing Industry Corp, Community Development Award for Design of Wah Luck House, 1982; Assn Builders & Contractors, Monumental Structure Award: Chinatown Archway; AS&U Magazine, Outstanding School, University Bldg: Aquinas College, Arts & Music Building; DC Downtown Partnership, 1984-93, 1985. **SPECIAL ACHIEVEMENTS:** Author: "Chinatown Design Guidelives & Streetscape Standards," Wash DC, 1985; "The Future of Washington's Chinatown: Extinction or Distinction," 1983; "The Timeless Art of China," The Herald, Aquinas College, 1962; Solo Art Exhibit, National Endowment for the Arts, 1977; featured as Chinese Architect & Artist, Channel 7 "Asian Minutes, The History We Are Proud Of.". **BIOGRAPHICAL SOURCES:** Patriots Magazine, Asian Pacific Heritage Month Issue, p 84, 1992. **BUSINESS ADDRESS:** President, AEPA Architects Engineers, PC, 2421 Pennsylvania Ave NW, Washington, DC 20037, (202)822-8320.

LIU, ANNE W.
Educator. Chinese American. **PERSONAL:** Born Jul 8, 1950, People's Republic of China; son of Polk Fay Ow and Amy Ow; children: Peter, Henry, Alice. **EDUCATION:** San Francisco State University, BS, 1972; University of Illinois, MS, 1975. **CAREER:** San Bernardino Valley College, Computer Science Dept, chairperson, 1976-. **BUSINESS ADDRESS:** Professor, San Bernardino Valley College, 701 S Mount Vernon, C126, San Bernardino, CA 92410, (909)888-6511.

LIU, BEN CHIEH
Educator. Chinese American. **PERSONAL:** Born Nov 17, 1938, Chung King, Szechuan, China; married Jill, 1965; children: Tina W Ting, Roger W Ming, Milton W Jung. **EDUCATION:** National Taiwan University, Taipei, BA, economics, 1961; Memorial University Newfoundland, Canada, MA, economics/resources, 1965; Washington University, MA, 1967, PhD economics, 1971. **CAREER:** St Louis Commerce & Growth Association, research project director, 1967-72; Midwest Research Institute, principal advisor, senior economist, 1972-79; Argonne National Laboratory, project manager, 1979-80; Oklahoma City University, professor of business/economics, 1981-82; United Nations, advisor to Jordan, China, etc, 1981-; Liu and Associates, Inc, president/project manager, 1981-; Chicago State University, management information systems, professor, 1982-. **ORGANIZATIONS:** Chinese Economic Association in North America, president, 1989-90; Chinese American Professional Association in Midwest America, president, 1985-86; US National Commission Library & Information Science, commissioner, 1991-94; Congressional Science & Technology Committee, Congressman Farwell, 1986-; committee member: American Statistical Association, American Economics Association, The Institute of Management Association, Operational; Society of America; International Statistical Institute, etc; National Heritage Groups Councip, vice president and president, 1987-. **HONORS/AWARDS:** Council for International Exchange of Scholars, Fulbright Award, 1991-92; Chinese National Science Council, Distinguished Professor Award, 1992; Chicago State University, Outstanding Performance/Excellence Awards and Professional Advancement Increase Award, 1984-90. **SPECIAL ACHIEVEMENTS:** 5 books: Quality of Life Indicators by State, Kansas City, MRI, 1975; Quality of Life Indicators for US Metro Areas, Praeger Pub, 1978, GPO, 1979; Air Pollution Damage Functions/Damage Estimates, 1979; Earthquake Risk & Damage Functions, Westview Publications, 1981; Energy, Income & Quality of Life Management, TanKang U Press, 1988; 180 articles in professional journals. **HOME ADDRESS:** 5360 Pennywood Dr, Lisle, IL 60532, (708)964-0236. **BUSINESS ADDRESS:** Professor, Chicago State University, 95th at King Dr, Chicago, IL 60628, (312)995-3951.

LIU, BEN SHAW-CHING
Educator. Taiwanese American. **PERSONAL:** Born Jul 12, 1955, Taipei, Taiwan; son of Bon-Fu and Lien-Chu Liu; married Li-Ling Liu, Jun 12, 1978; children: Megan. **EDUCATION:** National Cheng-Kung University, BSE, 1977; Tung Hai University, professional manager's certificate, 1984; State University of New York, Buffalo, PhD, 1991. **CAREER:** Chang-Shing Iron Works, sales engiener, 1979-81; ATW Electronics, marketing manager, 1981-83; General Instrument Microelectronics, purchasing supervisor, 1983-86; Teamwood Corp, managing director, 1983-86; SUNY at Buffalo, instructor, 1988-91; University of Illinois, assistant professor, 1991-. **ORGANIZATIONS:** American Marketing Association, 1988-; Institute for Management Science, 1988-; Association for Consumer Research, 1989-; International Association for Conflict Management, 1990-. **HONORS/AWARDS:** SUNY at Buffalo, PhD Student Achievement Award, 1992; NCKU, YMCA Scholarship, 1977; Ministry of Education, Taiwan, Thomas Edison's Award, 1973, Experimental Biochemistry Competition, 1972. **SPECIAL ACHIEVEMENTS:** With Bunn, Michele D, "Defining Purchases Types by Situational Assessment," American Marketing Association Educators' Winter Conference Proceedings, Chicago IL: American Marketing Association, 1993; "Emerging Topics in Marketing: A Behavioral Focus," panel member, The Haring Symposium, Indiana University at Bloomington, 1993; with Wai-Kwan Li, "Matching or Mismatching: Masculinity Matters," presented to Center for Conflict and Negotiation Research, University of Illinois at Urbana-Champaign, 1993; with Bunn, Michele D, "Elements of Situational Risk in Organizational Buying," Working Paper 0152-1993, College of Commerce and Business Adminstration, University of Illinois at Urbana-Champaign, 1993; numerous others. **MILITARY SERVICE:** Army, Taiwan, soldier. **BUSINESS ADDRESS:** Assistant Professor, University of Illinois, 1206 S Sixth St, 350 Commerce West Building, Champaign, IL 61820, (217)333-9003.

LIU, BENJAMIN Y. H.
Educator, engineer. Chinese American. **PERSONAL:** Born Aug 15, 1934, Shanghai, China; son of Dorothy Pao-ning Cheng and Wilson Wan-su Liu; married Helen Hai-ling Cheng, Jun 14, 1958; children: Lawrence A. S. **EDUCATION:** National Taiwan University, 1951-54; University of Nebraska, BSME, 1956; University of Minnesota, PhD, 1960. **CAREER:** Honeywell Co, Minneapolis, associate engineer, 1956; University of Paris, visiting professor, 1968-69; University of Minnesota, research assistant, instructor, 1956-60, assistant professor, 1960-67, associate professor, 1967-69, professor, 1969-,

Particle Tech Lab, director, 1973-. **ORGANIZATIONS:** ASME; ASHRAE; American Society of Engineering Education; Air & Waste Management Association; American Association for Aerosol Research, president, 1986-88; Chinese American Association, Minnesota, president, 1971-72; National Academy of Engineering. **HONORS/AWARDS:** Guggenheim Fellow, 1968-69; Alexander von Humboldt Foundation, Senior US Scientist Award, 1982-83. **SPECIAL ACHIEVEMENTS:** Contributing author: Aerosol Science, 1966; editor: Fine Particles, 1976; Application of Solar Energy for Heating and Cooling Buildings, 1977; Aerosols in the Mining and Industrial Work Environment, 1983; Aerosols: Science, Technology, and Industrial Application of Airborne Particles, 1984; editor-in-chief: Aerosol Science and Technology, 1982-; contributor to Encyclopedia of Chemical Technology; patentee in field. **BUSINESS ADDRESS:** Professor, Particle Tech Lab, University of Minnesota, 1111 Church St SE, Minneapolis, MN 55455. *

LIU, CHAO-NAN
Educator. Taiwanese American. **PERSONAL:** Born Dec 19, 1940, Taichung, Taiwan; son of Shouming Liu; married Doris C Liu; children: Sam, Dan. **EDUCATION:** Tunghai University, BA, 1964; Texas A&M University, PhD, 1976. **CAREER:** Trenton State College, professor of economics, 1981-. **ORGANIZATIONS:** Eastern Economic Association, 1990-; Economists of New Jersey, 1986-; Association for Comparative Economic Studies, 1984-; American Economic Association, 1977-87; Center for Modern China, 1992-. **HONORS/AWARDS:** Woodrow Wilson Foundation, fellowship, 1984. **SPECIAL ACHIEVEMENTS:** Articles published in Journal of Comparative Economics, Business Journal, Journal of Contemporary China. **BUSINESS ADDRESS:** Professor, Dept of Economics, Trenton State College, Bliss Hall, Rm 115, Trenton, NJ 08650-4700, (609)771-2240.

LIU, CHEN-CHING
Educator. Taiwanese American. **PERSONAL:** Born Dec 30, 1954, Tainan, Taiwan. **EDUCATION:** National Taiwan University, BSEE, 1976, MSEE, 1978; University of California, Berkeley, PhD, 1983. **CAREER:** University of California, research assistant, 1980-83; University of Washington, assistant professor, 1983-87, associate professor, 1987-91; professor, 1991-. **ORGANIZATIONS:** Proceedings of the IEEE, editorial board, 1989-; Power Engineering Society, history committee, chairman, 1992-, executive board, 1992-; working group on applications of AI, computer & analytic methods subcom, chairman, 1990-93; Seattle Section, treasurer, secretary, 1991-; CRL Publishing Ltd, Engineering Intelligent Systems, editor, 1993-; CIGRE-Conference Internationale des Grand Research, Electriques a Haute Tension, 1989; Taiwanese American Citizens League, Seattle chapter, president, 1991-92. **HONORS/AWARDS:** National Science Foundation, Presidential Young Investigator's Award, 1987; IEEE Student Chapter, University of Washington, Teacher of the Year Award; University of Tokyo, Japan, Tokyo Electric Power Chair, 1991; IEEE, Fellow. **SPECIAL ACHIEVEMENTS:** One of the first researchers in the world to apply modern expert system technologies to power system problems. **BUSINESS ADDRESS:** Professor, Dept of Electrical Engineering, University of Washington, FT-10, Seattle, WA 98195, (206)543-2198.

LIU, CHING-TONG
Research physiologist. Chinese American. **PERSONAL:** Born Oct 19, 1931, Tai-Shin, Jiangsu, China; son of Lien-yi Liu and Su-Ju (Ku) Liu; married In-May Liu, Feb 28, 1970; children: Rex F, Grace M, Jeannette M, Christine M. **EDUCATION:** National Taiwan University, BS, 1956; University of Tennessee Graduate School, MS, 1959, PhD, 1963. **CAREER:** National Taiwan University, teaching assistant, 1956-57; Sterling-Winthrop Research Inst, associate research biologist, 1965-66; Baylor College of Med, assistant professor, 1966-73, adjunct associate professor, 1973-79, adjunct professor, 1979-; US Army Medical Research Institute of Infectious Diseases, research physiologist, 1973-. **HONORS/AWARDS:** University of Tennessee, Full Scholarship, 1957-63; USAMRIID, Outstanding Performance Rating, 1976-77, Sustained Superior Performance Rating, 1980-81, Exceptional Performance Rating, 1982-84, PMRS Performance Award, 1985-92. **SPECIAL ACHIEVEMENTS:** Published 74 papers in the fields of physiology and pharmacology; published 75 abstracts. **BUSINESS ADDRESS:** Assistant Dept Chief, US Army Medical Research Inst of Infectious Diseases, Fort Detrick, Room 130, Bldg 1412, Frederick, MD 21702-5011, (301)619-2724.

LIU, CHUAN SHENG
Educator. Chinese American. **PERSONAL:** Born Jan 9, 1939, Chuan, Kwansi, China; son of Hsing-Chi Liu and Li-Wen Wang; married Jing Yi Hong; children: Albert, Benjamin, Jennifer, Anna. **EDUCATION:** Tunghai Univer-

sity, Taiwan, BS, 1960; University of California, Berkeley, MA, 1964, PhD, 1968. **CAREER:** University of California, Los Angeles, assistant professor in residence, 1968-70; General Atomic Co, visiting scientist, 1970-71, director of theoretical science division, 1981-85; Institute of Advanced Study, 1971-74; University of Maryland, professor of physics, 1974-, chairman of physics dept, 1985-90, 1993-. **ORGANIZATIONS:** American Physical Society, fellow, 1987, Division of Plasma Physics, chairman, 1992-93, vice chair, 1991-92; State of Maryland, Sister State Committee with Anhui Province, People's Republic of China, chairman, 1986-. **SPECIAL ACHIEVEMENTS:** More than one hundred research articles published in scientific journals. **HOME ADDRESS:** 524 Ridgewell Way, Silver Spring, MD 20902, (301)384-8636. **BUSINESS ADDRESS:** Professor and Chairman, Physics Dept, University of Maryland, College Park, MD 20742, (301)405-8054.

LIU, CHUNG-CHIUN
Educator. Chinese American. **PERSONAL:** Born Oct 8, 1936, Canton, Kwang Teing, China; divorced; children: Peter S. **EDUCATION:** California Institute of Technology, MS, 1962; Case Western Reserve University, PhD, 1968. **CAREER:** Case Western Reserve University, Chemical Engineering, professor, 1978-, Wallace R Persons Professor of Sensor Technology and Control, 1989-, Electronics Design Center, director, currently. **ORGANIZATIONS:** Committee on Solid-State Sensors and Actuators, Intl Coordinator, US delegate, 1990-; Intl Committee of Chemical Sensor Meeting, North American Region, steering committee, chairman, 1990-. **SPECIAL ACHIEVEMENTS:** Published extensively in technical journals on sensor technologies. **BUSINESS ADDRESS:** Professor, Case Western Reserve University, Electronics Design Center, Bingham Building, 10900 Euclid Avenue, Cleveland, OH 44106-7200, (216)368-2935.

LIU, DAVID TA-CHING (DAJING)
Librarian. Chinese American. **PERSONAL:** Born Dec 6, 1936, Zhong-Shan City, Guangdong, China; son of Chung-ling Liu and Ging-wa Vong Liu; married Agnete Mei-cheng Liu, Dec 15, 1962; children: Nadine, Austin W T. **EDUCATION:** Tamkang English College, Taiwan, 1954-55; National Taiwan University, BA, 1959; English Research Institute of National Normal University, Taiwan, 1960-61; University of Washington, Seattle, 1962; George Peabody College for Teachers Nashville, MALS, 1963. **CAREER:** Chinese Air Force Headquarters, Taipei, Taiwan, interpreter/officer, 2nd lieutenant, 1960-61; Chicago Public Library, cataloger, 1963-64; Joliet Public Library, chief of adult services, reader's adviser, 1964; Bay De Noc Community College, head librarian, asst professor of political science, 1964-73; Pharr Memorial Library, library director, 1973-. **ORGANIZATIONS:** Chinese-American Librarians Association, president, 1981-82; Pharr Rotary Club, secretary/treasurer, 1975-76; Escanaba Rotary Club, chair of international youth projects, 1972-73; Asian/Pacific-American Librarians Association, Recruitment and Scholarship Committee, chair, 1993-94. **HONORS/AWARDS:** Chinese-American Librarians Association, Distinguished Service Award, 1975. **SPECIAL ACHIEVEMENTS:** Author: Taiwan Revisited, China Friendship Publishing Company, Beijing, 1985; Library Journal of Bowler Co, book reviewer, 1969-70; Bay De Noc Community College, first professional librarian, 1964, built new library on North Campus, 1968; Pharr Memorial Library, first professional librarian, 1973, doubled its size, 1978. **HOME ADDRESS:** 311 S Cypress Circle, Pharr, TX 78577-5950, (210)787-4723. **BUSINESS ADDRESS:** Library Director, Pharr Memorial Library, 200 S Athol St, Pharr, TX 78577-4806.

LIU, DONALD JIANN-TYNG
Educator. Taiwanese American. **PERSONAL:** Born Sep 16, 1953, Taipei, Taiwan; son of David K Liu and Nancy W Liu; married Deedee M Liu, Mar 5, 1978; children: Dewitt Clearwell, Dustin Cleanwell. **EDUCATION:** University of Chinese Culture, Taipei, BS, 1975; California State University, Fresno, MS (with honors), 1980; University of Minnesota, Saint Paul, PhD, 1985. **CAREER:** University of Minnesota, research assistant, 1980-85; Cornell University, research associate, 1985-89; Iowa State University, assistant professor, 1990-. **ORGANIZATIONS:** American Agriculture Economics Association, 1985-; Western Agriculture Economics Association, 1990-. **HONORS/ AWARDS:** Northeastern Agriculture & Resource Econ Association, Journal Article of the Year, 1990. **SPECIAL ACHIEVEMENTS:** Published 15 journal articles, 2 book chapters, 4 popular press articles, 22 technical reports, and 46 presentations; selected by students as the best teacher within department several times. **MILITARY SERVICE:** Taiwanese Army, second lieutenant, 1975-77. **BUSINESS ADDRESS:** Professor, Iowa State University, Department of Economics, Heady Hall, Ames, IA 50011, (515)294-6176.

LIU, DWIGHT DAVIDSON
Bank executive. Chinese American. **PERSONAL:** Born Oct 25, 1958, Newark, NJ; son of David and Agnes; divorced; children: Marissa Lian. **EDUCATION:** Pepperdine University, BSM, 1981, MBA, 1983. **CAREER:** Union Bank, asst mgr, 1976-81; Crocker Bank, operations mgr, 1981-85; First Interstate Bank, finance mgr, 1985-90; US Trust Co, CFO, 1990-.

LIU, EDMUND K.
Chemical company manager. Chinese American. **PERSONAL:** Born Jun 7, 1951, Honolulu, HI; son of Young Wah Liu and Shuk Kwan Liu; married Edwina P Liu, Sep 6, 1980; children: Jennifer A, Katherine E. **EDUCATION:** University of Chicago, BS, 1973; Massachusetts Institute of Technology, PhD, 1977. **CAREER:** Los Alamos Scientific Laboratory, postdoctoral staff, 1977-79; Aerojet Corp Propulsion Divison, sr chemist, 1979-84, chemistry specialist, 1984-90, chemistry supervisor, 1990-91, chemistry manager, 1991-. **ORGANIZATIONS:** American Chemical Society, 1977-; Sigma Xi, 1973-; JANNAF. **HOME ADDRESS:** 904 Doheney Ct, Roseville, CA 95661, (916)782-2671. **BUSINESS ADDRESS:** Chemistry Manager, Aerojet Corp Propulsion Division, PO Box 13222, Sacramento, CA 95813, (916)355-5716.

LIU, EDWIN H.
Environmental scientist. Chinese American/Pacific Islander American. **PERSONAL:** Born Apr 11, 1942, Honolulu, HI; son of Margaret Y Liu and Edward F Liu; divorced. **EDUCATION:** Johns Hopkins University, AB, 1964; Michigan State University, PhD, 1971. **CAREER:** Michigan State University, research fellow, 1972-73; University of South Carolina, biology professor, 1973-81; California Regional Water Quality Control Board, Newport Bay coordinator, 1986-88; University of Georgia, research professor, 1981-86; Environmental Protection Agency, regional monitoring coordinator, 1988-. **ORGANIZATIONS:** Society for the Study of Evolution; Ecological Society of America; Sigma Xi. **HONORS/AWARDS:** University of South Carolina, Student Government Award, 1977; American Society of Plant Physiologists, Young Scientist Travel Award, 1975. **SPECIAL ACHIEVEMENTS:** 40 publications in the subjects of biochemistry, ecological genetics, and environmental management. **HOME PHONE:** (510)843-3548. **BUSINESS ADDRESS:** Regional Monitoring Coordinator, US Environmental Protection Agency, Region IX, 75 Hawthorne St, San Francisco, CA 94105, (415)744-2012.

LIU, ERIC P.
Government official. Chinese American. **PERSONAL:** Born Nov 1, 1968, Poughkeepsie, NY; son of Chao-Hua Liu and Julia Liu. **EDUCATION:** Yale College, BA, 1990. **CAREER:** Senate Select Committee on Intelligence, research assistant, 1990-91; US Senator David Boren, legislative assistant, 1991-93; The Next Progressive, editor & founder, 1991-; US Department of State, speechwriter, 1993-; National Security Council, legislative affirs director, 1993-. **ORGANIZATIONS:** Organization of Chinese Americans, 1992-; Asian-American Journalists Assn, 1991-. **HONORS/AWARDS:** Truman Scholarship Foundation, Harry S. Truman Scholarship, 1988; White House/ Public Allies, Tomorrow's Leaders Today, 1993. **SPECIAL ACHIEVEMENTS:** Editor & contributor, Next, an anthology of essays by young writers, W W Norton. **HOME ADDRESS:** 1400 20th St, NW #905, Washington, DC 20036, (202)775-4598.

LIU, FRANK YINING
Educator, library administrator. **PERSONAL:** Born Feb 7, 1943, Wu Ning, Jiangxi, China; married Heidi Liu; children: Alexander. **EDUCATION:** National Taiwan University, LLB, 1965; Yale Law School, graduate fellowship, 1966-67; University of Texas at Austin, MCJ, 1970, MLS, 1973. **CAREER:** University of Texas-Austin, asst law librarian, 1971-72; Villanova University Law School, asst law librarian, 1975-80; Duquesne University, Law Library, dir, 1980-, School of Law, prof, law, 1985-. **ORGANIZATIONS:** World Trade Center, board of directors, 1993-; Pennsylvania Humanities Council, 1991-94; Pittsburgh Folk Festival, board of directors, 1992-94; Western PA Asian American Coalition, president, 1992-93; American Assn of Law Libraries, steering committee co-chair, 1992-95; Organization of Chinese Americans, president, 1988-89; PA Heritage Affairs Commission, at-large commissioner, 1988-92; Mid-Atlantic Law Library Cooperative, founding member, 1981-. **HONORS/AWARDS:** China University of Political Science and Law, Honorary Professor, 1992; Duquesne University, President's Faculty Award for Excellence in Community Service, 1990; American Assn of Law Libraries, Executive Board Candidate, 1990. **SPECIAL ACHIEVEMENTS:** Initiated and concluded a faculty and library material exchange program, Duquesne University School of Law and China University of Political Science and Law-

Beijing, ROC, coordinator of program, 1991-. **BUSINESS ADDRESS:** Director and Professor of Law, Duquesne University Law Library, 900 Locust St, Hanley Hall, Rm 208, Pittsburgh, PA 15282, (412)396-5018.

LIU, GERALD HANMIN
Organization administrator, educator. Chinese American. **PERSONAL:** Born Aug 24, 1944, San Francisco, CA; son of Howard Y Liu and Patricia Marian Lee Low; married Jennifer Mei, Sep 6, 1969. **EDUCATION:** University of the Pacific, BA, 1966; New York University, DDS, 1970; Union for Experimenting Colleges and Universities, PhD, 1978. **CAREER:** Min An Health Center, executive director, board of directors, 1979-82, 1987-89; US-China Educational Institute, founder, president, board of directors, 1978-; San Francisco-Shanghai Friendship City Commission, 1983-89; W K Kellogg Foundation, MI, consultant, 1984-87, 1989-, Kellogg International, steering committee; MacArthur Foundation, Chicago, 1986-89; William T Grant Foundation, New York City, 1988-89; numerous other foundations. **ORGANIZATIONS:** AAAS; Omicron Kappa Upsilon. **HONORS/AWARDS:** Michigan State University, fellowship program, 1985-88; honorary adviser for: Shanghai Mental Health Center, China, 1987 and Beijing Medical University, Shanghai 1st People's Hospital, 1985; numerous grants from various foundations. **SPECIAL ACHIEVEMENTS:** Peace Corps, Cultural Training Program, coordinator, 1989-; Essential Book of Traditional Chinese Medicine, project director, V 1 & 2, 1986. **MILITARY SERVICE:** US Army, captain, 1971-73. **BUSINESS ADDRESS:** President, United States - China Educational Institute, 1144 Pacific Ave, San Francisco, CA 94133-4212, (415)775-1151. *

LIU, HANJUN
Chemist. Chinese American. **PERSONAL:** Born Feb 3, 1964, Zhongshan, Canton, People's Republic of China; son of Zhanping Liu and Wei Ping Chen; married Jiemin Wu, Apr 17, 1993. **EDUCATION:** South China Institute of Technology, Canton, BS, 1984; California State Polytechnic University, Pomona, MS, 1989. **CAREER:** Shiqi Chemical Factory, engr, 1984-88; Weck Laboratory Inc, analytical specialist, 1990-. **ORGANIZATIONS:** American Chemical Society, 1991-; Zhongshan Chemical Society, 1984-88. **HOME ADDRESS:** 3861 Sycamore St, West Covina, CA 91792, (818)965-7162.

LIU, HENRY
Educator. Chinese American. **PERSONAL:** Born Jun 3, 1936, Beijing, China; son of Yen-Huai Liu and Remei Bardina Liu; married Dou-Mei (Susie), Dec 16, 1964; children: Jerry B, Jason C, Jeffrey H. **EDUCATION:** National Taiwan University, BS, 1959; Colorado State University, MS, 1963, PhD, 1966. **CAREER:** National Taiwan University, visiting national scholar, 1980; University of Melbourne, visiting professor, 1980; University of Missouri, assistant professor, 1965-69, associate professor, 1969-75, professor, 1976-, Capsule Pipeline Research Center, director, 1991-. **ORGANIZATIONS:** International Freight Pipeline Society, president, 1989-94; American Society of Civil Engineers, pipeline research committee, chairman, 1991-95, aerospace division executive committee, chairman, 1988-89, aerodynamics committee, chairman, 1976-79; US Wind Engineering Research Council, board member, 1985-89 . **HONORS/AWARDS:** American Society of Civil Engineers, Bechtel Pipeline Engineering Award, 1992, Aerospace Sciences and Technology Award, 1983; International Freight Pipeline Society, Distinguished Lecture Award, 1982; State of Missouri, Energy Innovation Award, 1988; University of Missouri, Faculty/Alumni Award, 1993. **SPECIAL ACHIEVEMENTS:** Inventor: three US patents on capsule pipeline; author, Wind Engineering: A Handbook for Structural Engineers, Prentice Hall, 1991; editor, Freight Pipelines, Hemisphere Publishing, 1980; Wind Loads & Building Codes, University of Missouri, Extension, 1987. **BUSINESS ADDRESS:** Professor, Director, Capsule Pipeline Research Center, University of Missouri- Columbia, College of Engineering, E-2421 Engineering, Columbia, MO 65211-0002, (314)882-2779.

LIU, HONG
Educator. Chinese American. **PERSONAL:** Born Jul 17, 1957, Nanking, Jiangsu, People's Republic of China; daughter of Ruiyu Zhang and Kang Liu; married Xiaonan Lu, Jan 6, 1985; children: Charles Lu. **EDUCATION:** Hefei Polytechnic University, Anhui, China, BS, computer science and math (honors), 1982, MS, computer science, 1984; Polytechnic University, Brooklyn, PhD, computer science, 1990. **CAREER:** Hefei Polytechnic University, instructor, 1982-85; Computer Systems and Technology, system analyst, 1985-86; Polytechnic University, academic associate, 1987-89, visiting assistant professor, 1990; Columbia University, visiting scholar, summer 1992, summer 1993; University of Massachusetts, Dartmouth, assistant professor, 1990-.

ORGANIZATIONS: ACM/SIGCOMM, voting member, 1982-84, 1988-; IEEE/Communications Society, 1985-86, 1992-; Upsilon Pi Epsilon, 1987-. **HONORS/AWARDS:** University of Massachusetts, Dartmouth, Healy Award for Faculty Research, 1993; Polytechnic University, Pearl Brownstein Doctoral Research Award, 1989, Deborah Resenthal MD Award for Excellent Performance in PhD Qualifying Exams, 1987; Westinghouse, Westinghouse Research Grant for Women in EE or CS, 1986; Chinese Science & Technology, State 3rd Award for excellent master thesis & graphics research, 1985. **SPECIAL ACHIEVEMENTS:** Author of: "Software Engineering Practice in an Undergraduate Compiler Course," IEEE Tran on Education, 1993; "Models for T1 Problem," Proc of IEEE International Conference on Microw and Commun, 1992; "Visualization in Network Topology Optimization," Proc of ACM 20th CSC, 1992; "Artificial Intelligence Applications to Comm Network Design," Proc of ACM 20th CSC; "An Interactive Graphic System on Microcomputers," Mini-Micro Systems, 1985. **BUSINESS ADDRESS:** Professor, Dept of Computer & Information Science, University of Massachusetts, Dartmouth, Old Westport Road, North Dartmouth, MA 02747-2300, (508)999-8502.

LIU, HONG-TING
Educator. Chinese American. **PERSONAL:** Born Apr 20, 1932, Fuzhou, Fujian, China; son of Yi-Lian Liu & Shun-Hong Li; married Jean Yu, Dec 31, 1960; children: Mimi Y, Albert Y. **EDUCATION:** Zhejiang University, BS, 1952; Sian Institute of Metallurgy and Construction Engineering, post graduate program, 1962-65; University of Minnesota, PhD, 1984. **CAREER:** Fuzhou University, vice president of the Institute of Survey, Structural and Architectural Design, 1979-81, associate professor, 1979-81; California Polytechnic State University, lecturer, 1984-86, associate professor, 1986-90, professor, 1990-. **ORGANIZATIONS:** American Society of Civil Engineering, 1984-; American Concrete Institute, 1984-. **HONORS/AWARDS:** California Polytechnic State University, Meritorious Performance and Professional Promise Award, 1988. **SPECIAL ACHIEVEMENTS:** Author of several publications relating to civil engineering. **BUSINESS ADDRESS:** Professor, Dept of Architectural Engineering, California Polytechnic State University, San Luis Obispo, CA 93407, (805)756-2152.

LIU, HSIEN-TUNG
Educator. Chinese American. **PERSONAL:** Born Feb 17, 1935, Canton, China; son of Chiu-nan Liu and Shiu-fang Wu; married Li-Ping Hsieh, Jun 5, 1964; children: Benjamin, Lisa. **EDUCATION:** Natl Taiwan University, BA, 1958; California State University, Chico, MA, 1962; Claremont Graduate School and University Center, PhD, 1967. **CAREER:** California State University, Chico, asst professor, 1965-67; Point Park College, asst, assoc and full professor, 1967-91, vp and dean of faculty, 1987-91; Bloomsburg University, College of Arts and Sciences, dean, 1991-. **ORGANIZATIONS:** American Political Science Assn, 1967-; Intl Society for Educational, Cultural & Scientific Interchanges, editor, 1974-78; Intl Studies Assn; Global Awareness Society Intl, 1993-. **HONORS/AWARDS:** Natl Endowment for Humanities, Summer Award, 1975; Claremont Graduate School, Fellowship, 1962; Chico State College, Douglas MacArthur Scholarship, 1961; Alpha Chi, Honorary Member, 1991. **SPECIAL ACHIEVEMENTS:** Border Disputes between Imperial China and Tsarist Russia, 1968. **BUSINESS ADDRESS:** Dean, College of Arts & Sciences, Bloomsburg University, E 2nd St, Bloomsburg, PA 17815, (717)389-4410.

LIU, HSUN KAO
Educator. Chinese American. **PERSONAL:** Born Oct 16, 1945, China; son of H C & F J Liu; married Tenly Liu, Aug 21, 1971; children: Titi, Jojo. **EDUCATION:** Taiwan National Cheng Kung University, BSEE, 1968; University of Cincinnati, MSEE, 1971; State University of New York, Buffalo, PhD, 1976. **CAREER:** General Dynamics Corp, senior consultant, 1980-92; California Polytechnic University, professor, 1976-. **ORGANIZATIONS:** Association for Computing Machinery, 1971-. **HONORS/AWARDS:** Chinese American Professional Society, Outstanding Support, 1982; General Dynamics and California Polytechnic University, Outstanding Service, 1982. **SPECIAL ACHIEVEMENTS:** Three dimensional display of human organs from computed tomograms, 1979; shading models for computer displayed organ surfaces, Acta Cybernetica, 1978; "Dynamic Boundary Surface Detection," Computer Graphics & Image Processing, 1978; "Display of 3-Dimensional Information in Computed Tomography," Journal of Computer Assisted Tomography, 1977. **BUSINESS ADDRESS:** Professor, California Polytechnic University, 3801 W Temple Ave, Pomona, CA 91768, (909)869-3442.

LIU, JAMES P.

Educator. Chinese American. **PERSONAL:** Born Feb 10, 1936, Hupei, China; son of Sze-Hai Liu and Chin-Sha Wang; married Jenny, Oct 1971; children: Daniel. **EDUCATION:** National Taiwan University, BA, law, 1959; Virginia Polytechnic Institute and State University, MS, math, 1967, PhD, math, 1972. **CAREER:** Burroughs Corp (Unisys), systems specialist, 1974-78; Trenton State College, professor of business admin, 1978-81; AT&T Bell Laboratories, technical staff, 1981-84; Trenton State College, professor of business admin, 1984-. **ORGANIZATIONS:** Central Jersey Chinese-American Association, executive council, 1991-; Phi Kappa Phi, 1971-; Institute of Decision Sciences, 1984-. **SPECIAL ACHIEVEMENTS:** Published articles in Journal of Systems Management; American Economist; Proceedings of Northeast Decision Sciences and others. **BUSINESS ADDRESS:** Prof of Business Admin, School of Business, Trenton State College, Trenton, NJ 08650-4700.

LIU, JIANG BO

Educator. Chinese American. **PERSONAL:** Born Jan 28, 1952, WuHai, Hubei, People's Republic of China; son of Yi and Xiulai Han Liu; married Qin Wang Liu, Feb 1, 1979; children: Michael Y, Jessica H. **EDUCATION:** Nanking Institute of Aeronautical Technology, diploma, 1977; University of Science and Technology of China, graduate studies certificate, 1980; Washington University, MS, 1981, PhD, 1985. **CAREER:** Nanking Institute of Aeronautical Technology, instructor, 1977-78; Washington University at St Louis, research assistant, 1980-85; Indiana University at South Bend, assistant professor, 1985-87; Bradley University, assistant professor, 1987-90, associate professor, 1990-. **ORGANIZATIONS:** IEEE, 1985-; ACM, 1985-; ISCA, 1992-93. **HONORS/AWARDS:** Caterpillar Inc, Fellowship, 1991. **SPECIAL ACHIEVEMENTS:** Published over thirty technical papers. **BUSINESS ADDRESS:** Prof, Computer Sci & Information Systems Dept, Bradley University, 1501 W Bradley Ave, Peoria, IL 61625-0002, (309)677-2448.

LIU, JIE

Educator. Chinese American. **PERSONAL:** Born May 30, 1962, Gan Su, People's Republic of China; son of Quing-Luai Liu and Bao Ying Zhang; married Lan Chen, Mar 5, 1986; children: Sandy. **EDUCATION:** Northern Jiaotong University, BS, 1983; Oregon State University, MS, 1989, PhD, 1993. **CAREER:** Western Oregon State College, lecturer, 1989-93, assistant professor, 1993-. **ORGANIZATIONS:** ACM, 1989-. **BUSINESS ADDRESS:** Assistant Professor, Western Oregon State College, 345 N Monmouth Ave, ITC 306, Monmouth, OR 97361-1394, (503)838-8989.

LIU, JOHN J.

Educator. Chinese American. **PERSONAL:** Born Mar 22, 1951, Wuhan, Hubei, People's Republic of China; married Sherry S Liu, Dec 16, 1977; children: James X, Patrick Y. **EDUCATION:** Huazhong University of Science and Technology, MS, 1982; Stanford University, MS, 1983; Pennsylvania State University, PhD, 1986. **CAREER:** Huazhong University of Sci & Technology, lecturer, 1980-82; University of Wisconsin-Milwaukee, assistant professor of production, 1986-91, associate professor of production, 1992-. **ORGANIZATIONS:** American Production and Inventory Control Society, 1987-; National Association of Purchasing Management, PhD Committee, 1989-; Operations Research Society of America, 1984-; The Institute of Industrial Engineers, 1985-; Production/Operations Management Society, 1990-; Organization of Chinese Americans, 1988, Milw Chapter President, 1992. **HONORS/AWARDS:** UW-Milwaukee, Research Award, 1991, Graduate School Research Award, 1990. **BUSINESS ADDRESS:** Assoc Prof of Production & Management Science, School of Business Administration, University of Wisconsin-Milwaukee, Milwaukee, WI 53201, (414)229-3833.

LIU, JUANITA CHING

Educator. Chinese American. **PERSONAL:** Born Aug 9, 1947, Honolulu, HI; daughter of Albert Y A Ching and Winifred Lum Ching; divorced; children: Anthony K W, Deborah Y L. **EDUCATION:** University of Southern California, BA (magna cum laude), mathematics, 1969; University of Pennsylvania, MA, regional science, 1971, doctoral program, energy mgmt & policy, 1971-72; Simon Fraser University, PhD, geography, economics, 1979. **CAREER:** University of Hawaii, assistant professor, 1980-85, associate professor, 1985-89, professor, graduate chair, 1989-. **ORGANIZATIONS:** American Association of Geographers, 1979-; American Statistical Association, 1991-; Western Regional Science Association, 1980-; Travel and Tourism Research Association, 1987-. **HONORS/AWARDS:** University of Hawaii, Board of Regents Excellence in Teaching Award, 1993; BC Dept of Education, Grad Research Engineering and Technology Award, 1978-81; University of Southern Califor-

nia, Phi Beta Kappa, 1969, Distinquished Men and Women of Troy, 1969, Phi Kappa Phi, 1969. **SPECIAL ACHIEVEMENTS:** Published first tourism economic impact study for American affiliated Pacific Islands, 1987; published first tourism economic impact study for Western Canada, 1980; first woman to be promoted to full professor at the University of Hawaii, College of Business Administration, 1989. **BUSINESS ADDRESS:** Professor & Graduate Chair, School of Travel and Industry, University of Hawaii, 2560 Campus Rd, Honolulu, HI 96822, (808)956-6610.

LIU, JUN S.

Educator. Chinese American. **PERSONAL:** Born Apr 26, 1965, Beijing, People's Republic of China; son of Guopu Liu and Yuan Ge. **EDUCATION:** Beijing University, BS, 1985; Rutgers University; University of Chicago, PhD, 1991. **CAREER:** Harvard University, assistant professor, 1991-. **BUSINESS ADDRESS:** Assistant Professor, Dept of Statistics, Harvard University, 1 Oxford St, Science Center, 6th Floor, Cambridge, MA 02138-2901, (617)495-1600.

LIU, JYH-CHARN STEVE

Educator. Taiwanese American. **PERSONAL:** Born Dec 6, 1956, Kaohsiung, Taiwan; son of Gi-Chin Liu and Kim-Lien Chu Liu; married Bih-Yu Grace Liu, Dec 2, 1988; children: Brian Guan-Chun, Alexander Guan. **EDUCATION:** National Cheng-Kung University, Electrical Engineering Dept, BS, 1979, MS, 1981; University of Michigan, Ann Arbor, PhD, electrical engineering, 1989. **CAREER:** Sian-Teik Co., associate, 1983; University of Michigan, research associate, 1989; Texas A&M University, assistant professor, 1989-. **ORGANIZATIONS:** IEEE Computer Society, 1984-. **SPECIAL ACHIEVEMENTS:** "Area Wide Real-Time Traffic Control System, A New Concept for Traffic Control," IEEE Transaction Vehicle Technology, 1993; "A Tight Clock Synchronization Technique for Large Scale Parallel Processing System," Intl Journal on Circuit Theory and Applications, 1992; "An RAM Architecture for Concurrent Memory Accessing & Testing," IEEE Transactions on Computers, 1991; "Polynomial Testing of Padeet Switching Networks," IEEE Transactions on Computers, 1989; "A Cost-Effective Multistage Interconnection Network with Network Overlapping & Memory Interlearning," IEEE Transactions on Computers, 1985. **BUSINESS ADDRESS:** Asst Professor, Computer Science Dept, Texas A&M University, H R Bright Bldg, College Station, TX 77843, (409)845-8739.

LIU, KAREN CHIA-YU

Educator. Chinese American. **PERSONAL:** Born Jul 25, 1949, Taipei, Taiwan; daughter of Kuo-Yueh Liu and Hwa-Fong Liu; married Feng-Ou Frank Ko, Jul 29, 1974; children: William S Ko, Tiffany Ko. **EDUCATION:** National Taiwan Normal University, bachelor of education, 1972; Michigan State University, MA, 1976, PhD, 1982. **CAREER:** University of Minnesota-Waseca, associate professor, 1982-88; Indiana State University, associate professor, 1989-. **ORGANIZATIONS:** National Association for the Education of Young Children, 1982-; World Organization for Early Childhood Education, historian, 1989-; Indian Association for the Education of Young Children, board officer, 1989-; Association for Childhood Education International, research committee, 1990-; Indiana Association for Childhood Education International, board member, 1992-. **HONORS/AWARDS:** All-University Council on Aging, Research Grant Award, 1987; University of Minnesota, Personal Development Grant Award, 1985; Republic of China, National Development Foundation Fellowship Award, 1983, Outstanding Student Leadership Award, 1971. **SPECIAL ACHIEVEMENTS:** Author: "Early Experience of Cooperative Learning in Preschool," Contemporary Education, Vol LXIII, No 3, Spring 1992; "Children As Individual: Learning Styles and Ethnicity," Journal of the Ohio Elementary Kindergarten Nursery Educators, March 1992; "Multicultural Learning Styles," First Teacher, Vol 12, No 8, Sept/Oct, 1991; "Vive La Difference! Help Children Appreciate Racial and Cultural Differences," First Teacher, Vol 11, No 10, October, 1990. **BUSINESS ADDRESS:** Assoc Professor, Dept of Elementary and Early Childhood Educ, Indiana State University, 803 School of Education, Terre Haute, IN 47809, (812)237-2856.

LIU, KEH-FEI FRANK

Educator. Chinese American. **PERSONAL:** Born Jan 11, 1947, Beijing, China; son of Hsiang-Chang and Jui-Hua Liu; married Yao-Chin Liu, Apr 6, 1974; children: Helen, Alex. **EDUCATION:** Tunghai University, BS, 1968; SUNY, Stony Brook, MA, 1972, PhD, 1975. **CAREER:** CEN Saclay, visiting scientist, 1974-76; UCLA, postdoc, assistant professor, 1976-80; University of Kentucky, professor, 1980-. **ORGANIZATIONS:** American Physical Society, 1972-; European Physical Society, 1985-; Overseas Chinese Physicists Association, 1990-. **HONORS/AWARDS:** Humboldt Foundation, Alexander Von Humboldt Senior Scientist Award, 1990; University of Kentucky Research Professorship, 1992; Academia Sinica of China, First Prize in Theoretical Physics, 1987; DOE, Grand Challenge Award, 1988, 1989. **SPECIAL ACHIEVEMENTS:** Publications in refereed journals, 1974-; editor of review volume, Chiral Soliton, World Scientific. **BUSINESS ADDRESS:** Professor, University of KY, Dept of Physics & Astronomy, Lexington, KY 40506, (606)257-4849.

LIU, LEIGHTON KAM FAT
Educator. Chinese American. **PERSONAL:** Born Jul 23, 1944, Honolulu, HI; son of Edward Yet Far Liu & Margaret Yuen Soong Liu; married Wendie Shirley Liu, Aug 3, 1969; children: Marissa Noelle. **EDUCATION:** University of Hawaii, Manoa, BFA, 1968, MFA, 1971. **CAREER:** Leighton Liu Design, principal, 1968-88; Summer Day Camp, The American School in Japan, crafts specialist, English teacher, 1984-92; Design Strategies, principal, 1989-93; University of Hawaii, Department of Art, shop director, 1969-70, School of Architecture, instructor, shop director, 1971-76, assistant professor, 1976-83, associate professor, 1983-. **ORGANIZATIONS:** National Association for Museum Exhibition, 1992-94; National Trust for Historic Preservation, 1991-94; Historic Hawaii Foundation, 1991-94; Hawaii Museums Association, 1991-94; Design Communication Association, charter member, 1989-94; The Contemporary Museum, 1988-94; Honolulu Academy of Arts, 1990-94. **HONORS/AWARDS:** American Institute of Architecture Students, AIAS National Educator Honor Award, 1992; University of Hawaii, Merit Teaching Award, 1977, 1982, 1986, nominee, Excellence in Teaching Award, 1976, 1983; Flora Pacifica, Best of Show Design Excellence Award, 1974; Honolulu Academy of Arts, Purchase Award, 1971. **SPECIAL ACHIEVEMENTS:** Exhibition chair; exhibition designer; lecture series coordinator, "Contemporary Japanese Architecture," 1992; author, "Sequential Projects-Elements of Design," Representation Journal, 1991; designer, photographer, author, "The Principles of Design," series of 8 posters, 1989; producer, director, "Recognizing and Drawing Value," video, 17min, 1981; producer, director, "Selecting a Point of View for a Drawing," video, 21min, 1981. **BUSINESS ADDRESS:** Associate Professor, University of Hawaii, School of Architecture, 1859 East-West Rd, Honolulu, HI 96822-2287, (808)956-8311.

LIU, LILI
Student, community service worker. Taiwanese American. **PERSONAL:** Born Jul 2, 1971, Hsinchu, Taiwan; daughter of Chin Kwan Liu & Chun Jong Liu. **EDUCATION:** University of Washington, BS, psychology, 1993; Columbia University, post-baccalaureate pre-medical program, 1994. **CAREER:** Temple Day Care, assistant teacher, 1987-88; City of Seattle, head counselor, summer day camp, 1988-90; University of Washington, Central Animal Surgery, student helper, 1991, Medical Genetics, laboratory assistant, 1991-93. **ORGANIZATIONS:** Chinese Students Association, president, vice-president, secretary, 1990-92; Student Buddhism Association, founder, representative, finance & budget, 1989-92; Asian Students Commission, assistant director, 1992-93; Alpha Epsilon Delta Pre-Medical Honor Society, 1990-91; Mortar Board National Senior Honor Society, alumna, 1992-; Taiwanese Students Association, 1990-92; Children's Hospital and Medical Center, volunteer, 1985-86; University of Washington Medical Center, volunteer, 1989-90; St Luke's Roosevelt Hospital, volunteer, 1993-94. **HONORS/AWARDS:** University Lions Club, scholarship, 1989; John Margaret Nelson Fund, scholarship, 1989; PEMCO Financial Center, scholarship, 1992. **HOME ADDRESS:** 11404 Roosevelt Way NE, Seattle, WA 98125.

LIU, LILY PAO-IH
Educator. Chinese American. **PERSONAL:** Born Nov 4, 1941, Shanghai, China; daughter of C H Tsiang and S Y Zee Tsiang; married George S Liu, Aug 21, 1966; children: Pai Tse, Jan Tse. **EDUCATION:** Tokyo University of Arts; Ricks College; California College of Arts & Crafts, BFA. **CAREER:** Palo Alto Times, commercial artist, 1966-67; Micro Science Associates, technical illustrator, 1967-70; Star Photofabrication, graphic designer, 1970; Central Advertising Co, graphic designer, 1979-84; Oldsmobile Division-General Motors Corp, computer graphics, 1985; Lansing Community College, asst professor, 1986-. **ORGANIZATIONS:** National Computer Graphics Assn, 1989-; American Cancer Society, volunteer, 1990-; Ingham County Health Department Breast & Cervical Cancer Control Program, volunteer, 1992-; Arthritis Foundation, volunteer, 1988-90. **HONORS/AWARDS:** Lansing Community College, Certificate of Employee Recognition, 1992, Special Person Award, 1992; National Computer Graphics Educational Foundation, Full Scholarship, 1989; Clip Bits Magazine, Outstanding Creative Graphic Design, 1982, 1983; Na-

tional Comm Sign Design Contest, Fourth Place, 1980. **SPECIAL ACHIEVEMENTS:** Helped establish Computer Graphics Program, Lansing Community College, and organized cirriculum committee for program, 1986; presentations & lectures to Michigan Community College Educator's Conference, 1989. **BIOGRAPHICAL SOURCES:** Sing Tao Daily News, p 16, 1989; Open Line, LCC, p 12, 1989. **HOME ADDRESS:** 5110 Country Dr, Okemos, MI 48864, (517)347-0739. **BUSINESS ADDRESS:** Asst Professor, Lansing Community College, 315 N Grand Ave, Ace Bldg, Rm 310, Lansing, MI 48901, (517)483-1476.

LIU, LIN CHUN
Federal official. Taiwanese American. **PERSONAL:** Born Jul 21, 1963, Taipei, Taiwan; daughter of Shean Lun Liu and Swei Yu Chen Liu. **EDUCATION:** University of California, Berkeley, BA (with honors), 1986; Harvard University, Kennedy School of Government, MPP, 1989. **CAREER:** Congressman Norman Y Mineta, legislative correspondent, 1986-87; The Rand Corp, policy analyst, 1989-91; Office of Management & Budget, Executive Office of the President, policy analyst, 1991-. **ORGANIZATIONS:** Conference on Asian Pacific American Leadership, founding member, 1989-; Association of Public Policy Analysis & Management, 1987-. **HONORS/AWARDS:** Sloan Foundation/Association of Public Policy Analysis & Management, Fellow, 1987; OMB Performance Award, 1992. **SPECIAL ACHIEVEMENTS:** RAND note on the implementation of the State Legalization Impact Assistance Grant Program, 1991. **BUSINESS ADDRESS:** Policy Analyst, Office of Management & Budget, 725 17th St NW, New Executive Office Bldg, Rm 9215, Washington, DC 20009, (202)395-3442.

LIU, LOUIS F.
Print shop owner. Taiwanese American. **PERSONAL:** Born Jun 17, 1931, Kwang-Fu, Taiwan; son of Tien-Tai Liu and Si-Mei Teng; married Heidi Liu, Dec 2, 1979; children: Tod, Tony, Teddy. **EDUCATION:** Taiwan Normal University, bachelor's degree, English, 1955; University of Michigan, teaching English as a second language, 1962; Golden Gate University, MBA, accounting, 1969. **CAREER:** Ventura County Assessor, auditor, appraiser, 1972-82; Quick Printing Plus, owner, 1982-. **HONORS/AWARDS:** Fulbright Foundation, Fulbright Scholarship, 1961. **BUSINESS ADDRESS:** Owner, Quick Printing Plus, 6477 Telephone Rd, Ste 7, Ventura, CA 93003, (805)654-1707.

LIU, MAW-SHUNG
Educator. Taiwanese American. **PERSONAL:** Born Feb 2, 1940, Taiwan; son of Chao-Tung & Chian Hwang Liu; married Min-Chau Liu, Sep 15, 1966; children: Chien-Ye. **EDUCATION:** Kaohsiung Medical College, Taiwan, DDS, 1964; University of Kentucky, MSc, 1970; University of Ottawa, Canada, PhD, 1976. **CAREER:** Louisiana State University, School of Medicine, assistant professor, 1976-78; Bowman Gray School of Medicine, Wake Forest University, associate professor, 1978-82; St Louis University, School of Medicine, professor, 1982-. **ORGANIZATIONS:** Shock Society, 1978-; American Physiological Society, 1976-; International Society for Heart Research, 1978-. **HONORS/AWARDS:** HIH, Surgery, Anesthesiology, and Trauma Study Section, 1988-92; Nanjing Medical University, honorary professor, 1984; Hunan Medical University, honorary professor, 1988; visiting professor, Beijing Medical University, 1984, 1986, 1992, Zhejiang Medical University, 1986, 1988, Kovharing Medical College, 1989-; Chang Gung Medical College, 1989-. **SPECIAL ACHIEVEMENTS:** Editorial board, Circulatory Shock, 1980-; Shock, 1994-. **BIOGRAPHICAL SOURCES:** Published more than 60 full-length papers and 60 abstracts in areas of shock and trauma, in professional peer-reviewed journals. **BUSINESS ADDRESS:** Prof, Dept of Pharmacological & Physiological Science, St Louis University School of Medicine, 1402 S Grand Blvd, St Louis, MO 63104-1004, (314)577-8244.

LIU, MENGXIONG
Educator, librarian. Chinese American. **PERSONAL:** Born Dec 17, 1946, Shanghai, China; daughter of Tianxiong Liu and Xiaomeng Qin; married Tian Song, Sep 24, 1973; children: David Song. **EDUCATION:** Shanghai International Studies University, BA, 1968; University of Denver, MA, 1983; University of Michigan, PhD, 1990. **CAREER:** Taught courses at the Univ of California, Berkeley; Shanghai Light Industry Corp Lib, head librarian, 1968-77; Shanghai Research Inst of Pharmaceutical Industry, info spec, 1977-82; United Nations /UNFPA, interpreter, 1979-82; University Microfilms Int'l, research intern, 1985-87; Adult Learning Systems, information specialist, 1987-89; San Jose State University, School of Info & Lib Science, adjunct professor, Clark Library, engineering librarian, 1989-; University of Michigan, lecturer; University of California Berkeley Extension, lecturer. **ORGANIZA-**

TIONS: American Library Association, 1984-, Research and Statistics Committee, 1993-95; American Society for Information Science, 1987-; Association of Library & Information Science Education, 1988-; Chinese-American Librarians Association, CALA, newsletter editor, California Chapter, president, 1985-; Special Libraries Association, 1986-. **HONORS/AWARDS:** Beta Phi Mu International Library Science Honorary Society, life member, 1983-; SJSU Foundation, GSSP Grant and Affirmative Action, Faculty Development Grant, 1989-92; PEO, International Peace Scholarship, 1985; Barbour Scholarship for Oriental Women, 1984-86; American Association of University Women, fellowship, 1982. **SPECIAL ACHIEVEMENTS:** Publications on scientific citing process in information science prof journals, numerous presentations at professional conferences of ALA, ACRL, SLA, etc; proficient in Chinese. **BUSINESS ADDRESS:** Engineering Librarian, Clark Library, San Jose State University, One Washington Square, San Jose, CA 95192-0028, (408)924-2817.

LIU, MIN
Educator. Chinese American. **PERSONAL:** Born Jul 15, 1959, Shanghai, People's Republic of China; married. **EDUCATION:** East China Normal University, BA, 1982; West Virginia University, MA, 1990, EdD, 1992. **CAREER:** East China Normal University, instructor, 1982-86; West Virginia University, computer consultant at HRE Microlab, 1986-90, research assistant at Research & Training Center, 1987-90, assistant director of HRE Microlab, 1990-93; University of Texas, Austin, assistant professor, 1993-. **ORGANIZATIONS:** Phi Delta Kappa, newsletter editor, 1988-89; Eastern Educational Research Association, 1989-; American Educational Research Association, 1990-; Association for Advancement of Computing in Education, 1990-; Association for Development of Computer-Based Instructional System, 1989-; Computer Assisted Language Learning, 1990-; International Society for Technology in Education, 1989-. **HONORS/AWARDS:** Eastern Educational Research Association, Meritorious Research Award, 1993; Phi Delta Kappa, Outstanding Student Research Award, 1993. **SPECIAL ACHIEVEMENTS:** Author of several publications, including: "Hypermedia-assisted-instruction and Second Language Learning: A Semantic-network-based Approach," in Hypermedia in the Schools, Computers in the Schools, 1993; with W Michael Reed, "The Comparative Effects of BASIC Programming Versus HyperCard Programming on Problem-Solving, Computer Anxiety and Performance," in Hypermedia in the Schools, Computers in the Schools, 1993; co-author, "The relationship between the learning strategies and learning styles in a Hypermedia environment," Journal of Computers in Human Behavior, in press. **BUSINESS ADDRESS:** Asst Professor of Instructional Technology, Dept of Curriculum & Instruction, The University of Texas at Austin, Austin, TX 78712, (512)471-5211.

LIU, MING CHENG
Educator. Taiwanese American. **PERSONAL:** Born Nov 18, 1951, Hwa-Lien, Taiwan; son of Sui-An Liu and Ah-Jyu Liu; married Angel Wang Liu, May 8, 1953; children: David R, Kathy W. **EDUCATION:** Fu-Jen Catholic University, BS, 1974; Arizona State University, MS, 1978, PhD, 1987. **CAREER:** Arizona State University, visiting assistant professor, 1987-88; Wichita State University, assistant professor, 1988-. **ORGANIZATIONS:** Institute of Industrial Engineers, Wichita Chapter, 1986-, president, 1992-93; ASQC, 1987-. **HONORS/AWARDS:** Wichita State University, Dwane & Velma Wallace Teaching Award, 1993; IIE, Graduate Research Award, Adviser, 1992. **SPECIAL ACHIEVEMENTS:** ASOC Certified Quality Engineer, 1991; ASOC Certified Reliability Engineer, 1992. **BIOGRAPHICAL SOURCES:** Quality Engineering, vol 5, no 3, p 392, 1993. **BUSINESS ADDRESS:** Asst Professor, Dept of Industrial Engineering, Wichita State University, Wichita, KS 67260-0035, (316)689-3425.

LIU, MINI
Physician. Chinese American. **PERSONAL:** Born Apr 17, 1949, Minneapolis, MN. **EDUCATION:** Harvard University, BS, 1971; George Washington University, MD, 1978. **CAREER:** NENA Community Health Center, physician, 1981-88; Gouverneur Diagnostic & Treatment Center, attending physician, 1988-. **ORGANIZATIONS:** Asian American Union for Political Action, 1987-; Organization of Asian Women, 1982-. **BUSINESS ADDRESS:** President of the Board of Directors, Committee Against Anti-Asian Violence, 191 E 3rd St, New York, NY 10009, (212)473-6485.

LIU, NANCY SHAO-LAN
Artist, editor, writer. Chinese American. **PERSONAL:** Born Mar 8, 1932, Shanghai, China; daughter of Ching-Dea & Zao-Hwa Lee; married Rueywen

Liu, Aug 18, 1957; children: Alexander, Theodore. **EDUCATION:** University of California, Berkeley, BA, 1954, 1977-78; Harvard University, MEd, 1955; University of Illinois, MA, 1958. **CAREER:** Saint Mark's Social Center, preschool teacher, 1955-56; University of Illinois, Audio-Visual Department, editorial staff, 1958-59; National Taiwan University, lecturer in English department, 1969; Holy Cross College, professor, 1970-71; Indiana University, lecturer, 1975, 1976, continuing education instructor, 1979-89; Convergence Magazine, co-publisher, editor, writer, 1976-. **ORGANIZATIONS:** Saint Joseph Medical Center Auxiliary, financial secretary, 1989-90; Ladies of Notre Dame, director, 1993-95. **SPECIAL ACHIEVEMENTS:** 14th Biennial Michiana Regional Art Competition, 1986. **HOME ADDRESS:** 1929 Dorwood Dr, South Bend, IN 46617, (219)233-2914.

LIU, NORA M.
Housing development consultant. Chinese American. **PERSONAL:** Born Jun 10, 1956, Urbana, IL; daughter of Geoffrey Hao-Wen Liu & Lucille Chang Liu. **EDUCATION:** Harvard University, AB, 1978; University of Washington, MArch, 1990. **CAREER:** Wediko Children's Services, counselor, therapist, 1981-83; Preterm, health educator, counselor, 1982-83; Rich, Lang & Cote, designer, drafter, 1983-84; Lois Champy Design, designer, drafter, 1984-85; Geise Assoc in Architecture Inc, designer, drafter, 1985-87; Fremont Public Assn, housing project manager, 1991-. **ORGANIZATIONS:** Homestead Community Land Trust, board member, 1991-92; Tenants Union, board member, 1992-93. **HONORS/AWARDS:** Valley Scholarship; AIA Scholarship. **SPECIAL ACHIEVEMENTS:** Author: "Feminism & Domestic Architecture: Fact, Fiction & Fancy," thesis, 1990. **HOME ADDRESS:** 403 14th Ave E, Seattle, WA 98112.

LIU, PETER CHI-WAH
Educator. Hong Kong American. **PERSONAL:** Born Sep 1, 1957, Hong Kong; son of Hing Fun Liu and Hing Lam; married Wai H Yu, May 21, 1986; children: Nil. **EDUCATION:** Chinese University of Hong Kong, BS, 1982, MP, 1984; University of Florida, MA, 1989, PhD, 1989. **CAREER:** University of Miami, assistant professor, currently. **ORGANIZATIONS:** American Economic Association; Econometric Society; American Statistical Association. **SPECIAL ACHIEVEMENTS:** Published paper in: Journal of Intl Money & Finance, 1992; Empirical Economics, 1992; Weltwirtschaftliches Archiv, 1992; Statistical Papers, 1993; Economic Inquiry, 1994. **BUSINESS ADDRESS:** Assistant Professor, University of Miami, PO Box 248126, 517 Jenkins Bldg, Coral Gables, FL 33124, (305)284-5540.

LIU, PING
Educator. Chinese American. **PERSONAL:** Born Aug 27, 1959, Nankang, Jiangxi, People's Republic of China; son of Qianqiu Liu and Xinyin Li; married Susan X Shao, Aug 27, 1985; children: Annie. **EDUCATION:** Jiangxi Polytechnic Institute, BS (with distinction), 1982; Zhejiang University, MS, 1984; Iowa State University, PhD, 1991. **CAREER:** Zhejiang Institute of Technology, assistant professor, 1984-87; Eastern Illinois University, assistant professor, 1991-. **ORGANIZATIONS:** American Society for Mechanical Engineers, 1992-; American Society for Quality Control, 1992-; American Society for Metals, 1988-; Society of Manufacturing Engineers, 1991-. **HONORS/AWARDS:** American Society for Quality Control, Certified Quality Engineer. **SPECIAL ACHIEVEMENTS:** Author of 15 published papers on materials property, development and recycling. **BIOGRAPHICAL SOURCES:** "Professors Focus on Plastics," Charleston, IL, Times-Courier, p A8, Nov 30, 1992. **BUSINESS ADDRESS:** Assistant Professor, Eastern Illinois University, School of Technology, 101 Klehm, Charleston, IL 61920-3011, (217)581-6267.

LIU, PINGHUI VICTOR
Educator. Chinese American. **PERSONAL:** Born Feb 9, 1924, Fenshan, Taiwan; son of Chin-eng Liu and Chulan Liu; married Chiameng Judy Liu, Aug 10, 1959; children: Nancy J, Albert J. **EDUCATION:** Tokyo Jikei-kai School of Medicine, MD, 1947; Tokyo Medical College, Japan, PhD, 1957. **CAREER:** University of Louisville School of Medicine, professor of microbiology, currently. **BUSINESS ADDRESS:** Professor of Microbiology, University of Louisville Sch of Med, Health Science Center, Louisville, KY 40292, (502)588-5363.

LIU, QING-HUO
Research scientist. Chinese American. **PERSONAL:** Born Feb 4, 1963, Huian, Fujian, People's Republic of China; son of Yi-Kuan Liu and Le Wang; married Li-Tong Liu, Aug 22, 1987; children: Winston Jing-Yang. **EDUCATION:**

Xiamen University, BS, 1983, MS, 1986; University of Illinois, Urbana-Champaign, PhD, 1988. **CAREER:** University of Illinois, research assistant, 1986-88, research associate, 1989-90; Schlumberger-Doll Research, research scientist, 1990-. **ORGANIZATIONS:** IEEE, 1988-; SPWLA, 1991-; SEG, 1992-. **HONORS/AWARDS:** Xiamen University, Distinguished Student Award, 4 awards, 1980-83. **SPECIAL ACHIEVEMENTS:** Author, "A Modeling Study of EPT in Complicated Borehole Environments," Log Analyst, vol 30, p 424, 1989; "NMN Method for the Multi-Region, Vertically Stratified Media," IEEE Trans Antennas Propegat, 1990; "Surface Integral Equation Method for the Analysis of an Obliquely Stratified Half-Space," IEEE-April, 1990; "EM Field Generated by an Off-Axis Source in a Cylindrically Layered Medium," Geophysics, 1993; "Reconstruction of Two-Dimension Axisymmetric Media," IEEE Trans Geoscience Remote Sensing, 1993. **BIOGRAPHICAL SOURCES:** IEEE Trans Geoscience Remote Sensing, vol 289, p 313, 1991; IEEE Trans Microwave Theory Technology, vol 39, p 430, 1991. **BUSINESS ADDRESS:** Research Scientist, Schlumberger-Doll Research, Old Quarry Rd, Ridgefield, CT 06877, (203)431-5537.

LIU, RAY H. (JUEI-HO)
Educator. Taiwanese American. **PERSONAL:** Born Apr 3, 1942, Taitung, Taiwan; son of Ku Liu and Tsan Huang; married Hsiu-Lan, Dec 4, 1965; children: Yu-Ting, Eugene, Hubert. **EDUCATION:** Central Police College, Taiwan, LLB, 1965; Indiana University, Bloomington, 1969-71; Southern Illinois University, PhD, 1976. **CAREER:** University of Illinois at Chicago, assistant professor, 1977-80; US Enviromental Agency, Chicago, mass spectrometrist, 1980-82; US Department of Agriculture, Philadelphia, Research Center, mass spectrometrist, 1982-83; University of Alabama at Birmingham, associate professor, 1984-89, professor, 1989-, program director, 1991-. **ORGANIZATIONS:** American Academy of Forensic Sciences, fellow, 1977-; American Chemical Society, 1976-; American Society for Mass Spectrometry, 1981-; American Association for Clinical Chemistry, 1979-; Sigma Xi, 1976-. **HONORS/AWARDS:** Central Police College, Taiwan, Distinguished Alumni Award, 1991; Taiwanese National Science Council, visiting professorship, 1981, 1993; NASA, NASA Summer Faculty Fellowship, 1992; New York State Department of Health, Certificate of Qualification, lab director, 1989-; US Department of Health National Lab Certification Program, lab inspector, 1988-. **SPECIAL ACHIEVEMENTS:** Editor-in-chief, Forensic Science Review, 1989-; book author: Approaches to Drug Sample Differentiation, 1981; over 50 scientific articles published in refereed journals; 5 invited book chapters; over 60 scientific meeting presentations. **MILITARY SERVICE:** Army, Taiwan, lt, 1966-67. **BUSINESS ADDRESS:** Professor, Program Dir, Dept of Criminal Justice, University of Alabama at Birmingham, Graduate Program in Forensic Science, Birmingham, AL 35294, (205)934-2069.

LIU, RICHARD CHUNG-WEN
AIDS/HIV educator. Taiwanese American. **PERSONAL:** Born Jul 10, 1970, Annapolis, MD; son of Laurence Liu and Ling Ling Liu. **EDUCATION:** Drexel University, BA, 1994. **CAREER:** Livengrin Foundation, Inc, advertising, 1989-90; CoreStates Financial Corp, special events, 1991; Earle, Palmer, Brown & Spiro, public relations, 1992; AIDS Task Force of Philadelphia/Philadelphia Community Health Alternatives, special projects coordinator, 1991-. **ORGANIZATIONS:** Mayor's Commission on Sexual Minorities, City of Philadelphia, commissioner, appointed, 1992-; AIDS Information Network of Philadelphia, Executive Committee, Safeguards Project, 1991-92; Asian Americans United, 1992-; Sexual Minority Youth Roundtable of Philadelphia, chair, 1992-; Public Relations Society of America, 1990-; Bread and Roses Community Fund, Community Funding Board, member, 1993-. **HONORS/AWARDS:** Philadelphia Gay News Lambda Award, Outstanding Emerging Leader, 1992; Men of All Colors Together-Philadelphia, Dr Gerald L Mallon Resisting Racism Award, 1992. **HOME ADDRESS:** 21 S Strawberry St, Apt 4C, Philadelphia, PA 19106. **BUSINESS PHONE:** (215)545-8686.

LIU, SAMUEL HSI-PEH
Research scientist. Chinese American. **PERSONAL:** Born Apr 17, 1934, Taiyuan, China; married Annabel L Liu, 1961; children: Andrea, Clifton. **EDUCATION:** National Taiwan University, BS, 1954; Iowa State University, MS, 1958, PhD, 1960. **CAREER:** IBM Research Center, research staff, 1960-64; Iowa State University, associate professor, 1964-67, professor, 1967-81; Oak Ridge National Lab, senior scientist, 1981-89, corporate fellow, 1989-. **ORGANIZATIONS:** American Physical Society, 1959-66, fellow, 1966-, executive committee, 1985-87; American Association for the Advancement of Science, 1985-; Sigma Xi, 1959-.

LIU, SHIA-LING
Educator. Chinese American. **PERSONAL:** Born May 23, 1922, Hunan, China; married Lilyon C Liu, Jun 28, 1957; children: Alexander, Daniel, Vivian. **EDUCATION:** National Cheng Chi University, BA, 1945; University of Cincinnati, MA, 1949; New York University, 1949-52; University of North Texas, EdD, 1963. **CAREER:** Executive Yuan, ROC, staff, 1945-46; Yu Yao District Court, judge, 1946-47; National Cheng Chi University, associate professor, 1956-57; Chinese Journal, NYC, editor, 1950-56; Ministry of Education, ROC, committee, executive secretary, 1950-59; Jarvis Christian College, professor, 1959-63; Fayetteville State University, dept chairman, professor, 1963-92, professor emeritus. **ORGANIZATIONS:** Phi Delta Kappa, 1963-; Association of Chinese Studies, 1978-; Association of Asian Studies, 1972-; American Political Science Association, 1963-; Association of Chinese Social Scientists in North America, 1985-. **SPECIAL ACHIEVEMENTS:** Author: American Domestic and Foreign Policies, 1970, 1974; Adventures of Three American Presidents in Asia, 1983; American Domestic and Foreign Policies in the Last Decades of 20th Century, 1994; Democracy, Freedom and ROC-PRC Relations, 1994. **BUSINESS ADDRESS:** Professor Emeritus, Fayetteville State University, 1200 Murchison Rd, Fayetteville, NC 28301-4298.

LIU, SI-KWANG
Veterinary pathologist, educator. Taiwanese American. **PERSONAL:** Born in Kweshun, Kwangsi, China; son of Yeeshao & Shinwei; married Sing-ping Chueh, Dec 20, 1961; children: David, Earnest, Diana, Phillip. **EDUCATION:** Veterinary College of the Chinese Army, DVM; University of California, PhD; Veteran General Hospital, Bronx, New York, Pathology Fellow. **CAREER:** National Taiwan University, instructor & chief vet lab, 1956-59; University of California, School of Veterinarian Medicine, research assistant, 1959-64; National Science Council, ROC, visiting expert, 1976, 1983, 1988, 1991; National Taiwan University, visiting professor, 1976, 1983, 1988, 1991; The Animal Medical Center, pathologist, chairman, senior staff, 1964-; New York Zoological Society, consulting pathologist, scientific fellow, 1964-; Pig Research Institute, Taiwan, ROC, senior investigator & consultant, 1984-. **ORGANIZATIONS:** The Animal Medical Center, cardiovascular research, pathologist, 1964-; Animal Center, Bronx Zoo, training programs, head, 1967-, research programs, head, 1972-90, pathology training programs, head, 1965-; The Animal Medical Center Bone Research Program, head, 1970-; Pig Research Institute, Taiwan, cardiovascular research, 1984-; Cornell University, College of Medicine, molecular cardiology research, 1990-. **HONORS/AWARDS:** Ralston Purina Company, Feline Disease Research Excellence Award, 1982; Carnation Company, Outstanding Achievement in Vet Medicine, 1984; Beecham Award, Research Excellence, 1986; New York City & New York State Veterinary Association, Outstanding Service Awards, 1991; Chinese Veterinary Association, Outstanding Veterinary Research, 1993. **SPECIAL ACHIEVEMENTS:** First discovered heart muscle diseases in cats & dogs, 1970, 1975; first discovered vitamin E deficiency in zoo animals similar to human vitamin E deficiency, 1980; described animal models for human diseases, 1970-90; first discovered swine heart muscle diseases similar to human heart muscle disease, 1991; author, An Atlas of Cardiovascular Pathology, 1989, publication of over 150 papers. **MILITARY SERVICE:** Chinese Army, ROC, Veterinary Corps, major. **HOME ADDRESS:** 182-49 80th Road, Jamaica, NY 11432. **BUSINESS PHONE:** (212)838-8100.

LIU, STEPHEN SHU-NING
Educator. Chinese American. **PERSONAL:** Born Mar 16, 1930, Chungking, Sichuan, China; married Shirley, Dec 23, 1965; children: Miranda, April. **EDUCATION:** Nanking University, China, BA, Chinese, 1948; Wayland Baptist University, BA, English, 1956; University of Texas, MA, English, 1958; University of North Dakota, PhD, English, 1973. **CAREER:** Northern Montana College, assistant professor of English, 1966-69; Southwest Teachers University, visiting lecturer, 1980; Sichuan Teachers University, visiting lecturer, 1980; College of San Mateo, visiting lecturer, 1968; Baijing Normal University, visiting professor, 1989-90; University of North Dakota, teaching assistant, 1970-73; Community College of Southern Nevada, professor of English, 1973-. **HONORS/AWARDS:** Nevada Governor's Award for literature, 1985; MacDowell Colony, New Hampshire, Writing Fellow, 1984; Pen Syndicate Fiction Project, Short Fiction Contest, winner, 1983; National Endowment for the Arts, Creative-Writing Fellowship Grant for Poetry, 1981-82. **SPECIAL ACHIEVEMENTS:** Dream Journeys to China (bilingual format), 1992; poems appeared in college texts such as X J Kennys Literature, New Worlds of Literature, 1989, Literature, ed by Kirszner and Mandell, 1991. **BIOGRAPHICAL SOURCES:** China Today, May 1993; Chinese American Poetry, University of Washington Press, 1991; Desert Wood: An Anthology of

Nevadan Poetry, University of Nevada Press, 1991. **HOME PHONE:** (702)871-5987. **BUSINESS ADDRESS:** Professor of English, Community College of Southern Nevada, West Charleston Campus, 6375 W Charleston Blvd-WIA, Las Vegas, NV 89102-1124, (702)877-1133.

LIU, SU-FENG
Economist. Taiwanese American. **PERSONAL:** Born Dec 30, 1934, Chiayi, Taiwan; son of Chong and Tsai-Tzin Liu; married Mei-Li Kao, 1962; children: Wayne, Linda, Edward. **EDUCATION:** Chung-Hsing University, BSc, 1958; Research Institute of Agricultural Economics, MSc, 1960; University of Illinois, PhD, 1966. **CAREER:** University of Illinois, graduate assistant, 1962-66; Organization of American States, chief economist, 1966-. **ORGANIZATIONS:** American Economic Association. **BUSINESS ADDRESS:** Chief Economist, Dept of Economic and Social Affairs, Organization of American States, 1889 F Street, Room #320-A, Washington, DC 20006, (202)458-3136.

LIU, SUSANA JUH-MEI
Librarian. Chinese American. **PERSONAL:** Born Oct 16, 1942, Fuchien Province, China; daughter of Siyi & Karl Chen; married Gerald Chien-wu Liu, 1966; children: Lawrence Chia-lun, Michael Chia-ting. **EDUCATION:** National Chung Hsing University, BA, sociology and social work, 1963; Case Western Reserve University, MLS, 1966; San Jose University, MA, instructional technology, 1980. **CAREER:** Cleveland State University Library, catalog librarian, 1966; University of Missouri Library, catalog librarian, 1966-69; Rice University Library, catalog librarian, 1969-70; Texas A&M University Library, Catalog Maintenace Dept, head, 1970-74; Foothill College Library, acquistions librarian, 1974-75; Stanford University Library, catalog librarian, 1975-76; San Francisco City College Library, reference librarian, 1976-77; San Jose State University Library, Serials Dept, head, 1977-86, special services coordinator & ref librarian, 1986-. **ORGANIZATIONS:** Chinese American Economic & Technology Development Association, board of directors & treasurer, 1993-; Chinese-American Librarians Association, Awards Committee, chair, 1992-93, Public Relation Committee, chair, 1990-92, Constitution & Bylaws Committee, chair, 1987, board member, 1984-86, Books to China Project, chair, 1983-84, president, 1983; California Academic and Research Librarians, 1980-; California Library Association; California Society of Librarians, director, 1984-85, councilor, 1988-90, Technical Services Chapter, Program Planning Committee, 1984-86, Serials Discussion Group North, chair, 1984-86; American Library Association, 1966-; Texas Library Association, 1969-74; Missouri Library Association, 1966. **HONORS/AWARDS:** California State University: Award for Research, Scholarship and Creative Activities, 1990, Affirmative Action Faculty Development Program Grant Award, 1985, 1987; Meritorious Performance and Professional Promise Award, 1988, 1989; participant, National Development Seminar, Education Committee, Republic of China, 1988; San Jose State University, Faculty Development Travel Grant, 1988; South Bay Cooperative Library System, Meritorious Services Award for Multi-type Networking Activities, 1988. **SPECIAL ACHIEVEMENTS:** Author of: "East Asian Language Works in the San Jose State University Library," San Jose State University, 1988; library presentation to the People's Republic of China, sponsored by Library Association of Central Government Units & Scientific Research Networks and the National Central Library, sponsored by the Chinese Librarians Association and the National Central Library, Republic of China, 1988. **BUSINESS ADDRESS:** Special Service Coordinator & Reference Librarian, San Jose State University, Clark Library, One Washington Square, San Jose, CA 95192, (408)924-2805.

LIU, TALLY C.
Newspaper executive. **PERSONAL:** Born 1950. **EDUCATION:** Florida Atlantic University, Graduate School of Business Administration, 1977. **CAREER:** Knight-Ridder Inc, vice president, controller, currently. **ORGANIZATIONS:** American Institute of CPAs; International Newspaper Financial Executives, Minority Affairs Committee, cochairman. **BUSINESS ADDRESS:** VP/Controller, Knight-Ridder Inc, One Herald Plaza, Miami, FL 33132, (305)376-3800. *

LIU, TE-HUA
Physician. Chinese American. **PERSONAL:** Born Dec 21, 1924, Chun Chow, China; daughter of Zienchin Qian; married Chi-chien Kao, Apr 16, 1950; children: Diana K Chu, Frank F Kao, Winifred Kao. **EDUCATION:** National Shanghai Medical College, MD, 1950; Shanghai First Medical College, postgraduate radiology residency, 1950-54; Saint Luke's Roosevelt Hospital Center, 1980-83; Columbia University, College of Physicians and Surgeons, visiting clincial fellow, 1980-83. **CAREER:** Shanghai First Medical College,

attending radiologist, instructor, 1954-60, deputy director of department of radiology, teaching assistant professor, 1960-78, deputy director of research, 1968-80; Temple University, assistant professor, attending radiologist, 1983-87, associate professor, chief of neuroradiology, 1987-92, professor of radiology & neurosurgery, chief of neuroradiology, 1992-. **ORGANIZATIONS:** American Society of Neuroradiology, senior member, 1984-; Radiological Society of North America, 1980-; Eastern Neuroradiological Society, 1990-; Association of Program Directors in Radiology, 1992-. **SPECIAL ACHIEVEMENTS:** Books: co-editor, textbook of x-ray diagnosis for medical students, 1963; Diagnostic Radiology, main author and editor of vol 2, co-editor of vol 1 and vol 3; co-author, Magnetic Resonance Imaging & CT of Musculo-skeletal System; 25 articles published in radiological journals. **HOME PHONE:** (215)741-0269. **BUSINESS ADDRESS:** Professor of Radiology and Neurosurgery, Temple University Hospital, 3410 N Broad St, Parkinson Pavilion, Philadelphia, PA 19140, (215)707-4210.

LIU, THOMAS
Government official. Chinese American. **PERSONAL:** Born Jan 11, 1944, San Francisco, CA; son of Tso Nom Liu and Chin Shee Liu; married Lorelyn Allison Liu, Jun 12, 1966; children: Stephen Gregory. **EDUCATION:** City College of San Francisco, AA, history, 1965; San Francisco State college, BA, public administration, 1967. **CAREER:** Internal Revenue Service, revenue officer, 1968-78, group manager, 1978-83, regional analyst, 1983, branch chief, 1983-89, assistant division chief, 1989-92, regional problem resolution officer, 1992-94; executive assistant to the regional compliance officer, 1994-. **ORGANIZATIONS:** IRS, Speakers Panel, 1973-77, classroom instructor, 1975-80, upward mobility counselor, recruiter and career counselor, 1970-73, EEO complaints investigator, 1979-81; Northern California Oriental Peace Offficers Association, charter member, 1980-83; Villa Tahoe Condominium Association, board of directors, president, 1991-93. **HONORS/AWARDS:** Internal Revenue Service, Performance Award, Distinguished Rating, 1983-92, Special Act Award, 1969, Superior Performance Award, 1973, EEO Award of Excellence, 1988. **BUSINESS ADDRESS:** Executive Assistant to the Regional Officer, Internal Revenue Service-Western Regional Office, 1650 Mission St, Ste 410, San Francisco, CA 94103, (415)556-3035.

LIU, THOMAS JYHCHENG
Educator. Taiwanese American. **PERSONAL:** Born Sep 12, 1956, Keelung, Taiwan; son of Wen-Kwang Liu and Chiou-Shern Liu; married Yu-Chun Liu, Jul 17, 1988; children: Esther, Samuel. **EDUCATION:** Tatung Institute of Technology, BS, 1979; University of Illinois, Chicago, MS, 1983, 1985, PhD, 1988. **CAREER:** Tatung Institute of Technology, Taipei, teaching & research assistant, 1979-81; University of Illinois, Chicago, teaching assistant, 1983-84, research assistant, 1985-88; University of Florida, Gainesville, research scientist, 1988-90; Argonne National Laboratory, visiting scientist, 1993; Lebanon Valley College, professor, 1990-. **ORGANIZATIONS:** Tau Beta Pi; Phi Kappa Phi; I-EEE Computer Society; Electrochemical Society; National Association of Corrosion Engineers; American Mathematical Society; American Computing Machinery Society; Mathematical Association of America. **SPECIAL ACHIEVEMENTS:** Author: "Application of Kalman Filter in Modeling of Galvanostatic and Potentiostatic DC Transient Techniques for the Determination of Kinetic Parameter of Electrode Reactions," to be published; "Corrosion of Chromium Containing Alloys in Non-steady State Environments Containing Oxygen, Carbon, and Chlorine," J Physique, Oct, 1993; "Effects of Temperature Variations on Oxidation/Chlorination of Iron-Chronium Alloys," to be published; languages: Chinese, Japanese, German. **BUSINESS ADDRESS:** Professor, Lebanon Valley College, 101 N College Avenue, Annville, PA 17003-1400, (717)867-6085.

LIU, TSU-HUEI
Supervisory engineer. Chinese American. **PERSONAL:** Born Mar 10, 1943, Kwei-yang, Kwei-chou, China; daughter of Ke-chang Lee Liu and Chien Liu; married Kai-Hwa Ger, Jun 20, 1971; children: Kwang-yi Ger, Kwang-chien Ger. **EDUCATION:** Natl Taiwan University, BS, 1964; University of Oregon, PhD, 1969. **CAREER:** Portland State University, asst professor, 1969-75; Bonneville Power Administration, section chief, 1975-. **ORGANIZATIONS:** CAN/AM EMTP User Group, co-chairman, 1991-. **BUSINESS ADDRESS:** Chief, Planning Methods Section, Bonneville Power Administration, PO Box 3621 - EOHB, Portland, OR 97208, (503)230-4401.

LIU, WARREN KUO-TUNG
Computer software company executive. Chinese American. **PERSONAL:** Born Oct 26, 1952, Taipei, Taiwan; son of Calvin Liu and Yun-Mei Yao;

married Ingrid Liu, Dec 19, 1976; children: Amy, Alexander, Bernard. **EDU-CATION:** City College of New York, BS, 1975; University of Wisconsin, Madison, MS, 1976; Harvard Business School, MBA, 1981. **CAREER:** AT&T Long Lines, supervisor, market research, 1979; Lockheed/Cadam, planning and development manager, 1981-85; McDonnell Douglas, marketing and planning director, 1985-89; Warefront Technologies, international operations director, 1989-91; Schlumberger/Applicon, vice president, 1991-. **ORGANIZA-TIONS:** Harvard Business School Club of St Louis, board member, 1987-89; American Marketing Association, 1991-; Harvard Business School Club of St Louis, treasurer, 1989; USA-ROC Economics Council, technology committee member, 1993. **HONORS/AWARDS:** General Motors Corp, GM Fellow, 1980; Lockheed Management Institute, 1982; Lockheed Leadership Institute, 1984; McDonnell Douglas Advanced Management Conference, 1987; Schlumberger Forum, 1991. **SPECIAL ACHIEVEMENTS:** Grew Warefront Technologies' international business by 1000% in 18 months; fluent in Chinese; proficient in German. **BIOGRAPHICAL SOURCES:** World Journal, December 26, 1992, Sing Tao Daily, Nov 28, 1992; People's Daily Overseas Edition, Nov 20, 1992; Industry Week, p 42, Jan 4, 1993. **HOME ADDRESS:** 4701 Vorhies Rd, Ann Arbor, MI 48105, (313)665-2335. **BUSINESS AD-DRESS:** Vice President, Business Development, Schlumberger Measurement & Systems, 12, Lorong Bakar Batu #07-07/11, 65-746-9676.

LIU, WEI-MIN
Educator. Chinese American. **PERSONAL:** Born Dec 24, 1945, Shanghai, China; married Hao-Qing Chen, Sep 15, 1972; children: Jing. **EDUCATION:** Shanghai College of Mechanical & Electrical Engr, BS equivalent, 1968; Shanghai Institute of Biochemistry, MS, 1981; Cornell University, MS, 1986, PhD, 1987. **CAREER:** Shanghai Institute of Biochem, research assistant professor, 1982-83; University of Kentucky, visiting scholar, 1989; Indiana University-Purdue University at Indianapolis, assistant professor, 1987-93, associate professor, 1993-. **ORGANIZATIONS:** Society for Industrial & Applied Math, 1990-; Society for Mathematical Biology, 1987-. **HONORS/AWARDS:** International Center for Theoretical Physics, UNESCO, travel grants, 1981, 1986; Cornell University, Liu's Award for Outstanding Chinese Students, 1985, Mathematical Sciences Institute Fellowship, 1986-87; IUPUI, Summer Faculty Fellowship, 1988; Boston University, research awards, 1991, 1992. **SPECIAL ACHIEVEMENTS:** Mathematical models of chemical and biological problems; using graph-theoretical rules for calculations in quantum chemistry and chemical kinetics; using bifurcation theory to explain the origins of chirality of biomolecules; modeling recurrent outbreaks of infectious diseases; pharmacodynamical models; distance geometry. **BUSINESS AD-DRESS:** Professor, Dept of Math & Science, Indiana University-Purdue University at Indianapolis, 402 N Blackford St, LD 3224D, Indianapolis, IN 46202-3216.

LIU, WEI-YING
Banking executive. Chinese American. **PERSONAL:** Born in Shanghai, People's Republic of China; married James C Lok. **EDUCATION:** University of Maryland, BA, economics, 1974. **CAREER:** Abu Dhabi Intl Bank, asst vice pres, money market dealer, 1985-. **ORGANIZATIONS:** Assn Cambiste Internationale, Forex USA, 1985-. **BUSINESS ADDRESS:** Assistant Vice President, Abu Dhabi International Bank, 1020 19th St NW, Ste 500, Washington, DC 20036, (202)842-7980.

LIU, WING KAM
Educator. Hong Kong American. **PERSONAL:** Born May 19, 1952, Hong Kong; son of Yin Lam Liu and Chan Shiu Lin Liu; married Betty Hsia, Dec 12, 1986; children: Melissa Margaret, Michael Kevin. **EDUCATION:** University of Illinois, Chicago, BS (highest honors), engineering science, 1976; California Institute of Technology, MS, 1977, PhD, 1981. **CAREER:** University of Illinois at Chicago Circle, Material Engineering, research assistant, 1974-76; California Institute of Tech, Engineering & Applied Science, research assistant, 1976-80; Northwestern University, Mechanical & Nuclear Engineering, assistant professor, 1980-83; Civil Engineering, assistant professor, courtesy appt, 1982-83, associate professor, courtesy appt, 1983-88, associate professor, full professor, 1988-. **ORGANIZATIONS:** American Society of Civil Engineers, fellow, Computational Mechanics Committee, vice-chairman & chairman, 1987-91; American Society of Mechanical Engineers, fellow, Computing in Applied Mechanics Committee, vice-chairman & chairman, 1991-95; Journal of Pressure Vessel Technology, associate editor, 1989-95; United States Association for Computational Mechanics, member at large, 1991-; American Academy of Mechanics, treasurer, 1983-88; Journal of Applied Mechanics, associate editor, 1993-95. **HONORS/AWARDS:** American Society of Me-

chanical Engineers, Melville Medal, 1979, Pi Tau Sigma Gold Medal, 1985, fellow, 1990; American Society of Automotive Engineers, Ralph R Teetor Educational Award, 1983; International Association for Structural Mechanics in Reactor Technology, Thomas J Jaeger Prize, 1989; American Society of Civil Engineers, fellow, 1993. **SPECIAL ACHIEVEMENTS:** Published 5 books & over 200 papers in journals & proceedings; co-editor: Innovative Methods for Nonlinear Problem, 1984, Computational Mechanics of Probabilistic Reliability Analysis, pp 622, 1989; principal/co-principal investigator for projects sponsored by Natl Sci Foundation, US Army Research Office, NASA Langley & NASA Lewis, Office of Naval Research, Air Force Office of Scientific Research, General Electric Co & Chrysler Corp; consultant to Argonne Natl Lab, Hughes Inc, Battelle Columbus Labs, ZACE Svcs, Switzerland; Grumman Aerospace Corp, Centric Engineering Inc, Mitsubishi Heavy Industries, Japan, Kawasaki Heavy Industries, Japan. **BUSINESS ADDRESS:** Professor, Mechanical Engineering Dept, Northwestern University, 2145 Sheridan Road, Technological Institute, Evanston, IL 60208-3111, (708)491-7094.

LIU, XINGWU
Researcher, educator. Chinese American. **PERSONAL:** Born Aug 14, 1942, Heilongjiang, China; son of Jinhe Liu and Zixian Gao; married Lingjuan Liu, 1972; children: Yongsong. **EDUCATION:** Heilongjiang University, China, honors, 1965; Chinese Academy of Social Sciences, Graduate School, MA, 1981. **CAREER:** Ministry of Light Industry, China, project officer & interpreter, 1965-81; Institute of Nationality Studies, Chinese Academy of Social Sciences, associate research fellow, deputy director of global ethnic studies, 1981-; Oregon State University, visiting associate professor, 1989-90; DePaul University, associate professor, 1990-; World Culture Institute, China Programs, director, currently. **ORGANIZATIONS:** Development Innovations & Networks, board member, 1987-; Society for Applied Anthropology, honorary fellow, 1986-; American Anthropological Association, 1992-, fellow, 1993; Chinese Association for Global Ethnic Studies, deputy secretary general, 1986-90; Chinese Association for South Asian Studies, standing council member, 1987-. **HONORS/AWARDS:** Oregon State University, Outstanding Service Award, 1986. **SPECIAL ACHIEVEMENTS:** Author: Sri Lanka, Chinese language, 1984; contributions to Cihai (Great Lexicon of China), Encyclopedia Sinica, etc; numerous articles & papers; languages: Chinese, English; read French & Russian. **HOME PHONE:** (312)335-9236. **BUSINESS ADDRESS:** Director, China Programs, World Culture Institute, 135 NW 25th St, Corvallis, OR 97330, (503)752-5940.

LIU, YILU
Educator. Chinese American. **PERSONAL:** Born Jan 4, 1959, Chengdu, People's Republic of China; daughter of Zichen Feng and Xiulan Liu; married Fei Wang. **EDUCATION:** Xian Jiaotong University, BS, 1982; Ohio State University, MS, 1985, PhD, 1989. **CAREER:** General Electric, faculty intern, 1993; Virginia Polytechnic Institute & State University, assistant professor, 1990-. **ORGANIZATIONS:** IEEE, working group member, 1985-; Power Engineering Society. **HONORS/AWARDS:** National Science Foundation, Young Investigators Award, 1993. **SPECIAL ACHIEVEMENTS:** Published numerous research papers in IEEE Transactions and International Journals on V electrical power systems and energy systems. **BUSINESS ADDRESS:** Professor, Electrical Engineering, Virginia Tech, Blacksburg, VA 24061-0111, (703)231-3393.

LIU, YING
Educator. Chinese American. **PERSONAL:** Born Jun 29, 1961, Beijing, People's Republic of China; son of Guong Jun Liu and HuiQiong Xie Liu; married Gina Porter Liu, Dec 28, 1991; children: Tiffany Porter. **EDUCATION:** Lanzhou University, BS, physics, 1982; Carnegie-Mellon University, MS, physics, 1984, PhD, physics, 1988; University of South Carolina, MS, computer science, 1990. **CAREER:** Lanzhou University, physics program, 1978-82; Carnegie-Mellon University, physics program, 1982-88; University of South Carolina, computer science program, 1988-90; Savannah State College, assistant professor of computer science, 1990-. **ORGANIZATIONS:** Sigma Xi; IEEE Compute Society; IEEE Information Theory Society; IEEE System, Man & Cybernetic Society; International Society for Optical Engineering; International Society for Computing & Their Application. **SPECIAL ACHIEVEMENTS:** More than 50 conference and journal papers including: "Continuous-Tone Image Recognition Using Fractal Theory," Proc SPIE, Vol 2060, September, 1993; "Pattern Recognition Using Stochastic Neural Networks," Proc SPIE, Vol 2055, September, 1993; "Attractor Identification and Prediction for Iterative Dynamical Systems," Proc SPIE, Vol 2037, July, 1993;

"Image Compression Using Boltzmann Machines II," Proc SPIE, Vol 2032, July, 1993; "Image Compression Using Boltzmann Machines I," Proc World Congress on Neural Networks '93, July, 1993. **BUSINESS ADDRESS:** Professor, Dept of Math & Computer Science, Savannah State College, Savannah, GA 31404-9701, (912)356-2309.

LIU, YUAN HSIUNG
Educator. Taiwanese American. **PERSONAL:** Born Feb 24, 1938, Tainan Shen, Taiwan; son of Chun Chang Liu and Wong Kong Liu; married Ho Pe Tung, Jul 27, 1973; children: Joan Anshen, Joseph Pinyang. **EDUCATION:** National Taiwan Normal University, BEd, 1961; National Chengchi University, MEd, 1967; University of Alberta, MEd, 1970; Iowa State University, PhD, 1975. **CAREER:** Nan Ning Junior High School, teacher of industrial arts and mathematics; 1961-64; Chung-Cheng Institute of Technology, instructor of technical math, 1967-68; Sundstrand Hydro-Transmission Corporation, drafter, 1973-75; Fairmont State College, lead instructor of drafting/design program, 1975-80; Sinclair Community College, drafting instructor, 1985; Miami University, associate professor, 1980-85; Southwest Missouri State University, professor, 1985-. **ORGANIZATIONS:** Four-State Conference, trade & industrial program, co-chairperson, 1988, general session program, co-chairperson, 1989; American Design Drafting Association, 1975-86, 1992-; National Association of Industrial Technology, 1975-80, 1988-89; American Society for Engineering Education, 1980-. **HONORS/AWARDS:** Fairmont State College, West Virginia, Excellent Teaching in Drafting Award, 1978; National Chengchi University, Taiwan, National Long-Term Scientific Development Award, 1967, Dr C T Wu's Outstanding Scholastic Award, 1965. **SPECIAL ACHIEVEMENTS:** "Making Color Transparencies and Slides with Computer-Aided Drafting Equipment," School Shop/Tech Directions, vol 50, no 4, p 27, November, 1990; "Angle Ellipse vs Isometric Ellipse," Engineering Graphics Journal, pp 79-82, November 1989; "Give Drafting/Design Students Real-World Experiences In Industry," School Shop, pp 25-26, October 1988; "Challenge Students to Find Top and Right Side Views," School Shop, p 24, February 1985; "10 Steps To An Industry Project," VocEd, vol 60, p 23, January/February 1985. **MILITARY SERVICE:** The Infantry Army of the Republic of China, Taiwan, second lieutenant, 1962-63; Outstanding Military Skills and Knowledge Award, 1963. **BUSINESS ADDRESS:** Professor, Southwest Missouri State University, 901 S National, Kemper Hall, Room 103 Q, Springfield, MO 65804-0094, (417)836-5443.

LIU, YUNG SHENG
Scientist, consultant. Chinese American. **PERSONAL:** Born Sep 23, 1944, China; son of HC Liu & LW Wang Liu; married Ming Lee, Nov 22, 1969; children: Alan, Jenny. **EDUCATION:** National Taiwan University, Taiwan, BS, 1966; Cornell University, PhD, 1973. **CAREER:** Cornell University, research associate, 1968-72; General Electric, senior scientist, 1972-; SUNY at Albany, adjunct professor, 1986-. **ORGANIZATIONS:** IEEE, 1978-; Optical Society of America, 1972-; Materials Research Society, 1978-; American Physical Society, 1972-; National Development Conference, ROC, 1982, 1984. **HONORS/AWARDS:** General Electric, Outstanding Achievement Award, 1977, Gold Medal Patent Award, 1989, Publication Award, 1989; Cornell University, Cornell Fellow, 1970, AVCO Fellow, 1969. **SPECIAL ACHIEVEMENTS:** Max Planck Society, Germany, lecturer, 1989, 1991, UN Development Program, China, consultant, 1986. **MILITARY SERVICE:** Air Force ROC, lieutenant, 1966-67. **BUSINESS ADDRESS:** Senior Scientist, General Electric Co, 1 River Rd, Bldg KW, Rm B1307, Schenectady, NY 12301.

LIU, YUNG-WAY
Educator. Taiwanese American/Chinese American. **PERSONAL:** Born Jun 16, 1955, Taipei, Taiwan; son of Mr & Mrs T C Liu; married Chung-Yuan C Liu, Jun 1, 1981; children: Wei-Han Bobby, Wei-Ning Eddie. **EDUCATION:** National Taiwan University, BS, 1977; University of Delaware, MS, 1981, PhD, 1987. **CAREER:** University of Delaware, teaching assistant, 1979-87; Tennessee Technological University, assistant professor, 1987-92, associate professor, 1992-. **ORGANIZATIONS:** American Mathematical Society; Society for Industrial and Applied Mathematics; Mathematical Association of America. **SPECIAL ACHIEVEMENTS:** Author: A Boundary Integral Equation for the Two-Dimensional Floating-Body Problem, 1991; Rotatability Laws for N-Bar Kinematic Chains and Their Proof, 1991; Rotatability Laws for Spherical N-Bar Kinematic Chains, 1992. **BUSINESS ADDRESS:** Professor, Mathematics Dept, Tennessee Tech University, Box 5054, Cookeville, TN 38505-0001, (615)372-3564.

LIU, YUNG Y.
Engineer. Chinese American. **PERSONAL:** Born Mar 20, 1950, Taipei, Taiwan; son of Kan C and Mu-Wen Liu; married Teresa L Liu, Jan 4, 1975; children: Sharon H Y, Alvin H L. **EDUCATION:** National Tsing-Hua University, Taiwan, BS, 1971; Massachusetts Institute of Techonology, MS, 1976, ScD, 1978. **CAREER:** Entropy Limited, engineer, 1977-78; Argonne National Laboratory, assistant nuclear engineer, 1978-82, nuclear engineer, 1983-. **ORGANIZATIONS:** American Nuclear Society, 1978-; American Society for Metals, 1978-. **HONORS/AWARDS:** American Nuclear Society, Materials and Technology Division, Significant Contribution Award, 1992. **SPECIAL ACHIEVEMENTS:** Project Manager, behavior of metal fuels under simulated reactor accident conditions, 1988-; principal investigator, corrosion-erosion of materials in advanced fossil technologies, 1986-88; task manager, fusion solid breeder materials, 1982-86. **MILITARY SERVICE:** Air Force, Taiwan, ROC, 2nd lt, 1971-73. **HOME ADDRESS:** 333 Hampton Pl, Hinsdale, IL 60521, (708)986-5908. **BUSINESS PHONE:** (708)252-5127.

LIU, ZHUANG (LILY)
Educator. Chinese American. **PERSONAL:** Born Oct 24, 1932, Shanghai, China; daughter of Liu Ren Xi and Xiong You Cheng; married Li Yan Sheng, Apr 29, 1957; children: Li Yan, Li Lu. **EDUCATION:** Shanghai Conservatory of Music, BM, 1956, MM, 1958. **CAREER:** Central Philharmonic Orchestra of China, first class composer, 1969-89; Syracuse University, visiting Fulbright professor, 1989-91, adjunct professor, 1991-. **ORGANIZATIONS:** Musician Society of China, 1959-; Sino-American Music Research Society in China, council member, 1984-; Film Music Society in China, council member, 1982-; Phi Beta Delta, 1991-. **HONORS/AWARDS:** United States Information Agency, Fulbright Asian Scholar in Residence, 1989; Chinese Ministry of Culture, Creativity Award for Woodwind Quintet, 1982, National Symphonic Creativity Award for Symphonic Picture "Plum Blossom Triptych," 1981; Chinese Film Society, Best Motion Picture Award, Gold Rooster, 1986. **BIOGRAPHICAL SOURCES:** People's Daily of China, Pg 8, June, 1987; People's Music of China, Pg 24-28, Vol 8, 1987; Hong Kong New Evening News, Pg 24, Nov 6, 1992. **BUSINESS ADDRESS:** Adjunct Professor, School of Music, Syracuse University, 100 Crouse College, Syracuse, NY 13244-1010, (315)443-5895.

LIU, ZHUANGYI
Educator. Chinese American. **PERSONAL:** Born May 2, 1954, Shanghai, People's Republic of China; son of Shenxiang Liu and Ruilan Chen; married Junyi Tu Liu, Feb 25, 1992; children: Jieming. **EDUCATION:** Virginia Polytechnic Institute and State University, MS, 1986, PhD, 1989. **CAREER:** University of Minnesota, assistant professor, 1989-. **ORGANIZATIONS:** SIAM, 1988-. **SPECIAL ACHIEVEMENTS:** Approximations of thermoelastic and viscoelastic control systems, 1990; Exponential stability of semigroup associated with thermoelastic system, 1991; On the energy decay of a linear thermoelastic bar, 1992; Uniform exponential stability and approximation in control of thermoelastic systems, 1993; On the exponential stability of linear viscoelasticity and thermoviscoelasticity, 1993. **BUSINESS ADDRESS:** Assistant Professor, Department of Mathematics and Statistics, University of MN Duluth, 10 University Drive, 108 Heller Hall, Duluth, MN 55812-2496, (218)726-7179.

LO, CHI-YUAN
Telecommunication company administrator. Chinese American. **PERSONAL:** Born May 21, 1952, Hsinchu, Taiwan; son of Ching-Mou Lo; married Jan Lo, Aug 8, 1977; children: Lewen, Leyan, Justin. **EDUCATION:** National Taiwan University, China, BS, 1974; University of Texas, Austin, MS, 1978; Rutgers University, PhD, 1992. **CAREER:** Honckels Haas & Brown Inc, systems analyst, 1978-80; AT&T/Bell Laboratories, technical staff mbr, 1980-84, technical mgr, 1984-. **ORGANIZATIONS:** IEEE, 1978-; ACM, 1990-. **HONORS/AWARDS:** Best Paper Award nominee, for "Cell-Based Pitchmaking Compaction Using Minimal LP.". **SPECIAL ACHIEVEMENTS:** Author: over 20 technical publications on Very-Large Scale Integration Computer-Aided Design (VSLI CAD); with David Dutt, "Method of Integrated Circuit Manufacturing Including Cell Assembly," US Patent 5,229,231, July 20, 1993. **MILITARY SERVICE:** Republic of China Navy, ensign, 1974-76. **BUSINESS ADDRESS:** Technical Manager, AT&T/Bell Laboratories, 600 Mountain Ave, 3B 415, Murray Hill, NJ 07974.

LO, CHIEN-KUO
Educator. Chinese American. **PERSONAL:** Born Jul 9, 1946, Nanking, Chiang-su, China; son of Shou-yen Lo & Hwa-yin Chiang Lo; married Hsiao-

jung Yu, Aug 15, 1971; children: Leon Li-yen. **EDUCATION:** National Cheng Kung University, Taiwan, Republic of China, BS, 1969, MS, 1972; University of Iowa, PhD, hydraulics, 1981. **CAREER:** Hydro Research Science, hydraulic engineer, 1979-81; Bechtel Civil Co, hydraulic engineer, 1981-83; California Polytechnic State University, professor, 1983-. **ORGANIZATIONS:** American Water Resources Association, 1983-; Chi Epsilon, National Civil Engineers Honor Society, 1985-; Phi Beta Delta, Honor Society for International Scholars, 1989-. **HONORS/AWARDS:** Chi Epsilon, Chapter Honor Member, 1987. **SPECIAL ACHIEVEMENTS:** Publications of more than 30 papers and technical articles. **BUSINESS ADDRESS:** Professor, Civil & Environmental Engineering Dept, California Polytechnic State University, San Luis Obispo, CA 93407, (805)756-2947.

LO, HOWARD H.
Educator. Taiwanese American/Chinese American. **PERSONAL:** Born Sep 3, 1937, Hsinchu, Taiwan; married Polly B Lo, Dec 1965; children: Wilbur, Gilbert. **EDUCATION:** National Taiwan University, BS, 1960; University of Minnesota, MS, 1964; Washington University, PhD, 1970. **CAREER:** Geological Survey of Taiwan, junior geologist, 1960-62; University of Minnesota, research assistant, 1962-64; Opemiska Copper Mines, Ltd, mine geologist, 1964-65; Ottawa Collegiate Institute, Canada, instructor, 1965-67; Washington University, St Louis, research assistant, 1967-70; Cleveland State University, assistant professor, associate professor, professor, 1970-. **ORGANIZATIONS:** American Geophysical Union, honor member, 1968-; Ohio Academy of Science, vice president, 1991-93, membership coordinator, 1992; Chinese American Faculty Association, vice president, 1990-92, president, 1992-; Chinese Academy of Greater Cleveland, president, 1978-79; Taiwanese Association of Greater Clevelend, board officer, 1985-. **HONORS/AWARDS:** Washington University, University Fellowship, Wheeler Fellowship, 1967-70; National Science Foundation, COSIP, 1972-73; Cleveland State University, Class I Scholar Awards, 1979, 1981; Ohio Education, Economic Act Program, 1986-87; Ohio Department of Development, Thomas Alva Edison Program, 1988-91. **SPECIAL ACHIEVEMENTS:** "Contact Oxidatic Process. . .Textile Wastewater Treatment," Acta Hydrochim, 1988; "Optimizing Coagulation. . .for Turbidity Removal," International Journal Environment Studies, 1989; "Wastewater Treatment. . .Earth Materials as Coagulants," Journal Environment Health, 1990; "Utilization of Clays & Zeolites. . .Wastewater Treatment," Intl Journal Environment Studies, 1991; "Activated Sludge Treatment of Municipal Wastewater," Intl Journal Environment Studies, 1992. **BUSINESS ADDRESS:** Prof, Dept of Geological Sciences, Cleveland State University, Euclid Ave at East 24th St, Cleveland, OH 44115, (216)687-4821.

LO, KWOK-YUNG (FRED)
Educator. Chinese American. **PERSONAL:** Born Oct 19, 1947, Nanjing, Jiangsu, China; son of Pao-Chi Lu and Ju-hwa Hsu; married Helen Chen Lo, Jan 1, 1973; children: Jan-Hsin, Derek Pei-Hsin. **EDUCATION:** MIT, SB, 1969, PhD, 1974. **CAREER:** Caltech, research fellow, 1974-76, senior research fellow, 1978-80, assistant professor of radio astronomy, 1980-87; University of Illinois, professor of astronomy, 1987-. **ORGANIZATIONS:** American Astronomical Society, 1970-; International Astronomical Union, 1978-; American Association for Advancement of Science, 1989-. **HONORS/AWARDS:** University of California, Berkeley, Miller Institute, Miller Fellow, 1976-78; University of Illinois, Center for Advanced Study, Associate, 1991-92; Alexander von Humboldt Award, 1994-95. **SPECIAL ACHIEVEMENTS:** Over 100 publications, 1970-. **BUSINESS ADDRESS:** Professor, Astronomy Dept, University of Illinois, 1002 W Green St, Urbana, IL 61801, (217)333-9381.

LO, SAMUEL E.
Cleric. Taiwanese American. **PERSONAL:** Born Nov 23, 1931, Tainan City, Taiwan; son of Shiong and Khi Lo; married Charlotte M H Lo, Jul 23, 1983; children: Calvin Eric, Burton Judson. **EDUCATION:** Boston University, MDiv, 1962; Harvard University, certificate, 1963; New York University, PhD, 1968; Point Loma College, MA (magna cum laude), 1988; Somerset University, England, PhilD, 1989. **CAREER:** Various Presbyterian Churches, NY, pastor, 1960-68; Seton Hall University, professor, 1968-73; Tainan and Taiwan Theological Seminaries, professor, 1981-85; Flamingo Garden Inc, managing director, 1986-89; Canaan Christian Church, English pastor, 1989-91; Taiwanese Presbyterian Church, pastor, 1991-. **ORGANIZATIONS:** Council on Scientific Study of Religion, 1960-80; American Academy of Religion, 1960-80; Philosophical Association of America, 1960-80; American Association of University Professors, 1960-80; Association for Asian Studies, 1960-80; Presbytery of Newton, The Presbyterian Church, USA, 1969-. **HONORS/AWARDS:** New York University, Honors Scholar, 1968; American Historical Association, fellowships, 1970-71. **SPECIAL ACHIEVEMENTS:** Tillichian Theology and Educational Philosophy, Philosophical Library Inc, 1970; proficient in 4 languages. **HOME ADDRESS:** 4 Wenonah Ave, Lake Hiawatha, NJ 07034, (201)316-8126.

LO, SUZANNE J.
Librarian. Chinese American. **PERSONAL:** Born Apr 23, 1950, Berkeley, CA; daughter of Bock Seow Gee and Hong Ting Chin; divorced; children: Roxanne Lo. **EDUCATION:** University of California, Berkeley, BA, sociology, 1972, MLS, 1973. **CAREER:** San Francisco Public Library, adult reference librarian, 1974-76, children's librarian, 1976-83; Oakland Public Library, Asian Branch, senior librarian, 1983-. **ORGANIZATIONS:** Library Information Technology Association, OCLC Minority Scholarship Comm, 1992; American Library Association, Louise Giles minority scholarship commitee, 1993-94; Association of Library Service to Children, selection var culture comm, 1992-94; Library Administration Management Association, cultural diversity committee, 1993-95; Public Library Association, international relation committee, 1993-95; California Library Association, minority services committee, 1992-94; Chinese American Librarians Association, vice president, president, 1989-90, treasurer, 1992-94; University of California, Berkeley, Library School Alumni Association, board of directors, 1992-93. **HONORS/AWARDS:** East Bay Asian Local Development Corporation, Hearts of Gold, individual honoree, 1993; University of California, Los Angeles, GSLIS, California State Lib, transition into mgt scholarship, 1992; City of Oakland Volunteer Program, Service Award, 1991. **SPECIAL ACHIEVEMENTS:** "Asian Images in Children's Books," Emergency Librarian, May-June 1993; contributor: Global Voices, Global Vision, Bowker, 1994; Our Family, Our Friends, Our World, Bowker, 1992; Venture into Cultures, ALA, 1992; Developing Library Collections for California's Emerging Majority, BALIS, 1990. **BUSINESS ADDRESS:** Branch Senior Librarian, Asian Branch, Oakland Public Library, 449 9th St, Oakland, CA 94607, (510)238-3400.

LO, TOU GER (TONG)
Steel company machinist. Hmong American/Laotian American. **PERSONAL:** Born Sep 7, 1947, Lao People's Democratic Republic; son of Say Chou Lo; married May Lo, Feb 18, 1972; children: Lee, Davee, Lisa, John, Jeanie, Michael. **CAREER:** Twin City Shipyard, welder; Emery Corp, machinist, currently. **ORGANIZATIONS:** Hmong Assn of Long Beach, CA; Hmong Mission Church of North Carolina. **MILITARY SERVICE:** Laos Army, 1962-75. **BIOGRAPHICAL SOURCES:** National Geographic, 1986. **HOME ADDRESS:** 4138 Scott Rd, Morganton, NC 28655. **BUSINESS PHONE:** (704)433-1536.

LO, YAO
Association administrator. Laotian American. **PERSONAL:** Born Jan 1, 1950, Nonghet, Xieng Khouang, Lao People's Democratic Republic; son of Chia Lue Lo; married X Mai Kao Lo, Feb 1972; children: Cheng Seng, Ky, Julie, George. **EDUCATION:** St Paul Technical College, degree, 1979. **CAREER:** St Paul Technical College, interpreter, 1979-81; Lao Family Community, STRIDE coordinator, 1982-. **BUSINESS ADDRESS:** Coordinator, STRIDE, Lao Family Community of Minnesota, 976 W Minnehaha Ave, St Paul, MN 55104.

LO, YUEN-TZE
Electrical engineer. Chinese American. **PERSONAL:** Born Jan 31, 1920, China; married 1953; children: two. **EDUCATION:** Natl Southwest Assoc Unversity, BS, 1942; University of Illinois, MS, 1949, PhD, electrical engineering, 1952. **CAREER:** Tsinghua University, Radio Research Institute, asst, 1942-46, instructor, 1946-48; Yenching University, instructor, 1946-48; Channel Master Corp, project engineer, 1952-56; consultant at numerous companies, including: Westinghouse, 1957-58, Andrew Corp, 1963, Emerson Electric, 1968-69, IBM, 1969, Ford Aerospace, 1986, Lockheed; University of Illinois at Urbana-Champaign, Electromagnetics Lab, from asst professor to professor, 1956-90, director, 1982-90, professor emeritus, 1990-. **ORGANIZATIONS:** Northwest Telecommunications Engineering Institute, China, honorary professor; Northwest Polytech University, honorary professor; Sigma Xi; Natl Academy of Engineering; Intl Union Radio Science. **HONORS/AWARDS:** IEEE, John T Bolljahn Memorial Award, 1964, Centennial Medal, 1984; Halliburt Engineering, Education and Leadership Award, 1986. **BUSINESS ADDRESS:** Professor Emeritus, Dept of Electrical Engineering, University of Illinois, 1406 W Green St, Urbana, IL 61801. ∗

LOCK, CHUCK CHOI

Contractor, inventor, manufacturer. Chinese American. **PERSONAL:** Born Dec 30, 1930, Canton, Fat Sun, China; son of Sally Chan & Chee Park Lock; married Pearl Lock, Nov 23, 1963; children: Johnston Paul, Lewis Miles George. **EDUCATION:** University of Vancouver, 1952-53. **CAREER:** Lock Electro-Acupuncture Devices, owner, manufacturer, 1974-80; Lock Electric Company, president, owner, 1977-. **ORGANIZATIONS:** Asia Inc. **SPECIAL ACHIEVEMENTS:** First Asian to receive any patent in the United States for point finder, 1975, treatment machine, 1976. **HOME ADDRESS:** 144 Sixth Avenue, San Francisco, CA 94118.

LOCKE, GARY F.

County executive, state official. Chinese American. **PERSONAL:** Born Jan 21, 1951, Seattle, WA; son of James and Julie; divorced. **EDUCATION:** Yale University, AB, 1972; Boston University, JD, 1975. **CAREER:** King County Prosecutor's Office, deputy prosecutor, 1976-80; State Senate, staff attorney, 1981; Seattle Human Rights Dept, legal advisor, 1981-82; Garvey Shubert Adams and Barer, office counsel, 1984-85; US West Communications, community development manager, 1988-92; Washington State Legislature, state representative, 1983-93; King Co, Washington, county executive, currently. **ORGANIZATIONS:** Board member: United Way; Washington Wildlife and Recreation Coalition; Northwest Regional Educational Laboratory; Seattle Chongqing Sister City Foundation; Northwest AIDS Foundation, honorary; Planned Parenthood of Seattle-King County, 1989-; Market Foundation, 1988-. **HONORS/AWARDS:** Boy Scouts of America, Eagle Scout, Vigil Honor Member of the Order of The Arrow; Washington State Retired Teachers Association, Legislative Excellence Award, 1992; The ARC, Distinguished Community Service Award, 1992; Children's Hospital Medical Center, Appreciation Award, 1992; Issaquah Alps Trails Club, Outstanding Elected Official, 1991; Northwest AIDS Foundation, Friendship Award, 1992. **BUSINESS ADDRESS:** King County Executive, 400 King County Courthouse, 516 3rd Ave, Seattle, WA 98104-3271.

LODHI, M. A. K.

Educator. Pakistani American/Indo-American. **PERSONAL:** Born Sep 17, 1933, Agra, Uttar Pradesh, India; son of Addul Hakim Khan Lodhi; married Khalida, Jun 15, 1973; children: Asra, Saima, Sundus. **EDUCATION:** University of Karachi, BSc, 1952, MSc, 1956; Imperial College London, DIC, 1960; University of London, PhD, 1963. **CAREER:** Texas Tech University, professor, 1963-. **ORGANIZATIONS:** American Physical Society, 1970-. **HONORS/AWARDS:** American Association Muslim Scientists and Engineers, Al-Khawarzsni Award, 1988. **SPECIAL ACHIEVEMENTS:** One hundred-seventy professional articles and books, 1965-93. **HOME ADDRESS:** 5421 7th St, Lubbock, TX 79416, (806)799-7788. **BUSINESS ADDRESS:** Professor, Dept of Physics, Tex Tech University, Science Bldg Rm 111, Lubbock, TX 79409, (806)742-3778.

LOH, EUGENE C.

Educator. Chinese American. **PERSONAL:** Born Oct 1, 1933, Soochow, China; son of Hung-Yu Loh and Chen-Cheu Sun Loh; married Jocelyn D Loh, Dec 25, 1958; children: Stephen, Stanton, Stewart. **EDUCATION:** Virginia Polytechnic Institute, BS, 1955; MIT, PhD, 1961. **CAREER:** MIT, assistant professor, 1962-64; Cornell University, senior research associate, 1964-75; University of Utah, associate professor, 1975-77, professor, 1977-, Department of Physics, chairman, 1980-89, High Energy Astrophysics Institute, director, 1993-. **ORGANIZATIONS:** American Physical Society, fellow; European Physical Society; American Association of Physics Teachers; American Association of the Advancement of Science. **HONORS/AWARDS:** State of Utah, Governor's Medal of Science, 1987; University of Utah, Distinguished Researcher Award, 1993. **BUSINESS ADDRESS:** Professor, University of Utah, 311 JFB Building, Salt Lake City, UT 84112, (801)581-5505.

LOH, WALLACE D.

Educator, educational administrator. Chinese American. **PERSONAL:** Born Jan 26, 1945, China; son of S Y Loh and Lily Loh; married Barbara, 1985; children: Andrea. **EDUCATION:** Grinnell College, BA, 1965; Cornell University, MA, 1968; University of Michigan, PhD, 1971; Yale University, JD, 1974. **CAREER:** University of Washington, dean, professor of law, currently. **HONORS/AWARDS:** Grinnell College, Honorary Doctor of Laws, 1993. **SPECIAL ACHIEVEMENTS:** Social Research in the Judicial Process, Russell Sage Foundation Press, 1984. **BUSINESS ADDRESS:** Dean, Professor of Law, University of Washington, 1100 Northeast Campus Pky, Seattle, WA 98105.

LONG, GRACE FAN

Educator. Chinese American. **PERSONAL:** Born May 13, 1953, Shanghai, People's Republic of China; daughter of Bao-Xian Fan and You-Fang Shao; married Gordon Long, Oct 10, 1987; children: Nathaniel, Daniel. **EDUCATION:** Jiangxi Teachers' College, China, AA, 1980; Point Loma Nazarene College, BA, 1983; University of North Texas, MM, 1986, DMA, 1991. **CAREER:** Jiangxi Teachers' College, teaching assistant, 1979-80; University of North Texas, graduate teaching fellow, 1983-88; The Music Academy, Highland Park Presbyterian Church, piano instructor, 1988-91; self-employed music teacher, currently. **ORGANIZATIONS:** National Music Honor Society, Alpha Alpha Chapter, Pi Kappa Lambda, 1990; The Music Teacher National Association, 1985; American College of Musicians/National Guild of Piano Teachers, 1986. **HONORS/AWARDS:** University of North Texas, Elizabeth Cope Memorial Accompanying Scholarship, 1988-89, Graduate Teaching Fellowship, 1983-85, 1986-88; Point Loma Nazarene College, Music Scholarship, 1981-83. **SPECIAL ACHIEVEMENTS:** Point Loma Nazarene College, Guest Pianist in Solo Recital, 1990; Highlander Concert in Dallas, 1988; Soloist with the Point Loma Community Orchestra, 1983; Music Teachers Association, Juror for various Music Festivals, 1985-93. **HOME ADDRESS:** 4449 Cleveland Dr, Plano, TX 75093, (214)964-7723.

LOO, CYRUS W.

Physician. Chinese American. **PERSONAL:** Born Sep 10, 1918, Honolulu, HI; son of Ernest B Loo and Mary Kong Loo; married Amy, Jul 18, 1942; children: Chalsa, Dennis D, Patricia. **EDUCATION:** University of Virginia, MS, 1948; IGAS, MS, 1965. **CAREER:** University of Hawaii, professor of medicine, 1986; self employed, physician, 1943-. **ORGANIZATIONS:** Rotary International, board member; Waikiki Rotary; Waikiki Masonic Lodge, organist; Shriners-Aloha Temple; Rajah's National Sojourners Heroes of 76 Shriner's Band, Scottish Rite of Freemasonry; Hawaii Acupuncture Association, vice president; American Academy of Dermatology; Pacific Dermatological Association. **HONORS/AWARDS:** Outstanding Graphoanalyst in Nation, 1964; Hiram Award Recipient, 1986; music contest, first prize, 1936; World Peace Academy, State of Hawaii: consultant, University of HI, School of Nursing, Outstanding Lecturer, 1991. **SPECIAL ACHIEVEMENTS:** Author of 17 multiple publications on acupuncture, including: "Comparison of Western & Eastern Medicine," Am J of Acupuncture, June 1984; author of 10 western medicine articles including: "Deep Acne Pits Repaired by New Surgical Methods.". **MILITARY SERVICE:** US Army, Medical Corps, capt, 1952-54. **BIOGRAPHICAL SOURCES:** Midweek, cover story, Sept 20, 1989; Honolulu Star Bulletin, front page story, Oct 26, 1987; Buddy Hackett's Book, His Ups & Downs, p 54-55; Honolulu Magazine, p 34-35, Feb 1993. **HOME ADDRESS:** 2727 Kolonahe Place, Honolulu, HI 96813, (808)536-6383. **BUSINESS ADDRESS:** Physician, 321 N Kuakini St, Kuakini Medical Plaza, Honolulu, HI 96817, (808)537-4434.

LOO, TI LI

Educator. Chinese American. **PERSONAL:** Born Jan 7, 1918, Changsha, Hunan, China; son of Adrian Loo & Diane Lee Loo; married Marie Lee Loo, Jun 23, 1951; children: Michael D, Agnes D Carey, Jonathan D. **EDUCATION:** Tsing Hua University, BSc, 1940; Oxford University, DPhil, 1946, DSc, 1986. **CAREER:** University of Maryland, postdoctoral fellow, 1947-50; Christ Hospital Institute of Medical Research, research associate, 1950-55; National Cancer Institute, pharmacologist, 1955-65; University of Texas MD Anderson Cancer Center, professor of biochemistry, 1965-68, professor of pharmacology, 1968-80, Ashbel Smith Professor of therapeutics, 1980-85; GWU Medical Center, research professor of pharmacology, 1985-. **ORGANIZATIONS:** American Association for Cancer Research, 1962-; American Society of Clinical Oncology, 1970-; American Society for Pharmacol and Expt Therap, 1967-; American Society for Clinical Pharmacol and Therap, 1970-; American Association for Adv Science, fellow, 1960-; American Chemical Society, 1948-; Royal Society of Chemistry, 1945-; Association of Chinese Americans, president, Houston chap, 1978-80. **HONORS/AWARDS:** Japanese Society of Clinical Pharmacology, special lecturer, 1986; University of Texas Cancer Center, Gottlieb Award, 1988. **SPECIAL ACHIEVEMENTS:** About 150 scientific papers published; NIH consultant, 1970-90. **BUSINESS ADDRESS:** Professor, George Washington University Medical Center, 2300 Eye St NW, Ross Hall, Room 638A, Washington, DC 20037-2337, (202)994-2706.

LOOR, RUEYMING

Research and development manager. Taiwanese American. **PERSONAL:** Born Aug 16, 1948, Kaohsiung, Taiwan; son of Ho & Kan Loor; married

Chungpei Loor, Aug 28, 1976; children: Jeffrey. **EDUCATION:** National Chung Shing University, Taiwan, BS, 1970; University of Wisconsin, Superior, MS, 1974; State University of New York, Buffalo, PhD, 1978. **CAREER:** University of Chicago, research associate, 1978-80; Roswell Park Cancer Research Institute, senior scientist, 1980-82; BioRad Laboratories, senior chemist, 1982; Cetus Corp, scientist, 1982-86; Leeco Diagnostics Inc, assistant director, 1986-88; Microgenics Corp, manager, 1988-. **ORGANIZATIONS:** American Association for Cancer Research, 1978-; American Association for Clinical Chemistry, 1982-; American Society for Microbiology, 1986-. **HONORS/AWARDS:** National Cancer Institute, research grant, 1981; Clinical Ligand Assay Society, Best Abstract Award, 1991. **SPECIAL ACHIEVEMENTS:** 35 scientific papers published in various professional journals; 4 patents granted. **BUSINESS ADDRESS:** Manager of Research & Development, Microgenics Corp, 2380 A Bisso Ln, Concord, CA 94520, (510)674-0667.

LORD, BETTE BAO
Author, lecturer. Chinese American. **PERSONAL:** Born Nov 3, 1938, Shanghai, China; daughter of Sandys Bao & Dora Fang Bao; married Winston Lord, May 4, 1963; children: Elizabeth Pillsbury, Winston Bao. **EDUCATION:** Tufts University, BA, 1959; Fletcher School of Law and Diplomacy, MA, 1960. **CAREER:** University of Hawaii, East-West Cultural Center, assistant to director, 1961-62; Fulbright Exchange Program, program officer, 1962-63; modern dance performer and teacher, Geneva and Washington, 1964-73; National Conference for the Associated Councils of the Arts, conference director, 1970-71; freelance writer/lecturer, 1982-. **ORGANIZATIONS:** Freedom House, chairwoman, 1993-; Asia Society, board of trustees; Aspen Institute, board of trustees; Freedom Forum, board of trustees; Council on Foreign Relations; PEN; Authors Guild; Organization of Chinese Americans; Kennedy Center Community and Friends, board of trustees; National Portrait Gallery, board of trustees; Kennedy Center Community and Friends, board of trustees; National Portrait Gallery, board of trustees. **HONORS/AWARDS:** Skidmore College, honorary doctorate, 1992; Marymount College, honorary doctorate, 1992; Bryant College, honorary doctorate, 1990; Dominican College, honorary doctorate, 1990; University of Notre Dame, honorary doctorate, 1985; Tufts University, honorary doctorate, 1982; Barnard College Medal of Distinction, 1993; National Council of Women, Women of Honor Award, 1993; New York Public Library's Literary Lion, 1992; Women's Project and Productions, Exceptional Achievement Award, 1992; numerous others. **SPECIAL ACHIEVEMENTS:** Author: Legacies, A Chinese Mosaic, 1990; In the Year of the Boar and Jackie Robinson, 1984; Spring Moon, 1981; Eighth Moon, 1964. **BIOGRAPHICAL SOURCES:** (TV) CBS Evening News; Face the Nation; CNN; 20/20, Barbara Walters, 1987.

LOUGANIS, GREG E.
Actor, diver. Pacific Islander American. **PERSONAL:** Born Jan 26, 1960, San Diego, CA; son of Peter E and Frances I Scott Louganis. **EDUCATION:** University of Miami, 1978-80; University of California, Irvine, BA, drama, 1983. **CAREER:** US National Diving Team, beginning 1976; actor, currently. **HONORS/AWARDS:** Olympic medals: platform diving, silver, 1976, gold, 1984, 1988, springboard diving, gold, 1984, 1988; Olympic Games, James E Sullivan Award, 1984; Olympic Hall of Fame inductee, 1985; winner of 48 US national diving titles; World Diving Champion, platform and springboard, 1986; Jesse Owens Award, 1987; Pan Am Gold Medal, 1979, 1983, 1987. **SPECIAL ACHIEVEMENTS:** Played role of Darius in Greenwich Village play Jeffrey, 1993. **HOME ADDRESS:** PO Box 4130, Malibu, CA 90265-1430.*

LOUI, WARREN R.
Attorney. Chinese American. **PERSONAL:** Born Jul 1, 1956, Philadelphia, PA; son of Wallace Loui & Florence Chinn Loui; married Rose Chan, Aug 31, 1985; children: Nicholas, Ryan. **EDUCATION:** MIT, BS, 1977; Stanford University, MBA, 1981, JD, 1981. **CAREER:** Simpson Thacher & Bartlett, associate, 1981-86; O'Melveny & Myers, partner, 1986-. **ORGANIZATIONS:** California State Bar, corporations committee; LA County Bar; Joint Minority Bar Task Force, co-chair; Southern California Chinese Lawyers Association; Asian Business League. **HONORS/AWARDS:** Chi Epsilon. **SPECIAL ACHIEVEMENTS:** Stanford Law Review, 1979-81. **BUSINESS ADDRESS:** Partner, O'Melveny & Myers, 1999 Avenue of the Stars, Ste 700, Los Angeles, CA 90067, (310)246-6735.

LOUIE, AI-LING M.
Writer, librarian. Chinese American. **PERSONAL:** Born Jul 18, 1949, New York, NY; daughter of Lillian Dong Louie & Peter Dung Ock Louie; married Patrick Arthur Miller, Sep 5, 1971; children: Melanie Louie Miller, Wesley Louie Miller. **EDUCATION:** Sarah Lawrence College, BA, 1971; Wheelock College, MEd, 1977; Rutgers University, MLS, 1992. **CAREER:** Wilmington Public Schools, Massachusetts, elementary teacher, 1971-73; Brookline Public Schools, elementary teacher, 1973-77; Metuchen Public Library, children's intern, 1991-92; Monmouth County Libraries, children's librarian, 1992-. **ORGANIZATIONS:** 1st Unitarian Church of Monmouth County, race relations, co-chair, 1992-; New York Chinatown History Project, membership committee, 1988-89. **HONORS/AWARDS:** Wheelock College Centennial Alumni Award, 1988; Elegance Magazine of Hong Kong, Top 100 Women, 1985. **SPECIAL ACHIEVEMENTS:** Author: Yeh-Shen: A Cinderella Story from China, Philomel/Putnam, 1981, American Library Association Notable Book, International Reading Association Children's Choice Award; "Growing Up Asian American," Journal of Youth Services, vol 6, no 2, Winter 1993; "The Child and Picture Books," Records of the Boston Association for Education of Young Children, March 1978. **BIOGRAPHICAL SOURCES:** "Writer's Success Story Began with a Fairy Tale," Woodbridge, NJ, News Tribune, Jan 27, 1983; "Ai-Ling Louie, Author and Children's Librarian...," Allaire, NJ, Herald, Apr 2, 1993. **BUSINESS ADDRESS:** Children's Librarian, Monmouth County Libraries, State Hwy 35, Eastern Branch, Shrewsbury, NJ 07701, (908)431-7228.

LOUIE, ALAN C.
Acquisition services & property management company executive. Chinese American. **PERSONAL:** Born Apr 24, 1951, San Francisco, CA; married May MK Louie, Feb 14, 1976; children: Jennifer, Tiffany. **EDUCATION:** Santa Rosa Junior College, AA, 1971; College of San Mateo, AA 1983; California State University of Fresno, BS, 1974. **CAREER:** Pacific Gas & Electric Co, land technician, 1974-79, acquisition agent, 1979-93, land project manager, 1988-93; local communication company, site acquisition specialist, 1993; A C Louie Acquisition Services, sole proprietor, currently. **ORGANIZATIONS:** International Right of Way Association Chapter 2, 1979-, past president, 1993, president, 1992, vice president, 1991, secretary, 1990, luncheon chair, 1988-89, employee, 1986-87; American Congress in Surveying & Mapping, 1971-. **HONORS/AWARDS:** International Right of Way Association, Ch 2, Professional of the Year, 1992. **SPECIAL ACHIEVEMENTS:** Project manager for all real estate activities related Pacific Gas & Electric's Telecommunication microwave & mobil & base radio systems. **HOME ADDRESS:** 2481 Hallmark Dr, Belmont, CA 94002.

LOUIE, CLIFF
Planning and housing administrator. Chinese American. **CAREER:** Interim Community Development Assn, planner/housing developer, 1990-. **ORGANIZATIONS:** International Examiner, board of directors, currently; Intl Special Review District Board, chair, 1993; Denise Louie Education Center, board of directors; Intl District Housing & Social Services, board of directors. **BUSINESS ADDRESS:** Board of Directors, International Examiner, 622 S Washington St, Seattle, WA 98104, (206)624-3925.*

LOUIE, DAVID A.
Television news reporter/anchor. Chinese American. **PERSONAL:** Born Jun 19, 1950, Lakewood, OH; son of May and Troy Louie. **EDUCATION:** Northwestern University, BS, journalism, 1972. **CAREER:** KGO-TV San Francisco, reporter, 1972-77; WXYZ-TV Detroit, asst news director, 1977-79; KGO-TV San Francisco, reporter/anchor, 1979-. **ORGANIZATIONS:** Natl Academy of Television Arts & Sciences, natl vice chairman & member, Emmy Awards Committee, 1990-94, natl trustee, 1986-90; Asian American Journalists Assn, natl president, 1990-92. **HONORS/AWARDS:** Natl Academy of Television Arts & Sciences, Emmy Award, 1981, 1988; University of Georgia, member of the reporting team awarded the George Foster Peabody Award for coverage of the 1989 Loma Prieta/San Francisco Bay Area earthquake. **SPECIAL ACHIEVEMENTS:** Pioneer Asian American broadcast journalist in San Francisco. **BIOGRAPHICAL SOURCES:** Congressional Record, entry by Rep Tom Lantos of California, September 9, 1992. **BUSINESS ADDRESS:** Business Editor & Money Reporter, KGO-TV, Capital Cities/ABC, Inc, 900 Front St, San Francisco, CA 94111-1450, (415)945-7227.

LOUIE, DAVID H.
Restaurateur. Chinese American. **PERSONAL:** Born Sep 30, 1951, Portland, OR; son of Andrew and Amy; married Cindy, Jun 4, 1989. **EDUCATION:**

University of Oregon, BA, liberal arts, 1974. **CAREER:** Huber's Restaurant, owner, manager, 1974-. **ORGANIZATIONS:** Prince of Peace Church, Sunday school teacher, 1985-91; Refugee Loan Fund, board member, 1988-93; Multnomah County Rep Party, precinct person, 1992-93. **HONORS/ AWARDS:** Pacific Northwest Magazine, Best Business Lunch, 1987-88; Oregonian, 100 Years in Business. **BIOGRAPHICAL SOURCES:** Restaurant Management Magazine, p 36, 37, May 1988; Nation's Restaurant News, June 1989. **BUSINESS ADDRESS:** Owner, Huber's Restaurant, 411 SW Stark, Oregon Pioneer Bldg, Portland, OR 97204, (503)228-5686.

LOUIE, DAVID WONG

Author. Chinese American. **PERSONAL:** Born 1954, Rockville Centre, NY; married 1982; children: Julian. **EDUCATION:** Vassar College, BA, 1977; University of Iowa, MFA, 1981. **CAREER:** Teacher of creative writing, literature: University of California, Berkeley, 1988, Vassar College, 1988-92, University of California, 1992-; author, currently. **HONORS/AWARDS:** Art Seidenbaum Award, 1991; John C Zacharis First Book Award, 1991. **SPECIAL ACHIEVEMENTS:** The Best American Short Stories of 1989, 1989; The Big Aiiieeeee! An Anthology of Chinese American and Japanese American Literature, 1991; Pangs of Love, and Other Stories, 1991; Other Sides of Silence: A Ploughshares Anthology, 1993; Charlie Chan Is Dead: An Anthology of Contemporary Asian American Fiction, 1993; The Barbarians Are Coming, forthcoming; contributor to Chicago Review, Fiction Intl, Iowa Review, New York Times Book Review, Ploughshares. **BIOGRAPHICAL SOURCES:** New York Times Book Review, p 13, July 14, 1991; Time, p 66-67, June 3, 1991. **BUSINESS ADDRESS:** Author, Pangs of Love, Alfred A Knopf Inc, 201 E 50th St, New York, NY 10022.*

LOUIE, DICKSON LEW

Newspaper publishing executive. Chinese American. **PERSONAL:** Born Mar 18, 1958, Cleveland, OH; son of Richard & Nancy Louie. **EDUCATION:** California State University, Hayward, BS (high honors), 1980; University of Chicago, MBA, 1984. **CAREER:** Los Angeles Times, financial planning analyst, 1984-88, senior planning analyst, 1988-89, circulation planning manager, 1989-. **ORGANIZATIONS:** Los Angeles Times Management Conference, vice president, 1991-92; president, 1992-93; Asian American Journalists Assn, Los Angeles Chapter, treasurer, director, 1987-; Chinatown Service Center, director, 1991-; Project Literacy Los Angeles, trustee, 1991-; Unity Media Access Project, board member, 1993-. **HONORS/AWARDS:** White House Fellowships, national finalist, 1993, 1992; Council on General Mgmt Education, COGME Fellow, 1982; Newspaper Assn of America, Foundation Fellow, 1994. **HOME PHONE:** (310)478-7888. **BUSINESS ADDRESS:** Circulation Planning Manager, Los Angeles Times, Times Mirror Square, Rm 407, Los Angeles, CA 90053, (213)237-3197.

LOUIE, EMMA WOO

Nurse epidemiologist (retired). Chinese American. **PERSONAL:** Born Oct 18, 1926, Seattle, WA; daughter of Pang Shee and Key Sing Jew; married Paul Louie, Aug 1, 1948; children: Stephen John, David Mark, Lisa Jeanne, Alan Paul. **EDUCATION:** Santa Clara County Hospital School of Nursing, nursing, 1948; University of California at Berkeley, 1948-50; Los Angeles City College, AA, 1975. **CAREER:** Hospital nursing, 1966-71; University of Southern California, School of Medicine, nurse epidemiologist, 1971-88. **ORGANIZATIONS:** Chinese Historical Society of Southern California, charter mbr, life mbr, 1975-; American Name Society, 1977-; Organization of Chinese-American Women, 1980-; Chinese Historical Society of America, 1991-; Japanese-American National Museum, charter mbr; Wing Luke Asian Museum, 1980-; Chinatown History Museum, 1984-. **SPECIAL ACHIEVEMENTS:** Editor: Gum Saan Journal, Chinese Historical Society of Southern California, 1992-; articles and presentations: "Name Styles and Structure of Chinese American Personal Names," NAMES, vol 39, num 3, 1991; "Clues to Surname Ethnicity," Claremont McKenna College Conference on Chinese Americans, 1991; "Surnames as Clues to Family History," Chinese America: History and Perspectives, 1991; "History and Sources of Chinese American Family Names," Gum Saan Journal, vol 10, num 2, 1987; "A New Perspective on Surnames..." Amerasia Journal, vol 12, num 1, 1985-86. **HOME ADDRESS:** 1648 Redcliff St, Los Angeles, CA 90026-1650.

LOUIE, ERIC K.

Physician, educator. Chinese American. **PERSONAL:** Born May 17, 1951, Chicago, IL; son of David S Louie and Eleanor T Louie; married Karen G Louie, May 6, 1979; children: Andrew David, Steven Michael. **EDUCATION:** Harvard College, AB (summa cum laude), 1972; Harvard GSAS, 1974-95;

Harvard Medical School, MD, 1977. **CAREER:** Peter Bent Brigham Hospital, resident; University of Chicago, fellow, 1979-81; White House, assistant physician to President Ronald Reagan, 1981-84; National Institutes of Health, guest investigator, 1984-85; UNIF SVC University of Health Sciences, instructor, assistant professor, 1981-85; University of Illinois Medical Center, assistant professor of medicine, 1985-88; Loyola University Medical Center, associate professor of medicine, 1988-. **ORGANIZATIONS:** American College of Cardiology, fellow; American Heart Association, fellow; Chicago Heart Association, program council, chairman; Chicago Society of Echocardiography; University Club of Chicago; Harvard Medical Alumni Association; Phillips Academy, Andover Alumni Association. **HONORS/AWARDS:** Van Duzer Andover-Harvard Award, 1968; Harvard National Scholar, 1969-77; Phi Beta Kappa, 1972; Alpha Omega Alpha, 1977. **SPECIAL ACHIEVEMENTS:** Author of over 50 articles, book chapters and abstracts in the field of cardiovascular diagnosis and treatment. **MILITARY SERVICE:** US Navy, commander, 1981-91; Meritorious Service Medal, Presidential Services Badge. **BIOGRAPHICAL SOURCES:** References cited in Index Medicus. **BUSINESS ADDRESS:** Associate Professor of Medicine, Loyola University Medical Center, 2160 S First Ave, Maywood, IL 60153, (708)216-5043.

LOUIE, EUGENE H.

Photojournalist. Chinese American. **PERSONAL:** Born Jan 10, 1953, Los Angeles, CA; son of William & Yook Ying Louie; married Karenina Grun-Louie, Jun 12, 1983; children: Jonathan Scott. **EDUCATION:** Fullerton Community College, AA, radio & tv; California State University, Long Beach, BA, psychology. **CAREER:** El Paso Times, photographer, 1979-80; Longview Daily News, Washington, photographer, 1980-81; San Jose Mercury News, Picture Edition, photographer, 1981-. **ORGANIZATIONS:** National Press Photographers Association, currently; Asian American Journalists Association, currently; Region Clip Contest, chairman. **HONORS/AWARDS:** American Photographer Magazine, "New Faces," photojournalism, 1982; Pulitzer Prize, Eruption of Mt St Helens, staff award, 1981; Pulitzer Prize, Loma Preita Earthquake, staff award, 1989; Pictures of the Year, Editorial Illustration, first place; Region II, Pacific Northwest, Photographer of the Year. **SPECIAL ACHIEVEMENTS:** Fluent in Cantonese Chinese. **BIOGRAPHICAL SOURCES:** "A Mother's Touch," The Tiffany Callo Story, by Jay Matthews, p 116, 1992. **HOME ADDRESS:** 6448 Berwickshire Way, San Jose, CA 95120, (408)997-6142. **BUSINESS ADDRESS:** Staff Photographer, San Jose Mercury News, 750 Ridder Park Dr, Editorial Photography, San Jose, CA 95190, (408)920-5336.

LOUIE, GEORGE CHANG

Physical therapist (retired). Chinese American. **PERSONAL:** Born Jan 9, 1932, San Francisco, CA; son of Suey Chung Louie and Wong Shee Louie; married Joan L Louie, Jun 6, 1965; children: Glenna M, Gretta L. **EDUCATION:** University of California, San Francisco, BS, 1954. **CAREER:** Children's Hospital, San Francisco, staff, 1954; US Army, 5th General Hospital, staff, 1955-57; Mt Diablo Rehabilitation Center, staff, 1957-58; Ukiah Physical Therapy, owner, 1958-87. **ORGANIZATIONS:** American Physical Therapy Assn, 1954-; Glenna C Smith Memorial Trust, trustee, 1980-; Ukiah Rotary Club, 1964-80, director, 1967-68; Ukiah Community Concert Assn, director, 1966-82, president, 1969-70; Mendocino County Tuberculosis Assn, director, vice pres, 1965-70. **HONORS/AWARDS:** Ukiah Rotary Club, Merit Award, 1970, 1975. **SPECIAL ACHIEVEMENTS:** Inhome Health Care of Ukiah, consultant, 1974-; Chinese Methodist Church, San Francisco, organist, 1947-55, 1957-64; author: "A Table for Mechanically Resistive Exercise," Physical Therapy Review, Jun 1959; "Holding Strap," Physical Therapy Review, Oct 1960. **MILITARY SERVICE:** US Army, sp 3, 1955-57. **BIOGRAPHICAL SOURCES:** "Ukiah Musician's Program," Ukiah Daily Journal, May 4, 1968; "Health Care through Physical Therapy," Ukiah Daily Journal, p 5, Jul 20, 1987; "Ukiah Physical Therapy Cares," Ukiah Daily Journal, p 6, Oct 21, 1990. **HOME ADDRESS:** 3 Highland Dr, Ukiah, CA 95482-4637.

LOUIE, GILMAN G.

Computer company executive. Chinese American. **EDUCATION:** San Francisco State University, BS (magna cum laude), business administration. **CAREER:** Micro Programming Application Systems, partner, consultant, 1979-81; Voyager Software, partner, 1981-83; Nexa Corp, president, chairman of board, 1983-87; Sphere Inc, CEO, chairman of board; Spectrum HoloByte Inc, chairman, currently. **ORGANIZATIONS:** Delta Sigma Pi, president; San Francisco School Volunteers, president; San Francisco Unified School District, Propostition A&B, vice chairman, Health and Family Life Education, advisory sub-committee chairman, bilingual community council; Coleman Advocates

Advisory Board San Francisco; Community College San Francisco, former computer studies chairman; America Israel Friendship League, former board member; Chinese Newcomers Service Center, former board member. **HONORS/AWARDS:** Asian Business League of San Francisco, Distinguished Entrepreneur of the Year, 1993. **BIOGRAPHICAL SOURCES:** Forbes Magazine, Aug 1990. **BUSINESS ADDRESS:** Chairman of the Board, Spectrum HoloByte Inc, 2490 Mariner Sq Loop, Alameda, CA 94501, (510)522-3584.

LOUIE, JAMES SAM
Educator, physician. Chinese American. **PERSONAL:** Born Jun 23, 1940, Los Angeles, CA; son of Willie Way Louie & Janice Leong Louie; married Roella Hsieh Louie, Jul 23, 1967; children: John Corwin, Andrew David, Matthew James. **EDUCATION:** Tulane University, 1958-61; Washington University School of Medicine, MD, 1965. **CAREER:** Johns Hopkins Hospital, intern/resident, 1965-67; National Institutes of Health, sabbatical, 1979-80; UCLA Medical Center, fellow-rheumatology, 1969, chief resident, 1971-72, UCLA, Harbor chief-Rheumatology, 1972-; UCLA Medical School, professor, 1986-. **ORGANIZATIONS:** American College of Rheumatology, fellow, Educational Council,; American College of Physicians, fellow; American Board of Internal Medicine, subspeciality recertifying exam committee: Arthritis Foundation, research committee; Western Society Clinical Investigation; FDA-Arthritis Drugs, 1989-92; Southern California Rheumatism Society, president, 1985-86; American Lupus Society, medical advisory board, 1990-93. **HONORS/AWARDS:** Harbor-UCLA Medicine, Distinguished Teacher, 1982; Arthritis Foundation, Marilyn Magram Award for Medical Education, 1992; XV International Congress Rheumatology, Art Presentation, 1981. **SPECIAL ACHIEVEMENTS:** Lecturer "Renoir-His Art & His Arthritis," 1981-94; research in rheumatology; 40 publications-articles/chapters. **MILITARY SERVICE:** US Air Force, captain, 1967-69. **BUSINESS ADDRESS:** Chief, Division of Rheumatology, UCLA School of Medicine, Harbor-UCLA Medical Center, 1000 W Carson St, E2-South, Torrance, CA 90509, (310)222-3697.

LOUIE, MARVIN KIM
City official. Chinese American. **PERSONAL:** Born Sep 9, 1942, Los Angeles, CA; married Pansy Louie; children: Ken, Sheryl, David, Jennifer. **EDUCATION:** California State University, Los Angeles, BS, 1966. **CAREER:** City of El Monte, finance director, currently. **BUSINESS ADDRESS:** Finance Director, City of El Monte, 11333 Valley Blvd, El Monte, CA 91734.

LOUIE, PAUL
Cleric (retired), human relations commission consultant. Chinese American. **PERSONAL:** Born Sep 10, 1918, Seattle, WA; son of Mr and Mrs Louie Loy; married Emma Woo Louie, Aug 1, 1948; children: Stephen, David, Lisa, Alan. **EDUCATION:** Linfield College, AB, 1942; Harvard Divinity School, STM, 1945; Pacific School of Religion, 1950-55. **CAREER:** Chinese YMCA, San Francisco, program secretary, 1947-49; Chinese Presbyterian Church, Oakland, California, minister, 1950-55; various Presbyterian churches in California, Christian education minister, 1956-69; US Bureau of Census, Southern California Asian Community, rep, 1970; Los Angeles County Human Relations Commission, consultant, 1970-86. **ORGANIZATIONS:** Council of Oriental Organizations, president, 1970; National Asian Presbyterian Conference, secretary/treasurer, 1975; Chinatown Teen Post, Los Angeles, board of directors, 1971-93; Asian Presbyterian Council of Synod of Southern California and Hawaii, moderator, 1989-90; Asian Pacific Family Center, Pacific Clinics, community advisory council, 1989-93; Chinatown Community on Aging/Housing, board of directors, LA, 1991-93; Chinese Cultural and Community Center of Greater Los Angeles, vice chairman, 1992-93; Chinatown Advisory Community, Los Angeles Community Redevelopment Agency, secretary, 1993. **HONORS/AWARDS:** Asian Pacific Family Center, life time service award, 1989; Chinatown InterAgency Council, community service award, 1988. **SPECIAL ACHIEVEMENTS:** East Coat Chinese Christian Youth Conference, Silver Bay, New York, founder and chairman, 1944-46; Chinese Historical Society of Southern California, one of 3 Founders, 1975. **HOME ADDRESS:** 1648 Redcliff St, Los Angeles, CA 90026, (213)664-3808.

LOUIE, RUBY LING
Librarian, educator. Chinese American. **PERSONAL:** Born Apr 11, 1931, Chicago, IL; daughter of Tsin Nan Ling and Poo Tsui Ling; married Hoover J Louie, Jan 8, 1961; children: Leigh-Ellen, John. **EDUCATION:** University of California, Los Angeles, BA, 1956; Carnegie Institute of Technology, MLS, 1957; University of Southern California, PhD, 1976. **CAREER:** Greenwich Public Library, children's librarian, 1957-59; New York Public Library, senior

children's librarian, 1959-60; Los Angeles County Public Library, regional children's librarian, 1961-62; Long Beach Unified Sch Dist, elementary school librarian, 1963-70; Glendale Public Library, part-time librarian, 1983-88; California State University, Los Angeles, assistant professor, 1978-92; Los Angeles Unified Sch Dist, library media teacher, 1989-. **ORGANIZATIONS:** Library Journal, children's book reviewer, 1957-60; American Library Assn, Aurianne Book Award Committee, 1960-63; Castelar Elem School, 1st Community Advisory Council, chairperson, 1969-71; Los Angeles Council for Peace & Equality, board member, 1977-79; Friends of the Chinatown Library, founding president, 1976-83, 1986-90; 3rd Pacific Rim Conference on Children's Literature, board, 1986; Los Angeles Commission on the Bicentennial, 1st dist board member, 1987-91; United Way Literacy Task Force, board member, 1989-91. **HONORS/AWARDS:** White House Conference on Libraries & Information Services, elected California delegate, 1979; Chinese Historical Society of S California, Outstanding Chinese American Pioneer Women, 1984; Asian Pacific Women's Network, Woman Warrior, Community Service, 1986; Organization of Chinese American Women, Individual Community Service, 1991; Reader's Digest, American Heroes in Education, 1992. **SPECIAL ACHIEVEMENTS:** Author, dissertation, "Community Profile Approach for Expanding Public Library Services: Through Communication Survey Procedures Reaching Chinese Americans in Los Angeles Chinatown Community. . .," 1976; Los Angeles Chinatown Branch: A Working Model for a Library/School Joint Venture, Illinois Libraries, vol 67 no 1, p 25-30, 1985. **BUSINESS ADDRESS:** Reading Resource Librarian, South Gate Middle School, Los Angeles Unified School Dist, 4100 Firestone Boulevard, Library, South Gate, CA 90280, (213)567-1431.

LOUIE, SAMMY G.
Educator, chef. Chinese American. **PERSONAL:** Born Sep 11, 1932, Toy Sun Kwongtung, China; son of James & Lee Kan Louie; married Eleanor So-Lan Louie, Oct 11, 1965; children: Vivian, Spencer, Velma. **EDUCATION:** City College of San Francisco, AA, 1958; University of San Francisco, adult teaching, 1973-74, MA, 1981. **CAREER:** American President Line, cook, chef, 1964-69; Mark Hopkins Hotel, cook, chef, 1964-69; Trader Vic's, cook, chef, 1964-69; World Trade Club, cook, chef, 1964-69; Community College District Pacific Heights, general hospital food instructor; City College of San Francisco, instructor, 1972-; Chinatown American Cooks School Inc, executive chef, director, 1972-. **ORGANIZATIONS:** American Academy of Chef & Les Anis D'Escoffier; Chef Association of Pacific Coast, board of directors; Chinese American Citizen's Alliance, board of directors; Chinatown Resource Center, board member; Soo Yuen Senior Center, past president; Chinese American Missionary Society, board of directors; Louie, Fong, Kwong Benevolent Association, past president. **HONORS/AWARDS:** City of San Francisco Mayor, Outstanding Public Service, 1980; Board of Supervisors of San Francisco, Outstanding Public Service, 1977, 1980, 1984; Salvation Army, 1987; Chinese Progressive Association, Empowerment Working People, 1991. **SPECIAL ACHIEVEMENTS:** Soo Yuen Benevolent Senior Center, founder and instructor, 1970. **MILITARY SERVICE:** Army, sgt, 1952-54. **BIOGRAPHICAL SOURCES:** The Recipe for Success, San Francisco Examiner, p B1, June 7, 1992; Chinese Food in America, Asian Week, May 13, 1988. **BUSINESS ADDRESS:** Executive Director, Chinatown American Cooks School Inc, 1450 Powell St, San Francisco, CA 94133.

LOUIE, STEVEN GWON SHENG
Educator. Chinese American. **PERSONAL:** Born Mar 26, 1949, Canton, People's Republic of China; son of Art Louie and Kam Shui Lau Louie; married Jane Y Louie, Aug 3, 1975; children: Jonathan S, Jennifer Y, Sarah W. **EDUCATION:** University of California, Berkely, AB, physics & math, 1972, PhD, physics, 1976. **CAREER:** University of California, Berkeley, NSF postdoctoral fellow, 1976-77, associate professor of physics, 1980-84, professor of physics, 1984-; IBM Watson Research Center, postdoctoral fellow, 1977-79; AT&T Bell Labs, visiting technical staff member, 1979; University of Pennsylvania, assistant professor of physics, 1979-80; Lawrence Berkeley Lab, sr faculty scientist, 1993-. **ORGANIZATIONS:** American Physical Society, fellow, 1977-. **HONORS/AWARDS:** US Dept of Energy Award for Sustained Outstanding Research in Solid State Physics, 1993; Fourier University, France, municipal chair, visiting professor, 1990; JS Guggenheim Foundation, Guggenheim Fellowship, 1989-90; University of Tokyo, Japan, Eminent Visiting Scholar, 1989; Miller Inst for Basic Science, research professorship, 1986-87; American Physical Society, elected fellow, 1985; AP Sloan Foundation, Sloan Fellowship, 1980-82. **SPECIAL ACHIEVEMENTS:** Over 175 publications in scientific journals. **BUSINESS ADDRESS:** Professor of Physics, University of California, Berkeley, Berkeley, CA 94720, (510)642-1709.

LOUIS, LAWRENCE HUA-HSIEN

Educator (retired). Chinese American. **PERSONAL:** Born Apr 23, 1908, Canton, China; son of George Louis and Mary Lee Louis; married Isabelle Chao Louis, Mar 28, 1942; children: Mei-chen Waldon, Mei-chu O'Sullivan, Mei-lin Goff, Mei-yao Boerma. **EDUCATION:** University of Michigan, BS, chemistry, 1932, MS, chemistry, 1933, ScD, 1937; University of Berlin, Germany, postdoc, 1937-39. **CAREER:** University of Pennsylvania, fellow in physiology, 1940-41; University of Michigan, Biochemistry, res asst, 1941-46, instructor, 1946-48, asst prof, 1948-53, assoc prof, 1953-70, prof, 1970-78. **ORGANIZATIONS:** American Chem Soc; American Soc Biol Chem; AAAS. **MILITARY SERVICE:** US Army, office of scientific development, 1942-46; certificate of merit, 1946.

LOW, BOON-CHYE

Physicist. **PERSONAL:** Born Feb 13, 1946, Singapore; son of Kuei-Huat Lau & Ah-Tow Tee; married Daphne Nai-Ling Low, Mar 31, 1971; children: Yi-Kai Liu. **EDUCATION:** King's College, University of London, UK, BS, 1968; University of Chicago, MS, 1969, PhD, 1972. **CAREER:** High Altitude Obs, National Center for Atmospheric Research, scientist, 1981-87, senior scientist, 1987-, acting director, 1989-90. **ORGANIZATIONS:** NASA Mission Operation Working Group, Solar Physics, 1992-; Solar Physics Journal, editorial board, 1991-. **HONORS/AWARDS:** Japan Society for Promotion of Science, Fellow at University of Tokyo, 1978; NASA-NRC Senior Research Associate, 1980. **BUSINESS ADDRESS:** Senior Scientist, High Altitude Observatory, National Center for Atmospheric Research, PO Box 3000, Boulder, CO 80307, (303)497-1553.

LOW, HARRY WILLIAM

Judicial mediator. Chinese American. **PERSONAL:** Born Mar 12, 1931, Oakdale, CA; son of Tong Low and Ying Gong; married Mayling, Aug 24, 1952; children: Larry, Kathy, Allan. **EDUCATION:** Modesto Junior College, AA, 1950; University of California, Berkeley, BA (honors), political sci, 1952; University of California Law School, LLB, 1955. **CAREER:** Boalt Hall, teaching assoc, 1955-56; California Dept of Justice, deputy attorney general, 1956-66; Workers' Compensation Appeals Board, commissioner, 1966; San Francisco Municipal Court, judge, 1966-74, presiding judge, 1972-73; Juvenile Court, supervising judge, 1981-82; Superior Court, San Francisco, judge, 1974-82; California Court of Appeals, 1st district, presiding justice, 1982-92; San Fracniso Police Commission, president, 1992-; Judicial Arbitration and Mediation Services, member, 1992-. **ORGANIZATIONS:** American Bar Assn, Judicial Admin Div, Appellate Judges Conference, chairperson, 1990-92; Natl Ctr for State Courts, board member, 1987-; Institute for Chinese-Western History, University of San Francisco, pres, 1987-89; Chinese-American Citizens Alliance, San Francisco Lodge, pres, 1976-77, natl pres of the Grand Board, 1989-93; Senior Tutors for Youth in Detention, chairman, 1985-; Chinese-American Intl School, chairman, 1980-; Education Ctr for Chinese, chairman of the board, 1969-; US Military Acad, Board of Visitors, chairman, 1982; California Judicial Council, 1979-81; California Judges Assn, pres, 1978-79; San Francisco City College Foundation, pres, 1978-88; California Council on Criminal Justice 1976-86; San Francisco Bench/Bar/Media Com, co-chairman, 1974-75; Courts Commentary, editor, 1973-76. **SPECIAL ACHIEVEMENTS:** Contributor to numerous journals and publications. **BUSINESS ADDRESS:** Judicial Arbitration and Mediation Services, 111 Pine St #205, San Francisco, CA 94111.

LOW, LOH-LEE

Government research scientist. Malaysian American/Chinese American. **PERSONAL:** Born Jan 15, 1948, Kuala Lumpur, Malaysia; son of Yap Kim Hock; married Betty Low, Jul 16, 1983; children: Justin, Adam, Christina. **EDUCATION:** University of Washington, BS, fisheries science, 1970, MS, fisheries, 1972, PhD, 1974. **CAREER:** University of Washington, fishery biologist, 1972-74; US National Marine Fisheries Service, deputy division director, 1974-. **ORGANIZATIONS:** Pacific Fishery Biologist, 1974-. **BUSINESS ADDRESS:** Deputy Division Director, REFM, AFSC, National Marine Fisheries Service, 7600 Sandpoint Way NE, Bldg 4, Seattle, WA 98115-0070, (206)526-4190.

LOW, RANDALL

Physician. Chinese American. **PERSONAL:** Born Jun 24, 1949, San Francisco, CA; son of Huet Hee Low & Betty T Low; married Dorothy Low, May 4, 1975; children: Audrey, Madeleine, Jennifer. **EDUCATION:** City College of San Francisco, AA, 1969; University of California, Berkeley, BA, 1971; University of California, Davis, Medical School, MD, 1975. **CAREER:** St

Francis Memorial Hospital, San Francisco, active staff, 1981-; Chinese Hospital, San Francisco, active staff, 1981-; self-employed, physician, 1981-; Laguna Honca Hospital, San Francisco, cardiology consultant, 1981-. **ORGANIZATIONS:** Assoc Chinese Community Physicians, secretry, treasurer, 1986-89; American Heart Assoc, SF Chapter, board of governors, 1988-90; Chinese Hospital, San Francisco, Medical Staff, secretary, treasurer, 1989-90; Chinese Hospital, San Francisco, chief of medicine, 1991-92; Chinese Community Health Care Assoc, president, 1991-93; University of California, San Francisco, clinical instructor, 1988-. **HONORS/AWARDS:** University of California, Berkeley, Hearst Public Service Award, 1970. **BUSINESS ADDRESS:** Physician, 909 Hyde St, Ste 501, San Francisco, CA 94109, (415)956-8339.

LOWE, ROLLAND CHOY

Physician, association administrator. Chinese American. **PERSONAL:** Born Sep 29, 1932, San Francisco, CA; son of Lawrence Choy Lowe and Eva Chan Lowe; married Kathryn, Jan 7, 1957; children: Larry, Randall, Yvonne Uyeki. **EDUCATION:** University of California, Berkeley, AB, 1952; University of California, San Francisco, MD, 1955. **CAREER:** Self-employed physician, 1963-93; University of California, San Francisco, associate clin professor surgery, 1985-93; California Medical Association, first Asian vice chair, board of trustees, 1992-. **ORGANIZATIONS:** San Francisco Medical Society, first Asian president, 1982; San Francisco Foundation, first Asian member of the board of trustees, 1993; Chinese Hospital, chair, board of trustees; Chinese Culture Foundation, chair/president, board of trustees, 1975-88; Foundation for Chinese Democracy, president, 1989-93; City & County of San Francisco, civil service commissioner, 1979-80. **HONORS/AWARDS:** Chinese Culture Foundation, Distinguished Service/Culture Award, 1986; University of California, San Francisco, Chancellor's Award for Public Service, 1988; Asian Foundation for Community Development, Image Award, 1988; Chinatown Resource Center, Community Award, 1989; Courvoiser Leadership Award, Most Outstanding Chinese-American Professional, 1991. **MILITARY SERVICE:** US Army, captain, 1956-58. **BUSINESS ADDRESS:** Physician, 929 Clay St, Ste 401, San Francisco, CA 94108, (415)982-4100.

LU, DAVID YUN-CHEN

Physician. Chinese American. **PERSONAL:** Born Jul 29, 1954, Taipei, Taiwan; married. **EDUCATION:** MIT, BS, 1977; Yale, MD, 1981. **CAREER:** Washington VAMC, cath lab, director, 1989-. **ORGANIZATIONS:** ACP, 1989-; ACC, fellow, 1991-. **BUSINESS ADDRESS:** Director, Cath Lab, Washington Virginia Medical Center, 50 Irving St N W, 151-D, Washington, DC 20422, (202)745-8115.

LU, DONGHAO ROBERT

Educator. Chinese American. **PERSONAL:** Born Jan 25, 1956, Shanghai, People's Republic of China; son of Peishen Lu; married Feiwen Mao, Dec 27, 1985; children: Andrew, Michael. **EDUCATION:** Shanghai University, BS, 1982; South Dakota State University, MS, 1987; Purdue University, PhD, 1990. **CAREER:** Idaho State University, assistant professor, 1990-92; University of Georgia, assistant professor, 1992-. **ORGANIZATIONS:** American Association of Pharmaceutical Scientists, 1989-; Society for Biomaterials, 1989-; American Chemical Society, 1990-; American Association of Colleges of Pharmacy, 1990-. **SPECIAL ACHIEVEMENTS:** Author, Glucagon Adsorption on Polymer Surfaces with Alpha and Beta Conformations, 1993; Pharm K, an Interactive Pharmacokinetic Program for Mac, 1993; Boron Neutron Capture Therapy for Cancers (PBA Formulation Studies), 1993; Effect of Surface-Hydrophobicity on the Conformation Changes of Absorbed Protein, 1991; 18 other publications. **HOME ADDRESS:** 175 Wickersham Dr, Athens, GA 30606. **BUSINESS ADDRESS:** Assistant Professor, University of Georgia, College of Pharmacy, D W Brooks Dr, Pharmacy Bldg, Athens, GA 30602, (706)542-5331.

LU, FRANK KERPING

Educator. Chinese American/Taiwanese American/Singaporean American. **PERSONAL:** Born Oct 17, 1954, Taipei, Taiwan; son of Steve Lu and Nancy Mah; married Jean Yang, Oct 29, 1983; children: Richard. **EDUCATION:** Cambridge University, UK, BA (honors), 1976, MA, 1980; Princeton University, MSE, 1983; Pennsylvania State University, PhD, 1988. **CAREER:** Singapore Armed Forces, military officer, 1979-79; Republic of Singapore Air Force, admin asst, 1979; Princeton University, graduate research asst, 1979-82; ICOS Corp of America, project engineer, 1982-83; Penn State University, graduate reserach asst, 1984-87; University of Texas, Arlington, assistant professor, 1987-93, associate professor, 1993-. **ORGANIZATIONS:** American Institute of Aeronautics and Astronautics, senior member; ASEE; APS; ASME; American Academy Mechanics; Sigma Xi; Sigma Gamma Tau. **SPECIAL ACHIEVEMENTS:** Numerous technical papers, journals and conferences, 1983-; book reviewer; research for NASA, 1988-. **BUSINESS ADDRESS:** Associate Professor, Mechanical & Aerospace Engineering Dept, University of Texas, Arlington, Box 19018, Arlington, TX 76019-0018.

LU, I-TAI
Educator. Chinese American. **PERSONAL:** Born Oct 19, 1953, Taipei, Taiwan; son of Tu-Chen Lu & A-Min Chen; married Celine Lu, Jan 25, 1985; children: Enoch, Jonathan. **EDUCATION:** National Chiao Tung University, BSEE, 1976; National Taiwan University, MSEE, 1978; Polytechnic Institute of New York, PhD, 1985. **CAREER:** National Chiao-Tung University, Taiwan, instructor, 1978-80; Polytechnic Institute of New York, research fellow, 1980-85, research associate, 1985; Polytechnic University, research assistant professor, 1985-86, assistant professor, 1986-90, associate professor, 1990-. **ORGANIZATIONS:** IEEE; Acoustical Society of America; Optical Society of America; Sigma Xi; URSI, Commission B. **HONORS/AWARDS:** National Science Foundation, Engineering Initiation Award, 1987; Institute for Theory and Computation of the Electromagnetic Academy, 1990. **SPECIAL ACHIEVEMENTS:** Author: "A Hybrid Ray-mode-moment Method for Wave scattering from an Aperture Coupled System," 1990; "Intrinsic Modes in a Wedge-shaped Taper above Anisotropic Substrates," 1991; "Forward Modeling and Data Inversion for Beam Propagation in a Stratified Medium," 1992; "Localization of a Broadband Source Using a Matched Mode Procedure in Time-Frequency Domain," 1993; numerous others. **BUSINESS ADDRESS:** Associate Professor, Polytechnic University, Route 110, Farmingdale, NY 11735, (516)755-4226.

LU, JANET C.
Educator, librarian. Chinese American. **PERSONAL:** Born Apr 15, 1938, Shanghai, China; daughter of Mr & Mrs S Y Cheng; married Pau-Chang Lu, Sep 14, 1964; children: Jean, Lynn. **EDUCATION:** National Cheng-Kung University, BA, 1961; Case-Western Reserve University, MS, Library Science, 1967. **CAREER:** University of Mid-America, librarian, 1974-75; Southeast Community College, librarian, 1975-79; Nebraska Wesleyan University, head of public services, 1979-. **ORGANIZATIONS:** ALA; NLA, treasurer, 1990-92. **HONORS/AWARDS:** Nebraska Library Association, NEMRT, Mentor of the Year Award, 1992. **SPECIAL ACHIEVEMENTS:** Paper published in NLA conference proceedings, 1982, 1984, 1986, 1990. **BUSINESS ADDRESS:** Professor, Nebraska Wesleyan University, 5000 & St Paul Avenue, Lincoln, NE 68504, (402)465-2407.

LU, JANET Y. H.
Educator. Chinese American. **PERSONAL:** Born in Guangzhou, Guangdong, People's Republic of China; married Kim Man Lai. **EDUCATION:** College of Nazareth, BA; St Thomas University, MEd; University of Hawaii, MA. **CAREER:** Seattle Public Schools, bilingual/ESL teacher, 1972-77, Title VII Project Director, 1977-83; San Francisco Unified School District, education specialist, 1983-86; ARC Associates Inc, education specialist, 1986-. **ORGANIZATIONS:** National Association for Asian and Pacific American Education, secretary-treasurer, 1977-81, treasurer, 1987-91, vice president, 1991-93, president, 1993-95, national conference chair, 1990; California Association for Bilingual Education, 1983-, Presenters' Committee Chair, 1986, 1988; National Association for Bilingual Education, 1977-; California State Foreign Language Advisory Panel, 1990-. **HONORS/AWARDS:** Nazareth College, 4-year full scholarship; University of Hawaii, EPDA fellowship; Clark University, NDEA summer grant. **SPECIAL ACHIEVEMENTS:** A Resource Guide for Asian and Pacific American Students K-12, 1989, revised 1992. **BUSINESS ADDRESS:** Education Specialist, ARC Associates, Inc, 1212 Broadway, Ste 400, Oakland, CA 94612, (510)834-9455.

LU, JOHN Y.
Educator. Chinese American. **PERSONAL:** Born Dec 11, 1933, Tainan, Taiwan; son of Paul C Lu & Shuyin Lu; married Meijin H Lu, Dec 19, 1967; children: Andia, Wendy, Ken. **EDUCATION:** National Taiwan University, BS, 1957; University of Tennessee, MS, 1964; Purdue University, PhD, 1967. **CAREER:** Weichuan Foods Corp, biochemist, 1957-62; University of Tennessee, research assistant, 1962-64; Purdue University, research assistant, 1964-67; Russell Agr Research Center, USDA, food technologist, 1971; Tuskegee University, professor, food science and nutrition program, coordinator, 1967-. **ORGANIZATIONS:** Tuskegee University, The School Faculty Award Committee, chair, 1993, food and nutrition program, coordinator, 1993, Graduate Faculty Committee, chair, 1993, faculty senate, 1983-84, Chinese Student

Association, advisor, 1970-85; Chinese Association, Montgomery, Alabama, president, 1983-84; Dixie Institute of Food Technologists, employment/career guidance committee, 1981, awards committee, 1985. **HONORS/AWARDS:** Tuskegee University, The Faculty Performance Award, Research, 1987-88, 1992-93, Sigma Xi Research Award, 1988-89. **SPECIAL ACHIEVEMENTS:** More than 80 research papers, abstracts published in refereed journals and nomographs; received research grants from USAID, USDA, NIH, DOE, NASA; served in proposed review and evaluation committee for BARD; served in panel discussion on "Sweet Potato and Space Crop," in the symposium, Kagoshima City, Japan, December 1, 1992; speaks Japanese, Chinese, reads French and German. **BIOGRAPHICAL SOURCES:** Tuskegee Horizons, Food Agr Environment People, p8, Fall 1991; Agricultural Research, USDA, ARS, p11, May 1993. **HOME ADDRESS:** 101 Seminole Dr, Montgomery, AL 36117.

LU, JYE-CHYI
Educator. Taiwanese American. **PERSONAL:** Born Apr 1, 1957, Yi-Lan, Taiwan; son of Shao-Shin Lin; married Yih-Yuan Chiu, Jul 28, 1986; children: Stephanie. **EDUCATION:** National Chiao-Tung University, BS, 1979; University of Wisconsin-Madison, PhD, 1988. **CAREER:** University of Wisconsin-Madison, acting instructor, 1987-88; North Carolina State University, assistant professor, 1988-. **BUSINESS ADDRESS:** Asst Prof, Dept of Statistics, North Carolina State University at Raleigh, Box 8203, Raleigh, NC 27695-8203, (919)515-2532.

LU, KAU U.
Educator. Chinese American. **PERSONAL:** Born Jul 10, 1939, Canton, China; son of Shuk-to Lu and Shan Hwung; children: Pamela W. **EDUCATION:** National Taiwan University, BS, 1961; California Institute of Technology, PhD, 1968. **CAREER:** California State University, Long Beach, assistant professor, 1968-75, associate professor, 1975-80, professor, 1980-. **BUSINESS ADDRESS:** Professor, Dept of Mathematics, California State University, Long Beach, CA 90840.

LU, LE-WU
Educator. Chinese American. **PERSONAL:** Born Jun 5, 1933, Shanghai, China; son of W Y and C B Lu; married Dorothy C Lu, Aug 17, 1963; children: Julia Y, Paul Y. **EDUCATION:** National Taiwan University, BS, 1954; Iowa State University, MS, 1956; Lehigh University, PhD, 1960. **CAREER:** Iowa State University, graduate assistant, 1955-57; Lehigh University, research assistant, 1957-59, research associate, 1959-61, assistant professor, 1961-65, associate professor, 1965-69, professor, 1969-. **ORGANIZATIONS:** American Society of Civil Engineers, committee on tall buildings, chairman, 1978-82, committee on plastic design, chairman, 1966-70; Council on Tall Buildings and Urban Habitat, general secretary, 1970-76; Applied Technology Council, board member, 1987-90. **HONORS/AWARDS:** American Society of Civil Engineers, Leon S Moisseiff Award, 1967; Council on International Exchange of Scholars, Senior Fulbright-Hays Lectureship, 1975; Harbin Architectural and Civil Engineering Institute, honorary professorship, 1980. **SPECIAL ACHIEVEMENTS:** Numerous publications, including articles, monographs and books. **BUSINESS ADDRESS:** Professor, Dept of Civil Engineering, Lehigh University, Fritz Engineering Laboratory, 13 E Packer Ave, Bethlehem, PA 18015-3176.

LU, LINA
Educator. Chinese American. **PERSONAL:** Born Mar 6, 1950, Beijing, People's Republic of China; married Shuzhong Zhao, Oct 1, 1975; children: Hao Zhao. **EDUCATION:** Northeast Normal University, BA, 1973; Portland State University, MA, 1988, MA, 1992. **CAREER:** Portland State University, instructor, 1986; Reed College, instructor, 1987-89; Pacific University, instructor, 1991-. **ORGANIZATIONS:** Northwest Regional China Council. **BUSINESS ADDRESS:** Professor, Pacific University, 2043 College Way, Forest Grove, OR 97116, (503)357-6151.

LU, LINYU LAURA
Educator. Chinese American. **PERSONAL:** Born Dec 30, 1957, Taichung, Taiwan; daughter of Bing-Jing Lu and Jing-Po Chang; married HaoChun Chang, Sep 10, 1983; children: Wei-Jean Chang. **EDUCATION:** Fu-Jen Catholic University, BS, 1980; National Chung-Hsing University, MS, 1982; State University of New York at Stony Brook, PhD, 1988. **CAREER:** Chung-Hwa Institution for Economics Research, 1982-84; Plymouth State College, University System of New Hampshire, assistant professor, 1989-93; Long Island University, assistant professor, 1988-89, 1993-. **ORGANIZATIONS:**

The Association of Management, conference co-group chairperson, 1993, conference track chairperson, 1991; The American Economic Association, 1986-; Eastern Economics Association, 1989-; Western Economics Association, 1989-; Midwest Economics Association, 1991-; Midsouth Academy of Economics and Finance, 1991-. **SPECIAL ACHIEVEMENTS:** Author of several research papers and publications. **BIOGRAPHICAL SOURCES:** Plymouth State Update, vol VI, no 2, p 3, 1991, vol V, no 2, p 5, 1990. **BUSINESS ADDRESS:** Assistant Professor, Economics Dept, Long Island University, C W Post Campus, Brookville, NY 11548, (516)299-2369.

LU, LUO

Educator. Chinese American. **PERSONAL:** Born Jan 11, 1952, Shanghai, People's Republic of China; son of Zhen Tong Lu and Yu Ying Luo; married Xin Chun Shu, May 1, 1982; children: Victoria. **EDUCATION:** Shanghai 2nd Medical School, MD, 1983; University of Minnesota, PhD, 1988; Johns Hopkins University, postdoc, 1991. **CAREER:** University of Minnesota, research assistant, 1984-88; The Johns Hopkins University, postdoctoral fellow, 1988-91; Wright State University, assistant professor, 1991-. **ORGANIZATIONS:** American Physiological Society, 1992-; Biophysical Society, 1989-; Ohio Physiological Society, 1991-; FASEB, 1989-. **HONORS/AWARDS:** Minnesota Medical Foundation, Bacaner Basic Research Award, 1988; Wright State University, Research Challenge Award, 1991; National Science Foundation, research grant, 1992-95; National Institutes of Health, research grant, 1992-97; American Heart Association, Ohio, Grant In-Aid Award, 1992; numerous others. **SPECIAL ACHIEVEMENTS:** With T Yang, D Markakis, W B Guggino and R W Craig, "Alterations in Voltage-gated K + Currents Associated with an Early Stage in the Differentiation of Hematopoietic Myeloblasts," J of Membrane Biology, vol 132, p 267-274, 1993; with W B Guggino, "Regulation and Identification of Whole-Cell Cl and Ca2+ -activated K+ Currents in Medullary Thick Ascending Limb Cells," 135: 181-189, J of Membrane Biology, 1993; numerous others. **BUSINESS ADDRESS:** Asst Professor, Wright State University, School of Medicine, 011 D Medical Science Building, Dayton, OH 45435, (513)873-3858.

LU, MI

Educator. Chinese American. **PERSONAL:** Born in Si Chuan, People's Republic of China; daughter of Chong Pu Lu & Shu Sheng Fan. **EDUCATION:** Shanghai Institute of Mechanical Engineering, BS, 1981; Rice University, MS, 1984, PhD, 1987. **CAREER:** Shanghai Science & Technology Exchange Center, editor, 1976-77; Texas A&M University, asst prof, 1987-93, assoc prof, 1993-. **ORGANIZATIONS:** IEEE; Eta Kappa Nu Assn. **HONORS/AWARDS:** Natl Science Foundation, Research Initiation, 1988; Texas Higher Education Coordinating Board, Texas Advanced Technology, 1991. **SPECIAL ACHIEVEMENTS:** Publications: "Optimal Algorithms for Rectangle Problems on a Mesh-connected Computer," Jour of Parallel & Distributed Computing, 5, p154-171 1988; "Geometric Problems on Two-dimensional Array Processors," Circuits, Sys, & Signal Processing, 7:2 p191-211 1988; "Parallel Machine for the Unification Algorithm," IEEE Micro 10:4 p21-33 Aug 1990; "Solving Visibility Problems on MCC's of Smaller Size," Info Scis, v56 p163-192 Aug 1991; "Floating-point Numbers in Residue Number Sys," Computers & Mathematics with Applications, 22:10 p127-140 1991; "Parallel Square-root Algorithm for the Modified Extended Kalman Filter," IEEE Transactions on Aerospace & Electronics Sys, 28:1 p153-163 Jan 1992; "Parallel Computation of the Modified Extended Kalman Filter," Intl Jour of Computer Mathematics, v45 p69-87 1992; "Novel Division Algorithm for Residue Number Systems," IEEE Trans on Computers, 41:8 p1026-1032 Aug 1992; "Solution of Cache Ping-pong Problem in Multiprocessor Sys," Jour of Parallel & Distributed Computing, 16:2 p158-171 Oct 1992; "Applying Parallel Computer Sys to Solve Symmetric Tridiagonal Eigenvalue Problems," Parallel Computing, v18 p1301-1315 1992; "On the Optimal Reconfiguration of Multipipeline Arrays in the Presence of Faulty Processing & Switching Elements," IEEE Trans of VLSI Sys, 1:1 p76-79 Mar 1993; "Iteration Partition Approach for Cache & Local Memory Thrashing on Parallel Processing," IEEE Trans on Computers, 42:5 p529-546 May 1993. **BIOGRAPHICAL SOURCES:** IEEE Micro, 10:4, p33, 1990; IEEE Transactions on Aerospace & Electronics Systems, 28:1, p163, 1992; IEEE Transactions on Computers, 41:8, p1032, 1992, 42:5, p546, 1993. **BUSINESS ADDRESS:** Assoc Prof, Dept of Electrical Engineering, Texas A&M University, College Station, TX 77843, (409)845-3749.

LU, MICHAEL Y.

Computer company executive. Chinese American. **PERSONAL:** Born Sep 5, 1955, Canton, People's Republic of China; son of Guang Lu and Shi-Kwai Ng;

married Elizabeth Nadeau Lu, Oct 26, 1985; children: Juliet Nadeau, Vincent Nadeau. **EDUCATION:** Sun Yat-Sen University; University of Massachusetts, BS, 1985; Harvard University, MCS, 1990, ME, 1992. **CAREER:** No 4 Research Institute, engr, 1978; Comark Computer Corp, hardware engr, 1984; Honeywell, sr computer engr, 1985; Digital Equipment Corp, sr system engr, 1986-88; Prospects Corp, founder, sr vice pres, currently. **ORGANIZATIONS:** IEEE, voting mbr; ACM, voting mbr; Harvard Alumni Assn. **SPECIAL ACHIEVEMENTS:** Author: Computer-related research papers, ACM, numerous others. **HOME ADDRESS:** 17 Roby St, Nashua, NH 03060, (603)891-0524.

LU, MIN ZHAN

Educator. Chinese American. **PERSONAL:** Born Feb 6, 1946, Shanghai, China; daughter of Daisy & P K Loh; married Bruce Horner, Aug 12, 1984; children: Yvonne Hsu. **EDUCATION:** University of Pittsburgh, MA, 1983, PhD, 1989. **CAREER:** University of Pittsburgh, teaching assistant, 1981-88; Drake University, assistant professor, 1990-. **ORGANIZATIONS:** Conference of College Composition & Communication, executive committee, 1992-. **HONORS/AWARDS:** Mina P Shaughnessy Award, 1992; Andrew W Mellon Predoctoral Fellowship, 1987. **SPECIAL ACHIEVEMENTS:** "Conflict & Struggle: The Enemies of Preconditions of Basic Writing?," College of English, vol 54, p1-27, December, 1992; "A Pedagogy of Struggle: The Use of Cultural Dissonance," Journal of Teaching Writing, vol 11, no 1, p118, 1992; Fish, short story, Prairie Schooner, summer, 1991; "From Silence to Words: Writing as Struggle," College English, vol 49, p437-48, 1987; articles & chapters in Journal of Education, Journal of Basic Writing, Writing: The Translation of Memory, Critical Theory: Curriculum, Pedagogy, Politics, etc. **BUSINESS ADDRESS:** Assistant Professor of English, English Dept, Drake University, 320 Howard, Des Moines, IA 50311, (515)271-3973.

LU, PONZY

Educator. Chinese American. **PERSONAL:** Born Oct 7, 1942, Shanghai, China; son of Abraham Lu and Beth Chou Lu; married Heidi Fahl, Jan 13, 1975; children: Kristina. **EDUCATION:** California Institute of Technology, BS, 1964; MIT, PhD, 1970. **CAREER:** Arthritis Foundation postdoctoral fellow, Max Planck Inst, Germany, 1970-73; NIH, study section, 1982-86, 1992-96; University Space Research Assn/NASA Biotechnology Discipline Working Group, microgravity sci & applications div, 1986-91; University of Pennsylvania, Dept of Chem, asst prof, 1973-78, assoc prof, 1978-82, prof, 1982-. **ORGANIZATIONS:** American Soc of Biol Chemists; Biophys Soc; Sigma Xi. **HONORS/AWARDS:** NIH, Career Development Award, 1977-82. **BUSINESS ADDRESS:** Professor, Dept of Chemistry, University of Pennsylvania, Philadelphia, PA 19104.

LU, STEVEN ZHIYUN

Educator. Chinese American. **PERSONAL:** Born Nov 25, 1941, Shanghai, China; son of Hairu Lu and Lang Ying Chen; married Shiru Zhao, Sep 12, 1968; children: Tony, Zong. **EDUCATION:** QingLua University, China, BS, 1965; Cornell University, MS, 1984, PhD, 1986. **CAREER:** Cornell University, postdoctoral associate, 1986-87; Intellisys Corp, senior research engineer, 1987-90; New York Institute of Technology, associate professor, 1990-. **ORGANIZATIONS:** AIAA, 1990-. **HONORS/AWARDS:** National Science Foundation, SBIR Award, 1988. **SPECIAL ACHIEVEMENTS:** Published more than 20 papers; speak Chinese language (Mandarin) and English fluently. **HOME PHONE:** (516)248-4029. **BUSINESS ADDRESS:** Associate Professor, NY Institute of Technology, 268 Wheatley Rd, Henry Schure Hall, Old Westbury, NY 11568.

LUH, BOR SHIUN

Food science educator. Chinese American. **PERSONAL:** Born Jan 13, 1916, Shanghai, Jiangsu, China; son of Tsung Fong Luh and King Ying Chen Luh; married Bai Tsain Liu Luh, Nov 23, 1940; children: Janet Shirley. **EDUCATION:** Chiao Tung University, Shanghai, BS, chemistry, 1938; University of California, Berkeley, MS, food science, 1948, PhD, agrichemistry, 1952. **CAREER:** Chiao-Tung University, Shanghai, teaching assistant, 1938-41; Far Eastern Chemical Works, Shanghai, chemist, 1941-43; Maling Canned Foods Co, Shanghai, chief chemist, 1943-46; University of California, Davis, junior specialist, 1952-56, food technologist, 1957-63, associate food technologist, 1963-69, food technologist, 1969-. **ORGANIZATIONS:** Institute of Food Technologists, fellow, professional member, 1953-; American Chemical Society, 1965-; American Oil Chemists Society, 1968-; American Association of Cereal Chemists, 1970-; American Society of Horticultural Science, 1970-; Phytochemical Society of North America, 1970-. **HONORS/AWARDS:** Chinese American Food Society, Food Technology Achievement Award, 1984; Academic Staff Organization, University of California, Appreciation Award, 1986; Institute of Food Technologists, fellow, 1986; California League of Food Processors, Distinguished Service Award, 1994. **SPECIAL ACHIEVE-MENTS:** Publications include: Commerical Fruit Processing, Avi Pub Co, 1975, 1986; Commercial Vegetable Processing, Avi Pub Co, 1975, 1988; Rice Production & Utilization, Avi Pub Co, 1980; Rice Production, Van Nostrand Reinhold Co, 1991; Rice Utilization, Van Nostrand Reinhold Co, 1991. **BUSINESS ADDRESS:** Food Technologist, University of California, Davis, Dept of Food Science & Technology, Cruess Hall, Davis, CA 95616.

LUH, JIANG
Educator. Chinese American. **PERSONAL:** Born Jun 24, 1932, Haining, Chejiang, China; son of Hsieh-Tang Luh & Hsing-Su Wu; married Tsu-yunn Ma Luh; children: Albert Hung-Pei, Ellice Yeng, Michael Hung-Tai. **EDUCATION:** National Taiwan Normal University, BS, 1956; University of Nebraska, MS, 1959; University of Michigan, PhD, 1963. **CAREER:** Indiana State University, associate professor, 1963-65; Wright State University, associate professor, 1966-68; North Carolina State University, associate professor, 1968-70, professor, 1970-. **ORGANIZATIONS:** American Mathematical Society, 1961-; Mathematical Association of America, 1960-. **SPECIAL ACHIEVEMENTS:** More than 50 papers published in international mathematical journals; fluent in Chinese and English. **BUSINESS ADDRESS:** Professor, North Carolina State University, Box 8205, Raleigh, NC 27695-8205, (919)515-3261.

LUH, YUHSHI
Chemist. Taiwanese American. **PERSONAL:** Born Feb 14, 1949, Kaohsiung, Taiwan; son of Shui-Chien Luh & Chien-Gin Luh; married Beatrice K Luh, Aug 27, 1974; children: Esther G, Vivian J. **EDUCATION:** National Taiwan University, BS, 1971; Rice University, PhD, 1976. **CAREER:** MD Anderson Hospital & Tumor Institute, project investigator, 1977-78; Massachusetts Institute of Technology, NIH postdoctoral fellow, 1978-79; Mobil Oil Corp/Mobil Res & Development Co, res chemist, 1979-81; Gulf Oil Co/Gulf Science & Technology Co, res scientist, 1981-83; Mine Safety & Appliance Co, res chemist, 1983-84; American Cyanamid Co, sr research chemist, 1984-92; ITRI/Union Chemical Laboratories, manager specialty chemicals, 1993-. **ORGANIZATIONS:** American Chemical Society; Chinese Colloid and Interface Society, editor, 1993; Calvary Baptist Church, New Haven, chairman, board of deacons, 1992; Pittsburgh Chinese Church, chairman, board of trustees, 1983. **HONORS/AWARDS:** Welch Foundation, Welch Fund Award, 1974. **SPECIAL ACHIEVEMENTS:** ACS Symposium series #243, ''Xenobiotics in Foods and Feeds,'' 1982; US patents 4303411, 4370243, 4479894, 4873365; European patents, 366884A2, 5806A2; language proficiency: Chinese. **HOME ADDRESS:** 948 Red Fox Rd, Orange, CT 06477.

LUI, MEIZHU
Community organizer, labor leader. Chinese American. **PERSONAL:** Born May 8, 1945, Ann Arbor, MI; daughter of Lawrence Hua-Xian Louis & Isabelle Kuei-Ling Chao. **EDUCATION:** University of Michigan, BA, 1968. **CAREER:** Boston City Hospital, dietary worker, 1978-93; Health Care for All, Boston Health Access Project, coordinator, 1993-. **ORGANIZATIONS:** American Federation of State, County Municipal Employees Local 1489, Boston City Hospital, president, 1986-92, treasurer, 1982-86; Women of Colors Unified, co-chair, 1984-85; Asian Sisters in Action, 1981-93; Union Members for Jobs and Equality, co-chair, 1981-83. **HONORS/AWARDS:** Massachusetts Rainbow Coalition, Leadership, 1986; Boston Women's Fund, Leadership, 1991; Women's Law Caucus, New England School of Law, Social Justice, 1992; Pi Alpha Alpha, Suffolk University chapter, 1993; Massachusetts Commonwealth Coalition, administration coalition building, 1993. **BIOGRAPHICAL SOURCES:** A Troublemaker's Handbook, Dan LaBotz, A Labor Note Book, pp 63-64, 169-170, 1991. **BUSINESS ADDRESS:** Coordinator, Boston Health Access Project, Health Care for All, 30 Winter St, Ste 1007, Boston, MA 02108, (617)350-0178.

LUI, WAI MING
Engineer. Hong Kong American/Chinese American. **PERSONAL:** Born Oct 24, 1951, Hong Kong; son of Man Lui and Sze-Mui Lee; married Becky D Lui, Oct 20, 1990; children: Michael W. **EDUCATION:** University of Michigan, BSEE, 1978. **CAREER:** Bechtel Power Corporation, engineering group leader, 1978-87; Arizona Public Service, engineering supervisor, 1987-. **ORGANIZATIONS:** Instrument Society of America, senior member, 1991-.

HOME ADDRESS: 2135 E Cathedral Rock Dr, Phoenix, AZ 85044, (602)759-7302.

LUM, ALBERT C.
Attorney. Chinese American. **PERSONAL:** Born Jan 21, 1934, West Memphis, AR; son of Charlie Lum Sr and Bertha Wong Lum; married Theresa Cheng, Apr 16, 1960; children: Jennifer Theresa, Mina Lum Rubenstein, Albert Justin, Robert Charles. **EDUCATION:** Tulane University, BBA, 1958; University of Southern California, Law, 1965. **CAREER:** Self-employed attorney, 1963-92; Lum and Ku, senior partner, 1974-81; Lewis, D'Amato, Brisbois & Bisgarad, partner 1986-89; Djang, Lum & Ziemba, partner, 1993-. **ORGANIZATIONS:** Southern California Chinese Lawyers Association, founding president, 1976; Los Angeles Chinese Chamber of Commerce, president, 1985-86; Chinatown Advisory Council to CRA, chairman, 1983-85; Chinese American Citizens Alliance, citizenship committee, chairman, 1975-76; Los Angeles-Taipei Sister City Committee, chairman, 1992-93. **HONORS/AWARDS:** Chinese American Citizens Alliance, Outstanding Member, 1985. **SPECIAL ACHIEVEMENTS:** Lead counsel on behalf of Los Angeles Chinese Community redistrcting case, 1986; candidate for US Congress, California, 1992; attorney for Consolidated Benevolent Association in Year of the Dragon lawsuit, 1984. **MILITARY SERVICE:** US Army, sp-4, 1954-55. **BIOGRAPHICAL SOURCES:** Asian Week, San Francisco Weekly, 1980's, 1991-93. **BUSINESS ADDRESS:** Partner, Djang, Lum and Ziemba, 625 Fair Oaks Ave, Ste 358, South Pasadena, CA 91030.

LUM, DEAN SCOTT
Attorney. Chinese American. **PERSONAL:** Born Feb 20, 1958, Hong Kong; son of Abe & Helen Lum; married Elena Lum, Nov 16, 1991. **EDUCATION:** Pomona College, BA, 1980; University of Washington, JD, 1983. **CAREER:** King County Prosecutor's Office, deputy prosecuting attorney, 1983-90; Bliss Riordan, attorney, 1990-93; Forsberg & Umlauf, attorney, 1993-. **ORGANIZATIONS:** Asian Bar Association of Washington, president, 1992; National Network Against Anti-Asian Violence, 1992-; Washington State Bar Association, Young Lawyer's Division, trustee, 1992-. **HONORS/AWARDS:** Washington State Bar Association, Young Lawyer of the Year, 1993. **BUSINESS ADDRESS:** Attorney, Forsberg & Umlauf, 1191 2nd Ave, #1500, Seattle, WA 98101, (206)622-3790.

LUM, DOMAN
Educator, cleric. Chinese American. **PERSONAL:** Born Sep 23, 1938, Hamilton, OH; son of Edward Kam Wo Lum and Lillian Mee Hop Wong Lum; married Joyce Wong Lum, Jun 25, 1967; children: Lori, Jonathan, Amy, Matthew. **EDUCATION:** University of Hawaii, BA, 1960; Fuller Theological Seminary, MDiv, 1963; The School of Theology at Claremont, ThD, 1967; Case Western Reserve University, PhD, 1974. **CAREER:** Salvation Army Social Service Center, personnel coordinator, 1967-70; Makiki Counseling Center, Honolulu, director & counselor, 1967-72; Diamond Head Mental Health Center, clinical psychologist, 1970-71; Hawaii State Judiciary, Honolulu, director of volunteer services, 1971-72; University of Hawaii, clinical instructor of psychiatry, 1970-73; Case Western Reserve University School of Applied Social Sciences, instructor, 1973-74; California State University, Sacramento, professor, 1974-. **ORGANIZATIONS:** Lima Kukua Hawaii Association, president, 1979; Council of Social Work Education, House of Delegates, 1982-85; Journal of Social Service Research, review board member, 1987-90; Commission on Accreditation, Council on Social Work Education, commissioner, 1985-88; Journal of Social Work Education, consulting editor, 1988-95; American Cancer Society, CA Division, social work subcommittee member, 1980-85; Adopt A Child Abuse Caseworker Program, board member, 1992-94; Phi Beta Delta, Omicron chapter, 1992-; The Lim Foundation, Sacramento, CA, board president, 1993-. **HONORS/AWARDS:** Department of Health, Education, and Welfare, Doctoral Fellow, 1972, 1974; California State University, Sacramento, Meritorious Teaching Award, 1984, 1985; National Association of Social Workers, founder, ACBSW, certification, 1991. **SPECIAL ACHIEVEMENTS:** Author: Responding to Suicidal Crisis, Eerdmans, 1974; Author, Social Work Practice & People of Color, Brooks/Cole, 1986, 1992; The Pain of Suicide & The Healing Church, The Banner, 1993; ''Chinese-Americans'' in Encyclopedia of Social Work, 1994; Editor, Social Work and Health Care Policy, Allenheld, Osmun, 1982. **BUSINESS ADDRESS:** Professor of Social Work, Cal St University of Sacramento Business Building Room 3097, 6000 J St, Sacramento, CA 95819, (916)278-7189.

LUM, GEORGE
Television director, production manager (retired). Chinese American. **PERSONAL:** Born Mar 21, 1931, Des Moines, IA; son of Jack Lum and Ng Shee Lum; married Mary Ann Lum, Jun 15, 1952; children: Michael A, Lydia G Wong. **EDUCATION:** San Francisco State University, AB, radio-television, 1954, advanced graduate work, 1960-63. **CAREER:** KNBC-TV, news producer, programming, 1954-55; KPIX-TV, producer, director, 1955-59; KTVU-TV, staff director, production manager, 1959-88. **ORGANIZATIONS:** AFTRA, board mbr, 1965-88. **HOME ADDRESS:** 5531 Diamond Heights Blvd, San Francisco, CA 94131, (415)584-7556.

LUM, JEAN L. J.
Education. Chinese American. **PERSONAL:** Born in Honolulu, HI; daughter of Yee Nung & Pui Ki Young Lum. **EDUCATION:** University of Hawaii, Manoa, BS, 1960; University of California, San Francisco, MS, nursing, 1961; University of Washington, Seattle, MA, sociology, 1969, PhD, sociology, 1972. **CAREER:** Western Interstate Commission on Higher Education, Analysis & Planning Project, co-project director, 1978; University of Hawaii, Manoa, professor, 1961-, School of Nursing, dean, 1982-89. **ORGANIZATIONS:** National Advisory Council for Nursing Research, 1990-93; St Andrews Primary, board of trustees, 1983-; Straub Pacific Health Foundation, board of directors, 1991-; Hawaii Medical Service Assn, board of directors, 1985-92; County Public Health Facility, City and County of Honolulu, management committee, 1982-; Pacific Health Research Institute, board of directors, 1982-90; Advances in Nursing Science, reviewer, 1980-93; Scholarly Inquiry in Nursing Practice, reviewer, 1985-; National League for Nursing Council on Baccalaureate and Higher Degree Programs, review committee, 1980-87, chair and vice chair, 1984-87. **HONORS/AWARDS:** American Academy of Nursing, fellow, 1977; National Academies of Practice, Distinguished Practitioner in Nursing, 1986; Western Institute of Nursing, Jo Eleanor Elliott Leadership Award, 1991; US PHS, Centennial Medallion for Significant Contributions to Nursing, 1989; University of Hawaii, Manoa, Distinguished Alumnus, 1984. **SPECIAL ACHIEVEMENTS:** Many publications in nursing journals and book chapters. **BUSINESS ADDRESS:** Professor of Nursing, University of Hawaii at Manoa, Webster 409, 2528 The Mall, Honolulu, HI 96822-2277.

LUM, SHARON SHOU JEN
Physician. Chinese American. **PERSONAL:** Born Feb 9, 1967, St Louis, MO; son of Jon Tek Lum & Anna Tseng Lum; married Ahmed Abou-Zamzam Jr, May 23, 1992. **EDUCATION:** Harvard University, AB (cum laude), 1988; Washington University, School of Medicine, MD, 1992. **CAREER:** Oregon Health Sciences University, general surgery house officer, 1992-. **ORGANIZATIONS:** American Association of Women Surgeons, 1992-; American Medical Association, 1988-; American Medical Student Association, 1988-92. **HONORS/AWARDS:** Washington University, School of Medicine, Harvey Butcher Award, 1992. **SPECIAL ACHIEVEMENTS:** Post presentation, American Society of Human Genetics, 1992. **HOME ADDRESS:** 142 Willow Brook Dr, St Louis, MO 63146.

LUM, TAMMY KAR-HEE
Pianist, educator. Chinese American/Hong Kong American. **PERSONAL:** Born Sep 15, 1960, Hong Kong; daughter of Shoi Duen Lum and Shun Fat Lum. **EDUCATION:** The Eastman School, BA, 1983, MS, 1985; The Juilliard School, professional studies, 1985-86; Manhattan School of Music, PhD, 1993. **CAREER:** Nyack College, assistant professor, 1988-. **SPECIAL ACHIEVEMENTS:** New York Debut, Weill Recital Hall, 1990; Leschetizky Foundation, piano competition, winner, 1990; Five Town Arts Foundation, piano competition, winner, 1990; Manhattan School of Music, concerto competition, winner, 1988; William Boyd Competition, winner, 1987; Liederkanz Foundation Competition, prize winner, 1986. **BIOGRAPHICAL SOURCES:** American Keyboard Artist, 1988. **BUSINESS ADDRESS:** Asst Professor, Music Dept, Nyack College, Nyack, NY 10960, (914)358-1710.

LUM, VINCENT Y.
Educator. Chinese American. **PERSONAL:** Born Sep 26, 1933, Guangdong, China; son of Henry Lum & Ng Gum Lum; married Fay, May 10, 1960; children: Stacey, Esther, Spencer. **EDUCATION:** University of Toronto, BAppSc, 1960; University of Washington, MS, 1961; University of Illinois, Urbana, PhD, 1966. **CAREER:** IBM, engineer, 1962-63, research staff, project manager, 1966-82, Germany, project manager, 1982-85; Naval Post Graduate School, professor, chairman, 1985-88, professor, 1988-91; Chinese University of Hong Kong, professor, chairman of department, 1991-. **ORGANIZA-**

TIONS: IEEE, senior member, 1962-; IEEE-CS, T C chairman; ACM, 1962-91. **SPECIAL ACHIEVEMENTS:** Over 60 original research publications; language proficiency in English and Chinese.

LUO, SHEN-YI
Educator. Chinese American. **PERSONAL:** Born Jan 18, 1949, Chang Sha, Hunan, People's Republic of China; son of Dao Sheng Luo and Yao Xi Tang; married Ping Fang, May 5, 1978. **EDUCATION:** Tong Ji University, Shanghai, China, BS, 1982; University of Delaware, PhD, 1988, MS, 1986. **CAREER:** Shanghai Institute of Building Science, China, assistant engineer, 1982-; University of Delaware, Center for Composite Materials, visiting scientist, 1988-89; University of Nevada, Reno, assistant professor, 1989-. **ORGANIZATIONS:** American Society of Mechanical Engineers, Committee of Applied Mechanics on Composite Materials; Society for the Advancement of Material Process Engineers. **SPECIAL ACHIEVEMENTS:** More than twenty technical publications. **BUSINESS ADDRESS:** Mechanical Engineering Dept, University of Nevada, Reno, Reno, NV 89557-0154, (702)784-1456.

LUONG, SON N.
Educator. Vietnamese American. **PERSONAL:** Born Oct 23, 1961, Saigon, Vietnam. **EDUCATION:** University of Tennessee, MS, mathematics, 1989. **CAREER:** Dekalb College, math instructor, 1991-. **ORGANIZATIONS:** MAA, 1989-; AMATYC, 1989-. **HOME ADDRESS:** 568 Collingwood Dr, Decatur, GA 30032-1431, (404)498-6910.

LUU, LANG VAN
Business executive. Vietnamese American. **PERSONAL:** Born Sep 30, 1935, Saigon, Vietnam; son of Phai Luu and Hoi Luu; married Jacqueline Luu, Apr 29, 1961; children: Pierre, Michael, David, Hao, John. **EDUCATION:** Saigon University, School of the Law, LLB, 1966; Dalat University, MBA, 1970. **CAREER:** NCC, project manager, 1976-84; Action Building Systems Inc, operations manager, 1984-86; California Security Bank, San Jose, advisory director, 1990; Far East Maintenance Corp, dba First Pacific Inc, founder, CEO/president, 1986-. **ORGANIZATIONS:** Vietnamese Forum. **HONORS/AWARDS:** Asian American Heritage Council, State of Illinois, Asian Americans You Should Know, nominee, 1980. **SPECIAL ACHIEVEMENTS:** Helped company receive ranking as one of the largest janitorial services in Santa Clara County & Freemont. **BIOGRAPHICAL SOURCES:** Interview, Chicago Sun-Times, September 26, 1979. **BUSINESS ADDRESS:** President, CEO, First Pacific Maintenance Services Inc, 586 North First St, Ste 225, San Jose, CA 95112, (408)275-6670.

LY, KIEU KIM
Computer systems analyst. Chinese American/Vietnamese American. **PERSONAL:** Born Aug 24, 1965, Saigon, Vietnam; daughter of Tai and Muoi Ly. **EDUCATION:** Miami University, Ohio, BS, 1988. **CAREER:** Eli Lilly & Co, project leader, systems design analyst, 1988, Audit Services, lead auditor, currently. **ORGANIZATIONS:** National Assn for Female Executives, 1992-. **SPECIAL ACHIEVEMENTS:** Contributing writer: "A Taste of Reality," Model Voices, by Jeffrey Sommers, p 329, 1989. **BUSINESS ADDRESS:** Lead Auditor, Audit Services, Eli Lilly Company, Lilly Corporate Center, Drop 6267, Indianapolis, IN 46285, (317)276-3596.

LY, TAM MINH
Social worker, monk. Vietnamese American/Cambodian American. **PERSONAL:** Born Nov 8, 1961, Thu Duc, Gia Dinh, Vietnam; son of Tao Chu Ly & Nguyet Thi Huynh. **EDUCATION:** Renton Vocational Institute, certificate; Seattle Central Community College. **CAREER:** Buddhist Temple, monk, 1979-86; Community Mental Health, counselor assistant, 1986-87; Seattle Public Schools, tutor, 1987-88; Highline School District, tutor, 1988-89; Parklake Neighborhood House, social worker, 1989-. **BUSINESS ADDRESS:** Social Service Worker, Parklake Neighborhood House, 10041 6th Ave SW, Seattle, WA 98146, (206)461-4554.

M

MA, ALAN KING-YAN
Electrical engineer. Hong Kong American. **PERSONAL:** Born Aug 14, 1966, Hong Kong; son of Kin-Kwok Ma and Min-Yin Minnie Ho. **EDUCATION:** Northern Arizona University, BSEE (magna cum laude), 1988; University of Arizona, MSEE, 1991. **CAREER:** Northern Arizona University, tutor, 1988; University of Arizona, research assistant, 1990-91; Datatape Incorporated,

associate engr, 1991-. **ORGANIZATIONS:** IEEE, 1987-; Sigma Nu Fraternity, scholastic chairman, 1988; Overseas Chinese Student Union, 1989-91. **HONORS/AWARDS:** Golden Key, 1987; Phi Kappa Phi, 1987; Tau Beta Pi, 1987; National Dean's List, 1987, 1988. **SPECIAL ACHIEVEMENTS:** Thesis: Timing Recovery for Two-Dimensional Modulational Codes, 1991. **BUSINESS ADDRESS:** Associate Engineer, Technolgy Center, Datatype Inc, 3400 Garrett Dr, Santa Clara, CA 95054, (408)562-9858.

MA, CHEN-LUNG RINGO
Educator. Chinese American. **PERSONAL:** Born Oct 5, 1952, Ilan, Taiwan; son of Yung-Chih Ma and Hsiu-Wen Chang; married Shu-Wen Louisa Ma, Mar 29, 1979. **EDUCATION:** South Dakota State University, MA, 1984; University of Florida, PhD, 1987. **CAREER:** University College of Cape Breton, assistant professor, 1987-91; State University of New York, Fredonia, assistant professor, 1991-. **ORGANIZATIONS:** Speech Communication Association, 1985-; International Communication Association, 1989-; The Society for Intercultural Education, Training & Research, 1985-; World Communication Association, 1986-; Chinese Communication Association, 1991-; The Association for Chinese Communication Studies, 1991-. **SPECIAL ACHIEVEMENTS:** Author: "Contexts of Discontented Responses in Canadian and Chinese Cultures," Journal of Asian and African Studies, vol 27, 263-70, 1992; "The Role of Unofficial Intermediaries in Interpersonal Conflicts in the Chinese Culture," Communication Quarterly, vol 40, p 269-78, 1992; "Types of Responses to Conflicts in Chinese and North American Cultures," World Communication, vol 19, no 2, p 139-51, 1990; "An Exploratory Study of Discontented Responses in American and Chinese Relationships," Southern Communication Journal, vol 55, p 305-18, 1990. **BUSINESS ADDRESS:** Assistant Professor, State University of New York College at Fredonia, 322 McEwen Hall, Fredonia, NY 14063, (716)673-3260.

MA, CHING-TO ALBERT
Educator. Hong Kong American/Chinese American. **PERSONAL:** Born Mar 26, 1960, Hong Kong; son of Leung Ma and Hee-Ping Fan; married Kam-Ling Lucia Ma, Jan 3, 1984; children: Beatrice Long-Yee. **EDUCATION:** University of Hong Kong, BSocSc, 1982; University of Manchester, MA, economics, 1984; London School of Economics, PhD, 1988. **CAREER:** Boston University, economics, assistant professor, 1987-. **ORGANIZATIONS:** Econometric Society, 1985-. **SPECIAL ACHIEVEMENTS:** Author, "Bargaining with Deadlines and Imperfect Player Control," Econometrica, 1993; "Contract Penalties, Monopolizing Strategies and Antitrust Policy," Stanford Law Review, 1993; "Adverse Selection in Dynamic Moral Mazard," Quarterly Journal of Economics, 1991; "A Signaling Theory of Unemployment," European Economic Review, 1993; "Unique Implementation of Incentive Contracts with Many Agents," Review of Economic Studies, 1988. **BUSINESS ADDRESS:** Professor, Dept of Economics, Boston University, 270 Bay State Rd, Boston, MA 02215, (617)353-4010.

MA, FAI
Educator. Chinese American. **PERSONAL:** Born Aug 6, 1954, Canton, People's Republic of China; son of Rui-Qi Ma and Shao-Fen Luo. **EDUCATION:** University of Hong Kong, BS, 1977; California Institute of Technology, MS, PhD, 1981. **CAREER:** Weidlinger Associates, senior research, engineer, 1981-82; IBM Thomas J Watson Research Center, IBM research fellow, 1982-83; Standard Oil Company, senior engineer, 1983-86; University of California at Berkeley, associate professor, 1986-. **ORGANIZATIONS:** American Society of Mechanical Engineers, 1985-. **HONORS/AWARDS:** IBM, IBM Postdoctoral and Junior Faculty Fellowship, 1982; National Science Foundation, Presidential Young Investigator Award, 1987; Federal Republic of Germany, Alexander von Humboldt Fellowship, 1992. **SPECIAL ACHIEVEMENTS:** Contributing author of two books; author or co-author of more than 70 technical publications in Mechanical Vibrations and the Analysis of Random Systems. **BUSINESS ADDRESS:** Associate Professor, Dept of Mechanical Engineering, University of California, Berkeley, CA 94720.

MA, LAURENCE J. C.
Educator. Chinese American. **PERSONAL:** Born Jun 12, 1937, China; son of Shih I Ma and Chung-lan Kao Ma; married Florence D Ma, Dec 8, 1984; children: Amy. **EDUCATION:** National Taiwan University, BA, 1960; Kent State University, MA, 1968; University of Michigan, PhD, 1971. **CAREER:** University of Akron, professor, currently. **BUSINESS ADDRESS:** Professor, Dept of Geography, University of Akron, Akron, OH 44325, (216)972-6325.

MA, LI-CHEN
Educator. Chinese American. **PERSONAL:** Born May 10, 1941, Xian, Shanxi, China; son of Ho-tze Ma and Chin-fin Lin Ma; married Sue Ann Ma, Aug 20, 1968; children: Serena, Jennifer. **EDUCATION:** National Taiwan University, BS, 1963, MS, 1967; University of Georgia, PhD, 1972. **CAREER:** National Taiwan University, teaching assistant, instructor, 1965-68; University of Georgia, teaching & research assistant, 1968-72; Lamar University, assistant professor, 1972-80, associate professor, 1980-86, professor, 1986-. **ORGANIZATIONS:** Chinese Association of Southeast Texas, president, 1993; Mid-South Sociological Association, nomination committee, 1991-; Southwestern Social Science Association, nomination committee, 1990-91. **HONORS/AWARDS:** Lamar University, College of Arts & Sciences, Research Incentive Awards, 1984-89, Lamar Board of Regents, Faculty Development Awards, 1977, 1988. **SPECIAL ACHIEVEMENTS:** Articles published in: Journal of Social Psychology, Sociological Spectrum, others; visiting professorship at National Taiwan University, 1983; visiting lectureship at Social Science Academy of Harbin, China, 1987; visiting lectureship at Hohai University, Central China University of Science & Technology, China, 1989; invited overseas Chinese scholar for attendance at the National Construction Seminar by Republic of China Government in Taiwan, 1986. **BIOGRAPHICAL SOURCES:** Sociology, by John Macionis, Prentice-Hall, 4th edition, 1993, p 267; Haves and Have Nots, ed by James Curtis and Lorene Tepperman, Prentice-Hall, 1993, pp 334-39. **BUSINESS ADDRESS:** Prof of Sociology, Dept of Sociology, Social Work & Criminal Justice, Lamar University, M L King Blvd, Beaumont, TX 77710, (409)880-8545.

MA, MARK T.
Electronics engineer. Chinese American. **PERSONAL:** Born Mar 21, 1933, Salt City, Jiangsu, China; son of Hsin-fan & Mou-huan Ma; married Simone K Ma, Jul 18, 1959; children: Beverly, John. **EDUCATION:** National Taiwan University, BSEE, 1954; University of Illinois, MSEE, 1957; Syracuse University, PhD EE, 1961. **CAREER:** National Taiwan University, instructor, 1955-56; University of Illinois, research assistant, 1956-57; IBM Research & Development Lab, research engineer, 1957-58; Syracuse University, instructor, 1958-61; General Electric, engineer, 1961-64; National Institute of Standards & Technology, senior engineer, 1964-. **ORGANIZATIONS:** Institute of Electrical & Electronic Engineers, fellow, 1982-, fellow committee, 1990-. **HONORS/AWARDS:** National Electronics Conf, Best Original Paper Award, 1960; IRE Syracuse Chapter, Best Paper Award, 1961; US Dept of Commerce, Science & Technology Fellow Award, 1972, Special Achievement Award, 1974, 1975, Bronze Medal Award, 1990. **BUSINESS ADDRESS:** Senior Engineer, US Dept of Commerce, National Institute of Standards & Technology, 325 Broadway, Boulder, CO 80303, (303)497-3800.

MA, MICHAEL
Educator. Hong Kong American. **PERSONAL:** Born Sep 26, 1955, Hong Kong. **EDUCATION:** Caltech, BS, 1977; University of Illinois, PhD, 1983. **CAREER:** MIT, research associate, 1982-85; University of Cincinnati, assistant professor, 1985-91, associate professor, 1991-. **BUSINESS ADDRESS:** Assoc Professor, University of Cincinnati, Physics, ML 11, Cincinnati, OH 45221-0011, (513)556-0638.

MA, SHENG-MEI
Educator. Taiwanese American. **PERSONAL:** Born Jun 3, 1958, Taipei, Taiwan; married Lien Hsu, Oct 29, 1981. **EDUCATION:** Tamkang University, Taiwan, BA, English literature, 1980; Military Police Academy in Taiwan, 1982; Indiana University, Bloomington, PhD, English literature, 1990. **CAREER:** Indiana University, English Department, associate instructor, 1986-90; Wabash College, visiting instructor, 1989; James Madison University, assistant professor, 1990-. **ORGANIZATIONS:** Modern Language Assn of America, 1989-; Northeast Modern Language Association, 1990-; Association for Asian American Studies. **HONORS/AWARDS:** Pacific Cultural Foundation, Research Grant, 1992-93; NEH, Summer Institute, 1992; James Madison University, Teaching Academy Grant, 1992; James Madison University, Madison Fellowship, 1991-92. **SPECIAL ACHIEVEMENTS:** "Contrasting Two Survival Literatures," Holocaust and Genocides Studies, vol 2, p 81-93, 1987; Thirty, Left and Right, collection of poetry, Taipei, Shulin Publishers, 1989; "Obsession and Oblivion: Jewish & Chinese Genocide Literature," volume III, Vision in History, forthcoming; "Asian Immigrant: Confessions of a Yellow Man," in English Studies/Culture Studies, University of Illinois, forthcoming; "Orientalism in Chinese American Discourse: Body & Pidgin," in Modern Language Studies, xxiii:4, fall 1993, 104-107; "Interracial Eroticism in Asian American Literature: Male Subjectivity and White Bodies," The Journal of

American Culture, forthcoming; book in progress: Immigrant Subjectives in Asian American and Asian Emigre Literatures; assembly delegate for ethnic studies, Modern Language Association, 1994-96. **MILITARY SERVICE:** Military Police Academy, Taiwanese, sgt, 1980-82. **BUSINESS ADDRESS:** Assistant Professor of English, James Madison University, Harrisonburg, VA 22807, (703)568-3978.

MA, STEPHEN K.
Educator. Chinese American. **PERSONAL:** Born 1945, Shanghai, China; married Lee Anne T Ma; children: Royce T, Ryan T. **EDUCATION:** Shanghai Institute of Foreign Languages, BA, 1966; University of Alberta, Canada, MA, 1985, PhD, 1994. **CAREER:** California State University, Los Angeles, Dept of Political Science, assistant professor, 1989-. **ORGANIZATIONS:** American Political Science Association, 1987-; Association for Asian Studies, 1987-. **SPECIAL ACHIEVEMENTS:** Book reviewer (Chinese Politics) for Choice, 1989-; "A Dangerous Game: Deng & the Intellectuals," Journal of Contemporary China, Winter/Spring, 1993; "Chinese Bureaucracy & Post-Mao Reforms: Negative Adjustment," Asian Survey, November 1990; "Reform Corruption: A Discussion on China's Current Development," Pacific Affairs, Spring 1989; "A Comparison of Canadian & Chinese Systems of Ministerial Responsibility," Tansue yu Zhengming (in Chinese), no 5, 1988. **BUSINESS ADDRESS:** Professor, Dept of Political Science, California State University, 5151 State University Dr, Los Angeles, CA 90032, (213)343-2234.

MA, TAI-LOI
Librarian. Chinese American. **PERSONAL:** Born Oct 14, 1945, Canton, China; son of James C W Ma and Mary W Ma. **EDUCATION:** University of Hong Kong, BA (with honors), 1969; University of Chicago, MA, 1972, PhD, 1987. **CAREER:** Tsung Tsin College, prefect of studies, 1969-70; University of Chicago, East Asian Library, Chinese cataloger, 1972-78, head of cataloging, 1978-87, curator, 1987-. **ORGANIZATIONS:** Committee on East Asian Libraries, Subcommittee on Chinese Materials, chair, 1993, executive group, 1989-92; ALA, Comm on Cataloging: Asian & African Materials, 1985-89. **HONORS/AWARDS:** University of Chicago, International House Fellowship Award, 1970-72; ACLS, Mellon Grant, 1980; ACLS, China Conference Grant, 1983; University of Hong Kong, Sri Lo Man Dam/Jardine Scholarship Ward, 1967-69; Committee on Scholarly Communication with China, China Conference Grant, 1993. **SPECIAL ACHIEVEMENTS:** Presented papers at: Intl Workshop on the Dream of the Red Chamber, WI, 1980; 2nd Intl Conference on the History of Chinese Science, Hong Kong, 1983; Intl Conference on the Nan-fang ts'ao-mu chuang, China, 1983; Intl Conference on the History of the Ming-Ch'ing Periods, Hong Kong, 1985; Intl Conference on New Frontiers in Library and Information Services, Taiwan, 1991; Intl Conference on Traditional Chinese Fiction, China, 1993. **BUSINESS ADDRESS:** Curator, East Asian Library, University of Chicago, 1100 E 57th Street, Chicago, IL 60637, (312)702-8436.

MA, TSO-PING
Educator, researcher. Chinese American. **PERSONAL:** Born Nov 13, 1945, Lan-Tsou, Gansu, China; son of Liang-Kway & Zwey-Yueen Liu Ma; married Pin-fang Lin; children: Mahau, Jasmine. **EDUCATION:** National Taiwan University, BSEE, 1968; Yale University, MS, 1972, PhD, 1974. **CAREER:** Makong Airbase, electonics engineer, 1968-69; IBM, staff engineer, 1974-77; Yale University, research assistant, 1970-74, teaching assistant, 1970-74, assistant professor, 1977-80, associate professor, 1980-85, professor, 1985-, Department of EE, chairman, 1991-. **ORGANIZATIONS:** Organization of Chinese Americans; Materials Research Society; American Physical Society; Organization of Chinese Americans, New Haven chapter, president, 1988-90; Electrochemical Society; Connecticut Academy of Science and Engineering; Yale Figure Skating Club, vice president, 1991-93; Sigma Xi, Yale Chapter, vice president, 1986, president, 1987-88; IEEE, senior member, chairman, various committees, 1986-. **HONORS/AWARDS:** Connecticut Yankee Ingenuity Award, 1991; BF Goodrich Collegiate Inventors Advisor Award, 1993; Harding Bliss Award, 1974; GE Whitney Symposium Lecturer, 1985. **SPECIAL ACHIEVEMENTS:** Contributor of articles to professional journals; patentee in field. **BUSINESS ADDRESS:** Professor, Chairman, Dept of Electrical Engineering, Yale University, 15 Prospect St, Becton Center, New Haven, CT 06520-2157, (203)432-4211.

MA, TSU SHENG
Chemist, educator, consultant. Chinese American. **PERSONAL:** Born Oct 15, 1911, Canton, China; son of Shao-ching and Sze Mai Ma; married Gioh-Fang Dju, Aug 27, 1942; children: Chopo, Mei-Mei Ma Chao. **EDUCATION:** Tsing

Hua University, BS, 1931; University of Chicago, PhD, 1938. **CAREER:** University of Chicago, instructor, director of microchem lab, 1938-46; Peking University, China, professor, 1946-49; University of Otago, New Zealand, senior lecturer, 1949-51; New York University, assistant professor, 1951-54; City University of New York, Brooklyn College, professor, professor emeritus, 1954-. **ORGANIZATIONS:** New York Academy of Science, fellow; AAAS; American Institute of Chemists; Chem Society, London; American Chem Society; Am Microchm Society, Society Applied Spectroscopy; Sigma Xi. **HONORS/AWARDS:** US State Dept, Fulbright lecturer, 1961-62, 1968-69; Beneditti-Pichler Award in Microchemistry, American Microchem Society, 1976. **SPECIAL ACHIEVEMENTS:** Organic Functional Group Analysis, 1964; Microscale Manipulations in Chemistry, 1976; Organic Functional Group Analysis by Gas Chromatography, 1976; Quantitative Analysis of Organic Mixtures, 1979; Modern Organic Elemental Analysis, 1979; Organic Analysis Using Ion-Selective Electrodes, 1982. **HOME ADDRESS:** 7 Banbury Lane, Chapel Hill, NC 27514. **BUSINESS ADDRESS:** Professor, Dept of Chemistry, City University of New York, Brooklyn, NY 11210.

MA, WENHAI
Educator, artist, illustrator, designer. Chinese American. **PERSONAL:** Born Aug 17, 1954, Tailai, Heilongjiang, People's Republic of China; son of Longqi Ma & Min Qu; married Shu-Ching Ma, Dec 1, 1981; children: Dorothy. **EDUCATION:** The Central Academy of Dramatic Art, BFA, 1982; Carnegie Mellon University, MFA, 1984. **CAREER:** The Central Academy of Drama, lecturer, 1984-87; Duke University, assistant professor, 1987-. **ORGANIZATIONS:** China Theater Association, 1984-; China Theater Design Association, 1984-. **HONORS/AWARDS:** Central Academy of Drama, Hundred Flowers Design Award, 1980; Carnegie Mellon University, West Coast Drama Clan Award, 1983; Ministry of Higher Education, China, Model Young Teacher Award, 1987. **SPECIAL ACHIEVEMENTS:** The Painted Fan, a picture book, illustrator, William Morrow Children's Books; Swan's Gift, a picture book, illustrator, Candlewick Press; Red Means Good Fortune, one of the Once Upon America Series Books, Viking Children's books; illustrations in children's magazines, such as Calliope, Cricket, Ladybug, Odyssey and Spider. **BIOGRAPHICAL SOURCES:** "Ma Says Work at Duke Is His Most Exciting Period," Dialogue, Duke University, 1987; "Artist in Residence Blends Cultural Elements in Creations," The Chronicle, p 11, 1988; "Theater Design Captivates w/Illustrations," The Chronicle, Duke University, p 4, 1992. **BUSINESS ADDRESS:** Assistant Professor, Drama Program, Duke University, 206 Bivins Building, Durham, NC 27704, (919)684-8972.

MA, XIAOYUN
Educator. Chinese American. **PERSONAL:** Born Apr 2, 1945, Shanghai, China; daughter of Zhongjian Ma and Huiyun Gu; married Fuyun Ling, Jan 18, 1971; children: Jing Ling. **EDUCATION:** University of Science & Technology of China, BS, 1967; Shanghai Jiao Tong University, MS, 1982; Northeastern University, PhD, 1990. **CAREER:** ShenYang Institute of Computer Technology, assistant engineer; Marine Design & Research Institute of China, engineer; Northeastern University, teaching assistant; Harvard University, teaching assistant; University of Wisconsin, La Crosse, assistant professor, currently. **ORGANIZATIONS:** American Mathematical Society; Mathematical Association of America. **HONORS/AWARDS:** University of Wisconsin, LaCrosse, research grant, 1991, 1992, 1993, 1994. **SPECIAL ACHIEVEMENTS:** "The Laplacian on Complete Manifolds with Warped Cylindrical Ends," Comm in PDE, vol 16, no 10, pp 1583-1614, 1991; "Complete Conformal Metrics with Zero Scalar Curvature," Proceeding of AMS, vol 115, no 1, pp 69-77, May 1992; "Mathematics in Ancient China"; "Complete Conformal Metrics with Zero Negative and Prescibed Scalar Curvature. . ."; "Isometry," Journal of COMAP. **BUSINESS ADDRESS:** Assistant Professor, University of Wisconsin, La Crosse, 1725 State St, 1018 Cowley Hall, La Crosse, WI 54601, (608)785-6607.

MA, YAN
Librarian. Chinese American. **PERSONAL:** Born Apr 27, 1957, Hangzhou, Zhejiang, People's Republic of China; daughter of Chao-ying Ma and Ru-jin Chen. **EDUCATION:** Hangzhou University, BA, 1982; Kent State University, MLS, 1988; University of Wisconsin, Madison, post-MLS specialist, 1990, PhD, 1993. **CAREER:** Kent State University, graduate assistant, 1986-88; University of Wisconsin, Madison, reference librarian, project assistant, 1988-89, teaching assistant, 1989-91; Northwestern University, cataloging librarian, 1991-. **ORGANIZATIONS:** International Visual Literacy Association; Medical Library Association; Chinese-American Librarians Association; Association for Education Communications & Technology; American Educational

Research Association. **HONORS/AWARDS:** Kent State, School of Library Science, August Alpers Award, 1988; Professional Development Program, University of Chicago, University of Illinois at Chicago, Northwestern University, fellow, 1992-93. **SPECIAL ACHIEVEMENTS:** Author, "Chinese-American Newspapers and Periodicals in the United States," Ethnic Forum 9 (1-2), p 100-121, 1989; "A Comparison of the Effectivenss of DAPPOR, A Computer-Assisted Instruction Drill Program and a Print Drill Program for End-Users in Education of Dialog Command Language," Journal of Education for Library & Information Science; a reader response analysis of A Book from the Sky, University of Wisconsin, 1993. **HOME ADDRESS:** 2464 N Geneva Terrace #C3-4, Chicago, IL 60614, (312)327-8052. **BUSINESS ADDRESS:** Cataloging Librarian, Galter Health Sciences Library, Northwestern University, 303 3 Chicago Ave, Chicago, IL 60611-3008, (312)503-1913.

MA, YI HUA
Educator, educational administrator. Chinese American. **PERSONAL:** Born Nov 7, 1936, Nanking, China; son of Tzu-Liang Ma and Su-Yi Huang; married Maria C, Feb 23, 1963; children: Vivian, Yvette, Jeffrey. **EDUCATION:** National Taiwan University, BS, 1959; University of Notre Dame, MS, 1963; MIT, ScD, 1967. **CAREER:** Worcester Polytechnic Institute, assistant professor, 1967-71, assoc professor, 1971-76, department head, 1979-89, professor, 1976-, Center for Inorganic Membrane Studies, director, 1988-. **ORGANIZATIONS:** International Zeolite Association, vice president, 1989-92, council member, 1986-92; International Adsorption Society, board of directors, 1992-96; Separation Technology, international advisory board, 1990-; Journal of Adsorption, international editorial board, 1993-; New England Association of Chinese Professionals, president, 1993-95. **SPECIAL ACHIEVEMENTS:** Over 85 technical publications; edited four technical symposium series. **MILITARY SERVICE:** Army, Republic of China, lieutenant, 1959-61. **BUSINESS ADDRESS:** Professor, Dept of Chemical Engineering, Worcester Polytechnic Institute, 100 Institute Road, Worcester, MA 01609, (508)831-5398.

MA, YO-YO
Cellist. Chinese American. **PERSONAL:** Born Oct 7, 1955, Paris, France; son of Hiao-Tsiun and Marina Ma; married Jill Horner, May 20, 1978; children: Nicholas, Emily. **EDUCATION:** Juilliard School, 1964-71; Harvard University, BA, humanities, 1976. **CAREER:** Career as cellist began at age five and continues to perform with numerous orchestras, chamber groups, and own chamber ensembles; discography includes: Bach, Complete Suites for Cello; Barber, Concerto for Cello, 1988; Bolling, Suite for Cello and Jazz Piano; Dvorak, Trios No 3 and 4 for Piano, Violin, and Cello; Mozart, Adagio and Fugue in C Minor; Strauss, Don Quichotte; numerous others. **HONORS/AWARDS:** Avery Fisher Prize, 1978; Elgar Cello Concerts, Grammy Award, 1985. **SPECIAL ACHIEVEMENTS:** New York debut at age 15, Carnegie Hall, 1970; requested by Leonard Bernstein to perform at televised fund-raiser, Kennedy Center for the Performing Arts, Washington, DC, 1970. **BUSINESS ADDRESS:** Cellist, ICM Artists Ltd, 40 W 57th St, New York, NY 10019.*

MADAN, DWARKA NATH
Business executive. Indo-American/Pakistani American. **PERSONAL:** Born Sep 10, 1937, Lyallpur, Punjab, India; son of Dewan Chad Madan; married Saroj Madan; children: Vikram, Anuradha, Lalit. **EDUCATION:** Punjab University, Prabhakar (honor in Hindi), 1958. **CAREER:** Sonu Enterprises Ltd, president, 1958-. **ORGANIZATIONS:** Lions Club, Elmhurst; International Punjabi Society, life member; AWB Food Bank; Overseas Sindhu Sabha of New York; Hindu Temple Society of North America; Satya Narayana Mandhir. **BUSINESS ADDRESS:** President, Sonu Enterprises Ltd, 149-11 Sanford Ave, Flushing, NY 11355, (718)939-5270.

MADE GOWDA, NETKAL M.
Educator. Indo-American. **PERSONAL:** Born Apr 10, 1947, Netkal, Karnataka, India; son of Ningamma Made Gowda & M Made Gowda; married Bharathi; children: Nandini, Pavithra, Pallavi. **EDUCATION:** University of Mysore, India, BSc, 1969, MSc, 1971, PhD, 1978. **CAREER:** University of Mysore, India, Department of Chemistry, lecturer, 1971-79; University Texas Medical Branch, Galveston, postdoctoral fellow & research associate, 1979-86; Indiana University-Purdue University at Indianapolis, Department of Chemistry, assistant professor, 1986-87; Western Illinois University, Macomb, Department of Chemistry, assistant professor, 1987-88, 1989-92, assoc prof, 1992-; University of Tennessee, Knoxville, visiting summer faculty, 1988; University of Virgin Islands, St Thomas, assistant professor of chemistry, 1988-89. **ORGANIZATIONS:** American Chemical Society, 1982-; American Institute of Chemists, 1985-; International Union of Pure and Applied Chemistry, 1985-

90; Sigma Xi, 1979-86; Illinois Academy of Sciences, 1991-; International Journal of Chemical Kinetics, editorial advisory board member, 1994-. **HONORS/AWARDS:** Western Illinois University, Outstanding Faculty Research Award, 1992, Faculty Excellence Award, 1992, 1993; American Institute of Chemists, fellow, 1985. **SPECIAL ACHIEVEMENTS:** Career total of 78 research papers in national and international journals; published and presented 40 papers in scientific meetings and conferences. **BUSINESS ADDRESS:** Associate Professor, Dept of Chemistry, Western Illinois University, Currens Hall 332B, Macomb, IL 61455, (309)298-1760.

MAEDA, ROBERT J.
Educator. Japanese American. **PERSONAL:** Born Dec 6, 1932, El Centro, CA; son of Junichi Maeda & Tetsuye Maeda; married Nobuko Yamasaki Maeda, Mar 28, 1975; children: Kimi. **EDUCATION:** University of Illinois, BA, 1953; University of Michigan, MA, 1960; Harvard University, PhD, 1969. **CAREER:** Brandeis University, instructor of fine arts, 1967-70, assistant professor of fine arts, 1970-76, associate professor of fine arts, 1976-82, professor of fine arts, 1982-91, Robert B and Beatrice C Mayer professor of fine arts, 1991-. **ORGANIZATIONS:** College Art Association; JACL, president of New England Chapter, 1987-88; Asian American Resource Workshop. **HONORS/AWARDS:** UCLA Asian American Studies Center, Rockfeller Foundation Fellowship, 1992-93; Whiting Foundation, Fellowship, 1992-93; Brandeis University, Mazer Faculty Research Award, 1982; US Government, Fulbright Fellowship, Japan, 1964-66. **SPECIAL ACHIEVEMENTS:** Two Sung Texts on Chinese Printing and the Landscape Styles of the 11th and 12th Centuries, Gardner Press, 1978; "Spatial Enclosures: The Idea of Interior Space in Chinese Painting," Oriental Art, Winter, 1985-86; "The Water Theme in Chinese Painting," Artibus Asiae, vol XXXIII, 4, 1971. **MILITARY SERVICE:** US Army, sp3, 1954-56. **BUSINESS ADDRESS:** Robert B & Beatrice C Mayer Professor of Fine Arts, Brandeis University, Waltham, MA 02254, (617)736-2670.

MAEDA, SHARON
Businesswoman, federal government official. Japanese American. **PERSONAL:** Born 1945?, Milwaukee, WI; daughter of Milton Maeda (deceased) and Molly Kageyama Maeda. **EDUCATION:** Washington University; Harvard University. **CAREER:** Renton Middle School, art teacher, 1960s; public radio and television businesswoman, 1970s; Pacifica Radio Network, Pacifica Foundation, CEO, executive director, 1980s; Natl Park Service, director; Specta Communications, president, until 1993; US Dept of Housing and Urban Development, deputy asst secretary, 1993-. **HONORS/AWARDS:** American Public Radio, grant recipient, to produce 15 segments in US-Japan relations for the anniversary of the bombings of Hiroshima and Nagasaki, 1993. **BUSINESS ADDRESS:** Deputy Asst Secretary for Public Affairs, US Dept of Housing & Urban Development, 451 7th St SW, Rm 10132, Washington, DC 20410, (202)708-0980.*

MAEDA, YUTAKA
Manufacturing company manager. Japanese American. **PERSONAL:** Born Sep 2, 1955, Japan; married. **EDUCATION:** NEO College, A/ST, 1981. **CAREER:** Tri-Con Industries Ltd, plant manager, currently. **BUSINESS ADDRESS:** Plant Manager, Tri-Con Industries Ltd., 1215 Airport Rd, Livingston, TN 38570.

MAEDJAJA, DANIEL
Cleric. Indonesian American. **PERSONAL:** Born Apr 8, 1931, Ujung Pandang, Sulawesi, Indonesia; son of Tje Kok Soei and Tong Sioe Kie; married Esther K Maedjaja, Mar 26, 1956; children: Samuel, Febe Maedjaja-Handali. **EDUCATION:** Post, Telegraph & Telephone Academy, Indonesia, BTech, telecommunication, 1954; American Baptist Seminary of the West, MA, religion, 1984, MDiv, 1988; Fuller Theological Seminary, doctor of ministry, 1992. **CAREER:** Post, Telegraph & Telephone Company, Indonesia, telecommunication engineer, 1954-60, International Radio-Transmission-Station, head, 1960-64; PT Caltex Pacific Indonesia, Indonesia, superintendent communications, 1964-84; Gereja Oikumene Indonesia, pastor, 1988-. **HOME ADDRESS:** 1403 Marchbanks Dr #1, Walnut Creek, CA 94598, (510)932-6983.

MAENO, JOHN Y. *See* Obituaries.

MAEYAMA, KIKUKO
International civil servant. Japanese American. **PERSONAL:** Born Jul 22, 1957, Saga, Japan; daughter of Norimoto Maeyama and Atsuko Maeyama. **EDUCATION:** Showa Women's University, Tokyo, Japan, BA, 1980; Uni-

versity of California, Berkeley, MLIS, 1983; New York University, certificate, public relations, 1993. **CAREER:** Yamaha Motor Co, principal clerk, 1980-82; University of California at Berkeley, library assistant, 1983-87; San Francisco Japanese Language Class, teacher, 1984-87; United Nations, librarian, 1987-. **SPECIAL ACHIEVEMENTS:** Language proficiency: Japanese, English, Spanish; writer: "A Shortcut and a Detour to International Civil Servant," How to Become International Civil Servants, p 251-252; monthly article on contest/competitions in the US, Kobo Guide, 1989-92. **BUSINESS ADDRESS:** Assoc Librarian, Dept of Public Information, United Nations, L-329, New York, NY 10017, (212)963-0507.

MAGDAMO, PATRICIA L.
Educator. Myanmar American. **PERSONAL:** Born Jan 1, 1931, Yangon, Rangoon, Burma; daughter of Samuel C and Louise V Ling; married Benjamin V Magdamo, Oct 11, 1958; children: Christopher, Marco, Kirwan. **EDUCATION:** Eastern Baptist Theological Seminary, MRE, 1955; Columbia University Teacher's College, EdD, 1975. **CAREER:** Silliman University, asst prof, 1960-68; American Baptist Churches-USA, scty for intl issues, 1980-89; United Board for Christian Higher Education in Asia, vice pres, 1989-. **SPECIAL ACHIEVEMENTS:** Co-author: Christ in Philippine Context, college text, 1963. **BUSINESS ADDRESS:** Vice President, United Board for Christian Higher Education in Asia, 475 Riverside Dr, Rm 1221, New York, NY 10115, (212)870-2602.

MAH, RICHARD SZE HAO
Educator. Chinese American. **PERSONAL:** Born Dec 16, 1934, Shanghai, China; son of Fabian Soh Pai Mah and E Shang Chang Mah; married Shopin Stella Lee, Aug 31, 1962; children: Christopher. **EDUCATION:** University of Birmingham, BSc, 1957; DIC, PhD; University of London, Imperial Coll Sci and Tech, Leverhulme student, 1961. **CAREER:** APV Co, England, jr chem engineer, 1957-58; University of Minnesota, res fellow, 1961-63; Union Carbide, res engineer, 1963-67; Esso Maths & Systems, group head/sr proj analyst, 1967-72; CACHE Corp, trustee, 1974-, sec, 1978-80, vp, 1982-84, pres, 1984-86; Argonne Natl Lab, consultant, 1975-78; du Pont de Nemours & Co, consultant, 1981-89; Northwestern University, assoc prof, chem engineering, 1972-77, prof, 1977-. **ORGANIZATIONS:** American Chem Soc; American Soc Engineering Education; American Soc Quality Control; Tau Beta Pi. **HONORS/AWARDS:** American Inst Chem Engineers, fellow, Computing in Chem Engineering Award, 1981, E W Thiele Award, 1990; American Soc Quality Control, Youden Prize, 1986. **SPECIAL ACHIEVEMENTS:** Author and editor of 3 books and more than 75 scientific and engineering publications. **BUSINESS ADDRESS:** Professor, Northwestern University, McCormick School of Engineering, 2145 Sheridan Rd, Evanston, IL 60208, (708)491-5357.

MAHADEVAN, DEV
Engineer. Indo-American. **PERSONAL:** Born Jul 2, 1944, Madras, India; son of P V Balakrishnan and Kamakshi; married Lakshmi Mahadevan, Jan 21, 1974; children: Geetha, Pritha, Vinay. **EDUCATION:** University of Madras, India, BEngMech, 1967; IIT, Kanpur, India, MTechME, 1969; SUNY, Stoney Brook, MSME, 1972. **CAREER:** Davy McKee, piping engr, 1976-78; PDM Corp, piping engr, 1979-81; Gilbert Associates, stress analyst, 1983-85; Atlantic Tech, Virginia Power, stress analyst, 1985-87; Henkels & McCoy, sr mech engr, 1988-89; Quantum Resources, stress engr, Mobay Corp, 1989-91; Kadco, stress analyst, Litwin Engineers and Constructors Inc, 1991-. **ORGANIZATIONS:** PE, Ohio, Virginia; ASME. **HOME ADDRESS:** 6822 Fawncliff Dr, Houston, TX 77069, (713)537-6773.

MAHADEVAN, KUMAR
Marine laboratory executive. Indo-American. **PERSONAL:** Born Sep 29, 1948, Madras, Tamil Nadu, India; son of Pankajam & Sockalingam Ponnusamy Mahadevan; married Linda, Sep 27, 1980; children: Vijayan, Andrew, Alexander, Chad. **EDUCATION:** Madras University, BSc, 1967; Annamalai University, MSc, 1971; Florida State University, PhD, 1977. **CAREER:** Florida State University, research assistant, 1971-75; Conservation Consultants, marine scientist, 1975-78; Mote Marine Laboratory, division director/senior scientist, 1978-83, interim co-director, 1984-85, executive director, 1986-. **ORGANIZATIONS:** National Association of Marine Laboratories, president-elect, 1992-93, president, 1994-95; Southern Association of Marine Laboratories, 1984-, president, 1990; Association of Marine Laboratories of the Carbibean, 1984-, president, 1986; World Aquaculture Society, 1989-. **HONORS/AWARDS:** University Grants Commission, National Merit Scholar, 1969-71. **SPECIAL ACHIEVEMENTS:** Various publications on marine benthic ecology and environmental assessment. **BUSINESS ADDRESS:** Executive Direc-

tor, CEO, Mote Marine Laboratory, 1600 Ken Thompson Pky, Sarasota, FL 34236, (813)388-4441.

MAHAJAN, ANOOP KUMAR
Educator. Indo-American. **PERSONAL:** Born Aug 30, 1957, Delhi, India; son of Kailash Mahajan & Pratibha Mahajan; married Gyanam Mahajan, Feb 11, 1985; children: Ilica. **EDUCATION:** MIT, PhD, 1990. **CAREER:** UCLA, assistant professor, 1991-. **BUSINESS ADDRESS:** Asst Professor, University of California, Los Angeles, 405 Hilgard Ave, Campbell Hall, Linguistics, Los Angeles, CA 90024, (310)206-2662.

MAHAJAN, ARVIND
Educator. Indo-American. **PERSONAL:** Born Nov 24, 1951, Delhi, India; son of Vedavrata Mahajan and Shakuntala Mahajan; married Vanita, Jan 16, 1983; children: Aseem, Sia. **EDUCATION:** University of Delhi, India, BCom (with honors), 1972; University of Scranton, MBA, 1975; Georgia State University, PhD, finance, 1980. **CAREER:** Raisina Press, finance officer, 1972-73; Manufacturers Hanover Trust Co, senior consultant, 1987-88; Johannes Kepler Universitat, Austria, visiting professor, 1992; Texas A&M University, professor, 1980-, Center for International Business Studies, associate director, 1990-. **ORGANIZATIONS:** Associate editor, Journal of Multinational Financial Management, Journal of Intl Finance, North American Journal of Economics & Finance, Current Economic & Financial Issues of the North American & Caribbean Countries; North American Economics & Finance Assn, vp, , 1989; advisory board, executive committee, 1983-; Financial Management Assn, Intl Finance Track Chair, 1992 Program, Annual Meetings Program Committee, 1985-87, 1990-93; Academy of Intl Business, annual meetings review committee, 1987, 1990-92; American Finance Assn & Eastern Finance Assn, annual meetings program committee, 1990. **HONORS/AWARDS:** Texas A&M University, Jordan Faculty Fellow in International Business, 1989; University of Scranton, Distinguished Alumni Award, 1987; Association of Former Students of Texas A&M University, Distinguished Teaching Award, 1986; numerous others. **SPECIAL ACHIEVEMENTS:** Published numerous research articles in leading domestic & intl academic journals such as Journal of Money, Credit & Banking, Journal of Intl Business Studies, Columbia Journal of World Business, Journal of Banking & Finance, Journal of Financial Research, Financial Review, Journal of Intl Finance, Journal of Futures Markets, Intl Journal of Management, Journal of Business Strategies, North American Review of Economics & Finance, Indian Economic Journal, others. **BUSINESS ADDRESS:** Professor, Dept of Finance, Texas A&M University, College Station, TX 77843-4218, (409)845-4876.

MAHAJAN, HARPREET
Educator, educational administrator. Indo-American. **PERSONAL:** Born Nov 29, 1953, Simla, Himachal Pradesh, India; daughter of Jaspal Singh & Rajinder Kaur; married Gurinder B S Chhachhi, Dec 28, 1979. **EDUCATION:** Delhi University, Gargi College, BSc, 1973; Jawaharlal Nehru University, MA, 1975, MPhil, 1976, PhD, 1980; Columbia University, Southern Asian Institute, certificate, 1980; Columbia University, MPhil, political science, 1983. **CAREER:** Columbia University, SIPA, systems coordinator, 1986-87, director of computer lab, SIPA, 1987-89, assistant professor, political science, 1988-90, assistant professor, DIPA, 1990-93, associate professor, DIPA, 1994-, director of academic computing, SIPA, 1992-. **ORGANIZATIONS:** Columbia University, SIPA, Task Force on Computer Use, chair, 1992-93; Journal of International Affairs, technical consultant, 1989-; Southern Asian Institute, executive committee, 1993-. **HONORS/AWARDS:** University Grants Commission, JNU, India, research fellowship, 1975-79; Columbia University, Department of Political Science, fellow, 1979-80, President's Fellow, 1980-81, SIPA Student Association, award for service to the school of international & public affairs' community, fall 1990. **SPECIAL ACHIEVEMENTS:** Author, "Arms Transfer to India, Pakistan and the Third World," Young Asia, 1982; Modern Review, vol 144, nos 11-12, p 323-326, Dec 1980; Africa Quarterly, vol 17, no 4, p 46-66, 1978; Philosophy & Social Action, vol 4, no 4, p 31-38, 1979; Institute for Defence Studies & Analyses Journal, vol 11, no 4, p 329-419, 1979; Peace & Disputed Sovereignty, UPA & Col University, 1985; Public Opinion Quarterly, vol 50, 1986. **HOME ADDRESS:** 423 W 120th St, Apt 28, New York, NY 10027, (212)932-3017. **BUSINESS ADDRESS:** Director of Academic Computing, Associate Professor, Columbia University, School of International & Public Affairs, 420 W 118th St, Rm 1513B IAB, New York, NY 10027-6940, (212)854-8347.

MAHAJAN, JAYASHREE

Educator. Indo-American. **PERSONAL:** Born in Pune, Maharashtra, India; daughter of Captain and Mrs Y V Mahajan; married Asoo J Vakharia; children: Rohan A Vakharia. **EDUCATION:** Bombay University, BA (honors), 1977, MA, 1979; University of Windsor, MBA, 1981; University of Wisconsin, Madison, PhD, 1986. **CAREER:** University of Wisconsin, Madison, lecturer, 1984-85; University of Arizona, professor, 1986-94; University of Florida, professor, 1994-. **ORGANIZATIONS:** American Marketing Association, 1981-; The Institute of Management Sciences, 1987-; Association for Consumer Research, 1986-; Society for Judgment & Decision Making, 1992-. **HONORS/AWARDS:** National Science Foundation, Research Planning Grant, 1992; Marketing Science Institute, honorable mention in research competitions, 1984-91. **SPECIAL ACHIEVEMENTS:** Coauthor, "An Exploratory Investigation of the Interdependence of Marketing and Operations Functions in Service Firms," Intl Journal of Research in Marketing, 1993; "The Overconfidence Effect in Marketing Management Predictions," Journal of Marketing Research, 4, 329-342, August, 1992; "A Data Envelopment Analytic Model for Assessing the Efficiency of the Selling Function," European Journal of Operational Research, 53, 189-205, July 1991. **BUSINESS ADDRESS:** Assistant Professor, University of Florida, College of Business Administration, Bryan Hall, Gainesville, FL 32611, (904)392-0161.

MAHAJAN, ROOP L.

Educator, researcher. Indo-American. **PERSONAL:** Born Mar 15, 1943, Jassar, Punjab, India; son of Buta Mal Mahajan & Krishna Devi Mahajan; married Kavita D Mahajan, Jan 7, 1978; children: Neha, Shreya, Parag. **EDUCATION:** Punjab University, BSME, 1964, MSME, 1969; Cornell University, PhD, 1977. **CAREER:** American Refrigerator Co, Calcutta, mech engineer, 1964-65; Punjab Engneering College, Chandigarh, assistant professor, 1965-72; AT&T Bell Labs, Princeton, member technical staff, 1976-79, supervisor, 1979-91; University of Colorado, Boulder, professor, director, 1991-. **ORGANIZATIONS:** American Society of Mechanical Engineers, 1984-, executive committee, K-8 fundamental research, 1978-, executive committee, K-15 materials processing, 1989-. **HONORS/AWARDS:** AT&T Bell Labs, fellow, 1989, Great Boss Award, 1988; Cornell University, Allen Seymour Olmstede Fellowship, 1974. **SPECIAL ACHIEVEMENTS:** Co-author: Buoyancy Induced Flows & Transport, both reference and text; review article: "Instability and Transition in Buoyancy-Induced Flows," Advances in Applied Mechanics, 1982; over 70 papers in refereed journals; United Nations assignment to India as an expert in thermal management, 1988, 1993. **BUSINESS ADDRESS:** Professor, Director, Dept of Mechanical Engineering, University of Colorado, Campus Box 427, Boulder, CO 80309-0427, (303)492-7750.

MAHAJAN, SATISH MURLIDHAR

Educator. Indo-American. **PERSONAL:** Born Nov 12, 1955, Ahmednagar, Maharashtra, India; son of Murlidhar P and Prabhavati M Mahajan; married Shubhada S Mahajan, Aug 31, 1983; children: Priya, Sneha. **EDUCATION:** University of Poona, India, BE, 1978; State University of New York, Buffalo, MS, 1983; University of South Carolina, PhD, 1987. **CAREER:** Tennessee Technological University, associate professor, 1987-. **ORGANIZATIONS:** IEEE, 1982-; Tennessee Academy of Science, 1988-; Dielectric Engineer & Insulation Society, 1988-. **BUSINESS ADDRESS:** Associate Professor, Electrical Engineering Dept, Tennessee Technological University, Brown Hall, Cookeville, TN 38505, (615)372-3397.

MAHAJAN, VIJAY

Educator. Indo-American. **PERSONAL:** Born Apr 5, 1948, Jammu, Jammu and Kashmir, India; son of Mrs & Mr Shiv Saran Gupta; married Fawn, Jan 31, 1977; children: Ramin, Geeti. **EDUCATION:** Indian Institute of Technology, India, BS, 1965; University of Texas at Austin, MS, 1972, PhD, 1975. **CAREER:** State University of New York at Buffalo, 1975-78; Ohio State University, 1978-80; University of Pennsylvania, Wharton School, 1980-82; Southern Methodist University, 1982-90; University of Texas at Austin, John P Harbin Centennial Chair of Business, 1990-. **ORGANIZATIONS:** American Marketing Association, 1975-. **HONORS/AWARDS:** University of Texas at Austin, Graduate School of Business, Lifetime Outstanding Research Contributions, 1990, Maynard Award for best research article, 1990. **SPECIAL ACHIEVEMENTS:** Editor designate, Journal of Marketing Research American Marketing Association, 1994-97. **BIOGRAPHICAL SOURCES:** Perspectives on Strategic Market Planning, Allyn & Baum, 1990; Innovation Diffusion Models, Ballinger, 1986. **BUSINESS ADDRESS:** John P Harbin Centennial Chair, Professor of Business, Dept of Marketing, University of Texas, Austin, TX 78712, (512)471-1128.

MAHAJAN, Y. LAL

Educator. Indo-American. **PERSONAL:** Born Aug 16, 1938, Dina Nagar, Punjab, India; son of Amar & Sita; married Pinky, Jul 24, 1988; children: Tony, Jeffrey, David, Paul. **EDUCATION:** University of Chicago, MA, 1970; Northern Illinois University, PhD, 1976. **CAREER:** Northeastern University, assistant professor, 1976-79; Monmouth College, associate professor, 1979-. **ORGANIZATIONS:** AEA, AFA, ASA. **HOME ADDRESS:** 610 Carol Ave, Ocean, NJ 07712, (908)531-0145. **BUSINESS ADDRESS:** Associate Professor, Monmouth Col, Cedar & Norwood Ave, West Long Branch, NJ 07764-1898, (908)571-3647.

MAHALINGAM, R.

Educator, consultant. Indo-American. **PERSONAL:** Born in India; children: Ramesh. **EDUCATION:** Bombay University, BS (honors), 1957; Indian Institute of Science, Bangalore, India, Dip IISc, 1959; Purdue University, MS, 1963; University of Newcastle-Upon-Tyne, England, PhD, 1966. **CAREER:** Century Rayon Corp, development engineer, 1959-61; Monsanto Corp, development engineer, 1966-67; Scientific Design Co, development/design engineer, 1967-69; Washington State University, Chemical Engineering, professor, 1969-, Materials Science & Engg, adjunct professor, 1972-89, Civil & Env Engg, adjunct professor, 1987-, Env Science & Regional Planning, adjunct professor, 1993-; Battelle Labs, visiting scientist, summers, 1973, 1974; US Dept of Energy, visiting scientist, summers, 1979-80, 1989, 1991; Indian Institute of Technology, Madras, visiting professor, 1985; US Environmental Protection Agency, visiting scientist, 1992. **ORGANIZATIONS:** American Institute of Chemical Engineers, 1963-, research committee, 1980-, Environmental Division, secretary, 1985, Environmental Progress Journal, editorial board, 1983-; American Chemical Society, 1963-; Washington State University, Chemical Energy & Proc Res, head, 1975-80; Kiwanis Club, 1970-. **HONORS/AWARDS:** Sigma Xi, 1980; Phi Lambda Upsilon, 1962; American Institute of Chemical Engineers, Fellow, 1988; Washington State University College of Engineering, Faculty Research Excellence Award. **SPECIAL ACHIEVEMENTS:** About 150 reports, presentations, refereed articles, book chapters; consultancy assignments: Aerojet; Weyerhaeuser; Ashland Chemical; Battelle; Olin Corp; Ciba-Geigy; Hittman-Westinghouse; Dow Chemical; MarTech International; US Department of Energy, Burns & Roe; PRC; Consultech; United Nations, Tokten-India; World Environmental Center, ZCH-Poland; CheMet Engg Group Inc; Petro Bras-Brazil. **BUSINESS ADDRESS:** Professor of Chemical Engineering, Washington State University, Pullman, WA 99164-2710, (509)335-1304.

MAHANTHAPPA, KALYANA T.

Physicist, educator. Indo-American. **PERSONAL:** Born Oct 29, 1934, Hirehalli, Karnataka, India; son of Kalyana Thipperudraiah & Tippamma Maddanappa; married Prameela, Oct 30, 1961; children: Nagesh, Rudresh, Mahesh. **EDUCATION:** Central College, Mysore University, Bangalore, India, BSc (with honors), 1954; Delhi University, Delhi, India, MSc, 1956; Harvard University, PhD, 1961. **CAREER:** University of California, Los Angeles, research associate, 1961-63; University of Pennsylvania, assistant professor, 1963-66; International Centre for Theoretical Physics, Trieste, Italy, visiting scientist, 1970-71; University of Rome, 1970; Cambridge University, UK, 1976-77; University of Colorado, associate professor, 1966-69, professor, 1969-; NATO Advanced Study Institute in Elementary Particle Physics, director, 1979; Advanced Research Workshop on Superstings, director, 1987; Theoretical Advanced Study Institute in Elementary Particle Physics, director, 1989-. **ORGANIZATIONS:** American Physical Society, fellow, 1969-; AAAS, 1973-; Sigma Xi, 1975-. **HONORS/AWARDS:** University of Colorado, Faculty Fellowship, 1970, 1976, 1983, 1993; Scientific and Engineering Research Council, UK, Imperial College London, senior visiting research fellow, 1983. **SPECIAL ACHIEVEMENTS:** Published more than 100 physics research papers in professional journals. **HOME ADDRESS:** 2865 Darley Ave, Boulder, CO 80303-6307. **BUSINESS PHONE:** (303)492-8780.

MAHESH, VIRENDRA BHUSHAN

Educator. Indo-American. **PERSONAL:** Born Apr 25, 1932, Khanki, India; son of Narinjan Prasad and Sobhagyati Mahesh; married Sushila Kumari Mahesh, Jun 29, 1955; children: Anita Rani Schwarz, Vinit Kumar. **EDUCATION:** Patna University, BSc (with honors), 1951; Dehli University, MSc, 1953, PhD, 1955; Oxford University, DPhil, 1958. **CAREER:** Yale University, James Hudson Brown Memorial Fellowship, 1958-59; Medical College of Georgia, assistant professor of endocrinology, 1959-63, associate professor of endocrinology, 1963-66, professor of endocrinology, 1966-72, Department of Endocrinology, regents professor/chairman, 1972-86, Department of Physiology and Endocrinology, regents professor and chairman, 1986-. **ORGANIZA-TIONS:** National Institutes of Health, Reproductive Biology Study Section, 1977-81, Human Embryology Study Section, 1982-86, 1990-93, chairman, 1991-93. **HONORS/AWARDS:** Society for Study of Sterility, Rubin Award, 1963; American Medical Association, Billings Silver Medal, 1966; Association of Scientists of Indian Origin, Distinguished Scientist Award, 1989; Medical College of Georgia, School of Graduate Studies, Distinguished Faculty Award, 1981, School of Medicine, Distinguished Faculty Award, 1992. **SPECIAL ACHIEVEMENTS:** Co-editor of 7 books; author of 350 scientific publications in Reproductive Biology. **BUSINESS ADDRESS:** Regents Professor & Chairman, Dept of Physiology & Endocrinology, Medical College of Georgia, Augusta, GA 30912-3000, (706)721-2781.

MAHESHWARI, ARUN K.
Insurance company executive. Indo-American. **PERSONAL:** Born Nov 9, 1944, Jaipur, India; son of Chandmal Maheshwari and Kamala Maheshwari; married Vijaylakshmi, Jan 16, 1974; children: Aditi, Amit. **EDUCATION:** Rajasthan, BS, 1964; Columbia University, MBA, 1970; University of Pennsylvania, PhD, 1973; Stanford University, MS, 1977. **CAREER:** Tata Consultancy, consultant, 1974-76; McKinsey & Co, consultant, 1977-81; Reliance Insurance, asst vice pres, 1981-85; Continental Insurance Co, vice pres, 1985-. **ORGANIZATIONS:** India Temple, secretary, 1992-93; Indian Cultural Center, treasurer, 1992-93. **HOME ADDRESS:** 737 Brandywine Dr, Moorestown, NJ 08057, (609)231-0348.

MAHILUM, BENJAMIN C.
Farming and farm consulting, company executive. Filipino American. **PERSONAL:** Born Aug 9, 1931, Calatrava, Negros Occidental, Philippines; son of Hipolito P Mahilum & Basilia N Comawas; married Paulita M Mahilum, Jul 28, 1957; children: David M, Lourdes Mahilum Tapay, Junever M, Lyman M, Jorge M, Don M. **EDUCATION:** Cebu School of Arts and Trades, technical auto mechanics, 1952; Mindanao Agricultural College, BS (magna cum laude), agriculture, 1957; University of Hawaii-Manoa, MS, soil science, 1966; Oklahoma State University, PhD, soil science, 1971. **CAREER:** Negros Occidental National Agricultural School, vocational agricultural teacher, 1957-61; Mindanao Institute of Technology, college instructor, 1961-66, assistant professor III, 1966-73; University of Eastern Philippines, associate professor III and research coordinator, 1973-74; Visayas State College of Agriculture, associate professor VI, director, Regional Coconut Research Center, chairman, Department of Agronomy and Soils, 1974-76; Oklahoma State University, visiting assistant professor, 1977-79; University of Hawaii, Hilo, assistant professor of soil science, 1976-79; self employed, dba Trapag Hawaii, CEO/single proprietor, 1976-. **ORGANIZATIONS:** International Soil Science Society, 1964-86; Soil Science Society of America, 1964-86; American Society of Agronomy, 1967-86; Council for Agricultural Science and Technology, 1982-86; Philippine Association for the Advancement of Science, 1971-77; Philippine Society for the Advancement of Research, 1973-77; Soil Science Society of the Philippines, 1961-77; Philippine Council for Agriculture Resources Research, 1973-77; American Association for the Advancement of Science, 1968-86. **HONORS/AWARDS:** East-West Center, Scholarship Grant for MS, 1963-65; National Science Development Board, Scholarship for PhD, 1967-71; Oklahoma State University, Presidential Honor Award, 1970. **SPECIAL ACHIEVEMENTS:** Accelerated Research and Faculty Development at University of Eastern Philippines, 1973-74; established Dept of Agronomy and Soils, and Regional Coconut Research Center at Visayas State College of Agriculture, 1974-77; co-author of Organic Compounds in Soils: Movement, Degradation and Persistence, Ann Arbor Science Publishers, 1982; intensive farming through multicropping systems, 1986-. **HOME ADDRESS:** PO Box 1213, Honokaa, HI 96727, (808)775-9730.

MAI, HUGH D.
Physician. Vietnamese American. **PERSONAL:** Born Apr 22, 1959, Saigon, Vietnam; son of X H Mai and A D Lang; married Marianne Vu Mai, Apr 22, 1990; children: Nicholas V K. **EDUCATION:** San Diego State University, BS, 1981; University of Texas, San Antonio, MD, 1985. **CAREER:** St Paul Medical Center, Dallas, Texas, president, internal medicine, 1985-88; VA Medical Center, Phoenix, Arizona, fellow, gastroenterology, 1988-90; self-employed physician, 1990-. **ORGANIZATIONS:** American Gastroenterological Association, 1993-; American College of Gastroenterology, 1992-; American Society for Gastrointestinal Endoscopy, 1992-; American College of Physicians, 1989-; American Medical Association, 1986-. **HONORS/AWARDS:** University of Texas Medical School, San Antonio, Texas Legislative Merit Scholarship, 1985; Phi Beta Kappa, 1980; Phi Kappa Phi, 1980; San Diego State University, Outstanding Graduate Award in Chemistry, 1981. **SPECIAL ACHIEVEMENTS:** Diplomate of American Board of Internal Medicine, 1988; Diplomate of American Subspecialty Board of Gastroenterology, 1991; Gastrointest Endosc, Improved Patient Care Using the ASGE Guidelines On Quality Assurance: A Prospective Comparative Study, 1991; Regression of Duodenal Gastrinomas in a Patient with Multiple Endocrine Neoplasia Type I After Parathyroidectomy, 1992; numerous others. **BUSINESS ADDRESS:** Physician, 63 S 12th St, San Jose, CA 95112, (408)993-0636.

MAI, MARIANNE VU
Optometrist. Vietnamese American. **PERSONAL:** Born Dec 27, 1967, Saigon, Vietnam; daughter of Oanh N Vu and Anh Vu; married Hugh D Mai, Apr 22, 1990; children: Nicholas. **EDUCATION:** UC, Riverside, BS, 1983; Southern California College of Optometry, OD, 1993. **CAREER:** Optometrist, currently. **ORGANIZATIONS:** American Optometric Association. **BUSINESS ADDRESS:** Optometrist, 63 S 12th St, San Jose, CA 95112, (408)993-0636.

MAJ, NAWEED K.
Surgeon. Pakistani American. **PERSONAL:** Born Dec 2, 1945, Pakistan; son of Abdul Majid and Mahmooda Majid; married Zarmina, Jan 7, 1977; children: Nadia, Amer, Sonia. **EDUCATION:** Islamia College, Pechawar, Pakistan, FSc, 1962; King Edward Medical College, Lahore, Pakistan, MBBS, 1967. **CAREER:** Private practice, cardiovascular/thoracic surgeon, 1980-. **ORGANIZATIONS:** Barnert Hospital, bd of trustees, 1993-; Passaic General, Section of Cardiac Surgery, chief, 1992-; American Islamic Academy, chairman of the board, 1992; fellow: American College of Surgeons, American College of Chief Physicans, American College of Angiology, Intl College of Surgeons. **MILITARY SERVICE:** US Air Force, major, 1977-80. **BUSINESS ADDRESS:** Surgeon, 1031 McBride Ave, West Paterson, NJ 07424, (201)256-4880.

MAK, CHI HO
Educator. Hong Kong American. **PERSONAL:** Born Sep 1, 1963, Hong Kong; son of Wai-Lam Mak & Po-Tak Mak; married Muse T P Mak, Jul 27, 1991. **EDUCATION:** University of California, Berkeley, BS, 1984; Stanford University, PhD, 1988. **CAREER:** UC Berkeley, postdoctoral associate, 1988-90; University of Southern California, assistant professor of chemistry, 1990-. **ORGANIZATIONS:** American Chemical Society, 1986-; American Physical Society, 1986-. **HONORS/AWARDS:** UC Berkeley, Certificate of Distinction, 1984, Chemical Engineering, Departmental Citation, 1984; National Science Foundation, Predoctoral Fellow, 1984, Young Investigator Award, 1992; Dreyfus Foundation, New Faculty Award, 1990. **SPECIAL ACHIEVEMENTS:** A Dynamical Test of the Centroid Formulation of Quantum Transition Theory, 1993; Stochastic Method for Real-Time Path Integrations, 1992; Coherent-Incoherent Transitions and Relaxations in Condensed-Phase Tunneling Systems, 1991; Solving the Sign Problem in Quantum Monte Carlo Dynamics, 1990. **BUSINESS ADDRESS:** Assistant Professor, Dept of Chemistry, University of Southern California, Los Angeles, CA 90089-0482, (213)740-4101.

MAK, JAMES
Educator. Chinese American. **PERSONAL:** Born Feb 28, 1941, Macao; son of Eddie & Patty Mak; married Alice Wakukawa Mak, Aug 1975; children: Eric S, Christopher K. **EDUCATION:** Wilmington College, BS, 1964; Miami University, MA, 1966; Purdue University, PhD, 1970. **CAREER:** University of Hawaii, professor of economics, 1970-. **ORGANIZATIONS:** American Economic Association; Economic History Association; Hawaii Council on Economic Education; Western Economic Association. **HONORS/AWARDS:** State of Hawaii, House and Senate Concurrent Resolution, 1974; Hawaii Council on Economic Education, Jackstadt Award, 1991; Economic History Association, Cole Prize, 1973. **SPECIAL ACHIEVEMENTS:** With E Haites and G Walton, Western River Transportation During the Era of Early Internal Improvements, Baltimore, Johns Hopkins University Press, 1974; over 60 publications in economics. **BUSINESS ADDRESS:** Professor, Dept of Economics, University of Hawaii, Manoa, Porteus Hall, Rm 542, Honolulu, HI 96822, (808)956-8496.

MAK, PAUL P.
Association executive. Hong Kong American. **PERSONAL:** Born Jan 3, Hong Kong. **EDUCATION:** Hunter College, BA; New York University, certificate of association management. **CAREER:** Brooklyn Chinese-American Association, president, CEO, currently. **ORGANIZATIONS:** Red Cross of America,

board of directors; Sunset Park Family Health Network of Lutheran Medical Center; Brooklyn Community Board Seven; New York Police Department, Asian-American Advisory Council; Brooklyn District Attorney's Asian-American Advisory Council; Brooklyn Chinese American Business Association, consultant; Brooklyn Chinese American Voters Association, honorary chair. **HONORS/AWARDS:** New York City Transit Authority, community support and commitment; Chinese Language Journalists Association, contributions to Chinese community; New York City Police Department, Certificate of Appreciation, Certificate of Recognition; Brooklyn Community Board Twelve, Community Service Award; United States Bureau of Census, Outstanding Contributions; South West Brooklyn Industrial Development Corporation, Creating a Better Sunset Park Business Environment. **SPECIAL ACHIEVEMENTS:** Initiated and developed the Brooklyn Chinatown community in mid 1980's; initiated Annual Chinese New Year Parade in Brooklyn since 1988; initiated multiple human services to the Chinese population in Brooklyn since 1988; translated New York Police Department Safety Tips, 14 different types, into Chinese; initiated the first Chinese-American bilingual nurse training programs in New York City; established the first Chinese-American bilingual medical clinic in Brooklyn; established the first Chinese-American Senior Citizen and Youth Center. **BUSINESS ADDRESS:** President, CEO, Brooklyn Chinese-American Association Inc, 5313 8th Ave, Brooklyn, NY 11220, (718)438-9312.

MAK, SIOE THO
Scientist. Chinese American. **PERSONAL:** Born Sep 3, 1932, Medan, Sumatera Utara, Indonesia; son of Mak Boen Kit and Tjoa Tjioe Nio; married Jeanne Giok Nio, Jun 12, 1959; children: Sharleen Mak Ruddy, Shanta Mak Keeven. **EDUCATION:** Illinois Institute of Technology, PhD, electrical engineering, 1970. **CAREER:** Bandung Institute of Technology, Indonesia, senior lecturer, 1960-67; Washington University, St Louis, adjunct professor, 1975; Illinois Institute of Technology, instructor, 1967-78; Joslyn Mfg & Supply Company, senior scientist, 1971-78; Emerson Electric Co, staff scientist, 1978-89; Distribution Control Systems Inc, senior staff scientist, 1989-. **ORGANIZATIONS:** IEEE, senior member, 1971-, Power System Engineering Committee, Demand Side Management Subcommittee, Distribution Automation Working Group, Standardization of Interfaces Task Force, chairman. **HONORS/AWARDS:** The Agency for International Development, Research and Study Junior Fellowship, 1959-61; Illinois Institute of Technology, Teaching Fellowship, 1967-70; Emerson Electric Co, honorable mention in annual report; IEEE, honorable mention for working group activities. **SPECIAL ACHIEVEMENTS:** Publications in various journals, including: IEEE Transactions, International Symposium on Demand Side Management and Distribution Automation; organized and participated in several technical panel sessions at IEEE (USA) and IEE (United Kingdom); holds numerous patents (US and Foreign) in communications of data, algorithms for detection, etc. **BUSINESS ADDRESS:** Senior Staff Scientist, Distribution Control Systems Inc, 5657 Campus Pky, Hazelwood, MO 63042, (314)895-6459.

MAK, STANLEY M.
Import/export company executive. Chinese American. **PERSONAL:** Born Feb 17, 1949, Chengdu, Sichuan, People's Republic of China; son of Mak Fung and Yil Sui-Fun; married Suzanne Phelps, Jun 9, 1971; children: Justin, Kristin, Kathryn. **EDUCATION:** Eastern Washington State University, BA, 1992. **CAREER:** King Broadcasting Co, KREM, account exec, radio sales, 1972-75, King AM, account exec, radio sales, 1975-77, TV sales, King TV, account exec, 1977-79, KINK Radio, sales manager, 1979-82, KINK Radio, vice president, general manager, 1982-87, radio, senior vice president, 1987-92; Mak Pacific, Inc, president, currently. **ORGANIZATIONS:** Centrum, board of directors, 1993-; Seattle Youth Symphony Orchestra, executive board, board of directors, 1988-91; American Red Cross, Oregon, executive boad, boad of directors, 1985-87; Portland Traffic Safety Commission, board of directors, 1984-86. **BUSINESS ADDRESS:** President, Mak Pacific, Inc, 10900 NE Eighth St, Suite 900, Bellevue, WA 98004, (206)455-2638.

MAK, WILLIAM K.
Import company executive. Chinese American. **PERSONAL:** Born Mar 14, 1921, Canton, China; son of Kam Tai Mak and Yuk yu Mak; married Marion W Mak, May 26, 1951; children: Elise P Yau, Darrell J. **EDUCATION:** Dr Sun Yat Sen University, BA, 1943; New York University, MA, 1953. **CAREER:** Voice of America, newscaster, 1951-53, program producer, 1954-65, senior news editor, 1966-84; General Commodities Co, CEO/president, 1984-; Dragon Mustard Co of America, CEO, 1986-; Chinese American Marketing Co, CEO, 1990-. **ORGANIZATIONS:** American Economic Association,

1962-; Chinese Consolidated Benevolent Association, chairman, 1988-92; Montgomery County Economic Advisory Council, 1992-. **HONORS/AWARDS:** Voice of America, Service Award, 1984; Organization of American Chinese, Community Service Excellence Award, 1988; Carlos Rosario Adult Education Center, Education Leadership Award, 1991; The Republic of China, Government Honor Medal for Foreign Citizen, 1993; Chinese Consolidated Benevolent Association, Community Leadership Award, 1993. **SPECIAL ACHIEVEMENTS:** The Economic Policy of Wang An Shih, 1953; The Development of Chinese Ethnic Schools in America, 1953.

MAKHIJANI, SRICHAND. *See* Obituaries.

MAKINO, SEIICHI
Educator. Japanese American. **PERSONAL:** Born Jan 20, 1935, Tokyo, Japan; son of Fujio & Emiko Makino; married Yasuko Makino, Mar 24, 1963; children: Shigeki. **EDUCATION:** Waseda University, BA, 1958, MA, 1960; University of Tokyo, BA, 1962, MA, 1964; University of Illinois, Urbana-Champaign, PhD, 1968. **CAREER:** University of Illinois, Urbana-Champaign, professor of Japanese and linguistics, 1968-91; Princeton University, professor of Japanese and linguistics, director, Japanese Language, 1991-. **ORGANIZATIONS:** Association of Teachers of Japanese; Linguistic Society of America, 1968-; Association for Asian Studies, 1970-; Linguistic Society of Japan, 1960-; American Council on the Teaching of Foreign Languages, 1992-. **SPECIAL ACHIEVEMENTS:** Author, Some Aspects of Japanese Nominalizations, Tokyo, Tokai University Press, 1969; Kotoba to Kukan, Tokyo, Tokai University Press, 1978; Kurikaeshi no Bunpo, Tokyo, Taishukan Shoten, 1980; co-author, A Dictionary of Basic Japanese Grammar, Tokyo, The Japan Times, 1986. **HOME ADDRESS:** 7 Westwinds, Princeton Junction, NJ 08550. **BUSINESS PHONE:** (609)258-5365.

MAKINO, SHOJIRO (MIKE)
Chemical company executive. Japanese American. **PERSONAL:** Born Jun 5, 1929, Tokyo, Japan; married Sachi Makino, Apr 24, 1965; children: Genta. **EDUCATION:** Keio University, BA; University of Oregon, MBA. **CAREER:** Getz Bros, Shokai, salesman, 1951-55, Getz Bros & Co, Okinawa, Japan, mgr, industrial sales, 1955-59, San Francisco, mgmt trainee, 1959-61; Omark Industries Inc, sales representative, 1962-67, Omark Japan Inc, vice pres, general mgr, 1967-69; Grace Japan K K, vice pres, 1969-70, president, 1970-; W R Grace & Co, corporate vice pres, 1988-. **ORGANIZATIONS:** American Chamber of Commerce in Japan, bd of governors; Tokyo Chamber of Commerce and Industry; Japan-American Cooperative Committee, vice chmn; The America-Japan Society, counselor; Rotary Club of Tokyo East. **HOME ADDRESS:** 5-16-17-403 Roppongi, Minato-ku, Tokyo 106, Japan, 3-3583-1215.

MAKINO, YASUKO
Librarian. Japanese American. **PERSONAL:** Born Apr 8, 1937, Tokyo, Japan; daughter of Toshio & Itsuko Hosoya; married Seiichi Makino, Mar 24, 1963; children: Shigeki. **EDUCATION:** Tokyo Joshi Daigaku, Tokyo Woman's Christian University, 1961; University of Illinois, Urbana-Champaign, MA, 1970, MLS, 1972. **CAREER:** Higashimurayama Dai-2 Chugakko, Tokyo, 1961-64; University of Illinois, Urbana-Champaign, Japanese librarian, 1972-91; Columbia University, Japanese cataloger, 1991-92, Japanese Studies librarian, 1992-. **ORGANIZATIONS:** Association for Asian Studies, 1976-; American Library Association, 1985-, Cataloging Committee: Asia & Africa, 1992-94; Subcommittee on Japanese Materials of CEAL, chair, 1987-90; Japan Library Association, 1975-; Japan Society of Library Science, 1978-91; International Association of Oriental Librarians, 1985-; Asian/Pacific American Librarians Association, treasurer, 1991-93. **SPECIAL ACHIEVEMENTS:** Japanese Rare and Old Books: Annotated bibliographical guide of reference books, Tokyo, Hobundo, 1977, with publication grant from the Japan Foundation; Japan through Children's Literature: A Critical Bibliography, enlarged edition, Westport, CT, Greenwood Press, 1985; National Union List of Current Japanese Serials in East Asian Libraries of North America, with Mihoko Miki, Los Angeles, Subcommittee on Japanese Materials, AAS, 1992; Student Guide to Japanese Reference Books in Humanities, with Masaei Saito, Ann Arbor, Center for Japanese Studies, University of Michigan, 1994. **BUSINESS ADDRESS:** Japanese Studies Librarian, Columbia University, C V Starr East Asian Library, 300 Kent Hall, New York, NY 10027, (212)854-1506.

MAKINODAN, TAKASHI
Educator, health services administrator. Japanese American. **PERSONAL:** Born Jan 19, 1925, Hilo, HI; married Jane S Makinodan, Dec 19, 1954;

children: Ann Y Maser. **EDUCATION:** University of Hawaii, BS, 1949; University of Wisconsin, MS, 1951, PhD, 1953. **CAREER:** Oak Ridge National Laboratory, Lab of Radiation Immunology, chief, 1955-72; NICHD, NIH, Lab of Comp Physiology, chief, 1972-76; UCLA, professor of medicine, 1976-; Veterans Affairs Medical Center, GRECC, director, 1976-79, associate director, 1976-. **ORGANIZATIONS:** Am Assn of Immunologists, 1956-, program comm, 1972-75; Fed of Am Society Etptl Biology, 1956-, Public Infor Officer, 1973-77; Gerontology Society of America, 1971-, vp, 1974-75; White House Conf on Aging, consultant, 1970-80; Intl Assn Gerontology, council member, 1975-78; NIH Study Section, Immunobiol Sciences, 1978-82; Natl Science Foundation Adv Panel, regulatory biology, 1971-73. **HONORS/ AWARDS:** Veterans Affairs, Chief Medical Director, Commendation Award, Accomplishment in Aging Research, 1989; Gerontology Society of America, Kleemeier Award, 1988; UCLA, Arthur Cherkin Memorial Award, 1987; Beijing Medical University, visiting professor, 1988; Andrus Gerontology Ctr, University of Southern California, Biomedical Sciences Award, 1976. **SPECIAL ACHIEVEMENTS:** Peer-reviewed research papers: 135; reviews & book chapters: 105; books: 5. **BUSINESS ADDRESS:** Associate Director, Research, GRECC, VA Medical Center, West Los Angeles, Wilshire and Sawtelle Blvds, (11G), Los Angeles, CA 90073, (310)824-4301.

MAKO (MAKOTO IWAMATSU)

Actor. Japanese American. **PERSONAL:** Born Dec 10, 1932, Kobe, Japan; married Shizuko Hoshi; children: two. **EDUCATION:** Pratt Institute, architecture; Pasadena Playhouse, theatre studies. **CAREER:** Stage appearances: Pacific Overtures, 1967-68, 1976; A Banquet for the Moon, 1961; Yellow Fever, 1983; The Wash, 1985; Gold Watch, 1972; Station J, 1981; Hokusai Sketchbooks, 1967-68; Director: Fisher King, 1976; Music Lessons, 1980; FOB (Fresh Off the Boat), 1980; film appearances: An Unremarkable Life, 1989; Man and His Dream, 1988; Silent Assassins, 1988; The Wash, 1988; The Escape, 1986; Armed Response, 1986; numerous others; TV appearances: Hawaiian Heat, 1984; Alfred of the Amazon, 1967; Streets of San Francisco, 1972; Judge Dee in the Monastery Murders, 1974; Last Ninja, 1983; Ohara, 1987; Spenser: For Hire, 1987; Tour of Duty, 1987; Equalizer, 1988; Supercarrier, 1988; Paradise, 1990; MASH, 1974, 1976, 1980; Incredible Hulk, 1978-79; numerous others; East/West Players and the Children's Workshop, founder, artistic director, 1966-. **ORGANIZATIONS:** Actors' Equity Association; Screen Actors Guild; American Federation of Television and Radio Artists. **HONORS/AWARDS:** Had star installed in Hollywood Walk of Fame, 1994. **SPECIAL ACHIEVEMENTS:** Stage writings: Christmas in Camp, 1981; There's No Place Like a Tired Ghost, 1972; The Sand Pebbles, Academy Award Nominee for Best Supporting Actor, 1966; Pacific Overtures, Antoinette Perry Award Nominee for Best Actor in a Musical, 1976. **MILITARY SERVICE:** US Armed Forces. *

MALHOTRA, ANJU

Educator. Indo-American. **PERSONAL:** Born Jun 10, 1958, Kapurthala, Punjab, India; daughter of O P Malhotra & Vimla Malhotra; divorced. **EDUCATION:** Cornell University, BA, 1980; University of Michigan, MA, 1985, PhD, 1990. **CAREER:** University of North Carolina, post-doctoral fellow, 1990-91; University of Maryland, assistant professor, 1991-. **ORGANIZATIONS:** Population Association of America, 1983-; American Sociological Association, 1990-. **HONORS/AWARDS:** Rockefeller Foundation, Population Research Grant, 1992; NICHD, pre & post-doctoral fellowships, 1983-86, 1990-91; Population Council, pre-doctoral fellowship, 1987. **SPECIAL ACHIEVEMENTS:** "Gender and Changing Generational Relations: Spouse Choice in Indonesia," Demography, vol 28, p 4, November 1991; "Determinants of Contraceptive Method Choice in Sri Lanka: An Update from a 1987 Survey," Asian-Pacific Population Journal, vol 6, p 3, September 1991. **BUSINESS ADDRESS:** Professor, Dept of Sociology, University of Maryland, Art-Sociology Bldg, College Park, MD 20742-1315, (301)405-6417.

MALHOTRA, ASHOK K.

Educator. Indo-American. **PERSONAL:** Born Apr 1, 1940, Ferozepur, Punjab, India; son of Nihal C Malhotra and Vidya W Malhotra; married Nina J Finestone, Oct 24, 1966 (deceased); children: Raj K, Ravi K. **EDUCATION:** University of Rajasthan, India, BA, 1961, MA, 1963; University of Hawaii, PhD, 1969. **CAREER:** State University of New York, professor of philosophy, 1967-. **ORGANIZATIONS:** Society for Asian & Comparative Philosophy, vp, 1981-87, secretary, 1981-87, symposia chairperson, 1981-87; American Philosophical Assn, 1975-; Sartre Society, 1989-; Intl Phenomenological Society, 1988-; Assn for Asian Studies, 1988-. **HONORS/AWARDS:** SUNY, United University Professions Excellence in Teaching Award, 1991; University

of Hawaii, East West Center Award, 1963-67; NEH Grant, 1979; SUNY Press, Editorial Board Member, 1989-93. **SPECIAL ACHIEVEMENTS:** Author: Jean-Paul Sartre's Existentialism, 1978; Pathways to Philosophy, June 1994; translation of the Bhagavad Gita, Dec 1994; transcreation of the Tao Te Ching, used in television series "Kung-Fu the Legend Continues," 1993. **HOME PHONE:** (607)432-0496. **BUSINESS ADDRESS:** Professor, Dept of Philosophy, State University of New York, #513 Fitzelle Hall, Oneonta, NY 13820, (607)436-3220.

MALHOTRA, MANOHAR LAL

Industrial company executive. Indo-American. **PERSONAL:** Born Sep 12, 1939, Multan, Pakistan; son of Chetan Dass Malhotra (deceased) and Prakash Wati Malhotra; married Usha Malhotra, Jun 6, 1966; children: Ravi, Arun. **EDUCATION:** University of Delhi, India, MS, physics, 1963; Fairleigh Dickinson University, MS, physics, 1970; Banaras Hindu University, India, PhD, physics, 1972; University of Virginia, PhD, materials science, 1974. **CAREER:** National Physical Lab of India, research scientist, 1965-68; Degussa Corporation, dir of research, 1977-86; Argen Precious Metals Inc, vice pres, technology, 1987-. **ORGANIZATIONS:** Intl Assn for Dental Research, 1974-; Intl Precious Metals Institute, 1977-86; American Assn for Dental Research, 1974-; Sigma Xi; American Society for Metals. **HONORS/ AWARDS:** National Institutes of Health, postdoctoral research, 1975-77; National Science Foundation, postdoctoral research, 1974-75; Fairleigh Dickinson University, Research and Teaching Fellow, 1968-70. **SPECIAL ACHIEVEMENTS:** Published: over 25 research papers in national and intl magazines; lectured: national and intl dental research meetings; introduced cost-effective new palladium alloys to dental profession, 1981. **HOME PHONE:** (619)484-9246. **BUSINESS ADDRESS:** Vice President, Technology, Argen Precious Metals, Inc, 8380 Miralani Dr, San Diego, CA 92126, (619)549-7900.

MALHOTRA, OM P.

Educator. Indo-American. **PERSONAL:** Born Nov 9, 1930, Patiala, Punjab, India; son of B D & Maya Malhotra; married Vimla Malhotra, Jun 20, 1957; children: Anju, Meena Malhotra Punjabi, Sanjay. **EDUCATION:** Punjab University, India, BA, 1951, MA, English, 1954; Rajasthan University, India, BEd, 1968; State University of New York, Binghamton, PhD, 1981. **CAREER:** Government Colleges, India, senior lecturer, 1954-69; SUNY, Farmingdale, professor, chairman, 1974-. **ORGANIZATIONS:** MLA, 1973-; South Asian Literary Association, executive committee, 1982-; ADE, 1992-; United University Professions, 1974-. **HONORS/AWARDS:** Punjab University, Chancellor's Award, 1951; SUNY Binghamton, Teaching Assistantship, 1970-74. **SPECIAL ACHIEVEMENTS:** "Romantic Encounter with Hinduism: Southey," Dissertation, 1981; "Ambiguities of Southey's Prose Writings," SRA, 1984; "British Raj Revisited in Recent Films," MLA Convention, 1985; "Influence of Indian Thought in Eighteenth Century English Literature," MLA Convention, 1990; editor, newsletter of South Asian Literary Association, 1987-91. **BUSINESS ADDRESS:** Chairman, English/Humanities Dept, SUNY, College of Technology, 1250 Melville Rd, Knapp Hall, Farmingdale, NY 11735, (516)420-2050.

MALHOTRA, VIJAY K.

Educator. Indo-American. **PERSONAL:** Born Sep 23, 1946, Lahore, Punjab, India; son of Anand Kumar Malhotra and Swarn Kanta Malhotra; married Madhu Malhotra, Aug 18, 1973; children: Jaishri, Vivek, Vaishali. **EDUCATION:** Delhi University, BA, 1965; Meerut University, MA, 1968; Pepperdine University, MA, 1970; Nova University, EdD, 1994. **CAREER:** Lycee De Los Angeles, head of math dept, 1971-78; LA Trade Technical College, instructor of math, 1978-84; El Camino College, professor of mathematics, 1984-. **ORGANIZATIONS:** American Federation of Teachers; The Mathematical Association of America. **BUSINESS ADDRESS:** Professor of Mathematics, El Camino College, 16007 Crenshaw Blvd, Torrance, CA 90506, (301)715-3218.

MALIK, ANAND KUMAR

Educator. Indo-American. **PERSONAL:** Born Apr 10, 1944, Mian Channu, India; son of Malik Arjan Das & Kartar Kaur; divorced; children: Arun, Ashwin, Avinash. **EDUCATION:** Panjab University, BA (honors), MA; University of London, PGCE, DEd; Columbia University, New York, EdD. **CAREER:** University of Tennessee, Knoxville, professor of inter-cultural education, currently. **HONORS/AWARDS:** Columbia University, president's scholar; University of Saskatchewan, Humanities and Social Science Research Fund Award; University of Tennessee, Student Government, Best Teacher of the Year Award, Phi Kappa Phi Faculty Mace Bearer, post doctoral research at University of London. **SPECIAL ACHIEVEMENTS:** Books: One Thousand Moral Tales, Library of Congress; Social Foundations of Canadian Education, Prentice-Hall, both paperback and hardback editions; Current Themes in Philosophy of Education, University of Saskatchewan Publication no 198; numerous others; International Education, founder-editor, a bi-annual scholarly journal; chairperson, board of editors, The Londinian, Institute of Education Magazine, The University of London; over 150 articles, book reviews, etc, in various magazines and journals. **BUSINESS ADDRESS:** Professor of Intercultural Education, University of Tennessee, Knoxville, TN 37996-0003.

MALIK, HAFEEZ
Educator. Pakistani American. **PERSONAL:** Born Mar 17, 1930, Lahore, Pakistan; married Lynda P Malik; children: Cyrus, Dean. **EDUCATION:** Government College, Pakistan, BA, 1949; University of Punjab, Pakistan, diploma, journalism, 1952; Syracuse University, MS, journalism, 1955, MA, political science, 1957, PhD, politicl science, 1961. **CAREER:** Villanova University, political science, assistant professor, 1961-63, associate professor, 1963-67, professor, 1967-. **ORGANIZATIONS:** Association for Asian Studies; Pi Sigma Alpha; American Association of University Professors; American Political Science Association; American Historical Association; Asian Society, NY, Pakistan Council, chairman, 1971-76; Columbia University, The National Seminar on Pakistan, Bangladesh, 1970-75. **SPECIAL ACHIEVEMENTS:** Proficiency in English, Urdu, Punjabi, Hindi, Persian, Arabic, French languages; papers, articles, chapters, and books including: Central Asia: its Strategic Importance and Future Prospect, Macmillan, St Martin's Press, 1994; Soviet-Pakistan Relations and Post-Soviet Dynamics, Macmillan, St Martin's Press, 1994; Dilemmas of National Security and Cooperation in India and Pakistan, Macmillan, St Martin's Press, 1993. **BUSINESS ADDRESS:** Professor, Villanova University, 416 SAC, Villanova, PA 19085, (215)645-4738.

MALIK, NAEEM
Engineer. Pakistani American. **PERSONAL:** Born May 20, 1952, Karachi, Sind, Pakistan; son of Altaf-Ur-Rahman and Hamida Malik; married Lubna Malik, Dec 23, 1989; children: Najia. **EDUCATION:** DJ Science College, BS, physics, math, 1975; Fairleigh Dickinson University, BSEE, 1981, MSEE, 1983. **CAREER:** Prediction Systems Inc, director, manager; Union Technical Institute, department head. **ORGANIZATIONS:** IEEE; Armed Forces Communications and Electronics Assn; Society for Computer Simulation. **HOME ADDRESS:** 39 Schanck Rd, Holmdel, NJ 07733, (908)946-4799.

MALIK, SADIQ R.
Educator. Bangladeshi American. **PERSONAL:** Born Jul 11, 1944, Ibrahimpur, Chuadanga, Kushtia, Bangladesh; son of Khalil R & Saleha Malik; married Rehana Malik, Jun 15, 1968; children: Faris S, Fahim S. **EDUCATION:** Rajshahi University, Bangladesh, BS (with honors), physics, 1964, MS, electronics, 1965; Birmingham University, UK, MS, radiation tech, 1970, PhD, applied nuclear science, 1973. **CAREER:** Rajshahi University, assistant professor, 1967-75; Birmingham University, research fellow, 1973-75; Garyonis University, assistant professor, 1976-79; Kuwait University, assistant professor, 1979-85, associate professor, 1985-90; Columbia Union College, associate professor, 1990-93, professor, 1993-, Dept of Physics and Engineering, program chair, 1994-. **ORGANIZATIONS:** Institute of Physics, UK, 1974-81; Lunar Science Institute, 1971-75; International Center for Theoretical Physics, Italy, associate member, 1988-90; Ministry of Health, Kuwait, consultant on radiations, 1988-90. **HONORS/AWARDS:** Government of Bangladesh, Talent Scheme Scholarships, 1961-65; Common Scholarship Commission, UK & Association of Commonwealth University, Commonwealth Scholar, 1968-73. **SPECIAL ACHIEVEMENTS:** Proficient in Bengali, English, Urdu, Arabic. **BIOGRAPHICAL SOURCES:** The Bangladesh Observer, June 1, 1973; Columbia Reunion, winter 1991; Columbia Journal, Nov 19, 1990. **HOME ADDRESS:** 11806 Pittson Rd, Silver Spring, MD 20906, (301)933-0175.

MALIK, SAIED AHMAD
Military officer (retired), writer. Indo-American/Pakistani American. **PERSONAL:** Born Dec 19, 1922, Amritsar, Gurdaspur, India; son of Malik Aziz Ahmad and Begum Khurshid Malik; married Malik Shamim, Jun 8, 1930; children: Naveed Saeed, Javed Saeed, Shahid Saeed, Zahid Saeed, Amir Saeed, Hamid Saeed. **EDUCATION:** University of the Punjab, oriental languages (honors), 1942, BA, 1974. **CAREER:** Pakistan Army, officer, 1949-80. **SPECIAL ACHIEVEMENTS:** Language proficiency: Urdu language & literature. **MILITARY SERVICE:** Pakistan Army, infantry, lt colonel, 1949-80;

Sitara Harb, 1965, 1971. **HOME ADDRESS:** 7320 Beverly Park Dr, Springfield, VA 22150, (703)912-6304.

MALIK, TIRLOK N.
Filmmaker. Indo-American. **PERSONAL:** Born Dec 22, 1952, New Delhi, India; son of Amrit Malik & Tara Malik. **EDUCATION:** New School of New York, filmmaking, 1985; Actors Institute, acting; New Delhi, India, BA. **CAREER:** Westside Cafe Inc, vice president, 1984-; Apple Productions, president, 1986-. **HONORS/AWARDS:** Indian Ambassador, Pride of India, 1991; N R I Association, Glory of India International Award, 1993. **SPECIAL ACHIEVEMENTS:** Film, Lonely in America, dealing with the journey of an immigrant into American culture. **HOME ADDRESS:** 215 W 90th St, Penthouse B, New York, NY 10024, (212)877-3623. **BUSINESS PHONE:** (212)662-7200.

MALIK, ZAFAR A.
Educator. Indo-American. **PERSONAL:** Born Jan 22, 1931, India; son of M I Malik (deceased); married Sally, Jan 25, 1969; children: Saleem, Zaheer, Saira. **EDUCATION:** Institution of Mechanical Engineers, London, BSME, 1954; Union College, Schenectady, MS, OR, 1967; Rensselaer Polytechnic Institute, PhD, 1974. **CAREER:** Government of India Railway Service, senior manager, 1953-65; Union College, Schenectady, instructor, 1967-73; Rensselaer Polytechnic Institute, associate professor, MBA director, 1975; University of Southern California, assistant professor, 1975-79; Governors State University, Illinois, professor, 1982-. **ORGANIZATIONS:** American Society of Mechanical Engineers. **HOME ADDRESS:** 19141 Loomis Ave, Homewood, IL 60430, (708)798-5248. **BUSINESS PHONE:** (708)534-4953.

MALKANI, ROMA V.
Communications company executive. Indo-American. **PERSONAL:** Born Jun 4, 1949, Bombay, India; daughter of Nari Vaswani and Sheila Vaswani; married Prem Malkani, Apr 18, 1971; children: Arvin, Sabrina. **EDUCATION:** University of Virginia, BS, 1969; George Washington University, MS, 1971, PhD. **CAREER:** Communications Satellite Corp, programmer, 1969-70; American University, programmer/analyst, 1970-71; NASA, Goddard Space Flight Center, senior programmer analyst, 1971-73; Environmental Protection Agency, systems analyst, 1973; System Development Corp, senior systems analyst, 1973-75; US House of Representatives, planning & evaluation, technical adviser, 1976-79; Information Systems & Networks Corp, corporation president, 1980-. **ORGANIZATIONS:** IEEE, 1993; AFCEA, Washington Chapter, board of directors; Washington Adventist Hospital Board, founding board president; Federal Emergency Management Agency, national executive reserve board; Armed Forces Communications and Electronics Association, board of directors. **HONORS/AWARDS:** Ernst & Young, Inc Mag, Merrill Lynch Enterpreneur of The Year, 1993; George Washington University, Engineering Alumni Achievement Award, 1993; Washington Business Journal, Top 26 Women Business Owners, 1989; Arthur Young Inc Magazine, Greater Washington/Baltimore Entrepreneur of Year, 1989; Washington Technology, American Elec Association, KPMG, Peat Marwick, High Tech Entrepreneur of Year, 1989; Ernst and Young, Inc Magazine, Merrill Lynch, Washington Business Journal, Greater Washington Entrepreneur of the Year, Woman-Owned Category, 1993; National Association of Women Business Owners, Owner of the Year Award, 1993. **SPECIAL ACHIEVEMENTS:** Author: "Benchmark Test-Means & Analysis of Performance of a Twin IBM 370/158," Hardware Conf, vol 9, 1977; "Preliminary Report on Automatic Indexing Tools," 1978; "House Consideration of SCORPIO as an Info Retrieval System," 1978; "Model 204 Applications Performance Tests," 1977; "Computer Assisted Instructions Discussion Paper," 1977; "Performance Test Analysis Report, Model 204," 1977; "Technical Evaluation of The Pilot Member Info Network," 1976; "Options Paper on Computer Security in WWMCCS Environment," 1974; "Clustering Techniques Analysis," 1971. **HOME ADDRESS:** 10321 Holly Hill Pl, Potomac, MD 20854. **BUSINESS ADDRESS:** President, Information Systems & Networks Corp, 10411 Motor City Dr, Bethesda, MD 20817, (301)469-0400.

MALLICK, PANKAJ K.
Educator. Indo-American. **PERSONAL:** Born Feb 14, 1946, Hooghly, W. Bengal, India; son of P B & Ananda Mallick; married Sunanda Mallick, Aug 7, 1970; children: Samip. **EDUCATION:** Bengal Engineering College, BE, 1966; Illinois Institute of Technology, MS, 1970, PhD, 1973. **CAREER:** Hindustan Steel Ltd, 1967; American Can Co, 1974-75; Eagle International Corp, research engineer, 1976; Ford Motor Co, senior research scientist, 1976-79; University of Michigan, Dearborn, professor, 1979-. **ORGANIZATIONS:**

Society of Plastics Engineers; American Society of Mechanical Engineers; ASM International. **SPECIAL ACHIEVEMENTS:** Author, Fiber Reinforced Composites, textbook, 1988, 1993; author, editor, Composite Materials Technology, book, 1990. **BUSINESS ADDRESS:** Professor, University of Michigan-Dearborn, 4901 Evergreen Rd, Rm 228 FOB, Dearborn, MI 48128, (313)593-5580.

MAMIDALA, RAMULU
Educator. Indo-American. **PERSONAL:** Born Sep 19, 1949, Tharigoppula, Andhra Pradesh, India; son of Mamidala Somaiah and Mamidala Venkamma (deceased); married Vinati R Mamidala, Sep 6, 1985; children: M Manaswi, M Soumya, M Mourya. **EDUCATION:** Osmania University, India, BE, mech, 1974; Indian Institute of Technology, India, MTech, production, 1976; University of Washington, Seattle, PhD, 1982. **CAREER:** University of Washington, Seattle, research assistant professor, 1982-85, assistant professor, 1985-90, associate professor, 1990-. **ORGANIZATIONS:** ASME, Material Processing Committee, chair, 1992-, J of Engineering Materials and Technolgy, associate editor, 1992-; Society for Experimental Mechanics, Research Committee, chairman, 1992-; Society of Manufacturing Engineers, advisor to student chapter, 1986-; ASM; SAE; ASEE; AAM; WJTA; North American Manufacturing Institute of SME, elected member, 1993-; Tau Beta Pi, chief advisor to student chapter, 1984-. **HONORS/AWARDS:** University of Washington, Faculty Excellence Award, 1991, College of Engineering, Outstanding Teacher Award, 1985-86; National Science Foundation, Presidential Young Investigator Award, 1989; American Society for Engineering Education, AT&T Foundation Award, 1989; Society of Automotive Engineers, Ralph R Teetor Award, 1987;. **SPECIAL ACHIEVEMENTS:** Published over 100 technical papers in archival journals and conference proceedings. **BUSINESS ADDRESS:** Associate Professor, Dept of Mechanical Engineering, University of Washington, FU-10, Seattle, WA 98195, (206)543-5349.

MAMIYA, RON
Judge. Japanese American. **PERSONAL:** Born Apr 2, 1947. **CAREER:** Seattle Municipal Court, judge, 1987-. **BUSINESS ADDRESS:** Judge, Seattle Municipal Court, 600 3rd Ave, Seattle, WA 98104, (206)684-8709. ∗

MAMMEN, ABRAHAM
Restaurateur. Indo-American. **PERSONAL:** Born Dec 11, 1952. **CAREER:** Restaurant owner: Delhi Palace and Udipi Palace, currently. **ORGANIZATIONS:** Merchants' Association, executive committee; Jackson Heights Beautification Group, executive committee; New York City Mayor's Small Business Advisory Board. **HONORS/AWARDS:** Columbia University, Outstanding Performance Award. **BUSINESS ADDRESS:** Owner, Delhi Palace, 37-33 74th St, Jackson Heights, NY 11372, (718)507-0666. ∗

MAMMEN, THOMAS
Association administrator. Indo-American. **CAREER:** Federation of Indo-American Associations of Northern California, chairman; Live Community Church, San Francisco, senior minister, currently; organizational development specialist, currently. **BUSINESS ADDRESS:** Chairman, Federation of Indo-American Assns of Northern California, 3676 Delaware Dr, Fremont, CA 94538, (415)564-7535. ∗

MAN, CHI-SING
Mathematician, educator. Chinese American. **PERSONAL:** Born Aug 23, 1947, Hong Kong; son of Yip Man and Sau-Ying Leung; married May Lai-Ming Chan, Jul 5, 1973; children: Li-Xing, Yi-Heng. **EDUCATION:** University of Hong Kong, BSc, 1968, MPhil, 1976; Johns Hopkins University, PhD, 1980. **CAREER:** Hong Kong Baptist College, tutor of mathematics & physics, 1970-72, assistant lecturer of physics, 1972-76; Johns Hopkins University, postdoctoral fellow, 1980-81; University of Manitoba, assistant professor of civil engineering, 1981-85; University of Kentucky, assistant professor of mathematics, 1985-88, associate professor of mathematics, 1988-. **ORGANIZATIONS:** Society for Natural Philosophy, service member, arrangements committee, 1987-, secretary, 1992-93; American Mathematical Society, 1985-; International Society of Offshore and Polar Engineers, 1991-. **SPECIAL ACHIEVEMENTS:** Research on acoustoelastic measurement of residual stress, elasticity with initial stress, stress waves in lungs, constitutive equation for creep of ice, foundation of continuum thermodynamics and Gibbsian thermostatics. **BUSINESS ADDRESS:** Associate Professor, Dept of Mathematics, University of Kentucky, 715 Patterson Office Tower, Lexington, KY 40506-0027, (606)257-3849.

MANABE, SYUKURO
Meteorologist, climatologist. Japanese American. **PERSONAL:** Born Sep 21, 1931, Shingu-Mura, Uma-Gun, Ehime, Japan; son of Seiichi Manabe & Sueko Akashi Manabe; married Nobuko Manabe, Jan 26, 1962; children: Nagisa Manabe Bianchini, Yukari. **EDUCATION:** Tokyo University, BSc, 1953, MSc, 1955, DSc, 1958. **CAREER:** US Weather Bureau, General Circulation Section, research meteorologist, 1958-63; Environmental Science Services Administration, Geophysical Fluid Dynamics Laboratory, senior research meteorologist, 1963-68; Princeton University, lecturer with rank of professor, 1968-; National Oceanic and Atmospheric Administration, Geophysical Fluid Dynamics Laboratory, senior research meteorologist, 1968-; Senior Executive Service, USA, 1979-. **ORGANIZATIONS:** National Research Council, commission on geoscience, environment and resources, 1990-93; National Academy of Sciences, 1990-; American Geophysical Union, fellow; American Meteorological Society, fellow; Academia Europaea, foreign member, 1994-. **HONORS/AWARDS:** Japan Meteorological Society, Fujiwara Award, 1966; American Meteorological Society, Meisinger Award, 1967, 2nd-half Century Award, 1977, Rossby Award, 1992; Asahi Glass Founation, Blue Planet Prize, Academic Award, 1992; American Geophysical Union, Roger Revelle Medal, 1993; Dept of Commerce, Gold Medal, 1970; US President, Meritorious Executive Award, 1989. **SPECIAL ACHIEVEMENTS:** Prediction of Green House warming by Mathematical Models of Climate, 1967-. **HOME ADDRESS:** 8 Princeton Ave, Princeton, NJ 08540, (609)924-0734. **BUSINESS PHONE:** (609)452-6520.

MANANKIL, NORMA RONAS
Educator. Filipino American. **PERSONAL:** Born Jan 2, Angeles, Pampanga, Philippines; daughter of Roberto Ronas & Petronila G Ronas; married Conrado Manankil Jr, Feb 7, 1967; children: Mark, Dyan. **EDUCATION:** Elementary teachers certificate, 1953; BS, education, 1958; certificate in physical education, 1965; certificate and licensure in food sanitation, 1992. **CAREER:** St Giles School, teacher, 1970-. **ORGANIZATIONS:** Intl Foundation for the Homeless Children in Manila, Chicago chapter, fundraising chairman, 1991-; Mt Pinatubo Walkathon, coordinator, 1991; Mt Pinatubo Phoneathon, chairman, 1991; PACMAN Earthquake Fundraiser, chairman, 1989; Typhoon Ruby Phoneathon, chairman, 1988; Philippine Week Celebration, chairman, 1987; Philippine Week Parade, grand marshal, 1988; L Club, president and district I-A associate chairman 1975; Circulo Capampangan, president, 1985. **HONORS/AWARDS:** Intl Foundation for the Support & Education of Indigent Children, Philippines, Recognition Award, 1993; Filipino Image, One of the 20 Outstanding Fil-Americans in the US, 1992; Philippine Consulate, Service Award, 1991, Appreciation Award; Philippine Week Celebration, Achievement Award, chairman; Philippine Week Fundraising, Service Award, 1988-89; Circulo Capampangan Award, 1987; Lioness Intl Service Award, 1976; Lioness Intl Presidential Award, 1974. **SPECIAL ACHIEVEMENTS:** Author, My Favorite Lines, 1982, 1992; producer/director: Miss Chicago Philippines, 1974-; Chicago Philippine Gems Calendar, 1987-; Chicago Philippine Best Dressed, 1989-; social columnist: Philippine Herald, 1974; Philippine Tribune, 1981; Philippine News, 1985; Via Times, 1988-; television host, Eskwelahang Munti, 1974-75. **HOME ADDRESS:** 609 Independence Ave, Westmont, IL 60559, (708)920-0682.

MANE, SATEESH RAMCHANDRA
Scientist. Malaysian American. **PERSONAL:** Born Jun 26, 1959, Malacca, Malaysia; son of Ramchandra Mane and Kusum Mane; married Vibha R Mane, Oct 16, 1991. **EDUCATION:** Cambridge University, UK, BA (with honors), 1981; Cornell University, PhD, 1987. **CAREER:** University of Michigan, research associate, 1987; Fermi National Accelerator Lab, research associate, 1987-89; Brookhaven National Lab, physicist, 1989-. **ORGANIZATIONS:** American Physical Society, life member, 1984-. **BUSINESS ADDRESS:** Physicist, Brookhaven National Lab, Bldg 911, Upton, NY 11973-9999.

MANIWA, KAZ
Attorney, association administrator. Japanese American. **PERSONAL:** Born Dec 16, 1950, Berkeley, CA; son of Hitoshi Maniwa & Amy Maniwa; married Masako, Sep 21, 1986; children: Kenta. **EDUCATION:** University of California, Berkeley, BA, 1972; Hastings College of the Law, JD, 1975. **CAREER:** Neighborhood Legal Assistance, attorney, 1975-79; Law Offices of Kaz Maniwa, attorney, 1979-. **ORGANIZATIONS:** Japanese Cultural & Community Center of Northern California, president, 1990-; Kimochi Inc, president, 1983-86; Asian Bar Association, bd member, 1985-; S F Bar Association, 1975-; California State Bar, 1975-; Oakland International Foreign Trade and Investment Commission, 1992-; Japan Scholarship Fund, director, 1988-. **BUSI-**

NESS ADDRESS: Chairman, President, Japanese Cultural and Community Center, 1840 Sutter St, San Francisco, CA 94115, (415)921-9000.

MANNE, VEERASWAMY
Scientist. Indo-American. **PERSONAL:** Born Jun 1, 1952, Achanta, Andhra Pradesh, India; son of Gopalam and Subbalakshmi; married Rama, Nov 20, 1980; children: Kiran, Harika. **EDUCATION:** Andhra University, BS, 1972; University Mysore, MS, 1974; Indian Institute of Science, PhD, 1979. **CAREER:** University of Maryland, postdoctorate fellow, 1979-80; Roche Institute of Molecular Biology, research associate, 1980-84; Hoffmann La Roche, research associate, 1984-86; Wistar Institute, research associate, 1986-89; Bristol-Myers Squibb, senior research investigator, 1989-. **ORGANIZATIONS:** American Society for Biochemistry & Molecular Biology, 1989-; American Association for the Advancement of Science, 1986-. **HONORS/AWARDS:** Government of India, Hindi Scholarship for Non-Hindi speaking people, 1969-71, Ministry of Health and Family Planning, Merit Scholarship, 1972-74. **SPECIAL ACHIEVEMENTS:** Author and co-author of numerous publications including: "Identification and Preliminary Characterization of Protein Cystein Farnesyltransferase," Proc National Academy Science, vol 87, p 7541-7545, 1990; "Purified Yeast Protein Farnesyltransferase Is Structurally and Functionally Similar to Its Mammalian Counterpart," Biochemistry Journal, vol 289, p 25-31, 1993; patents include: Farnesyl-protein transferase assay for identifying compounds that block neoplastic transformation, US patent 5185248, 1992; Method for blocking neoplastic transformation of cells induced by ras oncogenes, 1991, and numerous others. **BUSINESS ADDRESS:** Senior Research Investigator, Bristol-Myers Squibb Pharmaceutical Research Institute, PO Box 4000, Princeton, NJ 08543, (609)252-5832.

MANSUR, IQBAL
Educator. Bangladeshi American/Indo-American. **PERSONAL:** Born Jun 11, 1955, Dhaka, Bangladesh; son of Faizul Hossain Mazumder and Jaibun Nessa Mazumder; married Nasima R Mansur, Jul 6, 1984. **EDUCATION:** Goshen College, BA, 1977; Western Michigan University, MS, 1979; University of Cincinnati, PhD, 1984. **CAREER:** Ashland College, assistant professor of economics, 1983-84; Widener University, associate professor of finance, 1985-. **ORGANIZATIONS:** Bangladesh Assn of Delaware Valley, vice president, 1990-93; American Finance Assn, 1990-; Financial Management Assn, 1986-; Midwest Finance Assn, 1984-; Southern Finance Assn, 1986-; Eastern Finance Assn, 1985-. **HONORS/AWARDS:** Lindback Outstanding Professor Award, 1992. **SPECIAL ACHIEVEMENTS:** Publications: co-author, "The Effects of FIRREA on the Equity Return Levels of Banks and Savings and Loans," Applied Financial Economics, forthcoming; author, "Covariability of Major Equity Markets Around the October 1987 Crash: Tests of Granger Causality," International Journal of Commerce and Management 1 & 2, 91-96, 1991; co-presenter, "Interest Rate Sensitivity on the Equity Returns of Financial Institutions during Economic Expansions and Contractions," Financial Management Association, 1992. **BIOGRAPHICAL SOURCES:** India West, p 96, Apr 16, 1993. **HOME ADDRESS:** 608 Meadowvale Lane, Media, PA 19063, (215)876-3460. **BUSINESS ADDRESS:** Associate Professor of Finance, Widener University, School of Management, One University Place, Chester, PA 19013, (610)499-4321.

MANTIL, JOSEPH CHACKO
Physician, educator, administrator. Indo-American. **PERSONAL:** Born Apr 22, 1937, Kottayam, Kerala, India; son of Chacko Manthuruthil and Mary Manthuruthil; married Joan, Jun 18, 1966; children: Ann, Lisa. **EDUCATION:** Poona University, BS, 1956; University of Detroit, MS, 1960; Indiana University, PhD, 1965; University of Juarez, MD, 1977. **CAREER:** US Government, research physicist, 1964-75; Good Samaritan Hospital, resident, 1977-80; University of Cincinnati, fellow in nuclear medicine, 1980-82; Kettering Medical Center, Wright State University, associate director, nuclear medicine, 1982-86, professor & director of mag res lab, 1985-, director nuclear medicine/PET, 1986-. **ORGANIZATIONS:** American Physical Society, 1964-; Society of Nuclear Medicine, 1982-; Society of Magnetic Resonance in Medicine, 1986-; Society of Magnetic Resonance Imaging, 1985-; Institute for Clinical PET, 1989-. **HONORS/AWARDS:** Served as session chairman, speaker, and co-organizer of 5 international conferences in USA, Western Europe & Far East. **SPECIAL ACHIEVEMENTS:** 40 publications in professional scientific refereed journals; 12 publications in professional scientific conference proceedings; 60 scientific papers presented at professional meetings; 2 books: Radioactivity in Nuclear Spectroscopy, volumes I & II. **HOME ADDRESS:** 6040 Mad River Road, Dayton, OH 45459, (513)435-8789. **BUSINESS ADDRESS:** Professor & Director, Nuclear Medicine Dept, Wright State University,

Kettering Medical Center, 3535 Southern Blvd, Kettering, OH 45429, (513)296-7211.

MAO, CHUNG-LING
Chemical company manager. Chinese American. **PERSONAL:** Born Apr 21, 1936, China; son of H Mao and Y Su Mao; married Leanne Hai-Ping Chou Mao, Dec 31, 1966; children: Kelvin K, Vivian H. **EDUCATION:** Cheng-Kung University, Taiwan, BS,chem engineering, 1959; Texas Tech University, MS, chem, 1964; Virginia Polytechnic Institute and State University, PhD, chem, 1967. **CAREER:** Duke University, research associate, 1967-69; Uniroyal, Inc, senior research scientist, 1969-80; Avery International, pressure sensitive adhesives, project manager, 1980-83; Air Products and Chemicals Inc, emulsions development, manager, 1983-. **HONORS/AWARDS:** Uniroyal Inc, Inventor Award, 1976; Air Products and Chemicals, Technology Innovation Award, 1989, 1992. **SPECIAL ACHIEVEMENTS:** Twenty-three publications on organic chemistry; 24 US patents in polymer chemistry, polyolefins, acrylics, polyurethane, polyvinyl acetate-ethylene adhesives, binders, powders, coatings, emulsion polymerizations, chemical engineering, and others. **MILITARY SERVICE:** Artillery Army, Chinese, Taiwan, second lieutenant, 1959-61. **BUSINESS ADDRESS:** Manager, Emulsions Dev, Polymer Chemicals Technology, Air Products and Chemicals, Inc, 7201 Hamilton Blvd, Allentown, PA 18195-1501, (215)481-6153.

MAO, HO-KWANG
Scientist. Chinese American. **PERSONAL:** Born Jun 18, 1941, Shanghai, China; son of Sen Mao and Tak-Chun Mao; married Agnes L Mao, Feb 10, 1968; children: Cyndy L, Linda L, Wendy L. **EDUCATION:** Taiwan University, BS, geology, 1963; University of Rochester, MS, geology, 1966, PhD, geology, 1968. **CAREER:** University of Rochester, research associate, 1967-68; Carnegie Institute of Washington, postdoctoral fellow, 1968-70, research associate, 1970-72, staff geophysicist, 1972-. **ORGANIZATIONS:** National Academy Sciences, 1993-; National Science Foundation, advisory committee for earth science, 1991-; Physics of Earth & Planetary Interiors, editorial board, 1979-; Journal of High Pressure Research, editorial board, 1988-. **HONORS/AWARDS:** American Geophysical Union, fellow; Mineralogical Society of America, Award, 1979; International Association for the Advancement of High Pressure Science & Technology, Bridgman Gold Medal Award, 1989; National Academy of Sciences, Arthur L Day Prize and Lectureship, 1990; Sigma Xi, National Lectureship, 1991-93. **BUSINESS ADDRESS:** Staff Geophysicist, Geophysical Laboratory, Carnegie Institution of Washington, 5251 Broad Branch Rd NW, Washington, DC 20015-1305, (202)686-2467.

MAO, JAMES CHIEH-HSIA
Scientist (retired). Chinese American. **PERSONAL:** Born Apr 3, 1928, Ningpoo, Chekiang, China; married Rose Mao, Jun 21, 1956; children: Gloria E, Victor H. **EDUCATION:** University of Wisconsin, PhD, 1963. **CAREER:** Abbott Laboratories, senior scientist, 1970-84, Volwiler Society member, 1985-89. **ORGANIZATIONS:** Chinese-American Education Foundation, president, 1970; Chinese-American Association of Lake County, president, 1982; American Chemical Society, 1965-; Federation of American Society of Experimental Biology, 1973; American Society for Microbiology, 1980; Sigma Xi; Phi Sigma; Phi Lambda Upsilon. **SPECIAL ACHIEVEMENTS:** Protein biosynthesis; biosynthesis of DNA and RNA; mode of action of antibiotics; mechanism of resistance to erythromycin; discover of anti-viral drugs. **HOME ADDRESS:** 134 Hamilton Road, Landenberg, PA 19350, (610)274-0657.

MAR, DAN K.
General contractor. Chinese American. **PERSONAL:** Born Aug 16, 1925, Seattle, WA; son of Mar Kim; married Edith, Feb 20, 1949; children: Susan, Marilyn, Donald, Douglas. **CAREER:** M W Blackstock Homes, production mgr, 1965-71; Pacific Components Inc, president/founder, 1971-93. **ORGANIZATIONS:** American Legion #186, executive bd; Seattle Chinatown Chamber of Commerce, president, 1993-94; Chinatown Business Improvement Area, steering comm; Chinatown International Dist Community Development Committee, steering comm, until 1993. **MILITARY SERVICE:** US Navy, EM/3/C, 1943-46; South Pacific Campaign Medals. **BUSINESS ADDRESS:** Chairman, Pacific Components Inc, 1227 S Weller, Seattle, WA 98144, (206)323-2700.

MAR, WILLIAM DAVID
Designer. Chinese American. **PERSONAL:** Born Oct 26, 1954, Salinas, CA; son of Mun K Mar and Yick May Mar. **EDUCATION:** University of California at Berkeley, BA, 1976. **CAREER:** Davy McKee Corp, illustrator, 1979-82;

Westinghouse Electric, commercial concept illustrator, 1982-85; William Mar Design, president, currently. **BUSINESS ADDRESS:** President, William Mar Design, 220 Montgomery St, Ste 608, San Francisco, CA 94104, (415)989-3935.

MARASIGAN, ROGELIO U. (ROGER)
Accountant. Filipino American. **PERSONAL:** Born Jan 3, 1934, Manila, Philippines; son of Crispulo M Marasigan and Teresa U Marasigan; married Cecilia B Marasigan, Jun 21, 1976; children: Robert J, Ronald J. **EDUCATION:** University of the East, Manila, Philippines, BSBA, accounting, 1954. **CAREER:** University of California at Berkeley, accountant, 1984-. **ORGANIZATIONS:** Vallejo-Filipino Club, 1980-; Philnabank Golf Club, 1960-75. **SPECIAL ACHIEVEMENTS:** Model: appeared in Manila newspaper, Shell Philippines; appeared in Philippine National Bank advertisment. **HOME ADDRESS:** 149 Creekview Dr, Vallejo, CA 94591-3642, (707)643-7421.

MARGALLO, LUCIO N., II
Physician, educator. Filipino American. **PERSONAL:** married Claudette Dinero; children: Farah, Justin, Christopher, Jonelle. **EDUCATION:** University of Santo Thomas School of Medicine, 1970; University of South Dakota School of Medicine, Internal Medicine, residency, 1980. **CAREER:** St Joseph Hospital, chief of staff; University of South Dakota School of Medicine, clinical assistant professor, currently, Cardio-Pulmonary Services, medical director, currently; Brady Memorial Home, medical director, currently; private practice, internist, currently. **ORGANIZATIONS:** Medical Society of South Dakota, 6th district, president, 1993-; South Dakota State Medical Assn, councilor; South Dakota Political Action Committee, director; South Dakota Medical Directors Assn; American Society of Internal Medicine; Filipino American Assn of Dakota & Minnesota. **HONORS/AWARDS:** American Colleges of International Physicians, fellow; South Dakota State Jaycees, Speak Up champion, 1975; US Jaycees, Presidential Award of Excellence, Achievements, and Merits; numerous others. **BUSINESS ADDRESS:** Clinical Asst Professor, University of South Dakota School of Medicine, 414 E Clark St, Vermillion, SD 57069, (605)677-5011.*

MARR, WILLIAM WEI-YI
Engineer, poet. Chinese American. **PERSONAL:** Born Sep 3, 1936, Taichung, Taiwan; son of Chieh-Ying Marr and Sai-Zhen Tsai; married Jane Jy-Chyun Liu, Sep 22, 1962; children: Dennis, Alvin. **EDUCATION:** Taipei Institute of Technology, BS equivalent, 1957; Marquette University, MS, 1963; University of Wisconsin, PhD, 1969. **CAREER:** Taiwan Sugar Corporation, assistant engineer, 1959-61; Allis-Chalmers Mfg Co, senior analyst, 1963-67; Argonne National Laboratory, staff engineer, 1969-. **ORGANIZATIONS:** Illinois State Poetry Society, president, 1993-; Chinese Artists Association of North America, board member, 1989-; First Line Poetry Society, 1988-; American Society of Mechanical Engineers, 1977-; Li Poetry Society, 1963-. **HONORS/AWARDS:** Taiwan Literature Association, New Poetry Award, 1981; Li Poetry Society, Translation Award, 1981, Creative Poetry Award, 1984; Chicago City, Outstanding New Citizen of Year Award, 1972. **SPECIAL ACHIEVEMENTS:** Eight books of poetry; four books of translations; editor, Contemporary Chinese Poetry, Modern Poetry in Taiwan, Forty Modern Poets from Taiwan. **BUSINESS ADDRESS:** Staff Engineer, Argonne National Laboratory, 9700 S Cass Avenue, 362/G212, Argonne, IL 60439, (708)252-3337.

MARSHALL, THURGOOD, JR.
Government administrator. Filipino American. **PERSONAL:** Born Aug 12, 1956, New York, NY; son of Thurgood Marshall Sr and Cecile Sucat Marshall; married Colleen, Sep 24, 1983; children: Thurgood William Marshall III. **EDUCATION:** University of Virginia, BA, 1978, School of Law, JD, 1981. **CAREER:** Judge Barrington D Parker, law clerk, 1981-83; Kaye Scholer Fierman Hays & Handler, attorney, 1983-85; Senator Albert Gore Jr, counsel and staff director, 1985-87; Senate Judiciary Committee, Senator Edward M Kennedy, counsel, beginning 1988; Office of Vice President Albert Gore Jr, director of legislative affairs, 1993-. **ORGANIZATIONS:** American Bar Association; District of Columbia Bar Association; Bars of the US District Court for the District of Columbia and the Second Circuit Court of Appeals. **SPECIAL ACHIEVEMENTS:** Coauthor, The Sony Betamax Case, Computers and the Law, 1984; contributing editor, The Nicaragua Elections: A Challenge of Democracy, 1989. **BUSINESS ADDRESS:** Director of Legislative Affairs, Offive of the Vice President, Old Executive Affairs Bldg, Washington, DC 20501, (202)224-3121.*

MARTIN, ABRAHAM NGUYEN
Civil engineer, general contractor. **PERSONAL:** Born Aug 20, 1946, Ninh-Binh, Vietnam; son of Nguyen Van Lien & Nguyen Thi Bay; married Anna Anh Martin, Sep 1, 1985; children: Alan John, Joanne, Giang Tran. **EDUCATION:** University of Michigan, certificate, 1965; Cambridge University, England, certificates of English, 1967; Cornell University, 1970; University of Hawaii, BS, civil engineering, 1971. **CAREER:** Glenn Construction, engineer assistant supt, 1972-73; Isemoto Contracting Co, assistant general supt, 1973-74; DMA/Pacific JV, general foreman, 1974-76; Swinnerton-Walberg, foreman, 1976-77; Cawdrey-Mars-General, assistant superintendent, 1977-78; Abraham Construction, president, 1978-. **ORGANIZATIONS:** General Contractors Association of Hawaii, 1979-; General Contractors Association of America, 1979-. **HONORS/AWARDS:** Safety awards, 1988. **SPECIAL ACHIEVEMENTS:** Expert in high-rise constr, vertical control, earth work, construction layout, planning, remodelling. **HOME ADDRESS:** 4580 Kilauea Ave, Honolulu, HI 96816, (808)735-5562. **BUSINESS PHONE:** (808)545-5944.

MARUMOTO, WILLIAM HIDEO
Management consultant. Japanese American. **PERSONAL:** Born Dec 16, 1934, Los Angeles, CA; son of Harry Y Marumoto & Mary Midori Marumoto; married Jean Masako Marumoto, Jun 14, 1959; children: Wendy M Vlahos, Todd M, Lani M Moore, J Tamiko Smith. **EDUCATION:** Whittier College, BA, 1957; University of Oregon, graduate studies, 1957-58. **CAREER:** Whittier College, director of alumni relations, 1958-65; UCLA, associate director of alumni & development, 1965-68; California Institute of the Arts, vice president for planning & development, 1968-69; Peat, Marwick, Mitchell & Co, sr consultant, 1969; US Department of Health, Education & Welfare, assistant to the secretary, 1969-70; The White House, special assistant to the president, 1970-73; The Interface Group Ltd, Boyden, chairman of the board, 1973-. **ORGANIZATIONS:** Whittier College, board of trustees, 1978-; Japanese American National Museum, board of trustees, 1979-; Leadership Education for Asian Pacifics, chairman, board of trustees, 1992-; Mexican American Legal Defense & Educational Fund, board of directors, 1989-93. **HONORS/AWARDS:** Whittier College, Distinguished Alumni Achievement Award, 1991, Alumni Service Award, 1978; Council for the Advancement and Support of Education, over 20 national awards, 1962-68; White House Civil Liberties Public Education Fund, board of directors, 1992. **SPECIAL ACHIEVEMENTS:** Reagan White House Personnel Task Force, 1980-88; White House Conferences on Small Business, delegate, 1986; named to the Career Makers: North America's Top Executive Recruiters, Harper & Row, 1990, 1992; Fifty Leading Retainer Search Firms in the US, Executive Recruiter News, four occasions. **BUSINESS ADDRESS:** Chairman of the Board, CEO, The Interface Group Ltd/Boyden, 1025 Thomas Jefferson St NW, Ste 410, East Lobby, Washington, DC 20007, (202)342-7200.

MARUR, HANUMAN
Engineer. Indo-American. **PERSONAL:** Born Nov 23, 1939, Marur, Bangalore, Karnataka, India; married Lalitha Marur, May 26, 1967; children: Surendra, Ravindra. **EDUCATION:** Mysore University, India, BE, civil engineering, 1963; Bangalore University, India, ME, struct engineering, 1966; Michigan State University, MSE, soils & highways, 1968. **CAREER:** RV College of Engineering, lecturer, 1965-67; Kraft Engineering, consulting engineer, 1969-76; Charter Township of Genesee, township engineer & director of public works, 1976-80; Trans Environmental Engineers, consulting engineer, 1981-, president, managing engineer, 1981-. **ORGANIZATIONS:** American Society of Civil Engineers, Michigan Section, director, 1977-78; KASI Sri Viswanatha Temple, president, managing trustee, 1981-; International Institute of Flint, director, 1984-92; Council of Hindu Temples in North America, director, 1984-; American Society of Civil Engineers, 1974-; National Society of Professional Engineers, 1972-. **BUSINESS ADDRESS:** President and Managing Engineer, Trans Environmental Engineers, 4296 Corunna Rd #3, Flint, MI 48532-4315, (313)743-2741.

MARUYAMA, KIYOSHI
Researcher, computer manufacturing company executive. Japanese American. **PERSONAL:** Born Dec 5, 1945, Kamisato, Nagano-Ken, Japan; son of Genichiro Maruyama and Mitsu Maruyama; married Michiko Maruyama, Mar 24, 1972; children: Yuki. **EDUCATION:** University of Illinois, MS, 1970, PhD, 1972. **CAREER:** IBM, Research Center, research staff mbr, mgr, 1972-89, IBM Asia-Pacific, director, 1989-90, IBM Japan, director, 1990-92, IBM T J Watson Research Center, senior consultant, 1992-. **ORGANIZATIONS:** IBM Academy of Technology, 1992-. **HONORS/AWARDS:** IBM, 2nd Inven-

tion Achievement Award, 1986, Corporate Award, 1984, Outstanding Innovation Award, 1979, 1981, 1st Invention Achievement Award, 1980. **SPECIAL ACHIEVEMENTS:** Numerous publications; three US patents. **BUSINESS ADDRESS:** Senior Consultant, IBM, T J Watson Research Center, PO Box 704, Hawthorne H1-D10, Yorktown Heights, NY 10598, (914)784-7256.

MARUYAMA, TAKASHI
Physicist. Japanese American. **PERSONAL:** Born Mar 26, 1950, Hirotani, Hyogo, Japan; son of Tatsunosuke and Tomoko Maruyama; married Harumi Maruyama, Aug 11, 1979; children: Christopher. **EDUCATION:** Osaka University, BS, physics, 1972; Tohoku University, MS, physics, 1974, PhD, physics, 1977. **CAREER:** Tufts University, research associate, 1978-81; University of Wisconsin, project associate, 1981-84, asst scientist, 1984-85, associate scientist, 1985-89; Stanford Linear Accelerator Center, staff physicist, 1990-. **ORGANIZATIONS:** American Physical Society; Physical Society of Japan. **SPECIAL ACHIEVEMENTS:** Numerous high-energy physics papers published: Physical Review Letters, Physical Review. **BUSINESS ADDRESS:** Staff Physicist, Stanford Linear Accelerator Center, 2575 Sand Hill Rd, Menlo Park, CA 94025, (415)926-3398.

MASAMUNE, SATORU
Educator. Japanese American. **PERSONAL:** Born Jul 24, 1928, Fukuoka, Japan; son of Hajime & Chikado Kondo Masamune; married Takako, Jul 25, 1956; children: Hiroko Masamune Cooper, Tohoru. **EDUCATION:** Tohoku University, Sendai, Japan, BSc, 1952; University of California, Berkeley, PhD, 1957; University of Wisconsin, Madison, PDA, 1956-59. **CAREER:** University of Wisconsin, Madison, lecturer, 1959-61; Mellon Institute, research fellow, 1961-64; University of Alberta, associate professor, 1964-67, professor of chemistry, 1967-79; Reaction Intermediates, editor, 1976-80; Organic Syntheses, editor, 1970-78; Massachusetts Institute of Technology, professor of chemistry, 1978-91, A C Cope Professor of Chemistry, 1991-. **ORGANIZATIONS:** Royal Society of Canada, fellow, 1975-; Chemical Society, London, fellow, 1956-; American Academy Arts & Sciences, fellow, 1987; American Chemical Society, 1956-. **HONORS/AWARDS:** American Chemical Society, Creative Work in Syn Org Synthesis, 1978, A C Cope Scholar Award, 1987; University of Nebraska, Hamilton Award, 1984; Chemical Society, London, Centenary Lecturer, 1980. **SPECIAL ACHIEVEMENTS:** Published over 215 scientific articles. **BUSINESS ADDRESS:** A C Cope Professor of Chemistry, Massachusetts Institute of Technology, 77 Massachusetts Ave, 18-311, Cambridge, MA 02139, (617)253-1846.

MASAOKA, MIYA JOAN
Musician, composer, association administrator. Japanese American. **PERSONAL:** Born Jan 3, 1958, Washington, DC; daughter of Tad & Helen Masaoka; married Jesse Drew, Jul 2, 1976; children: Mariko Drew. **EDUCATION:** San Francisco State University, BA (magna cum laude), music, 1990; Mills College, MA, music composition, 1994. **CAREER:** Tenderloin Reflection & Education Center, artistic director, music for homeless program, 1990-92; San Francisco Gagaku Society, director, 1991-. **ORGANIZATIONS:** Asian American Women Artists Association, 1991-93. **HONORS/AWARDS:** Mills College, Alumni Scholarship for Music Composition, 1993; Crothers Scholarship, 1992; Zellerbach Family Fund, 9066, commission for composition tape, 1992. **SPECIAL ACHIEVEMENTS:** Invitation to tour Japan with Ainu (Japanese indigenous) musicians, 1991, 1993; Asian Heritage Council, concert honoring creative Japanese-American women, 1993; Asian American Women in Jazz; AA Jazz Festival Concert, 1992; invited to tour Japan with Ethnic Music Festival, 1993, 1994; released solo CD, Compostions and Improvisations, Asian Improv Records. **BIOGRAPHICAL SOURCES:** San Francisco Examiner, p B-2, March 31, 1993; California Jazz Now, p 11, July 1992. **HOME ADDRESS:** 797 Hampshire St, San Francisco, CA 94110.

MATHAI, ANISH
Bank executive. Indo-American. **PERSONAL:** Born Feb 20, 1949, Tiruvalla, Kerala, India; son of Stephen and Susy; married Susan, Jul 14, 1980; children: Amreeta. **EDUCATION:** Keio University, Tokyo, Japan, 1968-69; St Stephen's College, BA (honors), 1968; Delhi University, MA, 1971; Harvard University, MBA, 1977. **CAREER:** Best & Co, Madras, India, computer executive, 1971-73; College of India, Hyderabad, India, admin staff consultant, 1973-75; Sysncsort Inc, NJ, marketing exec, 1977-81; Coopers & Lybrand, NY, sr consultant, 1981-83; European American Bank, NY, vice president, 1983-88; Bankers Trust Company, NY, managing director, 1988-. **ORGANIZATIONS:** Vellore Board, treasurer, 1993-; St Georges Church, finance committee, 1991-92; Harvard Club, NY, 1981-; HBSC, NY, 1981-90; ISFRC,

Boston, affiliate, 1993-. **SPECIAL ACHIEVEMENTS:** Proficient in Hindi, Malayalam, Japanese. **BUSINESS ADDRESS:** Mangaging Director, Bankers Trust Companpy, 280 Park Avenue, New York, NY 10019, (212)454-3062.

MATHAI-DAVIS, PREMA
Association executive. Indo-American. **PERSONAL:** Born Oct 28, 1950, Thiruvalla, Kerala, India; daughter of Stephen & Susy Mathai; married Wallace Mathai-Davis, Oct 15, 1978; children: Stephen, Lisa, Tara. **EDUCATION:** Delhi University, Lady Irwin College, India, BS, 1970, MS, 1972; Harvard University, EdD, 1979. **CAREER:** Hunter College Brookdale Center on Aging, Mt Sinai-Hunter Gerontology Center, director, 1979-81; Community Service Society, director of CASC, 1981-85; Community Agency for Senior Citizens, president & CEO, 1985-90; City of New York, NYC Department for the Aging, commissioner, 1990-; YWCA of the USA, national executive director, currently. **ORGANIZATIONS:** Metropolitan Transportation Authority, board member, 1991-; New York Academy of Medicine, fellow, 1992-; NY State Association of Area Agencies, board member, 1990-; Health Systems Agency of NYC, board member, 1991-; Asian American Federation of NY, board member, 1991-; Staten Island Hospital Organization, board member, 1989-90; S.I. Community Housing Resource Board, chairperson, 1987-90; Center for Policy on Aging of the NY Community Trust, advisory board member, 1990-. **HONORS/AWARDS:** Seniors Helping Seniors, Distinguished Service Award, 1992; Metropolitan NY Coordinating Council on Jewish Poverty, Community Service Award, 1992; Vichar March India Youth Association, Outstanding Role Model Award, 1992; Korean Association of Greater New York, Community Service Award, 1991; NY State Intergenerational Network, First Leadership Award, 1990; NY State Women's Political Caucus, Leadership Award, 1990; New York Urban League, Mills Skinner Health & Social Welfare Award, 1988; Staten Island Borough President, Medallion for Distinguished Service to the Community, 1986. **BUSINESS ADDRESS:** National Executive Director, YWCA of the USA, 726 Broadway, New York, NY 10003, (212)614-2700.

MATHEW, SARAMMA T.
Educator. Indo-American. **PERSONAL:** Born Jun 6, 1938, Kuzhikala, Kerala, India; daughter of Chandy Thomas & Saramma Thomas; married Thomas Mathew, Aug 5, 1963; children: Teki Susan, Thomas Jr, Alexander. **EDUCATION:** Kerala University, Jabalpur University, BSc, 1958, BT, 1959; Howard University, MA, 1968; University of Florida, PhD, 1981; University of Northern Iowa, post doctoral AA school psychology certification, 1982-84. **CAREER:** Basic Training School, Kerala Education System, teacher, 1959-60, 1963; George Washington University, Vanderbilt University, lab technician, 1965-68, 1969; University of Georgia, lab technician, 1973-76; University of Florida, graduate assistant, 1978-81; University of Northern Iowa, adjunct assistant professor, 1982-84; Department of Mental Health & Mental Retardation, psychologist, 1985-88; Troy State University, assistant professor, 1988-. **ORGANIZATIONS:** Kappa Delta Pi, 1981-; John Dewey Society, 1981-; Phi Delta Kappa, 1989-; Council for Exceptional Children, 1990-; Alabama Association of Women Educators, 1992-; Mid-South Sociological Association, 1992-; Alabama Academy of Science, 1993-. **SPECIAL ACHIEVEMENTS:** Author, abstract: A Creative Problem Solving Program for Emotionally Handicapped Children to Reduce Aggression, Journal of Creative Behavior, vol 18, no 4, p278, 1984; Creative Problem Solving: A Tool to Reduce the Aggression of Emotionally Handicapped Children, Alabama Council for Exceptional Children Journal, vol 9, no 1, p21-24, 1992. **BIOGRAPHICAL SOURCES:** "Saramma Made East Meet West," Troy Messenger, vol 23, p1, 3, 1990. **HOME ADDRESS:** 325 Oldfield Dr, Montgomery, AL 36117, (205)279-6200. **BUSINESS ADDRESS:** Asst Professor of Psychology, Coordinator of Master of Science in Foundation of Education, Troy State University, 4 McCartha Hall, Troy, AL 36082, (205)670-3362.

MATHEW, VALSA
Nurse. Indo-American. **PERSONAL:** Born Dec 29, 1947, Ayroor, Kerala, India; daughter of K T Thomas and Chinnamma Thomas; married T A Mathew, Jun 2, 1973; children: Abie, Toby, Shelby. **EDUCATION:** Byl Nair Hospital, Bombay, India, nursing, 1970. **CAREER:** John Sealy Hospital, nurse, 1970-72; St Joseph Hospital, registered nurse, 1972-. **ORGANIZATIONS:** TAP-PAN, 1990-; Trinity Mar Thoma Church, 1973-. **HOME ADDRESS:** 255 Castle Way Lane, Houston, TX 77015, (713)455-7469.

MATHEWS, PETER
Educator. Indo-American. **PERSONAL:** Born Nov 11, 1951. **CAREER:** College abroad, instructor, 1990; Cypress College, professor of political sci-

ence, currently. **SPECIAL ACHIEVEMENTS:** Candidate for US Representative, California, 1992. **BUSINESS ADDRESS:** Professor, Political Science Department, Cypress College, 9200 Valley View Cypress, Cypress, CA 90630, (714)826-2220. ∗

MATHIPRAKASAM, BALAKRISHNAN

Researcher. Indo-American. **PERSONAL:** Born Jan 3, 1942, Virudhunagar, Tamil Nadu, India; son of G Balakrishnan & B Rajammal; married Pavalamani Mathiprakasam, Sep 11, 1972; children: Murthy. **EDUCATION:** VSV Polytechnic, India, LME, 1961; University of Mysore, India, ME, 1976; Illinois Institute of Technology, PhD, 1980. **CAREER:** VSV Polytechnic, Mechanical Engineering, lecturer, 1961-68, shop superintendent, 1968-74; Midwest Research Institute, Kansas City, associate engineer, 1980-81, senior engineer, 1981-84, principal engineer, 1984-89, senior advisor for engineering, 1989-. **ORGANIZATIONS:** American Society of Mechanical Engineers, Heat Pump Executive Committee, Thermoelectric Executive Committee; International Thermoelectric Society, executive committee, society's treasurer. **HONORS/ AWARDS:** Research & Development Magazine, IR 100 Award, 1986, R&D 100 Award, 1988; Midwest Research Institute, President's Award, 1986; Council of Principal Scientists, Science Award, 1987; NASA, Cleveland, Certificate of Recognition, 1983. **SPECIAL ACHIEVEMENTS:** Published over 30 technical papers; holds 3 US patents. **HOME ADDRESS:** 8429 Broadmoor, Overland Park, KS 66212, (913)381-7316. **BUSINESS ADDRESS:** Senior Advisor for Engineering, Midwest Research Institute, 425 Volker Blvd, Kansas City, MO 64110, (816)753-7600.

MATHUR, ACHINT P. (JEFF)

Mechanical engineer. Indo-American. **PERSONAL:** Born Oct 30, 1945, Agra, Uttar Pradesh, India; son of Agam P Mathur and Prem Sakhi Mathur; married Shashi R Mathur, Jan 16, 1972; children: Vineesh. **EDUCATION:** Agra University, India, BSc, 1966; Villanova University, BS, 1969; MIT, MS, 1971; Duke University, PhD, 1976. **CAREER:** Linford Air and Refrigeration Co, design engr, 1971; University of Roorke, India, asst professor, 1971-73; Thomas & Olive Inc, design engr, 1974-76; Carrier Corp, senior engr, 1976-82; Tranter Inc, Texas Division, chief engr, 1982-. **ORGANIZATIONS:** ASHRAE, 1977; Sigma Xi, 1975; Tau Beta Pi, 1968; Pi Tau Sigma, 1967. **HONORS/AWARDS:** ASTM, Annual Student Award, 1968; Agra University, India, Gold Medal, 1966; Villanova University, dean's list, 1969; MIT, NASA Scholarship, 1970; Duke University, ASHRAE Scholarship, 1976. **SPECIAL ACHIEVEMENTS:** Five US patents, 1984-93; numerous publications, 1979-88; reviewer of technical papers, ASHRAE, 1978-93; registered professional engr, Texas, 1984. **HOME ADDRESS:** 4838 Rhea Rd, Wichita Falls, TX 76308, (817)691-0250. **BUSINESS ADDRESS:** Chief Engineer, Texas Div, Tranter Inc, PO Box 2289, Wichita Falls, TX 76308, (817)723-7125.

MATHUR, ADITYA P.

Educator. Indo-American. **PERSONAL:** Born Jul 30, 1948, Mathura, Uttar Pradesh, India; son of Shiva Prasad and Usha Prasad Mathur; married Jyoti I Mathur, Aug 29, 1976; children: Gitanjali, Ravishankar. **EDUCATION:** Birla Institute of Technology and Science, BE (with honors), 1970, ME (with honors), 1972, PhD, 1977. **CAREER:** Birla Institute of Technology of Science, associate professor, 1982-88; Georgia Institute of Technology, visiting associate professor, 1985-87; Purdue University, associate professor, 1987-. **ORGANIZATIONS:** IEEE; ACM. **SPECIAL ACHIEVEMENTS:** Over 35 research publications in journals and conference proceedings; Introduction to Microprocessors, Tata-McGraw Hill, 3rd edition, 1989; Introducion to Pascal, Tata-McGraw Hill, 1982. **BUSINESS ADDRESS:** Associate Professor, Computer Science, Purdue University, 1398 University St, West Lafayette, IN 47907, (317)494-7822.

MATHUR, BALBIR SINGH

Organization executive. Indo-American. **PERSONAL:** Born Dec 10, 1936, Bhatinda, Punjab, India; son of Umrao Singh Mathur & Sushila Tangri Mathur; married Treva Brown Mathur, Dec 21, 1966; children: Tara, Keir. **EDUCATION:** Allahabad University, India, BA, economics, history & political science, 1954; master's, political science, 1957; Wichita State University, mgmt, mkting courses, 1958-63. **CAREER:** International Bazaar, president, 1959-71; Intermark Inc, president, 1971-83; Trees for Life, president, 1984-. **ORGANIZATIONS:** Wichita Council of Foreign Relations, president, 1980-81. **HONORS/AWARDS:** Garden Club of America, Distinguished Service Award, 1992; The Giraffe Project, Giraffe Award, 1989; Charles A Lindbergh Fund, Lindbergh Grant Recipient, 1989; Arbor Day Foundation, International

Project Award, 1985; Searching for Success, Environmental Achievement Award, 1990. **SPECIAL ACHIEVEMENTS:** Conducted 8-country investigation on leather source for Genesco Inc, 1971; established joint-venture corporation for Afghan-US companies, 1972; international study in Zimbabwe, Mozambique & India for Garvey Industries, 1993; proficient in Hindustani, Urdu, Punjabi & English; host family for foreign students, 1970-80; assisted in relocating three Afghan families, 1979-80. **MILITARY SERVICE:** National Cadet Corps & Provincial Education, co commander, Allahabad Contingent, India, 1952-53; Best Cadet of College, 1952. **BIOGRAPHICAL SOURCES:** New York Times, October 17, 1988; Hinduism & Ecology; Seeds of Truth by Rachor Prime, 1992. **BUSINESS ADDRESS:** President, Trees for Life, 1103 Jefferson, Wichita, KS 67203, (316)263-7294.

MATHUR, HARBANS B.

Educator. Indo-American. **PERSONAL:** Born Jan 15, 1938, Agra, Uttar Pradesh, India; son of Sukhdeo Behari Mathur (deceased) and Gyanvati Devi Mathur (deceased); married Sumanlata Mathur, Dec 1, 1962; children: Anant B. **EDUCATION:** University of Allahabad, India, BS, 1956; University of Roorkee, India, BS electronics & comm, 1960, BS, electrical eng, 1964; University of Delhi, India, PG Diploma, marketing, 1974; Youngstown State University, MSEE, 1990. **CAREER:** Himalayan Radio Propagation Unit, Min of Def, R & D, India, junior executive offices, 1960-65; Gannon Dunkerley & Co Ltd, India, sales engineer, 1965-69; OEN India Ltd, Cochin, India, sales engineer, 1969-80; Wheatland Tube, inventory analyst, 1980-84; Kent State University, Trumbull Campus, assistant prof, 1984-. **ORGANIZATIONS:** IEEE; American Tech Edu Association. **BUSINESS ADDRESS:** Assistant Professor, Kent St University of Trumbull, 4314 Mahoning Ave N W, Warren, OH 44483, (216)847-0571.

MATHUR, IKE

Educator, educational administrator. Indo-American/Pakistani American. **PERSONAL:** Born Nov 22, 1943, Jamshedpur, India; son of Robert and Ivy Mathur; married Lynette L Mathur, Jul 11, 1981; children: Rebecca L Satterfield, Jason G. **EDUCATION:** Eastern Michigan University, BS, 1965, MBA, 1968; University of Cincinnati, PhD, 1974. **CAREER:** American Math Society, copy editor, 1965-69; University of Cincinnati, teaching fellow, 1969-72; University of Dayton, instructor, 1972-73; University of Pittsburgh, assistant professor, 1973-77; Southern Illinois University, interim dean, currently. **ORGANIZATIONS:** Haworth Press, series editor in international finance, 1991-; Journal of International Fin Markets, Inst & Money, editor, 1990-; Journal of Mult Fin Mgt, mng editor, 1990-; Phi Kappa Phi, president, 1992-93, vice president, 1991-92. **HONORS/AWARDS:** US Government, Fulbright Award for Finland, 1983, Fulbright Award for Portugal, 1993. **SPECIAL ACHIEVEMENTS:** Strategies for Joint Ventures in the Peoples Republic of China, 1987; Financial Management in Post-1992 Europe, 1993; Wealth Creation in Eastern Europe, 1992; Personal Finance, 1989; Cases in Managerial Finance, 1984. **HOME ADDRESS:** RR4, Union Hill, Carbondale, IL 62901. **BUSINESS ADDRESS:** Interim Dean, College of Business, Southern Illinois University, Carbondale, IL 62901, (618)453-3328.

MATHUR, KAILASH V.

Educator. Indo-American. **PERSONAL:** Born Feb 21, 1934, Jodhpur, Rajasthan, India; son of ViJey Mal Mathur (deceased) and Mohan Kaur (deceased); married Savita Mathur, Jul 29, 1964; children: Shikha Sinha, Sameer Mathur. **EDUCATION:** Jaswant College, Jodhpur, Rajasthan, India, BS, 1955; Veterinary College of Bikaner, Rajasthan, India, DVM, 1960; North Carolina State University, MS, 1964; University of Illinois, Urbana-Champaign, PhD, 1975. **CAREER:** Veterinary College, in charge of college clinics, 1960-65; Southeastern Consortium for International Development, technician, 1980-82; South Carolina State University, assistant professor of dairy science, 1965-71, project director, human nutrition research, professor of nutrition, 1971-80, nutritional sciences grad program, project coordinator, international dpv program, professor, advisor, 1982-. **ORGANIZATIONS:** American Dietetic Association; SC Dietetic Association, board of directors, 1986-87, 1990; American Heart Association, Orangeburg Division, board of directors, 1989-; Orangeburg/Calhoun Tech College, advisory board, 1985-; Orangeburg Rotary Club, Assoc Degree in Nursing program, board of directors, 1990-, International Project World Community Service, chairman, 1986-. **HONORS/ AWARDS:** SC State University, Dept of Home Economics, School of Human Services, Teacher of the Year, 1990, Endowed Distinguished Faculty Chair, 1991; State of SC, Governor's Distinguished Professor, 1991. **SPECIAL ACHIEVEMENTS:** "Effect of Nutrients on Hematcrit and Birth Weight in Orangeburg County," Journal of SC Medical Association, 1991; Nutrition and

Health, Eyertonian Egerton College, Kenya; "Hypertension, Hypercholesterol and Other Health Indices among Blacks of Hampton County," Journal of SC Medical Association, 1981; "Mercury and Lead Levels of Hampton County SC Residents," Journal of SC Medical Association, 1980; numerous others. **HOME ADDRESS:** 610 Alexander Drive, Orangeburg, SC 29115, (803)531-4555. **BUSINESS ADDRESS:** Prof/Adviser, Nutritional Scis Grad Program, South Carolina State University, 300 College Street NE, Orangeburg, SC 29117-0002, (803)536-7435.

MATHUR, KRISHAN D.
Educator. Indo-American. **PERSONAL:** Born Apr 22, 1928, Hyderabad, India; son of Rai Shiv Dayal and Sarjo Rani Mathur; children: Leila Rani, Roy K. **EDUCATION:** Osmania University, India, BSc, MSc, zoology; The George Washington University, MA, government, 1953, PhD, political science, 1958. **CAREER:** Georgetown University, Urdu Language & Indian History, lecturer; Library of Congress, Science and Technology Division, senior reference librarian; University of Maine, Presque Isle, Chemistry, assistant professor, Extension Center, International Relations & American Diplomate History, instructor; Central Washington University; Western Washington University; Howard University; University of the District of Columbia, professor, currently. **HONORS/AWARDS:** Osmania University, scholarship for obtaining highest grade in zoology; George Washington University, Phi Gamma Mu, Prof Society in Social Sciences. **SPECIAL ACHIEVEMENTS:** Impact of Buddhism on Indian Science and Politcs; The Origin of Observatories in India; India under Netaji, etc; Idealism and National Interest in India's Policies towards the United States; Science and Federal Government. **BUSINESS ADDRESS:** Professor, University of the District of Columbia, 4250 Connecticut Ave NW, Bldg 48, Rm 7107, Washington, DC 20008-1174.

MATHUR, RAGHU P.
Educator. Indo-American. **PERSONAL:** Born Sep 1, 1948, Banaras, Uttar Pradesh, India; son of Bindeshwari P and Radhey Mathur; married Karuna Mathur, Sep 4, 1971; children: Neil Manik, Shaun Akhil. **EDUCATION:** Banaras University, BSc (honors), 1966; California State University, Fresno, MS, 1970. **CAREER:** Irvine Valley College, School of Physical Sciences & Technologies, professor/chair, 1979-. **ORGANIZATIONS:** Kiwanis Club of Mission Viejo, 1983-. **HONORS/AWARDS:** Saddleback Valley Unified School District, board of trustees, 1983-92, elected official. **BUSINESS ADDRESS:** Professor/Chair, School of Physical Sciences & Technologies, Irvine Valley College, 5500 Irvine Center Dr, Irvine, CA 92720-4399, (714)559-3381.

MATSUDA, FAY CHEW
Museum administrator. Chinese American. **PERSONAL:** Born Apr 11, 1949, New York, NY; daughter of Chock Nom Chin and Bick Koon Dong Chin; married Karl Matsuda, May 22, 1980; children: Amy Lani. **EDUCATION:** Barnard College, AB, 1971; New York University, MSW, 1973. **CAREER:** Hamilton Madison House, Senior Services, director, 1973-86; Chinatown Health Clinic, director of education, 1986-88; Chinatown History Museum, executive director, 1989-. **ORGANIZATIONS:** Asian American Legal Defense & Education Fund, board of directors, 1980-. **HONORS/AWARDS:** Smithsonian Institution, Award for Museum Leadership Program, 1992; New York State Governor's Office, Governor's Arts Award, 1990. **BUSINESS ADDRESS:** Executive Director, Chinatown History Museum, 70 Mulberry St, 2nd Floor, New York, NY 10013, (212)619-4785.

MATSUDA, FUJIO
Research administrator. Japanese American. **PERSONAL:** Born Oct 18, 1924, Honolulu, HI; son of Yoshio Matsuda & Shimo Iwasaki Matsuda; married Amy Matsuda, Jun 11, 1949; children: Bailey, Thomas, Sherry Bumatai, Joan Brotman, Ann Sueoka, Richard. **EDUCATION:** University of Hawaii, 1943, 1946-47; Rose Polytechnic Institute, BS, civil engineering, 1949; Massachusetts Institute of Technology, ScD, civil engineering, 1952. **CAREER:** USGS, hydraulic engineer, 1949; Park and Yee Ltd, 1956-58; consulting structural engineer, 1958-60; Shimazu, Matsuda, Shimakuburo and Associates, president, 1960-63; Massachusetts Institute of Technology, research assistant, 1950-52, research engineer, 1952-54; University of Illinois, research assistant professor of civil engineering, 1954-55; University of Hawaii, assistant professor of engineering, 1955-57, associate professor of engineering, 1957-58, 1959-62, professor of engineering, 1962-65, 1974-84, department of civil engineering, chairman, 1960-63, engineering experiment station, director, 1962-63, vice president for business affairs, 1973-74, president, 1974-84, research corporation, executive director, 1984-. **ORGANIZATIONS:** C Brewer & Company

Ltd & Buyco Inc, director, 1973-; UAL Corporation, director, 1975-; First Hawaiian Bank, First Hawaiian Inc, director, 1984-; Rehabilitation Hospital of the Pacific Inc, director, 1990-; Maui Economic Development Board, director, 1990-; World Sustainable Agriculture Association, vice chairman of board, president, 1991-; Tampa Bay Lightning, director, 1992-; American Society of Civil Engineers, life member; National Ocean Resources Technology Corp, chairman, CEO, director, 1993-; Social Science Association of Honolulu, life member; Sigma Xi; Urasenke Hawaii Chapter, president, 1984-. **HONORS/AWARDS:** University of Hawaii, Distinguished Alumnus Award, 1974, 1991; Government of Japan, Order of the Sacred Treasure, Second Class, 1985; American Society of Civil Engineers, Parcel-Sverdrup Engineering Management Award, 1986. **MILITARY SERVICE:** Army, 1943-45. **BUSINESS ADDRESS:** Executive Director, Research Corp of University of Hawaii, 2800 Woodlawn Drive, Suite 200, Honolulu, HI 96822, (808)988-8311.

MATSUI, DORIS KAZUE OKADA
Governmental administrator, philanthropist. Japanese American. **PERSONAL:** Born Sep 25, 1944, Dinuba, CA; married Robert Takeo Matsui, Sep 17, 1966; children: Brian Robert. **EDUCATION:** University of California, Berkeley, BA, 1966. **CAREER:** Clinton/Gore Transition Team, board, 1992; The White House Office of Public Liaison, deputy director, deputy assistant to the President, 1993-. **ORGANIZATIONS:** Sacramento Symphony League, president; KVIE, Sacramento public television, president board of directors; Sacramento Science Center, board; Sacramento Junior League, board; Peace Links, co-leader; Congressional Wives for Soviet Jewry; Congressional Families for Drug Free Youth; House of Representatives Childcare Center, board of directors; Sidwell Friends Parents' Association, chairwoman; Christmas in April Foundation, national board of directors; Child Mental Health Interest Group; Congressional Club, past president, Project Awareness, chief sponsor, 1991; numerous others. **HONORS/AWARDS:** Sidwell Friends Parents' Association, Newmyer Award for Outstanding Volunteer Contribution; University of CAL, Rosalie Stern Award. **SPECIAL ACHIEVEMENTS:** Health care advocate for women and children; projects include establishing community projects throughout country to offer education regarding breast cancer and mammogram screening for low income women; appeared on NBC's Today Show, 1992. **BUSINESS ADDRESS:** Deputy Assistant for Public Liaison, President Bill Clinton, Executive Office Bldg, 1600 Pennsylvania Ave, Washington, DC 20006, (202)456-2930.

MATSUI, KEIKO
Musician. Japanese American. **PERSONAL:** Born Jul 26, 1961, Tokyo, Japan; daughter of Yoshihisa and Emiko Doi; married Kazu Matsui; children: Maya. **EDUCATION:** Japan Women's University, BA, children's culture. **CAREER:** Musician, CDs: A Drop of Water, Unity; Under Northern Lights, MCA; No Borders, MCA; Night Waltz, Sindrome; Cherry Blossom, Unity. **HONORS/AWARDS:** City of Reading, Honorable Citizen. **SPECIAL ACHIEVEMENTS:** Yamaha Music Foundation, selected for advanced music studies program & signed as an artist. **BIOGRAPHICAL SOURCES:** "Family Affair," Transpacific, Sep/Oct 1992, p27. **HOME ADDRESS:** 10291 Countess Dr #314, Huntington Beach, CA 92649.

MATSUI, MACHIKO
Educator. Japanese American. **PERSONAL:** Born May 18, 1950, Saijo, Ehime, Japan; daughter of Nobuhiro Matsui and Kazuko Matsui; married Zhao Yumin, Aug 18, 1990. **EDUCATION:** Nara National Women's University, Japan, BA, 1974, MA, 1977; State University of New York, Buffalo, MA, 1986, PhD, 1991. **CAREER:** Board of Education, Osaka, Japan, highschool teacher, 1977-82; SUNY/Buffalo, instructor, research assistant, 1985-89; Lanzhou Railway Institute, foreign expert, 1989-90; SUNY/Buffalo, lecturer, 1991-; Southern Methodist University, assistant professor, 1991-. **ORGANIZATIONS:** Association of Asian Studies, 1992-; National Women's Studies Association, 1993-; Southwest Caucus of Asian Studies, 1992-; Japan Women's Studies Society, 1992-; Japan Council SMU, 1991-; Asian Studies Council SMU. **HONORS/AWARDS:** Southern Methodist University, Faculty Excellence Award, 1993; SUNY/Buffalo, Diamond Research Grant, 1989. **SPECIAL ACHIEVEMENTS:** Author of: The Impact of Ryosai Kembo Ideology on Women's Education in Japan; A Search for Identity: Using the Mother-Daughter Dyad to Analyze Asian American Women's Literature; The Trend in American History Textbooks: Feminism & Racial Issues; Light & Shade of the Open Door Policy: Chinese Women at Present; Evolution of Feminist Movement in Japan; Making Asian Women Visable in the Curriculum; numerous others. **BIOGRAPHICAL SOURCES:** Bi-cultural Matsui promotes Womens Studies, The Daily Campus, vol 77 no 41 pp 1-2, Oct 31,

1991. **BUSINESS ADDRESS:** Director of Japanese Studies, Asst Prof, Dept of Foreign Languages & Literatures, Southern Methodist University, 309 Clements, Dedman College, Dallas, TX 75275, (214)768-3143.

MATSUI, NORIATSU
Educator. Japanese American. **PERSONAL:** Born 1945, Flushun, Manchuria, China; married. **EDUCATION:** Osaka University, BA, 1968; University of Hawaii, MA, 1972; Ohio State University, PhD, 1984. **CAREER:** Institute of Developing Economics, researcher, 1968-80; Kyoto University, research affiliate, 1969-70; Ohio State University, graduate associate, 1977-83; Kenyon College, assistant prof, 1983-85; Denison University, assistant prof, 1985-86; Earlham College, assistant prof, 1986-92, associate prof, 1992-. **ORGANIZATIONS:** American Economic Association. **BUSINESS ADDRESS:** Associate Professor of Economics, Earlham College, National Road West, Richmond, IN 47374, (317)983-1301.

MATSUI, ROBERT TAKEO
Congressman. Japanese American. **PERSONAL:** Born Sep 17, 1941, Sacramento, CA; son of Yasuji Matsui and Alice Magata Matsui; married Doris Kazue Okada Matsui, Sep 17, 1966; children: Brian Robert. **EDUCATION:** University of California, Berkeley, AB, political science, 1963; Hastings College of Law, JD, 1966. **CAREER:** Self-employed attorney, beginning 1967; Sacramento City Council, 1971-78, vice mayor, 1977; 96th-103d Congresses from 3rd California District, congressman, 1978-, committees include: House of Representatives Ways and Means Committee; Ways and Means Subcommittee on Human Resources; Ways and Means Subcommittee on Trade. **HONORS/AWARDS:** Honored by Children's Defense Fund, 1993; Claremont College, Outstanding Legislator, 1990, 1992; American Academy of Pediatrics, Excellence in Public Service Award, 1992; American Wind Energy Association, cited for environmental work; American Public Transit Association, recognized for promoting mass transit; Anti-Defamation League, Lifetime Achievement Award; Child Welfare League of America, Congressional Advocate of the Year; Yale University, Chubb Fellowship, 1989; numerous others. **SPECIAL ACHIEVEMENTS:** Democratic front runner for trade, tax policy, social security, health care and welfare reform; key administrator for North American Free Trade Agreement, 1993; guest on various news programs such as: Meet the Press, The CBS Evening News, MacNeil/Lehrer News Hour, C-SPAN, CNN's "Crossfire," "The Morning Business Report," and "Both Sides with Jesse Jackson"; responsible for Enterprise Capital Formation Act, 1992; numerous others. **BUSINESS ADDRESS:** Congressman, US Congress, 2311 Rayburn Bldg, Washington, DC 20515-0505, (202)225-7163.

MATSUMOTO, DONALD MICHIAKI
Optometrist, educator. Japanese American. **PERSONAL:** Born Aug 21, 1954, Gardena, CA; son of Akira Matsumoto & Mary Matsumoto; married Cynthia Matsumoto, Jun 22, 1985; children: Al. **EDUCATION:** University of California, Los Angeles, BA, economics, 1976; University of California, Berkeley, OD, 1980. **CAREER:** Matsumoto & Associates, optometrist/owner, 1980-88; California State Board of Optometry, expert examiner, 1992-; Pacific Eye Care Center, optometrist/owner, 1989-; Southern California College of Optometry, assistant professor, 1990-. **ORGANIZATIONS:** American Academy of Optometry, 1992-; Asian American Optometric Society, president, 1993; American Optometric Association, 1989-; California Optometric Association, 1989-; Colorado Optometric Association, trustee, 1987. **HONORS/AWARDS:** 20/20 Magazine, Best and the Brightest, 1992; University of California School of Optometry Alumni Association, Gold Retinoscope Award, 1980; Board of Supervisors, Boulder County, Colorado, Outstanding Volunteer, 1987. **SPECIAL ACHIEVEMENTS:** Chapter title, "Screening Principles," Community Health and Optometry, 1988; co-author, "Base Curve Measurement of Soft Contact Lenses," AAO Journal, 1980. **BUSINESS ADDRESS:** Optometrist, Pacific Eye Care Center, 12461 W Washington Blvd, Los Angeles, CA 90066, (310)390-6287.

MATSUMOTO, GEORGE
Architect, educator (retired). Japanese American. **PERSONAL:** Born Jul 16, 1922, San Francisco, CA; son of Manroku & Ise Matsumoto; married Kimi Nao, Dec 15, 1951; children: Mari-Jane, Kiyo-Ann, Kei-Ellen, Kenneth Manroku, Miye-Eileen. **EDUCATION:** University of California, Berkeley, 1939-42; Washington University, BArch, 1944; Cranbrook Academy of Art, MArch (honors), 1945. **CAREER:** Heathers Garden Devel Co, designer, 1941-42; George F Keck, designer, 1943-44; Skidmore, Owings & Merrill, sr designer, 1945-46; Saarinen & Swanson, sr designer/planner, 1946-47; Runnells, Clark, Waugh, Matsumoto, partner, 1947-48; University of

Oaklahoma, instructor, 1947-48; North Carolina State College, asst prof, 1948-51, assoc prof, 1951-57, prof, 1957-61; University of California, Berkeley, prof, 1961-67; architect: Oklahoma, 1947-48, North Carolina, 1948-61, San Francisco, 1962-92; George Matsumoto & Assocs, pres, 1992-. **ORGANIZATIONS:** Oakland Art Council, board of directors; Oakland Mus Assn, board of directors; Mich Soc Architects; Assn College Sch Architecture; Raleigh Council Architects; San Francisco Planning & Urban Renewal Assn; Natl Council Archtl Registration Bds; California Assn of Architects; Building Research Inst; Japanese-American Citizens League. **HONORS/AWARDS:** AIA, Fellow; Intl Inst Arts and Letters, Fellow; numerous awards, including: Washington University, Distinguished Alumni Award, 1960; AIA, Awards of Merit; American Institute of Landscape Architects, Award of Merit, 1984. **SPECIAL ACHIEVEMENTS:** Numerous articles in professional journals, including: House & Garden, May 1951, p128-133; Progressive Architecture, Jun 1948, p 59, Feb 1949, p 62-66, Apr 1949, p 66-69, Jul 1954, p 92-94; Architectural Record, Mar 1972, p 46.

MATSUMOTO, IKU
Educator (retired). Japanese American. **PERSONAL:** Born Aug 27, 1919, Seattle, WA; daughter of Ryotaro Nishikawa and Ichiyo Akita Nishikawa; married Sumio Matsumoto, Jan 21, 1943; children: Gary H, Ellen M Deleganes, Melissa M Koenig. **EDUCATION:** University of Washington, BA, 1940, MA, 1941; Holy Names College, BA, 1953. **CAREER:** Spokane School Dist 81, English teacher to foreign born, 1950-53, elementary teacher, 1963-67, secondary teacher, 1967-84. **ORGANIZATIONS:** Fujihana Kai, Japanese Classical Dance, translator, advisor, 1958-85; Eastern Washington Agency of Aging, trustee, 1980-83; Spokane Nishinomiya Sister City, education committee, 1970-93; Spokane Chapter Japanese American Citizens League, sec, 1963-93; Spokane Public Library, trustee, 1984-93; Japan Week, board, 1993. **HONORS/AWARDS:** Nishinomiya Ed Board, Certificate Promoting Good Will, 1990; Spokane Public Library, Recognition of Distinguish Service, 1993; Spokane City Govt, Appreciation of Voluntary Community Service, 1993; Washington State Educ Act, Study Grant at Sophia University, Tokyo, 1967, Fulbright Scholarship, 1970-; Women in Communication, Women of Distinction, 1990. **SPECIAL ACHIEVEMENTS:** Translator, Japanese Kabuki Dances, 1958-85; Facilicitator & Mistress of Ceremony; Japanese Conversation, Grammar, Teacher, 1967-84. **BIOGRAPHICAL SOURCES:** Spokesman Review, p F 7, Feb 10, 1991; Alki, vol 7, no 2 p 53, July 1991-. **HOME ADDRESS:** 2815 E 11th Avenue, Spokane, WA 99202, (509)534-9796.

MATSUMOTO, KEN
Chemist. Japanese American. **PERSONAL:** Born Sep 8, 1941, San Bernardino, CA; son of Gunichi & Shizuyo Matsumoto; married Yasuko Matsumoto, Jun 17, 1967; children: Alison S, Eric K. **EDUCATION:** Arizona State University, BS, 1963; University of California, Berkeley, PhD, 1967. **CAREER:** Eli Lilly and Co, senior organic chemist, 1969-74, research scientist, 1974-82, senior research scientist, 1982-. **ORGANIZATIONS:** American Chemical Society, 1963-; Sigma Xi, 1967-. **MILITARY SERVICE:** US Army, Chemical Corp, captain, 1967-69. **BUSINESS ADDRESS:** Senior Research Scientist, Lilly Research Labs, Lilly Corp Ctr, Indianapolis, IN 46285, (317)276-4724.

MATSUMOTO, MARK R.
Educator. Japanese American. **PERSONAL:** Born Jul 13, 1955, Washington, DC; son of Akio Matsumoto and Sachiye Sato Matsumoto; married Sherilynn, Jul 16, 1977; children: David, Julieanne, Janalee. **EDUCATION:** University of California, Irvine, BS, 1977; University of California, Davis, MS, 1980 PhD, 1982. **CAREER:** UC Riverside, visiting associate professor, 1992-93; SUNY Buffalo, assistant professor, 1983-89, associate professor, 1989-. **ORGANIZATIONS:** American Society of Civil Engineers, associate member, 1983-; Water Environment Federation, 1983-. **HONORS/AWARDS:** University of California, regents fellow, 1979, Earle C Anthony Graduate Fellow, 1980; Lilly Foundation, Lilly Teaching Fellow, 1987. **SPECIAL ACHIEVEMENTS:** Numerous articles in technical journals, 1982-. **BUSINESS ADDRESS:** Associate Professor, Dept of Civil Engineering, State University of New York, Buffalo, 212 Ketter Hall, Buffalo, NY 14260.

MATSUMOTO, NANCY K.
Journalist. Japanese American. **PERSONAL:** Born in Chicago, IL. **EDUCATION:** Pomona College, BA, 1980. **CAREER:** Freelance writer, 1986-90; Time-Warner, staff correspondent, People Magazine, 1990-. **ORGANIZATIONS:** Asian American Journalists Association, 1990-; Toastmasters International, 1993-; American Lupus Society, 1986-. **HONORS/AWARDS:** Arthri-

tis Foundation, Cecil Writing Award, 1992. **SPECIAL ACHIEVEMENTS:** Japanese language proficiency; American Lupus Society, support group leader, 1992-; "A Guide to Ethnic Groups in CA," associate editor, 1980. **BUSINESS ADDRESS:** Staff Correspondent, People Weekly, Time-Warner Inc, 10880 Wilshire Blvd, Ste 1700, Los Angeles, CA 90024, (310)824-7239.

MATSUMOTO, RANDALL ITSUMI
Company executive. Japanese American. **PERSONAL:** Born Jun 1, 1953, Honolulu, HI; son of Wallace Y Matsumoto (deceased) and Eunice T Matsumoto; married Taryn A Matsumoto, Mar 5, 1983; children: Daniel K, Alex A, Sean I. **EDUCATION:** Purdue University, BS, civil engineering, 1975. **CAREER:** Hawaiian Dredging Construction Co, civil construction superintendent, 1975-88; Hawaiian Bitumuls and Paving Co, vp of engineering, currently. **ORGANIZATIONS:** Hawaii Asphalt Paving Industry, State DOT Committee, treasurer, 1990-. **BUSINESS ADDRESS:** Vice President of Engineering, Hawaiian Bitumuls & Paving Co, 110 Puuhale Rd, Honolulu, HI 96819, (808)842-3227.

MATSUMOTO, RYUJIRO
Trading company executive. Japanese American. **PERSONAL:** Born Jan 18, 1964, Nagoya, Aichi, Japan; son of Toraji Matsumoto and Kazuko Matsumoto. **CAREER:** Transacta Corp, accountant; CMS Meisei, Japan, president; Matsumoto Research Service, Japan, president; UV Clothing Corp, president, currently. **HOME ADDRESS:** 2215 W 237th St, Torrance, CA 90501, (310)534-5785.

MATSUMOTO, TAKASHI
Lawyer. Japanese American. **PERSONAL:** Born Oct 8, 1943, Dandong, Manchuria, China; son of Hyogo Matsumoto and Kazuko Matsumoto; married Teruko Matsumoto, Oct 8, 1967; children: Shintaro, Kentaro. **EDUCATION:** Osaka University Faculty of Law, LLB, 1966; New York University, School of Law, LLM, 1990. **CAREER:** Itochu Corp, Domestic & International, Legal Dept, 1966-81; Itochu International, Legal Dept, manager, 1981-87; Sumitomo Trust Banking Co Ltd, senior vice president/general counsel, 1987-92; Mudge Rose Guthrie Alexander & Ferdon, partner, 1992-. **ORGANIZATIONS:** American Bar Association, 1986-; New York State Bar Association, 1986-; Inter-Pacific Bar Association, 1993-.

MATSUMOTO, TERUO
Educator. **PERSONAL:** Born Jan 2, 1929, Fukuoka, Japan; son of Yoshinari Matsumoto & Fumie Hayashi Matsumoto; married Mary Matsumoto, 1969; children: Michi, Chieko, Meiko, Tateru. **EDUCATION:** Kyushu University, BS, 1949, Medical School, MD, 1953, PhD, 1956. **CAREER:** US Army Hospital, Japan, general surgeon, 1961-65; Walter Reed Army Institute of Research, Department of Experimental Surgery, chief, 1965-68, Division of Surgery, director, 1965-69; US Army Research & Development Command, US Army Surgical Research, Paficie, director, 1968-69; Hahnemann University, School of Medicine, associate professor of surgery, division of surgical research, director, 1969-80, department of surgery, professor, chairman, 1975-90, division of vascular and laser surgery, professor, director, 1990-. **ORGANIZATIONS:** American Association for the Surgery of Trauma; American College of Surgeons; American Heart Association, fellow; American Society of Clinical Oncology; Collegium Internationale Chirvigae Digestives; International Cardiovascular Society; Society for Surgery of the Ailmentary Tract; Society for Vascular Surgery. **HONORS/AWARDS:** Southeastern Surgical Congress, Gold Medal Winner, 1968; American Medical Association, Golden Apple Award, 1972, numerous others. **SPECIAL ACHIEVEMENTS:** Over 300 publications in the surgical field of vascular, laser, oncological, trauma, GI and endocrine; visiting professorship in US and overseas, over 50 visits; editorships, national and international journals; grants private federal grants for surgical research. **MILITARY SERVICE:** US Army, Medical Corps, lt colonel, 1961-69; Army Commendation Medal, 1965, Army Certificate of Achievement, 1969, Outstanding Achievement. **BIOGRAPHICAL SOURCES:** I Was in the Middle of the Atomic Blast in Hiroshima, Military Medicine, Sept 1967. **BUSINESS ADDRESS:** Professor, Director, Division of Vascular & Laser Surgery, Hahnemann Hospital, Broad & Vine Sts, MS 468, Philadelphia, PA 19102, (215)762-8181.

MATSUO, PAUL T.
Administrator, engineer. Japanese American. **PERSONAL:** Born Jan 16, 1935, Lihue, Kauai, HI; son of Torakichi and Yasuko; married Grace; children: Lynn, Michael. **EDUCATION:** University of Hawaii, BSc, 1957. **CAREER:** Territorial Hwy Department, civil engineer, 1957-59; City & County of Honolulu,

civil engineer, 1959-61; Department of Land & Natural Resources, civil engineer, 1961-88; Division of Agricultural Resource Management, administrator, chief engineer, currently. **ORGANIZATIONS:** American Water Workers Association; American Society of Civil Engineers. **BUSINESS ADDRESS:** Administrator, Chief Engineer, Division of Agricultural Resource Management, 1428 S King St, Honolulu, HI 96814, (808)973-9473.

MATSUOKA, JAMES TOSHIO
Manufacturing company executive (retired). Japanese American. **PERSONAL:** Born Jan 20, 1920, Long Beach, CA; son of Kunizo Matsuoka and Hirano Kasahara; married Dassie Shigeko, 1942; children: Arlene Cole, Louise, Nancy Stern, Marie Ashmus, Marilyn Miyamoto. **CAREER:** Intercole Inc, senior vice pres, director; Intercole Bolling Corporation, president, CEO. **SPECIAL ACHIEVEMENTS:** Over 100 United States and foreign patents.

MATSUOKA, MATTHEW S.
Rubber manufacturing company manager. Japanese American. **PERSONAL:** Born Dec 10, 1957, Los Angeles, CA; son of Iwao (Matt) Matsuoka and Yoshie Matsuoka; married Yuka Matsuoka, Jun 24, 1989. **EDUCATION:** California State University, Los Angeles, BA, 1985. **CAREER:** Kokoku Rubber Inc, administrations manager, currently. **BUSINESS ADDRESS:** Administrations Manager, Kokoku Rubber Inc, 120 Hanger Circle, Richmond, KY 40475, (606)623-7096.

MATSUOKA, SHIRO
Research manager. Japanese American. **PERSONAL:** Born May 1, 1930, Kobe, Japan; son of Teikichi and Matsuko; married Norma L C Matsuoka, Aug 1, 1957; children: Tama, Bryce, Timothy. **EDUCATION:** Stevens Institute of Technology, ME, 1955; Princeton University, PhD, 1959. **CAREER:** Stevens Institute of Technology, visiting professor, 1963-73; Rutgers University, adjunct professor, 1973-; AT&T Bell Laboratories, technical staff member, supervisor, department head, 1959-. **ORGANIZATIONS:** American Physical Society, fellow, 1960-93; Society of Plastics Engineers, fellow, 1960-93; American Chemical Society, 1960-93; Society of Rheology, 1960-93; Society of Polymer Science, Japan, 1981-93. **HONORS/AWARDS:** National Academy of Engineering, membership, 1989; Society of Polymer Science, Japan, distinguished service, 1989; Society of Plastics Engineers, international award, engineering, 1980. **SPECIAL ACHIEVEMENTS:** Author, "Relaxation Phenomena in Polymers," Hanser Publishing, 1992, "Polymer Alloy," Polymer Society, 1992; over 150 publications in science and engineering of plastics. **HOME PHONE:** (908)647-1052. **BUSINESS ADDRESS:** Head, Plastics Research and Engineering, AT&T Bell Laboratories, 600 Mountain Ave Rm 7F-202, Murray Hill, NJ 07974-0636, (908)582-6840.

MATSUSHIMA, CHARLES HIROSHI
Business executive. **PERSONAL:** Born Sep 4, 1939, Portland, OR; son of Umata and Fumiko Matsushima; married Janie M Matsushima, Mar 10, 1968; children: Becky Fumiko, Darryn Hiroshi, Ryan Mitsuhiro. **EDUCATION:** University of Oregon, 1957-58; University of Portland, BBA, 1962. **CAREER:** Anzen Pacific Corp, partner, secretary-treasurer, vice pres, currently. **ORGANIZATIONS:** JACL; Japanese Ancestral Society. **MILITARY SERVICE:** US Air Force, ssgt, 1962-68; 5 year medal. **BUSINESS ADDRESS:** Vice President, Partner, Anzen Pacific Corporation, 736 NE Martin Luther King Jr Blvd, Portland, OR 97232.

MATSUSHIMA, JANIE MITSUYE
Business executive. Japanese American. **PERSONAL:** Born Nov 9, 1944, Tule Lake, CA; daughter of Frank and Mae Furukawa; married Charles Hiroshi Matsushima, Mar 10, 1968; children: Becky Fumiko, Darryn Hiroshi, Ryan Mitsuhiro. **EDUCATION:** Portland State University, BS, 1968, MEd, 1970. **CAREER:** Portland Public Schools, teacher; Anzen Pacific Corp, partner, owner, currently. **ORGANIZATIONS:** Boy Scouts of America, troop committee, FOS, 1985-; Cub Scouts of America, leader, chairman, treasurer, 1982-85; Tualatin Hills Water Polo Club, treasurer, 1991-93; Sunset Water Polo Club, 1990-93; Oregon Educators Assn, 1968-76; Oregon Historical Society, Japanese-American Women in America, panel member, 1991-92.

MAYELL, JASPAL SINGH
Scientist. Indo-American. **PERSONAL:** Born Jan 1, 1929, Sialkot, Punjab, Pakistan; son of Moti Singh Mayell and Harbans Kaur Mayell; married Parkash Kaur Mayell, Dec 11, 1955; children: Manvin Singh, Nita K Sabo. **EDUCATION:** Punjab University, India, BSc (honors), 1950, MSc, tech, 1952; University of Texas, Austin, PhD, 1962. **CAREER:** University of Texas, Austin,

teaching assistant, research fellow, 1958-61; American Cyanamid Co, research chemist, 1962-70; DuPont (Endo) Pharmaceutical, New York, senior scientist, 1971-76; Purdue Frederick, New York, assistant director, 1977-. **ORGANIZATIONS:** American Chemical Society; Electrochemical Society; American Pharmaceutical Society; Catalysis Society; Phi Lambda Upsilon, 1959-. **HONORS/AWARDS:** National Science Foundation, fellow, 1959; Welch Organization, Texas, fellow, 1959, 1960. **SPECIAL ACHIEVEMENTS:** Ten publications in national scientific journals; two patents; seven presentations at national scientific organizations. **HOME ADDRESS:** 40 Jay Rd, Stamford, CT 06905, (203)322-7229.

MCCARTHY, NOBU
Actress. Japanese American. **CAREER:** California State University, adjunct professor; East West Players, Los Angeles, artistic director, until 1993: As the Crow Flies, Sarcophagus, Come Back Little Sheba, Into the Woods; director, The Chairman's Wife; television appearances: China Beach, Magnum PI, Quincy, Farewell to Manzanar; movies: Geisha Boy, Wake Me When It's Over, Karate Kid II, Pacific Heights, The Wash. **HONORS/AWARDS:** Drama-Logue Award for As the Crow Flies. *

MCCARTY, FAITH B.
Advertising executive. Filipino American. **PERSONAL:** Born Aug 1, 1960, Philippines; married Robert McCarty, Aug 30, 1987; children: Amanda, Ariel. **EDUCATION:** BS, business administration. **CAREER:** San Diego Advertising Specialties, owner, currently. **ORGANIZATIONS:** State Assembly. **HONORS/AWARDS:** Small business awardee. **BUSINESS ADDRESS:** Owner, San Diego Advertising Specialties, 9420 Activity Road, Suite G, San Diego, CA 92126, (619)566-9247.

MCNEELY, JUNE
Accountant. Chinese American. **PERSONAL:** Born in People's Republic of China; married. **EDUCATION:** Shoreline Community College, AA, 1985; University of Washington, business economics, 1988. **CAREER:** Universal Freights Forwarder, accountant, 1989; Boeing, financial specialist, 1989-93, property manager, 1989-; Molbak's Greenhouse and Nursery, 1993-. **SPECIAL ACHIEVEMENTS:** Language proficiency: Chinese. **HOME ADDRESS:** 14140 76th Place NE, Bothell, WA 98011, (206)823-1436.

MEHRA, RAVINDER C.
Plastics labware company executive. Indo-American. **PERSONAL:** Born Oct 23, 1942, Amritsar, Punjab, India; son of Chaman Lal Mehra and Kamla Mehra; married Manju Mahra, Feb 3, 1969; children: Rahoul, Rohan. **EDUCATION:** BITS, Pilani, India, BSME, 1965; University of Wisconsin, MSME, 1967; Rochester Institute of Technology, MBA, 1973. **CAREER:** Webster Electric, engineer, 1967-68; DuPont Co, engineer, 1968-70; Nalge Co, senior vice president, vice president of engineering, 1970-. **ORGANIZATIONS:** Society of Plastic Engineers, past president & board of directors, 1968-; Association of Rotational Molders, past president & board of directors, 1980-. **BUSINESS ADDRESS:** Senior Vice President, Vice President of Engineering, Nalge Company, 75 Panorama Creek Dr, PO Box 20365, Rochester, NY 14602.

MEHROTRA, KISHAN GOPAL
Educator. Indo-American. **PERSONAL:** Born Dec 9, 1941, Kashipur, Uttar Pradesh, India; son of Ram Gopal Mehrotra; married Rama; children: Ateev, Manjaree. **EDUCATION:** University of Wisconsin, Madison, PhD, 1971. **CAREER:** Banaras Hindu University, lecturer; Syracuse University, professor, 1971-91; School of Computer and Information Science, professor, currently. **BUSINESS ADDRESS:** Professor, School of Computer and Information Science, 4-116 Center for Science and Technology, Syracuse, NY 13244-4100, (315)443-2811.

MEHROTRA, PREM N.
Consulting/engineering firm executive. Indo-American. **PERSONAL:** Born Oct 12, 1938, Etawah, Uttar Pradesh, India; son of Madhuri Mohan Mehrotra & Sumitra Devi Mehrotra; married Shashi Mehrotra, Aug 17, 1968; children: Neeraj, Rashmi. **EDUCATION:** Banaras Engineering College, India, BSME, 1960; Northwestern University, Kellogg Graduate School of Management, MM, 1977. **CAREER:** Blue Star Ltd, India, planning engineer, 1960-70; Holabird and Root, project engineer, 1970-71; Sargent and Lundy Engineers, project supervisor, 1971-81; Energy Resources & Planning Inc, senior vice president, 1981-85; General Energy Corp, founder, president, 1985-. **ORGANIZATIONS:** American Society of Heating, Refrigerating & Air Conditioning Engineers, 1972-; Association of Energy Engineers, 1989-; National Society of Professional Engineers, 1992-. **HONORS/AWARDS:** Ashrae Energy Award, for outstanding achievement in energy management and conservation design, 1984. **HOME ADDRESS:** 237 Stockport Ln, Schaumburg, IL 60193, (708)386-6000. **BUSINESS ADDRESS:** President, General Energy Corp, 230 Madison St, Oak Park, IL 60302, (708)386-6000.

MEHROTRA, SUDHIR CHANDRA
Company executive. Indo-American. **PERSONAL:** Born Nov 27, 1945, Bilgram, Uttar Pradesh, India; son of Shyam Nath & Mohini Mehrotra; married Usha Mehrotra, Jul 20, 1973; children: Surabhi, Shruti, Shakti. **EDUCATION:** Indian Institute of Technology, BS, 1968; University of Kansas, MS, 1971, PHD, 1977. **CAREER:** University of Kansas, research assistant, 1968-74, research associate, 1974-79; ViGYAN Inc, president, 1979-. **ORGANIZATIONS:** Hindu Temple of Hampton Roads, trustee, 1987-; American Institute of Aeronautics and Astronautics, associate fellow, 1976-; National Society of Professional Engineers, 1980-; National Contract Management Association, 1982-. **HONORS/AWARDS:** Peninsula Chamber of Commerce, Small Business Person of the Year, 1992; Small Business Administration, Minority Small Business Person of the Yer, 1989; NASA, Minority Contractor of the Year, company recognition, 1987. **BUSINESS ADDRESS:** President, ViGYAN Inc, 30 Research Dr, Hampton, VA 23666, (804)865-1400.

MEHTA, AJAI SINGH (SONNY MEHTA)
Publishing company executive. Indo-American. **PERSONAL:** Born 1943, New Delhi, India; married Gita. **EDUCATION:** Cambridge University, London. **CAREER:** Pan and Picador Publishers, London, publishing director, until 1987; Alfred A Knopf, president, editor-in-chief, 1987-. **BIOGRAPHICAL SOURCES:** "After a Year, Knopf Shows the Impact of a New Top Editor," New York Times, March 26, 1988, Sec A, p18, col 3. **BUSINESS ADDRESS:** President, Editor-in-Chief, Director, Alfred A Knopf Inc, 201 East 50th St, New York, NY 10022, (212)751-2600.*

MEHTA, AMARJIT (JEET)
Government official. Indo-American. **PERSONAL:** Born Oct 29, 1941, Bahawalpur, India; son of Sobhag Rai Mehta (deceased) and Shyama Rani Mehta; married Naomi Rae Vasbinder, Jan 15, 1961; children: Karuna, Christopher, Nishtha Burke. **EDUCATION:** Howard University, BSME, 1964. **CAREER:** Bechtel Power Corp, eng supv/project engr, 1964-80; Gibbs & Hill Inc, chief mech/nuc eng, 1980-83; Management Analysis Co, engineering mgmt consultant, 1983-85; self employed, engineering mgmt consultant, 1985-86; Wolf Creek Nuc Operating Corp, mgr, Systems Engineering, 1987-90; US Dept of Energy, division dir, 1990-. **ORGANIZATIONS:** Amer Mechanical Engineers, 1962-; American Nuclear Society, 1975-; Professional Engineer, CA, KS; National Council of Examiners for Engineers. **BUSINESS ADDRESS:** Division Director, US Dept of Energy, 1000 Independence Ave SW, Forrestal Bldg, Washington, DC 20585, (202)586-0199.

MEHTA, ASHOK V.
Pediatric cardiology educational administrator. Indo-American. **PERSONAL:** Born Jan 16, 1951, Bakor, Gujarat, India; son of Vallavdas H Mehta & Sushila V Mehta; married Pragna, Apr 2, 1978; children: Raj. **EDUCATION:** Baroda Medical College, India, MB, BS, 1974; Misericardia, MD, 1978; University of Miami, MD, 1981. **CAREER:** Temple University, pediatric cardiologist, 1976-81; East Tennessee State University, director, ped cardiology, 1986-. **ORGANIZATIONS:** American Heart Association, JC Chaper, board of directors; American College of Cardiology. **HONORS/AWARDS:** American Academy of Pediatrics, fellow, 1981; American College of Cardiology, fellow, 1983. **SPECIAL ACHIEVEMENTS:** Research published in several papers in the field of pediatric cardiology. **BUSINESS ADDRESS:** Director, Pediatric Cardiology, East Tennessee State University, Quillen College of Medicine, PO Box 70,578, Johnson City, TN 37614, (615)929-7755.

MEHTA, BHARAT V.
Physician. Indo-American. **PERSONAL:** Born Jan 26, 1930, Rajkot, India; son of Vrajlal C Mehta and Champaben V Mehta; married Asha, Oct 7, 1962; children: Maya. **EDUCATION:** University of Bombay, MD, BS, 1954; University of Liverpool, MCh, 1963. **CAREER:** Self-employed, orthopedic surgeon, 1972-73; Waterbury General Hospital, orthopedic surgeon, 1972-73; St Mary's Hospital, orthopedic surgeon, 1972-73; Danville Polyclinic Ltd, physician, 1973-. **ORGANIZATIONS:** Vermillion County Medical Society, 1973-; Illinois State Medical Society, 1973-; AMA, 1973; United Samaritans Medical Center, chief of staff, 1993; American Academy of Ortho, Surgeon Fellow,

1980; American Board of Ortho Surgeons, certified, 1974. **HONORS/ AWARDS:** Royal College of Surgeons, England, FRCS, 1959; Royal College of Surgeons, Edinburgh, 1960. **SPECIAL ACHIEVEMENTS:** University of Illinois, Champaign, clinical associate in surgery, 1975-. **BUSINESS ADDRESS:** Physician, Danville Polyclinic, Ltd., 200 S College, Danville, IL 61832, (217)446-6410.

MEHTA, GURMUKH DASS
Engineering manager. Indo-American. **PERSONAL:** Born Aug 27, 1945, India; son of Sham Sunder Mehta and Ishwar Dureja Mehta; married Veena Makhija Mehta, Jan 15, 1973; children: Rohini I, Rashi I, Rupal I. **EDUCATION:** Punjab University, India, BS, 1967; ITT Kanpur, India, MS, 1969; Brown University, PhD, 1974. **CAREER:** IIT Kanpur, senior research assistant, 1970-88; Brown University, research & teaching assistant, 1970-74; Hydronautics Inc, staff scientist, 1974-77; Intertechnology Corporation, director of technical operations, 1977-81; SAIC, assistant vice president & division deputy director, 1981-. **ORGANIZATIONS:** American Society of Mechanical Engineers, 1974-94; Journal of Membrane Science, tech reviewer, 1980-94; Simulation Management Board, 1989-93; Missile Simulation Control Panel, 1989-93; Tomahawk Missile Evaluation Team, 1989-92; American Solar Energy Society, 1977-81; American Institute of Aeronautics & Astronautics, 1974-85; American Institute of Chemical Engineers, 1977-82. **HONORS/ AWARDS:** US Navy, Atlas Award, 1985; NASA, cash award & certificate of recognition, 1980; SAIC, cash award & citation, 1986; Punjab University, Gold Medal, 1967; Brown University, research assistantship, 1970-74. **SPECIAL ACHIEVEMENTS:** Three US patents in the energy field; over 75 publications & reports in the technical area; proficient in Hindi, Urdu, Punjabi, and Multani. **HOME ADDRESS:** 3331 Monarch Lane, Annandale, VA 22003. **BUSINESS ADDRESS:** Asst Vice Pres, Div Deputy Director, Science Applications International Corporation, 1213 Jefferson Davis Highway, Suite #1300, Arlington, VA 22202, (703)553-6182.

MEHTA, JAWAHAR L. (JAY)
Physician. Indo-American. **PERSONAL:** Born Aug 10, 1946, Kahrore, Punjab, India; son of Ishwar Devi Mehta and Mohan Lal Mehta; married Paulette Mehta, Oct 20, 1977; children: Asha, Jason. **EDUCATION:** Panjab University, Chardigash, MBBS, 1967; Mt Sinai School of Medicine, resident in medicine, 1971-73; SUNY, Stony Brook, fellow in cardiology, 1973-75; University of Minnesota, research fellow, 1975-76; University of Uppsala, Sweden, PhD, medicine, 1991. **CAREER:** University of Florida, Dept of Medicine, assistant professor, 1976-81, associate professor, 1981-86, professor, 1986-. **ORGANIZATIONS:** American College of Cardiology, fellow, 1977-; American Heart Association, Council on Circulation, fellow, 1978-; American Society for Clinical Investigation, 1986. **HONORS/AWARDS:** Served on 2 NIH Research Review Committees, 1993; frequent invitee to national & international symposiums on cardiovascular disease, 1977-. **SPECIAL ACHIEVEMENTS:** Edited two books; Platelets & Prostaglandins in Cardiovascular Disease, Futura, New York, 1981; Thrombosis & Platelets in Myocardial Ischemia, FA Davis Co, Philadelphia, 1987; published over 500 papers and abstracts. **BUSINESS ADDRESS:** Professor of Medicine, University of Florida, Box 100277, JHMHC, Gainesville, FL 32610, (904)376-1611.

MEHTA, KAILASH
Plant manager. Indo-American. **PERSONAL:** Born Jul 18, 1948, Jodhpur, Rajasthan, India; son of Paras Mal Mehta and Sohan Kr Mehta; married Saroj Mehta, Jul 9, 1973; children: Shawna, Sachin. **EDUCATION:** Jodphur University, India, BSc, 1967, MSc, 1969; Miami University, Ohio, MS, 1975. **CAREER:** The Beckett Paper Co, quality control, 1972-73; Miami Valley Paper Co, plant manager, 1973-. **ORGANIZATIONS:** TAPPI, process committee, 1985-. **HONORS/AWARDS:** India Club, Dayton, various awards, 1985-. **BUSINESS ADDRESS:** Plant Manager, Miami Valley Paper Company Inc, 413 Oxford Rd, Franklin, OH 45005, (513)746-6451.

MEHTA, KAMLESH T.
Educator, educational administrator. Indo-American. **PERSONAL:** Born Nov 19, 1959, Jamnagar, Gujarat, India; son of Tansukhlal O Mehta & Kantaben T Mehta. **EDUCATION:** Maharaja Sayajirao University of Bavoda, India, BComm, 1981, MComm, 1983; Emporia State University, Emporia, KS, MBA, 1986; US International University, San Diego, CA, DBA, 1990. **CAREER:** State Bank of India, cashier, 1983-84; Bank of America, marketing representative, 1986; Chamber of Commerce, assistant to president, 1984-85; US International University, instructor, adjunct professor, 1987-88; St Mary's University, assistant professor, 1989-93, International Business Management, associate

professor, 1993-, Center for Global Business Studies, director, 1991-. **ORGANIZATIONS:** Southwest Region Decision Sciences Institute, vice president of programs, 1993-94; San Antonio World Trade Association, 1992-; San Antonio World Affairs Council, 1990-94; San Antonio Chamber of Commerce, 1992-; Music Society of San Antonio, 1992-94; Academy of International Business, 1990-; Decision Sciences Institute, 1988-. **HONORS/AWARDS:** Academy of International Business, Best Paper in Latin American Track, 1993. **SPECIAL ACHIEVEMENTS:** Contributor, Journal of Technical Writing and Communications, 1993; AIB Proceedings, DSI Proceedings, Midwest Review of Research in Business, Case Research Association of America. **BUSINESS ADDRESS:** Associate Professor, International Business Management, Director of Center for Global Business Studies, St Mary's University, 1 Camino Santa Maria, San Antonio, TX 78228, (210)431-2024.

MEHTA, KISHOR SINGH
Plastics company executive. Indo-American. **PERSONAL:** Born Jul 27, 1941, Jodhpur, Rajasthan, India; son of Ranjit Singh Mehta & Hem Kumari Singhvi; married Shashi Kala Jain, Dec 11, 1963; children: Amitabh Singh, Anurag Singh, Abhishek Singh. **EDUCATION:** University of Rajasthan, MS, mechanical engineering, 1962; University of Delaware, plastics engineering certificate, 1972; Rochester Institute of Technology, MBA, 1981. **CAREER:** Jayshree Plastics Pvt Limited, technical director, 1964-70; B K Plastics Pvt Limited, plant manager, 1964-70; American Can Company, senior engineer, 1970-73; Johnson & Johnson, senior engineer, 1973-74; Continental Group, senior advisory engineer, 1974-78; Xerox Corporation, Polymer Processing, manager, 1978-83; Miles Inc, Design Engineering, manager, 1983-. **ORGANIZATIONS:** Society of Plastics Engineers, Annual Technical Conference, chairman, 1985, treasurer, 1986-87, secretary, 1987-88, Seminar Board, adviser, 1983-86, Injection Molding Division, chairman, 1983-84, fellow, 1984. **HONORS/AWARDS:** Society of Plastics Engineers, Meritorious Services Award, 1985, Man of The Year Award, 1986; Xerox Corporation, Outstanding Achievement Award, 1981, Miles Inc, Quality Improvement Award, 1990, 1993. **SPECIAL ACHIEVEMENTS:** Published articles in leading plastics journals, including Plastics Design Forum, Nov-Dec 1986; Plastics Engineering, Sept 1992; presented papers at conferences; proficient in Hindi and German; three patents in plastics processing and part design, 1966-68. **HOME ADDRESS:** 408 Pine Villa Drive, Gibsonia, PA 15044. **BUSINESS ADDRESS:** Manager, Engineering, Miles Inc, Mobay Road, Polymers Division, Pittsburgh, PA 15205-9741.

MEHTA, KRISHNAKANT HIRALAL
Certified public accountant. Indo-American. **PERSONAL:** Born Mar 28, 1931, Ankleshwar, Gujarat, India; son of Hiralal T Mehta and Champa H Mehta; married Sudha; children: Samir K. **EDUCATION:** Sydenham College, BU, BCom, 1954, MCom, 1957; New Law College, BU, LLB, 1956; ACA, chartered accountant of India, 1960. **CAREER:** Institute of Bankers, asst secretary, 1961-64; Institute of Chartered Accountants of India, asst secretary, 1964-66; Hindustan Polymers, internal auditor, 1966-68; private practice, CPA, currently. **BUSINESS ADDRESS:** CPA, 1254 W Chester Pike, L & M Professional Bldg, Havertown, PA 19083, (610)789-0496.

MEHTA, MAHENDRA
Paper company manager. Indo-American. **PERSONAL:** Born Sep 28, 1952, Jodhpur, Rajasthan, India; son of Moti Mal Mehta & Pushpa Mehta; married Chandra Mehta, Apr 29, 1979; children: Shweta, Priyesh. **EDUCATION:** Jodhpur University, India, BSc, 1971, MSc, 1974, PhD, 1978. **CAREER:** Baylor University, postdoctoral research fellow, 1979-81; Gayford Research Institute, research fellow, 1981-84; Mead Corporation, research specialist, corporate R&D, 1984-88, senior research scientist, corporate R&D, 1988-90, director, R&D, speciality paper division, 1990-. **ORGANIZATIONS:** American Chemical Society; TAPPI. **SPECIAL ACHIEVEMENTS:** Many publications in international journals. **HOME ADDRESS:** 169 Mountain Dr, Pittsfield, MA 01201, (413)499-4052. **BUSINESS ADDRESS:** Director, Research and Development, Mead Paper, Speciality Paper Division, Rt 102, Willow St, South Lee, MA 01260, (413)243-1231.

MEHTA, MAHESH
Organization administrator, educator. Indo-American. **PERSONAL:** Born Nov 19, 1935, Bombay, India. **EDUCATION:** University of Bombay, India, BA, 1953, MA, 1955, LLB, 1957, PhD, Sanskrit, 1964. **CAREER:** Gujarat University, India, professor of Sanskrit, 1958-61; University of Bombay, lecturer, 1961-63; University of Pennsylvania, fellow, 1967-68, lecturer, 1968-69; University of Windsor, Dept Indian Philosophy & Religion, asst professor,

1969-73, associate professor, beginning 1973; Koch Membrane Systems, Research & Development, director, currently. **ORGANIZATIONS:** Vishwa Hindu Parishad of America, president, currently; Association Asian Studies; Canadian Society Asian Studies; Bhandarkar Orient Research Institute; numerous others. **SPECIAL ACHIEVEMENTS:** Author of numerous publications including, The Mahabharata: A Study of the Critical Edition, Bharatiya Vidya Bhavan; contributed several articles to professional journals. **BUSINESS ADDRESS:** Director, Research & Development, Koch Membrane Systems, 850 Main Street, Wilmington, MA 01887.*

MEHTA, MEHUL MANSUKH
Surgeon, educator. Indo-American. **PERSONAL:** Born Jan 8, 1958, Bombay, India; son of Mansukh H Mehta and Jayashree Mehta; married Claire, Jan 7, 1984; children: Nicola, Samir, Priya. **EDUCATION:** St Thomas Hospital Medical School, London, UK, MB, BSc, 1992. **CAREER:** St Helier Hospital, house officer, 1982-83; Derby City Hospital, house surgeon, 1983; Derby Royal Infirmary, senior house officer, 1984; Mt Sinai Hospital, resident, general surgery, 1984-89; Connecticut Combined Hand Surgery, fellow, hand surgery, 1989-90; Wayne State University, resident, plastic and reconstructive surgery, 1990-92, Harper Hospital, Division of Plastic Surgery, asst professor, currently. **ORGANIZATIONS:** American Society of Plastic and Reconstructive Surgeons, candidate mbr, 1992; American College of Surgeons, associate fellow, 1990; American Medical Assn; Oakland County Medical Society, 1993; Michigan State Medical Society, 1993. **SPECIAL ACHIEVEMENTS:** Hand Surgery Fellowship Program, director, 1992. **HOME ADDRESS:** 1052 Northlawn, Birmingham, MI 48009. **BUSINESS PHONE:** (313)745-8773.

MEHTA, MOHINDER PAUL
Educational administrator. Indo-American. **PERSONAL:** Born Sep 5, 1937, Lahore District, Pakistan; son of Mr & Mrs Sundar D Mehta; married Sudesh Sharma, Jan 16, 1963; children: Samita, Neal K. **EDUCATION:** Punjab University, India, BA, 1956, MA, English, 1960, MA, history, 1963; University of Montana, MA, English, 1968, EdD, 1970. **CAREER:** RSD College, Ferozepur City, Punjab, lecturer of English, 1961-64; Leask High School, Canada, teacher, 1964-68; Missoula County High School, teacher, 1969-70; Minot State University, professor, division chairman, education & psychology, school of education, acting dean, 1970-86; Prairie View A&M University, College of Education, dean, 1986-. **ORGANIZATIONS:** American Assn of Colleges for Teacher Education, board of directors, 1993-95, chairman advisory council of state representatives; The Holmes Group, treasurer, 1992-; Texas Assn of Colleges for Teacher Education, president, 1992-93; Assn of Deans of Education at Land Grant Universities, executive comm, 1991-94; American Educational Research Assn. **HONORS/AWARDS:** North Dakota Humanities Council, grant, 1972-73; Texas Higher Education Coordinating Board, Grant for Inservice of Elementary Teachers, 1987-88; Texas Education Agency, Grant for Center for Professional Develpment and Technology, 1992-94. **SPECIAL ACHIEVEMENTS:** Author of two chapters, Leadership in Teacher Education, 1974; co-producer of 16mm documentary, "A Measure of North Dakota-The Land & the People"; co-author of three publications on Governance Tenure and Academic Freedoms, published by Natl Educ Assn, 1982; co-author, Handbook on Evaluation for Growth. **HOME ADDRESS:** 7619 Creek Glen Dr, Houston, TX 77095.

MEHTA, PRAKASH V.
Research chemist. Indo-American. **PERSONAL:** Born Feb 23, 1946, Jhalod, Gujarat, India; son of Vithaldas P Mehta; married Pallavi P Mehta; children: Prapti, Purvi. **EDUCATION:** Sardar Patel University, India, BSc, MSc, 1966, 1969; Polytechnic Institute of Brooklyn, New York, MS, 1972, MS, 1974, 1977 PhD. **CAREER:** Kay Fries Inc, research chemist, 1978-82; Pace University, Pleasantville, associate professor, 1980-87; Dynamit Nobel, group leader, 1982-86; Huls America Inc, manager of R&D, 1986-. **ORGANIZATIONS:** India Cultural Society of Rockland, NY, vice president, 1979-80, president, 1980-81; Federation of Indian Association, board member, 1979-82; American Chemical Society, 1975-. **HONORS/AWARDS:** Kay Fries Inc, President Award, 1980; Huls America Inc, Huls Performance Award, 1992.

MEHTA, RAHUL
Educator. Indo-American. **PERSONAL:** Born Jan 12, 1949, Varanasi, Uttar Pradesh, India; son of Bhanu Shanker and Suhasini; married Kaberi, Dec 26, 1983; children: Paulomi, Devika. **EDUCATION:** Banaras Hindu University, BSc, 1969, MSc, physics, 1971; North Texas State University, PhD, physics, 1982. **CAREER:** Louisiana State University, teaching assistant, 1971-72; North Texas State University, teaching assistant, 1973-78, research fellow,

Welch, 1979-82, post doctoral fellow, 1983-84; University of Texas, Arlington, visiting assistant professor, 1983; East Carolina University, visiting assistant professor, 1984-90; University of Central Arkansas, assistant professor, 1990-92, associate prof, 1992- . **ORGANIZATIONS:** American Physical Society; Sigma Pi Sigma, 1976-; Society of Physics Students, president, local, 1973-90; Sigma Xi, life member; Arkansas Academy of Science, 1991-. **SPECIAL ACHIEVEMENTS:** M-Shell X-ray Production in 79Au 82Pb 83Bi & 92U by 1H 2He & 9F ions, 1982. **BUSINESS ADDRESS:** Associate Professor, Physics, University of Central Arkansas, Lewis Science Center, Room 103, Conway, AR 72035, (501)450-5906.

MEHTA, RAJ B.
Educator. Indo-American. **PERSONAL:** Born Jul 16, 1962, Ankleshwar, Gujarat, India; son of Bipinchandra C Mehta and Pramila B Mehta; married Sheela Mehta, Aug 5, 1987; children: Natasha. **EDUCATION:** Indian Institute of Technology, BTech, 1984; BK School of Management, MBA, 1986; University of Utah, PhD, 1991. **CAREER:** University of Cincinnati, assistant professor, 1990-. **ORGANIZATIONS:** American Marketing Association, 1990-; Institute of Management Science, 1990-; Cincinnati Chamber of Commerce, 1991-. **SPECIAL ACHIEVEMENTS:** "An Examination of the Use of Unacceptable Levels in Conjoint Analysis," Journal of Consumer Research, 1992; "Artifacts, Identity & Transition: Favorite Possessions of Indians and Indian Immigrants to the US," Journal of Consumer Research, 1991. **BUSINESS ADDRESS:** Asst Professor, University of Cincinnati, 326 Lindner Hall, Cincinnati, OH 45221-0145, (513)556-7116.

MEHTA, RAJENDRA G.
Educator. Indo-American. **PERSONAL:** Born Aug 31, 1947, Dabhoi, Gujarat, India; son of Govindlal H & Arvinda G Mehta; married Raksha Mehta, Feb 23, 1976; children: Sonkulp R, Prerak R. **EDUCATION:** Gujarat University, India, BSc, 1966, MSc, 1968; University of Nebraska, PhD, 1974. **CAREER:** University of Rochester, research associate, 1974-76; University of Louisville, research associate, 1976-77; IIT Research Institute, research scientist, 1977-79, senior scientist, 1979-90, scientific advisor, 1990-92; University of Illinois, College of Medicine, associate professor, 1992-. **ORGANIZATIONS:** American Association Cancer Research, 1980-; International Society Breast Cancer Research, 1987-; International Society Vitamins and Nutrition, 1988-; NIH Study Section, chartered member, 1989-93; American Cancer Society, committee member. **HONORS/AWARDS:** Japanese Cancer Institute, Distinguished Scientist. **SPECIAL ACHIEVEMENTS:** Author or co-author of over 100 publications and abstracts in peer reviewed journals or book chapters. **BUSINESS ADDRESS:** Professor, Cancer Center, University of Illinois, College of Medicine, 2201 W Campbell Park, M/C 454, Chicago, IL 60612, (312)413-1156.

MEHTA, SONNY. *See* MEHTA, AJAI SINGH.

MEHTA, SUNIL KUMAR
Physician. Indo-American. **PERSONAL:** Born Jan 26, 1939, Mandsaur, Madhya Pradesh, India; son of Chandmal Mehta and Zaver Bai Mehta; married Usha Mehta, May 24, 1967; children: Kiran, Prabhat, Nisha. **EDUCATION:** R R College, Bombay, India, BSc, 1957; MGM Medical College, Indore, India, MBBS, 1962, MD, 1967; American Board of Internal Medicine, 1976. **CAREER:** Private practice, physician, 1974-. **ORGANIZATIONS:** American Medical Assn; American Assn of Physicians From India. **BUSINESS ADDRESS:** Physician, 675 N Broad St Extension, Grove City, PA 16127.

MEHTA, UJJWAL J.
Pharmaceutical company executive. Indo-American. **PERSONAL:** Born Nov 2, 1944, Baroda, Gujarat, India; son of Janardan Mehta and Vinodini Mehta; married Smriti U Mehta, Apr 19, 1971; children: Moha, Anuja, Sheetal. **EDUCATION:** MSU of Baroda, India, BSME, 1966; Illinois Institute of Technology, Chicago, MSIE, 1968; Northwestern University, MBA, finance, 1971. **CAREER:** Union Carbide Corp, production engr, 1968-70, controller, 1970-72; Abbott Laboratories, senior cost accountant, 1972-74, Manufacturing Accounting, mgr, 1974-79, asst controller, 1979-83, Business Systems, dir, 1983-87, Corporate Strategic Systems Planning, dir, 1987-. **ORGANIZATIONS:** SIM; AIIM; PRISM. **HOME ADDRESS:** 1124 Kristin Dr, Libertyville, IL 60048, (708)367-7924.

MEHTA, VED (PARKASH)
Writer, educator. Indo-American. **PERSONAL:** Born Mar 21, 1934, Lahore, India; son of Amolak Ram and Shanti Mehra Mehta; married Linn Cary, 1983;

children: Sage, Natasha. **EDUCATION:** Arkansas School for the Blind, 1949-52; Pomona College, BA, 1956; Balliol College, Oxford, BA (honors), 1959, MA, 1962; Harvard University, MA, 1961. **CAREER:** The New Yorker magazine, staff writer, 1961-; Case Western Reserve University, visiting scholar, 1974; Bard College, professor of literature, 1985, 1986; Sarah Lawrence College, Noble Foundation Visiting Professor of Art & Cultural History, 1988; visiting fellow in literature: Balliol College, Oxford University; New York University, visiting professor of English, 1989-90; Yale University, Rosenkranz Chair in Writing, 1990-93, lecturer in history, 1990-92, lecturer in English, 1991-93; Berkeley College (Yale College), associate fellow, 1988-, residential fellow, 1990-93; Williams College, English, History, Arnold Bernhard Professor, 1994; Vassar College, Randolph Distinguished Professor, 1994. **ORGANIZATIONS:** Council on Foreign Relations, 1979-; American Heritage Dictionary, Usage Panel, 1982; New York Institute for the Humanities, fellow, 1988-92. **HONORS/AWARDS:** Balliol College, Oxford, visiting fellow, literature, 1988-89; Phi Beta Kappa, 1955; Hazen Fellow, 1956-59; Harvard Prize Fellow, 1959-60, Resident Fellow, Eliot House, 1959-61; Guggenheim Fellow, 1971-72, 1977-78; Ford Foundation Travel & Study Grant, 1971, 1976; Public Policy Grant, 1979-82; MacArthur Prize Fellow, 1982-87; Assn of Indians in America Award, 1978; Asian/Pacific American Library Assn, Distinguished Service Award, 1986; New York City Mayor's Liberty Medal, 1986; Pomona College, Centenary Barrows Award, 1987; New York Public Library Lion Medal, 1990; New York State Asian-American Heritage Month Award, 1991; honorary degrees: Pomona College, 1972, Bard College, 1982, Williams College, 1986, Stirling, Scotland, 1988. **SPECIAL ACHIEVEMENTS:** Author: Face to Face, 1957; Walking the Indian Streets, 1960; Fly and the Fly-Bottle, 1963; New Theologian, 1966; Delinquent Chacha, 1967; Portrait of India, 1970; John Is Easy to Please, 1971; Mahatma Gandhi & His Apostles, 1977; New India, 1978; Photographs of Chachaji, 1980; A Family Affair: India Under Three Prime Ministers, 1982; Three Stories of the Raj, 1986; Rajiv Gandhi and the Dynasty's Legacy, 1994; writer and narrator of television documentary film, "Chachaji, My Poor Relation," PBS, 1978, BBC, 1980, film received DuPont Columbia Award for Excellence in Broadcast Journalism, 1977-78. **BIOGRAPHICAL SOURCES:** Autobiographical series, Continents of Exile: Daddyji, 1972; Mamaji, 1979; Vedi, 1982; Ledge Between the Streams, 1984; Sound-Shadows of the New World, 1986; Stolen Light, 1989; Up at Oxford, 1993. **HOME ADDRESS:** 139 E 79th St, New York, NY 10021.

MEHTA, ZUBIN
Musical conductor. Indo-American. **PERSONAL:** Born Apr 29, 1936, Bombay, India; son of Mehli Nowrowji Mehta and Tehmina Daruvala Mehta; married Nancy Diane Kovack; children: Zarina, Merwan. **EDUCATION:** St Xavier's College, India, 1951-53; State Academy of Music, Austria, 1954-60; Sir George Williams University, Canada, LLD, 1965. **CAREER:** Montreal Symphony Orchestra, music director, 1961-67; Los Angeles Philharmonic Orch, music director, 1962-68; Israel Philharmonic, music director, 1969-; Vienna Philharmonic, conductor, currently; Israel Philharmonic, conductor, currently; New York Philharmonic, conductor, music director, 1978-; albums as recording artist for numerous labels, including: Decca, CBS, RCA, New World. **ORGANIZATIONS:** Occidental College, honorary DMus; numerous honorary doctorates; Met Opera, guest conductor; Salzburg Festival, guest conductor; Vienna Philharmonic, guest conductor; Berlin Philharmonic, guest conductor; La Scala, music director. **HONORS/AWARDS:** Liverpool Conductors Competition, First Prize, 1958. **BUSINESS ADDRESS:** Conductor, New York Philharmonic, 132 W 65th St, New York, NY 10023.∗

MEI, CHIANG CHUNG
Educator. Chinese American. **PERSONAL:** Born Apr 4, 1935, Wuhan, China; son of Ju Long Mei & Yu Ling Mei; married Caroline Jean Schmitt, May 29, 1965; children: Deborah. **EDUCATION:** National Taiwan University, BS, 1985; Stanford University, MS, 1958; California Institute Technology, PhD, 1963. **CAREER:** Massachusetts Institute of Technology, assistant professor, 1965-68, associate professor, 1968-74, professor, 1974-93, Edmund K Turner Professor, 1993-. **ORGANIZATIONS:** American Society Civil Engineers; Society Indust Appl Math; American Physical Society; American Geophy Union; Sigma Xi; National Academy of Engineering, 1986. **HONORS/AWARDS:** Academia Sinica, academician, 1992; University of Miami, Rosenstiel Award, 1987; American Society Civil Engineers, Moffat Nichols Award, 1992; British Institution of Civil Engineers, T K Hsieh Award, 1984. **SPECIAL ACHIEVEMENTS:** Book: Applied Dynamics of Ocean Surface Waves, 1983. **MILITARY SERVICE:** Army, Republic of China, 2nd Lt,

1955-57. **BUSINESS ADDRESS:** Edmund K Turner Professor, MIT, Dept of Engineering, 48-413, Cambridge, MA 02139, (617)253-2994.

MEI, JUNE Y.
Consultant, interpreter. Chinese American. **PERSONAL:** Born in New York, NY. **EDUCATION:** Bryn Mawr College, AB; Harvard University, MA, PhD. **CAREER:** University of California, Los Angeles, lecturer, research associate; National Committee on US-China Relations, program associate; independent consultant, interpreter, currently. **ORGANIZATIONS:** Office of the Mayor of New York, NYC Translators Certification Program, panel member. **HONORS/AWARDS:** Whiting Foundation Fellowship in the Humanities. **SPECIAL ACHIEVEMENTS:** Languages: English, Chinese (Cantonese & Mandarin); various reports and scholarly publications; envoy of the LA Olympic Organizing Committee to the People's Republic of China Delegation, 1984. **BUSINESS ADDRESS:** Independent Interpreter, 395 Broadway, Ste 8A, New York, NY 10013.

MEI, KENNETH K. (KWAN-HSIANG)
Educator. Chinese American. **PERSONAL:** Born May 19, 1932, Shanghai, China; son of Denis Y D Mei; married Huei-chun Chiu; children: Cynthia, Audrey, An Kai. **EDUCATION:** University of Wisconsin, Madison, BS, 1959, MS, 1960, PhD, 1962. **CAREER:** University of California, Berkeley, professor of electrical engineering & computer science, professor of buddhist study group, currently. **ORGANIZATIONS:** Institute of Electrical & Electronics Engineering; Union of Radio Science International. **HONORS/AWARDS:** Institute of Electrical & Electronics Engineering, Best Paper Award, 1967, Honorable Mention to Best Paper Award, 1974; University of Wisconsin, Centennial Medal, 1991. **SPECIAL ACHIEVEMENTS:** Over one hundred technical publications in the area of electromagnetic fields and waves, 1962-93. **BUSINESS ADDRESS:** Professor, Dept EECS, University of California, Berkeley, CA 94720, (510)642-4106.

MEI, WAI-NING
Educator. Chinese American. **PERSONAL:** Born Dec 31, 1949, Taipei, Taiwan. **EDUCATION:** Chinese University of Hong Kong, BS, 1972; State University of New York at Buffalo, PhD, 1979. **CAREER:** Purdue University, research associate, 1979-82; Naval Research Laboratory, research scientist, 1983-84; University of Wisconsin-Milwaukee, research associate, 1984-86; University of Nebraska at Omaha, associate professor, 1986-. **ORGANIZATIONS:** American Physical Society, 1974-. **BUSINESS ADDRESS:** Associate Professor, Dept of Physics, University of Nebraska at Omaha, Durham Science Center, 66 X Dodge St, Rm 124, Omaha, NE 68182-0266, (402)554-3729.

MELOOKARAN, JOSEPH
Certified public accountant. Indo-American. **PERSONAL:** Born Nov 4, 1955, Koratty, Kerala, India; son of George Melookaran & Anna Melookaran; married Jenny Melookaran, Jul 14, 1985; children: Ann, Roslyn. **EDUCATION:** Sri Sankara College, India, BCom, 1978; Institute of CAs, chartered accountant, 1981; Kansas State Board of Accountancy, CPA, 1986. **CAREER:** Abraham & Jose, senior auditor, 1978-81; Coopers & Lybrand, senior auditor, 1981-83; Sellers & Co, partner, 1984-88; Joseph-Wallace & Associates PC, co-founder, chairman, 1989-. **ORGANIZATIONS:** Indian American Forum for Political Education, president, 1992-; Child Abuse Prevention Coalition, financial consultant, 1991-93; All India Catholic University Federation, national committee, 1975-77; Rasana Magazine, editorial board member, 1972-82; Rally Magazine, Cochin correspondent, 1976; Intl Relations Council, board of directors, 1993; Rotary Club of Kansas City, MO, 1993; American Institute of Public Accountants, personal financial planning section, 1992; Christian Education Group of Kansas City, 1993; Christian College Management Board on India, student member, 1977. **HONORS/AWARDS:** Stallions Intl, Best Speaker, 1977; All India Catholic University Federation, Best Camper, 1975; Best Student of Archdiocese, 1973. **SPECIAL ACHIEVEMENTS:** Current firm is a multi-million dollar accounting and management consulting business employing over 100 professionals; edited Rasana Magazine (regional language of India) for 2 years. **BIOGRAPHICAL SOURCES:** Kansas City Globe, p 9, May 11, 1990; Kansas City Business Journal, p 44, March 30, 1987. **HOME ADDRESS:** 12910 Blue Jacket, Overland Park, KS 66213. **BUSINESS ADDRESS:** Co-Founder/Chairman, Joseph-Wallace & Associates PC, 10 E Cambridge Cir, Ste 310, Kansas City, KS 66103, (913)321-6633.

MENG, JAMES CHENG-SUN

Scientist, federal official. Chinese American. **PERSONAL:** Born Aug 1, 1943, Chung-King, Sichuan, China; son of Mark Ting-Fan Meng & Mary Ming-Wan Lee; married Lucy Chang Meng, Mar 22, 1968; children: Charis, Fleur, Justin. **EDUCATION:** National Taiwan University, BSME, 1965; University of California, Berkeley, MS, eng physics, 1967, PhD, aero engineering, 1969; Massachusetts Institute of Tech, Sloan School of Management, MS, management, 1994. **CAREER:** Physical Dynamics Inc, scientist, 1972-75; NASA, Marshall Space Flight Center, National Academy of Sciences, post doctoral associate fellow, 1970-72; Science Applications Inc, Fluid Dynamics Div, manager, 1976-81; Gould Electronics Inc, research director, 1981-87; US Naval Undersea Warfare Center, director of tech, code 801, 1987-. **ORGANIZATIONS:** National Science Foundation, advisory committee, 1985-87; Newport Hospital, board of trustees, 1987-90; Newport Health Foundation Inc, board of directors, 1990-91; Naval Hydrodynamics, Hydroacoustics Tech Center, technical committee, 1991-92. **HONORS/AWARDS:** Federal Executive Council, Professional Employee of the Year, 1991; NUWC, Excellence in Science & Engineering, 1990, Excellence in Technical Management, 1989. **SPECIAL ACHIEVEMENTS:** Publications in following journals: Journal of Fluid of Mechanics; Journal of Applied Optics; Journal of Computational Physics, 1970-89. **HOME ADDRESS:** 95 Holman St, Portsmouth, RI 02871-9013, (401)683-1820. **BUSINESS ADDRESS:** Director of Technology, US Naval Undersea Warfare Center, PO Box 5048, Code 801, Bldg 990, Newport, RI 02841-5047.

MENG, JIMMY Z.

Construction company executive. Chinese American. **PERSONAL:** son of Chuang-Chi Meng and Chang-Wei-Feng Meng; married Shiao-Mei Wang, Dec 29, 1974; children: Grace, Caroline, Andy. **EDUCATION:** National Taiwan Normal University, BA, 1963; Oklahoma State University, 1975. **CAREER:** New York Building Material Suppliers, associate president; HCM Manufacturing Co Inc, president; Team-System Business Corp; Queens Lumber Co Inc, president, currently. **ORGANIZATIONS:** New York Building Material Suppliers Association, president, 1990-; Queens Chinese American Voter Association, vice president, 1990-91; Chinese American Business Association. **HONORS/AWARDS:** Chinese American Business Association, Outstanding Businessman, 1992. **BIOGRAPHICAL SOURCES:** Lucky Men's World Co. **BUSINESS ADDRESS:** President, Queens Lumber Co Inc, 34-41 College Pt Blvd, Flushing, NY 11354, (718)539-0400.

MENG, QING-MIN

Artist. Chinese American. **PERSONAL:** Born Sep 7, 1954, Shanghai, People's Republic of China; son of Chu-Lin Meng & Zheng-Qing Zhou. **EDUCATION:** Shanghai Fine Art School, 1972-74; Shanghai Teachers' University, BFA, 1982; Miami University, MFA, 1988. **CAREER:** Shanghai Teachers' University, assistant professor of art, 1982-86; Southwest Texas State University, assistant professor of art, 1988-93; artist, currently. **ORGANIZATIONS:** National Drawing Association, 1990-. **HONORS/AWARDS:** Southwest Texas State University, Research Enhancement Grant, 1993; National Foundation for Advancement in the Arts, Resident Fellowship, 1993; Mid-America Arts Alliance, The National Endowment for the Arts, Fellowship Award in Painting and Works on Paper, 1992; Rockefeller Foundation, The National Endowment for the Arts, New Forms Regional Initiatives Grant, 1991. **SPECIAL ACHIEVEMENTS:** Solo exhibitions: Conduit Gallery, Dallas, TX, 1994, 1992; Kendall Gallery, Wellfleet, MA, 1994, 1993, 1992; Galveston Art Center, Galveston, TX, 1993; group exhibitions: New Works, Laguna Gloria Art Museum, Austin TX, 1992; Osaka Triennale '90, The International Triennial Competition of Painting Public Exhibit Space, Osaka, Japan, 1990. **BIOGRAPHICAL SOURCES:** "East Meets West on Meng's Canvas," Dallas Morning News, June 15, 1992; "New Strokes Are Brilliant," Austin American-Statesman, Sep 19, 1992. **HOME ADDRESS:** 1700-A, RR 12, San Marcos, TX 78666, (512)353-4441.

MENG, XIANNONG

Educator. Chinese American. **PERSONAL:** Born Dec 11, 1957, Suzhou, Jiangsu, People's Republic of China; married Hong Liu, Jun 28, 1986; children: Jennifer. **EDUCATION:** Nanjing Institute of Technology, China, BS, 1982; Worcester Polytechnic Institute, PhD, 1990. **CAREER:** Worcester Polytechnic Institute, visiting assistant professor, 1990; Bucknell University, visiting assistant professor, 1991-. **ORGANIZATIONS:** Association of Computing Machinery; Institute of Electrical and Electronics Engineering; USENIX Association. **BUSINESS ADDRESS:** Assistant Professor, Bucknell University, Lewisburg, PA 17837, (717)524-1782.

MENON, GOPINATH K.

Real estate company executive. Indo-American. **PERSONAL:** Born Sep 18, 1943, Trichur, Kerala, India; son of Gopala Menon and Kochammni Menon; married Leela Menon, Feb 3, 1971; children: Rajesh, Ramesh. **EDUCATION:** Fordham University, business administration, 1976. **CAREER:** Lincoln Hospital, hospital administrator, 1978-88; Menon Investments, president, 1988-. **ORGANIZATIONS:** Asian Americans of Rockland County, committee member, 1985-; Federation of Keralites in North America, 1982-. **HOME ADDRESS:** 85 River Rd, Grandview, NY 10960, (914)353-2939.

MERCHANT, ISMAIL NOORMOHAMED

Film producer. Indo-American. **PERSONAL:** Born Dec 25, 1936, Bombay, India; son of Noormohamed and Hazrabi Rehman. **EDUCATION:** Saint Xavier's College, Bombay, BA, 1958; NYU, MBA, 1960. **CAREER:** Film producer, films include: Heat and Dust, 1983; A Room with a View, 1986; Mr & Mrs Bridge, 1990; Howards End, 1992; Remains of the Day, 1993; director, In Custody, 1993. **HONORS/AWARDS:** British Academy of Film and Television Arts, Best Film for Howards End, 1993. **BUSINESS ADDRESS:** Film Producer, Merchant Ivory Productions, 250 W 57th St, Ste 1913A, New York, NY 10107, (212)582-8049.

MERCHANT, VASANT V.

Educator, consultant. Indo-American. **PERSONAL:** Born Sep 11, 1933, Bombay, Maharashtra, India; daughter of Ratanbai Vallabhdas Merchant and Vallabhdas Permanand Merchant. **EDUCATION:** University of Bombay, diploma in teaching, 1953, BA (honors), 1955, MA (honors), LLB, 1957; University of Minnesota, MA, 1960; University of Southern California, PhD, 1966. **CAREER:** University of Minnesota, professor, consultant, researcher, 1957-63; University of Southern California, World Campus Afloat, professor, researcher, 1963-66; University of Seven Seas, consultant, 1964-65; World Peace University, Academic Affairs, vice chancellor, 1980-82, distinguished professor; Northern Arizona University, Dept of Humanities and Religious Studies, consultant, researcher, 1966-, adjunct professor, researcher, consultant, 1987-; Intl Journal of Humanities & Peace, editor-publisher, 1983-. **ORGANIZATIONS:** World Peace University, intl advisory board; Intl Council of Psychologists; Natl Assn of Humanities Education, former president, board member; Arizona Humanities Assn, founder, president; Assn of Asian Studies; University of the Air, founder, co-director. **HONORS/AWARDS:** US President's Award, Outstanding Handicapped Professional Woman of Year, 1976; Key of Success, 1988; Acheivement in Research, 1988; Leader in Intl Education, 1990; Leader in World Religions, 1990; Woman of Year, 1991; Distinguished Service to Community, 1991; Natl Heart Foundation, Certificate of Appreciation; Soroptimist Intl of Arizona, Outstanding Contributions towards Intl Goodwill; Women of Distinction Award, 1993. **SPECIAL ACHIEVEMENTS:** Published extensively on topics including: health psychology, humanities, comparative philosophies, religions, values; books include: The True Role of Women; Sri Aurobindo's Philosophy for the Modern Age; numerous others. **HOME ADDRESS:** 1436 N Evergreen Dr, Flagstaff, AZ 86001, (602)774-4793.

MESHII, MASAHIRO

Educator. Japanese American. **PERSONAL:** Born Oct 6, 1931, Amagasaki, Hyogo, Japan; son of Masataro and Kazuyo Meshii; married Eiko Meshii, May 21, 1959; children: Alisa, Erica Meshii Myers. **EDUCATION:** Osaka University, Dept of Metallurgy, BS, 1954, MS, 1956; Northwestern University, Dept of Materials Science and Engineering, PhD, 1959. **CAREER:** Northwestern University, lecturer, 1959-60, assistant professor, 1960-64, associate professor, 1964-67, professor, 1967-88, Dept of Materials Science and Engineering, chairman, 1978-82, John Evans Professor, 1988-. **ORGANIZATIONS:** National Research Institute for Metals, Tokyo, visiting scientist, 1970-71; Osaka University, guest professor, 1985; ASM International, Materials Science Division, chairman, 1984-86, Seminar Committee, chairman, 1981-83; AIME-TMS, Chemistry and Physics of Metals, chairman, 1975-77, Chicago Section, chairman, 1983-84; Midwest Society of Electron Microscopists, president, 1973-74, 1983-84; Argonne National Laboratory, Electron Microscopy Center Committee, chairman, 1978-80; Acta/Scripta Metallurgica, lecturer, 1993-95. **HONORS/AWARDS:** Fulbright, grant recipient, 1956; Japan Society, fellow, 1958-59; ASM International, Henry Marion Gold Medal, 1968, fellow, 1983; Japan Institute of Metals, Koseki sho Meritorious Award, 1972; Japan Society for Promotion of Science, fellow, 1985; Midwest Society of Electron Microscopists, Founder's Award, 1987. **SPECIAL ACHIEVEMENTS:** Author or co-author of approximately 200 technical papers published in international journals, 1957-; editor or co-editor of 5 books published by Academic Press,

ASM International and AIME-TMS, 1965, 1978, 1979, 1982, 1989. **BIO-GRAPHICAL SOURCES:** Who's Who in Technology Today. **HOME ADDRESS:** 3051 Centennial Ln, Highland Park, IL 60035. **BUSINESS ADDRESS:** John Evans Professor of Materials Science and Engineering, McCormick School of Engineering and Applied Science, Northwestern University, Room 1129 MLSF, Evanston, IL 60208, (708)491-3213.

METHA, PRADIPKUMAR D.
Civil engineer. Indo-American. **PERSONAL:** Born Oct 28, 1940, Jhalod, Gujarat, India; son of Dalsukhdas P Mehta and Jashodaben D Mehta; married Ranjanben P Mehta, Jan 29, 1969; children: Devang. **EDUCATION:** Sardar Patel University, India, BE, civil engineering, 1964; New York State, professional license, 1980. **CAREER:** McKenzies Ltd, Bombay, India, junior engr, 1964-70; Shah Const Co, Bombay, India, civil engr, 1970-71; PWD, Govt of Gujarat, India, junior engr, 1971-75; City of New York, Dept of Environmental Protection, assistant civil engr, 1975-80; New York City Transit Authority, civil engr, 1980-. **HOME ADDRESS:** 79-05 270th St, New Hyde Park, NY 11040, (718)347-7705.

MIAH, ABDUL J.
Educational administrator, educator. Bangladeshi American/Pakistani American. **PERSONAL:** Born Jun 2, 1937, Dhaka, Bangladesh; married Sakina Miah, May 31, 1961; children: Azhar. **EDUCATION:** Karachi University, Pakistan, BA, 1961, DLS, 1963, LLB, 1964; Long Island University, MS, 1968; University of Wisconsin, MS, 1972; Virginia Polytechnic and State University, EdD. **CAREER:** Karachi University, circulation librarian, 1956-58; Pakistan Standards Institution, head librarian, 1958-59; United Nations Information Center, chief librarian, 1960-65; Brooklyn Public Library, intern librarian, 1966-68; Red River Community College, chief librarian, 1969-76; Hudson Valley Community College, associate director, 1977; J Sargeant Reynolds Community College, director, 1978-. **ORGANIZATIONS:** Asian/Pacific American Librarians Association, president; Virginia Library Association, Community College Section, chairman; American Library Association, cultural diversity committee; ACRL, nominations committee; LAMA, editorial board; Virginia Association of Community Colleges, LRC Commission, chair; Virginia Governor's Conference on Library Information Sciences, delegate. **SPECIAL ACHIEVEMENTS:** Automated Library Networking in Virginia's Community Colleges Learning Resources, article; Automated Library Networking in American Public Community Colleges; The Multimedia Career Resource Information Center at Red River; The Dag Hammarshjold Library, article. **BIOGRAPHICAL SOURCES:** People in the News, ACRL News, p 786, Sep 1990. **HOME PHONE:** (804)741-0984. **BUSINESS ADDRESS:** Director, Independent Studies & Learning Resources, J Sargeant Reynolds Community College, 700 E Jackson St, PO Box 85622, Rm 224, Richmond, VA 23285-5622, (804)786-5638.

MIAN, ATHAR S.
Broadband product manager. Pakistani American. **PERSONAL:** Born Jan 25, 1962, Lahore, Pakistan; son of Muhammad Saleem and Fehmeeda Qureshi. **EDUCATION:** University of Engineering & Technology, BSc (with honors), 1985; Columbia University, MS, 1987; Rensselaer Polytechnic Institute, PhD candidate, 1987-90. **CAREER:** AH Institute of Electronics, hardware engineer, 1985; NYNEX Science & Technology Inc, technical staff member, 1990-93; NYNEX Telesector Resources Group, associate director, 1993-. **ORGANIZATIONS:** American Mensa, 1985-; Columbia Club of New York, board of directors, 1993-95; Institute of Elect & Electronics Engineers, 1982-; Asian Association, NYNEX, 1991-. **HONORS/AWARDS:** NYNEX Corp, Standards Commendation Medal, 1991; IEEE, University of Engineering & Technology, Outstanding Student Secretary, 1984; Government of Pakistan, Science & Technology Graduate Fellowship, 1985-89. **SPECIAL ACHIEVEMENTS:** Series 7 and 63 licensed securities broker; Author, Poetry Collection (including Japanese-style Haiku), Echo, Lahore, 1981; magazine editor, Echo Magazine, 1982-83. **HOME ADDRESS:** 235 W 102nd St, Apt 11A, New York, NY 10025, (212)864-7634. **BUSINESS ADDRESS:** Associate Director, NYNEX Telesector Resources Group, 120 Bloomingdale Rd, Rm 279H, White Plains, NY 10605, (914)644-5290.

MIAN, WAQAR SAEED
Physician. Pakistani American. **PERSONAL:** Born Jul 20, 1958, Lahore, Punjab, Pakistan; son of Mian Mohammad Saeed and Surriya Saeed; married Rubeena H Mian, Dec 27, 1987; children: Amara W, Ayla W. **EDUCATION:** University of Punjab, Pakistan, BSc, 1979; Rawalpindi Medical College, Pakistan, MBBS, 1981; University of Manchester, England, MSc, 1990. **CAREER:**

Punjab Health Department, 1983-85; University of Chicago, Department of Surgery, research assistant, 1988-89; Weise Memorial Hospital, internal medicine resident, 1990-93; Humana Health Care Plans, doctor, currently. **ORGANIZATIONS:** Pakistan Medical Association, 1982-; British Association of Audiological Physicians, associate member, 1987-; American College of Physicians, associate member, 1990-. **HOME ADDRESS:** 5633 S Woodlawn, Chicago, IL 60637, (312)752-1122.

MIDORI (MIDORI GOTO)
Violinist. Japanese American. **PERSONAL:** Born Oct 25, 1971, Osaka, Japan. **EDUCATION:** Juilliard School of Music. **CAREER:** Violinist, has performed with orchestras and in recitals throughout the US and in Japan, 1981-. **HONORS/AWARDS:** Japanese Government, Best Artist of the Year, 1988; Los Angeles Music Center, Dorothy B Chandler Performing Arts Award, 1989; Ashani shimbun newspaper, Crystal Award, for contributions to the arts. **SPECIAL ACHIEVEMENTS:** Recordings: J S Bach: Concerto No 2; J S Bach: Concertos for Two Violins and Orchestra in D Minor; Dvorak: Concerto for Violin and Orchestra in A Minor; Dvorak: Romances for Violin and Orchestra in F Minor; Live at Carnegie Hall; contributor to Japanese teen magazine. **BIOGRAPHICAL SOURCES:** New York Times Biographical Service, 1991. **BUSINESS ADDRESS:** Violinist, c/o ICM Artists, 40 W 57th St, New York, NY 10019.*

MIHARA, NATHAN
Judge. **PERSONAL:** Born 1950?; married; children: one. **EDUCATION:** Hastings College of Law, graduate. **CAREER:** State of California, San Francisco, state deputy attorney general, 10 years; Municipal Court, judge, 1985-1988; Santa Clara County Superior Court, judge, beginning 1988; State of California, 6th District Court of Appeals, judge, 1993-. **BUSINESS ADDRESS:** Judge, 6th District Court of Appeals, 333 W Santa Clara St, Ste 1060, San Jose, CA 95113, (408)277-1004.*

MIN, DAVID ILKI
Educator. Korean American. **PERSONAL:** Born Apr 20, 1951, Seoul, Republic of Korea; son of Byung Yong Min and Sihun Min-Yoon; married Susanna Wallshin Min, Dec 1, 1976; children: David Kyungsoo, John Kyungho. **EDUCATION:** Seoul National University, BS, 1975; University of Minnesota, PharmD, 1987, MS, 1989. **CAREER:** Northeastern University, assistant professor, 1989; University of Iowa, assistant professor, 1992-. **ORGANIZATIONS:** American College of Clinical Pharmacy, 1988; American Society of Hospital Pharmacists, 1988; Korean-American Scientists & Engineers Association, 1990; University Bible Fellowship, 1976. **HONORS/AWARDS:** Massachusetts Society of Hospital Pharmacists, Excellent Research Award, 1991. **SPECIAL ACHIEVEMENTS:** Bioavailability and Patients Acceptance of Cyclosporine in Renal Transplant Patients, and many others, 1990. **BIOGRAPHICAL SOURCES:** The Annals of Pharmacotherapy, vol 26, p 175-179, 1992; American Journal of Hospital Pharmacists, vol 49, p 2964-2966, 1992. **BUSINESS ADDRESS:** Assistant Professor, University of Iowa, College of Pharmacy, 2267 Quad Bldg, Iowa City, IA 52242, (319)335-8839.

MIN, HOKEY
Educator. Korean American. **PERSONAL:** Born Jun 28, 1954, Seoul, Republic of Korea; son of Byungjoo Min and Hangwon Seo Min; married Christine K Min; children: Alexander S. **EDUCATION:** Yonsei University, Korea, MBA, 1980; University of South Carolina, MSBA, 1982; Ohio State University, MA, 1986, PhD, 1987. **CAREER:** Ohio State University, teaching associate, 1983-87; University of New Orleans, assistant professor, 1987-89; Northeastern University, assistant professor, 1989-92; Auburn University, assistant professor, 1992-. **ORGANIZATIONS:** Decision Sciences Institute, 1983-; Operations Research Society of America, 1983-; Institute of Management Science, 1983-; Council of Logistics Management, 1987-; Production and Operations Management Society, charter member, 1987-; National Association of Purchasing Managers, 1987-; American Production and Inventory Control Society, 1987-. **HONORS/AWARDS:** Auburn University, 1991-92, Most Outstanding Researcher Award in the College of Business, 1993; SE, TIMS, best student paper award, 1986; SE, DSI, Honorable Mention, third place, student paper award, 1986. **SPECIAL ACHIEVEMENTS:** Published 26 refereed journal articles in the management area, 1993; published over 10 refereed proceeding articles, 1993. **BUSINESS ADDRESS:** Assistant Professor, Dept of Marketing and Transportation, Auburn University, College of Business, Rm 238, Auburn, AL 36849.

MIN, K. JO (KYUNG)

Educator. Korean American. **PERSONAL:** Born Jul 3, 1961, Seoul, Republic of Korea; son of Wan Ki Min & Inhi Min Ahn; married Jae Kyong Chang. **EDUCATION:** UCLA, BS (summa cum laude), math-systems, 1984; University of California, Berkeley, MS, IEOR, 1985, PhD, IEOR, 1990. **CAREER:** University of California, Berkeley, teaching assistant, 1985-89, research assistant, 1987-89; State of California, Telecom Operating Cost Branch, intern, 1988; Iowa State University, assistant professor, 1990-. **ORGANIZATIONS:** Operations Research Society of America, 1987-; Institute of Management Science, 1990-; Institute of Industrial Engineers, 1993-. **HONORS/ AWARDS:** National Science Foundation, Research Initiation Award, 1991-94; University of California, Berkeley, Regent Fellowship, 1984-85; Phi Beta Kappa Honor Society, 1984-. **SPECIAL ACHIEVEMENTS:** Co-author, with S S Oren, "Economic Determination of Special Levels and Allocation Priorities of Semiconductor Products," IIE Transactions, 1994; author, "Inventory and Pricing Policies under Competition," OR Letters, 1992; "Inventory and Quantity Discount Pricing Policies under Profit Maximization," OR Letters, 1992; co-author, with C Chen, "Optimal Selling Quantity & Purchasing Price for Intermediary Firms," IJOPM, 1991. **BUSINESS ADDRESS:** Assistant Professor, Dept of IMSE, Iowa State University, 205 Engineering Annex, Ames, IA 50011-2234.

MIN, KYUNG HO (KEN)

Educator. Korean American. **PERSONAL:** Born Aug 14, 1935, Inchon City, Kyungki, Republic of Korea; son of Je-Yong Yoon and Un Ki Min; married Daphne Ann Nixon, Aug 13, 1966; children: Sylvia Je-Sun, Kwan Hong. **EDUCATION:** Korean Sports Science College, DPE, 1961; University of Georgia, MEd, 1966. **CAREER:** University of Montana, instructor, 1966-67; Eastern Montana College, professor, 1968-69; University of California, Berkeley, activity professor, 1970-, Martial Arts Program, director, 1970-. **ORGANIZATIONS:** United States Judo Federation, ed advisor, 1970-74; United States Collegiate Judo Association, president, 1972-76; United States Olympic Committee, Education Council, 1984-92; The World Taekwondo Federation, University Committee, chairman, 1978-; United States Collegiate Judo Coaches Association, president, 1990-; United States Taekwondo Union, president, 1974-78; World University Sports Federation, Technical Commission, 1989-. **HONORS/AWARDS:** Chung Nam National University, PhD, 1981; World Taekwondo Federation, 9th Dan Black Belt, 1991; Korea Judo Association, 8th Dan Black Belt, 1992; Korea Hapkido Association, 7th Dan Black Belt, 1989; Korea Kumdo Association, 3rd Dan Black Belt, 1987. **SPECIAL ACHIEVEMENTS:** 1st World Taekwondo Championship, Organizing Committee, chairman, 1986; 24th Olympics, Evaluation Committee, 1988; 25th Olympics, United States Taekwondo Team, head, 1992; editor, US Taekwondo Journal, editor, 1977-92; Judo-USA Quarterly Magazine, editor, 1974-79. **BIOGRAPHICAL SOURCES:** Martial Arts Encyclopedia, p 186-190, 1977; Taekwondo Instructors Handbook, p 4-9, 1992. **BUSINESS ADDRESS:** Professor, University of California, 103 Harmon Gym, Berkeley, CA 94720.

MIN, PYONG-GAP

Educator. Korean American. **PERSONAL:** Born Feb 18, 1942, Choong-Nam, Republic of Korea; son of Hong Sik & Nam Hee Min; married Hyun Suk Min, Sep 21, 1972; children: Jay, Michael, Tony. **EDUCATION:** Seoul National University, BA, history, 1970; Georgia State University, MAT, history, 1971, PhD, education, 1979, PhD, sociology, 1983. **CAREER:** Korea Herald, Seoul, general reporter, 1970-71; Dong-Book High School, Seoul, teacher of English, 1971-72; Georgia State University, instructor & research associate, 1983-87; Queens College, assistant professor, 1987-91, associate professor, 1992-. **ORGANIZATIONS:** American Sociological Association, 1983-; Korean-American Professors Association, 1987-; Korean American Cultural Education Association, president, 1992-; Korean Methodist Church and Institute, principal, The Korean Language School, 1990-. **HONORS/AWARDS:** New York City Comptroller, Asian and Pacific American Heritage Month Award, 1991; Social Security Administration, Pacific Asian American Advisory Committee Award, 1992. **SPECIAL ACHIEVEMENTS:** Editor, author of 3 chapters, Asian Americans: A Survey of Ethnic Groups, Sage Publications, 1994; Minority Groups in the US, Kanaan, 1990; Ethnic Business Enterprise: Korean Small Business in Atlanta, Center for Migration Studies, 1988; approximately 35 articles on Korean/Asian Americans published in scholarly journals. **HOME ADDRESS:** 210-17 38th Ave, Bayside, NY 11361. **BUSINESS PHONE:** (718)520-7389.

MIN, YONG SOON

Artist, educator. Korean American. **PERSONAL:** Born Apr 29, 1953, Bugok, Kyonggi, Republic of Korea; daughter of Kang Ja Lee Min and Tae Yong Min; married Allan deSouza, Oct 2, 1992. **EDUCATION:** University of California, Berkeley, BA, 1975, MA, 1977, MFA, 1979; Whitney Museum Independent Study Program, non-degree program, 1981. **CAREER:** California Institute of the Arts, lecturer, 1991; Rhode Island School of Design, visiting faculty, 1992; University of California, Irvine, assistant professor, 1993-. **ORGANIZATIONS:** Asian American Arts Alliance, board of directors, 1989-; Artists Space, board of directors, 1990-93; Women's Caucus for Art, board of directors, 1991-; College Art Association, 1980-; Godzilla Asian American Arts Network, 1990-; Seoro, Korean Cultural Network, advisory member, 1990-; Young Koreans United, 1985-87. **HONORS/AWARDS:** Organization of Independent Artists, Warren Tanner Memorial Fund, award for sculptor, 1992; National Endowment for the Arts, Visual Artists Fellowship Grant in New Genre, 1989; New York State Council on the Arts, Artist in Resident Grant, 1988-89; The Institute for Contemporary Art (PS1), National Studio Program, 1991. **SPECIAL ACHIEVEMENTS:** Exhibitions; University Art Museum, UC Santa Barbara & Museum Folkwang, Germany: Mistaken Identity, 1992; The Bronx Museum of the Arts, NY, solo installation, 1991; The Decade Show, The New Museum, Studio Museum of Harlem, Museum of Contemporary Hispanic Art, NY, 1990; Committed to Print, Museum of Modern Art, 1988. **BIOGRAPHICAL SOURCES:** Asian Americans: Comparative & Global Perspectives, p 277-287, 1990; Mixed Blessings: New American Art & the Cross-Cultural Process, p 190, 1990. **BUSINESS ADDRESS:** Assistant Professor, Dept of Studio Art, University of California at Irvine, Irvine, CA 92717, (714)856-4917.

MINAMOTO, JENNIFER NORIKO

Labor union executive. Japanese American. **PERSONAL:** Born May 12, 1950, Tokyo, Japan; daughter of Masanori Minamoto and Etsuko Oba Minamoto; divorced. **EDUCATION:** Colorado State University, BSBA, 1971; George Washington University, MBA, 1979. **CAREER:** Eastern Conference of Teamsters, research analyst, 1973-76, associate director of research, 1976-93, director of productivity studies, 1993-. **ORGANIZATIONS:** Industrial Relations Research Association, national member, 1972-; IRRA, Washington, DC Chapter, secretary, 1982-84, board member, 1981-84; Institute of Industrial Engineers, 1985-. **HONORS/AWARDS:** George Washington University, Sigma Epsilon Honorary Society, 1979; Colorado State University, Beta Epsilon Honorary Society, 1971. **SPECIAL ACHIEVEMENTS:** "Increasing Worker Productivity: Management's Failure to Manage," in Annual Conference Proceedings, Vol. II, Council of Logistics Management, 1989; various internal publications. **BUSINESS ADDRESS:** Director of Productivity Studies, Eastern Conference of Teamsters, 4641 Montgomery Ave, Bethesda, MD 20814, (301)656-6006.

MINETA, NORMAN YOSHIO

Congressman. Japanese American. **PERSONAL:** Born Nov 12, 1931, San Jose, CA; son of Kay Kunisaki and Kane Watanabe Mineta; divorced; children (previous marriage): David K, Stuart S; married Danealia Mineta; children: stepsons: Bob & Mark Brantner. **EDUCATION:** University of California, Berkeley, BS, 1953. **CAREER:** Mineta Insurance Agency, broker, 1956-89; San Jose Human Relations Commission, member, 1962; City Council of San Jose, Housing Authority, member; San Jose City Council, member, 1967, vice mayor, 1969, mayor, 1971; US House of Representatives, congressman, 1974-; New Members Caucus, chair; 103rd Congress, House Committee on Public Works and Transportation, chair, 1993-; past & present congressional services include: Budget Committee, 1977-82, Task Force on the Budget Process, 1979-80; Democratic Policy & Steering Comm, 1981-84; Deputy Whip, House Democratic Leadership, 1982-; Post Office and Civil Service Comm, 1975-76; Public Works & Transportation Comm: Surface Transportation Subcommittee, chair, 1989-92, Aviation Subcomm, chair, 1981-88, Investigations & Oversight Subcomm, chair, 1979-80, Public Buildings & Grounds Subcomm, 1977-78; Science, Space & Technology Comm, sr member, 1983-92; Select Comm on Intelligence, 1977-84. **ORGANIZATIONS:** Greater San Jose Chamber of Commerce; Rotary Club of San Jose; Jackson-Taylor Business and Professional Assn; Mexican American Community Services Agency, Santa Clara County; JACL; University of Santa Clara, board of regents; Washington, DC, Visitors Committee for Freer Gallery, chair, 1981-. **HONORS/AWARDS:** Honorary degrees include: Santa Clara University, Doctor of Public Service, 1989; National University, San Diego, Doctor of Humane Letters, 1987. **SPECIAL ACHIEVEMENTS:** Impetus for redress bill from his experience of incarceration as a child with other Japanese Americans during World War 2, succeeded during 100th Congress with the H R 442, Civil Liberties Act, 1988. **BUSINESS ADDRESS:** Congressman, US House of Representatives, 2221 Rayburn House Office Bldg, Washington, DC 20515-0515, (202)225-2631.

MING, WILLIAM PAUL. *See* **MINNIG, WILLIAM PAUL.**

MINK, PATSY TAKEMOTO
US representative. Japanese American. **PERSONAL:** Born Dec 6, 1927, Paia, HI; daughter of Mitama Tateyama Takemoto and Suematsu Takemoto; married John Francis Mink, Jan 28, 1951; children: Gwendolyn Matsu Rachel. **EDUCATION:** University of Hawaii, BA, 1948; University of Chicago Law School, LLD, 1951. **CAREER:** Territory of Hawaii, legislator, 1956-59; State of Hawaii, legislator, 1963-64; Univ of Hawaii, lecturer, 1960-62, 1980-81; US State Dept, OES, asst secretary of state, 1977-78; Honolulu city councilmember, 1983-87; US House of Representatives, 1965-77, 1990-. **ORGANIZATIONS:** Public Reporter, president, 1989-91; Americans for Democratic Action, national president, 1978-81; Public Citizen, past director; National Women's Law Center, past director. **HONORS/AWARDS:** YWCA, Honolulu, Distinguished Service Award, 1987; National JACL, Nisei of the Biennium Award; ABA, Margaret Brent Award, Woman Lawyer of Achievement, 1992; Honorary LLD: Syracuse Univ, 1976; Whitman College, 1981. **BUSINESS ADDRESS:** US Representative, US House of Representatives, 2135 Rayburn House Office Bldg, Washington, DC 20515, (202)225-4906.

MINNICK, SYLVIA SUN
City council member, publisher, state official. Chinese American. **PERSONAL:** Born Apr 26, 1941, Kuala Lumpur, Malaysia; daughter of Patrick Pichi Sun and May Lan Chew Sun; married Richard S Minnick, Nov 7, 1970; children: Donna Chan Forsch, Darcelle Chan. **EDUCATION:** San Joaquin Delta College, AA (high honors), 1978; California State University-Sacramento, BA (summa cum laude), history, 1980, MA, history, 1983. **CAREER:** Historian, writer, 1984-; Heritage West Books, owner, publisher, 1989-; City of Stockton, council member, 1990-; California State Parks and Recreation, deputy asst director, 1993-. **ORGANIZATIONS:** San Joaquin Historical Museum/Society, trustee, 1981-; Stkn Cultural Heritage Board, chair, 1984-89; San Joaquin Visitors Convention Bureau, dir, 1990-93; Chinese Historical Society of America, life member; Institute of Historical Studies, 1983-89. **HONORS/AWARDS:** Girl Scouts-Tierra del Oro Council, Female Role Award, 1991; City of Stockton, Capt Weber Award, Preservation Honoree, 1991; Asian Pacific Concerns, Asian Female of the Year, 1991; Asian Advisory Council, Women of the Year, 1993; California State University, Sacramento, Distinguished Service Award, 1994. **SPECIAL ACHIEVEMENTS:** Author, SAMFOW: The San Joaquin Chinese, Panorama West, 1988. **HOME ADDRESS:** 1404 N Commerce St, Stockton, CA 95202.

MINNIG, WILLIAM PAUL (WILLIAM PAUL MING)
International sales and marketing executive. Chinese American/Korean American. **PERSONAL:** Born Nov 18, 1950; married Mi Hwa Minnig, Jun 13, 1988. **EDUCATION:** California State University, BA, 1973, MA, 1978; University of Southern California, PhD, 1981. **CAREER:** GTE Sylvania, marketing manager, 1973-84; Hyundai Electrical Engineering, marketing vice president, 1984-87; Lotus Eng International, general manager, 1987-89; Power Control Inc, Sales & Marketing, vice president, 1989-91; Selco Products, general manager, 1991-. **HONORS/AWARDS:** Korea Minister of Post & Telecommunication, Special Service Award, 1988. **SPECIAL ACHIEVEMENTS:** Negotiating joint venture agreement between Hyundai of South Korea and General Electric; directed consortium of multi-national corporations; revamped negotiating techniques for Hyundai Corporation applying international market strategies; assembled and directed team of commercial, engineering and technical telecommunications experts selling central office switching equipment and manufacturing facilities in Shanghai and Henan Provinces. **BUSINESS ADDRESS:** General Manager, Selco Products Company, 7580 Stage Rd, Buena Park, CA 90621, (714)521-8673.

MINOCHA, HARISH C.
Educational administrator. Indo-American. **PERSONAL:** Born Aug 31, 1932, Shahpur City, India; son of Bishan Das Minocha and Ram Baye Ahuja Minocha; married Ved Minocha, Jul 11, 1955; children: Meena Khurana, Hans, Nick, Pam. **EDUCATION:** Agricultural University, India, DVM, 1955; Kansas State University, MS, 1963, PhD, 1967. **CAREER:** North Carolina State University, assistant professor, 1966-69; Kansas State University, associate professor, 1970-76, professor of virology, 1977-88, Research and Graduate Affairs, associate dean, 1989-. **ORGANIZATIONS:** American Society for

Microbiology; American Academy of Microbiology; American Veterinary Medical Association; American Association of Veterinary Medical Colleges. **HONORS/AWARDS:** National Institutes of Health, Animal Model to AIDS Virus, 1993-96, Fibroma Tumor Virus, 1967-71; USDA, NRICGP, 1987-94, Animal Health Program, 1972-93. **SPECIAL ACHIEVEMENTS:** Anti-idiotypie Mimicry & Receptor Interactions in Herpes Viruses; Large Animal Model Systems to AIDS Virus-study of Bovine Immunodeficiency Virus and Bovine Herpes Virus; Monoclonal Antibodies to Respiratory Disease Viruses; over 100 articles published on virus diseases and mechanism of virus disease. **BUSINESS ADDRESS:** Associate Dean for Research & Graduate Affairs, Kansas State University, College of Veterinary Medicine, Trotter Hall, Manhattan, KS 66506, (913)532-4002.

MIRCHANDANI, ARJUN SOBHRAJ (ART S.)
Engineer, real estate broker. **PERSONAL:** Born Sep 28, 1943, Hyderabad Sind, India; son of Sobhraj Mirchandani (deceased) and Putli Mirchandani (deceased); married Renu Mirchandani, Dec 3, 1978; children: Neeta, Neil. **EDUCATION:** Electronics, AS, 1973; Xerox Corp courses in communication skills, 1973-. **CAREER:** Xerox Corp, customer service engineer, 1973-; Four Seasons Realty, real estate broker, 1986-. **ORGANIZATIONS:** American Congress on Real Estate, 1989-. **HONORS/AWARDS:** Xerox Corp, outstanding co-operation with others to achieve Xerox goals, 1988; Exceptional Customer Satisfaction, 1989. **HOME ADDRESS:** 3575 Hillside Ct, Hoffman Estates, IL 60195, (708)934-7320.

MIRCHANDANI, GAGAN
Educator. Indo-American. **PERSONAL:** Born Oct 6, 1932, Mussurrie, Uttar Pradesh, India; married Alice. **EDUCATION:** Cornell University, PhD, EE, 1968. **CAREER:** University of Vermont, professor, 1968-. **ORGANIZATIONS:** IEEE, 1963-. **BUSINESS PHONE:** (802)656-3330.

MIRCHANDANI, PRAKASH
Educator. Indo-American. **PERSONAL:** Born Mar 28, Pune, Maharashtra, India; son of B S Mirchandani & Devaki B Mirchandani. **EDUCATION:** IIT, New Delhi, BTech, 1979; IIM, Ahmedabad, PGDM, 1983; MIT, PhD, 1989. **CAREER:** Telco, Pune, India, graduate engineer, 1979-81; A F Ferguson Co, New Delhi, India, consultant, 1983-85; University of Pittsburgh, assistant professor, 1989-. **ORGANIZATIONS:** Operations Research Society of America, 1986-. **HONORS/AWARDS:** Several scholastic awards. **BUSINESS ADDRESS:** Professor, Dept of Business Administration, University of Pittsburgh, 244 Mervis Hall, Roberto Clemente Drive, Pittsburgh, PA 15213, (412)648-1652.

MIRIKITANI, ANDY
City official, attorney. Japanese American. **PERSONAL:** Born Aug 25, 1955, New York, NY; son of Carl M Mirikitani & Hisa Yoshimura Mirikitani. **EDUCATION:** University of Southern California, BA (magna cum laude), 1978; University of Santa Clara Law School, JD, 1982. **CAREER:** Hawaii Judiciary, Intermediate Court of Appeals, State of Hawaii, law clerk to Chief Judge James S Burns, 1984-85; Case, Kay & Lynch, attorney, 1985-86; Dept of Commerce and Consumer Affairs, State of Hawaii, attorney, 1986-87; Char, Hamilton, Campbell & Thom, attorney, 1987-; Honolulu City Council, City and County of Honolulu, majority leader, 1990-92, council vice-chairman, chairman, Policy Committee, 1992-; Hawaii State Assn of Counties, Honolulu city council representative, 1992-. **ORGANIZATIONS:** Waialae-Kahala Neighborhood Board, chairman, 1989-90; East Diamond Head Community Association, president, 1989-90; Save Our Beach, president, 1987-90; Legal Aid Society of Hawaii, board of directors, 1988-90; Protection and Advocacy Agency of Hawaii, board of directors, 1988-89; United Japanese Society, vice-president, 1990-91; Save Diamond Head Beach Coalition, founder, 1993-; American Beltwrap Corporation, vice-president, director, 1985-; Hawaii Holocaust Project, board of directors, 1985-90. **HONORS/AWARDS:** University of Southern California, Phi Beta Kappa, 1978, Blackstonian National Honor Society, 1978, Alpha Mu Gamma, 1978; University of Santa Clara Law School, editor, Santa Clara Law Review, 1982. **SPECIAL ACHIEVEMENTS:** Co-patentee and holder of 4 US patents. **BUSINESS ADDRESS:** Council Vice-Chairman, Honolulu City Council, City and County of Honolulu, 530 S King St, Honolulu Hale-City Hall, Honolulu, HI 96813, (808)523-4787.

MISHRA, SHITALA P.
Educator. Indo-American. **PERSONAL:** Born Aug 13, 1938, Raipur, Uttar Pradesh, India; son of Chakra Manohar Mishra and Rani Mishra; married Satya Mishra, May 11, 1965; children: Sunita, Sangeeta, Sudeep. **EDUCATION:**

University of Lucknow, BSc, 1958, BEd, 1961, MEd, 1962; University of Oregon, MA, 1967, PhD, 1969. **CAREER:** University of Lucknow, lecturer in education, 1962-63; University of Oregon, research assistant, 1967-68; University of Arizona, Department of Educational Psychology, dept head, professor, 1968-. **ORGANIZATIONS:** American Psychological Association, 1969-; American Educational Research Association, 1969-. **HONORS/AWARDS:** Watumull Memorial, Dissertation Award, 1968; Asian American Faculty Association, Outstanding Faculty, 1990; Hispanic Administrators Association, Outstanding Minority Educator, 1991. **SPECIAL ACHIEVEMENTS:** Research work published in many professional journals; research studies on the topic of human memory, cognitive assessment and testing bias. **BUSINESS ADDRESS:** Professor & Head, Dept of Educational Psychology, University of Arizona, College of Education, Tucson, AZ 85721, (602)621-7825.

MISRA, ALOK C.
Computer scientist. Indo-American. **PERSONAL:** Born Sep 29, 1950, Kanpur, Uttar Pradesh, India; son of Prayag N Misra & Rama Misra; married Suniti Misra, Feb 9, 1981; children: Neil Anshu. **EDUCATION:** University of Kanpur, India, BS, 1969; University of Allahabad, India, BS, 1973; Worcester Polytechnic Institute, MS, 1978. **CAREER:** Continental Company, engineer, 1978-79; Computer Controls Corp, sr engineer, 1979-81; ACM Software, consultant, 1981-. **ORGANIZATIONS:** Association for Computing Machinery, 1978-; Institute of Electrical & Electronics Engineers, 1981-. **SPECIAL ACHIEVEMENTS:** Author, Languages for Computer Aided Instruction, 1978. **BUSINESS ADDRESS:** Consultant, ACM Software, 31 Barron Ave, Salem, NH 03079, (603)898-4881.

MISRA, DWARIKA NATH
Research scientist. Indo-American. **PERSONAL:** Born Mar 17, 1933, Sarai-Miran, Uttar Pradesh, India; son of Kanauji Lal Misra and Sanatani Devi Misra; married Chandra Kala Misra, Jun 10, 1954; children: Sunil, Vinod, Timir. **EDUCATION:** Lucknow University, UP, India, BS, 1951, MS, 1953; Howard University, PhD, 1963. **CAREER:** Regional Research Lab, Hyderabad, AP, India, research fellow, 1954-58; Hek Corp, senior research scientist, 1966-68; Howard University, visiting lecturer, 1969-71; ADAHF Paffenbarger Research Center, research associate, senior scientist, 1972-. **ORGANIZATIONS:** American Chemical Society, 1964-; Sigma Xi, 1962-. **HONORS/AWARDS:** Pennsylvania State University, NSF Postdoctoral Fellow, 1963-66. **SPECIAL ACHIEVEMENTS:** Published 55 scientific papers in peer-reviewed scientific journals; edited or co-edited two books. **BUSINESS ADDRESS:** Research Associate, Senior Scientist, ADA Health Foundation, Paffenbarger Research Center, National Institute of Standards and Technology, Gaithersburg, MD 20899, (301)975-6814.

MISRA, PRABHAKAR
Educator, researcher. Indo-American. **PERSONAL:** Born May 7, 1955, Lucknow, Uttar Pradesh, India; son of Prem Krishna Misra and Lakshmi Misra; married Suneeta Misra, Jun 13, 1981; children: Isha. **EDUCATION:** University of Calcutta, India, MSc, 1978; Carnegie-Mellon University, MS, 1981; Ohio State University, PhD, 1986. **CAREER:** Carnegie-Mellon University, graduate teaching, research assistant, 1979-81; Ohio State University, graduate teaching, research associate, 1981-86, postdoctoral research fellow, 1986-88; Howard University, assistant professor, 1988-92, associate professor, 1992-. **ORGANIZATIONS:** American Physical Society, 1984-; American Mensa, 1985; Sigma Pi Sigma Honor Society, 1991; American Chap of Indian Physics Association, 1989-. **HONORS/AWARDS:** Howard University, Graduate Researcher of the Month, April 1993, Research Grant, 1990-91; Wright-Patterson AFB, Research Grant, 1990-94; Strategic Defense Initiative Organization, Research Grant, 1990-91. **SPECIAL ACHIEVEMENTS:** Photochem Photobiol, vol 56, p 325-332, 1992; Journal Phys B: At Mol Opt Phys, vol 25, p 2343-2350, 1992; Appl Spectrosc, vol 46, p 797-799, 1992; Spectroscopy, vol 8 no 2, p 48-55, 1993; Spectroscopy Letters, vol 26, no 2, p 389-402, 1993. **HOME ADDRESS:** 8307 Satinleaf Ct, Bowie, MD 20715, (301)805-5889. **BUSINESS ADDRESS:** Associate Professor, Dept of Physics & Astronomy, Howard University, 2355 Sixth St NW, Thirkield Hall, #102, Washington, DC 20059, (202)806-4913.

MISTRY, JAYANTHI
Educator. Indo-American. **PERSONAL:** Born Nov 28, 1952, Colachel, Tamil Nadu, India; daughter of Devadason Sundaresan and Starry T Chelliah; married Jamshed Mistry, Dec 31, 1979; children: Ashti, Anushay. **EDUCATION:** Punjab Agricultural University, India, BS, 1973; M S University, India, MS, 1975; Purdue University, PhD, 1983. **CAREER:** University of Utah, postdoc-

toral fellow, 1983-85; Kamehameha Schools, associate researcher, 1985-90; Tufts University, assistant professor, 1990-. **ORGANIZATIONS:** Society for Research in Child Development, 1983-; International Society for the Study of Behavioral Development, 1993-; National Association for the Study of Young Children, 1993-. **HONORS/AWARDS:** Punjab Agricultural University, Gold Medal, 1973; M S University, Pramila Phaltrak Fellowship, 1975; AHEA USA, Ethel Parker Fellowship, 1980; NIMH, postdoctoral fellow, 1983-85. **SPECIAL ACHIEVEMENTS:** Co-author, "Guided Participation in Cultural Activity by Toddlers and Caregivers," SRCD Monograph, 1993; other publications in journals & books on human development. **BUSINESS ADDRESS:** Assistant Professor, Eliot-Pearson Dept of Child Study, Tufts University, 105 College Ave, Medford, MA 02155-5555, (617)627-3355.

MITAL, NAVEEN KUMAR
Engineering manager. Indo-American. **PERSONAL:** Born Apr 10, 1947, Hardwar, Uttar Pradesh, India; son of Narendra Kumar Mital and Jagwati Mital; married Pratibha Bhatia Mital, Jan 4, 1987; children: Narayani Naveen, Naren Bhatia. **EDUCATION:** Banaras Hindu University, BSME (honors), 1968; Indian Institute of Science, MEng (with distinction), 1970; The University of Michigan, MSME, 1972; Wayne State University, PhD, 1978; Rensselaer Business School, MBA, 1992. **CAREER:** The University of Michigan, research asst, 1972-73; Ford Motor Co, test engr, 1973; Wayne State University, research associate, 1973-79; General Motors, staff engr, 1979-. **ORGANIZATIONS:** Society of Manufacturing Engrs, certified mfg engr; American Society of Mechanical Engrs. **HONORS/AWARDS:** General Motors, Mgmt of Technology Certificate, 1992; Festival of India, Detroit, Distinguished Service to the Community, 1983. **SPECIAL ACHIEVEMENTS:** Licensed professional engr: State of Michigan; author: 18 technical papers, journals & conferences; producer: 12 research & product development reports, several universities & General Motors. **HOME ADDRESS:** 1042 Tiverton Trail, Rochester Hills, MI 48306-4068, (810)651-6823. **BUSINESS ADDRESS:** Staff Engineer, General Motors Corp, NAO Engineering Center, 30200 Mound Rd, Engineering Bldg (C1-W20), Warren, MI 48090-9010, (313)986-7409.

MITAMURA, RON W.
Computer programmer/analyst. Japanese American. **PERSONAL:** Born Jan 19, 1957, Denver, CO; son of Albert Mitamura and Mitsuko Tsutsumi. **EDUCATION:** Colorado School of Mines, 1975-76; University of Colorado, Denver, 1976-77; Community College of Denver, AS, 1983. **CAREER:** Center Rental & Sales, programmer/operator, 1985-90; The Denver Post, programmer/analyst, 1990-. **BUSINESS ADDRESS:** Programmer/Analyst, The Denver Post, 1560 Broadway, Information Services, Denver, CO 80202, (303)820-1905.

MITCHELL-ONUMA, SUSAN C.
Graphic design firm owner. Japanese American. **PERSONAL:** Born Apr 9, 1960, Tachikawa, Japan; daughter of Mr and Mrs Harold Mitchell Jr; married Kimon G Onuma, Jun 1, 1985; children: Aristotle Mitchell Onuma. **EDUCATION:** Abilene Christian University, BA, 1982. **CAREER:** Tobishima USA, administrative assistant, 1985-88; Onuma & Associates, 1988-93; The Aris Group, 1993-. **ORGANIZATIONS:** Pasadena Symphony Juniors. **HONORS/AWARDS:** Numerous Japanese singing contests, placing first. **SPECIAL ACHIEVEMENTS:** Fluent in Japanese. **BIOGRAPHICAL SOURCES:** Asahi Evening News, April 23, 1984; Abilene Reporter News, April 22, 1982. **BUSINESS ADDRESS:** Owner, The Aris Group, 140 S Lake Ave, Ste 208, Pasadena, CA 91101.

MITOMA, MIKE
Mayor. Japanese American. **PERSONAL:** Born Aug 3, 1943. **CAREER:** Pacific Business Bank, chairman, 1982-89; City of Carson City, mayor, currently. **BUSINESS ADDRESS:** Mayor, City of Carson City, City Hall, 701 E Carson St, Carson, CA 90745, (310)830-7600.∗

MITRA, GRIHAPATI
Educator. Indo-American. **PERSONAL:** Born Oct 29, 1927, Burdwan, W. Bengal, India; son of Rohinindra Lala Mitra and Surama Mitra; married Gayatri Mitra, Jun 1, 1958; children: Raman. **EDUCATION:** Calcutta University, BSc, 1947, MSc, 1949, DSc, 1954. **CAREER:** University of Washington, Seattle, postdoctoral chemistry, 1955-57; Pennsylvania State University, postdoctoral physics, 1960-61; King's College, professor, chemistry, 1961-. **ORGANIZATIONS:** American Chemical Society, 1956-; Rotary Club, 1966-80. **SPECIAL ACHIEVEMENTS:** Twenty-five scientific papers in chemistry;

two articles on Indian philosophy; languages: Hindu, Bergali, Sanskrit-moderate, French-very little. **HOME ADDRESS:** 161 Price St, Kingston, PA 18704, (717)288-5998. **BUSINESS ADDRESS:** Professor, Chemistry Dept, King's College, N River St, Wilkes Barre, PA 18711, (717)826-5900.

MITSUNAGA, JIMI
Attorney. Japanese American. **PERSONAL:** Born Mar 5, 1934, Salt Lake City, UT; son of Junsaku & Yasuko Mitsunaga; married Barbara, Feb 13, 1953; children: Janice Akiko Mitsunaga Matsui, Darrell Setsu, Tracy Koji, Hollis Kiku Mitsunaga Whitten. **EDUCATION:** University of Utah, JD, 1958. **CAREER:** Legal Defender's Office, director, 1965-68; self employed, attorney, currently. **ORGANIZATIONS:** Utah State Bar, Criminal Law Section, chairman, 1965-67; SL Legal Defenders Office, chairman of board of trustees, 1969-79, 1990-; Utah State Bar Committee to Revise Criminal Procedure Code, chairman; Governor's Committee on Children and Youth, 1970; Utah Asian Association, chairman, 1976-78; Utah Asian Advisory Committee, chairman, 1986-87; Salt Lake JACL, president. **HONORS/AWARDS:** Sugar House Jaycees, Outstanding Young Man of 1966, 1966; IDC, Japanese American of the Biennium Award, 1966-67; Asian Association of Utah, Dedication Award, 1981; Mt Olympus & Salt Lake JACL Award, Outstanding Service, 1987. **MILITARY SERVICE:** Reserve Branch JAG, Army, colonel, retired, 1953-87; Army Commendation Medal, 1981. **BUSINESS ADDRESS:** Attorney, 731 E South Temple, Salt Lake City, UT 84102, (801)322-3551.

MITTAL, KAMAL
Business executive. Indo-American. **PERSONAL:** Born Sep 27, 1940, Delhi, India; son of Sukhbir Prasad and Shanti Devi; married Mohini Mittal, May 11, 1967; children: Madhu, Sapna. **EDUCATION:** University of Delhi, India, BCom, 1959; post-graduate diploma in marketing, 1972. **CAREER:** Dalmia Cement Ltd, asst exec, 1959-62; Fried Krupp, trainee, 1963-64; Ciba of India, commercial assistant, 1965-66; State Trading Corp of India, Middle East, regional mgr, 1967-76; Sonnar Inc, vice pres, 1976-81; Camit Intl Inc, president, 1981-. **ORGANIZATIONS:** Delhi University Students Union, exec mbr, 1958-59. **SPECIAL ACHIEVEMENTS:** Goethe Institut, Munich, Certificate in German Language, 1962. **BUSINESS ADDRESS:** President, Camit International Inc, 9-11 Caesar Place, Moonachie, NJ 07074.

MITTAL, KASHMIRI LAL
Researcher, educator. Indo-American. **PERSONAL:** Born Oct 15, 1945, Kilrodh, Haryana, India; son of Parmanand Mittal & Bhagwan Dai Mittal; married Usha, Dec 30, 1970; children: Anita, Rajesh, Nisha, Seema. **EDUCATION:** Panjab University, BSc, 1964; Indian Institute of Technology, India, MSc, 1966; University of Southern California, PhD, 1970. **CAREER:** Pennsylvania State University, postdoctoral res associate, 1970-71; University of Pennsylvania, postdoctoral fellow, 1971-72; IBM Corp: San Jose, CA, 1972-74, Poughkeepsie, NY, 1974-77, E Fishkill, NY, 1977-84, Technical Education, 1984-92, Skill Dynamics, research educator, 1992-. **ORGANIZATIONS:** Fine Particle Society, Contamination Control Division, chairman; American Institute of Chemists, fellow; Indian Chemical Society, fellow. **HONORS/AWARDS:** American Society for Testing and Materials, Dudley Award, 1990; Society of Plastics Engineers, Mid-Hudson Section, Outstanding Contribution Plaque, 1984; Institute of Environmental Sciences, Certificate of Appreciation, 1979; Intl Surface and Colloid Community, Recognition Plaque, 1986. **SPECIAL ACHIEVEMENTS:** Editor, Intl Journal of Adhesion Science & Technology; member, editorial boards of a number of journals, magazines; editor of 43 published books in areas of surfactants, polymers, adhesion, & contamination & cleaning, & other books which are in process of publication; organizer & chairman of many intl symposia; chaired workshops for Natl Science Foundation; author/co-author of more than 60 pubs; invited as project specialist in area of materials science by Intl Advisory Panel & the Chinese Review Commission to visit Shanghai Jiao Tong University, 1985; invited under TOKTEN program to visit India to give series of lectures. **BUSINESS ADDRESS:** Skill Dynamics, an IBM Co, 500 Columbus Ave, Thornwood, NY 10594, (914)742-5747.

MITTER, SANJOY K.
Educator. Indo-American. **PERSONAL:** Born Dec 9, 1933, Calcutta, India; son of Protiva Mitter; married Adriana Mitter. **EDUCATION:** Imperial College of London, England, BSc, 1957, PhD, 1965. **CAREER:** Case Institute of Technology, assistant professor, 1965; Case Western Reserve University, associate professor, 1967; Center for Int Cont Systems, director, 1986; Massachusetts Institute of Technology, visiting associate professor, 1969, associate professor, 1970, professor, 1973-, LIDS, director, 1981, co-director, 1986.

ORGANIZATIONS: AHPCRC, University of Minnesota, advisory committee, 1991; ICASE, NASA, Langley, science council, 1992; IEEE Trans on Auto Con, associate editor at large, 1992. **HONORS/AWARDS:** Imperial College, London, Central Electricity Res Board Fellow, 1962; IEEE, fellow, 1979; National Academy of Eng. **BUSINESS ADDRESS:** Professor, Massachusetts Institute of Technology, 77 Massachusetts Ave, 33-304, Cambridge, MA 02139, (617)253-2160.

MIURA, GEORGE AKIO
Laboratory technician, armed forces member. Japanese American. **PERSONAL:** Born Aug 6, 1942, Honolulu, HI; son of Tsueno & Mildred Miura. **EDUCATION:** University of Hawaii, BS, 1964; Harvard University; Indiana University, PhD, 1968. **CAREER:** US Army, sr medical lab tech, 1977-. **ORGANIZATIONS:** Sigma Xi, 1982-. **MILITARY SERVICE:** Medical Corps, SFC, 1977-. **BUSINESS ADDRESS:** Sr Medical Lab Technician, Pathology Div, US Army Med Research Inst of Infectious Dis, Frederick, MD 21701, (301)698-7444.

MIURA, IRENE TAKEI
Educator. Japanese American. **PERSONAL:** Born Jul 18, 1939, Santa Cruz, CA; daughter of Jean Abe Takei and Iowa Takei; married Neal Isamu Miura, Jun 26, 1960; children: David Takei, Gregory Ross, Jennifer Ann. **EDUCATION:** University of California, Berkeley, BA, 1960; College of Notre Dame, MAT, 1981; Stanford University, PhD, 1984. **CAREER:** San Jose State University, professor of child development, 1984-. **ORGANIZATIONS:** American Psychological Association, 1982-; American Educational Research Association, 1982-; Society for Research in Child Development, 1982-; American Association for the Advancement of Science, 1984-. **BUSINESS ADDRESS:** Professor of Child Development, San Jose State University, One Washington Sq, 305 Sweeney Hall, San Jose, CA 95192-0075, (408)924-3718.

MIURA, KEN-ICHI
Educator. Japanese American. **PERSONAL:** Born Mar 16, 1963, Toyota, Aichi, Japan; son of Takeo & Shizuyo Miura. **EDUCATION:** Nanzan University, Japan, BA, 1986; University of Wisconsin, Madison, MA, 1990. **CAREER:** Middlebury College, assistant in Japanese, instructor; University of Wisconsin, Madison, teaching assistant; Northwestern University, lecturer, currently. **HONORS/AWARDS:** College of Art and Science, faculty honor roll, 1991-92, 1992-93. **BUSINESS ADDRESS:** Lecturer, Program of African and Asian Languages, Northwestern University, 1856 Sheridan Road, Evanston, IL 60208-0002, (708)467-1986.

MIURA, NOLAN A.
Petroleum company manager. Japanese American. **PERSONAL:** Born Aug 27, 1955, Los Angeles, CA; son of Toshio Miura and Ruri Miura. **EDUCATION:** California State University at Long Beach, BS, 1979; University of Southern California, MBA, 1987. **CAREER:** ARCO, senior analyst, 1982-84, senior financial analyst, 1984-85; Flying Rice, Inc, president, 1985-87; ARCO, manager, government compliance, 1985-87, manager, budgets and performance analysis, 1987-90; ARCO Marine Fuels, Inc, president, manager, planning evaluation & business development, 1990-93, manager, marketing analysis, 1993-. **ORGANIZATIONS:** Beta Gamma Sigma, 1978-. **HONORS/AWARDS:** ARCO, ATC President's Award, 1986, 1990, 1992. **HOME ADDRESS:** 9852 Hot Springs Dr, Huntington Beach, CA 92646, (714)968-5564. **BUSINESS ADDRESS:** Manager, Marketing Analysis, Atlantic Richfield Company, 1055 W Seventh St, PAC 815, Los Angeles, CA 90051-0570, (213)486-0688.

MIYA, WAYNE
Public utilities manager. Japanese American. **PERSONAL:** Born Oct 6, 1946, Ogden, UT; son of Minoru Miya and Ume Miya. **EDUCATION:** University of Utah, BA, mathematics, 1968, MBA, 1971. **CAREER:** Utah Power & Light, programmer, analyst, systems analyst, admin svcs mgr, policy & procedures coordinator, employee info spec, beginning 1969; PacifiCorp, employee mgr, 1990-. **ORGANIZATIONS:** Mental Health Services West, board mbr; Art Quake, board mbr; Echo- Volunteer Org, board mbr; Toastmasters, Salt Lake City, UT, past president, area governor; Salt Lake Area Postal Customer Council, past president; Junior Achievement, advisory board, president. **HONORS/AWARDS:** General Motors, Academic Scholarship, 1964-68. **HOME ADDRESS:** 15100 NW Oakmont Loop, Beaverton, OR 97006, (503)690-1731.

MIYAHARA, BRUCE
State government official. Japanese American. **PERSONAL:** Born Nov 16, 1951?. **CAREER:** Intl District Community Health Center, director; Seattle/ King County, Jail Health Services, administrator, Health Dept, deputy director, 1986-93; Dept of Health, State of Washington, secretary, 1993-. **BUSINESS ADDRESS:** Secretary, Washington State Dept of Health, 1112 SE Quince St, Olympia, WA 98504, (206)753-5871.*

MIYAHARA, PAUL MASAYOSHI
Government official. Japanese American. **PERSONAL:** Born Nov 2, 1945, Seattle, WA; son of Jimmy Satoshi and Miyoko Miyahara; married Wanda Seiko Miyahara, Jun 30, 1968; children: Trina Mihoko, Kelly Ayako. **EDUCATION:** Shoreline Community College, 1969-70; University of Washington, BA, 1971; Seattle University, Graduate School of Business, 1975-76. **CAREER:** US Treasury, IRS-CID, Seattle district, special agent, 1972-77, Los Angeles District, group manager, 1977-82, branch chief, 1982-83, San Jose district, chief, 1983-85, Western Region, executive assistant, 1985-88, assistant regional commissioner, 1988-. **ORGANIZATIONS:** San Gabriel Valley Japanese Community Center, 1978-83; Diablo Japanese American Community Center, 1984-; Northern California Asian Peace Officers Association, 1987-; Senior Executives Association, 1988-. **HONORS/AWARDS:** Internal Revenue Service, Distinguished Performance Awards, 1980-88, Outstanding Performance Awards, 1984, 1987, Special Achievement Awards, 1986, 1987, 1989, SES Distinguished Performance Awards, 1988-92. **SPECIAL ACHIEVEMENTS:** Completed executive selection and development program, 1990. **MILITARY SERVICE:** US Army, 1st lt, 1966-69; Officer's Candidate School, 1967; Army Commendation Medal, 1969. **BUSINESS ADDRESS:** Asst Regional Commissioner, Criminal Investigation Div, US Treasury, Internal Revenue Service, 1650 Mission St, Rm 508, Western Regional Headquarters, San Francisco, CA 94103, (415)556-0553.

MIYAKAWA, EDWARD T.
Union administrator. Japanese American. **PERSONAL:** Born Oct 5, 1939, Covina, CA; son of Chieko Miyakawa. **EDUCATION:** East Los Angeles College, AA, 1961. **CAREER:** United Food and Commercial Workers Union Local 770, director of special projects and organizing, 1973-. **ORGANIZATIONS:** Asian Pacific American Labor Alliance, 1991-. **SPECIAL ACHIEVEMENTS:** Coordinator of special projects with union, such as out-of-country union officials; direct organizing campaigns to organize nonunion workers. **HOME ADDRESS:** 1101 S Sandy Hook St, West Covina, CA 91790-4909, (818)337-1992.

MIYAKODA, KIKURO
Meteorologist, government official, educator. Japanese American. **PERSONAL:** Born Nov 7, 1927, Yonago, Tottori, Japan; son of Kanae and Kimiyo Miyakoda; married Toyoko Miyakoda, Jan 8, 1954; children: Noriko Miyakoda Hall. **EDUCATION:** University of Tokyo, BS, 1953, DSc, 1961. **CAREER:** University of Tokyo, associate professor, 1957-65; Geophysical Fluid Dynamics Laboratory, research meteorologist, 1965-79, supervisory meteorologist, 1979-. **HONORS/AWARDS:** American Meteorological Society, Carl-Gustav-Rossby Medal, 1991; US Department of Commerce, Gold Medal, 1972, 1988; Japan Meteorological Society, Society Award, 1956, Fujiwara Award, 1983. **HOME ADDRESS:** 110 Glen Valley Rd, Morrisville, PA 19067, (215)295-5547. **BUSINESS ADDRESS:** Supervisory Meteorologist, Geophysical Fluid Dynamics Laboratory/NOAA, Forrestal Campus, Princeton University, GFDL Bldg, Rm 320, Princeton, NJ 08542, (609)452-6540.

MIYAMOTO, LANCE
Human resources executive. Japanese American. **PERSONAL:** Born Jun 22, 1955, Baltimore, MD; son of Lanny Hideto Miyamoto and Ona May Miyamoto; married Donna Adams Miyamoto, Oct 27, 1990. **EDUCATION:** Harvard University, BA, 1977; University of Pennsylvania, Wharton School of Finance, MBA, 1979. **CAREER:** Exxon Research & Engineering, specialist, 1979-84; Wang Laboratories, director, 1984-87; Avon Product Inc, manager, 1987-89; Dun & Bradstreet, vice president, 1989-. **ORGANIZATIONS:** Organization Development Network, 1979-. **HONORS/AWARDS:** COGME, fellow, 1974; Harvard University, Ames Award Winner, 1977. **SPECIAL ACHIEVEMENTS:** Black Belt, Judo, 1974. **BUSINESS ADDRESS:** Vice President, Human Resources, Dun & Bradstreet Information Services, One Diamond Hill Rd, Murray Hill, NJ 07974, (908)665-5829.

MIYAMOTO, MICHAEL DWIGHT
Educator. Japanese American. **PERSONAL:** Born Apr 22, 1945, Honolulu, HI; son of Donald Masanobu Miyamoto and Chisako Moriwaki Miyamoto; married Janis W Miyamoto, Jun 16, 1973; children: Julie Lynn, Scott Michael. **EDUCATION:** Northwestern University, BA, 1966, PhD, 1970. **CAREER:** Rutgers Medical School, instructor of pharmacology, 1970-72; University of Connecticut, assistant professor of pharmacology, 1972-78; East Tennessee State University, associate professor of pharmacology, 1978-87, professor of pharmacology, 1987-. **ORGANIZATIONS:** American Society for Pharmacol & Exp Ther, 1975-; Society for Neuroscience, 1978-; American Association of University Professors, 1988-. **HONORS/AWARDS:** East Tennessee State University College of Med, Best Instructor Award, 1980; National Institutes of Health, research grant, 1975, 1978, 1988, 1992; Pharmaceutical Manufacturers Association Fndn, research starter Award, 1975; Epilepsy Foundation of America, research grant, 1976. **HOME ADDRESS:** 318 Baron Drive, Johnson City, TN 37601, (615)929-9419. **BUSINESS ADDRESS:** Professor, Dept of Pharmacology, East Tenn State University, Quillen College of Medicine, Box 70,577, Johnson City, TN 37614-0577.

MIYAMOTO, MICHAEL MASAO
Educator. Japanese American. **PERSONAL:** Born Jul 2, 1955, Gardena, CA; son of Tadashi and Marcella Miyamoto; married Michele R Tennant, Aug 8, 1982. **EDUCATION:** California State University, Dominguez Hills, BA, 1977; University of Southern California, PhD, 1982. **CAREER:** Wayne State University, research associate; University of Florida, associate professor, 1987-. **ORGANIZATIONS:** AAAS; Society of Systemic Biology; Society for the Study of Evolution. **HONORS/AWARDS:** National Science Foundation, Presidential Young Investigator, 1988-; Systemic Biology, editor, 1993-. **BUSINESS ADDRESS:** Associate Professor, Dept of Zoology, University of Florida, 223 Bartram, Gainesville, FL 32611-2002, (904)392-3275.

MIYAMOTO, SEIICHI
Educator, consultant. Japanese American. **PERSONAL:** Born Oct 1, 1944, Nagasaki, Japan. **EDUCATION:** University of California, Riverside, PhD, 1972. **CAREER:** Texas A&M University, assistant professor, 1976, associate professor, 1982, professor and graduate faculty, 1987-. **ORGANIZATIONS:** American Society of Agronomy, assoc editor; American Society for Horticultural Science; Soil Sciences Society of America. **SPECIAL ACHIEVEMENTS:** Professional publications: 121 articles; consultant to the World Bank; soil, water & irrigation consultant. **HOME ADDRESS:** 11417 Dean Refram, El Paso, TX 79936, (915)592-7577.

MIYAMOTO, WAYNE AKIRA
Educator, artist. Japanese American. **PERSONAL:** Born Sep 6, 1947, Honolulu, HI; son of James Miyamoto & Thelma K Miyamoto; children: Tyler, Akira Ruddle-Miyamoto, Yasuo Ruddle-Miyamoto. **EDUCATION:** RPI, 1965-68; University of Hawaii, BA, 1970, BFA, 1970, MFA, 1974. **CAREER:** University of Central Florida, assistant professor of art, 1976-78; California State University, Sacramento, visiting assistant professor, 1980-81; University of Hawaii, Hilo, lecturer in art, 1974, visting asst professor, 1976, professor of art, 1981-. **ORGANIZATIONS:** College Art Association, 1973-; Society of American Graphic Artists, 1992-; Southern Graphics Council, 1992-; Boston Printmakers Association, 1986-; Print Club of Philadelphia, 1986-; Northwest Print Council, 1987-; Florida Printmakers Association, 1989-; Honolulu Printmakers Association, 1969-, board, 1969-71. **HONORS/AWARDS:** The Printmaking Workshop, New York, fellowship, 1990; University of Hawaii Research Council, research grant, 1986, 1989; Moroccan, Ministry of Culture, fellowship, 1988; Hawaii State Foundation on Culture & Arts, project grants, 1981-. **SPECIAL ACHIEVEMENTS:** Exhibitions of Work: 44th North American Print Exhibition, Boston University, Massachusetts, 1993; Ottawa National Print Exhibition, Sylvania, Ohio, 1993; Sivermine International Print Exhibition, New Canaan, Connecticut, 1990, 1992; 2nd Bharat Bhavan International Biennial, Bhopal, India, 1991; Bradley National Print and Drawing Exhibition, Peoria, Illinois, 1988, 1990, 1991. **MILITARY SERVICE:** Army Reserves, E4, 1968-73. **BUSINESS ADDRESS:** Professor, Dept of Art, University of Hawaii at Hilo, Hilo, HI 96720, (808)933-3307.

MIYASAKI, GEORGE JOJI
Visual artist, educator. Japanese American. **PERSONAL:** Born Mar 24, 1935, Kalopa, HI; son of Uichi & Tsuyako Miyasaki (deceased); divorced; children: Julie, Farrell, Michael. **EDUCATION:** California College of Arts & Crafts, BFA, 1957, BA, education, 1957, MFA, 1958. **CAREER:** University of California, Berkeley, Art Department, professor, currently. **ORGANIZA-**

TIONS: National Academy of Design, associate member. HONORS/ AWARDS: John Hay Whitney Foundation, Opportunity Fellowship, 1957; John Simon Guggenheim Foundation, Fellowship, 1963; National Endowment for the Arts, Artists' Fellowship, 1980, 1985. SPECIAL ACHIEVEMENTS: Recent solo exhibitions: Klein Gallery, Chicago, Illinois, 1989; Stephen Wirts Gallery, San Francisco, California, 1992; Mary Ryan Gallery, New York, New York, 1993. BIOGRAPHICAL SOURCES: Printmaking Today, by Jules Heller, Holt, Rinehart & Winston, 1973, second edition, p 90, "The California Printmaker," A Conversation with George Miyasaki, by Linda Goodman, Spring, 1992. HOME ADDRESS: 2844 Forest Avenue, Berkeley, CA 94705, (510)841-4834.

MIYASHIRO, AKIHO
Geologist, educator. Japanese American. PERSONAL: Born Oct 30, 1920, Kasaoka, Okayama, Japan; son of Tsuneshi Miyashiro and Hideyo Shigemasa Miyashiro. EDUCATION: University of Tokyo, BSc, 1943, PhD, 1953. CAREER: University of Tokyo, associate professor, 1958-68; Columbia University, visiting professor, 1967-70; State University of New York, Albany, professor, 1970-90, professor emeritus, 1991-. ORGANIZATIONS: Mineralogical Society of America, life fellow, 1962-; Geological Society of America, life fellow, 1977-; Geological Society of London, honorary fellow, 1971-; Geological Society of France, honorary fellow, 1976-; Geological Society of Japan, honorary fellow, 1993-. HONORS/AWARDS: Geological Society of America, Arthur L Day Medal, 1977; Royal Academy of Belgium, Paul Fourmarier Medal, 1981; Asiatic Society, Calcutta, P Bose Memorial Medal, 1984; International Geological Congress, LA Spendiarov Prize, 1992. BIOGRAPHICAL SOURCES: Modern Scientists and Engineers, McGraw-Hill, vol 2, p 318-319, 1980. HOME ADDRESS: 14 Stonehenge Dr, Albany, NY 12203-2019, (518)482-0654.

MIYATA, KEIJIRO
Culinary art educator. Japanese American. PERSONAL: Born Mar 8, 1951, Tokyo, Japan; son of Yataro Miyata & Midori Hekkiken Choy Miyata; married Connie J Miyata, Mar 8, 1976; children: Michelle Akemi, Kelly Naeko, Adam Keijiro. EDUCATION: Culinary Institute of America, AOS, (with honors), 1972; Everett Community College, teaching certificate, 1982. CAREER: Waikiki Yacht Club, working chef, 1972-74; Rye Town Hilton Hotel, assistant pastry chef, 1976-77; Explorer Restaurant, executive chef, 1977-79; Holiday Inn Hoetl, executive chef, 1979-81; Mill Creek Country Club, executive chef, 1981; Everett Community College, instructor, 1981-85; North Seattle Community College, instructor, 1985-90; Seattle Central Community College, instructor, 1990-. ORGANIZATIONS: Washington State Chef Association, 1977-, board member officer, treasurer, 1979-88, certification chairman, 1988-91; National Ice Carving Association, 1992-; Food Service Executive Association of Hawaii, 1973-74; US Ice Carving Association, team captain, 1988. HONORS/AWARDS: Washington Federation of Teachers, Excellence in Education, 1992; Oregon and Washington Community College Councils, Educational Excellence Award, 1988-89; Washington State Chef Association, Chef of the Year, 1986; ACF American Seafood Challenge, ACF Silver Medals, 1989, 1990; World Culinary Olympics, Germany, Gold & Bronze, 1984, 1988; International Ice Sculpting Competition, Canada, 1st place, 1989-91, 1993; International Ice Carving Competition, Japan, 2nd place & Muzuda Award, 1988; National Ice Carving Championship, US, grand champion, 1986-87; ACF Portland Culinary Show, ACF Gold, four 1st-place awards, grand prize, 1983; ACF Cold Food Competitions, ACF Gold, Silver, Bronze, 1982-85, 1987, 1988. BUSINESS ADDRESS: Professor, Seattle Central Community College, 1701 Broadway, 2BE 2120, Seattle, WA 98122-2413, (206)344-4325.

MIYOSHI, DAVID MASAO
Attorney. Japanese American. PERSONAL: Born Jan 2, 1944, Overton, NV; son of Joseph Masaru Miyoshi and Jean Michiye Miyoshi; married Teruko Ochiai Miyoshi, Jul 18, 1977; children: Mark Masaharo, Brandon Kohei. EDUCATION: University of So California, BS, 1966; University of California, JD, 1973; Wasedo University, Japan, Certificate of Completion, 1976; Harvard University, MBA, 1978. CAREER: Matsuo & Kosugi, Tokyo, foreign liaison attorney, 1974-76; Mori & Ota, associate attorney, 1978-80; Morgan Lewis & Bockius, associate attorney, 1980-82; Trans-Continental Investment, president, 1982-84; Miyoshi & Associates, consultant, 1984-; Law Offices David Miyoshi Inc, senior attorney, 1983-. ORGANIZATIONS: California Bar Assn, 1973-; American Bar Assn, 1973-; Japanese American Bar Assn, 1978-; American Baptist Society, director, 1986-; Palos, Verdes Baptist Church, director, 1986-; Japanese American Republican, 1985-. SPECIAL ACHIEVEMENTS: US Condominiums, Regulations, 1976; US Trade Laws

Newsletter, 1978; US Real Property Investments Newsletter, 1986. MILITARY SERVICE: United States Marine Corp, captain, 1966-69; Naval Commendation Medal with combat V, 1970. BUSINESS ADDRESS: Attorney at Law, Law Offices of David M Miyosh Inc, 3250 Wilshire Blvd, Suite 1610, Los Angeles, CA 90010, (213)387-6223.

MIZUNO, NOBUKO SHIMOTORI
Research biochemist (retired). Japanese American. PERSONAL: Born Apr 20, 1916, Oakland, CA; daughter of Shinichiro & Kii Shimotori; married Walter Masami Mizuno, Mar 20, 1942 (deceased). EDUCATION: University of California, Berkeley, AB, 1937, MA, 1939; University of Minnesota, PhD, 1956. CAREER: University of California, Berkeley, research assistant, 1939-41; Macalester College, instructor, 1943-51; University of Minnesota, research associate, 1956-62; Minneapolis VA Medical Center, research biochemist, 1962-79. ORGANIZATIONS: American Society of Biochemistry & Molecular Biology, 1974-; American Institute Nutrition, 1963-; American Association Cancer Research, 1965-79; Society Experimental Biology Medicine, 1971-79; Phi Beta Kappa, 1936; Iota Sigma Pi, 1938-. HONORS/AWARDS: National Science Foundation, fellowship, 1955; National Institutes of Health, research grants, 1967-74. SPECIAL ACHIEVEMENTS: About 50 publications in national and international journals such as: Journal of Biological Chemistry, Biochimica Biophysica Acta, Biochemical Pharmacology, Chemical-Biological Interact, Science, Nature, Cancer Research, Cancer Chemotheraphy Reports, Journal of Nutrition, Blood, Journal of Medicinal Chemistry, Cell Tissue Research. HOME ADDRESS: 3628 Loma Way, San Diego, CA 92106, (619)222-6974.

MIZUTANI, SATOSHI
Research scientist. Japanese American. PERSONAL: Born Nov 19, 1937, Yokohama, Kanagawa-ken, Japan; son of Hideo Mizutani and Hiroko Mizutani; married Kaoruko K Mizutani, Jun 10, 1966; children: Takaharu. EDUCATION: Tokyo University of Agriculture and Technology, BS, 1962; University of Kansas, PhD, 1969. CAREER: Nippon Kayaku KK, research scientist, 1962-65; University of Wisconsin, instructor, assistant, associate scientist, 1971-80; Abbott Laboratories, sr molecular biologist, 1981-82; Merck Research Laboratories, associate director, senior research fellow, 1982-88; Wyeth-Ayerst Research, associate director, 1988-. ORGANIZATIONS: American Society for Microbiology, 1972; American Association for Advancement of Science, 1980; International Society for Antiviral Research, 1990; New York Academy of Science, 1992. HONORS/AWARDS: US-Japan Fulbright Committee, Fulbright Scholarship, 1965-71; University of Wisconsin Medical School, Charles & Dorothy Inbush Award, 1975; Leukemia Society of America, scholar award, 1973-78. SPECIAL ACHIEVEMENTS: Discovery of reverse transcriptase, 1970; discovery of protein deoxyguanidyl transferase of hepatitis B virus, 1991. BUSINESS ADDRESS: Associate Director, Wyeth-Ayerst Research, 145 King of Prussia Rd, Research Building, Room 2109, Radnor, PA 19087, (215)341-2047.

MO, HUGH H.
Attorney. Chinese American. PERSONAL: Born Nov 15, 1950, Shanghai, People's Republic of China; son of Mo Tze Shin; divorced; children: Elizabeth. EDUCATION: New York University, BA, political science, history, 1973; Boston University, JD, 1976. CAREER: New York County District Attorney's Office, assistant district attorney, 1976-84; New York City Police Department, deputy commissioner-trials, 1984-88; Whitman & Ransom, partner, 1988-93; Law Firm of Hugh H. Mo, sole partner, 1993-. ORGANIZATIONS: Association of the Bar of the City of New York, judiciary committee, criminal courts committee, 1991; Criminal Justice Advisory Council for Mayor David N Dinkins Campaign, chairman, Fall 1989; National Committee on United States-China Relations; Flushing Boys Club, director; Chinese American Planning Council Inc, board president, 1983-85; City Garment Industry Development Corp, first vice-chairman, 1984-86; Agency for Child Development, Child Abuse Task Force, 1985-86; Community Board No 1, Manhattan, 1978; New York County Lawyers Association, Supreme Courts Committee, 1982. HONORS/AWARDS: New York City Chinese Community Tribute, 1988; Chinese Methodist Center Corp, Man of the Year, 1987; Asian Jade Society, New York City Police Department, Man of the Year, 1985. SPECIAL ACHIEVEMENTS: Fluent in Chinese Mandarin. BUSINESS ADDRESS: Attorney, Law Firm of Hugh H. Mo, PC, International Plaza, 750 Lexington Ave, 15th Floor, New York, NY 10022, (212)750-8000.

MO, LUKE W.
Physicist, educator. Chinese American. **PERSONAL:** Born Jun 3, 1934, Shantung, China; son of Si-leng Mo (deceased) and Shu-feng Lo (deceased); married Doris Mo, Dec 31, 1960; children: Curtis L, Alice. **EDUCATION:** National Taiwan University, Taipei, Taiwan, BSEE, 1956; National Tsinghua University, Hsinchu, Taiwan, MS, physics, 1959; Columbia University, PhD, physics, 1963. **CAREER:** Columbia University, research associate, 1963-65; Stanford Linear Accelerator Center, research physicist, 1965-69; University of Chicago, assistant professor, 1969-76; Virginia Polytechnic Institute and State University, professor, 1976-. **ORGANIZATIONS:** American Physical Society, 1977-. **HONORS/AWARDS:** Guggenheim Foundation, fellow, 1981; Virginia Polytechnic Institute and State University, Alumni Award in Research Excellence, 1980; Fulbright Foundation, student scholarship, 1959. **SPECIAL ACHIEVEMENTS:** Research in high-energy physics. **BIOGRAPHICAL SOURCES:** Various articles in Physical Review Letters, Physical Reviews, Physics Letters. **BUSINESS ADDRESS:** Professor, Physics Dept, Virginia Polytechnic Institute and State University, 315 Robeson Hall, Blacksburg, VA 24061, (703)231-5423.

MO, SUCHOON
Educator. Korean American. **PERSONAL:** Born Apr 19, 1932, Nagoya, Aichi, Japan; son of Chihyun Mo and Monica Shin Kim; married Judith C Oslick Mo, Dec 1969; children: Blaise, Bernard, Sage, Daisy, Clifton. **EDUCATION:** Idaho State College, BS, 1959; University of Pennsylvania, PhD, 1968. **CAREER:** University of Detroit, 1967-73; University of Southern California, Department of Psychology, professor, 1973-. **ORGANIZATIONS:** American Psychological Association; American Association for Advancement of Science; New York Academy of Sciences; Sigma Xi. **HONORS/AWARDS:** Kukkiwon, First dan black belt, taekwondo, 1992. **SPECIAL ACHIEVEMENTS:** Numerous professional publications. **BUSINESS ADDRESS:** Professor, Dept of Psychology, University of Southern Colorado, Pueblo, CO 81001-4901.

MODI, SHAILESH (SONNY)
Audit manager. Indo-American. **PERSONAL:** Born Aug 8, 1963, Ahmedabad, Gujarat, India; son of Ramanlal Modi and Sitaben Modi; married Ketki Dalal Modi, Jul 23, 1988. **EDUCATION:** New York University-CBPA, BS, 1984; New York University-GBA, MBA, 1987. **CAREER:** Deloitte & Touche, audit manager, 1986-. **ORGANIZATIONS:** AICPA, 1991; New York SSCPA, 1991; New Jersey SCPA, 1991. **SPECIAL ACHIEVEMENTS:** Certified Public Accountant, 1991. **HOME ADDRESS:** 1804 Merrywood Dr, Edison, NJ 08817.

MODY, MUKUND V.
Pediatrician. Indo-American. **PERSONAL:** Born Feb 25, 1940, Dunger, Gujarat, India; son of Vrundavandas Harilal Mody and Pramila Mody; married Kokila Mukund Mody, Feb 20, 1967; children: Swati, Sushama. **EDUCATION:** Bombay University, MBBS, 1964. **CAREER:** Flushing Hospital Medical Center, 1967-68; Kings County Hospital, 1968-70; Queens General Hospital, 1970-71; Downstate Medical Center, 1971-73; Dr. Mukund Mody MD, PC, president, 1973-. **ORGANIZATIONS:** Overseas Friends of BJP, president, 1991-; American Association of Physicians from India, New York Chapter, president, 1988-90, natl chapter, chairman of political action committee, 1986-87; Federation of Indian Assns, New York, president, 1985-86; Friends of India Society International, secretary general, 1982-88; Friends of India Society International, vice president, 1979-82; Indians for Democracy, New York coordinator, 1976-78. **HOME ADDRESS:** 36 Merrick Ave, Staten Island, NY 10301, (718)273-1157.

MOHAN, CHANDRA
Educator, researcher. Indo-American. **PERSONAL:** Born Aug 3, 1950, Lucknow, Uttar Pradesh, India; son of Prithivi Nath and Tara Rani; married Nirmala Sharma, Jul 23, 1978; children: Deepak, Naveen. **EDUCATION:** Bangalore University, BS (honors), 1970, MS, 1972, PhD, 1976. **CAREER:** USC Medical School, research associate, 1978-83, assistant professor, 1983-. **ORGANIZATIONS:** American Institute of Nutrition, 1987-; New York Academy of Sciences, 1984-; Society for Experimental Biology & Medicine, 1983-; American Association for Advancement of Science, 1989-. **HONORS/AWARDS:** Biochemical Medicine and Metabolic Biology, associate editor, 1987-. **SPECIAL ACHIEVEMENTS:** Over 30 publications scientific journals. **HOME ADDRESS:** 13638 E Dicky Street, Whittier, CA 90605, (310)698-5962.

MOHANTY, SASHI B.
Educator. Indo-American. **PERSONAL:** Born Sep 4, 1932, Village-Durgapur, Orissa, India; son of Madhu Sudan Mohanty (deceased) and Narayani Mohanty; married Pranoti; children: Nibedita, Bibhu, Nihar, Puspamitra. **EDUCATION:** Utkal University, ISc, 1951; Bihar University, BVSc, 1956; University of Maryland, MS, 1961, PhD, 1963. **CAREER:** University of Maryland, graduate assistant, 1960-63, assistant professor, 1963-69, associate professor, 1969-74, professor, 1974-, associate dean, 1986-. **ORGANIZATIONS:** WHO/FAO, head of working team, Bovine, Equine, Porcine Picornaviruses, 1973-82; WHO, verterate virus subcommittee of the international committee on taxonomy of viruses, 1975-82; American Veterinary Medical Association; Maryland Vet Medical Association; American Society of Microbiology; Society for Experimental Biology & Medicine; Microscopy Society of America. **HONORS/AWARDS:** Alexander von Humboldt, Stiftung, Germany, fellow, 1972-73; American Academy of Microbiology, fellow, 1991-; Gold Medal for Highest Scholastic Achievement, BVSc, 3rd year, 1955. **SPECIAL ACHIEVEMENTS:** Research & teaching; more than 65 publications in scientific journals on bovine respiratory viruses, molecular biology, electron microscopy; author of 2 books, "Veterinar Virology," Electron Microscopy for Biologists. **BUSINESS ADDRESS:** Associate Dean, Regional College of Veterinary Medicine, University of Maryland, College Park, College Park, MD 20742, (301)935-6083.

MOHAPATRA, RABINDRA N.
Educator. Indo-American. **PERSONAL:** Born Sep 1, 1944, Musagadia, Orissa, India; son of Bidyadhar Mohapatra & Parbati Mohapatra; married Manju Mohapatra, Jul 19, 1969; children: Pramit, Sanjit. **EDUCATION:** Utkal University, India, BSc (with honors), 1964; Delhi University, India, MSc, 1966; University of Rochester, PhD, 1969. **CAREER:** SUNY at Stony Brook, research associate, 1969-71; University of Maryland, College Park, research associate, 1971-74, professor, 1983-; City University of New York, assistant professor, 1974-77, associate professor, 1977-79, professor, 1979-82. **ORGANIZATIONS:** American Physical Society, 1981-; National Academy of Science, India, 1987-. **HONORS/AWARDS:** American Physical Society, fellow, 1981; Indian National Academy of Science, fellow, 1987; Alexander von Humboldt, fellow, 1980-81; Sigma-Xi, 1969. **SPECIAL ACHIEVEMENTS:** Two books: Unification and Supersymmetry, Springer-Verlag, 1st ed, 1986, 2nd ed, 1992; "Massive Neutrinos in Physics and Astrophysics," World Scientific, 1991; edited two books; developed four theories for elementary particles: left-right symmetry theory, MAJORON theory, CP-Violation theory and theory of massive neutrinos. **BIOGRAPHICAL SOURCES:** MOSAIC, published by US NSF, spring issue, 1991; Physics Today, June 1982. **BUSINESS ADDRESS:** Professor, Dept of Physics, University of Maryland, College Park, MD 20742, (301)405-6022.

MOINUDDIN, MASOOD A.
Insurance agent. Indo-American. **PERSONAL:** Born Jun 26, 1963; son of Mahmood Moinuddin & Andrea M Moinuddin; married Barbara S Moinuddin, Jul 3, 1986; children: Katie M. **CAREER:** ABC Auto Insurance Agency, Inc, president, currently. **HOME ADDRESS:** 211 E Ridgewood Dr, Seven Hills, OH 44131, (216)524-8624.

MONDAL, KALYAN
Research & Development engineer. Indo-American. **PERSONAL:** Born Aug 17, 1951, Calcutta, W. Bengal, India; son of Dwijendra Nath (deceased) and Bijali Mondal; married Chitralekha Mondal, Aug 5, 1981; children: Indrani, Chandrani. **EDUCATION:** University of Calcutta, India, BSc, 1969, BTech, 1972, MTech, 1974; University of California at Santa Barbara, PhD, 1978. **CAREER:** University of California, Santa Barbara, lecturer, 1978-79; Lehigh University, assistant professor, 1980-83; AT&T Bell Labs, MTS, 1981-87, DMTS, 1987-. **ORGANIZATIONS:** IEEE, senior member, CAS Society, board of governors, 1990-92; Eta Kappa Nu, 1978-; Sigma Xi, 1978-; India Students Association, secretary, 1990-91; AT&T, 4A-PA, president, 1990-91. **HONORS/AWARDS:** University of Calcutta, India, Gold Medal, 1972, 1974; PA Power & Lights Co, Research Grant, 1981; AT&T Bell Labs, Exceptional Contribution Award, 1988, 1993. **BUSINESS ADDRESS:** Distinguished Member of Technical Staff, AT&T Bell Labs, 600 Mountain Ave, Room 2A-340A, Murray Hill, NJ 07974, (908)582-2511.

MONG, SEYMOUR
Industrial research company executive. Chinese American. **PERSONAL:** Born Oct 23, 1951, Taipei, Taiwan; son of Chau Sheck Mong and Wen-Yin Chu (deceased); married Shau-Ming Mong, Jul 5, 1977; children: Sandy, Cindy.

EDUCATION: National Taiwan University, BS, 1974; Baylor College of Medicine, PhD, 1980. **CAREER:** Baylor College of Medicine, research assistant, 1977-80; University of Pennsylvania, post-doctoral fellow, 1980-82; SmithKline & French Laboratory, asst director, 1982-86; SmithKline Beecham Inc, associate director, 1987-89; Fujisawa Pharmaceutic Co, director, 1990-92; Immuno Pharmaceutics Inc, vice pres, 1992-. **ORGANIZATIONS:** New York Academy of Sciences, 1992-; American Association for Cancer Research, 1992-; American Society for Clinical Pharmacology and Therapeutics, 1992-; Society of Toxicology, Midwest, 1991-; American Society of Toxicology, 1992-; San Diego Youth Symphony, treasurer, 1993-. **HONORS/AWARDS:** City of Taipei, Elite Student Award, 1974; SmithKline & French Laboratory, Scientific Achievement Award, 1986; National Institutes of Health, Post-Doctoral Fellowship, 1981. **SPECIAL ACHIEVEMENTS:** Language proficiency: Chinese, English; patent: "Pentamidine Meter Dose Inhaler," US IND, 35258, 1991; author: "Co-Expression of Receptors," Advanced Prost Leukemia Research, Raven Press, 1989; "Leukotriene Binding Assay," Methods in Enzymology, Acad Press, 1990. **HOME ADDRESS:** 10966 Autillo Way, San Diego, CA 92127, (619)673-1838. **BUSINESS ADDRESS:** Vice President, ImmunoPharmaceutics Inc, 11011 Via Frontera, San Diego, CA 92127, (619)451-8400.

MONTERO, JUAN MURILLO, II
Physician, surgeon. Filipino American. **PERSONAL:** Born May 18, 1942, Bayabas, Surigao del Sur, Philippines; son of Juan Ramirez & Felicitas Luna Montero; married Mary Ann Goodsell Montero, Jan 24, 1970; children: Daniel, Gregory, Andrew, Paul. **EDUCATION:** San Carlos University, BS, 1960; Cebu Institute of Technology, MD, 1965. **CAREER:** Chesapeake General Hospital, chief of surgery, 1979-80; self-employed, physician-surgeon, 1972-; Eastern Virginia Medical School, clinical instructor surgery, 1979-85, assistant professor surgery, 1985-. **ORGANIZATIONS:** Philippine Medical Association of Southeastern Virginia, president, 1978; Philippine American Community of Tidewater, president, 1979; Virginia Association of Philippine Physicians, president, 1980; Chesapeake Medical Society, president, 1983-84; Association of Philippine Practicing Physicians in America, board of governors, 1980-82, president, 1983-84; Society of Philippine Surgeons in America, board of governors, 1979-, president, 1986. **HONORS/AWARDS:** Association of Philippine Practicing Physicians, Community Service Award, 1979; Virginia Primary Care Association, Health Care Provider Award, 1984. **SPECIAL ACHIEVEMENTS:** Halfway Through, autobiography, Philippine Heritage Endowment Fund, Indiana University, 1982; "Where a Flashlight is Standard in the OR," Medical Economics, Aug 1982; "Alien Foreign Medical Graduates - A Vanishing Breed," Filipino American, Philippine News, Filipino Reporter, Feb 1984; "The Ultimate Solution: Statehood for the Philippines," Philippine News, July 1984; associate editor, Philippine American Medical Bulletin, 1981-; also several scientific papers and speaking engagements. **BUSINESS ADDRESS:** Surgeon, 2147 Old Greenbrier Rd, Chesapeake, VA 23320, (804)424-5485.

MOODERA, JAGADEESH SUBBAIAH
Scientist. Indo-American. **PERSONAL:** Born in Bangalore, Karnataka, India; son of Subbaiah Moodera and Muthavva Moodera; married Geetha P Berera. **EDUCATION:** Mysore University, India, BSc, 1971, MSc, 1973; Indian Institute of Technology, Madras, PhD, 1978. **CAREER:** Indian Institute of Technology, India, post doctoral fellow, 1978-; West Virginia University, research associate, 1979-81; Massachusetts Institute of Technology, research scientist, 1981-. **ORGANIZATIONS:** American Physical Society, 1980-; Materials Research Society, 1986-; Cryogenic Society of America, 1984-. **SPECIAL ACHIEVEMENTS:** Published over 70 research articles in physics in reputed journals, 1976-. **BUSINESS ADDRESS:** Research Scientist, Massachusetts Institute of Technology, 170 Albany St, NW14-2114, Cambridge, MA 02139, (617)253-5423.

MOON, BYUNG HWA
Cleric. Korean American. **PERSONAL:** Born Mar 10, 1956, Seoul, Republic of Korea; son of Han Ju Moon and Soon Y Moon-You; married Sung Ai Moon, May 23, 1981; children: Samuel Ha. **EDUCATION:** Korean Christian College, BA (summa cum laude), 1980; Freed-Hardeman University, BA (cum laude), 1983; Harding University Graduate School of Religion, MDiv, 1988, DMin candidate. **CAREER:** Go Gang Church, youth minister, 1976-79; Naesoo Church, education minister, 1980-82; Memphis Korean Church of Christ, visitation minister, 1984-86, sr minister, 1987-. **ORGANIZATIONS:** Leadership Training Program, co-president, 1991-; Christian Youth Camp, director, 1980-82; Society of Biblical Literature, 1992-. **HONORS/**

AWARDS: Korean-American Community, Outstanding Leadership Award, 1988, 1993. **SPECIAL ACHIEVEMENTS:** Editor: New Testament Church, quarterly; lecturer: Korean Mission Workshop, 1990-92; social worker: Korean-American Community, 1988-. **BIOGRAPHICAL SOURCES:** "Tradition Transition," The Commercial Appeal, Sep 1988; "Korean Congregation Sees Dream Come True," Tri-State Christian Observer, Nov 1993. **BUSINESS PHONE:** (901)360-9669.

MOON, CHUNG-IN
Educator. Korean American. **PERSONAL:** Born Mar 25, 1951, Cheju, Cheju, Republic of Korea; son of Tae Seng Moon & Yeo Jun Kim; married Jai-Ok Kim, Aug 9, 1978; children: Ki Hyun, Iris J. **EDUCATION:** Yonsei University, BA, 1977; University of Maryland, MA, 1981, PhD, 1984. **CAREER:** Williams College, assistant professor of political science, 1984-85; Inha University, University, assistant professor of political science, 1987-88; University of California, San Diego, visiting associate professor, 1993; University of Kentucky, Dept of Political Science, asst professor, 1985-87, associate professor, 1989-. **ORGANIZATIONS:** Korean American University Professors' Association, 2nd vice president, 1992-; Association of Korean Political Studies in North America, executive secretary, 1991-; Social Science Research Council, Korea committee, 1985-92. **HONORS/AWARDS:** International Studies Association, Distinguished Scholarship Award, nominated, 1986; US Institute of Peace, research fellowship, 1992; Institute for the Study of World Politics, doctoral dissertation fellowship, 1992; University of Kentucky, Special Faculty Incentive Award, 1988. **SPECIAL ACHIEVEMENTS:** Author, Alliance Under Tension, the Evolution of US-South Korean Relations, 1988; The US and the Defense of the Pacific, Westview Press, 1989; National Security in the Third World, E Elgar Press, 1988; Pacific Dynamics, Westview Press, 1989. **HOME PHONE:** (606)266-4081. **BUSINESS ADDRESS:** Professor, Dept of Political Science, University of Kentucky, Patterson Office Tower, Rm 1661, Lexington, KY 40506, (606)257-1771.

MOON, INSO JOHN
Retail hardware company executive. Korean American. **PERSONAL:** Born Jun 11, 1938, Seoul, Republic of Korea; son of Hojun Moon and Kyuke Yoon; married Yangja Elizabeth Moon, Oct 23, 1969; children: Sukhee Paul, Chulhee Charlie. **EDUCATION:** Konkuk University, BS, biology, 1964. **CAREER:** Pacific Architects & Engineering Inc, safety engr, 1965-70; Hunghwa Construction Co, safety engr, 1970-71; St Mary's Hospital, radiographic tech, 1971-74; Elmhurst General Hospital, radiographic tech, 1974-78; Zenith Wine & Liquor Inc, president, 1978-88; Hector Hardware Corp, president, chief exec officer, 1988-. **MILITARY SERVICE:** Army, ssgt, 1959-62. **HOME ADDRESS:** 375 Marlborough Rd, Cedarhurst, NY 11516, (516)374-1477.

MOON, JUNG SUK
Realtor. Korean American. **PERSONAL:** Born Jan 3, 1944, Kang-reung, Kang-won, Republic of Korea; son of Kyung In Moon & Eun Hae Moon; married In Sook Moon, Jun 30, 1973; children: Elisa, David, Michelle. **EDUCATION:** Yonsei University, BA, 1968; The American University, MA, 1976. **CAREER:** The Korea Tribune, editor, 1970-71; Overseas Employment & Information Service, manager, 1971-77; Colquitt-Carruthers, realtor, 1977-80; Merrill Lynch Realty, Maryland, realtor, 1980-89; The Prudential Preferred Properties, Maryland, realtor, 1989-. **ORGANIZATIONS:** National Association of Realtors, 1977-; Montgomery County Association of Realtors, 1977-; Washington, DC Association of Realtors, 1977-; Prince George's County Association of Realtors, 1977-; Northern Virginia Association of Realtors, 1990-. **HONORS/AWARDS:** Montgomery County Association of Realtors, Maryland, number 2 in sales, 1981; Merrill Lynch Realty, Eastern Region, number 2 in sales, 1981; Montgomery County Association of Realtors, Maryland, number 1 in sales, 1988; Merrill Lynch Realty, US top 10 sales agent, 1988; Montgomery County Association of Realtors, Maryland, top 10 in sales, 1981-90. **MILITARY SERVICE:** Republic of Korea Army, 1966-68. **BIOGRAPHICAL SOURCES:** The Korean-American Life, p 22-26, Nov. 1989; Realtor (Washington Area), p 61, June 1989; The Bethesda Gazette, April 13, 1989. **HOME ADDRESS:** 7200 Bradley Blvd, Bethesda, MD 20817-2128, (301)469-4969. **BUSINESS PHONE:** (301)652-0001.

MOON, KEE SUK
Educator. Korean American. **PERSONAL:** Born Mar 30, 1959, Sosan, Chungnam, Republic of Korea; son of Sung Hoon & Kyung Sook Moon; married Jin Hee Moon, Jan 22, 1983; children: Joshua Jehyung. **EDUCATION:** Korea University, BS, 1981, MS, 1983; University of Illinois, Chicago, MS, 1987, PhD, 1990. **CAREER:** Korea University, teaching assistant, 1981-

82; Jung-Kyung Junior College, instructor, 1983-84; University of Illinois, Chicago, teaching assistant, 1985-88; Northern Illinois University, instructor, 1989-90; Khan, Phillips & Associates, Inc, consultant, 1990; Michigan Technological University, assistant professor, 1990-. **ORGANIZATIONS:** Society of Manufacturing Engineers, 1991-; Institute of Industrial Engineers, 1990-; Operations Research Society of America, 1991-; Michigan Technological University, Korean Student Association, advisor, 1993-. **SPECIAL ACHIEVEMENTS:** Author, journal articles including: "A Stochastic Optimization of the Production Speed of Robots Based on Measured Geometric and Nongeometric Errors," International Journal of Production Research, vol 30, no 1, p 49-62, 1992; "Procrustes Analysis & Its Application to Sensor Integration," Trans of NAMRI, vol 20, p 347-354, 1992; "Development of a Magnetostriction Based Cutting Tool Micropoistioner," Trans of NAMRI, vol 21, 1993; "A Robust Control Scheme for Improved Machined Surface Texture," Trans of NAMRI, vol 21, 1993; "The Origin and Interpretation of Spatial Frequencies in a Turned Surface Profile," Journal of Engineering for Industry, Trans ASME, 1994. **BIOGRAPHICAL SOURCES:** Manufacturing Engineering, p 56, July 1993. **BUSINESS ADDRESS:** Assistant Professor, Dept of ME-EM, Michigan Technological University, 1400 Townsend Dr, Houghton, MI 49931-1295, (906)487-2541.

MOON, RONALD TAE-YANG

State supreme court justice. Korean American. **PERSONAL:** Born Sep 4, 1940; married Stella H Moon. **EDUCATION:** Coe College, BS, psychology, sociology, 1962; University of Iowa, JD, 1965. **CAREER:** US District Court, law clerk to Chief Judge Martin Pence, 1965-66; City and County of Honolulu, deputy prosecutor, 1966-68; Libkuman, Ventura, Ayabe, Chong & Nishimoto, associate, 1968-72, partner, 1972-82; Circuit Court, State of Hawaii, 9th division, 1st circuit, judge, 1982-90; University of Hawaii, adj professor, 1986-88; Hawaii Supreme Court, associate judge, 1990-93, chief justice, 1993-. **ORGANIZATIONS:** ABA; Hawaii Bar Association; Association of Trial Lawyers; American Board of Trial Advocates, president, 1986-, national secretary, 1989-; American Inn of Cts, IV, bencher, 1983-; American Judicature Society; Hawaii State Trial Judges' Association, seminar organization committee, 1987, executive committee, 1985-90, liaison supreme court, 1990-. **SPECIAL ACHIEVEMENTS:** Circuit court rules committee, 1983-89; Supreme Court committee on judiciary administration, 1987; committee to study and report on lawyer professionalism in Hawaii, 1988; appointed to court annexed arbitration program committee, 1985-90; study for judiciary's automation application transfer team, chairperson, 1985; arbitration judge 1st circuit, circuit court, 1986-90; Center for Alternative Dispute Resolution, board of directors, 1989; Judiciary Arbitration Committee, chairperson, 1986-90; guest speaker at numerous events. **BUSINESS ADDRESS:** Chief Justice, Supreme Court of Hawaii, PO Box 2560, Honolulu, HI 96804, (808)539-4700.*

MOON, YOUNG B.

Educator, engineer. Korean American. **PERSONAL:** Born May 1, 1958, Seoul, Republic of Korea; son of Hyun-Soon Moon & Ok-In Bae; married Hyune-Ju Kim, Aug 9, 1985; children: Timothy J, Deborah J. **EDUCATION:** Seoul National University, BS, 1981; Stanford University, MS, 1985; Purdue University, PhD, 1988. **CAREER:** Syracuse University, assistant professor, associate professor, 1988-; Hewlett-Packard Co, research staff, 1992; MIT, visiting scholar, 1993. **ORGANIZATIONS:** AAAI, 1988-; IEEE, 1989-; SME, 1988-; ASME, 1988-; ASA, 1992-. **SPECIAL ACHIEVEMENTS:** More than 30 published research papers, 1989-. **BUSINESS ADDRESS:** Assoc Professor, Dept of Mechanical Engineering, Syracuse University, 433 Link Hall, Syracuse, NY 13244, (315)443-2649.

MORI, JOHN P.

Educator, sculptor. Japanese American. **PERSONAL:** Born Nov 15, 1951, Albuquerque, NM; son of Perry T Mori & Chiyo Sato Mori; married Katie Mori, May 22, 1988; children: Kalee Yoshiko, Chelsea Hanako. **EDUCATION:** University of New Mexico, BFA, 1976; Southern Illinois University at Carbondale, MFA, 1980. **CAREER:** Memphis College of Art, visiting instructor, 1985-86; Arkansas Tech University, assistant professor, 1986-. **ORGANIZATIONS:** Arkansas River Valley Art Center, Visual Arts Committee, head board member, 1990-93. **SPECIAL ACHIEVEMENTS:** Various sculptures in the "Portal" series, 1993. **BIOGRAPHICAL SOURCES:** Arkansas: Year of American Craft, p 38, 39, 61, 1993. **BUSINESS ADDRESS:** Professor, Art Dept, Arkansas Tech University, Russellville, AR 72801, (501)968-0244.

MORI, SANDY OUYE

Health commissioner. Japanese American. **CAREER:** San Francisco City and County Health Commission, executive director, currently. **ORGANIZATIONS:** US-Japan Joint Commission on Aging, appointed member, 1992-. **BUSINESS ADDRESS:** Executive Director, San Francisco City & County Health Commission, 101 Grove, Rm 308, San Francisco, CA 94102, (415)554-2500.*

MORIBAYASHI, MIKIO (MIKE)

Plastic molding company executive. Japanese American. **PERSONAL:** Born Jan 1, 1940, Nagoya, Aichi, Japan; son of Sasuke Moribayashi and Hanako Moribayashi; married Noriko Moribayashi, Apr 19, 1970; children: Masako, Hideyuki. **EDUCATION:** Tokyo University of Foreign Studies, BA, Anglo-American studies, 1962. **CAREER:** Nichimen Corp, Tokyo, Japan, gen mdse dept, staff mbr, 1962-71, Kuala Lumpur branch office, rep, 1971-73, Tokyo plastics dept, staff mbr, 1973-75, asst mgr, 1975-82, mgr, 1982-83; Nichimen America Inc, chemicals plastics dept, gen mgr, vice pres, 1983-90, plastics dept, gen mgr, vice pres, 1989-90; American Fuji Seal Inc, vice pres, marketing, 1990, acting CEO, 1991, vice pres, marketing, resident bd dir, 1991-; Kyowa America Corp, Pennsylvania plant, vice pres, plant mgr, currently. **BUSINESS ADDRESS:** Vice President, Plant Manager, Kyowa America Corp, Pennsylvania Plant, 1000 E Roy Furman Hwy, Waynesburg, PA 15370, (412)627-4700.

MORISAWA, MARIE ETHEL

Educator (retired). Japanese American. **PERSONAL:** Born Nov 2, 1919, Toledo, OH; daughter of Ethel Anderson & Mitsuru Morisawa. **EDUCATION:** Hunter College, BA, 1937; Union Theological Seminary, MA, religious education, MA, 1945; University of Wyoming, MA, geology, 1952; Columbia University, PhD, geology, 1960. **CAREER:** Honolulu Council of Churches, religious education, instructor, 1946-49; Bryn Mawr College, instructor in geology, 1955-59; University of Montana, assistant professor of geology, 1959-61; US Geological Survey, geologist, 1961-62; Antioch College, associate professor of geology, 1963-69; State University of New York, professor of geology, 1970-90. **ORGANIZATIONS:** Geological Society of America, fellow, councillor, 1989-91, chairman of Membership Committee, associate editor of GSA Bulletin, 1982-87, Penrose Comm, 1982-84, vice chairman, chair of Quaternary Geology and Geomorphology Division, 1978-81, board member, 1972-74, 1976-78; American Association for Advancement of Science, fellow, councillor of Section E, 1988-89; Sigma Xi, vice president, president of Triple Cities Club, 1986-88, Visiting Scientist Program, 1970; American Geophysical Union. **HONORS/AWARDS:** University of Wyoming, Distinguished Alumna, 1992; Association of Women Geoscientists, Outstanding Educator, 1992; USIA, Fulbright Lecturer to India, 1987-88. **SPECIAL ACHIEVEMENTS:** Author, Streams: Their Dynamics and Morphology, McGraw Hill Book Co, 1968; Rivers, Longman Pub Group Ltd, 1985; Geomorphology Laboratory Manual, John Wiley, 1976; editor, Fluvial Geomorphology, Allen and Unwin, 1974; Tectonic Geomorphology, Allen and Unwin, 1986. **BIOGRAPHICAL SOURCES:** Physical Geology, J S Monroe and R Wicander, p384, 1992; Women in Geology, S D Halsey, B McCaslin, W L Carey and W D Romey, p21-23, 1976. **BUSINESS ADDRESS:** Professor, Dept of Geological Sciences, State University of New York, Vestal Parkway East, Binghamton, NY 13902-6000, (607)777-2837.

MORITA, ICHIKO T.

Librarian. Japanese American. **PERSONAL:** Born in Osaka, Japan; daughter of Ichita & Asa Takagi; married James R Morita, Oct 30, 1955; children: Louise Naomi Morita Landry, Carol Hiromi. **EDUCATION:** Okayama University, BA, 1954; University of Chicago, MA, 1964. **CAREER:** Chicago Loop College, Foreign Languages Department, instructor, 1968-69; University of Oregon, Department of Classics & Chinese, Japanese, instructor, 1969-72; Ohio State University Libraries, Processing Division, assistant head, 1972-76, instructor, 1972-74, assistant professor, 1975-82, Automated Processing Division, head, 1977-85, associate professor, 1983-92, Cataloging Department, head, 1986-, professor, 1993-. **ORGANIZATIONS:** American Library Association, council member, 1992-95; Academic Library Association of Ohio, president, 1988-89; Asian-Pacific American Librarians Association, president, 1988-89; OCLC, Cataloging Advisory Council, 1985-87, special consultant on bibliographic services in Japan, 1987; American Society of Information Science, Central Columbus Chapter, executive committee, 1982-83; Japan Information Center of Science & Technology, consultant, 1984-85; Japanese American Club of Columbus, president, 1981. **HONORS/AWARDS:** Japan Foundation, fellowship, 1979; Tokyo University, research fellow, 1979; US

Department of Commerce, NTIS Research Fellow, 1988. **SPECIAL ACHIEVEMENTS:** "Japanese Technical Information: It's Infrastructure," Encyclopedia of Libraries & Information Science, NTIS PB Report, 1991; "The Current Status of Science & Technology Gray Literature in Japan," 1988; "Japanese Characters, Computer Input of . . .," Encyclopedia of Computer Science & Technology, 1989; "Johoka Jidai Ni Taio Suru Amerika No Toshokan," Chi Shi Ki, 1985; "A Cost Analysis of OCLC On-Line Shared Cataloging System," LRTS, 1978. **BUSINESS ADDRESS:** Professor, Head, Cataloging Dept, Ohio State University Libraries, 1858 Neil Avenue Mall, William Oxley Thompson Library, Columbus, OH 43210-1286, (614)292-8114.

MORITA, JOHN TAKAMI

Artist. Japanese American. **PERSONAL:** Born Apr 10, 1943, Honolulu, HI; son of Takaichi & Miyako Morita. **EDUCATION:** Chaminade College, BA, history, 1965; San Francisco Art Institute, BFA, photography, 1974; San Francisco State University, MA, printmaking, 1976. **CAREER:** University of Hawaii, Manoa, lecturer in art, 1982-83; Windward Community College, lecturer in art, 1991-92; artist, solo exhibitions include: Honolulu Academy of Arts, 1977; San Francisco Museum of Modern Art, 1979; Alternative Museum, NY City, 1987; Intergrafik 90, Berlin, 1990; The Print Club, Philadelphia, 1990. **ORGANIZATIONS:** Kapiolani Community College, Art Program Advisory Board, board of directors, 1992-93; Honolulu Printmaking Work Shop, board of directors, 1992-93; Northwest Print Council, 1982, 1993; Los Angeles Printmaking Society, 1985, 1993. **HONORS/AWARDS:** National Endowment of the Arts, Fellowship in Printmaking, 1986; Intergrafik 87, International Print Trienniale, Berlin, First Prize, 1987; The Print Club, Philadelphia, Print Club Selection Award, 1988. **MILITARY SERVICE:** US Army, sp 5, 1966-69; First Prize, All Army, Second Prize, Interservice Phot ography Category, B & W Experimental, 1969. **BIOGRAPHICAL SOURCES:** Intergrafik 90, Internationale Triennale Engagierter Grafik in der Deutschen Demokratischen Republik, p 296-312, 1989. **HOME ADDRESS:** 1640 Ahihi St, Honolulu, HI 96819, (808)845-8003.

MORITA, PAT (NORIYUKI)

Comedian, actor. Japanese American. **PERSONAL:** Born 1932, Isleton, CA; married Yuki Morita, 1970; children: Tia, Aly. **CAREER:** Actor, comedian; television credits include: "Sanford and Son," 1974-75; "Happy Days," 1975-76, 1982-83; "Mr T and Tina," 1976; "Blansky's Beauties," 1977; "Ohara," 1987; television movies include: Vegas Strip War; Amos; Return to Manzanar; motion pictures include: Thoroughly Modern Millie, 1967; Midway, 1976; When Time Ran Out, 1980; Savannah Smiles, 1982; Jimmy the Kid, 1983; The Karate Kid, 1984; The Karate Kid Part II, 1986; Collison Course, 1987. **HONORS/AWARDS:** Assn of Asian/Pacific American Artists, lifetime achievement award, 1987; Academy Award nomination, for Karate Kid, 1985.*

MORITA, RICHARD YUKIO

Educator. Japanese American. **PERSONAL:** Born Mar 27, 1923, Pasadena, CA; son of Jiro and Reiko Morita; married Toshiko Nishihara Morita, Mar 14, 1953; children: Sally Jean, Ellen Jane Mitchell, Peter Wayne. **EDUCATION:** University of Nebraska, BS, 1947; University of Southern California, MS, 1949; University of California, Scripps Institute of Oceanography, PhD, 1954. **CAREER:** University of Houston, assistant professor, 1955-58; University of Nebraska, associate professor, 1958-62; Oregon State University, professor of microbiology & oceanography, 1962-89, professor emeritus 1989-; National Science Foundation, program director for biochemistry, 1968-69; James Cook University, Australia, visiting professor, 1973-74; Kyoto University, distinguished visiting professor, 1989; Florida Intl University, Glaser Visiting Professor, 1990; Banfield Marine Station, Canada, visiting professor, 1978. **ORGANIZATIONS:** American Society for Microbiology, 1948-, honorary member, 1990; American Society for Limnology and Oceanography, 1955-; Canadian Society for Microbiologists, 1966-90; Oceanographical Society of Japan, 1964-89; AAAS, 1963-89, fellow, 1981; Society for Industrial Microbiology, 1983-89. **HONORS/AWARDS:** Danish Crown, Galathea Medal and Ribbon, 1956; Australian Government, Senior Queen Elizabeth II Fellowship, 1975; Ministry of Education, Science and Culture of Japan, Special Foreign Guest Professorship, 1989; Phi Kappa Phi; Sigma Xi; Alpha Epsilon Delta, Texas chapter; Japan Society for Promotion of Science, Fellowship, 1978; American Society for Microbiology, Fisher Award, 1988; Oregon State University, Milton Harris Award in Basic Science, 1984. **SPECIAL ACHIEVEMENTS:** Books co-edited: 2; laboratory manuals co-edited: 2; chapters in books: 48; scientific articles in refereed profession journals: 132; US Govern-

ment publications: 2; scientific abstracts: 83; scientific review articles: 4; contributor to research articles: 4. **MILITARY SERVICE:** US Army, 442nd Regimental Combat Team, pfc, 1944-46. **BUSINESS ADDRESS:** Prof Emeritus of Microbio & Oceanography, Oregon State University, Nash Hall 220, Corvallis, OR 97331-3804, (503)737-1862.

MORIWAKI, CLARENCE

Press secretary. Japanese American. **CAREER:** Transition team for governor-elect Mike Lowry, spokesman; Washington state governor Mike Lowry, deputy press secretary, 1993-. **SPECIAL ACHIEVEMENTS:** Washington state senate candidate, 1992. **BUSINESS ADDRESS:** Deputy Press Secretary, Washington Governor Mike Lowry, Office of the Governor Legislature Bldg, Olympia, WA 98504-0002, (206)753-6780.*

MORIZUMI, S. JAMES

Scientist (retired). Japanese American. **PERSONAL:** Born Nov 13, 1923, San Francisco, CA; son of Mohei & Hatsue Morizumi (deceased); married Hiroko Morizumi, Nov 20, 1955; children: Michael Noriyuki. **EDUCATION:** Kumamoto University in Japan, BS, mechanical engineering, 1944; University of California, Berkeley, BS, mechanical engineering, 1955; California Institute of Technology, MS, aeronautics, 1957; University of California, Los Angeles, PhD, mathematics, 1970. **CAREER:** US Fifth Air Force, interpreter, translator, 1946-50; Douglas Aircraft Company, sr aerodynamicist, 1955-60; TRW (formerly Space Technology Laboratories), sr staff, 1960-81; HR-Textron Inc, director, 1981-82; Hughes Aircraft Company, sr staff, 1982-89; National University, professor, 1989-92. **ORGANIZATIONS:** American Institute of Aeronautics and Astronautics. **HONORS/AWARDS:** University of California, Tau Beta Pi, 1954; UCLA, Pi Mu Epsilon, 1969. **SPECIAL ACHIEVEMENTS:** An Investigation of Infrared Radiation by Vibration-Rotation Bands of Molecular Gases; presentations of tech papers: AIAA Aerospace Science Meeting, NY; Thermophysics Conference, Boston, 1974; Symposium on Radiation in The Atomphere, University of Munich, West Germany, 1976; AIAA 17th Aerospace Science Meeting, New Orleans, 1979; 36th International Congress of Astronautics, Stockholm, Sweden, 1985; Thermal Radiation from the Exhaust Plume of an Aluminized Comoposite Propellant Rocket, J of Spacecraft and Rockets, Sept 1964; Analytical Determination of Shape Factors from a Surface Element to an Axisymmetrical Surface, AIAA Journal, Nov 1964. **BIOGRAPHICAL SOURCES:** US Air Force Report on Thermal Radiation Model, NASA TM X-53579, by Lt Roshelle; proceedings of International Symposiums on Space Technology and Science, Japan, 1971, 1973, 1975, 1982, 1984, 1986, 1988, 1990, 1992; An overview of Nuclear Effects Phenomenology. **HOME ADDRESS:** 29339 Stadia Hill Lane, Rancho Palos Verdes, CA 90274, (310)541-2903.

MOTHKUR, SRIDHAR RAO

Radiologist, physician, educator. Indo-American. **PERSONAL:** Born Oct 5, 1950, Mothkur, Andhra Pradesh, India; son of Venkat Rao Mothkur & Laxmi Bai Gundepally Mothkur; married Sheila Ramarao Paga Mothkur, Nov 30, 1973; children: Swathi, Preethi, Venkat Krishna. **EDUCATION:** Osmamia University, Hyderabad, India, PUC, 1966, MBBS, 1972, DPH, 1974. **CAREER:** Louise Burg Hospital, Diagnostic Radiology, chairman and medical director, 1979-85; Shriners Hospital for Crippled Children, Diagnostic Radiology, chairman and medical director, 1986-88; Christ Hospital and Medical Center, special staff radiologist, 1988-89; Michigan City Radiologists, Inc, medical director, Magnetic Resonance Imaging and Interventional Radiology, 1989-; University of Illinois at Chicago, clinical assistant professor, 1990-; St Anthony and Memorial Hospital, Michigan City, Diagnostic Imaging, medical director, 194-. **ORGANIZATIONS:** American Medical Assn; Radiological Society of North America; American College of International Physicians; American College of Radiology; Society of Magnetic Resonance in Medicine; American Diabetes Assn; American College of Angiology; Osmania University Medical Alumni Assn; Telugu Assn of Greater Chicago; America Telugu Association; Tri State Telugu Assn; Telugu Assn of North America; International Society of Krishna Consciousness; American Society of Head and Neck Radiology; Society of Cardiovascular and Interventional Radiology; Chicago Medical Society; Illinois State Medical Society. **HONORS/AWARDS:** University of Illinois at Chicago, Fellowship in Imaging, 1988-89; American Association of International Physicians, FACIP; American Biographical Institute, FABI; American College of Angiology, FACA; International College of Angiology, FICA; American Board of Radiology, 1981-. **SPECIAL ACHIEVEMENTS:** "Advances in Diagnostic Radiology," Images, vol 1, no 6, Dec 1981; co-author, MRI and Potential Use of In-vivo H-1 Spectroscopy of Uveal Melanomas, exhibit at the seventh annual meeting of the Society of

Magnetic Resonance in Medicine, 1988; co-author, "Analysis of Neuroelectric Implant Integrity," Applied Neurophysiology, Journal of Stereotactic and Functional Neurosurgery, 1989; co-author, "Volume-selective Water-suppressed Proton Spectra of Human Tissues in Vivo," Abstract in Biophysical Journal, vol 55, 452a, 1989; language proficiencies: Hindi, Kannada and Telugu. **HOME ADDRESS:** 1018 Prestwick Drive, Frankfort, IL 60423. **BUSINESS ADDRESS:** Radiologist, Michigan City Radiologists Inc, 916 Washington St, Michigan City, IN 46360, (219)872-7268.

MOTIHAR, KAMLA MANSHARAMANI
Library director. Indo-American. **PERSONAL:** Born Aug 16, 1933, Sukkur, Sind, India; daughter of Gangaram Mansharamani (deceased) and Dadan Mansharamani; married Dewan Motihar, Feb 17, 1963 (divorced 1983). **EDUCATION:** DAV College, Kanpur, India, BA, 1952; Christ Church College, Kanpur, India, MA, sociology, 1955; Delhi University, Delhi, India, library science dip, 1957; Northwest Polytechnic, London, England, chartered librarian, 1973. **CAREER:** Delhi University Library, Delhi, technical processing, librarian, 1957-58; American Library, Delhi, circulation & reference, head, 1958-62; Library of Congress, Book Procurement Center, Delhi, cataloger, 1962-64; British Council, London, head, Asian & Pacific Region, 1964-73; Andrew W Mellon Foundation, director, library, 1974-. **ORGANIZATIONS:** American Library Association, 1993-; Special Libraries Association, chairperson, liaison education div to foreign relations committee, 1992-; British Library Association, 1964-; Indian Library Association, life member; Asian Indian Women of America, founder, treasurer, 1981-; Association of Indians in America, life member; Global Organization of People of Indian Origin, chairperson, cultural committee, first global convention, NYC, 1989; NYC Police Commissioner's Asian American Advisory Council, member, board of directors, Indian Cultural Center of NY, 1974-80. **SPECIAL ACHIEVEMENTS:** Contributed articles to professional journals; indexed books, eg, Bowen, W G, In Pursuit of PhD, Princeton, 1992; acted in an advisory capacity for some publications; speak, read and write English, Hindi, Sindhi; understand Bengali.

MOTILALL, MAKESHWAR FIP
Entrepreneur, chemical engineer. Indo-American. **PERSONAL:** Born Nov 2, 1961, Coretyne, Guyana; son of Motilall and Brijrani; married Irene, Feb 1, 1986 (deceased); children: Anastasia Kay, Stephanie Holly, Lorissa Renea. **EDUCATION:** Minneapolis Community College, AA, 1981; University of Minnesota, BSChE, 1983. **CAREER:** Hotel Seville, night mgr, 1981-83; Osmonics Inc, ultrapure water specialist, 1983-85, Osmonics Asia Pacific, managing dir, 1985-88; Aqua Media Intl, managing dir, 1986-88; Lazers H2O Inc, president, chief exec officer, 1988-. **ORGANIZATIONS:** American Electroplaters & Surface Finishers; American Society of Plumbing Engineers; Minnesota Hindu Dharmic Sabah. **BUSINESS ADDRESS:** President, Lazers H2O Inc, 3506 Bloomington Ave S, Minneapolis, MN 55407, (612)721-3874.

MOUDGIL, BRIJ MOHAN
Educator. Indo-American. **PERSONAL:** Born Aug 4, 1945, Pataudi, Haryana, India; son of Devki Nandan Moudgil (deceased) and Bhagawati Devi Moudgil (deceased); married Sheela Moudgil, Oct 1, 1973; children: Suniti, Sarika, Bharat. **EDUCATION:** Panjab University, BS, 1965; Indian Institute of Science, BE, 1968; Columbia University, MS, 1972, Eng ScD, 1981. **CAREER:** Occidental Research Co, research eng, 1976-78; Columbia University, research assistant, 1978-81; University of Florida, research engineer, 1973-76, professor & director, 1981-. **ORGANIZATIONS:** Society for Mining, Metallurgy and Exploration, Mineral Metallurgical Processing Division, chairman; American Ceramic Society; American Institute of Chemical Engineers; American Chemical Society; American Filtration Society; Sigma Xi. **HONORS/AWARDS:** NSF, US Presidential Young Investigator Award, 1984; Columbia University, Outstanding Graduate Studen Award, 1972; Hindustan Steel Ltd, Best Engineer Award, 1969. **SPECIAL ACHIEVEMENTS:** More than 120 technical publications; edited 5 books; 10 patents. **BUSINESS ADDRESS:** Professor, Dept of Materials Science & Eng, University of Florida, 161 Rhines Hall, Gainesville, FL 32611, (904)392-6670.

MOUDGIL, VIRINDER K.
Educator, research scientist. Indo-American. **PERSONAL:** Born in Ludhiana, Punjab, India; son of Shri Harbhagwan Moudgil and Shrimati Lajwanti Devi Moudgil; married Parviz G Moudgil; children: Sapna, Rishi. **EDUCATION:** Panjab University, India, BSc, 1967; Banaras Hindu University, India, MSc, 1969, PhD, 1972; Mayo Clinic, postdoctoral fellowship, 1973-76. **CAREER:** Oakland University, assistant professor, 1976-82, associate professor, 1982-87, professor, 1987-; Wayne State University, adj professor, 1989-. **ORGANIZA-**

TIONS: American Physiological Society; The Endocrine Society; American Association for Advancement of Science; American Society for Cell Biologists; American Association for University Professors; Sigma Xi; American Society for Biochemistry and Molecular Biology; Indian Society for the Study of Reproduction and Fertility, life member. **HONORS/AWARDS:** Mariam Wilson Award, 1986; National Institutes of Health, Physiological Sciences Study Section, 1988-92, 1993-96; Review Reserve of National Institutes of Health, 1992-93; Meadow Brook Conferences on Hormone Action, Scientific Committee, chairman. **SPECIAL ACHIEVEMENTS:** United Nations Consultant; editor of five books on hormone action; series editor, monographs on hormones in Health and Disease; speaker at several national and international scientific conferences; Journal of Experimental Endocrimology, editorial board; chaired numerous scientific sessions at national and international conferences. **BUSINESS ADDRESS:** Professor of Biological Sciences, Oakland University, Rochester, MI 48309-4401, (313)370-3553.

MOW, BILL
Fashion industry executive. Chinese American. **PERSONAL:** Born 1936, Hangchow, China. **EDUCATION:** Rensselaer Polytechnic Institute; Brooklyn Polytechnic, MS, 1961; Purdue University, PhD, 1967. **CAREER:** Brooklyn Polytechnic, Microwave Dept, research associate, 1961-63; Honeywell, Data Processing Division, senior logic engineer, 1963; Litton, Guidance and Control Division, program manager, 1967; Macrodata, co-founder, 1968; Dragon International, founder; Buckaroo International, founder; Bugle Boy Industries, founder, chairman, currently. **BUSINESS ADDRESS:** Chairman, Bugle Boy Industries, 2900 Madera Rd, Simi Valley, CA 93065, (805)582-1010.*

MOW, CHAO-CHOW
Development company executive. Chinese American. **PERSONAL:** Born Apr 28, 1930, NanKing, China; son of Mr & Mrs Pang-Tsu Mow; married Constance Mow, Jun 26, 1954; children: Barnum, Jacqueline, Bettina, Peter. **EDUCATION:** Rensselaer Polytechnic Institute, BME, 1953, MS, 1956, PhD, 1959. **CAREER:** Rensselaer Polytechnic Institute, instructor, 1953-59; The Mitre Corp, sub department head, 1960-63; The Rand Corp, director advance technology, 1963-78; Century West Development Inc, founder, CEO, COB, 1979-. **ORGANIZATIONS:** ASME, 1960-; Chinatown Service Center, board member, 1987-90; Center for Partially Sighted, board member, 1989-; Senior Peer Health Council, board member, 1985-88; Project Discuss Thrower, technical director. **HONORS/AWARDS:** Pi Tau Sigma, ASME honor society, 1953; Sigma Xi, Science Award, 1956; Phi Tau Phi, Chinese Science Society; Asian Business League, Asian Business Man of the Year, 1990. **SPECIAL ACHIEVEMENTS:** Development of more than 200 projects; extensive publications in Journal of Applied Mechanic Applied Physics; book: Stress Ware Propagation & Dynamic Stress Concentration. **HOME ADDRESS:** 20541 Rocachica Dr, Malibu, CA 90265. **BUSINESS PHONE:** (310)458-1631.

MOY, DONALD
Market development manager. Chinese American. **PERSONAL:** Born Aug 20, 1955, Hinsdale, IL; son of William C Moy and Beck Jan Moy; married Susan Moy, May 19, 1984; children: Stephen William. **EDUCATION:** Northern Illinois University, BS, finance, 1977. **CAREER:** Giesche's Shoe Store, stockperson, sales associate, 1971-77; Metropolitan Life, sales associate, 1977-78; Hinsdale-Oak Brook Associates, sale associate, mgr, 1978-82; Safeco Insurance Co, claims rep, marketing rep, 1982-87; Hanover Insurance Co, market development manager, 1987-. **ORGANIZATIONS:** Society of Certified Insurance Counselors, CIC, 1990-; Life Insurance Training Council, LUTC, 1977-; Phi Beta Lambda, Illinois state treasurer, 1976-77, local treasurer, 1975-76; United States Volleyball Assn, mbr, coach, 1991-; Amateur Athletic Union, mbr, coach, 1992-. **HOME ADDRESS:** PO Box 28, Downers Grove, IL 60515. **BUSINESS ADDRESS:** Market Development Manager, Hanover Insurance Company, 333 Pierce Rd, Ste 400, Itasca, IL 60143, (708)773-4266.

MOY, EDMUND
Law firm adviser. Chinese American. **PERSONAL:** Born Sep 12, 1957; married Karen Johnson, 1982. **EDUCATION:** University of Wisconsin, BA, economics, political science, international relations, 1979. **CAREER:** Office of Health Care Information, board member; Wisconsin Equal Rights Council, vice chairman; Blue Cross/Blue Shield United of Wisconsin, various sales and management positions, 1979-89; state of Wisconsin, adviser to secretary of health and human resources; Office of Managed Health Care Policy, head; Health Care Financing Administration, Medicare/Medicaid, overseas, senior executive; federal office of HMOs, director; Welsh, Carson, Anderson and

Stowe, private equity capital firm, adviser, 1993-. **ORGANIZATIONS:** Inter-Varsity Christian Fellowship, advisory council; National Managed Health Care Congress, advisory board; Volunteer Center of Greater Milwaukee, board; Tau Kappa Epsilon Fraternity, adviser. **BUSINESS ADDRESS:** 218 11th St, NE, Washington, DC 20002.*

MOY, GEORGE S.
Social worker. Chinese American. **PERSONAL:** Born Feb 1, 1939, New York, NY; son of Henry Moy and Ruth Pong Moy; married Gloria Moy, Sep 1, 1962; children: Kathy, Gregory. **EDUCATION:** New York Institute of Finance, 1960; Valparaiso University, 1958-59; Wagner College, BA, 1964. **CAREER:** Waukesha County Human Services, dispositional worker, juvenile probation officer, 1969-. **ORGANIZATIONS:** Wisconsin Juvenile Assn, 1975-; Chinese American Civic Club, 1986-; Wauwatosa Jaycees, director, 1969-71. **HONORS/AWARDS:** US National Jaycees, 2nd Place Mental Health Award, Community Service, 1971; Waukesha County Board, 25 Years of Dedicated Service Award, 1993. **BUSINESS ADDRESS:** Dispositional Worker/Juvenile Probation Officer, Waukesha County Human Services, 500 Riverview St, Waukesha, WI 53186.

MOY, HENRY
Museum director, educator. Chinese American. **PERSONAL:** Born Dec 8, 1955, Chicago, IL; son of Fook S Moy and Jennie S Moy (deceased). **EDUCATION:** University of Chicago, 1973-75; Beloit College, BA, 1977, MAT, 1978. **CAREER:** Jade by Chang Inc, assistant to president, 1978; University of Alabama, field archaeologist, 1979; State Historical Society of Wisconsin, archaeologist, 1979; Illinois State University, archaeological technician, 1979-80; Lakeview Museum, curator of collections, exhibitions, 1981-84; Beloit College, director of museums, Museum Studies Program, chair, 1985-. **ORGANIZATIONS:** Wisconsin Federation of Museums, president, 1988-; American Association of Museums, Committee on Museum Professional Training, board member, 1992-; Midwest Museums Conference, 1984-; Art League of Beloit, board member, 1986-, vice president, 1991-. **HONORS/AWARDS:** Beloit College, Von-Eschen Steele Award, 1993. **SPECIAL ACHIEVEMENTS:** Author of several papers, including "The Northern and Southern Schools of Chinese Painting," 1991; "Chinese Calligraphy and Painting: Contexts for the Work of Wang Lan Ruo," 1991; leader of several archaeological expeditions. **BUSINESS ADDRESS:** Director of Museums, Beloit College, 700 College St, Beloit, WI 53511.

MOY, JAMES S.
Educator. Chinese American. **PERSONAL:** Born Sep 12, 1948, Chicago, IL; son of Robert Fook Shew Moy & Ann Ngan Kwan Chin; married Penelope M Leavitt-Moy, Mar 4, 1978; children: Jennifer Leavitt-Moy. **EDUCATION:** University of Illinois, Chicago, AB, 1971, AM, 1973, Urbana, PhD, 1977. **CAREER:** University of Texas, Austin, instructor, 1977-79; University of Oregon, assistant professor, 1979-81; University of Wisconsin, associate professor, 1981-93, professor, 1994-. **ORGANIZATIONS:** Asian American Studies Association; American Society for Theatre Research; Association for Theatre in Higher Education. **SPECIAL ACHIEVEMENTS:** Marginal Sights: Staging the Chinese in America, University of Iowa Press, 1993; editor, Theatre Journal, Johns Hopkins University Press, 1982-85; numerous articles published in: Theatre Survey, High Performance, Theatre Quarterly, Theatre Research International, Themes in Drama, etc. **BUSINESS ADDRESS:** Professor, Dept of Theatre & Drama, University of Wisconsin, Madison, 821 University Ave, 6010 Vilas Hall, Madison, WI 53706, (608)263-3357.

MOY, JAMES YEE KIN
Cleric, church administrator. Hong Kong American. **PERSONAL:** Born Mar 15, 1934, New York, NY; son of Ruth Pong and Henry Moy; married Mabel Lai Ying Chin, Dec 21, 1957; children: James Blanchard, Thomas Michael. **EDUCATION:** Valparaiso University, BA, 1956; Lutheran Seminary, MDiv, 1960; Columbia University, MA, 1963; Ohio University, PhD, 1972. **CAREER:** Christ Lutheran Church, 1960-63; Macalester College, dean of men, 1963-66; Ohio University, director, West Green, 1967-69; Saint Paul Lutheran Church, pastor, 1969-71; Wartburg College, dean of students, 1971-76; Lutheran Community Service, executive director, 1977-83; Pacific NW Synod, LCA, assistant to bishop, 1984-87; Evangelical Lutheran Church in America, Leadership Dev, director, 1988-. **ORGANIZATIONS:** Columbia County Council of Churches, NY, vice president, 1963-63; Upper Hudson Area, New York State Council of Churches, chair, 1962-63; PTA, New Haven Elementary School, West Virginia, president, 1970-71; New Haven Parks & Recreation Commission, chair, 1970-71; Asian Caucas, Lutheran Church in America,

chair, 1982; American Personnel & Guidance Association; National Association Student Personnel Administrators. **HONORS/AWARDS:** Valparaiso University, Alumni Achievement Award, 1989; United Way, Community Service Award, 1981; Lutheran Social Services Award, 1983. **SPECIAL ACHIEVEMENTS:** Published doctoral dissertation in Journal of Experimental Education, winter 1972, "Leadership Behavior and Management Systems within a University's Residence Life System"; certified scuba diver; language proficiency: Greek, German, Spanish; certified master gardener. **MILITARY SERVICE:** US Navy, lt, 1969-72. **HOME ADDRESS:** 1252 Beechwood Ct, Schaumburg, IL 60193, (708)529-9309.

MOY, JEFFERY FEI
Retail executive. Chinese American. **PERSONAL:** Born Nov 29, 1962, Boston, MA; son of Ning Moy and Kwai Fung Moy; married M Margaret, May 2, 1992. **EDUCATION:** Boston University, BS, 1984; Massachusetts Institute of Technology, MBA, 1986. **CAREER:** Venture Resources, associate, 1986-87; Massachusetts Industrial Finance Agency, associate, 1987-89; Matuscha Venture Partners, associate, 1989-91; Keystone Mutual Funds, international equity analyst, 1991-92; Staples Inc, international joint ventures, 1992-. **ORGANIZATIONS:** Algonquin Club of Boston, marketing & entertainment committee, 1991-; Alumni Consulting Team, 1993-. **SPECIAL ACHIEVEMENTS:** Speaks Chinese and German. **HOME ADDRESS:** 25 Woodward Ave, Quincy, MA 02169.

MOY, MAMIE WONG
Educator. Chinese American. **PERSONAL:** Born Sep 4, 1929, San Antonio, TX; daughter of Tai Hay Wong and Chin Shee Wong; married Edward Yue-Quon Moy, Jul 6, 1958 (deceased); children: Clifford Keith. **EDUCATION:** University of Texas, Austin, BA, 1950; University of Houston, MSc, 1952. **CAREER:** University of Houston, professor, 1952-. **ORGANIZATIONS:** American Chemical Society, Minority Affairs Committee, 1993-, Membership Affairs Committee, 1990-, Southeastern Texas Section, councilor, 1981-, chair, 1983-; American Association Advancement of Science; Iota Sigma Pi, 1950-; Alpha Chi Sigma, 1975; Institute of Chinese Culture, Houston chair, board of trustees. **HONORS/AWARDS:** University of Houston, Teaching Excellence Award, 1977; American Chemical Society, Southeastern Texas Section, Southeastern Texas Section Award, 1988; Phi Kappa Phi. **BUSINESS ADDRESS:** Professor, Dept of Chemistry, University of Houston, Houston, TX 77204-5502, (713)743-2720.

MOY, NAOMI OGAWA
Librarian, educator. Japanese American. **PERSONAL:** Born Jun 19, 1949, Los Angeles, CA; daughter of Tatsuo Ogawa and Sadako June Ogawa; married Terrence C Moy, Aug 23, 1975; children: Ryan H. **EDUCATION:** University of Southern California, BA, 1971, MSLS, 1972, MA, 1977. **CAREER:** California State University, Dominguez Hills, reference librarian/professor of the library, 1972-. **ORGANIZATIONS:** American Library Association; California Academic & Research Libraries; California Clearinghouse on Library Instruction; California Faculty Association, librarian and library affairs committee; Chinese American Librarians Association; Southern California Association of Law Libraries. **HONORS/AWARDS:** Phi Beta Kappa, 1971; Phi Kappa Phi, 1971; Beta Phi Mu, 1973. **SPECIAL ACHIEVEMENTS:** Author, "American Minority Cultures: Asian-Pacific," Good Reading, 1985, 1990. **BUSINESS ADDRESS:** Reference Librarian & Professor, California State University-Dominguez Hills, 800 E Victoria St, Carson, CA 90747, (310)516-3718.

MOY, ROBERT CARL
Educator. Chinese American. **PERSONAL:** Born Jan 19, 1958, Minneapolis, MN; married. **EDUCATION:** University of Minnesota, BME, 1978; George Washington University, JD, 1983. **CAREER:** United States Court of Appeals, Federal Circuit, judicial law clerk, 1983-85; Max Plank Institute or Comparative Law, guest researcher, 1985-86; Merchant, Gold, Smith, Edell, PA, associate atty, 1986-91; William Mitchell College of Law, assistant professor, 1991-. **ORGANIZATIONS:** ABA, Intell Prop Section, 1991-, committee on patent legislation, chair, 1993-94; American Intellectual Prop Law Association, 1986-. **HONORS/AWARDS:** Order of the Coif, 1983. **SPECIAL ACHIEVEMENTS:** Numerous legal publications. **BUSINESS ADDRESS:** Assistant Professor, William Mitchell College of Law, 875 Summit Ave, Saint Paul, MN 55105.

MOY, STAN YIP
Architect. Chinese American. **PERSONAL:** Born Sep 15, 1948, Brooklyn, NY; son of Heung Shun Yip and How Gin Lee; married Pauline Moy, Jun 29, 1969; children: Christopher Yip, Meredith Yip. **EDUCATION:** CCNY, BArch, 1972. **CAREER:** Shreve Lamb Harmon, junior designer, 1972-73; F P Wiedersum Associates, designer, 1973-75; Board of Ed, NYC, assistant arch, 1975-77; Bank Bldg Corp, architect, 1977-78; Reel Grobman, senior associate, 1978-81; Finger & Moy, founder, president, 1981-. **ORGANIZATIONS:** Private Industry Council, SF, 1986-; SF Port Planning Committee, 1991-94; SF Rent Board, 1983-85; NCPC, 1992-93; CAABA, 1983-93; AAA/E, 1981-93; SF State Office Building, JPA, 1993-97. **SPECIAL ACHIEVEMENTS:** Design of BART, W Pittsburgh Station, 1993; design of Pullman Way Maintenance Facility, 1993. **BUSINESS ADDRESS:** President, Finger & Moy Architects, 231 Sansome Street, San Francisco, CA 94104, (415)956-5211.

MUDUNDI, RAMAKRISHNA RAJU
Radiation oncology researcher. Indo-American. **PERSONAL:** Born Jul 15, 1931, Pedamiram, Andhra Pradesh, India; son of Narashimha Raju Mudundi & Suramma; married Subhadra Devi Raju Mudundi. **EDUCATION:** Presidency College; Madras University; Andhra University; MIT, PhD. **CAREER:** Massachusetts General Hospital, fellow; Lawrence Radiation Lab, fellow; Los Alamos National Lab, fellow, currently. **BUSINESS ADDRESS:** Fellow, Los Alamos National Lab, Life Sciences, Los Alamos, NM 87544.

MUI, CONSTANCE L.
Educator. Chinese American. **PERSONAL:** Born Jun 20, 1959, Hong Kong; daughter of Lun Moy and Kit Fong Chung. **EDUCATION:** Loyola University of Chicago, BA, philosophy, 1982; BS, sociology, 1982; Brown University, MA, philosophy, 1984, PhD, philosophy, 1987. **CAREER:** Loyola University, New Orleans, associate professor of philosophy, currently. **ORGANIZATIONS:** Society of Women in Philosophy, 1985-; Sartre Society, central div executive committee, 1992-; American Phil Association, 1982-; Southern Society of Philosophy and Psychology, 1987-; Southwest Philosophical Society, 1989-; Louisiana Women's Studies Consortium, 1987-; National Women's Studies Association Journal, referee, 1988-. **HONORS/AWARDS:** Mellon Foundation, Award for Outstanding Achievement, 1982, first prize position paper, 1982; Midwest Sociological Society, first prize undergraduate paper, 1981; Brown University, teaching assistantships & fellowships, 1982-87. **SPECIAL ACHIEVEMENTS:** Author, "Sartre's Sexism Reconsidered," *Auslegung,* 1989; "Against Cartesian Dualism," *Southwest Phil Review,* 1991; "On The Empirical Status of Radical Feminism," *Journal of Applied Phil,* 1991; book reviews in: *Canadian Philosophical Review* & *National Women's Studies Association Journal.* **BUSINESS ADDRESS:** Professor, Dept of Philosophy, Loyola University, 6363 St Charles Ave, New Orleans, LA 70118-6195, (504)865-3050.

MUKAI, FRANCIS KEN
Attorney. Japanese American. **PERSONAL:** Born Aug 21, 1956, San Francisco, CA; son of Akira Mukai and Amy Mukai; married Phyllis Mukai, Aug 4, 1984; children: Susan. **EDUCATION:** California Institute of Technology, BS (with honors), engineering & applied science, 1978; Harvard Law School, JD, 1984. **CAREER:** Packard Electric, applications engineer, 1978-79; State of Hawaii Supreme Court, law clerk to Hon Justice Hayashi, 1985-86; Damon Key Char & Bocken, associate, 1986-90; Alexander & Baldwin, Inc, senior counsel, 1990-92, assistant general counsel, 1992-. **ORGANIZATIONS:** Hawaii Chamber of Commerce, 1991-; American Bar Association, 1984-; Hawaii State Bar Association, 1984-. **BUSINESS ADDRESS:** Assistant General Counsel, Alexander & Baldwin Inc, 822 Bishop St, Honolulu, HI 96813, (808)525-6620.

MUKAI, HIROAKI
Educator, educational administrator. Japanese American. **PERSONAL:** Born in Tochigui, Japan. **EDUCATION:** Waseda University, Tokyo, BEEE, 1969; University of California, Berkeley, MS, 1971, PhD, 1974. **CAREER:** University of California, Berkeley, assistant research engineer, 1975, visiting associate professor, 1982; Washington University, professor, 1975-, Master of Control Engineering, director, 1989-, SSM Undergraduate Program, director, 1993-. **ORGANIZATIONS:** IEEE, senior member, various positions, 1979-; Sigma Xi, 1977-80; Mathematical Programming Society; American Control Council, newsletter editor, 1982-87. **HONORS/AWARDS:** Engineering Students at Washington University, Professor of the Year, 1990, 1991; University of California, graduate fellowship, 1971, 1972; Waseda University, fellowship, 1969. **SPECIAL ACHIEVEMENTS:** Over 50 research publications, 1970-.

BUSINESS ADDRESS: Professor, Dept of Systems Science and Mathematics, Washington University, Campus Box 1040, St Louis, MO 63130, (314)935-6064.

MUKAI, ROBERT L.
Attorney, state official. Japanese American. **PERSONAL:** Born Nov 4, 1945, Detroit, MI; son of Cromwell D Mukai and Kyoko Hoshiga Mukai; divorced; children: Stephan. **EDUCATION:** University of California, Berkeley, BA, 1966; University of California, Davis, JD, 1972. **CAREER:** California Atty General, deputy attorney general, 1972-90, chief assistant attorney general, 1991-. **ORGANIZATIONS:** California State Bar, 1972-; Asian Bar Association of Sacramento. **BUSINESS ADDRESS:** Chief Assistant Attorney General, Civil Law Division, California Attorney General's Office, 1515 K St, Sacramento, CA 95814.

MUKAI, YOSHIKO
Government official. Japanese American. **PERSONAL:** Born Nov 7, 1941, Los Angeles, CA; daughter of Yoshio & Tomiko Mukai. **EDUCATION:** Pepperdine University, BS, 1978, MBA, 1980; USC, Seaport Management, certificate, 1980-81; UCLA, Extension-Engineering Management for Construction, certificate, 1984-85. **CAREER:** City of Los Angeles, Harbor Department, director of port construction and maintenance II, 1992-. **ORGANIZATIONS:** Los Angeles City Employee Association, vice chair, 1991-; Society of Port Engineers, 1990-; Japanese American National Museum, charter member, 1991-. **HONORS/AWARDS:** City of Los Angeles, Mayor's Office & Commission on the State of Women, Women of Achievement in a Non-Traditional Area Certificate, 1990. **BUSINESS ADDRESS:** Director, Port Construction & Maintenance, Los Angeles Harbor Department, Construction & Maintenance Div, Berth 161, Wilmington, CA 90744, (310)732-3555.

MUKERJEE, PASUPATI
Educator. Indo-American. **PERSONAL:** Born Feb 13, 1932, Calcutta, India; son of Nani Gopal Mukerjee and Provabati Mukerjee; married Lalita Mukerjee, Feb 29, 1964. **EDUCATION:** University of Calcutta, BSc, 1949, MSc, 1951; University of Southern California, PhD, 1957. **CAREER:** University of Southern California, research asst, 1953-36, lecturer, 1956-57, sr scientist, 1964-66; Brookhaven National Laboratory, research assoc, 1957-59; Indian Assn for the Cultivation of Science, reader, 1959-64; University of Wisconsin, professor, 1966-. **ORGANIZATIONS:** American Chemical Society, 1955-; Sigma Xi, 1955-; American Assn for the Advancement of Science, fellow, 1967-; American Institute of Chemists, Fellow, 1979-; Academy of Pharmaceutical Sciences, Fellow, 1985-; Intl Union of Pure and Applied Chemistry, assoc mbr of commission, 1975-83. **HONORS/AWARDS:** University of Oklahoma, J Clarence Karcher Lecturer, 1983; US Dept of Agriculture, Distinguished Lecturer, 1973; numerous invited lectures, presented nationally and internationally, 1959-. **SPECIAL ACHIEVEMENTS:** Author of 80 research articles, 1955-; research monograph, 1971. **BUSINESS ADDRESS:** Professor, University of Wisconsin, School of Pharmacy, 425 N Charter St, Madison, WI 53706, (608)262-7289.

MUKHERJEA, ARUNAVA
Educator. Indo-American. **PERSONAL:** Born Aug 14, 1941, Calcutta, W. Bengal, India; married Swapna Mukherjea, Aug 10, 1971; children: Ananya. **EDUCATION:** Wayne State University, PhD, 1967. **CAREER:** University of South Florida, professor, mathematics, 1969-. **ORGANIZATIONS:** American Mathematics Society; American Statistical Assn. **SPECIAL ACHIEVEMENTS:** Co-author: *Real and Functional Analysis,* vols I & II, 1st & 2nd ed, Plenum Publishing Co, *Measures on Topological Semigroups (Convolution Products and Random Walks),* Springer-Verlag, 1976; editor-in-chief: *Journal of Theoretical Probability,* Plenum Publishing Co. **BUSINESS ADDRESS:** Professor, Mathematics, University of South Florida, 4202 E Fowler Ave, Physics 327, Tampa, FL 33620-5700, (813)974-2664.

MUKHERJEE, BHARATI
Educator, author. Indo-American. **PERSONAL:** Born Jul 27, 1940, Calcutta, India; daughter of Sudhir Lal and Bina Banerjee Mukherjee; married Clark L Blaise, Sep 19, 1963; children: Bart Anand, Bernard Sudhir. **EDUCATION:** University of Calcutta, BA, 1959; Univ of Baroda, India, MA, 1961; University of Iowa, MFA, 1963, PhD, 1969. **CAREER:** McGill University, assistant professor, English, 1969-73, associate professor, 1973-78, professor, 1978-80; University of Iowa, visiting professor, 1979, 1982; Skidmore College, English, visiting professor, 1979-80, 1981-82; Emory University, visiting professor, 1983; Montclair State College, associate professor, 1984-87; CUNY, professor,

1987-89; University of California, Berkeley, professor, currently. **ORGANI-ZATIONS:** PEN. **HONORS/AWARDS:** National Book Critics Circle Award, for The Middleman, 1989; National Endowment for the Arts, 1986; Can Council of India, 1976; Guggenheim fellow, 1978. **SPECIAL ACHIEVE-MENTS:** Author: Jasmine, 1989; The Middleman, 1988; Darkness, 1985; Kautilya's Concept of Diplomacy, 1976; Wife, 1975; Tiger's Daughter, 1972; coauthor: The Sorrow and the Terror, 1988; Days and Nights in Calcutta, 1977, film script, 1989. **BUSINESS ADDRESS:** Professor, Dept of English, University of California, Berkeley, Berkeley, CA 94720, (510)642-3467.*

MUKHERJEE, TAPAN KUMAR
Government official. Indo-American. **PERSONAL:** Born Jan 5, 1929, Gorakhpur, Uttar Pradesh, India; married Gouri Mukherjee, Apr 6, 1957; children: Shamoli, Dipali. **EDUCATION:** Patna University, Patna, India, BSc, 1948, MSc, 1950 DSc, 1974; Wayne State University, PhD, 1956. **CAREER:** US Airforce Cambridge Research Lab, research scientist, 1962-74; National Science Foundation, program director, 1974-. **BUSINESS ADDRESS:** Program Director, National Science Foundation, 4201 Wilson Blvd, Arlington, VA 22230.

MUKHOPADHYAY, NIMAI C.
Educator. Indo-American. **PERSONAL:** Born Jan 17, 1942, Maharampur, W. Bengal, India; son of Ram C Mukhopadhyay and Ava Mukhopadhyay; married; children: Dipali, Piali. **EDUCATION:** University of Calcutta, India, BSc, (honors), 1963, MSc, 1965; University of Chicago, SM, 1970, PhD, 1972. **CAREER:** University of Maryland, CTP fellow, 1972-74; Cern, Geneva, Switzerland, visiting scientist, 1974-75; Swiss Inst for Nucl Res, physicist, 1975-80; Swiss Fed Reactor Res Inst, scientist, 1980-81; University of Virginia, visiting professor, 1988-89; Rensselaer Poly Inst, associate professor, 1981-86, professor, 1986-. **ORGANIZATIONS:** American Phys Society, 1981-92, fellow, 1992-; Sigma Xi, 1972; Hindu Temple Society, board of trustess, vice chair, 1993; College of Saint Rose, Interfaith Dialogue Com, 1992-;. **HONORS/AWARDS:** American Phys Society, fellowship, 1992; US Educational Foundation in India, Fulbright Grant, 1968. **SPECIAL ACHIEVEMENTS:** Author of one hundred professional papers, articles in books, 1968-. **BUSINESS ADDRESS:** Professor, Dept of Physics, Rensselaer Polytechnic Institute, Troy, NY 12180-3590, (518)276-6663.

MUNAKATA, GRACE MEGUMI
Artist, educator. Japanese American. **PERSONAL:** Born May 20, 1957, Monterey, CA; daughter of Yutaka & Martha Munakata; married Michael Tompkins, Aug 11, 1985. **EDUCATION:** University of California, Davis, BA, 1980; Skowhegan School of Painting & Sculpture, 1984; University of California, Davis, MFA, studio art, 1985. **CAREER:** Sierra College, lecturer, 1986; California State University, Hayward, assistant professor, 1987-; numerous exhibitions, including: "Small Things Come.," Braunstein/Quay Gallery, San Francisco, 1994; "North by Northeast," Richmond Art Center, CA, 1994; "Yellow Forest," SOMAR, San Francisco, 1994; "Landscapes & Still Lifes of the Sacramento Valley School," John Natsoulas Gallery, Davis, 1994; upcoming solo exhibit, Braunstein/Quay Gallery, San Francisco, 1994. **ORGANIZATIONS:** Phi Beta Kappa, Davis Chapter, 1980; Asian America Council, 1991-; Asian American Women's Art Association, 1994; Regional Center for the Arts, Bedford Gallery, advisory council, 1994. **HONORS/AWARDS:** California State University, Faculty Development Grant, 1991; University of California, Regents Fellowship, 1984, Teaching Award, 1985; University of California, Davis, Andy Warhol Scholarship, 1984. **BIOGRAPHICAL SOURCES:** "Strait Reflections," Diablo Arts Magazine, p18, May 1992; "Painters Attack Images. . .," San Francisco Chronicle, September 1, 1989; "Flatlanders: Sacramento Valley School," Artweek, 1994. **BUSINESS ADDRESS:** Assistant Professor, Art Dept, California State University, Hayward, Hayward, CA 94542, (510)881-3111.

MUNI, INDU A.
Biotechnology company executive. Indo-American. **PERSONAL:** Born Oct 24, 1942, Amereli, Gujarat, India; son of Atmaram Muni and Sarswaty Muni; married Gita, Jan 16, 1969; children: Neal, Sheel. **EDUCATION:** Nagpur University, India, BS, 1964; North Dakota State University, MS, 1966; University of Mississippi, PhD, 1969. **CAREER:** Bioassay Systems, executive vice president, 1981-85; DynaGen Inc, president, CEO, co-founder, 1988-. **ORGANIZATIONS:** AACC; ASM; Rho Chi; SOT. **BUSINESS ADDRESS:** President, CEO, DynaGen Inc, 99 Erie St, Cambridge, MA 02139, (617)491-2527.

MUNROE, TAPAN
Economist. Indo-American. **EDUCATION:** University of Allahabad, BS, physics, mathematics; University of New Hampshire, MA, economics; University of Colorado, PhD, economics. **CAREER:** MIT, Civil Engineering Department, visiting scholar; University of California Berkeley, Urban Studies & Regional Planning, adjunct professor; University of Pacific, Stockton, Department of Economics, former chairperson; Pacific Gas & Electric, chief economist, currently. **HONORS/AWARDS:** Pacific Rim Gala and Asian Pacific Leadership Awards, honoree, 1993. **BUSINESS ADDRESS:** Chief Economist, Pacific Gas & Electric Co, 245 Market St, San Francisco, CA 94105, (415)781-4211.*

MURA, DAVID
Author, arts administrator. Japanese American. **PERSONAL:** Born Jun 17, 1952, Great Lakes, IL; son of Tom K and Tesuko Mura; married Susan Sencer, Jun 18, 1983; children: Samantha Lyn. **EDUCATION:** Grinnell College, BA (honors), 1974; University of Minnesota-Twin Cities, graduate study, English, 1974-79; Vermont College, MFA, 1991. **CAREER:** COMPAS Writers-and-Artists-in-the-Schools, creative writing instructor, 1979-85, assoc director of literature program, 1982-84; The Loft, core faculty member, instructor in poetry & creative nonfiction, 1984-, board of directors, 1982-84, president, 1987-88, vp, 1988-89, Long Range Planning Committee head, 1982-84; St Olaf College, instructor, 1990-91; University of Oregon, visiting professor, 1991; Asian American Renaissance Conference, board of directors/development artistic director, 1991-. **ORGANIZATIONS:** Center for Arts Criticism, board of directors, 1990-, pres, 1991-92, vp, 1992-93; Jerome Foundation, board of directors, 1991-. **HONORS/AWARDS:** Minnesota State Arts Board, grant and fellowship, 1991; American Academy of Poets, Fanny Fay Wood Memorial Prize, 1977; Bush Foundation Fellowship, 1981; National Endowment for the Arts Literature Fellowship, 1985; New York Times Notable Book of the Year, for Turning Japanese, 1991; Loft McKnight Award of Distinction for poetry, 1992; numerous others. **SPECIAL ACHIEVEMENTS:** Works include: A Male Grief: Notes on Pornography & Addiction, 1987; After We Lost Our Way, poems, 1989; Turning Japanese, 1991; Listening; works represented in anthologies: Men & Intimacy: Personal Accounts Exploring the Dilemmas of Modern Male Sexuality; Breaking Silence: An Anthology of Contemporary Asian-American Poets, 1983; The Open Boat: An Asian American Poetry Anthology; contributor of poems & articles to Nation, New Republic, River Styx, New England Review, Quarry, American Poetry Review. **BUSINESS ADDRESS:** Author, c/o Amanda Urban, International Creative Mgmt, 40 W 57th St, New York, NY 10019.*

MURA, TOSHIO
Educator. Japanese American. **PERSONAL:** Born Dec 7, 1925, Kanazawa, Ishikawa, Japan; married Sawa Mura, May 3, 1955; children: Miyako Izzo, Nanako K Wasniewski. **EDUCATION:** University of Tokyo, BE, 1949, PhD, 1954. **CAREER:** Meiji University, assistant professor, 1954-58; Northwestern University, research assistant, 1958-61, professor, 1966-. **ORGANIZATIONS:** National Academy of Engineering; ASME, fellow; American Academy of Mechanics, fellow. **HONORS/AWARDS:** Japan Institute of Metals, honorary member; JSME, MMD Award of Merit, 1992. **HOME ADDRESS:** 2727 Orchard, Wilmette, IL 60091, (708)251-8230. **BUSINESS ADDRESS:** Walter P Murphy Professor, Dept of Civil Engineering, Northwestern University, Evanston, IL 60208, (708)491-4003.

MURAD, SOHAIL
Educator. Pakistani American. **PERSONAL:** Born May 4, 1953, Rawalpindi, Punjab, Pakistan; son of Ruhafza Murad and Akram Murad; married Penny Newland Murad, Dec 15, 1979; children: Adam, Anita. **EDUCATION:** University of Engineering, Pakistan, BS, 1974; University of Florida, Gainesville, MS, 1976; Cornell University, PhD, 1979. **CAREER:** US Army Ballistic Research Laboratory, research fellow, summer 1985; Exxon Research & Engineering, senior engineer, 1981-82; University of Illinois, assistant professor, 1979-86, associate professor, 1986-91; University of Illinois, professor, 1991-. **ORGANIZATIONS:** American Institute of Chemical Engineers, 1976-; American Chemical Society, 1981-; American Philatelic Society, 1986-; American Airmail Society, 1988-. **HONORS/AWARDS:** National Science Foundation, research grants, 1981-; Department of Energy, research grants, 1987-; North Atlantic Treaty Organization, research grants, 1985-. **SPECIAL ACHIEVEMENTS:** Over 40 technical publications in scientific/engineering journals, 1977-. **BUSINESS ADDRESS:** Professor of Chemical Engineering, University of Illinois, Chicago, 810 S Clinton Ave, Chicago, IL 60607, (312)996-5593.

MURAI, NORIMOTO
Educator. Japanese American. **PERSONAL:** Born Mar 4, 1944, Sapporo, Hokkaido, Japan; son of Nobuo Murai and Hideko Murai; married Andreana Lisca; children: Naoki. **EDUCATION:** Hokkaido University, BS, 1966, MS, 1968; University of Wisconsin-Madison, PhD, 1973. **CAREER:** University of Wisconsin-Madison, postdoctoral fellow, 1974-82; National Institute of Agrobiological Resources, Tsukuba, Japan, lab chief, 1983-84; Louisiana State University, assoc prof, 1985-92, prof, 1992-. **ORGANIZATIONS:** American Assn for the Advancement of Science, 1985-; American Society of Plant Physiologists, 1968-; Intl Society for Plant Molecular Biology, 1987-; Molecular Biology Society of Japan, 1984-; Crop Science Society of America, 1992-. **HONORS/AWARDS:** Fulbright Travel Grant, 1968; Phi Delta Kappa, Honor Researchers, 1989; Sigma Xi, 1992; Gamma Sigma Delta, 1988; Louisiana Education Quality Support Fund, Research Grants, 1988, 1989, 1991; Monsanto Co, Research Grants, 1992, 1993. **SPECIAL ACHIEVEMENTS:** Author: "Phaseolin Gene from Bean is Expressed after Transfer to Sunflower Via Tumor-Inducing Plasmid Vectors," Science, 222, p 476-482, 1983; "Cytokinin Biosynthesis in tRNA and Cytokinin Incorporation into Plant RNA," CRC Press, 1993. **BUSINESS ADDRESS:** Professor, Dept of Plant Pathology and Crop Physiology, Louisiana State University, LSU Agricultural Center, Life Sciences Bldg, Rm 302, Baton Rouge, LA 70808, (504)388-1380.

MURAKAMI, JEFFREY HISAKAZU
Educational administrator. Japanese American. **PERSONAL:** Born Oct 3, 1962, Los Angeles, CA; son of Douglas & Ruth Murakami; married Christine Murakami, Jun 25, 1989; children: Leilani Grace. **EDUCATION:** University of Southern California, BA, 1986. **CAREER:** United Church of Christ, Commission for Racial Justice, project coordinator, 1985, Sycamore Congregational Church, Youth Ministries, director, 1985-89; University of Southern California, APASS, director, 1990-. **ORGANIZATIONS:** Aisarema, board of directors, 1991-; Lotus Festival, advisory committee, 1991, 1993; United Ministry, USC, board of directors, 1991-; United Church of Christ, Council for Racial & Ethnic Ministries, 1986-89. **BUSINESS ADDRESS:** Director, USC Asian American Student Services, Student Union 410, Los Angeles, CA 90089-0890, (213)740-4999.

MURAKAMI, PAMELA S.
Educator. Japanese American. **PERSONAL:** Born Feb 22, 1951, Ewa, HI; daughter of Masaye & Hanako Murakami; married Charles Alexander, Dec 7, 1974; children: Nicholas Alexander. **EDUCATION:** University of Hawaii, BFA (distinction), 1973; University of the Philippines, MFA, 1981. **CAREER:** Monterey Peninsula College, ceramic instructor, 1989-91; Hartnell College, ceramics instructor, 1986-. **ORGANIZATIONS:** Ikenobo Ikebana, 1983-; Urasenke School of Chanoyu, 1983-. **SPECIAL ACHIEVEMENTS:** Ceramics Monthly, "Japanese Aesthetics," 1987; Archipelago Magazine, "Philippine Artistic Genius," 1979. **BIOGRAPHICAL SOURCES:** Northern California House & Garden Magazine, p 17, February 1993. **HOME ADDRESS:** 2438 San Juan Rd, Watsonville, CA 95076, (408)726-3352.

MURAKAMI, RICHARD M.
Government official. Japanese American. **PERSONAL:** Born Jan 29, 1932, Florin, CA; son of Kazuo and Yomiko Murakami; divorced. **EDUCATION:** University of Southern California, BS, 1959. **CAREER:** Department of Corporations, chief examiner, financial services division, 1979-86, assistant commissioner, financial services division, 1986-91, health care service plan division, assistant commissioner, 1991-. **ORGANIZATIONS:** National Association of State Credit Union Supervisors, president, 1991-92, board member, 1987-91; Optimist Club, Uptown Los Angeles, president, 1969-70; Optimist Club, Bella Vista, secretary, 1988-89; Nisei Week Japanese Festival, board member, chairman, parade & queen comm, vice chairman, 1977-88. **HONORS/AWARDS:** Optimist Club, Uptown Los Angeles, Optimist of the Year, 1971-72; Pacific Southwest Optimist International, Optimist of the Year, Zone 2, 1973-74; Nisei Week Japanese Festival, Grand Marshal, 1992. **MILITARY SERVICE:** US Army, cpl, 1953-55. **BUSINESS ADDRESS:** Asst Commissioner, Dept of Corporations, Health Care Service Plan Div, 3700 Wilshire Blvd, Los Angeles, CA 90010, (213)736-2776.

MURASE, MIKE
Attorney. Japanese American. **PERSONAL:** Born Jan 25, 1947, Tsuyama, Okayama, Japan; son of Hide Murase & Mitsuko Murase; married June Hibino, Jul 1, 1983; children: Sachi. **EDUCATION:** UCLA, BA, 1970; USC Law Center, JD, 1974. **CAREER:** Cultural Awareness Program, executive director, 1980-82; Visual Communications, writer, producer, 1983-84; Legal Aid Foundation, staff attorney, 1985-87; Jesse Jackson for President, campaign manager, 1987-88; California Rainbow Coalition, executive director, 1984-85, 1988-90; Project Build, director of special projects, 1988-92; US House of Reps, attorney, congressional aide, 1992-. **ORGANIZATIONS:** California Democratic Party, executive committee, 1989-91; Democratic National Convention, floor leader, 1988; Little Tokyo Service Center, president, board of directors, 1979-91. **SPECIAL ACHIEVEMENTS:** Author, book, Little Tokyo: One Hundred Years in Pictures, 1983; City of Los Angeles, Building & Safety Commission, president, 1986-87. **HOME PHONE:** (213)382-2357.

MURATA, MARGARET K.
Educator. Japanese American. **PERSONAL:** Born Jul 29, 1946, Chicago, IL; daughter of Yoshinori Murata and Mikiko Hayashida. **EDUCATION:** University of Chicago, AB, 1967, AM, 1971, PhD, 1975. **CAREER:** University of California, Irvine, professor, 1973-. **ORGANIZATIONS:** American Musicological Society, 1967-; College Music Society, 1980-; International Musicological Society, 1980-; Societa Ital di Musicologia, 1973-. **HONORS/AWARDS:** AAUW, diss award, 1972; Alumni Association, University of California, Irvine, Distinguished Teaching, 1979. **BUSINESS ADDRESS:** Professor, Dept of Music, University of California, Irvine, Music, #292, Irvine, CA 92717-2775.

MURATA, YUJI
Educator. Japanese American. **PERSONAL:** Born Jun 15, 1942, Higashisumiyoshi-ku, Osaka, Japan. **EDUCATION:** Osaka University Medical School, MD, 1967; University of Southern California, Obstetrics & Gynecology, residency, 1968-71, internship, 1975-76. **CAREER:** University of California, Irvine College of Medicine, associate professor, 1974-86, professor, 1986-; Nihon University School of Medicine, professor, 1990-; Miyazaki Medical College, professor, 1992-. **ORGANIZATIONS:** California Perinatal Association; Society of Ob/Gyn of Osaka, Japan; American Institute of Ultrasound in Medicine; Association of Professors of Ob/Gyn; American College of Ob/Gyn, fellow; International Correspondence Society of Obstetricians and Gynecologists; Japan Society of Obstetrics and Gynecology; Japan Society of Ultrasonics in Medicine; March of Dimes; Society for Gynecological Investigation; Society of Perinatal Obstetricians. **HONORS/AWARDS:** Senior Ob/Gyn Resident Award for Outstanding Independent Effort and Availability, 1985; also 7 grants. **SPECIAL ACHIEVEMENTS:** Published 52 abstracts, 100 articles, 13 book chapters, 187 presentations. **BUSINESS ADDRESS:** Professor, Maternal Fetal Medicine, University of California, Irvine Medical Center, College of Medicine, 101 The City Dr, Bldg 25, Orange, CA 92668, (714)456-6682.

MURIERA, HELEN BAUTISTA
Physician. Filipino American. **PERSONAL:** Born Dec 17, 1926, Corregidor, Cavite, Philippines; daughter of Frank Bautista Sr (deceased) and Severina Bautista; married Romulo O Muriera, Dec 20, 1958 (deceased); children: Ronald, Catherine Muriera Williams, Alan, Melanie Muriera Morrill. **EDUCATION:** University of Santo Tomas Philippines, AA, 1949, MD, 1954; Academy of Family Physician, fellow, 1985. **CAREER:** Euclid Glenville Hospital, internship, 1955-56, general practice, 1956-57; Bradford Hospital, medical resident, 1957-58; Gouveneur Hospital, NY, chief medical resident, 1958-59; St Francis Hospital, Trenton, NJ, chief medical resident, 1959-60; St Lukes Hospital, San Francisco, CA, medical resident, 1966-67; Golden Gate Hospital, CA, house physician, 1967-74; self employed physician, currently. **ORGANIZATIONS:** Masantolenos of San Francisco, president, 1985, adviser, 1986-; Filipino-American Star of the Sea Parish, public relation officer, 1974-; United Corregidorian of America, public relation officer, 1972-85, budget director, 1985-; Filipino-American Lions Club of San Francisco, board of directors, 1991-93, third vice president, 1993-94. **HONORS/AWARDS:** Filipino-American Women Action League, San Francisco, Humanitarian Committee Work in the Field of Medicine, 1989; Filipino-American Lion's Club of San Francisco, Lion of the Year, 1991-92; Arthritis Foundation, efforts in helping educate patients with arthritis, 1992-93; Lions Club International Foundation, Melvins Jones Fellow for Humanitarian Services, 1991-92; Lions Eye Foundation, Helen Keller Fellow, 1993-94; Masantolenos of San Francisco and Bay Area, Outstanding Mansantolenos in the Field of Medicine, 1989; United Corregidorian of America, untiring effort & dedication, 1992-93. **SPECIAL ACHIEVEMENTS:** Filipino-American Lions Club of San Francisco, barbers shop quartet, 1993, tail twisting, 1993. **HOME ADDRESS:** 751 17th Ave, San Francisco, CA 94121, (415)386-1029. **BUSINESS PHONE:** (415)387-8004.

MURTHY, A. KUMARESA S.
Manufacturing company executive. Indo-American. **PERSONAL:** Born Nov 24, 1943, Sivakasi, Tamil Nadu, India; son of K Andiappan and A Janaki; married Mohana Murthy, Apr 17, 1970; children: Rajan, Vale. **EDUCATION:** Indian Institute of Technology, BTech (with hons), 1966; Columbia University, MS, 1968, ScD, eng, 1974. **CAREER:** Digvijay Cement, India, process engineer, 1966-67; Allied Signal, Morristown, NJ, process engineer, 1968-76, manager, process, 1977-80, manager, r & d, 1980-89; Jacobs Engineering, process engineering, manager, 1990-93; BOC Group, technology, director, 1993-. **ORGANIZATIONS:** American Institute of Chemical Engineers, 1970-; American Chemical Society, 1978-82; American Association for Advancement of Science, 1975-81; NJ State Board of Professional Engineers, 1975-. **HONORS/AWARDS:** Indian Institute Chemical Engineers, P C Ray Award, 1966; Columbia University, New York, Graduate Citation, 1968. **SPECIAL ACHIEVEMENTS:** "Phase Equilibrium," Handbook of Chemical Engineering Calculations, 1984; Deposition of Thin Films Using Supercritical Fluids, US patent, 1988; Catalytic Process for the Production of Light Hydrocarbons by Treatment of Heavy Hydrocarbons with Water, US patent, 1988; co-author: High-Capacity Trays Improve RVP, 1993; numerous other patents and publications. **HOME ADDRESS:** 8 Pilgrim Court, Convent Station, NJ 07961, (201)267-2258.

MURTHY, SRINIVASA (K. R. S.)
Engineering and business manager, executive speaker. Indo-American. **PERSONAL:** Born Jun 12, 1949, Bangalore, Karnataka, India; son of Gowramma Kadur and Ramaswamy Kadur. **EDUCATION:** Bangalore University, BS, physics, 1967, MS, physics, 1969; Mysore University, MSEE, 1971. **CAREER:** Bharat Electronics Ltd, research engineer, 1969-71; Indian Space Research Organization, project manager, 1971-79; California State University, visiting professor, 1979-82; Systems & Applied Sciences Corp, project manager, 1980-83; IMR Systems Corp, division director, 1983-84; General Electric, general manager, 1984-85; AT&T Bell Labs, business & program manager, 1985-. **ORGANIZATIONS:** IEEE Engineering Management Society, governing board, vp, 1986-; IEEE Systems Management & Cybernetics Society, governing board, 1988-; IEEE Computer Society, technical & area activities board, 1986-89; IEEE Communications Society, founding member, 1987-, network magazine; IEEE Tencon Conference, program chair, advisory board, 1989-; National Engineering Consortium, advisor, evaluator, 1991-; IEEE International Engineering Management Conference, program chair, advisory board, 1989-; Bell Laboratories, Indian Subcontinent Club, founder. **HONORS/AWARDS:** Cultural Festival of India, Man of the Year, Science & Engineering, 1991; IEEE Engineering Management Society, Outstanding Achievement Award, 1990; AT&T Bell Labs, Exceptional Contribution Award, 1986; IEEE Computer Society, Exceptional Services Award, 1989, 1990, 1991; IEEE Aerospace & Electronics Systems Society, Outstanding Service, 1984; Government of India, Outstanding Contribution to Space Research, 1975. **SPECIAL ACHIEVEMENTS:** First person in India to: develop radar systems using digital circuits; use integrated circuits for industrial, space research and defense systems; developed the first star sensor with venier scale; developed on-board and ground check-out systems, and earth stations for the first Indian satellite; developed on-board and ground check-out systems for NASA's Shuttle Solar Back Scatter Ultra Violet experiment, for the first space shuttle; developed the first COMBAND cable TV converter in the world; invented a method to convert boolean logic expressions into arithmetic expressions; created an electronic mail news group presently used by over 200,000 readers around the world. **HOME ADDRESS:** 5 Polo Club Dr, Tinton Falls, NJ 07724, (908)389-2392. **BUSINESS ADDRESS:** Business and Program Manager, AT&T Bell Labs, 600 Mountain Ave, Rm 3B-329, Mountain View, NJ 07974, (908)582-5882.

MURTY, KATTA GOPALAKRISHNA
Educator. Indo-American. **PERSONAL:** Born Sep 9, 1936, Andhra Pradesh, India; son of Narayana Swamy Katta and Adilakshmi Katta; married Vijaya, Feb 2, 1964; children: Vani Sridevi Katta, Madhusri Katta. **EDUCATION:** University of Madras, BSc (with honors), 1952-55; Indian Statistical Institute, MStat, 1957; University of California, Berkeley, MS, 1966, PhD, 1968. **CAREER:** Indian Statistical Institute, India, assistant professor, consultant, 1957-65; University of California, Berkeley, instructor, junior specialist, 1965-68; Bell Labs, consultant, 1974; University of Texas, Dallas, visiting professor, 1982; KFUPM, Dhahran, Saudi Arabia, visiting professor, 1988-89; University of Michigan, professor, 1968-. **ORGANIZATIONS:** Mathematical Programming Society; Operations Research Society of America. **HONORS/AWARDS:** Alpha Pi Mu, Outstanding Faculty Member, 1978. **SPECIAL**

ACHIEVEMENTS: Four graduate texbooks in Optimization Algorithms, 1976-92; 1 undergraduate text in Optimization Methods, 1994; 50 research publications in refereed journals. **HOME ADDRESS:** 3311 Alton Ct, Ann Arbor, MI 48105, (313)995-3475. **BUSINESS ADDRESS:** Professor, Industrial & Operations Engineering Dept, University of Michigan, 1205 Beal, 232, Ann Arbor, MI 48109-2117, (313)763-3513.

MURTY, KOMANDURI SRINIVASA
Educator, educational administrator. Indo-American. **PERSONAL:** Born Jul 1, 1956, Rajahmundry, Andhra Pradesh, India; son of Komanduri Krishna Murty and Komanduri Andalamma; married Andal, Aug 23, 1986; children: Vandana, Chandana. **EDUCATION:** Andhra University, India, BS, 1975, MA, 1977; International Institute for Population Sciences, Bombay, diploma, 1979; Mississippi State University, PhD, 1984. **CAREER:** Andhra University, Population Research Center, research officer, 1979-81; Mississippi State University, Sociology Department, graduate assistant, 1981-84; Atlanta University, Department of Criminal Justice, residential counselor/adjunct professor, 1984-85, director of research, 1985-89, assistant professor, 1985-89; Clark Atlanta University, Department of Criminal Justice, acting chair & associate professor, 1989-90, chair & associate professor, 1990-. **ORGANIZATIONS:** International Journal of Comparative & Applied Criminal Justice, associate editor, 1989-; International Association for the Study of Organized Crime, 1990-; Mid-South Sociological Association, 1987-; American Statistical Association, 1986-; American Society of Criminology, 1984-. **HONORS/AWARDS:** Joint Secretary, Department of Higher Education, India, Man of Achievement, 1989. **SPECIAL ACHIEVEMENTS:** Author and coauthor of: The Place of Historically Black Colleges & Universities in US Higher Education, with Julian Roebuck, New York, Preager, 1993; book: The Drinking Driver: The DUI Offender as a Social Type, contract with the State University of New York Press, Albany, forthcoming; "Marielitos, Cuban Detainees and the Atlanta Riot: A Study in Social and Personal Identify," Studies in Symbolic Interaction, with Julian B Roebuck, 1993; "An Analysis of Crisis Calls by Battered Women in the City of Atlanta," Emilio C Viano, ed; Intimate Violence: Interdisciplinary Perspectives, with Julian B Roebuck, 1992. **BUSINESS ADDRESS:** Professor and Chairman, Criminal Justice Dept, Clark Atlanta University, James P Brawley Drive at Fair Street SW, Atlanta, GA 30314-4358, (404)880-8725.

MUSAPETA, HARI
Supply company executive. Indo-American. **PERSONAL:** Born Jun 6, 1952, Hyderabad, Andhra Pradesh, India; son of Veeraiah Musapeta and Venkatamma Musapeta; married Asha; children: Risha, Vinita. **EDUCATION:** Osmania University, BCom, 1972; AICWA, cost accounting, 1974; Oklahoma City University, MBA, 1980; Toastmaster International, CTM, 1992. **CAREER:** P&R Supply Co Inc, president, currently. **ORGANIZATIONS:** Toastmasters Club #148, president; Indian Association of Tulsa, president; Telugu Association of Oklahoma, president; Morton Clinic, board of director; Red Cross Minority Committee Governing Body; Executive Association of MBA Alumni of Oklahoma City University; Asian American Association. **HONORS/AWARDS:** Outstanding Small Business of the Year; Outstanding Community Service by Toastmasters International; India Association of Greater Tulsa, Outstanding Community Service Award; National Small Business Award nominee. **BUSINESS ADDRESS:** President, P&R Supply Co Inc, PO Box 690094, Tulsa, OK 74169.

MUSTAFA, SHAMS
Marketing executive. Pakistani American. **PERSONAL:** Born Oct 8, 1952, Karachi, Sind, Pakistan; son of Shaista Mustafa and Mustafa Hasan Zuberi; married Naheed S Mustafa, Apr 23, 1982; children: Adeel S, Shariq S. **EDUCATION:** Punjab University, BS (with honors), 1970, MS, 1971. **CAREER:** Associated Consulting Engineers, chief chemist/director, 1972-77; American Standards Testing Bureau Inc, chemist, 1977-79; Caleb Brett (USA) Inc, agri manager, 1979-89; E W Saybolt & Company, Inc, laboratory manager, 1989-92; Chemical Care Inc, vice-president, marketing, 1992-93; SGS Control Services, Inc, marketing director, agriculture division, 1993-. **ORGANIZATIONS:** AOCS, president roll, referee, 1980, 1986; AOAC, 1980; AIC, fellow, 1986; AMA, marketing executive, 1990; American Biographical Institute, research advisor, 1988-93, life fellow; Institute of Food Technologists; NOPA, certified chemist, 1985-92, ASTM, 1990; Sales and Marketing Executives International. **HONORS/AWARDS:** American Oil Chemists Society, Smalley Award, 1986, Doughtie Award, 1987, Certificate of Honor, 1984-88; American Institute of Chemists, fellow, 1986; American Institute of Chemical Engineers, 1988. **SPECIAL ACHIEVEMENTS:** Chartered Chemist: Royal Society of

Chemistry, 1991; translator of scientific books from English into Urdu; International Union of Pure & Applied Science, 1990. **HOME ADDRESS:** 2904 Plaza Drive, Woodbridge, NJ 07095, (908)636-8650. **BUSINESS ADDRESS:** Marketing Director, SGS Control Services, 20 Lafayette Street, Carteret, NJ 07008, (908)541-7200.

MUTHUKRISHNAN, SUBBARATNAM
Educator. Indo-American. **PERSONAL:** Born Dec 27, 1942, Madurai, Tamil Nadu, India; son of K V Subbaratnam and Rajam Subbaratnam; married Asha, Sep 15, 1977; children: Aravind, Ranjan. **EDUCATION:** University of Madras, BS, 1963, MS, 1965; Indian Institute of Science, PhD, 1970. **CAREER:** University of Chicago, research associate, 1971-73; Roche Institute of Molecular Biology, research fellow, 1973-76; National Institutes of Health, visiting scientist, 1976-80; Kansas State University, professor, 1980-. **SPECIAL ACHIEVEMENTS:** "5'-Terminal 7-Methyl Guanosine in Eukaryotic MRNA Is Required for Translation," Nature, vol 255, p33-37, 1975; "Hormonal Control of Alpha Amylase Gene Expression in Barley," Journal of Biological Chemistry, vol 258: p2370-2375, 1983; "Identification of an Endochitinase CDNA Clone from Barley Aleurone Cells," Plant Molecular Biology vol 12: p403-412, 1989; "Sequence of a CDNA and Expression of the Gene Encoding Epidermal and Gut Chitinases of Manduca Sexta," Insect Biochem Molec Biol, 1993. **BIOGRAPHICAL SOURCES:** "Enigma Variations of Mammalian Messenger RNA," Nature, vol 255, p 4, 1975. **BUSINESS ADDRESS:** Professor, Dept of Biochemistry, Kansas State University, Willard Hall, Manhattan, KS 66506, (913)532-6939.

MYER, YASH PAUL
Educator, researcher. Indo-American. **PERSONAL:** Born May 5, 1932, Jullundur City, Punjab, India; son of Bhagwan Das Myer and S Devi; married Ruth D Myer; children: Anita, Vic Evan. **EDUCATION:** Panjab University, India, BSc (honors), 1953, MSc (honors), 1955; University of Oregon, PhD, 1961. **CAREER:** Yale University, 1961-66; State University of New York at Albany, professor, 1966-. **ORGANIZATIONS:** Federation of Societies for Experimental Biology, 1963-; Biohysical Society, 1965-; Protein Society, 1991-; Sigma Xi, 1961-; American Association for the Advancement of Science, 1968-. **SPECIAL ACHIEVEMENTS:** Basic research in the field of protein structure-function, 1966-; circular dichroism spectroscopy. **BUSINESS ADDRESS:** Professor, Dept of Chemistry, State University of New York, 1400 Washington Ave, Albany, NY 12222, (518)442-4420.

MYINT, THAN HTUN (TRUETT HACKETT THAN PE)
Utilities and energy company manager. Myanmar American. **PERSONAL:** Born Jun 23, 1949, Taunggyi, Southern Shan State, Burma; son of U Than Pe and Daw Myat Tin; married Nang Htay Yin, Nov 2, 1974; children: Judy Htay, Samuel Than. **EDUCATION:** Taunggyi College, BS, 1968; Mandalay Arts & Science University, BS, 1971; Southern Illinois University, MS. **CAREER:** National Christian High School, teacher, 1971; Hopong State High School, teacher, 1972-76; Granite City Steel Co, Utilities/Energy Mgt, WWTP operator, 1977-. **ORGANIZATIONS:** First Baptist Church, diaconate brd, 1977-83, finance & trustees brd, 1985-91, chmn, 1991, mission committee chair, 1985-91; Illinois Water Pollution Control Assn, 1978-. **HONORS/AWARDS:** National Steel Co, Safety Olympic Award, 1984; Granite City Steel Co, Swanson Safety Awards, 1986-88, 1990. **BIOGRAPHICAL SOURCES:** "Highland Sesquicentennial Anniversary," Highland News Leader, p B1, Feb 21, 1987. **HOME ADDRESS:** #5 Petite Acres, Highland, IL 62249, (618)654-2506. **BUSINESS PHONE:** (618)451-3090.

MYODA, TOSHIO TIMOTHY
Consulting company executive. Japanese American. **PERSONAL:** Born Mar 17, 1929, Mukden, China; son of Kihachi Myoda & Hisako Kanda Myoda; married Lois Johnson Myoda, Jun 9, 1963; children: Samuel Peter, Paul Timothy. **EDUCATION:** Hokkaido College, Sapparo, Japan, BS, 1949, MS, 1952, PhD, 1954; Iowa State University, PhD, 1959. **CAREER:** Hokkaido University, Sapporo, instructor, 1954-59; Iowa State University, Ames, research assistant, 1956-59; National Research Coun, Saskatoon, Canada, research fellow, 1959-60; Western Res University, research fellow, 1960-64; Institute Microbial Chemistry, Tokyo, sr research fellow, 1964-66; La Rabida, University of Chicago Inst, instructor, research associate, 1966-67; Alfred I DuPont Institute of the Nemours Foundation, various positions, 1967-86; Valparaiso University, visiting professor, 1967; Uni-Tech Associates, USA Inc, president, 1985-; University of Delaware School Life and Health Sciences, adj professor, 1986-; Tokai University School Medicine, Isehara, Japan, professor, 1989-91; Margaronics Inc, director, science affairs, 1990-. **ORGANIZATIONS:**

AAAS; American Academy Microbiology; American Chem Society, biology chemistry div, fermentation div, del div; American Society Microbiology; Biochem Society, UK; Inst Food Tech; International Federation Advancement of Genetic Engineering and Biotechnology; Japan Association Microbiology; Japan Society Bioscience; Biotechnology and Agrochemistry, NY Academy Science; Society for Actinomycetes, Japan; Soc Indsl Microbiology; US Federation Culture Collections; Rotary Club; Rodney Square Club. **HONORS/ AWARDS:** Waksman Found, grantee, 1965; Japan Soc, scholarship, 1957; International Union Microbiology Socs, Distinguished Service Medal, 1958. **SPECIAL ACHIEVEMENTS:** Speaker to various symposia, universities and government; co-author, Perspectives in Culture Collections, no 1: Procurement of Patent Cultures, 1992; contributor, numerous articles to professional journals. **BUSINESS ADDRESS:** President, UNI-Tech Associates, USA, Inc, PO Box 354, Rockland, DE 19732-0354.

MYUNG, JOHN Y.
Attorney. Korean American. **PERSONAL:** Born Sep 21, 1964, Charleston, WV; son of John I and Okjoo Myung. **EDUCATION:** University of Denver, BSBA, 1986; University of Tulsa, MBA, 1989, JD, 1989. **CAREER:** SAFECO Life Insurance Company, attorney, 1990-. **ORGANIZATIONS:** Asian Bar Association of Washington, social chair, 1991, vice president, 1992, president-elect, 1993, president, 1993; Washington State Bar Association, 1990-; American Bar Association, 1990-; Seattle King County Bar Association, 1990-; SAFECO United Way Committee, appointment, 1992-; National Asian Pacific American Bar Association, 1991-. **HONORS/AWARDS:** University of Denver, Mortar Board, 1985, Order of Omega, 1985. **BUSINESS ADDRESS:** Attorney, SAFECO Life Insurance Co, 15411 NE 51st Street, Redmond, WA 98052, (206)867-6013.

N

NADKARNI, SUDHIR V. (NED)
Sales executive. Indo-American. **PERSONAL:** Born Apr 8, 1947, Lahore, Punjab, Pakistan; son of Vinayak V Nadkarni and Sumitrabai V Nadkarni; married Gita S Nadkarni, Jul 22, 1978; children: Gurudev S. **EDUCATION:** University of Cambridge, 1965; Forman Christian College, BS, 1968. **CAREER:** Pete Vrontikis & Son, sales associate, 1985-86; Intermountain Video, sales associate, 1987-90; Teletape Video Systems, president, 1990-. **BUSINESS ADDRESS:** President, Teletape Video Systems, 7127 S 400 West, # 5, Midvale, UT 84047, (801)562-8881.

NAG, RONJON
Business owner. Indo-American. **PERSONAL:** Born 1962?. **EDUCATION:** MIT, Sloan School of Management, MBA; Cambridge University, PhD, speech recognition. **CAREER:** Stanford University, Dept of Psychology, former teacher; Lexicus, co-founder, president, currently. **HONORS/AWARDS:** Harkness Scholar. **BUSINESS ADDRESS:** Co-Founder/President, Lexicus, 345 First St, Palo Alto, CA 94301, (415)323-8547.*

NAGAI, NELSON KEI
Educator. Japanese American. **PERSONAL:** Born Sep 11, 1950, Stockton, CA; son of Katsuto Kenneth Nagai and Grace Sumida Nagai; married Beverly Kordziel, Jun 2, 1975; children: Tyrone K, Tyree Ranko. **EDUCATION:** Stanford University, BA, political science, 1972; UC, Davis, MS, international agricultural development, 1978. **CAREER:** California Farm Bureau, general coordinator, 1974-76; Tri/Valley Growers, assistant production manager, 1979-82; University of the Pacific, instructor, education, 1982-89; San Joaquin Delta College, instructor, economics, 1989-. **ORGANIZATIONS:** Phi Delta Kappa, 1993; Japanese American Citizens League, board member, 1982-; Association of Asian American Educators, board member, 1982-; International Hotel Tenants Association, auditor, 1972-73; Stanford University, Asian Student Union, chairman, 1970-71; Yellow Seed, Constitutional Committee, chairman, 1969-72. **HONORS/AWARDS:** University of California, Bancroft Fellowship, 1978, Regents Fellowship, 1977; Japanese American Citizens League, National Scholarship, 1968. **SPECIAL ACHIEVEMENTS:** Nihonmachi Little Friends, San Francisco, founding member, 1975; Committee Against Nihonmachi Evictions, San Francisco, Legal Committee, chairman, 1973; Bay Area Asian Coalition Against the War, San Francisco, chairman, 1972; UC, Davis, Third World Forum, community editor, 1977-78. **BIOGRAPHICAL SOURCES:** Bancroftiana, Bancroft Library, UC, Berkeley, p 2-3, June 1977. **BUSINESS ADDRESS:** Professor, San Joaquin Delta College, 5151 Pacific Ave, Stockton, CA 95207, (209)474-5262.

NAGANO, KENT GEORGE
Musical conductor. Japanese American. **PERSONAL:** Born Nov 22, 1951, Morro Bay, CA; married Mari Kodama, 1992. **EDUCATION:** University of Oxford, 1969; University of California, Santa Cruz, BA, sociology, music, 1974; San Francisco State, MMusic, 1976; studied with Goodwin Sammel, Laszlo Varga and Seiji Ozawa. **CAREER:** Opera Company of Boston, 1977-79; Berkeley Symphony Orchestra, music director, 1978-; Opera de Lyon, chief conductor, 1989-. **HONORS/AWARDS:** Affiliate Artists, Seaver Conducting Award, co-recipient, 1985; Natl Syndicate of Music and Drama Critics, France, Personality of the Year, 1992. **SPECIAL ACHIEVEMENTS:** Ojai Music Festival, 1984; guest conductor with several orchestras in Europe and America; Erato recordings, 15 record contract, 1992. **BUSINESS ADDRESS:** Musical Director, Berkeley Symphony, 2322 Shattuck Ave, Berkeley, CA 94704, (510)841-2800.*

NAGANO, PAUL TATSUMI
Artist. Japanese American. **PERSONAL:** Born May 21, 1938, Honolulu, HI; son of Don Sakae Nagano and Masako Imamoto Nagano. **EDUCATION:** Columbia College, BA, 1960; Pennsylvania Academy of the Fine Arts, 1963-67. **CAREER:** Pucker Safrai Gallery, art director, 1967-89, exhibitions annually, 1976-88; Fenway Studio 406, Boston, "Nagano on Lipari," 1989; CSIS, Jakarta, "Indonesian Idylls," exhibition, 1990; Neka Museum, Ubud, Bali, "Two Visions: Paintings of Bali," exhibition, 1992; Fenway Studio 406, Boston, "Boston, Bali, and Between," 1993; Contemporary Museum Gallery, Honolulu, "The Diamond Head Series," 1994; Murals for the Campbell Estate, Kapolei, Hawaii, 1994. **ORGANIZATIONS:** Japan Society of Boston, 1970-; Art Institute of Boston, trustee, 1993-. **MILITARY SERVICE:** US Navy, lt, jg, 1960-63. **BIOGRAPHICAL SOURCES:** American Artist Magazine, p 48, May 1978, p 58, Mar 1985. **HOME ADDRESS:** 30 Ipswich St, #406, Boston, MA 02215-3616, (617)266-3509.

NAGAOKA, MICHAEL M.
Law enforcement manager. Japanese American. **PERSONAL:** Born Feb 22, 1946, Chicago, IL; son of Mits & Mae Nagaoka; married Sharon, Aug 12, 1990; children: Michael, Sherilynn. **EDUCATION:** East LA, AA; California State, LA, BS; Pepperdine University, master's; University of Redlands, master's. **CAREER:** Los Angeles County Sheriff's Department, captain, currently. **HONORS/AWARDS:** Rotarians, Paul Harris Fellow, 1992. **MILITARY SERVICE:** Army, sergeant, 1968-70. **BUSINESS ADDRESS:** Captain, Los Angeles County Sheriff's Department, 150 N Hudson Ave, City of Industry, CA 91715, (818)330-3322.

NAGARAJAN, RAMAKRISHNAN
Scientist, business executive. Indo-American. **PERSONAL:** Born May 14, 1931, Kodaikanal, Madras, India; son of Ramakrishnan & Thangam; married Alice, Jan 21, 1971; children: Ravi, Thara, Raju. **EDUCATION:** Delhi University, India, BSc (honors), 1953, MSc, 1955; McGill University, PhD, 1961. **CAREER:** Eli Lilly Co, senior research scientist, 1978-93. **ORGANIZATIONS:** National Federation of Indian American Association, vice president, 1986-88, joint secretary, 1988-90, secretary, 1990-92, board of directors, 1986-92, editor, 1989-92; International Center of Indianapolis Inc, chairman, 1986, board of directors, 1986-93; India Association of Indianapolis Inc, vice president, 1984, president, 1985, board of trustees, 1985-90, editor, 1987-89. **HONORS/AWARDS:** NRI Society, New Delhi, India, Hind Rattan, 1992; Sugar Research Institute, postdoctoral fellow, 1962-64. **SPECIAL ACHIEVEMENTS:** Author of numerous articles and publications referring to the pharmaceutical industry; editor, "Glycopeptide Antibiotics," Marcel Dekker, 1993; author of 40 original publications, 5 review articles, over 30 invited lectures, 1967-93. **HOME ADDRESS:** 5 West 79 St, Indianapolis, IN 46260-2978, (317)251-5398.

NAGATANI, SCOTT A.
Musician, composer. Japanese American. **PERSONAL:** Born Sep 25, 1956, Hanford, CA; son of John Nagatani and Diane Nagatani; married Kim Nagatani, Nov 7, 1981; children: Ayame, Alysa. **EDUCATION:** DeVry Institute of Technology, AA, 1977. **CAREER:** World Communications, field service engineer, 1981-91; Visual Communications, clerk, 1991-; musician, composer, musical director, currently. **ORGANIZATIONS:** Musician, composer, musical director: Japanese American National Museum, Japanese American Cultural & Community Center, East West Players, LA Children's Theatre. **SPECIAL ACHIEVEMENTS:** Composer, films & videos: Sprint commercial, Sho-Time! cable access; theater: First Annual Comedy One Act Festival, 1993, Beside Myself, 1993; musical director, theater: Into the Woods, 1992;

Comedy Sportz, 1992; keyboards/orchestrations, theater: Remember. . ., 1991, Canton Jazz Club, 1991; worked with Artsreach/California Youth Authority in developing musical theatre for juvenile inmates within state correctional institutions. **HOME ADDRESS:** 4400 1/4 Edenhurst Ave, Los Angeles, CA 90039, (213)667-3224.

NAGOSHI, DOUGLAS N.
Propane distribution company executive. Japanese American. **PERSONAL:** Born Mar 22, 1942, Kalaheo, Kauai, HI; son of Tetsuro Nagoshi and Shizue Nagoshi; married Pearl K Nagoshi, Jun 13, 1970; children: Matthew S H, Jennifer Y S. **EDUCATION:** University of Hawaii, BBA, 1965, CPC, 1966, MBA, 1972; US Army Officers' Candidate School, commissioned lieutenant, 1967. **CAREER:** Dillingham Corp, dir, planning & analysis, various other positions, 1969-78; Cal Gas Corp, vice pres of eastern marketing, asst to sr vice pres, 1978-81; Synergy Corp, vice pres of marketing, 1982; Hanson PLC, Suburban Propane Division, regional mgr, regional marketing mgr, beginning 1982, vice pres of marketing & customer service, area vice pres, 1993-. **ORGANIZATIONS:** National Propane Gas Assn, marketing development committee, 1991-; World Futures Society, 1970-; Kentucky Colonels, 1987-. **SPECIAL ACHIEVEMENTS:** Amateur radio operator, general license, 1958-. **MILITARY SERVICE:** US Army, lt, 1966-69; Bronze Star, 1969; Army Commendation Medal, 1969; Tet Campaign Medal, 1968; Vietnam Service Ribbon, 1969. **BUSINESS ADDRESS:** VP, Marketing & Customer Service, Suburban Propane Division, Hanson PLC, 240 Rte 10 West, PO Box 206, Whippany, NJ 07981-0206, (201)887-5300.

NAHATA, MILAP CHAND
Educator, researcher. Indo-American. **PERSONAL:** Born Oct 20, 1950, Sardar Shahr, Rajasthan, India; son of Bachh Raj Nahata and Ratani Devi Anchalia Nahata; married Suchitra Kothari Nahata, May 18, 1978; children: Leena. **EDUCATION:** University of Jodhpur, BS, chem, phys, math, 1970; University of Bombay, BS, pharmacy, 1973; Duquesne University, MS, pharmaceutics, 1975, Pharm D, 1977. **CAREER:** Wexner Institute for Pediatric Research Laboratory, director, 1989-; Ohio State University, assistant professor, 1977-83, associate professor, 1983-88, professor, 1988-. **ORGANIZATIONS:** American College of Clinical Pharmacy, president, 1991-92; American Association of Colleges of Pharmacy, chairman, 1990-91; American College of Clinical Pharmacy, board member, 1986-89, Research Institute, chairman, 1992-93; Annals of Pharmacotherapy, senior associate editor, 1993-; Journal of Clinical Pharmacy and Therapeutics, column editor, 1992-; University of Calcutta, India, external examiner, 1987-. **HONORS/AWARDS:** Ohio State University, Balshone Award-Distinguished Teaching, 1984, 1990, Alumni Distinguished Teaching Award, 1991; American Society of Hospital Pharmacy, Sustained Contributions to Literature Award, 1987; American College of Clinical Pharmacy, Education Award, 1990; American Association of Colleges of Pharmacy, Distinguished Educator Award, 1993; University of Texas, Robert G Leonard Memorial Award, 1988-89; elected fellow of five national scientific and professional organizations. **SPECIAL ACHIEVEMENTS:** Characterized absorption, distribution, metabolism and elimination pathways of medicines in neonates, infants and children; developed guidelines for optimal formulations, delivery and clinical use of medicines in pediatric patients; published over 250 refereed articles, 180 abstracts, and one book; served as editor of three journals and referee for 15 journals. **BIOGRAPHICAL SOURCES:** The Annals of Pharmacotherapy, vol 27, p 95-96, January 1993; On Campus, Ohio State University, vol 22, p 4, June 10, 1993. **BUSINESS ADDRESS:** Professor, College of Pharmacy, Ohio State University, 500 W 12th Ave, Columbus, OH 43210.

NAHATA, SUPARAS M.
Systems analyst. Indo-American. **PERSONAL:** Born Jan 2, 1943, Nirmali, Bihar, India; son of Sugan Chand Nahata and Kamala D Nahata; married Kiran Nahata, May 6, 1967; children: Vinni, Amit K. **EDUCATION:** Bihar Institute of Technology, Sindri Bihar, India, BSME, 1966; City College of New York, MSIE, 1971; New York University, computer programming, 1983. **CAREER:** V&G Mfg Co, industrial engr, 1973-74; St Johnsbury Trucking Co, resident industrial engr, 1974-79; Chase Manhattan Bank, cost analyst, 1979-83; A G Becker & Co, systems analyst, 1981-85; Ericsson Info System, systems analyst, 1985-86; Depository Trust Co, senior systems analyst, 1986-. **HOME ADDRESS:** 18 Ponderosa Ln, Old Bridge, NJ 08857, (908)360-2528.

NAHM, MOON H.
Educator, physician, scientist. Korean American. **PERSONAL:** Born Mar 23, 1948, Seoul, Republic of Korea; son of Chung C Nahm and Ai J Nahm; married

Chong K Nahm, Jan 22, 1983; children: Laura, Sarah. **EDUCATION:** Washington University, AB, 1970, MD, 1974. **CAREER:** Washington University, assistant professor, 1981-89, associate professor, 1989-. **ORGANIZATIONS:** American Immunology Association; American Society of Microbiologists; American Association of Clincial Chemists. **HONORS/AWARDS:** Phi Beta Kappa, 1969. **SPECIAL ACHIEVEMENTS:** About 90 scientific papers. **BUSINESS ADDRESS:** Associate Professor, Washington University, 660 S Euclid Ave, St. Louis, MO 63110.

NAIDU, SEETALA VEERASWAMY
Educator. Indo-American. **PERSONAL:** Born Jan 28, 1957, Akividu, Andhra Pradesh, India; son of Seetala Subbarao and Seetala Veerayamma; married Sailaja Seetala, Nov 25, 1987; children: Prasant Seetala. **EDUCATION:** Andhra University, BSc, 1978; Mysore University, MScEd, physics, 1980; Institute of Physics, Bhubaneswar, post MSc, Advanced Diploma, 1981; Saha Institute of Nuclear Physics, PhD, 1988. **CAREER:** Institute of Physics, research fellow, 1981-82; Saha Institute of Nuclear Physics, DST research fellow, 1982-83, senior research fellow, 1983-85; University of Texas, Arlington, Department of Physics, lecturer/postdoctoral research associate, 1986-88; Grambling State University, Department of Physics, assistant professor, 1988-. **ORGANIZATIONS:** American Physical Society, 1991; Sigma Pi Sigma, 1990; American Chapter of Indian Physics Association, 1990; Louisiana Academy of Science, 1989. **SPECIAL ACHIEVEMENTS:** Published over 25 research papers in international journals; presented over 30 research papers in conference proceedings; published 2 articles in reference books. **HOME PHONE:** (318)251-9266. **BUSINESS ADDRESS:** Assistant Professor, Dept of Physics, Grambling State University, Grambling, LA 71245, (318)274-2574.

NAIK, DATTA VITTAL
Educator. Indo-American. **PERSONAL:** Born Mar 5, 1947, Margao, Goa Daman and Diu, India; son of Vittal D & Sukanti V Naik; married Sushilata D Naik, Dec 11, 1971; children: Kimmy D, Neal A. **EDUCATION:** St Xavier's College, Goa, University of Bombay, BS (honors), 1967; University of Notre Dame, PhD, 1972. **CAREER:** University of Florida, College of Pharmacy, assistant professor, 1973-75; Manhattanville College, NY, assistant professor, 1975-77; Monmouth College, NJ, assistant professor, 1977-82, associate professor, 1982-90, Department of Chemistry & Physics, chairman, 1982-91, professor, 1990-. **ORGANIZATIONS:** American Chemical Society, 1971-, Monmouth County Section, chairman, 1981, treasurer, 1988-, Middle Atlantic Region, steering committee, chairman, 1990-91; Sigma Xi. **HONORS/AWARDS:** St Xavier's College, Goa, India, St Xavier's Medal for Academic Excellence, 1967; University of Notre Dame, Peter C Reilly Fellowship, 1972; NASA, Certificate of Recognition, 1986, 1987; Monmouth College, Distinguished Teacher Award, 1989. **SPECIAL ACHIEVEMENTS:** 36 research publications. **BUSINESS ADDRESS:** Prof of Chemistry, Dept of Chemistry & Physics, Monmouth College, E-243 Edison Science Bldg, Cedar Ave, West Long Branch, NJ 07764, (908)571-3436.

NAIK, TARUN RATILAL
Educator. Indo-American. **PERSONAL:** Born Apr 22, 1940, Ahmedabad, Gujarat, India; son of Gajaraben R Naik & Ratilal H Naik (deceased); married Irene de Venecia, Aug 20, 1966; children: Eela T, Nisha T. **EDUCATION:** Gujarat University, BE, 1962; University of Wisconsin, Madison, MS, civil engineering, 1964, PhD, civil engineering, 1972. **CAREER:** Civil engineering consulting companies in Chicago and Madison, structural engineer, 1964-67; University of Wisconsin, Madison, lecturer, researcher, 1966-72; Soils and Engineering Services, Inc, executive vice president, until 1975; University of Wisconsin, Milwaukee, director, Center for By-products Utilization, associate professor, 1975-. **ORGANIZATIONS:** American Concrete Institute, Wisconsin Chapter, past president; American Society of Civil Engineers, Legislative Affairs Committee of Wisconsin, past chairman; American Society for Testing Materials, ASTM Committee, past chairman; Society for Experimental Mechanics; National Society of Professional Engineers; Wisconsin Society of Professional Engineers, board of directors, past president. **HONORS/AWARDS:** American Society of Civil Engineers, Individual Achievement as an Engineer in Education, 1986; American Concrete Institute, elected fellow, 1988; Wisconsin Society of Professional Engineers, Outstanding Engineer in Education, 1989; Mexican Cement and Concrete Institute, Dedication to Concrete Education, 1989; College of Engineering & Applied Science, UWM, Outstanding Service, 1990. **SPECIAL ACHIEVEMENTS:** Conducted research as a result of grants provided by government agencies and companies in USA and Europe; published over 200 technical reports and papers in ASCE, ACI, ASTM, etc; lectured and made presentations in many countries including

South Africa, India, Mexico, & Norway, Hungary, Venezuela, etc. **HOME ADDRESS:** 622 N 72nd St, Wauwatosa, WI 53213, (414)453-6994. **BUSINESS ADDRESS:** Director, Center for By-Products Utilization, Associate Professor, CE & M Dept, University of Wisconsin-Milwaukee, PO Box 784, Milwaukee, WI 53201, (414)229-6696.

NAIR, CHANDRA K.
Physician, educator. Indo-American. **PERSONAL:** Born May 20, 1944, Trichur, India; married; children: 3. **EDUCATION:** Bombay University, BS (with honors), 1964, DMS, 1972; Armed Forces Medical College, India, MBBS, 1968. **CAREER:** Bombay University Affiliated Hospitals, cardiology, registrar, 1970-73; Creighton University Affiliated Hospitals, clinical instructor, 1977-78; Creighton University School of Medicine, asst professor, 1978-85, associate professor, 1985-90, professor of medicine, 1990-. **ORGANIZATIONS:** American Heart Assn, 1976-; American College of Physicians, 1977-; American Federation for Clinical Research, 1978-; Midwest Clinical Soc, 1978-; Cardiovascular Soc of Omaha, 1978-; Metro Omaha Medical Soc, 1979-; American Soc of Internal Medicine, 1979-; American Institute of Ultrasound in Medicine, 1982-87, senior member, 1987-; Council on Clinical Cardiology, 1983-; New York Academy of Sciences, 1991; Council on Geriatric Cardiology, 1991. **HONORS/AWARDS:** American College of Cardiology, fellow, 1981; American College of Physicians, fellow, 1982; American Heart Assn, fellow, 1982-; American College of Chest Physicians, fellows, 1983-; American College of Angiology, fellow, 1989; American College of Cardiology, Council on Geriatric Cardiology, fellow, 1990; Intl College of Angiology, fellow, 1991. **SPECIAL ACHIEVEMENTS:** 49 presentations & 84 publications including: "Mitral Annular Calcium in Patients with & without Rheumatic Heart Disease," Abstracts 58th Annual Scientific Assembly, Chest, vol 102, no 2, p 209S, 1992; "Diagnostic & Prognostic Value of ST Segment Changes Detected by Ambulatory ECG Monitoring in Unselected Patients with Chest Pain," Abstract, Chest, vol 103, no 3, p 152S, March 1993. **HOME ADDRESS:** 9929 Devonshire, Omaha, NE 68114. **BUSINESS ADDRESS:** Professor, Creighton University School of Medicine, 3006 Webster St, Omaha, NE 68131-2044.

NAIR, K. M.
Scientist. Indo-American. **PERSONAL:** Born Jan 1, 1933, Vaikam, Kerala, India; son of K Kumaran Nair and K Karthiyani Amma; married Xina Nair, Sep 22, 1970; children: M Natha. **EDUCATION:** University of Kerala, India, BSc, 1959, MSc, 1961; Pennsylvania State University, MS, 1964; University of Washington, PhD, 1969. **CAREER:** Government of India, scientist, 1961-62; Penn State University, research scientist, 1962-64; University of Washington, research scientist, NIH fellow, 1964-74; University of Cincinnati, faculty, 1974-78; E I du Pont de Nemours & Co, scientist, 1978-. **ORGANIZATIONS:** American Ceramic Society, 1978-, secretary, program chair, vice chair, chair, 1983-90, trustee, 1993-; Ideas Inc, president, 1989-. **HONORS/AWARDS:** Numerous international awards. **SPECIAL ACHIEVEMENTS:** Author: 21 technical publications; two dramas; editor, co-editor: 8 books; patents: 18 US; 14 European; 14 Japanese. **HOME ADDRESS:** 3350 Westminster Ln, Buckingham, Doylestown, PA 18901. **BUSINESS ADDRESS:** Scientist, E I du Pont de Nemours & Co, Inc, Experimental Station, Box 80334, Wilmington, DE 19880-0334, (302)695-8303.

NAIR, MIRA
Filmmaker. Indo-American. **PERSONAL:** Born 1957, Bhubaneswar, Orissa, India; married Mahmood Mamdani; children: Zohran. **EDUCATION:** Delhi University, sociology; Harvard University. **CAREER:** Filmmaker; works include: Jama Masjid Street Journal, 1979; So Far from India, 1982; India Cabaret, 1985; Children of a Desired Sex, 1987; Salaam Bombay!, 1988; Mississippi Masala, 1991; current projects include: The Perez Family; Kama Sutra. **ORGANIZATIONS:** Salaam Baalak Trust, co-founder. **HONORS/AWARDS:** Prix du Publique, most popular film shown at Cannes, for Salaam Bombay!; American Film Festival, best documentary award, for India Cabaret; Global Village Film Festival, best documentary award, for India Cabaret; Cannes Film Festival, Camarea d'Or, for Salaam Bombay!; Academy Award nomination, for Salaam Bombay!, 1988. **BIOGRAPHICAL SOURCES:** Current Biography Yearbook, 1993. **BUSINESS ADDRESS:** Filmmaker, International Creative Management, 8942 Wilshire Blvd, Attn: Bart Walker, Beverly Hills, CA 90211, (310)550-4000.*

NAIR, V. KRISHNAN
Cardiologist. Indo-American. **PERSONAL:** Born Dec 30, 1941, Neyyattinkara, India; son of A Velupillai-Bharathi; married Sathy, Apr 22, 1971;

children: Parvathy, Pradeep. **EDUCATION:** Kerala University, BSc, 1958, MB, 1961, BS, 1965, MD, 1970. **CAREER:** New York Medical College, assistant professor; Somerset Hospital, director of cardiology, 1980-; self-employed, cardiology, 1980-; Somerset Hospital, chief of staff, 1990-93. **ORGANIZATIONS:** American Heart Association, Somerset Division, board member, 1986-; PA Medical Society; Somerset County Medical Society, past president; Cardiac Club, Somerset, director. **HONORS/AWARDS:** American College of Cardiology, fellow, 1980; American College Physicians, fellow, 1993; American Board of Internal Medicine, 1976; American Board of Cardiology, 1979. **SPECIAL ACHIEVEMENTS:** Advanced Achievement of Internal Medicine, 1987. **HOME ADDRESS:** 620 Meadowrim Dr, Somerset, PA 15501, (814)443-1515. **BUSINESS ADDRESS:** Cardiologist, 223 S Pleasant Ave, Somerset, PA 15501, (814)445-7101.

NAITO, HERBERT K.
Chief, association executive. Japanese American. **PERSONAL:** Born Nov 25, 1942, Honolulu, HI; son of Yukio Naito & Elsie Naito; divorced. **EDUCATION:** University of Northern Colorado, BA, 1963; University of Northern Colorado, MA, 1965; Iowa State University of Science & Technology, PhD, 1971; The Cleveland Clinic Foundation, postdoctoral fellow, 1973; Lake Erie College, MBA, 1988. **CAREER:** Cleveland State University, adjunct assistant professor, 1973-75, clinical assistant professor, 1975-77, clinical associate professor, 1977-80, clinical professor, 1980-89; The Cleveland Clinic Foundation, Research Institute, senior scientist, 1973-89, head, Section of Lipids, Nutrition and Meatbolic Diseases, 1973-89, Dept of Cardiology, clinical consultant, 1986-89; Nichols Institute, academic associate, 1989-90; Cleveland VA Medical Center, chief, clinical chemistry, 1990-; National Center for Laboratory Accuracy and Standardization, Dept of Veterans Affairs, associate director, 1992-. **ORGANIZATIONS:** American Association for the Advancement of Science; American Heart Association, Council on Atherosclerosis, fellow; American College of Nutrition, fellow; National Academy of Clinical Biochemistry, fellow; American Association for Clinical Chemistry; American Society for Clinical Pathologists; Society for Experimental Biology and Medicine; American Institute of Nutrition; American Association of Experimental Pathologists; Endocrine Society; American Chemical Society; American Oil Chemists Society; Sigma Xi; Association of Clinical Scientists, fellow. **HONORS/AWARDS:** American Association for Clinical Chemistry, Young Investigator Award, 1977; National Academy of Clinical Biochemistry, George Grannis Award, 1981; American Association for Clinical Chemistry, Outstanding Speaker Award, 1987-88; Roche Diagnostic Award for Outstanding Contributions in selected area of research, 1987-88; Federal Executive Board Award for Outstanding Federal Service, 1992; US Congress Achievement Award, 1992. **SPECIAL ACHIEVEMENTS:** Books published: Nutritional Elements and Clinical Biochemistry, M A Brewster and H K Naito, (eds), 1980; Nutrition and Heart Disease, H K Naito (ed), 1982; Handbook of Electrophoresis: vol IV, Lipoprotein Studies of Nonhuman Species, 1983; Detection and Treatment of Lipid and Lipoprotein Disorders of Childhood, K Widhalm and H K Naito (eds), 1985; Recent Aspects of Diagnosis and Treatment of Lipoprotein Disorders: Impact on Prevention of Atherosclerotic Diseases, Widhalm K and Naito, H K (eds), 1987. **BUSINESS ADDRESS:** Chief & Assoc Dir, Dept of Veterans Affairs Med Ctr, Pathology and Laboratory Medicine Service, 10701 East Blvd, Rm 113W, Cleveland, OH 44106, (216)791-3800.

NAITO, MICHAEL K.
Law enforcement official. Japanese American. **PERSONAL:** Born Apr 8, 1948, Chicago, IL; son of Tony and Mary Naito; married Linda, Apr 20, 1974; children: Jason, Kristen. **CAREER:** City of Chicago, Chicago Police Dept, patrolman, police officer, currently. **ORGANIZATIONS:** Asian American Police Assn. **BUSINESS ADDRESS:** Patrolman, Chicago Police Dept - City of Chicago, 1940 W Foster, Chicago, IL 60656.

NAITO, SAMUEL TERUHIDE
Business executive. Japanese American. **PERSONAL:** Born Dec 10, 1921, Portland, OR; son of Hide & Fukiye Naito; married Mary, 1949; children: Lawrence, Ronald Verner. **EDUCATION:** University of Utah, BA, 1944; Columbia University, MSc, 1946. **CAREER:** Norcrest China Co, owner, CEO, currently. **ORGANIZATIONS:** Standard Insurance Co, board member; First Interstate Bank of Oregon, board member; Japanese Garden Society of Oregon, past president, chairman; Better Business Bureau; Oregon Historical Society; Japan-American Society; Lewis & Clark College, trustee; Medical Research Foundation; Oregon International Trade Committee; Portland-Sapporo Sister City Committee; International Trade Institute; First United Methodist Church. **HONORS/AWARDS:** American Institute of Architects, Civic Enrichment

Award; Chamber of Commerce, Annual Award for Business Property Improvements, 1975, 1976; Portland Beautification Award; Oregon Environmental Council, Richard L Neuberger Award; Portland Historical Landmark Committee, 1979; Lewis & Clark College, Aubrey Watzek Award, 1982; Portland Realty Board, First Citizen Award, 1983; National Minority Enterprise Award, 1983. **MILITARY SERVICE:** US Army, corp, 1944-46. **BUSINESS ADDRESS:** CEO, Norcrest China Co, 5 NW Front Ave, Portland, OR 97209, (503)228-7404.

NAJITA, TETSUO
Educator. Japanese American. **PERSONAL:** Born Mar 30, 1936, Honokaa, HI; son of Niichi and Kikuno Najita (deceased); married Elinor, Aug 2, 1958; children: Mie (deceased), Kiyoshi. **EDUCATION:** Grinnell College, BA, 1958; Harvard University, MA, 1960, PhD, 1965. **CAREER:** Carleton College, 1964-66; Washington University, 1966-68; University of Wisconsin, Madison, 1968; University of Chicago, Robert S Ingersoll Distinguished Service professor, 1969-; University of Hawaii, Manoa, John A Burns Distinguished Visiting Professor, 1994. **ORGANIZATIONS:** Association for Asian Studies, president, 1992-93, board of directors, 1991-95; American Council of Learned Societies, executive comm, 1993-96; American Historical Association; Chicago/Osaka Sister City Program, chair, Education Comm, 1992-. **HONORS/AWARDS:** Grinnell College, Honorary Doctorate of Law, 1989; Prefecture of Osaka, Yamagata Banto Prize, 1989; American Academy of Arts & Sciences, fellow, 1993. **SPECIAL ACHIEVEMENTS:** Book: Visions of Virtue in Tokugawa, Japan, The Kaitokudo Merchant/Academy. **BUSINESS ADDRESS:** Robert S. Ingersoll Professor, Dept of History, University of Chicago, 1126 East 59th St, Chicago, IL 60637, (312)702-8934.

NAKADEGAWA, ROY
Transportation administrator, civil engineer. Japanese American. **CAREER:** San Francisco Bay Area Rapid Transit, District 3, director, 1992-. **ORGANIZATIONS:** Institute of Transportation Engineers. **SPECIAL ACHIEVEMENTS:** Registered civil engineer; only person in country to be elected by the public to serve in three transit governing board positions, serving Oakland, Berkeley, and El Cerritos. **BUSINESS ADDRESS:** Director, District 3, San Francisco Bay Area Rapid Transit, 800 Madison St, Oakland, CA 94607, (510)464-6095. *

NAKAGAWA, CRESSEY
Attorney. Japanese American. **CAREER:** Attorney, currently. **ORGANIZATIONS:** Japanese American Citizens League, national president, 1992. **BUSINESS ADDRESS:** Attorney, #5 Third St, San Francisco, CA 94103, (415)421-6995.*

NAKAGUCHI, RICHARD T.
Promotion artist. Japanese American. **PERSONAL:** Born Feb 27, 1938, Sacramento, CA; son of Thomas I Nakaguchi and Ruth M Nakaguchi; married Louise K Nakaguchi, Jun 3, 1967; children: Shelley M, Russell K. **EDUCATION:** Fresno City College, AA, 1962; Fresno State University, AB, 1964. **CAREER:** Fresno Bee, editorial staff artist, 1964-90, marketing promotion artist, 1990-. **MILITARY SERVICE:** Army, SFC, 1960-66. **HOME ADDRESS:** 6043 N Harrison, Fresno, CA 93711, (209)431-4135. **BUSINESS ADDRESS:** Promotion Artist, The Fresno Bee, 1626 E St, Fresno, CA 93786, (209)441-6088.

NAKAHARA, SHOHEI
Scientist. Japanese American. **PERSONAL:** Born Jan 3, 1942, Hiroshima, Japan; son of Shinichi Nakahara and Yasuko Nakahara; married Hazel V Nakahara, Oct 7, 1978; children: Jay, Jonathan. **EDUCATION:** Hiroshima University, BEng, 1965, MEng, 1967; Stevens Inst of Tech, PhD, 1973. **CAREER:** AT&T Bell Labs, member of tech staff, 1973-. **ORGANIZATIONS:** Sigma Xi; Electrochem Soc. **HOME ADDRESS:** 114 Wildflower Dr, Allentown, PA 18104. **BUSINESS ADDRESS:** Member of Technical Staff, Solid State Tech Ctr, AT&T Bell Laboratories, 9999 Hamilton Blvd, Rm 2C-204, Breinigsville, PA 18031-9359, (215)391-2684.

NAKAJIMA, NOBUYUKI
Educator, educational administrator. Japanese American. **PERSONAL:** Born Nov 3, 1923, Tokyo, Japan; son of Kiyoshi Nakajima and Tomi Nakajima; divorced; children: Charles M, Leslie M, Eric T. **EDUCATION:** Toyko University, 1945; Polytechnic University of New York, MS, 1955; Case Western Reserve University, PhD, 1958. **CAREER:** Osaka Gas Company, production engineer, 1945-51; W R Grace & Company, research associates, 1960-66;

Allied Chemical Company, manager of research, 1966-71; B F Goodrich Company, research fellow, 1971-84; Institute of Polymer Engineering, The University of Akron, asst dir, professor, 1984-. **ORGANIZATIONS:** American Chemical Society, Rubber Division and Polymer Division, currently; American Physical Society; Society of Rheology; Sigma Xi; International Polymer Processing Society; Japanese Society of Rubber Industry, associate editor; Japanese Society of Polymer Science. **SPECIAL ACHIEVEMENTS:** Author of 140 publications. **BUSINESS ADDRESS:** Professor and Assistant Director, Institute of Polymer Engineering, University of Akron, Akron, OH 44325-0301, (216)972-6607.

NAKAJO, STEVE
Association administrator. Japanese American. **PERSONAL:** children: son. **CAREER:** City College of San Francisco, part-time teacher; Kimochi Inc, executive director, currently. **BUSINESS ADDRESS:** Executive Director, Kimochi Inc, 1840 Sutter St, Ste 208, San Francisco, CA 94115, (415)931-2294. *

NAKAMOTO, DONALD JIRO
Labor union official, editor. Japanese American. **PERSONAL:** Born Jan 8, 1955, Los Angeles, CA; son of Nobuo Nakamoto and Matsuye Nakamoto; married Sharon Lazo-Nakamoto, Nov 7, 1987; children: Alyssa. **EDUCATION:** University of Southern California, BA, 1976. **CAREER:** Dean Newspaper Group, reporter, 1978; Service Employees Intl Union, editor, 1979-88; Intl Assn of Machinists and Aerospace Workers, editor, research director, 1988-. **ORGANIZATIONS:** Alliance of Asian Pacific Labor, AFL-CIO, vice pres, 1990-93; Competitiveness Policy Council, Manufacturing Subcommittee, 1992; Project California, Human Resources Subcommittee, 1993. **HONORS/AWARDS:** Intl Labor Communications Assn, 15 awards for labor journalism excellence, 1980-91; Western Labor Press Assn, 24 awards for labor journalism excellence, 1980-91; Intl Assn of Machinists, 6 awards for labor journalism excellence, 1989-93. **HOME ADDRESS:** 3349 Pasadena Ave, Long Beach, CA 90807. **BUSINESS ADDRESS:** Editor, Research Director, Intl Assn of Machinists and Aerospace Workers, 2600 W Victory Blvd, Burbank, CA 91505.

NAKAMOTO, TETSUO
Educator. Japanese American. **PERSONAL:** Born Dec 20, 1939, Kure, Hiroshima-Ken, Japan; son of Takamori Nakamoto and Masae Nakamoto; married Lynda G Nakamoto, May 14, 1980; children: Andrew T, Christopher W T. **EDUCATION:** Nihon University School of Dentistry, DDS, 1964; University of Michigan, Ann Arbor, MS, 1966, MS, 1971; University of North Dakota, Grand Forks, MS, 1969; MIT, PhD, 1978. **CAREER:** Nihon University, Japan, visiting professor, 1987, School of Dentistry, visiting professor, 1992; Louisiana State University Medical Center, assistant professor of physiology, 1978-84, associate professor of physiology, 1984-91, professor of physiology, 1991-. **ORGANIZATIONS:** International Association for Dental Research; American Association for Dental Research; Sigma Xi; Society for Experimental Biology and Medicine; American Institute of Nutrition; The American Physiological Society. **SPECIAL ACHIEVEMENTS:** Contributor to professional journals. **BUSINESS ADDRESS:** Professor of Physiology, Louisiana State University Medical Center, 1100 Florida Ave, New Orleans, LA 70119, (504)948-8541.

NAKAMURA, KAREN TSUNEKO
General contractor. Japanese American. **PERSONAL:** Born Jul 2, 1944, Honolulu, HI; daughter of Paul T Nakagaki & Dorothy A Higuchi Nakagaki; married Bertram S Nakamura, Nov 28, 1964; children: Leinani Nakamura Malig, Bert Paul. **EDUCATION:** University of Hawaii, 1962-65. **CAREER:** Dorothy-Karen's Beauty Salon, 1965-68; Wallpaper Hawaii Ltd, stock clerk, 1959-68, president, CEO, 1981-. **ORGANIZATIONS:** National Association of Home Builders, board member, 1985-, National Remodelors Council, chairman, 1991, Advisory Sub-Committee, membership chairman, 1993; Building Industry of Hawaii, education committee, chairman, 1993; Aloha United Way, board member, 1992-94; YWCA, board member, 1992-93; Maryknoll Schools, chairman, board member, 1987-93; Rotary Club of Honolulu, 1990-. **HONORS/AWARDS:** NAHB-RC, National Remodelor of the Year, 1986; Building Industry of Hawaii, Builder of the Decade for the 1980's. **SPECIAL ACHIEVEMENTS:** First woman general contractor in the state of Hawaii, 1982; first woman president of Building Industry of Hawaii, 1986; first woman chairman of National Remodelors Council, NAHB, 1991. **MILITARY SERVICE:** Naval Reserves, seaman apprentice, 1962-64. **BIOGRAPHICAL SOURCES:** Honolulu Sunday Advertiser & Star Bulletin, front page, home section, B4, May 18, 1986, Dec 30, 1990; The Hawaii Herald, A14-15, March 1, 1991. **BUSINESS ADDRESS:** President, CEO, Wallpaper Hawaii Ltd, dba Remodeling Specialists Hawaii, 3160 Waialae Ave, Honolulu, HI 96816, (808)735-2861.

NAKAMURA, MICHAEL S.
Law enforcement official. Japanese American. **CAREER:** Honolulu Police Department, police chief, currently. **BUSINESS ADDRESS:** Police Chief, City of Honolulu Police Department, 1455 S Beretania St, Honolulu, HI 96814, (808)943-3162. *

NAKAMURA, MITSURU JAMES
Educator. Japanese American. **PERSONAL:** Born Dec 17, 1926, Los Angeles, CA; son of Jingo and Michie Nakamura; married Judith Ann, Dec 15, 1973; children: Monica Suzan, Nancy Midori, Mark James. **EDUCATION:** University of California at Los Angeles, AB, 1949; University of Southern California, MS, 1950; Boston University, School of Medicine, PhD, 1956. **CAREER:** University California, San Francisco, research assistant, 1950-52; Northeastern University, assistant professor & associate professor, 1952-56; University of Montana, associate professor to professor, chairman, 1956-92, professor emeritus, 1992-. **ORGANIZATIONS:** American Society of Microbiology, 1949-; American Society Trop Medicine and Hygiene, 1950-; American Association Advancement of Science, 1956-80; American Public Health Association, 1956-80; Commissioned Officers Association of USPHS, 1958-89; Sigma Xi, 1950-93; Royal Society of Tropical Medicine and Hygiene, 1958-80; Society for Experimental Biology and Medicine, 1956-80. **HONORS/AWARDS:** Albert Szent-Gyorgyi Medical University, Hungary, Honorary Doctor of Medical Sciences, 1991; National Academy of Sciences, travel grants to make scientific visits to: Poland, Yugoslavia, Hungary, Bulgaria, Czechoslovakia, 1976-90; National Institutes of Health: research grants in microbiology, 1958-76; postdoctoral fellowships to do advanced study at: University of Wisconsin, U Minnesota, Harvard University, University Virginia, Louisiana State University, University South Calif. **SPECIAL ACHIEVEMENTS:** Visiting professor to universities in Taiwan, Trinidad, Hungary, 1987-91; commissioned officer in the reserves of the US Public Health Service, lt jg to captain, 1959-93; over 70 publications in scientific journals, 1950-92. **MILITARY SERVICE:** US Army Military Intelligence Service Language School, Presidio of Monterey, sergeant; 1945-46; Good Conduct Medal, 1946, Victory Medal, 1946. **HOME ADDRESS:** 2612 Highwood Drive, Missoula, MT 59803, (406)251-3970.

NAKAMURA, PATRICIA AKEMI KOSUGI
Educator. Japanese American. **PERSONAL:** Born Sep 5, 1948, Stockton, CA; daughter of Frank & Tomiko Kosugi; married Robert, May 26, 1973; children: Darin Kei Kosugi, Clark Takeshi. **EDUCATION:** San Joaquin Delta College, AA, 1968; UC Berkeley, BA, 1970, MA, 1971, Secondary Teaching Credential, 1972. **CAREER:** Merritt College, art teacher, 1971-72; San Joaquin Delta College, art teacher, 1973-93. **ORGANIZATIONS:** California Teachers Assn; Japanese American Citizens League; Academic Senate, committee member; Alpha Rho Tau, art club advisor; SIDC Scholarship Foundation Association. **BUSINESS ADDRESS:** Teacher, Art Dept, San Joaquin Delta College, 5151 Pacific Ave, Stockton, CA 95207, (209)474-5209.

NAKAMURA, ROYDEN
Scientist, educator. Japanese American/Pacific Islander American. **PERSONAL:** Born Jun 13, 1939, Kohala, HI; son of Margaret & Tatsuichi Nakamura; divorced; children: Kuikahi, Randal L. **EDUCATION:** University of Hawaii, BA, 1961, MS, 1965; University of British Columbia, PhD, 1970. **CAREER:** Lummi Indian Tribal Council, director of aquaculture training programs, 1969-72; University of Massachusetts, Dartmouth, professor, 1972-78; California Polytechnic University, professor, 1979-. **ORGANIZATIONS:** American Society of Ichthyologist and Herpetologists, 1972-; American Fisheries Society, 1985-; World Aquaculture Society, contributing editor, Technology Transfer Committee, 1969; Western Society of Naturalists, 1990-. **HONORS/AWARDS:** International Council for Exchange of Scholars, fellow, 1980; US International Communications Agency, Senior Fulbright-Hays Scholar, 1980. **SPECIAL ACHIEVEMENTS:** Publications in various scientific journals on aquaculture, fisheries, marine biology; various research grant awards. **MILITARY SERVICE:** USAF/Hawaii Air National Guard, a2c, 1964-69; USAF Certification Weather Observer. **BUSINESS ADDRESS:** Professor, Biological Sciences Dept, California Polytechnic University, San Luis Obispo, CA 93407, (805)756-2788.

NAKAMURA, RUSSELL KOICHI
Beverage manufacturing company executive. Japanese American. **PERSONAL:** Born Sep 7, 1953, Amarillo, TX; son of Harry Nakamura and Myrtle Nakamura; married Lori J Otsuka, May 22, 1982. **EDUCATION:** NASA Radio School of Technology; Leeward College. **CAREER:** NASA, Bendix Field Engineering, radio/computer tech; Kauai Beverage/Ice Cream, sales mgr, general mgr, president, currently. **ORGANIZATIONS:** West Kauai Jaycees. **MILITARY SERVICE:** US Air Force, e-4, 1972-76. **BUSINESS ADDRESS:** President/General Manager, Kauai Beverage & Ice Cream Co, Ltd, PO Box 1889, Lihue, HI 96766.

NAKANISHI, DON TOSHIAKI
Research director, educator. Japanese American. **PERSONAL:** Born Aug 14, 1949, Los Angeles, CA; son of Tsugio Nakanishi and Miyoko Nakanishi; married Marsha Hirano-Nakanishi, Dec 28, 1974; children: Thomas. **EDUCATION:** Yale University, BA (cum laude), political science, 1971; Harvard University, PhD, political science, 1978. **CAREER:** University of California, Los Angeles, Graduate School of Education, associate professor, currently, Asian American Studies Center, director, currently. **ORGANIZATIONS:** Amerasia Journal, co-founder, publisher, 1970-75, editorial board, 1975-; Assn of Asian American Studies, national president, 1983-85; Natl Assn for Asian and Pacific American Education, executive board, vp, 1983-; The College Board, New York, advisory panel member on minority concerns, 1984-. **HONORS/AWARDS:** California Teachers Assn, John Swett Award, nominee, 1989; Asian American Legal Center of Southern California, Civil Rights Impact Award, 1989; recipient: Chancellor's Challenge Grant in Arts and Humanities, 1991, California Policy Seminar Grant, 1992, University of California Pacific Rim Studies Grant, 1992. **SPECIAL ACHIEVEMENTS:** Research specialist and author of over 50 articles and books on education policy issues facing Asian Pacific Americans and other minorities, minority political participation in the US; University of Michigan, Martin Luther King Jr Symposium, guest speaker, 1990; University of California, Berkeley, Ethnic Studies Program, review committee member, 1991; Yale University, Conference on Political Identity and American Thought, speaker, 1991. **BUSINESS ADDRESS:** Director, Asian American Studies Center, University of California, 3230 Campbell Hall, Los Angeles, CA 90024, (213)825-2974.

NAKANO, FRANCIS
Educator, assistant superintendent. Japanese American. **PERSONAL:** Born Mar 23, 1938, Los Angeles, CA; son of Art & Ruth Nakano; married Jane, Jun 1964; children: Eric, Michele. **EDUCATION:** California State University, Los Angeles, BA, 1962, MA, 1966; UCLA, MA, 1972; Claremont Graduate School, PhD, 1979. **CAREER:** Los Angeles Unified School District: teacher, 1962-69, consultant, 1969-76, dean of attendance, 1976-78, assistant principal, 1978-80, principal, 1980-87, region administrator of operations, 1988-89, assistant superintendent, 1989-. **ORGANIZATIONS:** Association of California School Administrators. **HONORS/AWARDS:** Executive Educator-100, USA; Chamber of Commerce, Principal of the Year Award; awards from city and state officials; award from county office of education; awards from community organizations. **SPECIAL ACHIEVEMENTS:** Created first film on Asian Americans, LAUSD; developed first professional library on Asian Americans; published magazine articles on safety in schools; written up in US News and World Report, Time Magazine, LA Times, national TV programs; Asian American Educators Association, organized and set the course of action, 1978; Alliance of Asian Pacific Administrators, organized and developed association, 1985. **BUSINESS ADDRESS:** Assistant Superintendent, Los Angeles Unified School District, 450 N Grand Ave, A-221, Los Angeles, CA 90012, (213)625-6251.

NAKANO, FRANK HIROSHI
Physician. Japanese American. **PERSONAL:** Born Dec 21, 1935, Modesto, CA; son of George Gonkichi Nakano and Haruko Harano; married Josephine van Nieuwpoort, Jul 25, 1979; children: Genji Chihiro, Bastiaan Gonkichi. **EDUCATION:** UC Berkeley and San Francisco School of Pharmacy, BS (honors), 1958; UCLA School of Medicine, MD, 1962. **CAREER:** UCLA School of Medicine, assistant clinical professor of Medicine; Los Angeles VA Center, attending cardiology services; Washington Medical Center, chief of staff, 1982-84, intensive care unit, director; West-Bay Medical Group, internist/cardiologist, 1970-71; self-employed private practice, cardiology, 1971-. **ORGANIZATIONS:** American Heart Association; American College of Cardiology; American Society of Echocardiography; Japanese-American Cultural & Community Center Ambassadors Council. **HONORS/AWARDS:** School of Pharmacy, Rho Chi, Bear Photo Award for Scholarship. **SPECIAL**

ACHIEVEMENTS: Los Angeles County Medical Assn, vp, Bay District div II, 1978-79; Board Certified Medical Board of Internal Medicine and Cardiovascular Disease; Council of Clinical Cardiology, American Heart Assn, fellow; American College of Cardiology, fellow; publications, co-author: "Fatal Lung Scan in a Case of Pulmonary Hypertension Due to Obliterative Pulmonary Vascular Disease," Chest, vol 67, p 308-310, 1975; "Computer Enhanced Digital Angiography," Clinical Cardiology, vol 5, p 318-326, 1982; "Computer Enhanced Digital Angiography," American Heart Journal, 1982. **MILITARY SERVICE:** Army, maj, 1967-69; Chief, Cardiology Service, US Army in Japan 106th General Hosp. **BUSINESS ADDRESS:** Cardiologist, 3831 Hughes Avenue, Ste 604, Culver City, CA 90232, (310)559-2627.

NAKANO, GEORGE
City government official. Japanese American. **CAREER:** City of Torrance, former mayor pro-tem, councilman, currently. **SPECIAL ACHIEVEMENTS:** Democratic National Committee, Asian Pacific Advisory Council Vote Headquarters, opening celebration, speaker, 1992. **BUSINESS ADDRESS:** City Councilman, Torrance City Council, 3031 Torrance Blvd, Torrance, CA 90503, (310)618-2801.*

NAKANO, MEI TAKAYA
Writer, editor, publisher. Japanese American. **PERSONAL:** Born Dec 1, 1924, Olathe, CO; daughter of Shika and Junsuke Takaya; married Shiro Nakano, Apr 25, 1943; children: Chris H, Nikki S Omi, Philip A. **EDUCATION:** California State University, Hayward, BA (summa cum laude), 1970, MA, 1974. **CAREER:** Laney Community College, English instructor, 1974-79; Diablo Valley Community College, English instructor, 1979-81; Mina Press Publishing/Consultants, editor, publisher, 1981-; writer, currently. **ORGANIZATIONS:** Japanese American Citizen's League, Sonoma County, executive board, 1979-; Women's Concerns Comm, organizing member/chair, 1985-87; KRCB, Public TV, Community Advisory Council, 1985-; Sonoma County Coalition for Human Rights, organizer/chair, 1991-92; Japanese American National Museum, Scholarly Advisory Committee, 1991-; Sonoma County Commission on Human Rights, executive board, 1993. **HONORS/AWARDS:** Sonoma County Japanese American Citizens League, JACLer of the Year, 1982; Women of Color Task Force, Sonoma County Commission on Status of Women, Award for Community Involvement, 1991; Santa Rosa Junior College Faculty Women, Political Women honoree, 1991; Sonoma County YWCA, Women of Achievement honoree, 1993; San Francisco Community Center, Literature and the Arts awardee, 1991. **SPECIAL ACHIEVEMENTS:** Riko Rabbit, folk tale, 1982; Japanese American Women: Three Generations, 1990, 1991, 1993; section, "Japanese American Women in WWII," in Women's Studies Encyclopedia, V, III, 1991; "Japanese American Women," in History News, for American Association for State & Local History, 1990; regular monthly column, Sidebar, for Pacific Citizen, newspaper. **BIOGRAPHICAL SOURCES:** "Profiles," Press Democrat newspaper, p D6, Sunday, March 11, 1990; story in Valiant Women, Sally Hayton-Keeva, ed, book, p 190, 1987. **BUSINESS ADDRESS:** Editor, Publisher, Mina Press Publishing and Consultants, PO Box 854, Sebastopol, CA 95473.

NAKASATO, GEORGE
Association administrator. Japanese American. **CAREER:** 442nd Veterans Club, association administrator, currently. **ORGANIZATIONS:** 442nd Regimental Combat Team, 50th Anniversary Celebration, general chairman, 1993. **BUSINESS ADDRESS:** Association Administrator, 442nd Veterans Club, 933 Wili Wili St, Honolulu, HI 96826, (808)949-7997.*

NAKASHIMA, MITSUGI
Educator (retired), educational administrator. Japanese American. **PERSONAL:** Born Aug 16, 1929, Hanapepe, Kauai, HI; son of Imakichi & Koto Nakashima; married Marjorie Mieko Nakashima, Jul 1, 1961; children: Mindy Miyoko, Marcia Mariko. **EDUCATION:** University of Hawaii, BEd, 1951, prof certificate, 1952; Colorado State College, MA, 1961; Michigan State University, EdD, 1967. **CAREER:** Hawaii Department of Education, teacher, 1955-59, counselor, 1959-60, 1961-62, principal, 1962-65, 1967-69, curriculum specialist, 1969-78, assistant superintendent, office of instr services, 1978-80, district superintendent, Kauai Schools, 1980-87, program specialist, 1987. **ORGANIZATIONS:** Association for Supv & Curric Development, 1969-; National Society for Study of Education, 1965-; Phi Delta Kappa, 1979-; National Association State Board of Education, 1988-, western region rep, 1988-, Pacific region rep, 1993-95; National School Board Association, 1988-; YMCA of Kauai, 1955-; Hawaii Board of Education, 1988-; National Assessment Governing Board, 1993-97. **HONORS/AWARDS:** Mott Foundation,

Mott Fellowship, 1965-66. **MILITARY SERVICE:** US Army, Hawaii Army NG, 1st lt, 1952-55, 1957-59. **HOME ADDRESS:** 4549-A Puuwai Rd, PO Box 612, Kalaheo, HI 96741, (808)332-8507.

NAKASHIMA, TOM VINCENT
Artist, educator. Japanese American. **PERSONAL:** Born Sep 4, 1941, Seattle, WA; son of Victor K & Kathleen S Nakashima; married Lindsey Hughes Nakashima, Aug 16, 1980; children: Lindsay Jean, Jay Thomas, Heidi Jean. **EDUCATION:** Loras College, BA, 1967; University of Notre Dame, MA, 1968, MFA, 1969. **CAREER:** Columbus College of Art & Design, head of printmaking, 1963-68; University of Notre Dame, summer program, assistant professor, 1971, 1972; West Virginia University, coordinator of painting, associate professor, 1973-80; Anton Gallery, director, 1981-83; Catholic University of America, professor, 1981-; University of Minnesota, summer, Split Rock Arts Program, 1992-93. **ORGANIZATIONS:** Washington Project for the Arts, board member, 1991-93; Japan Embassy, Information & Culture Cen, "Continumm," a cross-cultural art exhibition, exhibition director, 1993; Pyramid Atlantic, papermaking and printmaking workshop, board of directors, 1991-93. **HONORS/AWARDS:** AVA, 11 Awards in the Visual Arts Fellowship, 1992; Mid-Atlantic NEA, Painting Fellowship, 1992; Mayor Sharon Pratt Kelly, Mayor's Award for Excellence in an Artistic Media, 1991; DC Commission on the Arts, Indiv Artist Fellowship, 1984, 1988, 1989; Pyramid Atlantic, Artist in Residence, Glen Eagles Fellowship, 1989. **SPECIAL ACHIEVEMENTS:** Solo exhibitions: Washington Project for the Arts, 1990; Bernice Steinbaum Gallery, NYC, 1991; Yamanashi Prefectural Mus of Art, 1988; Anton Gallery, DC, 1984-93; group exhibitions: The Decade Show, Studio Mus in Harlem, New Mus & MOCHA, NYC, 1990; Relocation & Revision-Japanese American Internment Reconsidered, Long Beach Museum of Art, 1992; Washington Moscow Art Exchange, Tretyakov Museum Moscow, 1991. **MILITARY SERVICE:** US Army-Airborne, 101st Airborne Division, Sp-5, 1960-63. **BIOGRAPHICAL SOURCES:** "Art in America," Tom Nakashima at Bernice Steinbaum, Janet Koplos, p152-153, October 1991; "Tom Nakashima, 1984-1990," by Lynn Schmidt, catalog with several pages of text, Washington Project for the Arts. **HOME ADDRESS:** 436 M St NW, #9, Washington, DC 20001, (202)737-3623.

NAKASONE, ROBERT C.
Toy company executive. Japanese American. **PERSONAL:** Born 1947; married. **EDUCATION:** Claremont College, BA, 1969; University of Chicago, MBA, 1971. **CAREER:** Brighams Ice Cream Parlor & Sandwich Shops, 1979-82; Jewel Food Stores, vice president, general manager, 1982-84; Toys R Us, midwest stores, vice president, 1986-89, USA, president, vice chairman, 1989-, Worldwide Toy Stores, president, currently. **ORGANIZATIONS:** Toys R Us, Board of Directors, chairman, currently. **SPECIAL ACHIEVEMENTS:** US Pan Asian American Chamber of Commerce, Excellence 2000 Awards, keynote speaker, 1992. **MILITARY SERVICE:** US Army, first lt. **BUSINESS ADDRESS:** Vice Chairman/President, Toys R Us, 461 From Rd, Paramus, NJ 07652-3524, (201)262-7800.∗

NAKATA, HERBERT MINORU
Educator, educational administrator. Japanese American. **PERSONAL:** Born Mar 10, 1930, Pasadena, CA; son of Russell Kingo and Fusayo Nakata; married Barbara Ann, Apr 9, 1960; children: Stephen, Laura Nakata-Vannucci, Debra. **EDUCATION:** University of Illinois, BS, 1952, MS, 1956, PhD, 1959. **CAREER:** Washington State University, instructor, 1959-62, assistant professor, 1962-66, associate professor, 1966-71, professor, department chair, 1968-92, professor, 1971-93. **ORGANIZATIONS:** American Society for Microbiology, 1956-, Northwest Branch, 1960-, vice president, president, 1975-77, 1983-85, councilor, 1980-83; American Association for the Advancement of Science, 1965-; Nature Conservancy, 10 years; Sigma Xi, 1962-. **SPECIAL ACHIEVEMENTS:** Publications in professional journals. **MILITARY SERVICE:** US Army, s/sgt, 1952-54. **HOME ADDRESS:** NW 335 Janet St, Pullman, WA 99163, (509)332-3269.

NAKATANI, COREY
Jockey. Japanese American. **PERSONAL:** Born 1970?; son of Roy; married Michele Dollase; children: Brittany Marie, Matthew. **EDUCATION:** Graduated from jockey training school in Castaic, CA. **CAREER:** Worked at a thoroughbred farm near Palmdale, CA; thoroughbred jockey, 1989-. **HONORS/AWARDS:** Finished fourth in Kentucky Derby, 1991; Louisiana Derby winner; Hollywood Turf Cup winner, 1990; Kentucky Oaks winner, 1991; Santa Margarita Handicap, Santa Anita, winner, 1993; Charles H Straub Stakes at Golden Gate Fields, 1993. **SPECIAL ACHIEVEMENTS:** Has

earned over $16 million in career. **BUSINESS ADDRESS:** Jockey, Santa Anita Park, 285 Huntington Dr, Arcadia, CA 91007, (818)574-7223.∗

NAKATANI, HENRY MASATOSHI
Government engineering manager. Japanese American. **PERSONAL:** Born Feb 23, 1942, Honolulu, HI; son of Minoru & Teruko Nakatani; divorced; children: Janice. **EDUCATION:** University of Hawaii, BS, 1964, MS, 1966; San Jose State University, 1967-68. **CAREER:** Sandia Corp, technical staff member, 1966-69; Shimazu Shimabukuro & Fukuda Inc, structural engineer, 1969-71; University of Hawaii, College of Continuing Education and Community Service, lecturer, 1980-; Aloha Stadium, stadium engineer, 1978-81; State of Hawaii Public Works, structural engineer, 1971-78, 1981-. **ORGANIZATIONS:** American Public Works Association, awards chairman, 1990-; Structural Engineers Association of Hawaii, 1990-; Rainbow Camera Club, treasurer, 1971-75; American Society of Civil Engineers, 1967-72. **HONORS/AWARDS:** American Society of Civil Engineers, Outstanding Civil Engineering Senior, 1964; Chi Epsilon, 1963; Omicron Delta Kappa, 1964; Phi Kappa Phi, 1964; State of Hawaii, Achievement Award, 1989, 1993. **SPECIAL ACHIEVEMENTS:** Author, "Comparison of Wind Induced Vibrations of Structures Using Real and Pseudo Wind Records," Center for Engineering Research, University of Hawaii, 1966. **BUSINESS ADDRESS:** Design Branch Chief, State of Hawaii Public Works, 1151 Punchbowl St, Kalanimoku Bldg, Rm 431, Honolulu, HI 96813, (808)586-0433.

NAKATANI, ROY EIJI
Educator. Japanese American. **PERSONAL:** Born Jun 8, 1918, Seattle, WA; son of Ushinosuke and Fuku Nakatani; married Harue Nakatani, May 28, 1955; children: Ronald Lee, Dale Eiji, Scott M, Mika Lyn, Mark Isamu. **EDUCATION:** BS, fisheries, 1947; PhD, fisheries, 1960. **CAREER:** General Electric, biological scientist, 1959-60, aquatic biology manager, 1960-65; Battelle, NW ecology, manager, 1965-70; University of Washington, associate professor, 1970-73, professor, associate director, Fisheries, Research Institute, 1973-88, professor emeritus, 1988-. **ORGANIZATIONS:** International Academy of Fishery Scientists, fellow; American Association for the Advancement of Science, fellow; American Institute of Fishery Research Biologists, fellow, national secretary, 1986-91. **MILITARY SERVICE:** US Army, S/sg, 1941-46. **HOME ADDRESS:** 6719- 152nd Ave NE, Redmond, WA 98052. **BUSINESS ADDRESS:** Professor, University of Washington, Fisheries Research Institute, WH-10, Seattle, WA 98195, (206)543-4652.

NAKATSUKA, LAWRENCE KAORU
Journalist, government official (retired). Japanese American. **PERSONAL:** Born Jan 27, 1920, Hanalei, HI; son of Mr & Mrs Ichiro Nakatsuka; married Minnie Nakatsuka, Aug 5, 1948; children: Paul, Roy, Laura Carlucci. **EDUCATION:** Harvard University, fellowship, 1950-51; University of Hawaii, 1984-86. **CAREER:** Honolulu Star Bulletin, reporter, assistant city editor, 1939-53; Gov Samuel Wilder King, press secretary, 1953-57; Gov William F Quinn, press secretary, 1957-60; US Senate, legislative assistant to Sen Hiram Fong, 1963-76; Chamber of Commerce of Hawaii, legislative director, 1976-83. **ORGANIZATIONS:** Japanese-American Citizens League, Washington DC Chapter, president, 1974; Hawaii Hiroshima Heritage Study Group, president, 1985-86. **HONORS/AWARDS:** Nieman Foundation, Harvard University, 1950.

NAKAYAMA, HARVEY KIYOSHI
State government official. Japanese American. **PERSONAL:** Born Feb 23, 1944, Wahiawa, HI; son of Charles S Nakayama and Alice K Kozuma Nakayama; married Theresa; children: Lance K, Shannon M, Lisa M, Brent M, Reed A, Mark A, Amanda A. **EDUCATION:** Colorado State University, BS, 1967; University of Southern California, MSSM, 1976. **CAREER:** US Army, LTC, MSC, 1967-89; Colorado Department of Labor and Employment, Office of Info Systems, director, 1989-. **ORGANIZATIONS:** American Legion #185, 1993-94; Colorado Department of Labor & Employment, Annual Benefit Golf Committee, chair, 1993-94. **SPECIAL ACHIEVEMENTS:** Hawaii All-Star Baseball Electee, 1961. **MILITARY SERVICE:** Army, ltc, 1967-89. **BUSINESS ADDRESS:** Director, Office of Information Systems, Colorado Department of Labor and Employment, 600 Grant St, Ste 302, Denver, CO 80203, (303)837-3842.

NAKAYAMA, RANDALL SHIGE
Educator. Japanese American. **PERSONAL:** Born Aug 20, 1957, Oakland, CA; son of Shigenobu Nakayama and Helen Wada. **EDUCATION:** University of California-Berkeley, AB, 1979, MA, 1982, PhD, 1986. **CAREER:** San Jose

State University, visiting asst prof, 1988-90; San Francisco State University, asst prof, 1991-. **SPECIAL ACHIEVEMENTS:** Author: "Domesticating Mr Orton," Theatre Journal, 1993; author, editor: The Life and Death of Mrs Mary Frith, with introduction, Garland Publishing, 1993. **BUSINESS ADDRESS:** Dept of English, San Francisco State University, 1600 Holloway Ave, San Francisco, CA 94132, (415)338-7453.

NAKAZAWA, ANTHONY TADASHI
Educator, state official. Japanese American. **PERSONAL:** Born Aug 18, 1949, Kansas City, MO; son of Koki Nakazawa & Mitsueko Nakazawa; married Lynette Aiko Nakazawa, Jan 29, 1972; children: Amber Konno, Beryl Toki. **EDUCATION:** University of Hawaii, BA, economics, 1971; University of California, Santa Barbara, MA, urban economics, 1974; University of California, MS, agricultural & resource economics, 1977, PhD, agricultural & resource economics, 1979. **CAREER:** City of Santa Barbara, police officer, 1972-74; University of California, research assistant, 1974-77; Ketchikan Gateway Borough, economic devt specialist, 1977-79; University of Hawaii, Cooperative Extension Service, assistant professor, community devt, 1979-80; University of Alaska, Cooperative Extension Service, Community and Rural Development, associate professor, 1980-94; University of Petroleum, China, visiting professor, 1989; State of Alaska, Dept of Community & Regional Affairs, director of community & rural devt, 1992-. **ORGANIZATIONS:** Western Extension Community Devt Committee, chair, vice-chair, sec, 1982-84; Western Rural Development Center, advisory committee, 1984-92; Alaska Moving Arts Center, president and co-founder, 1985-; Alaska-Asian Cultural Center, board member, 1990-91; Rural Alaska Community Action Program, board member, 1992-; Alaska Job Training Council, board member, 1992-93; Consortium for Alaska Municipal Training, co-founder, 1982-; International Shotokan Karate Federation, Alaska region director, 1982-; Alaska JTPA, liaison, 1993-. **HONORS/AWARDS:** International Questar Award to Caribou People Video, 1993; US Int Film & Video Festival, Certificate for Creative Excellence to Caribou People, 1993; Am Ec Dev Council Best of Class for Caribou People Video, 1993; Japan Karate Association Sho-Dan Degree, 1980. **SPECIAL ACHIEVEMENTS:** Article, The Northern Review, summer, 1992; "The Regulation of Subsistence in Alaska; The State's Current Dilemma," 1992; video, Project coordinator & PI for Caribou People, a video on Arctic Village Alaska, 1992; editor, "Philosophy and History of Japanese Martial Arts," Journal of Asian Martial Arts, vol 1, 4, Oct 1992; Hosted the National ISKF & Collegiate Karate Tournament, Anchorage AK, 1992; "The Cooperative Extension Service and its Response to the Changing Needs of Rural America," presented at the 3rd Annual US Competition Conference, Phoenix, AZ, Nov 1992; University of Alaska Center for Economic Development, co-founder, co-PI, 1991-92. **HOME ADDRESS:** PO Box 774209, Eagle River, AK 99577, (907)694-4918. **BUSINESS PHONE:** (907)269-4500.

NAKAZONO, BENITO LOPEZ
Chemical engineer. Japanese American. **PERSONAL:** Born Oct 26, 1946, N Laredo, Tamaulipas, Mexico; son of Benito Lopez Ramos and Ayko Nakazono; married Anastacia, Jun 22, 1981; children: Benito Keizo, Tanzy Keiko, Aiko Michelle, Mayeli. **EDUCATION:** ITESM, BSChE, BS, industrial engineering, 1968; University of Houston, MSChE, 1971. **CAREER:** ITESM, chem engrng, professor, 1971-72; M W Kellogg, vessel analytical/process engr, 1973-79, sr vessel analytical engr, 1981-82; Ind Del Alcali, marketing mgr, 1980-81; Haldor Topsoe Inc, sr process engr, 1982-. **ORGANIZATIONS:** Sigma Xi; AIChE; TSRPE. **HOME ADDRESS:** 1805 Lanier Dr, League City, TX 77573.

NAKUJIMA, HIDEYUKI
Business executive. Japanese American. **CAREER:** Atari Games Corp, president, currently. **BUSINESS ADDRESS:** President, Atari Games Corp, 675 Sycamore Dr, Milpitas, CA 95035, (408)434-3700. ∗

NAM, SANGBOO
Physicist. Korean American. **PERSONAL:** Born Jan 30, 1936, Kyung-Nam, Republic of Korea; son of Sae-Hi Nam and Boon-Hi Kim Nam; married Wonki Kim Nam, Jun 1, 1969; children: Saewoo, Jean Ok. **EDUCATION:** Seoul National University, BS, physics, 1958; University of Illinois, MS, physics, 1961, PhD, physics, 1966. **CAREER:** Wright State University, professor, 1980-. **ORGANIZATIONS:** American Physical Society, fellow, 1977. **HONORS/AWARDS:** National Research Council, senior research fellow in physics, 1974-76; National Academy of Sciences, senior research fellow in physics, 1984-86. **SPECIAL ACHIEVEMENTS:** Publications in: Physical Review; Physical Rev Lett; J Math Phys; Appl Phys & Appl Phys Lett;, J

Korean Phys Soc., etc. Subjects include: superconductivity, semiconductor physics, solid state physics, low temp physics, etc. **HOME ADDRESS:** 7735 Peters Pike, Dayton, OH 45414.

NAM, SEHYUN
Research scientist. Korean American. **PERSONAL:** Born Feb 11, 1949, Seoul, Republic of Korea; son of Kidong Nam & Okjoon Park; married Kuisook Nam, Aug 13, 1975; children: Edwin T, Brian T. **EDUCATION:** Seoul National University, Korea, BSE, applied chemistry, 1971; Oregon State University, MS, chemical engineering, 1975; University of Michigan, MSE, materials & metallurgical engineering, 1978; University of Tennessee, PhD, polymer engineering, 1982. **CAREER:** Research teaching assistant: Oregon State University, University of Michigan, University of Tennessee, 1973-82; 3M Company, senior engineer, 1982-86, research specialist, 1986-. **ORGANIZATIONS:** Society of Rheology, 1980-; Society of Plastics Engineers, senior member, 1978-; International Polymer Processing Society, 1982-; Korean Scientists and Engineers Association, chapter chairman, 1975-. **HONORS/AWARDS:** Phi Lambda Upsilon, 1974; Alpha Sigma Mu, 1978; Phi Kappa Phi, 1977; Sigma Xi, 1981. **SPECIAL ACHIEVEMENTS:** Several publications in Polymer Processing, Polymer Rheology; two patents in pressure sensitive adhesives, thermoplastic elastomer; languages: Japanese, German, English and Korean. **BUSINESS ADDRESS:** Research Specialist, 3M Company, 201-1W-28, 3M Center, St Paul, MN 55144, (612)733-7287.

NAM, WONKI KIM
Cataloger. Korean American. **PERSONAL:** Born Jan 8, 1940, Seoul, Republic of Korea; married Sang Boo Nam, Jun 1, 1969; children: Sae Woo, Jean Ok. **EDUCATION:** Ewha Womens University, BA, 1962; Rutgers University, MLS, 1969. **CAREER:** H Q Brown Library, Central State University, cataloging department, head, currently. **ORGANIZATIONS:** American Library Association. **BUSINESS ADDRESS:** Head, Cataloging Dept, Central State University, H Q Brown Library, Bush Row Rd, Wilberforce, OH 45384, (513)376-6520.

NAMBU, YOICHIRO
Educator (retired). Japanese American. **PERSONAL:** Born Jan 18, 1921, Tokyo, Japan; son of Kichiro Nambu and Kimiko Kikuchi Nambu; married Chieko Hida, Nov 3, 1945; children: Jun-ichi. **CAREER:** University of Tokyo, research asst, 1945-49; Osada City University, physics professor, 1950-56; University of Chicago, research associate, 1954-56, faculty member, 1956-91, Dept of Physics, professor, 1958-1971, distinguished professor, 1971-91, professor emeritus, 1991-. **ORGANIZATIONS:** Institute of Advanced Study, 1952-52; Natl Academy of Sciences; American Academy of Arts and Sciences; American Physics Society. **SPECIAL ACHIEVEMENTS:** Contributor of scientific articles to numerous professional journals.∗

NANDA, NAVIN CHANDAR
Cardiologist, educator. Indo-American. **PERSONAL:** Born Jul 6, 1937, Kabarnet, Rift Valley, Kenya; son of Balwantrai Nanda (deceased) and Maya Vati Nanda; married Kanta Kumari Nanda, Sep 13, 1967; children: Nitin, Anil, Anita. **EDUCATION:** Bombay University, India, Inter-Science Certificate, 1956, MBBS, 1962, MD, 1967. **CAREER:** King George VI Hospital, Nairobi, resident house officer, 1962; King Edward Memorial Hosp, Bombay, medical registrar, 1963-64, sr medical registrar, 1964-67; Inst of Cardiology & Natl Heart Hosp, London, fellow in cardiology, 1967-68; Moorgate & Rotherham Hosps, Rotherham, England, sr house physician/registrar, 1968-71; Univ of Rochester Sch of Medicine, instructor & trainee in medicine, 1971-73, asst prof of medicine & radiology & assoc physician, 1973-79, assoc prof of med & dir of noninvasive cardiology labs, sr assoc physician, 1979-84; Genesee Hosp & Rochester General Hosp, consult in cardiology, 1979-84; Univ of Alabama at Birmingham Sch of Med, Div of Cardiovascular Disease, prof of med, dir of heart station & echocardiography-graphics labs, 1984-86, distinguished prof of medicine, 1986-. **ORGANIZATIONS:** American College of Angiology, fellow; American College of Cardiology, fellow; American College of Intl Physicians, fellow; American Heart Assn, Council on Clinical Cardiology, fellow, Council on Geriatric Cardiology, fellow; Intl College of Angiology, fellow. **HONORS/AWARDS:** Cardiology Soc of India, Award for Outstanding Contributions in Field of Cardiology, 1992; Fifth Brazilian Congress of Echocardiology, Brazilian Soc of Echocardiology, Dr Navin C Nanda Day of Echocardiography, 1993; Dr Navin C Nanda Natl Institute of Echocardiography & Cardiovascular Research, first institute of echocardiography to be established in southeast Asia, 1988; Chilean Soc of Cardiology, fellow, 1992; Chilean Soc of Echocardiography, honored for pioneering contributions, 1992; numerous

others. **SPECIAL ACHIEVEMENTS:** Author, Doppler Echocardiography, 1993; editor-in-chief, Echocardiography, 1989-; editorial bds, Alabama Journal of Medical Services, editor, Noninvasive Cardiology Section, 1984-; American Journal of Cardiology, 1982; American Journal of Non-Invasive Cardiology, 1985-; Cardiology Today, natl television series; Cardiology Trends, 1989-; co-editor, Advances in Echo Imaging Using Contrast Enhancement, 1993. **BUSINESS ADDRESS:** Professor of Medicine, Director, Heart Station/Echocardiography Laboratories, University of Alabama at Birmingham, 619 S 19th St, Heart Station SW/S102, Birmingham, AL 35233, (205)934-8256.

NANDA, RAVINDRA

Educator, educational administrator. Indo-American. **PERSONAL:** Born Feb 19, 1943, Layalpur, Punjab, India; son of Nand Lal Nanda and Dhan Devi Nanda; married Patricia Ann, May 3, 1986; children: Renu, Seema, Anjuli. **EDUCATION:** King Georges Medical College, BDS, 1964, MDS, 1966; University of Nymegen, PhD, 1969; University of Connecticut, Ortho Certificate, 1978. **CAREER:** Loyola University, assistant professor, 1970-72; Japan Promotion for Science, visiting professor, 1980; University of Connecticut, professor, head of orthodentics, 1972-. **ORGANIZATIONS:** American Association of Orthodontists, 1975-; American Dental Association, 1975-; European Orthodontic Society, 1969-. **BUSINESS ADDRESS:** Professor and Head of Orthodontics, University of Connecticut, School of Dental Medicine, Health Center, Farmington, CT 06030, (203)679-2349.

NANDA, VIR A.

Computer services company executive. Indo-American. **PERSONAL:** Born Sep 20, 1942, Gujerarrwala, Punjab, Pakistan; son of Sant Ram Nanda & Shanti Devi Nanda; married Lucille S Nanda, Jun 9, 1973; children: Aarti, Sameer. **EDUCATION:** Delhi University, BS, 1962, MS, 1964; Georgia Institute of Technology, MS, 1972. **CAREER:** First Financial Management, vice president, 1974-86; Intercept, vice president, partner, 1986-. **ORGANIZATIONS:** Asian Pacific American Council, president, 1992; India American Cultural Association, president, 1986; Nurgis Dult Memorial Foundation, president, 1993; APAC, board of directors, 1993; IACA, board of directors, 1986-88, 1993; High Museum of Arts, CRC, 1992-93; National Federation of Indian American Associations, Southeast Region, vice president, 1993. **BUSINESS ADDRESS:** Vice President, Intercept, 6611 Bay Circle, Ste 160, Norcross, GA 30071, (404)840-2731.

NANDKUMAR, NUGGEHALLI BALMUKUND

Manufacturing company executive. Indo-American. **PERSONAL:** Born Jan 18, 1949, Mysore, Karnataka, India; son of N S Balmukund and N B Rathna; married Premalatha Nandkumar, May 16, 1979; children: Darshun, Samantha. **EDUCATION:** Osmania University, Hyderabad, India, BE, 1972; Texas Tech University, MS, 1974. **CAREER:** Lubbock Manufacturing, industrial engr, 1974-75; Consolidated Casting Corp, chief engr, 1975-83; Bruce J Carter & Associates, sales engr; Universal SPC Inc, president, currently. **ORGANIZATIONS:** AIIE, 1973-79; Quality Circle, Texas Chapter, founding member, 1978-79. **BUSINESS ADDRESS:** President, Universal-SPC Inc, 412 N State St, Elgin, IL 60123, (708)742-8870.

NARAHARA, HIROMICHI T.

Public health research scientist. Japanese American. **PERSONAL:** Born Oct 24, 1923, Tokyo, Japan; son of U Narahara & Tama Narahara; married Ruth, Sep 16, 1954; children: John, Anne Bergman, David, Daniel. **EDUCATION:** Columbia College, BS, 1943; Columbia University College of Physicians & Surgeons, MD, 1947. **CAREER:** University of Washington, research fellow, instructor, 1953-58; Washington University, School of Medicine, assistant-associate professor, 1958-70; Albany Medical College, associate professor, adjunct, 1970-; NY State Department of Health, research physician, 1970-83, research scientist, 1983-. **ORGANIZATIONS:** American Diabetes Association, 1955-; Endocrine Society, 1955-; American Society Biochemistry & Molecular Biology, 1962-. **HONORS/AWARDS:** Columbia College, Phi Beta Kappa, 1943; College of Physicians & Surgeons, Alpha Omega Alpha, 1947. **SPECIAL ACHIEVEMENTS:** About 40 scientific publications in journals & books, 1947-89; certified by American Board of Internal Medicine, 1955. **MILITARY SERVICE:** US Army, Medical Corps, 1st lt, 1951-53; stationed in Japan & Korea. **BIOGRAPHICAL SOURCES:** American Board of Medical Specialties, Compendium of Certified Medical Specialists, 1992. **HOME ADDRESS:** 3 Wisconsin Ave, Delmar, NY 12054-3323.

NARAHASHI, TOSHIO

Educator. Japanese American. **PERSONAL:** Born Jan 30, 1927, Fukuoka, Japan; son of Asahachi Ishii & Itoko Ishii; married Kyoko Narahashi, Apr 21, 1956; children: Keiko, Taro. **EDUCATION:** University of Tokyo, DVM, 1948, PhD, 1960. **CAREER:** University of Tokyo, instructor, assistant professor, 1951-65, Duke University, assistant professor, 1965-67, associate professor, 1967-69, head of pharmacology division, 1970-73, Dept of Physiology and Pharmacology, vice chairman, 1970-73, professor, 1969-77; Northwestern University, professor and chairman, 1977-, Alfred Newton Richards Professor of Pharmacology, 1982-, John Evans Professor of Pharmacology, 1986-. **ORGANIZATIONS:** American Society for Pharmacology and Experimental Therapeutics; American Physiological Society; Society for Neuroscience; Biophysical Society; American Chemical Society; Society of Toxicology; New York Academy of Sciences; International Brain Research Organization;. **HONORS/AWARDS:** Japanese Society of Applied Entomology and Zoology, Society Award, 1955; Biophysical Society, The Cole Award, 1981; National Institutes of Health, Javits Neuroscience Award, 1986-93; American Chemical Society, Burdick & Jackson International Award for Research in Pesticide Chemistry, 1989; Society of Toxicology, The Merit Award, 1991; National Advisory Environmental Health Sciences Council, NIH, 1982-87; American Assoc for the Adv of Sci, fellow, 1985; Midwest Reg Chapter , Soc of Toxicology, DuBois Award, 1988. **SPECIAL ACHIEVEMENTS:** 327 scientific papers published in professional journals, 1950-; edited ten books, 1975-. **HOME ADDRESS:** 175 E Delaware Place, Unit 7911, Chicago, IL 60611, (312)337-0987. **BUSINESS ADDRESS:** Professor and Chairman, Dept of Pharmacology, Northwestern University Medical School, 303 E Chicago Ave, Chicago, IL 60611, (312)503-8284.

NARASIMHAN, SRIDHAR

Educator. Indo-American. **PERSONAL:** Born Feb 3, 1956, New Delhi, India; son of P V Narasimhan & J Narasimhan; married Aruna Srinivasan, May 28, 1983; children: Tarun Sai. **EDUCATION:** Birla Institute of Technology & Science, BE, 1977; Indian Institute of Management, MBA, 1981; University of Rochester, MS, 1984; The Ohio State University, PhD, 1987. **CAREER:** DCM Data Products, systems officer, 1977-79; University of Rochester, teaching associate, 1981-83; The Ohio State University, teaching associate, 1984-86; Georgia Tech, assistant professor, 1987-93, associate professor, 1993-. **ORGANIZATIONS:** Information Tech Management at Georgia Tech, area coordinator, 1988-; IEEE, 1987-; ORSA, 1987-; TIMS, 1987-. **HONORS/AWARDS:** Ohio State University, Presidential Fellowship, 1986-87; Society for Info Mgt, doctoral fellow, 1986; Indian Institute of Mgt, Gold Medal, 1981. **SPECIAL ACHIEVEMENTS:** Published refereed articles in journals such as: IIE Transaction; Decision Sciences; Computers & OR; IEEE Transactions on Communications; Computer Networks & ISDN Systems; Naval Research Logistics; Computer Communication; Management Science; ORSA Journal on Computing ; Annals of OR; also presented papers at numerous conferences. **BUSINESS ADDRESS:** Associate Professor, School of Management, Georgia Institute of Technology, Atlanta, GA 30332-0520, (404)894-4378.

NARASIMHAN, SUBHA

Educator, attorney. Indo-American. **PERSONAL:** Born May 9, 1948, Delhi, India; daughter of P S Narasimhan & Lakshmi; married Brian Bell, 1969. **EDUCATION:** Imperial College, London University, BS, 1970; Stanford University, MS, 1973, PhD, 1975; Columbia Law School, JD, 1980. **CAREER:** IBM, research scientist, 1975-77; Columbia University, assistant professor of law, associate professor of law, professor of law, 1980-. **SPECIAL ACHIEVEMENTS:** Author of publications in contract law. **BUSINESS ADDRESS:** Professor, Columbia Law School, Columbia University, 435 West 116th St, New York, NY 10027, (212)854-3092.

NARAYAN, KIRIN

Educator, novelist. Indo-American. **PERSONAL:** Born Nov 18, 1959, Bombay, India; daughter of Narayan Contractor and Didi Contractor; married Eytan Bercovitch, Aug 18, 1993. **EDUCATION:** Sarah Lawrence College, BA, 1980; UC, Berkeley, MA, 1982, PhD, 1987. **CAREER:** Middlebury College, assistant professor, 1987-88; Hampshire College, assistant professor, 1988-89; University of Wisconsin, Madison, assistant professor of anthropology, S Asian studies, 1989-. **ORGANIZATIONS:** American Folklore Society, State of the Profession Committee, 1992-94; Society for Humanistic Anthropology, Executive Committee, 1993-96; Association for Asian Studies, South Asia Council, 1993-96. **HONORS/AWARDS:** John Simon Guggenheim Memorial Foundation, fellowship, 1993; School of American Research, NEH Fellowship, 1993; Society for Humanistic Anthropology, Victor Turner Prize for Ethnographic Writing, 1990; American Folklore Society, Elsie Clews Parsons Prize for Folklore, 1990; National Endowment for the Humanities, fellowship, 1990. **SPECIAL ACHIEVEMENTS:** Storytellers, Saints & Sconndrels: Folk Narrative in Hindu Religious Teaching, 1989; Love, Stars & All That, novel, 1994; ed, with Smadar Lane & Renato Rosaldo, Creativity/Anthropology, 1993; "How Native is a Native Anthropologist?," American Anthropologist, 95, 1993; "Refractions of the Field at Home: Images of the Hindu Holy Man in America," Cultural Anthropology, 1993. **BUSINESS ADDRESS:** Professor, Anthropology Dept, University of Wisconsin, Madison, 1180 Observatory Dr, Anthrop 5240, Soc Sci Bldg, Madison, WI 53706-1320.

NARAYANAMURTI, VENKATESH

Educator. Indo-American. **PERSONAL:** Born Sep 9, 1939, Bangalore, Karnataka, India; son of Duraiswami Narayanamurti and Janaki Subramaniam Narayanamurti; married Jayalakshmi Krishnayya, Aug 23, 1961; children: Arjun, Ranjini, Krishna. **EDUCATION:** St Stephens College, India, BSc, MSc, 1958; Cornell University, PhD, 1965. **CAREER:** Cornell University, instructor, research associate, 1965-68; AT&T Bell Labs, member of technical staff, 1968-76, dept head, 1976-81, director, 1981-87; Sandia Natl Labs, vp of research, 1987-92; University of California, Santa Barbara, dean of engineering, 1992-. **ORGANIZATIONS:** Cornell University, College of Electrical Engineering, chairman of advisory board, 1989-90; Jet Propulsion Lab, microelectric board, 1988-90; Stanford Synchtron Lab, science board, 1989-92; Natl Science Foundation, engineering directorate advisory board, 1992-; Dept of Energy, Fermi award committee member, 1992-, inertial confinement fusion advisory committee, chair, 1992-; NAE; Royal Swedish Academy of Engineering Sciences. **HONORS/AWARDS:** IEEE, Fellow; AAAS, Fellow; American Physics Society, Fellow; Indian Academy of Sciences, Fellow. **SPECIAL ACHIEVEMENTS:** Author of over 100 articles in technical publications. **BUSINESS ADDRESS:** Dean of Engineering, University of California, Santa Barbara, 552 University Ave, Santa Barbara, CA 93106.*

NARAYANAN, A. SAMPATH

Educator. Indo-American. **PERSONAL:** Born Jan 14, 1941, Umayalpuram, Tamil Nadu, India; son of Appathurai & Lakshmi; married Lakshmi, Sep 7, 1975; children: Nandakumar, Madhu. **EDUCATION:** University of Madras, India, BS, 1961, MS, 1963, PhD, 1967. **CAREER:** University of Madras, Madas, India, Biochemistry Lab, research officer, 1965-67; University of Washington, Seattle, Dept of Pathology, research associate, 1971-75, Research Dept, assistant professor, 1975-78, associate professor, 1978-86, School of Medicine, Affiliate, Research Center in Oral Biology, professor, 1986-. **ORGANIZATIONS:** American Society of Biological Chemists; American Society for Cell Biology; International Association of Dental Research; NIH/NIDR, editorial board, 1986-; Gordon Research Conferences on Periodontal Disease, chairperson, 1981. **SPECIAL ACHIEVEMENTS:** Numerous scientific publications. **BUSINESS ADDRESS:** Research Professor, Dept of Pathology, University of Washington, Health Sciences Bldg, SM-30, Seattle, WA 98195, (206)543-6638.

NARAYANASWAMY, ONBATHIVELI S.

Consulting engineer. Indo-American. **PERSONAL:** Born May 13, 1936, Sriperumpudur, Tamil Nadu, India; son of Subrahmanya Ayyar & Akilandam Ammal; married Padmini, Jan 26, 1967. **EDUCATION:** University of Madras, India, BE, 1958; University of Saskatchewan, Canada, MS, 1962; Case Institute of Technology, PhD, 1965. **CAREER:** Atomic Energy Establishment, junior scientific officer, 1958-60; Indian Institute of Technology, lecturer, 1960-61; Ford Motor Co, associate staff scientist, principal research engineer, senior research engineer, 1965-86; Computer Simulations, president, currently. **ORGANIZATIONS:** American Ceramic Society; Society for Experimental Mechanics. **HONORS/AWARDS:** American Ceramic Society, Ross Coffin Purdy Award, 1973, fellow, 1979. **SPECIAL ACHIEVEMENTS:** Author, "A Model of Structural Relaxation in Glass," Journal American Ceramic Society, vol 54, p10, 1971; "Annealing of Glass," Science and Technology, chapter 5, Academic Press, vol 3, 1986. **HOME ADDRESS:** 26610 Hass Ave, Dearborn Heights, MI 48127, (313)563-1607. **BUSINESS PHONE:** (313)563-1607.

NARITA, GEORGE M.

Publishing company executive. Japanese American. **PERSONAL:** Born Sep 9, 1928, London, England; daughter of Tami and Masaaki; divorced; children: Ian. **EDUCATION:** Fordham University, BS, 1955; New York University, graduate studies. **CAREER:** University of Chicago Press, science editor, 1963-69; Van Nostrand Rheinhold, senior editor, 1970-77; Noyes Publications,

executive editor, vice pres, 1980-. **ORGANIZATIONS:** Intl Student Council of New York, president, 1953-55; Intl House, New York Chapter, executive board. **SPECIAL ACHIEVEMENTS:** Editor-in-chief: Grzimeks Animal Life Encyclopedia, 1976; Grzimeks Encyclopedia of Ecology, 1976; Grzimeks Encyclopedia of Evolution, 1976; Grzimeks Encyclopedia of Ethology, 1976; involved with creation acquisition and publishing of numerous scientific, medical, and engineering professional books and series. **BUSINESS ADDRESS:** Vice President/Executive Editor, Noyes Publications, 120 Mill Rd, Park Ridge, NJ 07656.

NARULA, SUBHASH CHANDER

Educator. Indo-American. **PERSONAL:** Born Jan 20, 1944, Bannu, NWFP, Pakistan; son of Har Dial Narula & Sumitra Narula. **EDUCATION:** University of Delhi, India, BE, mechanical engineering, 1964; University of Iowa, MS, industrial and management engineering, 1969, PhD, industrial and management engineering, 1971. **CAREER:** Hindustan Machine Tools Ltd, Pinjore, India, supervisor, 1965-68; State University of New York, Department of Industrial Engineering, assistant professor, 1971-77; Rensselaer Polytechnic Institute, School of Management, associate professor, 1977-83; Linkoping Institute of Technology, Department of Mathematics, professor of optimization, 1991-93; University of Statistics, University of Sao Paulo, Institute of Mathematics and Statistics, visiting professor, 1983-; Helsinki School of Economics, visiting professor, 1986-; University of Campinas, Department of Statistics, visiting professor, 1987-; Virginia Commonwealth University, School of Business, professor, 1983-. **ORGANIZATIONS:** American Statistical Association, fellow; American Society for Quality Control, fellow; International Society on Multiple Criteria Decision Making; International Statistical Institute; Royal Statistical Society, fellow; numerous others. **HONORS/AWARDS:** VCU, School of Business, Distinguished Research Award, 1984-85, 1987-90. **SPECIAL ACHIEVEMENTS:** Numerous refereed journal articles, proceedings; numerous presentations; editor, International Journal of Mathematical and Statistical Sciences, 1991-; associate editor, Studies in Locational Analysis, 1993-; associate editor, Journal of Quality Technology, 1989-91; co-author, "Testing Software for Robust Regression," L1-Statistical Data Analysis and Relate Methods, Y Dodge, editor, North-Holland, p361-369, 1992; numerous others. **HOME PHONE:** (804)740-4435. **BUSINESS ADDRESS:** Professor, Virginia Commonwealth Univ, School of Business, 1015 Floyd Ave, Richmond, VA 23284-4000, (804)367-7485.

NASH, PHILIP TAJITSU

Lawyer, journalist, educator, writer. Japanese American. **PERSONAL:** Born Dec 3, 1956, New York, NY; married. **EDUCATION:** New York University, BA, 1978; Rutgers University, School of Law, JD, 1982. **CAREER:** Education Law Center, 1981-83; Washington Coalition on Redress, 1983; District Council 37 Municipal Employees Legal Sevices Plan, 1983-84; New York University, assistant professor, 1984-85; Yale University, instructor, 1985-86; Asian American Legal Defense and Education Fund, 1984-92; City University of New York Law School, instructor, 1986-91; Georgetown University Law Center, adjunct professor, 1992-; National Asian Pacific American Legal Consortium, founding executive director, 1993-. **SPECIAL ACHIEVEMENTS:** Wrote weekly column, "Inter-Change," New York Nichibei, 1984-87; "Japanese American Redress Movement Wins and Loses," 114 New Jersey Law Journal, vol 117, 1984; "Moving for Redress: A Review of Tateishi's And Justice for All," 94 Yale Law Journal, vol 743, 1985; chapters in Asian Americans and the Supreme Court, Greenwood Press, 1991, and ESL Today: Myths and Realities, Heinemann Educ Books, 1990; numerous others. **BIOGRAPHICAL SOURCES:** Los Angeles Times, Washington Edition, p A6, May 13, 1993; New York Times, p B7, May 28, 1993; Washington Post, outlook section, p 7, June 14, 1992. **BUSINESS ADDRESS:** Executive Director, National Asian Pacific American Legal Consortium, 1629 K St NW, Ste 1010, Washington, DC 20006, (202)296-2300.

NATH, AMAR

Scientist, educator. Indo-American. **PERSONAL:** Born Nov 28, 1929, Agra, Uttar Pradesh, India; son of Prithvi Nath; married Pratibha, May 17, 1957; children: Anupam Lekha. **EDUCATION:** Agra University, India, MS, 1950, DSc, 1970; Moscow State University, PhD, 1961. **CAREER:** Bhabha Atomic Research Center, section head, 1951-58, 1961-66; University of California, Los Angeles, Nobel Laureate W F Libby visiting scientist, 1966-67, 1969-70; University of California, Berkeley, Nobel Laureate Melvin Calvin visiting scientist, 1967-69; Drexel University, professor, 1970-. **HONORS/AWARDS:** Indian Ministry of Education, Fellowship to Study in Russia, 1958-61. **SPECIAL ACHIEVEMENTS:** "Direct Observation of Isotopic Exchange in the

Solid State," Nature, vol 224, p 794, 1969; "Studies of Isotopic Exchange in Solids: Healing of Damaged Molecules," Acc Chem Research, vol 17, p 90, 1984; "Dynamics of the Cu-O Chain in Y Ba2Cu3O7 Emission Mossbauer Studies," Journal of Supercond, vol 3, p 433, 1990; "A Novel Class of Ferromagnetic Compounds," Mater Lett, vol 16, p 39, 1993; "Superparamagnetic Behavior in Nd2-xCexCu(570Co)O4," Phys Rev Lett, 3355, 1993. **BUSINESS ADDRESS:** Professor, Dept of Chemistry, Drexel University, 32nd & Chestnut, Philadelphia, PA 19104, (215)895-2648.

NATH, JOGINDER
Educator. Indo-American. **PERSONAL:** Born May 12, 1932, India; son of Moti Ram and Vira Wali Khorana; married Charlotte Reese Lynn; children: Pravene Alexander, Brian Anthony. **EDUCATION:** Panjab University, BS (w/ honors), 1953, MS (w/honors), 1955; University of Wisconsin, Madison, PhD, 1960. **CAREER:** American Foundation for Biol Research, research associate, 1960-63; Southern Illinois University, assistant professor, 1963-66; West Virginia University, assistant professor, 1966-67, associate professor, 1967-72, professor & chairman, 1972-. **ORGANIZATIONS:** Sigma Xi; Environmental Mutagen Society; Society for Cryobiology; Indian Society of Genetics and Plant Breeding. **HONORS/AWARDS:** NSF, Grant: Role of Purines in Cold Hardiness, 1967-70; NIOSH, Grant: Studies on Mutagenesis & Carcinogenesis, 1985-. **SPECIAL ACHIEVEMENTS:** Publications on: cryobiology, mutagenesis, cancer research, cytogenetics, and molecular mutagenesis. **BUSINESS ADDRESS:** Professor, Chair, Genetics & Developmental Biology, West Virginia University, Plant & Soil Sciences, College of Agriculture and Forestry, Morgantown, WV 26506-6108, (304)293-6256.

NATIVIDAD, IRENE
Company executive. Filipino American. **PERSONAL:** Born Sep 14, 1948; married Andrea Cortese; children: Carlo Natividad Cortese. **EDUCATION:** Long Island University, BA (summa cum laude), 1971; Columbia University, MA (with high honors), 1973, PhD, candidate (ABD), MPhil, orals (with high honors), 1976. **CAREER:** Columbia College, Lehman College, City University of New York, Columbia University, instructor, 1973-76; Long Island University, acting director of continuing education, 1976-78; William Paterson College, director of continuing education, 1978-85; National Women's Political Caucus, national chair, 1985-89; Natividad & Associates, principal, 1990-. **ORGANIZATIONS:** Women of Color for Change Committee for Clinton/ Gore, co-chair, 1992; Philippine American Foundation, executive director, 1990-; 1992 Global Forum of Women, director, 1990-; National Commission on Working Women, chair, 1991-; First World Summit on Women, international steering committee, 1990; Coalition for Women's Appointments, chair, 1988-89; Women's Roundtable, chair, 1987-89; National Network of Asian-Pacific American Women, founder, 1982; Asian American Professional Women Inc, founder, president, 1978-80; Democratic National Committee Asian Pacific Caucus, deputy vice chair, 1982-84; Global Summit of Women, program director, 1994. **HONORS/AWARDS:** Women's Congressional Council, Democratic Congressional Campaign, Women Making History Award, 1985; Long Island University, Honorary Doctorate of Humane Letters, 1989; Earthquake Relief and Rehabilitation Efforts in the Philippines, Presidential Recognition by President Corazon Aquino, 1990; Organization of Chinese Americans, Award for Outstanding Public Service, 1989; Asian American Legal Defense Fund, Justice in Action Award, 1988; Philippine National Day Celebration, People's Power Award, 1986; National Museum of Women in the Arts, trustee, 1993-; numerous others. **SPECIAL ACHIEVEMENTS:** Asian American Almanac, executive editor; Influence Magazine for Political Women, editorial advisory board; "US Media Ignore Human Suffering Caused by Volcanic Eruptions," USA Today; Another Voice: Mount Pinatubo, July 8, 1991; Do Women in Business Need a "Mommy Track?" The Denver Post, April 10, 1989; "Women of Color and the Campaign Trail," The American Woman; 1991-92, 1991; PBS television, "To the Contrary," regular panelist. **BIOGRAPHICAL SOURCES:** "74 Women Who Are Changing American Politics," Campaigns & Elections Magazine, 1993; "100 Most Important Women," Ladies Home Journal, 1988; Washington Woman Magazine, 1987; Reader's Choice Honors, 1987; "25 Most Influential People in Asian America," A. Magazine, 1993. **BUSINESS ADDRESS:** Principal, Natividad & Associates, 1000 Vermont Ave NW, Ste 605, Washington, DC 20005.

NATORI, JOSIE CRUZ
Apparel company executive. Filipino American. **PERSONAL:** Born May 9, 1947, Manila, Philippines; daughter of Felipe F Cruz and Angelita A Almeda Cruz; married Kenneth R Natori, May 20, 1972; children: Kenneth E F. **EDUCATION:** Manhattanville College, BA, economics, 1968. **CAREER:**

Merrill-Lynch, vice president, 1971-77; House of Natori, The Natori Co, co-founder, president, 1977-. **ORGANIZATIONS:** Dreyfus Third Century Fund, Calyx and Corolla, board of directors; Philippine American Foundation, board of directors; Junior Achievement, board of directors, 1992; Intl Women's Forum; Manhattanville College, trustee. **HONORS/AWARDS:** American Jewish Committee, Human Relations Award, 1986; Working Woman, Harriet Alger Award, 1987; Manhattanville College, Castle Award, 1988; US Pan Asian American Chamber of Commerce, Excellence 2000, 1992, Outstanding Asian American in Design and Business Award, 1992. **BUSINESS ADDRESS:** President, The Natori Co, 40 E 34th St, 18th Fl, New York, NY 10016-4501, (212)532-7796.*

NAVANGUL, HIMANSHOO VISHNU BHAT
Educator. Indo-American. **PERSONAL:** Born Dec 22, 1940, Wai, Maharashtra, India; son of Vishnu Narayan Bhat Navangul and Usha Vishnu Gokhale Navangul; married Neelarani Tilak Navangul, Oct 18, 1964; children: Sangeeta Devika Navangul-Ryan, Vikram Bharat. **EDUCATION:** University Pune, Maharashtra, S P college, BS, 1961, BSc, (with honors) 1962, MSc, 1963, PhD, 1967. **CAREER:** National Chem Lab, Pune, Bharat, jr/sr research fellow, 1963-67; University of Zurich, Switzerland, research fellow, 1967-69; University of Wyoming, research fellow, 1969-70; University of Missouri, research fellow, visiting asst professor, 1970-75; Northeast Missouri State University, visiting asst professor, 1975-76; Al-Fateh University, Tripoli, Libya, asst professor, 1976-79; Clemson University, visiting faculty, 1979-80; NC Wesleyan College, professor, 1980-; UNC Chapel Hill, visiting professor, 1989-90. **ORGANIZATIONS:** American Chem Society, 1970-; American Institute Chemistry, fellow, 1970-, secretary, local section (NCIC), 1993-. **HONORS/AWARDS:** Swiss Government, post-doctoral fellowship, 1967-69; Council of Scientific and Industrial Research, Sr Fellowship, 1967, Junior Fellowship, 1963-66. **SPECIAL ACHIEVEMENTS:** Numerous publications in the field of molecular quantum mechanics and UV-visible spectroscopy; language proficiency in: Marathi, Urdu, Hindi, Sanskrit, German, French and Arabic. **HOME ADDRESS:** 2800 Jason Drive, Rocky Mount, NC 27803-1612, (919)937-2026. **BUSINESS ADDRESS:** Professor, Dept of Chemistry, North Carolina Wesleyan College, 3400 N Wesleyan Blvd, Rocky Mount, NC 27804-8677, (919)985-5161.

NAYAK, BHAGCHAND D.
Architect. Indo-American. **PERSONAL:** Born Jan 1, 1937, Nagpur, Maharashtra, India; son of Deokaran D Nayak and Champa D Nayak; married Leela Nayak, May 26, 1966; children: Yoshika, Taniya. **EDUCATION:** Government Polytechnic, Nagpur, MS, India, diploma in architecture, 1960; VR College of Engineering, Nagpur, MS, India, BArch, 1967; Massachusetts Institute of Technology, MArch, 1970. **CAREER:** Master Sathe & Kothari Architects, New Delhi, India, architect, 1960-66; Paul Rudolph Architect, design manager, 1970-71; J Glenn Hugh Associates, design director, 1971-85; B D Nayak Architects & Planners Inc, president, 1985-. **ORGANIZATIONS:** American Institute of Architects; Boston Society of Architects. **HONORS/AWARDS:** Cape Cod & Island Board of Realtors Inc, Certificate of Recognition, 1992; Falmouth Council for Civic Beautification, Merit Award, 1992; MIT, scholarships, 1968-69, 1969-70. **SPECIAL ACHIEVEMENTS:** First in Order of Merit, Nagpur University BArch Program, 1967. **BUSINESS ADDRESS:** President, B D Nayak Architects & Planners, Inc, 220 Forbes Rd, Ste 115, Braintree, MA 02184, (617)843-1002.

NAYAK, TAPAN KUMAR
Educator. Indo-American. **PERSONAL:** Born Feb 21, 1957, Kalera, W. Bengal, India; son of Gati Sankar & Mridula Nayak; married Kaberi Nayak, Jun 12, 1985; children: Debojit. **EDUCATION:** Calcutta University, BS, 1976; Indian Statistical Institute, MStat, 1979; University of Pittsburgh, PhD, 1983. **CAREER:** RKMR College, lecturer, 1979-80; University of Pittsburgh, teaching/research assistant, 1980-83; Indian Statistical Institute, visiting scientist, 1990; George Washington University, visiting assistant professor, 1983-84, assistant professor, 1984-89, associate professor, 1989-. **ORGANIZATIONS:** American Statistical Association, 1983-; Washington Statistical Society, 1983-, methodology program director, 1991-92, methodology section chair, 1992-93. **HONORS/AWARDS:** Government of India, National Scholarship, 1973-76; Calcutta University, ranked 1st in BSc (honors in statistics), 1976; University of Pittsburgh, Mellon Predoctoral Fellowship, 1982-83. **SPECIAL ACHIEVEMENTS:** Published over 25 research articles in statistical journals; made original contribution in the areas of software reliability, income inequality, diversity analysis, and statistical methodology; proficient in English,

Bengali and Hindi. **BUSINESS ADDRESS:** Assoc Professor, Dept of Statistics, George Washington University, Washington, DC 20052, (202)994-6355.

NAYYAR, SARV P.
Engineer, company executive. Indo-American. **PERSONAL:** Born Aug 26, 1941, Lahore, India; son of Hazari Lal & Sarla Devi Nayyar; married Vichitra Nayyar, Jul 17, 1970; children: Anjali, Alka. **EDUCATION:** Punjab Engineering College, India, BS, civil engineering, 1965; Indian Institute of Technology, Chicago, MS, civil engineering, 1977; Illinois Institute of Technology. **CAREER:** Balmer Lawrie & Co, Calcutta, India, design & sales engineer, 1966-70; Dexion Inc, structural engineer, 1970-72; Acme Barrel Co, maintenance engineer, buying agent, 1972-73; Skidmore Owings & Merrill, project engineer, 1973-77, associate, senior structural engineer, 1978-85; Inryco Inland Steel, structural consultant, 1977-78; Nayyar & Nayyar, president, chief structural engineer, 1985-. **ORGANIZATIONS:** American Society of Civil Engineers, 1984-; American Concrete Institute, 1984-; Structural Engineers Association of Illinois, 1984-; American Institute of Steel Construction, 1984-. **SPECIAL ACHIEVEMENTS:** Successfully completed design of a shrine in Michigan, 1992-93; selected as structural peer reviewer for McCormick Place Expansion, Chicago. **HOME ADDRESS:** 1455 West Harrison, Chicago, IL 60607. **BUSINESS PHONE:** (312)431-1010.

NEE, MICHAEL WEI-KUO
Educator. Chinese American. **PERSONAL:** Born Apr 21, 1955, Berkeley, CA; son of David S Nee & Amy C H Sah. **EDUCATION:** University of Santa Clara, BS, 1977; California Institute of Technology, PhD, 1981. **CAREER:** University of California, Santa Barbara, postdoctoral research fellow, 1981-83; Oberlin College, associate professor of chemistry, 1983-. **ORGANIZATIONS:** American Chemical Society, 1977-; American Association for the Advancement of Science. **HONORS/AWARDS:** Phi Beta Kappa, 1977. **BUSINESS ADDRESS:** Associate Professor of Chemistry, Oberlin College, 130 West Lorain St, Kettering Hall, Oberlin, OH 44074.

NEWAZ, S. S.
Polymer/chemical company manager. Bangladeshi American. **PERSONAL:** Born May 21, 1945, Khulna, Bangladesh; son of S Wajed Ali & Sofia Ali; married Saeeda B Newaz, Jan 14, 1972; children: Rifi S. **EDUCATION:** University of Rajshahi, Bangladesh, BS, 1964, MS, 1966; University of Houston, PhD, 1973. **CAREER:** Aldrich Chemical Co, research chemist, 1976-79; Polaroid Corp, scientist, 1979-81; Miles Inc, Latex Development, manager, 1981-. **ORGANIZATIONS:** American Chemical Society, 1973-; Bangladesh Chemical & Biological Society of North America, vice president, 1988-. **HOME ADDRESS:** 8803 Hydethorpe, Houston, TX 77083, (713)933-4044. **BUSINESS ADDRESS:** Manager, Polysar Rubber Division, Miles Inc, 8701 Park Place Blvd, Houston, TX 77017, (713)477-8821.

NG, ANASTACIO C.
Physician. Filipino American. **PERSONAL:** Born Apr 15, 1933, Manila, Philippines; son of Gregorio Ng Gee and Maxima Chan; married Maria C Ng, Nov 30, 1963; children: Judith F, Jodie B. **EDUCATION:** University of Santo Tomas, AA, 1953, MD, 1958; Mercy Hospital, internship, 1958-59; Cook County Hospital, radiology residency, 1959-60; Washington University, radiology residency, 1960-63. **CAREER:** Homer G Phillips Hospital, asst radiologist, 1963-64; Regina General Hospital, Saskatchewan, Canada, radiologist, 1964-68; Indiana University Medical Center, assistant professor, 1968-70; Methodist Hospital of Indiana, radiologist, 1970-. **ORGANIZATIONS:** American College of Radiology, 1964-; Canadian Assn of Radiologists, 1965-; Royal College of Physicians & Surgeons of Canada, 1965-; Saskatchewan College of Physicians & Surgeons, 1966-; Regina Medical Soc, 1966-; Canadian Medical Assn, 1966-; Radiological Soc of North America, 1969-; American Assn for the Advancement of Science, 1970-; American Medical Assn, 1970-; Marion County Medical Soc, 1970-; Indiana State Medical Assn, 1970-; Indiana State Radiological Soc, 1973-; American Roentgen Ray Soc, 1976-; American Institute of Ultrasound in Medicine, 1980-; Soc of Radiologists in Ultrasound, 1992-. **HONORS/AWARDS:** AMA Physicians' Recognition Awards, 1974-93. **SPECIAL ACHIEVEMENTS:** Coauthor: "Nonfunctioning Paraganglioma of the Liver, Gallbladder and Common Bile Duct," Indiana Medicine, 83:822, 1990; "Obstruction of the Small Intestine: Accuracy and Role of CT in Diagnosis," Radiology, 1993; numerous others. **BUSINESS ADDRESS:** Physician, Methodist Hospital of Indiana, 1701 N Senate Blvd, Indianapolis, IN 46202.

NG, ASSUNTA C. M.
Publisher. Chinese American. **PERSONAL:** Born Oct 5, 1951, People's Republic of China; daughter of Hoi Sai Wong and Eric D Woo; married George Liu, 1974; children: Ho-Yin Liu, Ho-Ghan Liu. **EDUCATION:** University of Washington, BA, education, journalism, 1974, MA, business adminstration, speech communications, 1979. **CAREER:** University of Washington, newspaper reporter, library aide, 1974; Seattle Public School, teacher, 1974-79; Seattle Chinese Post, publisher, president, 1982-. **ORGANIZATIONS:** Seattle Rotary Club; Seattle Chamber of Commerce, board member. **HONORS/AWARDS:** Mayor Charles Royer Small Business Award, 1984; Esquire Magazine's, The Best of Men and Women under 40, 1984; Pacific Northwest Magazine's, The Brightest under 40, 1986; Network for Managerial and Professional Women, Mentor Award, 1989; Seattle Weekly, Influential People under 40, 1989; Women in Communications, Women of Achievement Award, 1990; Japanese American Citizens League, 1991; Nordstrom's Cultural Diversity Award, 1991; Avon & SBA, Women of Enterprise Award, 1991; Eastside Week's, Influential People under 40, 1991; International Women's Forum Award, 1992; SBA, Women Business Advocate of 1992, Minority Business Advocate of Year, 1992, Woman Business Advocate of Year, 1993. **SPECIAL ACHIEVEMENTS:** Numerous speaking engagements. **BIOGRAPHICAL SOURCES:** KCTS Channel 9, Sept 1993. **BUSINESS ADDRESS:** Publisher/President, Seattle Chinese Post/Northwest Asian Weekly, 414 8th Ave South, PO Box 3468, Seattle, WA 98104, (206)223-0623.

NG, DAVID
Seminary educator. Chinese American. **PERSONAL:** Born Sep 1, 1934, San Francisco, CA; son of Hing Ng & Chin Shee Ng; married Irene Young Ng, Jun 15, 1958; children: Stephen Paul, Andrew Peter. **EDUCATION:** Westminster College, Salt Lake City, BA, 1956; San Francisco Theological Seminary, MDiv, 1959. **CAREER:** Presbyterian Church in Chinatown, co-pastor, 1959-62; Mendocino Presbyterian Church, pastor, 1962-66; Program Agency, Presbyterian Church, secretary for youth resources, 1966-75; Austin Presbyterian Theological Seminary, associate professor of church program & nurture, 1975-81; National Council of Churches, associate general secretary for education, 1981-86; Program Agency, Presbyterian Church, educational development, 1986-88; San Francisco Theological Seminary, professor of Christian education, 1988-. **ORGANIZATIONS:** Association of Professors & Researchers in Religious Education, executive committee, 1975-; Religious Education Association, former vice president, 1975-; Pacific Asian American & Canadian Christian Education, liaison officer, 1978-; USA Committee for the United Nations, 1981-86; World Council of Churches, education sub-committee, 1982-88; Reformed Liturgy and Music Editorial Board, 1988-; Grand Jury, Mendocino County, California, 1966; Association of Presbyterian Church Educators, 1966-. **HONORS/AWARDS:** Association of Presbyterian Church Educators, Educator of the Year, 1991; Westminster College, Salt Lake City, Doctor of Divinity, 1966. **SPECIAL ACHIEVEMENTS:** Published 12 books on Christian education. **BIOGRAPHICAL SOURCES:** R Stephen Warner, New Wine in Old Wineskins: Evangelicals and Liberals in a Small Town Church, University of California Press, chapters 1, 4, 1988. **BUSINESS ADDRESS:** Professor of Christian Education, San Francisco Theological Seminary, 2 Kensington Rd, San Anselmo, CA 94960, (415)258-6579.

NG, FRANK MANG LEANG
Treasurer. Chinese American. **PERSONAL:** Born Feb 12, 1950, Shanghai, People's Republic of China; son of Hon Ping Ng and Fan Yang Ng; married Jeanne Ng, Jun 11, 1974; children: Michelle, Natalie, Elizabeth, Frank. **EDUCATION:** Northeastern University, BA, 1972; Western New England College, MBA, 1983. **CAREER:** Singer Sewing Machine, Brazil, inventory manager, 1974-77; Data General, cost accountant, 1977-78; Computervision, accounting manager, 1978-85; Avanti Inc, controller, 1985-87; Comprehensive ID, vice pres of operations, 1987-; Alpha Identification, treasurer, 1989-. **ORGANIZATIONS:** American Society for Industrial Security, 1991-. **BUSINESS ADDRESS:** Treasurer, Alpha Identification Inc, 7 Spanish River Rd, Grafton, MA 01519-1009, (508)839-6144.

NG, JEANNE H.
Photography supplies company executive. Chinese American. **PERSONAL:** Born Oct 15, 1950, Boston, MA; daughter of Slin Chu and Ong Chu; married Frank Ng, Jun 11; children: Michelle, Natalie, Elizabeth, Frank. **EDUCATION:** Northeastern University, BA, 1973. **CAREER:** Alpha Identification Inc, president, 1986-. **BUSINESS ADDRESS:** President, Alpha Identification Inc, 7 Spanish River Rd, Grafton, MA 01519, (508)839-6144.

NG, JEFFREY C. F.
Architect. Chinese American. **PERSONAL:** Born Aug 3, 1953, Kowloon, Hong Kong; son of Ting Wei Ng & Sin Poy Ng; married Winnie Y Yu, May 16, 1986; children: Thaddeus, Thomas. **EDUCATION:** Massachusetts Institute of Technology, BS, mathematics, 1974, BS, art and design, 1974; Princeton University, MArch, 1976. **CAREER:** Princeton University, teaching assistant, 1974-76; Skidmore Owings and Merrill, architect, 1976; Cossutta and Associates, architect, 1979-81, project architect, 1983-84; I M Pei and Partners, architect, 1981-83; Davis Brady Associates, project architect, 1985-89; Ehrenkrantz & Eckstut Architects, associate, 1990-. **ORGANIZATIONS:** American Institute of Architects; Connecticut Society of Architects; Arts Student League; Chinese Alumnae of MIT. **HONORS/AWARDS:** Westinghouse Science Talent Search, Scholarship Winner, 1970. **BUSINESS ADDRESS:** Associate, Ehrenkrantz & Eckstut Architects, 23 East Fourth Street, 5th Floor, New York, NY 10003.

NG, KAM WING
Government official. Hong Kong American. **PERSONAL:** Born Oct 26, 1951, Hong Kong; son of Wah and Kwon Ng; married Shirley Y Ng, Aug 18, 1974; children: Melissa Y, Janice Y. **EDUCATION:** Cooper Union, BE, 1973; Rensselaer Polytechnic Institute, MSME, 1975; University of Rhode Island, PhD, 1988. **CAREER:** Part & Whitney Aircraft, research engineer, 1973-78; ITT Grinnell Corp, project engineer, 1978-81; Naval Undersea Warfare Center, mechanical engineer, 1982-91; Office of Naval Research, program manager, 1991-. **ORGANIZATIONS:** Institute of Noise Control Engineering, 1980-, paper reviewer, 1990-; American Society of Mechanical Engineers, 1973-, paper reviewer, 1978-; Instrument Society of America, Subcommittee Sp75, 1980-, co-chairman, Sp75.07, 1980-82; US launcher specialist, Technical Cooperation Panel, 1989-; Institute of Vibration, steering committee, 1992-. **HONORS/AWARDS:** Naval Undersea Warfare Center, various superior performance awards, 1985-91. **SPECIAL ACHIEVEMENTS:** Holds 5 US patents in control valve, acoustic intensity probe, active control, noise and drag reduction, composite material; published 30 papers on jet noise, valve noise, launcher noise, active noise control, and flow-induced noise. **BUSINESS ADDRESS:** Program Manager, Office of Naval Research, 800 North Quincy St, Arlington, VA 22217, (703)696-0816.

NG, MARTIN K.
Data processing director. Hong Kong American. **PERSONAL:** Born Jun 15, 1952, Hong Kong; son of Gen-Wing Ng and Kok-Ying Tsang Ng; married Alice Au Ng, Dec 9, 1980; children: Charles, Jennifer. **EDUCATION:** University of Texas, Austin, BA, computer science, 1978; University of Houston, Clear Lake City, MS, computer science, 1981. **CAREER:** Texas Medical Center, system analyst, 1979-82, assistant director, 1983, computer services director, 1983-. **ORGANIZATIONS:** ACM, 1977-; IEEE, 1985-; Initiatives for Children Inc, board of directors, 1990-, business committee, chairman, 1991-, officers of the board, member-at-large, 1992-. **BUSINESS ADDRESS:** Director, Computer Services, Texas Medical Center, 406 Jesse Jones Library Building, Houston, TX 77030.

NG, MAY-MAY DONNA LEE
Insurance company executive, real estate officer. Taiwanese American/Hong Kong American. **PERSONAL:** Born Sep 26, 1952, Taipei, Taiwan; married Chi-Man William Ng, Mar 8, 1980; children: Timothy, Nicholas. **EDUCATION:** Illinois State University, BS, accounting, 1977; MBA, 1980. **CAREER:** State Farm Life Ins Co, sr accountant, 1978-82; Western Farm Bureau Management Co, asst vice pres, 1982-91; Central Life Assurance Co, vice pres, accounting, 1991-93, vice pres, internal auditing, 1993-. **ORGANIZATIONS:** AICPA; LOMA, cost accouting committee, 1989-92; Insurance Accounting & System Assn, Rocky Mountain Chapter, vice pres, 1989-91; Fellow of Life Management Institute, Colorado, vice pres, 1988. **HONORS/AWARDS:** Chartered Life Underwriter, 1982; Fellow of Life Management Institute, 1982; CPA, 1990. **BUSINESS ADDRESS:** Vice President, Internal Auditing, Central Life Assurance Company, 611 Fifth Ave, Des Moines, IA 50309, (515)242-4541.

NG, MICHAEL WAI-MAN
Civil engineer, manager. Chinese American. **PERSONAL:** Born Sep 1, 1960, Canton, People's Republic of China; son of Kock Poy Ng and Fung Sheung Ng; married Jenny J A Ng, Feb 4, 1992. **EDUCATION:** Northeastern University, BS (high honors), 1984. **CAREER:** HCH Partners, designer, 1984-86; VTN Southwest Inc, project engr, 1986-87; The McIntire Group, project engr, 1987-89; CMB & Associates, engineering manager, 1989-. **ORGANIZATIONS:** American Society of Civil Engineers, 1990-; National Society of Professional Engineers, 1990-. **SPECIAL ACHIEVEMENTS:** Registered civil engineer: California, 1989; Arizona, 1990; Nevada, 1991. **HOME ADDRESS:** 14393 La Harina Ct, San Diego, CA 92129, (619)484-0260.

NG, PATRICK
Business executive. Chinese American/Hong Kong American. **PERSONAL:** Born Mar 15, 1944, Hong Kong; son of Ng Bun Wah; married Bette Ng, Mar 27, 1973; children: Karen, Klara, Karine. **EDUCATION:** University of Illinois, BS, 1969. **CAREER:** Amdahl, systems analyst, 1979; IBM Corp, system engr, 1979-81; Reliance Technical Services, vice pres, 1981-. **ORGANIZATIONS:** SMTA; AAMA. **BUSINESS ADDRESS:** Vice President, Reliance Technical Services, Inc, 3100 Central Expressway, Santa Clara, CA 95051, (408)988-0888.

NG, PETER A.
Educator. Malaysian American. **PERSONAL:** Born Dec 31, 1941, Yong Peng, Johore, Malaysia; son of Kim Chong Peter Ng & Hwee Kuan Chua; married Ida Ah-Siew-Lim Ng, May 24, 1969; children: Eric Huai-Tsaw, Evan Hean-Tsaw. **EDUCATION:** St Edward's University, BS, mathematics, 1969; University of Texas, Austin, PhD, computer science, 1974. **CAREER:** CUNY, Hunter College, assistant professor, 1974-76; University of Missouri, Columbia, assistant professor, 1976-84, professor, chairman, 1984-86; University of North Texas, professor, chairman, 1986-87; New Jersey Institute of Technology, professor, chairman, 1987-. **ORGANIZATIONS:** IEEE, Computer Society, 1971-; ACM, 1971-; International Institute for Systems Integration, board member, 1993-; Software Engineering Strategies, board of advisors and contributors, 1993-. **SPECIAL ACHIEVEMENTS:** Co-author: "On Research Issues Regarding Uncertain Query Processing in an Office Document Retrieval System," Journal of Systems Integration, vol 3, no 2, pp 163-194, 1993; co-author, "Texpros: An Intelligent Document Processing System," International Journal on Software Engineering and Knowledge Engineering, vol 2, no 2, pp 171-196, June 1992; founder of International Conference on Systems Integration, 1990; Journal on Systems Integration, editor-in-chief, founder, 1991-. **BUSINESS ADDRESS:** Professor/Chairman, Dept of CIS, New Jersey Institute of Technology, University Heights, Newark, NJ 07102, (201)596-3387.

NG, REBECCA P.
Librarian. Chinese American. **PERSONAL:** Born Jul 8, 1962, Hong Kong; daughter of Kwong Piu Ng and Sau Ngor Fong. **EDUCATION:** Tam Kang University, BA, 1984; University of Hawaii at Manoa, MLS, 1988. **CAREER:** Lingnan College Library, catalog librarian, 1985-87; Library Management Systems, catalog librarian, 1989; Loyola Law Library, catalog librarian, 1990-. **ORGANIZATIONS:** American Library Association, 1990-; American Association of Law Libraries, 1990-. **SPECIAL ACHIEVEMENTS:** Fluent in Cantonese and Mandarin. **BUSINESS ADDRESS:** Catalog Librarian, Loyola Law Library, 1440 W 9th Street, Los Angeles, CA 90034, (213)736-1413.

NG, RICHARD
Consultant. Chinese American. **PERSONAL:** Born Dec 24, 1950, Boston, MA; son of Way Yee Ng & Got Gee Yee Ng; married Angela D Ng, May 12, 1979; children: Christina, Deanna, Michael, Laura, Stephen. **EDUCATION:** Tufts University, BS (cum laude), 1973, MS, 1974; Harvard University, MS, 1974; Indiana University, MBA, 1988. **CAREER:** Bethlehem Steel Corporation, senior env health engineer, 1976-86; Northrop Defense Systems Division, manager, safety/IH/env, 1986-88; Commodore Semiconductor Group, manager, safety/health/env, 1988-92; EHS Consultants, principal, 1992-. **ORGANIZATIONS:** American Industrial Hygiene Association, 1974-; American Academy of International Hygiene, 1979-; Semiconductor Safety Association, 1988-. **HONORS/AWARDS:** Beta Gamma Sigma, 1988. **SPECIAL ACHIEVEMENTS:** Certified industrial hygienist, 1979. **HOME ADDRESS:** 215 Valley View Circle, Phoenixville, PA 19460, (215)935-3291. **BUSINESS ADDRESS:** Principal, EHS Consultants, 215 Valley View Circle, Phoenixville, PA 19460, (215)935-3291.

NG, RICHARD YUT
Physician. Chinese American. **PERSONAL:** Born Jul 18, 1952, Detroit, MI; son of Yut Sun Ng and Yook Kum Ng; married Rosa Lynn Schindler, Jun 29, 1980; children: Garek Raymond, Laura. **EDUCATION:** Wayne State University, BS, 1977, MD, 1982. **CAREER:** Providence Medical Center, family practice specialist, currently. **BUSINESS ADDRESS:** Physician, Providence Medical Center, 47601 Grand River Ave, Ste A-115, Novi, MI 48374, (313)380-8270.

NG, RITA MEI-CHING
Educator. Hong Kong American. **PERSONAL:** Born Apr 21, 1958, Kowloon, Hong Kong; daughter of Ng Hin Hung and Chiu Kwan Fong. **EDUCATION:** Indiana University, BS, 1983, MA, 1985, PhD, 1989. **CAREER:** Indiana University, associate instructor, 1984-89; Sul Ross State University, assistant professor, 1989-90; Ferris State University, assistant professor, 1990-. **ORGANIZATIONS:** Speech Communication Association; International Listening Association. **HONORS/AWARDS:** Indiana University, teaching scholarship, 1984-89, research assistant, 1987. **SPECIAL ACHIEVEMENTS:** Paper: "The Social Acceptability for Compliance-gaining Strategies and Its Application to Competence Research," presented at the Speech Communication Annual Conference, 1992. **HOME ADDRESS:** 6017 W 32nd Ave, Wheat Ridge, CO 80033, (303)233-8249.

NG, TANG-TAT PERCY
Educator. Chinese American. **PERSONAL:** Born Jan 20, 1960, Hong Kong; son of Hee Ng and Lao Chan; married Tseng Shih Fong Ng, Jul 4, 1983; children: Paul, Peter. **EDUCATION:** National Taiwan University, BS, 1981; Carnegie-Mellon University, MS, 1983; Rensselaer Polytechnic Institute, PhD, 1989. **CAREER:** United Consultant Corp, engineer, 1984; Rensselaer Polytechnic Institute, post-doctoral, 1989-90; University of New Mexico, professor, 1990-. **ORGANIZATIONS:** American Society of Civil Engineering; American Society of Engineering Education. **SPECIAL ACHIEVEMENTS:** Co-author, works include: "Numerical Simulations of Monotonic and Cyclic Loading of Granular Soil," Journal of Geotechnical Engineering (ASCE), 120(2), 1994; "A Nonlinear Numerical Model for Soil Mechanics," Intl Journal for Numerical and Analytical Methods in Geomechanics, 16 (4), p 247-264, 1992; numerous others. **BUSINESS ADDRESS:** Professor, Dept of Civil Engineering, University of New Mexico, Albuquerque, NM 87131-0002, (505)277-4844.

NG, THOMAS
Fire commissioner. **CAREER:** San Francisco Fire Commission, commissioner, currently. **ORGANIZATIONS:** Chinese Hospital, board chairman. **BUSINESS ADDRESS:** Commissioner, San Francisco Fire Commission, 57 Waverly Place, San Francisco, CA 94108, (415)861-8000.*

NG, VINCENT W.
Hospital administrator. Chinese American. **PERSONAL:** Born Sep 11, 1954, Hong Kong; son of Jacob and Harline Ng. **EDUCATION:** University of Washington, BS, 1977; Trinity University, MS, 1979. **CAREER:** VA Medical Center, Portland, OR, executive assistant, 1979-81; VA Medical Center, Long Beach, CA, executive assistant, 1981-86; VA Medical Center, Dallas, TX, assistant director, 1986-87; VA Medical Center, Lebannon, PA, associate director, 1987-89; VA Medical Center, Philadelphia, PA, associate director, 1989-93; VA Medical Center, Newington, CT, director, 1993-. **ORGANIZATIONS:** American College of Health Care Executives, 1985-; Federal Manager Association, 1990-; Philadelphia Comfort House Inc, board member, 1992-; Senior Executive Association, board member. **HONORS/AWARDS:** Federal Executive Board, Manager of the Year, 1993; Pennsylvania Chamber of Commerce, Leadership Program, 1992. **SPECIAL ACHIEVEMENTS:** Participant in various leadership programs: Leadership VA; Leadership Lebanon Valley; Leadership Pennsylvania. **BUSINESS ADDRESS:** Director, Veterans Administration Medical Center, 555 Willard Ave, Newington, CT 06111, (203)667-2308.

NG, WING
Educator, engineer. Hong Kong American. **PERSONAL:** Born Sep 17, 1956, Hong Kong; married Lucy; children: Tracy, Yvonne. **EDUCATION:** Northeastern University, BS, mechanical engineering; MIT, MS, mechanical engineering, PhD, mechanical engineering. **CAREER:** GE Aircraft Engine Group; MIT, Gas Turbine Laboratory; NASA Langley Research Center; NASA Lewis; GE Corporate Research and Development; Virginia Tech, Mechanical Engineering Department, professor, currently. **ORGANIZATIONS:** ASME, executive committee, Aerospace Division, 1990-95, Propulsion Committee, Aerospace Division, chairman, 1991-92, Aircraft Engine, Turbomachinery & Education Committees, IGTI; AIAA, Airbreathing Propulsion Technical Committee, associate fellow, 1991-93; ASEE; International Society for Air Breathing Engines; SAE; Sigma Xi; Tau Beta Pi; Pi Tau Sigma. **HONORS/AWARDS:** Virginia Tech, Certificate of Teaching Excellence, 1985, 1988, Sporn Award, 1987; Society of Automotive Engineers, Ralph R Teetor Education Award, 1986. **SPECIAL ACHIEVEMENTS:** Registered professional engineer in Virginia. **BUSINESS ADDRESS:** Professor, Mechanical Engineering Dept, Virginia Tech, Randolph Hall, Blacksburg, VA 24061-0238, (703)231-7274.

NG, YUK-CHOW
Educator, researcher. Chinese American/Hong Kong American. **PERSONAL:** Born Feb 7, 1955, Canton, People's Republic of China; son of Kwok-Tin Ng; married Van-I Lam, Sep 1, 1984; children: Michelle Tsoek Kiu, Wesley Tsoek Jin. **EDUCATION:** Washington State University, BS, 1977, MS, 1979; Michigan State University, PhD, 1985. **CAREER:** Michigan State University, graduate assistant, 1980-84, research associate, 1985-86, research assistant professor, 1986-89; Pennsylvania State University, assistant professor, 1989-. **ORGANIZATIONS:** American Society for Pharmacology and Experimental Therapeutics, 1990-; International Society for Heart Research, 1989-; Sigma Xi, treasurer, 1990-; American Heart Association Basic Science Council, 1991-. **HONORS/AWARDS:** National Institute of Health, First Award, 1988. **SPECIAL ACHIEVEMENTS:** Author: Tissue-specific isoform regulatin of Na K-ATPase by thyroid hormone in the ferret, American Journal of Physiology, 1989; Expression of Na K-ATPase alpha 1 and alpha 3 isoforms in adult and neonatal ferret hearts, American Journal of Physiology, 1992. **BUSINESS ADDRESS:** Assistant Professor, Dept of Pharmacology, Pennsylvania State University, MS Hershey Medical Center, Hershey, PA 17033, (717)531-6027.

NGAI, KIA LING
Consultant. Chinese American. **PERSONAL:** Born May 20, 1940, Canton, China; son of Hei Ming Ngai & Hok Yee Cheung; married Linsen H Ngai, Dec 23, 1967; children: Sianne, Seagan, Serin. **EDUCATION:** University of Hong Kong, BS, 1962; University of Southern California, MS, math, 1964; University of Chicago, PhD, physics, 1969. **CAREER:** James Franck Institute, research associate, 1969; MIT Lincoln Lab, research staff, 1969-71; Naval Research Lab, section head, 1971-80, consultant, 1980-. **HONORS/AWARDS:** Department of Defense, Superior Civilian Service Award, 1978. **SPECIAL ACHIEVEMENTS:** Physics of relaxations in Complex Correlated Systems, 1979-. **BUSINESS ADDRESS:** Consultant, US Naval Research Laboratory, 4555 Overlook Ave SW, Washington, DC 20375-5000, (202)767-6150.

NG-BRECKWOLDT, MAY SUE
Systems analyst. Chinese American. **PERSONAL:** Born Jan 6, 1958, San Francisco, CA; daughter of Suet Kum Tsang Ng and William Ng; married Ken Breckwoldt, Sep 5, 1992. **EDUCATION:** Queens College, BA, 1981. **CAREER:** Kaiser Aluminum, assoc systems analyst, 1981-82; ESL, programmer, 1982-83; Grant County PUD, sr systems analyst, 1983-87; Paccar Inc, sr systems analyst, 1987-93; Advanced Tech Lab, sr systems analyst, 1993-. **BUSINESS ADDRESS:** Senior Systems Analyst, Advanced Technology Laboratories, PO Box 3003, Mailstop 270, Bothell, WA 98041-3003, (206)487-8142.

NGO, DAVID
Credit analyst. Vietnamese American. **PERSONAL:** Born Feb 29, 1960, Saigon, Vietnam; son of Ngo Xuan Trach and Ho Thi Ba. **EDUCATION:** Pima Community College, AG (with honors), general studies, 1987; The University of Arizona, BS, industrial engineering, 1990. **CAREER:** IBM Corp, data analyst, 1989-92; American Express, credit analyst, 1993-. **ORGANIZATIONS:** Institute of Industrial Engineers, 1987-.

NGOR, HAING S.
Author, actor, physician. Cambodian American. **CAREER:** Physician; actor: The Killing Fields, 1984; Eastern Condors, 1986; The Iron Triangle, 1989; Last Flight Out: A True Story, 1990; Vietnam Texas, 1990; In Love and War, 1991; Ambition, 1991. **HONORS/AWARDS:** The Killing Fields, Academy Award for Best Supporting Actor, 1984. **BIOGRAPHICAL SOURCES:** Autobiography, Haing Ngor: A Cambodian Odyssey, author, Macmillan Publishing Co, 1988. **BUSINESS ADDRESS:** Author, c/o Macmillan Publishing Co Inc, 866 Third Ave, 21st Fl, New York, NY 10022.*

NGUYEN, AN H.
Educator. Vietnamese American. **PERSONAL:** Born May 5, 1950, Quangnam, Vietnam; son of Nguyen Huu An & Hua Thi Mai; married Amy Pham Nguyen, Aug 23, 1977; children: Lisa Lilan, Nathan An Thien, Benjamin Duy Minh. **EDUCATION:** Tennessee Tech University, BS, 1974, MS, 1977; University of California, PhD, 1993. **CAREER:** Thoratec Laboratories Corp, consultant/senior engineer, 1980-92; University of California, research assistant/lab manager, 1983-90; San Jose State University, associate professor,

1990-. **ORGANIZATIONS:** San Jose State University, Computer Engineering Dept, departmental graduate committee, chm, 1991-93; Computer Society, adviser, 1993-; Vietnamese Student Association, adviser, 1990-. **HONORS/ AWARDS:** Phi Kappa Phi; Kappa Mu Epsilon, Mathematics. **SPECIAL ACHIEVEMENTS:** Model Control of Image Processing: Pupillometry, 1993; Top-Down Model Control of Image Processing for Telerobotics and Biomedical Instrumentation, 1993. **HOME ADDRESS:** 43943 Rosemere Dr, Fremont, CA 94539, (510)623-0610.

NGUYEN, ANH MAI (ANDY)
Mechanical engineer. Vietnamese American. **PERSONAL:** Born Oct 7, 1957, Saigon, Vietnam; son of Hai Xuan Nguyen and Gai Thi Vu; married Kim D Nguyen, Jul 24, 1982. **EDUCATION:** Ecole Polytechnique, Universite De Montreal, BSME, 1981; Penn State University, MSME, currently. **CAREER:** Exeltor Inc, R&D engr, 1981-82; AMP Inc, engr, 1984-85; MacBeth Engineering Corp, engr, 1986-87; Strato-Lift Inc, chief engr, 1987-. **BUSINESS ADDRESS:** Chief Engineer, Strato-Lift Inc, Twin Valley & Hemlock Rds, PO Box 220, Morgantown, PA 19543, (215)286-2014.

NGUYEN, BAN MAU. *See* **NGUYEN, BENJAMIN BAN.**

NGUYEN, BAO GIA
Educator. Vietnamese American. **PERSONAL:** Born Oct 29, 1954, Saigon, Vietnam; son of Thuong Nguyen and Loi Nguyen. **EDUCATION:** Brown University, AB, AM, 1980; UCLA, PhD, 1985. **CAREER:** Illinois Institute of Technology, assistant professor, 1988-. **ORGANIZATIONS:** American Mathematical Society, 1987-; Institute of Mathematical Statistics, 1987-. **SPECIAL ACHIEVEMENTS:** Articles published in: Communications in Mathematical Physics, 1985; Journal of Statistical Physics, 1987; Journal of Applied Probability, 1990; Illinois Journal of Mathematics, 1992; Annals of Probability, 1993. **BIOGRAPHICAL SOURCES:** Percolation by Grimmett, Springer-Verlag, p 184-185, 1989; Self Avoiding Random Walk, by N Madras and G Slade, Birkhäuser, p 169, 1993. **BUSINESS ADDRESS:** Professor, Dept of Mathematics, Illinois Institute of Technology, IIT Center, E1, Rm 213, Chicago, IL 60616, (312)567-8810.

NGUYEN, BAO T.
Federal government official. Vietnamese American. **PERSONAL:** Born in Phu-Tho, Vietnam; married Kim-Lien; children: Tien. **EDUCATION:** National Defense University; Syracuse University; Harvard University; Army War College; Naval War College; Air War College; University of Paris Law School, law, 1954; USC, MBA, 1960. **CAREER:** Caterpillar Tractor Dealership, Vietnam, managing director, 1960-63; Allis Chalmers Dealership, France, parts manager, purchasing officer, 1963-68; ITT Hartford Insurance Group, senior analyst, 1970-74; GEICO Insurance, data administrator, 1974-81; Naval Research Lab, senior analyst, 1981-84; Department of the Air Force, air force data administrator, 1984-93, assistant to deputy secretary, currently. **HONORS/AWARDS:** Data Administration Management Association, Data Administrator of the Year, 1992; General Services Administration, Excellence in Administration, 1992; Government Computer News, contribution to Improved Information Resource Management, 1989. **SPECIAL ACHIEVEMENTS:** Establishment of the data administration function in the Dept of the Air Force, the initiation of the $500,000,000.00 Joint Service Database Machine Requirement contract for the Dept of Defense, the successful development of the unique Air Force Intelligent Repository (a critical tool to manage information resources as a corporate asset). **MILITARY SERVICE:** Army, 2nd lt. **HOME ADDRESS:** 1611 Fremont Lane, Vienna, VA 22182.

NGUYEN, BENJAMIN BAN (BAN MAU NGUYEN)
Accountant. Vietnamese American. **PERSONAL:** Born Jan 29, 1933, Hue, Thua-Thien, Vietnam; son of Tung Mau Nguyen and Co Thi Ho; married Anne Tuyet-Hong Nguyen, Oct 20, 1958; children: Alexandre Huy, Paul Hoang, Joseph Binh, Christopher Minh, Nam Mau, Phuong-Lan Hong. **EDUCATION:** Thu Duc Officer Academy, Vietnam, reserve officer, 1953; The Infantry School, Fort Benning, BIOC, RMI, 1955; University of Saigon, LLM, 1964; University of Minnesota. **CAREER:** Fourth Region Military Court, Cantho, Vietnam, chief prosecutor, 1968-72; Saigon Military Court, Vietnam, staff judge advocate, 1972-75; The Pillsbury Company, 1975-79; Angleton General Mechanical Co, accountant, 1980-82; Way Engineering Co, accountant, 1982-83; Mekong Business Services, owner, manager, 1983-. **ORGANIZATIONS:** Assn of Thu Duc Former Officers, vice pres, 1979-; Hue Old Capital Mutual Assn, board of directors, 1983-; Nguyen Royal Assn, 1985-. **HONORS/ AWARDS:** City of Columbus, GA, Honorary Citizen of Georgia, 1955.

SPECIAL ACHIEVEMENTS: Pacific American National Bank (Proposed), board of directors, 1982; editor, writer: Vietnam Thoi Bao Magazine, 1983. **MILITARY SERVICE:** Directorate of Justice, Ministry of Defense, ARVN, lt col, 1967-75; 12 military medals, including 5th degree of National Order of VN Medal. **BIOGRAPHICAL SOURCES:** Vietnam Military Record, National Record Department; US Dept of Defense Record, State of Georgia; City of Columbus Record. **BUSINESS ADDRESS:** Owner/Manager, Mekong Business Services, 2908 San Jacinto, Houston, TX 77004, (713)650-6262.

NGUYEN, BONG VAN
Accounting supervisor. Vietnamese American. **PERSONAL:** Born Jun 25, 1954, Saigon, Vietnam; son of Ty Van Nguyen and Thinh Thi Nguyen; married Oanh Thai Nguyen, Feb 1, 1992; children: Patricia. **EDUCATION:** Howard College, AA (magna cum laude), 1977; The University of Texas, BBA, 1979. **CAREER:** Hunt Oil Co, revenue supervisor, 1980-90; Hunt Refining Co, accounting supervisor, 1990-. **ORGANIZATIONS:** Assn Oil Pipe Line, 1990-. **MILITARY SERVICE:** US Air Force, 2nd lt, helicopter pilot, 1972-75; Certificate of Achievement; Distinguished Pilot, 1974. **BUSINESS ADDRESS:** Supervisor, Accounting, Hunt Refining Company, 1445 Ross at Field, Dallas, TX 75202, (214)978-8817.

NGUYEN, CAM
Educator. Vietnamese American. **PERSONAL:** Born Jul 14, 1954, Vietnam; son of Suong Nguyen; married Diep Ngoc Tran, Jan 2, 1980; children: Uyen (Christine), Andrew. **EDUCATION:** California State Polytechnic University, BSEE, 1980; California State University, MSEE, 1983; University of Central Florida, PhD, EE, 1990. **CAREER:** ITT Gilfillan Co, design engineer, 1979-82; Hughes Aircraft Co, member of technical staff, 1982-83; TRW Inc, member of technical staff, 1983-86, senior staff engineer, 1989-90; Aerojet Electro Systems Co, technical specialist, 1986-87; Martin Marietta Corp, professional staff, 1987-89; Texas A&M University, assistant professor, 1991-. **ORGANIZATIONS:** IEEE, sr member, 1982-91, editorial board, MTT Transactions, 1991-. **HONORS/AWARDS:** Registered professional engineer in the state of Texas. **SPECIAL ACHIEVEMENTS:** Published 60 technical papers and 2 book chapters; technical reviewer for IEEE MTT Transactions, IEE Electronics Letters, & Microwave & Optical Technology Letters. **BUSINESS ADDRESS:** Assistant Professor, Dept of Electrical Engineering, Texas A & M University, College Station, TX 77843-3128, (409)845-7469.

NGUYEN, CAROLINE P.
Aerospace engineer. Vietnamese American. **PERSONAL:** Born 1962, Saigon, Vietnam. **EDUCATION:** University of California, Berkeley, BS, 1985; University of Washington, Seattle, MS, 1987. **CAREER:** Water Technology Center, assistant enr, 1985; University of Washington, research assistant, 1986-87; Lockheed Missiles & Space, spacecraft research engineer, 1988-91, material & process engineer, 1991-93, reliability engineer, 1993-. **ORGANIZATIONS:** American Institute of Aeronautics & Astronautics, assoc member, 1992; Society of Women Engineers, 1991; National Association of Female Executives, 1992. **HONORS/AWARDS:** Lockheed/NASA, Hubble Space Telescope Achievement Certificate, 1990; Richmond District, California, Special Art Award, 1980. **SPECIAL ACHIEVEMENTS:** Two patents pending, 1993. **HOME ADDRESS:** 4540 Romano Drive, Stockton, CA 95207, (408)246-2238.

NGUYEN, CHARLES C.
Engineering educator, researcher. Vietnamese American. **PERSONAL:** Born Jan 1, 1956, Danang, Vietnam; son of Buoi Nguyen & Tinh T Nguyen; married Kim-Bang T Nguyen, Aug 5, 1989; children: Carissa Thuy-Duong. **EDUCATION:** Konstanz University, Germany, diplom ingenieur, 1978; George Washington University, MS, 1980, DSc, 1982. **CAREER:** Rheinfelden Power Co, 1973; Siemens Corp, engineer, 1977; Liebherr Co, designer, 1977-78; George Washington University, Electrical Engineering and Computer Science, assistant professional lecturer, 1982; Catholic University of America, electrical engineering, assistant professor, 1982-87, electrical engineering, associate professor 1987-92, Robotics and Control Lab, School of Engineering, director, 1985-, electrical engineering, professor, 1992-. **ORGANIZATIONS:** Institute of Electrical & Electronic Engineers, senior member, Control System Society, Washington, DC Chapter, vp, 1985, treasurer, 1984, Intl Organizing Committee, Second Intl Symposium on Robotics & Manufacturing Research, Education & Applications, 1988, Intl Program Committee, ISMM Intl Conference on Computer Applications in Design Simulation & Analysis, 1989; Sigma Xi; Tau Beta Pi, chief faculty advisor; Intl Society for Mini & Microcomputers; American Biographical Institute, research board of advisors; Intl Biographical Centre,

advisory council; Society of Manufacturing Engineers, senior member; Robotics Intl, senior member; Intl Journal of Computers & Electrical Engineering, associate editor; numerous others. **HONORS/AWARDS:** Catholic University of America, Academic VP's Research Excellence Award, 1989; President of Konstanz University, Best University Graduate Award, 1978; NASA/ASEE Fellowship Awards, 1985-86; Natl Academy of Science, Senior Research Associate Award, 1990-91; Engineering Foundation, Research Initiation Grant, 1985. **SPECIAL ACHIEVEMENTS:** Co-author, "Adaptive Control of a Stewart Platform-based Manipulator," Journal of Robotic Systems, July 1993, "Autonomous Berthing/Unberthing of A Work Attachment Mechanism, Work Attachment Fixture," Report, NASA/ Goddard Space Flight Center, Aug 1992; guest editor, "Parallel Closed-Kinematic Chain Manipulators and Devices," Journal of Robotic Systems, 1993; author, "Application of Robotics to the NASA Space Program," IEEE, Washington Chapter, Industry Applications Society, Jan 1992. **BUSINESS ADDRESS:** Professor, Dept of Electrical Engineering, Catholic University of America, Pangborn Bldg, Rm 201, Washington, DC 20064.

NGUYEN, CHRIS CUONG MANH
Food company executive. Vietnamese American. **PERSONAL:** Born Sep 17, 1947, Vietnam; son of Thien T Nguyen. **EDUCATION:** Trinity University, BBA; University of Iowa, MBA candidate, 1971. **CAREER:** Lo-an/Florida Inc, chairman, CEO, 1971-90; first US Access Corporation, president, CEO, currently. **ORGANIZATIONS:** Institute of American Entrepreneurs, lifetime member. **HONORS/AWARDS:** Institute of American Entrepreneurs, Entrepreneur of the Year, 1988. **SPECIAL ACHIEVEMENTS:** Second Annual Symposium on Business Achievement, speaker, 1987. **BIOGRAPHICAL SOURCES:** Winners, by Carter Henderson, Holt Rinehart Winston, p136-142; Fortune, p156, Sept 12, 1988.

NGUYEN, CHUONG VAN
Educator. Vietnamese American. **PERSONAL:** Born May 7, 1957, Saigon, Vietnam. **EDUCATION:** Portland State University, BS, 1982, MS, 1986. **CAREER:** Portland State University, instructor; Palomar College, associate professor, currently. **BUSINESS ADDRESS:** Associate Professor, Mathematics Dept, Palomar College, 1140 West Mission Rd, E16, San Marcos, CA 92069-1487, (519)744-1150.

NGUYEN, CU D.
Government official. Vietnamese American. **PERSONAL:** Born Oct 15, 1954, Saigon, Vietnam; son of Tu Dinh Nguyen and Thai Thi Lu; married Thuy B Nguyen, Oct 10, 1975; children: Gabrielle Tu. **EDUCATION:** University of Missouri, Rolla, BS, mechanical engineering, 1981. **CAREER:** Oklahoma City Air Logistic Center, senior mechanical engineer, 1981-. **ORGANIZATIONS:** Oklahoma Volunteerism Advisory Council, appointed by senator Protem, currently; Oklahoma Task Force on Volunteerism, appointed by governor, currently; Oklahoma City Human Rights Commission, commissioner at large, currently; American Red Cross, Oklahoma City Chapter, board member, currently; National Conference of Christians and Jews, Oklahoma City Chapter, board member, currently; Urban League of Oklahoma City, board member, currently; Asia Society of Oklahoma, founder, board member, currently; Leadership Oklahoma, board member, 1990-91; numerous others. **HONORS/AWARDS:** Asian Society of Oklahoma, Outstanding Individual Member Award, 1990. **SPECIAL ACHIEVEMENTS:** Selected to be a class member of the Leadership Oklahoma Class III, 1989. **MILITARY SERVICE:** South Vietnamese Army, lt, 1972-75. **BIOGRAPHICAL SOURCES:** Tinker County Weekly, vol 18, no 66, p 4, Mar 2, 1993, vol 16, no 6, Jan 8, 1992; Oklahoma Gazette, p 1-4, April 11, 1990. **HOME ADDRESS:** 2616 SW 107th, Oklahoma City, OK 73170, (405)691-7194.

NGUYEN, CUONG PHU
Electronics engineer. Vietnamese American. **PERSONAL:** Born Jul 30, 1964, Danang, Vietnam; son of Du Nguyen and Lan Thi Huynh; married Maria-Nina V Nguyen, May 1, 1992. **EDUCATION:** Stevens Institute of Technology, BSEE, 1989. **CAREER:** Lorch Electronics, design engr, production engr, 1989-90; Mini-Circuits Labs, applications engr, 1990-. **HOME ADDRESS:** 2058 E 57th St, Brooklyn, NY 11234.

NGUYEN, DUC BA
Cosmetic processor. Vietnamese American. **PERSONAL:** Born Jun 19, 1963, Vietnam; son of Thien Nguyen. **EDUCATION:** Middlesex County College, associate degree, 1991. **CAREER:** Cosmair Inc, cosmetic processor, currently. **ORGANIZATIONS:** Vietnamese Catholic Community, vice leader of choir.

NGUYEN, DUNG DANG
Physician. Vietnamese American. **PERSONAL:** Born Dec 1, 1950, Hanoi, Vietnam; married Michelle Nguyen, May 1985; children: Daniel, Brian. **EDUCATION:** University of Saigon Medical School, MD, 1975. **CAREER:** New York Downtown Hospital, nephrologist, currently. **ORGANIZATIONS:** American College of Physicians, fellow, 1990; American Society of Nephrology. **SPECIAL ACHIEVEMENTS:** Publications; teachings. **BIOGRAPHICAL SOURCES:** ABMS Compendium of Certified Medical Specialist, Vol 2, 3rd edition, p 1370, 1990-91. **BUSINESS ADDRESS:** Physician, 254 Canal St, Ste 5001A, New York, NY 10013, (212)334-8108.

NGUYEN, HENRY THIEN (HUNG THIEN)
Educator, educational administrator. Vietnamese American. **PERSONAL:** Born Jan 7, 1954, Vinh Long, Vietnam; son of Nghiep Van Nguyen and Bay Thi Nguyen; married Jenny Lam, Dec 24, 1977; children: Davis, Francis. **EDUCATION:** University of Cantho, Vietnam, 1972-75; Penn State University, BS, 1977, MS, 1978; University of Missouri, PhD, 1982. **CAREER:** Penn State University, graduate research assistant, 1977-78; University of Missouri, graduate research assistant, 1978-82; Oklahoma State University, assistant professor, 1982-84; Texas Tech University, assistant professor, 1984-89, associate professor of genetics, 1989-, Biotechnology Institute, director, 1989-. **ORGANIZATIONS:** American Society of Agronomy, public relations committee; Crop Science Society of America, award committee; American Society of Plant Physiologists; Genetics Society of America; American Association for the Advancement of Science; Sigma Xi; Gamma Sigma Delta, president of Texas Tech University chapter. **HONORS/AWARDS:** Crop Science Society of America, Young Crop Scientist Award, 1990; National Science Foundation, Presidential Young Investigator Award, 1986. **SPECIAL ACHIEVEMENTS:** Discovery of the genetic diversity of heat shock protein synthesis in wheat and maize; isolation of heat and drought stress responsive genes in wheat and maize; molecular mapping of stress tolerance traits in cereal crops. **BUSINESS ADDRESS:** Professor, Dept of Agronomy, Texas Tech University, Mail Stop 2122, Lubbock, TX 79409.

NGUYEN, HIEN VU
Research scientist. Vietnamese American. **PERSONAL:** Born Dec 15, 1943, Saigon, Vietnam; married Emily, Dec 27, 1972; children: Hoai Andrew, Nam William, Phong Matthew. **EDUCATION:** Montana State University, BS, 1966; University of Wisconsin, PhD, 1970. **CAREER:** W R Grace & Company, research associate, 1976-78; Johnson & Johnson, Canada, senior development engineer, 1974-76, research fellow, 1978-. **ORGANIZATIONS:** American Chemical Society, 1978-; American Institute of Chemical Engineers, 1988-. **SPECIAL ACHIEVEMENTS:** Fifteen technical publications; nine US patents. **BUSINESS ADDRESS:** Research Fellow, Johnson & Johnson, 2351 US Route 130, Dayton, NJ 08810, (908)274-3131.

NGUYEN, HO NGOC
Educator, educational administrator. Vietnamese American. **PERSONAL:** Born Jul 15, 1946, Phat-Diem, Ninh-Binh, Vietnam; son of Andrew Nguyen & Mai-Nhu Tran; married Phuong-Loan Nguyen, Aug 5, 1972; children: Viet, Minh-Lann, Dao. **EDUCATION:** University of California, Santa Cruz, BA, 1969; University of Calgary, MA, 1971; Dalhousie University, PhD, 1976. **CAREER:** Defense Language Institute, instructor, 1968-69; Terre Des Hommes, social worker, 1969-70; Florida Institute of Technology, 1983-; Technical Consulting Inc, vice president, 1989-92; Aspen Research Inc, president, 1993-; St Mary's College of Maryland, division head/professor, 1979-. **ORGANIZATIONS:** American Economic Association, 1979-93; Canadian Economic Association, 1975-79; Eastern Economic Association, 1983-93; National Association of Economic Educators, 1982-93; Omicron Delta Epsilon, faculty advisor, 1993-. **HONORS/AWARDS:** Fulbright-Hays, Summer Grant, 1992. **BUSINESS ADDRESS:** Professor, Head, Division of History & Social Science, St Mary's College of Maryland, St Mary's City, MD 20686, (301)862-0408.

NGUYEN, HUE THI
Social work case manager. Vietnamese American. **PERSONAL:** Born Aug 18, 1951, Hungyen, Vietnam; daughter of Nguyen An and Nguyen Dai; married Ru Tran, Jun 20, 1972; children: Thuhang Tran, Caohung Tran, Tran Caohoan, Tran Hahang, Tran Xuan Hang. **EDUCATION:** Bunker Hill College, English, 1989-93. **CAREER:** Foreman, 1989-92; case manager, 1992-. **HOME ADDRESS:** 33 Buttonwood, Dorchester, MA 02125.

NGUYEN, KIM-OANH THI

Chemical engineer. Vietnamese American. **PERSONAL:** Born Oct 10, 1960, Saigon, Vietnam; daughter of Dat Van Nguyen and Phuc Thi Doan; married Hung Phi Vo, Jul 7, 1991. **EDUCATION:** Kansas State University, BSChE, 1981, MSChE, 1983. **CAREER:** Kansas State University, research assistant, 1981-84; AT&T, technical staff member, 1984-. **ORGANIZATIONS:** Bruce Junior High School, Science Club Program, volunteer, 1990-; Spar and Spindle Girl Scout Council, board of directors, 1989-92; Northeast Consortium of Colleges & Universities in Massachusetts, advisory council, 1987-89; Vietnamese Community Development Center, treasurer, 1986-90; Boy Scouts of America, coordinator, 1986-90; Kansas State University, student senator & graduate student council, 1981-83. **HONORS/AWARDS:** YMCA, Tribute to Women Industry Nominee, 1989; Society of Women Engineers, semifinalist on the National Speech Contest, 1981. **SPECIAL ACHIEVEMENTS:** "Cause of Elevated Ozone and Fine Particles Concentrations in SAW3 Cleanroom," 1993; "Particle in SAW III Cleanroom," 1991, 1992; "Elimination of Trichlorsethylene in SAW Devices," 1990; "Preparation and Characteristics of Alumina," 1983; "Semifluidized Bed Filtration," 1981. **BUSINESS ADDRESS:** Member of Technical Staff, AT&T, 1600 Osgood St, Dept 531210300, Chem Lab 32-AA4, North Andover, MA 01845, (508)960-2058.

NGUYEN, LONG

Artist. Vietnamese American. **PERSONAL:** Born Dec 23, 1958, Nha-Trang, Vietnam; son of Chinh Nguyen and Thuan Tran. **EDUCATION:** Christian Brothers College, BS, civil engineering, 1980; San Jose State University, MFA, 1985. **CAREER:** Artist, group exhibitions include: Intercessor, Allegra Gallery, 1989; Oakland's Artist '90, the Oakland Museum, 1990; Entre d'Arte, Michael Walls Gallery, New York, Artists from the South of the World, Galleria Civica d'Arte Contemporanian, Italy; Responsive Witness, Palo Alto Culture Center, 1991; Tale of Yellow Skin, San Francisco Art Commission Gallery, 1992; "12 Bay Area Artists," San Jose Museum of Art, 1993; solo exhibitions include: Master Gallery, San Jose State University, 1985; Studio One Gallery, 1986; Miller/Brown Gallery, 1987, 1988, 1989; d p Fong Galleries, 1990; "Open to the Four Winds," San Jose Institute of Contemporary Art, "Illumination," Works on Paper, Monterey Peninsula Museum, 1993; "Tales of Yellow Skin," d p Fong & Spratt Galleries, 1993; San Jose State University, part-time lecturer, 1988-91; UC Berkeley, lecturer, 1989-90; UC Davis, 1990-92, San Francisco Art Institute, part-time lecturer, 1993-. **HONORS/AWARDS:** Fleishacker Foundation, Eureka Fellowship, $15,000 Award (painting), 1993; National Endowment for the Arts, $5,000 Award (works on paper), 1989. **BIOGRAPHICAL SOURCES:** "The Art of His Life," by Kathleen Donnelly, Mercury News, cover story, art & book section, April 18, 1993; "Long Nguyen," by Casey Fitzsimmons, Artweek Magazine, March 19, 1992. **HOME ADDRESS:** 1050 47th Avenue #2, Oakland, CA 94601, (510)533-6225.

NGUYEN, LUU THANH

Engineer, educator. Vietnamese American. **PERSONAL:** Born Oct 11, 1954, Saigon, Vietnam; son of Luong T Nguyen and Cuc B Tran. **EDUCATION:** University of Southern California, BS, industrial and system engineering, 1976, MS, 1977; MIT, SM, mechanical engineering, 1979, PhD, 1984. **CAREER:** IBM T J Watson Research Center, research staff, 1984-88; Philips R&D Center, senior scientist, 1988-91; San Jose State University, adjunct professor, 1992-; National Semiconductor Corporation, program manager, 1991-. **ORGANIZATIONS:** ASME; IEEE; ISHM; Sigma Xi; Phi Kappa Phi; Tau Beta Pi. **HONORS/AWARDS:** MIT, ME Department, Outstanding Student Service Award, 1984, Karl Taylor Compton Prize, 1984; Community Service Fund Board, Service Award, 1982, 1983; NASA, Orbiter Design & Development Team Award, 1977, Certificate of Appreciation, for contributions to Viking, 1977; AAAS/Industrial Research Institute, Mass Media Science and Engineering Fellow Award; ISHM, Best Session Paper Award, 1992; Fannie and John Hertz Foundation Fellowship; AAAS Mass Media Science and Engineering Fellowship. **SPECIAL ACHIEVEMENTS:** Over 70 technical papers; over 15 invention disclosures; over 40 general science features; 7 patents; 4 book chapters; editor of 2 books. **BUSINESS ADDRESS:** Program Manager, Strategic Planning & Development, Natl Semiconductor Corp, PO Box 58090, M/S 29-100, Santa Clara, CA 95052, (408)721-4786.

NGUYEN, MANH-HUNG

Educator. Vietnamese American. **PERSONAL:** Born Mar 8, 1937, Hanoi, Vietnam; son of Quan-Chinh Nguyen & thi Tho Pham; divorced; children: Peter H, Patrick H. **EDUCATION:** LLB, law, 1960; international relations: MA, 1963, PhD, 1965. **CAREER:** National School of Administration, Viet-

nam, professor, 1965-75; George Mason University, associate professor, 1977-, Indo China Institute, director, 1980-. **ORGANIZATIONS:** National Congress of Vietnamese in America, board of directors, 1987-93; National Association for Vietnamese American Education, president, 1982-84; Vietnamese Lawyers Association, advisory board, 1979-80; Vietnam Foundation, vice-president, 1975-77; Vietnam Council on Foreign Relations, 1971-75; Vietnam Economic Association, vice-president, 1974-75; Association for Administrative Studies, general secretary, 1967-75. **HONORS/AWARDS:** Social Science Research Council, fellow, 1986; Smith Mundt-Fulbright, Scholar, 1960-62. **SPECIAL ACHIEVEMENTS:** Author, Introduction to International Relations, Saigon, 1971; co-author, Peace & Development in South Vietnam, Saigon, 1973; contributor, New Directions in the International Relations of Southeast Asia, Singapore University Press, 1973; contributor, Refugees in the United States, Greenwood Press, 1985; contributor, The American War in Vietnam, Greenwood Press, 1987; articles in scholarly journals. **BUSINESS ADDRESS:** Associate Professor, Dept of Public & Intl Affairs, George Mason University, Fairfax, VA 22030, (703)993-3722.

NGUYEN, MIKE CHI

Engineer. Vietnamese American. **PERSONAL:** Born Oct 30, 1956, Dalat, Vietnam; son of Ngoc Nguyen and Tuyet Bui; married Oanh Luu, Jan 1980; children: Anh, Thu, Catherine, Jacqueline. **EDUCATION:** Mission College, AS, 1984; University of California, Berkeley, BS, 1986. **CAREER:** Mentor Graphics, design verification engr, 1986-90; Panasonic, senior design engr, 1990-91; LSI Logic, senior design engr, 1991-. **HOME ADDRESS:** 2703 Glen Loman Way, San Jose, CA 95148.

NGUYEN, NGHIA VAN

Physicist. Vietnamese American. **PERSONAL:** Born Apr 6, 1941, Hanoi, Vietnam; son of Boi Van Nguyen & Tan Thi Do; married Thuy-Phuong T Nguyen, Aug 30, 1969; children: The-Hung. **EDUCATION:** Saigon University, Vietnam, 1960; Brandeis University, BA (cum laude), math, 1963; Tufts University, MS, physics, 1965, PhD, physics, 1968. **CAREER:** EPSCO Incorporated, sr system analyst, 1969-78; Charles S Draper Laboratory, Inc, group leader, 1978-. **HONORS/AWARDS:** Charles S Draper Laboratory, Performance Recognition Award, 1992; US Navy, US Fleet Ballistic Missile Ten Year Service Award, 1991. **SPECIAL ACHIEVEMENTS:** Co-author, "Death of a Software Manager, How to Avoid Career Suicide Through Dynamic Software Process Modeling," American Programmer, vol 6, no 5, p 10, May 1993. **BUSINESS ADDRESS:** Group Leader, Charles Stark Draper Laboratory Inc, 555 Technology Square-MS15, Cambridge, MA 02139, (617)258-4031.

NGUYEN, NGOC-DIEP THI

Educator. Vietnamese American. **PERSONAL:** Born May 3, 1958, Ho Chi Minh City, Vietnam; daughter of Dinh Ngoc Nguyen & Anh Lien Ly; married Billy Joe Shaw, Aug 6, 1983; children: Timothy Nguyen Shaw, Daniel Nguyen Shaw, Ian Nguyen Shaw. **EDUCATION:** West Virginia University, BS, 1979; Ohio State University, MA, 1981, PhD, 1989. **CAREER:** Saint Agatha Elementary School, teacher, 1979-81; Groveport-Madison Schools, teacher, 1981-83; Ohio State University, research & teaching associate, 1983-85; Ohio Department of Education, consultant, 1985-86; Mulitfunctional Resource Center, consultant, 1986-88; National Louis University, adjunct professor, 1988-; Illinois Resource Center, consultant, 1988-. **ORGANIZATIONS:** National Association for the Education and Advancement of Cambodian, Laotian & Vietnamese Americans, president, 1992-; National Council of Teachers of English, Mulitcultural Booklist Committee, 1990-93; Vietnamese Association of Illinois, board of directors, 1987-; Ohio Refugee Assistance Advisory Council, 1984-86. **HONORS/AWARDS:** National Association for Bilingual Education, semifinalist, Oustanding Dissertation Award, 1991; Mortar Board Honorary Society, 1979; Kappa Delta Pi, 1979. **SPECIAL ACHIEVEMENTS:** Proficient in Vietnamese, French & Spanish; presenter at national conferences on education. **BUSINESS ADDRESS:** Consultant, Illinois Resource Center, 1855 Mt Prospect Rd, Des Plaines, IL 60018, (708)803-3112.

NGUYEN, THUAN KE

Educator. Vietnamese American. **PERSONAL:** son of Ninh Van Nguyen and Hieu Thi Nguyen; married Bangtam Thi Le, Sep 12, 1981; children: An Le, Thuy Linh. **EDUCATION:** California State Polytechnic University, Pomona, BSc, chemical engineering, 1974; Princeton University, MA, chemical engineering, 1975, PhD, chemical engineering, 1979. **CAREER:** California State Polytechnic University, professor, 1979-. **ORGANIZATIONS:** Omega Chi Epsilon, 1980-. **HONORS/AWARDS:** California Polytechnic, Pomona, Meritorious Performance & Professional Promise Award, 1985. **SPECIAL**

ACHIEVEMENTS: "Numerical Solution for Film Evaporation of Spherical Liquid Droplet on an Isothermal and Adiabatic Surface," Int J Heat Mass Transfer, vol 30, 1987; "A Computer Program for Modeling Steady-State Combustion in a Pocket Engine Thrust Chamber," UFAF Report, SN75-02, 1984. **BUSINESS ADDRESS:** Professor, Chemical & Materials Engineering Dept, California State Polytechnic University, Pomona, 3801 West Temple Avenue, Bldg 13, Room 226, Pomona, CA 91768, (909)869-2631.

NGUYEN, TONY C.
Marketing administrator. Vietnamese American. **PERSONAL:** Born Aug 16, 1948, Saigon, Vietnam; son of Ho Nguyen; married Tanya Nguyen, Dec 1, 1980; children: Steven, Diana. **EDUCATION:** University of Cincinnati, BSME, 1981. **CAREER:** Texas Instruments Inc, engineer, 11 years; NSA Inc, national marketing director, 1991-. **HOME ADDRESS:** 828 Deerlake Dr, Allen, TX 75002-5055, (214)727-8209.

NGUYEN, TRI HUU
Educator. Vietnamese American. **PERSONAL:** Born Dec 25, 1936, Nhatrang, Khanh Hoa, Vietnam; son of Le Van Nguyen & Beo Ngoc Thi Pham; married Anh Tu Nguyen, Jun 7, 1963; children: Trang Thanh Thi, Nhan Huu, Bich Ngoc. **EDUCATION:** Miami University, BA, 1962; Georgetown University, MS, 1965, PhD, 1981. **CAREER:** University of Saigon, assistant professor, 1965-69; Northern Virginia Community College, professor, 1977-. **ORGANIZATIONS:** TESOL, currently; WATESOL, currently. **HONORS/AWARDS:** USAID, Leadership Training Scholarship; Asia Foundation Fellowship. **SPECIAL ACHIEVEMENTS:** Thang Ngo, a collection of short stories in Vietnamese, 1992. **BIOGRAPHICAL SOURCES:** Book review, A Review of Thang Ngo, Phu Nu Viet Magazine, p 31, May 23, 1993. **HOME ADDRESS:** 3614 Great Laurel Ln, Fairfax, VA 22033, (703)742-4055.

NGUYEN, VUNG DUY
Educator. Vietnamese American. **PERSONAL:** Born Dec 25, 1938, Nhatrang, Khanh Hoa, Vietnam; son of Con Duy Nguyen and Duc Thi Nguyen; married Quy Tran Nguyen, Nov 10, 1963; children: Khanh Duy, Phong Duy, Lam Duy, Linhda. **EDUCATION:** Saigon Science University, Certificate, physics, chemistry, biology, 1957; Interne Des Hopitaux, 1962-63; Saigon Medical School, MD (with honors), 1964; ECFMG Certificate, 1964; University of Texas Health Science Center, Diagnostic Radiology Board, 1979. **CAREER:** Tay Ninh Hospital, internist, 1965-67; Draftee Center, radiologist chief, 1967-69; Conghoa Hospital, staff radiologist, 1969-74; Saigon Medical School, radiology dept, assistant chief, 1974-75; University of Texas Health Science Center at San Antonio, instructor, 1977-79, assistant professor, 1980-84, associate professor, 1985-. **ORGANIZATIONS:** American Roentgen Ray Society, 1989-; Radiological Society of North America, 1988-; University Radiologists Association, 1981-; San Antonio Radiological Society, 1980-; Texas Vietnamese Association, 1980-; University of Texas Health Science Center at San Antonio, adviser to Vietnamese medical students, 1980-; International Skeletal Society, 1993. **HONORS/AWARDS:** Second Asian Congress on Oral and Maxillo-Facial Surgery, Taipei, Distinguished Speaker Award, 1993; VA Hospital, certificate of appreciation, 1991; People to People Ambassador Citizen Program, invited member, 1987, 1988; best teacher, 1981, 1983, 1984; AMA Physician Recognition Award, 1983; University of Texas Health Science Center at San Antonio, Radiology Dept, certificate of appreciation, 1979. **SPECIAL ACHIEVEMENTS:** Numerous articles in professional journals, including: Skeletal Radiology, Computerized Imag and Graphics, Radiology, Journal of Canadian Radiol Assn, AJNR, Gastro Intestinal Radiol, Australasian Radiol, Critical Rev in Diag Imag, Pediat Radiol, Southern Med Journal, JAMA; proficient in 3 languages: Vietnamese, French, English. **MILITARY SERVICE:** South Vietnam Army, major, 1958-74. **BIOGRAPHICAL SOURCES:** Journal of Japanese Orthopedic Association, Vol 66, 1992, Vol 65, 1991; Orthopedics, Rheumatology Digest, Netherlands, 1985; Diabetes Mellitus, Subis, Vol 2, 1993. **BUSINESS ADDRESS:** Associate Professor of Radiology, University of Texas Health Sciences Center At San Antonio, 7703 Floyd Curl Drive, MCH, Room 208, San Antonio, TX 78284, (210)567-6488.

NGUYEN, XE V.
Revenue analyst. Vietnamese American. **PERSONAL:** Born Jul 4, 1948, Can Tho, Vietnam; married Tam T Nguyen, 1968; children: 4. **EDUCATION:** Northern VA Community College, AA, 1982; National Louis University, BA, 1992; Everett Business College, MBA, 1994. **CAREER:** US Embassy, Saigon, assistant to the office of consulate general, 1968-75; US Congress, joint committee on taxation, revenue analyst, 1975-. **ORGANIZATIONS:** National and Northern Virginia Realtors Associations; National Association of Security

Dealers; Vietnamese Parents Association, president, 1984-88. **MILITARY SERVICE:** Vietnamese Army, special forces, 1966-68. **BIOGRAPHICAL SOURCES:** Regadier, p 8, 1986; Congressional Directory, 102 Congress, p 499, 1260. **HOME ADDRESS:** 4505 Deane Ct, Alexandria, VA 22312, (703)941-8791. **BUSINESS ADDRESS:** Revenue Analyst, Joint Committee on Taxation, United States Congress, 1015 LHOB, Washington, DC 20515, (202)226-7575.

NGUYEN-HUU, XUONG
Educator. Vietnamese American. **PERSONAL:** Born Jul 14, 1933, Thai Binh, Vietnam; son of Thu Nguyen; married Lan Nguyen-huu, Jun 30, 1979; children: Mai. **EDUCATION:** Ecole d'Electricite de Marseille, France, BSEE, 1955, MSEE, 1957; University of Paris, MS, Math, 1949; University of California, MA, PhD, physics, 1962. **CAREER:** University of California, assistant professor, chemistry and biology, 1962-70, associate professor, chemistry and biology, 1970-78, professor of physics, chemistry, and biology, 1978-. **ORGANIZATIONS:** American Crystallography Association, 1972-. **HONORS/AWARDS:** Guggenheim Fellowship, 1965-66; NATO, Fellowship, 1972; UCSD, Chancellor's Community Service Award, 1991. **SPECIAL ACHIEVEMENTS:** The Xuongs Machine, a high speed data collection system for protein crystallography, 1980. **BIOGRAPHICAL SOURCES:** Patriots, Asian Pacific Am Heritage Month, Commemorative Issue, p86, 1990. **BUSINESS ADDRESS:** Professor, Dept of Physics, Univ of California at San Diego, 9500 Gilman Dr, #0319, La Jolla, CA 92093-0319.

NI, PRESTON C.
Educator. Taiwanese American/Chinese American. **PERSONAL:** Born May 9, 1964, Taipai, Taiwan. **EDUCATION:** Academy of Art College, 1982; San Francisco State University, BS, 1987, MSBA, 1991; Eurocenter, Germany, 1987. **CAREER:** Asian Art Museum of San Francisco, audio visual coordinator, 1989-; Foothill College, speech communication, instructor, 1991-; Fine Arts Museums of San Francisco, audio visual coordinator, 1993-. **ORGANIZATIONS:** Stewitts Society, advisory board; San Francisco, school volunteer. **HONORS/AWARDS:** YMCA Stonestown, San Francisco, Volunteer Fundraising. **SPECIAL ACHIEVEMENTS:** Actor in dramatic film (lead male); songwriter; speaks Chinese Mandarin fluently; motivational public speaker. **BUSINESS ADDRESS:** Instructor of Speech Communication, Division of Language Arts, Foothill College, 12345 El Monte Road, Los Altos Hills, CA 94022, (415)949-7440.

NIETES, LINDA MARIA
Businesswoman. Filipino American. **CAREER:** Philippines Expressions Bookshop, businesswoman, currently. **BUSINESS ADDRESS:** Owner, Philippines Expressions Bookshop, 10717 Wilshire Blvd, Apt 702, Los Angeles, CA 90024-4425, (213)208-1890.*

NIIZUMA, MINORU
Sculptor. Japanese American. **PERSONAL:** Born Sep 29, 1930, Tokyo, Japan. **EDUCATION:** Tokyo University of Fine Arts of Music, BFA. **CAREER:** Sculptor; Brooklyn Museum Art School, instructor, 1964-69; Columbia University, adjunct professor, 1972-84. **ORGANIZATIONS:** Sculptors Guild. **SPECIAL ACHIEVEMENTS:** Works are at Solomon R Guggenheim Museum; Chase Manhattan Bank, NY; American Embassy, Tokyo; National Museum of Contemporary Art, Korea; Museum of Modern Art, New York, NY; exhibitions since 1968 include: Howard Wise Gallery; Rockefeller University; Center for Intl Arts Cultural Center in New York City; Galerie Nichido, Tokyo, 1989; Fnd Veranneman, Belgium, 1989; numerous others; one-man shows in: Tokyo and Osaka, Japan; Toronto, Ontario; Honolulu, HI; Zurich, Switzerland; Lisbon, Portugal; Mekler Gallery, Los Angles, CA.*

NING, TAK HUNG
Physicist. Chinese American. **PERSONAL:** Born Nov 14, 1943, Canton, China; son of Hong Ning and Kwai-Chan Lee Ning; married Yin Ngao Fan; children: Adrienne, Brenda. **EDUCATION:** Reed College, BA, physics, 1967; University of Illinois, MS, physics, 1968, PhD, physics, 1971. **CAREER:** IBM, Research Division, 1973-78, bipolar devices and cirs manager, 1978-82, Advanced Silicon Tech Lab, manager, 1982-83, silicon devices and tech manager, 1983-90, Research Div, VLSI design and tech manager, 1990-91, IBM fellow, 1991-. **ORGANIZATIONS:** IEEE, fellow, Trans on Electron Devices, associate editor, 1988-90; Natl Academy of Engineering. **HONORS/AWARDS:** IEEE, J J Ebers Award, 1989, Jack A Morton Award, 1991. **BUSINESS ADDRESS:** IBM Fellow, IBM Research Center, PO Box 218, Yorktown Heights, NY 10598.*

NINOMIYA, CALVIN
Attorney. Japanese American. **PERSONAL:** Born Jun 9, 1926, Seattle, WA; son of Kamesaku Ninomiya & Tetsu Uyeda Ninomiya; married Hannelore Sadezky Ninomiya, Aug 16, 1958; children: Lisa Cathryn, Roland Ban, Erik Friedrich. **EDUCATION:** University of Washington, Seattle, BA, 1949; University of Chicago, JD, 1952; University of Maryland, MA. **CAREER:** US Treasury, Bureau of Public Dept, chief counsel, 1975-. **ORGANIZATIONS:** Federal Bar Association; Senior Executive Service, Federal. **HONORS/ AWARDS:** US Treasury, Meritorious Service Award, 1973. **MILITARY SERVICE:** US Army. **BUSINESS ADDRESS:** Chief Counsel, Bureau of the Pubic Dept, US Department of the Treasury, 999 E St NW, Rm 504, Washington, DC 20239, (202)219-3320.

NIP, WAI-KIT
Educator. Chinese American. **PERSONAL:** Born May 5, 1941, Hong Kong; son of Chuck-Foon Nip (deceased) and Jean Sze Nip; married Li Liu, Oct 31, 1970; children: Jun-Yun, Jaime. **EDUCATION:** National Chung-Hsing University, Taiwan, BS, 1962; Texas A&M University, MS, 1965, PhD, 1969. **CAREER:** National Chung-Hsing University, associate professor, 1969-74; University of Wisconsin, research associate, 1974-76; University of Hawaii, assistant professor, 1976-82, associate professor, 1982-90, professor, 1990-. **ORGANIZATIONS:** Institute of Food Technologists, 1963; American Society of Horticultural Sciences, 1965-; American Association of Cereal Chemists, 1969-; World Aquaculture Society, 1978-; Chinese Institute of Food Sci Tech, life member, 1971-; Chinese Culture Service Center, Hawaii, second vice president, 1990-; Hawaii Chinese Association, past president, 1992-. **SPECIAL ACHIEVEMENTS:** Over 60 scientific publications including one patent. **BUSINESS ADDRESS:** Professor of Food Science, University of Hawaii at Manoa, 1920 Edmondson Road, Honolulu, HI 96822, (808)956-3852.

NISHIKAWA, DENNIS
Consultant. Japanese American. **CAREER:** City of Los Angeles, Public Works, commissioner; SEIU Local 347, consultant, currently. **BUSINESS ADDRESS:** Consultant, SEIU Local 347, 1015 Wilshire, Los Angeles, CA 90017, (213)482-6660.∗

NISHIMURA, JONATHAN SEI
Educator. Japanese American. **PERSONAL:** Born Sep 30, 1931, Berkeley, CA; son of Masamoto Nishimura and Kimi Ishihara Nishimura; married Marie Nishimura, Sep 8, 1955; children: Jon Scott, Wendy Leigh Kiniris. **EDUCATION:** University of California, AB, 1956, PhD, 1959. **CAREER:** Tufts University School of Medicine, senior instructor, 1962-64, assistant professor, 1964-69; University of Texas Health Science Center, San Antonio, assoc professor, 1969-71, professor, 1971-. **ORGANIZATIONS:** American Society for Biochemistry and Molecular Biology, 1968-. **MILITARY SERVICE:** United States Army Corps of Engineers, Corporal, 1952-54; UN Korean Service Medal, Good Conduct, 1954. **BUSINESS ADDRESS:** Professor of Biochemistry, University of Texas Health Science Center at San Antonio, 7703 Floyd Curl Dr, San Antonio, TX 78284-7760, (210)567-3757.

NISHIMURA, MIWA
Educator. Japanese American. **PERSONAL:** Born Sep 25, 1951, Tokyo, Japan; daughter of Toshiko & Seiji Nishimura. **EDUCATION:** Aogama Gakuin University, Tokyo, BA, 1975, MA, 1977; University of Pennsylvania, PhD, 1985. **CAREER:** San Diego State University, lecturer, 1984-85; Cornell University, visiting assistant professor, 1985-86; Georgetown University, assistant professor, 1986-92; American University, assistant professor, 1992-. **ORGANIZATIONS:** Linguistic Society of America, 1983-; Association for Asian Studies, 1982-; Association of Teachers of Japanese, 1985-. **BUSINESS ADDRESS:** Assistant Professor, American University, 4400 Massachusetts Ave, Washington, DC 20016, (202)885-2386.

NISHIMURA, TOM
Association administrator. Japanese American. **CAREER:** Western Adults Buddhist League, president, 1993-. **BUSINESS ADDRESS:** President, Western Adults Buddhist League, 1710 Octavia St, San Francisco, CA 94109, (415)776-5600.∗

NISHIMURA, WENDY NATSUE
Public relations executive. Japanese American. **PERSONAL:** Born Aug 19, 1955, Honolulu, HI; daughter of Shiro and Sueko Kondo; married Glenn K Nishimura, Aug 19, 1979; children: Lance Y, Jonathan S. **EDUCATION:** Cannon's International Business College of Honolulu, diploma, 1975. **CAREER:** Educators of the Pacific Inc, director of public relations, 1989-93; Heald Business College of Honolulu, director of public relations, currently. **ORGANIZATIONS:** Our Redeemer Lutheran Elementary School, PTO grade representative, 1991-93; board of education, 1991-92; Hawaii Business Education Association; Public Relations Society of America, Hawaii chapter. **HONORS/AWARDS:** Cannon's International Business College of Honolulu, Alumni Hall of Fame, 1992. **SPECIAL ACHIEVEMENTS:** Editor of school newsletter, Cannon's Courier. **BUSINESS ADDRESS:** Director of Public Relations, Heald Business College, 1500 Kapiolani Blvd, Honolulu, HI 96814-3797, (808)955-1500.

NISHINA, CLIFFORD M.
Public accountant, government official (retired). Japanese American. **PERSONAL:** Born Mar 27, 1912, Holualoa, HI; son of Nenohe Nishina and Tori Nishina; married Helen H Nishina; children: Vincent, Lloyd, Conrad, Amline Hayduk. **EDUCATION:** University of Hawaii, 1931-32; Honolulu Business College, diploma, 1934; La Salle University, higher education, accounting, 1934-35. **CAREER:** Army and Air Force Exchange, chief fin/accountant; Nishina Accounting Office, owner, public accountant, currently. **ORGANIZATIONS:** Hawaii Association of Public Accountant, president, director, honorary member for life, 1965-; National Society of Public Accountant, committee chair, board of governors, 1965-93; Palolo Lions Club, various positions, president, 1949-93; District 50 Lions International, various positions, deputy district governor, 1949-; Honpa Hongwanji Betsuin, board of directors, 1988-. **HONORS/AWARDS:** Hawaii Association of Public Accounting, life membership, 1991; National Society of Public Accountant, life membership, 1991; Lions International, life membership, 1993, LCIF, 1993. **HOME ADDRESS:** 1836-A Mahana St, Honolulu, HI 96816, (808)737-7780.

NISHIOKA, DAVID JITSUO
Educator. Japanese American. **PERSONAL:** Born Aug 12, 1945, Los Angeles, CA; son of Harry Yuzuru Nishioka and Grace Ayako Naura Nishioka. **EDUCATION:** California State University, Fullerton, BA, 1971, MA, 1972; University of California, Berkeley, PhD, 1976. **CAREER:** University of California, San Diego, postdoctoral fellow, 1976-77; Stanford University, postdoctoral fellow, 1977-78; Georgetown University, assistant professor, 1978-84, associate professor, 1984-91, professor, 1991-. **ORGANIZATIONS:** American Society for Cell Biology, 1978-; Society for Developmental Biology, 1978-; Sigma Xi, 1978-. **SPECIAL ACHIEVEMENTS:** Course lectures, 1978-; invited lectures, 1976-; 50 publications, 1976-. **MILITARY SERVICE:** US Army, sp5, National Defense Medal; Vietnam Service Medal; Vietnamese Campaign Medal; Good Conduct Medal; Army Commendation Medal; Presidential Unit Citation; Vietnamese Cross of Gallantry, 1967-69. **BUSINESS ADDRESS:** Professor, Dept of Biology, Georgetown University, Washington, DC 20057, (202)687-5888.

NISHIOKA, HAYWARD H.
Educator, actor. Japanese American. **PERSONAL:** Born Jan 4, 1942, Los Angeles, CA; son of Alice; divorced; children: Faith, Alicia, Eric. **EDUCATION:** LA City College, AA, 1968; California State University, LA, masters, physical education, 1975, masters, administrative ed, 1976. **CAREER:** California State University, Long Beach, instructor; Los Angeles City College, professor of PE education. **ORGANIZATIONS:** International Judo Federation "A" Referee; US Judo Inc, chairperson, PR, national coaching staff; Teaching Training Institute, promotion board; American Federation of Teachers; Screen Actors Guild; US Judo Federation and Association, life member. **HONORS/ AWARDS:** California State University, LA, Outstanding Alumni Award, 1989; International Judo Federation, Seventh Degree Blackbelt; US Judo Inc, National Champion, 1965, 1966, 1970; Pan American Judo Union, Olympic Committee; Pan American Games, medalist, 1967. **SPECIAL ACHIEVEMENTS:** Author of over 100 articles in various magazines and two books; produced several videos on judo. **BUSINESS ADDRESS:** Professor, Dept of Phys Ed, Los Angeles City College, 855 N Vermont Ave, Los Angeles, CA 90029.

NISHIURA, WAYNE IWAO
Marketing executive. Japanese American. **PERSONAL:** Born Jan 28, 1964, Palo Alto, CA; son of Franklin Mitsuo Nishiura and Kumiko Nishiura. **EDUCATION:** Cal Poly, BSEL, 1988. **CAREER:** Vector Marketing, district manager, 1990-. **HONORS/AWARDS:** Vector Marketing, Academy of Champions, 1991, Top 10 in Nation, 1991, President's Banquet, 1991, Top 10 Team Builder, 1991, $1,000,000 Plaque, 1992, #2 Rookie of the Year, 1991.

BUSINESS ADDRESS: District Manager, Vector Marketing, 917 SW Oak St, Ste 205, North Pacific Bldg, Portland, OR 97205, (503)241-1225.

NITTA, SANDRA HARUYE
Entrepreneur, olympic coach. Japanese American. **PERSONAL:** Born Apr 21, 1949, Burbank, CA; daughter of Jerry Jiro Nitta & Susie Nitta. **EDUCATION:** California State University, Los Angeles, BA, PE. **CAREER:** City of Commerce, supervisor of aquatics, 1964-80; owner, apartments, 1980-90, mobile home park, 1990-. **ORGANIZATIONS:** United States Water Polo Inc, Women's National Water Polo Team, head coach, 1980-94, Women's International Comm, chairperson, 1976-79, Women's Junior Team, head coach, 1979. **SPECIAL ACHIEVEMENTS:** US Olympic Team, swimming team member, 1964. **HOME PHONE:** (702)456-9568. **BUSINESS ADDRESS:** Owner, Polo Coach Mobile Home Park, 5959 Boulder Highway, Las Vegas, NV 89122.

NIZAMI, SHAFIQ AHMED
Retail corporate executive. Pakistani American. **PERSONAL:** Born Jan 1, 1956, Karachi-Sindh, Pakistan; son of Laiq A Nizami & Mehr Un Nisa; married Mahnaz Nizami, Sep 6, 1985; children: Saqib Ahmed, Maryam Ahmed. **EDUCATION:** University of Karachi, BS (with honors), 1976; University of New York, BS, 1986. **CAREER:** N&A Pharmacy Inc, district manager, 1977-86; Rock Bottom Stores Inc, manager, 1986-88; Lionel Kiddie City Toys, store manager, 1988-92; Conway Organization, general manager, 1992-. **HONORS/ AWARDS:** Kanachi, Lion Club, director, 1975. **HOME ADDRESS:** 2742 Amboy Rd, Staten Island, NY 10306, (718)987-4501.

NODA, TAKAYO
Artist. Japanese American. **PERSONAL:** Born Sep 20, 1934, Tokyo, Japan; daughter of Jun Tatebe and Hide Tatebe; married M Noda, Apr 12, 1958; children: K Noda. **EDUCATION:** Gakushuin University, Japan, 1953-55; Art Students League, 1979-83. **CAREER:** Self-employed artist, currently. **ORGANIZATIONS:** The National Arts Club; Audubon Artists, vice president for graphics section; Boston Printmakers; SAGA; Silvermine Guild Center for the Arts; National Association of Women Artists. **HONORS/AWARDS:** Audubon Artists, Gold Medal for Graphics, 1992, Silver Medal for Graphics, 1989; National Association of Women Artists, Elizabeth Morse Genius Award for Graphics, 1992; Silvermine Guild Center for the Arts, 1st Prize, 1983. **SPECIAL ACHIEVEMENTS:** Art exhibitions include: Trenton State College, 1988; Roopanker Museum of Fine Arts, India, 1989; National Academy, NYC, 1990; The Bergen Museum of Art & Science, 1991; Portland Art Museum, 1992; Pen & Brush, NYC, one person show, 1992. **BIOGRAPHICAL SOURCES:** Profile of Contemporary Art, The Early 80's in Japan & Korea, p 121, 1987. **HOME ADDRESS:** 5 Charles St, #2R, New York, NY 10014.

NOGA, AL
Professional football player. Pacific Islander American. **PERSONAL:** Born Sep 16, 1965, American Samoa. **EDUCATION:** Hawaii. **CAREER:** Defensive end: Minnesota Vikings, 1988-92; Washington Redskins, 1993-. **BUSINESS ADDRESS:** Professional Football Player, Washington Redskins, PO Box 17247, Dulles Airport, Washington, DC 20041.*

NOGUCHI, JOHN TAKEO
Governmental official. Japanese American. **PERSONAL:** Born Oct 4, 1960, San Francisco, CA; son of Moriaki and Nell Noguchi; married Diane Hayakawa, Aug 22, 1992. **EDUCATION:** University of California, Davis, BA, 1982; San Francisco State University, MPA, 1993. **CAREER:** Charles Schwab & Co, mutual funds trader, 1983-85; San Francisco Associates Financial Planning, account exec, 1985-87; City & Co of San Francisco, Recycling Program, commercial recycling coordinator, 1987-89; City and County of San Francisco, Convention Facilities Dept, asst director, 1989-. **ORGANIZATIONS:** City & Co of San Francisco, Disadvantaged/High Risk Youth Employment Task Force, 1993, Job Corps Task Force, 1993, Municipal Executives Association, 1991-; Japanese Cultural & Community Center of Northern California, chief financial officer, 1989-91, board member, 1988-; Kimochi, Inc, "Sansei Live!," board member, 1987-91; SF Cherry Blossom Festival, pageant treasurer, 1987-88, scholarship chair, 1989, program booklet chair, 1990. **BUSINESS ADDRESS:** Assistant Director, Convention Facilities Dept, City and County of San Francisco, Moscone Center, 747 Howard St, San Francisco, CA 94103, (415)974-4027.

NOMURA, KAWORU CARL
Physicist (retired), business executive. Japanese American. **PERSONAL:** Born Apr 1, 1922, Deer Lodge, MT; son of Kazuichi Nomura and Mizuko Takahashi Nomura; married Louise Takeda Nomura, Dec 23, 1947; children: Kathryn Madono, Teresa, John, David. **EDUCATION:** University of Minnesota, BPhys, 1948, MS, 1949, PhD, 1953; Harvard, AMP, 1972. **CAREER:** Physicist, 1953-60; Honeywell, various levels of management, 1960-82, Semiconductor Gr, senior vice president, 1982-85, corporate senior vice president, 1985-86; Skookum Ed Program Corporation, chairman of the board, 1992-. **ORGANIZATIONS:** American Physical Society, fellow, 1964. **HONORS/ AWARDS:** University of Minnesota, Distinguished Graduate/Outstanding Achievement Award, 1988, President's Club, 1992. **SPECIAL ACHIEVEMENTS:** Solid state research publications, 1953-60. **MILITARY SERVICE:** US Army, private first class, 1945-46. **BIOGRAPHICAL SOURCES:** Minneapolis Star Tribune, Minneapolis, MN, Dec 19, 1988; Port Townsend Leader, Port Townsend, WA, June 14, 1989. **HOME ADDRESS:** 363 Discovery Rd, Port Townsend, WA 98368, (206)385-5231.

NOMURA, MASAE GOTO
Retail florist. Japanese American. **PERSONAL:** Born Sep 4, 1911, Huntington Beach, CA; daughter of Miyo Ando and Yasako Goto; married Robert Nomura (deceased); children: Rod, Ouhe, Ann, Jay. **EDUCATION:** Pasadena City College, AA. **CAREER:** M's Flowers, florist, owner of 4 stores, 1929-. **ORGANIZATIONS:** M&B Womens Club; Chamber of Commerce; Ashiya Sister City; YMCA. **HONORS/AWARDS:** Montebello City, Pioneer Business Owner, 1991; Montebello School Dist, PTA, 1990; Professional Women Club, Business Women, 1988; American Legion, Women of Year, 1988; Senator Charles Calderon, Resolution, 1992. **BUSINESS ADDRESS:** Owner, M's Flowers, 801 W Washington Blvd, Montebello, CA 90640, (213)728-4604.

NOMURA, MASAYASU
Educator, research scientist. Japanese American. **PERSONAL:** Born Apr 27, 1927, Hyogo-Ken, Japan; son of Hiromichi & Yaeko Nomura; married Junko Hamashima, Feb 10, 1957; children: Keiko, Toshiyasu. **EDUCATION:** University of Tokyo, BS, 1951, PhD, 1957. **CAREER:** Inst Protein Research, Osaka, Japan, assistant professor, 1960-63; University of Wisconsin-Madison, genetics, associate professor, 1963-66, professor, 1966-70, genetics & biochemistry, Elvehjem Professor in Life Science, 1970-84, Inst for Enzyme Research, co-director, 1970-84; University of California-Irvine, Grace Bell Professor of Biological Chemistry, 1984-. **ORGANIZATIONS:** American Academy of Arts & Sciences, 1969-; Royal Danish Academy of Sciences & Letters, foreign member, 1977-; National Academy of Sciences, 1978-; American Association for the Advancement of Science, fellow, 1979-; Royal Netherlands Academy of Arts & Sciences, foreign member, 1989-. **HONORS/ AWARDS:** National Academy of Science, US Steel Award, 1971; Japanese Academy of Sciences, Japan Academy Award, 1972. **HOME ADDRESS:** 74 Whitman Court, Irvine, CA 92717. **BUSINESS ADDRESS:** Professor, Dept of Biological Chemistry, University of California, Med Sci I, Rm D240, Irvine, CA 92717-1700, (714)856-4564.

NOOJIBAIL, ESHWAR
Engineering and construction company executive. Indo-American. **PERSONAL:** Born Aug 10, 1937, Puttur, Karnataka, India; son of Gopal Krishnayya Noojibail and Devaki; married Judy A, Jun 17, 1967; children: Paul, Sheila, Jenny. **EDUCATION:** University of Madras, BS, 1956, BSME, 1960; University of Michigan, BSIE, 1964; Illinois Institute of Technology, MSIE, 1968. **CAREER:** Union Carbide, Industrial Engineering Dept, manager, beginning 1968; Felt Products, production control manager, beginning 1976; Commercial Engineering Corp, president, currently. **BUSINESS ADDRESS:** President, Commerical Engineering Corp, 2890 Dundee Rd, Northbrook, IL 60062, (708)205-1112.

NORI, DATTATREYUDU
Physician, educator. Indo-American. **EDUCATION:** Kurnool and Hyderabad, Andhra Pradesh, India, medicine. **CAREER:** New York University Medical Center, instructor, currently; Booth Memorial Center, Radiation Oncology Department, chairman, currently. **HONORS/AWARDS:** National Federation of Indian American Associations, Outstanding Achievement Award in Medicine, 1992. **SPECIAL ACHIEVEMENTS:** At Booth Memorial, provides direction for development of a comprehensive cancer program, and expansion of oncology education and research. **BUSINESS ADDRESS:** Chairman, Radiation Oncology Dept, Booth Memorial Center, 56-45 Main St, Flushing, NY 11355, (718)670-1021.*

NOZAKI, KENZIE
Chemist (retired). Japanese American. **PERSONAL:** Born Jun 1, 1916, Los Angeles, CA; son of Saihachi Nozaki & Kiku Ichimura; married Mary T Nozaki, Jan 27, 1944; children: Joan T Lee, Shirley A. **EDUCATION:** University of California, Los Angeles, BA, 1937, MA, 1938; Stanford University, PhD, 1940. **CAREER:** University of California, Davis, instructor of chemistry, 1940-42; WRA, Guayule Rubber, director, 1943-44; Harvard University, post-doctoral research associate, 1944-46; Shell Development Co, chemist, 1946-72; Shell Amsterdam, chemist, 1958-59; Shell Oil Co, consulting research chemist, 1972-79; Shell Dev Co, senior research associate, 1980-83. **ORGANIZATIONS:** American Chemical Society, 1943-92; Sigma Xi, 1950-60; SIRS, 1987-93; Sierra Club; Habitat for Humanity. **HONORS/AWARDS:** University of California, Los Angeles, Phi Beta Kappa, 1939; Stanford University, Franklin Fellow, 1938-40; Shell Dev, 1-year European sabbatical, 1958-59. **SPECIAL ACHIEVEMENTS:** More than 50 US patents granted, 1949-84; more than 15 papers in JACS and other publications, 1940-48; invited speaker at 3 Gordon Conferences and Faraday Society, 1947-55; toured Japanese universities and lectured, 1964. **HOME ADDRESS:** 1524 Madera Circle, El Cerrito, CA 94530, (510)235-1452.

NUON, SAMUEL
Cleric. Cambodian American. **PERSONAL:** Born Oct 20, 1945, Siemreap, Cambodia; son of Bun Seng Nuon and Pram Aing Nuon; married Chamroeun Chhuon, Feb 1970; children: Waddhana, Viriya. **EDUCATION:** Universite des Sciences Agronomiques, Cambodia, Ingenieur d'Agronomie, 1970; Baptist Theology Seminary at Richmond, MDiv, 1994. **CAREER:** Ministry of Agriculture, Pailin, Cambodia, chief of veterinary service, 1972-75; A H Robins Pharmaceutical Co, Dept of Pharmacology, biologist II, 1976-91; Derbyshire Baptist Church, Khmer Baptist Mission, pastor, currently. **ORGANIZATIONS:** Cambodian Southern Baptist Fellowship, vice pres, communication and fellowship; West Henrico Kiwanis Club, chmn, Community and Intl Relation Services; Toastmaster Intl Club, competent toastmaster; Leadership Metro Richmond, class 1991. **HONORS/AWARDS:** Cambodian Baptist Fellowship, Bridge of God, 1987; Paul Pathfinder, 1988. **SPECIAL ACHIEVEMENTS:** Thesis in French: "Contribution a l'etudes des Vaches laitieres au Cambodge," (Contribution of Study of Dairy cattle in Cambodia), 1975, submitted to Second Intl Animal Husbandry, Wageningen, the Netherlands, 1974. **HOME PHONE:** (804)740-0421. **BUSINESS ADDRESS:** Pastor, Derbyshire Baptist Church, 8800 Derbyshire Rd, Richmond, VA 23229.

O

O, CAO KINH
Social work administrator. Chinese American. **PERSONAL:** Born in Saigon, Vietnam. **EDUCATION:** Cornell University, BA, 1980; Hunter College School of Social Work, MSW, 1983. **CAREER:** Hamilton-Madison House, director of development, 1983-87; New York State Office of Mental Health, program specialist, 1987-88; United Way of New York City, consultant, 1988-90; Asian American Federation of NY, executive director, 1990-. **ORGANIZATIONS:** Asian American Legal Defense & Education Fund, board of directors, 1986-; Chinatown Voter Education Alliance, board of directors, 1984-; Hamilton-Madison House, board of directors, 1991-; Human Services Council of New York City, steering committee, 1990-, vice chair, 1993-. **HONORS/AWARDS:** President of City Council, Asian American Role Model Award, 1993; New York University Asian Clubs, Asian Pride Leadership Award, 1991. **BIOGRAPHICAL SOURCES:** Asian Americans, by Joann Faung Jean Lee, pg 104, 1991. **BUSINESS ADDRESS:** Executive Director, Asian American Federation of New York, 95 Madison Ave, Ste 1309, New York, NY 10016-7801, (212)725-3840.

O, SAN LUONG
Social worker, educator. Chinese American/Vietnamese American. **PERSONAL:** Born Sep 27, 1949, Saigon, Vietnam; daughter of Lam O and Muoi Luc. **EDUCATION:** Saigon University, BA, 1974; Columbia University of New York, BA, 1980; University of Chicago School of Social Service Administration, MSW, 1984. **CAREER:** Chan Trung High School, foreign language teacher, 1967-69; Vien Dong High School, foreign language teacher, 1969-75; Khai Duc Elementary School, principal, 1973-75; New York Association for New Americans, refugee specialist/translator, 1979-80; Asian Human Services, social worker, 1980-82; Truman College Adult Continuing Education Program, off-campus instructor, 1981-90; South-East Asia Center, director of programs, 1984-. **ORGANIZATIONS:** United Way, Discrimination Grants Committee,

1992-93; Chicago Public Library, board of directors, 1989-; Attorney General of Illinois, Asian American Advisory Council, 1988-. **HONORS/AWARDS:** City of Chicago, Women's Hall of Fame, 1990; Illinois Minority Women Caucus, Outstanding Service to the Asian Community, 1987; City of Chicago, Outstanding Service to the Southeast Asian Community, 1986. **SPECIAL ACHIEVEMENTS:** "Social Work Practice with Indochinese Refugees," 1989; "First lessons in the USA: A Vietnamese Refugee Tells Her Story," Response, 1977; University of Chicago School of Social Service Administration, featured in exhibit: SSA Alumni Visions of Helping Others, as part of school's centennial celebration, 1992. **BIOGRAPHICAL SOURCES:** "SSA Alumni: Visions of Helping Others," SSA Magazine, The University of Chicago, p26, Fall/Winter, 1992; "Refugee Now Helps Others Feel at Home," NewsStar, September 11-12, 1990. **BUSINESS ADDRESS:** Director of Programs, South-East Asia Center, 1124 W Ainslie, Chicago, IL 60640, (312)989-6927.

OBATA, GYO
Architect. Japanese American. **PERSONAL:** Born Feb 28, 1923, San Francisco, CA; son of Chiura Obata and Haruko Obata; children (previous marriage): Kiku, Nori, Gen; married Courtney, Nov 24, 1984; children: Max. **EDUCATION:** Washington University, BA, 1945; Cranbrook Academy of Art, master's of architecture and urban design, 1946. **CAREER:** Skidmore, Owings & Merrill, architect, until 1951; Hellmuth, Yamasaki & Leinweber, architect, 1951-55; Hellmuth, Obata & Kassabaum, architect, co-chairman, design, 1955-. **ORGANIZATIONS:** St Louis Art Museum, trustee; Presidio Council; Nature Conservancy; Opera Theatres of St Louis, board member. **HONORS/AWARDS:** American Institute of Architects, FAIA, 1969; Washington University, Doctor of Fine Arts, 1990; University of Missouri, Doctor of Fine Arts, 1991. **SPECIAL ACHIEVEMENTS:** Downtown St Louis Levee Stone Award, 1989; Asian American Architects/Engineers, recipient of 1st Annual Lifetime Achievement Award, 1993. **MILITARY SERVICE:** US Army, PFC, 1946-47. **BUSINESS ADDRESS:** Co-Chairman, Design, Hellmuth, Obata & Kassabaum Inc, One Metropolitan Square, St Louis, MO 63101, (314)421-2000.

OCHI, ROSE MATSUI
City government official. Japanese American. **EDUCATION:** University of California, Los Angeles, BS, 1959; California State University, Los Angeles, MA, 1967; Loyola Law School, Los Angeles, JD, 1972. **CAREER:** Los Angeles Unified School District and Montebello Unified School District, secondary teacher, 1961-1969; US Attorney, Central Dist of California, Loyola Clinical Program, law clerk summer intern, 1971-72; University of Southern California, Western Ctr on Law & Poverty, Reginald Heber Smith Fellowship, staff attorney, 1972-74; City of Los Angeles, Criminal Justice Planning Office, program coordinator, 1974, legislative and research coordinator, 1974-75, deputy director, 1975, director and executive asst to the mayor, 1975-. **ORGANIZATIONS:** Los Angeles County Bar Assn, 1972-; Japanese-American Bar Assn, organizing member, board of directors; Minority Bar Assn; California Leadership, board executive committee; Natl Institute against Prejudice & Violence, board of directors; Japanese American Citizens League, natl vp of membership. **HONORS/AWARDS:** Constitutional Rights Foundation, Certificate of Commendation for Service; Huuman Relations Commission, Achievement Award; Asian Pacific Family Ctr, Achievement Award; Asian American Leaders, White House Conference, Delegate; Los Angeles City Asian Employees Assn, Leader Award, 1987; US Dept of Justice, Award for Distinguished Public Service, 1988; LA Women's Commission, Asian Women Leaders Recognition, 1992. **BUSINESS ADDRESS:** Director of Criminal Justice Planning Office, Exec Asst to Mayor, Office of Mayor, City Hall, 200 N Spring St, Rm 1404, Los Angeles, CA 90012, (213)485-4425.

OCHIAI, SHINYA
Engineer. Japanese American. **PERSONAL:** Born Jun 6, 1935, Kofu City, Yamanashi-ken, Japan; son of Shinroku Ochiai and Takako Ochiai; married Hisako Ochiai, May 21, 1966; children: Mari. **EDUCATION:** Waseda University, Japan, BSME, 1960; Rice University, MSME, 1962; Purdue University, PhD, 1966. **CAREER:** Celanese Fibers Company, instrumentation development engineer, 1965-67, R&D engineer, 1967-68; Celanese Chemical Company, senior process system engineer, 1968-74; Texas A&M University, part-time visiting associate professor, 1974-75; Hoechst Celanese Chemical Group, engineering associate, 1974-90, senior engineering associate, 1990-. **ORGANIZATIONS:** Instrument Society of America, program coordinator, automatic control division, 1988-90, fellow, 1990-; Society of Instrument & Control Engineers, 1965-; American Institute of Chemical Engineers, 1991-; Sigma Xi,

1976-. **HONORS/AWARDS:** American Control Council, Schuck Award for Best Paper, 1975; Instrument Society of America, Automatic Control Division, Best Paper Award, 1987, Society Service Award, 1989. **SPECIAL ACHIEVEMENTS:** 17 publications on automatic controls in intl and natl journals, 1967-92; language proficiency, Japanese. **BUSINESS ADDRESS:** Senior Engineering Associate, Hoechst Celanese, Box 9077, Corpus Christi, TX 78469, (512)242-4176.

OCHOA, GLORIA MEGINA
Attorney. Filipino American. **PERSONAL:** Born in Manila, Philippines; children: Patric, Alejandro, Francisco. **EDUCATION:** University of California at Davis, BS, chemistry; University of California at Davis Law School, JD. **CAREER:** University of California at Davis, chemist, 8 years; private law practice, attorney; California Energy Resources, Conservation and Development Commission, public advisor; California Housing Dept, asst secretary; California State Judiciary Committee, counsel; County of Santa Barbara, county supervisor, beginning 1988; California 22nd Congressional District, Democratic party candidate, 1992.*

ODO, BLAIR M. T.
Educational administrator. Japanese American. **PERSONAL:** Born in Honolulu, HI; daughter of Mr & Mrs Tokiharu Takenaka. **EDUCATION:** University of Hawaii, BA, 1974, MEd, 1982; University of Oregon, PhD, 1985. **CAREER:** University of Hawaii, Manoa, Bureau of Student Activities, 1974-79, special assistant to the chancellor, 1979-81; Oregon Institute of Technology, executive assistant to the president, 1986-88; Japan-America Institute of Management Science, senior director fo academic affairs, 1988-. **ORGANIZATIONS:** Soroptimist International of the Americas, founder region, 1993-94, Dist VI Rep, YCA, TAP committee, 1992-94, Dist VI Rep, nominating committee, 1993-95; Soroptimist International of Honolulu, president, 1992-94, president-elect, fashion show chair, 1991-92; American Association for Higher Education, Women's Caucus, chair, 1988-90; Japanese Cultural Center of Hawaii, 1989-; Japanese Women's Society of Honolulu, 1990-. **HONORS/AWARDS:** National Center for Higher Education Management System, Research Assistantship, 1984-85. **SPECIAL ACHIEVEMENTS:** Salary Study of Oregon Educators, 1986; Budgetary Reallocation in Higher Education Management, 1985. **BUSINESS ADDRESS:** Senior Director of Academic Affairs, Japan-America Institute of Management Science, 6660 Hawaii Kai Dr, Honolulu, HI 96825, (808)395-2314.

ODO, FRANKLIN SHOICHIRO
Educator, educational administrator. Japanese American. **PERSONAL:** Born May 6, 1939, Honolulu, HI; son of Masaru & Betty Odo; married Enid Reid Odo, Sep 5, 1964; children: David Reid, Rachel Shizuka, Jonathan Shoji. **EDUCATION:** Princeton University, BA, 1961; Harvard University, MA, 1963; Princeton University, PHD, 1975. **CAREER:** Occidental College, instructor of history, 1968-70; UCLA, lecturer, 1970-72; Cal State University, Long Beach, Asian American studies, professor, 1972-78; University of Pennsylvania, American Civilization, visiting professor, 1993-94; Columbia University, History, visiting professor, 1993; University of Hawaii, Ethnic Studies, director, professor, 1978-. **ORGANIZATIONS:** Association for Asian American Studies, 1983, president, 1991-92; Japanese American Citizens League, 1975-. **HONORS/AWARDS:** Kaimuki High School, Outstanding Graduate, 1993; National Endowment for Humanities, Summer Institute, 1992. **SPECIAL ACHIEVEMENTS:** Author, Roots: An Asian American Reader, A Pictorial History of the Japanese in Hawaii.

OETTINGER, REENA
Investment executive. Indo-American. **PERSONAL:** Born Oct 28, 1967, Nabha, Punjab, India; daughter of Ved and Kailash Goyal; married James G Oettinger, Jan 16, 1993. **EDUCATION:** George Mason University, BS, accounting, 1988; Series 7, 1992. **CAREER:** Dalewood Walk-In Clinic, accountant, 1985-88; Keller Zanger Bissell, accountant, 1988-89; Hills Capital Parking, accounting mgr, 1989-91; Legg Mason, investment executive, 1991-. **ORGANIZATIONS:** Business and Professional Women's Club, 1993-. **HONORS/AWARDS:** Legg Mason, Pace Setter, 1993, 1994. **HOME ADDRESS:** 1717 Gosnell Rd #203, Vienna, VA 22182, (703)242-5176. **BUSINESS PHONE:** (703)821-9100.

OGATA, JEFFERY MORIMASA
Attorney. **PERSONAL:** Born Feb 23, 1954, Los Angeles, CA; son of Morito & Chizue Ogata; married Joanne Lowe, Feb 11, 1990. **EDUCATION:** Stanford University, BA, 1976; University of California, Davis, JD, 1979. **CAREER:**

Legal Services of N California, staff attorney, 1979-87; California Energy Commission, senior staff counsel, 1987-. **ORGANIZATIONS:** Sacramento Asian Community Resources Inc, president, 1977-92; Legal Center for the Elderly and Disabled, board member, 1988-; Asian Bar Association of Sacramento, past president, 1981-; United Way of Sacramento County, volunteer trainer, 1988-; State Bar of California, Legal Services Section, comm member, 1988-; Asian/Pacific State Employees Association, 1987-; Community Housing Resources Board, treasurer, 1986-92; Voluntary Legal Services Program, volunteer, 1988-. **HONORS/AWARDS:** State Bar, President's Pro Bono Service Award, 1988. **BUSINESS ADDRESS:** Attorney, California Energy Commission, 1516 9th St, Sacramento, CA 95814, (916)654-3963.

OGAWA, FRANK HIRAO
City official, wholesale nursery company executive. Japanese American. **PERSONAL:** Born May 17, 1917, Lodi, CA; son of Mr and Mrs Katsuichiro Ogawa; married Grace Ogawa, Jan 1939; children: Alan. **CAREER:** Frank H Ogawa Inc, president, currently; City of Oakland, city council, currently. **ORGANIZATIONS:** Lake Merritt Breakfast Club, past president; Optimist Club, past president; Bay Area Air Quality Management Board, past chairman; Central Chapter Nurseryman's Association, past president. **HONORS/AWARDS:** California State Polytechnic University, Honorary Garden Science Degree; Order of the Sacred Treasure, Japan, Medal of Honor; American Heart Association, East Bay Award. **BUSINESS ADDRESS:** Council Member-at-Large, City of Oakland, 505 14th St, Ste 642, Oakland, CA 94612, (510)238-3266.

OGAWA, JOSEPH MINORU
Educator (retired). Japanese American. **PERSONAL:** Born Apr 24, 1925, Sanger, CA; son of Joseph Shosaku Ogawa and Naomi Yamaka Ogawa; married Margie; children: Julie Ogawa Morison, Martin K, JoAnn Ogawa Ende. **EDUCATION:** University of Nebraska, Lincoln; University of California, Davis, BS, 1950, PhD, 1954. **CAREER:** FAO United Nations Development Program, Taiwan, 1967-68; Cornell University, New York Agricultural Experiment Station, Geneva, 1977; Hirosaki University, Japan, Japan Society for Promotion of Science, 1990; consultant, Iran, Iraq, Chile, Brazil, Mexico; University of California, professor and plant pathologist, 1954-91, professor emeritus, 1991-. **ORGANIZATIONS:** American Phytopathological Society, Pacific division, councilor, 1986-88, vp, 1984, president, 1985; California Aggie Alumni Association, 1950-, treasurer, 1955-70. **HONORS/AWARDS:** Monsanto Chemical Co, plaque, 1990; California Freezer's Association, plaque, 1962; San Joaquin Cherry Growers & Industry Foundation, plaque, 1972; California Pistachio Commission, plaque, 1985; APS, fellow, 1986, Pacific Division, Lifetime Achievement Award, 1991; California Aggie Alumni Association, Excellence Award, 1991. **SPECIAL ACHIEVEMENTS:** Co-author, Diseases of Temperate Zone Tree Fruit & Nut Crops, 1991; co-author, Fungal, Bacterial and Certain Nonparasitic Diseases of Fruit and Nut Crops, 1979; approximately 150 scientific publications; incarcerated in Poston, Arizona by the United States War Relocation Authority, 1942-44. **MILITARY SERVICE:** US Army, Counter Intelligence Corp, T/sgt, 1945-46. **HOME ADDRESS:** 806 Linden Ln, Davis, CA 95616, (916)753-2583.

OGAWA, PATRICK
County administrator. Japanese American. **CAREER:** Los Angeles County Department of Health Services, Alcohol and Drug Programs, acting chief of planning, program development and technical assistance, currently. **ORGANIZATIONS:** National Advisory Council for the Office of Substance Abuse Prevention; California Department of Alcohol and Drug Programs, Asian/Pacific American Committee. **BUSINESS ADDRESS:** Acting Chief, Los Angeles County Alcohol and Drug Programs, 714 W Olympic, Ste 1040, Los Angeles, CA 90015, (213)744-6516.*

OH, ANGELA
Attorney, association administrator. Korean American. **PERSONAL:** Born Sep 8, 1955. **EDUCATION:** UCLA, public health, bachelor's degree, master's degree; University of California, Davis, law degree, 1986. **CAREER:** Beck, De Corso, Barrera and Oh, criminal defense attorney, currently. **ORGANIZATIONS:** Assembly Special Committee on the Los Angeles City Crisis; Korean American Bar Association of Southern California, president, 1992-; chairperson for Senator Barbara Boxer's federal judicial nominations; Electoral College of California, 1992. **SPECIAL ACHIEVEMENTS:** Wrote article in Ms Magazine about the Los Angeles riots, July/August 1992; wrote commentaries in the Los Angeles Times and the Los Angeles Sentinel; worked pro bono for Korean businesses; testified before US Commission on Civil Rights, 1993.

BIOGRAPHICAL SOURCES: Glamour magazine, Aug 1992; "Giving Voice to the Hurt and Betrayal of Korean-Americans," New York Times, May 2, 1993, sec 4 p9 col 1.*

OH, CHAN SOO
Research scientist. Korean American. **PERSONAL:** Born Jul 4, 1938, Kwangju, Chonnam, Republic of Korea; married; children: Michael C, Susie C. **EDUCATION:** Seoul National University, BS, 1961; St John's University, MS, 1967, PhD, 1971. **CAREER:** RCA Res Center, member of tech staff, 1971; Beckman Instruments, principal research scientist, currently. **ORGANIZATIONS:** American Chemical Society, 1967-; Society for Information Display, 1975-. **HONORS/AWARDS:** Beckman Instruments Inventors Hall of Fame. **SPECIAL ACHIEVEMENTS:** Flat Panel Displays; Liquid Crystal Materials and Applications; Immunochemistry; Clinical Diagnostics Reagents; Organic Synthesis of Biological Applications. **BUSINESS ADDRESS:** Principal Research Scientist, Beckman Instruments, Inc, 200 S Kraemer Blvd, Brea, CA 92621, (714)961-3835.

OH, CHANG H.
Chemical engineer. Korean American. **PERSONAL:** Born Apr 28, 1946; son of Byung Rin Oh; married Theresa Boknam Oh, Mar 26, 1976; children: Paul, John. **EDUCATION:** Yonsei University, BSChE, 1969; University of Florida, MSChE, 1979; Washington State University, PhD, chemical engineering, 1985. **CAREER:** Dong-A Pharmaceutical Co, 1973-74; Korea Institute of Science & Technology, 1974-77; Ethyl Corporation, senior engr, 1979-82; University of Idaho, Chemical Engineering Dept, affiliated professor, 1989-; Idaho National Engineering Laboratory, EG&G Idaho, senior engineering specialist, 1985-. **ORGANIZATIONS:** AIChE, 1985-; ANS, 1985-; ASME, 1985-. **HONORS/AWARDS:** Tau Beta Pi Engineering Honor Society, 1984. **SPECIAL ACHIEVEMENTS:** Technical session chair, ANS conference, ASME conference. **BUSINESS ADDRESS:** Senior Engineering Specialist, Idaho National Engineering Laboratory, 2525 Fremont Ave, EROB, Idaho Falls, ID 83415.

OH, HARRY K.
Consulting engineer. Korean American. **PERSONAL:** Born Oct 3, 1935, Seoul, Republic of Korea; son of Soo-Young Oh and Kyung-Ja Park; married Soon Jean Oh, Dec 29, 1985; children: Richard Philip, John, Howard. **EDUCATION:** University of Pennsylvania, BS, 1958; George Washington University, MS, 1961; Harvard University, Graduate School of Design, 1981. **CAREER:** United Engineers & Contractors, electrical engineer, 1956-58; C N Bogan & Associates, electrical engineer, 1958-60; Kluckhuhn & McDavid Co, project engineer, 1960-63; Thomas B Burnes Associates, chief engineer, 1963-65; Harry K Oh & Associates, president, 1965-; Oh & Chen Associates, president, 1979-. **ORGANIZATIONS:** Korean-American Citizens Federation of Maryland, president, 1981-83, 1992-; Natl Society of Professional Engineers, 1965-; Maryland Society of Professional Engineers, 1965-. **HONORS/AWARDS:** Government of Republic of Korea, National Honor Medal, Order of Dongbak, 1975. **BUSINESS ADDRESS:** President, Oh & Chen Associates, 11900 Parklawn Dr, Ste 205, Rockville, MD 20852, (301)231-6006.

OH, JOSEPH
Business owner. Korean American. **PERSONAL:** Born Sep 21, 1943, Taegu, Republic of Korea; married Eazher Oh; children: Jane, Becky, Christin. **EDUCATION:** Young University, administration. **CAREER:** Peking Restaurant, 1975-86; Quik Pak Super Market, 1986-89; U D Cleaners, owner, 1989-; SNK Apts, owner, 1979-; Northwest Maintenance, president, currently. **MILITARY SERVICE:** I Corp 7, Seoul, Korea, int, sgt. **BUSINESS ADDRESS:** President, Northwest Maintenance, 7520 40th St West, Tacoma, WA 98466.

OH, KEYTACK HENRY
Educator. Korean American. **PERSONAL:** Born Mar 16, 1938, Hamduk, Cheju-Do, Republic of Korea; married Youngsim Lee Oh, Sep 15, 1967; children: Jeanne, Susan. **EDUCATION:** Hanyang University, BS, 1962; Oklahoma State University, MS, 1966; Ohio State University, PhD, 1974. **CAREER:** East Gate Telephone Exchange, telephone engineer, supervisor, 1960-62; Western Electric Co, operations research specialist, 1966-68, MIS, staff member, 1968-71; Ross Laboratories, staff logistics engineer, 1972-75; University of Missouri-Rolla, asst professor, 1975-81; North Carolina A&T State University, associate prof, 1982; University of Toledo, associate prof, 1982-. **ORGANIZATIONS:** Institute of Industrial Engineer, Toledo Chapter, president, 1984-85; American Society for Engineering Education, 92 conference planning committee, 1992; Decision Science Institute; American Society for Engineering Management; Korean Scientists and Engineers in America Assn,

St Louis Chapter, president, 1978-79; Anthony Wayne Toastmaster Club, president, 1993-94; Toastmaster Intl, District 28, area governor, 1993-94. **HONORS/AWARDS:** Oklahoma State University, Presidential Fellowship, 1964; Toastmasters Intl Best Speaker Award, Interclub speech contest of Anthony Wayne & Trend Setter Clubs, 1991. **SPECIAL ACHIEVEMENTS:** Expert Decision Systems, Decision Science Institute Conference Proceedings, 1992; productivity improvement strategy under uncertainity, productivity, Frontier IV, 1993; setting productivity goals for manufacturing operations, Productivity Frontier IV, 1991. **HOME ADDRESS:** 2817 Westchester, Toledo, OH 43615, (419)536-8172. **BUSINESS ADDRESS:** Associate Professor, Dept of Industrial Engineering, University of Toledo, 2801 W Bancroft St, Toledo, OH 43615, (419)537-4626.

OH, TAE HEE
Educator, anesthesiologist. Korean American. **PERSONAL:** Born Aug 4, 1939, Taegu City, Republic of Korea; married Vivian Oh; children: Peter, Jane. **EDUCATION:** SNU, MD, 1964, MS, 1969. **CAREER:** Yale University, School of Medicine, professor, currently. **HONORS/AWARDS:** Yale University, MA. **MILITARY SERVICE:** Korean Medical Corps, capt. **BUSINESS ADDRESS:** Professor, Yale University School of Medicine, 333 Cedar St, New Haven, CT 06525, (203)785-2802.

OH, TAESUNG
Aircraft inspector. Korean American. **PERSONAL:** Born Apr 6, 1947, Seoul, Republic of Korea; married Sungrye Oh, Feb 29, 1975; children: Jae Young. **EDUCATION:** Airport College, AA. **CAREER:** McDonnell Douglas Corp, aircraft inspector, currently. **SPECIAL ACHIEVEMENTS:** 6th Degree Black Belt, Tae Kwon Do. **MILITARY SERVICE:** US Army, sp-4. **BUSINESS ADDRESS:** Aircraft Inspector, McDonnell Douglas Corporation, 3855 Lakewood Blvd, Long Beach, CA 90846.

OHASHI, ALAN JOSEPH
Architect, furniture designer. Japanese American. **PERSONAL:** Born Mar 19, 1949, Los Angeles, CA; son of Joe and Yuki Ohashi; married Joy Ohashi, Sep 7, 1981; children: Adam Kenzo. **EDUCATION:** University of California, Los Angeles, BA, 1975, MFA, cinematography, 1977; University of California, Berkeley, MArch, 1983. **CAREER:** Visual Communications, principal, 1970-77; ELS Design Group, architect, 1980-84; Tanner & Van Dine Architects, architect, 1984-85; Ohashi Design, principal, owner, 1985-. **ORGANIZATIONS:** San Francisco Chamber of Commerce, Business Alliance, chmn, 1993; Japanese-American Citizens League, San Francisco Chapter, board member, 1993; The Japan Society, 1992-93; Oakland Chamber of Commerce, 1992-93. **HONORS/AWARDS:** American Film Institute, Young Filmmakers Award, 1976. **SPECIAL ACHIEVEMENTS:** Works featured: "Self-Appointed Chairpersons," SF Magazine, 1991; "Delicate Sensibilities," Northern California Home & Garden Magazine, 1991; "Everyday Objects," San Francisco Airport Commission Gallery, 1991. **HOME ADDRESS:** 5739 Presley Ave, Oakland, CA 94618. **BUSINESS PHONE:** (510)652-8840.

OHASHI, WATARU
Writer, association administrator. Japanese American. **PERSONAL:** Born Jun 11, 1944, Hiroshima, Japan; son of Sakei Ohashi & Yasuyo Sato Ohash; married Bonnie Harrington. **EDUCATION:** Chuo University, BA, 1965. **CAREER:** Shiatsu Education Center of America, founder, director, beginning 1974; Logan College for Chiropractic, guest instructor, 1975-76; Harrington-Ohashi Associates, literary agents, partner, beginning 1976; Ohashi Institute, director, currently. **SPECIAL ACHIEVEMENTS:** Guest speaker: ASPO/Lamaze Silver Anniversary Conference, 1985; Whole Life Expo, New York, 1983; author: Touch for Love, Ballantine Books: New York, 1986; Touching the Invisible: An Introduction to Oriental Diagnosis, Ohashi Institute, 1985; Natural Childbirth: the Eastern Way, Ballantine Books, 1983; Reading The Body: Ohashi's Book of Oriental Diagnosis, Arkana Books, 1991; creator producer, "Ohashiatsu for a Healthy and Happy Pregnancy," video cassette for parents and professionals, Ohashi Institute, 1986. **BUSINESS ADDRESS:** Director, Ohashi Institute, 12 W 27th St, New York, NY 10001.

OHNISHI, TOMOKO
Educator. Japanese American. **PERSONAL:** Born Jun 8, 1931, Kobe, Hyogo-ken, Japan; daughter of Ryogi Kirita and Tomie Kirita; married Tsuyoshi Ohnishi, Apr 26, 1958; children: Hiroshi, Noriko. **EDUCATION:** National Kyoto University, Japan, BS, 1956, MS, 1958, PhD, 1962. **CAREER:** University of Stockholm, research assoc, 1965-66; Phillips University, Germany, visiting prof, 1966; Cornell University, research assoc, 1966-67; University of

Pennsylvania, visiting asst prof, 1967-71, asst prof, 1971-77, research assoc prof, 1977-84, research prof, 1984-. **ORGANIZATIONS:** Biophysical Society, Bioenergetics Subgroup, chairperson, 1992-95; University of Pennsylvania Medical School, Biochemistry Graduate Group, Biophysics Graduate Group; Biophysical Society; American Society for Biological Chemistry; American Assn for the Advancement of Science. **HONORS/AWARDS:** Fogarty Intl Research Collaboration Award, 1993-96; NIH, Metallobiochemistry Section, regular member, 1989-93; Centre Nationale de Recherche Scientifique, Paris, scholar, 1983-84; Tokyo Metropolitan Institute of Medical Science, Invited Scholar, 1982; Organization of American States, Invited Professor, 1977. **SPECIAL ACHIEVEMENTS:** Author, scientific research on bioenergetics: 175 publications, in refereed journals, invited book chapters. **BIOGRAPHICAL SOURCES:** Cellular Membrane: A Key to Disease Processes, 1992; Journal of Bioenergetics and Biomembranes, mini-review special issue, 1993. **BUSINESS ADDRESS:** Research Prof, Dept of Biochemistry & Biophysics, University of Pennsylvania, 37th & Hamilton Walk, A606 Richards Bldg, Philadelphia, PA 19104-6089, (215)898-8024.

OHNO, MITSUGI

Glassblower. Japanese American. **PERSONAL:** Born Jun 28, 1926, Bato, Nasu-Gun Tochigi, Japan; married Kimiyo Ohno (died 1985); children: Tsutomu, Hiroko Prawl, Julie; married Nao Ohno, Jul 1986. **EDUCATION:** Hongo Seinen Night School. **CAREER:** Takagi Glass Corp, apprentice, 1939-45; Kitamukata Bato Nasu, family farm, 1945-47; Tokyo University, Dept of Chem, glassblower, 1947-60; Kansas State University, Dept of Physics, glassblower, 1961-83, Dept of Chem, glassblower, 1983-. **HONORS/AWARDS:** Yoshikawa-Eiji Prize for Cultural Merit, 1979; Kansas State University, Walter Morrison Award, 1979; Tokyo University, Citation from Head of the Dept of Chem, 1984; Governor of Prefecture, Tochigi, Japan, 1986; Mayor of Bato City, 1991. **BIOGRAPHICAL SOURCES:** A Glassblower's Experience, Chem and Industry, October 1989; The Glassblower's Life, 1993. **HOME ADDRESS:** 2808 Nevada St, Manhattan, KS 66502, (913)539-5013.

OHNO, PETER TAKESHI

Technical manager. Japanese American. **PERSONAL:** Born Jun 9, 1960, San Francisco, CA; married Midori Takeshima Ohno, Oct 16, 1993. **EDUCATION:** San Francisco State University, BS, business administration, 1986. **CAREER:** Relational Technology, customer account rep, 1988-89; Ingres Corp, technical staff, 1989-91, corp technical sales rep, 1991-92; ASK Group, Marketing Events and Promotions, technical manager, 1992-. **ORGANIZATIONS:** Commonwealth Club of California, 1988-89; San Francisco Ad Club, 1986-87; San Francisco Jr Ad Club, 1986-87; Asian Business Association, 1991-92. **SPECIAL ACHIEVEMENTS:** Drum Corps International World Champions, Santa Clara Vanguard, 1981. **BUSINESS ADDRESS:** Technical Manager, ASK Group, Marketing & Promotions, 1080 Marina Village Pkwy, Alameda, CA 94501, (510)748-3385.

OHTA, MASAO (MARTIN)

Chemist (retired). Japanese American. **PERSONAL:** Born May 4, 1919, Kobe, Japan; son of Shizuo Ohta and Kikuno Ohta; married Miwako, Feb 25. **EDUCATION:** Kyoto University, BS, 1943; University of California, Berkeley, MS, 1956; University of Akron, PhD, 1959. **CAREER:** Mitsui Chemical Co, research chemist, 1943-52; Monsanto Co, research specialist, 1959-72; Chemical Abstract Service, senior editor, 1972-84. **HOME ADDRESS:** 5945 NE 201st St, Seattle, WA 98155, (206)487-0431.

OHTA, SHIRLEY MAE

Steel service center executive. Japanese American. **PERSONAL:** Born May 7, 1945, Wailuku, Maui, HI; daughter of Bessie Ohta and Shigeyoshi Ohta. **EDUCATION:** Marymount College, BS, 1966. **CAREER:** US Army Reserve, 100th Division TNG, SSAA, 1976-82; Eagle Steel Products, Inc, vice president, administration, 1982-91, CEO, 1991-. **ORGANIZATIONS:** Kentuckiana Minority Purchasing Council, 1991-; Reserve Officer Association, 1971-; Steel Service Center Institute, 1991-. **MILITARY SERVICE:** US Army, colonel, 1966-89; Bronze Star, 1970; Meritorious Service Medal, 1989; Army Commendation Medal, 1969. **BUSINESS ADDRESS:** CEO, Eagle Steel Products, Inc, 5150 Utica Pike, Jeffersonville, IN 47130, (812)282-4770.

OHTAKE, TAKESHI

Meteorologist, consultant. Japanese American. **PERSONAL:** Born Jan 22, 1926, Abiko, Chiba prefecture, Japan; son of Sakae Ohtake (deceased) and Sumiko Ohtake (deceased); married Kumiko Ohtake, Jan 20, 1953; children: Tomoko, Atsuko, Tadahiro. **EDUCATION:** Meteorological College of Japan,

diploma, 1948; Tohoku University, BSc, 1952. **CAREER:** Tohoku University, research assoc, 1952-64; University of Alaska, prof, 1964-87; Colorado State University, visiting assoc prof, 1969-71; National Polar Research Institute, visiting prof, 1979-80; Air Force Geophysics Laboratory, visiting prof, 1985-87; Nagoya University, visiting prof, 1990-91; Alaska Environmental Service, Inc, owner, currently. **ORGANIZATIONS:** American Meteorological Society, Farthest North Chapter, president, 1971-72, 1984-85, cloud physics committee, 1973-75. **HONORS/AWARDS:** University of Alaska, Professor Emeritus, Physics, 1988; Royal Meteorological Society, Fellow, 1985; American Meteorological Society, Fellow, 1989; KL7YR, amateur radio operator, 1986. **SPECIAL ACHIEVEMENTS:** Author of numerous articles in professional journals. **BUSINESS ADDRESS:** Owner, Alaska Environmental Service Inc, 14250 W Warren Dr, Lakewood, CO 80228.

OISHI, SATOSHI

Civil engineer. Japanese American. **PERSONAL:** Born Jan 19, 1927, Katada, Mie-Ken, Japan; son of Mitsuhei Oishi and Yei Oishi; married Jeanette C, Jul 2, 1960; children: Michelle Yuki. **EDUCATION:** University of Connecticut, BSCE, 1949. **CAREER:** Edwards & Kelcey Inc, partner, vice president, executive vice president, 1965-86, president, CEO, 1987-90, chairman of the board, 1990-94, chairman emeritus. **ORGANIZATIONS:** American Society of Civil Engineers, vice president zone I and fellow, 1991-93, director district 1, 1987-90, president metropolitan section, 1985-86; American Institute of Architects, 1972-; New Jersey and New York Assn of Consulting Engineers, director, 1965-; American Consulting Engineers, council, fellow, 1965-; Regional Plan Association, New Jersey Committee, 1986-; Engineering Foundation, board and executive committee, 1987-90. **HONORS/AWARDS:** Chi Epsilon, New Jersey Institute of Technology, honor member, 1975; University of Connecticut, Engineering Alumni Award, 1986, Day-of-Pride Alumni Honoree, 1993; American Society of Civil Engineers, Harland Bartholomew Award, 1992, Citizen-Engineer Award, 1993; New Jersey Journal of Business, New Jersey's 10 Best Employers, 1990. **SPECIAL ACHIEVEMENTS:** Manhattan Bridge Rehabilitation, officer-in-charge, 1979-90; Penn-North Station, Baltimore, officer-in-charge & exec architect, 1978-83; author of Infrastructure Column, NY Construction News, 1990-; on Jury of Awards for Corps of Engineers, 1992, and American Institute of Steel Construction, 1976. **BUSINESS ADDRESS:** Chairman Emeritus, Edwards & Kelcey, Inc, 70 S Orange Ave, Livingston, NJ 07039, (201)994-4520.

OJIMA, IWAO

Educator, research director. Japanese American. **PERSONAL:** Born Jun 5, 1945, Yokohama, Japan; son of Masaharu Ojima and Sumiko Ojima; married Yoko Ojima, Apr 24, 1971. **EDUCATION:** University of Tokyo, BS, 1968, MS, 1970, PhD, 1973. **CAREER:** Sagami Institute of Chemical Research, research fellow, 1970-76, senior research fellow, Organometallic Group, leader, 1976-83; Tokyo Institute of Technology, adjunct lecturer, 1978; Tokyo University of Agriculture & Technology, adjunct lecturer, 1983; Universite Claude Bernard Lyon I, Lyon, France, visiting professor, 1989; State University of NY, Stony Brook, Chemistry Dept, associate professor, 1983, professor, 1984, leading professor, 1991-. **ORGANIZATIONS:** American Chemical Society, 1993; American Association for the Advancement of Science, 1993; American Peptide Society, 1993; NY Academy of Science, 1993; Sigma Xi, 1993; The Chemical Society of Japan, 1993; The Society of Synthetic Organic Chemistry, Japan, 1993; National Cancer Institute, Developmental Therapeutics Contracts Review Committee, 1993-. **HONORS/AWARDS:** Chemical Society of Japan for Excellent Young Investigators, 25th Progress Award, 1976; Royal Swedish Academy of Sciences, nominator for Nobel Prize in Chemistry, 1990; University of Kansas-Lawrence, Eli Lilly Lecturer, 1990; Taiwan, National Science Council Lecturer, 1990; University of Oklahoma, J Clarence Karcher Lecturer, 1992; American Chemical Society, Arthur C Cope Scholar, 1994, William and Florence Catacosinos Professor in Cancer Research, 1994. **SPECIAL ACHIEVEMENTS:** Published more than 200 papers and reviews in leading journals; more than 130 patents and patent applications; has given 32 plenary and invited lectures at international conferences and symposia; Advisory Committee member of the National Institutes of Health, Medicinal Chemistry Study Section, for the evaluation of research grants, 1988-92; US Department of Energy, Basic Energy Science Program, panel reviewer, 1992; National Science Foundation, REU Program, Chemistry Divsion, panel reviewer, 1992. **BUSINESS ADDRESS:** Leading Professor, Dept of Chemistry, State University of New York at Stony Brook, Chemistry Bldg, Stony Brook, NY 11794-3400, (516)632-7890.

OKA, CHRISTINE KAZUKO
Librarian. Japanese American. **PERSONAL:** Born Oct 24, Los Angeles, CA; daughter of Isao Oka & Sachiko Jean Oka. **EDUCATION:** UCLA, BA, 1975; Defense Language Institute, Russian Language Course, 1976-77; UCLA Graduate School of Library & Information Sciences, MLS, 1990. **CAREER:** UCLA Unicversity Research Library, library assistant, 1979-90; UCSB Library, reference librarian and coordinator of publications for refernce services, 1990-. **ORGANIZATIONS:** American Library Association, 1990-; Asian/Pacific American Librarians Association; Asian Pacific Americans in Higher Education, 1992-; Asian American Faculty Staff Association of UCSB, 1990-; Friends of the Goleta Public Library, executive board, 1990-. **SPECIAL ACHIEVEMENTS:** "Languages of the World on CD-ROM," CD-ROM Professional 5:5, p 134-5, Sept 1992; "CD-MARC Bibliographic, Commemorative Edition," CD-ROM Professional 5:3, p 11, May 1992; "Guinness Disc of Records, 1991 Edition," CD-ROM Professional 5:2, p 117-8, March 1992; "Mammals Encyclopedia on CD-ROM," CD-ROM Professional 4:5, p 122-3, Sept 1991; numerous others. **MILITARY SERVICE:** US Army, Military Intelligence Service, 1976-79. **BUSINESS ADDRESS:** Reference Librarian, University of California, UCSB Library, Santa Barbara, CA 93106, (805)893-3454.

OKA, TAKAMI
Scientist. Japanese American. **PERSONAL:** Born Jan 1, 1940, Tokyo, Japan; son of Kiyomi Oka & Fumi Oka; married Keiko, Apr 1, 1969; children: Hidemi, Tomomi. **EDUCATION:** Tokyo University, BS, 1963; Stanford University, School of Medicine, PhD, 1969. **CAREER:** National Institutes of Health, HHS, senior scientist, 1969-. **ORGANIZATIONS:** American Society of Biochemistry and Molecular Biology, 1973; American Society of Cell Biology, 1974. **SPECIAL ACHIEVEMENTS:** Scientific publications, 170 papers, 1969-. **BUSINESS ADDRESS:** Senior Scientist, National Institutes of Health, HHS, 90 Rockville Pike, Bldg 8, Rm 311, Bethesda, MD 20892, (301)496-1404.

OKABE, HIDEO
Educator. Japanese American. **PERSONAL:** Born Dec 13, 1923, Takatomachi, Nagano-ken, Japan; son of Tokujiro and Masu; married Tomoko Shoji, Mar 15, 1959; children: Ken, Aya, Naomi Hauschild. **EDUCATION:** University of Tokyo, BE, 1947; University of Rochester, PhD, 1957. **CAREER:** National Institute of Standards and Technology, 1959-83; Howard University, research professor, 1983-. **ORGANIZATIONS:** American Chemical Society, 1970-; Sigma Xi, 1973-; Washington Academy of Science, 1983-; Chemical Society of Japan, 1983-; Materials Science Society, 1990-. **HONORS/AWARDS:** Institute of Physical Chemistry, The University of Bonn, Germany, visiting scholar, 1963-65; Tokyo Institute of Technology, Japan, visiting scholar, 1978; NASA Goddard Space Flight Center, senior research associate, 1982-83; Institute of Molecular Science, Japan, visiting professor, 1985; Hokkaido University, Research Institute of Applied Electricity, Japan, visiting professor, 1990. **SPECIAL ACHIEVEMENTS:** Department of Commerce, Gold Medal, 1973; book, Photochemistry of Small Molecules, Wiley, 1978; about 75 publications in photochemistry and materials science, atmospheric chemistry. **BUSINESS ADDRESS:** Professor, Chemistry Dept, Howard University, 525 College St, Washington, DC 20059, (202)806-6895.

OKADA, CONNIE TOKIYE
Art librarian. Japanese American. **PERSONAL:** Born Apr 10, 1943, Hunt, ID; daughter of Yoshito Okada & Takayo Ota. **EDUCATION:** University of Washington, BA, 1964; University of California, Santa Barbara, ML, 1969, MS, 1982. **CAREER:** University of California, Santa Barbara, Book Order Dept, Library, assistant librarian, 1969-78; University of Washington, assistant art librarian, Art Library, 1978-83, head, Art Library, 1983-. **ORGANIZATIONS:** Art Libraries Society of North America, 1979-; American Library Association, 1983-. **BUSINESS ADDRESS:** Head, Art Library, University of Washington, School of Art, DM-10, Seattle, WA 98195, (206)543-0648.

OKADA, TONY MANABU
Student, athlete. Japanese American. **PERSONAL:** Born Jan 10, 1973, Anaheim, CA; son of Theodore & Carol Okada. **EDUCATION:** San Jose State University, physical therapy, currently. **CAREER:** Student, currently; athlete, currently. **ORGANIZATIONS:** OCBC Judo Club, assistant instructor, 1988-92; San Jose State Judo Club, 1993-. **HONORS/AWARDS:** ASCCS Tiger, High School All American Wrestler, first team, 1991; US Senior Nationals, Judo, first place, 1992, 1993; Olympic Sports Festival, Judo, second place, 1992; state champion, wrestling, high school, 132 lbs 1990, 135 lbs, 1991.

SPECIAL ACHIEVEMENTS: All American Wrestling Team, 2 times; Olympic Team member, judo, 60 kg, 1992. **HOME ADDRESS:** 10324 Ashdale, Stanton, CA 90680, (714)821-5397.

OKAMOTO, KENNETH WAYNE
Electronics manufacturing company executive. Japanese American. **PERSONAL:** Born May 31, 1947, Bridgeton, NJ; married Christine McCann Okamoto, Jun 27, 1970; children: Kelly, Erin, Michael. **EDUCATION:** Western Kentucky University, BA, psychology, 1970. **CAREER:** Savings Bank of Manchester, branch manager, 1970-72; Ted Trudon, Inc, sales rep, 1972-74; RCA-Solid State Division, industrial relations rep, administration compensation & organization design, manager employment, 1974-78; Harris Corp, manager compensation & benefits, human resources, director, 1978-. **ORGANIZATIONS:** Industrial Association of Quincy, president of executive board, 1993-, 1st vice president, 1992-93, sec/treas, 1991-92; United Way of Adams County, board of directors, 1990-; John Wood Community College, placement steering committee, 1992-; Quincy Public Schools, in-touch advisory council, 1989-. **BUSINESS ADDRESS:** Director of Human Resources, Harris Allied Broadcast Equipment, 3200 Wismann Ln, Quincy, IL 62305.

OKAMOTO, SHARI AKIKO
Magazine editor. Japanese American. **PERSONAL:** Born Aug 5, 1963, Torrance, CA; daughter of Ben & Joanne Okamoto. **EDUCATION:** El Camino College, 1981-83; University of Southern California, BA, 1985. **CAREER:** LA Times, intern, 1986; Daily Breeze, pop music columnist, 1987-91; Village View, contributor, 1990-91; Bam Magazine, contributor, LA assistant editor, 1989-. **ORGANIZATIONS:** Asian American Journalists Association, assistant executive director, 1986. **BUSINESS ADDRESS:** Assistant Editor, Bam Magazine, 6767 Forest Lawn Dr, Ste 110, Los Angeles, CA 90068, (213)851-8600.

OKAMURA, ARTHUR SHINJI
Artist, educator. Japanese American. **PERSONAL:** Born Feb 24, 1932, Long Beach, CA; son of Frank & Yukiko Okamura; married Kitty Wong Okamura, Feb 1, 1991; children: (from previous marriage) Beth, Jonathan, Jane Sanders, Ethan. **EDUCATION:** Art Institute of Chicago, diploma, 1954. **CAREER:** Academy of Art, San Francisco, instructor, 1958; Central YMCA College, Chicago, instructor, 1956-57; Evanston Art Center, instructor, 1956-57; School of Art Institute, Chicago, instructor, 1958; UC Santa Cruz, watercolor painting in Tahiti, teacher, 1987, watercolor painting in Bali, teacher, 1989-91; California College of Arts & Crafts, professor, 1966-. **ORGANIZATIONS:** California College of Arts & Crafts, Oakland, California, Diversity Task Force, co-chair, 1989-93; Commonweal, board of directors, 1993; Bolinas Museum, 1993. **HONORS/AWARDS:** University of Chicago, Religious Arts Award, 1953; Art Institute of Chicago, Martin Cahn Award, 1957; University of Illinois, Purchase Award, 1959; San Francisco Museum of Art, Schwabacher Frey Award, 1960; Whitney Museum of Art, Neysa McMein Purchase Award, 1960. **SPECIAL ACHIEVEMENTS:** Books published: 1,2,3,4,5,6,7,8,9,10, co-author, Robert Creeley, Shambala/Mudra, 1971; Basho, co-author Robert Bly, Mudra, 1972; Ox-Herding, co-author Joel Weishaus, Cranium Press, 1971; Passionate Journey, co-author Steve Kowit, City Miner Books, 1984; 10 Poems by Issa, co-author Robert Bly, Floating Island Publications, 1993. **MILITARY SERVICE:** US Army, pvt, 1955-56. **BIOGRAPHICAL SOURCES:** Art USA Now, text, Allen S Weller, edited, Lee Nordness, p 452, 1962; Views from Asian California, 1920-65, Michel Brown, p 49. **HOME ADDRESS:** 210 Kale Rd, PO Box 367, Bolinas, CA 94924.

OKANO, YUJI
Senior buyer. Japanese American. **PERSONAL:** Born Sep 4, 1932, Wheatland, CA; son of Masaichi Okano (deceased) and Matsuyo Okano (deceased); married Eimi Okano, Jul 31, 1960; children: Caroline Erickson, Garett, Kimberly. **EDUCATION:** University of California, Berkeley, BS, 1955. **CAREER:** Ampex Corp, production scheduler, 1959-60; General Electric Co, production control scheduler, 1960-65; Varian Associates, master scheduler, 1965-68; General Electric Co, senior buyer, 1968-. **ORGANIZATIONS:** California Business Alumni, 1960-; Palo Alto Buddhist Temple, board & other positions, 1968-; ELFUN. **SPECIAL ACHIEVEMENTS:** Starred in movie, Constitution and Military Power: Korematsu v. US, produced by Mass Communications of Columbia Press (New York Film Library), 1958. **MILITARY SERVICE:** US Army, Artillery, Anti Aircraft, 1st lt, 1956-58. **HOME ADDRESS:** 1301 Harker Ave, Palo Alto, CA 94301.

OKAZAKI, JAMES

City government official. Japanese American. **PERSONAL:** Born in Wakayama-ken, Japan; married Linda; children: Marc, Rick, Irene. **EDUCATION:** UCLA, School of Engineering, graduate, certificate in business management. **CAREER:** Dharma School, teacher, currently; City of Los Angeles Department of Transportation, chief of transit programs, currently. **ORGANIZATIONS:** Nisei Week Japanese Festival, vice chairman, 1992, chairman, 1993; Nisei Week Carnival, chairman, currently; Senshin Buddhist Temple, Sangha Teens Teen-Age Program, adviser, currently; Los Angeles City Employees Asian American Association; Asian Pacific Alumni Association of UCLA, board of directors. **BUSINESS ADDRESS:** Chief of Transit Programs, City of Los Angeles Department of Transportation, 200 N Spring St, Rm 1200, Los Angeles, CA 90012.∗

OKAZAKI, STEVEN

Filmmaker. Japanese American. **PERSONAL:** Born Mar 12, 1952, Venice, CA. **CAREER:** Filmmaker, director, producer, screenwriter; films/documentaries include: Survivors, 1982; Unfinished Business, 1985; Living on Tokyo Time, 1987; Days of Waiting, 1989; The Lisa Theory; Troubled Paradise, 1992; American Sons. **HONORS/AWARDS:** Visual Communications, Tatsukawa Award; Academy of Motion Picture Arts and Sciences, Oscar, Best Short Documentary, 1990; Asian CineVision, Asian American Media Award, 1991. **SPECIAL ACHIEVEMENTS:** Oscar winning documentary, Days of Waiting, released nationally on videocassette by Mouchette Films, 1992. **BUSINESS ADDRESS:** Filmmaker, 548 5th St, San Francisco, CA 94107.∗

OKI, SCOTT D.

Museum administrator, business executive. Japanese American. **PERSONAL:** Born 1948?. **EDUCATION:** University of Colorado, MBA. **CAREER:** Microsoft Corp, numerous positions ranging from marketing manager, special account manager, Intl Opertions, director, Sales, Marketing and Services, senior vice president, 10 years; Oki Developments Inc, founder, president; Oki Foundation, chief volunteer, founder, president, currently. **ORGANIZATIONS:** Japanese American Chamber of Commerce, board of directors; Asian MBA, board of directors; Japan American Society, board of directors; Children's Hospital Foundation, board of directors; Imperials Youth and Music, board of directors; numerous others. **SPECIAL ACHIEVEMENTS:** University of Washington Board of Regents, appointed regent, 1993; Japanese American Natl Museum, appointed trustee, 1992-. **BUSINESS ADDRESS:** President, Oki Foundation, 10838 Main St, Bellevue, WA 98004, (206)454-2800.∗

OKIHIRO, GARY YUKIO

Educator. Japanese American. **PERSONAL:** Born Oct 14, 1945, Aiea, HI; son of Alice Kakazu Okihiro and Tetsuo Okihiro; married Elizabeth Ritch, Nov 13, 1971; children: Sean Sachio Ritch, Colin Isamu Ritch. **EDUCATION:** Pacific Union College, BA, 1967; University of California, Los Angeles, MA, 1972, PhD, 1976. **CAREER:** Humboldt State University, assistant, associate professor, 1977-80; Santa Clara University, director Ethnic Studies, associate professor, 1980-89; Cornell University, director Asian American Studies, associate professor, 1990-. **ORGANIZATIONS:** Association for Asian American Studies, president, 1985-87; Japanese American Resource Center, San Jose, director, 1988-90; Asian Americans for Community Involvement, San Jose, chair of board, 1987-89. **HONORS/AWARDS:** Association for Asian American Studies, Outstanding Book Awards, 1987, 1992; Amherst College, John J McCloy '16 Professor of American Institutions and International Relations. **SPECIAL ACHIEVEMENTS:** Books: Cane Fires: The Anti-Japanese Movement in Hawaii, 1865-1945; Japanese Legacy: Farming and Community Life in California's Santa Clara Valley; ed, In Resistance: Studies in African, Caribbean, and Afro-American History. **BUSINESS ADDRESS:** Director, Asian American Studies Program, Associate Professor of History, Cornell University, McGraw Hall, Ithaca, NY 14853, (607)255-3320.

OKIMOTO, DANIEL IWAO

Educator. Japanese American. **PERSONAL:** Born Aug 14, 1942, Santa Anita, CA; son of Tameichi Okimoto and Kirie Okimoto; married Nancy Okimoto; children: Saya, Kevin. **EDUCATION:** Princeton University, BA, history, 1965; Harvard University, MA, East Asian studies, 1967; University of Tokyo, 1968-70; University of Michigan, PhD, political science, 1977. **CAREER:** Aspen Institute for Humanistic Studies, Mellon Foundation Fellow, 1977-78; Stanford University, Hoover Institute, national fellow, 1979-80, assistant professor, 1977-85; Stanford Center in Berlin, visiting professor, 1987-88; Stockholm School of Economics, visiting professor, 1988-; Stanford University,

professor, 1985-, A/PARC, co-director, 1990-. **ORGANIZATIONS:** Princeton University, Dept of Politics, advisory council, 1988-; National Research Council, Japan, 1990-; Council on Foreign Relations; Japan Society of San Francisco; World Affairs Council of N California; American Political Science Association; Association for Asian Studies. **HONORS/AWARDS:** Stanford University, Institute for International Studies, senior fellow; East-West Center international advisory panel. **SPECIAL ACHIEVEMENTS:** Inside the Japanese System, co-edited w/ T Rohlen, 1988; Between MITI & the Market: Japan Industrial Policy for High Tech, 1988; The Semiconductor Competition & National Security w/ Rowen, Dahl, 1987; American in Disguise, 1971. **BUSINESS ADDRESS:** Co-director, Asia/Pacific Research Center, Stanford University, 200 Encina Hall, Stanford, CA 94305-6055, (415)723-9744.

OKITA, DWIGHT HOLDEN

Playwright, poet. Japanese American. **PERSONAL:** Born Aug 26, 1958, Chicago, IL; son of Patsy Takeyo Okita and Fred Yoshio Okita. **EDUCATION:** University of Illinois at Chicago, BA, creative writing, 1983. **CAREER:** Playwright, poet; poetry: Crossing with the Light, Tia Chucha Press, 1992; plays: Dream/Fast, Igloo Theater, 1987; The Rainy Season, Zebra Crossing Theatre, 1993; The Salad Bowl Dance, Angel Island Asian American Theatre/Chicago Historical Society, 1993; "Crossing with the Light," poetry video, PBS-TV, 1988. **ORGANIZATIONS:** Chicago Dramatists Workshop, resident playwright, 1991-93; Tia Chucha Press, published poet, 1992; Chicago Historical Society, commissioned playwright, 1993. **HONORS/AWARDS:** Illinois Arts Council, Poetry Achievement Fellowship, 1988; Asian American Renaissance Conference, Featured Guest/Performer, 1992. **BIOGRAPHICAL SOURCES:** "The Asian American Dream," New City newspaper, cover story, May 5, 1993; Hyphen Magazine, cover story, Fall 1993; other feature stories & reviews. **HOME ADDRESS:** 426 W Surf, Apt 111, Chicago, IL 60657, (312)883-5219.

OKITA, GEORGE TORAO

Educator, researcher. Japanese American. **PERSONAL:** Born Jan 18, 1922, Seattle, WA; son of Kazue Okita and Fusao Muguruma Okita; married Fujiko Shimizu, Nov 29, 1958; children: Ronald Hajime, Glenn Torao, Sharon Mariko Chylack. **EDUCATION:** University of Cincinnati, 1943-44; Ohio State University, BA, 1948; University of Chicago, PhD, 1951. **CAREER:** University of Chicago, research associate, instructor, 1953-56, research associate, assistant professor, 1956-58; assistant professor, 1958-63; Northwestern University, associate professor, 1963-66, professor, 1966-90, acting chairman, 1968-70, 1976-77, professor emeritus, 1990-. **ORGANIZATIONS:** American Society Pharmacology and Expltl Therapeutics, 1958-; American Society Advancement Science, 1956-; Cardiac Muscle Society, 1978-; International Society Biochemical Pharmacology, 1968-80; Society of Toxicology, Midwest region, 1980-; Sigma Xi, 1952-; American Heart Association, 1958-; United States Pharmacopeial Convention, 1970-85. **SPECIAL ACHIEVEMENTS:** Author of 67 publications in various scientific biomedical journals; assistant editor, Journal of Pharmacology and Experimental Pharmacology, 1965-68. **MILITARY SERVICE:** US Army, technician, 4th grade, 1944-46. **HOME ADDRESS:** 8619 Vineyard Ridge Pl, San Jose, CA 95135.

OKUDA, YASUYORI (YURI)

Entertainment/information executive. Japanese American. **PERSONAL:** Born Jul 8, 1938, Tokyo, Japan; son of Ryozo Okuda & Shizuko Okuda; married Teruko Okuda, May 15, 1969; children: Haru. **EDUCATION:** University of Illinois, Champaign, BS, 1961; Harvard Business School, PMD, 1969. **CAREER:** Time-Life, Asia, joint ventures, director, 1974-76; Time-Life Books, mkg director, 1977-80, group product mgr, 1980-84, marketing director, 1984-88; Time-Life, New Product Develop, director, 1988-90; Time Inc, Europe, director of R&D, 1990-92; Time-Warner, director of operations, 1992-. **ORGANIZATIONS:** Direct Marketing Association, currently, DC; Japan-American Society; Japan Chamber of Commerce, Washington; Harvard Alumni Association, Washington; Harvard Club at National Press Club; Northern VA Youth Symphony Association, president, 1987. **SPECIAL ACHIEVEMENTS:** Language proficiency: Japanese. **BUSINESS ADDRESS:** Director of Operations, Time-Warner Inc, 777 Duke St, Alexandria, VA 22314, (703)838-7000.

OMATA, ROBERT ROKURO

Medical science administrator (retired). Japanese American. **PERSONAL:** Born Nov 3, 1920, Hanford, CA; son of George Jitsuzo & Kane Okazaki Omata; married Hiroko Kamikawa Omata, Nov 25, 1948; children: Douglas M, Roberta (Robin) Kane, Donna R. **EDUCATION:** University of California, BA,

1944; University of Minnesota, MS, 1946, PhD, 1949. **CAREER:** National Institute of Dental Research, research microbiologist, 1949-60; Division of Research Grants, executive secretary, fellowship sec, 1960-63; Office of International Research, fellowship section, asst chief, 1963-64; Pacific Office, Tokyo, asst chief, 1964-67, fellowship section, asst chief, 1967-68; Fogarty International Center, fellowship section, chief, 1968-74; National Cancer Institute, international program specialist, 1974-85. **ORGANIZATIONS:** American Society of Microbiology, 1946-63; American Association for the Advancement of Science, 1950-64; International Association for Dental Research, 1950-60. **HONORS/AWARDS:** National Institutes of Health, pre-doctoral fellowship, 1947-49; American Dental Association, post-doctoral fellowship, 1949-53. **MILITARY SERVICE:** US Public Health Service, captain, 0-6, 1953-85; Meritorious Service Medal, 1979; Commendation Medal, 1975. **HOME ADDRESS:** 314 Beech Grove Ct, Millersville, MD 21108, (410)987-8466.

OMORI, ALVIN I.
Government official. Japanese American. **PERSONAL:** Born Feb 4, 1948, Honolulu, HI; son of Kenneth H Omori and Agnes K Omori; married Julee I Omori, Aug 25, 1979. **EDUCATION:** University of Hawaii, BA, 1971, John A Burns School of Medicine, MD, 1977. **CAREER:** University of Hawaii, John A Burns School of Medicine, assistant professor; City and County of Honolulu, chief medical examiner, currently. **ORGANIZATIONS:** National Association of Medical Examiners, 1985-; American Academy of Forensic Sciences, 1985-; American Medical Association, 1985-; College of American Pathologists, 1985-. **HONORS/AWARDS:** American Academy of Forensic Sciences, Research Award, 1989; Phi Kappa Phi, 1970; Phi Beta Kappa, 1971. **SPECIAL ACHIEVEMENTS:** Contributing author, Suicidal Behavior in the Asia-Pacific Region, 1992; articles in Journal of Forensic Sciences, 1991, 1992; board certification: American Board of Pathologists, Forensic Pathology, 1987; American Board of Pathologists, Anatomic and Clinical Pathology, 1982. **BUSINESS ADDRESS:** Chief Medical Examiner, City and County of Honolulu, 835 Iwilei Rd, Honolulu, HI 96817, (808)527-6777.

OMORI, YOSHIAKI
Educator. Japanese American. **PERSONAL:** Born Jan 9, 1961, Kawasaki, Kanagawa, Japan; son of Fumio Omori & Takeko Omori; married Heajung Omori. **EDUCATION:** Sophia University, BA, 1983, MA, 1985; State University of New York, Stony Brook, PhD, 1990. **CAREER:** University of Connecticut, assistant professor. **ORGANIZATIONS:** American Economic Association, 1989-; Japan Society of Economics and Econometrics, 1983-. **BUSINESS ADDRESS:** Assistant Professor, Dept of Economics, University of Connecticut, U-63, Storrs Mansfield, CT 06269, (203)486-5267.

OMURA, MARK CHRISTOPHER
Law enforcement official. Japanese American/Chinese American. **PERSONAL:** Born Oct 12, 1956, Chicago, IL; son of Jimmy A Omura and Helen Shiu; married Elizabeth A Omura, Sep 1, 1984; children: Lauren Kinuko, Matthew Akio. **EDUCATION:** Culver-Stockton College, BS, 1978. **CAREER:** Illinois State Police, trooper, 1981-84, trooper 1st class, 1984-85, sergeant, 1985-92, acting master sergeant, 1992-93, master sergeant, 1993, Investigations, squad leader, 1993, Firearms Task Force, supervisor, 1994-. **ORGANIZATIONS:** Trooper's Lodge 41, 1981. **BUSINESS ADDRESS:** Sergeant, Illinois State Police, 9511 W Harrison St, Des Plaines, IL 60010, (708)294-4500.

ONG, BENG SOO
Educator. Malaysian American. **PERSONAL:** Born Jun 27, 1962, Penang, Malaysia; son of Ong Huck Keat and Lim Siew Eng; married Veen Chee Foong, Feb 6, 1992. **EDUCATION:** Warrensburg University, BS, 1985; Central Missouri State, BS, BA, 1985, MBA, 1986; University of Arkansas, PhD, marketing, 1992. **CAREER:** Central Missouri State University, library assistant, 1985-86; University of Arkansas, household research panel director, 1987-90; California State University, Fresno, associate professor, 1990-. **ORGANIZATIONS:** Phi Kappa Phi; Southern Marketing Association; Academy of Marketing Science. **HONORS/AWARDS:** California State University, Fresno, Faculty Educational Innovation Award, 1993, research minigrants, 1991-93; Purchasing Management Association of Arkansas Scholarship, Regents Scholarship, 1986, Sterne-Spaeth Scholarship, 1985, 1986. **SPECIAL ACHIEVEMENTS:** Seven articles published and consulted with seven different companies. **BUSINESS ADDRESS:** Assoc Professor, Dept of Marketing, California State University, Fresno, Sid Craig School of Business, M#7, Fresno, CA 93740, (209)278-2594.

ONG, CHEE-MUN
Educator. Malaysian American. **PERSONAL:** Born Nov 23, 1944, Ipoh, Perak, Malaysia; son of Chin Kok Ong & Say Choo Yeoh; married Penny, Jul 17, 1971; children: Yi-Ping, Yi-Ching, Chiew-Jen. **EDUCATION:** University of Malaya, BE (honors), 1967; Purdue University, MS, 1968, PhD, 1974. **CAREER:** Guinness Brewery, plant engineer, 1967; University of Malaya, lecturer, 1968-73, 1976-78; Purdue University, assistant professor, 1978-81, associate professor, 1981-85, professor, 1985-. **ORGANIZATIONS:** Institute of Electrical & Electronics Engineers, senior member, 1979-; Institution of Electrical Engineers, UK, Fellow, 1988-. **HONORS/AWARDS:** UNESCO, fellowship, 1969, 1970; Fulbright-Hays, scholarship, 1967, 1968; Perak Turf, scholarship, 1963, 1967. **SPECIAL ACHIEVEMENTS:** Published many papers on analysis, control design, modeling and simulation of adjustable speed drives, high voltage direct current transmission, and alternate energy source systems. **BUSINESS ADDRESS:** Professor, Purdue University, 1285 School of Electrical Engineering, West Lafayette, IN 47907, (317)494-3484.

ONG, CYNTHIA
State government official. Korean American. **PERSONAL:** Born Mar 7, 1931. **EDUCATION:** University of California, Los Angeles, bachelor's; UCLA Law School, JD, 1977. **CAREER:** Los Angeles Foundation of Legal Services, 1977-80; State Public Defender's Office, 1980-82; State Attorney General's Office, deputy state attorney general, 1982-. **ORGANIZATIONS:** City of San Francisco, Redevelopment Commission, appointed commissioner, 1992-; California State Bar Assn. **BUSINESS ADDRESS:** Deputy State Attorney General, State of California, 455 Golden Gate Ave, Ste 6200, San Francisco, CA 94102-3658, (415)703-1985.

ONG, CYNTHIA K. CHAR
Certified public accountant. Chinese American. **PERSONAL:** Born Sep 5, 1953, Honolulu, HI; daughter of Lloyd F and Aileen H Char; married Luke H Ong, Aug 29, 1975; children: Kathleen K, Michael A, Christopher L. **EDUCATION:** Stanford University, AB, 1975; University of Utah, MPrA, 1979. **CAREER:** Grant Thornton, tax manager, 1979-86; Luke H Ong, PC, tax consultant, 1987-. **ORGANIZATIONS:** Salt Lake City Public Library, board, 1985-94, chair, 1989-92; Children's Dance Theatre, board/treasurer, 1986-88; AWSCPA of Utah, 1985-, treasurer, 1986-87; Utah Association of CPAs, 1979-; American Institute of CPAs, 1979-; American Society of Women Accountants, 1979-; West High School, community council, 1992-94. **BUSINESS ADDRESS:** Certified Public Accountant, Luke H Ong, PC, 1200 Beneficial Life Tower, 36 S State Street, Salt Lake City, UT 84111-1401, (801)538-2345.*

ONG, EDWARD FRANK
Structural engineer. Chinese American. **PERSONAL:** Born Mar 19, 1952, Oakland, CA; son of Philip Ong and Helen Ong; married May L Ong, Jul 16, 1977; children: Markus D, Lianne J. **EDUCATION:** California Polytechnic State University, BS (w/honors), 1975; University of California, Berkeley, MS, 1976. **CAREER:** University of California, Berkeley, teaching assistant, 1975-76, research assistant, 1976-77; URS/Blume, assistant engineer, 1977-78; Paul F Fratessa Associates, manager of production/associate, 1978-86; Tulloch Construction, chief structural engineer, 1986-. **ORGANIZATIONS:** Huntington Park Homeowners' Association, president, 1987-88; Plum Manor Homeowners' Association, president, 1978-79; Chinese Christian School, board of governors, 1979-; Chinese Bible Church, deacon, 1979-80, trustee, 1978-79, 1982-84. **HONORS/AWARDS:** Tau Beta Pi, 1975; Phi Kappa Phi, 1975; Manpower Services, scholarship, 1970. **SPECIAL ACHIEVEMENTS:** Publications, The CAD CAM Journal, March/April 1987, May/June 1987; Macintosh Construction Forum, May 1993; interviewed by Architectural Record for a magazine article, 1992. **HOME ADDRESS:** 739 Flume Ct, San Leandro, CA 94578-4455, (510)357-8769. **BUSINESS ADDRESS:** Chief Structural Engineer, Tulloch Construction, Inc, 3428 Ettie St, Oakland, CA 94608, (510)655-3400.

ONG, GEORGINA
Company owner/executive. Chinese American. **PERSONAL:** Born Jan 15, 1946, San Francisco, CA; daughter of George W Ong and Rena C Ong. **EDUCATION:** Dental Assisting, AA, 1965. **CAREER:** Gump's, recruiter, 1986-88; Gateway Saving & Loan, recruiter, 1982-86; White Collar, recruiter, 1977-82; Positive Connections, president, owner, 1988-. **ORGANIZATIONS:** Mountain View Chamber, ambassador, 1992-93; Self Help for the Elderly, volunteer coordinator, 1988-89; 5th Asian New Year's Parade, Mtn View, coordinator, 1993; Chinese Ski Club, past board, social director; Chinese

Tennis Association, past board. **HONORS/AWARDS:** Mountain View Chamber, Ambassader of the Year, 1993; White Collar Recruiter of the Year, 1981. **BIOGRAPHICAL SOURCES:** Mountain View Town Crier, Asian Week, vol 2, no 7, Aug 21, 1992; Sunnydale Valley Journal, p 4, Aug 12, 1992; Trellis Singles Magazine, p 14, July/Aug 1992; Las Altos Town Crier, vol 45, no 6, Feb 12, 1992; San Jose Mercury, July 16, 1993, B section; SF Downtown, vol 2, mo 3, Feb 1994. **BUSINESS ADDRESS:** President, Positive Connections, 119 Easy St, Unit 6, Mountain View, CA 94043-3700, (415)961-5588.

ONG, JAMES M.

Enrolled Agent. Chinese American. **PERSONAL:** Born 1934, San Francisco, CA; son of Chester Ong; married Pinky Chan Ong; children: Jonathan, Jeffery. **EDUCATION:** Occidental College, BA, 1956; Golden Gate University, postgraduate studies; San Francisco State University, postgraduate studies; University of California, Berkeley, postgraduate studies. **CAREER:** Ong Associates, owner, 1958-. **ORGANIZATIONS:** Oakland Convention & Visitors Bureau, board chairman, 1992-94; Oakland Chinatown Chamber of Commerce, president, 1989-91; Oakland Assn of Insurance Agents, president, 1971; Kiwanis Club of Jack London Square, president, 1967; Independent Insurance Agents & Brokers of California, board, 1975-78; East Bay/San Francisco Assn of Enrolled Agents, president, 1981; California Society of Enrolled Agents, director, 1983; Natl Assn of Enrolled Agents, director, 1983-85; Oakland Boys Clubs, executive board, 1971-73: Children's Fairyland Anniversary, 1975; Alameda County Transportation Advisory, 1990-92; Boy Scouts, San Francisco Council, executive committee, 1967-70; Citizens Budget Advisory, Oakland, 1988-; Chinese Presbyterian Church, treasurer, 1959-; Oakland Economic Development Council, board, 1987-92. **HONORS/AWARDS:** Boy Scouts of America, Silver Beaver, 1975. **SPECIAL ACHIEVEMENTS:** Mayors Special Events & Sports Commission, 1989; Oakland Sharing the Vision, 1991-92. **MILITARY SERVICE:** US Navy, 1956-58. **BUSINESS ADDRESS:** Owner, Ong Associates, 701 Franklin St, Oakland, CA 94607, (510)893-7011.

ONG, NAI-PHUAN

Educator. Malaysian American/Chinese American. **PERSONAL:** Born Sep 10, 1948, Penang, Malaysia; son of Ong Chin Seng & P'ng Hooi-Kean; married Delicia Lai, Aug 12, 1982. **EDUCATION:** Columbia College, NY, BA, 1971; University of California, Berkeley, PhD, 1976. **CAREER:** University of Southern California, assistant professor of physics, 1976-83; Max Planch Institute, Stuttgart, visiting scientist, 1981; University of Southern California, associate professor of physics, 1983-85; Princeton University, professor of physics, 1985-. **ORGANIZATIONS:** American Physical Society, 1974-; Graduate Record Examination, committee member, 1985-87. **HONORS/AWARDS:** Alfred Sloan Foundation, Fellowship Award, 1982-84; American Physical Society, Elected Fellow, 1989. **SPECIAL ACHIEVEMENTS:** 28 invited talks at international conferences on superconductivity, 1988-; 105 professional articles in refereed journals, Physical Review, Nature etc, 1976-; US patent, awarded for growing high temperature superconductors, 1991; co-discoverer with Pierre Monceau of charge-denisty-wave conductivity in one-dimensional metals, 1976. **BIOGRAPHICAL SOURCES:** Science Citation Index, Institute for Science Info, 1980-; Mossaic Magazine, NSF, vol 15, 5, p 26, 1984. **BUSINESS ADDRESS:** Professor of Physics, Princeton University, PO Box 708, Princeton, NJ 08544, (609)258-4347.

ONG, OWH KIAN

Oil and gas company executive. Chinese American. **PERSONAL:** Born Apr 28, 1957, New York, NY; married Wing Y Lee-Ong; children: Quentin Lee. **EDUCATION:** Baruch College, City University of New York, BBA, 1979; Harvard Business School, MBA, 1988. **CAREER:** Peat, Marwick, Mitchell & Co, audit supervising senior, 1979-84; Amerada Hess Corporation, International Exploration & Production, senior acct, 1984-85, Abu Dhabi Acctg/Admin, superintendent, 1985-86, Retail Financial Control, supervisor, 1988-89, Marketing Planning & Control, manager, 1990, Refining, Planning & Control, manager, 1990-92, Operations Financial Controls, manager, 1993-. **ORGANIZATIONS:** Chinatown Planning Council, finance committee chairman, 1980-83. **HOME ADDRESS:** 879 River Rd, Chatham, NJ 07928. **BUSINESS ADDRESS:** Manager, Marketing Financial Controls, Amerada Hess Corporation, One Hess Plaza, Woodbridge, NJ 07095, (908)750-6973.

ONG, SING-CHEONG

Educator, mathematician. Chinese American/Malaysian American. **PERSONAL:** Born Jan 2, 1952, Yongchun, Fujian, People's Republic of China; son of Lian & Gau Lee (deceased); married Siu-Wah Chan Ong, Aug 12, 1982; children: Payton Pei-De, Luvena Le-Yun, Peijie. **EDUCATION:** Nanyang

University, Singapore, BSc, 1974, BSc (with honors), 1975; Dalhousie University, MA, 1976, PhD, 1979. **CAREER:** Dalhousie University, teaching assistant, 1975-79; University of Victoria, visiting assistant professor, 1979-80; University of Waterloo, postdoctoral fellow, lecturer, 1980-81; University of Toronto, research associate, lecturer, 1981-83; Central Michigan University, assistant professor, 1983-88, associate professor, 1988-92, professor, 1992-. **ORGANIZATIONS:** American Mathematical Society, 1977-; Mathematical Association of America, 1987-. **HONORS/AWARDS:** Nanyang University, Silver Medal, 1974; Dalhousie University, Killam Trust, Killam Memorial Scholarship, 1977-79; Central Michigan University, Research Professor, 1991-92. **SPECIAL ACHIEVEMENTS:** Research articles published in internationally-known journals, 1980-; article quoted in textbook, Topics in Matrix Analysis, by R Horn and C R Johnson, Cambridge University Press, p 340-341, 1991. **BUSINESS ADDRESS:** Professor of Mathematics, Central Michigan University, S Washington, Pearce Hall, Rm 206C, Mount Pleasant, MI 48859, (517)774-3622.

ONISHI, HIRONORI

Educator. Japanese American. **PERSONAL:** Born Feb 11, 1936, Nara, Japan; married Clara, Aug 22, 1964; children: Kristine, Karen. **EDUCATION:** Allegheny College, BS, 1957; MIT, MS, 1959, PhD, 1961. **CAREER:** City College of New York, professor of mathematics, currently. **ORGANIZATIONS:** American Mathematical Society; Mathematical Association of America; American Physical Society. **SPECIAL ACHIEVEMENTS:** Research in mathematics and physics. **BUSINESS ADDRESS:** Professor of Mathematics, City College of New York, 138th Street at Convent Avenue, R6/282, New York, NY 10031, (212)650-5137.

ONO, KANJI

Educator. Japanese American. **PERSONAL:** Born Jan 2, 1938, Tokyo, Japan; son of Saburo Ono and Yoshiko Ono; married Fumie, May 19, 1962; children: Kenji, Yuka, Kohji. **EDUCATION:** Tokyo Institute of Technology, BE, 1960; Northwestern University, PhD, 1964. **CAREER:** Northwestern University, research assistant, associate, 1960-65; University of California, assistant professor, 1965-70, associate professor, 1970-76, professor, chair, 1976-. **ORGANIZATIONS:** ASM International, 1963-; AIME, 1963-81, Southern California Section, chairman, 1973-74; AEWG, 1971-; ASNT, 1971-, awards committee, 1981-85; SAMPE, 1986-; ASTM, 1974-. **HONORS/AWARDS:** American Society for Metals, H M Howe Medal, 1968; American Society for Nondect Testing, Achievement Award, 1980; Acoustic Emission Working Group, Achievement Award, 1985, Gold Medal Award, 1991. **SPECIAL ACHIEVEMENTS:** Editor, Journal of Acoustic Emission, 1982-. **BUSINESS ADDRESS:** Professor & Chair, Dept of Materials Science and Engineering, University of California, Los Angeles, 405 Hilgard Ave, 6531 Boelter Hall, Los Angeles, CA 90024-1595, (310)825-5233.

ONO, RICHARD DANA

Biotechnology company general manager, consultant. Japanese American. **PERSONAL:** Born Jan 16, 1953, Bridgeton, NJ; son of Frank H Ono and Fumi Y Ono; married Anne Wagner, Oct 10, 1981; children: Alison Celia, Maxwell Wagner. **EDUCATION:** Johns Hopkins University, AB, 1975; Harvard University, AM, 1978, PhD, 1981. **CAREER:** Regis McKenna Inc, general manager, 1986-87; Integrated Genetics Inc, business development, director, 1987-89; Enzytech Inc, business development, vice president, 1989-91; Arcturus Pharmaceutical Corp, chief executive officer, 1991-92; The Celemax Group, president, 1992-. **ORGANIZATIONS:** Massachusetts Biotechnology Council Inc, founding director, 1984; Environmental Business Council Inc, founding member, 1992-; Harvard University, Dunster House Affiliate, advisory board, 1991-, Kennedy School of Govt, working group on biotechnology, 1991-; Museum of Comparative Zoology, Harvard, research associate, 1981-. **HONORS/AWARDS:** Society of Ichthyologists and Herpetologists, Raney Award, 1979. **SPECIAL ACHIEVEMENTS:** The Business of Biotechnology, Butterworth Publishers, 1991; Vanishing Fishes of North America, Stone Wall Press, 1983; Paintings of "Satsukimasu Salmon and Coelacanth" for JLB Institute of Ichthyology International Conservation Exhibition, 1993. **HOME ADDRESS:** 80 Woodside Lane, Arlington, MA 02174, (617)641-0729.

ONO, YOKO

Artist, musician, filmmaker. Japanese American. **PERSONAL:** Born Feb 18, 1933, Tokyo, Japan; daughter of Eisuke Ono and Isoko Yasuda Ono; married Toshi Ichiyanagi, 1957 (divorced 1964); married Anthony Cox, 1964 (divorced 1968); children: Kyoko; married John Ono Lennon, Mar 20, 1969 (died 1980); children: Sean. **EDUCATION:** Gakushuin University; Sarah Lawrence College. **CAREER:** Artist, author, activist, filmmaker, musician; works include: films, Bottoms, 1966; Smile, 1969; author, Grapefruit, 1964; solo albums, Yoko Ono, 1970; Fly, 1971; Feeling The Space, 1973; Starpeace, 1986; numerous others; with John Lennon, Unfinished Music 1: Two Virgins, 1968; Unfinished Music 2: Life with the Lions, 1969; Wedding Album, 1969; Double Fantasy, 1980; Milk and Honey, 1984; numerous others; Whitney Museum of American Art, New York, exhibit, 1989. **SPECIAL ACHIEVEMENTS:** Numerous contributions toward world peace including a section of New York's Central Park known as "Strawberry Fields" as a memorial to John Lennon's effort toward unity. **BIOGRAPHICAL SOURCES:** The Ballad of John and Yoko, 1982; Imagine, 1988; The Playboy Interviews with John Lennon and Yoko Ono, 1981. **BUSINESS ADDRESS:** Musician, c/o The Dakota, 1 West 72nd St, New York, NY 10033.∗

ORDANZA, BONAGRACE FRANCISCO
Facilities engineer. Filipino American. **PERSONAL:** Born Jul 29, 1965, Mandaluyong Rizal, Manila, Philippines; daughter of Josefa Reyes Francisco and Edilberto Trinidad Ordanza Sr. **EDUCATION:** San Jose State University, industrial & systems engineering, 1990. **CAREER:** San Jose State University, database analyst, 1987-89; Northern Telecom, facilities project engineer, 1989-. **ORGANIZATIONS:** International Facilities Management Association, currently; Institute of Industrial Engineers, 1988-90; Akbayan Filipino-American Club, secretary, 1984-89. **HONORS/AWARDS:** Akbayan Club, Scholarship, 1984; Northern Telecom, Spot Award-Support Services, 1992. **SPECIAL ACHIEVEMENTS:** Performed on Annual Cultural Night Akbayan for 2 years, 1985-86; worked on Special Projects at San Jose State University in areas of industrial engineering, 1988-90.

OSHIMA, EUGENE AKIO
Educator. Japanese American. **PERSONAL:** Born Jan 2, 1934, Kaneohe, HI; son of Paul T Oshima and Elsie H Oshima; married Dale Yasuko Miura, Jun 6, 1959; children: Lisa Mayomi Oshima Baugh, Barron Hideo, Kyle Yukio. **EDUCATION:** University of Hawaii, 1952; Colorado State College, BA, 1955; University of Northern Colorado, MA, 1956; Oklahoma State University, EdD, 1966. **CAREER:** University of Northern Colorado, graduate assistant, 1955; Decatur County High School, Kansas, head of science department, 1956-64; Oklahoma State University, special staff, 1964-66; Central Missouri State University, professor of biology/science education, 1966-. **ORGANIZATIONS:** Phi Delta Kappa, life member, 1956-; National Science Teachers Association, life member, 1956-; National Education Association, life member, 1956-; Phi Kappa Phi, executive committee, 1968-; Missouri Academy of Science, 1966-; Science Teachers of Missouri, 1983-. **HONORS/AWARDS:** Greater Kansas City Science and Engineering Fair, 15 Years of Service, 1993; Central Missouri State University, dedication to UNIV 1000, 1993, 25 Years of Service, 1991. **BUSINESS ADDRESS:** Professor of Biology/Science Education, Central Missouri State University, LOV 300G, Warrensburg, MO 64093-5086, (816)543-4930.

OSHIMA, HAROLD H.
Investment management company executive. Japanese American. **PERSONAL:** Born Dec 4, 1954, Los Angeles, CA; son of Haruto and Miyoko Oshima; married Anne K Oshima, Jun 10, 1984; children: Michael, Daniel, David, Kathleen. **EDUCATION:** Pomona College, BA, 1975; Harvard University, AM, PhD, 1981. **CAREER:** Oshima & Associates, Inc, president, CEO, 1981-; UMC Systems, Inc, director, 1987-. **BUSINESS ADDRESS:** President and CEO, Oshima & Associates, Inc, One Faneuil Hall Marketplace, 3rd Fl, Boston, MA 02109.

OSHIRO, KATHLEEN F.
Corporate executive. Japanese American. **PERSONAL:** Born in Honolulu, HI; daughter of George and Nora Sekigawa; married Herbert Y Oshiro Jr; children: Randy M Domingo. **EDUCATION:** Cannon's Business College. **CAREER:** C Brewer and Co, Ltd, utility secretary, 1975, senior secretary, 1976, executive secretary, 1978, administrative assistant, 1986, assistant vice president, corporate secretary, 1989-93; vice president, administration/corporate secretary, 1993-. **ORGANIZATIONS:** Hawaii Society of Corporate Secretaries, president, 1994-; International Association of Business Communicators, 1990-; Executive Women International, Honolulu Chapter, past president, 1986. **SPECIAL ACHIEVEMENTS:** C Brewer Today, editor. **BUSINESS ADDRESS:** Vice President, Administration & Corporate Secretary, C Brewer and Company, Ltd, 827 Fort St Mall, Honolulu, HI 96813, (808)544-6248.

OSHIRO, RENE KATSUKO
Educator. Japanese American. **PERSONAL:** Born in Lahaina, Maui, HI; daughter of Tokuzo Oshiro. **EDUCATION:** Parsons School of Fashion Design, 1963. **CAREER:** Sant Angelo, patternmaker/designer, 1969-75; Muney Design, fashion designer, 1975-83; Oshiro, president, 1983-86; Parsons School of Design, instructor, currently. **HOME ADDRESS:** 55 West 14th St, New York, NY 10011.

OSHIRO, ROY C.
Airlines executive. Japanese American/Pacific Islander American. **PERSONAL:** Born Sep 17, 1946, Wahiawa, HI; son of Henry Oshiro and Yoshiko Oshiro; married Patricia Maria, Apr 6, 1972; children: Lauren Ann. **EDUCATION:** University of Utah, BA, 1968; University of Houston, MBA, 1982. **CAREER:** Japan Airlines Co, Ltd, sales manager, 1970-. **SPECIAL ACHIEVEMENTS:** International trade export of high tech products to be manufactured overseas/off shore and returned for consumption. **HOME ADDRESS:** 4153 Byron St, Palo Alto, CA 94306.

OTA, DEAN
Manufacturing company executive. Japanese American. **PERSONAL:** Born Dec 22, 1950, Washington, DC; son of Robert Y and Toshiko Ota; divorced; children: Ryan Ota, Alicia Ota. **EDUCATION:** Montgomery College, 1969-71; Orange Coast College, 1981-82. **CAREER:** Quality Golf Products Inc, owner.

OTA, HENRY YASUSHI
Museum board director, attorney. Japanese American. **PERSONAL:** Born Dec 31, 1942, Gila River, AZ; son of Harry Toshio Ota and Tsuyoko Fukai Ota; married Patricia A Ota, Apr 28, 1970; children: Christine, Candace. **EDUCATION:** Dartmouth College, BA, 1964; University of Southern California, JD, 1969. **CAREER:** Mori and Ota, associate, partner, 1970-84; Kelley, Drye & Warren, partner, 1984-88; Baker & McKenzie, partner, 1988-. **ORGANIZATIONS:** Japanese American Natl Museum, chairman, trustee, 1992-; Japanese American Cultural and Community Center, board of directors; American Bar Assn; California Bar Assn; Los Angeles County Bar Assn. **BUSINESS ADDRESS:** Committee Chair, Japanese American National Museum, 369 E 1st St, Los Angeles, CA 90012-3901, (213)625-0414.∗

OTA, ISAAC I.
Automotive leasing company executive. Japanese American. **PERSONAL:** Born Dec 10, 1943, Kealakekua, HI; son of Kazuo & Yukie Ota; married Lorraine S, Jun 24, 1972; children: Kevin, Dan. **EDUCATION:** University of Hawaii, BBA, 1966. **CAREER:** First Hawaiian Bank, assistant branch manager, 1970-79; Service Lease Company, Division of Servco Pacific Inc, vice president, 1979-. **MILITARY SERVICE:** US Army, e-5, 1966-70; Commendation Medal, 1970. **BUSINESS ADDRESS:** Vice President, Service Lease Co, Div of Servco Pacific Inc, 2850 Pukoloa St, Ste 301, Honolulu, HI 96819, (808)831-5966.

OTA, MABEL TAKAKO
Elementary school teacher/administrator (retired). Japanese American. **PERSONAL:** Born Sep 13, 1916, San Diego, CA; daughter of Suezo Kawashima & Iyo Obonai Kawashima; married Fred Kaname Ota, Apr 7, 1940; children: Madeline Iyoko, Candice Kiyoko Ota Funakoshi. **EDUCATION:** UCLA, BA, 1939; CSU, Los Angeles, elem teaching credential, 1949; USC Graduate School, MS, elem adm credential, MS, education, 1956; Mt St Mary's Graduate School, general secondary & general administration, 1971. **CAREER:** Los Angeles Unified School District, elem classroom teacher, 1949-58, teachers' consultant, 1958-60, vice principal, 1960-62, principal, 1962-80. **ORGANIZATIONS:** LA City Commission on Disability, commissioner, vp; Asian Pacific Coalition for Aging, past president of board of directors; Seinan Senior Citizens Club, legislative chair, board of directors; Wilshire Japanese American Citizens' League, 1st vp; Los Angeles City Council on Aging, executive board; LA City Dept of Aging, advisory board; Rebuild LA, Housing Committee; UCLA Alumni Association, life member; Pi Lambda Theta; Los Angeles Retired Teachers Assn; California State Teachers Assn; Associated Administrators of Los Angeles; National JACL Century Club, life member; Exceptional Children's Foundation Associates Support Group. **HONORS/AWARDS:** Pacific Southwest District Council, JACL Certificate of Appreciation, 1985; Letter of Commendation from Pat Saiki, US Congresswoman, 1987; LA City Council Aging, Citation for Meritorious Service, 1990, Certificate of Appreciation, 1991-92; Mayor Richard Riordan, Certificate of Appreciation, 1993. **BIOGRAPHICAL SOURCES:** Congressional Record, Commission on

Wartime Relocation & Internment of Civilians, August 4, 1981; Nobuya Tsuchida: Asian and Pacific American Experiences: Women's Perspectives, p 102, University of Minnesota, 1982; Japanese American Women, by Mei Nakano, Mina Press Pub, p 149, 1990; And Justice for All, by John Toteishi. **HOME ADDRESS:** 3805 S Grayburn Ave, Los Angeles, CA 90008, (213)294-4522.

OU, CHING-NAN
Educator. Taiwanese American. **PERSONAL:** Born May 15, 1945, Kao Hsiung, Taiwan; son of Te-Chui Ou & Yu-Mei Ou; married Suh-Yun L Ou, Aug 16, 1971; children: Edwin Y, Peter S. **EDUCATION:** Chung-Hsing University, BS, 1967; Iowa State University, 1970-73; Texas Tech University, PhD, 1977. **CAREER:** Johns Hopkins University, postdoctoral fellow, 1977-78; Mayo Clinic, postdoctoral fellow, 1978-80; Baylor College of Medicine, assistant professor of clinical pathology, 1980-87, associate professor of clinical pathology, 1987-; Texas Childrens Hospital, assistant director of clinical chemistry, 1980-87, director of clinical chemistry, 1987-. **ORGANIZATIONS:** American Association for Clinical Chemistry, 1978-; National Academy of Clinical Biochemistry, fellow, 1987-; Academy of Clinical Lab Physicians & Scientists, 1979-; North American Chinese Clin Chemistry, 1980-, president, 1986; North American Taiwanese Professor Association, 1982-, treasurer, 1992. **HONORS/AWARDS:** ACLPS, Young Investigator Award, 1979. **SPECIAL ACHIEVEMENTS:** Diagnosis of Hemoglobinopathies & Thalassemias by HPLC, 1983-; Therapeutic Drug Monitoring, 1980-; Clinical Applications of HPLC, 1980-; Pediatric Clinical Chemistry, 1980-; published 55 articles and 64 abstracts. **BUSINESS ADDRESS:** Dept of Pathology, Director of Clinical Chemistry, Texas Children's Hospital, MC2-2261, Houston, TX 77030, (713)770-5107.

OU, HSIEN-WANG
Oceanographer, educator. Chinese American. **PERSONAL:** Born Sep 5, 1949, Hsinchu, Taiwan; son of Cheng-Tzu Ou and Hsiu-Ying Cheng; married Linda Ou, Jun 24, 1979; children: Melissa, Christina. **EDUCATION:** Florida State University, MS, 1975; MIT, WHOI, PhD, 1979. **CAREER:** MIT, post-doctoral investigator, 1980; Columbia University, associate research scientist, 1980-86, research scientist, 1986-89, senior research scientist, 1989-, adjunct professor, 1992-. **BUSINESS ADDRESS:** Professor, L-DEO of Columbia University, Oceanography Bldg, Rte 9W, Palisades, NY 10964, (914)365-8825.

OU, SHUKONG
Consultant. Chinese American. **PERSONAL:** Born Mar 7, 1952, Taipei, Taiwan; son of Shu-Huang Ou and Jane T Ou; married Joan M O'Connor, Jun 28, 1981; children: Katherine Mayling, Michal James Tunhwa. **EDUCATION:** Princeton University, BS, 1974; Massachusetts Institute of Technology, MS, 1976. **CAREER:** Research-Cottrell, Inc, engineer, 1976-81; Stone & Webster Engineering Corp, consultant, 1981-. **SPECIAL ACHIEVEMENTS:** Co-author, presenter, Designing, Operating and Maintaining a Highly Reliable Flue Gas Desulfurization System; co-author, "Increasing Flue Gas Desulfurization System Reliability," Power Engineering, May 1984; co-author, presenter, Upgrading Older Flue Gas Desulfurization Systems; co-author, presenter, DiBasic Acid Test and Chemical Process Evalution at Petersburg Unit 3 FGD System, Indianapolis Power & Light Co, Stone & Webster Engineering Corp, 1985. **HOME ADDRESS:** 4 Summit Ave, Winchester, MA 01890. **BUSINESS PHONE:** (617)589-2654.

OU, THUOK. *See* OUTHUOK, T.

OUTHUOK, T. (THUOK OU)
Broadcast journalist. Cambodian American. **PERSONAL:** Born Nov 28, 1940, Phnom Penh, Cambodia; son of Ou Khleang; married Hory, May 23, 1971; children: Thilda, Jamie. **EDUCATION:** University of Georgia, BS, forestry management, 1965. **CAREER:** Dept of Social Services, social worker, supervisor; Voice of America, international broadcaster, currently. **HOME ADDRESS:** 6616 Kerns Road, Falls Church, VA 22042, (703)532-7931.

OZAKI, YOJI
Community relations representative. Japanese American. **PERSONAL:** Born May 6, 1922, Los Angeles, CA; son of Kyujiro Ozaki and Tomino Tsuchihashi Ozaki; married Molly Mariko Ozaki, Apr 8, 1954; children: Julie Emiko Modaff, Janis Haru Matsuo. **EDUCATION:** Roosevelt College, BS, 1950; Roosevelt University, MS, 1955. **CAREER:** Jewish Vocational Service, vocational counselor, 1953-59; Japanese American Service Committee, executive

director, 1964-68; Illinois Dept of Mental Health, General Office, rehab dev, 1969-72, Reg II rehab coordinator, 1972-74; Illinois Inst for Developmental Disabilities, program dir, 1974-79; Asian Human Services, executive director, 1984-85; Northeastern Illinois Area Agency on Aging, community relations rep, 1985-. **ORGANIZATIONS:** Heiwa Terrace, board of directors, program committee chair, 1990-; Japanese American Service Committee, board of directors, 1991-; Illinois Alliance for Aging, board of directors, 1990-; AARP, National Legislative Council, 1989-. **HONORS/AWARDS:** Natl Rehabilitation Assn, Mary Switzer Scholar, 1986; Chicago Community Trust, Community Service Fellow, 1984; Asian American Coalition, Community Service Award, 1991; Operation ABLE, Senior Achievement Award, 1993; City of Chicago, Senior Hall of Fame, inductee, 1993. **SPECIAL ACHIEVEMENTS:** Established sheltered workshop for Issei elder, 1979; set up Cross Cultural Communication Program for conferences, 1991. **MILITARY SERVICE:** US Army, 442 RCT, s/sgt, 1944-46. **BIOGRAPHICAL SOURCES:** National Distinguished Registry: Medical & Vocational Rehabilitation, p214, 1987. **HOME ADDRESS:** 4954 N Monticello, Chicago, IL 60625. **BUSINESS ADDRESS:** Community Relations Representative, Northeastern Illinois Area Agency on Aging, 245 W Roosevelt Rd, Bldg 18, Ste 161, West Chicago, IL 60185, (708)293-5990.

OZATO, KEIKO
Immunologist. Japanese American. **PERSONAL:** Born Aug 25, 1941, Yamagata, Yamagata, Japan; daughter of Chiyo Naito & Masaru Naito; married Igor B Dawid, Apr 8, 1976. **EDUCATION:** Kyoto University, MS, 1968, PhD, 1973. **CAREER:** National Cancer Institute, visiting associate, 1978-81; National Institute of Child Health and Human Development, NIH, senior staff fellow, 1981-83, head, unit on molecular genetics of immunity, 1983-87, chief, section on molecular genetics of immunity, 1987-. **ORGANIZATIONS:** American Association of Immunologist, 1976. **HONORS/AWARDS:** NIH, Director's Award, 1993. **BUSINESS ADDRESS:** Chief, Section of Molecular Genetics of Immunity, National Institutes of Health, Child Health and Development, Laboratory of Molecular Growth Regulation, Bldg 6, Rm 2A01, Bethesda, MD 20892, (301)496-9184.

OZAWA, GALEN M.
State government official. Japanese American. **PERSONAL:** Born Sep 23, 1937, Turlock, CA; son of Sada M Ozawa and Alice M Ozawa; married Terrill V, Sep 28, 1968; children: Ken M. **EDUCATION:** UCLA, BA, 1962. **CAREER:** US Air Force, weather officer, 1962-68, intelligence officer, 1968-72, disaster prep specialist, 1977-82; Zody's, sales rep, 1983-84; State of Nevada, radiological/hazardous material officer, 1984-91, planner/analyst, 1991-. **MILITARY SERVICE:** US Air Force, captain, 1962-82; Vietnam Service, 1968; UN Expeditionary, 1971; Air Force Commendation, 1982. **BIOGRAPHICAL SOURCES:** Yamato Colony. **BUSINESS ADDRESS:** Planner/Analyst, Division of Emergency Management, State of Nevada, 2525 S Carson St, Carson City, NV 89710, (702)687-4240.

OZAWA, MARTHA NAOKO
Educator. Japanese American. **PERSONAL:** Born Sep 30, 1933, Ashikaga City, Tochigi Prefect, Japan; daughter of Tokuichi Ozawa and Fumi Ozawa; divorced. **EDUCATION:** Aoyama Gakuin University, BA, 1956; University of Wisconsin-Madison, MSSW, 1966, PhD, 1969. **CAREER:** Portland State University, assistant professor of social work, 1969-70, associate professor of social work, 1970-72, 1975-76; New York University, research associate professor of social work, 1972-75; Washington University, professor of social work, 1976-85, Bettie Bofinger Brown Professor of Social Policy, 1985-. **ORGANIZATIONS:** The Gerontological Society of America, fellow; National Association of Social Workers; Council of Social Work Education; Natl Academy of Social Insurance. **HONORS/AWARDS:** Washington University, Distinguished Faculty Award, 1988; University of California, Berkeley, Seabury Lecturer, 1985; North Carolina State University, Ellen Winston Lecturer, 1984; Adelphi University, Social Development, visiting fellow, 1982. **SPECIAL ACHIEVEMENTS:** Income Maintenance and Work Incentives, Praeger, 1982; Editor, Women's Life Cycle and Economic Insecurity, Greenwood, 1989; Editor, Women's Life Cycle: A Japan-US Comparison in Income Maintenance, University of Tokyo Press, 1989, 1992; numerous articles in journals and chapters in various books. **BUSINESS ADDRESS:** Bettie Bofinger Brown Professor of Social Policy, Washington University, George Warren Brown School of Social Work, One Brookings Dr, St Louis, MO 63130-4988, (314)935-6615.

OZAWA, SEIJI

Music director. Chinese American. **PERSONAL:** Born Sep 1, 1935, Shenyang, China; son of Kaisaku Ozawa and Sakura Ozawa; married Vera Motoki-Ilyin; children: Seira, Yukiyoshi. **EDUCATION:** Toho School of Music, Japan, 1953-59; has studied with Hideo Saito, Eugene Bigot, Herbert von Karajan, Leonard Bernstein; Tanglewood Music Center, student invited by Charles Munch, 1959. **CAREER:** New York Philharmonic, asst conductor, 1961-62; Ravinia Festival, music director of season, 1964-68; Toronto Symphony Orchestra, music director, 1965-69; San Francisco Symphony Orchestra, music director, 1970-76; Tanglewood Festival, appointed artistic adviser, 1970; Boston Symphony Orchestra, conductor, 1970, music adviser, 1972-73, music director, 1973-. **HONORS/AWARDS:** Evening at the Symphony, Emmy Award; Intl Competition of Orchestra Conductors, 1st Prize, 1959; Tanglewood Music Center, Koussevitzky Prize, 1960; named Laureate Fondation du Japon, 1988. **SPECIAL ACHIEVEMENTS:** Guest conductor for several major orchestras. **BUSINESS ADDRESS:** Director, Boston Symphony Orchestra, Symphony Hall, 301 Massachusetts Ave, Boston, MA 02115.*

OZAWA, TERUTOMO

Educator. Japanese American. **PERSONAL:** Born Jan 17, 1935, Yokohama City, Japan; son of Hanjiro & Tsuru Ozawa; married Hiroko Aoyama, Sep 2, 1967; children: Edwin Tomoya, Clare Risa. **EDUCATION:** Tokyo University of Foreign Studies, BA, 1958; Columbia University, MBA, 1962, PhD, 1966. **CAREER:** Massachusetts Institute of Technology, visiting research associate, 1975-76; Cambridge University, visiting scholar, 1982-83; United Nations Conference on Trade & Development, consultant, 1983-84; Organization of Economic Cooperation and Development, Paris, consultant, 1980-; Colorado State University, professor of economics, 1974-. **ORGANIZATIONS:** American Economic Association, 1966-; Academy of International Business, 1990-; Transnational Corporations (UN Journal), editorial advisory committee member, 1992-. **HONORS/AWARDS:** Colorado State University, Distinguished Service Award in scholarly & creative activities, 1985, Burlington Northern Faculty Achievement Award, 1993; Japan Foundation, Senior Professional Fellowship, 1987; Colorado School of Mines, John M Olin Distinguished Visiting Professorship, 1987. **SPECIAL ACHIEVEMENTS:** Books: Recycling Japan's Surpluses for Developing Countries, OECD, 1988; editor, The Role of General Trading Companies in Trade and Development, Tokyo, APO, 1987; co-author, Japan's General Trading Companies: Merchants of Economic Development, OECD, 1984; Multinationalism, Japanese Style, Princeton University Press, 1979; Japan's Technological Challenge to the West, 1950-74, MIT Press, 1974. **BUSINESS ADDRESS:** Professor, Dept of Economics, Colorado State University, Fort Collins, CO 80523, (303)491-6075.

P

PADRE, MARC CRUZ

Financial services administrator. Filipino American. **PERSONAL:** Born Jan 19, 1937, Llanera, Nueva Ecija, Philippines; son of Juan G Padre and Teodorica C Padre; married Josefina Morin Padre, Mar 31, 1964; children: Norman, Aaron, Macario Jr. **EDUCATION:** Wesleyan University, Philippines, BA, 1964; Mount Carmel College, BS, education, 1967; Far Eastern University, post graduate in administration, 1968; Compton Community College, respiratory therapy, 1975. **CAREER:** MLK-Drew Medical Center, institutional helper, 1973, intermediate clerk, 1973-75, patient admitting worker, 1975-78, patient financial services worker, 1979-. **ORGANIZATIONS:** United Methodist Church, Sunday school teacher, day preacher, 1973-. **SPECIAL ACHIEVEMENTS:** Language proficiency: Spanish.

PAEK, CHISUN JIM

Professional hockey player. Korean American. **PERSONAL:** Born Apr 7, 1967, Seoul, Republic of Korea; son of Pong H Paek & Kyu Hui Paek. **CAREER:** Pittsburgh Penguins, player, currently. **HONORS/AWARDS:** International Hockey League, Turner Cup, 1989; National Hockey League, Stanley Cup, 1991, 1992. **BUSINESS ADDRESS:** Professional Hockey Player, Pittsburgh Penguins, 300 Auditorium Pl, Pittsburgh, PA 15219.

PAEK, MIN

Broadcast journalist, association administrator. Korean American. **CAREER:** KTSF-TV, host, currently; graphic artist; writer. **ORGANIZATIONS:** Korean American Development Corporation, executive director, currently. **HONORS/AWARDS:** Office of San Francisco Mayor Frank Jordan, Certificate of Appreciation, for work as member of Citizen's Committee on Community Develop-

ment from 1988-92; State Senator Milton Marks, commendation, which declared Aug 28, 1992 as Min Paek Day. **SPECIAL ACHIEVEMENTS:** Author, children's book, Aekyung's Dream, 1988. **BUSINESS ADDRESS:** Executive Director, Korean American Development Corp, 745 Buchanan St, San Francisco, CA 94102, (415)252-1346.*

PAI, ANNA CHAO

Educator. Chinese American. **PERSONAL:** Born Jan 27, 1935, Peking, China; daughter of Huai Tung Chang and Shih Hui Chao; married David H Pai, Aug 29, 1959; children: Benjamin F H, Michael F C. **EDUCATION:** Sweet Briar College, BA, 1957; Bryn Mawr College, MA, 1959; Albert Einstein College of Medicine, PhD, 1964. **CAREER:** Moravian Seminary for Girls, teacher, 1959-60; Albert Einstein College of Medicine, instructor, 1965-66; Montclair State College, biology, professor, 1969-. **ORGANIZATIONS:** Sigma Xi; American Association for Advancement of Science; American Institute of Biological Sciences; National Association of Biology Teachers; New Jersey Academy of Sciences; Developmental Biology Society; New York, New Jersey Molecular Biology Club. **HONORS/AWARDS:** Phi Beta Kappa, 1972; Montclair State College, Merit Award, 1982. **SPECIAL ACHIEVEMENTS:** 5 publications in scientific journals; author, Foundations of Genetics, McGraw-Hill, 1st ed, 1975, 2nd ed, 1985. **BUSINESS ADDRESS:** Professor of Biology, Montclair State College, Normal Ave, 255 Mallory Hall, Upper Montclair, NJ 07043, (201)893-5101.

PAI, DAVID HSIEN-CHUNG

Engineering company executive. Chinese American. **PERSONAL:** Born Jan 7, 1936, Guilin, Guangxi Zuangzu, China; son of Chung-Hsi & Pei-Cheng Ma Pai; married Anna Chao Pai, Aug 29, 1959; children: Benjamin, Michael. **EDUCATION:** Virginia Military Institute, BS, civil engineering, 1958; Lehigh University, MS, civil engineering, 1960; New York University, ScD, structural mechanics, 1965. **CAREER:** Foster Wheeler Development Corp, FW Energy Applications, Inc, vice president, director of engineering, Nuclear and Special Products Department, Equipment Division, chief engineer, Solid Mechanics Department, senior research associate, assistant head, Analysis Section, research associate, head, Research Division, senior engineer, development engineer, chairman, president, currently. **ORGANIZATIONS:** ASCE; Sigma Xi; Manufacturings Alliance for Productivity and Innovation, Council on Engineering and Technology; China National Standards Committee on Pressure Vessels, consultant; Chinese Mechanical Engineering Society, senior advisor; ASME, fellow, Design and Analysis Committee, PVP Division, former chair, subcommittee on Elevated Temperature Design Pressure Vessel Research Committee, former chair. **HONORS/AWARDS:** ASME Medal for Pressure Vessel and Piping Technology, 1987. **SPECIAL ACHIEVEMENTS:** Author or co-author of more than 30 papers; editor of 2 books; holds 2 patents. **BUSINESS ADDRESS:** Chairman & President, Foster Wheeler Development Corp, 12 Peach Tree Hill Rd, Livingston, NJ 07039, (209)535-2309.

PAI, GREGORY GI YONG

Economist. Korean American. **PERSONAL:** Born Mar 4, 1945, Washington, DC; son of Ei Whan Pai and Inez Kong Pai; divorced. **EDUCATION:** University of Hawaii, BA, 1967; Harvard University, MArch, 1974; Massachusetts Institute of Technology, PhD, 1979. **CAREER:** Institute of Urban Studies and Development, Yonsei University, Korea, research director, 1970-72; United States Government, Dept of Commerce, Bureau of Economic Analysis, economist, 1979-82; First Hawaiian Bank, vice president, chief economist, 1983-89; State of Hawaii, special assistant to governor for economic affairs, 1989-. **ORGANIZATIONS:** Hawaii Korean Chamber of Commerce, president, 1987; American Statistical Association, Hawaii Chapter, president, 1989; Honolulu Symphony Orchestra, director, 1986; Hawaii Public Radio, director, 1993; Girl Scout Council of the Pacific, director, 1986; Catholic Diocese of Honolulu, Campaign for Human Development, director, 1988; State of Hawaii, Governor's Council on Revenues, 1993; Governor's Blue Ribbon Panel on Health Care, 1992. **HONORS/AWARDS:** National Science Foundation, National Needs Postdoctoral Fellowship, 1979; Harvard/MIT Joint Center for Urban Studies, Catherine Bauer Wurster Fellowship, 1978; MIT, Dept of Urban Studies and Planning, Bemis Fund Fellowship, 1978. **SPECIAL ACHIEVEMENTS:** United States Peace Corps, Seoul, Korea, 1969-72. **BUSINESS ADDRESS:** Special Asst to the Gov for Economic Affairs, Office of the Governor, Hawaii State Capitol, Honolulu, HI 96813, (808)587-2817.

PAI, K. VASANTH

Health care executive. Indo-American. **PERSONAL:** Born Jul 3, 1933, Mangalore, Karnataka, India; son of Kernire Upendra Pai and Sharada Bai; married Mala V Pai, Nov 18; children: Suresh V, Sunil K. **EDUCATION:** Madras University, Government College, India, BCom, 1955; Institute of Chartered Accountants, India, FCA, 1961; Institute of Certified Public Accountants, New York, CPA, 1975; Institute of Management, London, fellow, FI Mgt; Harvard Business School, AMP, 1979. **CAREER:** Blue Cross & Blue Shield of Illinois, vice president, 1970-79; Peat, Marwick & Mitchell, partner, 1980-81; Leader Group Inc, principal, 1981-93; Martha Washington Hospital, president/CEO, 1990-91; Hyde Park Hospital Inc, president/CEO, 1992-93; US Health Inc, president, 1993-. **ORGANIZATIONS:** American Konkani Association, president, 1984-. **HOME ADDRESS:** 535 Hamilton Wood, Homewood, IL 60430, (708)957-2845.

PAI, KENNETH Y.

Housing development company executive. Taiwanese American. **PERSONAL:** Born Jun 6, 1947, Keelung, Taiwan; married Katy M Pai, May 20, 1976; children: Jason M, John M, Tony M. **EDUCATION:** Taiwan Provincial College of Oceanic Technology, bachelor's degree, 1971; University of Wisconsin-Milwaukee, MS, 1973. **CAREER:** Group Development Corp, treasury/secretary, 1987; PT Pacific Corp, president, 1983; Dunes & Associates, principal, 1983; Edgewick & Associates, principal, 1986; Vistaview Associates, Ltd, treasurer/secretary, 1991; Parkridge Associates, Ltd, treasurer/secretary, 1991; Teamco Development, Inc, president, 1992-. **ORGANIZATIONS:** Taiwanese Chamber of Commerce of Seattle, secretary, 1991-93. **BUSINESS ADDRESS:** President, Teamco Development, Inc, 2688 74th Ave SE, Mercer Island, WA 98040, (206)232-0888.

PAI, LISA KOONGHUI KIM

Attorney. Korean American. **PERSONAL:** Born Feb 10, 1960, Seoul, Republic of Korea; daughter of Frederick Kim and Hyun Sook Ahn (deceased); married Edward Y H Pai, Apr 20, 1991; children: Grace Pai. **EDUCATION:** University of Chicago, BA, economics, 1981; UCLA School of Law, JD, 1990. **CAREER:** Thelen, Marrin, Johnson & Bridges, associate, 1990-. **ORGANIZATIONS:** Korean American Bar Association, community services committee, co-chair, special programs committee, co-chair; Asian Pacific Alumni of UCLA; WORK. **HONORS/AWARDS:** Asian Pacific American Legal Center of Los Angeles, Pro Bono Service Award, 1992; State Bar of California, The Wiley W Manuel Award for Pro Bono Legal Services, 1993. **SPECIAL ACHIEVEMENTS:** Languages: conversational Korean. **BUSINESS PHONE:** (213)621-9800.

PAI, SADANAND V.

Research and development manager. Indo-American. **PERSONAL:** Born Aug 13, 1937, Cochin, Kerala, India; son of Vittal and Radha Pai; married Hymavathy Pai, Aug 27, 1969; children: Sonia. **EDUCATION:** Madras University, BSc, 1957; Banaras Hindu University, BPharm, 1961, MPharm, 1962; Washington State University, PhD, 1968. **CAREER:** University of Illinois, research associate, 1967-69; McGill University, lecturer, 1969-76; Wastex Industries, lab director, 1976-79; Gulf South Research Institute, senior chemist, 1979-80; Allied-Signal Corp, envir chem, manager, 1980-86; Fujisawa USA, R & D, manager, 1986-. **ORGANIZATIONS:** American Chemical Society, 1968-; American Association for the Advancement of Science, 1968-92; American Association of Pharmaceutical Scientist, 1988-; Parenteral Drug Association, 1990-. **HONORS/AWARDS:** Rho Chi, 1965; Sigma Xi, 1966. **SPECIAL ACHIEVEMENTS:** BPharm Class, 1st in the University, 1960-61; Canadian Heart Foundation, Fellow, 1970-74; Quebec Heart Foundation, Research Award, 1972-74. **HOME ADDRESS:** 152 Post Road, Burr Ridge, IL 60521, (708)323-0758. **BUSINESS ADDRESS:** Manager, Fujisawa, USA, Inc, 2045 N Cornell Ave, Melrose Park, IL 60160, (708)547-2367.

PAI, VENKATRAO K.

Chemical company executive. Indo-American. **PERSONAL:** Born Jan 7, 1939, Coondapoor, Karnataka, India; son of U Krisharaya Pai & U Devaki Pai; married Vasanti Pai, Aug 28, 1977; children: Athma. **EDUCATION:** University of Bombay, India, BS, chem eng, 1961; Northwestern University, MS, chem eng, 1963, PhD, chem eng, 1965. **CAREER:** American Cyanamid Company, Cytec Industries, process development, director, currently. **ORGANIZATIONS:** AIChE; ACS. **BUSINESS ADDRESS:** Director, Process Development, American Cyanamid Co/Cytec Industries, 1937 W Main St, Stamford, CT 06904, (203)321-2582.

PAIK, HO JUNG

Educator. Korean American. **PERSONAL:** Born Mar 25, 1944, Seoul, Republic of Korea; son of In Kee Paik and Young Pal Choi; married Minja, Sep 6, 1969; children: Ellen, Terri. **EDUCATION:** Seoul National University, BS, physics, 1966; Stanford University, MS, physics, 1970, PhD, physics, 1974. **CAREER:** Stanford University, research associate, 1974-78; University of Maryland, assistant professor, 1978-83, associate professor, 1983-89, professor, 1989-. **ORGANIZATIONS:** American Physical Society, 1978-. **HONORS/AWARDS:** Alfred Sloan Foundation, Sloan Fellowship, 1981-83. **SPECIAL ACHIEVEMENTS:** 33 papers in refereed journals; 39 papers in conference proceedings; 9 papers in books; 2 patents. **BUSINESS ADDRESS:** Professor, Dept of Physics, University of Maryland, College Park, MD 20742, (301)405-6086.

PAIK, WOON KI

Educator. Korean American. **PERSONAL:** Born Mar 2, 1925, Naju-City, Chulla-Namdo, Republic of Korea; son of Nam-Sung Paik and Bu-Ik Kim Paik; married Sangduk Kim Paik, Jun 15, 1959; children: Margaret S Paik Blacker, Dean D, David C. **EDUCATION:** Yonsei University School of Medicine, Korea, MD, 1947; Dalhousie University, Canada, MSc, 1956. **CAREER:** National Institutes of Health, visiting scientist, 1958; University of Ottawa, associate professor, 1963; Temple University, professor, 1972-. **ORGANIZATIONS:** American Society of Biological Chemists; American Association of Cancer Research; American Association for the Advancement of Science; New York Academy of Science. **HONORS/AWARDS:** Korean Medical Association of America, Distinguished Scholar and Scientist Award, 1989; Korean Government, Prime Minister Award, 1991. **SPECIAL ACHIEVEMENTS:** Protein Methylation, John Wiley & Sons, 1980; Protein Methylation, CRC Press, 1990; over 220 refereed journal publications; organizing committee member for many international conferences for Formaldehyde or S-Adenosyl-L-methionine. **HOME ADDRESS:** 7818 Oak Ln Rd, Cheltenham, PA 19012, (215)635-5737.

PAK, KOON YAN

Biochemist. Chinese American. **PERSONAL:** Born Aug 9, 1950, Canton, People's Republic of China; son of Chi-Chung Pak and Siu So Mui; married Siu Chun Pak; children: Victoria, Edward. **EDUCATION:** SUNY, Plattsburgh, BA, 1974; University of Pittsburgh, MS, 1977; Memphis State University, PhD, 1981; University of Pennsylvania, postdoctoral, 1983. **CAREER:** Mallinckrodt, immuno chemist, 1983-85; Centocor, sr research scientist, 1985-89, Research & Development, asst dir, 1989-93; Molecular Targeting Technology Inc, co-founder, CEO, president, 1993-; Asia Mira, co-founder, CEO, president, 1993-. **ORGANIZATIONS:** Chinese-American Society of Nuclear Medicine, president, 1992-93, secretary-treasurer, 1990-92; Society of Nuclear Medicine, 1984-; Society of Clinical Bioscientists in America, 1989-. **SPECIAL ACHIEVEMENTS:** Co-inventor: 7 patents in New Radio Phamaceuticals; organizer: Second Sino-American Nuclear Medicine Conference, Beijing, China, 1991; World Chinese Conference of Nuclear Medicine, Wuxi, China, 1993. **HOME ADDRESS:** 41 Craig Lane, Malvern, PA 19355, (215)251-0574.

PAK, PETER HUI-MUN

Physician. Korean American. **PERSONAL:** Born Feb 13, 1963, Seoul, Republic of Korea; son of Chrysostom C & Marianne Y Pak. **EDUCATION:** Johns Hopkins University, BA, 1985; Harvard Medical School, MD, 1989. **CAREER:** Massachusetts General Hospital, medical resident, 1989-92; Saint Agnes Hospital, part-time attending physician, 1992-; Johns Hopkins Hospital, senior clinical fellow, 1992-. **ORGANIZATIONS:** American Medical Association, 1985-; Massachusetts Medical Society, 1985-. **HONORS/AWARDS:** Johns Hopkins University, Phi Beta Kappa, 1988; American College of Cardiology, Merck Fellow, 1994. **BUSINESS PHONE:** (410)955-3116.

PAK, RONALD YU-SANG

Educator. Chinese American. **PERSONAL:** Born Aug 23, 1957, Hong Kong; married Doris, Aug 1987. **EDUCATION:** California Institute of Technology, PhD, 1985. **CAREER:** University of Colorado, Boulder, assistant professor, 1985-91, associate professor, 1991-. **ORGANIZATIONS:** American Society of Civil Engineers; Organization of Chinese Americans. **HONORS/AWARDS:** National Science Foundation, Presidential Young Investigator, 1989; Association of Professional Engineers of Ontario, Gold Medal, 1979. **BUSINESS ADDRESS:** Professor of Civil Engineering, University of Colorado, Campus Box 428, Boulder, CO 80309-0428, (303)492-8613.

PAK, YONG CHIN

Educator. Korean American. **PERSONAL:** Born in Seoul, Republic of Korea; married Hye; children: Sue, Glen. **EDUCATION:** Korean Judo College, BA; Iowa State University, MA. **CAREER:** Iowa State University, professor, currently. **ORGANIZATIONS:** National Collegiate Tae Kwon Do Association, president; Sate of Iowa Tae Kwon Do Association, PR. **HONORS/ AWARDS:** Amoco Outstanding Teacher Award, 1983; Iowa State, Outstanding Faculty. **SPECIAL ACHIEVEMENTS:** Martial arts seminars, demos, clinic; author, "A Fighting Chance," Self Defense, p 29, January 6, 1991. **MILITARY SERVICE:** Korean Army. **HOME ADDRESS:** 3118 Eisenhower, Ames, IA 50010, (515)233-6844. **BUSINESS PHONE:** (515)294-5966.

PAKVASA, SANDIP

Educator, scientist. Indo-American. **PERSONAL:** Born Dec 24, 1935, Bombay, India; son of Sirish V Pakvasa and Sumitra S Pakvasa; married Heide-Marie, Nov 19, 1993. **EDUCATION:** M S University of Baroda, BSc, 1954, MSc, 1957; Purdue University, PhD, 1966. **CAREER:** Syracuse University, res assoc, 1965-67; University of Hawaii, assistant professor, 1968-70, associate professor, 1970-74, professor, 1974-; University of Wisconsin, Madison, visiting professor, 1978; CERN, Switzerland, visiting associate, 1982; KEK, National Lab for High Energy Phys, Japan, visiting professor, 1983, 1989; Tata Institute Fund Res, Bombay, visiting professor, 1983; University of Melbourne, Australia, visiting professor, 1986. **ORGANIZATIONS:** American Physical Society, fellow, 1976-; Sigma Xi, 1966-; Indian Physics Association. **HONORS/AWARDS:** Japan Society for Promotion of Science, fellowship, 1981, 1985. **SPECIAL ACHIEVEMENTS:** Over 100 publications in scientific journals, 1969-; over 30 publications in conference proceedings, 1970-; co-editor of 7 conference proceedings, 1967, 1975, 1977, 1979, 1985, 1992, 1993. **BUSINESS ADDRESS:** Professor of Physics, University of Hawaii, Watanabe Hall, 2505 Correa Rd, Honolulu, HI 96822, (808)956-2970.

PAL, PRATAPADITYA

Museum curator. Indo-American. **PERSONAL:** Born Sep 1, 1935, Sylhet, Bangladesh; son of Gopesh C Pal & Srimati Bidyut Kana Pal; married Chitralekha Pal, Apr 20, 1968; children: Shalmali, Lopamudra. **EDUCATION:** University of Delhi, St Stephen's College, BA, 1956; University of Calcutta, MA, ancient Indian history, 1958, DPhil, 1962; Cambridge University, Corpus Christi College, PhD, 1965. **CAREER:** American Academy of Benares, sr research associate, 1966-67; Museum of Fine Art, Boston, keeper of the Indian collection, 1967-69; Marg Magazine, general editor, 1993-; Los Angeles County Museum of Art, senior curator, 1970-. **HONORS/AWARDS:** Asiatic Society Calcutta, Bimala Churu Law Memorial Gold Medal, 1993; Association of Indians in America, Honoree, 1992; Asiatic Society Bombay, Honorary Fellowship, 1991; 11th Annual Conference of Bengalis, DC, Honoree, 1991; Calcutta University, Gold Medal, 1958. **BUSINESS ADDRESS:** Senior Curator, Los Angeles County Museum of Art, 5905 Wilshire Blvd, Los Angeles, CA 90036, (213)857-6091.

PALAMAND, KRISHNA

Company executive. Indo-American. **PERSONAL:** Born Jan 11, 1933, Bangalore, Karnataka, India; son of Hanumantha Rao Palamand and Sharadamma Palamand; married Leela, Feb 7, 1964; children: Venkatesh. **EDUCATION:** BM Sreenivasaiah College of Engineering, BSME, 1955. **CAREER:** Mysore Kirloskar Ltd, methods engineer, 1957-64; MICO (Division Robert Bosch Co), industrial engineer, 1967-70; ACF Industries, inductrial engineer, 1970-83; Palamand Corp, chief executive officer, 1983-. **SPECIAL ACHIEVEMENTS:** Bought an ongoing business, converted it from Jigs and Tools to a defense oriented industry manufacturing high precision parts for the aircraft industry. **BUSINESS ADDRESS:** CEO, Palamand Corp, 3216 Woodson Rd, St Louis, MO 63114, (314)427-7000.

PAN, DAWNING

Computer consultant. Chinese American. **PERSONAL:** Born May 31, 1945, Shanghai, China; son of Mr and Mrs Chia-Wang Pan; married Susan S Pan, Sep 16, 1972; children: Christina W, Alexander W. **EDUCATION:** University of California, Berkeley, BA, physics, 1968; Harvard University, MS, applied physics, 1969, PhD, applied physics, 1974. **CAREER:** IBM, advisory system engineer, 1974-. **ORGANIZATIONS:** Houston Chinese Community Center, board of directors, 1993-; Harvard Alumni Association, 1974-; Chinese Professional Club in Houston, 1985-; United States Tennis Association, 1990-; Phi Beta Kappa, 1968-. **HONORS/AWARDS:** IBM, several technical excellence awards; Harvard University, fellowships; University of California, scholar-

ships. **SPECIAL ACHIEVEMENTS:** Fluent in 3 Chinese dialects: Mandarin, Shanghainese, and Cantonese; Chinese American Petroleum Association, Technology Conference, 1993; papers: "An Overview of AIX," "IBM RISC System/6000 Workstations and Some Technical Applications.". **HOME ADDRESS:** 8810 Linkpass Ln, Houston, TX 77025, (713)660-0888. **BUSINESS PHONE:** (713)940-2643.

PAN, FUNG-SHINE

Educator. Taiwanese American. **PERSONAL:** Born Jul 4, 1951, Tainan, Taiwan, China; married. **EDUCATION:** National Taiwan University, Taipei, Taiwan, BA, 1973; National Chengchi University, Taipei, Taiwan, MBA, 1976; Northeastern University, MA, economics, 1980; University of California, Berkeley, PhD, finance, 1986. **CAREER:** University of Texas, Austin, assistant professor of finance, 1986-90; California State University, Hayward, associate professor of finance, 1990-. **BUSINESS ADDRESS:** Professor, Dept of Management and Finance, California State University, Hayward, CA 94542-3000, (510)881-3306.

PAN, WEI-PING

Educator. Taiwanese American. **PERSONAL:** Born Sep 9, 1954, Taipei, Taiwan; son of Ta-Ching Pan and Li-Chun Wong; married Nancy Pan, Dec 24, 1984; children: Gene, Alice. **EDUCATION:** Michigan Technological University, PhD, 1986. **CAREER:** Western Kentucky University, Chemistry Dept, Sumpter Professor, currently. **ORGANIZATIONS:** American Chemical Society; North American Thermal Analysis Society; Sigma Xi. **HONORS/ AWARDS:** Western Kentucky University, Research and Creative Award, 1991, Ward Sumpter Professorship, 1992. **SPECIAL ACHIEVEMENTS:** Author of 50 publications. **BUSINESS ADDRESS:** Sumpter Professor, Dept of Chemistry, Western Kentucky University, Bowling Green, KY 42101, (502)745-5322.

PAN, YUH-KANG

Educator. Chinese American. **PERSONAL:** Born Feb 14, 1936, Guangzhou, Guangdong, China; son of S Y Pan and L C Pan; married Su Chiang Pan; children: Irene, Elsie. **EDUCATION:** National Taiwan University, BSc, 1959; Michigan State University, PhD, 1966. **CAREER:** Harvard University, research associate, 1967-68; Stuttgart University, Germany, visiting professor, 1973-74; Max Planck Institute, Germany, visiting professor, 1974-75, 1978-79; Boston College, professor, 1967-. **ORGANIZATIONS:** National Association of Chinese Americans, president, 1986-90; Science Technology Review, editorial board, 1979-; Journal of Molecular Science, editorial board, 1982-. **HONORS/AWARDS:** Honorary Professor of 31 different universities and institutes, 1978-89. **SPECIAL ACHIEVEMENTS:** Over 100 scientific papers and four books, 1956-. **BUSINESS ADDRESS:** Professor, Dept of Chemistry, Boston College, 140 Commonwealth Ave, Chestnut Hill, MA 02167, (617)552-3631.

PANDE, GYAN SHANKER

Health care corporation executive. Indo-American. **PERSONAL:** Born Aug 5, 1932, Bareilly, Uttar Pradesh, India; son of K S Pande (deceased) & K D Pande; married Eva Pande, Jun 30, 1972; children: Wayne, Angel. **EDUCATION:** Agra University, India, BSc, 1951; Lucknow University, India, MSc, 1953, PhD, 1958. **CAREER:** University of Lucknow, India, assistant professor, beginning 1955, associate professor, until 1958; Roorkee University, India, lecturer in chemistry, 1958-60; University of Saskatchewan, Canada, research associate, 1960-65; Uniroyal Research Inc, Canada, R&D chemist, 1965-72; Conap Inc, USA, director, R&D, 1972-77; Cordis Corporation, manager, materials eng, 1977-85; Ednap Medical Inc, president, CEO, 1985-. **ORGANIZATIONS:** Biomaterial Society, 1977-; Society of Plastics Engineers, 1977-, chairman, medical plastics division, 1990; American Chemical Society, 1972-; Chemical Society of Canada, 1985-; SAMPE, 1993; IEEE, 1992-. **HONORS/ AWARDS:** SPE, Medical Plastics Division, Speaker's Award, 1989; American Chemical Society, Speaker's Award, 1984. **SPECIAL ACHIEVEMENTS:** Several publications on polymers for medical devices, chemical reactions, etc; several patents. **BUSINESS ADDRESS:** President and CEO, Ednap Medical Inc, 3759 NW 16th St, Bays 1 and 2, Lauderhill, FL 33311, (305)584-6630.

PANDE, KRISHNA P.

Engineering company executive. Indo-American. **PERSONAL:** Born Jan 3, 1946, Basti, Uttar Pradesh, India; son of Ram M Pandey & Sheetla Pandey; married Malti Pande, Jun 6, 1973; children: Aru, Pari. **EDUCATION:** Indian Institute of Technology, PhD, 1973. **CAREER:** Rensselaer Polytechnic Institute, research associate, 1975-79; Rutgers University, assistant professor, 1979-

81; Bendix/Allied-Signal, manager, technical staff member, 1981-86; Sperry/Unisys, director, 1986-88; COMSAT, associate executive director, executive director, 1988-93; Microwave Signal, Inc, executive vp, general manager, 1994-. **ORGANIZATIONS:** IEEE, fellow; APS; NY Academy of Science; NSF/ERC Technology, advisory committee; University of Cincinnati, engineering board; COMSAT Labs, quality council; Hexawave Corp, Howard County, Math/Science Advisory Commission, advisory board member. **HONORS/AWARDS:** Allied-Signal Chairman's Special Recognition Award, Inventor's Award; Sperry Semiconductor, Outstanding Contribution Award. **SPECIAL ACHIEVEMENTS:** Over 75 published papers in the area of semiconductors; three patents. **HOME ADDRESS:** 12200 Galesville Dr, Gaithersburg, MD 20878, (301)990-7526. **BUSINESS ADDRESS:** Executive VP, General Manager, Microwave Signal, Inc, 22300 Comsat Dr, Clarksburg, MD 20871, (301)428-5197.

PANDEY, RAS BIHARI
Educator. Indo-American. **PERSONAL:** Born Mar 31, 1953, Ballia, Uttar Pradesh, India; son of Ram Sagar Pandey and Samudra Pandey. **EDUCATION:** University of Allahabad, BS, 1972, MS, 1974; University of Roorkee, PhD, 1981. **CAREER:** North Carolina State University, visiting assistant professor, 1981-82; Cologne University, Germany, postdoc research associate, 1983; Cambridge University, UK, postdoc research associate, 1983-84; University of GA, postdoc research associate, 1984-85; Jackson State University, assistant professor, 1985-88; University of Southern Mississippi, associate professor, 1988-. **ORGANIZATIONS:** American Physical Society, lifelong member; American Association for the Advancement of Science, 1989-; Mississippi Academy for Science, 1990-; Sigma Xi, 1991-; Sigma Pi Sigma, 1992-. **HONORS/AWARDS:** Alexander von Humboldt Fellowship, 1988. **SPECIAL ACHIEVEMENTS:** Over 50 papers published in various journals. **HOME ADDRESS:** 407 Kensington Dr, Hattiesburg, MS 39402, (601)264-9410. **BUSINESS ADDRESS:** Associate Professor of Physics and Astronomy, University of Southern Mississippi, SS Box 5046, Hattiesburg, MS 39406-5046, (601)266-4485.

PANDIT, GRISH ROY
Business executive. Indo-American. **PERSONAL:** Born Nov 26, 1955, Tanga, United Republic of Tanzania; son of Mohinder and Asha; married Minakshi, Nov 30, 1978; children: Bhavna, Rajan. **EDUCATION:** University of London, associate law. **CAREER:** Eagle Import & Export Inc, president, 1982-. **ORGANIZATIONS:** American Association of Indian Professionals, joint secretary, 1991-92; Indian Business Association, vp, 1993-94, secretary, founding member, 1990-92. **HOME ADDRESS:** 170 Chateau Latour Dr, Kenner, LA 70065. **BUSINESS PHONE:** (504)835-4412.

PANDIT, SUDHAKAR MADHAVRAO
Educator. Indo-American. **PERSONAL:** Born Dec 3, 1939, Gherdi, Maharashtra, India; son of Madhavrao Dhondopant Pandit and Ramabai Madhavrao Pandit; married Maneesha Sudhakar Pandit, May 12, 1966; children: Milind Sudhakar, Devavrat Sudhakar. **EDUCATION:** Poona University, India, BE, mech, 1961; Pennsylvania State University, MS, ind eng, 1970; University of Wisconsin, Madison, MS, statistics, 1972, PhD, mech eng, 1973. **CAREER:** Kirloskar Oil Engines, Poona, trainee engineer, 1961; East Astatic Co Ltd, Bombay, trainee engineer, 1962; Heavy Engineering Corp, Ranchi, engineer, 1962-68; Penn State University, State College, teaching assistant, 1968-70; University of Wisconsin, Madison, res assistant, 1970-73, lecturer, 1973-76; Michigan Technological University, professor, 1976-. **ORGANIZATIONS:** American Society of Mech Engineers, 1976-; Society of Manufacturing Engineers, senior member, 1981-; Institute of Industrial Engineers, senior member, 1982-; Sigma Xi, 1973-. **HONORS/AWARDS:** National Science Foundation, Travel Award, 1977, 1986; Michigan Technological University, research fellowship, 1977-78; American Statistical Association, Senior Research Fellowship, 1993-94. **SPECIAL ACHIEVEMENTS:** Author, Time Series and System Analysis with Applications, J Wiley, 1983; Modal and Spectrum Analysis: Data Dependent Systems in State Space, Wiley Interscience, 1991. **BUSINESS ADDRESS:** Professor, ME-EM Dept, Michigan Technological University, 1400 Townsend Drive, Houghton, MI 49931-1295, (906)487-2153.

PANDYA, AMIT ANANT
Attorney, government official. Indo-American. **PERSONAL:** Born Jul 23, 1950, Rajkot, Gujarat, India; son of Anantprasad J Pandya and Hansaben Pandya; married Cecilia Muñoz, Sep 1, 1991; children: Cristina Muñoz Pandya. **EDUCATION:** Oxford University, BA, 1972; University of Pennsyl-

vania, MA, 1974, MA, 1976; Yale Law School, JD, 1980; Georgetown University, LLM, 1981. **CAREER:** Institute for Public Representation, fellow, 1980-81; National Center for Immigrants' Rights, research director, 1981-83; Political Asylum Project, ACLU, director, 1983-85; private practice of law, attorney at law, 1985-88; National Immigration, Refugee & Citizenship Forum, general counsel, 1988-89; House Government Operations Committee, counsel, 1989-91; House Foreign Affairs Committee, counsel, 1991-. **ORGANIZATIONS:** District of Columbia Bar, 1980-; Missouri Bar, 1987-; Journal of Asian and African Affairs, editorial board, 1989-; World News Report, Inc, board member, 1988-; Webster University, adjunct faculty, 1987-88; Washington University, visiting lecturer, 1988-90; National Immigration, Refugee & Citizenship Forum, board member, 1990-; El Rescate Nova, board member, 1983-85. **HONORS/AWARDS:** Thouron/University of Pennsylvania Fund, Thouron Scholar, 1972-75; New College, Oxford, Exhibition in History, 1969-72. **SPECIAL ACHIEVEMENTS:** Languages: French, Spanish, Hindi-Urdu, Gujarati, Mandarin Chinese; publications: Illegal Immigration—An Alternative Perspective, Georgetown University, 1981; Employer Sanctions—Discriminatory Effects, Georgetown University; The Hands That Feed Us, ACLU, 1986; Salvadorans in the US, ACLU, 1983; various papers on refugee & migration affairs in learned journals on South Asian legal, political & security issues. **BUSINESS ADDRESS:** Counsel, Subcommittee on International Operations, Committee on Foreign Affairs, 2103 Rayburn House Office Building, Washington, DC 20515, (202)225-3424.

PANDYA, DEEPAK N.
Educator, physician. Indo-American. **PERSONAL:** Born Dec 6, 1932, Mangrol, Gujarat, India; son of Narmadashanker Pandya & Rambhaben Pandya; married Bonnie, Nov 12, 1960 (deceased); children: Jay, Dina, Sunita. **EDUCATION:** Indiana State Medical Board, MD, 1963; Ohio State Medical Board, MD, 1964; Case Western Reserve University, postdoctoral fellowship, 1964-66; OHNA Medical College, Surat, India, MD, 1957. **CAREER:** Harvard University School of Medicine, professor of neurology, 1969-; Boston University School of Medicine, professor of anatomy and neurology, 1973-; Bedford VA Hospital, staff internist, professor, 1973-. **ORGANIZATIONS:** American Medical Association, currently; Society for Neuroscience; American Association of Anatomists. **HONORS/AWARDS:** Cajal Club, Outstanding Waste on Cerebal Cortex, 1973, senior scientist, 1990. **SPECIAL ACHIEVEMENTS:** Author, "Friedrich Sanlndes," Cortex 27, p 307-309, 1991; co-author, "Efferent Cortical Connections of Multimodel Cortex of Superior Temporal Sulcus in Rhesus Monkey," J Comp Neurol, 318, p 222-244, 1992; "Laminar Termination of Thalamic, Callosal, and Association Afferents in the Primary Auditory Cortex of the Rhesus Monkey," Experimental Neurol, 119, p 220-239, 1993; "Striatal Connections of the Parietal Association Cortices in Rhesus Monkeys," J Comp Neurol, in press; has carried out research on architecture and connections of cerebral cortex since 1964; published nearly 100 papers; presented studies internationally. **HOME ADDRESS:** 20 Whiting Way, Needham, MA 02192. **BUSINESS PHONE:** (617)275-7500.

PANG, CHAP AIK (JAMES PANG)
Systems analyst. Singaporean American. **PERSONAL:** Born Sep 18, 1959, Singapore, Singapore; son of Chee Poh Pang and Tai Hui Tan; married Ya-Mei Chang, Sep 18, 1988; children: Irene, Arthur. **EDUCATION:** Southern Illinois University, BA, 1985, MSc, 1987. **CAREER:** Hewlett Packard, associate program analyst, 1987-88; 3M Unitek Corp, senior systems analyst, 1989-. **ORGANIZATIONS:** APICS, 1992-. **HONORS/AWARDS:** Southern Illinois University, SIUC-Scholarship, 1984-87. **SPECIAL ACHIEVEMENTS:** Certified in production & inventory management, 1993. **BUSINESS ADDRESS:** Senior Systems Analyst, 3M Unitek Corp, 2724 S Peck Rd, 608 M/S 148, Monrovia, CA 91016, (818)574-4609.

PANG, JAMES. See **PANG, CHAP AIK.**

PANG, KEUM Y.
Educator. Korean American. **PERSONAL:** married Sunjoo Pang; children: David. **EDUCATION:** Yansei University, Korea, BSN, 1962; Royal College of Nursing, certificate, 1967; University of Washington, MA, 1972; Catholic University of America, PhD, 1983. **CAREER:** Niagara University, instructor, 1973-; Catholic University, lecturer, 1984; Howard University, College of Nursing, associate professor, 1984-, College of Medicine, assistant professor of psychiatry, 1992-. **HONORS/AWARDS:** American Anthropological Association, fellow, 1993; NIH, research, 1991-95. **SPECIAL ACHIEVEMENTS:** Book Korean Elderly Women in America, 1991; journal articles, 1989-93; Korean-language proficiency. **BIOGRAPHICAL SOURCES:** Medical An-

thropology Quarterly, Vol 6 (2), pp 178-180; June, 1992; Transcultural Psychiatric Research, Vol 30 (1), pp 71-73. **BUSINESS ADDRESS:** Professor, Howard University, 501 Bryant St, Freedmen Annex I, Washington, DC 20059-0002, (202)806-7459.

PANG, RUBYE-HUEY
Cleric. Chinese American. **PERSONAL:** Born May 18, 1929, Tacoma, WA; daughter of Eddie N Huey & Dorothy Lee Young Hing Huey; divorced; children: Lory Ann, Peter. **EDUCATION:** City University of Seattle, BS, business administration, 1979; Episcopal Diocesan School of Theology, certificate completion, 1990; Clinical Pastoral Education, Virginia Mason Hospital, Seattle, 1991; Pastoral Care, Swedish Hospital, Seattle, 1992; Pacific Institute, Seattle, certified as training facilitator, 1992. **CAREER:** Boeing Co, author-editor, 1959-91; Charismatic Catholic Church of America, priest, apostolic vicar, 1991-; Bellevue Business, freelance writer, 1984-. **ORGANIZATIONS:** City of Bellevue Probation, Bellevue District Court, vol probation counselor, 1988-; American Correctional Chaplains Association, 1991-; Chinese Nursing Home, board of directors, 1985-; Chinese Community & Cultural Center, vice president & board of directors, 1985-; Boeing Employees Good Neighbor Fund, board of trustees, alumni, 1980-; Church Women United, Greater Seattle Unit, 1991-; Church of Mary Magdalene, board of directors, 1992-; Breaking Barriers, Gordon Graham Associates, 1991-; Republican Washington Legislative District 41, precinct committeeman, 1964-94. **HONORS/AWARDS:** US West/King TV, YMCA, Making a Difference, 1988; Seattle Professional Engineering Employees Association, council rep, certificate, training achievement, 1985; King County Probation, Bellevue City Probation, assistant probation counselor, Volunteer Probation Counselor Service Awards, 1985-93; Breaking Barriers Program, Washington State Reformatory for Men, recognition plaque, 1992-93; Boeing Co, Boeing Employees Good Neighbor Fund, Special Service Award, recognition plaque, 1980. **SPECIAL ACHIEVEMENTS:** First Asian-Chinese-American female ordained priest in Catholic Charismatic Church, 1993; first Asian-Chinese-American female to seek Washington State legislative office, 1974; first Asian-Chinese-American female to serve as vp, president, Seattle South Convocation, Episcopal Church, Diocese of Olympia, 1987-88; chaplain for Immigration & Naturalization Service, Detention Center, 1991-; sponsor to United Asian Coalition, Washington State Reformatory for Men, 1989-. **BIOGRAPHICAL SOURCES:** Articles: "Spiritualized Journey...," The Source, Church Council, Seattle, Sept 1990; Washington Teamster, May 23, 1991; "Candidacy for Washington State Legislature," Bellevue Journal American, Republican Call, Sept 1974. **BUSINESS ADDRESS:** Apostolic Vicar, Diocese of the State of Washington, Charismatic Catholic Church of America, Emmaus Community, PO Box 697, Bellevue, WA 98009-0697, (206)746-8015.

PANG, SENG PUANG
Educator. Malaysian American/Chinese American. **PERSONAL:** Born Mar 14, 1953, Malaysia; daughter of King Quan Puang & Keng Hong Chan; married Victor Pang, May 21, 1988. **EDUCATION:** Assunta School of Nursing, Malaysia, nursing diploma, 1976; University of Missouri, Columbia, BSHE, food & nutrition, 1982, MEd, administration & teaching, 1984. **CAREER:** Truman Medical Center, staff nurse, patient education rehabilitation, 1983-84, clinical dietitian, 1984-87; University of Missouri Kansas City, School of Medicine, instructor of nutrition, 1984-87; Menorah Medical Center, assistant clinical nurse manager, 1987-88; MS Delta Community College, director, nursing instructor, 1988-. **ORGANIZATIONS:** MS Association of Practical Nurse Educators, member ar large, 1993-94, 1988-; Health Occupation Educators Association, 1988-, by-laws chairperson, 1993-94; Health Occupation Students Association, advisor, 1988-; Vocational Industrial Club of America, advisor, 1988-; American Dietetic Association, 1982-; American Vocational Association, 1988-; MS Faculty Association for Junior & Community Colleges, 1988-; Northwest District Dietetic Association, 1988-. **HONORS/AWARDS:** Kappa Delta Pi, Honor Society in Education, 1984; Curators Scholarship, 1982-84. **SPECIAL ACHIEVEMENTS:** Author, Why Won't Patients Do What is Best for Them?, Bi-Weekly Beeper, vol V, no 28, Aug 24, 1983; Home Care Manual for Tracheostomy Patients, Planned Patient Education Program, University of MO, 1983; Tube Feeding for Home Use, Planned Patient Education Program, University of MO, 1983; participant in health related community services; nutrition educator for non-English speaking Chinese immigrants. **HOME PHONE:** (601)627-5183. **BUSINESS ADDRESS:** Nursing Instructor/Director, MS Delta Community College, PO Box 1724, Clarksdale, MS 38614.

PANG, SU-SENG
Educator. Taiwanese American. **PERSONAL:** Born Jun 1, 1958, Pun U, Canton, People's Republic of China; son of Tak-Hong Pang & Hei Wong; married Ying-Ying Pang, Jul 20, 1985; children: Alice R, Richard R. **EDUCATION:** National Taiwan University, BS, mechanical engineering, 1980; University of Minnesota, MS, aerospace engineering & mechanics, 1982; University of California, Berkeley, PhD, mechanical engineering, 1987. **CAREER:** Southern University, mechanical engineering, adjunct assistant professor, 1990-91, adjunct associate professor, 1991-; Louisiana State University, mechanical engineering, assistant professor, 1987-91, associate professor, 1991-. **ORGANIZATIONS:** Society of Plastics Engineers, 1989-; American Society for Engineering Education, 1990-; The Association of American-Chinese Professionals, 1990-; The American Society of Mechanical Engineers, associate member, 1987-; Tau Beta Pi National Engineering Honor Society, faculty member, 1988-; Pi Tau Sigma National Mechanical Engineering Honor Society, faculty member, 1987-; Society of Plastics Engineers' Joining of Plastics & Composites Group, Technical Program Committee, 1991-94; The Association of American-Chinese Professionals, board of directors, 1993-. **HONORS/AWARDS:** National Taiwan University, ranked no 1 in mechanical engineering department, 1980; Pi Tau Sigma, Best Teaching Associate/Assistant in UC Berkeley ME Department, 1985-86; Louisiana State University, Ned Adler Award, Outstanding Faculty Award in ME Department, 1987; UC Berkeley Fellowship, 1984-85; International Rotary Club, scholarship, 1979-80. **SPECIAL ACHIEVEMENTS:** Published 44 technical papers in refereed journals and conference proceedings, 1985-; author/co-author of 21 technical reports, 1988-; co-author of 1 US patent, 1991; principal investigator/co-investigator for 13 research projects, with total grants exceeding $1.5 million, 1988-; chaired sessions in 6 technical conferences; reviewed technical papers, etc. **BUSINESS ADDRESS:** Associate Professor, Dept of Mechanical Engineering, Louisiana State University, Baton Rouge, LA 70803, (504)388-5892.

PANG, WILMA
Vocalist, music instructor. Chinese American. **PERSONAL:** Born Nov 22, 1940, Hong Kong; daughter of Chu Ching Pang and So Jun Pang; divorced; children: Gheeva Chung-Tom, Ghava Chung-Huie, Leeva Chung. **EDUCATION:** San Francisco State University, MA, 1974. **CAREER:** City College of San Francisco, music instructor, 1976-; San Francisco Arts Commission, neighborhood arts organizer, 1980-82; Sino Broadcasting Corp, English program director, 1988-; Music in Schools Today, music specialist, 1992-; California Arts Council, music specialist, 1992-. **ORGANIZATIONS:** Chinese Culture Center, 1990-93; Tung Sen Benevolent Association, English secretary, 1993; California Arts Council/State Local Partnership, multicultural committee, 1980-85. **HONORS/AWARDS:** California Arts Council, artist-in-residence, 1981-82, 1992-93; Sino Broadcasting Corp, Teacher of the Year, 1989. **SPECIAL ACHIEVEMENTS:** Languages: Mandarin, Cantonese: Radio On-Air English Instructor, 1988-; performer of Chinese traditional folksongs, US and China tour. **BIOGRAPHICAL SOURCES:** "Flying Dragon, Flowing Stream," R Riddle, UCLA, p 183; "Opera, West and East," Opera America. **HOME ADDRESS:** 958 Jackson Street, San Francisco, CA 94133, (415)296-8701.

PANJWANI, VISHNU
Export company executive. Indo-American. **PERSONAL:** Born Sep 16, 1950, Yamunanagar, Haryana, India; son of Hariram and Mohini; married Pooja, May 20, 1977; children: Christopher, Nicole. **EDUCATION:** Chemical Engineering Institute, PU Chandigarh, BSc, chemical engineering, 1972; Department of Management, PU Patiala, MBA, 1974; Eastern Michigan University, MSIS, 1984. **CAREER:** Domino's Pizza, project manager, 1984-89; Citizens Insurance Co, system analyst, 1990-92; ABC International Inc, president, currently. **ORGANIZATIONS:** Beta Gamma Sigma. **BUSINESS ADDRESS:** President, ABC International, Inc, 1145 Henlon Circle, Saline, MI 48176, (313)429-2203.

PANLILIO, ADELISA LORNA
Medical epidemiologist. Filipino American. **PERSONAL:** Born Jan 23, 1949, Manila, Philippines; daughter of Filadelfo Panlilio & Elsie Belle Nessia Panlilio; married Andrew Eilers, Jun 25, 1993. **EDUCATION:** Radcliffe College, AB, 1969; State University of New York, Downstate Medical College, MD, 1973; Harvard School of Public Health, MPH, 1988. **CAREER:** Columbia Presbyterian Medical Center, resident, 1973-75; State University of NY, Downstate Medical Center, fellow, 1975-77; American Red Cross Blood Services, Nashville, medical director, 1977-87; Centers for Disease Control & Prevention, medical epidemiologist, 1988-. **ORGANIZATIONS:** American

Association of Blood Banks, 1977-91; Physicians for Social Responsibility, 1982-; Nashville Academy of Medicine, 1977-87; Tennessee Medical Association, 1977-87. **HONORS/AWARDS:** Alpha Omega Alpha, 1972; American Medical Women's Association, scholastic achievement, 1973. **MILITARY SERVICE:** US Public Health Service, commander, 1988-; Commendation Medal, 1992. **BUSINESS ADDRESS:** Medical Epidemiologist, Centers for Disease Control and Prevention, 1600 Clifton Rd, NE, Mail Stop A-07, Atlanta, GA 30333, (404)639-1547.

PANNU, DAVE S.
Structural engineer. Indo-American. **PERSONAL:** Born Jan 15, 1941, Ballo, Panjab, India; son of Basant Singh Pannu and Laj kaur; married Adele M Pannu, May 18, 1983; children: John. **EDUCATION:** Panjab University College, FSc, 1960; Panjab Engineering College, BSc, civil engineering, 1964. **CAREER:** SGS (Iran Ltd), senior civil structural engineer, 1976-78; Sir M MacDonald & Partners, senior structural engineer, 1978-79; consultant, consulting engineer, 1981; independent consultant engineer, London, 1981-82; A&B Engineers, consulting structural engineer, 1982-. **ORGANIZATIONS:** Structural Engineering Association of California, 1985-. **HOME PHONE:** (310)513-6767. **BUSINESS ADDRESS:** Principal, A&B Engineers, 3423 Investment Boulevard, Suite 201, Hayward, CA 94545, (510)785-4896.

PAO, CHIA-VEN
Educator. Chinese American. **PERSONAL:** Born Aug 10, 1933, Ho-Hsien, An-Whei, China; married Mei-Shan Kao Pao, Apr 27, 1963; children: Gene S, Bing S, Phillip S. **EDUCATION:** National Taiwan University, BS, 1959; Kansas State University, MS, 1962; University of Pittsburgh, PhD, 1968. **CAREER:** Kansas State University, research assistant, 1961-62; Westinghouse Electric Corp, engineer, 1962-67; University of Pittsburgh, post doctorate, 1969; North Carolina State University, professor, 1969-. **ORGANIZATIONS:** Society for Industry and Applied Mathematics, 1969-; American Mathematical Society, 1969-78. **HONORS/AWARDS:** Principal lecturer at numerous universities in Europe and China; principal speaker at professional conferences. **SPECIAL ACHIEVEMENTS:** Author, Nonlinear Parabolic and Elliptic Equations, Plenum Press, 1992; more than one hundred papers published in various professional journals. **BIOGRAPHICAL SOURCES:** World Journal, Chinese, p A22, May 10, 1933. **BUSINESS ADDRESS:** Professor, Dept of Mathematics, North Carolina State University, Box 8205, Harrelson, Raleigh, NC 27695-8205, (919)515-7453.

PAPASANI, SUBBAIAH VENKATA
Educator. Indo-American. **PERSONAL:** Born Jul 1, 1943, Karumanchi, Andhra Pradesh, India; son of Papasani Ratnamma and Papasani Venkaiah; married Subbalakshmi, 1965. **EDUCATION:** Indian Institute of Science, Bangalore, PhD, 1971. **CAREER:** Rush Medical College, professor of medicine, 1985-. **ORGANIZATIONS:** American Heart Association; American Association for the Advancement of Science; American Chemical Society. **SPECIAL ACHIEVEMENTS:** Published over 60 papers on biochemistry of lipids and lipoproteins; grants from National Institutes of Health, American Heart Association, various others. **BUSINESS ADDRESS:** Professor of Medicine, Rush Medical College, 1653 West Congress Parkway, Chicago, IL 60612.

PARATE, NATTHU SONBAJI
Government official, educator, consultant. Indo-American. **PERSONAL:** Born Oct 17, 1936, Nagbhir, Maharashtra, India; son of Sonbaji Fagoji Parate and Bijabai Parate; married Pushpa, Aug 7, 1969; children: Sachin, Sanjay, Milind. **EDUCATION:** Saugar University, BE, 1961; Sheffield University, UK, MEng, 1965; Ministry of Power & Natl Coal Board, UK, CCM, 1967; Ecole Polytechnique Lab & Paris University, PhD, 1968. **CAREER:** Ecole Polytech Lab, Paris, res engineer geomech, 1968-69; Laval University, Canada, postdoctoral fellow, rock fracture, 1969-70; Can Intl Develop Agency & Govt, Niger, 1970-73; PNP Intl, sr engineer, 1973-75, consultant, 1979-82, currently, president, currently; Waterloo University, visiting prof, geomech & environ engineering, 1975-77; Pennsylvania Pub Utility Commission, mgt res assoc & engineer, 1977-79; Tennessee State University, assoc prof, 1982-86; TVA, prin investigator, 1984-85; Texas A&M University, Prairie View, visiting prof, 1986-; United Nations, consultant, infrastructure-environment-geotechnology, Maputo, Mozambique, 1993; NASA-MSFC, AL. **ORGANIZATIONS:** Intl Soc of Rock Mechanics; Assn of Geoscientists for Intl Development; American Soc of Civil Engineering. **HONORS/AWARDS:** Numerous professional and academic awards and prizes. **SPECIAL ACHIEVEMENTS:** Canadian and United Nations expert and adviser; speaks many languages; established a precedence in academic constitutional right for professors in grading students,

1989, Parate vs Isidor. **BUSINESS ADDRESS:** Consultant and President, PNP Intl, 7801 Shoal Creek Blvd #107, Austin, TX 78757.

PAREKH, NAVNIT M.
Company executive. Indo-American. **PERSONAL:** Born Aug 5, 1935, Bombay, India; married Saroj R Shah, Dec 31, 1961; children: Ketan, Renu Joshi, Bina Raghavan, Madhvi Oelerich. **EDUCATION:** Bombay University, India, BText, 1957; Lowell Institute of Technology, MS, engineering, 1958. **CAREER:** Paul Dosier Associates, dir, intl marketing, 1981-83; self-employed, investment and real estate company executive. **HOME ADDRESS:** 941 Dahlia Ave, Costa Mesa, CA 92626.

PARIKH, HEMANT BHUPENDRA
Chemical engineer. Indo-American. **PERSONAL:** Born May 11, 1951, Baroda, Gujarat, India; son of Bhupendra Parikh and Nirmala Parikh; married Sushma, May 1, 1977; children: Deepa, Riki. **EDUCATION:** M S University of Baroda, BSChE, 1973; New York University, MS, applied science, 1980; Polytechnic Institute of New York, MSChE, 1980; Fairleigh Dickinson University, MS, computer science, 1987. **CAREER:** GSFC, process design engineer, 1973-83; Stepan Co, proc/proj engineer, 1983-90; Henkel Corp, senior process engineer, 1990-91; International Specialty Products, GAF Chemicals, senior process engineer, 1991-. **ORGANIZATIONS:** AIChE, 1983-; ISA, 1989-. **HONORS/AWARDS:** Gujarat State, Merit Scholarship, 1967-73; New York University, research assistantship, 1978-80. **SPECIAL ACHIEVEMENTS:** Aerodynamics of Hypersonic Vehicle, AIAA, 1980; 2 patents. **BUSINESS ADDRESS:** Senior Process Engineer, International Specialty Chemicals, 1361 Alps Rd, Bldg 1, Wayne, NJ 07470, (201)628-3384.

PARIKH, INDU
Pharmaceutical executive. Indo-American. **PERSONAL:** Born Jan 20, 1937, Bhavnagar, India; married Emma Parikh; children: Rayan. **EDUCATION:** University of Zurich, PhD, 1965. **CAREER:** National Institutes of Health, 1968-70; Johns Hopkins School of Medicine, 1970-75; Burroughs Wellcome Co, 1975-86; Glaxo Inc, 1986-90; University of North Carolina School of Medicine, Department of Medicine, adjunct professor of pediatric endocrinology, 1987-92; Research Triangle Pharmaceuticals Ltd, vice president, 1990-. **ORGANIZATIONS:** American Chemical Society, 1968-90; American Society of Pharmacology and Experimental Therapeutics, 1972-; American Society for Biochemistry and Molecular Biology, 1978-; Controlled Release Society, 1978-; International Society for Biorecognition Technology, treasurer, 1979-91, executive council, 1979-; American Association of Pharmaceutical Scientists, 1990-; Association for Research in Vision and Ophthalmology, 1991-. **HONORS/AWARDS:** Monsanto Company, Postgraduate Fellowship Award, 1961-63; Geigy Co, Postgraduate Fellowship, 1963-65; Alopecia Areata Research Foundation, board of directors, 1983-; National Academy of Sciences, India, honorary member, 1989-; Society of Biological Chemistry, honorary life member, 1989. **SPECIAL ACHIEVEMENTS:** More than 100 scientific publications; co-editor of a book; served on the editorial boards of three scientific journals, 1987-92. **BUSINESS ADDRESS:** Vice President for Research and Development, Research Triangle Pharmaceuticals Ltd, 4364 S Alston Ave, Ste 201, Durham, NC 27713, (919)361-2277.

PARIKH, KIRIT GIRISHCHANDRA
Consulting company executive. Indo-American. **PERSONAL:** Born Sep 6, 1942, Rajpipla, Gujarat, India; son of Girishchandra Sakerlal Parikh and Chandramati Girishchandra Parikh; married Jyoti Kirit Parikh, Mar 31, 1970; children: Neil Kirit. **EDUCATION:** Birla Engineering College, BE, 1964; University of Wisconsin, Madison, MS, 1966. **CAREER:** Nassaux-Hemsley Corp, engr, 1966-67; Peter F Loftus Corp, engr, 1967-74; Bechtel Power Corp, sr engr, project engr, 1974-88; K&M Engineering & Consulting Corp, sr vice pres, 1988-. **ORGANIZATIONS:** National Society of Professional Engineers, 1993; State of Pennsylvania, registered professional engr, 1978. **HOME ADDRESS:** 8405 Plum Creek Dr, Gaithersburg, MD 20882, (301)869-6314. **BUSINESS ADDRESS:** Senior Vice President, K&M Engineering and Consulting Corp, 2001 L St NW, Ste 500, Washington, DC 20036, (202)728-0390.

PARIKH, PRAVIN P.
Auditor. Indo-American. **PERSONAL:** Born Sep 4, 1929, Baroda, Gujarat, India; son of Panalal K Parikh and Kalavatiben P Parikh; married Jyotsna P Parikh, Apr 24, 1956; children: Dipti, Nimisha, Prena, Shri, Krishna. **EDUCATION:** MS University, Baroda, BA, 1956; Gujarat University, Bcom; Appalachian State University, MA, accounting, auditing, 1970. **CAREER:** Chawnak Area Develop, administration aide, 1971; Agriculture T&T, business associate,

1972; North Carolina State, Office of Economic Opportunity, fiscal officer, 1972; Fayetteville State University, business instructor, 1973; North Carolina State, Department of Revenue, field auditor, 1974-. **ORGANIZATIONS:** Hindu Center, board of trustees, 1981-84, auditor, chairperson, 1980-81. **HOME ADDRESS:** 814 E Woodlawn Rd, Charlotte, NC 28209, (704)527-0192.

PARIKH, RAJEEV N.
Educator, educational administrator. Indo-American. **PERSONAL:** Born Oct 12, 1950, Bombay, Maharashtra, India; son of Natvarlal C Parikh & Gulab N Parikh; married Carol E McMahon, Aug 29, 1975; children: Monica. **EDUCATION:** Indian Institute of Technology, BTech (honors), 1972; SUNY, Buffalo, PhD, 1982; Institute of Management Accountants, CMA, 1987. **CAREER:** Carborundun Co, division controller, 1978-80; Cliffstar Corp, chief financial officer, 1980-82; St Bonaventure University, professor, 1982-, director, MBA Program, 1990-. **ORGANIZATIONS:** American Finance Association, 1975-; American Accounting Association, 1975-; Institute of Management Accountants, 1985-; Colden Zoning Board of Appeals, chair, 1989-; Financial Executives Institute, 1993-. **HONORS/AWARDS:** Institute of Management Accountants, Robert Beyer Gold Medal, 1987; Indian Institute of Technology, Silver Medal in General Proficiency, 1972. **SPECIAL ACHIEVEMENTS:** Co-author, World Accounting, vol I, II, III, Matthew Bender & Co, 1987, 1989, 1990. **BUSINESS ADDRESS:** Director, MBA Program, Professor, St Bonaventure University, PO Box 108, St Bonaventure, NY 14778-0108, (716)375-2277.

PARIKH, ROHIT J.
Educator. Indo-American. **PERSONAL:** Born Nov 20, 1936, Palanpur, Gujarat, India; son of Shashikala & Jivanlal Parikh; married Carol Parikh, May 15, 1968; children: Vikram, Uma. **EDUCATION:** Harvard College, AB, 1957; Harvard University, PhD, 1962. **CAREER:** Stanford University, instructor, 1961-63; Panjab University, reader, 1964-65; Bristol University, lecturer, 1965-67; Boston University, professor, 1967-82; City University of New York, distinguished professor, 1982-. **ORGANIZATIONS:** TARK Inc, president, 1992; LICS '89, program chair, 1988-89; TARK '89, program chair, 1988-89; International Journal of Foundations of Computer Science, managing editor, 1987-; Society of Indian Academics in America, executive committee, 1987-89, 1992-; Boston Logic Colloquium, director, 1972-80. **SPECIAL ACHIEVEMENTS:** Parikh's theorem cited in several text books; other well known work in nonstandard analysis, proof theory, dynamic logic and logic of knowledge; reading knowledge of six languages. **BUSINESS ADDRESS:** Professor, Dept of Computer Science, City University Graduate Center, 33 W 42nd St, New York, NY 10036.

PARIKH, RUPESH N.
Systems analyst. Indo-American. **PERSONAL:** Born Nov 23, 1963, Baroda, Gujarat, India; son of Naun Parikh and Mrudula Parikh; married Shilpa; children: Nisha. **EDUCATION:** University of California, San Diego, BS, chemical engineering, 1984. **CAREER:** EDS, systems engineer, 1985-88; self-employed, owner, 1989-91; IBM, project manager, system analyst, 1991-. **HOME ADDRESS:** 841 Ladera Corte, San Ramon, CA 94583.

PARK, BYUNGWOO
Educator. Korean American. **PERSONAL:** Born Oct 10, 1958, Seoul, Republic of Korea; son of Min Sik Park and Joon Soon Shin; married Kyunghee Ahn, Jun 12, 1984; children: Helen Hejin, James Eujin. **EDUCATION:** Seoul National University, BS (with honors), 1981; Pennsylvania State University, MS, 1984; Harvard University, PhD, 1989. **CAREER:** Pennsylvania State University, research assistant, 1982-84; Harvard University, research assistant, 1985-89; IBM, TJ Watson Research Center, post-doctoral research fellow, 1989-91; California Institute of Technology, research fellow, 1991-92; Georgia Institute of Technology, assistant professor, 1992-. **ORGANIZATIONS:** Materials Research Society; American Physical Society; The Minerals, Metal and Materials Society; ASM International. **HONORS/AWARDS:** Harvard University, Division of Applied Sciences Fellowship, 1984-85. **SPECIAL ACHIEVEMENTS:** Co-author: "Development of Fluctuations into Domains During Ordering in Fe3Al," Phys Rev Lett, 68:1742, 1992; "Comment on Calculation and Simulation of Chemical-Diffusion Coefficients: The Inadequacy of Mean-Field Theory," Phys Rev Lett, 68:1438, 1992; "Kinetics of True Mean-Field Ising Models and Langevin Equation: A Comparison," Phys Rev B, 46:5079, 1992. **BUSINESS ADDRESS:** Assistant Professor, Georgia Institute of Technology, School of Materials Science and Engineering, Bunger-Henry Bldg, Office 250, Atlanta, GA 30332, (404)894-2544.

PARK, CHAN HO
Professional baseball player. Korean American. **PERSONAL:** Born 1973?, Republic of Korea. **CAREER:** Los Angeles Dodgers organization, relief pitcher, 1994-. **BUSINESS ADDRESS:** Professional Baseball Player, Los Angeles Dodgers, 1000 Elysian Park Ave, Los Angeles, CA 90012.*

PARK, CHANG HO
Educator. Korean American. **PERSONAL:** Born in Seoul, Republic of Korea; married. **EDUCATION:** Seoul National University, BS, 1975; State University of New York at Buffalo, MS, 1985; Purdue University, PhD, 1989. **CAREER:** Honam Oil Refinery Co, engineer, 1980-82; University of Minnesota, assistant professor, 1989-. **ORGANIZATIONS:** AIChE, 1982-. **SPECIAL ACHIEVEMENTS:** 20 publications in refereed journals. **MILITARY SERVICE:** RO Korea Army, 1977-80. **BUSINESS ADDRESS:** Asst Prof, Dept of Agr Eng, University of Minnesota, 1390 Eckles Ave, St Paul, MN 55108, (612)625-5770.

PARK, CHUL
Engineer. Korean American. **PERSONAL:** Born Jun 8, 1934, Taegu, Kyongsangpukto, Republic of Korea; son of Hyunjin Park and Harwoon Ryang; married Chyon Sue Son Park, Aug 29, 1992; children: Sora, Pora, Marie. **EDUCATION:** Seoul National University, Seoul, Korea, BS, 1957, MS, 1960; Imperial College of Science and Technology, London, PhD, 1964. **CAREER:** Massachusetts Institute of Technology, visiting engineer, 1971-72; Stanford University, part-time lecturer, 1988-91; NASA Ames Research Center, staff scientist, 1964-. **ORGANIZATIONS:** American Institute of Aeronautics and Astronautics, associate fellow, 1980-. **HONORS/AWARDS:** NASA, Exceptional Scientific Achievement Award, 1990. **SPECIAL ACHIEVEMENTS:** Author, Nonequilibrium Hypersonic Aerothermodynamics. **MILITARY SERVICE:** Korean Air Force, first lieutenant, 1958-61.

PARK, CHUNG I.
Librarian, educator. Korean American. **PERSONAL:** Born Aug 25, 1938, Yongsam-Ri, Kyungnam, Republic of Korea; son of Zung Seek Park & Bong Yee Choo Park; married Jung Yol Yoo Park, Aug 30, 1969; children: Charlotte, Sue, Andrew. **EDUCATION:** Yonsei University, BA, 1961; University of Southern California, MSLS, 1971; University of Illinois, Urbana, post graduate, 1975. **CAREER:** Malcom X College, acquisitions librarian, associate professor, 1972-; Info Digest, editor, writer, 1978-88. **ORGANIZATIONS:** American Federation of Teachers, 1972-; American Library Association, 1971-; American Society for Information Science, 1978-88; World Future Society, 1978-88. **SPECIAL ACHIEVEMENTS:** Advertisement Digest: Library and Information Services, 1979; Bestsellers & Best Choices, annual, 1980-83; Best Books by Consensus, annual, 1984-88; The COINT Reports, Quarterly as reporter, writer, 1980-88; "What Makes a Good Book?," Catholic Library World, Sep/Oct 1987. **HOME PHONE:** (708)965-1456. **BUSINESS ADDRESS:** Librarian/Associate Professor, Malcolm X College Library, 1900 W Van Buren St, Chicago, IL 60612, (312)850-7250.

PARK, CHUNG UK
Educator. Korean American. **PERSONAL:** Born Jun 21, 1940, Jeonju, Cheonbuk, Republic of Korea; son of Chang Keun Park & Soon Duk Kim; married Oksoon Park, Dec 20, 1969; children: Charles, Christopher. **EDUCATION:** Georgetown College, BA, 1966; University of Missouri, Columbia, PhD, 1974. **CAREER:** University of Missouri, Columbia, visiting professor, adjunct professor of biology; Lincoln University, professor of biology, currently. **ORGANIZATIONS:** Missouri Academy of Science, president, president-elect, vice president, Collegiate Division director; University of Missouri, Columbia, Korean Scholarship Foundation, president; American Cancer Society, Missouri Division; American Association for Advancement of Science; Truman Institute for Asian Studies, advisory board; UMC, Alumni Association, Korean Chapter, scholarship fund, advisor. **HONORS/AWARDS:** University of Missouri, College of Arts & Science, Distinguished Service Award; Missouri Academy of Science, Outstanding Service Award; UMC, Korean Chapter, Outstanding Service Award. **SPECIAL ACHIEVEMENTS:** Proficient in Korean. **BIOGRAPHICAL SOURCES:** The Proceedings, Directory and Handbook, 1988-91. **BUSINESS ADDRESS:** Professor, Dept of Math & Science, Lincoln University, 820 Chestnut St, Jefferson City, MO 65101-3537, (314)681-5123.

PARK, DUK-WON

Educator. Korean American. **PERSONAL:** Born Mar 8, 1945, Kyong-buk, Republic of Korea; son of Sung-Ui Park and Sang Soon Han; married Sun-Ja Kim Park, Dec 6, 1975; children: Jeanie, Jason, Eunice. **EDUCATION:** Inha University, Korea, BS, 1967; University of Missouri, Rolla, MS, 1971, PhD, 1975. **CAREER:** D'Appolonia Consulting Engineers Inc, assistant project engineer, 1975-76; West Virginia University, assistant professor, associate professor, 1976-81; University of Alabama, associate professor, professor, 1981-. **ORGANIZATIONS:** Society for Mining, Metallurgy, and Exploration, 1973-; International Society of Rock Mechanics, 1982-. **HONORS/ AWARDS:** US Bureau of Mines, Research Grants, 1983-94; Pittsburg and Midway Coal Mining Company, Research Grants, 1988, 1990; Jim Walter Resources Inc, Research Grants, 1985. **SPECIAL ACHIEVEMENTS:** 73 technical publications, 1975-. **MILITARY SERVICE:** Korean Army, first lt, 1967-69. **BUSINESS ADDRESS:** Professor, Dept of Mineral Engineering, University of Alabama, Box 870207, 203 Bevill Bldg, Tuscaloosa, AL 35487-0207, (205)348-1679.

PARK, HOON

Educator. Korean American. **PERSONAL:** Born Nov 10, 1948, Mokpo, Chunnam, Republic of Korea; son of Pal Chun Park & Ok Yeon Hong; married Young Shim Park, Feb 2, 1980; children: Ki E, Sey H. **EDUCATION:** Hankuk University of Foreign Studies, BA, 1974; Florida State University, MBA, 1983; Georgia State University, PhD, 1988. **CAREER:** Hyundai Heavy & Shipbuilding Co, purchasing manager, 1974-75; East-West Petrochemical, purchasing manager, 1975-77; Dow Chemical, Korea, purchasing manager, 1977-81; Florida Stae University, 1981-83; Georgia State University, instructor, 1986-88; University of Central Florida, associate professor, 1988-. **ORGANIZATIONS:** Association for Global Business, Pacific Area Coordinator, 1990; Academy of International Business, 1986; Academy of Management, 1991. **SPECIAL ACHIEVEMENTS:** Many publications in refereed journals in the area of joint venture management and cross cultural communication & behaviors. **MILITARY SERVICE:** Korean Army, 1971-74. **HOME ADDRESS:** 714 Barrington Circle, Winter Springs, FL 32708, (407)366-2282.

PARK, HUN YOUNG

Educator. Korean American. **PERSONAL:** Born Jan 24, 1951, Seoul, Republic of Korea; son of Heung-Lim Park and Han-nam Cho; married Soo Eae Tae Park, Dec 19, 1976; children: Sung Bae, Christie Eae. **EDUCATION:** Seoul National University, BBA, 1974; Ohio State University, MBA, 1979, PhD, 1982. **CAREER:** Oriental Textile Corp, financial analyst, 1973-74; Ohio State University, instructor, 1980-82, research associate, 1981-82; University of Illinois, assistant professor, 1982-87, associate professor, 1987-; Seoul National University, visiting professor, 1988. **ORGANIZATIONS:** Bureau of Economics and Business Research, research professor, 1987-88; Center for Pacific-Basin Capital Markets, research fellow, 1990-; Center for Study of Futures Markets, research associate, 1988-; Korea-America Finance Association, executive board member, 1992-; Korean-American Economics Association, secretary general, 1994; American Finance Association, 1982-; Financial Management Association, 1982-; Western Finance Association, 1982-; European Finance Association, 1982-. **HONORS/AWARDS:** Chicago Board of Trade, Research Grant, 1985, 1988; Center for the Study of Futures Markets, Research Fellowship, 1988; Korean Securities Association, Research Grant, 1988; Pacific Basin Finance Conference, Best Research Award, 1990. **SPECIAL ACHIEVEMENTS:** Contributor, Economics and Finance Journals, 1982-; a number of invited presentations in the US and abroad, 1982-; introduced in a personal profile column by Korea Economic Newspaper, 1992; Futures Contracts, reported daily under five subtitles in Seoul Daily Economic Newspaper, 1988; developed a special seminar program, Financial Management in a Global Economy, 1992. **MILITARY SERVICE:** Korean Navy, lt, 1974-77. **BIOGRAPHICAL SOURCES:** "Futures Market," Korea Futures Trading Association, Sep 1988, June 1989; Korea Economic Newspaper, June 21, 1992. **HOME ADDRESS:** 2320 Hackberry Ct, Champaign, IL 61821, (217)359-6414. **BUSINESS ADDRESS:** Professor, University of Illinois at Urbana-Champaign, 1206 S 6th St, 340 Commerce W, Champaign, IL 61820-6915, (217)333-0659.

PARK, JAE YOUNG

Educator, nuclear physicist. Korean American. **PERSONAL:** Born May 4, 1930, Chochiwon, Chung-Nam, Republic of Korea; son of Byung-Joo Park and Eup Chu Kim; married Sue Oak, Oct 21, 1951; children: David, Measue Liotta, Paul. **EDUCATION:** Seoul National University, BS, 1952; Rensselaer Polytechnic Institute, MS, 1956; University of North Carolina, Chapel Hill, PhD,

1962. **CAREER:** North Carolina State University, assistant professor, 1962-68, associate professor, 1968-75, professor, 1975-. **ORGANIZATIONS:** American Physical Society, 1962-; American Association of Physics Teachers, 1962-; Korean Physical Society, fellow, 1952-; Sigma Xi, research, 1962-; Sigma Pi Sigma, 1962-; Korean Scientists and Engineers Association in America, past president, 1971-. **HONORS/AWARDS:** National Science Foundation, NATO Senior Fellow in Science, 1973. **SPECIAL ACHIEVEMENTS:** Over 200 publications, invited and contributed papers; over 70 invited talks; University of Giessen, Germany, guest professor, 1980; Kyoto University, Japan, guest scholar, 1982; North Carolina Japan Center, faculty fellow, 1982-; Pohomg Institute of Science and Technology, visiting professor. **MILITARY SERVICE:** Army, Rep of Korea, second lt, 1950-53. **BUSINESS ADDRESS:** Professor, Dept of Physics, North Carolina State University, Hillsborough St, Cox Hall 410C, Raleigh, NC 27695-8202, (919)515-3344.

PARK, JEANNIE

Magazine editor. Korean American. **PERSONAL:** Born 1962, Cincinnati, OH; daughter of Yoon Soo Park and Dju Hyun Park; married David H Chan, 1990. **EDUCATION:** Harvard-Radcliffe College, BA, 1983. **CAREER:** Korea Herald, Seoul, copy editor/reporter, 1984; Time Magazine, reporter/researcher, 1985-89; People Magazine, staff writer, 1989-90, senior writer, 1990-91, associate editor, 1991-92; Entertainment Weekly, senior editor, 1992-. **ORGANIZATIONS:** Asian American Journalists Association, 1987-, national secretary, 1991-93, national board member, 1987-93, New York chapter, founding president, 1987-89. **HONORS/AWARDS:** Phi Beta Kappa, elected member, 1983; Rotary Foundation, Graduate Fellowship, 1983. **BUSINESS ADDRESS:** Senior Editor, Entertainment Weekly, Time Inc, 1675 Broadway, 28th Floor, New York, NY 10019.

PARK, JINWOO

Educator. Korean American. **PERSONAL:** Born Mar 26, 1957, Seoul, Republic of Korea; son of Bong-Kil Park & Hee-Suk Suh; married Young-Eun Park, Nov 19, 1983; children: Jung-Hoon, Sae-Rom. **EDUCATION:** Hankuk University of Foreign Studies, BA, 1981; University of Illinois, Chicago, MBA, 1985; University of Iowa, PhD, 1990. **CAREER:** Federation of Korean Industries, research analyst, 1981-83; University of Iowa, instructor, 1988-90; Kansas State University, assistant professor, 1990-. **ORGANIZATIONS:** American Finance Association, 1987-; Financial Management Association, 1987-; Korean-American Finance Association, 1992-; Beta Gamma Sigma, 1990-; KSU Korean Student Association, advisor, 1992. **HONORS/AWARDS:** University of Iowa, Ponder Fellowship, 1987-88; Kansas State University, Faculty Development Award, 1992, 1993; University of Illinois, dean's list, 1984-85. **SPECIAL ACHIEVEMENTS:** Author, articles in Journal of Financial and Quantitative Analysis, Global Finance Journal, Research in International Business and Finance, and Pacific-Basin Finance Research; presentation of several papers at national or international conferences. **BUSINESS ADDRESS:** Professor, Dept of Finance, Kansas State University, Calvin Hall, Manhattan, KS 66506, (913)532-4372.

PARK, JOON B.

Educator. Korean American. **PERSONAL:** Born Jun 20, 1944, Pusan, Republic of Korea; son of Sung Sub & Jung Ju Park; married Bea Y, Sep 14, 1963; children: Misun, Yoon Ho, Yoon Li. **EDUCATION:** Seoul National University, Seoul, Korea; Boston University, BS (cum laude), 1967; MIT, MS, 1969; University of Utah, PhD, 1972. **CAREER:** University of Washington, Seattle, postdoctorate, 1972-73; University of Illinois, Urbana, visiting assistant professor, 1973-76; Clemson University, assistant professor/associate professor, 1976-81; Tulane University, professor, 1981-83; University of Iowa, professor, 1983-. **ORGANIZATIONS:** Society for Biomaterials, founding member, 1975-; Orthopedic Research Society, 1977-; Biomed Engineering Society, 1991-. **HONORS/AWARDS:** Clemson University, Quattlebaum Research Award, 1980. **SPECIAL ACHIEVEMENTS:** Author of 3 textbooks on biomaterials, by Plenim Publications; editorial board, Journ Biomedical Materials Research, 1980-, Journ Biomedical Materials & Engineering, 1990-, Journ Biomedical-Medinical Behavior, currently, Materials and Engineering, 1990-; editorial board member, Annals Biomedical Engineering, 1990-. **BUSINESS ADDRESS:** Professor, Dept of Biomedical Engineering, University of Iowa, 1212 EB, Iowa City, IA 52242, (319)335-5637.

PARK, KANG H.

Educator. Korean American. **PERSONAL:** Born Oct 14, 1946, Seoul, Republic of Korea; son of Su Kyung & Eui Hyang Park; married Seung H Park, Aug

1, 1974; children: Yung, Boyne. **EDUCATION:** Seoul National University, BA, law, 1969; University of Wisconsin, Madison, masters, public policy, 1975; Southern Illinois University, PhD, economics, 1981. **CAREER:** Economic Planning Board, Korean Government, assistant director, 1969-76; Southeast Missouri State University, professor of economics, 1979-. **HONORS/AWARDS:** National Endowment for Humanities, fellowship, 1985, 1989. **BUSINESS ADDRESS:** Professor of Economics, Southeast Missouri State University, 1 University Plaza, Cape Girardeau, MO 63701, (314)651-2942.

PARK, KAP YUNG
Merchant. Korean American. **PERSONAL:** Born Dec 19, 1957, Republic of Korea; son of Jae I Park & Nam J Park; married Myoung Hwa Park, Jun 2, 1983; children: Lydia Y, Joseph Y. **EDUCATION:** Anne Arundel Community College; RETS Institute of Tech, diploma. **CAREER:** 7-11, manager, 1984-87; Sam's Grocery, owner, 1987-. **ORGANIZATIONS:** Korean American Grocers Association, president, 1992-. **SPECIAL ACHIEVEMENTS:** 7-11, Top Manager in Maryland and Washington, DC, 1986. **HOME ADDRESS:** 7901 Colchester Ct, Pasadena, MD 21122, (410)360-1783.

PARK, LAURA HEYONG
Law student. Korean American. **PERSONAL:** Born Apr 16, 1969, Seoul, Republic of Korea; daughter of Lani B Park and Chun B Park. **EDUCATION:** University of California, Santa Barbara, BA, 1991; Loyola Law School, currently. **CAREER:** Bank of America, teller, customer service rep, 1987-89; Channel Counties Legal Services, legal intern, 1991; California Women's Law Center, summer associate, 1992; Contractors' Surety Co, law clerk, 1992; Horikawa, Ono & Yamamoto, law clerk, 1992-; Roxborough & Associates, law clerk, 1993-. **ORGANIZATIONS:** Korean American Bar Association, 1992-, Law Student Liaison Committee, co-chair, 1993; Korean American Coalition, volunteer, 1991-93; Women's Organization Reaching Koreans, board member, 1992-93; Media Action Network for Asian Americans, board member, 1992-93; Asian Concerns Committee, 1992-93; Japanese American Bar Association, 1992-93; Southern California Chinese Lawyers Association, 1992-93; Korean American Advocates for Justice, co-founder, president, 1993. **HONORS/AWARDS:** Loyola Law School, Loyola Diversity Scholarship, 1992, 1993, 1994; Women's Organization Reaching Koreans, WORK Scholarship, 1992; Korean American Bar Association, KABA Scholarship, 1992; Yong Yun Scholarship, 1990; University of California, Santa Barbara, Senior Excellence for Co-Curricular Activity Award, 1991. **SPECIAL ACHIEVEMENTS:** University of California, Santa Barbara Commencement Speaker, 1991; founder and chair of "Korean Studies Now," Committee, Advocated for and installed Korean studies courses into UCSB curriculum, 1990; several publications in KOREAM Journal, 1992-93; several appearances in American and Asian American media, advocating and representing Asian American issues, 1992-93. **HOME ADDRESS:** 3414 Jasmine Ave, #19, Los Angeles, CA 90034, (310)838-6906. **BUSINESS ADDRESS:** Law Clerk, Law Offices of Roxborough & Associates, 10866 Wilshire Blvd, Suite 1200, Los Angeles, CA 90024, (310)470-1869.

PARK, MYUNG KUN
Educator, author, scientist. Korean American. **PERSONAL:** Born Sep 30, 1934, Suhung, Hwanghae, Republic of Korea; son of Jungjin & Sonnyu; married Issun Kim Park, Jan 21, 1967; children: Douglas Yongwoon, Christopher Yongchul, Warren Yongsun. **EDUCATION:** Seoul National University, Seoul, Korea, premedical course, Diploma, 1956, MD, 1960. **CAREER:** University of Washington School of Medicine, instructor, 1966-68; University of Kansas Medical School, assistant professor, 1973-76; University of Texas Health Science Center, associate professor, 1976-83, professor, 1983-. **ORGANIZATIONS:** Society of Pediatric Research, 1977-; American Society of Pharmacology & Experimental Therapeutics, 1977-; Sigma Xi, 1979-; American College of Cardiology, fellow, 1976-; American Academy of Pediatrics, fellow, 1975-. **HONORS/AWARDS:** Seoul National University, Gold Medal for Academic Excellence, 1960; University of Texas Health Science Center, Excellence in Teaching Award, 1991. **SPECIAL ACHIEVEMENTS:** Books: How to Read Pediatric ECGs, Mosby-Year Book, 1982, 1992; Pediatric Cardiology for Practitioners, Mosby-Year Book, 1984, 1988; Pediatric Cardiology Handbook, Mosby-Year Book, 1991; over 100 publications in medical journals, text books, and biological journals. **BUSINESS ADDRESS:** Professor, Dept of Pediatrics, Head, Division of Cardiology, University of Texas Health Science Center, 7703 Floyd Curl Dr, San Antonio, TX 78284-7804, (210)567-5325.

PARK, OUNYOUNG
Educator. Korean American. **PERSONAL:** Born Mar 3, 1949, Taegu, Republic of Korea; son of Kyeyoon Park and Sunja Choi; married Hwasook Park, Nov 27, 1980; children: Changmo, Lionel. **EDUCATION:** Seoul National University, Korea, BS, 1972; University of Alabama, Huntsville, MS, 1986, PhD, 1988. **CAREER:** Agency for Defense Development, Korea, senior researcher, 1974-84; University of Alabama, Huntsville, research assistant, 1984-88, research associate, 1989; Alabama A&M University, assistant professor, 1990-. **ORGANIZATIONS:** AIAA, 1992-; SAE, 1991-; Korean Scientists & Engineers Association, 1984-. **HONORS/AWARDS:** University of Alabama, Huntsville, Departmental Honor, 1988; Agency for Defense Development, Honorable Achievement, 1980; Seoul National University, Korea, Scholastic Honor, 1972. **SPECIAL ACHIEVEMENTS:** MICOM Report on Combustion Instability, 1989; NASA Report on Combustion Dynamics, 1989; NASA Report on Combustion Dynamics Computer Program, 1988; AIAA paper 88-0542, 1988, 86-0566, 1986. **HOME ADDRESS:** 2605 Excalibur Drive, Huntsville, AL 35803, (205)881-8008.

PARK, SANG OH
Educator, educational administrator. Korean American. **PERSONAL:** Born Jul 23, 1930, Seoul, Republic of Korea; married Alice K Park; children: Diane Rose, David Lee. **EDUCATION:** Florida State University, BA, 1957, MA, 1959; University of North Carolina, PhD, 1962. **CAREER:** Austin College, assistant professor, 1962-63; Clemson University, associate professor, 1963-68; US Dept of Commerce, Bureau of Econ Analysis, senior economist, 1968-82; Christopher Newport University, School of Buiness & Economics, dean, 1989-90; Department of Economics & Finance, chairman, 1988-92, professor of economics, 1982-. **ORGANIZATIONS:** Virginia Consortium for Asian Studies, vice president, 1993-94; Christopher Newport University, Japanese Studies, director, 1988-; Association for Asian Studies, 1990-; Association for Comparative Econ Systems, 1990-; American Economics Association, 1990-; Korean-American Econ Association, board member, 1978-, president, 1971-78. **HONORS/AWARDS:** Earhart Foundation, Senior Fellowship, 1959-62; University of NC, Chapel Hill, Graduate Fellowship, 1961-62; Florida State University, Graduate Fellowship, 1958-59. **SPECIAL ACHIEVEMENTS:** Articles in Asian Economic Journal; book & monograph publications; T.V. presentations & appearances in local T.V. stations; speeches & presentations to various professional associations. **MILITARY SERVICE:** Adjutant General, captain, Bronz Star Medal, Presidential Ribbon, Citations, 1950-55. **BUSINESS ADDRESS:** Professor, Christopher Newport University, 50 Shoe Ln, Newport News, VA 23606, (804)594-7176.

PARK, SEUNG-KYOON
Physician, educator, educational administrator. Korean American. **PERSONAL:** Born Feb 27, 1936, Cholwon, Kang-Won-Do, Republic of Korea; son of Mr & Mrs Hyun-Yang Park; married Yonzi; children: Edward J S, Aileen M S. **EDUCATION:** Seoul National University, College of Arts & Sciences, BS, 1957, Medical School, MD, 1961, Graduate School, MS, 1963. **CAREER:** Erie County Medical Center, clinial director, 1975-79; SUNY, Buffalo, co-director, undergraduate education, 1975-79; Department of Psychiatry, clinical associate professor, 1975-, director, residency training, 1984-; Buffalo VA Hospital, chief, inpatient unit, 1992-. **ORGANIZATIONS:** American Psychiatric Association, fellow, 1967-; Western NY Psychiatric Society, president, 1987-88; American Association of Directors of Psychiatric Residency Training, 1984-; Association of Academic Psychiatry, 1989-; Dae Han Foundation, 1980-, board of directors. **SPECIAL ACHIEVEMENTS:** American Board of Psychiatry & Neurology, examiner, 1979-. **MILITARY SERVICE:** Korean Army, Medical Corps, captain, 1961-66. **BUSINESS ADDRESS:** Clinical Associate Professor, Director, Residency Training Program, SUNY at Buffalo Medical School, ECMC, 462 Grider St, Buffalo, NY 14215, (716)898-4221.

PARK, SIYOUNG
Educator. Korean American. **PERSONAL:** Born Nov 7, 1945, Seoul, Republic of Korea; daughter of Si-In Park; divorced; children: Henry Lee. **EDUCATION:** Seoul National University, BA, 1967, MA, 1970; University of Minnesota, MA, 1972, PhD, 1977. **CAREER:** Western Illinois University, assistant prof, 1977-83, assoc prof, 1983-88, professor, 1988-. **ORGANIZATIONS:** Association of American Geographers; Association of Asian Studies. **HONORS/AWARDS:** Fulbright scholar to China and to Korea. **BUSINESS ADDRESS:** Professor, Dept of Geography, Western Illinois University, Macomb, IL 61455-1328, (309)298-1648.

PARK, SU-MOON
Educator. Korean American. **PERSONAL:** Born Dec 1, 1941, Choong-Ju, Chungbuk, Republic of Korea; son of Haebong & Kannan Park; married Sunhee C Park, Oct 15, 1967; children: Hye-Sun, Min-Sun, Il-Sun Albert. **EDUCATION:** Seoul National University, BS, 1964; Texas Tech University, MS, 1972; University of Texas at Austin, PhD, 1975. **CAREER:** Chung-Ju Fertilizer Corp, Korea, chemist, 1964-67; Yong-Nam Chemical Co, Korea, lab supervisor, 1967-70; Texas Tech University, teaching and research assistant, 1970-72; University of Texas, Austin, research assistant, 1972-75; University of New Mexico, assistant prof, associate prof, professor, 1975-. **ORGANIZATIONS:** American Chemical Society, 1975-; Electrochemical Society, 1974-; Korean Chemical Society, 1967-; Korean Scientists & Engineers Society in America, 1974-. **HONORS/AWARDS:** Associated Western Universities, AWU Fellowship, 1992-93; University of Texas, Austin, Welch Research Fellowship, 1973-75; Texas Tech University, Welch Research Fellowship, 1971-72; Seoul National University, Sam-Sung Scholarship, 1963. **SPECIAL ACHIEVEMENTS:** Over 120 publications in chemistry journals, 1975-; two books published. **BUSINESS ADDRESS:** Prof, Dept of Chemistry, University of New Mexico, Albuquerque, NM 87131, (505)277-2505.

PARK, SUNG-IL (CHRIS)
Financial services company executive. Korean American. **PERSONAL:** Born Mar 21, 1940, Kimpo, Kyunggi-Do, Republic of Korea; son of Bum Ryong Park; married Bong-Im Kil, Aug 17, 1968; children: Kyung-Soo, Kyung-Ah. **EDUCATION:** Seoul National University, BC, 1962; University of Wyoming, Laramie, MS, 1965; University of Michigan, post-graduate studies. **CAREER:** Deloitte & Touche, partner, currently. **ORGANIZATIONS:** Seoul Sang Dae Alumni Association, president, 1980-85, chairman, 1986-90; US-Korea Business Council, 1992-; AICPA, 1971-; NYSSCPA, 1971-. **HONORS/AWARDS:** Korean Chamber of Commerce, Seoul, Award of Appreciation, 1988; Office of National Tax Administration, Korea, Award of Appreciation, 1990; Seoul National University, Award of Appreciation, 1989. **SPECIAL ACHIEVEMENTS:** First Korean immigrant to become partner of a big six accounting firm, 1978. **MILITARY SERVICE:** Military Intelligence Group, Korean Army, corporal, 1961-62. **BIOGRAPHICAL SOURCES:** Korea Economic Daily, numerous articles; Dong-A Daily. **BUSINESS ADDRESS:** Partner, Deloitte & Touche, One World Trade Center, New York, NY 10048, (212)669-5094.

PARK, SUNG-WON SAM
Educator. Korean American. **PERSONAL:** Born Jul 2, 1953, Bonghwa, Kyungbuk, Republic of Korea; son of Tae Ryong Park and Ok Hyang Kim; married Eun-kyung Kim Park, Dec 22, 1979; children: Kyo Hoon, Say Hoon. **EDUCATION:** Hanyang University, South Korea, BE, 1975; University of New Mexico, MS, 1982, PhD, 1985. **CAREER:** Auburn University, assistant professor, 1985-89; Texas A&M University, Kingsville, associate professor, 1989-. **ORGANIZATIONS:** Institute of Electrical and Electronics Engineers, 1985-. **HONORS/AWARDS:** University of New Mexico, Phi Kappa Phi, 1985. **SPECIAL ACHIEVEMENTS:** Registered Professional Engineer in Texas, 1991. **BIOGRAPHICAL SOURCES:** IEEE Transactions on Electromagnetic Compatibility, p 180, May 1988. **HOME ADDRESS:** 7421 Blue Lake Dr, Corpus Christi, TX 78413, (512)850-9220. **BUSINESS PHONE:** (512)595-2638.

PARK, TAE SUNG
Physician, educator. Korean American. **PERSONAL:** Born Jan 19, 1947, Seoul, Republic of Korea; son of Ha Jang Park and Yu Rae Kim; married Hyun Sook Kim, Mar 23, 1976; children: Martha Jefferson, Thomas Jefferson. **EDUCATION:** Yonsei University School of Medicine, MD, 1971. **CAREER:** University of Virginia, clinical professor of neurological surgery; Washington University School of Medicine, Neurological Surgery and Pediatrics, professor, currently; St Louis Children's Hospital, neurosurgeon-in-chief, currently. **ORGANIZATIONS:** American Association of Neurological Surgeons, Pediatric Section, executive committee, 1991-92; National Institutes of Health, neurology study group, 1987. **HONORS/AWARDS:** National Institutes of Health, Teacher-Investigator Development Award, 1984-89, One of the Best Doctors in America, 1993. **SPECIAL ACHIEVEMENTS:** Published 79 peer reviewed papers, 2 books and 20 invited chapters on cerebrovascular physiology and neurosurgery; Child's Nervous System Official Journal, International Society for Pediatric Neurosurgery, editorial board, 1993; published the first scientific paper about the role of adenosine in regulation of neonatal cerebral blood flow in piglets; Journal of Cerebral Blood Flow Metabolism, vol 8, p 822-828, 1988. **HOME ADDRESS:** #6 Brentmoor Park, Clayton, MO 63105, (314)862-0309.

BUSINESS ADDRESS: Professor of Neurological Surgery & Pediatrics, Washington University School of Medicine, St Louis Children's Hospital, One Children's Place, Saint Louis, MO 63110, (314)454-2811.

PARK, TED S.
Service company executive. Korean American. **PERSONAL:** Born Dec 3, 1956, Seoul, Republic of Korea; son of In-Kwan Park and Yeong-Ae Kim; married Jane Yoon, Nov 23, 1985; children: Michelle, Adrienne. **EDUCATION:** SUNY at Buffalo, BS, 1985. **CAREER:** Naval Surface Warfare Center, electrical engr, 1985-89; Professional Hearing Aid Service, hearing aid dispenser, 1989-, president, owner, currently. **BUSINESS ADDRESS:** President, Owner, Professional Hearing Aid Service, 2141 K St NW, Washington, DC 20037, (202)785-8704.

PARK, WON J.
Educator. Korean American. **PERSONAL:** Born Sep 18, 1935, Sunchun, Pyongbul, Republic of Korea; married Chung A Park, Sep 17, 1966; children: David W, Ronald S. **EDUCATION:** Seoul National University, Seoul, Korea, BS, engineering, 1957; University of California, MA, mathematics, 1966; University of Minnesota, PhD, mathematics, 1969. **CAREER:** Seoul National University, Seoul, Korea, visiting professor, 1979; Okayama University of Sciences, Okayama, Japan, visiting professor, 1985; Wright State University, Department of Mathematics & Statistics, assistant professor, 1969-73, associate professor, 1973-81, professor, 1981-. **ORGANIZATIONS:** American Statistical Association, 1970-; Institute of Mathematical Statistics, 1970-; IEEE, Reliability Society, 1988-. **SPECIAL ACHIEVEMENTS:** Author, "A Multi-Parameter Gaussian Process," Ann of Math Statistics 41, 1970; "Weak Convergence of Probability Measure on C[0,1]2," J of Multivariate Analysis 1, 1971; "The Law of Iterated Logarithm for Brownian Sheets," J of Applied Probability 12, 1975; "Symmetric Three Directional Optimal Laminate Design," J of Composite Material 21, 1986; "Goodness of Fit Test for the Power Law Process," IEEE Trans on Reliability, 41, 1992. **BUSINESS ADDRESS:** Professor, Dept of Mathematics and Statistics, Wright State University, Dayton, OH 45435.

PARK, YOUNG WHAN
Architect. Korean American. **PERSONAL:** Born Apr 13, 1936, Seoul, Republic of Korea; son of Wan Sik Park and Myung Soon Ahn; married Sun Kyung Park, Jun 19, 1965; children: Jean H. **EDUCATION:** Miami University, Ohio, BA, 1962; Catholic University of America, MA, 1970. **CAREER:** H D Nottingham & Assoc, Principal Architects, planner, 1969-78; Designtech-East, Ltd, Architects, Engineers, president 1978-. **ORGANIZATIONS:** American Institute of Architects, 1973-; American Institute of Planners, 1972-; American Society of Landscape Architects, 1970-; Korean American Scholarship Foundation, president, national board of directors, chairman; Wesley Foundation Housing Corp, board of directors. **HONORS/AWARDS:** Korean American Scholarship Foundation, Dist Service, 1991; Wesley Foundation, Housing Corp, Dist Service, 1992. **HOME ADDRESS:** 11501 Twining Lane, Potomac, MD 20854. **BUSINESS PHONE:** (301)881-8890.

PARKE, KEOL-BAI
Banker. Korean American. **PERSONAL:** Born Aug 13, 1946, Seoul, Republic of Korea; married Bock-hee Kim, Dec 12, 1976; children: Chong-Young, Chong-Suck. **EDUCATION:** Sung Kyun Kwan University, BA, 1973; California Western School of Law, MCL, 1993. **CAREER:** The Export-Import Bank of Korea, deputy director, legal officer, currently. **SPECIAL ACHIEVEMENTS:** Secured Transactions by Deed of Trust, 1983; ADL International Commercial Arbitration, 1993. **HOME ADDRESS:** 5235 Genesee Cove #45, San Diego, CA 92122, (619)453-4658.

PARKHIE, MUKUND R.
Federal government official, toxicologist. Indo-American. **PERSONAL:** Born Aug 4, 1933, Wardha, Maharashtra, India; son of Raghunath Shridhar Parkhie & Kamalabai Raghunath Parkhie; married Barbara Helene Parkhie, Feb 9, 1969; children: Ravi, Mira, Ram, Shyam. **EDUCATION:** University of Jabalpur, India, BVSc, 1957; Agra University, India, MVSc, 1960; University of Saskatchewan, Canada, MSc, 1963; University of Missouri, PhD, 1970; DVM, educational commission for foreign veterinary graduates, 1972. **CAREER:** Osmania University, India, assistant professor, 1960-61; University of Saskatchewan/Toronto Med School, world university scholar, NRC of Canada, res fellow, 1961-63; Ohio State University, research assistant, 1963-65; University of Missouri, research assistant, 1965-70; US NASA, Aeronautics Lab, National Academy of Sciences, fellow, 1970-72; US Matrix Corp, senior

scientist, 1972-74; US Food & Drug Administration, RDA, clinical pharmacol, toxicologist, 1974-. **ORGANIZATIONS:** US Center for Vet Med, chairperson, monitored adverse drug reaction committee, 1992-; Inter-Agency Committee on Drug Control, 1989-; American Academy of Vet & Comp Toxicology, fellow, 1982-; Sigma Xi, 1969-; American Vet Med Association, 1974-; Society of Toxicology, elected member; Regulatory Affairs Professional Society; Endocrine Society; Aerospace Med Association, associate fellow; Society for Study Reprod; Teratology Society; New York Academy Sciences. **HONORS/AWARDS:** US Food & Drug Administration, Group Recognition Award, 1993, cash performance awards, 1988-93, US National Academy of Sciences, post-doctoral res fellowship, 1970-72. **SPECIAL ACHIEVEMENTS:** Publications in Teratology, Neuroendocrinology, Drug-Interactions, & Comp-Drug Metabolism; ad-hoc reviewer: Teratology; J of the American College of Toxicology; contributed to World Health Organization's Monograph on the Evaluation of Carcinogenic Risk of Chemicals to Humans; proficient in Hindi, Marathi and Urdu; chairperson, Intl Symposium, Role of Trace Elements in Maternal and Child Health, 1993; sr visiting scientist, Medical Research Council, England, 1980-81. **HOME ADDRESS:** 15032 Joshua Tree Rd, North Potomac, MD 20878-2549. **BUSINESS ADDRESS:** Sr Toxicologist, US Food & Drug Administration, 7500 Standish Place, MPN-II, Rm 439E, HFV-216, Rockville, MD 20855, (301)295-1758.

PARK LI, GIMMY
Radio broadcasting administrator. Chinese American. **PERSONAL:** Born Dec 23, 1945, San Francisco, CA; daughter of Joe Park Li and Mae Wong Li; married Xing Chu Wang, Jan 27, 1990. **EDUCATION:** San Francisco State University, BA, English lit, 1968. **CAREER:** KNBR NBC Radio, promotion & merchandising, assistant, 1968-70, community relations, assistant, 1970-76, public service/audience relations, manager, 1977-83, public service, manager, 1983-89; KNBR/KFOG Radio, public service, manager, 1989-. **ORGANIZATIONS:** Asian American Journalists Association, secretary; Golden Gate National Recreation Area, citizens advisory commission; Clay Street Chinatown North Beach YWCA, committee of management; San Francisco County Democratic Central Committee; Chinese American Democratic Club, Inc, past president. **HONORS/AWARDS:** San Francisco Friends of the Human Rights Commission, Eugene Block Journalism Award, 1988, 1991, 1992. **BIOGRAPHICAL SOURCES:** Interview, Womenews, San Francisco Commission on the Status of Women; Asian Week; Directory of Significant 20th Century American Minority Women, Fisk University; Publicity Handbook, by David R Yale, Bantam, 1982. **BUSINESS ADDRESS:** Manager, Public Affairs, KNBR/KFOG Radio, 55 Hawthorne, #1100, San Francisco, CA 94105, (415)995-6829.

PARK-TAYLOR, SONYA SUNNAH
Policy analyst. Korean American. **PERSONAL:** Born Apr 26, 1967, Baltimore, MD; daughter of I James Park and Ock Ryang Pai Park; married Tedford James Park-Taylor, May 2, 1992. **EDUCATION:** Harvard-Radcliffe Colleges, BA, 1985. **CAREER:** Chesapeake Habitat for Humanity, executive director, 1990-92; Joint Commission on Health Care, health policy analyst, currently. **ORGANIZATIONS:** Baptist Center for Women, founding member, 1992-; Alliance of Baptists, board member, 1993-96. **BUSINESS ADDRESS:** Richmond, VA 23221.

PARTHASARATHY, SAMPATH
Scientist, educator. Indo-American. **PERSONAL:** Born Dec 27, 1947, Madras City, Madras, India; son of Kunnathur Sampath & Chella Sampath; married Kalyani Parthasarathy, Nov 24, 1974; children: Raghu, Bharath. **EDUCATION:** University of Madras, India, BSc, 1964-67, MSc, 1967-69; Indian Institute of Science, India, PhD, 1969-74; University of California, professional certificate in management, 1985-86. **CAREER:** University of California, San Diego, assistant professor, 1984-89, associate professor, 1989-92, professor of medicine, 1992-93; Emory University, professor of gynecology, obstetrics, professor of medicine, 1993-; Journal of Lipid Research, associate editor, 1993-. **ORGANIZATIONS:** American Heart Association, fellow, 1984-, grant review committee, 1994-; American Society for Cell Biology, 1980-; American Society for Investigative Pathology, 1993-; Society for Free Radical Research, 1985-; National Institutes of Health, review committee B, 1993-. **SPECIAL ACHIEVEMENTS:** Over 95 scientific publications; over 60 conferences as invited speaker, chairman from all over the world; National Institutes of Health, study section, 1993-; American Heart Association, review section, 1992-. **BUSINESS ADDRESS:** Professor, Dept of Gynecology & Obstetrics, Emory University School of Medicine, PO Box 21246, Atlanta, GA 30322, (404)727-8604.

PARTHASARATHY, TRIPLICANE ASURI
Scientist. Indo-American. **PERSONAL:** Born Apr 17, 1954, Madras, Tamil Nadu, India; son of T A G Krishnan and Vathsala Krishnan; married Shubha Parthasarathy, Jun 2, 1986; children: Sriya. **EDUCATION:** Indian Institute of Technology, Madras, India, BTech, 1976; Ohio State University, MS, 1982, PhD, 1983. **CAREER:** BHEL, India, development engineer, 1977-80; University of Illinois, Urbana-Champaign, assistant professor, 1984-88; UES Inc, senior scientist, 1988-93, principal scientist, 1993-. **ORGANIZATIONS:** The American Ceramic Society, 1988-; The Metallurgical Society, 1981-91; Materials Research Society, 1991-, publication committee, 1992. **HONORS/AWARDS:** Alpha Sigma Mu, elected honorary member, 1982; Phi Kappa Phi, elected honorary member, 1983; University of Illinois, Racheff Teaching Award, 1988. **SPECIAL ACHIEVEMENTS:** Over 50 publications in various materials journals, 1982-. **HOME ADDRESS:** 2493 Christalee Dr, Beavercreek, OH 45434, (513)427-0349. **BUSINESS ADDRESS:** Principal Scientist, UES Inc, 4401 Dayton-Xenia Rd, Dayton, OH 45432-1894.

PARTIDO, ROUSALYN BAUTISTA (ROZ)
State government consultant. Filipino American. **PERSONAL:** Born Sep 6, 1968, Manila, Philippines; daughter of Rogelio Guillermo Partido and Hospicia Bautista Partido. **EDUCATION:** University of California, Santa Cruz, BA, 1990; University of Texas, MPA, 1992. **CAREER:** Friends of Ben Menor, campaign consultant, 1991; Political Research Institute, research consultant, 1991; Creative Rapid Learning Center, program evaluator, 1992; Villa Mills & Associate, program evaluator, 1992-93; California State Legislature, associate consultant, 1993, legislative consultant, 1993-. **ORGANIZATIONS:** Asian Pacific Americans in Higher Education Inc, 1989-92; Council of Philipino-American Organizations Inc, 1992-; Filipinos for Affirmative Action Inc, 1992-; Asian Law Caucus, supporter, 1992-; Philippine Nurses Association, supporter, 1993; Filipino-American Democratic Club, vice president, 1993; Asian Pacific Islander Democratic Club, 1993; Leadership Education for Asian Pacifics, 1993; National Filipino American Council, delegate, 1993. **HONORS/AWARDS:** Alameda County Board of Supervisors, Commendation, 1989; University of California, Santa Cruz, Outstanding Undergraduate, 1989; Woodrow Wilson Foundation, scholarship, 1989-90, fellowship, 1990-92; University of Texas, Austin, Professional Award, 1991-92. **SPECIAL ACHIEVEMENTS:** In progress: Institutionalized Exclusion or Inclusion, BA thesis, 1990; The Hidden Vote: An Analysis of Filipino American Voter Turnout, MPA thesis, 1992. **HOME ADDRESS:** PO Box 721054, San Diego, CA 92172-1054.

PATEL, ANIL J.
Medical technologist. Indo-American. **PERSONAL:** Born Apr 24, 1952, Bhetasi, Gujarat, India; son of Jashbhai D Patel and Madhuben J Patel. **EDUCATION:** Sadar Patel University, V V Neigar, Gujarat, India, BSCh, 1973, MSCh, 1975. **CAREER:** Gujarat Agricultural University, Micronutrient Project, ICAR, sr res asst, 1976-80, soil chemist, asst res scientist, 1980-87; Osborn Lab Inc, lab tech, 1988-90, med tech, 1990-. **ORGANIZATIONS:** Staff Club, secretary, treasurer, 1980-87. **HONORS/AWARDS:** ASCP, 1990; CLA, 1991; Osborn Lab, Silver Award, 1993. **SPECIAL ACHIEVEMENTS:** Co-author: 10 research papers in various soil science journals in India. **HOME ADDRESS:** 13309 W 68th Terrace, Shawnee, KS 66216, (913)962-1478.

PATEL, ANIL S.
Research scientist. Indo-American. **PERSONAL:** Born Jun 28, 1939, Baroda, Gujarat, India; son of Shankerbhai Somabhai Patel and Gangaben Shankerbhai Patel; married Asha, Aug 22, 1992; children: Ravi, Sunil. **EDUCATION:** The M S University of Baroda, India, BS, 1960; Purdue University, MS, 1963; Northwestern University, PhD, 1966; Stanford University, The Graduate School of Business, Stanford Executive Program, 1993. **CAREER:** Northwestern University, postdoctoral fellow & lecturer, Biomedical Engineering Center, 1966-67; Baxter Travenol Laboratories Inc, senior research scientist, 1968-74; Cavitron Corporation, manager of advanced products research, chief scientist, 1974-83; Cooper Vision Inc, manager of advanced products research, chief scientist, 1983-86, director of advanced products research, chief scientist, 1986-89; Alcon Laboratories Inc, director of research, 1989-92, senior director of research, 1993-. **ORGANIZATIONS:** Assn for Research in Vision & Ophthalmology, 1985-; Intl Soc of Refractive Keratoplasty, 1988-; Soc of Biomaterials, 1988-; Assn of the Advancement of Medical Instrumentation, 1978-; American Assn for the Advancement of Science, 1974-; Institute of Electrical & Electronics Engineers, Biomedical Engineering Group, 1966-; American Soc for Lasers in Medicine & Surgery, founding research fellow, 1983-; American National Standard Institute; Intl Standards Organization, IOL Standards Committee,

technical expert, 1988-. **HONORS/AWARDS:** Institute of Neurological Diseases and Blindness, NIH, USA, doctoral and postdoctoral fellowships, 1963-67; University of California at San Francisco, Dept of Ophthalmology, Grand Round Lecture on Intraocular Lenses, 1988; Washington State Technology Center, Seattle, Advanced Bio-Material Research Program, industry consultant to review programs, 1989-92; International Standards Organzation, US representative for intraocular lens standards, 1992-93. **SPECIAL ACHIEVEMENTS:** Holder of 8 US issued patents and several in the IOL field, 1982-; presented and published more than fifty papers in the field of biomedical engineering, 1966-. **HOME ADDRESS:** 4202 Brownwood Ln, Arlington, TX 76017. **BUSINESS ADDRESS:** Senior Director of Research, Alcon Laboratories Inc, 6201 South Freeway, Mail Stop R5-12, Fort Worth, TX 76134-2099, (817)568-6439.

PATEL, APPASAHEB R.
Federal government official. Indo-American. **PERSONAL:** Born Sep 5, 1931, Baroda, Gujarat, India; son of Raojibhai M Patel (deceased) and Vimlaben R Patel (deceased); married Elsebet Wodschow Patel, Aug 1, 1946; children: Michael, Mark, Christopher, Anne, Catherine. **EDUCATION:** University of California, PhD, 1960. **CAREER:** University of California, teaching assistant, 1956-60; University of Virginia, postdoctoral research associate, 1963-; Leo Pharmaceuticals Products, Denmark, research chemist, 1963-64; University of Virginia, postdoctoral research associate, 1965-68; Meloy Laboratories Inc, supervisor, chemistry laboratory, 1968-77; National Cancer Institute, program director for diet/nutrition, 1977-. **HONORS/AWARDS:** National Institutes of Health, Merit Award, 1990. **BUSINESS ADDRESS:** Program Director for Diet/Nutrition, Division of Cancer Etiology, National Cancer Institute, 6130 Executive Boulevard, Executive Plaza North, #535, Rockville, MD 20852, (301)496-9600.

PATEL, ARVINDKUMAR MOTIBHAI
Engineer. Indo-American. **PERSONAL:** Born Oct 19, 1937, Isnav, Gujarat, India; son of Motibhai P Patel and Jibaben M Patel; married Varsha A Patel, May 19, 1963; children: Sandeep, Svasti, Shimman. **EDUCATION:** Sardar Vallabhbhai Vidyapeeth, India, BE, 1959; University of Illinois, MSEE, 1961; University of Colorado, PhD, EE, 1969. **CAREER:** IBM Corporation, fellow, 1986-. **ORGANIZATIONS:** Institute of Electrical and Electronics Engineers, fellow, 1984. **HONORS/AWARDS:** IBM Corporation, Outstanding Innovation Award, 1972, 1973, 1983, 1985, 1992. **SPECIAL ACHIEVEMENTS:** Many publications and patents in the field of coding and its applications to magnetic storage products. **HOME ADDRESS:** 6583 San Ignacio Ave, San Jose, CA 95119, (408)578-5267. **BUSINESS ADDRESS:** IBM Fellow, IBM Corporation, 5600 Cottle Rd, H18/025, San Jose, CA 95193, (408)256-2222.

PATEL, ASHOK R.
Company executive. Indo-American. **PERSONAL:** Born Nov 19, 1942, Napad, Gujarat, India; married Hansa A Patel, May 31, 1964; children: Nimeet, Nehal. **EDUCATION:** Vikram University, Ujjain, India, Bachelor Degree, business, 1962; Indore University, India, Master Degree, business, 1964. **CAREER:** Kiran Clothing Mfg Ltd, vice pres, 1964-68; Four Seasons Ltd, president, 1968-73; Bella Textile Ltd, president, 1973-75; V Y Investment Inc, vice pres, 1975-; Invamed Inc, president, 1983-. **ORGANIZATIONS:** India Cultural Society, 1987-, director, chmn, 1991; Rotary Club, 1985-, director, 1988, asst treasurer, 1989-90. **HONORS/AWARDS:** Rotary International, Paul Harris Fellow, 1993. **BUSINESS ADDRESS:** President, Invamed Inc, #2400, Rte 130 N, Dayton, NJ 08810, (908)274-2400.

PATEL, BHAGVAN H.
Business executive. Indo-American. **PERSONAL:** Born Dec 10, 1942, Gujarat, India; married Mangu B Patel; children: Madhu B, Rajendra B, Amit B. **EDUCATION:** California State University, BS, chemical engineering, 1970. **CAREER:** Amitron Corp, marketing director, printed circuit board, CEO, currently. **HOME ADDRESS:** 6 Stone Brook Ct, South Barrington, IL 60010, (708)426-0127.

PATEL, BHAGWANDAS MAVJIBHAI
Research and development scientist. Indo-American. **PERSONAL:** Born Nov 24, 1938, Rander-Surat, Gujarat, India; son of Mavjibhai Khushalbhai Patel and Diwaliben Mavjihbai Patel; married Manjula B Patel, May 13, 1964; children: Deepti B, Varsha B, Tejas B. **EDUCATION:** Gujarat University, India, BS, 1961, MS, 1963; University of Bombay, PhD, science, 1980. **CAREER:** Govt of India, Bhabha Atomic Research Center, Dept of Atomic Energy, sr scientist, r&d scientist, 1963-84; University of Florida, Gainesville, Dept of Chemistry,

postdoctoral research fellow, 1984-87; University of Florida, Dept of Food Science, research consultant, 1987-90; Texaco Inc, Research & Development Dept, tech coordinator, 1991-. **ORGANIZATIONS:** American Chemical Society, 1984-; Society for Applied Spectroscopy, 1984-. **HONORS/AWARDS:** Intl Atomic Energy Agency, Vienna, Austria, Fellowship, 1971-72; University of Florida, Gainesville, visiting scientist, 1971-72, postdoctoral research consultant, 1984-90; Texaco Inc, Outstanding Star Contributor, 1993. **SPECIAL ACHIEVEMENTS:** Spectrochemical Methods of Trace Analysis, PhD Thesis, 1980; research activities in analytical chemistry, atomic and molecular spectroscopy, chromatography, environmental and industrial applications; over 70 papers and presentations in scientific literature and at natl & intl conferences. **BUSINESS ADDRESS:** Research Scientist, R&D Dept, Texaco Inc, PO Box 1608, Port Arthur, TX 77641, (409)989-6411.

PATEL, BHARAT R.
Physician. Indo-American. **PERSONAL:** Born Apr 21, 1947, Surat, Gujarat, India; son of Ramchandra Patel and Savita Patel; married Vrunda Patel, May 1981; children: Kunjan, Punam. **CAREER:** Stamford Hospital, physician, currently. **ORGANIZATIONS:** American College of Emergency Physicians; AIA, Connecticut Chapter; Stamford Hospital, VIP Club. **HONORS/AWARDS:** American Academy of Family Physicians, fellow. **HOME ADDRESS:** 27 Meredith Ln, Stamford, CT 06903.

PATEL, BHULABHAI C.
Company executive. Indo-American. **PERSONAL:** Born Nov 24, 1948, Navsari, Gujarat, India; son of Chhotubhai M Patel and Jadavben C Patel; married Pushpa B Patel, Dec 14, 1974; children: Nimesh, Reena, Tina. **EDUCATION:** MS University of Baroda, India, DCE, 1969; Tennessee Technological University, MSCE, 1972. **CAREER:** Stone & Webster Engineering Comp, design engineer, 1973-78; Ebasco Engineering Service, design engineer, 1978-79; Neshco Corp, chairman, president, 1979-. **ORGANIZATIONS:** Gujarati Samaj of Atlanta, ex-president, director, 1993-; Indian American Cultural Association, life member; National Federation of Indian Association; Asian American Hotel Owners Association, founder, board of directors; Volunteers for Homeless, founder, board of directors; Summitt National Bank, founder, board of directors. **HONORS/AWARDS:** Stone & Webster Engineering Co, Distinguished Service Award, 1974; Morris Brown College, Minority Small Businessman Award, 1989; President Bush, Community Service Recognition, 1990. **SPECIAL ACHIEVEMENTS:** Co-author, The Management of Small Lodging Facilities, A Practical Guide, in progress. **HOME ADDRESS:** 2304 Ranch Tr, Norcross, GA 30071, (404)448-4832.

PATEL, BHUPEN N.
Government official. Indo-American. **PERSONAL:** Born Mar 21, 1941, Uvarsad, Gujarat, India; son of Nabhubhai Patel and Kankuben Patel; married Usha B Patel, May 1964; children: Parashar B, Abha B. **EDUCATION:** Sardar Patel University, BS, civil, 1964; University of Connecticut, MS, civil, transportation; Hartford Graduate Center/RPI, MS, mgmt, 1990. **CAREER:** Fadia Dalal & Company, project construction engineer, 1964-66; State of Gujarat Minor Irrigation Project, engineer, 1966-70; Purcell Associates, senior engineer, transportation, 1970-74; Capitol Region Council of Government, Hartford, senior transportation planner, 1974-76; Town of Granby, CT, director of community development, 1976-78; City of Hartford, CT, director of transportation, 1978-. **ORGANIZATIONS:** Institute of Transportation Engineer, 1970-; Urban Traffic Engineering Council, ex committee, 1988-89; Town of Newington Planning and Zoning Commission, commissioner, 1984-. **HOME ADDRESS:** 43 Green Ave, Newington, CT 06111. **BUSINESS PHONE:** (203)722-6215.

PATEL, CHANDRA KUMAR NARANBHAI
Educational administrator. Indo-American. **PERSONAL:** Born Jul 2, 1938, Baramati, India; son of Naranbhai Patel and Maniben Patel; married Shela Dixit Patel, Aug 20, 1961; children: Neela, Meena. **EDUCATION:** College of Engineering, Poona, India, BE, telecommunications, 1958; Stanford University, MSEE, 1959, PhD, electrical engineering, 1961. **CAREER:** AT&T Bell Labs, researcher in field of gas lasers, beginning 1963, Research, Materials Science, Engineering and Academic Affairs Div, executive director, until 1993; University of California, Los Angeles, vice chancellor of research, 1993-. **ORGANIZATIONS:** Natl Academy of Science, council member, 1988-91, executive committee, 1990-91, vp, currently, president, 1995; Natl Academy of Engineering; Indian Natl Science Academy, foreign fellow; Third World Academy of Sciences, associate fellow; IEEE, fellow; APS, fellow, council member, 1987-91, executive committee, 1987-90; OSA, fellow; American Academy of

Arts and Sciences, fellow; AAAS, fellow. **HONORS/AWARDS:** Optical Society of America, Lomb Medal, 1966, Towne's Medal, 1982, Ives Medal, 1989; Franklin Institute, Ballantine Medal, 1968; Coblentz Prize, 1974; Assn of Indians in America, Honor Award, 1975; IEEE, Lamme Medal, 1976, Medal of Honor, 1989; NAE, Zworykin Award, 1976; Laser Institute of America, Schawlow Award, 1987; American Physical Society, Pake Prize, 1988; New Jersey Institute of Technology, ScD, 1988. **SPECIAL ACHIEVEMENTS:** Discoverer of the laser action on the vibrational-rotational transitions of carbon dioxide, 1963; inventor of efficient vibrational energy transfer between molecules, 1964; over 180 publications in the field of lasers and applications of lasers to spectroscoopy, industry, pollution detection, and medicine; 37 patents in lasers and optics. **BIOGRAPHICAL SOURCES:** Laser Pioneers, by Jeff Hecht, Academic Press, p191-204. **BUSINESS ADDRESS:** Vice Chancellor of Research, University of California, Los Angeles, 405 Hilgard Ave, 2138 Murphy Hall, Los Angeles, CA 90024-1405, (310)825-7943.

PATEL, CHANDRAKANT B.
Geohydrologist, environmental consultant. Indo-American. **PERSONAL:** Born Sep 20, 1959, Navsari, Gujarat, India; son of Bhanabhai C Patel and Maniben B Patel; married Anjana C Patel, Nov 23, 1988. **EDUCATION:** Indiana University at Indianapolis, BS, geology, 1982. **CAREER:** VS Engineering, civil engineering consultant, 1986-90; Indiana Dept of Environmental Management, project mgr, 1990-92; Envirocorp, geohydrologist, 1992-. **ORGANIZATIONS:** National Groundwater Assn, 1991-; Gujarat Samaj of Houston, 1992-. **HOME ADDRESS:** 1371 Edenderry Lane, Missouri City, TX 77459, (713)261-5986. **BUSINESS ADDRESS:** Geohydrologist, Envirocorp Services and Technologies, Inc, 7020 Portwest Dr, Ste 100, Houston, TX 77024, (713)880-4640.

PATEL, CHANDRAKANT J.
Software development manager. Indo-American. **PERSONAL:** Born Jan 14, 1947, Nakuru, Kenya; son of Jashbhai Motibhai Patel; married Raksha, Nov 23, 1972; children: Zena C, Aneka C. **EDUCATION:** Lanchester Poly, BSc, 1970; Warwick University, MSc, 1972. **CAREER:** Marconi-Space & Defense, systems engineer, 1973-75; NEI-RP Automation, control system development designer, 1975-82; BNR/NT, S/W development designer, 1982-87, S/W/DMS development manager, 1987-. **ORGANIZATIONS:** IEEE, 1969-. **HOME ADDRESS:** 3605 Longbow Ln, Plano, TX 75023.

PATEL, CHANDU K.
Engineer. Indo-American. **PERSONAL:** Born Jul 1, 1931, Chikhodra, Gujarat, India; son of Kashibhai Mangalbhai Patel and Dahiben Kashibhai Patel; married Maniben Maganbhai, May 5, 1948; children: Geeta Mahesh, Kiran C, Tina Harshad. **EDUCATION:** Gujarat University, Birla Engineering (Birla Vishwakarma Mahavidyalay), BE, civil, 1956; Roorkee University, India, soil mech & foundation eng, 1961; McGill University, orthotropic struct & plastic design str. steel, 1970. **CAREER:** M N Dastur & Co Ltd, senior engr, 1956-65; Foundation of Canada Engr Co, section engr, 1965-74; C D Howe Co, senior engr, 1974-77; Stadler Hurter Ltd, senior engr, 1977-79; H K Ferguson, senior engr, 1979-82; G & T Associates Inc, president/CEO, 1982-. **HOME ADDRESS:** 19776 Braemar Way Oval, Strongsville, OH 44136, (216)572-0536. **BUSINESS ADDRESS:** President, CEO, G & T Associates Inc, 11925 Pearl Road, Suite 401, Strongsville, OH 44136, (216)572-0555.

PATEL, CHANDU M.
Auditor. Indo-American. **PERSONAL:** Born Dec 25, 1937, Narsanda, Gujarat, India; son of Maganbhai Patel; married Sharda, May 1962; children: Kaushika, Hitesh. **EDUCATION:** Vallabh Vidyanagar, BS, accounting, 1961; MS, advance accounting costing, 1963. **CAREER:** City of New York, accountant, 1973-80, associate management auditor, 1980-92, associate accountant, 1992-. **ORGANIZATIONS:** Cultural Heritage of India, vice president/treasurer, 1990-; Bochasanwasi Swaminarayan Sanstha, vice president/treasurer, 1977-; BSS, NJ, vice president/treasurer, 1991-92. **HOME ADDRESS:** 78-19 268th St, Floral Park, NY 11004, (718)470-0157.

PATEL, DEEPAK M.
Business manager. **PERSONAL:** Born Oct 17, 1948, Bombay, Maharashtra, India; son of Mohanlal M Patel; married Anjana D Patel, Apr 25, 1974; children: Sejal D, Tejas D. **EDUCATION:** Roosevelt University, MS, marketing communication, 1982. **CAREER:** Courtesy Manufacturing Co, purchase manager, 1984-. **ORGANIZATIONS:** Manav Seva Mandir, executive secretary, 1992-. **HONORS/AWARDS:** Courtesy Manufacturing Co, SPC Control,

1992. **HOME ADDRESS:** 1804 N Drury Ln, Arlington Heights, IL 60004, (708)392-8691.

PATEL, DILIPKUMAR Z.
Production manager. Indo-American. **PERSONAL:** Born Apr 30, 1957, Baroda, Gujarat, India; son of Zaverbhai M Patel; married Dakshaben D Patel, Oct 3, 1981; children: Rushin D. **EDUCATION:** M S University, Baroda, India, BS, 1979, MS, 1981. **CAREER:** Gujarat State, India, project officer; Nessor Alloy, QC inspector; Andin Intl, production mgr, currently. **HOME ADDRESS:** 958 Townley Ave, Union, NJ 07083, (908)964-8407.

PATEL, DINESH
Orthopaedic surgeon. Indo-American. **PERSONAL:** Born Jan 1, 1936, Sojitra, Gujarat, India; son of Gokalbhai Patel; married Kokila, Dec 1965; children: Neha, Mona, Paresh. **EDUCATION:** BJ Medical College, India, MBBS, 1962; Massachusetts General Hospital, Harvard Medical School, orthopaedic surgery residency, 1967-71. **CAREER:** Massachusetts Institute of Technology, lecturer; Harvard University, assistant clinical professor, orthopaedic surgery, currently; Massachusetts General Hospital, chief of arthroscopic surgery, 1978-. **ORGANIZATIONS:** Indian American Forum for Political Education, chairperson, 1992-94; Board of Registration in Medicine, chairperson, 1990-92; Federation of State Medical Brothers, board of directors, 1993. **HONORS/AWARDS:** Japanese Arthroscopic Society, 1st Official Foreign Guest, 1991; Gujarat Orthopaedic Society, honorary member, 1991; National Orthopaedic Society Mexico, Official Guest and Lecturer, "Orthopaedic 2001," 1991; Orthopaedic Society Brazil, Official Guest, 1991. **BUSINESS ADDRESS:** Physician, Massachusetts General Hospital, ACC 510, 15 Parkman St, Boston, MA 02114, (617)726-3555.

PATEL, HIREN S.
Bank executive. Indo-American. **PERSONAL:** Born Dec 27, 1950, Bombay, India; son of Sarabhai Patel. **EDUCATION:** Gaston College, electronics associate, 1971. **CAREER:** National Republic Bank of Chicago, bank chairman, currently. **BUSINESS ADDRESS:** Chairman, National Republic Bank of Chicago, 1201 W Harrison, Chicago, IL 60607, (312)738-4900.

PATEL, INDRAVADAN R.
Chemical company executive. Indo-American. **PERSONAL:** Born Nov 24, 1942, Ahmedabad, Gujarat, India; son of Ramanlal Patel; married Sushila, May 4, 1965; children: Bhrugang, Kesuri. **EDUCATION:** Gujarat University, BS, 1962, MS, 1964; Wayne State University, MS, 1966. **CAREER:** Abbott Chemical Co, chemist, 1967-70; Peerless Chemical Co, chemist, 1970-72; Foster Chemical Co, technology director, 1972-74; Abso-Clean Chemical Co, technology director, 1974-77; Labtech Corp, president, 1977-. **ORGANIZATIONS:** Gujarati Samaj of Detroit, 1977-; Jain Society of Detroit, 1981-; CSMA, 1981-93. **HONORS/AWARDS:** Dow Chemical, Certificate of Achievement, 1972. **BUSINESS ADDRESS:** President, Labtech Corporation, 7707 Lyndon, Detroit, MI 48238, (313)862-1737.

PATEL, JAY M.
Businessman. Indo-American. **PERSONAL:** Born Dec 9, 1953, Harare, Zimbabwe; son of Morarjibhai Patel & Madhuben Patel; married Ranjan, May 30, 1978; children: Jayesh, Sonica. **EDUCATION:** Indiana State University, BSc, accounting, 1980. **CAREER:** Deloitte & Touche, senior auditor, 1981-83; Coman Inc, president, 1983-. **ORGANIZATIONS:** US Field Hockey Association, vice president, teams, coaching, 1992-; Cheyenne Village Inc, president, 1991-92; North End Commercial Association, president, 1986; National Federation of Indian Associations, vice president, 1991; Early Bird Field Hockey Association, 1986-; American Institute of Certified Public Accountants, 1982-; Colorado CPA Society, 1983-; Asian American Hotel Owners Association, board member, 1993-. **HONORS/AWARDS:** El Paso County, District 11, Business School District Partnership, 1992-. **SPECIAL ACHIEVEMENTS:** Language proficiency in English, Gujerati, Hindi, and Shona; CPA, 1981. **BUSINESS ADDRESS:** President, Coman Inc, 4604 Rusina Rd, Colorado Springs, CO 80907, (719)599-7503.

PATEL, JAYANT P.
Company executive. Indo-American. **PERSONAL:** Born May 21, 1957, Kamuli, Bojoga, Uganda; son of Purshottam G Patel and Shantaben P Patel; married Kalpana J Patel, Feb 3, 1981; children: Monika, Nikki. **EDUCATION:** BJVM, Vidyanagar, India, BBA, 1978. **CAREER:** Milplex Circuits, president, 1981-. **HONORS/AWARDS:** BJVM, Gold Medal, 1st Class First, 1978; SP University, Gold Medal, 1st class first, 1978. **BUSINESS AD-**

DRESS: President, Milplex Circuits Inc, 1301 W Ardmore Ave, Itasca, IL 60143, (708)250-1580.

PATEL, JAYANTI R.
Engineer. Indo-American. **PERSONAL:** Born Jul 6, 1947, Nairobi, Kenya; son of Rambhai Patel; married Rama Patel, Feb 25, 1973; children: Amie, Aarti. **EDUCATION:** Poona Engineering College, BE, 1970; MIT, ME, 1972. **CAREER:** Rotron EG&G, aerodynamics engineer, 1972-77; IBM, staff engineer, 1978-82; Pall Corp, engineering group leader, 1983-. **HOME ADDRESS:** 110 West Tarpon Ave, Tarpon Springs, FL 34689, (813)937-6121. **BUSINESS ADDRESS:** Engineering Group Leader, Pall Corp, 10540 Ridge Rd, New Port Richey, FL 34654-5198, (813)849-9999.

PATEL, JITENDRA B (JAY)
Research scientist. Indo-American. **PERSONAL:** Born Apr 18, 1942, Bombay, India; son of Balkrishna R Patel; married Yogini, Jun 21, 1969; children: Neil, Rina. **EDUCATION:** LM College of Pharmacy, BS, 1965; University of Kansas, MS, 1968; St John's University, PhD, 1977. **CAREER:** Schering Plough, senior scientist, 1968-78; ICI Pharmaceutical, research scientist, 1978, senior scientist, 1980-87; Zeneca Pharmaceutical, principal scientist, 1987-. **ORGANIZATIONS:** American Society of Pharmacology & Exp Therapeutics, 1982; Society of Neuroscience, 1983; New York Academy of Science, 1982; Rho Chi, honorary Pharmacy Society. **SPECIAL ACHIEVEMENTS:** Registered pharmacist, NY and MA, 1975. **BUSINESS ADDRESS:** Principal Scientist, Zeneca Pharmaceutical Company, Concord Pike & Murphy Road, 212 BMRD, Wilmington, DE 19897, (302)886-8035.

PATEL, KALYANI
Physician. Indo-American. **PERSONAL:** Born Oct 15, 1965, Balisna, Gujarat, India; daughter of Harji and Narmada Patel. **EDUCATION:** State University of New York at Binghamton, BS, 1987; UMDNJ, Robert Wood Johnson Medical School, MD, 1991; Hospital of the University of Pennsylvania, 1992-. **CAREER:** University of Pennsylvania Hospital, physician, currently. **BUSINESS ADDRESS:** Physician, Dept of Anesthesia, Hospital of the University of Pennsylvania, 3400 Spruce St, Philadelphia, PA 19104.

PATEL, KAMLA
Government official. Indo-American. **PERSONAL:** Born Nov 19, 1929, Lonavla, Maharashtra, India; daughter of Madhuram Kapur and Sadakaur Kapur; married Chandrakant Baburao Patel, Jan 17, 1953 (divorced); children: Anil, Arun. **EDUCATION:** University of Poona, India, BS, philosophy, (honors), 1951, MS, experimental psychology, 1954; University of Calcutta, India, PhD, psychology, 1964; University of Georgia, 1978; University of Utah, 1981; National Defense University, executive programs, 1991-92; University of Pennsylvania, executive programs, 1991-92, Cambridge University, England, Merit University Scholarships, four year scholar. **CAREER:** State of Utah, consultant, 1979-81; US Dept of Army, program mgr, 1981-83, operations research analyst, 1983-87, director, information management, 1989-91, special asst, office of CIO, 1991-92, special asst, business re-engineering, 1992-; US Army Corps of Engineers, chief, information management, 1987-89. **ORGANIZATIONS:** Intl Organization for Giftedness, Research Council, chairman; Indian Applied Psychology Association, regional president. **HONORS/AWARDS:** US Army, Exceptional Performance and Sustained Superior Performance Awards; Fulbright Hays, US Government Senior Fulbright Fellow; Ford Foundation, fellow; Cullum Foundation, fellow; United Nations Educational, Scientific & Cultural Organization, fellow; American Association of University Women, International Woman of the Year, Ida Hayes Award; Utah State Women's Legislative Council; Cambridge University, England, Merit University Scholarships, four year scholar. **SPECIAL ACHIEVEMENTS:** Over 80 publications, reports and presentations in professional career. **HOME ADDRESS:** 1950 Kirby Rd, Mc Lean, VA 22101.

PATEL, KANTI L.
Real estate company executive. Indo-American. **PERSONAL:** Born Feb 17, 1951, Morogoro, United Republic of Tanzania; son of Labbubhai Patel & Laxmiben Patel; married Mradula Patel, Mar 11, 1978; children: Rupal, Nehal. **EDUCATION:** Norwich City College, England, ACII, 1971. **CAREER:** Elkay Enterprises, owner/principal, currently. **ORGANIZATIONS:** FIA, Hotel & Motel Committee, chair; City of Oakland, International Trade, commissioner, CEDAC, commissioner; India Club, SF; Commonwealth Club, SF; Oakland Board of Realtors; Oakland Chamber of Commerce, board of directors; First Indo-American Bank, SF, board of directors. **HONORS/AWARDS:** Mayor of Oakland, NFIA, special recognition, 1992. **SPECIAL ACHIEVE-**

MENTS: Distributed blankets to earthquake victims, Oct 1989; housed refugees from Uganda during 1972 exodus in UK; participant in the festival American Folk Life, 1776-1976; Bicentennial held at Washington DC, 1976. **HOME ADDRESS:** 7716 Skyline Blvd, Oakland, CA 94611.

PATEL, KANTILAL P.
Auditor. Indo-American. **PERSONAL:** Born Feb 14, 1935, Viramgam, Gujarat, India; son of Punjabhai H Patel and Maniben P Patel; married Sushila K Patel, Dec 7, 1958; children: Sameer K, Anish K. **EDUCATION:** University of Bombay, India, BA, 1956, MA, 1958, LLB, 1959; University of Scranton, MBA, 1977. **CAREER:** NY State Dept of Social Services, auditor, 1977-78; US Dept of Commerce, auditor, 1978-85; US Dept of Education, auditor, 1985-. **ORGANIZATIONS:** Assn of Government Accountants & Auditors, New York Chapter, 1978-. **HOME ADDRESS:** 94-18 134th St, South Richmond Hill, NY 11419-1630, (718)526-3956. **BUSINESS ADDRESS:** Auditor, US Dept of Education, Office of Inspector General, 26 Federal Plaza, Rm 3739, New York, NY 10278, (212)264-6584.

PATEL, KIRAN K.
Chemical company director. Indo-American. **PERSONAL:** Born Dec 29, 1955, Baroda, Gujarat, India; son of Kantibhai M Patel and Indumat K Patel; married Sukirtee K Patel, Oct 23, 1983; children: Ruchita, Paven. **EDUCATION:** SP University, India, BS, 1976, MS, 1978. **CAREER:** Eastern Resins & Chemical, chemist, 1982-85, 1986-88; NY City Narcotics Laboratory, chemist, 1985-86; TACC International, sr chemist, 1988-91; Bacon Industries, technical director, 1991-. **BUSINESS ADDRESS:** Technical Director, Bacon Industries, 192 Pleasant St, Watertown, MA 02172, (617)926-2550.

PATEL, KISHOR N.
Laboratory director. Indo-American. **PERSONAL:** Born Mar 4, 1955, Ambach, Gujarat, India; son of Naranji Patel and Divaliben Patel; married Nutan Patel, Dec 6, 1976; children: Nima, Nikesh. **EDUCATION:** South Gujarat University, BSc, 1975; Bombay School of Medical Technology, MLt, 1976; University of Long Island, 1987. **CAREER:** Alvin Last Inc, chemical service manager, 1978-83; Ecometics Inc, lab director, 1983-. **ORGANIZATIONS:** Society of Cosmetic Chemists, 1991-. **BUSINESS ADDRESS:** Laboratory Director, Ecometics Inc, 19 Concord St, South Norwalk, CT 06854, (203)853-7856.

PATEL, MITESH K.
Printing company executive. Indo-American. **PERSONAL:** Born Jul 29, 1965, Nairobi, Kenya; son of Kanubhai A Patel and Savitaben K Patel; married Dipti Patel, Aug 31, 1988; children: Dipali. **EDUCATION:** Chetana College, bachelor of commerce, 1985; London College of Printing, masters in printing, 1988. **CAREER:** Infinity USA Inc, controller, beginning 1988; Dipali Enterprises Inc, president, currently. **ORGANIZATIONS:** Gujarati Samaj of New York Inc, secretary, 1992; Viashnav Temple of New York, 1990-; Federation of Indian Associations, head of float committee, 1992-. **HONORS/AWARDS:** Federation of Indian Associations, Plaque for heading float committee for 1992, 1993. **SPECIAL ACHIEVEMENTS:** Editor of Kalam Magazine. **BIOGRAPHICAL SOURCES:** Kalam, pp 1-12, April 1993. **BUSINESS ADDRESS:** President, Dipali Enterprises Inc, 261-15 69th Ave, Floral Park, NY 11004, (718)343-9315.

PATEL, MUKESH M. (MIKE)
Electronic cable company executive. Indo-American. **PERSONAL:** Born Feb 5, 1950, Ahmedabad, Gujarat, India; son of Manibhai S Patel and Leelavati M Patel; married Usha G Patel, Jul 30, 1971; children: Aakash M, Sagar M. **EDUCATION:** University of Bombay, India, BSc, 1968; Illinois Institute of Technology, BS, 1970, MS, 1972; Worcester Polytechnic Institute, MBA, 1987. **CAREER:** Essex Group, process engr, 1973-75, technical superintendent, 1976-80, product engrng mgr, 1980-81; Madison Cable Corp, Mfg Support, mgr, 1981-83, plant mgr, 1983-85, Mfg, vice pres, 1985-87, Technical Services, vice pres, 1987-. **ORGANIZATIONS:** Wire Assn International, electrical management committee, 1984-87. **BUSINESS ADDRESS:** Vice President, Technical Services, Madison Cable Corporation, 125 Goddard Memorial Dr, Worcester, MA 01603, (508)752-7320.

PATEL, MUKUL B.
Engineer. Indo-American. **PERSONAL:** Born Oct 23, 1954, Baroda, Gujarat, India; son of Bipin Patel and Suryabala Patel; married Sujata M Patel, Feb 12, 1985; children: Trushna M, Anjli M. **EDUCATION:** Electrical engineering degree, 1977. **CAREER:** Dill Products, engineering technician, 1979-80;

Maxwell Ind Inc, manufacturing engineer, 1981-89; Papizal Idea Inc, service engineer, 1989-92; Maxwell Dynamometer Systems, chief service engineer, 1992-. **HOME ADDRESS:** 2805 Sandpiper Dr, Audubon, PA 19403, (215)666-5720. **BUSINESS ADDRESS:** Chief Service Engineer, Maxwell Dynamometers Systems, 1 E Uwchlan Ave, Ste 401, Exton, PA 19341, (215)363-0314.

PATEL, MUKUND R.

Electrical engineer, researcher. Indo-American. **PERSONAL:** Born Apr 21, 1942, Bavla, Gujarat, India; son of Ranchhodlal N Patel and Shakariben M Patel; married Sarla Shantilal, Nov 4, 1967; children: Ketan, Bina, Vijal. **EDUCATION:** Sardar University, Vidyanagar, India, BE (with distinction); Gujarat University, Ahmedabad, India, ME (with honors); Rensselaer Polytechnic Institute, Troy, New York, PhD, engineering, 1972. **CAREER:** Sardar University, Vidyanagar, India, lecturer electrical engineering, 1965-66; General Electric Co, Pittsfield, Massachusetts, senior development engineer, 1967-76; Bharat Bijlee (Siemens) Ltd, Bombay, manager, research & development, 1976-80; National Productivity Council, consultant, 1976-80; Westinghouse Research & Development Center, fellow engineer, 1980-84; Westinghouse Senate, member, 1982-84; Induction General Inc, president, 1984-86; General Electric Co Space Center, principal engineer, 1986-. **ORGANIZATIONS:** IEEE Insulation Magazine, associate editor; Institution of Mechanical Engineers, fellow; IEEE; American Society of Scientific Research; Tau Beta Pi; Eta Kappa Nu; Omega Rho; Elfun Society of Volunteers; International Congress on Large High Voltage Electric Power Systems, 1981-85. **HONORS/AWARDS:** Patents and invention awards for electromechanical design of superconducting generators; NASA award for research on space power systems. **SPECIAL ACHIEVEMENTS:** Research work on electrical and mechanical design of space power systems; international authority in the area of electromechanical design of large power transformers; contributed articles to national and international professional journals. **HOME ADDRESS:** 1199 Cobblestone Ct, Yardley, PA 19067-4751, (215)321-0899.

PATEL, NAGIN K.

Educator. Indo-American. **PERSONAL:** Born Jun 17, 1932, Navsari, Gujarat, India; son of Keshavbhai B Patel and Deviben K Patel; divorced; children: Robin N, Janice Elaine, Harish David. **EDUCATION:** Gujarat University, L M College of Pharmacy, B Pharm, 1954; Temple University, School of Pharmacy, MS, 1957; University of Maryland, School of Pharmacy, PhD, 1962. **CAREER:** Temple University, instructor of pharmacy, 1961-62; Duquesne University, assistant professor of pharmaceuticals, 1962-63; University of Manitoba, assistant professor, 1963-66; University of Alberta, associate professor of pharmaceuticals, 1966-69; Frank W Horner Inc, Montreal, group supervisor, pharm-dev, 1969-80; McNeil Consumer Products Co, group leader, 1980-81; Long Island University, AMS College of Pharm, professor, 1981-. **ORGANIZATIONS:** Indo-American Pharmaceutical Association, executive committee member, 1992-; Par Pharmaceutical, Inc, board of directors, 1989-92; Montreal Pharmaceutical Discussion Group, secretary, 1976-78. **HONORS/AWARDS:** Grant-in-aid awards for research: National & Medical Research Councils of Canada, 1963-69; Smith Kline & French Inter-American Pharm Corp, 1965-69; Warner-Lambert Co, Warner-Lambert Foundation Grants, 1983, 1992, 1993. **SPECIAL ACHIEVEMENTS:** Drug in a Bead Form and Process for Preparing Same, Canadian patent, 1990, US patent, 1989; Aspirin or Acetaminophen in Bead Form and Process for Preparing Same, UK patent, 1989; author of over 30 publications, 1957-; co-author, chapter, The Theory and Practice of Industrial Pharmacy, Lea & Febiger, p 479-501, 1986. **HOME ADDRESS:** 256F Bennett Road, Matawan, NJ 07747, (908)290-8143. **BUSINESS PHONE:** (718)488-1630.

PATEL, NARAYAN G. (ANIL)

Scientist, business executive. Indo-American. **PERSONAL:** Born May 5, 1928, Sinaj Na Pura, Viramgam, Gujarat, India; son of Ganesh H Patel; divorced; children: Niel, Ulka Russell. **EDUCATION:** College of Agriculture, Anand, India, BSc, 1950; Poona University, India, MSc, 1952; University of Minnesota, Saint Paul, PhD, 1959. **CAREER:** University of Poona, entomological officer, 1951-55; University of Minnesota, research fellow, 1956-64; Case-Western Reserve University, research associate, 1964-69; E I Du Pont De Nemours & Co, research associate, 1969-86; University of Delaware, adjunct professor, 1976-; Monell Chemical Senses Center, scientist, 1987-89; Institute of Natural Products, president, director, 1985-; International Health Products, president, research director, 1985-. **ORGANIZATIONS:** American Association for Advancement of Sciences, 1964-; Developmental Biology, 1964-69; Earthwatch, PI/leader, 1985-87; Entomological Society of

America, editorial board, 1952-; Sigma Xi, Res Counc America, Du Pont Chapter, president, 1972-75; University of Minnesota Toast Masters International, graduate faculty, president, 1957; Akhil Bharitya Vanaushdhi Sansodhan Mandal, 1985-. **HONORS/AWARDS:** NIH/NSF, research grant, 1962, 1969; Ben Franklin Research Center, Innovation Award, 1992; Du Pont Co, Seed Grant Award, 1991; University of Minnesota, Foreign Student Scholarship, 1956-60; Royal Jelly Foundation, Research Award, 1963. **SPECIAL ACHIEVEMENTS:** Over 70 publications: agriculture entomology, natural products, 1951-; patents: antivirals, insecticides, muscular dexterity, 1969, 1984. **BIOGRAPHICAL SOURCES:** Earthwatch, Ayurvedic Medicinal Plants, p19, 1985; Plant-Medicine Study Returns Scientist to His Roots, Sunday News Journal, Wilmington, Delaware, October 27, 1985. **BUSINESS ADDRESS:** President, Research Director, International Health Products Inc, 3624 Market St, University City Science Center, Philadelphia, PA 19104, (215)662-0867.

PATEL, NARENDRA D.

Dentist. Indo-American. **PERSONAL:** Born Apr 4, 1949, Kampala, Uganda; son of Dahyabhai and Vimlaben; married Jayshoce Patel, May 23, 1974; children: Niseet, Mitul. **EDUCATION:** Government Dental College & Hospital, Bombay, India, BDS, 1973. **CAREER:** Self-employed, dentist, currently. **ORGANIZATIONS:** American Dental Association; Indian Dental Association. **HOME ADDRESS:** 31 Woodward St, Roslyn, NY 11576. **BUSINESS ADDRESS:** Dentist, 146-02 89th Ave, Jamaica, NY 11435, (718)523-8438.

PATEL, PRATIBHA A.

Pediatrician. Indo-American. **EDUCATION:** Medical school graduate, 1971. **CAREER:** Baltimore City Hospital, three-year pediatric residency; Buffalo Children's Hospital, fellowship training, research; La Palma Intercommunity Hospital, chief of staff, until 1993, pediatrician, 1994-. **ORGANIZATIONS:** South Asian Help-Line and Referral Agency, president, 1991-. **HONORS/ AWARDS:** American Academy of Pediatrics, fellow. **SPECIAL ACHIEVEMENTS:** Parenting in the 90s, lecture, La Palma Intercommunity Hospital, 1993; conducted research in clinical infectious diseases, Buffalo Children's Hospital. **BUSINESS ADDRESS:** Pediatrician, La Palma Intercommunity Hospital, 7901 Walker St, La Palma, CA 90623, (714)670-7400.*

PATEL, RAKESH

Production manager. Indo-American. **PERSONAL:** Born in Baroda, Gujarat, India; son of J Patel. **EDUCATION:** Kansas State, 1982-83; Rutgers University, MBA/MS, 1985. **CAREER:** New York Folding Box Co, production manager, 1984-. **BUSINESS ADDRESS:** Production Manager, New York Folding Box Co, 129 Christie SE, Newark, NJ 07105, (201)589-0654.

PATEL, RAMESH D.

Engineer. Indo-American. **PERSONAL:** Born Nov 13, 1937, Nadiad, Gujarat, India; son of Dahyabhai B Patel; married Usha R Patel, Jun 2, 1959; children: Pradeep R, Roopalee Patel Allis. **EDUCATION:** Gujarat University, BSCE, 1961; University of Kentucky, MSCE, 1963. **CAREER:** Gannon Dunkerley Co, resident engineer, 1961-62; J S Kenney & Co, civil engineer, 1962-63; Howard K Bell Inc, structural engineer, 1963-64; O O McKinley Co, chief engineer, 1964-65, 1966-67; Gherzi Eastern Ltd, structural engineer, 1965-66; M W Inc, project engineer, 1967-68; City of Indianapolis, project coordinator, 1968-69; James Associates, project engineer, 1969-79; Superior Engineering, chief structural engineer, 1979-83; James Architecture & Engineering, chief structural engineer, 1983-89; BSA Design, chief structural engineer, 1989-. **ORGANIZATIONS:** India Association of Indiana, member and founder, 1967-; Gujarati Association of Indianapolis, Sandesh, trustee. **HONORS/ AWARDS:** Indian Concrete Journal, Honorarium, 1965; State of Indiana, professional engineer; State of Illinois, structural engineer. **HOME ADDRESS:** 6126 Ashway Ct, Indianapolis, IN 46224, (317)291-9191.

PATEL, RAMESH P.

Manufacturing company executive. Indo-American. **PERSONAL:** Born Mar 14, 1944, Karamsad, Gujarat, India; son of Purushottam N Patel and Shanaben P Patel; married Hansa R Patel, Jun 12, 1971; children: Milan R, Kanak R. **EDUCATION:** SVP University, VV Nagar, Gujarat, India, BEngMech, 1965; University of Tennessee, MSIE, 1968; Mount Saint Mary's College, MBA (with honors), 1993. **CAREER:** Grove Worldwide, sr project engr, 1973-77, project mgr, 1977-80, chief engr, 1980-87, engineering director, 1987-90, vice pres, product marketing, 1990-. **SPECIAL ACHIEVEMENTS:** Several US patents; registered professional engineer, State of Ohio, 1972-. **HOME ADDRESS:** 20230 Beaver Creek Rd, Hagerstown, MD 21740, (301)714-1429.

BUSINESS ADDRESS: Vice President, Product Marketing, Grove Worldwide, Box 21, Shady Grove, PA 17256, (717)597-8121.

PATEL, RAMESH V.
Business executive. Indo-American. **PERSONAL:** Born Oct 30, 1951, Pati, Gandevi, Gujarat, India; son of Vadanji D Patel and Laxmiben V Patel; married Sheela R Patel, Feb 14, 1982; children: Raj. **EDUCATION:** Sonegate College, England, AA, 1970; California State University, Los Angeles, BS, 1977, MBA, 1984. **CAREER:** International Magnetics, jr engr, 1976-77; Standard Industries, engr, 1977-79, engineering mgr, 1980-86, vice pres, engineering, 1986-. **ORGANIZATIONS:** IEEE, 1980-. **BUSINESS ADDRESS:** Vice President, Engineering, Standard Industries, 14250 Gannet St, La Mirada, CA 90638.

PATEL, RAY J.
Architectural company executive. Indo-American. **PERSONAL:** Born in India; married Meena Patel; children: Samir, Neha. **EDUCATION:** University of Baroda, BArch, 1963; St. Jacinto College, RE, law, 1978. **CAREER:** DMP Architects Inc, pres, 1978-. **ORGANIZATIONS:** Am Institute of Architects, 1978-; Commissioner, City of Sugar Land, TX, secretary, 1989-; Cental Appraisal Dist, Ft Bd, TX, director/secretary, 1990-; Water Board #2, director/secretary, 1986-. **HONORS/AWARDS:** Vedant School, Chinmaya Mission, Excellence in Architectural Design; City of Pasadena, Senior Citizens' Center, Excellence in Architectural Design; Manor House, Low Income Housing, Outstanding Architectural Design Award. **BUSINESS ADDRESS:** President, DMP & Architects, Inc, AIA, 6776 Southwest Fwy #285, Houston, TX 77074.

PATEL, RAY L.
Business executive. Indo-American. **PERSONAL:** Born 1945, Gujarat, India; married Manju, 1964; children: Amit, Prakash. **EDUCATION:** Gujarat University, BS, 1966; University of Toledo, BSME, 1969, MBA, 1976. **CAREER:** Bendix, Toledo Stamping, exec vice pres, 1982-85; Andrews Corp, president, 1985-87; Johnston Filtration Systems, president, 1988-91; Wheelabrator Engrd Systems Inc, president, CEO, 1992-. **ORGANIZATIONS:** Society of Manufacturing Engineers, 1968-83; Society of Automotive Engineers, 1971-83, steering committee, 1976-78. **SPECIAL ACHIEVEMENTS:** Author: Automation, SME publication, 1982; Rocker Arm, SAE publication, 1975; patents: several US, including: "Intake-Exhaust Rocker Arm Design-Function". **BUSINESS ADDRESS:** President, CEO, Wheelabrator Engineered Systems Inc, PO Box 64118, St. Paul, MN 55164-0118, (612)636-3900.

PATEL, ROGER
Business executive. Indo-American. **PERSONAL:** Born Jul 23, 1950, India; married Baby Patel, Dec 31, 1974; children: Sheila, Nina, Shawn. **EDUCATION:** Gujarat, India, BSChE. **CAREER:** Martin Lane Partnership, general partner, currently; Pho-Tronics, NTW Inc, president, owner, currently; National Technology Inc, president, owner, currently. **BUSINESS ADDRESS:** President, National Technology Inc, 1101 Carnegie St, Rolling Meadows, IL 60008, (708)506-1300.

PATEL, SANJAY VRAJLAL
Accountant. Indo-American. **PERSONAL:** Born Aug 24, 1964, Calcutta, W. Bengal, India; son of Vrajlal D Patel and Vanita V Patel; married Jayna Patel, Feb 21, 1990. **EDUCATION:** University of Calcutta, BAcc, BBM; Breward Community College, micro computer application, 1990. **CAREER:** Industrial Tools Supply Corp, gen mgr, 1985-90; Ocean Avenue Mfg Inc, accountant, 1990; K-Mart, cash room clerk, 1990-91; Abraham Reily & McNamara Printers, full-charge bookkeeper, 1991-92; Unitex Intl Inc, full-charge bookkeeper, 1992-. **HOME ADDRESS:** 3622-B Meadowglen Village, Doraville, GA 30340, (404)270-0195.

PATEL, SARLA M.
Electrical engineer, researcher. Indo-American. **PERSONAL:** Born Oct 10, 1939, Vaso, Gujarat, India; daughter of Shantilal Patel & Kantaben Patel; married Mukund R Patel, Nov 4, 1967; children: Ketan, Bina, Vijal. **EDUCATION:** Sardar University, India, BSEE, 1963; University of Michigan, MSEE, 1965; University of Pittsburgh, MS, engineering management, 1983. **CAREER:** General Electric Co, system engineer, 1967-76; Westinghouse Electric Corp, senior research engineer, 1980-84; Induction General Inc, NASA project director, 1984-87; Ketron Inc, senior reliability engineer, 1987-88; TKLP Architects & Engineers, senior project engineer, 1988-. **ORGANIZATIONS:** Gujarati Association of Philadelphia Area, president, 1992-, board of directors, 1988-92; Instrument Society of America, senior member, 1988-; Institute of Electrical & Electronics Engineers, 1967-88. **HONORS/AWARDS:** Univer-

sity of Pittsburgh, Omega Rho, 1983; NASA recognition for contribution to the design and research for the space station Freedom, 1987. **SPECIAL ACHIEVEMENTS:** Several research publications in the Journal of the Instrument Society of America. **HOME ADDRESS:** 1199 Cobblestone Ct, Yardley, PA 19067-4751, (215)321-0899.

PATEL, SHAILESH R.
Financial services company executive. Indo-American. **PERSONAL:** Born Sep 22, 1953, Samarkha, Gujarat, India; son of Rameshbhai M Patel & Shardaben R Patel; married Jaymini S Patel, May 27, 1978; children: Avani S, Timir S. **EDUCATION:** SP University, India, advanced accounting & auditing degree, 1975; Houston Community College, MS-DOS I, certificate, 1989, business bookkeeping certificate, 1983; H&R Block, 1990. **CAREER:** Spicy Food USA Inc, fall charge bookkeeper, 1985-78; Unical, accounts payable, 1990-91; Stop & Go, assistant manager, 1989-90; Fuller Interest Ltd, accounts receivable, 1991-92; Path Finance, accounting assistant, 1992-93; GECO Pailal, accounts payable, 1993; ATJ Minority Enterprise, owner, currently. **HOME ADDRESS:** 3730 Embarcadero Dr, Houston, TX 77082, (713)558-1335.

PATEL, SHIRISH A.
Chemist. Indo-American. **PERSONAL:** Born May 30, 1942, Kampala, Uganda; son of Vimladen; married Bharti, May 10, 1966; children: Nainasri, Leena. **EDUCATION:** University of Bombay, BS, 1966; University of London, MS, 1968. **CAREER:** Kilembe Mines Ltd, chemist/geologist, 1969-72; Chemex Lab, geo-chemist, 1972-79; Rhone Poulenc, chemist, 1981-. **ORGANIZATIONS:** American Chemical Society; ASQC. **HOME ADDRESS:** 2710 Oak Hill Dr, Missouri City, TX 77459-2532, (713)499-9920. **BUSINESS PHONE:** (409)233-7871.

PATEL, VIPIN A.
Civil engineer. Indo-American. **PERSONAL:** Born Aug 9, 1939, Ahmedabad, Gujarat, India; son of Ambalal F Patel and Savitaben A Patel; married Hansa V Patel, May 30, 1962; children: Archana R, Ilaxi P, Devesh V. **EDUCATION:** SSCE Board, Ahmedabad, India, SSc, 1956; Gujarat University, Ahmedabad, India, ISc, 1958; Government Polytechnic, Ahmedabad, India , DCE, 1961. **CAREER:** Patel Engineers, partner, 1962-67; Shilpavin & Co, president, 1967-72; Addison Engineering, partner, 1972-76; Collins, Patel & Associates, president, 1976-90; Patel & Giannetti Const, Inc, president, 1985-. **ORGANIZATIONS:** Lions Club of Naroda, charter member, 1962; Chamber of Commerce of Addison, charter member, 1974; Addison Industrial Association, charter member, 1974; Old Mill PTA, president, 1975-77; Village of Addison, Public Committee, 1976; Shakti Mandir, Chicago, Atlanta, founder-president, 1984; Kalaniketan, Chicago, founder-president, 1982; Manav Seva Mandir, Chicago, founder-trustee, 1985. **SPECIAL ACHIEVEMENTS:** Registered professional engineer, 1972, Illinois, Wisconsin, Arizona; registered land surveyor, 1982, Arizona; registered real estate salesman, 1978. **HOME ADDRESS:** 177 E Drummond Ave, Glendale Heights, IL 60139, (708)752-8771.

PATEL, VIRENDRA CHATURBHAI
Educator, engineer. Indo-American. **PERSONAL:** Born Nov 9, 1938, Mobasa, Kenya; son of Chaturbhai S Patel and Kantaben N Rai Patel; married Manjula, May 29, 1966; children: Sanjay, Bindiya. **EDUCATION:** Imperial College, England, BSc (with honors), 1962; Cambridge University, England, PhD, 1965. **CAREER:** Cambridge University, senior research asst, 1965-69; Indian Institute of Technology, visiting professor, 1966; Lockheed Co, consultant, 1969-70; University of Iowa, faculty member, 1971-, Dept of Mechanical Engineering, professor, 1975-, division chairman, 1976-82, dept chairman, 1978-82, Iowa Institute of Hydraulic Research, research engineer, 1971-; University Karlsruhe, Germany, visiting professor, 1980-81; Ecole Nationale Superieure de Mechanique, France, visting professor, 1984. **ORGANIZATIONS:** American Society of Mechanical Engineers, fellow; AIAA, associate; American Society of Engineering Education; Society of Naval Architectural Marine Engineers; Sigma Xi; Pi Tau Sigma; Iowa Governors Science Advisory Council, 1977-83; International Towing Tank Conference, resistance committee, 1978-87. **HONORS/AWARDS:** University of Iowa Foundation, Distinguished Professor, 1990-; Chalmers Institute of Technology, Jubilee Professor, 1988; Alexander von Humboldt Foundation, Senior Scientist Award, 1980, 1993. **SPECIAL ACHIEVEMENTS:** Author: Three Dimensional Turbulent Boundary Layers, 1972; AIAA Journal, associate editor, 1987-; numerous articles in professional journals. **BUSINESS ADDRESS:** Professor, Dept of Mechanical Engineering, University of Iowa, Iowa City, IA 52242-1585.

PATHAK, SEN

Researcher. Indo-American. **PERSONAL:** Born Jul 13, 1940, Sur Hur Pur, Azamgarh, Uttar Pradesh, India; son of Shri Baij Nath Pathak & Smit-Bhago Pathak; married Raj Kumari Pathak, Mar 13, 1958; children: Shalaish K, Sudha Mishra, Radha R, Sanjay K. **EDUCATION:** Banaras Hindu University, India, BS, 1961, MS, 1963, diploma in German, 1966, PhD, 1967. **CAREER:** Baylor College of Medicine, visiting professor of medicine, 1985-; National Academy of Sciences, fellow, 1985-; University of Texas MD Anderson Hospital & Tumor Institute, Houston, geneticist, associate professor of genetics, 1985-86; University of Texas MD Anderson Cancer Center, Houston, primary appointment, geneticist, professor of cell biology, 1986-; Southwest Foundation for Biomedical Research, scientist adjunct, Department of Genetics, 1991-; University of Texas Health Science Center, Houston, Genetics Center, Program in Genetics, faculty member, 1992-. **ORGANIZATIONS:** American Association for the Advancement iof Science; Texas Genetics Society; Tissue Culture Association, Texas Branch; American Society of Human Genetics; Southwest Pediatric Oncology Group; Metastasis Research Society; Indian Society of Human Genetics; American Association for Cancer Research; Asian Zoological Society; Incian Association for Cancer Research. **HONORS/AWARDS:** Banaras Hindu University, University Prize, 1962-63; Council of Scientific and Industrial Research, Junior Research Fellowship, 1963; University Grants Commission, Senior Research Fellowship, 1967; Baylor College of Medicine, Robert A Welch Foundation, 1970; University of Texas Health Science Center Graduate School of Biomedical Sciences, Houston, Dean's Teaching Excellent List, 1986-89; received 6 grants. **SPECIAL ACHIEVEMENTS:** Published 219 articles, numerous abstracts and presentations. **BUSINESS ADDRESS:** Professor, Chief, Cellular Genetics Lab, University of Texas, MD Anderson Cancer Center, 1515 Holcombe Blvd, Houston, TX 77030, (713)792-2582.

PATI, A. KUMAR

Publisher. Indo-American. **PERSONAL:** Born Jan 6, 1954, Calcutta, India; son of Sudarsan Pati and Sabitri Pati. **EDUCATION:** J B Ray State Medical College, MD. **CAREER:** Holistic Health Medicine, publisher; Asian Pacific Naval, publisher; Health World, publisher, currently. **ORGANIZATIONS:** Human Energy Press, secretary. **BUSINESS ADDRESS:** Publisher, Health World, 1540 Gilbreth Rd, Burlingame, CA 94010, (415)697-8038.

PATIL, POPAT N.

Educator. Indo-American. **PERSONAL:** Born in Chinchkhede, Maharashtra, India; married B Patil; children: three. **EDUCATION:** Gujarat University, India, BPharm, 1956; Ohio State University, MS, 1960, PhD, 1963. **CAREER:** Ohio State University, College of Pharmacy, professor, 1972-. **ORGANIZATIONS:** American Society for Pharmacology and Experimental Therapeutics; American Association for the Advancement of Science; The Ohio Academy of Sciences, life member; American Foundation for Pharmaceutical Education, life member; Indian Pharmacological Society. **HONORS/AWARDS:** Humboldt Foundation, Humboldt Award, 1980-81. **SPECIAL ACHIEVEMENTS:** Many publications, book chapters, and reviews on sterochemical aspects of drug action, ocular pharmacology with special reference to drug melanin interactions. **BUSINESS ADDRESS:** Professor, College of Pharmacy, Ohio State University, Parks Hall, 500 West 12th Ave, Columbus, OH 43210.

PATIL, PRALHAD T.

Electrical engineer. Indo-American. **PERSONAL:** Born Apr 1, 1943, Jalgaon, Maharashtra, India; son of Tukaram & Bhagirithi Patil; married Hemlata P Patil, Feb 19, 1972; children: Ohe Anand. **EDUCATION:** University of Poona, BSc, physics, 1965, C Wadia Maharashtra State, DERE, diploma in electronics & radio engineer, 1968; Chicago Technical College, BSEE, 1970. **CAREER:** Rock-ola Manufacturing Corp, quality manager, 1973-89; Unity Manufacturing Co, Quality Dept, electrical engineer, currently. **ORGANIZATIONS:** American Society for Quality Control. **HONORS/AWARDS:** University of Illinois, Chicago, Parents Organization, director & founder, 1991; Maharashtra Mandal, Chicago, vice president, 1991, president, 1992, trustee, 1993-95; World Vision 2000, programs vice president, 1993; Federation of Indian Organizations, Chicago, vice president, 1993. **HOME ADDRESS:** 824 E Heatherstone Dr, Schaumburg, IL 60173, (708)619-3968.

PATNAIK, AMIYA K.

Educator, researcher, pathologist. Indo-American. **PERSONAL:** Born Mar 19, 1930, Cuttack, Orissa, India; son of Gokulananda Patnaik; married Kabita R Patnaik, Aug 3, 1955; children: Mamata, Sujata, Asis, Asit. **EDUCATION:** Madras Veterinary College, India, BVSc, 1951, MVSc, 1962; The Animal Medical Center, residency, 1967. **CAREER:** State Government of Orissa, India, various positions, 1952-64; The Animal Medical Center, pathologist, 1964-. **ORGANIZATIONS:** American Veterinary Medical Association, 1985-; NY State Veterinary Medical Association, currently; New York City Veterinary Medical Association, currently. **HONORS/AWARDS:** Ralston Purina, Small Animal Research Award, 1984; Beecham Veterinary Research Award, 1987; Charles Davis DVM Foundation, Journal Scholarship Award, 1990. **SPECIAL ACHIEVEMENTS:** Over 100 publications dealing with comparative oncologic pathology; chapters in books. **HOME ADDRESS:** 503 Bryant Place, Rivervale, NJ 07675. **BUSINESS ADDRESS:** Senior Staff Pathologist, Dept of Pathology, The Animal Medical Center, 510 E 62nd St, New York, NY 10021, (212)838-8100.

PAZ, JENNIFER C.

Actress. Filipino American. **PERSONAL:** Born in Manila, Philippines; daughter of Auring Cube and Tony Paz. **EDUCATION:** University of Washington; Northwest Actors' Studio. **CAREER:** Actress; credits include: SiningKilUSAn stage group, Across Oceans of Dreams; Miss Saigon, national touring company, alternate, 1992-93, main role, 1993-. **SPECIAL ACHIEVEMENTS:** Member of first national touring company of Miss Saigon, 1992-. **BIOGRAPHICAL SOURCES:** Philippine News, p 3, May 5-11, 1993. **BUSINESS ADDRESS:** Actress, Miss Saigon National Tour, c/o Orpheum Theatre, 910 Hennepin Ave, Minneapolis, MN 55403.*

PE, MAUNG HLA

Educator. Myanmar American. **PERSONAL:** Born Nov 14, 1920, Mandalay, Burma; son of U Soe Min and Daw Tin; married Ma Tin Hlyne, Apr 16, 1957. **EDUCATION:** Rangoon University, Burma, BSc, math, physics, 1946; Lehigh University, MS, electrical engineering, 1951; Polytechnic University of New York, MS, applied mathematics, 1952; New York University, MNE, 1957; Lehigh University, PhD, electrical engineering, 1957. **CAREER:** City University of New York, electrical engineering, lecturer, 1957-61; Manhattan College, assistant professor of physics, 1961-64, associate professor of physics, 1964-91, associate professor emeritus of physics, 1991-. **HONORS/AWARDS:** Columbia University, NSF Faculty Fellowship in Space Science, 1965; NATO, Fellowship Grant, 1966; Centro De Investigacion Y de Estudios Avanzados del Instituto Politecnico Nacional, Visiting Professor of Physics. **SPECIAL ACHIEVEMENTS:** A Unifying Concept for Disease Processes: A Physicist's Point of View, 125th Anniversary Special Faculty Issue, 1979; Magnetic Bottle, Academic American Encyclopedia; Magnetohydrodynamics, Academic American Encyclopedia. **HOME ADDRESS:** 240 W 261st St, Bronx, NY 10471, (718)549-4306.

PEI, I. M. (IEOH MING)

Architect. Chinese American. **PERSONAL:** Born Apr 26, 1917, Canton, China; son of Tsu Yee Pei and Lien Kwun Chwong; married Eileen Loo, Jun 20, 1942; children: T'ing Chung, Chien Chung, Li Chung, Liane. **EDUCATION:** MIT, BArch, 1940; Harvard University, MArch, 1946. **CAREER:** Architecture practice, New York, NY, 1939-42; Harvard Grad School of Design, assistant professor, 1945-48; Webb and Knapp Inc, architectural division, director, 1948-55; Pei, Cobb, Freed and Partners, president, 1955-. **ORGANIZATIONS:** National Institute of Arts and Letters; American Academy of Arts and Sciences; Royal Institute of British Architects; NAD; Urban Design Council; National Council on the Arts, 1980-. **HONORS/AWARDS:** Honorary DFA, Dartmouth College, 1991, Northeastern University; American University of Paris, LHD, 1990; MIT, traveling fellow, 1940; ASID, honorary fellow; Medal of French Legion of Honor, 1988; National Medal of Art, 1988; Praemium Imperiale Japan Art Association, 1989; UCLA Gold Medal, 1990; Calbert Foundation, First Imperial Award for Excellence, 1991, Excellence 2000 Award; AIA, fellow; numerous others. **SPECIAL ACHIEVEMENTS:** Projects include: National Center for Atmospheric Research, Boulder, Colorado; Mile High Center, Denver, Colorado; Dallas City Hall; John F Kennedy Library, Boston, Massachusetts; Canadian Imperial Bank of Commerce Complex, Toronto, Ontario; Chinese Banking Corp Center, Singapore; National Gallery of Art, East Bldg, Washington; Louvre Museum, Paris, expansion and modernization; Creative Arts Agency, Beverly Hills, CA; Rock n Roll Hall of Fame and Museum, Cleveland, OH; S W Washington Redevelopment Plan; numerous others. **BUSINESS ADDRESS:** President, Pei, Cobb, Freed and Partners, 600 Madison Ave, New York, NY 10022-1615, (212)751-3122.*

PEI, LOWRY CHENG-WU
Educator, author. Chinese American. **PERSONAL:** Born Sep 24, 1946, Chicago, IL; son of Ching Pong Pei & Marjorie Nelle Lowry; married Vaughn J Sills, Jun 6, 1993; children: Matthew Abrams. **EDUCATION:** Harvard University, BA, 1967; Stanford University, MA, 1969, PhD, 1975. **CAREER:** University of Missouri, adjunct instructor, 1971-72; University of California, San Diego, lecturer, assistant professor, 1974-78; Harvard University, preceptor in writing, 1978-85; Simmons College, associate professor, director of writing, 1985-. **ORGANIZATIONS:** National Council of Teachers of English; Association of Writing Program Administrators. **SPECIAL ACHIEVEMENTS:** Author, "The Cold Room," Best American Short Stories, 1984; "Naked Women," The American Story: The Best of Story Quarterly, 1990; Family Resemblances, Random House, 1986, Vintage Contemporary, 1988. **BUSINESS ADDRESS:** Professor, English Dept, Simmons College, 300 The Fenway, Boston, MA 02115, (617)521-2216.

PEI, RICHARD Y.
Engineer. Chinese American. **PERSONAL:** Born Jul 24, 1927, Suzhou, Jiangsu, China; son of Tseziang & Shihju Pei; married Paula Pei, Dec 3, 1951; children: Gabriel, Raphael, Michael. **EDUCATION:** Rensselaer Polytechnic Institute, PhD, 1964. **CAREER:** Blaw Knox Co, Copes-Vulcan Division, engineer, 1955-56; General Electric Co, program supervisor, 1956-62; Neptune Research Lab, technical director, 1962-64; Bellcomm Inc, staff, 1964-67; Institute for Defense Analysis, staff, 1967-69; TRW, technical director, 1969-71; The RAND Corporation, program director, 1985-90, senior engineer, 1971-. **HOME ADDRESS:** 1474 Waggaman Circle, Mc Lean, VA 22101. **BUSINESS PHONE:** (202)296-5000.

PEII, AHMAD OSNI
Sculptor. Indonesian American. **PERSONAL:** Born Sep 7, 1930, Palembang, Sumatra, Indonesia; son of B D Shawal. **EDUCATION:** Pacific Western University, BFA, 1984, DFA candidacy. **CAREER:** Craft Student League, New York YWCA, art instructor, 1972-74; New England Art Center, art instructor, 1977-78; Wadsworth Atheneum, 1978; University of Connecticut, 1978; Johnson & Wales College, art instructor, 1978-79; Wesleyan University, educator, 1979; New School for Social Research, culinary instructor, 1979-81; sculptor, exhibitions include: United Nations, UNICEF, 1967-70; Lever House, 1970; Brooklyn Museum, 1973; Silvermine Guild of Arts, 1974; Slater Memorial Museum, 1976; New York Botanical Garden, Schulman Sculpture Garden; Hudson River Museum, New York, 1988; Cast Iron Gallery, New York, 1991; Bradley International Airport, 1991; Connecticut Commission on the Arts, New Canaan Library. **ORGANIZATIONS:** Sculptors Guild New York, exhibition chairman, 1970-74; International Society for Education through Arts; International Art Collective, Barcelona, Spain. **HONORS/AWARDS:** The New School for Social Research, New York, Grant, 1967; Artist-Craftsman of New York, 1972-74; Connecticut Commission on the Arts, 1978; World of Poetry, 1986, 1989. **SPECIAL ACHIEVEMENTS:** Author, "Should the Public Get the Art It Likes?," Norwich Bulletin, June 1979; "Art as an Elevation of Life," Norwalk News, March 1982; "The Denomination of an Artwork Amidst the Confusing Diversity of Mannerism and Movement in Comtemporary Arts," The Toth-Maathian Review, 1985. **MILITARY SERVICE:** Revolutionary Army, Indonesia, 1947-49. **HOME PHONE:** (203)966-6772. **BUSINESS ADDRESS:** Sculptor, PO Box 613, New Canaan, CT 06840-0613.

PEMMARAJU, NARASIMHA RAO
Scientist. Indo-American. **PERSONAL:** Born Dec 20, 1928, Rajahmundry, Andhra, India; son of Pemmaraju Rama Rao and Pemmaraju Lakshmi Narasamma; married Suvarna Rani Pemmaraju, Jun 26, 1953; children: Uma Devi, Ramakrishna, Sankar. **EDUCATION:** Andhra University, BS, 1948, MS, 1950; Calcutta University, PhD, 1954. **CAREER:** Southwest Foundation for Biomedical Research, research associate, biochemistry, 1958-62, associate foundation scientist, org chem, 1962-67, foundation scientist, org chem, 1967-77, chairman, org chem, 1977-. **ORGANIZATIONS:** Incarnate Word College, adjunct professor, 1983-; St Marys University, research professor of chemistry, 1960-. **HONORS/AWARDS:** Government of India Senior Research Scholar; Fulbright Postdoctoral Research Fellowship, 1950, 1953, 1954; United Nations, Transfer of Know How Through Expatriate Nationals, 1982; US India Cultural, Educational, and Scientific Cooperation, visiting scientist, 1988. **SPECIAL ACHIEVEMENTS:** Over 100 publications on: organic chemistry, steroid hormone chemistry research, metabolism and development of immunoassay procedures, 1954-. **BUSINESS ADDRESS:** Chairman, Dept of Organic

Chemistry, Southwest Found Biomed Res, PO Box 28147, San Antonio, TX 78228-0147, (210)670-3214.

PENG, CHANG-SHYH
Educator. Taiwanese American. **PERSONAL:** Born Jul 8, 1961, Taipei, Taiwan; son of Nien Peng & Chang Ching-Chih Peng; married Ming-Ju Lee Peng, Aug 3, 1985; children: Joshua Hao-En. **EDUCATION:** National Taiwan University, BS, 1983; University of Texas at Dallas, MS, 1987, PhD, 1990. **CAREER:** University of Texas at Dallas, teaching/research assistant, 1986-90; Creighton University, assistant professor, 1990-. **ORGANIZATIONS:** Association of Computing Machinery, voting member, 1990-. **SPECIAL ACHIEVEMENTS:** Fuzzy Network Flow, 1993; Extending the DOS, 1993; Simulation among Parallel Networks, 1992; Fuzzy Graphs, 1992. **BUSINESS ADDRESS:** Asst Professor, Dept of Math/Computer Science, Creighton University, California at 25th St, Omaha, NE 68178-2090, (402)280-3053.

PENG, DACHUNG PAT
Business executive. Taiwanese American/Chinese American. **PERSONAL:** Born Jan 5, 1946, Tringtao, China; married; children: Eric, Jeffery. **EDUCATION:** National Taiwan University, BS, 1967; University of Connecticut, MS, 1970; Lehigh University, PhD, 1974; University of Illinois, MBA, 1978. **CAREER:** Monsanto Company, program director, 1987-90, Monsanto Fellow, 1980-93; Pacific International, CEO, president, currently. **ORGANIZATIONS:** OCA, national vice president, 1988-90; American Petroleum Institute, director, 1992-93; ASME, fellow, 1990-93; ASTM, 1990-93; ROC-USA Trade Association. **HONORS/AWARDS:** Floral Design Winner. **SPECIAL ACHIEVEMENTS:** 101 technical publications; Chinese novel, Light Circle; Chinese book, Five-Hundred Years Ago; advisor in Life & Universe. **BUSINESS ADDRESS:** President & CEO, Pacific International, Monsanto Fellow, 12965 Olive St Rd, St. Louis, MO 63141, (314)878-4774.

PENG, GEORGE TSO CHIH
Educator, city planner, architect. Chinese American. **PERSONAL:** Born Feb 25, 1928, Yuhsien, Hunan, China; son of Tsu-wen Peng and Hwei-yin Chen; married Marianne Gerads Peng, Nov 11, 1960; children: Georgianna Peng Chen, Sonia Peng Wierzba, Claudia Peng Gorman. **EDUCATION:** National Sun Yat-sen University, China, BS, architecture, 1949; University of Illinois, Urbana, MA, architecture, 1954; Technische Hochschule (now Universitaet), Germany, Dr-Ing, Staedtebau, 1960. **CAREER:** Siegfried Reitz Architekt BDA, Germany, architect, 1959; Shenango Valley Regional Planning Commission, chief planner, 1960-62; City of Allenton, executive director of city planning, 1962-65; University of Nebraska, professor & head of urban design, 1965-71; Urban Rural Planning and Design Inc, president, 1971-75; Texas Tech University, College of Architecture, professor, 1975-, Institute for Urban Studies International, director, 1984-. **ORGANIZATIONS:** American Society of Planning Officials, 1961; American Institute of Planners, 1968; American Planning Association, 1976; American Institute of Certified Planners, charter member, 1978; International Federation for Housing and Planning, 1968; American Association of University Professors, 1966. **HONORS/AWARDS:** US Department of State, Educational Exchange Award, 1952; Deutscher Akademischer Austauschdienst, Germany, Stipendium Award, 1958. **SPECIAL ACHIEVEMENTS:** The Philosophy of the City Design of Peking, Ekistics, 33/195, 1972; Organiedualism: A Theory for Planning and Design, IFHP Proceedings, 1977: Die Rolle der chinesischen Philosophien fur die Gestaltung von Architektur, Landschaft und Stadt, Daidalos 12, Berlin, 1984; 3x3 as a Model in the Design of Housing, Neighborhood, and City, IUSI, 1993. **HOME ADDRESS:** 5403 16th Place, Lubbock, TX 79416, (806)792-0267.

PENG, JEN-CHIEH
Research scientist. Chinese American. **PERSONAL:** Born Jan 14, 1949, Canton, Kwang-Tung, People's Republic of China; son of Chan-Chang Peng & Ai-Shen Yao Peng; married Tze-huey Chiou-Peng, Jul 5, 1975; children: Chih-Cheng. **EDUCATION:** Tunghai University, BS, 1970; University of Pittsburgh, PhD, 1975. **CAREER:** Center of Nuclear Study at Saclay, France, research associate, 1975-77; University of Pittsburgh, senior research associate, 1977-78; Los Alamos National Lab, technical staff member, 1978-. **ORGANIZATIONS:** American Physical Society, 1977-; Physical Review Letters, reviewer of manuscripts, 1985-; National Science Foundation, reviewer of research proposals, 1985-. **HONORS/AWARDS:** Tunghai University, fellowship, 1967; Fermi National Accelerator Lab, guest scientist, 1992-; Academia Sinica, research fellow, 1992. **SPECIAL ACHIEVEMENTS:** Author or co-author of approx 100 papers in scientific journals, 1973-; author of approx 30 invited talks in international physics conferences, 1980-; leader of

approx 5 high-energy physics experiments, 1984-. **MILITARY SERVICE:** Marine, lt, 1970-71. **BUSINESS ADDRESS:** Research Scientist, Los Alamos National Lab, Mail Stop D456, Los Alamos, NM 87545, (505)667-9431.

PENG, SYD S.
Educator. Chinese American. **PERSONAL:** Born Jan 27, 1939, China; married Felicia, Jun 15, 1968; children: Stanford, Wildon. **EDUCATION:** Taipei Institute of Technology, diploma, 1959; South Dakota School of Mines, MS, 1967; Stanford University, PhD, 1970. **CAREER:** Sinchu Coal Mine, Taiwan, mining engineer, 1959-65; US Bureau of Mines, laboratory head, 1970-74; West Virginia University, chairman of mining engineering, 1974-, distinguished professor, 1987-. **ORGANIZATIONS:** Society of Mining Engineers, 1968-; International Bureau of Strata Mech, 1987-. **HONORS/AWARDS:** Society of Mining Engineer, Rock Mehanics Award, 1987; Pittsburgh Coal Mining Institute of America, Education Excellence Award, 1988; British Institution of Mining Engineers, Oversea Award, 1992. **SPECIAL ACHIEVEMENTS:** SME, Surface Subsidence Engineering, p 161, 1992; Longwall Mining, Wiley, p 708, 1984; Coal Mine Ground Control, Wiley, p 491, 1978, 1986; 183 papers in professional journals and conference proceedings; 125 research reports. **MILITARY SERVICE:** Chinese Army, 2nd lt, 1959-61. **BUSINESS ADDRESS:** Professor, Dept of Mining Eng, West Virginia University, PO Box 6070, 365 Comer Bldg, Morgantown, WV 26506, (304)293-7680.

PENG, YING-SHIN CHRISTINE
Educator. Chinese American. **PERSONAL:** Born Dec 26, 1945, Harbin, China; daughter of Mr and Mrs F Liu; married Raymond K Peng, Sep 7, 1974; children: Phyllis H, Leslie H. **EDUCATION:** National Taiwan University, BS, 1968; University of Manitoba, PhD, 1973. **CAREER:** University of Manitoba, postdoctoral, 1973-74; University of California, Davis, professor, 1975-. **ORGANIZATIONS:** Entomological Society of America, 1975-; International Bee Research Association, 1975-; Professional Apicultural Research Association, 1985-; Eastern Apicultural Society, 1989-; International Social Insect Association, 1983-. **HONORS/AWARDS:** National Research Council of Canada, Postdoctoral Fellowship, 1973; California State Beekeepers Association, Distinguished Service Award, 1989; Eastern Apiculture Society, J I Hambleton Award, Outstanding Research Award, 1990. **SPECIAL ACHIEVEMENTS:** Conducting research in honey bee gamete biology, gamete interactions, and honey bee pathology and parasitic mites. **BUSINESS ADDRESS:** Professor, Dept of Entomology, University of California, Davis, 162 Briggs Hall, Davis, CA 95616-5224, (916)752-0490.

PETERSON, INDIRA VISWANATHAN
Educator, educational administrator. Indo-American. **EDUCATION:** Harvard University, PhD, Sanskrit and Indian studies. **CAREER:** Mount Holyoke College, Asian Studies Program, associate professor, chair, currently. **BUSINESS ADDRESS:** Assoc Professor/Chair, Asian Studies Program, Mount Holyoke College, South Hadley, MA 01075-1411, (413)538-2000.*

PHAM, DANNY
Engineer. Vietnamese American. **PERSONAL:** Born Jan 25, 1963, Vietnam; son of Quy Pham (deceased) and Khue Pham; married Trang Pham, Dec 18, 1982; children: Martin. **EDUCATION:** Long Beach State College, BA (w/ honors), computer science, 1986. **CAREER:** Pro Computer Sciences, Inc, programmer analyst, 1985-88; Electronic Data Systems Corp, senior engineer, 1988-. **BUSINESS ADDRESS:** Engineer, Electronic Data Systems Corp, 10824 Hope St, Cypress, CA 90630, (714)952-5665.

PHAM, HENRY TUOC VAN (XUAN-TUOC PHAM)
Educator, novelist. Vietnamese American/Chinese American. **PERSONAL:** Born May 31, 1920, Hiep-hoa, My-tho, Vietnam; son of Dang Van Pham and Chinh Thi Trinh; married Hai Thi Le, Jan 1, 1949; children: Hoa Xuan, Trung Quang, Huong Flanagan, Mary-Ann Ha Xuan, Truc Trung, Martin D, Hao Xuan Vu. **EDUCATION:** Academy of Paris, France, degree. **CAREER:** Denver Public Schools, tutor; Aurora Public Schools, tutor; Berlitz School of Languages of America, Vietnamese teacher; Van-nghe Tien-phong Magazine, novelist, 1977-; Tu-Do Magazine, novelist, 1990-. **ORGANIZATIONS:** Vietnamese American Cultural Alliance of Colorado, president, 1980-. **HONORS/ AWARDS:** Republic of S Vietnam, Education & Culture Medal; Freedoms Foundation at Valley Forge, PA, award, 1983; Onizuka Award, 1987; Colorado Senate, Golden Poet Award, 1991; World of Poetry, Golden Poet Award, 1991; National Library of Poetry, Editor's Award, 1993. **SPECIAL ACHIEVEMENTS:** Works for the refugee and Vietnamese community in Colorado and

in the US; many novels published (in Vietnamese); speaks Vietnamese, English, French, and Chinese; has written articles, letters in the Huntsville Times, AL, in the Denver Post and Rocky Mountain News. **BIOGRAPHICAL SOURCES:** Articles published in the Denver Post and Rocky Mountain News. **BUSINESS ADDRESS:** President, Vietnamese American Cultural Alliance of Colorado, 986 S Ventura Way, Aurora, CO 80017, (303)368-0657.

PHAM, HUNG DO
Pharmacist. Vietnamese American. **PERSONAL:** Born May 21, 1940, Hanoi, Vietnam; son of Ngoc Do Pham and Bao Thi Tran; married Loan Tu Nguyen Pham, Dec 31, 1965; children: Quyen Anh Do Pham, Cuong Anh Do Pham. **EDUCATION:** Saigon University, BS, pharmacy, 1965, MS, pharmacy, 1970; State of California, license, clinical laboratory technologist, 1977; Temple University, BS, pharmacy, 1985. **CAREER:** Pham Do Pharmacy, Vietnam, chief pharmacist, 1965-75; Public Hospitals, Vietnam, pharmacy dir, chief medical technologist, 1965-75; Saigon University, School of Pharmacy, instructor, 1968-75; Galieno Pharmaceutical Lab, general dir, technical manager, 1970-75; Creighton University, School of Medicine, research asst, 1975-77; 3M Clinical Laboratory, clinical lab technologist, 1978-82; Ellis Pharmacy, pharmacist-in-charge, 1987-. **ORGANIZATIONS:** Vietnamese Pharmacists Assn in Vietnam, vice secretary, 1968-70, adviser, 1970-72; Vietnamese Assn of Pharmaceutical Laboratories in Vietnam, adviser, 1972-75; Vietnamese Veterans Assn, Inc, USA, board director, 1989-; California Pharmacists Assn, 1988-; Vietnamese Elderly Mutual Assistance Assn in San Francisco, vp, 1988-; Northern California Vietnamese Pharmacists Assn, president, CEO, 1990-; Vietnamese Pharmacists Assn of the Free World, CEO, 1992-. **HONORS/AWARDS:** Galieno Pharmaceutical Laboratory, Vietnam, Honorable Awards; Pham Do Pharmacy, Vietnam, Honorable Awards; Vietnamese American Scholarship Foundation of Northern California, Award, 1991; Ellis Pharmacy, Honorable Awards. **SPECIAL ACHIEVEMENTS:** Study of Histamine in Some Vietnamese Foods, School of Pharmacy, Saigon University, 1972-75; co-author, Effects of Various Drugs on the Histamine Skin Reaction in Rats, Creighton University, 1977; Production of Reaginic Antibody in Mice, Creighton University, 1977; poems & songwriting. **MILITARY SERVICE:** Vietnamese Medical Army, capt, 1966-68; Vietnamese Army Honors, Awards, 1967. **BUSINESS ADDRESS:** Phamacist-in-Charge, Ellis Pharmacy, 468 Ellis St, San Francisco, CA 94102, (415)441-5088.

PHAM, KIEN TRUNG
Educator. Vietnamese American. **PERSONAL:** Born Jun 19, 1952, Vinh Long, Vietnam; son of Thao Ngoc Pham & Nhiem Thi Pham; married Huong Lam Bui, Jul 4, 1987. **EDUCATION:** University of Texas, El Paso, BS, chemistry, 1974, M Ed, ed psych, 1976; University of Texas, Austin, PhD, curr & inst, 1989. **CAREER:** Defense Language Institute, instructor, 1969-70; El Paso Natural Gas, chemist, 1974-75; University of Texas, El Paso, teaching assistant, 1975-76; Research & Development Center, UT, Austin, research associate II, 1977-80; Bilingual Resource Center, consultant, 1980-83; Austin Ind School District, teacher, 1985-90; California State University, Fresno, assistant professor, 1990-. **ORGANIZATIONS:** National Council of Teachers of Mathematics, 1980-; Association for Supervision & Curriculum Development, 1991-; California Mathematics Council, 1990-; American Education Research Association, 1991-; National Association for Bilingual Education, 1980-; National Association for Vietnamese & American Educators, 1980-; Kappa Delta Pi, faculty advisor, area rep, 1980-; Computer Using Educators, 1991-. **HONORS/AWARDS:** Kappa Delta Pi, Area Representative, 1991-; University of Texas, Austin, Henderson Scholarship, 1979; California State University, Fresno, Affirmative Action Grant, 1992-93. **SPECIAL ACHIEVEMENTS:** Proficient in Vietnamese, English, French; diversity coordinator, San Joaquin Valley Math Project, 1991-94; presenter at national & regional conferences on mathematics education & education technology; consultant, National Literacy Project for young adults. **BUSINESS ADDRESS:** Asst Professor, School of Ed & Human Dev, California State University, Fresno, 5310 N Campus Dr, Fresno, CA 93740-0002, (209)278-2172.

PHAM, VIET VAN
Educator. Vietnamese American. **PERSONAL:** Born Jan 23, 1967, Saigon, Vietnam; son of Pham Van Soan and Nguyen Thi Ngo; married Amy Roberts Pham, Aug 17, 1990. **EDUCATION:** University of Massachusetts at Amherst, BS, biochem, 1990. **CAREER:** Worthington City Schools, science teacher, currently. **HOME ADDRESS:** 4464 Zeller Rd, Columbus, OH 43214, (614)784-8727. **BUSINESS ADDRESS:** Educator, Science Dept, Worthington City Schools, 300 Dublin-Grandville Rd, Worthington, OH 43085, (614)431-6565.

PHAM, XUAN-TUOC. *See* **PHAM, HENRY TUOC VAN.**

PHAN, SEM HIN
Educator. Chinese American. **PERSONAL:** Born Sep 15, 1949, Jakarta, Indonesia; son of Joek Sloe Phan and Hong Tek Hauw; married Katherine A Phan, Jun 19, 1976; children: Nicholas, Louis. **EDUCATION:** Indiana University, BSc, 1971, PhD, 1975, MD, 1976. **CAREER:** University of Connecticut Health Center, pathology resident & postdoctoral fellow, 1976-80; University of Michigan, assistant professor, 1980-86, associate professor, 1986-92, professor, 1992-. **HONORS/AWARDS:** American Heart Association, Established Investigator Award, 1984-89; Veterans Administration, Career Development Award, 1980-83; National Institutes of Health, Research Grants, 1983-. **SPECIAL ACHIEVEMENTS:** Author or co-author of numerous scientific publications and book chapters. **BUSINESS ADDRESS:** Professor, Dept of Pathology, University of Michigan, M0602, Ann Arbor, MI 48109-0602, (313)764-3190.

PHAN, TRUNG HUYNH
Association administrator. Vietnamese American. **PERSONAL:** Born Aug 15, 1952, Vientiane, Laos; son of Sang H Phan and Lang T Huynh; married Linda Suong Phan; children: Michael, Rene, Tam, Trang. **EDUCATION:** University of Paris, licencie es-lettres, 1977, MSoc Admin (summa cum laude), 1979; University of St Thomas, mini-MBA, 1992. **CAREER:** Credit Commercial de France, foreign exchange clerk, 1979-80; Chemical Bank International of San Francisco, foreign exchange clerk, 1980; Arkansas Refugee Health Program, administrative assistant, 1982-84; Fort Smith Public Schools, consultant/supervisor, 1984-90; Intercultural Mutual Assistance Association, administrator/supervisor, 1990-; Language Services, director, 1990-; Am-Viet Marketing Co, vp, 1990-. **ORGANIZATIONS:** Rochester Human Rights Commission, commissioner, 1991, 1992; Leadership Fort Smith, 1988, 1989, 1990. **HONORS/AWARDS:** Westark Community College/Fort Smith Chamber of Commerce, Leadership Award, 1989. **SPECIAL ACHIEVEMENTS:** Language proficiency: English, French, Lao & Vietnamese. **HOME ADDRESS:** 3528 8th St NW, Rochester, MN 55901, (507)287-6626. **BUSINESS ADDRESS:** Administrator of Programs, Supervisor, Intercultural Mutual Assistance Association, 16 SW 7th Ave, Rochester, MN 55902, (507)289-5960.

PHO, HAI B.
Educator. Vietnamese American. **PERSONAL:** married Lan. **EDUCATION:** Boston College, BA, history, 1960; Boston University, MA, political science, 1964, PhD, political science, 1972. **CAREER:** University of Lowell, professor, currently. **ORGANIZATIONS:** American Political Science Association; Association for Asian Studies; International Studies Association; Massachusetts Governor's Advisory Council for Refugees & Immigrants. **SPECIAL ACHIEVEMENTS:** Author, Vietnamese Public Management in Transition, University Press of America, 1990; "The Politics of Refugee Resettlement in Massachusetts," Migration World, vol XIX, no 4, fall 1991. **BUSINESS ADDRESS:** Professor, Political Science Dept, University of Massachusetts, 1 University Ave, Lowell, MA 01854-2893, (508)934-4256.

PHOMMASOUVANH, BANLANG
Educator. Laotian American. **PERSONAL:** Born May 10, 1946, Samneua, Hoa Phan, Lao People's Democratic Republic; daughter of Phouang Luangvija and Kham Luangvija; married Bounlieng, Nov 1970; children: Arounthit, Souksathit, Lela. **EDUCATION:** Ecole Nomale des Filles, Bordeaux; Talence University, France, AA, 1970; Southen Illinois University, BA, 1974; Ball State University, MAE, 1985; Hamline University, bilingual education license, 1990. **CAREER:** Washington High School, Iowa, bilingual teacher, 1982-84; Ball State University, bilingual education coordinator, 1985-86; Community University Health Care Center, senior social worker, 1986-87; Hamline University, Southeast Asian ethnography instructor, 1989-90; Henry High School, French, bilingual teacher, 1990-91; Folwell Junior High, Minneapolis, French teacher, 1992-; Roosevelt High School, bilingual teacher, 1987-90, French, bilingual teacher, 1991-92, instructor, currently. **ORGANIZATIONS:** Lao Parent and Teacher Association, builder, executive director, 1988-; Southeast Asian Legal Education and Advocacy Project, 1990; Black, Indian, Hispanic and Asian Women in Action, 1989; Women of Colors Health Alternative Network, vice president, 1992; Asian Women Study Group, 1991-93; Centre for Asian Pacific Islanders, vp, 1989-92. **HONORS/AWARDS:** Minnesota Governor's Commendation, Assisting the Pacific Minnesotans, State Council of Asia, 1990; Urban Coalition, Coalition Builder Award, 1992; American Association of Teachers of French, Professeur du Laureat, 1992; State of Minnesota Governor's Office, Certificate of Commendation, 1990; BIHA,

Outstanding Contribution to the Community, 1989. **SPECIAL ACHIEVEMENTS:** Assists the Lao PTA in promoting Lao culture, language and arts through various classes and support services. **BIOGRAPHICAL SOURCES:** "Woman Instills Pride in Lao Children," Metropolitan Council, Nov 5, 1989; "Honors 16 Women," St Paul Pioneer Press, March 2, 1989; "Heritage through Dance," Colors, Sept 1993. **HOME ADDRESS:** 1396 Michelle Dr, Eagan, MN 55123, (612)454-7185. **BUSINESS PHONE:** (612)627-2658.

PHUNG, DOAN LIEN (PHUNG LIEN DOAN)
Consulting company executive. Vietnamese American. **PERSONAL:** Born Jan 1, 1940, Battrang, Gialam Hanoi, Vietnam; son of Thanh Van Phung and Phong Thi Le; married Thu Le Doan, Jun 28, 1970; children: Thu-Trang L, Thu-Anh. **EDUCATION:** Florida State University, BA, physics, math, 1961; Massachusetts Institute of Technology, MS, nuclear engineering, 1964, MS, physics, 1964, PhD, nuclear engineering, 1972. **CAREER:** Vietnam Atomic Energy Office, scientist, 1964-66; United Engineers & Constructors, engineering consultant, 1966-75; Oak Ridge Associated Universities, chief scientist, 1975-83; PAI Corp, president, CEO, 1983-. **ORGANIZATIONS:** American Nuclear Society, 1966-; American Association for Advancement of Science, 1970-83; New York Academy of Science, 1978-88. **HONORS/AWARDS:** Sigma Xi, Research Excellence, 1972; Phi Beta Kappa, Academic Excellence, 1961; Phi Kappa Phi, Academic Excellence, 1961; Pi Mu Epsilon, Math Excellence, 1960; Sigma Pi Sigma, Physics Excellence, 1960. **SPECIAL ACHIEVEMENTS:** More than 100 technical reports & articles, 1964-84; book, The Second Nuclear Era, co-author, 1983; theory, Cost-Energy Dynamics, 1980; book, The Special and General Theory of Relativity, 1966, translation into Vietnamese of Einstein's book; registered professional engineer, State of Pennsylvania, 1974-, State of Tennessee, 1986-, State of Florida, 1993-. **BUSINESS ADDRESS:** President, CEO, PAI Corp, 116 Milan Way, Oak Ridge, TN 37830, (615)483-0666.

PIAN, CARLSON CHAO-PING
Research laboratory executive. Chinese American. **PERSONAL:** Born Dec 31, 1945, Beijing, China; son of Charles H C Pian and Juliette Fan Pian; married Sally Tseng Pian, Aug 23, 1969; children: Kevin, Phillip, Timothy. **EDUCATION:** University of Michigan, BS, 1968, MS, 1969, PhD, 1974. **CAREER:** University of Michigan, instructor, 1965-74, research assistant, 1971-74; Eindhoven Technical University, visiting scientist, 1974-75; NASA Lewis Research Center, research engineer, 1975-79; Avco Research Laboratory, principal research engineer, 1979-88; Textron/Avco Research Laboratory, director, 1988-. **ORGANIZATIONS:** American Institue of Aeronautics & Astronautics, 1969-; Journal of Propulsion and Power, associate editor, 1992-; Symposium of Engineering Aspects of MHD, board of directors, 1988-. **HONORS/AWARDS:** American Institute of Aeronautics & Astronautics, Space Shuttle Flag Award, 1984; American Society of Mechanical Engineers, Advanced Energy Division, J F Louis Memorial Award, 1989. **SPECIAL ACHIEVEMENTS:** Contributed over sixty technical papers to professional and/or refereed journals, 1979-. **HOME ADDRESS:** 38 Kenmore Street, Newton, MA 02159.

PIAN, THEODORE HSUEH-HUANG
Educator, engineering consultant. Chinese American. **PERSONAL:** Born Jan 18, 1919, Shanghai, China; son of Chao-Hsin Shu-Cheng Pian and Chih-Chuan Yen Pian; married Rulan Chao Pian, Oct 3, 1945; children: Canta Chao-Po. **EDUCATION:** National Tsing Hua University, Kunmin, China, BS, 1940; Massachusetts Institute of Technology, MS, 1944, ScD, 1948. **CAREER:** Central Aircraft Manufacturing Co, Loiwing, China, junior engineer, 1940-42; Chengtu Glider Manufacturing Factory, engineer, 1942-43; Curtiss Aircraft Division, stress analyst, 1944-45; Massachusetts Institute of Technology, teaching assistant, 1946-47, research associate, 1947-52, assistant professor, 1952-59, associate professor, 1959-66, professor of aeronautics & astronautics, 1966-89, professor emeritus, 1989-. **ORGANIZATIONS:** National Academy of Engineering, 1988-; American Institute of Aeronautics, fellow, 1988-, AIAA Journal, associate editor, 1943-45; International Association for Computational Mechanics, honorary associate member of general council, 1991-, member of the council, 1985-91. **HONORS/AWARDS:** American Society of Mechanical Engineers, honorary member, 1985-; TRE Corp, Beverly Hills, California, von Karman Memorial Prize, 1974; American Institute of Aeronautics and Astronautics, Structures, Structural Dynamics and Materials Award, 1975; Beijing University of Aeronautics and Astronautics, Honorary Doctor, 1990; Shanghai University of Technology, Honorary PhD, 1991. **SPECIAL ACHIEVEMENTS:** Pioneering the hybrid finite element model in computational structural mechanics. **BIOGRAPHICAL SOURCES:** Early FEM Pioneers by

John Robinson, Robinson & Associates, pp 155-172, 1985. **HOME ADDRESS:** 14 Brattle Circle, Cambridge, MA 02138-4625, (617)876-9036. **BUSINESS ADDRESS:** Professor Emeritus, Dept of Aeronautics & Astronautics, Massachusetts Institute of Technology, 77 Massachusetts Ave, Rm 9-347, Cambridge, MA 02139, (617)253-2425.

PIEN, EDWARD H.
Physician. Chinese American. **PERSONAL:** Born Nov 25, 1955, Washington, DC; son of Pao Chi Pien and Yu Ming Pien; married Danielle Monique Schor, Sep 1983; children: Lisa, Margot. **EDUCATION:** Georgetown University, BS, 1977; Georgetown University Medical School, MD, 1981. **CAREER:** Patuxent Medical Group, Radiology, vice chmn, 1991-92, physician, currently. **ORGANIZATIONS:** RSNA, 1986; AIUM, 1988-; ACR, 1986-. **BUSINESS ADDRESS:** Physician, Patuxent Medical Group, 2 Knoll North Dr, Columbia, MD 21045, (410)964-4532.

PILLAI, UNNIKRISHNA S.
Educator. Indo-American. **PERSONAL:** Born May 6, 1955, Quilon, Kerala, India; son of P Sreedharan Pillai & B Saraswathy Amma; married Indira, Aug 11, 1987. **EDUCATION:** Institute of Technology, India, BTech, electronics engineering, 1977; Indian Institute of Technology, MTech, electrical engineering, 1982; Moore School of Electrical Engineering, University of Pennsylvania, PhD, systems engineering, 1985. **CAREER:** Bharat Electronics Ltd, India, deputy engineer, 1978-80; Polytechnic University, Brooklyn Polytechnic, assistant professor, 1985-89, associate professor, electrical engineering, 1989-. **ORGANIZATIONS:** IEEE, senior member, 1985-. **SPECIAL ACHIEVEMENTS:** Author, book, Array Signal Processing, Springer-Verlag, 1989; book, Spectrum Estimation & System Identification, with T I Shim, Springer-Verlag, 1993; over 15 journal publications and 30 conference publications related to electrical engineering/signal processing. **BUSINESS ADDRESS:** Assoc Prof, Dept of Elec Eng, Polytechnic University, 5 Metro Tech Center, Brooklyn, NY 11201, (718)261-3732.

PILLAI, VIJAYAN K.
Educator. Indo-American. **PERSONAL:** Born Apr 17, 1949, Kajang, Selangore, Malaysia; son of C K Unnikrishna Pillai & J Chandramathi; married Ann C Kelley, May 22, 1982. **EDUCATION:** University of Kerala, India, BSc, 1970; University of Indore, India, MA, 1972; School of Planning, Ahmedabad, India, graduate diploma in planning, 1974; University of Iowa, PhD, 1983. **CAREER:** University of Iowa, research associate, 1983-85, 1987-89; University of Zambia, lecturer, 1985-86; University of North Texas, assistant professor, 1989-. **ORGANIZATIONS:** Population Association of America, 1989-; International Union for Scientific Study of Population, 1990-. **SPECIAL ACHIEVEMENTS:** With Jay Weinsten, "Ahmedabad: An Ecological Perspective," Third World Planning Review, 1979; "Postwar Rise and Decline of American Fertility," Journal of Family History, 1992; with C K Umari, "Fertility and Social Development in Africa," Population Review, 1987, 1992; with M Conaway, "Immunization Coverage in Lusaka, Zambia," Journal of Biosocial Science, 1992; with T Barton, "An Evaluation of a Prototype Jobs Program," Evaluation Review, 1993. **BUSINESS ADDRESS:** Asst Prof, Dept of Sociology, University of North Texas, PO Box 13675, Chilton Hall, Denton, TX 76203-3675.

PILLAY, MULLAYIL K. G. (KEN)
Social service administrator, association executive. Indo-American. **PERSONAL:** Born Apr 19, 1924, Aroor, Kerala, India; son of Gopal Pillai & Gowri Amma; married Ann Rebeiro, Nov 1951 (deceased); children: Prem, Sunil. **EDUCATION:** Madras University, Maharajas College, Ernakulam, Kerala, India, FA, 1944; Punjab University, private study, BA, 1956; Delhi University, Delhi School of Economics, DBM, MBA, 1959. **CAREER:** Indian Air Force, logistics supervisor, 1944-59; Indian Institute of Technology, materials management, assistant registrar, 1960-65; Hindustan Aeronautics Ltd, purchasing manager, 1965-69; AFPrint Nigeria Ltd, materials controller, 1970-74; Waltham & Elgin Watch Co, distribution, supervisor, 1975-79; Cook County Hospital, materials management, divisional director, 1981-91; Indo American Center, president, CEO, 1991-, founder. **ORGANIZATIONS:** Indo American Center, volunteer, 1990-; Federation of Indian Associations, president, 1984; National Federation of Indian American Associations, treasurer, 1990-92; Malayales Association of Chicago, president, 1983; National Federation of Kerala Associations in America, treasurer, 1982; Geethamandalam, Chicago, board member, 1993-94; SPACE, board member, 1991-92; AARP, Chapter 4629, president, 1993-. **HONORS/AWARDS:** City of Chicago, Hall of Fame, senior citizens, 1990; National Federation of Kerala Associations, Distin-

guished Service, 1991; Federation of India Associations, Distinguished Service Award, 1990; India Tribune, Gandhi Award, 1983. **SPECIAL ACHIEVEMENTS:** Writes frequently for ethnic newspapers & journals, 1970-; organized first India Day Parade in Chicago, 1985. **MILITARY SERVICE:** Indian Air Force, 1944-60; honors/awards: War, Independence, Kashmir, etc. **BIOGRAPHICAL SOURCES:** Profiles and tributes appeared in News India, India Tribune, Spotlight, etc. **BUSINESS ADDRESS:** President, CEO, Indo-American Center, 2538 W Devon Ave, Chicago, IL 60659.

PILLAY, SIVASANKARA K. K.
Laboratory manager. Indo-American. **PERSONAL:** Born Jan 28, 1935, Puliyoor, Kerala, India; son of Mr & Mrs T N Raman Pillay; married Revathi K Pillay, Mar 24, 1964; children: Gautam Pillay. **EDUCATION:** University of Mysore, India, BSc, (honors), 1955, MSc, 1956; Pennsylvania State University, PhD, 1965. **CAREER:** Penn State University, teaching assistant, 1960-65; Argonne National Lab, research associate, 1965-66; Western New York Nuclear Research Center, senior scientist, 1966-71; Penn State University, assistant & associate professor, 1971-81; Los Alamos National Lab, tech staff member, 1981-92, program manager, 1992-. **ORGANIZATIONS:** American Chemical Society, 1962-; American Nuclear Society, numerous positions, 1965-; American Association for Advancement of Science, 1967-; American Institute of Chemists, fellow, 1971-; Institute of Nuclear Materials Managers, 1982-; American Society for Testing Materials, 1989-; New York Academy Science, 1967-. **HONORS/AWARDS:** Government of India, Merit Scholar, 1952-56; Kopper Chemical Co, fellow, 1962, 1963; ERDA, fellow, 1976. **SPECIAL ACHIEVEMENTS:** 125 technical publications including 2 books, chapters in topical publications, journal articles and technical reports, 1965-. **BUSINESS ADDRESS:** Program Manager, Waste Minimization, Los Alamos National Laboratory, Nuclear Materials Technology Division, Mail Stop: E-500, Los Alamos, NM 87545, (505)667-2556.

PINDIPROLU, MANJULA
Government official. Indo-American. **EDUCATION:** Montgomery Community College, AA, 1985; University of Maryland, University College, BS, 1987; George Washington University, MBA, 1989. **CAREER:** US Credit Corp, marketing specialist, 1989; Lovell International Inc, marketing, vice president, 1990-92; Peace Corps, minority recruitment specialist, 1992-. **ORGANIZATIONS:** George Washington University MBA Association, 1987-89, International Students Association, 1987-89; American Marketing Association, 1988-92. **BUSINESS ADDRESS:** Minority Recruitment Specialist, Peace Corps, 1990 K St NW, Rm 9334, Washington, DC 20526, (202)606-3387.

PINTO, JAMES J.
Electronics company executive. Indo-American. **PERSONAL:** Born Dec 6, 1937, Bangalore, India; son of Albert M Pinto & Rosalie Pinto; married Rosa; children: David, Christopher, Rosalie. **EDUCATION:** Mysore University, India, BSc (honors), 1957, MSc, physics, 1958. **CAREER:** Action Instruments Inc, president & founder, 1971-. **ORGANIZATIONS:** Instrument Society of America, fellow, 1992-, 1970-; MENSA, 1972-. **HONORS/AWARDS:** Instrument Society of America, Douglas Annin Award, 1991; US Small Business Administration, SBA Small Businessman of the Year for California, 1980. **SPECIAL ACHIEVEMENTS:** Over 50 technical articles in several industry journals; 4 patents. **BIOGRAPHICAL SOURCES:** Industry Week article, "Manager for All Seasons," June 1992; Inc Magazine article, "A Call to Action," January 1981. **BUSINESS ADDRESS:** President, Action Instruments Inc, 8601 Aero Dr, San Diego, CA 92123, (619)279-5726.

POC, SORYA
State official. Cambodian American. **PERSONAL:** Born in Phnom-Penh, Cambodia; married Thieun Lo Poc, Jan 16, 1958 (deceased); children: Vannadevi Nina Poc Underwood, Maya Watson. **EDUCATION:** Notre-Dame Du Lang-Biang Dalat, South Vietnam, French Baccalaureat 2nd part, 1951; University Catholic, Paris, France, 1953-54. **CAREER:** State of Colorado, Department of Social Services, Refugee Services Program, employment case manager, 1982-. **ORGANIZATIONS:** Cambodian Buddhist & Christian Society of Colorado, coordinator, 1980-87; All Denver Women, steering committee, 1984; International Women's Club, Seoul, Korea, president, 1973-74. **HONORS/AWARDS:** US Department of Justice, Community Relations Service, 1989; Causes & Effects in Child Abuse, Jean Mathews-Powers Identification, 1988; Pacific Institute, Investment in Excellence, 1986. **SPECIAL ACHIEVEMENTS:** Fluent in French, Cambodian and Vietnamese. **HOME ADDRESS:** 2950 S Willow St, Denver, CO 80231. **BUSINESS PHONE:** (303)863-8216.

PONG, SCHWE FANG
Pharmaceutical researcher. Taiwanese American. **PERSONAL:** Born Jun 4, 1936, Hsin-Chu, Taiwan; married Yuh Ing Pong, Dec 30, 1964; children: Amy, Cindy, Kathy. **EDUCATION:** National Taiwan University, BS, pharmacy, 1963; University of Tennessee, MS, pharmacognosy, 1966; University of Mississippi, PhD, pharmacology, 1970. **CAREER:** Texas Research Institute of Mental Sciences, research specialist I, 1971; Indiana University Medical Center, Institute of Psychiatric Res, research associate, 1973- 74; Procter & Gamble Pharmaceuticals, 1974-. **HONORS/AWARDS:** Institute of Psychiatric Research, Indiana University Medical Center, NIMH Postdoctoral Fellow, 1971-73. **SPECIAL ACHIEVEMENTS:** More than 50 publications. **MILITARY SERVICE:** Nationalist Chinese Navy, second lieutenant, 1962-63. **BUSINESS ADDRESS:** Procter & Gamble Pharmaceuticals, PO Box 191, Norwich, NY 13815-0191, (607)335-2580.

PONG, TING-CHUEN
Educator. Chinese American. **PERSONAL:** Born Jun 27, 1957, Hong Kong; son of Wai-Tong Pong & Yin-Chor Li Pong; married Carmen Pong, Aug 1, 1981; children: Terrence, Tiffany. **EDUCATION:** University of Wisconsin-Eau Claire, BS, mathematics & physics, 1978; Virginia Polytechnic Institute & State University, MS, computer science, 1981, PhD, computer science, 1984. **CAREER:** Virginia Tech, Department of Computer Science, teaching assistant, 1979-80, Spatial Data Analysis Lab, research assistant, 1980-84; Hong Kong University of Science & Technology, senior lecturer, 1991-92; University of Minnesota, Department of Computer Science, assistant professor, 1984-90, associate professor, 1990-. **ORGANIZATIONS:** Institute of Electrical & Electronics Engineers, 1984-; Association of Computing Machinery, 1984-; Hong Kong Institute of Science, founding member, 1992-; IEEE International Conference on Robotics & Automation, program committee member, 1993; Asian Conference on Computer Vision, program committee member, 1993. **HONORS/AWARDS:** Pattern Recognition Society, Annual Pattern Recognition Society Award, 1990, Honorable Mention Award, 1986; IEEE, certificate of recognition and appreciation, 1988. **SPECIAL ACHIEVEMENTS:** Excellent Awards Paper: "Shape from Shading Using the Facet Model," Pattern Recognition, 1989; "Shape Estimation from Topographic Primal Sketch," Pattern Recognition, 1985; Pattern Recognition Journal, associate editor, 1991-. **BIOGRAPHICAL SOURCES:** Pattern Recognition Journal, vol 22, no 6, p 695, 1989; IEEE Transactions on Systems, Man, and Cybernetics, vol 19, no 2, p 276, 1989. **BUSINESS ADDRESS:** Associate Professor, Computer Science Dept, University of Minnesota, 4-192 EE/CSci Bldg, 200 Union St SE, Minneapolis, MN 55455, (612)625-4097.

POON, CHI-SANG
Research scientist. Hong Kong American. **PERSONAL:** Born Nov 12, 1952, Kowloon, Hong Kong; son of Chee-Kong Poon & Man-Hing Wong; married Sau-Chun Ng, Aug 12, 1978; children: Ivan Yun-Wye. **EDUCATION:** University of Hong Kong, BSc, engineering, 1975; Chinese University of Hong Kong, MPhil, 1977; University of California, Los Angeles, PhD, 1981. **CAREER:** North Dakota State University, assistant professor, electrical engineering, 1981-85, associate professor, electrical engineering, 1985-89; MIT, visiting associate professor, 1988-89, principal research scientist, 1989-. **ORGANIZATIONS:** Institute of Electrical Engineers, senior member, 1976-; Biomedical Engineering Society, senior member, 1983-; American Physiological Society, 1983-; Neural Network Society, 1988-; American Association for the Advancement of Science, 1986-; CRC Press, Editor, Neural Networks book series, 1991-; American Journal of Physiology, editorial board, 1988-90. **HONORS/AWARDS:** University of California, Education Abroad Program Scholarship, 1977, Regent's Fellowship, 1978, Hortense Fishbaugh Memorial Scholarship, 1980; US Department of State, Exchange Scholarship, 1977; Biomedical Engineering Society, Harold Lamport Award, 1983; National Institutes of Health, New Investigators Award, 1983; Sigma Xi, outstanding research award, 1987. **SPECIAL ACHIEVEMENTS:** Over 50 scientific publications and 2 patents. **BUSINESS ADDRESS:** Principal Research Scientist, Massachusetts Institute of Technology, 77 Massachusetts Ave, Rm 20A-126, Cambridge, MA 02139.

POONI, AMARDEEP SINGH. *See* Obituaries.

POSEY, SANDRA MIZUMOTO
Writer, storyteller. Japanese American. **PERSONAL:** Born Aug 18, 1966, Harbor City, CA; daughter of Calvert and Akiko Posey. **EDUCATION:** CSU Long Beach, BA (magna cum laude), comparative literature, 1990; UCLA, folklore & mythology, currently. **CAREER:** Writer, storyteller, currently.

ORGANIZATIONS: Nisei Week Japanese Festival, storytelling chairperson, 1993; National Association for the Preservation & Perpetuation of Storytelling, 1988-; Community Storytellers, 1992-; Society of Children's Book Writers & Illustrators, 1991-; Southcoast Storytellers Guild, master teller, 1993-. **HONORS/AWARDS:** James Irvine Foundation, Dorland Mountain Arts Colony Fellowship, 1993; James Clavell American Japanese National Literary Award, Honorable Mention, 1992; N/W Asian American Theatre's Playwright Contest, Honorable Mention, 1992; JACL & AAPAA National Short Story Contest, Second Place, 1991; CSU Long Beach, Outstanding Graduate in Comparative Literature, 1990. **SPECIAL ACHIEVEMENTS:** Publications include: folk retelling, The Rafu Magazine, Dec 18, 1993; short story, Mid-American Review, Fall 1993; short story and comics, Art Spiral, fall 1993; comic: LA Times, April 19, 1993; weekly comic: Rafu Shimpo, 1992-; short story: Pacific Citizen, Dec 1991; performances include: Japanese American National Museum, California Afro-American Museum, International Festival of Masks, NISEI Week/Mattel Multicultural Storyfest, producer; Highways Women's Festival; Summer Solstice Music, Dance, & Storytelling Festival; Lotus Festival. **BIOGRAPHICAL SOURCES:** "Passing on History through Stories," Rafu Shimpo, pg 1, Aug 6, 1993; "Low Pressure Story Meetings: Storytellers Make Their Own Words, Backstage West, Oct 8-14, 1993. **HOME PHONE:** (310)834-3877.

POUW, STANLEY SIONG-IN
Architect. Chinese American. **PERSONAL:** Born Oct 2, 1942, Sukabumi, Java, Indonesia; son of George B G Pouw and Sylvia L Pouw; married Rebecca Ann Pouw, Jun 13, 1970; children: Bryson J, Wesley M, Shalisa S. **EDUCATION:** University of Kentucky, BArch, 1969; University of Michigan, MLA, 1971. **CAREER:** Seracuse Lawler & Partners, architect/designer, 1971-77; Pouw & Associates, Inc, president, 1977-. **ORGANIZATIONS:** Asian Cultural Center, president, 1989-; Mayor's Asian Advisory Council, chair, 1993-; Colorado Scholarship Coalition, chairman, 1992-; Kindred Spirits DCPA, vice chair executive committee, 1992-; University of Colorado, Denver, minority advisory committee, 1992-; New World Airport Commission, 1992-; Stapleton 2000 Citizen Advisory Board, 1993-; The Denver Museum of Natural History, board of trustees, 1994-. **HONORS/AWARDS:** Denver Chamber of Commerce & Denver Post, Minority Business of the Year, 1992; American Institute of Architects, National & Denver AIA Award for Limon Fire & Rescue Station, 1992; Denver Entrepreneur of the Year, Finalist, 1993. **SPECIAL ACHIEVEMENTS:** AIA Denver, Design Merit Award, Hunter Douglas Headquarters, 1992; American Concrete Institute, Award, 1992, for 198 Inverness Office Building; language proficiency in English, Bahasa Indonesia, and Dutch. **BUSINESS ADDRESS:** President, Pouw & Associates Inc, 1860 Blake St, Ste 200, Denver, CO 80202, (303)296-4343.

PRABHAKAR, ARATI
Federal government official. Indo-American. **PERSONAL:** Born 1959, New Dehli, India. **EDUCATION:** Texas Tech University, BS, electrical engineering, 1979; California Institute of Technology, MS, electrical engineering, 1980, PhD, applied physics, 1984. **CAREER:** Defense Department, Advanced Research Projects Agency, Microelectronics Technology Office, director, 1986-88; National Institute of Standards and Technology, director, 1993-. **ORGANIZATIONS:** American Physical Society; Institute of Electrical & Electronics Engineers, senior member. **HONORS/AWARDS:** Office of Technology Assessment, Congressional Fellow, 1984-86; Eta Kappa Nu; Tau Beta Pi; Bell Laboratories Graduate Research Program for Women, fellowship. **BUSINESS ADDRESS:** Director, National Institute of Standards & Technology, A - 1134, Gaithersburg, MD 20899-0001, (301)975-2300.

PRABHU, R. D.
Pulmonologist, activist. Indo-American. **CAREER:** The Lung Institute, pulmonologist, currently. **ORGANIZATIONS:** Indian American Forum for Political Education, past president. **HONORS/AWARDS:** Honored at 10th annual Indian American Forum for Political Education, 1992. **BUSINESS ADDRESS:** Pulmonologist, The Lung Institute, 5701 W Charleston, Suite 210, Las Vegas, NV 89102, (702)877-9514.*

PRABHUDESAI, MUKUND M. (MUKUND M. DESAI)
Laboratory director, researcher, educator. Indo-American. **PERSONAL:** Born Mar 17, 1942, Goa, India; son of Madhav R Prabhudesai & Kusum M Prabhudesai; married Sarita Prabhudesai, Feb 1, 1972; children: Nitin. **EDUCATION:** IY College, India, BM, 1962; GS Medical College, India, 1962-67, MBBS, 1967; Saint Joseph Hospital, rotating internship, 1968-69; Albert Einstein College of Medicine, pathology residency, 1969-72, chief, resident

pathology, 1972-73. **CAREER:** Fordham Hospital, assistant pathologist, 1973-74, associate pathologist, 1974-76; Lincoln Medical & Mental Health Center, associate director of clinical pathology, 1976, deputy director of pathology, 1977-79; Bronx County, deputy assistant coroner, 1972-73; University of Illinois, College of Medicine, clinic associate professor, 1983-, clinical associate, 1988; VA Medical Center, chief, pathology & lab medical service, Peoria Clinic, 1979-, coordinator, research & development service, 1983-. **ORGANIZATIONS:** College of American Pathologists, fellow, 1979-; Illinois Society of Pathologists, board of directors, 1986-; American Association of Physician Executives, 1990-; Illinois State Society of Pathologists, membership committee, chair, 1989-; College of American Pathologists, delegate to the house, 1991-, inspector, 1980-; University of Illinois, College of Medicine, executive committee, 1987-91; promotions committee, 1992-, research committee, 1984-89, senator, Chicago campus, 1982-83; American Cancer Society, Vermilion Co, vice president, 1982-86, president, 1986-88, Early Detection & Prevention Committee, chair, 1987-88. **HONORS/AWARDS:** University of Bombay, Final MD Gold Medal, 1967; VA Medical Center, Central Office, Cost Containment Suggestion Award, 1982; American Cancer Society, Vermilion Co, Certificate of Recognition, 1986; VA Medical Center, University of Illinois, director, associate director, dean's letter of commendation, 1988; College of American Pathologists, I/A Program, letter of commendation from chairman, 1993. **SPECIAL ACHIEVEMENTS:** Competitive research grant funds, 1980-82; published 9 journal articles, 1976-93; presented 21 posters/abstracts, 1976-93; most cost effective, complex quality laboratory in peer group comparison by VA standards, Pathology VACA Monographs. **HOME ADDRESS:** 319 Fletcher, Danville, IL 61832, (217)446-0530. **BUSINESS ADDRESS:** Chief, Pathology & Laboratory Medicine Service (113), VA Medical Center, 1900 E Main St, Bldg 58, Danville, IL 61832, (217)442-8000.

PRADHAN, SHEKHAR
Educator. Indo-American. **PERSONAL:** Born Mar 6, 1953, Allahabad, Uttar Pradesh, India; son of Udar Nath Pradhan and Tara Pradhan; married Savita Pradhan, Feb 12, 1978; children: Shilpi, Anupam K, Kunwarji. **EDUCATION:** Banaras H University, BTechEE, 1974; University of Cincinnati, MSEE, 1988, PhD, 1990. **CAREER:** University of Cincinnati, lecturer, 1985-90; Lafayette College, asst professor, 1990-91; University of North Carolina, associate professor, professor, 1991-. **ORGANIZATIONS:** IEEE, 1985-; American Physical Society. **SPECIAL ACHIEVEMENTS:** Over 20 publications in refereed journals, 1985-. **HOME ADDRESS:** 9124 Sandburg Ave, Charlotte, NC 28213, (704)548-1918.

PRAKASH, SHAMSHER
Educator. Indo-American. **PERSONAL:** Born Jan 3, 1933; married. **EDUCATION:** University of Roorkee, India, BE, civil engineering, 1954, PG Dip, 1959; University of Illinois, MS, 1961, PhD, 1962. **CAREER:** Panjab PWD, India, assistant engineer, 1954-57; Roorkee University, lecturer, 1957-62; University of Illinois, TCM research fellow, 1959-62; University of Roorkee, reader, 1962-66, professor, 1966-78, Civil Engineering Department, professor and head, 1982-83; Roorkee, India, director, 1983-85; University of Missouri-Rolla, associate professor, 1978-80, professor, 1980-. **ORGANIZATIONS:** International Society of Off Shore and Polar Eng, co-chair, 1992-; ASCE, 1984, 1989-; ASTM, 1980-; International Journal of Soil Dynamics and Earthquake Engineering, editorial board, 1982-; Egyptian Society of Earthquake Engineering, editorial board, 1991-; ISSMFE, 1991-; International Committee for Numerical Methods in Rock Mechanics, 1976-90. **HONORS/AWARDS:** International Conference on Soil Mech & Found Engg, co-general reporter, 1989; SM & FE, disc leader, 1985, panel reporter, 1981, co-reporter, 1977, chairman, 1973; Invited SOA Speaker, 1992. **SPECIAL ACHIEVEMENTS:** Published 13 books in USA and India; edited 6 books; wrote 215 papers, 89 presentations, and 94 reports. **HOME ADDRESS:** 1111 Duane Avenue, Rolla, MO 65401, (314)364-5572. **BUSINESS ADDRESS:** Professor of Civil Engineering, University of Missouri-Rolla, Rolla, MO 65401-0249, (314)341-4489.

PRASAD, MAREHALLI GOPALAN
Educator. Indo-American. **PERSONAL:** Born Jul 22, 1950, Hassan, Karnataka, India; son of M G Shakunjala and M S Gopalan; married Geetha Prasad, May 20, 1976; children: Yashaswi, Tejaswi. **EDUCATION:** University College of Engineering, India, BE, 1971; Indian Institute of Technology, India, MS, 1974; Purdue University, PhD, 1980. **CAREER:** Indian Institute of Technology, research scholar, 1972-74; Hindustan Aeronautics, engineer, 1974-77; Purdue University, graduate instructor, 1978-80; Stevens Institute of Technology, assistant/associate professor, 1980-. **ORGANIZATIONS:** Institute of Noise Control Engineering, vp, ext aff, 1990-92; American Society of

Mech Engineers, Tech Committee, chairman, 1988-92, associate editor, 1989-. **HONORS/AWARDS:** Nelson Ind, Acoustical Paper Award, 1986; INCE, Best Paper Award for Dr Prasad's Student, 1989. **SPECIAL ACHIEVEMENTS:** Acoustical Source Characterization in Duct Systems, 1991; Four Load Method for Source Impedance, 1987; research results published in books by other authors. **BUSINESS ADDRESS:** Professor, Dept of Mechanical Engineering, Stevens Inst of Technology, Castle Point on The Hudson, Hoboken, NJ 07030, (201)216-5571.

PRASAD, RAMESHWAR
Educator. Indo-American. **PERSONAL:** Born Jul 3, 1936, Sayadpur, Uttar Pradesh, India; son of Ganesha Nand (deceased) and Krishna Kumari (deceased); married Mithilesh Prasad, Dec 8, 1961; children: Roli, Rachna. **EDUCATION:** Lucknow University, India, BS, 1954; Allahabad University, India, MS, 1956, PhD, 1959, DSc, 1967. **CAREER:** Panta University, reader in chemistry, 1968-70; University of Illinois, faculty positions, 1972-, associate professor of pathology, currently. **ORGANIZATIONS:** American Association for Clinical Chemistry, 1984-; National Academy Clinical Biochemists, fellow, 1984-; Indian Science Congress, life member, 1992-; National Academy Science, India, fellow, 1960. **HONORS/AWARDS:** Allahabad University, Sa Hill Memorial Prize. **SPECIAL ACHIEVEMENTS:** Over 60 publications. **BUSINESS ADDRESS:** Associate Professor of Pathology, University of Illinois, College of Medicine, 1853 W Polk Street, Chicago, IL 60612, (312)996-7182.

PREMRAJ, A. N.
Engineer. Indo-American. **PERSONAL:** Born Nov 29, 1945, Madras, India; son of A Gopal; married Shirley, May 23, 1971; children: Michael, Julia. **EDUCATION:** University of Toronto, Canada, MBA program, 1969-72; Madras University, India, BME, 1968. **CAREER:** Douglas Aircrafts Co, Toronto, Canada, design engineer; Picker & X Ray Mfg, Toronto, mfg engineer; Burnside Equipment Ltd, Toronto, Canada, vp, mfg; IBM, R&D group; Prem Ind Inc, president; SP Technologies Inc, vp; Wintech Aerospace & Defense, engineer, currently. **BUSINESS ADDRESS:** Engineer, Wintech Industries Inc, 3103 E Chamber St, Phoenix, AZ 85040, (602)270-6046.

PUI, CHING-HON
Physician, educator. Hong Kong American. **PERSONAL:** Born Aug 20, 1951, Hong Kong; son of Y T Bay. **EDUCATION:** National Taiwan University, MD, 1976. **CAREER:** Saint Jude Children's Research Hospital, Departments of Hematology-Oncology & Pathology and Laboratory Medicine, assistant member, 1982-86, associate member, 1986-89, member, 1990-, vice chairman, 1994-; University of Tennessee, professor of pediatrics, 1990-, Center for Pediatric Pharmacokinetics & Therapeutics, member, 1991-; Saint Jude Children's Research Hospital, professor, Lymphoid Disease Progam, director, 1992-. **ORGANIZATIONS:** American Academy of Pediatrics, fellow, 1988-; American Society of Clinical Oncology, 1982-; American Association for Cancer Research, 1983-; American Society of Hematology, 1983-; Pediatric Oncology Group, principal investigator, 1985-; Society for Pediatric Research, 1987-; American Association for the Advancement of Science, 1992-. **HONORS/AWARDS:** National Taiwan University, Book Coupon Award, 1971, 1974, 1975. **SPECIAL ACHIEVEMENTS:** Over 200 articles & chapters published in medical journals, 1980-; Beijing Children's Hospital, China, visiting professor, 1991; National Taiwan University, visiting professor, 1992; National Pediatric Institute, visiting professor, 1993; University of Hong Kong, honorary professor, 1993. **BUSINESS ADDRESS:** Professor of Pediatrics, St Jude Children's Research Hospital, 332 N Lauderdale, PO Box 318, Memphis, TN 38101, (901)522-0335.

PUJARA, SUBHASH SOMABHAI
Radiologist. Indo-American. **PERSONAL:** Born Apr 24, 1946, Mahisa, Gujarat, India; son of Somabhai G Pujara; married Jayshree, Oct 15, 1975; children: Priya, Vishal. **EDUCATION:** BJ Medical College, Ahmedabad, Gujarat, India, MBBS, 1969; NYU, St Vincent's Hospital, radiology, 1973-76; VA, UAB at Birmingham, chief resident, nuclear medicine, 1976-78. **CAREER:** Community Hospital, radiologist, 1978-85; Dorn VA Hospital, radiologist, 1985-89; Eisenhower Army Medical Center, radiologist, 1989-. **ORGANIZATIONS:** American College of Radiology; Radiology Society of North American; Society of Nuclear Medicine. **HONORS/AWARDS:** American College of Radiology, Board Certification, 1976; Society of Nuclear Medicine, Board Eligible, 1978. **BIOGRAPHICAL SOURCES:** Radiology Journal, May 1978; Journal of Nuclear Medicine, 1977. **HOME ADDRESS:** 55 Old Still Rd, Columbia, SC 29223, (803)736-6329.

PULIGANDLA, VISWANADHAM
Materials scientist. Indo-American. **PERSONAL:** Born Jan 12, 1938, Vijayawada, Andhra Pradesh, India; son of P V Raman & Venkata Ratnamma; married Santhy, Aug 10, 1962; children: Usha Robillard, Ramana Sayi. **EDUCATION:** Sri Venkateswara University, India, BSc, 1957; Saugor University, India, MSc, 1959; University of Toledo, PhD, 1974. **CAREER:** India Meteorlgy Dept, sr technical asst, 1959-68; University of Toledo, grad asst, 1969-74; Ohio Dominican College, asst professor, 1974-78; Montana State University, asst res chemist, 1978-79; IBM Corp, advisory engr/scientist, Rochester, MN, 1979-85, Endicott, NY, 1991-92, Austin, TX, 1985-. **ORGANIZATIONS:** India Community Centre, Austin, Texas, chairperson, 1990; Indian Classical Music Circle of Austin, Texas, chairperson, 1993-94. **HONORS/AWARDS:** IBM, First Invention Achievement Award, 1990. **SPECIAL ACHIEVEMENTS:** Published over 60 articles in professional journals in chemistry, materials science, electronic packaging; author of 13 invention disclosures; two patents, one in corrosion control, one on nickel plating; author of chapters in 2 books. **HOME ADDRESS:** 2147 Surrender Ave, Austin, TX 78728, (512)251-3928.

PULIJAL, MADHU V.
Beverage company executive. Indo-American. **PERSONAL:** Born Feb 8, 1949, Hyderabad, India; married Aruna Pulijal, Apr 14, 1956; children: Pooja, Gautham. **EDUCATION:** Osmania University, BSc, 1970, MBA, 1972. **CAREER:** Prime Foods Inc, president, 1985-. **BUSINESS ADDRESS:** President, Prime Foods Inc, 4-40 44th Dr, Long Island City, NY 11101.

PUN, PATTLE PAK-TOE
Educator. Chinese American. **PERSONAL:** Born Sep 30, 1946, Hong Kong; son of Sak-Chi Pun and Ngan-Chu Kwan; married Gwen Yam Qun Chiu, Aug 22, 1970; children: Patrick, Benjamin. **EDUCATION:** San Diego State University, BS, chemistry (with high honors), 1969; State University of NY at Buffalo, MA, biology, 1972, PhD, biology, 1974; Wheaton College, MA, theology, 1985. **CAREER:** Wheaton College, professor of biology, 1973-; Argonne National Laboratory, resident associate, 1974-76; University of Illinois College of Medicine, research associate, 1980-81, 1992-93; American Critical Care, Inc, visiting scientist, 1984; Northern Illinois University, visiting microbiologist, summers 1985-88, fall 1987. **ORGANIZATIONS:** American Scientific Affiliation, member/fellow, 1971-; NY Academy of Science, 1975-; American Society for Microbiology, 1973-. **HONORS/AWARDS:** Robert Shields Foundation, scholarship, 1968-69; National Science Foundation, Undergraduate Research Award, 1969, Research Opportunity Award, 1985-88, 1992-93; Research Corp, Cottrell Science grant, 1975-76, 1979-80, 1982-83. **SPECIAL ACHIEVEMENTS:** 50 professional articles, including two books in English and in Chinese, 1974-93. **BIOGRAPHICAL SOURCES:** Who's Who in Technology. **BUSINESS ADDRESS:** Professor of Biology, Wheaton College, Seminary Rd, Armending 316, Wheaton, IL 60187, (708)752-5303.

PUNWANI, DHARAM VIR
Research and development executive. Indo-American. **PERSONAL:** Born Aug 23, 1942, Multan, India; son of Bhagwan Das & Gyan Devi Punwani; married Kiran, Feb 19, 1970; children: Vipul, Amit. **EDUCATION:** Indian Institute of Technology, Bombay, BS, 1964; Illinois Institute of Technology, MS, 1967; Loyola University, MBA, 1974. **CAREER:** Institute of Gas Technology, vice president, 1966-. **ORGANIZATIONS:** American Institute of Chemical Engineers, 1967-; Hindu Temple of Greater Chicago, education committee, 1992-. **HONORS/AWARDS:** State of Kentucky, Kentucky Colonel, 1989. **SPECIAL ACHIEVEMENTS:** Energy and environmental research; coal gasification; synthetic fuels production from coal and oil shale; biotechnological research; peat and biomass processing. **HOME ADDRESS:** 427 Prairie Knoll Dr, Naperville, IL 60565, (708)357-5532. **BUSINESS ADDRESS:** Vice President, Process Technology R & D, Institute of Gas Technology, 3424 S State St, Chicago, IL 60616, (312)949-3713.

PURI, PRATAP
Educator. Indo-American. **PERSONAL:** Born Mar 15, 1938, Lahore, Punjab, India; son of Kidar Nath Puri & Shakuntala Devi Puri; divorced; children: Amrita, Salil. **EDUCATION:** Camp College, Panjab University, BA (honors), 1957; Delhi University, MA, 1959; Indian Institute of Technology, Kharagpur, MTech, 1960, PhD, 1965. **CAREER:** IIT Bombay, associate lecturer, 1962-63, lecturer, 1963-68; University of New Orleans, assistant professor, 1968-71, associate professor, 1971-76, professor, 1976-. **ORGANIZATIONS:** SIAM; AAM; Calcutta Math Society. **BUSINESS ADDRESS:** Professor of Mathe-

matics, University of New Orleans, 2000 Lakeshore Dr, 245 Math Bldg, New Orleans, LA 70148, (504)286-6331.

PUROHIT, MILIND VASANT
Educator. Indo-American. **PERSONAL:** Born Aug 16, 1957, Delhi, India; son of Sudha & Vasant Purohit; married Uma M Purohit, Mar 3, 1986; children: Ashwin, Priya. **EDUCATION:** Indian Institute of Technology, Delhi, MS, 1978; California Institute of Technology, PhD, 1983. **CAREER:** Fermilab, research associate, 1983-86, Wilson fellow, 1986-88; Princeton University, assistant professor, 1988-. **ORGANIZATIONS:** American Physical Society, 1983-. **HONORS/AWARDS:** Fermilab, Wilson Fellow, 1986; US Dept of Energy, Outstanding Junior Investigator, 1989. **SPECIAL ACHIEVEMENTS:** Author of numerous publications. **BUSINESS ADDRESS:** Professor, Physics Dept, Princeton University, PO Box 708, Princeton, NJ 08544, (609)258-5852.

Q

QASIM, SYED REAZUL
Educator. Indo-American. **PERSONAL:** Born Dec 1, 1938, Allahabad, Uttar Pradesh, India; son of Syed Zamir Qasim and Fakhra Begum Qasim; married Mujtaba Begum Qasim, Dec 17, 1966; children: Zeba Saira, Saba Bano. **EDUCATION:** Aligarh Muslim University, India, BS, civil engineering, 1957; West Virginia University, MSCE, 1962, PhD, 1965. **CAREER:** Municipal Corporation, Allahabad, India, assistant district engineer, 1959-60; Indian Agricultural Research Institute, pool officer, 1965-66; Alden E Stilson and Associates, civil engineer, 1966-68; Battelle Memorial Institute, senior civil engineer, 1968-70; Polytechnic Insitute of New York, Dept of Civil Engineering, associate professor, 1971-73; University of Texas at Arlington, Dept of Civil Engineering, associate professor, 1973-78, professor, 1978-. **ORGANIZATIONS:** American Society of Civil Engineers, national and Texas, 1972-; American Society of Professional Engineers, national and Ohio, 1969-71; Water Environment Federation, national and Texas, 1965-; Technology Transfer Society, 1989-; American Waterworks Association, national and Texas, 1990-; Tau Beta Pi, 1974-; Chi Epsilon, 1972-; Sigma Xi, 1965-. **HONORS/AWARDS:** US Information Service, Fulbright Fellowship, 1986; Faculty of College of Engineering, The Halliburton Award for Excellence in Research, 1988-89; The University of Texas at Arlington, Distinguished Research Award, 1900-91; United Nations Development Program of CSIR, India Tokten consultant, 1992. **SPECIAL ACHIEVEMENTS:** Author, Wastewater Treatment Plants: Planning Design and Operation, Holt, Rinehart and Winston, 1985; numerous book chapters, journal articles and tecnical reports. **BUSINESS ADDRESS:** Professor, Dept of Civil Engineering, PO Box 19308, University of Texas at Arlington, Arlington, TX 76019, (817)273-2665.

QUAN, HANSON WAYNE
Design engineer. Chinese American. **PERSONAL:** Born Nov 29, 1965, Los Angeles, CA; son of Henry Sun Quan and Willa Fung Quan. **EDUCATION:** Occidental College, Advanced BA, physics, 1987; UC at Irvine, MSEE, 1989. **CAREER:** Jet Propulsion Laboratory, technical staff, 1985-87; professional photographer, 1990-; Western Digital Corporation, design engr, 1989-. **ORGANIZATIONS:** Society of Physics Students, 1986-87; UC at Irvine Engineering Alumni Society, treasurer, 1990-. **HONORS/AWARDS:** Sigma Pi Sigma, 1986; Occidental College, Departmental Honors, Physics, 1987. **SPECIAL ACHIEVEMENTS:** Language proficiency: French.

QUAN, KATIE
Labor union official. Chinese American. **PERSONAL:** Born Oct 27, 1952, Oakland, CA; daughter of Jack T Quan and June M Quan; children: Eric Takakuwa. **EDUCATION:** University of California, Santa Cruz, 1970-72; Chinese University of Hong Kong, 1973; University of California, Berkeley, BA, 1974; Cornell Institute of Labor Relations, 1984-86; Columbia University, 1988-89. **CAREER:** Oakland Public Schools, bilingual teacher's assistant, 1974-75; various other sewing factories, seamstress, 1975-79; Kin Yip Sportswear, seamstress, 1979-83; Asian American Legal Defense, administrative assistant, 1983; International Ladies' Garment Workers' Union, educator, researcher, 1984-86, organizer, 1986-89, district manager, 1990-. **ORGANIZATIONS:** Asian Pacific American Labor Alliance, AFL-CIO, vice president, founding chair, 1992-; San Francisco Labor Council, executive commitee, 1990-; We Do The Work, Labor TV Show, board of directors, 1991-; New York Chinatown History Museum, board of directors, 1987-; Coalition of Labor Union Women, 1984-; Asian American Federation of Union Members,

1990-; City of Hope, 1990-. **HONORS/AWARDS:** University of California, Phi Beta Kappa, 1974; KGO-TV, Channel 7, Profile of Excellence, 1991; Asian American Federation of Union Members, Labor Award, 1990; Mayor of San Francisco, Certificate of Appreciation, 1990; National Organization for Women, Honors Certificate, 1991. **SPECIAL ACHIEVEMENTS:** Proficient in Cantonese, Mandarin, Taishanese and Chinese. **BIOGRAPHICAL SOURCES:** Women and Unions, by Cobble, 1993; "Garment Workers Union Focuses on Asians," SF Chronicle, Jan 15, 1990. **BUSINESS ADDRESS:** Manager, Pacific Northwest District Council, International Ladies' Garment Workers' Union, 660 Howard Street, San Francisco, CA 94105, (415)543-9990.

QUAN, WILLIAM CHUN
Industrial designer. Chinese American. **PERSONAL:** Born Mar 10, 1953, Oakland, CA; son of Ann Quan. **EDUCATION:** University of California at Berkeley, 1971-73; Art Center College of Design, BS, 1976. **CAREER:** General Motors Design Staff, sr designer, 1976-86; Walter Dorwin Teague Assoc, sr designer, 1986-. **ORGANIZATIONS:** Industrial Designers Society of America, 1976-; Chinese American Assn for Professionals, vice pres, 1988-; Municipal League of King County, bd member, 1990-. **BUSINESS ADDRESS:** Senior Designer, Walter Dorwin Teague Assoc, 14727 NE 87th St, Redmond, WA 98052, (206)883-8684.

QUAN, XINA
Scientist. Chinese American. **PERSONAL:** Born Dec 23, 1957, Gloucester, NJ; daughter of Kuo-Kong Quan and Jean Li Quan; married Charles Roxlo, Jun 29, 1980; children: Thomas Roxlo. **EDUCATION:** Massachusetts Institute of Technology, SB, chem engineering, 1979, SM, chem engineering, 1980; Princeton University, PhD, chem engineering, 1986. **CAREER:** AT&T Bell Laboratories, assoc MTS, 1980-83, MTS, 1983-91, distinguished member of technical staff, 1991-. **ORGANIZATIONS:** American Chem Soc; American Phys Soc. **BUSINESS ADDRESS:** Distinguished Member of Technical Staff, AT&T Bell Laboratories, 600 Mountain Ave, Rm 7F-212, Murray Hill, NJ 07974.

QUEROL MORENO, CHERIE M.
Journalist. Filipino American. **PERSONAL:** Born Sep 15, Lucena, Quezon, Philippines; married Miguel; children: Juan Miguel Q. **EDUCATION:** BA, communication arts, 1974. **CAREER:** Lourdes Esclamado, general manager, 1985-; Philippine News, managing editor, currently. **ORGANIZATIONS:** Westmoor High School PTSA, membership committee, 1992-93; Likha Arts, publicity director, 1987-88; Children's Walkathon, advisory board, 1993; Asian American Journalists Association, 1988-89; Sampaguita, Video Project, advisory board, 1992. **HONORS/AWARDS:** Asian Foundation, Woman Warrior Nominee. **SPECIAL ACHIEVEMENTS:** Volunteer work to promote Filipino culture with Likha Organization, 1988; Advocacy of Youth, Women's Issues. **BUSINESS ADDRESS:** Managing Editor, Philippine News, 156 South Spruce Avenue, Suite 207, South San Francisco, CA 94080, (415)872-3000.

QUIMPO, RAFAEL GONZALES
Educator. Filipino American. **PERSONAL:** Born Mar 23, 1938, Ibajay, Aklan, Philippines; son of Manual R Quimpo & Consuelo Gonzales; married Vanida Suriyakham-Quimpo, Dec 28, 1963; children: Rafael Jr, Veronica Quimpo-Roberson, Carlos Manuel, Vanessa. **EDUCATION:** Feati University, Philippines, BSCE, 1959; SEATO Graduate School of Engineering, Thailand, MEng, 1962; Colorado State University, PhD, 1966. **CAREER:** Colorado State University, graduate research assistant, 1963-66; University of Pittsburgh, assistant professor, 1966-70, associate professor, 1970-75, professor, 1975-. **ORGANIZATIONS:** International Association of Hydrologic Sciences, secretary, Committee on Math Models, 1976-79; American Geophysical Union, Committee on Urban Hydrology, 1983-85; American Society of Civil Engineering, chairman, Surface Water Hydrology Committee, 1988-92, Committee on Research Hyd, 1989-, chairman, Committee on Education, 1988-91. **HONORS/AWARDS:** University of Pittsburgh, Beitle-Veltri Teaching Excellence, 1984; ASCE Pittsburgh Section, Professor of the Year, 1985; National Science Foundation, research grants, 1970-76, 1979-80, 1984-88, 1990-91, travel grants, 1971, 1976, 1980, 1983, 1986. **SPECIAL ACHIEVEMENTS:** Author, textbook on hydrology and hydraulics, 1986; published more than 70 papers in journals of ASCE, AGU and IASH, 1968-. **BUSINESS ADDRESS:** Prof, Dept of Civil Eng, University of Pittsburgh, 940 Benedum Hall, Pittsburgh, PA 15261, (412)624-9873.

QUISMORIO, FRANCISCO P., JR.
Physician, educator, researcher. Filipino American. **PERSONAL:** Born Jan 21, 1941, San Fernando, La Union, Philippines; son of Francisco N Quismorio & Cristina L Parpana; married Violeta Consolacion, Jun 1972; children: James Patrick, Anne Violet. **EDUCATION:** University of Philippines, BA, 1960, MD, 1964; University of Pennsylvania, fellowship in rheumatology, 1966-68; University of Southern California, fellowship in rheumatology & immunology, 1969-70. **CAREER:** Los Angeles County-University of Southern California Medical Center, physician specialist, unit chief, clinical rheumatology laboratory, 1978-; University of Southern California, School of Medicine, professor of medicine, vice chief, Division of Rheumatology & Immunology, 1983-, professor of pathology, 1986-. **ORGANIZATIONS:** American College of Physicians, fellow, 1977-; American College of Rheumatology, fellow; American Association of Immunologists; Clinical Immunology Society; New York Academy of Science; Southern California Rheumatology Society, president, 1983-84; Association of Philippine Physicians in America; Philippine Medical Association of Southern California. **HONORS/AWARDS:** Southern California Rheumatology Society, Research Award, 1969, 1970; Philippine Medical Society of Southern California, Award for Excellence in Academic Medicine, 1982; Arthritis Foundation, Service Award, 1983; University of the Philippines, Outstanding Alumnus, 1989; American Lupus Society, Fleur De' Lis Award, 1991. **SPECIAL ACHIEVEMENTS:** Editorial board, Postgraduate Medicine, 1991-; commissioner, oral examinations, California State Medical Board, 1981-; associate editor, Lupus Erythematosus, book, 4th edition, 1993; author of over 100 medical and scientific articles in peer-reviewed publications. **BUSINESS ADDRESS:** Prof, Medicine & Pathology, Vice Chief, Div of Rheumatology & Immunology, Univ of Southern California, Sch of Med, 2025 Zonal Ave, Hoffman Bldg, Rm 715, Los Angeles, CA 90033, (213)342-1946.

QUON, CHECK YUEN
Research director. Chinese American. **PERSONAL:** Born Nov 15, 1949, Canton, Kwang Tung, People's Republic of China; married Wailan Louie Quon; children: Nicole, Daniel, Justin. **EDUCATION:** UCLA, BS, chemistry, 1972, PhD, pharmacology, 1977; University of Wisconsin, postdoctoral studies, 1977-79. **CAREER:** Arnar Stone, research investigator, drug metabolism, 1979-81; American Critical Care, Drug Metabolism, sr research investigator, 1981-83, section head, 1984-86; DuPont Critical Care, Clinical Pharmacology and Drug Metabolism, section head, 1986-88; DuPont Merck, director of drug metabolism and pharmaco kinetics, 1988-. **ORGANIZATIONS:** American Association for Pharmacology & Experimental Therapeutics, 1986-; International Society for Study of Xenobiotics, 1987-; American Association of Pharmaceutical Sciences, 1988-; American Chemical Society, 1979-89; Pharmaceutical Manufacturers Association, steering comittee, 1991-95. **HONORS/AWARDS:** UCLA, Departmental Honor in Chemistry, 1972; American Association for Pharmacology & Experimental Therapeutics, elected member, 1986. **SPECIAL ACHIEVEMENTS:** Thirty-six manuscripts and forty abstracts in areas of drug metabolism and pharmacokinetics; two book chapters on cardiovascular drugs. **BUSINESS ADDRESS:** Director, Drug Metabolism & Pharmacokinetics, DuPont Merck Pharmaceutical Co, Stine-Haskell Research Center, PO Box 30, Elkton Rd, Bldg 115, Rm 54, Newark, DE 19714, (302)366-5405.

QUON, SHUN WING
Pharmacist. Hong Kong American. **PERSONAL:** Born May 24, 1950, Hong Kong; son of Mrs S Y Quon; married Jane J Quon, Aug 11, 1974; children: Justin, Suzanne. **EDUCATION:** University of Mississippi, BA, 1972, Pharmacy School, BS, pharmacy, 1978. **CAREER:** Roy's Prescription Shop, staff pharmacist, 1977-78; Hub City Pharmacy, pharmacist, manager, 1978-82; Super D Drugs, pharmacist, manager, 1982-84; Longs Drugs, staff pharmacist, 1984-85; Payless Drugs, staff pharmacist, 1984-85; Wapples Pharmacy, staff pharmacist, 1984-85; Forest Ave Pharmacy, pharmacists, owner, 1985-. **ORGANIZATIONS:** Santa Clara County Pharmacists Association, president, 1992-93, board member, continuing education administrator, 1990-92; California Pharmacists Association, 1985-94; American Pharmaceutical Association, 1974-94; National Association of Retail Druggist, 1985-94. **MILITARY SERVICE:** US Army, specialist 5, 1972-74. **BUSINESS ADDRESS:** Pharmacist, Forest Ave Pharmacy, 2039 Forest Ave, Ste 202, San Jose, CA 95128, (408)295-8100.

QURESHI, MUQUARRAB AHMED
Educator. Pakistani American. **PERSONAL:** Born Nov 4, 1953, Sargodha, Punjab, Pakistan; son of Abdur Razaq; married Raana Qureshi, Oct 24, 1975; children: Taiyyaba A. **EDUCATION:** University of Agriculture, Faisalabad,

Pakistan, DVM, 1974, MS, 1977; Cornell University, PhD, 1986. **CAREER:** University of Agri, Pakistan, lecturer, 1975-81; Cornell University, research assistant, 1981-86; NC State University, associate professor, 1987-. **ORGANIZATIONS:** American Association of Immunologists, 1990-; Poultry Science Association, 1987-. **HONORS/AWARDS:** Cornell University, Bruckner Memorial, 1986. **SPECIAL ACHIEVEMENTS:** Published over 100 scientific papers, 1975-93. **BIOGRAPHICAL SOURCES:** Poultry Science, 70: p 530-538, 1991. **BUSINESS ADDRESS:** Associate Professor, North Carolina State University, Scott Hall, Room 360, Raleigh, NC 27695, (919)515-5388.

QURESHI, QADEER AHMAD
Computer engineer. Pakistani American. **PERSONAL:** Born Mar 29, 1957, Rawal Pindi, Pakistan; son of Munir Ahmad Qureshi and Anwar Sultana; married Samina Q Qureshi, May 10, 1985; children: Haris A, Haseeb A, Habib A. **EDUCATION:** University of Engineering & Technology, BSEE, 1980; Texas A&M University, MSEE, 1985. **CAREER:** Schlumberger Wireline, instrument engineer, 1981-83; Texas A&M University, lecturer, 1985; Micon Engineering, design engineer, 1985-90; Texas Instruments, systems engineer, 1990-. **ORGANIZATIONS:** Texas Society of Professional Engineers, 1990-. **HOME ADDRESS:** 6801 Vero Dr, Plano, TX 75023.

R

RAB, MIRZA M.
Engineer. Indo-American. **PERSONAL:** Born Oct 6, 1940, Hyderabad, India; son of Mirza A Rab and Sajida Sultana; married Zia Rab, Mar 22, 1980; children: Mubeen, Diba, Aqil, Aliyah. **EDUCATION:** Osmania University, Hyderabad, India, BSEE, 1961; University of Strathclyde, Glasgow, Scotland, MSEE, 1969. **CAREER:** Pahlavi University, Iran, instructor in elec eng, 1969-71; Sargent and Lundy Engineers, engineer, 1971-73; Bechtel Power Corp, senior engineer, 1973-78; CDA engineering, partner/supervising engineer, 1978-87; Multi Tech Resources, president, 1987-. **ORGANIZATIONS:** Michigan Education Council, trustee/secretary, 1991-; Wayne State University Islamic Center, trustee, 1990-. **BUSINESS ADDRESS:** President, Multi Tech Resources, 32950 Five Mile Rd, Livonia, MI 48154, (313)261-7096.

RADHAKRISHNAMURTHY, BHANDARU
Educator. Indo-American. **PERSONAL:** Born Jul 1, 1928, Vemulapalli, Andhra Pradesh, India; son of Rajeswararao Bhandaru and Sathyavathi Bhandaru; married Sakuntala, Sep 5, 1953 (deceased); children: Rajeswararao, Uma Kalagnanam, Hema, Srinivas; married Sulochana, Feb 20, 1983. **EDUCATION:** Nizam College, India, BS, 1951; Osmania University, India, MS, 1953, PhD, 1958. **CAREER:** Sirsilk Ltd, India, chemist, 1953-54; Osmania University, India, lecturer, 1955-61; Louisiana State University, instructor, professor, 1961-92; Tulane University, professor, 1992-. **ORGANIZATIONS:** American Society of Biochemists & Molecular Biologists; American Chemical Society; American Assn for the Advancement of Science; American Heart Assn, Council of Atherosclerosis; Southern Society for Clinical Investigations; Sigma Xi; Society for Complex Carbohydrates; Hindu Temple Society, New Orleans, president, 1979-89. **HONORS/AWARDS:** Osmania University, Merit Scholarship, 1953; Fulbright, travel grant, 1961; Louisiana Heart Assn, research grant, 1972; National Institutes of Health, research grants, 1972-. **SPECIAL ACHIEVEMENTS:** About 200 research articles published in scientific journals on biomedical mechanisms of arteriosclerosis, diabetes, chronic lung diseases. **BUSINESS ADDRESS:** Professor, School of Public Health & Tropical Medicine, Tulane University, 1501 Canal St, Rm 310, New Orleans, LA 70112, (504)585-7195.

RAGHAVAN, SRIDHAR A.
Software technology consultant. Indo-American. **PERSONAL:** Born May 12, 1950, Kumbakonam, Tamil Nadu, India; son of Pankajam and Raghavan; married Sandhya, Aug 26, 1981; children: Vasanthi, Ananth. **EDUCATION:** Bombay University, BEE, 1972; Indian Institute of Technology, MTech, 1974; Georgia State University, PhD, 1984. **CAREER:** Data Consultancy Services, senior software engineer, 1974-79, software consultant, 1980-84; Information Systems America, Information Systems, consultant, 1984-85; Wang Institute, assistant professor of software eng, 1985-87; Bentley College, assistant professor of CIS, 1987-91; Digital Equipment, senior staff, 1991-. **ORGANIZATIONS:** New Hampshire Association of Asian Indians, president, 1992-; Journal of Info Technology Management, member of editorial board, 1988-; International Workshop on Computer-Aided Software Eng, program committee, 1992, 1993, 1995; Prism, Task Force on DSS Workbenches, 1990, 1991;

Wang Institute, Corporate Association Program, faculty director, 1985-86; Mini Track on DSS Workbenches, coordinator, 1992-93; ACM; IEEE; TIMS; AAAI. **HONORS/AWARDS:** Bentley College, Research Publication Award, 1989, 1990, Research Fellowship, 1988-89, 1989-90; Georgia State University, Teaching Fellowship, 1979-84; State of Maharashta, Government Scholarship, 1969-72. **SPECIAL ACHIEVEMENTS:** Research papers on software engineering, 1985-; professional development tutorials, ACM, IEEE, 1985-87; Colloquium on Decision Support to Chinese Economic Delegation, Lowell, 1987; Colloquium, Tutorial on Expert Systems, COSTED, United Nations Agency, Madras, India, 1987. **BIOGRAPHICAL SOURCES:** Peterson's Guide, Wang Institute, 1985-87; IEEE Software, July 1989. **BUSINESS ADDRESS:** Senior Staff, Digital Equipment Corporation, 110 Spitbrook Road, ZK02-1/Q18, Nashua, NH 03062.

RAGUDOS, JOHN L.
Youth agency executive. Filipino American. **PERSONAL:** Born Nov 3, 1948, Seattle, WA; son of Johnny B Ragudos; married Elizabeth S Ragudos, May 8, 1971; children: Jon Frederic, Dante Mateo, Tavia Elyse. **EDUCATION:** Seattle Central Community College, 1966-68; Seattle University, 1971, 1992. **CAREER:** City of Seattle, outreach worker, 1972-73; Filipino Youth Activities, administrative secretary, 1971-72, program coordinator, 1973-75, administrative coordinator, 1975-77, executive director, 1977-. **ORGANIZATIONS:** Asian Pacific Executive Directors Coalition, 1991-; Minority Executive Directors Coalition, 1983-; Veterans of Foreign Wars, 1971-; Seattle Central Community College Asian Advisory Board, 1978-79; Seattle Metro Softball Umpires Assn, 1982-; Filipino American Natl Historical Society, Seattle, 1993. **HONORS/AWARDS:** Filipino American National Historical Society, Seattle, Very Impressive Pinoy, 1993; Washington Outstanding Filipino-Americans, Community Service Award, 1990. **SPECIAL ACHIEVEMENTS:** Presidential Appointment, American Bicentennial, Asian Advisory Committee, 1974-76. **MILITARY SERVICE:** US Army, sgt (E-5), 1969-71, Vietnam Veteran/Army Commendation Medal, 1970. **BUSINESS ADDRESS:** Executive Director, Filipino Youth Activities, Inc, 810-18th Ave Ste 200, Seattle, WA 98122, (206)461-4870.

RAHMAN, YUEH-ERH (JADY)
Educator, educational administrator. Chinese American. **PERSONAL:** Born Jun 10, 1928, Guang Zhou, Guangdong, China; daughter of Li; married Anees Rahman, Nov 3, 1956 (deceased); children: Aneesa Rahman Scandalis. **EDUCATION:** Universite de Paris, BS, pre-med, 1950; Universite de Louvain, Belgium, MD (magna cum laude), 1956, postdoctoral fellow, 1959-60. **CAREER:** University of Utrecht, Netherlands, visiting scientist, 1968-69; Northern Illinois University, adjunct professor, 1971-85; Argonne National Laboratory, numerous positions, 1964-85; University of Minnesota, director of graduate studies, 1989-92, Department of Pharmaceutics, professor, 1985-, head, 1991-. **ORGANIZATIONS:** International Society for Cell Biology; American Society for Cell Biology; New York Academy of Science; American Association of Pharmaceutical Scientists; American Institute of Biological Sciences; American Association for the Advancement of Science; Radiation Research Society; Association for Women in Science, Chicago chapter president, 1978-79, nominating committee, nationals, 1982-85; International Committee on Oral Chelation, 1993-. **HONORS/AWARDS:** IR-100 Award for Liposome Encapsulation of Drugs, 1976; awarded three patents; NIH, Experimental Therapeutic Study Section, 1979-83; American Association of Pharmaceutical Scientists, fellow, 1992. **SPECIAL ACHIEVEMENTS:** Fluent in written and spoken French and Chinese; "Liposomes as Carriers for Chelators," Liposome Letters, A D Bangham, ed, Academic Press Inc, p 335-340, 1983; "Liposome Targeted to Cellular Receptors," Investigation of Membrane Located Receptors, E Reid, GMW Cook and DJ Moore, editors, Plenum Publishin Corp, p 317-330, 1984; "Liposomes in Metal Poisoning and Metal Storage Diseases," in Liposomes and Drug Carriers: Trends and Progress, G Gregoriadis, editor, John Wiley and Sons Ltd Publishing, p 485-496, 1988. **BUSINESS ADDRESS:** Professor, University of Minnesota, 308 Harvard St SE, HSU-F, 9-112, Minneapolis, MN 55455, (612)626-2678.

RAI, AMARENDRA KUMAR
Scientist. Indo-American. **PERSONAL:** Born Oct 20, 1952, Varanasi, Uttar Pradesh, India; son of Dina Nath Rai (deceased) and Asharfi Rai (deceased); married Urmila Rai, Jun 29, 1971. **EDUCATION:** Gorakhpur University, BSc, 1970; Banaras Hindu University, MSc, 1972, PhD, 1977. **CAREER:** North Carolina State University, research associate, 1979-81; UES Inc, research scientist, 1981-85, senior scientist, 1985-. **ORGANIZATIONS:** American Physical Society, 1981-; American Society of Metals, 1989-; SAMPE, 1992-.

HONORS/AWARDS: Council of Sci & Ind Res, India, Junior Research Fellow, 1972, Senior Research Fellow, 1974, Post-doctoral Fellow, 1977. **SPECIAL ACHIEVEMENTS:** Published over 90 research papers in scientific journals; invited by scientific journals to be contributor. **BUSINESS ADDRESS:** Senior Scientist, Universal Energy Systems Inc, 4401 Dayton-Xenia Rd, Dayton, OH 45432, (513)426-6900.

RAI, ARTI K.
Attorney. Indo-American. **PERSONAL:** Born Nov 17, 1966, India; daughter of Jagdish Bains & Jagdishwar Srinastava. **EDUCATION:** Harvard College, AB, 1987; Harvard Medical School, 1988; Harvard Law School, JD, 1991. **CAREER:** Judicial Clerk to Federal District Judge Marilyn Hall Patel, 1991-92; Jenner & Block, attorney, 1992-. **ORGANIZATIONS:** Harvard Civil Rights Civil Liberties Law Review, executive editor, 1990-91. **HONORS/AWARDS:** Harvard Law School, Ames Most Court Competition Winner, 1990. **SPECIAL ACHIEVEMENTS:** Cost-Benefit and Cost-Effectiveness Analysis in the Medical Literature: Are the Methods Being Used Correctly?, 116 Annals of Internal Medicine, vol 3 p 238-244, 1992. **HOME ADDRESS:** 1735 1/2 Corcoran St NW, Apt A, Washington, DC 20009, (202)986-0483. **BUSINESS ADDRESS:** Attorney, Jenner & Block, 601 13th St, 12th Fl, Washington, DC 20005, (202)639-6048.

RAI, ARUN
Educator. Indo-American. **PERSONAL:** Born Sep 28, 1963, Kanpur, Uttar Pradesh, India; son of Hashmat Rai (deceased) & Sudarshan Rai; married Sujata, Jun 27, 1990. **EDUCATION:** Birla Institute of Technology & Science, India, MS, 1985; Clarion University of Pennsylvania, MBA, 1987; Kent State University, PhD, 1990. **CAREER:** Gwalior Rayons, India, engineer trainee, 1984-85; The Systems Group, India, systems consultant, 1985-86; Clarion University of Pennsylvania, graduate assistant, 1986-87; Kent State University, research and teaching fellow, 1987-90; Southern Illinois University, assistant professor, 1990-. **ORGANIZATIONS:** Beta Gamma Sigma, 1990-; Institute of Management Sciences, 1989-; Decision Sciences Institute, 1988-. **HONORS/AWARDS:** Southern Illinois University, College of Business, Researcher of the Year, 1993, Graduate Teaching Honor Roll, 1992, 1993; Kent State University, Dissertation Research Award, 1990, University Fellowship, 1990. **SPECIAL ACHIEVEMENTS:** Published several articles in leading journals and conference proceedings in the area of management information systems. **BUSINESS ADDRESS:** Assistant Professor, Dept of Management, Southern Illinois University, College of Business and Administration, Carbondale, IL 62901.

RAI, GAURI S.
Educator. Indo-American. **PERSONAL:** Born Jan 24, 1944, Varanasi, Uttar Pradesh, India; son of Sri Vishwa Nath Rai; married Krishna K Rai, Mar 15, 1964; children: Saroj, Anjoo, Taruna, Sumita, Anita. **EDUCATION:** Kashi Vidyapith University, India, BA, 1962, MAS, 1964; St Louis University, MSW, 1970; Rutgers University, PhD, 1976. **CAREER:** Rutgers University, assistant professor, 1976-78; State University College, Buffalo, associate professor, 1978-80; University of Akron, Ohio, professor, 1980-. **ORGANIZATIONS:** National Association of Social Workers; Council on Social Work Education. **HONORS/AWARDS:** License independent social worker, 1987-. **BIOGRAPHICAL SOURCES:** Reducing Bureaucratic Inflexiblity, Social Service Review, vol 57, no 3, pp 44-58, 1983; Control Structure and Conflict in Public Agencies, Administration in Social Work, vol 9, pp 75-87, 1985-86. **HOME PHONE:** (216)686-2458. **BUSINESS PHONE:** (216)972-6190.

RAI, VIJAI NARAIN
Government official. Indo-American. **PERSONAL:** Born Nov 19, 1941, Malsa, Ghazipur, Uttar Pradesh, India; son of Kamala and Nagita Rai; married Sherry Louise Rai, Jul 29, 1977; children: Mira Lynn, Nisha Ann. **EDUCATION:** Banaras Hindu University, Varanasi, UP, India, BS, 1961, MS, 1963; Mackay School of Mines, University of Nevada, Reno, MS, 1968, PhD, 1972. **CAREER:** California State University, San Jose, assistant professor of geology, 1970-71, 1977-78; California State University, Chico, lecturer in geology, 1972-76; Mackay School of Mines, University of Nevada, lecturer in geology, 1978-79; Engineering & Val Branch (IRS), US Dept of the Treasury, mining engineer, 1979-84; Energy & Minerals (BIA), US Dept of the Interior, staff geologist, 1984-1987; Office of Surface Mining, US Dept of the Interior, geologist, 1987-90; Office of the Secretary, US Dept of the Interior, chief, Mineral Resources Division, 1990-. **ORGANIZATIONS:** Society for Mining, Metallurgy, and Exploration Inc, 1987-; Am Inst of Mining, Metallurgy & Petroleum Engineers, Washington, DC chapter, 1990-. **HONORS/AWARDS:**

Office of the Secretary, US Dept of The Interior, Performance Award, 1991, 1992, 1993; Office of Surface Mining, US Dept of the Interior, Citation for Special Act or Service, 1990; Internal Revenue Service, US Dept of the Treasury, Certificate of Award for Sustained Superior Performance, 1983, 1984; Mackay School of Mines, University of Nevada, Research Award, 1969-90. **BUSINESS ADDRESS:** Chief, Mineral Resources Division, Office of Env Policy & Compliance, Office of the Secretary, US Dept of the Interior, 1849 C St, MS 2340, Main Interior Bldg, Washington, DC 20240, (202)208-6661.

RAIMUNDO, CRIS C.
Educational administrator. Filipino American. **PERSONAL:** married Evelyn; children: Maria Rocio, Antonio. **CAREER:** Varian Associates, Corporate Audit, manager, currently. **ORGANIZATIONS:** Fremont Unified School District, school board member, 1990-; Lahi, organizer. **BUSINESS ADDRESS:** Board Member, Fremont Unified School District, PO Box 5008, Fremont, CA 94537, (510)657-2350.*

RAINA, ASHOK K.
Research entomologist. Indo-American. **PERSONAL:** Born Feb 28, 1942, Srinagar, Jammu and Kashmir, India; son of Sarwanand Raina and Leelawati Raina; married Santosh Raina, Sep 26, 1960; children: Rakesh, Seema Raina Kak. **EDUCATION:** Jammu & Kashmir University, BSc, 1961; Aligarh Muslim University, MSc, 1967; North Dakota State University, PhD, 1974. **CAREER:** Commonwealth Institute Biological Control, field assistant, 1962-65; US Aid-India, sr res assistant, 1967-70; Minot State University, assistant professor biology, 1974-75; Virginia State University, res associate, 1975-77; International Center of Insect Physiology & Ecology, res scientist, 1978-80; University of Maryland, sr res associate, 1981-85; USDA Agric Res Ser, res entomologist, 1986-. **ORGANIZATIONS:** Entomological Soc of India, fellow, life member; Entomological Society of America, 1974-; International Society Chem Ecology, 1984-; Kashmir Overseas Association, Washington chapter, past president; Indo-American Kashmir Forum, board of directors, currently. **HONORS/AWARDS:** University Maryland, College Park, Outstanding Invention of 1989, 1990; Entomol Society America, L O Howard Distinguished Award, 1991; ESA, Eastern Branch, J E Bussart Award Nominee, 1993; USDA, ARS, nine merit awards, 1989-93. **SPECIAL ACHIEVEMENTS:** Discovered a neuropeptide hormone that controls sex pheromone production in moths, 1989; four papers in science, three senior author, 1984, 1989, 1990, 1992. **BUSINESS ADDRESS:** Research Entomologist, USDA, ARS, Insect Neurobiol & Hormone Lab, Room 313, Bldg 306, BARC-East, Beltsville, MD 20705.

RAJ, HARKISAN D.
Educator. Indo-American. **PERSONAL:** Born Jan 1, 1926, Sehwan, Sindh, Pakistan; son of Dunichand C Tejwani & Moar N Chandanani; married Anita H Raj, Sep 1, 1956; children: Robin C, Arnaz K (sons). **EDUCATION:** University of Bombay, India, BS (with honors), 1947; University of Pune, India, MS, 1952; PhD, 1955. **CAREER:** Public Health Service, Pune & Bombay, India, bacteriologist, 1948-56; A&M University of Texas, postdoctoral fellow, 1956-57; Oregon State University, postdoctoral fellow, 1957-58; Public Health Service, Seattle, Washington, bacteriologist, 1958-59; University of Washington, asst professor, 1959-62; California State University, Long Beach, professor, 1962-92. **ORGANIZATIONS:** American Society for Microbiology, 1960-; Canadian Society for Microbiology, 1960-80; California Society for Electron Microscopy, 1962-85; American Institute of Food Technology, 1960-65. **HONORS/AWARDS:** Sigma Xi, Research Recognition, 1958; American Academy of Microbiology, elected fellow, 1993; various research grants from state, federal agencies and private corporations, 1959-. **SPECIAL ACHIEVEMENTS:** Over 50 scientific research publications, review articles & reports covering bacterial physiology, structure and taxonomy in national and international microbiology journals, 1953-90; served as an editorial referee for various manuscripts for publication in various journals; discovered 3 new bacteria, author of their nomenclature at genus and species levels, 1964-90; new bacteria deposited with American Type Culture Collection, Washington DC; consultant to various private corporations & FAO of the United Nations, Rome, Italy, 1967-89. **HOME PHONE:** (714)846-0718.

RAJA, RAJENDRAN
High energy physicist. Indo-American. **PERSONAL:** Born Jul 14, 1948, Guruvayur, Kerala, India; son of P K S Raja & Chandramathi Raja; married Selitha Raja, Jul 24, 1976; children: Anjali. **EDUCATION:** University of Cambridge, England, BA (with honors), 1970, PhD, 1975. **CAREER:** Fermi Lab, research associate, 1975-78, associate scientist, 1978-83, scientist I, 1983-

88, scientist II, 1988-. **ORGANIZATIONS:** American Physical Society. **HONORS/AWARDS:** Trinity College, University of Cambridge, exhibitioner, 1968, senior scholar, 1969, fellow, 1973. **SPECIAL ACHIEVEMENTS:** Published 80 papers in top journals on high energy experiemental particle physics, 1975-; organized conferences, editor of proceedings; playing a leading role in an experiment at Fermi Lab to discover Top Quark. **BUSINESS ADDRESS:** Scientist II, Fermi National Accelerator Laboratory, PO Box 500, Batavia, IL 60510, (708)840-4092.

RAJAGOPAL, KUMBAKONAM RAMAMANI
Educator. Indo-American. **PERSONAL:** Born Nov 24, 1950, New Delhi, India; son of Kumbakonam Rajagopal Ramanani & Hemalata Ramamani; married Chandrika, Jul 14, 1975; children: Keshava, Sudarshan. **EDUCATION:** Indian Institute of Technology, BTech, 1973; Illinois Institute of Technology, MS, 1974; University of Minnesota, PHD, 1978. **CAREER:** University of Michigan, postdoctoral lecturer, 1978-80; Catholic University, assistant professor, 1980-82; University of Pittsburgh, professor, 1982-. **ORGANIZATIONS:** American Society Mech Engineer, fellow, fluid mechanics committee, constitutive equations committee, 1980-; American Academy Mech, 1986-; Society for National Philosophy, past chairman, 1980-. **HONORS/AWARDS:** ASME, fellow, 1991; University of Pittsburgh, Chancellors Distinguished Research Award, 1990. **SPECIAL ACHIEVEMENTS:** Editorial Board: Archive for Rational Mechanics & Analysis, Intl Journal of Engineering Science, Intl Journal of Non-Linear Mechanics, Mecanica, Continuum Mechanics & Thermodynamics, Stability and Applied Analysis of Continua, Mathematical Models & Methods in Applied Sciences, Journal of Mathematical & Physical Sciences. **BUSINESS ADDRESS:** Professor, University of Pittsburgh, 637 Benedum Hall, Pittsburgh, PA 15261, (412)624-9799.

RAJAN, FREDERICK E. N.
Church administrator. Indo-American. **PERSONAL:** Born Oct 15, 1949, Neyyoor, Tamil Nadu, India; son of Frederick Raj & Daisy Frederick Raj; married Sheila Rajan, Nov 24, 1976. **EDUCATION:** Annamalai University, BA, 1972; Madras University, MA, 1974; Faith Lutheran Seminary, MDiv, 1979, MTH, 1981. **CAREER:** India Youth for Christ, area director, 1974-76; Faith Lutheran Seminary, administrative assistant, 1978-81; Holy Trinity Lutheran Church, Irving, Texas, pastor, 1984-87; Evangelical Lutheran Church in America, director for multicultural mission strategy, 1988-91, executive director, comm for multicultural ministries, 1992-. **ORGANIZATIONS:** Asian Lutheran Association, editor, 1985-87, president, 1986-88; Clergy and Laity Concerned, board member, 1992-; Interdenominational Multicultural Education and Training, board member, 1992-. **SPECIAL ACHIEVEMENTS:** Author, Eternal River: Asian Cultural Awareness, 1986. **BUSINESS ADDRESS:** Exec Dir, Commission for Multicultural Ministries, Evangelical Lutheran Church in America, 8765 W Higgins Rd, Chicago, IL 60631, (312)380-2841.

RAJAN, PERIASAMY KARIVARATHA
Educator, educational administrator. Indo-American. **PERSONAL:** Born Sep 20, 1942, Karur, Tamil Nadu, India; son of K S Periasamy Gounder & Ponnamal; married Visalakshi, Jan 31, 1971; children: Raj. **EDUCATION:** University of Madras, India, BS, 1966; IIT, Madras, India, MTech, 1969, PhD, 1975. **CAREER:** Regional Engineering College, Trichy, associate lecturer, 1969-70; IIT Madras, India, associate lecturer, lecturer, 1970-77; State University College, Buffalo, assistant professor, 1978-80; North Dakota State University, associate professor, 1980-83; Tennessee Technological University, associate professor, 1983-85, professor, 1985-, chairperson, 1992-. **ORGANIZATIONS:** IEEE, senior member; ASEEE. **HONORS/AWARDS:** Tennessee Technological University, Caplenor Research Award, 1990. **SPECIAL ACHIEVEMENTS:** More than 45 articles published in reviewed engineering journals. **HOME ADDRESS:** 852 Lone Oak Dr, Cookeville, TN 38501, (615)528-6075. **BUSINESS PHONE:** (615)372-3397.

RAJAN, RAGHURAM GOVIND
Educator. Indo-American. **PERSONAL:** Born Feb 3, 1963, Bhopal, Madhya Pradesh, India; son of R Govindarajan and M Sarangapany; married Radhika Puri, Aug 21, 1989. **EDUCATION:** Indian Institute of Technology, B Tech, 1985; Indian Institute of Management, MBA, 1987; Massachusetts Institute of Technology, PhD, 1991. **CAREER:** Tata Administrative Service, officer, 1987; University of Chicago, assistant professor, 1991-. **HONORS/AWARDS:** American Finance Association, Smith Breeden Prize, 1992; Western Finance Association, Treffstz Award, 1991; Small Firm Financial Research

Association, Best Paper Award, 1993. **SPECIAL ACHIEVEMENTS:** Articles in various scholarly journals and newspapers. **BUSINESS ADDRESS:** Assistant Professor, University of Chicago, Graduate School of Business, 1101 E 58th St, Chicago, IL 60637-1511, (312)702-9299.

RAJANI, PREM RAJARAM
Transportation company financial executive. Indo-American. **PERSONAL:** Born Nov 9, 1949, Bombay, Maharashtra, India; son of Devibai Rajani and Rajaram Rajani; married Rekha, Apr 21, 1977; children: Anand, Harshada. **EDUCATION:** Indian Institute of Technology, Bombay, BTech, chemical engineering, 1973; Columbia University, MBA accounting, finance, 1975. **CAREER:** Pfizer Inc, New York, senior operations auditor, 1975-78; Sea-Land Industries, senior projects financial analyst, 1978-80, financial manager joint ventures, 1980-81, manager, corp planning & analyst, 1981-84; Sea-Land Corp, manager of corp finance, 1984-87, assistant treasurer, international, 1987-88; Sea Land Service, assistant treasurer, domestic, 1988, staff vice president & treasurer, 1988-. **ORGANIZATIONS:** National Association of Corp. Treasurers, 1988-; Society of International Treasurers, 1988-. **BUSINESS ADDRESS:** Staff Vice-President and Treasurer, Sea-Land Service, Inc, 150 Allen Rd., Liberty Corner, NJ 07938, (908)604-3362.

RAJASEKHAR, AMAR
Financial analyst. Indo-American. **PERSONAL:** Born Jul 27, 1963, Kolar Gold Fields, Karnataka, India; son of Choodappa Rajasekharaiah and Devarathva Rajasekharaiah. **EDUCATION:** Indian Institute of Technology at Madras, BTech, 1986; University of Texas, Austin, MS, 1988; University of Virginia, Darden School, MBA, 1993. **CAREER:** University of Texas, teaching assistant, 1986-88, research assistant, 1986-88; Aerostructures Inc, project engineer, 1988-91; IBM, financial analyst, 1992; Pratt & Whitney, financial analyst, 1993-. **ORGANIZATIONS:** AIAA, 1991-; IIT Alumni Association, 1986-. **HOME ADDRESS:** 58 Robin Ct, Middletown, CT 06457, (203)632-2780.

RAJENDRAN, VAZHAIKKURICHI M.
Scientist. Indo-American. **PERSONAL:** Born Dec 2, 1952, Vazhaikkurichi, Tamil Nadu, India; son of S G Muthukumarasamy and Sreeniammal Muthukumarasamy; married Vanathy Rajendran, Jun 1, 1984; children: Nithya, Lavanya. **EDUCATION:** University of Madras, BS, 1974, MS, 1977, PhD, 1981. **CAREER:** University of Pittsburgh, postdoctoral fellow, 1982; University of South Carolina, postdoctoral fellow, 1982-83; Medical College of Wisconsin, research associate, 1983-85; Yale University, associate research scientist, 1985-90, research scientist, 1990-. **BUSINESS ADDRESS:** Research Scientist, Yale University School of Medicine, 333 Cedar St, 89 LMP, New Haven, CT 06510, (203)785-4131.

RAJU, SESHADRI
Physician. Indo-American. **PERSONAL:** Born Jul 13, 1939, India; married Sybil Fredericks Raju; children: Ravi, Arun. **EDUCATION:** Christian Medical College, India, 1962; Madras University, India, 1967; University of Mississippi Medical Center, 1971. **CAREER:** University of Mississippi Medical Center, professor of surgery, currently. **ORGANIZATIONS:** Mississippi State Medical Association; National Society for Medical Research; Sigma Xi; Southeastern Organ Procurement Foundation, bd of directors, 1980-; United Network for Organ Sharing, bd of directors, 1984-86; American Venous Forum, executive committee, treasurer, 1989-92; Transplantation Society; The Floyd Spence Foundation, advisory board, 1989-; XII World Congress of L'Union Internationale de Phlebologie, international scientific advisory committee, 1993-95; Macmillan Healthcare Information, editorial advisory board, 1993-. **HONORS/AWARDS:** American College of Chest Physicians, fellow; American College of Surgeons, fellow. **BUSINESS ADDRESS:** Professor of Surgery, University of Mississippi Medical Center, 2500 North State St, Jackson, MS 39216, (601)984-5060.

RAJU, SOLOMON NALLI, SR.
Educator. Indo-American. **PERSONAL:** Born May 3, 1934, Mori, Andhra Pradesh, India; son of Anandam Nalli and Subbamma Nalli; married Jessy F Raju, Sep 16, 1953; children: Solomon Darwin, Paul, Justus, Jashuva, Nazarene. **EDUCATION:** Andhra University, Waltair, India, BSc (honors), 1958, MSc, 1959, PhD, 1963; Scripps Institution of Oceanography, University of California, San Diego, postdoctoral. **CAREER:** University of California, San Diego, assistant research biologist, 1968-70; Simpson College, associate professor, 1970-83; University of San Francisco, adjunct professor, 1982-83; City College of San Francisco, professor, 1983-. **ORGANIZATIONS:** FASEB,

1991-; Mission Comp Inc, founder-president, 1981-; Project India, founder-president, 1981-. **HONORS/AWARDS:** Scripps Institution of Oceanography, University of California, San Diego, Post-Doctoral Award, 1973, Outstanding Educators of America, 1968; Council of Scientific & Industrial Research Award, Delhi, India, 1967; University Grant Commission Award, New Delhi, India, 1966; Government of India, Federal Scholarship, 1959-66. **SPECIAL ACHIEVEMENTS:** Author of 11 papers published in USA, Europe and India, inclucing: "Congrid Eels & Leptocephali of the Eastern Pacific," US Fish Bulletin, 1985. **BUSINESS ADDRESS:** Professor of Biology, City College of San Francisco, 50 Phelan Ave, San Francisco, CA 94112.

RAKAMOTO. *See* **SHIMAMOTO, SCOTT SEIYA.**

RAMACHANDRA, SRINIVAS R. (RAM)
Physician. Indo-American. **PERSONAL:** Born Jul 15, 1950, Salem, Tamil Nadu, India; son of V S Raghavan and Kanakavalli Raghavan; married Pramela Ramachandra, Apr 3, 1980; children: Arun, Tara. **EDUCATION:** Bangalore Medical College, MBBS, 1972. **CAREER:** Permanente Medical Group, surgeon, chief of surgery, 1982-. **ORGANIZATIONS:** American College of Surgeons, 1983-; Hahnemann Surgical Society, 1983-. **BUSINESS ADDRESS:** Chief of Surgery, Permanente Medical Group, 27400 Hesperian Blvd, Hayward, CA 94545.

RAMACHANDRAN, NADARAJA
Economist. Sri Lankan American. **PERSONAL:** Born Oct 23, 1934, Jaffna, Sri Lanka; son of Vytialingah Nadaraja and Nesammah Nadaraja; married Malathi Rajendra, Oct 28, 1967; children: Ganeshan, Ravi, Shanthi. **EDUCATION:** University of Ceylon, BA (with honors), economics, 1957; London School of Economics, post-graduate certificate in business administration, 1959, PhD, 1962. **CAREER:** Central Bank of Ceylon, research economist, 1962-65; Ministry of Planning and Economic Affairs, Sri Lanka, director of economic affairs, 1965-72; OECD Development Center, Paris, consultant, 1972-73; World Bank, Washington, DC, senior economist, 1973-81; World Bank, Government of Liberia, team leader/macro-economic planner, 1981-84; World Bank, Bangladesh, senior macro economist, 1988-91; World Bank, Venezuela, Caribbean & South Asia, senior economist, 1984-88, 1991-. **ORGANIZATIONS:** University of Ceylon, Sports Council, captain of tennis, 1956; National Savings Bank, Sri Lanka, director, 1970; United Nations, Liberia, community warden, 1983. **HONORS/AWARDS:** University of Ceylon, Pestonjee Gold Medal for Economics, 1957; Government of Ceylon, Post-Graduate Research Scholarship at LSE, 1958; Asian Productivity Organization, Japan, First in APO International Essay Contest, 1970. **SPECIAL ACHIEVEMENTS:** Publications: Foreign Plantation Investment in Ceylon, 1963; Role of Productivity in Asian Economic Growth, 1970; Agricultural and Industrial Development Policies in Turkey, 1974; St Lucia: Economic Performance & Prospects, 1985; Policy Reform and Renewed Growth in Trinidad & Tobago, 1988. **HOME ADDRESS:** 7604 Geranium St, Bethesda, MD 20817, (301)229-2503. **BUSINESS ADDRESS:** Senior Economist, World Bank, 1818 H St NW, Washington, DC 20433, (202)458-0440.

RAMACHANDRAN, RITA
Banker. Indo-American. **PERSONAL:** Born Apr 28, 1963, Bangalore, Mysore, India; daughter of K S Ramachandran. **EDUCATION:** Pennsylvania State University, BA, finance, 1986. **CAREER:** Chase Manhattan Bank, credit officer, 2nd vice president, 1986-. **BUSINESS ADDRESS:** Second Vice President, Credit Officer, The Chase Manhattan Bank, 2099 Broadway, 2nd Fl, New York, NY 10023, (212)580-3808.

RAMADHYANI, SATISH
Educator. Indo-American. **PERSONAL:** Born Aug 1, 1949, Bangalore, Karnataka, India; son of K R Keshavachar and Padma Keshavachar; married Rachel B Ramadhyani, Jun 17, 1979. **EDUCATION:** Indian Institute of Technology, Madras, BTech, 1971; University of Minnesota, MS, 1977, PhD, 1979. **CAREER:** Motor Industries Co, Bangalore, India, research engineer, 1971-75; Tufts University, mechanical engineering, assistant professor, 1979-83; Purdue University, School of Mechanical Engineering, professor, 1983-. **ORGANIZATIONS:** American Society of Mech Engineers, Heat Transfer Division, committee member, 1986-; American Society of Engineering Educators, 1985-; American Institute of Aeronautics and Astronautics, 1986-; Sigma Xi, 1986-. **HONORS/AWARDS:** Phi Kappa Phi, 1979; Tau Beta Pi, 1982; President of India Medal for the best performance in the BTech degree program, 1971. **SPECIAL ACHIEVEMENTS:** Published more than seventy technical papers in archival professional journals and professional conference

proceedings, 1977-. **BUSINESS ADDRESS:** Professor, Purdue University, School of Mechanical Engineering, West Lafayette, IN 47907.

RAMAKRISHNA, KILAPARTI
International environmental lawyer. Indo-American. **PERSONAL:** Born in India; married Anjali; children: Ujwala. **EDUCATION:** Andrhra University, College of Arts & Sciences, Rajahmundry, BSc, 1973, College of Law, Waltair, BL, general laws, 1976; Jawaharlal Nehru University, New Delhi, MPhil, international law, 1978, PhD, international law of environment, 1985. **CAREER:** Indian Journal of International Law, assistant editor, 1980-85; Indian Academy of International Law & Diplomacy, assistant professor, 1980-85; Woods Hole Oceanographic Institute, fellow & guest investigator, 1986-89; Boston University, visiting professor, lecturer, 1987-88, 1991; The Woods Hole Research Center, senior associate, 1987-. **ORGANIZATIONS:** Sigma Xi; International Council of Environmental Law; American Society of International Law, life member; International Law Association; Indian Society of International Law & the Indian Law Institute, life member; Indian Academy of Environmental Law, Policy and Administration; Supreme Court Bar Association. **HONORS/AWARDS:** UNCED, Special Guest of Maurice Strong Secretary General of the Conference, 1992; UN INC/FCCC, Special Advisor, 2nd, 3rd, 4th, 5th sessions; Rapporteur of Forests Task Group, Second World Climate Conference, 1990. **SPECIAL ACHIEVEMENTS:** East-West Center, visiting research fellow, summer 1987; Harvard Law School, Fulbright Visiting Scholar, 1985-87; various articles published in law reviews. **BUSINESS ADDRESS:** Senior Associate for International Environmental Law, Director, Program on Science in Public Affairs, The Woods Hole Research Center, 13 Church St, PO Box 296, Woods Hole, MA 02543, (508)540-9900.

RAMAKRISHNAN, TERIZHANDUR S.
Research scientist. Indo-American. **PERSONAL:** Born Nov 13, 1958, Madras, India; married Malini Ramakrishnan; children: Shwetha. **EDUCATION:** Indian Institute of Technology, BTech, 1980; Illinois Institute of Technology, PhD, 1985. **CAREER:** Schlumberger-Doll Research, research scientist, 1985-. **ORGANIZATIONS:** Indian Institute of Chemical Engineer, 1978-; American Institute of Chemical Engineers, 1981-; Society of Petroleum Engineers, 1986-; Sigma Xi, 1984-. **HONORS/AWARDS:** Indian Institute of Technology, The Institute Sliver Medal, 1980; Indian Institute of Chemical Engineers, P C Ray Award, 1980. **SPECIAL ACHIEVEMENTS:** Publications on interfacial phenomena, fluidized beds, flow through porous media, enhanced oil recovery, 1983-; proficient in Tamil and Hindi languages. **BUSINESS ADDRESS:** Research Scientist, Schlumberger-Doll Research, Old Quarry Rd, Ridgefield, CT 06877, (203)431-5000.

RAMAKUMAR, RAMACHANDRA GUPTA
Educator, electrical engineer. Indo-American. **PERSONAL:** Born Oct 17, 1936, Coimbatore, Tamil Nadu, India; son of G Ramachandra Gupta & S Saraswathi Bai; married Gokula Ramakumar, Jun 13, 1963; children: Sanjay, Malini. **EDUCATION:** Government College of Technology, Coimbatore, BE, 1956; Indian Institute of Technology, Kharagpur, MTech, 1957; Cornell University, PhD, 1962. **CAREER:** Coimbatore Institute of Technology, Electrical Engineering Department, assistant lecturer, 1957-59, lecturer on study leave, 1959-62, assistant professor, 1962-67; Oklahoma State University, School of Electrical and Computer Engineering, visiting associate professor, 1967-70, associate professor, 1970-76, professor, 1976-, engineering energy lab, director, 1987-, PSO/Albrecht Naeter Professor, 1991-. **ORGANIZATIONS:** Institute of Electrical & Electronics Engineers, fellow, 1994; Power Engineering Society, awards committee, energy development and power generation committee, chairman of the awards working group, energy development subcommittee, photovoltaics working group, administrative committee; Oklahoma State University, Student Branch, faculty advisor, 1975-77; American and International Solar Energy Societies; American Society for Engineering Education. **HONORS/AWARDS:** University of Madras, First Rank in Electrical Engineering, 1956; Oklahoma Society of Professional Engineers, Outstanding Engineer Achievement, 1972; Oklahoma State University, Outstanding Electrical Engineer Professor, 1975, Halliburton Outstanding Engineering Faculty, 1992; Burlington Northern Foundation, Faculty Achievement Award, 1993. **SPECIAL ACHIEVEMENTS:** Textbook: Engineering Reliability: Fundamentals and Applications, Prentice Hall, 1993; US patents, 3663945, 3703976, 3727122, 4657681; chapters in 4 books, sections in 4 handbooks on the subject of energy systems; over 140 publications in journals, transactions, national and international conference proceedings; developer of the concept of and design procedures for integrated renewable energy systems; listed in 8 different biographical reference sources; registered professional engineer, State of Okla-

homa. **HOME ADDRESS:** 2623 N Husband St, Stillwater, OK 74075, (405)372-7886. **BUSINESS ADDRESS:** PSO/Albrecht Naeter Professor, Director of Engineering Energy Lab, Oklahoma State University, 216 Engineering South, Stillwater, OK 74078, (405)744-5157.

RAMALINGAM, MYSORE LOGANATHAN
Research scientist. Indo-American. **PERSONAL:** Born Dec 12, 1954, Mysore, Karnataka, India; son of Mysore Laxmanaswamy & Arunachalam Sundarabat Loganathan; married Samyuktha Ramalingam, Jun 22, 1981; children: Suraj Kumar, Shyma. **EDUCATION:** University Visveshwariah College of Engineering, India, BS, 1975; Indian Institute of Science, MS, 1977; Arizona State University, PhD, 1986. **CAREER:** Jyothi Pumps Inc, assistant engineer, 1977; ISRO Satellite Centre, India, engineer SC, 1977-80, engineer SD, 1980-81; UES, Inc, research scientist, 1986-89, senior scientist, 1989-91, principal research scientist, 1991-. **ORGANIZATIONS:** ASME, AESD, DTPCTM Technology Committee, chairperson, 1992-; Space Nuclear Power Symposium, steering committee, 1992-; IECEC, session chairperson, 1989-; AIAA, associate fellow, 1991-; ASME, 1987-. **HONORS/AWARDS:** UES,Inc, Top 5 Most Profitable Managers, 1990, Top 10 Most Profitable Managers, 1991; AIAA, nominated for outstanding scientist in Dayton, 1993. **SPECIAL ACHIEVEMENTS:** Published over 80 technical papers in the areas of heat pipes, thermionic energy conversion and high temperature materials. **BIOGRAPHICAL SOURCES:** Journal of Less Common Metals, p 153, 1986; Mechanical Engineering, 1993. **BUSINESS ADDRESS:** Principal Research Scientist, Universal Energy Systems Inc, 4401 Dayton-Xenia Rd, Bldg 3, Dayton, OH 45432, (513)253-3986.

RAMAN, ARAVAMUDHAN
Educator. Indo-American. **PERSONAL:** Born Oct 13, 1937, Madras State, India; son of Aravamudha Iyengar and Pankajam Aravamudhan; married Edelgard Raman, Jan 15, 1965; children: Vasudevan, Padhmavathi, Lakshmi-Kala. **EDUCATION:** Jamal Mohammed College, Tiruchirapalli, University of Madras, India, 1953-55; St Joseph's College, Tiruchirapalli, University of Madras, India, MA, phys, 1958; Indian Institute of Science, Dept of Metallurgy, Bangalore, India, BE, metallurgy, 1960; Technical University of Stutgart, Max Planck Institute for Metal Research, metallurgy program, DrN, 1964. **CAREER:** University of Illinois, Dept of Metallurgy, res associate, 1964-65; University of Texas, Chem Eng Dept, postdoctoral fellow, 1965-66; Louisiana State University, asst prof, beginning 1966, assoc prof, 1969, professor, 1975-. **ORGANIZATIONS:** NACE, chair, T-3R, T3A-15. **HONORS/AWARDS:** USSR Academy of Sciences, Moscow, invitation, 1990. **SPECIAL ACHIEVEMENTS:** Approx 75 professional refereed publications on metals science, 1965-; 2 books published, one text book; one book edited. **HOME ADDRESS:** 6919 N Rothmer Dr, Baton Rouge, LA 70808, (504)766-0530. **BUSINESS ADDRESS:** Professor, Dept of Mechanical Engineering, Louisiana State University, Baton Rouge, LA 70803, (504)388-5910.

RAMANATHAN, VEERABHADRAN
Educator, scientist. Indo-American. **PERSONAL:** Born Nov 24, 1944, Madras, India; married Girija; children: Nithya, Dhakshin, Tara. **EDUCATION:** Annamalai University, BE, 1965; Indian Institute of Science, MS, 1970; State University at Stony Brook, PhD, 1973. **CAREER:** NASA, ERBE Science Team, principal investigator, 1979-; University of Chicago, professor, geophysical sciences, 1986-90; Scripps Inst of Oceanography, Alderson Professor of Ocean Sciences, 1990-, CEPEX Project, chief scientist, 1993, director, C4 center, 1991-. **ORGANIZATIONS:** Science, board of reviewing editors, 1992-; NASA, engineer review advisory committee, 1991-; NOAA, panel on climate and global change; NAS, board on global change; DOE, space initiative technology oversight group; University of Alaska, advisory panel; UCSD, committee on faculty research lecturer. **HONORS/AWARDS:** NASA, Medal for Exceptional Scientific Achievement, 1989; SUNY, Distinguished Alumnus Award, 1984; NASA, Special Achievement Award, 1975; American Association for the Advancement of Science, fellow, 1988. **BUSINESS ADDRESS:** Professor, Scripps Institution of Oceanography, 9500 Gilman Dr, SIO-0239, La Jolla, CA 92093, (619)534-8815.

RAMASWAMI, VAIDYANATHAN (RAM)
Corporate executive. Indo-American. **PERSONAL:** Born Feb 24, 1950, Badagara, Kerala, India; son of Bhuvaneswari and L V Vaidyanathan; married Soundaram Ramaswami, Aug 26, 1977; children: Priya, Prem. **EDUCATION:** University of Madras, India, BSc, 1969, MSc, 1971; Purdue University, MS, 1976, PhD, 1978. **CAREER:** Loyola College, Madras, India, lecturer, 1971-74; Drexel University, asst professor of mathematics, 1978-82; Bell Laborato-

ries, technical staff, 1982-84; Bell Communications Res Inc, technical staff, 1984-90, director, 1990-. **ORGANIZATIONS:** IEEE, senior member, 1992-. **SPECIAL ACHIEVEMENTS:** Over 40 published papers in Journal of Applied Probability, Advances in Applied Probability, IEEE Transactions, Stochastic Models; Communications in Statistics; Stachastic Models editor, 1986-. **BUSINESS ADDRESS:** Director, Network Services Performance and Control, Bell Communications Research, 331 Newman Springs Rd, NVC 2X-151, Red Bank, NJ 07701.

RAMCHANDANI, RAJ S.
Educator, consultant. Indo-American. **PERSONAL:** Born Jun 6, 1941, Hydrabad, Pakistan; son of Shamdas B & Kishni U Bharwani Ramchandani; married Sheila Nagrani, Jun 3, 1971 (deceased); children: Suneil, Nina. **EDUCATION:** Birla Institute of Technology, BS, engineering, 1964; Pennsylvania State University, MS, 1966; Ohio State University, PhD, 1975. **CAREER:** NCR Co, staff engineer, 1966-69; Ohio State University, research assoc, 1969-71; Ohio Institute of Tech, asst professor, electronic engineering, 1971-74; University of Toledo, visiting asst professor, EE, 1974-75; Owens Tech College, asst professor, EE, 1975-76; CSU Los Angeles, professor, EE, 1976-, CSULA Adopt-A-School program, director, 1986-; consultant: LA Dept of Water & Power, and Pacific Gas & Electric, principal investigator for electric power studies, 1981-85; Los Angeles DWP, consultant, 1981-85; General Dynamics, Pomona, 1979-80; Jet Propulsion Lab, 1976-78. **ORGANIZATIONS:** IEEE, 1966; American Soc Engineering Educators, 1971-; Power Engineering Society. **HONORS/AWARDS:** Ind Council of San Gabriel, appreciation certificate, 1986; CSULA, MPPA Award, 1989. **BUSINESS ADDRESS:** Professor, Elec Eng Dept, California State University, Los Angeles, 5151 University Dr, Los Angeles, CA 90032.

RAMIL, MARIO R.
State government official, judge. Filipino American. **PERSONAL:** Born Jun 21, 1946, Quezon City, Philippines; son of Quentin A Ramil & Fausta Reyes; married Judy Wong Ramil, Nov 6, 1971; children: Jonathan Wong, Bradley Russel. **EDUCATION:** California State University, Hayward, BA, political science, 1972; Hastings College of the Law, San Francisco, JD, 1975. **CAREER:** San Francisco Neighborhood Legal Aid Foundation, law clerk, 1973-75; Sandigan-Newcomers Services Inc, legal counsel, 1975-76; Department of Labor and Industrial Relations, deputy attorney general, 1976-79; University of Hawaii, Central Administration, deputy attorney general, 1979-80; Hawaii House Majority Attorney's Office, staff attorney, 1980; private law practice, 1980-82; State of Hawaii, Administrative Division, deputy attorney general, 1982-84; Hawaii State Insurance Commissioner, 1984-86; Hawaii State Department of Labor and Industrial Relations, director, 1986-91; Lyons, Brandt, Cook and Hiramatsu, of counsel, 1991-93; Hawaii Supreme Court, associate justice, 1993-. **ORGANIZATIONS:** Advisory Council on Housing and Construction; Hawaii Non-profit Housing Corporation, president, director; Oahu Filipino Community Council, executive secretary; Administrative Budget Committee, chairman; Palama Settlement, board member. **SPECIAL ACHIEVEMENTS:** Bar admissions: State of California Supreme Court; State of Hawaii Supreme Court; US District Court, Hawaii; US District Court for the Northern District of California; 9th Circuit Court of Appeals. **BUSINESS ADDRESS:** Associate Justice, Hawaii Supreme Court, 417 South King St, Honolulu, HI 96813.

RANA, GURINDER MOHAN SINGH
Engineer. Indo-American. **PERSONAL:** Born Sep 25, 1946, Sialkot, India; son of Jaswant K Rama & Monmohan S Rana; married Sandra L Rana, Jun 17, 1972; children: Renee K, Rich S. **EDUCATION:** Indian Institute of Technology, India, BOT, civil engineering, 1962-67; Colorado State University, MS, civil engineering, 1967-69. **CAREER:** Pennsylvania Department of Transportation, design engineer, 1969-70; University of Akron, OH, teaching assistant, 1970-72; CJ Messmore & Associates, project manager, 1972-76; Industrial Inspection Ind, senior geotechnical engineer, 1976-80; R&R International Inc, president, 1980-. **ORGANIZATIONS:** National Society of Professional Engineers; Association of Soil & Foundation Engineers; Ohio Association of Minority Architects & Engineers; EPA Board, State of Ohio, committee chairman; Rotary Club of Northeast Ohio. **HONORS/AWARDS:** US Small Business Administration, Cleveland District, Minority Small Business Person of the Year, 1992; Weatherhead 100, One of the Fastest Growing Firms in Northeast Ohio, 1991. **SPECIAL ACHIEVEMENTS:** Co-author, "Groundwater Influence on Highway Slope Stability," 39th Annual Highway Geology Symposium, p 214-35, 1988; co-author, abstract, A Geotechnical Investigation of the Miles Road Landslide area, Cuyahoga County, Ohio, Vol 24, no 7, 1992.

BUSINESS ADDRESS: President, R&R International, Inc, 1234 S Cleveland-Massillon Rd, Akron, OH 44321, (216)666-2200.

RANA, MOHAMMED WAHEED-UZ-ZAMAN
Educator. Pakistani American/Indo-American. **PERSONAL:** Born May 28, 1934, Lahore, Pakistan; son of Mohammed Nizam-ud-Din Rana and Zainab Bibi; married Janice Wolford Rana, Aug 21, 1965; children: Jamil, Aneesa, Omar, Nadia. **EDUCATION:** Olivet College, BA, 1964; Wayne State University, MS, 1966, PhD, 1968. **CAREER:** St Louis University School of Medicine, associate professor, 1968-. **ORGANIZATIONS:** American Association of Anatomists, 1968-; National Conference of Christians & Jews, board of directors, 1987-; Islamic Center, second Imam, 1969-. **SPECIAL ACHIEVEMENTS:** Key Facts in Embryology, 1983; 60 publications in professional journals, including religious journals. **HOME ADDRESS:** 2750 Yaeger Rd, Saint Louis, MO 63129, (314)894-0346. **BUSINESS ADDRESS:** Associate Professor, Anatomy Dept, St Louis University School of Medicine, 1402 South Grand, Saint Louis, MO 63104, (314)577-8271.

RANADE, D. G. (RAJA)
Environmental scientist. Indo-American. **PERSONAL:** Born Mar 24, 1947, Bombay, India; son of Gopal A Ranade and Lila G Ranade; married Anita D Ranade, Jun 14, 1989; children: Amit, Nikhil, Sameer, Rahul. **EDUCATION:** University of Bombay, India, BS, 1966, MS, 1969; University of Minnesota, MS, 1973, MPH, 1975. **CAREER:** Midwest Research Institute, junior chemist, 1975; Kansas City Testing Laboratory, senior chemist, 1975-78; Johnson County Health Department, director, environmental health, 1978-85; Kansas City, MO, Health Department, public health engineer, 1985-88; Environmental Audit Inc, technical director, 1988-90; John Mathes & Associates, group leader, environmental audit, 1990; Westinghouse Hanford Co, principal scientist, 1991-. **SPECIAL ACHIEVEMENTS:** Registered Environmental Assessor, state of California, 1989-. **HOME ADDRESS:** 1611 S Sheppard St, Kennewick, WA 99337.

RANADE, MADHUKAR G.
Steel company executive. Indo-American. **PERSONAL:** Born Sep 8, 1953, Bombay, Maharashtra, India; son of Govind Waman Ranade (deceased) & Shalini Govind Ranade; married Karen B Ranade, Aug 25, 1979; children: Brian Naveen, Erica Sonia. **EDUCATION:** Indian Institute of Technology, BTech, 1975; University of California, Berkeley, MS, 1977. **CAREER:** Inland Steel Co, Research & Development, engineer, 1977-79, research engineer, 1979-82, senior engineer, 1982-85, section manager, 1985-89, manager, 1989-93, Op Tech & Research & Development, manager, 1993-. **ORGANIZATIONS:** Iron & Steel Society, program committee, 1983-, Liaison-Process Technician Division, 1987-; American Society for Testing & Materials, 1981-, leader of US delegation, 1982, Iron & Steel Institute of Japan, 1982-; Calumet Region Montessori School, board of directors, 1989-. **HONORS/AWARDS:** Iron & Steel Society, J E Johnson Award, 1989; ITT-Bombay, Silver Medal, 1975; University of California, Berkeley, Jane Lewis Fellowship, 1976. **SPECIAL ACHIEVEMENTS:** 17 technical articles in professional journals & conferences, 1977-; University of Minnesota, invited lecturer, 1987; McMaster University, Hamilton, Ontario, invited lecturer, 1992. **BUSINESS ADDRESS:** Manager, Operating Technology, Inland Steel Co, Ironmaking & Process Research, 3001 E Columbus Dr, R&D 9-000, East Chicago, IN 46312, (219)399-6202.

RANGASWAMY, THANGAM (SAM)
Consulting engineer. Indo-American. **PERSONAL:** Born Jun 12, 1942, Arakkankottai, Tamil Nadu, India; son of Venkalappalayam Kailasam Thangamuthu and Ottarkarattuppalayam Ramaswamy Ramakkal; married Kohilam Murugaiya, Sep 21, 1970; children: Chandhiran. **EDUCATION:** University of Madras, BE, 1964; University of California, Berkeley, MS, 1966; University of Kentucky, PhD, 1970. **CAREER:** Public Works Dept, Tamil Nadu, India, junior engineer, 1964; University of California, Berkeley, teaching assistant, 1964-66; Brighton Engineering Company, design engineer, 1966; Watkins and Associates Inc, project engineer, 1966-68; University of Kentucky, research assistant, 1968-70; Senler, Cambell and Associates, structural engineer, 1970-74; Rangaswamy and Associates Inc, president, 1974-. **ORGANIZATIONS:** National Society of Professional Engineers; Kentucky Society of Professional Engineers, bldg code committee chairman; American Institute of Steel Construction; International Conference of Bldg Officials; Structural Engineers Association of Illinois; Structural Engineers Association of Southern California; Structural Engineers Assoc of KY, organizer, secretary, incorporator; South Louisville Rotary Club; Society of American Military Engineers.

HONORS/AWARDS: US Small Business Administration, Minority Small Business Person of the Year; Louisville Minority Business Development Center, Outstanding Contractor; Associated Builders and Contractors, Inc, Award of Excellence; Kentuckiana Masonry Institute, Excellence in Masonry Design; Commonwealth of Kentucky, Kentucky Colonel. **SPECIAL ACHIEVEMENTS:** ACI Design Handbook, volume 2, Columns per ACI 318-77, 1978; ACI Design Handbook, Slab Design in Accordance with ACI 318-77, 1978; Dale Carnegie courses, certified instructor, 1983-; yoga teacher at Hindu Temple of Kentucky, 1989-; proficient in Tamil Language. **BIOGRAPHICAL SOURCES:** Who's Who in Technology Today, 1982. **HOME ADDRESS:** 10404 Scarlet Oaks Court, Louisville, KY 40241-1714. **BUSINESS PHONE:** (502)589-2212.

RANHOTRA, GURBACHAN S.
Researcher, educator. Indo-American. **PERSONAL:** Born Aug 8, 1935, Abbotabad, NW Frontier Prov, India; married Tejinder, May 27, 1960; children: Gurdeep, Anita. **EDUCATION:** Agra University, BS/MS, 1960; University of Minnesota, PhD, 1964. **CAREER:** Kansas State University, adjunct professor, 1978-; American Institute of Baking, director, 1969-. **ORGANIZATIONS:** American Institute of Nutrition, 1969-; Institute of Food Technologists, 1970-; American Association of Cereal Chemists, 1969-. **HONORS/AWARDS:** Several. **SPECIAL ACHIEVEMENTS:** Over 100 publications in nutrition & food science. **BUSINESS ADDRESS:** Dir, Nutrition Research, American Institute of Baking, 1213 Bakers Way, Manhattan, KS 66502, (913)537-4750.

RAO, ANANDA G.
Medical researcher, biochemist. Indo-American. **PERSONAL:** Born Dec 27, 1930, Quilon, Kerala, India; son of Govinda Vadhyar and Sundari Bai; married Syamala A Rao, Aug 31, 1962; children: Gita V Pai, Veena A, Vivek A. **EDUCATION:** University of Kerala, BSc, 1952, MSc, 1954; University of Texas, PhD, 1966. **CAREER:** Sree Sankara College, Kerala, chemistry, lecturer, 1954-55; Government of India, research scholar, 1955-58, assistant research officer, 1958-59; Christian Medical College Hospital, India, research assistant, 1959-62; Southwestern Medical School, research fellow, 1962-67; Texas A&M University, research scientist, 1967-71; Northern California System of Clinics, Dept of Veterans Affairs, research biochemist, 1971-. **ORGANIZATIONS:** American Institute of Nutrition; International Society for Biomedical Research on Alcoholism; Biochemical Archives, editor; Journal of Optimal Nutrition, editorial board. **HONORS/AWARDS:** Scholastic Achievements, Gold Medal, 1952, 1954; National Institutes of Health, research grant, 1970-73; Department of Veterans Affairs, Research Grant, 1971-, Performance Awards, 1976-81, 1983-85, 1988, 1991. **SPECIAL ACHIEVEMENTS:** 230 papers published in scientific journals and abstracts, presentation in national and international scientific meetings; reviewer of scientific articles for many journals; research in intestinal absorption of fat, lipid synthesis, mammary neoplasia, iron deficiency, and alcohol effects. **HOME ADDRESS:** 10 Hargate Ct, Pleasant Hill, CA 94523, (510)933-4358. **BUSINESS ADDRESS:** Research Biochemist, Dept of Veterans Affairs, Northern California System of Clinics, 150 Muir Road, Research Service, 151 H, Martinez, CA 94553, (510)372-2763.

RAO, ANGARA KONETI
Physician. Indo-American. **PERSONAL:** Born Dec 22, 1950, Madras, India; son of A Seshagiri Rao and A Lakshmil Rao; married Vijay M Rao, May 10, 1974; children: Deepak, Gita. **EDUCATION:** Hindu College, University of Delhi, pre-medical, 1968; All India Institute of Medical Sciences, MBBS, 1973. **CAREER:** Temple University School of Medicine, assistant professor of medicine & thrombosis research, 1981-84, deputy director for clinical research, thrombosis research center, 1983-, associate professor of medicine & thrombosis research, 1984-91, professor of medicine & thrombosis research, 1991-, professor of pathology, 1992-. **ORGANIZATIONS:** American College of Physicians, fellow, 1984-; American Federation for Clinical Research; International Society of Thrombosis and Hemostasis, 1985-; AAAS; American Society of Hematology; Philadelphia Hematology Society, president, 1990-91; American Heart Association, PA Chapter, Research Peer Review Committee, 1989-; Council on Thrombosis and Hermostarsc. **HONORS/AWARDS:** National Institutes of Health, Academic Award in Vascular Disease, 1992-97, National Research Service Award, 1979-81; Platelets Journal, principal editor, 1989-. **SPECIAL ACHIEVEMENTS:** Total of 49 original publications in peer reviewed medical journals in the areas of hemostasis and thrombosis; research area: normal and abnormal platelet function, inherited platelet bleeding disorders, thrombolytic therapy. **BUSINESS ADDRESS:** Professor of Med, Thrombosis Res & Pathology, Temple University School of Medicine,

3400 N Broad St, Medical Research Building, Room 112, Philadelphia, PA 19140, (215)221-4684.

RAO, BARRY
Company executive. Indo-American. **PERSONAL:** Born May 31, 1953, Bombay, India; son of Mukund Rao and Kanaklata Rao; married Christine, Dec 26, 1975; children: Dave, Neil. **EDUCATION:** New York University, BA, 1971. **CAREER:** Dane Corp, CEO; Skyline Properties, CEO; National Paper Corp, CEO; Galaxy International, CEO; American Scholar, CEO, currently. **BUSINESS ADDRESS:** CEO, American Scholar, 200 Candlewood Rd, Bay Shore, NY 11706, (516)273-6550.

RAO, BHAMIDIPATY KAMESWARA
Educator. Indo-American. **PERSONAL:** Born Aug 1, 1955, Vijayawada, Andhra Pradesh, India; son of Rama Krishna Rao and Subba Lakshmi; married Vijaya Lakshmi, Aug 22, 1984; children: Gayatri and Keshava. **EDUCATION:** Regional Engineering College, B Tech, 1977; Indian Institute of Science, ME, 1982; University of Illinois, PhD, 1986. **CAREER:** BHEL, India, stress analysis engineer, 1977-80; Indian Institute of Science, research associate, 1980-82; University of Illinois, postdoctoral fellow, 1986-88; Idaho State University, associate professor, 1988-. **ORGANIZATIONS:** ASME, 1982-; AIAA, 1982-; ANS, 1982-; NSPE, 1989-; ISES, 1983-; Combustion Institute, 1987-; Society of Rheology, 1983-; ASEE, 1988- . **HONORS/AWARDS:** Idaho State University, Outstanding Engineering, 1993; GRE, Examiner; Indian Institute of Science, State Merit Fellowship, 1980-82; SRR & CVR College, Gold Medal (Best Student), 1972. **SPECIAL ACHIEVEMENTS:** Language proficiency: German, Sanskrit; more than 12 technical publications in thermal fluids area. **BUSINESS ADDRESS:** Professor, Idaho State University, College of Engineering, 833 S 8th Ave, Colonial Hall Rm #4, Pocatello, ID 83209, (208)236-2324.

RAO, DABEERU C.
Educator, researcher. Indo-American. **PERSONAL:** Born Apr 6, 1946, Santhabommali, Andhra Pradesh, India; son of D Ramarao Patnaik and D Venkataratnam; married Sarada Rao, Jul 31, 1974; children: Ravi, Lakshmi. **EDUCATION:** Indian Statistical Institute, Calcutta, India, BStat, 1968, MStat, 1969, PhD, 1971. **CAREER:** University of Sheffield, postdoctoral, 1971-72; University of Hawaii, assistant geneticist, 1972-78, associate geneticist, 1978-80; Washington University School of Medicine, associate professor, director, 1980-82, professor, director, 1982-. **ORGANIZATIONS:** Biometric Society, 1980-; American Statistical Association, 1980-; Royal Statistical Society, fellow, 1990-; Society for Epidemiological Research, 1986-; American Society of Human Genetics, 1972-; Indian Society of Human Genetics, 1978-; International Genetic Epidemiology Society, founding member, 1991-. **HONORS/AWARDS:** American Biographical Institute, Most Admired Man of the Decade, 1992; Telugu Association of North America and World Telugu Conference, Chetana, 1993. **SPECIAL ACHIEVEMENTS:** Principal investigator of research grants from National Institutes of Health; author: A Source Book for Linkage in Man, 1979; Methods in Genetic Epidemiology, 1983; Genetic Epidemiology of Coronary Heart Disease, 1984; author of over 200 research publications in journals, 1970-; founding editor-in-chief, Genetic Epidemiology, 1984-91. **BUSINESS ADDRESS:** Professor, Director, Divison of Biostatistics, Washington University School of Medicine, 660 S Euclid Ave, Box 8067, Old Shriners Rm 1100, St Louis, MO 63110-1010, (314)362-3606.

RAO, GANDIKOTA VENKATA
Educator, educational administrator. Indo-American. **PERSONAL:** Born Jul 15, 1934, Vizianagram, Andhra Pradesh, India; son of Gandikota Babu Rao and Seetha; married Vidya, Jun 23, 1965; children: Madhu, Anita. **EDUCATION:** Andhra University, BSc (with honors), 1954, MSc, 1955; Indian Institute of Technology, Kharagpur, MTech, 1958; University of Chicago, PhD, 1965. **CAREER:** University of Chicago, research assistant, post doctoral, 1959-65; University of Miami and National Hurricane Research Laboratory, assistant professor, 1965-68; Meteorological Service of Canada, post doctoral, 1968-70; University of Waterloo, postdoctoral, 1970-71; St Louis University, Department of Earth and Atmospheric Sciences, assistant professor, beginning 1971, associate professor of meteorology to professor of meteorology, currently, director of meteorology, 1980-. **ORGANIZATIONS:** American Meteorological Society, 1960-; American Geophysical Union, 1973-; Sigma Xi, 1973-; Missouri Academy of Science, 1985-. **HONORS/AWARDS:** St Louis University, Senior Grantwinner Award, 1984. **SPECIAL ACHIEVEMENTS:** Published 40 articles, 2 book reviews. **BUSINESS ADDRESS:** Professor and

Director of Meteorology, Saint Louis University, 3507 Laclede Ave, Macelwane Hall, Rm 310, St Louis, MO 63103, (314)658-3115.

RAO, GOPAL SUBBA
Electronic products company executive. Indo-American. **PERSONAL:** Born Aug 12, 1938, Mangalore, Karnataka, India; son of Gopal and Sharada Rao; married Harsha, 1972; children: Raveen. **EDUCATION:** Madras University, BS, 1958; Howard University, MS, 1964; University of Michigan, PhD, 1969. **CAREER:** Public Health Institute, India, chemist, 1958-61; Howard University, instructor, 1962-64; University of Michigan, research fellow, 1964-69; National Institute of Health, research fellow, 1969-74; American Dental Association Research Institute, director of research, 1974-85; Loyola University Dental School, professor, 1985-; Multitek Circuitronics, Inc, president, 1985-. **ORGANIZATIONS:** American Chemical Society; Federation of American Societies for Experimental Biology; Chicago Printed Circuit Association, 1985-; Society of Toxicology; American Society for Pharmacology & Experimental Therapeutics, 1969-; Association of Scientists of Indian Origin, founding council member, 1980-82, secretary/treasurer, 1983-84, Chicago Section, council member, 1985-89; Association of Indians in America, high school award committee, 1989; International Association of Dental Research, local host committee, 1982-84; Festival of India at Museum of Science & Industry, Chicago, science and technology seminars host, 1986. **HONORS/AWARDS:** University of Michigan, research fellowships, 1964-69; Eli Lilly Endowment Fellowship, 1965-68; Horace H Rackham Graduate School Fellowship, 1969; National Institute of Health, International Fellowship, 1970; numerous research grants from National Institutes of Health, Americal Dental Health Foundation Smokeless Tobacco Research Council, etc, 1969-. **SPECIAL ACHIEVEMENTS:** Published over 100 original research papers in professional journals in the field of biochemical toxicology and occupational medicine, including chapters in text books, 1961-; invited speaker at numerous national/international professional meetings/symposia. **BUSINESS ADDRESS:** President, Multitek Circuitronics, Inc, 2900 Soffel Ave, Melrose Park, IL 60160, (708)343-3815.

RAO, GOPALAKRISHNA M.
Government official. Indo-American. **PERSONAL:** Born Mar 17, 1944, Udupi, Karnataka, India; son of Sarswathi and Lakshminarayana; married Kavitha G Rao, Oct 19, 1975; children: India G. **EDUCATION:** Mahatma Gandhi Memorial College, India, BSc, 1964; Mysore University, India, MSc, 1966; Memorial University of Newfoundland, Canada, PhD, 1973. **CAREER:** Stanford University, research associate, 1978-81; Unidad Merida, Mexico, visiting professor, 1984; Dow Chemical Company, research specialist, 1981-86; Rice University, visiting scholar, 1986-87; Advanced Clinical Products, R & D, director, 1987-88; US Air Force, guest scientist, 1988-89; NASA, Energy Storage Section, head, 1989-. **ORGANIZATIONS:** NASA, battery steering committe, 1989-; Inter Agency Advanced Power Group, 1989-; Electrochemical Society, 1975-; American Chemical Society, 1975-. **HONORS/AWARDS:** NASA, Special Act Award, 1992, Group Awards, 1989-, Performance Incentive Award, 1993; several prizes, merit awards, and fellowships received in USA, Canada and India, 1961-. **SPECIAL ACHIEVEMENTS:** Published 40 technical papers in reviewed journals; author: NASA Handbook for Nickel-Hydrogen Batteries, NASA Reference Publications, 1993; NASA Handbook for Handling and Storage of Nickel Cadium Batteries: Lessons Learned, NASA Reference Publications, 1994; invited speaker in international, national and academic meetings, 1971-. **BUSINESS ADDRESS:** Head, Energy Storage Section, NASA, Goddard Space Flight Center, Code 734.5, Bldg 11, Greenbelt, MD 20771, (301)286-6654.

RAO, GOTTIPATY N.
Educator. Indo-American. **PERSONAL:** Born Apr 7, 1936, Peyyeru, Andhra Pradesh, India; son of Gottipaty Kotaiah; married Saraswathi; children: Venkateshwar, Krishna, Archana. **EDUCATION:** Aligarh University, PhD, 1963. **CAREER:** Adelphi University, physics department, professor, chair, currently. **ORGANIZATIONS:** American Physical Society. **HOME PHONE:** (516)538-9534. **BUSINESS ADDRESS:** Professor and Chair, Physics Dept, Adelphi University, South Ave, Blodgett Hall, Rm 202, Garden City, NY 11530, (516)877-4877.

RAO, GUNDU H. R.
Educator. Indo-American. **PERSONAL:** Born Apr 17, 1938, Tumkur, India; son of H V Rama Rao and T S Annapoornamma; married Yashoda T R Rao, Jun 11, 1965; children: Anupama T R, Prashanth T R. **EDUCATION:** University of Mysore, India, BSc, 1957; University of Poona, India, BSc (with

honors), 1958, MSc, 1959; Kansas State University, PhD, 1968. **CAREER:** University of Minnesota, Laboratory Medicine & Pathology, assistant professor, 1975-81, associate professor, 1981-88, professor, 1988-. **ORGANIZATIONS:** American Heart Association, National Thrombosis Council; The Biochemical Society, London; American Association of Pathologists; American Association Biological Chemists & Molecular Biologists; American Association of Cell Biologists; New York Academy of Sciences; Association of Scientists of Indian Origin; Asian Society on Atherosclerosis and Thrombosis, founding member, secretary. **SPECIAL ACHIEVEMENTS:** Author, co-author of over 200 publications in national and international journals. **HOME ADDRESS:** 9333 Hyland Creek Road, Bloomington, MN 55437. **BUSINESS ADDRESS:** Professor, Laboratory Medicine and Pathology, University of Minnesota, 420 Deleware SE, Heart and Lung Institute (KE/HS 231b), PB 198 UMHC, Minneapolis, MN 55455, (612)626-2717.

RAO, K. L. SESHAGIRI
Educator. Indo-American. **PERSONAL:** Born Oct 14, 1929, Mulbagal, Mysore, India; son of K Lakshminarayana Rao and Kamakshamma; married Saraswati Rao, May 20, 1954; children: Niranjan, Nanda Kumar, Santosh, Sudhir. **EDUCATION:** University of Mysore, BA, 1950, MA, 1951; Gandhi Peace Foundation, fellow, 1962; Harvard University, PhD, 1967. **CAREER:** Chattisarh College, Raipur, India, 1951-60; Gandhi Peace Foundation, New Delhi, India, 1960-62; Punjabi University, Patiala, India, 1967-71; University of Virginia, Department of Religious Studies, professor, 1971-. **ORGANIZATIONS:** International Association of Gandhian Studies, president, 1982; Quest Institute, vice-president, 1986; World Hindu Federation, Nepal, vice-president, 1989. **HONORS/AWARDS:** International Para-Psychology Association, Hall of Fame Anim Award, 1983; Integral Yoga Association, Ecumenical Studies Award, 1986; College of Natural Law, Consciousness Studies Award, 1983; University of Virginia, Sesquicentennial Award, 1976; Fulbright Grant, 1962. **SPECIAL ACHIEVEMENTS:** Chief editor, Encyclopedia of Hinduism, 1988; editor, World Faiths Insight, London, 1978; The Concept of Sraddha, Motilal Banarasidas, India, 1969; Gandhi and Andrews, A Study in Hindu-Christian Dialogue, 1970; World Religions and Human Responsibility: Gandhian Perspectives, 1988; Mahatma Gandhi and Comparative Religion, Delhi, 1978; general editor, Hinduism, Buddhism, Sikhism, Islam, Patiala, 1970. **HOME ADDRESS:** 1050 Lyons Run Rd, Trafford, PA 15085.

RAO, KAMESWARA KOLLA (KAMESH)
Director of design. Indo-American. **PERSONAL:** Born Jul 28, 1944, Kasimkota, Andhra Pradesh, India; son of Kolla Subbarao and Kolla Ammaji; married Vasavi K Rao, Nov 17, 1972; children: Swathi, Sandhya, Preethi, Srinivas. **EDUCATION:** Andhra University, Waltair, India, BSc (w/honors), 1963, MSc, 1964, PhD, 1968; University of Wisconsin, Madison, PhD, 1975. **CAREER:** Western Michigan University, Kalamazoo, assistant professor of physics, 1979; National Semiconductor, staff engineer, 1979-81; Signetics, section head, 1981-83; Intel, project manager, 1983-86; Catalyst Semiconductor, director of design, 1986-. **HOME ADDRESS:** 1172 Arlington Ln, San Jose, CA 95129, (408)257-3720. **BUSINESS ADDRESS:** Director of Design, Catalyst Semiconductor, 2231 Calle de Luna, Santa Clara, CA 95054, (408)764-0240.

RAO, KONERU RAMAKRISHNA
Educator. Indo-American. **PERSONAL:** Born Oct 4, 1932, Vijayawada, Andhra Pradesh, India; son of Koneru Nagabhushanam and Koneru Annapurna; married Sarojini Devi, May 5, 1950; children: Rani Rao Gargavarapu, Vani Rao Chilukuri, Sarat Koneru. **EDUCATION:** University of Chicago, AM, 1960; Andhra University, PhD, 1962, DLit, 1976. **CAREER:** Andhra University, lecturer, 1953-60, professor, 1968-76, vice chancellor, 1984-87; Duke University, research associate, 1962-65; Institute for Parapsychology, director, 1977-84; Foundation for Research on the Nature of Man, executive director, 1987-. **ORGANIZATIONS:** American Psychological Association, 1976-; American Association for the Advancement of Science, 1977-; Indian Academy of Applied Psychology, president, 1986, 1987; Parapsychological Association, president, 1965, 1978, 1990. **HONORS/AWARDS:** Nagarjuna University, honorary degree, 1987; Kakatiya University, honorary degree, 1989; Andhra University, honorary degree, 1991. **SPECIAL ACHIEVEMENTS:** Experimental Parapsychology, 1966; Gandhi and Pragmatism, 1968; Mystic Awareness, 1972; J B Rhine on the Frontiers of Science, ed, 1982; Cultivating Consciousness, ed, 1993. **BIOGRAPHICAL SOURCES:** The Encyclopedia of Parapsychology and Psychial Research, p 349-350, 1991; Encyclopedia of Psychology, vol 3, p 205, 1984; Biographical Dictionary of Parapsychology, p 263-264, 1964. **BUSINESS ADDRESS:** Executive Director, Foundation for Research on the Nature of Man, 402 N Buchanan Blvd, Durham, NC 27707, (919)688-8241.

RAO, MADHUSUDANA N.
Educator. Indo-American. **PERSONAL:** Born Dec 2, 1956. **EDUCATION:** Jawaharlal Nehru University, New Delhi, India, MPhil, 1980; Kent State University, PhD, 1988. **CAREER:** Kent State University, part-time faculty, 1983-85; University of Akron, lecturer, 1983-89; Bridgewater State College, assistant professor, 1989-. **ORGANIZATIONS:** American Society for Photogrammetry & Remote Sensing; American Congress on Surveying and Mapping; Association of American Geographers. **HONORS/AWARDS:** Several grants. **BUSINESS ADDRESS:** Assistant Professor, Earth Sciences & Geography, Bridgewater State College, Bridgewater, MA 02325, (508)697-1390.

RAO, MAHESH K.
Semiconductor manufacturing executive. Indo-American. **PERSONAL:** Born Nov 29, 1959, Mysore, India; son of Sripathi Rao; married Vijaya Rao, Jan 16, 1985; children: Akhil. **EDUCATION:** University of Mysore, India, BE, 1981; University of Windsor, MASc, EE, 1984; University of Wyoming, PhD, EE, 1988. **CAREER:** University of Nevada, instructor, 1987-88, assistant professor, 1988-92; INTEL, sr tech mktg engineer, 1992-. **ORGANIZATIONS:** IEEE, 1982-; ISMM, 1989-. **SPECIAL ACHIEVEMENTS:** 20 publications in periodicals of: IEEE, IAS, IES, ISMM, etc. **HOME ADDRESS:** 406 S Lexington Dr, Folsom, CA 95630.

RAO, MENTREDDI ANANDHA (ANDY)
Educator. Indo-American. **PERSONAL:** Born Jul 4, 1937, Dornakal, Andhra Pradesh, India; son of M S Prakasa Rao (deceased) and M Sathya Narayanamma (deceased); married Janet Saine Rao, Jul 25, 1970; children: Hari Andre. **EDUCATION:** Osmania University, BChE, 1958; University of Cincinnati, MS, 1963; Ohio State University, PhD, 1969. **CAREER:** Wright-Patterson AFB, research associate, 1963-65; American-Standard Inc, research scientist, 1969-71; University of Caminas, Brazil, professor, 1971-73; Cornell University, assistant professor, beginning 1973, associate professor, professor, currently. **ORGANIZATIONS:** Am Inst Chem Engineers, 1966-; Society of Rheology, 1970-; Institute of Food Technologists, 1972-; Sigma Xi, 1969-. **HONORS/AWARDS:** Council of Exchange of Scholars, Fulbright Research/ Teaching, 1980-81, 1988-89. **SPECIAL ACHIEVEMENTS:** Books: co-editor, Viscoelastic Properties of Foods, Elsevier, London, 1992; co-editor, Engineering Properties of Foods, Marcel Dekker, New York, 1986. **BUSINESS ADDRESS:** Professor, Cornell University, PO Box 462, Geneva, NY 14456-0462, (315)787-2266.

RAO, NAGARAJA R.
Utility company coordinator. Indo-American. **PERSONAL:** Born Nov 7, 1942, Cuddapah, Andhra Pradesh, India; son of R Govinda Rao (deceased) & R Kamala Bai (deceased); married Kanchana Rao, Feb 19, 1980; children: Devii, Iishwara, Maheshwara, Uma. **EDUCATION:** AM Yoga Society, India, Avadhuta, 1963-66; KG Polytechnic, CE. **CAREER:** AMPS Yoga, international president, 1966-71; Youth for an Orderly Universe, Inc, president, 1971-78; Pacific Gas and Electric Co, engineering data coordinator, 1979-. **ORGANIZATIONS:** County Democratic Central Committee, 1990-; State Democratic Party, 1990-, executive board member, 1994-; 14th Assembly District, steering committee, 1990-; Hindu Community and Cultural Center Inc, chairman, human services, 1988-; Richmond Democratic Club, president, 1991; Richmond Neighbors, chairman, 1991-; NAACP; Federation of Indian Associations; AARP; International Brotherhood of Electrical Workers, 1971-, shop steward, 1979-; City of Richmond Parks and Recreation Commission, chairman, 1992-94; Asian Pacific Islander Caucus of California Democratic Party, treasurer, 1992-94; Bayarea Association; Tamil Association; Malayalee Association. **HONORS/AWARDS:** United Nations, Philippines, Golden Medallion, Exemplary Citizen of the World and a Dedicated Friend of Humanity, 1969; Intl Academy of Leadership, Honorary Doctorate in Humanities, 1970; delegate to the Democratic National Conventions, 1988-92; state senator's voluntary legislative assistant, 1989-91; assemblyman's alternate to county central committee, 1990-91. **SPECIAL ACHIEVEMENTS:** Author, Yogamritam-The Nector of Yoga, 1978. **BIOGRAPHICAL SOURCES:** Manila Times, May 24, 1969; Manila Daily Bulletin, Feb 3, 1968; Fabulous Hong Kong, Oct 1967; Southern Illinoisan, Sept 30, 1969; Harvard Crimson, April 9, 1990; The Wichita Eagle, Nov 30, 1969. **HOME ADDRESS:** 4724 Castilla Ave, Richmond, CA 94804, (510)235-1184. **BUSINESS PHONE:** (415)973-2705.

RAO, PAPINENI S.

Educator. Indo-American. **PERSONAL:** Born Apr 19, 1937, Vetapalam, Andhra Pradesh, India; son of Umamaheswara Rao and Sesharatnam; married Uma R Rao, Jul 19, 1967; children: Karuna, Rajani, Sobha. **EDUCATION:** Andhra Veterinary College, BVSc, 1959; University of Missouri, MS, 1961, PhD, 1965. **CAREER:** University of Missouri, research assistant, 1961-65, research associate, 1965-66; Saint Louis University, instructor, 1966-69, assistant professor, 1969-72, associate professor, 1972-79; University of South Florida, associate professor to professor, 1979-. **ORGANIZATIONS:** American Physiological Society, 1969-; Society for the Study of Reproduction, 1968-; American Association for the Advancement of Science, 1967-; Circulatory Shock Society, 1981-; American Association of University Professors, 1979-; International Endotoxin Society, 1985-. **HONORS/AWARDS:** University of Missouri, Charles Kiepe Scholarship, 1961-62, Curators Scholarship, 1961-65. **SPECIAL ACHIEVEMENTS:** Septic Shock in Obstetrics and Gynecology, book, 1977; 8 chapters or segments of books, 1973-88; several publications in refereed journals. **BUSINESS ADDRESS:** Professor, Dept of Obstetrics & Gynecology, College of Medicine, University of South Florida, 12901 Bruce B Downs Blvd, Box 18, Tampa, FL 33612, (813)254-6900.

RAO, POTARAZU KRISHNA

Government official. **PERSONAL:** Born Mar 26, 1930, Andhra Pradesh, India; son of Potarazu Satyanarayana and Potarazu Annapoorna; married Potarazu Rukmini, Aug 8, 1954; children: Ramanarayan Potarazu, Sreedhar Potarazu. **EDUCATION:** Andhra University, India, BS, 1950, MS, 1952; Florida State University, Tallahassee, MS, 1960; New York University, PhD, 1968. **CAREER:** World Meteorological Organization, Geneva, Switzerland, advisor to sec general, WMO, 1974-76; National Oceanic and Atmospheric Administration, director of Satellite Applications Lab, 1980-85, director of the Office of Research and Applications, 1985-. **ORGANIZATIONS:** NOAA Climate and Global Change Program, Board of Directors, 1988-; NOAA Cooperative Institute, advisory committee, 1985-. **HONORS/AWARDS:** American Meteorological Society, Fellow, 1988; Royal Meteorological Society, Fellow, 1957; New York Academy of Sciences, Fellow, 1977. **SPECIAL ACHIEVEMENTS:** Published over sixty papers in scientific Journals; principal editor of a book on weather satellites. **BUSINESS ADDRESS:** Director, Office of Research and Applications, Natl Environmental Satellite, Data & Info Service, NOAA, World Weather Bldg, Rm 701, Washington, DC 20233.

RAO, RAGHAV H.

Educator. Indo-American. **PERSONAL:** Born Jan 2, 1958, Bangalore, India; son of H S Rao & Lakshmi Rao; married Sabitha, Aug 23, 1985; children: Ashwin, Lavanya. **EDUCATION:** IIT, Kanpur, India, B Tech, 1979; University of Delhi, India, MBA, 1981; Purdue University, PhD, 1987. **CAREER:** Indiana University, lecturer, 1986-87; State University of New York at Buffalo, associate prof, currently. **ORGANIZATIONS:** IEEE, 1987-; ACM, 1987-; AAAI, 1987-; Tims/Orla, 1987-. **HONORS/AWARDS:** Midwest Business Association, Distinguished Paper Award, 1988; National Science Foundation Award, 1990. **SPECIAL ACHIEVEMENTS:** 25 journal papers, 1988-; chaired sessions of international & national conferences; published in journals such as: Discrete Applied Mathematics, Applied Artificial Intelligence, MIS Quarterly, Communications of the ACM. **BUSINESS ADDRESS:** Associate Professor, State University of New York at Buffalo, Putnam Way, 325 G Jacobs Center, Amherst, NY 14260, (716)645-3245.

RAO, RAMESH K. S.

Educator. Indo-American. **PERSONAL:** Born Mar 12, 1952, Madras, Tamil Nadu, India; son of K S Srinivasa Rao and Akhila Rao; married Anita, Dec 26, 1975; children: Nikhil. **EDUCATION:** Indian Institute of Technology, Madras, BTech, 1974; Indiana University, MBA, 1976, DBA, 1978. **CAREER:** University of Texas, Austin, Graduate School of Business, professor, 1978-. **ORGANIZATIONS:** American Finance Association, 1978-; Financial Management Association, 1978-; SGT International, director. **HONORS/ AWARDS:** University of Texas, Excellence in Education Award, 1993, Jack Taylor Award, 1987, Joe Beasley Award, 1985, Outstanding Professor Award, 1984. **SPECIAL ACHIEVEMENTS:** Author, Financial Management Concepts and Applications, 2nd ed, Macmillan Publishing Co, New York, 1992; author, Fundamentals of Financial Management, Macmillan, New York, 1989; various academic publications in financial economics. **BUSINESS ADDRESS:** Professor of Finance & CBA Foundation Fellow, University of Texas, Austin, Graduate School of Business, CBA 6-222C, Austin, TX 78712, (512)471-4368.

RAO, RAMGOPAL P.

Medical instrument company executive. Indo-American. **PERSONAL:** Born Aug 15, 1942, Hyderabad, Andhra Pradesh, India; son of Seshgir and Arya; married Sandhya, Jun 15, 1969; children: Sameer, Sushant, Neeraj. **EDUCATION:** Regional Engineering College, BSEE, 1965; Oklahoma State University, MSEE, 1966; Massachusetts Institute of Technology, 1966-68; Northeastern University, MBA, 1972. **CAREER:** Digilab Inc, director of r&d, 1974-78, vice president of manufacturing, 1978-82; BioRad Laboratories, Inc, division manager, 1982-90; Tomey Technology, Inc, president, 1990-. **ORGANIZATIONS:** National Society to Prevent Blindness, president, 1990-92, director, currently; IEEE, senior member, 1967-; AMA, 1992-; Japan Society of Boston, 1991-. **HOME ADDRESS:** 31 Stewart Rd, Needham, MA 02192, (617)449-3264. **BUSINESS ADDRESS:** President, Tomey Technology, Inc, 325 Vassar St, Cambridge, MA 02139, (617)864-6488.

RAO, SADASIVA MADIRAJU

Educator. Indo-American. **PERSONAL:** Born Jul 24, 1953, Hyderabad, Andhra Pradesh, India; son of M Sita Rama Rao & M Rangamma; married Kalyani M Rao, Nov 14, 1986; children: Yeshaswi M, Siri M. **EDUCATION:** Osmania University, BE, 1974; Indian Institute of Science, ME, 1976; University of Mississippi, PhD, 1980. **CAREER:** Rochester Institute of Technology, assistant professor, 1980-85; Osmania University, senior scientist, 1985-87; University of Houston, visiting associate professor, 1987-88; Auburn University, professor, 1988-. **ORGANIZATIONS:** IEEE, senior member. **BUSINESS ADDRESS:** Professor, Dept of Electrical Engineering, Auburn University, 200 Braun Hall, Auburn, AL 36849, (205)844-1876.

RAO, SINGIRESU SAMBASIVA

Educator. Indo-American. **PERSONAL:** Born Apr 9, 1944, Mangalagiri, Andhra Pradesh, India; son of Singiresu Narasimham and Singiresu Manikyamma; married Kamala, Jan 31, 1968; children: Sridevi, Shobha. **EDUCATION:** Andhra University, Waltair, India, BE (with honors), 1965; Indian Institute of Technology, Kanpur, MTech, 1968; Case Western Reserve University, PhD, 1971. **CAREER:** Indian Institute of Technology, Kanpur, India, professor of mechanical engineering, 1971-81; San Diego State University, professor of mechanical engineering, 1981-85; Purdue University, professor of mechanical engineering, 1985-. **ORGANIZATIONS:** American Society of Mechanical Engineers, 1983-; American Institute of Aeronautics and Astronautics, 1993-. **HONORS/AWARDS:** Andhra University, Vepa Krishna Murty Gold Medal, 1965, Lazarus Prize, 1965; James F Lincoln Arc Welding Foundation, First Prize for Best Graduate Research Paper, 1971; Telugu Association of North America, Best Researcher Award, 1987. **SPECIAL ACHIEVEMENTS:** Books: Optimization: Theory & Applications, 2nd edition, Wiley, 1984; The Finite Element Method in Engineering, 2nd edition, Pergamon Press, 1989; Mechanical Vibrations, 2nd edition, Addison-Wesley, 1990; Reliability-Based Design, McGraw-Hill, 1992. **BUSINESS ADDRESS:** Professor, School of Mech Engineringing, Purdue University, Rm ME-304, West Lafayette, IN 47907-1288.

RAO, SPUMA M.

Educator. Indo-American. **PERSONAL:** Born Jan 12, 1947, Vijaywada, Andhra Pradesh, India; son of S P Ramalingeswar Rao & S P Sakvntala; married Spnirvpama Rao, Oct 15, 1975; children: Spvijay. **EDUCATION:** Andhra University, BSc, mathematics, 1964; Osmania University, BE, mechanical, 1968; University of Wisconsin, MBA, 1984; MSU, PhD, 1988. **CAREER:** APSRTC, district manager, 1969-81; University of Southwestern Louisiana, associate professor, 1988-. **ORGANIZATIONS:** FMA, 1988-; Southwest Decision Sciences, 1988-; Southwestern Society of Economists, 1988-; Western Decision Science, 1988-; Beta Gamma Sigma, 1984-. **SPECIAL ACHIEVEMENTS:** Six publications on investments; proficient in English, Telugu, Hindi languages. **HOME ADDRESS:** 100 McDonald, Apt J 11, Lafayette, LA 70506, (318)989-8431. **BUSINESS ADDRESS:** Associate Professor, Finance, University of Southwestern Louisiana, PO Box 44570, Lafayette, LA 70504, (318)231-6099.

RAO, SRIKUMAR S.

Educator, educational administrator, consultant. Indo-American. **PERSONAL:** Born Apr 11, 1951, Bombay, India; married Meenakshi S Rao, Jun 26, 1981; children: Gowri S, Gautam S. **EDUCATION:** Indian Institute of Management, Ahmedabad, MBA, 1972; Columbia University, Graduate School of Business, MPhil, 1980, PhD, 1982. **CAREER:** Data Resources Inc, marketing research, associate director, 1978-80; Baruch College, CUNY, assistant professor, 1983-85; Long Island University, Dept of Marketing, chairman,

1985-. **ORGANIZATIONS:** MENSA, marketing advisor; American Management Association, seminar leader. **SPECIAL ACHIEVEMENTS:** Success Magazine, contributing editor. **HOME ADDRESS:** 25 Shirley Court, Commack, NY 11725, (516)864-3146. **BUSINESS ADDRESS:** Chairman, Dept of Marketing, Long Island University, 302 Roth Hall, Brookville, NY 11548, (516)299-2143.

RAO, T. K. SREEPADA
Physician, educator. Indo-American. **PERSONAL:** Born Jun 4, 1944, Kolar, Karnataka, India; son of T K Krishna Murthy Rao (deceased) & Nagamma (deceased); married Pushpa Rao, Mar 9, 1972; children: Kiran, Sheethal. **EDUCATION:** National College, Bangalore, India, PUC, 1959; Bangalore Medical College, India, MBBS, 1966; Fellow of American College of Physicians, 1976. **CAREER:** Kings County Hospital, director of hemodialysis, 1973-; State University of New York, professor of medicine, 1974-. **ORGANIZATIONS:** Karnataka State Medical & Dental Alumni Association, board of trustees; Nargis Dutt Memorial Foundation, 2nd vice president; American Association of Physicians from India, patron; Long Island Indian Association, life member; American & International Society of Nephrology; American & International Society of Artificial Organs; International Society of Transplantation; National Kidney Foundation. **HONORS/AWARDS:** Madras Medical College, honorary fellow, 1984; Manipal Medical College, honorary fellow, 1985; New York Asian-American Lions Club, Meritorious Award, 1980; Long Island Indian Association, special honoree, 1993. **SPECIAL ACHIEVEMENTS:** Member of editorial board, Medical Journals; "HIV Nephorpathy," Annual Review of Medicine, vol 42, p 391-401, 1991; "What Role for Hemodialysis in HIV Seropositive Patients? Can It Improve Outcome?," Journal of Critical Illness, vol 7, no 1, p 16-17, 1992; "Renal Insufficiency in HIVAN, Can It Be Prevented?," Journal of Critical Illness, vol 8, no 3, p 326-327, 1993; numerous others. **BUSINESS ADDRESS:** Professor of Medicine, SUNY-HSC at Brooklyn, 450 Clarkson Ave, Box 52, Brooklyn, NY 11203-2098, (718)270-1394.

RAO, TARAMANOHAR B.
Educator. Indo-American. **PERSONAL:** Born Dec 8, 1933, Hyderabad, Andhra Pradesh, India; son of Sudershan & Lakshmi; married Premila, Dec 17, 1961; children: Pravin, Protima, Himavantha Prashanth. **EDUCATION:** Osmania University, Hyderabad, India, BA, 1953; Calcutta University, India, MA, 1956; University of Missouri, PhD, 1974. **CAREER:** Ferris State University, professor, 1980-. **HOME ADDRESS:** 112 W Bridge, Big Rapids, MI 49307.

RAO, TEJASWINI
Educator. Indo-American. **PERSONAL:** Born Oct 23, 1949, Madras, Tamil Nadu, India; daughter of C R Rao & C Bhargavi Rao. **EDUCATION:** Penn State University, PhD, 1975. **CAREER:** Buffalo State College, associate professor, 1976-93. **ORGANIZATIONS:** American Dietetic Association; Institute of Food Technology. **HOME PHONE:** (716)836-5989. **BUSINESS ADDRESS:** Associate Professor, Buffalo State College, 205 Caudell Hall, 1300 Elmwood Ave, Buffalo, NY 14222, (716)878-4333.

RAO, VAMAN
Educator. Indo-American. **PERSONAL:** Born in Gogi, Karnataka, India; son of Venkatesh Rao and Bhima Bai; married Geetha V Rao, Dec 5, 1963; children: Kavita Rao Dhanwada, Anita. **EDUCATION:** Osmania University, India, BSc, BA, BEd, MA, econ; University of Missouri, PhD, econ, 1973. **CAREER:** Government College of Education, lecturer; Osmania University, Hyderabad, senior lecturer, 1965-70; University of Missouri-Columbia, research assistant, 1970-73; University of Missouri-Rolla, assistant professor of economics, 1973-79; Western Illinois University, associate professor, 1979-82; Soochow University, Taipei, visiting professor, 1982-83; Western Illinois University, professor of economics, 1982-. **ORGANIZATIONS:** Association of Indian Economic Studies, chairperson, 1991-95, executive committee, 1979-95; Indian Econometric Society, 1975-; Missouri Valley Economic Association, director, 1991-93; AIES Newsletter, editor, 1981-91; International Journal of Indian Studies, associate/book review editor, 1991-; Journal of Social Economics, book review editor, 1986-; Journal of Developing Areas, editorial board, 1986-. **HONORS/AWARDS:** Western Illinois University, WIU BGU Distinguished Professor Award, 1993, Annual Faculty Lecturer, 1991, Faculty Excellence Awards, 1986-93, Presidential Merit Award, 1981-83; Osmania University, College of Education, Gold Medal for Excellent Teacher, 1957. **SPECIAL ACHIEVEMENTS:** More than 75 publications in books and professional journals, such as: American Journal of Agricultural Economics,

The Journal of Economics, International Journal of Indian Studies, Studies in Comparative Economic Development, Journal of Energy Economics, and others; more than 15 monographs; more than 100 presentations at professional conferences. **HOME PHONE:** (309)833-5184. **BUSINESS ADDRESS:** Professor of Economics, Western Illinois University, 442 Stipes Hall, Macomb, IL 61455, (309)298-1321.

RAO, VENIGALLA BASAVESWARA
Researcher, educator. Indo-American. **PERSONAL:** Born Jun 10, 1954, Donepudi, Andhra Pradesh, India; son of Venigalla Koteswara Rao and Venigalla Janaki Devi; married Mangala Rao, Aug 20, 1982; children: Prashant Arkalgud, Vishnu-Prakash Venigalla. **EDUCATION:** Andhra University, BSc, 1974, MS, 1976; Indian Institute of Science, PhD, 1982. **CAREER:** University of Maryland Medical School, research associate, 1980-88, research assistant professor, 1988-89; The Catholic University of America, assistant professor, 1989-. **ORGANIZATIONS:** American Association for Microbiology; American Association for Advancement of Science; Sigma Xi. **HONORS/AWARDS:** Department of Energy, research grant, 1990-93. **SPECIAL ACHIEVEMENTS:** Sixteen publications in professional peer-reviewed journals, original research articles related to biochemistry of enzymes, virology, and molecular biology. **HOME ADDRESS:** 607 Hyde Rd, Silver Spring, MD 20902, (301)593-7985. **BUSINESS ADDRESS:** Assistant Professor, Dept of Biology, Catholic University of America, 620 Michigan Ave NE, 103 McCort Ward Hall, Washington, DC 20064, (202)319-5271.

RAO, YALAMANCHILI KRISHNA
Educator. Indo-American. **PERSONAL:** Born May 9, 1941, Andhra Pradesh, India; son of Y V Subba Rytu Rao and Y Kamalamma; married Y Padmavathi Rao, Jul 23, 1969; children: Ram Prasad, Vijay Mohan, Rupa. **EDUCATION:** Andhra University, Waltair, India, IASc, 1958; Banaras Hindu University, Varanasi, India, BSc, 1962; University of Pennsylvania, PhD, 1965. **CAREER:** Banaras Hindu University, lecturer, 1962; Inland Steel Co, research engineer, 1965-67; Corning Glass Works, research metallurgist, 1967-68; Columbia University, assistant professor & associate professor, mnl engineeringng, 1968-76; University of Washington, metallurgical engineering, associate professor, beginning 1976, professor, currently. **ORGANIZATIONS:** The Minerals, Metals and Materials Society, Inc, 1963-; American Chemical Society, 1971-; The Institution of Mining and Metallurgy (UK), fellow, 1980-; The Indian Institute of Metals, 1988-. **HONORS/AWARDS:** Banaras Hindu University, Distinguished Alumnus, 1984. **SPECIAL ACHIEVEMENTS:** Alumina Chlorination, US Patent No 4565674, 1986; slag use in continuous casting of steel, US Patent No 3704744, 1972; continuous casting slag and method of making, US Patent No 3649249, 1972; author, Stoichiometry and Thermodynamics of Metallurgical Processes, 1985. **BUSINESS ADDRESS:** Professor, University of Washington, FB-10, 302K Roberts Hall, Seattle, WA 98125, (206)543-2620.

RASHEED, SURAIYA
Educator. Pakistani American. **PERSONAL:** Born Sep 2, 1936, Hyderabad, India; daughter of M Yaseen Alvi & Mehrunnisan Begum Alvi; married Nasir Rasheed, Jan 4, 1958; children: 2. **EDUCATION:** Osmania University, BSc, 1953, MSc, 1955, PhD, 1958; London University, England, PhD, 1964. **CAREER:** Mt Vernon Hospital, research associate, 1964-70; University of Southern California, Pathology, instructor, 1970-72, assistant professor, 1972-76, associate professor, 1976-82, professor, 1982-. **ORGANIZATIONS:** International Association for Comparative Research in Leukemia and Related Diseases; American Society of Virologists; American Society for Microbiology; American Association for the Advancement of Science; American Association of University Professors; International AIDS Society. **HONORS/AWARDS:** USC, Faculty Research and Innovation Award, 1983, Outstanding Service Award, 1989; Eisenhower Medical Ctr Annenberg Ctr for Health Services, Distinguished Speaker Award, 1987; First Medical Univ of Shanghai, Honorary Professorship, 1988-92; Zhejiang Medical Univ, Honorary Professorship, 1988-92; Institute of Basic Medical Sciences, Honorary Professorship, 1988-92; Commandant Armed Forces Medical College, honorary plaque, 1989; ICSC, Achievement Award, 1992; Pakistan Assn of Pathologist, plaque, 1992; Biomerieux Behring Progressive Medicals, gold medal, 1992; Medal of Honor for Distinguished Lifelong Achievements, 1993; Royal College of Pathologists, London, Fellow, 1993; numerous research grants, 1970-96. **SPECIAL ACHIEVEMENTS:** Published: 38 books & chapters, 97 abstracts, 122 presentations & 90 journal articles. **BUSINESS ADDRESS:** Professor of Pathology, School of Medicine, University of Southern California, 1840 N Soto St,

Rm 103, Edmondson Research Bldg, Los Angeles, CA 90032-3626, (213)224-7415.

RATH, NIGAM PRASAD

Educator. Indo-American. **PERSONAL:** Born Mar 24, 1958, Berhampur, Orissa, India; son of Satyabadi Rath and Urmila Rath; married Suchitra Rath, May 29, 1985; children: Niharika. **EDUCATION:** Khallikote College, India, ISc, 1975; Berhampur University, India, BSc (with honors), 1977, MSc, 1979; Oklahoma State University, PhD, 1985. **CAREER:** University of Notre Dame, research associate, 1986-87, assistant faculty fellow, 1987-89; University of Missouri, research assistant professor, 1989-. **ORGANIZATIONS:** American Crystallography Association; American Chemical Society. **SPECIAL ACHIEVEMENTS:** 50 publications in refereed journals, 1985-. **BUSINESS ADDRESS:** Research Assistant Professor of Chemistry, University of Missouri, 8001 Natural Bridge Rd, St Louis, MO 63121, (314)553-5333.

RATHBONE, SUSAN WU

Community activist, association executive. Chinese American. **PERSONAL:** Born Oct 29, 1922, China; married Frank Rathbone, Aug 20, 1945; children: Frank, Edward. **EDUCATION:** City University of New York, BA, 1984. **CAREER:** Queens Chinese Women's Association, founder, chairperson, currently; Chinese Immigrants Service, Auntie Wu's Hotline, chairperson, founder, currently. **ORGANIZATIONS:** American-Chinese Businesswomen's Association, founder; Anhwei Provincial Association, founder, honorary lifetime president. **HONORS/AWARDS:** National Organization of Women, Susan B Anthony Award, 1987; City of New York Ethnic Award, 1984; Council of the City of New York, Unsung Heroine Award, 1987; City of New York, Mayor Dinkins Award, 1990; Queens Federation of Churches, Outstanding Leadership, 1991. **SPECIAL ACHIEVEMENTS:** Assisting Chinese immigrants with life in the USA, 1947-93; executive editor, Women's Voice Magazine, 1993. **BIOGRAPHICAL SOURCES:** Life Overseas, p 14, Aug 1992; The Flushing Times, p 1, Nov 12, 1992. **HOME ADDRESS:** 26-10 Union St, Flushing, NY 11354, (718)461-3044. **BUSINESS ADDRESS:** Chairperson, Queens Chinese Women's Association, Chinese Immigrants Service, 135-17 40 Rd, 3rd Fl, Flushing, NY 11354, (718)353-0195.

RATTI, RAKESH KUMAR

Writer. Indo-American. **PERSONAL:** Born Sep 27, 1959, Jama Rai, Punjab, India; son of Ram N Ratti & Tara W Ratti. **EDUCATION:** California State University, Sacramento, BA, psychology, 1981; California State University, Los Angeles, MA, psychology, 1989; Georgia State University, PhD, currently. **CAREER:** Georgia Mental Health Institute, behavior specialist, 1991-. **ORGANIZATIONS:** Trikone, San Francisco, board of directors, founding member, 1986-89, Los Angeles, founding member, 1987-90; Los Angeles Gay & Lesbian Alliance Against Defamation, speaker, 1989-90; Atlanta Gay & Lesbian Alliance Against Defamation, board of directors, 1992-93; Project Open Hand, volunteer, 1992-93. **SPECIAL ACHIEVEMENTS:** Proficient in Hindi, Punjabi, and Spanish; editor, A Lotus of Another Color: An Unfolding of the Gay & Lesbian South Asian Experience, 1993; short story, "Promenade," Indivisible, 1991; poems: "The Greater God," Boyhood Experiences, 1993; "White Wrinkles on Smooth Brown Skin," Samar, 1992; graphic artist. **BIOGRAPHICAL SOURCES:** Time, international edition, p 50, May 17, 1993; India Today, North American edition, p 60B, May 31, 1993. **HOME PHONE:** (404)688-8126.

RAU, A. RAVI PRAKASH

Educator. Indo-American. **PERSONAL:** Born Aug 9, 1945, Calcutta, W. Bengal, India; son of M Anantaswamy Rau and Vijayalakshmi Rau; married Luba M Witer, Jun 28, 1969 (died 1981); married Dominique G Homberger, May 16, 1985; children: Nicholas N, Alexander V. **EDUCATION:** Delhi University, India, BSc (honors), 1964, MSc, 1966; University of Chicago, PhD, 1970. **CAREER:** New York University, assoc research scientist, 1970-72; Tata Inst of Fundamental Research, Bombay, India, visiting fellow, 1972-73; Louisiana State University, professor, 1974-. **ORGANIZATIONS:** American Physical Society, fellow. **HONORS/AWARDS:** Louisiana State University, Distinguished Research Master, 1987; Alfred P Sloan Foundation, Sloan Fellowship, 1977. **SPECIAL ACHIEVEMENTS:** Yale University, 13th Hannan Rosenthal Memorial Lecture, 1985; co-author of book: Atomic Collisions and Spectra, Academic Press, 1986; approx 100 physics publications in international refereed journals, 1967-. **BUSINESS ADDRESS:** Professor, Dept Physics, Louisiana State University, Baton Rouge, LA 70803-4001, (504)388-6841.

RAUT, KAMALAKAR BALKRISHNA

Educator. Indo-American. **PERSONAL:** Born Aug 10, 1920, Bombay, India; son of Balkrishna Ramchandra Raut and Rukhmini; married Savita, Feb 21, 1945; children: Pravin, Madhuri Vidmer, Chandrakala Jenkins, Seema Csukas, Rajesh. **EDUCATION:** University of Bombay, India, BSc, 1941, BA (with honors), 1942, MSc, 1946; University of Oklahoma, PhD, 1959. **CAREER:** University of Oklahoma, teaching and research assistant, 1955-59; East Texas State University, visiting instructor, 1959-60; Central Drug Research Institute, Govt of India, scientific officer, 1960-61; Indian Institute of Technology, Kanpur, India, assistant professor, 1962-69; NATO Advanced Study Institute, Norduikjhout, Netherlands, 1973; Savannah State College, professor, 1964-91, professor, emeritus of chemistry, 1991-. **ORGANIZATIONS:** American Chemical Society, alternate councilor, 1992-94; Georgia Academy of Science, chairman and secretary; American Association of University Professors, 1977-93; International Union of Pure and Applied Chemistry, 1987-92; Optimist International, charter member, 1976-; United States Chess Federation, life member. **HONORS/AWARDS:** Chemical Abstract Service, Certificate of Recognition, 1976; American Chemical Society, Service of Merit, 1978; Georgia Science and Engineering Fair, trophy, 1980; American Chemical Society, Award Certificate, 1991; Savannah State College, Department of Chemistry, award, 1991. **SPECIAL ACHIEVEMENTS:** Over 50 publications in the field of organic chemistry, computer assisted instructions and solid waste; air pollution, medical waste disposal. **HOME ADDRESS:** 708 Penn Waller Rd, Savannah, GA 31410, (912)897-1437.

RAVINDRA, NUGGEHALLI MUTHANNA (RAVI)

Educator. Indo-American. **PERSONAL:** Born Oct 1, 1955, Hyderabad, Andhra Pradesh, India; son of Nuggehalli Garudachar Muthanna & Padma Muthanna; married Pushpa Ravindra; children: Krishna, Pradeep, Jayant. **EDUCATION:** Bangalore University, India, BS (with honors), 1974, MS, 1976; University of Roorkee, India, PhD, 1982. **CAREER:** Indian Institute of Science, research fellow, 1976-77; University of Roorkee, research fellow, 1977-82; CNRS (France), ICTP (Italy), fellow, 1982-85; North Carolina State University, visiting scientist, 1985-86; Vanderbilt University, research associate professor, 1986-87; New Jersey Institute of Technology, associate professor, 1987-. **ORGANIZATIONS:** IEEE, 1987-; APS, 1990-92; SPIE, 1987-90; MRS, 1986-92; ECS, 1988-92; Sigma Xi, 1987-90. **HONORS/AWARDS:** CSIR, India, Research Fellowship, 1977-82; IPA, India, 2nd Prize, Best Essay, All India Competetion, 1976. **SPECIAL ACHIEVEMENTS:** Ravindra Relation, Refractive Index-energy Gap Relationship for Semiconductors, 1978; Si $SiO2$ interfaces, evolution with oxide thickness, 1986; formation of shallow junctions, implantation through metals, 1986-90; formation of buried oxides in germanium, 1987-90. **BIOGRAPHICAL SOURCES:** "Energy Gap, Refractive Index Relations in Semiconductors," Physica Status Solidi, by T S Moss, (b), vol 131, p 415-435. **BUSINESS ADDRESS:** Associate Professor, Dept of Physics, New Jersey Institute of Technology, Tiernan Bldg, #452, Newark, NJ 07102, (201)596-3278.

RAVINDRAN, NAIR N.

Imaging technology researcher (retired). Indo-American. **PERSONAL:** Born Nov 25, 1934, Vechoor, Kerala, India; children: Pramod K. **EDUCATION:** Purdue University, PhD, 1972. **CAREER:** Eastman Kodak Co, research associate, 1974-91. **ORGANIZATIONS:** American Chemical Society; Society of Motion Picture and Television Engineers. **SPECIAL ACHIEVEMENTS:** Several publications in many international chemistry journals, including JACS, JOC; one US patent. **HOME ADDRESS:** 220 Pennels Drive, Rochester, NY 14626, (716)225-9194.

RAWAT, ARUN KUMAR

Health services administrator. Indo-American. **PERSONAL:** Born Sep 19, 1945, Agra, Uttar Pradesh, India; son of P L Rawat and S L Rawat; married Anuradha Sharma, Jul 26, 1974; children: Atul Sharma, Angeli. **EDUCATION:** University of Lucknow, India, BSc, 1962, MSc, 1964; University of Copenhagen, Denmark, DSc, 1969. **CAREER:** Mt Sinai Medical School, instructor, medicine, 1970-71; Downstate Medical Center, SUNY, assistant professor, 1971-73; Medical College of Ohio, associate professor, 1973-78; University of Toledo, associate professor, 1978-82, professor, pharmacology, 1983-; Ohio Department of Mental Health, chief, research and evaluation, 1979-82, Midwest Institute, director, 1983-. **ORGANIZATIONS:** Medical College of Ohio, Research Committee Psychiatry, head, 1976-78; Ohio Governor's Task Force for Minority Health, 1982; Ohio Department of Health, advisory committee, childhood lead poisoning prevention, 1993; Human Ethics and Research Committee, ODMH, 1975-82; Ohio Department of Mental

Health, Clinical Executive Committee, 1979-82; American College of Toxicologists, 1982; American Society of Neurochemistry, 1974; American Society of Biochemical Molecular Biology, 1974; American Society Clinical Research, 1971; American Medical Education Research Society on Alcoholism, 1975. **HONORS/AWARDS:** NRI Association, India, Hind Rattan Award, 1993. **SPECIAL ACHIEVEMENTS:** Contributor to the following publications: Advances in Experimental Medicine & Biology, 1974, 1979, International Reviews of Neurobiology, 1978, Neurobehavioral Toxicology, 1980, DHEW Monograph, Washington, DC, 1982, Ohio State Medical Journal, 1978. **HOME ADDRESS:** 521 Greenfield Dr, Maumee, OH 43537, (419)893-7228. **BUSINESS ADDRESS:** Director, CEO, Midwest Institute, University Park W, PO Box 5888, Toledo, OH 43613-0888, (419)536-5151.

RAWAT, BANMALI SINGH
Educator. Indo-American. **PERSONAL:** Born Jul 2, 1947, Garhwal, Uttar Pradesh, India; son of Dilwan Singh Rawat and Narda Rawat; married Shanti Rawat, Feb 6, 1977; children: Manita, Sahit. **EDUCATION:** Banaras Hindu University, BSEE, 1968, MSEE, 1970; Sri Venkateswara University, PhD, 1976. **CAREER:** West Coast Paper Mill Ltd, instrumentation engineer, 1971-72; Defense R&D Organization, senior scientist, 1975-78; MMM Engineering College, associate professor, 1978-80, professor and head, 1980-81; University of North Dakota, associate/professor, 1981-88; University of Nevada, professor and head, 1988-91, professor, 1991-. **ORGANIZATIONS:** IEEE Red River Valley, secretary/treasurer, 1987, vice-chairman, 1988; IEEE Northern Nevada, chairman, 1989-90, 1993-94; ISRAMT, Advisory Committee, chairman, 1989-, Technical Program Committee, chair, 1989-; ICOMM-90, advisory committee, 1990; AYSO, governing board, 1990. **HONORS/AWARDS:** Banaras Hindu University, Gold Medal, 1970; IETE, India, fellow, 1985; CIE, fellow, 1993. **SPECIAL ACHIEVEMENTS:** Large number of publications in microwave journals, 1975-; founder of ISRAMT Conference, 1986; proficiency in Russian, German, Hindi. **BUSINESS ADDRESS:** Professor, Electrical Engineering Dept, University of Nevada, SEM/260, Reno, NV 89557, (702)784-6927.

RAWLINGS, NOELLA A.
Attorney. Japanese American. **PERSONAL:** Born Dec 24, 1955, Honolulu, HI; daughter of Harold and Patricia Hashimoto; married Leslie H Rawlings, Oct 5, 1991; children: Alexandra, Daniel. **EDUCATION:** University of Hawaii, BA, 1977; University of Washington, JD, 1980. **CAREER:** Evergreen Legal Services, staff attorney, 1980-81; Physicians Insurance, vice president & general counsel, 1989-92; Attorney General's Office, assistant attorney general, 1981-89, 1992-. **ORGANIZATIONS:** Asian Bar Association of Washington, president, 1993, president elect, 1992-93, Judicial Evaluation Committee, past chair; Washington State Bar Association, 1980-; Seattle-King County Bar Association, 1989-; National Association of College & University Attorneys, 1987-89, 1992-; American Academy of Hospital Attorneys, 1987-92. **SPECIAL ACHIEVEMENTS:** Published chapter in Family Law Deskbook, Washington State Bar Association Publication, 1989, 1992. **BUSINESS ADDRESS:** Assistant Attorney General, Attorney General's Office, 900 Fourth Ave #1800, Seattle, WA 98164, (206)587-5090.

RAWN, BYUNG SOON
Company executive. Korean American. **PERSONAL:** Born Aug 10, 1936, Republic of Korea; daughter of Park; married William L Rawn, Jul 23, 1957 (deceased); children: Mary L Peterson, Joyce A, Margaret E. **EDUCATION:** Pearce College, 1975-80. **CAREER:** Reseda Rubber Stamp, president, 1982-. **BUSINESS ADDRESS:** President, Reseda Rubber Stamp, 7327 Reseda Blvd, Reseda, CA 91335.

RAY, SIBA PRASAD
Engineer, scientist. Indo-American. **PERSONAL:** Born Jan 4, 1944, Dinhata, W. Bengal, India; son of Nilmony Prasad and Bina Pani Ray; married Lipika Ray; children: Sourav, Leena. **EDUCATION:** Calcutta University, India, BE, 1964; Columbia University, New York, MS, 1970, Dr Engg Sc, materials science, 1974. **CAREER:** Bhabha Atomic Research Centre, scientist, 1964-69; Pennsylvania State University, research associate, 1975-76; Alcoa Laboratories, scientist, 1977-78, sr scientist, 1978-81, senior scientific associate, 1991-. **ORGANIZATIONS:** American Ceramic Society, 1977; Minerals Metals and Materials Society, 1979-; Sigma Xi, 1974-. **HONORS/AWARDS:** Columbia University, Krumb Fellowship, 1969. **SPECIAL ACHIEVEMENTS:** 12 patents in the area of non-consumable anodes for aluminum electrolysis, 1981-86; 3 patents on ceramic matrix composites, 1987-90; 2 patents on high temperature ceramic superconductors, 1989-91; 4 patents on reaction sintering of interwoven composites (SHS reactions), 1984-87. **HOME ADDRESS:** 6007 Pilgrim Ct, Murrysville, PA 15668, (412)327-2903. **BUSINESS ADDRESS:** Senior Scientific Associate, Aluminum Company of America, 100 Technical Dr, Alcoa Technical Center, Alcoa Center, PA 15069, (412)337-2803.

RECANA, MEL RED
Judge. Filipino American. **PERSONAL:** married Rory. **EDUCATION:** University of the East, Philippines, JD, 1964; University of Southern California, post-graduate; Harvard University, Kennedy School of Government, master's, public administration. **CAREER:** Recana & Associates, attorney, 1974-77, 1980-81; County of Los Angeles, deputy district attorney, 1977-80; Pacific Coast University, asst professor of law, 1981-; Los Angeles Judicial District, municipal court judge, 1981-. **ORGANIZATIONS:** Judges Association; Los Angeles Municipal Court Judges Association; Pilipino American Bar Association. **HONORS/AWARDS:** Philippine Counsel General, Los Angeles, Recognition Award, 1990; Internal Revenue Service, Dept of Treasury, Certificate of Recognition, 1989, 1982; Los Angeles Damayan Lions Club, Commendation, 1988; Alpa Phi Omega Alumni Association, Commendation, 1988. **SPECIAL ACHIEVEMENTS:** California Center for Judicial Education and Research, certificates of completion, Voir Dire and Trial Management, 1990, Judicial Fact-Finding and Decision-Making, 1990, Jurisprudence II, 1989, Jurisprudence, I, 1989. **BUSINESS ADDRESS:** Municipal Judge, Los Angeles Municipal Court, 110 N Grand Ave, Los Angeles, CA 90012.

REDDY, BANDARU S.
Scientist. Indo-American. **PERSONAL:** Born Dec 30, 1932, Nellore, Andhra Pradesh, India; son of Ramamma & Bandaru Venkatasubba Reddy; married Subhashini Reddy, Dec 22, 1962; children: Sudhakar, Sada, Srikanth. **EDUCATION:** Madras University, India, DVM, 1955; University of New Hampshire, Durham, MS, 1960; Michigan State University, PhD, 1963. **CAREER:** University of Notre Dame, assistant research professor, 1965-68, associate research professor, 1968-71; New York Medical College, research professor, 1976-; American Health Foundation, acting chief, division of nutrition, 1971-80, associate chief, 1980-90, chief of nutritional carcinogenesis, 1990-. **ORGANIZATIONS:** American Association for Cancer Research; American Association for Investigative Pathology; American Institute for Nutrition; Society for Experimental Biology and Medicine; Society of Toxicology; American Association for Advancement of Science; American Gastroenterological Association; Association of Gnotobiotics, president, 1983-84. **HONORS/AWARDS:** Sigma Xi; Association of Gnotobiotics, president, 1979-80; Lobund Lab, University of Notre Dame, advisory board member, 1980-84; Japan Bifidus Foundation Award, 1990. **BIOGRAPHICAL SOURCES:** Published 250 scientific papers in peer-reviewed scientific journals. **BUSINESS ADDRESS:** Chief, Division of Nutritional Carcinogenesis, American Health Foundation, One Dana Rd, Valhalla, NY 10595, (914)789-7149.

REDDY, C. SUBBA
Educator, researcher. Indo-American. **PERSONAL:** Born Jul 1, 1942, Ananthasagaram, Andhra Pradesh, India; son of Chinthagunta Subba Reddy and Chinthagunta Ankamma; married Vasantha Y Reddy, Aug 31, 1969; children: Srikanth C, Sathya C, Chakradhar C. **EDUCATION:** Srivenkateswara University, India, BE, 1963; Indian Institute of Tech, India, post graduate certificate, 1972; University of Hawaii, MS, 1973; Clarkson University, PhD, 1976. **CAREER:** Design engineer, lecturer, etc, 1964-76; Clarkson University, postdoctoral associate, 1976-77; Old Dominion University, assistant professor, 1977-82; University of Alabama, associate professor, 1982-85; State University of New York, associate professor, 1985-88, department chairman, 1987-88; Union University, associate professor, 1988-92; VA State University, associate professor, 1992-. **ORGANIZATIONS:** American Society of Mech Engineers, Mohawk Valley Section, NY, treasurer, 1987-88, secretary, 1986-87; Virginia Academy of Sciences, Aeronautical Section, chairman, 1981-82, secretary, 1980-81; ASME, 1975-. **HONORS/AWARDS:** NASA-ASEE, Langley Research Center, fellowship, 1993; DOE, fellowships to conduct research at Oak Ridge National Laboratory, 1985, 1988; scholarships, awards, prizes, essay contest, etc. **SPECIAL ACHIEVEMENTS:** Published 43 papers and reports in national and international journals and conference proceedings. **BUSINESS ADDRESS:** Professor, Engineering Dept, Viginia State University, Box 9032, Petersburg, VA 23806.

REDDY, CHILEKAMPALLI ADINARAYANA
Educator. Indo-American. **PERSONAL:** Born Jul 1, 1941, Nandimandalam, Cuddapah, Andhra Pradesh, India; son of C Narayana Reddy and C Balamma Reddy; married Sasikala C Reddy, Oct 9, 1972; children: Sumabala C. **EDU-**

CATION: Sri Venkateswara University, India, BVSc, 1962; University of Illinois, Urbana-Champaign, MS, 1967, PhD, 1970. **CAREER:** Government of Andhra Pradesh, India, veterinary assistant surgeon, 1962-65; University of Illinois, research assistant, 1965-70; University of Georgia, research associate, 1970-72; Michigan State University, assistant professor, 1972-77, associate professor, 1977-85, professor, 1985-. **ORGANIZATIONS:** American Academy of Microbiology, elected fellow; American College of Veterinary Microbiolgy, diplomate; American Society for Microbiology; Society for Industrial Microbiology; American Veterinary Medical Association; Conference of Research Workers in Animal Diseases, elected member; American Association for the Advancement of Science. **HONORS/AWARDS:** Michigan State University, Smithkline Beecham Award for Research Excellence, 1991; Sigma Xi; research grants from: NIH, DOE, NSF, USDA. **SPECIAL ACHIEVEMENTS:** Contributed to approximately 100 publications in scientific journals and proceedings; citation, Hot Paper, Scientist; author, editor of four books; reviewer of various journals. **BUSINESS ADDRESS:** Professor of Microbiology, Michigan State University, East Lansing, MI 48824-1101, (517)355-6499.

REDDY, CHURKU MOHAN
Educator. Indo-American. **PERSONAL:** Born Aug 3, 1942, Kothapalli, India; son of Krishna C Reddy; married Rema C Reddy, 1948; children: Hemelatha, Rajender. **EDUCATION:** Osmanis University, 1966, MBBS, 1966; American Board of Pediatrics, diplomate, 1975; American Board of Ped Endocrinology, diplomate, 1983. **CAREER:** Downstate Medical Center, assistant, 1971-75; Meharry Medical College, assistant professor, 1975-77, director, pediatric endocrinology, 1975-, associate professor, 1977-82, professor, 1982-. **ORGANIZATIONS:** American Academy of Pediatrics; Tennessee Medical Association. **HONORS/AWARDS:** American Academy of Pediatrics, Fellow. **SPECIAL ACHIEVEMENTS:** Published several articles in the field of pediatrics. **BUSINESS ADDRESS:** Professor of Pediatrics, Meharry Medical College, 1005 David B Todd Blvd, Nashville, TN 37208, (615)327-6112.

REDDY, DHANIREDDY RAMALINGA (RAMALINGA REDDY DHANIREDDY)
Aerospace engineer. Indo-American. **PERSONAL:** Born Sep 6, 1949, Yerragudi, Andhra Pradesh, India; son of Dhanireddy Linga Reddy and Dhanireddy Veeramma; married Geeta, Jun 18, 1975; children: Soni, Swati, Srikant. **EDUCATION:** S V University, India, BE, mech, 1971; Indian Institute of Science, Bangalore, ME, aero, 1974; University of Cincinnati, PhD, aero, 1983. **CAREER:** Defense Research and Development Lab, India, senior scientist, 1974-79; University of Cincinnati, research assistant & associate, 1980-84; General Motors Corp, Allison Gasturbine Division, senior project engineer, 1984-87; Sverdrup Technology, Inc, supervisor, turbomach analysis, 1987-91; NASA, Lewis Research Center, chief, computational fluid dynamics branch, 1991-. **ORGANIZATIONS:** American Institute of Aeronautics and Astronautics, 1984-; American Management Association, 1989-90; NASA, Lewis Asian American Association, 1989-. **HONORS/AWARDS:** Government of India, National Merit Scholarship, 1966-71; University of Cincinnati, Research Assistantship, 1980-83. **SPECIAL ACHIEVEMENTS:** Published refereed journal articles in scientific journals; presented research work at technical conferences; speak, read and write three Indian languages: Hindi, Telugu, Kannada; read and write French. **HOME ADDRESS:** 17043 Beaver Circle, Strongsville, OH 44136, (216)238-0482. **BUSINESS ADDRESS:** Chief, Computational Fluid Dynamics Branch, NASA Lewis Research Center, 21000 Brookpark Rd, Bldg 5, Rm 200E, MS 5-11, Cleveland, OH 44135, (216)433-8133.

REDDY, EASHWER K.
Physician. Indo-American. **PERSONAL:** Born May 10, 1944, Nawabpet, Andhra Pradesh, India; son of Venkat & Radha Reddy; married Parwathi, May 7, 1971; children: Sridevi, Sushruth, Sushma. **EDUCATION:** Kakathiya Medical College, MD, 1968. **CAREER:** University of Kansas Med Ctr, professor, 1975-. **HONORS/AWARDS:** American College of Radiology, Fellow, 1990. **HOME ADDRESS:** 11618 Pennsylvania Ave, Kansas City, MO 64114.

REDDY, GUDIGOPURAM BHASKAR
Educator. Indo-American. **PERSONAL:** Born Jan 5, 1945, Hyderabad, Andhra Pradesh, India; son of Ranga G Reddy and Kamala G Reddy; married Rajitha G Reddy, Nov 12, 1975; children: G Chetan, G Divya. **EDUCATION:** A P AGRI University, BS, agriculture, 1966, MS, agriculture, 1968; University of Georgia, PhD, 1974. **CAREER:** Rockefeller Foundation, research associate, 1968-70; University of Georgia, laboratory coordinator, extension, 1975-79; North Carolina A&T State University, professor, grad coordinator, 1979-.

ORGANIZATIONS: International Soil Science Society; Sigma Xi; Gamma Sigma Delta; American Society of Microbiology; Soil Science Society of America. **HONORS/AWARDS:** Environmental Pollution Editorial Board, Best Research Award, 1990; ARD Symposium, Blue Ribbon Panel Member. **BUSINESS ADDRESS:** Grad Cordinator/Prof, Natural Resources & Env Sci, North Carolina A&T State University, E Market St, Carver Hall, Greensboro, NC 27411.

REDDY, GUNDA
Research toxicologist. Indo-American. **PERSONAL:** Born in Cheekod, Andhra Pradesh, India; son of Raja Reddy Chlukala; married Vijaya Reddy, Mar 24, 1976; children: Samatha. **EDUCATION:** Osmania University, Hyderabad, India, BS, 1960, MS, 1963, PhD, 1968. **CAREER:** University of Kentucky, postdoctorate fellow, 1969-70; Rice University, research associate, 1970-71; Marquette University, visiting fellow, 1971-73, research associate, 1976-78; University of Illinois, research associate, 1973-76; University of Wisconsin, research associate, 1978-83; US Army Biomedical Research & Developemnt Lab, pharmacologist, 1983-. **ORGANIZATIONS:** American Board of Toxicology, 1984; Society of Toxicology, 1980; American Society for Pharmacology and Experimental Therapeutics, 1991; American College of Toxicology, 1981; Association of Government Toxicologist; Indian Science Congress, life member, 1970; ASTM, 1992. **HONORS/AWARDS:** Undergraduate Riyathi Scholarship, 1957-60; University Merit Scholarship, 1960-61; Rotary Club, Merit Scholarship, 1960-61; Council of Scientific and Industrial Research, fellow, junior and senior, 1963-69. **SPECIAL ACHIEVEMENTS:** Pharmacologist, Toxicity and Metabolism of Munition Compounds, 1983-; Carcinogenicity and Metabolism of PCBS, 1978-83; Mode of action and metabolism of juvenile hormones, 1976-78; Toxicity and Metabolism of Pesticides, 1970-76; numerous others. **HOME PHONE:** (301)695-7459. **BUSINESS PHONE:** (301)619-7526.

REDDY, INDRA KARAN
Educator. Indo-American. **PERSONAL:** Born Oct 1, 1958, Nizamabad, Andhra Pradesh, India; son of Krishna K Reddy and Kausalya K Reddy; married Neelima K Reddy, Jun 28, 1989. **EDUCATION:** Kakatiya University, India, BPharm, 1981; Sagar University, India, MS, 1984; University of Florida, PhD, 1989. **CAREER:** Center for Drug Design & Delivery, research associate, 1989-90; St Johns University, assistant professor of industrial pharmacy, 1990-. **ORGANIZATIONS:** American Association of Pharm Scientists, 1989-; American Association of Colleges of Pharm, 1990-; American Pharm Association, 1990-; Pharm Manufacturers Visiting Scientists, 1991-; Industrial Pharmacy Congress, 1984-; Controlled Release Society Inc, 1992-; American Chemical Society, 1990-. **HONORS/AWARDS:** University of Florida, Excellence in Graduate Research, 1988; AAPS, Excellence in Graduate Research, 1988; St Johns University, Faculty Merit Award, 1991-92, 1992-93; St Johns Student Government, Teacher of the Year, 1992-93. **SPECIAL ACHIEVEMENTS:** Editor, Ocular Drug Delivery: A Multi-disciplinary Approach; author and co-author of many chapters; corresponding author on more than 10 research articles; consultant to three major pharmaceutical companies in US; investigator on many grants, federal & private. **BUSINESS ADDRESS:** Assistant Professor of Industrial Pharmacy, St John's University, Grand Central & Utopia Pkwys, St Albert Hall, Rm 103, Jamaica, NY 11439-1001, (718)990-6679.

REDDY, JUNUTHULA N.
Educator. Indo-American. **PERSONAL:** Born Aug 12, 1945, Warangal, Andhra Pradesh, India; son of Mr & Mrs J Keshava Reddy; married Aruna, Jun 21, 1962; children: Anita, Anil. **EDUCATION:** Osmania University, Hyderabad, India, BE, 1969; Oklahoma State University, MS, 1970; University of Alabama, Huntsville, PhD, 1973. **CAREER:** University of Texas, Austin, postdoctoral fellow, 1973-74; Lockheed Missiles and Space Co, research scientist, 1974-75; University of Oklahoma, assistant and associate professor, 1975-80; Virginia Polytechnic Institute, Clifton C Garvin professor, 1980-92; Texas A & M University, Oscar S Wyatt endowed chair, 1992-. **ORGANIZATIONS:** American Society of Mechanical Engineers, fellow, 1970-; American Society of Civil Engineers, fellow, 1982-; American Academy of Mechanics, fellow, 1980-; American Institute of Aeronautics and Astronautics, 1992-; Aeronautical Society of India, fellow, 1991-; Society of Engineering Science, board of governors, 1978-. **HONORS/AWARDS:** American Society of Civil Engineers, Walter Huber Research Prize, 1983; American Society of Automotive Engineers, Ralph R Teetor Award, 1976; University of Oklahoma, College of Engineering Research Award, 1979; Virginia Polytechnic Institute, Alumni Research Award, 1985; American Society of Mechanical Engineers, Worcester

Warner Medal, 1992. **SPECIAL ACHIEVEMENTS:** Author of eight books on engineering analysis and applied mechanics; author of over 200 publications in archival journals and books. **BUSINESS ADDRESS:** Oscar S Wyatt Endowed Professor, Dept of Mechanical Engineering, Texas A & M University, College Station, TX 77843-3123, (409)862-2417.

REDDY, KAPULURU CHANDRASEKHARA
Educational administrator. Indo-American. **PERSONAL:** Born Aug 20, 1942, Nellore, India; married 1967; children: one. **EDUCATION:** V R College, India, BA, 1959; Sri Venkateswara University, India, MSc, 1961; Indian Institute of Technology, MTech, 1962, PhD, applied mathematics, 1965. **CAREER:** Indian Institute of Technology, associate lecturer, math, 1964-65; University of Maryland, College Park, instructor, aerospace engineering, 1965-66; Lockheed Electronics Co, staff engineer, 1969-70; US Army Research Office, consultant, 1973; Lockheed Georgia Co, consultant, 1976; Arco Inc, Calspan, Arnold Eng Development Center, research engineer, 1977-; University of Tennessee Space Institute, assistant professor, beginning 1966, associate professor, until 1975, professor, math, 1975-, dean, academic affairs, 1990-. **ORGANIZATIONS:** American Institute of Aeronautics and Astronautics; Sigma Xi; Society for Industrial and Applied Mathematics. **BUSINESS ADDRESS:** Dean, Academic Affairs, University of Tennessee Space Institute, Space Institute Campus, Tullahoma, TN 37388-9100.*

REDDY, NALLAPU NARAYAN
Economist. Indo-American. **PERSONAL:** Born Jun 22, 1939, Nagaram, Andhra Pradesh, India; son of Nallapu Narasimha Reddy and Nallapu Shanthamma Reddy; married Saroja, Jun 1, 1957; children: Lata N, Mala N. **EDUCATION:** Michigan Technological University, BS, 1961; University of Missouri, MS, 1963; University of Notre Dame, MA, 1973; The Pennylvania State University, PhD, 1967. **CAREER:** General Dynamics, assistant project engineer, 1961-62, special projects engineer, 1963-64; Clarkson University, assistant professor of economics, 1967-72, associate professor of economics, 1972-74; The University of Michigan, associate professor of economics, 1974-79, professor of economics, 1979-, chair, Dept of Economics, 1981-84, 1993-96. **ORGANIZATIONS:** American Economic Association; Eastern Economic Association; Western Economic Association; Southern Economic Association; Midwest Economic Association. **HONORS/AWARDS:** Phi Kappa Phi, 1966; Omicron Delta Epsilon, 1966; The University of Michigan, Distinguished Professor Award for Excellence in Teaching, 1979. **SPECIAL ACHIEVEMENTS:** Publications in professional journals and books. **HOME ADDRESS:** 6250 Kings Shire Rd, Grand Blanc, MI 48439, (810)694-7062. **BUSINESS ADDRESS:** Professor and Chair, Dept of Economics, University of Michigan, Flint, MI 48502-2816, (810)762-3280.

REDDY, NARENDER PABBATHI
Educator, engineer. **PERSONAL:** Born May 5, 1947, Karimnagar, Andhra Pradesh, India; son of Pabbathi Lakshma Reddy and Pabbathi Rathnamma Reddy; married Swarna-Latha, Feb 1976; children: Haricharan, Vishnukrupa. **EDUCATION:** Osmania University, India, BE, 1969; University of Mississippi, MS, 1971; Texas A&M University, PhD, 1974. **CAREER:** Texas A&M University, research associate, 1974-75; Baylor College of Medicine, research associate, 1975-77; University of California, San Francisco, post-graduate research physiologist, 1977-78; Helen Hayes Hospital, senior research associate, 1978-81; University of Akron, professor, 1981-. **ORGANIZATIONS:** American Society Engineering Education, Biomed Engr-Division, newsletter editor, 1987-91, chairman, 1994, Awards Comm, 1992-93; Biomedical Engineering Society, BED, Awards Committee, 1988-91; American Society of Mechanical Engineers, Bioengineering Division, Membership Committee, 1990-92. **HONORS/AWARDS:** Chaired numerous scientific sessions at various national and international professional meetings. **SPECIAL ACHIEVEMENTS:** Published 60 papers; presented more than 100 papers at various professional meetings; one US patent. **HOME ADDRESS:** 1231 Millhaven, Akron, OH 44321. **BUSINESS ADDRESS:** Professor, Dept of Biomedical Engineering, University of Akron, Akron, OH 44325-0302, (216)972-6653.

REDDY, PANNALA SATHYANAHAYANA
Educator. Indo-American. **PERSONAL:** Born Nov 19, 1950, Hyderabad, India; son of Pannala Anantha Reddy; married Thawna Pannala, Jun 6, 1979; children: Naga Pannala. **EDUCATION:** Osmania University, Hyderabad, India, BS, 1970; Bangalore University, Bangalore, India, BE, 1974; diploma in materials management, Hyderabad, India, 1981; Jackson State University, MS, 1983. **CAREER:** Hyderabad Allcoyn Ltd, purchasing officer, 1976-82; Jackson State University, graduate assistant, 1982-83; Wiley College, instructor/

chairperson, 1983-87; University of Arkansas, assistant professor, 1987-. **ORGANIZATIONS:** Association for Computing Machinery, 1987-; Arkansas Computer Science Association, 1989-; ASCIT, Education Advisory Committee, 1992-; Beta Kappa Chi, 1986-87. **HOME ADDRESS:** 4321 Olive St, #66, Pine Bluff, AR 71603, (501)541-9355. **BUSINESS ADDRESS:** Assistant Professor, Dept of Mathematical Science, University of Arkansas, Pine Bluff, 1200 N University Dr, Pine Bluff, AR 71601-2799, (501)543-8789.

REDDY, PRADEEP K.
Physician. Indo-American. **PERSONAL:** Born May 26, 1954, Hyderabad, Andhra Pradesh, India; son of Ramkrishna Reddy and Ahalya Devi; married Hema Reddy, 1984; children: Rakesh, Rajesh. **EDUCATION:** Kakatya Medical College, Waraugal, India, MBBS, 1979; Salem Hospital, MD, 1992. **CAREER:** Harvard School of Public Health, research, 1987-88; Lown Cardiovascular, cardiology research fellow, 1988-89; Salem Hospital, resident physician, 1989-92; Framingham Heart Study, fellow, 1992-93. **ORGANIZATIONS:** AMA; MMS; GBPSR; IPPNW. **HOME ADDRESS:** 6 McDewell Ave, #17, Danvers, MA 01923.

REDDY, PRATAP P.
Educator. Indo-American. **PERSONAL:** Born Jun 6, 1950, Musthial, Andhra Pradesh, India; son of P Narsi Reddy and P Ramamma Reddy; married Balamani Reddy, May 31, 1971. **EDUCATION:** Osmania University, AP, India, MS, nuclear physics, 1973; Pratt Institute, Brooklyn, NY, MS, comp sci, 1981; Walden University, MN, PhD, higher ed, 1994. **CAREER:** Raritan Valley Community College, instructor, 1982-87, assistant professor, 1987-93, associate professor, 1993-. **ORGANIZATIONS:** Community College Computer Consortium, NJ, president, 1992-93. **BUSINESS ADDRESS:** Associate Professor, Raritan Valley Community College, PO Box 3300, North Branch, NJ 08876, (908)526-1200.

REDDY, RAJ
Educator. Indo-American. **PERSONAL:** Born Jun 13, 1937, Katoor, India; married 1966; children: two. **EDUCATION:** University of Madras, BE, 1958; University of New South Wales, MTech, 1961; Stanford University, PhD, computer science, 1966. **CAREER:** IBM Corp, Australia, applied science rep, 1960-63; Stanford University, assistant professor, computer science, 1966-69; consultant to numerous companies and societies, including Litton Ind, 1968-69, NSF, 1972-76, Jet Propulsion Labs, 1978-79, others, 1978-; Carnegie-Mellon University, associate professor, beginning 1969, professor, 1984-, Robotics Institute, director, 1980-. **ORGANIZATIONS:** World Center for Computer Science and Human Resources, vp, chief scientist, 1982-; American Association for Artificial Intelligence, president, 1987-89; National Academy of Engineering; Association for Computing Machinery; Association for Computer Ling. **HONORS/AWARDS:** John Guggenheim Fellow, 1975-76; Acoustical Society of America, fellow; IEEE, fellow. **BUSINESS ADDRESS:** Professor, School of Computer Science, Carnegie-Mellon University, 5000 Forbes Ave, Pittsburgh, PA 15213.*

REDDY, RAMAKRISHNA P.
Research geneticist. Indo-American. **PERSONAL:** Born Jun 30, 1936, Kalwakurthy, Andhra Pradesh, India; son of Pashuvula China Baswa Reddy; married Kranthi Reddy, May 4, 1961; children: T Vasantha, Sudhir. **EDUCATION:** Osmania University, India, BVSc, AH, 1959; IVRI, India, MVSc, 1968; Virginia Polytechnic Institute & State University, MS, 1974, PhD, genetics, 1976. **CAREER:** Aminal Husbandry Department, AP, India, veterinary surgeon, 1959-71; VPI & SU, research assistant, 1972-76; Peterson Industries Inc, director of research, 1976-85, vice president, director, research & development, 1986-. **ORGANIZATIONS:** Poultry Breeders of America, president, 1986; National Breeder's Roundtable, chairman, 1988; PSA, Broiler Research Award Committee, chairman, 1991. **HONORS/AWARDS:** VPI & SU, Gamma Sigma Delta, 1974; Phi Kappa Phi, Blacksburg, VA, 1973; Sigma Xi, 1975. **SPECIAL ACHIEVEMENTS:** Published 10 research papers; more than 50 professional talks to industry groups, 1975-93, both national and international; invited to present paper at 1992 World Poultry Congress in Amsterdam, Holland. **HOME ADDRESS:** 261 Oak Ave, Decatur, AR 72722, (501)752-3550. **BUSINESS ADDRESS:** Vice Pres & Dir, Research & Development/Avian Health, Peterson Industries Inc, First & Main, PO Box 248, Decatur, AR 72722, (501)752-5000.

REEVES, KEANU
Actor. Pacific Islander American/Chinese American. **PERSONAL:** Born Sep 2, 1964, Beirut, Lebanon. **CAREER:** Actor, film appearances include: Prodi-

gal, Flying (Canadian films); Youngblood; River's Edge, 1987; Permanent Record, 1988; The Night Before, 1988; Prince of Pennsylvania, 1988; Dangerous Liaisons, 1988; Bill and Ted's Excellent Adventure, 1989; Parenthood, 1989; I Love You to Death, 1990; Tune in Tomorrow, 1990; Bill and Ted's Bogus Journey, 1991; Point Break, 1991; Bram Stoker's Dracula, 1992; numerous others; television appearances include: Act of Vengeance; Under the Influence; Babes in Toyland; stage appearances include: Wolf Boy; For Adults Only; Romeo and Juliet. **BUSINESS ADDRESS:** Actor, c/o Creative Artists Agency, 9830 Wilshire Blvd, Beverly Hills, CA 90212.*

REN, SHANG YUAN
Physicist. Chinese American. **PERSONAL:** Born Jan 10, 1940, Chongqing, Sichuan, China; son of Jicheng Ren and Shujuan Yang; married Weimin Hu, Jul 7, 1968; children: Yujian Ren, Yuhui Ren. **EDUCATION:** Peking University, BS, 1963, PhD, 1966. **CAREER:** Beijing Second Semiconductor Factory, engineer, 1968-73; Stanford University, visiting scholar, 1978-80; University of Illinois, Urbana-Champaign, research associate, 1980-81; University of Science and Technology, China, teacher to associate professor, 1973-85, professor, 1985-; University of Notre Dame, faculty fellow, 1987-90; Arizona State University, research professor, 1991-. **ORGANIZATIONS:** Superlattices and Microstructures, editorial board, 1985-; American Physical Society, 1987-. **SPECIAL ACHIEVEMENTS:** More than 70 research papers on physics published, 1980-. **BUSINESS ADDRESS:** Research Professor of Physics, Dept of Physics and Astronomy, Arizona State University, Tempe, AZ 85287-1504, (602)965-2993.

RENGE, I. BETH
Investment banking company executive. Japanese American. **PERSONAL:** Born Feb 3, 1959, Fresno, CA; daughter of Nancy & Nobuo Renge. **EDUCATION:** University of the Pacific, BS, business administration, 1981. **CAREER:** Kidder, Peabody & Co Inc, sales assistant, 1981, vice president, 1985-91; Dean Witter Reynolds, assistant vice president, 1982-85; Renge Securities & Co Inc, president, 1991-. **ORGANIZATIONS:** California School of Professional Psychology, board member, 1993-; California Leadership, board member, 1992-; Social Venture Network, 1993-; Japan Society, board member, 1990-92; American Red Cross, board member, 1988-91; YWCA, board member, 1985-86; Japanese American Citizens League Legacy Fund, trustee & chairperson, 1991-. **HONORS/AWARDS:** Invited by pres-elect Bill Clinton to participate in his Economic Conference, Dec 1992. **SPECIAL ACHIEVEMENTS:** Asian American Manufacturers Assn, Asian Financing for Emerging Companies, sponsor coordinator for Sources, 1990. **BUSINESS ADDRESS:** President, Renge Securities & Co Inc, 44 Montgomery St, Ste 500, San Francisco, CA 94104, (415)955-2627.

RESPICIO, ELSA TOJE
Company executive. Filipino American. **PERSONAL:** Born Jan 21, 1945, Bayombong, Nueva Vizcaya, Philippines; daughter of Elizabeth Respicio and Florante Respicio (deceased). **EDUCATION:** St Mary's College, BSc, accounting, 1965; Far Eastern University, MSBA, economics, 1973; Center for Training & Careers, computer assisted accounting, 1992. **CAREER:** National Food Authority, Philipines, economist, 1973-82; Solectron Corp, administrative assistant, 1982-83; Anacomp Corp Xidex, product operator, 1983-91; Akashic Memories, visual inspector, 1993-. **HOME ADDRESS:** 2504 Glen Elm Way, San Jose, CA 95148, (408)270-5977.

REYES, ADELAIDA (ADELAIDA SCHRAMM)
Educator. Filipino American. **PERSONAL:** Born Apr 25, 1930, Manila, Philippines; daughter of Cesar E Reyes and Adelaida Nava; married N Katigbak, 1953 (divorced); children: Maria Corazon, Stephen Katigbak; married Harold Schramm, 1968 (deceased). **EDUCATION:** St Scholastica's College, BM (cum laude), 1951; Columbia University, PhD, music, 1975. **CAREER:** Jersey City State College, professor of music, 1970-; Columbia University, visiting professor, lecturer, 1975-86, 1991; New York University, visiting professor, 1987, 1989, 1991; Juilliard School of Music, visiting professor, 1989, 1991. **ORGANIZATIONS:** International Institute of NJ, board member, 1985-89; Society for Ethnomusicology, council member, 1976-78, ethics committee, 1979-81; International Council for Traditional Music, Program Committee, chair, 1982-83; National Endowment for Folk Arts, panel member, 1987-90. **HONORS/AWARDS:** Oxford University, research fellow, 1990; 1993; National Endowment for the Humanities, Grant Award, 1983-84; 1992-93; Columbia University, Presidential Fellowship, 1987; Rockefeller Foundation, PhD Distinction Fellowship for Music Criticism, 1964-66, 1975. **SPECIAL ACHIEVEMENTS:** Ed & Intro, Music and the Refugee Experience, Berlin,

1990; "Music & Tradition. . .," Yearbook for Traditional Music, 1989; "Tradition in the Guise of Innovation," Yearbook for Traditional Music, 1986; Guest Editor, Yearbook for Traditional Music, volume 16; music & book reviews. **BUSINESS ADDRESS:** Professor, Jersey City State College, Kennedy Blvd, Rossey 206, Jersey City, NJ 07305, (201)200-3280.

REYES, HERNAN M.
Pediatric surgeon. Filipino American. **PERSONAL:** Born Apr 5, 1933, Alicia, Isabela, Philippines; son of Leonor B Reyes & Anacleta Macaballug Reyes; married Dolores, Feb 27, 1960; children: Cynthia, Michael, Maria, Patricia, Catherine. **EDUCATION:** University of the Philippines, pre med, 1949-51; University of Santo Tomas, Philippines, MD, 1957. **CAREER:** Stritch School of Medicine, Loyola University, clinical assistant, 1964-65, 1968-69; University of Santo Tomas College of Medicine, Manila, instructor in surgery, chief, 1966-67; Pritzker School of Medicine, University of Chicago, assistant professor, 1969-73, acting chief of section, 1973-76, associate professor, 1973-76; Cook County Graduate School of Medicine, lecturer, 1972-; University of Illinois, College of Medicine, Chicago, division of pediatric surgery, chief, 1976-90, professor of surgery, 1976-, professor of clinical pediatrics, 1982-; Cook County Hospital, 1959-65, research fellow, 1964-65, cairman, div of pediatric surgery, 1976-92, chairman, Department of Surgery, 1987-. **ORGANIZATIONS:** American Academy of Pediatrics; American Association for the Surgery of Trauma; American Association of University Professors; American College of Surgeons; American College of Surgeons, Chicago Committee on Trauma; American Medical Association; American Pediatric Surgical Association; Association for Academic Surgery; American Association for the Advancement of Science; American Trauma Society; Central Surgical Association; Chicago Surgical Society; Eastern Association for the Surgery of Trauma; Western Surgical Association; Society International de Chirurgie; NY Acad of Sci; American College of Physician Executives; others. **HONORS/AWARDS:** Many honors including: University of Chicago, Pritzker School of Medicine, awards, 1974, 1975, 1976; Radiological Society of North American, Certificate of Merit, 1981; USTMMA, Distinguished Alumnus Award, 1987; American College of Surgeons, Scientific Exhibit, Certificate of Appreciation, 1989; University of Illinois, Distinguished Award, 1988, 1989; Philippine Medical Association of Northern California, Distinguished Recognition Award, 1990. **SPECIAL ACHIEVEMENTS:** Published 21 chapters, 39 abstracts, numerous presentations, 56 journal articles including: "A One-Antibiotic Regimen for Ruptured Appendix," Emergency Medicine, p 200, Jan 15, 1992; "Traumatic Death in Urban Children, Revisited," American Journal of Diseases of Children, Jan 1993; "Effects of High-Dose Vitamin C Administration on Postburn Microvascular Fluid and Protein Flux," Journal of Burn Care & Rehabilitation, vol 13, no 5, p 56-566, Sept 1992; "Caustic Stricture of the Esophagus," Common Problems Pediatric Surgery, 175-183; Mosby-Year-Book, 1991; others. **MILITARY SERVICE:** Armed Forces of the Philippines, University of the Philippines, ROTC, 1949-51. **BUSINESS ADDRESS:** Professor, Chairman, Dept of Surgery, Cook County Hospital, 1835 W Harrison St, M-2201, Chicago, IL 60612, (312)633-8207.

RHA, CHOKYUN
Educator. Korean American. **PERSONAL:** Born Oct 5, 1933, Seoul, Republic of Korea; daughter of Sea Zin & Young Soon Choi; married Anthony John Skinskey, Aug 22, 1969; children: Jae Minn Song, Ribf Uj Lee. **EDUCATION:** Massachusetts Institute of Technology, BS, life sciences, 1962, MS, food technology, 1964, MS, chemical engineering, 1966, ScD, food sciences, 1967. **CAREER:** Anheuser-Busch Inc, senior research engineer, 1967-69; University of Massachusetts, Food & Biology Process Engineering, assistant professor, 1969-73; Massachusetts Institute of Technology, Food Process Engineering, associate professor, 1974-82, Biomaterials Science & Engineering, 1982-90, Biomaterials Science & Engineering, professor, 1990-; Rha-Sinskey Association, president, 1972-; XGen Inc, president, 1992. **ORGANIZATIONS:** Genzyme, science advisory bd, 1985-; Bioinfo Association, prin, 1980-; American Flavor Inc, board member, 1993-; Carbohydrate Polymers, Food Hydrocolloids, editorial board; American Institute Chemical Engineer; Institute Food Technologists; Society of Rheology; Sigma Xi. **SPECIAL ACHIEVEMENTS:** Contributor of over 120 articles and scientific papers to scientific journals; author, editor, Theory: Determination and Control of Physical Properties of Food Materials, 1975; achievements including patents for numerous patents. **HOME ADDRESS:** 285 Commonwealth Ave, Boston, MA 02115, (617)536-7828. **BUSINESS ADDRESS:** Professor, Biomaterials Science and Engineering Laboratory, Massachusetts Institute of Technology, Bldg 56, Rm 137, Cambridge, MA 02139, (617)253-3493.

RHEE, CHASE CHONGGWANG

Educator, businessman. Korean American. **PERSONAL:** Born Feb 26, 1942, Boryong, Choongnam, Republic of Korea; son of Jongbae Rhee and Moohee Rhee; married Socorro, Jun 26, 1971; children: Tammie, Jennifer, Doreen. **EDUCATION:** Seoul National University, BA, 1968; American Graduate School of International Management, MA, 1971; United States International University, DBA, 1991. **CAREER:** Ameriko Inc, CEO, 1972; UCLA Extension, adjunct professor, 1991-; California State University, LA, adjunct professor, 1992-. **ORGANIZATIONS:** Korean Chamber of Commerce of Los Angeles, president, 1986-87; Los Angeles Olympic Lions Club, president, 1980-81; California State University, LA, president's advisory board, 1986-. **HONORS/ AWARDS:** Republic of Korea, President's Award, 1987; City of Los Angeles, Mayor's Award, 1987. **SPECIAL ACHIEVEMENTS:** Import/Export: A Fundamental Guide to International Trade. **BUSINESS ADDRESS:** CEO, Ameriko Inc, 170 N Fair Oaks Ave, Ste 200, Pasadena, CA 91103-3639, (818)795-7988.

RHEE, HAHN-KYOU

Educator. Korean American. **PERSONAL:** Born Dec 25, 1954, Andong, Kyungsangbookdo, Republic of Korea; son of Hun-Moon Rhee and Eun-Sook Rhee; married Chae-Ran Rhee, Apr 12, 1983; children: John, Jane. **EDUCATION:** Hanyang University, Korea, BE, 1978; University of Florida, MS, 1985, PhD, industrial engineering, 1989. **CAREER:** Agency for Defense Development, Korea, researcher, 1978-83; University of Florida, graduate assistant, 1984-89, instructor, 1987-88; University of Missouri, Columbia, assistant professor, 1989-. **ORGANIZATIONS:** Operations Research Society of America; Korean Scientists and Engineers Association in America. **HONORS/AWARDS:** University of Missouri, Columbia, Summer Research Fellowship, 1993; Hanyang University, University Scholarship, 1976-77, Sungsan Scholarship, 1978. **SPECIAL ACHIEVEMENTS:** "Mission Effective Analysis of an Aircraft Attacking Passive Target," European Journal of Operational Research, 1990; "Distribution of the Busy Period in a Controllable M/M/2 Queueing System Operating under the Triadic (O,K,N,M) Policy," Journal of Applied Probability, 1990; "An Assembly Sequence Generation Procedure," Computers in Industrial Engineering, 1991; "Analysis of Flexible Machines," AMSE Press, 1991. **BUSINESS ADDRESS:** Assistant Professor, Dept of Engineering, University of Missouri, Columbia, 113 Engineering Building West, Columbia, MO 65211, (314)882-9567.

RHEE, HANG YUL

Educator. Korean American. **PERSONAL:** Born Sep 29, 1938, Seoul, Republic of Korea; son of Chang Ik Rhee; married Sung Mi Rhee, Jun 20, 1968; children: Eleanor. **EDUCATION:** Seoul National University, College of Law, LLB, 1961; Columbia University, MA, 1963; American University, PhD, 1977; Johns Hopkins University, post-doctoral study, 1978. **CAREER:** Debevoise, Plimpton, Lyons & Gates, research assistant, 1963-65; Muskingum College, assistant professor, 1967-68; Shepherd College, chair & professor, 1968-. **ORGANIZATIONS:** Assn of Korean Political Studies in the US, president, 1987-89; Intl Studies, Steering Committee, 1990-; Research Institute of Korean Problems, co-chairman, 1986-; Council of the Peaceful Unification for Korea, governing board, 1984-; Intl Research Assn, research fellow, 1964; American Political Science Association. **HONORS/AWARDS:** Clark University, John F Donnelly Fellow; National Endowment for Humanities Scholarship, 1978. **SPECIAL ACHIEVEMENTS:** Author, Political Behavior of the Citizenry of Seoul 1952-71, 1977; "Urbanization: Communication & Economic Inequality," Journal of World Affairs, 1981; "Some Thoughts on the Approaches to Inter-Korean Dialogue," 1989. **HOME ADDRESS:** 1021 St Clair St, Hagerstown, MD 21742. **BUSINESS PHONE:** (304)876-2511.

RHEE, JHOON GOO

Educator, foundation administrator. Korean American. **PERSONAL:** Born Jan 7, 1932, Asan, Choongham, Republic of Korea; son of Jin Hoon Rhee; married Han Soon Rhee, Jul 10, 1966; children: Joanne Oh, James, Chun, MeMe. **EDUCATION:** Southwest Texas State College, 1958-60; University of Texas, 1960-62. **CAREER:** Jhoon Rhee Institute of Tae Kwon Do Inc, founder, president, CEO, 1962-91; Jhoon Rhee Seminar Co, president, CEO, 1985-; World Martial Arts Congress for Education Inc, founder, president, 1985-; Jhoon Rhee Foundation, founder, president, CEO, 1991-. **ORGANIZATIONS:** US Congress Gymnastics, karate, tae kwon do, instructor, 1965-; Fulbright, associate member, 1992-; President's Council on Physical Fitness & Sports, special advisor; July 4th Nation's Birthday Celebration, chairman, 1983. **HONORS/AWARDS:** Washington Touch Down Club, Martial Arts Man of the Century Award, 1976; President George Bush, Thousand Points of

Light Award, 1992; Excellence in Community Service, 1992, Asian Pacific American Heritage Presidential Dinner, 1992; Excellence 2000 Award, 1993. **SPECIAL ACHIEVEMENTS:** Leading actor in 2 movies; invented martial arts safety equipment; founder of martial arts ballet; 60 Jhoon Rhee Tae Kwon Do studies in USA, 65 in the former Soviet Union; conducted over 100 Born To Be Healthy & Happy Seminars; volunteer work: Joy of Discipline, program in 8 DC public elementary schools. **MILITARY SERVICE:** Korean Army, 1st lt, 1952-57. **BIOGRAPHICAL SOURCES:** Awaken the Giant Within, Anthony Robbins, p 9; US Congressional Record, p 973-987, April 24, 1990. **BUSINESS ADDRESS:** President, CEO, Jhoon Rhee Foundation for Intl Leadership, 4068 Rosamora Court, Mc Lean, VA 22101.

RHEE, KHEE CHOON

Educator. Korean American. **PERSONAL:** Born Jun 25, 1938, Seoul, Republic of Korea; son of In Mook Rhee and Ki Nam Song; married Ki Soon Rhee, Apr 24, 1964; children: Vincent I, Raymond M. **EDUCATION:** Seoul National University, BS, 1961, MS, 1964; Michigan State University, PhD, 1969. **CAREER:** Seoul National University, research assistant, 1962-64; Michigan State University, research assistant, 1966-69; Brown University, postdoctoral fellow, 1969-70; Texas A&M University, research associate, 1970-73, assistant/associate professor, 1973-78, professor/associate director, 1978-. **ORGANIZATIONS:** American Chemical Society, 1969-; American Association of Cereal Chemists, 1969-; American Oil Chemists' Society, 1969-; Institute of Food Technologists, 1969-; Korean Society of Food Science & Technology, 1969-; Korean Scientist & Engineers Association, 1972-. **HONORS/ AWARDS:** Sigma Xi, Graduate Research Award, 1968; Texas Engineering, fellow, 1984, 1985; Experiment Station, senior fellow, 1987. **SPECIAL ACHIEVEMENTS:** 100 publications; 4 patents. **MILITARY SERVICE:** Korean Army, 1957. **BUSINESS ADDRESS:** Professor, Food Protein R&D Center, Texas A&M University, Cater Mattil Hall, College Station, TX 77843-2476.

RHEE, PHILLIP

Actor, film producer/director. Korean American. **PERSONAL:** Born 1960, Seoul, Republic of Korea; son of Min Ho; married Amy (Mi-sun Yoon), 1991. **CAREER:** Actor: Kentucky Fried Movie; Fistful of Yen; Ninja Turf, writer, producer; Silent Assassins, producer; Best of the Best, co-producer, 1989; Best of the Best II, producer, director, actor; Ballistic, producer; Creative Film Concepts, partner, producer, currently. **SPECIAL ACHIEVEMENTS:** Martial arts, instructor.*

RHEE, SANG FOON

Journalist. Korean American. **PERSONAL:** Born Dec 23, 1963, Seoul, Republic of Korea; son of Jin Woo & Kumja Rhee. **EDUCATION:** Duke University, AB,(magna cum laude), history, 1984. **CAREER:** The Charlotte Observer, Mecklenburg Neighbors, reporter, 1984, Catawba Valley Bureau, 1984-87, city hall reporter, 1987-91, Raleigh Bureau, reporter, 1992-. **HONORS/ AWARDS:** Freedom Forum, Fellowship in Asian Studies, 1991-92; Historical Society of North Carolina, Hugh T Leflen Award, 1984. **SPECIAL ACHIEVEMENTS:** "Vanguards and Violence: A Comparison of the US and Korean Student Movements," Korean Studies, vol 17, Spring 1993. **BUSINESS ADDRESS:** Reporter, The Charlotte Observer, Raleigh Bureau, 19 W Hargett St, Ste 507, Raleigh, NC 27601, (919)834-8471.

RHEE, SONG NAI

Educator, educational administrator. Korean American. **PERSONAL:** Born Sep 10, 1935, Namwon, Republic of Korea; son of Byung Hong Rhee & Choon Kil Shin; married Margaret Sue, Jul 19, 1963; children: Pamela Elling, Kathleen, Kristine Womack. **EDUCATION:** Northwest Christian College, BTh, 1958; Butler University, BA, 1960, MA, 1960; Dropsie University for Hebrew & Cognate Learning, PhD, 1963; University of Oregon, MA, MA, 1969, MS, 1979, PhD, 1984. **CAREER:** Northwest Christian College, ancient Near East studies, professor, 1963-, academic vice president, 1984-. **ORGANIZATIONS:** Assn for Asian Studies, 1984-; American Anthropological Assn, 1984-; Assn for Ancient Historical Studies, Korea, 1986-; Korean Archaeological Society, Korea, 1986-; Biblical Archaeology Society, 1976-. **HONORS/ AWARDS:** Northwest Christian College, President Award, 1958, nominated, Outstanding College Teacher of Year Award, 1983; Butler University, Indianapolis Hebrew Congregation Award, 1959; Dropsie University for Hebrew & Cognate Learning, Doctoral Fellow, 1960-63; US State Dept, New York University, Fellowship for Study in Israel, 1964; Ford Foundation, University of Oregon, Grant for Study in Japan, 1967, 1968; Interfaith Bible Conference, Oregon, Outstanding Contributions to Biblical Scholarship in Archaeology,

1991. **SPECIAL ACHIEVEMENTS:** Articles include: author, "Origins and Evolution of Korean Bronze Age," Kaoguhsue Wenhua Lunchi, vol 4, China, 1991; "Emergence of Complex Society in Prehistoric Korea," coauthor, J of World Prehistory, vol 6, no 1, Plenum Press, 1992; co-editor, Pacific Northeast Asia in Prehistory, Washington State University, 1993; "Prehistoric Burial Systems of Korea and Their Social and Ethnic Significance," Korean Culture, Korean Cultural Center, California, 1993; numerous others. **BUSINESS ADDRESS:** Vice President of Academic Affairs, Northwest Christian College, 828 E 11th St, Eugene, OR 97401-3727, (503)343-1641.

RHEE, SUSAN BYUNGSOOK
Educator, counselor. Korean American. **PERSONAL:** Born Oct 16, 1937, Seoul, Republic of Korea; daughter of Dr & Mrs Kap Soo Lee; married Charles Hangtai Rhee, Mar 17, 1961 (deceased); children: Ronald Eungjoo, Sandra Haejoo, Robert Yungjoo. **EDUCATION:** MacMurray College, BA, sociology, 1960; George Williams College, MS (honors), counseling psychology, 1971; Northern Illinois University, EdD, counseling, 1993. **CAREER:** George Williams College, Counseling and Human Relations Center, counselor, career specialist, 1971-81, Graduate Department of Counseling Psychology, graduate faculty, 1975-81; College of DuPage, counselor, instructor, 1976-83, professor, counselor, 1983-; Ball Foundation, director of career counseling, 1979-81, consultant, 1981-85; Alma College, adviser to president on Korean Affairs, 1987-. **ORGANIZATIONS:** ICA, human rights chair, 1994; ACCA, award committee, 1992-94; AACD, women's committee, 1989-90-91; AMCD, taskforce, 1990-91; Korean-American Community Service, board member, 1989-; Illinois Assn for Multicultural Counseling & Development, president, 1989-90, co-chair, 1989; ACA; APA; ACPA; IACD. **HONORS/AWARDS:** Northern Illinois University, Outstanding Dissertation in Counseling, 1993; Kappa Delta Pi, 1989; AACD, Distinguished Service Award, 1988; Phi Gamma Mu; Phi Beta Kappa. **BUSINESS ADDRESS:** Professor/Counselor, College of DuPage, Central Campus Counseling, 22nd St & Lambert Rd, Glen Ellyn, IL 60137, (708)858-2800.

RHEE, YOUNG EUN
Physician. Korean American. **PERSONAL:** Born Dec 12, 1941, Seoul, Republic of Korea; son of Eung Joon Rhee; married Angela Myung, Jun 23, 1967; children: Paul Hyung, Peter Hyung. **CAREER:** Physician, currently. **ORGANIZATIONS:** International College of Surgeons, fellow; American Society of Abdominal Surgeons, fellow; Society of Laparoendoscopic Surgeons; AMA; California Medical Association; Santa Clara County Medical Association; Korean Surgical Society. **HONORS/AWARDS:** Korean American Services Inc, chairman, CEO; Korea Vision Inc, board of directors. **BUSINESS ADDRESS:** Physician, 1150 Scott Blvd, D-2, Santa Clara, CA 95050.

RHIM, AESOP
Artist. Korean American. **PERSONAL:** Born Jul 20, 1933, Chosan, Republic of Korea; son of Mr & Mrs Yong Gap Rhim; married Sunhee Rhim, Jul 30, 1966; children: Janice, Joanne. **EDUCATION:** Seoul National University, Fine Arts College, Korea, BA, 1959; IIT, Institute of Design, MA, 1970. **CAREER:** Aesop Display Studio Inc, president, currently. **BUSINESS ADDRESS:** President, Aesop Display Studio Inc, 1741 N Western Ave, 1st fl, Chicago, IL 60647, (312)772-8482.

RHIM, JOHNG SIK
Physician, researcher. Korean American. **PERSONAL:** Born Jul 24, 1930, Kwang Ju, Republic of Korea; son of Hac Woon Rhim and Moo Duc Choi; married Mary Margaret Lytke, Aug 25, 1962; children: Jonathan, Christopher, Peter, Andrew, Michael, Kathleen. **EDUCATION:** Seoul National University, MD, 1957; Seoul National University Hospital, intern, 1957-58. **CAREER:** Children's Hospital Research Foundation, Cincinnati, research fellow, 1958-60; Baylor University, research fellow, 1961; University of Pittsburgh, research fellow, 1962; Louisiana State University, research associate, 1962-64; National Institute Allergy & Infectious Disease, visiting scientist, 1964-66; Microbiological Association, cancer research, project director, 1966-78; Georgetown Medical Center, adjunct professor, 1988-; National Cancer Institute, senior investigator, 1978-. **ORGANIZATIONS:** AAAS; American Association Cancer Research; AMA; Society Experimental Biology and Medicine; International Association Comp Leukemia Research; American Society of Virology; Winchester School SS Md, board of directors. **HONORS/AWARDS:** Editorial Academy of Int Journal of Oncology, 1993. **SPECIAL ACHIEVEMENTS:** More than 200 research papers published in virus and cancer-related journals; numerous chapters in books; a book published on neoplastic transformation of human cells culture, 1991. **HOME ADDRESS:** 11455 South Glen Rd, Poto-

mac, MD 20854, (301)299-5668. **BUSINESS ADDRESS:** Senior Investigator, National Cancer Institute, Bldg 37, Rm 1C03, Bethesda, MD 20892, (301)496-5990.

RIKHIRAJ, SADHU SINGH
Engineer. Indo-American. **PERSONAL:** Born Sep 15, 1942, Dosanjh, Punjab, India; son of Badan Singh and Basant Kaur; married Tirlochan Kaur Rikhiraj, Jun 1963; children: Inder Kaur, Harvind Kaur, Hardeep Kaur Singh. **EDUCATION:** Thapar Polytechnic, Patiala, India, diploma, civil engineering, 1962; University of Ottawa, Canada, BS, civil engineering, 1979. **CAREER:** Ministry of Transportation, India, 1962-70; Ministry of Natural Resources, Ontario, 1972-80; MacLaren Plansearch, engineer, 1980-83; Delon Hampton & Associates, vice president, mgr, 1983-92; Singh & Associates, Inc, president, 1992-. **ORGANIZATIONS:** American Society of Civil Engineers; Illinois Society of Professional Engineers. **BUSINESS ADDRESS:** President, Singh & Associates Inc, 300 West Adams St, Chicago, IL 60606, (312)629-0240.

RINPOCHE, GELEK
Religious leader. Tibetan American. **PERSONAL:** Born in Tibet; married. **EDUCATION:** Drepung Loseling Monastery, Lhasa, Tibet. **CAREER:** Former Buddhist monk; Jewel Heart, lama, spiritual head, currently. **SPECIAL ACHIEVEMENTS:** Travels around the world to lecture on Buddhist principles. **BUSINESS ADDRESS:** Lama, Jewel Heart, 5501 Morgan Rd, Ypsilanti, MI 48197, (313)994-3387.*

RIO-JELLIFFE, REBECCA
Educator. Filipino American. **PERSONAL:** Born Aug 9, 1922, Talisay, Negros Occidental, Philippines; daughter of Domingo E Rio & Paz Dianala Rio; married Robert A Jelliffe, Apr 1, 1950 (deceased); children: Angela, Cynthia Rio Brown. **EDUCATION:** Central Philippine University, BA, BSE (magna cum laude), 1946; Oberlin College, MA, English, 1950; University of California, Berkeley, PhD, English, 1964. **CAREER:** Central Philippine University, high school teacher, 1945-47; Kobe College, lecturer in English, 1953-56; University of Redlands, English Department, chair, 1974-77, professor of English, 1958-. **ORGANIZATIONS:** PMLA, 1970-; Association of Departments of English, lecturer on internships, 1975-78; Teacher Partners Program, director, 1993-. **HONORS/AWARDS:** Fulbright Program of the Philippines, Fulbright Scholar, 1948-50; Oberlin College Scholarships, 1948-50; Danforth Foundation, Danforth Teacher, 1960-64, Summer Grant, 1964; NEH Research Award, 1982-83, College Teachers Seminar, 1977; Yale University, Department of English, Postdoctoral Fellow, 1977-82. **SPECIAL ACHIEVEMENTS:** Mortarboard Distinguished Teacher Award, 1969; University of Redlands, Distinguished Teacher Award, 1982, 1991; publications on William Cullen Bryant, and William Faulkner; internship programs in English; in progress: William Faulkner's Theory & Practice; The Language of Time in Fiction. **BUSINESS ADDRESS:** Professor of English, University of Redlands, Redlands, CA 92373, (909)793-2121.

RISHI, SATCHIDANAND RAAM
Company executive. Indo-American. **PERSONAL:** Born Feb 22, 1933, Mahidpur, Madhya Pradesh, India; son of Raam and Leela Rishi Indore; married Usha, May 25, 1957; children: Smeeta, Aruna Joglexar, Nandini Kolimas, Jayashree Kathardekar. **EDUCATION:** VJTI, Bombay, 1958. **CAREER:** Westinghouse Ele Corp, mfg engineering, 1966-78; Westhill Industries, Inc, president, currently. **HOME ADDRESS:** 2460 Heilman Dr, Ford City, PA 16226, (412)763-2593.

RIVERA, EVELYN MARGARET
Educator. Filipino American. **PERSONAL:** Born Nov 10, 1929, Hollister, CA; daughter of Atanacio Rivera & Anselma Dangtayan; divorced. **EDUCATION:** University of California, Berkeley, AB, 1952, MA, 1960, PhD, 1963. **CAREER:** University of Reading, National Institute for Research in Dairying, postdoctoral fellow, 1963-65; Michigan State University, assistant professor of zoology, 1965-68, associate professor of zoology, 1968-72, professor of zoology, 1972-. **ORGANIZATIONS:** Tissue Culture Association, 1965-, newsletter, editor, 1986-90; American Association for the Advancement of Science, life member, fellow, 1966-; American Association for Cancer Research, 1975-; British Society for Endocrinology, 1964-; Society for Experimental Biology and Medicine, 1966-; American Women in Science, 1991-; Sigma Xi, 1965-; Mid-Michigan Asian Pacific American Association, 1991-; Asian Pacific American Women's Association in the Greater Lansing Area, president, 1990-93. **HONORS/AWARDS:** UNESCO, travel award, 1965; National Institutes of Health, Career Development Award, 1967-72; National

Cancer Institute, National Research Service Award, 1978-79; Michigan State University Faculty Professional Women's Association, outstanding woman faculty award, 1992. **SPECIAL ACHIEVEMENTS:** More than 50 publications in professional journals and books, 1959-; service on numerous national and university committees, 1965-. **HOME PHONE:** (517)351-1823. **BUSINESS ADDRESS:** Professor, Dept of Zoology, Michigan State University, 203 Natural Science Bldg, East Lansing, MI 48824-1115, (517)353-5164.

RIVERS, MAVIS. *See* Obituaries.

RODIS, RODEL E.
Attorney, journalist. Filipino American. **PERSONAL:** Born Nov 7, 1951, Manila, Philippines; son of Hermilo V Rodis & Teofila A Elepano; married Edna V Austria, Jul 22, 1979; children: Carlo, Daniel, Eric. **EDUCATION:** New College of California, School of Law, JD, 1980. **CAREER:** San Francisco State University, Filipino American Studies Program, American Studies Department, School of Ethnic Studies, lecturer, 1972-78; Philippine News, columnist, 1987-; self-employed, lawyer, 1980-. **ORGANIZATIONS:** San Francisco Community College, board member, 1991-; San Francisco United Way, board of directors, 1991-; San Francisco World Affairs Council, board of trustees, 1990-; New College of California, board of trustees, 1992-; Filipino American Political Association, general counsel, 1987-. **HONORS/AWARDS:** St Paul of the Shipwrecked, Martin Luther King Award, 1992. **SPECIAL ACHIEVEMENTS:** Author, Telltale Signs of Filipinos in America, 1991. **BUSINESS ADDRESS:** Attorney, Law Offices of Rodel Rodis, 2429 Ocean Ave, San Francisco, CA 94127, (415)334-7800.

ROHATGI, PRADEEP K.
Educator. Indo-American. **PERSONAL:** Born Feb 18, 1943, Kanpur, Uttar Pradesh, India; son of H S Rohatgi & Bimla Rohatgi; married Kalpana Rohatgi, Dec 13, 1968; children: Rajat, Sonali. **EDUCATION:** Banaras Hindu University, India, BS, 1961; MIT, MS, 1963, DSc, 1964. **CAREER:** Merica Research Lab International, researcher, 1964-; IIT Kanpur, visiting faculty, 1968-69; Homer Research Lab, researcher, 1969-72; India Institute of Science, professor, 1972-77; Council of Scientific & Industrial Research, director, 1977-85; University of Wisconsin, Milwaukee, Ford/Briggs & Stratton Professor, Director, 1986-. **ORGANIZATIONS:** ASM, fellow; AAAS, fellow; TWAS, fellow; Institute of Engineering, fellow; Institute of Ceramics, fellow. **HONORS/AWARDS:** Banaras University, Gold Medal of Outstanding Performance, 1961; National Metallurgists Day Award, 1976; Indian Research Centre, Gold Medal Award for Technology for the Future, 1981; Indian Institute of Metals, Binani Gold Medal, 1988; University of Wisconsin, Milwaukee, Outstanding Research Award from UWM, 19891 CEAS, Outstanding Service Award, 1992. **SPECIAL ACHIEVEMENTS:** 350 research publications; 6 books; 10 patents. **HOME PHONE:** (414)962-3428. **BUSINESS ADDRESS:** Professor, Dept of Materials Engineering, University of Wisconsin, Milwaukee, CEAS, PO Box 784, Milwaukee, WI 53201, (414)229-4987.

ROHATGI, UPENDRA SINGH (KUMAR)
Mechanical engineer. Indo-American. **PERSONAL:** Born Mar 3, 1949, Kanpur, Uttar Pradesh, India; son of Jitendra Singh Rohatgi & Bimala Rohatgi; married Charu Rohatgi, Jun 26, 1975; children: Ruchi, Udai Singh. **EDUCATION:** Indian Institute of Technology, Kanpur, BTech, 1970; Case Western Reserve University, MS, 1972, PhD, 1975. **CAREER:** Brookhaven National Lab, group leader, 1975-. **ORGANIZATIONS:** American Society of Mechanical Engineers, multiphase flow committee, vice chair, 1992-94, chair, 1994-; gas-liquid flow subcommittee, chair, 1984-91, Journal of Fluids Engineering, associate editor, 1988-91. **HONORS/AWARDS:** US Nuclear Regulatory Commission, appreciation award, 1989; American Society of Mechanical Engineer, certificate, 1990. **SPECIAL ACHIEVEMENTS:** Over 80 publications in the area of two-phase flow, turbomachinery & reactor safety. **BUSINESS ADDRESS:** Mechanical Engineer, Brookhaven National Laboratory, Bldg 475 B, Upton, NY 11973, (516)282-2475.

ROHATGI, VIJAY K.
Educator, consultant. Indo-American. **PERSONAL:** Born Feb 1, 1939, Delhi, India; son of Behari Lal & Motal Devi; married Bina, Dec 15, 1971; children: Sameer. **EDUCATION:** Delhi University, BSc, 1958, MA, 1960; University of Alberta, MSc, 1964; Michigan State University, PhD, 1967. **CAREER:** Catholic University, associate professor, 1967-72; Independence One, consultant, 1987-; Michigan National Bank, senior analyst, 1989; Bowling Green State University, professor, graduate coordinator, 1972-. **ORGANIZATIONS:** International Statistics Institute, 1973-; American Statistics Association, 1972-;

Institute Math Statistics, 1963-. **HONORS/AWARDS:** BGSU, Special Achievements, 1974-75. **SPECIAL ACHIEVEMENTS:** Introduction to Probability & Statistics, Wiley, 1975; Probability Theory, Wiley, 1979; Statistical Inference, Wiley, 1984; Contributions to Probability, Ac Press, 1981. **BUSINESS ADDRESS:** Professor, Grad Coordinator, Math Sciences, Bowling Green State University, Bowling Green, OH 43403, (419)372-7470.

ROHILA, PRITAM KUMAR
Clinical neuropsychologist. Indo-American. **PERSONAL:** Born Sep 25, 1935, Jagadhari, Haryana, India; son of Krishan Chandra and Champa Wati Rohila; married Kundan, Nov 17, 1983; children: Arun, Vineeta Andrews, Snehal Shah, Shilpa Gorajia. **EDUCATION:** Government College, Rupar, Panjab, India, BA, 1954; DM College, Moga, Panjab, India, BT, 1957; Panjab University Camp College, New Delhi, MA, 1960; Central Institute of Education, Delhi, India, diploma, educational & vocational guidance, 1962; University of Oregon, PhD, 1969. **CAREER:** National Institute of Education, New Delhi, counselor, 1962-67; University of Oregon, graduate research assistant, 1967-69; Western State Hospital, clinical psychologist, 1969-73; private practice, clinical psychologist, 1970-79, clinical neuropsychologist, 1982-; Oregon State Hospital, clinical neuropsychologist, 1979-85, senior clinical psychologist, geropsychology, 1983-85. **ORGANIZATIONS:** International Neuropsychological Society, 1989-; National Academy of Neuropsychology, 1989-; Oregon Psychological Association, 1980-, chair, prof affairs, 1984-86; American Psychological Association, 1973-; Association for Communal Harmony in Asia, president, 1993-; Mid-Valley Arts Council, board of directors, 1983-84; Unity of Salem, board of directors, 1983-84; Pierce County Growth Council, Human Resources Group, chair, 1977-78; South Sound Psychological Association, 1975-79, president, 1975; Washington State Psychological Association, 1970-79, continuing education committee, 1978-79. **HONORS/AWARDS:** American Board of Professional Disability Consultants, diploma, 1990-; National Register of Health Service Providers in Psychology, 1975-; Central Institute of Education, Delhi, Distinction, 1962. **SPECIAL ACHIEVEMENTS:** Co-author: Neuropsychological Test Batteries: Review of Research and Description, Milap Institute of Human Development, 1977; "Time Perspectives of American and Indian Adolescents," Journal of Cross Cultural Psychology, vol 3, pp 293-302, 1972. **BUSINESS ADDRESS:** Clinical Neuropsychologist, 831 Lancaster Dr NE, Ste 214, Salem, OR 97301-2930, (503)362-4635.

ROSER, CE
Artist. Chinese American. **PERSONAL:** Born in Philadelphia, PA; daughter of Emma & Chou Kwong Shue; married Harold Roser; children: Lorin. **EDUCATION:** Hoch Schule fur Bildende Kunst, Germany. **CAREER:** Self-employed artist, currently. **ORGANIZATIONS:** Women in the Arts Foundation, founding member, first executive coordinator; New York Cultural Center, organizer and juror, first all-women artists exhibition: Women Choose Women; Asian American Art Center, advisory board Womens Caucus for Art and American Abstract Artists. **SPECIAL ACHIEVEMENTS:** Producer, narrator, editor, color-video documentary, "The Circle of Charmion von Wiegand," shown on Channel 13, 1978. **BIOGRAPHICAL SOURCES:** Women artists series, Scarecrow Press, 1994. **BUSINESS ADDRESS:** 355 Riverside Dr, New York, NY 10025.

ROUF, MOHAMMED ABDUR
Educator. Bangladeshi American. **PERSONAL:** Born May 2, 1933, Dhaka, Bangladesh; son of Kafiludden Sarder and Nadia Sarder; married Reena, Sep 30, 1973; children: Arman, Alia. **EDUCATION:** University of Dacca, Bangladesh, BS (w/honors), 1954, MS, 1955; University of California, Davis, MS, 1959; Washington State University, PhD, 1963. **CAREER:** University of Dacca, director, survey of medic plants, 1955-56; University of Wisconsin-Oshkosh, asst professor, 1964-66, associate professor, 1966-68, professor & chairman, 1968-; consultant to several NYSE listed corporations on microbiological quality control and packaging. **ORGANIZATIONS:** American Society for Microbiology; ASM-North Central Branch, president, 1991-92; Sigma Xi; American Chemical Society; Wisconsin Academy of Arts & Science. **HONORS/AWARDS:** Wisconsin State University, Board of Regents Grant, 1969-70; University of Wisconsin-Oshkosh, Institutional Grant, 1970-72, Faculty Development Grant, 1979-80, 1982-86, James F. Duncan Research Award, 1985; National Science Foundation, Microbial Ecology, 1976-78, Small Business Innovative Research, 1980-81, Faculty Fellow, 1976-78; American Academy of Microbiology, Fellow; American Institute of Chemists, Fellow. **BUSINESS ADDRESS:** Chairman, Dept of Biology & Microbiology, University of Wisconsin-Oshkosh, 800 Algoma Blvd, Halsey Science Center 142, Oshkosh, WI 54901-8640.

ROY, DEV KUMAR
Mathematician, educational administrator. Indo-American. **PERSONAL:** Born Jul 15, 1951, Patna, Bihar, India; son of Sukumar and Renuka Roy; married Maneck Daruwala, Aug 4, 1985. **EDUCATION:** Indian Institute of Technology, MSc, 1973; University of Rochester, PhD, 1980. **CAREER:** University of Wisconsin, Milwaukee, lecturer, 1979-81; Florida International University, assistant professor, 1981-86, associate professor, 1986-, Department of Math, chairman, 1987-. **ORGANIZATIONS:** Association for Symbolic Logic, 1976-. **HONORS/AWARDS:** Government of India, Science Talent Scholar, 1968-73. **SPECIAL ACHIEVEMENTS:** Author of various research publications. **BUSINESS ADDRESS:** Chairman, Dept of Mathematics, Florida International University, Miami, FL 33199, (305)348-2743.

ROY, PRADIP KUMAR
Scientist, engineer. Indo-American. **PERSONAL:** Born Feb 27, 1943, Hazaribagh, Bihar, India; son of B N Roy and H Roy; married Maria, 1968; children: Milan, Jason, Michael. **EDUCATION:** Indian Institute of Technology, India, BTech (with honors), 1964; University of Alberta, Canada, MSc, English, 1967; Columbia University, PhD, 1973. **CAREER:** National Metallurgical Lab, senior research fellow, 1964-66; IBM Research Center, postdoctoral fellow, 1973-76; SES, Shell Inc, senior scientist, 1976-81; AT&T Bell Labs, member of technical staff, 1982-. **ORGANIZATIONS:** IEEE, 1989-; AVS/APS, 1980-; MRS, 1990-; ACBL, life master, 1975-; AVS, fellow, 1993. **HONORS/AWARDS:** AT&T Microelectronics, Shared Valves Gold Triangle, sustained innovations, 1989; AT&T VLSI Tech Lab, Bell Llabs, 1991 Affirmative Award, 1992; US Patent & Trademark Office, replica of the first US patent, thin oxide tech, 1989; AT&T's 1993 nominee, NSF's National Medal of Science, nominee, National Inventors Hall of Fame, 1993. **SPECIAL ACHIEVEMENTS:** "Pioneering Work in Thin Stacked Oxide Technology," US patents 4,851,370 & 5,153,701, IEDM Tech Digest, Dec 1988; "Layering Process in Semiconductors," US patents 4,631,804, 4,742,020, 5,147,820, MRS Sympo Proc, fall 1992; "Thin Film Solar Photovoltaics," US patent 4,260,428, 15th IEEE Photovoltaic Specialists Conf, p 1025, 1981; seminal work in thin oxide and layering process. **BIOGRAPHICAL SOURCES:** "Thin Oxide Breakthrough Strengthens Our Hand," AT&T Technical Rep, p 1, July-Aug 1988, p 2, June-July 1989; "Patents and Other Awards," AT&T Asian Americans News & Views, vol 1, June 1989, April 1993. **BUSINESS ADDRESS:** Member of Technical Staff, AT&T Bell Labs, 555 Union Blvd, 2A-253, Allentown, PA 18103, (215)439-7878.

ROY-BURMAN, PRADIP
Educator, scientist. Indo-American. **PERSONAL:** Born Nov 12, 1938, Comillah, Bengal, India; son of Prafulla N Roy-Burman and Mrinalini (Barman) Roy-Burman; married Sumitra (Ghosh) Roy-Burman, Nov 26, 1963; children: Arup, Paula. **EDUCATION:** Calcutta University, India, BSc (with honors), chemistry, 1956, MS, 1958, PhD, 1963. **CAREER:** University of Southern California, assistant professor of biochem, 1967-70, assistant professor of biochem & pathology, 1970-72, associate professor of pathology & biochemistry, 1972-78, professor of pathology & biochemistry & molbiol, 1978-, vice-chairman, Dept of Pathology, 1987-, chairman, Biomed Research Support Grant Commission, 1984-. **ORGANIZATIONS:** American Cancer Society, California Division, special grant committee, 1974-78; Hematological Oncology, editorial board, 1987-; NIH Study Section, Pathology B, DRG, 1990-; NIH NINDS Extramural Research Program, special review committee, 1992-; American Society for Microbiology, 1992-; American Society for Biological Chemists & Molecular Biologists, 1973-; American Society of Virology, 1983-; International Asst for Company Research on Leukemia & Related Diseases, 1973-; American Association for Cancer Research, 1993-. **HONORS/AWARDS:** University of Southern California, Robert S Clelland Excellance in Teaching Award, 1982, 1990; National Institutes of Health, principal investicator of research grants, 1970-; American Cancer Society, Senior Fellow in Oncology, 1966-71; International Organizations, travel grants, 1976-79, 1988, 1994. **SPECIAL ACHIEVEMENTS:** Molecular genetics of feline leukemia viruses, many publications, ongoing research; co-convenor, Symposium on Oncogenes and Tumor Suppressor Genes, 16th International Congress of Biochem & Molecular Biology, 1994; co-chairman, Symposium on Retroviral Carcinogenesis, XVI Intl Cancer Congress, 1994; Molecular Genetics of Human Cancer, publication, ongoing research; "Recombinant Feline Leukemia Virus Genes Detected in Naturally Occurring Feline Lymphosarcomas," Journal Virol, vol 67, p 3118-3125, 1993; "Workshop Report," Cancer Research, vol 51, p 5440-5444, 1991. **BUSINESS ADDRESS:** Professor of Pathology, Biochemistry & Molecular Biology, Vice Chmn, Dept

of Pathology, University of Southern California, 2011 Zonal Ave, HMR 209, Los Angeles, CA 90033, (213)342-1184.

RU, WESLEY
Business executive. Chinese American. **PERSONAL:** Born Dec 9, 1954, Taipei, Taiwan; son of Matthew D J Ru and Maylin C Ru; divorced; children: Nathaniel. **EDUCATION:** California State University at Los Angeles, BS, 1977; Corro Foundation, 1983. **CAREER:** Mandarin Realty, sales, 1977-82; Flying Tiger Line, intl sales, 1977-83; Triad Intl Trade Consultants, president, 1977-; Western Badge & Trophy Co, president, 1984-; Plastic Graphics, principal, 1987-; All American Pin, principal, 1990-; Promotional Graphics, principal, 1990-. **ORGANIZATIONS:** Los Angeles County Dept of Children Services, director, 1991-; Asian Youth Center, director, 1992-; Pacific Clinic, director 1993-; Asian American Economic Development Council, advisory bd, 1993; Los Angeles County Commission on Insurance, commissioner, 1992-; Los Angeles Chamber of Commerce, 1986-; California Chamber of Commerce, 1992-. **SPECIAL ACHIEVEMENTS:** Language proficiency: English, Mandarin, Spanish. **BUSINESS ADDRESS:** President, Western Badge and Trophy Co, 1716 W Washington, Los Angeles, CA 90007, (213)735-1201.

RUSTAGI, RAVINDER KUMAR
Physician. Indo-American. **PERSONAL:** Born Jul 10, 1951, New Delhi, India; son of Ram Kishore Rustagi and Kapoori Devi Rustagi; married May 26, 1985; children: Akshay, Ankush. **EDUCATION:** Maulana Azad Medical College, MBBB, 1976. **CAREER:** Irwin Hospital, New Delhi, India, house physician, 1976-77; Prince George's General Hospital, resident, 1976-81; Deborah Heart & Lung Center, fellow, cardiology, 1981-83; Ravinder K Rustagi MD, PA, president, cardiologist, 1983-. **ORGANIZATIONS:** American College of Physicians, 1980-. **BUSINESS ADDRESS:** President, Ravinder K. Rustagi MD, PA, Cheverly Hills Medical Center, 6132 Landover Rd, Cheverly, MD 20785, (301)386-2666.

RYU, DEWEY DOO YOUNG
Educator. Korean American. **PERSONAL:** Born Oct 27, 1936, Republic of Korea; children: Mina L, Regina P. **EDUCATION:** Massachusetts Institute of Technology, BS, 1961, PhD, 1967. **CAREER:** Squibb Institute for Medical Research, Bristol-Myer Squibb, senior research engineer, 1967-72; The Korea Advanced Institute of Science, Seoul, professor, chair, 1973-81; Massachusetts Institute of Technology, visiting professor, 1972-73; University of California, Davis, professor, director, 1982-. **ORGANIZATIONS:** American Institute of Chemical Engineers; American Chemical Society; American Society for Microbiology; American Association for the Advancement of Science; American Institute of Medical and Biological Engineering. **HONORS/AWARDS:** The President of Korea, National Civil Merit Award, 1980. **SPECIAL ACHIEVEMENTS:** 176 original research papers, 1965-92; 18 US and other invention patents. **HOME ADDRESS:** 658 Portsmouth Ave, Davis, CA 95616. **BUSINESS ADDRESS:** Professor, Director of Biochemical Engineering Program, University of California, Davis, Davis, CA 95616, (916)752-8954.

S

SABHARWAL, KULBIR
Food company executive. Indo-American. **PERSONAL:** Born Jan 5, 1943, Punjab, India; son of Shri Faqir Chand Sabharwal & Kesar Devi Sabharwal; married Karuna Sabharwal; children: Sabina, Avnish. **EDUCATION:** Punjab Agricultural University, India, BSc, agriculture, 1964, MSc, agriculture, 1966; Ohio State University, MS, 1969, PhD, 1972. **CAREER:** Fisher Cheese Company, research and development, director, 1972-86, Gilardi Foods Company, technical services, director, 1987-90; Galaxy Food, vice president, technical services, 1991-. **ORGANIZATIONS:** Institute of Food Technologists, professional member, 1972-; American Dairy Science Association, 1968-86. **HONORS/AWARDS:** American Oil Chemists' Society, honored student award, 1972; Gamma Sigma Delta, honored member, 1969. **HOME ADDRESS:** 8210 Ambrose Cove Way, Orlando, FL 32819, (407)354-5439. **BUSINESS ADDRESS:** Vice President, Technical Services, Galaxy Food Company, 2441 Viscount Row, Orlando, FL 32809, (407)855-5500.

SABNIS, GAJANAN M.
Educator. Indo-American. **PERSONAL:** Born Jun 11, 1941, Belgaum, India; son of Mahadeo A Sabnis and Shantabai M Sabnis; married Sharda G Sabris, May 7, 1969; children: Rahul G, Madhavi G. **EDUCATION:** University of Bombay, BE, 1961; Indian Institute of Technology, Bombay, MTech, 1963;

Cornell University, PhD, 1967. **CAREER:** Cornell University, research assistant, 1964-67; University of Pennsylvania, postdoctoral fellow, 1967-68; American Cement Corp, structure research engineer, 1968-69; Bechtel Power Corp, group supervisor, 1970-74; KC Engineering, PC, president, 1983-; Howard University, Washington, DC, professor, civil engineering, 1974-. **ORGANIZATIONS:** American Society of Civil Engineering, fellow; American Concrete Institute, ACI, fellow; American Society for Engineering Education; Institute of Engineers, India; Prestressed Concrete Institute; Experimental Stress Analysis. **HONORS/AWARDS:** ACI, Chapter Activities Award, 1976; University of Bombay, James Berkeley Gold Medal, 1961. **SPECIAL ACHIEVEMENTS:** Author of 10 books; author of over 100 research papers related to reinforced and prestressed concrete, rehabilitation of concrete structures, and other engineering topics, 1966-93. **HOME ADDRESS:** 13721 Townline Rd, Silver Spring, MD 20906-2113. **BUSINESS PHONE:** (202)806-6580.

SABNIS, SUMAN TRIMBAK
Entrepreneur. Indo-American. **PERSONAL:** Born Nov 27, 1935, Rajkot, Gujarat, India; son of Trimbak Sitaram Sabnis and Indira Trimbak Sabnis; married Vasumati Suman Sabnis, Aug 13, 1960; children: Samir Suman, Sushil Suman, Kalpana Suman. **EDUCATION:** Christ Church College, BS, 1954; H B Technological Institute, AHBTI, ChE, 1957; Lehigh University, MS, ChE, 1960, PhD, ChE, 1967; Rutgers University, MS, applied and mathematical statistics, 1964. **CAREER:** Union Carbide Corp, chemical engineer, 1960-63; Monsanto Co, group leader, research and development, 1966-74; Kerite Co, manager, process development, 1974-81; Laribee Wire Manufacturing Co, vice president, engineering sales, 1981-88; KSS Associates, owner, currently. **ORGANIZATIONS:** American Institute of Chemcial Engineers, 1960-74; American Chemical Society, Rubber Division, 1974-; IEEE, 1974-; Sigma Xi, 1967-; Society of Plastic Engineers, president, 1981-82; Jaycees, Springfield, MA, president, 1970-71; National Epilepsy Foundation, Springfield, MA, president, Better Dental Health, vice president, 1971-72; Orange Rotary, director community projects, 1991-. **HONORS/AWARDS:** JC International, JCI Senator, 1972; Springfield Jaycees, Jaycee of the Year, 1973. **SPECIAL ACHIEVEMENTS:** Established commercial feasiblity in US for special process for manufacturing rubber insulated power cables. **BUSINESS ADDRESS:** Owner, KSS Associates, 843 Garden Rd, Orange, CT 06477-1513, (203)799-2309.

SACHAN, DILEEP SINGH
Educator. Indo-American. **PERSONAL:** Born Dec 18, 1938, Makhauli, Kanpur, Uttar Pradesh, India; son of Sri Jagdeo Prasad Sachan & Smt Parag Sachan; married Cheryl L, Nov 2, 1968; children: Rashmi D, Ravi C, Vinay K. **EDUCATION:** Jabalpur University, MP Veterinary College, BVSc, 1961, MVSc, 1963; University of Illinois, MS, 1966, PhD, 1968. **CAREER:** University of Illinois, research assistant, 1964-69; Case Western Reserve University Medical School, research associate, 1969-71; Meharry Medical College, assistant professor, 1971-76; Veterans Admin Hospital, research chemist, 1976-78; Vanderbilt University Medical School, nutr & GI fellow, pathology, instructor, 1978-79; University of Tennessee, professor, 1979-. **ORGANIZATIONS:** American Institute of Nutrition; American College of Nutrition; American Society of Clinical Nutrition; International College of Nutrition; Gamma Sigma Delta, 1967-; Sigma Xi, 1967-; Phi Zeta, 1983-. **HONORS/AWARDS:** Phi Kappa Phi, 1993-; Jabalpur University, Gold Medal, 1961. **SPECIAL ACHIEVEMENTS:** Research papers, symposium, invited presentations at national and international meetings of nutrition, biochemistry, physiology, pharamacology and toxicology, etc, in the area of nutrition in alcoholism, cancer, environmental toxicology, drug metabolism and chronic disease. **HOME ADDRESS:** 921 Parrish Road, Knoxville, TN 37923, (615)690-0733. **BUSINESS ADDRESS:** Professor/Director, Nutrition Institute, Dept of Nutrition, University of Tennessee, 1215 Cumberland Ave, Knoxville, TN 37996-1900, (615)974-6257.

SACHDEV, RAMESH KUMAR
Purchasing agent. Indo-American. **PERSONAL:** Born Apr 2, 1944, Allahabad, Uttar Pradesh, India; son of Sri J R Sachdev and Thakuri Sachdev; married Bharati Sachdev, Oct 15, 1972; children: Pallavi, Shwetank. **EDUCATION:** University of Allahabad, MS, 1965; Institute of Chartered Accountants, 1965-69. **CAREER:** Vardhaman Spg & General Mills Ltd, corporate branch manager, 1982; Warsha Burners Put Ltd, finance, chief exec, 1985-; Nassau Lens Co Inc, chief purchasing agent, 1988-. **ORGANIZATIONS:** Gas Stove Mfrs Org, co-chairman, 1986; Steel Wire Mfr Association, vice president, 1982. **HONORS/AWARDS:** Western India Accountants Association, Most Valu-

able Person, 1983. **HOME ADDRESS:** 201 Henmarken Dr, Northvale, NJ 07647-1705, (201)784-6013.

SADANA, AJIT
Educator. Indo-American. **PERSONAL:** Born Feb 14, 1947, Rawalpindi, India; son of Jai Chand Sadana and Jinder Sadana; married Lopa M Sadana, Jan 16, 1973; children: Neeti, Richa. **EDUCATION:** Indian Institute of Technology, Kanpur, BTech, 1969; University of Delaware, MChE, 1972, PhD, 1975. **CAREER:** National Chemical Lab, Poona, India, senior scientific officer, 1975-80; Auburn University, chem engineering, visiting associate professor, 1980-81; University of Mississippi, chemical engineering, associate professor, 1981-90, chem engineering, professor, 1990-. **SPECIAL ACHIEVEMENTS:** Biocatalysis: Fundamentals of Enzyme Deactivation Kinetics, Prentice Hall, 1991; Bioseparations: Fundamentals of Protein Quality Control, Prentice Hall, 1994. **HOME ADDRESS:** 229 St Andrews Circle, Oxford, MS 38655, (601)234-0859. **BUSINESS ADDRESS:** Professor of Chemical Engineering, University of Mississippi, Rebel Dr, 134 Anderson Hall, University, MS 38677-9740, (601)232-7023.

SAEKI, HIROKO YODA
Art dealer. Japanese American. **PERSONAL:** Born Oct 11, 1936, Toyko, Japan; daughter of Takayoshi and Ayako Yoda; divorced; children: Rei. **EDUCATION:** Toyoeiwa College, Tokyo, Japan, 1956. **CAREER:** Hiroko Saeki Inc, currently. **ORGANIZATIONS:** Private Art Dealers Assn. **BUSINESS ADDRESS:** President, Hiroko Saeki Inc, 45 E 89th St, New York, NY 10128, (212)876-8804.

SAFDARI, YAHYA BHAI
Educator. Indo-American. **PERSONAL:** Born Jul 25, 1930, Amravati, Maharashtra, India; son of Asghar & Batul Safdari; married Saeeda S Safdari, Dec 23, 1962; children: Imran, Yusuf, Fawzia, Muhammad. **EDUCATION:** Aligarh Muslim University, India, BSME, 1952, BSEE, 1953; University of Washington, MSME, 1959; NMSU, DSc, 1964. **CAREER:** Delhi Cloth Mills, India, 1954-56; University of Washington, grad assistant, 1956-59; Refrigeration Engineering Co, 1959-61; New Mexico State University, instructor/research, 1961-64; Bradley University, professor, 1969-. **ORGANIZATIONS:** Solar Energy Industry Association, governor, 1974-79, founding father, life membership, standards committee, process heat div, chairman, 1977-79; State of Illinois, Inter-Universities Energy Organization Comm, State of Illinois Solar Energy Panel; Illinois Solar Energy Industries Assn, pres, 1977-82; Bradley University Senate, 1991-93; University Senate Executive Comm, 1991-93; University Sabbatical Leave Comm, chairman, 1990-91; University Comm on Tenure, Promotion & Dismissal; Sigma Xi; American Society of Mechanical Engineers; Intl Solar Energy Society; Solar Energy Industry Association, life member; American Solar Energy Soc; ASHRAE; Bradley University ASME Student Section, faculty advisor, 1968-76. **SPECIAL ACHIEVEMENTS:** Co-author, "Photovoltaic Power for Remote Applications, Design Cost, and Future," Proceedings: Alternative Energy in the Midwest, 1987, "Two Dimensional Transient Analysis for the Solar Heating of a Fluid by a Partially Radiation Absorbing Medium," ISES, 1991, Solar World Congress, Denver, Aug 1991, "Analysis of Failure in a Partially Solar Radiation Absorbing Medium Due to Thermal Stress," ASME International Solar Energy Conference, Hawaii, April 1992; Solar Air Collector, US Patent No 4,019,494; proficient in English, Urdu, Arabic. **BUSINESS ADDRESS:** Professor, Bradley University, 1501 W Bradley Ave, Jobst Complex Rm 110, Peoria, IL 61625, (309)677-2708.

SAGAMI, KIM
Dancer. Japanese American. **CAREER:** Joffrey Ballet, dancer, currently. **SPECIAL ACHIEVEMENTS:** Performances include: Empyrean Dances, written by Edward Stierle, 1992. **BUSINESS ADDRESS:** Dancer, Joffrey Ballet, 130 W 56th St, New York, NY 10019-3885, (212)265-7300.*

SAGAWA, SHIRLEY SACHI
Government official. Japanese American. **PERSONAL:** Born Aug 25, 1961, Rochester, NY; daughter of Hidetaka Sagawa and Patricia Ford Sagawa; married Gregory Baer; children: Jackson Ford Baer. **EDUCATION:** Smith College, AB, 1983; London School of Economics, MSc, 1984; Harvard Law School, JD, 1987. **CAREER:** Senate Labor and Human Resources Committee, chief counsel for youth policy, 1987-91; National Women's Law Center, senior counsel, 1991-93; White House, special assistant to the President for domestic policy, 1993-. **ORGANIZATIONS:** Commission on National and Community Service, board of director, vice chair, 1991-; Organization of Pan Asian Ameri-

can Women, executive board, 1987-89; Women's Information Network, 1992-. **HONORS/AWARDS:** Truman Scholarship, 1981; American Association of University Women, Fellowship, 1986; Smith College Alumnae Association, Fellowship, 1983; Center for the Advancement of Citizenship, McGance Award, 1991. **SPECIAL ACHIEVEMENTS:** Drafted National and Community Service Act of 1990; drafted National and Community Service Trust Act of 1993; author, Visions of Service: The Future of the National and Community Service Act, 1993, "Batson v Kentucky: Will It Keep Women on the Jury?'', 3 Berkeley Women's Law Journal, vol 14, 1987-88, Women in The Military, Issue Papers Series, 1992. **BUSINESS ADDRESS:** Special Assistant for the President for Domestic Policy, The White House, West Wing, Washington, DC 20500.

SAGAWA, YONEO
Educator. Japanese American. **PERSONAL:** Born Oct 11, 1926, Olaa, HI; son of Chikatada Sagawa (deceased) & Mume Kuno Sagawa (deceased); widowed; children: Penelope Toshiko, Irene Teruko. **EDUCATION:** Washington University, St Louis, AB, 1950, MS, 1952; University of Connecticut, PhD, 1956. **CAREER:** Brookhaven National Lab, research associate, 1955-57; University of Florida, assistant, associate professor, 1957-64; University of Hawaii, professor, 1964-, director, Lyon Arboretum, 1967-91. **ORGANIZATIONS:** Phi Kappa Phi, past chapter president, vp, councillor; International Association of Plant Tissue Culture; American Association for the Advancement of Science; Botanical Society of America; American Institute of Biological Sciences; American Society for Horticultural Science; International Association for Horticultural Science; International Palm Society; Consultant: NASA Biosatellite Project, 1966-67; UNFAO, 1971; USAID-ASAP, 1992-93; UNDP-UNISTAR, 1993; VOCA, 1993; Instituut voor Toepassing van Atoomenergie and Agricultural University, Wageningen, The Netherlands 1979-80; Bishop Museum, research associate. **HONORS/AWARDS:** American Anthurium Society, honorary life; American Orchid Society, honorary life; Honolulu Orchid Society, honorary life; Kaimuki Orchid Society, honorary life; Garden Club of Honolulu, honorary life. **SPECIAL ACHIEVEMENTS:** Na Okika O Hawaii, Hawaii Orchid Journal, editor, 1972-; Pacific Orchid Society Bulletin, editor, 1966-71. **BIOGRAPHICAL SOURCES:** From Hiroshima to the Moon, by Daniel Lang, Simon & Schuster, p410-428, 1959. **BUSINESS ADDRESS:** Professor, Horticulture Dept, University of Hawaii, Manoa, 3190 Maile Way, Rm 102, Honolulu, HI 96822.

SAH, CHIH-TANG
Engineer, educator. Chinese American. **PERSONAL:** Born Nov 10, 1932, Beijing, China; son of Adam Peng-tung Sah and Shu-shen Huang Sah; married Linda Chang, Nov 29, 1959; children: Dinah Wenyee, Robert Lie-Yuan. **EDUCATION:** University of Illinois, BS, physics, BEE, 1953; Stanford University, MEE, 1954, PhD, 1956. **CAREER:** Stanford Electronics Lab, research associate, 1956; Shockley Transistor Corp, technical staff, senior member, 1957-59; Fairchild Semiconductor Lab, Physics Dept, head manager, 1959-64; Fairchild Semiconductor Corp, first generation Si, VLSI tech, program director, manager, 1959-64; University of Illinois, Urbana, physics and electrical engineering, professor, 1962-68, Illinois Solid State Electronics Lab, director, 1962-68; consultant: Jet Propulsion Laboratory, Dept of Energy, 1976-85, Harry Diamond Lab, 1974-75, IBM Corp, 1967-69, numerous others, 1964-68; University of Florida, Gainesville, Pittman Eminent Scholar chair, graduate research professor, chief scientist, College of Engineering, 1988-. **ORGANIZATIONS:** National Academy of Engineering; Materials Research Society; Electrochemical Society. **HONORS/AWARDS:** Univ Louvain, Beligium, D honoris causa, 1975; Asian American Manufacturing Association, first high tech award, 1982; IEEE, fellow, IRE Browder I Thompson Prize, 1963, J J Ebers Award, 1980, Jack Morton Award, 1989; American Physical Society, Franklin Institute, Certificate of Merit Award, 1975. **SPECIAL ACHIEVEMENTS:** Author, Fundamentals of Solid-State Electronics, 1991; codeveloper, complementary metal-oxide semiconductor circuit, 1962; 250 articles to journals; codiscoverer, Si P-N Junction Diode Recombination Phenomena, Sah-Noyce-Shockley Theory, 1957. **BUSINESS ADDRESS:** Professor, Dept of Electrical Engineering, University of Florida, 216 Larsen Hall, Gainesville, FL 32611, (904)392-8914.*

SAHA, GOPAL BANDHU
Chemist. Bangladeshi American. **PERSONAL:** Born Apr 30, Chittagong, Bangladesh; son of Hriday Ranjan Saha and Charubala Saha; married Sipra Saha, Aug 11, 1965; children: Prantik, Trina. **EDUCATION:** Dacca University, Bangladesh, BSc (with honors), 1959, MSc, 1960; McGill University, PhD, 1965. **CAREER:** Purdue University, 1965-66; McGill University, re-search associate, 1966-69; Royal Victoria Hospital, associate scientist, 1970-76; University of Arkansas for Medical Sciences, professor of radiology, 1976-82; University of New Mexico, professor and director of radiopharmacy, 1982-84; Cleveland Clinic, director of nuclear chemistry and pharmacy, 1984-. **ORGANIZATIONS:** Society of Nuclear Medicine, 1970-; American Chemical Society, 1970-; American Association for the Advancement of Science, 1984-; Radiological Society of North America, 1985-; American Association for Physicists in Medicine, 1985-. **SPECIAL ACHIEVEMENTS:** Author, Fundamentals of Nuclear Pharmacy, 1st ed, 1979, 2nd ed, 1984, 3rd ed, 1992; Essentials of Nuclear Medicine Science, 1987; Physics and Radiobiology of Nuclear Medicine, 1993; 75 publications. **BUSINESS ADDRESS:** Director of Nuclear Chemistry and Pharmacy, Cleveland Clinic Foundation, 9500 Euclid Ave, Gb-3, Cleveland, OH 44195, (216)444-2777.

SAHNI, SHAM L.
Travel company executive. Indo-American. **PERSONAL:** Born Aug 24, 1951, Ambala City, Haryana, India; son of Ram Murti Sahni and Rukmani Devi Sahni; married Madhu Sahni, May 4, 1978; children: Nikhil, Neha. **EDUCATION:** Regional Engineering College, Kurukshetra, India, electrical engineer, 1972; University of Vermont, business, 1975. **CAREER:** New Mother India, president, currently; Travel Arrangement, president, currently. **BUSINESS ADDRESS:** President, The Travel Arrangement, 394 Lowell St, Ste 5, Lexington, MA 02173, (617)862-8400.

SAHNI, VIRAHT
Educator. Indo-American. **PERSONAL:** Born Dec 31, 1944, Lahore, Pakistan; son of Harbans Lal & Hema Lal; married Catherine, Nov 16, 1991; children: Vishal, Vikram. **EDUCATION:** Indian Institute of Technology, BTech, electrical engineering, 1965; Polytechnic Institute of Brooklyn, MS, electrical engineering, 1968, PhD, physics, 1972. **CAREER:** Pratt Institute, instructor of electrical engineering, 1968-70; Brooklyn College of CUNY, postdoctoral associate, 1972-74; assistant professor of physics, 1974-78, associate professor of physics, 1979-81, professor of physics, 1982-. **ORGANIZATIONS:** American Physical Society, 1972-; Sigma Xi, 1972-. **HONORS/AWARDS:** Various research awards from the National Science Foundation, American Chemical Society, and Research Foundation of CUNY. **SPECIAL ACHIEVEMENTS:** Over 60 publications on theoretical physics. **BUSINESS ADDRESS:** Professor, Dept of Physics, Brooklyn College of the City University of New York, 2900 Bedford Ave, Rm 1407A Ingersoll, Brooklyn, NY 11210, (718)951-5785.

SAIKI, PATRICIA F.
Former government administrator. Japanese American. **PERSONAL:** Born May 28, 1930, Hilo, HI; daughter of Kazuo and Shizue Inoue Fukuda; married Stanley Mitsuo Saiki, Jun 19, 1954; children: Stanley Mitsuo, Sandra Saiki Williams, Margaret C, Stuart K, Laura H. **EDUCATION:** University of Hawaii, Manoa, BA, 1952. **CAREER:** Teacher of US history: Punahou School, Kaimuki Intermediate School, Kalani High School, 1952-54; Hawaii State Senate, research assistant, 1966-68; Hawaii House of Representatives, representative, 1968-74; Hawaii State Senate, senator, 1974-82; US Congress, congresswoman, 1987-91; US Small Business Administration, administrator, 1991-93. **ORGANIZATIONS:** Republican Party in Hawaii, secretary, 1964-66, vice chairman, 1966-68, 1982-83, chairman, 1983-85; President's Advisory Council on Status of Women, 1969-76; Natl Commission of International Women's Year, 1969-70; Western Interstate Commission on Higher Education; Kapiolani Hospital Auxilary; Federation of Republican Women; Boys and Girls Clubs of Hawaii, past board of governors; ARC, advisory council; Natl Fund for Improvement of Post-Secondary Education, past board of directors; Straub Medical Research Foundation, past board of directors; Hawaii Visitors Bureau, 1983-85. **HONORS/AWARDS:** Rutgers University, Eagleton Institute of Politics, fellow, 1970; US Small Business Association, Asian American of the Year, 1992; Hawaii Pacific College. trustee; University of Hawaii Foundation, trustee, 1984-86. **SPECIAL ACHIEVEMENTS:** Hawaii Constitutional Convention, delegate, 1968; Republican National Convention, alternate delegate, 1968, delegate, 1984; Republican nominee for lt governor of Hawaii, 1982.*

SAITO, SEIJI
Sculptor. Japanese American. **PERSONAL:** Born Jun 8, 1933, Utsunomiya, Tochigi Pref, Japan; son of Eiji Saito and Shimo Saito; married Kuni Saito; children: Ghen. **EDUCATION:** Brooklyn Museum Art School, 1961-68; studied techniques of granite carving with Mr Odilio Beggi, 1962; Tokyo University of Art, BFA, 1958, MFA, stone carving, 1960; Warabi Art Studio, Saitama

Pref, Japan figure drawing. **CAREER:** Brooklyn Museum Art School, instructor of sculpture, 1974, 1976, 1984, 1985; free-lance sculptor, currently. **ORGANIZATIONS:** National Sculpture Society, fellow, 1970-, committee, 1985, 1986; Sculpture for Audubon Artists Inc, awards jury, 1973; CAPS Sculpture Panel, NY, fellowship, 1975; Exhibition of Salmagundi Art Club, NY, award jury, 1982, 1984, 1985; Exhibition of Bergen Museum of the Art and Science, NJ, selection and award jury, 1985. **HONORS/AWARDS:** NSS of 53rd Annual Show, NY, Maurice B Hexter Prize, 1986; 1st Kotaro Takamura Grand Prize Show, Japan, Kasakusho Award, 1980; The Annual Show of National Academy of Design, NY, Certificate of Merit, 1973; Kaikan Gallery, Japan, Certificate of Merit, 1958; The Annual Art Festival Show at Tochigi, Outstanding Prize. **SPECIAL ACHIEVEMENTS:** Muse, marble figure, Pepsico Collection, 1968; Pensive, bronze figure, Pepsico Collection, 1970; Mother and Child, granite, Methodist Hospital of Brooklyn, NY, 1968; Stream, marble and bronze figure, Tochigi Museum, Japan, 1975; Crouch, marble figure, Nezu Museum, Tokyo, Japan, 1990. **BIOGRAPHICAL SOURCES:** Expressions, MacMillan Publishing Co Inc, NY, p 40-42, 1980; Media: NBC-TV News Report, Mr Robert Potts, 1970, 1978. **BUSINESS ADDRESS:** Sculptor, Studio, 566 President St, 1st Fl, Brooklyn, NY 11215, (718)852-6830.

SAITO, THEODORE TERUO
Scientific manager. Japanese American. **PERSONAL:** Born Sep 9, 1942, Poston, AZ; son of Frank Hideo Saito and Akiko Tsuboi Saito; married Diane Gail Saito, Aug 31, 1968; children: Jennifer Akiko, Paul Hideo. **EDUCATION:** US Air Force Academy, BS, 1964; Massachusetts Institute of Technology, SM, 1966; University of New Mexico, 1967; Pennsylvania State University, PhD, 1970. **CAREER:** Air Force Weapons Lab, program coordinator, group leader, 1970-77; Air Force Materials Lab, technical area mgr, 1977-80; USAF Academy, FJ Seiler Research Lab, commander, 1980-84; Lawrence Livermore National Laboratory, Precision Engineering Program, acting leader, deputy leader, Optics Group, leader, Defense Science Dept, deputy dept head, 1984-. **ORGANIZATIONS:** SPIE, president, vice pres, secretary, chmn, publications fellow, 1972-; American Society for Precision Engineering, 1985-; Optical Society of America, fellow, R W Wood Comm, chair, 1966-; American Physical Society, 1965-67; Assn of Federation Technology Transfer Executives, board of directors, 1992-. **HONORS/AWARDS:** USAF Academy, Lt Gen Chennault Award, 1966; SPIE, Governors Award, 1979, Technical Achievement Award, 1980; R&D Magazine, IR100 Award, 1979; FJ Seiler Research Lab, Lowell King, 1982; NASA, Certificate of Recognition, 1986. **SPECIAL ACHIEVEMENTS:** 96 publications including: 34 refereed articles in the areas of lasers, optics, laser damage, laser spectroscopy, precision engineering, materials, technology transfer & metrology. **MILITARY SERVICE:** US Air Force, lt col, 1960-84; Air Force Commendation Medal, 1977; Meritorious Service Medals, 1974, 1980, 1984. **BUSINESS ADDRESS:** Acting Program Leader, Lawrence Livermore National Laboratory, PO Box 808, L-644, Livermore, CA 94551, (510)422-1553.

SAITO, THOMAS E.
Law librarian. Japanese American. **PERSONAL:** Born Jul 8, 1948, Glendale, CA; son of George Saito & Sachiko Tsuchiya; married Marie, Apr 8, 1972; children: Andrew. **EDUCATION:** UCLA, BA, 1970. **CAREER:** Mitchell, Silberberg & Knupp, assistant librarian, 1979-90; Hill Wynne Troop & Meisinger, librarian, 1990-. **ORGANIZATIONS:** UCLA Alumni Association; American Association of Law Libraries; Southern California Association of Law Libraries. **BUSINESS ADDRESS:** Librarian, Hill Wynne Troop & Meisinger, 10940 Wilshire Blvd, Suite 800, Los Angeles, CA 90024-3902, (310)443-7643.

SAITO, WALTER MASAO
Organization executive. Japanese American. **PERSONAL:** Born Aug 14, 1929, Waipahu, HI; son of Kanichi Saito and Fumiyo Saito; married Kathleen A Saito, Feb 7, 1954; children: Michael M, Charlene M Kimura, Susan M. **CAREER:** Boise Cascade, sales manager, 1957-83; Yukon Office Supply, branch manager, 1983-85; NBI The Office Place, vice president/general manager, 1985-89; Office Depot-Hawaii, store manager, 1990-91; Japanese Cultural Center of Hawaii, executive director, currently. **ORGANIZATIONS:** Kuakini Health System, trustee, 1984-; Kuakini Medical Center, board of directors, 1988-; Honolulu Japanese Chamber of Commerce, chairman of the board, 1979-80, board of directors, 1974-; Japanese Cultural Center of Hawaii, board of governors, 1989-92; Chamber of Commerce of Hawaii, vice president, 1979-81; Sales & Marketing of Executive Hawaii, treasurer, 1978-79. **MILITARY SERVICE:** US Army, sgt, 1951-53; Commendation Ribbon with

Metal Pendant. **BUSINESS ADDRESS:** Executive Director, Japanese Cultural Center of Hawaii, 2454 S Beretania St, Honolulu, HI 96826, (808)945-7633.

SAITO, YOSHIO
Educator. Japanese American. **PERSONAL:** Born Jul 6, 1949, Tokyo, Japan; son of Toshicko & Sukeyoshi Saito; married Dorcas Grigg-Saito, Mar 29, 1975; children: Katrina Toshicko, Emily Melia. **EDUCATION:** Nihon University, Tokyo, BS, 1968; Emerson College, Boston, MA, 1975. **CAREER:** Free lance photographer, 1973-85; University of Massachusetts, Media Production, supervisor, 1978-81, Media & Instructional Development, director, 1981-83; Multi Media International, director/producer of video production, 1983-85; Newbury College, adjunct professor for photography & television productions, 1982-85; Boston College, Slavic Eastern Languages, adjunct professor, 1986-, audio visual services director, 1986-. **ORGANIZATIONS:** Asian American Civic Association, board member; Association for Educational Communication & Technology; International Communication Industry Association; Emerson College Graduate Alumni Council; Newbury College, media advisory board; Commonwealth of Massachusetts Board of Regents of Higher Education, advisory council on affirmative action; Society for Applied Learning Technology. **HONORS/AWARDS:** WEEI AM-FM, Boston, Photography Contest, First Prize, 1976. **SPECIAL ACHIEVEMENTS:** Theory vs "Real Life" Instructional Media Design, 1982; Video Taping as a Viable Teaching Strategy in Education, 1980; proficient in Japanese & Spanish languages; producer, "China in the 80's," video program on location in China, 1986; producer, "Cuba's Progress in the 80's," video program on location in Cuba, 1988. **BUSINESS ADDRESS:** Adjunct Professor, International Technology Director, Boston College, Chestnut Hill, MA 02167, (617)552-4500.

SAJI, KIYOTAKA
Statistician. Japanese American. **PERSONAL:** Born May 30, 1942, Tokyo, Japan; son of Seima and Misao Saji; married Noboko Saji, Aug 20, 1966; children: Kenneth. **EDUCATION:** University of Florida, BS, 1965, MS, 1968; New York University, PhD, 1977. **CAREER:** Consultant; educator; IBM, senior statistician, currently. **ORGANIZATIONS:** American Statistical Assn. **SPECIAL ACHIEVEMENTS:** Develops math and statistical models for use in electronics packaging and manufacturing; implements statistical process control in electronics packaging and semiconductor manufacturing lines. **BUSINESS ADDRESS:** Senior Statistician, IBM, Rt 52, B/334, Hopewell Junction, NY 12533.

SAKAGAWA, RICHARD MASARU
Insurance company executive. Japanese American. **PERSONAL:** Born Nov 3, 1943, Honolulu, HI; son of Hiroshi Sakagawa and Beatrice Sakagawa; married Sharon A Sakagawa, Feb 4, 1967; children: Anten H, Taina M. **EDUCATION:** Colorado State University, BS, 1966, MEd, 1968. **CAREER:** The Capitol Life Insurance Co, actuarial student, 1968-71, reinsurance mgr, 1971-77, financial analyst, 1977-83, invt acctng and opr, mgr, 1983-84, investments, mgr, 1984-85, asst vice pres, 1985-89, vice pres, 1989-. **ORGANIZATIONS:** FLMI Society of Colorado, 1986-. **HONORS/AWARDS:** LOMA, FLMI, 1974. **BUSINESS ADDRESS:** Vice President, The Capitol Life Insurance Company, 1741 Cole Blvd, Ste 150, Golden, CO 80401, (303)273-9303.

SAKAI, MICHAEL H.
Manufacturing company executive, attorney. Japanese American. **PERSONAL:** Born Dec 27, 1950, Cleveland, OH; son of Hideo and Yoshiye Sakai; married Kathleen, Sep 26, 1980. **EDUCATION:** Ohio University, BBA, 1973; Cleveland Marshall College of Law, JD, 1978. **CAREER:** Hand Screw Machine Co, president, currently. **BUSINESS ADDRESS:** President, Hand Screw Machine Co., 17703 Pennsylvania Ave, Maple Heights, OH 44137, (216)475-0220.

SAKAI, VICTORIA K.
Dietitian. Japanese American. **PERSONAL:** Born Apr 14, 1943, Honolulu, HI; daughter of Mitsu Sakai and Sataro Sakai (deceased). **EDUCATION:** University of Hawaii, BS, 1965. **CAREER:** New York State Dept of Mental Hygiene, sr dietitian, 1966-69; ARA, supervising dietitian, 1969-72; Queen's Medical Ctr, food and nutritional services, director, currently. **ORGANIZATIONS:** Hawaii Dietetic Assn, 1977-; American Dietetic Assn, 1966-; Hawaii Society for Hospital Administrators, 1989-; Hawaii Foundation for Dietetics, president, 1992-93. **BUSINESS ADDRESS:** Director, Food and Nutritional Services, The Queen's Medical Center, 1301 Punchbowl St, Honolulu, HI 96813, (808)547-4255.

SAKAMOTO, ARTHUR, JR.
Educator. Japanese American. **PERSONAL:** Born Mar 30, 1959, New York, NY; son of Arthur & Charlene Sakamoto; married Meichu Chen, Jun 1, 1984; children: Arthur Hsiao-Ho. **EDUCATION:** Harvard College, BA (magna cum laude), economics, sociology, 1981; Sophia International University, Tokyo, Japan, 1983; University of Wisconsin, Madison, MS, sociology, 1985, PhD, sociology, 1988. **CAREER:** Numazu, Japan, English teacher, 1981-83; NICHHD Center for Demography & Ecology, trainee, 1983-88; University of Texas, Austin, assistant professor of sociology, 1989-94, associate professor of sociology, 1994-. **HOME ADDRESS:** 12406 Deer Falls Dr, #A, Austin, TX 78729-7204. **BUSINESS ADDRESS:** Associate Professor of Sociology, University of Texas, Austin, Burdine Hall 336, Austin, TX 78712-1088.

SAKAMOTO, CLYDE MITSURU
Educational administrator. Japanese American. **PERSONAL:** Born Jul 31, 1943, Honolulu, HI; son of Tadashi & Aiko Sakamoto; married Gerrianne, Mar 17, 1984. **EDUCATION:** University of Hawaii, BA, political science, 1965; Institute of World Affairs, 1965; University of Santa Clara Law School, 1966; University of Hawaii, MEd, 1987; George Washington University, EdD, 1987. **CAREER:** Peace Corps, India, volunteer, 1966-68; English Language Lab, director, instructor, 1969-70; International Language Institute, director, instructor, 1970-72; International Marketing Educators of the Pacific, vice president, 1972-75; Office of Senator Daniel K Inouye, congressional fellow, 1985-87; Office of International Services, American Association of Community and Junior Colleges, director, 1984-86; Maui Community College, dean of students, 1973-80, dean of instruction, 1973-90, provost, 1991-. **ORGANIZATIONS:** Maui Economic Development Board, 1990-; Hawaii Community Services Council, 1988-; Decisions Maui, co-chair, 1988-; ASK-2000, steering committee, 1990-; Maui Rehabilitation Center, board member, 1974-; Phi Kappa Phi, 1972-; Big Brothers of Maui, 1973-. **HONORS/AWARDS:** Maui Jaycees, Outstanding Young Educator Award, 1976. **SPECIAL ACHIEVEMENTS:** Exchange, editor, 1984-86; International Trade Education: Issues and Programs, 1985; The Next Challenge: Balancing International Competition and Cooperation, 1987. **BUSINESS ADDRESS:** Provost, Maui Community College, 310 Kaahumanu Ave, Kahului, HI 96732-2132, (808)242-1213.

SAKAMOTO, KATSUYUKI
Educational administrator. Japanese American. **PERSONAL:** Born Oct 24, 1938, Los Angeles, CA; son of Yoshio & Asako Sakamoto-Masui and Frank Masui (stepfather); married Edna C Sakamoto, Nov 27, 1967; children: David K, Bryce Y. **EDUCATION:** California State University, Fresno, BA, 1961, MA, 1968; Southern Illinois University, Carbondale, PhD, 1971. **CAREER:** Army Education Center, Munich, Germany, instructor, 1962-63; Fresno County Public Welfare, welfare officer, 1963-64; Salvation Army Men's Social Service Center, social worker, 1964-66; Keuka College, chair behavorial science, 1971-78; Eastern Oregon State College, associate dean academic affairs, 1978-85; Indiana University-East, vice chancellor academic affairs, 1985-91; California School of Professional Psychology, Alameda, chancellor, 1991-. **ORGANIZATIONS:** American Association of University Administrators, past vp, 1991-93; Rotary International-Alameda, 1991-; City of Alameda Library Board, 1991-; Asian American Psychological Association, president, 1987-91; American Association of Higher Education, 1985-; Whitewater Opera Board, president, 1990-91; Asian Community Mental Health Board, 1991-; American Psychological Association, 1991-. **HONORS/AWARDS:** USPHS, Special Doctoral Award, 1968-70; Southern Illinois University, Special Doctoral Award, 1971. **MILITARY SERVICE:** US Army, Spc4, 1961-63. **BUSINESS ADDRESS:** Chancellor, California School of Professional Psychology, Alameda, 1005 Atlantic Ave, Alameda, CA 94501, (510)521-4964.

SAKAMOTO, LYNN
City government official. Japanese American. **EDUCATION:** Los Angeles Harbor College; El Camino College; University of Southern California, journalism. **CAREER:** Los Angeles County Supervisor Kenneth Hahn, press deputy, 1987-93; City of Gardenia, director of public information, 1993-. **BUSINESS ADDRESS:** Director of Public Information, City of Gardena, 1700 W 162nd St, Gardena, CA 90247, (310)217-9500.*

SAKHARE, VISHWA M.
Educator. Indo-American. **PERSONAL:** Born Aug 28, 1932, Belgaum, Karnataka, India; son of M R Sakhare (deceased) and P M Sakhare; married Sheela V Sakhare, Dec 6, 1956; children: Raj, Ravi, Anil. **EDUCATION:** Karnatak University, India, B Sc, 1951; Cambridge University, BA, MA, 1954; University of Tennessee, PhD, 1973. **CAREER:** East Tennessee State University, professor, 1965-. **ORGANIZATIONS:** MAA, 1965-. **HOME ADDRESS:** 1623 Seward Drive, Johnson City, TN 37604, (615)929-2616.

SAKIMOTO, PHILIP JON
Government official, scientist. Japanese American. **PERSONAL:** Born Jan 21, 1954, Los Angeles, CA; son of Jimmy Sachio Sakimoto (deceased) and Amy Emi Sakimoto; married Susan Hubbard Sakimoto, Dec 31, 1988. **EDUCATION:** Pomona College, BA, physics, 1976; University of California, Los Angeles, MA, astronomy, 1977, PhD, astronomy, 1985. **CAREER:** Compton Community College, instructor, 1976-77; Terminal Island Federal Correctional Institution, instructor, 1978-79; University of California, Los Angeles, research associate, teaching fellow, 1979-85; Whitman College, visiting assistant professor, 1985-89; Johns Hopkins Space Grant Consortium, assistant director, 1989-90; NASA/Goddard Space Flight Center, university affairs officer, 1990-. **ORGANIZATIONS:** American Astronomical Society; Astronomical Society of the Pacific; Center for Theology and the Natural Sciences. **HONORS/AWARDS:** University of California, Los Angeles, Regents fellowship, 1976; NASA/Goddard Space Flight Center, summer faculty fellow, 1986; Phi Beta Kappa. **BUSINESS ADDRESS:** University Affairs Officer, NASA/GSFC, Code 160, Greenbelt, MD 20771, (301)286-8733.

SAKITA, BUNJI
Physicist, educator. Japanese American. **PERSONAL:** Born Jun 6, 1930, Inami, Toyama-ken, Japan; son of Eiichi Sakita and Fumi Morimatsu; divorced; children: Mariko Mozeson, Taro. **EDUCATION:** Kanazawa University, BS, 1953; Nagoya University, MS, 1956; University of Rochester, PhD, 1959. **CAREER:** University of Wisconsin, physics, assistant professor, 1963-64; Argonne National Laboratory, associate physicist, 1964-66; University of Wisconsin, professor, 1966-70; City College of New York, physics, distinguished professor, 1970. **ORGANIZATIONS:** American Physical Society, fellow. **HONORS/AWARDS:** Guggenheim, fellowship, 1970-71; Japan Society for Promotion of Science, fellowship, 1975, 1980, 1987; Nishina, prize, 1974. **SPECIAL ACHIEVEMENTS:** 100 publications in professional journals on the research of elementary particles physics. **BUSINESS ADDRESS:** Distinguished Professor of Physics, City College of New York, CUNY, Convent Ave & 138th St, Science Bldg, Rm 312, New York, NY 10031, (212)650-6888.

SAKODA, JAMES MINORU
Educator. Japanese American. **PERSONAL:** Born Apr 21, 1916, Lancaster, CA; son of Kenichi Sakoda & Tazu Kihara Sakoda; married Hatsuye Sakoda; children: William J. **EDUCATION:** University of California, Berkeley, AB, psychology, 1942, PhD, psychology, 1949. **CAREER:** University of California, Evacuation and Resettlement Study, research assistant, 1942-47; Brooklyn College, Department of Psychology, assistant professor, 1949-52; University of Connecticut, Department of Psychology, assistant professor, 1952-57, associate professor, 1957-62; Brown University, Department of Sociology, professor, 1962-81. **ORGANIZATIONS:** Friends of the Origami Center of America; Nippon Origami Association; British Origami Society. **HONORS/AWARDS:** First International Paper Airplane Contest, Origami Design Prize, 1967. **SPECIAL ACHIEVEMENTS:** Author: Modern Origami, Simon and Schuster, 1969. **BIOGRAPHICAL SOURCES:** Views From Within, Yuji Ichioka, UCLA, pp219-81, 1989. **HOME ADDRESS:** 411 County Rd, Barrington, RI 02806, (401)245-8779.

SAKURAI, FRED YUTAKA
Physician. Japanese American. **PERSONAL:** Born Jun 19, 1927, Tokyo, Japan; son of Kikuzo and Fumiko Sakurai; widowed; children: George, Jennifer. **EDUCATION:** Tokyo College, BS, 1948; Keio University Medical School, MD, 1952. **CAREER:** New York Medical College, Metropolitan Medical Center, residency in surgery; US Army Hospital, Fort MacArthur, chief of surgery, 1961; American Board of Surgery, 1961; Community Hospital of Gardena, chief of surgery, 1980, board of trustees, chairman, 1992, chief of staff, 1993; Fred Y Sakurai, MD, PC, president, currently. **ORGANIZATIONS:** International College of Surgeons, fellow; American Society of Abdominal Surgeons, fellow; American Academy of Family Physicians; American Medical Association; California Medical Association; LA County Medical Association; Japanese American Cultural & Community Centre, senior vice president, 1993-; Japanese Chamber of Commerce of Southern California, vice president, 1993-; Japan America Society, advisor, 1989-93; Chamber Music Society of Los Angeles, chairman, 1992-; Japan America Symphony Association, 1992-; Japanese American Medical Association, 1993. **HONORS/AWARDS:** Honored by the Japanese American Medical Association, 1993.

MILITARY SERVICE: US Army Medical Corps, major, 1959-62. **BUSINESS ADDRESS:** President, Fred Y Sakurai, MD, PC, 1141 W Redondo Beach Blvd, Suite 302, Gardena, CA 90247.

SALONGA, LEA
Actress. Filipino American. **PERSONAL:** Born 1971?; daughter of Ligaya Salonga. **CAREER:** Actress: Miss Saigon, lead female role of Kim; Les Miserables, role of Eponine, 1993; singer: Academy Awards, Whole New World, from the Aladdin soundtrack; concerts of a repertoire of Broadway hits from musicals; Atlantic Records, recording artist, 1992. **HONORS/AWARDS:** Museum of Modern Arts, sang the part of Jasmine for the Disney movie premiere of Aladdin; Tony Award, Miss Saigon, Best Actress in a Musical, 1991. **BUSINESS ADDRESS:** Actress, c/o William Morris Agency, 151 El Camino Dr, Beverly Hills, CA 90212, (310)274-7451.*

SALUJA, JAGDISH KUMAR (JACK)
Engineering company executive. Indo-American. **PERSONAL:** Born Jan 14, 1934, Jhelum, Pakistan; son of Kirpa Ram & Raksha Devi Saluja; married Subhashini (Guddie) Saluja, Jun 9, 1967; children: Sunil, Samir. **EDUCATION:** St Xavier College, India, BSc, physics, 1955; University of Michigan, BSE, 1957, BSE, mathematics, 1958, MSE, nuclear engineering, 1959; University of Florida, Gainesville, PhD, nuclear engineering, 1966. **CAREER:** Argonne National Lab, nuclear engineer, 1959-62; Westinghouse Electric, sr engineer, 1967-77; Vikinig Systems International, president & CEO, 1978-. **ORGANIZATIONS:** American Nuclear Society, 1959-; National Coal Association, 1989-; Society of Manufacturing Engineers, 1989-93. **HONORS/AWARDS:** Presidential Order of Merit, 1991; presidential commission conferred, 1986. **SPECIAL ACHIEVEMENTS:** Author: Considerations of Industrial & Agricultural Byproducts as Potential Energy Feedstocks to Displace Petroleum Fuels in the US, presented at International Energy Congress, Turkey, 1981; preparation of design operations and maintenance manuals and hazards report, Juggernaut Reactor, ANL, 1960, 1961, 1962; author: NERVA Flight Engine Control Systems Design, ANS Transactions, Oct 1971; preparation of an International Coal Data Base, DOE Report, 1986; development of environmentally acceptable and commercially viable technologies in the emerging national energy systems, presented at 3rd Intl Symposium on World Energy Sytems, Ukraine, 1993. **BIOGRAPHICAL SOURCES:** "Defense Contracting: Still a Good Offense," Technology, Aug, 1991; "Programmable Mobile Robot," India West, July 26, 1991. **BUSINESS ADDRESS:** President & CEO, Viking Systems International Inc, 2070 Wm Pitt Way, Pittsburgh, PA 15238, (412)826-3355.

SALUNKHE, DATTAJEERAO K.
Educator. Indo-American. **PERSONAL:** Born Nov 7, 1925, Kolhapur, Maharashtra, India; son of Mr & Mrs K D Salunkhe; married Urmilla, Apr 18, 1955; children: Kirti Bhonsle. **EDUCATION:** Poona University, India, BSc, 1949; Michigan State University, MS, 1951, PhD, 1953. **CAREER:** Utah State University, professor, 1953-90. **ORGANIZATIONS:** Institute of Food Technologists, 1955-. **HONORS/AWARDS:** IFT, Fellow, 1980. **SPECIAL ACHIEVEMENTS:** Author or co-author of over 400 scientific publications; author or co-author of 25 books. **BUSINESS ADDRESS:** Professor, Dept of Nutrition, Utah State University, Logan, UT 84322-8700, (801)750-2110.

SAMPANG, CONRADO CARRIEDO
Military official, educator, laboratory officer. Filipino American. **PERSONAL:** Born Jan 4, 1952, Baguio City, Philippines; son of Valeriano D Sampang Sr and Felisa G Sampang; married Georgie C Sampang, Jun 18, 1979; children: Bradnell-Shawn, Jazel-Marie, Darryl-Conrad. **EDUCATION:** George Washington University, AS, 1979; Norfolk State University, BSMT (cum laude), 1983; Golden Gate University, MPA, health serv mgt, 1988. **CAREER:** US Navy, med lab tech, 1973-83, Reserves, med lab tech, 1983-85; VA Bch Gen Hosp, staff, med tech, 1983, 1987, evening supervisor, 1987, 1989; US Army, Reserves, med tech, lab officer, 1985-89; SMG, Minot AFB, chief lab svcs, 1989, 1992; US Air Force, lab officer, captain, 1989-; 382 MTS/BTL, Sheppard AFB, intermediate supv, 1992-. **HONORS/AWARDS:** Alpha Kappa Mu, 1984. **MILITARY SERVICE:** US Air Force, Commendation Medal, 1992. **BUSINESS ADDRESS:** Intermediate Supervisor, 382 Medical Training Squadron/BTL, US Air Force, 917 Missile Rd, Ste 3, Sheppard AFB, TX 76311, (817)676-3871.

SANADI, D. R.
Scientist, administrator, educator. Indo-American. **PERSONAL:** Born Aug 8, 1920, Mangalore, Karnataka, India; son of Lakshman and Amba; married Mary

Jane, Mar 12, 1950; children: Clyde, Mara Wagner. **EDUCATION:** University of Madras, BS, (honors), 1941, MS, 1945; University of California, Berkeley, PhD, 1949. **CAREER:** University of Wisconsin, assistant professor, 1951-55; University of California, assistant professor, 1955-58; NIH, National Heart Institute, section chief, 1958-66; Harvard University Medical School, associate professor, 1975-; Boston Biomedical Res Institute, director, 1966-. **ORGANIZATIONS:** American Society Biol Chemistry, 1952-; American Chemical Society, 1950-; Gerontology Society, fellow, 1950-; AAAS, 1950-. **SPECIAL ACHIEVEMENTS:** Over 200 research articles in primary scientific journals; editor, Current Topics in Bioenergetics Research, 1966-83; editor, Journal of Bioenergetics, 1975-91, editorial board, 1989-; Archives Biochemistry and Biophys, 1970-76; NIH, Study Section, 1970-73; NIA, study section, 1974-75; Gordon Res Conf, chairman, 1969, 1974, 1975; NSF, Metabolic Biol Panel, 1971-74. **BUSINESS ADDRESS:** Director, Dept of Cell and Molecular Biology, Boston Biomed Research Institute, 20 Staniford St, Boston, MA 02114.

SANDHU, RANBIR SINGH
Educator. **PERSONAL:** Born Jan 19, 1928, Lyallpur, Punjab, Pakistan; married Surinder K Sandhu, Oct 4, 1957. **EDUCATION:** University of Punjab, Lahore, BA (with honors), mathematics, 1946; East Punjab University, Solan, BSc, (with honors), civil engineering, 1949; University of Sheffield, UK, MEng, 1962; University of California, Berkeley, PhD, 1968. **CAREER:** Irrigation Department, Punjab, assistant engineer, dep director, designs, sr design enr, 1950-63; Punjab Engineering College, associate professor, 1963-65; University of California, Berkeley, junior specialist, 1965-68; John A Blume Associates, senior engineer, 1968; Harza Engineering Co, senior engineer, 1968-69; Ohio State University, associate professor, 1969-73, professor, 1973-. **ORGANIZATIONS:** American Society of Civil Engineers, fellow, life member, 1961-. **HONORS/AWARDS:** Ohio State University, College of Engineering, MacQuigg Award for Distinguished Teaching, 1991, research award, 1989, Department of Civil Engineering, Lichtenstein Award for Faculty Excellence, 1984, 1991; University of Stuttgart, Germany, guest professor, 1980; Royal Norwegian Research Council, Senior Scientist Fellowship, 1977. **SPECIAL ACHIEVEMENTS:** Over 100 publications. **BUSINESS ADDRESS:** Professor, Dept of Civil Engineering, Ohio State University, 2070 Neil Ave, 470 Hitchcock Hall, Columbus, OH 43210, (614)292-7531.

SANDHU, SHINGARA SINGH
Educational administrator, educator. Indo-American. **PERSONAL:** Born Oct 10, 1932, Amritsar, Punjab, India; son of S Jagir Singh & Kartar K Sandhu; married Jind K Sandhu, Mar 13, 1960; children: Jeet, Manider, Neeta, Guri. **EDUCATION:** Punjab University, India, BS, 1952, MS, 1954; Utah State University, PhD, 1970. **CAREER:** Punjab Agricultural University, India, assistant professor, chemistry, lieutenant, ROTC, acquisition officer, Division of Chemistry, 1955-65; Claflin College, professor of chemistry, principal investigator, 1969-80, Natural Sciences and Mathematics Div, Dept of Chemistry, chairman, 1981-87, Division of Natural Sciences and Mathematics, chairman, 1987-93, director of research and grants, Distinguished Professor of Research, 1993-. **ORGANIZATIONS:** American Chemical Society, program chair, 1970-, SC committee, 1991-93; American Association for the Advancement of Science, 1971-80; Smithsonian Associate, 1973-78. **HONORS/AWARDS:** Delegation to People's Republic of China, International Environmental Health, 1992; Goal Five Task, National Education Goals Panel, co-leader, 1993; Claflin College, Presidential Citation, Leadership Award, 1993; SSETP Parents/Students Service, Dedication Award, 1990; 3rd Biennial Research Symposium, Best Paper Award, 1976; USU Logan, Research Fellowship Award, 1965. **SPECIAL ACHIEVEMENTS:** A total of 50 publications, five latest: "Degradation Mechanisms of Tetraphenylboron," symposium, 1993; "Effects of Leacheate from Coal-Ash Basins of Varying Age on Groundwater," 1993; "Leachability of Ni, Cd, Cr, and As from Coal Ash Impoundments," book chapter, 1992; "Trace Element Distributing in Various Phases of SRS Aquatic System," book chapter, 1992; "Mechanisms of Mobilization and Attenuation of Inorganic Pollutants," book chapter, 1991. **MILITARY SERVICE:** Indian Army Infantry, lieutenant, 1962-65. **BIOGRAPHICAL SOURCES:** Times and Democrat Daily, June, 1989, 1993. **BUSINESS ADDRESS:** Director of Research and Grants, Distinguished Professor of Research, Claflin College, College Ave, JST 125, Orangeburg, SC 29115.

SANDRAPATY, RAMACHANDRA RAO
Educator. Indo-American. **PERSONAL:** Born Feb 15, 1942, Eluru, Andhra Pradesh, India; son of Venkata Subbarao Sandrapaty and Annapoornamma Sandrapaty; married Kalyani K Sandrapaty, Apr 7, 1966; children: Ravichandra Kumar, Kiran Kumar. **EDUCATION:** Andhra University, India, BE, ME

(honors), 1963; University of Roorkee, India, ME, production & ind engg, 1965; University of South Carolina, MSME, 1971, PhD, 1974. **CAREER:** S G K R Mill-B, Eluru, India, business partner, 1965-66, production engineer, 1967-69; Central Mechanical Engineering, Research Institute, Durgapur, India, production div, project engineer, 1966-67; South Carolina State University, professor and chairman, 1973-. **ORGANIZATIONS:** Institute of Industrial Engineers; South Carolina Academy of Science SCSU representative; American Society of Mechanical Engineers; Air and Waste Management Association; American Society for Engineering Education; American Association of University Professors; South Carolina Technical Education Association; South Carolina Energy Research Institute, adjunct staff member. **HONORS/AWARDS:** Govt of India, Post-Matriculation Merit Scholar, 1957-63, Junior Research Fellow, 1963-65; South Carolina State University, Distinguished Faculty Chair, 1987, 1990, 1991. **SPECIAL ACHIEVEMENTS:** Language proficiency: Telugu, Hindi; publications: Assessment of After Treatment Devices for the Control of Diesel Particulate Matter, Cambridge, MA, 1980; "Parametric Study of Three-Dimensional Gas Turbine Combustor Model," Cleveland, Ohio, NASA, 1982; "On Production Policies for a Linearly Increasing Demand and Finite, Uniform Production Rate," Computers and Industrial Engineering, vol 18, no 2, pp 119-27, 1990; review panel for the US Dept of Energy, Historically Black Colleges & Universities, Nuclear Energy Training Program; ASEE Journal of Engineering Technology, reviewer. **HOME ADDRESS:** 2688 Lakeside Drive N E, Orangeburg, SC 29115-1814, (803)534-0552. **BUSINESS ADDRESS:** Professor & Chairman, South Carolina State University, 300 College Street N E, HC 102, POB #8164, Orangeburg, SC 29117-8164, (803)536-7164.

SANI, BRAHMA P.
Senior scientist. Indo-American. **PERSONAL:** Born Sep 13, 1937, Trichur, Kerala, India; son of B L Porinchu & T V Annam; married Alice Celine Sani, Nov 27, 1967; children: Anita Damian, Renju. **EDUCATION:** Saint Thomas College, Trichur, India, BS, 1960; Holkar Science College, Indore, India, MS, 1962; Indian Institute of Science, PhD, 1967; Retina Foundation, postdoctoral fellowship, 1968-71. **CAREER:** Indian Institute of Science, Bangalore, research scholar, 1962-67, senior research fellow, 1967-68; Retina Foundation, Boston, research fellow, 1968-71; Institute for Cancer Research, Pennsylvania, research associate, 1971-74; Southern Research Institute, Birmingham, AL, senior scientist, 1974-, section head, 1979-. **ORGANIZATIONS:** American Association Cancer Research, 1975-; American Society Biochemistry Molecular Biology, 1978-; Indian Association Cancer Research, 1991-; Human Tissue Procurement Comm, University of Alabama, Birmingham, 1978-86. **HONORS/AWARDS:** National Cancer Institute, research grant, 1975, 1977, 1985, 1992; World Health Organization, research grant, 1983-87; Tobacco Research Council, research grant, 1983-87; American Institute Cancer Research, research grant, 1994-97. **SPECIAL ACHIEVEMENTS:** Discovered a specific retinoic acid-binding protein that may mediate the cellular transport of retnoids to their nuclear acceptor sites, 1974; "Binding Affinities of Retinoids to Their Binding Proteins and Receptors, & Their Biological Activities," Retinoids: Progress in Research and Clinical Applications, pp 237-248, 1993. **BUSINESS ADDRESS:** Section Head and Senior Staff Scientist, Southern Research Institute, 2000 9th Ave S, Birmingham, AL 35255.

SAN JUAN, E.
Educator. Filipino American. **PERSONAL:** Born Dec 29, 1938, Manila, Philippines. **EDUCATION:** University of the Philippines, AB, 1958; Harvard University, PhD, 1965. **CAREER:** Brooklyn College, CUNY, professor of comparative literature, 1977-79; University of Connecticut, professor of English, 1967-. **ORGANIZATIONS:** National Association of Ethnic Scholars, 1992-93; International Gramsci Society; Modern Language Association of America. **HONORS/AWARDS:** Institute of Humanities, Fellow, 1993, University of Edinburgh; Fulbright Lectureship, 1987-88; Association for Asian American Studies, National Book Award, 1993; Gustavus Myers Center, Human Rights Award, 1993. **SPECIAL ACHIEVEMENTS:** The Arkansas Quarterly, advisory editor, 1991-; Nature, Society, Thought, associate editor, 1989-. **BUSINESS ADDRESS:** Professor, Dept of English, University of Connecticut, Storrs, CT 06268, (203)486-3273.

SANKARAN, AIYLAM P.
Financial planner. Indo-American. **PERSONAL:** Born Aug 1, 1939, Madras, India; married. **EDUCATION:** Oklahoma State University, MSIE, 1965; Polytechnic of NY, MSOR, 1976; Institute of Certified Financial Planners, CFP, 1987. **CAREER:** Strategic Financial Planning, owner, currently. **ORGANIZATIONS:** American Institute of Individual Investors; Intl Assn of Financial

Planners; Carnatic Music Assn of North America, patron. **HOME ADDRESS:** 24 Manor Ct, Glen Rock, NJ 07452, (201)447-3495.

SANTHANAM, RADHIKA
Educator. Indo-American. **PERSONAL:** Born Aug 27, 1959, Bombay, India; daughter of K V Santhanam & Vasantha Santhanam; married Krish Muralidhar, Jul 15, 1984; children: Pavitra Muralidhar. **EDUCATION:** University of Madras, India, BSc, 1978; University of Bombay, India, MMS, 1983; Texas A&M University, MS, 1986; University of Nebraska, PhD, 1989. **CAREER:** Florida International University, assistant professor, 1989-. **SPECIAL ACHIEVEMENTS:** Published research in several journals. **BUSINESS ADDRESS:** Asst Professor, Decision Sciences, Florida International University, College of Business, Miami, FL 33199-0400, (305)348-2160.

SANTOS, MARIO ALBAN
Estate planner, insurance company executive. Filipino American. **PERSONAL:** Born Oct 19, 1947, Manila, Philippines; son of Felix Arriola Santos and Maria Alban Santos; married Marylou Garlitos, Jun 16, 1971; children: Martia Garlitos. **EDUCATION:** Polytechnic University of the Philippines, BSc, advertising marketing, 1969; Ateneo Graduate School of Business, MBA, academics, 1978. **CAREER:** Polytechnic University of the Phils, college instructor, 1969-72; Mario A Santos & Associates, president, 1980-; Surety Life Insurance Co, regional director, 1989-. **ORGANIZATIONS:** Peninsula Association of Life Underwriters, board of directors, 1993-94; Filipino-American Lions of SF, board of directors, 1991-93, parliamentarian, 1992-93, bulletin editor, 1992-93; San Mateo County Human Relations Commission, commissioner, 1989-92; Life Underwriters Training Council, moderator, 1992-93. **HONORS/AWARDS:** Surety Life Insurance, Fast Start Regional Director, 1992, executive council, 1990; Polytechnic University of the Phils, Student Leader of the Year, 1969; Million Dollar Round Table, qualifying member, 1979. **SPECIAL ACHIEVEMENTS:** Concert singer, Tony Toledo Productions, 1989. **BUSINESS ADDRESS:** President, Mario A Santos & Associates, PO Box T, Daly City, CA 94017, (415)991-2217.

SARATHY, PARTHA R.
Engineering/technology manager. Indo-American. **PERSONAL:** Born Mar 18, 1942, Ranipet, Tamil Nadu, India; son of Komalam and Rangachari; married Padmaja, Aug 22, 1965; children: Shobita, Suhas. **EDUCATION:** Madras University, India, BSChE, 1963; Indian Institute of Science, MSChE, 1965; Leeds University, England, Diploma, chemical engineering, 1966, MPhil, 1968. **CAREER:** Oxley Engineering Group, chemical engineer, 1968-70; Procon Inc, senior process engineer, 1970-77; HRI Inc, manager of process analysis, 1977-87; Bechtel Inc, chief process engineer, 1987-90; John Brown Inc, manager of technology, 1990-93; ABS Consulting Services Inc, director, 1993-. **ORGANIZATIONS:** American Institute of Chemical Engineers, 1968-; American Chemical Society, 1993-. **SPECIAL ACHIEVEMENTS:** Numerous publications/presentations: Hydrocarbon Processing Magazine, Fuel Reformulation Magazine, American Institute of Chemical Engineers National Meetings, World Conference on Refinery Processing & Reformulated Gasoline, National Petroleum Refiners Association Annual Meeting, 1977-. **HOME ADDRESS:** 4805 Valerie St, Bellaire, TX 77401-5705, (713)432-0825.

SARIN, HARRY C.
Engineer. **PERSONAL:** Born Oct 4, Amritsar, India. **EDUCATION:** Institution of Mechanical Engineers, London, chartered engineer, 1956; Institution of Chemical Engineers, London, GI chem eng, 1969. **CAREER:** Sarin and Son, Inc, president, currently. **ORGANIZATIONS:** NASA-LBJ Space Ctr, president, coordinating of bldg 2 activities; Shell Chemical Co, president, coordinated effluent facilities; W R Grace, Deer Park, president, coordinator, system hydraulics. **SPECIAL ACHIEVEMENTS:** Wisconsin Society of Prof Engineers, PE, mech eng, 1970; Texas State Bd of Prof Engineers, PE, chem eng, 1989. **BUSINESS ADDRESS:** President, Sarin and Son, 7900 North Stadium Dr, Ste 56, Houston, TX 77030, (713)795-4414.

SARKAR, FAZLUL H.
Educator. Indo-American. **PERSONAL:** Born Jan 26, 1952, Naroshingapur, W. Bengal, India; son of Patanuddin Sarkar and Allaya Sarkar; married Arfatun H Sarkar, Apr 3, 1983; children: Sarah, Sanila H. **EDUCATION:** Calcutta University, BS, 1971; Aligarh Muslim University, MS, 1974; Banaras Hindu University, PhD, 1978. **CAREER:** Memorial Sloan Kettering Cancer, Center, research associate, 1978-84; Oakland University, assistant professor, 1984-86; Oxford Biomedical, director of research, 1986-88; Henry Ford Hospital, tumor biology, director, 1988-90; Harper Hospital, molecular biology, director,

1990-; Wayne State University, associate professor, 1990-. **ORGANIZA-TIONS:** American Association of Cancer Research, 1988-; New York Academy of Science, 1979-; American Society for Biochemistry and Molecular Biology, 1989-; American Association for the Advancement of Science, 1989-. **HONORS/AWARDS:** National Institutes of Health, funded grants, 1988-. **SPECIAL ACHIEVEMENTS:** Seventy-five research articles and book chapters, 1975-. **BUSINESS ADDRESS:** Associate Professor, School of Medicine, Wayne State University, 540 E Canfield Ave, 9374 Scott Hall, Detroit, MI 48201, (313)745-1418.

SARKAR, NITIS (NITISH SIRCAR)
Research scientist. Indo-American. **PERSONAL:** Born Dec 1, 1938, Guwahati, Assam, India; son of Srish Chandra Sarkar (deceased) and Nalini Prova Sarkar; married Chandana Sarkar, Jan 18, 1970; children: Richik, Prateek. **EDUCATION:** University of Gauhati, BSc (honors), 1957; University of Calcutta, MSc, tech, 1960; Massachusetts Institute of Technology, ScD, 1965. **CAREER:** Dow Chemical Company, associate scientist, 1965-. **ORGANIZATIONS:** American Chemical Society, 1970-; Society of Rheology, 1991-. **HONORS/AWARDS:** Dow Chemical Company, Michigan Division, R&D Scientists, Scientists Award, 1983. **SPECIAL ACHIEVEMENTS:** Publications: "Structural Interpretation of the Interfacial Properties of Aqueous Solutions of Methycellulose and Hydroxypropyl Methylcellulose," Polymer, vol 25, pp 481-486, 1984; co-author, "Utilizing Cellulose Ethers as Suspension Agents in the Polymerization of Vinyl Chloride," J. Vinyl Technology, vol 13, no 2, p26, 1991; patents: co-holder, Water Insoluble, Crosslinked Sulfonated Aromatic Polyamide, no 4,824,916, 1989, Water Soluble Aromatic Polyamides and Polyureas, no 4,895,660, 1990; several other publications and patents. **HOME ADDRESS:** 4507 Oakridge Dr, Midland, MI 48640, (517)839-0476. **BUSINESS ADDRESS:** Associate Scientist, Dow Chemical Company, 1604 Bldg, Midland, MI 48674, (517)636-2163.

SARKAR, SANTANU KUMAR
Mechanical engineer. Indo-American. **PERSONAL:** Born Oct 31, 1942, Calcutta, W. Bengal, India; son of Kali Das Sarkar (deceased) and Bimala Sarkar (deceased); married Bhabani, Dec 8, 1971; children: Sanjib, Sumit. **EDUCATION:** Jadavpur University, Calcutta, India, BSME, 1965. **CAREER:** Phillips Petroleum, process engr, 1973-74; Bechtel, mech engr, 1974-75; Vitok, mech engr, 1975-77; MW Kellogg, equipment engr, 1977-79; Catalytic, supervising engr, 1979-85; Day Engineering Co, mech engr I, 1985-. **HONORS/AWARDS:** State of Kentucky, Professional Engineer, 1975; State of Texas, Professional Engineer, 1978. **HOME ADDRESS:** 5624 Ryder Ave, Charlotte, NC 28226, (704)541-3451.

SARKER, BHABA RANJAN
Educator. Bangladeshi American. **PERSONAL:** Born Jan 1, 1949, Dasmina, Barisal, Bangladesh; son of Manoranjan Sarker & Bakul Prova Sarker; married Lopa M Sarker, Jul 7, 1982; children: Joyatee M, Aneek Uttam. **EDUCATION:** University of Dhaka, Bangladesh, BA, math, 1972; Bangladesh University of Engineering & Technology, BScEng, 1974; Indian Institute of Technology, Kharagpur, India, MTech, 1976; Syracuse University, MS, 1979, ind engineer, 1982; Texas A&M University, PhD, 1989. **CAREER:** Oklahoma State University, research assistant, 1981-82; World Bank, systems analyst, 1983; University of Oklahoma, research assistant, 1983-84; Centralia College, instructor, 1984-85; University of Texas, instructor, 1986-87; Texas A&M University, assistant professor, 1989-90; Louisiana State University, assistant professor, 1990-. **ORGANIZATIONS:** Operations Research Society of America, 1980-; Institute of Industrial Engineers, 1980-; Institute of Management Science, 1980-; Decision Science Institute, 1989-; Production and Operations Management Society, 1990-; American Association of Bangladesh Engineers, 1990-. **HONORS/AWARDS:** Institute of Industrial Engineers, Best Dissertation Award, 1991; Production & Operations Management Society, Best Dissertation Award, 1990; Decision Science Institute, Best Dissertation Award, 1990; Louisiana State University, Baton Rouge, IE Professor of the Year, 1992, Dean's Citation for Teaching Excellence, 1991; Texas A&M University, Most Valuable Professor, 1989. **SPECIAL ACHIEVEMENTS:** IIE Transactions, associate editor; Production Planning & Control, member of the editorial board; Production & Operations Management, member of the review board; reviewer of more than ten journals; published more than 40 refereed articles in many journals. **MILITARY SERVICE:** US Army Corps of Engineers, Mobility Systems Div, civilian, Waterways Experiment Station, summer 1993, summer faculty fellowship, 1993. **BUSINESS ADDRESS:** Asst Prof, Dept of Industrial & Manufacturing Systems Engineering, Louisiana State University, 3128 CEBA Bldg, Baton Rouge, LA 70803-6409, (504)388-5370.

SARKER, BIMAL. *See* Obituaries.

SASAHARA, ARTHUR ASAO
Physician, educator. Japanese American. **PERSONAL:** Born May 11, 1927, Del Ray, CA; son of Harold Hango Sasahara and Blanche Yukiye Takayama; married Alice Guenther Sasahara, Apr 2, 1955; children: Ann Mariko Sasahara-Lane, Claire Michiko, Ellen Reiko, Karen Hideko, Mark Tadao. **EDUCATION:** Oberlin College, AB, 1951; Case-Western Reserve University School of Medicine, MD, 1955. **CAREER:** West Roxbury Veterans Administration Medical Center, medicine, asst chief, cardiopulmonary laboratory, chief, cardiology, chief, 1960-74; Brockton/West Roxbury Veterans Affairs Medical Ctr, Veterans Administration, medical service, chief, 1974-87; Harvard Medical School, professor of medicine, 1974-; Brigham and Women's Hospital, sr physician, 1982-; Abbott Laboratories, thrombolytics research, senior venture head, 1987-. **ORGANIZATIONS:** American Heart Assn, Boston Chapter, board of directors, 1962-78, exec committee, 1967-74, president, 1971-73, Council on Thrombosis, exec committee, 1971-75; Veterans Administration, chiefs of medicine advisory group, chmn, 1979-80, District I chiefs of medicine committee, chmn; National Heart, Lung and Blood Institute, thrombosis advisory board, 1972-76, task force on respiratory diseases, consultant, 1972-74; fellow: American College of Physicians, American College of Cardiology, American College of Chest Physicians; International Society of Thrombosis; International Society for Fibrinolysis and Thrombolysis. **HONORS/AWARDS:** Alpha Omega Alpha Honor Medical Society, 1955; The Hamann Honor Medical Society, Case Western Reserve University, 1955; Harvard University, Honorary AM Degree, 1982. **SPECIAL ACHIEVEMENTS:** Author, Pulmonary Embolic Disease, Grune & Stratton Inc, 1965; Pulmonary Emboli, Grune & Stratton Inc, 1975; 300 scientific articles. **MILITARY SERVICE:** US Army Medical Department, sgt, 1945-47. **BIOGRAPHICAL SOURCES:** Reflections and Reminiscences of an Academic Physician, p 42, 207, Lea and Febiger, 1993; Fibrinolysis, Thrombosis and Hemostasis, p 101, Lea and Febiger, 1992. **HOME ADDRESS:** 1094 Linda Lane, Glencoe, IL 60022. **BUSINESS PHONE:** (708)937-8933.

SASAKI, BETTY GAIL
Educator. Japanese American. **PERSONAL:** Born Aug 20, 1957, Reedley, CA; daughter of Viola and George Sasaki. **EDUCATION:** Universidad Complutense, Madrid, Spain, 1978-79; University of California, Santa Barbara, BA, Spanish, Portuguese, 1981; University of California, Berkeley, MA, 1983, PhD, 1992. **CAREER:** UC Berkeley, teaching associate, Spanish, 1981-87; College of Preparatory School, Spanish teacher, 1987-91; Colby College, assistant professor, 1991-. **ORGANIZATIONS:** Modern Language Association, 1991-; Midwest Modern Lang Assn, 1992-; American Assn of University Women, 1993. **HONORS/AWARDS:** Colby College, Humanities Research/Travel Grant, 1992, 1993. **SPECIAL ACHIEVEMENTS:** Dissertation: "The Artifice of Ethics: Reading Strategies in Seventeenth Century Spanish Poetry," 1992; language proficiency: Spanish and Portuguese. **HOME ADDRESS:** 47 Redington St, #3, Waterville, ME 04901. **BUSINESS ADDRESS:** Asst Professor of Spanish, Dept of Romance Languages and Literatures, Colby College, Waterville, ME 04901, (207)872-3121.

SASAKI, CHIYO KATANO
Nursing educator (retired). Japanese American. **PERSONAL:** Born Jun 2, 1925, Delano, CA; daughter of Fuku Yamaguchi & Ryuzo Harry Katano; children: Kenneth Michael, David Edward. **EDUCATION:** St Mary's School of Nursing, Quincy, IL, RN, 1947; Loyola University, Chicago, BSN, 1952; UCLA, MSNEd, 1964. **CAREER:** Michael Reese Hospital, Chicago, staff nurse, 1949-52; Mercy Hospital, Urbana, clinical instructor, head nurse pediatric unit, 1952-55; Riverside Community College, assistant professor of nursing, 1977-84, associate professor of nursing, 1984-91. **ORGANIZATIONS:** California Nurses Association, district finance committee, 1975-93; California Teachers Association, 1975-91; JACL, charter member, scholarship committee chair, recording secretary, 1968-93; Habitat for Humanity, selection committee, 1991-92; Hospice Riverside, volunteer, 1983-90; Calvary Presbyterian Church, mothers council, newsletter editor, 1959-93, Sunday school teacher, Deacon; North High School, PTA, health committee, recording secretary, board member, 1979-83; Highland Elementary School, PTA, health committee, 1977-78. **HONORS/AWARDS:** Riverside JACL, Certificate of Appreciation Founding Chair Education Committee, 1976; Riverside Community College, President's Grant Program, Instructional Development Grant, 1989; Employment Training, Chancellor's Office, Sacramento, Vocational Instructor and Career Counselor In-Service Training Project, 1986; Association Students of RCC, Outstanding Advisor, 1987; RCC Recognintion of Outstanding Service,

Certificate of Excellence, 1987, 1990; RCC Club Advisor, Outstanding Achievement Award, 1987, 1989. **BIOGRAPHICAL SOURCES:** Teaching Excellence at RCC, p 17, 1990; RCC Commencement, p 10, 1991. **HOME ADDRESS:** 2664 Laramie Rd, Riverside, CA 92506.

SASAKI, DALE I.
Attorney. Japanese American. **PERSONAL:** Born Feb 21, 1948, San Jose, CA; son of George Sasaki and Toshiko Sasaki; married Mary M Sasaki, Jun 29, 1972; children: Darla M, Russell K. **EDUCATION:** San Jose State University, BA, 1970, MS, 1972; Santa Clara University, JD, 1982. **CAREER:** Sasaki & Knopf, attorney, 1982-. **ORGANIZATIONS:** San Jose Japanese Community Youth Services, 1989-; Santa Clara County Planned Parenthood, 1991-; Planned Parenthood Advocates, 1992-; San Jose Taiko, 1991-; San Jose Zebras, 1991-; Santa Clara County Bar Association, 1982-; American Bar Association, 1983-92; Wesley United Methodist Church Endowment Committee, 1991-. **BUSINESS ADDRESS:** Attorney, Sasaki & Knopf, 4 N Second St, Ste 1215, San Jose, CA 95113-1307, (408)993-8777.

SASAKI, HIDEO
Landscape architect, educator. Japanese American. **PERSONAL:** Born Nov 25, 1919, Reedley, CA; son of Kaichiro Sasaki and Kiyome Ogasawara; married Kisa Noguchi Sasaki, Dec 23, 1951; children: Rin, Ann. **EDUCATION:** Reedley Junior College, AA, 1939; University of California, Los Angeles, Berkeley, 1939-41; University of Illinois, BFA (highest honors), 1946; Harvard Graduate School of Design, MLA, 1948. **CAREER:** University of Illinois, dept of landscape architecture, instructor, assistant professor, 1948-50; Harvard Graduate School of Design, dept of landscape architecure, professor, chairman, 1950-68; Sasaki Associates Inc, president, chairman of board, 1954-80. **ORGANIZATIONS:** US COmmission of Fine Arts, appointed by Presidents John F Kennedy and Lyndon Johnson, 1961-71; John F Kennedy Memorial Library, advisory committee on arts and architecture, 1964-65; Harvard Graduate School of Design, visiting committee, 1981-86; University of Colorado, design review board, 1961-; University of Arizona, design review board, 1982-89; University of California, design review board, 1989-91; ASLA, fellow; Vietnam Memorial Competition, juror, 1981; Astronaut Memorial Competition, juror, 1989. **HONORS/AWARDS:** ASLA, ASLA Medal, 1971; AIA, Allied Professions Medal, 1973; Arizona State University, Centennial Medal, Citation for Contributions to Excellence of Design, 1989; University of Colorado, Award for Urban Design, 1984; Asian American Architects & Engineers Assn, Outstanding Achievement Award, 1993; numerous honorary degrees from various universities. **BIOGRAPHICAL SOURCES:** Contemporary Architects, St Martins Press, MacMillan, p 709-710, 1990. **HOME ADDRESS:** 4 Mount View Lane, Lafayette, CA 94549. **BUSINESS PHONE:** (617)926-3300.

SASAKI, RAYMOND TOSHIAKI, JR.
Fashion director/coordinator. Japanese American. **PERSONAL:** Born Aug 13, 1944, Honolulu, HI; son of Raymond Toshiaki Sasaki and Mildred Tatsuko Sasaki. **EDUCATION:** Princeton, MBA, 1968. **CAREER:** Producer, director, coordinator, commentator for fashion shows and fashion events; fashion consultant; fashion writer; ADR Productions Inc, ADR Model & Talent Agency, president, currently. **ORGANIZATIONS:** Hawaii Fashion Industry Assn, board director, 1992-94; Hawaii Film and Video Assn, scy, board director, 1993. **HONORS/AWARDS:** California Fashion Creators, World Award, Globe Award, 1983. **SPECIAL ACHIEVEMENTS:** Governor's fashion director for promotions overseas, 1982-. **HOME ADDRESS:** 2350 Makiki Heights Dr, Honolulu, HI 96822.

SASAKI, RUTH A.
Writer. Japanese American. **PERSONAL:** Born Oct 31, 1952, San Francisco, CA; daughter of Shigeru Sasaki and Tomiko Sasaki. **EDUCATION:** University of Kent, Canterbury, 1972-73; University of California, Berkeley, BA, English, 1974; San Francisco State University, MA, English/creative writing, 1988. **CAREER:** Author, works include: The Loom and Other Stories, Graywolf Press, 1991; "Harmony," Story Magazine, 1993; short fiction has appeared on NPR's "Selected Shorts," 1994, and in numerous anthologies including Growing Up Asian-American, 1993, Making Waves, 1989, and Growing Up Female, 1993. **HONORS/AWARDS:** Pushcart Press, Pushcart Prize, for The Loom, reprinted in Pushcart Prize XVII: Best of the Small Presses, 1992; 1992; American Japanese National Literary Award, 1983. **BIOGRAPHICAL SOURCES:** "Weaving Traces, "The World & I, Washington Times, pp 346-350, March 1992; "Loom Weaves Stories about Japanese-American Experience," Oakland Tribune, p 11, Dec 8, 1991; "Threads

from the Immigrant's Loom," San Francisco Chronicle, Review section, p 4, Feb 16, 1992; Multicultural Review, vol 1, no 1, 1992; "Fashioned Out of Silence," Intersect, pp 28-30, Oct 1992; "A Talent for Battling Cultural Amnesia," San Jose Mercury News, June 28, 1992; "Growing Up Japanese or American?," American Book Review, Oct-Nov 1992; "A New Generation of Writers," Pacific Citizen, Jan 3-10, 1992; "Sansei Author Writes from Experience," Northwest Nikkei, Jan 1992. **HOME ADDRESS:** 1500 C Cedar St, Berkeley, CA 94703. **BUSINESS ADDRESS:** Author, Graywolf Press, 2402 University Ave, Ste 203, St Paul, MN 55114, (612)641-0077.

SASSA, SHIGERU
Biochemist. Japanese American. **PERSONAL:** Born Mar 3, 1935, Tokyo, Japan; son of Heiji Sassa and Fuki Sassa; married Reiko Sassa, Nov 10, 1963; children: Junko, Osamu. **EDUCATION:** University of Tokyo, MD, 1961, PhD, 1966. **CAREER:** Cornell University Medical College, lecturer, 1976-88, adjunct associate professor, 1983-; Rockefeller University, associate professor/physician, currently. **HONORS/AWARDS:** Health Research Council of NY, career scientist, 1973-75; American Cancer Society, research grant, 1974-77; US Public Health Service, research grant, 1970-; American Porphyria Foundation, research grant, 1992-. **SPECIAL ACHIEVEMENTS:** Approximately 250 publications related to the biology of heme biosynthesis, gene defects of heme biosynthesis. **BUSINESS ADDRESS:** Head of Laboratory (Biochemical Hematology), Rockefeller University, 1230 York Ave, New York, NY 10021, (212)327-8497.

SATHYAVAGISWARAN, LAKSHMANAN
Physician. Indo-American. **PERSONAL:** Born Mar 17, 1949, Madras, India; son of Brig L S Easwaran (deceased) and Ashokam S Easwaran; married Vijay Lakshmanan, Aug 1978; children: Ashwini Lakshmanan. **EDUCATION:** Loyola College, Madras University, 1965; Madras University, Stanley Medical College, India, 1971. **CAREER:** Training, Stanley Hospital, India, rotating intern, 1971-72; Jewish Hospital of Brooklyn, medical intern, 1972-73; Columbia University, St Luke Hospital, anatomic & clinical pathology, 1973-77; Brooklyn Cumberland Hospital, senior residency in medicine, 1980-81; Harlem Hospital, Columbia University, fellow, infectious disease, 1981-82; King Drew Medical Center, fellow, infectious disease, 1982-83; Los Angeles County, Coroner Office, forensice pathology training, 1977-78, medical examiner, 1977-. **ORGANIZATIONS:** College of American Pathologists, fellow; Infectious Disease Society of America; American Academy of Forensic Sciences, fellow; American College of Physicians, fellow; Royal College of Physicians and Surgeons of Canada, Division of Medicine; National Academy of Sciences, Institute of Medicine, 1993, committee member. **HONORS/AWARDS:** Government Stanley Medical College, Madras University, Prizes in Surgery, Medicine, Forensic Medicine and Preventive Medicine, Gold Medal in Anatomy, Honor Certificates in Physiology, Bacteriology, Pharmacology, Anatomy and Forensic Medicine; Indian Medical Association of Southern California, Distinguished Physician Award, 1992. **SPECIAL ACHIEVEMENTS:** 16 sessions and abstracts; 9 publications; licensure/board certification: New York, MD, 1975, California, physician/surgeon, 1976; American Board of Pathology; Canadian Royal College of Physicans/Surgeons, certification in pathology, 1979; internal medicine, 1983; geriatric medicine, 1992; American Board of Internal Medicine. **BIOGRAPHICAL SOURCES:** "New Coroner," LA Times, page 1, Feb 12, 1992; "New Coroner Moves into Office," County Digest, p1, 3, April 6, 1992. **BUSINESS ADDRESS:** Medical Examiner/Coroner, County of Los Angeles, 1104 N Mission Rd, Los Angeles, CA 90033, (213)343-0522.

SATO, FREDERICK AKIRA
Computer programmer, computer systems analyst. Japanese American. **PERSONAL:** Born Feb 21, 1946, Los Angeles, CA; son of Anthony Tokuye Sato and Fusako Sally Sato; married Bobbie Yuriko Sato, Mar 6, 1976; children: Erick Yoshiharu. **EDUCATION:** El Camino College, AA, 1966; California State University at Long Beach, BS, IT, 1969. **CAREER:** Rockwell International, B-1 Div, sr mfg engr, 1972-77, master scheduler, 1977-81, sr mgt systems analyst, 1981-83, programmer analyst, 1983-84; Northrop, B-2 Div, sr programmer analyst, 1984-90, database administrator, 1990-91, project leader, 1991-. **ORGANIZATIONS:** Natl Management Assn, 1976-84, board of directors, treasurer, 1979-81; American Society for Metals, 1966-70; Japanese-American League, 1966-70. **HONORS/AWARDS:** Natl Management Assn, Booster Honor Award, 1979. **SPECIAL ACHIEVEMENTS:** Completion of the workshop for NMA instructors, 1978. **MILITARY SERVICE:** US Army, spf-4, 1969-71. **HOME ADDRESS:** 21122 Woodland Court, Walnut, CA 91789-5005.

SATO, GARY TERUO
Chiropractor. Japanese American/Chinese American/Filipino American. **PERSONAL:** Born Jan 2, 1955, Honolulu, HI; son of Richard Sato and Elissa Sato; married Sandra K Rasmussen, Mar 27, 1993; children: Andrew Ryan. **EDUCATION:** Santa Monica College, 1973-74; University of CA Santa Barbara, 1974-77; Pepperdine University, BS, kinesiology, 1978; Los Angeles College of Chiropractic, DC, 1992. **CAREER:** USA Olympics, Volleyball, asst men's volleyball coach, 1985-88, 1992; self-employed, chiropractor, currently. **ORGANIZATIONS:** American Chiropractic Association, 1993; US Volleyball Association. **HONORS/AWARDS:** Federation of International Volleyball, Most Valuable Coach, World Cup, 1985. **SPECIAL ACHIEVEMENTS:** Two time USA Olympic coach, 1988, 1992. **BUSINESS ADDRESS:** Chiropractor, Billauer-Sato Chiropractic, 1027 Swarthmore Ave, Pacific Palisades, CA 90272, (310)459-4600.

SATO, IRVING SHIGEO
Educator, educational administrator. Japanese American. **PERSONAL:** Born Sep 4, 1933, Honolulu, HI; son of Jusaku Sato (deceased) and Matsuyo Uchida Sato; married Helen Hatsuko Sato, Aug 18, 1956. **EDUCATION:** University of Hawaii, BE, education, 1955, fifth-year diploma, education, 1960; University of Southern California, MS, 1962. **CAREER:** Hawaii Dept of Education, classroom teacher, 1957-58; Pasadena City Schools, California, classroom teacher, dept chairman, 1958-66; Colorado Dept of Education, gifted and creative student programs, consultant, 1966-68; California Dept of Education, education of mentally gifted, consultant, 1968-72; Ventura County Schools, National/State Leadership Training Institute on Gifted and Talented, director, 1972-93; IDEAS Unlimited Inc, director, 1993-. **ORGANIZATIONS:** Phi Delta Kappa, national educational fraternity, 1955-92; Council of State Directors of Programs for the Gifted, 1966-, president, 1969-71; The Association of the Gifted, 1964-94, Standing Committee, chairman, 1970-71; California Association for the Gifted, 1970-94; National Association for Gifted Children, 1975-; Association for Supervision and Curriculum Development, 1981-; World Council on the Gifted, 1975-; member of the following advisory boards: Torrance Studies for Gifted, Creative, and Future Behaviors, 1984-; Gifted Children's Association of San Fernando Valley, 1970-82; Gifted Children's Association of Los Angeles, 1968-77. **HONORS/AWARDS:** Phi Kappa Phi, 1954; National Association or Gifted Children, Citation of Merit, 1973; State of Louisiana, Honorary Colonel, 1974; State of Kentucky, Honorary Colonel, 1975-; US Office of Education, Office of Gifted and Talented, Certificate of Recognition, 1974; California Association for the Gifted, Educator of the Year, 1976; Association for the Gifted, Certificate of Appreciation, 1982; National Association for Gifted Children, Distinguished Service Award, 1982; California Association for the Gifted Children, Ruth Martinson Memorial Past Presidents' Award, 1987; Consortium of Ohio Coordinators for the Gifted, Honorary Member, 1992; Colorado Academy of the Gifted, Talented and Creative, Honorary Member, 1992; Texas Association for the Gifted, President's Award, 1992; New Jersey Association for Gifted and Talented, Special Award, 1994. **SPECIAL ACHIEVEMENTS:** Author: "N/S-LTI-G/T From the 1970's into the 1990's: Upgrading the Education of the Gifted/Talented through Human Resources Development," 1993; "Problems in the Development of Programs and Science Curricula for Student Gifted/Talented Areas Other than Science," NSTA Yearbook, 1989; editor: Realms of Meaning, by Philip Phenix, 1986; coeditor, with James J. Gallagher & Sandra N Kaplan: Promoting the Education of the Gifted Talented: Strategies for Advocacy, 1983. **MILITARY SERVICE:** Medical Service Corps, 1st lt, 1955-57. **HOME ADDRESS:** 1744 Via Del Rey, South Pasadena, CA 91030, (213)257-0702. **BUSINESS PHONE:** (213)257-0702.

SATO, KEIKO
Musician. Japanese American. **PERSONAL:** Born Jan 28, 1959, Tokyo, Japan; daughter of Eiichi & Atsuko Sato; married Ohad Bar-David, Sep 11, 1988; children: Benjamin, Erika. **EDUCATION:** Curtis Institute, BM, 1982; Yale University, MM, 1985. **CAREER:** Yale University, jr faculty, 1985-87; Curtis Institute, currently. **BUSINESS ADDRESS:** Musician, Curtis Institute of Music, 1726 Locust St, Philadelphia, PA 19103, (215)893-5252.

SATO, MASAHIKO
Biologist. Japanese American. **PERSONAL:** Born Aug 19, 1955, Kyoto, Japan; son of Hidemi and Yukiko Sato; married Joan Sato, Sep 1, 1979; children: Michael, Amy. **EDUCATION:** University of Pennsylvania, BA, 1978; Dartmouth, PhD, 1983. **CAREER:** Merck, research fellow, 1986-91; Eli Lilly and Company, senior cell biologist, 1991-. **ORGANIZATIONS:** American Society for Cell Biology, 1981-; American Society for Bone and Mineral

Research, 1986-; Microscopy Society of America, 1987-. **HONORS/AWARDS:** Dartmouth, Nathan Jenks Award, 1979, Albert Cass Award, 1982; NIH Trainee, MBL physiology course and post course, 1980; Muscular Dystrophy Association, Johns Hopkins School of Medicine, post doc fellow, 1985-86. **SPECIAL ACHIEVEMENTS:** Characterization of visco-elastic properties of living cells and cytoplasmic proteins, 1983-88; characterization of mechanisms important in osteoclastic resorption of bone, 1989-. **BUSINESS ADDRESS:** Senior Cell Biologist, Dept Skeletal Diseases, Eli Lilly and Company, MC 620, Indianapolis, IN 46285, (317)276-8046.

SATO, PAUL TOSHIO
Educator, computer scientist. Japanese American. **PERSONAL:** Born Aug 22, 1932, Yokohama, Kanagawa-ken, Japan; son of Shigezo and Kikuyo; married Mariko, May 12, 1958. **EDUCATION:** Aoyama Gakuin University, Tokyo, Japan, BA, 1960, MA, 1964; Harvard University, PhD, 1977. **CAREER:** Harvard University, teaching fellow in linguistics, 1970-72; Boston University, lecturer of Japanese, 1972-76; University of Massachusetts, Amherst, visiting instructor of Japanese linguistics, 1976-78; Occidental College, associate professor of Japanese, 1978-85; Widner Communications Corp, computational linguist, 1985-87; North Central College, assoc prof of computer science & linguistics, 1987-. **ORGANIZATIONS:** Association for Computational Linguistics; Association for Computing Machinery; Linguistic Society of America. **HONORS/AWARDS:** US State Dept, Fulbright-Hays All-Expense Grant, 1966-67; ACLS, Fellowship in Linguistics, 1967. **SPECIAL ACHIEVEMENTS:** Over 40 papers and articles in academic and professional journals; "A Common Parsing Scheme for Left- and Right-Branching Languages," Computational Linguistics, 14:1, p20-30, 1988. **HOME ADDRESS:** 925 Springhill Dr, Northbrook, IL 60062. **BUSINESS ADDRESS:** Professor of Computer Science and Linguistics, North Central College, 30 N Brainard St, Naperville, IL 60566-7063, (708)420-3400.

SATO, SHIGETADA
Architect. Japanese American. **PERSONAL:** Born Jun 19, 1940, Tokyo, Japan; son of Shigeyuki Sato and Chitose Sato; married Nobuko Sato, Sep 1, 1973; children: Masanao. **EDUCATION:** Kogakuin University, architecture, 1966. **CAREER:** Weiss Whelan Edelbaum Webster Architects, 1970-74; Joseph Fuchida Architects, 1974-76; Swanke Hayden Connell Architects, designer, 1976-77; Marcel Breuer Associates, designer, 1977-82; Atelier-254 New York, Inc, president, 1982-. **ORGANIZATIONS:** Japanese Community Club, committee member, 1982-. **HOME ADDRESS:** 67 Bar Beach Rd, Port Washington, NY 11050. **BUSINESS PHONE:** (212)213-1691.

SATO, TOMMY M.
Utilities company executive (retired). Japanese American. **PERSONAL:** Born Jun 21, 1931, Kahului, HI; married Jane, Oct 21, 1957; children: Creighton, Laurel Moriguchi, Lisa Endo. **EDUCATION:** Milwaukee School of Engineering, electrical engineering, 1957. **CAREER:** Wynn Nakamura-Elec, consultant, 1957-58; Maui Electric Co, Engineering, mgr, 1958-86. **ORGANIZATIONS:** Lions Club of Kahului, 1971-; Maui County Planning Commission, chmn, 1984-90; Maui County Bd of Variance Appeals, chmn, 1979-83; Maui County Subdivision Standards Committee; Maui County Street Lighting Committee. **MILITARY SERVICE:** US Army, corporal, 1950-53; Combat Infantry Badge, 1951. **HOME ADDRESS:** 617 Imi Dr, Wailuku, HI 96793, (808)244-3675.

SATO, WALTER N.
Government official. Japanese American. **PERSONAL:** Born Dec 11, 1946, Brigham City, UT; son of Nobuichi Sato and Amy Yagi Sato; married Karen Kunimoto Sato, Jul 10, 1967; children: Stephanie Kunie, Heather Miyuki. **EDUCATION:** University of Utah, BSME, 1970, MSME, 1971. **CAREER:** US Dept of Energy, engineer, 1971-78, Loss of Fluid Test, project manager, 1978-87, Nuclear Safety Branch, chief, 1987-89, Environmental Restoration, program manager, 1989-92, Waste Management Division, director, 1992-. **ORGANIZATIONS:** National Ski Patrol System, national appointment, 1978-. **HOME ADDRESS:** 2081 Balboa Dr, Idaho Falls, ID 83404, (208)529-8499. **BUSINESS ADDRESS:** Director, Waste Management Division, US Dept of Energy, Idaho Operations Office, 785 DOE Place, Idaho Falls, ID 83402, (208)526-0193.

SATO, WILLIAM K.
Educator. Japanese American. **PERSONAL:** Born in Poston, AZ; married Alexandra W Saur; children: Rose Sachi. **EDUCATION:** University of California-Berkeley, AB; Cal-State University at Hayward, MA. **CAREER:** Uni-

versity of California, Santa Cruz Extn, adjunct prof, 1971; San Jose State University, asst prof, 1970-72; Peralta Community College, professor, 1971-93; Laney College, professor, currently. **ORGANIZATIONS:** Peralta Asian Pacific American Assn, president, 1992-94; City of Berkeley, Human Relations & Welfare Commission, chair, 1987-89; National Japanese American Historical Society, 1987-94; Chinese Historical Society of America, 1987-92; National Asian-American Telecommunications Assn, 1986-94; Friends of the Asian Library, board member, 1977-82. **HONORS/AWARDS:** NIH, National Endowment for the Humanities, Summer Seminar Awards, 1978, 1981. **SPECIAL ACHIEVEMENTS:** Participant: Human Rights Tour of Japan, 1991; Hiroshima-Nagasaki Peace Delegation to Japan, 1983. **BUSINESS ADDRESS:** Professor, Laney College, 900 Fallon St, Oakland, CA 94607, (510)464-3192.

SATOW, STUART ALAN
Television director. Japanese American. **PERSONAL:** Born Jun 8, 1956, Munich, Germany; son of Oscar and Lillian Satow; married Arlayne, Sep 4, 1982; children: Sarah, Daren, Ashley, Victoria. **EDUCATION:** California State University, BA (w/honors), communication studies, 1979. **CAREER:** KTXL, sports assistant, sports producer, photographer, 1975-79; KNTV, sports anchor, sports reporter, 1979; KXTV, spotscaster, sports director, 1980-. **BUSINESS ADDRESS:** Sports Director, KXTV, 400 Broadway, Sacramento, CA 95812, (916)441-2345.

SATYAPRIYA, COIMBATORE K. (C. K.)
Consulting engineer. Indo-American. **PERSONAL:** Born Jan 27, 1949, Bangalore, Karnataka, India; son of C V Keshavamurthy and C V Vedamma; married Indira M Satyapriya, Nov 1, 1976; children: Ajay, Anand, Divya. **EDUCATION:** Bangalore University, BE, civil engineering, 1969, ME, soil mechanics and foundation engineering, 1971; Worchester Polytechnic Institute, MS, marine geomechanics, 1974. **CAREER:** Mason & Ray Inc, staff engr, 1976-77; Resource Intl, sr geotech engr, 1977-79; CTL Engineering, vice pres, 1979-82, exec vice pres, 1982-85, president, 1985-. **ORGANIZATIONS:** American Society of Civil Engineers, fellow, 1993, Soil Placement & Improvement, 1984-93; American Society of Testing Materials, 1982-93; Asian Indian American Business Grp, vice pres, 1992. **SPECIAL ACHIEVEMENTS:** Coauthor: Densification on Soft Soils by the Use of Prefabricated Vertical Drains, presented, 1987; Stability of Black Bottom Soil with Lime and Rice Husk Ash, presented, 1982; Marine Geomechanics Overview and Projections, 1973; author: Consolidated Vane Shear Test, MS thesis, 1974. **HOME ADDRESS:** 8015 Flint Rd, West Worthington, OH 43235. **BUSINESS ADDRESS:** President, CTL Engineering, Inc, 2860 Fisher Rd, Columbus, OH 43204, (614)276-8123.

SAWATARI, TAKEO
Physicist, research and development company executive. Japanese American. **PERSONAL:** Born Feb 7, 1939, Yanahara, Okayama, Japan; son of Kentaro and Kimiko Sawatari; married Yoshiko Sawatari, Feb 7, 1966; children: Atomu, Ken, Yoh. **EDUCATION:** Waseda University, BS, 1962, PhD, 1970. **CAREER:** Canon Camera, researcher, 1962-65; University of Tokyo, research associate, 1965-66; Optics Technology Inc, physicist, 1966-70; Bendix Research Lab, principal physicist, 1970-77; Bendix Advanced Technology Ctr, member of technology staff, 1977-81; Sentec Corporation, president, 1981-. **ORGANIZATIONS:** Optical Society of America, 1967-; NASA Minority Business Resource Advisory Committee, 1992-. **HONORS/AWARDS:** Bendix, Corporate Technical Award, 1979; State of Michigan, Research & Development Small Business Award, 1992. **SPECIAL ACHIEVEMENTS:** Published over 50 technical papers and contributed to two fiber optics text books; research fields are optics, signal processing, and laser applications. **BUSINESS ADDRESS:** President, Sentec Corporation, 2000 Oakley Park Rd, Ste 205, Walled Lake, MI 48390, (810)960-1020.

SAWHNEY, AJAY
Insurance company manager. Indo-American. **PERSONAL:** Born Jan 23, 1953, New Delhi, India; son of Sheila & Dev Raj Sawhney; married Sang Ita, Sep 17, 1987; children: Kabir. **EDUCATION:** St Stephen's College, Delhi University, BA (honors), 1973; Columbia University, MBA, 1975. **CAREER:** Data Resources Inc, managing consultant, 1973-79; McKinsey & Co, senior engagement manager, 1979-86; Prudential Insurance Company of America, managing director, 1981-. **HONORS/AWARDS:** Industry of Chartered, Financial Analysts, CFA, 1991. **BUSINESS ADDRESS:** Managing Director, The Prudential Insurance Company of America, 100 Mulberry St, Newark, NJ 07102.

SAWHNEY, GURJEET SINGH (GARY)
Computer analyst. Indo-American. **PERSONAL:** Born Sep 23, 1955, Ludhiana, Punjab, India; son of S Mohan Singh Sawhney; married Sangeeta Sawhney, Aug 6, 1989; children: Sumit. **EDUCATION:** Punjab Agricultural University, BS (with honors), 1977, MS, 1979. **CAREER:** Homestead AFB Federal Credit Union, lead operator, 1984-86; Florida Power & Light Group, computer operations analyst, 1986-. **ORGANIZATIONS:** Sikh Society of Florida, 1982-. **HOME ADDRESS:** 13700 SW 106th St, Miami, FL 33186, (305)387-0882. **BUSINESS ADDRESS:** Computer Operations Analyst, Florida Power & Light Group, Computer Center, General Office, 9250 W Flagler, Miami, FL 33174, (305)552-4928.

SAXENA, BRIJ B.
Educator. Indo-American. **PERSONAL:** married Anjali Saxena; children: Ranjeet, Sanjeet. **EDUCATION:** Lucknow University, India, DPhil, 1954; University Muenster, Germany, DSc, 1957; University of Wisconsin, PhD, 1961. **CAREER:** New Jersey College of Medicine, Biochem & Endocrinology, assistant professor, associate professor, 1966-74; Cornell University Medical College, biochemistry, associate professor, 1974-, endocrinology, Department of Medicine, professor, 1974-, div reproductive endocrinology, Department of Ob/Gyn, director, 1981-. **ORGANIZATIONS:** Royal Soc Medicine, London, fellow; American Society of Biological Chemistry; AAAS; Endocrine Society; Harvey Society; American Physiological Society; American Chemical Society. **HONORS/AWARDS:** NYC Health Council, Career Scientist Award Recipient; Upjohn Research Award; Campoz da Pasz Award. **SPECIAL ACHIEVEMENTS:** Language proficiency in: English, Hindi, French, & German; 200 articles in professional journals. **BUSINESS ADDRESS:** Professor of Endocrinology, Department of Medicine, Director, Division of Reproductive Endocrinology, Department of Ob/Gyn, Cornell University Medical College, 1300 York Avenue, Room A-265, New York, NY 10021, (212)746-3065.

SAXENA, SATISH CHANDRA
Educator. Indo-American. **PERSONAL:** Born Jun 26, 1934, Lucknow, Uttar Pradesh, India; son of Raja Ram Sinha & Vidya Wati Saxena; married Asha Saxena, Feb 16, 1964; children: Alka, Alok, Anup, Anil. **EDUCATION:** Lucknow University, Lucknow, BSc, 1951, MSc, 1953; Calcutta University, PhD, 1956; University of Maryland, Columbia, Yale University, postdoctoral, 1956-59. **CAREER:** Bhabha Atomic Research Center, research officer, 1959-61; University of Rajasthan, reader, 1961-66; Purdue University, associate professor, 1966-68; University of Illinois, Chicago, professor, 1968-; Banaras Hindu University, visiting professor, 1986-87. **ORGANIZATIONS:** National Chemical Laboratory, Pune, guest scientist, 1987; NASA Ames Research Laboratory, CA, sr research associate, 1987, 1988; Argonne National Laboratory, faculty research fellow, 1977; Pittsburgh Energy Technology Center, faculty research participant, 1983, 1984; Morgantown Energy Technology Center, faculty research participant, 1979, 1980, 1981; consultant to: CINDAS; Purdue University; General Electric Co; Argonne National Laboratory: Dupont, Delaware; Ortho Mc; Huazhong University of Science and Technology, Wahan, China, National Key Coal Combustion Lab, 1991. **HONORS/AWARDS:** Oak Ridge Associated Universities, Faculty Travel Scholar, 1979-90; Huazhong University of Science & Technology, China, consulting professor, 1991; Government of India, Pomersary Scholarship, 1951-53, Research Scholarship, 1953-56. **SPECIAL ACHIEVEMENTS:** Author and co-author of numerous publications including: Thermal Conductivity of Nometallic Liquids and Gases, Plenum Press, 1970; Viscosity, Plenum Press, 1975; Thermal Accommodation and Adsorption Coefficients of Gases, Hemisphere Publishing Corporation, 1979, 1981. **HOME ADDRESS:** 8321 Kilbourn Avenue, Skokie, IL 60076-2636, (708)679-4147. **BUSINESS ADDRESS:** Professor, Dept of Chemical Engineering, University of Illinois at Chicago, Box 4348, Chicago, IL 60680, (312)996-2341.

SAXENA, SUBHASH CHANDRA
Mathematician, educator. Indo-American. **PERSONAL:** Born in Etawah, Uttar Pradesh, India; son of Prem Narain Saxena and Hansmukh Rani Kudsia Saxena; married Pushpa Rani Saxena; children: Anita Saxena Ginski, Anil. **EDUCATION:** University of Delhi, BA (with honors), 1952, MA, 1954, PhD, 1958. **CAREER:** Defense Academy, India, instructor, 1958; University of Delhi, postdoctoral fellow, 1958-59; Atlanta University, assistant & associate professor, 1959-63; Northern Illinois University, associate professor, 1963-68; University of Akron, associate professor, 1968-73; Coastal Carolina University, professor, 1973-, chair, 1987-. **ORGANIZATIONS:** American Mathematical Society, 1963-; Mathematical Association of America, 1962-; National

Council of Teachers of Mathematics, 1990-; American Association of University Professors, 1987-; Pi Mu Epsilon, faculty advisor, 1987-. **HONORS/AWARDS:** University of Delhi, Sir Maurice Gwyer Research Scholarship, 1954-55; Government of India, Government of India Scholarship, 1955-57; Council of Scientific & Industrial Research, Senior Post-Doctoral Fellow, 1958; Coastal Carolina University, Outstanding Teacher, 1985; University of South Carolina, USC System AMOCO Foundation, Teaching Award, 1985. **SPECIAL ACHIEVEMENTS:** Author, book, Intro to Real Variable Theory, 1972, 1980; research paper, "Portugaliae Mathematica," 1975; research paper, Indian Journal of Pure & Applied Mathematics, 1985; expository research, American Mathematical Monthly, 1970; expository research, Mathematics Magazine, 1973. **HOME ADDRESS:** 4407 Greenbay Trail, Myrtle Beach, SC 29577. **BUSINESS ADDRESS:** Professor and Chair, Dept of Mathematics, Coastal Carolina University, PO Box 1954, Wall Bldg, 124-D, Conway, SC 29526, (803)349-2076.

SAY, ALLEN
Children's book author and illustrator. Japanese American. **PERSONAL:** Born Aug 28, 1937; son of Masako Moriwaki; married Deirdre Myles, Apr 18, 1974; children: Yuriko. **EDUCATION:** Aoyama Gakuin, Japan, 3 years; Chouinard Art Institute, 1 year; Los Angeles Art Center School, 1 year; University of California, Berkeley, 2 years; San Francisco Art Institute, 1 year. **CAREER:** EIZO Press, publisher, 1968; commercial photographer, illustrator, 1969-; writer. **HONORS/AWARDS:** Horn Book Honor List, 1984; Christopher Award, 1985; Boston Globe/Horn Book Award, 1988; Caldecott Honor Book, 1989. **SPECIAL ACHIEVEMENTS:** Writer and illustrator: Dr Smith's Safari, 1972; Once under the Cherry Blossom Tree: An Old Japanese Tale, 1974; The Feast of Lanterns, 1976; The Innkeeper's Apprentice, 1979; The Bicycle Man, 1982; A River Dream, 1988; The Lost Lake, 1989; El Chino, 1990; Grandfather's Journey, 1993; illustrator: A Canticle to the Waterbirds, 1968; Two Ways of Seeing, 1971; Magic and Night River, 1978; The Lucky Yak, 1980; The Secret Cross of Lorraine, 1981; How My Parents Learned to Eat, 1984; The Boy of the Three Year Nap, 1988. **BIOGRAPHICAL SOURCES:** Contemporary Authors, New Revision Series, Vol 30, 1990; Something about the Author, Vol 28, 1982. **BUSINESS ADDRESS:** Author, Grandfather's Journey, c/o Houghton Mifflin, 222 Berkeley St, Boston, MA 02116, (617)725-5000.*

SAYALA, CHHAYA
Federal government official. Indo-American. **PERSONAL:** Born Apr 16, 1950, Bangalore, Karnataka, India; daughter of T Janakiram and Sundari Janakiram; married Dash Sayala, May 3, 1978; children: Seema D. **EDUCATION:** Bangalore University, India, BS, 1970, MS, 1972; Indian Institute of Technology, India, PhD, 1976. **CAREER:** Diablo Valley College, lecturer, 1984; Ohlone College, lecturer, 1985; Northern Virginia Community College, lecturer, 1987-89; George Mason University, lecturer, 1986-88; Patent & Trademark Office, patent examiner, 1989-. **ORGANIZATIONS:** Patent & Trademark Office Society, 1990-. **HONORS/AWARDS:** Council of Scientific & Industrial Research, India, PhD and Postdoctoral Fellowship, 1972-78; Katholieke University, Nijmegen, The Netherlands, Postdoctoral Fellowship, 1978; Virginia State Science & Engineering Fair, judge, 1989-; Patent & Trademark Office, six various awards for performance, productivity and special achievements, 1990-92. **SPECIAL ACHIEVEMENTS:** "Complexes of Te(IV), Te(II) and Se(II) with 2.2'-iminodiethanoldithiocarbamate," with B G Sejekan and G Aravamudam, in J Inorg Nuel Chem, 40, 211, 1978; "Complexes of Morpholine 4-thiocarbonic acid anilide with Te(IV) and Te(II)," with G Aravamudan, in Current Science, 47, 22, 851, 1978; Complexes of Carboxin With Copper (II), report; "Complexes of Te(IV), Te(II) an Se(II) with Methyl-Beta hydroxyethl-dithiocarbamate," with G Aravamudan and B G Sejekan, in Phosphorus and Sulfur, 5, 1985, 1978; "Nickel(II) Complexes of Deprotonated Thiourea, Crystal Structures Ni(C6 H5)NC(S)N(C2H4Z 0)2," with W P Boxman, J Willemse and J A Cras, in Reel Trav Chim Pays-Bas, 99, 314, 1980. **BIOGRAPHICAL SOURCES:** Westlife, The Daily Sentinel, Grand Junction, Co, vol 92, no 53, p 9, January 18, 1984. **BUSINESS ADDRESS:** Patent Examiner, Patent & Trademark Office, Jefferson Davis Highway, 11B07 CMI, Washington, DC 20231.

SAYALA, DASH
Environmental scientist. Indo-American. **PERSONAL:** Born Sep 12, 1943, Hyderabad, Andhra Pradesh, India; son of Veeraiah Sayala; married Chhaya Sayala, May 1978; children: Seema. **EDUCATION:** Osmania University, BSc, 1962, MS, 1964; University of New Mexico, MS, 1972; George Washington University, PhD, 1978. **CAREER:** Uranium King Corp/American Ura-

nium Corp, senior program manager, 1972-79; Bendix Field Engineering Corp, advanced research geoscientist, manager of technology integration, 1979-84; Woodward-Clyde Consultants, senior scientist, 1984-85; MITRE Corp, staff scientist, 1985-91; SAIC, senior scientist/senior program manager, 1991-. **ORGANIZATIONS:** Smithsonian Associates, 1974-; National Geographic Society, 1970-; National Well Water Association, 1991-; Virginia State Science & Engineering Fair, judge, 1991-. **HONORS/AWARDS:** Dept of Energy, certificate of appreciation, 1986; MITRE Corp, achievement award, 1987. **SPECIAL ACHIEVEMENTS:** Published several papers on uranium exploration, environmental assessments and geology/geochemistry . **BUSINESS ADDRESS:** Senior Scientist, Senior Program Manager, Science Applications International Corp, 11251 Roger Bacon Dr, MS R-1-3, Reston, VA 22090, (703)318-4644.

SAYAPHUPHA, ROBERT BOUAKHAM
Law enforcement official. Laotian American. **PERSONAL:** Born Aug 12, 1963, Savanaketh, Lao People's Democratic Republic; son of Pong & Kim Sayaphupha; married Rose Hoa Ma, Oct 13, 1988; children: Elaine Sayaphupha Ma. **CAREER:** Oakland Police Department, police officer, currently. **ORGANIZATIONS:** Asian Youth Services Committee, co-founder; Asian Advisory Committee on Crime, sergeant-at-arms; Northern Asian Peace Officer's Association, board of directors. **HONORS/AWARDS:** East Bay Asian Development Corp, Individual of the Year, 1991. **SPECIAL ACHIEVEMENTS:** Read & write Chinese, Mandarin, speak Lao, Chio Chow; in charge of training & supervising the Asian Youth Services Committee Lion Dance Group. **BUSINESS ADDRESS:** Police Officer, Oakland Police Department, 455 7th St, Rm 313, Oakland, CA 94607, (510)238-3066.

SCHRAMM, ADELAIDA. *See* **REYES, ADELAIDA.**

SEHGAL, OM PARKASH
Educator. Indo-American. **PERSONAL:** Born Jul 22, 1932, Rawal Pindi, Punjab, India; son of B L Sehgal and Savitry Sehgal; married Santosh Sehgal, Dec 24, 1963; children: Ravi, Ritu. **EDUCATION:** Agra University, BSc, 1951; Lucknow University, India, MSc, 1953; University of Wisconsin, Madison, PhD, 1961. **CAREER:** University of Arizona, post-doctoral fellow, 1961-63; University of Missouri, assistant professor, 1963-68, associate professor, 1969-75, professor, 1976-. **ORGANIZATIONS:** American Society for Virology, 1982-; American Society for Advancement of Science, 1965-; American Phytopathological Society, 1958-; Indian Virological Society, 1988-; North-Central Division, American Phytopathological Society, president, 1984. **HONORS/AWARDS:** Indian Virological Society, fellow, 1991; Lucknow University, Birbal Sahni Gold Medalist, 1953; National Science Foundation, India-Exchange Scientist, 1976; FAO/UN, consultant, 1991. **SPECIAL ACHIEVEMENTS:** Over sixty research publications in the field of plant virology. **HOME ADDRESS:** 500 Rothwell Dr, Columbia, MO 65203. **BUSINESS ADDRESS:** Professor, Dept of Plant Pathology, University of Missouri, 108 Waters Hall, Columbia, MO 65211, (314)882-7060.

SEHGAL, RAJ K.
Business owner. Indo-American. **PERSONAL:** Born Dec 9, 1946, Delhi, Delhi, India; son of Jag M Sehgal; married Poonam Sehgal, Oct 11, 1980; children: Payal, Karneek, Kaveesh. **EDUCATION:** Delhi Polytechnic, diploma in pharmacy, 1968. **CAREER:** Sehgal's International, owner, currently. **BUSINESS ADDRESS:** Owner, Sehgal's International, 6222 Richmond Ave, Ste 390, Houston, TX 77057, (713)785-7252.

SEID, ALLAN
Association administrator, psychiatrist. **PERSONAL:** married Mari; children: Mark, Arlene, Marcine. **CAREER:** Self-employed, psychiatrist. **ORGANIZATIONS:** Asian Americans for Community Involvement, founder, 1973, executive director, 1982-. **HONORS/AWARDS:** AACI, honorable mention, 1992. **BUSINESS ADDRESS:** Executive Director, Asian Americans for Community Involvement, 232 E Gish Rd, Ste 200, San Jose, CA 95112, (408)452-5151.*

SEKI, AKIRO
Stamping company executive. Japanese American. **PERSONAL:** Born Dec 1, 1943, Nara, Nara, Japan; son of Kanzo Seki and Shizu Seki; married Izumi Seki, Jul 12, 1970; children: Shotaro, Sunske. **EDUCATION:** Osaka University, law, 1964-68. **CAREER:** Mazda Corp, Japan, manager purchasing, 1986; Mazda Motor Manufacturing, US Corp, purchasing manager, 1987-88; Lenawee Stamping, general manager of sales & purchasing, 1988-89, vice

president of manufacturing, 1989-91, executive vice president, 1991-. **BUSINESS ADDRESS:** Executive Vice President, Lenawee Stamping Corp, 1200 E Chicago Blvd, Tecumseh, MI 49286, (517)423-2400.

SEN, ARUN
Remodeling company executive. Indo-American. **PERSONAL:** Born Mar 15, 1933, Varanasi, Uttar Pradesh, India; son of Dinesh Chandra Sen and Kanak Lata Sen; married Bharati, Jan 22, 1965; children: Baishali Rinku, Chaitali. **EDUCATION:** Varanasi University, BS, 1954; Technical University, Stuttgart, Germany, Diploma, 1962. **CAREER:** Kanak Home Remodeling, president, 1980-. **HOME ADDRESS:** 130 Lions Dr, Morrisville, PA 19067, (215)295-8800. **BUSINESS ADDRESS:** President, Kanak Home Remodeling Inc, 415 W Lincoln Hwy, Penndel, PA 19047, (215)752-0555.

SEN, ARUN KUMAR
Government official. Indo-American. **PERSONAL:** Born Jul 25, 1938, Calcutta, India; son of Atul Chandra Sen & Renu Sen; married Lourminia; children: Anita, Monina. **EDUCATION:** Bihar Agricultural College, India, BSc, agriculture, 1959; Oregon State University, MS, 1963, PhD, 1968. **CAREER:** Basic Vegetable Products, plant pathologist/nematologist, 1968-72; State of California, senior pesticide evaluation scientist, 1972-. **ORGANIZATIONS:** Entomological Society of America, 1972-; American Phytopathological Society, 1978-; Society of Nematologists, 1968-; Toastmasters International, board of directors, 1968-; California Multicultural Park Foundation, board of director, 1990; Davis Human Relations Commission, chair, 1994; International Agricultural Center, Wageningen, fellow, 1963. **HONORS/AWARDS:** Toastmasters International, Distinguished Toastmaster, 1975; Trans-Sierra District, H A Yarbrough Sustained Service Award, 1989; Jaycees Intl Senator, 1972. **SPECIAL ACHIEVEMENTS:** 10 publications in scientific journals. **HOME ADDRESS:** 422 Fiesta Ave, Davis, CA 95616. **BUSINESS PHONE:** (916)324-3559.

SEN, ASHISH KUMAR
Educator. Indo-American. **PERSONAL:** Born Jun 8, 1942, Delhi, India; son of Ashoka K Sen and Arati Sen; married Colleen Taylor, Apr 8, 1972. **EDUCATION:** Calcutta University, India, BS (with honors), 1962; University of Toronto, MA, 1964, PhD, 1971. **CAREER:** Northwestern University, research associate, lecturer in geography, 1967-69; University of Illinois, Chicago, College of Urban Sciences, assistant professor, 1969-73, associate professor, 1973-78, acting dean, 1977, School of Urban Sciences, director, 1977-78, School of Urban Sciences, acting director, 1992, professor of urban planning, 1978-. **ORGANIZATIONS:** Chicago Board of Education, 1991-, Facilities Committee, chairman, 1991-92, Finance Committee, chairman, 1992-; Asian Institute, board of trustees; Indo American Center, board of trustees; Royal Statistical Society, fellow; American Statistical Association. **SPECIAL ACHIEVEMENTS:** Author of many articles in the fields of transportation, urban planning, statistics, and medicine; coauthor of the monograph, Statistical Regression: Theory, Practice, and Applications. **BUSINESS ADDRESS:** Professor, University of Illinois, Chicago, PO Box 4348, Chicago, IL 60680.

SEN, KARABI
Educator. Indo-American. **PERSONAL:** Born in Meherpur, W. Bengal, India; children: Satadru, Santanu, Indumati, Aparajito, Priyodarshi. **EDUCATION:** Calcutta University, BA, 1962, MA, 1964, PhD, 1976; San Francisco State University, multiple subject teaching credential, 1987; California State Dept of Education, language development specialist, 1990. **CAREER:** Burdwan University, Burdwan, lecturer, reader, professor, dept of philosophy, head, 1965-83; California Institute of Integral Studies, dept of philosophy and religion, professor, 1984-85, ESL, teacher, 1993; San Francisco Unified School District, resource teacher, 1986-87; Modesto City Schools, Modesto City Adult Education Center, sheltered classroom teacher, 1987-. **ORGANIZATIONS:** Northern California Geographic Alliance, consultant teacher, 1992-94; National Educators' Association, 1987-94; California Teachers' Association, 1987-94; Modesto Teachers' Association, 1987-94, Modesto City Poet's Corner, active participant in poetry writing, recitals and publications; CSPCA, 1962-72; Animal Welfare Society, India, 1962-73. **HONORS/AWARDS:** Calcutta University, five gold medals, one silver medal, 1962-64; Modesto City Poet's Corner, Contest Winner in Poetry, 1987-93; Women for Peace, Peace Essay Contest Winner, 1990. **SPECIAL ACHIEVEMENTS:** Author: When Stevenson Left Soksomoeun, Vantage Press; 8 stories in A Treasury of Wise Actions-An Anthology of Jataka Tales, Dharina Publishers, 1993; editor and contributor, Her Story, An Anthology of Essays in Women's Studies, Pragati Publishers, 1984; Art, Education and Crime in a Changing Society, Burdwan University

Publications, 1983; Values and Their Significance, Burdwan University Publications, 1980; Dimensions of Causality and the Philosophy of Speciesism, Sanskrit Pustak Bhandau, 1980; An Introduction to a Scientific Philosophy & Ethics, Sanskrit Pustak Bhandar, 1978. **BUSINESS ADDRESS:** Teacher, Modesto City Schools, 426 Locust, Modesto, CA 95351.

SEN, MIHIR
Educator. Indo-American. **PERSONAL:** Born Jan 17, 1947, Calcutta, W. Bengal, India; son of Santi Bhusan Sen and Anima Sen; married Beatriz Sen, Dec 26, 1972; children: Pradeep, Maya. **EDUCATION:** Indian Institute of Technology, Madras, India, BTech, 1968; MIT, ScD, 1975. **CAREER:** National University of Mexico, professor, 1975-85; Cornell University, visiting professor, 1985-86; University of Notre Dame, associate professor, 1986-. **ORGANIZATIONS:** ASME; ASEE; SIAM. **SPECIAL ACHIEVEMENTS:** 50 journal papers. **HOME ADDRESS:** 52833 Sporn Dr, South Bend, IN 46635. **BUSINESS PHONE:** (219)631-5975.

SEN, PABITRA NARAYAN
Physicist, researcher. Indo-American. **PERSONAL:** Born Sep 5, 1944, Calcutta, India; son of Bibudh N & Uma Sen; married Susan Shu, Feb 18, 1984; children: Indra, Maya. **EDUCATION:** Calcutta University, MS, 1966; University of Chicago, PhD, 1972. **CAREER:** Xerox, profl staff, 1973-76; Xonics, senior scientist, 1976-78; University de Provence, Marseille, France, visiting professor, 1985; Royal Society Eng, guest rsch fellow, 1988-89; Schlumberger-Doll Research, sci adv, 1978-. **ORGANIZATIONS:** Am Phys Society, fellow. **SPECIAL ACHIEVEMENTS:** Explanation of laws of conduction in porous media. **BUSINESS ADDRESS:** Science Advisor, Schlumberger-Doll Research, Old Quarry Rd, Ridgefield, CT 06877-4108.

SEN, TAPAS K.
Business executive. Indo-American. **PERSONAL:** Born Mar 1, 1933, Calcutta, W. Bengal, India; son of Pulin Behari Sen (deceased) and Parul Bala Sen (deceased); married Sondra, Jul 3, 1966; children: Raji, Monisha. **EDUCATION:** Calcutta University, BSc, 1951, MSc, 1954; Johns Hopkins University, PhD, 1963. **CAREER:** Bell Laboratories, technical staff, 1963-72; AT&T, work relationships/human resources planning, dist mgr, 1973-78, empl participation, div mgr, 1979-91, quality/employee relations director, 1992-. **ORGANIZATIONS:** Human Factors/Ergonomics Society, fellow, 1980-; American Psychological Association, 1963-; Association of Asian Indians in America, founder, co-chairman, 1967-68, life member, 1967-; Human Factors Society, Metropolitan Chap, president, 1970; Kennedy School, Harmon Program, advisory board, 1989-91; Work in America Institute, advisory board, 1986-; NY State Governor's Excelsior Committee, executive committee member, Public Sector, co-chair, 1991-93. **HONORS/AWARDS:** Toastmasters International, Distinguished Governor, 1967. **SPECIAL ACHIEVEMENTS:** Several publications in psychology and management journals. **HOME ADDRESS:** 29 Arden Road, Mountain Lakes, NJ 07046. **BUSINESS PHONE:** (201)898-8543.

SENGUPTA, DIPAK LAL
Educator. Indo-American. **PERSONAL:** Born Mar 1, 1931, East Bengal, Bangladesh; son of Jayanta Kumar Sengupta & Pankajini Sengupta; married Sujata Sengupta, Aug 31, 1962; children: Sumit, Mita. **EDUCATION:** University of Calcutta, India, BSc, 1950, MSc, 1952; University of Toronto, PhD, 1958. **CAREER:** Harvard University, electronics, research fellow, 1958-59; University of Michigan, res physicist, 1959-63; University of Toronto, assistant professor, 1963-64; Central Electronics Eng Res Institute, Pilani, India, assistant director, 1964; University of Michigan, electrical engineering, research scientist & professor, 1965-86; University of Detroit Mercy, EE & Physics Dept, professor & chair, 1986-. **ORGANIZATIONS:** IEEE, Southeastern Michigan Section, treasurer, vice-chairman, chairman, 1976-78; IEEE Transactions on Antennas and Propagation, associate editor, 1976-78; URSI Commission B, secretary, 1976-78; US Department of Energy Wind Turbine Site Selection Committee, 1978-80; EMI Group of International Energy Association, US delegate, 1989; International Symposium on Micromme Comm, Khargpr, India, technical program committee, 1981. **HONORS/AWARDS:** IEEE, Certificate of Achievement for Outstanding Contribution, 1969, Certificate of Recognition for Outstanding Services, 1979, Fellow, 1988; Fulbright Foundation, Fulbright Visiting Lecturer in India, 1992-93. **SPECIAL ACHIEVEMENTS:** Numerous research publications and books. **BUSINESS ADDRESS:** Professor, Dept of Elec Eng and Physics, University of Detroit-Mercy, 4001 W McNichols Rd, Detroit, MI 48219-3599, (313)993-3365.

SENZAKI, MIYO
Association administrator. Japanese American. **CAREER:** Japanese American Citizens League, Pacific Southwest Regional Office, Pasadena Chapter, president, 1993-. **BUSINESS ADDRESS:** President, Pasadena Chapter, Japanese American Citizens League, 244 S San Pedro Ste 507, Pacific Southwest Regional Office, Los Angeles, CA 90012, (213)626-4471. *

SENZAKI, RANDALL KIYOMI
Educational administrator, musician. Japanese American. **PERSONAL:** Born May 19, 1943, Rohwer, AR; son of Ben T and Miyo Senzaki; divorced; children: Miles, Marissa. **EDUCATION:** California State University, Los Angeles, BA, psychology, 1967; San Francisco University, MA, ethnic studies, education, 1993. **CAREER:** US Public Health Service, Centers for Disease Control, research & development analyst, 1967-71; Measurement Research Center, Westinghouse Learning Corp, exercise administration, 1971-72; California State University, Los Angeles, placement advisor, 1972-73; UCLA, career counselor, foreign student specialist, 1974-75, career counselor, minority affairs rep, 1975-76; Asian American Communities for Education, 1979-80; San Francisco State University, EOP director, 1980-. **ORGANIZATIONS:** Asian & Pacific Americans in Higher Education, founding board member; Western Association of Educational Opportunity Programs; Community Colleges EOPS Association; CSU Asian Pacific American Education, advisory committee; Japanese American Citizens League, executive national director, currently. **HONORS/AWARDS:** State of California, Senate, Rules Committee, Commendation, Resolution, 1989, Assembly, Commendation, Resolution, 1989; City & County of San Francisco, Board of Supervisors, Board of Education, Certificates of Honor, 1989; San Francisco State University, Associated Students, Certificate of Appreciation, 1987. **SPECIAL ACHIEVEMENTS:** Performed saxophone in Asian American Jazz Festival, San Francisco, 1985; recorded with Jon Jang, "Are You Chinese or Charlie Chan?", 1984; recorded with Bob Matsueda, "Live in J-Town," 1985. **BUSINESS ADDRESS:** Executive National Director, Japanese American Citizens League, 1765 Sutter St, San Francisco, CA 94115, (415)921-5225.

SESHADRI, KAL S.
Research chemist. Indo-American. **PERSONAL:** Born May 11, 1924, Jagalur, Karnataka, India; son of Kal Srinivasa & Kankamma Srinivasa; married Champaka L, May 11, 1951; children: Viji R, Veena. **EDUCATION:** University of Mysore, BSc (with honors), 1945, MSc, 1947; Oregon State University, PhD, 1960. **CAREER:** University of Mysore, lecturer, 1945-60; National Research Council, Canada, post-doctoral fellow, 1960-62; Ohio State University, research associate, 1962-66; Gulf R&D Center, senior research chemist, 1966-83; University of Pittsburgh, consultant, 1983-85; EG&G, Washington Analytical Service Center, scientist, 1985-. **ORGANIZATIONS:** American Chemical Society, 1963-. **SPECIAL ACHIEVEMENTS:** Author of approximately 60 publications. **BUSINESS ADDRESS:** Scientist, EG&G, Washington Analytical Service Center, 3610 Collins Ferry Rd, Morgantown, WV 26505, (304)291-4680.

SETH, ARUN K.
Cancer research scientist. Indo-American. **PERSONAL:** Born Jul 16, 1953, New Delhi, India; son of Manohar Lal Seth and Shanti Devi Seth; married Indu Seth, Jun 4, 1981; children: Rishie Manohar, Sachin Arun. **EDUCATION:** Meerut University, India, BSc, 1973, MSc, 1975; University of New Brunswick, Canada, PhD, 1981. **CAREER:** University of New Brunswick, research associate, 1980-81; Bethesda Research Laboratories, staff scientist, 1981-82; Georgetown University, School of Medicine, research asst professor, 1982-83; Organon Teknika, scientist, 1983-87; National Cancer Institute, research associate, 1983, staff scientist, 1987-. **ORGANIZATIONS:** Chemical Institute of Canada, 1979-81; American Assn for Advancement of Science; American Assn for Cancer Research. **HONORS/AWARDS:** Meerut University, Chemistry Honors, 1973; University of New Brunswick, Research Fellowship, 1976-81, Teaching Assistantship, 1976-81; Journal of Viral Diseases, editorial board; Oncology Reports, editorial board. **SPECIAL ACHIEVEMENTS:** Author of 75 research (cancer) papers in peer reviewed journals and books, 1979-. **HOME ADDRESS:** 23 Burnt Woods Ct, Germantown, MD 20874, (301)540-2099. **BUSINESS ADDRESS:** Research Scientist, National Cancer Institute, Frederick Cancer and Development Center, Bldg 469, Rm 211, Frederick, MD 21702, (301)846-5997.

SETH, SHYAM S.
Engineer. Indo-American. **PERSONAL:** Born Dec 1, 1943, Punjab, India; son of C L Seth and Saraswati Devi Seth; married Kiran Seth, Jun 6, 1973; children:

Rohit K (Tony), Geeta, Rajeev K. **EDUCATION:** Ranchi University, Bihar, India, BScE, 1965; LaSalle Extension University, Chicago, business management, 1973; Western Michigan University, MTech, industrial engineering, 1975. **CAREER:** SMC Inc, chief engineer, 1990-. **ORGANIZATIONS:** AIIE, 1976-; ASME, 1980-; HAWT, 1990-. **HOME ADDRESS:** 6001 Mecca St, Odessa, TX 79762, (915)368-0703.

SETHI, ISHWAR KRISHAN
Educator. Indo-American. **PERSONAL:** Born Jan 30, 1948, Muzaffar Nagar, Uttar Pradesh, India; son of Faqir Chand Sethi and Janak Sethi; married Suman Sethi, Sep 20, 1974; children: Rahul, Saurabh. **EDUCATION:** Indian Institute of Technology, India, BS, 1969, MS, 1971, PhD, 1977. **CAREER:** Indian Institute of Technology, assistant professor, 1977-82; Wayne State University, Dept of Computer Science, professor, 1982-. **ORGANIZATIONS:** IEEE, senior member, 1977; International Neural Network Society, 1987. **HONORS/AWARDS:** National Science Foundation, research grants, 1985-86, 1991-93; Pattern Recognition Journal, associate editor, 1990. **SPECIAL ACHIEVEMENTS:** Co-editor, Artificial Neural Networks and Statistical Pattern Recognition, North-Holland Publishing, 1991. **BUSINESS ADDRESS:** Professor, Dept of Computer Science, Wayne State University, 424 State Hall, Detroit, MI 48202, (313)577-0730.

SETHI, NARESH KUMAR
Research scientist. Indo-American. **PERSONAL:** Born Nov 26, 1961, New Delhi, Delhi, India; son of C L Sethi and S R Sethi; married Videsha Sethi, Dec 30, 1989. **EDUCATION:** University of Delhi, India, BS, 1982; University of Utah, Salt Lake City, PhD, 1988. **CAREER:** University of Utah, teaching asst, 1983-84, graduate research asst, 1984-88; Amoco Oil Co, postdoctoral fellow, 1988-89; Amoco Corp, research scientist, 1989-. **SPECIAL ACHIEVEMENTS:** Several scientific papers in technical journals. **HOME PHONE:** (708)369-4548. **BUSINESS ADDRESS:** Research Scientist, Amoco Research Center, 150 W Warrenville Rd, MS B-5, Naperville, IL 60566, (708)420-3769.

SETO, BELINDA P.
Science administrator. Chinese American. **PERSONAL:** Born Jul 25, 1948, Canton, China; daughter of Chun Tak Seto and Nancy So Ying Seto; married William G Coleman Jr, Oct 13, 1974; children: Melissa, Alicia, Natasha. **EDUCATION:** University of California, Davis, BS (summa cum laude), 1970; Purdue University, PhD, 1974. **CAREER:** Purdue University, teaching assistant, 1970-71; Food and Drug Administration, research group leader, 1980-89; Public Health Service, senior health policy analyst, 1991-92; National Institutes of Health, staff fellow, 1974-77, senior staff fellow, 1977-80, scientific review administrator, 1989-91, deputy director, 1992-. **ORGANIZATIONS:** American Society for Biochemistry and Molecular Biology; Phi Kappa Phi; Alpha Gamma Sigma; Organization of Chinese Americans. **HONORS/AWARDS:** Office of the Assistant Secretary for Health, Special Recognition Award, 1992; DHHS Secretary, Award for Exceptional Achievement, 1985; NIH, Traineeship, 1971-74. **SPECIAL ACHIEVEMENTS:** Two patents; service on several federal committees including: NIH Committee on the Recruitment of Minority Individuals; PHS Executive Task Force on AIDS; proficient in Chinese. **BUSINESS ADDRESS:** Deputy Director, Office of Research on Minority Health, National Institutes of Health, 9000 Rockville Pike, Building 1, Room 255, Bethesda, MD 20892, (301)402-2515.

SETO, BENJAMIN S. F.
Journalist. Japanese American. **EDUCATION:** University of Hawaii, BA, journalism, 1986. **CAREER:** San Francisco Examiner, banking reporter, currently. **ORGANIZATIONS:** Asian American Journalists Association, chapter president. **BUSINESS ADDRESS:** Banking Reporter, San Francisco Examiner, 110 5th St, San Francisco, CA 94103, (415)777-2424. *

SETO, JOSEPH TOBEY
Virologist. Japanese American. **PERSONAL:** Born Aug 3, 1924, Tacoma, WA; son of Mr and Mrs Toraichi Seto; married Grace K Seto, Aug 9, 1959; children: Susan Lynn, Steven Fred. **EDUCATION:** University of Minnesota, BS, 1949; University of Wisconsin, MS, 1955, PhD, 1957. **CAREER:** Institute for Virology, University of Giessen, Germany, guest professor; San Francisco State University, assistant professor, 1959-60; California State University, Los Angeles, professor, 1960-. **ORGANIZATIONS:** American Society for Microbiology, 1953-93; Society for General Microbiology, 1953-93, Electron Microscope Society of America, 1960-93; American Association Advancement of Science, 1960-; Sigma Xi, 1956-; New York Academy of Sciences, 1960-90. **HONORS/AWARDS:** American Society for Microbiology, Fellow; World

Health Organization; Humboldt Award; Humboldt Medal; NATO, Senior Scientist Award. **SPECIAL ACHIEVEMENTS:** Many publications in scientific journals such as Virology, Journal of Virology, Journal of Gen virology, Archieves of Virology, 1953-. **MILITARY SERVICE:** US Army, sgt, 1945-46. **BUSINESS ADDRESS:** Professor, Dept of Microbiology, California State University of Los Angeles, Biological Science 105, Los Angeles, CA 90032-8205.

SETO, ROBERT MAHEALANI MING
Federal judge. Chinese American/Pacific Islander American. **PERSONAL:** Born May 12, 1936, Canton, China; son of Mr & Mrs Yuen Jan Seto; married Elizabeth Marie Everhart, Nov 12, 1977; children: Craig K, Michelle Leilani Horack, Jeff K, Pamela B, Scott David. **EDUCATION:** St Louis University, BS, 1962, Law School, JD, 1968; George Washington University Law School, LLM candidate, 1993. **CAREER:** Monsanto Company, patent attorney, 1968-69; Corporation Counsel's Office, Honoloulu, Hawaii, attorney, 1969-70; US States Senate, Special Committee on Aging, Judiciary Committee & Office of Senator Hiram L Fong, minority counsel, 1971-76; US International Trade Commission, senior attorney, 1976-81; US Court of Claims, federal trial judge, 1981-82; US Court of Federal Claims, federal judge, 1982-87; US Dept of Agriculture, federal administrative judge, 1987-. **ORGANIZATIONS:** American Bar Association, Public Contract Section, 1968-; Hawaii Bar Association, 1971-; Missouri Bar Association, 1968-; DC Bar Association, 1978-. **HOME ADDRESS:** 4511 Fidelity Court, Annandale, VA 22003, (703)425-9414. **BUSINESS ADDRESS:** Federal Judge, US Dept of Agriculture, 1400 Independence Avenue SW, Rm 2912, South Bldg, Washington, DC 20250, (202)720-2066.

SETO, THELMA G.
Writer. Japanese American. **PERSONAL:** Born May 9, 1954, Aleppo, Syrian Arab Republic; daughter of Paul Susumu Seto and Genevieve Reynolds; children: Hayden Susumu. **EDUCATION:** Antioch College, BA, literature, 1977. **CAREER:** Writer, currently. **ORGANIZATIONS:** California Arts Council, panelist. **HONORS/AWARDS:** JACL/AAPAA, first place in fiction contest, 1992. **SPECIAL ACHIEVEMENTS:** Work appears in the following publications: Rafu Shimpo, Amerasia Journal, Portland Review, Bridge, Mothering, Sinister Wisdom, Xenophilia, Westword, Pacific Citizen, High Performance Magazine; contributor, Two Worlds Walking, 1994; Asian American Anthology, Greenfield Review Press, 1995. **BUSINESS ADDRESS:** PO Box 411292, San Francisco, CA 94141-1292.

SETO, THEODORE PAUL
Educator. Japanese American. **PERSONAL:** Born Feb 18, 1951, Kermanshah, Iran; son of Paul Susumu Seto and Genevieve Reynolds; married Lenore Trina Rothman, Aug 2, 1980; children: Kira Rothman. **EDUCATION:** Harvard College, BA, 1973; Harvard Law School, JD, 1976. **CAREER:** US Court of Appeals, Second Circuit, NY, clerk to the honorable Walter R Mansfield, 1976-77; Foley, Hoag & Eliot, associate, 1977-83; Drinker Biddle and Reath, associate, 1983-86, partner, 1986-91; Loyola Law School, associate professor, 1991-. **ORGANIZATIONS:** American Bar Association, Tax Section, 1977-, Advisory Committee, 1990-91; article editor, The Tax Lawyer, 1986-90, Partnership Committee, 1987-, Environmental Tax Committee, 1990-, Affiliate and Related Corporations Committee, 1984-86; Pennsylvania Bar Association, Tax Section, 1983-; Philadelphia Bar Association, Tax Section, 1983-91, council member, 1988-91, federal tax committee, 1987-91; National Asian Pacific American Bar Association, 1988-; Asian American Bar Association of the Delaware Valley, Executive Committee, 1990-91; Harvard Law School Association, executive committee, 1987-91, treasurer, 1987-89, vice president, 1989-91. **BUSINESS ADDRESS:** Associate Professor, Loyola Law School, 1441 W Olympic Blvd, Los Angeles, CA 90015, (213)736-1154.

SHA, JI-PING
Educator. Chinese American. **PERSONAL:** Born Aug 16, 1957, Nanjing, People's Republic of China; son of Yujun Sha and Shugui Chen; married Jinping Dai, Dec 31, 1983; children: Fern. **EDUCATION:** University of Science and Technology of China, BS, 1982; State University of New York, Stony Brook, PhD, 1986. **CAREER:** Institute for Advanced Study at Princeton, visiting member, 1986-87; University of Chicago, Dickson Instructor, 1987-89; Indiana University, assistant professor, 1989-93, associate professor, 1993-. **ORGANIZATIONS:** American Mathematical Society, 1984-. **BUSINESS ADDRESS:** Professor, Dept of Mathematics, Indiana University, Bloomington, IN 47405-1101, (812)855-1113.

SHA, SHUNG-TSE (PHILIP WEI HUA, QIAODA SHA)
Educator. Chinese American. **PERSONAL:** Born May 15, 1929, Hailun County, Heilongjiang, China; son of Sha Guangren and Yu Jingxin; married Sun Kai, Jun 18, 1955; children: Sha Xin-Wei, Sha Hsin-Ru, Sha Hsing-Min. **EDUCATION:** Hailun Military and Political Academy, 1946; Belont Abbey College, BA, 1954; Georgetown University, MA, 1957, PhD, 1960. **CAREER:** Christian Brothers College, Memphis, assistant professor and chairman, 1960-62; University of Dayton, assistant and associate professor, 1962-69; University of the District of Columbia, History Department, professor and chairman, 1969-. **ORGANIZATIONS:** Northeast China Studies Association, founding member, 1992-93; American Historical Association, local arrangement committee, 1992; Association for Asian Studies, 1962-93; National Association of Chinese-Americans, local committee; Asian Studies Committee, Miami Valley Consortium of Colleges and Universities, chairman of the committee, 1966-69; Chinese Cultural and Educational Center, Washington, DC, founder 1972; National Council of Social Studies. **HONORS/AWARDS:** Jilin Academy of Social Sciences, Best Essay on Dongbei Literature, 1991; National Endowment of Humanties Faculty, grants, 1978, 1984; Council of International Education, faculty seminar in Taiwan, 1968. **SPECIAL ACHIEVEMENTS:** "Chinese Communism and Christianity," China Today, July, 1965; "Studies in Japanese Culture," Thought, Summer, 1965; "Ideology and Politics: An Analysis of the Proletarian Cultural Revolution in China," University of Dayton Review, November 13, 1968; "Porcelain Route: China's Maritime Relations," Papers in Social Sciences, Volume III (1983), pp29-36. **BIOGRAPHICAL SOURCES:** American Scholars: History, 1968. **HOME ADDRESS:** 10402 Great Arbor Drive, Potomac, MD 20854. **BUSINESS PHONE:** (202)274-5146.

SHA, WILLIAM T.
Engineer. Chinese American. **PERSONAL:** Born Sep 13, 1928, Kiangsu, China; son of Mr & Mrs Chin Fung Sha; married Joanne Y Sha, Jul 20, 1957; children: Andrea E, Beverly E, William C. **EDUCATION:** Polytechnic University, BS, mechanical engineering, 1958; Columbia University, PhD, nuclear engineering, 1964. **CAREER:** Combustion Engineering Inc, 1957-60; Westinghouse Electric Corp, senior scientist, 1960-67; Argonne National Laboratory, director of Multiphase Flow Research Institute, 1967-. **ORGANIZATIONS:** American Nuclear Society, fellow, 1960-; Phi Tau Phi, Midwest Chapter, president, 1986. **HONORS/AWARDS:** Argonne National Laboratory, Pace Setter Award for Exceptional Job Performance, 1989. **SPECIAL ACHIEVEMENTS:** Author of more than two hundred technical journal papers, 1965-. **BIOGRAPHICAL SOURCES:** Handbook for Heat and Mass Transfer. **HOME ADDRESS:** 2823 Meyers Rd, Oak Brook, IL 60521, (708)655-2257.

SHAH, ABHAY
Educator. Indo-American. **PERSONAL:** Born Jun 5, 1956, Almora, Uttar Pradesh, India; son of Madhuri Shah and Jagdish Lal Shah. **EDUCATION:** St Xaviers College, BA, 1980; University of Evansville, MBA, 1983; Oklahoma State University, PhD, 1991. **CAREER:** Oklahoma State University, teaching assistant, 1985-88; University of Southern Colorado, assistant professor, 1988-. **ORGANIZATIONS:** American Marketing Association, 1986-. **HONORS/AWARDS:** Alpha Mu Alpha, 1988. **BUSINESS ADDRESS:** Assistant Professor of Marketing, University of Southern Colorado, 2200 Bonforte Blvd, Pueblo, CO 81001, (719)549-2128.

SHAH, AHMER
Electrical engineer. Pakistani American. **PERSONAL:** Born Aug 26, 1965, Karachi, Sind, Pakistan; son of Mohammed Shah (deceased) and Fahmida Shah; married Mary Leavins Shah, May 23, 1987. **EDUCATION:** University of South Alabama, BSEE. **CAREER:** DELCO, consultant; Uniway Management Corp, consultant; James River Corp, project engr, electrical & instrumentation, currently. **ORGANIZATIONS:** Carmel Property Owner's Assn, president; Lake Forest Country Club; Lake Forest Yacht Club; Financial Planning Associates; Ducks Unlimited; Tau Beta Pi; IEEE. **HONORS/AWARDS:** Uniway Management Corp, President's 200 Club, 1988, 1989. **SPECIAL ACHIEVEMENTS:** Language proficiency: Urdu, Arabic. **HOME ADDRESS:** 6050 Grelot Rd, Mobile, AL 36609-3616, (205)342-2503.

SHAH, AMAR M.
Consulting engineer. Indo-American. **PERSONAL:** Born Mar 14, 1959, Ahmedabad, Gujarat, India; son of Manubhai Shah and Ramaben Shah; married Krupa A Shah, Dec 22, 1983; children: Neel A, Saagar A. **EDUCATION:** St Xavier's College, FYSc, 1977; LD College of Engineering, BSCE, 1981; New Jersey Institute of Technology, MSCE, 1984. **CAREER:** Perliter &

Ingalsbe, senior engineer, 1985-. **ORGANIZATIONS:** ASCE, 1992-. **BUSINESS ADDRESS:** Senior Engineer, Perliter & Ingalsbe, 1461 E Chevy Chase Dr, Glendale, CA 91206, (213)245-5785.

SHAH, AMIT
Editor, marketing specialist. Indo-American. **PERSONAL:** Born Apr 1, 1950, Calcutta, W. Bengal, India; son of Amal Shah & Aruna Dutt Shah; married Lisa Elaine Samson (divorced); children: Arnav Delaney Samson; partner: Pamela Jane Marshall. **EDUCATION:** Saint Stephen's College, Delhi University, BA (with honors), history, political science, 1970; Columbia University, School of General Studies and School of International Affairs, 1971-73; New York University, continuing education, 1980, 1981, 1983. **CAREER:** Delilah Books, managing editor, 1981-82; Saint Martin's Press, senior production editor, 1984-87; Basic Books, managing editor, 1991-92; Turnstile Magazine, founder, editor, 1986-; Prentice Hall Travel, senior editor, 1987-91; Prentice Hall/Paramount Publishing, senior editor and marketing specialist, 1992-. **ORGANIZATIONS:** Paramount Publishing, Multicultural Program Council, soc studies representative, 1993-; Multicultural Link, editorial board, 1993-; Multicultural Review, editorial advisory board, 1991-; Women's Action Alliance, consultant, 1976. **SPECIAL ACHIEVEMENTS:** Turnstile Literary Magazine has won NYSCA, NEA, CCLMP Awards, 1986, 1987, 1990, 1992, 1993; founder, Sprout House, Preschool Community Development Project, 1974; Fodor's India and Nepal, principal writer, 1988. **BIOGRAPHICAL SOURCES:** Turnstile, editorial, issue no 2, vol 2, 1990. **HOME ADDRESS:** 9 Dimick St, Somerville, MA 02143-4348, (617)625-6805. **BUSINESS ADDRESS:** Senior Editor & Marketing Specialist, Education Group, Prentice Hall/Paramount Publishing, 160 Gould St, Needham Heights, MA 02194-2310, (617)455-1317.

SHAH, AMITKUMAR L.
Textile company executive. Indo-American. **PERSONAL:** Born Oct 11, 1957, Mombasa, Kenya; son of Liladhar Raishi Shah and Kasturben L Shah. **EDUCATION:** University of Washington, BA, economics, political science, 1978. **CAREER:** International News Inc, executive vice president, 1983-; Zebra Club Inc, vice president, 1986-; Shah Safari Inc, executive vice president, 1986-. **ORGANIZATIONS:** Commission Asian American Affairs, State of Washington, 1991-; Washington South Asian Council, 1986-. **BUSINESS ADDRESS:** Executive Vice President, International News Inc, 19226 70th Ave S, Kent, WA 98032, (206)872-3542.

SHAH, ARVIND K.
Engineer. Indo-American. **PERSONAL:** Born Feb 23, 1939, Akrund, Gujarat, India; son of Keshavlal V Shah and Champaben K Shah; married Daksha A Shah, May 25, 1962; children: Kaushik A. **EDUCATION:** MS University of Baroda, BECE, 1960; Oklahoma State University, MSStE, 1965; Indiana Northern University, MBA, 1973. **CAREER:** SSOE Inc, project engr, 1969-72, mgr of structural eng, 1972-78, vice pres, mgr of production systems, 1978-89, Automotive Division, president, 1989-91, vice president, dir of operations, 1991-. **ORGANIZATIONS:** American Society of Civil Engineers, secretary, vice pres, president, 1978-85; Intergraph Computer Users Group, secretary, treasurer, vice pres, president, chmn, 1979-92; India Assn of Toledo, president, 1972, 1978; Gujarati Samaj, Detroit Branch, trustee, 1988-90; Automated Procedures For Engineering Consultants, trustee, 1986-, treasurer, president, currently. **SPECIAL ACHIEVEMENTS:** Presented papers: Implementation of Interactive Computer Graphic, Detroit Engineering Society, 1981; Soft Benefits vs Hard Benefits, APEC Inc, 1985; Dollars & Sense, Consulting Engineers, 1988. **HOME ADDRESS:** 6905 Underhill Dr, Lambertville, MI 48144, (313)856-1237. **BUSINESS ADDRESS:** Vice President, Director of Operations, SSOE Inc, Engineers, Architects & Planners, 1001 Madison Ave, Toledo, OH 43624, (419)255-3830.

SHAH, BHUPENDRA P.
Engineer. Indo-American. **PERSONAL:** Born Oct 14, 1934, Baroda City, Gujarat, India; son of Panalal Girdharlal Contractor and Sulaxana P Contractor; married Devyani, Nov 16, 1959; children: Nayan, Shailan. **EDUCATION:** Baroda University, India, BE (honors), 1956; Indian Institute of Science, India, ME (distinguished), 1958; Syracuse University, MEE, 1966. **CAREER:** Syracuse University, research asst, 1958-61; Catholic University, asst prof, 1961-67; CEIR, Control Data Corp, senior analyst, 1967-69; Singer-SISCO, prgm analyst, 1969-70; CIA, computer specialist, 1983-85, 1987-92; University of DC, assoc prof, 1970-. **ORGANIZATIONS:** IEEE, 1960-; NSPE-DCSPE, 1968-; Natl Federation of Indian American Assns, national executive director, 1984-; India House of Worship, secretary, 1974-; Alumni of Baroda University,

president, 1988-. **HONORS/AWARDS:** Sigma Xi, 1965. **SPECIAL ACHIEVEMENTS:** Editor: Samskar, quarterly journal, India House of Worship, 1981-. **HOME ADDRESS:** 1428 Chilton Dr, Silver Spring, MD 20904, (301)384-4090. **BUSINESS ADDRESS:** Associate Professor, Electrical Engineering Technology, University of the District of Columbia, 4200 Connecticut Ave NW, Bldg 42, Rm 109, Washington, DC 20008, (202)274-6307.

SHAH, CHANDU M.
Chemical engineer. Indo-American. **PERSONAL:** Born Oct 28, 1944, Bombay, Maharashtra, India; son of Maganlal S Shah and Shantaben M Shah; married Pushpa C Shah, Mar 6, 1973; children: Nirav, Nirali. **EDUCATION:** University of Bombay, BSc, chemistry, 1966; State University of New York, Buffalo, BSCE, 1971; Rutgers University, MBA, 1975. **CAREER:** BASF, group leader, 1973-79; Sun Chemical, process control manager, 1975-80; Hercules Pigment, owner, 1980-86; Sun Chemical process control superintendent, 1986-. **ORGANIZATIONS:** Jain Center of Cincinnati & Dayton, president, 1992-93. **HOME ADDRESS:** 7810 Albritton Pl, West Chester, OH 45069, (513)779-2013. **BUSINESS ADDRESS:** Process Control Superintendent, Sun Chemical Corp, 4526 Chickering Ave, Cincinnati, OH 45232, (513)681-5950.

SHAH, CHIMANLAL KESHAVLAL
County government official, engineer. Indo-American. **PERSONAL:** Born May 19, 1930, Samlod, Broach Dist, Gujarat, India; son of Keshavlal Maganlal Shah and Kamala (Shivlal) Shah; married Kalavati; children: Piyushkumar, Pallavi, Nitinkumar, Meeta. **EDUCATION:** Maharaja Sayajirao University of Baroda, India, BE (honors), civil, 1955; University of Roorkee, India, PGD, photogrammetric engineering, 1961. **CAREER:** Cook County, Department of Highways, highway engineer II, 1974-81, highway engineer III, 1981-89, highway engineer IV, 1989-. **ORGANIZATIONS:** Life member: Gujarati Samaj Chicago, Jain Society of Chicago. **SPECIAL ACHIEVEMENTS:** Department of Registration & Education, Licensed Professional Engineer, 1974-. **HOME ADDRESS:** 4825 W Davis St, Skokie, IL 60077, (708)677-4437.

SHAH, DHIRAJ HARILAL
Physician. Indo-American. **PERSONAL:** Born May 23, 1943, Mandvi-Kutch, Gujarat, India; son of Harilal Mavji Shah and Prabhaben Harilal Shah; married Pratima Dhiraj Shah, May 14, 1970; children: Nealesh D, Mitul D. **EDUCATION:** Gujarat University, RR Lalan College, inter science, 1963, NHLM Medical College, MBBS, 1969; SUNY at Buffalo, EJ Meyer Hospital, American Board of Radiology, diplomat, 1975. **CAREER:** VS Hospital, intern, 1969-70; Euclid General Hospital, intern, 1970-71; EJ Meyer Memorial Hospital, resident, 1971-74; Dhiraj Shah MD PC, president, 1975-. **ORGANIZATIONS:** American Medical Assn, 1975-; New York State Medical Society, 1975-; Niagara County Medical Society, 1975-; American College of Radiology, 1975-; Asian American Physicians from India, 1985-; Buffalo Radiological Society, 1975-; Rotary Club of Niagara Falls, World Comm Service, chmn, 1975-77; Federation of Jain Assns in North America, World Comm Service, chmn, 1991-. **HONORS/AWARDS:** Rotary Club of Niagara Falls, Service Award, 1977; Federation of Jaina, Jaina Ratna Award, 1993; Democratic National Convention, delegate, 1992; Hindu Cultural Society of W NY, trustee, 1991; Citi Mission of Buffalo, honorary director, 1991. **SPECIAL ACHIEVEMENTS:** Paper: Use of Indium I in Detection of Abscess, III Prize Winner, Research, 1973; invited to the White House by President Clinton to attend the Rose Garden signing ceremony of the Religious Freedom Restoration Act of 1993. **BIOGRAPHICAL SOURCES:** Buffalo News, p B4, Feb 22, 1993; India West, Jun 26, 1992, Mar 5, 1993; India Tribune, Nov 28, 1992; India Today, p 44h, Apr 15, 1993; Guj Samachar, p 16, Apr 4, 1993; India Abroad, p 12, June 12, 1992, p 34, Oct 4, 1991. **HOME ADDRESS:** 135 Morningside Dr, Grand Island, NY 14072, (716)773-1314. **BUSINESS ADDRESS:** President, Dhiraj Shah MD, PC, 817 Main St, Niagara Falls, NY 14301, (716)285-8438.

SHAH, DHIREN BHAWANJI
Government scientist. Indo-American. **PERSONAL:** Born Jun 7, 1936, Bombay, Maharashtra, India; son of Bhawanji H Shah & Laxmi B Shah; married Sheela, Nov 9, 1967; children: Neel, Jai. **EDUCATION:** University Bombay, BSc (with honors), 1956; University of Wisconsin, PhD, 1962; Johns Hopkins University, 1962-63, 1968-72; Justus Liebig University, W Germany, 1966-67. **CAREER:** Johns Hopkins University, research associate, 1968-72; University of Kentucky Medical School, assistant professor, 1972-79; US Food & Drug Administration, branch chief, microbial biochemistry, 1981-89, branch

chief, microbial ecology, 1989-92, director, division microbiological studies, 1992-. **ORGANIZATIONS:** American Society for Microbiology, 1982-; Sigma Xi, 1962-. **SPECIAL ACHIEVEMENTS:** Over 50 publications, presentations in peer-reviewed journals, natl & intl societies; grant, reviews. **BUSINESS ADDRESS:** Director, Division of Microbiological Studies, Food & Drug Administration, 200 C St SW, Washington, DC 20204, (202)205-4981.

SHAH, DINESH OCHHAVLAL
Educator. Indo-American. **PERSONAL:** Born Mar 31, 1938, Bombay, India; son of Ochhavalal Shah and Shardaben O Shah; married Suvarna Shah, Apr 6, 1968; children: Bijal D, Prerak D. **EDUCATION:** University of Bombay, BS, physics-mathematics, 1959, MS, biophysics, 1961; Columbia University, PhD, biophysics, 1965. **CAREER:** Columbia University, research associate, 1965-67, 1968-70; NASA Ames Research Center, research associate, 1967-68; University of Florida, asst prof, 1970-72, assoc prof, 1972-75, prof, 1975-, Center for Surface Science & Engineering, director, 1984-. **ORGANIZATIONS:** India Cultural & Education Ctr, founding president, 1992; American Inst of Chemical Engineers, 1970-; American Chemists Soc, 1970-; American Assn for the Advancement of Science, 1970-. **HONORS/AWARDS:** Swami Narayan Sanstha, Pride of India Award, 1993; Vishwa Gurjari Intl Award for Outstanding Achievement, 1992; University of Florida, Florida Blue Key Distinguished Faculty Award, 1992, President's Medallion for Excellence in Teaching & Scholarship, 1985, Teacher/Scholar of the Year, 1984-85. **SPECIAL ACHIEVEMENTS:** Author: Parab Tara Pani - A Book of Songs and Poems, 1986; 250 publications in surface chemistry aspects of engineering and biomedical systems, 1970-. **HOME ADDRESS:** 2615 SW 21st St, Gainesville, FL 32605, (904)378-3242. **BUSINESS ADDRESS:** Professor & Director, Center for Surface Science & Engineering, University of Florida, 425 Chemical Engineering, PO Box 116005, Gainesville, FL 32611-2002, (904)392-0877.

SHAH, GHULAM MOHAMMAD
Educator. Indo-American. **PERSONAL:** Born May 22, 1937, Srinagar, Jammu and Kashmir, India; son of Mohammad Hussain Shah and Zaina Shah; married Zubeda Shah, Oct 6, 1962; children: Fasahat Hussain, Sabahat Hussain, Shujahat Hussain. **EDUCATION:** Jammu and Kashmir University, BA, 1956; Aligarh Muslim University, MA, 1958, LLB, 1958; University of Wisconsin, PhD, 1966. **CAREER:** American Singh College, India, lecturer in mathematics, 1958-60; Regional Engineering College, India, lecturer in math, 1960-63; University of Wisconsin-Milwaukee, assistant professor, 1966-70; University of Wisconsin Centers, associate professor, 1970-75, professor, 1975-. **ORGANIZATIONS:** American Mathematical Society, 1965-73. **HONORS/AWARDS:** Aligarh Muslim University, India, Zia-Ud-din Medal, 1958. **SPECIAL ACHIEVEMENTS:** Several articles regarding geometry of zeros of polynomials and univalent functions in: Proceedings of American Mathematical Society, Transactions of American Mathematical Society, Illinois Journal of Mathematics, Pacific Journal of Mathematics, Indian Journal of Mathematics, Journal of Math & Science. **BUSINESS ADDRESS:** Professor of Mathematics, University of Wisconsin Centers, Waukesha County, 1500 University Dr, Northview Hall, Waukesha, WI 53188, (414)521-5537.

SHAH, HARIKRISHNA D. (HARISH)
Analytical chemist. Indo-American. **PERSONAL:** Born Jan 19, 1937, Bombay, Maharashtra, India; son of Dahyabhai B Shah and Vijyalaxmi D Shah; married Smita H Shah, Dec 20, 1965; children: Sejal, Suken, Samit. **EDUCATION:** L M College of Pharmacy, BS, 1964; Duquesne University, MS, industrial pharmacy, 1968. **CAREER:** Lannett Pharmaceutical, chemist, 1968-69; Merck and Co, senior chemist, 1969-. **ORGANIZATIONS:** Indo-American Club, chairperson for education, scholarship chairman, 1987-88; Gujarati Samaj, volunteer, 1970-; American Cancer Society, volunteer, 1991; Share and Care Foundation, volunteer, 1990-; Hare Krishna Temple, donation committee, volunteer, 1992-; Earthquake Relief Fund, 1993; ISKCON Temple, trustee, 1994. **HONORS/AWARDS:** Duquesne University, School of Pharmacy, Academic Excellence Honor Award, 1968; Water Associates, Excellence in Liquid Chromotography Award, 1980. **SPECIAL ACHIEVEMENTS:** North Penn High School Regional Science Fair Competition, Judge; Regional Math Counts Competition, Judge; Montgomery County Science Fair, Judge, March 1994; Delaware County Science Fair, Judge, April 1994; proficient in three languages; publications: Evaluation of Selected Parameters Affecting the Release of Insulin from Suppository Bases, 1968. **HOME ADDRESS:** 1142 Scobee Drive, Lansdale, PA 19446, (215)368-3218.

SHAH, HARISH S.
Educator. Indo-American. **PERSONAL:** Born Nov 19, 1943, Baroda, Gujarat, India; son of Shah Shantilal Maganlal & Shah Vinodben S; married Shah Rupam, Oct 18, 1972; children: Gopi, Neha. **EDUCATION:** Gujarat University, MSc, 1968; MTI, Texas, diploma, electronics, 1982. **CAREER:** North Harris College, program coordinator, HVAC&R currently. **BUSINESS ADDRESS:** Program Coordinator, HVAC&R Dept, North Harris College, 2700 W W Thorn Rd, WN 260L, Houston, TX 77073, (713)443-5672.

SHAH, HARNISH V.
Research chemist. Indo-American. **PERSONAL:** Born May 18, 1953, Rajpipla Broach, Gujarat, India; son of Vallabhdas H Shah and Manherben V Shah; married Madhvi H Shah, Jan 27, 1981; children: Rita H, Anita H. **EDUCATION:** Saurashtra University, Rajkot, India, BS, 1973, MS, 1975. **CAREER:** Columbia Organics, chemist, 1978-82; Cardinal Stabilizers, Inc, R&D manager, 1982-. **ORGANIZATIONS:** American Chemical Society, 1983-. **SPECIAL ACHIEVEMENTS:** US patent on manufacture of organotin compounds, 1989. **HOME ADDRESS:** 835 Knollwood Dr, Columbia, SC 29209, (803)776-7841.

SHAH, HASMUKH N.
Research scientist. Indo-American. **PERSONAL:** Born Mar 25, 1934, Radhanpur, Gujarat, India; son of Navinchandra M Shah; married Hansa Shah, Dec 25, 1959; children: Saumil, Viral. **EDUCATION:** Bombay University, India, BS (with honors), 1955, Department of Chemical Technology, BSTech, plastics, 1957, MSTech, research, 1960; South German Plastic Center, Wurzburg, diplom, engineering, 1970. **CAREER:** GAF Corp, research & development engineer; Into-Chem Akzo Inc, research & development engineer; Bectron Dickinson, research engineer; Johnson & Johnson, consultant; Convatec Bristol Myers & Squibb, research scientist, 1990-. **ORGANIZATIONS:** Society of Plastics Engineering, senior member, 1975-; American Association for the Advancement of Science, 1978; Society of Chemical Engineers, 1990; Society for the Advancement of Medical Products & Designing Engineering. **HONORS/AWARDS:** Material of Engineering, Citation Award for Heat Sinking Panels, 1980; Government of India, scholar for research for MS in technology of plastics, 1958-60; Government of India, scholar for studies at South German Plastic Institute, Wurzburg, 1968-70. **SPECIAL ACHIEVEMENTS:** Disposable Cassette for Insulin Pump, patent, 1983-84; Heat Sinking Panels, patent pending; Disposable Kit for Surgical Sharps, patent, 1970; Rigid PVC, Bombay Technologist Centenany issue, 1969-70; Painting and Decoration on Polystyrene, annual issue, Popular Plastics, 1970. **HOME ADDRESS:** 10 Landing Ln, #7G, New Brunswick, NJ 08901, (908)249-4807. **BUSINESS PHONE:** (908)281-2638.

SHAH, JAYPRAKASH BALVANTRAI
Consulting engineering company executive. Indo-American. **PERSONAL:** Born Nov 2, 1946, Jamshedpur, Bihar, India; son of Balvantrai & Mangala Shah; married Bharti, Nov 29, 1972; children: Bejal, Rupal. **EDUCATION:** Walchand College/Shivaji University, India, bachelor of civil engineering, 1969; Wayne State University, MSCE, 1970; University of Detroit, MBA, 1981. **CAREER:** Oakland County, operations engineer, 1971-79; Spalding, DeDecker & Associates Inc, vice chairman, 1979-. **ORGANIZATIONS:** American Society of Civil Engineers, fellow, 1971-, 1995 Specialty Conference, chairman, 1993-95; Consulting Engineers Council, MI, Transportation Comm, 1991-93; Water Environment Federation, 1993-; American Arbitration Assn, Construction Panel, 1985-; Waterford Township, planning commissioner, 1987-, Zoning Board of Appeals, 1988-93; Oakland County Economic Dev Corp, vice chairman, 1982-. **HONORS/AWARDS:** ASCE, Semibranch Outstanding Engineer of the Year, 1993. **SPECIAL ACHIEVEMENTS:** Michigan Soc of Planning Comm, GIS/Mapping for Planners, 1991. **BUSINESS ADDRESS:** Vice Chairman, Assistant CEO, Spalding DeDecker & Associates Inc, 655 W 13 Mile Rd, Madison Heights, MI 48071, (313)585-5545.

SHAH, MAYANK H.
Travel agency owner. Indo-American. **PERSONAL:** Born Mar 21, 1951, Bombay, Maharashtra, India; son of Himmatlal Shah and Vasant Shah; married Mita Shah, Jul 6, 1974; children: Aalok, Shamin. **EDUCATION:** University of Rhode Island, BS, 1974. **CAREER:** Devoe Travel Svc, owner, manager, 1989-. **HOME ADDRESS:** 1834 E. Nanette Ave, West Covina, CA 91792. **BUSINESS ADDRESS:** Owner/Manager, Devoe Travel Service, 6229 Bristol Parkway, Culver City, CA 90230.

SHAH, MINAL J.
Physician. Indo-American. **PERSONAL:** Born Jun 14, 1956, Kalol, Gujarat, India; married Neeta Shah, Feb 7, 1987; children: Neil, Devan. **EDUCATION:** Queens College, BA, 1980; JN Medical College, India, MBBS, 1987; Winthrop University Hospital, New York, MD, 1992. **CAREER:** Self-employed, physician, 1992-. **ORGANIZATIONS:** AMA, 1990-; ASIM, 1990-. **HOME ADDRESS:** 7773 N State St, Lowville, NY 13367, (315)376-5255. **BUSINESS ADDRESS:** Physician, Beaver River Health Center, Route 126, Beaver Falls, NY 13305, (315)346-6824.

SHAH, MIRZA MOHAMMED
Engineer. Indo-American. **PERSONAL:** Born Aug 11, 1941, Delhi, India; son of Mirza Iqbal Shah and Kishwar Jehan Begam; married Gulrukh Shah, Oct 27, 1977; children: Alvira Sultana, Mirza Akbar. **EDUCATION:** Aligarh Muslim University, India, BS, 1959, BSME, 1963; California State University, Los Angeles, MSME, 1973. **CAREER:** Central Mechanical Engineering Research Institute, India, scientist-in-chg, 1964-68; Institute of Refrigeration, Norway, scientist, 1968-69; Bechtel Power Corp, mech engr, 1973; United Engineers, engr, 1974-76; Gilbert Commonwealth, sr engr, 1976-78; Ebasco Services, principal engr, 1978-89, 1991-93; self-employed, consulting engineer, 1994-. **ORGANIZATIONS:** American Society of Heating and Air-Conditioning Engineers, 1969-, chmn handbook sub-committee of technical committee 8.4, 1979-83; American Society of Mechanical Engineers, Long Island Chapter, chmn, heat transfer technical committee, 1978-. **HONORS/AWARDS:** National Science Foundation, Research Grant, 1986. **SPECIAL ACHIEVEMENTS:** Author of more than 50 publications about engineering, including: research papers, handbook chapters, trade journal articles; contributing writer: ASHRAE Handbook, 1983; General Electric Heat Transfer & Fluid Flow Data Book, 1981-86. **HOME ADDRESS:** 10 Dahlia Ln, Redding, CT 06896, (203)938-2539. **BUSINESS ADDRESS:** Consulting Engineer, 10 Dahlia Ln, Redding, CT 06896, (203)938-2539.

SHAH, MOWAHID HUSSAIN
Attorney, editor, speaker. Pakistani American. **PERSONAL:** Born Jan 18, 1949, Rawalpindi, Pakistan; son of Amjad Hussain Sayed and Samin Sayed; married Dayna Kinnard, Apr 7, 1978. **EDUCATION:** Punjab University, Lahore, BA, 1968; Punjab University Law College, LLB, 1970; George Washington University, National Law Center, LLM, intl law, 1976. **CAREER:** American-Arab Anti Discrimination Committee, consultant, 1980-81; Abourezk, Sobd, & Tristu, of counsel, 1981-85; The Muslim (daily), dep editor/editor designate, 1986-87; Hassan & Hassan, Advocates, advocate, 1988; Hon Nawaz Sharif, former Prime Minister of Pakistan, 1993 election strategist, 1993; Eastern Times, editor, 1989-. **ORGANIZATIONS:** US Supreme Court Bar, 1983-; Foreign Correspondents Association, vice president, 1992; District of Columbia Bar, 1980-; High Court Bar, Lahore, Pakistan, 1970-. **HONORS/AWARDS:** National Institute of Trial Advocacy, Diplomate in Trial Advocacy, 1982. **SPECIAL ACHIEVEMENTS:** US State Dept, Foreign Service Institute, guest lecturer, 1983-; Harvard University, panel speaker, 1993; C-SPAN, featured guest, 1990; author, "Pakistan, Islam, & Politics of Muslim Unrest," Change and the Muslim World, 1981, over 100 articles. **BUSINESS ADDRESS:** Editor, Eastern Times, 933 N Kenmore Street, Suite 400, Arlington, VA 22201, (703)243-5585.

SHAH, MUBARAK ALI
Educator. Pakistani American. **PERSONAL:** Born Oct 14, 1954, Lakhi, Sindh, Pakistan; son of Hakim Ali Sham & Hashmat Jahan; married Becky J Lee, Jun 1986; children: Sono Lee. **EDUCATION:** NCET, Karachi, Pakistan, BE, 1979; Wayne State University, Detroit, MS, 1982, PhD, 1986. **CAREER:** University of Central Florida, assistant professor, 1986-91, associate professor, 1991-. **ORGANIZATIONS:** IEEE; ACM; SPIE. **HONORS/AWARDS:** Ministy of Education, Pakistan, Quad-er Azam Scholarship, 1981-86. **SPECIAL ACHIEVEMENTS:** 25 research papers published in Comupter Vision, 1986-93. **BUSINESS ADDRESS:** Associate Professor, Computer Science Dept, University of Central Florida, Orlando, FL 32816.

SHAH, NAGAMBAL DEEPAK
Educator. Indo-American. **PERSONAL:** Born Nov 20, 1944, Perumannore, Kerala, India; daughter of Mr and Mrs P S Narayana Iyer (both deceased); children: Ashok, Anand. **EDUCATION:** University of Kerala, India, BSc, 1964, MSc, 1966; University of Windsor, Ontario, MS, 1968, PhD, 1970. **CAREER:** Michigan Technological University, assistant professor of math, 1969-71; Florida Institute of Technology, assistant professor of math-sciences, 1971-72; Spelman College, Dept of Math, professor, 1972-. **ORGANIZA-**

TIONS: American Statistical Association, 1968-; Pi Mu Epsilon; GA Heart Association's High School Blood Pressure Education Program Committee, 1977-81. **HONORS/AWARDS:** Government of India, Merit Scholarship, 1964-66; His Highness Maharajah Scholarship, 1961-64; US Delegate, WHO Interregional Conference on Teaching Statistics to Medical Undergraduates, Karachi, Pakistan, 1978; CHANCE Project, with Dartmouth College, 1992-94; Province of Ontario, merit scholarship, 1968-69. **SPECIAL ACHIEVEMENTS:** "A Retrospective Study of Shift in Staff from Predominantly White to Black as Relates to Surgical Care," JAMA, vol 72, no 7, 1980; "On Multiplying a Polykay by Ploykay Products of Weigal-5," Canadian Journal of Stats, vol 2, no 2, 1974; contributions to products of polykays, PhD thesis, 1970. **BUSINESS ADDRESS:** Professor of Mathematics, Spelman College, 350 Spelman Ln, Box 272, Atlanta, GA 30314.

SHAH, NAGIN B.
Aerospace hardware company executive. Indo-American. **PERSONAL:** Born May 17, 1946, Mozambique, Magudo, Mozambique; son of Bachubhai & Banuvanti Shah; married Priya Shah, Nov 30, 1973; children: Ronak, Rachana. **EDUCATION:** University of Bombay, BCom, 1968; University of Scranton, MBA, 1970; University of Pennsylvania, postgraduate courses, 1972. **CAREER:** Impex International, president, currently. **ORGANIZATIONS:** IRMSDC, MIC chairman, 1985-; Rotary, committee chairman, 1985-. **HONORS/AWARDS:** Westinghouse Electric Co, Best Supplier, 1990; Paul Harris Fellow. **BUSINESS ADDRESS:** President, Impex International, Inc, 810 W State Blvd, Fort Wayne, IN 46808.

SHAH, NANDLAL CHIMANLAL
Physician. Indo-American. **PERSONAL:** Born Jul 3, 1933, Sadra, Gujarat, India; son of Chimanlal Devchanddas Shah and Dahiben Chimanlal Shah; married Indira N Shah, May 15, 1960; children: Sandip, Tushar. **EDUCATION:** BJ Medical College, Ahmedabad, India, MB, BS, 1957; Gujarat University at Ahmedabad; Albert Einstein College of Medicine, MD, board certificate, physical medicine and rehabilitation, 1974. **CAREER:** Family & General Practice, India, 3 years, Kenya, 10 years; Yonkers General Hospital, intern, 1970; St Barnabas Hospital, internal medicine resident, 1971; Albert Einstein College of Medicine, PM & R residency, 1971-74; Institute of Physical Medicine and Rehabilitation, staff physiatrist, 1974-79; Thomas Rehabilitation Hospital, medical director, 1979-81; Charlotte Rehab Hospital, staff physiatrist, 1981; Carolina Rehabilitation Clinic, Physical Medicine & Rehab, physician, owner, 1981-; local Charlotte Hospital, consultant, currently. **ORGANIZATIONS:** American Medical Association, 1974-81; Mecklenburg County Medical Association, 1981-84; American Congress of Rehabilitation, 1974-81. **SPECIAL ACHIEVEMENTS:** American Board of PM & R, passed board exam, certificate, 1977; American Board of Quality Assurance and Utilization Physicians, certified, 1993. **BUSINESS ADDRESS:** Owner, Physician, Carolina Rehabilitation Clinic, 230 Baldwin Ave, Charlotte, NC 28204-3110.

SHAH, NAREN N.
Cardiologist. Indo-American. **PERSONAL:** Born Jan 12, 1934, Ahmedabad, India; son of Natwarlal G Shah and Kanta M Shah; married Mary Ann Iafolla; children: Jennifer, Jeffrey, Jason. **EDUCATION:** MG Science Institute, Ahmedabad, 1951; BJ Medical College, MD, 1957; Elgin General Hospital, St Thomas, ON, Canada, intern, 1959-60. **CAREER:** Union Memorial Hospital, Baltimore, resident in medicine, 1960-62; Hahnemann Medical Center, Philadelphia, resident in cardiology, 1963-64, fellow in kidney disease, 1964-65; Philadelphia General Hospital, resident in cardiology, 1965-66; Hamilton General Hospital, fellow in medicine, 1966-67; St Michael's Hospital Toronto, fellow in cardiology, 1967-68; Group Health Association, 1968-72; Lincoln Hospital, Bronx, attending cardiologist, 1972-73; Metropolitan Hospital, Manhattan, 1973-80; New York Medical College, Valhalla, clinic associate, 1980-; VA Medical Center, Montrose, NY, chief medicine, 1980-. **ORGANIZATIONS:** American College Physicians, fellow; American College Angiology; American College Cardiology; American Society Echocardiography; American Heart Association; New York Medical Society. **HONORS/AWARDS:** AMA, Physician's Recognition Award, 1979-. **MILITARY SERVICE:** US Army, lt col, 1980-. **BUSINESS ADDRESS:** Chief of Medicine, VA Medical Center, Montrose, NY 10548.

SHAH, NARENDRA M.
Engineer. Indo-American. **PERSONAL:** Born Oct 9, 1937, Ahmedabad, Gujarat, India; son of Mohanlal P Shah and Hiraben Shah; married Anila N Shah, Dec 28, 1962; children: Sonya, Munier. **EDUCATION:** Gujarat University, BSEE, 1960; Illinois Institute of Technology, MSEE, 1962. **CAREER:**

Bechtel Corp, cost & schedule supervisor, 1962-. **ORGANIZATIONS:** IEEE, 1964-. **HONORS/AWARDS:** Cousteau Society, Certificate of Appreciation, 1982; Republican National Committee, Presidential Achievement Award, 1983; Ellis Island Foundation Inc, Certificate of Appreciation, 1984; March of Dimes, Certificate of Appreciation, 1984, 1985; Bechtel Corp, Special Olympics Mini Marathon Volunteer, 1992. **BUSINESS ADDRESS:** Cost & Schedule Supervisor, Bechtel Corp, 9801 Washington Blvd, Gaithersburg, MD 20878, (301)417-3000.

SHAH, NARENDRA N.
Physician. Indo-American. **PERSONAL:** Born Feb 4, 1948, Baroda, Gujarat, India; son of Natverlal Shah and Icchaben Shah; married Alka, Mar 16, 1975; children: Neelay, Ashish. **EDUCATION:** MS University of Baroda, pre med, 1965-66; Medical College, Baroda, MBBS, 1972; Jewish Hospital of Brooklyn, residency, 1973-76. **CAREER:** TBK Clinic, anesthesiologist, 1976-80; Associated Anesthesiology Services, president, 1980-85; Midland Empire Anesthesiology Inc, president, anesthesiologist, 1986-90; Heartland Anesthesiology Inc, anesthesiologist, 1990-. **ORGANIZATIONS:** American Society of Anesthesiologists, 1973-; Missouri Society of Anesthesiologists, 1976-; Buchanan County Medical Services, 1976-. **MILITARY SERVICE:** US Air Force, lt col, 1986-92; Missouri Air National Award. **BUSINESS ADDRESS:** Anesthesiologist, Dept of Anesthesiology, Heartland Hospitals, 5325 Faraon, St Joseph, MO 64506.

SHAH, NILESH D.
Educator, consultant. Indo-American. **PERSONAL:** Born Apr 15, 1960, Bombay, Maharashtra, India; son of Dhiraj B Shah & Hansa D Shah; married Prena Shah, Mar 5, 1988; children: Naman N. **EDUCATION:** Regional Institute of Technology, Jamshedpur, India, BS, electrical engineering, 1983; New Jersey Institute of Technology, Newark, MS, CIS, 1987. **CAREER:** UNC-Charlotte, instructor, 1987-88; Monroe College, professor, acting chairperson, computer science, 1988-; DeVry Tech Institute, adjunct professor, 1991-93. **HOME ADDRESS:** 94 Brandywine Road, Fords, NJ 08863, (908)225-3662.

SHAH, NITIN J.
Chemist. Indo-American. **PERSONAL:** Born Nov 30, 1948, Bombay, India; son of Jayantilal Shah; married Meena Shah, Mar 18, 1954; children: Michelle, Jessica, Jamie. **EDUCATION:** MSc, organic chemistry, 1970. **CAREER:** Chem-Impex, owner, president, currently. **BUSINESS ADDRESS:** Owner, President, Chem-Impex, 825 Dillon, Wood Dale, IL 60191, (708)766-2112.

SHAH, PARTH J.
Educator. Indo-American. **EDUCATION:** Auburn University, PhD, 1990. **CAREER:** University of Michigan, Dearborn, assistant professor, currently. **ORGANIZATIONS:** Mackinac Center for Public Policy, board of advisors; Heartland Institute, board of advisors. **SPECIAL ACHIEVEMENTS:** Publications on monetary theory, money and banking, economic development, and Austrian economics. **BUSINESS ADDRESS:** Asst Prof, Economics, Dept of Social Sciences, University of Michigan-Dearborn, Dearborn, MI 48128-1491, (313)593-5096.

SHAH, PIYUSH A.
Textile company executive. Indo-American. **PERSONAL:** Born Sep 14, 1939, Ahmedabad, Gujarat, India; son of Ajitbhai and Indiraben; married Abantika, Apr 11, 1968. **EDUCATION:** MS University, Baroda, India, BS, textile technology, 1961; Lowell Tech Institute, MS, textile engineering, 1965. **CAREER:** Fabric Development Inc, president, currently; Textile Products, Inc, president, currently. **ORGANIZATIONS:** SAMPE. **BUSINESS ADDRESS:** President, Fabric Development Inc & Textile Products Inc, 1217 Mill St, Quakertown, PA 18951.

SHAH, PRADYUMNA R.
Company executive. Indo-American. **PERSONAL:** Born Jul 29, 1941, Baroda, Gujarat, India; son of Ratilal Shah and Shantaben Shah; married Ramola, Feb 9, 1969; children: Rupl, Minal. **EDUCATION:** MS University of Baroda, India, MS, 1964; Indian Institute of Management, Ahmedabad, India, diploma, 1968; Rutgers University, MBA, 1976. **CAREER:** American Express, assistant accountant, 1971-72; Amerada Hess Corp, staff accountant, 1972-74; Northeast Container, controller, vice president, 1975-. **ORGANIZATIONS:** India Cultural Association of Central Jersey, founding and executive member, 1980-; VHP of America, 1982-. **HONORS/AWARDS:** MS University of Baroda, Silver Medalist, 1964. **BUSINESS ADDRESS:** Controller, Vice President,

Northeast Container Corp, 161 Woodbine St, Bergenfield, NJ 07621, (201)385-6200.

SHAH, PRAVIN M. (PAUL)
Roofing company executive. Indo-American. **PERSONAL:** Born Feb 14, 1950, Chotila, Gujarat, India; son of Mansukh M Shah and Kamala M Shah; married Jyotsna P Shah, Jan 27, 1975; children: Dipak P, Chirag P. **EDUCATION:** University of Missouri, Columbia, BS, 1972; Northern Illinois University, MBA, 1977; State of Illinois, Department of Professional Regulation, PE, 1979. **CAREER:** Pioneer Systems, Inc, engineer, 1972-75; Crowther, Inc, estimator, 1975-79; Anderson & Shah Roofing, Inc, president, 1980-. **ORGANIZATIONS:** Chicago Roofing Contractors Association, board of directors, 1988-90, vp, 1991, director, 1992-, Contract Review Committee, chairman, 1990-; Jain Society of Chicago, Construction Committee, 1990-. **HONORS/AWARDS:** Big Bropthers/Big Sisters of Will County, volunteer tutor, 1990-. **BIOGRAPHICAL SOURCES:** Chicago Tribune, Southwest Tempo Section, Big Brothers/Big Sisters, photograph, p 9, April 19, 1993. **BUSINESS ADDRESS:** President, Anderson & Shah Roofing, Inc, 23900 County Farm Rd, Joliet, IL 60436, (815)741-0909.

SHAH, RAJANI C.
Engineering manager. Indo-American. **PERSONAL:** Born in Palej, Gujarat, India; son of Chandulal M Shah (deceased) and Hiraben C Shah (deceased); married Asmita R Shah, Jan 19, 1978; children: Rishita, Ajita, Rupesh. **EDUCATION:** M Sayajirao University of Baroda, BE, 1972; Polytechnic Institute of New York, MS, 1975. **CAREER:** Liberty Heat Treating Inc, production mgr, 1975-78; GTE Corp, sr engr, 1978-84; IBM Corp, sr associate engr, 1984-88, staff engr, 1988-90, advisory engr, 1990-93; Sematech/IBM, project mgr, 1993-, program mgr, 1994-. **ORGANIZATIONS:** ASM, organizing committee, Electronics Materials and Packaging Conference, 1990-93, chmn, York, PA Chapter, 1984-85; Lions Club, Fishkill-EF, president, 1989-90, dir, Austin, TX Chapter, 1993-94. **HONORS/AWARDS:** IBM, Formal/Informal Awards, 1988-92. **SPECIAL ACHIEVEMENTS:** Language proficiency, speaks, reads, writes: English, Hindi, and Gujarati. **HOME ADDRESS:** 1304 Dusky Thrush Trail, Austin, TX 78746, (512)329-0320. **BUSINESS PHONE:** (512)356-3439.

SHAH, RAMESH KESHAVLAL
Auto company executive. Indo-American. **PERSONAL:** Born Sep 23, 1941, Bombay, India; son of Keshavlal M & Hiraben K Shah; married Rekha R Shah, Jan 22, 1968; children: Nilay R, Nirav R. **EDUCATION:** Gujarat University, India, BE, 1963; Stanford University, MS, 1964, engineering, 1970, PhD, 1972. **CAREER:** Air Preheater Co, Wellsville, NY, project engineer, 1964-66; Avco Lycoming, Charleston, SC, project engineer, 1968-69; GMC, Harrison Division, Lockport, NY, research engineer, 1971-76, technical director of research, 1976-83, staff development engineer, 1983-89, senior staff research scientist, 1989-; State University of New York at Buffalo, adjunct professor, 1978-. **ORGANIZATIONS:** American Society of Mechanical Engineers, fellow, 1966-; Society of Automotive Engineers, 1972-; Indian Society for Heat and Mass Transfer, life member, 1981-; Niagara Frontier Association of R&D Directors, 1989-, vice president, 1993-94; ASME Heat Transfer Division, executive committee, 1982-87, chairperson, 1985-86; Assembly of World Conferences on Experimental Heat Transfer, Fluid Mechanics and Thermodynamics, president, 1988-; Journal of Heat Transfer, technical editor, 1981-86; Experimental Thermal and Fluid Science, editor in chief, 1988-. **HONORS/AWARDS:** ASME Region III, Technical Achievement Award, 1979; General Motors, Outstanding Achievement Award, 1986; ASME Heat Transfer Division, Valued Service Award, 1986, 1987, 1991, 50th Anniversary Award, 1988; ASME & Pai Tau Sigma, Charles Russ Richards Memorial Award, 1989. **SPECIAL ACHIEVEMENTS:** Published 68 technical papers, 11 books and 12 symposium volumes that covers the research areas of compact heat exchangers, process heat exchangers, internal laminar and turbulent flow forced convection, and heat transfer in manufacturing and matyerials processing. **BUSINESS ADDRESS:** Senior Staff Research Scientist, Harrison Division, General Motors Corp, 200 Upper Mountain Rd, Bldg 6, Lockport, NY 14094-1896, (716)439-3020.

SHAH, RAMESH V.
Roofing company executive. Indo-American. **PERSONAL:** Born Jul 17, 1940, Baroda, Gujarat, India; son of Vadilal Shah and Kamlabeh Shah; married Shehlata Shah, Jun 2, 1967. **EDUCATION:** Secondary School Certificate Board, Poona, SSC, 1957; MS University of Baroda, BE, civil engineering, 1963. **CAREER:** Gujarat Refinery, IOC Ltd, engineering assistant, 1963-65;

Instrumentation Ltd, assistant engineer, 1965-68; U J Bhatt Consulting Engineering, senior engineer, 1968-70; Engineers India Ltd, asst engineer, 1970-73, executive engineer, 1974-77, senior engineer, 1977-80; Anup Contracting, estimator, 1981; City of New York, Div of Real Property, associate, 1981-82; K G Roofing Corp, project manager/vice president, 1982-. **BUSINESS ADDRESS:** Vice President, K G Roofing Corp, 103-07 Plattwood Ave, Ozone Park, NY 11417, (718)843-0700.

SHAH, SARJU S.
Physician. Indo-American. **PERSONAL:** Born Dec 1, 1965, Ahmedabad, Gujarat, India; son of Mr and Mrs Suresh A Shah; married Shreya S Shah, Dec 13, 1991. **EDUCATION:** Government Medical College, Surat, Gujarat, India, MBBS, 1989. **CAREER:** Oakwood Hospital, house officer III, family practice, currently. **ORGANIZATIONS:** American Academy of Family Physicians, 1991-; Michigan Academy of Family Physicians, 1991-; Gujarat Medical Council, India. **HONORS/AWARDS:** National Kidney Foundation, Scholarship, 1991-92, 1992-93. **SPECIAL ACHIEVEMENTS:** Author: Neonatal Sephcaenia Due to H-Influenzae Acquired from Mother, case report research, 1993. **HOME ADDRESS:** 170 E. Tami Circle, Apt G306, Westland, MI 48185, (313)728-4311.

SHAH, SHAILESH R.
Arts and crafts company executive. Indo-American. **PERSONAL:** Born Jul 17, 1946, Baroda, Gujarat, India; son of Rajnikant Shah; married Bharti Shah, May 8, 1977. **EDUCATION:** MS University of Baroda, BCom, 1967; Columbia University, MBA, 1974. **CAREER:** Pearl Art & Craft Supplies Inc, president, CEO, currently. **ORGANIZATIONS:** Indian Cultural Association, trustee, 1991-; Kala Kondra, 1969-. **HOME ADDRESS:** 481 Grove Ave, Edison, NJ 08820.

SHAH, SHEILA
Physician. Indo-American. **PERSONAL:** Born Mar 14, 1945, Zanzibar, United Republic of Tanzania; daughter of Mr & Mrs H D Shah; married Upendra V Pai, Dec 29, 1973; children: Sona Pai, Neil Pai. **EDUCATION:** Bombay University, Elphinstone College, int science, 1964, Seth GS Medical College, MBBS, 1969; West Virginia University Medical, pathology residency, 1970-74. **CAREER:** West Virginia University, assistant professor pathology, 1974-79, associate professor pathology, 1979-80; Northwest Missouri Pathologist, MD, PC, vice president, 1980-. **ORGANIZATIONS:** Buchanan County Medical Society, president, 1993; Missouri State Medical Association, 1980-; American Medical Association, 1980-; International Academy Pathology, 1974-; American College of Pathology, 1990-; ASCP, 1975-. **HONORS/AWARDS:** West Virginia University, MacLachlan Award for Excellence in Teaching in the Basic Medical Sciences, 1979. **SPECIAL ACHIEVEMENTS:** Scientific publications: Cancer vol 51, p 509-520, 1983; "Epstein-Barr Virus, Fatal Infectious Monomucleosis," in American Journal of Clinical Pathology, vol 78, no 5, Nov 1982. **BIOGRAPHICAL SOURCES:** Buchanan County Medical Society Bulletin, vol 45, p 10-11, Feb 1993; St Joseph News Press, Gazette, Dec 1, 1992; St Joseph Telegraph, no 7, Feb 18, 1993. **BUSINESS ADDRESS:** Vice President, Dept of Pathology, Northwest Missouri Pathologists, 5325 Faraon St, St Joseph, MO 64506, (816)271-6170.

SHAH, SHIRISH
Plating business owner. Indo-American. **PERSONAL:** Born Mar 22, 1944, Sojitra, Gujarat, India; son of Kantilal C Shah and Shardaben K Shah; married Gita Shah, May 15, 1971; children: Niva. **EDUCATION:** Gujarat University, BS, 1965, MS, 1967; SP University, PhD, 1971. **CAREER:** Victor Comp, chemist, 1976; Nobert Plating, chemist, 1983; Omega Plating, president, currently. **SPECIAL ACHIEVEMENTS:** IR & UV spectroscopic studies on acetoacet arylamide and their sodium comp, 1970; arylamides of 6 nitro, 1-2 benzisoxazole-3 carboxylic acid, 1971; synthesis of B-(2-4 dinitrophenoxy) croton arylamid, 1971. **HOME ADDRESS:** 16924 Pineview, Lockport, IL 60441, (815)485-1954.

SHAH, SHIRISH K.
Educator. Indo-American. **PERSONAL:** Born May 24, 1942, Ahmedabad, Gujarat, India; son of Sushilaben and Kalyanbhai Shah; married Kathleen, Jun 28, 1973; children: Lawrence. **EDUCATION:** Gujarat University, St Xavier's College, BSc, chemistry, phys, 1962; University of Delaware, PhD, physical chemistry, 1968; University of Virginia, certificate business management, 1986. **CAREER:** Washington College, assistant professor of chemistry, 1967-68; Vita Foods Inc, director of quality control, 1968-72; Chesapeake College, Marine Science and Food Science, administrator, associate professor of sci-

ence, 1968-76; Community of College of Balitmore, Dept of Science & Technology, professor, Dept of Computers & Technology, chairman, 1976-91; College of Notre Dame, associate professor of chemistry, 1991-. **ORGANIZATIONS:** American Chemical Society, Maryland Section, chair, education committee, 1991-; National Association of Industrial Technology, board of accreditation, 1988-; American Association of Tech Education, 1985-; American Institute of Chemists, fellow, 1985-; American Lung Association of Maryland, board member, 1971-80; Baltimore City's Vocational Advisory Council, 1983-91; Maryland Association of Community and Junior Colleges, president, 1978-91; Baltimore City's Apprenticeship Council, consultant, 1980-91. **HONORS/AWARDS:** Republican Presidential Task Force, Gold Medal from President Bush, 1990; World University, PhD, Cultural Education, 1986. **SPECIAL ACHIEVEMENTS:** Built computer aided design lab through private and public grants, 1988-90; developed and implemented telecommunications program with significant assistance from MCI Inc, 1985-88; developed marine science & food science curriculum through grants, 1972-75; "The Radiation Chemistry of Nitro & Nitrose Compounds," PhD thesis, 1968. **HOME ADDRESS:** 5605 Purlington Way, Baltimore, MD 21212-2950. **BUSINESS ADDRESS:** Associate Professor of Chemistry, College of Notre Dame of Maryland, 4701 N Charles St, Baltimore, MD 21210, (410)532-5712.

SHAH, SYED M.
Editor. Pakistani American. **PERSONAL:** Born Nov 25, 1945, Shahbazpur, Pakistan; son of Fazal H Shah & Noor Jehan; married Nishat Shah, Jan 19, 1974; children: Shabnam B, Asad A. **EDUCATION:** Peshawar University, Pakistan, MS, chemistry, 1969; Queens College, CUNY, MLS, 1976. **CAREER:** New York Public Library, librarian trainee, 1974-76; HW Wilson Co, Biological & Agricultural Index, editor, 1976-. **ORGANIZATIONS:** Special Library Association, membership committee, 1992-; American Library Association, 1977-. **HONORS/AWARDS:** Peshawar University, Gold Medal in Chemistry, 1969. **SPECIAL ACHIEVEMENTS:** Language proficiency in Urbu, Punjabi; thesis: Protoberberine Alkaloids in Berberis Lycium. **BUSINESS ADDRESS:** Editor, Biological & Agricultural Index, HW Wilson Co, 950 University Ave, Bronx, NY 10452, (718)588-8400.

SHAH, UMA
Association administrator. Indo-American. **CAREER:** Asian-Indian Women in America, president, currently. **BUSINESS ADDRESS:** President, Asian-Indian Women in America, RD 1, Box 98, Palisades, NY 10964, (914)365-1066.*

SHAH, YOGESH K.
Engineer. Indo-American. **PERSONAL:** Born May 1, 1945, Ahmedabad, India; son of Kantilal N Shah and Sharda K Shah; married Rupa Y Shah, Dec 30, 1972; children: Anup Y, Arti Y. **EDUCATION:** Gujarat University, BSEE, 1967; Polytechnic Institute of New York, MSEE, 1977. **CAREER:** ITT, engineer II, 1977-78, senior engineer, 1980-82; Western Electric, senior engineer, 1978-80; Northern Tele, senior engineer, 1982-84; CDI Corp, senior system analyst, 1984-85; GSA, electronics engineer, 1986-92, sup electronics engineer, 1992-. **ORGANIZATIONS:** IEEE. **SPECIAL ACHIEVEMENTS:** Speaker of a session on an "ISDN in FTS2000" in ISDN '91; chaired session "Govt Applications of ISDN" in ISDN '92, conference & seminar, 1992; speaker on "ISDN and the Integrated Federal Telecommunication System" at COS conference, 1991. **BUSINESS ADDRESS:** Sup Electronics Engineer, General Services Adm/FTS2000, 7980 Boeing Ct, Vienna, VA 22182, (703)760-7754.

SHAHZAD, FARHAT
Music company executive, poet. Indo-American. **PERSONAL:** Born Oct 17, 1955, Dera Ghazi Khan, Punjab, Pakistan; son of Shahkat Ali; widowed; children: Shahnit. **EDUCATION:** University of Karachi, Pakistan, MA, 1976; Computer Learning Center, diploma, 1981; Fontbonne College, MBA, 1986. **CAREER:** Author, currently; Ethereal Vibes, CEO, currently. **HONORS/AWARDS:** Urdu Markaz, Best Book of the Year, 1991. **SPECIAL ACHIEVEMENTS:** Two Urdu/Hindi Poety books, 1991, 1993. **HOME ADDRESS:** 545 Maple Meadows Dr, Arnold, MO 63010, (314)296-1181. **BUSINESS ADDRESS:** Chief Executive, Ethereal Vibes, 51 Teasdale Street, Thousand Oaks, CA 91360, (805)374-6780.

SHAIKH, ABDUL HAMID
Educator, educational administrator. Pakistani American. **PERSONAL:** Born Jul 4, 1944, Bombay, India; son of Suleman Ahmed Shaikh; married Najma Hamid Shaikh, Sep 9, 1991; children: Irfan Ahmed. **EDUCATION:** University

of Karachi, Pakistan, BS, (honors), 1965, MSc, biochemistry, 1967; Medical College of Georgia, MS, endocrinology, 1972. **CAREER:** Medical College of Georgia, associate professor, director of graduate program, currently. **ORGANIZATIONS:** Georgia Society for Medical Technologists, District I, director; American Society for Medical Technologists; American Association of Clinical Chemists; American Society of Clinical Pathologists. **HONORS/AWARDS:** Alpha Eta Honor Society, 1976; Georgia Society for Medical Technology, Gloria F Gilbert Achievement Award, 1993; Medical College of Georgia, Outstanding Faculty Award, 1993. **SPECIAL ACHIEVEMENTS:** Published about 25 articles and abstracts in medical technology professional journals concerning cholesterol screening, instrument selection for clinical labs, and safety in clinical labs. **BUSINESS ADDRESS:** Assoc Prof & Graduate Program Director, Dept of Medical Technology, Medical College of Georgia, 15th St, Augusta, GA 30912-1003, (706)721-3046.

SHAIKH, SAEED AHMAD

Educational administrator. Pakistani American. **PERSONAL:** Born Jan 1, 1953, Hyderabad, Sind, Pakistan; son of Bashir Ahmad Shaikh; married Rizwana Shaheen, Aug 31, 1989; children: Sidrah, Shaikh Jr. **EDUCATION:** Miami Dade, AS, electronics, 1978; FIU, BSEE, 1981; US, MSE, 1987. **CAREER:** Harris, process control engineer, test engineer, 1987; IMC, design engineering, director, 1991; MDCC, Electronic/Electrical Engineering Department, chairman, currently. **ORGANIZATIONS:** Common Course Committee, Florida Department of Education, currently; Education in Electronics, Miami, advisory board, 1981; FACC, 1985; Computer Designers & Users, 1984. **HONORS/AWARDS:** Harris Comm Division, Engineer of the Year, 1986; Florida Department of Education, Outstanding Support Communication, 1988. **SPECIAL ACHIEVEMENTS:** Principal Electrical Circuit, book, 1991; Use Spanish Language in Computer Repair, 1989; Industrial Electronics, 1988. **BUSINESS ADDRESS:** Chairman, Electronic/Electrical Engineering Dept, Miami-Dade Community College, 11380 NW 27th Ave, Rm 3242-88, Miami, FL 33168, (305)237-1240.

SHAIKH, ZAHIR A.

Educator, educational administrator. Pakistani American. **PERSONAL:** Born Mar 31, 1945, Jullundur, Punjab, India; son of Zafer A and Mehmooda Chohan Shaikh; married Mary, Aug 23, 1993; children: Faraz, Kashan, Summur. **EDUCATION:** Karachi University, Pakistan, BS, 1965, MS, 1967; Dalhousie University, Canada, PhD, 1972. **CAREER:** University of Oklahoma, Department of Environmental Health, research associate, 1972-73; University of Rochester, Dept of Pharmacology and Toxicology, senior postdoctoral fellow, 1973-75, assistant professor, 1975-81, Division of Toxicology, associate professor, 1981-82; University of Rhode Island, Dept of Pharmacology and Toxicology, associate professor, 1982-85, professor and chairman, 1985-. **ORGANIZATIONS:** Society of Toxicology, 1977-; American Society of Pharmacology and Experimental Therapeutics, 1977-; American Association for the Advancment of Science, 1975-. **HONORS/AWARDS:** National Institutes of Health, postdoctoral research fellowship, 1973-75, research grants, 1976-; Society of Toxicology, Metals Specialty Section, president, 1980-81. **SPECIAL ACHIEVEMENTS:** Publications in professional journals, 1971-. **BUSINESS ADDRESS:** Professor and Chairman, Dept of Pharmacology & Toxicology, University of Rhode Island, Kingston, RI 02881-0809, (401)792-2362.

SHAM, LU JEU

Educator. Chinese American. **PERSONAL:** Born Apr 28, 1938, Hong Kong; son of T S Shen and Cecilia Siu Shen; married Georgina Bien Sham, Apr 25, 1965; children: Kevin Shen, Alisa Shen. **EDUCATION:** University of London, BS, 1960; University of Cambridge, PhD, 1963. **CAREER:** University of California, Irvine, assistant professor of physics, 1966-67; Queens College, London, reader in applied math, 1967-68; University of California, San Diego, assistant research physicist, 1963-66, professor of physics, 1968-. **ORGANIZATIONS:** American Physical Society, fellow, 1968-; AAAS, 1985-; International Union of Pure and Applied Physics, chair of semiconductor commission, 1990-. **HONORS/AWARDS:** Guggenheim Foundation, Guggenheim Fellow, 1984; Humboldt Foundation, Senior Scientist Award, 1978; Imperial College, London, Governors Prize in Mathematics, 1960; Churchill College, research student, 1960-63. **BUSINESS ADDRESS:** Professor, Dept of Physics, University of California San Diego, 9500 Gilman Dr, 0319, La Jolla, CA 92093-0319, (619)534-3269.

SHAN, ROBERT KUOCHENG

Educator. Chinese American. **PERSONAL:** Born Nov 9, 1927, Gaoan, Jiangxi, China; married Lily Chen, Sep 7, 1963; children: Tony Donguang. **EDUCATION:** Taiwan Normal University, BS, 1956; University of British Columbia, MS, 1962; Indiana University, PhD, 1967. **CAREER:** National Taiwan University, Zoology, instructor, 1956-59; Indiana University, postdoctoral research associate, 1967-69; Fairmont State College, Biology, professor, 1969-. **ORGANIZATIONS:** American Institute of Biological Sciences, 1963-; American Society of Umnology and Oceanography, 1963-; Ecological Society of America, 1963-; Sigma Xi, 1965-. **HONORS/AWARDS:** Fairmont State College, Faculty Achievement, 1989. **SPECIAL ACHIEVEMENTS:** Animal Population, Ecology, Science Press, 1983; "Pleuroxus Denticulatus and P Procurvus, Cladocera, Chydoridae, in North America," Canadian Journal of Zoology, 1983. **BUSINESS ADDRESS:** Professor of Biology, Fairmont State College, Fairmont, WV 26554, (304)367-4495.

SHANG, BERNARD Y.

Educator. Taiwanese American. **PERSONAL:** Born Apr 16, 1941, Chia-Yi, Taiwan; married Grace Mei-Ying Shang, Jul 12, 1970; children: Ameca Ellis. **EDUCATION:** Chinese Culture University, BS, 1969; University of Southern Mississippi, MEd, 1978, Education Specialist, 1986, PhD, 1992. **CAREER:** Chia-Yi Branch, China Youth Corp, coordinator of social services & educational services, 1969-74; University of Southern Mississippi, instructor of beginning Chinese, 1987-89; Ellisville State School, special education teacher III, 1976-. **ORGANIZATIONS:** Mississippi Educator Association, 1989-92; Chinese Student Association, University of Southern Mississippi, consultant, 1986-; Summer & Winter Youth Self-Strength Activities Organization, director, 1969-71; Association of Urban Planning & Administration, 1965-69. **HONORS/AWARDS:** University of Southern Mississippi, Gamma Beta Phi Society, 1991. **SPECIAL ACHIEVEMENTS:** Dissertation title: "The Effects of Tangible and Social Rewards on a Selected Motor Activity Performance of Institutionalized Mentally Retarded," 1992. **MILITARY SERVICE:** Mandatory Chinese Army Service, sergeant, 1962-65. **HOME ADDRESS:** 3017 Mesa Dr, Hattiesburg, MS 39402, (601)268-6313.

SHANG, STELLA I-HUA

Librarian. Chinese American. **PERSONAL:** Born Oct 31, 1944, Shanghai, China; daughter of Wang Shang and Jeannan Shang; married Daniel Jia-Cheng Yen, Feb 14, 1978; children: Cornelius Li-Sen Yen. **EDUCATION:** National Taiwan University, BA, 1965; Case Western Reserve University, MSLS, 1968; Miami University, Ohio, Center for Management Development, certificate, 1990. **CAREER:** New York Public Library, librarian, 1968-, Allerton Branch, supervising branch librarian, 1980-88, North Bronx Region, regional librarian, 1989-. **ORGANIZATIONS:** ALA; EMIERT, executive board, membership committee; PLA, awards committee; PLA-CIS, education and training committee; CALA, professional development task force. **SPECIAL ACHIEVEMENTS:** Fluent in Chinese. **BUSINESS ADDRESS:** Regional Librarian, Baychester Regional Library, The New York Public Library, 2049 Asch Loop North, Bronx, NY 10475, (718)379-6733.

SHANG, WEIJIA

Educator. Chinese American. **PERSONAL:** Born Apr 9, 1956, Sichuan, People's Republic of China; daughter of Zhifen Shang and Shiliang Fu; married Yi Xiang Wang, Aug 23, 1993; children: Jim Min Wang, Sumin Weijia Wang. **EDUCATION:** Changsha Institute of Technology, BS, 1982; Purdue University, MS, 1984, PhD, 1990. **CAREER:** Purdue University, tutor, 1984, grader, 1984-85, research assistant, 1985-90; University of Southwest Louisiana, assistant professor, 1990-. **ORGANIZATIONS:** Phi Kappa Phi, 1988; IEEE, 1988-; ACM, 1988-. **HONORS/AWARDS:** NSF, Research Initiation Awards, 1991; Changsha Institute of Technology, Distinguished Student, 1978, 1979; Chinese Academy of Sciences, Scholarship, 1983, 1984. **SPECIAL ACHIEVEMENTS:** Co-author, "Independent Partitioning of Uniform Dependency Algorithms," IEEE Trans on Computers, vol 41, no 2, pp 190-206, Feb 1992; co-author, "Time Optimal Linear Schedules for Algorithms with Uniform Dependencies," IEEE Trans on Computers, vol 40, no 6, pp 723-42, June 1991; co-author, "On Mapping of Uniform Dependence Algorithms into Lower Dimensional Processor Arrays," IEEE Trans on Parallel and Distributed Systems, vol 3, no 3, pp 350-63, May 1992; co-author, "On Loop Transformations for Generalized Cycle Shrinking," accepted by IEEE Trans on Parallel and Distributed Systems. **BUSINESS ADDRESS:** Professor, Center for Advanced Computer Studies, University of Southwestern Louisiana, Lafayette, LA 70504-4330, (318)231-6608.

SHANKAR, SRINIVASAN

Aerospace company executive. Indo-American. **PERSONAL:** Born Nov 20, 1950, Tiruchy, Tamil Nadu, India; son of Panchapakesa Srinivasan and Savitri Srinivasan; married Padmini Shankar, Aug 30, 1979; children: Vikram, Rekha. **EDUCATION:** Indian Institute of Technology, Madras, India, BTech, 1973; State University of New York at Stony Brook, PhD, 1977. **CAREER:** Howmet Corp, mgr, coating development, 1977-82; Turbine Components Corp, vice pres, engineering & technology, 1982-. **ORGANIZATIONS:** American Society of Metals, 1974-; American Society of Mechanical Engrs, 1988-; Intl Gas Turbine Institute, MMM committee, 1983-, chairman, 1990-92. **HONORS/ AWARDS:** Several academic awards. **SPECIAL ACHIEVEMENTS:** Several publications and patents. **BUSINESS ADDRESS:** Vice President, Engineering and Technology, Turbine Components Corp, 2 Commercial St, PO Box 801, Branford, CT 06405, (203)481-5371.

SHANKAR, SUBRAMONIAN

Personal computer program and components manufacturing company executive. Indo-American. **CAREER:** American Megatrends, president, founder, 1985-. **SPECIAL ACHIEVEMENTS:** Company ranked second on Inc Magazine's list of the top 500 fastest-growing privately held US companies, 1991. **BUSINESS ADDRESS:** President, American Megatrends, 6145-F Northbelt Pkwy, Norcross, GA 30071-2972, (404)263-8181.

SHARMA, ANIL F.

Educator, international trade consultant. Indo-American. **PERSONAL:** Born Sep 26, 1960, Bhavnagar, Gujarat, India; son of Faqirchand Sharma & Lilavati Sharma; married Fariba, May 24, 1987; children: Rohan. **EDUCATION:** Gujarat University, H L College of Commerce, BComm, 1980; Marshall University, West Virginia, MBA, 1983; United States International University, California, DBA, 1990. **CAREER:** Komal Raj Transport Co, managing partner, 1976-81; Telitronix Systems, salesperson, 1981; Capt D's Seafood Restaurant, assistant manager, 1983-84; US International University Bookstore, assistant manager, 1985-86; Marshall University, assistant professor, 1986-87; Frostburg State University, assistant professor, beginning 1986, associate professor, currently, ex-chair, 1987-; Global Marketing Systems Inc, president, 1990-. **ORGANIZATIONS:** National Business Honor Society, faculty advisor, 1987-; American Marketing Association, 1988-; Southern Marketing Association; Academy of International Business; University of Maryland International Faculty & Administration. **HONORS/AWARDS:** Direct Marketing Educational Foundation, fellowship, 1989; DMEF & DMAW, fellowship, 1989; Frostburg State University, research grant, 1990, faculty lecture series, 1990; Center for International Business Education & Research, research grant, 1991. **SPECIAL ACHIEVEMENTS:** Author of numerous presentations. **BIOGRAPHICAL SOURCES:** Marketing Theory and Practice: Developments for the 90's, proceedings, vol V, p 215-217, 1989; conference proceedings: Association for Global Business, p 305-311, 1989; "Small Firms Face Impediments in Exporting," Cumberland Times-News, September 9, 1989; numerous others. **HOME PHONE:** (301)722-0236. **BUSINESS ADDRESS:** Associate Professor, Dept of Business Administration, Frostburg State University, Frampton Hall, Frostburg, MD 21532, (301)689-4052.

SHARMA, ARUN

Educator. Indo-American. **PERSONAL:** Born Aug 19, 1957, Sheffield, England; son of Prem Swarup Sharma and Prem Lata Sharma; married Anita Sharma, Dec 26, 1986; children: Avani. **EDUCATION:** Rajastan University, BS, engineering, 1978; Indian Institute of Management, Calcutta, India, MBA, 1980; University of Illinois, PhD, 1988. **CAREER:** Indian Communications Network, India, product manager, 1980-83; University of Miami, assistant professor, beginning 1987, associate professor, currently. **ORGANIZATIONS:** American Marketing Association; Academy of Marketing Science; The Institute of Management Science. **HONORS/AWARDS:** University of Miami, School of Business, excellence in teaching, 1990; McLamore Award in Business and Social Sciences, 1989, 1991, 1992. **SPECIAL ACHIEVEMENTS:** Author, "The Persuasive Effect of Salesperson Credibility: Conceptual and Empirical Examination," The Journal of Personal Selling and Sales Management, Vol 10, No 4, fall 1990; with Douglas M Lambert, "Using Salespeople to Collect Customer Service Information," International Journal of Physical Distribution and Logistics Management, Vol 21, No 6, 1991; reviewer, "Marketing High Technology by William Davidson," International High Technology Marketing Review, August 1987; presenter, "Organizational Culture and Adoption of High Technology Products," presented at the 1993 American Marketing Association Winter Educators Conference; ad-hoc reviewer: The Journal of the Academy of Marketing Science. **BUSINESS AD-**

DRESS: Associate Professor, Dept of Marketing, University of Miami, PO Box 248147, Coral Gables, FL 33124-6554, (305)284-5935.

SHARMA, BHUDEV

Educator. Indo-American. **PERSONAL:** Born Jun 21, 1938, Bankpur, Bijnor, Uttar Pradesh, India; son of Janki Prasad Sharma and Shanti Devi Sharma; married Kusum Lata Sharma, Jul 9, 1959; children: Ritu, Swati, Harsh Dev. **EDUCATION:** Agra University, Hindu College, BSc, 1955; Agra University, Meerut College, MSc, 1957; University of Delhi, PhD, 1971. **CAREER:** N.A.S. College, Meerut, India, lecturer in math, 1957-63; Municipal College, Mussoorie, India, department of math, head, 1963-64; Vaish College, Shami, India, dept of math, head, 1964-66; University of Delhi, lecturer in math, assistant professor, 1966-72, reader in math, associate professor, 1972-79; University of West Indies, Trinidad, professor of math, 1979-88; Xavier University, Louisiana, professor of math, 1988-. **ORGANIZATIONS:** Forum for Interdisciplinary Math, president, 1987-91, general secretary, 1976-87, vice president, 1991-; Calcutta Math Society, vice president, 1986-90; Bharatiya Association of Caribbean, president, 1984-86; Hindi Nidhi, Trinidad, vice president/chairman, acad committee, 1986-89; Hindu Educational & Reli Society, president/director, 1992-; Maharishi Vedic University, LA, director, 1993-; Society Indian Academics in America, national representative, 1993-. **SPECIAL ACHIEVEMENTS:** Chief editor, Journal of Combinatorics, Information & System Science, 1976-; editor, Journal of the Calcutta Math Society; Journal of the Ramanujan Math Society, Caribbean Journal of Mathematics; advisory editor, Journal of Information and Optimization Sciences, 1978-; editor-in-chief, Vishva-Vivek, international Hindi magazine; advisor, India Times, fortnightly. **HOME PHONE:** (504)454-6348. **BUSINESS ADDRESS:** Professor of Mathematics, Xavier University of LA, 7325 Palmetto St, Academic SC Complex, 204G, New Orleans, LA 70125-1056.

SHARMA, BRIJ LAL

Electrical engineer, business executive. Indo-American. **PERSONAL:** Born Jul 19, 1946, Uddowali, Punjab, India; son of Banarsi Lal Sharma and Mangli Devi Sharma; married Vijay K; children: Ajay Kumar. **EDUCATION:** Panjab Engineering College, Chandigarh, India, BSc, engineering, 1969. **CAREER:** Advani-Oerlikon, Ltd, engineer, 1970-71; Carl Kloos, KG, West Germany, engineer, 1971-73; Brown Boueri, Brazil, engineer, 1973-74; Siemens, Brazil, sales manager, 1974-83; Autotech Corp, director marketing, 1983-91; PowerVolt Inc, owner, president, 1991-. **SPECIAL ACHIEVEMENTS:** Language proficiency: German, Portuguese, English. **BUSINESS ADDRESS:** President, PowerVolt, Inc, 409 E Myrtle St, Elizabeth, IL 61028, (815)858-2248.

SHARMA, DEVA DATTA

Educator. Indo-American. **PERSONAL:** Born Jan 15, 1942, Shikoi, Uttar Pradesh, India; son of Mohan Lal Sharma and Gomti Sharma; married Vimla Sharma, May 20, 1964; children: Venita Sharma Mishra, Anita. **EDUCATION:** ASJ College, Lakhaoti, 1957-59; DAV College, Dehradun, BS, 1961, MS, 1963; University of Nevada, Reno, PhD, 1971. **CAREER:** RK College, Shamli, UP, lecturer, 1963-64; CSIO Chandigarh Pb, research fellow, 1964-67; University of Nevada, Reno, teaching fellow, 1967-71; Barber-Scotia College, assistant professor, 1972-77; Duke Power Co, health physicist, 1977-78; Livingstone College, associate professor, 1978-79; Winston-Salem State University, professor, 1979-. **ORGANIZATIONS:** American Association of Physics Teachers, 1968-79; Sigma Pi Sigma, 1970-93; DECUS, 1974-80; Indu-US Cultural Association, president, 1985, vice president, 1984, secretary, 1983; Hindu Society of North Carolina, 1975-93. **HONORS/AWARDS:** Hindu Society of North Carolina, fund raising, 1989; Friends of O'Kelley Library, 1990; NSF, Dept of Education, research grants, 1980-93. **SPECIAL ACHIEVEMENTS:** Longitudinal Polarization of Electrons, 1971; Static Measurement of Beam Profile, 1972; Analysis of Asbestos Minerals, 1973; Electron Capture Decay, 1976; Range Energy Tables for Electrons, 1992. **BUSINESS ADDRESS:** Professor, Winston-Salem State University, 601 M L King Dr, Hill Hall 118, Winston-Salem, NC 27110, (919)750-2544.

SHARMA, GHANSHYAM D.

Educator. Indo-American. **PERSONAL:** Born Feb 28, 1931, Delhi, India; son of Ram Chandra Bharadwaja and Kalawati; divorced; children: Arun K. **EDUCATION:** Benaras Hindu University, India, BSc, 1952; Swiss Fed Inst of Technology, Switzerland, diploma, 1958; University of Michigan, PhD, 1961. **CAREER:** University of Michigan, research assistant, 1959-61; Sinclair Research Inc, research engineer, 1961-63; University of Alaska, Fairbanks, professor & director, 1963-91, emeritus professor & director, 1991-; Rogaland

University Centre, professor, 1990-. **ORGANIZATIONS:** American Association of Petroleum Geologists, 1966-; Alaska Geological Society, 1971-74; American Geophysical Union, 1970-86; International Association of Sedimentologists, 1975-88; Journal of Geology, 1984-88; Society of Economic Paleontologists & Mineralogists, 1968-88; Society of Petroleum Engineers, 1986-; Science 80, charter member, 1980-83. **HONORS/AWARDS:** University of Michigan, University Scholar, 1960-61; American Association of Petroleum Geologists, President's Award, 1968; 14th Alaska Legislature, honoring and commendation, 1986, honoring, 1992; University of Alaska Fairbanks, Appreciation for Dedicated Service, 1990. **SPECIAL ACHIEVEMENTS:** Author of The Alaskan Shelf, Springer-Verlag, 1979; Particle Technology & Surface Phenomena in Petroleum & Minerals, Plenum Pub Corp, 1992; contributions to 8 books, journals, newspapers; numerous interviews. **BIOGRAPHICAL SOURCES:** American Association of Petroleum Geologist Bull, 527, p 1342, 1968. **BUSINESS ADDRESS:** Director Emeritus & Professor Emeritus, Petroleum Development Laboratory, University of Alaska Fairbanks, PO Box 755880, Fairbanks, AK 99775-5880, (907)474-7743.

SHARMA, GOVIND CHANDRA
Educator. **PERSONAL:** Born Mar 3, 1944, Udaipur, Rajasthan, India; son of Jagdeesh C Sharma and Manorama Sharma; married Prabha, Aug 25, 1968; children: Manan. **EDUCATION:** University of Udaipur, BS, agriculture; University of Florida, MAg, fruit crops; Kansas State University, PhD, horticulture. **CAREER:** University of Florida, pesticide analyst, 1965-66; General Dynamics Corp, agricultural training coordinator, 1966; Alabama A&M University, associate professor, 1970-73; professor and chairman, 1973-; plant science journals, technical reviewer, 1985-; academic programs area junior and senior colleges, consultant, 1980-88. **ORGANIZATIONS:** Huntsville Botanical Garden, board member, 1988-92; American Society of Horticulture Science, 1968-; American Society of Agronomy, 1970-. **HONORS/AWARDS:** American Society Horticultural Science, Outstanding Graduate Student Research, 1971; Alabama A&M University, Outstanding Teacher Award, 1988. **SPECIAL ACHIEVEMENTS:** Published over 50 papers in technical and scientific journals; received over 5 million dollars in research and teaching grant program funds; expanded academic program offerings to MS and PhD levels in plant and soil science; languages: Hindi, Urdu. **BUSINESS ADDRESS:** Professor & Chairman, Dept of Plant & Soil Science, Alabama A&M University, PO Box 1208, Normal, AL 35762.

SHARMA, HARI CHAND
Researcher, educator. Indo-American. **PERSONAL:** Born Mar 22, 1949, Ghansui, Himachal Pradesh, India; son of Ram Ditta and Manso Devi; married M Veena Sharma, Feb 7, 1976; children: Seema, Kiran, Nikki, Jay D. **EDUCATION:** Punjab Agricultural University, BS, 1970; Indian Agricultural Research Institute, MS, 1976; University of California, PhD, 1980. **CAREER:** Department of Agriculture, HP, India, county agent, 1970-73; University of California, research assistant, 1976-80; Kansas State University, postdoctoral fellow, 1980-83; Monsanto Company, senior research biologist, 1983-86; Purdue University, research agronomist, 1986-. **ORGANIZATIONS:** American Society of Agronomy, 1984-85, 1987-; Crop Science Society of America, 1984-85, 1987-; Indian Society of Genetics & Plant Breeding, 1980-, fellow, 1984-; Greater Lafayette Volunteer Bureau, volunteer, 1989; Punjab Agri University, Palampur Campus, captain, volleyball, 1970. **HONORS/AWARDS:** University of California, Phi Beta Kappa Award, 1979; Indian Agri Res Institute, fellowship, 1973-75; Punjab Agri University, Gold Medal, Honors, fellowship, 1967-70; US Dept of Agri, USAID, competitive research grant awards, 1983, 1987-. **SPECIAL ACHIEVEMENTS:** "Variability in Primitive and Wild Wheats for Useful Genetic Character," Crop Sci, 1981; "Production, Morphology and Cytogenetic Analysis of Elymus Caninus x Triticum. . .," Theoretical and Applied Genetics, 1986; "Chromosome Doubling and Aneuploidy in Anther Culture. . .," Genome, 1988; "Response of Wheatgrasses and Wheat & Wheatgrass Hybrids to BYDU," Theor Appl Gen, 1989; "Crossability and Embryo Rescue Enhancement in Wide Crosses. . .," Euphytica, 1990. **HOME ADDRESS:** 525 N 7th, Lafayette, IN 47901-1087, (317)742-8696. **BUSINESS ADDRESS:** Research Agronomist, Dept of Agronomy, Purdue University, West Lafayette, IN 47907-1150, (317)494-4787.

SHARMA, HARI M.
Physician. **PERSONAL:** Born Jan 16, 1938, Aligarh, Uttar Pradesh, India; son of Ram K Sharma & Shiv-Devi Sharma; married Indu B Sharma, Nov 23, 1957; children: Regni Pahouja, Shree, Micky, Nick. **EDUCATION:** K G Medical College, Lucknow, India, MBBS, 1961, MD, 1965; Ohio State University, College of Medicine, MSc, 1969; Royal College of Physicians & Surgeons of

Canada, Fellowship in Medicine, 1970; American Board of Pathology, certification, 1970. **CAREER:** Jewish General Hospital, assistant pathologist, 1970-71; Indiana University, School of Medicine, assistant professor, 1971-72; Ohio State University, assistant professor, 1972-73, associate professor, 1973-1980, professor of pathology, 1980-; Cancer Prevention & Natural Products Research, director, 1990-. **ORGANIZATIONS:** College of American Pathologists, fellow, 1973-; Royal College of Physicians of Canada, fellow, 1972-; Intl Academy of Pathology, 1972-; Intl Society of Nephrology, 1975-; American Society of Nephrology, 1975-; American Society Expt Pathology, 1975-. **HONORS/AWARDS:** Global Director, Maharishi Ayur-Ved Research Programs, 1990. **SPECIAL ACHIEVEMENTS:** Author, book, Freedom from Disease; over 95 publications in the areas of pathology, medicine, Maharishi Ayur-Ved, cancer, immunity, and free radicals. **BUSINESS ADDRESS:** Professor of Pathology, Director, Cancer Prevention & Natural Products Research, Ohio State University, College of Medicine, 320 W 10th Ave, M-376SL, Columbus, OH 43210, (614)293-3886.

SHARMA, JANDHYALA L.
Educator. Indo-American. **PERSONAL:** Born in India; son of Jandhyala V Somayajulu; married Udaya; children: Rajakumari, Meenakshi. **EDUCATION:** Andhra University, Waltair, India, MCom, BCom (honors), 1961; Madras University, India, LLB, 1963; University of Arkansas, MBA, 1971, PhD, 1974. **CAREER:** Western Carolina University, 1975-78; National Credit Union Administration, 1978-79; Cleveland State University, associate professor of finance, 1979-. **ORGANIZATIONS:** American Finance Association; American Economic Association; Ohio State Bar Association; Western Finance Association; Financial Management Association. **HONORS/AWARDS:** AACSB, Federal Faculty Fellowship Award, 1978-79. **SPECIAL ACHIEVEMENTS:** Attorney, admitted to the Supreme Court of Ohio. **BUSINESS ADDRESS:** Associate Professor, College of Business, Cleveland State University, E22/Euclid, Cleveland, OH 44115-1123, (216)687-3687.

SHARMA, M. P.
Educator. Indo-American. **PERSONAL:** Born Jan 14, 1947, Gaya, India; son of Sidheshwar & Prarad Sinha; married Geeta Sharma; children: Maneesh. **EDUCATION:** BIT, Sindri, BSc, ME, 1967; IIT, Kanpur, MS, ME, 1970; Washington State University, PhD, ME, 1977. **CAREER:** Case Western Reserve University, postdoctoral research associate, 1977; Babcock and Wilcox Research Center, senior research engr, 1978-81; Shell Oil Company, senior research engineer, 1981-82; University of Wyoming, Laramie, assistant professor, 1982-87, associate professor, 1987-92, professor, 1992-. **ORGANIZATIONS:** American Society of Mechanical Engineers; Society of Petroleum Engineers; American Society of Engineering Education. **HONORS/AWARDS:** Pi Epsilon Tau, National Petroleum Engineering Honor Society, Outstanding Contribution to Petroleum Industry, 1987. **SPECIAL ACHIEVEMENTS:** Many research papers. **BUSINESS ADDRESS:** Professor, Petroleum Engineering Dept, University of Wyoming, Engineering Building, Laramie, WY 82071, (307)766-6317.

SHARMA, MUKUL MANI
Educator. Indo-American. **PERSONAL:** Born Aug 11, 1959, Benaras, Uttar Pradesh, India; son of S Sharma and A Sharma; married Suman Sharma; children: D Sharma, T Sharma. **EDUCATION:** Indian Institute of Technology, BTech, 1980; University of Southern California, MS, chemical engineering, 1981, PhD, engineering, 1985. **CAREER:** University of Southern California, research engineer, 1981-83; Chevron Oilfield Research Co, research engineer, 1984; University of Texas, Austin, assistant professor, 1985-90, associate professor, 1990-. **ORGANIZATIONS:** Society of Petroleum Engineers of AIME; American Geophysical Union; American Chemical Society; Pi Epsilon Tau; Sigma Xi. **HONORS/AWARDS:** Engineering Foundation Faculty Leadership Award, 1987; Sun E&P Co Centennial Fellowship, 1986-92; Shell Oil Foundation Faculty Fellowship, 1985-88; SPWLA Education Foundation Award, 1986; ARCO Foundation Doctoral Fellowship, 1983-85. **SPECIAL ACHIEVEMENTS:** 55 refereed publications; 26 conference proceedings; 19 invited presentations; The Log Analyst, associate editor, 1992-; Society of Petroleum Engineers Journal, technical editor, 1991-. **BUSINESS ADDRESS:** Associate Professor, Dept of Petroleum Engineering, University of Texas, Austin, Austin, TX 78712-1104, (512)471-3257.

SHARMA, MUTYAM V.
Physician. Indo-American. **PERSONAL:** Born Aug 9, 1930, Bellary, Karnataka, India; son of Mutyam Sitarama Sharma and Saraswati Sharma; married Regina Michael Ann Sharma, Apr 28, 1964. **EDUCATION:** Royal

College of Surgeons, England, FRCS, 1958; Royal College of Surgeons, Edinburgh, FRCS, 1958; Royal College of Surgeons, Glasgow, FRCS, 1958; Diplomate American Board of Emergency Physicians, diplomate, 1982. CAREER: Mutyam V Sharma Professional Service Corp, president, 1974-. ORGANIZATIONS: Royal College of Surgeons, England, fellow, 1958; Royal College of Surgeons, Edinburgh, fellow, 1958; Royal College of Surgeons, Glasgow, fellow, 1958; International College of Surgeons, US, fellow, 1964; American College of Emergency Physicians, fellow, 1982.

SHARMA, ONKAR PRASAD

Educational administrator, educator. Indo-American. PERSONAL: Born Mar 3, 1937, Birupur, Bihar, India; son of Ramswaroop Prasad Sharma (deceased) and Ramdulari Sharma; married Urmila Sharma, Jun 13, 1956; children: Renu Sinha, Rashmi, Ragini Singh, Abinash, Ashish. EDUCATION: Bihar University, BSc, 1959; University of California, Berkeley, MS, 1968; New York University, PhD, 1971. CAREER: State Electricity Board, Bihar, India, assistant electrical engineer, 1959-60; Bihar Institute of Technology, India, assistant professor of electrical engineering, 1960-66; City College/City University of New York, assistant professor of computer science, 1970-75; international training consultant, Burbank, CA, deputy, managing director, education and training, Tehran, Iran, 1976-78; Moorhead State University, professor of computer science, 1979-86; Marist College, Division of Computer Science & Math, Div of Computer Science and Math, chair, 1986-. ORGANIZATIONS: Association for Computing Machines, 1971-; Computer Science Accreditation Commission, program evaluator, 1987-93; Eastern Small College Computing Conference, steering committee, 1986-; New York State Education Dept, program evaluator, 1990-92. HONORS/AWARDS: Moorhead State University, Merit Award for Academic Accomplishments and Outstanding Teaching Achievements, 1980; New York University, Founders Day Award for Evidence of Outstanding Scholarship, 1971; Government of Bihar, India, Overseas Scholarship for Higher Studies, 1966. SPECIAL ACHIEVEMENTS: Coauthor, 3 textbooks in computer science, Prentice-Hall, 1986; 12 conference presentations and Publications at Small College Computing Conference/Symposium, SIGESE Technical Symposium, and Journal of Franklin Institute/Computer Languages. HOME ADDRESS: 28 Hart Dr, Poughkeepsie, NY 12603. BUSINESS ADDRESS: Chair, Division of Computer Science & Math, Marist College, 290 North Rd, Lowell Thomas Communication Center, Rm 109, Poughkeepsie, NY 12601-1387.

SHARMA, PARASHU RAM

Educator. Indo-American. PERSONAL: Born May 4, 1946, Jodhpur, Rajasthan, India; son of Vasudev and Sooraj Kunwar; married Indu, Feb 19, 1973; children: Saurabh. EDUCATION: Birla Institute of Technology & Science, India, BE, chemical engineering, 1969, ME, chemical engineering, 1972; University of Roorkee, India, PhD, chemical engineering, 1977; University of Karlsruhe, Germany, postdoctoral diploma, chemical engineering, 1984. CAREER: University of Roorkee, India, research associate, 1977, lecturer, 1979-85; Birla Institute of Technology & Science, India, lecturer, 1978; Karlsruhe University, Institute of Technical Thermodynamics & Refrigeration, postdoctoral, 1983-84; Argonne National Laboratory, summer research scientist, 1989; Grambling State University, associate professor, math, computer science, 1985-. ORGANIZATIONS: American Institute of Chemical Engineers, 1986-90; American Mathematical Society, 1985-87; Mathematical Association of America, 1987-90; National Council of Teachers of Mathematics, 1992-; Louisiana Academy of Sciences, 1989-; Indian Institute of Chemical Engineers, associate member, 1982-85, Indian Association of Quality and Reliability, 1982-84. HONORS/AWARDS: National Science Foundation, grant, 1991-93; Institute of Engineers, India, technical paper award, 1979. SPECIAL ACHIEVEMENTS: Published 20 articles on nucleate pool boiling heat tr, 1979-93; co-author, monograph on process utility services, 1985; proficient in German and Hindi; author of several grant proposals, 1989-93; reviewed books on Fortran and calculus, 1992-93; Louisiana Systemic Initiative Program, to enhance middle school math education, 1992. BUSINESS ADDRESS: Associate Professor, Dept of Mathematics & Computer Science, Grambling State University, Main St, Carver Hall, Rm 137/113-C, Grambling, LA 71245-3090, (318)274-2278.

SHARMA, PUNEET

Process/safety engineer. Indo-American. PERSONAL: Born Mar 18, 1967, New Delhi, India; son of P C Sharma and Nirmal Sharma. EDUCATION: Texas A&M, BS, chemical engineering, 1988; University of Houston, EMBA, 1994. CAREER: Brown & Root Braun, process/process safety engineer, 1989-. ORGANIZATIONS: American Red Cross, volunteer WSI, 1985-.

BUSINESS ADDRESS: Process Engineer, Brown & Root Braun, 10200 Bellaire, Bldg 91, Rm ISE15B, Houston, TX 77072, (713)575-4854.

SHARMA, RAGHUBIR PRASAD

Educator. Indo-American. PERSONAL: Born Sep 7, 1940, Bharatpur, Rajasthan, India; son of Rammurti & Ramdulari Sharma; married Lalita, Dec 13, 1958; children: Rajesh, Sanjeev. EDUCATION: University of Rajputana, BVS, 1959; University of Minnesota, PhD, 1968. CAREER: Government of Rajasthan, India, veterinarian, 1959-60; Rajasthan Veterinary College, instructor, 1960-61; G B Pant Agricultural University, India, assistant professor, 1961-64; University of Minnesota, research fellow, 1964-69; Utah State University, professor, 1969-. ORGANIZATIONS: American Society of Pharmacology and Experimental Therapeutics, 1974-; Society of Toxicology, 1970-. HONORS/AWARDS: National Institutes of Health, several research grants, 1970-. SPECIAL ACHIEVEMENTS: Editor of books: Immunologic Considerations in Toxicology, Vol I & II, 1981; Mycotoxins and Phytoalexins, 1991; Dietary Factors and Birth Defects, 1993; over 200 research publications in scientific journals and texts. BUSINESS ADDRESS: Professor, Director-Center for Environmental Toxicology, Utah State University, UMC 5600, Logan, UT 84322-5600, (801)750-1890.

SHARMA, RAMESH

Educator. Indo-American. PERSONAL: Born May 10, 1953, Chittaranjan, W. Bengal, India; son of Jagannath Sharma (deceased) and Ramdasi Devi; married Sushma Sharma, Mar 8, 1976; children: Richa, Sweta. EDUCATION: Banaras Hindu University, India, BSc (with honors), 1974, MSc, 1976, PhD, 1980; University of Windsor, Canada, PhD, 1986. CAREER: University of Windsor, teaching & research assistant, 1981-87; Michigan State University, instructor, 1987-88; University of New Haven, assistant professor, 1988-92, associate professor, 1992-. ORGANIZATIONS: American Math Society, 1984-; Math Association of America, 1993-; International Committee on Gen Relativity & Gravitation, 1984-86. HONORS/AWARDS: Banaras Hindu University, BHU Prize, 1974; University of Windsor, CP Crowley & UOW Scholarships, 1982-85; University of New Haven, Faculty Fellowship & Research Fund, 1991, Faculty Travel Award, 1993; Connecticut Space Grant College Consortium, NASA, Travel Fellowship, 1993. SPECIAL ACHIEVEMENTS: 34 research papers published in refereed journals, recent ones: "On the Curvature of Contact Manifolds," to appear in Journal of Geometry; "Proper Conformal Symmetries of Spacetimes with Divergence-free Weyl Conformal Tensor," Journal of Mathematical Physics 34, p 3582-3587, 1993; 10 papers presented at conferences/universities, recent one: Ricci Curvature Inheriting Symmetry of Semi-Riemannian Spaces; invited paper at a special session of the joint meeting of the American and Canadian Mathematical Societies, Vancouver, Aug 1993; paper presentations at conferences/universities; refereed 3 papers for International Journal Math and Sciences; reviewed 1 paper for Journal of Mathematical Physics. BUSINESS ADDRESS: Associate Professor, University of New Haven, 300 Orange Ave, Maxcy Hall 321, West Haven, CT 06516-1916, (203)932-7292.

SHARMA, RAVINDRA NATH

Library administrator. Indo-American. PERSONAL: Born Oct 22, 1944, Kartar Pur, Panjab, India; son of Baikunth Nath and Gyan Devi; married Mithlesh Sharma, Jul 8, 1972; children: Nalini, Mohini. EDUCATION: University of Delhi, India, BA (honors), 1963, MA, 1966; North Texas State University, MLS, 1970; State University of New York at Buffalo, PhD, 1982. CAREER: College of the Ozarks, assistant librarian, 1970-71; Colgate University, reference librarian, 1971-81; Pennsylvania State University, Beaver, head librarian, 1981-85; University of Wisconsin, Oshkosh, assistant director for public services, 1985-89; University of Evansville, University Libraries, director, 1989-. ORGANIZATIONS: Asian/Pacific American Librarians Association, president, 1993-94, vice president, 1992-93; ALA/IRC, First American/South Asian Librarians Conference Committee, chair, 1989-93; Research & Academic Librarians: A Global View Conference, 1990-92; Book Donation Committee, IRC/ALA, 1989-92; ACRL/Research Conference Committee, chair, 1989-93; Country Resource Committee for India, ALA Standing Committee on Education, chair, 1989-. HONORS/AWARDS: APALA Certificate of Appreciation, 1991; Indiana Library Association, delegate to Governor's Conference on Library & Information Science, 1991; University of Wisconsin, Rider Award, 1988. SPECIAL ACHIEVEMENTS: S R Ranganathan and the West, Sterling Publishers, 1992; Indian Academic Libraries and Dr S R Ranganathan, Sterling Publishers, 1986; Indian Librarianship: Perspectives and Prospects, Kalyani Publishers, 1981; Library Times International, editor, 1984-; published over 150 articles, editorials, reports, interviews, & book reviews; won many grants. **HOME ADDRESS:** 8128 Briarwood Drive, Evansville, IN 47715, (812)473-2420. **BUSINESS ADDRESS:** Director, University Libraries, University of Evansville, 1800 Lincoln Ave, Evansville, IN 47722, (812)479-2485.

SHARMA, SANTOSH DEVRAJ
Educator. Indo-American. **PERSONAL:** Born Feb 24, 1934, Kisumu, Kenya; daughter of Devaraj Sharma and Lakshmi Devi Sharma. **EDUCATION:** BJ Medical School, India, MD, 1960; Royal College Obstetrics and Gynecology, MRCOG, 1966; American Board Obstetrics & Gynecology, 1977; American Board Obstetrics & Gynecology, recertification, 1991. **CAREER:** Makerere University Medical School, lecturer, 1967-68, senior lecturer, 1968-72; Howard University Medical School, assistant professor, 1972-74; University of Hawaii, Department OB/GYN, associate professor, 1974-78, professor, 1978-. **ORGANIZATIONS:** American College of OB/GYN, fellow, 1973-; Royal College of OB/GYN, fellow, 1979-; American Medical Association, 1976-; American Society Colposcopy & Cervical Pathology, fellow, 1980-; International Menopausal Society, 1980-; North American Menopausal Society, 1990-. **HONORS/AWARDS:** Association of Professors of OB/GYN, Excellence in Teaching Award, 1993; American Society for Colposcopy & Cervical Pathology, Colposcopy Recognition Award, 1992; Royal College of OB/GYN Leader, fellow, 1979. **SPECIAL ACHIEVEMENTS:** "Maternal Physiology in Pregnancy," chapter, Concise Textbook of Obstetrics, edited by Drs Hale & Krieger, 1987; "Cancer of the Cervix," chapter, Concise Textbook of Gynecology, edited by Drs Hale & Krieger, 1982; Induction of Labor at Term with Prostaglandin, 1977. **BUSINESS ADDRESS:** Professor, John A Burns School of Medicine, University of Hawaii at Manoa, 1390 Punahou Street, #824, Honolulu, HI 96826, (808)956-7457.

SHARMA, SAROJ
Educator. Indo-American. **PERSONAL:** Born Feb 22, 1945, Punchcula, Chandigarh, India; daughter of Payare Lal Jain and Pushpa Wati Jain; married Prem Lal Sharma, Apr 26, 1974; children: Upma, Umang, Arun. **EDUCATION:** Delhi University, BA, 1965, MA, 1967; Rutgers University, PhD, 1973. **CAREER:** Delhi University, lecturer, 1968-69; SIU, lecturer, 1973-75; University of Kansas, Lawrence, lecturer, 1976-77; UMR, lecturer, 1978-79, 1980-81; UAPB, associate professor, 1983-85; Butler University, assistant professor, 1985-. **ORGANIZATIONS:** Kappa Mu Epsilon; Mathematical Association of America. **HONORS/AWARDS:** UGC Summer Institute, Dehli, Outstanding Participant, 1968; National Meeting of the AMS, session chair, 1974. **SPECIAL ACHIEVEMENTS:** Research citied in Von Neumann Regular Rings, by K R Goodearl, 1979. **BUSINESS ADDRESS:** Assistant Professor, Butler University, 4600 Sunset Ave, Indianapolis, IN 46208-3443, (317)283-9559.

SHARMA, SATANAND (STAN)
Health services administrator. Indo-American. **PERSONAL:** Born May 17, 1948, Suva, Fiji; son of Ram Sharma and Bidya Sharma; married Cynthia; children: Seanjay. **EDUCATION:** University of California, Los Angeles, BS, 1969; California State University, Los Angeles, MS, 1971; University of California, Irvine, PhD, 1973. **CAREER:** University of California, Los Angeles, associate professor, 1969-79; Inglewood Medical Health Services, executive director, 1980-. **BUSINESS ADDRESS:** Executive Director, Inglewood Medical & Mental Health Services, 4450 W Century Blvd, Inglewood, CA 90304.

SHARMA, SATISH
Educator, social worker. Indo-American. **PERSONAL:** Born Apr 2, 1941, Batala, Punjab, India; son of Shiv Dass Sharma and Kaushalya Sharma; married Asha Sharma, Jul 8, 1967; children: Ashish, Anu. **EDUCATION:** Panjab University, India, MA, 1964; University of Iowa, Iowa City, MSW, 1980; Ohio State University, PhD, 1974. **CAREER:** Punjab Agri University, India, assistant professor, 1966-71; Ohio State University, graduate research associate, 1971-74; University of Northern Iowa, assistant professor, 1974-79; University of Iowa, assistant professor, 1979-80; Adult Care Inc, Iowa, area manager, 1980-82; University of Nevada-Las Vegas, associate professor, 1982-86, director, professor, 1986-. **ORGANIZATIONS:** Inter-University Consortium for Intl Social Development, vp, 1989-; Canadian Peace Research & Education Association, 1988-; Indian Sociological Society, life member, 1964-; Council on Social Work Education, 1980-; Natl Assn of Social Workers, 1980-; Intl Community Education Assn, 1988-; American Rural Sociology Society, 1974-. **HONORS/AWARDS:** Natl Assn of Social Workers, Certificate of Service, 1991; UCCSN Board of Regents, Outstanding Professor, 1990; University of Iowa, Outstanding Alumnus, 1990; University of Nevada-Las Vegas,

Barrick Scholar Award, 1988, William Morris Teaching Award, nominee, 1988. **SPECIAL ACHIEVEMENTS:** Author, Gandhi, Women, and Social Development, 1982; Modernism and Planned Social Change, 1982; monograph, Migratory Workers and Their Socio-Cultural Adjustment, 1964. **BUSINESS ADDRESS:** Director & Professor, School of Social Work, University of Nevada-Las Vegas, 4505 Maryland Pky, Las Vegas, NV 89154, (702)895-1038.

SHARMA, SHRI C.
Pharamceutical and food company executive. Indo-American. **PERSONAL:** Born Jun 18, 1945, Sangwari, Haryana, India; son of Saraswati & Suraj Bhan Sharma; married Pushp L Sharma, Jun 4, 1975; children: Anu, Samar, Rupa. **EDUCATION:** Indian Institute of Technology, Kharagpur, BTech (with honors), 1967; University of Wisconsin, MS, 1970; Rutgers University, PhD, 1974. **CAREER:** CPC International, research manager, 1975-79; Pepsi Co Inc, associate director, 1979-82; Warner Lambert Co, senior director, 1982-85; Nutrition Tech Corp, vice president, 1985-88; Nutra Lab Inc, president, 1988-. **ORGANIZATIONS:** American College of Nutrition, fellow, 1991-; Institute of Food Technologists, professional member, 1975-; National Confectioners Association, tech committee, 1985-88; Grocessary Manufacturers Association, tech committee, 1985-88; American Society of Parental & Enteral Nutrition, 1988-92. **HONORS/AWARDS:** American Society of Ag Engineers, Paper Award, 1977; Pepsi Co, Scientific Excellence, 1981. **SPECIAL ACHIEVEMENTS:** 45 patents, 1977-93; 18 publications, various journals; 65 products, food & pharmaceutical. **HOME ADDRESS:** 5400 Indian Heights Dr, Cincinnati, OH 45243, (513)561-8011.

SHARMA, SUBHASH C.
Educator. Indo-American. **PERSONAL:** Born Oct 27, 1951, New Delhi, India; married Kusum; children: Amit, Sheena. **EDUCATION:** University of Delhi, BA, mathematics (with honors), 1973, MA, mathematical statistics, 1975; University of Kentucky, MS, statistcs, 1979, PhD, statistics, 1983. **CAREER:** Southern Illinois University, assistant professor, 1983-87, associate professor, 1987-93, professor of economics, 1993-. **SPECIAL ACHIEVEMENTS:** "The Interest-Rate Management and Sterilization Hypotheses for the UK: Under Fixed Exchange Rates," Applied Economics, vol 23, no 4B, pp 821-838, April 1991; "New Jacknife Tests for Grouped Heteroscedasticity," Journal of Quantitative Economics, vol 8, no 2, p 309-326, 1992; "Robustness to Non-Normality of the Durbln-Watson Test for Autocorrelation," Journal of Econometrics, vol 57, 1993; numerous others. **BUSINESS ADDRESS:** Professor of Economics, Southern Illinois University, Carbondale, IL 62901-4399, (618)453-5079.

SHARMA, SURENDRA P.
Government official. Indo-American. **PERSONAL:** Born Feb 3, 1943, Gorakhpur, Uttar Pradesh, India; son of Suresh dutt Sharma & Dhanpatti Devi; married Prabha Durgapal, May 12, 1983; children: Seema. **EDUCATION:** University of Gorakhpur, India, BS, 1962; PFU, Moscow, MS, 1968; Massachusetts Institute of Technology, DS, 1978. **CAREER:** Naval Postgraduate School, adjunct professor, 1979; University of Tennessee, Space Int, engr, 1979-81; Brown & Roof, Inc, senior engr, 1981-82; Sii Drilco, senior engr, 1982-85; NASA Ames Research Center, research scientist, 1986-. **ORGANIZATIONS:** American Institute of Aeronautics & Astronautics, associate fellow, 1988-; Sigma Xi, 1973-; PTA, Cupertino, CA, 1990. **HONORS/AWARDS:** NASA Ames, Outstanding Performance, 1987, 1988, 1990; AIAA, Best Thermophysics Paper, 1992, Special Citation for Survey Paper, 1990. **SPECIAL ACHIEVEMENTS:** Co-author, "Rate Parameters in Coupled Vibration-Dissociation in a Generalized SSH Approximation," Journal of Thermophysics and Heat Transfer, vol 6, no 1, p 9-21, March, 1992; "Assessment of Nonequilibrium Radiation Computation Methods for Hypersonic Flows," International Journal of Modern Physics C, Physics and Computers, also NASA TM-103994, January, 1993; co-author, "Time-dependent Simulations of Reflected Shock/Boundary Layer Interactions," AIAA Paper 93-0480; and others; over 30 technical papers. **BUSINESS ADDRESS:** Research Scientist, NASA Ames Research Center, M/S 230-2, Moffett Field, CA 94035-1000, (415)604-3432.

SHARMA, UDHISHTRA DEVA
Veterinarian, educator. Indo-American. **PERSONAL:** Born Aug 16, 1928, Amritsar, Punjab, India; son of Pt Harcharn Das; married Sarla Sharma, Jan 16, 1959; children: Sadhana Sharma Swaroop. **EDUCATION:** Haryana Agricultural University, Hissar, India, BVSc, 1948; University of Illinois, Urbana, MS, 1954, PhD, 1957. **CAREER:** Indian Veterinary Research Institute, UP, India,

research assistant, 1949-53; University of Illinois, department of dairy science, research assistant, fellow, 1953-57; American Foundation for Biological Research, research associate, 1957-58; Postgraduate College of Animal Sciences Indian Veterinary Research Institute, Izatnagar, India, Animal Genetics, professor, 1958-64; Haryana Agricultural University, professor of animal husbandry, 1964-65, department of anatomy, veterinary college dean, professor, head animal husbandry department, 1964-65; University of Arkansas Medical Center, Department of Anatomy, visiting professor, 1965-66; Alabama State University, professor of biology, 1966-. **ORGANIZATIONS:** American Veterinary Medical Association, 1983-; Central Alabama Veterinary Medical Association, 1975-; Hindu Society of Alabama, 1981-, Hindu Temple, board member, 1992-. **HONORS/AWARDS:** University of Illinois, research fellowships, 1954-57. **SPECIAL ACHIEVEMENTS:** More than 30 research papers on semen physiology and physiology of reproduction published in national and international journals, 1953-66; research in mammalian germ cell physiology, 1949-66. **HOME ADDRESS:** 4438 Eley Court, Montgomery, AL 36106, (205)272-0980. **BUSINESS ADDRESS:** Professor of Biology, Alabama State University, South Jackson St, Science Bldg, Rm 214, Montgomery, AL 36101, (205)293-4448.

SHAW, FRED. *See* **HSIAO, FENG.**

SHEIKH, GHAFOOR A.
Financial analyst. Pakistani American/Indo-American. **PERSONAL:** Born Jul 4, 1947, Amritsar, India; son of Mohammed H Sheikh; married Florence; children: Aysha, Omar, Laila. **EDUCATION:** St Joseph's College, BSc, 1974; Temple University, MBA, 1978. **CAREER:** Boston Gas, personnel specialist, 1978-80; Raytheon Company, program analyst, 1980-84; US Air Force, operations research analyst, 1984-90, financial analyst, 1990-. **ORGANIZATIONS:** Society of Cost Estimating and Analysis, 1987-. **HONORS/AWARDS:** SCEA, Professional Cost Estimator, certification, 1987. **HOME ADDRESS:** 26 Sewell St, Framingham, MA 01701-6001, (508)626-0776.

SHEN, BENJAMIN SHIH-PING
Scientist, educator. Chinese American. **PERSONAL:** Born Sep 14, 1931, Hangzhou, Zhejiang, China; son of Nai-Cheng Shen and Chen-Chiu Sun; married Lucia Elisabeth Simpson, 1971; children: William, Juliet. **EDUCATION:** Assumption College, AB, 1954; Clark University, AM, physics, 1956; University of Paris, DSc d'Etat, physics, 1964. **CAREER:** New York University, associate professor of space science, 1964-66; University of Pennsylvania, associate professor, 1966-68, professor, 1968-72, Department of Astronomy and Astrophysics, chairman, 1973-79, Council of Graduate Deans, chairman, 1979-81, provost, 1980-81; US National Science Board, 1990-; University of Pennsylvania, Reese W Flower Professor of Astrophysics, 1972-. **ORGANIZATIONS:** US National Science Board Task Force on Scientific Literacy, chairman, 1992-; American Physical Society, fellow; Royal Astronomical Society, fellow; International Astronomical Union; AAAS, fellow. **HONORS/AWARDS:** Republic of France, Ordre des Palmes Academiques, 1993; Societe d'Encouragement au Progres, Vermeil Medal for Science, 1978. **SPECIAL ACHIEVEMENTS:** Numerous publications. **BUSINESS ADDRESS:** Professor, University of Pennsylvania, David Rittenhouse Laboratory, Philadelphia, PA 19104-6394.

SHEN, CHIA THENG
Association executive. Chinese American. **PERSONAL:** Born Dec 15, 1913, Hangchow, CheKiang, China; son of Foo Sheng and Wen Hsia; married Woo Chu Ju, Apr 21, 1940 (deceased); children: Maria May Shen Jackson, May Shen George, David Chuen Tsing, Freda Foh. **EDUCATION:** Chiao Tung University, Shanghai, China, BEE, 1937. **CAREER:** Central Electric Mfg Works, manager, 1937-44; National Resources Com Dept, dept head, 1945-47; China Trading Co, president, 1947-53; Transatlantic Financing Corp, president, 1954-62; Marine Transport Lines, senior vice president, 1958-70; American Steamship Co, chairman, CEO, 1971-80. **ORGANIZATIONS:** Buddhist Association of the United States, trustee, vice president, 1964-; China Institute in America, trustee, executive committee, chairman 1963-84; Chinese Institute of Engineering, 1964-; Institute for Advance Studies of World Religion, president, trustee, 1970-. **HONORS/AWARDS:** St John's University, LittD, 1973. **SPECIAL ACHIEVEMENTS:** Books published in Chinese and English; lectures on Buddhism. **HOME ADDRESS:** RD 2, Route 301, Carmel, NY 10512, (914)225-1737. **BUSINESS ADDRESS:** President, Institute for Advanced Studies of World Religions, RD 2, Rt 301, Carmel, NY 10512.

SHEN, CHUNG YU (TONY C. Y.)
Chemical engineer, business executive. Chinese American. **PERSONAL:** Born Dec 15, 1921, Beijing, China; son of Chia-I Shen and Yi Ting Shen; married Colleen N Shen, Jun 10, 1954; children: Sheldon, Vincent, Anthony. **EDUCATION:** National SW Association University, Kunming, China, BS, 1942; University of Louisville, MChE, 1950; University of Illinois, PhD, 1954. **CAREER:** Tung-Li Oil Works, ChungKing, China, group leader, 1942-45; Central Chemical Works, Shanghai, China, section chief, 1945-49; Institute of Industrial Research, senior engineering, 1949-52; Monsanto Co, senior fellow, 1954-86; Shen and Shen, Inc, vice president, 1987-. **ORGANIZATIONS:** American Institute of Chemical Engineering, fellow; American Oil Chemical Society; American Association for Advancement of Science; Sigma Xi. **SPECIAL ACHIEVEMENTS:** Over 65 US patents, 1956-92; over 23 professional articles and book chapters, 1960-82. **HOME PHONE:** (314)434-2183. **BUSINESS ADDRESS:** Vice President, Shen and Shen, Inc, 5 Mason Ridge Ct, St Louis, MO 63141.

SHEN, GRACE LIU (WEI LIU)
Organization executive. Chinese American. **PERSONAL:** Born Mar 24, 1941, Shantung, China; daughter of Tao-yuan Liu & Su Kuei Y Liu; married Liang Chi Shen, Jun 26, 1965; children: Michael Koping, Eugene Liu. **EDUCATION:** Tunghai University, Taiwan, BS, 1962; Wellesley College, 1962-64. **CAREER:** Harvard University, research assistant, 1964-66; Saint Agnes Academy, science teacher, 1973-85; Chinese Community Center, executive director, 1989-. **ORGANIZATIONS:** United Way of the Texas Gulf Coast, Asian Marketing Committee, chair, 1992-94; Chinese Writers' Assn, board member, 1991-; Evergreen Chinese School, founder, board, board chair, principal, 1983-91. **SPECIAL ACHIEVEMENTS:** Proficient in Chinese; writer, columnist, public speaker on education; book, Education Guide for Chinese American Youth, Chinese, 1989; TV hostess, "Mrs Shen's Time," on Texas Chinese TV, 1990-; newspaper columnist, Mrs Shen's Mailbox, on World Journal, the largest Chinese newspaper in the US; apply government & foundation funding to assist in the assimilation of Asian immigrants. **BIOGRAPHICAL SOURCES:** "Evergreen School Keeps Chinese Traditions Alive," Houston Post, March 31, 1985; "Solve Problems for the Immigrant Youths," World Journal, May 30-31, 1991. **BUSINESS ADDRESS:** Executive Director, Chinese Community Center, 5855 Sovereign Dr, Houston, TX 77036, (713)271-6100.

SHEN, HAO-MING
Engineer. Chinese American. **PERSONAL:** Born Nov 5, 1933, Chang-Zhou, Jiangsu, China; son of Zhi-Yang Shen and You-Lan Chai; married De-Wei Chen, Oct 17, 1959; children: Hong-Hui, Wei-Hui, Qing-Hui. **EDUCATION:** Beijing University, BS, physics, 1958; Chiaotung University, PhD, 1966. **CAREER:** Beijing University, teaching assistant, 1958-63; Harbin Civil Engineering College, lecturer, 1966-78, associate professor, 1978-79; Harvard University, visiting scholar, 1979-83, research associate, 1986-; Academy of Science, China, associate professor, 1983-86, professor, 1986-. **ORGANIZATIONS:** Chinese Institute of Electronics, 1985-; IEEE, 1985-; International Union of Radio Science, committee member, 1985-. **HONORS/AWARDS:** IEEE, EMC Society, Prize Paper Award, 1983. **BUSINESS ADDRESS:** Research Associate, Harvard University, Nine Oxford St, Gordon McKay Laboratory, Cambridge, MA 02138, (617)495-4464.

SHEN, HSIEH WEN
Educator. Chinese American. **PERSONAL:** Born Jul 13, 1931, Peking, China; married 1956. **EDUCATION:** University of Michigan, BS, 1953, MS, 1954; University of California, Berkeley, PhD, hydraulics, 1961. **CAREER:** US Army Corps of Engineers, hydraulic engineer, 1955-56; Giffels & Vallet Inc, structural engineer, 1956; University of California, Institute Eng Research, hydraulic research engineer, 1956-61; Harza Engineering Co, hydraulic engineer, 1961-63; Colorado State University, Fort Collins, Hydraulic Engineering, associate professor, 1964-68, professor, 1968-. **ORGANIZATIONS:** Natl Academy of Engineering. **HONORS/AWARDS:** American Society of Civil Engineers, Freeman fellow, 1965-66, Einstein Award, 1990-91; Guggenheim fellow, 1972; Humboldt Foundation, Germany, Senior Research Award, 1990-91; American Geophysics Union, Horton Award. **BUSINESS ADDRESS:** Professor of Hydraulic Engineering, University of California, Berkeley, 412 O'Brien Hall, Berkeley, CA 94720, (510)642-6777.*

SHEN, I-YAO
Librarian, historian, educator. Chinese American. **PERSONAL:** Born Nov 9, 1926, China; married Verna Shen, Nov 6, 1962. **EDUCATION:** Zhongshan

University, China, BA, 1949; Columbia University, MA, 1960; Rutgers University, MLS, 1961. **CAREER:** University of Maryland, librarian, 1961-71; Library of Congress, librarian, 1971-72; Teachers College of DC, librarian II, assistant professor, 1972-77; University of The District of Columbia, librarian III, professor, 1978-. **ORGANIZATIONS:** NEA, 1978-; ALA, 1975-; DCLA, 1979-; Chinese American Forum, board of directors, 1987-; Yellow River University, co-founder, 1984-. **HONORS/AWARDS:** Overseas Chinese Histroical Association, Honorable Director, 1983; Jiaying University, Honorable Professor, 1985; Southwestern Agricultural University, Honorable Professor, 1986. **SPECIAL ACHIEVEMENTS:** Author, A Century of Chinese Exclusion Abroad, 1970, 1980, 1985, 1993; Confucian Analects: Selected Readings, 1987-1993; Southeast Asia: Overseas Motherland, 1985; Standard Code of Parliamentary Procedure, 1987, 1993; Library Modernization in China: Collected Works, 1989. **BIOGRAPHICAL SOURCES:** A Profile of 50 Celebrated Chinese-Americans, Beijing, pp 251-254, 1987; Dictionary of Overseas Chinese, Beijing, pp 410, 672-673, 1993. **HOME ADDRESS:** 9005 Acredale Ct, College Park, MD 20740, (301)935-0653. **BUSINESS ADDRESS:** Professor, Librarian, University of the District of Columbia, 4200 Conn Ave N W, Bldg 39, Rm Bo8A, Washington, DC 20008, (202)274-6118.

SHEN, LIANG CHI

Educator. Chinese American. **PERSONAL:** Born Mar 17, 1939, China; son of Kuang Hai & Ting Chin Shen; married Wei Grace Liu, Jun 26, 1965; children: Michael, Eugene. **EDUCATION:** National Taiwan University, BSEE, 1961; Harvard University, PhD, applied physics, 1967. **CAREER:** Gulf, research consultant, 1981-82; ARCO, research fellow, 1990-91; University of Houston, professor and chairman, 1977-81, professor, director, well logging lab, 1978-. **ORGANIZATIONS:** IEEE, fellow, 1987-, Geoscience, associate editor, 1986-;SPE; SPWLA; SEG; American Geophysical Union. **HONORS/AWARDS:** University of Houston, College of Engineering, Excellence in Research, 1982. **SPECIAL ACHIEVEMENTS:** Author, Applied Electromagnetism, Shen & Kong, PWS Publishing, 1987; more than 70 technical papers in tech journals; fluent in Chinese. **BUSINESS ADDRESS:** Professor, Electrical Engineering Dept, Director, University of Houston, Well Logging Lab, Houston, TX 77204-4793, (713)743-4420.

SHEN, SHAN-FU

Educator, consultant, engineer. Chinese American. **PERSONAL:** Born Aug 31, 1921, Shanghai, China; son of Tsu-Wei Shen and Sien-Hwa New Shen; married Ming-Ming, Dec 16, 1950; children: Hseuh-Yung, Hsueh-Lang. **EDUCATION:** National Central University, China, BS, aeronautical engineering, 1941; MIT, DSc, aeronautical engineering, 1949. **CAREER:** Bureau of Aero Research, Chinese Air Force, assistant research scientist, beginning 1941, associate research scientist, until 1945; MIT, mathematics dept, research associate, 1948-50; University of Maryland, College Park, assistant professor, beginning 1950, professor, until 1960; visiting professor, Univ of Paris, 1964-65, 1969-70, Tech Univ, Austria, 1977, Univ of Tokyo, 1984-85; Cornell University, aerospace engineering, professor, 1961-78, John Edson Sweet Professor of Engineering, beginning 1978, professor emeritus, currently. **ORGANIZATIONS:** International Academy of Astronautics; NAE; Academia Sinica of Taiwan. **HONORS/AWARDS:** Washington Academy of Science, Engineering Award, 1958; Guggenheim Fellow, 1957; Humboldt Foundation, Republic of West Germany, Senior Scientist Award, 1985. **SPECIAL ACHIEVEMENTS:** Author, over 100 journal articles. **BUSINESS ADDRESS:** Professor Emeritus, Sibley School of Mechanical and Aerospace Engineering, Cornell University, Upson Hall, Ithaca, NY 14853, (607)255-2000.*

SHEN, SHELDON SHIH-TA

Educator. Chinese American. **PERSONAL:** Born Nov 22, 1947, Shanghai, China; son of Tony Cy Shen; married Virginia Lee Geary, Jun 16, 1979; children: Christopher, Molliarda, Camille. **EDUCATION:** University of Missouri, Columbia, BS, 1969; University of California, Berkeley, PhD, 1974. **CAREER:** Iowa State University, professor, 1989-. **HOME ADDRESS:** 3700 Fuller Rd, West Des Moines, IA 50265-5332, (515)224-9914. **BUSINESS ADDRESS:** Professor, Dept of Zoology & Genetics, Iowa State University, 339 Science II, Ames, IA 50011-3211, (515)294-8435.

SHEN, TEK-MING

Scientist. Chinese American/Hong Kong American. **PERSONAL:** Born Jan 6, 1949, Hong Kong; married Ho-Lan Shen; children: Isabel, Vincent. **EDUCATION:** University of Hong Kong, physics/math (1st class honor), 1972, physics, BSc (special), 1973; UC, Berkeley, California, PhD, physics, 1979.

CAREER: AT&T Bell Labs, DMTS, 1980-. **ORGANIZATIONS:** LEOS; IEEE, senior member, 1980-. **BUSINESS ADDRESS:** Scientist, AT&T Bell Laboratories, 600 Mountain Avenue, Room 2D-352, Murray Hill, NJ 07974, (908)582-2903.

SHEN, THOMAS T.

Government official, educator. Chinese American. **PERSONAL:** Born Aug 14, 1926, Jiaxing, Zhejiang, China; son of Jing-Chiu Shen and Fong Chen; married Cynthia Shen, Jun 24, 1959; children: Grace Shen Law, Joyce Shen Shavers. **EDUCATION:** St John's University, BSc, civil eng, 1948; Northwestern University, MSc, sanitary engineering, 1960; University of Southern California, air pollution control instructor, 1966; Rensselaer Polytechnic Institute, PhD, env eng, 1971. **CAREER:** The Boeing Co, associate engineer, 1960-62; Washington State Government, Department of Health, sanitary engr, 1962-66; New York State Government, Department of Health, senior engineer, 1966-70, Dept of Env Conservation, senior scientists, 1970-92; Columbia University, School of Public Health, adjunct professor, 1981-; The United Nations, consultant, env training & projects, 1983-; US EPA Science Advisory Board, consultant, 1987-92. **ORGANIZATIONS:** Air & Waste Mgt Association, chairman, several committees, 1962-; Am Society of Civil Engineers, New York State Council, chairman; Am Academy of Environmental Engineers, Air Pollution Committee, chairman, 1989-92; Phi Tau Phi, East US, president; Oversea Chinese Env Engineers & Scientists Association, president; Chinese American Academic & Professional Society, board director, 1990-; Delmar Rotary International, president; American Bureau Medical Aid to China, board director, 1986-. **HONORS/AWARDS:** Phi Tau Phi, Service Award, 1986; Pollution Engineering Magazine, Outstanding Editorial Contribution, 1978, 1981; Overseas Chinese Env Engrs & Scientists Association, Service Award, 1990; President Bush's Environment & Conservation Council, Awards Reviewer, 1991, 1992. **SPECIAL ACHIEVEMENTS:** Books: Assessment and Control of VOC Emissions from Waste Treatment and Disposal Facilities, Van Nostrand Reinbold, New York, 1992; Air Pollution and Its Control, Chinese Env Sc Press, 1985; "Land Disposal," Chapter 20, Air Pollution Eng Manual, USEPA/AWMA, 1991; "Air Quality Impact Assessment," Chapter 1, Encyclopedia Env Control Tech, vol 2, 1989. **MILITARY SERVICE:** Chinese Air Force, Engineering Corps, major, 1948-50. **HOME ADDRESS:** 146 Fernbank Ave, Delmar, NY 12054, (518)439-2362.

SHEN, WU-MIAN

Research scientist. Chinese American. **PERSONAL:** Born Aug 23, 1942, Shanghai, China; son of An-zhi Shen & Jia-bao Hu; married Li-li Yang, Jan 1, 1974; children: Zong-jing. **EDUCATION:** Shanghai Jiao-Tong University, BE, electrical engineering, 1964, ME, polymer science, 1981; City University of New York, PhD, solid state physics, 1991. **CAREER:** Tianjin Electronic Wire & Cable Co, engineer, 1964-78; Shanghai Jiao-Tong University, lecturer in applied chemistry department, 1981-83; Brooklyn College, Physics Department and Applied Sciences Institute, visiting scholar, 1983-84, research assistant, 1984-91, research associate, 1991-. **ORGANIZATIONS:** American Physical Society, 1985-; The Electrochemical Society, 1987-; Sigma Xi, 1992-. **SPECIAL ACHIEVEMENTS:** More than 20 research papers published in professional journals such as Journal of Applied Physics and Journal of Electrochemical Society, 1985-. **BUSINESS ADDRESS:** Research Associate, Physics Dept, Brooklyn College of CUNY, 2900 Bedford Ave, Brooklyn, NY 11210, (718)951-4738.

SHEN, XIAO-YAN (CHEYENNE CHEN)

Educator, librarian. Chinese American. **PERSONAL:** Born Feb 21, 1963, Nanjing, Jiangsu, People's Republic of China; daughter of JingBo Shen and DeLan Gao; married Chien Chen, Nov 27, 1987. **EDUCATION:** Peking University, BA, 1986; University of Wisconsin-Milwaukee, MLIS, 1990. **CAREER:** University of Mississippi, science librarian, bibliographer, assistant professor, 1990-91; University of the Pacific Systems, librarian, assistant professor, 1991-. **ORGANIZATIONS:** American Library Association, committee vice chair, 1989-; California Library Association, committee member, 1991-. **HONORS/AWARDS:** Journal Communications, research assistantship, 1989-90. **SPECIAL ACHIEVEMENTS:** Co-editor, plot locator, Garland Publishing, 1991; language proficiency, Chinese. **BUSINESS ADDRESS:** Systems Librarian, Assistant Professor, University of the Pacific, 3601 Pacific Ave, Library, Stockton, CA 95211, (209)946-2029.

SHEN, YUEN-RON

Educator. Chinese American. **PERSONAL:** Born Mar 25, 1935, Shanghai, China; married Hsiao-Lin Shen, Oct 21, 1982; children: Kerry Kai, Pearl Hao,

Alex Ming. **EDUCATION:** National Taiwan University, BS, 1956; Stanford University, MS, 1959; Harvard University, PhD, 1963. **CAREER:** Hewlett-Packard Co, research assistant, 1959; Harvard University, research fellow, 1963-64; Lawrence Berk Lab, principal investigator, 1964-; University of California Berkeley, assistant professor, 1964-67, associate professor, 1967-70, professor, 1970-. **ORGANIZATIONS:** American Phys Society, fellow; Optical Society of America, fellow; American Academy Arts & Sciences. **HONORS/AWARDS:** Sloan Fellow, 1966-68; Guggenheim Foundation Fellow, 1972-73; Charles Hard Townes Award, 1986; Arthur L Schawlow Prize, 1992; DOE-MRS Research, Outstanding research in solid state physics, 1983. **SPECIAL ACHIEVEMENTS:** Author: The Principles of Non Linears Optics, 1984; more than 350 publications. **BUSINESS ADDRESS:** Professor, Physics Dept, University of California Berkeley, Berkeley, CA 94720.

SHENDRIKAR, ARUN D.
Environmental chemist. Indo-American. **PERSONAL:** Born Jul 10, 1938, Gwlberga, Karnataka, India; son of Dhondopant Shendrikar & Vachala Bai Shendrikar; married Rajani Shendrikar, Sep 23, 1966; children: Rita, Atul. **EDUCATION:** Osmania University, Hyderabad, India, MSc, 1961; Durham University, England, PhD, 1966. **CAREER:** Oil Shale Corp, senior research chemist, 1974-78; Meteorology Research Inc, technical staff specialist, 1978-80; Research Triangle Institute, senior chemist, 1980-82; Compuchem Labs, inorganics manager, 1982-86; Beta Labs, general manager, 1986-88; EIRA Inc, Analytical Services, manager, 1988-89; Litho Industries Inc, Environmental Affairs, director, 1989-. **ORGANIZATIONS:** Royal Institute of Chemistry; American Chemical Society; Sigma Xi; ASTM-D 22/04, Sulfur Compounds, chairman, Committee on Conference, chairman. **HONORS/AWARDS:** North Carolina's Governor Award for Excellence in Wast Management. **SPECIAL ACHIEVEMENTS:** Colorado Governor's Air Pollution Control Commission, advisory committee. **HOME ADDRESS:** 1011 W Saint Helena Place, Apex, NC 27502, (919)387-0440.

SHENG, BRIGHT
Composer, pianist, conductor. Chinese American. **PERSONAL:** Born Dec 6, 1955, Shanghai, People's Republic of China; son of David Cheng & Alice Cheng. **EDUCATION:** Shanghai Conservatory of Music, BA, 1982; Queens College, CUNY, MA, 1984; Columbia University, DMA, 1993. **CAREER:** Lyric Opera of Chicago, composer-in-residence, 1989-; San Francisco Symphony, artistic director of Wet Inc 93 Festival, 1993; Seattle Symphony, composer-in-residence 1992-94; Santa Fe Chamber Music Festival, composer-in-residence, 1993; La Jolla Chamber Music Summerfest, composer-in-residence, 1993; co-composer, The Song of Majhun, opera; recordings include: Arias and Barcarolles, H'UN, Two Folk Songs from Chinhai. **HONORS/AWARDS:** Columbia University, Pulitzer Prize in Music, first runner up, 1989, 1991; Guggenheim Foundation, fellowship award, 1990; The National Endowment for the Arts, fellowship award, 1987, 1990; The Rockefeller Foundation, residency award, 1991; The American Academy & Institute of Arts and Letters, Charles Ives Prize, 1984. **BUSINESS ADDRESS:** Composer, c/o G Schirmer Inc, 254 Park Ave South, New York, NY 10010.

SHENG, PING
Physicist. Chinese American. **PERSONAL:** Born Jul 1, 1946, Shanghai, China; son of Sherman Tse-Min Sheng and Vena Yin Sheng; married Deborah Wen, Jun 6, 1970; children: Ellen, Ada. **EDUCATION:** California Institute of Technology, BS, physics, 1967; Princeton University, PhD, physics, 1971. **CAREER:** Institute for Advanced Study, visiting scholar, 1971-73; RCA David Sarnoff Research Center, research staff, 1973-79; Exxon Research & Engineering, senior research associate, 1979-. **ORGANIZATIONS:** Exxon Research & Engineering, group head, 1982-86. **HONORS/AWARDS:** American Institute of Physics, American Physical Society, fellow, 1987; University of California Irvine, Regent Lecturer, 1990; Universite Pierre et Marie Curie, Paris, France, University Professor, 1992; Fudan University, China, Honorary Professor, 1987. **SPECIAL ACHIEVEMENTS:** Author of 150 technical publications; 9 US & foreign-filed patents; editor of 4 books; proficient in Chinese & English. **BUSINESS ADDRESS:** Dept of Physics, Hong Kong University of Science & Technology, Clearwater Bay, Kowloon, Hong Kong.

SHENG, TONY L.
Corporate executive. Chinese American. **PERSONAL:** Born Feb 28, 1935; married Ke-Ling Sheng, May 22, 1960; children: James, Lambert, Raymond. **EDUCATION:** Brooklyn Polytechnical Institute, master's, 1969. **CAREER:** Kotow Inc, president, currently. **ORGANIZATIONS:** Society of Plastic Engineers. **SPECIAL ACHIEVEMENTS:** Fluent in: Chinese, French, English.

BUSINESS ADDRESS: President, Kotow Inc, 244 Dukes St, Kearny, NJ 07032.

SHENOI, B. A.
Educator. Indo-American. **PERSONAL:** Born Dec 23, 1929, Belle, Karnataka, India; married Suman. **EDUCATION:** University of Madras, BSc, 1951; Indian Institute of Science, Bangalore, DIISc, 1956; University of Illinois, Urbana, PhD, 1962. **CAREER:** University of Minnesota, EE, assistant professor, 1962-66, associate professor, 1966-71, professor, 1971-86; Wright State University, EE, chairman, 1986-92, professor, currently. **ORGANIZATIONS:** IEEE, Fellow, 1978-; Circuits & Systems Society, president, 1975, secretary, 1972-73, Trans on Circuits & Systems, associate editor, 1973-75; IETE, Fellow, 1988. **HONORS/AWARDS:** National Cheng-Kung University, honorary professor, 1988; IEEE, Circuits & Systems Society, Meritorious Service Award, 1992. **SPECIAL ACHIEVEMENTS:** Publication of more than 50 papers in professional journals. **BUSINESS ADDRESS:** Professor of Electrical Engineering, Wright State University, 311 Russ Center, Dayton, OH 45435.

SHENOY, NARASIMHA B.
Engineer. Indo-American. **PERSONAL:** Born May 25, 1949, Athikaribettu, Mysore, India; son of Santhappa & Sumithra Shenoy; married Aruna, Apr 24, 1972; children: Maya, Priya. **EDUCATION:** West Virginia Institute of Technology, BSEE (magna cum laude), 1976; West Virginia College of Graduate Studies, MSEE, 1980; Drexel University, MBA, 1986. **CAREER:** West Virginia Engineering Co, engineering supervisor, 1976-80; Bechtel Corp, test director, 1980-84; General Electric Co, chief engineer, 1984-92; Railway Systems Design, technical director, 1992-; S & G Electric Co, president, 1993-. **ORGANIZATIONS:** Council of Indian Organization, president, 1992-; Asian American Voter Coalition, vice chair, 1992-; Asian American National Republican Association, vice chair, 1991-92; National Federation of Indian Associations, board member, 1992-; Pennsylvania Heritage Affairs Commission, 1992-; Mayor's Commission on Asian Affairs, Philadelphia, 1990-. **SPECIAL ACHIEVEMENTS:** Met with President George Bush in the oval office, 1992. **BIOGRAPHICAL SOURCES:** "Asian Americans Forge Ahead," India-West, p 17, Nov 1991. **HOME ADDRESS:** 25 Mill Ln, Frazer, PA 19355.

SHETH, ASHVIN C.
Gem business executive. Indo-American. **PERSONAL:** Born May 30, 1935, Gondal, Gujarat, India; son of Chhaganlal V Sheth and Nandkunvar C Sheth; married Tarlika; children: Hemang, Deepan. **EDUCATION:** Gujarat University, India, BA, 1959, MA, 1962, BEd, 1963; Tulsa University, MTA, 1965. **CAREER:** Vallabhvidyanagar S V Patel University, professor, 1966-69; College of Education, professor, 1969-72; Various Education Trust, principal, 1972-74; J V U K M Trust, principal, 1974-82; Tru Gems, proprietor, currently. **HONORS/AWARDS:** Shru Morarjeebhai Desai, former prime minister of India, honored for work as chief of various health camps. **BUSINESS ADDRESS:** Proprietor, Tru Gems, PO Box 380903, Duncanville, TX 75138, (214)780-0725.

SHETH, ATUL CHANDRAVADAN
Educator. Indo-American. **PERSONAL:** Born Dec 2, 1941, Bombay, Maharashtra, India; son of Chandravadan and Tanman; married Sheila, Feb 16, 1965; children: Roma, Archana. **EDUCATION:** University of Bombay, India, BS, 1964; Northwestern University, MS, 1969, PhD, 1973. **CAREER:** Esso Standard Eastern, Inc, production supervisor, 1964-67; Riker Laboratories, chemical operator, 1967; Armour Industrial Chemicals Co, process engineer, 1969; Charlotte Charles, Inc, assistant plant manager, 1971-72; Argonne National Laboratory, chemical engineer, 1972-80; Exxon Research & Engineering Co, staff chemical engineer, 1980-84; University of Tennessee Space Institute, professor, 1984-. **ORGANIZATIONS:** Air & Waste Management Association, 1989-; Sigma Xi, 1968-; American Institute of Chemical Engineers, 1969-. **HONORS/AWARDS:** ASME/AIAA, Best Posters at Symposium on Engineering Aspects of Magnetohydrodynamics meetings, 1991, 1992; The Elphinstone College, Anil P Desai Prize, 1960. **SPECIAL ACHIEVEMENTS:** Four US patents (#5,059,406, #5,057,294, #4,917,874, & #4,309,398), 1982-91. **BUSINESS ADDRESS:** Professor, University of Tennessee Space Inst, B H Goethert Parkway, F-248, Tullahoma, TN 37388-8897, (615)393-7427.

SHETH, KETANKUMAR KANTILAL
Mechanical engineer. Indo-American. **PERSONAL:** Born Jan 21, 1959, Gondal, Gujarat, India; son of Kantilal C Sheth and Sudha K Sheth; married

Rita, Aug 30, 1987; children: Dhara. **EDUCATION:** Sardar Patel University, BEME, 1980; Texas A&M University, MS, 1985. **CAREER:** TATA Chemicals, India, maintenance engineer, 1980-82; Texas A&M University, research associate, 1984-85; Centrilift, senior associate engineer, 1985-87, staff engineer, 1987-89, project engineer, 1989-90, engineering supervisor, 1990-. **ORGANIZATIONS:** Society of Professional Engineers, Oklahoma, professional engineer, 1990; ASME, 1985; SPE, 1991; Tulsa Jain Sangh, 1991; India Association of Tulsa, 1985; Hindu Society of Oklahoma, 1985. **SPECIAL ACHIEVEMENTS:** US Patent No 4838758, 1989; US Patent No 5207810, 1993; author, "Slip Factors of Centrifugal Slurry Pump," Journal of Fluid Engineering, vol 109, pp 312-318, Sep 1987; "Elbow Flowmeter Calibrations for Slurries," Chemical Engineering Communications, vol 63, Jan 1988. **HOME ADDRESS:** 8810 S 73 E Ave, Tulsa, OK 74133, (918)250-3075. **BUSINESS PHONE:** (918)342-8249.

SHETH, KISHOR C.
Educator, business executive. Indo-American. **PERSONAL:** Born Sep 19, 1943, Palitana, Gujarat, India; son of Chunilal V Sheth; married Kalpana, 1968; children: Nirav, Kanan. **EDUCATION:** MBA, 1970. **CAREER:** Delaware State University, Business & Economic Studies, professor, currently; 1st State Mortgage Inc, president, currently. **ORGANIZATIONS:** Dover Chamber of Commerce, president elect; American Heart Association, Kent County, past president; American Cancer Society, Dover, director; Delaware Dev Corporation, commissioner. **HONORS/AWARDS:** Businessman of the Year, 1985. **BUSINESS ADDRESS:** President, 1st State Mortgage Inc, PO Box 086, Dover, DE 19903, (302)678-2772.

SHETH, NAVIN D.
Construction company executive. Indo-American. **PERSONAL:** Born Jan 15, 1946, Palitana, Gujarat, India; son of Dalichand V Sheth and Gunvanti D Sheth; married Sucheta, Dec 20, 1973; children: Kevin N, Kinjal N. **EDUCATION:** Bombay University, BS, 1967; Atlanta University, MBA, 1971. **CAREER:** Stamie E Lyttle Co Inc, vice pres of finance, 1972-. **ORGANIZATIONS:** Hindu Center of Virginia, executive committee, 1989-. **HOME ADDRESS:** 5331 Sunbeam Rd, Richmond, VA 23234, (804)271-8670.

SHETTY, ANIL N.
Research scientist. Indo-American. **PERSONAL:** Born Mar 21, 1952, Bombay, India; son of Narsinha S Shetty and Soarojini N Shetty; married Renu Shetty, Jul 9, 1984; children: Nikhil, Rohan, Tushar. **EDUCATION:** Bombay University, MSc, 1974; Kent State University, MA, 1978, PhD, 1982; University of Pennsylvania, post doctoral, 1988. **CAREER:** University of Pennsylvania, post-doctoral fellow, 1986-88; Siemens Medical Systems, research scientist, 1988-91; William Beaumont Hospital, Dept of Radiology, chief, 1991-. **ORGANIZATIONS:** Society of Magnetic Resonance in Medicine; Association of American Physicists in Medicine. **HONORS/AWARDS:** Siemens Medical Systems, research merit, 1987. **HOME ADDRESS:** 4655 Bentley Dr, Troy, MI 48098. **BUSINESS ADDRESS:** Chief, Dept of Radiology, William Beaumont Hospital, 3601 W 13 Mile Rd, Royal Oak, MI 48073.

SHEU, BING J.
Educator. Taiwanese American. **PERSONAL:** Born Oct 26, 1955, Hsin-Chu, Taiwan; son of So Paul Sheu and Wang Da Sheu; married Shelley Sheu, 1985. **EDUCATION:** National Taiwan University, BSc, electrical engineering, 1978; University of California, Berkeley, MSc, electrical engineering, 1983, PhD, electrical engineering, 1985. **CAREER:** University of California, Berkeley, teaching assistant, 1981-82, graduate research assistant, 1982-85; University of Southern California, assistant professor, 1985-91, associate professor, 1991-. **ORGANIZATIONS:** Institute of Electrical and Electronics Engineers, 1985-91, senior member, 1991-, International Conference on Neural Networks, Technical Program Committee, 1993; International Neural Networks Society, 1991-; Association of Computing Machinery, 1987-88. **HONORS/AWARDS:** University of California, Berkeley, Tse-Wei Liu Memorial Fellowship, 1980, Stanley M Tasheria Scholarship, 1981; National Science Foundation, Engineering Initiation Award, 1987; IEEE, Best Presenter Award, 1991, 1992; National Chiao Tung University, Honorary Consulting Professor, 1992. **SPECIAL ACHIEVEMENTS:** Publication of more than 130 technical papers in scientific journals & conferences; author, Hardware Annealing in Analog VLSI Neurocomputing, Kluwer Academic Publishers, 1991; Neural Information Processing and VLSI, Kluwer, 1994; IEEE Transactions on VLSI Systems, associate editor, 1993; IEEE Transactions on Neural Networks, associate editor, 1993. **MILITARY SERVICE:** Army of Taiwan, 2nd lt, 1978-80. **BUSINESS**

ADDRESS: Assoc Professor, Dept of Electrical Engineering, University of Southern California, PHE-604, Los Angeles, CA 90089-0271, (213)740-4711.

SHEU, LIEN-LUNG
Chemical engineer. Taiwanese American. **PERSONAL:** Born Apr 15, 1959, Kaohsuing, Taiwan; son of Yao-Kai Sheu and Yu-Lan Lin Sheu; married Pey-Hwa Lee Sheu, Jul 11, 1987; children: Ashley Shaomin. **EDUCATION:** National Taiwan University, BS, 1981; Northwestern University, PhD, 1989. **CAREER:** National Taiwan University, research assistant, 1983-85; Northwestern University, research associate, 1986-89, post doctoral research associate, 1989; The BOC Group, Inc, senior engineer, 1989-. **ORGANIZATIONS:** American Society of Testing and Material, committee member, 1991-; Applied Catalysis, referee, 1991-; American Institute of Chemical Engineers, 1989-; North American Catalysis Society, 1989-. **SPECIAL ACHIEVEMENTS:** Published more than 10 technical papers and had 1 international patent issued, 2 US patents, 1985-; developed new processes for anhydride and special chemical productions, 1989-; synthesized Pd carbonyl inside zeolite cages at room temp, 1988-89; found a universal relationship between nobel metal particles and their absorbed CO's IR spectra, 1988-89; synthesized a new type metal boride catalysts, 1984-85. **BUSINESS ADDRESS:** Senior Engineer, The BOC Group, Inc, 100 Mountain Ave, Rm B1-3, Murray Hill, NJ 07974, (908)771-6183.

SHEVDE, KETAN
Anesthesiologist. Indo-American. **PERSONAL:** Born Jan 14, 1943, Karachi, Sindh, Pakistan; son of Usha Shevde and Wasudeo Damodar Shevde; married Nirmala Shevde, Mar 27, 1971; children: Nishad Raj. **EDUCATION:** Makerere Medical School, Uganda, MBChB, 1968. **CAREER:** Jewish Hospital of Brooklyn, internship, 1969-70, internal medicine, resident, 1970-71; Mount Sinai School of Medicine, anesthesia, resident, 1971-73, critical care, fellow, 1973-74; New York University Medical Center, staff anesthesiologist, 1974-82; Maimodides Medicial Center, cardiac anesthesia, director, 1982-87, Dept of Anesthesia, chairman, 1987-. **ORGANIZATIONS:** ASA, Scientific Exhibit Committee, 1992-93; Society of Cardiovascular Anesthesia, 1980-; Society for Education in Anesthesia, 1990-; New York State Society of Anesthesiologists, 1975-, Scientific Workshop Committee, 1992-93; Society of Critical Care Medicine, 1985-. **SPECIAL ACHIEVEMENTS:** Headache Prevention Following Accident Dural Puncture in Obstetric Patients, 1993; Adenosine and Myocardial Protection, 1992; Intraoperative Diagnosis of Free-Floating Atrial Thrombus, 1992; Discrepancies in Upper-limb Blood Pressure & Their Impact on Internal Mammary Artery-Coronary Artery Grafting, 1992; A Survey of 800 Patients' Knowledge, Attitudes, and Concerns Regarding Anesthesia, 1991; Prevention of Pulmonary Artery Rupture with the Use of Pressure Relief Balloon, 1993; invention, radial artery catheter; board certification: anesthesiology, 1975; critical care, 1989; CDQ, 1993. **BUSINESS ADDRESS:** Chairman, Dept of Anesthesiology, Maimonides Medical Center, 4802 10th Ave, Brooklyn, NY 11219.

SHIANG, ELAINE
Physician. Chinese American. **PERSONAL:** Born Mar 21, 1950, Malden, MA; daughter of Flora Wang Shiang and Si Ta Shiang; married Frederick P Li. **EDUCATION:** Wellesley College, BA, 1972; Harvard Medical School, MD, 1976. **CAREER:** Massachusetts Institute of Technology, physician, currently. **BUSINESS ADDRESS:** Physician, Massachusetts Institute of Technology, 77 Massachusetts Ave, E23, Cambridge, MA 02139.

SHIAO, DANIEL DA-FONG
Chemist, business executive. Chinese American. **PERSONAL:** Born Apr 6, 1937, China; son of Mr & Mrs E K Shiao; married Jeanne Shiao, Mar 2, 1974; children: Nara, Lena, David. **EDUCATION:** National Taiwan University, BS, 1958; New Mexico Highlands University, MS, 1963; University of Minnesota, PhD, 1968. **CAREER:** Kodak Research Labs, research associate, 1970-91; Rohai Technology Inc, president, currently. **ORGANIZATIONS:** American Chemical Society; Society for Imaging Science and Technology. **HONORS/AWARDS:** The Society for Imaging Science and Technology Journal, Honorable Mention, 1991. **SPECIAL ACHIEVEMENTS:** 13 publications in the field of biophysical chemistry; 10 publications in the field of photographic science; 4 patents in the field of photographic technology; fluent in Chinese. **BIOGRAPHICAL SOURCES:** The Theory of Photographic Process, p 430, 459, 1977. **HOME ADDRESS:** 1009 Whalen Rd, Penfield, NY 14526, (716)377-0185. **BUSINESS PHONE:** (716)377-7370.

SHIBATA, EDWARD ISAMU
Physicist, educator. Japanese American. **PERSONAL:** Born Mar 1, 1942, Gallup, NM; son of Edward Lawrence Shibata and Toshie Jean Shibata; married Frances Hatch Shibata, May 26, 1973. **EDUCATION:** Massachusetts Institute of Technology, SB, 1964, PhD, 1970. **CAREER:** Northeastern University, research associate, 1970-72; Purdue University, assistant professor, 1972-78, associate professor, 1978-84, professor, 1984-. **ORGANIZATIONS:** American Physical Society, 1970-; American Association of Physics Teachers, 1985-; Institute of Electrical and Electronic Engineers, 1991-. **HONORS/ AWARDS:** Purdue University Class of 1941, Innovative Teaching Award, 1991; Tippecanoe County Historical Association, Preservation of Historical Architecture, 1988. **SPECIAL ACHIEVEMENTS:** Over 130 publications on research in experimental high energy physics; development of a computerized physics laboratory for over 2000 students/year at Purdue University. **BUSINESS ADDRESS:** Professor, Purdue University, 1396 Physics Bldg, West Lafayette, IN 47907, (317)494-5193.

SHIEH, JOHN TING-CHUNG
Educator, entrepreneur. Chinese American. **PERSONAL:** Born Oct 11, 1935, Nanchang, Jiangxi, China. **EDUCATION:** National Chunghsing University, BS, 1956; Kansas State University, MS, 1960; University of California, Riverside, MA, 1970; University of Southern California, DBA, 1981. **CAREER:** California State Polytechnic University, professor of economics, 1967-. **ORGANIZATIONS:** American Economic Assn; Omicron Delta Epsilon. **HONORS/AWARDS:** NSF, fellowships, 1970s; Fulbright Fellow, 1989. **BUSINESS ADDRESS:** Professor of Economics, California State Polytechnic University, 3801 W Temple Ave, Pomona, CA 91768-4070, (909)869-3858.

SHIEH, RONG CHUNG
Engineer. Taiwanese American. **PERSONAL:** Born Jun 24, 1933, Kuang-Fu, Taiwan; married Kui Mei Shieh, Aug 8, 1960; children: Leon Lan, Devin Liang-Yi. **EDUCATION:** National Taiwan University, Bs, 1956; University of Michigan, MS, 1963; University of Illinois, PhD, 1968. **CAREER:** New York City Government, assistant structural engineer, 1963-65; University of California at San Diego, assistant research engineer, 1967-68; NASA-Langley Research Center, postdoctoral research associate, 1968-70; Cornell Aeronautical Laboratory Research, mechanical engineer, 1971-75; US Nuclear Regulatory Commission, GS 14, structural engineer, 1975-80; MRJ, Inc, technical staff, program manager, 1980-. **ORGANIZATIONS:** American Society of Mechanical Engineers, 1976-; American Institute of Aeronautics and Astronautics, 1988-; Taiwanese Professors Association of North America, 1986-. **HONORS/AWARDS:** Perkin-Elmer Corporation, Best Technical Paper Award, 1988. **SPECIAL ACHIEVEMENTS:** Wrote and published 40 technical papers; won highly competitive Small Business Innovation Research Contracts, 3 contracts in the past three years from NASA, Langley and Lewis Research Centers and DOD, 1990-93, Phase 2, from NASA/Lewis, 1994-96. **BUSINESS ADDRESS:** Member of the Technical Staff, MRJ, Inc, 10455 White Granite Drive, Oakton, VA 22124.

SHIEH, TSAY-JIU BRIAN
Educator. Taiwanese American. **PERSONAL:** Born Sep 20, 1953, Chiang-Hwa, Taiwan; son of Wan-Chi Shieh and Chi-Chu Tsai Shieh; married Lily Sun, Nov 2, 1978; children: Conan, Stefenie. **EDUCATION:** National Taiwan University, BS, physics, 1976; University of Cincinnati, MSEE, 1983, PhD, 1985. **CAREER:** University of Texas, Arlington, assistant professor, 1985-90, associate professor, 1990-. **ORGANIZATIONS:** IEEE Electron Device Society, Dallas Section, vice chairman, 1988-90; Chinese Institute of Engineers, DFW Chapter, treasurer, 1989-90, board of directors, 1991-93. **HONORS/ AWARDS:** University of Texas, Arlington, Halliburton Outstanding Young Faculty Research Award, 1990. **SPECIAL ACHIEVEMENTS:** NSF Industry/University Cooperative Research Center for Advanced Electron Devices and Systems, University of Texas, founding faculty member, received over $1 million, research contracts; published four engineering design software and over 20 technical papers; areas of focus include: compound semiconductor device modeling, processing development, vacuum microelectronics. **HOME ADDRESS:** 1710 Martinique Ct, Arlington, TX 76012. **BUSINESS PHONE:** (817)273-3479.

SHIEH, WUN-JU
Physician. Taiwanese American. **PERSONAL:** Born May 23, 1954, Taipei, Taiwan; son of The-Jen Shieh and A-Fong Shieh; married Pei-Chou Shieh; children: Joseph, Jocelyn, Jonathan. **EDUCATION:** Taipei Medical College, MD, 1979; Harvard University, School of Public Health, MPH, 1987; Vanderbilt University, PhD, microbiology 1992. **CAREER:** Taipei Medical College Hospital, medical staff, 1981-82; Cathay General Hospital, Taipei, medical staff, 1983-86; Vanderbilt Medical Center, pathology, medical staff, 1992-. **BUSINESS ADDRESS:** Physician, Vanderbilt Medical Center, 1301 22nd Ave South, Rm 4605 TVC, Nashville, TN 37232, (615)343-9166.

SHIEH, YUCH-NING
Educator. Taiwanese American. **PERSONAL:** Born Feb 15, 1940, Changhwa, Taiwan; son of Min-chu and Hwei-Tsao Shieh; married Tiee-Leou Ni Shieh, Sep 10, 1966; children: Lisa, Mae-Mae. **EDUCATION:** National Taiwan University, BS, 1962; California Institute of Technology, PhD, 1969. **CAREER:** McMaster University, post-doctoral fellow, 1968-72; Purdue University, professor, 1972-. **ORGANIZATIONS:** The Geochemical Society, 1969-; American Geophysical Union, 1969-; The Geological Society of China, 1962-. **SPECIAL ACHIEVEMENTS:** Published about 40 papers on oxygen, hydrogen, carbon and sulfur isotope geochemistry in rocks, minerals, coals, geothermal systems, and ore deposits. **MILITARY SERVICE:** National Army in Taiwan, 2nd lieutenant, 1961-62. **BUSINESS ADDRESS:** Professor, Dept Earth & Atmospheric Sciences, Purdue University, Civil Engineering Bldg, Rm 3271, West Lafayette, IN 47907, (317)494-3272.

SHIGEMASA, THOMAS KEN
Law enforcement official. Japanese American. **PERSONAL:** Born Sep 23, 1945, Waipahu, HI; son of Ruth Shigemasa and James Shigemasa; married Sue, Jun 21, 1967; children: Lei, Carie. **EDUCATION:** San Jose State University, BA, 1965-67; California Poly, Pomona, traffic program management institute 1979; California State University, Sacramento, narcotic command, 1980; University of Virginia, Charlottesville, FBI national academy, 1983. **CAREER:** San Jose Police Department, officer, 1967-71, sergeant, 1972-78, lieutenant, 1978-84, captain, 1985-92, Bureau of Administration, deputy chief, 1992-93, chief of detectives, 1993-. **ORGANIZATIONS:** Japanese American Citizens League, S J Chapter, delegate to district executive board, 1992-, president, 1990, 1991; Asian American City Emp Organization, co-founder, board member, 1990-; Coalition of Asian Americans for Public Safety, co-founder, past president, 1989-; North California Asian Peace Officers Association, South Bay Chapter, co-founder, 1990-; S C Co Law Enforcement Executive Committee, board member, 1992-. **HONORS/AWARDS:** Santa Clara County Human Relations Commission, Special Recognition, 1992; Northern California Asian Peace Officers Association, First Asian SJPD Deputy Chief, 1992; San Jose Police Department, Employee Recognition Award, 1991; City Council of San Jose, Resolutions for Specific Work, 1987-93; US Drug Enforcement Administration, Special Recognition, 1984. **BUSINESS ADDRESS:** Deputy Chief of Police, San Jose Police Department, 201 W Mission, San Jose, CA 95110, (408)277-4147.

SHIGIHARA, PATRICIA
Dentist, state government official. **CAREER:** Self-employed, dentist, currently. **ORGANIZATIONS:** State of Washington, Board of Dental Examiners, 1993-97. **BUSINESS ADDRESS:** Dentist, 907 N 130th St, Seattle, WA 98133-7502, (206)362-1121.*

SHIH, ARNOLD SHANG-TEH
Physicist. Chinese American. **PERSONAL:** Born May 17, 1943, Shanghai, China; son of Samuel L Shih and Sally Y P Shih; married Mary W Shih, Jun 28, 1969; children: Tina T Y, Michelle M Y. **EDUCATION:** University of California, Berkeley, AB, 1965; Columbia University, PhD, 1972. **CAREER:** National Bureau of Standards, research physicist, 1972-74; Naval Research Lab, research physicist, 1975-. **ORGANIZATIONS:** American Physical Society; American Vacuum Society. **BUSINESS ADDRESS:** Research Physicist, Naval Res Lab Code 6840, 4555 Overlook Ave, Washington, DC 20375-5000, (202)767-2260.

SHIH, CHIA C.
Educator. Chinese American. **PERSONAL:** Born Apr 18, 1939, China; son of Shau Chang Shih & Hen Fung Wen; married Linlin Shen, Feb 11, 1967; children: Connie K. **EDUCATION:** National Taiwan University, BS, 1961; Cornell University, PhD, 1967. **CAREER:** Brookhaven National Lab, research associate, 1967; Carnegie Mellon University, research associate, 1969; Los Alamos National Lab, visiting scientist, 1983; University of Arizona, visiting professor, 1988; University of Marburg, visiting professor, 1989; University of Tennessee, professor, 1971-. **ORGANIZATIONS:** American Physical Society, 1965-. **BUSINESS ADDRESS:** Professor, Dept of Physics, University of Tennessee, Knoxville, Knoxville, TN 37996-1200, (615)974-7806.

SHIH, CHIANG
Educator. Chinese American. **PERSONAL:** Born Aug 30, 1956, Taipei, Taiwan; son of Chi-ling Shih and Tze-Lan Shen; married Ya-Li Shih, Jun 25, 1980; children: Jonathan. **EDUCATION:** Tsing-Hua University, Taiwan, 1978; Louisiana State University, MSc, 1982; University of Southern California, PhD, 1988. **CAREER:** University of Southern California, research assistant, research associate, 1982-88; Florida State University, assistant professor, 1988-. **BUSINESS ADDRESS:** Assistant Professor, College of Engineering, Florida St University, 2525 Pottsdamer St, Rm 229, Tallahassee, FL 32316, (904)487-6321.

SHIH, CHILIN
Educator. Chinese American. **PERSONAL:** Born Mar 8, 1955, Taipei, Taiwan; daughter of Hung-Ta Shih and Yu Lui Yeh Shih; married Richard Sproat, Aug 14, 1987. **EDUCATION:** Taiwan University, BA, 1977; University of Hawaii, Manoa, MA, 1979; University of California, San Diego, PhD, 1986. **CAREER:** AT&T, postdoctoral, 1986-87; Cronell University, assistant professor, 1987-89; Rutgers University, assistant professor, 1989-. **ORGANIZATIONS:** Linguistic Society of America; International Association of Chinese Linquistics. **HONORS/AWARDS:** National Science Foundation, Grant, 1991-93; Rutgers University, Henry Rutgers Fellow, 1989-91. **SPECIAL ACHIEVEMENTS:** Built a Chinese Text-to-Speech System (Chinese Speech Synthesizer), 1987; Tone and Intonation in Mandarin, 1988; A Statistical Method for Finding Word Boundaries in Chinese Text, 1990; Prosodic Structure in Language Understanding, 1989; Variations of Mandarin Rising Tones, 1992. **BUSINESS ADDRESS:** Professor, Rutgers University, College Avenue, 327 Scott Hall, New Brunswick, NJ 08903, (908)932-7383.

SHIH, FRED F.
Research chemist. Chinese American. **PERSONAL:** Born Dec 11, 1936, Nanking, China; married Betty Y Shih; children: Cheryl, Danny. **EDUCATION:** National Taiwan University, BA, 1958; Kansas State University, MS, 1966; Louisiana State University, PhD, 1976. **CAREER:** Maryville College, associate professor, 1967-72; US Department of Agriculture, research chemist, 1976-. **ORGANIZATIONS:** American Chemical Society, Louisiana Section, auditor, executive committee, 1991-94; Institute of Food Technologists, Gulf Coast Section, treasurer, 1991-93; Chinese Academy of New Orleans, executive committee secretary, 1992-93, chairman, 1993-94; Sigma Xi, treasurer, 1991-92. **HONORS/AWARDS:** Kansas State University, fellowship, 1965; USDA, Superior Performance Award, 1987, Service Award, 1992, Invention award, 1989. **SPECIAL ACHIEVEMENTS:** Fluent in Chinese and English; durable press textile research: two patents, 15 published papers; food protein research: one patent, 25 publications; 35 publications on chemical research in scientific journals and presentations. **BUSINESS ADDRESS:** Research Chemist, USDA-ARS-SRRC, PO Box 19687, New Orleans, LA 70179, (504)286-4354.

SHIH, HONG-YEE
Educator. Chinese American. **PERSONAL:** Born Mar 23, 1957, Taipei, Taiwan; son of Chen-Shu Shih & Ching-Hsiang Lee Shih. **EDUCATION:** Chung-Yuan University, bachelor's, ME, 1979; University of Nebraska, Lincoln, master's, ME, 1984. **CAREER:** Hsian Hao Primary School, instructor, 1979; Goshen Industrial Co Ltd, design engineer, 1981-82; Lincoln Manufacturing Co Ltd, draftsman, 1984; Shung Ye Co Ltd, development engineer, 1986; Sun Metal Co Ltd, design engineer, 1987; Oregon Institute of Technology, associate professor, 1984-. **ORGANIZATIONS:** American Society for Engineering Education, 1990-91. **HONORS/AWARDS:** Oregon Institute of Technology, Faculty Excellence Award, 1990. **SPECIAL ACHIEVEMENTS:** Paper, CAD in Mechanical Engineering Technology at OIT, 1989. **MILITARY SERVICE:** Army, 1979-81. **HOME ADDRESS:** PO Box 2014, Klamath Falls, OR 97601. **BUSINESS ADDRESS:** Associate Professor, Oregon Institute of Technology, 3201 Campus Dr, Klamath Falls, OR 97601, (503)885-1406.

SHIH, JASON CHIA-HSING
Educator. Chinese American. **PERSONAL:** Born Oct 8, 1939, Chian-Chen, Hunan, China; married Jane C H Shih, Aug 31, 1966; children: Giles C, Tim C. **EDUCATION:** National Taiwan University, Taipei, Taiwan, BS, 1963, MS, 1966; Cornell University, PhD, 1973. **CAREER:** University of Illinois, research associate, 1973-75; Cornell University, senior research associate, 1975-76; North Carolina State University, assistant professor, 1976-80, associate professor, 1980-88, professor, 1988-. **ORGANIZATIONS:** American Institute of Nutrition, 1978-; American Society for Microbiology, 1980-; Poultry Sci-

ence Association, 1977-; Society of Chinese Bioscientists in America, 1984-; American Heart Association, 1991-; Triangle Area Chinese American Society, 1978-, president, 1982-83, chairman of the board, 1992-93. **HONORS/AWARDS:** Pew Charitable Trusts, Pew Fellowship, 1991; UNDP Specialist, United Nation Development Program, 1987-93; American Institute of Nutrition, travel awards, 1981, 1989; Cardiff University College, visiting fellowship, 1983; Shenyang Agricultural, science advisor, 1985-; recipient of 18 competitive grants, 1977-94. **SPECIAL ACHIEVEMENTS:** Inventor of 5 US patents, 1990-93; publication of 110 scientific papers and articles, 1968-94; coordinator of NCSU China Programs, 1987-94. **BUSINESS ADDRESS:** Professor, Dept of Poultry Science, North Carolina State University, Scott Hall, Raleigh, NC 27695-7608, (919)515-5521.

SHIH, JOAN FAI
Artist. Chinese American. **PERSONAL:** Born Sep 4, 1932, Shantou, Guangdong, China; daughter of Henry Hen-Wai and Laura Chen Shuk-Wai. **EDUCATION:** Art Students League of New York, 1953; Kansas City Art Institute, BFA, 1956, MFA, 1961; Pennsylvania Academy of the Fine Arts, 1957-59, 1961-63. **CAREER:** Kansas City Art Institute, instructor, 1959-61; Converse College, instructor, 1966-67; Rosemont College, lecturer, 1969-88. **ORGANIZATIONS:** Hong Kong Art Club, 1952; The Pennsylvania Academy of the Fine Arts, fellowship, 1962-; Philadelphia Watercolor Club, 1976-; National Association of Women Artists, 1978-. **HONORS/AWARDS:** Plastic Club All Media Art Exhibition, first prize, Philadelphia, 1990, Marion Cohee Memorial Award, Philadelphia, 1989; National Association of Women Artists, Elizabeth Erlanger Memorial Prize, New York City, 1980; D W Newcomer's Sons Annual Exhibition, first prize and purchase award, Kansas City, 1960; Kansas City Art Institute, Fireside Committee, Four-Year Honor Scholarship, 1953-56, Two-Year Teaching Fellowship, 1959-61. **SPECIAL ACHIEVEMENTS:** Solo exhibition, Danville Museum of Fine Arts, VA, 1986; solo exhibition, British Council, Gloucester Bldg, Hong Kong, 1956; group exhibition, Woodmere Art Museum, Philadelphia, 1979, 1981, 1987, 1992; group exhibition, Huntington Museum, New York City, 1981; group exhibition, National Academy of Design, New York City, 1978; various others. **HOME ADDRESS:** 2013 Locust St, Philadelphia, PA 19103, (215)567-1529.

SHIH, JOHN CHAU
Engineer, business executive. Taiwanese American. **PERSONAL:** Born Jan 9, 1939, Taipei, Taiwan; son of Lieh-Shong Shih and Gien-Lien Shih; married Jean Chen Shih, May 11, 1968; children: Jeffrey C, Jack C. **EDUCATION:** National Taiwan University, BSEE, 1961; UCLA, MS, computer science, 1965, PhD, computer science, 1968. **CAREER:** TRW, senior staff, 1968-80; Compunet, executive vice president, 1980-83; Titan System Inc, vice president, 1983-86; S Y Technology Inc, president, 1986-. **ORGANIZATIONS:** AIAA, 1964-; Society of Computer Simulation, 1989-; Organization of Chinese-American Entrepreneur's Advisory Network, chairman of the board. **BUSINESS ADDRESS:** President, S Y Technology Inc, 15643 Sherman Way, Ste 440, Van Nuys, CA 91406, (818)904-0201.

SHIH, KO-MING
Educator. Taiwanese American. **PERSONAL:** Born Nov 17, 1953, Taipei, Taiwan; son of Gen-Ling & Lee-Yu-Geng Shih; married Jui-Chiu Shih, Dec 10, 1979; children: Chih-Yu, Karen. **EDUCATION:** National Taiwan Normal University, BS, 1977; Washington University, MS, 1983; Louisiana State University, MSEE, 1985; University of Texas, Arlington, PhD, 1990. **CAREER:** University of Texas, Arlington, graduate research, 1985-90; Mercer University, electrical and computer engineering, assistant professor, 1990-. **ORGANIZATIONS:** IEEE, 1990-; ASEE, 1990-. **HONORS/AWARDS:** Robert Leroy Foundation, scholarship, 1987-89; Tatung Foundation, fellowship, 1974-76. **HOME ADDRESS:** 4823 Oxford Rd, Macon, GA 31210, (912)471-9488. **BUSINESS ADDRESS:** Assistant Professor, Electrical & Computer Engineering, Mercer University, 1400 Coleman Ave, School of Engineering, Macon, GA 31207, (912)752-2213.

SHIH, MING-CHE
Educator. Taiwanese American. **PERSONAL:** Born Aug 23, 1953, Keelung, Taiwan; married Hsiao-Ping Peng, Aug 25, 1979; children: Joshu, Jopei. **EDUCATION:** Tunghai University, Taiwan, BS, 1976; University of Iowa, PhD, 1983. **CAREER:** Harvard Medical School, post-doctoral research fellow, 1984-88; University of Iowa, assistant professor, 1988-. **ORGANIZATIONS:** Genetics Society of America, 1989-; American Society of Plant Physiologists, 1989-. **HONORS/AWARDS:** NIH, ROI Research Award, 1989-; Phi Tau Phi

Scholastic Society, 1976. **BUSINESS ADDRESS:** Assistant Professor, Dept of Biological Sciences, University of Iowa, Iowa City, IA 52242, (319)335-2071.

SHIH, PHILIP C.
Librarian. Chinese American. **PERSONAL:** Born Jul 6, 1943, Hunan, China; married Catholing L Shih, Aug 1972; children: Evangeline L. **EDUCATION:** Tunghai University, BS, 1965; Florida State University, MS, 1969. **CAREER:** Wichita State University, reference librarian, 1969-73; Logansport-Cass Public Library, director, 1974-. **ORGANIZATIONS:** American Library Association, 1976-; Rotary Club International, 1976-. **HOME ADDRESS:** 2020 Westgate Drive, Logansport, IN 46947.

SHIH, STEPHEN CHINGYU
Educator. Taiwanese American. **PERSONAL:** Born Sep 25, 1957, Pingtung, Taiwan; son of Yao-ming Shih & Yin Shih; married Shiowyun Su Shih, Jan 15, 1985. **EDUCATION:** Tunghai University, BS, 1981; University of Missouri-Columbia, MS, 1987; Pennsylvania State University, PhD, 1992. **CAREER:** Sampo Elec Co, Taiwan, industrial engineer, 1982-84; University of Missouri-Columbia, teaching assistant, 1985, research assistant, 1986; The Pennsylvania State University, research assistant, 1987-90; St Cloud State University, assistant professor, 1990-93; Auburn University at Montgomery, assistant professor, 1993-. **ORGANIZATIONS:** Institute of Industrial Engineers, 1992-; Society of Manufacturing Engineers, 1987-; IEEE Computer Society, 1990-; NACISPA, 1992-. **HONORS/AWARDS:** St Cloud State University, Q7 Acceleration Grant, 1993; Pennsylvania State University, Ben Franklin Partnership Fund, 1987-90; University of Missouri, Memorial Hospital Partnership Fund, 1985-86. **SPECIAL ACHIEVEMENTS:** Papers: "Hybrid Feature-based CAD Modeling & Intelligent Database Systems for Generative Part Family Formation and CIM Integration," "An Architecture of Integrated Object-Oriented Database Expert Systems & Neural Networks for Intelligent Manufacturing Information Systems," numerous others. **HOME ADDRESS:** 155 Sylvest Drive, Montgomery, AL 36117, (205)279-9689. **BUSINESS PHONE:** (205)244-3373.

SHIH, TOM I-PING
Educator. Chinese American. **PERSONAL:** Born Dec 16, 1952, Tainan, Taiwan; son of Soh-Chao Shih and Sze G Sun; married Audrey Chiu-Hsiao Shih, May 29, 1977; children: Marie Che-Chin, George Che-Fu. **EDUCATION:** West Virginia University, 1971-72; National Cheng Kung University, BSE, 1976; University of Michigan, Ann Arbor, MSE, 1977, PhD, 1981. **CAREER:** NASA-Lewis Research Center, mechanical engineer, 1981-82; University of Florida, assistant professor, 1982-87, associate professor, 1987-88; Carnegie Mellon University, associate professor, 1988-93, professor, 1993-. **ORGANIZATIONS:** American Institute of Aeronautics and Astronautics, 1979-; American Society of Mechanical Engineers, 1980-; Society of Automotive Engineers, 1980-88; Sigma Xi, 1980-88, 1990-; New York Academy of Sciences, 1984-85; Pi Tau Sigma, 1984-; Institute for Liquid Atomization and Spray Systems, 1992-. **HONORS/AWARDS:** Society of Automotive Engineers, Ralph R Teetor Award, 1986; University of Florida, Tau Beta Pi Teacher of the Year Award, 1988. **SPECIAL ACHIEVEMENTS:** Over 50 publications on computational fluid dynamics, propulsion, and aerodynamics in journals and conference proceedings; 8 computer programs for calculating two- and three-dimensional flowfields in propulsion and aerodynamics. **BUSINESS ADDRESS:** Professor, Dept of Mechanical Engineering, Carnegie Mellon University, 5000 Forbes Ave, Pittsburgh, PA 15213-3890, (412)268-2503.

SHIH, TSUNG-MING ANTHONY (TONY)
Federal executive, pharmacologist. Chinese American. **PERSONAL:** Born Oct 8, 1944, Taipei, Taiwan; son of Robert C Shih and Jean Su Shih; married Hui-Mei Wang, Mar 31, 1987; children: Liane, Jason. **EDUCATION:** Kaohsiung Medical College, Kaohsiung, Taiwan, BS, pharmacy, 1967; University of Pittsburgh, PhD, pharmacology, 1974. **CAREER:** Columbia University, teaching assistant, 1968-69; University of Pittsburgh, teaching assistant, 1969-71, NIH predoctoral fellow, 1972-74, research assistant III, 1974-76, research associate, 1976-78; US Army Medical Research Institute Chemical Defense, pharmacologist, 1978-, Applied Pharmacology Branch, chief, 1993-. **ORGANIZATIONS:** Towson State University, Master's Degree Advisory Committee, 1979-83; US Army Med Rsch Institute Chemical Defense, Institute Lab Animal Care & Use Committee, 1980-85; University North Carolina, Chapel Hill, PhD Degree Advisory Committee, 1984-89; Chinese Language School of Baltimore, dean, 1982-84, principal, 1984-87, board of trustees, 1982-, chairman, 1991-; Organization of Chinese Americans, Northern Maryland chapter, board of directors, 1992-; Asian Arts Center, Towson State University, Sup-

porting Committee, 1992-. **HONORS/AWARDS:** China Department of Education, Distinguished Youth Award, 1967; USA Army, Research & Development Achievement Award, 1983. **SPECIAL ACHIEVEMENTS:** Author, chapters in professional books: numerous articles submitted to professional journals. **BUSINESS ADDRESS:** US Army Medical Research Institute of Chemical Defense, SGRD-UV-PB, Building E-3100, Aberdeen Proving Ground, MD 21010-5425, (410)671-1943.

SHIH, WEI
Educator. Chinese American. **PERSONAL:** Born May 16, 1933, Fuzhou, China; son of Fa-Rong Shih (deceased) and Ping-Chi Chen Shih (deceased); married Susan Shih, Sep 11, 1962; children: Koyin, Milton, Andrew. **EDUCATION:** Natl Taiwan University, BA, 1956; Baruch College, CUNY, MBA, 1964; NYU, Stern School of Business, PhD, 1970. **CAREER:** Iona College, graduate div, statistics lecturer, 1967; NYU, Stern School of Business, visiting asst professor of management science, 1972; University of Rhode Island, assistant professor of management science, 1970-72; US Social Security Administration, Office of Advanced Systems, operations research analyst, 1979-80; Shandong University, China, Dept of Economics, visiting professor/Fulbright Sr Scholar; Bowling Green State University, Dept of Applied Statistics & Operations Research, professor, 1979-, chairman, 1990-. **ORGANIZATIONS:** Decision Science Institute, meeting and programs committee, 1992-; America Chinese Management Educators Assn, president, 1988-89; Institute of Management Service, 1968-; Operations Research Society of America, 1968-; Beta Gamma Sigma, 1968-; Phi Kappa Phi, 1991-; Operational Research Society of Great Britain, 1974-. **HONORS/AWARDS:** Bowling Green State University, College of Business, Patton Scholarly Achievement Award, 1990; US Informatiion Agency, Fulbright Sr Scholar, 1983; American Assembly of Collegiate Schools of Business, Federal Faculty Fellow, 1978; NYU, Founders Day Award, 1972; Ford Foundation/NYU, Ford Foundation Fellowship, 1965-67. **SPECIAL ACHIEVEMENTS:** Author, "Optimal Forecast Biasing in Theoretical Inventory Systems," Intl J of Production Research, 1989; "A Constraint Selection Technique for a Class of Linear Programs," Operations Research Letters, vol 7, no 4, 1988; "Modified Stepping-stone Method as a Teaching Aid for Capacitated Transportation Problems," Decision Science, 1987; "A General Decision Model for Cost-Volume-Profit Analysis Under Uncertainty," Accounting Review, Oct 1979; "Dynamic Course Scheduling for College Faculty Via Zero-One Programming," Decision Science, vol 8, no 4, 1977. **MILITARY SERVICE:** ROTC, ROC, 2nd lt, 1956-58. **BUSINESS ADDRESS:** Professor/Chair, Dept of Applied Stats & Operations Research, Bowling Green State University, Bowling Green, OH 43403-0001.

SHIM, EUN SUP
Educator. Korean American. **PERSONAL:** Born Jan 7, 1957, Kang-Nung, Kang-Won Do, Republic of Korea; son of Sang Ki Shim & Soon Ja Choi; married Sung Jip Choi, Oct 1, 1981; children: Arthur J, Lynda Jaehyang, Paul Jaewoo. **EDUCATION:** Dong-Guk University, Seoul, Korea, BS, 1978; Philadelphia College of Textile & Science, MBA (with highest honors), 1985; Rutgers University, MBA, 1989, PhD, 1992. **CAREER:** Dong-Sung Corp, assistant manager, 1979-81; Rutgers University, lecturer, 1987-90; Saint Joseph's University, professor, 1990-. **ORGANIZATIONS:** American Institute of CPAs, 1990-93; Institute of Certified Management Accountants, 1990-93; American Accounting Association, 1987-93; Institute of Management Accountants, campus coordinator, 1990-93; National Honor Society in Business Administration, 1985; Ilsan Handicapped Children Support Organization of Philadelpia, secretary general. **HONORS/AWARDS:** Rutgers University, Teaching and Research Assistantship, 1985-. **SPECIAL ACHIEVEMENTS:** Principal, First Korean Language School of Philadelphia, for second generation Korean Americans, voluntary position. **BIOGRAPHICAL SOURCES:** St Joseph's University Magazine, p 6, Winter, 1993; Kang-Won Daily News, p 9, February, 13, 1993, in Korean; Dong-Ah Daily News, Philadelphia, p 6, October 9, 1991, p 7, October 10, 1992, in Korean; Maple Newtown News, Newtown Square, PA, May 2, 1985. **BUSINESS ADDRESS:** Professor, Dept of Accounting, Saint Joseph's University, 5600 City Ave, Philadelphia, PA 19131, (215)660-1660.

SHIM, JAE K.
Educator, author, consultant. Korean American. **PERSONAL:** Born Jul 4, 1943, Seoul, Republic of Korea; married Chung Hi Shim, Jun 19, 1970; children: Christine, Allison. **EDUCATION:** Seoul National University, BS, 1965; University of California, Berkeley, MBA, 1968, PhD, 1973. **CAREER:** Queens College of NY, Department of Economics, visiting professor, 1979-81; CUNY, Department of Accounting and Information Systems, professor, 1973-

81; California State University, Long Beach, College of Business Adm, professor, 1981-. **ORGANIZATIONS:** Los Angeles County, financial consultant, 1982-; City of New York, financial consultant, 1976-79. **HONORS/AWARDS:** Credit Research Foundation, Outstanding Paper Award, 1982. **SPECIAL ACHIEVEMENTS:** Author, Financial Management, Barron's; The Vestpocket CPA, Prentice-Hall; Strategic Business Forecasting, Probus, 1994; The Vestpocket MBA, 1986; Encyclopedia of Accounting and Finance, Prentice-Hall; over 50 refereed articles and scholarly papers; over 40 college and professional books. **HOME ADDRESS:** 3941 Myra Avenue, Los Alamitos, CA 90720. **BUSINESS PHONE:** (310)985-8609.

SHIM, JUNG P.
Educator. Korean American. **PERSONAL:** Born Sep 3, 1947, Daegu, Republic of Korea; son of Dr & Mrs Jae Wan Shim; married Susan J Shim, Aug 14, 1980; children: Julie, John J. **EDUCATION:** Seoul National University, MBA, 1973; University of Nebraska, Lincoln, PhD, 1983. **CAREER:** University of Nebraska, Lincoln, graduate assistant, 1978-82; University of Wisconsin, La-Crosse, assistant professor, 1982-84; Mississippi State University, associate professor, 1984-89, professor, 1989-. **ORGANIZATIONS:** Decision Sciences Institute, advisory committee, numerous other committees, 1982-; The Institute of Management Science, committee member, 1980-; Korean American MIS Association, president, 1992-. **HONORS/AWARDS:** Mississippi State University, Outstanding Faculty Award, 1992, Outstanding Research Award, 1990, Outstanding Service Award, 1993; National Science Council, Taiwan, invited scholar, 1992; George State University, Bell South, invited participant, 1989. **SPECIAL ACHIEVEMENTS:** Readings in MIS, 1993; Micro Management Science, 1986, 1990; Micro Manager, 1986, 1990; Mississippi State University, International Business Strategy Program, 1992, 1993. **BIOGRAPHICAL SOURCES:** Socio-Economic Planning Science, vol 25, no 3, p 248, 1991. **BUSINESS ADDRESS:** Professor, Dept of Management & Information Systems, Mississippi State University, Drawer MG, Mississippi State, MS 39762, (601)326-1994.

SHIM, SANG KYU. *See Obituaries.*

SHIM, SOOK CHIN (SHIRLEY)
Nurse. Korean American. **PERSONAL:** Born Sep 20, 1939, Daejeoun, Choong Nam Province, Republic of Korea; daughter of Hyang Bong Kim; married Jae Yong Shim, Nov 5, 1967; children: Edward Seongwook, Jewel Jiryung. **EDUCATION:** Seoul Adventist Hospital School of Nursing, 1958-61; National Psychiatric Hospital Psychiatric Clinic, Seoul, Korea, 1973; Kalamazoo Valley Community College, 1987; Kellogg Community College, 1988. **CAREER:** Seoul Adventist Hospital, registered nurse, 1961-65; Portland Adventist Hospital, registered nurse, 1973-74; Saint Joseph Hospital, registered nurse, 1974-75; Fairfield Community Hospital, registered nurse, 1975-76; Terrace Nursing Home, registered nurse, 1977-80; Michael Reese Hospital, registered nurse, 1989-92; Saint Mary Hospital, staff/registered nurse, 1992-. **ORGANIZATIONS:** Korean Nurse Association, 1961-73; Calhoun County Medical Society Auxiliary, 1980-82; Korean American Medical Association of Seventh-day Adventist, 1981-; Wisconsin Nurse Association, 1992-; Battle Creek Academy, school board, 1983-84; Battle Creek, Korean Seventh-day Adventist Church, Dorca Society, chair, 1981-82; Battle Creek Tabernacle of Seventh-day Adventists, Social Committee, 1983. **SPECIAL ACHIEVEMENTS:** Community service work, chairwoman, Dorca Society of Battle Creek Tabernacle of Seventh-day Adventist Participant, Battle Creek Korean Seventh-day Adventist Church, 1981-82; participated in fund-raising for Battle Creek Academy, 1980-89. **HOME ADDRESS:** RR 5, Box 274KB, Tomah, WI 54660, (608)372-0779.

SHIM, WALTON KENN TSUNG
Pediatric surgeon, educator. Chinese American. **PERSONAL:** Born May 15, 1931, Honolulu, HI; son of Wai On & Esther Fo Shim; married Sandra Yee, Apr 14, 1971; children: Jennifer, Jonathan, Elizabeth, Christopher. **EDUCATION:** Dartmouth College, AB (summa cum laude), 1953; Dartmouth Medical School, Graduate School, 1954; Columbia University College of Physicians & Surgeons, MD, 1956. **CAREER:** New York Hospital, Cornell Medical Ctr, surgical intern, 1956-57, surgical resident, 1957-58; E J Meyer Memorial Hosp, surgical resident, 1958-62; Kirk Army Hosp, consult in surgery, 1962-64; Children's Memorial Hosp, surgical resident, 1964-65; Northwestern University, instructor in surgery, 1965-67; Kauikeolani Children's Hosp, Birth Defects Ctr, Natl Foundation, asst dir, 1967; University of Hawaii Medical Sch, asst clinical prof of surgery, 1967-71, assoc clinical prof of surgery, 1971-72, assoc prof of surgery, 1971-87, prof of surgery, 1987; Kauikeolani Children's

Hosp, chief of surgery, 1971-77, chief of staff, 1981-83, dir of surgical education, 1972-; Kapiolani Medical Ctr for Women & Children, chief of surgery, 1983-85, 1992-; pediatric surgeon, 1966-; University of Hawaii, Dept of Genetics, affiliate faculty, 1967-; Hawaii Transplant Foundation, 1970-; Tripler Army Medical Ctr, surgical consult, 1973-. **ORGANIZATIONS:** Alpha Kappa Kappa; Phi Beta Kappa; Hawaii Medical Assn; American Medical Assn; American College of Surgeons, fellow; British Assn of Pediatric Surgeons, 1971-; Pacific Coast Surgical Assn, 1990-; Pan-Pacific Surgical Assn, board of trustees, 1984-. **SPECIAL ACHIEVEMENTS:** American Bd of Surgery, 1963; American Bd of Pediatrics Surgery, 1975; recertification, 1985. **MILITARY SERVICE:** US Army, Chemical Research & Development Laboratory, captain, 1962-64. **BUSINESS ADDRESS:** President, Children's Surgery Ltd, 1319 Punahou St, Ste 100, Honolulu, HI 96826, (808)947-2611.

SHIMA, JOHN DAVID
Sports trainer, business owner. Japanese American. **PERSONAL:** Born Apr 30, 1957, Chicago, IL; son of Arthur T Shima and Rose T Shima; married Cecilia Vazquez, Feb 14, 1989. **EDUCATION:** Trinity University, BS, psychology, 1981. **CAREER:** Merchants Group Intl, commodity trader, 1982-83; Kolar Arms, vice pres, 1985-89; Bender-Smith Shooting Clinics, partner, 1992-. **SPECIAL ACHIEVEMENTS:** Five-time World Champion Skeet Shooter, 1977-82; one of two people to ever win 12-gauge world title back-to-back. **BUSINESS ADDRESS:** Partner, Bender-Shima Shooting Clinics, 217 Linden Ave, Oak Park, IL 60302, 800-438-7340.

SHIMADA, KATSUNORI
Engineer. Japanese American. **PERSONAL:** Born Mar 12, 1922, Tokyo, Japan; son of Katsujiro Shimada and Mume Shimada; married Ikuko Shimada, Oct 30, 1975; children: Karl, Keiko Stearns. **EDUCATION:** Tokyo University, Japan, BSEE, 1945; University of Minnesota, Minneapolis, MSEE, 1954, PhD, 1958. **CAREER:** Toshiba/Kawasaki, Japan, engineer, 1945-50; University of Minnesota, Minneapolis, instructor, 1950-58; Boeing Co, consultant, 1960-63; University of Washington, associate professor, 1958-64; Jet Propulsion Lab, Research Group, supervisor, 1964-80, Field Center Integ Task, manager, 1980-85; Celestial Senoro Group, supervisor, 1985-89; NASDA, Los Angeles, consultant, 1989-93. **HONORS/AWARDS:** NASA, Certificate of Recognition, 1973, 1977, 1978, 1981-83; Toshiba, patents, 1946, 1948; Tokyo University, invited professor at ISAS, 1973; NEDO, Japan, invited lecturer, 1983. **SPECIAL ACHIEVEMENTS:** Author of more than 60 publications in technical journals, conference proceedings and JPL Technical Reports; "Astros: High Performance CCD Tracker for Spacecraft," Advances in the Astronautical Sciences, vol 63, pp 117-137, 1987; co-author, Photovoltaics in Japan, 1983. **HOME ADDRESS:** 3840 Edgeview Dr, Pasadena, CA 91107.

SHIMADA, YOSHIKI
Attorney. Japanese American. **PERSONAL:** Born Jul 25, 1960, New York, NY; son of Naoki & Eiko; married Katharine, Aug 19, 1989. **EDUCATION:** Cornell University, College of Art & Sciences, AB, 1982; Harvard Law School, JD, 1985. **CAREER:** Brown & Wood, partner, currently. **ORGANIZATIONS:** New York State Bar, 1986-; District of Columbia Bar, 1987-; New Jersey Bar Association, 1987-; Federal District Bar Association, 1988-; American Bar Association, 1986-. **HONORS/AWARDS:** Phi Beta Kappa, 1982. **SPECIAL ACHIEVEMENTS:** Fluent in Japanese language; law review article entitled, "A Comparison of Securities Regulation in the US and Japan," published by the Columbia Journal of Transnational Law of Columbia Law School, January, 1992. **BUSINESS ADDRESS:** Associate, Brown & Wood, 1 World Trade Center, 58th Fl, New York, NY 10048, (212)839-5859.

SHIMAMOTO, SCOTT SEIYA (RAKAMOTO)
Rapper, musician, song writer, radio show host. Japanese American. **PERSONAL:** Born Aug 25, 1960, Los Angeles, CA; son of Seiya Roy Shimamoto & Peggy Kinuko Tsutsumida Shimamoto. **EDUCATION:** University of Southern California, BS, 1982. **CAREER:** "Out Front-Radio Show," host, 1993-. **ORGANIZATIONS:** Asian American Advertising and Public Relations Alliance, 1993-. **SPECIAL ACHIEVEMENTS:** The Banzai Beat!, rap music CD, 1992; various performances around Los Angeles; radio show, "Asian Understanding," hosted by John Kobara, 1993; TV show, "Shotime," hosted by Amy Hill and Marilyn Tokuda, 1993. **HOME ADDRESS:** 4076 Rosemead Blvd, Pico Rivera, CA 90660, (310)695-4266.

SHIMIZU, GORDON TOSHIO
Educator. Japanese American. **PERSONAL:** Born Oct 9, 1945, Honolulu, HI; son of Richard J Shimizu and Doris M Shimizu; married Michi, Aug 15, 1970;

children: Trevor K. **EDUCATION:** California State University, San Jose, BA, industrial studies, 1970, STD, teach credential, 1971; University of San Francisco, MA, counseling, psychology, 1992. **CAREER:** Lockheed Research Labs, research technician, 1967-70; Santa Rosa City Schools, high school teacher, 1971-78; Santa Rosa Junior College, instructor, 1978-. **ORGANIZATIONS:** Northern California Comm College Computer Consortium, 1985-; Council on Math, California Comm College, 1989-. **SPECIAL ACHIEVEMENTS:** Electronic text: Electronic Fabrication, 1989. **BUSINESS ADDRESS:** Instructor, Santa Rosa Junior College, 1501 Mendocino Ave, Analy Temp Bldg A, Santa Rosa, CA 95401-4332, (707)527-4340.

SHIMIZU, NOBUMICHI

Scientist. Japanese American. **PERSONAL:** Born Feb 4, 1940, Tokyo, Japan; son of Shigemichi & Mitsuko Shimizu; married Kazuko Shimizu, Nov 12, 1965; children: Taku, Shu. **EDUCATION:** University of Tokyo, BSc, 1963, MSc, 1965, DSc, 1968. **CAREER:** University of Tokyo, instructor, 1968-75; Carnegie Institute, Washington, research associate, 1971-74; Universite de Paris 6, associate physicist, 1974-78; Massachusetts Institute Technology, senior research scientist, 1978-88; Woods Hole Oceangraphic Inst, senior scientist, 1988-. **ORGANIZATIONS:** American Geophysical Union, 1981-; Geochemical Society, 1981-. **SPECIAL ACHIEVEMENTS:** More than 50 scientific articles published in international journals, 1964-. **BUSINESS ADDRESS:** Senior Scientist, Dept of Geology and Geophysics, Woods Hole Oceanographic Institution, Clark Laboratory 102, Woods Hole, MA 02543, (508)457-2000.

SHIMIZU, SCOTT EDWARD

Textile company executive. Japanese American. **PERSONAL:** Born Aug 30, 1953, Chicago, IL; son of Frank A Shimizu and Yoshiko Shimizu; married Lorraine, Jun 29, 1985; children: Amanda. **EDUCATION:** Illinois State University, BS, 1975, MBA, 1977. **CAREER:** Springs Mill, sales rep, 1977-82; Pillowtex Corp, sales rep, 1982-84, sales mgr, 1984-87, vice pres, 1987-88, exec vice pres, 1988-. **HONORS/AWARDS:** Springs Mills, Salesman of the Year, 1980, 1981. **HOME ADDRESS:** 1812 Manor Lane, Plano, TX 75093. **BUSINESS PHONE:** (214)333-3225.

SHIMIZU, TAISUKE

Bank executive. Japanese American. **PERSONAL:** Born Apr 8, 1936, Osaka, Japan; married Tomoko Shimizu; children: Yumi, Megumi, Toru. **EDUCATION:** University of Tokyo, BF. **CAREER:** Bank of Tokyo, beginning 1959, Brussels office, general manager, 1982, Europe and Africa division, general manager, 1984-85, overseas division, general manager, 1987-88; California First Bank, San Francisco, exec vp, chief financial officer, 1985-87; Union Bank, San Francisco, vice chairman, director, 1988-90, president, CEO, 1990-. **ORGANIZATIONS:** Japanese Chamber of Commerce of Northern California, former president. **SPECIAL ACHIEVEMENTS:** Under Shimizu's presidency, Union Bank pledged $150,000 to the Library Foundation of San Francisco, 1993. **BUSINESS ADDRESS:** President/CEO, Union Bank, 350 California St, PO Box 7104, San Francisco, CA 94120-7104, (415)705-7000.*

SHIMIZU, TAK

Business executive. Japanese American. **PERSONAL:** Born Feb 13, 1946, Fukuoka, Japan; son of Kiyoshi Shimizu and Sue Shimizu; married Kuni Shimizu, Jun 10, 1970; children: Yoshi, Tsuneo, Miki. **EDUCATION:** Sophia University, Tokyo, Japan, BA,1969. **CAREER:** Fanon/Courier Corp, vice president of operations, 1978-81; Taxan USA Corp, president/CEO, 1981-87; Goldstar Technology, president/CEO, 1988-92; Tak & Associates, president, currently. **BUSINESS ADDRESS:** President, Tak & Associates, 13610 Saratoga Vista Ave, Saratoga, CA 95070-4938, (408)246-0260.

SHIMIZU, TORU

Fresh fruit exporting company executive. Japanese American. **PERSONAL:** Born Oct 20, 1947, Tokyo, Japan; son of Ryoichi Shimizu and Tsuru Shimizu; married Dianna, Aug 24, 1972; children: Jamie, Marika, Erik. **EDUCATION:** Hokkaido University, BEc, 1972. **CAREER:** Nichimen Corp, Toyko, Japan; Jaspo Inc, president, currently. **BUSINESS ADDRESS:** President, Jaspo Inc, 550 Industry Dr, Seattle, WA 98188, (206)575-0870.

SHIMOKIHARA, STANLEY SHIGEO

Aircraft dispatcher (retired). Japanese American. **PERSONAL:** Born Dec 31, 1937, Honolulu, HI; son of Wakasuke Shimokihara and Haruyo Shimokihara; married Tomoe Shimokihara, Aug 5, 1960; children: Andy Shigeru, Stacy Shigeki, Margie Sayuri, Janice Yuri. **EDUCATION:** Honolulu Technical School, 1961-62. **CAREER:** Japan Airlines, senior dispatcher, flight operations, 1962-93. **ORGANIZATIONS:** American Association of Retired Persons, associate member; United States Golf Association, individual/associate member; Navy League of the United States. **SPECIAL ACHIEVEMENTS:** FAA Aircraft Dispatcher Certificate; Japan Civil Aeronautics Board, aircraft dispatcher certificate, 1964. **MILITARY SERVICE:** United States Air Force, airman first class, 1956-61. **HOME ADDRESS:** 2483 Komo Mai Place, Pearl City, HI 96782.

SHIMOMURA, YUKIO

Human resources manager. Japanese American. **PERSONAL:** Born Apr 16, 1935, San Francisco, CA; son of Joe Toshinaga & Taka Shimomura; married Chizuko, Jul 5, 1958; children: Douglas, Scott, Tamiko. **EDUCATION:** Utah State University, BS, manufacturing engineering, 1965. **CAREER:** Fujitsu Ltd Subsidiaries: Microelectronic Inc, manager, compensation/benefits, 1985-87, Systems of America, director, human resources, 1987-93, compound semiconductor, manager, human resources, 1993-. **ORGANIZATIONS:** Society of Human Resource Management; American Compensation Association; Asians for Miracle Marrow Matches, vice chair, 1991-93; Corporation Action Committee, San Diego Blood Bank, chair, 1992, increase minorities in the national registry, bone marrow donor program. **HONORS/AWARDS:** National Marrow Donor Program, National Trailblazer Award, 1992; KGTV, San Diego, Leadership Award, 1991. **MILITARY SERVICE:** US Army, specialist, 1953-55. **HOME ADDRESS:** 394 Darryl Dr, Campbell, CA 95008, (408)378-4477. **BUSINESS ADDRESS:** Manager, Fujitsu Compound Semiconductor Inc, 50 Rio Robles, San Jose, CA 95134, (408)922-9585.

SHIMOOKA, RUSSELL

Television journalist. Japanese American. **PERSONAL:** Born Feb 15, 1960, Honolulu, HI; son of Raymond Shimooka and Ruth E Moniz; married Kimberly Faubert Shimooka, Feb 14, 1992; children: Summit. **EDUCATION:** New Mexico Military Institute, AA, 1980; University of Hawaii, BA, 1982. **CAREER:** KITV-TV, sportscaster, 1981-89; CBS Inc, tv sportscaster, 1989-91; KGO-TV, sportscaster, 1991-94; KARE-TV, sports director, currently. **ORGANIZATIONS:** American Federation of Radio & Television Artist, 1981-; Screen Actors Guild, 1987-; National Academy of Television Arts & Science, 1992-. **MILITARY SERVICE:** US Army Reserve, captain, 1980-; Expert Infantryman, Airborne Honor Graduate. **BUSINESS ADDRESS:** Sports Director, KARE-TV, 8811 Olson Memorial Hwy, Minneapolis, MN 55427, (612)546-1111.

SHIMOURA, JAMES

Attorney. Japanese American. **PERSONAL:** Born 1953?, Michigan. **CAREER:** Kemp, Klein, Umphrey & Endelman, shareholder, attorney, minority counsel practice group, currently. **ORGANIZATIONS:** American Citizens for Justice, past president. **BIOGRAPHICAL SOURCES:** "Have Asian Americans Arrived Politically? Not Quite," Governing, vol 4, p 32, November 1990. **BUSINESS ADDRESS:** Attorney, Kemp, Klein, Umphrey & Endelman, Columbia Center, Ste 600, 201 W Big Beaver, Box 4300, Troy, MI 48099-4300, (313)528-1111.*

SHIN, DOUG YONG

Educator. Korean American. **PERSONAL:** Born Mar 28, 1950, Gabchon, Kangwon, Republic of Korea; son of Dong Ha Shin and Hee Peel Chung; married Sook Kyung Shin, Oct 9, 1976; children: Jae Won C, Jae Yong. **EDUCATION:** University of Iowa, PhD, business, 1989. **CAREER:** Bank of Korea, economist, 1973-82; University of Pittsburgh, assistant professor, 1989-. **HONORS/AWARDS:** Ministry of Economic Planning Board, Korea, Minister's Award, 1978. **BUSINESS ADDRESS:** Assistant Professor, University of Pittsburgh, 220 Mervis Hall, Pittsburgh, PA 15260.

SHIN, ERNEST EUN-HO

Research physicist. Korean American. **PERSONAL:** Born Dec 31, 1935, Chindo Island, Chonnam, Republic of Korea; son of Hyung Sik Shin & Ok Bin Lim; married Shin Ai Shin, Jul 27, 1963; children: Irene, Juliet, Mariette, Michelle. **EDUCATION:** Carnegie Institute of Technology, BS, 1957; Harvard University, AM, 1959, PhD, 1961. **CAREER:** Harvard University, teaching fellow, 1958-60; Arthur D Little, Inc, research physicist, 1960-62; Massachsetts Inst of Technology, research physicist, 1962-66; University of Miami, professor of physics, 1966-73; Korea Atomic Energy Institute, visiting scientist, 1973-74; Yulsan America Inc, chairman/CEO, 1974-89; Chestnut Hill Institute, director, 1984-. **ORGANIZATIONS:** American Physical Society, life member, 1968-; New York Academy of Sciences, 1984-; Sigma Xi, 1968-;

American Mathematical Honor Society, 1957-. **HONORS/AWARDS:** Harvard University, Woodrow Wilson Fellow, 1959. **SPECIAL ACHIEVEMENTS:** Theory of Optical Properties of Metals, 1961; Quantum Theory of Transport, 1966; more than 100 research papers published in professional journals and in proceedings of meetings, 1961-. **HOME ADDRESS:** 3400 Redwood Rd, Napa, CA 94558. **BUSINESS ADDRESS:** Director, Chestnut Hill Institute, PO Box 3510, Napa, CA 94558, (707)253-8058.

SHIN, HUNG SIK
Educator. Korean American. **PERSONAL:** Born Nov 11, 1950, Inchon, Republic of Korea; son of Young Won Shin and Bok Young J Shin; married Young Oak L Shin, Nov 22, 1975; children: Susie. **EDUCATION:** Yon Sei University, BA, 1976; University of Alabama, MBA, 1981; Pennsylvania State University, PhD, 1991. **CAREER:** Sam-Bo Securities Co, Korea, manager, 1975-79; Pennsylvania State University, instructor, 1985-91; Frostburg State University, assistant professor, 1991-. **ORGANIZATIONS:** International Student Council at Penn State University, president, 1985-86; Korean Association of State College, PA, president, 1984-85. **SPECIAL ACHIEVEMENTS:** "An Analysis of Interday and Intraday Return Volatility-Evidence from the Korea Stock Exchange," Pacific Basin Finance Journal, May 1993; "Characteristics of the Korea Fund Premium," Research in International Business and Finance, JAI Press Inc, vol 10, 1993. **BUSINESS ADDRESS:** Professor, Department of Business Admin, Frostburg State University, Frostburg, MD 21532, (301)689-7269.

SHIN, IN-SOOK JEONG
Physician, educator. Korean American/Japanese American. **PERSONAL:** Born May 3, 1949, Kwangju, Chonnam, Republic of Korea; daughter of Yoon Hwa Jeong & Po-Bul-ee-Kang; married Kwang Ho Shin, Jun 1974; children: Daniel E, Cynthia S. **EDUCATION:** Chonnam National University, BA, MD. **CAREER:** State University of New York, Buffalo, clinical associate professor of neurology; Erie County Medical Center, attending physician, currently. **ORGANIZATIONS:** American Academy of Neurology; American Electroencephalographic Society. **BUSINESS ADDRESS:** Physician, EEG Lab, Dept of Neurology, Erie County Medical Center, 462 Grider St, Buffalo, NY 14215, (716)898-3371.

SHIN, KILMAN
Educator. Korean American. **PERSONAL:** Born in Yeosu-city, Geonnam, Republic of Korea; son of Yunchan Shin and Bon Shim Ju. **EDUCATION:** Waseda University, Tokyo, BA, 1956, MA, 1958, PhD, 1978; Brown University, MA, 1963; University of Connecticut, PhD, 1965. **CAREER:** Ferris State University, professor of management and finance, 1988-. **ORGANIZATIONS:** American Economic Association; American Finance Association. **HOME ADDRESS:** 521 Fuller Ave, 301A, Big Rapids, MI 49307, (616)796-4256. **BUSINESS ADDRESS:** Professor of Management and Finance, Ferris St University, College of Business, 119 S State St, Big Rapids, MI 49307-2295, (616)592-2474.

SHIN, MYUNG SOO
Physician, educator. Korean American. **PERSONAL:** Born May 5, 1930, Seoul, Republic of Korea; married Soon Cha (Betty) Shin, Jul 1, 1960; children: Joseph H, Jordan T, Joel L. **EDUCATION:** Seoul National University, School of Medicine, MD, 1956, DMSc, 1967. **CAREER:** University of Alabama, School of Medicine, Department of Radiology, assistant professor, 1969-70, associate professor, 1970-75, professor, 1975-. **ORGANIZATIONS:** American Medical Association, 1969-; American College of Radiology, fellow, 1969-; Radiological Society of North America, 1969-; Association of University Radiologists, 1972-; American Roentgen Ray Society, 1975-; Society of Thoracic Radiology, 1982-; American College of Chest Physicians, fellow, 1986-. **SPECIAL ACHIEVEMENTS:** Published 120 scientific papers in major American medical journals; presented 25 scientific papers in the field of radiology. **HOME PHONE:** (205)870-4383. **BUSINESS ADDRESS:** Professor of Radiology, School of Medicine, University of Alabama, Birmingham, 619 South 19th St, Birmingham, AL 35233, (205)934-3240.

SHIN, PAULL H.
Educator, state representative. Korean American. **PERSONAL:** Born Sep 27, 1935, KyongKi-Do, Republic of Korea; married Donna. **EDUCATION:** Brigham Young University, BA, 1962; University of Pittsburgh, MPIA, 1964; University of Washington, MA, 1970, PhD, 1980. **CAREER:** Brigham Young University, Hawaii Campus, assistant professor, 1964-67; University of Maryland, Hawaii Campus, part-time faculty, 1965-67; Shoreline Community College, professor of history, 1969-88, 1991-; Shin & Shin Inc, 1980-; APS Investment, 1981-; Transpacific Telecommunications Inc, chairman of the board, 1992-; Washington State House of Representatives, state representative, 1993-. **ORGANIZATIONS:** United Way of Sachomish County, board of directors, 1993-; Washington State International Trade Fair, board of directors, 1993-; TRADE Development Alliance of Greater Seattle, advisory committee, 1993-; Church of Jesus Christ of Latter Day Saints, mission president, 1988-91; Washington State Korean Association, chairman of board, 1875-77, president, 1983-84; Commission on Asian American Affairs, advisor to the Governor of Washington, 1976-84; Peaceful Reunification Committee of the Republic of Korea, advisory board, 1983-88, NW Region, chairman, 1983-88; Boy Scouts of America, International & Seattle Chapters, board memeber, 1984-87. **HONORS/AWARDS:** President of South Korea, Distinguished Service Award. **MILITARY SERVICE:** Army, E-5, 1958-60. **BUSINESS ADDRESS:** Representative, Washington State House of Representatives, John L O'Brien Bldg, #405, Olympia, WA 98504.

SHIN, SOONMI
Financial services company executive. Korean American. **PERSONAL:** Born May 13, 1953, Seoul, Republic of Korea; daughter of Mr and Mrs Hyun Joon Shin; married Raul Pelaez, Jul 24, 1993; children: Yoon Soo Byun. **EDUCATION:** New York University, BA, 1976; George Washington University, MBA, 1984. **CAREER:** TRS, Korea, mgmt trainee, 1984-85, funding & planning, mgr, 1985-86, International Financial Analysis, mgr, 1986-87, director, 1987-89, Worldwide Marketing, director, 1989-91, New Business Partnership, director, 1991-93, vice pres, 1993-. **BUSINESS ADDRESS:** Vice President, American Express TRS Co Inc, American Express Tower, World Financial Center 2700, New York, NY 10285, (212)640-1742.

SHIN, YOUNG
Association administrator. **CAREER:** Asian Immigrant Women's Advocates, executive director, currently. **BIOGRAPHICAL SOURCES:** Mother Jones, p 25, January 1989. **BUSINESS ADDRESS:** Executive Director, Asian Immigrant Women's Advocates, 310 8th St, Ste 301, Oakland, CA 94607, (510)268-0192.*

SHIN, YUNG C.
Educator. Korean American. **PERSONAL:** Born Mar 28, 1953, Kyungsan, Republic of Korea; son of Hyun-dong Shin and Soon-nam Shin; married Hwasoon Shin, Oct 25, 1980; children: Andrea S, Eric Y. **EDUCATION:** Seoul National University, BS, 1976; Korea Advanced Institute of Science, MS, 1978; University of Wisconsin, Madison, PhD, 1984. **CAREER:** Korea Institute of Machinery & Metals, research engineer, 1978-81; General Motors, senior project engineer, 1984-88; Pennsylvania State University, assistant professor, 1988-90; Purdue University, assistant professor, beginning 1990, associate professor, currently. **ORGANIZATIONS:** American Society of Mech Engineers, 1984-; Sigma Xi, 1984-; American Society of Metals, 1993-; Society of Manufacturing Engineering, 1984-. **BUSINESS ADDRESS:** Associate Professor, Purdue University, 1288 Mechanical Engineering, West Lafayette, IN 47907, (313)494-9775.

SHINAGAWA, LARRY
Educator. Japanese American. **CAREER:** Sonoma State University, Dept of American Studies, professor, currently, Institute for Cultural Diversity Research, director, currently; California State University System, Census Info Center, director, currently. **HONORS/AWARDS:** Voting Rights Program Southern Regional Council, grant recipient to study voting patterns of Asian Americans in San Francisco and Daly City, California. **BUSINESS ADDRESS:** Professor, Dept of American Studies, Sonoma State University, 1801 E Cotati Ave, Rohnert Park, CA 94928-3613.*

SHINOZUKA, MASANOBU
Engineer, educator. Japanese American. **PERSONAL:** Born Dec 23, 1930, Tokyo, Japan; son of Akira and Kiyo Shinozuka; married Fujiko Sakamoto, Oct 25, 1954; children: Rei, Naomi, Megumi. **EDUCATION:** Kyoto University, Japan, BS, 1953, MS, 1955; Columbia University, PhD, 1960. **CAREER:** Columbia University, civil engineering, research assistant, 1958-61, assistant professor, 1961-65, associate professor, 1965-69, professor, 1969-88, Renwick Professor, 1977-88; Modern Analysis Inc, president, 1972-; Princeton University, professor, 1988-, Sollenberger Professor, civil engineering, 1989-, on leave, 1990-; SUNY, Buffalo, Dept of Civil Engineering, visiting Capen Professor of Structural Engineering, 1990-, National Center for Earthquake Engineering Research, director, 1990-. **ORGANIZATIONS:** US Panel on

Structural Control Research, steering committee, 1990-; NAE; ASCE; ASME; AIAA; Japan Society of Civil Engineers; Sigma Xi. **HONORS/AWARDS:** Wessex Institute of Technology, medal, 1991; NSF, grantee, 1968-; ASCE, Moisseiff Award, 1988, C Martin Duke Award, 1991. **SPECIAL ACHIEVE-MENTS:** Reliability Approach in Structural Engineering, editor, 1975; ASCE Symposium on Probabilistic Methods in Structural Engineering, proceedings, coeditor, 1981. **BUSINESS ADDRESS:** Professor, Civil Engineering Dept, Princeton University, Princeton, NJ 08540, (609)258-3000.∗

SHINSATO, FRANCIS G.

Electronics manufacturing company executive. Japanese American. **PERSONAL:** Born Jan 22, 1951, Wahiawa, HI; son of Yoshitoshi Shinsato; divorced. **EDUCATION:** California Polytechnic University at Pomona, BSEE, 1972; University of Southern California, MSEE, 1974; Harvard Business School, MBA, 1976. **CAREER:** Rockwell International, technical staff, engineer, 1972-74, financial management administrator, 1976-78; Price Waterhouse, management consultant, manager, 1978-83; Bell Helmets Inc, vice president of finance, 1983-85; Newport Electronics Inc, vice president, controller, 1985-. **ORGANIZATIONS:** Harvard Business Association of Orange County, treasurer, 1992-93. **SPECIAL ACHIEVEMENTS:** Certified Public Accountant, State of California; professional engineer, State of California. **BUSINESS ADDRESS:** Vice President, Controller, Newport Electronics Inc, 2229 South Yale Street, Santa Ana, CA 92704, (714)540-4914.

SHIRAI, AKIKO

Artist, educator. Japanese American. **PERSONAL:** Born in Dairen, Manchuria, China; daughter of Takashi & Yoshiko Shirai; married Atsuyoshi Takayama, Jun 12, 1968; children: Suzanna, Cecilia. **EDUCATION:** Tokyo National University of Fine Arts, BA, oil painting, 1959, MA, printmaking, 1964. **CAREER:** Kyoto Seika University, Department of Fine Arts, professor, 1993-. **ORGANIZATIONS:** Society of American Graphic Artists; Japan Print Association, jury. **HONORS/AWARDS:** Rockefeller Foundation, fellowship, 1966; S Soma Foundation, scholarship, 1991. **SPECIAL ACHIEVEMENTS:** 5th Mainichi Contemporary Japan Art Exhibition, 1962; 7th Shell Contest, Tokyo, 1963; 5th Tokyo International Biennial Exhibition of Print, 1966; 9th San Paulo International Biennial Exhibition, 1967; Twentieth Century American Woodcuts, AAA Gallery, NY, 1985. **BIOGRAPHICAL SOURCES:** Special feature of Akiko Shinai, Hangwa Geijutsu, vol 22, 1978; special feature of Akiko Shinai, Monotype, Hangwa Geijutsu, vol 42, 1983. **HOME ADDRESS:** 905 Madison Ave, New York, NY 10021.

SHIRAKAWA, GEORGE

City government official. Japanese American. **PERSONAL:** Born Nov 18, 1939, Hanford, CA; son of Josephine Alvarez Esparza Shirakawa & Masaji J Shirakawa; married JoAnn, Aug 12, 1961; children: George Jr, Navette Heberling, Kenley. **EDUCATION:** San Jose State University, BA, 1968, MA, 1977, teacher credential, 1970, counseling credential, 1977, administrative services credential, 1982. **CAREER:** Farmworker, 1942-57; truck driver, 1957-62; small businessman, 1970-90; teacher, 1970-77; counselor, 1974-80; administrator, 1980-90; City of San Jose, city council member, 1990-. **ORGANIZATIONS:** St Mark's Child Care Center, board of directors, 1988; Community Coordinated Child Care of Santa Clara County, board of directors, 1988-; National Conference of Christians and Jews Conference for Santa Clara County, representative/presenter, James and Holden Ranch facilities, wards of the court, 1985-86; US Dept of Education, field reader consultant, 1983-86; Chicano Assn of School Administrators & the East Side Assn of Latino Educators, president, vp, treasurer, 1975-90. **HONORS/AWARDS:** Santa Clara Co Office of Education, Bilingual Education Award, 1993; SJ City College Latino Education Assn, LEA Community Award, 1993. **MILITARY SERVICE:** US Army, specialist, 4th class, 1962-64. **BUSINESS ADDRESS:** Council Member, City of San Jose, 801 N 1st St, Rm 600, San Jose, CA 95110, (408)277-5226.

SHISHIDO, CALVIN M.

State government manager. Japanese American. **PERSONAL:** Born Aug 24, 1933, Honolulu, HI; son of Isamu & Kane Shishido; divorced; children: Dale, Neala Shishido-Bovard. **EDUCATION:** Florence State College, BS (honors), 1961. **CAREER:** Internal Revenue Service, special agent, 1962-65; Federal Bureau of Investigation, special agent, 1965-84; IDS, financial planner, 1985-86; Galiher-de Robertis, investigator, 1988-89; State of Hawaii, Dept of Transportation, special assistant, 1989-91, Dept of Public Safety, sheriff, 1991, special projects manager, 1991-. **ORGANIZATIONS:** Society of Former Special Agents of the FBI, president, 1987-88; Lions Club, San Francisco,

program chairman, 1970-71; Junior Chamber of Commerce, 1961-62; National Sheriffs Association, 1991-; Hawaii State Law Enforcement Association, 1991-. **MILITARY SERVICE:** US Air Force, s/sgt, 1952-57. **HOME ADDRESS:** 45-800 Puupele Street, Kaneohe, HI 96744.

SHIVANANDAN, KANDIAH

Scientist. Malaysian American. **PERSONAL:** Born Aug 22, 1929, Parit Buntar, Parak, Malaysia; married Mary Shivanandan, Sep 22, 1960; children: John Suri, Marianne Gauri. **EDUCATION:** University of Melbourne, Australia, BSc, physics, 1955; University of Toronto, Canada, MS, physics, 1958; MIT, PhD, physics, 1963. **CAREER:** Oak Ridge Institute of Nuclear Studies, research physicist, 1956-58; MIT, research physicist, 1958-61; Goddard Space Flight Center, research scientist, 1961-63; Naval Research Laboratory, research physicist, 1963-91; General Research Corp, chief scientist, 1991-. **ORGANIZATIONS:** American Physical Society, 1968; Royal Astronomical Society, fellow, 1978-85; New York Academy of Science, fellow, 1985-90; International Astronomical Union, 1985-; Indian Physical Society, 1985-90; Asian Physical Society, 1985-; Scientific Research Society of America, 1983-. **HONORS/AWARDS:** Fulbright Scholar, 1957-58; Colombia Plan Fellow, 1954-56. **SPECIAL ACHIEVEMENTS:** Focal Plane Array Technology, 1990; Indo-US Science & Technology, 1985-90; US-Australia Initiative in Science and Technology, 1993. **BIOGRAPHICAL SOURCES:** Violent Universe. **HOME ADDRESS:** 4711 Overbrook Rd, Bethesda, MD 20816, (301)652-4536.

SHOHARA, SEI

Religious leader. Japanese American. **PERSONAL:** Born Dec 28, 1930. **CAREER:** Buddhist Churches of America, president, 1992-94. **BUSINESS ADDRESS:** Religious Leader, Buddhist Churches of America, 18350 Clifftop Way, Malibu, CA 90265.∗

SHON, KYO KWA

Orientation and mobility specialist. Korean American. **PERSONAL:** Born May 5, 1956, Pusan, Republic of Korea; son of Jin Soo Shon and Yeon Ja Ji; married Jong Hyee Shon, Apr 5, 1982; children: Dong Jin. **EDUCATION:** Pusan National University, bachelor's, English, 1980; Lehman College, Cuny, bachelor's, computer science, 1988; Florida State University, master's, visual disabilities, 1991. **CAREER:** Haewoondae Girls' High School, English teacher, 1984-86; Pinellas Center for the Visually Impaired, O&M team leader, 1991-. **ORGANIZATIONS:** Golden Key National Honor Society, 1987-; Pi Mu Epsilon, 1988-. **HONORS/AWARDS:** Korean Government, Korean Honor Scholarship, 1990; Lehman College, Lehman College Scholarship, 1987, Dean's List, 1987. **MILITARY SERVICE:** ROK Air Force, Korea, 1st lt, 1980-84; Honor of the Base Commander, 1983. **HOME ADDRESS:** 661-77th Ave N, # 309, St Petersburg, FL 33702.

SHRIVASTAVA, SATYENDRA P.

Company executive. Indo-American. **PERSONAL:** Born Jul 17, 1939, Darbhanga, Bihar, India; son of Kusheswar P. (deceased) and Lakshmi Devi Shrivastava; married Sudha, Jul 2, 1965; children: Sumeet, Amar, Nitika. **EDUCATION:** Patna University, BEE, 1963; University of North Carolina, MS, 1974; Marymount University, MBA, 1982. **CAREER:** Bihar College of Engineering, lecturer, 1963-64; Government of India, Ministry of Irrigation, asst dir, 1964-70; University of North Carolina, teaching asst, 1970-72; Elizabeth City State University, NC, lecturer, 1972-73; Potomac Electric & Power, mgr, engineering computer systems, 1973-81; GTE Telenet, Computer Applications Division, dir, 1981-83; Anstec Inc, founder, president, chief executive officer, 1983-. **ORGANIZATIONS:** Minority Business Assn of North Virginia, chairman, 1992-; Armed Forces Communications and Electronics Assn, 1987-; IEEE, 1976-; Natl Security Industrial Assn, 1993-; American Assn for Artificial Intelligence, 1987-; Air Traffic Control Assn, 1993-; Assn for Computing Machinery, 1983-; Virginia Regional Minority Assn, 1988-. **HONORS/AWARDS:** US Small Business Administration, Minority Entrepreneur of the Year, 1993; Natl Security Agency, Contractor Excellence Award, 1990; NASA Goddard Space Flight Center, TQM Certificate of Appreciation, 1991; Inc Magazine, Inc 500 Award, ranked #36, 1993; Washington Technology, Fast 50 Award, ranked #7, 1993. **BUSINESS ADDRESS:** President, CEO, Anstec Inc, 10530 Rosehaven St, Ste 600, Fairfax, VA 22030, (703)591-4000.

SHROFF, ARVIN P.

Government official. Indo-American. **PERSONAL:** Born Jul 2, 1933, Surat, Gujarat, India; son of Pranlal B Shroff; married Theresa, Jul 2, 1991; children: Susan Asha, Sarah Ann. **EDUCATION:** M.S. University of Baroda, BSc,

1954; Duquesne University, MS, 1958; University of Maryland, PhD, 1963. **CAREER:** Ortho Pharmaceutical Corp, research chemist, 1963-74; US Food & Drug Administration, review chemist, 1974-76, product surveillance research, chief, 1976-80, division of field science, director, 1980-86, regional operations, deputy director, 1986-91, enforcement, deputy director, 1991-. **ORGANIZATIONS:** Association of Food and Drug Officials, Science & Technical Committee, chairperson, 1987-91. **HONORS/AWARDS:** U.S. Food & Drug Administration, Commissioner's Special Citation, 1989, Award of Merit, 1989, commendable service, 1978; Ortho Pharm, Philip B. Hoffman, 1972; Merril Dow, Lunsford Richardson, 1961. **SPECIAL ACHIEVEMENTS:** Author, 45 scientific and technical papers; chapter, Analytical Profiles of Drug Substances; 30 US and foreign patents; synthesized contraceptive, Norgestimate marketed by Ortho Pharmaceutical Corp as "Ortho Tri-Cyclen.". **BUSINESS ADDRESS:** Deputy Director, Office of Enforcement, Food and Drug Administration, 5600 Fishers Lane, Rm 12-A-55 (HFC-201), Rockville, MD 20857, (301)443-7400.

SHUKLA, SHIVENDRA D.
Educator. Indo-American. **PERSONAL:** Born Oct 11, 1951, Mirzapur, Uttar Pradesh, India; son of Vidya Sagar Shukla; married Asha Shukla; children: Roshni, Sundeep, Bivek. **EDUCATION:** University of Liverpool, PhD, 1977. **CAREER:** Banaras Hindu University, lecturer, 1971-73; University of Birmingham, England, research fellow, 1976-80; University of Texas Health Science Center, research assistant professor, 1980-83; University of Missouri Columbia, professor, 1984-. **ORGANIZATIONS:** American Heart Association; American Society of Biochem & Mol Biol; American Society for Pharmacology & Exp Ther; New York Acad Sci; Physiological Society of India; Indian Science Congress Association; Sigma Xi; NIH, Study Section, reviewer. **HONORS/AWARDS:** Atomic Energy Commission, fellowship, 1968; Banaras Hindu University, Gold Medal, 1970; National Institutes of Health, Research Career Development Award, 1989. **SPECIAL ACHIEVEMENTS:** Over 100 scientific publications; editor, Platelet Activating Factor Receptor, CRC Press, 1993. **BIOGRAPHICAL SOURCES:** Several new bulletins of Missouri University; Columbia Missourian Newspaper, section C, February 8, 1989. **BUSINESS ADDRESS:** Professor, Pharmacology, University of Missouri, School of Medicine, 1 Hospital Dr, Columbia, MO 65212, (314)882-2740.

SHUM, ALEX C.
Engineer. Hong Kong American. **PERSONAL:** Born Aug 6, 1953, Hong Kong; married Loretta Shum, Nov 15, 1978; children: Victoria. **EDUCATION:** University of Houston, BSIE, 1979; University of Southern California, MSSM, 1986. **CAREER:** US Army, Engineering Resource Mgmt Division, chief, 1981-89, Mgmt Engineering & Systems Branch, chief, 1989-. **ORGANIZATIONS:** Society of Military Engineers, San Antonio Post, treasurer, 1992-; Institute of Industrial Engineers, San Antonio Branch, board of directors, 1992-; Texas State Board of Registration for Professional Engineers, professional engr, currently. **BUSINESS ADDRESS:** Chief, Management Engineering & Systems Branch, U.S. Army, Bld 4196, DEH, Fort Sam Houston, TX 78234.

SHUM, WILLIAM
Banking executive. Chinese American. **PERSONAL:** Born Feb 6, 1957, Hong Kong; married Helen King Shum; children: William Alexander. **EDUCATION:** Capital Radio Engineering Institute, AAS, 1979; Baruch College, BBA, 1985; Pace University, MBA, 1990. **CAREER:** Metropolitan Transit Authority, safety compliance officer, 1981-85; Internal Revenue Service, revenue agent, 1985-86; Morgan Stanley, tax accountant, 1986-89; Deloitte & Touche, tax mgr, 1989-91; Bayerische Landesbank, tax/regulatory compliance director, vice pres, 1991-. **ORGANIZATIONS:** American Institute of Certified Public Accountants; New York State Society of Certified Public Accountants; Asia Society; China Institute; US Tax Committee of German Banks; Committee of Banking Institutions on Taxation; Phi Beta Kappa; Asian Financial Society. **SPECIAL ACHIEVEMENTS:** Bankers Monthly, May 1990. **MILITARY SERVICE:** US Air Force, ssgt, 1976-81; Commendation Medal, 1981, Good Conduct Medal, 1981, Service Medal, 1981. **BUSINESS ADDRESS:** Vice President, Bayerische Landesbank-New York Branch, 560 Lexington Ave, 22nd Fl, New York, NY 10022, (212)310-9812.

SHWE, HLA
Educator, educational administrator. Chinese American/Myanmar American. **PERSONAL:** Born May 2, 1934, Rangoon, Burma; son of Boon-Chin Chiong and Chye-Har Teoh; married Sara Shwe, Jun 23, 1962; children: Walter,

Michael, Helen. **EDUCATION:** university of California, Berkeley, AB, 1958, MA, 1959, PhD, 1962. **CAREER:** Lawrence Berkeley Laboratory, research physicist, 1962-64; Ripon College, assistant professor of physics, 1963-69, associate professor of physics, 1972-73; Argonne National Laboratory, research physicist, 1967-69; East Stroudsburg University of Pennsylvania, professor of physics, 1969-, dean of arts and sciences, 1974-83, director of honors program, 1989-. **ORGANIZATIONS:** American Association of Physics Teachers, 1963-; American Physical Society, 1959-; Society of Physics Students, president, 1976-80; Pennsylvania Junior Academy of Science, advisory board, chair, 1983-; Rotary International, District 7410, governor, 1990-91; North-East Region, National Collegiate Honors Council, executive secretary, treasurer, 1993-96. **HONORS/AWARDS:** Phi Beta Kappa, 1957; Sigma Xi, 1957; Ripon College, Excellence in Teaching, 1967; Rotary Club, 1978. **HOME ADDRESS:** 143 Berwick Heights Road, East Stroudsburg, PA 18301, (717)424-1871. **BUSINESS ADDRESS:** Professor of Physics, Director of Honors Program, East Stroudsburg University, Prospect and Normal Streets, Gessner Science Hall, East Stroudsburg, PA 18301, (717)424-3655.

SIBAL, NICOLAS VILLADOLID
Architect. Filipino American. **PERSONAL:** Born Jan 14, 1960, Quezon City, Philippines; son of Felix Sibal and Lydia Sibal. **EDUCATION:** University of Maryland at College Park, BAr, 1982. **CAREER:** The Design Collaborative Architects, intern architect, 1983-85; Williams & Tazewell Architects Engineer, intern architect, 1985-86; GMR Architects Engineers, designer architect, 1986-90; Ellerbe Becket Architects, project architect, currently. **ORGANIZATIONS:** American Institute of Architects, 1987-; Tanshalang Pilipino, 1986-. **BUSINESS ADDRESS:** Project Architect, Ellerbe Becket Architecture, 1875 Connecticut Ave NW, Ste 600, Washington, DC 20009, (202)986-9115.

SIDDIQUI, ALEEM ABDUL
Educator. Indo-American. **PERSONAL:** Born Dec 23, 1948, Khammam, Andhra Pradesh, India; son of Mohammad Abdul Khader and Mujeebunnisa; married Julie Ann, Jan 1988; children: Sara-Jann. **EDUCATION:** Osmania University, India, BS, MS, 1966; Oregon State University, MS, 1971; University of Kansas Medical School, PhD, 1976. **CAREER:** University of Colorado Medical School, postdoctoral fellow, 1976-78; Stanford University, postdoctoral fellow, 1978-81; University of Colorado Medical School, assistant professor, 1982-87, associate professor, 1988-92, professor, 1992-. **HONORS/AWARDS:** American Cancer Society, faculty research award, 1988-93. **BUSINESS ADDRESS:** Professor, Microbiology Dept, University of Colorado Medical School, 4200 E 9th Ave, BRB 302, B172, Denver, CO 80262.

SIDDIQUI, EHTISHAM UDDIN AHMAD
Business development executive. Pakistani American. **PERSONAL:** Born Mar 29, 1954, Karachi, Sind, Pakistan; son of Nizam U A Siddiqui and Seyeda K Siddiqui; married Sadia; children: Saba Ahmad. **EDUCATION:** University of Karachi, BS, 1974; Syracuse University, MS, 1976, PhD, 1979. **CAREER:** GE Electrical Systems, des/dev engr, 1979-84, mgr, engrng, 1984-87, GE Aircraft Engines, mgr, hypersonic prop marketing, 1987-88, mgr, IR&D and resource plans, 1988-80; GE Aircraft Controls, mgr, business dev, 1990-93; Martin Marietta, director, business dev, 1993-. **ORGANIZATIONS:** ASME, 1976-. **HONORS/AWARDS:** General Electric, Engineer of the Year, 1980; University of Karachi, Valedictorian, 1974. **BUSINESS ADDRESS:** Director, Business Development, Martin Marietta Control Systems, 600 Main St, Rm 151, Johnson City, NY 13790, (607)770-2446.

SIDDIQUI, FARUQ MAHMUD ANAM
Educator. Bangladeshi American. **PERSONAL:** Born Jan 27, 1951, Rangpur, Bangladesh; son of M Faizul Anam Siddiqui and Mahmuda Begum Siddiqui; married Shahida N Siddiqui, Mar 12, 1977; children: Naasiha, Faiza. **EDUCATION:** Bangladesh University of Engineering & Technology, Dhaka, Bangladesh, BSCE, 1976; University of Pittsburgh, MSCE, 1979, PhD, 1981. **CAREER:** Bangladesh University of Engineering & Technology, Dhaka, lecturer in civil engineering, 1976-77; University of Pittsburgh, teaching fellow/assistant, research assistant, 1977-81, lecturer in civil engineering, 1982; Swarthmore College, assistant professor of engineering, 1982-88, associate professor of engineering, 1988-. **ORGANIZATIONS:** American Society of Civil Engineers, 1982-; American Society for Engineering Education, 1992-; Sigma Xi, 1986-; American Concrete Institute, 1991-; American Association of Bangladesh Engineers, treasurer, secretary, 1984-. **HONORS/AWARDS:** Chi Epsilon Civil Engineering Honor Society, 1981; Tau Beta Pi Engineering Honor Society, 1987; University of Pittsburgh Engineering Graduate Student Board, Outstanding Graduate Student, 1981. **SPECIAL ACHIEVEMENTS:**

Publications: "LRFD Aid for Tubeshaped Beams," Engineering Journal, AISC, vol 27, no 2, 1990; "Stress Concentration Factors in Angled Flexural Members of Rectangular Cross-Section," Journal of Vibrations, Acoustics, Stress and Reliability in Design, vol III, Oct 1989; "Simplified Analysis Method for Multistory Base Isolated Structures," Earthquake Engineering & Structural Dynamics, vol 18, no 1, 1989. **BUSINESS ADDRESS:** Associate Professor of Engineering, Swarthmore College, 500 College Ave, Hicks Hall 305, Swarthmore, PA 19081-1397, (610)328-8074.

SIDDIQUI, HABIB
Research engineer. Bangladeshi American. **PERSONAL:** Born Jul 14, 1953, Khulna, Bangladesh; son of Nazrul Islam Siddiqui; married Sakkar Ara Eva, Aug 29, 1982; children: Hassan Ismail. **EDUCATION:** Bangladesh University of Engineering & Technology, BS, chem eng, 1977; University of Saskatchewan, MS, chem eng, 1980; University of California, Santa Barbara, MS, nuc eng, 1983; University of Southern California, PhD, chem eng, 1989. **CAREER:** Rohm and Haas Co, research engineer, 1989-. **ORGANIZATIONS:** AIChE, 1978-82; CIChE, 1979-82; AIChEJ, reviewer, 1992-; CJChE, reviewer, 1993-. **HONORS/AWARDS:** University of Southern California, Certificate of Merit, 1988, Academic Achievement Award, 1988, University of Saskatchewan, University Graduate Fellowship, 1980, Thoruldson Scholarship, 1978-80; University of California, Los Angeles, Engineering Management Scholarship, 1983, University of Southern California, Student Leadership Award, 1988. **BUSINESS ADDRESS:** Research Engineer, Rohm & Haas Co, PO Box 219, Bldg 147C, Bristol, PA 19007, (215)785-8850.

SIDHU, GURMEL SINGH
Research scientist, educator. Indo-American. **PERSONAL:** Born May 23, 1943, Jullunder, Punjab, India; married Baljeet Kaur Sidhu, Mar 23, 1979; children: Vikram S, Rupinderpal S. **EDUCATION:** Punjab University, Chandigharh, India, BSc, 1962; University of British Columbia, MSc, 1968, PhD, 1972. **CAREER:** Simon Fraser University, postdoctoral fellow, 1972-75, research scientist, 1975-80; University of Nebraska, assistant professor, 1980-86; Germain's Inc, research pathologist, 1992-; California State University, Fresno, adj professor, 1987-. **ORGANIZATIONS:** American Phytopathological Society, 1975-86; Genetics Society of America, 1975-80; American Association for Advancement of Science, 1990-; Genetics Society of Canada, 1980-90; Phytopathology, associate editor, 1980-86; Crop Science of India, associate editor, 1979-86; Sahitya Samachar, editor, 1965-67. **HONORS/AWARDS:** Punjab Agricultural University, visiting professorship, 1979; University of Nebraska, research fellowship at Wisconsin, 1986. **SPECIAL ACHIEVEMENTS:** Author: Genetics of Plant-Pathogenic Fungi, Academic Press, 1989; six poetry books in Punjabi language, 1975-84. **HOME PHONE:** (209)292-4861. **BUSINESS ADDRESS:** Professor, Biology Dept, California State University, Shaw/Cedar, Fresno, CA 93740-0072, (209)278-4366.

SIEU, BENNY LOU
Photojournalist. Chinese American. **PERSONAL:** Born Oct 5, 1951, Chicago, IL; son of Sing K Sieu and Sun Tam. **EDUCATION:** University of Illinois, Champaign-Urbana, BS, engineering, 1973. **CAREER:** San Pedro News-Pilot, photographer, 1976-77; Milwaukee Sentinel & Journal, photojournalist, 1977-. **ORGANIZATIONS:** Wisconsin News Photographers Association; National Press Photographers Association. **HONORS/AWARDS:** Milwaukee Press Club, 1st Place, Picture Story, 1993; Wisconsin News Photographers Association, Best of Show, 1993, 1st Place, Feature Photo, 1993, 1st Place, Sports Action, 1993, 1st Place, News Picture Story, 1993. **SPECIAL ACHIEVEMENTS:** Recent assignments include: Democratic & Republican National Conventions; starvation in Somalia; Operation Desert Shield in Persian Gulf; pictures published in Newsweek, People, Vanity Fair, Audubon. **BUSINESS ADDRESS:** Photojournalist, Photo Dept, Milwaukee Sentinel, 918 N 4th St, Milwaukee, WI 53202, (414)224-2766.

SIHAG, RAM K.
Educator. Indo-American. **PERSONAL:** Born Jan 1, 1950, Hissar, India; married Christine Ptak. **EDUCATION:** Jawaharlal Nehru University, New Delhi, PhD, 1977. **CAREER:** University of Connecticut, Health Center, postdoctoral research associate, 1981-84; Harvard Medical School, research associate in biological chemistry; McLean Hospital, assistant biochemist, 1985-89; Harvard Medical School, McLean Hospital, associate biochemist, assistant professor, 1991-. **ORGANIZATIONS:** American Society for Cell Biology; American Society for Biochemistry and Molecular Biology; The Protein Society; The American Association for the Advancement of Science.

HONORS/AWARDS: National Science Foundation, Research Grant, 1991; National Institute of Health, Research Grant, 1989; American Federation of Aging Research, Research Grant, 1992; Study neuronal plasticity, protein phosphorylation and neuronal cytoskeleton structure and function. **SPECIAL ACHIEVEMENTS:** Several publications on the role of phosphorylation on the dynamics of neuronal cytoskeleton; regulation of protein synthesis; regulation of nitrate metabolism in scientific journals; review articles & book chapters. **BUSINESS ADDRESS:** Assistant Professor of Biochemistry, Dept of Psychiatry, Harvard Medical School, McLean Hospital, 115 Mill St, Belmont, MA 02178, (617)855-3567.

SIKAND, CHANDER KUMARI
Physician. Indo-American. **PERSONAL:** Born Oct 28, 1923, Hazro, District Campbellpur, Pakistan; daughter of Gokal Chand Shah and Shakuntala Devi; married Harcharan Das Sikand, Apr 26, 1947; children: Ravindar, Ashok, Vijay, Rajindar. **EDUCATION:** MD, 1946. **CAREER:** Westchester County, New York, child psychiatry chief, 1970-80; St. Joseph's Medical Center, Yonkers, New York, assistant, 1970-80; DCMH Westchester County, New York, psychiatrist II, 1980-86. **ORGANIZATIONS:** Psychiatric Society of Westchester County, 1970-; American Psychiatric Association, 1970-; American Academy of Child Psychiatry, 1970-; Psychiatric Society of New York Medical College, 1970-; American Association of Psychiatrists from India, 1970-. **HOME ADDRESS:** 43 Beechwood Rd., Irvington, NY 10533, (914)591-6461.

SILAO, RAY A.
Physician. Filipino American. **PERSONAL:** Born Dec 7, 1967, Dearborn, MI; son of Narciso & Virginia Silao; married Nora Silao. **EDUCATION:** Loma Linda University, BA, biology, 1985, MD, 1990. **CAREER:** Loma Linda University Medical Center, physician, currently. **BUSINESS ADDRESS:** Physician, Loma Linda University Medical Center, 11234 Anderson St, Loma Linda, CA 92354, (909)824-0800.

SIM, JOHN KIM-CHYE
Cleric. Singaporean American. **PERSONAL:** Born Feb 28, 1957, Singapore, Singapore; son of Hai Yong Sim and Ah Soon Quek; married Ammelia Beng-Geok Tan, Sep 4, 1978; children: Samuel. **EDUCATION:** Tung Ling Bible School, diploma (with honors), 1981; Christ for the Nations Institute, AA, 1982; Evangelical Teachers Training Assn, teacher's diploma, 1985; Life Bible College, BA (with honors), 1985; Alliance Theological Seminary, MDiv, 1990; Princeton Theological Seminary, ThM, 1993; Fuller Theological Seminary, DMin candidate, 1993-. **CAREER:** Hilton Intl, Singapore, sr sales executive, 1979-80; Church of Our Savior, pastoral staff, 1980-81; Chapel of the Resurrection, pastoral staff, 1985-87; Tung Ling Bible School, adjunct lecturer, 1985-87; Toledo Chinese Alliance Church, pastor, 1990-93; Irvine Canaan Christian Community Church, pastor, 1993-. **ORGANIZATIONS:** Christian and Missionary Alliance, 1990-. **HONORS/AWARDS:** International Biographical Center, Intl Man of the Year, 1993. **HOME ADDRESS:** 28046 Marguerite Parkway #N, Mission Viejo, CA 92692.

SIMUNEK, LINDA A.
Educational administrator. Filipino American. **CAREER:** Chicago State University, School of Nursing, dean, professor; Florida International University, School of Nursing, founder, dean, professor. **BUSINESS ADDRESS:** Dean, Professor, School of Nursing, Florida Intl University, 3000 NE 145th St, North Miami, FL 33181-3600. *

SINCO, VICTOR
Architect. Filipino American. **PERSONAL:** Born Feb 17, 1958, Dumaguete, Negros Oriental, Philippines; son of Leandro Sinco and Edelmira Sinco; married Dianne, Dec 1983; children: Christopher, Patrick, Stephen. **EDUCATION:** University of Washington, architecture, 1980. **CAREER:** Trans Oceanic Architecture Design, project manager, 1980-83; Norman Lacayo, project manager, 1983-85; Okita, Kummitsu & Associates, associate, 1985-88; AM Partners, Inc, associate, 1988-91; Entheos, owner, 1991-. **ORGANIZATIONS:** American Institute of Architects, 1980-. **BUSINESS ADDRESS:** President, Entheos, 1453 Alencastre St, Honolulu, HI 96816, (808)737-1871.

SING, LILLIAN K.
Judge. Chinese American. **PERSONAL:** Born Nov 13, 1942, Shanghai, China. **EDUCATION:** Occidental College, BS, 1964; Columbia University, MSW, 1966; University of California, Hastings College of Law, JD, 1975; CJER California Continuing Judicial Studies, 1982, 1984. **CAREER:** Chinese New

Comer Service Center, associate director, 1969-71; Simmons & Ungar, attorney at law, 1975-77; Solo Practitioner, attorney at law, 1977-81; SF Municipal Court, 1981-, presiding judge, 1988-89. **ORGANIZATIONS:** California Women Lawyers Association, 1982-; Assn of Immigration/Naturalization Lawyers, SF Chapter, liaison chair, 1980; SF Bar Association Endowment, board member, 1987, 1989; SF Institute for Criminal Justice, board member, 1990, 1991; Asian American Bar Association, Trial Practice Clinic, judge, 1982-; SF Municipal Court, Administrative Committee, chair, 1986-89, Reorganization Committee, chair, 1987-92; California Asian Judges Association, state chair, 1986, 1994. **HONORS/AWARDS:** SF Women Lawyers Alliance, Outstanding Jurist Award, 1993; Lawyers' Club of San Francisco, Presiding Judge Award, 1989; Trial Lawyers Association, San Francisco, Trial Judge of the Year Award, 1989; Asian American Bar Assn, Honoree, First Asian Women Judge in N California, 1985; Congresswoman Barbara Boxer, Women Making History Award, 1982. **SPECIAL ACHIEVEMENTS:** Chinese for Affirmative Action, founding member, 1971; Gay Asian Pacific Alliance, Community HIV Project, board member, 1993-; San Francisco Civil Service Commission, vice-chair, 1978; San Francisco Human Rights Commission, commissioner, 1975; SF Community College Governing Board, president, 1979. **BUSINESS ADDRESS:** Judge, San Francisco Municipal Court, 400 Van Ness, City Hall, Rm 300, San Francisco, CA 94102.

SINGH, AJAIB
Chemical company executive. Indo-American. **PERSONAL:** Born Jan 14, 1935, Dholanhithar, Punjab, Pakistan; son of Aroor Singh and Ram Kaur; married Manjit I Singh, Jan 24, 1964; children: Surveen Kaur, Dinesh, Parveen Kaur. **EDUCATION:** Punjab University, India, BSc, 1954, BSc (honors), 1956, MSc (honors), 1958; University of California, PhD, 1961. **CAREER:** Harvard University, research fellow, 1961-62; American Cyanamid Co, research group leader, 1962-78; Uniroyal Chemical Co, research director, 1978-. **ORGANIZATIONS:** American Chemical Society, 1960-; Polyurethane Manufacturer's Association, director, 1978-; Garden State Sikh Association, 1974-. **HONORS/AWARDS:** American Cyanamid Co, research fellowship, 1968-69. **SPECIAL ACHIEVEMENTS:** Expertise in polymer technology; recognized expert in polyurethane technology: publications, patents. **HOME ADDRESS:** 58 Autumn Ridge Rd, Shelton, CT 06484, (203)929-4865.

SINGH, AJAIB
Government official. Indo-American. **PERSONAL:** Born Jul 15, 1940, Paitiala, Punjab, India; married Kuldeep Bajwa; children: Navneet, Navtej. **EDUCATION:** Panjab University, BVSc, AH, 1962, MSc, 1965; University of Wisconsin, Madison, PhD, 1983. **CAREER:** Panjab University, Chandigarh, lecturer; University of Wisconsin, postdoctoral; Montana State University, adjunct assistant professor; Delaware Health Department, microbiologist; Milwaukee Health Department, chief microbiologist, currently. **BIOGRAPHICAL SOURCES:** Environmental Microbiology, John Wiley & Sons, p 125-56, 1992; Drinking Water Microbiology, Springer-Verlag, p 368-79, 1990. **BUSINESS ADDRESS:** Chief, Division of Microbiology, Milwaukee Health Department, 841 N Broadway, Rm 308, Milwaukee, WI 53202, (414)278-3935.

SINGH, AMARJIT
Scientist. Indo-American. **PERSONAL:** Born Nov 19, 1924, Ramdas, Punjab, India; son of Jagdish Singh and Ishar Kaur; married Surinder Kaur Dewan, Nov 21, 1953; children: Harinder J, Narinder J, Arvind J. **EDUCATION:** Punjab University, Lahore, MSc, 1945; Ohio State University, 1945-46; Harvard University, ME, Engg Sc, 1947, PhD, 1949. **CAREER:** University of Delhi, India, lecturer in radio physics, 1949-53; National Physical Laboratory, New Delhi, India, scientific officer, 1953-1957; Central Electronics Engineering Research Institute, Pilani, Raj, India, assistant/deputy director, 1957-62, director, 1963-84; University of Michigan, research engineer, 1962-63; Bell Telephone Laboratories, research engineer, 1963; United Nations Development Program, national chief project coordinator, 1984-87; University of Maryland, College Park, visiting scientist, 1987-. **ORGANIZATIONS:** Institute of Electrical and Electronics Engineers, senior member, 1954-74, fellow, 1974-89, life fellow, 1989-; Institute of Electrical and Telecommunications Engineers, New Delhi, India, distinguished fellow, 1974-; Indian Academy of Sciences, Bangalore, India, fellow, 1976-. **HONORS/AWARDS:** Punjab University, Patiala, DSc, 1980; President of India, PADMA BHUSHAN, 1985; Institute of Electrical and Electronics Engineers, name in publication, The Century of Honors, 1985. **SPECIAL ACHIEVEMENTS:** Co-editor, Microwave Integrated Circuits, 1976; about 80 publications in scientific journals; Central Electronics Engineering Research Institute, Gold Shield, Inventions Promotion

Board, India, during term as director, 1978. **HOME ADDRESS:** 5803 Cherrywood Terrace, #301, Greenbelt, MD 20770. **BUSINESS ADDRESS:** Visiting Scientist, Laboratory of Plasma Research, University of Maryland, 1201 P Energy Res Bldg, College Park, MD 20742, (301)405-4916.

SINGH, BALDEV
Research scientist. Indo-American. **PERSONAL:** Born Jan 9, 1939, Takhtupura, Punjab, India; son of Bhajan Singh and Bhagwan Kaur; married Nakshatar Kaur Singh, Oct 29, 1967; children: Amrita Kaur, Nimrta Kaur. **EDUCATION:** State University of New York at Buffalo, PhD, 1967. **CAREER:** Sterling Winthrop, Pharmaceuticals Research Division, fellow, 1967-. **ORGANIZATIONS:** American Chemical Society. **SPECIAL ACHIEVEMENTS:** Forty publications and fifty US patents in the field of medicinal chemistry. **HOME ADDRESS:** 316 R Glad Way, Collegeville, PA 19426, (215)454-1079. **BUSINESS ADDRESS:** Fellow, Sterling Winthrop, Pharmaceuticals Research Division, Collegeville, PA 19426, (215)983-5367.

SINGH, BALWANT (BUNT)
Consulting company executive. Indo-American. **PERSONAL:** Born Jan 21, 1934, India; son of Dr & Mrs Autar Singh; married Joyce Brengarth, Dec 27, 1971; children: Tejpal, Prem, Davinder. **EDUCATION:** Aligarh University, India, BSc, 1953; Mathura Veterinary College, BVSc, AH, 1957; University of Missouri, MS, 1963, PhD, 1965. **CAREER:** Veterinary asst surgeon, director, 1957-61; University of Pittsburgh, research associate, 1966-72, research assistant professor, 1972-77, research associate professor, 1977-86; Maximed Corporation, vice president, 1986-88; Health Resources International Inc, president, 1981-; Sci-Tech Corporation, president, 1986-. **ORGANIZATIONS:** American Society for Microbiology, 1966-; American Public Health Association, 1968-; American Venereal Disease Association, 1970-82; Conference of Public Health Veterinarians, 1972-; International Health Society, life member, 1974-; International Epidemiological Association, 1975-; Rotary International Club, president, 1988-89, governor, 1995-96; United Nations Association, board directors, 1990-; WHO Collaborating Center, associate director, 1977-85; International Health Society, chairman, Res Com, 1979-81; Brother's Brother Foundation, trustee, 1980-. **HONORS/AWARDS:** Sigma Xi, elected, 1967; National Academy of Veterinary Sciences, fellow, 1993; Mother of India Award, Glory of India Award, selected 1992; Gamma Sigma Delta, elected, 1964. **SPECIAL ACHIEVEMENTS:** Author of numerous publications.

SINGH, GURDIAL
Research scientist (retired). Indo-American. **PERSONAL:** Born Aug 15, 1934, Punjab, India; son of Foja Singh (deceased) and Nikko; married Nirmal K Singh, Mar 6, 1960; children: Balvinder, Gurinder, Ravinder. **EDUCATION:** PhD, 1964. **CAREER:** E I Du Pont de Nemours and Co, senior research scientist, until 1993. **HOME ADDRESS:** 1829 Graves Road, Hockessin, DE 19707, (302)239-3189.

SINGH, HARPAL
Educator. Indo-American. **PERSONAL:** Born Aug 16, 1941, India; son of Prem Singh (deceased) & Harbans Kaur; married Harbhajan Kaur; children: Reema, Arvinpal, Amitpal. **EDUCATION:** Punjab University, India, BS, zoology, MS, zoology, 1962; University of Tennessee, PhD, biological sciences, 1970, MPH, 1974. **CAREER:** Savannah State College, professor of biology, MARC Program, director, medical technology, coordinator, 1974-. **ORGANIZATIONS:** Env Health Society of America; Reproductive Toxicology Society. **HONORS/AWARDS:** NIH-NIGMS-MARC, Honors Undergraduate Research Award, 1985-95; NIH, Minority Biomedical Research Grant, 1977-87; Tennessee Governor, Honorary Citizen Award, 1970. **SPECIAL ACHIEVEMENTS:** Twenty-five publications on reproductive toxicology. **BUSINESS ADDRESS:** Professor of Biology, Savannah State College, PO Box 20425, Drew Griffith Bldg, Room 118, Savannah, GA 31404, (912)356-2313.

SINGH, JAGBIR
Educator. Indo-American. **PERSONAL:** Born Jan 2, 1940, Baraut, Uttar Pradesh, India; son of Birbal Singh and Hoshiari Singh; married Veena Singh, Aug 25, 1968; children: Rajesh, Seema, Sapna, Sikha. **EDUCATION:** Agra University, BSc, 1958; Muslim University, Aligarh, MS, statistics, 1960; Florida State University, PhD, statistics, 1967. **CAREER:** Ohio State University, assistant professor, 1967-74; Indian Agricultural Research Statistics Institute, New Dehli, India, senior professor, 1977-78; Meerut University, India, Institute of Advanced Studies, professor, 1983-84; Temple University, associate professor, 1974-77, professor, 1978-. **ORGANIZATIONS:** Editorial Board of the

Journal of Sensory Studies; International Statistical Institute, 1983. **HONORS/ AWARDS:** Aligarh University, Gold Medal for 1st position in MSc, 1960; Temple University, Excellent Employee Award, 1989, Stauffer Award, 1993. **SPECIAL ACHIEVEMENTS:** Over 30 research publications in refereed journals on statistical methods; author, Statistical Methods in Food and Consumer Research, Academic Press, 1983. **BUSINESS ADDRESS:** Professor of Statistics, Temple University, Speakman Hall, Philadelphia, PA 19122, (215)204-5069.

SINGH, KIM
Computer entrepreneur, community activist. Indo-American. **PERSONAL:** Born Aug 23, 1957, New Delhi, India; son of Rajendar Jolly & Surjit Singh Teja Singh. **EDUCATION:** University of Bombay, BS, physics, math, 1977, MBA, 1985; Indian Institute of Science, BE, computer science, 1980; University of Oregon, computer graphics, 1990; University of California, Los Angeles, communications, 1992. **CAREER:** Unisys Corp, software systems, computer engineer, 1980-82; Sheraton Hotels, systems manager, 1983-85; The CAD Source, president, 1986-; South Asian AIDS Action, director, 1992-. **ORGANIZATIONS:** Stonewall Democratic Club, Political Affairs, vice president; California Democratic Party, Asian Pacific Caucus, Southern California, secretary, currently; South Asian AIDS Action, director; 47th Assembly District, secretary; People of Color Public Policy Institute, co-chair. **HONORS/ AWARDS:** University of Bombay, Gold Medal for Securing Highest Rank in University, 1985; The CAD Source, Outstanding Achievement Award, Sales, 1992; Indian Institute of Science, awards for debate, dramatics and art, 1980. **SPECIAL ACHIEVEMENTS:** Lives on the Line, play, actor, 1993; conference of Indian Activists, Chicago, attendee, 1992; Democratic National Convention, New York, delegate, 1992; International AIDS Conference, Amsterdam, delegate, 1992; Creating Change Conference, Los Angeles, Host Committee, 1992. **HOME ADDRESS:** 12228 Venice Blvd, Ste 171, Los Angeles, CA 90066, (310)390-2193. **BUSINESS ADDRESS:** President, The CAD Source, 6245 Bristol Parkway, Suite 214, Culver City, CA 90230, (310)281-5909.

SINGH, MADAN MOHAN
Consulting engineer. Indo-American. **PERSONAL:** Born Nov 8, 1933, Quetta, Baluchistan, Pakistan; son of Mohan Singh and Inder Kaur; married Sartaj I Singh, Aug 19, 1964; children: Aman. **EDUCATION:** Indian School of Mines and Applied Geology, AISM, 1956; University of Illinois at Urbana-Champaign, MS, 1957; Pennsylvania State University, PhD, 1961. **CAREER:** Gulf Research and Development Co, mechanics laboratory research engineer, 1961-63; Pennsylvania State University, asst prof, director, rock mechanics laboratory, 1963-66; IIT Research Institute, senior engineer, rock mechanics, 1966-68, manager, soil and rock mechanics, 1968-74; Foundation Sciences Inc, vice president, 1974-75; Engineers Interntional Inc, president, 1975-. **ORGANIZATIONS:** Society for Mining, Metallurgy, & Exploration, numerous committees & positions, 1956-; American Institute of Mining, Metallurgical, & Petroleum Engineers, 1956-; Consulting Engineers Council of Illinois; ASCE, 1973-; AAAS, life member, 1965-; Institute of Shaft Drilling, charter member, 1982-; International Society for Rock Mechanics, 1964-; British Tunneling Society, 1977-; American Underground-Space Associate, 1976-; Illinois Mining Institute, 1956-. **HONORS/AWARDS:** US National Committee for Rock Mechanics, 1977-80; Intrepretion/Scaling of Laboratory, subpanel, co-chair, 1979-81; US National Committee on Tunneling Technology, 1974-76; ASCE, fellow, 1985; Illinois Minority and Female Business Enterprise Council, Minority Vendor of the Year, 1990; Society for Mining, Metallurgy, and Exploration Inc, Graduate Division Student Paper Prize, 1958. **SPECIAL ACHIEVEMENTS:** Published over 100 technical publications; presented several lectures in the US and abroad; chaired 6 national conferences, including the Silver Anniversary Rock Mechanics Symposium. **BUSINESS ADDRESS:** President, Engineers International Inc, 2764 Golfview Dr, Naperville, IL 60563-9199, (708)527-2430.

SINGH, MADHO
Educator. Indo-American. **PERSONAL:** Born Apr 25, 1936, Mandha, Rajasthan, India; son of Shri Kalyan Singh and Gulab K Singh; married Keshar K Singh, Feb 5, 1957; children: Indira, Vidhyotma, Vijaya, Jyotsana, Krishna Kumar. **EDUCATION:** University of Rajasthan, BScAg, 1954; Agra University, MScAg, 1956; University of Minnesota, PhD, 1965; University of Chicago, post-doctorate, 1966. **CAREER:** University of Minnesota, research assistant, 1961-64; University of Texas, Austin, research associate, 1968-69; University of Chicago, research scientist, 1965-66; Udaipur University, reader, 1966-68; State University of New York, assistant professor, 1969-73, associate

professor, 1974-87, professor, 1988-. **ORGANIZATIONS:** Genetics Society of America; Human Genetics Society of America; Biometrics Society; Society for the Study of Evolution; New York Academy of Sciences. **HONORS/ AWARDS:** University of Rajastham, Gold Medal, 1955; Rajastham University, Merit Scholarships, 1952-56; SUNY Research Foundation, Research Award, 1970, 1971. **SPECIAL ACHIEVEMENTS:** University of Hawaii, Honolulu, Medical School, visiting professor, 1974; Cornell University, visiting fellow, 1976. **BUSINESS ADDRESS:** Professor, Dept of Biology, State University of New York, Science 1, Oneonta, NY 13820, (607)436-3705.

SINGH, NATASHA. *See* Obituaries.

SINGH, PRITHIPAL
Medical diagnostic devices company executive. Indo-American. **PERSONAL:** Born Apr 6, 1939, Amritsar, Punjab, India; married Rajinder, Mar 14, 1963; children: Satinder, Bobby. **EDUCATION:** Punjab University, India, BS, 1959; Benaras University, India, MS, chemistry, 1961; University of Toronto, Canada, PhD, 1967; University of Southampton, England, postdoctorate, 1969. **CAREER:** Syva, A Syntex Co, vice president, 1970-85; Idetek, Inc, senior vice president & director, 1985-88; ChemTrak, Inc, president & CEO, 1988-93, chairman & CEO, 1993-. **ORGANIZATIONS:** American Chemical Society; American Society of Clinical Chemists; Royal Chemical Society, London; Commonwealth Club. **HONORS/AWARDS:** British Council, England, fellowship, 1969; Canada, Commonwealth Scholarship, 1967. **SPECIAL ACHIEVEMENTS:** Invented key technologies and implemented programs to develop, manufacture and market commercially successful novel diagnostic products; holder of over one hundred patents; various publications; director of privately- and publicly-held companies. **BUSINESS ADDRESS:** Chairman & CEO, ChemTrak, Inc, 929 E Arques Ave, Sunnyvale, CA 94086, (408)773-8156.

SINGH, RAJENDRA
Educator. Indo-American. **PERSONAL:** Born Feb 13, 1950, Dhampur, Uttar Pradesh, India; son of Raghubir Singh and Ishwar Kali; married Venna Singh, Jun 24, 1979; children: Rohit, Arun. **EDUCATION:** Birla Institute, Pilani, India, BS, 1971; University of Roorkee, India, MS, 1973; Purdue University, PhD, 1975. **CAREER:** Purdue University, graduate instructor, 1973-75; Syracuse University, adjunct lecturer, 1977-79; Carrier Corp, sr engineer, 1975-79; University of California, Berkeley, visiting professor, 1987-88; Ohio State University, assistant professor, associate professor, professor, 1979-, Acoustics and Dynamics Laboratory, director, currently. **ORGANIZATIONS:** American Society of Mechanical Engineers, fellow; Acoustical Society of America, fellow; Institute of Noise Control Eng, noise control methods committee, chair; National Conference Fluid Power, board of governors; American Society of Heating, Refrig, & Air-Cond Engineers; Applied Acoustical Journal, advisory board; Marcel Dekker, advisory board. **HONORS/AWARDS:** Am Soc Eng Educ, George Westinghouse Award, 1993; Inst Noise Control Eng, Excellence in Education, 1989; Ohio State University, Harrison Faculty Award, 1990, Research Awards, 1983, 1987, 1991; Purdue University, R H Kohr Award, 1975. **SPECIAL ACHIEVEMENTS:** 1 patent; published over 70 journal articles; 25 papers in refereed proceedings & books; 65 conference papers; 1 book, proceedings editor, 1973-. **HOME ADDRESS:** 4772 Belfield Ct, Dublin, OH 43017, (614)761-8855. **BUSINESS ADDRESS:** Professor of Mechanical Engineering, Director of Acoustics and Dynamics Laboratory, The Ohio State University, 206 W 18th Ave, 1065 Robinson Lab, Columbus, OH 43210-1107, (614)292-9044.

SINGH, SANT P.
Physician, educator, health services administrator. Indo-American. **PERSONAL:** Born Oct 2, 1936, Anokh Singhwala, Punjab, India; son of Jarnail Singh & Harbans Kaur; married Satinder K Singh, Apr 28, 1968; children: Kiran P. **EDUCATION:** Punjab University, Chandigarh, India, MBBS, 1959; McGill University, MSc, 1973. **CAREER:** Bergen Pines County Hospital, resident, medicine, 1961-63; Philadelphia General Hospital, endocrinology fellow, 1963-64, 1964-65; Downstate Medical Center, endocrinology fellow, 1965-66; Royal Victoria Hospital, McGill University, research fellow, 1966-70; Brooklyn-Cumberland Medical Center, endocrinologist, 1970-73; VA Medical Center, associate chief of staff, 1973-; Chicago Medical School, professor, Division of Endocrinology-Metabolism chief, 1974-. **ORGANIZATIONS:** American College of Physicians, fellow; American Diabetes Association; Endocrine Society. **HONORS/AWARDS:** Chicago Medical School, Lawrence R Medoff Award, 1990; Veterans Administration, Performance Award, 1976; American College of Physicians, fellowship, 1973; Medical

Research Council of Canada, research fellowship, 1970. **HOME PHONE:** (708)295-7754. **BUSINESS ADDRESS:** Chief, Division of Endocrinology-Metabolism, Professor of Medicine and Physiology, Chicago Medical School, 3333 Greenbay Rd, North Chicago, IL 60064, (708)688-1900.

SINGH, SHARON
Community liaison. Indo-American. **PERSONAL:** Born Jan 24, 1965. **CAREER:** California Democratic Women's Caucus, officer, currently; Vic Fazio, congressman 3rd district, community liaison, currently. **HONORS/AWARDS:** Unruh Assembly Fellow, 1989-90. **SPECIAL ACHIEVEMENTS:** First person of Indian descent to be officer of California Democratic Women's Caucus. **BUSINESS ADDRESS:** Community Liaison, Vic Fazio - Congressman, 722 Main St Ste B, Woodland, CA 95695, (916)666-5521. *

SINGH, SURENDRA PAL
Educator, physicist. Indo-American. **PERSONAL:** Born Jun 24, 1953, Mawana, Uttar Pradesh, India; son of Kharak Singh & Shanti Devi; married Reeta Vyas; children: Savith R Chauhan. **EDUCATION:** Banaras Hindu University, Varanasi, BSc (honors), 1973, MSc, 1975; University of Rochester, PhD, physics, 1982. **CAREER:** University of Arkansas, professor, 1982-. **ORGANIZATIONS:** American Physical Society; Optical Society of America; Indian Physics Association. **HONORS/AWARDS:** Joint Institute for Lab Astrophysics, visiting fellow, 1989-90; University of Rochester, Dexter Award, 1982. **SPECIAL ACHIEVEMENTS:** More than 50 refereed publications in scientific journal and books, 1978-; proficiency in English and Hindi. **BUSINESS ADDRESS:** Professor, Dept of Physics, University of Arkansas, Fayetteville, AR 72701, (501)575-5930.

SINGH, VIJAY P.
Educator. Indo-American. **PERSONAL:** Born Jul 15, 1946, Agra, Uttar Pradesh, India; son of Gurdayal Singh and Bhagwan Kumari; married Anita Singh; children: Vinay, Arti. **EDUCATION:** U P Agricultural University, BS, 1967; University of Guelph, MS, 1970; Colorado State University, PhD, 1974. **CAREER:** New Mexico Tech, assistant professor, 1974-77; George Washington University, associate research professor, 1977-78; Mississippi State University, associate professor, 1978-81; Louisiana State University, professor and coordinator, 1981-. **ORGANIZATIONS:** American Institute of Hydrology, Louisiana Section, president, 1988-; US CID, Crop Water Use Committee, vice chairman, 1991-; AWRA; ASCE; IAH; American Biographical Institute, advisor, 1981-; American Engineering Collegiate Award, nominator, 1992-; consultant to state, local, natl and intl organizations. **HONORS/AWARDS:** Various conferences/symposiums, director; 3 professional organizations, fellow; Australia, India, Italy, Switzerland, visiting professor; conference keynote speaker, session chairman, panelist; recipient of 10 awards. **SPECIAL ACHIEVEMENTS:** Author of 3 books; editor of 9 books on hydrology and water; author/co-author of 350 journal articles, book reviews, technical reports; editor/editorial boards of 7 journals, and book series. **HOME ADDRESS:** 1043 Beckenham Dr, Baton Rouge, LA 70808, (504)769-7404. **BUSINESS ADDRESS:** Professor, Dept of Civil Engineering, Coordinator, Water Resources Program, Louisiana State University, 3509 Ceba Bldg, Baton Rouge, LA 70803-6405, (504)388-6697.

SINGH, VIJAY PAL
Educator. Indo-American. **PERSONAL:** Born Jul 25, 1947, New Delhi, India; son of Sh Ram Pal Singh & Smt Kala Devi; married Carolyn Diana Singh, Dec 22, 1972; children: Vincent Ajay, Gordon Ranjeet. **EDUCATION:** Indian Institute of Technology, Delhi, BTech, electrical engineering, 1968; University of Minnesota, Minneapolis, MS, electrical engineering, 1970, PhD, electrical engineering, 1974. **CAREER:** University of Delaware, research assistant professor, 1974-76; Photon Power Inc, research engineer, 1976-80; Photon Energy Inc, research manager, 1980-83; University of Texas, El Paso, professor, 1983-. **ORGANIZATIONS:** IEEE; SID. **HONORS/AWARDS:** 6th International Workshop on Electroluminescence, technical program chairman, May 11-13, 1992. **SPECIAL ACHIEVEMENTS:** Author of many patents and publications. **BUSINESS ADDRESS:** Professor, Dept of Electrical Engineering, University of Texas, El Paso, El Paso, TX 79968, (915)747-6972.

SINGHA, NABAGHANA SHYAM
Choreographer, performer, educator. Indo-American. **PERSONAL:** Born Sep 11, 1939, Silchar, Dt Cachar, Assam, India; son of Gour Mohan Singha (deceased) & Atolai Devi (deceased); married Christel Stevens, Sep 25, 1982; children: Kamallata, Francisca Noopur, Nabeen Leigh. **EDUCATION:** Sri Sri Govindajee Nartanalaya, Imphal, Manipur, Jyotirmoy Degree, 1954; Manipuri

Nartanalaya, Calcutta, Nartanacharya Degree, 1991. **CAREER:** Maryland National Capital Park and Planning Commission, Arts Division, featured performer: "Arts Alive!" (series of cultural arts assemblies bringing music and dances of India to students in Maryland). **HONORS/AWARDS:** Maryland State Arts Council, Choreography Award, 1990; Prince George's Arts Council, Choreography Award, 1989, 1990, 1993. **HOME ADDRESS:** 4216 Underwood St, University Park, MD 20782, (301)864-6976.

SINGHAL, AVINASH CHANDRA
Educator, research administrator. Indo-American. **PERSONAL:** Born Nov 4, 1941, Aligarh, Uttar Pradesh, India; son of Shiam Sunder Singhal and Pushpa Lata Singhal; married Uma, Sep 5, 1967; children: Ritu Chanchal, Anita, Neil Raj Dave. **EDUCATION:** Massachusetts Institute of Technology, ScD, 1964. **CAREER:** Central Bldg Research, director, 1992-93; Arizona State University, professor, 1977-. **ORGANIZATIONS:** American Society of Civil Engineer, fellow, 1977. **HONORS/AWARDS:** Institute of Civil Engineers, Dennison Scholar, 1960; MIT, McLintock Fellow, 1960-62; Institute of Structural Engineers, London, Henry Adams Medal, 1972. **MILITARY SERVICE:** National Cadet Corp, 1953-57. **HOME ADDRESS:** 2631 South El Marino, Mesa, AZ 85202-7302, (602)839-1652. **BUSINESS ADDRESS:** Professor, Dept of Civil Engineering, Arizona State University, ECE 5306, Tempe, AZ 85287-5306, (602)965-6901.

SINGHVI, SAMPAT M.
Pharmaceutical company executive. Indo-American. **PERSONAL:** Born Oct 14, 1947, Jodhpur, Rajasthan, India; son of Manakchand R Singhvi and Jethi Singhvi; married Usha Singhvi, Jul 17, 1971; children: Nikmil S, Nilima S. **EDUCATION:** Birla Institute of Technology & Science, BPharm, 1967; Philadelphia College of Pharmacy & Science, MS, 1970; State University of New York, Buffalo, PhD, 1974; Ridger College, MBA, 1979. **CAREER:** E R Squibb & Sons, research investigator, 1974-78, senior research investigator, 1978-79, research group leader, 1979-88, associate director, 1988-89; Bristol-Myers Squibb, associate director, 1989-. **ORGANIZATIONS:** American Association of Pharmaceutical Scientists, founder, executive council, chair, reg aff section, 1992-93; American Pharmaceutical Association, 1975-; International Soc Study of Xenobiotics, 1985-; Drug Information Association, 1988-; American Society Pharmacol & Exprmntl Therap, 1979-; Regulatory Aff Prof Society, 1988-. **HONORS/AWARDS:** Pharmacy Honor Society, Rho Chi, 1970; Birla Institute of Tech & Science, Gold Medal of the University, 1967. **BUSINESS ADDRESS:** Associate Director, Bristol-Myers Squibb, PO Box 4000, Princeton, NJ 08543-4000, (609)252-4443.

SINGPURWALLA, NOZER DARABSHA
Educator. Indo-American. **PERSONAL:** Born Apr 8, 1939, Hubli, Karnataka, India; son of Darabsha Singpurwalla and Goolan Singpurwalla; married Norah Jackson Singpurwalla, Jun 15, 1969; children: Rachel Goolcher Kathleen, Darius Jonathan Nozer. **EDUCATION:** Karnatak University, int science, 1956; B V Bhoomraddi College, BS, 1959; Rutgers University, MS, 1964; New York University, PhD, 1968. **CAREER:** Stanford University, visiting professor of statistics, 1978; Carnegie Mellon University, visiting professor of statistics, tech staff member (software inst), 1990; Virginia Polytechic Institute, C C Garvin Professor of Computer Science and of Statistics, 1991; George Washington University, professor of operation research, statistics, distinguished research professor, 1969-. **ORGANIZATIONS:** American Stat Association, fellow, 1974; Institute of Math Stat, fellow, 1982; Intl Stat Inst, 1978; Army Research Office, Wilks Award, 1984; George Washington University, Trachtenberg Prize for Scholarship, 1991. **SPECIAL ACHIEVEMENTS:** Co-author "Methods for Statistics Anal of Reliability Data," 1974; co-author "Reliability and Fault Trees," 1978; author/co-author of over 125 publications in engineering, statistics, mathematics & operation research journals. **BIOGRAPHICAL SOURCES:** Reliability Review, vol 8, no 2, p 11, 1988; REAJ (in Japanese) vol 7, p 40-47, 1985. **BUSINESS ADDRESS:** Professor of Operations Research & Statistics, George Washington University, 707 22nd St NW, Staughton Hall, Washington, DC 20052, (202)994-7515.

SINHA, AKHOURI A.
Educator, federal official. Indo-American. **PERSONAL:** Born Dec 17, 1933, Charamanpur, Bihar, India; son of Mr & Mrs Akhouni Chandra B Sinha; married Dorothy Pamer Sinha, Sep 29, 1979. **EDUCATION:** University of Allahabad, India, BS, 1954; University of Patna, India, MS, 1956; University of Missouri, PhD, 1965; University of Wisconsin, Madison, postdoctorate, 1965. **CAREER:** Veteran Affairs Medical Center, research scientist, 1969-; University of Minnesota, professor, 1981-. **ORGANIZATIONS:** American Associa-

tion for Cancer Research, 1990-; Indian Science Congress; American Society for Cell Biology; Society for Basic Urologic Research; International Society of Differentiation, American Association of Anatomists; Society for the Study of Reproduction. **HONORS/AWARDS:** US, NSF sponsored expedition to Antarctica, 1972, 1974. **SPECIAL ACHIEVEMENTS:** The Anatomical Record, associate editor, 1990-; Microscopy Research Technique, guest editor, 1993; about 70 published papers, book chapters on prostate cancer research; biology of reproduction research; proficient in English & Hindi. **BIOGRAPHICAL SOURCES:** 151 Science Citation Index, 1993. **HOME PHONE:** (612)724-4871. **BUSINESS ADDRESS:** Professor, Genetics and Cell Biology, University of Minnesota, VA Medical Center, One Veterans Drive, Bldg 70, Research Service (151), Minneapolis, MN 55417, (612)725-2000.

SINHA, DIPEN N.
Physicist. Indo-American. **PERSONAL:** Born Mar 9, 1951, Mosaboni Mines, Bihar, India; son of Mrigen Sinha (deceased) & Narayani Sinha; married Barbara Ann Sinha, Sep 27, 1975; children: Naveen Neil. **EDUCATION:** St Xavier's College, BSc (with honors), 1970; Indian Institute of Technology, Kharagpur, MSc, 1972, DIIT, 1973; Portland State University, PhD, 1980. **CAREER:** Rockwell International, member of technical staff, 1983-86; Los Alamos National Lab, post-doctoral fellow, 1980-83, physicist, 1986-. **ORGANIZATIONS:** American Physical Society, 1975-. **HONORS/AWARDS:** Research & Development Magazine, R&D 100 Award, 1991; Popular Science, 100 Award, 1992. **SPECIAL ACHIEVEMENTS:** Over 40 publications; 2 patents granted and 3 pending; developer of the Acoustic Resonance Spectroscopy Technique for the use in chemical weapons treaty verification, both bilateral US-Russia and international. **BUSINESS ADDRESS:** Physicist, Los Alamos National Lab, MS D429, Los Alamos, NM 87545, (505)667-0062.

SINHA, NIRMAL K.
Engineer, community activist. Indo-American. **PERSONAL:** Born Sep 17, 1939, Dangarpar, Faridpur, Bangladesh; son of Nanigopal and Bela; married Tripti, Jan 22, 1965; children: Tanima, Tanushree. **EDUCATION:** Presidency College, Calcutta, India, intermediate science, 1958; Jadavpur University, Calcutta, India, BMechE, 1962; Polytechnic Institute of New York, MMechE, 1975; Ohio State University, mgmt, 1985. **CAREER:** Lynx Machinery Ltd, Indian, engineer, 1962; Mining Machinery Co, India, exec engr, 1963-70; Robins Engineers, design engineer, 1970-72; American Electric Power Service Corp, sr engr, 1972-93; State of Ohio, Civil Rights Commission, commissioner, 1991-. **ORGANIZATIONS:** American Society of Mechanical Engineers, 1978-; American Society of Testing & Materials, 1978-; Engineering and Business Consultant, 1993-; March of Dimes, Central Ohio, director, 1989-; International Centerboard, director, 1990-; Main Street Business Association, director, 1989-; Columbus International Program, director, 1990-; National Federation of Indian American Association, director, 1988-; Indian American Forum for Political Education, 1992-; Federation of Asian Indiansof Central Ohio, president, 1988, 1989, board of directors, 1990-92; Asian Indian Alliance of Ohio, 1993-. **HONORS/AWARDS:** Governor of Ohio, Ohio Civil Rights Comm, appointed commissioner, 1991; Federation of Asian Indian Associations of Central Ohio, Outstanding Achievement Award, 1990; India League of Ohio, Outstanding Contribution Award, 1992; Global Organization of People of Indian Origin, Founder Member Award, 1989. **SPECIAL ACHIEVEMENTS:** Civil rights article in journals, 1991-92; active in getting minority status for Asian Indians in Ohio, 1992; selected US Delegates to China & Soviet Union as a materials handling expert, 1985-90. **BIOGRAPHICAL SOURCES:** An Intrepid Spirit, Lotus, Aug 1991; various other articles. **HOME ADDRESS:** 6470 Meadowbrook Circle, Worthington, OH 43085, (614)846-4638.

SINHA, SUNIL KUMAR
Researcher, research manager. Indo-American. **PERSONAL:** Born Sep 13, 1939, Calcutta, India; son of Sushil Kumar & Romola Sinha; married Lonny Sinha, Jan 27, 1962; children: Arjun, Ranjan. **EDUCATION:** Cambridge University, BA, 1960, PhD, physics, 1964. **CAREER:** Iowa State University, physics, assistant professor, 1966-68, associate professor, 1968-73, professor, 1973-75; Argonne National Laboratory, neutron scattering, senior physicist, group head, 1975-82; Brookhaven National Laboratory, x-ray physics, group leader, 1989-90; Exxon Research & Engineering Co, condensed matter research, section head, senior research associate, 1983-. **ORGANIZATIONS:** American Physical Society, fellow, 1982-, Division of Condensed Matter Physics, executive committee, 1988-91; Materials Research Society, 1984-; American Crystallographic Association, 1988-; Indian Physics Association. **HONORS/AWARDS:** Guggenheim Foundation, Fellowship, 1983; US De-

partment of Energy, Outstanding Research Award, 1981; Japan Society for Promotion of Science, Visiting Fellowship, 1977. **SPECIAL ACHIEVEMENTS:** Theory of Diffuse X-ray Scattering from Rough Surfaces, 1988; Discovery of Antiferromagnetism in High-Tc materials, 1987; Theory of Scattering by Fractals, 1984; Existence of Magnetism & Superconductivity in Magnetic Superconductors, 1980; Measurement of Phonon Dispersion in Quantum Crystals, 1972. **BUSINESS ADDRESS:** Senior Research Associate, Corporate Research, Exxon Research & Engineering, Rte 22E, Annandale, NJ 08801, (908)730-2875.

SINHA, UDAY K.
Metallurgist. Indo-American. **PERSONAL:** Born Jan 5, 1938, Aurangabad, Bihar, India; son of Muneshwar Prasad (deceased) and Sunder Devi (deceased); married Geeta Sinha, Jun 18, 1962; children: Ashok, Anjale, Kalpana Rekha. **EDUCATION:** Bihar Institute of Technology, Sindri, India, BSc, metallurgy, 1960; New Mexico Institute of Mining & Technology, MS, 1970; Iowa State University, Ames, PhD, 1974. **CAREER:** Durgapur Steel Plant, India, foreman, 1961-67; Central Engineering & Design Bureau, India, design engineer, 1967-69; Ames Laboratory, ISU, research assistant, 1970-74; Southwire Co, senior consulting metallurgist, 1974-. **ORGANIZATIONS:** American Society for Metals, 1969-; Professional Engineer, Georgia, 1977-; BIT Alumni Association of North America, organizer. **SPECIAL ACHIEVEMENTS:** BIT Alumni Association of North America and offers 30 scholarships to students at BIT, Sindri, India; provide financial help to students of BIT Sindri coming to North American universities for graduate studies; received seven US patents related to developments in steel, copper, and alumnium making technology; published several technical papers. **HOME ADDRESS:** 145 Camp Dr, Carrollton, GA 30117, (404)834-8252. **BUSINESS PHONE:** (404)832-5035.

SINHA, YAGYA NAND
Scientist. Indo-American. **PERSONAL:** Born Oct 21, 1936, Rohua, Muzaffarpur, Bihar, India; son of Baidyanath Prasad & Rajeshwari Sinha; married Savitri, May 28, 1958; children: Manjula Pandey, Anita Verma, Suman Kumar, Arun Kumar. **EDUCATION:** Bihar Veterinary College, GBVC, 1957; Michigan State University, MS, 1964, PhD, 1967. **CAREER:** Bihar State Government, veterinary assistant surgeon, 1957-59; Livestock Research Station, Patna, research assistant, 1959-61; Michigan State University, graduate assistant, 1962-67; Cornell University, research associate, 1967-69; Scripps Clinic and Research Foundation, assistant member II, 1969-81; Whittier Institute, director of animal resources, 1982-, senior member, 1982-. **ORGANIZATIONS:** The Endocrine Society, 1973-; Society for Experimental Biology and Medicine, 1977-; American Association for the Advancement of Science, 1968-. **HONORS/AWARDS:** NIH, research grants. **SPECIAL ACHIEVEMENTS:** Over 100 scientific publications. **HOME ADDRESS:** 8385 Aries Rd, San Diego, CA 92126, (619)566-0073. **BUSINESS ADDRESS:** Senior Member, Whittier Institute for Diabetes & Endocrinology, 9894 Genesee Ave, La Jolla, CA 92037, (619)450-1280.

SIRCAR, RINA SCHYAMCHARAN
Educator, nun. Myanmar American/Indo-American. **PERSONAL:** Born Oct 23, 1938, Rangoon, Burma; daughter of Schyamcharan Sircar and Shnehalata. **EDUCATION:** Rangoon University, BA, Oriental studies, 1959, MA, Oriental phil, 1961, BL, law, 1963; Gujarat University, PhD, phil, 1974; California Institute of Asian Studies, PhD, Buddhist studies, 1976. **CAREER:** Rangoon University, professor, Oriental studies, 1959-71; Gujarat University, visiting professor, 1971-73; California Institute of Asian Studies, professor, 1974-80; California Institute of Integral Studies, professor, 1980-; Theravada Buddhist nun, currently. **ORGANIZATIONS:** Taungpulu Kaba-Aye Monastery, co-founder, 1981-. **HONORS/AWARDS:** World Buddhist Council of India, Dhammavidasanachariya, 1981, Dhammaratana, 1981; California Institute of Integral Studies, Haridas Chaudhuri Professor of South Asian and Comparative Philisophy, 1989. **SPECIAL ACHIEVEMENTS:** Publications: Buddha the Messenger of Hope, 1984; The Efficacy of Taking Refuge, 1983; "What We Need Now," in Voices of the Future, 1993; speaks Burmese, Hindi, Bengali, English, Pali; meditation teacher in the Burmese forest tradition of mahasatipatthanavipassana; established first Buddhist forest monastery in the United States; teaches and practices healing in the Buddhist tradition.

SISON, FREDILYN
Attorney, federal official. Filipino American. **PERSONAL:** Born Feb 13, 1963, Tarlac, Tarlac, Philippines; daughter of Linda Cruz Sison & Alfred Ibanez Sison. **EDUCATION:** Cornell University, BA, 1985; New York University School of Law, JD, 1988. **CAREER:** Ramsey County, Public De-

fender's Office; Hennepin County Attorney's Office; Oppenheimer Wolff & Donnelly; US Department of Justice, special assistant to the assistant attorney general, currently. **ORGANIZATIONS:** MN Minority Lawyers Association, president; National Lawyers Guild; MN Advocates for Human Rights; MN Hispanic Bar Association; MN Asian Pacific American Bar Association; Minnesota Women Lawyers. **HONORS/AWARDS:** MMLA, Community Service Award, 1990, Distinguished Service Award, 1993. **BUSINESS ADDRESS:** Spec Asst to Asst Attorney General, US Dept of Justice, Criminal Div, 10th & Constitution Aves NW, Rm 2116, Washington, DC 20530, (202)514-9541.

SIU, NANCY (NANCY SIU CHANG)

Mortgage company accountant. Chinese American. **PERSONAL:** Born Jun 16, 1940, Oriente, Cuba; daughter of Amanda Tamayo Barcelo and Siu Tu-Yi; married Manuel Fu-Kin Chang (divorced); children: Merida M Chang. **EDUCATION:** Escuela Profesional De Comercio, bachelor's degree, accounting; University of Miami, J J Koubek M Center, corporate & personal income taxes, 1975-76; Century 21, real estate license, 1986. **CAREER:** C Lao & Associates FNC, accountant, office mgr, 1973-90; Sanson, Kline, Sacomino & Co, accountant, 1990; Prime Mortgage Investors, chief financial officer, secretary, 1990-. **ORGANIZATIONS:** Cuban Accountants in Exile. **HOME ADDRESS:** 6471 SW 20th St, Miami, FL 33155.

SIU, YUM-TONG

Educator, researcher. Chinese American. **PERSONAL:** Born May 6, 1943, Canton, Quandong, China; son of Hok-Chow Siu and Siu-Har Lee; married Sau-Fong Selina Wong, Jun 17, 1967; children: Brian Yu-Cheng, Alan Yu-Hao. **EDUCATION:** University of Hong Kong, BA, 1963; University of Minnesota, MA, 1964; Princeton University, PhD, 1966. **CAREER:** Purdue University, asst prof of mathematics; University of Notre Dame, asst prof of mathematics, 1967-70; Yale University, assoc prof of mathematics, 1970-72, assoc prof of mathematics, 1972-78; Stanford University, prof of mathematics, 1978-82; Gottingen Academy of Sciences, Gauss Visiting Prof, 1980; Harvard University, prof of mathematics, 1982-. **ORGANIZATIONS:** Hong Kong University of Science & Technology, science advisory committee, 1990-94; University of Hong Kong, external examiner in mathematics, 1991-94; University of Malaysia, external examiner in mathematics, 1973; Natl Academy of Science, committee on mathematics, 1985; Journal of Differential Geometry, editor, 1986-89; Annals of Mathematics, associate editor, 1980-83. **HONORS/ AWARDS:** Sloan Foundation, Fellow, 1971-73; Guggenheim Foundation, Fellow, 1985-86; University of Hong Kong, Honorary Doctor of Science degree, 1990; Gottingen Academy of Sciences, corresponding member, 1993; Stefan Bergman Trust, Stefan Bergman Prize, 1993. **SPECIAL ACHIEVEMENTS:** Co-author, Gap Sheaves & Extension of Coherent Analytic Subsheaves, 1971; author, Techniques of Extension of Analytic Objects, 1974; lectures on Hermitian-Einstein Metrics for Stable Bundles and Kahler-Einstein Metrics, 1987. **BUSINESS ADDRESS:** William Elwood Byerly Professor of Mathematics, Harvard University, Science Center, 1 Oxford St, Cambridge, MA 02138, (617)495-3790.

SIY, JAMES ANDREW

Physician. Chinese American/Filipino American. **PERSONAL:** Born Jun 4, 1967, Manila, Philippines; son of Lucio Co Siy and Conchita Gue Siy. **EDUCATION:** University of Wisconsin, BS, economics, 1988; University of Wisconsin Medical School, MD, 1992. **CAREER:** Mayo Clinic, resident, internal medicine, 1992-. **ORGANIZATIONS:** AMA. **HONORS/AWARDS:** Phi Beta Kappa, 1988. **HOME ADDRESS:** 1151 Plummer Circle, Rochester, MN 55902, (507)288-2775.

SO, MAGDALENE YEE-HUEN

Scientist, educator. Chinese American. **PERSONAL:** Born Aug 16, 1949, Hong Kong; daughter of Patrick Kwok-Chu So (deceased) and Josephine Hung-Kwan Yu-So (deceased); divorced. **EDUCATION:** University of California, Berkeley, BA, bacteriology, 1971; University of Washington, PhD, microbiology, 1976. **CAREER:** Cold Spring Harbor Labs, NY, sr scientist, 1980-83; Scripps Clinic & Research Foundation, La Jolla, associate mbr, 1983-91; Oregon Health Sciences University, Dept of Microbiology & Immunology, chmn, professor, 1991-. **ORGANIZATIONS:** American Society for Microbiology. **SPECIAL ACHIEVEMENTS:** Over 50 publications in major scientific journals. **BUSINESS ADDRESS:** Chairperson, Dept of Microbiology & Immunology, Oregon Health Sciences University, 3181 SW Sam Jackson Park Rd, L220, Portland, OR 97201-3098.

SO, RONALD MING CHO

Educator. Hong Kong American. **PERSONAL:** Born Nov 26, 1939, Hong Kong; son of Tsang Yee So and Grace W K Chen So; married Mabel Y M Wu So, Aug 17, 1968; children: Winnie W N, Nelson S K. **EDUCATION:** University of Hong Kong, BSc (with honors), Engineering, 1962; McGill University, M Eng, 1966; Princeton University, MA, 1968, PhD, 1971. **CAREER:** Princeton University, research assistant, 1966-70; Union Camp Corporation, research scientist, 1970-72; Rutgers University, post-doctoral fellow, assistant research professor, 1972-76, Union College, adjunct professor, 1977-79; General Electric Co, mechanical engineer, 1976-81; Arizona State University, associate professor, 1981-83, professor, 1983-. **ORGANIZATIONS:** Institution of Mechanical Engineers, fellow; American Society of Mechanical Engineers, fellow; American Institute of Aeronautics and Astronautics, associate fellow; New York Academy of Sciences; Arizona-Nevada Academy of Sciences; Sigma Xi. **HONORS/AWARDS:** Commonwealth Scholarship, 1964-66; General Electric, Publication Award, 1981; Institution of Mechanical Engineers, London, England, Dugald Clerk Prize, 1990; University of Hong Kong, Honorary DSc Degree, 1993. **SPECIAL ACHIEVEMENTS:** Special Editor of: Combustion Science and Technology, 1988; Editor of: Near Wall Turbulent Flows, published 1993; associate editor: AIAA Journal, 1993-95; numerous other publications. **BUSINESS ADDRESS:** Professor, Dept of Mech & Aero Eng, Arizona State University, Tempe, AZ 85287-6106, (602)965-4119.

SO, YING HUNG

Chemical company researcher. Chinese American. **PERSONAL:** Born Apr 8, 1948, Hong Kong; son of Wah So and Yun-Yee Siao; married Dora Tsui Bing So, Apr 22, 1978; children: Albert Jin-Zen, Lisa Ming-Wai. **EDUCATION:** Chinese University of Hong Kong, Chung Chi College, BS, 1971; Colorado State University, PhD, 1977. **CAREER:** The Dow Chemical Co, sr research chemist, 1981-84, project leader, 1984-89, research leader, 1989-93, research associate, 1993-. **ORGANIZATIONS:** American Chemical Society, 1974-, Division of Polymer Chemistry, Division of Polymeric Materials Science & Engineering, Division of Organic Chemistry; The Chinese American Chemical Society, secretary, 1990-93. **SPECIAL ACHIEVEMENTS:** Author, numerous publications include: "Novel Thermoset Polybenzimidazoleamides," Macromolecules, p 516-520, vol 25, 1992; "Pyrolytic Preparation of Benzocyclobutenes in the Presence of a Diluent," Industrial & Engineering Chemisty Research, 1993; 5 patents, including: "Improved Process for Synthesis of Rigid Rod Heterocyclic Polymers," assigned to the Dow Chemical Company, 1993. **BUSINESS ADDRESS:** Research Associate, The Dow Chemical Company, 1702 Bldg, Midland, MI 48674, (517)636-9279.

SOGI, FRANCIS Y.

Attorney, museum board member. Japanese American. **PERSONAL:** Born Jun 9, 1923, Kona, HI. **EDUCATION:** University of Hawaii, BA, 1949; Fordham University School of Law, JD, 1952; Chuo University, Tokyo. **CAREER:** Kelley Drye & Warren, senior partner, currently; Tsuchiya Sakuragi & Sogi, Tokyo, senior partner, currently. **ORGANIZATIONS:** Pocantico Hills School District, board of education, 1974-82, president, 2 years; Japanese American Assn of New York, president, 1983-86, honorary president, 1986-, bd member, 25 years; Japanese American National Museum, Los Angeles, chairman of bd of trustees, currently, Natl Campaign Steering Committee; Asian American Federation of New York, board of directors; Whytes Trust Co Ltd, chairman of bd; Sogi Foundation, founder, trustee; Japanese American Citizen League Legacy Fund Investment Committee; PanAmerican Nikkei Assn; Sky Club; Japanese Chamber of Comerce & Industry; Nippon Club, NY; Tokyo American Club, Japan; American Bar Assn; Federal Bar Assn; New York Bar Assn; Washington DC Bar Assn; First Tokyo Bar Assn; Inter-Pacific Bar Assn; Intl Bar Assn; New York-Tokyo Sister City Committee. **HONORS/AWARDS:** Government of Japan, Order of Sacred Treasures, gold with rosettes, 1990. **SPECIAL ACHIEVEMENTS:** Representative of the East Coast of the US at the Enthronement Ceremonies of Emperor Akihito. **MILITARY SERVICE:** US Army, Occupation Forces, Counter Intelligence Corp, captain, World War II. **BUSINESS ADDRESS:** Senior Partner, Kelley Drye & Warren, 101 Park Ave, New York, NY 10178, (212)808-7850.

SOH, JOONG MIN (JAY)

Chemical company engineer. Korean American. **PERSONAL:** Born Oct 10, 1945, Inchun, Republic of Korea; son of Byung-Joo Soh and Hyesook Park; married Misook L Soh, Jan 18, 1975; children: Lawrence, Clara. **EDUCATION:** Seoul National University, BSME, 1972; Lehigh University, MSME, 1974. **CAREER:** Catalytic Inc, mech engr, 1974-77; National Airoil Co, director, R&D, 1977-79; Arco Chemical Co, sr consultant, 1979-92, engineering advisor, 1993-. **ORGANIZATIONS:** ASME, 1975-; AFRC, 1980-. **BUSINESS ADDRESS:** Engineering Advisor, Arco Chemical Co, 3801 Westchester Pike, Newtown Square, PA 19073, (610)359-4730.

SOHAL, HARJIT SINGH

Engineer. Indo-American. **PERSONAL:** Born Jan 5, 1944, Jullundur, Punjab, India; son of Gurbhajan Singh Sohal and Narinder Kaur Sohal; married Jagmani Sohal, Feb 28, 1971; children: Harjyot Singh, Gurjyot Kaur. **EDUCATION:** Punjab University, BScEng, 1965; University of Houston, MBA, 1976. **CAREER:** Crompton Greaves Ltd, asst branch mgr, 1965-72; Todd Shipyards Corp, electrical section head, 1973-76; Brown & Root Inc, lead electrical engr, 1976-78; Jacobs Engineering Group Inc, project mgr, 1978-. **ORGANIZATIONS:** State Board of Professional Engineers, registered, 1976-; IEEE, 1976-78; Society of Naval Architects & Marine Engrs, 1976-78; National Society of Professional Engrs, 1977-79; Texas Society of Professional Engrs, 1978. **SPECIAL ACHIEVEMENTS:** Author: "Hydrocutting," Hydrocarbon Processing Magazine, 1989. **BUSINESS ADDRESS:** Project Manager, Jacobs Engineering Group Inc, 4848 Loop Central Dr, Houston, TX 77081.

SOHN, DAVID YOUNGWHAN

Communications executive. Korean American. **PERSONAL:** Born Feb 8, 1943, Chung-Nam, Republic of Korea; son of Kum Sohn & Joon P Sohn; married Kim Mokjah, Jun 15, 1968; children: Gene Pyoung, Edward Genesuk. **EDUCATION:** Korean Military Academy, BS, elec eng, 1963; Rutgers University, MS, elec eng, 1972; Harvard University, Owner Management Program, 1991. **CAREER:** Varityper Word Processing Systems, software project manager, 1972-75; Lockheed Electronic Co, sr programmer, analyst, 1975-79; Computer Science Corp, principal engineer, 1979-80; Planning Research Corp, software manager, 1980-81; International Comp & Tele, president, CEO, chairman, 1981-. **ORGANIZATIONS:** International Computer & Tele, board member, 1981-; Montgomery County High Tech Council, board member, 1989-; Asian Pacific Council, board member, 1989-; Korean-American Scholarship Foundation, board member, 1990-; Montgomery United Way, council member, 1992-; Asian American Business Development Council, council member, currently; Korean Scientists & Engineers Association, 1975-; American Chamber of Commerce in Korea, 1991-. **HONORS/AWARDS:** Montgomery County High Tech Council, Jos A Sciulli Entrepreneur of Year, 1992; Asian Pacific American Heritage Council, Outstanding Asian Pacific American Achievement, 1990; Premiere of Republic of Korea, Award for Excellent Business, 1991; Prime Minister of Republic of Korea, Outstanding Korean-American Achievement, 1991; Ernst & Young Inc, Entrepreneur of the Year Finalist, 1989, 1990. **SPECIAL ACHIEVEMENTS:** Published The Korean American Life Magazine; published The Link, a newsletter for Asian Pacific Council Inc; founded Mainstream America Awards for Excellence ceremonies; guest speaker for Asian-American Youths; scholarship awards to Asian-American student. **BIOGRAPHICAL SOURCES:** "Hard Work Makes ICT Entrepreneur's Dreams Come True," The Montgomery Journal, May 27, 1992; "Korean's American Dream Rests on Involvement in Mainstream," The Washington Times, May 11, 1992; "Entrepreneur of the Year Lives Dream," Gazette, 5-6-92. **BUSINESS ADDRESS:** President, CEO, Chairman, International Computers and Telecommunications Inc, 18310 Montgomery Village Avenue, #610, Gaithersburg, MD 20879, (301)948-0200.

SOHN, HONG YONG

Educator. Korean American. **PERSONAL:** Born Aug 21, 1941, Kaesung, Kyunggi-do, Republic of Korea; son of Chong-Ku Sohn and Soon-Deuk Woo; married Victoria, Jan 28, 1971; children: Berkeley Jihoon, Edward Jihyun. **EDUCATION:** Seoul National University, Korea, BS, chemical engineering, 1962; University of New Brunswick, MS, chemical engineering, 1966; University of California, Berkeley, PhD, chemical engineering, 1970. **CAREER:** Cheil Sugar Co, engineer, 1962-64; State University of New York, Buffalo, research associate, lecturer, 1971-73; DuPont Co, research engineer, 1973-74; Lawrence Livermore National Laboratory, summer professor, 1975-77; University of Utah, professor, 1974-. **ORGANIZATIONS:** Minerals, Metals and Materials Society, chair of several committees, 1975-; American Institute of Chemical Engineers, AIChE journal review board, 1975-; Korean Institute of Chemical Engineers, permanent member, 1976-. **HONORS/AWARDS:** Camille and Henry Dreyfus Foundation, Teacher Scholar Awrd, 1977; Fulbright Commission, Distinguished Lecturer, 1983; Japan Society for Promotion of Science, Research and Lecture Fellowship, 1990; Minerals, Metals and Materials Society, Extractive Metallurgy Lecturer Award, 1990, Extractive Metallurgy Science Award, 1990, 1994, Champion H Mathewson Gold Medal,

1993. **SPECIAL ACHIEVEMENTS:** Monograph: Gas-Solid Reactions, with J Szekely and J W Evans, Academic Press, 1976; edited monograph: Rate Processes of Extractive Metallurgy, with M E Wadsworth, Plenum, 1979; 8 edited books; 200 technical articles; 1 patent; 16 technical reports; 100 invited lectures world-wide; 100 meeting presentations. **BUSINESS ADDRESS:** Professor, University of Utah, 412 WBB, Salt Lake City, UT 84112-1183, (801)581-5491.

SOHN, SO YOUNG

Educator. Korean American. **EDUCATION:** Yonsei University, BS, mathematics, 1981; Korea Advanced Institute Science & Tech, MSc, indust eng, 1983; Imperial College of Sci & Tech, University of London, MS, mgt sci, 1987; University of Pittsburgh, MA, applied stat, 1989, PhD, indst eng. **CAREER:** KIDA, researcher, 1983-85; University of Pittsburgh, graduate teaching assistant/research, 1987-89; Bureau of Labor Stat, researcher, 1990; Naval Postgraduate School, assistant professor, 1990-. **ORGANIZATIONS:** TIMS, 1988-; ASA, 1988-. **HONORS/AWARDS:** British Foreign & Commonwealth Office Awards, 1985-86; ASA, NSF, BLS: research associateship, 1990. **BUSINESS ADDRESS:** Assistant Professor, Dept of Operations Research, Naval Postgraduate School, Monterey, CA 93943-5000, (408)656-3300.

SOMANI, ARUN K.

Educator. Indo-American. **PERSONAL:** Born Jul 16, 1951, Beawar, Rajasthan, India; son of Kanwarlal Somani & Dularj Devi Somani; married Manju Somani, Jul 6, 1987; children: Ashutosh, Paritosh, Anju. **EDUCATION:** Birla Institute of Technology, India, BE (honors), 1973; Indian Institute of Technology, India, MTech, 1979; McGill University, Canada, MSEE, 1983, PhD, 1985. **CAREER:** Electronics Corp of India, technical officer, 1973-74; Department of Electronics, India, scientist, 1974-82; University of Washington, assistant professor of EE, 1985-90, associate professor of EE & CSE, 1990-. **ORGANIZATIONS:** HTCCPN, treasurer, 1990-92, vice chair, 1992-93, chair, 1993-; IEEE, 1985-89, senior member, 1989-; ACM, 1988-; HKN, 1988-; IAWW, jt sec, 1993-. **HONORS/AWARDS:** Government of Canada, Commonwealth Scholarship, 1982-85; Government of India, Merit Scholarship, 1967-77; McGill University, dean's honor list, 1983, 1985. **SPECIAL ACHIEVEMENTS:** About 80 technical papers, book chapters, patents in field. **BIOGRAPHICAL SOURCES:** IEEE Transactions on Computers, 1989. **HOME ADDRESS:** 16609 126th Ave NE, Woodinville, WA 98072, (206)488-2901. **BUSINESS ADDRESS:** Assoc Prof, Dept of Electrical Engineering, University of Washington, FT-10, Seattle, WA 98195, (206)685-1602.

SOMANI, PITAMBAR (PETER)

Government official. Indo-American. **PERSONAL:** Born Oct 31, 1937, Chirawah, Rajasthan, India; son of Narendra Kumar Somani and Sarla Maheshwari; married Kamlesh, May 5, 1960; children: Anita Richardson, Alok, Jyoti. **EDUCATION:** G R Medical College, Gwalior, India, MD, 1960; Marquette University, PhD, 1965. **CAREER:** Medical College of Wisconsin, assistant professor, 1966-69, associate professor, 1969-72; Abbott Laboratories, manager, general pharmacology, 1972-74; University of Miami School of Medicine, professor, 1974-80; Medical College of Ohio, professor, director, clinical pharmacology, 1980-90; Ohio Department of Health, assistant director, 1991-92, director, 1992-. **ORGANIZATIONS:** American Society Pharmacology & Exper Therapeutics, 1969-; American Medical Association, 1977-; American Federation of Clinical Research, 1969-92; American Society of Clinical Pharmacology, 1977-; American Heart Association, NW Ohio Chapter, president, 1989-90. **HONORS/AWARDS:** Wisconsin Heart Association, fellow, 1964-66. **SPECIAL ACHIEVEMENTS:** Publications: more than 100 scientific papers in professional peer-reviewed journals; United Nations Development Program, Tokten Fellow, 1988-89, Special Program Advisor to Government of Thailand, 1989-90; first Asian-American to be appointed cabinet member in Ohio. **BUSINESS ADDRESS:** Director, Ohio Dept of Health, 246 N High St, Columbus, OH 43266-0588, (614)644-8595.

SOMASUNDARAN, PONISSERIL

Educator, educational administrator. Indo-American. **PERSONAL:** Born Jun 28, 1939, Annallur, Kerala, India; son of M G Kumara Pillai & K P Lakshmikutty Amma; married Usha, May 25, 1966; children: Tamara. **EDUCATION:** Kerala University, BS, 1958; Indian Institute of Science, BE, 1961; University of California, Berkeley, MS, 1962, PhD, 1964. **CAREER:** International Minerals & Chem Corp, 1965-67; R J Reynolds Industries Inc, 1967-70; Columbia University, Mineral Engineering, associate professor, 1970-78, division head, 1975-78, professor, 1978-83, La Von Duddleson Krumb Professor, 1983-; Langmuir Center for Colloids & Interfaces, director, 1987-, Henry

Krumb School, chairman, 1988-. **ORGANIZATIONS:** National Academy of Engineering, 1985; Engineering Foundation, board member, 1990, Conference Committee, chairman, 1988, board chairman, 1993-. **HONORS/AWARDS:** Numerous awards and honors, including: Engineering Foundation Conference, Frank F Aplan Award, 1992; Indian Institute of Science, Most Distinguished Alumnus Award, 1990; The Association of Indians in America, Honor Award, 1988; Ellis Island Medal. **SPECIAL ACHIEVEMENTS:** Editor-in-chief, Colloids and Surfaces, 1979-; associate editor, Minerals and Metallurgical Processing, 1983-; associate editor, International Journal of Mineral Processing, 1977-; over 270 publications, including 11 books; 115 invited lectures in various national and international symposia, universities and industries in 17 countries; additional 150 lectures presented at meetings of professional societies. **BUSINESS ADDRESS:** La Von Duddleson Krumb Professor, Chairman, Henry Krumb School, Columbia University, New York, NY 10027.

SONG, CHOAN-SENG
Educator. Taiwanese American. **PERSONAL:** Born Oct 19, 1929, Taiwan; son of Chu-Khim Song & Chin-Ti Wu Song; married Mei-Man Chen Song, Aug 10, 1962; children: Ju-Ping, Ju-Ying. **EDUCATION:** National Taiwan University, BA, 1954; University of Edinburgh, BD, 1958; Union Theological Seminary, PhD, 1965. **CAREER:** Tainan Theological College, professor & principal, 1965-70; Reformed Church in America, secretary for Asian ministries; World Council of Churches, associate director of faith and order commission, 1973-82; World Alliance of Reformed Churches, director of studies, 1982-85; Pacific School of Religion, professor of theology, 1985-. **SPECIAL ACHIEVEMENTS:** Lecturer on numerous subjects, 1972-94; author of 9 books. **BUSINESS ADDRESS:** Professor of Theology and Asian Cultures, Pacific School of Religion, 1798 Scenic Ave, Berkeley, CA 94709-1323, (510)848-0528.

SONG, IL-YEOL
Educator. Korean American. **PERSONAL:** Born Mar 10, 1953, An-Dong, Kyung-Book, Republic of Korea; son of Hee-Sik Song & Seung-Hyang L Song; married Young C Song, Mar 11, 1979; children: Jae Won, Sharon J. **EDUCATION:** Han-Yang University, BE, 1975; Louisiana State University, MS, 1984, PhD, 1988. **CAREER:** Agency for Defense Development for Korea, senior researcher, 1975-82; Louisiana State University, teaching assistant, 1982-88; Drexel University, assistant professor, associate professor, 1988-. **ORGANIZATIONS:** Association for Computing Machinery, 1983-; IEEE Computer, 1992-. **HONORS/AWARDS:** Drexel University, Exemplary Teaching Award, 1992; Drexel Research Scholar Award, 1992, First Prize Award by 4th Scientific Research Symposium of Sigma Xi, 1992; Agency for Defense Development for Korea, Research Contribution Award, 1980; National Institute of Standards and Technology, research project, 1992. **SPECIAL ACHIEVEMENTS:** "Intentional Query Processing in Deductive Database Systems," PhD dissertation, 1988; "Design and Implementation of a Three Step Intentional Query Processing Scheme," Journal of Database Administration, vol 2, no 2, p 23-35, spring 1991; "A Knowledge Based System Converting ER Model into an OODB Schema," DASFAA '93, 1993; "Schema Conversion Rules between EER and NIAM," in 10th International Conf on ER Approach, pp 425-444, 1991; "Object-Oriented Database Design Methodologies," Information and Knowledge Management, Lecture Notes in Computer Science, vol 752, p 115-142. **BUSINESS ADDRESS:** Associate Professor, Drexel University, College of Information Studies, 32nd and Chestnut Streets, CIS 10, Philadelphia, PA 19104, (215)895-2489.

SONG, JOHN D.
Printing company executive, association executive. Korean American. **PERSONAL:** Born Mar 20, 1935, Seoul, Republic of Korea; son of I & S Song; married Soo Song, Dec 28, 1968; children: George, Cindy. **EDUCATION:** Yonsei University, Korea, BA, 1959; Loyola University, MA, 1970; Claremont Graduate School, PhD, 1973. **CAREER:** Moonhwa Broadcasting Company, Korea, announcer, 1959-65; LA Unified School District, psychologist, 1972-76; CA State University, Long Beach, professor, 1975-79; Keimyung University, Korea, visiting professor, 1979-81; AA-1 Printing Company, president, 1981-. **ORGANIZATIONS:** Korean American Student Guidance Center, director, 1972-79; Korean Association of Southern California, vice president, 1974-75; Korean School of Southern California, principal, 1974-75; Asian American Education Commission, 1974-76; The Association for Korean Studies, president, 1975-91. **SPECIAL ACHIEVEMENTS:** Theory of Adolescence, Keimyung University Press, 1980; Education Psychology, Keimyung University Press, 1982. **HOME ADDRESS:** 30104 Avenida Tranquila, Rancho Palos Verdes, CA 90274, (310)544-1267.

SONG, JOHN S.
Plastic products manufacturing executive. Chinese American. **PERSONAL:** Born Mar 6, 1921, An-Hsin, Hebei, China; son of S P Song and Y Z Song; married Helen S Song, Feb 8, 1958; children: Jordan E. **EDUCATION:** Tsing-Hwa University, BS, 1942; Cornell University, MS, 1945. **CAREER:** Magnesium Co of America, design engineer, 1950-58; Continental Can Co, R&D, supervisor new products, 1959-66; MOI Realty, president, founder, 1985-; Magenta Corporation, founder, president, chairman, 1968-. **ORGANIZATIONS:** Plastic Engineering Society, 1980-; Packaging Institute, speaker, 1959-66; Tissue Culture Association, 1982-; Tsing-Hwa Alumni Association, 1949-; Lincoln Park Zoological Society, inner circle, 1985-87; Evanston Art Center, 1978-89; Magenta Profit Sharing Fund, trustee, 1974-. **HONORS/AWARDS:** Packaging Magazine, Innovator's Gold Award, 1989. **SPECIAL ACHIEVEMENTS:** Several plastic closure patents. **BIOGRAPHICAL SOURCES:** Article, IBM Think Magazine. **BUSINESS ADDRESS:** Chairman of the Board, Magenta Corporation, 3800 N Milwaukee Ave, Chicago, IL 60641, (312)777-5050.

SONG, JOSEPH M.
Pathologist, educator. Korean American. **PERSONAL:** Born May 11, 1927, Pyongyang, Republic of Korea; son of Ha-Ju Song and Wha-Soon Koh; married Kumsaen Ryn Song, Apr 12, 1958; children: Patricia H, Michael J, Jeff J. **EDUCATION:** Seoul National University School of Medicine, MD, 1950; University of Tennessee, MS, 1956; University of Arkansas School of Medicine, MD, 1965. **CAREER:** University of Tennessee, Pathology, instructor, 1952-56; State of Rhode Island, Department of Health, Cancer Detection, director, 1956-59; University of Arkansas, Pathology, associate professor, 1959-64; Mercy Hospital, Des Moines, IA, director of path, 1965-92; Creighton University Medical School, professor of pathology, 1968-. **ORGANIZATIONS:** AMA, 1952; American College of Physicians, fellow, 1968; College of American Pathologists, fellow, 1956; American Society of Clinical Pathologists, fellow, 1959; American Society of Pathologists, 1954; American Association of Cancer Research, 1962; Mercy Hospital Medical Staff, president, 1981. **HONORS/AWARDS:** Southern Christian Leadership Conference, Martin Luther King Medical Achievement Award, 1972; American Academy of Medical Administrators, Statesmanship Award, 1987. **SPECIAL ACHIEVEMENTS:** The Human Intern, Charles C Thomas Publisher, 1964; Pathology of Sickle Cell Disease, Charles C Thomas Publisher, 1971. **MILITARY SERVICE:** Medical Corps, major, MP, 1951-52. **HOME ADDRESS:** 2345 Park Avenue, Des Moines, IA 50321, (515)243-7748.

SONG, RALPH H.
Educator (retired). Korean American. **PERSONAL:** Born Nov 15, 1926, Kang-Won-Do, Republic of Korea; son of Paul Song & Mary Lee; married Agnes Y Bae Song, Jul 28, 1968 (deceased); children: Lisa, Sandra, Thomas; married Grace Kim, Sep 5, 1992. **EDUCATION:** University of Fribourg, Switzerland, Diploma, 1951; Holy Ghost College, Korea, BA, 1954; Seton Hall University, MA, 1958; Catholic University of America, Washington, DC, JCD, 1962; St Johns University, Jamaica, NY, PhD, 1968. **CAREER:** St Teresa's High School, Korea, German teacher, 1955; Caldwell College, psychology lecturer, 1966-67; University of Wisconsin, Whitewater, Wisconsin, professor of psychology, 1968-92. **ORGANIZATIONS:** American Psychological Association; American Board of Professional Psychology; Asian American Psychological Association. **HONORS/AWARDS:** American Board of Professional Psychology, 1988; The State of Wisconsin Governor's Special Award; Board of Regents of the University of Wisconsin System, 1992. **SPECIAL ACHIEVEMENTS:** "Development of a Vocational Adjustment Rating Scales for the Retarded," J of Counseling Psychology, vol 18, no, 2, p 173-176, 1971; "The Bender Gestalt Test with BIP on Mental Retardates," J of Clinical Psychology, vol 25, no 1, p 69-71, Jan 1969; many other research articles. **HOME ADDRESS:** 8234 Forest Lake Dr, Conway, SC 29526, (803)347-0588.

SONG, SHIN-MIN
Educator. Taiwanese American. **PERSONAL:** Born Aug 12, 1951, Taipei, Taiwan; son of Ching-Kuo and Ai-Hwa Sung; married Sheng-Yeh Song, Dec 9, 1984; children: Joy, Grace, Joseph. **EDUCATION:** Tatung Institute of Technology, BSME, 1973; Ohio State University, MSME, PhD, mech eng, 1984. **CAREER:** Tatung Company, mfg engr, 1975-76, group leader, 1976-78, deputy R&D mgr, 1978-79; University of Illinois at Chicago, asst prof, 1984-90, assoc prof, 1990-. **ORGANIZATIONS:** American Society of Mechanical Engineers, 1984-; IEEE, 1990-. **HONORS/AWARDS:** National Science Foundation, Presidential Young Investigator Award, 1987; Applied Mecha-

nisms Conference, Best Paper Award, 1983. **SPECIAL ACHIEVEMENTS:** Author of more than 80 technical papers; Machines That Walk: The Adaptive Suspension Vehicle, MIT Press, 1989. **MILITARY SERVICE:** Armor Force, ROC, 2nd lt, 1973-75. **BUSINESS ADDRESS:** Assoc Professor, Dept of Mechanical Engineering, M/C 251, University of Illinois at Chicago, 842 W Taylor St, 2039 ERF, Chicago, IL 60607-7022, (312)996-2427.

SONG, XUESHU
Educator. Chinese American. **PERSONAL:** Born Jun 14, 1955, Beijing, People's Republic of China; son of Hui-Jun Liu and Zhen Song; married Ping Wang, Jan 30, 1984; children: Dan Yu. **EDUCATION:** Beijing University of Aeronautics and Astronautics, MS, engineering, 1983; Pennsylvania State University, PhD, 1989; Temple University, postdoctoral fellow, 1989-90. **CAREER:** Beijing Automobile Manufactory, technician, 1972-77; Beijing Research Institute of Aeronautic Manufacturing Technology, research engineer, 1983-85; Beijing Institute of Light Industry, lecturer, 1984-85; Northern Illinois University, assistant professor, 1990-. **ORGANIZATIONS:** American Society of Engineering Education, 1991-; American Welding Society, 1992-; National Association of Industrial Technology, 1990-. **HONORS/AWARDS:** International Honorary Professional Fraternity for Education in Technology, Exemplary Initiation, 1991. **SPECIAL ACHIEVEMENTS:** "Computer Simulation in Eye-hand Coordination Training: A Welding Lab on Disk," J of Educational Technology Systems, 1992; "Southwell's Relaxation Search in Computer-Aided Advising: An Intelligent Information System," International J of Instructional Media, 1992; "Key Course Development in Today's Computer Integrated Curriculum in Engineering Technology," J of Engineering Technology, 1993; "Exploring Future Engineering Education: The Theory and Design of Flexible Education System," J of Research in Higher Education, National State Commission of Education of China, 1993; "Implications of Emerging Market Economy: Thoughts and Suggestions on Chinese High Education Reform," J of Chinese Higher Education, Research Institute of High Education in China, 1993; "New Model Development and Validation in Shear Angle Prediction: A Synthetical and Statistical Approach," Journal of Materials and Technology, The American Society of Mechanical Engineers, 1994. **BIOGRAPHICAL SOURCES:** "Song Presenter at National Meeting," Northern Today, vol 10, no 16, p 6, Jan 19, 1993. **HOME PHONE:** (815)748-5958. **BUSINESS ADDRESS:** Assistant Professor, Northern Illinois University, College Ave, Still Hall, Rm 105, De Kalb, IL 60115-2853, (815)753-1345.

SONG, YANGSOON
Educator. Korean American. **PERSONAL:** Born Jan 3, 1948, Taejun, Republic of Korea; son of Jong-Kyu Song and No-Wan Park; married Jaimin Song, May 24, 1974; children: Jason, John, David. **EDUCATION:** Seoul National University, BE, 1971; Korea University, MBA, 1979; Pennsylvania State University, PhD, business administration, 1988. **CAREER:** Korea Institute of Science and Technology, research in techno-economics group, 1973-77; Electro-Technology and Telecommunication & Research Institute, technology analysis section, head, 1977-81; Pennsylvania State University, assistant professor of management science, 1986-93; Coppin State College, assistant professor of management science, currently. **ORGANIZATIONS:** Institute of Management Science, 1984-; Journal of Decision Sciences Institute, 1986-; American Production and Inventory Control Society, 1992-; Beta Gamma Sigma, 1987-. **HONORS/AWARDS:** Ministry of Education, Korea, scholarship, 1981-84. **SPECIAL ACHIEVEMENTS:** "Pricing Policing for Procurement Contract under Incomplete Information," Journal of Purchasing Management; "Bidding Strategies for Competitive Procurement Contract under Incomplete Information," Proceedings of Decision Sciences Institute, pp 547-549, Nov 1992. **MILITARY SERVICE:** Korean Army, 1st lt, 1971-73. **BUSINESS ADDRESS:** Assistant Professor of Management Science, Coppin State College, 2500 W North Ave, Baltimore, MD 21216, (410)383-5594.

SONG, YO TAIK
Government official. Korean American. **PERSONAL:** Born Feb 23, 1932, Kyunggi-Do, Republic of Korea; son of Song Moon Young; married Docil Song, Apr 6, 1960; children: Unmi, Una, Lee. **EDUCATION:** Yon Sei University, BE, 1954; University of Illinois, MS, 1962, PhD, 1968. **CAREER:** Korean Air Force Academy, instructor, 1954-57; Korean Atomic Energy Research Institute, engineer, 1959-60; Naval Civil Engineering Laboratory, research physicist, 1963-67; University of Tennessee, faculty, 1967-70; University of Colorado, faculty, 1970-72; Naval Surface Warfare Center, physicist, 1972-79; US Department of Energy, project manager, 1979-. **ORGANIZATIONS:** American Nuclear Society, 1963-; Korean American Scholarship Fund, board member, 1974-, past chairman of the board, president; Korean

Scientists and Engineers Association, 1972-. **SPECIAL ACHIEVEMENTS:** Journal of American Nuclear Society, NS&E; many technical reports, US Navy. **MILITARY SERVICE:** Korean Air Force, first lt, 1954-57. **HOME ADDRESS:** 14209 Woodwell Terr, Silver Spring, MD 20906, (301)460-8512.

SONG, YONG CHOL
Dentist. Korean American. **PERSONAL:** Born May 23, 1959, Seoul, Republic of Korea; son of Daniel Song; married Esther, Jun 4, 1988; children: Paul, Grace. **EDUCATION:** Baylor College of Dentistry, DDS, 1990. **CAREER:** Private practice, dentist, currently. **ORGANIZATIONS:** American Dental Assn; Texas Dental Assn; Dallas County Dental Society. **BUSINESS ADDRESS:** Dentist, 364 Park Forest S/C, Dallas, TX 75229, (214)350-8608.

SONI, NARENDRA
Travel business executive. Indo-American. **PERSONAL:** Born Mar 7, 1934, Ahmedabad, Gujarat, India; son of Jekishandas Soni and Samrat Soni; married Daksha Vyas, Nov 26, 1978; children: Reshma Soni. **EDUCATION:** Gujarat University, BSc, 1956; Carnegie Institute of Technology, 1959-60; Cornell University, 1960-61; University of Michigan, 1963. **CAREER:** Calico Mills, salesman, 1958-59; Amstadter Brothers, bookkeeper, 1963-64; Countriside Press, bookkeeper, 1963-64; Topco Associates, accountant, 1966-67; Hevi-Duty Heating Co, accountant, 1964-66; Seeburg Corp, accountant, 1967-69; Natural Gas Pipeline Co, accountant, 1969-71; Patson Enterprises, president, 1971-81; Khyber India Restaurant, president, 1975-81; Gaylord India Restaurant, director, 1975-; India Times, Chicago, publisher, 1977-79; Travel Center, managing director, 1982-. **ORGANIZATIONS:** Rotary Club #1, 1979-; India Association of Metro Chicago, president, 1967-68; India League of America, 1969-72. **HOME ADDRESS:** 330 W Diversey Pkwy, Apt 1008, Chicago, IL 60657. **BUSINESS PHONE:** (312)726-0088.

SOO, BILLY S.
Educator. Filipino American/Chinese American. **PERSONAL:** Born Mar 25, 1961, Manila, Philippines; son of Soo Wan and Sy Sam; married Lisa R Soo, Apr 6, 1990; children: Mark William. **EDUCATION:** University of the Philippines, BS, 1983; Northwestern University, MS, 1988, PhD, 1991. **CAREER:** SGV & Co, CPAS, staff auditor, 1983-84; University of the Philippines, instructor, 1984-85; Northwestern University, instructor, 1989-90; Boston College, asst professor, 1990-. **ORGANIZATIONS:** Philippine Institute of CPAs, 1983-; American Accounting Association, 1989-. **BUSINESS ADDRESS:** Assistant Professor, Dept of Accounting, Boston College, School of Management, Chestnut Hill, MA 02167, (617)552-3963.

SOO, CHARLIE H.
Association director, consultant. Chinese American. **PERSONAL:** Born Mar 24, 1945, Hawaii. **EDUCATION:** College of Emporia; University of Illinois; Roosevelt University, BA, business, 1963. **CAREER:** Chicago International Management Firm, president, 1960-64; Illinois Economic Development Commission, appointed by the Governor, commissioner, 1964-68; Chicago Economic Development Corp, director, 1964-68; Asian American Small Business Association, director, 1968-93. **ORGANIZATIONS:** Serves on the boards of: Chicago School Board Nominating Commission (appointed by the Mayor), advisory board, CTA; Chicago Access Corp, Asian American Advisory Council, Illinois Attorney General's Office, advisory council; Truman College, Bank of Chicago, US Presidential Commissions. **HONORS/AWARDS:** Illinois Future Business Leaders of America, Businessman of the Year, 1964; Chicago Jaycees, Chicago's Ten Outstanding Young Leaders, 1967; Illinois Senate Resolution of Outstanding Leaders and Service to the City/State, 1967. **BUSINESS ADDRESS:** Director, Asian American Small Business Association of Chicago, 5023 N Broadway, Chicago, IL 60640.

SOOD, DEVINDER KUMAR (DEVINDER KUMAR SUD)
Educator. Indo-American. **PERSONAL:** Born Jun 1, 1944, Moga, Punjab, India; son of Mangatu Ram Sood and Shanti Devi Sood; married Suman Sood, Apr 20, 1974; children: Monica, Mohit, Priya. **EDUCATION:** Punjabi University Patiala, India, MSc, 1970; University of Windsor, Canada, BEd, 1977; Control Data Institute, diploma in computers, 1981. **CAREER:** SD College, Ambala, India, professor, 1970-72; Windsor Board of Education, teacher, 1977-81; DeVry Technical Institute, professor, 1981-90, dean of info system, 1990-. **ORGANIZATIONS:** Lion's Club International, Canada, 1972-80; DPMA International, secretary, 1983-93. **HONORS/AWARDS:** DPMA, Continuous Service Award, 1992. **SPECIAL ACHIEVEMENTS:** Hindu Society of Essex County Annual Function, Master of Ceremony, 1986-89. **HOME ADDRESS:** 16 Heritage Dr, Howell, NJ 07731, (908)905-9379. **BUSINESS**

ADDRESS: Dean of Information Systems, DeVry Technical Institute, 479 Green St East, Woodbridge, NJ 07095, (908)634-3460.

SOOD, MOHAN K.
Educator, educational administrator. Indo-American. **PERSONAL:** Born Apr 17, 1941, Manpur Nagaria, Uttar Pradesh, India; son of Prem Nath Sood & Gunvanti; married Joginder, 1965; children: Sanjay, Rishi. **EDUCATION:** Panjab University, Chandigarh, India, MSc, 1963; University of Western Ontario, London, Canada, MSc, 1968, PhD, 1969. **CAREER:** Northeastern Illinois University, asst professor, 1970-73, associate professor, 1973-76, professor, 1976-, University Honors Program, coordinator, 1985-90, dean, graduate college, 1991-. **ORGANIZATIONS:** Honors Council of Illinois Region, president, 1990-91; National Collegiate Honors Council, research committee, 1987-88, honors ed committee, 1988-90, conference committee, 1990-91, planning committee. **HONORS/AWARDS:** Northeastern Illinois University, Faculty Excellence Award, 1989, Presidential Merit Award, 1984; University Foundation, Award for Research, 1983. **SPECIAL ACHIEVEMENTS:** Author, book, Modern Igneous Petrology, John Wiley & Sons, 1981; coauthor: "Petrogenetic Evolution of the Proterozoic Wausau Igneous Complex, Wisconsin," Proc Institute of Lake Superior Geology, vol 35, pt 1, pp18-21, 1989; "Geochemistry and Mineralogy of the Athelsthane Granite, Marinnette County, Wisconsin," Proc Institute of Lake Superior Geology, vol 34, pt 1, pp114-116, 1988; presentations at professional meetings: with T L Patton, "Mineral Chemistry and Petrogenesis of the Proterozoic Wausau Igneous Complex, Wisconsin," Geol Soc Am Abst, vol 21, p 44, 1989. **BUSINESS ADDRESS:** Dean, Graduate College, Northeastern Illinois University, 5500 N St Louis Ave, CLS 4029, Chicago, IL 60625, (312)794-2801.

SOOD, RAVINDER SINGH (SHASHI)
Book wholesale and export company executive. Indo-American. **PERSONAL:** son of Jagjit Singh Sood and Sudershan Rani Sood; married Sapna Sood, Aug 20, 1988; children: Samantha, Rohan, Shivani. **EDUCATION:** Delhi University, Faculty of Law, India, LLB, 1977. **CAREER:** Soothe Co, Stamford Books, president, currently. **HOME ADDRESS:** 163 Woodridge Dr S, Stamford, CT 06902.

SOO HOO, ERIC RANDOLPH
Physician. Chinese American. **PERSONAL:** Born Feb 3, 1951, Winslow, AZ; married Peggy; children: Cheryl, Christina, Carrie. **EDUCATION:** University of Arizona, BS, 1973, MD, 1976; Medical College of Wisconsin, MPH, 1993. **CAREER:** Self employed, 1979-80; University of Arizona, assistant professor, 1980-86; Western Occupational Health Center, president, 1986-. **ORGANIZATIONS:** American College of Occupational and Environmental Medicine, 1990-; American Academy of Family Practice, 1979-; Pima County Medical Society, 1991-. **BUSINESS ADDRESS:** President, Western Occupational Health Center, 2800 E Ajo Way, Tucson, AZ 85713, (602)573-2864.

SOO HOO, KAREN
Pediatrician. Chinese American. **PERSONAL:** Born Apr 13, 1960, Los Angeles, CA; daughter of Irene Soo Hoo and Don Soo Hoo; married Stephen Chang, May 2, 1987; children: Matthew Chang, Catherine Chang. **EDUCATION:** Harvard University, BA, 1981; Baylor College of Medicine, MD, 1987. **CAREER:** Sharp Rees Stealy Medical Group, pediatrician, 1990-. **ORGANIZATIONS:** American Academy of Pediatrics, 1987-. **HOME ADDRESS:** 9838 Via Caceres, San Diego, CA 92129.

SOOHOO, LEO, JR.
Audiologist. Chinese American. **PERSONAL:** Born May 16, 1956, Chicago, IL; son of Leo SooHoo Sr and Mae SooHoo; married Ruth Kuniyo SooHoo, May 19, 1990. **EDUCATION:** Illinois State University, BS, 1978; Michigan State University, MA, 1982; Lewis & Clark College, 1988-89. **CAREER:** Des Moines Independent Community School District, audiologist, 1982-84; Southard's Hearing Aid Center, audiologist, 1985-86; Health Evaluation Programs Inc, audiologist, 1987-89; self-employed, industrial audiologist, consultant, 1989-; Purdue University, staff audiologist, 1989-. **ORGANIZATIONS:** American Speech-Language-Hearing Association, 1982-; Hear-Indiana, chapter co-ordinator, 1989-; Indiana Speech-Language-Hearing Association, 1989-; Council Accreditation, occupational hearing conservation, 1991-; National Hearing Conservation Association, 1992-; American Academy of Audiology, 1993-. **HONORS/AWARDS:** Optimists Club of America, Civic Recognition, 1977. **SPECIAL ACHIEVEMENTS:** Signing Exact English II Workshop, 1992. **BUSINESS ADDRESS:** Staff Audiologist, Audiology & Speech Sciences,

Purdue University, 1353 Heavilon Hall, West Lafayette, IN 47907-1353, (317)494-3805.

SOO HOO, RICHARD
Certified public accountant. Chinese American. **PERSONAL:** Born Sep 2, 1950, Salem, MA; son of Wing K Soo Hoo and Ngontuey Wong; married Suzanne, Jun 1977; children: Claudia. **EDUCATION:** Harvard University, BA, 1972; Stanford University, MBA, 1974. **CAREER:** Coopers & Lybrand, cpa, 1974-76; Texas Instruments, senior financial analyst, 1976-77; Millipore, finance manager, 1977-80; Wang, division controller, 1980-. **ORGANIZATIONS:** Harvard Alumni Association, 1972-; Stanford Alumni Association, 1974-; Andover Chinese Clutural Exchange, vice president, 1991-; International Institute, board of trustees, 1992-; Shaughnessey Hospital, board of trustees, 1981-83. **HONORS/AWARDS:** COGME, fellowship, 1972-74. **SPECIAL ACHIEVEMENTS:** Languages: French, German, Cantonese, Spanish. **BUSINESS ADDRESS:** Accountant, Wang, 17 Wolcott Ave, Andover, MA 01810, (508)470-2293.

SOOHOO, RICHARD ALLEN
Controller. Chinese American. **PERSONAL:** Born Sep 6, 1948, Portland, OR; son of Sam P Soohoo (deceased) and Wilma D Soohoo; divorced; married Irene Doris Lei, Jan 25, 1994. **EDUCATION:** University of Houston, BA, 1974; Portland State University, 1983-84. **CAREER:** Alief Hastings High School, math teacher, 1974-75; Alief Elsik High School, math teacher, 1975-80; Portland Public Schools, math teacher, 1981-82; Hansen, Walden & Hunter PC, staff accountant, 1985-87; Huber's Inc, controller, 1980-. **ORGANIZATIONS:** National Restaurant Assn, 1987-; Oregon Society of CPA's, 1985-89; Texas State Teachers Assn, 1974-80; Alief Education Assn, 1974-80. **HONORS/AWARDS:** American Contract Bridge League, lifemaster, 1981-. **SPECIAL ACHIEVEMENTS:** Work with low-level math students was instrumental in getting Alief Independent School District to change their curriculum, 1980. **MILITARY SERVICE:** US Air Force, ssgt, 1967-71; National Defense Medal, Good Conduct Medal. **BUSINESS ADDRESS:** Controller, Huber's, Inc, 320 SW Stark, Rm 205, Portland, OR 97204, (503)228-5686.

SOO HOO, WILLIAM FONG
State government official. Chinese American. **PERSONAL:** Born May 4, 1948, Canton, China; son of Bing Yee Soo Hoo and Yit Jin Soo Hoo; divorced. **EDUCATION:** University of California, Berkeley, BA, economics, 1970, Davis, JD, 1977. **CAREER:** California Dept of Rehabilitation, staff attorney, 1978-80; Attorney General, deputy attorney general, 1980-86; Dept of Health Services, chief counsel and enforcement coordinator, 1986-90; Department of Toxic Substances Control, chief counsel and enforcement coordinator, 1990-91, director 1991-. **ORGANIZATIONS:** State Bar of California; Asian Bar Association of Sacramento. **SPECIAL ACHIEVEMENTS:** "Generations, Storage, Treatment, and Disposal of Haz Waste," California Environmental Law and Land Use Practice, Mathew Bender 8 Co, 1989; "Cleanup of Hazardous Waste," CA Env Law and Land Use Practice, Mathew Bender 8 Co, 1989; Evidence of Subsequent Repair: Yesterday, Today and Tomorrow; 9 UC Davis Law Review 421. **BUSINESS ADDRESS:** Director, Department of Toxic Substances Control, 400 P St, 4th Fl, PO Box 806, Sacramento, CA 95814, (916)322-3100.

SOONG, ARTHUR J.
Attorney. Chinese American. **PERSONAL:** Born May 7, 1951, New York, NY; son of Eugene Soong and Nancy Li Soong; married Barbara Ho Soong, Sep 11, 1977; children: Melissa, Audrea. **EDUCATION:** Amherst College, BA, 1974; Brooklyn Law School, JD, 1977. **CAREER:** MFY Legal Services, staff attorney, managing attorney, 1977-83; Soong & Liu, partner, 1983-. **ORGANIZATIONS:** Asian American Legal Defense and Education Fund, president, 1980-88, board of directors, 1980-; Opportunity to Learn, board of directors, 1990-, treasurer, 1992-. **BUSINESS ADDRESS:** Partner, Soong & Liu, 305 Broadway, Ste 802, New York, NY 10007, (212)608-3700.

SORIANO, LEE G.
Insurance company executive. Filipino American. **PERSONAL:** Born May 9, 1938; married Cora. **CAREER:** John Hancock Mutual Life Insurance Co, 1971-87; Surety Life Insurance Co, insurance executive, 1987-. **HONORS/AWARDS:** John Hancock, President's Honor Club, 1972-87, President's Cabinet Club, 1974-87; Million Dollar Round Table Award, 1972-91; Court of the Table Award, 1975-91; Top of the Table Club Award, 1975-91; Surety Insurance Co, Agent of the Year, 1988, President Council Award, 1988-91, Super

Achiever Award, 1989-92; Hall of Fame Award, 1993. **SPECIAL ACHIEVE-MENTS:** Convention, program, resource and sales congress, speaker, 1973-91. **BUSINESS ADDRESS:** Insurance Executive, Surety Life Insurance Co, 1929 Taravel, San Francisco, CA 94116, 800-669-7789.*

SREENIVASAN, KATEPALLI RAJU
Educator, engineer. Indo-American. **PERSONAL:** Born Sep 30, 1947, Kolar, India; married 1980; children: two. **EDUCATION:** Bangalore University, India, BE, 1968; Indian Institute of Science, ME, 1970, PhD, aeronautical engineering, 1975. **CAREER:** University of Sydney, Australia, fellow, 1975; University of Newcastle, fellow, 1976-77; Johns Hopkins University, research asssociate, 1977-79; Indian Institute of Science, visiting scientist, 1979, visiting professor, 1982; DFVLR, Germany, visiting scientist, 1983; California Institute of Technology, visiting professor, 1986; Rockefeller University, visiting professor, 1989; Jawaharlal Nehru Center for Advancement of Scientific Studies, visiting professor, 1992. Yale University, asst professor/associate professor, 1982-85, Dept of Mechanical Engineering, professor, 1985-, dept of mechanical engineering, chairman, 1987-92, council of eng, acting chairman, 1988, Harold W Cheel Professor, 1988-, physics professor, 1990-, applied physics professor, 1993-. **ORGANIZATIONS:** American Society of Mechanical Engineers, fellow; American Phys Society, fellow, fluid dynamics division, chairman, 1991; AIAA, associate fellow; Mathematics Society; Conn Academy of Science and Engineering; Sigma Xi. **HONORS/AWARDS:** Indian Institute of Science, Narayan Gold Medal, 1975, Distinguished Alumnus Award, 1992; Humboldt Foundation, fellow, 1983; Guggenheim Fellow, 1989. **SPECIAL ACHIEVEMENTS:** Research includes: origin and dynamics of turbulence, fractals. **BUSINESS ADDRESS:** Harold W Cheel Professor, Dept of Mechanical Engineering, Yale University, M6 ML, New Haven, CT 06520.

SREEVALSAN, THAZEPADATH
Educator. Indo-American. **PERSONAL:** Born Jan 25, 1935, Kanjiramattom, Kerala, India; son of Mr & Mrs E Achutha Panickar; married Sandra Sreevalsan, Mar 21, 1989. **EDUCATION:** University of Kerala, BSc, 1953, MSc, 1956; University of Texas, PhD, 1964. **CAREER:** High School, Kanjiramattom, teacher, 1954-56; Pasteur Institute India, research teacher, 1956-61; University of Texas, research associate, 1964-66; EI DuPont de Nemours, chemist, 1966-69; Georgetown University, assistant professor, 1969-74, associate professor, 1974-80, professor, 1980-. **ORGANIZATIONS:** American Society for Microbiology; American Society for Virology; American Association for Advancement of Sciences. **HONORS/AWARDS:** National Institutes of Health, research grant, 1970-77, 1983-86; American Cancer Society, 1979-81. **SPECIAL ACHIEVEMENTS:** University of Texas, Dept Microbiology, OB William Outstanding Student Award, 1963; Post Graduate Medicine, William Peck Outstanding Young Researcher Award, 1972; Fogarty International Fellow, 1978. **BUSINESS ADDRESS:** Professor, School of Medicine, Georgetown University, 3900 Reservoir Road NW, Med-Dent Bldg, NE 323, Washington, DC 20007, (202)687-1139.

SRINIVAS, RAMACHANDRA (SRINI)
Aerospace engineer. Indo-American. **PERSONAL:** Born May 31, 1944, Bangalore, India; son of U V Ramachandra Murthy and Vimala Bai; married Chitra Srinivas, Jan 26, 1973. **EDUCATION:** Bangalore University, India, BE, mech, 1966; Indian Institute of Technology, India, MTech, mech, 1970; McMaster University, Canada, ME, mech, 1971; University of Toronto, Canada, 1985. **CAREER:** SPAR Aerospace Ltd, staff engr, 1971-80; Sundstrand Corp, sr control sys engr, 1980-81; Teledyne Brown Engineering, sr sys engr, 1981-. **ORGANIZATIONS:** AIAA, 1980-; IEEE, 1980-; Assn of Professional Engrs, Ontario Branch, professional engr, 1977. **HONORS/AWARDS:** SPAR Aerospace Ltd, Outstanding Contribution to Shuttle Remote Manipulator System Program, 1979; NASA, JSC, Outstanding Contribution to Shuttle Program and Crew Training, 1981, MSFC, Certificate of Appreciation for Exceptional and Dedicated Support, 1991, Outstanding Support to the First United States Microgravity Mission, 1992. **SPECIAL ACHIEVEMENTS:** 26 technical paper publications. **BUSINESS ADDRESS:** Senior Systems Engineer, Teledyne Brown Engineering, 300 Sparkman Dr, Bldg 3, MS 128, Huntsville, AL 35807-7007, (205)726-2843.

SRINIVASAN, GUNUMAKONDA RAMASWAMIENGAR
Research scientist. Indo-American. **PERSONAL:** Born in Mysore, India; son of G N Ramaswamy Iyengar & Ranganayaki; married Alisan, Dec 4, 1968; children: Sandhya Gates, Leela Breithaupt, Nina, Neil. **EDUCATION:** University of Mysore, BSc, 1954, BSc (honors), 1956; Indian Institute of Science, Dipl, IISc, 1958; Colorado School of Mines, MS, 1958; University of Illinois,

PhD, 1966. **CAREER:** University of Illinois, research assistant, 1961-66; Cornell University, research faculty, 1966-68; Catholic University of America, assistant professor, 1968-71, associate professor, 1971-74; IBM Corp, advisory scientist, 1974-82, development manager, 1982-85, senior engineering manager, 1986-92, senior scientist, 1992-. **ORGANIZATIONS:** Electrochemical Society, executive comm, 1980-, technical planning comm, 1983-, comm on European affairs, 1982-90, program comm, international chemical vapor dep conf, 1991, editor & chairman of International Conference on Process, physics and modeling, 1987, 1990, 1993; Metallurgical Society, physical met comm, 1972-77. **HONORS/AWARDS:** Outstanding Technical Achievement, 5 Invention Achievement Awards, 3 Publication Awards. **SPECIAL ACHIEVEMENTS:** Published over 100 journal articles, 1960-; 11 USA patents, 1979-; division editor, Journals of Electrochemical Society, 1986-90. **HOME PHONE:** (914)454-3874. **BUSINESS ADDRESS:** Senior Scientist, IBM Semiconductor R&D Center, East Fishkill, Z/AE1, B/640-1, Hopewell Junction, NY 12533, (914)892-4064.

SRINIVASAN, RAMACHANDRA SRINI
Scientist. Indo-American. **PERSONAL:** Born Mar 16, 1939, Madurai, Tamil Nadu, India; son of N Ramachandran and S Abirami (both deceased); married Prabha, Jun 6, 1971; children: Karthik Ram. **EDUCATION:** Govt College of Tech, Coimbatore, India, BE, 1960; Indian Institute of Science, Bangalore, India, ME, 1962; Purdue University, MSEE, 1965; California Institute of Tech, PhD, 1969. **CAREER:** Rice University, research associate, 1970-72; Baylor College of Med, instructor, res associate, 1972-75; Abbott Labs, biomed engineer, 1975-77; Med University of SC, assistant professor, 1977-80; GE Govt Services, biomed research engineer, 1980-85, senior project scientist, 1986-87; Krug Life Sciences, senior research scientist, 1987-. **ORGANIZATIONS:** Biomedical Engineering Society, senior member; Institute of Electrical & Electronic Engineers; Sigma Xi. **HONORS/AWARDS:** General Electric Co, Professional Recognition Award, 1984, featured in National Engineers' Week, 1982; Metabolic Dynamics Foundation, Annual Award, 1969. **SPECIAL ACHIEVEMENTS:** Over seventy publications: articles, reports, abstracts and presentations. **BUSINESS ADDRESS:** Senior Research Scientist, Krug Life Sciences, 1290 Hercules Dr, Ste 120, Houston, TX 77058, (713)212-1440.

SRINIVASAN, THIRU R.
Pharmaceutical company executive. Indo-American. **PERSONAL:** Born Aug 7, 1945, Kakinda, Andhra Pradesh, India; son of T V Rama Chandran and T Seetha Lakshmi; married Sudha Srinivasan, Mar 19, 1979; children: Sruthi, Sharan. **EDUCATION:** Osmania University, BS, 1966; Texas A&I University, 1974. **CAREER:** Bristol Myers Squibb Co, district sales mgr, currently. **ORGANIZATIONS:** Balaji Temple, asst treasurer. **SPECIAL ACHIEVEMENTS:** Language proficiency: Tamil, Teluau, Kannada, and Hindi. **HOME ADDRESS:** 6910 Robey Ave, Downers Grove, IL 60516, (708)969-2979.

SRIRAMA, MALINI
Dance company director, educator. Indo-American. **PERSONAL:** Born in Bangalore, Karnataka, India; daughter of M D Parthasarathy and Sushila Parthasarathy; married M K Srirama; children: Madhanika, Rohith. **EDUCATION:** University of Mysore, India, MSc, zoology, 1968; Drexel University, MS, library and information science, 1972. **CAREER:** Seton Hall University, librarian, 1972-78; Washtenaw Community College, dance instructor, 1981-; Malini's Dances of India, artistic director, currently. **HONORS/AWARDS:** Washtenaw Council for the Arts, Michigan, Annie Awards for the Performing Arts, 1991; Bangalore, India, Natya Kala Kovide, 1964, Abhinaya Uisharade, 1982. **SPECIAL ACHIEVEMENTS:** Choreographer, dancer, and producer of many dance works, including: Lotus Blossom, Nritya Ganga, The Heroine, and videotapes on dance. **HOME PHONE:** (313)994-3167.

SRIVASTAVA, OM P.
Electronic instrumentation company executive. Indo-American. **PERSONAL:** Born Jan 8, 1939, Allahabad, Uttar Pradesh, India; son of J P Srivastava (deceased) and Vidya Devi Srivastava (deceased); married Joan Srivastava, Jun 1, 1968; children: Anjali, Sanjay. **EDUCATION:** University of Allahabad, MS, 1960; Michigan State University, 1963; Illinois Institute of Technology, 1970. **CAREER:** Gulton Graphic Industries, Instruments Division, engineer, 1964-69, quality assurance mgr, 1969-73, mfg mgr, 1973-78, director, engineering/QA, 1979-82, vice pres, 1982-. **ORGANIZATIONS:** ISHM; IEEE. **BUSINESS ADDRESS:** Vice President, Gulton Graphic Instruments Div, A Danaher Co, 212 Durham Ave, Metuchen, NJ 08840, (908)548-6500.

SRIVASTAVA, PRAKASH NARAIN

Educator. Indo-American. **PERSONAL:** Born Dec 7, 1929, Allahabad, Uttar Pradesh, India; son of G D Srivastava (deceased); married Krishna, Jun 29, 1955; children: Sunita Nigam, Sujata Raslogi, Shikha, Nalink. **EDUCATION:** KK College, Lucknow, inter science, 1947; Lucknow University, BS, 1949, MS, 1951; Cambridge University, PhD, 1965. **CAREER:** Government of India, assistant physiologist, 1952-68; University of Georgia, professor, 1969-. **ORGANIZATIONS:** American Society of Biochem & Molecular Biology, 1975-; American Physiological Society, 1975-; American Cell Biology Society, 1990-; Society of the Study of Reproduction, 1969-; Society for the Study of Fertility, UK, 1964-; NIH Study Section, 1990-94. **HONORS/AWARDS:** WHO, fellowship, 1975; UNDP, expert, 1988; speaker at the Nobel Symposium, 1970. **SPECIAL ACHIEVEMENTS:** Research papers, 1953-93. **BIOGRAPHICAL SOURCES:** Male Reproductive Function, by professor T R R Mann & C L Mann, p 225, 1981. **HOME ADDRESS:** 150 Spalding Circle, Athens, GA 30605, (706)353-8903. **BUSINESS ADDRESS:** Professor, Dept of Biochemistry, University of Georgia, Life Science Bldg, Athens, GA 30602, (706)542-1775.

SRIVASTAVA, SADANAND

Educator. Indo-American. **PERSONAL:** Born Jun 1, 1936, Gorakhpur, Uttar Pradesh, India; son of L B Srivastava (deceased) and Sarasvati Srivastava; married Veena Srivastava, Jun 8, 1969; children: Ritu, Nupur, Rahul. **EDUCATION:** University of Gorakhpur, UP, India, MS, 1958; University of Toronto, Canada, MA, 1965; University of Windsor, Canada, PhD, 1968. **CAREER:** St Andrews College, lecturer, 1958-62; MMM Engineering College, asst prof, 1962-64; University of Toronto, research asst, 1964-66; University of Windsor, research asst, 1966-68; University of Baghdad, asst prof, 1969-70; Bowie State University, professor, math & computer science, 1970-. **ORGANIZATIONS:** MAA; AMS; AAAI; Indian Math Society. **HONORS/AWARDS:** Govts of India & Canada, Commonwealth Fellowship, 1964-68; NASA, several grants, 1971-93. **BUSINESS ADDRESS:** Professor, Math and Computer Science, Bowie State University, Bowie, MD 20715.

SU, CHEH-JEN

Real estate executive. Taiwanese American. **PERSONAL:** Born Jun 11, 1934, Taipei, Taiwan; son of Ar-Ting Su and Wan-Shi Su; married Hsiu-Hua C Su, Jul 8, 1968; children: Albert, Steven, Kenneth. **EDUCATION:** Taipei Institute of Technology, diploma, 1955; North Carolina State University, BS, 1961; State University of New York, MS, 1963. **CAREER:** Continental Can Co, senior research scientist, 1967-76; Johnson & Johnson, research engineer, 1976-79; Masonito Corp, senior chemist, 1980-82; American Can Co, scientist, 1982-85; Jen Realty, president, 1985-. **ORGANIZATIONS:** Taipei Institute of Technology, Alumni Association of the Midwest, president, 1991-; Taiwanese Association of America, Chicago chapter, 1982-84; American Chemical Society, 1967-85; Formosan Association of Public Affairs, 1980-. **HONORS/AWARDS:** Taiwanese Cultural Society, successfully organized first Taiwanese musical performance in Chicago, 1983. **SPECIAL ACHIEVEMENTS:** Author of 10 publications in polymer, pulp & paper, 1967-80; 5 patents, 1968-85. **MILITARY SERVICE:** Army, 1955-56. **HOME ADDRESS:** 4151 Roslyn Rd, Downers Grove, IL 60515, (708)852-6964.

SU, JUDY YA-HWA LIN

Pharmacologist, educator. Chinese American. **PERSONAL:** Born Nov 20, 1938, Hsin-Chu, Taiwan; daughter of Ferng-Nian Lin and Chiu-Chin Lin; married Michael W Su, Aug 11, 1962; children: Marvin D. **EDUCATION:** National Taiwan University, BS, 1961; University of Kansas, Lawrence, MS, 1964; University of Washington, Seattle, PhD, 1968. **CAREER:** University of Alabama, assistant professor, 1972-73; University of Washington, research associate, 1976-77, acting assistant professor, 1977-78, research assistant professor, 1978-81, research associate professor, 1981-89, research professor, 1989-. **ORGANIZATIONS:** American Association for the Advancement of Science, 1976-; Biophysical Society, 1976-; American Society for Pharmacol & Exp Ther, 1980-; American Soc of Anesthesiologists, 1988-; American Physiological Society, 1989-. **HONORS/AWARDS:** San Diego Heart Association, research fellowship, 1970-72, Max-Planck Inst fellowship, 1982-83; National Institutes of Health, Research Career Dev Award, 1982-87; American Heart Association, basic science council, 1981-; Janssen Pharmaceutica, grant, 1980-; Anaquest, grant, 1987-; numerous others. **SPECIAL ACHIEVEMENTS:** Author of 52 abstracts and 35 publications, including: "Effects of Alfentanil on Isolated Cardiac. . .," Anesth Analg, 71:268-274, 1990; "Influence of Caffeine, Ca2 and Mg2 on. . .," Pflugers Arch, 421:1-6, 1992; "Left Ventricular Hypertrophy in Rabbits. . .," Anesthesiology, 77:513-521, 1992;

"Mechanisms of Action of 7-0-Ethyl Tetradine. . .," Naunyn-Schmiedeberg's Arch Pharmacol, 347:445-451, 1993. **BUSINESS ADDRESS:** Research Professor, Dept of Anesthesiology, University of Washington, 1959 N E Pacific Street, RN-10, Seattle, WA 98195, (206)543-2475.

SU, JULIE CHU-CHU

Librarian. Chinese American. **PERSONAL:** Born Dec 17, 1943, Szuchuan, China; daughter of Chen-Yu Tao and Patricia Kao; married Kenneth Su, Jul 11, 1970; children: Mark, Michelle. **EDUCATION:** National Taiwan University, bachelor, library science, 1965; University of California, Berkeley, master of librarianship, 1966; Indiana University, specialist degree, library & informations sciences, 1987. **CAREER:** Fresno State College Library, acquisitions librarian, 1966-67; University of California, Berkeley, East Asiatic Library, Chinese cataloger, 1967-69; Chicago State College, West Center Library, Cataloging Department, head, 1969-70; University of Wisconsin, School of Pharmacy Library, assistant librarian, 1970-71; Indianapolis Museum of Art Library, cataloging librarian, 1972-88; IUPUI University Libraries, serials cataloging librarian, 1988-. **ORGANIZATIONS:** American Library Association, 1985-; Association for Asian Studies, 1982-; North American Serials Interest Group, 1989; Indiana Library Federation, 1984-; Ohio Valley Group of Technical Services Librarians, 1988-. **HONORS/AWARDS:** Beta Phi Mu, 1988. **SPECIAL ACHIEVEMENTS:** Publications: "Indiana Chinese American Resources Directory," co-author with Ming-ming Kuo, InfoNet, 1992; "Library Services in an American Context," in press; contributing chapter, Diversity and Multiculturalism in Libraries, JAI Press, 1994. **BUSINESS ADDRESS:** Serials Cataloging Librarian, IUPUI, University Libraries, 755 W Michigan St, UL #1113G, Indianapolis, IN 46202, (317)274-0480.

SU, KWEI LEE

Forensic scientist. Taiwanese American. **PERSONAL:** Born Mar 18, 1942, Kaohsiung, Taiwan; married Philu Su, Oct 19, 1968; children: Jennifer. **EDUCATION:** University of Minnesota, PhD, 1971. **CAREER:** University of Minnesota, assistant professor, 1971-75; University of Missouri, assistant professor, 1975-76; Missouri State Highway Patrol, forensic scientist, 1976-87; Mid America Labs & Forensic Consultants, director, CEO, 1988-. **ORGANIZATIONS:** American Academy of Forensic Sciences, fellow, 1989-; Missouri Academy of Science, 1976-; Midwestern Association of Forensic Scientist, 1976-; Zonta Club, president, 1988-89; Cole County Medical Alliance, president, 1992-93. **HONORS/AWARDS:** AAUW, Women of Achievement, 1987. **BUSINESS ADDRESS:** Director, Mid America Labs & Forensic Consultants, 2712 Plaza Drive, Jefferson City, MO 65109, (314)893-4118.

SU, TIMOTHY C.

Educator. Chinese American. **PERSONAL:** Born Mar 10, 1944, Fukien, China; son of Tzyy Chin Su and Anna Pan; married Madeline Su, Aug 8, 1981; children: Synny, Kristin, Gregory. **EDUCATION:** Hope College, BA, 1967; University of Kansas, 1967-69; Wayne State University, PhD, 1971. **CAREER:** University of California, Santa Barbara, postdoctoral, instructor, 1971-74; Bowling Green State University, assistant professor of chemistry, 1974-75; University of Massachusetts, assistant professor of chemistry, 1975-79, associate professor of chemistry, 1979-84, professor of chemistry, 1984-. **ORGANIZATIONS:** American Chemical Association, 1968-; American Society for Mass Spectrometry, 1971-. **SPECIAL ACHIEVEMENTS:** Author of 48 publications, including: co-author, "Positive Ion-Molecule Reactions in Perfluoropropane," Journal Chem Phys, vol 54, p 4871, 1971; co-author, "Matasable Ions in C2F6 and C3F8," Intl Journal Mass Spectry Ion Phys, vol 11 p 57, 1973; co-author, "Effect of Dipole-Induced Dipole Potential on Ion-Polar Molecule Collision Rate Constants," Journal Chem Phys, 96, 5550, 1992. **BUSINESS ADDRESS:** Professor, Dept of Chemistry, University of Massachusetts, Dartmouth, North Dartmouth, MA 02747-2300, (508)999-8238.

SU, TSUNG-CHOW JOE

Engineer, educator. Taiwanese American. **PERSONAL:** Born Jul 9, 1947, Taipei, Taiwan; son of Chin-shui Su and Chen-ling Shih Su; married Hui-Fang Angie Huang Su, Dec 26, 1976; children: Julius Tsu-Li, Jonathan Tsu-wei, Judith Tsu-Te, Jessica Tsu-Yun. **EDUCATION:** National Taiwan University, BS, 1968; Cal Tech, MS, 1970, AeE, 1973; Columbia University, ScD, engineering, 1974. **CAREER:** Cal Tech, teaching assistant, research assistant, 1971-72; Columbia University, research assistant, 1972-73; John J McMullen Associates, Inc, naval architect, 1974-75; Texas A&M University, Civil Engineering, assistant professor, 1976-82; Florida Atlantic University, Ocean Engineering, associate professor, 1982-87, Ocean Engineering, professor, 1987-92, Mechanical Engineering, professor, 1992-. **ORGANIZATIONS:** ASCE,

Fluids Committee, chair, 1992-94; ASME, 1982-94; AIAA, 1972-94. **HONORS/AWARDS:** ASCE, fellow; AIAA, associate fellow. **SPECIAL ACHIEVEMENTS:** Over 60 technical publications, 1973-92; associate editor, ASCE Journal of Engineering Mechanics, 1992-94. **MILITARY SERVICE:** Chinese Army, 2nd lt, 1968-69. **BUSINESS ADDRESS:** Professor, Dept of Mechanical Engineering, Florida Atlantic University, 500 NW 20th St, Boca Raton, FL 33431-6498, (407)367-3896.

SU, TUHUEI
News film editor, educator. Taiwanese American. **PERSONAL:** Born Mar 31, 1931, Chia-Yi, Taiwan; son of Mon-Li Su and Su Lin Su; married Hueimei Su, 1964; children: Amanda. **EDUCATION:** National Taiwan University, BA, 1955; Western State College of Colorado, MA, 1959; University of Southern California, 1959-61; University of California at Los Angeles, MA, 1990. **CAREER:** Vi-Way Productions, cameraman, editor, 1961-67; National Broadcasting Co, newtork news editor, 1968-; Pepperdine University, instructor of Japanese, 1991-. **ORGANIZATIONS:** National Association of Broadcast Employees & Technicians, 1968-; Association of Teachers of Japanese, 1990-; National Academy of Television Arts and Science, 1975-85. **HONORS/AWARDS:** National Academy of Television Arts in Science, Emmy Award for Outstanding News Film Editing, 1973; Cine Award for editing, "The Captain's Courageous Climbers, " documentary, 1990. **BUSINESS ADDRESS:** Network News Editor, National Broadcasting Co, 3000 W Alameda Ave, Network News, Burbank, CA 91523.

SU, ZHIXIN
Educator. Chinese American. **PERSONAL:** Born Jan 1, 1956, Wuhan, Hubei, People's Republic of China; daughter of Yuexin Mo & Yongqin Su; divorced; children: Jeannie Yujing Chen. **EDUCATION:** Shanghai Foreign Studies University, BA, 1978; University of Washington, MED, 1985, PhD, 1989. **CAREER:** Chinese National Ministry of Education, program officer, 1981-84; University of Washington, research associate, 1984-90; University of California, Los Angeles, instructor, 1990-92; California State University, Northridge, assistant professor, 1990-93, associate professor, 1993-. **ORGANIZATIONS:** California State University, Northridge, China Institute, executive committee, 1992-; American Educational Research Association, 1987-; National Society for the Study of Education, 1989-; Phi Delta Kappa, 1987-; Comparative & International Education Society, 1989-; American Educational Studies Association, 1990-. **HONORS/AWARDS:** California State University, Northridge, Faculty Development Award for Research, 1991, 1992, Creativity & Research Competition Award, 1993, China Institute Research Award, 1992; UNESCO, educational research grant, 1983. **SPECIAL ACHIEVEMENTS:** Publication of research reports on teacher socialization in Oxford Review of Education, 1990; International Review of Education, 1991; Phi Delta Kappan, 1990; Journal of Research in Teaching, 1992; Journal of Research & Development in Education, 1993; numerous other articles and book chapters. **BIOGRAPHICAL SOURCES:** Special reports in International Daily, 1992, 1993; special report in Vancouver Sun, 1988. **BUSINESS ADDRESS:** Associate Professor, School of Education, California State University, Northridge, 18111 Northridge, Northridge, CA 91330, (818)885-3801.

SUBBASWAMY, KUMBLE RAMARAO
Educator, physicist, educational administrator. Indo-American. **PERSONAL:** Born Mar 18, 1951, Soraba, Karnataka, India; son of Kumble Ramarao and Mysore Gowramma; married Malathi Basral, Aug 18, 1986; children: Apurva. **EDUCATION:** Bangalore University, India, BSc (honors), 1969; Delhi University, India, MSc, 1971; Indiana University, Bloomington, PhD, 1976. **CAREER:** University of California, Irvine, research associate, 1976-78; University of Kentucky, assistant and associate professor, 1978-88, associate dean of arts & sciences, 1991-93, professor of physics, 1988-, Department of Physics and Astronomy, chair, currently. **ORGANIZATIONS:** American Physical Society, fellow, 1992-. **HONORS/AWARDS:** Research grants from NSF, DOE. **SPECIAL ACHIEVEMENTS:** Co-author: Local Density Theory of Polarizability, Plenum, 1990; over 50 research articles. **BUSINESS ADDRESS:** Chair, Professor, Dept of Physics & Astronomy, University of Kentucky, Chem-Phys 177, Lexington, KY 40506-0055, (606)257-6722.

SUBRAMANI, SURESH
Educator. Indo-American. **PERSONAL:** Born Feb 21, 1952, Jabalpur, Madhya Pradesh, India; married Feroza; children: Anand, Praveen. **EDUCATION:** Fergusson College, Pune, India, BSc, 1972; Indian Institute of Technology, Kandur, India, MSc, 1974; University of California, Berkeley, PhD, 1979; Stanford University, Stanford, post-doctorate, 1982. **CAREER:** University of

California, San Diego, assistant professor, 1982-87, associate professor, 1987-91, professor, 1991-. **HONORS/AWARDS:** National Science Talent Scholar, India, 1969-74; India, National Scholarship, 1972; Jane Coffin Childs Fund, fellow, 1979-81; Searle Scholar, 1982-85; National Cancer Institute, Research Career Development Award, 1985-90; India, Dr Narayana Memorial Lecturer, IISc, 1990; John Simon Guggenheim Fellow, 1993. **BIOGRAPHICAL SOURCES:** Who's Who in Technology, 1989. **BUSINESS ADDRESS:** Professor, Dept of Biology, University of California, San Diego, 0322 Bonner Hall, Room 3226, La Jolla, CA 92093-0322, (619)534-2327.

SUBRAMANIAM, PRAMILLA N.
Physician, educator. Indo-American. **PERSONAL:** Born Dec 24, 1953, Madras, India; daughter of C H & Yamuna Narayanan; married C V Subramaniam, 1976; children: Akila, Venkat, Ambika. **EDUCATION:** University of New Orleans, BS, 1974; LSU Medical Center, MD, 1977. **CAREER:** Ocshner Medical Foundation, fellowship, 1981-83; LSU Medical Center, internship, residency, 1977-80, assistant professor, 1983-89, associate professor, 1989-. **ORGANIZATIONS:** American Medical Association; American Heart Association; American College of Cardiology, fellow; Council on Clinical Cardiology; American Society of Echocardiography; Louisiana State Medical Society; American Association of Indian Physicians. **HONORS/AWARDS:** Comparison of the Effects of Eminase (APSAC) to those of tPA on Morbidity in Patients with Acute Myocardial Infarction, Multicenter Study, principal investigator, award $10,300, 1992. **SPECIAL ACHIEVEMENTS:** Publications: co-author, "Prenatal Cocaine Exposure: Developmental Neurobehavioral Deficits as Predictors of Cardiovascular Effects," abstract & poster presentation, Third LSU Neuroscience Retreat, 1991; "ISIS-3-Collaborative Group," Lancet, vol 339, p 753-770, March 1992; Pharmacology Clinical Correlation Lecture, 1992; guest lecturer to emergency medicine residents, topic: Acute Myocardial Infarction Management, 1992; Fourth International Study of Infarct Survival, ISIS-4, 1992-. **BUSINESS ADDRESS:** Associate Professor, Louisiana State University Medical Center, 1542 Tulane Ave, New Orleans, LA 70112-2865, (504)568-6895.

SUBRAMANIAN, SRIBALA (BONNIE)
Journalist. Indo-American. **PERSONAL:** Born Jun 29, 1962, Southampton, England; daughter of M R & Indu Subramanian; married Arvind Raghunathan, Aug 26, 1992. **EDUCATION:** Bangalore University, BCom, business, 1984; California State University, Fresno, MS, mass communication, 1987; Syracuse University, journalism, currently. **CAREER:** Time Magazine, reporter, 1989-. **ORGANIZATIONS:** Kappa Tau Alpha, 1986-. **BUSINESS ADDRESS:** Reporter, Time Magazine, 1271 6th Ave, Time Life Bldg, #2551C, New York, NY 10020, (212)522-3596.

SUBRAMANYA, SHIVA
Engineer, manager, scientist. Indo-American. **PERSONAL:** Born Apr 8, 1933, Hole-Narasipur, Karnataka, India; son of Srikantaiah; married Lee, Mar 3, 1967; children: Paul Kailas, Kevin Shankar. **EDUCATION:** Mysore University, BSc, 1956; Karnataka University, MSc, 1962; Clark University, PhD work, physics, 1963-64; California State University, Dominguez Hills, MBA, 1976; Nova University, PhD, mgt, 1986. **CAREER:** Defense Research Lab, inspector, 1956; Indian Telephone Industries, inspector, 1956-60; Atomic Energy Estb, senior scientific officer, 1962-63; Transcom Elex, chief engr, production manager, 1964-67; General Dynamics, principal engr, 1967-72; General Instrument, engineering consultant, 1972-73; TRW, assistant project manager, 1973-. **ORGANIZATIONS:** Indian Professional Forum, president, 1980-93; Vishwa Hindu Parishad of America, vice president, 1984-90; AFCEA, 1983-93; American Institute of Physics, 1963-70; IEEE, 1963-70; Association of Old Crows, 1968-73. **HONORS/AWARDS:** AFCEA, Meritorious Service Award, 1986, Medal of Merit, 1989; Atomic Energy Estb, scholarship, 1960-62; over 150 other awards from defense industry and/or DOD. **SPECIAL ACHIEVEMENTS:** Technical papers in Space C3I, over 30 published, 1970-92; technical papers in C3I, over 60 published, 1963-77; management papers, over 30 published, 1975-86; papers on philosophy and/or religion, over 20 published, 1975-93. **HOME ADDRESS:** 2115 Shelburne Way, Torrance, CA 90503, (310)533-4193.

SUBUDHI, MANOMOHAN
Engineering scientist. Indo-American. **PERSONAL:** Born Sep 27, 1946, Daspalla, Orissa, India; son of Brindabana Subudhi (deceased) and Paluni Subudhi (deceased); married Shantilata Subudhi, Jul 2, 1971; children: Sumit K, Mili (deceased). **EDUCATION:** Banaras Hindu University, India, BSc, 1969; Massachusetts Institute of Technology, SM, 1970; Polytechnic Institute

of New York, PhD, 1974. **CAREER:** Nuclear Power Services, engineer, 1974-75; Bechtel Power, engineer, 1975-76; Brookhaven National Lab, engineering scientist, 1976-. **ORGANIZATIONS:** ASME, 1975. **HONORS/AWARDS:** Prince of Wales Medal, Best Graduate in BSc, 1969. **BUSINESS ADDRESS:** Engineering Scientist, Brookhaven National Laboratory, Building 130, Upton, NY 11973, (516)282-2429.

SUDA, TATSUYA
Educator. Japanese American. **PERSONAL:** Born Aug 20, 1953, Fukushima, Fukushima, Japan; son of Toshiko and Tatsuo Suda; married Miyuki Suda, Sep 5, 1982; children: Kentaro, Shotaro. **EDUCATION:** Kyoto University, BS, 1977, MS, 1979, PhD, 1982. **CAREER:** Columbia University, researcher, 1982-84; University of California, professor, 1984-. **BUSINESS ADDRESS:** Professor, Dept of Information & Computer Science, University of California, Irvine, Irvine, CA 92717-3425, (714)856-5474.

SUDAN, RAVINDRA NATH
Electrical engineer, physicist, educator. Indo-American. **PERSONAL:** Born Jun 8, 1931, Chineni, Kashmir, India; son of Brahm Nath & Shanti Devi (Mehta) Sudan; married Dipali Ray, Jul 3, 1959; children: Rajani, Ranjeet. **EDUCATION:** University of Punjab, BA, 1948; Indian Institute of Science, diploma, 1952; Imperial College, London, diploma, 1953; University of London, PhD, 1955. **CAREER:** British Thomson-Houston Co, Rugby, England, engineer, 1955-57; Imperial Chemical Industries, Calcutta, India, engineer, 1957-58; Cornell University, research associate, 1958-59, Electrical Engineering, assistant professor, 1959-63, associate professor, 1963-68, professor, 1968-75, IBM Professor of Engineering, 1975-, Cornell Lab Plasma Studies, director, 1975-85, Cornell Theory Center, deputy director, 1985-87. **ORGANIZATIONS:** National Research Council, Plasma Science Committee, chairman, 1992-94; American Physical Society, Division of Plasma Physics, executive committee, 1971-72; University Fusion Associates, founder and chairman, 1979-80; IEEE Plasma Science Division, founding committee. **HONORS/AWARDS:** Naval Research Laboratory, Outstanding Publication Award, 1974; American Physical Society, Maxwell Prize, 1989, fellow; IEEE, fellow; AAAS, fellow; Czech Republic, Gold Medal of Academy of Sciences, 1993. **SPECIAL ACHIEVEMENTS:** Author of over 210 scientific publications on research in plasma physics, thermonuclear fusion, space and solar physics, intense beams, and plasma turbulence in related journals; co-editor, vols I & II, Handbook of Plasma Physics; served on editorial boards: Nuclear Fusion, Physics of Fluids, Physics Reports; DOE National Laboratories, consultant; 2 US patents. **BUSINESS ADDRESS:** Professor, Cornell University, Laboratory of Plasma Studies, 369 Upson Hall, Ithaca, NY 14853, (607)255-4127.

SUDARSHAN, T. S.
Engineer. Indo-American. **PERSONAL:** Born Dec 25, 1955, Madras, India; son of Mr and Mrs T R Srinivas; married Chitra Sudarshan, Mar 25, 1993. **EDUCATION:** Indian Institute of Technology, Madras, BTech, 1976; Virginia Polytechnic Institute & State University, MS, 1978, PhD, 1984. **CAREER:** Synergistic Technologies Inc, R&D, director, 1984-86; Materials Modification Inc, technical director, 1987-. **ORGANIZATIONS:** The Metallurgical Society chairman, SMACT, 1993-94. **HONORS/AWARDS:** SME Outstanding Young Manufacturing Engineer, 1990. **SPECIAL ACHIEVEMENTS:** Over 80 publications in refereed journals; 9 books; editor of Materials and Manufacturing Processes; editor of Materials Technology. **BIOGRAPHICAL SOURCES:** Surface Modification Technologies, TMS, Warrendale, PA, 1989-90. **BUSINESS ADDRESS:** Technical Director, Materials Modification Inc, 2929-P1 Eskridge Road, Fairfax, VA 22031, (703)560-1371.

SUELTO, TEEM D.
Financial sevices counselor. Filipino American. **PERSONAL:** Born Mar 28, 1928, Manila, Philippines; daughter of Pedro Diaz (deceased) & Ines Lano (deceased); divorced; children: Rowena, Edgar D, Imelda, Jose D. **EDUCATION:** University of the East, Manila, BBA, 1952, certified public accountant, 1953, masters in economics, 1962; American College, CHFC, 1993. **CAREER:** University of New Mexico Hospital, accountant, 1974-78; self-employed accountant and financial counselor, 1979-; Money Concepts Capital Corp, New Mexico regional vice president, currently. **BUSINESS ADDRESS:** New Mexico Regional V P, Money Concepts Capital Corp, 619 San Mateo NE, Money Concepts Plaza, Albuquerque, NM 87108-1432, (505)255-8068.

SUEN, CHING-YUN
Educator. Chinese American. **PERSONAL:** Born Mar 23, 1951, Taichung, Taiwan; son of Chia-Chih Suen and Min-Sha Suen; married Shi-Hang Huang, Apr 2, 1977; children: Karen. **EDUCATION:** National Tsing Hua University, MS, 1978; University of Houston, PhD, 1983. **CAREER:** Texas A&M University, visiting assistant professor, 1983-84; Texas A&M University, Galveston, assistant professor, 1983-89; Texas A&M University, associate professor, 1990-. **ORGANIZATIONS:** Computer Committee, chairman, 1987-92; Computer Task Force Committee, 1992-; Scholarship and Award Committee, 1987-88; Faculty Research Advising Committee, 1989-91; American Mathematical Society, 1983. **HONORS/AWARDS:** Texas A&M University, Galveston, CD Mickey Award, 1986; College of Geosciences and Maritime Studies, Texas A&M University, Distinguished Teaching Award, 1992. **SPECIAL ACHIEVEMENTS:** "On Representations of Completely Bounded Maps," Journal of Math Analysis and Applications, 154, p 212-225, 1991; "An NXN Matrix of Linear Maps of C-Algebra," Proc American Math Society, 112, pp 709-712, 1991; "The Numerical Radius of a Completely Bounded Map," Acta Mathematical Hungarica, 59, pp 283-89, 1992; "Representations of an NXN Matrix of Linear Maps on a C-Algebra," Math Japonica, 1993; "The Minimum Norm of Certain Completely Positive Maps," Proc American Math Society, 1993. **BIOGRAPHICAL SOURCES:** "Completely Bounded Maps and Dilations," Pitman Research Notes in Math, vol 146, Longman, London, pp 117-118, 1986. **BUSINESS ADDRESS:** Associate Professor of Mathematics, Dept of General Academics, Texas A&M University, Galveston, College of Geosciences and Maritime Studies, PO Box 1675, Galveston, TX 77553-1675, (409)740-4523.

SUGANO, KATSUHITO
Physicist. Japanese American. **PERSONAL:** Born May 25, 1948, Fukushima, Japan; son of Toshie Sugano; married Ayako Sugano, 1979; children: Mary Sakiko. **EDUCATION:** University of Tokyo, BS, 1972, MS, 1974, PhD, 1979. **CAREER:** Fermilab, research associate, 1979-83; Argonne National Lab, assistant physicist, 1983-90; UCSC, research associate, 1990-. **ORGANIZATIONS:** Physical Society of Japan, 1974-92; American Physical Society, journal referee (pr, prl), 1979-. **SPECIAL ACHIEVEMENTS:** A review article in International Journal of Modern Physics, 1988; more than 100 articles & papers, 1972-. **HOME ADDRESS:** 239 Cardiff Pl, Santa Cruz, CA 95060. **BUSINESS ADDRESS:** Research Associate, University of California, Santa Cruz, High St, NS II, Santa Cruz, CA 95064, (408)459-3038.

SUGANO, MIYOKO
Educator. Japanese American. **PERSONAL:** Born May 3, 1932, Honolulu, HI; daughter of Jujiro Sugano & Itoyo Kuromoto Sugano (both deceased). **EDUCATION:** University of Hawaii, Manoa, BA, 1954; University of Michigan, MA, 1956. **CAREER:** Emma Willard School, educator, 1956-58, 1962-63; Honolulu Business College, educator, 1958-60; Kapiolani Community College, educator, 1964-67; Keaukaha Language Project, specialist, 1967-69; University of Hawaii, Hilo, educator, 1969-. **ORGANIZATIONS:** Hawaii Literary Arts Council, board member, 1990-; Association of Asian American Studies, 1989-. **HONORS/AWARDS:** University of Hawaii Board of Regents, Excellence in Teaching, 1990; Kumu Kahua, UH, Manoa, Annual Playwriting Award, 1991. **SPECIAL ACHIEVEMENTS:** Poems published in Sister Stew: Fiction and Poetry by Women, 1991; Kanilehua, 1991; Bamboo Ridge, Fall 1991; award winning play by UHH Theater, spring, 1994. **BUSINESS ADDRESS:** Associate Professor of English, University of Hawaii, Hilo, 200 Kawili St, Humanities Division, EKH 214, Hilo, HI 96720-4091, (808)933-3463.

SUGAWARA, SANDRA LEE
Journalist. Japanese American. **PERSONAL:** Born Aug 15, 1953, Cincinnati, OH; daughter of Hoshiko and Hisashi Sugawara; married Louis Levy, Dec 30, 1987; children: Matthew, Megan. **EDUCATION:** Wellesley College, BA, 1975. **CAREER:** Rep Norman Mineta, legislative aide, 1975-77; UPI, reporter, 1977; States News Service, reporter, 1978-81; Washington Post, reporter, 1981-. **BUSINESS ADDRESS:** Reporter, Washington Post, 1150 15th St NW, Washington, DC 20071, (202)334-6000.

SUGIHARA, JAMES MASANOBU
Educational administrator. Japanese American. **PERSONAL:** Born Aug 6, 1918, Las Animas, CO; son of William Bansaku & Takeyo Kubota Sugihara; married May Murakami Sugihara, Jun 4, 1944; children: John, Michael. **EDUCATION:** University of California, Berkeley, BS, 1939; University of Utah, PhD, 1947. **CAREER:** University of Utah, chemistry instructor, 1944-47,

assistant professor, 1947-48, associate professor, 1949-54, professor, 1954-64; North Dakota State University, dean college of chemistry and physics, 1964-73, dean college of science and math, 1973-74, 1985-86, dean graduate school and director of research, 1974-85, acting academic vice president, 1984, professor of chemistry, 1964-89, emeritus professor, 1989-. **ORGANIZATIONS:** American Chemical Society, 1944-, Red River Valley Section, chairman, 1970-71; Cass-Clay United Way, board of directors, 1980-86, president of board, 1984-85; Southeast Area Health Education Center of the North Dakota School of Medicine, steering committee, 1975-82. **HONORS/AWARDS:** North Dakota State University, Blue Key Doctor of Service Award, 1972. **SPECIAL ACHIEVEMENTS:** 56 research publications; principal advisor to 27 PhD recipients and 11 masters recipients; research grants from American Petroleum Institute, National Science Foundation, Petroleum Research Fund, and others; consultant to Sun Oil Co, 1964-73, Exxon, 1973, American Gilsanite Co, 1960-64; member of US delegation from Department of Energy which met with USSR oil experts on geochemistry and properties of petroleum in USSR, 1978. **HOME ADDRESS:** 1001 Southwood Dr, Fargo, ND 58103, (701)235-8266.

SUGIHARA, JARED GENJI

Physician. Japanese American. **PERSONAL:** Born Dec 2, 1941, Honolulu, HI; son of Clarence Y Sugihara & Chieno Sugihara; married Valerie, Oct 10, 1970; children: Robin Emi, Rebecca Mie. **EDUCATION:** Yale University, BA, 1963; Harvard Medical School, MD, 1967. **CAREER:** Straub Clinic & Hospital, 1974-77; John Burns School of Medicine, assistant professor of medicine, 1976-; Nephrology Consultants, physician, 1977-; St Francis Renal Institute, medical director, 1990-. **ORGANIZATIONS:** American College of Physicians, fellow; American Society of Nephrology; International Society of Nephrology; International Society of Peritoneal Dialysis. **MILITARY SERVICE:** USAR, cpt, 1969-71. **BUSINESS ADDRESS:** Physician, Nephrology Consultants, 1380 Lusitana Street, Suite 814, Honolulu, HI 96813, (808)521-3802.

SUGIOKA, MICHAEL HIROYUKI

Educational administrator. Japanese American/Filipino American. **PERSONAL:** Born May 11, 1948, Laupahoehoe, HI; son of Tokuo Sugioka and Conchita Santos; married Yvonne C Sugioka, May 17, 1986; children: Shannon K, Sheldon K; stepdaughter: Mena R Brown. **EDUCATION:** Southwest Texas State University, BAAS, 1987; Webster University, MA, 1989. **CAREER:** US Army, personnel officer, 1967-89; Southwest Texas State University, coordinator, testing services, 1989-. **ORGANIZATIONS:** Retired Officers Association, member, 1989-; Texas Association of College Testing Pers, member, 1989-. **MILITARY SERVICE:** US Army, Bronze Star Medal, Meritorious Service Medal, Army Commendation Medal. **HOME ADDRESS:** 926 Lazy Trail, New Braunfels, TX 78130, (210)625-0464.

SUGIYAMA, ALAN

Educational administrator. Japanese American. **CAREER:** Center for Career Alternatives, executive director, currently. **ORGANIZATIONS:** Seattle School Board, 1989-, president, 1992; Asian Pacific Islander Taskforce for Youth. **BUSINESS ADDRESS:** Executive Director, Center for Career Alternatives, 3700 Rainier Ave S, Seattle, WA 98144, (206)723-2286.*

SUH, BERNADYN KIM

Educator. Korean American. **PERSONAL:** Born Dec 4, 1940, Wahiawa, HI; daughter of Bernie and Dora Kim; married Paul Suh, Aug 15, 1964; children: Christopher H, Jonathan I. **EDUCATION:** University of Hawaii, BEd, 1962; Columbia University Teachers College, MA, 1963, professor diploma, 1967, EdD, 1970. **CAREER:** Hofstra University, assistant professor, 1965-70; St Johns University, assistant professor, 1970-75; Dowling College, associate professor, 1975-. **ORGANIZATIONS:** Kappa Delta Pi, Xi Chi Chapter, counselor, currently; Pi Lambda Theta, Alpha Epsilon Chapter, currently; Delta Kappa Gamma, Alpha Upsilon Chapter, currently; Newsday, advisory board, currently; Association of Supervisors and Curriculum Developers; Dowling College, Personnel Committee, faculty chairperson, 1991-93. **HONORS/AWARDS:** Kappa Delta Pi, Achievement Award, Chairperson of a National Committee, 1985; Delta Kappa Gamma, Alice Pierce Award. **SPECIAL ACHIEVEMENTS:** Publications: "Quantitative and Qualitative Eval of Soc St Textbook Contents," ERIC and Research in Ed, 1974; International Study of the Learning Styles of Korean Gifted Adolescents, Praeger Press, 1993; "Releasing Child Power," Delta Kappa Gamma Bulletin, 1975. **BUSINESS ADDRESS:** Associate Professor, Dowling College, Idle Hour Blvd, Science Bldg, Room 305, Oakdale, NY 11769.

SUH, BYUNGSE (BING)

Educator, physician. Korean American. **PERSONAL:** Born Mar 6, 1941, Ansung, Republic of Korea; son of Sang Keun and Chongsang Suh; married Youngjoo Lee Suh, Dec 21, 1974; children: Jason, Jessica, Janice. **EDUCATION:** Chungang University, BS, pharmacy, 1962; University of Kansas, MA, microbiology, 1967, PhD, microbiology, 1969; University of Miami School of Medicine, MD, 1973. **CAREER:** University of Wisconsin Medical School, housestaff, 1973-76, fellow, 1976-78; Temple University School of Medicine, assistant professor of medicine, 1978-83, associate professor of medicine, 1983-90, professor of medicine, 1990-. **ORGANIZATIONS:** Infectious Disease Society of America, fellow, 1976-; American College of Physicians, fellow, 1978-; American Society for Microbiology, 1964-; Philadelphia College of Physicians, 1988-; American College of Clinical Pharmacology, 1983p. **HONORS/AWARDS:** Chungang University, Most Distinguished Alumnus of the Year, 1989; Alpha Omega Alpha, Epsilon Chapter, honorary member. **SPECIAL ACHIEVEMENTS:** 50 scientific articles and book chapters. **BUSINESS ADDRESS:** Professor of Medicine, Section of Infectious Diseases, Temple University Health Sciences Center, Broad and Ontario Sts, Parkinson Pavilion, Ste 500, Philadelphia, PA 19140, (215)707-3603.

SUH, DAE-SOOK

Educator. Korean American. **PERSONAL:** Born Nov 22, 1931, Republic of Korea; married Yun-ok Suh; children: Maurice, Kevin. **EDUCATION:** Texas Christian University, BA, 1956; Indiana University, MA, 1958; Columbia University, PhD, 1964. **CAREER:** University of Houston, 1965-72; University of Hawaii, professor of political science, 1972-. **ORGANIZATIONS:** American Political Sciences Association, life member; Association for Asian Studies, 1964-. **HONORS/AWARDS:** Research Grants from: East-West Center, Columbia University, Ford Foundation, Fulbright, Woodrow Wilson Center for International Scholars, Smithsonian Institution. **SPECIAL ACHIEVEMENTS:** Books, Kim Il Sung: The North Korean Leader, Columbia University Press, 1988; Korean Communism: Reference Guide to the Political System, University of Hawaii, 1981; Documents of Korean Communism, Princeton University Press, 1971; The Korean Communist Movement, Princeton University Press, 1967. **BUSINESS ADDRESS:** Professor, Dept of Political Science, University of Hawaii, Honolulu, HI 96822-2281, (808)956-7041.

SUH, NAM PYO

Educator. Korean American. **PERSONAL:** Born Apr 22, 1936, Republic of Korea; son of Doo Soo Suh and Joon Joo Lee Suh; married Young Ja Suh, 1960; children: Mary, Helen, Grace, Caroline. **EDUCATION:** Massachusetts Institute of Technology, BS, 1959, MS, 1961; Carnegie-Mellon University, PhD, 1964; Worcester Polytechnic Institute, DEng 1986. **CAREER:** Guild Plashes, Inc, devt engineer, 1958-61; USM Corp res engineer, project mgr, 1961-65; University of South Carolina, assistant professor, 1965-68, associate professor, 1968-69; MIT, associate professor of mech engr, 1970-75, professor of mech engr, 1975-; NSF, assistant director for engineering (presidential appointee), 1984-88, Ralph E & Eloise F Cross Professor, 1989-, Department of Mechanical Engineering, head, 1990-, Manufacturing Institute, director, currently. **ORGANIZATIONS:** ASME, fellow; ASEE; SPE, CIRP, 1978; Royal Swedish Academy of Engineering Sciences, 1989. **HONORS/AWARDS:** ASME, The Gustus L Larson Memorial Award, 1976; ASME, The Blackall Award, The William T Ennor Manufacturing Technology Award, 1993; SME, FW Taylor Research Award; NSF, Distinguished Service Award, 1987; University of Massachusetts-Lowell, LHD, 1988; ASEE, Centennial Medal, 1993. **SPECIAL ACHIEVEMENTS:** Over 200 papers & 40 patents; author: The Principles of Design, Oxford University Press, 1990; Tribophysics, Prentice-Hall, 1986; Elements of Mechanical Behavior of Materials, McGraw-Hill, 1975; editor-in-chief, Robotics and Computer-Integrated Mfg. **BUSINESS ADDRESS:** Professor, Massachusetts Institute of Technology, Room 3-173, Cambridge, MA 02139, (617)253-2225.

SUH, YUNG-HO

Educator. Korean American. **PERSONAL:** Born Nov 15, 1956, Seoul, Republic of Korea; son of Suk-Don Suh and Young-Soon Kwon; married Hyewon Suh; children: Lina, Hannah, Brittany. **EDUCATION:** Seoul National University, BBA, 1979; Korean Advanced Institute of Science, MS, 1981; Syracuse University, PhD, MIS, 1990. **CAREER:** Korean Institute of Defense Analysis, researcher, 1981-84; Syracuse University, teaching instructor, 1986-90; University of Wisconsin-Eau Claire, assistant professor, 1990-. **ORGANIZATIONS:** ACM, 1988-92; Decision Sciences Institute, 1988-. **HONORS/AWARDS:** University of Wisconsin-Eau Claire, Summer Research Grant, 1993; Korean Institute for Defense Analysis, Superior Research Award, 1982.

SPECIAL ACHIEVEMENTS: Numerous papers presented and published in the area of expert systems verification and neural networks. **BUSINESS ADDRESS:** Assistant Professor, School of Business, University of Wisconsin-Eau Claire, Park and Garfield Ave, Eau Claire, WI 54702, (715)836-5968.

SUI, ANNA
Fashion designer. Chinese American. **PERSONAL:** Born 1955?, Dearborn Heights, MI; daughter of Paul and Grace Sui. **EDUCATION:** Parsons School of Design. **CAREER:** Lei, fashion magazine, stylist; Simultanee, designer; fashion designer, currently. **HONORS/AWARDS:** Perry Ellis Award for New Fashion Talent, 1992. **BIOGRAPHICAL SOURCES:** Current Biography Yearbook, 1993. **BUSINESS ADDRESS:** Fashion Designer, c/o Jill Nicholson, 853 7th Ave, Ste 10-A, New York, NY 10019, (212)582-3473.∗

SUM, GRACE C. K.
Association executive. Chinese American. **CAREER:** Pearl S Buck Foundation, executive director, currently. **BUSINESS ADDRESS:** Executive Director, Pearl S Buck Foundation, Green Hills Farm - Box 181, Perkasie, PA 18944-0181, (215)249-0100.∗

SUMARTOJO, JOJOK
Geologist. Indonesian American. **PERSONAL:** Born Jul 5, 1937, Surabaya, Java, Indonesia; son of Moedjono and Sasmini Surodikromo; married Esther Marie Davenport, Dec 22, 1966; children: Ekashanti, Widyarini. **EDUCATION:** Bandung Institute of Technology, Indonesia, mining engineer, 1961; University of Kentucky, MSc, geology, 1966; University of Cincinnati, PhD, geology, 1974. **CAREER:** University of Adelaide, Australia, demonstrator in geology, 1969-75; Vanderbuilt University, assistant professor of geology, 1975-80; Exxon Production Research Company, senior research specialist, 1980-86; Independent Consulting, Ekos consultants, 1986-88; EA Engineering, Science & Technology, senior geologist, 1988-89; Law Environmental Inc, senior geologist, 1989-91; UST Environmental Services, vice president/partner, 1991-. **ORGANIZATIONS:** Atlanta Geological Society, secretary, 1992-; Houston Geological Society, 1982-; Clay Minerals Society, 1978-; American Association of Petroleum Geologists, 1982-. **HONORS/AWARDS:** US State Dept/AID, graduate study in geology, 1962; Houston Geological Society, Environmental Geology, 1988; US Dept of Energy, Oakridge Associated University, Faculty Fellowship, 1976-78. **SPECIAL ACHIEVEMENTS:** Research in petroleum geology, 1975-86; academic teaching & research; published papers in precambrian geology; consulting in environmental assessments and remediation, 1986-; languages: Javanese, Indonesian, English, fluent written and oral; German, French, Dutch reading knowledge. **HOME ADDRESS:** 2236 Carlyle Drive, Marietta, GA 30062. **BUSINESS PHONE:** (404)955-2966.

SUMIDA, JON TETSURO
Educator. Japanese American. **PERSONAL:** Born Jul 7, 1949, Washington, DC; son of Theodore T & Sumi W Sumida; married Janet Marie, Aug 25, 1975; children: Madeline Claire, Lauren Michelle. **EDUCATION:** University of California, Santa Cruz, BA, 1971; University of Chicago, MA, 1974, PhD, 1982. **CAREER:** Roosevelt University, lecturer, 1980; University of Maryland, lecturer, 1980-82, assistant professor, 1982-88, associate professor, 1988-. **ORGANIZATIONS:** Journal of Military History, editorial advisory board; Society of Military Historians; International Naval Research Organization; United States Naval Institute; American Historical Association. **HONORS/AWARDS:** US Naval Historical Center, Hooper Research Grant, 1992; Guggenheim Foundation, fellowship, 1990-91; Wilson Center, fellowship, 1986; Churchill College, fellow-commoner, 1983. **SPECIAL ACHIEVEMENTS:** Author, In Defense of Naval Supremacy: Finance, Technology and British Naval Policy, 1889-1914, Boston, Unwin Hyman, 1989, Routledge paperback, 1993, The Pollen Papers: The Privately Circulated Printed Works of Arthur Hungerford Pollen, 1901-1916, London, George Allen & Unwin, for Navy Records Society, 1984. **BUSINESS ADDRESS:** Associate Professor, Dept of History, University of Maryland, College Park, MD 20742.

SUMIDA, KENNETH DEAN
Scientist, educator. Japanese American. **PERSONAL:** Born Dec 5, 1958, Pasadena, CA; son of Bill & Ruby Sumida. **EDUCATION:** University of Southern California, BS, 1981, PhD, 1993; California State University, Long Beach, HCA certificate, 1984; Chapman University, MS, 1987. **CAREER:** Chapman University, graduate assistant, 1985-86, faculty, 1986-87, assistant professor, 1994-; University of Southern California, teaching assistant, 1987-93, assistant lecturer, 1993-. **ORGANIZATIONS:** American College of Sports

Medicine, 1986-; American Physiological Society, 1991-. **HONORS/AWARDS:** American Physiological Society, Graduate Student Award, 1992. **SPECIAL ACHIEVEMENTS:** American College of Sports Medicine, Exercise Specialist Certification, 1988; American Journal of Physiology, vol 258, p R770-R776, 1990; Journal of Applied Physiology, vol 74, no 2, p782-787, 1993. **HOME ADDRESS:** 501 E Simmons Ave, Anaheim, CA 92802.

SUMII, TAKAO
Television company executive. Japanese American. **PERSONAL:** Born Jan 3, 1936, Toyko, Japan; son of Kohei Sumii and Tamako Sumii; married Misako Sumii, Jan 27, 1968; children: Asako. **EDUCATION:** International Christian University, bachelor's degree, 1958. **CAREER:** Nippon Television Network, sr correspondent for intl affairs, 1958-86; NTV Intl Corp, president, 1986-. **SPECIAL ACHIEVEMENTS:** Right to Know, 1980; Children and Television, 1978; The Front Line of the News Media Technology, 1983; Television in US, I, 1988, II, 1993. **BUSINESS ADDRESS:** President, NTV International, 50 Rockefeller Plaza, Ste 940, New York, NY 10020, (212)489-8390.

SUMISAKI, ROY
Law enforcement official. Japanese American. **CAREER:** Gilroy Police Department, chief of police, currently. **BUSINESS ADDRESS:** Chief of Police, Gilroy Police Department, 7370 Rosanna, Gilroy, CA 95020, (408)848-0300.∗

SUN, CHANG-TSAN
Educator. Chinese American. **PERSONAL:** Born Feb 20, 1928, Shen-Yang, Liaoning, China; son of Sun Yao-Tsung and Lee Chung-Shuan; married Jenny M Sun, Aug 17, 1963; children: Barry I-Lung, Karen I-Teh, Nancy I-Huei. **EDUCATION:** Taiwan University, 1953; Stevens Institute of Technology, 1960; Yale University, Doctor of Engineering, 1964. **CAREER:** Atomic Power Development Associates, 1964-65; Iowa State University, 1965-79; General Motors Research Laboratories, 1977-79; University of Florida, professor, 1979-. **ORGANIZATIONS:** American Society of Mechanical Engineers; American Society of Composites; Sigma Xi, Nu Society; Yale Engineering Association. **BUSINESS ADDRESS:** Professor, Dept of Aerospace Engg, Mechanics & Engg Sci, University of Florida, Aerospace Building, Gainesville, FL 32611, (904)392-8157.

SUN, CHIH REE
Educator. Chinese American. **PERSONAL:** Born May 6, 1923, Shuchen, Anhui, China; son of Fuling Sun & Chi Lan Pan; married Felicia Pu-Feng Sun, Dec 27, 1982; children: Lena, Eugene, Anna Vanacore. **EDUCATION:** University of Calcutta, BSc, 1947; UCLA, MS, 1951, PhD, 1956. **CAREER:** Princeton University, research staff member, 1956-62; Northwestern University, assistant professor, 1962-65; Queens College, associate professor, 1965-68; Princeton University, consultant, 1968-69; SUNY, Albany, professor, 1968-. **ORGANIZATIONS:** American Physical Society; American Association of University Professors. **HONORS/AWARDS:** Sigma Xi, 1951; Sigma, 1951; Frank Hsu Fellowship, 1954-56; SUNY, Albany, Presidential Award on Excellence in Research, 1986. **SPECIAL ACHIEVEMENTS:** Published over two hundred research papers in the fields of nuclear physics, elementary particles, higher energy physics detectors, nuclear instruments, particle accelerators, bubble chambers high energy channeling in Physics Rev Letters, Physical Review. **BUSINESS ADDRESS:** Professor, Dept of Physics, SUNY, Albany, 1400 Washington Ave, Albany, NY 12222, (518)442-4543.

SUN, FRANK F.
Scientific researcher. Chinese American. **PERSONAL:** Born Jul 26, 1938; married. **EDUCATION:** University of Texas, PhD, 1966. **CAREER:** The Upjohn Company, senior scientist, currently. **BUSINESS ADDRESS:** Senior Scientist, The Upjohn Company, 301 Henrietta St, Kalamazoo, MI 49001, (616)385-7917.

SUN, HUGO SUI-HWAN (SHU HUAN)
Educator. Chinese American. **PERSONAL:** Born Oct 19, 1940, Hong Kong; son of Jun T Sun and Sarah H Sun; married Ixin Wen, Jun 6, 1989. **EDUCATION:** University of California, Berkeley, BA, 1963; University of Maryland, College Park, MA, 1966; University of New Brunswick, Fredericton, Canada, PhD, 1969. **CAREER:** University of New Brunswick, assistant professor of math, 1969-70; California State University, Fresno, professor of mathematics, 1970-. **ORGANIZATIONS:** American Math Society, 1970-. **HONORS/AWARDS:** World Congress of Poets, First Anthology Award, 1981. **BUSINESS ADDRESS:** Professor, Mathematics Dept, California State University, Fresno, CA 93740-0108, (209)278-4633.

SUN, RICHARD C.

Metallurgical engineer. Chinese American. **PERSONAL:** Born Jan 5, 1935, Nanking, China; son of Kung-Yu Sun and Ta-Chen C Sun; married Shirley Sun, Sep 10, 1966; children: Juliana L, William C. **EDUCATION:** Taipei Institute of Technology, Taipei, AA, 1956; Missouri School of Mines, BS, 1959; Northwestern University, MS, material science, 1962; The University of Wisconsin, PhD, metallurgical engineering, 1967. **CAREER:** Cabot Corp, 1966-79; Certified Alloy Products, 1979-81; Smith Tool, 1982; Coast Cast, 1983-84; V&W Castings, technical director, 1984-86; American Racing Equipment Inc, Foundry R&D, technical director, currently. **ORGANIZATIONS:** American Foundrymen's Society; American Society for Metals; SAE, The Engineering Society for Advancing Mobility: Land, Sea, Air and Space. **HONORS/AWARDS:** Sigma Xi; Phi Kappa Phi. **SPECIAL ACHIEVE-MENTS:** 5 publications; language proficiency: Chinese. **MILITARY SERVICE:** Chinese Nationalist Army, 2nd lt, 1956. **HOME ADDRESS:** 2562 E Riles Circle, Anaheim, CA 92806, (714)533-4207. **BUSINESS PHONE:** (310)761-4946.

SUN, SAMUEL SAI-MING

Educator. Chinese American. **PERSONAL:** Born Sep 15, 1942, Canton, China; son of Keung Sun and Siu-Ying Wong; married Piera S Sun, May 25, 1974; children: Bryan. **EDUCATION:** Chinese University of Hong Kong, BSc, 1966, University of Hong Kong, BSc (honors), 1969, MSc, 1971; University of Wisconsin-Madison, PhD, 1974. **CAREER:** University of Wisconsin, postdoc associate, 1975-79, assistant scientist, 1979-80; ARCO Plant Cell Res Institute, senior and principal scientist, 1980-86; Shanghai Jiao University, visiting scholar, 1984; Plant Cell Research Institute, director, mol biology, 1986-87; Beijing Agriculture University, visiting professor, 1989-; University of Hawaii, associate professor, 1987-91, professor, 1992-. **ORGANIZA-TIONS:** International Society for Plant Molecular Biology, 1984-; American Society for Plant Physiologists, 1971-; American Association for the Advancement of Science, 1988-; Society of Chinese-American Bioscientists in America, 1987-. **HONORS/AWARDS:** Hong Kong Government, scholarship, 1962-66; New Asia College, distinction scholarship, 1966; ARCO, distinguished research award, 1984. **SPECIAL ACHIEVEMENTS:** Representative publications: "Intervening Sequence in a Plant Gene," Nature, 1981; "Enhancement of Methionine Content of Seed Protein," Plant Mol Biol, 1989; "Arcelin Seed Protein," Science, 1988; "Phosphoenolpyruvate Carboxylase Gene," Plant Mol Biol, 1992; "Transgenic Plants for Improving Seed Protein", book chapters, 1992. **HOME ADDRESS:** 7008 Niumalu Loop, Honolulu, HI 96825. **BUSINESS PHONE:** (808)956-6893.

SUN, TUNG-TIEN

Educator. Taiwanese American. **PERSONAL:** Born Feb 20, 1947, ChungKing, China; son of Chung-Yu Sun and Wen Lin; married Brenda S Y Sun; children: I-Hsing, I-Fong. **EDUCATION:** National Taiwan University, Taipei, BS, agricultural chem, 1967; University of California, Davis, PhD, biochemistry, 1974; Massachusetts Institute of Technology, postdoctoral, 1978. **CA-REER:** Massachusetts Institute of Technology, biology, research associate, 1974-78; Johns Hopkins University Medical School, dermatology & cell biology, assistant professor, 1978-81; cell biology, dermatology, ophthalmology, associate professor, 1981-82; New York University Medical School, dermatology and pharmacology, associate professor, 1982-86, pharmacology and dermatology, professor, 1986-, dermatology, Rudolf L Baer Professor, 1990-; University Pennsylvania Medical School, adjunct professor of dermatology, 1992-. **ORGANIZATIONS:** Society of Chinese Bioscientists in America, councilor, 1988-90; Cell Biology Study Section, National Institutes of Health, 1984-88; International Society Differentiation, board of directors, 1985-88, editorial board, 1984-; Society of Investigative Dermatology, board of directors, 1993-, associate editor, 1990-; Journal of Epithelial Cell Biology, editorial board, 1990-; Journal of Dermatological Science, editorial board, 1992-; Hair Research Society, board of directors, 1992-. **HONORS/AWARDS:** National Eye Institute, Research Career Development Award, 1978-82; Monique Weill-Caulier Career Scientist Award, 1984-89; University of Toronto Medical School, Canada, Angus Lecturer, 1986; American Academy Dermatopathologists, Pinkus Lecturer, 1986; Stanford Medical School, Liu Lecturer, 1987; Society of Invest Dermatology, Montagna Lecturer, 1989; Harvard Medical School, Swerling Lecturer, 1991; American Association for the Advancement of Science, Fellow, 1992; Alcon Award for Outstanding Research in Ophthalmology, 1993. **SPECIAL ACHIEVEMENTS:** Studies on epithelial growth and differentiation. **BUSINESS ADDRESS:** Rudolf L Baer Professor of Derm & Pharm, New York University Medical School, 560 First Ave, Tisch Hospital, Rm 359, New York, NY 10016, (212)263-5685.

SUN, WEN-YIH

Educator. Taiwanese American. **PERSONAL:** Born Oct 4, 1945, I-Lan, Taiwan; son of Dong-Liang and Ah-Chun Sun; married Rueen-yuh Lee, Nov 1973; children: Ming-Teh, Ming-Hwi. **EDUCATION:** National Taiwan University, BS, 1968; The University of Chicago, MS, 1972, PhD, 1975. **CAREER:** University of Chicago, research associate, 1975; University of Illinois, research assistant professor, 1975-78; Princeton University, visiting scientist, 1978-79; Purdue University, professor, 1979-. **ORGANIZATIONS:** American Meteorology Society; North American Taiwanese Professors' Association, vice president, 1992-93., president, 1993-94. **HONORS/AWARDS:** NSF, research grants, 1982-; NASA, research grant; US Army, research grant; DOE, research grants. **SPECIAL ACHIEVEMENTS:** Scientific papers published in: Journal of Atomspheric Sciences, 1975-; Journal of Applied Meteorology; Monthly Weather Review; Journal of Computational Physics, Beitrage zur Physik der Atmosphere; Atmospheric Environment; Boundary Layer Meteor, Terrestrial, Atmospheric and Oceanic Sciences; Foundation Louis De Broglic, Quarterly Journal of the Royal Meteorlogical Society, and book chapters; Terrestrial, Atmospheric and Oceanic Sciences, associate editor; Laboratory for Atmospheric Research, Army, consultant. **MILITARY SERVICE:** Taiwan Air Force, second lt, 1968-69. **BUSINESS ADDRESS:** Professor, Dept of Earth & Atmospheric Sciences, Purdue University, Civil Engineering Bldg, West Lafayette, IN 47907, (317)494-7681.

SUNAIDA, MARI

Actress, writer. Japanese American. **PERSONAL:** Born in Santa Monica, CA; married John Snyder. **CAREER:** Director, Seoul to Soul; produced spoken word compact disc portion, "The Verdict and the Violence," High Performance; co-writer, production, We've Come This Far; actress, writer, Hybrid Vigor, 1992. **SPECIAL ACHIEVEMENTS:** Pacific Asian American Women Writers - West, reader at International Women's Month Celebration, 1993. **BIOGRAPHICAL SOURCES:** "Seoul to Soul: Art as a Force for Social Change," Los Angeles Times, section F, p 6, March 14, 1992.*

SUNDARAM, KALYAN

Research scientist. Indo-American. **PERSONAL:** Born Nov 22, 1932, Hyderabad, Andhra Pradesh, India; son of Shamrao and Savitri; married Kathleen, Apr 29, 1967; children: Shaker Sean, Debra Jean. **EDUCATION:** Omaria University, Hyderabad, BVSc, 1956; University of Manitoba, MSc, 1963; Purdue University, PhD, 1966. **CAREER:** Goot of Andram, Pradesh, India, vet suregon, 1956-61; Sloan Kettering Institute, fellow, 1966-67; The Population Council, scientist, 1967-90, senior scientist, 1990-. **ORGANIZATIONS:** Society of Toxicology, 1988-93; The Endocrine Society, 1975-93; Society of the Study of Reproduction, 1976-93; American Society of Andiology, 1980-93. **SPECIAL ACHIEVEMENTS:** Diplomate, American Board of Toxicology, 1987. **BUSINESS ADDRESS:** Senior Scientist, The Population Council, 1230 York Ave, New York, NY 10021, (212)327-8743.

SUNDARAM, MEENAKSHI R.

Educator, engineer. Indo-American. **PERSONAL:** Born Jun 20, 1942, Salem, Tamil Nadu, India; son of R N Ramalinga Mudaliar and R Rengathayee Ramalingam; married Kalavathy Sundaram, Jun 10, 1971; children: Brintha M, Karthik M. **EDUCATION:** Madras University, BE, 1963, MSc, 1967; Texas Tech University, PhD, 1976. **CAREER:** Government of India, special grade apprentice, 1963, superintendent, grade I, 1964-65; College of Engineering, Guindy, Madras, India, lecturer in mechanical engineering, 1967-73; Old Dominion University, assistant professor, 1976-78; SUNY College of Technology, associate professor, 1979; Tennessee Tech University, professor of industrial engineering, 1980-. **ORGANIZATIONS:** Institute of Industrial Engineers, senior member, 1976-; Society of Manufacturing Engineers, senior member, 1976-; American Society of Mechanical Engineers, 1986-. **HONORS/AWARDS:** Alpha Pi Mu, 1977; Commonwealth of Virginia, Professional Engineer, 1979. **SPECIAL ACHIEVEMENTS:** Over 50 publications and four books. **HOME PHONE:** (615)432-4828. **BUSINESS AD-DRESS:** Professor of Industrial Engineering, Tennessee Technological University, Box 5011, Cookeville, TN 38505, (615)372-3790.

SUNDARESAN, GLORIA MARQUEZ

Government employee, research chemist. Filipino American. **PERSONAL:** Born Aug 30, 1940, Iloilo City, Panay Island, Philippines; daughter of Visitacion Beciete Marquez and P Marquez; married Peruvemba Ramnathan Sundaresan, Dec 23, 1970; children: Sita Marquez, Ramesh Marquez. **EDU-CATION:** University of San Agustin, Philippines, BS, 1960. **CAREER:** Massachusetts General Hospital, chemist, 1966-69; Tufts New England Medical Center, chemist, 1969-70; St Joseph Research Institute, research associate, 1970-78; National Institutes of Health, chemist, 1982-89; Food & Drug Administration, chemist, 1978-82, research chemist, 1989-. **ORGANIZATIONS:** American Association of Pharmaceutical Sciences, 1991-93; Federal Asian Pacific American Council, recording secretary, 1990-91, vice chair, 1992-93, chair, 1993-94, national conference coordinator, 1990-91, National Training Conference, treasurer, 1990-91, national chapter, chairperson, 1992-93, congressional liaison, White House liaison and adviser for congressional reception, training conference and job fair, 1994; FDA, Asian Representative, 1992-94, Asian Pacific American Advisory Forum, vice chair, 1990-93. **HONORS/ AWARDS:** National Institutes of Health, Appreciation, Recognition Special Award, 1984; FDA, Asian Pacific American Advisory Forum, Leadership, Superior Services, 1992; Fed Asian Pacific American Council, Outstanding Achievement, 1992, 1993; Lancaster PA art show for "Leaves", which was chosen as the favorite oil painting, 1977; area speech contest winner, 1985. **SPECIAL ACHIEVEMENTS:** Work for civil rights and employment rights of Asian Pacific American federal employees. **BUSINESS ADDRESS:** Chairperson, Federal Asian Pacific American Council, PO Box 23184, Washington, DC 20026-3184, (202)205-4295.

SUNDARESAN, P. RAMNATHAN
Research scientist. Indo-American. **PERSONAL:** Born Aug 11, 1930, Madras, Tamil Nadu, India; son of P A & Saraswathi Ramanathan; married Gloria M Sundaresan, Dec 23, 1970; children: Sita, Ramesh. **EDUCATION:** University of Banaras, BSc, 1950, MSc, 1953; Indian Institute of Science, Bangalore, PhD, 1959. **CAREER:** Council of Science & Industrial Research, New Delhi, senior research fellow, 1959-61; University of Illinois, research associate, 1961-62; Massachusetts Institute of Technology, research associate, 1962-64; US Army Research Institute of Environmental Medicine, visiting scientist research associate, 1964-66, research biochemist, 1966-68; St Joseph Hospital, Lipids Lab, chief, 1968-77; Food and Drug Administration, review scientist in toxicology, 1977-82, research chemist, nutrient toxicity, 1982-92, research chemist, DSAT, OSN, CFSAN, 1992-. **ORGANIZATIONS:** American Institute of Nutrition; American Society Biochemistry & Molecular Biology; American College of Toxicology; American Institute Chemists; Biochemical Society, England; International Association for Nutrition & Cancer; Sigma Xi, FDA Chapter. **HONORS/AWARDS:** Council of Science & Industrial Research, New Delhi, Senior Research Fellow, 1959; National Academy of Science, National Research Council, Visiting Scientist Research Associate, 1964-66; National Institutes of Health, Research Grantee, 1970-77. **SPECIAL ACHIEVEMENTS:** Millersville State College, research consultant & adjunct associate professor, 1972-77; Veterans Administration Medical Center, Washington, DC, consultant, biochemistry, 1973-77; Lipid Research Lab, Veterans Administration Medical Center, consultant, 1983; Foodsci, Technology, Nutrition Panel, AID, Off Scientific Adviser, Washington, DC, 1990; National Cancer Institute, SEG, Bethesda, MD, 1988. **BUSINESS ADDRESS:** Research Chemist, Div of Science & Appl Technology, Off Spec Nutritionals/Ctr Food Safety & Appl Nutrition, US Food & Drug Administration, 8301 Muirkirk Rd, MOD1, Rm G313, Laurel, MD 20708, (301)594-6009.

SUNG, BETTY LEE
Professor emerita, author. Chinese American. **PERSONAL:** Born Oct 3, 1924, Baltimore, MD; married Charles C M Chung; children: Tina, Victor, Cynthia, Alan, Wilma, Cathie, Vivian, Calvin. **EDUCATION:** University of Illinois, BA, 1948; Queens College of CUNY, MLS, 1968; City University of New York, Graduate Center, PhD, 1983. **CAREER:** Army Map Service, Chinese transliterator, 1942-45; Voice of America/US Information Service, radio script writer, 1949-54; housewife & mother, 1954-60; Islands in the Sun Club Magazine, assoc editor, 1960-61; Doubleday Educ Div, chief copy editor, 1962-64; Crowell Collier Pub Co, assoc editor, 1964; McGraw Hill, Doubleday, et al, free-lance editor; Queens Borough Public Lib, librarian, 1965-70; City University of New York, Bd of Higher Educ, chancellor's fellow, 1981-82; Princeton University, visiting prof, 1989; City College of New York, instructor, beginning 1970, Dept of Asian Studies, prof & chair, until 1992. **ORGANIZATIONS:** Asian American Studies Assn; Organization of Chinese Americans; Asian American Advisory Comm for 1980 Census, 1977-80; Chancellor's Asian Pacific American Advisory Council, NY Bd of Educ, 1992-; Ctr for Migration Studies Advisory Bd, 1991-. **HONORS/AWARDS:** Phi Beta Kappa; Phi Kappa Phi; Alpha Kappa Delta; Asian American Studies, Outstanding Service Award, 1989; Asian Pacific American Librarians Association, Distinguished Service Award, 1990; Choice Magazine, Outstanding Book of 1976 for: A Survey of Chinese American Manpower & Employment. **SPECIAL ACHIEVEMENTS:** Author, books, including: Mountain of Gold,

1967; Survey of Chinese American Manpower & Employment, 1976; Statistical Profiles of Chinese in the US, 1979; Adjustment Experience of Chinese Immigrant Children in New York City, 1987; Chinese American Intermarriage, 1990; Overseas Chinese Research Assn, Canton, China, speaker: "Overview of the Chinese in the US," 1993; initiated first courses in Asian American Studies in the entire Eastern seaboard at City College of New York, 1970. **HOME ADDRESS:** 165 Park Row, Apt 20F, New York, NY 10038.

SUNG, CHI CHING
Educator. Chinese American. **PERSONAL:** Born Mar 5, 1936, Nanking, China; married Janet, 1968; children: Eric, Julie. **EDUCATION:** National Taiwan University, BSc, 1959; Washington University, St Louis, MS, 1960; University of California, Berkeley, PhD, 1965. **CAREER:** Ohio State Univ, assistant professor, 1969-73; University of Al, Physics Department, associate professor, 1973-78, professor, 1978-. **ORGANIZATIONS:** Am Opt Society, 1980-, fellow, 1993-. **BUSINESS ADDRESS:** Professor, Physics Department, University of Alabama, Huntsville, AL 35899, (205)895-6276.

SUNG, LAWRENCE M.
Attorney. Taiwanese American. **PERSONAL:** Born Oct 18,1965, Quebec; son of Cheng-Po Sung and Chiu-Mei Sung. **EDUCATION:** University of Pennsylvania, BA, 1985; US Dept of Defense, Uniformed Services University of the Health Sciences, PhD, 1990; American University, Washington College of Law, JD, 1993. **CAREER:** Finnegan, Henderson, Farabon, Garrett & Dunner, summer associate, law clerk, 1991-93; US Court of Appeals for the Federal Circuit, law clerk, currently. **ORGANIZATIONS:** Asian-Pacific American Law Students Assn, Washington College of Law, co-chairperson, 1991-92; American Assn for the Advancement of Science, 1987-; American Society for Microbiology, 1985-. **HONORS/AWARDS:** American University Law Review, Federal Circuit Editor, 1992-93; Graduate Research Colloquium, Outstanding Performance Commendation, 1988. **SPECIAL ACHIEVEMENTS:** Co-author, works include: "Will You Be Liable for Patent Infringement?," 5 BioPharm 26, 1992; author: "Intellectual Property Protection or Protectionism?: Declaratory Judgment Use by Patent Owners Against Prospective Infringers," 42 Am U L Rev 239, 1992. **HOME ADDRESS:** 5301 Westbard Circle, #415, Bethesda, MD 20816-1428, (301)654-2123. **BUSINESS ADDRESS:** Law Clerk to Judge Raymond C Clevenger, III, US Court of Appeals for the Federal Circuit, 717 Madison Pl NW, Washington, DC 20439, (202)633-5909.

SUNG, ZINMAY RENEE
Educator. Chinese American. **PERSONAL:** Born Feb 16, 1947, Shanghai, China; married Nelson N H Teng, Mar 6, 1974. **EDUCATION:** University of California, Berkeley, PhD, 1973. **CAREER:** University of California, Berkeley, assistant professor, 1976-83, associate professor, 1983-89, professor, 1989-. **SPECIAL ACHIEVEMENTS:** Co-author, "EMF, an Arabidopsis Gene Required for Vegetative Shoot Development," Science, 258, 1645-1647, 1992. **BUSINESS ADDRESS:** Professor, Dept of Plant Biology, University of California, 111 Kashland Hall, Berkeley, CA 94720, (510)642-6966.

SUNOO, BRENDA PAIK
Journalist. Korean American. **PERSONAL:** Born Feb 13, 1948, Los Angeles, CA; daughter of Edward & Katherine Paik; married Jan Jung-min Sunoo, Sep 20, 1969; children: David, Tommy. **EDUCATION:** UCLA, BA, 1970. **CAREER:** East West Newspaper, freelance reporter, 1984-85; Orange County Register, reporter, 1986-87; Rice Magazine, features editor, 1988; Korea Times, English Edition, news editor, staff writer, 1988-93. **ORGANIZATIONS:** Asian American Journalists Association, 1985-; UCLA Amerasia Journal, Media Advisory Committee, 1985-. **HONORS/AWARDS:** California Teachers Association, John Swett Award, Certificate of Merit, 1987.

SURTI, TARUN NATWARLAL
Business executive. Indo-American. **PERSONAL:** Born Feb 8, 1950, Vyara, Gujarat, India; son of Natwavlal M Tailor and Dhanuben N Tailor; married Lata T Surti, Sep 11, 1980; children: Vivek T, Zarna T. **EDUCATION:** Gandhi College of Engineering & Technology, electrical, 1971, mechanical, 1972. **CAREER:** American Ribbon Technology, president; ARTE Corp, president, currently. **ORGANIZATIONS:** India Association of Nashville, president; NFIA, regional vice president; Indo-American Hospitality Association, conuenor. **HOME ADDRESS:** 899 S Curtiswood Ln, Nashville, TN 37204-4320. **BUSINESS PHONE:** (615)832-8800.

SURYANARAYANAN, RAJ GOPALAN

Educator. Indo-American. **PERSONAL:** Born Apr 19, 1955, Cuddalore, Tamil Nadu, India; son of Pushpa Rajagopalan & Natesan Rajagopalan; married Shanti Suryanarayanan, Nov 24, 1985; children: Priya M, Meera S. **EDUCATION:** Banaras Hindu University, BPharm, 1976, MPharm, 1978; University of British Columbia, MSc, 1981, PhD, 1985. **CAREER:** Indian Drugs and Pharmaceuticals Ltd, management trainee, 1978; Roche Products Limited, production supervisor, 1979; University of British Columbia, teaching assistant, 1979, 1982-83; University of Minnesota, assistant professor, 1985-92, associate professor, 1992-. **ORGANIZATIONS:** American Pharmaceutical Association, 1985-86; American Association of Pharmaceutical and Scientists, 1986-; American Association of Colleges of Pharmacy, 1986-; American Association for the Advancement of Science, 1991-. **HONORS/AWARDS:** Banaras Hindu University, Aruna & Malaviya Gold Medal, 1976, BHU Gold Medal, 1976; Indian Drug Manufacturers Association, IDMA-GP Nair Award, 1976; Science Council of British Columbia, Graduate Research in Engineering and Technology Award, 1979-82; numerous others. **SPECIAL ACHIEVEMENTS:** Author or co-author of: "Modified USP Assay of Calcium Gluceptate," J Pharm Sci, vol 70, p 968, 1981; "The Precipitation of Calcium Gluceptate from Aqueous Solutions," J Pharm Sci, vol 73, p 78-82, 1984; "Evaluation of Two Concepts of Crystallinity Using Calcium Gluceptate as a Model Compound," Int J Pharm, vol 24, p 1-17,1985; numerous others. **BIOGRAPHICAL SOURCES:** "Minnesota Pharmacy Prof Received Top Award," Pharmacy Times, pages 42-50, May 1993. **BUSINESS ADDRESS:** Associate Professor, College of Pharmacy, Univ of Minnesota, 308 Harvard St SE, 9-127B Health Sciences Unit F, Minneapolis, MN 55455, (612)624-9626.

SUZAWA, NAOKO M.

Interpreter. Japanese American. **PERSONAL:** Born Feb 16, 1959, Mitoyo-gun, Hagawa-ken, Japan; daughter of Nobuyoshi and Miyoko Matsuda; married Shoichi Suzawa, Dec 25, 1991. **EDUCATION:** Sophia University, BA, 1982. **CAREER:** American Foreign Insurance Assn, exec secretary, 1983-84; United Nations, Public Information Dept, secretary, 1984-85; Salomon Brothers, Asia, sales/trading assistant, 1985-88; free-lance translator/coordinator, services for: Honda of America, Nippon Steel, Asahi Glass, 1988-91; TS Trim Industries, interpreter, 1991-. **HOME ADDRESS:** 290 Glen Village Ct, Powell, OH 43065, (614)436-4948.

SUZUKAWA, STEVEN

Judge. Japanese American. **PERSONAL:** Born 1954?. **CAREER:** Municipal Court, judge, 1989-92; California Superior Court, judge, 1992-. **BUSINESS ADDRESS:** Judge, Superior Court of Los Angeles, 200 W Compton Blvd, Compton, CA 90220, (916)322-5957.*

SUZUKI, BOB H.

Educational administrator. Japanese American. **EDUCATION:** University of California, Berkeley, bachelor's and master's degrees, mechanical engineering; California Institute of Technology, PhD, aeronautics. **CAREER:** University of Southern California, School of Engineering, instructor, 1967-71; University of Massachusetts, Amherst, Division of Education Policy, administration and research, professor, School of Education, assistant dean for administration, 1971-74; California State University, Los Angeles, dean of graduate studies and research, 1981-85; California State University, Northridge, vice president of academic affairs, 1985-91; California State Polytechnic University, Pomona, president, 1991-. **HONORS/AWARDS:** National Education Association, Human Rights Award for Leadership in Asian Pacific Island Affairs, first recipient. **SPECIAL ACHIEVEMENTS:** Asked to serve on Council of Advisors by chair of President-elect Bill Clinton's Education Transition Team, 1993; appointed to the national board of the Fund for Improvement of Postsecondary Education, 1994; author, numerous articles on Asian Americans and education; specialist in multicultural education. **BUSINESS ADDRESS:** President, California State Polytechnic University, Pomona, 3801 W Temple Ave, Pomona, CA 91768-2557.*

SUZUKI, HOWARD KAZURO

Sculptor. Japanese American. **PERSONAL:** Born Apr 3, 1927, Ketchikan, AK; son of George Kichijro Suzuki and Tsuya Suzuki; married Tetsuko Suzuki, Aug 11, 1952; children: Georgeanne Joan Hart, James, Stanley. **EDUCATION:** Marquette University, BS, 1949, MS, 1951; University of Michigan, 1949-51; Tulane University, PhD, 1955. **CAREER:** Yale University, anatomy instructor, 1955-58; University of Arkansas, assistant to professor anatomy, 1958-70; University of Florida, associate health related professor, 1970-72, professor of anatomy, 1970-90, dean, health related professor, 1972-79;

Aquatic Life Sculptures, owner, currently. **ORGANIZATIONS:** American Artists Prof League, 1991-; Civitans Regional Blood Center, board member, 1977-. **HONORS/AWARDS:** Netherlands Antiles, Bonaire Foundation for Arts, intern exchange artist, 1991; Arkansas Wildlife Federation, conservation educator, 1967; American Association Adv Science, fellow, 1967. **SPECIAL ACHIEVEMENTS:** Numerous contributions to scientific journals. **BUSINESS ADDRESS:** Owner, Aquatic Life Sculptures, 4331 NW 20th Pl, Gainesville, FL 32605, (904)372-5661.

SUZUKI, MASAO FRED

Educator. Japanese American/Filipino American. **PERSONAL:** Born May 21, 1955, San Francisco, CA; son of Mary Irene Bonzo Suzuki and Iwao Lewis Suzuki; married Susan Midori Nakamura, Aug 24, 1991. **EDUCATION:** University of California, Berkeley, AB, economics, 1983; Stanford University, PhD, economics, 1994. **CAREER:** UC Berkeley, tutor, 1982-84, principal clerk, 1984-87; Stanford University, teaching assistant, 1988-91, instructor, 1990-92, teaching assistant coordinator, 1992-93; Mills College, Department of Economics, assistant professor, 1993-. **ORGANIZATIONS:** American Economic Association, 1988-; Economic History Association, 1988-; Nihonmachi Outreach Committee, 1989-; Association for Asian American Studies, 1990-; Japanese American Citizens League, 1991-. **HONORS/AWARDS:** Phi Beta Kappa, 1983. **BUSINESS ADDRESS:** Assistant Professor, Dept of Econ, Mills College, 5000 MacArthur Boulevard, Oakland, CA 94613, (510)430-2346.

SUZUKI, MICHIO (MIKE)

Federal social work executive. Japanese American. **PERSONAL:** Born Oct 26, 1928, Oakland, CA; son of George Kanichiro Suzuki and Haruko Suzuki; married Namiko H Suzuki, Oct 29, 1955; children: Peter Michiro, Linda Haruko. **EDUCATION:** University of California, Berkeley, AB, 1949, School of Social Work, MSW, 1952. **CAREER:** Jewish Family Services of NYC, caseworker, 1952-55; Shonien/Japan, American Comm Services, director, 1958-63; California Department of Social Welfare, director of social services, 1963-72; US Department of Health and Human Services, senior executive services, 1972-. **ORGANIZATIONS:** National Association of Social Workers, 1957-; Academy of Certified Social Workers; National Council on Aging; American Public Welfare Association; US Committee-International Council on Social Welfare; American Society on Aging. **BUSINESS ADDRESS:** Director, Office of Policy Coordination and Analysis, Administration on Aging, US Department of Health and Human Services, 330 Independence Ave SW, Cohen Bldg, Rm 4254, Washington, DC 20201, (202)619-2615.

SUZUKI, PAUL TED

Attorney. Japanese American. **PERSONAL:** Born Dec 18, 1948, Los Angeles, CA. **EDUCATION:** UCLA, BA, public service, 1971, JD, 1974. **CAREER:** Suzuki & Ito, attorney, currently. **ORGANIZATIONS:** Asian Business Association, president, 1992, board of directors, 1993; Japanese American Bar Association, board of governors, 1984; Japanese American Democrats, president, 1982; ACLU, Riverside Chapter, president, 1976; JACL, Marina Chapter, president, 1975. **HONORS/AWARDS:** LA Business Journal, Outstanding Business Leader, 1993; Asian Business Association, Outstanding Leadership Award, 1992; Riverside Legal Aid, Community Legal Advocate, 1974. **BUSINESS ADDRESS:** Attorney, Suzuki and Ito Law Offices, 2975 Wilshire Blvd, #425, Los Angeles, CA 90010, (213)306-6850.

SUZUKI, TSUNEO

Scientist, educator. Japanese American. **PERSONAL:** Born Nov 23, 1931, Nagoya, Aichi, Japan; son of Morichika Suzuki and Toshiko Suzuki; widowed; children: Riichiro, Aijiro, Yozo. **EDUCATION:** Tokyo University, MD, 1957; Hokkaido University, Japan, PhD, 1969. **CAREER:** University of Kansas Med Ctr, assistant professor, 1970-79, associate professor, 1979-83, professor, 1983-. **ORGANIZATIONS:** NIH Experimental Immunology Study Section, 1983-87; American Association of Immunologists, 1970-; American Society for Leukocyte Biology, 1980-; American Society for Biochemisty and Molecular Biology, 1986-. **HONORS/AWARDS:** Fulbright Scholarship, 1962; American Society for Biochemistry and Molecular Biology, travel grant, 1988; University of Kansas Med Ctr, Senior Investigation Award, 1990. **BUSINESS ADDRESS:** Prof, Dept of Microbiology, Molecular Genetics and Immunology, University of Kansas Medical Center, 3901 Rainbow Blvd, Kansas City, KS 66160-7420, (913)588-6724.

SWAROOP, ANAND
Scientist, educator. Indo-American. **PERSONAL:** Born Jan 14, 1957, Turrah, Uttar Pradesh, India; son of Shanti Sarup and Dharamvati Sarna; married Manju Swaroop, Dec 11, 1982; children: Alok, Kanchan. **EDUCATION:** Meerut University, India, BSc, 1975; GB Pant University, Pantnagar, India, MSc, 1977; Indian Institute of Science, Bangalore, India, PhD, 1982. **CAREER:** Yale University, post doctoral associate, 1982-86, associate research scientist, 1986-90; University of Michigan, Ann Arbor, assistant professor, 1990-. **ORGANIZATIONS:** American Association for the Advancement of Science; American Society for Microbiology; American Society of Human Genetics; Association for Research in Vision and Ophthalmology; National Institute of Health, Mammalian Genetics Study, 1992; National Eye Institute, Special Review Committee, 1993; Michigan Human Genome Center Executive Committee, 1990-. **HONORS/AWARDS:** National Society to Prevent Blindness, Virginia Boyce Award, 1988; Retinitis Pigmentosa Foundation, Young Investigator Award, 1990. **SPECIAL ACHIEVEMENTS:** Approximately 30 research publications in peer-reviewed journals; Research Grants from National Eye Institute and RP Foundation. **HOME ADDRESS:** 3481 Yellowstone Dr., Ann Arbor, MI 48105. **BUSINESS ADDRESS:** Assistant Professor, University of Michigan, 1000 Wall St., 540 Kellogg Eye Center, Ann Arbor, MI 48105, (313)936-9547.

SY, ANTONIO NGO, JR.
Information systems analyst. Chinese American/Filipino American. **PERSONAL:** Born Aug 28, 1964, Manila, Philippines; son of Antonio A Sy and Mary N Sy. **EDUCATION:** University of the Philippines, BS, industrial engineering, 1987; University of Illinois at Champaign-Urbana, MBA, 1991. **CAREER:** Sycip, Gorres, Velayo & Co, technical analyst, 1987-88; Marton Mfg, Phils, plant mgr, 1988-89; General Electric Co, information systems analyst, 1991-. **ORGANIZATIONS:** Fil-Am Society of Kentuckiana, 1991-; Wire Assn Intl, 1989-; Society of Mfg Engineers, 1992-. **HONORS/AWARDS:** General Electric Co, Managerial Award, 1992.

SY, BON KIEM
Educator. Hong Kong American. **PERSONAL:** Born Dec 27, 1961, Hong Kong, People's Republic of China; son of Gui Hong Sy and Pil Wan Hui. **EDUCATION:** Hong Kong Polytechnic, higher diploma, 1983, associateship, 1984; Northeastern University, MSc, 1986, PhD, 1988. **CAREER:** Northeastern University, research & teaching assistant, 1985-88; New England Medical Center, consultant, 1987-88; City University of New York, assistant professor, 1988-. **ORGANIZATIONS:** American Association on Artifical Intelligence, 1988-; Institute of Electrical and Electronics Engineers, 1983-; American Society of Acoustics, 1988-; Association for Computing Machinery, 1988-. **SPECIAL ACHIEVEMENTS:** "A Recurrence Local Computation Approach towards Ordering Computer Hypotheses," International Journal of Approximate Reasoning, January 1993; "Reasoning Composite Beliefs Using Qualitative Approach," Annals of Mathematics and Artifical Intelligence, Vol 4, 1991; "AI-Based Communication System for Non-verbal, Motor Disabled: Design Methodologies and Prototype Testing," IEEE Trans on Biomedical Engineering, May 1989; "A Frame Architecture for a Certain Class of Graph Search Algorithm," IEEE Trans on Systems, Man & Cybernetics, Sep 1988; "Reasoning MPE to Multiply Connected Belief Networks Using Message Passing," Proc of the 10th National Conference on Artifical Intelligence, July 1992. **BUSINESS ADDRESS:** Asst Professor, Dept of Computer Science, Queens College, City University of New York, 65-30 Kissena Blvd, NSB A202, Flushing, NY 11367, (718)997-3500.

SY, FRANCISCO S.
Educator, epidemiologist. Filipino American/Chinese American. **PERSONAL:** Born Feb 12, 1949, Manila, Philippines; son of Sy Hack Chan & Elena Santos; divorced. **EDUCATION:** University of the Philippines, BS, 1970, MD, 1975; Harvard University, MS, 1981; Johns Hopkins University, DrPH, 1984. **CAREER:** University of the Philippines, assistant professor of parasitology, 1978-84; University of South Carolina, associate professor of epidemiology, 1985-. **ORGANIZATIONS:** American College of Preventive Medicine, fellow, 1993-; Royal Society of Tropical Medicine & Hygiene, fellow, 1981-; American College of Allergy & Immunology, scientific fellow, 1987-; American College of Epidemiology, 1988-; International Society for AIDS Education, founding president, 1987-; National Council for International Health, 1985-; American Public Health Association, 1985-; American Medical Association, 1985-; Mortar Board College Senior Society, honorary member, 1988-; Delta Omega Honor Society, 1987. **HONORS/AWARDS:** University of South Carolina, J Keith Outstanding Teaching Award, 1991; Johns Hopkins

University, Outstanding Alumnus in Public Health, 1990; University of the Philippines, Outstanding Medical Alumnus in Medical Education, 1993. **SPECIAL ACHIEVEMENTS:** Publications on AIDS, parasitic diseases, tuberculosis and other infectious diseases; AIDS Education & Prevention-An Interdisciplinary Journal, editor, 1988-. **BUSINESS ADDRESS:** Associate Professor, Grad Dir, Dept of Epidemiology & Biostatistics, University of South Carolina School of Public Health, Columbia, SC 29208, (803)777-7353.

SY, JOSE
Educator. Chinese American. **PERSONAL:** Born Dec 10, 1944, Sorsogon, Philippines; son of Sy Hai and Yu Pec Sian; married Sharon Yu; children: Theodore, Michael, Aileen. **EDUCATION:** Adamson University, Philippines, BS, 1965; Duke University, PhD, 1970. **CAREER:** Rockefeller University, assistant professor, 1976-80, associate professor, 1980-85; University of California, Irvine, visiting professor, 1990-92; California State University, Fresno, professor of chemistry, 1985-. **ORGANIZATIONS:** American Society of Biochemistry and Molecular Biology; Protein Society. **SPECIAL ACHIEVEMENTS:** Author of numerous publications. **BUSINESS ADDRESS:** Professor, Dept of Chemistry, California State University at Fresno, Fresno, CA 93740, (209)278-4756.

SYAL, SHANTA
Manufacturing company executive. Indo-American. **PERSONAL:** Born Sep 2, 1948, New Delhi, India; daughter of Mr and Mrs Sajjan Singh Duggal; married Jang Syal, Jan 31, 1992. **CAREER:** S K Merchandising Corp, president, owner, 1980-. **SPECIAL ACHIEVEMENTS:** Invented metal point correction pen unique to industry; US patent. **BUSINESS ADDRESS:** President, S K Merchandising Corp, Mid-Valley Industrial Park, Olyphant, PA 18447, (717)383-3062.

SYED, KARAMAT A.
Computer consultant. Pakistani American/Indo-American. **PERSONAL:** Born 1939, Delhi, Uttar Pradesh, India; son of Mr and Mrs Riasat Ali Syed; married Husna, 1972; children: Four. **EDUCATION:** Karachi University, Pakistan, MA, mathematics, 1963; IBM Education Center, London, systems engineering, 1967; Pittsburgh University, MS, computer science, 1970. **CAREER:** University of Sind, Pakistan, lecturer, mathematics, 1963-65; IBM, World Trade Corp, Pakistan, systems engr, 1966-69; IBM, New York, mgmt science analyst, 1970-71, project leader, 1972-76, advisory systems analyst, 1977-81, I/S development mgr, 1982-88, I/S Financia Planning, program manager, 1988-90; IBM CHQ, Financial Systems, program mgr, systems assurance, 1989-. **ORGANIZATIONS:** MSA, Pittsburgh Chapter, president, 1968-70; Islamic Society of Westchester, NY, president, 1990-91; Westchester Muslim Center, chairman, 1993-95. **HONORS/AWARDS:** Karachi University, Pakistan, 2nd Position in MA (mathematics), 1963. **HOME PHONE:** (914)271-6436. **BUSINESS ADDRESS:** Program Manager, Systems Assurance, IBM CHQ Financial Systems, 150 Kettletown Rd, Southbury, CT 06488.

SZE, CHIA-MING
Architect. Chinese American. **PERSONAL:** Born Jun 6, 1937, Shanghai, China; son of Szeming Sze & Yioh-Ching Li Sze; married Judith, Sep 9, 1961; children: David, Sarah. **EDUCATION:** Yale College, BA, 1959; Yale School of Architecture, MArch, 1966. **CAREER:** Chia-Ming Sze Architects Inc, president, 1972-. **ORGANIZATIONS:** Wang Center, trustee, 1992-; Center House, board of directors, 1992-; Community Music Center, board of directors, 1990-; First Night Boston, board of directors, 1989-92; Boston Zoning Board, 1984-93; Asian American Bank & Trust, incorporator and director, 1993-. **BUSINESS ADDRESS:** President, Chia-Ming Sze Architects Inc, 326 A St, Boston, MA 02210, (617)451-2727.

SZE, MORGAN CHUAN-YUAN
Engineer (retired). Chinese American. **PERSONAL:** Born May 27, 1917, Tientsin, China; children: three. **EDUCATION:** Massachusetts Institute of Technology, SB, 1939, ScD, chemical engineering, 1941. **CAREER:** Universal Trading Corp, chemical engineer, 1941-42; Belle Works, E I du Pont de Nemours and Co Inc, process engineer, 1942-44; Hydrocarbon Res Inc, process engineer, 1944-45, senior process engineer, 1947-53, Process Engineering Dept, director, 1953-59, tech director, 1959-61; Foster Wheeler Corp, process engineer, 1945-47; Lummus Co, executive staff engineer, 1961-64, Engineering Development Center, manager, 1964-71, research and development, vice president, 1971-80; Signal Comp Inc, Adv Tech Group, vice president, 1980-85. **ORGANIZATIONS:** National Academy of Engineering; American Insti-

tute of Chemical Engineers; AAAS; Sigma Xi; American Chemical Society. **BUSINESS ADDRESS:** 4 Regina Rd, Portsmouth, NH 03801. *

SZE, PAUL Y.
Scientist, educator. Chinese American. **PERSONAL:** Born Jun 7, 1938, Shanghai, China; son of K M Sze and Y F Wong-Sze. **EDUCATION:** University of Chicago, PhD, 1968. **CAREER:** University of Connecticut, assistant professor & professor, 1969-84; Chicago Medical School, professor, 1984-. **ORGANIZATIONS:** Society for Neuroscience, 1971-; International Society for Neurochemistry, 1971-; American Society for Neurochemisty, 1991-; International Brain Research Organization, 1975-. **SPECIAL ACHIEVEMENTS:** Author of more than 80 research articles, 1965-; National Institutes of Health, Neurology: A Study Section, 1980-84, General Research Support Review Committee, 1985-89, Behavioral Neuroscience Review Committee, 1990-; editorial board, several research journals. **BUSINESS ADDRESS:** Professor of Pharmacology and Molecular Biology, Chicago Medical School, 3333 Green Bay Rd, North Chicago, IL 60064, (708)578-3000.

SZETO, ERIK K.
Physician. Chinese American. **PERSONAL:** Born Sep 17, 1949, Hong Kong; son of Yat Szeto & Siu Fong Szeto; divorced; children: Matthew, Eileen, Amanda, Jacob. **EDUCATION:** University of Oregon, BA, 1972; Yale University, MS, 1974; Kirksville College of Osteopathic Medicine, DO, 1978. **CAREER:** Private practice, physician, 1979-. **ORGANIZATIONS:** Family Care PCO of Oregon, Quality Assurance Committee, chairman, 1991-; Evergreen PCO of Oregon, Quality Assurance Committee, chairman, 1991-; Governor Roberts Transitional Team, Health Committee, 1990; Chinese Social Service Center, board of directors, chairman, founder, 1983-; Chinese Community Development Corporation, chairman, founder, board of directors, 1991-; Asian-American Coalition, Executive Committee, chairman, 1992-. **HONORS/AWARDS:** Oregon Chinese Community, Friends of the Chinese Community, 1990. **SPECIAL ACHIEVEMENTS:** Chinese Social Service Center, founder; Chinese Community Development Corporation, non-profit low income housing, founder; Asian-American Coalition, executive committee, chairman, social equality, civil rights, advancement, political involvement. **BIOGRAPHICAL SOURCES:** The Oregonian, p C2, May 23, 1990. **BUSINESS ADDRESS:** Physician, 4130 SE Division St, Portland, OR 97202, (503)239-5836.

T

TA, TAI VAN
Attorney, educator. Vietnamese American. **PERSONAL:** Born Apr 16, 1938, Ninh Binh, Vietnam; son of Ta Van Duong; married Lien-Nhu Tran, Oct 23, 1967; children: Becky (Bich-Thuyen), John (Chuong), Khuong, Dora (Dao). **EDUCATION:** Saigon University of Law School, LLB, 1960; University of Virginia, MA, 1964, PhD, 1965; Harvard Law School, LLM, 1985. **CAREER:** Saigon Law School, professor, 1965-75; Vietnam National School of Administration, professor, 1965-75; Tang thi Thanh Trai/Ta Van Tai Law Firm, partner, 1967-75; Reed Smith Shaw & McClay, researcher, 1975; Harvard Law School, research associate, 1975-; self-employed, Attorney-at-law, 1986-; Massachusetts Governor's Asian-American Commission, commissioner, 1992-. **ORGANIZATIONS:** Vietnamese Community of Western Massachusetts, counsel, 1993; Vietnamese Refugee Association of Massachusetts, vice president, 1976-82; Vietnamese Lawyers Association, Washington, DC, 1982-84, Southern California, 1990-; Association of Translators and Interpreters, Massachusetts, 1990-; Association of Former Members of Hue University, Van Hanh University, Law School, Saigon University Vietnam National School of Adminstration. **HONORS/AWARDS:** Fulbright Program, Award, 1960-62; Asia Foundation, Asia Foundation Grant for Scholar, 1972, 1974; Ford Foundation, Fellowship for Indochinese Refugee Intellectual, 1975-76. **SPECIAL ACHIEVEMENTS:** Vietnamese Tradition of Human Rights, 1988; Investment Law and Practice in Vietnam, 1990; The Le Code: Law in Traditional Vietnam (3v), 1987; Doing Business in Vietnam, Saigon; Vietnam Council on Foreign Relations, 1970, 1974; languages include: Vietnamese, Chinese, French, English. **MILITARY SERVICE:** Vietnam Infantry Basic Training, private, 1968. **HOME ADDRESS:** 145 Naples Rd, #2, Brookline, MA 02146, (617)734-1315. **BUSINESS ADDRESS:** Research Associate, Harvard Law School, 1563 Massachusetts Avenue, Pound Hall, Room 423, Cambridge, MA 02138, (617)495-1726.

TABUCHI, SHOJI
Musician. Japanese American. **PERSONAL:** Born 1944?, Daishoji, Ishikawa Prefecture, Japan; son of Shigeru and Yukie; married MaryJo (divorced); children: Shoji John; married Dorothy, 1981; children: Christina. **EDUCATION:** St Andrew's College, BE. **CAREER:** Osaka Okies, musician; Starlite Club, fiddler; Grand Ole Opry, performer; St Francis Hospital, radiology department, orderly; Western Swing Club, performer; David Houston and the Persuaders, performer, 1970-75; Country Music World, 1985-88; Shoji Tabuchi Theater, owner, performer, 1990-. **SPECIAL ACHIEVEMENTS:** Guest appearances on Lifestyles of the Rich and Famous, The Today Show, and Inside Edition. **BUSINESS ADDRESS:** Musician, Shoji Tabuchi Theatre c/o Shoji Entertainment Inc, Shepherd of Hills Expressway HCR 2, PO Box 2323, Branson, MO 65616, (417)334-7469. *

TAGASHIRA, GAIL S.
Journalist. Japanese American. **PERSONAL:** Born May 4, 1948, Honolulu, HI; daughter of Mamoru Tagashira & R Patsy Gomez. **EDUCATION:** San Jose State University, BA, journalism, 1972; University of California, Berkeley, post-graduate, political science, Santa Cruz, dance history. **CAREER:** Honolulu Star Bulletin, reporter, 1968-69; San Jose Mercury News, reporter, 1969-82; Times Mirror Videotex, 1983-86; Los Angeles Herald Examiner, copy editor, 1986; Los Angeles Times, Calendar, assistant news editor, 1986-. **ORGANIZATIONS:** Dance Critics Association, voting member, currently; Asian American Journalists, 1986-; Japanese American Citizens League, San Jose Chapter, board member, 1983-86; Bay Area Women in Music, 1980-86. **HONORS/AWARDS:** East-West Center, Jefferson Fellow, 1986; National Endowment for the Arts, Dance Critics Seminar participant, 1972. **SPECIAL ACHIEVEMENTS:** Participant, Poynter Institute Seminar design and graphics for copy editors, 1992, management, 1991. **BUSINESS ADDRESS:** Assistant News Editor, Calendar, Los Angeles Times, Times Mirror Square, Los Angeles, CA 90053, (213)237-4593.

TAGAWA, CARY-HIROYUKI
Actor. Japanese American. **PERSONAL:** Born Sep 27, 1950, Japan; married Sally Phillips; children: Calen, Brynne. **EDUCATION:** University of Southern California. **CAREER:** Actor, films: Big Trouble in Little China, extra; Armed Response; The Last Emperor, 1987; Last Warrior, 1989; Showdown in Little Tokyo, 1991; American Me, 1992; Rising Sun, 1993; television: Space Rangers, 1993. **BUSINESS ADDRESS:** Actor, c/o Innovative Artists, 1999 Avenue of the Stars, Ste 2850, Los Angeles, CA 90067. *

TAHARA, MILDRED MACHIKO
Educator. Japanese American. **PERSONAL:** Born May 15, 1941, Hilo, HI; daughter of Charles Satoru and Toshie. **EDUCATION:** University of Hawaii, BA, 1963, MA, 1965; Columbia University, PhD, 1970. **CAREER:** University of Hawaii at Manoa, assistant professor, 1969-76, associate professor, 1976-. **ORGANIZATIONS:** American Literary Translators Association; American Translators Association; Modern Language Association; Association for Asian Studies; American Association for University Women; The Japanese American National Museum; Hawaii Literary Arts Council; Hawaii Committee for the Humanities, secretary-treasurer, 1992-94. **SPECIAL ACHIEVEMENTS:** "Ariyoshi Sawako: The Novelist," Chapter 8, pp 297-322, Heroic with Grace, edited by Chieko Mulhern, M E Sharpe, 1991; Her Highness Princess Kazu, Translation, Columbia University, Vol xvii, Fall 1986, 164-183; trans of novels by Ariyoshi Sawako: The Twilight Years, The River Ki, Kodansha Intl, 1980; Tales of Yamato: A Tenth-Century Poem-Tale, University of Hawaii Press, 1980. **BUSINESS ADDRESS:** Assoc Prof of Japanese Literature, East Asian Langs & Literatures Dept, University of Hawaii at Manoa, 1890 East West Rd, Moore Hall 382, Honolulu, HI 96822, (808)956-2058.

TAHILIANI, JAMNU H.
Engineer. Indo-American. **PERSONAL:** Born Feb 20, 1936, Navsharo, Sind, India; married Savi J Tahiliani, Nov 19, 1965; children: Nisha Sundram, Meena, Priya. **EDUCATION:** Maharaja Sayajirao University, Banada, India, BS, engineering, 1957; Memphis State University, MS, engineering, 1970. **CAREER:** Pickering Engineering Inc, chief engineer, 1969-79; Jamnu H Tahiliani & Associates Inc, president, 1979-. **ORGANIZATIONS:** American Consulting Engineers Council, 1975-; American Concrete Institute, 1980-.

TAHILIANI, VASU HARIRAM
Electrical distribution research manager. Indo-American. **PERSONAL:** Born Oct 26, 1942, Baroda, Gujarat, India; son of Hariram Hazarimal Tahiliani and Bhagwani H Tahiliani; married Kiran, Dec 21, 1970; children: Mamta,

Radhika, Diya. **EDUCATION:** MS University, Baroda, BSEE, 1964; West Virginia University, MSEE, 1970. **CAREER:** McGraw Edison, design engineer, 1966-71; ITE Imperial Corp, project manager, 1971-76; EPRI, senior project manager, 1977-84, tech transfer administrator, 1984-87, program mgr tech transfer, 1988-90, sr programs mgr, distribution pgm, 1991-. **ORGANIZATIONS:** IEEE Power Engineering Society, PES, chairman, 1991-92, WG Standards Department, secretary, 1971-76, 1966-; CIGRE, 1978-; CIRED, contributing member, 1991-; State of California, professional engineer, 1977-. **HONORS/AWARDS:** CIGRE, Expert Advisor, 1979-. **SPECIAL ACHIEVEMENTS:** Published over 30 technical papers in IEEE, CIGRE, and other professional organizations; 5 US patents granted, many are pending. **BUSINESS ADDRESS:** Senior Program Manager, EPRI, 3412 Hillview Ave, Palo Alto, CA 94304, (415)855-2315.

TAI, C. STEPHEN
Educator. Korean American. **PERSONAL:** Born Oct 15, 1940, Seoul, Republic of Korea; son of Hyung-Kyoon Tai (deceased) and Ock-Hee Tai; married Susan, Aug 28, 1965; children: Isabella, Elizabeth, Michael. **EDUCATION:** Yonsei University, BA, 1963; Illinois State University, MA, 1972; Northwestern University, MA, 1972, PhD, 1974. **CAREER:** Northwestern University, lecturer, 1974-75; University of Arkansas, Pine Bluff, assistant professor, 1976-80, associate professor, 1980-86, professor, 1986-. **ORGANIZATIONS:** International Center for Asian Studies, fellow; American Political Science Association; Arkansas Political Science Association; Association for Asian Studies; Association of Korean Political Studies in North America; University of Arkansas, Pine Bluff, International Faculty Club, president. **HONORS/ AWARDS:** Arkansas Endowment for the Humanities Award, 1980; National Endowment for the Humanities Fellowship Award, 1980; Fulbright-Hays Award for Faculty Seminar in China, 1985; Southwestern International Studies Consortium Award for Faculty Seminar in Mexico, 1986. **SPECIAL ACHIEVEMENTS:** Numerous articles published in professional journals, 1974-. **MILITARY SERVICE:** Republic of Korea Air Force, first lieutenant, 1963-67. **HOME ADDRESS:** 11324 Hickory Hill Road, Little Rock, AR 72211. **BUSINESS ADDRESS:** Professor, University of Arkansas at Pine Bluff, North University, 227 Childress Hall, Pine Bluff, AR 71601-2799, (501)543-8189.

TAI, CHEN TO
Educator. Chinese American. **PERSONAL:** Born Dec 30, 1915, Soochow, Kiangsu, China; married Chia Ming Shen, Apr 28, 1941; children: Arthur, Bing, Julie, David, James. **EDUCATION:** Tsing Hua University, BS, 1937; Harvard University, DSc, 1947. **CAREER:** Stanford Research Institute, senior scientist, 1949-54; Technical Institute of Aeronautics, professor, 1956-60; Ohio State University, professor, 1960-64; University of Michigan, Ann Arbor, professor, 1964-, professor emeritus, 1986-. **ORGANIZATIONS:** IEEE Antennas/Propagation Society, president, 1971-72; National Academy of Engineering, 1987. **HONORS/AWARDS:** University of Washington, Walker-Ames Professorship, 1973; University of Michigan, Distinguished Faculty Achievement Award, 1975; IEEE, Centennial Award, 1984; Antennas/Propagation Society, Distinguished Achievement Award, 1986. **SPECIAL ACHIEVEMENTS:** Author of: Dyadic Green's Functions in Electromagnetic Theory, Intext Publishers, 1971; Generalized Vector and Dyadic Analysis, IEEE Press, 1992. **BUSINESS ADDRESS:** Professor Emeritus, Dept of EECS, University of Michigan, Radiation Lab, Ann Arbor, MI 48109.

TAI, HSIN-HSIUNG
Educator. Taiwanese American. **PERSONAL:** Born May 30, 1941, Kaohsiung, Taiwan; son of Ming-Chuan Tai and Tu Lee Tai; married Chen Ling Tai, Oct 11, 1969; children: Jed Daniel, Ray Peter. **EDUCATION:** National Taiwan University, BS, 1964; University of Wisconsin, MS, 1967, PhD, 1970; Harvard University, postdoctorate, 1970-71. **CAREER:** New York University Medical Center, instructor, 1971-72, assistant professor of medicine, 1972-73; University of Rochester Medical Center, assistant professor of medicine, 1973-77; University of North Texas, Texas College of Osteopathic Medicine, associate professor of biochemistry, 1977-81; University of Kentucky, professor of medicinal chemistry, 1981-. **ORGANIZATIONS:** American Society of Biochemistry and Molecular Biology, 1978-; American Society for Pharmacology and Experimental Therapeutics, 1982-; American Association of Colleges of Pharmacy, 1989-; American Association for the Advancement of Science, 1981-; Kentucky Heart Association, research review subcommittee, 1981-86; National Institutes of Health, neurological disorders study section, 1993-97. **HONORS/AWARDS:** National Institutes of Health, Research Career Development Award, 1981; American Heart Association, Estab-

lished Investigatorship, 1981; New York Heart Association, Senior Investigatorship, 1972; University of Kentucky, University Research Professorship, 1986. **MILITARY SERVICE:** Republic of China Army, 1964-65. **BUSINESS ADDRESS:** Professor of Medicinal Chemistry, University of Kentucky, College of Pharmacy, 900 Rose St, Rm 527, Pharmacy Bldg, Lexington, KY 40536-0082, (606)257-1837.

TAI, JULIA CHOW
Educator. Chinese American. **PERSONAL:** Born Dec 15, 1935, Shanghai, China; daughter of Mr and Mrs Fei-chen Chow; married Hung-chao Tai, Aug 14, 1960; children: Eve, Helen, Michael. **EDUCATION:** National Taiwan University, BS, 1957; University of Oklahoma, MS, 1959; University of Illinois, Urbana, PhD, 1963. **CAREER:** Wayne State University, research associate, 1963-68; National Taiwan University, visiting associate professor, 1968-69; University of Michigan, Dearborn, assistant professor, 1969-73, associate professor, 1973-79, professor, 1979-. **ORGANIZATIONS:** American Chemical Society; Michigan College Chemistry Teachers Association; Council on Undergraduate Research; American Association of University Women. **SPECIAL ACHIEVEMENTS:** Published in: Journal of American Chemical Society; Journal of Chemical Physics; Tetrahedron; Journal of Computational Chemistry. **BUSINESS ADDRESS:** Professor, Dept of Natural Sciences, University of Michigan-Dearborn, 4901 Evergreen, Dearborn, MI 48128, (313)593-5166.

TAI, PETER Y. P.
Plant geneticist. Chinese American. **PERSONAL:** Born Jul 6, 1937, Chutung, China; son of Yu shu Tai & Chomay Tai; married Rosie P Tai, Jan 30, 1964; children: Robert H, Thomas H. **EDUCATION:** Taiwan Institute of Agriculture, diploma, 1958; National Taiwan University, BS, 1961; Texas A&M University, MS, 1966; Oklahoma State University, PhD, 1972. **CAREER:** University of Georgia, research associate, 1972-77; USDA-ARS, research geneticist, 1977-. **ORGANIZATIONS:** Astronomy Society of America, 1970-; Crop Science Society of America, 1970-; American Society of Sugar Cane Technologists, 1977-. **HONORS/AWARDS:** Florida Sugar Cane League, 1992, 1993. **SPECIAL ACHIEVEMENTS:** Plant breeding and plant genetics. **BUSINESS ADDRESS:** Research Geneticist, Agricultural Research Service, US Department of Agriculture, Star Route Box 8, Canal Point, FL 33438, (407)924-5227.

TAI, WILLIAM P.
Venture capitalist. Taiwanese American. **PERSONAL:** Born May 29, 1962, Pittsburgh, PA; son of W T Tai & L S Tai. **EDUCATION:** University of Illinois, BS, electrical engineering, 1984; Harvard Graduate School of Business, MBA, 1987. **CAREER:** LSI Logic Corp, marketing executive, 1984-87; Alex Brown & Sons, vice president, 1987-91; The Walden Group, general partner, 1991-; Integrated Circuit Works, director, 1992-93; Auravision Corp, director, 1992-93. **ORGANIZATIONS:** Harvard Business School Association, chairman, 1992-93; American Red Cross, associate leadership cabinet; Tour De Grapevine, co-chairman, 1988-93. **HONORS/AWARDS:** Harvard Business School Association, Entrepreneur of the Year, 1992-93. **BIOGRAPHICAL SOURCES:** Venture Capital Journal, Feb 1993. **BUSINESS ADDRESS:** General Partner, The Walden Group, 750 Battery St, #7F, San Francisco, CA 94111.

TAIRA, MASA MORIOKA
Homemaker, civic volunteer. Japanese American. **PERSONAL:** Born Nov 25, 1923, Kagoshima City, Kagoshima-Ken, Japan; daughter of Kin Masuda Morioka Uyeno and Masakiyo Morioka; married Tom Keizo Taira, Aug 7, 1954; children: Mikilani. **EDUCATION:** Madison College, BS, 1944; George Peabody Teachers College; University of California, Los Angeles, MS, 1953; University of Hawaii, Manoa. **CAREER:** Madison College & Sanitorium, 1943-47; Washington Sanitorium and Hospital, 1947-49; White Memorial Hospital, Los Angeles, therapeutic dietition, 1949-51; University of California, Los Angeles, nutritionist, 1951-53; Frances Stern Food Clinic NE MC, Boston Dispensary, nutritionist, 1954-56; Chicago Board of Health, nutritionist, 1956-58; Queen's Medical Center, nutritionist instructor, 1963-65. **ORGANIZATIONS:** American Dietetic Assn, 1954-65; Hawaii Dietetic Assn, 1963-65; Queen's Medical Center Auxilary, volunteer, 1975-; Queen's Medical Center Auxilary Board, 1976-; Queen Emma Gallery, director, 1976-; National Museum Women Artists, charter member, 1991; Hawaii Artists' League, 1985-86; Honolulu Printmakers, 1977-80. **HONORS/AWARDS:** Hawaii Committee for Humanities, Grant Award, 1984-87. **SPECIAL ACHIEVEMENTS:** Hawaii Committee for Humanities Publication & Interpretive Exhibition, Human

Form: From Egypt to the Renaissance Traveling Exhibition, 1984-85; Monouri, Street Venders of Japan, 1985; Kumulipo, Hawaiian Chant of Creation, 1987. **BUSINESS ADDRESS:** Director, Queen Emma Gallery, 1301 Punchbowl St, c/o Volunteer Service, Honolulu, HI 96813, (808)547-4397.

TAIRA, TOY-PING CHAN
Government official, educator. Chinese American. **PERSONAL:** Born Oct 18, 1937, New Haven, CT; daughter of Helen Chan; divorced; children: Gregg S, Helene S, Kelly H. **EDUCATION:** George Washington University, BA, 1959; Johns Hopkins University, MS, 1992. **CAREER:** US HHS, Hospital Care Statistics, NCHS branch chief, Inpatient Care Statistics, IHS branch chief, before 1975; US GAO, National Health Ins Task Force, technical director, 1975-80; US EPA, supervisory statistician, project director, 1980-81; US Dept of Commerce, NOAA, senior management analyst, 1981-88; Potomac Change Management, president/proprietor, 1992-; US FDA, Management Systems & Analysis, branch chief, 1988-89, Pilot Drug Evaluation Staff, deputy director, 1989-; Johns Hopkins University, Applied Behavioral Sciences, Master's Degree Program, adjunct faculty member, 1992-. **ORGANIZATIONS:** National Association of Professional Asian American Women, 1992-; Kaleidoscopic Options, charter member, 1992-; Johns Hopkins Alumni, 1992-; Chesapeake Bay Organization Development Network, 1992-. **HONORS/AWARDS:** US FDA, FDA Commendable Service Award, 1989; US Dept of Commerce, Bronze Medal Award, 1988; merit performance bonuses, 1980-. **SPECIAL ACHIEVEMENTS:** Article, "Asian Americans in the Workplace," Managing in the Age of Change, 1994. **BUSINESS ADDRESS:** Deputy Director, Pilot Drug Evaluation Staff, US Food & Drug Administration, Center for Drug Evaluation & Research, 5600 Fishers Lane, Parklawn Bldg, Room 9B45, Rockville, MD 20854, (301)443-4250.

TAJIMA, TOSHIKI
Educator. Japanese American. **PERSONAL:** Born Jan 18, 1948, Nagoya, Japan; son of Fumiko Tajima (deceased) and Hidetoshi Tajima; married Fumiko Chiba, Jul 7, 1972; children: Mika Robin, Yuhki John. **EDUCATION:** University of Tokyo, BS, 1971, MS, 1973; University of California, Irvine, PhD, 1975. **CAREER:** University of California, Los Angeles, research physicist, 1976-80; University of California, Berkeley, visiting scientist, 1989; Superconducting Super Collider, member, 1990-93; Japan Atomic Energy Research Institute, group leader, 1993-; University of Texas, Austin, assistant professor, associate professor, professor, 1980-. **ORGANIZATIONS:** American Physical Society, fellow, 1973-; Physical Society of Japan, 1971-; American Geophysical Union, 1977-; National Research Council, National Academy of Science, 1978-; American Astronomical Society, 1983-; Beta Alpha Phi, 1985-; Japan America Society of Austin, director of board, 1992-; US Department of Energy Tokamak Consortium, steering member, 1992-; Texas High Energy Physics Committee, steering member, 1989-. **HONORS/AWARDS:** American Physical Society, fellowship, 1986; Japan Society for Promotion of Science, fellowship, 1973, 1974. **SPECIAL ACHIEVEMENTS:** Author, Computational Plasma Physics, Addison-Wesley, book, 1989; co-editor, with F Matsen, Supercomputers, University Texas Press, book, 1986; co-editor, with Y H Ichikawa, Nonlinear Dynamics and Particle Acceleration, American Institute of Physics, book, 1991. **BUSINESS ADDRESS:** Professor of Physics, Dept of Physics, University of Texas, Austin, TX 78712, (512)471-4574.

TAKAGI, DANA Y.
Educator. Japanese American. **PERSONAL:** Born Jul 22, 1954, Los Angeles, CA; daughter of Paul Takagi and Mary Anna Takagi. **EDUCATION:** UC, Berkeley, BA, mathematics, 1976, PhD, sociology, 1986. **CAREER:** University of California, Irvine, assistant professor, 1986-87; University of California, Santa Cruz, associate professor, 1987-. **ORGANIZATIONS:** American Sociological Assn, 1977-, chair of committee on minority fellowship program, 1993-94. **HONORS/AWARDS:** Rockefeller Foundation, Rockefeller Humanities Fellowship, 1990-91; Institute of American Cultures, post-doctoral fellow, 1991-92. **SPECIAL ACHIEVEMENTS:** The Retreat from Race: Asian American Admissions and Racial Politics, 1993; "Asian Americans and Racial Politics: A Postmodern Paradox," Social Justice, 1993; "From Discrimination to Affirmative Action," Social Problems, 1990. **BUSINESS ADDRESS:** Assoc Professor, Dept of Sociology, University of California, Santa Cruz, Stevenson College, Santa Cruz, CA 95064.

TAKAGI, NORIO (KEN)
Electronics/electrical company manager. Japanese American. **PERSONAL:** Born Apr 3, 1947, Shizuoka, Shizuoka, Japan; son of Fumio Takagi and Kyoko Takagi; married Keiko Takagi, Apr 29, 1973; children: Junichiro, Tomoko.

EDUCATION: Waseda University, MS. **CAREER:** Matsushita America Semiconductor Company, director; Panasonic Industrial Co, Semiconductor Business Group, general manager, currently. **HOME ADDRESS:** 53 Hubbardton Rd, Wayne, NJ 07470. **BUSINESS PHONE:** (201)348-5254.

TAKAHASHI, ABRAHAM TOMIO
Government official (retired), association administrator. Japanese American. **PERSONAL:** Born Jul 15, 1939, Waipahu, Oahu, HI; son of Harry Toshio Takahashi (deceased) & Edith Tomiko Mizuno; married Patsy Joyce Story, Apr 4, 1964. **EDUCATION:** Michigan State University, BA, 1961. **CAREER:** Michigan Department of Mental Health, management trainee to administrative officer, 1961-75; Michigan State Police, division director, deputy director, bureau director, 1975-91. **ORGANIZATIONS:** Association of Mental Health Administrators, 1962-75; Michigan Association of Chiefs of Police, 1980-93; International Association of Chiefs of Police, 1980-91; Governor's Advisory Commission on Asian American Affairs, 1988-90; Council on Asian American Affairs, 1991-; Mid-Michigan Asian Pacific American Association, member & secretary, 1987-90, chairperson, 1992, 1993, Lao Hmong Family Community, board of volunteers, chair, 1991-. **HONORS/AWARDS:** Michigan Council on Asian American Affairs, recognition, 1991; American Citizens for Justice, recognition, 1992; Michigan Legislature, special tribute & concurrent resolution, 1991. **HOME ADDRESS:** 5705 Lake View Dr, Perry, MI 48872. **BUSINESS ADDRESS:** Chairperson, Mid-Michigan Asian Pacific American Association, 735 East Michigan Ave, Old State Library, 2nd Fl, Lansing, MI 48912, (517)482-4434.

TAKAHASHI, JOSEPH S.
Educator, educational administrator. Japanese American. **PERSONAL:** Born Dec 16, 1951, Tokyo, Japan; son of Shigeharu & Hiroko Hara Takahashi; married Barbara P S Takahashi, Jun 28, 1985; children: Erika Sachiko. **EDUCATION:** Swarthmore College, BA, 1974; University of Oregon, Eugene, PhD, 1981; National Institutes of Health, postdoctoral fellow, 1981-83. **CAREER:** Institute of Neuroscience, acting associate director, 1988-; Northwestern University, assistant professor, 1983-87, Department of Neurobiology and Physiology, associate professor, associate chair, 1987-91, acting chair, 1991-92, professor, associate chair, 1991-. **ORGANIZATIONS:** American Association Advancement of Science, 1976-; Society for Neuroscience, 1981-; Association Research in Vision Ophthalmology, 1983-; Society for Research on Biological Rhythms, advisory committee, 1986-; International Mammalian Genome Society, 1993-; Task Force on Biological Rhythms and Psychopathology, 1992-; NIMH Psychobiology and Behavior Review Committee, 1988-92. **HONORS/AWARDS:** Honma Foundation, Honma Prize in Biological Rhythms Research, 1986; NSF, Presidential Young Investigator Award, 1985-90, Graduate Fellowship, 1976-79; Chicago Community Trust, Searle Scholars Award, 1985-88; Alfred P Sloan Foundation, Sloan Research Fellowship in Neuroscience, 1983-85. **SPECIAL ACHIEVEMENTS:** Over 60 publications in scientific journals, over 60 published abstract presentations at national meetings; over 90 presentations and seminars at meetings and universities. **BUSINESS ADDRESS:** Prof/Assoc Chair, Dept of Neurobiology & Physiology, Northwestern University, 2153 N Campus Dr, Evanston, IL 60208-3520, (708)491-4598.

TAKAHASHI, KEN M.
Chemical engineering. Japanese American. **PERSONAL:** Born Jul 7, 1959, Baltimore, MD; son of Yasuo Takahashi & Betty M Takahashi. **EDUCATION:** Massachusetts Institute of Technology, BS, 1981; University of Illinois, MS, 1983, PhD, 1986. **CAREER:** AT&T Bell Laboratories, member technical staff, 1986-. **ORGANIZATIONS:** American Institute of Chemical Engineers, 1986-; Tau Beta Pi; Phi Lambda Upsilon. **SPECIAL ACHIEVEMENTS:** Published in more than 13 scientific publications. **BUSINESS ADDRESS:** Member Technical Staff, AT&T Bell Laboratories, 600 Mountain Ave, MH ID-328, Murray Hill, NJ 07974.

TAKAHASHI, KOZO
Educator. Japanese American. **PERSONAL:** Born Jan 17, 1948, Kagawa, Japan; son of Yoshitaka & Mitsuko Takahashi; married Kayoko Takahashi, Oct 10, 1971; children: Alexander Shiro, Eileen Sarah. **EDUCATION:** Houkaido University, BA, 1972; University Washington, BSc, 1975, MSc, 1977; MIT, PhD, 1981. **CAREER:** University of California, San Diego, assistant professor geologist, 1982-84; Woods Hole Oceanographic Institution, assistant scientist, 1984-86, associate scientist, 1986-92; Hokkaido Tokai University, professor, 1992-. **ORGANIZATIONS:** Hokkaido University, visiting professor, 1990-; Woods Hole Oceanographic Institution, 1992-. **HONORS/AWARDS:** Woods

Hole Oceanographic Institution, Post Doctoral Scholar, 1981-82. **SPECIAL ACHIEVEMENTS:** 50 publications in refereed journals and books; presentations in international and domestic conferences; fluent in Japanese & English. **BUSINESS ADDRESS:** Professor, Hokkaido Tokai University, Minamisawa 5-1-1-1, Minamiku, Sapporo 005, Japan.

TAKAHASHI, LOREY K.
Researcher, educator. Japanese American. **PERSONAL:** Born Jul 25, 1953, Honolulu, HI; son of George H and Margie Y Takahashi; married Chintana Y Takahashi, Aug 22, 1982; children: Edwin A, Cyrus G. **EDUCATION:** University of Hawaii, Manoa, BA, 1975, MA, 1978; Rutgers University, PhD, 1982; Princeton University, postdoctoral research. **CAREER:** University of Hawaii, Department Psychology, graduate resident assistant, 1975-78; Rutgers University, Department Psychology, undergraduate teaching assistant, 1978-82; Princeton University, Department Biology, NIMH neurosci postdoc trainee, 1982-83, NIMH postdoct fellow, 1983-85; University of Wisconsin Medical School, Department Psychiatry, assistant scientist, 1986-90, assistant professor, 1990-. **ORGANIZATIONS:** American Association Advancement of Science, 1980-; American Psychological Association, 1983-; American Soc Zool, 1984-; Animal Behavior Society, 1981-; International Brain Research Organization, 1985-; Sigma Xi, 1979-; Society of Neurosci, 1987-; Society for the Study of Reproduction, 1993-. **HONORS/AWARDS:** Japanese National Student Exchange Research Fellow, 1977. **SPECIAL ACHIEVEMENTS:** Numerous publications in scientific journals. **HOME ADDRESS:** 6406 Olympic Dr, Madison, WI 53705, (608)833-0603. **BUSINESS ADDRESS:** Assistant Professor, Dept of Psychiatry, University of Wisconsin Medical School, 600 Highland Ave, Madison, WI 53792-2475, (608)263-6063.

TAKAHASHI, MASATO
Physician, educator. Japanese American. **PERSONAL:** Born Feb 10, 1933, Tokyo, Japan; son of Noboru and Fujiko Takahashi; married Marcia P Takahashi, Jan 16, 1966; children: Rumi Anne, Yuki Lynn. **EDUCATION:** Wabash College, AB, 1956; Indiana University School of Medicine, MD, 1960. **CAREER:** Children's Hospital of Los Angeles, attending physician, 1968-; USC School of Medicine, professor of pediatric cardiology, currently. **ORGANIZATIONS:** American Heart Association, Committee on Rheumatic Fever, Endocarditis and Kawasaki Disease, 1991-. **SPECIAL ACHIEVEMENTS:** Research in Kawasaki Syndrome, 1979-. **BUSINESS ADDRESS:** Professor of Pediatrics, USC School of Medicine, Children's Hospital of Los Angeles, 4650 Sunset Blvd, Los Angeles, CA 90027-6016, (213)669-4634.

TAKAHASHI, RITA
Library administrator, educator. Japanese American. **CAREER:** San Francisco State University, School of Behavioral and Social Sciences, professor. **ORGANIZATIONS:** Japanese American National Library, vice president, secretary, board member, president, currently. **BUSINESS ADDRESS:** President, Japanese American National Library, PO Box 590598, San Francisco, CA 94159-0598, (415)567-5006.*

TAKAHASHI, TARO
Educator, scientist. Japanese American. **PERSONAL:** Born Nov 15, 1930, Tokyo, Japan; son of Takezo Takahashi III & Tama Takahashi; married Elaine Ache Takahashi, Apr 29, 1966; children: Timothy Taro, Suzanne Eileen. **EDUCATION:** University of Tokyo, BE, 1953; Columbia University, PhD, 1957. **CAREER:** University of Rochester, from assistant professor to professor, 1962-70; Queens College, CUNY, distinguished professor, 1971-77; Lamont-Doherty Earth Observatory of Columbia University, associate director, Doherty Senior Scientist, 1977-. **ORGANIZATIONS:** National Academy of Science, Committee on Ocean Carbon, chairman, 1991-; Geochemical Society, secretary, 1980-83. **HONORS/AWARDS:** National Oceanographic & Atmospheric Administration, Distinguished Author Award, 1991. **SPECIAL ACHIEVEMENTS:** Author, Carbon Dioxide in the Oceans, 1970-; Crystals Under Very High Pressure, 1958-77. **BUSINESS ADDRESS:** Associate Director, Doherty Senior Scientist, Lamont-Doherty Earth Observatory of Columbia University, Route 9W, Palisades, NY 10964, (914)365-8537.

TAKAKI, RONALD
Educator. Japanese American. **PERSONAL:** Born Apr 12, 1939, Honolulu, HI; son of Catherine Okawa Takaki & Toshio Harry Takaki; married Carol Rankin Takaki, Jun 12, 1961; children: Dana, Troy, Todd. **EDUCATION:** College of Wooster, BA, history, 1961; UC Berkeley, MA, American history, 1962, PhD, American history, 1967. **CAREER:** UCLA, professor, 1967-72; UC Berkeley, professor, 1972-. **HONORS/AWARDS:** Cornell University,

Messenger Lectureship, 1993, Goldwin Smith Lectureship, 1988; UC Berkeley, Distinguish Teaching Award, 1980; nominated for a Pulitzer Prize, for Strangers from A Different Shore. **SPECIAL ACHIEVEMENTS:** Author, A Different Mirror: A History of Multicultural America, 1993; Strangers from a Different Shore: A History of Asian Americans, 1987; From Different Shores: Perspectives on Race and Ethnicity in America, 1987; Pau Hana: Plantation Life and Labor in Hawaii, 1983; Iron Cages: Race and Culture in 19th-Century America, 1979; Violence in the Black Imagination, Essays and Documents, 1972, 1993; A Pro-Slavery Crusade, The Agitation to Reopen the Slave Trade, 1971. **BUSINESS ADDRESS:** Professor of Ethnic Studies, University of California, Berkeley, Asian American Studies, Berkeley, CA 94707, (510)642-2289.

TAKAKOSHI, WILLIAM K.
Military official. Japanese American. **CAREER:** Under Secretary of the US Army, special assistant, currently. **BUSINESS ADDRESS:** Special Assistant, Under Secretary of the US Army, Dept of the Army, 102 Army Pentagon, Washington, DC 20310, (703)695-3317.*

TAKAMI, DAVID A.
Public information officer. Japanese American. **PERSONAL:** Born Feb 9, 1957, Glen Cove, NY; son of Alyce S Takami and Suyehiro Takami; married M Wingate Packard, May 23, 1987. **EDUCATION:** University of Washington, BA, English, 1980. **CAREER:** Japan Times, copy editor, 1982-84; Seattle Times, copy editor, 1985-87; Tacoma News Tribune, copy editor, 1987; City of Seattle, Dept of Community Development, public information officer, 1987-92, Dept of Parks and Recreation, public information officer, 1992-. **ORGANIZATIONS:** International Examiner, board of directors, president, 1991-; Society of Professional Journalists, 1988-; Asian American Journalists Association, 1988-. **HONORS/AWARDS:** City Hall Public Information Awards Competition, National Award of Merit, 1989; Society of Professional Jounrnalists, Third Prize, news features, 1988. **SPECIAL ACHIEVEMENTS:** Wrote exhibit catalogue for Executive Order 9066, 1992; wrote Shared Dreams, History of Asians in Washington State, 1989. **BIOGRAPHICAL SOURCES:** "Nikkei Journalist," Northwest Nikkei newspaper, p 2, Spt 1991. **HOME ADDRESS:** 9404 42nd Avenue NE, Seattle, WA 98115, (206)527-3021. **BUSINESS PHONE:** (206)233-7929.

TAKAMI, HIDEKI
Restaurateur. Japanese American. **PERSONAL:** Born Mar 3, 1943, Yokohama, Kanagawa, Japan; son of Kojiro and Kiri Takami. **EDUCATION:** City University of New York, Bernard Baruch College, BBA, 1975. **CAREER:** Hotel New Otani, asst mgr, 1964-67; Igor Stravinsky, personal chef, 1967-70; Ishizuka CPA, sr accountant, 1970-73; La Maison Japonaise, president, 1973-93. **SPECIAL ACHIEVEMENTS:** Originated first Franco-Japonaise restaurant in US, 1973; personal chef and butler to Igor and Vera Stravinsky, 1967-70. **BIOGRAPHICAL SOURCES:** And Music at the Close, L Libman, p 331-32, 1971; Retrospectives and Conclusions, Igor Stravinsky & R Craft, p 29, 1968. **HOME ADDRESS:** 123 E 39th St, New York, NY 10016, (212)986-0224. **BUSINESS ADDRESS:** President, La Maison Japonaise, 125 E 39th St, New York, NY 10016, (212)682-7375.

TAKANO, MARK ALLAN
High school teacher, community college trustee. Japanese American. **PERSONAL:** Born Dec 10, 1960, Riverside, CA; son of William Tadao Takano & Nancy Tsugiye Takano. **EDUCATION:** Harvard College, AB, 1983; University of California, Riverside, teaching credential, 1988. **CAREER:** Rialto High School, English and social studies teacher, 1988-; Riverside Community College, board of trustees, 1990-. **ORGANIZATIONS:** California Democratic Party, 43rd Congressional District Nominee, 1992-, Candidate Recruitment Committee, co-chair, 1993-; Riverside Urban League, board member, 1989-; California Teachers Association/National Teachers' Association, 1988-. **SPECIAL ACHIEVEMENTS:** Created social studies curriculum on the history of the Vietnam War, 1989-90. **BIOGRAPHICAL SOURCES:** "Why Teach," Los Angeles Times Magazine, cover story, Nov 26, 1989; A variety of press articles documenting political career, 1990-. **BUSINESS ADDRESS:** Trustee, Riverside Community College, 4800 Magnolia Ave, Riverside, CA 92506, (909)684-3240.

TAKANO, MASAHARU (MARK)
Consultant. Japanese American. **PERSONAL:** Born Jan 20, 1935, Tainan, Taiwan; son of Syuzo and Misao Takano; married Hiroko Takeshita, Aug 27, 1965; children: Kentaro, Jojiro, Miwako. **EDUCATION:** Hokkaido Univer-

sity, Sapporo, Japan, BS, 1957; University of Tokyo, MS, 1959, DSc, 1963; McGill University, postdoctoral research, 1963-67. **CAREER:** Takasago Rubber Co, research consultant, 1960-63; University of Tokyo, postdoctoral fellow, 1962-63; McGill University, postdoctoral fellow, 1963-67; Monsanto Co, senior process consultant, 1967-90; Takano International, president, owner, 1991-. **ORGANIZATIONS:** American Chemical Society, 1967-; American Institute of Chemists, fellow, 1970-; American Physical Society, 1970-; Society of Rheology, 1965-; Japan Society of Polymer Science, 1959-; Japanese American Citizens League, 1970-; Japan America Society, 1980-; World Affairs Council, 1993-; Foundation of County Soccer Association, West St Louis County, participant. **HONORS/AWARDS:** National Research Council of Canada, postdoctoral fellowship, 1963, 1964; Japan Association for Promotion of Science, postdoctoral fellowship, 1962, 1963; American Institute of Chemists, Certificate of Professional Chemist. **SPECIAL ACHIEVEMENTS:** Contribution of articles to professional journals, 1963-75; government reports on high performace composites, manufacturing process, 1967-72; started a Japanese festival in St Louis as board member of JACL, 1975; research and development of biotechnologies to produce animal growth hormones, 1982-90. **HOME ADDRESS:** 13146 Roundstone Ct, St. Louis, MO 63146-3642, (314)878-8896. **BUSINESS PHONE:** (314)997-6093.

TAKASAKI, RICHARD SADAJI

Educator (retired). Japanese American. **PERSONAL:** Born Apr 1, 1918, Honolulu, HI; son of Jutaro and Tome Takasaki; married T Rose Takasaki, Dec 23, 1945. **EDUCATION:** University of Hawaii, BS, 1940; Columbia University, MA, 1949; Harvard University, MPA, 1960; Brandeis University, 1969-70. **CAREER:** State of Hawaii, Department of Public Welfare, chief of research & statistics, 1951-56, chief management division, chief budget examiner, 1956-61; City and County of Honolulu, director of finance, 1961-63; University of Hawaii, vice-president for business affairs, professor of social work, acting president, chancellor, 1963-73; Bishop Estate, director of finance, 1973-78; East West Center, vice-president for administration, 1978-83. **ORGANIZATIONS:** Hawaii Humane Society, Campaign Committee, chairman, 1979; City & County of Honoluu Charter Commission, 1970-71; National Center for Higher Education Commission, board of directors, 1971-73; Kamehameha Schools, board of governors, 1971-73; Liliuokalani Trust Child Welfare Department, Advisory Committee, chairman, 1968-69; City and County of Honolulu Planning Commission, 1962-63; Hawaii Visitors Bureau, board of directors, 1962-63, Honolulu Health and Community Services, board of directors, 1959-60. **HONORS/AWARDS:** McKinley High School, Hall of Honor, 1990; University of Hawaii, Outstanding Alumni Award, 1966; Phi Beta Kappa, 1964; American Society for Public Administration, Annual Award, 1964; Harvard University, Littauer Fellow, 1960. **MILITARY SERVICE:** US Army Military Intelligence Service, 1944-46. **HOME ADDRESS:** 3247 Melemele Place, Honolulu, HI 96822.

TAKASAKI, WILLIAM YOSHI TSUGU

Government official. Japanese American. **PERSONAL:** Born Dec 28, 1939, Honolulu, HI; son of David & Helen Takasaki; married Susanna S Takasaki, Sep 13, 1958; children: Cherie Lyn Celli, Kenneth, Joann. **EDUCATION:** University of Maryland, BA, 1972; Central Michigan University, MA, 1974; Industrial College of the Armed Forces, National Def University, DIP, 1980; Air War College, DIP, 1989. **CAREER:** USA Strategic CMD-Hawaii, maintenance mgmt spec, 1972-74; US Army Comm Cmd, Ft Huachuca, AZ, plans officer, 1974-75; United Nations CMD/Eight US Army, supervisor, resource management, 1975-78; 1st Signal Brigade, Rep of Korea, director of Logistics, 1978-80; National Oceanic & Atmospheric Admin, director, Spt Svcs, 1980-82; Dept of Defense Dependent Schs-Germany, comptroller, 1982-88; Defense Log Svcs Center, deputy commander, 1988-. **ORGANIZATIONS:** Masonic; Scottish Rite; Shrine, 1967-; Salvation Army, advisory board, 1991-; Battle Creek Schools, Math & Science Center Advisory Committee, 1989-; Pi Sigma Alpha, National Honor Society, Pol Science, 1972-; Academy of Political Science, 1970-; Special Olympics, head of Committee for Logistics, Germany, 1985-86; US Army Europe Track and Field Officials Union, 1984-88; Far East US Secondary Schools Coaches Committee, 1977-79. **HONORS/AWARDS:** Special Olympics Program, Certificate of Appreciation, 1985, 1986; Seoul American High School, Medal for Outstanding Coaching, 1978; Republic of China Government, Medal for Outstanding Service, 1970. **SPECIAL ACHIEVEMENTS:** Logistics support for overseas schools, booklet used by the Dept of Defense, 1983; Career Program Guide for Quality Assurance Specialist, US Army, 1974; Development of tools to use in alignment of High Freq Output transmitters, 1964; proficient in Chinese Mandarin & Japanese.

MILITARY SERVICE: US Army, pfc, 1957-60. **HOME ADDRESS:** 316 Eaton St, Battle Creek, MI 49017.

TAKASHIMA, SHIRO

Educator (retired). Japanese American. **PERSONAL:** Born May 12, 1923, Tokyo, Japan; son of Atsuharu Takashima and Yoshie Takashima; married Yuki; children: Nozomi Miazzo, Makoto. **EDUCATION:** University of Tokyo, BS, 1947, PhD, 1955. **CAREER:** University of Minnesota, post doctoral fellow, 1955-57; Osaka University, associate professor, 1959-62; University of Pennsylvania, research associate, 1957-59, assistant professor, 1963-70, associate professor, 1979-78, professor, 1970-92, professor emeritus, currently. **ORGANIZATIONS:** Biophysical Society, senior member; AAAE; IEEE, senior member. **HONORS/AWARDS:** University of Genoa, visiting professor; Osaka University, visiting professor; Kyoto University, visiting professor. **SPECIAL ACHIEVEMENTS:** Author of more than 100 scientific papers, including book chapters; author of Electrical Properties of Biopolymers and Membrances, book; many invited lectures and presentations; languages: Japanese, English, French, German. **BUSINESS ADDRESS:** Professor Emeritus, University of Pennsylvania, 240 S 33rd Street, Hayden Hall, Philadelphia, PA 19104-6392, (215)898-8537.

TAKASUGI, NAO

State government official. Japanese American. **PERSONAL:** Born Apr 5, 1922, Oxnard, CA; son of Shingoro Takasugi & Yasuye Hayashi Takasugi (both deceased); married Judith Shigeko, Mar 23, 1952; children: Scott, Russell, Ronald, Tricia, Lea. **EDUCATION:** Ventura College, AA, 1941; Temple University, BS, 1945; University of Pennsylvania, MBA, 1946. **CAREER:** City of Oxnard, councilman, 1976-82, mayor, 1982-92; State of California, assembly member, 1992-. **ORGANIZATIONS:** State of California, United Nations representative, 1991; Optimist Club of Oxnard, 1965-91; Japanese American Citizens League, Ventura Co Chapter, 1948-. **HONORS/AWARDS:** Government of Japan, 4th Order of Sacred Treasure, 1992. **SPECIAL ACHIEVEMENTS:** Speaker, National Republican Conventions, New Orleans, 1988, Houston, 1992. **BUSINESS ADDRESS:** Assembly Member, State of California, Capitol Bldg, Rm 2016, Sacramento, CA 95814, (916)445-7827.

TAKASUGI, ROBERT M.

Judge. Japanese American. **PERSONAL:** Born Sep 12, 1930, Tacoma, WA; son of Hidesaburo Takasugi (deceased) and Kayo Takasugi (deceased); married Dorothy, Mar 30, 1958; children: Jon Robert, Lesli Mari. **EDUCATION:** University of California, Los Angeles, BS, 1963; University of Southern California Law Center, JD, 1959. **CAREER:** Self-employed, Velarde & Takasugi, partner, 1960-73; State of California, East Los Angeles Municpal Court, judge, 1973-75, Los Angeles Superior Court, judge, 1975-76; US Government, US district judge, 1976-. **ORGANIZATIONS:** JACL, national legal counsel, 1971; commissioner, civil rights, human relations, 1963-76; Southern California Law Review, editorial board; numerous court committees, 1976-. **HONORS/AWARDS:** East Los Angeles, Montebello Bar Association, Judge of the Year, 1974; Mexican American Bar Association, Judge of the Year, 1974; Japanese American Bar Association, Judicial Excellence, 1982; Japanese American Cultural Center, Judicial Excellence, 1986; Criminal Courts Bar Association, Judicial Excellence, 1990; Pro Bono Bar Review, Judicial Excellence, 1993. **SPECIAL ACHIEVEMENTS:** Has written and published numerous legal opinions and legal articles, 1973-. **MILITARY SERVICE:** US Army, cpl, 1953-55; Military Man of Year, Far East, 1954, 1955. **BUSINESS ADDRESS:** US District Judge, United States Courthouse, 312 N Spring St, Courtroom 22, Los Angeles, CA 90012, (213)894-2370.

TAKAYAMA, AKIRA

Educator. Japanese American. **PERSONAL:** Born Jun 28, 1932, Yokohama, Japan; son of Tsunaki and Shoko Takayama; married Machiko Takayama, Jan 31, 1970. **EDUCATION:** International Christian University, Tokyo, Japan, BA, 1957; University of Rochester, MA, 1960, PhD, 1962; Hitotsubashi University, Tokyo, Japan, doctor of economics, 1964. **CAREER:** International Christian University, lecturer & assistant professor, 1962-64; University of Manchester, England, fellow in economic statics, 1964-65; University of Minnesota, visiting associate professor of economics, 1965-66; Purdue University, from associate professor to professor of economics, 1967-78; Texas A&M University, professor of economics, 1978-82; University of Kyoto, professor of economics, 1982-85; Southern Illinois University at Carbondale, Vandeveer Professor of Economics, 1983-. **ORGANIZATIONS:** American Economic Association; Econometric Society; Japan Association of Economics and Econometrics; Japan Center for Economic Research, special member. **HONORS/ AWARDS:** Japan Center for Economic Research, The Best Books of the Year Award in Economics and Management, for Nikkeisho, 1975; Journal of International Economics Integration, Daeyang Prize, 1991. **SPECIAL ACHIEVEMENTS:** Kokusai Keizaigaku, International Economics, Tokyo, Toyo Keizai Shimposha, 1963; International Trade: An Approach to the Theory, Holt, Rinehart & Winston, 1972; Mathematical Economics, Cambridge University Press, second ed, 1985; Analytical Methods in Economics, University of Michigan Press, 1993; coeditor, Economic Development in East and Southeast Asia, Singapore, Institute of Southeast Asian Studies, 1990; coeditor, Trade, Policy and International Adjustments, Academic Press, 1991; over 100 articles in professional journals. **BUSINESS ADDRESS:** Vandeveer Professor of Economics, Southern Illinois University at Carbondale, Carbondale, IL 62901, (618)453-2827.

TAKAYAMA, GREGG

State government official. Japanese American/Chinese American. **PERSONAL:** Born Sep 3, 1952, Honolulu, HI; son of Robert and Lena Takayama; married Linda Chu Takayama, Nov 1, 1975; children: Kelly Jean Kikukawa, Teal, Sage. **EDUCATION:** Lewis and Clark College, 1970-72; University of Hawaii, BA, journalism, 1974. **CAREER:** Honolulu Star-Bulletin, news reporter, 1974-78; US Sen Daniel K Inouye, press secretary, 1978-90; US Sen Daniel Akaka, communications director, 1990-91; Lt Governor Benjamin Cayetano, communications director, 1991-. **HOME ADDRESS:** 1639 Hoolana St, Pearl City, HI 96782, (808)456-7151.

TAKEDA, YASUHIKO

Physician, researcher, educator. Japanese American. **PERSONAL:** Born Mar 16, 1927, Liyama, Nagano, Japan; son of Hideyoshi Takeda and Hana Takeda; married Tamako Takeda, May 5, 1958; children: James, Basil, Mary Takeda Stephens, Clara Takeda Waddington. **EDUCATION:** Shinshu University, Japan, 1945-48; University of Chiba, School of Medicine, Japan, MD, 1948-52; Sacred Heart Hospital, WA, anat pathology residency, 1954-56; University of Colorado, School of Medicine, clin pathology residency, 1956-58; American Board of Pathology, Diplomate, 1970. **CAREER:** Canadian Res Council, research fellow, 1960-63; University of Colorado, School of Medicine, research fellow, 1958-60, instructor, 1963-64, assistant professor, 1965-69, associate professor, 1969-78, professor, 1979-88, emeritus professor, 1988-. **ORGANIZATIONS:** College of American Pathologists (FCAP); American Society of Clinical Pathologists (FASCP); American Physiological Society; International Society on Thrombosis & Hemostasis; American Heart Association, Thrombosis Council; American Association for the Advancement of Sciences; Central Society for Clinical Investigation; Western Society for Clincial Investigation. **HONORS/AWARDS:** American Heart Association, Advanced Research Fellow, 1964-66; NIH, Career Development Award, 1967-72, reserach grants, 1969-80. **SPECIAL ACHIEVEMENTS:** 50 original publications in the area of blood coagulation, especially regarding purification and metabolism of albumin, fibrinogen, prothrombin, Factor X, antithrombin III, plasminogen and tissue thromboplastins. **HOME ADDRESS:** 635 Dexter, Denver, CO 80220, (303)399-0168.

TAKEI, GEORGE HOSATO

Actor. Japanese American. **PERSONAL:** Born Apr 20, 1937, Los Angeles, CA; son of Fumiko Emily Nakamura and Takekuma Norman Takei. **EDUCATION:** UCLA, BA, 1960, MA, 1964. **CAREER:** T G H Bldg Management, president, 1964-; Golden Security Thrift and Loan, director, chairman, 1981-; actor; films include: Green Berets, 1967; Star Trek, 1979; Star Trek 2, 1982; Star Trek 3, 1984; Star Trek 4, 1986; Star Trek 5, 1989; Star Trek 6, 1991; Blood Oath, 1990; Return from River Kwai, 1989; plays include: Macbeth, 1972; Year of the Dragon, 1974; Undertow, 1988; Wash, 1990; television shows include: ''Playhouse '90,'' 1959; ''Star Trek,'' 1966-69. **ORGANIZATIONS:** Japanese American National Museum, Los Angeles Theatre Center, trustee, 1984-; NATAS, Blue Ribbon Committee, 1976-; SAG; Association of Asian Pacific American Artists; American Cinemateque. **HONORS/ AWARDS:** US Pan Asian American Chamber of Commerce, Excellence 2000 Award, Outstanding Asian American in the Arts, 1992; Asian American Legal Defense and Education Fund, Justice in Action Award, 1992; National Asian Pacific American Committee for Clinton-Gore, honorary co-chair, 1992. **SPECIAL ACHIEVEMENTS:** Panelist, How the Media Affects the Perceptions of Asian Americans, panel discussion of the Association of Asian Pacific American Artists, 1992. **BUSINESS ADDRESS:** Actor, c/o Gerler/Stevens, 3349 Cahuenga Blvd W, Ste 1, Los Angeles, CA 90068, (213)850-7386.✱

TAKEI, RICHARD

Government official. Japanese American. **PERSONAL:** Born Mar 26, 1947, Oakland, CA; son of Akira Takei (deceased) and Marion Takei; married Lily S Takei, Jan 16, 1978; children: Sandra. **EDUCATION:** California State University at Hayward, BS, physical education, 1969, BBA, 1976. **CAREER:** US Census Bureau, district office manager, 1980 Census, 1979-80, evaluations section, chief, 1980-82, survey statistician, 1982-84, assistant branch chief, 1984-88, branch chief, 1988-, assistant regional census manager, 1988-91, program coordinator, currently. **MILITARY SERVICE:** US Air Force, sgt, 1970-74, Airman of Month, Sept 1970. **BUSINESS ADDRESS:** Program Coordinator, US Bureau of Census, 15350 Sherman Way, Ste 300, Van Nuys, CA 91406-4224, (818)904-6109.

TAKEKAWA, THOMAS TSUYOSHI

Social worker. Japanese American. **PERSONAL:** Born Nov 5, 1933, Seattle, WA; married Kiyomi K Takekawa, May 18, 1966; children: Lisa Mari, Michael Thomas. **EDUCATION:** University of Minnesota, BA, sociology, 1956; Case Western Reserve University, MSW, 1964. **CAREER:** Olmsted County Community Services, social worker, mgr, 1964-92. **ORGANIZATIONS:** NASW, 1963-. **HONORS/AWARDS:** Council on Asian Pacific Minnesotans, member appointed by governor, 1993-96. **SPECIAL ACHIEVEMENTS:** NASW, ACSW, 1966-. **MILITARY SERVICE:** US Army, Spc 4, 1957-58, Korea. **HOME ADDRESS:** 2304 Stanley Lane NW, Rochester, MN 55901-2100.

TAKEMORI, AKIRA EDDIE

Educator. Japanese American. **PERSONAL:** Born Dec 9, 1929, Stockton, CA; son of Matsutaro Takemori and Haruko Teshima Takemori; married Valerie Williams Takemori, Jun 22, 1958; children: Tensho, Rima. **EDUCATION:** University of California, Berkeley, AB, 1951, San Francisco, MS, 1953; University of Wisconsin, Madison, PhD, 1958. **CAREER:** Upstate Medical Center, Syracuse, instructor, 1959-61; SUNY, assistant professor, 1961-63; University of Minnesota, assistant professor, 1963-65, associate professor, 1965-69, professor, 1969-. **ORGANIZATIONS:** American Society for Pharmacology & Experimental Therapeutics, 1961-, president, 1992-93; American Association for the Advancement of Science, 1959-; American Association of University Professors, 1960-; American College of Neuropsychopharmacology, 1980-; College on Problems of Drug Dependence, charter fellow, 1992-; Society for Experimental Biology & Medicine, 1961-; Sigma Xi, 1957-; American Chemical Society, Medical Chem Division, 1965-. **HONORS/ AWARDS:** National Academy of Science, International Travel Award, 1962, 1965; China Medical Board Inc, The Alan Gregg Fellowship in Med Educ, 1971; Japan Society for the Promotion of Science, Visiting Scientist Award, 1971; Committee on Problems of Drug Dependence, Nathan B Eddy Award, 1991. **SPECIAL ACHIEVEMENTS:** Approximately 425 research papers in scientific journals, 1952-; two US patents (897920, 914448), 1993; speaks Japanese. **MILITARY SERVICE:** US Army, Medical Service Corporation, sp3, active service, 1953-55, inactive service 1956-61. **BUSINESS ADDRESS:** Professor, University of Minnesota, 435 Delaware St SE, 3-249 Millard Hall, Minneapolis, MN 55455, (612)625-3248.

TAKENAKA, MAKOTO B.

Pianist, educator. Japanese American. **PERSONAL:** Born Jul 1, New Haven, CT; son of Masao Takenaka and Fumiko Takenaka; married Noriko Takenaka, Jul 1, 1987; children: Mio, Kyoko. **EDUCATION:** International Christian University, BA, education, 1976, MA, education, 1978; Berklee College of Music, BA (magna cum laude), music, 1982. **CAREER:** International Christian University, instructor, teaching assistant, 1976-80; Ichikawa High School, instructor, 1976-80; Massachusetts Institute of Technology, instructor, 1989-91; Northeastern University, instructor, 1988-; Berklee College of Music, assistant professor, 1989-93, associate professor, 1993-. **ORGANIZATIONS:** Japanese Association of Greater Boston, 1980-; Japan Society, Boston, 1989-; Japan Club of Berklee, adviser, 1990-. **HONORS/AWARDS:** Berklee College of Music, Publishing Essays, 1993. **SPECIAL ACHIEVEMENTS:** Concert, Boston Pops Memorial at Charles River Esplanade, every summer at the Hatch Shell, 1988-; concerts at Harvard, MIT, BU, Berklee Performance Center, 1981-; Chords and Scales, book; played on TV (CBS, ABC, NBC, Cable TV), and on radio (WGBH, WMJX, WBUR, WERS, etc); concert tours to Japan, Korea, Taiwan, Costa Rica, US. **BIOGRAPHICAL SOURCES:** Boston Globe; Boston Phoenix; Cambridge Chronicle; Newton Graphic; Asahi; Mainichi; New England Notes. **HOME PHONE:** (617)527-5150. **BUSINESS ADDRESS:** Associate Professor, Berklee College of Music, 1140 Boylston St, Faculty Box 228, Boston, MA 02215, (617)266-1400.

TAKESHITA, KENICHI

Hematologist, educator. Japanese American. **PERSONAL:** Born Mar 16, 1957, Tokyo, Japan; son of Tsuneichi Takeshita and Yoshiko Takeshita; married Mayumi Kittaka, Oct 10, 1992. **EDUCATION:** Harvard University, AB (magna cum laude), 1979; Yale University, MD, 1984. **CAREER:** Yale-New Haven Hospital, resident, internal medicine, 1984-88; University of Tokyo, visiting scientist, 1991-92; Yale University, postdoctoral fellow, 1988-91, research scientist, 1992-93, instructor, 1993-94; NYU, assistant professor of medicine, 1994-. **ORGANIZATIONS:** American Federation of Clinical Research, 1984-. **HONORS/AWARDS:** Japan Society for Promotion of Science, Research Award, 1991; National Institutes of Health, Physician-Scientist Award, 1988; Yale University, Louis Nahum Prize, 1984; Japanese Medical Society of New York, Hiromi Shinya Award, 1981; Harvard University, Phi Beta Kappa, 1979; Yale University, Dean's Young Faculty Award, 1993; Donaghue Foundation, New Investigator Award, 1993. **SPECIAL ACHIEVEMENTS:** Scientific research publications in professional journals. **BUSINESS ADDRESS:** Associate Professor of Medicine, Hematology Div, NYU School of Medicine, Dept of Internal Medicine, 550 First Avenue, New York, NY 10016, (212)263-6268.

TAKEUCHI, ESTHER KIYOMI

Teaching assistant. Japanese American. **PERSONAL:** Born Dec 30, 1941, Watsonville, CA; daughter of Isamu Okano & Lillian Okano (deceased); married Ronald Hatsuo Takeuchi, Jun 15, 1963; children: Marcy Ayako, Kevin Hatsuo. **EDUCATION:** Contra Costa College, ECE, 1985; Armstrong Business College, AA, 1992. **CAREER:** American Red Cross, executive secretary, 1962-64; West Contra Costa Unified School District, teaching assistant, 1975-. **ORGANIZATIONS:** Richmond-Shimada Friendship Commission, delegate to Japan, 1992; Contra Costa Japanese American Citizens League, editor, 1985; Fairmede Vista Hills PTA, president, 1976; Troop 146 Boy Scouts of America, secty, treasurer, comm member, 1976-; Japanese American Seniors of the East Bay, BINGO Vol, 1988-; Sakura Kai Senior Center, health fair volunteer, 1985-. **HONORS/AWARDS:** 11th Assembly Dist, Woman of the Year, 1992; RBPW, International Women of the Year, 1993; Contra Costa JACL, Community Service Award, 1993; Troop 146, Scouter of the Year, 1987; Fairmede Vista Hills PTA, Honorary Service Award, 1976. **HOME ADDRESS:** 3008 Phillip Ct, Richmond, CA 94806-2745, (510)223-2258.

TAKEUCHI, KENJI

Engineer. Japanese American. **PERSONAL:** Born Dec 11, 1934, Tokyo, Japan; son of Eiji Takeuchi and Ayako Takeuchi; divorced; children: Makoto J, Yoshimi R, Yoshitoshi H. **EDUCATION:** Tokyo Institute of Technology, BS, 1958; University of Michigan, PhD, 1967. **CAREER:** Argonne National Laboratory, research associate, 1966-70; University of Manchester, England, research fellow, 1970-73; Westinghouse Electric Corp, fellow engineer, 1973-. **ORGANIZATIONS:** American Nuclear Society, 1973-; American Physical Society, 1965-. **SPECIAL ACHIEVEMENTS:** More than 60 publications in Nuclear Physics Theory, Fluid Structure Interaction, Two Phase Flow Dynamics, and Nuclear Safety Evaluation. **BUSINESS ADDRESS:** Engineer, Westinghouse Electric Corp, PO Box 355, WECE-513B, Pittsburgh, PA 15230, (412)374-4263.

TAKEUCHI, KENNETH JAMES

Educator. Japanese American. **PERSONAL:** Born Sep 27, 1953, Cincinnati, OH; son of James Minoru Takeuchi and Haruko Ruth Takeuchi; married Esther Sans Takeuchi, May 15, 1982. **EDUCATION:** University of Cincinnati, BS, 1975; Ohio State University, PhD, 1981. **CAREER:** University of North Carolina, postdoctoral researcher, 1981-83; State University of New York at Buffalo, assistant professor, 1983-90, associate professor, 1990-. **ORGANIZATIONS:** American Chemical Society, 1977-, symposium organizer, 1989-90, Western New York Region, executive committee, 1989; Phi Beta Kappa, 1975-; Phi Eta Sigma, 1987-, SUNY at Buffalo Chapter, 1986. **HONORS/AWARDS:** SUNY at Buffalo, EOP, Friend of the EOP, 1993; SUNY at Buffalo Student Association, Milton Plesur Teaching Award, 1989, Award for Excellence in Teaching, 1985, Chancellor's Award for Excellence in Teaching, 1986. **SPECIAL ACHIEVEMENTS:** Lilly Teaching Fellow, three video tapes of inorganic chemists, 1988-89; total of 40 publications in refereed journals, author or co-author; total of 38 presentations at colleges and universities; over 100 presentations at conferences. **BUSINESS ADDRESS:** Associate Professor, Dept of Chemistry, State University of New York at Buffalo, Buffalo, NY 14214, (716)829-2512.

TAKEUCHI, TAKAO

Educator. Japanese American. **PERSONAL:** Born Feb 16, 1945, Nagoya, Japan; son of Masataka & Kinko Takeuchi; married Keiko Takeuchi, Dec 26, 1983; children: Kazumasa, Takahiro. **EDUCATION:** Nagoya University, BS, 1967; Kanazawa University, MS, 1970; University of North Carolina, Chapel Hill, PhD, 1976. **CAREER:** Kanazawa University, visiting lecturer, 1970; Komatsu Technical College, visiting lecturer, 1970; North Carolina Central University, assistant professor, 1976-83; State University of New York, assistant professor, 1983-88, associate professor, 1988-. **ORGANIZATIONS:** American Physical Society; Physical Society of Japan. **SPECIAL ACHIEVEMENTS:** Author of: "Temperature Dependence of Cation Concentrations in $RbAg_4I_5$," Physica Stat Solidi, p 132, k7, 1992; "Electronic Structure of F-Center in LIH by the SCF X Method," Physica Stat Solidi, p 277, 158, 1990; "Electronic Structure of $CuCl_4$ -3, $CuCl_4$ -4, and $CuCl_4$ -2 Cluster," Physica Stat Solidi, p 579, 149, 1988; "Note on MD Calculation of $RbAg_4I_5$," Physica Stat Solidi, p 147, K9, 1988; "Absorption Transition Energies in F-type Centers in MgO," Physica Stat Solidi, p 140, K113, 1987. **BUSINESS ADDRESS:** Associate Professor, Physics Dept, SUNY, College of Technology, Alfred, NY 14802, (607)587-4598.

TAKIGUCHI, MASAKO

Organization administrator. Japanese American. **PERSONAL:** Born Jan 5, 1932, Seattle, WA; daughter of Tomigoro Takatsui & Koyuwa Nakano; married Minoru Takiguchi, Jul 27, 1958; children: Joyce Emi Takiguchi Mella, Ilene Yumi, Susan Sue. **CAREER:** Japanese American Citizens League, Arizona Chapter, president, 1983; commissioned to the Arizona Governor Rose Mofford's Japanese Baseball Committee, 1989, 1990; Mayor's Phoenix Pride Commission, Phoenix Pacific Rim Advisory Council, 1991; Arizona Gakuen School, board member, 1991; Phoenix Japanese Friendship Garden Fundraising Committee, founder, vice chair, 1991; Phoenix Sister Cities Commission, Himeji chairperson, 1991-93; Arizona America Japan Week, honorary co-chair, 1993. **ORGANIZATIONS:** Japanese American Citizens League, 1960-, board member, 1980, cultural chair, 1980; Phoenix Matsuri Steering Committee, 1985-; International General Federation of Women's Club, 1980-; Glendale Historical Society, Glendale arts council; Japan America Society of Phoenix-Charter; Arizona State University, West Provost's Club, 1989; Phoenix Japanese Friendship Garden Fundraising committee, founder, 1990. **HONORS/AWARDS:** Arizona America Japan Week, 1993; Phoenix Mayor Johnson, Sunday on Central, Participation Ceritificate, 1992; Glendale's 1992 Centennial Celebration, Certificate of Appreciation, 1992; Phoenix Parks, Recreation and Library Department, One Hundred Volunteer Award, 1990, Recreational Enrichment of the Community, 1988; Japanese American Citizens League, Arizona Chapter Award, Chapter Past President Award, 1989. **SPECIAL ACHIEVEMENTS:** Fluent in Japanese; instructor in Sekishu School Tea Ceremony; professional volunteer. **HOME ADDRESS:** 5702 West Northern Ave, Glendale, AZ 85301.

TAKIMOTO, HIDEYO HENRY

Chemist (retired). Japanese American. **PERSONAL:** Born Aug 14, 1928, Vacaville, CA; son of Jihei Takimoto and Hayae Takimoto; married Mitzi Takimoto, Jun 22, 1957; children: Chris Hidemi, Corey Kenji. **EDUCATION:** University of California, Berkeley, BS, 1952; University of California, Los Angeles, PhD, 1957. **CAREER:** Hughes Aircraft Co, group leader, 1956-60; The Aerospace Corp, senior staff scientist, 1960-93. **ORGANIZATIONS:** American Chemical Society. **HOME ADDRESS:** 3612 Coolidge Ave, Los Angeles, CA 90066.

TAKIMOTO, MABEL YAYOKO (YOKO)

Association administrator, department store manager. Japanese American. **PERSONAL:** Born in Brighton, CO; married Toshio Takimoto, 1942; children: Dick. **CAREER:** Bullock's Century City, dressmaker, beginning 1971, Alteration Dept, manager, currently. **ORGANIZATIONS:** San Fernando Valley Japanese American Community Center, president, 1993, secretary, currently; board member; Nikkei Village Board, chairperson, currently; San Fernando Valley Japanese American Citizens League, president, 1961, 1971; Pacific Southwest District Council, Japanese American Citizens League, board member, currently; San Fernando Valley Holiness Church, charter board of trustees, currently. **HONORS/AWARDS:** Japanese American Citizens League, Downtown Chapter, Nanka Nikkei Fujinkai, Women of the Year honoree, 1993. **SPECIAL ACHIEVEMENTS:** First woman president of San Fernando Valley Japanese American Community Center, 1993. **BUSINESS ADDRESS:** Secretary, San Fernando Valley Japanese American Community Center, 12953 Branford St, Pacoima, CA 91331, (818)834-2740.*

TAKUMI, ROY M.
Legislator. Japanese American. **PERSONAL:** Born Oct 13, 1952, Honolulu, HI; son of Hideo Takumi and Muriel Takumi; married Wanda A Kutaka, Mar 26, 1976; children: Aisha K, Jaron K. **EDUCATION:** Friends World College, BA, 1990; University of Hawaii, Manoa, MPA, 1993. **CAREER:** American Friends Service Committee, program director, 1984-90; Hawaii State AFL-CIO, communications specialist, 1990-; Hawaii State Legislature, representative, 1992-. **ORGANIZATIONS:** Hawaii Job Training Coordinating Council, 1990-92; State Commission on Employment and Human Resources, commissioner, 1990-92; Labor Education Advisory Council, vice chair, 1990-92; US-Japan Committee for Racial Justice, 1988-; Hawaii Democratic Movement, board member, 1990-. **HONORS/AWARDS:** University of Hawaii, Manoa, Herman Doi Fellowship, 1991. **MILITARY SERVICE:** Hawaii Air National Guard, ssgt e-5, 1970-77; outstanding honor graduate, 1970, distinguished graduate, 1976. **BUSINESS ADDRESS:** Representative, Hawaii State Legislature, 235 S Beretania Street, Room 1011, Honolulu, HI 96813, (808)586-6170.

TALWANI, MANIK
Educator. Indo-American. **PERSONAL:** Born Aug 22, 1933, Patiala, Punjab, India; son of Bir Sain Talwani & Saraswati Khosla Talwani; married Anni Fittler Talwani, Apr 3, 1958; children: Rajeev Manik, Indira, Sanjay. **EDUCATION:** Delhi University, Delhi, India, BS (with honors), 1951, MS, 1953; Columbia University, New York, PhD, 1959. **CAREER:** Lamont-Doherty Geological Observatory of Columbia University, research scientist, senior research associate, associate professorf, 1959-70, directory, 1972-81; Columbia University, professor of geophysics, 1970-82; Gulf Research & Development Co, Center for Marine Crustal Studies, director 1981-83, chief scientist, 1983-85; Rice University, Schlumberger Professor of Geophysics, 1985-; Geotechnology Research Institute, Houston Advanced Research Center, director, 1985-. **ORGANIZATIONS:** Sigma Xi; Geological Society of America, fellow; Society of Exploration Geophysicists; American Geophysical Union, fellow; American Association for the Advancement of Science, fellow; American Association of Petroleum Geologists; Houston Geophysical Society, honorary member; Norwegian Academy of Arts and Sciences; Russian Academy of Natural Sciences; Houston Philosophical Society. **HONORS/AWARDS:** Indian Geophysical Union, First Krishnan Medal, 1965; American Geophysical Union, Sixth James B Macelwane Award, 1967; NASA, Exceptional Scientific Achievement Award, 1973; Guggenheim, fellowship, 1973-74; Fulbright-Hays Grant, 1973-74; American Geophysical Union & US Navy, 6th Maurice Ewing Award for Oceanography, 1981; University of Oslo, Norway, Honorary Doctorate of Philosophy, 1981; Geological Society of America, Second George P Woollard Award, 1984; University of Tel Aviv, Israel, Sackler Distinguished Lecturer, 1988; Natl Institute of Oceanography, Goa, India, Unesco Tokten Award, 1990; Russian Academy of Natural Sciences, Foreign Member, 1992; European Union of Geoscience, Alfred Wegener Medal, 1993; Geophysical Society of Houston, honorary member. **SPECIAL ACHIEVEMENTS:** Handbook of Physical Properties of Rocks, advisory bd, 1977-; Atlantic & Pacific Geophysical Atlas, Intl Oceanographic Commission, editorial bd, 1982-; books, co-editor: Ocean Floor, 1982; Structure & Development of the Greenland Scotland Ridge: New Methods & Concepts, 1983; atlases: Geophysical Atlas of the Norwegian-Greenland Sea, Lamont-Doherty Geological Observatory, 1978; Intl Geolog-Geophys Atlas of the Indian Ocean, Intergovernmental Oceanographic Commission, UNESCO, Moscow, 1975; Intl Geolog-Geophys Atlas of the Atlantic Ocean, Intergovernmental Oceanographic Commission, UNESCO, Moscow, 1989-90; more than 120 publications in refereed journals; marine geophysical researcher in all oceans of the world; inventor of instrumentation for improving marine gravity measurements; principal investigator of first gravity measurements of the moon. **HOME ADDRESS:** 1111 Hermann Dr, #10-D, Houston, TX 77004.

TAM, CHRISTOPHER KWONG-WAH
Educator. Chinese American. **PERSONAL:** Born Oct 22, 1939, Macao, Macao; son of Bak-Hung Tam and Sui-Fong Au-Yeung; married Delia Tam, Dec 20, 1969; children: Brian, Tobey. **EDUCATION:** McGill University, BEng, 1962; California Institute of Technology, MS, 1963, PhD, 1966. **CAREER:** California Institute of Technology, research fellow, 1966-67; Massachusetts Institute of Technology, assistant professor, 1967-71; Florida State University, professor, 1971-. **ORGANIZATIONS:** American Physical Society, fellow; American Institute of Aeronautics & Astronautics, associate fellow; Society for Industrial and Applied Mathematics; American Acoustical Society. **HONORS/AWARDS:** Lockheed Aircraft Co, Disclosure of Invention Award, 1981; AIAA, Space Shuttle Flag Plaque Award, 1984, Aeroacoustics Award,

1987; Florida State University, Distinguished Research Professor Award, 1991. **BUSINESS ADDRESS:** Professor, Dept of Mathematics, Florida State University, Tallahassee, FL 32306-3027, (904)644-2455.

TAM, ERIC TAK-KEUNG
Environmental laboratory executive. Chinese American. **PERSONAL:** Born Jun 19, 1962, Kowloon, Hong Kong; son of Yue Tung Tam and Fung King Tse; married Connie S Tam, Nov 19, 1986; children: Nicole Brittany, Janice Ellen. **EDUCATION:** University of California, Berkeley, BS, 1985. **CAREER:** Anresco Inc, senior chemist, section head, 1985-87; ChromaLab Inc, president, lab director, 1987-. **ORGANIZATIONS:** American Chemical Society, 1987-. **BUSINESS ADDRESS:** President, ChromaLab, Inc, 2239 Omega Rd, Unit #1, San Ramon, CA 94583, (510)831-1788.

TAM, FRANCIS MAN KEI
Educator. Macanese American. **PERSONAL:** Born Dec 7, 1938, Macao; son of Anthony Wai Chiu Tam and Agatha Yeung Tam; married Margaret McGann Tam, Sep 28, 1976; children: Mary Christina, Peter Anthony, Matthew Philip. **EDUCATION:** Ying Wah College, Hong Kong, GCE, cert of matriculation, 1959; University of California, Berkeley, AB, 1963; University of Minnesota, MS, 1967. **CAREER:** Salesian Institute, Macao, high school teacher, 1959-60; University of California, Berkeley, reader, 1962-63; University of Minnesota, teaching assistant, 1963-65, research associate, 1965-67; Frostburg State University, assistant professor of physics, 1967-. **ORGANIZATIONS:** American Geophysical Union, 1967-; American Meteorological Society, 1975-; American Association of Physics Teachers, 1967-, chair of committee on minority education, 1989-91, Appalachian Section, secretary, 1981-91, section representative, 1991-; Mary, Servant of the Lord Community, pastoral leader, 1977-80. **HONORS/AWARDS:** Appalachian Section of American Association of Physics Teachers, Distinguished Service Award, 1991; Westinghouse Corp, grant, 1990. **SPECIAL ACHIEVEMENTS:** Thunderstorm Electrification, author, 1972; Snowrollers, Weatherwise, 1982; Chinese proficiency. **HOME ADDRESS:** 33 Teaberry Lane, Frostburg, MD 21532. **BUSINESS ADDRESS:** Assistant Professor of Physics, Frostburg State University, Frostburg, MD 21532, (301)689-4165.

TAM, HENRY
Aerospace engineer. Chinese American. **PERSONAL:** Born Mar 24, 1965, Kowloon, Hong Kong; son of Sze Keung Tam and Chow Ho Tam. **EDUCATION:** California State University, Long Beach, BA, 1988. **CAREER:** Hughes Aircraft Co, development engr, 1989-. **HONORS/AWARDS:** Bank of America, Award of Excellence in the field of social studies, 1983. **MILITARY SERVICE:** US Navy Reserve, E-5, 1987-93; Sailor of Quarter; Good Conduct Medal, 1991; National Defense Medal, 1991. **HOME ADDRESS:** 5322 Belgrave Ave, Garden Grove, CA 92645.

TAM, JAMES PINGKWAN
Educator, scientist. Hong Kong American. **PERSONAL:** Born Mar 25, 1947, Hong Kong; son of Bing-Cho Tam and So-Ching Liu; married Sylvaine, Aug 1; children: Greta, Jonathan. **EDUCATION:** University of Wisconsin, Eau Claire, BSc, 1971, Madison, PhD, 1976. **CAREER:** Rockefeller University, assistant professor, 1980-82, associate professor, 1982-92; Vanderbilt University, professor, 1992-. **ORGANIZATIONS:** American Chemical Society; American Association for the Advancement of Science; American Society for Biochemistry & Molecular Biology; Protein Society; American Peptide Society, councilor, 1991-97. **HONORS/AWARDS:** Triton Sciences Inc, Presidential Award, 1986; The Vincent du Vigneaud Award for Young Investigators in Peptide Research, 1986. **SPECIAL ACHIEVEMENTS:** 154 published articles; holder, co-holder of 9 US patents. **BUSINESS ADDRESS:** Professor, Dept of Microbiology and Immunology, Vanderbilt University, A5321 MCN, Nashville, TN 37232, (615)343-1465.

TAM, LEO
Life insurance company executive. Chinese American. **PERSONAL:** Born Apr 24, 1955, Kwong Chow, Canton, People's Republic of China; son of Yiu Tam and Yan-Qi Tam; married Cinda Tam, May 3, 1979; children: Ho-Yin, Wai-Yin, Lick-Kong. **EDUCATION:** The American College, diploma, financial planning, 1991; Life Underwriters Training Council, LUTCF, 1992. **CAREER:** MetLife, branch mgr, 1988-. **ORGANIZATIONS:** National Assn of Life Underwriters, 1986-. **HONORS/AWARDS:** General Agents and Managers Assn, Bronze Management Award, 1993; Natl Assn of Life Underwriters, National Quality Award, 1990. **BUSINESS ADDRESS:** Branch Manager,

Metropolitan Life Insurance Co, 65 Harrison Ave, Rm 401, Boston, MA 02111, (617)451-0912.

TAM, SANG WILLIAM
Pharmaceutical company executive. Chinese American. **PERSONAL:** Born Nov 26, 1953, Macao; married Coretta C Tam; children: Brian K, Karen M. **EDUCATION:** University of Wisconsin, Oshkosh, BS, 1974; University of Nebraska, Lincoln, MS, 1976; SUNY, Downstate Medical Center, PhD, 1979; Yale University School of Medicine, postdoctoral, 1979-81. **CAREER:** E I du Pont Co, research pharmacologist, 1981-86, senior research pharmacologist, 1986-88, neuroscience research, group leader, 1988-89, Du Pont Merck Pharmaceutical Co, senior group leader, 1990-91, associate director, 1991-92, acting director, 1992-. **ORGANIZATIONS:** American Society of Pharmacology & Exp Therapeutics, 1985-; Society for Neuroscience, 1986-; Society of Chinese Bioscientists in America, life member, 1987-; Mid-Atlantic Pharmacology Society, 1988-; Chinese American Community Association, board member, 1990-93. **SPECIAL ACHIEVEMENTS:** 156 scientific papers and abstracts published, 1974-93; 14 patents awarded or pending. **BUSINESS ADDRESS:** Acting Director, CNS Disease Research, DuPont Merck Pharmaceutical Co, PO Box 80400, Experimental Station, E400/4352, Wilmington, DE 19880-0400, (302)695-7223.

TAM, SIMON M. W.
Company executive. Hong Kong American. **PERSONAL:** Born Dec 21, 1960, Hong Kong; married Amy C Tam, Sep 27, 1986; children: Esther B Y. **EDUCATION:** Pasadena City College, AA, 1981; California State University, Los Angeles, BS (with honors), 1983. **CAREER:** Grace Home Centers West, accounting manager, 1983-85; Simon M Tam, CPA Consulting, owner, self employed, 1985-88; Hacienda Mexican Food Products, vice president, finance, 1988-89; National Media Inc, vice president, chief financial officer, 1989-. **ORGANIZATIONS:** California Society of Certified Public Accountants, 1991-; Board of Accountancy, California, 1988-; American Institute of Certified Public Accountants, 1988-92; Hollywood Chamber of Commerce, finance committee, 1992-. **HONORS/AWARDS:** Alpha Gamma Sigma, 1981. **BUSINESS ADDRESS:** Vice President, Chief Financial Officer, National Media Inc, Los Angeles Independent Newspapers, 4201 Wilshire Blvd, Ste 600, Los Angeles, CA 90010, (213)932-6397.

TAM, THOMAS KWAI-SANG
Real estate appraiser/consultant. Chinese American. **PERSONAL:** Born Mar 24, 1942, Kwei-Lin, Kwangsi, China; son of Kwong-Wah Tam and Wai-Man Kwan Tam; married Susan Yang Tam, Jul 18, 1970. **EDUCATION:** National Taiwan University, BA, 1965; University of Oklahoma, MLS, 1968; Harvard University, MPA, 1988. **CAREER:** New York Public Library, senior librarian, 1968-87; Appraisal Advisory Group, Ltd, appraisal consultant, 1989-. **ORGANIZATIONS:** Chinese-American Planning Council, board member, 1973-; Organization of Chinese Americans, board member, 1992-; Chinese American Voters Association, board member, 1992-. **HOME ADDRESS:** 153-23C 82nd St, Howard Beach, NY 11414, (718)738-3362.

TAMAKI, JEANNE KEIKO
Aerospace engineer. Japanese American. **PERSONAL:** Born Nov 9, 1954, Los Angeles, CA; daughter of Jiro Tamaki and Michiko Tamaki. **EDUCATION:** University of Southern California, 1970-71; UCLA, BA (summa cum laude), 1973; MIT, PhD, 1977. **CAREER:** Tufts University, visiting assistant professor, 1978; Tulane University, assistant professor, 1978-80; Jet Propulsion Lab, senior engineer, summer 1980; University of Santa Clara, assistant professor, 1980-82; Naval Ocean Systems Center, consultant, summers 1981, 1982; TRW, staff engineer, 1982-. **HONORS/AWARDS:** UCLA, Paul Daus Award, 1973; National Science Foundation, Theoretical Computer Science Grant, 1978. **BUSINESS ADDRESS:** Staff Engineer, TRW, One Space Pk, Redondo Beach, CA 90278, (310)814-2988.

TAMHANE, AJIT C.
Educator. Indo-American. **PERSONAL:** Born Nov 12, 1946, Bhiwandi, Maharashtra, India; son of Chintaman & Sarla; married Meenal, Jun 18, 1975; children: Shalaka, Salil. **EDUCATION:** Indian Institute of Technology, Bombay, B Tech, 1968; Cornell University, MS, 1973, PhD, 1975. **CAREER:** Larsen & Toubro Ltd, design engineer, 1968-70; Northwestern University, professor, 1975-. **ORGANIZATIONS:** American Stat Association, 1972-, NE Illinois Chapter, president, 1993; Institute of Math Stat, 1973-; Biometrics Society, 1976-; Amer Society for Quality Control, 1983-. **HONORS/AWARDS:** American Stat Association, fellow, 1991; ASQC, Chem Proc Div,

WJ Youden Award, 1985. **SPECIAL ACHIEVEMENTS:** Multiple Comparisons Procedures, co-author with Y Hochberg, publisher: John Wiley, 1987. **BUSINESS ADDRESS:** Professor, Industrial Engg & Statistics, Northwestern University, 2006 Sheridan Road, Evanston, IL 60208, (708)491-3577.

TAN, AMY RUTH (AN-MEI)
Author. Chinese American. **PERSONAL:** Born Feb 19, 1952, Oakland, CA; daughter of John Yuehhan (deceased) and Daisy Tu Ching Tan; married Louis M DeMattei, Apr 6, 1974. **EDUCATION:** Linfield College, 1969; San Jose City College; San Jose State University, BA, linguistics, English, 1973, MA, linguistics, 1974; University of California, Berkeley, postgraduate work, medicine, 1974-76. **CAREER:** Alameda County Association for Mentally Retarded, language development specialist, 1976-80; MORE Project, project director, 1980-81; Emergency Room Reports, reporter, managing editor, associate publisher, 1981-83; works include: Endgame; Waiting Between the Trees; Joy Luck Club, 1989; "Mother Tongue," The Threepenny Review, fall 1990, Best American Essays, 1991; The Kitchen God's Wife, 1991; The Moon Lady, 1992; works represented in: State of the Language, 1989; Best American Essays, 1991; contributor to periodicals, including Atlantic Monthly, McCall's, Seventeen; Joy Luck Club movie, screenwriter, producer, 1993. **ORGANIZATIONS:** Squaw Valley Community of Writers, 1985; writers' group, led by Molly Giles, currently; Fool and His Money, currently, cofounder. **HONORS/AWARDS:** Booklist editor's choice, Bay Area Book Reviewers Award, both for The Kitchen God's Wife, 1991; all for Joy Luck Club, 1989: Commonwealth Club Gold Award, for fiction; Bay Area Book Reviewers Award, for fiction; American Library Association, Best Book for Young Adults Award; National Book Critics Circle Award, for best novel; Los Angeles Times Book Award nominee; Asian Perinatal Advocates, honoree, 1992. **SPECIAL ACHIEVEMENTS:** The Joy Luck Club appeared on the New York Times bestseller list from April to November, 1989; member of Rock Bottom Remainders, a rock 'n' roll band that raises money for charities. **BIOGRAPHICAL SOURCES:** "Thirty Minutes with Amy Tan: Chinese American Writer Is Her Mother's Daughter," Asian Week, Feb 25, 1994, p80.*

TAN, BARRIE
Educator. Chinese American. **PERSONAL:** Born Oct 7, 1953, Ipoh, Perak, Malaysia; son of C L Tan and T E Too; married Elizabeth B Tan, Aug 12, 1990. **EDUCATION:** University of Otago, New Zealand, BS, 1975, PhD, 1979; Auburn University, postdoctoral, 1979-81. **CAREER:** Carotech Associates, vice president, 1988-; University of Massachusetts, Department of Food Science, adjunct professor, 1989-, Department of Chemistry, assistant professor, 1982-90. **ORGANIZATIONS:** American Chemical Society, Analytical, Agricultural, Chromatography, 1979-; American Oil Chemical Society, 1988-; Institute of Food Technology, Nutritional, 1989-. **HONORS/AWARDS:** Numerous university awards; numerous outside grants and funds. **SPECIAL ACHIEVEMENTS:** Over 35 publications. **BIOGRAPHICAL SOURCES:** American Chemical Society, Faculty Research Texts, circa 1990. **BUSINESS ADDRESS:** Adjunct Professor, Dept of Science, University of Massachusetts, Chenoweth Labs, Amherst, MA 01003, (413)253-3449.

TAN, CHENG IMM
Clergyman. Malaysian American/Chinese American. **PERSONAL:** Born Jan 19, 1958, Penang, Malaysia. **EDUCATION:** Dickinson College, BA (summa cum laude), 1981; Harvard Divinity School, MDiv, 1986. **CAREER:** City Mission Society, volunteer co-director, 1983-84; Ecumenical Society Action Committee, assistant teacher, 1985-86; Unitarian Universalist Ministry, associate minister, 1986-; Asian Women's Project, director & founder, 1989-. **ORGANIZATIONS:** Asian Task Force against Domestic Violence, chair & founder, 1987-; International Refugee Women's Coalition, co-chair, 1990-; Unitarian Universalists Acting against Domestic Violence, founder & co-convenor, 1991-92; Battered Women Fighting Back, advisory board member, 1992-; Jane Doe Safety Fund, advisory board member, 1992-; State-wide Women's Legislative Network, board member, 1993-. **HONORS/AWARDS:** Boston Jaycees, 10 Outstanding Young Leaders, 1991; Festival of Hope '92, Peace Award, 1992; YWCA, Cambridge, Outstanding Women of Achievement, 1992; MA House of Representatives, violence prevention, 1992; Patriots Girl Scouts, Leading Women, 1992. **SPECIAL ACHIEVEMENTS:** Author: "Confronting Domestic Violence in Asian Communities," Sojourner, 1992; "What the Wars Have Done to Southeast Africa," Present Time, April 1992; "When Knowing the Language is Crucial to Survival," Foundations/Corporate Philanthropy News, 1991; "Asians Confronting Domestic Violence," Sampan, December 1991; "Impressions of the UN Decade for Women, Nairobi Conference," Que Pasa, 1986; Holding Up More Than Half the Heaven: Domestic

Violence in Our Communities, a Call for Justice, The State of Asian America, Activism and Resistance in the 90s, 1994. **BUSINESS ADDRESS:** Director, Asian Women's Project, PO Box 73, Boston, MA 02120, (617)739-6696.

TAN, CHENG-PHENG
Educator. Malaysian American. **PERSONAL:** Born Nov 17, 1953, Sungei Patani, Kedah, Malaysia; son of Tan Kee Lim and Geam Swee Ngoh. **EDUCATION:** Gallaudet University, BA, 1982, MS, 1986; Catholic University of America, MS, 1994. **CAREER:** Gallaudet University, instructor, 1985-89; Southwest Collegiate Institute for the Deaf, assistant professor, 1989-. **ORGANIZATIONS:** Highland Council for the Deaf, treasurer, 1990-. **BUSINESS ADDRESS:** Assistant Professor, Southwest Collegiate Institute for the Deaf, Avenue C, Big Spring, TX 79720-7299, (915)264-3700.

TAN, CHIN AN
Educator. Hong Kong American/Chinese American. **PERSONAL:** Born Jun 8, 1961, Hong Kong; son of Yu Hian Tan and Ah Wah Hui; married Flora Mei-Wah Tan, Aug 12, 1989. **EDUCATION:** University of California, Berkeley, BSc (highest honors), 1982; Caltech, MSc, 1983; University of California, Berkeley, PhD, 1989. **CAREER:** Wayne State University, assistant professor, 1989-. **HONORS/AWARDS:** Caltech, Donald Wills Douglas Prize Fellowship, 1982; University of California, Berkeley, Distinguished Teaching Assistant Award, 1984; Wayne State University, ANR Faculty Research Award, 1990, 1991. **HOME ADDRESS:** 6067 Ledwin Drive, Troy, MI 48098, (810)879-3205. **BUSINESS ADDRESS:** Assistant Professor, Wayne State University, 5050 Anthony Wayne Drive, 2137 Engineering Bldg, Detroit, MI 48202, (313)577-3888.

TAN, CHOR WENG
Educator, association administrator. Chinese American. **PERSONAL:** Born Apr 20, 1936, Swatow, Canton, China; son of Ee Hock Tan and Tung Hong Khor; married Yulin L Tan, Jun 8, 1963; children: Stephen, Reynold. **EDUCATION:** University of Evansville, BS, 1959; University of Illinois, Urbana, MS, 1961, PhD, 1963. **CAREER:** Cooper Union, assistant, associate & professor of engineering, 1963-91, School of Engineering, dean, 1975-87; National Science Foundation, director, program, 1987-89; American Society of Mechanical Engineers, managing director, education, 1991-. **ORGANIZATIONS:** NY City Commission on the Year 2000, 1986-90; NY City Commission for Science & Technology, 1986-91; NY City Chancellor's Asian American Advisory Council E, 1992-. **HONORS/AWARDS:** National Science Foundation, citation, 1989; The Cooper Union, citation, 1987; University of Illinois, Distinguished Alumni Award, 1976. **SPECIAL ACHIEVEMENTS:** Contributed over 50 refereed technical papers published in technical professional journals. **HOME ADDRESS:** 76 Echo Bay Drive, New Rochelle, NY 10805. **BUSINESS PHONE:** (212)705-7058.

TAN, COLLEEN WOO
Educator. Chinese American. **PERSONAL:** Born May 6, 1923, San Francisco, CA; daughter of Mr & Mrs S H Ng Quinn; married Tanny Kok Joon Tan, Aug 21, 1948; children: Lawrence Leo, Lance C. **EDUCATION:** Indiana University, BA, English & American literature, 1950, MA, English & American literature, 1952; UC, Berkeley, post grad studies, English literature, 1952-53; Whittier College, MA, speech arts, 1972. **CAREER:** UC, Berkeley, teaching assistant, 1952-53; Whittier High School, English & social studies teacher, 1957-60; Mt San Antonio College, English professor, 1960-69, speech communication, 1969-. **ORGANIZATIONS:** American Association of University Women, California State Division; Delta Kappa Gamma International, committee worker; Whittier Community Theater, supporter; Whittier Cultural Arts, supporter; Chinese American Faculty Association; Organization of Chinese American Women, supporter. **HONORS/AWARDS:** Indiana University, Phi Beta Kappa, 1950; AAUW, Education Foundation Award, 1974, Las Distinguidas Award, 1992-93; Mt San Antonio College, Outstanding Educator of America, nominee, 1972, Outstanding Educator Award, nominee, 1990, 1991, 1992;. **SPECIAL ACHIEVEMENTS:** Mt San Antonio College, department chair, 1972-80, director of forensics, 1969-80, started: 3 student groups, SPEAK!, Mountie Oracles, Chinese club for speech students. **BIOGRAPHICAL SOURCES:** AAUW Whittier Branch Newsletter, April 1993. **BUSINESS ADDRESS:** Professor, Dept of Communication, Mt San Antonio College, 1100 N Grand Avenue, Walnut, CA 91789-1397, (714)594-5611.

TAN, ERIC TUANLEE
Real estate administrator. Singaporean American. **PERSONAL:** Born Mar 1, 1945, Singapore; married Mary H S Chua, Oct 20, 1974; children: Dylan H.

EDUCATION: Singapore Polytechnic, Associate's degree, electrical engineering, 1965. **CAREER:** Texas Instruments, staff engr, 1972-84; UTC-Mostek, staff engr, 1984-87; Conner Peripherals/Archive, corporate facilities, director, 1987-. **ORGANIZATIONS:** Intl Facilities Management Assn, 1988-; American Institute of Plant Engineers, 1984-. **HOME ADDRESS:** 22281 Platino, Mission Viejo, CA 92691.

TAN, HENRY S. I.
Educator. Indonesian American/Chinese American. **PERSONAL:** Born Mar 26, 1932, Bandung, Indonesia; son of Kay Toeng Tan and Hwie Nio Lie; married Hetty G H Tan, 1958. **EDUCATION:** University of Indonesia, BS, pharmacy, 1954, MS, pharmacy, 1956; University of Wisconsin, Madison, certificate of accomplishment, 1962; University of Kentucky, PhD, pharmacy science, 1971. **CAREER:** Bandung Institute of Technology, assistant professor, associate professor, 1957-66; University of Kentucky, research assistant, 1967-71; University of Cincinnati Medical Center, assistant professor, 1971-76, associate professor, 1976-82, professor of pharmaceutical chemistry, 1982-. **ORGANIZATIONS:** American Association of Pharmaceutical Scientists, chairman membership committee, 1991-93, Analysis & Pharmaceutical Quality Section, Undergraduate Research Award Committee, chairman, 1991; United States Pharmacopeial Convention, 1985-; Kappa Psi Pharmaceutical Fraternity, 1975-. **HONORS/AWARDS:** Lederle Faculty Award, 1976, 1977; United States Pharmacopeia, Committee of Revision, elected, 1990-; American Chemical Society, 25 Year Recognition with Chemical Abstract Services, 1992; Rho Chi Pharmaceutical Honor Society, 1970. **SPECIAL ACHIEVEMENTS:** Published two editions of Laboratory Manual for Pharmaceutical Analysis; published over 65 research articles in various pharmaceutical refereed journals. **BUSINESS ADDRESS:** Professor, University of Cincinnati Medical Center, College of Pharmacy, 3223 Eden Ave, Mail Loc 4, Cincinnati, OH 45267-0004, (513)558-0729.

TAN, JACK SIM EDDY
Educator. Singaporean American/Chinese American. **PERSONAL:** Born Apr 13, 1958, Singapore; married Michelle Torres-Tan, Nov 16, 1990. **EDUCATION:** University of Minnesota, MS, 1986, PhD, 1990. **CAREER:** University of Houston, assistant professor, 1990-. **ORGANIZATIONS:** IEEE, 1986-; IEEE Computer Society, 1986-. **SPECIAL ACHIEVEMENTS:** Published works in many computer-related journals/conference proceedings. **BUSINESS ADDRESS:** Asst Professor, Computer Science Dept, University of Houston, 4800 Calhoun Blvd, Houston, TX 77204-3475, (713)743-3340.

TAN, KIM HOWARD
Educator. Indonesian American. **PERSONAL:** Born Mar 24, 1926, Jakarta, Indonesia; married Yelly A Tan, Dec 2, 1959; children: Budi Spencer. **EDUCATION:** University of Indonesia, MS, agronomy, 1955, PhD, soil science, 1958; NC State University, Raleigh, postdoctoral, 1960; Cornell University, Ithaca, NY, postdoctoral, 1961. **CAREER:** Rubber Plantation, assistant manager, 1955-56; University of Indonesia, Dept of Soil Science, chairman, 1965-67, professor, 1964-67; USDA-ARS, Ft Collins, CO, soil scientist, 1967-68; University of Georgia, assistant professor, 1968-73, associate professor, 1973-77, professor, 1977-. **ORGANIZATIONS:** American Society of Agronomy, translation committee, 1973-77; Soil Science Society of America, Div S-9 Conference, Anaheim, CA, chairman, 1982, Las Vegas, NV, 1983; Soil & Crop Science Society of Florida, editorial board, 1989-; International Journal of Tropical Agriculture, editorial board, 1989-; University of Malaysia, PhD program, oversears examiner, 1990-92; University of Calcutta, PhD program, overseas examiner, 1990-92; International Humic Acid Society, Session 1A Intern Meeting, Italy, chairman, 1992. **HONORS/AWARDS:** University of Georgia, Horticulture Club, Outstanding Teacher College Agri, 1972, AG Alumni Association, Distinguished Faculty Award, 1972, D W Brooks Award for Excellence in Teaching, 1982; Gamma Sigma Delta, Distinguished Teaching Award, 1986; American Society of Agronomy, fellow, 1984; Soil Science Society of America, fellow, 1984. **SPECIAL ACHIEVEMENTS:** Research in soil clay mineralogy, soil organic matter, humic acid chemistry, soil chemistry and its effect on plant growth and the environment; pedology of soils in temperate and tropical regions; author, 12 books, 10 book chapters, 112 refereed journal articles, and a great number of abstracts.

TAN, LAWRENCE W.
Food company executive. Chinese American. **PERSONAL:** Born Oct 9, 1964, Chicago, IL; son of John S Tan and Rhea L Tan. **EDUCATION:** Northwestern University, BA, political science, international politics, 1986; UCLA, MA (with honors), Latin American studies, 1992. **CAREER:** RTA International,

account executive, 1986-88; Wah King Noodle Co, exec vice pres, 1988-. **ORGANIZATIONS:** Chinese-American Voters League, 1992-, treasurer, 1986; Asian-American Voters Coalition, regional co-chair, 1992-93; Asian-American Christian Fellowship, Northwestern Chapter, founder, 1984-86; Evergreen Baptist Church, 1988-; The Navigators, Asian-American Ministry, associate staff, 1988-90; Chinese-American Civic Council, 1992-. **SPECIAL ACHIEVEMENTS:** Language proficiency: Cantonese, Spanish, Mandarin, Portuguese, Biblical Greek. **BUSINESS ADDRESS:** Executive Vice President, Wah King Noodle Co Inc, 2211 E Seventh St, Los Angeles, CA 90023, (213)268-0222.

TAN, MARY
Physician. Indonesian American. **PERSONAL:** Born May 30, 1929, Pakan Baru, Indonesia; daughter of Oei Beng Jau & Sit Goet Lan; divorced; children: Lian, Indriati, John, James. **EDUCATION:** Medical School, Indonesia, MD, 1959. **CAREER:** VA, Hines, Illinois, attending physician, 1979-91; VA, Big Spring, Texas, chief, Rehabilitation Medicine Service, chief, 1991-. **ORGANIZATIONS:** American Congress of Rehabilitation Medicine; American Paraplegic Society; Illinois Society of Rehabilitation Medicine. **BUSINESS ADDRESS:** Chief, Rehabilitation Medicine, VAMC Big Spring Hospital, 2400 S Gregg St, Big Spring, TX 79720.

TAN, NADY
Public administrator. Cambodian American. **PERSONAL:** Born May 31, 1936, Prey Veng, Cambodia; son of Tan So Boun & Kau Sam Ol; married Saramanya Tan, Nov 19, 1958; children: Saravuth, Saravath, Sarady, Saradan, Vinita. **EDUCATION:** Portland State University, MPA, 1989. **CAREER:** Cambondian Air Force, wing and air base commander, 1959-75; Indochinese Cultural and Service Center, deputy director, 1976-82; Southeast Asian Refugee Federation, executive director, 1982-84; IRCO, executive director, 1984-. **ORGANIZATIONS:** Santepheap Khmer, president, 1980-; Nike, minority advisory board, 1991-; Refugee Policy Group, advisory board, 1987-; City of Portland Economic Development, board member, 1985-; Governor's Higher Education Commission, currently; Portland State University, minority board member, currently. **HONORS/AWARDS:** Portland State University, Outstanding Services to the Community, 1989. **MILITARY SERVICE:** Cambodian Air Force, 1959-75, Lt General; Military Cross, Gold Palm Leaves (6), 1970-75. **BUSINESS ADDRESS:** Executive Director, IRCO, 1336 E Burnside St, Portland, OR 97214, (503)234-1541.

TAN, S. Y.
Educator. Singaporean American. **PERSONAL:** Born Sep 27, 1946, Singapore; married Alexandria; children: Leilani, Quincy. **EDUCATION:** McGill University, MD, 1970; University of Hawaii, School of Law, JD, 1986. **CAREER:** University of Hawaii, professor of medicine, 1988-, adjunct professor of law, 1994-; Saint Francis Medical Center, director of medical education, currently. **ORGANIZATIONS:** Organization of Chinese Americans, Hawaii branch, board member, 1993-; American College of Physicians, fellow; American College of Legal Medicine, fellow. **HONORS/AWARDS:** University of Hawaii, School of Medicine, commencement speaker, 1990, 1992; John A Burns School of Medicine. **BUSINESS ADDRESS:** Director of Medical Education, Saint Francis Medical Center, 2230 Liliha St, Honolulu, HI 96817, (808)547-6497.

TAN, SINFOROSA G. (ROSE TAN KAUNG)
Educator. Chinese American. **PERSONAL:** Born Jul 7, 1943, Lugait, Misamis Oriental, Philippines; daughter of Tan Eh Bon and Go Gun; married William H P Kaung, Jul 21, 1973. **EDUCATION:** University of San Carlos, BSChE, 1965; Cornell University, MST, mathematics, 1970; Syracuse University, PhD, curriculum, 1975. **CAREER:** Iligan Capitol College, mathematics, chemistry teacher, 1965-68; Crouse-Irving Memorial Hospital, School of Nursing, resident assistant, 1970-73; Syracuse University, graduate assistant, 1973-75; Mount Vernon Board of Education, consultant, substitute teacher, 1975-76; Bronx Community College, metric program director, 1976-77; Mercy College, adjunct math facutly, 1976-78; Westchester Community College, math professor, 1977-. **ORGANIZATIONS:** Philippines Library Materials Project Foundation, book drive coordinator, 1988-; Pi Lambda Theta, chapter president, vp, secretary, region rep, 1973-; New York State Math Assn of Two Year Colleges, executive board, newsletter editor, committees, 1979-; College Board, SAT committee, 1990-93; Natl Council of Teachers of Math, life member, 1971-; MAA, AMATYC, NSSE, ASCD, AERA; Literacy Volunteer of America, volunteer, 1976-77; Our Lady of Perpetual Help Church, choir member, 1987-. **HONORS/AWARDS:** The Foundation for Westchester Community College,

Medallion Award, 1993; WCC Student Senate, Advisors Recognition Award to the Student Body, 1993, Outstanding Advisor Award, 1987; University of Texas, National Teaching Excellence Award, 1989; Pi Lambda Theta, Westchester Area Chapter, Distinguished Service Award, 1985; State University of New York, Chancellors Excellence in Teaching Award, 1983. **SPECIAL ACHIEVEMENTS:** Has presented papers, led workshops and spoken at numerous conferences: international, national, regional, statewide, and local levels; chaired committees of professional organizations and WCC Collegewide and departmental faculty committees; wrote numerous internal reports and grants proposals; tutorial coordinator, syllabi revision, innovations; "Project Select," Community, Technical and Senior College Journal, Feb-March 1990; "Alternative to Computer Assisted Instruction," Communicator, A Publication of the California Mathematics Council, June 1987; Westchester Education Coalition, IN, scholar-in-residence, 1994; director of several funded projects. **BUSINESS ADDRESS:** Professor, Mathematics, Westchester Community College, 75 Grasslands Rd, Technology Bldg 139A, Valhalla, NY 10595-1636, (914)785-6788.

TAN, TJIAUW-LING
Educator, psychiatrist. Indonesian American/Chinese American. **PERSONAL:** Born Jun 2, 1935, Pemalang, Central Java, Indonesia; son of Ping-Hoey Tan and Liep-Nio (Liem) Tan; married Esther Joyce Tan, Aug 27, 1961; children: Paul Budiman, Robert Yuling, Alice Ayling. **EDUCATION:** University of Indonesia, MD, 1961; University of California, Los Angeles, psychiatry, 1967-71; Pennsylvania State University, psychiatry, 1971-72. **CAREER:** University of Indonesia, resident in psychiatry, 1961-65, asst prof, 1965-67; Santa Monica Hospital Medical Ctr, medical intern, 1969-70; University of California, resident in psychiatry, 1970-71, postdoctoral fellow, 1967-69, asst research psychiatrist, 1969-70; Pennsylvania State University, associate prof, 1971-. **ORGANIZATIONS:** American Psychiatric Assn, Fellow, 1969; Assn for Advancement of Behavior Therapy, 1972; Assn of Applied Psychophysiology & Biofeedback, 1974; Soc of Behavioral Medicine, 1976; American Assn for Geriatric Psychiatry, 1986; American Geriatric Soc, 1986; American Academy of Sleep Disorder Medicine, 1988; Pennsylvania Psychiatric Soc, 1971. **HONORS/AWARDS:** American Board of Psychiatry & Neurology, Diplomate in Psychiatry, 1973; American Board of Psychiatry and Neurology, Diplomate in Psychiatry with Added Qualifications in Geriatric Psychiatry, 1991; Indonesian Board of Psychiatry & Neurology, Diplomate in Psychiatry, 1965. **SPECIAL ACHIEVEMENTS:** Contribution of articles in professional journals & book chapters in the field of eating disorders, sleep disorders, geriatric psychiatry, etc. **HOME ADDRESS:** 1478 Bradley Ave, Hummelstown, PA 17036-9143, (717)566-3009. **BUSINESS ADDRESS:** Pennsylvania State University College of Medicine, 500 University Dr, Box 850, Hershey, PA 17033-0850, (717)531-8207.

TAN, WAI-YUAN
Educator. Chinese American. **PERSONAL:** Born Aug 14, 1934, Hunan, China; son of Chan-Lee Tan and Shiw-Jen Lai Tan; married Shiow-Jen Tan, Nov 12, 1964; children: Emy Tan Musik, Eden. **EDUCATION:** National Taiwan University, Taipei, Taiwan, MS, agronomy, 1959; University of Wisconsin, Madison, MS, math, statistics, 1963, PhD, statistics, 1964. **CAREER:** Institute of Botany, Academia Sinica, Taiwan, associate res fellow, 1964-66, research fellow, 1966-68; University of Wisconsin, Madison, asst prof, 1969-72; Washington State University, associate prof, 1973-75; Memphis State University, prof, 1975-91; NCI/NIH, cancer expert, 1984-85; CDC, math statistician, 1990; Emory University, visiting professor, 1990; Memphis State University, research professor, 1991-. **ORGANIZATIONS:** Royal Statistical Soc, 1971-; ASA, 1989-, Western Tennessee chapter, president, 1991-93; Biometric Society, 1969-; IMS, 1969-; Chinese Statistical Soc, council member, 1991-; American Assn for Cancer Res, 1992-; Canadian Statistical Society, 1972-89; AIDS/NIH, peer review, 1989-. **HONORS/AWARDS:** Chinese Government of Taiwan, Sun-Yat Sun Distinguished Award, 1967; MSU, Distinguished Research Award, 1983, 1989, Superior Research Award, 1984, 1988, 1990, 1991, 1993. **SPECIAL ACHIEVEMENTS:** Published three books; published over 130 research papers. **HOME ADDRESS:** 8031 Brooxie Cove, Germantown, TN 38138. **BUSINESS ADDRESS:** Professor, Dept of Mathematical Sciences, Memphis State University, Memphis, TN 38152, (901)678-2492.

TAN, ZOE
Researcher. Chinese American. **EDUCATION:** Tunghai University, Taiwan, BA, 1976; University of Hawaii, MA, 1980; University of Michigan, PhD, 1987. **CAREER:** University of Texas, Austin, assistant professor, 1987-90;

KSCI-TV 18, director of research, 1991-. **HONORS/AWARDS:** University of Michigan, Dissertation Award, 1987; International Communication Association, USA, Top 3 Division Paper, 1989; Association for Education in Journalism, Top Student Paper, 1988. **SPECIAL ACHIEVEMENTS:** "Mass Media and Insurgent Terrorism: A Twenty-Year Ballance Sheet," Gazette International Journal of Mass Communication Research, vol 42, p 3-32, 1988; "The Role of Mass Media in Insurgent Terrorism: Issues and Perspectives," Gazette International Journal of Mass Communication, vol 44, p 45-54, 1989; "Receiver Prejudice and Model Ethnicity," Journalism Quarterly, p 267-274, winter 1990. **BUSINESS ADDRESS:** Director of Research, KSCI-TV 18 & International Channel Network, 12401 W Olympic Blvd, Los Angeles, CA 90064, (310)478-1818.

TANA, AKIRA
Musician, producer. Japanese American. **PERSONAL:** Born Mar 14, 1952, San Jose, CA; son of Daisho Tana & Tomoe Hayashima Tana; married Marjorie Fujiki, Sep 26, 1987; children: Kyle, Ryan. **EDUCATION:** Harvard University, BA, East Asian studies, 1974; New England Conservatory of Music, BM, percussion, 1979; private studies with: Vic Firth of the Boston Symphony Orchestra, drummer Alan Dawson, Fred Buda of the Boston Pops. **CAREER:** TanaReid Quintet, co-leader, currently; TanaReid's recordings include: "Yours and Mine," "Passing Thoughts," "Blue Motion"; works produced include: "Sound Circle/Asian American Trio," A Tribute to Wes Montgomery/Kenny Burrell, "Spanish Treasure/Tetemontoliu"; drummer, currently. **ORGANIZATIONS:** New York State Council of the Arts, panelist auditor, 1992-93. **HONORS/AWARDS:** Harvard University, scholarship, 1970-74; New England Conservatory, scholarship, 1976-79; Music Festival, Tanglewood, fellowship, 1979. **SPECIAL ACHIEVEMENTS:** Has worked with many musicians including: Lena Horne, Dizzy Gillespie, Manhattan Transfer; performed at many international jazz festivals, including Montreaux, Switzerland; Nice, France; Red Sea Jazz Festival, Israel; conducted workshops and clinics at numerous US colleges and universities; product endorser for Yamaha Drums, Sabian Cymbals, Vic Firth Sticks, Remo Drumheads. **BIOGRAPHICAL SOURCES:** "Akira Tana," Modern Drummer, p 30, Nov 1991. **BUSINESS ADDRESS:** Musician, Producer, Acannatuna Music/TanaReid Productions, 243 W 99th St, Ste 7B, New York, NY 10025, (212)662-7476.

TANA, PHONGPAN
Healthcare administrator, nurse. Thai American. **PERSONAL:** Born Sep 16, 1946, Nakhon Rajsima, Thailand; daughter of Tavee Saifag and Sageum Saifag; married Pachon Tana, Jun 20, 1969; children: Naran. **EDUCATION:** Nakhon Rajsima College of Nursing, diploma, 1968. **CAREER:** Memorial Hospital Medical Center, charge nurse, 1973-76; Casa De Belita Conv Hosp, dir of nurses, 1976-83; Hillcrest Conv Hosp, dir of nurses, 1983-. **ORGANIZATIONS:** American Nurses Assn, 1983. **SPECIAL ACHIEVEMENTS:** Certified by California State Dept of Education, Bureau of Industrial Educ, 1978 to teach nursing and was received from UCLA. **BUSINESS ADDRESS:** Director of Nurses, Hillcrest Convalescent Hospital, 3401 Cedar Ave, Long Beach, CA 90807, (310)426-4461.

TANABE, GEORGE JOJI, JR.
Educator. Japanese American. **PERSONAL:** Born Dec 15, 1943, Waialua, HI; son of George J Tanabe Sr and Ethel Y Tanabe; married Willa Jane Tanabe, Jun 12, 1967; children: Gen Shotaro. **EDUCATION:** Union Theological Seminary, MDiv, 1969; Columbia University, MA, 1974, PhD, 1983. **CAREER:** University of Hawaii, associate professor, department chairman, 1977-. **ORGANIZATIONS:** Association for Asian Studies, 1980-; American Academy of Religion, 1980-; Hawaii Committee for the Humanities, chair, 1990-91. **HONORS/AWARDS:** Columbia University, President's Fellow, 1973; Japan Foundation, fellowship, 1976; Ford Foundation, Foreign Area Fellowship, 1974-76; Social Science Research Council, grant, 1984. **SPECIAL ACHIEVEMENTS:** Myoe the Dreamkeeper, Harvard University Press, 1992; Nihon Bukkyo no saisei, Tokyo, Kosei Shuppan, 1990; over 35 journal articles, reviews, and translations, 1973-; organized fourteen international conferences on Buddhism, 1980-. **BUSINESS ADDRESS:** Assoc Prof & Chairman, Dept of Religion, University of Hawaii, 2530 Dole St, Sakamaki Hall A-303, Honolulu, HI 96822, (808)956-4204.

TANADA, TAKUMA
Plant scientist. Japanese American. **PERSONAL:** Born Oct 30, 1919, Honolulu, HI; son of Gehei Tanada & Tora Takamura; married Toshiye Shimizu, Feb 21, 1947 (deceased); children: Juliet T Vesely. **EDUCATION:** University of Hawaii, BS, 1942, MS, 1944; University of Illinois, PhD, 1950. **CAREER:** US Army, scientific consultant, 1946-47; USDA, plant physiologist, 1950-57; International Cooperation Adm, research advisor, 1957-60; US Department of Agriculture, senior research plant physiologist, 1960-84. **ORGANIZATIONS:** American Association of Plant Physiologists, 1950-85; Botanical Society of America, 1950-70. **HONORS/AWARDS:** Phi Kappa Phi, 1942; Phi Beta Kappa, 1942. **SPECIAL ACHIEVEMENTS:** Research in radiation damage, photosynthesis, growth. **MILITARY SERVICE:** US Army, T/4, 1944-46. **HOME ADDRESS:** 19 Skycrest Way, Napa, CA 94558.

TANAKA, EDDY SEI
Public social services director. Japanese American. **PERSONAL:** Born Apr 12, 1934, Walnut Grove, CA; son of Yeichi Tanaka (deceased) & Aiko Tanaka; married Barbara, Apr 16, 1960; children: Steven, Laura, David. **EDUCATION:** University of California, Berkeley, BS, 1956. **CAREER:** Office of the LA County Assessor, head administrative assistant, 1965-67; Office of the LA County CAO, principal administrative analyst, 1969-71, chief analyst, 1971-74, division chief, 1974-77; LA County DPSS, various assignments, 1958-64, deputy district director, 1964-65, budget services, head, 1967-68, division chief, 1968-69, chief deputy director, 1977-79, director, 1979-. **ORGANIZATIONS:** National Association of Counties, Human Services Steering Committee, Income Maintenance Subcommittee; National Association of County Human Service Administrators; American Public Welfare Association; Council of Local Human Services Administrators; County Welfare Director's Association of California, executive committee, board of directors; Los Angeles County Inter-Agency Council on Child Abuse and Neglect; Los Angeles County Red Cross Emergency Services Advisory Committee; Los Angeles County Charitable Giving Task Force; Southern Counties Welfare Directors Group; Los Angeles County Management Council, executive committee; Los Angeles County Emergency Management Council; Los Angeles County Committee on Aging; Countywide Contracting Advisory Board, chairman; Los Angeles County Roundtable for Children; Los Angeles County Technology and Systems Advisory Body, executive board. **MILITARY SERVICE:** US Army, e-5, 1956-58. **BUSINESS ADDRESS:** Director, Dept of Public Social Services, Los Angeles County, 12860 Crossroads Pkwy South, City of Industry, CA 91746-3411, (310)908-8383.

TANAKA, GARY ALAN SHINICHI
Real estate company executive. Japanese American. **PERSONAL:** Born Jun 15, 1954, Honolulu, HI; son of Gary N and Akiko K Tanaka; married Grace N Tanaka, Mar 16, 1986; children: Amanda Akiko. **EDUCATION:** University of Hawaii, BBA, 1976. **CAREER:** Realty Partners Inc, president, 1986-92; Realty Edge Inc, vice president, 1993-. **ORGANIZATIONS:** Honolulu Board of Realtors, 1980-; National Board of Realtors, 1980-; Hawaii Numismatic Assn, 1972-. **BUSINESS PHONE:** (808)593-9999.

TANAKA, JAMES JUNJI
Construction company executive. Japanese American. **PERSONAL:** Born Sep 1, 1940, Sacramento, CA; son of Roy Tanaka and Nobuko Tanaka; married Dale A Tanaka, Nov 12, 1966; children: Douglas S. **CAREER:** Aerojet, senior engrng project clerk, 1961-64; PMI Corp, purchasing agent, 1964-68; Murchison Construction, estimator, 1968-72; P&T Construction, general partner, 1972-74; Paschal & Tanaka Inc, president, 1974-. **ORGANIZATIONS:** Kiwanis Club, Carmichael, 1989-, treasurer, 1990-91; Sacto General Contractors' Assn, 1978-85, president, 1980-81; Boy Scouts of America, Troop 55, 1981-91, asst scoutmaster, 1985-86, scoutmaster, 1986-91, Pack 55, 1981-91, den leader, 1981-84; El Camino High School Booster Club, 1987-91, PTSA, 1987-91. **MILITARY SERVICE:** US Army, SP-4, 1958-61, Reserves, E-4, 1961-64; Good Conduct Ribbon, 1961. **HOME PHONE:** (916)489-0166. **BUSINESS ADDRESS:** President, Paschal & Tanaka, Inc, 3928 California Ave, Carmichael, CA 95608, (916)944-4140.

TANAKA, JOHN
Educator. Japanese American. **PERSONAL:** Born Jun 18, 1924, San Diego, CA; son of Keinosuke Tanaka & Tokuko Tanaka; married Patricia Louise, Aug 14, 1959; children: Peter Mark, Paul Michael. **EDUCATION:** UCLA, BA, 1951; Iowa State, PhD, 1956. **CAREER:** South Dakota State, associate professor of chem, 1956-63; University of Connecticut, professor of chemistry, 1965-. **ORGANIZATIONS:** American Chemical Society; IEEE/DEIS, president, 1985-87, vice president admin, 1983-85, vice president tech, 1981-83. **HONORS/AWARDS:** IEEE, fellow, 1990; DEIS/IEEE, service award, 1988; Paul Sabatier University, honorary doctorate, 1983; Elec/Electronics Insul Conf, Hall of Fame, 1991. **SPECIAL ACHIEVEMENTS:** Author of 85

papers and 60 conference papers; IEEE/DEIS, EI Magazine, editor, 1987-. **BUSINESS ADDRESS:** Professor, University of Connecticut, 215 Glenbrook Rd, UCONN, Chem, U-60, Rm 151, Storrs, CT 06268, (203)486-2443.

TANAKA, KOUICHI ROBERT
Educator, educational administrator. Japanese American. **PERSONAL:** Born Dec 15, 1926, Fresno, CA; son of Kenjiro Tanaka and Teru Tanaka; married Grace, Oct 23, 1965; children: Anne, Nancy, David. **EDUCATION:** Wayne State University, BS, 1949, MD, 1952. **CAREER:** Los Angeles County General Hospital, rotating intern, 1952-53; Detroit Receiving Hospital, resident in pathology, 1953-54, fellow and resident in medicine, 1954-57; Harbor-UCLA Medical Center, chief, division of hematology, 1961-, acting chair, department of medicine, 1992-; UCLA School of Medicine, instructor, assistant professor, associate professor, 1957-68, professor of medicine, 1968-. **ORGANIZATIONS:** Los Angeles Society of Internal Medicine, president, 1971; American College of Physicians, SC Region I, governor, 1993-97; American Journal of Hematology, associate editor, 1975-; Blood, editorial board, 1979-83; NIH Hematology Study Section, 1978-82, 1986-89; National Committee for Clinical Laboratory Standards, subcommittee for cellular enzymology, chairman, 1977-92; American Society of Hematology, subcommittee on red cells, chairman, 1976. **HONORS/AWARDS:** Alpha Omega Alpha, 1950; Sigma Xi, 1950; American College of Physicians, Laureate Award, 1992; Wayne State University School of Medicine Alumni Award, 1952, Distinguished Alumni Service Award, 1981; UCLA School of Medicine, S M Mellinkoff Faculty Award, 1986. **SPECIAL ACHIEVEMENTS:** 132 research papers published; 130 book chapters, reviews, abstracts published. **MILITARY SERVICE:** US Army, T4, 1946-48. **BUSINESS ADDRESS:** Professor, Harbor-UCLA Medical Center, 1000 W Carson St, Box 400, Torrance, CA 90509, (310)222-2404.

TANAKA, RICHARD I.
Company executive. Japanese American. **PERSONAL:** Born Dec 17, 1928, Sacramento, CA; son of G and Kei Tanaka; married Edith Arita Tanaka, Aug 18, 1951; children: Steven Richard, Jean Elizabeth, John Richard, Anne Mariko. **EDUCATION:** University of California, Berkeley, BSEE, 1950, MSEE, 1951; California Institute of Technology, PhD, 1958. **CAREER:** Hughes Aircraft, tech staff, 1954-57; Lockheed Missiles & Space Co, senior research & dept mgr, 1957-65; California Computer Products, Inc, senior vice president, 1966-77; International Technology Resources, president, 1977-80; Systonetics, Inc, CEO & president, 1980-86; Lundy Electronics & Systems, president, 1986-89; Scan-Optics, Inc, chairman, CEO & president, 1989-. **ORGANIZATIONS:** International Federation for Info Processing, president, 1974-77, US Delegate, 1971-79; Am Federation of Info Processing Societies, president, 1969-71; IEEE Computer Society, president, 1965-66. **HONORS/AWARDS:** International Federation for Info Processing, honorary member, 1979; Am Federation of Info Proc Soc, distinguished service, 1983; IEEE, fellow, 1977, Centennial Medal, 1980; Phi Beta Kappa, Eta Kappa Nu, Tau Beta Pi. **SPECIAL ACHIEVEMENTS:** Author: Residue Arithmetic and Its Applications to Computer Technology, McGraw-Hill, 1967. **BUSINESS ADDRESS:** Chairman of the Board, CEO & President, Scan-Optics, Inc, 22 Prestige Park Circle, East Hartford, CT 06108, (203)289-6001.

TANAKA, S. KEN
Microbiologist. **PERSONAL:** Born Dec 23, 1951, Seattle, WA; married Chris Nakamura Tanaka. **EDUCATION:** University of Washington, BS, 1974; Northwestern University, PhD, 1978. **CAREER:** E R Squibb and Sons, 1981-87; Schwarz Pharma, 1987-91; Abbott Laboratories, clinical microbiologist, 1991-. **BUSINESS ADDRESS:** Anti-Infective Microbiology, Abbott Laboratories, 1 Abbott Park Rd, D47T/AP9A, Abbott Park, IL 60064, (708)937-4087.

TANAKA, TY SKIP
Insurance sales associate, musician. Japanese American. **PERSONAL:** Born Feb 17, 1952, Chicago, IL; son of Eddie Tanaka and Mei Tanaka; married Sandy, Mar 25, 1972; children: Paul Steven, Heather Michelle. **EDUCATION:** American College, CLU, 1982. **CAREER:** Silver Mfg, inventory control mgr, 1973-76; Modern Woodmen of America, salesman, 1976-83; Connecticut Mutual, salesman, chartered life underwriter, 1983-. **ORGANIZATIONS:** American Society of CLU, 1982-; National Association of Life Underwriters, 1976-. **HONORS/AWARDS:** Connecticut Mutual, Leaders Club, 1991; Million Dollar Round Table, 1985; Principal Financial Group, Group Millionaire, 1991. **SPECIAL ACHIEVEMENTS:** Musician with Snooze Brothers Band: "Beeper Ball and Chain," cassette, CD, 1991; American Cancer Society, Knoxville Telethon, 1992. **HOME ADDRESS:** 8904 Barlow Circle, Knox-

ville, TN 37923, (615)691-1426. **BUSINESS ADDRESS:** Salesman, Chartered Life Underwriter, Connecticut Mutual, 2222 Plaza Tower, Knoxville, TN 37929, (615)637-9931.

TANAKA, WAYNE D.
Attorney. Japanese American. **PERSONAL:** Born Jan 14, 1950, Lufkin, TX; son of Mitsuko & Harry Tanaka; married Jan C H Tanaka, Sep 18, 1976; children: Ryan, Kelly. **EDUCATION:** Harvard University, AB, 1972; University of Washington Law School, JD, 1975. **CAREER:** Ogden, Murphy, Wallace, partner, 1975-. **ORGANIZATIONS:** Bellevue School Board, director, 1989-; Washington State Association of Municipal Attorneys, 1975-; American Bar Association, 1975-; Seattle King County Bar Association, 1975-; Washington State Bar Association, 1975-.

TANDON, ANAND
Finance manager. Indo-American. **PERSONAL:** Born Apr 20, 1949, New Delhi, India; married. **EDUCATION:** Indian Institute of Technology, BTech, 1971; Harvard Business School, MBA, 1980. **CAREER:** Philips India Ltd, materials manager, 1972-78; Commodities Corp, commodities analyst, 1980-82; Digital Equipment Corp, finance manager, 1982-. **BUSINESS ADDRESS:** Finance Manager, Digital Equipment Corporation, 4851 LBJ Freeway, Suite 1100, Dallas, TX 75244, (214)702-4157.

TANDON, RAJIV
Educator, consultant. Indo-American. **PERSONAL:** Born May 9, 1944, Allahabad, Uttar Pradesh, India; son of Jagdish Bihari Tandon and Vimla Tandon; married Priti Tandon, Sep 21, 1969; children: Ribhu Dev, Veeti. **EDUCATION:** Indian Institute of Technology, Kharagpur, BTech (with honors), 1966; University of Minnesota, MS (OR), 1970, MBA, 1972, PhD, 1987. **CAREER:** Kumardhubi Eng Works, prod control officer, 1966-69; University of Minnesota, instructor, 1969-71; National Car Rental, 1971-74, fin an, dir, 1971-86, mgr, OR, 1974-77, MIS & plan, corp vice pres, 1977-80, corp vice pres, general mgr, 1980-86; University of St Thomas, Inst for Venture Mgt, director, 1988-. **ORGANIZATIONS:** ORSA, 1972-, Midwest Chapter, president, 1978; TIMS, 1972-; ASME, 1972-; NASCP, 1972-; AFA, 1972-; AMA, 1980-; Planners League, president, 1980; American Car Rental Assn, 1980-86, president, 1985. **HONORS/AWARDS:** Price-Babson Program, Edwin M Appel Prize, 1992; UST, Business Programs, Excellence in Teaching, 1992. **BUSINESS ADDRESS:** Director, Institute for Venture Management, University of St Thomas, 1000 La Salle Ave, 100 MPL, Minneapolis, MN 55403, (612)962-4406.

TANG, ALEX YING HO
Financial controller. Hong Kong American. **PERSONAL:** Born Jan 22, 1960, Hong Kong; son of Wong Fai Tang and Yuk Chuk Tang; married Annie Lam, May 24, 1986; children: Alvin. **EDUCATION:** University of Hawaii at Manoa, Bachelor Degree, marketing, 1983, Master Degree, accounting, 1986. **CAREER:** Terry Wong CPA, auditor, 1985-86; Citicorp-Citibank, planning and controller mgr, 1986-87; Gannett Outdoor of Southern California, sr accountant, 1987-89, asset mgt and financial analysis, supvr, 1989-90, assistant financial controller, 1990-. **ORGANIZATIONS:** Institute of Management Accountants, 1991-. **HONORS/AWARDS:** Gannett Inc, Unsung Hero, Runner-Up, 1993. **BUSINESS ADDRESS:** Assistant Financial Controller, Gannett Outdoor of Southern California, 1731 Workman St, Los Angeles, CA 90031, (213)222-7171.

TANG, AMERICA
Fencing company executive. Chinese American. **PERSONAL:** Born Jun 6, 1955, Lima, Peru; daughter of Antonio K Y Tang and Yong Tang; divorced; children: Amy Tsui, Annette Tsui, Michael. **EDUCATION:** California State University, Los Angeles, BS, intl business, 1979. **CAREER:** Berge SA, Spain, exec scy, 1973-74; Bank of America, stenotypist, 1974-75; Algert Co, Import/Export Co, scy, 1975-77; Los Angeles Times, Composing Dept, leadperson, 1976-82; Mandarin Realty, sales agent, 1980-82; Handfore Realty Corp, broker, vice pres, 1982-; Ace Fence Co, president, 1988-. **ORGANIZATIONS:** Natl Assn of Women Business Owners, 1991-; US Chamber of Commerce; Industry City Council; West SG Valley Bd of Realtors. **HONORS/AWARDS:** Mayor Tom Bradley, Top 100 Women Owned Businesses in LA County, 1991; LA Business Journal, Top 100 Women Owned Businesses in LA County, 1989, 1990, 1991. **SPECIAL ACHIEVEMENTS:** Language proficiency, speaks fluently: Chinese-Cantonese, Spanish. **BIOGRAPHICAL SOURCES:** "Making It," Success Stories of Minority and Women Owned Businesses, 1/2

hr television program, Sep 1991. **BUSINESS ADDRESS:** President, Ace Fence Co, 15135 Salt Lake Ave, City of Industry, CA 91746, (818)333-0727.

TANG, ANDREW HING-YEE
Research scientist. Chinese American. **PERSONAL:** Born Feb 10, 1936, Canton, China; married Irene L Tang, Aug 21, 1964. **EDUCATION:** Purdue University, MS, 1962, PhD, 1964. **CAREER:** The Upjohn Co, senior scientist, 1964-. **ORGANIZATIONS:** American Society for Pharmacology and Experimental Therapeutics, 1970-; Society for Neuroscience, 1980-. **BUSINESS ADDRESS:** Research Scientist, Upjohn Co, 301 Henrietta St, Kalamazoo, MI 49001, (616)385-7594.

TANG, ASSUMPTA
Educator. Chinese American. **PERSONAL:** Born Apr 12, 1934, Port of Spain, Trinidad and Tobago; daughter of Doris Chung Tang and Hector Tang. **EDUCATION:** Salve Regina University, BS, 1988, MS, 1989; Walden University, PhD candidate, administration/management, regional planning, 1994. **CAREER:** Sodality of the Children of Mary, Trinidad, spiritual directress, 1959-60; St Bernadette's Hostel and David Hostel, Guyana, administrator, 1965-70; Ministries of Regional Planning & Finance, Guyana, community development officer, 1972-79; Govts of Guyana & the Netherlands, District Hospital, project supervisor, 1979-82; State Planning Secretariat, Guyana, regional planner; Salve Regina University, tutor, 1986, director of academic computer labs, 1987-91, part-time faculty, 1987-91, instructor, 1991-; Walden University, assistant professor, currently. **ORGANIZATIONS:** Corpus Christi Carmelite Sisters. **HONORS/AWARDS:** Medal of Service/Award of Excellence, Guyana, 1976; Sigma Phi Sigma, Salve Regina College Chapter, Honorary Award, 1987-88; National Deans Award, 1986-87. **BUSINESS ADDRESS:** Instructor, Geography Dept, Salve Regina University, Ochre Point Ave, Newport, RI 02840.

TANG, CHARLES CHAU CHING
Illustrator, artist. Hong Kong American/Chinese American. **PERSONAL:** Born Oct 5, 1948, Hong Kong; son of Sophie Tai and Wai Tong Tang; married Susan Crocca Tang, Aug 28, 1971; children: Nicholas, Lucian. **EDUCATION:** Pratt Institute, BFA (summa cum laude), 1992. **CAREER:** Cover illustrator, publishers include: Albert Whitman & Co, Harper, Dell Publishing, Ballantine Books, Scholastic Inc; self-employed, artist, book illustrator, currently. **ORGANIZATIONS:** Trenton Artist's Workshop Assn; Lawrence Hamnett Soccer Assn, coach; Washington Crossing Audubon Society; Trinity Church, Princeton, graphic art committee. **SPECIAL ACHIEVEMENTS:** Group show: Mercer County Library, 1991, 1992; two-person show: St Francis Medical Center, 1993; cover paintings: The Boxcar Children, series, all titles; Lois Duncan's Suspense Series, all titles; A Touch of Chill, anthology, Joan Aiken; The Accident, Todd Strasser; The Wendy Puzzle, Florence Perry Heide; numerous others. **BIOGRAPHICAL SOURCES:** Contemporary Authors Series, Gale Research Inc. **HOME ADDRESS:** 40 Winthrop Rd, Lawrenceville, NJ 08648-1559, (609)896-3046.

TANG, CHIK-KWUN
Physician, educator. Chinese American. **PERSONAL:** Born Jul 14, 1941, Macau, Portugal; married; children: Two. **EDUCATION:** National Defense Medical Center, Bachelor of Medicine, 1967. **CAREER:** The New York Hospital, instructor, 1973-74; Cornell Medical College, assistant professor of pathology, 1974-75; University of Maryland School of Medicine, assistant professor of pathology, 1976-79, associate professor of pathology, 1979-83; Temple University Hospital and School of Medicine, chief of surgical pathology, professor of pathology, 1983-. **ORGANIZATIONS:** National Defense Medical Center Alumni Society; US-Canadian Division, International Academy of Pathology; American Association for Advancement of Science; Arthur Purdy Stout Society. **SPECIAL ACHIEVEMENTS:** Co-author, Anaplastic Carcinoma of Urinary Bladder with Oat Cell Features, 1986; co-author, Desmoplastic Fibroma Associated with Paget's disease of Bone, 1988; co-author, Does Antibiotic Peritoneal Lavage Cause Peritoneal Adhesion Formation?, 1989; co-author, Vasovasostomy in Dogs Using the Carbondioxide Milliwatt Laser, 1990; "Disorders of the Vermiform Appendix," Pathology of the Gastrointestinal Tract, chapter 33, 1992. **BUSINESS ADDRESS:** Professor of Pathology, Chief of Surgical Pathology, Temple University School of Medicine and Hospital, 3401 N Broad St, Philadelphia, PA 19140, (215)707-8253.

TANG, CHUNG LIANG
Engineer. Chinese American. **PERSONAL:** Born May 14, 1934, Shangai, China; married 1958; children: three. **EDUCATION:** University of Washington, BS, 1955; California Institute of Technology, MS, 1956; Harvard University, PhD, applied physics, 1960. **CAREER:** Raytheon Co, research staff member, 1960-61, sr res scientist, 1961-63, principal res scientist, 1963-64, consultant res div, 1964-72; Cornell University, Spencer T Olin Professor of Engineering, 1968-; Ithaca Research Corp, president. **ORGANIZATIONS:** Natl Academy of Engineering; Journal of Quantum Electronics, IEEE, associate editor, 1969-. **HONORS/AWARDS:** Institute of Electrical & Electronics Engineers, Fellow; American Phys Soc, Fellow; Optical Soc of America, Fellow. **BUSINESS ADDRESS:** Spencer T Olin Professor of Engineering, Dept of Electrical Engineering, Cornell University, 418 Phillips Hall, Ithaca, NY 14853.*

TANG, CHUNG-SHIH
Educator. Chinese American. **PERSONAL:** Born Jan 8, 1938, Tongcheng, Anhui, China; son of Chuan-Chi & I-Chuan H Tang; married Wen-Jing Y Tang, Jan 31, 1965; children: Annie, Nina, Michele. **EDUCATION:** National Taiwan University, BS, 1960, MS, 1962; University of California, Davis, PhD, 1967. **CAREER:** University of California, Davis, Department of Food Science & Technology, graduate assistant, 1963-67, Department of Environmental Toxicology, research associate, 1967-68; University of Hawaii, Department of Environmental Biochemistry, assistant professor, 1968-73, associate professor, 1974-79, chairman, 1988-92, professor, 1979-. **ORGANIZATIONS:** American Chemical Society, 1964-; International Society of Chemical Ecology, 1984-; Phytochemical Society of North America, 1985-; American Society of Pl Physiolosts, 1970-88; Chinese American Chemical Society, 1980-. **HONORS/AWARDS:** Gamma Sigma Delta, Research Award of Merit, 1988; South China Institute of Botany, honorary professor, 1986-; Kumming Institute of Botany, honorary professor, 1988-; South China Agricultural University, honorary professor, 1992-. **SPECIAL ACHIEVEMENTS:** The Science of Allelopathy, co-editor, John Wiley & Sons, 1986. **BUSINESS ADDRESS:** Professor, Dept of Environmental Biochemistry, University of Hawaii, 1800 East-West Rd, Henke Hall, Honolulu, HI 96822, (808)956-6005.

TANG, DAVID KWONG-YU
Attorney. Chinese American. **PERSONAL:** Born Apr 29, 1953, Hong Kong; son of Philip Tang & Phyllis Tang; married Daphne C P W Tang, Aug 1977; children: Jonathan M E, Kirsten M T. **EDUCATION:** Harvard University, AB (magna cum laude), 1975; Hague Academy of International Law, 1976; Columbia University School of Law, JD, 1979; Parker School of Foreign and Comparative Law, 1979. **CAREER:** Preston Thorgrimson, attorney, partner, 1979-. **ORGANIZATIONS:** University of Washington, School of Law, adjunct professor, 1985-; Higher Education Coordinating Board of Washington, 1989-; Epiphany School, board of trustees, president, 1989-; The Evergreen State College, board of trustees, chairman, 1986-89; Pacific Science Center, board of directors, secretary, 1991-; American Bar Association, Section of Real Property Law, council, 1991-, Section of International Law, chairman, International Commercial Transactions, 1990-93; American College of Real Estate Lawyers, 1990-; Council on Foreign Relations, New York, chairman, term membership, 1991-; Seattle Art Museum, board of trustees, 1994-. **SPECIAL ACHIEVEMENTS:** "Foreign Investors as Joint Venture Partners," Foreign Investment, 1990; "Public/Private Joint Ventures," ABA National Institute, 1990; "Economic and Trade Organizations in China," Doing Business in China, 1989; "Wholly Foreign-Owned Enterprise Law," Journal of Chinese Law, 1988. **BUSINESS ADDRESS:** Partner, Preston Thorgrimson, 701 Fifth Ave, 5000 Columbia Center, Seattle, WA 98104, (206)623-7580.

TANG, EUGENIA C. G.
Librarian. Chinese American. **PERSONAL:** daughter of T K Ying; married Yi-Noo Tang, Sep 5, 1964; children: Irwin A B, Irene A L. **EDUCATION:** National Taiwan University, BA, 1961; Eastern Mennonite College, 1962; George Peabody College, MALS, 1964. **CAREER:** Saint Louis Public Library, cataloger, 1964; Southern California College, senior descriptive cataloger, 1965-67; Texas A&M University, catalog maintenance librarian, 1968-70, technical reports cataloger, 1976-90, doc/microtext reference librarian, 1990-. **ORGANIZATIONS:** Special Library Association, 1977-82; American Library Association, 1983-; Chinese American Librarians Association, 1980-; Texas Library Association, 1986-87, 1991-. **BUSINESS ADDRESS:** Reference Librarian, Texas A&M University, Evans Library, College Station, TX 77840, (409)845-2551.

TANG, JIANXIN
Educator. Chinese American. **PERSONAL:** Born Dec 21, 1952, Hepu, Guangxi Zhuangzu, People's Republic of China; son of Jingzhi Tang & Ping Wang; married Heli Dong, Jan 31, 1981; children: Ling, Shirley D. **EDUCATION:** Guangxi University, BS, 1976; University of Bridgeport, MS, 1984; University of Connecticut, PhD, 1989. **CAREER:** Guangxi University, instructor, 1978; University of Connecticut, teaching assistant, 1986; Alfred University, assistant professor, 1989-. **ORGANIZATIONS:** IEEE, 1984. **HONORS/AWARDS:** University of Conn, predoctoral fellowship, 1984, Dissertation Preparation Fellowship, 1988; Alfred University, research grant on power system scheduling, 1990; National Science Foundation, research grant on power system scheduling, 1993, research grant on control system laboratory, 1993. **SPECIAL ACHIEVEMENTS:** Author: "A Decomposition Method for Generation Scheduling of Hydro Systems with Delays and Unpredictable Changes in Natural Inflow," Computer and Industrial Engineering, Vol 22, No 2, pp 147-155, 1992; "The Mixed Coordination Method for Long Horizon Optimal Control Problems," International Journal of Control, Vol 53, No 6, pp 1395-1412, 1991. **HOME ADDRESS:** 45 Sayles Street, Alfred, NY 14802. **BUSINESS ADDRESS:** Professor, Division of Electrical Engineering, Alfred University, Alfred, NY 14802, (607)871-2130.

TANG, JULIE MONG-SEE
Municipal court judge. Hong Kong American. **PERSONAL:** Born Oct 22, 1949, Hong Kong; daughter of Dr & Mrs P Y Tang; divorced; children: Louis Kon-Wai Lee. **EDUCATION:** University of San Francisco, BA, 1972; Stanford University, MA, 1973; Hastings College of Law, JD, 1982. **CAREER:** San Francisco Unified School District, counselor, 1975-76; Canada Community College, counselor, 1973-75; San Francisco Community College, counselor, 1976-79; San Francisco District Attorney's Office, assistant district attorney, 1983-90; San Francisco Municipal Court, judge, 1991-. **ORGANIZATIONS:** Chinese American Voters Education Committee, chair, 1978-79; Chinese American Democratic Club, board of directors, 1977-90; San Francisco Community College District, board of governor, 1981-90, president of board of governors, 1981, 1985, 1989; KQED Channel 9 Public Television, board of directors, 1978-79; Democratic County Central Committee, vice chair, 1979-81. **BUSINESS ADDRESS:** Judge, San Francisco Municipal Court, Hall of Justice, 850 Bryant St, San Francisco, CA 94103, (415)554-6869.

TANG, KIN LING
Educator. Chinese American. **PERSONAL:** Born Jul 5, 1936, Nanking, China; daughter of H S Chow & S T Chen; married Sing C Tang, Aug 29, 1964; children: Wayne, Terry, Gale. **EDUCATION:** Taiwan Normal University, BA, 1959; Marquette University, MEd, 1961; Michigan State University, PhD, 1965. **CAREER:** Eastern Michigan University, visiting lecturer, 1968-77; Schoolcraft College, adjunct faculty, 1979-89, assistant professor, 1990-. **ORGANIZATIONS:** American Psychological Society, 1993-; American Pshychological Association, affiliate member, 1991-; National Education Association, 1979-; Michigan Education Association, 1979-; Michigan Developmental Ed Consortium, 1990-. **HONORS/AWARDS:** Schoolcraft Connection, Favorite Instructor Contest winner, 1992; Schoolcraft College, Presidential Recognition Award for Teaching Excellence, 1993. **SPECIAL ACHIEVEMENTS:** "Paired Classes for Success," AACJC Journal, 1991. **BUSINESS ADDRESS:** Assistant Professor, Schoolcraft College, 18600 Haggerty Rd, Liberal Arts LA565, Livonia, MI 48152-2696, (313)462-4400.

TANG, KLAIRON KIT-LING
Librarian. Chinese American. **PERSONAL:** Born in Hong Kong; daughter of Bing Ki Hui and Siu Fong Ng; married Raymond Tang, 1986. **EDUCATION:** University of Washington, BA, music, 1981, BA, psychology, 1981; Louisiana State University, MLS, 1985, MPA, 1987. **CAREER:** East Baton Rouge Parish Library, librarian I, 1987-89; Bellaire City Library, head of technical services, cataloger, 1989-. **ORGANIZATIONS:** American Library Association, 1985-; Texas Library Association, 1990-; Houston Online Users Group, 1991-; Special Library Association, 1991-92. **HONORS/AWARDS:** American Library Association, Student Award for attending the 1985 ALA Annual Conference, 1985. **SPECIAL ACHIEVEMENTS:** Co-author: "A Collection of Papers on Economic Development," prepared for Senator Samuel B Nunez Jr and Representative John Alario, April 1987. **BUSINESS ADDRESS:** Head of Technical Services, Bellaire City Library, 5111 Jessamine St, Bellaire, TX 77401, (713)662-8163.

TANG, KWEI
Educator. Taiwanese American. **PERSONAL:** Born Aug 26, 1953, Pingtang, Taiwan; son of Shan Tang and Wen-Ching Cheng; married Anna K Tang, Jul 16, 1981; children: Nina, Daniel, David, Jonathan. **EDUCATION:** National Chiao Tung University, Taiwan, BS, 1976; Bowling Green State University, MS, 1981; Purdue University, PhD, 1984. **CAREER:** Louisiana State University, assistant/associate professor, 1984-91, professor/chairman, 1991-. **ORGANIZATIONS:** IIE Transactions, associate editor, 1991-; ASQC, 1987-; Institute of Management Science, 1982-. **HONORS/AWARDS:** NSF, Presidential Young Investigator Award, 1988. **SPECIAL ACHIEVEMENTS:** 40 academic papers published, 1984-93. **BUSINESS ADDRESS:** Professor/ Chmn, Dept of Quantitative Business Analysis, Louisiana State University, 3190 CEBA, Baton Rouge, LA 70803, (504)388-2126.

TANG, LILLIAN Y. D.
Pharmacist. Chinese American. **PERSONAL:** Born Nov 16, 1923, Nanking, Jiangsu, China; daughter of Thomson Eason Mao and Chuan-Hwei Tai Mao; married Yu-Sun Tang, Jun 9, 1950; children: Paul C, Elaine Tang Lee, John C. **EDUCATION:** West China Union University, BS, pharm, 1946; charter of SUNY, Buffalo, BS, pharm, 1946; National CheKiang University, BS, chem, 1947; University of Wisconsin, Madison, MS, pharm, 1949; University of Florida, pursued PhD, 1949-52. **CAREER:** Indiana University, Medical Center, pharmacist, 1961-66; Thrift Drug Co, retail pharmacist, 1968-70; Mayer's Drug Store, pharmacist, 1971-78; Meisner Pharmacy, pharmacist, 1978-81; Ta-Kung Po, Medical/Drug Info Update, writer, 1982-85; Methodist Home, Mt Lebanon, relief pharmacist, 1984-86; Pharmacist Relief Service, Consultants Inc, Latrobe, relief pharmacist, 1986-90: Baldwin Court Pharmacy Inc, relief pharmacist, 1991-. **ORGANIZATIONS:** American Pharmaceutical Association, 1948-65; Organization of Chinese Americans, 1976-. **HONORS/ AWARDS:** West China Union University, Canadian Red Cross Fellowship, 1948-49. **SPECIAL ACHIEVEMENTS:** Author: "A Study of Native Chenopodium Oil," Journal of Chinese Pharmacy; "Identification of Osthole in Hseh Tsuang Seed," Journal of American Pharm Association, vol 39, no 2, 1950; drug adviser to Organization of Chinese Americans, Pittsburgh section, 1972-. **HOME ADDRESS:** 1552 Holly Hill Dr, Bethel Park, PA 15102-3508, (412)835-2198.

TANG, MARK GIAKHY
Educator. Chinese American. **PERSONAL:** Born Aug 27, 1956, Vientiane, Lao People's Democratic Republic; son of Suyming Tang; married Stacy Chunglan Yu, Aug 28, 1990; children: Christopher Hanson. **EDUCATION:** National Taiwan University, BA, 1979, MBA, 1983; University of Alabama, Tuscaloosa, MS, 1986; Indiana University, PhD, 1990. **CAREER:** Indiana University, associate instructor, 1985-89; Morgan State University, lecturer, 1989-90, assistant professor, 1990-. **ORGANIZATIONS:** Decision Sciences Institute, 1988-; Operations Research Society of America, 1990-; American Statistics Association, 1992-; The Institute of Management Science, 1988-. **HONORS/AWARDS:** Beta Gamma Sigma, Outstanding Scholastic Achievement, 1990; Mu Sigma Rho, Outstanding Graduate Student, 1985. **SPECIAL ACHIEVEMENTS:** "A Stochastic Version Machine Maintenance and Sale Model: Results with Different Production Functions", 1993. **BIOGRAPHICAL SOURCES:** MSR Taiwan Army, private, 1975; Model Soldier Award. **BUSINESS ADDRESS:** Assistant Professor, Morgan State University, 1700 E Cold Spring Lane, Campus Box 441, Baltimore, MD 21239-4001, (410)319-3160.

TANG, MING-JE
Educator. Chinese American. **PERSONAL:** Born Dec 26, 1953, Taipei, Taiwan; son of Wei-Shen Tang and Tze-Ching Lou; married Yenhwa Tang-Yan, Jul 1979; children: Hanlin Tang, Hayden Tang. **EDUCATION:** National Taiwan University, BS, 1975; National Chengchi University, MBA, 1979; Massachusetts Institute of Technology, PhD, 1985. **CAREER:** MIT, research assistant, 1979-85; University of Illinois, assistant professor, 1985-91, associate professor, 1991-. **ORGANIZATIONS:** Strategic Management Society, 1985-; Academy of Management, 1985-. **SPECIAL ACHIEVEMENTS:** Author, "Foreign Entry Strategy," Management Science, 1990; "Competition Under Continuous Tech Change," Managerial & Decision Economics, 1992; "Escalating Commitment," Strategic Management Journal, 1988. **BUSINESS ADDRESS:** Professor, University of Illinois at Urbana-Champaign, 1206 Sixth St, 350 Commerce West, Champaign, IL 61820, (217)333-4260.

TANG, PAUL CHI LUNG
Educator. Chinese American. **PERSONAL:** Born Jan 23, 1944, British Columbia; son of Pei-Sung Tang & Violet Wong Tang (deceased). **EDUCATION:** University of British Columbia, Vancouver, BS, 1966; Simon Fraser University, Vancouver, MEd, 1971; Washington University, MA, 1975, PhD, 1982. **CAREER:** Simon Fraser University, teaching asst, 1969-71; St Louis Community College at Meramec, instructor, 1975-82; Washington University, St Louis, lecturer, instructor, 1972-76; Southern Illinois University at Edwardsville, visiting lecturer, 1978-79; Harris-Stowe State College, adjunct asst professor, 1980-82; Grinnell College, asst professor, 1982-85; California State University, Long Beach, associate to professor, dept chair, 1985-. **ORGANIZATIONS:** American Philosophical Assn, 1982-; Philosophy of Science Assn, 1982-; History of Science Assn, 1985-; Philosophy of Science Journal, asst editor, 1972-75; Philosophy of Science Assn Newsletter, editor, 1986-90; New York Academy of Science, 1993-; American Society for Aesthetics, 1992-; Kennedy Institute of Ethics, Georgetown University, 1988-; numerous others. **HONORS/AWARDS:** California State University, Long Beach, Phi Beta Delta, 1986, Summer Research Fellowship, 1988; National Endowment for the Humanities, Summer Seminar Fellowship, 1988; California State University, Long Beach, Meritorious Performance Award, 1986, 1988, 1990, Award for Internationalizing the Curriculum, 1993. **SPECIAL ACHIEVEMENTS:** Coauthor, LSAT Study Guide, REA, 2nd ed, 1992; numerous articles published in such books as: Proceedings of the Philosophy of Science Assn, 1984; Recent Developments in Epistemology & Philosophy of Science; Philosophy of Natural Science; & in such journals as: Journal of Chinese Philosophy; Isis; Journal of Aesthetic Education; publications: The Philosophy of Natural Science, 1989; Intl Journal of Intelligent Systems, 1988; Conceptus: Zeitschrift fur Philosophie, 1990; numerous music reviews and music articles in periodicals. **BUSINESS ADDRESS:** Professor, Dept of Philosophy, California State University, Long Beach, 1250 Bellflower Blvd, Long Beach, CA 90840, (310)985-7675.

TANG, ROGER Y. W.
Educator. Chinese American. **PERSONAL:** Born Feb 19, 1947, Fuhai, Yunnan, China; son of V H Tang & Y H Liu Tang; married Ann Tang, Dec 24, 1974; children: Sherri, Kevin. **EDUCATION:** National Taiwan University, BA, 1968; Eastern New Mexico University, MBA, 1974; University of Nebraska, PhD, 1977. **CAREER:** University of Nebraska, instructor, 1974-77; McGill University, assistant professor, 1977-80; University of Calgary, associate professor, 1980-88; Western Michigan University, professor and Upjohn Chair, 1988-. **ORGANIZATIONS:** Academy of International Business; American Accounting Association; Association for Asia Studies; Institute of Internal Auditors; Institute of Management Accountants; Portales Chapter of Phi Kappa Phi, 1973. **HONORS/AWARDS:** National Taiwan University, Honor Student Award, 1968; National Association of Accountants, Winner of a Certificate of Merit, 1978, 1979. **SPECIAL ACHIEVEMENTS:** Transfer Pricing Practices in the United States and Japan, Praeger, 1979; Multinational Transfer Pricing, Butterworths, 1981; Transfer Pricing in the 1990s, Quorum, 1993; "The Automobile Industry in Indonesia," Columbia Journal of World Business, winter 1988; "Audit of Collective Bargaining," Internal Auditor, April 1993. **BUSINESS ADDRESS:** Professor, Upjohn Chair, Haworth College of Business, Western Michigan University, 1201 Oliver Street, Kalamazoo, MI 49008, (616)387-5247.

TANG, SHERMAN
Library administrator. Chinese American. **PERSONAL:** Born Aug 1, 1936, Hankow, China; married Jean Tang; children: Nelson, Philip. **EDUCATION:** Tunghai University, Taichung, Taiwan, BA, 1959; Florida State University, Tallahassee, Florida, MS, 1963; New York University, PhD, 1979. **CAREER:** Queens Borough Public Library, Central Library, director, currently. **ORGANIZATIONS:** American Library Association. **BUSINESS ADDRESS:** Director, Central Library, Queens Borough Public Library, 89-11 Merrick Blvd, Jamaica, NY 11432, (718)990-0753.

TANG, THOMAS
US circuit judge. Chinese American. **PERSONAL:** Born Jan 11, 1922, Phoenix, AZ; son of Tang Shing & Lucy Yee Sing; married Pearl Mao Tang, Jul 10, 1947; children: Carol Suzanne, Richard Thomas. **EDUCATION:** University of Santa Clara, BS, 1947; University of Arizona, College of Law, LLB, 1950. **CAREER:** Maricopa County, deputy county attorney, 1953-57; State of Arizona, assistant attorney general, 1957-59; Phoenix, Arizona, city council member, 1960-62; Superior Court, Maricopa County, Arizona, judge, 1963-70; US Court of Appeals, ninth circuit, judge, 1977-. **HONORS/AWARDS:** University of Santa Clara, doctor of laws, 1977. **MILITARY SERVICE:** United States Army, first lieutenant, 1942-46, 1951-52. **BUSINESS ADDRESS:** United States Circuit Judge, United States Court of Appeals, Ninth Circuit, United States Courthouse, 230 North First Ave, #6412, Phoenix, AZ 85025, (602)514-7210.

TANG, THOMAS LI-PING
Educator. Taiwanese American. **PERSONAL:** Born Jun 1, 1949, Taipei, Taiwan; son of Kuan Ying Tang and Fang Chen Chu Tang; married Theresa Li-Na Tang, Aug 4, 1973; children: Cindy S, David S. **EDUCATION:** Chung Yuan University, BS, 1971; Case Western Reserve University, MA, 1977, PhD, 1981. **CAREER:** Psychological Research Services of CWRU, research assistant, 1974-78; Joseph Gallagher Jr High School, counselor/tutor, 1978-81; National Taiwan University, visiting associate professor, 1982; Self-Esteem X Effort = Success, president, 1988-; Middle Tennessee State University, Department of Psychology, assistant/associate professor, 1983-91, associate professor, management, 1991-. **ORGANIZATIONS:** American Psychological Association, 1983-; Academy of Management, 1983-; International Association of Applied Psychology, 1981-; Society of Human Resource Management, 1983-; Society for Industrial and Organizational Psychology, 1983-; Southern Management Association, 1991-; Southeastern Psychological Association, 1985-; American Chinese Management Educators Association, 1991-. **HONORS/AWARDS:** Middle Tennessee State University Foundation, Outstanding Research Award, 1991. **SPECIAL ACHIEVEMENTS:** Publications appearing in: Journal of Applied Psychology, 1984; Personnel Psychology, 1987; Journal of Management, 1989; Journal of Organizational Behavior, 1992-93; Public Personnel Management, 1992; Human Resource Development Quarterly, 1993; Personnel Administrator, 1987; Journal of Social Psychology, 1987, 1988, 1990, 1991, 1993, and numerous others; language proficiency in Chinese. **MILITARY SERVICE:** Chinese Army, Republic of China, 2nd lt, 1971-73; Golden Statue Award, 1972; Singing Contest, 1972. **BUSINESS ADDRESS:** Professor, Dept of Management and Marketing, Middle Tennessee State University, College of Business, East Main St, Murfreesboro, TN 37132-0002, (615)898-2005.

TANG, THOMAS TZE-TUNG
Physician, educator. Chinese American. **PERSONAL:** Born Nov 11, 1920, Peking, China; married Georgeen H Tang, Nov 3, 1959; children: Thomas T. **EDUCATION:** National Central University, Chungking, China, 1940-43; St Mary's College, BS, 1949; George Washington University, PhD, 1954, MD, 1958. **CAREER:** George Washington University, DC, instructor of biochemistry, 1951-55; University of Wisconsin, Madison, instructor of pathology, 1963-64; Children's Hospital of Wisconsin, pathologist, 1965-; Medical College of Wisconsin, professor of pathology, 1988-. **ORGANIZATIONS:** American Society of Clinical Pathologists, fellow, 1966-; College of American Pathologists, fellow, 1965-; Society of Nuclear Medicine, fellow, 1975-; American Medical Association, 1965-. **HONORS/AWARDS:** Bugamor International, Honorarium, 1993; Annual Review of Hydrocephalus, Recognition, 1993. **SPECIAL ACHIEVEMENTS:** Sixty publications on pediatric pathology & health science; bilingual in English & Chinese with high proficiency; board certified in anatomic pathology, clinical pathology, nuclear medicine and radioisotopic pathology. **MILITARY SERVICE:** Chinese Nationalist Army, lt colonel, 1943-46; Veteran's Medal, 1975. **BIOGRAPHICAL SOURCES:** ABMS Compendium of Certified Medical Specialists, 3rd ed, vol 3, p 381, 1990-91; vol 4, p 552, 1990-91. **BUSINESS ADDRESS:** Physician, Children's Hospital of Wisconsin, PO Box 1997, Milwaukee, WI 53201.

TANG, VICTOR K. T.
Analyst. Chinese American. **PERSONAL:** Born Mar 13, 1929, Peiping, China; married. **EDUCATION:** National Taiwan University, BA, 1955; University of Washington, MA, 1963; Iowa State University, PhD, 1971. **CAREER:** Humboldt State University, assistant professor, associate professor, professor, 1963-85, professor emeritus, 1985-; Center For Naval Analysis, analyst, 1985-. **ORGANIZATIONS:** American Statistical Association, 1963-; Institute of Mathematical Statistics, 1963-. **BUSINESS ADDRESS:** Center For Naval Analysis, 4401 Ford Ave, Alexandria, VA 22302-0268, (703)824-2215.

TANG, WALLACE T. Y.
Business executive. Hong Kong American. **EDUCATION:** Harvard College, AB, 1985. **CAREER:** Laserlith Corp, general manager, research director, 1985-; Endpoint Technologies Inc, CEO, 1992-; Endorobotics Corp, president, 1993-. **ORGANIZATIONS:** Organization of Chinese-American Entrepreneurs' Advisory Network, 1990-92; Bay Area Chrome User Group, 1989-; Photomask Standards Committee, Semiconductor Equipment and Materials

International, 1989-; Society of Photo-Optical Instrumentation Engineers, 1989-90. **SPECIAL ACHIEVEMENTS:** Author of various publications in the semiconductor processing technologies field, 1989-. **BUSINESS ADDRESS:** CEO, Endpoint Technologies Inc, PO Box 4408, Warren, NJ 07059, (908)271-9088.

TANG, WEN
Educator. Chinese American. **PERSONAL:** Born Sep 19, 1921, Nanking, China; son of Mr & Mrs Cheng-Far Tang; married Wendy H Tang, Oct 24, 1948; children: Cha-Mei, Cha-Rie, Cha-Min, Cha-Nan, Joyce, Jessamy. **EDUCATION:** National Central University, BS, 1945; New York University, MS, 1958, PhD, 1960. **CAREER:** Taipi, International Airport Weather Station, chief scientist, 1953-56; New York University, College of Eng, research assistant, research associate, 1956-60; GCA Corp, senior scientist, scientist, 1960-68; University of Massachusetts, professor, 1968-; Institute of Storm Research, Houston, Texas, consultant, 1969-; Ecological Corp, Redford Massachusetts, consultant, 1973. **HONORS/AWARDS:** NYU, Achievement Award, 1960; University of Lowell, University of Massachusetts, Research Achievement, 1974. **SPECIAL ACHIEVEMENTS:** Proficient in speaking & writing Chinese; Chinese brush painting & calligraphy. **MILITARY SERVICE:** Nationalist Chinese Air Force, major, 1946-56. **BUSINESS ADDRESS:** Professor, University of Massachusetts/Lowell, 1 University Ave, Rm OH-101-C, Earth Sciences, Lowell, MA 01854.

TANG, WILSON HON-CHUNG
Educator. Hong Kong American. **PERSONAL:** Born Aug 16, 1943, Hong Kong; son of Shu Chun Tang and Shui Kuen Chan Tang; married Bernadette Yim, Jul 29, 1969; children: Tze John, Joyce Wing-Yi. **EDUCATION:** Massachusetts Institute of Technology, BS, 1966, MS, 1967; Stanford University, PHD, 1969. **CAREER:** Fay, Spofford and Thorndike, structural engineer, 1966; Sargent and Lundy, consulting engineer, 1971; Norwegian Geotechnical Institute, visiting professor, Guggenheim Fellow, 1976-77; Imperial College, visiting professor, Guggenheim Fellow, 1976-77; National University of Singapore, visiting professor, 1983; University of Illinois, Urbana-Champaign, assistant professor, 1969-74, associate professor, 1974-80, professor, 1981-, Department of Civil Engineering, associate head, 1989-91. **ORGANIZATIONS:** American Soc of Civil Engineers, fellow; Journal of Structural Safety, editorial bd; National Research Council, geotechnical bd; National Research Council Committee for Workshop on Reliability Methods for Risk Mitigation in Geotechnical Engineering, chair; ASCE Technical Committee on Geotechnical Reliability, co-chair; Intl Soc of Soil Mechanics and Foundation Engineering; American Soc of Engineering Educ; Intl Geostatistical Assn; Intl Assn for Structural Safety and Reliability; Intl Assn for Civil Engineering Reliability and Risk Analysis; Chinese-American Assn of Natural Disaster Mitigation Research. **HONORS/AWARDS:** Urbana-Champaign Campus Award, Excellence in Undergraduate Instruction, 1991; ASCE, Regional Scholarship, 1963, State of the Art Civil Engineering Award, 1990; Civil Engineering Outstanding Teaching Award, 1980; John Simon Guggenheim Fellowship, 1976; Engineering Joint Council, Engineers of Distinction, 1970; Phi Tau Phi, Tau Beta Pi; Sigma Xi; Chi Epsilon. **SPECIAL ACHIEVEMENTS:** Over 100 books & technical papers; co-author, "Reliability Evalution of Idealized Tunnel Systems," Structural Safety, vol 11, pp 81-93, 1992; co-author, "Optimal Importance-Sampling Density Estimator," Journ of Engineering Mechanics, ASCE, vol 118, no 6, pp 1146-1163, June 1992; co-author, "Uncertainty of Mobilised Undrained Shear Strength," Soils & Foundations, vol 32, no 4, pp 107-116, Dec 1992; co-author, "Site Exploration Strategy for Geologic Anomaly Characterization," Journal of Geotechnical Engineering, ASCE, vol 119, no GT2, Feb 1993; author, "Recent Developments in Geotechnical Reliability," Probabilistic Methods in Geotechnical Engineering, K S Li & S-C R Lo, editors, Balkema, 1993. **HOME ADDRESS:** 310 Willard, Urbana, IL 61801, (217)344-8771. **BUSINESS PHONE:** (217)333-6954.

TANG, YI-NOO
Educator. Chinese American. **PERSONAL:** Born Feb 28, 1938, Hubei, China; son of Kwan-Nan Tang and Chan Chin Tang; married Eugenia C G Tang, Sep 4, 1964; children: Irwin, Irene. **EDUCATION:** Chung Chi College, Hong Kong, BS, 1959; University of Kansas, PhD, 1964. **CAREER:** Texas A&M University, professor, 1967-. **ORGANIZATIONS:** American Chemical Society, 1962-. **HONORS/AWARDS:** Texas A&M University, Faculty Distinguished Achievement Award in Teaching, 1975, College of Science Distinguished Teaching Award, 1986. **SPECIAL ACHIEVEMENTS:** 62 published articles in chemistry journals; coordinator of the First Year Chemistry Lecture Program at Texas A&M University, the largest freshman chemistry program in

the country, with 4500 students each semester. **BUSINESS ADDRESS:** Professor, Dept of Chemistry, Texas A&M University, College Station, TX 77843, (409)845-3755.

TANG, YINGCHAN EDWIN
Educator. Taiwanese American. **PERSONAL:** Born Apr 1, 1953, Hsih-chi, Taipei, Taiwan; son of Hsiu-Yan Tang; married Chih-Ping Wang, May 21, 1988; children: Jame Devon, Deborah Charlotte. **EDUCATION:** National Cheng-chi University, Taiwan, BA, 1976; Texas Tech University, MS, management, 1984; University of Texas, Dallas, PhD, 1989. **CAREER:** Starch INRA, research analyst, 1978-80; International Advertising Agency, account executive, 1980-81; University of Texas, Dallas, teaching fellow, research assistant, 1984-88; North Carolina State University, assistant professor, 1988-. **ORGANIZATIONS:** American Marketing Association; Institute of Management Science; Academy of Management; North Carolina State University, graduate faculty associate membership, 1990. **HONORS/AWARDS:** Southwestern Doctoral Symposium, Best Research Paper Award, 1987; University of Texas, Dallas, graduate student scholarship, 1984-88. **SPECIAL ACHIEVEMENTS:** Co-author: "Advertising's Effect on the Product Evolutionary Cycle," Rutgers University, Journal of Marketing, July 1990; papers presented at the Marketing Science Conference, 1988-92. **MILITARY SERVICE:** Taiwan Marine Corps, 1978; special recognition for exemplary service. **HOME ADDRESS:** 104 Kirkfield Dr, Cary, NC 27511, (919)859-4764. **BUSINESS ADDRESS:** Assistant Professor, Dept of Business Management, North Carolina State University, PO Box 7229, 145 E Nelson Hall, Raleigh, NC 27695, (919)515-6954.

TANG, YU-SUN
Engineering consultant. Chinese American. **PERSONAL:** Born Oct 24, 1922, Nanjing, Jiangsu, China; son of Chian-Chung Tang and Shiu-Lang Han Tang; married Lillian Yu-Djang Tang, Jun 9, 1950; children: Paul C, Elaine T Lee, John C. **EDUCATION:** Chinese National Central University, BS, ME, 1944; University of Wisconsin, Madison, MS, ME, 1948; University of Florida, PhD, ChE, 1952. **CAREER:** Westinghouse Electric Corp, steam division, senior devel engineer, 1956-59; General Motors Corp, Allison division, principal scientist, 1959-66; Westinghouse, Astronucl Laboratory, advisory engineer, 1966-71, advanced reactors divison, advisory engineer, 1971-84; University of Pittsburgh, adj associate professor, 1984-86, adj research professor, 1987-90; Tang's Consulting Engr, consulting engineer, 1987-. **ORGANIZATIONS:** Am Association Advancement of Science, fellow; Am Institute Chm Engineers, fellow, energy transfer com, chairman, 1976-80, nuclear energy com, chairman, 1988-90; Am Nuclear Society; Am Society of Mech Engineers; Orgn of Chinese Americans. **SPECIAL ACHIEVEMENTS:** More than 40 articles on heat transfer and reactor thermohydraulics; US patent in a heat removal apparatus; coauthor, Thermal Analysis of Liquid Metal Fast Breeder Reactors, Radioactive Waste Management; visiting professorships to: National Central and National Tsing Hua Universities in Taiwan and Nanyang Tech University in Singapore. **HOME ADDRESS:** 1552 Holly Hill Dr, Bethel Park, PA 15102-3508, (412)835-2198.

TANIGUCHI, ALAN Y.
Architect, educator. Japanese American. **PERSONAL:** Born Sep 13, 1922, Stockton, CA; son of Isamu Taniguchi and Sadayo Miyagi; married Leslie H Taniguchi, Apr 29, 1947; children: Evan Key, Keith. **EDUCATION:** University of California, Berkeley, BA, architecture, 1949. **CAREER:** University of Texas, Austin, assistant professor, associate professor, professor, 1961-72, School of Architecture, dean, 1967-72; Rice University, School of Architecture, director, 1972-74, professor, 1974-79; Alan Y Taniguchi, Architect and Associates, president, 1979-. **ORGANIZATIONS:** American Institute of Architects, FAIA, 1958-; Texas Society of Architects, vice president, 1972; Association of Collegiate Schools of Architecture, 1961-78, president, 1972; National Architectural Accrediting Board, 1968-74; Texas Committee for the Humanities, 1974-80, chair, 1978-80; Huston-Tillotson College, trustee, 1990-. **HONORS/AWARDS:** American Institute of Architects, College of Fellows, 1971; University of Texas, Austin, Student Association Teaching Excellence, 1961, 1962; University of Virginia, Thomas Jefferson Professor, 1970; Universidad Autonoma de Guadalajara, Mexico, Distinguished Professor, 1975. **SPECIAL ACHIEVEMENTS:** Texas Society of Architects, 8 Design Awards, 1960-82; AIA, Austin Chapter, 9 Design Awards, 1963-92; Progressive Architecture Magazine Design Award, 1978. **BUSINESS ADDRESS:** President, Alan Y Taniguchi, Architect and Associates, 1609 W Sixth St, Austin, TX 78703, (512)474-7079.

TANIGUCHI, ROBERT IWAO
Educator. Japanese American. **PERSONAL:** Born Jan 12, 1945, Price, UT; son of Fred Taniguchi and Ferry Taniguchi; married Nancy J Taniguchi, Jul 13, 1973; children: Dashiell, Darcy. **EDUCATION:** University of Utah, BS, 1967; Utah State University, MEd, 1968. **CAREER:** Clark County School District, NV, teacher, 1968-73; International School, Kuala Lampur, Malaysia, teacher, 1973-76; Carbon School District, UT, teacher, 1976-79; College of Eastern Utah, math instructor, 1979-89; Merced College, math instructor, 1990-, athletic director, currently. **ORGANIZATIONS:** Japanese American Citizens League; National Council of Teachers of Mathematics; Association of Two-Year Colleges. **HONORS/AWARDS:** College of Eastern Utah, Outstanding Teacher Award, 1983, 1984, Teacher of the Year Award, 1982. **MILITARY SERVICE:** US Army, cpl, 1970-71. **BUSINESS ADDRESS:** Professor, Merced College, 3600 M St, Science Bldg, Merced, CA 95348, (209)384-6364.

TANNAN, ASHOK
Mechanical engineer. Indo-American. **PERSONAL:** Born Nov 11, 1942, Jullundar City, Punjab, India; son of Om Prakash Tannan & Sarla Tannan; married Ashi Tannan, Jul 14, 1973; children: Neil, Jay. **EDUCATION:** Jiwaji University, India, BSME, 1966; Ohio University, MSME, 1969; University of Wisconsin, MBA, 1980. **CAREER:** August Winter & Sons, project manager, 1978-85; Tannan Engineering Inc, president, 1985-. **ORGANIZATIONS:** American Society of Heating, Refrigeration & Air Conditioning Engineers, NE chapter, president, 1985-, vice president, 1984-, secretary, 1983-, treasurer, 1982-. **BUSINESS ADDRESS:** President, Tannan Engineering Inc, 1313 Palisades Dr, Appleton, WI 54915, (414)731-2897.

TANOUYE, MARK ALLEN
Educator. Japanese American. **PERSONAL:** Born Oct 14, 1950, San Jose, CA; son of Kiyoshige Tanouye & Misao Nakano Tanouye; married Ellen Kazuko Tanouye, Jun 23, 1973; children: Matthew, Adam, David. **EDUCATION:** Stanford University, BS, 1973, MA, 1973; Yale University, PhD, 1978; California Institute of Technology, postdoctoral, 1978-83. **CAREER:** California Institute of Technology, assistant professor, 1983-90; University of California, Berkeley, acting associate professor, 1990-92, professor, 1992-. **ORGANIZATIONS:** University of California, Berkeley, College of Natural Resources, Faculty Research Committee, chairman, 1992-, Faculty Executive Committee, 1992, Asian American Affairs, chair, 1993-, Chancellor's Advisory Committee; National Institutes of Health, Neurology C Study Section, 1993-; Society of Neuroscience, Minority Education, Training, and Professional Advancement Committee, 1988-. **HONORS/AWARDS:** Alfred P Sloan Foundation, fellow, 1984; McKnight Foundation, fellow, 1983. **HOME ADDRESS:** 1831 Hamlet St, San Mateo, CA 94403, (415)345-9260. **BUSINESS ADDRESS:** Professor, Dept of Entomology and Dept of Molecular & Cell Biology, University of California, Berkeley, Berkeley, CA 94720, (510)642-9404.

TAO, STEPHEN G.
Film studio executive. Chinese American. **PERSONAL:** Born Sep 24, 1963, Palo Alto, CA; son of Helen & George Tao. **EDUCATION:** Claremont McKenna College, BA, 1985; UCLA, MBA, 1989. **CAREER:** Boston Consulting Group, associate, 1985-87; Permut Presentations, creative intern, 1988-89; Walt Disney Pictures, director, creative affairs, 1989-. **HONORS/AWARDS:** Phi Beta Kappa, UCLA, 1987. **BUSINESS ADDRESS:** Director, Creative Affairs, Walt Disney Pictures, 500 S Buena Vista St, Team Disney, 308L, Burbank, CA 91521.

TASHIMA, A. WALLACE
Judge. Japanese American. **PERSONAL:** Born Jun 24, 1934, Santa Maria, CA; married. **EDUCATION:** University of California, Los Angeles, AB, 1958; Harvard Law School, LLB, 1961. **CAREER:** State of California, deputy attorney general, 1961-67; Amstar Corp, attorney, 1968-72, general attorney, vice president, 1972-77; Morrison & Foerster, partner, 1977-80; US District Court, US district judge, 1980-. **SPECIAL ACHIEVEMENTS:** Co-author, Federal Civil Procedure Before Trial, 2 vols, The Rutter Group, 1989, updated annually; author of articles on federal practice. **MILITARY SERVICE:** US Marine Corps, sgt, 1953-56. **BUSINESS ADDRESS:** US District Judge, US District Court, 312 N Spring St, Los Angeles, CA 90012, (213)894-4203.

TAURA, RICHARD BILL
Graphic design company executive. Japanese American. **PERSONAL:** Born Aug 9, 1953, Chicago, IL; son of Masayasu B Taura and Martha Masako Sugimoto; married Joni L Taura, Aug 27, 1988; children: Joseph Dillon, Jacob Masayasu. **EDUCATION:** University of Illinois, Champaign, Urbana, BS,

marketing, 1976. **CAREER:** Pillsbury Co, sales rep, 1977-79; Coca-Cola USA, sales manager, 1979-81; Make Ready Inc, president, 1981-91, general manager, beginning 1991; Performance Communications Group, account executive, currently. **BUSINESS ADDRESS:** Account Executive, Performance Communications Group, 312 W Randolph St, Chicago, IL 60606, (312)419-0735.

TAZOI, NORMA
Association administrator. Japanese American. **CAREER:** Atascadero State Hospital, appointed by Governor Deukemejian to state advisory board; Japanese American Republicans, president, currently. **ORGANIZATIONS:** Organization of State Hospital Advisory Boards.*

TCHEN, JOHN KUO WEI (JACK)
Educational administrator. Chinese American. **PERSONAL:** Born Aug 23, 1951, Madison, WI; married Judy Susman; children: Sara Tchen-Susman. **EDUCATION:** CIDOC, Mexico, alternatives in education, 1971; University of Wisconsin-Madison, BA, 1973, MA, modern Chinese history, 1975; New York University, MA, American history, 1987, PhD, American history, 1992. **CAREER:** Asian American Resources Center, Basement Workshop, coordinator, 1975-78, executive director, 1978-79; Hunter College, CUNY, Dept of Black & Puerto Rican Studies, Asian American Studies, instructor, 1976-78; Center for Community Studies, New York Chinatown History Project, co-founder, executive director, historian, 1980-86, dba Chinatown History Museum, historian, 1986-; Queens College, CUNY, Asian/American Center, associate director, historian, 1987-90, acting director, historian, 1990-92, director, 1992-, Dept of Urban Studies, assistant professor, 1992-. **ORGANIZATIONS:** American Studies Assn; Assn of American Museums; Assn of Asian American Studies; Intl Oral History Assn; Organization of American Historians; numerous conferences, boards, and committees, including: CUNY Graduate Center, PhD Degree Program, Ethnic & Intercultural Studies, planning committee, 1993-94; Queens College, CUNY, Affirmative Action, comm member, 1990-94, Asian/American Center, Asians Reshaping Higher Education, planning comm, 1991-92, interdisciplinary major comm, 1993-94; Organization of American Historians, annual conference, planning comm, 1991-93; Smithsonian Institution, Arthur M Sackler Gallery, visiting comm, 1992-, Smithsonian Council, 1991-; New York State Archives and Records Administration, advisory board, 1991-93. **HONORS/AWARDS:** City of New York, Mayor's Award of Honor, for Arts & Culture, 1993; National Endowment for the Humanities, Charles Frankel Prize, 1991; New York State, Governor's Art Award, for New York Chinatown History Project, 1990; Columbia University, Charles H Revson Fellow, 1986-87; Organization of Chinese Americans, Champion of Excellence Award, 1986-87; Before Columbus Foundation, American Book Award, for Genthe's Photographs of San Francisco's Old Chinatown, 1985; Municipal Arts Society, Recognition Award, for New York Chinatown History Project, 1984; New York Historical Resources Center, Cornell University, historian-in-residence fellow, 1980. **SPECIAL ACHIEVEMENTS:** Editor, author of introduction: Chinese Laundryman: A Study of Social Isolation, 1987; author: Genthe's Photographs of San Francisco's Old Chinatown, 1895-1906, 1984; "Conjuring Ghosts in a Journey to the East," 1993 Proceedings of the Assn of the Asian American Studies Annual Conference, 1994; "Rethinking Who 'We' Are: A Basic Discussion of Basic Terms," Voices from the Battlefront, Achieving Cultural Equity, 1993; various other books & essays; curator of several exhibitions & productions. **BUSINESS ADDRESS:** Director, Asian/American Center, Professor, Dept of Urban Studies, Queens College, CUNY, 65-30 Kissena Blvd, Flushing, NY 11367, (718)997-3050.

TENG, ANTHONY YUNG-YUAN
Educator. Chinese American. **PERSONAL:** Born Oct 20, 1939, Hankow, China; son of Kuen-tien Teng (deceased) and Lien-chen Wang Teng (deceased); married Grace H Teng, 1967; children: Betty P. **EDUCATION:** Tunghai University, Taichung, Taiwan, BA, 1962; Occidental College, MA, 1966; University of Wisconsin-Madison, PhD, 1972. **CAREER:** Occidental College, research assistant, 1964-66; University of Wisconsin, teaching assistant, 1967-68; Rhode Island College, assistant professor, 1969-72, associate professor, 1972-. **ORGANIZATIONS:** Association For Asian Studies, 1967-; Phi Alpha Theta, 1969-; New England Historical Society, 1969-; New England Chinese Professional Society, vice-president, 1985-; RI Chinese-American Association, 1975-; New England Asian Studies Association, 1969-. **HONORS/AWARDS:** Occidental College, Chevalier Graduate Scholarship, 1964-66; The California China Foundation Award, 1965-66; RIC Faculty Research Grant, 1973, 1975; International Oriental Studies Travel Grant, 1975. **SPECIAL ACHIEVEMENTS:** "The Concept of International Interests: A Time

for New Approaches," Chen Chung Translation Series, Cheng Chung Book Co., Taipei, Taiwan, 1979; "A Strategic Triangle of Two and A Half Power," Cheng Chung Translation Series, Cheng Chung Book Co., Taipei, Taiwan, Jan 1980; Leung, Edwin P, ed, Historical Dictionary of Revolutionary China, 1839-1976, Greenwood Press, pp 211-212, 441-443. **BIOGRAPHICAL SOURCES:** Historical Dictionary of Revolutionary China, ed by Edwin P Leung, Greenwood Press, p xi, 1992. **BUSINESS ADDRESS:** Assoc Professor, History Dept, Rhode Island College, 600 Mt Pleasant Ave, 212 Gaige Hall, Providence, RI 02908, (401)456-9751.

TENG, HENRY SHAO-LIN
Company executive. Chinese American. **PERSONAL:** Born Mar 12, 1947, New York, NY; son of Yen-lin Teng and Helen Chung Teng; married Joan Chang-hou Teng, Oct 17, 1977. **EDUCATION:** University of Science and Technology of China, 1978-80; Northeastern University, BS, computer science, 1984; Worcester Polytechnic Institute, MS, computer science, 1987; University of Massachusetts at Lowell, MA, PhD candidate. **CAREER:** Academia Sinica, Institute of Chemistry, staff, 1975-78; General Electric Company, scientific programmer, 1981; Digital Equipment Corp, principal software engr, 1982-92, software engr manager, 1992-; Northeastern University, Boston, part-time instructor, 1990-; Asia & America Technology Inc, president, 1990-, CEO, currently. **ORGANIZATIONS:** Tau Beta Pi, 1983-; Phi Kappa Phi, 1984-; DEC Artificial Intelligence Technology Center Senior Technical Forum, 1990-91; DEC Computer & Network Security Tools Task Force, chairperson, 1989. **HONORS/AWARDS:** Northeastern University, William Hotchkin Scholarship, 1980, Outstanding Academic Achievement Award, 1984, Sears B Conduct Honor Award, 1984; Digital Equipment Corp, DIS Achievements Award with Distinction, 1988; DEC AI Technology Center, Quarterly Award, 1991. **SPECIAL ACHIEVEMENTS:** Author: "An Expert System Approach to Security Inspection of a VAX/VMS System in a Network Environment," presented, 10th National Computer Security Conference, 1987; "Security Audit Trail Analysis Using Inductively Generated Predictive Rules," presented, 6th IEEE Conference on Artificial Intelligence Applications, 1990; "Adaptive Real-time Anomaly Detection Using Inductively Generated Sequential Patterns," presented, IEEE Symposium on Research in Security & Privacy, 1990; "XSAFE: A Prototype Expert System for Security Inspection of a VAX/VMS System in a Network Environment," presented, 2nd International Conference on Applications of Artificial Intelligence in Engineering, 1987; patent: System Including Inductive Learning Arrangement for Adaptive Management of Behavior of Complex Entity, US Patent Office, #5,034,898, 1991; patent: Rule Invocation Mechanism for Inductive Learning Engine, US Patent Office, #5,222,197, 1993; 1 patent pending. **BIOGRAPHICAL SOURCES:** "Couple Reunited with Boy," Palm Beach Post, Sep 5, 1980; Cyberpunk, Katie Hafner and John Markoff, p 124, Touchstone, 1992. **BUSINESS ADDRESS:** President, Asia & America Technology, Inc, 8 Concetta Circle, Acton, MA 01720, (508)897-8639.

TENG, HSI CHING
Physician. Chinese American. **PERSONAL:** Born Aug 7, 1919, Wuxi, Jiangsu, China; son of Mr and Mrs Z S Teng; married Catherine Teng, Oct 26, 1948; children: Ray, Jay, Neal, Leland. **EDUCATION:** St John's University, China, BS, 1942; St John's University Medical School, MD, 1945. **CAREER:** St Paul Hospital, medical intern, resident, 1948-51; University of Texas Southwestern Medical School, medical research fellow, instructor, 1951-59, clinical assistant professor of medicine, 1966-; self employed, physician, 1959-. **ORGANIZATIONS:** New York Academy of Sciences, 1957-; American Medical Association, 1959-90; Texas Medical Association, 1959-; Texas Chinese Association, president, 1973-74; American College of Chest Physicians, fellow, 1974-; Chinese Chapel, First Baptist Church of Dallas, steering committee chair, 1974-90; First Chinese Baptist Church of Dallas, deacon, 1987-90, 1992-93. **HONORS/AWARDS:** St Paul Medical Center, Dallas, Honorary (Emeritus) Medical Staff, 1984, Award of Honor, 1985; First Chinese Baptist Church of Dallas, Distinguished Service Award, 1993. **SPECIAL ACHIEVEMENTS:** 15 Research articles published in medical journals, 1953-60. **HOME ADDRESS:** 4056 Fawnhollow, Dallas, TX 75244. **BUSINESS PHONE:** (214)620-9669.

TENG, LEE CHANG-LI
Physicist. Chinese American. **PERSONAL:** Born Sep 5, 1926, Beijing, Hebei, China; son of Tsuy-Ying Teng & Chien-Min Ho; married Nancy Lai-Shen Huang, Sep 21, 1961; children: Michael Nan-Hao. **EDUCATION:** Fu Jen University, Peking, BS, physics, 1946; University of Chicago, MS, physics, 1948, PhD, physics, 1951. **CAREER:** University of Chicago, teaching assis-

tant, 1948-49, cyclotron assistant, 1949-51; University of Minnesota, assistant professor, 1951-53; Wichita State University, associate professor, 1953-55; Fermi National Accelerator Lab, Accelerator Theory Section, head, 1967-72, Advanced Projects Department, head, 1974-79, Accelerator Division, associate head, 1972-76, Accelerator Physics Department, head, 1986-87, directors office special projects, 1987-89; Synchrotron Radiation Research Center, Taiwan, director, 1983-85, board of directors, 1983-; Argonne National Lab, Accelerator Theory Group Particle Accelerator Division, leader, 1955-62, Particle Accelerator Division, director, 1962-67, Advanced Photon Source Project, Accelerator Physics Dept, head, 1989-. **ORGANIZATIONS:** Chinese Chamber of Commerce and Professions, board chairman, 1988-; Midwest Chinese Student and Alumni Services, president, 1973-74; Mid-American Chapter, Phi Tau Phi, president, 1963-64; Sigma Xi, president, 1954-55; Academician, Academia Sinica. **HONORS/AWARDS:** American Physical Society, fellow; Argonne National Lab, fellow, 1985-87; Fu Jen Alumni Association, honorary chairman, 1984-; Beijing Normal University, honorary professor; Chinese Academy of Sciences, honorary advisor; Chinese Ministry of Education, Gold Medal of Achievement, 1956; Immigrants Service League, Distinguished Service Award, 1963. **SPECIAL ACHIEVEMENTS:** Achievements in accelerator technology include: resonant extraction and injection of beam from circular accelerator; RF capture during injection; space charge detuning of elliptical beam; extension of isochronous sector-focusing field to high energies; 4 patents. **HOME ADDRESS:** 400 E Eighth St, Hinsdale, IL 60521, (708)655-2827. **BUSINESS ADDRESS:** Senior Scientist, Argonne National Laboratory, 9700 S Cass Ave, Bldg 360, F201, Argonne, IL 60439, (708)252-3405.

TENG, MABEL SIK MEI
Organization executive. Chinese American. **PERSONAL:** Born May 1, 1953, Hong Kong; daughter of C C Teng & Molly C Teng; married Richard Joseph Yuen, Dec 10, 1983; children: Tania Yuen, Leticia Yuen. **EDUCATION:** University of Massachusetts, BA (with honors), biology, 1975. **CAREER:** Michael Angelo Elementary School, teacher, 1975-77; Harvard University Medical School, research associate, 1977-80; City College of San Francisco, instructor, 1980-91; Career Resources Development Center, executive director, 1991-. **ORGANIZATIONS:** Chinese Progressive Association, board of directors, 1984-86; Chinese American Democratic Club, board of directors, 1990-; San Francisco College Governing Board, board of trustees, 1990-. **HONORS/AWARDS:** California State Legislature, Exemplary Record of Service, 1993; City College of San Francisco, Board of Trustees, Outstanding Leadership Award, 1992; Council on Black American Affairs, Award of Honor, 1991; Chinese Progressive Association, Outstanding Leadership Award, 1992; Chinatown Youth Center, Award of Honor for Services to Youths, 1991; Pacific and Asian American Women of Bay Area, Outstanding Contribution in Politics and Community Advocacy, 1985. **SPECIAL ACHIEVEMENTS:** Conceptualized & developed a national model workplace literacy program, Department of Education Award; designed & implemented a bilingual vocational training program, Department of Education Award. **BIOGRAPHICAL SOURCES:** Asian Week Newspaper; San Francisco Independent Newspaper; San Francisco Examiner; San Francisco Journal. **BUSINESS ADDRESS:** Executive Director, Career Resources Development Center, 655 Geary St, San Francisco, CA 94102, (415)775-8880.

TENG, TSUCHI PAUL
Government official. Chinese American/Taiwanese American. **PERSONAL:** Born Apr 3, 1939, Ngochen, Hupei, China; son of Ting-yuan Teng and Chientau Tu Teng; married Margurita M Teng, Oct 11, 1969; children: Stephanie A, Scott M. **EDUCATION:** Chung Yuan University, Taiwan, BSCE, 1962; University of Mississippi, MSCE, 1966; Mississippi College, MBA, 1978. **CAREER:** Mississippi State Hwy Department, assistant R&D division engineer, 1970-74, R&D division engineer, 1974-81; Federal Hwy Administration, R&D program manager, 1981-83, management procedures team leader, 1983-86, asphalt pavements team leader, 1986-87, pavement design & rehabilitation branch chief, 1987-91, long term pavement performance division chief, 1991-. **ORGANIZATIONS:** American Society of Civil Engineers, committee chair; American Society for Testing and Materials, committee member; Transportation Research Board, National Research Council, committee chair; American Association of State Hwy and Transportation Officials. **HONORS/AWARDS:** Chi Epsilon National Honorary Civil Engineering Fraternity, 1966, University of Mississippi Chapter, Honor Member, 1985. **SPECIAL ACHIEVEMENTS:** Commendation letters from AASHTO, AGC, ARTBA, SASHTO, TRB, FHWA, states and numerous industry groups; technical publications in ASCE, ACI, ASTM and TRB journals; exceptional performance ratings, 1981-82, 1984, 1986, 1990-92, US government service;

outstanding performance ratings 1983, 1985, 1987, US government service; Federal Hwy Administration Superior Achievement Award, 1986. **BIO-GRAPHICAL SOURCES:** The University of Mississippi Alumni Association, p 521, 1991. **BUSINESS ADDRESS:** Chief, Long Term Pavement Performance Division, Federal Highway Administration, 6300 Georgetown Pike, HNR-40, Mc Lean, VA 22101, (703)285-2355.

TERAJI, THOMAS SHUICHI

Educator (retired). Japanese American. **PERSONAL:** Born May 16, 1919, Huntington Park, CA; son of Densuke Teraji (deceased) & Shina Teraji (deceased); married Lily Yuriko Teraji, Oct 19, 1946; children: Alan Robert, James Thomas, David George, Barbara Ann. **EDUCATION:** Los Angeles City College, associate in arts, 1940; George Williams College, BS, 1945, MS, 1948; University of Chicago, post graduate, 1955-56. **CAREER:** Los Angeles Unified School District, playground director, 1940-42; Manzanar Relocation Center, recreation director, 1942; Olivet Institute, groupwork/community organization, 1943-50; Department of Army, civil affairs, public welfare advisor, Japan, 1950-51, military history, Japan & Korea, 1951-52; Chicago Board of Education, Ray School, 1952-57, Washington School, 1957-61, Sherwood School, assistant principal, 1961-63, Hyde School, assistant principal, 1963-66, director of planning school attendance, 1966-76, Dept of Facilities, dept director, 1976-80, Dept of Maintenance and Rehabilitation, Bureau of Facilities, director, 1980-85, Operation Analysis, dept director, 1985-88. **ORGANIZA-TIONS:** Phi Delta Kappa, Professional Fraternity, 1975-88; Council of Educational Facility Planning, Midwest rep, 1973-80; America Association of School Administrators, 1973-88; Asian American Educators Association of Illinois, 1975-88; Japanese American Service Committee, vice president, 1973-76, president, 1976-80; JASC Housing Corporation, Retirement Home, Heiwa Terrace, board president, 1976-81, 1989-93; State of Illinois Asian American Advisory Council to the Governor, 1989-91; Chicago Japanese American Council, board of directors, vice president, 1983-93; JASC Keiro Extended Care Center Committee, charman, 1987-94. **HONORS/AWARDS:** Japanese American Citizens League, Brotherhood Award, 1967; Japanese American Service Committee Award, Outstanding Award, for service to the community, 1981; Chicago Nisei Athletic Association Award, 1970; United Way of Chicago, Silver Award, for outstanding service to the people of community, 1986; Annual Asian American Coalition Award, 1989; City of Chicago, Senior Citizens Hall of Fame Award, 1985; Order of the Rising Sun, Gold and Silver Rays Award, 1992; Chicago Area Council, Boy Scouts of America, Silver Beaver Award, 1978. **HOME ADDRESS:** 895 S Dwyer Ave, Arlington Heights, IL 60005, (708)577-7916.

TERAMOTO, YOSHITSUGU

Surgeon, health services administrator. Japanese American. **PERSONAL:** Born Dec 5, 1931, Honokaa, HI; son of Kaichi Teramoto and Tsugi Horita Teramoto; married Jill, Aug 11, 1973; children: Gregory, Jason, Jennifer. **EDUCATION:** Hiram College, BA, 1959; Hahnemann Medical College and Hospital, MD, 1963. **CAREER:** Highland Alameda County Hopital, rotating intern, 1963-64, surgery, resident, 1964-68; private practice, general surgeon, 1968-; East Bay Med/Surg Ctr, general partner 1986-, surgical director, 1993-. **ORGANIZATIONS:** Castro Valley Chamber of Commerce; Federated Ambulatory Surgery Assn; California Ambulatory Surgery Assn. **MILITARY SERVICE:** US Army, cpl, 1949-53. **BUSINESS ADDRESS:** General Partner, Surgical Director, East Bay Medical/Surgical Center, 20998 Redwood Rd, Castro Valley, CA 94546, (510)538-2828.

TEWARSON, REGINALD P.

Educator. Indo-American. **PERSONAL:** Born Nov 17, 1930, Pauri, Garhwal, Uttar Pradesh, India; son of Seth Narottam & Chand Mani Tewarson; divorced; children: Anita, Monique. **EDUCATION:** Lucknow University, BSc (with honors), 1950; Agra University, MSc, 1952; Boston University, PhD, 1961. **CAREER:** Lucknow Christian College, India, lecturer, 1951-57; Honeywell EDP Division, Wellesley Hill, Mass, senior scientist, 1960-64; State University of New York, assistant professor, 1964-66, associate professor, 1966-69, professor, 1969-89; leading professor, 1989-. **ORGANIZATIONS:** American Math Society, 1964-; Society of Ind & Applied Math, 1965-; Society for Math Biology, 1978-; International Conference Math Modeling, organizing committees, 1987, 1989, 1991. **HONORS/AWARDS:** Crusade Scholar, 1957-59; recipient of several merit awards; editorial board, Applied Math Letters, Math & Computer Modeling, Pan American Math Journal; NIH, consultant, 1973-80; several research grants. **SPECIAL ACHIEVEMENTS:** Author of the first book on "Sparse Matrices"; published 101 papers in refereed journals; fluent in English, Hindi, Urdu. **BUSINESS ADDRESS:** Leading Professor, Dept of

Applied Math & Statistics, State University of New York, Stony Brook, NY 11794-3600, (516)632-8368.

THADANI, RAJU

Airline company project manager. Indo-American. **PERSONAL:** Born Mar 19, 1965, Hyderabad, Andhra Pradesh, India; son of J H Thadani and S J Thadani; married Anuradha Thadani, Jul 3, 1989. **EDUCATION:** Mercy College, BS, 1989. **CAREER:** British Airways, pc specialist, 1989, pc/lan consultant, 1989-90, project manager, 1990-. **ORGANIZATIONS:** Communication Manager's Association, 1990-; Mercy College Alumni Association. **HONORS/AWARDS:** British Airways, Award for Excellence, 1992; Mercy College, Scholarship, 1986-88. **SPECIAL ACHIEVEMENTS:** Proficiency in Hindi Certificates 1 & 2, 1980. **HOME ADDRESS:** 53 Christie Ave, River Edge, NJ 07661, (201)261-1858. **BUSINESS ADDRESS:** Project Manager, British Airways, 75-20 Astoria Blvd, Jackson Heights, NY 11370, (718)397-4044.

THADHANI, KALOO C.

Research scientist. Pakistani American. **PERSONAL:** Born Dec 30, 1925, Hyderabad, Sind, Pakistan; son of Chandiram Jethmal Thadhani and Sitabai Chandiram Thadhani; married Rekha, Jan 15, 1959; children: Savita, Suresh. **EDUCATION:** Bombay University, BSc, 1947; Bombay University, Indian Institute of Science, PhD, 1951; University of Emory, 1959-60; University of Chicago, 1960-65. **CAREER:** Indian Institute of Science, India, research associate, 1950-52, Haffkine Institute, Bombay, research fellow, 1952-54; CIPLA Laboratories, Bombay, chief biochemist, 1954-59; Food Research Institute, research scientist, professor, 1960-65; Emory University, Dept of Microbiology, research fellow, 1959-60; TB Research Institute, chairman, research scientist, 1965-70; Christ Hospital, Dept of Pathology, immuno-microbiologist, 1970-78, chief pathologist, 1970-74; Cook County Hospital, director and chairman, Inf Disease Lab, 1978-. **BUSINESS ADDRESS:** Director, Infectious Disease Laboratory, Cook County Hospital, Hektoen Bldg, 1835 W Harrison St, Rm 605, Chicago, IL 60612.

THAKKAR, PRAVIN ASHARAM

Electronics company administrator. Indo-American. **PERSONAL:** Born Nov 18, 1946, Ahmedabad, Gujarat, India; son of Asharam Mohanlal Ghorkhoda Thakkar and Santok Ranchoddas Mulani Thakkar; married Premila; children: Sonal, Rakesh, Sima. **EDUCATION:** Detroit Institute of Technology, BSEE, 1974. **CAREER:** Self-employed, designer, printed circuit, 1974-81; Welex, Halliburton Co, drafting, supervisor, 1981-82; Baker-Hughes, team leader, documentation, 1982-85; Cummins Electronics, team leader, documentation, 1985-90, team leader, harness engineering, 1990-. **ORGANIZATIONS:** Society of Automotive Engineering, 1985-; Gujarati Samaj of Houston, treasurer, 1981-82. **HOME ADDRESS:** 4529 Post Horn Ct, Columbus, IN 47203-3215, (812)372-7050. **BUSINESS PHONE:** (812)377-5048.

THAKOR, NITISH VYOMESH

Educator. Indo-American. **PERSONAL:** Born Feb 19, 1952, Nagpur, India; son of Vyomesh H Thakor & Jayshree V Thakor; married Ruchira N Thakor, Dec 17, 1983; children: Mitali N, Milan N. **EDUCATION:** Indian Institute of Technology, Bombay, BTech, 1974; University of Wisconsin-Madison, MS, 1978, PhD, 1981. **CAREER:** Philips India Ltd, electronics engineer, 1974-76; University of Wisconsin, research asst, 1976-81; Northwestern University, assistant professor, 1981-83; Johns Hopkins Medical School, associate professor, 1983-. **ORGANIZATIONS:** IEEE, senior member, 1981-; Biomedical Engineering Society, 1991-. **HONORS/AWARDS:** National Science Foundation, Presidential Young Investigator Award, 1985; National Institutes of Health, Research Career Development Award, 1985-90; Fulbright Award, 1987; University of Wisconsin, Centennial Certificate, 1991; IIT, Bombay, National Merit Scholar, 1974. **SPECIAL ACHIEVEMENTS:** 60 scientific publications in international journals, 1981-93; books: Frontiers of Computers in Biomedical Eng, IEEE Press, 1994; Neuroengineering, Springer Verlag, to be published. **BUSINESS ADDRESS:** Associate Professor, Biomedical Eng Dept, Johns Hopkins University, 720 Rutland Ave, 701 Traylor Bldg, Baltimore, MD 21205, (410)955-7093.

THAKORE, KILLOL J.

Physician. Indo-American. **PERSONAL:** Born May 1, 1960, Jasdan, Gujarat, India; son of Jagdishchandra R Thakore and Pushpa J Thakore. **EDUCATION:** St Xavier's Science College, Gujarat, India, BSc, 1977; B J Medical College, Gujarat, India, MBBS, 1982; Sheth K M School of Post-graduate Medicine and Research & Sheth V S General Hospital, Gujarat, India, MD, radiology, 1988.

CAREER: Gujarat State Health and Medical Services Referral Hospital, medical officer, 1983-84; Sheth K M School of Post-graduate Medicine and Research and Sheth L G General Hospital, assoc radiologist, 1988-89; Metpath Inc, Department of Virology, research assoc, 1990; Michigan State University, McLaren Regional Medical Center, Department of Internal Medicine, PGY-I resident physician, 1990-91; Emory University School of Medicine, Department of Radiology, Division of Nuclear Medicine, PGY-IV, resident physician, 1991-93; Louisiana State University Medical Center, Department of Radiology, resident physician, 1993-. **ORGANIZATIONS:** American College of Physicians, associate; Society of Nuclear Medicine, cardiovascular council; Indian Radiological and Imaging Assn; Medical Council of India; Radiological Society of North America; American Roentgen Ray Society. **HONORS/ AWARDS:** National Scholar, 7 years. **SPECIAL ACHIEVEMENTS:** Author, works include: "Effects of Different ROIs for Background Correction on Relative Function on Kidneys in Patients with Unilateral Nephrectomy," presented, Society of Nuclear Medicine, 1992; "Pre-operative Localization of Parathyroid Tissue with Te-99m Sestamibi and I-123 Substraction Scanning: The Emory Experience," presented, American Federation of Clinical Research, 1993; "The Effects of Different ROIs for Background Correction on Relative Renal Function in Patients with Unilateral Nephrectomy," presented, Society of Nuclear Medicine, 1993; language proficiency: Gujarati, Hindi, spoken and written Sanskrit. **HOME ADDRESS:** 1201 West Esplanade Ave, Apt 805, Kenner, LA 70065. **BUSINESS ADDRESS:** Physician, Dept of Radiology, LSU Medical Centertals, 1542 Tulane Ave, New Orleans, LA 70112, (504)568-4646.

THAKORE, KIRIT JAMIYATRAM
Architect. Indo-American. **PERSONAL:** Born Apr 3, 1941, Gandevi, Gujarat, India; son of Jamiyatram and Kaushalya Ben; married Daya, Apr 26, 1970; children: Bhoomi. **EDUCATION:** BArch, 1964. **CAREER:** H M Patel, architect, 1965-70; Peter Seidner, architect, draftsman, 1970-71; J Glenn Hughes, architect, designer, 1972-73; Austin, architect, 1973-74; Sagent & Lundy, sr architect, designer, 1974-83; McGee Corp, architect, designer, 1983-; Random House, president, currently. **ORGANIZATIONS:** Associate of the Indian Institute of Architects; Royal Institute of British Architects. **HOME PHONE:** (708)544-5623. **BUSINESS ADDRESS:** President, Random House, 4205 St Charles Rd, Bellwood, IL 60104, (708)544-5585.

THAKUR, MANISH
Investment banker, journalist. Indo-American. **PERSONAL:** Born Nov 20, 1966, London, England; son of Dina Nath Thakur and Bimla Thakur. **EDUCATION:** University of London, BSc (honors), economics; Columbia University, School of Business, MBA. **CAREER:** Hong Kong and Shanghai Bank, Hong Kong, intl officer, 1989-90; Merrill Lynch, associate, 1992-. **ORGANIZATIONS:** University of London India Society, president, 1988; Beta Gamma Sigma; USA-India Foundation; IMPACT. **SPECIAL ACHIEVEMENTS:** Journalist, various articles in: Wall Street Journal, Asian Wall Street Journal, 1990. **BUSINESS ADDRESS:** Associate, Merrill Lynch & Co, World Financial Center, North Tower, New York, NY 10281-1330, (212)449-1437.

THANGARAJ, SANDY
Chemical engineer. Indo-American. **PERSONAL:** Born Dec 3, 1934, Madras, India; son of Sankarnarayan Iyer (deceased) & Chinnathai Ammal (deceased); married Jarka Kauchner Thangaraj, Aug 9, 1980; children: Neena, Paula-Milena Castano (step-daughter). **EDUCATION:** University of Madras, BS, chemistry, 1954, MS, chem engineer, 1956, PhD, chem engineer, 1966; National College of Rubber Technology, diploma, 1958. **CAREER:** Plastics & Rubber Inds, East Africa, plant manager, chief chemist, 1966-71; East Africa Globe Superior Inc, R&D chemist, 1971-72; Avonsole Company, technical director, 1972-75; Teknor Apex Co, Process Products Rubber Division, manager, 1975-79; Industrias Modernas, Colombia-South America Mfg & Technical, director, 1979-80; O'Sullivan-Vulcan International, R&D and Process, manager, 1982-87; Rubber Inds Inc, vice-president/technical, 1988-. **ORGANIZATIONS:** American Chemical Society, 1972-; Rubber Division-American Chemical Society, 1972-; American Institute of Chemists, fellow, 1972-89, 1991; Twin Cities Rubber Group, 1988-; American Society of Testing Material, 1993-; International Union of Pure & Applied Chemistry, affiliate member, 1993. **HONORS/AWARDS:** Dictionary of African Biography, Merit Certificate, 1970; Twin Cities Rubber Group, Membership Generation Plaque, 1993. **SPECIAL ACHIEVEMENTS:** Languages: Spanish, Swahili. **BUSINESS ADDRESS:** Vice President Technical, Rubber Industries Inc, 200 Cavanaugh Dr, Shakopee, MN 55379, (612)445-1320.

THAN PE, TRUETT HACKETT. *See* **MYINT, THAN HTUN.**

THAO, CHRISTOPHER TENG
Litigation attorney. Chinese American/Hmong American. **PERSONAL:** Born Jul 6, 1957, Xiengkhouang, Lao People's Democratic Republic; son of Wa Moua Thao and Xia Yang; married Sylvia X Thao, Jun 1981; children: Pajjar, Gao-Jai, Mitchia, Ho-Shia, Ho-Seng. **EDUCATION:** Hamline University, BA, political science, 1983; William Mitchell College of Law, JD, 1986. **CAREER:** Nilva & Frish, PA, attorney, 1986-89; Robins, Kaplan, Miller & Ciresi, attorney, 1989-91; Thao & Associates, attorney, 1991-. **ORGANIZATIONS:** Hmong American Partnership, co-founder & past chairman, 1990-; MN Attorney General's Hmong Working Group, 1990-91; City of St Paul Southeast Asian Working Group, 1990; MN State Bar Association; MN Trial Lawyer Association; National Asian-Pacific American Bar Association; Hennepin County Bar Association. **HONORS/AWARDS:** Council on Asian Pacific Minnesotans Distinguished Service, 1993. **SPECIAL ACHIEVEMENTS:** Published numerous articles in MN Bench & Bar, Hmong World, Haiv Hmoob Magazine. **BIOGRAPHICAL SOURCES:** USA Today Newspaper; Almanac-TV2, St Paul; KSTP-TV, Minneapolis; St Paul Pioneer Press, 1986; Minneapolis Star & Tribune; Today Show; Baltimore Sun; William Mitchell Magazine; Christian Science Monitor-TV. **BUSINESS ADDRESS:** Attorney, Thao & Associates, 7038 Brooklyn Blvd, Minneapolis, MN 55429-1370, (612)560-1185.

THIRUVATHUKAL, KRIS V.
Educator. Indo-American. **PERSONAL:** Born May 1, 1925, Shertalla, Kerala, India; son of Mr and Mrs George K Thiruvathukal; divorced; children: George K, Maria K, Cheryl K. **EDUCATION:** University of Kerala, India, BSc; Boston College, MS; St Louis University, PhD. **CAREER:** Duquesne University; Lewis University, professor, currently. **ORGANIZATIONS:** Sigma Xi. **BIOGRAPHICAL SOURCES:** Author, Digestive tract of painted turtle, Chrysemys picta, Anima Morph & Phys, 1960; Histology of the pancreas of Chrysemys picta, Amer Micro Soc, 1960. **HOME ADDRESS:** 2213 Arden Place, Joliet, IL 60435-5401, (815)725-7028.

TIANGCO, EDDIE EUGENIO
Sales manager. Filipino American. **PERSONAL:** Born Mar 26, 1941, Manila, Philippines; son of Clint N Tiangco and Angelina E Tiangco (deceased); married Lettie Ong Tiangco, May 26, 1976; children: Angeline O, Andrew J. **EDUCATION:** Far Eastern University, BSC, accounting, 1962; Lyceum of the Philippines, marketing, 1964; Mt St Antonio College, MS, 1981. **CAREER:** Stetson-Creative, manager, 1970-76; Cert-Fresh Foods, chief financial officer, controller, 1986; Gesuetti Bros Seafoods, controller, 1976-86; Red Chamber Co, financial consultant, 1987; Escuadro Food Sales Inc, chief financial officer, controller, 1987-91; Orient Fisheries Inc, general mgr, sales, 1992-. **ORGANIZATIONS:** Parents United, vice pres, 1981, Exec Committee, director. **HOME ADDRESS:** 1708 E Almanac Dr, West Covina, CA 91791, (818)918-6369. **BUSINESS ADDRESS:** General Manager, Orient Fisheries, Inc, 1912 E Vernon Ave, Ste 110, Vernon, CA 90058, (213)231-1600.

TIEN, CHANG-LIN
Educational administrator. Chinese American. **PERSONAL:** Born Jul 24, 1935, Wuhan, China; son of Yun-Di Lee and Yun-Chien Tien; married Di-Hwa Tien, 1959; children: Norman Chihnan, Phyllis Chihping, Christine Chihyih. **EDUCATION:** National Taiwan University, BS, 1955; University of Louisville, MME, 1957; Princeton University, MA, 1959, PhD, 1959. **CAREER:** University of California, Irvine, executive vice chancellor, distinguished professor, 1988-90; University of California, Berkeley, mechanical engineering, acting asst professor, 1959-60, asst professor, 1960-64, associate professor, 1964-68, professor, 1968-89, 1990-, Thermal Systems Division, chair, 1969-71, Department of Mechanical Engineering, chair, 1974-81, vice chancellor, research, 1983-85, A Martin Berlin Chair Professor, 1987-88, 1990-, chancellor, 1990-. **ORGANIZATIONS:** ASME, Basic Engineering, vice president, 1988-90, honorary member, 1993; Asian Law Journal, Boalt Hall, board of advisors, 1993-; Aspen Institute Domestic Strategy Group, 1992-; Princeton University, board of trustees, 1991-; Wells Fargo Bank, board of directors, 1991-; numerous industrial, governmental and educational organizations, consultant, 1971-; American Association for the Advancement of Science, fellow, 1991, board of directors, 1992-; American Society for Engineering Education, National Advisory Council, 1993; Northeastern University, China, board of trustees, 1994; AIAA, fellow, 1985. **HONORS/AWARDS:** ASME Heat Transfer Div, Best Paper of the Year Award, 1993; Society of Hong Kong Scholars, Most Distinguished Chinese Scholar, 1989; AIChE-ASME, Max

Jakob Memorial Award, 1981; Japan Society for the Promotion of Science, Senior US Scientist Fellowship, 1980; Alexander von Humbolt Foundation, West Germany, Senior US Scientist Award, 1979; Guggenheim Fellow, 1965; numerous honorary degrees and fellowships. **SPECIAL ACHIEVEMENTS:** Journal of Quantitative Spectroscopy & Quantitative Transfer, associate editor, 1971-; International Journal of Heat and Mass Transfer, editor, 1981-; International Communications in Heat and Mass Transfer, editor, 1981-; Experimental Heat Transfer, editor-in-chief, 1987-; one book, seven edited volumes, nineteen review and monograph articles, over 260 refereed research papers. **BUSINESS ADDRESS:** Chancellor, University of California, Berkeley, Office of the Chancellor, 200 California Hall, Berkeley, CA 94720, (510)642-7464.

TIEN, H. TI
Educator. Chinese American. **PERSONAL:** Born Jan 17, 1938, Beijing, China; son of F C Tien and W-T Chow; married Angelica Leitmannova; children: Stephen, David, Adrienne, Jennifer. **EDUCATION:** University of Nebraska, BS, chem eng, 1953; Temple University, PhD, 1963. **CAREER:** Allied Chemical Corp, chemical engineer, 1955-57; Eastern Pennsylvania Psychiatric Institute, senior researcher, 1957-63; Northeastern University, associate professor, 1963-66; Michigan State University, professor, 1966-, Biophysics Dept, chairman, 1978-82. **ORGANIZATIONS:** ACS; AAAS. **HONORS/AWARDS:** Academia Sinica, honorary member, 1979-; Center for Interface Sciences, STU, external director, 1992-. **SPECIAL ACHIEVEMENTS:** Bilayer Lipid Membranes (BLM): Theory & Practice, 1974; Membrane Photochemistry & Biophysics, 1989; BLM-based Biosensors, 1992. **BUSINESS ADDRESS:** Professor, Physiology Dept, Michigan State University, 111 Giltner Hall, East Lansing, MI 48824, (517)355-6475.

TIEN, PING KING
Electronics engineer. Chinese American. **PERSONAL:** Born Aug 2, 1919, Chekieng, China; son of N S & C S Yen Tien; married Nancy N Y Chen, Apr 19, 1952; children: Emily-Ju-Psia, Julia Ju-Wen. **EDUCATION:** National Central University, China, BS, 1942; Stanford University, MS, 1948, PhD, 1951. **CAREER:** Stanford University, research associate, 1951-52; Bell Tel Labs, technical staff member, 1952-59, Department of Electron Physics Research, head, 1959-84, Department of High Speed Electronics, head, 1985-91, Photonics Research Lab, fellow emeritus, 1990-. **ORGANIZATIONS:** National Academy of Science; National Academy of Engineering; Institute of American Physics; Acad Sci Republic of China; Academic Sci of Third World; Sigma Xi. **HONORS/AWARDS:** Chinese Institute of Engineers, Achievement Award, 1966; AT&T Labs, fellow, 1983; IEEE, Morris N Liebmann Award, 1979, fellow; Optical Society of America, fellow. **SPECIAL ACHIEVEMENTS:** Contributor of scientific and technical articles to professional journals; researcher for the following areas: device physics; microwave electronics; electron dynamics; wave propagation; noise; ferrites; acoustics in solids; gas lasers; superconductivity; integrated optics. **BUSINESS ADDRESS:** Fellow Emeritus, Photonics Research Lab, Bell Telephone Labs Inc, 101 Crawford Corner Rd, Holmdel, NJ 07733.*

TIKOO, MOHAN L.
Educator. Indo-American. **PERSONAL:** Born Feb 15, 1943, Srinagar, Kashmir, India; son of Sri Kantha Tikoo and Prabha Vati Tikoo; married Jaikishuri Tikoo, Jun 2, 1969; children: Sonia. **EDUCATION:** University of Kashmir, BA, 1960, MA, 1963; University of Kansas, MA, 1980, PhD, 1984. **CAREER:** University of Kashmir, assistant professor, 1966-78; University of Kansas, assistant instructor, 1978-84; Southeast Missouri State University, assistant professor, 1984-88, associate professor, 1988-93, professor, 1993-. **ORGANIZATIONS:** American Mathematical Society, 1980-; Mathematical Association of America, 1988-; Planetary Society, 1983-; International Platform Society, 1992-; National Geographic Society, 1992-. **HONORS/AWARDS:** University of Kansas, Florence Black Teaching Award, 1982, May Landis Fellowship, 1981, graduate school fellowship, 1982, 1983; Southeast Missouri State University, Merit Award, 1987, 1989. **SPECIAL ACHIEVEMENTS:** Contributor to research journals; reviewer for Mathematical Reviews; co-director: Saturday College for gifted high school students, 1986, 1987, 1988, 1991. **HOME ADDRESS:** 2409 Lynnwood Drive, Cape Girardeau, MO 63701, (314)335-1181. **BUSINESS ADDRESS:** Professor, Southeast Missouri State University, One University Plaza, 211 Johnson Hall, Cape Girardeau, MO 63701, (314)651-2778.

TIN, BO
Industrial engineer. Myanmar American. **PERSONAL:** Born Jul 20, 1936, Pyinmana, Myanmar; son of U Tin Ohn and Daw Ngwe Kyin; married Iris Tin,

Apr 3, 1966; children: Kyaw Soe, Moe Thant, Thu Ra, Kyaw Myo. **EDUCATION:** Montana State University, BSIE, 1960; University of Rangoon, LLB, 1964. **CAREER:** Productivity Center, Myanmar, productivity engr, 1960-65; Industrial Training Center, Myanmar, training director, 1965-68; Rubber Industry, Myanmar, factory mgr, 1968-75; Leather Works Factory, Myanmar, factory mgr, 1975-79; Ministry of Industry, Myanmar, Leather Factories, project director, 1978-80; Northrop Corp, Aircraft Division, industrial engrng specialist, 1981-. **ORGANIZATIONS:** AIIE, senior member, 1965-; Burmese Assn of Scientists and Engineers, 1989-. **HONORS/AWARDS:** Northrop Corp, Industrial Engineering Excellence through Achievement Award, 1984; Myanmar State Govt, Scholarship to Study in USA, 1955; Rangoon University, Collegiate Scholarship, 1953. **SPECIAL ACHIEVEMENTS:** Language proficiency: read, write, speak fluently, Myanmar. **BUSINESS ADDRESS:** Industrial Engineer Specialist, Aircraft Division, Northrop Corporation, One Northrop Ave, M/S D.5026/56, Hawthorne, CA 90250, (310)332-5718.

TING, JAN C.
Educator. Chinese American. **PERSONAL:** Born Dec 17, 1948, Ann Arbor, MI; son of Sik Woo Ting and Ging Mei Kang Ting; married Helen Page Ting, Jul 17, 1971; children: Margaret P, Mary J. **EDUCATION:** Oberlin College, BA, 1970; University of Hawaii, MA, 1972; Harvard Law School, JD, 1975. **CAREER:** Pepper, Hamilton & Scheetz, attorney at law, 1975-77; Temple University, professor of law, 1977-; Widener University, visiting professor, 1985-86, 1990; US Dept of Justice, INS, director of international affairs, 1990-93. **ORGANIZATIONS:** East-West Center, board of governors, 1984-90; Civil Rights Reviewing Authority, US Dept of Educ, 1982-84; Delaware State Personnel Commission, chairman, 1986-90; Republican National Convention, delegate, 1988. **BUSINESS ADDRESS:** Professor, School of Law, Temple University, 1719 N Broad St, Philadelphia, PA 19122, (215)204-8020.

TING, JOSEPH K.
Mechanical engineer, educator. Chinese American/Japanese American/Filipino American. **PERSONAL:** Born Jan 23, 1950, Manila, Luzon, Philippines; married Monique; children: Audrey Adrienne, William Alexander. **EDUCATION:** De La Salle University, BS, mech engineering, 1972; Massachusetts Institute of Technology, MS, mech engineering, 1974; University of Ottawa, MBA program, financial mgt, 1981-86. **CAREER:** Brier Manufacturing Co, product engineer, 1974, plant manager, 1975; Natl Research Council (Canada), assoc engineer, 1975-86; Rensselaer Polytechnic Institute, adjunct professor, 1992-; New York State Dormitory Authority, sr mech engineer, 1986-. **ORGANIZATIONS:** American Soc of Heating, Refrigerating & Air Conditioning Engineers, Northeast Chapter, president, 1991-92, Region I, director & regional chairman, 1994-97, asst regional chm, 1992-94; Massachusetts Inst of Tech Alumni Club, president, 1992-94; Chinese Community Center, president, 1992-94; US Natl Committee, Intl Inst of Refrigeration, 1992; Who's Who in Environmental Registry, 1992. **HONORS/AWARDS:** ASHRAE, Outstanding Performance, 1988, 1991, Black Ink Award, newsletter editor, 1990; Chinese Community Center, Distinguished Service, 1991. **SPECIAL ACHIEVEMENTS:** Projects: conversion of Rolls Royce RB211 jet engine to gas pumping engine, research engineer, gas as an alternative to fuel, 1975-78; design of textile machinery for blended fabric (man-made with natural), research engineering student, new set of blended fabrics for civilian & military apparel, 1972-76; publications, contributor to: Essentials of Engineering Economics, 1983; Canadian Financial Management, 1983; Case Study for Canadian Financial Mgt, 1983; Computer-Aided Design Drafting, 1987; ASHRAE Standard 15, (Safety Code for Mech Refrigeration), 1992; Proficient in English, French, Mandarin, Tagalog, Spanish. **HOME ADDRESS:** PO Box 234, Delmar, NY 12054.

TING, LEE HSIA
Educator. Chinese American. **PERSONAL:** Born Feb 7, 1923, Yangchow, Jiangsu, China; daughter of Sing-Wu Hsu & Su-Cheng Huang Hsu; married Nai-tung Ting, Nov 11, 1948 (deceased). **EDUCATION:** National Central University, BA, 1944; Mount Holyoke College, MA, 1948; University of Texas, Austin, MLS, 1964; University of Chicago, PhD, 1969. **CAREER:** Edinburg, Texas, Independent School District, librarian, 1959-61; Harlingen Public Schools, librarian, 1961-65; Pharr-San Juan-Alamo Public Schools, librarian, 1965-66; University of Chicago, lecturer, 1969-71; Northern Illinois University, associate professor, 1973-77; Western Illinois University, associate professor, beginning 1977, professor, 1981-. **ORGANIZATIONS:** Chinese-American Librarians Association, director, 1978-82, vice president, 1979-80, president, 1980-. **HONORS/AWARDS:** Fulbright Senior Scholars Program, 1985-86. **SPECIAL ACHIEVEMENTS:** Author, Government Control of the

Press in Modern China: 1900-1949, Harvard University, 1974; Chinese Folk Narratives: A Bibliographical Guide, 1974; dozens of articles published in professional journals. **HOME ADDRESS:** 10 Woodland Ln, Macomb, IL 61455, (309)837-3803.

TING, ROBERT YEN-YING
Government official, educator. Chinese American. **PERSONAL:** Born Mar 8, 1942, Kwei-Yang, China; son of Chi-yung Ting and Shou-feng Ting; married Teresa Y Ting, Jun 3, 1967; children: Paul H, Peggy Y. **EDUCATION:** National Taiwan University, BS, 1964; MIT, MS, 1967; University of California, San Diego, PhD, 1971. **CAREER:** MIT, research staff, 1967-68; University of California, San Diego, research assistant, 1968-71, research staff, 1971; Naval Research Lab, research engineer, 1971-77, supervisory engineer/section head, 1977-80, supervisory physicist/section head, 1980-87, supervisory physicist/branch head, 1987-, professor, currently. **ORGANIZATIONS:** Acoustical Society of America, fellow, 1985-; American Chemical Society, 1974-86; American Ceramics Society, 1987-; American Institute of Chemical Engineers, 1975-81; Society of Rheology, 1973-81. **HONORS/AWARDS:** George Washington University, Professional Lectureship, 1974-80; Acoustical Society of America, Fellow, 1989; NRL, Excellence in Leadership for Technology Transfer, 1991. **SPECIAL ACHIEVEMENTS:** More than 100 publications in refereed journals in polymer science, chemical engineering, materials science and acoustics. **BUSINESS ADDRESS:** Professor, Naval Research Laboratory, USRD, PO Box 568337, Code 5910, Orlando, FL 32856-8337, (407)857-5156.

TING, SAMUEL C. C.
Educator, physicist. Chinese American. **PERSONAL:** Born Jan 27, 1936, Ann Arbor, MI; son of Kuan H & Jeanne Wong Ting; married Susan Carol Marks, Apr 28, 1985; children: Jeanne Min, Amy Min, Christopher M. **EDUCATION:** University of Michigan, BS, engineering, 1959, MS, 1960, PhD, 1962. **CAREER:** Columbia University, instructor of physics, 1964, assistant professor, 1965-67; Deutsches Elektronen-Synchroton, Hamburg, 1966; Massachusetts Institute of Technology, Department of Physics, associate professor, 1967-68, professor, 1969-, Thomas Dudley Cabot Institute professor, 1977-. **ORGANIZATIONS:** Natl Academy of Science; Pakistani Academy of Science, foreign member; Soviet Academy of Science, USSR, foreign member; Academia Sinica, foreign member. **HONORS/AWARDS:** Nobel Prize in Physics, 1976; Beijing Normal College, Honorary Prof, 1987; Jiatong University, Shanghai, Honorary Prof, 1987; University of Bologna, Italy, Honorary Prof, 1988; Ford Foundation, CERN, European Organization for Nuclear Research, fellow, 1963; American Academy of Science and Arts, fellow, 1975; honorary degrees: University of Michigan, ScD, 1978; Chinese University, Hong Kong, ScD, 1987; University of Bologna, Italy, 1988; Columbia University, 1990; Moscow State University, 1991. **SPECIAL ACHIEVEMENTS:** American Physical Society, Div Particles & Fields, program consultant, 1970; editorial board, Nuclear Instruments and Methods, Mathematical Modeling; advisor, Journal of Modern Physics A; Italian Republic, De Gasperi Prize, for science, 1988; US Government, Ernest Orlando Lawrence Award, 1976; Society of Engineering Science, A E Eringen Medal, 1977; Science City of Brescia, Italy, Gold Medal in Science, 1988; Town of Taormina, Golden Leopard Award, 1988; contributor to Physical Review and Physical Review Letters. **BUSINESS ADDRESS:** Professor, Dept of Physics, Massachusetts Institute of Technology, 77 Massachusetts Ave, Cambridge, MA 02139.*

TING, SANDRA
Company executive. Chinese American. **PERSONAL:** Born Nov 7, 1960, New York, NY; daughter of Er-Yi Ting and Theresa Ting. **EDUCATION:** Mount Holyoke College, BA, 1984; University of Southern California, School of Law, JD, 1987. **CAREER:** Inner City Broadcasting Corp, assistant to the president, 1982; Rockamerica Music Video Seminar, coordinator, 1983; 20th Century Fox Film Corp, legal affairs extern, 1986-87; Wyman, Bautzer, Kuchel & Silbert, entertainment, corporate associate, 1987-90; Hill, Wynne, Troop & Meisinger, entertainment associate, 1990-91; Media Assets, assistant vice president, acquisitions, 1993; Satellite Television Asian Region Ltd, assistant vice president, 1993-94; Orbit Communications Co, director of business affairs & production, 1994-. **ORGANIZATIONS:** American Bar Association, 1987-; Los Angeles County Bar Association, 1987-90; California State Bar, 1988-91, 1994-. **HONORS/AWARDS:** Mount Holyoke College, Abbey Howe Turner Award for Excellence in Biology, 1983. **SPECIAL ACHIEVEMENTS:** Fluent in Manadarin Chinese; literate in French. **HOME ADDRESS:** 1131 Alta Loma Rd, Los Angeles, CA 90069. **BUSINESS ADDRESS:** Director of Business Affairs & Production, Orbit Satellite Television & Radio Network, Via Raffaele Costi 60, 00155 Rome, Italy, 396-40796310.

TING, SHIH-FAN
Educator (retired). Chinese American. **PERSONAL:** Born Sep 27, 1917, Changde, Hunan, China; son of Zhi-Jun Ting and Shan Lun Hu Ting; married Teh-Fin Liu Ting, Nov 12, 1947; children: Grace. **EDUCATION:** National Zhejiang University, BS, chemistry, 1941; University of Alabama, MS, 1957, PhD, 1960. **CAREER:** Fisk University, asst prof of chemistry, 1960-65; Duquesne University, post-doctoral research fellow, 1965-66; Millersville State College, assoc prof of chemistry, 1966-69, prof of chemistry, 1969-83. **ORGANIZATIONS:** American Chemical Soc, 1960-; Sigma Xi, 1960-. **SPECIAL ACHIEVEMENTS:** Author, articles: Talanta, 3:240, 1960, 7:269, 1961; Inorg Chem, 5:696, 1966; Can J Chem, 45:425, 1967; J Chem Educ, 60:375, 1983. **HOME ADDRESS:** 777 E Valley Blvd, #102, Alhambra, CA 91801, (818)576-7168.

TING, T. C.
Educator. Chinese American. **PERSONAL:** Born Feb 8, 1935, China; married Shirley Ting, Sep 3, 1967; children: Lena, Yvonne. **EDUCATION:** Taiwan Normal University, BEd, 1962; Central Washington State College, MEd, 1965; Washington State University, MS, 1968, PhD, 1969. **CAREER:** Virginia Polytechnic Institute and State University, assistant professor, 1969-72; George Institute of Technology, associate professor, 1972-78; National Bureau of Standards, computer scientist, 1978-81; Worchester Polytechnic Institute, Computer Science Department, head, 1981-87; University of Connecticut, Engineering, associate dean, 1987-. **ORGANIZATIONS:** UPE, Honor Society for Computing Science, president, 1985-90; Association for Computing Machinery, 1967-. **HONORS/AWARDS:** Department of Commerce, Distinguished Service Award, 1980. **SPECIAL ACHIEVEMENTS:** Published three books, five book chapters, and over seventy papers and conference presentations in computer science. **BUSINESS ADDRESS:** Associate Dean and Professor, University of Connecticut, School of Engineering, Storrs Mansfield, CT 06269-0001, (203)486-5462.

TING, THOMAS CHI TSAI
Educator. Chinese American. **PERSONAL:** Born Feb 9, 1933, Taipei, Taiwan; son of Pai Kou Ting and Shan Lee; married Romana T K Ting, Dec 31, 1962; children: Albert, Bennett. **EDUCATION:** National Taiwan University, BS, 1956; Brown University, PhD, 1962. **CAREER:** Brown University, research associate, 1962-63, assistant professor, 1963-65; University of Illinois at Chicago, assistant professor, 1965-66, associate professor, 1966-70, professor, 1970-; Stanford University, visiting professor, 1972-73. **BUSINESS ADDRESS:** Professor, University of Illinois Chicago, 842 W Taylor St, CEMM Dept (M/C246), Chicago, IL 60607-7023.

TING, YING JI
Librarian. Chinese American. **PERSONAL:** Born Feb 15, 1927, Lanchow, Kansu, China; son of Yao-Shi Ting and Chün-chih Chen; married Lisa Ting, Mar 15, 1958; children: Martha Lusk, David. **EDUCATION:** UCLA, BA, 1956; USC, MSLS, 1959, MS, 1969. **CAREER:** Rand Corp, Oriental Collections, librarian, 1968-70; UCLA Library, cataloger. **ORGANIZATIONS:** ALA, 1960-; CLA. **HOME ADDRESS:** 1595 Fulton Ave, Monterey Park, CA 91755, (818)573-1988.

TING CANG-KIM, DONNA MARIE
Account executive. Filipino American/Japanese American/Chinese American. **PERSONAL:** Born Jul 14, 1957, Honolulu, HI; daughter of Dyniscio Ting Cang and Theodora M Ting Cang; children: Vince E Parengit, Vanessa E Parengit. **EDUCATION:** University of Hawaii, BS, 1978. **CAREER:** Professional Career Dev, sr consultant, 1985-88; Centex Telemanagement Inc, sr membership director, 1988-90; Business Telemanagement Inc, sr marketing mgr, 1990-91; Telwest Communications, sr acct exec, 1991-. **ORGANIZATIONS:** South OC Chamber; NAFE; Women in Sales. **HOME ADDRESS:** 22912 Leo Lane, Lake Forest, CA 92630, (714)770-1450. **BUSINESS ADDRESS:** Senior Account Executive, Telwest Communications, 51 Columbia, Ste 200, Aliso Viejo, CA 92656, (714)362-4080.

TOBA, HACHIRO HAROLD
Researcher. Japanese American. **PERSONAL:** Born Aug 24, 1932, Puunene, HI; son of Jinsaburo Toba and Haru Uemae Toba; married Matsuko Matsuura, Sep 6, 1958; children: Wynne, Rhonda, Luanne. **EDUCATION:** University of Hawaii, BS, 1957, MS, 1961; Purdue University, PhD, 1966. **CAREER:** US Department of Agriculture, research entomologist, 1965-. **ORGANIZATIONS:** American Association for the Advancement of Science; Entomological Society of America; South Carolina Entomological Society;

Sigma Xi. **HONORS/AWARDS:** Purdue University, Purdue Research Foundation Graduate Fellowship, 1964. **SPECIAL ACHIEVEMENTS:** 106 publications in entomology. **MILITARY SERVICE:** US Army, sp-3, 1952-54; Meritorious service w/metal pendant. **HOME ADDRESS:** 771 Ames Rd, Selah, WA 98942. **BUSINESS ADDRESS:** Research Entomologist, USDA Agricultural Research Service, 3706 W Nob Hill Blvd, Yakima, WA 98902, (509)575-5877.

TODA, HAROLD KEIJI
Insurance executive (retired), CPA (retired). Japanese American. **PERSONAL:** Born Nov 6, 1925, Honolulu, HI; son of Sukeichi Toda & Kikuyo Yamamoto; married Sali, Sep 27, 1968; children: Caia Keiko Maglinao. **EDUCATION:** Harvard Business School, 1954; University of Hawaii. **CAREER:** Connecticut General Life, assistant manager, 1965-73; Mutual Life Insurance Co of New York, assistant manager, 1973-76; Aetna Life Insurance Co, Honolulu, assistant manager, 1976-80; N America Insurance Agency Ltd, manager, 1980-84; TNT Assoc Inc, president, 1982-. **ORGANIZATIONS:** American Association CPA/Hawaii ACPA, 1975-; National Association Life Underwriters, 1965-; MENSA, proctor coordination, 1981-; American Diabetes Association, volunteer, 1983-; PSI World, instructor, 1976-. **MILITARY SERVICE:** Army, e-4, 1945-47. **BUSINESS ADDRESS:** President, TNT Associates Inc, 1040 South King, #101, Honolulu, HI 96814, (808)536-7005.

TODD, KATHRYN DOI
Judge. Japanese American. **PERSONAL:** Born Jan 14, 1942, Los Angeles, CA; daughter of Noboru Doi & Fumiye Kawamura Doi; divorced; children: Mia Doi. **EDUCATION:** Stanford University, AB, 1963; Loyola Law School, JD, 1970. **CAREER:** Los Angeles, private practice, 1971-77; Los Angeles Municipal Court, judge, 1978-81; Los Angeles Superior Court, judge, 1981-. **ORGANIZATIONS:** California Judges Association, 1978-; California Asian Judges Association, president, 1980; Los Angeles County Law Library, trustee, 1990-, president, 1993; National Association of Women Judges, founding member; Japanese American Cultural and Community Center, vice president; Judical Council Advisory Comm on Gender Bias in the Courts, Crimnial and Juvenile Court Subcommittee, chair, 1987-90. **BUSINESS ADDRESS:** Judge, Los Angeles Superior Court, 111 N Hill St, Department 25, Los Angeles, CA 90012-3117, (213)974-5627.

TODO, SATORU
Surgeon, educator. Japanese American. **PERSONAL:** Born Oct 30, 1947, Kogoshima, Japan; son of Mansaku Todo and Hatsue Uto; married Noriko, May 12, 1974; children: Akira, Tsuyoshi, Takashi. **EDUCATION:** Kyushu University, MD, 1972. **CAREER:** Kyushu University, resident, 1972-75, research fellow, 1975-80, assistant, 1980-84; University of Pittsburgh, research fellow, 1984-85, visiting assistant professor of surgery, 1985-87, associate professor of surgery, 1987-. **ORGANIZATIONS:** Japan Surgical Society; Japanese Society of Gastroenterological Surgery; Japanese Society of Hepatology; Japanese Society of Clinical Electron Microscopy; American Society of Transplant Surgeons; Society of University Surgeons; Transplantation Society of Australia & New Zealand. **SPECIAL ACHIEVEMENTS:** Over 300 articles published in scientific journals. **BUSINESS ADDRESS:** Associate Professor of Surgeory, University of Pittsburgh, 3601 Fifth Ave, 5C Falk Clinic, Pittsburgh, PA 15213, (412)624-0112.

TOKUDA, WENDY
Broadcast journalist. Japanese American. **PERSONAL:** Born 1950, Seattle, WA; daughter of George & Tama Tokuda; married Richard Hall, May 1979; children: Mikka Rose, Maggie. **EDUCATION:** Whitman College, 1968-69; University of Washington, political science. **CAREER:** King TV, Seattle, Public Affairs Department, secretary, 1974-75, on-air reporter, 1975, weekend anchor, 1976-77; KPIX, reporter, 1978-80, 6 & 11 pm news broadcasts, lead anchor, 1980-87, 6 pm news broadcast, lead anchor, 1987-91; KNBC-TV, co-anchor, 1991-. **HONORS/AWARDS:** Emmy Award recipient. **SPECIAL ACHIEVEMENTS:** Asian Pacific American Legal Center of Southern California Seventh Annual Awards Dinner, emcee, 1992; co-author: Humphrey the Humpback Whale, 1987; Shiro in Love, 1989; founder, monthly reading group; founder, Asian American Journalists Association, Bay Area Chapter. **BUSINESS ADDRESS:** Anchorwoman, Six O'Clock News, KNBC-TV, 3000 W Alameda Ave, Burbank, CA 91523, (818)840-4444.*

TOKUNAGA, HOWARD TAIRA
Educator. Japanese American. **PERSONAL:** Born Sep 17, 1957, San Jose, CA; son of Katsumi Tokunaga and Grayce Tokunaga; married Anna Sala, Dec

24, 1992; children: Stephanie Sala, Andre Sala, Nicolas Sala, Megan. **EDUCATION:** University of California, Santa Cruz, BA, psychology, 1979; University of California, Berkeley, PhD, psychology, 1989. **CAREER:** University of California, Berkeley, graduate teaching assistant, 1981-89, visiting instructor, 1987-89; San Jose State, professor of psychology, 1989-. **ORGANIZATIONS:** American Psychological Association, 1984-; Society for Industrial Organization Psychology, 1992-; American Educational Research Association, 1988-90. **HONORS/AWARDS:** University of California, Berkeley, Outstanding Graduate Student Instructor, 1987; University of California, Santa Cruz, Crown Service Award, 1979. **SPECIAL ACHIEVEMENTS:** Co-author, Introduction to Design and Analysis, Freeman, 1992; author, "The Use and Abuse of Credit," Journal of Economic Psychology, 1993; co-author, "Empirical Test of the Glass Ceiling," SIOP, 1993; author, "Ethical Issues in Consultation," Professional Psychology, 1984. **BUSINESS ADDRESS:** Professor, San Jose State University, One Washington Sq, DMH 157, San Jose, CA 95192-0120, (408)924-5649.

TOKUNAGA, KATSUMI
Insurance agent. Japanese American. **PERSONAL:** Born Jun 22, 1923, Clarksburg, CA; son of Moju Tokunaga & Tamoki Ozawa Tokunaga; married Miyoko Grayce Tokunaga, Sep 11, 1954; children: Pamela, Paul, Susan, Howard, Kevin. **EDUCATION:** Duluth Junior College, AA, 1945; University of California, Davis, BS, 1950; University of Minnesota, graduate studies, 1951-52. **CAREER:** Franklin Life Insurance Co, special agent, district manager, 1953-54, Golden Gate Agency, agency manager, 1954-. **ORGANIZATIONS:** Fuji Towers, San Jose, community relations, vice president, 1975-; San Jose Buddhist Church, vice president, president, 1971-75; Buddhist Churches of America, vice president, president, 1976-78; Fraternal Benefit Association, president, 1971-; Society for Advancement of Buddhist Understanding, president, 1978-; Sumitomo Bank of California, advisory board of directors, 1971-; Boy Scouts of America, 1st class; Amache, Colorado Concentration Camp, sports editor of camp paper, 1942. **HONORS/AWARDS:** Franklin Million Dollar Conference; Franklin Life Insurance Co, honor clubs: 60 Club, Key Club, Diplomat Club; National Association of Life Underwriters; National Sales Achievement Award; National Quality Award; Million Dollar Round Table. **SPECIAL ACHIEVEMENTS:** Many articles in life insurance journals; represented USA at World Buddhist Conference in Japan, 1978. **MILITARY SERVICE:** US Army, staff sergeant, 1946-48; Sharpshooter, 1947. **BIOGRAPHICAL SOURCES:** New Zealand Life Underwriter's Association Magazine, article, 2nd edition. **HOME ADDRESS:** 860 Monica Lane, Campbell, CA 95008, (408)378-0167.

TOKUUKE, TERRANCE KATSUKI
Cleric. Japanese American. **PERSONAL:** Born Nov 29, 1954, Hilo, HI; son of Katsumi Tokuuke and Gladys Tokuuke. **EDUCATION:** California Polytechnic State University, BS, 1983, MBA, 1992, MA Ed candidate, currently. **CAREER:** Monastery de San Luis Obispo, abbot, 1991-. **ORGANIZATIONS:** Monastery General Council, chairman, 1993; IEEE; MBA Assn; San Luis Obispo Chamber of Commerce; Hui O' Hawaii. **BUSINESS ADDRESS:** Abbot, Monastery de San Luis Obispo, PO Box 13915, San Luis Obispo, CA 93406-3915.

TOLENTINO, VIRGINIA CANTOR
Librarian. Filipino American. **PERSONAL:** Born May 4, 1940, Manila, Philippines. **EDUCATION:** Far Eastern University, Manila, BSEd, 1963; San Diego State University, MAEd, 1981. **CAREER:** San Diego Public Library, librarian, 1984-88; San Diego Unified School District, school librarian, 1975-88; Eastside Union HS District, school librarian, 1988-. **ORGANIZATIONS:** CMLEA, 1975-; FAEAC, 1988-; FAME, 1988-. **HONORS/AWARDS:** San Diego State University, Teacher Training Program Fellowship; Asian American Parents Forum, Youth Task Force, advisor.

TOM, ANGELO C.
Federal government official. Chinese American. **PERSONAL:** Born Jun 29, 1956, San Francisco, CA; son of T Y Tom and K F Tom; married Ro-Anne M Tom, Jun 18, 1983; children: Antonio, Alisa. **EDUCATION:** San Francisco State University, BA (magna cum laude), 1979, MA, 1985, MBA, 1985. **CAREER:** US Department HUD, community planning and development representative, 1980-82, economic development specialist, 1982-83, financial analyst, 1984-88, program support division, director, 1988-. **ORGANIZATIONS:** HUD, diversity advisory committee, 1993-, Asian Pacific American Heritage Committee, chair, 1991-; Chinese for Affirmative Action, 1989-; Lawton Alternative School, Parents/Teachers Club, 1991-; American Chinese Associa-

tion, 1989-; Earthsave Foundation, 1991-; Asian Law Caucus, 1992-; Psi Chi, 1981. **BIOGRAPHICAL SOURCES:** Asian Week, 1989, 1990; World Journal, 1989; Transpacific, 1992. **BUSINESS ADDRESS:** Division Director, US Department of Housing and Urban Development, 450 Golden Gate Ave, Phillip Burton Federal Building, San Francisco, CA 94102-3448, (415)556-0392.

TOM, LELAND B.
State government official. Chinese American. **PERSONAL:** Born May 3, 1932, Marysville, CA; son of Poy June Tom and Helen D Tom; married M Elizabeth Tom, Nov 30, 1953; children: Daphne Lee Tom Quist. **EDUCATION:** Golden Gate College, BBA, 1953. **CAREER:** State of California, Dept of Mental Health, administrator, 1962-. **SPECIAL ACHIEVEMENTS:** Fluent in Cantonese. **MILITARY SERVICE:** US Army, cpl, 1953-56; National Defense Service Medal, Korean Service Medal, United Nations Service Medal, Good Conduct Medal. **HOME ADDRESS:** 1179 Cedar Tree Way, Sacramento, CA 95831.

TOM, MELVIN GEE LIM
Environmental services company administrator. Chinese American. **PERSONAL:** Born Aug 2, 1950, Honolulu, HI; son of Mr and Mrs Stanley Y K Tom; married June, Aug 19, 1973; children: Lara, Brenton. **EDUCATION:** Seattle University, BA, 1972. **CAREER:** Pacific Concrete & Rock, supervisor, 1978-84; Grace Pacific Corp, supervisor, 1984-87; Ameron HC&D, superintendent, 1987-93; Pacific Thermal Services, manager, 1993-. **MILITARY SERVICE:** US Army, capt, 1972-78; Army Commendation Medal, 1978; Airborne, 1972; Expert, 1972. **HOME ADDRESS:** 1324 Kina St, Kailua, HI 96734, (808)262-1986.

TOM, PING
Food company executive. Chinese American. **PERSONAL:** Born Apr 15, 1935, Chicago, IL; son of Tom Y Chan and Lillian Tom Chan; married Valerie, Oct 11, 1958; children: Darryl, Curtis. **EDUCATION:** Northwestern University, BA, 1956, JD, 1958. **CAREER:** Chinese Noodle Co, president, 1966-; Chinese Trading Co, president, 1966-; Mah Chena Corp, president, 1980-; Chinese American Development Co, president, 1984-. **ORGANIZATIONS:** Chinatown Chamber of Commerce, counselor/founding president, 1983; Southside Planning Board, director; Planetarium Museum, director; Lincoln Academy, director; Channel 11 TV, trustee; Chicago Economic Development Commission, commissioner; Illinois Economic Development Commission, commissioner; Asian Bar Association. **HONORS/AWARDS:** Chicago Commission on Human Relations, 1987; OCA, Outstanding Citizen, 1986; Chinatown Chamber of Commerce, Community Service Award, 1986; Asian Human Service, Distinguished Service Award, 1988; Chicago Certificate of Merit, 1992. **BUSINESS ADDRESS:** President, Chinese Noodle Company, 2263 Wentworth Ave, Chicago, IL 60616, (312)842-2820.

TOMITA, TAMLYN NAOMI
Actress. Pacific Islander American/Japanese American/Filipino American. **PERSONAL:** daughter of Shiro & Asako. **EDUCATION:** University of California, Los Angeles. **CAREER:** Actress, films include: The Karate Kid, Part II, 1986; Come See the Paradise, 1989; The Joy Luck Club, 1993; Picture Bride, 1993; Notes on a Scale, 1993; plays include: Winter Crane, 1990; Don Juan: A Meditation, 1991; Nagasaki Dust, 1992; Day Standing on its Head, 1993-94. **ORGANIZATIONS:** The Antaeus Project, charter member, 1990-. **HONORS/AWARDS:** Drama-Logue, Best Actress Performance Award, 1990-91. **BUSINESS ADDRESS:** Actress, The Artist's Group Ltd, 1930 Century Blvd W, Ste 403, Los Angeles, CA 90067.

TOMOMATSU, HIDEO
Scientist. Japanese American. **PERSONAL:** Born Jun 8, 1929, Tokyo, Japan; son of Shinsai Tomomatsu and Sumako Tomomatsu; married Yuko Ito Tomomatsu, Nov 12, 1967; children: Tadao. **EDUCATION:** Waseda University, BS, chemical engineering, 1952; University of the Pacific, MSc, 1960; Ohio State University, PhD, 1964. **CAREER:** Hodogaya Chemical Company, research chemist, 1952-59; Texaco Chemical Company, senior res chemist, 1964-72; Quaker Oaks Company, principal scientist, 1972-. **ORGANIZATIONS:** American Chemical Society, 1960-; Institute of Food Technologists, 1980-; American Association of Cereal Chemists, 1993-. **SPECIAL ACHIEVEMENTS:** 21 US and foreign patents; 9 publications; proficient in Japanese; US patent agent (No 31,309); Registered Professional Engineer, State of Texas (No 33875). **BUSINESS ADDRESS:** Principal Scientist, The Quaker Oats Company, Research Laboratories, 617 W Main Street, Barrington, IL 60010, (708)381-1980.

TONAI, ROSALYN
Association administrator. Japanese American. **CAREER:** National Japanese American Historical Society, executive director, currently. **BUSINESS ADDRESS:** Executive Director, National Japanese American Historical Society, 1855 Folsom St, #161, San Francisco, CA 94103, (415)431-5007.*

TONEGAWA, SUSUMU
Educator. Japanese American. **PERSONAL:** Born Sep 5, 1939, Nagoya, Japan; son of Tsutomu and Miyoko Masuko Tonegawa; married Mayumi Yoshinari, Sep 28, 1985; children: Hidde, Hanna. **EDUCATION:** Kyoto University, Japan, BS, 1963; University of California, San Diego, PhD, 1968. **CAREER:** University of California, San Diego, research assistant, 1963-64; teaching assistant, 1964-68; Basel Institute of Immunology, Switzerland, staff, 1971-81; Massachusetts Institute of Technology, Biology Department, professor, 1981-. **ORGANIZATIONS:** Natl Academy of Science, foreign member; American Association of Immunologists, honorary member; Scandinavian Society of Immunology, honorary member; Journal of Molecular and Cellular Immunology, editorial board member. **HONORS/AWARDS:** Nobel Prize, for Physiology or Medicine, 1987; Emperor of Japan, Decorated Order of Culture; Cloetta Prize, 1978; Gesselschaft fur Immunologie, Avery Landsteiner, 1981; Columbia University, Louisa Gross Horwitz Prize, 1982; Gardiner Foundation International, Canada, award, 1983; Federal Republic of Germany, Robert Koch Prize, 1986; Albert Lasker Medical Research Award, co-recipient, 1987; Japanese Government, Person with Cultural Merit, 1983. **BUSINESS ADDRESS:** Professor, Dept of Biology, Massachusetts Institute of Technology, Center for Cancer Research, 77 Massachusetts Ave, Bldg E17, Rm 353, Cambridge, MA 02139-4307, (617)253-8000.*

TONG, ALEX WAI MING
Research scientist. Hong Kong American. **PERSONAL:** Born Apr 8, 1952, Kowloon, Hong Kong; son of Agnes & Robert Tong; divorced; children: Nicole L. **EDUCATION:** University of Oregon, Eugene, BA, 1973; Oregon Health Sciences University, Portland, PhD, 1980. **CAREER:** Oregon Health Sciences University, research associate, 1975-82; Baylor University, Medical Center, associate director, Immunol Lab, 1982-; Baylor University, associate professor, 1989-. **ORGANIZATIONS:** University of Texas Southwestern Medical Center, Immunology Graduate Program, adjunct member, 1982-; American Association of Immunologists, 1985-; American Association for Cancer Research, 1985-; American Society of Hematology, 1988-; Clinical Immunology Society, 1990-. **HONORS/AWARDS:** Medical Research Foundation of Oregon, Tartar Research Fellow, 1981-83. **SPECIAL ACHIEVEMENTS:** Co-author, "Augmentation of Lymphokine-activated Killer Cell Cytotoxicity by Monoclonal Antibody Against Human Small Cell Lung Carcinoma," Cancer Research, vol 49, p 4103-4108, 1989; co-author, "Fluorescent Probes for Cancer Detection," J Clin Laser Med & Surgery, vol 8, p 39-41, 1990; co-author, "Heterotransplantation of Human Multiple Myeloma Cell Lines in Severe Combined Immunodeficiency Mice," Anti-Cancer Research, vol 13, 1993; numerous others. **BUSINESS ADDRESS:** Associate Director, Cancer Immunology Research Lab, Baylor University Medical Center, 3500 Gaston Ave, 530 Sammons Tower, Dallas, TX 75246.

TONG, ALVIN H.
Business executive. Chinese American. **PERSONAL:** Born Jan 10, 1939, Chung-King, Sichuan, China; son of David T Tong; married Anna Tong, Jun 19, 1965; children: Tony, Scott. **EDUCATION:** National University of Taiwan, BSEE, 1961; University of Minnesota, PhD, electrical engineering, 1967. **CAREER:** Hsin-Chu Science-Based Industrial Park Administration, deputy director general, 1980-82; Asian Chemical Corp, president, 1983-84; New Dev Corp, president, 1984-86; Acer Inc, exec vice pres, 1986-90; independent consultant, 1990-92; Global Vantage Inc, president, chief exec officer, 1992; Vic Braden Global, president, chief exec officer, 1992-. **HOME ADDRESS:** 7156 Las Ventanas Dr, Austin, TX 78731, (512)795-9502.

TONG, BENJAMIN (BINH)
Software engineer. Vietnamese American. **PERSONAL:** Born Feb 19, 1966, Long Khanh, Vietnam; son of Hoang Van Tong and Mai Thi Bui; married Xuan-Hanh Nguyen-Le, Jul 28, 1992. **EDUCATION:** University of Lowell, BSEE (cum laude), 1991. **CAREER:** Polaroid Corp, software test engineer, 1992-. **ORGANIZATIONS:** National Engineer Honor Society, 1991-; Electrical Engineer Honor Society, 1991-. **HOME ADDRESS:** 1750A Middlesex St, Lowell, MA 01851, (508)453-5397. **BUSINESS PHONE:** (617)386-4565.

TONG, BENJAMIN ROBERT
Psychologist, educator, actor, director. Chinese American. **PERSONAL:** married Loretta H F Tong; children: Erik Morgan. **EDUCATION:** San Francisco State University, BA, sociology, 1965, MA, counseling, 1970; University of California, Berkeley, doctoral studies in sociology, 1970-71; California School of Professional Psychology, Berkeley, PhD, clinical psychology, 1974. **CAREER:** Private-practice psychotherapist & organizational consultant, 1975-; San Francisco State University, lecturer in Asian American studies, 1975-; University of California, Berkeley, Institute for the Study of Social Change, research associate, 1980-; California Institute of Integral Studies, associate professor of clinical psychology, 1991-. **ORGANIZATIONS:** International Karen Horney Society, steering committee, 1992-; Institute of Cross-Cultural Research, executive director, 1987-; Chinese for Affirmative Action, 1985-; Asian American Psychological Association; Asian American Theater Workshop, 1973-77. **HONORS/AWARDS:** National Institute of Mental Health, Community Psychology Training Grant, 1972-74; UCLA/NIMH, Drug Treatment Program Grant, 1974; University of California, Santa Cruz, Ethnic Studies Curriculum Grant, 1983-84; State of California, Curriculum Enrichment Project Grant, San Francisco State University AAS, 1989. **SPECIAL ACHIEVEMENTS:** Author: "Asian American Domestic Violence: A Critical Psychohistorical Approach," in Domestic Violence and Men of Color, Springer Publications, 1993; "The Tao of Chaos," The Social Dynamicist, 3(4), 9-10, 1992; others. **BIOGRAPHICAL SOURCES:** Karin Meissenburg, The Writing on the Wall: Socio-Historical Aspects of Chinese American Literature, 1900-80, Frankfurt, Germany: Verlag fur Interkulturelle Kommunkikation, 1987. **BUSINESS ADDRESS:** Associate Professor, Clinical Psychology Program, California Institute of Integral Studies, 765 Ashbury St, San Francisco, CA 94117-4094, (415)753-6100.

TONG, DOUGLAS L.
Market manager. Chinese American. **PERSONAL:** Born May 13, 1955, New York, NY; son of Wai Hoo Tong & Mayeross Lau Tong; married Alethea R Tong, May 25, 1979. **EDUCATION:** Northwestern University, BSChE, 1977. **CAREER:** DuPont AGCHEM, engineer, assistant to operations, 1977-79, process engineer, mfg, 1979-80; DuPont Agriculture Dept, process supervisor, mfg, 1980-83; DuPont Chemicals, area supervisor, mfg, 1983-86; DuPont Performance Products, sr account manager, 1986-89; DuPont Petroleum Additives, product planner, 1989-91; DuPont Petroleum Products, market manager, 1991-. **ORGANIZATIONS:** American Institute of Chemical Engineers, 1977-80; Belle Works, Softball League, president, 1980; Society of Automotive Engineers, 1990-; National Petroleum Refiners Association, 1991-; American Society of Testing Materials, 1991-. **HONORS/AWARDS:** DuPont Chemicals: Cetane Improver Market Success, Marketing Excellence Award, 1992, Next Generation Detergent Introduction, Marketing Excellence Award, 1991, Customer of the Quarter-Marketing Initiative, 1984; DuPont Specialty Chemicals, Continous Improvement Cash Flow, 1991, Working Capital-Supply Chain Success, 1990. **SPECIAL ACHIEVEMENTS:** Industrial Hygiene, Personal Monitoring at a Manufacturing Site, 1979-80; Northwestern University, Delaware Valley, Alumni Interviewer, 1991-; Belle Works Employee, Candidate Program, 1978-80. **BUSINESS ADDRESS:** Market Manager, DuPont Chemicals, 1007 Market St, Brandywine 12379, Wilmington, DE 19801, (302)774-3213.

TONG, FRANKLIN FUK-KAY
Research scientist. Chinese American/Hong Kong American. **PERSONAL:** Born Feb 18, 1956, Hong Kong; son of Man-Ping and Yuen Wah; married Mansze, Jun 11, 1986; children: Janyu, Wenting. **EDUCATION:** University of California, San Diego, BA, 1980; University of California, Santa Barbara, MA, 1982; Columbia University, PhM, 1987, PhD, 1987. **CAREER:** MIT, Lincoln Lab, research associate, 1982-87; IBM, Almaden Research Center, visiting scientist, 1987-89, T J Watson Research Center, research staff member, 1989-. **ORGANIZATIONS:** OSA; IEEE; LEOS; COMSOC; Chinese Photonics Society. **SPECIAL ACHIEVEMENTS:** Over 50 journals and conference publications, 1982-. **BUSINESS ADDRESS:** Research Staff Member, IBM, T J Watson Research Center, PO Box 704, Yorktown Heights, NY 10598, (914)784-7024.

TONG, JENNIE S.
Broadcast journalist, advertising company executive. Chinese American/Hong Kong American. **PERSONAL:** Born Mar 28, 1952, Hong Kong; daughter of Harry Tong & Tong Kwok Ying. **EDUCATION:** Queens College, BA, mass communication; New York University, MA, liberal studies/journalism. **CAREER:** OECD, researcher in tv & radio dept, 1978-79; TVB, Hong Kong

associate producer; Chung Hwa Broadcasting, anchor, producer, 1979-82; NBC News, researcher, field producer, associate producer, 1982-86; Lee Liu & Tong Advertising, CEO, 1987-; WNYC-TV, anchor, 1991-. **ORGANIZATIONS:** NY Minority Women Business Enterprise, Advisory Board to Mayor; Advertising Research Foundation, ethnic research committee, 1990-; Asian American Journalist Association, associate member; American Women Economic Development, round table, chief executive, 1990-; Manhattan Neighborhood Renaissance, loan credit committee, 1992-. **HONORS/AWARDS:** NBC Religion Unit, Emmy & Gabriel Awards, for "Chagall's Journey," 1986, Silver Angel, for "Father Serra & the American West," 1986; NYC Comptroller's Office, 1993 Outstanding Asian American. **SPECIAL ACHIEVEMENTS:** Developed and headed a successful Asian-language advertising agency with annual billings in excess of 10 million dollars; fluent in English, French and Chinese, Mandarin, Cantonese, Shanghainese. **BIOGRAPHICAL SOURCES:** Crains New York Business, special edition, page 30, 1992; numerous other articles. **BUSINESS ADDRESS:** Chief Executive Officer, Owner, Lee Liu & Tong Advertising, 580 Broadway, 8th Fl, New York, NY 10012, (212)941-6633.

TONG, LIK KUEN
Educator. Chinese American. **PERSONAL:** Born Oct 26, 1935, Hong Kong; son of Big Chuen Tong (deceased) and Miu Yin Chung (deceased); married Yu Hou Tong, Jul 15, 1969; children: Celia, Thalia, Arnold. **EDUCATION:** National Taiwan University, 1954-55; Hwa Kiu University, 1955-56; New York University, BS, 1958; New School for Social Research, PhD, 1969. **CAREER:** City University of New York, lecturer, 1967; Fairfield University, assistant professor, 1967-74, associate professor, 1974-78, professor, 1978-. **ORGANIZATIONS:** International Society for Chinese Philosophy, vice president, 1986-87, president, 1988-89, executive director, 1990-; American Philosophical Association; Society for Asian and Comparative Philosophy; International Society for the I Ching. **HONORS/AWARDS:** New York University, Founders Day Award, 1959; New School for Social Research, Kurt Riezler Memorial Award, 1969; Fairfield University, Outstanding Educator of America, 1975. **SPECIAL ACHIEVEMENTS:** The Word and Other Poems, Hong Kong, Chinese Cultural Enterprise Co, 1969; Between Chou-I and Whitehead, An Introduction to the Philosophy of Field-being, Taipei Li Min Cultural Enterprise Co, 1989. **BUSINESS ADDRESS:** Professor, Dept of Philosophy, Executive Director, International Society for Chinese Philosophy, Fairfield University, Fairfield, CT 06430-7524.

TONG, SUN-DE
Chemist. Chinese American. **PERSONAL:** Born Oct 4, 1950, Taipei, Taiwan; daughter of Nei-Hung Mo and Hung Loh Mo; married Wen-How Tong; children: Nathan, Stephanie. **EDUCATION:** National Taiwan University, BS, 1972; Ohio State University, MS, 1973. **CAREER:** Baxter Healthcare, chemist, currently. **HOME ADDRESS:** 13 Stonewall, Irvine, CA 92720.

TONG, TS'ING H.
Educator. Chinese American. **PERSONAL:** Born Sep 9, 1923, Kiading, Jiangsu, China; son of Yu-Nong Tong and Tse-Feng Tchang; married Chi-Hang Tong, 1970; children: Christopher, Anthony. **EDUCATION:** Southern Illinois University, BA 1961; DePaul University, MS, 1963. **CAREER:** Illinois College, Department of Mathematics, associate professor, 1964-. **ORGANIZATIONS:** Mathematical Association of American, 1964-. **BUSINESS ADDRESS:** Associate Professor, Mathematics, Illinois College, Jacksonville, IL 62650-2299, (217)245-3000.

TONG, WEN-HOW
Engineer. Chinese American. **PERSONAL:** Born Feb 9, 1949, Shanghai, China; son of Shao-Hong Tong and Yuan-Chien Tong; married Sun-De Tong, Oct 31, 1973; children: Nathan, Stephanie. **EDUCATION:** National Taiwan University, BS, 1973; Massachusetts Institute of Technology, MS, 1975. **CAREER:** EQE International, technical manager, currently. **HOME ADDRESS:** 13 Stonewall, Irvine, CA 92720. **BUSINESS PHONE:** (714)833-3303.

TOY, MADELINE SHEN (SIAO-FANG SHEN)
Scientist. Chinese American. **PERSONAL:** Born Nov 6, 1926, Shanghai, China; daughter of Zee Shen and She-ven Huang Shen; married Stephen M Toy, Dec 26, 1951; children: Stephanie M. **EDUCATION:** College of Saint Teresa, BS, 1949; University of Wisconsin, Madison, MS, 1951; Ohio State University, MS, 1957; University of Pennsylania, PhD, 1959. **CAREER:** Freelander R&D Lab of Dayco Corp, organic lab, manager, 1959-60; ITT Federal Lab, staff member, 1961-63; McDonnell Douglas Corp, section chief,

research scientist, 1964-70; SRI International, senior polymer chemist, 1971-75; Science Applications International Corp, head of chemistry lab, 1975-89; Carter Analysis Lab, senior scientist, 1989-91; Balazs Analysis Lab, senior scientist, 1991-93; Interscience Lab, consultant, 1994-. **ORGANIZATIONS:** American Chemical Society, 1955-, Fluorine Division, executive committee, 1972-75, Polymer Division, Polymer Materials Science and Engineering Division, Environmental Division; American Institute of Chemists, Golden Gate Chapter, secretary & treasurer, 1972-73; Chemical Society, fellow, 1964-. **HONORS/AWARDS:** NASA-JPL, NASA New Technology Awards, 1977; NASA-JSC, NASA Certificates of Recognition, 1978-80; McDonnell Douglas Corp, Professional Achievements & Value in Performance Awards, 1965-67; Science Applications International Corp Patent Awards, Ten Year Service Award, 1983-85. **SPECIAL ACHIEVEMENTS:** Contributed eight chapters to technology books; 15 US patents; contributing author to over 60 technology publications; principal investigator of numerous R&D contracts from various government agencies, commercial firms, and associations. **BIOGRAPHICAL SOURCES:** "Materials Applications on New Fluorocorbon Coatings, Protect A Wide Variety of Metalalloys from Harsh Environment," Industrial Research, p 35-36, March 1968; "Bonus from Space Research on New Fluoropolymers," Chemical Week, p 51, November 30, 1968.

TOYAMA, FRANK KENICHI
Business owner, machinist. Japanese American. **PERSONAL:** Born Jul 16, 1930, Los Angeles, CA; son of Matsuji Toyama & Natsu Toyama; married Yoshiko Toyama, Dec 4, 1952; children: Kathryn Kinuko, Stanley Nobuyuki, Vincent Shinichi, Diana Sumiyo Fletcher. **EDUCATION:** AA, 1958. **CAREER:** Milo Harding Co, machinist apprentice, 1953-55; Tools Inc, machinist apprentice, 1955-58; Calinoy, Illinois Tool Works, machinst, 1958-60; Sierra Electric Corp, machinist, 1960-62; TRW Operation & Support Group, experimental machinist, 1962-66; Frank K Toyama Company, owner, 1966-. **MILITARY SERVICE:** US Army, infantry, interpreter, private first class, 1951-53; Korean Svc Medal, UN Svc Medal.

TOYAMA, JEAN YAMASAKI
Educator. Japanese American. **PERSONAL:** Born Jan 14, 1942, Honolulu, HI; daughter of Fumie & Tsutomu Yamasaki; married Dennis Kazuo Toyama, Aug 28, 1966. **EDUCATION:** University of Hawaii, BA, 1964; Purdue University, MA, 1967; University of California, Irvine, PhD, 1975; Keio University, International Center, 1986-87. **CAREER:** University of Hawaii, French Divison, chair, 1980-83, 1987-93, professor, 1973-. **ORGANIZATIONS:** Governor's Advisory Council on Foreign Languages & International Studies, acting executive secretary, 1984; Hawaii Committee for the Humanities, 1982-89, chair, 1988-89, sec-treas, 1985-86, Proposal Review Committee, chair, 1986-88. **HONORS/AWARDS:** College of Language, Linguistics & Literature, Excellence in Teaching Award, 1989. **SPECIAL ACHIEVEMENTS:** Author, Beckett's Game: Self and Language in the Trilogy, Peter Lang Pub, 1991; co-editor, with Nobuko Ochner, Literary Relations East & West, Ult Press, 1990; author, What the Kite Thinks, Linked Verse With Ooka Makoto, Wing Tek Lum, & Joseph Stanton, winter, 1994; also poetry and short stories. **BUSINESS ADDRESS:** Professor, Dept of European Languages & Literature, University of Hawaii, 1890 East-West Rd, Moore Hall 485, Honolulu, HI 96822, (808)956-4185.

TOYOTA, MICHAEL DOUGLAS
Supply company manager. Japanese American. **PERSONAL:** Born Apr 30, 1965, Ontario; son of Roy Chikicu Toyota and Elizabeth Annie Toyota; married Frances Carlyle Toyota, Oct 24, 1987; children: Zackary Ryan, Tyler Michael. **EDUCATION:** US Army, Sniper School; 2 yrs college, BCC, business/construction, 1989. **CAREER:** Valmor Distributors, general manager, 1987-92; JWI Supply, branch manager, 1992-. **MILITARY SERVICE:** US Army, sgt, 1983-87; Z-Arcom, EIB, Air Assault, Service Award. **HOME ADDRESS:** 909 NW 107th Ave, Pembroke Pines, FL 33026. **BUSINESS ADDRESS:** Branch Manager, JWI Supply Inc, 3901 SW 47th Ave, Ste 405, Fort Lauderdale, FL 33314.

TRAN, DOROTHY N.
Auto repair business owner, nurse. Vietnamese American. **PERSONAL:** Born Feb 15, 1957, Saigon, Vietnam; daughter of Leon & Ernestine Nguyen; married Tran Chi, Jul 18, 1976; children: Steve, Scott, Shawn. **EDUCATION:** St Petersburg Junior College; Tomlinson Adult School of Nursing, license. **CAREER:** USCC, translator, counselor; Humana Hospital, nurse, 1978; Refugee Clinic, translator, counselor, 1980-90; Woodlawn Elementary School, bilingual teaching assistant, 1990-; Professional Auto Repairs, Inc, owner, currently.

ORGANIZATIONS: Woodlawn Elementary School, ESOL Program. **HONORS/AWARDS:** Home Health Agency, Employee of the Year; Pinellas County School Board, Employee of the Year nominee, plaque. **BIOGRAPHICAL SOURCES:** St Petersburg Times, 1989, 1990; St Petersburg Evening Independent, 1986. **BUSINESS ADDRESS:** Owner, Professional Auto Repairs, Inc, 2285-1st Ave N, St Petersburg, FL 33713, (813)321-3290.

TRAN, HONG-Y THI
Business owner. Vietnamese American. **PERSONAL:** Born May 8, 1959, Kien Giang, Vietnam; daughter of Lai Trai and Anh Tran; married Dan Nguyen, Jan 5, 1978; children: Daniel, Donna, Dolly, Dinah. **CAREER:** Quality Sewing Industries Inc, owner. **BUSINESS ADDRESS:** Owner, Quality Sewing Industries Inc, 8900 NE Vancouver Way, Portland, OR 97211-1395, (503)735-0000.

TRAN, HUYEN LAM
Language specialist, educator. Vietnamese American. **PERSONAL:** Born Apr 1, 1946, Nam Dinh, Vietnam; son of Tran Van Tu and Nguyen Thi Lam; married Tran Thi Thu-Thuy, Nov 29, 1972; children: Lam Xuan Giang, Lam Xuan Uyen. **EDUCATION:** Saigon University, Vietnam, BA, 1968; Gifu University, Japan, MA, 1977. **CAREER:** Can Tho University, school instructor, 1968-74; Salem Kaiser Public School, native language specialist, currently. **SPECIAL ACHIEVEMENTS:** Language proficiency: Vietnamese, Japanese. **HOME ADDRESS:** 4842 Future Dr NE, Salem, OR 97305.

TRAN, LA DINH
Hotel manager. Vietnamese American. **PERSONAL:** Born Jun 10, 1956, Khanh Hoa, Vietnam; son of Van Thong Tran; married Phu Nguyen Tran, 1981; children: Bao, Billy. **EDUCATION:** New York University, accounting, 1986; John Jay College, high-rise safety, 1990. **CAREER:** Hotel Opera, night manager; Intl Consumer Product, shipping manager; Park Lane Hotel, Hemsley, chief auditor; Visa Intl Hotel, auditor; Alphonse Hotel Corp, general manager, currently. **BUSINESS ADDRESS:** General Manager, Alphonse Hotel Corporation, 250 W 43rd St, Manager's Office, New York, NY 10036, (212)944-6000.

TRAN, LOC BINH
Educator. Vietnamese American. **PERSONAL:** Born May 1, 1946, Hanoi, Vietnam; son of Can Van Tran and Khang Bich Trinh; married Ai-Hanh N Tran, May 22, 1976; children: Eric, Jana, Austin, Ethan. **EDUCATION:** University of Saigon, Vietnam, BS, 1970, MS, 1972; University of Oklahoma, MS, 1978, PhD, 1981. **CAREER:** University of Oklahoma, postdoctoral research associate, 1981-84; Kansas Wesleyan University, physics, associate professor, 1984-. **HONORS/AWARDS:** University of Oklahoma, Department of Physics, Nielsen Award, Outstanding Graduate Student, 1981. **SPECIAL ACHIEVEMENTS:** Publications: Journal Chemical Phys Letters, vol 76, no 7, p 3839, 1982, Journal Chemical Physics, vol 77, no 11, p 5624, 1982; Journal Mathematical Physics, vol 24, no 2, p 397, 1983; Journal Mol Spectroscopy, vol 164, p 393, 1987; Journal Solution Chemistry, vol 18, no 7, p 675, 1989; Solutions of General Physics Problems, in Vietnamese, vols 1 and 2, Lightsource Publishers, Saigon, Vietnam. **BUSINESS ADDRESS:** Associate Professor of Physics, Kansas Wesleyan University, 100 E Claflin, Salina, KS 67401, (913)827-5541.

TRAN, LOI HUU
Retail store manager. Vietnamese American. **PERSONAL:** Born Dec 20, 1939, Hung-Yen, Vietnam; son of Tran Dinh Chuc and Ngo Thi Van; married Nguyen Thi Hoan; children: Ha, Thanh, Hai, Binh. **EDUCATION:** University of Hue, Vietnam, 1959-61. **CAREER:** Order From Horder, sales clerk; General Telegraph, electronic technician; Rauland Borg, electronic technican; Tan A Restaurant, manager; Children's Wear Outlet, manager, currently. **ORGANIZATIONS:** VAI; Vietnamese Catholic Group, Chicago; Vietnamese Chamber of Commerce. **MILITARY SERVICE:** US/VN Special Forces, specialist, 1962-70. **BIOGRAPHICAL SOURCES:** "New Comer," Sun Times, Jul 1975; Tribune, Jul 1975. **BUSINESS ADDRESS:** Manager, Children's Wear Outlet, 2050 W Peterson, Chicago, IL 60659.

TRAN, LONG TRIEU
Engineer. Vietnamese American. **PERSONAL:** Born Oct 10, 1956, Saigon, Vietnam; son of Nguyen Dinh Tran and Thiet Thi Nguyen; married Khanh Thi Hong Phan, Aug 3, 1988. **EDUCATION:** University of Kansas, BS (honors), mechanical engineering, 1976; University of California, Berkeley, 1977; Massachusetts Institute of Technology, MS, mechanical engineering, 1980; Univer-

sity of Louisville, MBA (honors), 1993. **CAREER:** University of California, Berkeley, teaching asst, 1977, Lawrence Berkeley Laboratories, research asst, 1977; Massachusetts Institute of Technology, research assistant, 1977-80; General Electric, production programming engineer, 1980-81, advanced manufacturing engineer, 1981-82, quality systems engineer, 1982-84, quality control engineer, 1984-86, senior quality information equipment engineer, 1986-89, senior quality industrial engineer, 1990-. **ORGANIZATIONS:** New York Academy of Sciences, 1989-; American Society for Quality Control, 1990-; Computer and Automated Systems Association, charter member, 1976-; Robotics International, charter member, 1976-; Society of Manufacturing Engineers, senior member, 1976-; American Society of Mechanical Engineers, 1976-; Industrial Computing Society, founding member, 1991-; Instruments Society of America, 1991-. **HONORS/AWARDS:** Pi Tau Sigma, 1975; Tau Beta Pi, 1975; Phi Kappa Phi, 1976; Sigma Xi, 1977; General Electric, Outstanding Contribution Award, 1980, 1982, 1988. **SPECIAL ACHIEVEMENTS:** Kansas Engineer-in-Training Certificate, 1976; executive advisor, Junior Achievement of Louisville, 1983-84; Dale Carnegie graduate, 1991; certified manufacturing engineer, 1991-94; certified quality engineer, 1991-94. **HOME ADDRESS:** 3423 Brookhollow Dr, Louisville, KY 40220. **BUSINESS ADDRESS:** Senior Quality Industrial Engineer, General Electric Co, Appliance Pk, AP5-1NC, Louisville, KY 40225, (502)452-7082.

TRAN, MYLUONG THI
Educator. Vietnamese American. **PERSONAL:** Born in Hanam, Phuly, Vietnam; daughter of Van Long Tran (deceased) and Yen Sam Bui (deceased); married Haplong H Tran, Oct 1981. **EDUCATION:** University of Paris, France, AAS, translation/interpretion, 1966; Marymount, New York, BA (with honors), English, 1971; Southern Illinois University, MA, English, 1974, PhD, higher education, 1979. **CAREER:** Southern Illinois University, adult education specialist, 1974-81; San Diego State University, College of Education, associate professor, 1981-. **ORGANIZATIONS:** American Educational Research Association, 1984-; National Education Association, 1985-; Vietnamese American Parent Teacher Association, vice president, 1983-. **HONORS/AWARDS:** Full scholarhips: BA, MA, PhD; San Diego State University, New Teacher Retention Project, 1988; San Diego County, Board of Supervisors, Outstanding Contribution on Public Welfare Advisory Board, 1984; Laubach Literacy International, National Affiliation for Literacy Advance, 1978. **SPECIAL ACHIEVEMENTS:** Author of: "Bridging Cultural Values Gaps;" "Maximizing the Vietnamese Parents Involvement in Schools;" "Teaching Reading to Vietnamese Bilingual Children;" proficiency in: English, Vietnamese, French; functionally bilingual in Spanish. **BIOGRAPHICAL SOURCES:** Social Education, April/May 1990; National Association for Secondary School Principals, Bulletin, Jan 1992; "Who Really Discovered Aspirin?" Science Teacher, May 1992; "Beyond Chopsticks and Dragons: Selective Asian American Literature for Children," The Reading Teacher, Nov 1992, vol 46, no3; "Passionate Commitment to a Multicultural Society," Equity and Excellence in Education, 1994. **BUSINESS ADDRESS:** Associate Professor, Teacher Education, College of Education, San Diego State University, Hardy Avenue, Campanile Dr #5300, San Diego, CA 92182-0002, (619)594-2918.

TRAN, NHUT VAN
Electronics technician. Vietnamese American. **PERSONAL:** Born Dec 17, 1935, Saigon, Vietnam; son of Tran Van Ngo and Huynh Thi Liên; married Kim Lang Tran, Nov 27, 1957; children: Nguyen, Nghia, Nga, Ngan. **EDUCATION:** College in Dalat, 1954. **CAREER:** Williams Brother, Bakersfield, oil refinery, 1978-79; Todd Pacific Shipyard, shipbuilder, 1979-86; Emulex Corp, repair technician, 1987-92. **ORGANIZATIONS:** Dalat Military Academy Association, president, 1988-89; International Committee for Free Vietnam, honorary member; Vietnam Community in Southern California, president, 1989-92; National Council for the Vietnamese American Community in the USA, president; Alliance for Democracy in Vietnam, board of representatives, chairman, 1993-97. **HONORS/AWARDS:** Letters of Recognition from City Mayor, Assemblymen, Congressman, OC Supervisor Board. **MILITARY SERVICE:** Vietnam Marine Corps/Army, brig general, 2nd Division ARVN commander, 1972-75; 2 US Silver Stars, 2 Bronze Stars with V, 1 US Army Commendation w/V. **HOME ADDRESS:** 1425 W Moore St, Santa Ana, CA 92704, (714)754-1125.

TRAN, PHUOC HUU
Educator. Vietnamese American. **PERSONAL:** Born Dec 12, 1939, Dalat, Vietnam; son of Bao V Tran and Manh T Mai; married Trinh Thuc Tran, Sep 23, 1967; children: Tri, Thuc, Thuy-Duong, Tin. **EDUCATION:** Catholic

University, Dalat, Vietnam, BS, 1964; University of Nebraska, MS, 1978; Kennedy-Western University, PhD, 1993. **CAREER:** Private high school, AN-MY, Binh Duong, Vietnam, principal, 1960-62; Mission Culturelle Francaise, Saigon, teacher, 1962-75; University of Nebraska, director of math lab, 1982-1988; Bellevue College, assistant professor, chairman, 1988-. **HONORS/AWARDS:** Dean Ralph G.K. Beach Distinguished Professorship nominee. **SPECIAL ACHIEVEMENTS:** Solution de math et physic du baccalaureat, 1961; La litterature Francaise du 18 siecle, 1962; Keys to success in teaching & learning math, 1993. **HOME ADDRESS:** 3520 N 66th St, Omaha, NE 68104, (402)554-8545. **BUSINESS PHONE:** (402)293-3754.

TRAN, QUI-PHIET
Educator. Vietnamese American. **PERSONAL:** Born Jan 6, 1937, Dalat, Langbian, Vietnam; son of Qui-But Tran and Anh Thi Nguyen Tran; married Ngan Thi Vo, Aug 30, 1963; children: Thuy, Long, Kien. **EDUCATION:** University of Hue, Vietnam, BA, 1960; University of Texas, MA, 1974, PhD, 1977. **CAREER:** University of Hue, Vietnam, English, instructor, 1965-72; University of Texas, English, instructor, 1978-79; Congressional Information Service Inc, document analyst, 1979-80; Arlington County Public Schools, resource specialist, 1980-81; Schreiner College, English, assistant professor, 1982-87, associate professor, 1987-90, professor, 1990-. **ORGANIZATIONS:** Modern Language Association; South Central Modern Language Association; Society for the Study of Narrative Literature; Association for Asian American Studies. **HONORS/AWARDS:** National Endowment for the Humanities, Summer Stipend, 1983, 1989; Mellon Foundation, Summer Stipend, 1983; Schreiner College, Faculty Development Grant, 1988, 1992; American Council of Learned Societies, Research Fellowship, 1984. **SPECIAL ACHIEVEMENTS:** Author, book: William Faulkner and the French New Novelists, 1980; articles: "The Question of Suicide in 'The Sound and the Fury'," 1987; "Vietnamese Artists & Writers in America, 1975 to the Present," 1989; "Vietnamese Americans in Tran Dieu Hang's Fiction," 1992; "Exile and Home in Contemporary Vietnamese Feminine Writing," 1994; articles in The Asian American Encyclopedia, 1994. **BUSINESS ADDRESS:** Professor, English Dept, Schreiner College, 2100 Memorial Blvd, Kerrville, TX 78028, (210)896-5411.

TRAN, THANG NHUT
Government official. Vietnamese American. **PERSONAL:** Born Feb 18, 1941, Cantho, Vietnam; son of Nghia Van Tran; married Rong Le Tran; children: Thien Huong, Long. **EDUCATION:** National Institute of Administration, Vietnam, BA, public adm, 1964, MPA, 1968; Catholic University of Washington, DC, MA, business accounting, 1981;. **CAREER:** Information Ministry, general secretary, Vietnam, 1969-74; Dept of Social Services, Arlington, social worker, 1979-85; Commissioner of The Revenue, Arlington, senior tax auditor, 1985-. **ORGANIZATIONS:** National Council for Vietnamese-American Community of USA, vice president, 1992-93; Vietnamese Community of Washington DC, Maryland, Virginia, president, 1990-92; National Institute of Admin Alumni, East Coast, USA, president, 1988-91; First Vietnamese Baptist Church of Maryland, deacon and Sunday school director, 1990-93. **HONORS/AWARDS:** Fairfax County Board, Recognition Certificate, 1991, 1992; Arlington County Board, Recognition Certificate, 1992. **HOME ADDRESS:** 9913 Woodstream Court, Lanham, MD 20706.

TRAN, THINH QUY
Business executive. Vietnamese American. **PERSONAL:** Born 1954?, Vietnam; married; children: three sons. **EDUCATION:** University of Wisconsin, BS, electrical engineering, 1974; Stanford University, MS, electrical engineering, 1975. **CAREER:** Amdahl Corporation, Engineering; Triology Systems Corporation, Engineering; Sigma Designs, co-founder, president, CEO, 1982-. **ORGANIZATIONS:** Asian American Manufacturers Assn, board of directors, first Vietnamese American president, 1993-. **HONORS/AWARDS:** Business Week, ranked among Top 100 Best Small Corporations, 1987-89; MacUser Magazine, Best Display Product of 1990, for L-View Multi-Mode display system, 1991; Computer Personlich Magazine, Best Product Award, for Sigma VGA Legend, 1991; Asian American Manufacturers Association, Entrepreneur of the Year, 1989. **BUSINESS ADDRESS:** President, CEO, Sigma Designs, 47900 Bayside Pky, Fremont, CA 94538-6477, (510)770-0100. *

TRAN, THOMAS
Engineer. Vietnamese American. **PERSONAL:** Born Mar 15, 1968, Saigon, Vietnam; son of Tham Tran Ngoc and Huong Thi Nguyen; married Jennifer Le L, Sep 26, 1992. **EDUCATION:** Southeastern Oklahoma State University, BS, computer science, 1989, BSEE, 1989. **CAREER:** IBM Corp, Memory Subsys-

tems Design Engineering, engr, 1990-. **BUSINESS ADDRESS:** IBM Corporation, 11400 Burnet Rd, Internal Zip 9620, Austin, TX 78758, (512)838-5793.

TRAN, THUAN VAN
Attorney, pharmacist. Vietnamese American. **PERSONAL:** Born Apr 17, 1948, Saigon, Vietnam; son of Phan Van Tran and Bao Thi Tran; married May Yeu Tran, Jul 22, 1972; children: Mila S, Annlan V. **EDUCATION:** Srisavangvong University, Vietiane, Laos, BS, pharm, 1971; Duquesne University, School of Pharmacy, BS, 1979; University of Denver, School of Law, JD, 1990. **CAREER:** BGL, Laos, quality control manager, 1973-75; Thrift Drug Co, management trainee, 1976-79, pharmacist, manager, 1979-81; Tran's Pharmacy, pharmacist, owner, 1981-87; Thuan Van Tran, PC, attorney-at-law, 1991-. **ORGANIZATIONS:** American Bar Association, 1990-; Utah State Bar Association, 1991-; Asian Association of Utah, board chairman, 1991-; New Hope Refugee Friendship, board chairman, 1991-; Vietnamese Association of Utah, vice chair, 1992-. **BUSINESS ADDRESS:** Attorney at Law, 357 S 200 E, ste 300, Salt Lake City, UT 84111, (801)359-9300.

TRAN, TRI K.
Military official. Vietnamese American/Chinese American. **PERSONAL:** Born Aug 3, 1960, Saigon, Vietnam; son of Tran Ca Quan and Duong Lang; married Maria B Tran, Apr 24, 1988; children: Patricia A. **EDUCATION:** University of Houston, 1979; US Air Force, computer technical/maintenance training, 1980, leadership/management training, 1986, Non-Commissioned Officer Academy, 1992. **CAREER:** US Air Force, computer maintenance apprentice, 1979-82, mobile communication specialist, 1982-85, communication technician, 1985-90, work center supervisor, technical sgt, 1990-. **ORGANIZATIONS:** Air Force Assn, life member, 1979-; Noncommissioned Officers Assn, 1992-; Air Force Sergeant's Assn, 1991-; Asian-Pacific, steering committee, 1989-. **SPECIAL ACHIEVEMENTS:** Language proficiency: French, Vietnamese, Chinese/Cantonese. **MILITARY SERVICE:** US Air Force, Air Force Commendation Medal, 1982; Air Force Achievement Medals, 1987.

TRAN, TUYET-NHUNG T.
State government official. Vietnamese American. **PERSONAL:** Born May 10, 1948, Hue, Vietnam; daughter of Tanh Thanh Tran and Thua Thi Nguyen; married Tuan Anh Le, Jan 20, 1990. **EDUCATION:** Institution of Business Administration, BS (with honors), 1969, MS (with honors), 1972; San Francisco State University, BS (summa cum laude), 1984. **CAREER:** Central Logistics Agency, South Vietnam, financial analyst, 1972-75; Ministry of Finance, Vietnam, financial officer, 1975-80; Faulkner Color Lab, accountant, 1984-86; State of California, Dept of Health Services, auditor, 1986-. **ORGANIZATIONS:** Alpha Beta Psi, 1982-84. **HONORS/AWARDS:** National Bank of South Vietnam, Best Thesis Award, 1972; San Francisco State University, McDale Award, 1983, American Women of Accounting Society Award, 1982. **BIOGRAPHICAL SOURCES:** Difficulties and Problems in Developing Vietnamese Industry, 1972. **HOME ADDRESS:** 72 Fairfield, Foothill Ranch, CA 92610.

TRINH, EUGENE
Astronaut. Vietnamese American. **CAREER:** NASA, California Institute of Technology, Jet Propulsion Lab, astronaut, currently. **HONORS/AWARDS:** Asian Pacific Council, Mainstream America Award for Excellence, for science and technology, 1992. **BUSINESS ADDRESS:** Astronaut, NASA, c/o California Inst of Technology, Jet Propulsion Lab, MS-183/401, 4800 Oak Grove Dr, Pasadena, CA 91101, (818)354-7125.∗

TRINH, HOANG HUY
Engineer. Vietnamese American. **PERSONAL:** Born Jan 2, 1958, Saigon, Vietnam; son of Huynh Khac Trinh and Mien Thi Nguyen; married Ngoc Thanh Trinh, Jul 3, 1989; children: Thao Ngoc, Joseph Hoang-Nam. **EDUCATION:** University of Oklahoma, BSEE, 1987; Southern Methodist University, MSEE, 1993. **CAREER:** General Dynamics, senior engr, 1992-; Lockheed Fort Worth Co, senior engr, 1993-. **HOME ADDRESS:** 8700 N Normandale, #138, Fort Worth, TX 76116. **BUSINESS PHONE:** (817)762-0583.

TRINH, NAM KY
Mechanical engineer. Vietnamese American. **PERSONAL:** Born Jul 5, 1961, Da-Nang, Vietnam; son of Hach D Trinh and My T Luu; married Thanh-Huong T Trinh, Jul 26, 1986; children: Nichole Hoang-Yen. **EDUCATION:** Valencia Community College, AA, 1980; University of Florida, BS, 1982; University of Central Florida, MS, 1985. **CAREER:** Naval Coastal Systems Station, me-

chanical engineer, 1985-. **ORGANIZATIONS:** ASME, 1986-; NRA, 1990-. **MILITARY SERVICE:** US Naval Reserve, lt, 1990-; National Defense Service Medal, 1991. **HOME ADDRESS:** 226 Scooter Dr, Panama City, FL 32408-5538. **BUSINESS PHONE:** (904)234-4546.

TRIPATHI, GORAKH NATH RAM
Educator. Indo-American. **PERSONAL:** Born Jan 1, 1944, Gorakhpur, Uttar Pradesh, India; son of Vishwanath Ram and Ramdasi Devi; married Poonam Tripathi, Jun 8, 1962; children: Pratibha, Pradeep, Amit. **EDUCATION:** University of Gorakhpur, India, PhD, 1968. **CAREER:** University of Gorakhpur, India, lecturer, reader, 1965-83; University of Manchester, UK, commonwealth senior academic staff fellow, 1976-77, Institute of Science and Technology, visiting senior lecturer, 1976-77; University of Notre Dame, Radiation Laboratory, senior scientist, faculty member, 1978-. **SPECIAL ACHIEVEMENTS:** Author of over 100 papers in the subjects of molecular spectroscopy, chemical physics and solid state physics. **BUSINESS ADDRESS:** Sr Scientist, Radiation Lab, University of Notre Dame, Notre Dame, IN 46556, (219)631-5514.

TRIPATHI, RAMESH CHANDRA
Ophthalmologist, researcher, educator. Indo-American. **PERSONAL:** Born Jul 1, 1936, Jamira, India; son of Arjun & Gandhari Tripathi; married Brenda Jennifer Lane, May 20, 1969; children: Anita, Paul. **EDUCATION:** Univ of Agra, India, MD, 1959; Lucknow Univ, India, MS, ophthal, 1963; Royal Coll of Physicians & Surgeons, England, DORCP & S, 1965; Univ of London, Institute of Ophthal, PhD, 1970; Royal Coll of Pathologists, London, FRCPath, 1974; Intl Coll of Surgeons, FICS, 1981; Natl Academy of Sciences, India, FNASc, 1987; Coll of Ophthalmologists, London, FCCphth, 1988; American Coll of Surgeons, FACS, 1990. **CAREER:** GSVM Medical College Hospitals, Lucknow Univ, India, resident house surgeon in ophthal, 1959-50, demonstrator, resident ophthalmic surgeon, 1960-62; Rly Hosp, Divisional Railway Hosp, Delhi, asst surgeon, medical officer in charge of Casualty Dept, 1963-64; Univ Eye Clinic, Belgium, 1964-65; SW Middlesex Hosp, Engl, ophthalmic registrar, 1965-67; Univ of London, Inst of Ophthalmology, Faculty of Medicine, lecturer, clinical sr lecturer, 1967-77, Bd of Studies in Pathology, recognized teacher/mbr, 1968-77, Academic Bd, 1968-77, Academic Council, 1974-77; Moorfields Eye Hosp, London, Hayward Fellow, registrar, chief clinical asst, 1967-71, consultant ophthalmologist, pathologist, 1972-77; Univ of Chicago, prof of ophthal & visual sci, 1977-, Eye Pathology Lab, director, 1977-, prof, 1979-; Univ of Chicago Hosps, attending ophthalmologist, eye pathologist, medical staff mbr, 1977-; Oak Forest Hosp, consult/attending ophthalmologist, 1986-. **ORGANIZATIONS:** Intl Soc of Ocular Toxicology, secretary-treasurer, 1993-; Southeastern Branch of Chicago Medical Soc, pres, 1993-; Chicago Medical Soc, vp, 1993-; American Academy of Ophthalmology, faculty mbr, Basic & Clinical Science Course, 1991-; Illinois Medical Soc, alternate delegate from Southeastern Branch, CMS, 1991-; Intl College of Surgeons in Ophthalmology, vice-regent, 1984-; numerous others. **HONORS/AWARDS:** Royal Soc of Medicine, Ophthalmological Prize, 1971; Ophthalmological Soc of UK, Royal Eye Hospital, London, Prize, 1976; Assn of Indians in America, Honor Award, 1983; American Academy of Ophthalmology, Honor Award, 1984; Indo-American Ctr, Achievement Award, 1991; numerous others. **SPECIAL ACHIEVEMENTS:** Over 400 pubs & 34 monographs & chapters in scientific journals & books encompassing: pathophysiology & anatomy of the eye; disorders of conjunctiva, cornea, contact lenses, & ocular adnexa; glaucoma; cataract; retinal vasculopathies; drug-induced & toxic diseases; genetically determined disorders of eyes; & medical surgical treatment of eye diseases; delivered over 275 presentations at scientific meetings & symposia, many as invited speaker & honored guest. **BUSINESS ADDRESS:** Professor of Ophthalmology & Visual Science, University of Chicago, 939 E 57th St, Visual Sciences Ctr, Rm 107, Chicago, IL 60637, (312)702-1981.

TRIPATHI, SATISH CHANDRA
Scientist, consultant. Indo-American. **PERSONAL:** Born May 15, 1956, Gwalior, Madhya Pradesh, India; son of Shiv Narayan Tripathi & Shanti Tripathi; married Guari S Tripathi, Jun 20, 1986; children: Pooja. **EDUCATION:** Jiwaji University, India, BS, 1975, MS, 1977; Bhopal University, India, MPhil, 1978; University of Glasgow, Scotland, PhD, 1984. **CAREER:** Government Postgraduate College, India lecturer, 1978-80; JNK University, India, assistant professor, 1980-85; Medical College of Wisconsin, res scientist, 1985-87; Emory University, visiting scientist, 1987-89; Massachusetts Institute of Technology, post doctoral scientist/res fellow, 1989-92; IIT Research Institute, staff biologist, 1990-. **ORGANIZATIONS:** Regulatory Affairs Professionals

Society; American Society for Cell Biology; American Association for Advancement of Science; Cell Kinetics Society; British Society for Cell Biology; Indian Society for Cell Biology. **HONORS/AWARDS:** University of Glasgow, Maitland Award, 1983-84. **SPECIAL ACHIEVEMENTS:** Works include: over thirty publications including scientific articles, book chapters, and conference presentations in cell and molecular biology, biotechnology, and public policy. **HOME ADDRESS:** 9643 Karlov Avenue, Skokie, IL 60076, (708)933-1528. **BUSINESS ADDRESS:** Staff Scientist, Dept of Life Sciences, IIT Research Institute, 10 W 35th St, Chicago, IL 60616, (312)567-4539.

TRIPATHI, SATISH K.
Educator, educational administrator. Indo-American. **PERSONAL:** Born Jan 20, 1951, Faizabad, Uttar Pradesh, India; son of Rajendranath Tripathi and Gaura Tripathi; married Kamlesh, May 13, 1970; children: Manish, Aashish. **EDUCATION:** Banaras Hindu University, BSc, 1968, MSc, statistics, 1970; University of Alberta, MS, statistics, 1974; University of Toronto, PhD, computer science, 1979. **CAREER:** ISI, Calcutta, research scholar, 1970-71; Electronic Corp, India, technical officer, 1971-72; University of Alberta, teaching assistant, 1972-74; University of Toronto, research assistant, 1974-78; University of Erlangen, visiting professor, 1985; University of Paris-SUD, visiting professor, 1984-85; University of Maryland, computer science professor, chairman, 1978-. **ORGANIZATIONS:** IEEE, 1984-, senior member, 1986-; ACM, 1978-; many international program committees. **SPECIAL ACHIEVEMENTS:** Published more than 60 articles in various international journals and conference proceedings. **BUSINESS ADDRESS:** Professor and Chairman, Dept of Computer Science, University of Maryland, College Park, MD 20742, (301)405-2662.

TRIPATHI, VIJAI KUMAR
Educator. Indo-American. **PERSONAL:** Born Dec 23, 1942, Kanpur, India; son of Tara Devi and Shivalal Tripathi; married Emma Tripathi, Apr 24, 1968; children: Sanjai, Ajai. **EDUCATION:** Agra University, BSc, 1958; Allahabad University, MSc Tech, 1961; University of Michigan, MSEE, 1964, PhD, 1968. **CAREER:** IIT, Bombay, sr research assistant, 1961-63; University of Michigan, res associate, 1966-67; University of Oklahoma, assistant professor, 1968-73; Oregon State University, asst professor, 1974-77, assoc professor, 1978-84, professor, 1985-. **ORGANIZATIONS:** Institute of Electrical & Electronic Engineers, 1968-, sr member, 1987-; Intl Society for Hybrid Microelectronics, committee chair, 1992-; SPIE, 1991. **HONORS/AWARDS:** IEEE, Fellow, 1993. **SPECIAL ACHIEVEMENTS:** "Transmission Line & Wave Propagation," CRC Press, 1992; "Emerging Optoelectronics," 1993; Guest Editor; IEEE, SPIE; over 150 technical papers in journals and conference proceedings. **BUSINESS ADDRESS:** Professor, Electrical & Computer Engineering, Oregon State University, ECE 220, Corvallis, OR 97331, (503)737-2988.

TRIPATHY, DEOKI N.
Educator. Indo-American. **PERSONAL:** Born Jul 1, 1933, Dwarahat, District Almora, Uttar Pradesh, India; son of Mathura Datt Tripaty & Kala Devi Tripathy; married Vidya D Tripathy, Jan 19, 1969; children: Sandeep K, Neena. **EDUCATION:** UP Agricultural University, Pantnagar, India, BSc & AH, 1964; University of Illinois, Urbana, MS, 1967, PhD, 1970. **CAREER:** University of Illinois, research assistant, 1965-70, research associate, 1970-72, teaching associate, 1972-73, assistant professor, 1973-77, associate professor, 1977-83, professor, 1983-. **ORGANIZATIONS:** International Committee for the Taxonomy of Viruses, poxvirus study group, 1984-93; American Lepropirosis Research Conference, 1972-93, president, 1983; American Society for Microbiology, 1970-92; American Association of Avian Pathologists, 1974-93; American Veterinary Medical Association, 1975-93; US Animal Health Association, 1976-93. **HONORS/AWARDS:** UP Agricultural University, Merit Scholarship, 1962-63, 1963-64, Vice Chancellor's Gold Medal, 1965; Commonwealth Bureau of Animal Health Prize, 1963; University of Illinois, fellowship, 1964-65. **SPECIAL ACHIEVEMENTS:** American College of Veterinary Microbiologists, Specialty Board, Diplomate, 1972; American College of Poultry Veterinarians, Specialty Board, Diplomate, 1992; selected publications from over 85: Pox Viruses of Veterinary Importance, 1981; Genomic and Antigenic Characterization of Avianpox Viruses, 1988; Pox in Diseases of Poultry, 9th ed, 1991; Swine Pox in Current Veterinary Therapy: Food Animal Practice 3, 1993. **HOME ADDRESS:** 104 W McHenry, Urbana, IL 61801, (217)344-0345. **BUSINESS ADDRESS:** Professor, Dept of Veterinary Pathobiology, University of Illinois, Urbana, College of Veterinary Medicine, 2001 S Lincoln Ave, 2641 Veterinary Medicine Basic Sciences Bldg, Urbana, IL 61801, (217)333-6141.

TRIVEDI, KISHOR S.
Educator. Indo-American. **PERSONAL:** Born Aug 20, 1946, Bhavnagar, Gujarat, India; son of Shridharbhai Trivedi and Jayaben Trivedi; married Kalpana, Jun 24, 1973; children: Kavita, Smita. **EDUCATION:** Indian Institute of Technology, BTech, 1968; University of Illinois, MS, 1972, PhD, 1974. **CAREER:** Duke University, asst professor, 1975-79, associate professor, 1979-83, professor, 1983-. **ORGANIZATIONS:** IFIP. **HONORS/AWARDS:** IEEE Computer Society, Meritorious Service Award, fellow. **SPECIAL ACHIEVEMENTS:** Author and coauthor of: Probability and Statistics with Reliability, Queuering, and Computer Science Applications, Prentice Hall, 1962; "Performance & Reliability Analysis Using Directed Acyclic Graphics," with R Sahner, IEEE trans on Software Engineering, vol SE-14, no 10, p 1105-1114, 1987; "Analytic Queuering Models for Programs with Internal Concurrency," with P Heidelberger, IEEE Trans on Compilers, vol C-32, no 1, p 73-82, 1983. **HOME ADDRESS:** 1713 Tisdale Street, Durham, NC 27705, (919)493-6563. **BUSINESS ADDRESS:** Professor, Dept of Electrical Engineering, Duke University, Box 90291, Durham, NC 27707, (919)660-5269.

TRIVEDI, MOHAN MANUBHAI
Engineering researcher, educator. Indo-American. **PERSONAL:** Born Oct 4, 1953, Wardhan, Maharashtra, India; son of Manubhai Jayashankar Trivedi & Tanugauri Manubhai Trivedi; married Nayana M Mehta Trivedi, Aug 22, 1982; children: Amruta, Aditi. **EDUCATION:** Birla Institute of Tech & Science, Pilani, India, BE (w/honors), 1974; Utah State University, ME, 1976, PhD, 1979. **CAREER:** Utah State University, research/assistant teaching, 1975-79; Louisiana State University, associate professor, 1979-86; University of Tennessee, professor, 1986-. **ORGANIZATIONS:** International Society for Optical Eng, fellow; IEEE, senior member. **HONORS/AWARDS:** Utah State University, Distinguished Alumni, 1993; IEEE Comp Society, Pioneer Award, 1988, Meritorious Service Award, 1989; SPIE, fellow, 1990. **SPECIAL ACHIEVEMENTS:** Over 150 publications in robotics, machine vision and human-machine systems fields; Image Analysis Applications, Marcel Dekker, editor, 1990; Digital Image Processing, Spie Press, editor, 1991; Pattern Recognition, IEEE Trans SMC, Machine Vision, associate editor. **HOME ADDRESS:** 749 Cherokee Blvd, Knoxville, TN 37919. **BUSINESS ADDRESS:** Professor, Electrical & Computer Engineering Dept, University of Tennessee, Computer Vision & Robotics Research Lab, Knoxville, TN 37996-2100, (615)974-5450.

TRIVEDI, NAYAN B.
Food company executive. Indo-American. **PERSONAL:** Born Feb 13, 1947, Kapadwanj, Gujarat, India; son of Bhaktiprasad M Trivedi and Kusumben B Trivedi; married Surbhi N Trivedi, Nov 4, 1970; children: Harsh, Nina. **EDUCATION:** Gujarat University, India, BSc, 1967; MS University of Baroada, India, MSc, 1969; University of SW Louisiana, PhD, 1974; University of Wisconsin, Milwaukee, MBA, 1990. **CAREER:** Arroyo Pharmaceutical/Chase Chemical, 1973-76; Schering Corp, scientist, 1976; Nabisco Brands, section mgr, R&D, 1977-81; Universal Foods Corp, research director, 1981-90, general mgr, WJCC, 1990-. **ORGANIZATIONS:** American Chemical Society, 1973-; American Society for Microbiology, 1974-; Institute for Food Technologists, 1988-; Society for Cosmetic Chemists, 1991-. **SPECIAL ACHIEVEMENTS:** Several scientific publications in the field of biotechnology, food technology; several biotech patents. **HOME ADDRESS:** 33 Parkview Road, Cranbury, NJ 08512, (609)395-9547. **BUSINESS PHONE:** (908)757-4500.

TRIVEDI, NAYANA MOHAN
Physician. Indo-American. **PERSONAL:** Born May 3, 1959, Bombay, India; daughter of Niranjanbhai Ratilal Mehta and Veenaben N Mehta; married Mohan Manubhai Trivedi, Aug 22, 1982; children: Amruta, Aditi. **EDUCATION:** University of Miami, Mt Sinai Medical Center, internal medicine residency; Government Medical College; South Gujart University, India, MD, 1982. **CAREER:** Mt Sinai Medical Center, resident, 1985-88; Lillicamp Hospital, emergency room physician, 1987-88; Knox County Health Department, primary care physician, 1988-. **ORGANIZATIONS:** Americal Medical Association; American College of Physicians; Tennessee Medical Association; Knoxville Medical Association. **HONORS/AWARDS:** President, India, Silver Medal. **SPECIAL ACHIEVEMENTS:** South Gujart University, 8 Gold Medals, 1st standing in the University, 1983. **HOME ADDRESS:** 749 Cherokee Blvd, Knoxville, TN 37919. **BUSINESS ADDRESS:** Physician, Knox County Health Department, Cleveland Place, Knoxville, TN 37996-2100.

TRIVEDI-DOCTOR, MINAKSHI DIPAK

Educator. Indo-American. **PERSONAL:** Born Sep 5, 1956, London, England; daughter of Kishore Trivedi and Pushpa Trivedi; married Dipak Pravin Doctor, Aug 18, 1985; children: Arjun, Avni. **EDUCATION:** Delhi University, BS, 1976, MS (academic distinction), 1978; BK School of Business Management, MBA, 1984; University of Texas at Dallas, PhD, 1991. **CAREER:** SIES College of Arts and Sciences, teacher, 1979-80; GLS School, teacher, 1981-82; Torrent Pharmaceuticals, distribution manager, 1984; University of Texas at Dallas, teaching assistant, 1985-89; SUNY at Buffalo, assistant professor, 1989-. **ORGANIZATIONS:** American Marketing Association, 1987-; The Institute of Management Science, 1987-90. **HONORS/AWARDS:** Faculty Research Awards Committee, Summer Research Grant, 1993; NYS/UUP Professional Development & QWL Committee, Faculty Development Grant, 1990, 1993, University at Buffalo Foundation, Inc, featured in annual report, 1991-92; Faculty Research Awards Committee, Joseph T J Stewart Fellowship, 1992; Office of Teaching Effectiveness, Faculty Development Grant, 1990; American Marketing Association, Consortium Fellow, 1988; BK School of Business Management, Merit Scholarship, 1983-84. **SPECIAL ACHIEVEMENTS:** Published: "An Investigation of the Relationship Between the MECCS Model and Advertising Affect," Cognitive and Affective Responses to Advertising, 1989; conference presentations (4) on various marketing issues, at ORSA/TIMS National Meetings, and Marketing Science Conferences, 1990, 1991, 1992. **BUSINESS ADDRESS:** Assistant Professor, State University of New York at Buffalo, North Campus, School of Management, Jacobs Center, Buffalo, NY 14260-0001, (716)645-3261.

TRUONG THI, HOA-DIEN

Company executive. Vietnamese American. **PERSONAL:** Born Mar 3, 1923, Vietnam; daughter of Truong-Nhu Hy and Tran-Thi Thuan; married Nguyen-Duy-Thu-Luong (divorced); children: Tuong Van, Tuong-Anh, Nguyen Duy Tuan, Nguyen-Duy Linh. **EDUCATION:** Hautes Etudes Commerciales, Paris, MBA, 1954; Harvard University International Marketing Institute, 1967. **CAREER:** Blue Mountain Inc, president, 1980-; The Sugar Maples Resort, president, 1977-. **ORGANIZATIONS:** New York Hotel Motel Association; Elka Park Club Association; Buddhist Association of Massachusetts. **BUSINESS ADDRESS:** President, The Sugar Maples Resort, Main St, Maplecrest, NY 12454.

TSAI, BETTY L.

Educator, librarian. Taiwanese American. **PERSONAL:** Born in Taipei, Taiwan; daughter of Kun-San Lin and Pao-Tien Lin; married Kuo-Yuan Tsai; children: Wendy, Anita. **EDUCATION:** National Taiwan University, BA, 1962; Rutgers University, MLS, 1965. **CAREER:** SUNY at Stony Brook, serials librarian, 1965-68; Trenton State College, catalog librarian, 1968-69; Bucks County Community College, assistant professor, 1970-71, assistant director, 1971-79, senior associate professor, tech serv librarian, 1979-93, professor, systems librarian, 1993-. **ORGANIZATIONS:** Asian/Pacific American Librarians Association, president, 1987-88; Chinese American Librarian Association, president, 1993-94; OCLC Users Council, alternate delegate, 1986-90, delegate, 1990; American Library Assn, various committees. **HONORS/AWARDS:** ALA Bogle International Library Travel Grant, 1988; BCCC Foundation, grants, 1988, Cultural Incentive Grant, 1991, Key Resource Faculty, 1991-; WTTM, Consumer Award, 1993; Middle States Assn of Colleges Evaluation Teams, 1986-. **SPECIAL ACHIEVEMENTS:** "Chinese People," a Hypercard program, 1991; "Quality Control of the Online Public Access Catalog," Proceedings of the International Symposium of New Technologies, Xian, China, 1988; Asian/Pacific American Librarians Association, in ALA Yearbook, 1988; book reviews in LISCA and ARBA, 1988-91. **BUSINESS ADDRESS:** Professor, Systems Librarian, Bucks County Community College Library, Swamp Rd, Newtown, PA 18940, (215)968-8010.

TSAI, BILIN PAULA

Educator. Chinese American/Japanese American. **PERSONAL:** Born May 23, 1949, Seattle, WA; daughter of Ai Chih Tsai & Ryo Morikawa Tsai; married Donald Poe, Dec 17, 1977; children: Sarah, Michael. **EDUCATION:** University of Chicago, SB, 1971; University of North Carolina, Chapel Hill, PhD, 1975. **CAREER:** University of Nebraska, Lincoln, postdoctorate associate, 1975-76; NIST (NBS), visiting research chemist, 1987-88; University of Minnesota, Duluth, associate dean, 1983-87, associate professor, assistant professor, 1976-92, professor and head, 1992-. **ORGANIZATIONS:** AAHE Asian Caucus, past chair, chair, chair elect, 1991-94; American Chemical Society, Women's Chemists Committee, 1989-. **HONORS/AWARDS:** University of Minnesota, Bush Sabbatical Award, 1987-88. **SPECIAL ACHIEVEMENTS:**

Author: "Spectroscopic and Ab Initio Studies of Difluoromethly Radicals and Cations," J Phys Chem, vol 96, p 585-94, 1992; "Experimental and Ab Initio Studies of Electronic Structures of the lcL3 Radical and Cation," J Am Chem Soc Vol 112, p 5763-5772, 1990; "Multiphoton Ionization of SiH3 and SiD3 Radicals: Electronic Spectra, Vibrational Analyses of the Ground and Rydberg States, and Ionization Potentials," J Chem Phys, Vol 91, 1990; "Electronic Spectra of CF2 CL and CFCL2 Radicals Observed by Resonance Enhanced Multiphoton Ionization," J Phys Chem, Vol 93, p 5334-36, 1989. **BUSINESS ADDRESS:** Professor and Head, Dept of Chemistry, University of Minnesota, Duluth, 10 University Avenue, Duluth, MN 55812, (218)726-7220.

TSAI, BOR-SHENG

Educator. Chinese American/Taiwanese American. **PERSONAL:** Born Apr 8, 1950, Kaohsiung, Taiwan; son of Yu-shiu and Huo-chu Tsai; married Shiu-hwa Yu Tsai, Feb 7, 1977; children: Shengdar. **EDUCATION:** Fu-jen Catholic University, library science, 1974; Case Western Reserve University, MSIS, 1979, PhD, information science, 1987. **CAREER:** Nan-ya Plastics Techniques Library, cataloger, 1973; National Central Library, Taiwan, Republic of China, acquisitions librarian, 1976-77; Case Western Reserve University, reference librarian, 1981; Cleveland Public Schools, Multicultural Bilingual Education, designer, instructor, 1985-86; Wayne State University, assistant professor, 1987-. **ORGANIZATIONS:** American Society for Information Science, 1987-, Education/Research Committee, 1993-, Michigan Chapter Steering Committee, 1991-92, representative, Chapter Assembly, 1992-93; Association of Library and Information Science Education, 1987-; American Library Association, 1987-; Chinese-American Librarians Association, Publication Committee, editor, E-Mail Committee, chair, 1991-; Michigan Library Association, 1987-; American Association of University Professors, 1987-. **HONORS/AWARDS:** Multicultural/Bilingual Education Program, Cleveland Public Schools, Oustanding Service, 1986; Wayne State University, nominee, WSU President's Award for Excellence in Teaching, 1993; Martha Holden Jennings Foundation, research grant for developing Computer-Assisted Tutorial System, 1985-86; National Science Foundation, funding for paper presentation at 3rd International Conf on Informetrics, India, 1991. **SPECIAL ACHIEVEMENTS:** Designer: Library of Plastics Techniques-Classification Scheme and Tables, 1973; designer: Computer-Assisted Tutorial Systems, 1986; designer: Animation-Supported Navigation System, 1993; "The Development of Theory & Practice of Cognitive Computing-based Automatic Instruction," paper contributed to the 1993 International Symposium on the Development of Theory and Practice of Lib & Inf Sci, Wuhan, PRC, May, 1993, others. **MILITARY SERVICE:** ROTC, infantry, political warfare, Taiwan, ROC, first lieutenant, 1974-76. **BUSINESS ADDRESS:** Asst Prof, Library & Info Sci Program, Wayne State University, 315 Kresge Library, Detroit, MI 48202, (313)577-6202.

TSAI, CHESTER

Educator. Chinese American. **PERSONAL:** Born Mar 7, 1935, Amoy, Fujian, China; son of W T Tsai and S M Wu; married Yen-Ying Tsai, Jun 16, 1962; children: Vivian Tsai Chin, Eugene, Renee. **EDUCATION:** National Taiwan University, BA, 1957; Marquette University, MS, 1961; Illinois Institute of Technology, PhD, 1964. **CAREER:** Michigan State University, professor, 1964-. **HOME ADDRESS:** 5419 Amber Dr, East Lansing, MI 48823, (517)337-7475. **BUSINESS ADDRESS:** Professor, Michigan State University, D216 Wells Hall, East Lansing, MI 48824, (517)353-3833.

TSAI, CHIA-YIN

Educator. Taiwanese American. **PERSONAL:** Born Dec 15, 1937, Taichung, Taiwan; son of Hsi-Keng Tsai and Chin-Ko Huang Tsai; married Hsueh-Chiao Tsai, Sep 9, 1967; children: Henry, Susan. **EDUCATION:** National Taiwan University, BS, 1960; Purdue University, PhD, 1967. **CAREER:** Academia Sinica, Taiwan, visiting professor, 1976; National Taiwan University, Taiwan, visiting professor, 1992; Purdue University, research associate, 1967-69, assistant professor, 1969-74, associate professor, 1974-80, professor, 1980-. **ORGANIZATIONS:** Sigma Xi; American Society of Plant Physiologists; Crop Science Society of America; MADICA, Italy, editorial board, 1975-78; NIH, USA, study section, 1981-85; North America Taiwanese Professors Association, president, 1981-82; Allied Corporation, consultant, 1983-84; Asgrow Seed Co, consultant, 1985-87. **HONORS/AWARDS:** National Science Council, Taiwan, distinguished service, 1976. **SPECIAL ACHIEVEMENTS:** Published more than 100 articles, in scientific journals; related to carbon and nitrogen metabolism in maize. **BUSINESS ADDRESS:** Professor of Genetics, Dept of Botany and Plant Pathology, Purdue University, 1155 Lilly Hall of Life Sciences, West Lafayette, IN 47907, (317)494-4640.

TSAI, CHON-KWO
Engineer. Chinese American. **PERSONAL:** Born Dec 7, 1955, Taipei, Taiwan; son of Y E Tsai and Whe-Jen Wang Tsai; married Charlotte H Y Chen-Tsai, Jul 30, 1983; children: Michele S, Emily P. **EDUCATION:** National Tsing Hua University, BS, 1978; Massachusetts Institute of Technology, MS, 1982, PhD, 1985. **CAREER:** Westinghouse Elec Corp, senior engineer, 1985-. **ORGANIZATIONS:** American Nuclear Society, 1980. **HONORS/AWARDS:** Westinghouse Elec Corp, Signature Award of Excellence, 1989, General Manager E-Award, 1988. **SPECIAL ACHIEVEMENTS:** Developed and licensed the first US best-estimate large break loss of coolant accident safety analysis methodology, 1988. **BUSINESS ADDRESS:** Senior Engineer, Westinghouse Elec Corp, PO Box 598, Pittsburgh, PA 15230-0598, (412)733-6538.

TSAI, CHUANG CHUANG
Physicist. Taiwanese American. **PERSONAL:** Born Jan 25, 1950, Taipei, Taiwan. **EDUCATION:** University of Chicago, PhD, 1978. **CAREER:** Xerox Corp, Palo Alto Research Center, physicist, currently. **BUSINESS ADDRESS:** Physicist, Xerox Corp, Palo Alto Research Center, 3333 Coyote Hill Rd, Palo Alto, CA 94304, (415)812-4515.

TSAI, FRANK Y.
Government official. Chinese American. **PERSONAL:** Born Feb 6, 1934, Tsingtao, China; married Julie Chou; children: Audrey, Antoinette. **EDUCATION:** National Taiwan University, BS, 1955; University of Minnesota, MS, 1960, PhD, 1968; New York University, 1973-74. **CAREER:** St Anthony Hydraulic Lab, research assistant, 1958-60; University of Minnesota, research fellow, 1960-68; Iowa State University, assistant professor, assistant dept head, 1968-72; EBASCO, senior engineer and section chief, 1972-75; HUD, senior engineer, 1975-79; FEMA, senior technical advisor, 1979-. **ORGANIZATIONS:** ASCE; The Tsunami Society; Sigma Xi; Federal Asian Pacific American Council; OCA; NoVAACC; IACWD; ECCFA; CAREN Inc. **BUSINESS ADDRESS:** Senior Technical Advisor, Federal Insurance Admin, FEMA, 500 C St, Federal Center Plaza, Rm 423, Washington, DC 20472, (202)646-2753.

TSAI, GOW-JEN (GORDON)
Biochemical engineer. Taiwanese American. **PERSONAL:** Born Apr 22, 1955, Tainan, Taiwan; son of Shih-Ching Tsai and Min-Shang Lee Tsai; married Chen-Yin Lai Tsai, May 22, 1985; children: Victor, Stephanie. **EDUCATION:** National Cheng Kung University, BS, 1977; National Taiwan University, MS, 1979; Purdue University, PhD, 1986. **CAREER:** Purdue University, research engineer, 1986-91; Lederle Labs, American Cyanamid Co, senior research biochemical engineer, 1991-. **ORGANIZATIONS:** American Chemical Society; American Institute of Chemical Engineers. **HONORS/AWARDS:** Tau Beta Pi, 1984; Phi Kappa Phi, 1985; Phi Tau Phi, 1977. **SPECIAL ACHIEVEMENTS:** Process developments of microbiological processes, 1991-; Research in enzyme and microbiological technologies, 1986-91. **BUSINESS ADDRESS:** Senior Research Biochemical Engineer, Lederle Laboratories, American Cyanamid Co, N Middletown Rd, Bldg 130, Rm 607, Pearl River, NY 10965, (914)732-4221.

TSAI, JAMES H.
Educator. Chinese American. **PERSONAL:** Born Jun 10, 1934, Fuzhou, Fujian, China; married Sue C Tsai, Aug 1, 1960; children: Cynthia, Julie. **EDUCATION:** National Chung Hsing University, BS, 1957; Michigan State University, MS, 1967, PhD, 1969. **CAREER:** International Institute of Tropical Agricu, scientist, 1969-70; Michigan State University, research assoc, 1970-73; University of Florida, professor, 1973-. **ORGANIZATIONS:** Entomological Society of America, subsection chairman, 1979-86; American Phytopathological Society, 1973-; Entomological Society of China, honorary member, 1978-. **HONORS/AWARDS:** National Science Foundation, international travel grants, 1976, 1980; National Academy of Sciences, research grant, 1980; USDA Competitive, research grants, 1988, 1989, 1991; USDA Tropical Agriculture research grants, 1981, 1987, 1990, 1993; USAID, competitive grants, 1990. **SPECIAL ACHIEVEMENTS:** Research on plant viruses and prokaryotic agents transmitted by the insects; published over 80 refereed articles in plant pathological and entomological journals; 10 book chapters; one monograph. **BUSINESS ADDRESS:** Professor, University of Florida, 3205 College Ave, Fort Lauderdale, FL 33314, (305)475-8990.

TSAI, JEFFREY J. P.
Educator. Taiwanese American. **EDUCATION:** Northwestern University, PhD, 1986. **CAREER:** University of Illinois, associate professor, 1991-. **OR-**GANIZATIONS: IEEE, senior member, 1990-; Mid-American Chinese Science and Technology Assn, board director, 1991-; Mid-American Chinese Science & Technology Association, vice president, 1993-94. **HONORS/AWARDS:** IEEE and Engineering Foundation Society, Research Award, 1988, Distingushed Visitor, 1993-. **SPECIAL ACHIEVEMENTS:** Publication: 1 book; over 100 papers in journals and conference proceedings in the area of artifical intelligence and software engineering. **BUSINESS ADDRESS:** EECS Dept, University of Illinois, 851 S Morgan St, M/C 154, Chicago, IL 60607, (312)996-9324.

TSAI, JEN-SAN
Physicist. Taiwanese American. **PERSONAL:** Born Aug 6, 1943, Koashing, Taiwan; son of High-Tong Tsai; married Lorraine Tsai, Jan 18, 1971; children: Jack, Andrea. **EDUCATION:** National Chao-Tung University, BS, electrophysics, 1968; University of Kansas, MS, nuclear physics, 1972; University of Toronto, PhD, atomic and nuclear physics, 1980. **CAREER:** University of Toronto, Dept of Chem Eng, postdoc, 1980-81; McMaster University, Dept of Physics, research associate, 1981-87; Harvard Medical School, postdoctoral fellow, 1987-89, instructor, 1989-91; Tufts - New England Med Ctr, asst professor, clinic physicist, 1991-. **ORGANIZATIONS:** American Assn of Physicists in Medicine, 1988-. **HONORS/AWARDS:** University of Toronto, Steven Nuclear Science Award, 1973-76. **SPECIAL ACHIEVEMENTS:** Areas of specialization: Stereotactic radiosurgery, radiation therapy treatment planning, quality assurances in radiotherapy, neutron capture nuclear reactions, photo neutron reactions, positron annihilation in atomic collisions, 1987-. **HOME PHONE:** (617)489-0529. **BUSINESS ADDRESS:** Assistant Professor, Dept of Radiation Oncology, Clinic Physicist, Tufts - New England Medical Center, 750 Washington St, #246, Boston, MA 02111.

TSAI, JIR-SHIONG
Educator. Taiwanese American. **PERSONAL:** married. **CAREER:** New York University Medical Center, associate professor, currently. **ORGANIZATIONS:** Endocrine Society; American Thyroid Association; American College of Physicians, fellow. **BUSINESS ADDRESS:** Associate Professor, New York University Medical Center, 530 First Ave, New York, NY 10016, (212)263-7043.

TSAI, KUEI-WU
Educator. Chinese American. **PERSONAL:** Born Jan 22, 1941, Pei-Kang, Taiwan; son of Chang-Pei Tsai & Teh Huang; married Leslie Wang Tsai, Feb 2, 1969; children: Felix, Gordon. **EDUCATION:** National Taiwan University, BSCE, 1962; Princeton University, MSCE, 1965, MA, 1965, PhD, 1967. **CAREER:** Engineering consultant 1968-; San Jose State University, chairman of civil engineering, 1981-89, professor, 1967-. **ORGANIZATIONS:** American Society of Civil Engineers, fellow, 1985-, San Jose Branch, president, 1978-79; Chinese Institute of Engineers, USA, chairman of national council, 1990, San Francisco Bay Area Chapter, president, 1981-82, chairman, 1988-89; Chinese American Economic & Technology Development Association, president, 1985-87; Chinese Cultural Association in USA, president, 1975. **HONORS/AWARDS:** San Jose State University, Outstanding Professor, 1992, Meritorious Performance and Professional Promise Awards, 1986, 1988, 1990; Chi-Epsilon Civil Engineering Honor Society, James M Robbins National Outstanding Teaching Award, 1993, Excellence-In-Teaching Award for the Pacific District, 1993, chapter honor member, 1987; Chinese Institute of Engineers, Institute Award, 1987. **SPECIAL ACHIEVEMENTS:** Publications on strength and consolidation characteristics of soft soils, penetrometer, land reclamation and development, settlement and stability of construction and structures on soft soils, diaphragm wall. **BIOGRAPHICAL SOURCES:** Who's Who in Technology Today. **BUSINESS ADDRESS:** Professor of Civil Engineering, San Jose State University, San Jose, CA 95192, (408)924-3902.

TSAI, LIN
Research chemist. Chinese American. **PERSONAL:** Born May 30, 1922, Hong Kong. **EDUCATION:** Chinese National Southwest Association University, BS, 1946; University of Oregon, MA, 1949; Florida State University, PhD, 1954. **CAREER:** Ohio State University, research associate, 1954-57; Worcester Foundation, research scientist, 1957-59; National Institutes of Health, visiting scientist, 1959-62, organic chemist, 1962-74, research scientist, 1974-. **ORGANIZATIONS:** American Chemical Society; Royal Society of Chemistry, London; American Society for Biochemistry and Molecular Biology; Alpha Phi Sigma; Sigma Xi; Phi Kappa Phi. **BUSINESS ADDRESS:** Research Chemist, National Institutes of Health, Bldg 3, Rm 110, Bethesda, MD 20892.

TSAI, LUNG-WEN
Educator. Taiwanese American. **PERSONAL:** Born Feb 20, 1945, Taipei, Taiwan; son of Chung-Ming Tsai and Kuy C Tsai; married Lung-Chu Tsai; children: Jule A, David J. **EDUCATION:** National Taiwan University, BS, 1967; State University of New York, Buffalo, MS, 1970; Stanford University, PhD, 1973. **CAREER:** Hewlett-Packard Co, r&d eng, 1973-78; General Motors Research, senior staff research eng, 1978-86; University of Maryland, professor, 1986-. **ORGANIZATIONS:** ASME, fellow, Mechanisms Committee, 1972-; SAE. **HONORS/AWARDS:** ASME, Melville Medal, 1985; SAE, Arch T Colwell Award, 1988; General Motors, John Campbell Award, 1986; Procter & Gamble Co, Procter & Gamble Award of Merit, 1984, 1989, 1991; ASME, ASME Mechanisms Best Paper Award, 1984. **SPECIAL ACHIEVEMENTS:** Over sixty archival journal and conference proceedings papers; four US patents, 1982, 1984; two patents pending, 1993; proficient in Chinese. **BUSINESS ADDRESS:** Professor, Institute for Systems Research, University of Maryland, College Park, College Park, MD 20742, (301)405-6629.

TSAI, MARK F.
Physician. Taiwanese American. **PERSONAL:** Born Nov 26, 1950, Chia Yi, Taiwan; son of Tien Tsai and Sheng Wu; married Ying C Tsai, Jan 24, 1978; children: Franklin C, Benjamin C, Joseph C. **EDUCATION:** National Taiwan University, MD, 1977; Harvard University, MPH, 1979. **CAREER:** University of Missouri, instructor of clinical medicine, 1982-84; Texas A & M University, assistant professor of medicine, 1984-87. **ORGANIZATIONS:** American College of Gastroenterology, fellow; American College of Physicians; American Society of Gastrointestinal Endoscopy; American Gastroenterological Association. **BUSINESS ADDRESS:** Physician, 18350 Roscoe Blvd, Ste 307, Northridge, CA 91325, (818)772-2798.

TSAI, MICHAEL MING-PING
Physician. Chinese American. **PERSONAL:** Born Mar 28, 1939, Chiayi, Taiwan; son of Y M Tsai and H W Tsai; married Pi-Zu, Apr 27, 1968; children: Patricia Julin. **EDUCATION:** Kaohsiung Medical College, MD, 1965; Methodist Hospital of Brooklyn, intern, 1966-67; Philadelphia State Hospital, resident in psychiatry, 1968-69; VA Hospital, resident in psychiatry, 1969-71; Hillside Hospital, fellow, child & adolescent psychiatry, 1971-72. **CAREER:** New Jersey Neuro-Psychiatric Institute, clinical psychiatrist, 1972-75; private practice, Indiana, PA, psychiatrist, 1975-78; Metropolitan State Hospital, staff psychiatrist, 1978-. **HONORS/AWARDS:** American Board of Psychiatry and Neurology, board certified, 1978. **BUSINESS ADDRESS:** Physician, 1878 Calle La Paz, Rowland Heights, CA 91748, (818)810-4303.

TSAI, MING-DAW
Educator. Chinese American/Taiwanese American. **PERSONAL:** Born Sep 1, 1950, Taiwan; son of Hui-jan Tsai and Wuchen Tsai; married Roa-Tong Tsai, Aug 27, 1976; children: Joyce C, Christopher M, Eric M. **EDUCATION:** National Taiwan University, BS, 1972; Purdue University, PhD, 1978. **CAREER:** Purdue University, visiting assistant professor, 1979-80; Rutgers University, assistant professor of chemistry, 1980-81; Ohio State University, assistant professor of chemistry, 1981-86, associate professor of chemistry, 1986-90; University of Wisconsin, biochemistry, visiting professor, 1989-90; Ohio State University, professor of chemistry, 1990-92, professor of chemistry and biochemistry, 1992-. **ORGANIZATIONS:** American Chemical Society; American Society of Biochemistry and Molecular Biology; American Association for the Advancement of Science; Protein Society; Sigma Xi. **HONORS/AWARDS:** Alfred P Sloan, fellow, 1983-85; Ohio State Chapter of Sigma Xi, Faculty Research Award, 1985; Camille and Henry Dreyfus Foundation, Teacher-Scholar Award, 1985-90; Ohio State University, Distinguished Scholar Award, 1992; American Association for the Advancement of Science, elected fellow, 1992. **SPECIAL ACHIEVEMENTS:** Published 85 research articles in primary chemistry and biochemistry journals. **MILITARY SERVICE:** Chinese Army (Taiwan), 2nd lieutenant, 1972-74. **BUSINESS ADDRESS:** Professor of Chemistry and Biochemistry, The Ohio State University, 120 West 18th Avenue, 100 New Chemistry, Columbus, OH 43210-1173.

TSAI, STANLEY
Engineer. Chinese American/Myanmar American. **PERSONAL:** Born Jul 26, 1950, Rangoon, Burma; son of Kun Hui Tsai and Tzeu Lyan Tzau; married Sharon L Tsai, Jun 16, 1976; children: Frederick H. **EDUCATION:** National Taiwan University, 1976; George Washington University, 1984. **CAREER:** Bell Sales, engr, 1979-81; Energy Mgt Corp, project engr, 1981-84; Catalyst Research, process engr, project engr, 1984-88; Whitman Requandt & Associates, engr, 1989-90; MD Dept of the Environment, public health engr, 1990-.

ORGANIZATIONS: Chemical Engineering, product research. **HONORS/AWARDS:** MD Dept of the Environment, Merit Award, 1992. **SPECIAL ACHIEVEMENTS:** Language proficiency: English, Chinese & Burmese. **BUSINESS ADDRESS:** Public Health Engineer, HWC, Maryland Dept of the Environment, 2500 Broening Hwy, Hazardous Waste Program, Baltimore, MD 21224, (410)631-3400.

TSAI, STEPHEN WEI-LUN
Educator. Chinese American. **PERSONAL:** Born Jul 6, 1929, Beijing, China; son of Stephen Tsai and Lily Tsai; married Iris Lee Tsai, Jun 20, 1954; children: Stephen Ming-Hsi, Ming-Hao Clayton. **EDUCATION:** Yale University, BE, 1952, DEng, 1961. **CAREER:** Foster Wheeler Corp, project engineer, 1952-58; Philco-Ford, manager, 1961-66; Washington University, professor, 1966-68; USAF Materials Lab, chief scientist, 1968-72, director of mechanics, 1972-90; Stanford University, research professor, 1990-. **ORGANIZATIONS:** ASME, fellow, 1952-; SAMPE, 1980-. **HONORS/AWARDS:** Tau Beta Pi, Engineering Society, 1952; Sigma Xi, Engineering Society, 1961. **SPECIAL ACHIEVEMENTS:** Editor-in-chief, Journal of Composite Materials, 1967-; editor-in-chief, Journal of Reinforced Plastics, 1982-; co-author, Introduction to Composite Materials, 1980; co-author, Composites Design, 4th ed, 1988; author, Theory of Composites Design, 1992. **BUSINESS ADDRESS:** Professor, Dept of Aeronautics and Astronautics, Stanford University, Durand Bldg, Stanford, CA 94305-4035.

TSAI, THEODORE F.
Physician. Chinese American. **PERSONAL:** Born Oct 10, 1948, Nanking, China; son of Wen-tchih & Janet Wu Tsai; married Sherry, Jun 24, 1976; children: Tobias, Elizabeth. **EDUCATION:** Antioch College, BA, 1969; University of Pennsylvania, MD, 1974; Johns Hopkins University, MPH, 1981. **CAREER:** Johns Hopkins Hospital, 1974-76, 1978-79; National Institutes of Health, medical officer, 1992-93; Centers for Disease Control, medical officer, 1976-78, 1980-92, asst division director, 1993-. **ORGANIZATIONS:** Infectious Disease Society of America, fellow, 1991-; Society for Pediatric Research, fellow, 1991; Pediatric Infectious Diseases Society, 1991. **HONORS/AWARDS:** University of Pennsylvania of Medicine, Alpha Omega Alpha, 1974; Centers for Disease Control, Alexander Langmuir Prize, co-author, 1976; USPHS, Outstanding Service Medal, 1987, 1990, Commendation Medal, 1989, Unit Commendation Medal, 1993; American Society for Microbiology, fellow, 1993. **BUSINESS ADDRESS:** Medical Officer, Centers for Disease Control, Fort Collins, CO 80522, (303)221-6407.

TSAN, MIN-FU
Researcher, government official. Taiwanese American. **PERSONAL:** Born Jan 27, 1942, Tainan, Taiwan; son of Tswan-De Tsan & Der-Han Huang Tsan; married Linda W Chen Tsan, May 24, 1975; children: Gloria L, Grace L. **EDUCATION:** National Taiwan University Medical College, MD, 1967; Harvard University Graduate School of Arts & Sciences, Medical Division, PhD, 1971. **CAREER:** Johns Hopkins University School of Medicine, assistant professor, medicine & radiology, 1975-79, associate professor, medicine & radiology, 1979-82; Stratton VA Medical Center, associate chief of staff for research & development, 1982-; Albany Medical College, professor of medicine & physiology, 1982-; Albany Research Institute, president, 1989-. **ORGANIZATIONS:** American Association for the Advancement of Science, 1970-; American Federation of Clinical Res, 1975-; American Society for Hematology, 1976-; American Society of Nuclear Medicine, 1977-91; Chinese Medical & Health Association, 1975-; Society Exp Biol & Medicine, 1989-; Chinese American Society Nuclear Medicine, 1982-; Sigma Xi, 1990-. **HONORS/AWARDS:** Harvard University, University Scholarship, 1968-71; NIH Research Career Development Award, 1977-82; Chinese American Med Society, Scientific Award, 1990; American Board of International Medicine, Diplomate, 1975; Amer Board of Nuclear Medicine, Diplomate, 1976; ABIM, Subspeciality Hematology, Diplomate, 1978. **SPECIAL ACHIEVEMENTS:** Published over 100 original papers in peer-reviewed scientific journals and over 10 book chapters. **BUSINESS ADDRESS:** Associate Chief of Staff for Research & Development, Samuel S Stratton VA Medical Center, 113 Holland Ave, Albany, NY 12208, (518)462-3311.

TSANG, BION YU-TING
Musician. Chinese American. **PERSONAL:** Born May 4, 1967, Lansing, MI; son of Paul J Tsang & Helena R Lit Tsang. **EDUCATION:** Harvard University, BA, 1988; Yale University, MM, 1991, MMA, doctoral candidate, 1993. **CAREER:** Self-employed, Columbia Artists management, cellist, currently. **HONORS/AWARDS:** Avery Fisher Career Grant, 1991; Musician Emer-

gency Fund Career Grant, 1990; IX International Tchaikovsky Competition in Moscow, Bronze Medal, 1990; Piatigorsky Memorial Prize, 1981; Artist International Award, 1984. **SPECIAL ACHIEVEMENTS:** Solo appearances with: New York Philharmonic, Atlanta Symphony Orchestra, National Symphony Orchestra, Stuttgart Chamber Orchestra, Moscow Philharmonic, Taiwan National Symphony; Chamber music appearances with: violinists Cho-Liang Lin and Pamela Frank, also Boston Chamber Music Society; further appearances: Wolf Trap, Marlboro Music, Portland Chamber Music Festival; Laurel Festival of Arts, PA, director of chamber music. **BIOGRAPHICAL SOURCES:** Various reviews and feature articles in The New York Times, Boston Globe, Washington Post, Washington Times, Los Angeles Times, New York Times Magazine, Strad Magazine, Strings Magazine. **BUSINESS ADDRESS:** Cellist, Columbia Artists Management Inc, c/o Ronald A Wilford & Laurence E Tucker, 165 W 57th St, New York, NY 10019.

TSANG, CHIU
Educational administrator. Chinese American. **CAREER:** Career Resources Development Center, executive director; City College of San Francisco, Vocational Education, dean, 1992-. **ORGANIZATIONS:** California Association for Asian Pacific Bilingual Education, president. **SPECIAL ACHIEVEMENTS:** Career Resources Development Center, July Graduation Ceremony, speaker, 1992. **BUSINESS ADDRESS:** Dean, Vocational Education, City College of San Francisco, 33 Gough St, San Francisco, CA 94103, (415)239-3000.*

TSANG, DEAN ZENSH
Electrical engineer. Chinese American. **PERSONAL:** Born Aug 13, 1952, Detroit, MI; son of Chi Mou Tsang & Chin Chow Nien. **EDUCATION:** Massachusetts Institute of Technology, SBEE, 1974, ScD, 1981; University of Illinois, Urbana-Champaign, MS, 1976. **CAREER:** LTV Aerospace, engineering aide, 1973; University of Illinois, research assistant, teaching assistant, 1974-75; MIT Lincoln Lab, research assistant, 1975-81, staff member, 1981-, program manager, 1990-. **ORGANIZATIONS:** Institute of Electrical and Electronic Engineers, Lasers and Electrooptics Society, membership chairman, 1991-, LEOS chapters committee, 1988-92, LEOS engineers committee, 1989-92, Boston chapter LEOS, chairman, 1988, Boston chapter LEOS, secretary-treasurer, 1987; Optical Society of America, 1989-; Sigma Xi, board of electors, 1985-. **HONORS/AWARDS:** IEEE, senior member, 1988. **SPECIAL ACHIEVEMENTS:** "Optical Interconnections for Digital Systems," IEEE Aerospace and Electric Systems, vol 7, p 10, 1992; "Optical Interconnections in Digital Systems Status and Prospects," Optics and Photonics News, vol 1, p 23-29, 1990; "One Gigabit per Second Free Space Optical Interconnection," Applied Optics, vol 29, p 2034-2037, 1990; co-author, IEEE Trans Comp, Hybrids Manufacturing Technology, vol 15, p 451-456, Aug 1992; "Optical Interconnections for Digital Systems," IEEE AES Systems Magazine, vol 7, p 10-15, Sep 1992; numerous others. **HOME ADDRESS:** 26 Beacon St, Apt 34F, Burlington, MA 01803. **BUSINESS ADDRESS:** Program Manager, Staff Member, MIT Lincoln Laboratory, 244 Wood St, C-213, Lexington, MA 02173.

TSANG, WAI LIN
Engineer. Chinese American. **PERSONAL:** Born Jun 3, 1951, Toishan, Kwantung, People's Republic of China; son of Tse Kwan Tsung and Bick Lin Chin-Tsung; married Rose Pui-shan, Aug 3, 1985; children: Pamela Chi-Ping, William Chi-Kern. **EDUCATION:** Northeastern University, BScEE (with honors), 1974, MScEE, 1975, PhDEE, 1981. **CAREER:** Northeastern University, assistant professor, 1980-81; Intermetrics, Incorporate, systems engineer, 1981-82; GTE Sylvania, research engineer, 1982-86; MITRE Corporation, member of technical staff, 1986-88; Science Applications International Corporation, senior engineer, currently. **ORGANIZATIONS:** American Institute of Aeronautics & Astronautics, senior member, 1970-; Institute of Electrical and Electronics Engineers, senior member, 1970-; Association for Computing Machinery, 1990-; Institute of Navigation, 1980-; Radio Technical Commission for Aeronautics, 1980-; Airlines Electrical Engineering Committee, 1990-; Air Traffic Technical Committee, 1990-; Civil GPS Service Interface Committee, 1992-; AFCEA, 1991-. **HONORS/AWARDS:** Massachusetts Board of Higher Education, Scholarship, 1969-75; Eta Kappa Nu; Tau Beta Pi; Northwestern University, Honorary BSCEE, 1974. **SPECIAL ACHIEVEMENTS:** Global Positioning System, numerous articles/publications, IEEE, ION; adaptive filtering, IEEE; systems theory, IEEE, proficiency in Chinese. **HOME ADDRESS:** 13198 Pleasant Glen Court, Herndon, VA 22071. **BUSINESS PHONE:** (703)448-6397.

TSAO, FRANCIS HSIANG-CHIAN
Scientist. Chinese American. **PERSONAL:** Born Jul 22, 1936, Nanjing, China; married Susan Schwarz-Tsao, Dec 27, 1989. **EDUCATION:** Chung Hsing University, BS, chemistry, 1961; Dalhousie University, MS, organic chemistry, 1966; Iowa State University, PhD, biochemistry, 1972. **CAREER:** University of Wisconsin, Madison, Dept of Pediatrics, senior scientist, currently.

TSAO, GEORGE T.
Educator, chemical engineer. Chinese American. **PERSONAL:** Born Dec 4, 1931, Nanking, China; married 1960; children: three. **EDUCATION:** National Taiwan University, BSc, 1953; University of Florida, MSc, 1956; University of Michigan, PhD, chemical engineering, 1960. **CAREER:** Olivet College, Physics Dept, assistant professor, 1959-60; Merck & Co, Inc, chemical engineer, 1960-61; Tennessee Valley Authority, research chemist, 1961-62; Miles Labs, Inc, Union Starch & Refining Co, Inc Div, Research Dept, Hydrolysis & Fermentation, section leader, 1962-65, assistant research director, 1965-66; Iowa State University, Chemical Engineering Dept, associate professor to professor, 1966-77; Purdue University, Chemical Engineering Dept, professor, 1977-. **ORGANIZATIONS:** American Chemical Society; American Institute of Chemical Engineers; American Society of Engineering Education. **SPECIAL ACHIEVEMENTS:** Researcher for the following areas: biological technology; fermentation; agricultural and natural products utilization; waste disposal; organic synthesis; industrial carbohydrates; process development; enzyme engineering. **BUSINESS ADDRESS:** Professor, Chemical Engineering, Purdue University, School of Eng Chem, West Lafayette, IN 47907-9980.*

TSE, CHARLES JACK-CHING
Investment and real estate development company executive. Chinese American. **PERSONAL:** Born Feb 12, 1952, Hong Kong; son of Bruce Man-Hing Tse & Mee-Loo Kain Tse; married Chih-Chen Lee Tse, Dec 26, 1978. **EDUCATION:** McGill University, university scholar, 1969-70; Massachusetts Institute of Technology, BS, 1972, MS, 1973, ScD, 1979. **CAREER:** The Charles Stark Draper Lab Inc, summer staff, 1974-79, technical staff, 1979-92; Winfair Group of Companies, principal, 1992-. **ORGANIZATIONS:** Sigma Xi, 1977; Tau Beta Pi, 1972; Sigma Gamma Tau, 1971; AIAA, 1976. **SPECIAL ACHIEVEMENTS:** A Guidance and Navigation System for Continuous Low-Thrust Vehicles, 1973; Minimum Time Attitude Control of a Spacecraft Spinning at a Constant Rate About Its Axis of Symmetry, 1979; a number of classified publications in the defense communities. **HOME ADDRESS:** 51 Sanderson Rd, Lexington, MA 02173, (617)863-1098.

TSE, FRANCIS LAI-SING
Pharmaceutical scientist. Chinese American. **PERSONAL:** Born Jan 20, 1952, Hong Kong; son of Yuen-Hong Tse and Lee-Ing Shone; married Irene Chow Tse, Mar 23, 1979; children: Clara. **EDUCATION:** University of Wisconsin, Madison, BS, pharmacy, 1974, MS, 1975, PhD, 1978. **CAREER:** Rutgers University, assistant professor of pharmaceutics, 1978-80; Sandoz Pharmaceuticals Corp, associate director, drug metabolism, 1981-. **ORGANIZATIONS:** American Pharmaceutical Association; American Association of Pharmaceutical Scientists; American Society for Clinical Pharmacology and Therapeutics; New York Academy of Sciences; International Society for the Study of Xenobiotics. **HONORS/AWARDS:** American College of Clinical Pharmacology, fellow, 1988; Academy of Pharmaceutical Research and Science, fellow, 1990. **SPECIAL ACHIEVEMENTS:** Published over 60 research articles in reference journals; co-author, editor of 4 books: Pharmacokinetics of Cardiovascular, Central Nervous System, and Antimicrobial Drugs, Royal Society of Chemistry, London, 1985; Pharmacokinetics: Regulatory-Industrial-Academic Perspectives, Marcel Dekker, New York, 1988; Preclinical Drug Disposition: A Laboratory Handbook, Marcel Dekker, New York, 1991; Pharmaceutical Bioequivalence, Marcel Dekker, New York, 1991. **BUSINESS ADDRESS:** Associate Director, Sandoz Research Institute, Route 10, Bldg 404/2, East Hanover, NJ 07936, (201)503-8538.

TSE, HARLEY YAU-SHUIN
Educator. Chinese American. **PERSONAL:** Born Jul 17, 1947, ShanTou, Guangdong, China; son of Tse Ton Cheuk and Choy Hou Ying; married Kwai-Fong Chui, Jan 13, 1979; children: Kevin, Alan, Leslie. **EDUCATION:** California Institute of Technology, BS (with honors), 1972; University of California at San Diego, PhD, 1977; Rutgers University, School of Business, MBA, 1986. **CAREER:** Arthritis Foundation, fellow, 1977-80; Merck & Co, senior research immunologist, 1980-86; Wayne State University, associate professor, 1986-. **ORGANIZATIONS:** Chinese Social Service Center, board member, 1975-76; Chinese Student Association of UCSD, president, 1973-75;

American Association of Immunologists, 1978-; Society of Chinese Bioscientists in America, life member, 1984-; Detroit Immunological Society, president, 1988-90; International Society for Neuroimmunology, 1989-; Autumn Immunology Conference, council member, 1990-. **HONORS/AWARDS:** University of California, University Scholarship, 1975, Chancellor's Scholarship, 1976; Arthritis Foundation, fellowship, 1977-80; National Institutes of Health, Research Career Development Award, 1992-97. **SPECIAL ACHIEVEMENTS:** Over 40 scientific publications in peer-reviewed scientific journals. **HOME ADDRESS:** 5393 Tequesta Drive, West Bloomfield, MI 48323, (313)681-6909. **BUSINESS ADDRESS:** Associate Professor, Dept of Immunology and Microbiology, Wayne State University School of Medicine, 540 E Canfield Ave, Scott Hall, Rm 8245, Detroit, MI 48201, (313)577-1564.

TSE, JOHN YUNG DONG (YONG TANG ZHU)
Educator. Chinese American. **PERSONAL:** Born Mar 25, 1924, Shanghai, China; son of Koong Yang Tse & Yu Jin Hwa; married Emma K C Tse, Aug 15, 1953; children: Robert C Y, Frank C W. **EDUCATION:** St John's University, Shanghai, BSCE, 1944; Stanford University, MBA, 1951; Harvard University, DCS, 1957. **CAREER:** Purdue University, professor of management, 1957-88, professor emeritus, 1988-. **ORGANIZATIONS:** University of Birmingham, England, visiting professor; Princeton University, Ford Foundation, visiting fellow; Jiangsu Center for Science and Technology Exchange with Foreign Countries; United Nations, consultant; Mayor's Commission on Human Relations, West Lafayette, Indiana, chairman, 1969-70. **HONORS/AWARDS:** Purdue University, Krannert Graduate School of Management, Distinguished Krannert Professor; Purdue University President's Council, Distinguished Fellow Member. **SPECIAL ACHIEVEMENTS:** Purdue University's Krannert Graudate School of Management, founder, 1962; West Lafayette Hilt Inn, first atrium garden hotel in Indiana, owner/developer, 1981-85; author: Profit Planning through Volume-Cost Analysis, Macmillan; I Budget Flessibili, Etas Kompass, Italy; On the Theory to My Country, poetry, Jiangsu People's Press, China; Tracing to my Ancestor Zhu Xi (1130-1200 AD), to the Beginning of Zhu (487 BC) and Beyond to Yellow Emperor (2398-2298 BC); Selected Poems by the Resident of Thatched House. **BIOGRAPHICAL SOURCES:** Krannert Portfolio, p 2-3, spring 1987. **HOME ADDRESS:** 2183 Tecumseh Park Ln, West Lafayette, IN 47906, (317)463-9758.

TSE, MING-KAI
Equipment manufacturing company executive, consultant. Chinese American. **PERSONAL:** Born May 14, 1953, Hong Kong; married Ananna See Tse; children: Yung-Wei. **EDUCATION:** Cornell University, BSc, 1975; Massachusetts Institute of Technology, MSc, 1977, PhD, 1981. **CAREER:** American Can Co, director of productivity programs, 1981-82; Massachusetts Institute of Technology, Mechanical Engineering, assistant professor, 1982-87, associate professor, 1987-88; Quality Engineering Associates Inc, founder, president, 1987-. **ORGANIZATIONS:** American Society of Mechanical Engineers, co-editor of special volume on sensors for manufacturing; American Society for Nondestructive Testing, acoustic emission and ultrasonics handbook committee; Society for Manufacturing Engineers; Institute of Electrical and Electronic Engineers; Optical Society of America; Acoustic Emission Working Group. **HONORS/AWARDS:** Massachusetts Institute of Technology, Young Faculty Chair in Mechanical Engineering, 1982; MIT Graduate Student Council Teaching Award, 1987. **SPECIAL ACHIEVEMENTS:** Two patents based on work in the sensor and quality technology areas, 1982, 1989; several other patents pending in similar fields. **BUSINESS ADDRESS:** President, Quality Engineering Associates Inc, 25 Adams St, Burlington, MA 01803, (617)221-0080.

TSE, SAU P.
Bank loan officer. Chinese American. **PERSONAL:** Born Dec 13, 1964, New York, NY; daughter of Shek Chuen Tse and Chui Lin Lee Tse. **EDUCATION:** Bernard M Baruch College, BBA, intl marketing, 1986; Long Island University, MBA, public accounting, 1991. **CAREER:** The Green Point Saving Bank, assistant mortgage loan officer, 1986-; Michael D Tucker CPAs, accountant, 1993-. **ORGANIZATIONS:** New York State Society for CPA Candidates, 1992. **HONORS/AWARDS:** Long Island University, Certificate for Excellence in Accounting, 1991; New York State Society of CPAs, Superior Scholastic Acievement Award in Accounting, 1991. **SPECIAL ACHIEVEMENTS:** Proficient in Chinese, Cantonese, Toi San. **HOME ADDRESS:** 343 E 30 St, Apt 4L, New York, NY 10016.

TSE, STEPHEN
Artist, educator. Hong Kong American. **PERSONAL:** Born Oct 20, 1938, Hong Kong; son of Tse Kwan Young; married May Tse, Mar 1973; children:

Lisa. **EDUCATION:** Washburn University of Topeka, BFA, 1965; University of Idaho, MFA, 1967. **CAREER:** Big Bend Community College, chairman of art dept, 1966-. **ORGANIZATIONS:** Big Bend Faculty Association, 1966-. **HONORS/AWARDS:** Carnegie Art Center, Painting Award, Juried Art Show, 1993, 1990, 1989; Larson Gallery, Central Washington Artist Exhibition, Painting Award, 1984; Wing Luke Memorial Museum, Asian/American Artists Exhibition, Best of the Show, 1983, Invitational Art Exhibition, First Award, Painting, 1979; Wenatchee Valley College, NCW Bicentennial Art Exhibition, First Place Award, 1977. **SPECIAL ACHIEVEMENTS:** Kirsten Gallery, one-man show, Seattle, WA, 1985, 1982, 1980, 1978, 1977; Prichard Art Gallery, one-man show, University of Idaho, 1986; Compton Union Gallery, one-man show, Washington State University, 1983; Whatcom Museum, one-man show, Bellingham, WA, 1980; Museum of Art, one-man show, University of Oregon, 1977. **HOME ADDRESS:** 957 Garden Dr, Moses Lake, WA 98837.

TSE DINH, YUK-CHING (YUK-CHING TSE DINH)
Biochemist, educator. Chinese American. **PERSONAL:** Born May 21, 1956, Hong Kong; daughter of Chu Tse & Yee-Lan Lam; married Steven M Dinh, Jun 17, 1982; children: Kate, Alex. **EDUCATION:** Hollins College, BA, 1977; Harvard University, PhD, 1982. **CAREER:** E I duPont, principal investigator, 1982-88; New York Medical College, assistant professor, 1988-91, associate professor, 1991-. **ORGANIZATIONS:** American Chemical Society, 1991-; NIH, study section, 1991-94. **HONORS/AWARDS:** Sigma Xi, 1977; Phi Beta Kappa, 1977. **BUSINESS ADDRESS:** Associate Professor, Dept of Biochemistry & Molecular Biology, New York Medical College, Valhalla, NY 10595, (914)993-4061.

TSEN, MAY F.
Medical researcher. Chinese American. **PERSONAL:** Born Dec 31, 1933, Guangdong, China; daughter of Mieng Ba Sam and Tri Khanh Vuong; married Chunfu Weng, Apr 26, 1972; children: Xiaofeng Weng. **EDUCATION:** Peking University, Peking Medical School, China, Doctor of Medical & Health Science, 1955; El Centro College, associate's degree, 1989. **CAREER:** Institute of Parasitic Disease at Shanghai, Academy of Medical Science of China, Malaria Lab, researcher, 1955-60, Ankylostomiasis Lab, researcher, 1960-72; Shanghai Hygiene & Anti-Epidemic Center, researcher, supervisor, 1972-82; University of Texas Southwestern Medical Center at Dallas, research assistant, 1989-. **ORGANIZATIONS:** American Society of Clinical Pathologists, 1989-. **HOME ADDRESS:** 2723 Pinery Lane, Richardson, TX 75080, (214)480-8162.

TSEN, MENG CHI
International trade consultant. Hong Kong American. **PERSONAL:** Born Oct 15, 1934, Hong Kong; son of Tsong Ming Tsen & Tchun Pi Fan Tsen; married Susan White Hastings Tsen, Sep 7, 1987. **EDUCATION:** Virginia Military Institute, BSEE, 1955; University of Illinois, MSEE, 1958; Harvard University, 1960-62. **CAREER:** Northeastern University, assistant professor, EE, 1963-72; Analog Devices, international sales engineer, 1972-76; Datel Systems, international manager, 1976-80; Nashua Corporation, Asia-Pacific area manager, 1980-85; self-employed, consultant, 1986-. **ORGANIZATIONS:** Tau Beta Pi, 1955-; Eta Kappa Nu, 1955-. **SPECIAL ACHIEVEMENTS:** Fluent in English, Chinese, French, German; Amassed the largest collection of British Victorian military & court uniforms, headdresses, accoutrements, and arms in America, all catalogued and displayed in personal museum. **HOME PHONE:** (508)371-7031.

TSENG, BEATRICE SHAN-YI
Educator. Taiwanese American. **PERSONAL:** Born Mar 22, 1966, Taipei, Taiwan; daughter of Tseng Pin-hsiang & Chen Shu-huei. **EDUCATION:** UCLA, BA (summa cum laude), Spanish & Portuguese literature, 1988, MA (with honors), Spanish Literature, 1991. **CAREER:** EF Institute for Cultural Exchange, tour director, spring 1987; 20th World Conference, interpreter & translator, August 1987; English Conversation School, ESL instructor, fall 1988; UCLA Education Abroad Program Office, intern, 1987-88, Spanish & Portuguese Department, teaching assistant, 1989-90; Pilgrim School, Spanish teacher, spring 1991; Irvine Valley College, Spanish professor, 1991-. **ORGANIZATIONS:** Phi Beta Kappa, 1988-; Sigma Delta, 1986-; Alpha Lambda Delta Scholastic Honor Society, 1988-; The Golden Key National Honor Society, 1988-; Faculty Association of California Community Colleges, 1991-; California Community College Foreign Language Council, 1993-; California Foreign Language Teachers Association, 1993-; Irvine Valley College Chinese Cultural Association, advisor, 1992-. **HONORS/AWARDS:** UCLA, Faculty

Excellence Award, nominee, 1992, Teaching Assistantship Award, 1989-91, fellowship, 1989-91, Del Amo Scholarship, 1986-87, The Regents of the University of California Scholarship, 1985-87. **SPECIAL ACHIEVE-MENTS:** Language proficiency: English, Spanish, Portuguese, Mandarin & Taiwanese; developed the study abroad program at Irvine Valley College, fall 1992. **BIOGRAPHICAL SOURCES:** "Learning Spanish, Costa Rica Style: New Course Designed by B Tseng," The Voice, p 3, March 15, 1993; "New Faculty & Staff at IVC," Issues, p 4, vol IV, no IV, Nov 1991. **BUSINESS ADDRESS:** Professor, School of Humanities and Languages, Irvine Valley College, 5500 Irvine Center Dr, Irvine, CA 92720, (714)559-3343.

TSENG, HUAN-CHI CHRIS
Educator. Taiwanese American. **PERSONAL:** Born Aug 2, 1957, Taipei, Taiwan; son of Tung-Hiu Tsang & Suet-Kiu Yeung; married Heun Jane Tung, Dec 1991; children: Eden. **EDUCATION:** National Taiwan University, BS, 1982; University of Illinois, Urbana-Champaign, MS, 1984, PhD, 1988. **CAREER:** Tamkang University, teaching assistant, 1982-83; University of Illinois, teaching assistant, 1983-84, research assistant, 1984-88; Santa Clara University, assistant professor, 1988-. **ORGANIZATIONS:** IEEE Santa Clara Valley Control System Society, vice chairman, 1992-93, chairman, 1993-. **HONORS/AWARDS:** National Taiwan University, Distinguished Book-Coupon Award, 1978; Santa Clara University, David Packard Fellow, 1988-90. **SPECIAL ACHIEVEMENTS:** Author of several articles relating to electrical engineering; languages: Mandarin, Cantonese, Taiwanese. **BIOGRAPHICAL SOURCES:** Santa Clara Spectrum, p 3, February 1989. **BUSINESS ADDRESS:** Professor, Electrical Engineering Dept, Santa Clara University, Santa Clara, CA 95053, (408)554-6804.

TSENG, JAMES H. W.
Educator, administrator, engineer. Chinese American. **PERSONAL:** Born May 27, Ts'ao Hsien, Shantung, China; son of Mo-Tang Tseng and Mei-Rong Zhou Li-Zeng Zhou; married Nancy Hui Rong Tseng, Aug 16, 1991; children: Jennifer Ching-Ning, Amanda Ching-Shiang, Diana Jia-ying Tan. **EDUCATION:** Southern Methodist University, LLM, 1957, PhD, 1978; Illinois Institute of Technology, BSEE, 1964, MSEE, 1966. **CAREER:** Consultant for various public/private organizations; Advance Ross Electronics Corp, R&D engineer; Northern Indiana Public Service Company, test engineer; Purdue University, Calumet Campus, assistant professor, 1966-69; University of Minnesota, Duluth, Computer Engineering Department, founding head, 1984-87; California Polytechnic State University, Electronic/Electrical Engineering, professor, 1969-; Lim Brothers International Inc, senior consultant, 1992-. **ORGANIZATIONS:** Institute of Electronics & Electrical Engineers, Transaction on Education, 1966-, reviewer; Assn for Computing Machinery, 1976-; American Society for Engineering Education, 1985-90, 1992-; Academic Senate, Cal Poly, School of Engineering, caucus chairman, university budget comm, senate executive comm, 1981-83; School of Engineering & Technology Council, Cal Poly, faculty rep, 1982-83; San Luis Obispo, Citizens Advisory Comm, 1978-81; California Polytechnic State University, comms: affirmative action, scheduling & registration, equal opportunity advisory council; Mentally Gifted Minors' Parent Assn, San Luis Coastal District, founding member, vp, comm chair, 1978-79. **HONORS/AWARDS:** Southwest Legal Foundation, fellowship, 1956; Southern Methodist University, Merle Collins Foundation Grant, 1976-77; NSF Grant, Worchester Polytechnic Institute, Summer Institute for College Teachers, 1970; University of Michigan, Faculty Advancement Program, grant, 1969; Taiwan Regional Development Institute, Taichung, fellow, 1992-. **SPECIAL ACHIEVEMENTS:** State Board of Registration for Professional Engineers, registered professional engineer, Texas, 1977-; "A Comparative Study in Digital and Voice Load Over Telecommunications Systems," 1977; initiated and taught the first senior/grad course in telecommunications at Cal Poly; initiated and taught the first non-Intel microprocessor/microcomputer application senior grad course at Cal Poly; "Microprocessor/Microcomputer Based Design in Telecommunications System," PhD dissertation; textbook: Logic/Switching Design Using Integrated Circuits—An Application of SSI, MSI, LSI, and VLSI. **BIOGRAPHICAL SOURCES:** Teaching Well—A Guide for New Undergraduate Engineering and Technology Faculty, IEE Transaction on Education, p 26, Feb 1987; Opportunities in Computer Engineering, IEEE Potential, Feb 1987; Minnesota Technology, fall 1986. **HOME ADDRESS:** PO Box 16132, San Luis Obispo, CA 93406-6132, (805)549-9923.

TSENG, LEON F.
Educator. Taiwanese American. **PERSONAL:** Born Nov 20, 1937, Tainan City, Taiwan; married Grace Tseng, Sep 3, 1965; children: Joshua, Daniel,

Joseph, Esther. **EDUCATION:** National Taiwan University, BS, pharmacy, 1961, MS, pharmacology, 1964; University of Kansas Medical Center, PhD, pharmacology, 1970. **CAREER:** National Taiwan University, Department of Pharmacology, instructor, 1966-67; University of California, San Francisco, Department of Psychiatry and Pharmacology, assistant professor, 1975-78; Medical College of Wisconsin, Department of Pharmacology, assistant professor, 1978-81, associate professor, 1981-89, professor, 1989-. **SPECIAL ACHIEVEMENTS:** Research: study of the mechanism of action of elapid snake venoms, study of the mechanism of action of amphetamines, study of the neural mechanisms of action of opioids and opiosdo peptides-induced analgesia; about 120 publications. **HOME PHONE:** (414)784-7844. **BUSINESS ADDRESS:** Professor, Dept of Pharmacology, Medical College of Wisconsin, 8701 Watertown Plans Rd, Milwaukee, WI 53213, (414)257-8625.

TSENG, LOUISA
Librarian. Taiwanese American. **PERSONAL:** Born Apr 24, 1944, Tou Liu, Taiwan; daughter of W C Yuan and Helen Liu Yuan; married Henry Tseng, Sep 23, 1972; children: Edward, Sharon. **EDUCATION:** TamKang University, BA, English; University of Kentucky, College of Library & Information Science, MLS; Atlanta University, School of Education, MA, education psychology; Emory University, Division of Librarianship, medical librarian certificate. **CAREER:** Mount Vernon Christian Academy, librarian, 1975-78; Atlanta University, catalog librarian, 1971-93; Morehouse School of Medicine, medical librarian, cataloging, 1978-79; University of Massachusetts, Boston, librarian, 1979-; Glover Memorial Hospital, director of medical library, 1988-. **ORGANIZATIONS:** The Academy of Health Sciences Information Professionals, senior member; National Education Association; Medical Library Association, 1988-; American Library Association, 1974, 1988-; The Association of Colleges & Research Libraries; Massachusetts Health Science Library Network; North Atlantic Health Science Libraries; National Taiwanese Women Association. **HONORS/AWARDS:** University of Kentucky, International Student Scholarship, 1969-70. **SPECIAL ACHIEVEMENTS:** TamKang University, visiting faculty, 1985-86; TamKang University, Library, visiting librarian, 1985-86; Bridgewater State College, Consultant to China Program, 1985, to teach students the Chinese language and culture. **BUSINESS ADDRESS:** Librarian, University of Massachusetts, Boston, 6000 Morrissey Blvd, Healey Bldg, 4th Fl, Boston, MA 02125, (617)287-5924.

TSENG, MOU-SIEN
Artist. Chinese American. **PERSONAL:** Born Aug 19, 1936, Taipei, Taiwan; son of E-Hwa Tseng & Lin-Lou Tseng; married Jean Tseng, Dec 24, 1966; children: Grace, Ivy. **EDUCATION:** National Taiwan Normal University, BA, 1963. **CAREER:** Self-employed, artist/illustrator, currently. **HONORS/AWARDS:** National Children's Book Contest, ROC, Golden Book Award, first prize, 1971; Chinese Art Society, ROC, Gold Goblet Award for Chinese painting, 1990. **SPECIAL ACHIEVEMENTS:** Classic Chinese painting, Man and Saddle. **HOME ADDRESS:** 31 Viola Dr, Glen Cove, NY 11542, (516)671-6830.

TSENG, MUNA SIU-CHUK
Dance company executive. Chinese American. **PERSONAL:** Born Aug 10, 1953, Hong Kong; daughter of Ronald Tseng and Stella Woo; married Issac Davidor, Sep 27, 1988. **EDUCATION:** University of British Columbia, Canada, BRE, 1975. **CAREER:** Theater of the Open Eye, dance soloist, 1978-85; Rutgers University, SUNJ, adjunct dance faculty, 1979-82; Queens College, CUNY, founder, director, summer dance residency, 1980-83; Muna Tseng Dance Projects, artistic director, 1988-. **ORGANIZATIONS:** Dance Theater Workshop, 1979-; Asian American Arts Alliance, 1990-; Asia Society, 1990-; Society for Nanlaoshu, 1992-. **HONORS/AWARDS:** National Endowment for the Arts, choreographic fellowship, 1987-88; New York Foundation for the Arts, choreographic fellowship, 1992-90; New York State Council for the Arts, choreographic commission, 1987-86; Manhattan Community Arts Fund, 1983, 1984, 1985, 1990, 1991; Meet the Composer, choreographic commission, 1992, 1993; New York City Council president, Chinese American Cultural Pioneer Award, 1993. **SPECIAL ACHIEVEMENTS:** Performances of dance with commissioned music, 1988-; master classes in dance, currently. **BIOGRAPHICAL SOURCES:** New York Times, numerous reviews, 1978-; Village Voice, Dance Magazines & other publications on dance. **BUSINESS ADDRESS:** Artistic Director, Muna Tseng Dance Projects Inc, 115 Christopher St, 4th Fl, New York, NY 10014, (212)627-5638.

TSENG, ROSE Y. L.

Educational administrator. Chinese American. **PERSONAL:** Born Feb 3, 1943, Shan-tung, People's Republic of China; daughter of En Shu and Li Kwan Chang; married Raymond C Tseng, Jun 25, 1966; children: Jennifer, Frank. **EDUCATION:** Kansas State University, BS, chemistry, 1964; University of California, Berkeley, MS, nutrition, 1966, PhD, 1968. **CAREER:** University of California, Berkeley, postgraduate research nutritionist, 1969; San Jose State University, Home Economics Department, lecturer, 1970-74, assistant professor, 1974-76, associate professor, 1977-93, Dietetics Program, coordinator, 1977-79, Department of Nutrition, Foods, & Dietetics, chairman, 1979-93, Division of Health Professions, director, College of Applied Sciences and Arts; San Jose City College, Physical Science Department, instructor, 1972-73; Fu Jen University, Taiwan, Nutrition and Food Science, visiting professor, 1982; West Valley-Mission Community College District, chancellor, 1993-. **ORGANIZATIONS:** American Dietetics Association; Society for Nutrition Education; Institute of Food Technology; California Nutrition Council; Nutrition Today Society; Phi Upsilon Omicron. **HONORS/AWARDS:** San Jose State University, Home Economics Professor Award, 1977-78. **SPECIAL ACHIEVEMENTS:** San Jose State University: counseled students, faculty; established student scholarships, internships; launched various university-community partnerships; San Jose University Foundation, research grantee, 1974, 1975; NASA Ames-University Consortium, grantee; California State Department of Education, grantee, 1978, 1979; contributor to professional journals. **BUSINESS ADDRESS:** Chancellor, West Valley-Mission Community College District, 14000 Fruitvale Av, Saratoga, CA 95070-5698, (408)867-2200.∗

TSENG, S. C.

Educator. Taiwanese American. **PERSONAL:** Born Jan 14, 1935, Tainan, Taiwan; son of Picheng Tseng and Chaoliu Wang Tseng; married Evelina M Tseng; children: Elaine E. **EDUCATION:** National Taiwan University, BA, 1957, MA, 1963; University of Oklahoma, PhD, 1972. **CAREER:** Cooperative Bank of Taiwan, chief economist; Provincial Govt of Taiwan, Bureau of Taxation, dir; University of Oklahoma, instructor; Georgia Southern University, asst professor, economics; Catawba College, professor, business and economics, currently. **ORGANIZATIONS:** Catawba College, faculty senator, 1989-92; Tsengs Intl, president, 1989-93. **HONORS/AWARDS:** Catawba College, Sayakini Award, 1978; Academia Sinica/Ford Foundation, Outstanding Research Fellowship Award, 1962-63. **SPECIAL ACHIEVEMENTS:** Author: "The Demand for Higher Education, A Theoretical Analysis," Intl Journal of Social Economics, vol III, num III; Successful Investment Strategies, American Prudential Enterprises; "Options As an Investment Strategy," Journal of Banking and Finance; several other presented papers. **BUSINESS ADDRESS:** Professor, Dept of Business & Economics, Catawba College, Ketner School of Business, #318, Salisbury, NC 28144-2488, (704)637-4407.

TSENG, WAN CHI

Financial analyst. Taiwanese American. **PERSONAL:** Born Jul 25, 1952, Taipei, Taiwan; daughter of Cheng Hsiu Shuai and Lung Chu Cheng Shuai; married Hsing Huang Tseng, Jun 19, 1976; children: Michael Hau-Tien, Diane Wen. **EDUCATION:** National Cheng-Chi University, bachelor in commerce, 1974; Rider College, MBA, 1981. **CAREER:** First Commercial Bank of Taiwan, bank officer, 1974-76; McGraw-Hill Inc, divisional accountant, 1982-85; Texas Department of Insurance, financial analyst, 1988-. **BUSINESS ADDRESS:** Financial Analyst, Texas Department of Insurance, 333 Guadalupe, Hobby Bldg III, 3rd Fl, Rm 330 N, Austin, TX 78701, (512)322-5002.

TSO, L. HILARY

Educator. Taiwanese American. **PERSONAL:** Born Jun 17, 1961, Taipei, Taiwan; daughter of Chen-nan Wang and Yuan-Fen Lee Wang; married Andy Tso, Jun 27, 1992. **EDUCATION:** Chinese Culture University, Taiwan, BS, 1983; Texas Tech University, MS, 1985; Cornell University, PhD, 1991. **CAREER:** Texas Tech University, research assistant, 1984-85; Cornell University, teaching/research assistant, 1986-89; University of New Hampshire, assistant professor, 1989-. **ORGANIZATIONS:** American Council of Consumer Interests, 1985-; American Home Economics Association, 1983-; International Federation of Home Economics, 1989-. **HONORS/AWARDS:** Center for Health Promotion and Research at University of New Hampshire, Research Fellow/Fellowship, 1992. **SPECIAL ACHIEVEMENTS:** Research articles published in various conference proceedings; fluent in Chinese. **BUSINESS ADDRESS:** Asst Professor, Dept of Family Studies, University of New Hampshire, 214b Pettee Hall, Durham, NH 03824, (603)862-2153.

TS'O, PAUL ON PONG

Educator. Hong Kong American. **PERSONAL:** Born Jul 17, 1929, Hong Kong. **EDUCATION:** Lingan University, China, BS, chemistry and biology, 1949; Michigan State University, MS, physiology and biochemistry, 1951; California Institute of Technology, PhD, biochemistry & chemistry, 1955. **CAREER:** California Institute of Technology, senior research fellow, 1961-62; Johns Hopkins University: associate professor of biophysical chemistry, 1962-67, professor, 1967-73; professor of biochemistry, 1973-; Dept Biochemistry and Div Biophysics, professor and director, 1973-90; professor of environmental health sciences, 1980-; Div Toxicological Sciences, interim director, 1987-88. **ORGANIZATIONS:** American Association for Cancer Research; American Chemical Society, senior grade; Biophysical Society, Public Science Policy Committee, chairman, 1972-76; American Society of Biological Chemistry, membership committe, 1976-80; Sigma Xi; American Association for the Advancement of Science, fellow, 1966; American Society for Microbiology; Academia Sinica, Taiwan, 1972; European Academy of Arts, Sciences and Humanities, 1980; American Society for Cell Biology. **HONORS/AWARDS:** China Institute of America, Frank Hsu Scholarship, 1954. **SPECIAL ACHIEVEMENTS:** Research Citation Index, 1 of 1,000 scientists whose publications were most cited during the period 1965-78. **BUSINESS ADDRESS:** Professor, Dept of Biochemistry, The Johns Hopkins University, School of Hygiene & Public Health, 615 N Wolfe St, Rm 3102, Baltimore, MD 21205, (410)955-3172.

TSO, TIEN CHIOH

Phytochemist. Chinese American. **PERSONAL:** Born Jul 25, 1917, Hupeh, China; married Margaret Lu, Aug 28, 1949; children: Elizabeth, Paul. **EDUCATION:** Nanking University, China, BS, 1941, MS, 1944; Pennsylvania State University, PhD, 1950. **CAREER:** Ministry Social Affairs, China, supt exptl farm, 1944-46; Tobacco Improvement Bur, exec sec, 1946-47; General Cigar Res Lab, res chemist, 1950-51; University of Maryland/US Dept of Agric, 1952-59; USDA, Agric Res Service, Crop Research Div, princ plant physiologist, 1959-60, Tobacco & Sugar Crops Res Br, tobacco quality investigation, leader, 1966-71, Tobacco Lab, chief, 1972-83, Senior Executive Service, 1977-83; consultant to: Dept of Health & Human Services, Office of Smoking & Health, Natl Heart Lung & Blood Inst, Natl Cancer Inst, 1968-; Institute of Intl Development & Education in Agriculture & Life Science, executive director, 1983-; USDA, Tobacco & Health, Agric Research Service, collaborator, 1984-. **ORGANIZATIONS:** AAAS, fellow; Agronomy Soc, fellow; American Intl Chemists, fellow; Phytochemical Soc of N America, fellow; American Chem Soc; American Soc Plant Physiol; and others. **HONORS/AWARDS:** Cigar Manufacturers Assn, Distinguished Science Achievement Award, 1971; Intl Congress of Tobacco Sci, Distinguished Scientific Achievement Award, 1978; US Presidential Rank Award, 1984; Chinese Academy of Agriculture Science, Honorary Research Fellow; State Science & Technology Commission Award, for International Cooperation, 1993. **SPECIAL ACHIEVEMENTS:** Author, Physiology & Biochemistry of Tobacco Plants, 1972; Production; Physiology & Biochemistry of Tobacco Plant, 1991; 6 US patents; 46 foreign patents. **BUSINESS ADDRESS:** Executive Director, IDEALS, 5010 Sunnyside Ave, Rm 9, Bldg 005, Beltsville, MD 20705, (301)504-5422.

TSUANG, MING T.

Psychiatrist, educator, researcher. Taiwanese American. **PERSONAL:** Born Nov 16, 1931, Taipei, Taiwan; son of Ping Tang & Chhun Kuei Lin T; married Snow H Tsuang, Nov 24, 1958; children: John, Debby, Grace. **EDUCATION:** National Taiwan University, MD, 1957; University of London, PhD, 1965, DS, 1981. **CAREER:** Natl Taiwan Univ Hospital, chief resident, 1956-61, staff psychiatrist, assoc prof, 1961-71; Washington Univ School of Medicine, visiting assoc prof of psychiatry, 1971-72; Univ of Iowa College of Medicine, assoc prof, 1972-75, prof of psychiatry, 1975-82; Brown Univ, prof, vice chr, sect of psychiatry & human behavior, 1982-85; Harvard Univ Medical School & Harvard School Public Health, prof of psychiatry, Psychiatric Epidemiology Prog, 1985-, dir, 1993-; Brockton/West Roxbury VA Medical Ctr, chief, psychiatry service & chr, Ctr for Mental Health & Behavioral Sciences, 1985-; Harvard Medical School at Brockton/West Roxbury VA Medical Ctr, Dept of Psychiatry, head, 1991-, Stanley Cobb Professor of Psychiatry, 1993-; Harvard Medical School at Massachusetts Mental Health Center, Department of Psychiatry, head, 1993-; Harvard Institute of Psychiatric Epidemiology and Genetics, director, 1993-. **ORGANIZATIONS:** NIMH, Epidemiology Studies Review Comm, 1976-79, Research Scientist Development Review Comm, chr, 1982-86, Epidemiologic Studies Review Comm, chr, 1989-90, Extramural Science Advisory Bd, 1990-; Veterans Health Services & Research Admin, VA Central

Office, Medical Research Service Planning Council, 1990-; Psychiatric Research Soc; American Psychopathological Assn, fellow; American Medical Assn & Massachusetts Medical Soc, fellow; American Psychiatric Assn, fellow; Massachusetts Psychiatric Soc; Soc of Biological Psychiatry; Behavior Genetics Assn; Soc for Life History Research in Psychopathology; American Assn for the Advancement of Science; American Academy for Clinical Psychiatrists, fellow; American Public Health Assn; American College of Psychiatrists, fellow; Assn of Clinical Psychosocial Research; Deutsche Gesellschaft fur Psychiatrie und Nervenheilkunde, honorary member; Royal College of Psychiatrists, fellow. **HONORS/AWARDS:** Chinese Natl Council Science Development, Research Fellow, 1966-70; University of Oxford, Josiah Macy Faculty Scholar, 1979-80; American Academy Clinical Psychiatrists, Clinical Research Award, 1983; American Public Health Association, Rema Lapouse Award, 1984; NIMH Merit Award, 1988-98; American College Psychiatrists, Stanley Dean Award for Research on Schizophrenia, 1989; Royal College of Psychiatrists, England, 67th Annual Maudsley Lecture, 1991; Center for Advanced Study in the Behavioral Sciences, Fritz Redlich Fellow, 1991-92; Royal College of Psychiatrists, UK, fellow, 1992. **SPECIAL ACHIEVEMENTS:** 201 papers published in peer review journals; 57 chapters in books; 10 books and monographs; publications are in the area of: psychiatric epidemiology, diagnostic classification, psychiatric genetics, nosology of major psychoses, psychopharmacology, alcohol and drug abuse, study design & methodology. **BUSINESS ADDRESS:** Stanley Cobb Professor of Psychiatry, Director of Psychiatric Epidemiology and Genetics, Brockton VA Medical Center, Harvard University, 940 Belmont St, #116A, Brockton, MA 02401, (508)583-4500.

TSUEI, Y. G.
Educator. Chinese American. **PERSONAL:** Born Feb 25, 1932, Anhui, China; married Judy, Jun 23, 1962; children: Betty, Karen, Jennifer, Stephanie. **EDUCATION:** Cheng Kung University, BSCE, 1956; Colorado State University, PhD, 1963. **CAREER:** National Cheng Kung University, professor, 1992; University of Cincinnati, professor emeritus, 1992. **ORGANIZATIONS:** AIAA; ASME; ASCE; Sigma Xi. **SPECIAL ACHIEVEMENTS:** Associate editor of International Journal of Modal Analysis.

TSUHA, WALLACE K., JR.
Electronics supply company executive. Japanese American. **PERSONAL:** Born 1943?, Hawaii; children: Jennifer, Christopher. **CAREER:** TRW, manager in transportation electronics; Saturn Electronics & Engineering, owner, founder, 1985-. **HONORS/AWARDS:** US Small Business Administration, Midwest Regional and Michigan Minority Small Business Person of the Year, 1993, Michigan Small Business Person of the Year, 1994; Master Entrepreneur of the Year; Minority Entrepreneur of the Year, 1991. **BUSINESS ADDRESS:** President, Saturn Electronics & Engineering, Inc, 2119 Austin Ave, Rochester Hills, MI 48309-3668, (313)852-2120.*

TSUHA, WALLACE KOICHI
Photographer (retired). Japanese American. **PERSONAL:** Born May 6, 1914, Waipahu, HI; son of Uto Tsuha (deceased) and Kame Tsuha (deceased); married Ai Kimiko Tsuha, Aug 20, 1957; children: Walter Shigeharu, Kurtis Keiichi. **CAREER:** Self-employed, photographer, 1938-80. **ORGANIZATIONS:** United Okiwawan Assn of Hawaii. **HOME ADDRESS:** 94-122 Haaa St, Waipahu, HI 96797, (808)677-5182.

TSUI, ANNIE
Association administrator, educator. Chinese American. **CAREER:** National Association of Asian American Professionals, president. **BUSINESS ADDRESS:** President, Natl Assn of Asian American Professionals, PO Box 772, New York, NY 10002, (212)514-8191.*

TSUI, CHERYL WAI-KUEN
Television reporter. Hong Kong American. **PERSONAL:** Born Aug 16, 1962, Hong Kong; daughter of Ki Tsui; married Oliver Ko, Sep 26, 1992. **EDUCATION:** Chu Hai College, Hong Kong, BA, 1987; University of South Carolina, MA, 1989. **CAREER:** Radio Television Hong Kong, broadcaster, 1986-87; KTSF, Lincoln Broadcasting Co, reporter/assignment coordinator, 1990-. **ORGANIZATIONS:** The Society of Professional Journalists, 1989-; South Carolina Philharmonic Chorus, 1987-89; Hong Kong Journalists Association, 1985-87. **HONORS/AWARDS:** Joey Award, 1990. **SPECIAL ACHIEVEMENTS:** Master's thesis, "Freedom of Press in Hong Kong Towards 1997," included in the journalism abstracts, 1990. **BUSINESS ADDRESS:** Reporter/

Assignment Coordinator, KTSF, Lincoln Broadcasting Company, 100 Valley Dr, Brisbane, CA 94005, (415)468-2626.

TSUI, DANIEL CHEE
Educator. Chinese American. **PERSONAL:** Born Feb 28, 1939, Henan, China; married 1964; children: two. **EDUCATION:** Augustana College, BA, 1961; University of Chicago, MS, 1967, PhD, physics, 1967. **CAREER:** University of Chicago, research associate, 1967-68; Bell Labs, member of technical staff, 1968-82; Princeton University, Arthur Legrand Doty Professor of Electrical Engineering, 1982-. **ORGANIZATIONS:** National Academy of Science. **HONORS/AWARDS:** American Physical Society, Oliver E Buckley Condensed Matter Physics Prize, 1984. **SPECIAL ACHIEVEMENTS:** Research on electronic properties of metals, surface properties of semiconductors, low temperature physics. **BUSINESS ADDRESS:** Professor, Electronic Engineering Dept, Princeton University, Princeton, NJ 08544, (609)258-3500.*

TSUI, PAULINE WOO
Association administrator. Chinese American. **PERSONAL:** Born Oct 2, 1920, Nanking, China; daughter of John Y and Sarah K Woo; married Tswen Ling Tsui, Jul 26, 1947; children: Lynnette Tsui Lee, Garrick C Y. **EDUCATION:** St John's University, BA, 1943; Columbia University, MA, 1947. **CAREER:** Army Map Service, Washington, geographic names specialist, 1951-62; Hydrographic Topographic Center, Defense Mapping Agency, cartographer, 1963-75, tech information specialist, 1975-76, Federal Women's Program, equal employment opportunity specialist, manager, 1976-80; Chinese American Women Educational Equity Program, beginning 1981. **ORGANIZATIONS:** US Civil Rights Commission, DC adv com, 1974-78; Brookmont Learning Tree Child Care Center, founding director, 1979-; National Commission for Responsive Philanthropy, board of directors, 1980; Organization of Chinese American Women, founding national president, 1977-; Federal Organizations for Professional Women, executive council member, 1980. **BUSINESS ADDRESS:** Executive Director, Organization of Chinese American Women, 1300 N St NW, Ste 100, Washington, DC 20005, (202)638-0330.*

TSUI, SUSAN LEE
Librarian, educator. Chinese American. **PERSONAL:** Born Jan 11, 1938, ChungKing, Sichuan, China; married James Bao-yen Tsui, May 19, 1965; children: David, Lisa Tsui Diller. **EDUCATION:** National Taiwan University, BS, foreign literature, 1961; University of Illinois, MLS, 1964. **CAREER:** Miami University, bibliographer/instructor, 1964-65; University of Dayton, Bibliographic Control, coordinator/associate professor, 1965-. **BUSINESS ADDRESS:** Coordinator/Associate Professor, University of Dayton Library, 300 College Park, Roesch Library, Rm 104B, Dayton, OH 45469-1360, (513)229-4268.

TSUJI, KIYOSHI
Scientist. Japanese American. **PERSONAL:** Born May 31, 1931, Kyoto, Japan; son of Takeshiro Tsuji and Sai Mukudai; married Ruriko Ikenami Tsuji, Jun 14, 1958; children: Shoko Barnes, Hiroshi, Jun. **EDUCATION:** Kyoto University, Japan, BS, 1954; University of Massachusetts, Amherst, MS, 1956, PhD, 1959. **CAREER:** Rutgers University, post-doctoral fellow, 1959-60; National Canners Association, research associate, 1960-63; MIT, Nutrition and Food Science Dept, research associate, 1963-64; The Upjohn Co, research scientist, 1964-73, senior scientist, 1973-92, senior scientist V, 1992-. **ORGANIZATIONS:** Journal of Laboratory Robotics and Automation, associate editor; Journal of Radiation Sterilization, associate editor; The Upjohn Co, Quality Control Academy; American Chem Soc; American Soc Microbiology; Inst Food Technologist; Sigma Xi; Phi Tau Sigma. **HONORS/AWARDS:** The Upjohn Company, Wm E Upjohn Award, 1971, Nicolas Copernicus Award, 1985, Upjohn Achievement in Science and Medicine Award, 1988, Laboratory Automation, Pioneer of Lab Robotics Award, 1985. **SPECIAL ACHIEVEMENTS:** GLC and HPLC Determination of Therapeutic Agents, vols I, II, & III, 1979-80; more than 100 publications in scientific journals; proficient in Japanese. **HOME ADDRESS:** 5616 Saddle Club Drive, Kalamazoo, MI 49009. **BUSINESS ADDRESS:** Senior Scientist V, The Upjohn Company, 7000 Portage Road, Mail Stop 4862-259-277, Kalamazoo, MI 49001, (616)323-5493.

TSUKAHIRA, TOSHIO GEORGE
Government official, educator, consultant. Japanese American. **PERSONAL:** Born Dec 22, 1915, Los Angeles, CA; son of Kuhei Tsukahira and Kikue Akazawa Tsukahira; married Lilly Yuriko Fujioka Tsukahira, Apr 4, 1942; children: Margaret Mine Norris, Peter Ken. **EDUCATION:** Meiji University,

Tokyo, AA, 1936; University of California, Los Angeles, AB, 1939, MA, 1941; Harvard University, PhD, 1951. **CAREER:** Harvard University, instructor in history, 1951-54; University of California, Berkeley, assistant professor of history, 1954-55; US Department of State, foreign service officer (Japan, Thailand), 1955-75; Princeton University, Woodrow Wilson School, visiting professor, 1976; US Foreign Service Institute, Japan-Korea area studies courses, chairman, 1980-82; US Department of State, foreign affairs consultant, 1982-; TGT Consulting, lecturer/consultant on Japanese affairs, 1977, president, 1977-. **ORGANIZATIONS:** Japan-America Society of Washington, DC, 1976-, trustee, 1980-86; Japanese American National Museum, 1992; Japanese American Veterans Assn of Washington, DC, 1992; Harvard Club of Washington, DC. **SPECIAL ACHIEVEMENTS:** Author: "Foreign Relations" chapter in Japan: A Country Study, Washington, DC, Foreign Area Studies, American University, 1982; Feudal Control in Tokugawa Japan: The Sankin Kotai System, Cambridge, Massachusetts, Harvard University Press, 1966; Postwar Development of Japanese Communist Strategy, Cambridge, Massachusetts, Center for International Studies, MIT, 1954. **MILITARY SERVICE:** US Army, captain, 1944-47. **HOME ADDRESS:** 6505 Pyle Rd, Bethesda, MD 20817-5451, (301)320-3978. **BUSINESS PHONE:** (301)320-3978.

TSUKAMOTO, JACK TORU

Educator, librarian. Japanese American. **PERSONAL:** Born Jan 3, 1931, Marugame, Kagawa-Ken, Japan; son of Shigeru Tsukamoto & Kinue Tsukamoto; divorced. **EDUCATION:** Shikoku Christian College, BA, 1954; Austin College, BA, 1955; University of Texas, Austin, MLS, 1962, PhD, 1976. **CAREER:** University of Texas, catalog librarian, 1961-63; Monmouth College, assistant librarian, 1963-66; Washington University, assistant professor, 1968-71; Tamagawa in the USA, founder, director, 1965-69; Ball State University, associate professor, 1971-92; Sasakawa Peace Foundation USA Library, chief librarian, 1992-. **ORGANIZATIONS:** American Library Association, 1961-; Linguistic Society of America, 1968-; Asian Pacific American Librarians Association, secretary, 1986-87; Association of College and Research Libraries, 1971-; Association for Asian Studies, 1963-; Ohio Valley Group of Technical Services Librarians, 1971-; Special Libraries Association, 1992-. **HONORS/AWARDS:** Presbyterian Church of the US, fellowship, 1954-57; University of Texas, NDEA Title IV Fellowship, 1969-71; Asian Pacific American Librarians Association, Distinguished Service, 1991. **SPECIAL ACHIEVEMENTS:** "Tamagawa in the USA-Its Academic Program," 1966; "Tamagawa in the USA: a Bridge to Cultural Understanding," 1968; Library Instruction and Faculty Development, 1980. **HOME ADDRESS:** 2004 17th St NW, Washington, DC 20009, (202)462-6650. **BUSINESS ADDRESS:** Chief Librarian, Sasakawa Peace Foundation USA Library, 1819 L St NW, Washington, DC 20009, (202)296-8245.

TSUKAMOTO, MARY TSURUKO

Educator (retired). Japanese American. **PERSONAL:** Born Jan 17, 1915, San Francisco, CA; married Alfred I Tsukamoto, 1936; children: Marielle. **EDUCATION:** University of Pacific, 1933-36; California State University, BS, 1951. **CAREER:** Elementary school teacher, 1949-76. **ORGANIZATIONS:** Florin United Methodist Church, 1947-; Florin Japanese American Citizens League, 1936-; Florin Historical Society; Elk Grove Historical Society. **HONORS/AWARDS:** Mary Tsukamoto Elementary School, 1992; Assemblymen Norm Waters, CA, Woman of the Year, 1990; California School Boards Association, Hall of Fame, 1989; National Educator's Association, Ellison Onizuka, Memorial Award, 1992; University of Pacific Alumni Association, Distinguished Public Service Award, 1993; numerous others. **SPECIAL ACHIEVEMENTS:** Author, We The People, A Story of Internment in America, Laguna Publishers, 1987. **BIOGRAPHICAL SOURCES:** Featured on Today Show, 1987; Dignity, University of Michigan Press, 1985; And Justice for All, Random House, 1984; Making Do, how women survived the 30s, 1976. **HOME ADDRESS:** 9132 Doc Bar Ct, Elk Grove, CA 95624, (916)685-6747.

TSUKUNO, PAUL

Attorney. Japanese American. **PERSONAL:** Born 1951?, Chicago, IL; married; children: two sons. **CAREER:** Illinois State Attorney's Office, 1979-, Arson Unit, supervisor, felony trial wing supervisor, Municipal Division, chief, 1993-. **SPECIAL ACHIEVEMENTS:** Has tried over 55 felony jury trials and 250 felony bench trials; lecturer; teacher; Cook County Circuit Court, associate judge candidate, 1990; highest ranking Asian American, State Attorney's Office, currently. **BUSINESS ADDRESS:** Chief, Municipal Division, State Attorney Office, 500 Richard J Daley Center, Chicago, IL 60602, (312)443-5440.*

TSUNEISHI, WARREN MICHIO

Library administrator (retired). Japanese American. **PERSONAL:** Born Jul 4, 1921, Monrovia, CA; son of Sho Murakami and Satoru Tsuneishi; married Betty Takeuchi, Nov 16, 1946; children: David, Kenneth, Julia Tsuneishi Jordan. **EDUCATION:** Syracuse University, BA, 1943; Columbia University, MA, 1948, MS, library science, 1950; Yale University, PhD, 1960. **CAREER:** Yale University Library, cataloger/research associate, 1950-52, Far Eastern Collection, curator, 1953-57, East Asian Collection, curator, 1960-66, area studies director, 1978-89; Yale University, Dept of Political Science, lecturer, 1963-64; University of Hawaii, Graduate Library School, lecturer, 1967-68, 1971; University of Chicago, Institute for Far Eastern Librarianship, lecturer, 1969; Library of Congress, Far Eastern Language Section, head, 1957-60, Orientalia Division, chief, 1966-78, Asian Division, chief, 1989-92. **ORGANIZATIONS:** Japan-America Society, board of trustees, 1968-72; ALA; Association for Asian Studies; International Association of Orientalist Librarians, president, 1983-. **HONORS/AWARDS:** Library of Congress, Superior Service Award, 1979, 1989. **SPECIAL ACHIEVEMENTS:** Author, Japanese Political Style, 1966; coeditor, University and Research Libraries, 1972, Issues in Library Administration, 1974. **MILITARY SERVICE:** US Army, 1943-46; Bronze Star, 1945.*

TSUSAKA, JUN

Investment banking executive. Japanese American. **PERSONAL:** Born Mar 25, 1961, Tokyo, Japan; son of Akira Tsusaka and Reiko Tsusaka; married Miki Uchida Tsusaka, Jun 16, 1985; children: Mia Uchida. **EDUCATION:** Harvard University, BA (cum laude), 1983, MBA (with distinction), 1988. **CAREER:** Merrill Lynch, associate, 1983-86; Goldman, Sachs & Co, vice president, 1988-. **HONORS/AWARDS:** Harvard College, Harvard College Scholarship, 1980-83. **BUSINESS ADDRESS:** Vice President, Goldman, Sachs & Co, 85 Broad St, 23rd Fl, New York, NY 10004, (212)902-5557.

TSUTAKAWA, GEORGE

Educator, artist (retired). Japanese American. **PERSONAL:** Born Feb 22, 1910, Seattle, WA; married Ayame; children: Gerard, Mayumi, Deems, Marcus. **EDUCATION:** University of Washington, BFA, 1936, MFA, 1950. **CAREER:** University of Washington, instructor of Japanese, School of Art, instructor, 1947-76, professor emeritus, 1976-. **HONORS/AWARDS:** Washington State Historical Society, Centennial Hall of Honor Award, 1981; Seattle University, Honorary Doctorate of Humanities, Honoris Causa, 1986; Whitman College, Walla Walla, honorary degree, Doctor of Fine Arts, 1986; Broadway High School Alumni Association, Distinguished Alumnus Award, 1988; JACL, Seattle Chapter, Lifetime Dedication of Art, 1993; Seattle Wing Luke Asian Museum, Contribution to the Community, 1993; American Society of Interior Designers, Design Achievement Award, 1994. **SPECIAL ACHIEVEMENTS:** Exhibitions include: One Man Show, Foster/White Gallery, Seattle, 1988; Sumi Paintings, group show, Bellevue Art Museum, 1988; Seattle Style, sumi-e group show/touring exhibit in France, 1988; commissions include: Water Department Building No 2, Sapporo, Japan, 1987; Garden of the Fukuyama Fine Art Museum, Japan, 1988; Central Plaza, Seattle University, 1989; slide lectures: Fountain Design, Washington Athletic Club, Seattle, Washington, February 13, 1985; Designing Fountains, Seattle Sunset Club, February 27, 1985. **MILITARY SERVICE:** US Army, served during WWII. **BIOGRAPHICAL SOURCES:** Fifty Northwest Artists, Chronicle Books; Sculpture in Public Places, Contemporary Sculpture Center, Tokyo, 1983; numerous feature articles and critical reviews in The Seattle Times, The Seattle Post Intelligencer, Seattle Weekly.

TSUTAKAWA, GERARD K.

Sculptor. Japanese American. **PERSONAL:** Born Nov 8, 1947, Seattle, WA; son of George & Ayame Tsutakawa; married Judith. **CAREER:** Sculptor. **SPECIAL ACHIEVEMENTS:** Exhibition: Bronze and Wood, Foster/White Gallery, Seattle, October 1992.

TSUTSUI, JAMES HARUO, JR.

Company manager. Japanese American. **PERSONAL:** Born Dec 16, 1952, Los Angeles, CA; son of James Haruo Tsutsui and Jeanne Chiemi Tsutsui; married Vicki Misaye Tsutsui, Jul 27, 1980; children: Christopher Mihoru, Alison Chiemi. **EDUCATION:** University of California, Irvine, BS, 1974, BA, 1976, MA, 1979. **CAREER:** Koho Hawaii Restaurant, waiter, 1974-79; University of California, Irvine, art instructor, 1978-79; Sunland Nurseries, cost estimator, 1979-80; Hunsaker & Associates, cost estimator, 1980-82, Covoc Corp, cost estimator, 1982-83; Hunsaker & Associates, manager of cost estimating, 1983-. **ORGANIZATIONS:** Landmark Education, seminar leader, 1989-92, introduction to the forum leader, 1981-, self-expression/leadership program leader, 1993-; Education Network, team leader, natl attendance project, 1989-91; Hunger Project, fund raiser, contributor, 1977-; Breakthrough Foundation, volunteer, contributor, 1980-88; Werner Erhard & Associates, team leader, 1980-90. **HONORS/AWARDS:** Bank of America, Achievement Award in Art, 1970; Education Network, Fund Raising, 1989. **SPECIAL ACHIEVEMENTS:** Thesis Show, Fine Arts Gallery, University of California, irvine, "Con with Myself Yia", 1979; Thesis Show 2, Fine Arts Gallery, University of California, Irvine, "Naked Japanese Girls, Art Guns", 1979. **HOME ADDRESS:** 22536 Caminito Pacifico, Laguna Hills, CA 92653, (714)837-5132.

TU, CHARLES W.
Educator. Taiwanese American. **PERSONAL:** Born Jan 1, 1951, Taipei, Taiwan; son of Tsuchih & Lichu Tu. **EDUCATION:** McGill University, BSc, 1971; Yale University, MPhil, 1972, PhD, 1978. **CAREER:** Yale University, lecturer, 1978-80; AT&T Bell Labs, member of technical staff, 1980-88; University of California, San Diego, professor, 1988-. **ORGANIZATIONS:** US Molecular Beam Epitaxy MBE Workshop, advisory board, 1990-; Electronic Material Conference Committee, 1991-; Materials Research Society, symposium organizer, 1989, 1992, 1994; Fourth International Conference on CBE, conference co-chair, 1993; Sixth International Conference on MBE, organization chair, 1990; Seventh International Conference on MBE, program committee, 1992; American Vacuum Society, executive board, Electronic Material Process Division, 1989-91. **HONORS/AWARDS:** United Nations, Development Program Award, 1991; AT&T Bell Labs, Distinguished Member of Technical Staff, 1987, Exceptional Contribution Award, 1985-87. **SPECIAL ACHIEVEMENTS:** More than 175 publications; 3 edited conference proceedings: "Semiconductor Heterostructures for Electronic and Photonic Applications," Materials Research Society Symposium Proceedings, vol 28, 1993; "III-V Heterostructures for Electronic, Photonic Devices," MRS Symposium Proceedings, vol 145, 1989; "Sixth International Conference on Molecular Beam Epitaxy," Journal Crystal Growth, vol 111, 1991. **BUSINESS ADDRESS:** Professor, Dept of Electrical and Computer Engineering, University of California, San Diego, Engineering Bldg Unit 1, Rm 4408, La Jolla, CA 92093-0407, (619)534-4687.

TU, CHING-I
Educator. Chinese American. **PERSONAL:** Born May 13, 1935, Nanking, China; son of Show-Mei & I-Fang Tu; married Sabrina S Tu, Jun 1970; children: Stephen S C, Sylvia. **EDUCATION:** National Taiwan University, BA, 1958; University of Washington, PhD, 1967. **CAREER:** University of Hawaii, visiting associate professor, 1971-72; National Taiwan university, visiting professor, 1974-75; Rutgers University, Department of Comparative Literature and Oriental Languages, professor & chair, 1979-82, director of Asian Studies, 1987-. **ORGANIZATIONS:** Association for Asian Studies, 1966; American Association for Chinese Studies, 1980; Association of Department of Foreign Languages, 1981; Chinese-American Academic and Professional Society, 1989; Assn for Asian Studies, Mid-Atlantic Region, 1988. **HONORS/AWARDS:** University of Washington, D Johnsonne Fund Prize, 1965; National Commission on Science, ROC, Research Grant, 1974-75; NJ Department of Higher Education, grants, 1984-90. **SPECIAL ACHIEVEMENTS:** Poetic Remarks in the Human World, Taipei, 1970; Anthology of Chinese Literature, Taipei, 1972; Reading in Classical Chinese Literature, New Brunswick, NJ, 1981; Tradition and Creativity: Essays on East Asian Civilization, New Brunswick, NJ, 1989. **BUSINESS ADDRESS:** Professor & Chair, Dept of East Asian Languages & Cultures, Rutgers University, College Avenue, Scott Hall, Rm 330, New Brunswick, NJ 08903, (908)932-7605.

TU, HAROLD KAI
Educator. Chinese American. **PERSONAL:** Born May 6, 1948, Shanghai, China; son of Sieu Mei Tu and Joseph Zung Tu; married Patricia Kay Tu, Aug 8, 1973; children: Travis, Andrew. **EDUCATION:** Linfield College, BA, 1971; University of Oregon Dental School, DMD, 1977; University of Nebraska Medical Center, MD, 1979; Fellow American College of Surgeons, 1992. **CAREER:** Omaha Veteran's Administration Medical Center, staff, 1982-; Nebraska Methodist Children's Hospital, staff, 1982-; MedCenter One, staff, 1987-; University of Nebraska Medical Center, staff, 1982-. **ORGANIZATIONS:** MediQual Systems Inc, consultant, 1990-; American Association of Oral Maxillofacial Surgeons, Committee on Scientific Sessions, 1988-; Physician Payment Review Commission Panel for Global Coding, 1988-; Special Commission on Value of Care and PPRC Task Force, 1988-; American Academy of Facial Plastic and Reconstructive Surgery, fellow, 1987-; American Medical Association, 1980-; American Dental Association, 1974-.

HONORS/AWARDS: Numerous professional awards and certificates. **SPECIAL ACHIEVEMENTS:** Book: Anesthesia for Facial Plastic Surgery, 1993; book chapter, Residents Manual: Oral and Maxillofacial Surgery, 1989; book chapter, The Team Physician's Handbook, Maxillofacial Injuries, 1990; book chapter, Textbook of Oral and Maxillofacial Surgery, Traumatic Injuries to the Teeth and Jaws, 1993; article, "Hematologic Management of a Patient with Fanconi's Anemia...," 1992. **BUSINESS ADDRESS:** Associate Professor, Oral and Maxillofacial Surgery, University of Nebraska Medical Center, 600 S 42nd St, UMA, Rm 4554, Omaha, NE 68198-3010, (402)559-4285.

TU, SAMSON W.
Researcher. Taiwanese American. **PERSONAL:** Born Jan 31, 1954, Taipei, Taiwan; son of Grant T Tu and Lillian L Tu; divorced. **EDUCATION:** Harvard University, AB, 1977; Stanford University, MS, 1985. **CAREER:** Stanford University, research associate, currently. **ORGANIZATIONS:** American Association of Artificial Intelligence; Association of Computing Machinery. **HOME ADDRESS:** 2180 Coolidge Dr, Santa Clara, CA 95051. **BUSINESS ADDRESS:** Research Associate, Stanford University, Section on Medical Information, Medical School Office Building, Stanford, CA 94305.

TU, SHENGRU
Educator. Chinese American. **PERSONAL:** Born Jan 26, 1950, Shanghai, People's Republic of China; son of Nian-Yong Tu & Xiang-Zhen Liu; married Qing Yang Tu, Oct 3, 1983; children: Chen-Guang. **EDUCATION:** Shanghai University of Technology, BS, 1981, MS, 1984; University of Illinois, Chicago, PhD, 1991. **CAREER:** Shanghai University of Technology, lecturer, 1984-87; University of California at Berkeley, visiting research fellow, 1987-88; University of Illinois, research engineer, 1988-90, research assistant, 1990-91; University of New Orleans, assistant professor, 1991-. **ORGANIZATIONS:** IEEE Computer Society, 1992-; Association for Computing Machinery, 1990-, SIGCSE, 1991-, SIGSOFT, 1991-, SIGOPS, 1992-. **HONORS/AWARDS:** University of New Orleans, Summer Scholar Award, 1991. **SPECIAL ACHIEVEMENTS:** Author: "Design and Implementation of a Petri Net-Based Toolkit for Ada Tasking Analysis," IEEE Trans on PDS, 1990; "Applying Petri Net Reduction to Support Ada-Tasking Deadlock Detection," Proceedings of ICDCS, 1990; "Automated Visualization of Tasking Behavior for Ada Programs," Proceedings of SEKE, 1991; "Linear Programming Supporting Static Analysis of Concurrent Programs," Proceedings of SEKE, 1991; "Supporting Inheritance in Relational Database Systems by Using Constraints," Proceedings of SEKE, 1992. **BUSINESS ADDRESS:** Asst Professor, Dept of Computer Science, University of New Orleans, 2300 Lakeshore Dr, Math Bldg, #321, New Orleans, LA 70148, (504)286-7108.

TU, SHIAO-CHUN (DAVID TU)
Educator. Chinese American. **PERSONAL:** Born Dec 29, 1943, Henan, China; married Teresa R H Tu, Jun 20, 1970; children: Elizabeth Kuang-I. **EDUCATION:** National Taiwan University, BS, agricultural chemistry, 1966; Cornell University, MNS, nutritional biochemistry, 1969, PhD, biochemistry, 1973. **CAREER:** Harvard University, research fellow, 1973-77; University of Houston, assistant professor of biochemical and biophysical sciences, 1977-82, associate professor of biochemical and biophysical sciences, 1982-85, professor of biochemical and biophysical sciences, 1985-, Institute for Molecular Biology, 1987-, chairman of Department of Biochemical and Biophysical Sciences, 1989-93, Institute for Molecular Design, 1993-, professor of chemistry, 1993-. **ORGANIZATIONS:** NIH Physical Biochemistry Study Section, 1984-88, 1993-97; Society of Chinese Bioscientists in America, life member, 1987-, newsletter editor, 1988-90, vice president of Houston chapter, 1992, president of Houston chapter, 1993, Nomination Committee, 1994-96; Photochemistry and Photobiology, associate editor, 1985-92; American Association for the Advancement of Science; American Chemical Society; American Society for Biochemistry and Molecular Biology; American Society for Photobiology; Sigma Xi. **HONORS/AWARDS:** The United Nations Development Program, TOKTEN Award, 1987; Sigma Xi Society, University of Houston Chapter, Faculty Award, 1982; National Institutes of Health, Research Career Development Award, 1981; University of Houston, Mortar Board National Senior Honor Society, Outstanding Educator, 1980; National Institutes of Health, National Research Service Award, 1975; Cornell University, DuPont Teaching Award, 1972. **SPECIAL ACHIEVEMENTS:** Over 70 scientific publications. **BUSINESS ADDRESS:** Professor, Dept of Biochemical and Biophysical Sciences, University of Houston, Houston, TX 77204-5934, (713)743-8359.

TU, SHU-CHEN H.
Librarian. Taiwanese American. **PERSONAL:** Born in Tou-nan, Yun-lin County, Taiwan; daughter of Ching-yuan Hung and Yu-fong L Hung; married Po-tung Tu, Apr 21, 1974; children: Wayne W. **EDUCATION:** National Taiwan University, BA, 1970; University of North Carolina at Chapel Hill, MSLS, 1985; Harvard University, MA, 1993. **CAREER:** Tou-nan Junior High, teacher/guidance counselor, 1970-72; Mackay Hospital, Taipei, social worker, 1972-75; Bridgewater State College, librarian, 1985-. **ORGANIZA-TIONS:** American Library Association, 1985-; ACRL, New England chapter, 1990-. **BIOGRAPHICAL SOURCES:** Directory of Library & Information Professionals, p1261, 1988. **BUSINESS ADDRESS:** Associate Librarian, Maxwell Library, Bridgewater State College, Shaw Road, Bridgewater, MA 02325, (508)697-1394.

TUAN, DEBBIE FU-TAI
Educator. Chinese American. **PERSONAL:** Born Feb 2, 1930, KiangSu, China; daughter of Shian-gien Tuan and Chin Lee Tuan; married John W Reed, Aug 15, 1987. **EDUCATION:** National Taiwan University, BS, 1954, MS, 1958; Yale University, MS, 1960, PhD, 1961. **CAREER:** Yale University, postdoctoral research fellow, 1961-64; University of Wisconsin, project associate, 1964-65; Yeshiva University, visiting scientist, summer 1966; Academic Sinica of China, National Taiwan University, Tsing-Hwa University, visiting professor, summer 1967; Harvard University, research fellow, 1969-70; SRI International, visiting scientist, 1981; Cornell University, research associate, 1983; Ohio State University, visiting professor, 1993; Kent State University, assistant professor, 1965-70, associate professor, 1970-73, professor, 1973-. **ORGANIZATIONS:** American Chemical Society, 1960-; American Physical Society, 1960-; Sigma Xi, 1961-. **HONORS/AWARDS:** National Taiwan University, scholarships, 1951-54; Chinese Women Association, President Chiang Kai-Shek Scholarship, 1954, 1958; China Foundation, Graduate Scholarship in Humanity and Science, 1955; Yale University, F W Heyl-Anong F Fellowship, 1960-61; Kent State University, Faculty Research Fellowship, 1966, 1968, 1971, 1985. **SPECIAL ACHIEVEMENTS:** Publications in: Journal of Chinese Chem Society, Annual Reviews of Physical Chemistry; J Physical Chemistry; J Chemical Physics; Chemical Physics, letters; J Inorganic Chemistry; J Molecular Structure; J Molecular Structure-Therochem, 1958-. **BUSINESS ADDRESS:** Professor, Chemistry Dept, Kent State University, Kent, OH 44242, (216)672-2995.

TUAN, SAN FU
Educator. Chinese American. **PERSONAL:** Born May 14, 1932, Tientsin, China; son of Mao Lan and Lu Kung (Tao) Tuan; married Loretta Kan, Dec 15, 1963; children: Katherine Tsung Yen, Melinda Tsung Tao, Priscilla Tsung Pei, David Tsung Lien. **EDUCATION:** Oxford University, BA, 1954, MA, 1958; University of California, Berkeley, PhD, 1958. **CAREER:** University of Chicago, research assoc, 1958-60; Brown University, asst prof, 1960-62; Purdue University, assoc prof, 1962-65, visiting prof, 1973; Princeton, Inst Adv Study, 1966, 1972; Beijing University/Institute of Theoretical Physics (Academia Sinica, China), visiting prof, 1979-80; University of Wisconsin-Madison, visiting prof, 1982; University of Hawaii, visiting prof, 1965-66, prof of theoretical physics, 1966-. **ORGANIZATIONS:** American Math Soc; American Physical Soc, fellow, 1969-; Oxford Union; Phi Beta Kappa. **SPECIAL ACHIEVEMENTS:** Co-editor, Proceedings of Second and Third Hawaii Topical Conferences in Particle Physics, 1967, 1969; editor, Modern Quantum Mechanics, 1985. **BUSINESS ADDRESS:** Professor, Dept of Physics & Astronomy, University of Hawaii at Manoa, 2505 Correa Rd, Watanabe Hall, Honolulu, HI 96822, (808)956-7391.

TULI, JAGDISH K.
Scientist. Indo-American. **PERSONAL:** Born Aug 7, 1941, Lahore, Punjab, India; son of Iqbal Singh & Shanti Devi Tuli; married Kiran Tuli, Mar 8, 1975; children: Neal, Nevin. **EDUCATION:** Agra University, BS, 1958; Delhi University, India, MS, 1965; Indiana University, MS, 1969, PhD, 1971. **CAREER:** Indiana University, research associate, 1971-73; Lawrence Berkeley Lab, research associate, 1976-77; Brookhaven National Lab, physicist, 1977-. **ORGANIZATIONS:** American Physical Society, 1977-. **BUSINESS ADDRESS:** Physicist, Brookhaven National Laboratory, 197 D, Upton, NY 11973, (516)282-5080.

TUN, HARRY T. (CHU-MIN CHENG)
Electrical engineer. Chinese American. **PERSONAL:** Born Nov 9, 1918, Kwonghai, Kwangtung, China; son of Bak Yee Tun and Pang Shee Tun; married Florence L Tun, May 20, 1948; children: Elaine Tun Chow, Daniel E,

Walter J. **EDUCATION:** Illinois Institute of Technology, BS, 1948. **CAREER:** Commonwealth Edison Co, supervising engineer, 1948-83. **ORGANIZATIONS:** Chinese American Civic Council, president, 1967, 1978; Chinese Consolidated Benevolent, English secretary, 1978-80. **HONORS/AWARDS:** City of Chicago, Senior Citizens Hall of Fame, 1988. **SPECIAL ACHIEVEMENTS:** Chinese American Progress, Chinese American Civic Council Publication, 1967-84. **MILITARY SERVICE:** US Army, Air Force, major, 1942-46, South Pacific, Asiatic Theatre Service Awards. **HOME ADDRESS:** 3824 W Eddy St, Chicago, IL 60618.

TUNG, HSI-TANG
Veterinarian. Taiwanese American. **PERSONAL:** Born Oct 20, 1939, Tainan, Taiwan; son of Ping-ting & Shin-yen Tung; married Shuling Tung, Aug 23, 1969; children: Gene Fong. **EDUCATION:** National Taiwan University, DVM, 1966; North Dakota State University, MS, bacteriology, 1969; North Carolina State University, PhD, microbiology, 1972. **CAREER:** Maag & Easterbrooks Inc, research bacteriologist & quality control manager, 1972-73; Vineland Laboratory, technical director, 1973-77; Abbott Laboratory, senior microbiologist, 1977-79; Beecham Laboratory, research director, 1979-82; American Animal Health, vice president & partner, 1983-. **ORGANIZATIONS:** American Association of Service Practitioners, 1980-; American Veterinary Medical Association, 1973-; American Society for Microbiologists, 1970-; American Association for Asian Pathologists, 1974-; Chinese Independent Businessman Association, board director, 2nd vice president, 1988-; Taiwanese Chamber of Commerce of North America, DFW Chapter, board director, 1991-. **HONORS/AWARDS:** Abbott Laboratory, Presidential Award, 1980. **MILITARY SERVICE:** The Canine Corp, Taiwan National Security Guard, 2nd lt, 1966-67. **BIOGRAPHICAL SOURCES:** AVMA Directory, p 409, 1991; ASM Directory, 1992. **HOME ADDRESS:** 3406 Ainsworth Court, Arlington, TX 76016, (817)496-9243. **BUSINESS ADDRESS:** Vice President, American Animal Health Inc, 2619 Skyway Dr, Grand Prairie, TX 75051, (214)641-2918.

TUNG, JOHN
Real estate company executive. Chinese American. **PERSONAL:** Born May 5, 1952, Taiwan; son of Shiu Kang Tung and Lee Wei Tung; married Susan P, Jun 5, 1982; children: Michael N, Brian N. **EDUCATION:** Princeton University, BSE, 1974; University of Chicago, MBA, 1976. **CAREER:** Chase Manhattan Bank, vice president, 1976-80; International Petroleum Refining & Supply, vice president, CFO, 1980-82; Kuo International, executive director of investments, 1982-87; Draper & Kramer, senior vice president, 1987-. **ORGANIZATIONS:** Urban Land Institute; Princeton Club of Chicago; Union League Club. **SPECIAL ACHIEVEMENTS:** "Required Rates of Return in Commercial Mortgage Market," Journal of Real Estate Research; "The Elusive Benefits of Convertible Debt," Real Estate Review, "The Cost of the Prepayment Privilege;" "An Alternative View of the Incremental Cost of Capital," Journal of Real Estate Finance. **HOME ADDRESS:** 1691 Lowell Ln, Lake Forest, IL 60045. **BUSINESS PHONE:** (312)346-8600.

TUNG, KO-YUNG
Attorney. Chinese American. **PERSONAL:** Born Feb 20, 1947, Beijing, China; son of H F Tung; married Alison Heydt Tung, Feb 2, 1975; children: Vanessa, Adrian, Cameron, Gregory. **EDUCATION:** Harvard College, BA (magna cum laude), physics, 1969; University of Tokyo, faculty of law, fellow, 1971-72; Harvard Law School, JD, 1973. **CAREER:** Debevoise & Plimpton, associate, 1973-76; Tung, Drabkin & Boynton, partner, 1976-85; O'Melveny & Myers, Global Practice Group, chairman, 1985-. **ORGANIZATIONS:** Trilateral Commission; East-West Center; Council on Foreign Relations; The Brookings Institute, council member; Japan Society Public Affairs and Corporate Program Committee; Overseas Development Council; US National Committee for Pacific Economic Corporation; Asian American Legal Defense Educational Fund; Institute for Asian Studies, advisory board; Asian American Bar Association of New York; Asian Partners Roundtable; Association of the Bar of the City of New York, Committee on the United States in a Global Economy. **HONORS/AWARDS:** Harvard College, Detur Prize, Phi Beta Kappa. **BIOGRAPHICAL SOURCES:** "Heavy Hitter, O'Melveny's Tokyo Connection," The American Lawyer, October, 1991; "100 Greats," Transpacific Magazine, p 30, Nov/Dec, 1991. **BUSINESS ADDRESS:** Chairman, Global Practice Group, O'Melveny & Myers, 153 East 53rd St, Citicorp Center, New York, NY 10022, (212)326-2001.

TUNG, MING SUNG
Research chemist. Taiwanese American. **PERSONAL:** Born Feb 25, 1942, Taichung, Taiwan; son of Mu-Zon Tung and Chen S Tung; married Su-fan Tung, Jun 13, 1970; children: Wayne T, Jayne T. **EDUCATION:** Cheng-Kung University, Taiwan, BS, 1964; Brown University, PhD, 1973. **CAREER:** Brown University, teaching/research assistant, 1965-72; University of Maryland, post doctoral fellow, 1972-74, visiting professor, 1974; American Dental Assn; NIST, Paffenbarger Research Center, project leader, 1974-. **ORGANIZATIONS:** North American Taiwanese Professors Assn, 1985-; Sigma Xi, 1972-; American Assn for Dental Research, 1975-; International Assn for Dental Research, 1975-; Taiwanese American Assn, 1975-. **HONORS/AWARDS:** International Association for Dental Research, E H Hatton Award, 1976. **SPECIAL ACHIEVEMENTS:** New inventions of chewing gum, toothpaste and mouth rinses for prevention of dental cavity and dentin sensitivity, 1991; "Developments to Watch," Business Week, p 110, April 19, 1993; "The Cutting Edge," Washington Post Health, p 5, March 30, 1993; TV news, radio interviews, national and international. **BIOGRAPHICAL SOURCES:** "People to Watch," Asiaweek, p 68, Dec 11, 1992; "New Technology Can Remineralize Teeth," ADA News, p 27, Oct 5, 1992. **BUSINESS ADDRESS:** Project Leader, Paffenbarger Research Center, National Institute of Standards and Technology, A153/224, Gaithersburg, MD 20899, (301)975-6823.

TUNG, THEODORE H.
Bank executive. Chinese American. **PERSONAL:** Born Aug 28, 1934, Beijing, China; married Patricia, 1966; children: Candice, Roderick. **EDUCATION:** National Taiwan University, BA, 1957; University of Oklahoma, MBA, 1962; University of Pennsylvania, Wharton School, PhD, 1965. **CAREER:** Bank of New York, sr economist, 1968-70; Continental Bank, vice pres, economist, 1971-80; Central National Bank, vice pres, chief economist, 1980-83; National City Corporation, sr vice pres, economist, 1983-. **ORGANIZATIONS:** National Assn of Business Economists; American Economic Assn; American Bankers Assn. **SPECIAL ACHIEVEMENTS:** Fluent in Chinese; author: Financial Market Outlook, monthly, 1983-; numerous professional articles; co-author of a book. **BUSINESS ADDRESS:** Senior Vice President, Economist, National City Corporation, 1900 E Ninth St, Loc #01-1408, Cleveland, OH 44114, (216)575-3269.

TUNG, WU-KI
Educator. Chinese American. **PERSONAL:** Born Oct 16, 1939, Kunming, Yunnan, China; son of Tung-ho Tung and Shou-ching Wang Tung; married Beatrice S Tung, Aug 24, 1963; children: Lei Hsin, Bruce Y. **EDUCATION:** National Taiwan University, BS, 1960; Yale University, PhD, 1966. **CAREER:** State University of New York, Stony Brook, research associate, 1966-68; Institute of Advanced Study, Princeton, member, 1968-70; University of Chicago, assistant professor, 1970-75; Illinois Institute of Tech, professor, 1975-92; Michigan State University, professor, 1992-. **ORGANIZATIONS:** American Physical Society, fellow. **SPECIAL ACHIEVEMENTS:** Author, Group Theory in Physics, World Scientific, 1985. **BUSINESS ADDRESS:** Professor, Dept of Physics/Astronomy, Michigan State University, East Lansing, MI 48824, (517)336-3624.

TUNG, YEOU-KOUNG
Educator. Taiwanese American/Chinese American. **PERSONAL:** Born Mar 4, 1954, Taiwan; son of Hsiang-Hiu Tung and Hong-Jen Hshue Tung; married Be-Ling Lee, Sep 18, 1977; children: Shue-Fen, Shue-Wen, Shue-Fei, Shue-Ting. **EDUCATION:** Tamkung University, Taiwan, BS, 1976; University of Texas, Austin, MS, 1978, PhD, 1980. **CAREER:** University of Texas, Austin, research associate, 1980; University of Nevada, Reno, assistant professor, 1981-84; University of Wyoming, professor, 1985-. **ORGANIZATIONS:** American Society of Civil Engineers; International Association of Hydraulic Research; International Water Resources Association; American Statistical Association. **HONORS/AWARDS:** American Society of Civil Engineers, Collingwood Prize, 1978; International Association of Hydraulic Research, Ippen Award, 1993. **SPECIAL ACHIEVEMENTS:** Specialization: probabilistic analysis and system analysis of hydraulic and water resource related problems. **HOME ADDRESS:** 1472 N 22nd St, Laramie, WY 82070, (307)742-8081. **BUSINESS ADDRESS:** Professor, University of Wyoming, Wyoming Water Resources Center, Laramie, WY 82071, (307)766-2143.

TUREK, LAURA KIM
Physician. Korean American. **PERSONAL:** Born Jan 27, 1967, Washington, DC; daughter of Charles Y C & Jane E Pak; married Paul J Turek, Apr 17, 1993. **EDUCATION:** Harvard University, BA, English, 1989; University of

Pennsylvania, School of Medicine, MD, 1993. **CAREER:** Baylor University, teaching fellow, anatomy, 1993; Texas Heart Institute, research fellow, cardiac transplant, 1993-94. **SPECIAL ACHIEVEMENTS:** "Testicular Histology in Prune Belly Syndrome: Just Another Intraabdominal Testis?," Journal of Urology, forthcoming; "Brain & Bone Aluminum: A Comparison of Aluminum Intake in Rats," Environmental Toxicology & Chemistry, 1992; "Calcium Citrate without Aluminum Antacids Does Not Cause Aluminum Retention in Patients with Functioning Kidneys," Bone & Mineral, 1993; chapter entitled "Allograft Vascular Disease," Heart Transplantation and Cardiovascular Support, forthcoming; "Are Two Hearts Better than None?: Heterotopic Heart Transplantation Revisited," in progress; "Use of Low-dose Cyclosporine with Aortic Allografts in Dogs," Texas Heart Institute Journal, forthcoming. **HOME ADDRESS:** 2701 Revere St, #250, Houston, TX 77098, (713)523-9158. **BUSINESS ADDRESS:** Research Fellow, Cardiac Transplant, Texas Heart Institute, Ste P357, 1101 Bates, Houston, TX 77225.

TYE, BIK-KWOON YEUNG
Educator, research scientist. Hong Kong American/Chinese American. **PERSONAL:** Born Jan 7, 1947, Hong Kong; daughter of Yeung Ngo and Ching-Yu Ma; married Henry Sze-Hoi Tye, Jun 25, 1971; children: Kay, Lynne. **EDUCATION:** Wellesley College, AB, 1969; University of California, San Francisco, MS, 1971; Massachusetts Institute of Technology, PhD, 1974; Stanford University, postdoc, 1974-77. **CAREER:** Cornell University, assistant professor, 1977-1984, associate professor, 1984-90, professor, 1991-. **ORGANIZATIONS:** NIH, grant review panel, 1984-88. **HONORS/AWARDS:** Fudan University, consulting professor, 1993-; Helen Hay Whitney Foundation, postdoctoral fellowship, 1974-77. **SPECIAL ACHIEVEMENTS:** 47 publications in 16 science journals, 1974-93. **BUSINESS ADDRESS:** Professor, Biochemistry, Molecular & Cell Biology, Cornell University, 325 Biotechnology Bldg, Ithaca, NY 14853, (607)255-2445.

TYE, SZE-HOI HENRY
Educator. Hong Kong American/Chinese American. **PERSONAL:** Born Jan 15, 1947, Shanghai, China; son of Heng-Shan Tye and Oi-Ching Cheng; married Bik-Kwoon Tye, Jun 25, 1971; children: Kay, Lynne. **EDUCATION:** Caltech, BS, 1970; MIT, PhD, 1974. **CAREER:** Stanford Linear Accelerator Center, researh associate, 1974-77; Fermi National Laboratory, research associate, 1977-78; Cornell University, research associate, 1978-80, senior research associate, 1980-87, physics professor, 1987-. **ORGANIZATIONS:** American Physical Society, 1977-; Overseas Chinese Physics Association, 1991-. **BUSINESS ADDRESS:** Professor of Physics, Cornell University, Newman Laboratory, Ithaca, NY 14853, (607)255-3360.

TZENG, KENNETH KAI-MING
Educator. Chinese American. **PERSONAL:** Born Aug 6, 1937, Kaifeng, Henan, China; son of Chen-Hua and Meng-Hua Hsiao; married Marjorie K, Aug 6, 1961; children: Todd Ching-Tien, Ted Ching-Yue. **EDUCATION:** National Taiwan University, BSEE, 1959; University of Illinois, Urbana, MSEE, 1962, PhD, EE, 1969. **CAREER:** IBM, jr engineer, 1962-63; NCR, electrical research engineer, 1963-65; University of Illinois, research assistant, 1965-69; Southwestern Jiaotung University, China, consulting professor, 1987-; Lehigh University, assistant professor, 1969-73, associate professor, 1973-77, interim chair, 1991-93, professor, 1977-. **ORGANIZATIONS:** Institute of Electrical and Electronics Engineers, senior member. **HONORS/AWARDS:** National Science Foundation, research grants, 1970-71, 1973-1976, 1976-79, 1988-1991, 1991-1994; NASA Faculty Fellow, 1976. **SPECIAL ACHIEVEMENTS:** Author of publications in: IEEE Transactions on Information Theory; Information and Control. **BUSINESS ADDRESS:** Professor, Dept of Electrical Engineering & Computer Science, Lehigh University, 19 Memorial Drive West, Packard Laboratory, Bethlehem, PA 18015-3084, (215)758-4076.

U

UBA, GEORGE R.
Educator. Japanese American. **PERSONAL:** Born in Chicago, IL. **EDUCATION:** University of Southern California, BA, 1969; University of Michigan, MA, 1970; UCLA, PhD, 1982. **CAREER:** California State University, Northridge, associate professor of English, 1987-. **ORGANIZATIONS:** Modern Language Assn of America, 1979-, Executive Committee of Asian American Literature Discussion Group, 1986-90, chair, 1990; Assn for Asian American Studies, 1989-; Society for the Study of Multi-Ethnic Literatures of the US,

1992-; American Culture Assn, 1992-. **HONORS/AWARDS:** California State University, Northridge, Meritorious Performance Awards, 1986, 1989, University Research Grants, 1987-88, 1990; UCLA, Academy of American Poets Prize, 1980. **SPECIAL ACHIEVEMENTS:** Selected critical publications in: Journal of American Culture, 1993; Reading the Literatures of Asian America, 1992; Asian America, 1992; Essays in Literature, 1990; MELUS, 1988; South Atlantic Quarterly, 1986; Amerasia Journal, 1985-86; Journal of Ethnic Studies, 1985; selected poems published in: Ploughshares, 1992; Quarry West, 1991; The Seattle Review, 1988-89; Southern (Australia) Review, 1988; The Jacaranda Review, 1986; Journal of Ethnic Studies, 1986; Carolina Quarterly, 1985; Breaking Silence, 1983; director, Japanese American San Fernando Oral History Project, 1993. **BUSINESS ADDRESS:** Associate Professor of English, California State University, Northridge, 18111 Nordhoff St, Northridge, CA 91330, (818)885-3431.

UBHAYAKAR, SHIVADEV K.
Manager. Indo-American. **PERSONAL:** Born Feb 14, 1946, Madras, Tamil Nadu, India; son of Krishna Rao & Chandrabhaga Devi Ubhayakar; married Jayalata, May 25, 1972; children: Savita S, Sonali S. **EDUCATION:** Bangalore University, BS, 1966; Indian Institute of Science, MS, 1968; Harvard University, PhD, 1973. **CAREER:** Harvard University, teaching assistant, 1968-73; University of California, San Diego, research engineer, 1973-75; Avco Everett Research Laboratory, senior scientist, 1975-78; Rockwell International, project engineer, 1978-80; Jaycor, senior project engineer, 1980-81; TRW Inc, division project manager, sr staff engr, etc, 1981-. **ORGANIZATIONS:** The Combustion Institute, 1973-; TRW Company, satisfaction committee, 1993. **HONORS/AWARDS:** The Electrochemical Society, Young Author Award, 1976; Harvard University, R H Watson Fellowship, 1968; Govt of India, Merit Scholarship, 1961-66. **SPECIAL ACHIEVEMENTS:** Over 20 technical presentations and papers, 1973-; completed Los Angeles marathon, 1992; TRW IR&D Roll of Honor, 1987; five patents in robotic arms, 1989-91; language proficiency: 3 Indian languages and German. **HOME ADDRESS:** 28325 Hazelridge Dr, Rancho Palos Verdes, CA 90274.

UCHIDA, RICHARD NOBORU
Fishery research biologist (retired). Japanese American. **PERSONAL:** Born Sep 4, 1929, Honolulu, HI; son of Kinji & Koyo Uchida; married Marilyn Tsutae Uchida, Aug 6, 1955 (deceased); children: JoAnn M Takeuchi, Dean Y, Gail C; married Frances Kazusa Maruyama. **EDUCATION:** University of Hawaii, 1947-49; University of Washington, BS, fisheries, 1951; Honolulu Business College, 1952; University of Hawaii, 1955-67. **CAREER:** National Marine Fisheries Service, 1954. **ORGANIZATIONS:** Hawaiian Science & Engineering Fair, associate and chief judges, 1973-83; American Institute of Fishery Research Biologist, fellow, 1983-84; Seamount Resources Planning Team, chairman, 1977-83; Environment and Resources of Seamount, Workshop, co-chairman, 1984; FAO of the United Nations, fishery consultant, 1977; SPC Regional Technical Meeting on Fisheries, consultant, 1979; Spiny Lobster Planning Team, 1977-84; American Fisheries Society, certified fishery scientist, 1968-84. **HONORS/AWARDS:** National Marine Fisheries Service, Superior Performance Awards, 1962, 1969, 1978, 1980, Special Achievement Awards, 1974, 1976, Federal Employee of the Year, 1975, Federal Manager of the Year, 1980, Certificate of Recognition for Best Publication in Marine Fisheries Review, 1984. **SPECIAL ACHIEVEMENTS:** Development in Fisheries for Skipjack Tuna, FAO Technology Rep, 1975; Estimates of Fishing Effort & Apparent Abundance of Skipjack Tuna, US Fishery Bulletin, 1976; symposium paper on biology of spiny lobster in NWHI, University of Hawaii Sea Grant, 1984; Groundfish Fisheries & Research, Marine Fishery Reivew, 1984; Fishery Atlas of the Northwestern Hawaiian Islands, NOAA Tech Rep, 1986. **MILITARY SERVICE:** Adjutant General's Staff, corp, 1952-54. **HOME ADDRESS:** 1586 Hoolehua St, Pearl City, HI 96782, (808)455-3598.

UCHIDA, YOSHIHIRO
Business executive. Japanese American. **PERSONAL:** married Mae. **CAREER:** San Jose State University, instructor, coach; Physician's Laboratory, owner, 1957-89; San Jose Savings and Loan, founder, 1966-; American Bank & Trust, founder, chairman of the board, 1974-; San Jose Nihonmachi Corp, founder, 1988-; Uchida Enterprises, founder, president, 1989-. **ORGANIZATIONS:** Affiliate and/or board member with over 30 organizations; US Olympic Committee, chair, 1960; US Olympic Judo Team, first coach, 1964. **HONORS/AWARDS:** Asian Americans for Community Involvement, 6th Annual Freedom Award, 1992; San Jose State University, Tower Award, 1992; Emperor of Japan, Kun Santo Jyuho-Sho Medal. **BUSINESS ADDRESS:** President, Uchida Enterprises, 50 W San Fernando St, San Jose, CA 95113, (408)298-7551. *

UCHIDA, YOSHIKO. *See* Obituaries.

UCHIMOTO, DENNIS D.
Graphic arts company executive. Japanese American. **PERSONAL:** Born Oct 30, 1945, Chicago, IL; son of Tadashi Ted Uchimoto and Hamako Waverly Oye Uchimoto; married Elisabeth Dorothy, Jul 19, 1987; children: David, Daniel. **EDUCATION:** Washington University, BSBA, 1967, MBA, 1969. **CAREER:** R R Donnelley, customer service rep, 1969-72; Associated Milk Producers, assistant to controller, 1972-73; Keebler Co, product profit analyst, 1973-75; General Mailing Service Inc, vice president, 1975-85; Bindery & Distribution Service, president, 1985-. **ORGANIZATIONS:** Graphic Finishing Industries, president, board of directors, 1984, 1976-85; Printing Industries of Illinois, board of directors, 1984; Binding Industries of America, board of directors, 1978-85; National Association of Sec Dealers, 1976-; Tau Kappa Epsilon, 1964-67; Alpha Kappa Psi, 1966-67. **HONORS/AWARDS:** University of Illinois, CPA, 1976; AICPA Society, 1976; Illinois CPA Society, 1976. **SPECIAL ACHIEVEMENTS:** Language proficiency in Japanese, Spanish; licensed insurance broker, 1975- ; licensed NASD broker. **MILITARY SERVICE:** US Army, field artillery, lt, 1969-75. **BUSINESS ADDRESS:** President, Bindery & Distribution Service Inc, 1138 S Falmore, Palatine, IL 60067, (708)550-7000.

UCHIMOTO, WILLIAM WARREN
Attorney. Japanese American. **PERSONAL:** Born Dec 29, 1955, Alameda, CA; son of Dan & Elsie Uchimoto; married Marsha Kay Uchimoto, Oct 29, 1988; children: Adam Daniel, Audrey Michelle. **EDUCATION:** University of California at Davis, BA, 1978; University of California, Hastings College of Law, JD, 1981. **CAREER:** US Securities & Exchange Commission, attorney, 1981-86; Philadelphia Stock Exchange, general counsel, 1986-; Temple University School of Law, securities regulation, lecturer, 1989-. **ORGANIZATIONS:** California Bar Association, 1981-. **SPECIAL ACHIEVEMENTS:** Temple International Law Journal Book Review, 1992. **BUSINESS ADDRESS:** Vice President & General Counsel, Philadelphia Stock Exchange, Inc, 1900 Market St, Philadelphia, PA 19103, (215)496-5208.

UCHIMURA, BRUCE JIRO
Educator. Japanese American. **PERSONAL:** Born Jan 25, 1959, Honolulu, HI; son of Paul Tatsuo Uchimura and Mavis Toyoko Uchimura; married Susan Y Wiersma, Aug 24, 1985; children: Melanie Michiko. **EDUCATION:** Juilliard School of Music, BMus, cello performance, 1981; Cleveland Institute of Music, MMus, cello performance, artist's diploma, 1983. **CAREER:** Michigan State University, visiting prof of music, 1983-84; Augusta Symphony Orchestra, principal cellist, associate conductor, 1984-87; Western Michigan University, associate prof of music, 1987-. **ORGANIZATIONS:** Michigan Cello Society, vice pres, 1989; Kalamazoo Chamber Music Society, board of directors, 1988-; Bullock Performance Institute, 1987-90; American Federation of Musicians, 1983-90; American Assn of University Professors, 1987-; American String Teachers Assn, 1988-; Music Teachers National Assn, 1989-. **HONORS/AWARDS:** Pi Kappa Lambda, 1983. **SPECIAL ACHIEVEMENTS:** Carnegie Hall Recital Debut, Merling Trio (Piano, Violin, & Cello), 1993. **HOME ADDRESS:** 3923 Stonegate Rd, Kalamazoo, MI 49004. **BUSINESS ADDRESS:** Associate Professor of Music - Cello, Western Michigan University, School of Music, Dalton Center, Kalamazoo, MI 49008.

UDA, ROBERT TAKEO
Aerospace company manager. Japanese American. **PERSONAL:** Born Aug 1, 1942, Honolulu, HI; son of Masao Uda & Irene Kuualoha Waipa Uda; married Karen Elizabeth Rowland Uda, Jun 8, 1968; children: Atom Richard, Marc Edward, Heather Ann. **EDUCATION:** University of Oklahoma, BS, aerospace engineering, 1966; Air Force Institute of Technology, MS, astronautics, 1968; University of the State of New York, BS, general business, 1988; University of LaVerne, California, MBA, 1993. **CAREER:** Planning Research Corp, principal engineer, lead sr design engr, 1974-77; Hamilton Standard Div of UTC, sr preliminary design engineer, 1977-78; TRW Inc, Defense & Space Systems Group, project engineer, 1978-79; HR Textron Inc, general manager, product line mgr & program mgr, 1979-83; North American Manufacturing Corp, vice pres & general manager, 1983; Apollo Systems Technology Inc, chairman, president & CEO, 1983-87; Rockwell International Corp, project manager, program development mgr, mgr of adv progs, proj mgr, sr engrg spec, 1987-. **ORGANIZATIONS:** Association of Proposal Management Professionals,

charter member, 1990-; Regents College Alumni Association, 1988-; American Astronautical Society, senior member, 1974-; British Interplanetary Society, fellow, 1968-; Air Force Association, 1966-; American Institute of Aeronautics and Astronautics, associate fellow, 1959-; Church of Jesus Christ of Latter-day Saints, 1950-, bishop, 1989-. **HONORS/AWARDS:** Sigma Tau, National Honorary Engineering Fraternity, 1963; Hawthorne Jaycees, Jaycee of the Year, 1970-71; Sunnyvale Jaycees, Jaycee of the Year, 1969-70. **SPECIAL ACHIEVEMENTS:** "A Shock Tube Study of the Ignition Limit of Boron Particles," master's thesis, 1968; National University, adjunct faculty, 1987; AIAA Missile Systems Engineering Standardization Committee, chairman, 1985-89; AIAA Standard Technical Council, 1986-; AIAA Space Launch Vehicles Committee on Standards, 1991-. **MILITARY SERVICE:** United States Air Force, captain, 1966-74; Meritorious Service Medal, 1974; SAMSO Jr Officer of the Year, 1971. **HOME ADDRESS:** 19544 Delight Street, Canyon Country, CA 91351, (805)251-2316. **BUSINESS ADDRESS:** Project Manager, Rockwell International Corporation, Space Systems Division, 12214 Lakewood Boulevard, Downey, CA 90241, (310)922-3205.

UDANI, KANAK H.
Health care company manager. Indo-American. **PERSONAL:** Born Dec 4, 1936, Rajkot, Gujarat, India; son of Harilal Udani and Suraj Udani; married Joan Marilyn Udani, Mar 25, 1966; children: Sanjay, Rajiv. **EDUCATION:** Gujarat University, BS (with honors), 1957; University of Bombay, BS, technology, 1959; University of Illinois, MS, 1962, PhD, 1965. **CAREER:** H J Heinz Co, senior food scientist, 1965-68; Kraft General Foods, senior scientist, 1968-83, research coordinator, 1983-90; Baxter Healthcare Corp, program manager, 1990-. **ORGANIZATIONS:** Institute of Food Technology, 1963-, Chicago Section, chairman, employment committee, 1970-90; American Association of Pharmaceutical Chemists, 1992-93. **BUSINESS ADDRESS:** Program Manager, Baxter Healthcare Corp, 1620 Waukegan Rd, Bldg R, Mc Gaw Park, IL 60085, (708)473-6329.

UEDA, CLARENCE TAD
Educator, educational administrator. Japanese American. **PERSONAL:** Born Jul 6, 1942, Kansas City, MO; son of Don Takao (deceased) and Grace Yukiko Ueda; married Judith Katsuko Yokoyama Ueda, Feb 20, 1971; children: Kimi Rei, Marc Ryan. **EDUCATION:** Contra Costa College, AA, 1963; University of California, School of Pharmacy, PharmD, 1967, San Francisco, PhD, 1974. **CAREER:** University of Nebraska, College of Pharmacy, pharmaceutics, assistant professor, 1974-77, associate professor, 1977-85, professor of pharmaceutical sciences, 1985-, department of pharmaceutics/pharmaceutical sciences, chairman, 1976-88, dean, 1986-. **ORGANIZATIONS:** American Pharmaceutical Association, 1964-; American Association of Pharmaceutical Scientists, 1987-; American College of Clinical Pharmacology, fellow, 1976-; American Society of Clinical Pharmacology & Therapeutics, 1978-; American Association of Colleges of Pharmacy, various committee chairs, committee membership, 1974-; United States Pharmacopeial Convention, committee of revision, elected, 1990-95; American Society of Hospital Pharmacists, 1990-; Rho Chi. **HONORS/AWARDS:** American College of Clinical Pharmacology, fellow, 1977; University of Nebraska Medical Center, Distinguished Teaching Award, 1984. **SPECIAL ACHIEVEMENTS:** Published over 50 scientific articles and book chapters, 1976-; 30 abstracts and numerous professional and scientific presentations, 1974-. **BUSINESS ADDRESS:** Dean & Professor, University of Nebraska, College of Pharmacy, 600 S 42nd St, Omaha, NE 68198-6000.

UEMOTO, KAREN
Postal official. Japanese American. **CAREER:** US Postal Service, transportation manager, currently. **SPECIAL ACHIEVEMENTS:** One of the three highest-ranking Japanese Americans in US Postal Service. **BUSINESS ADDRESS:** Transportation Manager, United States Postal Service, 475 L'Enfant Plaza SW, Washington, DC 20260-2100, (202)268-2000.*

UEMURA, JOSEPH NORIO
Educator. Japanese American. **PERSONAL:** Born Jul 3, 1926, Portland, OR; son of Hana Morishita and Seijiro Uemura; married Maye Mitsuye Oye, Sep 10, 1949; children: Wesley Makoto, Charissa Keiko. **EDUCATION:** Denver University, BA, 1946; Iliff School of Theology, ThM, 1949; Columbia University, PhD, philosophy, 1958. **CAREER:** Westminster College, professor, philosophy/religion, 1953-59; Morningside College, professor, philosophy, 1959-66; Hamline University, professor, philosophy, 1966-. **ORGANIZATIONS:** American Philosophical Association, Eastern Division, 1957-; Rocky Mountain Annual Conference, United Methodist Church, 1947-. **HONORS/**

AWARDS: Phi Beta Kappa, 1946; Omicron Delta Kappa, 1946; Westminster College, Sheldon Jackson Chair in Philosophy/Religion, 1955-59; Hamline University, Paul & Jean Hanna Chair in Philosophy, 1987-; Whitney Foundation Fellowship; NEH Fellowship; Eliz, Warren Fellowship; Carnegie Foundation Fellowship. **SPECIAL ACHIEVEMENTS:** Author, Seven Dialogues on Goodness, 1986; Six Dialogues of Plato: An Interpretation, 1991; editor, The Hamline Review, 1969-. **BIOGRAPHICAL SOURCES:** Essays in Honor of Joseph Norio Uemura, book, Cady & Beanblossom, eds, 1992. **HOME ADDRESS:** 1641 Stanbridge Ave, St Paul, MN 55113-1431, (612)633-2925. **BUSINESS ADDRESS:** Professor, Philosophy Dept, Hamline University, Hewitt at Snelling, Box 56, Giddens Hall 137, St Paul, MN 55104-1284, (612)641-2385.

UENG, CHARLES EN-SHIUH
Educator. Chinese American. **PERSONAL:** Born Sep 8, 1930, Yangchow, Jiangsu, China; son of San-Yu and Shu-Chi Ueng; married Shirley Wen-Hwa Chen Ueng, Oct 20, 1962; children: Vivian, Grace. **EDUCATION:** National Cheng-Kung University, BS, 1953; Kansas State University, MS, 1960, PhD, 1963. **CAREER:** Taiwan Power Company, assistant structural engineer, 1953-58; Kansas State University, assistant professor, 1963-64; Georgia Institute of Tech, assistant professor, 1964-67, associate professor, 1967-77, professor, 1977-. **ORGANIZATIONS:** American Society of Civil Engineers, awards comm, chairman, Aerospace Div, 1983-88, Structures and Materials, chairman, Aerospace Division, comm, 1980-83; American Society for Engineering Education, 1964-; Society of Engineering Science, 1967-. **HONORS/AWARDS:** American Society of Civil Engineers, Service Award, 1988. **SPECIAL ACHIEVEMENTS:** Research grants from: NSF, 1967, 1977, NASA, 1968, 1970, Society of Manufacturing Engineers, 1982, FHWA, 1992; published 66 refereed articles in professional journals. **BUSINESS ADDRESS:** Professor, Georgia Institute of Technology, School of Civil Engineering, Atlanta, GA 30332-0355, (404)894-2769.

UENO, TAKEMI
Attorney. Japanese American. **PERSONAL:** Born Jun 8, 1966, Brooklyn, NY; daughter of Hiromi Ueno & Ryuko Kobayashi Ueno. **EDUCATION:** Harvard & Radcliffe Colleges, AB, 1987; London School of Economics & Political Science, MA, 1988; Columbia University, M Phil, 1990; Harvard Law School, JD, 1993. **CAREER:** Winthrop, Stimson, Putnam & Roberts, associate, 1993-. **ORGANIZATIONS:** American Bar Association, 1992-; Radcliffe Club of New York, 1993-; Association of the Bar of the City of New York, 1993-; New York County Lawyers Association, 1993-. **HONORS/AWARDS:** Phi Beta Kappa, 1986; Mellon Fellowship in the Humanities, 1987. **SPECIAL ACHIEVEMENTS:** "Defining a 'Business Trust', Proposed Amendment of Section 101(9) of the Bankruptcy Code," Harvard Journal on Legislation, vol 30, no 2, p 499-518, 1993. **BIOGRAPHICAL SOURCES:** "For She's a Jolly Good Fellow," Harvard Crimson, June 11, 1987. **HOME ADDRESS:** 161 W 61st Street #14C, New York, NY 10023. **BUSINESS ADDRESS:** Associate, Winthrop, Stimson, Putnam & Roberts, One Battery Park Plaza, New York, NY 10004-1490, (212)858-1000.

UEOKA, MEYER MASATO
Attorney. Japanese American. **PERSONAL:** Born Jul 4, 1920, Paia, HI; son of Sokyo Ueoka (deceased) and Tomiyo Ueoka (deceased); married Yukie Hirano Ueoka, Aug 30, 1949; children: Ladd M, Celia C Suzuki, Janice T Kemp. **EDUCATION:** University of Nebraska, BA, 1947; Washburn University, School of Law, JD, 1949. **CAREER:** County of Maui, deputy county attorney, 1952-59; State of Hawaii, magistrate, 1967-72; Hawaii State legislature, member, House of Representatives, 1976-78; Ueoka & Ueoka, partner, 1959-. **ORGANIZATIONS:** Hawaii Constitutional Convention, delegate, 1968; Hawaii State Board of Education, 1964-66, 1980-; Maui County School Advisory Council, chairman, member, 1959-63; Maui County Council Boy Scouts of America, former president, 1977-79; Maui Japanese Community Association, president, 1991-; Maunaolu College, board of trustees. **HONORS/AWARDS:** Washburn University, Doctor of Laws, 1983; Boy Scouts of America, Silver Beaver, 1977, Silver Antelope, 1991, Distinguished Eagle Scout, 1985; Maui Community College, Honorary Licensed Practical Nurse, 1990. **MILITARY SERVICE:** US Army, 2nd lt, 1943-46, 1950-53. **BUSINESS ADDRESS:** Partner, Ueoka & Ueoka, 2103 Wells St, M Ueoka Bldg, Ste A, Wailuku, HI 96793, (808)244-7914.

ULLAH, M. RIFAT
Engineering scientist. Bangladeshi American. **PERSONAL:** Born Nov 1, 1957, Dhaka, Bangladesh; son of M Hedayetullah and Setara Hedayet; married

Seema R Ullah, Jul 18, 1983. **EDUCATION:** Bangladesh University of Engineering & Technology, BSc, 1980; Texas A&M University, MS, 1982, PhD, 1986. **CAREER:** Bangladesh University of Engineering & Technology, lecturer, 1980; Texas A&M University, lecturer, 1982-86; Allied Signal Auxiliary Power, sr engrng scientist, 1986-. **ORGANIZATIONS:** American Society of Mech Engrs; Garrett Employees Flying Club, secretary, 1987-89; Bangladesh Assn at College Station, president, 1981-82; Tau Beta Pi; Scottsdale Memorial Hospital, volunteer, 1990. **HONORS/AWARDS:** Texas A&M University, Amoco Foundation Teaching Award, 1983; Allied Signal, Recognition for Technical Excellance, 1993; ASME, IE Grant for Outstanding Technical Paper, 1985. **SPECIAL ACHIEVEMENTS:** Language proficiency: Spanish, Bengali, Urdu; several scholarly publications in refereed journals. **HOME ADDRESS:** 4109 E Mountain Sage Rd, Phoenix, AZ 85044-6166, (602)759-5493.

UMALI, FILEMON J.

Obstetrician, gynecologist. Filipino American. **PERSONAL:** Born Aug 8, 1925, Manila, Philippines; son of Francisco A Umali & Maria de Jesus Umali; married Nancy Jane Criswell, Jun 11, 1961 (deceased); children: Glenda, Donna Ruth, Eric F, Holli Vandeman; married Nancy Fuller-Vandeman, Sep 12, 1986. **EDUCATION:** Fairview Park Hospital, rotating intern, 1955-56; Manila Central University, Philippines, MD, 1956; Wichita General Hospital, general practice residency, 1956-57; Madison Hospital, general practice residency, 1957-59; St Thomas Hospital, general surgery residency, 1959-60; Regina General Hospital, Canada, Ob/Gyn residency, 1961-62; Columbia Hospital for Women, Ob/Gyn residency, 1963-66. **CAREER:** Obstetrician/Gynecologist at following: Wytheville Sanitarium & Hospital, 1967-85; Wythe County Hospital; Doctors Hospital, 1985; Glendora Community Hospital, 1985-; Covina Valley Community Hospital, 1985-; Intercommunity Medical Center, 1988-; Terrace Plaza Medical Center, 1989. **ORGANIZATIONS:** American Society of Abdominal Surgeons, fellow, 1976; Society of Philippine Surgeons of America, fellow, 1976; American Fertility Society, 1978; American Association of Gynecologic Laparoscopists, 1989. **HONORS/AWARDS:** Passed test for the educational council for Foreign Medical Graduates, 1962; Philippine Medical Boards, passed, 1962; Virginia Boards of Medical Examiners, passed, 1967; Georgia Boards of Medical Examiners, passed, 1970; California Medical Boards, Board of Medical Quality Assurance, passed, 1981. **SPECIAL ACHIEVEMENTS:** American Association of Sex Educators, Counselors, Therapists, certificates, 1979; European Sterility Congress, Madrid, Spain, certificate, 1975; Continuing Medical Education, Leningrad/Moscow, Russia, certificate; Karolinska Institute, Stockholm, Sweden, certificate; Continuing Medical Education, Beijing University, China, certificate; Women's Hospital, Shanghai, China; proficient in English, Tagalog, Spanish; played violin solo and won 2nd place in musical competition in Manila, Philippines, 1953; played "Habanera No 2," composed by violinist Ernesto Vallejo; first Filipino Adventist Missionary teacher in the island of Guam, 1949-52. **HOME ADDRESS:** 1347 Candish Ave, Glendora, CA 91740, (818)914-3618.

UN, HOWARD HO-WEI

Marketing manager. Chinese American. **PERSONAL:** Born Jun 8, 1938, Hong Kong; son of Mr & Mrs K P Un; married Mary Cheng, May 27, 1967; children: Caroline L, Kathleen K. **EDUCATION:** Beloit College, Wisconsin, BS, 1960; University of Michigan, MSchem, 1963, PhD, 1965. **CAREER:** DuPont Polymers, research chemist, Teflon, 1965-68, technical representative, Teflon, 1968-70, sr marketing rep, Teflon, 1970-77, product coordination supervisor, 1977-80, international sales manager, 1980-83; DuPont Wire & Cable, Asia Pacific, development manager, 1983-92; DuPont Fluoroproducts, international programs, development manager, 1992-. **ORGANIZATIONS:** American Chemical Society, 1959-; Phi Lambda Upsilon, 1963; Sigma Xi, 1963. **SPECIAL ACHIEVEMENTS:** Author, article, J Polymer Sci, vol A3, 3117, 1965; coauthor, US patent, 3855191, 1974. **BUSINESS ADDRESS:** Development Manager, E I DuPont De Nemours & Co Inc, PO Box 80711, Chestnut Run Plaza, Building 711, Wilmington, DE 19880-0711, (302)999-3661.

UNAKAR, NALIN JAYANTILAL

Educator. Indo-American. **PERSONAL:** Born Mar 26, 1935, Karachi, Sindh, Pakistan; son of Jayantilal Virshankar Unakar and Malati Jayantilal Unakar; married Nita Nalin Unakar, Jun 22, 1962; children: Rita Unakar Antani, Rupa Nalin. **EDUCATION:** Gujarat University, India, BS, 1955; Bombay University, India, MS, 1961; Brown University, PhD, 1965. **CAREER:** Indian Cancer Research Center, research assistant, 1955-61; Brown University, USPHS

trainee, 1961-65; University of Toronto, research associate, 1965-66; Oakland University, professor, 1966-. **ORGANIZATIONS:** American Association for the Advancement of Science, 1961-; American Society for Cell Biology, 1964-; Association for Research in Visual & Ophthalmology, 1970-; Sigma Xi, 1963-. **HONORS/AWARDS:** COOP Cataract Research Group, 1977-; Visual Science Study Section, National Institutes of Health, 1982-86; Lehigh University, visiting board, 1986-89. **SPECIAL ACHIEVEMENTS:** NIH, National Cancer Institute, research grant, 1967-70, National Eye Institute, research grant, 1976-. **BUSINESS ADDRESS:** Professor, Dept of Biological Sciences, Oakland University, Rochester, MI 48309-4401, (313)370-3577.

UNDERWOOD, ROBERT ANACLETUS

Government official. Pacific Islander American. **PERSONAL:** Born Jul 13, 1948, Tamuning, Guam; son of John Martinez Underwood and Esther Flores Taitano; married Lorraine Aguilar, Jun 15, 1968; children: Sophia Rosario, Roberto, Ricardo, Ramon, Raphael. **EDUCATION:** California State University, Los Angeles, BA, 1969; University of Southern California, EdD, 1987. **CAREER:** University of Guam, College of Education, dean, 1988-90, academic vice president, 1990-92; US House of Representatives, member, delegate, 1993-94. **ORGANIZATIONS:** Pacific Islands Bilingual Association, pres, 1980-81; National Association of Bilingual Education, 1979-; Organization of People for Indigenous Rights, 1981-. **SPECIAL ACHIEVEMENTS:** Chamorro Speaker; Chamorro Language Commission, chair, 1978-89; Guam Review Board of Historic Preservation. **BUSINESS ADDRESS:** Congressman/Delegate, US House of Representatives, Cannon HOB 507, Washington, DC 20515, (202)225-1188.

UNO, ANNE QUAN

Certified financial planner, entrepreneur. Chinese American. **PERSONAL:** Born Feb 27, 1942, Ukiah, CA; daughter of Dock Quan; divorced; children: Kiri, Marili. **EDUCATION:** UCLA, BS, 1964; Texas A&M, College Station, MEd, 1973; College for Financial Planning, CFP, 1983. **CAREER:** Waco Independent School District, teacher, 1969-77; Financial Associate Tax Service Inc, planner, 1983-. **ORGANIZATIONS:** NAIC, director, treas, 1979-; North Virginia Society ICFP, program chair, 1992-93; Mid Atlantic Retreat, 1992-93. **HONORS/AWARDS:** NAWPAW, Outstanding Service, 1990; NAIC, Service Award 15 years, 1993. **SPECIAL ACHIEVEMENTS:** Book, Aesthic Activities for Exceptional Children, 1976. **BUSINESS ADDRESS:** President, Financial Associates Tax Services Inc, 933 N Kenmore #217, Clarendon Office Bldg, Arlington, VA 22201, (703)522-3111.

UNO, HIDEO

Pathologist. Japanese American. **PERSONAL:** Born Nov 28, 1929, Tokyo, Japan; son of Yoshinori & Hana Uno; married Shoko Uno, Apr 1, 1956; children: Takeshi Uno, Yayoi Uno. **EDUCATION:** Yokohama Medical College, MD, 1955, PhD, 1961. **CAREER:** Yokohama City University, assistant professor of pathology, 1961-64; Jefferson Med College, instructor of pathology, 1964-66; Oregon Primate Center, visiting scientist, 1966-68; Yokohama City University, associate professor of pathology, 1967-70; Oregon Primate Center, scientist, 1970-79; Wisconsin Primate Center, senior scientist, 1979-; University of Wisconsin, adjunct professor of pathology, 1982-. **ORGANIZATIONS:** American Association of Pathologists, 1976-; Society for Investigative Dermatology, 1980-; US & Canadian Academy of Pathology, 1980-; Society of Neuroscience, 1975-; International House of Japan, 1968-. **HONORS/AWARDS:** Med Res Foundation of Oregon, Research Grant, 1976; NIH, Pathology Division of Wisconsin Primate Center, 1980-; Upjohn Company, Research Grant, 1982-87; Proctor and Gamble, Research Grant, 1989-; Shiseido Laboratory, Research Grant, 1985-. **SPECIAL ACHIEVEMENTS:** Histopathology of Hair Loss, Scope Publ, Upjohn, 1988; Models in Dermatology, vol 3, 1987; Models for Hair Growth, NY Acad of Sci, vol 642, 1991; Cerebral B-amyloidosis of Aged Monkey, NY Acad of Sci, 1993. **BIOGRAPHICAL SOURCES:** Brain damage by dexamethasone, Devel Brain Res, vol 53, p 157, 1990; Chemical Agents and Peptides Affect Hair Growth, J Invest Dermatol, vol 101, p 143S, 1993. **HOME ADDRESS:** 3722 Ross St, Madison, WI 53705, (608)233-3763. **BUSINESS ADDRESS:** Senior Scientist, Adjunct Professor of Pathology, University of Wisconsin-Madison, Regional Primate Research Center, 1223 Capitol Ct, Rm 203, Madison, WI 53715, (608)263-3529.

URANO, MUNEYASU

Researcher, educator. Japanese American. **PERSONAL:** Born Apr 21, 1936, Osaka, Japan; son of Iekazu Urano & Shizuyo Urano; married Michiyo Urano, Mar 2, 1963; children: Shin-ichi, Ju. **EDUCATION:** Kyoto Prefectural University of Medicine, MD, 1961, PhD, 1968. **CAREER:** Kyoto Prefectural University of Medicine, assistant professor, 1968-71; National Institute of Radiological Sciences, staff scientist, radiologist, 1971-77; Harvard Medical School, associate professor, 1977-88; Massachusetts General Hospital, associate professor, 1977-88; University of Kentucky College of Medicine, professor of radiation medicine, 1989-. **ORGANIZATIONS:** Radiation Research Society, 1977-; American Association of Cancer Research, 1977-; American Society of Therapeutic Radiology and Oncology, 1977-; North American Hyperthermia Society, 1980-; American Association of Advance Sciences, 1980-; Japanese Society of Cancer Research, 1968-. **SPECIAL ACHIEVEMENTS:** Radiation biology, specifically tissue radiation biology; thermal biology; editor, Hyperthermia and Oncology, three volumes; approximately 150 publications, reviewed journals only. **BIOGRAPHICAL SOURCES:** Frontiers in Science and Technology. **BUSINESS ADDRESS:** Professor, Dept of Radiation Medicine, University of Kentucky Medical Center, 800 Rose St, Lexington, KY 40536-0084, (606)257-5537.

USUI, KIICHI
Curator, painter. Japanese American. **PERSONAL:** Born Dec 2, 1931, Tokyo, Japan; married Betty T Usui. **EDUCATION:** Tokyo University of Arts, 1951-54; Art Student League of New York, 1955-60; University of Michigan, MA, 1970. **CAREER:** Oakland University, Meadow Brook Art Gallery, curator, director, 1971-. **BIOGRAPHICAL SOURCES:** The Official Museum Directory. **BUSINESS ADDRESS:** Curator, Meadow Brook Art Gallery, Oakland University, Rochester, MI 48309.

UY, WILLIAM C.
Research and development executive. Chinese American. **PERSONAL:** Born Feb 11, 1940, Manila, Philippines; son of Raymond Uykeeyao & Mary Cheng Uy; divorced; children: Michael, Steven, Stephanie, Alexander. **EDUCATION:** De La Salle College, BSChE (magna cum laude), 1965; Northwestern University, MSChE, 1967, PhDChE, 1970. **CAREER:** DuPont Company, research engineer, 1970, senior research engineer, 1972, research associate, 1983, senior research associate, 1986-. **ORGANIZATIONS:** Sigma Xi; American Chemical Society; SAMPE; Society of Rheology. **HONORS/AWARDS:** De La Salle College, Jose Rizal Honor Society, 1965; Northwestern University, Walter P Murphy Fellowship, 1965-67, ARPA/NSF/ACS fellowship, 1967-70. **SPECIAL ACHIEVEMENTS:** 7 patents on fiber finishes & fiber processes, 1978-93; 16 publications and/or presentations, 1969-90. **HOME ADDRESS:** PO Box 730, Hockessin, DE 19707-0730, (302)239-9565. **BUSINESS ADDRESS:** Senior Research Associate, DuPont Company, PO Box 80302, Experimental Station, Wilmington, DE 19880-0302, (302)695-2866.

UYEDA, ARTHUR ASA
Psychologist. Japanese American. **PERSONAL:** Born Sep 26, 1925, San Bernardino, CA; son of Fusajiro Uyeda and Hide Sawada; married Sumiko Kato Uyeda, Jul 23, 1960; children: Stanley Kei, Susan Asako. **EDUCATION:** San Diego State College, BA (with honors), 1951; UCLA, MA, 1958, PhD, 1960. **CAREER:** UCLA, post doctoral fellow, 1960-62, research psychologist, 1962-70; Sonoma State Hospital, research psychologist, 1970-73; Napa State Hospital, psychologist, 1973-87. **ORGANIZATIONS:** American Psychological Association, 1960; Western Psychological Association, 1960; Society for Neurosciences, 1972. **HONORS/AWARDS:** American Psychological Foundation, Pre-Doctoral Award, 1958; Mental Health Training Program, Post-Doctoral Training, 1960-62; NIMH, Research Awards, 1964-67, 1975-77. **SPECIAL ACHIEVEMENTS:** Several scientific publications, 1960-70. **MILITARY SERVICE:** US Army, corporal, 1952-54. **HOME ADDRESS:** 1500 Tanager Lane, Petaluma, CA 94954.

UYEDA, CLIFFORD I.
Physician (retired). Japanese American. **PERSONAL:** Born Jan 14, 1917, Olympia, WA; son of Matsutaro & Kimiyo Uyeda; married Helen Sachie, Oct 14, 1956 (died 1992). **EDUCATION:** University of Wisconsin, BA (cum laude), 1940; Tulane University School of Medicine, MD, 1945; Haravard Medical School, pediatrics, 1948-51. **CAREER:** Harvard Pediatric Study, clinical & reserach fellow, 1948-49; Harvard Medical School, residency & teaching fellow in pediatrics, 1949-51; Kaiser-Permanente Group, San Francisco, staff pediatrician, 1953-75. **ORGANIZATIONS:** Japanese American Citizens League, national president, 1978-80; Westside Community Mental Health Inc, San Francisco, board member, 1968-70; Center for Japanese American Studies, secretary, 1969-; World Affairs Council, 1976-88, program committee, 1981; National Japanese American Historical Society, 1984-, president, 1988-94; Japanese American Citizens League National Redress, chair,

1977-78. **SPECIAL ACHIEVEMENTS:** National committee for Iva Toguri, "Tokyo Rose," to regain her citizenship which she lost in 1949 when wrongly convicted, 1975-77; National campaign through Japanese American Citizens League to support the moratorium on commerical whaling, 1972-78, and to oppose the attempted government relocation of Navajo Indians, 1984-86. **MILITARY SERVICE:** US Air Force, captain, 1951-53. **BUSINESS ADDRESS:** President, National Japanese American Historical Society, 1855 Folsom Streeet, 161, San Francisco, CA 94103, (415)431-5007.

UYEDA, ROGER MAKOTO
Hospital supervisor, medical technologist. Japanese American. **PERSONAL:** Born Oct 18, 1940, Watsonville, CA; son of Frank J Uyeda and Nora N Uyeda; divorced; children: Brian David. **EDUCATION:** San Jose State College, BA, 1967. **CAREER:** Self-employed, professional archer, 1965-68; The Clinical Laboratory Medical Group, medical technologist, 1969-70, assistant supervisor chemistry, 1970-74, supervisor of hematology, 1974, chief technologist, 1974; Methodist Hospital of Southern California, research and development supervisor, 1984, hematology supervisor, 1987-. **ORGANIZATIONS:** Professional Archers of California, 1966-68; Registry of Medical Technologist of the American Society of Clinical Pathologist, 1969-. **HONORS/AWARDS:** Numerous archery awards, including: CSAA, 1st place, AA Professional Men's Championship, 1965; Black Mt Bowmen, 1st place, San Jose Open Professional Champion, 1966; Hunza Hunters Club, 1st place, AA Professional Sunnyvale Open, 1967. **SPECIAL ACHIEVEMENTS:** California State Archery Association, Professional Champion, 1965; invented and named archery bow parts for Hoyt Archery Co, modular weights, torque tubes, static counter balance, interchangeable dovetail handle grips, use of magnesium riser, dovetail take down bow limbs. **BIOGRAPHICAL SOURCES:** Register-Pajaronian Newspaper, Watsonville, CA, p1, Oct 5, 1965; Pacific Citizen, sport section, Dec 19, 1965. **HOME ADDRESS:** 2004 Fulton Ave, Monterey Park, CA 91754, (213)721-1719.

UYEHARA, CECIL H.
Consulting firm executive. Japanese American. **PERSONAL:** Born in London, England; married; children: two. **EDUCATION:** Keio University, Japan, BA, political science, 1948; University of Minnesota, MA, political science, economics, 1951; Harvard University, economics, science, public policy, 1963-64; Federal Executive Institute, senior management training, 1978. **CAREER:** USAF, OMB, AID (State Dept), 1964-80; Library of Congress, consultant on Japanese calligraphy, 1984-87; Japan-American Student Conference Inc, president, chairman, 1984-89; Precision Nesting Systems Inc, marketing consultant, 1987-88; US Foreign Service Institute, US-Japan Science and Technology Exchange, lecturer, 1982, 1988, 1990; Loyola College, Japanese Technical Evaluation Center, senior consultant, 1990-; Uyehara International Associates, president, currently. **ORGANIZATIONS:** Japan-American Society of Washington, DC, board member, 1977-83; Japan-America Student Conference Inc, board member, 1979-89; Columbia University, Seminar on Modern Japan, 1972-; Assn of Asian Studies, 1948-; Urasenke School of Tea, vp, 1979-; ACLU, life contributor, 1973-; Intl Society for Japanese Philately, 1983-. **HONORS/AWARDS:** Natl Institute of Public Affairs, Career Education Award, 1963-64; Ford Foundation, research grants, 1955-58; American Philosophical Society, research grants, 1953, 1955, 1962; University of Minnesota, Shevlin Fellowship, 1949-51. **SPECIAL ACHIEVEMENTS:** Japan-America Society of Washington, US-Japan Science and Technology Exchange Symposium, organizer, 1981, 1986; worked with US House of Reps Science and Tech subcommittee, 1982-84; consultant to Yomiuri Shimbun, Japan, brought first major exhibition of living Japanese calligraphers to US, 1983-84; AID Mission to Afghanistan, asst director, 1968-72; publications include: Meiko and the Fifth Treasure, illustrator, Putnam, 1993; Japanese Calligraphy: A Bibliographic Study, University Press of America, 1991; proficient in speaking, reading and writing Japanese. **BUSINESS ADDRESS:** President, Uyehara International Associates Inc, 7614 Arnet Ln, Bethesda, MD 20817, (301)229-3184.

UYEMATSU, AMY
Educator, writer. Japanese American. **PERSONAL:** Born in Los Angeles, CA. **CAREER:** UCLA, Asian American Studies Center, staff member, 1969-74; Grant High School, Van Nuys, mathematics teacher, currently; co-editor, Roots: An Asian American Reader; published poet, 1985-, works include: 30 Miles from J-Town, Story Line Press, 1992; "A Recent Conversation with My Grandmother," Los Angeles Times, Sunday Book Review Section, Jan 10, 1993. **ORGANIZATIONS:** Pacific Asian American Women Writers-West. **HONORS/AWARDS:** Nicholas Roerich Poetry Prize, 1992. **SPECIAL**

ACHIEVEMENTS: Asian Pacific Women's Network/Pacific Asian American Women's Writers-West, reading from book, 30 Miles from J-Town, 1993. **BUSINESS ADDRESS:** Math Teacher, Grant High School, 13000 Oxnard St, Van Nuys, CA 91401, (818)781-1400. *

UYESHIMA, MARY
Volunteer medical worker (retired). Japanese American. **PERSONAL:** Born Mar 3, 1923, Hollister, CA; daughter of Gozaimon Wada & Hatsu Wada; married Ikuo Uyeshima, Jul 15, 1945 (deceased); children: David, Don, Debra Uyeshima Dillard, Dale (deceased). **CAREER:** San Gabriel Valley Medical Center, volunteer, 6 years. **HONORS/AWARDS:** San Gabriel Valley Medical Center, Volunteer of the Year, 1993. **SPECIAL ACHIEVEMENTS:** Hearts & Soles, walking program, organizer. **HOME ADDRESS:** 401 W Glendon Way, San Gabriel, CA 91776, (818)571-7321.

V

VADLAMUDI, SRI KRISHNA
Supervisory scientist. Indo-American. **PERSONAL:** Born Aug 15, 1927, Moparru, Tenali, Andhra Pradesh, India; son of Venkataratnam Vadlamudi (deceased) and Pitchamma Yelavarti Vadlamudi (deceased); married Jamuna Bai Narra Vadlamudi, Oct 14, 1954; children: Anula Durga Gogineni, Nagarjuna, Venkataratnam, Gautam Kishore. **EDUCATION:** Andhra University, Waltair, India, inter arts & science, 1945; Madras University, India, BVSc, DVM, 1952; University of Wisconsin, Madison, MS, 1959, PhD, 1963; American Veterinary Medical Association, ECFVG, DVM, 1973. **CAREER:** Govt of Andhra Pradesh, Hyderabad, India, research veterinarian, 1952-57; University of Wisconsin, Department of Veterinary Science, project associate, 1957-62; Abbott Laboratories, senior research scientist, 1963-65; Microbiological Assoc Inc, Cancer Chemotherapy Research Division, director, 1965-75; FDA/BMD, executive secretary, immunology, toxicology panels, 1975-91; FDA/CDRH/ODE, chief, immunology branch, 1978-91, supervisory science expert, 1991-. **ORGANIZATIONS:** American Association for Cancer Research; Sigma Xi; American Society for Microbiology; American Society for Pathology, FASEB, president, ICCC, 1989; Indian Veterinary Medical Association, director, GWTCS, 1973-93; Madras Veterinary Students Association, general secretary, director, TANA, 1976-82; Andhra Pradesh Veterinary Medical Association, steering committee. **HONORS/AWARDS:** Food & Drug Administration, Outstanding Performance Association, 1978, Community Service Award, 1991; Govt of Madras, Merit Scholarship, 1946-51. **SPECIAL ACHIEVEMENTS:** Published about 60 papers in national and international science journals; presented about 70 papers before national & international science organizations; invited to preside or present science papers before several organizations in US, Sweden, former USSR, France, Germany, India, etc. **HOME PHONE:** (301)989-0863. **BUSINESS ADDRESS:** Supervisory Scientist, CDRH/FDA, 1390 Piccard Dr, Piccard Bldg, Rm 150 K, Rockville, MD 20850, (301)427-1084.

VAID, JYOTSNA
Educator. Indo-American. **PERSONAL:** Born in New Delhi, India; married. **EDUCATION:** Vassar College, BA, 1976; McGill University, MA, 1978, PhD, 1982. **CAREER:** Michigan State University, postdoctoral fellow, 1982-83; University of California, San Diego, and The Salk Institute for Biological Studies, research associate, 1983-85; Texas A&M University, assistant professor, 1986-91, associate professor, 1991-. **ORGANIZATIONS:** Committee on South Asian Women, founding member, 1983-; American Psychological Society, 1988-. **HONORS/AWARDS:** Council for International Exchange of Scholars, Indo-American Advanced Research Fellowship, 1985-86; American Institute of Indian Studies, Professional Development Fellowship, 1984. **SPECIAL ACHIEVEMENTS:** Co-editor, Women, Communities and Cultures: South Asians in America, 1994; The Bilingual Aphasia Test: Hindi/English, 1990; co-author, South Asian Women at Home and Abroad: A Guide to Resources, 1984; numerous others. **BUSINESS ADDRESS:** Assoc Professor, Dept of Psychology, Texas A&M University, College Station, TX 77843, (409)845-2576.

VAIDHYANATHAN, VISHNAMPET S.
Educator. Indo-American. **PERSONAL:** Born Dec 15, 1933, Madras, Tamil Nadu, India; son of Vishnsmpet Sivaramakrishnan; married Virginia, Aug 1965; children: Siva, Mehala snf Vedana. **EDUCATION:** Annamali University, India, BSc, 1953, MA, 1954; Illinois Institute of Technology, PhD, 1961. **CAREER:** University of Kansas, research associate, 1960-62; University of

Arkansas Medical Center, assistant professor; VA Hospital, Little Rock, Arkansas, Research Support Center, 1962-66; SUNY, associate professor biophysics, 1966-86, professor of biophysics, 1986-. **ORGANIZATIONS:** AAAS; Biophysical Society. **HONORS/AWARDS:** EMBO Fellow, 1969; Illinois Institute, Fellow, 1959-60; E O Freund, Fellow, 1958. **SPECIAL ACHIEVEMENTS:** Author of recent monograph on regulation and control in biological systems; about 100 scientific papers; 10 review articles; work cited in many books. **BUSINESS ADDRESS:** Professor of Biophysics, School of Medicine, State University of New York, 114 Cary Hall, S Campus, Buffalo, NY 14214, (716)829-2415.

VAIDYA, KIRIT RAMESHCHANDRA
Physician. Indo-American. **PERSONAL:** Born Feb 20, 1937, Sihor, Gujarat, India; son of Rameshchandra and Kanta; married Rashmi, Feb 22, 1966; children: Kaushal, Sujal. **EDUCATION:** Gujarat University, BS, 1959; Kasturba Medical Colege, MBBS, 1965. **CAREER:** Boston City Hospital, anesthesiologist, 1973-79; Bridgeport Hospital, anesthesiologist, 1979-. **ORGANIZATIONS:** CAPI, board member, 1991-93; AAPI, patron memeber, 1991-. **HOME ADDRESS:** 54 Quail Trail, Trumbull, CT 06611.

VALDERRAMA, DAVID MERCADO
State government official. Filipino American. **PERSONAL:** Born Feb 1, 1933, Manila, Philippines; son of Benita Mercado Valderrama and Nicasio Valderrama; married Nelia Valderrama, Apr 24, 1969; children: Kriselda, Emma Vida. **EDUCATION:** Far Eastern University, AA, 1952, LLB, 1956; Central Bank of the Philippines, bank management, 1958; Natl College for Probate Judges, probate judge, 1986; George Washington University, LLM, comparative law, 1988. **CAREER:** Bank of the Philippines, vp; Library of Congress, sr legal specialist, 1962-74; US Information Agency, tv correspondent, 1966-76; TV News, Rockville, Wheaton, Kennsington, publisher/editor, 1979-81; Democratic Central Committee, PG Co, vice-chair, elected member, 1982-85; 21st Century Communications, board chair, 1983-85; Orphans Court, PG Co, probate judge, 1985-90; Law office, intl relations consultant, 1991; Maryland General Assembly, delegate, 1990-. **ORGANIZATIONS:** Southeast Asian Refugee Task Force, chair; Asian Pacific American Chamber of Commerce, chair, co-founder; Asian Business Beat, chamber publication, editor-in-chief; SCLC, PG County, exec board member; Philippines Lawyers Assn, president, 1980-82; Philippine Heritage Federation, president, 1981-83; PG County Minority Business Procurement Task Force, 1984; NAACP, Common Cause, Port America Adv, exec board member; Prince Georgians on Camera, board member; Greater Southeast Community Hospital, board member; Metropolitan Washington Council of Governments, board member. **HONORS/AWARDS:** Philippine Heritage Federation, Most Outstanding Filipino; Americans by Choice, Honored American Award; Maryland State Democratic Central Committee, Dedicated Service; Progressive Alliance of Filipinos & Americans, highest ranking Filipino elected official, first Filipino State Assemblyman in Mainland US; recipient of over 100 other awards given by various local, natl and intl organizations. **SPECIAL ACHIEVEMENTS:** Co-author, A Revised Guide to the Law and Legal Literature of Mexico, 1973; author, A Revised Guide to the Law and Legal Literature of Peru, 1976; author, editorial piece on Simpson-Mazoli Immigration Bill, Washington Post, April 24, 1982; author, "A Revolutionary Returns to the Philippines," Quarterly Journal of the Library of Congress, January, 1982. **BIOGRAPHICAL SOURCES:** The Maryland Manual, A Guide to Maryland Government, various pages, 1990-93. **BUSINESS ADDRESS:** Delegate, 26th Legislative District of the Maryland General Assembly, 205 Lowe House Office Bldg, Annapolis, MD 21401, (301)858-3012.

VALMONTE, ARNEL ELVAMBUENA
Architect. Filipino American. **PERSONAL:** Born Aug 18, 1965, Plaridel, Bulagan, Philippines; son of Feligene G Valmonte and Leandro O Valmonte; married Frances V Valmonte, Dec 22, 1990. **EDUCATION:** University of Washington, architecture, 1988; Everett Community College, aerospace engineering, 1989. **CAREER:** Boeing Commercial Airplane Group, plant planner, 1989-. **HOME ADDRESS:** 505 164th Pl SE, Bothell, WA 98012. **BUSINESS PHONE:** (206)226-4555.

VAN, THANHTAN C.
Engineer. Vietnamese American. **PERSONAL:** Born Dec 11, 1961, Saigon, Vietnam; daughter of Phuoc C Van and Thuy Tien T Nguyen. **EDUCATION:** University of Maryland, BS, 1983. **CAREER:** US Department of Agriculture, 1983-85; US Information Agency, general engineer, 1985-90; US Department of Energy, general engineer, 1990-92, Configuration and Data Management

Branch, chief, 1992-. **ORGANIZATIONS:** Association for Configuration and Data Management, 1993-; OCA-DC Toastmasters, president, 1992; Federally Employed Women, secretary, 1984-85. **HONORS/AWARDS:** US Department of Energy, Performance Award, 1991, 1992; US Information Agency, Performance Award, 1987, 1988, 1989. **SPECIAL ACHIEVEMENTS:** Board for Architects, Professional Engineers, Land Surveyors and Landscape Architects, professional engineer license, 1990. **BUSINESS ADDRESS:** Chief, Configuration Management Branch, US Dept of Energy, 1000 Independence Ave SW, Forrestal Bldg, 7F-052, Washington, DC 20585, (202)586-1715.

VANCHIASONG, SIONG KOUA
Community service agency administrator. Laotian American/Hmong American. **PERSONAL:** Born Sep 10, 1944, Xieng Khouang, Lao People's Democratic Republic; son of Wang Chia Siong and Say Kue; married Pang Vanchiasong; children: Dua, Phoua, May, La, Kou, Maysy, Kong, Rosalie. **CAREER:** Asian Community Services, executive director, currently. **HONORS/AWARDS:** HHS, Asian Community Services, 1985-87, 1989-91. **SPECIAL ACHIEVEMENTS:** Social Services, 1984-93; planned secondary resettlement, 1985-92. **BIOGRAPHICAL SOURCES:** Atlanta Magazine, 1985; Atlanta Constitution, p C1-C5, September 3, 1992. **BUSINESS ADDRESS:** Executive Director, Asian Community Services, Inc, 145 New St, Decatur, GA 30030, (404)370-0113.

VAN HOUTEN, DAVID J.
Multimedia specialist, systems analyst. Korean American. **PERSONAL:** Born Feb 27, 1955, Republic of Korea; married; children: Two. **CAREER:** Los Angeles Times, editorial systems analyst, technical editor, currently. **ORGANIZATIONS:** Multimedia Development Group. **BUSINESS ADDRESS:** Editorial Systems Analyst, Technical Editor, Los Angeles Times, Times Mirror Square, Los Angeles, CA 90053, (213)237-7198.

VARGHESE, PHILIP LESLIE
Educator. Indo-American. **PERSONAL:** Born Sep 20, 1955, New Delhi, India; son of Thomas Koshy Varghese and Bertha Varghese; married Mae Daniller, Jul 15, 1984; children: Drew Daniller, Max Daniller. **EDUCATION:** Indian Institute of Technology, Madras, BTech, 1976; Syracuse University, MS, 1977; Stanford University, PhD, 1983. **CAREER:** SRI International, postdoctoral fellow, 1983; University of Texas, Austin, associate professor, 1983-. **ORGANIZATIONS:** American Institute of Aeronautics and Astronautics, 1988-; American Society of Mechanical Engineers, 1983-; Combustion Institute, 1983-; Optical Society of America, 1983-; America Physical Society, 1983-. **HONORS/AWARDS:** J William Fulbright Foreign Scholarship Board, Fulbright Senior Scholar, 1993; The University of Texas, Austin, W J Murray Centennial Fellowship in Engineering #3, 1992, Engineering Foundation Award for Outstanding Teaching by an Assistant Professor, 1988, Engineering Foundation, Faculty Excellence Award, 1987; ASME, Central Texas Section, Continous Outstanding Service Awards, 1987, 1986. **SPECIAL ACHIEVEMENTS:** Coauthor: "Directionally Adaptive Finite Element Method for Multidimensional Euler and Navier-Stokes Equations," AIAA 11th Computational Fluid Dynamic Conference, July 6-9, 1993; "Evaluation of Simple Rate Expressions for Vibration-Dissociation Coupling," J Thermophysics and Heat Transfer, February, 1993; numerous others. **BUSINESS ADDRESS:** Associate Professor, ASE-EM Dept, University of Texas, Austin, WR Woolrich Hall, Austin, TX 78712, (512)471-3110.

VARGHESE, RAJU MOLETHU
Insurance company manager. Indo-American. **PERSONAL:** Born May 6, 1947, Adur, Kerala, India; son of Y Varghese and Maria Varghese; married Alice, Oct 27, 1974; children: Rina, Ranita, Gregory. **EDUCATION:** Institute of Marketing Management, New Delhi, diploma, 1969; Punjab University, BA, 1973; American College, CLU studies, currently. **CAREER:** New York Life Insurance Co, general manager, 1983-. **ORGANIZATIONS:** General Agents & Manager Association, South Jersey Chapter, president, 1989-91; Council of Indian Organizations in Greater Philadelphia, president, 1988-90. **HONORS/AWARDS:** CJO, Community Service, 1989. **SPECIAL ACHIEVEMENTS:** Adviser to Rajani Publication, 1992-. **BIOGRAPHICAL SOURCES:** New York Life Publication. **HOME ADDRESS:** 11 Alton Ave, Voorhees, NJ 08043. **BUSINESS PHONE:** (609)488-6900.

VARGHESE, THOMAS K.
Accountant. Indo-American. **PERSONAL:** Born Nov 11, 1953, Meenadom, Kerala, India; son of Ouseph Varghese and Mary Varghese; married Gracy, Sep 15, 1980; children: Anita, Philip. **EDUCATION:** University of Kerala, India, BCom, 1976; Central State University, BS, accounting, 1987. **CAREER:** Midfirst Bank, staff accountant, 1985-89; BancFirst, staff accountant, 1989-; certified public accountant, sole proprietor, currently. **ORGANIZATIONS:** Oklahoma Society of CPAs, 1991-. **HOME PHONE:** (405)324-2382. **BUSINESS ADDRESS:** Staff Accountant, BancFirst, 101 N Broadway, Oklahoma City, OK 73102.

VARMA, ASHA
Government official. Indo-American. **PERSONAL:** Born Mar 19, 1942, Bareilly, Uttar Pradesh, India; married Vinod Shanker Agarwala, Feb 14, 1967; children: Veena Vinod Agarwala, Vinay Agarwala. **EDUCATION:** Agra University, BSc, 1958, MSc, 1960; Banaras Hindu University, PhD, 1963. **CAREER:** Postdoctoral fellow, 1963-66; assistant director, forensics, 1966-68; University of Connecticut, senior res fellow, 1973-77; University of Pennsylvania, supervisor, An Lab, 1977-82; US Navy, group leader, 1983-88, assistant director, Naval Air Warfare Center, currently. **ORGANIZATIONS:** American Institute of Chemists, Relations Committee, chair, 1993-94; National Certification Board, 1990-94; Federally Employed Women, president, 1986; Federal Women's Program Committee, chair, 1988; Navy, R&D Information Exchange Conference, chair & organizer, 1990-93, ACS; Coblentz Society; ECS; fellow: AIC & various non-scientific associations. **HONORS/AWARDS:** Office of Personnel Management, Special Achievement, 1988, Performance Award, 1977-93. **SPECIAL ACHIEVEMENTS:** Over 60 publications; speak Hindu, Urdu & Panjabi; author, CRC Publisher; Handbook of Atomic Absorption Spectroscopy, 1984; Handbook of Atomic Furnace Spectroscopy, 1989; Handbook of Inductively Coupled Plasma Spectroscopy, 1990. **HOME ADDRESS:** 1006 Marian Road, Warminster, PA 18974-2728. **BUSINESS PHONE:** (215)441-3975.

VARMA, RAJENDER S.
Research scientist. Indo-American. **PERSONAL:** Born Jul 26, 1951, New Delhi, India; son of Raj Mal Varma and Roopvati Varma; married Manju Varma, Dec 18, 1977; children: Abhishek, Prashant. **EDUCATION:** Punjab University, India, BSc, chemistry, physics, math, 1970; Kurukshetra University, India, MSc, organic chemistry, 1972; Delhi University, India, PhD, natural products chemistry, 1976; Norwegian Institute of Technology, post graduate diploma, pulp & paper technology, 1978. **CAREER:** Gwalior Rayons Silk Manufacturing Co Ltd, research scientist, 1976-77; Norwegian Institute of Technology, Norway, NORAD fellow, 1977-78; The University, Liverpool, England, postdoctoral research fellow, 1979-82; University of Tennessee, Knoxville, senior research associate, 1983-86; Houston Biotechnology Inc, group leader, 1986-90; Baylor College of Medicine, assistant professor, 1986-93; Houston Advanced Research Center, DNA Technology Laboratory, research scientist, 1993-. **ORGANIZATIONS:** American Chemical Society, 1985-, Organic Chemistry Division, 1985-, Medicinal Chemistry Division, 1985-; Education for Tomorrow Alliance, Local Area High School/Colleges, mentor, 1992-; Senior College Students Summer Training Program, mentor, 1992-. **HONORS/AWARDS:** Council of Scientific & Industrial Research, research fellowship, 1973-75; Center of Advanced Studies in Chemistry, senior research fellowship, 1976; Norwegian Government, NORAD Fellowship, 1977-78; National Institutes of Health, grantee, co-principal investigator, 1989-; American Cancer Society, grantee, principal, co-principal investigator, 1988. **SPECIAL ACHIEVEMENTS:** Published approx 90 research papers in peer-reviewed international journals; several patents issued or pending in the design & synthesis of novel anti-tumor agents, for ophthalmic disorders and novel oligonucleotide therapeutics, several reviews in international journals; chapter in multivolume series Comprehensive Organic Synthesis, Pergamon Press, vol 8, p 363, 1991; chapter in forthcoming series, Encyclopedia of Molecular Biology: Fundamentals & Applications, VCH Publishers, 1993-94. **HOME ADDRESS:** 8 Spurwood Ct, The Woodlands, TX 77381-2526, (713)292-2758. **BUSINESS ADDRESS:** Research Scientist, DNA Technology Laboratory, Houston Advanced Research Center, 4800 Research Forest Dr, The Woodlands, TX 77381, (713)364-4054.

VARMA, RAKESH
Healthcare company financial executive. Indo-American. **PERSONAL:** Born Apr 13, 1954, Ambala, Haryana, India; son of Dev B Varma and Pusupa Varma; married Abha Varma, Jan 26, 1988; children: Ruchi Priya, Noor Kashish. **EDUCATION:** University of Illinois, BS, 1976; University of California, Los Angeles, MBA, 1990. **CAREER:** Deloitte & Touche, senior accountant, 1977-79; G E Capital, account executive, 1979-81; Warner Communications, Inc, manager, 1981-85; First Interstate Bancorp, vice president,

director, 1983-91; CareAmerica Health Plans, vice president, controller, 1991-. **ORGANIZATIONS:** American Institute of CPAs, 1983-; California Society of CPAs, 1983-. **HONORS/AWARDS:** California State Board of Accountancy, CPA, 1983; Institute of Internal Auditors, CIA, 1983. **HOME ADDRESS:** 20252 Hemmingway St, Winnetka, CA 91306-2259, (818)882-9986.

VARMA, USHA
Physician. Indo-American. **PERSONAL:** Born Nov 8, 1942, Srinagar, Jammu and Kashmir, India; daughter of Somnath Wanchoo and Sooma Wati Wanchoo; married Dhirendra K Varma, Oct 11, 1967; children: Anisha, Vikas. **EDUCATION:** Government College for Women, pre-medical, 1961; Government Medical College, Srinagar, Kashmir, India, MBBS, 1966. **CAREER:** Private practice, physician, 1973-; Maryland General Hospital, director of endoscopic surgery, currently, associate chief of OB/GYN, currently. **HOME ADDRESS:** 5 Old Lyme Rd, Lutherville, MD 21093, (410)252-4760. **BUSINESS PHONE:** (410)383-2072.

VARMA, VISHWA K.
Environmental consulting/engineer company executive. Indo-American. **PERSONAL:** Born Jun 25, 1948, Delhi, India; son of Sonu Ram Varma & Kaushalya Devi Varma; married Katherine B Varma, Oct 25, 1975; children: Jaya K, Ravi P. **EDUCATION:** Indian Institute of Technology, Kanpur, BTech, 1970; Vanderbilt University, MBA, 1972. **CAREER:** Metro Govt of Nashville, Davidson County, director of environment, 1972-76; American Consulting Services, regional manager, 1976-77; Harmon Engineering, executive vice president, 1977-83; ATC Inc, president & chairman, 1983-88; Roy F Weston Inc, vice president, 1988-, member, board of directors, 1993-. **ORGANIZATIONS:** Auburn Center for Developing Industries, chairman of the board, 1987-; Auburn Industrial Development Board, board of directors, 1989-; Child Care Resources Center Inc, board of directors, 1990-; India Cultural Association of East Alabama, president, 1992; Auburn Chamber of Commerce, board of directors, 1989; Auburn Kiwanis Club, board of directors, 1985; Auburn Arts Association, president, 1989; Auburn United Way, board of directors, 1987. **HONORS/AWARDS:** Govt of India, National Science Talent Scholarship; Vanderbilt University, Houston Scholarship; Roy F Weston Inc, President's Award. **BIOGRAPHICAL SOURCES:** "Vish Varma's ATC Environmental Leader," in Auburn Bulletin, Auburn, AL, 1987. **BUSINESS ADDRESS:** Vice President, Roy F Weston Inc, 1635 Pumphrey Ave, Auburn, AL 36830, (205)826-6100.

VASAN, SRINI VARADARAJAN
Engineer. Indo-American. **PERSONAL:** Born Aug 24, 1956, Trivandrum, Kerala, India; son of Krishna Varadarajan and Srinivasan Ambujam; divorced. **EDUCATION:** IIT, Madras, India, BTech, 1979; Clarkson College of Technology, MS, 1983; Clarkson University, PhD, 1986. **CAREER:** Grindwell Norton Ltd, India, 1979-80; Hindustan Polymers, India, 1980-81; IBM, staff engineer, 1986-91; Motorola, senior staff (process), 1991-. **HONORS/AWARDS:** US Patent & Trademarks Office, US Patent #5,197,655, 1993, #5,004,508, 1991. **SPECIAL ACHIEVEMENTS:** Co-author: journals publications, "Crosslinking. . .", Photog Science Eng, 28, p175, 1984; "A Simple. . .," IEEE Trans Electr Dev, ED32, p1896, 1985; "Thermal Degradat. . .," Polym J, 17, p525, 1985; "Effect of . . .," Polym Degrad Stab, 13, p77, 1985; "Optical Density. . .," Proc SPIE, 539, p361, 1985; "Simulation of. . .," Proc 7th Intl Symposium Plasma Chem, 7, p1405, 1985; "Characterization. . .," J Imag Technol, 11, p168, 1985; "Modeling the. . .," Proc SPIE, 631, p268, 1986; "Effect of. . .," J Electrochem Soc, 133, p1686, 1986; "Excimer Laser. . .," J Applied Phys, 59, p3861, 1986, Proc MRS, 75, p 433, 1987. **HOME ADDRESS:** 12001 North Oaks Dr, Austin, TX 78753-2314, (512)834-8205.

VEDAMUTHU, EBENEZER RAJKUMAR
Research microbiologist. Indo-American. **PERSONAL:** Born Jun 23, 1932, Vellore, Tamil Nadu, India; son of D R Vedamuthu (deceased) and K Vedamuthu; married Judith Ann Vedamuthu, Aug 17, 1963; children: Jonathan J, Daniel S. **EDUCATION:** Madras University, BSc, 1953; National Dairy Research Institute, India, dairy diploma, 1956; University of Kentucky, MS, 1962; Oregon State University, PHD, 1965. **CAREER:** Government of Madras, dairy assistant, 1957-59; Oregon State University, research assistant, 1961-65, research associate, 1965-66, assistant professor, 1971-72; Iowa State University, research associate, 1966-67, assistant professor, 1967-71; Quest International, research microbiologist, 1972-. **ORGANIZATIONS:** American Dairy Science Association, research committee, currently, journal editorial board, 1988-; American Association Advancement of Science, 1973-; Ameri-

can Society Microbiology, 1972-; International Association Milk, Food and Environmental Sanitarians, 1974-. **HONORS/AWARDS:** University of Kentucky, Haggin Fellowship; International Association Milk, Food and Environmental Sanitarians, Best Paper Published on Dairy Foods, 1992; American Dairy Science Association, Diary Food Association Research Award in Dairy Foods Processing, 1993. **SPECIAL ACHIEVEMENTS:** 12 US patents; over 60 publications in research journals; 6 chapters in technical books. **BUSINESS ADDRESS:** Chief Research Microbiologist, Quest International, Bioproducts Group, 1833 57th St, Sarasota, FL 34243, (813)351-9453.

VELORIA, VELMA ROSETE
State legislator. Filipino American. **PERSONAL:** Born Oct 22, 1950, Philippines; daughter of Apelino and Patrocinio. **EDUCATION:** San Francisco State College, BS, 1976. **CAREER:** Washington Legislature, state rep, currently. **BUSINESS ADDRESS:** State Representative, Washington Legislature, John L O'Brien Bldg, Room 403, Olympia, WA 98504, (206)786-7862.

VEMULA, SUBBA RAO
Engineer, government official. Indo-American. **PERSONAL:** Born Dec 30, 1924, Andhra Pradesh, India; son of Anjaneyulu & Mahalakshmamma; married Sarojini; children: Naga Venkateswara Rao, Naga Venkata Krishna Rao. **EDUCATION:** Rensselaer Polytechnic Institute, MA, civil engineering, 1968, PhD, mechanics, 1974. **CAREER:** New York State Dept of Transportation, civil engineer, currently. **ORGANIZATIONS:** American Society of Mechanical Engineers. **HOME ADDRESS:** 27 Pinehurst Ave, Albany, NY 12205, (518)438-2336.

VENKATA, SUBRAHMANYAM SARASWATI
Educator. Indo-American. **PERSONAL:** Born Jun 28, 1942, Nellore, Andhra Pradesh, India; son of Ramiah Saraswati Venkata & Lakshmi Alladi Venkata; married Padma Subrahmanyam Mahadevan, Sep 3, 1971; children: Sridevi Saraswati, Harish Saraswati. **EDUCATION:** Andhra University, Waltair, India, BSEE, 1963; Indian Institute Technology, Madras, India, MSEE, 1965; University of South Carolina, PhD, 1971. **CAREER:** Coimbatore Institute Technology, lecturer in electrical engineering, 1965-66; South Carolina Electric & Gas, planning engineer, 1969-70; University of South Carolina, postdoctoral fellow, 1971; University of Massachusetts, instructor in electrical engineering, 1971-72; West Virginia University, assistant professor, 1972-75, associate professor, 1975-79; University of Washington, professor, 1979-. **ORGANIZATIONS:** Institute of Electrical & Electronics Engineers, fellow, 1989; CIGRE, 1990; Tau Beta Pi, 1983; Sigma Xi, Eta Kappa Nu, 1973; Hindu Temple & Cultural Center of Pacific NW, secretary, 1990, chairman, 1991; Explorer's Club, advisor, 1976-78; Jaycees, 1972-74. **HONORS/AWARDS:** West Virginia University Foundation, WVU Associates Award, 1974, 1978; IEEE, Best Paper Award, 1985, 1988, 1991. **SPECIAL ACHIEVEMENTS:** Author, book, Introduction to Electric Energy Devices, 1987; 2 inventions, Adaptive VAR Compensator, 1987, 1992. **BIOGRAPHICAL SOURCES:** IEEE Membership Directory, p 268-269, 1990. **HOME ADDRESS:** 14520 183rd Ave NE, Woodinville, WA 98072-9377. **BUSINESS ADDRESS:** Professor, Dept of Electrical Engineering, University of Washington, FT-10, Seattle, WA 98195, (206)543-2157.

VENKATARAMANAN, RAMAN (VENKAT)
Educator, researcher. Indo-American. **PERSONAL:** Born Aug 30, 1951, Kallal, Tamil Nadu, India; son of Rajalakshmi Raman and Venkatesa Raman; married Padma Venkataramanan, May 27, 1984. **EDUCATION:** University of Madras, India, BPharm, 1972; Birla Institute of Technology & Science, India, MPharm, 1974; University of British Columbia, Canada, PhD, 1979. **CAREER:** University of Washington, post-doctoral research associate, 1978-80; University of Pittsburgh, 1981-, professor, 1991-. **ORGANIZATIONS:** American Association of Pharmaceutical Scientists, 1986-; American College of Clinical Pharmacology, 1987-; American Association of Colleges of Pharmacy, 1982-; Cell Transplant Society, 1992-; Rho Chi Society, 1981-. **HONORS/AWARDS:** American College of Clinical Pharmacology, fellow, 1989; Medical Research Council, Canada, Special Visiting Scientist, 1990; Alberta Heritage Foundation, Canada, Visiting Scientist, 1985. **SPECIAL ACHIEVEMENTS:** Author of more than 140 publications in scientific literature; contributed chapters to 10 books; over 50 presentations at national/international symposiums. **BUSINESS ADDRESS:** Professor, University of Pittsburgh, 3501 Terrace St, 718 Salk Hall, Pittsburgh, PA 15261, (412)648-8547.

VERMA, AJAY
Neurologist. Indo-American. **PERSONAL:** Born 1962?, New Delhi, India. **EDUCATION:** University of Maryland (magna cum laude); Johns Hopkins University, MD, PhD, neurotoxicology. **CAREER:** Walter Reed Army Medical Center, neurology resident, currently. **SPECIAL ACHIEVEMENTS:** Coauthor: "Carbon Monoxide: A Putative Neural Messenger," Science, Jan 15, 1993; Johns Hopkins University School of Medicine, further research on carbon monoxide, 1993-. **BUSINESS ADDRESS:** Neurology Resident, Walter Reed Army Medical Center, 6825 16th St NW, Washington, DC 20307, (202)576-3000.*

VERMA, AJIT K.
Educator. Indo-American. **PERSONAL:** Born Aug 9, 1944, Jallandar, Punjab, India; married. **EDUCATION:** Punjab Agricultural University, BSc, biochemistry, 1966, MSc (honors), biochemistry, 1968; Flinders University of South Australia, PhD, biochemistry, 1972-76. **CAREER:** Flinders University of South Australia, teaching assistant, 1972-76; University of Wisconsin, Madison, postdoctoral fellow, 1976-81, assistant scientist, 1981-82, associate scientist, 1982-84, assistant professor, 1984-88, associate professor, 1988-92, Comprehensive Cancer Center, Department of Human Oncology, professor, 1992-. **ORGANIZATIONS:** American Association for Cancer Research, 1978-; American Association for the Advancement of Science, 1978-; American Society of Biological Chemists, 1983-; International Association for Vitamin and Nutritional Oncology, 1985-. **HONORS/AWARDS:** Government of India, National Merit Scholarship, 1962-67; Punjab Agricultural University, Merit Scholarship, 1967-68; Flinders University of South Australia, Merit Scholarship, 1972-76. **SPECIAL ACHIEVEMENTS:** Chairperson and plenary speaker at several international seminars; author of influential papers on cancer research; ranked first in MSc and Gold Medal in BSc. **BUSINESS ADDRESS:** Professor, Dept of Human Oncology, University of Wisconsin, Comprehensive Cancer Center, 600 Highland Ave, K4/532, CSC, Madison, WI 53792, (608)263-9136.

VERMA, ANIL K.
Psychiatrist. Indo-American. **PERSONAL:** Born Oct 28, 1958, New Delhi, India; son of Dhani Ram Verma and Harbai Devi Verma; married Susama Verma, Apr 2, 1986; children: Bianca A, Shawn S. **EDUCATION:** Vaish College, Bhiwani, Haryana, pre-medical, 1976; Medical College and Hospital, Rohtak, Haryana, MD, 1980; Mount Sinai-Elmhurst Hospital, residency, 1987. **CAREER:** Willard Psychiatric Center, psychiatrist, 1987-90; Columbia University, lecturer, 1989-90; Auburn Memorial Hospital, psychiatrist, 1990-91; Cayuga County, MHC, psychiatrist, 1990-; private practice, psychiatrist, 1993-. **ORGANIZATIONS:** American College of International Physicians, life fellow, 1989; American Medical Association, 1984-89; American Psychiatric Association, 1984-89. **HONORS/AWARDS:** Harvard Medical School, Gaebler Center, Fellowship, 1985. **SPECIAL ACHIEVEMENTS:** American Journal of Psychiatry, "Absence of Cognitive Impairment after more than 100 Life Time ECT," 1991. **BUSINESS ADDRESS:** Physician, Auburn Professional Building, Suite 10, 33 William Street, Auburn, NY 13021, (315)258-8167.

VERMA, DHANI RAM
Librarian. Indo-American. **PERSONAL:** Born Sep 20, 1929, Rohtak, Haryana, India; son of Ganpat Ram (deceased) and Sunder Devi; married Harbai Devi, Feb 3, 1949; children: Raj, Madhu Malwal, Anil, Arun. **EDUCATION:** Panjab University, India, BA, 1951; Ministry of Education, Govt of India, BLib, 1953; Panjab University, India, MA, political science, 1959; Simmons College, MLS, 1982. **CAREER:** Cabinet Secretariat, Govt of India, New Delhi, JCEC library gr III, librarian, 1953-55; Ministry of Education, Govt of India, librarian gr II, 1955-58; National Gallery of Art, New Delhi, India, Art Reference Library, librarian, 1958-70; Cabinet Secretariat, Govt of India, librarian, 1971-76; Dept of Culture, Govt of India, CSL, librarian, 1976-79, assistant director, 1979-80; Boston College, senior copy cataloger, 1980-. **ORGANIZATIONS:** ALA, Support Staff Interests Round Table, steering committee member, 1993-94; Council on Library/Media Technicians, 1990-, treasurer, 1992-94, Constitution Committee, chair, 1991-92; American Library Association, 1993-; United India Association of NE, president, 1991-92; International Federation of Library Associations, 1979-80; Government of India Libraries Association, vice president, 1979-80, secretary, 1977-79; US Postal Services, advisory council member, 1993-. **HONORS/AWARDS:** International Federation of Library Associations, 26th IFLA Congress, guest speaker from developing countries. **SPECIAL ACHIEVEMENTS:** Author, Indian Painting: Aspects of Indian Culture, A Select and Annotated Bibliography, Indian Council for Cultural

Relations, 1966; Directory of Central Government Employees of India Residing in Tagore Garden, New Delhi, India, 1975/1976, CGEWA, Tagore Garden, 1976; also numerous papers, articles, and seminars, 1963-93. **BIOGRAPHICAL SOURCES:** India Abroad, Vol XXII, No 45, p 44, Aug 7, 1992; India News, Vol 22, No 35, p 44, Aug 8, 1992; Library Mosaics, p 18, May/June, 1993, p 19, Jan/Feb, 1992; Library & Information Abstracts, Index, 1962-. **HOME ADDRESS:** 49 Fellsview Avenue, Medford, MA 02155, (617)395-3480.

VERMA, RAM SAGAR
Scientist, educator. Indo-American. **PERSONAL:** Born Mar 3, 1946, Vill Moradabad, Lucknow, Uttar Pradesh, India; son of Moonga Devi Verma (deceased) & Gaya Prasad Verma; married Shakuntala Devi Verma, May 4, 1962; children: Harendra K, Narendra K. **EDUCATION:** Agra University, India, BSc, agriculture, 1965, MSc, quantitative genetics, 1967; University of Western Ontario, PhD, cytogenetics, 1972; University of Colorado, post-doctoral research associate, 1973-76; The Royal College of Pathologists, London, DCC, 1984. **CAREER:** SUNY at Brooklyn, Dept of Medicine, instructor, 1976, assistant professor, 1976-79, associate professor, 1979-85, professor, 1985-; The Jewish Hospital and Medical Center of Brooklyn, chief of cytogenetics, 1978-79; Interfaith Medical Center, Division of Cytogenetics, chief, 1980-88; Long Island College Hospital, Division of Genetics, chief, 1986-. **ORGANIZATIONS:** American Association for the Advancement of Science, fellow; American Association for Clinical Research; American Federtion for Clinical Research; American Genetic Association, life member; American Society for Cell Biology; American Society of Human Genetics, life member; Association of Clinical Scientists, fellow; Clinical Genetic Society, life member; European Society of Human Genetics; Federation of American Scientists; Genetic Society of America; Genetic Society of Canada; Indian Society of Human Genetics, life member; Institute of Biology, fellow; International Association of Human Biologists; New York Academy of Sciences, fellow; New York Academy of Medicine, fellow; Society for Experimental Biology and Medicine; Royal College of Pathologists, UK. **HONORS/AWARDS:** University of Aeterna Lucina Vitma, Manly, Australia, honorary diploma of Clinical Cytogenetics, 1989; World Health Organization, Geneva, Switzerland, consultant, 1982; numerous others. **SPECIAL ACHIEVEMENTS:** Heterochromatin: Molecular and Structural Aspects, Cambridge University Press, 1988; Human Chromosomes Manual of Basic Techniques, Pergamon Press, 1989; The Genome, VCH Publishers Inc, 1990; Human Chromosomes Manual of Basic Techniques, McGraw Hill, 1992. **HOME ADDRESS:** 45-38 Springfield Blvd, Bayside, NY 11361, (718)631-2958. **BUSINESS ADDRESS:** Chief, Division of Genetics, Long Island College Hospital, Hicks St at Atlantic Ave, Brooklyn, NY 11201, (718)780-1401.

VERNEKAR, ANANDU DEVARAO
Educator. Indo-American. **PERSONAL:** Born Jul 5, 1932, Karwar, Karnataka, India; son of Devarao V Vernekar and Devaki D Vernekar; married Sharada A Vernekar, Dec 24, 1959; children: Anita Vernekar Shankar, Sunil A, Nutan A. **EDUCATION:** University of Poona, BSc (honors), 1956, MSc, 1959; University of Michigan, MS, 1963, PhD, 1966. **CAREER:** University of Michigan, assistant research meteorologist, 1961-66; Travelers Research Center, research scientist, 1967-69; University of Maryland, professor, 1969-. **ORGANIZATIONS:** American Meteorological Society, 1962-; American Geophysical Union, 1962-. **HONORS/AWARDS:** American Meteorological Society, Fellow, 1986. **SPECIAL ACHIEVEMENTS:** Meteorological Monograph, 1972; 35 articles in refereed journals. **BUSINESS ADDRESS:** Professor, University of Maryland, Space Sciences Bldg, Rm 2249, College Park, MD 20742, (301)405-5385.

VIET-CHAU, NGUYEN DUC
Foundation executive. Vietnamese American. **PERSONAL:** Born Dec 25, 1935, Vietnam; son of Van Nguyen. **EDUCATION:** University of Frubourg, STD, 1972, MA, 1975. **CAREER:** Vietnamese Catholic Federation in USA, president; DAN CHUA Catholic Magazine, publisher, editor, currently. **BUSINESS ADDRESS:** Publisher, Editor, DAN CHUA Media, PO Box 1419, Gretna, LA 70054, (504)392-1630.

VIJAYENDRAN, BHIMA R.
Chemical company executive. Indo-American. **PERSONAL:** Born Jun 16, 1941, Bangalore, India; son of Bhima Rao Sirsi & Sanrja Sirsi; married Levi, Aug 8, 1970; children: Ravi, Anie. **EDUCATION:** University of Madras, MTech, 1965; University of Southern California, PhD, 1969; University of New Haven, MBA, 1978. **CAREER:** RJ Reynolds Tobacco, postdoctoral

fellow, 1969-70; Pitney Bowes, group leader, 1970-76; Celanese Research, research associate, 1976-83; Air Products & Chemicals, manager, 1973-91; PPG Industries, associate director, 1991-. **ORGANIZATIONS:** American Chemical Society, 1971-; TAPPI, secretary, 1983-; Society of Plastic Engineers, advisory committee, 1985-; Sigma Xi, 1970-; Commercial Development Association, 1993-. **HONORS/AWARDS:** TAPPI, best speaker, 1984; Gorden Conference, symposium chairman, 1983; Air Products, Innovation Award, 1991. **SPECIAL ACHIEVEMENTS:** Over 80 publications, patents in the field of Applied Polymer/Surface Science. **HOME ADDRESS:** 109 Bel-Aire Dr, Monroeville, PA 15146, (412)856-5858. **BUSINESS PHONE:** (412)325-5310.

VIKRAM, CHANDRA SHEKHAR
Educator. Indo-American. **PERSONAL:** Born Oct 31, 1950, Payagpur, Uttar Pradesh, India; son of Pratap Singh (deceased) & Kailash Vati Singh; married Bina Singh, Jan 15, 1975; children: Preeti Singh, Tushar Singh. **EDUCATION:** Agra University, India, BSc, 1966; Indian Institute of Technology, Kanpur, MSc, 1968; Indian Institute of Technology, Delhi, MTech, 1970, PhD, 1973. **CAREER:** Indian Institute of Technology, senior research fellow, 1970-75, pool officer, 1975-77; Pennsylvania State University, research associate, 1977-82, senior research associate, 1982-89; University of Alabama, Huntsville, senior research scientist, 1989-93, research professor, 1993-. **ORGANIZATIONS:** Optical Society of America, fellow, 1984-; International Society for Optical Engineering, fellow, 1993-; Institute for Advanced Studies in Life Support, founding member, 1990. **SPECIAL ACHIEVEMENTS:** Books: Particle Field Holography, Cambridge University Press, 1992; Selected Papers on Holographic Particle Diagnostics, 1990; more than 100 journal articles. **BUSINESS ADDRESS:** Research Professor, Center for Applied Optics, University of Alabama, Huntsville, Optics Bldg, Rm 400-C, Huntsville, AL 35899, (205)895-6030.

VILLANUEVA, CHRIS
City council member. Filipino American. **CAREER:** Vallejo City Council, council member, currently. **BUSINESS ADDRESS:** Councilman, City of Vallejo, 555 Santa Clara St, Vallejo, CA 94590, (707)648-4527.*

VILLANUEVA, MARIANNE DEL ROSARIO
Author, educational administrator. Filipino American. **PERSONAL:** Born Jul 14, 1958, Manila, Philippines; daughter of Generoso Villanueva & Natividad Del Rosario; married Simeon De Jesus III, Feb 5, 1983; children: Andrew De Jesus. **EDUCATION:** Ateneo de Manila, BA, Philippine studies, 1979; Stanford University, MA, East Asian studies, 1981, MA, English, 1985. **CAREER:** Stanford University, Center for Infant Studies, research assistant, 1988, Center for East Asian Studies, 1988-90, East Asian Resource Center, project coordinator, 1990-93, Humanities and Sciences, Dean's Office, program & budget administrator, 1993-. **ORGANIZATIONS:** Filipino Staff Forum, public affairs officer, 1992-; Asian Women United, 1993-; International Pen, Western chapter, 1992-93. **HONORS/AWARDS:** California Arts Council, Literary Fellowship, 1993; Bread Loaf Writers Conference, Margaret Bridgman Scholar in Fiction, 1993; Stanford University Creative Writing Center, scholarship for creative writing, 1983-85; University of the Philippines, National Writing Fellow, 1976. **SPECIAL ACHIEVEMENTS:** Author: Bad Thing, short story, in anthology Home to Stay II, Greenfield Review Press, forthcoming; Lenox Hill, short story, in anthology Charlie Chan is Dead, Penguin Books, Dec 1991; Ginseng & Other Tales from Manila, short story collection, Calyx Books, 1991; Siko, short story, in anthology The Forbidden Stitch: An Asian American Women's Anthology,; Ginseng, short story, in Story Quarterly, vol 20. **BIOGRAPHICAL SOURCES:** "Area Author Speaks to Students," in Philippine News, section B1, Oct 20-26, 1993; "Review of Ginseng & Other Tales form Manila," Utne Reader, p 120, Jan/Feb, 1992. **HOME ADDRESS:** 2431 Hopkins Ave, Redwood City, CA 94062.

VILLA-REAL, OLIVIA CANCHELA (OLIVIA VILLA-REAL JACOBSEN)
Instructor, musician. Filipino American. **PERSONAL:** Born Jun 17, 1948, Manila, Philippines; daughter of Osmundo Canela Villa-Real and Isidra Canchela Villa-Real; married Carl Edward Jacobsen, Jun 16, 1979; children: Marc-Anthony Villa-Real Alabanza, Bella-Olivia Villa-Real Alabanza, Donna-Carole Villa-Real Jacobsen. **EDUCATION:** Santa Isabel College, music, 1963; Far Eastern University, MA, 1968; California State University, music, 1987; University of Southern California, music, 1988. **CAREER:** Villa Cabrini Academy, teacher, English department head, 1969; LA Harbor College, English professor, 1972; LA Trade Tech, English professor, 1974; LA City

College, English professor, 1971-89; Glendale College, English professor, 1988-89; self-employed, professor, piano and voice, 1969-; Creative Spectrum Enterprises, founder, president, currently. **ORGANIZATIONS:** Music Teachers' Association, Glendale Branch, 1992-; American Society of Composers, Authors and Publishers, 1976-; American Guild of Variety Artists, 1977-; Screen Actors Guild, 1980-; American Federation of Television and Radio Artists, 1978-; American Federation of Musicians, 1977-. **SPECIAL ACHIEVEMENTS:** Major solo concerts: Dorothy Chandler Pavilion, LA Music Center, soprano, pianist, composer, lyricist and dancer, 1977, 1991; recital soloist and guest artist in local symphonies; author, I Shouldn't Enter Your World, Rock Me Gently; composer of 58 original songs, 4 choral music and many poems and essays; two long-playing albums, six singles; currently working on a CD release; languages: speak Filipino, Spanish; read and sing in Italian, French, German and Latin. **BIOGRAPHICAL SOURCES:** "The Gift of Love," Philippine News Magazine, p 21, Sep 16-22, 1992; "Olivia Villa-Real Sets Concert," California Examiner, p 13-15, August 21-27, 1992. **HOME ADDRESS:** 5163 Ellenwood Dr, Los Angeles, CA 90041, (213)254-3060.

VIRJI, NAZNEEN
Wholesale company general manager. Indo-American. **PERSONAL:** Born May 22, 1951, Dar es Salam, United Republic of Tanzania; married Aniz Virji, Jun 27, 1970; children: Naushad, Azad, Ayaz. **CAREER:** Africana Gifts & Shells Inc, general manager, cur. **BUSINESS ADDRESS:** General Manager, Africana Gifts & Shells, Inc, PO Box 1830, Fort Myers, FL 33902, (813)731-1500.

VIRK, MUHAMMAD YAQUB
Real estate & investment management company executive, government manager. Pakistani American. **PERSONAL:** Born Apr 9, 1937, Rasulpur, Punjab, Pakistan; son of Muhammad Hussain & Zainib Bibi Virk; married Zubaida Yaqub Virk, Jun 2, 1967; children: Irfan G, Rizwan Q, Samina F, Adnan F. **EDUCATION:** University of Punjab, Lahore, Pakistan, BA, economics & sociology, 1968, MA, economics, 1970; Universite de Paris, Sorbonne, PhD, financial economics, 1973; University of Detroit, MBA, finance, 1977. **CAREER:** American Natural Gas Co, economic analyst, 1974-80; Ministry of Planning, Saudi Arabia, economist, 1980-81; TM Band of Chippewa Indians, director, mineral, oil & gas management, 1981-83; TM Community College, management specialist, 1983-84; US Department of Interior, natural resources officer, 1984-86; Michigan Department of Transportation, property manager, 1987-90; Michigan State Housing Development Authority, financial manager, housing management officer, 1990-94; Virk Enterprises, president, currently. **ORGANIZATIONS:** Detroit Rotary Club, 1991-92; South Lansing Rotary Club, 1990-91; Downriver Board of Realtors, 1987-90; Michigan Association of Realtors, 1987-90; National Association of Realtors, 1987-90. **HONORS/AWARDS:** Republican Presidential Task Force, Award of Merit. **SPECIAL ACHIEVEMENTS:** Testified before US Senate sub committee on Indian Affairs, 1982; testified, in writing, before US Senate Committee on energy & minerals, 1983; economic advisor, United Nations Development Program, NY, 1981. **HOME ADDRESS:** 22255 Crestwood St, Woodhaven, MI 48193-5246, (313)692-8174. **BUSINESS PHONE:** (313)692-8174.

VISWANADHAM, RAMAMURTHY K.
Engineer. Indo-American. **PERSONAL:** Born Jul 16, 1946, Tiruvur, Andhra Pradesh, India; son of Viswanatha Ramamurthy and Natesa Chellammal; married Subhadra Viswanadham, Jun 25, 1970; children: Madhuri, Srikant. **EDUCATION:** Osmania University, Regional Engineering College, Warangal, BE, 1968; University of Illinois, Urbana-Champaign, MS, 1970, PhD, 1973. **CAREER:** Martin Marietta Labs, senior scientist, 1975-79, staff scientist, 1986-88; Reed Tool Company, Materials Research, supervisor, 1979-84, R&D, manager, 1984-86; Multi-Metals, Engineering R&D, director, 1988-. **ORGANIZATIONS:** American Powder Metallurgy Institute, 1979-; American Society for Materials, 1979-; The Minerals, Metals & Materials Society, 1975-; Materials Research Society, 1990-. **HONORS/AWARDS:** Martin Marietta Labs, Robert Lye Memorial Award, 1977, 1981. **SPECIAL ACHIEVEMENTS:** Conference chairman, First International Conference on the Science of Hard Materials; editor, Science of Hard Materials, Plenum, NY, 1983. **BUSINESS ADDRESS:** Director of Engineering, R&D, Multi-Metals, 715 E Gray Street, Louisville, KY 40202, (502)587-5632.

VISWANATH, RAMPUR S.
Environmental scientist. Indo-American. **PERSONAL:** Born Sep 16, 1940, Rampur, Karnataka, India; son of Suryanarayana Setty and Bhagyalakshmi;

married Treja, Aug 18, 1971; children: Seetal, Sharat. **EDUCATION:** Mysore University, BS, 1961; Bangalore University, MS, 1967; University of Detroit, PhD, 1979. **CAREER:** Renukacharya College, instructor, assistant professor, 1961-71; R V College for Women, assistant professor, head of chemistry, 1971-76; University of Detroit, teaching assistant, 1976-79; Midstates Laboratory, project chemist, 1980-82; Tulsa City-County Health, senior environmental research chemist, 1982-. **ORGANIZATIONS:** American Chemical Society, 1979-, awards committee/chas, 1992-; Society for Applied Spectroscopy, 1979-; Air & Waste Management Association, 1992-; American Industrial Hygiene Association, 1992-; Institute of Hazardous Materials Management, 1992-; Tulsa Central Rotary Club, treasurer, board of directors, 1991-. **HONORS/AWARDS:** National Registry of Environmental Professionals, REM, 1992; Institute of Hazardous Materials Management, CHMM, 1992. **SPECIAL ACHIEVEMENTS:** Characteristics of Oilfield Emissions (submitted), 1993; Vibrational Spectra of Alkali Hydrogen Selenites, 1978; Infrared and Laser Raman Studies of Hydrogen Bonding, 1979; Infrared Overtone Spectra of KDP, RDP, & H2SeO3, 1979; High Temperature Phase Transition in NH4H2PO4, 1979. **HOME ADDRESS:** 13223 E 38th St, Tulsa, OK 74134, (918)622-7969. **BUSINESS ADDRESS:** Senior Environmental Research Chemist, Tulsa City-County Health Department, 4616 E 15th St, Tulsa, OK 74112, (918)744-1000.

VISWANATHAN, BYRAVAN
Physician. Indo-American. **PERSONAL:** Born Dec 23, 1939, Madras, Tamil Nadu, India; son of M Viswanathan and Meenakshi Viswanathan; married Lakshmi, Aug 23, 1967; children: Srilatha, Savitha, Sandya. **EDUCATION:** G R Medical College, India, MBBS, 1963. **CAREER:** Park Ave Hospital, physician, 1972-73; Memorial Hospital, physician, internist, 1973-81; VA Medical Center, physician, internist, 1981-86; self-employed, physician, internist, 1986-. **ORGANIZATIONS:** Pennsylvania Med Society, 1981-; American Medical Association, 1988-; Adams County Medical Society, 1986-. **HONORS/AWARDS:** American College of Physicians, fellow, 1981. **BUSINESS ADDRESS:** Physician, 124 W High St, Gettysburg, PA 17325, (717)334-8165.

VO, D. BRIAN
Electrical engineer. Vietnamese American. **PERSONAL:** Born Mar 12, 1957, Hue, Vietnam; son of Sinh Vo & Chanh Ta; married Kim C Vo, Jul 11, 1987; children: Kevin Minh-Duc. **EDUCATION:** Portland Community College, AS, 1978; University of Portland, BSEE, 1983. **CAREER:** Puget Sound Naval Shipyard, electrical engineer, 1983-85; Pacific Engineering, electrical engineer, 1985-87; Portland General Electric, electrical engineer, 1987-88; Port of Portland, electrical project engineer, 1988-. **ORGANIZATIONS:** The Institute of Electrical & Electronics Engineers, 1987-; Illuminating Engineering Society of North America, 1987-. **SPECIAL ACHIEVEMENTS:** Registered professional engineer, State of Oregon, 1991. **HOME ADDRESS:** 5025 SW Baird St, Portland, OR 97219-5122, (503)246-9917.

VO, JIMMY
Engineer. Vietnamese American. **PERSONAL:** Born Apr 28, 1955, Khanh Thien, Binh Thuan, Vietnam; son of Co Vo & Hoa Thi Nguyen; married Mary Vo, Oct 5, 1985; children: Julie P, Rocky. **EDUCATION:** Oklahoma State University, BA, 1984. **CAREER:** Tinker A F B, aerospace engineer, currently. **ORGANIZATIONS:** B1-B, Bomber Engineering Division. **HOME ADDRESS:** 1326 Hillcross Ct, Oklahoma City, OK 73159, (405)691-5422. **BUSINESS ADDRESS:** Aerospace Engineer, Tinker Air Force Base, 3001 Staff Dr, Ste 2AC 84A, Oklahoma City, OK 73145-3006, (405)736-7452.

VO, VAN TOI
Educator. Vietnamese American. **PERSONAL:** Born Jul 27, 1949, Saigon, Vietnam; son of Van Trinh Vo & Thi Khai Pham Vo; married Dominique Lemarquis, Jun 10, 1951; children: Xuan Mai, Anh Tuan. **EDUCATION:** Ecole Polytechnique Federale De Lausanne, Switzerland, PhD, 1982. **CAREER:** Tufts University, professor, 1984-. **ORGANIZATIONS:** Association for Research in Vision and Ophthalmology, 1987; Optical Society of America, 1990; Tau Beta Pi, 1990; Sigma Xi, 1991. **SPECIAL ACHIEVEMENTS:** Language proficiency: Vietnamese, French, English; two patents. **BUSINESS ADDRESS:** Professor, Electrical Engineering Dept, Biomedical Engineering Laboratory, Tufts University, Halligan Hall, Medford, MA 02155, (617)627-3217.

VOHRA, INDU
Educator, state government administrator. Indo-American. **PERSONAL:** Born Oct 20, 1951, Jammu, Jammu and Kashmir, India; daughter of Pishorilal Vohra and Ram Piyari Vohra; married Sunil K Sahu, Dec 17, 1977; children: Munjot Sahu, Punita Sahu. **EDUCATION:** Government College for Women, India, BA, 1970; University of Jammu of Kashmir, India, MA, 1972; Jawaharlal Nehru University, India, PhD, 1978; Indiana State University, MPA, 1994. **CAREER:** University of Delhi, India, assistant professor of political science, 1976-78; University of Illinois at Chicago, research curator/director of documentation center, 1979-84; Chicago State University, instructor in political science, 1985-88; Columbia College, Chicago, instructor in Liberal Arts, 1986-88; DePauw University, assistant professor, 1989-93; State of Indiana, Equal Employment Opportunity Compliance, specialist, 1993-. **ORGANIZATIONS:** Asian/Pacific Educators, 1982-84; Pi Sigma Alpha, 1993-; Association of Indian Women in North America, 1981-84. **HONORS/AWARDS:** Pi Sigma Alpha, 1993; Indiana State University, Dean's Scholarship, 1993-94; University Grants Commission, India, National Doctoral Fellowship, 1972-77; University of Jammu and Kashmir, Merit Scholarship for Collegiate Studies, 1967-70. **SPECIAL ACHIEVEMENTS:** "Pacific/Asian American Research: An Annotated Bibliography," 1981; "Pacific/Asian American Research: A Selected Bibliography," 1983; five articles in the Encyclopedia on Human Rights History, 1992; several civil rights articles in: African-American Encyclopedia, 1993; Encyclopedia on Asian-Americans, 1994; Ethnicity and Ethnic Groups; Encyclopedia on Multiculturalism, 1994. **BUSINESS ADDRESS:** State of Indiana Government, 100 N Senate Ave, N855, Indianapolis, IN 46204-2249, (317)232-8043.

VOHRA, RANBIR
Educator. Indo-American. **PERSONAL:** Born in Lyallpur, Punjab, India; son of D R Vohra; married Meena, Jan 14, 1954; children: Carin. **EDUCATION:** Government College, Lahore, BA (honors), 1946; Beijing University, diploma (Chinese), 1959; Harvard University, MA, 1965, PhD, 1969. **CAREER:** Government of India, program officer, all India radio, 1947-64; Harvard University, instructor, lecturer, 1969-71; University of Calgary, associate professor, 1971-73; Amherst College, visiting professor, 1974; Trinity College, associate professor, 1973-75, Department of Political Science, chair, 1973-85, 1993-96, Charles A Dana Professor of Political Science, 1975-. **ORGANIZATIONS:** Association of Asian Studies, 1969-; International Polictical Science Association, 1975-; India International Center, 1980-. **HONORS/AWARDS:** Ford Foundation, fellowship, 1964-68; Harvard University, research fellowship, 1968-69; SSRC, research grant, 1971; Trinity College, research grant, 1988; Harvard University, JKF Center, visiting scholar, 1989-90. **SPECIAL ACHIEVEMENTS:** Author of: Lao She And the Chinese Revolution, Harvard University Press, 1974; "The Chinese Revolution," Houghton Mifflin Press, 1974; "China's Path to Modernization," Prentice Hall, 2nd edition, 1992; China: The Search for Justice and Democracy, Penguin-Viking, 1991. **HOME ADDRESS:** 4 Shepard Rd, West Hartford, CT 06110, (203)561-3879. **BUSINESS PHONE:** (203)297-2496.

VORA, NARENDRA MOHANLAL
Rubber and chemical company administrator. Indo-American. **PERSONAL:** Born Dec 12, 1947, Bombay, India; son of Mohanlal D Vora; married Jyoti, May 2, 1974; children: Tejas, Niraj. **EDUCATION:** University of Bombay, India, BSc, 1968; University of Scranton, MS, 1972. **CAREER:** Onyx Chemical Co, QC chemist, 1972-76; Arkansas Chemical Co, QC supv, 1976-77; Singer Co, analytical chemist, 1977-81; Ciba-Geigy, sr analytical chemist, 1981-82; Louisiana Dept of Environmental Quality, lab supv, 1982-88; Agribusiness Marketers Inc, lab supv, 1988-90; Copolymer Rubber and Chemical Corp, lab mgr, 1990-. **ORGANIZATIONS:** American Chemical Society, 1977-; American Society of Quality Control, 1989-. **HOME ADDRESS:** 15018 Currency Dr, Baton Rouge, LA 70817, (504)752-3739.

VORA, PRAMATHESH S.
Food company executive. Indo-American. **PERSONAL:** Born Oct 24, 1946, Ahmedabad, Gujarat, India; son of Shashikant G Vora & Vasantben S Vora; married Bela P Vora, Dec 14, 1972; children: Jay P, Jill P. **EDUCATION:** Gujarat University, BS, 1967; Mississippi University, BS, 1970; Penn State University, MS, 1974. **CAREER:** SUN Co, Product Development, research engineer; MacAndrews & Forbes, Sales/Marketing/R&D/QC, senior vice president, currently. **ORGANIZATIONS:** Institute of Food Technologists; American Society of Chemical Engineers. **HONORS/AWARDS:** Tau Beta Kappa, honor society, 1969; Tobacco Intr, Best Presentation, 1985. **SPECIAL ACHIEVEMENTS:** Publications in: AOAL Journal, 1980-82; Tobacco Inter-

national, 1985; Tobacco Research Conference, 1986. **HOME ADDRESS:** 12 Bunker Hill Rd, Sewell, NJ 08080. **BUSINESS ADDRESS:** Senior Vice President, MacAndrews & Forbes Co, 3rd St & Jefferson Ave, Camden, NJ 08104, (609)968-4072.

VOVAN, BA
Administrator, educator. Vietnamese American. **PERSONAL:** Born Mar 2, 1952, Danang, Vietnam; son of Vovan Nhan & Pham Thi Ly; married Anna M Vovan, Jul 13, 1992; children: Man Tiep, Tran Chau, Kieu Chau, Robert. **EDUCATION:** Metropolitan State College of Denver, BAEd, recertification, 1981; University of Colorado, Denver, MAEd, 1987; University of Denver, administrator certificate, 1989. **CAREER:** Metropolitan State College, instructor, 1982-84; Asian Chamber of Commerce, executive director, 1989; Denver Public Schools, teacher, 1976-81, administrator, currently. **ORGANIZATIONS:** Colorado Association of School Executives, 1987-; Association for Supervision and Curriculum Development, 1987-; Colorado Refugee Advisory Council, chairman, 1989; Asian Cultural Center, board member, 1989-; Denver Mayor's Advisory Council, 1987-; Asian Chamber of Commerce, board member, 1990-; State of Colorado, Amer-Asian Advisory Council, board member, 1990-; Asian American Education Alliance, board member, 1991-. **HONORS/AWARDS:** City & County of Denver, Volunteer Award, 1978; Denver Public Library's Volunteer Award, 1988; Lupus Foundation of America, President Award, 1987; Colorado Association of Bilingual Bicultural Education, Community Service Award, 1983; received 25 certificates of appreciation for special contributions and community services. **SPECIAL ACHIEVEMENTS:** Contributor, "The Vietnamese Community," Friends of Children of Various Nations News, Summer 1987; "Understanding Vietnamese Students and Their Families," COTESOL, vol 10, no 2, 1987; co-author, "Understanding Culturally and Linguistically Different Students," Denver Public Schools, 1979; Vietnamese materials: 15 chemistry units, 15 physical science units, 30 life science units, 60 math units, 30 industrial arts units. **BUSINESS ADDRESS:** Administrator/Educator, Denver Public Schools, 900 Grant St, Rm 406, Denver, CO 80203, (303)764-3583.

VU, JOSEPH
Educator. Vietnamese American. **PERSONAL:** Born Mar 13, 1952, Vietnam; son of Phuong Vu and Nhan Vu; married Huyen-Tran Vu, Jul 1, 1978; children: Christine, Daniel. **EDUCATION:** Ohio University, 1973; University of Chicago, MBA, 1975, PhD, 1984. **CAREER:** University of Illinois, Chicago, professor, 1985-88; De Paul University, professor, 1988-. **ORGANIZATIONS:** Vietnamese Association of Illinois, president. **BUSINESS ADDRESS:** Professor, De Paul University, 1 E Jackson Blvd, Chicago, IL 60604, (312)362-5121.

VU, LIEM T.
Chemical engineer. Vietnamese American. **PERSONAL:** Born Jan 5, 1964, Camau, Vietnam; son of Dinh V Vu. **EDUCATION:** Tufts University, BSCE, 1987, MSCE, 1989. **CAREER:** Tufts University, staff asst, 1986-89; Merix Corp, sr engr, 1989-. **BUSINESS ADDRESS:** Senior Engineer, Merix Corp, 77 Charles St, Needham, MA 02194, (617)455-8877.

VU, QUANG
Publisher, editor. Vietnamese American. **PERSONAL:** Born Jan 1931, Hadong, Vietnam; married. **EDUCATION:** Metropolitan State University, BA. **CAREER:** Control Data Corp, technical writer, 1976; Honeywell, Inc, sr technical writer, 1982; Turck Multiprox Inc, advertising manager, 1983; Sick-Optic Electronic, marketing support mgr, 1988; Ngay Nay Minnesota, publisher, editor, currently. **ORGANIZATIONS:** The Fellowship of Vietnam Armed Forces Servicemen in Minnesota, president, 1978-87; The Vietnam Cultural Association, founder, 1979. **HONORS/AWARDS:** McKnight Human Services Award, 1992. **BIOGRAPHICAL SOURCES:** Minneapolis Star and Tribune, Dec 9, 1992. **BUSINESS ADDRESS:** Publisher, Editor, Ngay Nay Minnesota, PO Box 1149, Maple Grove, MN 55311, (612)559-6396.

VYAS, GAURANG RAJNIKANT
City official. Indo-American. **PERSONAL:** Born May 15, 1955, Poona, Maharashtra, India; son of R D Vyas & S R Vyas; divorced. **EDUCATION:** Rice University, BA, economics bus mgmt, 1978; Lehman College, MS, business education, currently. **CAREER:** Aramco, systems analyst, 1978-81; Chrysler Credit, collection manager, 1981-85; City of New York, assessor, 1985-. **SPECIAL ACHIEVEMENTS:** City of New York, Dept of Finance, acknowledged for having over 100 hours of community service in 1992, 1993; NYC Public Library, tutor in the adult literacy program, (voluntary), for those

who are functionally illiterate, 1993. **HOME ADDRESS:** 815 W 181st St #4B, New York, NY 10033-4529, (212)781-2090.

VYAS, GIRISH N.
Educator. Indo-American. **PERSONAL:** Born Jun 11, 1933, Aglod, Gujarat, India; son of Rukshmani Vyas and Narmadashankar Vyas; married Devi G Vyas, Apr 3, 1962; children: Jay, Shrikrishna. **EDUCATION:** St Xaviers College, BS, (with honors), 1954; University of Bombay, Seth G S Medical College, MS, 1956, PhD, 1964. **CAREER:** Bombay Municipal Blood Center, officer-in-charge, 1964-65; Western Reserve University, postdoctoral fellow, 1965-67; University of California, director of blood bank, 1969-88, assistant professor of lab medicine, 1969-73, associate professor of lab medicine, 1973-77, professor of lab medicine, 1977-, director of transfusion research program, 1985-. **ORGANIZATIONS:** American Society of Hematology, Transfusion Medicine Subcommittee, chair, 1990-91; National Research Council, Committee on Viral Hepatitis, 1974-76; American Association of Blood Banks, Scientific Program Committee, 1974-78; International Society of Blood Transfusion, Best Task Force, 1991-95; FDA, Blood Products Advisory Committee, 1983, acting chairman, 1991; NIH Consenus Conference on Red Cell Transfusion, 1990; International Symposium on Hepatitis and Liver Disease, chair, 1972-84; WHO Biostandards IABS, council member, 1992-96. **HONORS/AWARDS:** Mayor of Oakland, Outstanding Immigrant in Bay Area Communities, 1970; International Society of Blood Transfusion, Jean Julliard Prize, 1969. **SPECIAL ACHIEVEMENTS:** Viral Hepatitis and Liver Disease, 1978, 1984; Viral Hepatitis and Blood Transfusion, 1972; Membrane Structure and Function of Human Blood Cells, 1976; Laboratory Diagnosis of Immunologic Disorders, 1975; over 200 original papers published in peer-reviewed journals. **BUSINESS ADDRESS:** Professor, Director of Transfusion Research Program, University of California School of Medicine, 513 Parnassus Ave, Medical Sciences, Rm S-555, San Francisco, CA 94143-0134, (415)476-4678.

VYAS, PREMILA HARIPRASAD
Educator. Indo-American. **PERSONAL:** Born Aug 19, 1928, Dholka, Gujarat, India; daughter of Bhimshanker M & Pramoda B Oza; married Hariprasad D Vyas, May 2, 1957 (deceased). **EDUCATION:** Bombay University, India, BA (honors), 1950; M S University, Baroda, India, BEd, 1954; London University, UK, diploma, 1960; University of Houston, Texas, EdD, 1967. **CAREER:** Pioneer High School, India, teacher, 1950-57; Pear Tree High School, UK, 1960-62; Teachers' Training College, M S University, Baroda, 1963-64; Houston Community College, professor, 1975-78; Texas Southern University, professor, 1993-. **ORGANIZATIONS:** National Asian Pacific Americans Against Substance Abuse, Steering Committee, Regional Conference, 1993; Joyti Hindu Workshop Society, editor; Advisory Committee for Doctoral Dissertation, graduate; Gulf Schools Supplementary Education Center, research fellow; Texas Southern University, Faculty Research Council, director. **HONORS/AWARDS:** Fulbright Hays Award, Haiti, 1981; Texas State Teachers, scholarship, 1967; Alpha Teachers Sorority, scholarship, 1966-67; Altruso International, scholarship, 1965-66; Oberholtor, scholarship. **SPECIAL ACHIEVEMENTS:** Author of several articles published in journals. **HOME ADDRESS:** 4038 O'Meara, Houston, TX 77025, (713)661-8411. **BUSINESS ADDRESS:** Professor, Dept of Psychology, Texas Southern University, College of Education, 3100 Cleburn St, Houston, TX 77004-4501, (713)527-7344.

VYAS, UDAYKUMAR DAYALAL
Educator. Indo-American. **PERSONAL:** Born Nov 17, 1940, Bilkha, Gujarat, India; son of Dayalal L Vyas and Saraswati D Vyas; married Pragna U Vyas, May 28, 1967; children: Kalpesh, Avani. **EDUCATION:** Gujarat University, India, BSc, 1962, MSc, 1964; Madurai University, India, MPhil, 1973; Bhavnagar University, India, PhD, 1981. **CAREER:** Sir P P Institute of Science, Bhavnagar University, India, associate professor, 1964-83; Tongaloo College, assistant professor, 1983-84; Winston-Salem State University, associate professor, 1984-. **ORGANIZATIONS:** American Mathematical Society; Indian Mathematical Society, life member; Gujarat Mathematics Association, life member. **HONORS/AWARDS:** Tongaloo College, Instructor of the Year, 1984. **SPECIAL ACHIEVEMENTS:** Published research articles; author and editor of books and popular articles. **HOME ADDRESS:** 1841 Greencedar Ln, Winston-Salem, NC 27127, (919)785-7406. **BUSINESS ADDRESS:** Associate Professor, Math Dept, Winston-Salem State University, Winston-Salem, NC 27110-0001, (919)750-2491.

W

WADA, DEBRA SADAKO
Legislative assistant. Japanese American. **PERSONAL:** Born Oct 31, 1962, Honolulu, HI; daughter of Stanley S Wada and Aileen Y Wada. **EDUCATION:** Drake University, BA, 1984; American University, 1985-86. **CAREER:** Senator Daniel K Akaka, legislative assistant, 1987-. **BUSINESS ADDRESS:** Legislative Assistant to Senator Daniel K Akaka, US Senate, 720 Hart Senate Office Bldg, Washington, DC 20510-1103.

WADA, PATRICIA
Association administrator. Japanese American. **EDUCATION:** University of California, Berkeley, BA; California State University, Hayward, teaching credentials. **CAREER:** Hokubei Mainichi, English section, former associate editor; Doishisha Girls' Junior High School, Japan, English language, instructor; Japanese American Citizens League, Northern California-Western Nevada-Pacific District Council, regional director, 1992-. **ORGANIZATIONS:** National Japanese American Historical Society, board of directors, currently; California Japanese American Alumni Association, board of trustees, currently; Japanese American AIDS Project, advisory committee member, currently; Amerasia Journal, Community Media Advisory Council. **BUSINESS ADDRESS:** Regional Director, Japanese American Citizens League, 1765 Sutter St, San Francisco, CA 94115, (415)921-5225.*

WADA, TOSHIMASA FRANCIS
Conductor, educator. Japanese American. **PERSONAL:** Born Jan 5, 1945, Kiryu, Gunma, Japan; son of Motoharu and Fusa Wada; married Nancy J Wada, Oct 16, 1970; children: Merrycarol Yumi, Christina Naomi, Paul Kazutoshi, Daniel Kenji, Laura Kimi. **EDUCATION:** Catholic University of America, MM, 1972, BM, 1971; Loma Linda University, 1981-82. **CAREER:** Chatham Borough Schools, music teacher, 1972-78; Platte Valley Academy, chairman, music dept, 1978-79; Union College, assistant professor of music, 1979-83; Clark University, director, chamber orchestra, 1989-92; College of Holy Cross, director, chamber orchestra, 1988-93; Atlantic Union College, associate professor of music, 1992-; Thayer Sym Orch, music director, conductor, 1983-. **ORGANIZATIONS:** Massachusetts Cultural Council, panelist, 1993; North Central Massachusetts Chamber of Commerce, director, 1991-. **HONORS/AWARDS:** Governor Wm Weld, citation, 1992; Massachusetts senators, citation, 1992; Massachusetts House of Representatives, citation, 1992; Mayor of Fitchburg, citation, 1992; Mayor of Leominster, citation, 1992. **SPECIAL ACHIEVEMENTS:** CD recording on Neuma Label, 1991; Heartquake, biography by Lylie Wagner, 1983; finalist, International Conductor's Institute, 1981, 1982. **MILITARY SERVICE:** Japan Ground Defense Force, pfc, 1963-65; Highest Honor, 1964. **BUSINESS ADDRESS:** Music Director, Conductor, Thayer Symphony Orchestra, Main Street, South Lancaster, MA 01561, (508)368-0041.

WAIHEE, JOHN DAVID
Governor. Pacific Islander American. **PERSONAL:** Born May 19, 1946, Honokaa, HI; married Lynne Kobashigawa; children: John David, Jennifer. **EDUCATION:** Andrews University, BA, history, business, 1968; Central Michigan University, postgraduate studies, 1973; University of Hawaii, JD, 1976. **CAREER:** Benton Harbor Area Schools, Michigan, Community Education, coordinator, 1968-70, assistant director, 1970-71; Honolulu Model Cities Program, program evaluator, administrative assistant to directors, planner, 1971-73; City and County of Honolulu, Office of Human Resources, sr planner, 1973-74, program manager, 1974-75; Shim, Sigal, Tam, & Naito, Honolulu, associate, 1975-79; Waihee, Manuia, Yap, Pablo, & Hoe, Honolulu, partner, 1979-82; Hawaiian House of Representatives, representative, 1980-82; State of Hawaii, lt governor, 1982-86, governor, 1986-. **ORGANIZATIONS:** Constitutional Convention, delegate, 1978; Kalihi-Palama Community Council, director, past president; Goals for Hawaii Organization, steering committee, Land Use Goals Committee, past chairperson, Outreach Committee, past co-chairperson; Hawaii Sr Citizens Travel Board, past board of directors; State Council on Housing and Construction Industry; Kalihi-Palama Hawaiian Civic Club; Legal Aid Society of Hawaii, past board of directors; Alu Like, past board of directors; ABA; University of Hawaii Law School Alumni; Filipino Chamber of Commerce; Kalakaua Lions; Asian Pacific American Committee. **BUSINESS ADDRESS:** Governor, State of Hawaii, State Capitol Bldg 15th Fl, Honolulu, HI 96813, (808)586-0034.*

WAKABAYASHI, RON
Government official. Japanese American. **PERSONAL:** Born Nov 13, 1944. **CAREER:** City of Los Angeles, Human Relations Commission, executive director, currently. **ORGANIZATIONS:** Asian Drug Abuse Program, former director; Japanese American Citizens League, past natl president; United Way, former vp for planning & public policy. **BUSINESS ADDRESS:** Executive Director, Human Relations Commission, City of Los Angeles, City Hall, Rm 1000, 200 N Spring St, Los Angeles, CA 90012, (213)485-4495. *

WAKAMATSU, DON
Professional baseball player. Japanese American. **PERSONAL:** Born 1962?, Hood River, OR; married Laura, 1989; children: one. **EDUCATION:** Arizona State University. **CAREER:** Chicago White Sox, baseball catcher, 1991; Albuquerque Dukes, baseball catcher, 1992-93; Texas Rangers, baseball catcher, non-roster invitee, 1994. **SPECIAL ACHIEVEMENTS:** Played around 130 games per year in both JACL and regular baseball leagues while also attending high school; baseball player, Arizona State University, College World Series. **BUSINESS ADDRESS:** Catcher, Texas Rangers, PO Box 90111, Arlington Stadium, Arlington, TX 76004, (817)273-5222.*

WALIA, HARJEET ROSIE
Physician. Indo-American. **PERSONAL:** Born Apr 18, 1950, New Delhi, India; daughter of Diyal Singh Ahluwalia and Parduman Kaur; married Surendra K Gupta, Dec 11, 1979; children: Sangeeta Gupta, Seema Gupta. **EDUCATION:** Ottawa University, BSc (cum laude), 1973, MD (cum laude), 1977. **CAREER:** Ottawa Civic Hospital, family practice resident, 1977-79; Health Central, staff physician, 1979-83; self-employed, physician, 1983-; HCA Medical Center, Plano, active staff physician, 1986-, vice chief of family medicine, 1991-92, chief of family medicine, 1992-93. **ORGANIZATIONS:** Plano Independent School District, advisory board member, 1990-93; Collin County MHMR, advisory board member, 1986-89; American Academy of Family Practice, fellow, 1986-; College of Canadian Family Physicians, certificant, 1979-; Texas Medical Association, 1983-. **BUSINESS ADDRESS:** Physician, 1200 Coit Rd, Ste 105, Plano, TX 75075, (214)985-8393.

WALIA, JASJIT SINGH
Educator. Indo-American. **PERSONAL:** Born Mar 19, 1934, Lahore, Punjab, India; son of Harkishan Singh Ahluwalia and Harbhajan Kaur Ahluwalia; married Parveen Singh Walia, Jan 9, 1966; children: Sunila, Suneeta. **EDUCATION:** Punjab University, India, BS (with honors), 1955, MS (with honors), 1956; University of Southern California, PhD, 1960. **CAREER:** University of Southern California, teaching assistant, 1956-59, research associate, 1960; Massachusetts Institute of Technology, research associate, 1960-61; Punjab University, scientific officer, 1961-62; Banaras Hindu University, lecturer, 1962-66; Loyola University, associate professor, 1966-73, professor, 1973-. **ORGANIZATIONS:** American Chemical Society, 1958-; Royal Society of Chemistry, 1966-; Sigma Xi, 1961-; Sikh Society of South Inc, founder, 1979, chairman, board of directors, 1979-88, president, 1979-87. **HONORS/AWARDS:** Loyola University, Dux Academicus Award, 1982; Outstanding Educators of America Inc, Outstanding Educator of America Award, 1974; Punjab University, Professor Prem Singh Medal, 1955; American Chemical Society, award, 1964-66. **SPECIAL ACHIEVEMENTS:** Author, Some Aspects of Modern Organic Chemistry, 1964; 34 research publications, 1957-. **HOME ADDRESS:** 7225 Benson Ct, New Orleans, LA 70127. **BUSINESS ADDRESS:** Professor, Dept of Chemistry, Loyola University, 6363 St Charles Ave, New Orleans, LA 70118, (504)865-3275.

WAN, DAVID A.
Publishing company executive. Chinese American. **PERSONAL:** Born Jun 10, 1954, New York, NY; son of Su Yuen Wan and Shen Wu Wan; married Cindy Horowitz, May 1, 1982; children: Tiffany, Melissa. **EDUCATION:** Yale University, BA, 1976; Harvard University, MBA, 1981. **CAREER:** Andersen Consulting, consulting manager, 1981-84; Pepsico Inc, business planner, 1984-86; Paine Webber, corp vice president, 1986-88; Salomon Brothers, vice president, finance, 1988-89; Simon & Schuster, Finance Division, vice president, 1989-90, Education Group, senior vice president, 1990-93, Strategic Planning, senior vice president, 1993-. **ORGANIZATIONS:** Yale Westchester Alumni, 1989-; Yale Football Association, 1979-. **BUSINESS ADDRESS:** Senior Vice President, Paramount Publishing/Simon & Schuster, 1230 Avenue of the Americas, New York, NY 10020, (212)698-7033.

WAN, FREDERIC YUI-MING

Educator, government official. Chinese American. **PERSONAL:** Born Jan 7, 1936, Shanghai, China; son of Wai-Nam Wan (deceased) and Olga Pearl Jung Wan (deceased); married Julia C, Sep 10, 1960. **EDUCATION:** MIT, SB, math, 1959, SM, math, 1963, PhD, math, 1965. **CAREER:** MIT Lincoln Lab, staff member, 1959-65; MIT, Cambridge, math instructor, 1965-67, asst professor, 1967-69, associate professor, 1969-74; University of British Columbia, Institute of Applied Mathematics and Statistics, math professor, director, 1974-83; University of Washington, Seattle, Dept of Applied Mathematics, professor of math, 1983-, chairman, 1984-88, College of Arts and Sciences, associate dean, 1988-92; NSF, Division of Math Sci, program director, 1986-87, division director, 1993-. **ORGANIZATIONS:** MIT Educational Council for BC Area of Canada, 1974-83; associate editor: Journal of Applied Mechanics, Canadian Applied Mathematics Quarterly, Studies in Applied Mathematics; Canadian Applied Mathematics Society, council member, 1980-83, president, 1983-84; American Mathematics Society; Mathematics Assn of America; American Academy Mechanics, president, 1992-93, fellow, 1982-. **HONORS/AWARDS:** Sloan Foundation, award, 1973, Killam Senior Fellow, 1979; ASME, fellow; Sigma Xi; Canadian Applied Mathematics Society, Arthur Beaumont Distinguished Service Award, 1991. **SPECIAL ACHIEVEMENTS:** Contributor to articles in numerous professional journals; industrial firms and governmental agencies, consultant. **BUSINESS ADDRESS:** Professor, Dept of Applied Mathematics, University of Washington, FS-20, Seattle, WA 98195.

WAN, JAMES X.

Educator. Chinese American. **PERSONAL:** Born Sep 10, 1957, Nanjing, Jiangsu, People's Republic of China; married Meng Cai, Sep 8, 1988. **EDUCATION:** East China University of Water Resources, BS, 1981; University of California, Santa Barbara, MA, 1985, PhD, 1990. **CAREER:** Long Beach City College, department of mathematics, instructor, 1991-. **ORGANIZATIONS:** California Community College Association. **SPECIAL ACHIEVEMENTS:** Inference on semiparametric models, PhD dissertation, 1990. **BUSINESS ADDRESS:** Instructor, Dept of Math, Long Beach City College, 4901 E Carson St, Long Beach, CA 90808-1780, (310)420-4427.

WAN, PETER J.

Agriculture science and processing researcher. Chinese American. **PERSONAL:** Born Jan 29, 1943, Wei Hai Wey, Shantong, China; son of Hung Mao Wan & Maria H Meng; married Catherina C Wan, Jan 4, 1970; children: Anne C, Ellen Y. **EDUCATION:** Cheng Kung University, Taiwan, BSE, 1965; Illinois Institute of Technology, MS, 1970; Texas A&M University, PhD, 1973. **CAREER:** Food Protein R&D Center, Texas A&M University, project leader, 1975-79; Best Foods, CPC International, senior research material scientist, 1979-80; Anderson Clayton Foods, new technology director, 1980-87; Kraft-General Foods, technology manager, 1987-90; ARS, USDA, research leader, 1990-. **ORGANIZATIONS:** American Chemical Society; American Association Cereal Chemists; American Institute of Chemical Engineers; American Oil Chemists Society, former governing board member, former chairman of protein & co product division; Chinese American Food Society, past president, secretary, treasurer. **HONORS/AWARDS:** Chinese American Food Society, Outstanding Service Award, 1984-86; Chinese Lion Club, Dallas, Outstanding Service Award, 1985-87; UNIDO/UNDP, grant of $25,000 to train visiting scientists from Beijing, 1990-91; Cotton Incorporated, grant of $25,000 per year to conduct research in cottonseed, 1993-; USDA, 1890 school grant sponsor and advisor for grant to Alcorn State University, 1994-96. **SPECIAL ACHIEVEMENTS:** Served as a member of advisory team to Beijing and Jilin, China, for soybean utilization, 1984; served as a United Nations advisor to Beijing Food Additive Research Center, 1988; member of a special advisor team to Taiwan, Rep of China, 1989-90; UNIDO, Vienna, served as a technical advisor to Beijing, China, 1990-91. **MILITARY SERVICE:** Military Service in Taiwan, Rep of China, 2nd Lt, 1965-66. **HOME ADDRESS:** 5300 Washingtonian Dr, Metairie, LA 70003. **BUSINESS PHONE:** (504)286-4450.

WAN, STEPHEN SAMKONG

Physician. Chinese American. **PERSONAL:** Born Jan 5, 1958, Hong Kong; son of Chen Sien Wan and Zing Ying Young; married Eva Wan, Jul 10, 1982; children: Nicholas, Justin. **EDUCATION:** University of Wisconsin-Madison, BS, 1980; MIT, MS, 1982; Mount Sinai School of Medicine, NY, MD, 1986. **CAREER:** Physician. **ORGANIZATIONS:** American Medical Assn; American College of Ob & Gyn, fellow; Chinese American Medical Society. **HONORS/AWARDS:** American Board of Ob & Gyn, Diplomate, 1992.

BUSINESS ADDRESS: Physician, 19 Bowery, New York, NY 10002, (212)431-4333.

WAN, SZE-KAR

Educator. Chinese American. **PERSONAL:** Born Apr 23, 1954, Changsha, People's Republic of China; son of Chi-Lai Wan & Chui-Ying Tam. **EDUCATION:** Brandeis University, BA, 1975; Gordon-Conwell Theological Seminary, MDiv, 1982; Harvard University, ThD, 1992. **CAREER:** TMI Corp, computer programmer, 1975-76; Harvard University, research assistant, applied physics, 1976-77, teaching fellow, 1985-89; Raytheon Corp, research assistant, medical electronics, 1978; S and S Associates, Software Consultant, president, 1990-; Andover Newton Theological School, assistant professor, 1990-. **ORGANIZATIONS:** Society of Biblical Literature, 1985-; American Academy of Religion, 1985-. **HONORS/AWARDS:** Gulbenkian Travel Portugal Fellowship, Travelling Fellow to Isreal, 1988; Harvard University, Sinclair Kennedy Fellow, 1989-90; Dutch Government, NWO Research Fellow in Holland, 1990; Association of Theological Schools in North America, fellowship, 1993-94; Lady Davis Fellowship, Jerusalem, postgraduate fellow, 1993-94. **SPECIAL ACHIEVEMENTS:** Proficient in: Taishanese, Cantonese, Mandarin, Modern Armenian (Western), Hebrew; reading & writing: French, German, Classical Hebrew, Classical Greek, Latin. **HOME ADDRESS:** 42 Browning Rd, Somerville, MA 02145, (617)776-4214.

WANG, ALAN P.

Educator. Chinese American. **PERSONAL:** Born Mar 1, 1930, Shanghai, China; son of Jung-Liang Wang and Jia Yin Pan; married Cecilia Y Wang, Aug 31, 1957; children: Geoffrey, James, Eugene. **EDUCATION:** Washington State University, BS, 1954; University of Southern California, MS, 1957; University of California, Los Angeles, PhD, 1964. **CAREER:** Fleur Corp, engineer, 1954-58; Northrop Corp, senior research engineer, 1958-63; Hughes Air Craft, assistant project manager, 1965-70; IBM, senior consultant, 1970-76; Arizona State University, professor, 1970-. **ORGANIZATIONS:** Sigma Xi, 1962-; American Math Society, 1962-; American Astrophysics Society, 1962-. **BUSINESS ADDRESS:** Professor, Dept of Mathematics, Arizona State University, Tempe, AZ 85287-1804.

WANG, ALBERT S. D. (SHOW-DWO)

Educator. Chinese American. **PERSONAL:** Born Jul 13, 1937, Yantai, Shandong, China; son of Kung-Nan Wang and Wen-Lan Lin; married Monica M Huang, Dec 16, 1967; children: Arthur L, Mark L. **EDUCATION:** National Taiwan University, BS, 1959; University of Nevada, MS, 1963; University of Delaware, PhD, 1967. **CAREER:** Drexel University, applied mechanics, assistant professor, 1967-72, associate professor, 1972-77, professor, 1977-92, Albert and Harriet Soffa Professor of Mechanical Engineering, 1992-. **ORGANIZATIONS:** American Society of Mechanical Engineers; American Society for Testing Materials; Society for the Advancement of Materials and Proccessing Engineers; American Academy of Mechanics; Sigma Xi; American Liver Foundation, Philadelphia Chapter, board member; United Way of Southeastern Pennsylvania, board member. **HONORS/AWARDS:** Drexel University, Outstanding Research Award, 1981; US Academy of Science, Research Associateship Award, 1986; University of Delaware, Distinguished Visiting Professorship, 1990. **SPECIAL ACHIEVEMENTS:** Research and development of fiber-reinforced materials for precision structures; published over 100 archival papers in the Mechanics of Materials. **HOME ADDRESS:** 904 Drexel Ln, Bryn Mawr, PA 19010. **BUSINESS ADDRESS:** Professor, Dept of Mechanical Engineering, Drexel University, 32nd and Chestnut Sts, Philadelphia, PA 19104, (215)895-2297.

WANG, ARTHUR C.

Government official. Chinese American. **PERSONAL:** Born Feb 4, 1949, Boston, MA; son of Kung Shou Wang and Lucy Chow Wang; married Nancy J Norton, Sep 1, 1985; children: Alexander Xinglin, Sierra Xinan. **EDUCATION:** Franconia College, BA, 1970; University of Puget Sound Law School, JD (summa cum laude), 1984. **CAREER:** Tacoma Community House, VISTA, project coordinator, 1973-76; Washington House of Representatives, research analyst, 1977-80, state rep, 1981-; Davies Pearson, PC, attorney, 1984-; University of Puget Sound Law School, adjunct professor, 1987-. **ORGANIZATIONS:** House Capital Budget Committee, chair, 1993-; House Revenue Committee, chair, 1989-93; House Commerce & Labor Committee, chair, 1985-89; Legislative Evaluation & Accountability Program, chair, 1992-; Asian Caucus, Democratic National Convention, chair, 1976; Pacific/Asian Coalition National Board, treasurer, 1975-. **HONORS/AWARDS:** Washington Health Care Association, Legislator of Year, 1992; Seattle Chinese Post, Chinese American

Man of the Year, 1991. **SPECIAL ACHIEVEMENTS:** University of Puget Sound Law Review, associate editor, 1983-84. **HOME ADDRESS:** 3319 N Union, Tacoma, WA 98407, (206)752-1714. **BUSINESS ADDRESS:** State Representative, Washington House of Representatives, John L O'Brien Bldg, Olympia, WA 98504, (206)786-7974.

WANG, BEE-LAN CHAN
Writer, business administrator. Chinese American/Malaysian American. **PERSONAL:** Born Jan 23, 1949, Georgetown, Penang, Malaysia; married Timothy Wang, May 27, 1972; children: Stephen S, Jason C, Paul C. **EDUCATION:** Harvard University, AB, 1970; University of Chicago, PhD, 1975. **CAREER:** Science University of Malaysia, assistant lecturer, 1971-72; Wheaton College, assistant professor of sociology, 1974-82; Northern Illinois University, visiting assistant professor, 1982-83; Valley Medical & Cardiac Clinic, administrator, 1983-. **ORGANIZATIONS:** InterVarsity Christian Fellowship, Missions Advisory Board, 1987-93; District Parent Teacher Organization, co-chair, 1990-92; Curriculum Advisory Council, 1989-93; First Baptist Church of Geneva, Christian Education Board. **HONORS/AWARDS:** University of Chicago, Susan Colver Rosenberger Prize, 1976. **SPECIAL ACHIEVEMENTS:** "Affirmative Action," The Intl Encyclopedia of Education, supp vol two, Oxford: Pergamon, 1990; "Population and Hunger," Christian Perspectives on Social Problems, Indianapolis, Wesley, 1992; Should You Be The Working Mom? A Guide for. . ., Elgin, IL, Scripture Press, 1987; "Positive Discrimination in Education," "Sex and Ethnic Differences in Educational Investment," and many others in Comparative Education Review, 1977-83. **HOME ADDRESS:** 4N804 Grandma's Ln, St Charles, IL 60175, (708)377-0988. **BUSINESS PHONE:** (708)377-1810.

WANG, BEN
Educator. Taiwanese American/Chinese American. **PERSONAL:** Born Nov 4, 1954, Taichung, Taiwan; son of Pi-Chieh Wang and Chang C K Wang; married Lin H Wang, May 27, 1979; children: Annie, Mark. **EDUCATION:** Tunghai University, BS, industrial engineering, 1976; Pennsylvania State University, MS, industrial engineering, 1985, PhD, industrial engineering, 1986. **CAREER:** State University of New York, Buffalo, assistant professor, 1987-90; University of Iowa, associate professor, 1990-93; FAMU/FSU College of Engineering, professor and chair, 1993-. **ORGANIZATIONS:** Institue of Industrial Engineers, 1983-; Society of Manufacturing Engineers, 1983-. **HONORS/AWARDS:** Society of Manufacturing Engineers, Outstanding Young Manufacturing Engineer Award, 1990, Eugene Merchant Textbook of the Year Award, 1992; Institute of Industrial Engineers, Book of the Year Award, 1992. **SPECIAL ACHIEVEMENTS:** Author of over 60 technical papers and 20 book chapters, 1986-; 3 books, 1990, 1991, 1992. **BUSINESS ADDRESS:** Professor and Chair, Dept of Industrial Engineering, Florida A&M University, Florida State University, 2525 Pottsdamer Street, PO Box 2175, Tallahassee, FL 32316-2175, (904)487-6346.

WANG, BIN
Educator, researcher, scientist. Chinese American. **PERSONAL:** Born Oct 25, 1944, Qingdao, Shandong, China; son of Shuli Wang and Jin Liu; married Bin Wang, Jan 22, 1971; children: Datong, Duzhi. **EDUCATION:** Ocean University of Qingdao, BS, 1966; University of Science and Technology of China, MS, 1982; Florida State University, PhD, 1984. **CAREER:** Shandong Weather Services, meteorologist, 1968-75; Ocean University of Qingdao, lecturer, 1975-78; Chinese Academy of Sciences, assistant researcher, 1978-81; Florida State University, research assistant, 1981-84; Princeton University, visiting scientist, 1984-86; University of Hawaii, professor, 1987-. **ORGANIZATIONS:** American Meteorological Society, 1983-; American Geophysical Union, 1983-; Royal Meteorological Society, 1987-; Equatorial Pacific Ocean Climate Study, council member, 1987-; Tropical Ocean-Global Atmosphere/Coupled Ocean/Atmosphere Experiment, subscientific steering committee; Joint Institute of Marine Atmospheric Research, council member, 1987-. **SPECIAL ACHIEVEMENTS:** Forty scientific papers published in Journal Atmospheric Sciences, Journal of Climate, Tellus, Monthly Weather Review, Quarterly Journal of Royal Meteorological Society, Meteorology and Atmospheric Physics. **BUSINESS ADDRESS:** Professor, Dept of Meteorology, University of Hawaii, 2525 Correa Road, Honolulu, HI 96822, (808)956-2563.

WANG, C. H. (JIM)
Educator. Taiwanese American. **PERSONAL:** Born Sep 14, 1939, Kaohsiung, Taiwan; son of Chi Wang and Chung C Wang; married Lirong, Apr 16, 1963; children: Nency Y, Jenny Y, Elaine, Wilson. **EDUCATION:** National Taiwan University, BS, 1961; Utah State University, MS, 1964; Massachusetts Institute

of Technology, PhD, 1967. **CAREER:** Bell Laboratories, tech staff, 1967-69; University of Utah, professor, 1969-89; University of Nebraska-Lincoln, professor, 1989-. **HONORS/AWARDS:** Alexander von Humboldt Foundation (Germany), US Senior Scientist Award, 1984; Alfred P Sloan Foundation, Fellow, 1972; University of Utah, David P Gardner Fellow, 1981. **SPECIAL ACHIEVEMENTS:** Publication, Condensed Phase Spectroscopy, 1985; Author of over 200 scientific articles in refereed journals. **BIOGRAPHICAL SOURCES:** American Chemical Society Graduate Research Directory. **BUSINESS ADDRESS:** Professor, University of Nebraska-Lincoln, Hamilton 632, Lincoln, NE 68588, (402)472-5346.

WANG, CARL C. T.
Medical instrument company executive. Chinese American. **PERSONAL:** Born Dec 2, 1935, Hankow, Hubei, China; son of Joseph T F Wang and Mona M Y Wang; married Linda Y H Wang, Jul 26, 1963; children: Paul, Andrew, David Chen. **EDUCATION:** Taiwan University, 1953-54; University of Illinois, BSEE, 1958, MSEE, 1959, PhD, 1964. **CAREER:** IBM, research staff, 1964-67; Columbia University, research staff, 1967-69; MicroBit Corp, section manager, 1969-75; Berkeley Bio-Engineering, Inc, R&D, vice president, 1975-79; Cooper Medical Devices, Inc, Science & Technology, vice president, 1979-81; Alcon Surgical, Instrument Research, vice president, 1985-90; Medical Instrument Development Labs, Inc, president, 1981-85, 1991-. **ORGANIZATIONS:** IEEE, 1962-, section chairman, 1979-80; New York Academy of Science, 1970-71; NIH, special consultant, 1983-86; NIMH, special consultant, 1968-71; National Eye Institute, special consultant, 1985; Chinese-American Ophthalmological Society, founding member, 1988-; American Academy of Ophthalmology, 1989-; World Eye Foundation, US/China coordinator, 1985-. **HONORS/AWARDS:** Awarded memberships in the following honor societies: Sigma Tau, Tau Beta Pi, Phi Kappa Phi, Eta Kappa Nu, Pi Mu Epsilon and Sigma Xi; University of Illinois, Dean's List, University Key, Graduate Fellowship Award, 1958-64. **SPECIAL ACHIEVEMENTS:** Granted 9 US patents, 1983-92; founded Ophthalmic Training Center in Hang Zhou, China, 1992; principal, Chinese Language School, Lexington, Massachusetts, 1972-75; approximately 50 professional publications, papers & lectures, 1964-; approximately 20 seminars, workshops & surgical demonstrations in China, 1979-. **MILITARY SERVICE:** Taiwan Military Officer's School, 1954-55. **BIOGRAPHICAL SOURCES:** 2 newspaper interviews, 1 radio station interview, 1990-93; 2 national television appearances in China, 1991, 1992. **BUSINESS ADDRESS:** President, Medical Instrument Development Laboratories, Inc, 2235 Polvorosa Ave, Ste 200, San Leandro, CA 94577, (510)357-3952.

WANG, CHAO-CHENG
Educator. Chinese American. **PERSONAL:** Born Jul 20, 1938, China; son of N S Wang and W T Hsieh Wang; married Sophia C L Wang, Aug 24, 1963; children: Ferdinand T, Edward T. **EDUCATION:** National Taiwan University, BS, 1959; Johns Hopkins University, PhD, 1965. **CAREER:** Johns Hopkins University, assistant professor, associate prof, 1966-68; Rice University, professor, 1968-79, Noah Harding Professor, 1979-, Math Sci Dept, chairman, 1983-89, ME/MS Dept, chairman, 1991-. **ORGANIZATIONS:** State of Texas, professional engineer, 1991-. **HONORS/AWARDS:** Maryland Academy of Science, Distinguished Young Scientist Award, 1968. **SPECIAL ACHIEVEMENTS:** Publications include five books and seventy papers, 1965-. **BUSINESS ADDRESS:** Professor, Dept Mechanical Engineering & Mat Science, Rice University, South Main Street, Houston, TX 77251-1892, (713)285-5259.

WANG, CHARLES B.
Computer company executive. Chinese American. **PERSONAL:** Born Aug 19, 1944, Shanghai, China. **EDUCATION:** Queens College, BS, 1967. **CAREER:** Columbia University, computer programmer; New York City computer service bureau, software sales; Computer Associates, chairman, CEO, 1976-. **BIOGRAPHICAL SOURCES:** "Charles Wang and His Thundering Nerds," Forbes, July 11, 1988, p118. **BUSINESS ADDRESS:** CEO & Chairman of the Board, Computer Associates International, Inc, 1 Computer Associates Plaza, Islandia, NY 11788-7000, (516)342-5224.*

WANG, CHARLES CHEN-DING
Educator, researcher, company executive. Chinese American. **PERSONAL:** Born Sep 4, 1933, Hankow, Hubei, China; son of Pei-hua Wang & Jing-hua Huang Wang; married Yanlin Wang, Aug 27, 1989; children: Paul, Yolanda, Helena. **EDUCATION:** Taiwan College of Engineering, BS, 1957; Brown University, MS, 1958; Stanford University, PhD, 1960. **CAREER:** University of Washington, assistant professor, 1960-63; Philco Research Laboratory, re-

search specialist, 1963-66; Ford Motor Company, principal research physicist, 1966-87; Wayne State University, adjunct professor of physics and electrical engineering, 1978-87; University of Michigan, adjunct professor of physics, 1980-; Peninsula Technologies, president, 1987-. **ORGANIZATIONS:** American Physical Society, fellow, 1963-. **HONORS/AWARDS:** Chinese Academy of Sciences, Honorary Research Professor, 1980. **SPECIAL ACHIEVEMENTS:** Leading contributor in lasers, laser spectroscopy, and nonlinear optics. **MILITARY SERVICE:** Chinese Army, Taiwan, 2nd lt, 1955-57. **BUSINESS ADDRESS:** President, Peninsula Technologies Inc, PO Box 25-0463, Franklin, MI 48025, (810)626-3638.

WANG, CHARLES CHIMING
Business executive. Taiwanese American. **PERSONAL:** Born Dec 14, 1952, Taipei, Taiwan; son of Yung-Lung Wang and Kuo-Jui Liu Wang; married Aichung Wang, Jul 14, 1979. **EDUCATION:** National Chiao-Tung University, Taiwan, BS, 1974; UCLA, MS, 1977, PhD, 1985. **CAREER:** Lin Com Corp, 1979-81; Jet Propulsion Labortory, 1981-89; H and W Investment, Inc, president, 1987-; Everspring Development Inc, president, 1989-; TriLite Technology Corp, president, 1993-. **ORGANIZATIONS:** Phi Tau Phi Scholastic Honor Society, 1974-. **HONORS/AWARDS:** NASA, Six Certificates of Recognition, 1987-92; Alhambra Beautiful Committee, Certification of Commendation, 1987; California Legislature Assembly, Certification of Recognition, 1987. **SPECIAL ACHIEVEMENTS:** Patent granted on land-mobile satellite communication system, 1992. **BUSINESS ADDRESS:** President, Everspring Development Inc & TriLite Technology Corp, 701 S 1st Ave, #285, Arcadia, CA 91006, (818)446-4529.

WANG, CHARLES PEI
Government official. Chinese American. **PERSONAL:** Born Nov 20, 1939, Ta Tien, China; son of Chia Ming Wang and Sue Yen Hsing Wang; married Rita Yen Wang, Dec 25, 1965; children: Angelina. **EDUCATION:** National Cheng Chi University, Taiwan, BA, Chinese language, 1964; St John's University, MA, Asian history, 1967; New York University, certificate, public administration, 1986. **CAREER:** Riverdale Children's Association, caseworker, 1967; Childville, Inc, caseworker, 1968; Chinese American Planning Council, executive director, 1968-89; China Institute of America, president, 1989-93; US Commission on Civil Rights, commissioner, currently. **ORGANIZATIONS:** US Bureau of Census, Asian Pacific Islander Advisory Committee, chair, 1990; United Way of New York City, secretary, 1990-; Human Services Council of New York City, co-chair, 1990-; New York City Partnership, 1987-; Asian American Federation of New York City, vice president, 1990-; New York Govenor's Asian American Advisory Committee, 1987. **HONORS/AWARDS:** National Ethnic Coalition, Ellis Island Medal of Honor, 1990; Borough President, Staten Island Medal of Honor, 1988, Charles Wang Day in Manhattan, 1989; NAACP, New York Chapter, Dynamic Mover's Award, 1987; Organization of Chinese Americans, Man of the Year, 1989. **SPECIAL ACHIEVEMENTS:** Author, Civic Rights Issues of Aging Asian Americans in the 1990's, 1992; Asian Americans in New York, 1974; various newspaper and magazine articles regarding New York Chinatown, 1969-. **BUSINESS ADDRESS:** Commissioner, US Commission on Civil Rights, 624 Ninth St NW, Rm 700, Washington, DC 20425, (202)376-7700.

WANG, CHARLES PING
Scientist. Chinese American. **PERSONAL:** Born Apr 25, 1937, Shanghai, China; son of Kuan-Ying Wang and Ping-Lu Ming Wang; married Lily L Lee, Jun 29, 1963. **EDUCATION:** Taiwan University, BSME, 1959; Tsinghua University, MS, 1961; California Institute of Technology, MS, aeronautics, 1963, PhD, aeronautics, 1967. **CAREER:** Bellcomm, member technical staff, 1967-69; University of San Diego, Dept of Applied Mechanics and Engineering Sciences, research engineer, 1967-74; Aerospace Corp, starting 1974, Aerophysics Laboratory, senior scientist, 1976-86; University of California, San Diego, adjunct professor of engineering physics, 1979-90; Optodyne Inc, president, 1986-. **ORGANIZATIONS:** Chinese-American Engineers and Scientists Assn of Southern California, president, 1979-81; Intl Conference of Lasers, China, program chair, 1979-80; Lasers Conference, organizer, session chair, 1981-84, program chair, 1985; Series in Laser Technology, editor-in-chief, 1983-; American Institute of Aeronautics and Astronautics, AIAA Journal, associate editor, Plasmadynamics and Lasers Technical Committee; American Physics Society; Optical Society of America. **HONORS/AWARDS:** California Institute of Technology, scholar, 1965; American Optical Assn, fellow, 1982; Chinese Academy of Science, honor professor. **SPECIAL ACHIEVEMENTS:** Contributor of articles to professional journals; inventor of discharge excimer laser; developed cw 150-W argon-ion laser, 1972. **BUSINESS AD-**

DRESS: President, Optodyne Inc, 1180 Mahalo Pl, Compton, CA 90220, (310)635-7481.

WANG, CHI-HUA
Educator, chemist. Chinese American. **PERSONAL:** Born 1923, Beijing, China; married Nancy Yang Wang, Aug 9, 1949; children: Fong. **EDUCATION:** St John's University, Shanghai, BS, 1945; Fu-Jen University, Beijing, MS, 1946; St Louis University, PhD, 1951. **CAREER:** Brandis University, instructor, 1951-53, assistant professor, 1953-58, associate professor, 1958-62; Arthur D Little Inc, senior scientist, 1962-64; Wellesley College, associate professor, 1964-68; University of Massachusetts, professor, 1968-. **ORGANIZATIONS:** American Chemical Society, 1955-80; Sigma Xi, 1949-. **SPECIAL ACHIEVEMENTS:** Teaching and research in free radial chemistry; publications: 35 articles; books: Introduction to Physical Org Chemistry (in Chinese), Monographics in Theoretical Organic Chemistry, Chinese Acad of Science. **HOME ADDRESS:** 106 Pleasant Street, Lexington, MA 02173. **BUSINESS PHONE:** (617)287-6148.

WANG, CHI-SUN
Research biochemist. Chinese American. **PERSONAL:** Born Oct 8, 1942, Shanghai, China; son of Po-Jong Wang and Yu-Fu Yang Wang; married Nancy Tao Wang, Oct 27, 1973; children: Christy Pei-Ling. **EDUCATION:** National Taiwan University, Taipei, BS, 1966; University of Oklahoma School of Medicine, PhD, 1971. **CAREER:** University of Oklahoma School of Medicine, adjunct associate professor, 1985-; Oklahoma Medical Research Foundation, postdoctoral fellow, 1971-74, staff scientist, 1974-75, assistant member, 1975-82, associate member, 1982-. **ORGANIZATIONS:** Sigma Xi; American Chemical Society; American Association for the Advancement of Science; American Society for Biochemistry and Molecular Biology; American Oil Chemists Society. **HONORS/AWARDS:** Eason Oil Co, Eason Award, 1977; Oklahoma Medical Research Foundation, Merrick Award, 1981. **SPECIAL ACHIEVEMENTS:** Author of 77 articles published in scientific journals and books. **BUSINESS ADDRESS:** Associate Member, Oklahoma Medical Research Foundation, 825 NE 13th St, Mail Stop #23, Oklahoma City, OK 73104, (405)271-7284.

WANG, CHIEN YI
Government official. Taiwanese American. **PERSONAL:** Born Nov 22, 1942, Fengshan, Taiwan; son of Weng-Yi Wang and Sue-Nee Wang; married Shiow Ying Wang, Nov 30, 1968; children: Jean S, Ken S. **EDUCATION:** National Taiwan University, BS, 1964; Oregon State University, PhD, 1969. **CAREER:** Oregon State University, research assistant, 1965-69; Mid-Columbia Experiment Station, research associate, 1969-76; US Department of Agriculture, research horticulturist, 1976-. **ORGANIZATIONS:** American Society for Horticultural Science, 1969-; American Society of Plant Physiologists, 1969-. **HONORS/AWARDS:** National Academy of Science, Invited Lecturer on Postharvest Physiology, 1984; United Nations Industrial Development Organization, Expert in CA Storage, 1988; Office of International Cooperation and Development, Technical Advisor on chilling injury of fruits and vegetables, 1987; Agency for International Development, Scientic Review Panel, 1986. **SPECIAL ACHIEVEMENTS:** Chairman, Postharvest Working Group of the American Society for Horticultural Science; editor, Chilling Injury of Horticultural Crops; One of the authors of the World Book Encyclopedia. **BUSINESS ADDRESS:** Research Horticulturist, US Department of Agriculture, 10300 Baltimore Ave, Bldg 002, BARC-W, Beltsville, MD 20705-2350, (301)504-6128.

WANG, CHIH-CHUNG
Metallurgist. Chinese American. **PERSONAL:** Born Mar 8, 1922, Wusih, China; son of Chun-Hao and Chinyeh Loh Wang; widowed; children: Clement, Cheryl. **EDUCATION:** Chiao-Tung University, BS, mining & metallurgy, 1945; Illinois Institute of Tech, MS, metallurgy, 1950; MIT, ScD, metallurgy, 1953. **CAREER:** Sylvania Electric Prod Inc, senior engineer, 1953-55; Clerite Transistor Prod Inc, Materials & Metallurgy Department, director, 1955-63; Kennecott Copper Corporation, senior scientist, 1963-78, metal products, manager, 1978-80; Duracell Inc, chief metallurgist, 1981-. **ORGANIZATIONS:** American Institute of Mining, Metallurgical & Petroleum Engineers, 1949-; American Soc Metals, 1953-. **BUSINESS ADDRESS:** Chief Metallurgist, Duracell Inc, 37 A St, Needham, MA 02194, (617)455-9607.

WANG, CHIH H.
Educator (retired). Chinese American. **PERSONAL:** Born Sep 20, 1917, Shanghai, Jiangsu, China; son of Tie-Ya Wang and Yon-Lan Liu; married

Louise M Wang, Jun 30, 1956; children: Deying. **EDUCATION:** Shandong University, Tsingtao, China, BS, 1937; Oregon State University, MS, 1947, PhD, 1950. **CAREER:** Oregon State University, professor of chemistry, 1958-85, director, radiation center, 1962-85, department of nuclear engineering, head, 1972-85. **ORGANIZATIONS:** American Nuclear Society, fellow, 1968-; AAAS, fellow, 1960-; American Chemical Society, 1950-. **HONORS/AWARDS:** Oregon State University, Distinguished Professor, 1976; Oregon Museum of Science, Distinguished Scientist, 1978. **SPECIAL ACHIEVEMENTS:** Oregon Nuclear and Thermal Energy Council, chair, 1970. **BUSINESS ADDRESS:** Professor, Oregon State University, Radiation Ctr, 35th and Jefferson Sts, Corvallis, OR 97331, (503)737-2341.

WANG, CHING CHUNG
Educator, biochemist. Chinese American. **PERSONAL:** Born Feb 10, 1936, Beijing, China; son of Shou-Kang Wang and Frances Tsao Wang; married Alice Lee Wang, Apr 6, 1963; children: Charlotte I-Ting. **EDUCATION:** National Taiwan University, BSc, chemistry, 1958; University of California, Berkeley, PhD, biochemistry, 1966. **CAREER:** Columbia University, research associate, 1966-67; Princeton University, research associate, 1967-69; Merck, Sharp & Dohme Research Laboratory, senior investigator, 1969-81; University of California, San Francisco, professor, 1981-. **ORGANIZATIONS:** American Society of Parasitologists, Northern California Chapter, president, 1985-86; Society of Chinese Bioscientists in America, president, 1986-87; Chinese American Chemical Society, chairman of the board, 1987-88; National Institutes of Health Study Section, 1984-88; World Health Organization, Steering Committees, chairman, 1985-; Intl Laboratory Research Animal Diseases, Nairobi, Kenya, board of directors, 1989-; Golden Gate Regional Center for Develop Handicapped, San Francisco, board of trustees, 1982-88. **HONORS/AWARDS:** Burroughs Wellcome Fund, Molecular Parasitology Award, 1983-88; University of California, San Francisco, Distinction in Teaching Award, 1984-85; American Association Adv Sci, fellow, 1989; Academia Sinica, Taiwan, 1992. **SPECIAL ACHIEVEMENTS:** Coauthor, "An Additional Step in the Transport of Iron Defined by the Ton B Locus of E coli," J Biol Chem, 246, 2147-2151, 1971; "Biochemistry and Physiology of Coccidia," Biology of the Coccidia, chapter 5, pp 167-228, edited by P L Long, University Park Press, 1982; Molecular and Biochemical Parasitology, managing editor, 1988-. **BUSINESS ADDRESS:** Professor of Chemistry and Pharmaceutical Chemistry, University of California, San Francisco, Parnassus St and 3rd Ave, Health Science East, Rm 1199, San Francisco, CA 94143-0446, (415)476-1321.

WANG, CHING-HUA
Educator. Chinese American. **PERSONAL:** Born Sep 30, 1951, Beijing, People's Republic of China; daughter of Lee Wang and Zhi Zhao; married Nian-Sheng Huang, May 25, 1981; children: Sha L Hwang, Enid C Hwang. **EDUCATION:** Beijing Medical College, MD, 1978; Beijing Medical University, MS, 1981; Cornell University, PhD, 1986. **CAREER:** Cornell University, research associate, 1986-90; California State University, assistant professor, 1990-. **ORGANIZATIONS:** American Association of Immunologists, 1990-; American Association for the Advancement of Science, 1990-; Phi Kappa Phi, 1983. **HONORS/AWARDS:** Cornell University, Sage Fellowship, 1983, Graduate Research Fellowship, 1981-86. **SPECIAL ACHIEVEMENTS:** Publications in: Experimental Parasitology, vol 61, p 76-85, 1986, Parasite Immunology, vol 9, p 465-475, 1987, Immunology, vol 71, p 166-175, 1990, Journal of Immunology, vol 145, p 1021-1028, 1990, Cellular and Molecular Biology, vol 38, p 311-325, 1992. **BUSINESS ADDRESS:** Asst Professor, School of Natural Sciences, California State University, 5500 University Pkwy, San Bernardino, CA 92407-2318, (909)880-5365.

WANG, CHRISTINE A.
Scientist. Chinese American. **PERSONAL:** Born Sep 20, 1955, Providence, RI; daughter of James K C Wang and Sui Yen Wang; married Norman F Sheppard, Sep 6, 1980; children: Sarah E Sheppard, Peter A Sheppard. **EDUCATION:** Massachusetts Institute of Technology, BS, 1977, MS, 1978, PhD, 1984. **CAREER:** MIT Lincoln Laboratory, staff scientist, 1984-. **ORGANIZATIONS:** American Association of Crystal Growth, 1984-; Optical Society of America, 1991-; Institute of Electrical and Electronics Engineers, 1992-; Tau Beta Pi, 1977; Sigma Xi, 1977. **HONORS/AWARDS:** ASME, Morris Cohen Metallurgy Award, 1976; MIT, Alumnae Award, 1977; IBM, Pre-Doctoral Award, 1983. **SPECIAL ACHIEVEMENTS:** Over 50 publications; awarded 3 patents. **BUSINESS ADDRESS:** Staff Scientist, MIT, Lincoln Lab, 244 Wood St, #C-119, Lexington, MA 02173, (617)981-4466.

WANG, DAJIN
Educator. Chinese American. **PERSONAL:** Born Nov 27, 1958, Shanghai, People's Republic of China; married. **EDUCATION:** Shanghai University of Science & Technology, BE, 1982; Stevens Institute of Technology, PhD, 1990. **CAREER:** Montclair State College, assistant professor, 1990-. **BUSINESS ADDRESS:** Professor, Dept of Math & Computer Science, Montclair State College, Upper Montclair, NJ 07043, (201)655-7615.

WANG, DANIEL I.-CHYAU
Educator. Chinese American. **PERSONAL:** Born Mar 12, 1936, Nanking, China; son of Shou Chin Wang & Ling Nyi Vee Wang; married Victoria D Wang, Aug 27, 1966; children: Keith F. **EDUCATION:** Massachusetts Institute of Technology, BS, 1959, MS, 1961; University of Pennsylvania, PhD, 1963. **CAREER:** Esso Res & Dev Co, process engineer, 1963; US Army Biological Laboratory, process engineer, 1963-65; Massachusetts Institute of Technology, professor, 1965-. **ORGANIZATIONS:** American Institute of Chemical Engineering, 1965-; American Chemical Society, 1965-; American Society for Microbiology, 1966-92; Institute of Food Technology, 1965-91; Tau Beta Pi, 1959-; American Association for Advancement of Science, 1965-90. **HONORS/AWARDS:** National Academy of Engineering, fellow, 1986; American Academy of Arts & Sciences, fellow, 1985; American Institute for Medical & Biological Engineering, fellow, 1992; Academia Sinica, fellow, 1992; American Institute of Chemical Engineering, Food, Pharmaceutical Bio Eng Award, 1983. **SPECIAL ACHIEVEMENTS:** 200 papers in scientific journals, 1965-; 4 books, 1978-92; 12 patents, 1959-. **MILITARY SERVICE:** US Army, captain, 1963-65, Commendation Medal. **BUSINESS ADDRESS:** Chevron Professor of Chemical Engineering, Massachusetts Institute of Technology, 18 Vassar St, Bldg 20A, Rm 207, Cambridge, MA 02139, (617)253-2126.

WANG, DAVID EDWARD
Lawyer. Chinese American. **PERSONAL:** Born Sep 22, 1964, Camden, NJ; son of Michael Wang and Josephine Wang; married Michelle Robin Wang, May 31, 1992. **EDUCATION:** University of California at Berkeley, 1982-84; University of Southern California, BSEE, 1987, MSEE, 1990, JD, 1993. **CAREER:** Stanford University Linear Accelerator Center, engineering intern, 1986; Xerox Corp, member programming staff, 1987-90; DEW Consultants, president, 1990-92; Morrison & Foerster, summer law associate, 1992; Lyon & Lyon, associate, 1993-. **ORGANIZATIONS:** Southern California Interdisciplinary Journal, staff, 1991-92; Intellectual Property Society, president, 1990-92; Eta Kappa Nu, officer, 1986-87; Tau Beta Pi, 1985-87; American Bar Association, 1993-; Beta Omega Phi, officer, 1984-86; Southern California Chinese Lawyers Association, 1991-. **HONORS/AWARDS:** USC Law Center, Legion Lex Merit-Based Scholarship, 1990-93; Xerox Corp Scholarship, 1987-90; Powell Foundation Scholarship, 1985-87; Occidental College Math Competition Medalist; National Deans' List, American Jurisprudence Awards, 1991; University of California Berkeley Alumni Scholar. **SPECIAL ACHIEVEMENTS:** Judicial Extern for Judge Edward Rafeedie, US District Court, 1992; invited to join Law Center Hale Moot Court for oral advocacy, 1991; California real estate salesperson license. **BUSINESS ADDRESS:** Lawyer, Lyon & Lyon, 611 W Sixth St, Ste 3400, Los Angeles, CA 90017, (213)489-1600.

WANG, DAZONG
Auto company manager. Chinese American. **PERSONAL:** Born May 15, 1954, Jing de Zheng, People's Republic of China; son of Fan Wang and Qing Fang; married Mary, Aug 1980; children: Andy, Amy. **EDUCATION:** Huazhong University of Science & Technology, China, ME, 1981; Cornell University, MS, 1983, PhD, 1985. **CAREER:** Huazhong University of Science & Technology, lecturer, 1980; Cornell University, research assistant, 1981; General Motors Research Labs, senior research engineer, 1985; General Motors, staff research engineer, 1988; General Motors Systems Engineering, section head, senior staff research scientist, 1991-. **ORGANIZATIONS:** Chinese Association of Greater Detroit, president, 1992; American Society of Mechanical Engineers, Simulation Committee, chairman, 1990; Society of Automotive Engineers, 1985; Operations Research Society of America, 1992. **BUSINESS ADDRESS:** Section Head, General Motors Corp, 1151 Crooks Rd, Troy, MI 48084, (313)280-6611.

WANG, DEANE
Educator. Chinese American. **PERSONAL:** Born Mar 8, 1951, New York, NY; son of Derek Wang and Dee Wang; married Carolynne R Norman, Jul 4, 1975; children: Carolynne T L, Diane T M. **EDUCATION:** Harvard College,

BA, 1973; Cornell University, MS, 1977; Yale University, PhD, 1984. **CA-REER:** Roy F Weston Inc, associate research scientist, 1975-78; Yale University, associate in research, 1982-85; University of Washington, assistant professor, 1985-87; University of Vermont, associate professor, 1989-. **ORGANIZATIONS:** Ecological Society of America; Soil Science Society of America; International Association of Landscape Ecologists. **SPECIAL ACHIEVEMENTS:** Co-author, "Comparison of Nutrient-Use Efficiency of Biomass Production in Five Tropical Tree Taxa," For Ecology Management, vol 46, p 1-21, 1991; co-author, "Air Pollution Impacts on Plants: Current Challenges," ISI Atlas of Science, vol 1, no 1, pp 33-39, 1988. **BUSINESS ADDRESS:** Associate Professor, University of Vermont, Aiken Center, Burlington, VT 05405-0001, (802)656-4057.

WANG, DON J.
Banker. Chinese American. **PERSONAL:** Born Apr 29, 1944, Tainan, Taiwan; son of Chen Wang; married Ming Wang; children: Emily, Michael. **EDUCATION:** National Chung Sheng University, BS, 1969; Utah State University, MS, 1972; PhD candidate, 1972-74. **CAREER:** United Oriental Capital Corp, SBA licensee for Minority Enterprise, Small Business Investments Co, president, 1982-88; New Era Life Insurance Co, chairman of the board, 1989-; MetroBank, chairman of the board, 1987-. **ORGANIZATIONS:** Houston Chinese Chamber of Commerce, president, 1987-88; Houston Chinese American Lions Club, first vice president, 1987-88; Houston Police Advisory Committee, mayoral appointee, 1986-91; Texas Department of Commerce Product Commercialization, advisory board, 1990-92; Small Business Development Co of Houston, chairman of the board, 1990-; Greater Houston Partnership, board of directors, 1991-; Asian Chamber of Commerce, board of directors; Taiwanese Chamber of Commerce of North America, president, 1991-92. **HONORS/AWARDS:** Entrepreneur of the Year Award, nominee, 1991; Houston's Entrepreneur of the Year, finalist, 1991. **SPECIAL ACHIEVEMENTS:** Don Wang's Day proclaimed by Houston City Mayor, April, 29 1993. **BIOGRAPHICAL SOURCES:** Houston Post Business Section, Dec 6, 1992; Houston Chronicle, May 21, 1993. **BUSINESS ADDRESS:** Chairman of the Board, Metrobank, NA, 9600 Bellaire Blvd, #101, Houston, TX 77036, (713)776-3876.

WANG, DONG-PING
Educator. Chinese American. **PERSONAL:** Born Sep 12, 1948, Shanghai, China; son of Tien-Hsin Wang and Shen-Bai Wang; married Sheue-Jiau, Oct 11, 1975; children: Ronald, Joanne. **EDUCATION:** Tsinhua University, BS, 1970; University of Miami, PhD, 1975. **CAREER:** Johns Hopkins University, scientist, 1976-80; Argonne National Laboratory, oceanographer, 1980-85; SUNY, Stony Brook, professor, 1985-. **ORGANIZATIONS:** American Geophysics Union, 1976-. **BUSINESS ADDRESS:** Professor, Marine Sciences Research Center, State University of New York, Stony Brook, NY 11790, (516)632-8691.

WANG, DORA CHIA-CHI
Marketing executive. Chinese American. **PERSONAL:** Born Nov 30, 1961, Honolulu, HI; daughter of Jaw-Kai Wang & Kwang Mei Wang. **EDUCATION:** University of Hawaii, 1978-79; Pomona College, BA, 1983; MIT, Sloan School of Management, SM, 1987. **CAREER:** Massachusetts Dept of Public Health, research assistant, 1983-85; Baxter International, business analyst, 1986; Hewlett-Packard Co, financial analyst, 1987-89, financial reporting manager, 1989-90, Hewlett-Packard Singapore, market development manager, 1991-93, Hewlett-Packard Co, product manager, 1993-. **ORGANIZATIONS:** Singapura Ohana, founder, 1991-93. **HONORS/AWARDS:** Shell Oil Co, Shell Oil Century III Leaders Scholar, 1979. **SPECIAL ACHIEVEMENTS:** Fluent in Chinese (Mandarin); Nanjing University, exchange program, 1982. **HOME ADDRESS:** 204 Beacon St #2F, Boston, MA 02116. **BUSINESS ADDRESS:** Product Manager, Hewlett-Packard Co, 3000 Minuteman Rd, Andover, MA 01810, (508)659-4627.

WANG, FA-CHUNG (FRED)
Educator. Chinese American. **PERSONAL:** Born Mar 2, 1939, Chungking, China; son of S H Wang & W F Fan Wang; married Cecilia J Wang, Nov 23, 1969; children: Dean, Jennifer. **EDUCATION:** Tunghai University, BS, 1962; Texas A&M University, MS, 1968, PhD, 1972. **CAREER:** Texas A&M University, Physics Department, postdoctorate, 1980-83; Prairie View A&M University, Physics Department, assistant prof, 1983-88, associate prof, 1988-, Lab for Radiation Studies, associate dir, 1993-. **ORGANIZATIONS:** American Physical Society, 1981-; Prairie View A&M University, research committee, 1991-92, Lab for Radiation Studies, steering committee, 1991-92; faculty

senate, 1987-89; science seminars for junior high students, initiator, coordinator, 1981-83. **SPECIAL ACHIEVEMENTS:** Featured speaker: Understanding and Communicating—A Look At Issues Concerning Asians in America, NASA/GSFC Asian American Career Development Workshop, 1993; reviewer, Fundamentals of Physics, 4th ed, 1993; review panelist, NSF Young Scholar Programs, 1987. **BUSINESS ADDRESS:** Associate Professor of Physics, Prairie View A&M University, PO Box 2724, Harrington Science Bldg, Rm 107D, Prairie View, TX 77446, (409)857-4510.

WANG, FEI-YUE
Educator. Chinese American. **PERSONAL:** Born Nov 2, 1961, Qingdao, Shandong, People's Republic of China; son of Shui-Gan Wang and Mei-Lan Xu; married Wei Xie, Mar 11, 1986; children: Lin. **EDUCATION:** Shandong Institute of Chemical Engineering, Qingdao, Shandong, China, BE, 1981; Zhejiang University, Hangzhou, Zhejiang, China, MS, 1984; Rensselaer Polytechnic Institute, PhD, 1990. **CAREER:** Zhejiang University, instructor, 1984-86; NASA Center for Intelligent Robotic Systems for Space Exploration, research assistant, 1988-90; University of Arizona, assistant professor, 1990-. **ORGANIZATIONS:** Institution of Electrical and Electronics Engineers, 1988-; Association for Computing Machinery, 1990-. **HONORS/AWARDS:** China, Pao Yu-Kong and Pao Zao-Long Scholarship, 1986. **SPECIAL ACHIEVEMENTS:** Co-author, Coordination Theory of Intelligent Machines: Applications in Intelligent Robotic Systems and CIM Systems, Kluwer Academic Publishers, 1993; more than 40 refereed journal papers and more than 30 conference papers. **BUSINESS ADDRESS:** Professor, Dept of Systems & Industrial Engineering, University of Arizona, Old Engineering Bldg, Rm 103, Tucson, AZ 85721, (602)621-6558.

WANG, FRANCIS WEI-YU
Government official. Taiwanese American. **PERSONAL:** Born Jul 21, 1936, Peikang, Taiwan; son of Ying-Kwei Wang and Tsai-Wei Tseng Wang; married Susan Liao Wang, Jun 18, 1966; children: Anthony F, Andrea S, Edwin F. **EDUCATION:** California Institute of Technology, BS, chemical engineering, 1961, MS, chemical engineering, 1962; University of California, San Diego, PhD, physical chemistry, 1971. **CAREER:** National Inst of Stds & Technology, Polymers Division, group leader, supervisory research chemist, 1972-. **ORGANIZATIONS:** American Chemical Society, 1971-; American Physical Society, 1972-. **HONORS/AWARDS:** US Department of Commerce, Bronze Medal Award, 1985; US Public Health Service, Post Doctoral Fellowship, 1971. **SPECIAL ACHIEVEMENTS:** More than 70 publications in polymer science & engineering and in fluorescence spectroscopy, 1971-. **HOME ADDRESS:** 19505 Tiber Court, Gaithersburg, MD 20879. **BUSINESS ADDRESS:** Group Leader, National Institute of Standards and Technology, Routes 117 & 124, Building 224, Room B320, Gaithersburg, MD 20899, (301)975-6726.

WANG, FREDERICK ANDREW
Computer industry executive. Chinese American. **PERSONAL:** Born Sep 12, 1950, Boston, MA; son of An Wang & Lorraine C Wang; married Laurel A O'Connor, Oct 5, 1985; children: Andrea Katharine, Allison Sarah. **EDUCATION:** Brown University, ScB, applied math, 1972; Harvard University, John F Kennedy School of Government, MA, public administration, 1991. **CAREER:** Wang Laboratories, president, COO, 1986-89; Wang & Associates, Inc, director, 1989-, president, 1993-. **ORGANIZATIONS:** Museum of Science, Boston, overseer, 1981-; New England Medical Center, governor, 1990-; John F Kennedy Library Foundation, Inc, director, 1980-; 1000 Friends of Massachusetts, vice chairman, 1992-; Wang Center for the Performing Arts, trustee, 1983-. **BUSINESS ADDRESS:** President, Wang & Associates, Inc, 454 Grove St, Needham, MA 02192, (617)237-2695.

WANG, GARY S. H.
Company executive. Singaporean American. **PERSONAL:** Born Jul 13, 1960, Singapore; married Dawn Marie, Mar 31, 1992; children: Alexis Aisha. **EDUCATION:** Brighton College, A level, 1978; California State Polytechic, BS, finance (w/honors), 1988. **CAREER:** Cambridge Systems Group, marketing, 1982-86; ASCOM Communications, Inc, director of regulatory affairs, 1989-; Integrated Communications Corp, executive vice president, currently. **ORGANIZATIONS:** Florida Pay Telephone Association, legal committee, 1992-93; American Public Communications Council, 1989-93. **MILITARY SERVICE:** Singapore Armed Forces, Signals, corporal, 1978-80. **BUSINESS ADDRESS:** Executive Vice President, Integrated Communications Corp, 600 W Hillsboro Blvd, Ste 316, Deerfield Beach, FL 33441, (305)420-5500.

WANG, GENE
Software company executive. Chinese American. **PERSONAL:** Born May 5, 1957, Ann Arbor, MI; son of William S-Y Wang and Josephine Szeto; widowed; children: Gina. **EDUCATION:** University of California, Berkeley, BS, computer science, 1979. **CAREER:** Gold Hill Computers, vice president, founder, 1983-88; Borland, vice president, general manager, 1988-92; Symantec, executive vice president, 1992-. **BUSINESS ADDRESS:** Executive Vice President, Products, Symantec, 10201 Torre Ave, Cupertino, CA 95014.

WANG, GEORGE H.
Attorney. Chinese American. **PERSONAL:** Born Feb 12, 1952, New York, NY; son of Thomas Wang and En-Ming Chen; married Kyung, Sep 2, 1989. **EDUCATION:** Cornell University, BS, 1973; Massachusetts Institute of Technology, SM, 1975; Cornell Law School, JD, 1978. **CAREER:** Breed Abbott & Morgan, attorney; Ruffa & Hanover, attorney, until 1988; Sutherland Asbill & Brennan, partner, 1988-. **ORGANIZATIONS:** National Association of Securities Dealers, Inc, arbitrator, 1988-; MIT, Board of Educational Counselors, Educational Counselor, 1985-; Association of the Bar of the City of New York, 1979-. **BUSINESS ADDRESS:** Partner, Sutherland, Asbill and Brennan, 1270 Ave of the Americas, New York, NY 10020, (212)332-3000.

WANG, GEORGE HUNG-KAI
Government official. Chinese American. **PERSONAL:** Born Dec 22, 1939, China; son of Ping Yueh Wang & Gloria Lee Wang; married Susana C Wang, Jan 15, 1968; children: Connie Y, Greg S. **EDUCATION:** Taiwan Chung-Hsing University, BS, 1963; Northern Illinois University, MA economics, 1969; Iowa State University, PhD, statistics and economics, 1976. **CAREER:** Transportation System Center, US DOT, senior economist and econometrician, 1974-83; Federal Home Loan Bank Board, senior financial economist, 1983-87; George Mason University, visiting professor of finance, 1989-90; Commodity Futures Trading Commission and Econometrician, senior econometrician, financial economist, 1987-. **ORGANIZATIONS:** American Statistical Association; American Finance Association; Financial Management Association; Mu Sigma Rho; Omicron Delta Epsilon. **SPECIAL ACHIEVEMENTS:** Co-author: "Estimation of Seemingly Unrelated Regression with Lagged Dependent Variables and Autocorrelated Errors," Journal of Statistical Computation and Simulation, vol 10, p 133-146, 1980; "A Study of Leading Economic Indicators in Rail Freight Traffic Cycles: 1950-1976," Transportation Research, Part B: Methodological Issue, 15B, p 391-405, December 1981; "A Time Series Analysis of the Relationship Between Capital Stock and Federal Debt," Journal of Money, Credit and Banking, vol 18, no 4, p 527-538, Nov 1986; "Examination Ratings and the Identification of Problem/Non-problem Thrift Institutions," Journal of Financial Service Research, vol 2, p 319-342, 1989; "Empirical Analysis of the Liquidity of the S & P 500 Index Future Market During October 1987 Market Break," in Advances in Futures and Options Research, vol 4, edited by Frank J Fabozi, JAI Press Inc, p 191-218, 1990; "Determinants of the ARM Share of National and Regional Lending," Journal of Real Estate Finance and Economics, p 219-234, 1992. **BUSINESS ADDRESS:** Sr Financial Economist, Div of Economic Analysis, Commodity Futures Trading Commission, 2033 K St, NW, Washington, DC 20581, (202)254-6990.

WANG, GEORGE MAOSUE
Educator. Taiwanese American. **PERSONAL:** Born Sep 2, 1933, Chunghua, Taiwan; son of Hsiang-Hsue Wang and Cho Miang Wang; married Maria M Wang, Dec 2, 1962; children: John J, Nancy M. **EDUCATION:** Chung Hisng University, Taiwan, BA, 1960; University of Idaho, MA, 1966; University of Oklahoma, MLS, 1969. **CAREER:** Eastern State Hospital, institution counselor, 1966-67; New Mexico Highlands University, asst librarian, 1969-88, asst professor, 1976-. **ORGANIZATIONS:** American Library Association, 1994-; New Mexico Library Assn, 1970-, Conference Site Committee, 1991-; Natl Educ Assn, 1975-; New Mexico Educ Assn, 1975-; New Mexico Highlands University, Intl Students Club, asst to foreign students adviser, 1988-, Alumni Assn, 1987-, Library Committee, 1992-. **HONORS/AWARDS:** New Mexico Library Assn, Poster Contest Initiator, 1986-87, NMLA Conference, conference site initiator and planner, 1993; New Mexico Highlands University, Person of the Week, Oct 1988. **SPECIAL ACHIEVEMENTS:** Author, "Government Documents Can Help," La Mecha, 54:23, 1980; "Welcome to Las Vegas, New Mexico," NMLA Newsletter, 20:3, Sep 1992; "NMLA Conference in Las Vegas, 1993," NMLA Newsletter, 21:3, Sept 1993; language proficiencies: Chinese, English. **MILITARY SERVICE:** ROTC (Military Acad), Taiwan, lieutenant, 1955-56. **BUSINESS ADDRESS:** Asst Profes-

sor, Education Dept, New Mexico Highlands University, National Ave, Las Vegas, NM 87701, (505)454-3536.

WANG, GING-LONG
Physician. Taiwanese American. **PERSONAL:** Born Nov 20, 1938, Feng-Shang, Taiwan; son of Ming-Shun Wang and Fang C Wang; married Athena T Wang, Aug 6, 1965; children: Mona C, Philein D, Areta E. **EDUCATION:** National Taiwan University, MD, 1964; University of Michigan, Rackham Graduate School, MMedSc, 1971, School of Public Health, MPH, 1972. **CAREER:** SF Chinatown Child Development Center, program director, 1973; UCSF Langley Porter Psychiatric Institute, associate clinical professor of psychiatry, 1986-; CPC Walnut Creek Hospital, program director, children's unit, 1992-; private practice of psychiatry & child psychiatry, 1972-. **ORGANIZATIONS:** American Psychiatric Association, 1972-; American Academy of Child and Adolescent Psychiatry, fellow, 1977-; California Medical Association, 1972-; Chinese-American Physicians Society, 1977-; Northern California Taiwan Medical Association, 1987-. **HONORS/AWARDS:** American Board of Psychiatry and Neurology, examiner, oral section for certifcation of child psychiatry, 1980. **SPECIAL ACHIEVEMENTS:** Author, "Current Theory and Practice of Psychiatry in America," vol 7, Essays on Contemporary Social and Behavioral Sciences in USA, public 12-73, Chinese. **MILITARY SERVICE:** Military Medical Services, Chinese Army, Taiwan, second lieutenant, 1964-65. **BUSINESS ADDRESS:** Physician, 20081 Lake Chabot Road, Castro Valley, CA 94546, (510)886-1736.

WANG, GUO-HUA
Library coordinator. Chinese American. **PERSONAL:** Born Nov 26, 1955, Suzhou, Jiangsu, People's Republic of China; daughter of Zhen-Tin Wang and Su-Zhen Xu; married Haian Fu, Jul 27, 1983; children: Robert Wang Fu. **EDUCATION:** Anhwei University, BA, 1982; Rosary College, MLS, 1987; University of Wisconsin, Madison, specialist, 1989. **CAREER:** Harvard University, Fine Art Library, supervisor, 1989-90; Boston University, Mugar Library, search unit coordinator, 1990-. **ORGANIZATIONS:** American Library Association, 1990-; Beta Phi Mu Honorary Society in Library Science, 1991-. **HONORS/AWARDS:** Beta Phi Mu, Honorary Society in International Library and Information Science. **BUSINESS ADDRESS:** Search Unit Coordinator, Boston University Mugar Library, 771 Commonwealth Ave, Boston, MA 02215, (617)353-8906.

WANG, GWO-CHING
Educator. Chinese American. **PERSONAL:** Born Oct 10, 1946, In-Chen, Hu-Pei, China; daughter of Wen-Chang Wang and Hua-Sin Yang Wang; married Toh-Ming Lu, Jan 8, 1980; children: Victor. **EDUCATION:** Cheng-Kung University, Taiwan, BS, 1968; Northern Illinois University, MS, 1973; University of Wisconsin-Madison, PhD, 1978. **CAREER:** National Bureau of Standards, post doc, 1978-80; Oak Ridge National Lab, staff scientist, 1980-84; Rensselaer Polytechnic Institute, associate professor, 1984-91, professor, 1991-. **ORGANIZATIONS:** American Vacuum Society, 1980-, TN chapter, secretary, 1978; Physical Electronics Conference, general committee, 1983-86; 53rd Physical Electronics Conference, local chair, 1993; Chinese Community Center, school principal, 1992-93; American Physics Society, 1978; Material Research Society, 1984. **HONORS/AWARDS:** Rensselaer Polytechnic Institute, early career award, 1988; 38th Physical Electronic Conference, Nottingham Award, 1978. **SPECIAL ACHIEVEMENTS:** Over 90 refereed papers; co-author, Diffraction from Rough Surfaces and Dynamic Growth Front, book, 1993; proficient in Chinese. **BUSINESS ADDRESS:** Professor, Rensselaer Polytech Institute, 110 8th St, 1W02 Science Center, Troy, NY 12180-3590, (518)276-8387.

WANG, GWO-JAW
Physician, educator. Chinese American/Taiwanese American. **PERSONAL:** Born Feb 9, 1940, Taipei, Taiwan; son of Yao-Tung Wang & Chon-T Tsai-Wang; married Chen-Mei Amy Wang, Feb 24, 1969; children: Lillian I L, Margaret L L, Thomas L. **EDUCATION:** Kaohsiung Medical School, MD, 1966; Virginia Medical School, MD, orthopedic surgery, 1974. **CAREER:** University of Virginia, assistant professor, 1975-79, associate professor, 1979-84, professor, 1984-93, professor, chair, 1993-. **ORGANIZATIONS:** American Medical Association, 1975; American Academy of Orthopedic Surgery, 1977; Orthopedic Research Society, 1977; American College of Surgeons, 1977; Cervical Spine Research Society, 1979; American Orthopedic Association, 1985; Hip Society, 1990. **HONORS/AWARDS:** West Suburban Hospital, Outstanding Intern Award, 1970; University of Virginia, Outstanding Attending Award, 1981; Hip Society, AAOS, Stinchfield Award, 1986, Otto

Anfranc Award, 1992; Kaohsiung Medical School, Outstanding Alumni Award, 1993. **SPECIAL ACHIEVEMENTS:** Publication of 65 papers involving fracture healing and bone circulation. **MILITARY SERVICE:** Air Force, 2nd lt, 1966-67. **BUSINESS ADDRESS:** Professor, Chairman, Dept of Orthopedic Surgery, University of Virginia Hospital, Jefferson Park Ave, Box 159, Charlottesville, VA 22908, (804)924-5508.

WANG, H. E. FRANK
Aerospace engineer manager. Chinese American. **PERSONAL:** Born Oct 23, 1929, China; married Ming-Min, Aug 27, 1955; children: Joseph, Joyce. **EDUCATION:** National Taiwan University, BS, 1952; Bucknell University, MS, 1954; Brown University, PhD, 1959. **CAREER:** Boeing Co, research associate, 1958-60; The Aerospace Corp, principal director, 1960-92; Industrial Technology Research Institute, Taiwan, deputy general director, 1992-93. **ORGANIZATIONS:** American Institute of Aeronautics & Astronautics, associate fellow, 1968; Chinese-American Engineers & Scientists Association of Southern California, president, 1984-85, chairman, 1987-88. **HONORS/ AWARDS:** The Aerospace Corp, Asian-Pacific American of the Year, 1985; CESASC, service award, 1990. **SPECIAL ACHIEVEMENTS:** Managed the successful Space Test Program for ten years at the Aerospace Corp.; participated in the success of space shuttle mission 39, April-May, 1991. **HOME ADDRESS:** 27241 Sunnyridge Rd, Palos Verdes Peninsula, CA 90274, (310)377-7053.

WANG, HAI-TAO
Engineer. Chinese American. **PERSONAL:** Born Dec 16, 1954, Taipei, Taiwan; son of Chau-Yueh and Chi-Mei Wang; married Brenda S L Wang, Jul 15, 1978; children: Charlene, Tiffany. **EDUCATION:** Massachusetts Institute of Technology, BS, 1976, MS, 1978. **CAREER:** Sikorsky Aircraft, engineer, 1978-79; Control Data Corp, sr structure engineer, 1979-80; CIBA-Geigy Corp, sr research engineer, 1980-84; Swedlow Inc, sr project engineer, 1984-91; ASTECH/MCI Mfg Inc, engineering structures specialist, 1991-. **ORGANIZATIONS:** Society for the Advancement of Material and Process Engineering, 1986-; American Society of Mechanical Engineers, 1978-. **SPECIAL ACHIEVEMENTS:** Articles: "Interlaminar Crack Growth in Fiber Reinforced Composite During Fatigue," Transactions of the ASME, Journal of Engineering Materials and Technology, vol 101, No 1, Jan, 1979; "Silicone Interlayer Adhesion Characteristics," Conference on Aerospace Transparent Materials and Enclosures. **BUSINESS ADDRESS:** Engineering Structures Specialist, ASTECH/MCI Manufacturing, Inc, 3030 Red Hill Avenue, Santa Ana, CA 92705.

WANG, HELEN HAI-LING
Pathologist. Chinese American. **PERSONAL:** Born Apr 6, 1950, Taipei, Taiwan; daughter of Teh-Lung Wang and Tien Yuan Wang. **EDUCATION:** National Taiwan University, College of Medicine, MD, 1975; Harvard University, School of Public Health, MPH, 1976, DrPH, 1979. **CAREER:** Beth Israel Hospital, associate pathologist, 1989-; Harvard Medical School, assistant professor, 1989-. **BUSINESS ADDRESS:** Associate Pathologist, Assistant Professor, Beth Israel Hospital, 330 Brookline Avenue, Boston, MA 02215.

WANG, HENRY YEE-NEEN
Educator. Chinese American. **PERSONAL:** Born Jul 22, 1951, Shanghai, People's Republic of China; married Evangeline Cesar, Mar 1983; children: Stephanie. **EDUCATION:** Iowa State University, BS, 1972; MIT, SM, 1974, PhD, 1977. **CAREER:** Merck & Co, engineering associate, 1977-78; Schering Plough, senior scientist, 1978-79; University of Michigan, professor of chemical engineering, 1979-. **ORGANIZATIONS:** AIChE; ACS; ASM; SIM; AAAS. **HONORS/AWARDS:** ACS, Peterson Award, 1975; University of Michigan, DuPont Faculty Award, 1979. **SPECIAL ACHIEVEMENTS:** Author of over 80 publications; consultant of various companies; proficient in Chinese. **HOME ADDRESS:** 1215 Bardstown Trail, Ann Arbor, MI 48105, (313)996-1512. **BUSINESS ADDRESS:** Professor, Dept of Chemical Engineering, University of Michigan, Ann Arbor, Ann Arbor, MI 48109-2136, (313)763-5659.

WANG, HOWARD H.
Educator. Chinese American. **PERSONAL:** Born Jan 24, 1942, Shanghai, China; son of Charles & Lola Wang; married Judith, Aug 17, 1963; children: Maureen, Kevin. **EDUCATION:** California Institute of Technology, BS, 1963; University of California, Los Angeles, PhD, 1968. **CAREER:** Stanford University, visiting professor, 1985-87; University of Utrecht, The Netherlands, visiting professor, 1976-77; Lawrence Radiation Laboratory, chemist,

1968-69; Massachusetts Institute of Technology, resident scientist, 1969-70; University of California, Santa Cruz, professor, 1970-. **ORGANIZATIONS:** AAAS; Society for Neuroscience; Biophysical Society. **BUSINESS ADDRESS:** Professor, Dept of Biology, University of California, Santa Cruz, CA 95064, (408)459-4593.

WANG, HSUEH-HWA
Researcher, educator. Chinese American. **PERSONAL:** Born Jul 10, 1923, Peking, China; daughter of Shih-Chiek Wang and Teh-hwa Hsiao; married Shih-hsun Ngai, Nov 6, 1948; children: Mae, Janet, John. **EDUCATION:** National Central University, Nanking, China, MB, 1946. **CAREER:** Columbia University, professor, pharmacology, 1980-90, professor emeritus, 1990-. **ORGANIZATIONS:** Chinese American Medical Society, president, 1982, executive director, 1986-. **HONORS/AWARDS:** Outstanding Woman Scientist Award (AWIS), 1991. **SPECIAL ACHIEVEMENTS:** Research in cardiovascular physiology and pharmacology, especially central nervous system control of circulation, regulation of coronary circulation and effects of autacoids on peripheral circulation. **HOME ADDRESS:** 281 Edgewood Avenue, Teaneck, NJ 07666, (201)833-1506.

WANG, HUAQING
Educator. Chinese American. **PERSONAL:** Born Apr 18, 1949, Wuhan, Hubei, People's Republic of China; son of Yusan Wang and Geizheng Yu; married Sanyuan Hu; children: Ying, Sally. **EDUCATION:** Huazhong University of Science & Technology, diploma, 1977; Case Western Reserve University, PhD, 1988. **CAREER:** Huazhong University of Science & Technology, faculty member, 1977-83; California State University, Bakersfield, associate professor, 1988-. **SPECIAL ACHIEVEMENTS:** Two papers on database query language published in IEEE magazines, several others published by different sources. **BIOGRAPHICAL SOURCES:** "A Relational Calculus with Set Operators, Its Safety, and Equivalent Graphical Language," IEEE Transaction on Software Engineering, pp 1038-1052, Sept 1988; "Example-Based Graphical Database Query Language," IEEE Computer, pp 25-38, May 1993. **BUSINESS ADDRESS:** Assoc Professor, California State University, Bakersfield, 9001 Stockdale Hwy, Science Bldg, #404, Bakersfield, CA 93311-1099, (805)664-2357.

WANG, I-CHIH
Educator. Chinese American. **PERSONAL:** Born Apr 9, 1930, Peking, China; son of Shih-Chai Wang & Ray-Lane Yeh; married Venetia Wang, Jun 17, 1960; children: Albert, Linda Wang Cyr. **EDUCATION:** National Taiwan University, BS, 1955; University of Illinois, MS, 1960, PhD, 1963. **CAREER:** University of Cincinnati, professor, 1966-93. **ORGANIZATIONS:** ASME, 1963-93. **HOME ADDRESS:** 12 Far Hills Dr, Cincinnati, OH 45208, (513)321-2112. **BUSINESS ADDRESS:** Professor, University of Cincinnati, Mail Loc #72, 590 Rhodes Hall, Cincinnati, OH 45221, (513)556-2726.

WANG, I-SHOU
Educator, educational administrator. Chinese American. **EDUCATION:** National Taiwan University, BS, 1961; University of Minnesota, MA, 1966, PhD, 1971. **CAREER:** California State University, Academic Planning & Resources, associate vice president, currently. **BUSINESS ADDRESS:** Associate Vice President for Academic Planning & Resources, California State University, Northridge, 18111 Nordhoff St, Northridge, CA 91330.

WANG, JAMES C. F.
Educator. Chinese American. **PERSONAL:** Born Apr 4, 1926, Nanling, Anhui, China; married Sally C Wang, May 6, 1960; children: Sarah O, Eric K. **EDUCATION:** Oberlin College, BA, 1950; University of Hawaii, PhD, 1971. **CAREER:** East-West Center, Honolulu; University of Hawaii, professor, political science & intl studies, currently. **ORGANIZATIONS:** Asian Studies Assn; Law of the Sea Institute. **HONORS/AWARDS:** American Assn of Libraries, Outstanding Academic Book, 1993. **SPECIAL ACHIEVEMENTS:** Author: book on ocean politics and law. **BUSINESS ADDRESS:** Professor, Political Science Dept, University of Hawaii at Hilo, Hilo, HI 96720-4091.

WANG, JAMES CHOU
Educator. Chinese American. **PERSONAL:** Born Nov 18, 1936, Kiangsu, China; son of Chin Wang and H-L Shih Wang; married Sophia Shu-lan Hwang; children: Janice S, Jessica A. **EDUCATION:** National Taiwan University, Taipei, Taiwan, BS, 1959; University of South Dakota, MA, 1961; University of Missouri, PhD, 1964. **CAREER:** National Taiwan University, assistant

instructor, 1959-60; California Institute of Tech, chemistry research fellow, 1964-66; University of California, Berkeley, Chemistry Department, assistant professor, 1966-69, associate professor, 1969-74, professor, 1974-77; Harvard University, professor of biochemistry & molecular biology, 1977-88, Mallinckrodt Professor of Biochemistry & Molecular Biology, 1988-. **HONORS/ AWARDS:** US National Academy of Sciences, Molecular Biology Award, 1983; University of California, Berkeley, Chancellor's Distinguished Lectureship, 1984; The Guggenheim Foundation, Guggenheim Fellowship, 1986-87; University of Texas, MD Anderson Cancer Center, Distinguished Faculty Lecturer, 1989; University of Missouri, Distinguished Alumnus Award, 1991.

WANG, JASON T. L.
Educator. Taiwanese American. **PERSONAL:** Born Nov 23, 1958, Taiwan; son of Pao-Chieh Wang and Tzu-Chen Yen; married Lynn Yin-Hsung Wang, Dec 23, 1988; children: Tiffany. **EDUCATION:** National Taiwan University, BS, 1980; Memphis State University, MS, 1985; New York University, MS, 1988, PhD, 1991. **CAREER:** NCC, Taipei, application programmer, 1982-83; Memphis State University, teaching assistant, 1983-85; New York University, teaching assistant, 1985-88; New York Institute of Technology, adjunct instructor, 1988-89; New York University, research assistant, 1988-91; New Jersey Institute of Technology, assistant professor, 1991-. **ORGANIZATIONS:** Association for Computing Machinery, 1984-; Institute for Electrical and Electronic Engineers, 1987-; American Association for Artificial Intelligence, 1993. **HONORS/AWARDS:** Courant Institute, New York University, fellowship recipient, 1985-89; New Jersey Institute of Technology, Two Step Merit Increase Award, 1993; National Science Foundation, grantee, 1993-96. **SPECIAL ACHIEVEMENTS:** "A System for Approximate Tree Matching," IEEE Trans on Knowledge & Data Engineering, 1994; "On Research Issues Regarding Uncertain Query Processing," J Systems Integration, 1993; "TEXPROS: An Intelligent Document Processing System," Int J Software Engineering & Knowledge Engineering, 1992; "Optimizing Equi-Join Queries in Distributed Databases," ACM Transactions Database Systems, 1991; "New Techniques for Best-Match Retrieval," ACM Transactions on Information Systems, 1990; "Exact and Approximate Algorithms for Unordered Tree Matching," IEEE Trans on Systems, Man and Cybernetics, 1994; "Approximate Tree Matching in the Presence of Variable Length Don't Cares," Journal of Algorithms, 1994. **BIOGRAPHICAL SOURCES:** ACM Computing Reviews, vol 32, June 1991. **BUSINESS ADDRESS:** Professor, Dept of Computer and Info Science, New Jersey Institute of Technology, University Heights, Newark, NJ 07102, (201)596-3396.

WANG, JAW-KAI
Educator. Chinese American. **PERSONAL:** Born Mar 4, 1932, Nanjing, China; son of Shu-Ling Wang and Hsi-Ying Lo; divorced; children: Angela Chia-Chen, Dora Chia-Chi, Lawrence Chia-Yen. **EDUCATION:** National Taiwan University, BS, 1953; Michigan State University, PhD, 1958. **CAREER:** University of Hawaii, assistant professor, 1959-64, associate professor, Agricultural Engineering Department, chairman, 1964-68, professor, Agricultural Engineering, chairman, 1968-75, professor of biosystems engineering, 1975-, Aquaculture Program, CTAHR, director, 1990-; Aquaculture Technology, president, founder, 1990-. **ORGANIZATIONS:** American Society of Agricultural Engineering, Aquacultural Eng Comm, chairman, 1977-79, 1989-91, Graduate Instruction Comm, chairman, 1971-73, vice chairman, 1970-71, various technical committees, 1969-; United States-Japan National Res, aquaculture panel, 1992; Aquacultural Engineering, editorial board, 1982-; FAO, United Nations, expert panel on agricultural mechanization, 1984-1990; registered professional engineer. **HONORS/AWARDS:** American Society of Agricultural Engineering, Pacific Region, Engineer of the Year, 1976, Kishida International Award, 1991, fellow, 1980; State of Hawaii, Exemplary State Employee, 1986, Governor's Award for Distinguished State Service, 1990; American Institute for Medical and Biological Engineering, fellow, 1994. **SPECIAL ACHIEVEMENTS:** Over 120 technical papers published; Phase I and Phase II recipient, Small Business Innovative Research/USDA Grants; scientific research leadership via various grants at University of Hawaii; proficiency in Chinese. **BUSINESS ADDRESS:** Professor, Dept of Biosystems Engineering, University of Hawaii, 3050 Maile Way, 110 Gilmore Hall, Honolulu, HI 96822, (808)956-8154.

WANG, JEN-YU
Educator, business executive. Chinese American. **PERSONAL:** Born Mar 3, 1915, China; son of Ji-Chuan Wang and Yu-Chi Wu Wang. **EDUCATION:** Fujian Christian University, BS, physics, 1938; University of Wisconsin, MS, meterology, 1955, PhD, meterology, 1958. **CAREER:** Fujian Christian Uni-

versity, dean and professor, 1947-48; University of Chicago, research assistant, 1951-53; University of Wisconsin, research associate, 1953-55, assistant professor, 1955-64; San Jose State College, associate professor, 1964-67; San Jose State University, professor, 1967-; Environmental Sciences Institute, director, 1968-71; Milieu Information Service, Inc, president, currently. **ORGANIZATIONS:** US Weather Bureau, consultant, 1957; Natl Science Foundation, guest lecturer, 1963; Standard Research Institute, research consultant, 1966-67, Economic Dept, consultant, 1972-73; ARI, Natl Academy of Science, consultant, 1968-69; WMO, United Nations, 1970; Sino-American Institute, vice president, 1972-85; John Mowlem Inc, London, UK, consultant, 1982-83. **HONORS/AWARDS:** Fujian Christian University, Alumni Gold Medal, 1938; Assn of Distinguished American Scientists, honorary president, 1972; University of Wisconsin, doctor of philosophy, 1958. **SPECIAL ACHIEVEMENTS:** "A Computerized Weather Monitoring Unit for Farm Operation," Interciencia, vol 6, no 4, pp 254-256; Agriculture and Its Environment-Prediction and Control, Kendall Hunt Publishing Co, 1984; Exploring Man's Environment, Cummings Publishing Co, Inc, 1973; "Methods of Agrometeorology," in: Agricultural Meteorology, WMO, United Nations, 1972; Instruments for Physical Environmental Measurements, vol I & II, Kendall Hunt, 1983. **BIOGRAPHICAL SOURCES:** "As It Looks to Me," by John Carew, Michigan State University, in Vegetable Grower, p 22, May 1961; "Crowding into Cities Is Nation's Biggest Crime," East San Jose Sun, p 8, Sep 16, 1970. **BUSINESS ADDRESS:** President, Milieu Information Service, Inc, 1966 Meridian Ave, San Jose, CA 95125-5543, (408)723-2167.

WANG, JI-PING
Researcher, pharmacist. Chinese American. **PERSONAL:** Born Sep 13, 1948, Tang-Shan, Hebei, China; daughter of Shao-Hsun Wang and Liang-Shon Hu; married Si Luo, Feb 16, 1977; children: Lai, Laura, Luo. **EDUCATION:** University of Washington, BS, pharmacy, (magna cum laude), 1987, MS, 1992. **CAREER:** Beijing Municipal Institute of Drug Inspection, pharmacist, 1978-81; Luke's Pharmacy, Seattle, pharmacist, 1988-91; University of Washington, research scientist, 1991- . **ORGANIZATIONS:** American Pharmaceutical Association, 1984-91; Washington State Pharmacists Association, 1992-. **HONORS/AWARDS:** University of Washington, Scholastic Achievement Award, 1985, Merck Award, 1986. **SPECIAL ACHIEVEMENTS:** Co-author, Simple & Rapid, HPLC Assay for Zidovudine in Plasma and Urine, Journal of Chrometography, vol 430, p 420-423, 1988; co-author, Dose Ranging Pharmacokinetics of Zidovudine National Pharmaceutical Research, vol 6, no 8, p 734-36, 1989; first author, Disposition of Drugs in Cystic Fibrosis IV, Clinical Pharmacology and Therapeutics, vol 54, p 323-328, 1993; co-author, Disposition of Drugs in Cystic Fibrosis V, Clinical Pharmacology & Therapeutics, vol 54, p 293-302, 1993. **BUSINESS ADDRESS:** Research Scientist, Dept of Pharmaceutics, University of Washington, BG-20, Seattle, WA 98195-0001, (206)685-0901.

WANG, JIA
Educator. Chinese American. **PERSONAL:** Born Jan 17, 1954, Shanghai, People's Republic of China; son of Li Wang and Geng Xiang; married Yuan Li Yan; children: Kang. **EDUCATION:** Fu Dan University, diploma, 1980; California State University, Fresno, MBA, 1988; University of Tennessee, PhD, 1991. **CAREER:** Shanghai Science & Technology Committee, manager, 1980-84; University of Tennessee, research assistant, 1988-91; California State University, professor, 1991-. **ORGANIZATIONS:** Academy of Management, 1988-; Strategic Management Society, 1988-; Phi Kappa Phi, 1989-. **SPECIAL ACHIEVEMENTS:** Coauthor, "The Fortune Corporate Reputation Index: Reputation for What?," Journal of Management, 1994; "Boards of Directors and Hostile Takeovers, Journal of Managerial Issues, 4: 269-287, 1992; Board Composition and Corporate Philanthropy," Journal of Business Ethics, 11: 771-778, 1992; "Boards of Directors and Stakeholder Orientation," Journal of Business Ethics, 11: 115-123, 1992, Proceedings of the 1991 Southern Management Meeting, 1991; Outside Director Composition and Corporate Performance: A Model and Propositions, Proceedings of the 1990 Southern Management Meeting, 1990. **BUSINESS ADDRESS:** Professor, California State University of Fresno, 5245 N Backer, Fresno, CA 93740-0007, (209)278-4977.

WANG, JIE
Educator. Chinese American. **PERSONAL:** Born Aug 28, 1961, Guangzhou, Guangdong, People's Republic of China; son of Yue-Yun Wang and Lian-Fang Hu; married Hong H Zhao, Dec 26, 1986; children: Jesse. **EDUCATION:** Zhongshan University, Guangzhou, China, BS, 1982, ME, 1984; Boston University, PhD, computer science, 1990. **CAREER:** Zhongshan University,

instructor, 1984-86; Boston University, lecturer, 1989-90; Wilkes University, assistant professor, 1990-93; University of North Carolina, assistant professor, 1993-. **ORGANIZATIONS:** Association for Computing Machinery, 1988-; IEEE Computer Society, 1992-; Special Interest Group on Algorithms and Computation Theory, 1988-; European Association of Theoretical Computer Science, 1990-. **HONORS/AWARDS:** National Science Foundation, Research Initiation Award, 1991-94; Wilkes University, Outstanding Faculty Designation, 1992; Boston University, Presidential University Teaching Fellow, 1989-90; The Higher Educational Council of Guangdong Province, China, Scientific Award, 1986. **SPECIAL ACHIEVEMENTS:** Published research papers in SIAM Journal on Computing, Theoretical Computer Science, Mathematical Sytems Theory, Information Processing Letters, Information and Computation; Lecture Notes in Computer Science, IEEE proceedings of Structure in Complexity Theory, Dagstuhl Volume on Complexity Theory; DIMACS Volume on Advances in Computational Complexity Theory. **BUSINESS ADDRESS:** Professor, Dept of Mathematics, University of North Carolina, 383 Bryan Bldg, Greensboro, NC 27412.

WANG, JIH MING (JIM)
Educator. Chinese American. **PERSONAL:** Born Aug 27, 1932, Kiangsu, China; son of Ching-Chen Wang; married Luan S Wang, Aug 20, 1968; children: Warren. **EDUCATION:** National Taiwan University, BS, 1955; Kansas State University, MS, 1959. **CAREER:** University of South Carolina, assistant professor of chemistry, currently. **ORGANIZATIONS:** American Chemical Society, 1959-. **HOME ADDRESS:** 414 Catawba, Union, SC 29379, (803)427-4486.

WANG, JIN
Educator. Chinese American. **PERSONAL:** Born Jul 18, 1955, Taiyuan, Shanxi, People's Republic of China; married Yijun Miao, Nov 9, 1982; children: Xiaoyin, Xiaoyu. **EDUCATION:** Zhongshan University, BA, 1981; Ohio University, MA, 1984; Kansas State University, PhD, 1989. **CAREER:** Eureka College, assistant prof, 1989-92; University of Wisconsin-Stevens Point, assistant prof, 1992-. **ORGANIZATIONS:** American Economics Association; Midwest Economics Association; Illinois, Economics Association. **HONORS/AWARDS:** National Association of State Colleges & Universities, 1993; National Faculty Development Foundation Fellowship; Prochnow Foundation, 1990. **SPECIAL ACHIEVEMENTS:** Chinese and English Languages; articles and conference papers. **BUSINESS ADDRESS:** Professor, Div of Business & Economics, University of Wisconsin-Stevens Point, Stevens Point, WI 54481, (715)346-4358.

WANG, JIN-LIANG (JIM)
Chemical corporation project administrator. Taiwanese American. **PERSONAL:** Born Aug 18, 1937, Chunan, Taiwan; son of Tian-Chu Wang and Chou Chen Wang; married Grace Y K Feng; children: Lucy Halpern, Samuel, Eliza. **EDUCATION:** Taipei Institute of Technology, diploma, 1958; Kent State University, MS, 1966; University of Akron, PhD, 1971. **CAREER:** Huamin Paper Mill, Analytical Laboratory, supervisor, 1960-61; Taiwan Provincial Tobacco & Wine Monopoly Bureau, senior research chemical engineer, R&D and production, 1961-63; The Goodyear Tire & Rubber Co, senior research chemist, R&D, 1966-87; Great Lakes Chemical Corp, project leader, R&D, 1988-. **ORGANIZATIONS:** International Institute, trustee, 1981-88; American Chemical Society, 1966-; Sigma Xi, 1967-; Chinese ACS, currently; Mid-America Chinese Science and Technology Association, currently. **HONORS/AWARDS:** Kent State University, Academic Achievement Award, 1965; Great Lakes Chemical Corp, Achievement Award, 1992. **SPECIAL ACHIEVEMENTS:** Synthesis, Characterization and Application of Dibromostyrene & Butadiene Copolymers; Synthesis, Characterization and Application of Dibromostyrene, Styrene & Butadiene Terpolymers, Vol 34, no 1, pp 558, 560, 1993, respectively; "Changing the Reaction Paths of a Metathesis Catalyst," J Org Chem, vol 40, p 2983, 1975; patents: Olefin Metathesis Catalyst, Olefin Isomerization Process, Metathesis of Olefins, Interpolymer of Nitrile, Vinylidene Chloride and Acrylate Monomers, Laminates of PVC and Acrylonitrile/Alkyl Acrylate Copolymers, Olefin Metathesis Process, Fire Retardant Acrylic Terpolymer and Films, Laminate Preparing method, Flame Retardant Brominated Styrene-based Coatings. **BUSINESS ADDRESS:** Project Leader, Great Lakes Chemical Corp, US Hwy 52, NW, West Lafayette, IN 47906, (317)497-6116.

WANG, JING
Educator. Chinese American. **PERSONAL:** Born Jul 5, 1950, Taipei, Taiwan; divorced; children: Candice Rong-Rong Wei. **EDUCATION:** National Tai-

wan University, BA, 1972; University of Michigan, MA, 1975; University of Massachuetts, Amherst, PhD, 1985. **CAREER:** Middlebury College, instructor, 1982-85; Duke University, associate professor, director, 1985-. **HONORS/AWARDS:** National Humanities Center, fellowship, 1992-93; Duke Alumni Distinguished Teaching Award, 1987. **SPECIAL ACHIEVEMENTS:** Books: The Story of Stone: Intertextuality, Ancient Chinese Stone Lore and the Stone Symbolisum of Dream of the Red Chamber, Water Margin, and Journey to the West; Culture Politics of Post-Mao China: Six Essays on the 1980s; articles: "Romancing the Subject: Utopian Moments in the Chinese Aesthetics of the 1980s"; "The Mirage of Chinese Postmodernism"; "Modern Sinology in America: A Theoretical Proposal". **BUSINESS ADDRESS:** Dir and Associate Prof, Asian and African Lang and Lit, Duke University, 2101 Campus Drive, PO Box 90414, Durham, NC 27706-7706.

WANG, JOHN CHIANG
Hotel manager. Taiwanese American. **PERSONAL:** Born 1965, Taiwan. **EDUCATION:** California State University, Los Angeles, BBa, 1990. **CAREER:** Comfort Inn, general mgr, currently. **ORGANIZATIONS:** Intl Operating Council, advisory board, 1991. **HOME ADDRESS:** 5460 Ave Del Tren, Yorba Linda, CA 92687-4900.

WANG, JUN
Educator. Chinese American. **PERSONAL:** Born Jul 11, 1954, Dalian, Liaoning, People's Republic of China; son of Jingxian Wang & Shuofang Qi; married Li Jin, Jun 30, 1984; children: Shuo. **EDUCATION:** Dalian University of Technology, BS, 1982, MS, 1985; Case Western Reserve University, PhD, 1991. **CAREER:** Dalian University of Technology, instructor, 1985-86; Case Western Reserve University, teaching and research assistant, 1986-89; Zagar Inc, programmer, 1989-90; University of North Dakota, assistant professor, 1990-93, associate professor, 1993-. **ORGANIZATIONS:** Institute of Electrical & Electronics Engineers, 1989-; Operations Research Society of America, 1989-; International Neural Network Society, 1991-; Institute of Industrial Engineers, 1991-; Decision Sciences Institute, 1992-; International Technology Education Association, 1991-. **SPECIAL ACHIEVEMENTS:** 25 journal publications in: IEEE Transactions on Circuits and Systems, Neural Networks, International Journal of Production Research, Computers & Operations Research, Computers & Industrial Engineering, Computers & Mathematics with Applications, International Journal of Pattern Recognition and Artificial Intelligence, Information Sciences, Journal of Intelligent Manufacturing, etc; editor of two books on neural nets. **BIOGRAPHICAL SOURCES:** Computers and Operations Research, p151, 1992, p297, 1992. **BUSINESS ADDRESS:** Associate Professor, Dept of Industrial Technology, University of North Dakota, PO Box 7118, Starcher Hall, Rm 139, Grand Forks, ND 58202-7118, (701)777-2201.

WANG, JUNPING
Educator. Chinese American. **PERSONAL:** Born Nov 21, 1962, Xingtang, Hebei, People's Republic of China; son of Zhenhe Wang and Yanling Meng; married Lingxia Li, Jan 15, 1985; children: Zhaohui (Carrie), Meiyi, Boyang (Charles). **EDUCATION:** Hebei Teacher's University, BS, 1982; Institute of Systems Science, Academia Sinica, MS, 1984; University of Chicago, MS, 1986, PhD, 1988. **CAREER:** Cornell University, postdoctoral associate, 1988-89; University of Wyoming, assistant professor, 1989-93, associate professor, 1993-. **ORGANIZATIONS:** SIAM, 1989-; IMACS, technical committee, 1991-. **HONORS/AWARDS:** Academia Sinica, First Prize of Research in Natural Sciences, 1989; College of A&S, University of Wyoming, Outstanding Researcher, 1993. **SPECIAL ACHIEVEMENTS:** Sharp maximum norm error estimate of the finite element approximations for the stokes problem in 2-D, 1988; a superconvergence for mixed finite element methods on rectangular domains, 1989; convergence estimates for product iterative methods with applications to domain decomposition, 1991. **BUSINESS ADDRESS:** Associate Professor, Dept of Mathematics, University of Wyoming, PO Box 3036, Laramie, WY 82071, (307)766-4368.

WANG, K. P. (KUNG-PING)
Consultant, company executive. Chinese American. **PERSONAL:** Born Mar 11, 1919, Benxi near Shenyang, China; son of C F and F H Wang; married Rose K Wang, Jun 4, 1966; children: Michael C. **EDUCATION:** Qinghua University, Beijing, 1936-37; Yenching University, Beijing, BSCh, 1940; Missouri Schl of Mines, BS, mining, BS, metallurgy, 1942; Columbia University, MS, mining, 1943, PhD, mining, 1946. **CAREER:** Various US mining companies, engr, 1942-46; Family Mines, chief engr, asst gen mgr, late 1940's; Peiyang University, Tientsin, prof, mining, late 1940's; Columbia University, assoc

adjunct prof, late 1960's; US Bureau of Mines, chief specialist, Asian minerals, 1950's-70's; US Dept of Interior, Science Office, advisor, early 1970's; Pennzoil Co, consultant to president, 1980-85; Kreri Co, Korea, consultant, 1993-; K P Wang Assoc, president, 1980's-. **ORGANIZATIONS:** Organization of Chinese-Americans, founding mbr, early officer; Rotary Club of Potomac. **HONORS/AWARDS:** Missouri School of Mines, Honorary Engineer of Mines, 1961; Industrial College of the Armed Forces, Resident Graduate, 1961; Phi Kappa Phi; Sigma Xi; Tau Beta Pi. **SPECIAL ACHIEVEMENTS:** Author, numerous publications on mineral resources of Far East, including: China, A New Industrial Power, 1978; US mining representative, 100-man delegation for science, Geneva, 1973; US representative, numerous United Nations mineral conferences in Asia, 1950's-70's. **MILITARY SERVICE:** US Marine Corps, 1945. **HOME ADDRESS:** 1573 Warrington St, Winter Springs, FL 32708. **BUSINESS ADDRESS:** President, K P Wang Associates, 1573 Warrington St, Winter Springs, FL 32708.

WANG, KO
Educator. Taiwanese American. **PERSONAL:** Born Jun 28, 1955, Keelung, Taiwan; son of Yu Chu Wang & Chu Der Lee; married Su Han Chan, Nov 28, 1989. **EDUCATION:** Chinese Culture University, LLB, 1977; University of Texas, Austin, MS, community and regional planning, 1982, MBA, 1984, PhD, 1988. **CAREER:** Rudy Robinson & Associates Inc, director of investment analysis, 1984-87; McCluskey & Jenkins Appraisal Inc, partner, 1987-89; University of Texas, Austin, assistant professor, 1988-89; California State University, Fullerton, associate professor, 1989-92, professor, 1992-. **ORGANIZATIONS:** American Real Estate and Urban Economics Association, 1988-; American Real Estate Society, 1988-. **HONORS/AWARDS:** American Association of Individual Investors, best paper on investments, 1990; Texas Real Estate Research Center, Dissertation Award, 1988. **SPECIAL ACHIEVEMENTS:** Published 12 articles in the Journal of Financial Economics, AREUEA Journal, Journal of Urban Economics, Journal of Real Estate Finance and Economics, and Journal of Real Estate Research, 1990-94. **MILITARY SERVICE:** Chinese Air Force, 2nd lt, 1977-79. **BUSINESS ADDRESS:** Professor, Dept of Finance, California State University, Fullerton, School of Business Administration and Economics, Fullerton, CA 92634, (714)773-2217.

WANG, KUAN
Educator. Chinese American. **PERSONAL:** Born Sep 9, 1945, Shensi, China. **EDUCATION:** National Taiwan University, BS, 1967; Yale University, PhD, 1974. **CAREER:** American Heat Association, established investigator, 1984-89; University of Texas, Department of Chem & Biochem, assistant professor, 1977-82, associate professor, 1983-89, professor, 1989-. **ORGANIZATIONS:** American Association for the Advancement of Science; American Society for Biochem & Molecular Biology; American Society for Cell Biology; Biophysical Society; Chinese American Biophysical Society. **HONORS/AWARDS:** Yale University, Yale University Fellowship, 1970-71; National Institutes of Health, Postdoctoral Fellow, 1975-76. **MILITARY SERVICE:** Republic of China, lieutenant. **BUSINESS ADDRESS:** Professor, Dept of Chemistry & Biochemistry, University of Texas at Austin, Welch Hall 4.230C, Austin, TX 78712, (512)471-4065.

WANG, KUNG-LEE
Businessman, association administrator. Chinese American. **PERSONAL:** Born 1925, China. **EDUCATION:** Yenching University, China, BA, economics; Brown University, MA, economics; Columbia University, MBA, business economics; Harvard University, MPA, political economy/government, 1965. **CAREER:** CEIR, Inc, economist-operations analyst, 1955-60; US Dept of Interior, economist, 1960-66, senior economist, 1966-82, Bureau of Mines, Quantitiative Economics, chief, 1970-82; Chinatown Development Corp, co-founder, 1982, director/officer, 1983-; KLW Intl, Inc, president, 1982-. **ORGANIZATIONS:** Organization of Chinese Americans, founder, natl pres, 1973-77, natl board member, 1973-91, Business Advisory Council, coordinator, 1983-; AIME, Washington DC Mineral Economics Section, founder, pres, 1975-78, Council of Economics, natl chairman, 1980-81; US-China Capital Cities Friendship Council, chairman, 1987-; US-China Council for Intl Exchange, founder/president, 1988-; Asian American Voters Coalition, co-founder; Natl Council of Chinese American Voters League; co-founder, Asian Pacific American Heritage Council; co-founder; Assn of Chinese Schools, co-founder; Committee of 100, board of directors, 1990-, executive director, 1993-. **HONORS/AWARDS:** Ford Foundation/US Civil Service Commission, Career Education Award, 1964; Natl Inst of Public Affairs, Fellow, 1966; AIME-Washington DC Section, Engineer of the Year, 1976, Mineral Econo-

mist of the Year, 1984; Asian & Pacific American Civil Rights Alliance, Civil Rights Award, 1988; Ellis Island Medal of Honor, 1993. **SPECIAL ACHIEVEMENTS:** Numerous monographs, articles and book sections on mineral economics and input-output analysis. **BUSINESS ADDRESS:** Founder, Organization of Chinese Americans, 11228 Georgia Ave, Ste 9, Wheaton, MD 20902-4694, (301)946-4516.

WANG, KUO CHANG
Educator. Chinese American. **PERSONAL:** Born Nov 9, 1924, Anhui, China; married Betty S P Wang, Jun 15, 1958; children: Edward S J, Joyce S L, Philip S L. **EDUCATION:** Ordinance College, China, BS, 1947; Virginia Polytechnic Institute, MS, 1954; Rensselaer Polytechnic Institute, PhD, 1961. **CAREER:** Chinese Arsenal, engineer, 1947-53; Martin-Baltimore Division, research scientist, 1961-66; Research Institute for Advanced Studies, research scientist, 1967-72, senior scientist, 1973-79; San Diego State University, professor, 1980-. **ORGANIZATIONS:** American Institute of Aeronautics and Astronautics, 1963-; Sigma Xi; Phi Kappa Phi. **HONORS/AWARDS:** AIAA, San Diego section, Outstanding Contribution to Aerospace Engineering, 1981; Martin Marietta Corporation, Honor Award, 1974. **SPECIAL ACHIEVEMENTS:** Research publications in prestigious journals relating to the fields of fluid mechanics, applied mathematics and aerospace engineering; pioneering contribution to three-dimensional boundary layer theory and separated flow structure and in high-temperature gas flow and low aspect-ratio wing theory. **HOME ADDRESS:** 7273 Alliance Court, San Diego, CA 92119, (619)462-8314.

WANG, KUO KING
Educator. Chinese American. **PERSONAL:** Born Oct 8, 1923. **EDUCATION:** National Central University, Nanking, China, BS, 1947; University of Wisconsin-Madison, MS, 1962, PhD, mechanical engineering, 1968. **CAREER:** Taiwan Shipbuilding Corp, engineer, 1947-57; Ingalls-Taiwan Shipbuilding Corp, engineer, manager, 1957-60; United Tanker Corp, supervisor, shipbuilding, 1960-61; Walker Manufacturing Co, project engineer, 1962-66; University of Wisconsin-Madison, assistant professor, mechanical engineering, 1968-70; Cornell University, associate professor, 1970-77, professor, mechanical engineering, beginning 1977, professor emeritus, currently. **ORGANIZATIONS:** American Society of Mechanical Engineers; Natl Academy of Engineering. **HONORS/AWARDS:** American Society of Mechanical Engineers, Blackall Award, 1968; American Welding Society, fellow. **BUSINESS ADDRESS:** Professor Emeritus, Sibley School of Mechanical and Aerospace Engineering, Cornell University, 105 Upson Hall, Ithaca, NY 14853-0001, (607)255-5255.∗

WANG, LAWRENCE KONGPU
Consulting engineer. Chinese American. **PERSONAL:** Born Nov 20, 1940, Chekiang, China; son of Pu Chen Wang and Shu Yu Chu; married Muhao Sung Wang, Jun 8, 1968; children: John, Norman, Betty. **EDUCATION:** National Cheng Kung University, BS, 1962; University of Missouri, MSCE, 1965; University of Rhode Island, MS, 1967; Rutgers University, PhD, 1972. **CAREER:** Calspan-Arvin Inc, environmental engineer, 1970-73; Rensselaer Polytechnic Institute, assistant professor, 1973-77; Stevens Institute of Technology, associate professor, 1977-81; Rockland Chinese School, principal, 1980-81; Lenox Institute & Krofta Engineering Corp, director, 1981-88; International Environmental Systems Inc, Zorex Corporation, vp, 1988-93; University of Illinois at Urbana-Champaign, professor, 1993-. **ORGANIZATIONS:** American Water Works Association, Standard Method Committee, chairperson, 1990-91; American Institute of Chemical Engineers, Northeast Region, treasurer, 1989-90; Overseas Chinese Environmental Engineers & Scientists Association, president, 1990-92; Mainland-Taiwan Environmental Technology Seminar, founder, 1992-; National Cheng Kung University, professor, 1978-81. **HONORS/AWARDS:** New York Water Pollution Control Association, Kenneth Allen Research Award, 1978; Pollution Engineering Magazine, Five-Star Engineering Award, 1982; Korea Society of Water Pollution Research and Control, Research Award, 1991; Overseas Chinese Environmental Engineers & Scientists Association, Outstanding Service Award, 1991, 1992; American Academy of Environmental Engineers, Diplomate, 1981. **SPECIAL ACHIEVEMENTS:** Handbook of Industrial Waste Treatment, Marcel Dekker Inc, 1992; Air and Noise Pollution Control, Humana Press, 1979; Solid Waste Processing and Resource Recovery, Humana Press, 1980; Biological Waste Treatment Processes, Humana Press, 1986; Water Resources and Natural Control Processes, Humana Press, 1986; Marcel Dekker Inc, handbook, editor-in-chief, 1989-; Humana Press Inc, handbook, editor-in-chief, 1976; US patent awards, 1976, 1990-94. **BUSINESS ADDRESS:** Professor, Dept of Agricul-

tural Engineering, University of Illinois at Urbana-Champaign, 1304 West Pennsylvania Ave, Urbana, IL 61801, (217)333-7143.

WANG, LEON RU-LIANG
Educator. Chinese American. **PERSONAL:** Born Jun 15, 1932, Canton, China; son of Huai-Kao Wang (deceased) and Yuen-Chin Ho Wang (deceased); married Joyce Chieh-Chun Wang, Jul 22, 1961; children: Frank Yu-Heng, Mark Yu-Da, Cindy Chi-Wen. **EDUCATION:** Cheng-Kung University, Taiwan, BS, 1957; University of Illinois, MS, 1961; Massachusetts Institute of Technology, ScD, 1965. **CAREER:** Rensselaer Polytechnic Institute, assistant professor of civil eng, 1965-69, associate professor of civil eng, 1969-80; University of Oklahoma, professor of civil eng, 1980-84; Old Dominion University, professor of civil eng, 1984-, chairman of civil eng, 1984-90. **ORGANIZATIONS:** American Society of Civil Engineers, fellow, 1990-, Technical Council on Lifeline Earthquake Engineering, secretary, 1991-92; Earthquake Engineering Research Institute, 1977-; Eastern Virginia Chapter of Organization of Chinese Americans, president, 1990-91; Chinese Association of Greater Oklahoma City, president, 1982-84; Chinese Community Center, chairperson, 1978-79; Chinese-American Association of National Hazards Reduction, director, 1990-93; professional engineer, in states of Virginia, Oklahoma, and New York, 1967-. **HONORS/AWARDS:** National Science Foundation, numerous research awards, 1976-; Japanese Ministry of Education, Distinguished Foreign Professor, 1986; Old Dominion University, Outstanding Faculty, 1986, 1988. **SPECIAL ACHIEVEMENTS:** Co-author, book, Numerical Analysis and Modeling of Soil-Structure Interaction, Elsvier Publisher Inc, 1993; co-editor, Proceedings of Seismic Ground Motions and Response, ASME, 1992; editor, Proceeedings of NSF Research Grantee Workshop, 1992; editor, Proceedings of US-Taiwan Joint Seminar on Multiple Hazards Mitigation, 1984. **BUSINESS ADDRESS:** Professor of Civil Engineering, Old Dominion University, Hampton Blvd, KDH 133C, Norfolk, VA 23529-0241, (804)683-3764.

WANG, LI-SHING
Educational administrator. Taiwanese American. **PERSONAL:** Born Feb 6, 1960, Taipei, Taiwan; married Yaw Chang; children: Michael H Chang. **EDUCATION:** Johns Hopkins University, MA. **CAREER:** UNC-Wilmington, Student Life Studies, director, Department of Political Science, lecturer, currently. **ORGANIZATIONS:** NASPA, representative of NC in research and program development, Region III; North Carolina Association for Institutional Research; Association for College Personnel Administration; North Carolina Association for Women in Education; APSA; Association for Asian Studies. **BUSINESS ADDRESS:** Director for Student Life Studies, University of NC at Wilmington, 601 S College Rd, Westside Hall, Wilmington, NC 28403-3201, (919)395-3735.

WANG, LIH-JAU
Educator. Taiwanese American. **PERSONAL:** Born Apr 1, 1959, Taipei, Taiwan; daughter of Ching-Shou Wang and Ko-Mei Wang; married Shagi-Di Shih, Jan 10, 1992; children: Natalie Shih. **EDUCATION:** Tunghai University, Taiwan, BS, economics, 1981; National Cheng-Chi University, Taiwan, MA, economics, 1983; University of California, San Diego, PhD, economics, 1990. **CAREER:** University of Wyoming, assistant profesor, 1990-. **ORGANIZATIONS:** American Economics Association; Econometric Society. **BUSINESS ADDRESS:** Asst Professor, Dept of Economics and Finance, University of Wyoming, PO Box 3985, Univ Station, Laramie, WY 82071, (307)766-3143.

WANG, LILY L.
Engineer. Chinese American. **PERSONAL:** Born Jan 19, 1937, Checkaing, China; married Charles P Wang, Jun 29, 1963. **EDUCATION:** Chenkung University, Taiwan, BSEE, 1959; Oklahoma State University, Stillwater, MSEE, 1962; University of California at San Diego, PhD, electrical engineering, 1973. **CAREER:** TRW, member of technical staff, 1973-74; Aerospace Corp, section mgr, 1974-82; Global Technology Inc, president, 1982-. **ORGANIZATIONS:** IEEE, member. **SPECIAL ACHIEVEMENTS:** Founder: Global Technology, 1979; Optodyne Inc, 1986; research and development: Image processing and pattern reconstruction, 1973-85. **BUSINESS ADDRESS:** President, Global Technology, Inc, 1180 Mahalo Place, Compton, CA 90220, (310)635-7106.

WANG, LING JUN
Educator. Chinese American. **PERSONAL:** Born Dec 4, 1946, Feng Chen, Jiangxi, China; son of Bo Ling Wang & Yuhong Xiong Wang; married Bihua Liu Wang, 1977; children: Peter Ziyuan, Amy Elizabeth Ninyuan. **EDUCA-**

TION: Southeastern Massachusetts University, MS, 1981; University of Delaware, PhD, 1984. **CAREER:** Wesleyan University, research associate, 1984-86; Oak Ridge National Lab, research associate, 1986-87; Vanderbilt University, research assistant professor, 1987-90; Battelle Pacific Northwest, visiting scientist, 1990; Argonne National Lab, visiting scientist, 1991; ORNL, visiting scientist, 1992; University of Tennessee, Chattanooga, associate professor of physics, 1990-. **ORGANIZATIONS:** American Physical Society, referee, 1986-; Chattanooga Chinese Association, officer, 1991-; US-China Friendship Association, 1992-; Tennessee Academy of Sciences, 1991-; Chinese Academic and Professional Association of Southeastern US, 1992-. **HONORS/AWARDS:** University of Delaware, Graduate Competitive Fellow, 1982; Oak Ridge National Lab, Publication Award, 1988. **SPECIAL ACHIEVEMENTS:** Publication of 12 articles in physics; 3 political essays on democratic reform in China; language proficiency: Chinese, English, Japanese, Russian. **BUSINESS ADDRESS:** Assoc Professor, Dept of Physics, University of Tennessee, Chattanooga, 615 McCallie Ave, Grote Hall, Rm 346, Chattanooga, TN 37403, (615)755-5248.

WANG, LOUIE KEHLUH
Educator. Chinese American. **PERSONAL:** Born Nov 1953, Hsinchu, Taiwan; son of Y T Wang and C C Wang; married Jane Wang, Sep 1981; children: Alvin, Stanley. **EDUCATION:** National Taiwan University, BS, 1976; National Cheng Chi University, MBA, 1980; Northwestern University, PhD, 1989. **CAREER:** Bank of America, assistant loan officer, 1980-81; Rainier National Bank, assistant manager, 1981-82; Loyola University of Chicago, instructor, 1986-88; Tennessee Technological University, assistant professor, 1988-93; associate professor, 1993-. **ORGANIZATIONS:** American Finance Association, 1988-; Financial Management Association, 1988-; American Real Estate Association, 1992-; Treasury Management Association, 1992-. **SPECIAL ACHIEVEMENTS:** Author: "A Simplified Model for Fixed-Rate Mortgage Selection," 1993; "Asymmetric Information, Self Selection and Debt," 1993; "Secured Loan and Banking Relationship," 1993; certified cash manager. **BUSINESS ADDRESS:** Associate Professor of Finance, Tennessee Technological University, PO Box 5083, College of Business Administration, Cookeville, TN 38505-0001, (615)372-3879.

WANG, LOUISA HO-CHING
Educator. Chinese American. **PERSONAL:** Born Jan 29, 1941, Shanghai, China; daughter of T H & K T Fong; married Edward K C Wang, Jun 24, 1967 (deceased); children: Carolyn. **EDUCATION:** National Taiwan University, BA, 1963; University of San Francisco, 1965; University of California at Los Angeles, MBA, 1968. **CAREER:** University of California at Los Angeles, research assistant, 1966-68; National Taiwan University, lecturer, 1968-69; University of Illinois, systems analyst, 1969-74; California State Chico, assistant to the dean, 1975-79; Rolm, programming supervisor, 1979-80; Lockheed, consultant, 1980-81; San Jose State University, assistant director of systems, 1991-; H&R Block, quality control inspector, 1992-. **ORGANIZATIONS:** Data Processing Management Association, 1981-; South Bay Chinese Gospel Church, 1979-; Chinese Faculty Association, 1981-; Faculty/Staff of Asian Americans, 1991-; Parent/Faculty Club of Piedmont HS, parent member, 1988-92; UCLA Annual Fund, contributor, 1992-; St. Jude's Hospital, contributor, 1990-; Santa Clara American Cancer Society, contributor, 1992-; Summerdale School Parent Volunteers, volunteer, 1981-85; Harker Academy Parents Club, 1979-81. **HONORS/AWARDS:** University of San Francisco, Honors Student, 1965; National Taiwan University, Graduated Honors, 1963; San Jose State University, Certificate of Teamwork and Leadership, 1985. **SPECIAL ACHIEVEMENTS:** Michigan English Proficiency Test, 1964; IBM Training Certificate in Networking, 1989; IBM Training Certificate in Job Control, 1990; IBM Training Certificate in Language (CICS), 1990; IBM Training Certificate in DBase3, 1991; H&R Block Tax Preparation License, 1992. **BIOGRAPHICAL SOURCES:** Taiwan University Directory Catalogue, 1963; Operation Research Principles, 1969. **HOME ADDRESS:** 1478 Mardan Dr., San Jose, CA 95132. **BUSINESS PHONE:** (408)924-2007.

WANG, LUOYONG
Educator, actor. Chinese American. **PERSONAL:** Born Dec 24, 1958, Louyang, Henan, People's Republic of China; son of Zhao Quan Wang and Cheng Pu Qing; married Ning Ding, May 12, 1991. **EDUCATION:** Wu Han Conservatory of Music, Certificate, 1978; Shanghai Drama Institute, BA, 1985; Boston University, School of Theatre Arts, MFA, 1989. **CAREER:** Shiyan Dame Co, dancer, 1971-74; Shiyan Theatre Co, actor, 1975-78; Wu Han Theatre Co, actor, 1978-80; Shanghai Drama Institute, assistant professor, 1985-88; Miss Saigon First National Touring Co, actor, 1992-93; University of

Wisconsin,-Milwaukee, assistant professor, 1989-. **ORGANIZATIONS:** Shanghai Theatre Association, 1985-87; Actors' Equity Association, 1991-; Screen Actors Guild, 1992-. **HONORS/AWARDS:** Shanghai Drama Institute, Outstanding Graduate, 1984; Shanghai Theatre Fes, Best Acting Team, 1984. **SPECIAL ACHIEVEMENTS:** Played: Hamlet, "Hamlet," Shanghai Drama Institute, 1984; Song Liling, "M Butterfly," Oregon Shakespeare Fes, 1990, Song Liling, "M Butterfly" Seattle Repertory Theatre Co, 1991; Yep Man, "Dragon," Universal Picture, 1992; Engineer, Miss Saigon First National Touring Co, 1993. **BUSINESS ADDRESS:** Assistant Professor, Dept of Theatre & Dance, University of Wisconsin-Milwaukee, PO Box 413, Milwaukee, WI 53201, (414)229-4947.

WANG, MARGARET K.
Librarian. Chinese American. **PERSONAL:** Born Sep 13, 1940, Kumming, Yunnan, China; daughter of Chin-yao Kuo and Hsueh-hsi Kuo; married James C H Wang, Nov 11, 1972. **EDUCATION:** National Taiwan University, BA, 1963; Texas Woman's University, MLS, 1965; University of Delaware, computer technology certificate, 1977. **CAREER:** Chemical Abstracts Service Library, serials cataloger, 1967-69; University of Delaware Library, head of serials cataloging section, cataloging department, 1969-71, first assistant to the head of cataloging department, 1971-81, coordinator of serials cataloging, 1981-85, coordinator of original cataloging & authority control, 1985-. **ORGANIZATIONS:** American Library Association, ACRL representative to Association for Asian Studies, 1990-92, ACRL/Asian & African Section Conference Program Committee, 1989-90; Chinese-American Librarians Association, Mid-Atlantic Chapter, president, 1986-87; North American Serials Interest Group, 1992-; ACRL, Delaware Valley Chapter, 1992-; Delaware Library Association, treasurer, 1982-84. **SPECIAL ACHIEVEMENTS:** Co-editor, Directory of Delaware Libraries, 3rd edition, 1982, 4th edition, 1985; "Bibliographies by and about Wang Kuo-Wei," in Bibliography Quarterly 14, pp 105-108, 1980. **BIOGRAPHICAL SOURCES:** Directory of Ethnic Professionals in LIS, Four-G Publishers, 1991; Biographical Directory of Librarians in US & Canada, 5th edition, under maiden name, Margaret J Kuo, 1970; Directory of Library & Information Professionals, Research Publications, 1988. **BUSINESS ADDRESS:** Coordinator of Original Cataloging & Authority Control, University of Delaware Library, Newark, DE 19717-5267, (302)831-8223.

WANG, MAY X.
Educator. Chinese American. **PERSONAL:** Born May 12, 1960, Beijing, People's Republic of China. **EDUCATION:** Beijing University, China, BS, 1983; Michigan State University, MA, 1989, PhD, 1991. **CAREER:** Michigan State University, instructor, 1988-90; Missouri Southern State College, assistant professor, 1990-. **ORGANIZATIONS:** American Psychological Association, 1990-; Society for Research in Child Development, 1990-. **HONORS/AWARDS:** Michigan Psychological Association, Student Paper Award, 1988. **SPECIAL ACHIEVEMENTS:** Fitzgerald, Harris, Barnes, Wang, Cornell, et al, The Organization of Lateralized Behavior during Infancy, 1990; H E Fitzgerald, Lester, B M, & Yogman, M W, Theory and Research in Behavioral Pediatrics, Plenum, vol 5, 1990. **BUSINESS ADDRESS:** Assistant Professor, Dept of Psychology, Missouri Southern State College, E 3950 Newman Rd, Joplin, MO 64801, (417)625-9315.

WANG, MING-YU RACHEL
Educator. Chinese American. **PERSONAL:** Born Nov 29, 1951, Taipei, Taiwan; daughter of Kwei-Joeu Wang & Yet-Ken Tu. **EDUCATION:** National Taiwan University, Taipei, Taiwan, BS, 1973; University of Chicago, MS, 1974; Northwestern University, PhD, 1979. **CAREER:** Whitworth College, associate professor, 1979-85; Eastern Washington University, associate professor, 1986-87; Church in Spokane, full-time worker, 1987-88; Pathology Associates Medical Laboratories, toxicologist, 1989-90; Spokane Community College, instructor, 1990-. **ORGANIZATIONS:** American Chemistry Society, 1974-86, local section officer, 1982-85; Washington Chemistry Teachers Assn, 1992-. **HONORS/AWARDS:** National Taiwan University, Dr Sun-Yet Sen Award, 1972; Whitworth College, Distinguished Services to the Students, 1982. **SPECIAL ACHIEVEMENTS:** Numerous publications in chemistry journals; fluent in Chinese. **BUSINESS ADDRESS:** Chemistry Instructor, Spokane Community College, N 1810 Greene St, 7-121 MS2070, Spokane, WA 99207, (509)533-8826.

WANG, MOLLY M.
Indexer. Taiwanese American. **PERSONAL:** Born Nov 15, 1940, Tainan, Taiwan; daughter of Jon Tai Huang and Lanyin Huang; married Carl C Wang,

Jul 4, 1966; children: Nancy, William. **EDUCATION:** Taiwan Normal University, Taipei, Taiwan, BA, education, 1964; University of Michigan, MA, education/library media, 1973; Queens College/CUNY, management/supervision certificate program, 1993. **CAREER:** OVS Georgia Department of Human Resources, library associate, 1977; Atlanta Public Library, Aquisition Department, library associate, 1977-80; Adelphi University, Swinbul Library, cataloger, 1980-81; SUNY, College at Old Westbury, library technical assistant, 1981-83; The H W Wilson Co, indexer, humanities index, education index, 1983-. **ORGANIZATIONS:** American Library Association, ACRL, RASD, LAMA, 1983-; American Society of Indexers, 1993-; Taiwanese American Citizens League, New York, president, board of directors, 1990-93; International Immigrants Foundation/NGO Economic and Social Council, United Nations, coordinator, 1989-; Olympic Plaza Condominium, board of management, executive secretary, 1991-. **HONORS/AWARDS:** Government Scholarship Foundation, Taipei, National Taiwan Normal University, Academic Award, 1962-63; University of Michigan, PASE Scholarship, 1972-73. **SPECIAL ACHIEVEMENTS:** State of Maryland, Montgomery County Health Department, Early Childhood Education Certificate, 1974; State of Georgia, Real Estate Commission, Certificate of Real Estate Salesperson, 1978; State of Georgia, State Board for the Certification of Libarian, Certificate of Librarianship, 1980. **HOME ADDRESS:** 139-35 35th Ave, 3C, Flushing, NY 11354, (718)461-6762. **BUSINESS ADDRESS:** Indexer, The H W Wilson Co, 950 University Ave, Humanities Index, Bronx, NY 10452, (718)588-8400.

WANG, N. T.
Educator. Chinese American. **PERSONAL:** Born in Shanghai, China; son of P Y Wang and Suteh Wang; married Mabel U; children: June, Kay, Cynthia, Geraldine, Newton. **EDUCATION:** Columbia University, AB; Harvard University, AM, PhD. **CAREER:** Shanghai University of Finance and Economics, 7 other universities, honorary professor; World Bank, consultant; United Nations, assistant dir, CDPPP, director, United Nations Center on TNC; Columbia University, adj prof, senior res scholar, China Intl Business Project, director, currently. **ORGANIZATIONS:** Committee of 100; OCA; American Economic Association; Royal Economic Society; Chinese Economic Association. **HONORS/AWARDS:** International Academy of Management, Fellow; Committee on Scholarly Communication with China, Distinguished Scholar; Phi Beta Kappa. **SPECIAL ACHIEVEMENTS:** Books: Taiwan's Enterprises in Global Perspective, 1992; Transnational Corporations and China's Open Door Policy, 1988; China's Modernization and Transnational Corporations, 1984; Taxation and Development, 1976; Cooperation for Economic Development of Eastern Africa, Report of the Eastern Africa Team, 1971. **BIOGRAPHICAL SOURCES:** World Journal, January 24, 1993, January 31, 1993, February 7, 1993. **BUSINESS ADDRESS:** Dir, China International Business Project, Columbia University, 420 W 118 St, 925 1AB, New York, NY 10027, (212)854-4677.

WANG, NAM SUN
Educator. Chinese American. **PERSONAL:** Born Nov 10, 1956, Taipei, Taiwan; son of Show Kang Wang & Yip Kuin Sung Wang; married Patricia Gail Wang, May 24, 1980; children: Alexander Ande, Nicholas Anping. **EDUCATION:** University of California, Berkeley, BS, 1979; California Institute of Technology, MS, 1982, PhD, 1989. **CAREER:** University of Maryland, College Park, instructor, 1986-88, assistant professor, 1988-. **ORGANIZATIONS:** American Institute of Chemical Engineers; American Chemical Society; Society of Industrial Microbiology. **HONORS/AWARDS:** American Society of Engineering Education, JJ Martin Best Paper Award, 1988; Society of Industrial Microbiology, Best Paper Award, 1992; Allied-Signal, Faculty Award, 1986. **SPECIAL ACHIEVEMENTS:** "Cell Inactivation in the Presence of Sparging and Mechanical Agitation," Biotech Bioeng, 40, p 806-816, 1992; "Oxygen Mass Transfer Enhancement via Fermentor Headspace Pressurization," Biotechnol Progress, 8, p 244-251, 1992; "A Comparison of Neural Networks and Partial Least Squares for Deconvoluting Fluorescence Spectra," Biotechnol Bioeng, 40, p 53-62, 1992; "Alpha-Amylase Fermentation with Bacillus Amyloliquefaciens in an Aqueous Two-Phase System," Biotechnol Progress, 7, p 439-444, 1991; "Characterization of an On-Line Commercial Fluorescence Probe," Biotechnol Bioeng, 38, p 1292-1301, 1991. **BUSINESS ADDRESS:** Asst Professor, Chemical Engineering Dept, University of Maryland, College Park, MD 20742, (301)405-1910.

WANG, NANCY Y.
Chemist (retired). Chinese American. **PERSONAL:** Born Jan 20, 1925, Beijing, China; daughter of Yang & Wang; married Chi-Hua Wang, Aug 9, 1949; children: Fong. **EDUCATION:** Fu-Jen University, Beijing, BS, 1945; Saint

Louis University, MS, 1951; Boston University, PhD, 1965. **CAREER:** MIT, postdoctoral fellow, 1964-68; Retina Foundation, research associate, 1968-71; University of Massachusetts, lecturer, research associate, 1971-80. **ORGANIZATIONS:** Sigma Xi, 1951. **SPECIAL ACHIEVEMENTS:** Research in physical and synthetic organic chemistry, 1964-80. **HOME ADDRESS:** 106 Pleasant St, Lexington, MA 02173.

WANG, ORRIN NAN CHUNG
Educator. Chinese American. **PERSONAL:** Born Oct 10, 1957, Corvallis, OR; son of Samuel Wang and Betty Wang; married Marianne Conroy, Aug 23, 1991. **EDUCATION:** Reed College, BA, 1979; University of Chicago, MA, 1984, PhD, 1989. **CAREER:** University of Maryland, College Park, assistant professor of English, 1989-. **ORGANIZATIONS:** Washington Area Romanticist Group, co-director, 1992-; Keats Shelley Association, 1991-; Modern Language Association, 1987-. **HONORS/AWARDS:** American Council of Learned Societies, fellowship, 1993; University of Chicago, Galler Dissertation Award, 1990, Whiting Fellowship, 1988, Trustee Fellowship, 1983. **SPECIAL ACHIEVEMENTS:** Work in fields of British Romantic Literature & Literary Theory; completing book project, Fantastic Modernity: Dialectical Readings in Romanticism & Theory; published in Criticism (forthcoming); English Literary History or ELH, fall 1990; Yale Journal of Criticism, fall 1990; Clio, spring 1990. **BUSINESS ADDRESS:** Assistant Professor of English, University of Maryland, College Park, College Park, MD 20742-0001.

WANG, PAO-KUAN
Educator. Taiwanese American. **PERSONAL:** Born Dec 1, 1949, Tainan, Taiwan; son of Shou Wang and Luan-Chao Chiu Wang; married Li-Bi Wang; children: Lawrence C Y, Victor C M. **EDUCATION:** National Taiwan University, BS, 1971; University of California, Los Angeles, MS, 1975, PhD, 1978. **CAREER:** University of California, research assistant, 1973-78, research atmospheric physicist, 1978-80; University of Wisconsin, Madison, assistant professor, 1980-84, associate professor, 1984-88, professor, 1988-. **ORGANIZATIONS:** American Meteorological Society, Cloud Physics Committee chairman, 1991-93, 1974-; American Geophysical Union, 1980-; Royal Meteorological Society, UK, foreign member, 1988-; Midwest Association for Cloud and Aerosol Physics, founding member, 1988-. **HONORS/AWARDS:** Alexander von Humboldt Foundation, Senior Research Award, 1993. **SPECIAL ACHIEVEMENTS:** Published widely in scientific journals in the fields of aerosol physics, cloud physics and dynamics, atmospheric electricity, fluid mechanics, and filter modeling. **BUSINESS ADDRESS:** Professor, Atmospheric and Oceanic Sciences, University of Wisconsin, Madison, 1225 W Dayton St, Madison, WI 53706, (608)263-6479.

WANG, PAUL WEILY
Educator. Chinese American. **PERSONAL:** Born Nov 4, 1951, Kao-hsiung, Taiwan; son of Yaw-wen Wang & Yu-hua Lo; married Diana Chow Wang, Jun 9, 1979; children: Agnes, Carol, Alfred. **EDUCATION:** National Taiwan Normal University, BS, 1974; State University of New York at Albany, MS, 1981, PhD, 1986. **CAREER:** State University of New York at Albany, postdoctorate, 1986; Vanderbilt University, research assistant professor, 1986-90; University of Texas at El Paso, Department of Physics, assistant professor, 1990-. **ORGANIZATIONS:** American Ceramic Society; American Physical Society; Materials Research Society; Optical Society of America; International Society for Optical Engineering; Sigma Xi; Sigma Pi Sigma. **HONORS/AWARDS:** SUNY/Albany, Outstanding Teaching Assistant Award, 1980; Institute for the Study of Defects in Solids, fellow. **SPECIAL ACHIEVEMENTS:** "Hypervelocity Particle Penetration in Multi-Layered Thermal Blankets on LDEF," Scripta Metallurigica et Materialia, vol 28, p 377, 1993; "Some Effects of 5eV Photons on Defects in SiO2," J Non-Crys Solid, vol 149, p 122, 1992; "Luminescence in Silicas Stimulated by Low Energy Ions," Nuclear Instru and Met B59/60, p 1317, 1991; "KrF Laser Interaction with Intrinsic Defects in Silicas," SPIE Proceeding, vol 1327, pp 50-59, 1990; "Defect Formation in Fused Silicas due to Photon Irradiation at 5 and 50 ev," Lasers, 1989, p 1020. **BUSINESS ADDRESS:** Assistant Professsor, University of Texas at El Paso, 500 W University Ave, Physical Science Bldg, Room 215 B, El Paso, TX 79968, (915)747-7549.

WANG, PING H.
Physician. Taiwanese American. **PERSONAL:** Born Oct 29, 1957, Chia-Yi, Taiwan; son of Ying-Shih Wang and Mei-Man Lee; married Pauyu Lee Wang, Feb 1989; children: Jason, Candice, Natalie. **EDUCATION:** Kaohsing Medical College, MD, 1984; Harvard University, SM, 1985. **CAREER:** Boston VA Medical Center, resident, 1989-91; Brigham and Women's Hospital, physician,

1991-; Joslin Diabetes Center, fellow, 1985-88, physician, 1991-. **ORGANIZATIONS:** Harvard Medical School, fellow, 1991-; American Medical Association, 1990-; American Diabetes Association, 1987-; Massachusetts Medical Society, 1990-. **HONORS/AWARDS:** Juvenile Diabetes Foundation, Research Fellowship Award, 1992. **SPECIAL ACHIEVEMENTS:** Research article published in the Journal of Clinical Investigation, 1989; research article published in the Lancet, 1993; specialization: endocrinology. **BUSINESS ADDRESS:** Physician, Research Division, Joslin Diabetes Center, One Joslin Pl, Boston, MA 02215, (617)732-2597.

WANG, QUN
Educator. Chinese American. **PERSONAL:** Born Apr 28, 1956, Beijing, People's Republic of China; son of Yi Wang & Huiying Jian; married Lori A Lee, Sep 12, 1986; children: Sophia L. **EDUCATION:** East China Normal University, Shanghai, BA, 1978, MA, 1982; University of Oregon, PhD, 1990. **CAREER:** East China Normal University, Foreign Language Dept, instructor, 1978-82; University of Oregon, Dept of English, teaching assistant, 1985-90; University of Wisconsin-River Falls, Dept of English, assistant professor, 1990-. **ORGANIZATIONS:** Modern Language Association of America; Society for the study of the Multi-Ethnic Literature of the United States; University of Wisconsin-River Falls, Faculty Senate, secretary, executive committee member. **HONORS/AWARDS:** University of Oregon, E G Moll Scholarship, 1984; Ford Foundation, CSBLAC Fellowship, 1991; UW System Institute, Course Development Grant on Race and Ethnicity, 1992. **SPECIAL ACHIEVEMENTS:** Author: On the Dramatization of the Illusory World in Tennessee Williams, Arthur Miller and Edward Albee's Major Plays, University Microfilms International, 1990; "Theodore Dreiser, Richard Wright, Ralph Ellison, and Joseph Heller," An Anthology of 20th-Century American Fiction, vol 1 & 2, 1981-82; articles in Marshall Cavendish's Asian American Encyclopedia; regular reviwer, Magill's Literary Annual; contributor, St. James Press's Reference Guide to American Literature. **BUSINESS ADDRESS:** Professor, Dept of English, University of Wisconsin, 310 Fine Arts, River Falls, WI 54022, (715)425-3124.

WANG, RICHARD HSU-SHIEN
Chemist. Chinese American. **PERSONAL:** Born Jan 2, 1932, Anqing, Anhui, China; son of Tsung & Ging-Wen Hsia Wang; married Josephine Ti-Sun, Aug 11, 1962; children: Joseph, Christine, Dorothy. **EDUCATION:** National Taiwan University, BS, 1956; University of Illinois, MS, 1961; University of Kansas, PhD, 1968. **CAREER:** National Taiwan University, research assistant, 1957-58; National Survey of Illinois, research assistant, 1961-63; Eastman Chemical Company, research associate, 1968-. **ORGANIZATIONS:** American Chemical Society, 1968-. **HONORS/AWARDS:** Phi Lambda Upsilon, 1967; Anhui University, honorary professor, 1989; Eastman Chemical Company, Inventor Appreciation Award, 1993. **SPECIAL ACHIEVEMENTS:** 52 US patents in the fields of stabilization of polymer against UV light and thermal autoxidation, plastics additives and organic syntheses, 1968-93. **HOME ADDRESS:** 1414 Fairidge Dr, Kingsport, TN 37664, (615)247-1043.

WANG, RITA
Association administrator. Chinese American. **PERSONAL:** Born Aug 5, 1938. **CAREER:** Chinese Information and Service Center, executive director, currently. **BUSINESS ADDRESS:** Executive Director, Chinese Information and Service Center, 409 Maynard Ave S, 2nd Fl, Seattle, WA 98104, (206)624-5633.*

WANG, ROBERT T.
Physician. Chinese American. **PERSONAL:** Born Jan 29, 1949, Taipei, Taiwan; married Eva Dohrn. **EDUCATION:** MIT, BS, 1969; California Institute of Technology, PhD, 1976; University of Miami, MD, 1978. **CAREER:** Self-employed, physician, 1983-. **BUSINESS ADDRESS:** Physician, 2080 Century Pk E, Ste 1410, Los Angeles, CA 90067, (310)551-1200.

WANG, SAMUEL T. M.
Educator. Chinese American. **PERSONAL:** Born Apr 4, 1939, Peking, China; son of C C Wang & Anna Wang; married Linda, Jul 1970. **EDUCATION:** Augustana College, BA, 1964; University of Iowa, MFA, 1966. **CAREER:** Clemson University, professor, 1966-. **ORGANIZATIONS:** Society for Photographic Education, 1966-; Guild of South Carolina Artists, 1968-; Southeastern College Art Conference, 1975-. **HONORS/AWARDS:** Southern Arts Federation/NEA, fellowship, 1987; AAUP, Clemson, Professor of Merit, 1985. **HOME ADDRESS:** 108 Poole Lane, Clemson, SC 29631, (803)654-5456.

BUSINESS ADDRESS: Professor, Art Dept, Clemson University, Lee Hall, Box 340509, Clemson, SC 29634-0509, (803)656-3924.

WANG, SHAOGUANG
Educator. Chinese American. **PERSONAL:** Born Jan 31, 1954, Wuhan, People's Republic of China. **EDUCATION:** Peking University, LLB, 1981; Cornell University, MA, 1984, PhD, 1990. **CAREER:** Yale University, assistant professor, 1990. **ORGANIZATIONS:** American Political Science Association, 1990; Association for Asian Studies, 1990. **BUSINESS ADDRESS:** Professor, Dept of Political Science, Yale University, 124 Prospect St, New Haven, CT 06520, (203)432-5262.

WANG, SHAW S.
Educator. Chinese American. **PERSONAL:** Born in Taipei, Taiwan. **EDUCATION:** Rutgers University, PhD, 1970. **CAREER:** Rutgers University, professor, currently. **HONORS/AWARDS:** National Research Council, Taiwan, ROC, invited lectureship, 1990; Chinese American Food Society, Achievement Award, 1989. **BUSINESS ADDRESS:** Professor, Chemical Engineering, Rutgers University, New Brunswick, NJ 08903.

WANG, SHEN K.
Orthopedic surgeon. Chinese American/Malaysian American. **PERSONAL:** Born Sep 5, 1922, China; married Eleanor, 1946; children: Catherine S, Colbert L, Candace D, Christine C. **EDUCATION:** National Central University; Harvard Medical School, MD, 1957. **CAREER:** Self-employed, orthopedic surgeon, currently. **ORGANIZATIONS:** American College of Surgeons, fellow; American Academy of Orthopedic Surgeons, fellow. **BUSINESS ADDRESS:** Physician, Orthopedic Clinic, 1345 Locust Avenue, Fairmont, WV 26554-1497, (304)366-5050.

WANG, SHI-HWA
Educator. Taiwanese American. **PERSONAL:** Born Feb 5, 1961, Keelung, Taiwan; son of Ming-Song Wang and Jing-Cheu Yang; married Yu-Jane Yang, May 21, 1988. **EDUCATION:** Soochow University, Taiwan, BA, 1983; University of Illinois, Urbana-Champaign, MM, 1986, DMA, 1990. **CAREER:** Ann Arbor Symphony Orchestra, principal second violin, 1988-90; Scandinavian Symphony Orchestra, concertmaster, 1989-90; Wayne State University, artist-in-residence, 1989-90; Ballet West Symphony Orchestra, associate concertmaster, 1990-; New American Symphony Orchestra, concertmaster, 1990-; American String Workshop at University of Michigan, faculty, 1992-; Weber State University, assistant professor, 1990-. **ORGANIZATIONS:** Phi Kappa Phi, Scholastic Honor Society, 1989; American String Teachers Association, 1990; Student Chapter of the American String Teachers Association at WSU, sponsor, 1991-; Chinese Club Association, Weber State University, sponsor, 1993-; Asian Study Alliance, Weber State University, faculty, 1993-. **HONORS/AWARDS:** Paul Rolland Music Competition, second prize, 1985; Concerto Competition, Soochow University, winner, 1983; University of Illinois, graduate teaching assistantship, 1984-88; Chow's Scholarship for Music and Literature, winner, 1982; Soochow University, Top of the Class Honor, 1981-83. **SPECIAL ACHIEVEMENTS:** Dissertation: "A Study of Violin Sonatas, by Lalo, Lekeu, and D'Indy with Focus on the Compositional Employment of 'Cyclic Treatment,'" University of Illinois, 1989; soloist, Tchaikovsky Violin Concerto with the New American Symphony Orchestra, 1993; concertmaster in 12 different symphony orchestras. **BUSINESS ADDRESS:** Assistant Professor, Weber State University, 455E Browning Center, Ogden, UT 84408-1905, (801)626-6929.

WANG, SHIEN TSUN
Educator. Chinese American. **PERSONAL:** Born Aug 24, 1938, Changsha, Hunan, China; son of Yuan Kang Wang and Hwa-Ying Liu Wang; married Lung-chu S Wang; children: Alan, Stephen. **EDUCATION:** National Taiwan University, BSCE, 1960; Michigan State University, MS, 1964; Cornell University, PhD, 1969. **CAREER:** National Taiwan University, teaching assistant, 1961-62; Michigan State University, research assistant, 1962-64; Cornell University, research assistant, 1964-68; instructor, research associate, 1968-69; University of Kentucky, assistant professor, 1969-75, associate professor, 1975-82, professor, director of grad studies, 1982-. **ORGANIZATIONS:** Chi Epsilon; Tau Beta Pi; Sigma Xi; American Society of Civil Engineers; American Society of Engineering Education; International Structural Stability Research Council; American Academy of Mechanics; Cornell Society of Engineers; American Society of Civil Engineers, subcommittees and task committees, chairman, national committees; Structural Stability Research Council, task group and subcommittee, chairman. **HONORS/AWARDS:** Uni-

versity of Kentucky, Outstanding Civil Engineering Professor Award, 1985; Lincoln Arc Welding Foundation, Outstanding Achievement in Engineering Education Award, 1985; International Journal of Thin Walled Structures, editorial board. **SPECIAL ACHIEVEMENTS:** Over 40 publications in professional journals and conference proceedings. **MILITARY SERVICE:** Military Police, lieutenant, 1961-62. **BUSINESS ADDRESS:** Professor, Director of Graduate Studies, Dept of Civil Engineering, University of KY, S Limestone Rd, 233 Anderson Hall, Lexington, KY 40506-0001, (606)257-4916.

WANG, SHIH-CHUN
Physiologist, educator. Chinese American. **PERSONAL:** Born Jan 25, 1910; son of Yen Sun Wang and Hsi (Han) Wang; married Mamie Kwoh, Jan 10, 1939; children: Phyllis M, Nancy E. **EDUCATION:** Yenching University, BS, 1931; Peking Union University, Medical College, MD, 1935; Northwestern University, PhD, 1940. **CAREER:** Peiping Union Med College, asst, physiology, 1935-37; China Medical Board, fellow, 1937-40; Northwestern University, instructor, 1938-40; Columbia University, instructor, asst prof, assoc prof, prof of physiology, 1941-54, prof of pharmacology, 1954-74, Gustavus A Pfeiffer prof, 1974-79, Pfeiffer prof emeritus, 1979-. **ORGANIZATIONS:** Acad Sinica; American Physiol Soc; American Pharmacol Soc; NY Acad Scis; NY Acad Medicine; Assn for Research on Nervous and Mental Diseases; Soc Experimental Biology & Medicine; AAAS; NY State Medical Soc; Sigma Xi. **SPECIAL ACHIEVEMENTS:** Numerous publications on physiology and pharmacology of automatic nervous system. **HOME ADDRESS:** 18 Kent Rd, Tenafly, NJ 07670.

WANG, SHIH-HO
Educator. Chinese American/Taiwanese American. **PERSONAL:** Born Jun 29, 1944, Kiangsu, China; son of Mr and Mrs C C Wang. **EDUCATION:** National Taiwan University, BS, 1967; University of California, Berkeley, MS, 1970, PhD, 1971. **CAREER:** University of Colorado, assistant professor of elec eng, 1973-77; University of Maryland, assistant professor of elec eng, 1977-78, associate professor of elec eng, 1978-84; University of California, Davis, professor of ECE, 1984-. **HONORS/AWARDS:** IEEE Control System Society, Honorable Mention, 1975. **SPECIAL ACHIEVEMENTS:** Over 80 publications in control and robotics areas, 1970-. **MILITARY SERVICE:** Chinese Air Force, Republic of China, 2nd lt, 1967-68. **BUSINESS ADDRESS:** Professor, Dept of ECE, University of California, Davis, CA 95616, (916)752-7390.

WANG, SHIH-LIANG
Educator. Chinese American. **PERSONAL:** Born May 27, 1955, Sanchung, Taiwan; son of Chin-Chin and Yu-Hua Wang; married Yue-Min Wang, May 16, 1981; children: Harris, Christine. **EDUCATION:** National Tsing Hua University, BS, 1977; Ohio State University, MS, 1983, PhD, 1986. **CAREER:** Industrial Technology Research Institute, engineer, 1979-81; Ohio State University, graduate research associate, 1982-86; NC A&T State University, associate professor, 1986-. **ORGANIZATIONS:** American Society of Mechanical Engineers, secretary, Carolina Section, 1991-92; Sigma Xi. **HONORS/AWARDS:** American Society of Engineering Educators, Dupont Fellow, 1991. **SPECIAL ACHIEVEMENTS:** Pioneering research on robots with linkage structures, 1989-; contributor: ASME Journal of Mechanical Design, and International Journal of Robotics and Automation, 1985-; visiting scientist, Oak Ridge National Lab, 1989. **MILITARY SERVICE:** Army, Republic of China, 2nd lieutenant, 1977-79. **BUSINESS ADDRESS:** Associate Professor, Mech Engr Dept, NC A&T State University, 1601 E Market St, McNair 635, Greensboro, NC 27411, (919)334-7620.

WANG, SHIQING
Educator. Chinese American. **PERSONAL:** Born Oct 6, 1959, Beijing, People's Republic of China; son of DaLai Wang and YiYi Chen; married Shirley Wang, Jul 31, 1984; children: Janice, Alicia. **EDUCATION:** University of Chicago, PhD, 1987. **CAREER:** UCLA, postdoctoral; Case Western Reserve University, assistant professor, currently. **BUSINESS ADDRESS:** Professor, Case Western Reserve University, 2232 Circle Dr, Olin Bldg, Rm 701, Cleveland, OH 44106, (216)368-6374.

WANG, SHO-YA
Educator. Taiwanese American. **PERSONAL:** Born Jan 9, 1951, Lukang, Taiwan; married Ging Kuo Wang; children: Winston, Steven. **EDUCATION:** SUNY at Stony Brook, PhD, 1981. **CAREER:** SUNY at Albany, assistant professor, 1986-92, associate professor, 1992-. **ORGANIZATIONS:** American Association for Cancer Research, currently. **HONORS/AWARDS:** NIH,

The First Award, 1986. **BUSINESS ADDRESS:** Associate Professor, Dept of Biology, SUNY at Albany, 1400 Washington Ave, Albany, NY 12222, (518)442-4355.

WANG, SHOU-LING (DANIEL)

Engineer, educator (retired). Chinese American. **PERSONAL:** Born Oct 17, 1924, Shanghai, China; son of Pah-Yuen Wang & Su-Teh Tu; married Nilcea Muniz, Feb 21, 1986; children: Michael, Lawrence, Caroline. **EDUCATION:** St John's University, BS, 1946; Yale University, ME, 1948; University of Illinois, PhD, 1952. **CAREER:** DB Steinman, structural engineer, 1952-55; Clarkson College of Technology, assistant professor, 1955-57; University of Missouri, associate professor, 1957-60; North Carolina State University, visiting associate professor, 1960-67; David Taylor Research Center, group leader, Ship Protection Division, 1967-92. **HONORS/AWARDS:** David Taylor Research Center, Outstanding Performance Rating, 1970, 1978, Sustained Superior Performance Award, 1981, Group Achievement Award, 1981, MPS Top Rating and Cash Award, 1983, Meritorious Civilian Service Award, 1985. **SPECIAL ACHIEVEMENTS:** Published papers: Journal of the Structural Division, ASCE, 1963, 1966; Computers and Structures Journal, 1972; presented and published papers in 4th & 6th IEP ABCA-7 Quadripartite Conferences, 1974, 1983; presented and published papers at 2nd International Conference on Computational Methods, 1984; published about 70 reports at David Taylor Research Center, 1967-91. **BIOGRAPHICAL SOURCES:** Bridge Convention Complete, WANG Trump Asking Bids, p 400, 1990. **HOME ADDRESS:** 9132 Kirkdale Rd, Bethesda, MD 20817, (301)530-7957.

WANG, SHU-HSIA

Dentist. Chinese American. **PERSONAL:** Born Feb 21, 1955, Taipei, Taiwan; daughter of C T Wang and T Y Chang Wang; married Paul C Wang, Jun 23, 1984; children: Christine, Paula. **EDUCATION:** Tufts Dental School, DMD, 1983. **CAREER:** Private practice, dentist, 1985-. **ORGANIZATIONS:** American Dental Assn. **BUSINESS ADDRESS:** Dentist, 16037 Comprint Circle, Gaithersburg, MD 20877, (301)977-8383.

WANG, SHUJEN

Educator. Taiwanese American. **PERSONAL:** Born May 9, 1963, Tao-Yuan, Taiwan; daughter of Chieh Wang & Chung-Hsieu Kuo Wang. **EDUCATION:** Chinese Culture University, BA, 1985; Indiana University, Bloomington, MS, 1987; University of Maryland, College Park, PhD, 1991. **CAREER:** University of Maryland, graduate teaching assistant, 1987-91; News Mirror Weekly, free-lance writer, 1989-; Southeastern Louisiana University, assistant professor, 1991-93; Westfield State College, assistant professor, 1993. **ORGANIZATIONS:** Association for Education in Journalism & Mass Communications, 1987-; International Communication Association, 1990-; Speech Communication Association, 1990-; Eastern Communication Association, 1990-; Chinese Communication Association, 1990-. **HONORS/AWARDS:** Southeastern Louisiana University, Grant, 1992; Eastern Comm Association, Political Comm Division, Top Three Paper Winner, 1992; AEJMC, International Comm Division, third place paper winner, 1991; Chiang Ching-Kuo Foundation for International Scholarly Exchange, $12,000 Disseration Scholarship, 1991. **SPECIAL ACHIEVEMENTS:** Author, "Ideology and Foreign News Coverage: Propaganda Model Re-examined," chapt, Political Communication, Public Opinion, and the Media: US and International Issues edited by Yonah Alexander & Robert Deutsch, 1993; "The New York Times and Renmin Ribao's News Coverage of the 1991 Soviet Coup," text, 1993; "Factors Influencing Cross-National News Treatment of a Critical National Event," Gazette, 1992; "Credible News Source vs Propaganda Tool," Media Asia, 1992. **BUSINESS ADDRESS:** Asst Professor, Mass Communication Dept, Westfield State College, Westfield, MA 01086, (413)572-5746.

WANG, STANLEY

Business executive. Chinese American/Taiwanese American. **PERSONAL:** Born Dec 8, 1942, Chungking, Sichuan, China; married Franny Wang, Aug 23, 1969; children: Nina, Melissa. **EDUCATION:** National Taiwan University, BS, 1965; Temple University, MBA, 1971. **CAREER:** Philco Ford, 1970-73; Pantronix Corp, president, 1974-. **ORGANIZATIONS:** Monte Jade Science & Technology Association, chairman of the board, founder, board member, 1990-; CIE, board member, 1991-92; AAMA, board member, 1987-88. **BUSINESS ADDRESS:** President, Pantronix Corp, 145 Rio Robles Dr, San Jose, CA 95134-1994, (408)432-1890.

WANG, STUART SUI-SHENG

Educator. Chinese American. **PERSONAL:** Born Jul 28, 1946, Canton, Kwang-tung, China; son of Yin Chih Fong; married Margaret Wang, Jul 22, 1972; children: Elizabeth, Diana, Sarah. **EDUCATION:** National Taiwan University, BS, 1968; Cornell University, MS, 1971, PhD, 1975. **CAREER:** University of Oklahoma, instructor, 1975-76; Texas Tech University, visiting lecturer, 1976-78; Purdue University, visiting associate professor, 1984-86; Cornell University, visiting associate professor, 1988-89; Oakland University, assistant professor, 1978-83, associate professor, 1983-91, professor, 1991-. **ORGANIZATIONS:** American Mathematical Society; Mathematical Association of America. **BUSINESS ADDRESS:** Professor, Oakland University, Rochester, MI 48309-4401, (313)370-3441.

WANG, SU-SU

Educator. Chinese American. **PERSONAL:** Born May 10, 1948, Nanking, China; married Diana; children: Daniel. **EDUCATION:** National Cheng-Kung University, BS, 1968; National Taiwan University, MS, 1970; Massachusetts Institute of Technology, ScD, 1974. **CAREER:** MIT, research assistant, 1971-74, research associate, 1974-77; University of Illinois, assistant professor, 1977-80, associate professor, 1980-84, professor, 1984-90, National Center for Composite Materials, director, 1985-90; University of Houston, professor, 1990-. **ORGANIZATIONS:** ASME, 1972-; AIAA, 1974-; ASTM, 1974-; American Academy of Mechanics, 1974-; American Society of Composites, 1974-. **HONORS/AWARDS:** Alcoa Foundation, Faculty Research Award, 1986; University of Illinois, Best Faculty Research Award, 1984; Shell Foundation, Faculty Research Award, 1986-87; International Conf on Cryogenic Matls, Best Paper Award, 1980. **SPECIAL ACHIEVEMENTS:** Published over 130 papers in refereed journals and books; co-editor, two technical journals; served on various governmental and industrial committees on advanced materials and mechanical and aerospace engineering. **BUSINESS ADDRESS:** Distinguished University Professor, Mech Eng Dept, University of Houston, 4800 Calhoun Rd, Engineering Bldg, Rm N 216, Houston, TX 77204, (713)743-4515.

WANG, SUE S.

Computer programmer. Taiwanese American. **PERSONAL:** Born Feb 1, 1958, Kaohsiung, Taiwan; daughter of Yen-Lin Yeh and Yueh-Hsia Wu Yeh; married Lawrence S Wang, Mar 12, 1983; children: Crystal, Amethyst. **EDUCATION:** Tamkang University, BS, 1980; City University of New York, graduate school, 1982-83; Greater Hartford Community College, certificate, 1986. **CAREER:** Kaohsiung City Government, construction division, 1980-81; Greater Hartford Community College, supervisor, 1985-86; Judicial Information Systems, State of Connecticut, programmer I, 1986-87; Barry's Jewelers Inc, senior programmer analyst, 1987-90; Information Concept Inc, senior programmer analyst, 1990-91; PacTel Cellular Inc, consultant, 1992; PacifiCare Health Systems Inc, senior programmer analyst, 1992-. **ORGANIZATIONS:** Global Soto Enterprise, president, 1992-; Rowland Heights Chorus Group, vice president, 1991-93; Rowland Heights Chinese Association, 1992-93; Rowland District School Unified Parents Association, counselor, 1993; Hacienda Heights Chinese School Parents Association, counselor, 1993; New York Taiwan Hsian-Yin Chorus Group, 1981. **HONORS/AWARDS:** Outstanding Master of Cermonies, 1992; Miss New York Double-Tenth Contest, Miss Friendship, 3rd prize, 1981; Tamkang University, Chinese Calligraphy, 3rd prize, 1979. **HOME ADDRESS:** 17511 Rio Court, Rowland Heights, CA 91748, (818)810-6242.

WANG, SUOJIN

Educator. Chinese American. **PERSONAL:** Born Nov 16, 1959, Zhejiang, People's Republic of China; son of Chaogeng Wang and Yao Zhan; married Suqing Xia, Jun 24, 1985; children: Adam S, Jessica S, Diana S. **EDUCATION:** Hangzhou University, China, BA, 1982; University of Texas, Austin, PhD, 1988. **CAREER:** Hangzhou University, teaching assistant, 1982-83; University of Texas, Austin, teaching assistant, 1983-85, assistant instructor, 1985-88; Southern Methodist University, visiting assistant professor, 1988-90; Texas A&M University, assistant professor, 1990-93, associate professor, 1993-. **ORGANIZATIONS:** American Statistical Association, 1988-; Southeast Texas Chapter of American Statistical Association, vice president, 1992-93, president elect, 1993-94; Institute of Mathematical Statistics, 1990-. **HONORS/AWARDS:** University of Texas, University Fellowship, 1985. **SPECIAL ACHIEVEMENTS:** Over 20 research publications in refereed statistical and mathematical journals. **BUSINESS ADDRESS:** Associate Professor, Dept of Statistics, Texas A&M University, College Station, TX 77843-3143.

WANG, SYLVIA
Educator. Chinese American/Malaysian American. **PERSONAL:** Born Aug 5, 1960, Penang, Malaysia; daughter of Leon Wang and Soei-Ien Tan; married Jan Keith Weller, Mar 21, 1993. **EDUCATION:** Royal Academy of Music, London, England, diploma, 1981; Eastman School of Music, University of Rochester, MM, 1985, DMA, 1987. **CAREER:** University of Iowa, assistant professor of music, 1987-90; Present Music, core member, 1993-; Samaris Piano Trio, artistic director, 1987-; Northwestern University, director of chamber music, assistant professor, 1990-. **ORGANIZATIONS:** Music Teachers National Association, 1988-; Chamber Music America, 1989-; Pi Kappa Lambda, 1993-. **HONORS/AWARDS:** Chamber Music Yellow Springs, First Prize, 1990; Ohio Arts Council, Touring Grant, 1991-92; Eastman-Godowsky Competition, First Prize, 1986; Johann Sebastian International Bach Competition, finalist, 1992; Naumburg Chamber Music Competition, finalist, 1993. **SPECIAL ACHIEVEMENTS:** Performances throughout United States, Canada, England, France, Germany, Costa Rica, Malaysia, Singapore; broadcasts: WQXR-New York, Public Radio, Radio London; television: WHDH-Boston, Massachusetts, Asian Focus, Costa Rican Television; Recording: Northeastern label, 1994. **BUSINESS ADDRESS:** Assistant Professor of Piano, Northwestern University, 711 Elgin Road, Evanston, IL 60208, (708)491-3906.

WANG, TIXIANG
Educator. Chinese American. **PERSONAL:** Born Aug 27, 1946, Shanghai, China; married Aihua Zhou, Jan 1, 1971; children: Wengi, Minlan Zhou. **EDUCATION:** Nanjing University, BS , 1968, MS, 1981; University of Connecticut, PhD, 1986. **CAREER:** No 8 Metal Co, China, engineer, 1969-78; Nanjing University, instructor, 1981-84, associate professor, associate director, 1987-89; University of Connecticut, assistant professor, 1986-87, associate professor, 1990-. **ORGANIZATIONS:** American Mathematical Association, 1984-; Mathematical Association of China, 1981-; Mathematical Association of America, 1992-. **SPECIAL ACHIEVEMENTS:** Twenty publications. **BUSINESS ADDRESS:** Associate Professor, Dept of Mathematics, University of Connecticut, 1084 Shennecossert Rd, AA-208, Groton, CT 06340, (203)445-3429.

WANG, TON-LO
Educator. Taiwanese American. **PERSONAL:** Born May 17, 1953, Taipei, Taiwan; son of Shi-Geng Wang and Sun In Wang; married Yung-Hsun Tsao, Apr 26, 1986; children: Esther M, Joyce M. **EDUCATION:** Chung-Yuan University, BS, 1975; Illinois Institute of Technology, MS, 1979, PhD, 1984. **CAREER:** Illinois Institute of Technology, teaching assistant, 1979-82, research assistant, 1982-83; Association of American Railroads, assistant research engineer, 1983-85; Florida International University, associate professor, 1985-. **ORGANIZATIONS:** American Society of Civil Engineers, 1986-; Transportation Research Board, 1992-; International Association for Bridge and Structural Engineering, 1993-; American Railway Engineering Association, 1993-; American Society of Engineering Education, 1993-; Chinese-American Scholars Association of Florida, 1990-; North America Chinese Transportation Professionals Association, 1993-. **HONORS/AWARDS:** Association of American Railroads, Graduate Fellowship, 1982; Florida International University, Summer Research Award, 1988, Minority Faculty Development Award, 1990, Outstanding Achievement Award, 1990, Outstanding Research Award, 1992. **SPECIAL ACHIEVEMENTS:** Twenty-five papers in refereed journals; seventeen papers in conference proceedings. **BUSINESS ADDRESS:** Assoc Prof, Dept of Civil Engineering, Florida International University, VH 160, Miami, FL 33199, (305)348-3054.

WANG, TSUEY TANG
Investment company executive, educator. Taiwanese American. **PERSONAL:** Born Nov 12, 1932, Tainan, Taiwan; son of Shih Neng & Tsun Chen Wang; married Meitieh Lin Wang, Jun 12, 1965; children: David, Marjorie, Vanessa. **EDUCATION:** Cheng Kung University, BSc, 1955; Brown University, PhD, 1965. **CAREER:** Polytechnic University of New York, assistant professor, 1965-67; AT&T Bell Labs, distinguished member of technical staff, 1967-88; Rutgers University, visiting professor, 1988-; Transpac Capital Corp, president, CEO, 1988-. **ORGANIZATIONS:** National Association of Investment Companies, director of board, 1990-; American Physical Society, fellow, 1982-; National Center for Composite Materials, University of Delaware, industrial advisory board, 1986-89; Materials Research Society, 1991-; Formosan Association of Public Affairs, director of board, 1992-; North American Taiwanese Professors' Association, NY/NJ chapter president, 1984-85. **HONORS/AWARDS:** Japan Ministry of Education, Foreign Special Invited Professor, 1992; AT&T Bell Labs, Distinguished Member of Staff Award, 1983; Ameri-

can Physical Society, fellowship, 1982. **SPECIAL ACHIEVEMENTS:** Author of more than 80 technical papers; editor, The Applications of Ferroelectric Polymers, Blackie & Sons, 1988; contributing author, Optical Telecommunications, Academic Press, 1979; contributing author, Polymer Blends, Academic Press, 1978; read and speak Chinese, Japanese, and Taiwanese. **BUSINESS ADDRESS:** President, CEO, Transpac Capital Corporation, 1037 Rt 46E, C-201, Clifton, NJ 07013.

WANG, VERONICA C.
Educator. Chinese American. **PERSONAL:** Born Oct 11, 1936, Penglai, Shantung, China; daughter of C Y Chow; married Alfred S Wang, Sep 2, 1961; children: Dorothy, Lisa. **EDUCATION:** Queens College, AB, 1959; Tulane University, MA, 1964, PhD, 1967. **CAREER:** Southern University in New Orleans, assistant professor, 1965-67; East Carolina University, assistant professor, 1967-73, associate professor, 1973-. **ORGANIZATIONS:** Tar River Civitan Club, president, 1981; Melus Sessions, chair, 1993; Samla, 1984. **SPECIAL ACHIEVEMENTS:** Articles/essays on Asians, 1990; American lit published in Melus and South Dakota Reviews, 1985. **BUSINESS ADDRESS:** Associate Professor, Dept of English, E Carolina University, Greenville, NC 27858.

WANG, VICTOR SHENG
Educator. Chinese American. **PERSONAL:** Born Apr 28, 1956, Qiqihaer, Heilongjiang, People's Republic of China; son of Wang Wen Lin and Xue Qun; married Lucy X Liu, Dec 28, 1984; children: Connie K. **EDUCATION:** College of Education, Qiqihaer, AA, 1977; Lu Xun Academy of Fine Arts, BFA, 1983; Fontbonne College, Fine Arts Department, MFA, 1990. **CAREER:** Visual Teaching Centre, Qiqihaer, illustrator, 1977-79; Lu Xun Academy of Fine Art, assistant professor, 1983-88; St Louis Community College, Meramec, instructor, 1990-91; Webster University, assistant professor, 1990-91; Fontbonne College, assistant professor, 1990-91, assistant professor, 1991-. **ORGANIZATIONS:** Art St Louis Forum Committee, 1992; CAA, 1991-92; National Oil and Acrylic Painters' Society, 1992-93. **HONORS/AWARDS:** National Drawing Competition, 25th Annual National Drawing and Small Sculpture Exhibition, second prize, 1991; St Louis Artists' Guild, Regional Portrait Competition, first prize, 1990, first prize, 1991; Garret Gallery, St Louis, national juried competition, first prize, oil painting. **SPECIAL ACHIEVEMENTS:** "My Creative Idea," in Fine Arts, 1984. **BIOGRAPHICAL SOURCES:** "Gallery Shows Work of Chinese Painter," by Paul Harris, St Louis Post-Dispatch, 1992; "Eastern Ideas, Western Methods," in American Artist, pp 56-61, June, 1992; "Victor Wang's Paintings Are Studies in Contrast," in St Louis Post-Dispatch, August, 1991. **HOME ADDRESS:** 249 Cleta Ct, Ballwin, MO 63021, (314)256-6835.

WANG, WAYNE
Movie director. Chinese American. **PERSONAL:** Born Jan 12, 1949, Hong Kong; married Cora Miao. **EDUCATION:** Foothill College, two years; California College of Arts and Crafts, BFA, painting; California College of the Arts, MA, film, television. **CAREER:** Film director, works include: A Man, A Woman, and a Killer, 1975; Chan Is Missing, 1982; Dim Sum: A Little Bit of Heart, 1985; Slamdance, 1987; Eat a Bowl of Tea, 1989; Life Is Cheap. . . But Toilet Paper Is Expensive, 1990; The Stranger, 1992; Joy Luck Club, 1993. **HONORS/AWARDS:** Visual Communication, Steve Tatsukawa Memorial Award, 1992. **BUSINESS ADDRESS:** Film Producer, Director, c/o William Morris Agency, 151 El Camino Dr, Beverly Hills, CA 90212, (310)274-7451.∗

WANG, WEI
Table tennis competitor. Chinese American. **PERSONAL:** Born Mar 21, 1961, Beijing, People's Republic of China; daughter of Wang Jin Zhang and Qiao Shu Rui; married Diego Schaaf, Mar 16, 1989. **CAREER:** United States Table Tennis Association, women's team member, 1991-94. **HONORS/AWARDS:** US Table Tennis Assn, Women's Table Tennis Champ, 1990; Mayor Tom Bradley of Los Angeles, Asian Pacific Heritage Month, Recognition of Outstanding Contribution in Athletics, 1992. **SPECIAL ACHIEVEMENTS:** Women's Doubles Table Tennis US Champion (with Lily Yip), 1993; Women's Singles US Table Tennis Champion, 1991. **BIOGRAPHICAL SOURCES:** Asian Week, May 29, 1992. **BUSINESS ADDRESS:** Table Tennis Competitor, PO Box 51103, Pasadena, CA 91115.

WANG, WILLIAM KAI-SHENG
Educator. Chinese American. **PERSONAL:** Born Feb 28, 1946, New York, NY; son of Yuan-Chao Wang & Julia Ying-Ru Li Wang; married Kwan Kwan Tan Wang, Jul 29, 1972; children: Karen Y C. **EDUCATION:** Amherst

College, BA, 1967; Yale Law School JD, 1971. **CAREER:** Gruss & Co, assistant to managing partner, 1971-72; University of California, School of Law, Davis, visiting professor, 1975-76; University of San Diego, School of Law, assistant professor, associate professor, professor, 1972-81; White House Domestic Policy Staff, full-time consultant, 1979; University of California School of Law, Los Angeles, visiting professor, 1990; Hastings College of Law, professor, 1981-. **ORGANIZATIONS:** American Law Institute, 1990-; State Bar of California, 1972-; Asian American Bar Association of the Greater Bay Area, 1981-; American Bar Association, 1990-. **HONORS/AWARDS:** Phi Beta Kappa, 1966; Woodrow Wilson Foundation, Honorary Graduate Fellowship, 1967. **SPECIAL ACHIEVEMENTS:** Various articles in legal journals, newspapers, magazines, etc. **MILITARY SERVICE:** United States Army, Spc4, 1968-74. **HOME ADDRESS:** 455 39th Ave, San Francisco, CA 94121-1507, (415)668-3520. **BUSINESS ADDRESS:** Professor, Hastings College of Law, 200 McAllister St, San Francisco, CA 94102-4978, (415)565-4666.

WANG, WILLIAM S-Y.
Educator. Chinese American. **PERSONAL:** married; children: Eugene, Yulun, Yumei, Yusi. **EDUCATION:** University of Michigan, PhD, 1960. **CAREER:** University of California, Berkeley, professor, currently. **ORGANIZATIONS:** International Association of Chinese Linguistics, president, 1992. **HONORS/ AWARDS:** Guggenheim Foundation, 1978; Center for Advanced Studies in Behavioral Sciences, 1969, 1983; Rockefeller Center for Advanced Studies, 1991; Fulbright Senior Lecturer, Sweden, 1971. **SPECIAL ACHIEVE-MENTS:** Academia Sinica, 1992. **BUSINESS ADDRESS:** Professor, University of California, Berkeley, 2222 Piedmont Ave, Berkeley, CA 94720.

WANG, XIAOHAN
Physicist, scientist, engineer. Chinese American. **PERSONAL:** Born Jan 20, 1958, Beijing, People's Republic of China; married Daiqing Mou; children: Kailly. **EDUCATION:** China University of Science & Technology, BS, 1982; University of Michigan, MSEE, 1985, PhD, 1991. **CAREER:** University of Michigan, research assistant, 1985-90, research associate, 1991-92; Medasys, Inc, software engineer, 1992; Adac Labs, Inc, physicist, 1992-. **ORGANIZATIONS:** Tau Beta Pi, 1986-; IEEE, 1989-; Society of Nuclear Medicine, 1992-. **SPECIAL ACHIEVEMENTS:** Author and co-author of 16 scientific papers and abstracts in IEEE Transactions, Journal of Nuclear Medicine, and other publications; inventor and co-inventor of 2 US patents. **BUSINESS ADDRESS:** Physicist, Adac Labs, 540 Alder Dr, Milpitas, CA 95035, (408)321-9100.

WANG, XIAOPING
Educator. Chinese American. **PERSONAL:** Born Oct 5, 1956, Changchun, Jilin, People's Republic of China; daughter of Zhifang Wang and Mingfen Fan; married Ge Wu, Aug 2, 1983; children: Fangbai Wu. **EDUCATION:** Northeast Teachers University, BA, 1978, MA, 1982; East Tennessee State University, EdD, 1991. **CAREER:** Northeast Teachers University, instructor, 1978-79, lecturer, 1982-85; North China University of Technology, lecturer, 1985-87; East Tennessee State University, doctoral fellow, 1987-90; Northeast State Technical Community College, professor, 1990-. **ORGANIZATIONS:** American Ed Research Association, 1989-; Mid-South Ed Research Association, 1989-; PDK, 1989-. **HONORS/AWARDS:** East Tennessee State University, Outstanding Scholastic Achievement, 1991, 1990, Outstanding Academic Achievement, 1989, 1988. **SPECIAL ACHIEVEMENTS:** Fluent in Chinese; author: A Practical Course of English Pronunciation, Northeast Teachers University Press, 1986. **BUSINESS ADDRESS:** Professor, Northeast State Technical Community College, PO Box 246, Blountville, TN 37617-0246, (615)282-0800.

WANG, XINGWU
Educator. Chinese American. **PERSONAL:** Born Feb 19, 1953, Hangzhou, Zhejiang, People's Republic of China; son of Jinguang Wang & Xiuying Lin; married Changjiang Xu, Aug 6, 1986; children: Changcheng John. **EDUCATION:** Harbin Naval Engineering Institute, BS, electrical engineering, 1978; Hangzhou University, MS, physics, 1981; SUNY, Buffalo, PhD, physics, 1987. **CAREER:** State University of New York, Buffalo, teaching assistant, 1982-84, research assistant, 1984-87, postdoctoral research associate, 1987-88; Argonne National Lab, summer faculty, 1992, 1993; US Air Force, summer faculty, 1992, 1993; Alfred University, assistant professor of electrical engineering, 1988-93, associate professor of electrical engineering, 1993-. **HONORS/AWARDS:** Center for Advanced Research of New York, research grant, 1988-93; US Air Force, research grant, 1993; Argonne National Lab,

research grant, 1992-93; National Science Foundation Center for Glass Research, research grant, 1991, 1993; New York State Institute on Superconducting, research grant, 1989-90. **SPECIAL ACHIEVEMENTS:** More than 60 papers published in Physical Review, Applied Physics, etc; 13 US patents applied. **BUSINESS ADDRESS:** Associate Professor, Dept of Electrical Engineering, Alfred University, 26 N Main St, Alfred, NY 14802, (607)871-2130.

WANG, XUE-SEN
Educator. Chinese American. **PERSONAL:** Born Sep 20, 1961, Nanjing, Jiangsu, People's Republic of China; son of Chuan-song Wang and Fu-zhen Chen; married Jeanne Qing Cai, Feb 9, 1988. **EDUCATION:** Fudan University, BS, 1982; University of Maryland, College Park, PhD, 1990. **CAREER:** University of Maryland, graduate research assistant, 1984-90; University of California, Santa Barbara, postdoctoral research, 1990-92; University of Oklahoma, Norman, visiting assistant professor, 1993-. **ORGANIZATIONS:** American Physical Society, 1985-; American Vacuum Society, 1993-. **HONORS/AWARDS:** Maryland Graduate School, Fellowship, 1984-86. **SPECIAL ACHIEVEMENTS:** Constructing instruments for surface science research, including the scanning tunneling microscope; studies of physical and chemical properties of various semi-conductor surfaces. **BUSINESS PHONE:** (405)325-4323.

WANG, XUEFENG
Educator. Chinese American. **PERSONAL:** Born Apr 23, 1963, Zigong, People's Republic of China; married Lingyan Shu. **EDUCATION:** Peking University, BS, 1984; University of Minnesota, PhD, 1990. **CAREER:** Tulane University, assistant professor of mathematics, 1990-. **HONORS/AWARDS:** National Science Foundation, Research Grant, 1991-95.

WANG, XUN-LI
Scientist. Chinese American. **PERSONAL:** Born Dec 23, 1964, Harbin, Heilongjiang, People's Republic of China; son of Jin-Zhen Wang and Shu-Jin Liu; married Haiyi Xiao, Dec 25, 1987. **EDUCATION:** Beijing University, BS, 1985; Iowa State University, PhD, 1992. **CAREER:** Iowa State University, Argonne National Laboratory, graduate student, 1988-92; Oak Ridge National Laboratory, research associate, 1992-. **ORGANIZATIONS:** Materials Research Society, 1993-; American Ceramic Society, 1993-; American Physical Society, 1988-92; Neutron Scattering Society of America, 1992-. **HONORS/AWARDS:** United States Department of Energy, Postgraduate Fellowship, 1992; State Commission of Education of PR China, CUSPEA Scholarship, 1986. **BUSINESS ADDRESS:** Research Associate, Oak Ridge National Laboratory, Bldg 4515, MS 6064, Oak Ridge, TN 37831, (615)574-9164.

WANG, YAN
Economist, educator. Chinese American. **PERSONAL:** Born Sep 7, 1953, Beijing, People's Republic of China; daughter of Weili Xu and Dagang Wang. **EDUCATION:** The People's University of China, BA, 1982; Cornell University, MA, 1986, PhD, 1989. **CAREER:** Eastern Kentucky University, assistant professor, 1991-; The World Bank, consultant, 1989-91, economist, 1993-. **ORGANIZATIONS:** American Economic Association, 1987-; American Council of Consumer Interest, 1987-; Chinese Economic Society, 1986-; North America Economic & Finance Association, 1991-. **HONORS/AWARDS:** The World Bank, McNamara Fellowship, 1988-89; American Council of Consumer Interest, Best Dissertation Award, 1990; USIA, Fulbright Scholarship, 1983-84. **SPECIAL ACHIEVEMENTS:** "Inequality and Poverty in China," The World Bank Economic Review, May 1991; "Saving and Wealth Accumulation of Chinese Rural and Urban Hosehold," Tenth Anniversary Publication, The World Bank, 1991; American Consumption Pattern and the Price of Time, Journal of Consumer Affairs, winter 1990; "Effects of the Price of Time on Household Savings: A Life Cycle Consistent Model and Evidence from Microdata," Southern Economic Journal, April 1994; "Government Policies and Productivity Growth," Lessons of East Asia, The World Bank, Washington, DC; "Modern Securities and Futures Markets," The People's Publishing House, Shanghai, Oct 1993. **HOME PHONE:** (703)319-0661. **BUSINESS ADDRESS:** Economist, The World Bank, 1818 H St NW, E10-029 EAPVP, Washington, DC 20433, (202)458-1411.

WANG, YANG
Educator, physician. Chinese American. **PERSONAL:** Born May 12, 1923, Tangshan, China; married Helen, 1966; children: Dale, Cynthia, Jennifer, Heather. **EDUCATION:** National Medical College of Shanghai, China, MB, 1948; Harvard Medical School, MD, 1952; Massachusetts General Hospital,

residency in internal medicine; Massachusetts General Hospital & Mayo Clinic, Rochester, Minnesota, Cardiology Fellowship. **CAREER:** Instructor to professor of medicine, cardiology, 1959-; University of Minnesota Medical School, professor of medicine, currently. **ORGANIZATIONS:** American College of Physicians, fellow; American Association for the Advancement of Science, fellow; Association of University Cardiologists, Inc; Central Society for Clinical Research; American Federation for Clinical Research; American Heart Association, fellow; American College of Cardiology, fellow. **HONORS/AWARDS:** Alpha Omega Alpha. **SPECIAL ACHIEVEMENTS:** Over 100 publications in the field of cardiovascular disease and physiology. **MILITARY SERVICE:** US Air Force, captain, 1955-57. **BUSINESS ADDRESS:** Professor of Medicine, University of Minnesota Medical School, 420 Delaware St SE, PO Box 83, Minneapolis, MN 55455-0392, (612)625-9100.

WANG, YI-TIN
Educator. Chinese American. **PERSONAL:** Born Jan 17, 1952, Taiwan; son of S H Wang & C T Wang; married Yuh-Lang Wang, Dec 26, 1984; children: Andrew W, Jonathan C. **EDUCATION:** National Chung-Hsing University, BSCE, 1974; National Taiwan University, MSCE, 1976; University of Delaware, MCE, 1981; University of Illinois at Urbana-Champaign, PhD, 1984. **CAREER:** University of Illinois, research associate, 1984-85; University of Kentucky, assistant professor, 1986-91, associate professor, 1991-. **ORGANIZATIONS:** Water Environment Federation Program Committee, 1993-98; American Society of Civil Engineers, 1982-; American Water Works Association, 1982-; Association of Environmental Engineering Professors, 1986-; International Association on Water Pollution Research and Control, 1990-92. **HONORS/AWARDS:** University of Delaware, Graduate Fellowship, 1978; University of Kentucky, Summer Faculty Research Fellowship, 1988; US Environmental Protection Agency, Research Grant, 1990. **SPECIAL ACHIEVEMENTS:** "Anaerobic Degradation of Indole to Methane," Appl Environ Microbial, 1984; "Kinetics of an Expanded-Bed Methanogenic Reactor," J Environ Eng, 1986; "Methanogen Degradation of Ozonation Products," Water Res, 1990; "Inhibition of Acetate Methanogenesis by Phenols," 1991; "Biological Reduction of Hexavalent Chromium," J Environ Eng, 1993. **BUSINESS ADDRESS:** Associate Professor, Dept of Civil Engineering, University of Kentucky, 365 Civil Engineering Building, Lexington, KY 40506, (606)257-5937.

WANG, YI T'UNG
Educator (retired). Chinese American. **PERSONAL:** Born Oct 11, 1914, Jiang-Yin, Jiangsu, China; married An-chi Lou, Jul 3, 1947 (deceased); children: Selina Louis, Theodore. **EDUCATION:** Yenching University, BA, 1937, MA, 1941; Harvard University, PhD, 1949. **CAREER:** Nanking University at Chengtu, assistant professor, 1941-44; University of Chicago, visiting assistant professor, 1949-50; University of Wisconsin, visiting assistant professor, 1950-52; Harvard University, research fellow, 1952-57; University of British Columbia, associate professor, 1957-62; University of Pittsburgh, professor, 1962-85, professor emeritus, currently; University of Michigan, visiting professor, 1967; Indiana University, visiting professor, 1968; University of Minnesota, visiting professor, 1970; National Taiwan University, visiting professor, 1979; National Tsing-hua University, visiting professor, 1985-87. **HONORS/AWARDS:** Harvard-Yenching Institute, Fellowship, 1938-41, 1944-49; Fulbright-Hays, Research Grant, 1964-65, 1979-81; National Endowment for the Humanities, Research Grant, 1979-81. **SPECIAL ACHIEVEMENTS:** Author, Official Relations between China and Japan, Harvard UP, 1953; Influential Clans of the Southern Dynasties, 2 vols, revised ed, Chinese University of Hong Kong, 1978; translator, A Record of Buddhist Monasteries in Lo-Yang, Princeton University, 1984; author, Where Literature and History Converge: Selected Articles and Essays of Wang Yi-T'ung, 2 vols, Taipei, 1988. **HOME ADDRESS:** 615 Driftwood Dr, Pittsburgh, PA 15238.

WANG, YIJIANG
Educator. Chinese American. **PERSONAL:** Born May 5, 1953, Jiahe County, Hunan, People's Republic of China; son of Zizhen Wang and Chenqi Li; married Yunhui Peng, Aug 1982; children: Charles, Susan. **EDUCATION:** Peking University, BA, 1982, MA, 1985; Harvard University, PhD, 1991. **CAREER:** World Bank, consultant, 1989; Harvard University, teaching fellow, 1990-91; University of Minnesota, assistant professor, 1991-. **ORGANIZATIONS:** American Economic Association, 1992-; Chinese Economists Society, 1986-. **HONORS/AWARDS:** Harvard-Yenching Institute, visiting fellowship, 1985-86, Doctoral Scholaraship, 1986-90; Harvard University, GSAS, Scholarship, 1990-91. **SPECIAL ACHIEVEMENTS:** Publications of papers on: the inflationary monetary policy in China, 1991, firm's asset liquidation rules, 1992, the timing of privatization in transitional economies, 1993, institutional development, 1993. **BUSINESS ADDRESS:** Asst Professor, University of Minnesota, Industrial Relations Center, 271 19th Ave S, Rm 515, Minneapolis, MN 55455, (612)624-6814.

WANG, YONG TAI
Educator. Chinese American. **PERSONAL:** Born Sep 1, 1955, Hengyang, Hunan, People's Republic of China; son of Zhi-kang Wang & Li-jun Yi; married Wei Shi, Jun 15, 1984; children: Shi-Jun John, Stanley. **EDUCATION:** Wuhan Institute of Physical Education, BS, exercise science, 1982, MS, exercise science, 1985; Ball State University, MA, biomechanics & computer science, 1988; University of Illinois, Urbana-Champaign, PhD, biomechanics, 1991. **CAREER:** Wuhan Institute of Physical Education, instructor, 1984-85; Ball State University, research assistant, 1985-87; University of Illinois, Urbana-Champaign, instructor, 1987-91; Auburn University, assistant professor, 1991-. **ORGANIZATIONS:** American Alliance for Health PE, Recreation and Dance, presider of the biomechanics section, energetics, 1994; American College of Sports Medicine, paper presentation, 1993; PhD Student Committee, biomechanics chairperson, 1993-. **HONORS/AWARDS:** Auburn University, Research Grant-in-Aid, 1992; University of Illinois, Urbana-Champaign, Laura J Huslster Scholarship Award, 1991; UIUC-HINES, VA Hospital Research Grant, 1990; University of Illinois, College Set-Aside Fund, 1988; Wuhan Institute of PE, China, honorary associate professor, 1993. **SPECIAL ACHIEVEMENTS:** Book reviewer: Kinesiology Scientific Basis of Human Movement, 1993; development of a new video motion analysis system used in the biomechanical analysis of human movement, 1992. **BUSINESS ADDRESS:** Assistant Professor, Auburn University, 2050 Joel H Eaves Memorial Coliseum, Auburn, AL 36849-5323, (205)844-1468.

WANG, YU
Engineer. Chinese American. **PERSONAL:** Born Jan 22, 1962, Yining, Xinjiang Uygur Zizhigu, People's Republic of China; son of Shang-Li Wang and Wen-Jun You; married Huiping Qin, Aug 12, 1985; children: Jean, Edward Yu. **EDUCATION:** South China Institute of Technology, BS, 1982, MS, 1985; University of Pennsylvania, PhD, 1990. **CAREER:** South China Institute of Technology, assistant professor, 1985-87; University of Pennsylvania, research associate, 1987; Holtec International, senior engineer, 1988-90, project manager/ principal engineer, 1990-. **ORGANIZATIONS:** American Society of Mech Engineers, 1992-, associate member, 1990-92, student member, 1987-90. **HONORS/AWARDS:** USIA, Short Term Enrichment Program, 1988. **SPECIAL ACHIEVEMENTS:** Project management with the total contract value over $10 million; published over 10 tech papers; proficiency in Chinese, English languages. **BUSINESS ADDRESS:** Principal Engineer, Holtec International, 2060 Fairfax Ave, Cherry Hill, NJ 08003, (609)424-0999.

WANG, ZHI QIANG
Educator. Chinese American. **PERSONAL:** Born May 21, 1958, Qiqihar, Heilongjiang, People's Republic of China; married Li Ma, Jan 20, 1987. **EDUCATION:** Jilin University, China, BS, 1982; Institute Math, The Chinese Academy of Sciences, MS, 1984, PhD, 1986. **CAREER:** Peking University, China, postdoctor & lecturer, 1986-88; Institute Math, The Chinese Academy of Sciences, research associate professor, 1988-91; Courant Institute of Math Science, New York University, visiting member, 1988-89; University of Utah, assistant professor, 1989-90; University of Wisconsin at Madison, assistant professor, 1990-91; Utah State University, assistant professor, 1991-. **ORGANIZATIONS:** World Congress of Nonlinear Analysts, 1992-; World Federation of Scientists, 1993-. **HONORS/AWARDS:** Award for best thesis in math, China, 1987. **SPECIAL ACHIEVEMENTS:** Published seventeen papers in professional mathematical journals. **BUSINESS ADDRESS:** Assistant Professor, Dept of Math, Utah State University, Logan, UT 84322-3900, (801)750-3529.

WANI, MANSUKHLAL CHHAGANLAL
Chemist. Indo-American. **PERSONAL:** Born Feb 30, 1925, Nandurbar, Maharashtra, India; son of Chhaganlal K Wani and Maniben C Wani; married Ramila M Wani, Dec 4, 1954; children: Bankim M. **EDUCATION:** Bombay University, India, BSc, 1947, MSc, 1950; Indiana University, PhD, 1962. **CAREER:** Bhavan's College, lecturer, 1951-58; Indiana University, research assistant, 1958-61; University of Wisconsin, research associate, 1961-62; Research Triangle Institute, principal scientist, 1962-. **ORGANIZATIONS:** American Society of Pharmaconosy, 1972-; American Chemical Society, 1962-; American Association for Advancement of Science, 1983-; New York Academy of Science, 1993-; Sigma Xi, 1962-; Hindu Society of North Caro-

lina, 1976-; Association of Indians in America, 1970-; Indo American Forum for Political Education, 1989-. **HONORS/AWARDS:** Research Triangle Institute, Professional Development Award, 1983; Bochasanwasi Swaminarayan Sanstha, Pride of India Award, 1992; Indo-American Pharmaceutical Society, Award for Taxol Discovery, 1993; American Association for Cancer Research, thirteenth annual Bruce F Cain Memorial Award, recipient, 1994. **SPECIAL ACHIEVEMENTS:** Co-discover of Taxol, one of the most promising anticancer drugs to be dicovered in the last two decades, 1992. Taxol was approved by FDA for the treatment of refractory ovarian cancer. It has been marketed in USA since December 1992 by Bristol-Meyers Squibb. **BIOGRAPHICAL SOURCES:** India Abroad, p 24, Nov 8, 1991 & p 33, Feb 12, 1993; Life Magazine, p 73, May, 1992; Chemical and Engineering News, p 12, September, 1991. **HOME ADDRESS:** 2801 Legion Ave, Durham, NC 27707, (919)489-2573. **BUSINESS ADDRESS:** Principal Scientist, Research Triangle Institute, 304 W Cornwallis Road, Bay 2, Building 11, Research Triangle Park, NC 27709-2194, (919)541-6685.

WARASHINA, M. PATRICIA
Artist, educator. Japanese American. **PERSONAL:** Born Mar 16, 1940, Spokane, WA; daughter of Aiko Konzo Warashina and Heijiro Warashina; married Robert H Sperry, Jul 9, 1976; children: Gretchen Yayoi Bauer Ramels, Lisa Midori Bauer. **EDUCATION:** University of Washington, BFA, 1962, MFA, 1964. **CAREER:** Wisconsin State University, instructor, 1964; Eastern Michigan University, instructor, 1965-68; University of Washington, professor of art, 1970-. **HONORS/AWARDS:** National Endowment for the Arts, Visual Artist Fellowship, 1975, 1986; Governor's Award of Special Commendation for Art, 1980; Seattle Arts Commission, NW Special Collections Award, 1984; King County Arts Commission, Honors Program Award, 1992; University of Washington/Arts, Humanities Faculty Scholar Award, 1992. **SPECIAL ACHIEVEMENTS:** Sculpture, A Procession, 72 NW Artists, Seattle Opera House; sculpture installed, Meden Bauer Convention Center, Bellevue, Washington, fall 1993. **BIOGRAPHICAL SOURCES:** Ceramics in the Pacific NW, La Mar Harrington, 1979; 50 NW Artists, Bruce Guenther, 1983. **HOME ADDRESS:** 120 E Edgar, Seattle, WA 98102.

WASAN, DARSH T.
Educator. Indo-American. **PERSONAL:** Born Jul 15, 1938, Saraisalah, Hazara District, Pakistan; son of Tilakchand G Wasan and Ishari Devi Wasan; married Usha D Wasan; children: Ajay, Kern. **EDUCATION:** University of Illinois, Champaign/Urbana, BS, 1960; University of California, Berkeley, PhD, 1965. **CAREER:** Illinois Institute of Tech, professor, 1964, provost, 1991-, academic vp, currently. **ORGANIZATIONS:** Am Institute of Chem Engrs, Interfacial Phenomenon Committee, chairman, 1980-85; Am Chem Society, Colloid and Surface Chemistry Division, 1980 Society of Rheology, 1980-; Fine Particle Society, 1971-; American Society for Engineering Education, 1976-. **HONORS/AWARDS:** Syracuse University, Stevens Gauge Award, 1991; Am Society for Eng Education, 3M Lectureship Award, 1991, Westen Electric Award, 1972; Am Institute of Chem Engs, Chicago section, F. W. Thiele Award, 1989; National Science Foundation, Special Creativity Award, 1988; Federation of Asian Indians in North America, Enginering Excellence Award, 1988. **SPECIAL ACHIEVEMENTS:** Over 240 technical papers published in professional journals; 3 U.S. patents. **HOME ADDRESS:** 8705 Royal Swan Lane, Darien, IL 60561. **BUSINESS PHONE:** (312)567-3001.

WASSERMAN, FUMIKO HACHIYA
Judge. Japanese American. **PERSONAL:** Born Feb 15, 1947, Torrance, CA; married Ronald T Wasserman; children: Gavin Hachiya, Steven Itano. **EDUCATION:** University of California, Los Angeles, AB, anthropology, 1968; Loyola University, Los Angeles, School of Law, JD, 1978. **CAREER:** Torrance Unified School District, teacher, 1969-73; University of Santa Clara, Summer Institute for the Council Legal Educational Opportunity, teaching asst, 1975; Okamoto & Wasserman, law clerk, 1978-79; Los Angeles City Attorney's Office, deputy city attorney, 1979-80; US District Judge Terry J Hatter, judicial clerk, 1980-81; Adams Duque & Hazeltine, associate, 1981-82; Central District of California & Ninth Circuit Court of Appeals, asst US attorney, 1982-86; Los Angeles Municipal Court, 1986-87; South Bay Municipal Court, asst presiding judge, presiding judge, 1987-89; Los Angeles Superior Court, judge, 1989-. **ORGANIZATIONS:** California Elected Women's Assn for Education & Research, board member; Torrance Unified Sch District, bd of trustees, pres & vp; South Bay Trustees & Administrators Assn, pres; Natl Assn of Women Judges; California Judges Assn; Los Angeles Co Municipal Court Judges' Assn; California Asian Judges' Assn; American Bar Assn; Federal Bar Assn; California Women Lawyers; Japanese American Bar Assn. **HONORS/**

AWARDS: Center for Judicial Education & Research, New Trial Judges Orientation Program, faculty member, 1993. **SPECIAL ACHIEVEMENTS:** Author, Judicial Perspectives for CEB Action Guide, "Defending Your Client in a Misdemeanor Case," revised 1993; co-author, Municipal Court Judges' Assn Legislation Digest, 1988. **BUSINESS ADDRESS:** Judge, Los Angeles Superior Court, 7281 E Quill Dr, Dept 252, Downey, CA 90242, (310)940-8841.

WATAI, MADGE S.
Judge. Japanese American. **PERSONAL:** Born Dec 17, 1927, Honolulu, HI; daughter of Mr & Mrs Harry M Goto; married George, Jul 7, 1952; children: Jay, Karen. **EDUCATION:** Eastman School of Music, University of Rochester, BMus, 1949; Northwestern School of Music, MMus, 1950; Loyola University School of Law, JD, 1967. **CAREER:** Self employed, instructor in piano, 1950-54; Pacific Telephone, secretary, 1953-57; Geo Watai, legal secretary, 1960-63; self employed, attorney, 1968-78; Municipal Court, judge, 1978-81; Superior Court of Los Angeles County, judge, 1981-. **ORGANIZATIONS:** Sigma Alpha Iota, 1947-; Women Lawyers of LA, board committees, 1970-; LA County Bar, immigration committee, 1970-; South Bay Women Lawyers, 1980-; Soroptimist Intl of Gardena, 1979-; Gardena Valley YWCA, advisory board, 1975-; UGA of United Way, committee chair, 1987-; United Way, regional board, 1993; Japanese American Bar Association, 1978-; California Women Lawyers Assn; National Assn of Women Judges, 1979-; Asian Pacific Women's Network. **HONORS/AWARDS:** City of Gardena, Community Service Award, 1977; TELACU, Women's Achievement Award, 1977; Soroptimist, Women's Achievement Award, 1980; Asian Pacific Women, Outstanding Achievement & Servie Award, 1981; Optimist Club, Respect for Law & Services Award, 1984; El Camino Lions, Community Recognition Award, 1985; Women Lawyers of LA, Ernistine Stahlhut Award, 1988. **BUSINESS ADDRESS:** Judge, Superior Court of Los Angeles County, 111 N Hill St, Los Angeles, CA 90012.

WATANABE, CLYDE KAZUTO
Military officer. Japanese American. **PERSONAL:** Born May 20, 1953, Wahiawa, HI; son of Sadao Watanabe and Yukino Watanabe; married Faye S Watanabe, Aug 18, 1984; children: Lynne E, Wayne S. **EDUCATION:** US Coast Guard Academy, BSE, 1975; Purdue University, MSEE, 1980. **CAREER:** US Coast Guard, ensign to commander, 1975-. **ORGANIZATIONS:** Wild Goose Association, 1991-93. **MILITARY SERVICE:** Coast Guard Achievement Medal, 1978; Coast Guard Commendation Medal, 1990, 1991; CMDT LTR Commendation, 1980. **BUSINESS ADDRESS:** Commander, US Coast Guard, 7323 Telegraph Rd, Alexandria, VA 22310-3998, (703)313-5872.

WATANABE, JOHN MAMORU
Educator. Japanese American. **PERSONAL:** Born Dec 19, 1952, Vallejo, CA; son of David J Watanabe & Meriko M Matsushita Watanabe; married Deborah L Nichols; children: Aaron Ethan. **EDUCATION:** University of California, Santa Cruz, BA, 1975; Harvard University, MA, 1978, PhD, 1984. **CAREER:** Harvard University, teaching fellow, 1976-82; University of Michigan, Dearborn, lecturer, 1985; Eastern Michigan University, lecturer, 1985; University of Illinois, Champaign-Urbana, visiting assistant professor, 1985-86; University of Michigan, Ann Arbor, Michigan Society of Fellows, postdoctoral fellow, 1986-89; Dartmouth College, assistant professor, 1989-93, associate professor, 1993-. **ORGANIZATIONS:** American Anthropological Association, fellow, 1993; American Anthropologist, American Ethnologist, Man, Ancient Mesoamerica, Mesoamerica, journal manuscript reviewer, 1986-; University of Texas Press, book manuscript reviewer, 1993-; Social Science Research Council, Selection Committee for Dissertation Fellowships in Latin America and the Caribbean, 1993-94; University of Michigan, Ann Arbor, Horace H Rackham School of Graduate Studies, Distinguished Dissertations Award Committee, chair, 1986-89. **HONORS/AWARDS:** Dartmouth College, Goldstein Prize, 1993, Walter Burke Research Initiation Award, 1989-92; University of Michigan, Michigan Society of Fellows, postdoctoral fellowship, 1986-89; National Science Foundation, research grant, 1983; Harvard University, Frederick Sheldon Traveling Fellowship, 1978, Summer Travelling Fellowship, 1977; University of California, Santa Cruz, Holmes History Prize, 1975. **SPECIAL ACHIEVEMENTS:** Books: Maya Saints and Souls in a Changing World, University of Texas Press, 1992; Reader in Comparative Religion: An Anthropological Approach, 4th edition, Harper and Row Inc, 1979; also 13 articles, 19 papers & 8 book reviews. **BUSINESS ADDRESS:** Professor, Dept of Anthropology, Dartmouth College, 6047 Carpenter hall, Hanover, NH 03755-3570.

WATANABE, MARK HISASHI
Editor. Japanese American. **PERSONAL:** Born Dec 1, 1953, Wahiawa, HI; son of Atsushi Watanabe and Kimie Watanabe; married Jennifer L Watanabe, Jun 22, 1991; children: Samuel. **EDUCATION:** Northwestern University, BSJ, 1975; University of California, Los Angeles, MA, 1976. **CAREER:** Suburban Tribune, copy editor, 1977-78; Advertising Age, various editor positions, 1978-85; Chicago Times Magazine, business/production mgr, 1987-89; The Seattle Times, copy editor, 1985-87, newsfeatures special projects editor, 1989-. **ORGANIZATIONS:** Asian American Journalists Assn, Seattle Chapter, treasurer, 1989-; Japanese American Citizens League, 1992-.

WATANABE, MIKE
Social services administrator. Japanese American. **PERSONAL:** Born Aug 23, 1946, Hawaii; son of Iwao Osaka and Koyoshi Osaka; married Suzanne Watanabe. **EDUCATION:** California State University, Northridge, BA, 1973; UCLA, School of Social Welfare, MSW, 1976. **CAREER:** AADAP Inc, coordinator of residential svcs, 1975-77, director of treatment svcs, 1977-82, executive director, 1982-. **ORGANIZATIONS:** APPCON Ad Hoc Committee on Transitions, chair, 1992-; State Asian Pacific Islander Advisory Committee, chair, 1992-93; Alternative Allocations Methodology Committee, 1991-; National Asian Pacific American Families Against Substance Abuse, treasurer, 1988-; Asian Pacific Health Care Venture, board member, 1986-; Asian Pacific Planning Council, 1979-, president, 1984-86. **HONORS/AWARDS:** Search to Involve Philippino Americans, Bayanihan Award, 1993; Leadership Education for Asian Pacifics, Leadership Award, 1993; City of Los Angeles, Commendation, 1992; County of Los Angeles, Commendation, 1992; Asian Pacific Planning Council, Leadership Award, 1992. **SPECIAL ACHIEVEMENTS:** Initiated and worked to get the Deddeh Bill and the Becerra Bill through the California legislature. **MILITARY SERVICE:** US Army, Sgt, 1969-72. **BUSINESS ADDRESS:** Executive Director, Asian American Drug Abuse Program Inc, 5318 S Crenshaw Blvd, Los Angeles, CA 90043, (213)293-6284.

WATANABE, PAUL YASHIHIKO
Educator, political analyst. Japanese American. **PERSONAL:** Born Mar 14, 1951, Murray, UT; son of Hikomune Watanabe and Ida Watanabe; married Gloria Gustafson Watanabe, Aug 28, 1975; children: Joanna Stahr, Benjamin Gustafson. **EDUCATION:** University of Utah, BS, 1972; Harvard University, MA, 1975, PhD, 1980. **CAREER:** Harvard University, teaching fellow and tutor, 1973-77; University of Massachusetts, Boston, associate professor, 1978-, Institute for Asian American Studies, co-director, 1993-. **ORGANIZATIONS:** Massachusetts Immigrant and Refugee Advocacy Coalition, board member, 1992-; New England Political Science Association, council member, 1991-93; John F Kennedy Library Academic Advisory Committee, 1991-; Harvard Community Health Plan Board of Overseers, 1984-91; American Political Science Association, 1973-; Phi Beta Kappa, 1972; Phi Kappa Phi, 1972. **SPECIAL ACHIEVEMENTS:** Author, Ethnic Groups, Congress and American Foreign Policy, 1984. **HOME ADDRESS:** 65 Torrey St, South Weymouth, MA 02190, (617)337-6128. **BUSINESS ADDRESS:** Assoc Professor, Dept of Political Science, University of Massachusetts, Boston, 100 Morrissey Blvd, Boston, MA 02125, (617)287-5650.

WATANABE, ROBERT. *See* Obituaries.

WATANABE, SUWAKO
Educator. Japanese American. **PERSONAL:** Born Jun 12, 1959, Fukushima, Japan; daughter of Kazuo Ishii & Reiko Ishii; married Osamu Watanabe, Jan 21, 1986. **EDUCATION:** Hosei University, BA, law, 1982; Georgetown University, MS, linguistics, 1986, PhD, linguistics, 1990. **CAREER:** Portland State University, Dept of Foreign Language and Literature, asst professor, 1990-. **ORGANIZATIONS:** Linguistic Society of America, 1991; Association for Asian Studies, 1991; Association for Teachers of Japanese, 1990; ACTFL, The American Council on the Teaching of Foreign Languages, 1992; The Society for International Education, Training and Research, 1990. **HONORS/ AWARDS:** Portland State University, Faculty Development Award, 1991, 1993. **BUSINESS ADDRESS:** Asst Professor, Dept of Foreign Lang & Lit, Portland State University, PO Box 751, Portland, OR 97207-0751, (503)725-5284.

WATANABE, YUKI
Music producer, computer technician. Japanese American. **PERSONAL:** Born Jan 17, 1952, Gitu-City, Gitu-ken, Japan; son of Sumiko Watanabe; married Mayumi Watanabe, Jun 19, 1992. **EDUCATION:** Nanzan University, BA, 1975; New York University, graduate, 1984. **CAREER:** Doorknob Publishing Agency, president/director, 1979-; YWA Productions Inc, president/director, 1981-; Sumitomo One World College Pop Festival, overseas producer, 1989-; Nightclub Project "MARS!," producer/director, 1989-91; Nightclub project "QUICK!," producer/director, 1990-91. **SPECIAL ACHIEVEMENTS:** Video Performance Collaboration, Good Morning Mr Owell, 1984. **BUSINESS ADDRESS:** Producer, YWA Productions Inc, 580 Broadway, #301, New York, NY 10012, (212)966-0158.

WEGLYN, MICHI NISHIURA
Costume designer (retired), author, artist. Japanese American. **PERSONAL:** Born Nov 29, 1926, Stockton, CA; married Walter Weglyn. **CAREER:** Theatrical costume designer for Broadway, television, night clubs, retired; author; artist. **HONORS/AWARDS:** California State University, College of Arts, Honorary LHD, 1993. **SPECIAL ACHIEVEMENTS:** Author, works include: Years of Infamy: The Untold Story of America's Concentration Camps. **BUSINESS ADDRESS:** Author, c/o Morrow & Co, Inc, 1350 Avenue of the Americas, New York, NY 10019. *

WEI, ANTHONY YUEH-SHAN
Educator. Chinese American. **PERSONAL:** Born Jul 5, 1933, Cheung-chow, Hunan, China; son of Simon Wei and Martha Hsu; married Aimee Chen, May 21, 1971; children: Manuela, Ivanna, Erika. **EDUCATION:** Salesian University, Italy, BA, 1958, MA, 1962; Biblical Institute, Italy, MA, 1964, ABD, 1967; University of Freiburg, Switzerland, PhD, 1969; University of Pittsburgh, MLS, 1971. **CAREER:** L'Istituto per il Estremo Oriente, lecturer, 1969-62; Fu-jen University, assistant professor, 1964-66; St Francis College, chairman, assistant professor, 1969-71; The College of St Francis, adjunct professor, 1978-; Governors State University, professor, 1971-, assistant dean, 1974-76, university professor, 1977-. **ORGANIZATIONS:** American Academy of Religion, 1972-; Illinois Philospohical Association, 1972-. **SPECIAL ACHIEVEMENTS:** Life and Thought of Dieriech Bonheoffer, Universitas, 1967; Towards a Philosophy of Academic Libraranship, Library and Information Sciences Journal, 1980; fluent in Chinese, English, French, German, Italian; reads Classical Greek, Classical Hebrew, Spanish. **BUSINESS ADDRESS:** Professor, Governors State University, E 1503, University Park, IL 60466, (708)534-4588.

WEI, BENJAMIN MIN
Educator. Chinese American. **PERSONAL:** Born Aug 11, 1930, Hebel, China; son of Wei Fu Shuen (deceased); married Diana Yun-Dee Fan; children: Victor Mark. **EDUCATION:** Taiwan, BS, 1953; Canada, MS, 1970; Penn State University, PhD, 1981. **CAREER:** Ordance Corps Arsenal, Taiwan, mech engineer liaison, 1953-59; Wenshan Sr H S, Taiwan, teacher, 1960-61; New Brunswick University, teaching assistant, 1961-62; Kruger Paper & Pulp, industrial eng, 1962-64; Domtar Construction, supervisor, 1964-66; McGill University, consultant, 1966-67; University of Montreal, computer programmer, 1967-68; Sir George Wm University, researcher, 1968-70; Baldwin-Cartier School Commission, instructor, 1970-73; Norfolk State University, professor, 1974-. **ORGANIZATIONS:** US Senatorial Club; Republican Presidential Task Force. **HONORS/AWARDS:** Norfolk State University, Teacher of the Year Award, 1983; Rep Pres Task Force, US Medal of Merit, 1984; Taiyuan University, Hon Professorship, 1985; American Biographical Center Research Assn, Deputy Governor; Intl Hall of Fame, elected member. **SPECIAL ACHIEVEMENTS:** Author of numerous papers in various journals. **HOME ADDRESS:** 1152 Janaf Place, Norfolk, VA 23502, (804)461-5842.

WEI, CHAO HUI (CAROLINE)
Scientist. Chinese American. **PERSONAL:** Born Oct 10, 1956, Taipei, Taiwan; married. **EDUCATION:** National Taiwan University, BS, 1978; Yale University, MS, 1980; Carnegie-Mellon University, PhD, 1986. **CAREER:** Alcoa Research Center, scientist, 1986-89; Himont USA Research Center, scientist, 1989-. **ORGANIZATIONS:** American Chemical Society, 1978-; Society of Plastics Engineers, 1986-; Society for Advanced Materials Processing & Engineering, 1986-. **SPECIAL ACHIEVEMENTS:** Author of numerous publications. **HOME ADDRESS:** 10401 Regent Cir, Naples, FL 33942-1571.

WEI, JAMES
Educator, educational administrator. Chinese American. **PERSONAL:** Born Aug 14, 1930, Macao; son of Hsiang-chen Wei and Nuen Kwok Wei; married Virginia Hong, Nov 4, 1956; children: Alexander, Christina, Natasha, Randolph (deceased). **EDUCATION:** Georgia Institute of Technology, BSCE, 1952; MIT, MS, 1954, ScD, 1955; Harvard, advanced management program,

1969. **CAREER:** Mobil Oil Corp, research engineer to research associate, 1956-62, senior scientist, 1963-68, Corporate Planning, manager, 1969-70, consultant; University of Delaware, Allan P Colburn Professor, 1971-77; California Institute of Technology, visiting professor, 1965, Sherman Fairchild Distinguished Scholar, 1977; MIT, Warren K Lewis Professor, 1977-91, Dept of Chemical Engineering, head, 1977-88; Princeton University, visiting professor, 1962-63, Pomeroy and Betty Smith Professor of Chemical Engineering, 1991-, School of Engineering and Applied Science, dean, 1991-. **ORGANIZATIONS:** Natl Academy of Science, Comm on Motor Vehicle Emissions, consultant, 1972-74, 1979-80; EPA, science advisory board, 1976-79; Presidential Private Sector Survey Task Force on Dept of Energy, 1982-83; Chemical Engineering Communications, editor, 1972-; McGraw-Hill Chemical Engineering series, editor, 1964-; American Academy of Arts and Sciences; Academica Sinica of Taiwan; Sigma Xi; Natl Academy of Engineering, nominating committee, 1981, peer committee, 1980-82, membership committee, 1983-85. **HONORS/AWARDS:** American Academy of Achievement, Golden Plate Award, 1966; American Institute of Chemcial Engineers, Professional Progress Award, 1970, Walker Award, 1980, Lewis Award, 1985, Founders Award; American Chemcial Society, Award in Petroleum Chemistry, 1966. **SPECIAL ACHIEVEMENTS:** Contributor of papers and monographs to professional journals, including: The Structure of Chemical Processing Industries, 1979. **BUSINESS ADDRESS:** Dean, School of Engineering, Princeton University, Engineering Quadrangle, Princeton, NJ 08544-1099.

WEI, KUO-YEN
Educator. Chinese American. **PERSONAL:** Born Feb 5, 1953, I-Lan, Taiwan; son of Yang-Sien Wei & Ming-Yin Kao; married Yang Yu; children: Leonard, Julia. **EDUCATION:** National Taiwan University, BS, geology, 1975, MS, geology, 1978; University of Rhode Island, PhD, oceanography, 1987. **CAREER:** University of Rhode Island, research assistant, 1980-87; University of California, post doc researcher, 1987-88; Yale University, assistant professor, 1988-94, assoc professor, 1994-. **ORGANIZATIONS:** Peabody Natural History Museum, faculty affiliate, 1989-; American Geophysical Union, 1986-; Paleontological Society of America, 1992-; International Association of Nannoplankton, 1986-; Chinese American Academic & Professional Society, 1992-; International Chinese Statistical Association, 1991-. **HONORS/AWARDS:** Yale University, Yale Junior Faculty Fellowship, 1993-94. **BUSINESS ADDRESS:** Associate Professor, Dept of Geology and Geophysics, Yale University, PO Box 6666, New Haven, CT 06511-8130, (203)432-3150.

WEI, ROBERT
Educator. Korean American. **PERSONAL:** Born Apr 16, 1939, Republic of Korea; married Soraya N Wei; children: Yasmin N, Jiyan N. **EDUCATION:** George Washington University, BS, 1962, PhD, 1972; Georgetown University, MS, 1969. **CAREER:** Cleveland State University, associate professor, currently. **ORGANIZATIONS:** American Board of Clinical Chemistry; Society of Environmental Toxicology and Chemistry. **MILITARY SERVICE:** US Army, 1962-64. **BUSINESS ADDRESS:** Associate Professor, Dept of Chemistry, Cleveland State University, Euclid Ave, E 24th St, Cleveland, OH 44115-1123, (216)687-2421.

WEI, SUSANNA
Educator. Taiwanese American. **PERSONAL:** Born Aug 23, 1946, Tao-Yuan, Taiwan; daughter of Mr and Mrs Lang-han Fan-Chiang; married William Wei, Jul 4, 1971; children: Stephen, Stanley, Jessica. **EDUCATION:** University of Wisconsin, Madison, BA, 1974, MS, 1976; University of Pennsylvania, MSE, 1984, PhD, 1990. **CAREER:** University of Pennsylvania, visiting researcher, 1990-; Towson State University, assistant professor, 1990-92; Saint Joseph's University, assistant professor, 1992-. **ORGANIZATIONS:** IEEE/IEEE Computer Society; ACM/ACM SIGGRAPH; International AVS User Group. **HONORS/AWARDS:** US Army Chemical Research, Development and Engineering Center, Summer Faculty Research Fellow, 1991, 1992. **SPECIAL ACHIEVEMENTS:** "Strength Guided Motion," Computer Graphics, vol 24, pp 253-262, 1990; "Graphical Displays of Human Strength Data," Journal of Visualization and Computer Animation, vol 3, pp 13-22, 1992. **BUSINESS ADDRESS:** Assistant Professor, Saint Joseph's University, 5600 City Ave, Philadelphia, PA 19131-1395, (215)660-1563.

WEI, WEI
Science reference librarian. Chinese American. **PERSONAL:** Born Oct 27, 1952, People's Republic of China; daughter of Yong Da Wei and Rong Hua Shi; married Terry A Neudorf, May 30, 1986. **EDUCATION:** University of Nebraska, MA, 1986; University of Michigan, MALS, 1988. **CAREER:** University of Michigan, library associate, 1986-88; University of California, science reference librarian, 1988-. **ORGANIZATIONS:** American Libraries Association, 1987-; Special Libraries Association, 1987-; Asian American Librarians Association, 1989-. **SPECIAL ACHIEVEMENTS:** Author, "Preparing Academic Research Librians Today: The Library Associate Program at the University of Michigan," Journal of Educational Media & Library Sciences, vol 30, no 1, 1992. **BIOGRAPHICAL SOURCES:** Lincoln Star, p 1, Nov 25, 1985. **BUSINESS ADDRESS:** Science Librarian, Science Library, University of California, Santa Cruz, Santa Cruz, CA 95064, (408)459-3582.

WEI, WEI-ZEN
Research scientist. Chinese American/Taiwanese American. **PERSONAL:** Born May 1, 1951, Tainan, Taiwan; daughter of Chen-Hwa Lin and Shen-Hung Lin; married Kuang-Chung Wei, Aug 12, 1973; children: John Brown, Benjamin. **EDUCATION:** National Taiwan University, Taipei, Taiwan, BS, 1973; Upstate Medical Center, SUNY Syracuse, MS, 1975; Brown University, PhD, 1978. **CAREER:** Ohio State University, Department of Pathology, instructor, 1981-82; Michigan Cancer Foundation, Department of Immunology, Breast Cancer Biology Program, scientist, 1983-86, assistant member, 1986-91, associate member, 1991-, E Walter Albachten Department of Immunology, leader, 1991-; Wayne State University, Cancer Biology Program, Department of Pharmacology, adjunct assistant professor, 1983-. **ORGANIZATIONS:** American Association of Immunologists, 1981-; American Association for Cancer Research, 1984-; Society of Chinese Bioscientists in America, 1986-; Women in Cancer Research, 1988-; National Institutes of Health, Experimental Immunology Study Section, 1992-96. **HONORS/AWARDS:** National Institutesof Health, Research Awards, 1987-. **SPECIAL ACHIEVEMENTS:** Co-author, Two-dimensional gel analysis of polypeptides from normal, preoplastic and neoplastic mouse mammary tissues, Cancer Immunol Immunother, vol 30, pp 367-373, 1990; co-author, Elimination of VB2 bearing T cells in BALB/c mice implanted with syngeneic preoplastic and neoplastic mammary lesions, Cancer Research, vol 51, pp 3331-3333, 1991; co-author, Adoptive transfer of BB2 deleting activity with host cells from mice implanted with C4 preoplastic hyperplastic alveolar nodules, Cancer Research, vol 52, pp 5183-5263, 1992. **BUSINESS ADDRESS:** Associate Member/Leader, Dept of Immunology, Michigan Cancer Foundation, 110 E Warren Ave, Detroit, MI 48201-1379, (313)833-0715.

WEI, WILLIAM
Educator. Chinese American. **PERSONAL:** Born Jan 18, 1948, Tinghai, China; son of Ling Ching Wei & Lee Cha Wei; divorced; children: Leslie Ann. **EDUCATION:** Marquette University, BA, 1969; University of Michigan, Ann Arbor, MA, 1971, PhD, 1978. **CAREER:** Ann Arbor Public Schools, Multi-Ethnic Curriculum Revision Project, Title III, Asian American curriculum specialist, 1974; University of Illinois, Department of Policy Studies, Illinois/Chicago Project for Inter-Ethnic Dimensions in Education, Title IX, curriculum development coordinator, 1975; Indiana State University, professor of history, 1978-79; University of Colorado, Center for the Study of Race and Ethnicity in America, assistant professor, 1980-86, Asian American studies coordinator, 1987-92, Critical Studies of the Americas Book Series, managing editor, 1992-93, associate professor of history, 1987-, chancellor's special assistant, equity for matters, 1993-. **ORGANIZATIONS:** Association for Asian Studies, International Center for Asian Studies, fellow, 1983-86; Historical Society for 20th Century China in North America, board of directors, 1990-93; Association for Asian American Studies. **HONORS/AWARDS:** Minority Issues Coalition, Champions Award, 1990; mentor, NEH/Reader's Digest Teacher-Scholar Award recipient, 1989; University of Colorado Student Union, Outstanding Faculty Member of Color, UJIMA, Collective Work and Responsibility Conference, 1988; University of Colorado at Boulder, Faculty Award for Equity and Excellence, 1988; Rockefeller Foundation, research fellowship, 1986-87. **SPECIAL ACHIEVEMENTS:** Numerous publications, including: author, Asian American Movement, Asian American History & Culture Series, Temple University Press, 1993; Counterrevolution in China: The Nationalists in Jiangxi during the Soviet Period, Michigan Studies on China Series, University of Michigan Press, 1985. **BUSINESS ADDRESS:** Associate Professor, Dept of History, University of Colorado, Campus Box 234, Boulder, CO 80309, (303)492-7655.

WEI, WILLIAM WU-SHYONG
Educator. Taiwanese American. **PERSONAL:** Born Jun 2, 1940, Hsin-chu, Taiwan; son of Mr & Mrs A-Chen Wei; married Susanna Wei, Jul 4, 1971; children: Stephen, Stanley, Jessica. **EDUCATION:** National Taiwan University, BA, 1966; University of Oregon, BA, 1969; University of Wisconsin,

Madison, MS, 1972, PhD, 1974. **CAREER:** Temple University, assistant professor, 1974-78, associate professor, 1978-86, chair of statistics department, 1982-87, professor, 1986-. **ORGANIZATIONS:** Journal of Forecasting, associate editor, 1985-; Journal of Applied Statistical Science, associate editor, 1992-; International Chinese Statistical Association, board member, 1990-; American Statistical Association; Institute of Mathematical Statistics; Royal Statistical Society. **HONORS/AWARDS:** International Statistical Institute, elected member. **SPECIAL ACHIEVEMENTS:** "Effect of Temporal Aggregation on Dynamic Relationships of Two Time Series Variables," Biometrika, vol 63, pp 513-523, 1976; "The Effect of Systematic Sampling and Temporal Aggregation on Causality," Journal of American Statistical Association, 77, pp 316-319, 1982; "Disaggregation of Time Series Model," Journal of the Royal Statistical Society, B, 52, pp 453-47, 1990; Time Series Analysis: Univariate & Multivariate Methods, Addison-Wesley Publishing Co, 1990. **BUSINESS ADDRESS:** Professor, Temple University, North Broad & Montgomery, Speakman Hall, Philadelphia, PA 19122-2595, (215)204-8459.

WEI, YEN
Educator, researcher. Chinese American. **PERSONAL:** Born Sep 1, 1957, Linchuan, Jiangxi, People's Republic of China; son of Renzheng Wei and Wenqing Wei; married Jane Y Cai, Mar 25, 1986; children: Elizabeth Y, Robert Y. **EDUCATION:** Peking University, BS, 1979, MS, 1981; City College of New York, MA, 1984; City University of New York, PhD, 1986. **CAREER:** Massachusetts Institute of Technology, postdoctoral associate, 1986-87; Drexel University, assistant professor, 1987-91, DuPont Associate Professor, 1991-. **ORGANIZATIONS:** American Chemical Society, Polymer Group in Philadelphia Section, chairman, 1984; Sigma Xi, 1986; American Association for the Advancement of Science, 1989; Philadelphia Organic Chemist's Club, 1989; National Association for Thermal Analysis, 1988; Phi Lambda Upsilon, 1991. **HONORS/AWARDS:** E I du Pont de Nemours Co, du Pont Young Faculty Award, 1991; Drexel University, Drexel Research Scholar Award, 1988; The Li Foundation, USA, Li Fellowship Award, 1981. **SPECIAL ACHIEVEMENTS:** Over 60 research publications and patents in the field of polymer and materials chemistry, particularly in electrically conductive polymers, stereochemistry and mechanism of polymerization, organic-inorganic hybrid materials, solid state organic chemistry, high temperature superconductors, and organic magnetic materials. **BUSINESS ADDRESS:** Professor, Dept of Chemistry, Drexel University, 32nd and Chestnut Sts, Philadelphia, PA 19104, (215)895-2650.

WEN, SHIH-LIANG
Educator, educational administrator. Chinese American. **PERSONAL:** Born in Kanhsien, Jiangxi, China; divorced; children: Dennis Y, Andy Y. **EDUCATION:** National Taiwan University, BS, 1956; University of Utah, MS, 1961; Purdue University, PhD, 1968. **CAREER:** Boeing Co, associate research engineer, 1961-63; US Air Force, Applied Math Lab, research analyst, 1972; New York University, visiting research scientist, 1978-79; Ohio University, professor, 1968-, chairman, 1985-. **ORGANIZATIONS:** American Mathematical Society; Mathematical Association of America; Society for Industrial and Applied Mathematics. **HONORS/AWARDS:** Jiangxi University, honorary professor, 1985; Lanzhou University, Distinguished Professor, 1988. **SPECIAL ACHIEVEMENTS:** Author of numerous research articles published in mathematical journals and proceedings in the United States and abroad. **BUSINESS ADDRESS:** Professor and Chairman, Dept of Mathematics, Ohio University, Athens, OH 45701-2979, (614)593-1254.

WEN, WEN-YANG
Educator. Taiwanese American. **PERSONAL:** Born Mar 7, 1931, Shin-tsu, Taiwan; son of Chi Wen and Yu Wen; married Sue Liu Wen, Aug 1, 1959; children: Lilian Wen Klapper, Alvin. **EDUCATION:** National Taiwan University, BS, 1953; University of Pittsburgh, PhD, 1957. **CAREER:** DePaul University, assistant professor, 1960-62; Clark University, assistant professor, 1962-66, associate professor, 1966-74, professor, 1974-. **ORGANIZATIONS:** American Chemical Society, 1957-; American Association for the Advancement of Science, 1960-; New York Academy of Sciences; First Baptist Church of Worcester, Massachusetts, 1962-. **HONORS/AWARDS:** Humboldt Stiftung, Germany, Humboldt Dozenten, 1970-71, summer 1974. **SPECIAL ACHIEVEMENTS:** More than 60 publications in refereed scientific journals; language proficiency in Japanese, Chinese, Taiwanese; Kyoto University and Toyama Medical & Pharmaceutical University, visiting professor, 1991. **BUSINESS ADDRESS:** Professor, Chemistry Dept, Clark University, 950 Main St, Worcester, MA 01610, (508)793-7117.

WENG, WU-TSUNG
Physicist. Taiwanese American. **PERSONAL:** Born Aug 11, 1944, Hu-Wei, Taiwan; son of Gin-Shen and Chen Shur-Er Weng; married Chan Chuan Weng, Sep 17, 1967; children: Elaine, Helen. **EDUCATION:** National Taiwan University, BSEE, 1966; National Tsing-Hua University, MS, 1968; SUNY, Stony Brook, PhD, 1974. **CAREER:** Brookhaven National Lab, accelerator physicist, 1977-83; Stanford Linear Accelerator, accelerator physicist, 1983-87; Brookhaven National Lab, booster project manager, 1987-91, accelerator division head, 1990-. **ORGANIZATIONS:** American Physical Society, fellow, 1974-; IEEE, senior member, 1989-; NPSS/IEEE, chairman, Particle Accelerator Science and Technology Committee, 1989-. **BUSINESS ADDRESS:** Accelerator Division Head, Brookhaven National Laboratory, Bldg 911-B, Upton, NY 11973, (516)282-2135.

WHANG, BENJAMIN
Engineer, educator. Korean American. **PERSONAL:** Born Jun 17, 1937, Seoul, Republic of Korea; son of Andrew C K Whang and Hyun Sook Kim Whang; married Young Bo Kim Whang, Jun 17, 1961; children: Suzanne, Julie. **EDUCATION:** Polytechnic Institute of Brooklyn, BCE, 1959, MCE, 1961; Massachusetts Institute of Technology, PhD, 1969. **CAREER:** George Washington University, School of Engineering and Applied Science, adjunct professor, currently; Naval Surface Warfare Center, Carderock Division, research structural engineer, structural engineer, 1961-, supervisory structural engineer, supervisor, naval architect, structures, head, submarine survivability group, currently. **ORGANIZATIONS:** American Society of Civil Engineers, 1959-; Sigma Xi, 1968-. **HONORS/AWARDS:** DOD, Navy, scholarship, with salary, 1965-67; Navy's Meritorious Civilian Service Award, 1981; Civil Service, Group Achievement Awards. **SPECIAL ACHIEVEMENTS:** Research in: design of ships and submarines against weapons effects, fluid-structure interaction shock response of submarine pressure hulls and equipment, finite element method, design procedures, etc, computer code validation and certification in structural dynamics and hydrodynamics, 1961-. **BUSINESS ADDRESS:** Head, Submarine Survivability Group, Carderock Division, Naval Surface Warfare Center, Bethesda, MD 20084-5000, (301)227-1734.

WHANG, ROBERT
Physician executive, educator, educational administrator. Korean American. **PERSONAL:** Born Mar 7, 1928, Honolulu, HI; son of Won Tai & Grace Maria Whang; married May Taeko Whang, Jun 3, 1956; children: Charleen R, David D, Cynthia C Uptmore, Lisa A. **EDUCATION:** St Louis University, BS, 1952, School of Medicine, MD, 1956. **CAREER:** Veterans Administration, chief of metabolism, 1963-71, chief of staff, 1971-78, chief of medicine, 1978-92, chief of staff, 1992-; University of New Mexico, assistant to associate professor, 1963-71; University of Connecticut, professor of medicine, associate dean, 1971-73; Indiana University, professor of medicine, assistant dean, 1973-78; University of Oklahoma, professor of medicine, vice chair, 1978-92; University of Hawaii, professor of medicine, assistant dean, 1992-. **ORGANIZATIONS:** Central Society for Clinical Research, editorial board; American College of Nutrition, vice president, president, editorial board; American College of Physicians, fellow; Gordon Research Conference on Magnesium, vice chairman, chairman. **HONORS/AWARDS:** American College of Physicians, W O Thompson Travelling Scholar, 1967, fellow, 1967. **SPECIAL ACHIEVEMENTS:** Certified by American Board of Internal Medicine, 1965; certified by American Board of Internal Medicine in subspecialty of nephrology, 1972; published 77 articles, 19 book chapters. **MILITARY SERVICE:** 1946-48 US Army (RA); 1958-64, Army Natl Guard; 1985-, US Army Reserve, Colonel; 1985 "A" Professional Designation. **BUSINESS ADDRESS:** Chief of Staff, Veterans Administration Medical and Regional Office Center, 300 Ala Moana Blvd, PO Box 50188, Honolulu, HI 96850, (808)541-1600.

WHANG, SEUNGJIN
Educator. Korean American. **PERSONAL:** Born May 4, 1952, Seoul, Republic of Korea; son of Inock Whang and AeYang Ma; married Moon Kyung Whang, Dec 15, 1973; children: Jieun, Jihye. **EDUCATION:** Seoul National University, BE, 1974; University of Rochester, MA, 1983, PhD, 1988. **CAREER:** Stanford University, assistant professor, 1987-91, associate professor, 1991-. **ORGANIZATIONS:** Pi Systems, board member, 1991-. **HONORS/AWARDS:** Stanford University, Fletcher Jones Scholar, 1989, Bob & Marilyn Jaedicke Scholar, 1991. **SPECIAL ACHIEVEMENTS:** Papers: "Contracting for Software Contracting," Management Science, 1992; "The Impacts of Information Systems on Organizations and Markets," Communications of the ACM, 1991; "Cost Allocation Revisited," Management Science, 1989. **BUSI-**

NESS ADDRESS: Assoc Professor, Graduate School of Business, Stanford University, Stanford, CA 94305, (415)723-4756.

WHANG, SUKOO JACK

Pathologist. Korean American. PERSONAL: Born Feb 3, 1934, Seoul, Republic of Korea; son of Seung Il Whang and Young Sook Kim; married Chung A Whang, Nov 30, 1963; children: Selena, Stephanie, John. EDUCATION: Oregon State University, BS, 1957; UCLA, MS, 1960, PhD, 1963; Korea University, MD, 1972. CAREER: California State University, Pomona, assistant professor, 1963-64; Pacific Union College, adjunct professor, 1977-87; White Memorial Medical Center, Infection Control Committee, chairman, 1977-87, School of Medical Technology, program director, 1977-87, pathologist, 1977-. HOME ADDRESS: 1325 Via Del Rey, South Pasadena, CA 91030, (213)258-4765.

WHANG, UN-YOUNG

Educator. Korean American. PERSONAL: Born Feb 22, 1954, Seoul, Republic of Korea; daughter of Sun Soo Whang and Kewha Whang. EDUCATION: The Juilliard School, BM, MM, 1979; Columbia University, EdM, 1984, EdD, 1986. CAREER: Full Gospel Korean Church in New York, pianist, 1976-79; Trinity Korean Presbyterian Church, pianist, organist, 1981-83; Hudson Korean Church, Presbyterian, pianist, organist, 1983-86; Teachers College, Columbia University, part-time instructor, 1985-87; Queens Korean Church, pianist, 1986-87; Korean Central Covenant Church, pianist, 1989-91; Moody Bible Institute, associate professor, 1987-. ORGANIZATIONS: Music Educators National Conference, 1984-87; College Music Society, 1986-; Music Educators National Association, 1987-. HONORS/AWARDS: The Juilliard School, scholarships, 1968-79, 1st prize, piano concerto competition, 1970; Helena Rubinstein, scholarships, grants, 1970-76; Seoul Symphony Orchestra, Ewha Girls School, 1st prize winner of concerto competition, 1964; Republic of Korea, Presidential Award, 1968; Kappa Delta Pi, 1983-88. SPECIAL ACHIEVEMENTS: Numerous concerts in major concert halls in Korea, solo recitals, soloist with orchestras, 1964-68; numerous appearances on radio and TV programs in Korea, 1964-68; various solo & chamber concerts in New York area, including a recital in Carnegie Recital Hall and appearance with the Juilliard Pre-College Orchestra in Lincoln Center, 1970-85; performances in churches and Christian conferences in Chicago area, 1987-; MTNA Certified College Teacher, 1993. BUSINESS ADDRESS: Associate Professor of Music, Moody Bible Institute, 820 N LaSalle Dr, Chicago, IL 60610-3276, (312)329-4092.

WHANG, YUN CHOW

Educator. Chinese American. PERSONAL: Born Dec 13, 1933, Foochow, Fukien, China; married Yeong-Ping Chu; children: Ruth, Joyce, Kenneth. EDUCATION: Taiwan College of Engineering, BME, 1954; University of Minnesota, PhD, 1962. CAREER: Catholic University of America, professor, currently. HOME ADDRESS: 8003 Grand Teton Dr, Potomac, MD 20854.

WHANGBO, MYUNG-HWAN

Educator. Korean American. PERSONAL: Born Oct 21, 1945, Republic of Korea; married Jin-Ok Lee Whangbo, May 1, 1971; children: Jennifer Sung, Albert Jun. EDUCATION: Seoul National University, BS, 1968, MS, 1970; Queen's University, PhD, 1974. CAREER: Queen's University, postdoctoral fellow, 1975-76; Cornell University, postdoctoral associate, 1976-77; North Carolina State University, assistant professor, 1978-81, associate professor, 1981-87, professor, 1987-. ORGANIZATIONS: American Chemical Society, 1978-. HONORS/AWARDS: North Carolina State University, Alumni Associations Outstanding Research Award, 1988; Dreyfus Foundation, Camille and Henry Dreyfus Teacher-Scholar Award, 1980-85; Sigma Xi, Research Award, 1981. SPECIAL ACHIEVEMENTS: Over 200 publications in refereed journals, 2 books published, 1978-. HOME ADDRESS: 3731 Swift Dr, Raleigh, NC 27606, (919)851-6053. BUSINESS ADDRESS: Professor, Dept of Chemistry, North Carolina State University, Raleigh, NC 27695-8204, (919)515-3464.

WHITE, CEDINA MIRAN KIM

Attorney. Korean American. PERSONAL: Born Apr 5, 1963, Hollywood, CA; daughter of See Myun Kim and Ock Ja Kim. EDUCATION: Harvard University, AB, 1985; Boston College Law School, JD, 1988. CAREER: Shin & Kim, summer associate, 1986; Peabody & Arnold, summer associate, 1987; Bronson, Bronson & McKinnon, associate, 1988-90; Sees Color Textiles, attorney advisor, 1990-91; US Department of Health & Human Services, attorney advisor, 1991-93. HONORS/AWARDS: International Honors Pro-

gram Participant, 1984. BIOGRAPHICAL SOURCES: Martindale-Hubbell Directory; West Publication of California Lawyers. HOME ADDRESS: 235 E 22nd St, #2-S, New York, NY 10010.

WING, CHARMEEN HAH-MING

Association administrator. Chinese American. PERSONAL: Born Aug 9, 1958, Palo Alto, CA; daughter of Henry & Wanda Wing. EDUCATION: University of California, Los Angeles, BA, economics, 1982. CAREER: Kern/Mathai Advertising Co, assistant account executive, 1982-84; KLSX-FM, Greater Media Inc, public affairs director, 1984-85; Los Angeles Regional Foodbank, development manager, 1986-88; Southmark Pacific Leasing/So Pac Commercial Real Estate, leasing representative, 1988-89; Coldwell Banker Commercial Real Estate, sales associate, 1990; East West Players, managing director, 1990-91; Jefferson Center for Character Education, executive vice president, 1992-. ORGANIZATIONS: Asian Pacific Women's Network, board of directors, 1984-, public relations chair, 1985-86; Asian Rehabilitation Services, chair of the board, 1984-90, board of directors, 1990-; Big Sisters of Los Angeles, Asian Pacific Advisory Council, founding member, 1988-; Girl's Club of Santa Monica, advisory board, 1985-; Los Angeles Women's Foundation, Grants Review Committee, 1992-; National Society of Fundraising Executives, 1986-88, 1991-; Public Interest Radio and Television Educational Society, 1984-, board of directors, 1984-89, Scholarship Committee, 1986-, scholarship chair, 1986-88; United Way, Los Angeles Corp Office, Chinese Business Initiative Committee, co-chair, 1992-. BUSINESS ADDRESS: Executive Vice President, Jefferson Center for Character Education, 2700 E Foothill Blvd, Ste 302, Pasadena, CA 91107, (818)792-8130.

WING, JAMES

Chemist. Chinese American. PERSONAL: Born Jul 8, 1929, Highland Park, MI; son of Henry Richard Wing; married Dorothy Chi-Ching Lee Wing, Aug 10, 1957; children: Kimberly Jo Wing Parker, Jonathan Joe. EDUCATION: University of Tennessee, BS, chemistry, 1951; Purdue University, MS, chemistry, 1953, PhD, chemistry, 1956. CAREER: Argonne National Laboratory, associate chemist, 1955-69; National Bureau of Standards, research chemist, 1969-75; US Nuclear Regulatory Commission, reliability and risk analyst, 1975-. ORGANIZATIONS: American Chemical Society, 1951-; American Scientific Affiliation, 1986-. HONORS/AWARDS: Board of Foreign Exchange Scholars, Fulbright Scholarship, 1964-65; University of Tennessee, Honor Chemistry Senior, 1951. HOME ADDRESS: 15212 Red Clover Dr, Rockville, MD 20853.

WING, JEANNETTE M.

Educator. Chinese American. PERSONAL: Born in Newark, NJ; daughter of Omar Wing and Camella Wing. EDUCATION: Massachusetts Institute of Technology, SB, SM, 1979, PhD, 1983. CAREER: University of Southern California, assistant professor of computer science, 1983-85; Massachusetts Institute of Technology, visiting associate professor of computer science, 1992; Carnegie Mellon, assistant and associate professor of computer science, 1985-. ORGANIZATIONS: IEEE, 1977-; ACM, 1977-; Sigma Xi, 1979. HONORS/AWARDS: Academia Sinica, consultant, 1988; Phi Beta Kappa, 1979; Tau Beta Pi, 1977; Eta Kappa Nu, 1976. SPECIAL ACHIEVEMENTS: Book chapters, editor of book, many journal and conference publications, technical reports; service to national educational and research grantory institutes and committees. BUSINESS ADDRESS: Associate Professor, Computer Science Dept, Carnegie Mellon University, 5000 Forbes Ave, Pittsburgh, PA 15213-3891, (412)268-3068.

WINICK, TRANQUILINA RIOS (LYNN)

Company executive. Filipino American. PERSONAL: Born Jun 18, 1938, Sarrat, Ilocs Norte, Philippines; daughter of Godofredo & Aurelia Rios; married David F Winick, Jan 30, 1965; children: Wayne, Mark, Anthony. EDUCATION: Philippine Women's University, BS, pharmacy, 1960. CAREER: Philippine Drugstore, founder, owner, manager, 1962-70; Donaldson Dept Store Pharmacy, sales, 1970-72; Aero-space Computer Supplies, accounts receivable, 1981-83; Aero Assemblies Inc, president, CEO, 1983-. ORGANIZATIONS: American Red Cross, Greater Mpls Area, board member, 1988-93, assistant to mil fam committee, 1988-; Asian American Chamber of Commerce, board of directors, 1990-, task force in organizing chamber; Cultural Society of Fil-Americans, board of directors, 1990-, various positions; Boy Scouts of America, volunteer leader, 1973-90; United States Naval Academy, Parents Club of MN, president, 1989-90; Philippine-Minnesota Chamber of Commerce, board of directors, 1993-. HONORS/AWARDS: Ernst & Young/Merrill Lynch/Gray, Plant, Mooty, finalist, Minority Entrepreneur of the Year,

1991; Governor's Certificate of Commendation, 1990; Metropolitan Economic Development Association, Certificate of Commendation, 1990. **BUSINESS ADDRESS:** President, CEO, Aero Assemblies Inc, 12012 12th Avenue S, Burnsville, MN 55337.

WONG, ALAN S.
Educator. Chinese American. **PERSONAL:** Born Feb 28, 1954, Lahad Datu, Sabah, Malaysia; son of Wong Fen Hoi; married Lian Wong, Dec 20, 1982; children: Melissa, Jeremy, Janelle. **EDUCATION:** Spicer Memorial College, India, BA, 1977; Andrews University, MBA, 1981; University of North Texas, PhD, 1986. **CAREER:** Sabah Adventist Secondary School, teacher, 1977-78; University of North Texas, full-time instructor, 1985; Indiana University Southeast, associate professor of finance, 1986-. **ORGANIZATIONS:** ACCEPT (non-profit consumer credit counseling organization), advisory board, 1992-93; Financial Management Association; Midwest Finance Association; Indiana Academy of the Social Sciences; Indiana University Southeast, head, Student Recruitment & Retention Committee, 1992-93, Faculty Senate, 1988-89, 1993-94. **HONORS/AWARDS:** Phi Eta Sigma, Honorary Member, 1993; Beta Gamma Sigma, 1992. **SPECIAL ACHIEVEMENTS:** "Efficiency of the Treasury Bill Futures Market: Regression & Volatility Tests," Review of Business & Economic Research, 1990; "An Applied Ethical Analysis System in Business," Journal of Business Ethics, 1992; "Sensation-Seeking & Financial Risk-Taking in Everyday Money Matters," Journal of Business & Psychology, 1991; "Empirical Investigation of the Characteristics of Successful Accounting Researchers," Atlantic Economic Society Best Papers Proceedings, 1992. **BUSINESS ADDRESS:** Professor, Business & Economics, Indiana University Southeast, New Albany, IN 47150, (812)941-2423.

WONG, ALBERT
Educator, chemist. Chinese American. **PERSONAL:** Born Feb 8, 1938, Hanover, Jamaica; son of Charlie & Urcella Wong. **EDUCATION:** Mico Teachers College, teachers diploma, 1960; University of West Indies, BSc, 1970; St Thomas University, MS, 1985; Pacific Western University, PhD, 1988. **CAREER:** University of West Indies, lab superintendent, 1972-73; National Water Authority, Jamaica, chemist, 1979-71; Ministry of Education, Nassau, Bahamas, Prince Williams High School, chemistry teacher, 1970-72, York Castle High School, science chairperson, 1973-80; Rochester Public Schools, 1982-83; Dade County Schools, chemistry teacher, 1984-. **ORGANIZATIONS:** American Chemical Society, 1970-93; Chemical Society of Great Britain, 1970-86; Dade County Chamber of Commerce, 1989-93; United Teachers of Dade, 1984-; Florida Teachers Association, 1984-; Miami Chamber of Commerce, 1988-. **HONORS/AWARDS:** Hugh Clarke Scholarship, 1964; Miami Jackson Senior School, Outstanding A P Teacher, 1989; Chemical Society of Great Britain, fellow, 1972-; Miami Jackson High School, award for teaching advanced placement chemistry. **SPECIAL ACHIEVEMENTS:** Author, Methodologies in Endocrine Research, 1973; dissertation: "Teaching Chemistry to Advanced Placement Students," 1988; Productive Uses of the Castor Bean; Hormonal Changes in the Scarids. **MILITARY SERVICE:** Jamaica Combined Cadet Force, lt, 1973-81. **HOME ADDRESS:** 12515 NW 21st Place, Miami, FL 33167, (305)685-2802.

WONG, ALBERT Y.
Educator. Chinese American. **PERSONAL:** Born Feb 22, 1947, Nanjing, China; son of Frank Wong & Anna Wong; married Monica Wong, Sep 1, 1972; children: Ting. **EDUCATION:** Columbus College of Art and Design, BFA, 1970; Kent State University, MFA, 1974. **CAREER:** Varsity House Inc, artist, 1970-71; Structural System Consultants, artist, 1972-75; Dice Corp, designer, 1975-76; West Virginia Arts Council, artist-in-residence, 1976-78; Lincoln College, assistant professor, 1978-82; Western Kentucky University, associate professor, 1982-86; University of Texas, associate professor, 1986-. **ORGANIZATIONS:** Graphic Arts Society, vice president, 1992-, treasurer, 1991-92, secretary, 1990-91. **HONORS/AWARDS:** Print Magazine, honorable award, 1986. **SPECIAL ACHIEVEMENTS:** Solo exhibitions: Deming Art Center Gallery, 1993, Auburn University Gallery, 1992, Evansville Museum of Art, 1986. **HOME ADDRESS:** 1019 Esplanada Circle, El Paso, TX 79932, (915)584-3879. **BUSINESS ADDRESS:** Associate Professor, University of Texas, El Paso, 500 W University Ave, Fox Fine Arts, El Paso, TX 79968, (915)747-7841.

WONG, ALEXIUS YU-MING
Pianist, educator. Malaysian American. **PERSONAL:** Born Oct 17, 1965, Kuala Lumpur, Malaysia; son of Micheal & Teresa Wong. **EDUCATION:** Memphis State University, BA, 1987, BMus, 1989; University of Maryland,

College Park, MMus, 1991. **CAREER:** International Piano Archives, archive assistant, 1991; Field School, music director, 1991-92; Holton-Arms School, piano teacher, 1992-93; Elizabeth Seton High School, Spanish/piano teacher, 1993-; Pan-American Symphony Orchestra, principal pianist, 1992-. **ORGANIZATIONS:** Music Teachers National Association, 1993-; National Spanish Society, 1986-. **HONORS/AWARDS:** National Spanish Society, Member Award, 1986; Arkansas State University Piano Competition, 1st prize, 1989; Memphis State University Piano Concerto Competition, 2nd prize, 1988. **HOME ADDRESS:** 8669 Ritchboro Rd, Forestville, MD 20747.

WONG, ALFRED
Federal official. Chinese American. **PERSONAL:** Born Mar 25, 1919, New York, NY; son of John & Kate Wong; married Nora Wu Wong; children: 3 daughters. **EDUCATION:** Fordham University, BS, ed, 1950. **CAREER:** US Secret Service, dept assistant director, 1951-75; Supreme Court of the US, marshal, 1975-. **ORGANIZATIONS:** International Association Chiefs of Police, life member; Association Former Agents of Secret Service, 1975; American Society for Industrial Security, life member. **SPECIAL ACHIEVEMENTS:** Oversees operation of the Supreme Court, both administratively and for security. **MILITARY SERVICE:** US Army, 1943-45, Bronze Star medal, Combat Infantry Badge. **BUSINESS ADDRESS:** Marshal, Supreme Court of the United States, 1 First St, NE, Washington, DC 20543, (202)479-3200.

WONG, ALVIN C. P.
Banker. Chinese American. **PERSONAL:** Born Oct 26, 1950, Honolulu, HI; son of Wellington C Wong and Choi Yuk Wong; married Donna C Wong, Jan 19, 1980; children: Timothy G, Christie S. **EDUCATION:** University of Hawaii, BBA, 1972; Chaminade University, MBA, 1980. **CAREER:** Bank of Honolulu, assistant vice president, 1979-89; Hawaii National Bank, vice president, 1989-. **ORGANIZATIONS:** Chinese Chamber of Commerce of Hawaii, director, 1990; Manoa Jaycees, 1979-89; United Church of Christ, 1950-; Beta Gamma Sigma, 1972. **MILITARY SERVICE:** US Army, cpl, 1972-74. **BUSINESS ADDRESS:** Vice President, Hawaii National Bank, 45 N King St, Honolulu, HI 96817.

WONG, ANGELA MA
Author, educator, entrepreneur, publisher, intercultural consultant. Chinese American. **PERSONAL:** Born Feb 7, 1947, Nanking, China; daughter of Shiu Tong Ma and Renee Cheng Ma; married Norman Mun Fai Wong, Sep 2, 1967; children: S Jason, Wendy C, Jamie M, Steven D. **EDUCATION:** Virginia Polytechnic Institute & State University, 1964-67; University of Southern California, BA, 1968; California State University, Teaching Credential, 1968-69; UCLA, 1969-70. **CAREER:** KFI, Los Angeles, administrative assistant; Los Angeles Unified School District; instructor/advisor/couns, 1969-72, refugee advisory/admin, 1972-79, employment counselor, 1976-79, public relations, coordinator, 1980-86, 1986-; Pacific Heritage Books, president, currently. **ORGANIZATIONS:** Palos Verdes Chamber of Commerce, director, 1990-; Chinese Hist Society of So Calif, past president, 1975-; Organization of Chinese Amer Women, 1980-; Asian Business Association, 1989-; Asian American Public Relations & Advert Alliance, 1992-; Asian American Democratic Task Force, 1991-92; Chinese Amer Association of So Calif, 1986-; Chinese American Bicentinnial Committee, 1988-89. **HONORS/AWARDS:** City of Los Angeles, Commendation, 1993; California State Assembly, Certificate of Recog, 1993; Coordination Council for North Amer Affairs, Distinguished Service Award, 1993; Dept of Treasury, Cert of Recognition, 1993; City of LA, Resolution, 1989. **SPECIAL ACHIEVEMENTS:** Author: Target: The US Asian Market, 1993; Developer, The Practical Feng Shui Chart, 1992; Sane Motherhood, 1982. **BIOGRAPHICAL SOURCES:** Personnel Journal, pp 79-89, May 1993; Asia Week, May 20, 1992, 93; Atlantic Monthly, pp 146-151, November 1992; Palos Verdes Review, September 1992; News Pilot, Daily News, July 1992; LA Times, July 18, 1993; Downtown News, pp 75-92, May 22, 1993; Rafu Shimpo, June 16, 1993, p 1; World Journal (Chinese), May 20, 1993; Asian Week, June 25, 1993; International Daily News (Chinese), May 28, 1993, p K1, K6. **BUSINESS ADDRESS:** President/Intercultural Consultant, Pacific Heritage Books, PO Box 3967-WW, 28928 Crestridge Road, Palos Verdes, CA 90274-9547, (310)541-8818.

WONG, ANNA CLARA
Economic development coordinator. Chinese American. **PERSONAL:** Born Jan 14, 1959, Hong Kong; daughter of Kee-Tung Fok and Choy-Ying Fok; married Tony Kin Wong, Apr 27, 1980; children: Victoria, Florence, Candace, Curran. **EDUCATION:** Fashion Institute of Design & Merchandising, AA, 1980; Golden Gate University, BS (summa cum laude), 1991. **CAREER:**

Hang Ten, children's assistant designer, 1979-80; San Francisco Municipal Railway, assistant to director of planning, 1980-87; San Francisco Bureau of Claims & Contracts, asst to bureau manager, 1987-88; San Francisco Utilities Engineering Bureau, asst to bureau manager, 1988-93; Chinatown Economic Development Group, coordinator, 1993-. **ORGANIZATIONS:** San Francisco Unified School District, Bilingual Community Council, 1992-; SF Commission on the Status of Women, Women in the Workforce Committee, 1991-; SFUSD, Bilingual Advisory Committee, 1991-, District Advisory Committee, 1991-92. **HOME ADDRESS:** 7919 Potrero Ave, El Cerrito, CA 94530. **BUSINESS ADDRESS:** Coordinator, Chinatown Economic Development Group, City Hall, Rm 156, 400 Van Ness Ave, San Francisco, CA 94102, (415)554-6492.

WONG, ANTHONY JOSEPH (TSI LUN)
City law enforcement official. Chinese American. **PERSONAL:** Born Apr 17, 1928, Philadelphia, PA; son of Char Li and Glarice; married Dorothy, May 15, 1952; children: Bonita, Anthony, Ana Mai. **EDUCATION:** University of Vienna, 1948-49; University of Pennsylvania, 1956-59. **CAREER:** City of Philadelphia, Police Dept, chief inspector, 1953-. **ORGANIZATIONS:** Delaware Valley Chief of Police Association; Pan Asian Association; Southeastern Police Chiefs Association; Leon Lee Chinese American Legion Post 774; International Association of Chiefs of Police; Pennsylvania Chiefs of Police Association; Korean Community Center; Pennsylvania Municipal Police Officers Education and Training Commission, former commissioner, advisor, currently; On Lok Senior Citizens, board of directors; Nationalities Service Center; Philadelphia Chinatown Development Corporation. **HONORS/ AWARDS:** Pan Asian Association of Greater Philadelphia, Service and Achievement Award, 1990. **MILITARY SERVICE:** Army, 1946-51. **BUSINESS ADDRESS:** Chief Inspector, Information Systems Bureau, Philadelphia Police Department, 800 Race Street, Rm 212, Philadelphia, PA 19106, (215)592-5779.

WONG, B. D.
Actor, playwright. Chinese American. **PERSONAL:** Born Oct 24, 1962, San Francisco, CA; son of Roberta Christine Leong and William D Wong. **EDUCATION:** Studied acting with Don Hotton and voice with Tony McDowell. **CAREER:** Actor; stage credits include: Androcles and the Lion, 1982; M Butterfly, 1988; The Tempest, 1989; A Chorus Line; La Cage Aux Folles; film credits include: The Karate Kid II, 1986; Family Business, 1989; The Freshman, 1990; Mystery Date, 1991; Father of the Bride, 1991; television movies include: Goodnight Sweet Wife: A Murder in Boston; Crash Course; others; Royce Carlton Inc Speakers, lecturer, 1991-. **ORGANIZATIONS:** Actors Equity Association; Screen Actors Guild; American Federation of Television and Radio Artists; Asian Pacific Alliance for Greater Equality, founder; Alliance of Resident Theatres, board of directors. **HONORS/AWARDS:** Antoinette Perry Award, Drama Desk Award, Clarence Derwent Award, Outer Critics Circle Award, Theatre World Award, all for M Butterfly, 1988; Asian Pacific Council, 1992 Mainstream America, entertainment category. **BUSINESS ADDRESS:** Playwright, Actor, c/o Agency for the Performing Arts, 888 Seventh Ave, New York, NY 10019.*

WONG, BACKMAN
Engineer (retired). Chinese American. **PERSONAL:** Born Jan 24, 1927, Boston, MA; son of Young Jung Wong and Yee Shee; married Gloria Lee Wong, Jul 3, 1954; children: Malcolm Stephen, Cary Lee, Darrell Lee, Andrea Joyce, Janice Ellen. **EDUCATION:** MIT, BSME, 1948; Johns Hopkins University, 1953-54. **CAREER:** Bendix Radio, project engineer, 1952-57; Koppers, staff engineer, 1957-62; Standard Thomson, engineering & development, manager, 1962-92. **ORGANIZATIONS:** SAE, Systems Committee, 1962-93; ASME, 1964-93; NSPE, 1979-93. **HOME ADDRESS:** 49 Jeffrey Rd, Wayland, MA 01778, (508)358-2579.

WONG, BARRY
Photojournalist. Chinese American. **PERSONAL:** Born Apr 17, 1954, San Francisco, CA; son of Dick Keong Wong and Jean Fong; married Katherine Michiko Iritani, Aug 13, 1989. **EDUCATION:** Syracuse University, BA, 1977. **CAREER:** The Fresno Guide, photojournalist, 1978-79; The Seattle Times, photojournalist, 1979-. **ORGANIZATIONS:** Asian American Journalists Association; National Press Photographers Association. **HONORS/ AWARDS:** Gannett Foundation, Asian Studies Fellowship, Gannett Fellow, 1987; Pictures of the Year Competition, Food Photography, 2nd place, 3rd place, 1981. **BUSINESS ADDRESS:** Staff Photographer, The Seattle Times, PO Box 70, Seattle, WA 98111, (206)464-2297.

WONG, BENEDICT DING CHUNG
Educator. Hong Kong American. **PERSONAL:** Born Aug 1, 1955, Hong Kong; son of Ting Wong and Wai Yuen Lee. **EDUCATION:** University of Hawaii, BS, 1978, MS, 1980; University of Illinois, PhD, 1985. **CAREER:** University of Hawaii, research assistant, 1975-80; University of Illinois, graduate research assistant, 1980-85, post-doc research associate, 1985-86; Sub-Land Inc, engineer, 1986-87; Accugraph/Holguin Corp, senior software engineer, 1987-88; Caliber, principal/owner, 1988-90; University of North Texas, assistant professor, 1990-. **ORGANIZATIONS:** University of North Texas, in charge of CAD Lab, coordinator for the Mechanical Design Engineering Technology Program, Intl Education Committee, University Curriculum Committee; American Geophysical Union, life member; Operations Research Society of America, currently; Institute of Management Sciences, currently; Association for Computing Machinery, currently; Institute of Electrical & Electronics Engineers Computer Society, currently; Institute of Industrial Engineers, currently; Chi Epsilon. **SPECIAL ACHIEVEMENTS:** Author/co-author of more than 10 papers and technology reports; papers appeared in journals such as Water Resources Research, 19:5, Oct 1983, p 1127-1138, and conference proceedings, such as the Proceedings of the Second International Symposium on Uncertainty Modeling & Analysis (IEEE-Computer Society, Apr 1993), and Optimization Techniques and Applications, Vol 1 (World Scientific Publishing Co, June, 1992). **BIOGRAPHICAL SOURCES:** InHouse-UNT Monthly Newsletter-various issues; Accugraph/Holguin Corp. Newsletter. **HOME ADDRESS:** PO Box 2987, Denton, TX 76202. **BUSINESS ADDRESS:** Assistant Professor, Dept of Engineering Technology, University of North Texas, PO Box 13198, Denton, TX 76203, (817)565-2022.

WONG, BENSON D.
Attorney. Chinese American. **PERSONAL:** Born Nov 30, 1952, Seattle, WA; son of Allan F Wong and Elaine M Wong; married Terry M Mark, Mar 6, 1982; children: Trevor M, Brittney M. **EDUCATION:** Yale University, BA, 1976; University of Pennsylvania Law School, JD, 1979. **CAREER:** Foster, Pepper & Riviera, associate, 1979-82; Keller Rohrback, partner, 1982-. **ORGANIZATIONS:** King County Bar Association, treasurer, 1991-93, Young Lawyers Divsion, trustee, 1986-88, treasurer, 1988; American Immigration Lawyers Association, 1989-; Asian Counseling & Referral Service, board member, 1984-86, president, 1986; Chinese Nursing Home Society, board member, 1985-90, president, 1988. **BUSINESS ADDRESS:** Partner, Keller Rohrback, 1201 Third Avenue, Suite 3200, Seattle, WA 98101, (206)623-1900.

WONG, BERNARD P.
Anthropologist, educator. Chinese American. **PERSONAL:** Born Feb 12, 1941, Kwanchauwan, Kwangtung, China; son of Maurice S Wong and Teresa S Chau; married Rosemarie Deist, Apr 14, 1973; children: Veronica, Alexandra. **EDUCATION:** Berchman College, Philippines, BA, 1966; Ateneo de Manila University, postgraduate, 1968; University of Wisconsin, Madison, MA, 1971, PhD, 1974. **CAREER:** Wah Yan College, Hong Kong, deputy assistant principal, 1968-69; University of Wisconsin, Madison, Dept of Anthropology, teaching assistant, 1971-73, assistant professor, 1974-81, associate professor, 1981-86; San Francisco State University, Dept of Anthropology, professor, chair, 1986-. **ORGANIZATIONS:** American Anthropological Association, fellow, 1974-; Society for Applied Anthropology, fellow, 1974-; Society for Urban Anthropology, fellow, 1987-; Association for Asian Studies, 1974-89; American Ethnological Society, 1987-; Chinese Historical Society of America, 1987, board director, 1989; The Organization of Chinese Americans, Wisconsin Chapter, board director, 1980-83. **HONORS/AWARDS:** University of Wisconsin, Ford fellow, 1971-73; Ford Foundation, fellowship, 1972-73; National Science Foundation, Doctoral Research Grant, 1972-73; American Philosophical Society, Postdoctoral Research Grant, 1978; Japan Ministry of Education, Grant-in-Aid for Scientific Research, 1992-94. **SPECIAL ACHIEVEMENTS:** A Comparative Study of the Assimilation of the Chinese in New York City and Lima Peru, 1978; A Chinese American Community: Ethnicity and Survival Strategies, 1979; Chinatown, 1982; Patronage, Brokerage, Entrepreneurship and the Chinese Community of New York, 1989; "Ethnicity and Family Business," Family Business Review, 1992. **BIOGRAPHICAL SOURCES:** Journal of Asian Studies, vol 50 #3, Aug 1991, p 672. **BUSINESS ADDRESS:** Professor, Dept of Anthropology, San Francisco State University, 1600 Holloway Ave, San Francisco, CA 94132, (415)338-7518.

WONG, BING K.
Educator. Chinese American. **PERSONAL:** Born Oct 4, 1938, Shanghai, China; married. **EDUCATION:** Pittsburgh State University, Kansas, AB, 1961; University of Illinois, Urbana-Champaign, MA, 1963, PhD, 1966. **CA-**

REER: Wilkes University, professor of mathematics, 1968-, Dept of Mathematics & Computer Science, chairman, 1968-84, 1990-92, School of Science & Engineering, associate dean, 1992-. **ORGANIZATIONS:** Mathematical Association of American, Eastern Pennsylvania & Delaware Section, president, 1983-85; American Mathematical Society; Association for Computing Machinery. **BUSINESS ADDRESS:** Associate Dean, School of Science and Engineering, Wilkes University, Stark Learning Center, Wilkes-Barre, PA 18766, (717)831-4803.

WONG, BRADLEY D.
Physician, educator. Chinese American. **PERSONAL:** Born May 6, 1949, Honolulu, HI; son of Harriet Wong and Robert Wong; divorced; children: Carly, Dustin. **EDUCATION:** Yale University, BA, 1971; Jefferson Medical College, MD, 1975; University of Hawaii, School of Medicine, post-doctorate surgical residency, 1975-80. **CAREER:** University of Hawaii, John H Burns School of Medicine, assistant professor of surgery, 1982-; Queen's Medical Center, Surgical Education, director, 1992-. **ORGANIZATIONS:** American College of Surgeons, Hawaii Chapter, president, 1993-; Aloha Medical Commission, board of directors, 1991-. **BUSINESS ADDRESS:** Physician, 1329 Lusitana St, #805, Honolulu, HI 96813, (808)528-4144.

WONG, BRYAN ALLEN
Law enforcement official. Chinese American. **PERSONAL:** Born May 30, 1958, Oakland, CA; son of James Wong and Katherine Wong. **EDUCATION:** California State University, Sacramento, BA, 1980. **CAREER:** Los Angeles Police Dept, vice officer, 1981-, patrol officer, 1988, detective, 1988-89, patrol sergeant, 1989-91, gang supervisor, 1991-. **ORGANIZATIONS:** So California Asian Gang Investigators Assn; California Gang Investigators Assn; California Peace Officers Assn. **HONORS/AWARDS:** LAPD, Unit Citation Medal, 1983. **BUSINESS ADDRESS:** Sergeant, Los Angeles Police Dept, 150 N Los Angeles St, c/o Operations-Central Bureau CRASH, Los Angeles, CA 90012, (213)485-6888.

WONG, BUCK W.
Electronics company exexutive. Chinese American. **PERSONAL:** Born Jun 24, 1933, Newcastle, CA; married Aurora Jose Wong; children: Lawrence T, Nancy C. **EDUCATION:** US Merchant Marine Academy, BS, 1954; Stanford Graduate School of Business, MBA, 1959. **CAREER:** ULTEK Corporation, corp secretary/mfg mgr, 1959-63; ICORE Industries, vice president, 1963-69; Veeco/Andar, vice president, 1969-72; Veeco Instruments Inc, operations mgr, 1972-73; Arcata Management Inc, managing director, 1973-78; Arcata Associates Inc, president, CEO, founder, 1978-92, chairman of the board, 1993-. **ORGANIZATIONS:** US-ASIA Institute, board of directors, 1983-86; TFT Inc, board of directors, 1979-85; North Las Vegas Chamber of Commerce, board member, president, 1992-; Nevada Industry, Science Engineering and Technology, board member, 1990-; National Association of Ministry Business, board member, 1991. **HONORS/AWARDS:** SBA, Administrators Award of Excellence, 1992; NASA, Small Disadvantaged Business of the Year Award, 1990. **MILITARY SERVICE:** US Naval Reserve, lt, 1954-61. **BUSINESS ADDRESS:** Chairman of the Board, Arcata Associates Inc, 4220 Arcata Way, North Las Vegas, NV 89030, (702)642-9500.

WONG, BYRON F.
Attorney. Chinese American. **PERSONAL:** Born Dec 14, 1948, San Francisco, CA; son of Harlin S Wong and Basalle T Wong; married Donna Scott Wong, Sep 27, 1985; children: Cynthia, Byron Jr, Alison, Matthew. **EDUCATION:** Baylor University, 1967-68; University of California, Berkeley, AB, 1971; Hastings College of Law, JD, 1974. **CAREER:** District Attorney's Office of San Francisco, assistant district attorney, 1975-81; Law Offices of Gordon Lau, attorney, 1981-86; Law Offices of Byron F Wong, 1986-. **ORGANIZATIONS:** California Democratic Party, executive board, 1990-, affirm action committee, chair, 1990-, Asian Pacific Caucus, chair, currently; Democratic Central Committee of Marin, vice-chair, 1992-; Human Rights Committee of Marin County, chair, 1992-; Human Rights Resource Center of Marin, board of directors, 1989-; Tiburon Baptist Church, board of trustees; Northern California Asian Peace Officers Assn, president; Natl Asian Peace Officers Assn, incorporator, board member; Asian American Federation of Union Members, incorporator, board member; Chinese American Cooks Training School, chair. **BUSINESS ADDRESS:** Attorney, Law Offices of Byron F Wong, 2543 Clement Street, San Francisco, CA 94121-1817, (415)434-2233.

WONG, CHARLES FOO, JR. (CHARLES FOO)
Attorney. Chinese American. **PERSONAL:** Born Oct 26, 1922, Oroville, LA; son of Charlie Foo & Leung You; married Sue G Wong. **EDUCATION:** Hastings Law, JD, 1948. **CAREER:** Self employed, attorney, 1949-93. **ORGANIZATIONS:** San Francisco Lion's Club, president, 1955-75; Ronald Reagan's Committee for Governor, 1966. **SPECIAL ACHIEVEMENTS:** Chinese Translator, 1945; Intesified Japanese, 1943-44. **MILITARY SERVICE:** US Army, s-sgt, 1943-45. **HOME ADDRESS:** 532 Merritt Ave, Oakland, CA 94610. **BUSINESS ADDRESS:** Attorney, 1042 Grant Ave, Great Western Bank Bldg, #401, San Francisco, CA 94133, (415)392-4622.

WONG, CHIN SIONG (JAMES)
Educator. Malaysian American. **PERSONAL:** Born Nov 3, 1962, Paka, Terengganu, Malaysia; son of Swee Leung Wong and Ah Bee Gan. **EDUCATION:** University of Toronto, BS, 1984; Southwest Texas State University, MS, 1986; University of Texas, Dallas, PhD, 1990. **CAREER:** University of Texas, Dallas, research assistant, 1987-90, instructor, 1988; San Francisco State University, assistant professor, 1990-; Computer Curriculum Corp, researcher, 1992-. **ORGANIZATIONS:** Association for Computing Machinery; IEEE, Technical Committee of Operating Systems, Technical Committee of Real-Time Systems. **HONORS/AWARDS:** Dallas Chinese Lions Club Scholarship, 1990; SWTSU, The Best Student Award, 1986, Outstanding Achievement and Leadership Award, 1986; University of Toronto, Entrance Scholarship, 1981. **SPECIAL ACHIEVEMENTS:** Co-author: "Algorithms for Minimizing Mean Flow Time with Error Constraint," 3rd International Conference for Young Computer Scientists, 1993; "Minimizing the Number of Late Jobs with Release Time Constraints," Journal of Combinatorial Mathematics and Combinatorial Computing, 1992; "Packing Squares into a Square," Journal of Parallel and Distributed Computing 10, 1990; with J Leung, "Minimizing the Number of Late Jobs with Error Constraint," Information and Computation, pp 83-109, Sept 1993. **BUSINESS ADDRESS:** Assistant Professor, Dept of Computer Science, San Francisco State University, 1600 Holloway Ave, San Francisco, CA 94132-1722, (415)338-2858.

WONG, CLARK CHIU-YUEN
Library administrator. Chinese American. **PERSONAL:** Born Oct 9, 1937, Canton, Kwong Tung, China; son of Ling-Kui Wong & Miu-Yim Wu; married Rosalyn, Aug 9, 1964; children: Nanette, Stephanie. **EDUCATION:** National Chengchi University, Taiwan, BA, 1960; University of Nevada, Reno, MA, 1964; University of Michigan, MLS, 1965; University of Colorado, Boulder, PhD, 1975. **CAREER:** Oriental College, Hong Kong, English teacher, 1960; Reno High School, librarian, 1965-69; Community College of Denver, part-time instructor, 1969-71, Learning Materials Center, assistant director, 1969-73, director, 1973-80; California State University, Northridge, university library director of finance and personnel, 1980-. **ORGANIZATIONS:** American Library Association, 1975-, Standards Committee, 1987-90; Association for Educational Communications & Technology, 1966-, Conference Evaluation Committee, 1987-, Post Secondary Standards Committee, 1990-; Chinese American Librarian Association, 1987-, executive board, finance committee chair, 1987-90; California Library Association, 1980-, councilor, 1989-91. **HONORS/AWARDS:** Golden Key National Honor Society, honorary member, 1988; National Librarians Association, California Chapter, president, 1985-86. **SPECIAL ACHIEVEMENTS:** "Job Search Strategies," Ohio Media Spectrum, Miami University, 1988; "The Apple Computer & Library Operations," Association of Research Libraries, 1981; "Comparative Effectiveness of Two Approaches for Learning Materials Center Orientation," University Microform International, 1976; "Effect of Programmed Learning on Self-Concept," University of Nevada, 1964. **BIOGRAPHICAL SOURCES:** Directory of Library & Information Professionals, 1988; International Directory of Distinguished Leadership, 2nd edition, 1989. **HOME ADDRESS:** 22320 Heritage Pass Place, Chatsworth, CA 91311, (818)773-8032. **BUSINESS ADDRESS:** Director of Finance and Personnel, University Library, California State University, Northridge, 18111 Nordhoff St, University Library/OLIB, Northridge, CA 91330-8326, (818)885-2273.

WONG, CLIFFORD S.
Law enforcement official. Chinese American/Pacific Islander American. **PERSONAL:** Born Aug 3, 1939, Honolulu, HI; son of Clifford T Wong and Ella L Wong; married Ruth, Aug 6, 1967; children: Vikeni, Kalani, Kelii. **EDUCATION:** East Los Angeles College, AA, 1982. **CAREER:** Los Angeles Police Department, sergeant, supervisor, pilot, currently. **ORGANIZATIONS:** Monterey Park Masonic Lodge, head master, 1977; City of Monterey Park, park commissioner, 1972-73. **SPECIAL ACHIEVEMENTS:** First Chinese Amer-

ican on the Los Angeles Police Department; first Chinese helicopter airplane commercial law enforcement pilot in United States. **MILITARY SERVICE:** US Army, pfc, 1957-60. **HOME ADDRESS:** 415 Cumbre St, Monterey Park, CA 91754, (213)268-0121.

WONG, DANIEL W.
Educator. Hong Kong American/Chinese American. **PERSONAL:** Born Aug 6, 1953, Hong Kong; son of Ping Wong and Loy Tai Chan; married Lucy Wong-Hernandez, Apr 18, 1992. **EDUCATION:** University of North Texas, BA, 1979, MS, 1981; University of Northern Colorado, PhD, 1987. **CAREER:** University of North Texas, assistant professor, 1987-91; San Jose State University, associate professor, 1991-93; Hofstra University, assistant professor, 1993-. **ORGANIZATIONS:** American Rehabilitation Counseling Association, chair, research committee, 1992-; American Counseling Association, 1987-; United States Council on International Rehabilitation, 1991-. **HONORS/AWARDS:** American Counseling Association, research award, 1992; National Council on Rehabilitation Education, Young Educator of the Year Award, 1991. **SPECIAL ACHIEVEMENTS:** Author of: Toward the Development of a Second Generation Computerized Job-Matching System for Persons with Disabilities: A Conceptual Framework, Journal of Rehabilitation, 1992; Evaluating Rehabilitation Caseload Management Skills Through Computer Simulation, Journal of Counseling & Development, 1993. **BUSINESS ADDRESS:** Assistant Professor, Dept of Counseling, Research, Special Education & Rehabilitation, Hofstra University, Hempstead, NY 11550-0001, (516)463-5782.

WONG, DAVID CRAIG
Military officer. Chinese American. **PERSONAL:** Born Sep 1, 1966, West Islip, NY; son of Herbert Cy Wong and Theresa Ann Wong; married Magdalene Claire Danner (Wong), Apr 30, 1994. **EDUCATION:** Marquette University, BS, 1988. **CAREER:** US Marine Corps, forward observer, 1989-90, platoon commander, 1990-91, logistics officer, 1991-92, chief, testing management section, 1992-93, artillery officer, 1988-, operations officer, 1993-. **MILITARY SERVICE:** United States Marine Corps, Captain, 1988-; Sea Service Ribbon, National Defense Medal, South West Asia Medal, Kuwait Liberation Medal, Navy Unit Commendation, Combat Action Ribbon, 1991; Joint Service Achievement Medal, 1993; Navy Commendation Medal, 1993; Honor Graduate-Field Artillery Officer Basic Course, 1989; Saint Barbaras Medal, 1991. **HOME ADDRESS:** 537 Moores Court, Brentwood, TN 37027. **BUSINESS ADDRESS:** Operations Officer, Nashville Military Entrance Processing Station, 4751 Trousdale Dr, Nashville, TN 37220.

WONG, DAVID TAI WAI
Educator. Chinese American/Hong Kong American. **PERSONAL:** Born Apr 26, 1954, Hong Kong; son of Henry & Lina O-Young; married Alexandra Lichauco Wong. **EDUCATION:** Simon Fraser University, BSc, 1979; University British Columbia, DMD, 1981; Harvard School of Dental Medicine, certificate, oral pathology, 1985; Harvard University, DMSc, 1985. **CAREER:** Harvard School of Dental Medicine, associate professor of oral pathology, 1986-. **ORGANIZATIONS:** American Association of Science, 1984-; American Association of Dental Research, 1985-. **HONORS/AWARDS:** American Cancer Society, Cancer Research Scholar Award, 1987; National Institutes of Health, Research Career Development Award, 1991; Harvard School of Dental Medicine, Distinguished Faculty Award, 1993. **BUSINESS ADDRESS:** Associate Professor, Harvard School of Dental Medicine, 188 Longwood Ave, Rm 214, Boston, MA 02115, (615)432-1834.

WONG, DAVID TAIWAI
Biochemist, neuropharmacologist. Chinese American. **PERSONAL:** Born Nov 6, 1935, Hong Kong; son of Chi-Keung Wong and Pui-King Wong; married Christina Lee Wong, Dec 28, 1963; children: Conrad, Melvin, Vincent. **EDUCATION:** Seattle Pacific University, BS, 1961; Oregon State University, MS, 1964; University of Oregon, PhD, 1966. **CAREER:** University of Pennsylvania, post-doctoral fellow, 1966-67; Lilly Research Laboratories, senior biochemist, 1968-72, research scientist, 1973-77, senior research scientist, 1978-89, research advisor, 1990-; Indiana University Med Sch, adjunct professor of biochemistry, 1986-, adjunct professor of neurobiology, 1991-. **ORGANIZATIONS:** American College of Neuropsychpharmacology, 1994-; American Society of Pharmacology and Experimental Therapeutics; Society for Neuroscience; American Society of Neurochemistry; Intl Society of Neurochemistry; Sigma Xi; Indianapolis Association of Chinese Americans, president, 1987; Chinese Academic and Professional Association in Mid-America; Indiana Association of Chinese Professionals, treasurer, 1990-92; First Presby-

terian Church of Southport, Indiana, elder, 1985-87. **HONORS/AWARDS:** Chinese Neuroscience Society, Scientist of the Year, President's Award, 1991; Pharmaceutical Manufacturers Association, Discoverers Award, 1993; Seattle Pacific University, fellow, 1990-. **SPECIAL ACHIEVEMENTS:** Over 100 publications in scientific journals; over 10 patents; discoverer of antidepressant drug Fluoxetine (Prozac) and antidepressant candidate Duloxetine and development of anti-Parkinson's disease drug, Pergolide (Permax). **BUSINESS ADDRESS:** Research Advisor, Lilly Research Laboratories, Eli Lilly and Company, Lilly Corporate Center, Indianapolis, IN 46285, (317)276-4178.

WONG, DAVID YUE
Educator, educational administrator. Chinese American. **PERSONAL:** Born Apr 16, 1934, Swatow, China; son of Fan Wong and Tsang Wen Wong; married Elizabeth Wong, Mar 26, 1988; children: Amy Wong Nunez, Eric. **EDUCATION:** Hardin Simmons, BA, 1954; University of Maryland, PhD, 1957. **CAREER:** University of California, San Diego, assistant professor, physics, 1960-63, associate professor, physics, 1963-67, professor, physics, 1967-, chair, dept of physics, 1977-80, provost, Warren College, 1985-. **ORGANIZATIONS:** American Institute of Physics; American Physical Society; Sigma Pi; Sigma Xi. **HONORS/AWARDS:** Sloan Foundation, fellow, 1966-68. **SPECIAL ACHIEVEMENTS:** Author of numerous publications. **BUSINESS ADDRESS:** Provost, Warren College, University of California, San Diego, 9500 Gilman Dr, La Jolla, CA 92093-0422, (619)534-1710.

WONG, DEBORAH ANNE
Ethnomusicologist, educator. Chinese American. **PERSONAL:** Born Feb 25, 1959, New York, NY; daughter of John and Jean Wong. **EDUCATION:** University of Pennsylvania , BA, 1982; University of Michigan, MA, 1990, PhD, 1991. **CAREER:** Pomona College, assistant professor of music, 1991-93; University of Pennsylvania, assistant professor of music, 1993-. **ORGANIZATIONS:** Society for Ethnomusicology, council member, 1992-95. **HONORS/AWARDS:** Association for Asian Studies, small grant, 1993; Association of American University Women, dissertation grant, 1989; Social Science Research Council, dissertation fellowship, 1988; Asian Cultural Council, 1988; Fulbright IIE, 1986. **SPECIAL ACHIEVEMENTS:** "Threshold to the Sacred: The Overture in Thai and Javanese Ritual Performance," 1992; "Thai Cassettes and Their Covers: Two Case Histories," 1990. **BUSINESS ADDRESS:** Professor, Dept of Music, University of Pennsylvania, 201 S 34th St, Philadelphia, PA 19104, (215)898-7544.

WONG, DESMOND C.
Retail trade business executive. Chinese American. **PERSONAL:** Born Oct 4, 1950, Hong Kong. **EDUCATION:** Indiana University, BS, 1973; Harvard Business School, MBA, 1977. **CAREER:** Peat, Marwick, Mitchell & Co, audit supervisor, audit senior, audit staff, 1977-78, management consulting manager, 1979-82; Sears, Roebuck and Co, corporate finance manager, 1983-85, corporate finance director, 1985-92, assistant treasurer, 1992-. **ORGANIZATIONS:** Indiana University Foundation, Finance Committee, chairman, Audit, Investment and Managed Business Committees; Harvard Club of Chicago, treasurer and director; Harvard Business School Club of Chicago, advisory director. **HONORS/AWARDS:** Certified public accountant, Illinois, 1974; fluent in Chinese. **SPECIAL ACHIEVEMENTS:** The Grace Commission, appointed Presidential Commission staff, develop cost controls, improve operating efficiencies at US Treasury Dept; recommendations part of $424 billion cost saving proposal presented to President Ronald W Reagan, 1982-83.

WONG, DOLORES
Community volunteer. Chinese American. **PERSONAL:** Born Sep 24, 1921, Vallejo, CA; daughter of Fung Wing & Mary Bowen; married Delbert E Wong, Mar 28, 1942; children: Shelley Wong Pitts, Duane, Kent, Marshall. **EDUCATION:** University of California, Berkeley, BA, 1942; Smith College, MSS, 1946. **CAREER:** New Orleans Child Guidance Clinic; State of California Mental Hygiene Clinic, retired. **ORGANIZATIONS:** Asian American Pacific Artists Association, advisory board; Asian Pacific American Friends of the of Music Center, first president; Junior League of Los Angeles, advisory board; Asian Pacific American Heritage Week, first committee; Chinatown Democratic Club, charter member, Friends of Chinatown Library, founding member, 1971-. **HONORS/AWARDS:** LA Employees Asian American Association, Achievement and Service Award, 1978; Honored by Governor Jerry Brown, "Salute to Women" breakfast, 1979; KUSC-FM, Woman of Achievement Award; YWCA Women in Leadership, Volunteer Category Award, 1981; California State University, honored in conjunction with exhibit opening: Chinese-American Women of America, 1984; Chinese Interagency Council,

Asian Pacific Americans Week, 1985; Asian Pacific Women's Network, Community Leader of the Year, 1987; Channel 4 TV, Neighborhood Hero, 1986; State Senate President Pro Tem David Roberti, "Woman of the Year," from the 23rd Senate District, 1989; Organization of Chinese American Women, "Individual Community Service Award," 1990; YWCA of Los Angeles, "Lifetime Volunteer and Community Involvement," Athena Award, the highest honor, 1990; Honored by Senator Barbara Boxer, "Women Making History," 1993.

WONG, DORIS NING

Physician. Chinese American. **PERSONAL:** Born May 26, 1940, Chungking, China; married Chuen Wong, Apr 2, 1966; children: Michael, Christopher. **EDUCATION:** Miami University, Oxford, OH, Western College for Women, AB, 1962; Case Western Reserve University, MD, 1966; Harvard University, School of Public Health, MPH, 1981. **CAREER:** Pediatrician, currently. **ORGANIZATIONS:** American Academy of Pediatrics; Massachusetts Medical Society; Chinese American Medical Society. **HOME ADDRESS:** 6 Demar Rd, Lexington, MA 02173. **BUSINESS ADDRESS:** Pediatrician, 280 Beach St, Revere, MA 02151, (617)289-5057.

WONG, DOROTHY

Health services administrator. Chinese American. **PERSONAL:** Born Mar 30, 1952, Vallejo, CA; daughter of Poy Sun Wong and Wai Kuen Wong. **EDUCATION:** University of California, Berkeley, BA, 1974; San Francisco State University, MBA, 1982. **CAREER:** Westside Comm Mental Health Center, secretary to office manager, 1975-81; SFMCOIP Inc, admin assistant, 1981-87; Potrero Hill Health Center, clinic manager, 1987-88; SFDPH AIDS Office, contract specialist, 1988-90; Asian AIDS Project, director, 1990-92; International District CHC, executive director, 1992-. **ORGANIZATIONS:** NARAL, 1993; Region X PHS, HIV/AIDS Conference Planning Committee, 1991; Asian Pacific AIDS Council, board of directors, 1993; Cross Cultural Health Care, advisory board, 1993; National Minority AIDS Council, advisory board, 1992; Multicultural Liaison Board, 1991-92; POC Advisory Board, co-chair, 1990-92; ASPA, board of directors, 1991-92; YWCA North Beach, Committee of Management, 1976-82. **SPECIAL ACHIEVEMENTS:** Multicultural liaison board report to California State Office of AIDS, 1992; cultural competency assessment tool for SFDPH AIDS Office, 1992. **BIOGRAPHICAL SOURCES:** University of California, Berkeley Alumni Director, 1993. **BUSINESS ADDRESS:** Executive Director, International District Community Health Center, 416 Maynard Ave S, Seattle, WA 98104, (206)461-3617.

WONG, DOROTHY PAN

Educator. Chinese American. **PERSONAL:** Born in Nanking, China; daughter of Ting Kwan Pan; married Eugene Y Wong, Jun 22, 1968. **EDUCATION:** University of Oklahoma, BS, 1957; University of Minnesota, MS, 1959; Case Institute of Technology, PhD, 1964. **CAREER:** Continental Oil Co, assistant analytical chemist, 1957; University of Chicago, Airforce Midway Lab, 1959-60; Princeton University, research associate, 1965-66; California State University, Fullerton, professor, 1964-. **ORGANIZATIONS:** Iota Sigma Pi, National Honorary Chemistry Society for Women; American Chemical Society; American Physical Society; Sigma Xi; Chinese-American Society for Scientists & Engineers in Southern CA; Chinese-American Professors Association of Southern CA. **HONORS/AWARDS:** California State University, Fullerton, Special Research Leave Grant to UCLA, 1967, Small Research Project, 1970, 1971, Chancellor's Office, mini-grant, 1976; Research Corp, Frederick G Cottrell Research Grant, 1967-70, 1970-77. **SPECIAL ACHIEVEMENTS:** Co-author, several publications including: "Electronic Structure & Geometry of Hydrogen Cyanide," Journal Chemical Phys, vol 46, p 1797, 1967; "Internal Rotation Barriers for Hydrazine & Hydroxylamine from Ab Initio LCAO-MO-SCF Wave Function," Journal Chem Phys, vol 47, p 895, 1967. **BUSINESS ADDRESS:** Professor of Chemistry, California State University, Fullerton, 800 N State College Blvd, Fullerton, CA 92634-9480, (714)773-2184.

WONG, EARL GAR, JR.

HVAC/mechanical engineer. Chinese American. **PERSONAL:** Born Aug 15, 1963, Helena, MT; son of Earl G Wong Sr and Shirley Wong. **EDUCATION:** University of Portland, BSME, 1986. **CAREER:** United Engineers Stears-Roger, mechanical engineer V, 1988-92; United Engineers, West Office, mechanical engineer IV, 1991-93; Raytheon Engineers, HVAC/mechanical engineer III, 1993-. **ORGANIZATIONS:** ASHRAE, 1990-. **HONORS/AWARDS:** State of Colorado, EIT, 1991. **BUSINESS ADDRESS:** HVAC/Mechanical Engineer, Raytheon Engineers & Constructors, 5555 Greenwood Plaza Blvd, Plaza Marin B2-8F, Englewood, CO 80111, (303)843-2619.

WONG, EUGENE

Educator. Chinese American. **PERSONAL:** Born Dec 24, 1934, Nanking, China; son of May Yang and Jennings Wong; married Joan Chang, Sep 8, 1956; children: Linda, Michael, David. **EDUCATION:** Princeton University, BS, 1955, AM, 1958, PhD, 1959. **CAREER:** IBM Corp, staff researcher, 1960-62; Ampex Corp, consultant, 1963-79; Computer Corp of America, consultant, 1976-80; Relational Tech Inc, founder, consultant, 1980-; University of California, Berkeley, assistant professor, electrical engineering, 1962-65, associate professor, 1965-69, professor, 1969-83, Miller professor, 1983-, Dept of Electrical Engineering and Computer Science, 1985-. **ORGANIZATIONS:** Association for Computing Machinery; National Academy of Engineering. **HONORS/AWARDS:** Guggenheim fellow, 1968; Science Research Council, senior fellow, 1973; Vinton Hayes Fellow, 1976; IEEE, fellow. **SPECIAL ACHIEVEMENTS:** Author, Introduction to Random Processes, 1983; Stochastic Processes, 1971. **BUSINESS ADDRESS:** Prof/Chm, Dept of Elec Eng and Comp Sci, University of California, Berkeley, 207 Cory Hall, Berkeley, CA 94720, (510)642-3068.*

WONG, EUGENE G. C.

Physician. Chinese American. **PERSONAL:** Born Apr 5, 1940, Honolulu, HI; son of Wah Hin & Kim Oi Wong; married Deborah, Dec 6, 1988; children: David J S, Christie Ann L L. **EDUCATION:** Washington University, MD, 1965. **CAREER:** Straub Clinic, physician, 1971-77; John A Burns School of Medicine, associate professor of medicine, 1971-; Nephrology Consultants of Hawaii, physician, 1985-; Nephrology Associates, physician, 1977-85. **MILITARY SERVICE:** US Navy, lt commander, 1967-69. **BUSINESS ADDRESS:** Physician, Nephrology Consultants of Hawaii, 1380 Lusitana St, Ste 814, Honolulu, HI 96813, (808)521-3802.

WONG, EUGENE HANLAI

Educator. Hong Kong American. **PERSONAL:** Born Feb 22, 1964, Los Angeles, CA; son of Fook H Wong and Lai H Wong; married Suzanne L Wong, Dec 21, 1992. **EDUCATION:** University of California, Los Angeles, BA, 1986; University of California, Riverside, MA, 1989, PhD, 1991. **CAREER:** University of California, Riverside, master teaching assistant, 1990-91, visiting assistant professor, 1992; California State University, San Bernardino, lecturer, 1991-92; University of Maine, Farmington, asst professor, 1992-. **ORGANIZATIONS:** Society for Research on Child Development, 1992-; Association for the Advancement of Applied Sport Psychology, 1989-. **HONORS/AWARDS:** University of California, Riverside, Outstanding Teaching Assistant, 1989; University of Maine, Farmington, Outstanding Faculty Member, 1992. **SPECIAL ACHIEVEMENTS:** Author of numerous publications and presentations; recipient of several grants. **BUSINESS ADDRESS:** Asst Professor, Dept of Psychology, University of Maine at Farmington, 62 High St, Farmington, ME 04938, (207)778-7497.

WONG, EVELYN

Educational administrator. Chinese American. **CAREER:** West Los Angeles College, president, currently. **BUSINESS ADDRESS:** President, West Los Angeles College, 4800 Freshman Dr, Culver City, CA 90230-3519, (310)287-4200.*

WONG, FRANK F.

Educator. Chinese American. **PERSONAL:** Born Mar 21, 1935, Beloit, WI; son of Mr & Mrs Charles T Wong; married Cynthia T Wong, Sep 2, 1967; children: Christopher, Timothy. **EDUCATION:** Harvard University, BA, 1957; University of Wisconsin, MS, 1961, PhD, 1965. **CAREER:** Antioch College, professor, dean of the faculty, 1963-79; Beloit College, dean of the college, vice president for academic affairs, 1979-87; University of Redlands, provost, vice president for academic affairs, 1987-. **ORGANIZATIONS:** Association of American Colleges, board of directors, 1992-96; American Conference of Academic Deans, advisory board, 1986-89; Ford Foundation, cultural diversity consultant, 1992; Dana Foundation, cultural diversity consultant, 1991; Western Association of Schools & Colleges, diversity consultant, 1990-93; Western Interstate Commission on Higher Education, diversity consultant, 1992-93; National Security Education, program consultant, 1993. **HONORS/AWARDS:** Harvard University, Harvard National Scholarship, 1953-57; Ohio State Historical Society, Outstanding Historical Paper, 1968. **SPECIAL ACHIEVEMENTS:** Author, "Community and Diversity: Right Objectives, Wrong Arguments," Change Magazine, July/August, 1991; "Diversity and Our Discontents," Swarthmore Papers, Vol I, 1992; "Liberal Education and Today's World," Liberal Education, 1984. **BUSINESS ADDRESS:** Provost and Vice President for Academic Affairs, University of Redlands, 1200 E Colton Ave, Redlands, CA 92373, (909)793-2121.

WONG, FRANK VAN
Educational administrator. Chinese American. **PERSONAL:** Born Mar 12, 1939, Brooklyn, NY; son of Fong Wong and Loy Wong; married Marcia Lee Wong, Jan 19, 1963; children: Kenneth, Michael, Cathryn, Glenn. **EDUCATION:** City College of New York, BS, education, 1960, MS, education, 1964. **CAREER:** City College of New York, lecturer, 1960; Bronx Community College, associate professor of health & physical education, beginning 1963, associate professor, until 1990, associate dean of administration, 1990-. **ORGANIZATIONS:** International Tai Chi Institute, teaching faculty, 1991-; Bronx Community College, athletic director, 1965-75; Metropolitan Community College Athletic Conference, president, 1971-73; American Red Cross, aquatic trainer, 1980-92. **HONORS/AWARDS:** Bergen County Community College, International Studies Program, Outstanding Contribution Award, 1991; City University of New York Athletic Conference, Distinguished Service, 1987; National Junior College Athletic Conference, Service Award, 1977. **SPECIAL ACHIEVEMENTS:** Tai Chi instructor, solo, 2 man forms, weapons, meditation & massage, 1974-; Swim Coach: coached 2 national medal winners: NJCAA Michigan Championships, 1967; NJCAA at Florida Championships, 1969. **MILITARY SERVICE:** US Army, spec 4, 1962, 6 years reserve training; Outstanding Technician. **BUSINESS ADDRESS:** Associate Dean of Administration, Bronx Community College, City University of New York, 181st St and University Ave, Bronx, NY 10453, (718)220-6042.

WONG, FREDERICK
Artist, teacher, writer. Chinese American. **PERSONAL:** Born May 31, 1929, Buffalo, NY; son of Kim Lee Wong and Poy Wong; married Yvonne C Wong, Jun 10, 1967; children: Mary Kendall, Kim Meredith. **EDUCATION:** University of New Mexico, BFA, 1951, MA, 1952. **CAREER:** Free-lance writer and artist, currently; Frederick Wong Studio, owner, currently. **ORGANIZATIONS:** American Watercolor Society, 1961-; Allied Artists of America, 1963-; Audubon Artists, 1993. **HONORS/AWARDS:** National Arts Club, Gold Medal, 1961; Artists in Action, Hawaii, Gold Medal, 1960; Silvermine Guild, Connecticut, Gold Medal, 1963; Mainstreams, Ohio, Excellence, 1969; American Watercolor Society, Excellence, 1961, 1976. **SPECIAL ACHIEVEMENTS:** Author, Oriental Watercolor Techniques, Watson-Guptill Publishing, 1977; author, The Complete Calligrapher, Watson-Guptill Publishing, 1980; painting collections: Irving Trust Bank, American Express, US Summit, Pfizer International Corp, The Roy Neuberger Collection, The Smithsonian Institution. **MILITARY SERVICE:** US Army, cpl, 1952-54. **BIOGRAPHICAL SOURCES:** American Artist Magazine, p 42, 1978, Watercolor '90, p 116, 1990. **BUSINESS ADDRESS:** Owner, Frederick Wong Studio, 77 Chambers St, 5th Fl, New York, NY 10007, (212)233-6186.

WONG, GEORGE
Military officer. Chinese American. **PERSONAL:** Born May 5, 1955, Hong Kong; son of Chick Sheu Wong and Beck Sheu Wong. **EDUCATION:** Miami-Dade Community College, AA, 1976; University of Maryland, University College, BA, 1991. **CAREER:** US Marine Corps, captain, 1977-. **ORGANIZATIONS:** Marine Corps Association, 1980-; US Field Artillery Association, 1988-. **HOME ADDRESS:** 7422 NW 47th Place, Lauderhill, FL 33319, (305)748-4647.

WONG, GREGORY DEAN
Accountant, consultant. Chinese American. **PERSONAL:** Born Jul 31, 1957, Culver City, CA; son of Gage Jr & Betty Wong. **EDUCATION:** USC, BS, 1979; Price Waterhouse, CPA, 1982. **CAREER:** Price Waterhouse, staff accountant, 1979-82; Rockwell International, manager trainee, 1983-84; Allied Signal, cash manager, 1984-88; LORAL Aerospace, finance manager, 1988-91; Watkins-Johnson Aerospace/Environmental, finance manager, 1991-93; ENV America Environmental, controller, 1993-. **HOME ADDRESS:** 30011 Monteras St, Laguna Niguel, CA 92677, (714)363-0664.

WONG, GREGORY STERLING
Journalist. Chinese American. **PERSONAL:** Born Oct 16, 1946, Minneapolis, MN; son of Roy and Mabel Wong; married Donna V Wong, Mar 25, 1979. **EDUCATION:** University of Minnesota, BA, 1969. **CAREER:** St Paul Pioneer Press, sports reporter, 1969-. **ORGANIZATIONS:** US Tennis Writers Association, 1973-; Football Writers of America, 1972-; Professional Football Writers of America, 1982-; Baseball Writers Association of America, 1985-; College Baseball Writers Association, 1975-; North American Ski Journalists Association, 1971-; Asian American Journalists Association, 1993-. **HONORS/AWARDS:** Associated Press, Sports Spot News, first place, 1984; Newspaper Guild, Sports News Series, first place, 1975; NW Tennis Association, Special Award, 1988; Lynnhurst Area Recreation Council, Man of the Year, 1968. **MILITARY SERVICE:** US Army, spec 4, 1969-71; ARCOM, 1971; Special Proficiency, 1970. **BUSINESS ADDRESS:** Sports Reporter, St Paul Pioneer Press, 345 Cedar St, St Paul, MN 55101, (612)228-5508.

WONG, HAROLD H.
Real estate company executive. Chinese American. **PERSONAL:** Born Nov 14, 1958, San Francisco, CA; son of Lem S Wong and Annie Y Wong; married Helen Chue, May 11, 1991; children: Lauren I C. **EDUCATION:** Saint Mary's College, BS, 1981; Golden Gate University, MBA, 1985. **CAREER:** Pacific Land Co, vice president, currently. **ORGANIZATIONS:** Asian Business League, treasurer, 1989-; Sacred Heart College Prep, board of regents, 1986-; Russian Hill Neighbors, treasurer, 1982-91; Old First Concerts, board of directors, 1988-92; St Mary's College, chapter president, alumni assn, 1987-89. **BUSINESS ADDRESS:** Vice President, Pacific Land Co, 1204 Pacific St, San Francisco, CA 94109, (415)863-6070.

WONG, HARRY YUEN CHEE
Educator. Chinese American. **PERSONAL:** Born Oct 23, 1916, Kapaa, HI; son of Wong Sam; married Mabel Liu Wong, Jun 24, 1943; children: William James, Donald, Carol Jean Wong-Hastilow. **EDUCATION:** Oklahoma State University, BS, 1942; University of Southern California, MS, 1947, PhD, 1950. **CAREER:** Andrews University, associate professor of zoology, 1949-51; Howard University, College of Medicine, professor, 1951-. **ORGANIZATIONS:** Endocrine Society, 1957-, associate head teller, 1970-71; American Physiological Society, 1956-; Council on Arteriosclerosis, fellow, 1957-; Washington Heart Association, 1955-, Scientific Council, chairman, 1960-61. **HONORS/AWARDS:** FDA, Letter of Commendation, 1962; Chinese Embassy, One of the Outstanding Chinese-American Scholars, 1966; Howard University, Distinguished Faculty Award for Outstanding Research, 1982, College of Medicine, Magnificent Professor, 1992; Shanghai Medical University, PRC, visiting professor of biochem & physiology, 1988-89; Chinese Academy of Medical Sciences, PRC, visiting professor, 1982; Hormon Labor II Medizinsche Universitats-Klinik, Hamburg, Germany, visiting professor, 1969-70. **SPECIAL ACHIEVEMENTS:** Hawaii Heart Association, keynote speaker, 1958; New Jersey Heart Association, keynote speaker, 1959; 146 peer reviewed articles on stress, hormonal & metabolic changes, etc, 1951-; International Symp on Lipids & Post-Natal Development, Milan, Italy, lecturer, 1972; Organizing Comm & guest lecturer V International Symp on Drugs Affecting Lipid Metabolism in Italy; same for VIII Mtg, Florence, Italy, 1986. **MILITARY SERVICE:** United States Air Force, Surgeon General Off, col, 1951-72; consultant to Surgeon General USAF, 1972-; Outstanding Medical Service Liason Officer, 1969. **BUSINESS ADDRESS:** Professor, Howard University College of Medicine, 520 W St NW, Numa P G Adams Bulding, Room 2414C, Washington, DC 20059, (202)806-6330.

WONG, HENRY H.
Networking systems integration company executive. Hong Kong American. **PERSONAL:** Born May 2, 1951, Hong Kong; son of Kau Kuen Wong; married. **EDUCATION:** University of Utah, finance/mktg, 1979; Golden Gate University, MBA, 1982. **CAREER:** Burroughs Corp, sales, 1979-82; IBM-Rolm, mktg rep, 1982-83; DEC, sr sales executive, 1983-85; Wang-Telenova, director, 1985-88; CNet Technology Inc, executive vice president, currently. **BUSINESS ADDRESS:** Executive Vice President, CNet Technology Inc, PO Box 2834, Saratoga, CA 95070, (408)954-8000.

WONG, HENRY L.
Bank executive, economist. Myanmar American. **PERSONAL:** Born Nov 3, 1940, Rangoon, Burma; son of Chew King Wong and Jenny Yu Wong; married Laurie Yap, Apr 11, 1968; children: Rachael S Y, Remle S W. **EDUCATION:** Waynesburg College, BS, 1965; University of Hawaii, MS, 1968, PhD, 1968. **CAREER:** US Dept of Agriculture, Econ Research Service, economist, 1969-70; Hawaii Dept of Budget & Finance, economist, 1970-73; Hawaii Dept of Planning & Econ Development, Hawaii film office director, 1973-84; CB Bancshares, Inc, office of chairman, vice chairman, executive vice president, 1984-; Hawaii Strategic Development Corp, vice chairman, director, 1991-. **ORGANIZATIONS:** Friends of East West Center, vice president, board of directors, 1983-84; NDEA, fellow, 1965-69; Association Film Commrs, president, 1980, member, currently; American Economic Association; American Agricultural Economics Association; Hawaii International Film Festival; Chi-

nese Chamber of Commerce; Lanakila Rehab Center, trustee. **BUSINESS ADDRESS:** Executive Vice President, Chief Administrator, CB Bancshares, Inc, 201 Merchant St, Honolulu, HI 96813-2929, (808)546-3940.

WONG, HENRY SIK-YIN

Electronics company executive. Chinese American. **PERSONAL:** Born Feb 2, 1942, China; son of Kwan Tsui Shueng; children: Julie, Allen. **EDUCATION:** California State University, BS, electrical engineering, 1969; University of Southern California, MBA, 1973. **CAREER:** Sigma Electronics Inc, president, 1974-; (now Trans-Global Enterprises Inc). **ORGANIZATIONS:** IEEE, 1969-74; Southern California Engineering Association, vice president, 1970-72; National Burglar & Fire Alarm Association, 1976-80; NBFA of LA, director, 1978; Honeywell Corp, security protection consultant. **HONORS/AWARDS:** Involved in management, development of alarm products, computer automation programs for security field. **SPECIAL ACHIEVEMENTS:** Many articles in security alarm field, specialize in fiber optic use in medical, industrial and advertizing fields. **BUSINESS ADDRESS:** President, Trans-Global Enterprises Inc, 5935 E Washington Blvd, Los Angeles, CA 90040, (213)721-2662.

WONG, JACQUELINE JEANNE

Attorney. Chinese American. **PERSONAL:** Born Mar 24, 1951, Brooklyn, NY; daughter of Philip Wong and Theresa Wong. **EDUCATION:** Douglas College, Rutgers University, BA, 1972; Harvard Graduate School of Business Administration, 1977-78; Seton Hall Law School, JD (honors), 1979; New York University Law School, LLM, 1984. **CAREER:** AT&T, IMDP participant & manager, 1971; New Jersey Bell Telephone Co, EDP systems analyst, 1972-78; McCarter & English, associate, 1978-81; Proskauer, Rose, Goetz & Mendelsohn, associate, 1981-84; Morgan, Lewis & Bockius, London Office, associate, 1984-84; Curtis, Mallet-Prevost, Colt & Mosle, associate, 1985-86; Whitman & Ransom, partner & co-chair, structured finance, 1986-93; US Department of Treasury, senior advisor, tax policy, 1993-. **ORGANIZATIONS:** TIGAAR, the national Asian Pacific American Political Committee, co-founder, first treasurer; Asian Partners Roundtable, appointments Comm, co-chair, currently; National Asian Pacific American Bar Association; New York City Bar Association; Chinatown Health Clinic, special counsel; Asian Americans for Equality, annual event planning committee, 1993; NYS Clinton for President, Asian Pacific American committee chair, 1991-92; New York State Bar Association, below market loans ad hoc committee, 1990-91. **HONORS/AWARDS:** Seton Hall Law School, Award in Excellence for Conflicts of Law, 1979; Alfred R Mugel National Tax Moot Court Competition, winner, 1977; COGME Fellow for graduate management studies, 1977; National Merit Scholar, 1968. **SPECIAL ACHIEVEMENTS:** Speaker: Transfer Pricing, American Bar Association National Institute, 1992; Foreign Investments in Real Property, World Trade Institute, 1986; Proposed Branch Taxes, World Trade Institute, 1985; Offshore Tax Planning for Private Clients, Legal Studies & Svcs, Ltd, 1985; author, New Tests in The USA On Alien Residency Status, Intl Tax Report, 1984. **BUSINESS ADDRESS:** Senior Advisor, Tax Policy, US Department of Treasury, Room 3045-MT, 1500 Pennsylvania Ave NW, Washington, DC 20220, (202)622-0160.

WONG, JADE SNOW

Writer. Chinese American. **PERSONAL:** Born Jan 21, 1922, San Francisco, CA; daughter of Hing Kwai Tong and Hong Wong; married Woodrow Ong, Aug 29, 1950; children: Mark Stuart, Tyi Elizabeth, Ellora Louise, Lance Orion. **EDUCATION:** San Francisco Junior College, AA, 1940; Mills College, BA, 1942. **CAREER:** Secretary, San Francisco, 1943-45; ceramics gallery, proprietor, 1946-; travel agency, co-owner, 1957-; writer; works include: Fifth Chinese Daughter, 1950; The Immigrant Experience, 1971; No Chinese Stranger, 1975. **ORGANIZATIONS:** International Air Traffic Association; Norcal Pacific Area Travel Association; Museum Society. **HONORS/ AWARDS:** California State Fair, award for pottery, 1947, award for enamel, 1949; Mademoiselle, Silver Medal for craftmanship; Commonwealth Club of San Francisco, Silver Medal for nonfiction, for Fifth Chinese Daughter, 1976; Mills College, LHD, 1976. **SPECIAL ACHIEVEMENTS:** Author of column, San Francisco Examiner; contributor to periodicals, including Holiday and Horn Book. **BUSINESS ADDRESS:** Author, c/o Curtis Brown Agency, 575 Madison Ave, New York, NY 10022.*

WONG, JAMES H.

Financial consultant. Chinese American. **PERSONAL:** Born Jan 2, 1964, Penang, Malaysia; son of Ngoi Siok Wong and Yoke Noi Chan. **EDUCATION:** Arkansas State University, BS, math, 1988. **CAREER:** Craighead Electric Cooperative Corp, billing accounts clerk, 1984-87; Warsalls, Melville

Corp, retail customer service rep, 1992-93; IBM Corp, financial consultant, 1992-. **ORGANIZATIONS:** Sigma Pi Fraternity, secretary, social chairman, 1984-88; Yale University Art Gallery, associate member, 1992-. **HOME ADDRESS:** 4 Hawthorne Dr, Cheshire, CT 06410, (203)250-9279.

WONG, JANET S.

Certified public accountant. Chinese American. **PERSONAL:** Born Jul 17, 1958, Shreveport, LA; daughter of Joe S & Mae P Wong; married Ronald L Mullins, Aug 30, 1980. **EDUCATION:** Louisiana Tech University, MAcc, 1981; Golden Gate University, MTX, 1993. **CAREER:** Touche Ross & Co, manager, 1983-85; KPMG Peat Marwick, senior manager, 1985-. **ORGANIZATIONS:** Tax-Aid, vice president, board of directors, 1991-; Asian Business League, 1990-; Institute of Management Accountants, board member, 1983-; California Society of CPAs, accounting careers committee, 1992-93; American Institute of CPAs, 1983-; World Affairs Council, 1991-. **SPECIAL ACHIEVEMENTS:** Published articles in technical magazine; "Taxation for Accountants," Feb 1986, Feb 1988. **BUSINESS ADDRESS:** Certified Public Accountant, Senior Manager, KPMG Peat Marwick, 3 Embarcadero Ctr, Ste 2100, San Francisco, CA 94111-4003, (415)951-7613.

WONG, JANINE MEI-CHIAO

Educator. Chinese American. **PERSONAL:** Born Apr 12, 1956, Boston, MA; daughter of George Warren Wong and Madeleine Yip Wong; married James Stroud, Oct 25, 1989; children: James Ryder Stroud. **EDUCATION:** Cornell University, BArch, 1980; Yale University, MFA, 1984. **CAREER:** Skidmore, Owings & Merrill, 1980; Portland School of Art, 1983-84; Vesti Corp, 1985; Huygens, DiMella Shaffer Assoc, Inc, 1985-88; Bortell/Stroud Assoc, 1989-92; University of Massachusetts, Dartmouth, associate professor, 1990-. **ORGANIZATIONS:** Boston Society of Architects; American Institute of Architects. **HONORS/AWARDS:** Yale University, Carl Purington Rollins Fellowship, 1983; Cornell University, Traveling Fellowship, 1980, New York Council for Creative & Performing Arts, 1980. **SPECIAL ACHIEVEMENTS:** "Lofty Ideas," Christine Temin, Boston Globe, Oct 15, 1992; "Ski House," Margo Miller, Boston Globe, June 26, 1992; "The Poetics of Space," Victoria Giebel, Metropolis, Sept 1987. **BUSINESS ADDRESS:** Associate Professor, College of Visual and Performing Arts, University of Massachusetts, Dartmouth, North Dartmouth, MA 02747-2300, (508)999-8562.

WONG, JOHN A.

Computer company executive. **PERSONAL:** Born Jun 1, 1948, Portland, OR; son of G C Wong & Sue Wong; married Paula, Feb 14, 1972; children: Mark, Michelle. **EDUCATION:** MIT, SB, 1970. **CAREER:** Tektronix, info systems manager, 1974-82; Bethany Data Systems, president, 1982-. **ORGANIZATIONS:** NW China Council, board of directors, 1990-93. **BUSINESS ADDRESS:** President, Bethany Data Systems Inc, 3805 NW 166th Dr, Beaverton, OR 97006.

WONG, JOHN BULLITT

Insurance company executive. Chinese American. **PERSONAL:** Born Aug 16, 1959, Ashfield, MA; son of Pao Tee Wong and Ling Ying Wong; married Kathy Newton Wong, Oct 12, 1985; children: Priscilla Ling, Michael Bullitt. **EDUCATION:** Northeastern University, BS, business administration, accounting, 1982; Pace University, MBA, finance, 1991. **CAREER:** American International Group, 1975-77; IBM, co-op student, 1979-80; Continental Forest Industry, co-op student, accountant, 1980-81; Chesebrough Ponds, co-op student, planning, 1981-82; General Electric, accountant, 1982-83; Penn Central Corp, senior accountant, 1983-87; NAC Re Corp, accounting officer, 1987-93, asst vp, 1993-. **HONORS/AWARDS:** C V Starr Foundation, scholarship, 1977-82. **BUSINESS ADDRESS:** Assistant VP, NAC Re Corporation, One Greenwich Plaza, Greenwich, CT 06836.

WONG, JOHN D.

Educator. Chinese American. **PERSONAL:** Born Mar 14, 1962, Wichita, KS; son of David Y Wong & Phyllis B Chin. **EDUCATION:** Wichita State University, BBA, 1982, MA, 1984; Washburn University, JD, 1986; Northeastern University, PhD, 1990. **CAREER:** Wichita State University, instructor of economics, 1987-90, assistant professor public admin, 1990-. **BUSINESS ADDRESS:** Professor, Wichita State University, 1845 Fairmont, Center for Urban Studies, Wichita, KS 67260-0061, (316)689-3737.

WONG, JOHN LAP

Landscape architect. Hong Kong American/Chinese American. **PERSONAL:** Born Oct 10, 1951, Hong Kong; son of Lawrence Wong and Maria Lai Wong;

married Mildred Sum-Wong, Apr 24, 1982. **EDUCATION:** City College of San Francisco, AA, 1971; University of California, Berkeley, BS (honors), landscape architecture, 1974; Harvard University, Graduate School of Design, master of landscape architecture in urban design, 1978. **CAREER:** Sasaki, Walker Associates Inc, senior staff, 1973-74; Pod Inc, designer, 1974-76; The SWA Group East, principal, 1976-80; University of California, Berkeley, visiting lecturer, 1987-91; Harvard University, Graduate School of Design, visiting critic, 1979, 1984, 1985, 1990; The SWA Group, managing principal, 1980-. **ORGANIZATIONS:** American Academy in Rome, fellow, regional coordinator, 1981; American Society of Landscape Architects, 1980-; The Urban Land Institute, associate member, 1984-; Institute for Urban Design, 1982-; San Francisco Museum of Modern Art, 1988-; Headland Center for the Arts, 1989-; Registered Landscape Architect, State of California, #1766, 1974-. **HONORS/AWARDS:** American Academy in Rome, Rome prize in landscape architecture, fellow, 1981; American Soc of Landscape Architects, Merit Award, 1972, 1985, 1988, 1990; ASLA Boston Soc of Landscape Architects, Honor Award, 1984, 1985; ASLA Southern California Chapter, Honor Award, 1984, 1986; ASLA, Florida Chapter, Award of Excellence, 1986; ALSA, Northern California Chapter, Honor & Merit Awards, 1990, 1992; Napa County Museum Design Competition, finalist, 1990; Harbor Island Hotel Competition, San Diego, California, first prize, 1990; Todos Santos Plaza Design Competition, Concord, California, finalist, 1987; Pershing Square Natl Design Competition, Los Angeles, finalist, 1986; Copley Square Natl Design Competition, Boston, finalist, 1984; New Shanghai Civic District Competition, winner, 1994. **BIOGRAPHICAL SOURCES:** Process Architecture-Landscape Design and Planning at the SWA Group, May, 1992; Harvard Magazine, May-June, 1982. **BUSINESS ADDRESS:** Managing Principal, The SWA Group, 2200 Bridgeway Blvd, Sausalito, CA 94965, (415)332-5100.

WONG, JOHNNY S.
Educator. Hong Kong American. **PERSONAL:** Born Dec 11, 1954, Kowloon, Hong Kong; son of Sui Ho; married Camilla S Ho. **EDUCATION:** University of Hong Kong, BS (first class honor), 1977; University of Sydney, MS, 1982, PhD, 1987. **CAREER:** Iowa State University, assistant professor, 1986-93, associate professor, 1993-. **ORGANIZATIONS:** Chinese E-Free Church of Ames, 1986-. **HONORS/AWARDS:** Iowa State University, Teaching Excellence Award, 1989; University of Sydney, Telecom Research Award, 1986. **BUSINESS ADDRESS:** Associate Professor, Dept of Computer Science, Iowa State University, 205 Atanasoff Hall, Ames, IA 50011, (515)294-2586.

WONG, K. C.
Educator. Taiwanese American. **PERSONAL:** Born Sep 28, 1954, Taipei, Taiwan; son of Shih Wong and Tsung-Rong Wong; married Linda Wong, Aug 28, 1977; children: Margaret. **EDUCATION:** National Central University, Taiwan, BS, 1977; University of Colorado, MS, 1984; State University of New York, Binghamton, MS, 1985; PhD, 1989. **CAREER:** Clinton Taiwan Corporation, design/applications engr, 1979-82; University of Colorado, research assistant, 1982-84; SUNY, Binghamton, graduate assistant, 1985, academic consultant, 1986, teaching assistant, 1987-88; University of Akron, assistant professor, 1989-91; Governors State University, professor, 1991-. **SPECIAL ACHIEVEMENTS:** Directory Replication in Distributed Systems, 1989; Automatic Determination of Language Versions in Distributed Systems, 1990; Generalization of the Language Version Determination Problem, 1990; Detection of Version Features in Distributed Systems, 1991; Feature Inversion: A Practice on Language Versions Determination, 1992; Determing the Shortest Process Migration Paths for Program Compilation Using a Dynamic Programming Approach, 1993. **MILITARY SERVICE:** ROC Army, lieutenant, 1977-79. **BUSINESS ADDRESS:** Professor, Governors State University, Division of Sciences, University Park, IL 60466, (708)534-4544.

WONG, KAR-YIU
Educator. Chinese American. **PERSONAL:** Born Sep 19, 1950, Canton, People's Republic of China; married. **EDUCATION:** Hong Kong University, BS, eng, 1972; Chinese University of Hong Kong, MPhil, economics, 1979; Columbia University, PhD, 1983. **CAREER:** University of Washington, Dept of Economics, associate professor, currently. **ORGANIZATIONS:** American Economic Association; Chinese Economic Association in North America. **BUSINESS ADDRESS:** Associate Professor, Dept of Econ, University of Washington, D K-30, Seattle, WA 98195-0001, (206)685-1859.

WONG, KARL
Plant manager. Chinese American. **PERSONAL:** Born Jun 12, 1967, Kowloon, Hong Kong; son of Andrew and Han Fong Wong. **EDUCATION:**

Cal Poly San Luis Obispo, BSME, 1992. **CAREER:** Fortune Cookie Factory, plant mgr, currently. **ORGANIZATIONS:** ASME; SPE; AFM. **SPECIAL ACHIEVEMENTS:** EIT, 1991. **BUSINESS ADDRESS:** Plant Manager, Fortune Cookie Factory, 261 12th St, Oakland, CA 94607, (510)832-5552.

WONG, KAU FUI
Educator. Chinese American/Malaysian American. **PERSONAL:** Born Nov 22, 1949, Segamat Johore, Malaysia. **EDUCATION:** University of Malaya, BE, 1973; Case Western Reserve Univ, MS, 1975, PhD, 1977. **CAREER:** National Electricity Board, assistant engineer, 1973, research engineer, 1976-79; University of Miami, assistant professor, 1979-83, associate professor, 1983-; director of graduate studies, 1990-. **ORGANIZATIONS:** Malaysian Student Association, faculty advisor, 1980-; Pi Tau Sigma, 1987; Castle Condo Inc, board of directors, 1982-83; ASME; AIAA. **HONORS/AWARDS:** ASME, Innovation Honorable Mention, 1990. **SPECIAL ACHIEVEMENTS:** Numerous articles in professional journals. **HOME ADDRESS:** 8215 SW 48th St, Miami, FL 33155. **BUSINESS ADDRESS:** Director of Graduate Studies, University of Miami, PO Box 240001, Miami, FL 33124, (305)284-2571.

WONG, KENNETH K.
Educator. Hong Kong American. **PERSONAL:** Born May 11, 1955, Hong Kong; son of H C Wong and C K Man; married Michelle A Chu, 1979; children: Ellen E. **EDUCATION:** University of Chicago, BA (with honors), 1977, MA, 1980, PhD, 1983. **CAREER:** University of Oregon, assistant professor, 1983-88; University of Chicago, assistant professor, 1988-93, associate professor, 1993-. **ORGANIZATIONS:** American Educational Research Association, co-chair of Affirmative Action Committee in Division G, 1992-93; American Political Science Association, Nominating Committee in Urban Politics, Policy Section, 1991-92; Association for Policy Analysis and Management; Midwest Political Science Association. **HONORS/AWARDS:** National Academy of Education, Spencer Fellow, 1989-90; Benton Center, Research Grants, 1990-93; Institute for Poverty Research, Research Grant, 1990-91; Spencer Foundation, Research Grant, 1992-93; Social Science Research Council, Research Grant, 1991-93. **SPECIAL ACHIEVEMENTS:** Author, City Choices-Education and Housing, 1990; co-author, When Federalism Works, 1986; editor, Politics of Policy Innovation in Chicago, 1992; co-editor, Politics of Urban Education, 1992; series editor, Advances in Educational Policy, 1994-. **BUSINESS ADDRESS:** Associate Professor, Dept of Education, University of Chicago, 5835 Kimbark Ave, Chicago, IL 60637-1608, (312)702-1559.

WONG, KENNETH P.
Development executive. Chinese American. **PERSONAL:** Born Jun 9, 1956, New York, NY; son of Pershing Wong & Mary Pang Wong; married Christina F Petra, Sep 23, 1983; children: Mae Ling Petra-Wong, Perry Li Petra-Wong. **EDUCATION:** University of California, Berkeley, AB (highest honors), 1977; Massachusetts Institute of Technology, MArch, 1982, MCP, 1982. **CAREER:** Real Property Research Corp, project manager, 1981-82; Graham Gund Associates Inc, project manager, 1982-83; Gerald D Hines Interests, Hines Industrial, project manager, 1984-86; Himmel/Miller-Klutznick-Davis-Gray, executive vice president, 1986-91; Disney Development Co/The Walt Disney Co, senior vice president, 1991-. **ORGANIZATIONS:** UNICEF, Los Angeles Leadership Committee, 1993-; Amory Center for the Arts, board of directors, 1993-; Urban Land Institute, full member, council member, 1986-; Asian Business League of LA, 1992-; National Association of Industrial Parks, 1982-; Institute for Urban Design, 1988-; International Council of Shopping Centers, 1988-. **HONORS/AWARDS:** University of California, Berkeley, College of Env Design, Dean's Certificate as Outstanding Scholar, 1977, AIA Foundation Scholar, 1977, Marshall Scholar Finalist, 1977; MIT, HUD Internship, 1978-81, co-founder, elected member, governing committee for graduate students. **SPECIAL ACHIEVEMENTS:** Proficient in French; active and frequent guest lecturer at university; frequent public speaker; childhood television star, original cast of NBC series "Take a Giant Step," and other children's specials, 1971-72; taught graduate level courses in real estate finance and development at MIT, Harvard, Continuing Education, Massachusetts Bar Association, and American Legal Institute. **HOME ADDRESS:** 2110 Homet Rd, San Marino, CA 91108. **BUSINESS ADDRESS:** Senior Vice President, Disney Development Company/The Walt Disney Company, 500 S Buena Vista St, Burbank, CA 91521-6400, (818)955-6753.

WONG, KENT DOUGLAS

Educational administrator, educator, attorney. Chinese American. **PERSONAL:** Born May 27, 1956, Los Angeles, CA; son of Delbert and Dolores Wong; married Jai Lee Wong, Oct 26, 1980; children: Ryan Lee, Robin Philip. **EDUCATION:** University of California, Santa Cruz, 1973-74, Berkeley, 1975-77; Peoples College of Law, JD, 1983. **CAREER:** Asian Pacific American Legal Center, staff attorney, 1984-85; Service Employees International Union #660, staff attorney, 1985-91; numerous southern California universities, instructor, labor studies and ethnic studies, currently; UCLA, ethnic studies, labor studies, instructor, currently, Labor Center, director, 1991-. **ORGANIZATIONS:** Asian Pacific American Labor Alliance, president, 1992-; University & College Labor Education Association, executive comm, 1991-; Human and Civil Rights Comm, American Federation of Teachers, 1992-; Los Angeles County Federation of Labor, delegate, 1991-; Asian Pacific American Legal Center, volunteer attorney, 1985-; Harry Bridges Institute, board member, 1993-; Liberty Hill Foundation, Community Funding Board, 1987-89. **HONORS/AWARDS:** Kellogg Foundation, National Fellowship Program, 1989-92; Coro Foundation, Leadership Training Program, 1985. **SPECIAL ACHIEVEMENTS:** Author of numerous articles on labor and ethnicity; served as legal counsel for several precedent-setting class action discrimination cases; traveled to South Africa, Chile, Mexico & Eastern Europe to meet with labor leaders. **BUSINESS ADDRESS:** Director, UCLA Labor Center, 1001 Gayley Ave, 2nd Fl, Los Angeles, CA 90024, (310)794-0385.

WONG, KIN FAI

Government official. Chinese American. **PERSONAL:** Born Nov 6, 1944, Toishan, Kwangtung, China; son of Tung Wong and Seung Ching; married Yen-i, Jan 16, 1971; children: Vivian, Eric. **EDUCATION:** Arizona State University, Tempe, BSE (summa cum laude), 1965; University of Illinois, Urbana, MS, 1967, PhD, 1970. **CAREER:** Stauffer Chemical Co, senior research engineer, 1970-79; US Environment Protection Agency, project officer, 1979-; US Bureau of Mines, program manager, 1993-. **ORGANIZATIONS:** American Institute Chemical Engineers, National Capital Section, secretary, 1984-85; Tau Beta Pi, Arizona Beta Chapter, secretary, 1964; Sigma Xi, 1965-; American Chemical Society, 1965-85; Society Manufacturing Engineers, 1986; USEPA, Review Panel Research Grants, 1980-81. **HONORS/AWARDS:** Arizona State University, Foreign Student Scholarship, 1962-65; American Society Testing Materials, Student Prize, 1964; US Environmental Protection Agency, Bronze Medals, 1988, 1990, 1991. **SPECIAL ACHIEVEMENTS:** Solution Thermodynamics and Kinetic Solvent Effects, Faraday Society, 1970; Selection of Chemical Protection Clothing, 2nd International Sym CPC, Tampa, FL, 1987; Occupational Exposure Estimation Methods, US-OECD Joint Workshop, Orlando, 1992. **BUSINESS ADDRESS:** US Bureau of Mines (MS-6205), 801 Seventh St, NW, Washington, DC 20241, (202)501-9273.

WONG, KIN-PING

Educator, biotechnology researcher, science administrator. Chinese American. **PERSONAL:** Born Aug 14, 1941, Guangzhou, Guangdong, China; son of Yuan-Kwan Loo Wong & Kwok-Keung Wong; married Anna S K Koo Wong, Sep 16, 1968; children: Voon-Chung, Ming-Chung. **EDUCATION:** Grantham Teachers College, Hong Kong, teacher diploma, 1959; UC, Berkeley, BS, 1964; Purdue University, PhD, 1968; Duke University Medical Center, post-doctoral, 1968-70. **CAREER:** University of South Florida, assistant & associate professor of chemistry, 1970-75; Max Planck Institute for Molecular Genetics, Berlin, Germany, visiting scientist, 1972; University of Uppsala, Uppsala, Sweden, visiting professor, 1975; University of Kansas, associate professor, professor of biochemistry, 1975-83, graduate studies, dean, 1980-83; University of Tokyo, visiting professor of biochemistry & biophysics, Japan, 1979; National Science Foundation, program director of biophysics, 1981-83; Stanford University Medical Center, visiting professor of biochemistry, 1986-; University of California Medical Center, adjunct professor of medicine, 1986-, adjunct professor of biochemistry & biophysics, 1987-; University of California, San Francisco, Fresno, trustee, 1987-; Shantou University Medical School, People's Republic of China, honorary professor of medical biochemistry, 1987-; Chinese University of Hong Kong, Hong Kong, professor of biotechnology, 1982-; RiboGene Inc, founder, chairman, CEO, 1989-90, scientific board of advisors, chairman, 1989-91; Moss Landing Marine Laboratories, board of governors, 1983-; Hong Kong Institute of Biotechnology, Shatin, Hong Kong, managing director, CEO, 1992-93; California State University, science dean & professor, 1983-. **ORGANIZATIONS:** American Society of Biological Chemists, 1976-; American Association for the Advancement of Science, 1975; American Chemical Society, 1978-; Biophysical Society, 1970-; Biotechnol-

ogy Subcommittee Department of Industry, Hong Kong, 1993-. **HONORS/AWARDS:** Pepperdine University, Scholarship for Presidential/Key Executive MBA Program, 1986-88; Department of Commerce, California Sea Grant, 1987-90; American Institute of Chemists, fellow, 1987-; Royal Society of Chemistry, London, England, fellow, 1988-. **SPECIAL ACHIEVEMENTS:** Over 50 major research articles and 33 research abstracts, including: with J C Corton, "The Prediction of a Three-Dimensional Model of Ribosomal Protein S7," International Journal of Peptides and Proteins, 1989; with J C Corton, "The Structural Domains of Ribosomal Protein L7/L12: Proteolytic Dissection and Characterization of Fragments," Biophysical Journal, vol 51, p 374a, 1987, submitted to Biochemistry, 1989; with L S Nguyen, "The Unfolding and Refolding of Phenylalamine t-RNA from Yeast," Thirteen International Congress of Biochemistry, Amsterdam, 1985; foreign languages: German, written, fluent in Chinese, both written and spoken, 3 dialects. **BUSINESS ADDRESS:** Dean and Professor, School of Natural Sciences, California State University, 2555 E San Ramon Ave, Fresno, CA 93740-0090, (209)278-3936.

WONG, KING-LAP

Physicist. Chinese American. **PERSONAL:** Born Jan 6, 1946, China. **EDUCATION:** Chinese University of Hong Kong, BS, 1968; University of Delaware, MS, 1970; University of Wisconsin-Madison, PhD, 1975 . **CAREER:** Columbia University, research associate, 1975-76; Princeton University, research associate, 1976-78, research staff, 1978-80, research physicist, 1980-86, principal research physicist, 1986-. **ORGANIZATIONS:** American Physcial Society, fellow. **SPECIAL ACHIEVEMENTS:** Research work on plasma physics and fusion energy, 1970-; over 100 refereed articles published. **BUSINESS ADDRESS:** Principal Research Physicist, Plasma Physics Lab, Princeton University, Princeton, NJ 08543, (609)243-2567.

WONG, KUANG CHUNG

Physician, educator. Chinese American. **PERSONAL:** Born Nov 12, 1936, Chung King, China; son of Yeu Wah Wong and Lily Chang Wong; married Pey Chen Wong, Sep 3, 1989; children: Jade Loy, Shale Ling, Amber Li. **EDUCATION:** Iowa State University, BS, 1959; University of Iowa, School of Medicine, MS, 1962; University of Nebraska, School of Medicine, PhD, 1966, MD, 1968. **CAREER:** University of Nebraska, assistant professor of pharm, 1965-68; University of Washington, School of Medicine, associate professor of anes & pharm, 1970-74; University of Utah, School of Medicine, professor & chair, anes, 1976-, professor of pharmacology, 1980-. **ORGANIZATIONS:** American Heart Association; American Medical Association; American Society of Anesthesiologists; American Society of Clinical Pharmacology and Chemotherapy; American Society of Clinical Pharmacology and Experimental Therapeutics; Association of Cardiac Anesthesiologists; Association of Cardiac Anesthesiologists; Association of University Anesthetists; International Anesthesia Research Society; Salt Lake County Medical Society; Sigma Xi; Utah Heart Association; Utah State Medical Society; Utah State Society of Anesthesiologists. **HONORS/AWARDS:** Dr Ernest Tibbets Manning Memorial Scholarship, 1955-66; University of Nebraska, Upper Regents Scholarship, 1966-67; Mead Johnson's SAMA Scientific Forum-Honorable Mention, 1965; Pharmaceutical Manufacturers Association Foundations, traineeship, 1967-68; Midwest Anesthesiology Resident Conference, First Place, 1969; American Society of Anesthesiologists, Second Place Essay, 1969; Alpha Omega Alpha, 1990; also numerous grants, 1967-85. **SPECIAL ACHIEVEMENTS:** Has written 104 publications, 11 book chapters, 58 abstracts; course speaker on numerous occasions. **MILITARY SERVICE:** National Reserve, sp-3, 1955-63. **BUSINESS ADDRESS:** Professor & Chairman of Anesthesiology, University of Utah School of Medicine, 50 N Medical Dr, Salt Lake City, UT 84132-1001, (801)581-6115.

WONG, KWAN P.

Government official. Hong Kong American/Chinese American. **PERSONAL:** Born Aug 14, 1962, Hong Kong. **EDUCATION:** University of Washington, BA (with honors), 1985; University of Chicago, MA, 1987. **CAREER:** City of Seattle, senior analyst, 1988-. **ORGANIZATIONS:** Chinese Information & Service Center, president, board of directors, 1989-93; Kin-on Nursing Home, board of directors, 1989-91; Northwest Asian Weekly, community liaison, 1991-; Washington State Asian Elected Officials, 1991-. **HONORS/AWARDS:** Alfred P Sloan Foundation, APPAM Fellowship, 1988. **SPECIAL ACHIEVEMENTS:** Editor: ASUW Faculty Evaluation, University of Washington, 1986. **BIOGRAPHICAL SOURCES:** Northwest Asian Weekly, p 6-9, Sep 23, 1993; International Examiner, Sept 18, 1993. **BUSINESS ADDRESS:** Senior Analyst, City of Seattle, PO Box 3151, Seattle, WA 98114, (206)608-1337.

WONG, KWOK-FAI MATTHEW
Educator. Hong Kong American. **PERSONAL:** Born Mar 5, 1961, Hong Kong; son of Tat Wong and Yin Wong. **EDUCATION:** Acadia University, Canada, BA, economics, 1982; University of Manitoba, MBA, 1984; University of Mississippi, PhD, 1990. **CAREER:** St John's University, assistant professor of finance, 1989-. **ORGANIZATIONS:** American Finance Association, 1984-89; Financial Management Association, 1984-; International Association for Financial Engineers, 1991-92; Association for Investment & Management Research, 1992-. **HONORS/AWARDS:** AIMR, CFA, Accreditation Achievement Award, 1993; St John's University, Faculty Merit Award, 1992; Business Research Institute, research grant awards, 1990-93. **SPECIAL ACHIEVEMENTS:** Author, "Stock Returns and Monetary Aggregates," *Journal of Applied Business Research*, 1989; "Are Stock Returns Invariant to the Day of the Week in Pacific Basin Markets?," *Journal of Global Business*, 1991; "Tests of Inflation and Industry Portfolio Stock Returns," *Journal of Economics & Business*, 1992; "Seasonality and Interest Rate Swaps Pricing," *Review of Business Studies*, 1994. **HOME ADDRESS:** 59-22 Gates Ave 3F, Ridgewood, NY 11385, (718)497-6802. **BUSINESS ADDRESS:** Assistant Professor, Dept of Economics and Finance, St John's University, Jamaica, NY 11439, (718)990-6161.

WONG, LILIANE R.
Architect. Chinese American. **PERSONAL:** Born Oct 13, 1959, Hong Kong; daughter of Peter Wei Yang Wong and Winnie Yu Wong; married Daniel W Halston. **EDUCATION:** Vassar College, BA, 1981; Harvard University, MArch, 1985. **CAREER:** Perry, Dean, Rogers & Partners, associate/project architect, 1985-. **ORGANIZATIONS:** AIA, 1989-93; Boston Society of Architects, 1989-93; Vassar Club of Boston, board member, 1990-. **HONORS/AWARDS:** Boston Society of Architects, Women in Architecture, 1991; Historic Neighborhood Foundation, Winner, Competition for Bulfinch Architects, 1987. **SPECIAL ACHIEVEMENTS:** Design team, Architectural Record for Design of American Embassy at Perry, Dean, 1993; exihibition, Women in Architecture, 1991-92. **HOME ADDRESS:** 45 Sacramento St, Cambridge, MA 02138. **BUSINESS ADDRESS:** Associate, Perry, Dean, Rogers & Partners, 177 Milk St, 7th Fl, Boston, MA 02109.

WONG, LINDA J.
Association administrator. Chinese American. **PERSONAL:** Born May 27, 1949, Sacramento, CA; daughter of Howard & Lola Wong. **EDUCATION:** University of Southern California, BA, political science, 1971, JD, 1976. **CAREER:** Legal Aid Foundation of Los Angeles, staff attorney, 1978-79; Law Office of Kwoh and Ono, partner, 1979-81; Mexican American Legal Defense & Educational Fund, Southern California regional counsel, Immigrant Civil Rights Program, national director, 1981-88; California Tomorrow, executive director, president, 1988-91; The Achievement Council, executive director, president, 1991-93; Rebuild Los Angeles, co-chair, 1993-. **ORGANIZATIONS:** California Postsecondary Education Commission, commissioner, 1993-; California Higher Education Policy Center, board of directors, 1993-; Commission on Innovation for California Community Colleges, commissioner, 1991-93; National Civic League, board of directors, 1993-; Goldman Foundation Environmental Prize Jury, juror, 1989-; United Way, Los Angeles, chair of agency relations, board of directors, 1992-; Leadership Southern California, board of directors, 1991-; Educational Testing Service board of directors, 1994-; Pacific Bell Telecommunications Consumer Advisory Board, 1994-; California Wellness Foundation's Violence Prevention Institute, national advisory board committee, 1993-. **HONORS/AWARDS:** Edmund G (Pat) Brown Institute of Public Affairs, California State University, Los Angeles, Horizons Leadership Award, 1993; Asian Pacific Women's Network, Woman Warrior Award for Public Service, 1993; Mexican American Legal Defense & Educational Fund, Legal Service Award, 1992; Los Angeles County Human Relations Commission, professional service in field of human relations, 1991; National Lawyers Guild, Los Angeles Chapter, commitment to equity and civil rights, 1990. **SPECIAL ACHIEVEMENTS:** Co-founder of Coalition for Humane Immigrant Rights of Los Angeles, 1987; bilingual in Spanish, English. **BUSINESS ADDRESS:** Co-Chair, Rebuild LA, 1000 W 8th Place, Los Angeles, CA 90017, (213)489-9675.

WONG, MARTHA
City council member. Chinese American. **PERSONAL:** Born 1939?; widowed; children: three. **CAREER:** Houston Community College system, administrator; Houston City Council, council member, 1994-. **ORGANIZATIONS:** Organization of Chinese Americans, board member; Asian American Coalition, founder, former chair; American Red Cross, board member; Texas

Lion's Eye Bank; Houston Municipal Pension Fund; Greater Houston Women's Foundation. **SPECIAL ACHIEVEMENTS:** First Asian American elected to City Council of Houston. **BUSINESS ADDRESS:** City Council Member, Houston City Council, PO Box 1562, Houston, TX 77251-1562, (713)247-2004. *

WONG, MARTIN DING-FAT
Educator. Chinese American. **PERSONAL:** Born Oct 21, 1956, Canton, People's Republic of China; son of Po-Shin Wong & Po-Ping Cheung; married Jing Li, Dec 9, 1989; children: Michelle. **EDUCATION:** University of Toronto, Canada, BSc, 1979; University of Illinois, Urbana-Champaign, MS, 1981, PhD, 1987. **CAREER:** University of Illinois, Urbana-Champaign, visiting research assistant professor, 1987; University of Texas, Austin, assistant professor, 1987-93, associate professor, 1993-. **ORGANIZATIONS:** Institute of Electrical and Electronic Engineers, 1988-; Association of Computing Machinery, 1983-; Society of Industrial and Applied Mathematics, 1992-. **HONORS/AWARDS:** ACM SIGDA Design Automation Fellowshp, 1991-92; National Science Foundation Research Initiation Award, 1989-92; IBM Faculty Development Award, 1989-91; numerous others. **SPECIAL ACHIEVEMENTS:** Author: with H W Leong, C L Liu, Simulated Annealing for VLSI Design, book, Kluwer Academic Pub, 1988; with T C Wang, "Optimal Floorplan Area Optimization," IEEE Transactions on Computer-Aided Design, vol 11, no 8, p 992-1002, 1992; with T W Her, "Cell Area Minimization by Transistor Folding," Proceedings of the EuroDAC, 1993; numerous others. **BUSINESS ADDRESS:** Associate Professor, Dept of Computer Sciences, University of Texas at Austin, Taylor Hall 2124, Austin, TX 78712, (512)471-9527.

WONG, MAYWOOD
Government official. Chinese American. **PERSONAL:** Born May 11, 1949, Los Angeles, CA; son of Tim Wong and Sau Wong; married Patricia Martin, Oct 8, 1983; children: Elizabeth Ann. **EDUCATION:** UCLA, BS, 1971; Pepperdine University, MBA, 1991. **CAREER:** Board of Equalization, principal compliance supervisor, currently. **BUSINESS ADDRESS:** Principal Compliance Supervisor, Board of Equalization, 28 Civic Center Plaza, PO Box 12040, Santa Ana, CA 92712, (714)558-4090.

WONG, MEL
Artist, educator. Chinese American. **PERSONAL:** Born Dec 2, 1938, Oakland, CA; son of Tom Wong and Louise Lee Wong; married Constance Kreemer, Aug 1984; children: Anika Kreemer, Kira Kreemer, Suzanna Kreemer. **EDUCATION:** San Francisco State University, BA, 1965; Mills College, MFA, 1967; University of California, Los Angeles, 1967-68. **CAREER:** Merce Cunningham Dance Company, dancer, 1968-72; Cornell University, teacher, 1972-74; S.U.N.Y. College at Purchase, teacher, 1974-87; Arizona State University, guest artist, 1985-86; Hong Kong Academy for Performing Arts, guest artist, 1987-88; University of Colorado at Boulder, co-director, 1988-89; Mel Wong Dance Company, artistic director, 1975-; University of California at Santa Cruz, professor, 1989-. **HONORS/AWARDS:** Guggenheim Fellowship in Choreography, 1983-84; National Endowment for the Arts, Choreographic Fellowship, 1986-87; New York State Council on the Arts, 1986-87; Foundation for Contemporary Performing Arts, 1980. **SPECIAL ACHIEVEMENTS:** Growing Up Asian American in the Fifties, performance, 1989-93; Buddha Meets Einstein at the Great Wall, dance, New York City, 1985; Streams, 1980; Shuttle, 1981; Peaks, 1979. **MILITARY SERVICE:** United States Navy, seaman, 1958-60. **BIOGRAPHICAL SOURCES:** Further Steps, Fifteen Choreographers on Modern Dance, Kreemer Connie, ed, Harper & Row, 1987. **BUSINESS ADDRESS:** Professor, Theatre Arts, University of California, 1156 High St, Porter College D123, Santa Cruz, CA 95064-1026.

WONG, MORTON MIN-FONG
Chemical engineer (retired). Chinese American. **PERSONAL:** Born Oct 2, 1924, Zhongshan, Guangdong, China; son of Ngok Fong Wong & Hankue Low Wong; married Eunice Elizabeth Wong, May 23, 1956; children: Nancy Fong, Lawrence Brandon, Tracey Wong Briggs, Douglas. **EDUCATION:** University of California, Berkely, BS, 1951. **CAREER:** American Potash & Chemical, chemical engineer, 1951-53; US Bureau of Mines, project leader, 1953-62, research supervisor, 1962-69, research director, 1969-71, research supervisor, 1971-82; Unocal, senior engineering associate, 1982-91. **ORGANIZATIONS:** AIME, chairman, Reactive Metals Committee, chairman, Extractive Metallurgical Paper Awards Committee, Board of Review, Transactions of AIME, 1964-91. **HONORS/AWARDS:** Unocal, F L Hartley Research Award, 1988; International Lead Consortium, Hoffman Prize, 1982; US Dept of Interior, Distinguished Service Award, 1981, Meritorious Service Award, 1976. **SPE-**

CIAL ACHIEVEMENTS: Mineral Processing Environmental Protection Research, 1982-91; Non-Smelting Technology for Lead Production, 1976-82; Electrolytic Processing of Titanium, Beryllium and Rare Earths, 1953-74; over 80 technical papers and publications, over 14 patents, 1958-93; co-editor, Rare Earths, 1989. MILITARY SERVICE: US Army, cpl, 1943-46. HOME ADDRESS: 413 Lavender Lane, Placentia, CA 92670, (714)996-3064.

WONG, NELLIE
Educational administrator, poet. Chinese American. PERSONAL: Born Sep 12, 1934, Oakland, CA; daughter of Seow Hong Gee & Suey Ting Yee Gee; divorced. EDUCATION: San Francisco State University, candidate, creative writing. CAREER: Bethlehem Steel Corp, executive secretary, 1964-82; University of California, San Francisco, senior affirmative action analyst, currently. ORGANIZATIONS: Poets & Writers, NY, 1980-; Radical Women, executive committee, 1990-; National Asian American Telecommunications Association, 1991-; University Professional & Technical Employees, CWA, 1991-. HONORS/AWARDS: San Francisco Women's Foundation, Women of Words Award, 1989. SPECIAL ACHIEVEMENTS: Author, Dreams in Harrison Railroad Park, poetry, 1977; author, The Death of Long Steam Lady, poetry, prose, 1986; co-featured in documentary film, Mitsuye & Nellie, Asian American Poets, 1981; delegate, first US Women Writers Tour to China, 1983; University of Minnesota, Minneapolis, visiting professor in women studies, 1985. BIOGRAPHICAL SOURCES: The Open Boat, an anthology; Poems from Asian America, poetry; Dissident Song: A Contemporary Asian American Anthology, p 125, 1991. HOME PHONE: (415)826-8322. BUSINESS ADDRESS: Senior Affirmative Action Analyst, University of California, San Francisco, 145 Irving St, Rm 102, San Francisco, CA 94143-0988.

WONG, NICOLE ANNA
Editor. Chinese American. PERSONAL: Born Oct 22, 1968, San Diego, CA; daughter of Patricia & Richard Wong. EDUCATION: Georgetown University, BA, 1990; University of California, Berkeley, currently attending. CAREER: US Representative Jim Bates, San Diego, intern, 1987; Commission for the Study of International Migration, research associate, 1989-90; Guangdong Experimental Middle School, PR China, teacher, 1990-91; American Consulate General, PR China, newsletter editor, 1990-91; Littler Mendelson Fastiff & Tichy, summer associate, 1992; Anchorage Daily News, metro intern reporter, 1993; Asian Law Journal, editor-in-chief, founder, 1991-. ORGANIZATIONS: Asian American Law Students Association, 1993-; Asian American Journalists Association, student member, 1987-. HONORS/AWARDS: Folger Shakespeare Library, Lannan Literary Fellowship in Poetry, 1990; Wellesley College, Wellesley Book Award, 1986. SPECIAL ACHIEVEMENTS: "The Color of Justice," symposium: examining Asian American-African American relations, host org, 1992; "Labor, Language, and Limits," symposium: Asian American labor issues, host org, 1993; contributor, Asian American Almanac, 1994. BIOGRAPHICAL SOURCES: "Two New Law Journals Plan to Focus on Asian Americans," NY Times, January 29, 1993; "UC Students Produce First Asian Law Journals," Asian Week, January 1, 1993. BUSINESS ADDRESS: Editor-in-Chief, Asian Law Journal, University of California, Berkeley, Boalt Hall, School of Law, Rm 33, Berkeley, CA 94720, (510)643-9643.

WONG, NORMAN ZAW
Business executive. Myanmar American. PERSONAL: Born Oct 14, 1941, Yenan Gyang, Burma; son of U Ah Hain. EDUCATION: University of Rangoon; Salem-Teikyo University, BS, 1966; University of Houston, graduate studies. CAREER: Zisco Inc, owner, currently. BUSINESS ADDRESS: Owner, Zisco, Inc, PO Box 79084, Houston, TX 77279, (713)531-5666.

WONG, OVID K.
Educator, educational administrator. Chinese American. PERSONAL: Born Mar 9, 1946, Bandung, Indonesia; son of Matthew Wong and Mary Wong; married Ada H Hu, Jul 5, 1975; children: Jonathan, Nathaniel. EDUCATION: University of Alberta, Canada, BSc, 1970, DipEd, 1971; University of Washington, MEd, 1972; University of Illinois, Urbana-Champaign, PhD, 1977. CAREER: National Louis University, asst prgm dir, 1982-84; Board of Education, School District #65, curriculum spclst, 1985-90, School District #2, principal, curriculum dir, 1990-92, School District #89, supvr, 1992-. ORGANIZATIONS: Assn for Supervision and Curriculum Development, currently; National Science Teachers Assn, currently; Illinois Science Teachers Assn, currently; Illinois Assn of Bilingual Bicultural Education, 1982-90; American Educational Research Assn, 1982-84; Chicago Heart Assn, board, 1990-92. HONORS/AWARDS: Reading Roundtable of Chicago, Midwest

Book Author, 1986-88, 1991; National Science Foundation, Outstanding Science Teacher, Illinois, 1989; National Science Teachers Assn, Science Teaching Achievement Recognition (STAR), 1989; University of Alberta, Distinguished Alumni (first recipient), 1992. SPECIAL ACHIEVEMENTS: Author: 8 children's science books, Greenwood Press, HK, Childrens Press, Chicago, Franklin Watts, NY, 1986-; delegation leader: environmental studies, Soviet Union, 1990. HOME ADDRESS: 572 Montego Dr, Elk Grove Village, IL 60007.

WONG, PABLO JOSE
Government official. Chinese American. PERSONAL: Born Dec 15, 1956, Managua, Nicaragua; son of Juan & Pina Wong; married Khena Wong, May 30, 1993. EDUCATION: University of Hawaii, BS, ag econ, 1979; CORO Foundation, City Focus, 1990. CAREER: NCI Real Estate, broker/owner, 1987-91; California Department of Real Estate, industry/consumer liaison, currently. ORGANIZATIONS: SF Republican County Central Committee, vice chair, 1989-90; SF Association of Realtors, board of directors, 1991; Richmond Neighborhood Center, board of directors, 1990-91; Meda, board of directors, 1993. SPECIAL ACHIEVEMENTS: What You Should Know of Private Mortgage Loans, 1992. BIOGRAPHICAL SOURCES: "DRE Protects the Public...," El Bohemio News, Jan 13, 1993; "Nicaraguan Designated by Governor...," Avance Magazine, May 1, 1993; also featured in Tsing Tao, Chinese Times and Asian Week. HOME ADDRESS: 1803 30th Ave, #303, San Francisco, CA 94122. BUSINESS PHONE: (415)904-5903.

WONG, PAT CHUNG
Educator. Chinese American. PERSONAL: Born Jul 9, 1956, Hong Kong; son of Hok-Chee Wong & Shing-Nam Leung; married Stella S Leung, Jun 3, 1989. EDUCATION: University of Rochester, BA, psychology, 1978; Washington University, MSW, 1982; University of Wisconsin, Madison, PhD, social welfare, 1988. CAREER: University of Texas, assistant professor, 1988-94, associate professor, 1994-. ORGANIZATIONS: Asian American Alliance. HONORS/AWARDS: University of Texas, Texas Excellence in Teaching Award, 1989. SPECIAL ACHIEVEMENTS: Child Support and Welfare Reform, Garland Press, 1993; articles and book chapters on child support, child care, and family and children's services. BUSINESS ADDRESS: Associate Professor, University of Texas, LBJ School of Public Affairs, Austin, TX 78731.

WONG, PAUL
Educator, consultant, educational administrator. Chinese American. PERSONAL: Born Jan 10, 1944, Kwangsi, China; married. EDUCATION: University of California, Berkeley, BA, 1964, MA, 1966, PhD, 1971. CAREER: University of California, Berkeley, assistant professor, 1968-71; University of Illinois, Urbana, assistant professor, 1971-73; University of California, San Diego, assistant professor, 1973-76; Arizona State University, professor, PhD program chair, 1979-92; Washington State University, chair, comparative cultures, professor, 1993-. BUSINESS ADDRESS: Chair, Dept of Comparative American Cultures, Washington State University, Pullman, WA 99164, (509)335-2605.

WONG, PAUL K.
Artist. Chinese American. PERSONAL: Born Oct 30, 1951, Fargo, ND; son of Philip L Wong and Jean Mah Wong. EDUCATION: Moorhead State University, BA, 1973; University of Wisconsin, Madison, MFA, 1976. CAREER: Dieu Donne, artistic director, 1978-93; Delaware Divison of Arts Individual Artist Fellowship Program, juror/evaluator, 1992; University of Iowa, Paper and Book Intensive, works on paper instructor, 1992; Rugg Road Paper and Prints, lecturer; New York Institute of Technology, lecturer; artist, exhibitions include: 11th Annual Metro Show, City Without Wall Gallery, Newark NJ, 1993; 360 Degrees, Pino Modino Gallery, Rome, 1993; The Essential Material: Book Projects at Dieu Donne, Harper-Collins Exhibition Space, NYC, 1993; 360 Degrees, Pino Modino Gallery, NYC, 1992; Guilding Hands, Center for Book Arts Faculty Exhibition, CBA, NYC, 1992; Dieu Donne: 15 Years, CBA Gallery, NYC, curated by Paul Wong and Mina Takehashi, 1991; Paperworks, Castle Gallery, New Rochelle College, NY, 1991. ORGANIZATIONS: Friends of Dard Hunter, 1991-; IAPMA, 1991-; Center for Book Arts, 1988-. HONORS/AWARDS: NEA, Apprenticeship Grant, 1979; LC Tiffany Foundation, Apprenticeship Grant, 1978. BIOGRAPHICAL SOURCES: Artforum, Ronny Cohen, p 109, Nov 1985; "Paper's Third Dimension", Patricia Malarcher, New York Times, Bergen Museum, 1987; "In This Show, Paper Sheds Its Surface Image," Edward Sozanski, The Philadelphia Enquirer, p 7E, 1990; "With Paper as a Starting Point," WC, Vivian Raynor, New York

Times, p 24, 1991; American Artist, A Resource for Handmade Papers by Margaret Mathews-Berenson, p 42, Nov 1991. **HOME ADDRESS:** 40 N Moore St, 2W, New York, NY 10013, (212)431-5989.

WONG, PAUL WING KON
Physician, educator. Chinese American. **PERSONAL:** Born Jun 12, 1932, Hong Kong; married. **EDUCATION:** Hong Kong University, MD, 1958; University of Manchester, England, MSc, 1967. **CAREER:** Chicago Medical School, professor, 1967-73; University of Illinois, professor, 1973-76; Rush-Presbyterian-St Luke's Medical Center, professor, 1976-. **ORGANIZA-TIONS:** ASP; SPR; ASHG; Central Society; SIMD. **SPECIAL ACHIEVE-MENTS:** Genetic research, 1963-. **BUSINESS ADDRESS:** Professor, Rush-Presbyterian-St Luke's Medical Center, 1750 W Harrison St, Chicago, IL 60612, (312)942-6298.

WONG, PETER ALEXANDER
Educator. Chinese American. **PERSONAL:** Born Apr 9, 1941, Honan, China; son of Chai-Hee Wong; married Dixie Lee Barber, Aug 21, 1966; children: Lenson Patrick. **EDUCATION:** Rensselaer Polytechnic Institute, PhD, 1969. **CAREER:** Andrews University, professor of chemistry, 1969-. **ORGANIZA-TIONS:** American Chemical Society, 1969-; Sigma Xi, 1978-. **BUSINESS ADDRESS:** Professor, Chemistry Dept, Andrews University, Berrien Springs, MI 49104, (616)471-3259.

WONG, PETER M. C.
Educator. Hong Kong American. **PERSONAL:** Born Jul 18, 1953, Hong Kong; son of Man-To Wong & Mei-Sha Mary Wong; married Siu-Wah Chung, Aug 25, 1989; children: Benjamin S. **EDUCATION:** McGill University, BSc, 1977, PhD, 1983. **CAREER:** UCSF, visiting scientist, 1983; BC Cancer Research Ctr, NCI of Canada, junior fellow, 1983-85; National Institutes of Health, NCI of Canada, senior fellow, 1985-88; State University of New York, assistant professor, 1988-93; Temple University, associate professor, 1993. **ORGANIZATIONS:** AAAS, 1985-; A S Hematology, 1989-. **HONORS/ AWARDS:** Hanover Trust, Sinsheimer Scholar, 1990-93; NCI of Canada, Junior Fellow, 1983-85, Senior Fellow, 1985-88. **SPECIAL ACHIEVE-MENTS:** 25 scientific publications. **BUSINESS ADDRESS:** Associate Professor, Fels Institute for Cancer Research & Molecular Biology, Temple University, 3420 N Broad St, Rm 552, AHB, Philadelphia, PA 19140, (215)221-8361.

WONG, PETER P.
Educator. Chinese American. **PERSONAL:** Born Dec 12, 1941, Shanghai, China; son of Zun-Ken Wong and Chi Fong Wong; married Susan Wong, Jan 30, 1964; children: Athena L, Cliff N. **EDUCATION:** Oregon State University, BS, 1967, PhD, 1971. **CAREER:** University of Wisconsin, postdoctoral fellow, 1970-72; Washington State University, research assistant professor, 1972-76; Kansas State University, professor, 1976-. **ORGANIZATIONS:** United States Department of Agriculture, principal investigator of research grants, 1978-; National Science Foundation, principal investigator of research grants, 1975-82. **SPECIAL ACHIEVEMENTS:** Published many scientific papers on biochemistry and physiology of plants; recognized expert in nitrogen fixation research. **BUSINESS ADDRESS:** Professor, Division of Biology, Kansas State University, Ackert Hall, Manhattan, KS 66506, (913)532-6651.

WONG, PHILIP
Engineer. Chinese American. **PERSONAL:** Born in Boston, MA; son of Edward and Helen Wong; married Joy; children: Daniel. **EDUCATION:** MIT, BS, 1959. **CAREER:** Army Research Lab, ceramic engineer, 1960-. **ORGA-NIZATIONS:** National Association of Professional Engineers, 1970-93; American Ceramic Society, 1965-93; American Society for Metals, 1960-93. **HONORS/AWARDS:** Dept of Defense, R&D Achievement Award, 1974, 1983. **BUSINESS ADDRESS:** Ceramic Engineer, Army Research Laboratory, 405 Arsenal St, Watertown, MA 02172, (617)923-5324.

WONG, PHILIP T.
Commercial real estate, finance. Chinese American. **PERSONAL:** Born Apr 17, 1953, Boston, MA; son of George & Suey Soo Wong; married Carleen; children: Natalie Jessica. **EDUCATION:** Cornell University, BS, 1975, ME, 1976; Harvard Business School, MBA, 1982. **CAREER:** E F Hutton & Co, investment banker, 1982-85; Capital Markets Group, principal, 1986-. **ORGA-NIZATIONS:** Marin Montessori School, treasurer, volunteer on board of directors, 1993.

WONG, PO KEE
Research company executive, educator, entrepreneur. Chinese American. **PERSONAL:** Born May 5, 1934, Canton City, Kwangtung, China; son of Kum Fun Wong & Wai Chi Lum; married Ruby Ching Wong, Aug 18, 1965; children: Adam E, Anita. **EDUCATION:** Taiwan Provincial Cheng Kung University, BSc, mechanical engineering, 1956; University of Utah, MSc, mechanical engineering, 1961; California Institute of Technology, engineer's degree, applied mechanics, 1966; Stanford University, PHD, aeronautics & astronautics, 1970. **CAREER:** Lockheed Missle and Space Co, senior scientist, 1966-68; Stanford University, 1968-70; General Electric Breeder Reactor Department, 1972-73; Nuclear Services Co, specialist engineer, 1973; Stone and Webster Engineering Co, engineer, 1974-75; Boston Public Schools, tenured teacher, 1979-; Systems Research Co, president, CEO, 1976-. **ORGANIZA-TIONS:** ASME, 1967-; AAAS, 1988-; New York Academy of Sciences, 1991-; International Association of Structural Mechanics in Reactor Technology, 1990-; Mathematical Association of America, 1992-; Association for Supervision and Curriculum Development, 1993-. **HONORS/AWARDS:** Sigma Xi, 1972-; University of Utah, scholarship, teaching and research assistantships, 1959-61; China Institute in America, CT Loo Fellowship, 1961-62; California Institute of Technology, Graduate Scholarship, Teaching Assistantship, 1961-66; Lockheed, Stanford Honor Program Fellowship, Stanford Graduate Fellowship, 1968-70. **SPECIAL ACHIEVEMENTS:** Inventor, Trajectory Solid Angle, US patent 5,084,232, 1974-92; author, "A Unique Algorithm for Solving Nonlinear Structural Systems with Applications," 1978; "High Speed Rotating Shafts Design Algorithm with Applications," 1972; "The Formulation and Solution of the Governing Equations of Viscoelastodynamcis," 1970; "Unified General Solutions of Linear Wave Motions of Thermoelastodynamics & Hydrodynamics," 1968. **HOME ADDRESS:** 50 Bradley St, Somerville, MA 02145-2924, (617)628-8157.

WONG, PUI KEI
Educator. Chinese American. **PERSONAL:** Born Nov 7, 1935, Canton, China; married Vivian L Wong, Sep 2, 1967; children: Jean. **EDUCATION:** Pacific Union College, BS, 1956; Carnegie Institute of Technology, MS, 1958, PhD, 1962. **CAREER:** Carnegie Institute of Technology, instructor, 1960; Lehigh University, assistant professor of mathematics, 1962; Michigan State University, assistant professor of mathematics, 1964, associate professor of mathematics, 1967, professor of mathematics, 1972, associate dean, natural sciences, 1990-. **HOME ADDRESS:** 1247 Mizzen Dr, Okemos, MI 48864.

WONG, RAY G. L.
Systems editor. Chinese American. **PERSONAL:** Born Jan 9, 1950, Winslow, AZ; son of Wong Moy and Ong Oy Wong; married Martha Ann Fones, May 22, 1982. **EDUCATION:** Arizona State University, BS, journalism, 1972; University of Missouri, Coumbia, MA, journalism, 1974. **CAREER:** Columbia Missourian, picture editor, sports, 1972-74; Philadelphia Inquirer, photographer, 1973; Toronto Star, picture editor, 1974-76; The Clarion-Ledger, picture editor, director of graphics, 1976-82; The Tennessean, systems editor/ graphics editor, 1982-. **ORGANIZATIONS:** Asian American Journalists Association, 1982-; Society of Newspaper Design, 1978-; National Press Photographers Association, 1973-; Leadership Nashville Alumni Association, 1985-. **HONORS/AWARDS:** Gannett Foundation, Gannett Fellowship in Asian Studies, 1989-90. **SPECIAL ACHIEVEMENTS:** Pictures of the Year, winner, 1973. **BUSINESS ADDRESS:** Systems Editor, The Tennessean, 1100 Broadway, Nashville, TN 37203, (615)259-8098.

WONG, RAYMOND Y.
Educator. Chinese American. **PERSONAL:** Born Dec 15, 1938, Hong Kong; son of Tai-Yiu Wong and Ying-Ngor Dang; married Rose Marie Wong; children: Andre, Stephanie. **EDUCATION:** Hong Kong Baptist College, BS, 1961; Louisiana State University, Baton Rouge, PhD, 1966. **CAREER:** University of California, Los Angeles, NSF fellow & visiting assistant professor, 1966-67; University of Washington, Seattle, office of naval research fellow, visiting assistant professor, 1967-68; University of California, Santa Barbara, professor, 1968-. **ORGANIZATIONS:** American Math Society, 1964-; Math Association of America, 1980-. **HONORS/AWARDS:** UCLA, National Science Foundation, postdoctoral fellow, 1966-67; University of Washington, Seattle, Office of Naval, research fellow, 1967-68; NSF, research grant, 1972-76. **SPECIAL ACHIEVEMENTS:** Published over 35 research articles in mathematics, including: "Homeomorphisms of Certain Infinite Dimensional Spaces," Trans AMS, vol 128, pp 148-54, 1967; "Toplogical Equivalence of Dimensional Linear Spaces," Trans AMS, vol 137, pp 551-60, 1969; "Peridioc Actions on the Hilbert Cube," Fund Math, pp 203-10, 1974; "Homeomorphis

Spaces of Hilbert Manifolds," Proc AMS, vol 89, pp 693-704, 1983; "Manifold Subgroups of the Homeomorphism Group of a Compact Q-Manifold," Pacific Journal of Math, vol 147, p 165-85, 1991; "On Infinite-Dimensional Manifold Triples," Trans American Math Society, vol 318, p 545-55, 1990. **BUSINESS ADDRESS:** Professor, Dept of Mathematics, University of California, Santa Barbara, Santa Barbara, CA 93106, (805)893-3239.

WONG, RICHARD GENE
Management consultant. Chinese American. **PERSONAL:** Born Aug 4, 1939, Fresno, CA; son of Raymond A Wong and Ruth M Wong; divorced; children: Nicole Anna, Scott Kelly. **EDUCATION:** University of Southern California, BA, 1962; United States International University, MA, 1970. **CAREER:** US Department of Labor, assistant director, 1965-69; Ralston Purina Co, manager, 1969-79; Loyola Marymount University, Center for Industrial Recreations, instructor, 1970-82; TRW, manager, 1979-83; Smith International, director, 1983-86; American Express Co, senior vice president, 1986-89; ARC International, vice president, 1989-91; Alexander Consulting Group, senior consultant, 1991-93; Richard G. Wong & Co, president, currently. **ORGANIZATIONS:** Pasadena Community Access Corp, board member, 1993-96. **SPECIAL ACHIEVEMENTS:** The Outplacement Solution, co-author, 1988; "1-in-5's: Group Sensing," Organization Development Strategies for Future, co-author, p 67-71; Presenter to National Asia Conferences, 1980, 1988; Hong Kong Management Council, 1989. **BIOGRAPHICAL SOURCES:** EEO Bimonthly, "Managing Cultural Diversity in the Workplace," p 6-7, 10, May-June 1992.

WONG, RITA F.
Educator. Chinese American. **EDUCATION:** San Franciso State University, BA, French; University of California, Berkeley, 1970; University of Michigan, MA, linguistics, 1973. **CAREER:** San Francisco Unified School District, teacher, 1969-71; University of Toronto, instructor, 1975-76; San Francisco Community College District, instructor, 1976; University of California, Berkeley, associate, 1976-77; American Language Institute, San Francisco State University, assistant director, 1977-91; United States Information Agency, academic specialist, 1983-; Foothill College, ESL instructor, 1991-. **ORGANIZATIONS:** USIA, English Advisory Panel, 1991-93; TESOL, executive board, 1989-92, TESOL, quarterly advisory board, 1983-85; CATESOL, president, 1986-87, vice president, 1985-86, secretary, 1979-80, newsletter editor, 1980-85. **HONORS/AWARDS:** CATESOL, Outstanding Service Award, 1990. **SPECIAL ACHIEVEMENTS:** Author, Teaching Pronunciation: Focus on English Rhythm and Intonation, 1987; Becoming a Writer: Developing Academic Writing Skills, 1987; invited speaker, Symposium on Pronunciation, Carolina TESOL, Chapel Hill, NC, 1992, keynote; South African Applied Linguistics Association/South African Association for Language Teachers Conference, Potchefstrom, South Africa, 1988; presentation, Defense Language Institute, English Language Center, Lackland AFB, 1986. **BIOGRAPHICAL SOURCES:** New Generation, EFL Gazette, London, p 6, Jan 1991; UNAH y la U Pedagogica auspiciaron curso de fonetica y fonologia del ingles, Tribuna, Honduras, Aug 13, 1992. **BUSINESS ADDRESS:** ESL Instructor, Foothill College, 12345 El Monte Rd, Los Altos, CA 94022, (415)949-7459.

WONG, SAMUEL T.
Orchestra conductor. Hong Kong American. **PERSONAL:** Born Apr 12, 1962, Hong Kong, Hong Kong; son of John T O Wong and Emily S P Wong; married Hae-Young Ham, Oct 27, 1991. **EDUCATION:** Harvard University, AB, 1984, MD, 1988. **CAREER:** Harvard University, Bach Society Orchestra, music director, 1982-84; New York Youth Symphony, music director, 1988-93; New York Philharmonic, assistant conductor, 1990-; Ann Arbor Symphony, music director, 1992-. **SPECIAL ACHIEVEMENTS:** Conducting debut with New York Philharmonic at age 28, substituting for Leonard Bernstein and Zubin Mehta; guest conductor, orchestras of Toronto, Montreal, Vancouver, Calgary, Edmonton, Ottawa, New Orleans, San Antonio, Tampa, Brussels, Prague, Tokyo, Hong Kong, Mexico City. **BIOGRAPHICAL SOURCES:** An Emergency Call from the Philharmonic, New York Times, p B3, Jan 17, 1991. **HOME ADDRESS:** 67 Riverside Dr, #8A, New York, NY 10024.

WONG, SHAWN HSU
Writer, educational administrator. Chinese American. **PERSONAL:** Born 1949, Oakland, CA. **EDUCATION:** San Francisco State University, graduate; University of California, Berkeley, graduate. **CAREER:** University of Washington, Asian American Studies Program, assistant professor, Ethnic-American Studies, Undergraduate Studies, director, currently; works include: Homebase, 1979, Baum Des Himmels (German edition), 1982; Aiiieeeee!, An Anthology

of Asian American Writers, coeditor, 1974; Wooden Fish Songs, 1983; The Big Aiiieeeee!, 1991. **ORGANIZATIONS:** Before Columbus Foundation, board of directors; Combined Asian-American Resources Project, co-director; MultiCultural Review, editorial advisory board, 1992. **HONORS/AWARDS:** Pacific Northwest Bookseller's Award, Washington State Governor's Writers Day Award, both for Homebase; National Endowment for the Arts Creative Writing Fellowship Grant, for fiction, 1981. **SPECIAL ACHIEVEMENTS:** Coedited, special edition of Bulletin of Concerned Asian Scholars, Yardbird Reader; poems, essays and reviews published in various journals. **BUSINESS ADDRESS:** Director, Ethnic-American Studies Program, University of Washington, G N-80, Seattle, WA 98195-0001, (206)543-2100.*

WONG, SIU G.
Optometrist, government administrator, educator. Chinese American. **PERSONAL:** Born Feb 21, 1947, San Francisco, CA; daughter of Edwin K Wong and Loo Yod Yung Wong; married William L Jones, May 12, 1979. **EDUCATION:** University of California, Berkeley, BS, 1968, OD, 1970, MPH, 1972. **CAREER:** St Louis University, School of Medicine, research associate, 1972-73; University of Houston, College of Optometry, assistant professor, 1973-78, adjunct professor, 1978-; US Public Health Service, Indian Health Service, director, division of eye care, 1978-, chief of optometry, 1985-91; Southern California College of Optometry, adjunct professor, 1978-; New England College of Optometry, adjunct professor, 1978-. **ORGANIZATIONS:** American Optometric Association, Council on Clinical Optometric Care, 1986-91, chairperson, 1988-90, Quality Assurance Committee, chair, 1988-89, Primary Care Committee, 1990-92; American Public Health Association, Committee on Affiliates, 1992-, Committee on Women's Rights & Human Rights, 1985-86; Beta Sigma Kappa, vice president, 1993-; Council on Optometric Education, surveyor, 1992. **HONORS/AWARDS:** US Public Health Service, Traineeship Award, 1971-72; Beta Sigma Kappa, Noteworthy Practitioner, 1977; New Mexico Women Optometrist, 1984. **SPECIAL ACHIEVEMENTS:** Published over 15 articles in books and journals; presented over 30 papers nationally and internationalally; book chapter: "The Federal Sole," Public Health & Community Optometry, 1990; lecture: "Current Concepts in Quality Assurance," 8th Asian-Pacific Optometric Congress, Bali, 1991; lecture: "Quality Assurance & Its Impact in the 90's," American Optometry Association, Montreal, Quebec, 1992. **MILITARY SERVICE:** US Public Health Service, captain 06, 1978-; Outstanding & Meritorious USPHS Commendation, Achievement, 3 Unit Commendations. **BIOGRAPHICAL SOURCES:** American Optometric Association News, p 2, May 15, 1989. **BUSINESS ADDRESS:** Director, Division of Eye Care, US Public Health Service, Indian Health Service, 505 Marquette Ave NW, Ste 1502, Albuquerque, NM 87102-2162, (505)766-5507.

WONG, SOPHIE CHAO
Entrepreneur, public relations/marketing consultant. Chinese American. **PERSONAL:** Born May 20, 1927, Nanking, China; daughter of Calvin Chao and Faith C Chao; married Norman J Wong, Aug 8, 1959; children: Cheryl Wong Schulte, Debora A. **EDUCATION:** Los Angeles City College. **CAREER:** Golden Security Thrift & Loan, director, CFO/past chairman of the board, founding member, 1982-; American Realty, principal, 1985-; Pan Pacific Enterprises, principal, 1988-; Sophie C Wong & Associates, president, 1994-. **ORGANIZATIONS:** Alhambra City & High School Districts, Bd of Education, governing member, 1990-94; Los Angeles County Republican Central Committee, 49th Assembly District, 1992-94; California Asian American Pacific Islander Board Members Assn, pres-elect, 1993-; California School Board Assn, assembly delegate, 1992-94, Annual Conference Planning Comm, 1994; Asian Business Assn, pres-elect, 1994; Alhambra Chamber of Commerce, director, 1993-; Leadership California, director, 1993; Chinese PTA of Southern California, 1992-; Monterey Park Asian Youth Center Honorary Advisory Bd, 1989-; US Small Business Admin, natl steering comm, 1988-; Monterey Park Chamber of Commerce, 1985-; Natl Assn of Chinese-American Bankers, director/chm, 1988-; Alhambra Chamber of Commerce, 1985-; Council of Asian Republican Elected & Senior Officials, 1991-. **HONORS/AWARDS:** Natl Assn of Women Business owners, Applauding LA Business Women Award, 1994; California School Board Assn, Master of Boardsmanship Award, CMBA, 1993; Chinese American Parents & Teachers Assn of S California, award, 1993; City of Monterey Park, Mayor's Award for Community Involvement, 1985. **BUSINESS ADDRESS:** President, Sophie C Wong & Associates, 618 W Main St, Ste D, Alhambra, CA 91801, (818)289-9288.

WONG, STEVEN DALE

State government official. Chinese American. **PERSONAL:** Born Apr 21, 1949, Napa, CA; son of William S Wong and Bessie T Wong; married Paula H, Sep 10, 1972; children: Robert W, David T. **EDUCATION:** Napa Junior College, AA, science, 1969; California State University, Sacramento, BA, biology, 1972. **CAREER:** California Department of Food & Agriculture, inspector, 1973-76, registration specialist, 1976-78, supervisor of registration, 1978-86, program supervisor, 1986-89, branch chief, 1989-. **ORGANIZATIONS:** Association of American Feed Control Officials, board of directors, chairman, two standing committees, served on two task forces, 1986-; Association of American Plant Food Control Officials, three standing committees; Sacramento Chinese Sportsmans Club, president, 1980. **MILITARY SERVICE:** California Air National Guard, tech sgt, 1971-77. **BUSINESS ADDRESS:** Branch Chief, California Department of Food & Agriculture, 1220 N St, Rm A372, Sacramento, CA 95814, (916)654-0574.

WONG, STEVEN W.

Educator. Chinese American. **PERSONAL:** Born Oct 24, 1946, Honolulu, HI; son of Gerald Y K Wong and A Gwendolyn Wong; married Sandra L McCullough-Wong, Nov 26, 1992. **EDUCATION:** Clairmont Men's College, BA, economics, 1968; San Diego State College, MA, economics, 1969; Southern Illinois University, MBA, Finance, 1976. **CAREER:** Self-employed financial consultant, 1976-83; Merritt College, professor of accounting, 1983-88; San Joaquin Delta College, division chair, business, 1988-90; San Jose City College, professor of accounting, 1990-. **HOME ADDRESS:** 34303 Mimosa Terrace, Fremont, CA 94555-1811. **BUSINESS ADDRESS:** Professor, Business Division, Accounting Dept, San Jose City College, 2100 Moorpark Ave, San Jose, CA 95128-2723, (408)298-2181.

WONG, SUK YEE

Software developer. Hong Kong American. **PERSONAL:** Born Dec 24, 1968, Kowloon, Hong Kong; daughter of Wai Ho Wong and Yun Ying Lam Wong. **EDUCATION:** New York University, BA, 1990; Stevens Institute of Technology, 1992-. **CAREER:** Bellcore, member of technical staff, 1990-. **HONORS/AWARDS:** Phi Beta Kappa Society, 1990. **BUSINESS ADDRESS:** Member of Technical Staff, BellCore (Bell Communications Research), 44 Hoes Ln., RRC 4D-672, Piscataway, NJ 08854, (908)699-2185.

WONG, TERRY CHEN YI

Physician. Chinese American. **PERSONAL:** Born Oct 6, 1938, Honolulu, HI; son of Mr & Mrs Vincent T Wong; married Kathleen Kwai Lin Wong, Jul 3, 1967; children: Lisa, Kristina, Lara, Jeffrey. **EDUCATION:** Johns Hopkins University, BA, 1961; University of Washington, School of Medicine, MD, 1965; Philadelphia General Hospital, internship, 1965-66; Mayo Graduate School of Medicine, residency & fellowship, 1969-73. **CAREER:** The Honolulu Medical Group, physician, 1973-77; private practice, physician, 1977-. **ORGANIZATIONS:** American College of Physicians, fellow, currently. **MILITARY SERVICE:** US Navy, lt commander, 1967-69. **BUSINESS ADDRESS:** Physician, Terry C Y Wong, MD Inc, 1380 Lusitana St, Ste 506, Honolulu, HI 96813-2475, (808)524-6922.

WONG, TOM

Broadcasting company executive. Chinese American. **PERSONAL:** Born Feb 28, 1928, Los Angeles, CA; son of Yin Wong and Woo Shee Wong; married Lisa Wong, May 15, 1975. **EDUCATION:** USC, 1951. **CAREER:** KCOP-TV, production/stage manager, 1952-. **ORGANIZATIONS:** Chinese Citizen Association, 1958; Asian Teaching, 1967. **MILITARY SERVICE:** Army, t/s, 1944-46; European African Campaign Medal; Army of Occupation Medal. **HOME ADDRESS:** 1530 W 211th St, Torrance, CA 90501.

WONG, VERNON D. B.

Government official. Chinese American. **PERSONAL:** Born Feb 22, 1937, Honolulu, HI; son of Buck Tim Wong and Edna Chun Wong; married Audrey, Jun 28, 1987; children: Vincent, Frederic. **EDUCATION:** University of Hawaii, BA, zoology, 1960; Central Michigan University, MA, pub adm, 1975. **CAREER:** City & County of Honolulu, budget analyst, 1971-76, property manager & training counselor, 1976-81; Kapiolani Community College, auxiliary services officer, 1981-. **ORGANIZATIONS:** Hawaii Association of Physical Plant Administrators, pres, vice president, secretary, 1987-; US China People's Friendship Association, travel comm, chair, 1978-80; Hon Community Gardens Council, president, vice president, 1972-80; Kapahulu Neighborhood Board, president, 1978-82. **MILITARY SERVICE:** US Air Force, captain, 1961-71; bronze medal. **HOME ADDRESS:** 855 Olokele Avenue

#403, Honolulu, HI 96816, (808)735-2762. **BUSINESS ADDRESS:** Auxiliary Services Officer, Kapiolani Community College, 4303 Diamond Head Rd, Ilima Bldg, Room 203, Honolulu, HI 96816, (808)734-9111.

WONG, VICTOR KENNETH

Physicist, educational administrator. Chinese American. **PERSONAL:** Born Nov 1, 1938, San Francisco, CA; son of Bow Chee Wong and Tse Shee Wong; married Nancy Low Wong, Nov 7, 1964; children: Cassandra, Lianna, Pamela. **EDUCATION:** University of California, Berkeley, BS, engin phys, 1960, PhD, physics, 1966. **CAREER:** University of Michigan, Dearborn, associate professor of physics, 1976-82, professor of physics, 1982-86, dean, College of Arts, Sciences & Letters, 1983-86; University of Michigan, Flint, provost & vice chancellor, Academic Affairs, 1986-, professor of physics, 1986-; University of Michigan, Ann Arbor, assistant professor of physics, 1969-76, adjunct professor of physics, 1992-. **ORGANIZATIONS:** American Physical Society, 1966-; American Assn for Higher Education, 1986-, Asian Pacific American Caucus, founding chair, 1986-88, secretary, 1993-; Natl University Cont Educ Assn, Committee on Minority Leadership, 1989-90; North Central Assn of Colleges & Schools, consultant-evaluator, 1986-. **HONORS/AWARDS:** University of California, Berkeley, Honorable Mention for Most Distinguished Graduate, 1960; National Science Foundation, Post-doctoral Fellowship, 1966-68; Organization of Chinese Americans, Distinguished Service in Higher Education, 1986; Ohio State University, Keynote Leadership for Asian Awareness Week, 1993. **SPECIAL ACHIEVEMENTS:** Publications in the following physics journals: Physical Review Letters, Physical Review, Annals of Physics, Low Temp Physics, American Journal of Physics. **BUSINESS ADDRESS:** Provost and Vice Chancellor for Academic Affairs, University of Michigan, Flint, 229 University Pavilion, Office of the Provost, Flint, MI 48502-2186, (313)762-3177.

WONG, WENDELL P.

Physician, surgeon. Chinese American. **PERSONAL:** Born May 16, 1953, Chicago, IL; son of Warren H Wong and Pauline P Wong; married Vicki. **EDUCATION:** Northwestern University, BA, 1973; University of Illinois College of Medicine, MD, 1977; USC Medical Center, LA County General Hospital, internship, 1978; University of Illinois Eye-Ear Infirmary, residency, 1981. **CAREER:** International Eye Care Foundation, founder & medical director, 1987-92; Destiny, Inc, chairman & CEO, 1988-; California Center for Eye Surgery, Inc, founder & surgeon director, 1985-; California Center for Eye Care, chief of laser microsurgery, 1990-. **ORGANIZATIONS:** National Board of Medical Examiners, diplomate; American Academy of Ophthalmology, diplomate, fellow; YMCA, board of managers; International Society of Refractive Keratoplasty; American Association of Cataract & Refractive Surgery; Asian American Physicians Association; AMA; California Medical Assn; Los Angeles Medical Assn; MGMA; OOSS. **HONORS/AWARDS:** YMCA, Outstanding New Major Gifts Campaigner, 1992, Top Experienced Major Gifts Campaigner, 1993. **BIOGRAPHICAL SOURCES:** Transpacific Magazine, p 20, May 1993; Asiam Magazine, seven articles. **BUSINESS ADDRESS:** Chief of Laser Microsurgery, California Center for Eye Care, 3445 Pacific Coast Hwy, Ste 200, Torrance, CA 90505, (310)784-2020.

WONG, WILLIAM

Newspaper columnist. Chinese American. **PERSONAL:** Born Jul 7, 1941, Oakland, CA. **EDUCATION:** University of California, Berkeley, BA; Columbia University, Graduate School of Journalism, MS, 1970. **CAREER:** University of California, Berkeley, Graduate School of Journalism, instructor; San Francisco State University, Asian American studies, journalism, instructor; Wall Street Journal, Cleveland, San Francisco, staff reporter, 1970-79; Asian Week, columnist, currently; Oakland Tribune, business editor, assistant managing editor, ombudsman, associate editor, 1979-88, columnist, 1988-. **ORGANIZATIONS:** Asian American Journalists Association, national vice president. **HONORS/AWARDS:** National Conference of Christians and Jews, Certificate of Recognition, 1991; Media Alliance Meritorious Achievement Award for Print Journalism, 1990; Asian American Journalists Association, Special Recognition Award, Print-Asian American Issues category, second place, both 1990; World Affairs Council of Northern California, Thomas Storke International Journalism Awards, for columns on the Chinese democracy movement, 1989; San Francisco Press Club awards, Humor or Light Subject category, second place, 1989; East-West Center, Jefferson Fellowship, 1983. **SPECIAL ACHIEVEMENTS:** Frequent speaker to community, civic and education groups; numerous guest appearances on radio and television shows, including: ''John Hockenberry Show,'' National Public Radio; ''Forum,'' ''This Week in Northern California,'' KQED; ''Bay Sunday,'' KPIX;

"It Matters to You," KMTP-TV, 1992; Peace Corps volunteer to Philippines, 1960-64. **BUSINESS ADDRESS:** Columnist, Oakland Tribune, 66 Jack London Sq, Oakland, CA 94607-3731, (510)208-6300.

WONG, WILLIAM K. C.
Government official. Chinese American. **PERSONAL:** Born Oct 10, 1941, Honolulu, HI; son of Chip Tong Wong & Shiu Inn Chang Wong; married Amy Choy, Aug 8, 1976; children: Christy, Matthew. **EDUCATION:** California State College, Long Beach, BS, 1967. **CAREER:** Hawaii Department of Health, engineer III, supervisor, engineering section, 1987, Safe Drinking Water Branch, program manager, 1990. **ORGANIZATIONS:** American Water Works Association, currently. **BUSINESS ADDRESS:** Program Manager, Department of Health, 1250 Punchbowl St, Honolulu, HI 96813.

WONG, WILLIAM WAI-LUN
Scientist, educator. Hong Kong American. **PERSONAL:** Born Dec 4, 1948, Kowloon, Hong Kong; son of Sui Chuen Wong and Suk Ying Ng; married Susannah L Wong; children: Christina W, Princeton C. **EDUCATION:** Texas Lutheran College, BS, 1972; Texas A&M University, MS, 1974, PhD, 1976. **CAREER:** Texas A&M University, Department of Plant Sciences, postdoctoral fellow, 1976-78, Robert A Welch Foundation, postdoctoral fellow, 1978; Global Geochemistry Corp, research scientist, 1978-80; Baylor College of Medicine, Department of Pediatrics, instructor, 1980-82, assistant professor, 1982-88, associate professor, 1988-; USDA/ARS Children's Nutrition Research Center, associate professor, currently. **ORGANIZATIONS:** American Institute of Nutrition, 1988-; American Society for Clinical Nutrition, 1988-; Society for Pediatric Research, 1989-; European Society for Pediatric Research, 1992-; American College of Nutrition, fellow, 1993-; Chinese Professional Club, 1993-. **HONORS/AWARDS:** American Society for Mass Spectrometry, Award for Poster Presentation, 1986; Children's Nutrition Research Center, Young Investigator Award, 1985; United Soybean Board, $400,000, Research Grant Award, 1993-95. **SPECIAL ACHIEVEMENTS:** Ad hoc reviewer for numerous scientific journals, 1986-; ad hoc reviewer for National Science Foundation, 1980-; ad hoc reviewer for USDA Committee to Review Competitive Grants & Awards, 1988-; training of postdoctoral and medical fellows in nutrition research, 1982-; published 66 peer-reviewed articles, 19 book chapters, and 87 abstracts, 1974-. **BUSINESS ADDRESS:** Associate Professor, USDA/ARS Children's Nutrition Research Center, 1100 Bates St, Houston, TX 77030-3411, (713)798-7168.

WONG, WILLIAM WAI-LUN
Educator. Hong Kong American. **PERSONAL:** Born Jul 11, 1955, Hong Kong; son of Thomas Y Wong and Shun Kwong; married Amelia S Wong, Aug 23, 1986; children: Gabriella M. **EDUCATION:** Ohlone College, AA, 1980; Gallaudet University, BA, 1985; San Francisco State University, MA, 1989. **CAREER:** Laney College, math instructor, 1985-90; Ohlone College, math instructor, 1985-. **ORGANIZATIONS:** Access Silent Asian Conference Committees, Workshop, Cultural Entertainment, 1992-; Evangelical Free Fellowship of the Deaf, board member, secretary, 1988-. **BUSINESS ADDRESS:** Math Instructor, Ohlone College, College Deaf Center, 43600 Mission Blvd, Fremont, CA 94555, (510)659-6269.

WONG, WILLIE
Mayor. Chinese American. **PERSONAL:** Born Oct 12, 1948, Mesa, AZ. **CAREER:** Auto parts store, owner; City of Mesa, mayor, 1992-. **BUSINESS ADDRESS:** Mayor, City of Mesa, 55 N Center St, PO Box 1466, Mesa, AZ 85211-1466, (602)644-2011.*

WONG, WING Y. (WYNN)
Banker/auditor. Chinese American/Malaysian American. **PERSONAL:** Born Aug 1, 1941, Kuala Lumpur, Malaysia; married Mong C Yang, Dec 27, 1973; children: Wiyan. **EDUCATION:** Fujen the Catholic University of Taiwan, BA, economics, 1970; Michigan State University, MA, economics, 1976; ABA National Compliance School, 1992. **CAREER:** China Development Corp, Taiwan, investment analyst, 1970-73; Bank of America, Taiwan Branch, economist/financial planner, 1977-84; Kong Ming Bank Group, Malaysia, manager, internal audit, 1985-88; United National Bank, Los Angeles, vice president, audit/planner, 1988-. **ORGANIZATIONS:** Malaysian Economic Association; Nanyang Siangpao Business Daily, business columnist, 1989-. **BUSINESS ADDRESS:** United National Bank, 631 South Olive St, Crown Plaza, Los Angeles, CA 90014, (213)627-7888.

WONGANANDA, BOONDHARM
Physician. Thai American. **PERSONAL:** Born Apr 8, 1935, Chalung, Satul Province, Thailand; son of Mr & Mrs Boon-nak Wongananda (deceased); married Duangpranee Wongananda, Jan 20, 1968; children: Taan Joe, Tee Jack. **EDUCATION:** Chulalongkorn University, Thailand, BS, 1954; Mahidol Medical School, Thailand, MD, 1959; Baylor College of Medicine, plastic surgery training, 1973. **CAREER:** Self-employed, plastic surgeon, 1977-. **ORGANIZATIONS:** American Society of Plastic & Rec Surgery, 1976; American College of Surgeons, fellowship, 1980; MedChi, 1977; National Capital Society of Plastic Surgery, 1977; Montgomery County Medical Society, 1977; Laurel Medical Society, 1977; Thais for Thai Association, executive director, 1990. **BIOGRAPHICAL SOURCES:** AMBS Compendium of Certified Medical Specialists, p 190, 1990-91. **BUSINESS ADDRESS:** Medical Doctor, 2101 Medical Park Dr, Ste 204, Silver Spring, MD 20902, (301)565-5220.

WOO, BENSON K.
Automobile company executive. Chinese American. **PERSONAL:** Born 1954, San Francisco, CA. **EDUCATION:** Massachusetts Institute of Technology, BSEE, 1976; Harvard University, MBA, 1979. **CAREER:** General Motors Corp, since 1979: manager-Overseas Financing, 1981-84, director-Worldwide Banking & US Cash Management, 1984-87, treasurer-GM/Suzuki joint venture, 1987-88, treasurer-GM Brazil, 1988-91, finance director-GM Credit Card, 1992-. **BUSINESS ADDRESS:** Finance Director, GM Credit Card Operations, General Motors Corporation, 3044 W Grand Ave, General Motors Bldg, Detroit, MI 48202.

WOO, CELESTE KIMBERLEE
Real estate asset manager. Chinese American/Korean American. **PERSONAL:** Born Apr 24, 1956, Palo Alto, CA; daughter of Jeannette S J Gong & Chauncey F Woo; married Darrell G Lew, Oct 25, 1987. **EDUCATION:** California College of Arts & Crafts, BFA, 1978. **CAREER:** Ferguson-Hildreth, Inc, showroom sales, 1980-84; Sierra Capital Companies, assistant regional asset manager, 1984-91; Meridian Point Properties, Inc. assistant vice president, 1991-. **ORGANIZATIONS:** Institute of Real Estate Management, 1993-; Women in Real Estate, 1991-; International Council of Shopping Centers, 1986-. **BUSINESS ADDRESS:** Assistant Vice President, Asset Management, Meridian Point Properties Inc, 50 California St, Ste 1600, San Francisco, CA 94111, (415)956-3031.

WOO, CHUNG S. H.
Senate committee counsel. Korean American. **PERSONAL:** Born Aug 23, 1962, Busan, Republic of Korea; married Insook Chung, Nov 3, 1990; children: John. **EDUCATION:** MIT, AFROTC; Harvard University, BA, 1985; Widener University School of Law, JD, 1990. **CAREER:** US Senate, Republican staff counsel, committee on governmental affairs, currently. **BUSINESS ADDRESS:** Republican Staff Counsel, Committee on Governmental Affairs, United States Senate, 350 Dirksen Senate Office Bldg, Washington, DC 20510, (202)224-2627.

WOO, EDWARD D.
Medical instruments company manager. Chinese American/Hong Kong American. **EDUCATION:** University of Iowa, BS, 1978; Case Western Reserve University, MS, 1981. **CAREER:** Case Western Reserve University, research assistant, 1978-80; Medtronic, Inc, software verification manager, 1980-. **ORGANIZATIONS:** Medtronic Forum, vice president, 1991, secretary, 1990; Medtronic Asian Employee Resource Group, task force member, 1992-; Cantonese Cultural Center, task force member, 1988; IEEE, 1980-; AAMI, 1980-. **HONORS/AWARDS:** Tau Beta Pi, 1977; Phi Eta Sigma, 1975. **SPECIAL ACHIEVEMENTS:** Proficient in Chinese, Cantonese, & Mandarin. **BUSINESS ADDRESS:** Software Verification Manager, Medtronic, Inc, 7000 Central Ave NE, MS T405, Minneapolis, MN 55432, (612)574-4984.

WOO, HENRY
Telecommunications company software manager. Chinese American. **PERSONAL:** Born Apr 2, 1964, Hempstead, NY. **EDUCATION:** Massachusetts Institute of Technology, SB, 1986; University of Pennsylvania, MSE, 1987. **CAREER:** Bellcore, director, 1986-. **HOME ADDRESS:** 224 Hampshire Ct, Piscataway, NJ 08854. **BUSINESS ADDRESS:** Director, Bellcore, 33 Knightsbridge Road, PY4 4H-304, Piscataway, NJ 08854, (201)699-5936.

WOO, JAMES T. K.
Chemist. Chinese American. **PERSONAL:** Born Jun 7, 1938, Shanghai, China; son of Charles Y K Woo and Grace M T Dow; married Liisa Mikkola,

Jun 10, 1967; children: Alex, Anton, Alicia. **EDUCATION:** Wabash College, BA, 1961; University of Maryland, PhD, 1967. **CAREER:** Dow Chemical Co, research chemist, 1967-71; Horizons Research Inc, senior chemist, 1971-72; Glidden Co, senior scientist, 1972-. **ORGANIZATIONS:** Akron Polymer Lecture Group, Program Chairman; American Chemical Society; American Institute of Chemists. **SPECIAL ACHIEVEMENTS:** 30 US patents; 21 publications. **HOME ADDRESS:** 6551 Spieth Rd, Medina, OH 44256.

WOO, LECON
Scientist. Chinese American. **PERSONAL:** Born Sep 9, 1945, Chung King, China; son of Allen K Woo and Rijan Chu Woo (deceased); married Hung Lo Woo, Jan 17, 1978; children: Eileen, Raymond. **EDUCATION:** Kansas State University, BS, 1967; The University of Chicago, MS, 1973, PhD, 1973. **CAREER:** E I Dupont, senior dev chemist, 1973-78; Arco Chemical Company, senior scientist, 1978-82; Baxter Healthcare, senior scientist, 1982-84, technical director, 1984-92, Baxter Distinguished Scientist, 1992-. **ORGANIZATIONS:** Society of Plastics Engineers, sr member, 1975-; American Chemical Society, sr member, 1973-; AAAS, 1983-; American Institute of Physics, 1978-; Sigma Xi, 1982-. **HONORS/AWARDS:** Baxter, Outstanding Technical Achievement, 1990; Arco, Most Creative Employee Award, 1982; Ind Research Magazine, IR 100 Award, 1977. **SPECIAL ACHIEVEMENTS:** More than 50 technical publications, book chapters; more than 12 US and foreign patents issued. **HOME ADDRESS:** 1013 Shari Ln, Libertyville, IL 60048. **BUSINESS PHONE:** (708)270-4442.

WOO, MICHAEL K.
Lecturer, political activist. Chinese American. **PERSONAL:** Born Oct 8, 1951, East Los Angeles, CA; son of Wilbur and Beth Woo; married Susan Fong, 1986. **EDUCATION:** University of California, Santa Cruz, urban planning degree; University of California, Berkeley, masters in urban planning. **CAREER:** Worked briefly in a youth and unemployment office; California State Senator David Roberti, from student intern to top aide, speechwriter, policy adviser, 1981-85; worked for a nonprofit urban planning research center; Los Angeles City Council, 13th district, councilman, 1985-93; Harvard University, urban politics, acting lecturer, 1993-; candidate for office of secretary of state, California, 1994. **ORGANIZATIONS:** Los Angeles City Council, Ethics Ad Hoc Committee, former chairman. **HONORS/AWARDS:** Asian Business Association, Public Service Award, 1992. **SPECIAL ACHIEVEMENTS:** First Asian American elected to Los Angeles City Council; as a Los Angeles councilman: successfully pushed for the legalization of street vending; responsible for ethics reform package, as chair of Ethics Ad Hoc Committee; cocreator of Hollywood Development Project; helped form the Chinese American Political Internship Project. **BUSINESS ADDRESS:** Candidate, Mike Woo for Secretary of State, 601 N Vermont, Ste 101, Los Angeles, CA 90004, (213)644-1055.*

WOO, MICHAEL T.
Federal government administrator. Chinese American. **EDUCATION:** University of Chicago, MA, public policy, MS, physical chemistry. **CAREER:** Chicago Board of Education, consultant, 1977-78; University of Chicago, Resource Analysis Group, research technician, 1975-78; Sobottka & Co, consultant to US Dept of Energy, 1980; US House of Representatives, Subcommittee on Energy & Power, research asst, 1977, research analyst, 1978-81, Committee on Energy & Commerce, professional staff member, 1981-. **ORGANIZATIONS:** Natl Energy Resources Org, board of directors; Atlantic Council's Working Group on US Energy Policy for the 1990s. **SPECIAL ACHIEVEMENTS:** Co-author, Methodology for Energy Analysis, Proc Intl Conf on Energy End-Use Management, p 649, 1977. **BUSINESS ADDRESS:** Professional Staff Member, Committee on Energy & Commerce, US House of Representatives, 2125 Rayburn House Office Bldg, Washington, DC 20515-6115, (202)225-2927.

WOO, P. T.
Engineering consultant. Chinese American. **PERSONAL:** Born in China; married Helen. **EDUCATION:** University of Illinois, BS, 1949; Massachusetts Institute of Technology, ScD, 1955. **CAREER:** Chevron Corp, sr engineering associate, 1955-85; Technology Consultants, Inc, president, 1985-. **BUSINESS ADDRESS:** President, Technology Consultants Inc, 1401 Las Lomas Dr, Brea, CA 92621, (310)691-2541.

WOO, ROBERT KEN, JR.
Attorney. Chinese American. **PERSONAL:** Born Nov 20, 1967, Atlanta, GA; son of Robert K Woo Sr & Sally Lam Woo. **EDUCATION:** Harvard College,

AB, 1989; Harvard Law School, JD, 1994. **CAREER:** Honorable Stanley F Birch, judicial clerk, 1994-95; King & Spalding, associate, 1995-. **HONORS/AWARDS:** Harvard Law Review, editor, 1992-94; Harvard College, Graduate National Scholarship, 1991-94, John Harvard Scholar, 1988-89, Harvard College Scholar, 1986-88, Honorary National Scholar, 1985; Rotary International, Graduate Foundation Scholarship, University of Auckland, New Zealand, 1990; White House, US Presidential Scholar, 1985; State of Georgia, Star Student, 1985. **SPECIAL ACHIEVEMENTS:** Designated 200 millionth American featured on the cover of Life magazine, 1967; "Bobby Woo—200 Millionth American," The Atlanta Journal and Constitution Magazine, p 12-13, Dec 31, 1967. **BIOGRAPHICAL SOURCES:** "Win, Place, Show in the Population Sweepstakes," Life, vol 63, no 22, p 26, Dec 1, 1967; From Cotton Fields to High Technology in Tucker, GA, Dewey L Turner, pp 126-128, 1986. **HOME ADDRESS:** 3897 Allsborough Dr, Tucker, GA 30084. **BUSINESS ADDRESS:** Attorney, King & Spalding, 191 Peachtree St, Atlanta, GA 30303, (404)572-4600.

WOO, S. B. (SHIEN-BIAU WOO)
Educator. Chinese American. **PERSONAL:** Born Aug 13, 1937; son of C K and Kuo-Ying Chang Woo; married Katy K N Wu, Jul 20, 1963; children: Chih-I, Chih-Lan. **EDUCATION:** Georgetown College, BS (summa cum laude), physics and mathematics; Washington University, physics, MS, PhD, 1964. **CAREER:** University of Delaware, physics, professor, 1966-; State of Delaware, lieutenant governor, 1985-89. **ORGANIZATIONS:** AAAS; American Phys Soc; Sigma Xi; Organization of Chinese Americans, board of directors, 1977-79, natl president, 1990. **HONORS/AWARDS:** Asian American High Tech Conv, Highest Achievement Award, 1985; Natl Sci Foundation, grant, 1978-81. **SPECIAL ACHIEVEMENTS:** As lieutenant governor was highest-ranked Chinese American ever elected to statewide office; candidate for US senate, 1988; Democratic candidate for US House of Representatives, 1992. **BUSINESS ADDRESS:** Physics Professor, University of Delaware, Hullian Hall, Newark, DE 19716.*

WOO, SAVIO LAU-CHING
Educator. Hong Kong American. **PERSONAL:** Born Dec 20, 1944, Shanghai, China; married Emily Helen Chun-Van Woo, Jul 14, 1973; children: Audrey Chuan-Chu, Brian Yee-Huong. **EDUCATION:** Loyola College, BSc, honors chemistry, 1966; University of Washington, PhD, biochemistry, 1971. **CAREER:** Baylor College of Medicine, professor, 1973-, Howard Hughes Medical Institute, investigator, 1976-. **ORGANIZATIONS:** American College of Medical Genetics; American Society for Cell Biology; American Society of Human Genetics; American Society of Biochemistry and Molecular Biology; Society for the Study of Inborn Errors of Metabolism; Society of Inherited Metabolic Disorders; American Federation for Clinical Research; Human Genome Organization; American Association for the Advancement of Sciences. **HONORS/AWARDS:** UNICEF, Research for Development Award, 1989; NIH, Merit Award, 1988; honorary membership in the Japanese Society of Inherited Metabolic Disease, 1986; Society for Study of Inborn Errors of Metabolism, Noel Rain Memorial Award, 1983; March of Dimes, Houston Chapter, board of directors, 1979-87. **SPECIAL ACHIEVEMENTS:** Published over 250 articles in various scientific journals, 1970-; director of Baylor College of Medicine's Center for Gene Therapy, 1991-; member of 7 editorial boards for different journals. **BUSINESS ADDRESS:** Professor, Dept of Cell Biology & Molecular Genetics, Baylor College of Medicine, Howard Hughes Medical Institute, 1 Baylor Plaza, Room T721, Houston, TX 77030, (713)798-6080.

WOO, VERNON YING-TSAI
Attorney. **PERSONAL:** Born Aug 7, 1942, Honolulu, HI; son of Shu-Bin Woo and Hilda Woo; married; children: Christopher Shu-Bin, Lia Gay. **EDUCATION:** University of Hawaii, BA, 1964, MA, 1966; Harvard Law School, JD, 1969. **CAREER:** First District, Honolulu, Par Diem Judge, 1978-84; First Circuit, Honolulu, Adjunct Arbitrator, Judiciary, 1984-; Private Practice Attorney, 1971-. **ORGANIZATIONS:** Boys & Girls Club of Honolulu, past president and current director; Hawaii Bar Association; American Bar Association; Pacific Club; Waihihi Yacht Club. **BUSINESS ADDRESS:** Attorney At Law, 1019 Waimanu St #205, Honolulu, HI 96814, (808)522-0044.

WOO, WILLIAM FRANKLIN
Newspaper editor. Chinese American. **PERSONAL:** Born Oct 4, 1936, Shanghai, China; son of Elizabeth Louise Hart and Kyatang Woo; married Patricia Ernst, Dec 18, 1964 (divorced 1980); married Martha Richards Shirk, Sep 15, 1981; children: Thomas Shenton, Bennett Richards, Peter Snowdon. **EDUCA-**

TION: University of Kansas, BA, 1960. **CAREER:** Kansas City Star, Missouri, reporter, 1957-62; St Louis Post-Dispatch, feature writer, 1962-68, editorial writer, 1968-73, assistant editor, 1973-74, editorial page editor, 1974-86, editor, 1986-. **ORGANIZATIONS:** American Society of Newspaper Editors, board of directors, 1993-. **HONORS/AWARDS:** Harvard University, Nieman fellow, 1966-67. **MILITARY SERVICE:** US Air Force Reserves, staff sargeant, 1962. **BUSINESS ADDRESS:** Editor, St Louis Post-Dispatch, 900 N Tucker Blvd, St Louis, MO 63101-1099, (314)622-7000. *

WOODY, A-YOUNG MOON
Educator. Korean American. **PERSONAL:** Born Mar 7, 1934, Pyungyang, Pyungahn-Namdo, Republic of Korea; daughter of John Myung-Wan Moon & Soon-Hae Choi; married Robert W Woody, Jan 30, 1965; children: Michael R, David M. **EDUCATION:** University of California, Berkeley, BS, 1959; Cornell University, PhD, 1964. **CAREER:** Cornell University, postdoc, 1964-65; University of Illinois, research associate, 1965-69; Arizona State University, faculty research associate, 1972-75; Colorado State University, research associate, 1976-87; Colorado State University, research associate professor, 1988-. **ORGANIZATIONS:** American Chemical Society, 1959-; American Society for Biochemistry & Molecular Biology, 1991-. **BUSINESS ADDRESS:** Professor, Dept of Biochem & Molecular Bio, Colorado State University, MRB Bldg, Rm 330, Fort Collins, CO 80523, (303)491-0436.

WU, ALFRED CHI-TAI
Physicist. Chinese American. **PERSONAL:** Born Jan 24, 1933, Ningpo, Chekiang, China; son of Tsung-Hsien and Shu-Yung Wu; married Corinne Huang, Jul 22, 1967; children: Veda, Yvette. **EDUCATION:** National Taiwan University, 1950-52; Wheaton College, BS, 1955; University of Maryland, PhD, 1960. **CAREER:** Institute Theor Phys, University Lund, Sweden, visiting fellow, 1958-59; Institute Theor Phys, ETH, Zurich, Switzerland, visiting fellow, 1959-60; Institute for Advanced Study, Princeton, NJ, 1960-62; University of Michigan, assistant professor to professor, 1962-. **ORGANIZATIONS:** American Physical Society, 1956-. **HONORS/AWARDS:** John Simon Guggenheim Memorial Foundation, Fellow, 1968-69. **SPECIAL ACHIEVEMENTS:** Work in quantum field theory, particle physics and applications of group theory. **BUSINESS ADDRESS:** Professor, Dept of Physics, University of Michigan, 3038 Randall Lab of Physics, Ann Arbor, MI 48109-1120, (313)764-3455.

WU, ANGELA YUEN
Educator. Chinese American. **PERSONAL:** Born Jul 1, 1949, Hong Kong; daughter of Tai Yuen; married Eu S Wu, Aug 1973; children: Michael C, Michelle Y. **EDUCATION:** Villanova University, BS, 1970; Cornell University, MS, 1972; University of Maryland, College Park, PhD, 1978. **CAREER:** University of Maryland, College Park, visiting professor, 1978-; University of Maryland, Baltimore County, assistant professor, 1978-80; The American University, professor of computer science, 1980-. **ORGANIZATIONS:** ACM, 1977-; IEEE, senior member, 1985-; Sigma Xi, 1988-. **HONORS/AWARDS:** Woodrow Wilson Foundation, Woodrow Wilson Fellow, 1970. **SPECIAL ACHIEVEMENTS:** More than 35 publications in the field of computer vision, algorithms and parallel computing in various journals: IEEE, PAMI, IEEE Transition Computers, pattern recognition. **BUSINESS ADDRESS:** Prof, Dept of Computer Science & Info Systems, The American University, 119 Clark Hall, Washington, DC 20016, (202)885-1476.

WU, ANNA CHAOYING
Librarian. Chinese American. **PERSONAL:** Born Jan 8, 1958, Beijing, People's Republic of China; daughter of Songlian Wu and Yuzhen Wang; married Bob Xiaofen Ren, Aug 14, 1991; children: William. **EDUCATION:** Beijing Chemical Engineering College, BS, 1982; Brigham Young University, MS, 1987, MLS, 1990. **CAREER:** Beijing Chemical Company, engineer, 1982-84; George Mason University Fenwick Library, physical sciences reference librarian, 1990-. **ORGANIZATIONS:** American Library Association, 1989-; IEEE, 1992. **HONORS/AWARDS:** International Library Science, Beta Phi Mu, 1990; Dynix, Dynix Scholarship, 1989-90. **SPECIAL ACHIEVEMENTS:** Publication: "Formula-Based Subject Allocation: A Practical Approach," Collection Management 17, 1993; publication: "A Report to the Director of Librarians on Table of Contents Service & Document Delivery for George Mason University's Fenwick Library," Information Reports and Bibliographies, 1993. **BUSINESS ADDRESS:** Physical Sciences Reference Librarian, George Mason University Fenwick Library, 4400 University Drive, Fairfax, VA 22030, (703)993-2213.

WU, ANNA FANG
Physician, educator. Chinese American. **PERSONAL:** Born Mar 25, 1940, Chengtu, China; daughter of Tsun Chun Fang and Chu Chi Fang; married Tai Te Wu, Apr 16, 1966; children: Richard. **EDUCATION:** Cornell University, BA, 1962; Massachusetts Institute of Technology, PhD, 1967; University of Chicago, MD, 1974. **CAREER:** Muscle Institute, research associate, 1967-68; Columbia University, Department of Biochemistry, research associate, 1968-71; Northwestern Memorial Hospital, physician, director of employer health, 1979-92; Northwestern Medical Faculty Foundation, physician, assistant professor of medicine, 1977-. **ORGANIZATIONS:** American College of Physicians, 1976-; American Medical Association, 1992-; American College of Occupational Medicine, 1980-; Central States, American College of Occupational Medicine, 1980-, board of governors, 1985-88; Medical Directors Club of Chicago, secretary, treasurer, 1991-92. **BUSINESS ADDRESS:** Assistant Professor of Medicine, Northwestern Internists, 676 N St Clair, Ste 415, Chicago, IL 60611, (312)335-1133.

WU, CHERRY. *See* **WU, HSIU-YING.**

WU, CHIEN-SHIUNG
Educator (retired). Chinese American. **PERSONAL:** Born May 31, 1912, Shanghai, China; married 1942; children: one. **EDUCATION:** National Central University, China, BS, 1934; University of California, PhD, 1940. **CAREER:** University of California, research fellow, lecturer, 1940-42; Smith College, assistant professor, 1942-43; Princeton University, instructor, 1943-44; honorary professor, People's Republic of China, Nanking University, Beijing University, Science and Tech University, Tsao Hwa University, Nan Kai University, Italy, Padua University; Columbia University, senior scientist, 1944-47, associate, 1947-52, associate professor, beginning 1952, professor, until 1972, Pupin Professor of Physics, 1972-81. **ORGANIZATIONS:** American Physical Society; National Academy of Science; Chinese Academy of Science. **HONORS/AWARDS:** Honorary DSc degrees from: Princeton University, 1958; Smith College, 1959; Yale University, 1967; Harvard University, 1974; American Physical Society, Tom Bonner Prize, 1975; National Science Medal, 1975; Wolf Prize in Physics, 1978; Royal Society of Edinburgh, honorary fellow; AAAS, fellow; numerous others. **SPECIAL ACHIEVEMENTS:** Asteroid named in honor, 1990. *

WU, CHIEN-YUN (JENNIE)
Nurse, educator. Chinese American. **PERSONAL:** Born Dec 5, 1943, China; daughter of Wen-yu Yuan & Chao-yu Yuan; married Chieh Wu; children: Lawrence, David, James. **EDUCATION:** Taipei National College of Nursing, diploma, 1964; Villanova University, BS, nursing, 1973; George Mason University, MS, nursing, 1982, PhD, nursing, 1990. **CAREER:** Taiwan Gen Veterans Hospital, nurse, 1964-66; Burlington Co Memorial Hosp, nurse, 1967-68; Hosp of the Univ of Pennsylvania, nurse, 1969-70; Cherry Hill Medical Ctr, nurse, 1971-73, dir of education, 1973-75; Magee's Rehabilitation Hosp, supvr, 1976; Jackson Osteopathic Hosp, supvr, 1977; Medical Personnel Pool, nurse, 1979-80; George Mason University, teaching asst, 1981-82, consult, 1984, lecturer, 1985-86, 1988, asst prof, 1989-; UN Development Prog, consult, 1990, 1992, 1993; Fair Oaks Hosp, nurse, 1983-91; Cheng-de Health Sch, consult, 1990-; Taipei Natl Jr College of Nursing, Taiwan, visiting assoc prof, consult, 1992; Chinese Assn English Nursing Schs, consult, 1992-; Arlington Hosp, nursing supvr, 1992-. **ORGANIZATIONS:** Epsilon Zeta Chapter of Sigma Theta Tau, faculty adviser, 1991-; Research Comm of Arlington Hosp, faculty member, 1991-; Washington Urban League, Aging Services Div, adviser, 1991-92; Chinese Nurses Assn, honor member, 1993; American Nurses Assn; Virginia Nurses Assn; Sigma Theta Tau; American Assn of Critical Care Nurses. **HONORS/AWARDS:** George Mason University, research grant, 1993, Outstanding Undergraduate Faculty Award, 1990; Epsilon Zeta Chapter of Sigma Theta Tau, research grant, 1991; editor, Videotape, Confidence and a Better Life: How to Prevent and Cope with Cardiovascular Disease, Washington Urban League, 1992. **SPECIAL ACHIEVEMENTS:** Editor, Textbook of Nursing in English, Assn of Chinese English Nursing Schools, 1993; author, "Profile of Non-Nurse College Graduates Enrolled in Accelerated Baccalaureate Nursing Programs," Journal of Professional Nursing, vol 8, no 1, p35-40, 1992. **BUSINESS ADDRESS:** Assistant Professor, George Mason University, College of Nursing and Health Science, 4400 University Dr, Robinson Bldg, Fairfax, VA 22030, (703)993-1900.

WU, CHIH
Educator. Chinese American. **PERSONAL:** Born Apr 13, 1936, Changsha, Hunan, China; son of K T Wu and D R Yang; married Ho Ying Wu, Feb 4,

1975; children: Anna, Joy, Sheree, Patricia. **EDUCATION:** Cheng Kung University, BS, 1957; University of Illinois, PhD, 1966. **CAREER:** Johns Hopkins University, professor, 1969-; US Naval Academy, professor, 1966-. **HONORS/AWARDS:** USNA, Research Excellence, 1991; US Navy, Meritorious Service, 1991. **SPECIAL ACHIEVEMENTS:** Published 2 books, and more than 400 journal articles and conference papers. **BUSINESS ADDRESS:** Professor, Dept of Mechanical Engineering, US Naval Academy, Annapolis, MD 21402-5042, (410)267-3186.

WU, CHING-SHENG
Educator, research scientist. Chinese American. **PERSONAL:** Born Nov 11, 1929, Nanjing, China; married Lucia Wu, Aug 12, 1962; children: Bryant C. **EDUCATION:** National Taiwan University, BS, 1954; Virginia Polytechnical Institute, MS, 1956; Princeton University, PhD, 1959. **CAREER:** Jet Propulsion Laboratory, California Technology, senior scientist, member of technical staff, 1959-68; University of Maryland, research professor, 1968-. **ORGANIZATIONS:** American Physical Society; American Geophysical Union; Sigma Xi; New York Academy of Sciences; Intl Union Radio Science, US National Committee of Commission H; Chinese Association of Space Science. **HONORS/AWARDS:** University of Electronic Science and Technology of China, Chengdu, Sichuan, honorary professorship, 1992; New York Academy of Sciences, elected fellow, 1987; American Physical Society, elected fellow, 1984; Chinese Academy of Sciences, honorary professorship, 1979. **SPECIAL ACHIEVEMENTS:** Numerous achievements, including: Journal of Geophysical Research, associate editor, 1984-86; National Natural Science Foundation of China, guest consultant, 1986; Federal University of Rio Grande de Sol, visiting scientist, 1988. **BUSINESS ADDRESS:** Professor, University of Maryland, Institute for Physical Science and Technology, College Park, MD 20742.

WU, CHING-YONG
Research scientist. Taiwanese American. **PERSONAL:** Born Oct 6, 1931, Taipei, Taiwan; married Teng-Mei Wu; children: George, James, Andrew. **EDUCATION:** National Taiwan University, BS, 1954; University of Pittsburgh, PhD, 1961. **CAREER:** Gulf Res & Development Company, senior res chemist, 1965-83; Koppers Company Inc, senior scientist, 1983-88; INDSPEC Chemical Corporation, senior scientist, 1988-. **ORGANIZATIONS:** American Chemical Society; North American Catalysis Society. **SPECIAL ACHIEVEMENTS:** 31 US Patents; author of 20 scientific publications. **BUSINESS ADDRESS:** Senior Scientist, INDSPEC Chemical Corporation, 1010 William Pitt Way, Pittsburgh, PA 15238, (412)826-3679.

WU, CHIVEY DRAGENSON LUNG
Educator. Chinese American. **PERSONAL:** Born Mar 6, 1952, Shanghai, People's Republic of China; son of Xiyuan Wu and Minhua Xu; married Karen Yeeping Chyan, Jul 4, 1977; children: Mandarin Shaoching, Eric Changling. **EDUCATION:** National Cheng Kung University, Taiwan, BS, 1976; University of Illinois, Urbana-Champaign, MS, 1979, PhD, 1983. **CAREER:** Chillip Kwan & Associates, draftsman, 1971-72; Cheng Kung University, teaching assistant, 1976-77; University of Illinois, teaching, research assistant, 1977-83; California State University, assistant professor, 1983-87, associate professor, 1987-92, professor, 1992-. **ORGANIZATIONS:** American Institute of Aeronautics & Astronautics, 1984-; American Society of Engineering Education, 1992-; California Faculty Association, 1984-; American Society of Mechanical Engineers, 1983-; ASME, Los Angeles Section, director, 1991-. **HONORS/AWARDS:** California State University, Engineering Student Council, Outstanding Professor, 1993; American Society of Mechanical Engineers, Certificate of Appreciation, 1991; California State University, Certificate of Recognition, 1991; NASA, Certificate of Recognition, 1991, 1992; US Navy, Certificate of Appreciation, 1986. **SPECIAL ACHIEVEMENTS:** Involved in solar-powered cars development projects, 2 prototypes built, 1989-93; conducted research projects for NASA, 1991-; conducted research projects for Lockheed Aeronautical Systems Co, 1990-91; taught martial arts classes at East Los Angeles College, 1984-93, and the Chinese Cultural Center, Los Angeles, 1993-. **BIOGRAPHICAL SOURCES:** Chinese Daily News, World Journal, April 6, 1993, Nov 9, 1992, May 24, 1990; International Daily News, May 24, 1990, May 5, 1990. **BUSINESS ADDRESS:** Professor of Mechanical Engineering, California State University, 5151 State University Dr, Los Angeles, CA 90032, (213)343-4489.

WU, CHRISTINE A.
Marketing manager, apparel designer. Chinese American. **PERSONAL:** Born Aug 31, 1961, Taipei, Taiwan; daughter of Philip S Wu and Virginia S Wu; married William W Jacobson Jr, Nov 25, 1988; children: Maile-Marie. **EDUCATION:** University of Washington, BS, 1983. **CAREER:** Union Bay Sportswear, designer, 1986-88; Converse, merchandiser, designer, 1988-90; Reebok International, marketing manager, 1990-. **SPECIAL ACHIEVEMENTS:** Employee of Reebok, an official sponsor of the US Olympic Team for the '92 Olympic Games, provided performance products and was responsible for the merchandising of apparel and award suits, 1991-92. **HOME ADDRESS:** 205 High St, Westwood, MA 02090.

WU, CHRISTOPHER N.
Attorney, association executive. Chinese American. **PERSONAL:** Born Sep 7, 1957, Kansas City, MO; son of William Q Wu and Cecile Franking Wu; married Jennifer S Wu, Aug 8, 1981; children: Michael Milton. **EDUCATION:** Shimer College, BA, humanities, 1978; San Francisco State University, 1979-80; University of California, Boalt Hall School of Law, 1983-84; University of Michigan School of Law, JD, 1984. **CAREER:** Tonsing and Heimann, associate attorney, 1984-86; Law Offices of Christopher N Wu, attorney, 1986-87; Legal Services for Children, staff attorney, 1987-89, executive director, 1989-93, managing attorney, 1994-. **ORGANIZATIONS:** National Center for Youth Law, director, 1988-; National Association of Counsel for Children, 1988-, director, 1989-91; Asian American Bar Association of the San Francisco Bay Area, 1985-; California Child Welfare Strategic Planning Committee, commissioner, 1989-91; Foster Care Advisory Committee, Little Hoover Commission, 1991; California Children's Justice Act Task Force, 1993-; California Judicial Council, Juvenile and Family Law Advisory Committee, 1993-. **SPECIAL ACHIEVEMENTS:** Served as Judge ProTem, San Francisco Superior Court, 1991. **HOME ADDRESS:** 34 Anelda Dr, Pleasant Hill, CA 94523, (510)680-0683. **BUSINESS ADDRESS:** Managing Attorney, Legal Services for Children Inc, 1254 Market St, 3rd Fl, San Francisco, CA 94102, (415)863-3762.

WU, CHUAN-FU
Research and development manager. Taiwanese American. **PERSONAL:** Born Mar 1, 1955, Kaohsiung, Taiwan; married Bijou Wu, Sep 7, 1981; children: Sarah, Gary. **EDUCATION:** National Tsing-Hua University, Taiwan, BS, 1977, MS, 1979; Massachusetts Institute of Technology, PhD, 1987. **CAREER:** Institute of Nuclear Energy Research, research scientist, 1981-84; Massachusetts Institute of Technology, teaching assistant, 1985, research assistant, 1985-87; Oak Ridge National Laboratory, applied health physicist, 1988-89; Westinghouse Electric Corp, dosimetry manager, 1989-90, dosimetry & analytical technology manager, 1990-. **ORGANIZATIONS:** Department of Energy, Laboratory Accreditation Program Assessor, 1993-; Westinghouse Electric Corp, Saving through Sharing Steering Committee, 1993-; American Nuclear Society, Carlsbad Section, chairman, 1992-93; American Health Physics Society, 1988-; Sigma Xi, 1985-; New Mexico Academy of Sciences, 1992-; American Board of Health Physics, 1990-. **HONORS/AWARDS:** Westinghouse Electric Corp, Total Quality Award, 1990, 1993; Massachusetts Institute of Technology, Thompson Fellowship, 1985-86. **SPECIAL ACHIEVEMENTS:** American Board of Health Physics, certified, 1990; 22 papers and articles, 1979-; 24 presentations at conferences or meetings, 1979-; invited speaker at universities and scientific institutions, 1991-; chairman of technical sessions at conferences and meetings, 1991-. **HOME ADDRESS:** 806 Merion Dr, Carlsbad, NM 88220, (505)887-5707. **BUSINESS ADDRESS:** Manager, Dosimetry and Analytical Technology, Westinghouse Electric Corp, PO Box 2078, Carlsbad, NM 88221, (505)234-8384.

WU, CHUN-FANG
Educator. Chinese American/Taiwanese American. **PERSONAL:** Born Feb 4, 1947, Fujien, China; son of Chung-Chiun Wu and Yun Chen Wu; married Mei-Lien Lin Wu, Sep 25, 1971; children: Daw-An, Yusing, Dawin. **EDUCATION:** Tunghai University, Taichung, Taiwan, BS, 1969; Purdue University, PhD, 1976. **CAREER:** California Institute of Technology, research associate, 1976-79; University of Iowa, assistant professor, associate professor, 1979-89, professor, 1989-; National Taiwan University, visiting professor, 1987; University of Tokyo, visiting professor, 1988. **ORGANIZATIONS:** AAAS, 1973-; Biophysical Society, 1983-; New York Academy of Science, 1986-91; Society for Neuroscience, 1979-; Sigma Xi, 1989-; Society Chinese Bioscientists in America, 1986-. **HONORS/AWARDS:** National Institutes of Health, Research Career Development Award, 1982-87, Research Grants, 1979-; Searle Scholar Program, Chicago Community Trust, Scholar, 1981-86; Japan Society Promotion of Science, Fellow, 1988. **SPECIAL ACHIEVEMENTS:** NIH, adhoc reviewer, 1989-; Journal of Neurogenetics, associate editor, 1989-; Asia Pacific Journal of Pharmacology, Singapore, editorial board, 1987-; contributor

of numerous articles to professional journals. **BUSINESS ADDRESS:** Professor, Dept of Biological Sciences, University of Iowa, Iowa City, IA 52242.

WU, CHUNG-HSIU
Physician, educator. Taiwanese American. **PERSONAL:** Born Oct 10, 1936, Taitung, Taiwan; son of Ta-Tsang Wu and Tswei-Fong Chiang; married Fang-Rong Chen Wa, Oct 20, 1963; children: Sun-ching, Samuel, Sandra. **EDUCATION:** National Taiwan University, School of Medicine, MD, 1962; University of Pennsylvania, School of Medicine, 1965-67. **CAREER:** University of Pennsylvania, assistant professor, 1972-77, associate professor, 1977-80; University of Pennsylvania Hospital, attending physician, 1972-80; Thomas Jefferson University Hospital, attending physician, 1980-; director of Reproductive Endocrinology, 1980-87; Thomas Jefferson University, professor, 1980-. **SPECIAL ACHIEVEMENTS:** More than 100 scientific papers and 70 presentations in field of reproductive Endocrinology, 1965-93; languages: Chinese, Taiwanese, Japanese, English. **MILITARY SERVICE:** Chinese Army, Taiwan, second lt, 1962-63. **BUSINESS ADDRESS:** Professor, Dept of Ob & Gyn, Thomas Jefferson University, 1025 Walnut Street, Ste. 310, Philadelphia, PA 19107, (215)955-6930.

WU, DAN QING
Chemist. Chinese American. **PERSONAL:** Born Jul 18, 1960, Fujian, People's Republic of China; married Juliet Wu, Aug 7, 1992. **EDUCATION:** University of Science & Technology of China, BS, 1982; State University of New York at Stony Brook, PhD, 1990. **CAREER:** DuPont Co, division chemist, 1989-. **ORGANIZATIONS:** American Chemical Society, 1984-; American Physical Society, 1985-; Materials Research Society, 1987-90; Organization of Chinese Americans, 1991-, Delaware Chapter, vice president, 1993. **HONORS/AWARDS:** Materials Research Society, Graduate Student Award, 1989; Organization of Chinese Americans Delaware Chapter, Member of the Year, 1992. **SPECIAL ACHIEVEMENTS:** Over 30 publications in scientific journals on researches of macromolecules, 1985-. **BUSINESS ADDRESS:** Division Chemist, E I du Pont de Nemours & Company, Inc, Experimental Station, PO Box 80228, Wilmington, DE 19880-0228, (302)695-3516.

WU, DAVID (SZU-YUNG)
Educator. Taiwanese American. **PERSONAL:** Born Feb 25, 1959, Taipei, Taiwan; son of You-Jen Wu and Shi-Chow Wang; married Sheau-Ping Wu, Aug 10, 1983; children: Allison P, Brian J. **EDUCATION:** Tunghai University, BS, 1981; Pennsylvania State University, MS, 1984, PhD, 1987. **CAREER:** Pennsylvania State University, research assistant, 1983-87; GCA Corporation, systems specialist, 1985; Lehigh University, instructor, 1987, industrial eng, assistant professor, 1987-92, associate professor, 1992-. **ORGANIZATIONS:** Institute of Industrial Engineers, chapter vice president, 1988-90, senior member, 1983-; Operations Research Society of American, 1985-; American Association of Artificial Intelligence, 1984-89; Society of Manufacturing Engineers, 1983-89. **HONORS/AWARDS:** National Science Foundation, Research Initiation Award, 1990; Institute of Industrial Eng, Outstanding Dissertation Award Finalist, 1988; Pennsylvania State University, Graduate Research Competition, 1985. **SPECIAL ACHIEVEMENTS:** Published more than 40 articles on technical journals, books and proceedings, 1986-; conducted research funded by National Science Foundation; conducted research funded by UNISYS Corp; conducted reserach funded by Center of Manufacturing Systems Engineering; conducted research funded by Ben Franklin Advanced Technology Center. **BUSINESS ADDRESS:** Professor, Dept of Industrial Engineering, Lehigh University, 200 W Packer Ave, Mohler Lab, Bethlehem, PA 18015-3044, (215)758-4028.

WU, DE TING
Educator. Chinese American. **PERSONAL:** Born Jan 9, 1938, Shanghai, China; son of Robert P H Wu and W F Zhang (Wu); married Pei Hua Zhang (Wu), Jul 16, 1974; children: Yin. **EDUCATION:** Peking University, BA, 1962; University of Georgia, MA, 1983, PhD, 1988. **CAREER:** Shanghai Textile College, instructor, 1963-71; Shanghai #12 Textile Factory, worker, 1971-78; Shanghai Textile College, senior lecturer, 1978-81; University of Georgia, teaching assistant, 1981-88; Morehouse College, professor of mathematics, 1989-. **ORGANIZATIONS:** Shanghai Mechanics Association of General Mechanics, group member, 1980-81; American Mathematic Society, 1982-88; Mathematical Association of America, 1988-; American Association of University Professors, 1991-; Learned Society of Faculty of Atlanta University Center, charter member, 1990-; Organization of Chinese American, board of directors, 1992-. **HONORS/AWARDS:** Mainland China Monthly, Award for

Better Work, 1989; University of Georgia, graduate scholarship, 1981-88. **SPECIAL ACHIEVEMENTS:** Modern Science-Technology Dictionary, 1980; Selected Problem from Theoretical Mechanics, 1981; 4 articles in newspapers, 1988-89; "On Unification and Modernization of China," 1989; representation of "Using a Graphic Calculator to Teach Newton's Method," 1992; representation of "Stability of Approximate Solutions of Second Orders Ito Equation," 1993; Conference papers, 1978-81: "Analysis to the motion of a vibrating ring;" "Another proof of the equilibrium equations with two moments of the system of plane forces;" "About the equilibrium of the system of forces in space;" others. **BUSINESS ADDRESS:** Professor of Mathematics, Morehouse College, 830 Westview Dr SW, #328 Dansley Hall, Atlanta, GA 30314-3799, (404)681-2800.

WU, DIANA TING LIU
Educator. Chinese American. **PERSONAL:** Born Dec 24, 1936, Shanghai, China; daughter of Robert & Alice Liu; married George, Feb 6, 1960; children: Gloria, Greta, Daniel. **EDUCATION:** New York University, MBA, 1961; Wright Institute of Berkely, PhD, 1980. **CAREER:** University of Berkeley Students Co-op, chief accountant, general mgr, 1961-70; Wright Institute, asst to pres, 1970-79; John F Kennedy University, asst to pres, 1979-81; Saint Mary's College, lecturer, 1981, dept chair, 1986-94, prof, 1994-. **ORGANIZATIONS:** Acad of Mgt; American Mgt Assn; American Psychological Assn; Stanford Ctr for Entrepreneurship; American Assn of University Women; Asian Americans in Higher Education; Intl Soc for the Study of Chinese Overseas; Soc of Women Accountants; Natl Assn for Female Executive; Shanghai Enterprise & Mgt Assn; World Affairs Council; New China Foundation; Amnesty Intl. **SPECIAL ACHIEVEMENTS:** Publications include: "Is Romance Un-Chinese?," "Living through China's Whirlwind Years," "A Woman Warrior's Life in China," San Francisco Chronicle, "Chinese Women in Their Organizations" series, Sep 1981; Global Entrepreneurs, St Mary's College, 1993; "St Mary's College & the Study of Asian Americans," Chinese Journal, KTSF TV, June 1993. **BIOGRAPHICAL SOURCES:** Asian Week; Contra Costa Times; Contra Costa Sun; Oakland Tribune; San Francisco Chronicle; and others. **BUSINESS ADDRESS:** Professor, Dept of Business Administration, St Mary's College, St Mary Rd, Moraga, CA 94575, (510)631-4000.

WU, EN SHINN
Educator. Chinese American. **PERSONAL:** Born Apr 20, 1943, Kwangtung, China; son of Hsieh-Tang Wu and Shih-Ho Wu; married Angela Y Wu, Aug 4, 1973; children: Michael Chiao-An, Michelle Yuen-ting. **EDUCATION:** National Taiwan University, BS, 1965; Cornell University, PhD, 1972. **CAREER:** University of Maryland, assistant professor, 1974-80, associate professor, 1980-. **ORGANIZATIONS:** Optical Society of America. **BUSINESS ADDRESS:** Associate Professor, Dept of Physics, University of Maryland, Baltimore County, 5401 Wilkins Ave, Ste E, Catonsville, MD 21228, (410)455-2526.

WU, FA YUEH
Educator, researcher. Chinese American. **PERSONAL:** Born Jan 5, 1932, China; son of Chia Yu Wu and Yu Shih Lo Wu; married Jane, Apr 6, 1963; children: Yvonne, Yolanda, Yelena. **EDUCATION:** Chinese Naval College, BS, 1954; National Tsing Hua University, MS, 1959; Washington University, PhD, 1963. **CAREER:** Virginia Polytecnic Institute, assistant professor, 1963-67; National Science Foundation, program director, 1983-84; Northeastern University, assistant professor, 1967-69, associate professor, 1969-75, professor of physics, 1975-89, university distinguished professor, 1989-93; Matthews Distinguished Professor, 1993-. **ORGANIZATIONS:** American Physical Society, fellow. **HONORS/AWARDS:** Fulbright Scholar, 1973. **SPECIAL ACHIEVEMENTS:** 160 publications on statistical physics and condensed matter physics, 1962-93. **BUSINESS ADDRESS:** Matthews Distinguished Professor, Northeastern University, 360 Huntington Ave, 119 Dana, Boston, MA 02115, (617)373-2925.

WU, FANG-SHENG
Educator, biologist. Taiwanese American. **PERSONAL:** Born May 4, 1941, Taiwan; son of Shu-Sheng Wu and Yueh-Chieh Cheng Wu; married Melanie C Wu, 1975; children: Minming, Helen, Constance, Eaming. **EDUCATION:** National Taiwan Normal University, BS, 1967, MS, 1972; Michigan State University, PhD, 1977. **CAREER:** Institute of Botany Academia Sinica, assistant research fellow, 1972-73; Michigan State University, graduate assistant, 1974-77; University of Connecticut, postdoctoral fellow, 1977-79; Upstate Medical Center, SUNY, research assistant professor, 1979-81; Sandoz-Zeocon

Research Institute, senior scientist, 1981-88; Virginia Commonwealth University, associate professor, 1988-. **ORGANIZATIONS:** Phillip Morris USA, consultant, 1990-; Agency for International Development, review panel, 1989-93; National Science Foundation, review panel, 1988; American Association of Advanced Sciences, 1989-; American Tissue Culture Association, 1981-93; American Society of Plant Physiologists, 1983-93. **HONORS/AWARDS:** Michigan State University, Bessey Award, 1977. **SPECIAL ACHIEVEMENTS:** Twenty publications in selected journals or books including: J of Biol Chem, vol 256, p 5309-5312, 1981; Plant Physiology, vol 79, p 301-305, 1985; Planta, vol 171, p 346-357, 1987; Plant, Cell and Environment, vol 15, p 685-692, 1992; Biotechnology in Agriculture and Forestry, vol 9, p 197-216, 1989. **BUSINESS ADDRESS:** Associate Professor, Dept of Biology, Virginia Commonwealth University, 816 Park Ave, Box 2012, Richmond, VA 23284-2012, (804)367-1562.

WU, FRANCIS TAMING
Educator. Chinese American. **PERSONAL:** Born May 27, 1936, Shanghai, China; son of Tao Yi Wu and Ni Tse Su; married Miriam, Dec 17, 1966; children: Allison. **EDUCATION:** National Taiwan University, BS, 1959; California Institute of Technology, PhD, 1966. **CAREER:** California Institute of Tech, research fellow, 1966-68; Boston College, asst professor, 1968-69; State University of NY, Binghamton, assistant professor, 1970-72, assoc professor, 1972-76, chairman, dept geol sci, 1989-92, professor, 1976. **ORGANIZATIONS:** American Geophysical Union, 1965-; Seismological Society of America, 1965-, board of advisors, 1986-92; Institute of Earth Sciences, Academia Sinica, Taipei, board of advisors, 1985-, corresponding member, 1986-. **BUSINESS ADDRESS:** Professor, Dept of Geol Sci, State University of New York at Binghamton, Vestal Pkwy E, SI/G60, Binghamton, NY 13902-6000.

WU, FRANK I.
Financial consultant. Chinese American. **PERSONAL:** Born Dec 28, 1958, Corvallis, OR; son of Arthur S H Wu and Show Yong Wu. **EDUCATION:** Oregon State University, BSEE, 1982; Pepperdine University, MBA, 1989. **CAREER:** McDonnell Douglas Space Systems, engineer/specialist, 1982-92; Smith Barney Shearson, financial consultant, 1992-. **ORGANIZATIONS:** Saddleback Valley Lions Club; Chinese Chamber of Commerce, Orange County; Asian Business League; Orange County Sigma Chi Alumni; United States Tennis Association. **HONORS/AWARDS:** Southern California Tennis Association, #3 ranking, men's singles, 4.5 tennis, 1992; McDonnell Douglas, General Managers Award, 1991. **HOME ADDRESS:** 24206 Sparkling Spring, Lake Forest, CA 92630, (714)830-9334. **BUSINESS PHONE:** (714)641-7720.

WU, FREDERICK H.
Educator. Taiwanese American. **PERSONAL:** Born Oct 20, 1938, Tainan, Taiwan; married Winnie H Wu, Jan 5, 1967; children: Wilfred W, Christina H. **EDUCATION:** National Taiwan University, BA, 1961; University of California, Berkeley, MBA, 1966; Texas Tech University, PhD, 1975. **CAREER:** Pfizer Ltd, controller, 1967-70; Wichita State University, assistant, associate professor, 1974-84; Southern Illinois University at Carbondale, professor, director, 1984-93; University of North Texas, professor, chairman, 1993-. **ORGANIZATIONS:** Federation of Schools of Accountancy, Standards Committee, chair, 1987-; American Accounting Association, 1984-; Institute of Management Accounting, 1975-. **HONORS/AWARDS:** Institute of Management Accounting, Manuscript Competition Award, 1974, 1975. **SPECIAL ACHIEVEMENTS:** Accounting Information Systems: Theory and Practice, published by McGraw-Hill, Accounting Information Systems, published in Chinese in Taiwan. **BUSINESS ADDRESS:** Professor, Chairman, Dept of Accounting, University of North Texas, College of Business Administration, Denton, TX 76203, (817)565-3077.

WU, GEORGE
Educator. Chinese American. **PERSONAL:** Born Oct 25, 1963, Philadelphia, PA; son of Wei-ping Wu and Lily Shu-li Wu. **EDUCATION:** Harvard College, AB, applied mathematics, 1985; Harvard University, SM, applied mathematics, 1987, PhD, decision sciences, 1991. **CAREER:** Procter & Gamble, analyst, 1985-86; University of Pennsylvania, lecturer, 1991; Harvard Business School, assistant professor, 1991-. **HOME ADDRESS:** 4 Forest St, Cambridge, MA 02140, (617)354-9587. **BUSINESS ADDRESS:** Assistant Professor, Harvard Business School, Morgan 327, Boston, MA 02163, (617)495-6614.

WU, GEORGE K.
Company executive. Taiwanese American. **PERSONAL:** Born Jul 27, 1951, I-Lan, Taiwan; married Sheena Wu, Sep 30, 1977; children: Kevin, Shera, Jennifer. **EDUCATION:** Tankang University, International Trade Department, bachelor's degree, 1974. **CAREER:** SJA Industries Inc, CEO, currently. **BUSINESS ADDRESS:** CEO, SJA Industries Inc, 9344 Glenoaks Blvd, Sun Valley, CA 91352, (818)768-8011.

WU, HAI-SHENG
Educator. Taiwanese American. **PERSONAL:** Born Jun 22, 1947, Shanghai, China; son of Tsan-Hua Wu and Fang Chin Ann Wu; married Shiu-Jung Shih, Mar 25, 1972; children: Kuan-Chuen, Wan-Yin, Kuan-Jei. **EDUCATION:** National Taiwan Normal University, BS, 1970; Mankato State University, MA, 1982; Iowa State University, PhD, 1988. **CAREER:** Tai Chung Youth High School, physics teacher, 1972-77; Taipei Chin-Mei Municipal Girls High School, physics teachers/chief registrar, 1977-79; Mankato State University, teaching assistant, 1980-82; Iowa State University, research assistant, 1983-88; Mankato State University, associate professor of physics, 1988-. **ORGANIZATIONS:** American Physical Society; Sigma Xi, vice president of Mankato State University Club; American Vacuum Society; Society of Physics Students, Mankato State University Chapter, adviser; Minnesota American Association of Physics Teachers. **HONORS/AWARDS:** National Science Foundation, Improvement of Laboratory Instrumentation Grant, 1989; NASA, Jove (Joint Venture) Research Program, 1990; Mankato State University, Q-7 Critical Thinking Curriculum Development, 1993. **SPECIAL ACHIEVEMENTS:** Papers on amorphous semiconductors, superconductor thin films were published in several refereed journals. **MILITARY SERVICE:** Taiwan Army, lt, 1970-71. **HOME ADDRESS:** 1323 Warren St, Mankato, MN 56001-4948, (507)388-1608. **BUSINESS PHONE:** (507)389-1316.

WU, HARRY PAO-TUNG
Library administrator. Chinese American. **PERSONAL:** Born May 1, 1932, Jinan, Shandong, China; son of James Ching-Mei Wu and Elizabeth Hsiao Lu; married Irene Sun, Jun 23, 1961; children: Eva Pei-Chen, Walter Pei-Liang. **EDUCATION:** National Taiwan University, Taipei, Taiwan, BA, 1959; Ohio State University, 1962; Kent State University, MLS, 1966. **CAREER:** Massillon Public Library, reference librarian, 1964-65, acting assistant director, head of adult services, 1965, assistant director, 1966; Flesh Public Library, director, 1966-68; St Clair County Library System, director, 1968-; Blue Water Library Federation, founder, director, 1974-. **ORGANIZATIONS:** American Library Association, 1969-; Blue Water Reading Council, board member, 1987-88; Library of Michigan, board member, 1992-; Michigan Library Association, 1969-, Library Sytems Roundtable, chair, 1974-75; Michigan Waterways Council of Girl Scouts, board member, 1985-86; Port Huron International Club, 1968-, president, 1988; Port Huron Rotary Club, 1969-, board member, 1972-74, 1988-90; Chinese American Librarians Association, 1992-, Midwest Chapter Michigan Contact, 1993-; Michigan Library Film Circuit, president, 1977-79. **HONORS/AWARDS:** The Rotary Foundation of Rotary International, Paul Harris Fellow, 1988. **SPECIAL ACHIEVEMENTS:** Author, "Public Libraries Need Everyone's Support," The Times Herald, Sunday, p 7B, January 22, 1984. **HOME ADDRESS:** 1518 Holland Avenue, Port Huron, MI 48060. **BUSINESS ADDRESS:** Library Director, St Clair County Library System, 210 McMorran Boulevard, Port Huron, MI 48060-4098, (810)987-7323.

WU, HO-MOU
Educator. Chinese American. **PERSONAL:** Born Sep 26, 1952, Taichung, Taiwan; married Pyng Chern Wu, Jul 25, 1976; children: Hochong, Howei, Hoyu. **EDUCATION:** Stanford University, MA, 1980, PhD, 1982. **CAREER:** Rutgers University, assistant professor, 1982-83; Tulane University, assistant professor, 1983-89, visiting associate professor of finance, 1990-91, associate professor, 1989-; Vanderbilt University, visiting assistant professor, 1988; Stanford University, visiting associate professor, 1991-. **ORGANIZATIONS:** Chinese Economics Association of North America, program committee, 1990-; Econometric Society, 1982-; American Eonomics Association, 1982-. **HONORS/AWARDS:** Chiang-Ching Kuo Foundation, Research Grant, 1991. **SPECIAL ACHIEVEMENTS:** Works published in Economic Journal, Journal of International Economics, Journal of Mathematical Economics, Economics Letters, etc. **BUSINESS ADDRESS:** Professor, Dept of Economics, Stanford University, Stanford, CA 94305, (415)725-3266.

WU, HOFU
Educator. Taiwanese American. **PERSONAL:** Born Mar 28, 1949, Taipei, Taiwan; son of Rev and Mrs. Yung-Hwa Wu and Chin-Chau Huang; married Meina Lin, Jul 30, 1983; children: Anne, Michelle, Tiffany. **EDUCATION:** Tamkang University, Taipei, Taiwan, BArch, 1971; Illinois Institute of Technology, Grad School, 1973; University of Illinois, MArch, 1975; University of Michigan, DArch, 1988. **CAREER:** Office of Mies Van der Rohe, Chicago, arch designer, 1973; Kenyon & Associates, Peoria, Illinois, project architect, 1975-77; Colvin-Robinson Associates, Ann Arbor, project architect, 1978-81; University of Michigan, lecturer, assistant professor, 1978-83; Arizona State University, associate professor, 1984-90; Wu and Associates, Architect, principal, 1980-; California State Polytechnic University, Architecture, associate professor, 1990-. **ORGANIZATIONS:** American Institute of Architects, 1980-; American Society of Heating, Refrigeration, and Air-Conditioning Engineers, 1978-; International Solar Energy Society, 1979-; Association of Collegiate School of Architecture, 1981-; Society of Building Science Educators, 1984-, secretary, 1988. **HONORS/AWARDS:** All-Union Association of Building Engineers, Russia, ABOK, 1990; US Dept of Energy, Lawrence Berkeley Lab, research fellow, 1989; Associated Western University, Faculty Res Travel Fellowship, 1988; Ma's Architectural Design Award, 1969; Tamkang University, Arch Design Award, 1970. **SPECIAL ACHIEVEMENTS:** Numerous research papers presented in ASHRAE Transaction on Architectural Integration and Evaporative Cooling System Design and Performance, 1984-; Moisture Up-Take and Energy Efficiencies Associated with the Use of Evaporative Coolers; report to US DOE and Brookhaven Natl Lab, Arizona State University, 1990. **HOME ADDRESS:** PO Box 5051, Diamond Bar, CA 91765-3659, (909)396-1218. **BUSINESS ADDRESS:** Professor, Dept of Architecture, California State Polytechnic University, 3801 West Temple Avenue, Pomona, CA 91768-4048, (909)869-4527.

WU, HSIN-I (WALLY WU)
Educator. Chinese American. **PERSONAL:** Born May 25, 1937, Tokyo, Japan; son of Ti-cheng Wu & Ling-tuan Wu; married Sancy Yue-hsien Kiang Wu, May 2, 1964; children: Vernon Chao (deceased), Tammy Lynn. **EDUCATION:** Tunghai University, Taiwan, BS, 1960; University of Missouri, Columbia, MS, 1964, PhD, 1967; Texas A&M University, MS, 1977. **CAREER:** Southeast Missouri State University, associate professor of physics, 1967-76; Texas A&M University, professor, 1976-, professor of bioengineering, 1987-. **HONORS/AWARDS:** Fulbright Foundation, Senior Fulbright Scholar, 1992; Texas Engineering Experiment Station, fellow, 1990; UNDP, China, TOKTEN, 1986-88. **SPECIAL ACHIEVEMENTS:** Author of: Ecological Field Theory, Ecological Modelling, 1985; Nearest Neighbor Distribution for Individuals of Finite Sizes, Ecological Modelling, 1987; Simulation of Two-dimensional Patterns, 1987; Age-Size Population Dynamics, Computer & Mathematics with Application, 1987; "Plant Cell Wall Elasticity," J Theoretical Biology, 1988. **BUSINESS ADDRESS:** Professor, Dept of Industrial Engineering, Texas A&M University, Center for Biosystems Modelling, Wisenbaker Engineering Research Center, Rm 214P, College Station, TX 77843-3131, (409)845-5540.

WU, HSIU-YING (CHERRY WU)
Social worker. Taiwanese American. **PERSONAL:** Born Aug 26, 1962, Kaohsiung, Taiwan; daughter of Ming-Fa Wu & Pin-Lien Lin; married Chang-Yun Liu, Nov 26, 1988. **EDUCATION:** Tunghai University, Taiwan, BSW, 1985, MSW, 1987; San Jose State University, MSW, 1991. **CAREER:** Tunghai University, research assistant, 1986-87; Family & Youth Center, social worker, 1987-89; Asian Americans for Community Involvment, senior program director, 1991-. **ORGANIZATIONS:** Tunghai University Student Body Association, vice chairman, 1986; Asian Concerned Ethnic Chinese, 1991-; National Association of Social Work, 1991-; Chinese Senior Alliance, steering committee head, 1991-. **HONORS/AWARDS:** Wu Tsuen Shian Culture & Education, scholarship, 1987; Youth National Salvation Corps, scholarship, 1987. **BUSINESS ADDRESS:** Senior Program Director, Asian Americans for Community Involvement, 232 E Gish Rd, #200, San Jose, CA 95112, (408)452-5151.

WU, HUNG-HSI
Educator. Chinese American. **PERSONAL:** Born May 25, 1940, Hong Kong; son of Tsao-Chih Wu and Mary Tsun Auyang; married Kuniko Weltin-Wu, Aug 9, 1976; children: Colin Weltin-Wu. **EDUCATION:** Columbia College, AB, 1961; MIT, PhD, 1963. **CAREER:** MIT, research associate, 1963-64; Institute of Advanced Study, 1964-65; University of California, Berkeley, assistant professor of math, 1965-68, associate professor of math, 1968-73,

professor of math, 1973-. **BUSINESS ADDRESS:** Professor, Dept of Mathematics, University of California, Berkeley, CA 94720.

WU, ISHIUNG J.
Mineral exploration company executive. Taiwanese American. **PERSONAL:** Born Mar 6, 1945, Chia-Yi, Taiwan; son of Wu Wen-Li and Cheng Hun; married Priscilla Barton Wu, Jan 2, 1974; children: Jessica, Paloma. **EDUCATION:** National Taiwan University, BS, 1968; Harvard University, MA, 1971, PhD, 1975. **CAREER:** Kennecott Exploration Inc, research geochemist, 1974-77; Exxon Minerals Company, senior geologist, 1977-80; Chevron Resources Co, exploration manager, Chile, 1981-82, staff geologist, district geologist, 1983-90, exploration manager, US, 1991; IW Exploration Co, president, 1992-. **ORGANIZATIONS:** Society of Economic Geologists, fellow, 1977-; Society for Mining, Metallurgy & Exploration, 1989-; Geological Society of Nevada, 1984-; Northwest Mining Association, 1988-. **SPECIAL ACHIEVEMENTS:** Co-author: "Geochemistry of Tetrahedrite-Tennantite at Casapalca, Peru," Economic Geology, vol 72, 1977; "Mercury in Soils Geochemistry on Massive Sulfide Deposits in Arizona," Geochemical Exploration, Association Exploration Geochemists, 1978; "The Bournonite-Seligmannite Solid Solution," Am Mineralogist, 1977; "Tetrahedrite at Casapalca and Its Application in Mineral Exploration," Geol Soc America Annual Meeting Abs, vol 6, no 7, 1974; accepted invitations to present papers: Gold Exploration at Chinkuashih Copper-Gold Deposit, Taiwan, National Western Mining Conference and Exhibition, Denver, CO, 1994; Gold Exploration Potential in China and Taiwan, Association of Professional Engineers and Geologists, annual general meeting, 1994. **BUSINESS ADDRESS:** President, IW Exploration Company, 3537 Brighton Way, Reno, NV 89509.

WU, JEAN YU-WEN SHEN
Educator, educational administrator. Chinese American. **PERSONAL:** Born Jun 30, 1948, Nanjing, China; daughter of William Tien-te Wu and Lucy Li-woo Shen Wu. **EDUCATION:** Harvard University, EdM, 1975, EdD, 1984. **CAREER:** Harvard University, senior counselor, 1975-82, associate director, 1982-85; Brown University, associate dean of the college, lecturer, 1985-89; University of Pennsylvania, visiting professor, 1990-92; Bryn Mawr College, dean and director, Division of General Studies, 1989-, lecturer, human development and psychology, 1990-. **ORGANIZATIONS:** Asian American Studies Association, 1990-; Asian Americans United, board of directors, 1991-; The Painted Bride Multicultural Arts Center, advisory board, 1993-; Asian American Curriculum Task Force, Philadelphia School District, 1991-; ALANA, Bryn Mawr, Haverford, and Swarthmore Colleges, founding member, 1992-. **SPECIAL ACHIEVEMENTS:** Numerous presentations and workshops on the following topics: multicultural curriculum and pedagogy, Asian Americans in the schools and workplace, curriculum combatting anti-Asian violence, creating a pluralistic campus, comparative American cultures; publications: "Breaking Silence and Finding Voice: The Emergence of Meaning in Asian American Inner Dialogue and a Critique of Current Psychological Literature," Harvard GSE, 1984. **BUSINESS ADDRESS:** Dean and Director, Division of General Studies, Bryn Mawr College, 101 N Merion Avenue, Canwyll House, Bryn Mawr, PA 19010-2899, (610)526-7350.

WU, JENNIFER LEE
Librarian. Chinese American. **PERSONAL:** Born Mar 10, 1945, Canton, Guangdong, China; daughter of Yam-Nam Lee and Pauline Wei; married Stanley Lau-Po Wu, Dec 28, 1968; children: Jason Yee-Chien, Jeremy Yee-Tze. **EDUCATION:** Chinese University of Hong Kong, 1964-66; California State University, Chico, BA, sociology, 1967; University of Oregon, MLS, 1968. **CAREER:** Seattle Public Library, librarian, 1968-73; Lagos, Nigeria, and Rio de Janeiro, Brazil, interpreter, instructor of English as a second language, 1973-77; American International School, Lagos, Nigeria, managing librarian, 1978; Seattle Central Community College, librarian/member of faculty, 1985-. **ORGANIZATIONS:** Asian Pacific American Labor Alliance, Seattle Chapter, senior trustee, 1993-; Faculty Association of Community and Technological Colleges, vice president, 1993-; American Society for Information Science; American Library Association; Association of College and Research Libraries; Community College Librarians and Media Specialists; Asian Pacific American Librarians Association. **SPECIAL ACHIEVEMENTS:** Multicultural Review, Asian/Asian-American Studies editor and reviewer; contributor to: PC Consultant; FACTC Focus; Gamut; Information Literacy: Developing Students as Independent Students, Jossey-Bass, 1992; workshop presenter on cultural pluralism, information technology and information literacy; language proficiency: Chinese (four dialects), Portuguese. **BUSINESS AD-**

DRESS: Librarian/Member of the Faculty, Seattle Central Community College, 1701 Broadway Ave, 2BE2101, Seattle, WA 98122, (206)587-4069.

WU, JEREMY S.
Government official, educator. Chinese American. **PERSONAL:** Born Aug 8, 1953, Hong Kong; son of Yee Chi Wu and Shar Ching Dai; married Deanie P Wu, Feb 14, 1980. **EDUCATION:** George Washington University, BA, 1974, MA, 1976, PhD, 1983. **CAREER:** George Washington University, professorial lecturer, 1978-; USDA, Statistics, branch chief, 1983-. **ORGANIZATIONS:** American Statistical Association; International Chinese Statistical Association. **BUSINESS ADDRESS:** Statistics Branch Chief, USDA/AMS/SD, PO Box 96456, Rm 0603-South, Washington, DC 20090-6456, (202)720-7318.

WU, JIE
Educator. Chinese American. **PERSONAL:** Born Jul 5, 1961, Shanghai, People's Republic of China; son of Zengchang Wu & Yieyi Shao; married Ruiguang Zhang, Nov 16, 1986; children: Stephanie. **EDUCATION:** Shanghai University of Science & Technology, BS, 1982, MS, 1985; Florida Atlantic University, PhD, 1989. **CAREER:** Shanghai University of Science and Technology, lecturer, 1985-87; Georgia Institute of Technology, visiting professor, 1991; Florida Atlantic University, assistant professor, 1989-. **ORGANIZATIONS:** Institute of Electrical & Electronics Engineers, 1990-; Upsilon Pi Epsilon Honor Society, 1990-; Canadian Society for Electrical and Computer Engineering, 1990-. **HONORS/AWARDS:** Florida High Tech & Industrial Council, Grant, 1989-90; IBM, Boca Baton, Grant, 1990-. **SPECIAL ACHIEVEMENTS:** Over 50 technical publications, including 12 referenced journal publications; associate editor of one book and co-author of one book chapter; program committee of one international conference and session chair of several international conferences. **BUSINESS ADDRESS:** Asst Prof, Dept of Computer Science and Eng, Florida Atlantic University, 500 NW 20th St, Boca Raton, FL 33431, (407)367-3491.

WU, JIN ZHONG
Scientist. Chinese American. **PERSONAL:** Born Jan 5, 1945, Chengdu, Sichuan, China; daughter of Chieh Wu and Shuying Zhang; married Yue Ping Lu, Feb 18, 1976; children: Ying Jie Lu. **EDUCATION:** Beijing University, BS, physics, 1967; University of Science & Technology of China, MS, electronic engineering, 1981; University of Cincinnati, MS, physics, 1983, PhD, physics, 1988. **CAREER:** Beijing Semiconductor Devices Institute, Beijing, associate engineer, 1970-79; Institute of Semiconductors, Chinese Academy of Sciences, assistant researcher, 1981; University of Florida, Quantum Theory Project, postdoctoral associate, 1988-91, assistant scientist, 1991-. **ORGANIZATIONS:** American Physical Society. **HONORS/AWARDS:** University of Cincinnati, graduate fellowship, 1987-88, University Research Council, student summer research fellowship, 1984, 1985, 1987. **SPECIAL ACHIEVEMENTS:** Developed films stopping code for stopping calculation, calculated the stopping of swift projectiles in material thin films; four publications in International Journal of Quantum Chemistry, Nuclear Instruments and Methods in Physics Research; calculated electronic and structure properties of thin films; four publications in Physical Review B, International Journal of Quantum Chemistry; produced the first quantitative theory of the caliper dimeter of the Fermi surface of a two dimensional anisotropic degenerate electron gas in semiconductor inversion layers and quantum wells, 1983-. **BUSINESS ADDRESS:** Assistant Scientist, University of Florida, Williamson Hall, Gainesville, FL 32611-8435, (904)392-8113.

WU, JOSEPH M.
Educator. Chinese American. **PERSONAL:** Born Aug 1, 1947, Shanghai, China; son of Eisen Wu and Yui-Wei Chang; divorced; children: Amy H, Mary H. **EDUCATION:** McGill University, BS, 1970; Florida State University, MS, 1972, PhD, 1975. **CAREER:** New York Medical College, assistant professor, 1978-82, associate professor, 1982-87, professor, 1987-. **HOME ADDRESS:** 15 Andrea Ln, Thornwood, NY 10594, (914)747-3849. **BUSINESS ADDRESS:** Professor, Dept of Biochemistry, New York Medical College, Basic Sciences Bldg, Rm 127, Valhalla, NY 10595-1600.

WU, JULIA LI
Educational administrator. Chinese American. **PERSONAL:** Born Jul 2, 1936, Nankin, China; daughter of Tee Chuan Yu and Tze Kee Li; married Alfred Yung-Hsiang Wu, Jun 1, 1963; children: Alexander Alfred, Kelly King, Julius Jay. **EDUCATION:** National Taiwan Normal University, BA, English, 1958; Immaculate Heart College, MA, library science, 1962; California State University, Los Angeles, MA, education, 1976. **CAREER:** Minister of Education,

Republic of China, asst, 1958-69; Voice of America, US Information Agency, West Coast correspondent, 1961-72; Los Angeles County Library, asst regional librarian, 1961-69; Virgil Jr High School, head librarian, beginning 1969; Los Angeles City College, English instructor, beginning 1972; Los Angeles Unified Schools, Indo-Chinese Children's Program, coordinator; Los Angeles Community Colleges Board of Trustees, 1987-, vp, 1989-91, president, 1991-92, Community Affairs & Public Relations Committee, chair, currently. **ORGANIZATIONS:** California Community Colleges Board of Governors, 1992-; US Natl Commission on Libraries and Information Science, commissioner, 1973-; US Dept of Education Advisory Council on Bilingual Education; US Commission on Libraries; Asian-American Education Commission, LA Board of Education; AFT; CTA; UTLA; ALA; CLMEA; Asian/Pacific Librarians Assn; Chinese History Museum, board of directors; LA Chinatown Center, honorary adviser. **HONORS/AWARDS:** Asian/Pacific American Librarians Assn, Outstanding Service Award, 1984, 1990; Monterey Park City Council, California, Distinguished Service Award. **SPECIAL ACHIEVEMENTS:** Holds life credentials for California community college teaching, standard secondary teaching, standard education administration; fluent in seven Chinese dialects, accomplished in French and Spanish; during tenure, Los Angeles Community Colleges Board of Trustees, author of 40 adopted resolutions, adapted board committee structure into public forum. **BUSINESS ADDRESS:** Member, Board of Trustees, Los Angeles Community Colleges, 2383 West Silver Lake Dr, Los Angeles, CA 90039, (213)891-2044.

WU, JULIAN JUH-REN
Mathematician, government official. Chinese American. **PERSONAL:** Born Jun 15, 1935, Shanghai, China; son of Ta-yu Wu and Chi-su Liang Wu; married Joyce Forville Wu, Aug 26, 1967. **EDUCATION:** National Taiwan University, BS, civil engineering, 1958; Rice University, MS, civil engineering, 1960; Columbia University, MS, applied math, 1966; Rensselaer Polytechnic Institute, PhD, mechanics, 1970. **CAREER:** AVCO Advanced Technology Co, senior scientist, 1966-67; Teledyne Materials Research, project engineer, 1967-68; Benet Weapons Lab, Watervliet Arsenal, senior engineer & mathematician, 1971-84; Rensselaer Polytechnic Institute, adjunct professor, 1976-83; US Army European Research Office, branch chief of physics & mathematics, 1984-87; Duke University, adjunct professor, 1987-; US Army Research Office, program manager for applied mathematics, 1987-. **ORGANIZATIONS:** American Society for Mechanical Engineers, 1971; American Academy of Mechanics, 1979-; New York Academy of Sciences, 1987-. **HONORS/AWARDS:** US Army Research Office, Distinguished Performance Award, 1990, 1991, 1992; US Army European Research Office, Distinguished Service Award, 1986; Benet Weapons Lab, Superior Service Award, 1976, 1981. **SPECIAL ACHIEVEMENTS:** Publication of 40 technical papers on nonlinear vibrations, structural stability, finite elements, continuum mechanics, 1971-; co-editor, Composites Materials: Response, Constitutive Relations . . ., Elsevier, 1988; author, Modern Theory in Anisotropic Elasticity & Applications, SIAM Press, 1991. **BUSINESS ADDRESS:** Program Manager for Applied Mathematics, US Army Research Office, 4300 S Miami Blvd, PO Box 12211, Research Triangle Park, NC 27709-2211, (919)549-4332.

WU, JUN-RU
Educator. Chinese American. **PERSONAL:** Born Apr 5, 1944, Shanghai, China; married Yi ying L Wu, Jan 28, 1975; children: Jane, Kathy. **EDUCATION:** University of California, Los Angeles, MS, 1981, PhD, 1985. **CAREER:** University of California, postdoctoral associate, 1985; University of Vermont, assistant professor, 1987, associate professor, 1993-. **ORGANIZATIONS:** Acoustical Society of America, 1983, fellow, 1992; IEEE, 1987; American Institute of Ultrasound in Medicine, 1991. **HONORS/AWARDS:** UCLA, Teaching Assistant Award, 1984. **SPECIAL ACHIEVEMENTS:** More than 50 publications. **BUSINESS ADDRESS:** Associate Professor, Dept of Physics, University of Vermont, Cook Bldg, Burlington, VT 05405-0001, (802)656-8357.

WU, KIM
Office supply company executive. Taiwanese American. **PERSONAL:** Born Dec 7, 1951, Kaohsiung, Taiwan; married Pei-Hsun Wu; children: Tina, Alice. **EDUCATION:** Fu Jen Catholic University, BA, 1975; Monmouth College, MBA, 1977. **CAREER:** MBA Office Supply, president, currently. **BUSINESS ADDRESS:** President, MBA Office Supply, 460 Trimble Rd, San Jose, CA 95131, (408)954-1500.

WU, KINGSLEY K.
Educator, artist, design consultant. Chinese American. **PERSONAL:** Born Aug 24, 1934, Shanghai, China; son of Chauncey K Wu & Amy H Wu; married Susan A Wu, Feb 14, 1959; children: K Chauncey. **EDUCATION:** Brandeis University, 1954-55; University of Washington, BA, 1962; Pratt Institute, MFA, 1964. **CAREER:** Trenton Junior College, Art Department, instructor, 1963-66; California State Fullerton, Art Department, assistant professor, 1966-67; Texas Woman's University, Art Department, assistant professor, 1967-69; professional design consultant, 1967-; University of Georgia, Art Department, assistant professor, 1969-71; Purdue University, Visual & Performing Arts, associate professor, 1971-, Interior Design, chair, 1971-83; Shenzhen University, Architecture Department, visiting professor, 1985-86. **ORGANIZATIONS:** Interior Design Educators Council, 1968-, national treasurer, 1971-73, newsletter editor, 1969-72; Environmental Design Research Association, 1990-; Foundation for Interior Design Education Research, board of visitors for accreditations, 1984-88; Indiana Vocational Technical Institute, curriculum advisory board, 1976-78, Kokomo region, 1980-82. **HONORS/AWARDS:** US-Spain Joint Committee for Cultural & Educational Cooperation, research grant, 1988-89; Pratt Institute, graduate fellow, 1962-63. **SPECIAL ACHIEVEMENTS:** Designer, Japanese Garden, Fort Worth Botanic Gardens, Texas, 1968-69; author: Freehand Sketching in the Architectural Environment, Van Nostrand Reinhold, 1990; other art work in water colors, pen & ink; architectural design projects in US and abroad; language proficiency in Chinese (Mandarin, Shanghai, Cantonese), Spanish, some French. **MILITARY SERVICE:** US Army Reserve, cpl, 1959-64. **HOME ADDRESS:** 1431 Woodland Avenue, West Lafayette, IN 47906, (317)463-7945. **BUSINESS ADDRESS:** Associate Professor, Dept of Visual and Performing Arts, Purdue University, 1352 Creative Arts Bldg 1, West Lafayette, IN 47907-1352, (317)494-3058.

WU, KONRAD T.
Educator. Chinese American. **PERSONAL:** Born Jul 1, 1948, Canton, China; son of Whey-Yuen Wu and Rey-Jen Tan Wu; married Angela L Wu, Apr 13, 1974; children: Sabrina F, Bandon M. **EDUCATION:** Fu-Jen Catholic University, Taiwan, BS, 1970; State University of New York Albany, PhD, 1976. **CAREER:** University of Texas, research associate, 1976-77; Columbia University, research associate, 1977-78; Mount Sinai School of Medicine, chemist, 1978-80; State University of New York, Old Westbury, professor, 1980-. **ORGANIZATIONS:** American Chemical Society, 1974-; American Physical Society, 1974-; Sigma Xi, 1976-; Council on Undergraduate Research, 1989-; The International Biographical Society, fellow, 1985-; Chinese Cultural Association of Long Island, president, 1990-93; Association of Chinese Schools, president, 1993-94. **SPECIAL ACHIEVEMENTS:** Published more than 20 scientific papers. **BUSINESS ADDRESS:** Professor, State University of NY, Old Westbury, P.O. Box 210, Old Westbury, NY 11568-0210, (516)876-2747.

WU, KUNG CHRIS
Educator. Taiwanese American. **PERSONAL:** Born Oct 15, 1959, Taipei, Taiwan; son of Chen-Kao Wu and C L Wu; married Donna W C Wu, Jul 1990; children: Kevin. **EDUCATION:** University of Texas at El Paso, BSME, 1984; Rice University, MSME, 1986, MEE, 1989, PhD, 1990. **CAREER:** Genosys Biotech Inc, R&D mgr, 1989-91; University of Texas at El Paso, professor, 1991-. **ORGANIZATIONS:** State of Texas, professional engr, 1993; Sigma Xi, 1992; Pi Tau Sigma, 1984; IEEE, 1992. **BUSINESS ADDRESS:** Professor, Dept of Industrial & Mech Engineering, University of Texas at El Paso, 500 W University, El Paso, TX 79968, (915)747-7997.

WU, LYN XILING
Economic consultant, economist, statistician. Chinese American. **PERSONAL:** Born Dec 16, 1956, Chongqing, Sichuan, People's Republic of China; married Gelie, Jul 1, 1985; children: Andrew, Kevin. **EDUCATION:** Southwestern Agricultural University, China, BS, 1982; Michigan State University, MS, 1985; University of Florida, PhD, 1988. **CAREER:** University of Georgia, research associate, 1988-89; Sparks Companies Inc, senior economist, 1990-; A&K International, president, CEO, 1992-. **ORGANIZATIONS:** American Association of Agricultural Economics, 1986-. **HONORS/AWARDS:** Lambda & Sigma Agricultural Honor Society, 1986-. **SPECIAL ACHIEVEMENTS:** The first person from communist China to receive a PhD in agricultural economics in the US; author of numerous publications in agricultural economics & related fields. **BUSINESS ADDRESS:** Senior Economist, Sparks Companies, Inc, 889 Ridge Lake Blvd, Memphis, TN 38120, (901)766-4515.

WU, MICHAEL MING-KUN
Software company manager. Taiwanese American. **PERSONAL:** Born Dec 20, 1958, Taoyuan, Taiwan; son of Pei-Rin & Susan Wu; divorced. **EDUCATION:** Harvard College, AB, 1980; University of Tokyo, Brain Research Institute, 1985-86; University of Pennsylvania, PhD, 1990. **CAREER:** MIT Lincoln Lab, assistant staff, 1979-82; Laboratory Technologies Corp, Engineering Services, manager, 1990-. **ORGANIZATIONS:** IEEE, 1990-; Biophysical Society, 1987-; ACM, 1990-; Harvard Club of Concord, interviewer, 1992-; Society of General Physiologists, 1989-92. **HONORS/AWARDS:** Ministry of Science, Education & Culture, Japan, Monbusho Fellowship, 1984-86. **SPECIAL ACHIEVEMENTS:** "Cerebellar Granule Cells in Culture: Monosynaptic Connections with Purkinje Cells and Ionic Currents," Proceedings of the National Academy of Sciences, 1986; "Voltage Dependence of the Na, K-Exchange Pump of RANA Ogeytes," Journal of Membrane Biology, 1991. **HOME ADDRESS:** 6D N Commons Rd, Lincoln, MA 01773, (617)259-4412.

WU, NAN-RAY
Engineer. Chinese American. **PERSONAL:** Born Nov 3, 1949, Pinton, Taiwan; married Jennifer B L Leu Wu, Dec 26; children: Enoch. **EDUCATION:** National Chiao Tung University, BS, 1971; National Taiwan University, MS, 1975; University of California, Berkeley, PhD, material science, 1983. **CAREER:** Gould AMI, senior process engineer, 1983-86; ICT, senior product engineer, 1986-88; AMER, vice president of operation, 1988-89; IDT, product engineering manager, 1989-. **ORGANIZATIONS:** IEEE, 1978-. **MILITARY SERVICE:** 3rd Armor, Taiwan, lt, 1971. **HOME ADDRESS:** 46457 Paseo Padre Pkwy, Fremont, CA 94539, (510)651-1207.

WU, NANCY NAN-HWA
Physician. Chinese American. **PERSONAL:** Born Oct 1, 1919, Jiujiang, Jiangxi, China; daughter of Kwang-Tsu Wu and Jean-hsia Yu; married Tse-Tsung Chow, Mar 1958; children: Lena J Chow, Genie A Chow. **EDUCATION:** West China Union University, Medical College, MD, 1945. **CAREER:** University of Texas, Southwestern Medical School, Department of Anesthesiology & Pain Management, clinical associate professor; VA Medical Center, part-time staff anesthesiologist, currently. **ORGANIZATIONS:** AMA; ASA; IASP; APS. **BUSINESS ADDRESS:** Dept of Anesthesiology, VAMC, 4500 S Lancaster, Dallas, TX 75216.

WU, NORMAN B.
Government official. Chinese American. **PERSONAL:** Born Feb 13, 1925, Boston, MA; son of Wu Yee Bing and Rose Lee Wu. **EDUCATION:** Tufts University College of Engineering, BSc, 1974. **CAREER:** City of Boston, Veterans Services Department, deputy commissioner, 1975-. **ORGANIZATIONS:** American Legion Post 328, life member; Museum of Fine Arts, associate member; Massachusetts Social Workers, licensed certified social worker. **MILITARY SERVICE:** US Army, master sgt, 1944-66; Purple Heart, Commendation Medal. **BUSINESS ADDRESS:** Deputy Commissioner, Veterans' Services Dept, City of Boston, 20 Church St, Boston, MA 02116, (617)635-3713.

WU, RICHARD L. C.
Principal research scientist. Taiwanese American. **PERSONAL:** Born Aug 21, 1940, Tainan, Taiwan; son of Mr & Mrs Mar-Tar Wu; married Spring C C Wu, Dec 28, 1968; children: Joyce S. **EDUCATION:** National Cheng-Kung University, Taiwan, BS, 1963; University of Kansas, Lawrence, PhD, 1971. **CAREER:** University of Kansas, research associate and assistant, 1965-71; Wright-Patterson AFB, visiting scientist, 1971-72; SRL Inc, senior research scientist, 1972-75; Wright State University, adjunct and research professor, 1975-86; UES Inc, principal research scientist, 1986-. **ORGANIZATIONS:** American Chemical Society; American Material Research Society; Phi-Lambda Upsilon; Sigma Xi; American Association for the Advancement of Science; American Society for Mass Spectrometry. **SPECIAL ACHIEVEMENTS:** Published about 80 papers in various journal articles and book chapters; "Deposition of Diamond-like Carbon Films," US patent no 4,490,229, 1993; "Nucleation Enhancement of Diamond with Amorphous Films," Appl Phys Lett, 1993; "Physical and Tribological Properties of Rapid Thermal Anneded Diamond-like Carbon," 1992; "Environmental Effects on Friction and Wear of Diamond and Diamond-like Carbon Coatings," 1992; "Diamond Films for Thermionic Applications," 1992. **BUSINESS ADDRESS:** Principal Research Scientist, UES Inc, 4401 Dayton-Xenia Road, Dayton, OH 45432, (513)426-6900.

WU, ROY S.

Health scientist administrator. Chinese American. **PERSONAL:** Born Nov 15, 1944, Shangei, China; son of Lung Chung Wu and Chia Ling Shen Wu; married Irene C Liang, Jun 8, 1982; children: Michelle. **EDUCATION:** University of California, Berkeley, AB, 1967; Albert Einstein College of Med, PhD, 1972. **CAREER:** University of California, Berkeley, Dept of Zoology, lecturer/postdoctoral fellow, 1972-75; Biotech Research Labs, sr scientist, 1975-79; Natl Cancer Inst, Div Cancer Treatment, sr staff fellow, 1979-82, health scientist administrator cancer therapy evaluation, 1986-; Lab of Molecular Pharmacology, cancer expert, 1982-86. **ORGANIZATIONS:** AAAS; American Soc for Biochemistry & Molecular Biology; American Assn Cancer Research; Soc of Chinese Bioscientists in America, executive secretary, 1989-93; Sigma Chi. **HONORS/AWARDS:** NSF, peer reviewer, 1981, 1990; NIH, peer reviewer, 1981; Formosan Med Assn, travel grant, 1988. **SPECIAL ACHIEVEMENTS:** Research in assay for 0 to the 6th degree-alkylguanine-DNA alkyltrasferase using restriction enzyme inhibition. **BUSINESS ADDRESS:** Health Scienttist Administrator, Cancer Therapy Evaluation Program, DCT/NCI, 6130 Executive Blvd, Ste 734, Executive Plaza N, Bethesda, MD 20892, (301)496-8866.

WU, SAM. *See* WU, SHIEN-MING in the Obituaries.

WU, SAU LAN YU

Educator. Hong Kong American. **PERSONAL:** Born in Hong Kong; married Tai Tsun Wu. **EDUCATION:** Vassar College, BA, physics (summa cum laude), 1963; Harvard University, MA, physics, 1964, PhD, physics, 1970. **CAREER:** Harvard University, research assistant, 1965-70; MIT, research associate, 1970-72, research physicist, 1972-77; CERN, Geneva, Switzerland, visiting scientist, 1975-77; DESY, Hamburg, West Germany, visiting scientist, 1977-86; CERN, Geneva, Switzerland, visiting scientist, 1986-; University of Wisconsin-Madison, assistant professor, 1977-80, associate professor, 1980-83, professor, 1983-90, Enrico Fermi Distinguished professor of physics, 1990-. **ORGANIZATIONS:** CERN Users, advisory committee, 1989-93; DOE review committee on SLAC programs for SLC and SLD, 1992; DOE annual review committee on SLAC programs, 1993. **HONORS/AWARDS:** American Physical Society, fellow; US Department of Energy, Outstanding Junior Investigator Award, 1980; University of Wisconsin, Madison, Romnes Faculty Award, 1981; 17 honorary degrees. **SPECIAL ACHIEVEMENTS:** 18 review articles; 178 publications in refered journals; 40 invited talks in conferences; 100 colloquia and seminars. **BIOGRAPHICAL SOURCES:** "The God Particle," by Leon Lederman, p337, 1993; "Interactions," by Sheldon L Glashow, p545, May 1988; "Hunting of the Quark," by Michael Riordan, p348, 1987. **BUSINESS ADDRESS:** Professor, CERN, PPE Division, Bldg 32, RA05, CH-1211 Geneva 23, Switzerland.

WU, SHI TSAN

Educator, educational administrator. Chinese American. **PERSONAL:** Born Jul 31, 1933, Nanchang Kiawgsi, China; son of Shu Zee Wu and Duan Ming Pao Wu; married Mai San Kao Wu, Sep 5, 1964; children: Cheyenne, Roslind, Patricia. **EDUCATION:** National Taiwan University, BS, mechanical eng, 1955; Illinois Institute of Technology, MS, mechanical eng, 1959; University of Colorado, PhD, aerospace eng, 1967. **CAREER:** LaTrobe University, Australian/American Ed Foundation, professor of physics, 1975-76; Tel Aviv University, PhD examiner, foreign correspondence, 1982; University of Sci and Technology of China, visiting professor, 1982; Wu-Han University, visiting professor, 1982-; Acta Astrophysica Sinica, correspondence editor, 1985-; Center for Space Plasma and Aeronomic research, director, 1986-; University of Alabama, HSV, distinguished professor, currently. **ORGANIZATIONS:** Conf on Earth to Orbit Propulsion Technology, co-chairman, 1986-92; NASA Advanced Solar Observatory, Scientific Working Group, secretary, 1981-; Society of Mechanical Engineers, 1979-; 19th AIAA Fluid Dynamics, Plasma Dynamics, & Lasers Conf, co-chairman, 1987; SCOSTEP, bureau membership; US-Japan Seminar on Heliomagnetictosphere, co-chairman, 1984; AIAA/Alabama & Mississippi Section, chairman, 1984, director, 1980-82-, 1987-. **HONORS/AWARDS:** AIAA-AL/MS, Martin Schilling Award, 1987; Alabama Academy of Science, Wright Gardner Award, 1986; AIAA-AL/MS, Herman Oberth Award, 1983; Sigma Xi/UAH, Researcher of the Year, 1979; Senior Fulbright-Hays Scholar, Australia, 1975-76. **SPECIAL ACHIEVEMENTS:** Publication of more than 175 articles in the fields of plasma physics, solar physics, upper atmospheric physics, MHD flows, solar energy fundamentals and numerical methods in the Journals of Solar Physics, JGR, AIAA J, ASME J, Planet and Space Science, Ap J, ZAMP, International J on Numerical Methods, J of Applied Physics, J of Solar Energy, J of Computational Physics,

and International J of Computers and Fluids. **BUSINESS ADDRESS:** Professor, University of Alabama, CSPAR, EB 157f, Huntsville, AL 35899, (205)895-6413.

WU, SHIEN-MING. *See* Obituaries.

WU, SHIH-YEN

Educator. Chinese American. **PERSONAL:** Born Mar 26, 1929, Taigu, Shansi, China; son of Wei-Ching Wu and Kwei-lan Wu; married Margaret; children: Jennifer, Gregory. **EDUCATION:** Oberlin College, BA, 1954; Northwestern University, PhD, 1961. **CAREER:** University of Minnesota, lecturer, 1958-59; Los Angeles State College, associate professor, 1959-64; University of Iowa, professor, 1964-. **ORGANIZATIONS:** American Economic Review, editorial board, 1978-80; Managerial and Decision Economics, editorial board, 1989-. **HONORS/AWARDS:** Nankai University, guest professor, 1988. **SPECIAL ACHIEVEMENTS:** Author: Production, Entrepreneurship and Profits, Blackwell, 1989; Introduction to Demand Theory, Random House, 1967; more than forty refereed publications. **BUSINESS ADDRESS:** Professor of Economics, University of Iowa, Iowa City, IA 52242, (319)335-0846.

WU, STAN

City government administrator. Chinese American. **EDUCATION:** University of Washington, PhD, electrical engineering. **CAREER:** Worked as telecommunications consultant in many countries; City of Seattle, director of communications, currently. **HONORS/AWARDS:** Evergreen Chapter Public Service Recognition Award, 1993. **BUSINESS ADDRESS:** Director of Communications, City of Seattle, 710 2nd Ave, Rm 1350, Seattle, WA 98104, (206)684-0554.∗

WU, SYLVIA CHENG

Restaurateur. Chinese American. **PERSONAL:** Born in China; married King; children: Patrick, George. **CAREER:** Madame Wu's Garden Restaurant, owner, 1963-. **ORGANIZATIONS:** Los Angeles Music Center, Blue Ribbon 400 Committee; ARCs; UCLA, College of Letters and Science, Dean's Council; Loyola-Marymount University, Fine Arts Council; KCET, board of directors; ChildHelp Village. **HONORS/AWARDS:** California Restaurant Writers Association, Restaurateur of the Year; Columbia Teacher's College, honorary MA; The League for Crippled Children's Auxiliary of the Los Angeles Orthpaedic Hospital's, Woman of the Year; City of Hope Hospital, Woman of the Year, 1990. **SPECIAL ACHIEVEMENTS:** Books, Madame Wu's Art of Chinese Cooking; Memories of Madame Sun; Cooking with Madame Wu: Yin and Yang Recipes for Health and Longevity, 1993; cooking demonstrations at MGM Hotel, George V Hotel, Paris, Hotel Mediterraneo, Rome; TV appearances and speaking. **BUSINESS ADDRESS:** Madame Wu's Garden Restaurant, 2201 Wilshire Blvd, Santa Monica, CA 90403, (310)828-5656.

WU, TAI TE

Educator. Chinese American. **PERSONAL:** Born Aug 2, 1935, Shanghai, China; married Anna Fang Wu, Apr 16, 1966; children: Richard. **EDUCATION:** Hong Kong University, MB, BS, 1956; University of Illinois, BS, 1958; Harvard University, SM, 1959, PhD, 1961. **CAREER:** Harvard University, research fellow, 1961-63; Brown University, assistant professor, 1963-65; Harvard Medical School, research associate, 1965-66; Cornell University Medical College, associate professor, 1967-70; Northwestern University, professor, 1970-. **ORGANIZATIONS:** Association Biochem Mol Biol, currently; Biophys Society, currently; American Society Microbio, currently; Chicago Association Immunol, currently. **HONORS/AWARDS:** NIH, Research Career Developement Award, 1974-79. **SPECIAL ACHIEVEMENTS:** Publications in professional journals, 1961-. **BUSINESS ADDRESS:** Professor, Northwestern University, Evanston, IL 60208, (708)491-7849.

WU, THEODORE YAO-TSU

Educator. Chinese American. **PERSONAL:** Born Mar 20, 1924, Changchow, Kiangsu, China; son of Ren Fu and Gee-Ing Shu Wu; married Chin-Hua Shih, Jun 17, 1950; children: Fonda Bai-yueh, Melba Bai-chin. **EDUCATION:** Chiang-Tung University, BS, 1946; Iowa State University, MS, 1948; California Institute of Technology, PhD, 1952. **CAREER:** California Institute of Technology, faculty member, 1952-, associate professor, 1957-61; professor of engineering science, 1961-; Hamburg University, Germany, visiting professor, 1964-65. **ORGANIZATIONS:** AIAA; Sigma Xi; National Academy of Engineering; Phi Tau Phi. **HONORS/AWARDS:** Guggenheim Fellow, 1964-65; American Physical Society, fellow. **SPECIAL ACHIEVEMENTS:** Advances in Applied Mechanics Series, editorial board; consultant to a number of industrial firms; contributor to professional journals. **BUSINESS ADDRESS:** Professor, Dept of Engineering & Sci, California Institute of Technology, 104-44, Pasadena, CA 91125, (818)395-6811.∗

WU, TIEE-JIAN
Educator. Taiwanese American. **PERSONAL:** Born Sep 16, 1949, Kaohsiung, Taiwan; son of Ji-Ming Wu and Hui Hsu; married Chung-Li Yuan, May 23, 1982; children: Cindy. **EDUCATION:** National Cheng-Kung University, Tainan, Taiwan, BS, math, 1972; Wake Forest University, MA, math, 1976; Indiana University, MS, computer sciences, 1983, PhD, math, 1982. **CAREER:** Institute of Statistical Sciences, Academia Sinica, Taiwan, visiting expert, 1987-88, visiting research associate professor, 1990-91; Queen's University, Department of Mathematics & Statistics, visiting scholar, 1988; University of Houston, Department of Computer Sciences, lecturer, 1983, Dept of Mathematics, asst professor, 1983-89, associate professor, 1989-. **ORGANIZATIONS:** Institute of Mathematical Statistics, 1984-; American Statistical Association, 1985-; International Chinese Statistical Association, permanent member, 1990-. **HONORS/AWARDS:** University of Houston, Research Initiation Grant, 1984; National Science Council, Taiwan, Visiting Expert Grant, 1987-88, Visiting Research Associate Professor Grant, 1990-91; University of Houston, President Research Enhancement Fund, 1992. **SPECIAL ACHIEVEMENTS:** Co-author, "The Order of Normal Approximation for Signed Rank Statistics," Theory of Probability and Its Application, vol 31, pp 145-151, 1987; co-author, "Some Results on Sequential Unbiased Estimation of a Binominal Parameter," Theory of Probability and Its Application, vol 36, pp 411-419, 1992; co-author, "Time Integrated LSE of Regression Parameters of Independent Stochastic Processes," Stochastic Processes and Their Applications, vol 35, pp 141-148, 1990; Statistical Consulting & Analysis of Past Global Changes Program, IGBP, under a grant from Natl Science Council of Taiwan, May-Aug 1993. **MILITARY SERVICE:** Chinese Navy, Taiwan, ensign, 1971-72. **BUSINESS ADDRESS:** Associate Professor, Dept of Mathematics, University of Houston, 4800 Calhoun, 669 PGH, Houston, TX 77204-3476, (713)743-3452.

WU, TING-WEN
Educator. Chinese American. **PERSONAL:** Born Jul 30, 1957, Taipei, Taiwan; son of Ging-Ching Wu and Lo Tsai Wu; married Yu-Fen Chen Wu, Jan 1, 1986; children: Jason, Connie. **EDUCATION:** National Taiwan University, BS, 1979; University of Texas, Austin, MS, 1984, PhD, 1987. **CAREER:** University of Kentucky, research associate, 1987-89, assistant professor, 1989-. **ORGANIZATIONS:** The Acoustical Society of America, 1989-; The American Society of Mechanical Engineers, associate member, 1990-. **HONORS/ AWARDS:** National Science Foundation, Engineering Initiation Award, 1990. **SPECIAL ACHIEVEMENTS:** Co-Author, "Numerical Modeling of Acoustic Radiation and Scattering from Thin Bodies," J Acoustical Society of America, vol 92, p 2900-2906, 1992; co-author, "A Weighted Residual Formulation for the Chief Method in Acoustics," J Acoustical Society of America, vol 90, p 1608-1614, 1991. **MILITARY SERVICE:** Republic of China, Taiwan Navy, 2nd lt, 1979-81. **BUSINESS ADDRESS:** Asst Professor, Dept of Mechanical Engineering, University of Kentucky, CRMS 514E, Lexington, KY 40506, (606)257-5748.

WU, TUNG
Educator. Chinese American. **PERSONAL:** Born Nov 7, 1941, Shanyan, Hubei, China; son of C T Wu and P C Wu; married Ming C Wu, Sep 5, 1970; children: James, Daniel. **EDUCATION:** National Taiwan University, BS, 1965; New Mexico Institute of Mining & Technology, MS, 1968; University of Rhode Island, PhD, 1972. **CAREER:** University of Rhode Island, postdoctorate, 1972-73; Smithsonian Institution, chemist, 1973-81; Georgia Tech, scientist, 1981-83; Coppin State College, professor, 1983-. **ORGANIZATIONS:** American Institute of Chemists, fellow, 1986-; America Chemical Society, 1971-; American Society for Mass Spectrometry, 1992-. **HONORS/ AWARDS:** Smithsonian Institution, Academic Achievement, 1973. **SPECIAL ACHIEVEMENTS:** Smithsonian Institution, delegation member to China, 1980; thirty papers in the area of environmental research and pesticides. **MILITARY SERVICE:** Taiwan Military Police, second lieutenant, 1965. **BUSINESS ADDRESS:** Professor, Coppin State College, 2500 W North Ave, Baltimore, MD 21216-3698, (410)383-5484.

WU, WALLACE C.
Physician. Hong Kong American/Chinese American. **PERSONAL:** Born Jun 27, 1942, Chengtu, China; son of Y F Wu and C C Wu; married Mona Wu, Jan 5, 1971; children: David C, Brandon C. **EDUCATION:** University of Hong

Kong, MB, BS, 1966. **CAREER:** Bowman Gray School of Medicine, assistant professor of medicine, 1974-80, associate professor of medicine, 1980-87, professor of medicine, 1987-. **ORGANIZATIONS:** American Society for Gastrointestinal Endoscopy, chairman, membership committee, 1988-91, councillor, governing board, 1991-. **SPECIAL ACHIEVEMENTS:** Edited two books, 12 book chapters, and over 100 articles in the field of gastroenterology. **BUSINESS ADDRESS:** Professor of Medicine, Bowman Gray School of Medicine, Medical Center Blvd, Winston Salem, NC 27157-1048, (910)716-4603.

WU, WALLY. *See* **WU, HSIN-I.**

WU, WEI-HSIUNG (KITTY)
Educator. Chinese American. **PERSONAL:** Born Oct 4, 1937, Nanch'ang, Chiang-shi, China; daughter of Chih-Chi Chou & Ming-huei Yu Chou; divorced; children: Anna Chia-shan, Joy Chia-mei. **EDUCATION:** Soochow University, Taiwan, BA, English (honors), 1961; UCLA, certificate in TESOL, 1963; University of California, Los Angeles, MA, English, 1966; University of Maryland, PhD, English, 1989. **CAREER:** Soochow University, Department of English, teaching assistant, 1961-62; UCLA, Department of Public Health, translator/researcher, 1964-66; Anne Arundel County Board of Education, Head Start, teacher, 1966-67; The Evening Capital Publishers, librarian, 1970; University of Maryland, lecturer, East Asian Languages and literature, 1976; Bowie State University, associate professor of English, 1970-. **ORGANIZATIONS:** College Board, ATP Committee for English Composition/Writing, 1990-; College English Association, Middle Atlantic Group, executive board, 1988-; Taiwan Friendship Committee, 1988-92; Modern Language Association, 1977-; Asian American Studies Association, 1989-; Multicultural Literature of the United States, 1988-; Society for the Study of Narrative Literature, 1988-; Sigma Tau Delta, 1984-. **HONORS/AWARDS:** US Dept of Education, Fulbright Travel Grant, 1962; Soochow University, Phi Tau Phi, 1961; National Endowment for the Humanities, Fellowship Award, 1980, Dissertation Fellowship, 1984-85, Fulbright-Hayes Fellowship, 1991. **SPECIAL ACHIEVEMENTS:** 2 articles, one on Diana Chang and one on Bette Bao Lord, to be published in The Oxford Companion to Women's Writings in the United States; an article on Ama Ata Ado, "Devouring Gods and Sacrificial Animals: Male-Female Relationship in Ama Ata Aidoo's Changes: A Love Story," will be published in Arms Akimbo: Africana Women in Literature; areas of specialization: test development, program evaluation, American literature, Asian American concentration. **BUSINESS ADDRESS:** Associate Professor, Dept of Humanities and Fine Arts, Bowie State University, Jerico Park Rd, Bowie, MD 20715, (301)464-7295.

WU, WEI-PING
Educator, historian, economic consultant. Chinese American. **PERSONAL:** Born Jul 26, 1932, Fuan, Fujian, China; son of Wen-kai Wu & Yun-o Wu; widowed; children: George, Frank. **EDUCATION:** National Taiwan University, BA, 1955, MA, 1958; Harvard University, MA, 1960; University of Pennsylvania, PhD, 1969. **CAREER:** Wesleyan University, 1961-63; University of Arizona, instructor of Oriental studies, 1965-67; Wittenberg University, assistant professor of history, 1967-70; University of Bridgeport, assistant professor of history to Littlefield Professor of History and Economics, 1970-92; Institute of World History, The Chinese Academy of Social Sciences, senior corresponding fellow and project consultant, 1993-; Chimex Development, president, 1992-. **ORGANIZATIONS:** American Historical Association; Association of Asian Studies; The Dushkin Publishing Group, advisory board, 1984-; American Economics Association. **HONORS/AWARDS:** National Endowment for Humanities, fellowship, 1977; Harvard University Faculty of Arts and Sciences, fellowship, 1958-60, Harvard-Yenching Fellowship, 1958-60; Academia Sinica, Doctor Fu Ssu-nien Prize, 1957. **HOME ADDRESS:** 246 Linley Dr, Fairfield, CT 06430, (203)336-3195. **BUSINESS PHONE:** (203)336-3195.

WU, WILLIAM GAY
Educator (retired). Chinese American. **PERSONAL:** Born Feb 5, 1931, Portland, OR; son of George P Wu and Ida L Wu; married Gladys Kam Min Wu, Jan 5, 1957; children: Jeffrey S, Randall K, Mitchel G. **EDUCATION:** Oregon State University, BS, 1954, MS, 1960; University of Utah, PhD, 1962. **CAREER:** University of California, Davis, junior engineer, 1954-56; Oregon State University, research associate, 1957-59; University of Utah, graduate assistant, research assistant, 1959-62; San Francisco State University, assistant professor of biology, 1962-65, associate professor of biology, 1965-69, professor of biology, 1969-91, professor emeritus, 1991-. **ORGANIZATIONS:**

American Society for Microbiology, 1960-; American Association for Advancement of Science, 1965-; American Association of Immunologists, 1972-91; Northern California American Society for Microbiology, 1962-, president, 1976-79, national councilor, 1982-85. **HONORS/AWARDS:** Public Health Service Development of Advanced Medical Technology, Education and Training Program, 1967-71; NIH, Co-PI, Virulence Mechanisms of Klebsiella Pneumionial, 1987. **SPECIAL ACHIEVEMENTS:** Author, Medical Microbiology: A Laboratory Study, 2nd edition, Star Publishing Co, 1987, 3rd edition, 1994; sample publication, co-author, Immune Paralysis induced by Pneumococcal Polysacchaside I, Journal Immunology, vol 107, p 154-162, 1971; co-founder, Center for Advanced Medical Technology, San Francisco State University, 1968. **BUSINESS ADDRESS:** Professor Emeritus of Biology, San Francisco State University, 1600 Holloway Ave, San Francisco, CA 94132, (415)338-1222.

WU, WU-NAN
Pharmaceutical chemist. Taiwanese American. **PERSONAL:** Born Mar 16, 1938, Kaohsiung, Taiwan; son of Fu-Tien Wu & Kong-Chiew Lin Wu; married Anna Wu, Aug 11, 1946; children: Ernie J, Jonathan C. **EDUCATION:** Kaohsiung Medical College, BS, pharmacy, 1961; Ohio State University, PhD, pharmacy, 1972. **CAREER:** Taipei Medical College, instructor, 1962-64; Bristol Research Institute of Taiwan, specialist, 1965-67; Ohio State University, College of Pharmacy, research associate, 1967-72, post doctoral researcher, 1974-77; University of Florida, College of Pharmacy, research fellow, 1973-74; McNeil Pharmaceutical, principal scientist, 1978-89; R W Johnson Pharmaceutical Research Institute, research fellow, 1992-. **ORGANIZATIONS:** American Chemical Society, 1978-; American Society of Pharmacognosy, 1971-; American Association of Pharmaceutical Scientists, 1985-; International Society for the Study of Xenobiotics, 1990-; American Society for Mass Spectrometry, 1992-. **HONORS/AWARDS:** Rho Chi Pharmacy Society, Honor Award, 1970. **SPECIAL ACHIEVEMENTS:** 80 publications and 2 patents regarding drug metabolism and natural product studies;, language proficiency: English, Chinese, Japanese, French, German. **BUSINESS ADDRESS:** Research Fellow, R W Johnson Pharmaceutical Research Institute, McKean & Welsh Rds, Spring House, PA 19477, (215)628-5562.

WU, XIAN
Educator. Chinese American. **PERSONAL:** Born Jun 20, 1954, Jiangsu, People's Republic of China; son of He Wu and Wenhua Ma; married Yang Yang Xing, Jun 8, 1985; children: James, Jennifer. **EDUCATION:** Qinghua University, Beijing, China, BS, 1981; Harvard University, MS, 1985, PhD, 1986. **CAREER:** UCLA, Department of Math, assistant professor, 1986-88; USC, Department of Math, assistant professor, 1988-. **BUSINESS ADDRESS:** Asst Professor, Dept of Mathematics, University of South Carolina, Columbia, SC 29208.

WU, XIAN CONNIE
Information specialist. Chinese American. **PERSONAL:** Born Aug 20, 1954, Suzhou, Jiangsu, People's Republic of China; daughter of Chang Yi Wu and Xue Yu Zheng. **EDUCATION:** Beijing University of Posts & Telecommunications, BS, 1977; Brigham Young University, MLIS, 1987. **CAREER:** Automobile Manufacture of MPTC, China, technician, 1970-74; Beijing Research Institute of Postal Technology, engineer, designer, project manager, 1977-83; Patent Office of China, patent examiner, 1983-85; Brigham Young University, research assistant, librarian assistant, 1985-87; Rutgers University, engineering information specialist, assistant professor, 1988-. **ORGANIZATIONS:** Chinese American Librarians Association, president, Northeast Chapter, 1990-91, national membership chair, 1990-91; American Library Association, STS committee, 1989-92; American Society for Engineering Education, Literature Guides Subcommittee, 1992-; American Association of University Professors, 1988-; Patent Documentation Society, 1989-. **HONORS/AWARDS:** NTLA, CUS, Research Award, 1993; ALA, Whitney-Carnegie Awards, 1991, Institute of International Education, Grant, 1987. **SPECIAL ACHIEVEMENTS:** Papers were published in Special Libraries, Research Strategies, UK Online User Group Newsletter, ERIC and other publications; chapter in Advances in Publisher/Vendor/Library Relations, JAI Press. **BUSINESS ADDRESS:** Assistant Professor/Engineering Information Specialist, Rutgers University, Busch Campus, Library of Science & Medicine, Piscataway, NJ 08855-1029, (908)932-4728.

WU, Y. C. L. SUSAN
Small business executive. Chinese American. **PERSONAL:** Born Jun 23, 1932, Beijing, China; daughter of Chi-yu Lin; married Jain-Ming Wu, Jun 13,

1959; children: Ernest H, Albert H, Karen H. **EDUCATION:** National Taiwan University, BS, mechanical engineering, 1955; Ohio State University, MS, aeronautical engineering, 1959; California Institute of Technology, PhD, aeronautics, 1963. **CAREER:** Electro-Optics System, senior engineer, 1963-65; University of Tennessee Space Institute, professor, 1965-88; ERC, Inc, president & CEO, 1988-. **ORGANIZATIONS:** American Society of Mechanical Engineers, fellow; American Institute of Aeronautics and Astronautics, associate fellow; Sigma Xi; Society of Women Engineers, life member. **HONORS/AWARDS:** Amelia Earhart Fellowship, 1958, 1959, 1962; AIAA, Tennessee Section, General H H Arnold Award, 1984; Society of Women Engineers, Achievement Award, 1985, honors, National Science Foundation during Asian Week, 1987. **SPECIAL ACHIEVEMENTS:** Published over 100 technical papers in journals, symposia and meetings proceedings. **BUSINESS ADDRESS:** President & CEO, ERC, Inc, 205 Research Park Dr, PO Box 417, Tullahoma, TN 37388, (615)455-9915.

WU, YAO HUA
Chemist, consultant. Chinese American. **PERSONAL:** Born Jul 16, 1920, Soochow, China; son of Kenshen and Chenhua Wu; married Peiyu Huang, Jul 23, 1980; children: David, Helen Duncan. **EDUCATION:** Chiao-Tung University, BSc, 1943; University of Nebraska, PhD, 1951. **CAREER:** International Chemical Works, Shanghai, chemist, 1943-47; Dorsey Laboratories, chemist, 1951-53; Mead Johnson Res Ctr, director of chemical research, 1953-87; Bristol-Myer, Squibb Co, senior research consultant, 1987-. **ORGANIZATIONS:** American Chemical Society, emeritus member; American Association for the Advancement of Science; Swiss Chemical Society. **HONORS/AWARDS:** Tri-State Coun for Sci and Eng, Achievement Award, 1971. **SPECIAL ACHIEVEMENTS:** Inventor of Buspirone, an antianxiety agent; inventor of Methedilazine, an antiprurite agent; 46 US patents; 19 scientific papers. **BUSINESS ADDRESS:** Sr Research Consultant, Mead Johnson Nutritional Group, Bristol-Myers, Squibb Co, 2404 W Lloyd Expwy, Evansville, IN 47721.

WU, YAU
Educator, company executive. Chinese American. **PERSONAL:** Born Dec 3, 1932, Shou, Anhui, China; son of K K Wu; married Louise C Wu, Feb 27, 1965; children: Victoria Anne, Kevin E. **EDUCATION:** National Taiwan University, BS, 1955; University of Illinois, MS, 1958; Massachusetts Institute of Technology, SM, 1960; New York University, PhD, 1964. **CAREER:** Princeton University, research associate, 1964-66; University of Illinois, assistant professor, 1966-67; Virginia Polytechnical Institute, associate professor, 1967-73; MIT, visiting associate professor, 1973-74; Kaman Sciences Corp, senior staff scientist, 1974-75; Boston University, professor, 1975-81; Dynamic Analysis Corp, president, 1978-. **ORGANIZATIONS:** AIAA; APS; AAAS; Sigma Xi; New York Academy of Science; SAE. **HONORS/AWARDS:** New York University, Founder's Day Award, 1964. **SPECIAL ACHIEVEMENTS:** Proposed a new ultra-high molecular pump, 1960, 1965; discovered the revised law of thermal transpiration, 1964, 1967; developed a dusty model of kinetic theory of rarefied gas, 1972; revised the theory of absolute manometer and radiometer, 1967, 1968; proposed a new high-speed ground transportation vehicle (linear Air Turbine and Air Cushion Vehicle), 1971; developed a mathematical model of automobile collision (IMPACT), 1980; proposed a new high-speed ground transportation vehicle (Linear Air Turbine and Air Cushion Vehicle), 1971. **MILITARY SERVICE:** Air Force, Taiwan, ROTC, 1955-56, 2nd lt, 1955-65. **HOME ADDRESS:** 201 Indian Pipe Ln, Concord, MA 01742, (508)369-8053. **BUSINESS ADDRESS:** President, Dynamic Analysis Corporation, 201 Indian Pipe Ln, Concord, MA 01742, (508)369-8266.

WU, YEN
Educator. Chinese American. **PERSONAL:** Born Dec 3, 1934, China; son of K K Wu & S C Wu; married Yueh-shiou H Wu, Jun 11, 1966; children: Cynara C, Alex C. **EDUCATION:** National Taiwan University, BS, 1958; Virginia Tech, MS, 1963, PhD, 1969. **CAREER:** American Association Railroad, tank-car engineering, 1975-76; Northern Virginia Community College, professor, 1969-. **BUSINESS ADDRESS:** Professor, Northern Virginia Community College, 8333 Little River TP, CT305F, Annandale, VA 22003, (703)323-3187.

WU, YENNA
Educator. Chinese American. **PERSONAL:** Born 1957, Kaohsiung, Taiwan; married. **EDUCATION:** Natl Taiwan University, BA, 1978; UCLA, comp lit, 1978-79, MA, East Asian languages & culture, 1981; Harvard University, PhD, 1986. **CAREER:** Harvard University, teaching fellow, 1983-85; University of Vermont, asst professor & director of Chinese Language Program, 1986-92;

University of California, Riverside, asst professor of Chinese, 1992-. **ORGANIZATIONS:** Assn for Asian Studies; Chinese Language Teachers Assn. **HONORS/AWARDS:** University of California, Riverside, Center for Ideas & Society, Fellowship, 1993-94, Research Grant, 1992, 1993; University of Vermont, Research Grant, 1987, 1991-92; Pacific Cultural Foundation Research Grant, 1991; Geraldine R Dodge Foundation Scholarship, Chinese Pedagogy Workshop, Middlebury College, 1986; NCR Scholarship, summer dissertation research in China, 1984; Harvard University, Graduate Fellowships, 1981-86. **SPECIAL ACHIEVEMENTS:** Refereed articles: "Zhenshun jielie zugou ma?—you nu'er shu kan gudai dui youzhi funu zhi zhongshi," (Is Being Chaste & Submissive Sufficient?—On the High Regard for Women of Wisdom in Traditional Educational Handbooks for Women), Chinese Culture Quarterly, p123-28, 1992; "Interweaving of Sex & Politics in Zhang Xianliang's Half of Man Is Woman," Journal of the Chinese Language Teachers Assn, 1992, p1-27; "Women as Sources of Redemption in Chang Hsien-liang's Camp Fiction," Asia Major, IV, pt 2, p115-131, 1991; "Repetition in Xinqshi yinyuan zhuan," Harvard Journal of Asiatic Studies, p55-87, 1991. **BUSINESS ADDRESS:** Professor, Dept of Literature and Languages, University of California, Riverside, Riverside, CA 92521-0321.

WU, YING-CHAN FRED
Educator. Taiwanese American. **PERSONAL:** Born Feb 24, 1958, Taipei, Taiwan; son of Tieh-Hui Wu and Hui-Jen Wu; married Li-Chu Wu, Dec 23, 1986. **EDUCATION:** Tatung Institute of Technology, BS, 1980; Iowa State University, MS, 1984, PhD, 1988. **CAREER:** University of Miami, Dept of Electrical Engineering, assistant professor, 1988-. **ORGANIZATIONS:** IEEE, voting member, 1988-; ACM, voting member, 1989-; State of Flordia Dept of Professional Regulation, registered professional engineer, 1990-. **HONORS/AWARDS:** College of Engineering, University of Miami, Best Paper Award, 1993; University of Miami, General Research Support Award, 1991, 1993, Summer Research Award, 1989. **SPECIAL ACHIEVEMENTS:** "A Neural Network Design for Event-Related Potential Diagnosis," Computers in Biology and Medicine, vol 23, no 3, 1993; "A PC-based Neural Network for On-line Measurement of CBF," Computers in Biology and Medicine, vol 22, no 1, 1992; "Dynamic Commutation Voltages in a Reciprocating Linear Inductor Alternator," IEEE Trans Aerospace, vol 28, 1992; "Algorithms for Simple Object Reconstruction Using the Largest Possible Object Approach," Robotica, vol 10, 1992. **BUSINESS ADDRESS:** Ass Prof, Dept of Elec & Comp Eng, University of Miami, PO Box 248294, Rm 514, Coral Gables, FL 33124, (305)284-3323.

WU, YING VICTOR
Scientist. Chinese American. **PERSONAL:** Born Nov 1, 1931, Peking, Hopei, China; son of Hsien Wu and Daisy Yen Wu; married Mildred Ling, Jun 18, 1960; children: Julia. **EDUCATION:** University of California, Berkeley, 1949; University of Alabama, Tuscaloosa, BS, 1953; Massachusetts Institute of Technology, PhD, physical chemistry, 1958. **CAREER:** Massachusetts Institute of Technology, research assistant, 1953-57, postdoctoral fellow, 1957-58; Cornell University, postdoctoral research associate, 1958-61; National Center for Agricultural Utilization Research, research chemist, 1961-. **ORGANIZATIONS:** American Chemical Society, 1952-; American Association of Cereal Chemists, 1971-; Institute of Food Technologists, 1974-; Protein Society, 1988-; American Association for the Advancement of Science, 1968-; Alpha Chi Sigma, 1952-. **HONORS/AWARDS:** Gamma Sigma Epsilon, 1951; Pi Mu Epsilon, 1951; Sigma Pi Sigma, 1952; Sigma Xi, 1956; American Society of Biochemistry and Molecular Biology, 1967. **SPECIAL ACHIEVEMENTS:** Contributing author: Protein Resources and Technology, 1978; Nutritional Evaluation of Food Processing, 3rd edition, 1988; Wheat is Unique: Structure, Compostition, Processing, End-Use Properties and Products, 1989; Encyclopedia of Food Science and Technology, 1991; Quality Protein Maize, 1992; author of about 100 scientific journal publications. **BUSINESS ADDRESS:** Research Chemist, US Department of Agriculture, Natl Ctr for Agricultural Utilization Research, 1815 N University St, Peoria, IL 61604, (309)681-6364.

WU, ZHIJIAN
Educator. Chinese American. **PERSONAL:** Born Apr 6, 1961, Fuzhou, Fujian, People's Republic of China; son of Hanguang Wu; married Yanling Chen, Aug 7, 1987; children: Robin L, Kevin L. **EDUCATION:** Wuhan College of Geology, China, BA, 1982; Beijing University, China, MS, 1984; University of South Carolina, 1985-86; Washington University, PhD, 1990. **CAREER:** University of Alabama, assistant professor, 1990-. **ORGANIZATIONS:** American Mathematical Society, 1985-. **HONORS/AWARDS:** Washington Univer-

sity, Scholarship, 1986-90, University Fellowship, 1986-87; Royal Institute Mittag-Leffler, Sweden, researcher, 1991; Macquarie University, Australia, visiting fellow, 1992; University of Alabama, research grant, 1992. **SPECIAL ACHIEVEMENTS:** 14 papers published in math journals, 3 in Chinese, others in English. **BUSINESS ADDRESS:** Assistant Professor, Dept of Mathematics, University of Alabama, Tuscaloosa, AL 35487, (205)348-1963.

X

XIA, YUN
Librarian. Chinese American. **PERSONAL:** Born Jan 16, 1953, Beijing, People's Republic of China; daughter of Kaiqi Xia & Yuying Liu; married. **EDUCATION:** Peking University, Department of Library Science, BA, 1982, MA, 1984, Graduate School of Library and Information Science, 1988; University of Illinois, Urbana-Champaign, Certificate of Advanced Study. **CAREER:** Peking University, China, faculty member, 1984-86; University of Illinois, GSLIS, research assistant, 1987-88; East Stroudsburg University, library systems manager, 1989-. **ORGANIZATIONS:** Chinese Information Science Society, 1984-; Beta Phi Mu International Library Science Honor Society, 1989-; American Library Association, 1989-. **SPECIAL ACHIEVEMENTS:** Author: "Achievements and Influence of Colon Classification; and comments on the limitations of hierarchical classification," Information Science, Vol 3, No 5, pp 64-75, Oct, 1982; "Bibliographical Facilities in the United States: Current Developments and Trends," Information Services, vol 1, No 2, p 75-81, 1982; Database Conversion, Insider's Guide to Library Automation, Greenwood Press, 1993; "The US Congressional Research Service: A Remarkable Reference Service," Information Services, No 11, p 33, 1983; numerous others. **BUSINESS ADDRESS:** Library Systems Manager, East Stroudsburg University, Kemp Library, East Stroudsburg, PA 18301, (717)424-3827.

XIONG, LEE PAO
Social services administrator. Laotian American/Hmong American. **PERSONAL:** Born Sep 5, 1966, Long Cheng, Xieng Khouang, Lao People's Democratic Republic; son of Song Khoua Xiong & Mee Vang Xiong; married Yer Suzanne Xiong, Mar 15, 1990; children: Sophie Hli. **EDUCATION:** University of Minnesota, BA, political science, 1990; Hamline University, MPA, currently. **CAREER:** US Senate, legislative intern, 1988; Minnesota State Senate, legislative clerk, 1990; Hmong Youth Association of Minnesota, youth counselor, 1990-91, executive director, 1991-93; Minneapolis Community College, consultant, 1991-92; Hmong American Partnership, executive director, 1993-. **ORGANIZATIONS:** Full-Circle Program, Channel 11, steering committee, co-host, 1991-; Headwaters Funds, grants committee, 1991-; FR Bigelow Foundation's CFCI Fund, steering committee, 1992-; The St Paul Foundation, diversity fund, steering committee, 1992-; Minneapolis Foundation, board of trustees, 1993-. **HONORS/AWARDS:** University of Minnesota, Asian/Pacific American Student Leadership Award, 1987-88. **SPECIAL ACHIEVEMENTS:** Language proficiency in Hmong; one of 25 people chosen in nationwide competetion to attend International Peace and Justice Seminar, 1988. **BIOGRAPHICAL SOURCES:** HAP Welcomes New Director, The HAP Voice, vol 4, no 1, p 1 & 9, Jan/Feb 1993; St Paul Pioneer Press, "New Leader of Hmong Partnership Seeks More Cooperation Less Rivalry," p 14A, Feb 7, 1993. **BUSINESS ADDRESS:** Executive Director, Hmong American Partnership, 450 N Syndicate, Ste 35, St Paul, MN 55104, (612)642-9601.

XIONG, WILLIAM JOUA
Counselor. Chinese American/Laotian American/Hmong American. **PERSONAL:** Born May 3, 1963, Vang Vieng, Lao People's Democratic Republic; son of You Thao Xiong and Mao Thao Xiong; married Herlo X Xiong, Nov 20, 1990; children: Peggy Paajkub, Alfred Tub. **EDUCATION:** University of Wisconsin, Green Bay, BS, 1986; University of Wisconsin, Madison, MS, 1989. **CAREER:** United Nations High Commissioner for Refugees, teacher, grades 1-6, 1977-79; US Embassy, Bangkok, Thailand, interpreter, translator, 1979; Manitow Public Schools, English as a second language teacher, 1980-84; Madison Metropolitan School District, bilingual guidance counselor, 1987-89; self-employed, book store co-owner, 1983-, apartment owner, 1987-; Milwaukee Public Schools, guidance counselor, 1990-. **ORGANIZATIONS:** Hmong American Student Assn, University of Wisconsin, Madison, president, 1987-88; Shee Yee Community of Milwaukee Inc, president, 1991-93; Dept of Public Instruction, state superintendent's advisory council on ESL/bilingual education, 1990-93, linguistically culturally distinct project committee, 1991-; Wisconsin Counselor Assn, 1987-; American Psychological Assn, various affiliations, 1986-89; University of Wisconsin, Green Bay, Student Ambassa-

dor, 1985-86; Hmong Mutual Assistance Assn, board member, 1982-84. **HONORS/AWARDS:** Hmong Student Advancement Inc, Outstanding Board Member, 1993; National Education Assn, Award of Recognition, leadership training participation, 1992; Hmong Council, Certificate, 1989; Madison Metropolitan School District, human relations, Recognition for Outstanding Community Service, 1989. **SPECIAL ACHIEVEMENTS:** Language proficiency: Hmong (native), Lao, Thai, English, and some French; co-author, The English-Mong-English Dictionary, 1983. **BIOGRAPHICAL SOURCES:** Chiv Keeb, Shee Yee Community quarterly newsletter, p 2, March 1993. **HOME ADDRESS:** 1261 S 34th St, Milwaukee, WI 53215, (414)645-2578.

XU, CHIA-YI
Educator. Chinese American. **PERSONAL:** Born Jun 26, 1950, Semarang, Java, Indonesia; son of Ping Sum Xu; married Zhu Ying He, 1980. **EDUCATION:** Zhong Shan University, Guang Zhou, PRC, BA, 1976; City College of New York, MA, 1984. **CAREER:** Electronic Institute of Academia of Sinica Peking, PRC, engr, 1977-80; CUNY, GSUC, teaching/research assistant, 1981-83; Borough of Manhattan Community College, Math Dept, professor, 1984-. **HOME ADDRESS:** 50-51 Cloverdale Blvd, Flushing, NY 11364.

XU, JINYI. *See* **CHEE, CHENG-KHEE.**

Y

YADEN, SENKA LONG
Educator. Indo-American. **PERSONAL:** Born Apr 21, 1935, Mokokchung, Nagaland, India; son of Takojungba Yaden; married Theola Thedford, Dec 4, 1981. **EDUCATION:** Wilson College, Bombay, India, BSc, 1956; University of Bombay, India, MSc, 1959; University of Minnesota, PhD, 1965. **CAREER:** Jarvis Christian College, associate professor of biology, 1967-75, Division of Science & Math, chair, 1976-78, professor of biology, 1979-81; Texas College of Osteopathic Medicine, associate, 1981-84; Parker College, Basic Science, associate professor, 1984-86; Talladega College, associate professor of biology, 1987-88; Wiley College, professor of biology, 1988-93; Texas College, professor of biology, 1993-. **ORGANIZATIONS:** American Institute of Biological Science, currently; American Association for the Advancement of Sciences; American Association for University Professors; New York Academy of Science; Texas Academy of Science; Beta Kappa Chi, college sponsor; Naga-American Foundation, president, 1989-. **SPECIAL ACHIEVEMENTS:** Many scientific publications. **BUSINESS ADDRESS:** Professor of Biology, Texas College, 2404 N Grand Ave, Tyler, TX 75702.

YAGI, FUMIO
Educator, aerospace engineer (retired). Japanese American. **PERSONAL:** Born Jul 14, 1917, Seattle, WA; son of Saihichiro Yagi and Kima Okabe Yagi; married Shizuko Yagi, Jun 24, 1954. **EDUCATION:** University of Washington, BS, 1938, MS, 1941; Massachusetts Institute of Technology, PhD, 1943. **CAREER:** University of Washington, asst prof, 1946-53; Ballistic Research Lab, appl math, 1953-56; Jet Propulsion Lab, research specialist, 1956-63; Grumman Aerospace, group head, 1963-77. **ORGANIZATIONS:** American Mathematical Society, 1938-. **HONORS/AWARDS:** Massachusetts Institute of Tech, graduate scholarship, 1941-42; Institute for Advanced Study, postdoctoral asst, 1943; University of Washington, teaching fellow, 1940-41. **MILITARY SERVICE:** US Army, t4 sgt, 1944-46. **BIOGRAPHICAL SOURCES:** Yankee Samurai. **HOME ADDRESS:** 2914 Sahalee Dr E, Redmond, WA 98053, (206)868-7161.

YAGI, HARUHIKO
Scientist. Japanese American. **PERSONAL:** Born Jun 27, 1939, Sendai, Miyagi Prefecture, Japan; son of Seibei Yagi and Yoshi Yagi; married Yoko Yagi, Jun 27, 1969; children: Keiichi, Mary J. **EDUCATION:** Tohoko University, Pharmaceutical Institute, BS, 1963, MS, 1965, PhD, 1968. **CAREER:** Tohoku University, Pharmaceutical Institute, associate, 1968-72; Connecticut University, Chemistry Department, research assistant, 1969-70; Johns Hopkins University, Chemistry Dept, research associate, 1970-71; National Institutes of Health, scientist, 1971-. **ORGANIZATIONS:** American Chemical Society; Pharmaceutical Society of Japan. **SPECIAL ACHIEVEMENTS:** More than 270 publications; scientific articles, 1973-94. **BUSINESS ADDRESS:** Scientist, National Institutes of Health, Wisconsin Avenue, Bldg 8, Room 1A01, Bethesda, MD 20892, (301)496-1839.

YAMADA, DAVID TAKAO
Educator. Japanese American. **PERSONAL:** Born Aug 25, 1937, Riverside, CA; son of Harry G Yamada and Faith H Yamada; married Katherine K Yamada, Sep 4, 1960; children: Justin M, Jena M. **EDUCATION:** University of California, Berkeley, BA, 1959, MA, 1962; University of California, Santa Barbara, PhD, 1975. **CAREER:** Allan Hancock College, professor, 1969-71; Monterey Institute of International Studies, adjunct professor, 1979-87; Monterey Peninsula College, professor, 1971-, Political Science Department, chair; Hiroshima University, Fulbright visiting professor, 1986-87. **ORGANIZATIONS:** Northern California Political Science Association, executive council, 1975-; American Political Science Association, 1969-85; Academy of Political Science, 1986-; Japanese American Citizens League, president, board member, 1974-, Northern California-W Nevada Pacific District, executive board member, 1980-81; Pi Sigma Alpha, 1958-. **HONORS/AWARDS:** JUSEC, Fulbright, 1986-87; Community Foundation for Monterey Co, Allan Griffin Award for Teaching Excellence, 1984; JACL, NCWNP-District, Arigato Award, 1983. **SPECIAL ACHIEVEMENTS:** Two articles in Asian American Encyclopedia, Salem Press, 1994; "Rearming Japan? A Militech Society," Current Politics and Economics of Japan, vol 1, no 1, pp 13-20, fall 1991; Japanese Americans of the Monterey Peninsula, 1994; Internment: The Cherokee & Japanese American Experience, 1995. **MILITARY SERVICE:** US Army, Active & Reserves, e-4, 1962-68. **BUSINESS ADDRESS:** Professor, Chairperson, Political Science Dept, Monterey Peninsula College, 980 Fremont Blvd, Social Science Bldg, Monterey, CA 93940-4799, (408)646-4160.

YAMADA, KAY MATAYOSHI
Educator (retired). Japanese American. **PERSONAL:** Born Oct 28, 1926, Koloa, Kauai, HI; daughter of Butaro & Kama Tengan Matayoshi; married Edward Takeshi Yamada, Nov 17, 1962. **EDUCATION:** University of Hawaii, BEd, 1968, MA, 1969. **CAREER:** UH-Leeward Community College, instructor, 1969-91, professor, 1992. **ORGANIZATIONS:** ASCD, 1989-; HASCD, 1989-; Speech Association of America, 1969-; NCTE, 1991-; HCTE, 1988-; Hui O Laulima, Scholarship Committee, chair, 1993-94. **HONORS/AWARDS:** University of Hawaii Board of Regents, Excellence in Teaching Award, 1988, Dean's List, 1968-69. **SPECIAL ACHIEVEMENTS:** Coordinator: speech, communication, & journalism; author: "They Came for Different Reasons," 1988; "SS City of Tokio, the Beginning," 1985; "TESL and Speech Communication," 1971; several articles for local papers. **HOME ADDRESS:** 1144-C Lunalile St, Honolulu, HI 96822, (808)533-3304.

YAMADA, MITSUYE MAY
Educator, poet, writer. Japanese American. **PERSONAL:** Born Jul 5, 1923, Fukuoka, Kyushu, Japan; daughter of Hide & Jack Kaichiro Yasutake; married Yoshikazu Yamada, Aug 25, 1950; children: Jeni, Stephen Yamada-Heidner, Kai, Hedi Yamada Mouchard. **EDUCATION:** Columbia University; New York University, BA, 1947; University of Chicago, MA, 1953. **CAREER:** Cypress College, professor of English, 1968-89; California State University, Long Beach, lecturer, 1981-82; University of Illinois, Chicago, resource scholar, 1983; California Poets in the Schools, consultant, 1986-; Pitzer College, Claremont, visiting poet, 1987; University of California, Los Angeles, visiting professor, 1991; San Diego State University, visiting professor, 1993-94. **ORGANIZATIONS:** California Council for the Humanities, board member, 1993-96; Amnesty International, national board, 1987-92, committee on international development, 1987-; Multicultural Women Writers, founder/coordinator, 1980-; California Poets in the Schools, area coordinator, 1985-; Multiethnic Literature of the US, newsletter ed, 1986-88; Community Support for Academic Relevance. **HONORS/AWARDS:** Center for Women Policy Studies, Washington, DC, Jessie Bernard Wise Women Award, 1992; Rancho Santiago Foundation, Women of Achievement, 1991; Multi-Ethnic Literature of the US, Contributions to Ethnic Studies, 1989; North Orange County Community College, Distinguished Merit, 1988. **SPECIAL ACHIEVEMENTS:** Publications: Camp Notes & Other Poems, 1976; Desert Run: Poems & Stories, 1988; co-editor, Sowing Ti Leaves, Writings by Multicultural Women, 1990; film: Mitsuye and Nellie: Two American Poets, 1981. **BIOGRAPHICAL SOURCES:** A Gulf So Deeply Cut, Susan Schweik, p 197, 1991. **HOME ADDRESS:** 6151 Sierra Bravo Rd, Irvine, CA 92715, (714)856-8699.

YAMADA, YOZO
Accountant (retired), educational administrator. Japanese American. **PERSONAL:** Born Apr 22, 1927, San Francisco, CA; son of Saburo Yamada and Toshiko Yamada; married Toshi Yamada, Jun 12, 1953; children: David H. **EDUCATION:** Waseda University, Tokyo, Japan, AA, 1948; California State

University, Sacramento, BS, 1975. **CAREER:** US Air Force, Accounting and Finance Division, deputy chief, 1979-87; Rissno Japanese Language School, founder, 1977, principal, currently. **ORGANIZATIONS:** Air Force Assn, 1983-87; DOD Comptrollers Assn, 1983-87. **HONORS/AWARDS:** Air Force Assn, Conrad Peterson Award for Outstanding Accounting and Finance Civilian, 1983, Meritorious Service Award, 1984. **MILITARY SERVICE:** US Army, ssgt, 1948-51; Korean Campaign Ribbon. **HOME ADDRESS:** 26 Parklite Cir, Sacramento, CA 95831, (916)428-4554.

YAMAGA, CHESTER KIYOSHI

Safety and health consultant. Japanese American. **PERSONAL:** Born May 13, 1945, Denver, CO; son of Henry Yamaga and Dorothy Yamaga. **EDUCATION:** University of Hawaii, BBA, 1973. **CAREER:** Hawaii Insurance Bureau, 1973-78; Industrial Indemnity, 1978-84; Fidelity Risk Management, 1985; private business consultant, 1986-. **ORGANIZATIONS:** American Society of Safety Engineers; American Industrial Hygiene Association; American Fire Protection Association. **MILITARY SERVICE:** US Army, Vietnam, sgt, 1966-69; Army Commendation, 1968. **BUSINESS ADDRESS:** Safety & Health Consultant, 725 Kapiolani Blvd, Ste 307, Honolulu, HI 96813-5800, (808)591-8111.

YAMAGUCHI, KO

Import company executive. Japanese American. **PERSONAL:** Born Apr 3, 1934, Long Beach, CA; son of Seiji Yamaguchi (deceased) and Hide Yamaguchi; married Mary Sumiko Yamaguchi; children: Stanley Seiji, Keith Mase, Natalie Hideko Ziegler, Timothy Ko. **EDUCATION:** Pasadena City College, AA, 1952; Loyola Marymount, 1952-53. **CAREER:** New York Merchandise Co, general mgr, 1953-83; ICI Worldwide Inc, president, 1983-. **BUSINESS ADDRESS:** President, ICI Worldwide Inc, 175 W Bonita, PO Box 8, San Dimas, CA 91773, (909)592-6431.

YAMAGUCHI, KRISTINE TSUYA (KRISTI)

Professional figure skater. Japanese American. **PERSONAL:** Born Jul 12, 1971, Hayward, CA; daughter of Jim Yamaguchi and Carole Yamaguchi. **CAREER:** Professional figure skater, currently. **ORGANIZATIONS:** American Lung Association, Christmas Seal spokesperson, 1992-93; National Make-A-Wish Foundation, affiliation through fundraiser with Stars on Ice shows; Fremont Education Foundation, honorary board of directors; Women's Sports Foundation, athletes advisory board; 100th/442nd Veterans Association; Japanese American Citizens League, Fremont Chapter. **HONORS/AWARDS:** Taiwanese American Citizens League, Outstanding Asian American, 1989; Japanese American Citizens League, Japanese American of the Biennium, 1990-92; Nikkei Foundation of America, Outstanding Japanese American Award, 1991; United States Pan Asian American Chamber of Commerce, Excellence 2000 Award. **SPECIAL ACHIEVEMENTS:** US National Figure Skating Champion, 1992; World Champion, 1992; Olympic Gold Medalist, 1992; World Professional Champion, 1992. **BIOGRAPHICAL SOURCES:** International Management Group, Yuki Saegusa; Current Biography, vol 53, no 6, p56, 1992. **BUSINESS ADDRESS:** Figure Skater, 36520 Montecito Drive, Fremont, CA 94536, (510)713-1005.

YAMAGUCHI, MICHAEL J.

Attorney. Japanese American. **PERSONAL:** Born Mar 31, 1950, St Paul, MN. **EDUCATION:** UCLA, BA, 1972; USF School of Law, JD, 1978; NYU School of Law, LLM, 1979. **CAREER:** US Dept of Justice, assistant US attorney, 1980-93, US attorney, 1993-. **ORGANIZATIONS:** SF Juvenile Probation Commission, president, 1990. **MILITARY SERVICE:** USAR JAG, capt, currently. **BIOGRAPHICAL SOURCES:** Warlords of Crime, p 216-220, 225-26. **BUSINESS ADDRESS:** US Attorney, US Attorney's Office, US Dept of Justice, 450 Golden Gate Ave, Box 36055, Federal Bldg, 11th Fl, San Francisco, CA 94102, (415)556-1328.

YAMAKAWA, DAVID KIYOSHI, JR.

Attorney, consultant. Japanese American. **PERSONAL:** Born Jan 25, 1936, San Francisco, CA; son of David Kiyoshi Yamakawa and Shizu Negishi Yamakawa. **EDUCATION:** University of California, Berkeley, BS, 1958; Coro Foundation, Fellows Program, 1959-60; University of California, Berkeley, Institute for International Studies, School of Law, postdoctoral study, 1963. **CAREER:** Law Offices of David K Yamakawa Jr, principal, 1964-; San Francisco Community Action Agency, deputy director, 1968-69; City and County of San Francisco, City Demonstration Agency, director, 1969-70. **ORGANIZATIONS:** San Francisco Human Rights Commission, chair, 1977-80; United Neighborhood Centers of America, board member, 1977-83; National

Mental Health Association, Region IX, vice president, 1981-83; Japanese Cultural and Community Center of Northern Cal, vice president, 1981-85; United Way of the Bay Area, trustees chair, 1983-85; National Conference on Social Welfare, second vice president, 1983-; Independent Sector, board of directors, 1986-92; Non-Profit Services Inc, chair, 1990-. **HONORS/ AWARDS:** United Way of the Bay Area, Outstanding Volunteer Award, 1985; San Francisco Foundation, The San Francisco Foundation Award, 1985; David Yamakawa Day proclaimed by mayor of San Francisco, 1985; American Bar Association, Liberty Bell Award, 1986; San Francisco Mental Health Association, First Mental Health Awareness Award, 1990. **SPECIAL ACHIEVEMENTS:** Hiker and Camper of the Soviet Union, conferred title, 1958. **MILITARY SERVICE:** United States Army Reserves, Infantry, captain, 1959-67. **BUSINESS ADDRESS:** Principal, Law Offices of David K Yamakawa Jr, 582 Market St, Ste 410, San Francisco, CA 94104, (415)956-7300.

YAMAKAWA, KAZUO ALAN

Physicist (retired). Japanese American. **PERSONAL:** Born Jun 18, 1918, San Jose, CA; married Shizuko Linda, Aug 27, 1957. **EDUCATION:** Stanford University, MD, 1942; Princeton University, PhD, 1949. **CAREER:** Aberdeen Proving Ground Research Lab, department head, 1950-55; Pacific Semiconductors, MTS, 1955-57; Hughes Research Lab, group systems, 1957-60; Electro-Optical Systems, department head, 1960-; Jet Propulsion Lab, technical staff, 1971-82. **HONORS/AWARDS:** Stanford University, Phi Beta Kappa, 1940, John Switzer Fellow, 1942; Princeton, 1860; Exp Physics, fellow, 1945. **SPECIAL ACHIEVEMENTS:** Approx 12 scientific publications.

YAMAKI, MICHAEL ROGER

Police commissioner, attorney. Japanese American. **PERSONAL:** Born Nov 18, 1947, Los Angeles, CA; married. **EDUCATION:** UCLA, BA, 1971; University of West Los Angeles, JD, 1977. **CAREER:** State of California, California Council, Criminal Justice Dept, administrative coordinator, Narcotics Information Clinic, 1973; self employed, attorney at law, 1977-; City of Los Angeles, police commissioner, 1991-. **ORGANIZATIONS:** Los Angeles Police Commission, 1991-; Blue Cross of California, public advisory director, 1989-; University of West Los Angeles, School of Law, board of trusteees, 1992-; State Bar of California, Committee of Bar Examiners, vice-chair, 1987-89, Ethnic Minority Relations Committee, 1984-85; City of Los Angeles, Mayor's Advisory on Urban Housing & Community, Development, co-chair, 1974-76; Japanese American Bar Association, president; California Attorneys for Criminal Justice, board of governors. **HONORS/AWARDS:** YMCA, Outstanding Community Worker, 1970; PTA, honorary life membership, 1971; City of Los Angeles, Mayor Tom Bradley, Community Service Award, 1975; State Bar, delegate to State Bar, 1981, 1982, delegate to Democratic Convention, Congressional District 25, 1984; Criminal Courts Bar Association, Morton Herbert Award, 1993. **SPECIAL ACHIEVEMENTS:** Certified by State Bar of California as a criminal law specialist, 1985; Rated AV by Martindale-Hubbell, 1992. **BUSINESS ADDRESS:** Attorney at Law, 333 South Grand Avenue, 37th fl, Los Angeles, CA 90071-1599, (213)626-1082.

YAMAMORI, TETSUNAO (TED)

International relief and development executive. Japanese American. **PERSONAL:** Born Nov 12, 1937, Nagoya, Japan; son of Yasumitsu and Yaeki Yamamori; married Julia Yamamori, Aug 20, 1967; children: Kelli, Steven. **EDUCATION:** Northwest Christian College, BA, 1962; Texas Christian University, BD, 1964; Duke University, PhD, 1970. **CAREER:** McMurray College, professor, 1970-72; Milligan College, dean of students, 1972-76; Northwest Christian College, dean, 1976-77; Institute for American Church Growth, vice president, 1977-79; Biola University, Intercultural Studies, professor, director, 1979-81; Food for the Hungry International, president, 1981-. **ORGANIZATIONS:** Phoenix Committee on Foreign Relations. **HONORS/ AWARDS:** Warner Southern College, LLD, 1987; Sterling College, DLitt, 1993. **BUSINESS ADDRESS:** President, Food for the Hungry International, 7729 E Greenway Rd, Scottsdale, AZ 85260, (602)998-3100.

YAMAMOTO, ERIC K.

Educator. Japanese American. **PERSONAL:** Born Sep 10, 1952, Honolulu, HI; son of George Yamamoto and Tamiko Yamamoto; married Joan Ishibashi, Aug 1991. **EDUCATION:** University of Hawaii, Manoa, BA, 1975; University of California, Berkeley, JD, 1978. **CAREER:** Case & Lynch, attorney, 1978-85; University of Hawaii Law School, professor of law, 1985-. **ORGANIZATIONS:** Native Hawaiian Advisory Council, litigation advisor, 1991-; Native Hawaiian Legal Corp, bd of dir, 1986-91; Legal Aid Society of Hawaii, bd of dir, 1991-; Matsunaga Peace Institute, bd of dir, 1980-83, 1990-92;

Advocates for Public Interest Law, bd of dir, 1989-; Judiciary Committee on Racial Fairness, 1992-; American Association Law Schools, executive committee, civil procedure, 1992-. **HONORS/AWARDS:** University of Hawaii, Presidential Citation, 1991; University of Hawaii Law School, Outstanding Law Professor, 1986; Phi Beta Kappa, 1975; Phi Kappa Phi, 1974; Judiciary History Project, Humanities Scholar, 1990. **SPECIAL ACHIEVEMENTS:** Co-counsel to Fred Korematsu in reopening of WWII Japanese American Internment case, Korematsu v US, which laid the legal foundation for reparations; counsel to numerous Asian American community groups and individuals. **BUSINESS ADDRESS:** Professor of Law, University of Hawaii Law School, 2515 Dole Street, #247, Honolulu, HI 96822, (808)956-6548.

YAMAMOTO, JOHN HIROSHI

Engineering and real estate development company executive. Japanese American. **PERSONAL:** Born Jun 10, 1940, Tokyo, Japan; son of Thomas Yamamoto and Judy Yamamoto; married Cheri, Jun 11, 1991; children: Jeanne-Marie Yamamoto Sabate, Tamiko Ann Yamamoto Broms, Julianne Akiko, Kimiko Eleanor. **EDUCATION:** Manhattan College, BCE, 1963; St John's University, MBA, 1966. **CAREER:** Tippetts, Abbet, McCarthy, Stratton Project engineer, 1963-66; C W Riva Co Inc, chief engineer, 1966-69; C E Maguire Inc, vice president, 1969-74, 1981-85; Orgonics Inc, vice president, 1975-81; PAL International Hawaii Ltd, president, 1988-; PEMCO, Ltd, president, 1985-. **ORGANIZATIONS:** American Academy of Environmental Engineers, diplomate, 1982-; National Society of Professional Engineers, treasurer, 1980-; Construction Management Association of America, 1990-; ARE, life member, 1988-. **HONORS/AWARDS:** Naval Facilities Engineering Command, Certificate of Appreciation, 1982, 1989. **SPECIAL ACHIEVEMENTS:** Environmental Management Journal, Springer-Verlag, 1977-79; various articles in professional journals, 1975-92. **BUSINESS ADDRESS:** President/CEO, Pacific Engineering Management Company, dba Pemco, Ltd, 1600 Kapiolani Blvd, Ste 1306, Honolulu, HI 96814, (808)949-0414.

YAMAMOTO, KEITH ROBERT

Educator. Japanese American. **PERSONAL:** Born Feb 4, 1946, Des Moines, IA. **EDUCATION:** Iowa State University, BSc, 1968; Princeton University, PhD, biochemical science, 1973. **CAREER:** Iowa State University, Dept of Biochemistry & Biophysics, research assistant, biochemistry, 1967-68; Princeton University, NIH trainee, biochemical science, 1968-73; University of California, San Francisco, Lab Gordon M Tomkins, biochemistry, fellow, 1973-75, assistant professor, beginning 1976, associate professor, until 1983, professor of biochemistry, 1983-, Dept of Biochemistry and Biophysics, vice chairman, 1985-. **ORGANIZATIONS:** NIH, Molecular Biology Study Section, chair, 1987-90, Natl Adv Council for Human Genome Research, 1990-92; Natl Academy of Sciences; American Soc for Biological Chemists; American Soc for Developmental Biology; American Soc for Microbiology; AAAS; American Soc for Cell Biology; American Soc for Biochemistry & Molecular Biology; numerous others. **HONORS/AWARDS:** Greg Pincus Medal, 1990; American Academy of Arts and Sciences, fellow; Dreyfus Teacher Scholar Award, 1982-86; Harvard Medical School, Markey Lecturer, 1990; Weitzmann Institute, Lindner Lecturer, 1990; numerous others. **BUSINESS ADDRESS:** Vice Chairman, Dept of Biochem & Biophysics, University of California, San Francisco, 513 Parnassus Ave, San Francisco, CA 94143, (415)476-4324.＊

YAMAMOTO, MICHAEL TORU

Journalist. Japanese American. **PERSONAL:** Born Jul 9, 1960, San Francisco, CA; son of Harry Yamamoto and Noriko Yamamoto; married Marianne Chin, Oct 9, 1993. **EDUCATION:** San Francisco State Univ, BA, journalism, 1981, BA, psychology, 1981. **CAREER:** Hayward Daily Review, news editor, 1979; San Francisco State University Phoenix, editor, 1980; Long Beach Press Telegram, news editor, 1981; Los Angeles Times, national desk editor, 1981-85, Washington Bureau, investigative projects editor, night news editor, 1986-88; San Francisco Chronicle, city editor, executive projects editor, deputy city editor, 1989-. **ORGANIZATIONS:** Asian American Journalists Association, 1981-; White House Correspondents Association, 1986-89; Society of Professional Journalists, 1980-81. **HONORS/AWARDS:** Society of Professional Journalists, San Francisco State Univ, Outstanding Graduate in Journalism, 1981; Dow Jones Newspaper Fund Scholarship, 1980. **BUSINESS ADDRESS:** City Editor, San Francisco Chronicle, 901 Mission St, San Francisco, CA 94103, (415)777-7100.

YAMAMOTO, ROGER MASAAKI

Company executive. Japanese American. **PERSONAL:** Born Jul 6, 1943, Kyoto, Japan; son of Thomas Yamamoto and Jeanne Marie Yamamoto; married Catherine, Aug 10, 1977; children: Christopher, Emiko. **EDUCATION:** Mount St Mary's College, BA, 1966; Northwestern University, MBA, 1978. **CAREER:** Amerada Corp, international accountant, 1968-72; US Industries, international group controller, 1972-90; Bijur Lubricating Corp, vice president, finance & administration, 1980-. **BUSINESS ADDRESS:** Vice President, Finance & Administration, Bijur Lubricating Corp, 50 Kocher Dr, Bennington, VT 05201.

YAMAMOTO, TOSHIAKI

Engineer. Japanese American. **PERSONAL:** Born Apr 9, 1943, Tokyo, Japan; son of Keijiro Yamamoto; married Toshiko Yamamoto, Aug 25, 1972; children: Satoko, Riichi. **EDUCATION:** Sophia University, BS, 1967, MS, 1969; University of Illinois, MS, 1972; Ohio State University, PhD, 1979. **CAREER:** United McGill Corp, research engr, 1973-81; University of Denver, research engr, 1981-84; Research Triangle Institute, sr research engr, 1984-. **ORGANIZATIONS:** Sigma Xi; American Assn of Mechanical Engineers; American Assn for Aerosol Research; The Institute of Electrostatics, Japan; Japan Assn of Aerosol Science and Technology; Institute of Environmental Sciences, senior mbr. **HONORS/AWARDS:** IEEE Industry Applications Society James Melcher Prize Award, 1993; Institute of Environmental Sciences, Maurice Simpson Technical Editor's Award, 1990; RTI, Professional Development Award, 1989; United McGill, Research Grant Award, 1975. **SPECIAL ACHIEVEMENTS:** Copyright: user-friendly software, 1979, 1990, 1991; journal publications: 32; book chapters: 6; technical reports: 92; presentations: 29; author: "Control of Volatile Organic Compounds by an AC Energized Ferroelectric Pellet Reactor and a Pulsed Corona Reactor," IEEE Transactions on Industry Applications, p 528, May/Jun 1992; "Model Study of Contaminant Flow in the Vicinity of Semiconductor Process Equipment," J of the IES, vol. 33, July/August, 1990, p.25. **BUSINESS ADDRESS:** Senior Research Engineer, Research Triangle Institute, PO Box 12194, Research Triangle Park, NC 27709, (919)541-5810.

YAMAMOTO, Y. STEPHEN

Editor. Japanese American. **PERSONAL:** Born Aug 6, 1943, Topaz, UT; son of Shinji & Hifumi Yamamoto; married Mary Ellen Murphy, Sep 1977 (divorced); children: Michael K. **EDUCATION:** University of Wisconsin, BS, chemistry, 1965; Pennsylvania State University, PhD, organic chemistry, 1971. **CAREER:** Eastman Kodak, senior research chemist, 1971-78; Rochester Institute of Technology, associate professor, coordinator of experiential learning, 1978-83; VCH Publishers, senior editor, 1983-88; DuPont, information specialist, 1988-91, patent liaison, 1991-92, editor, 1992-. **ORGANIZATIONS:** American Chemical Society, 1965-; DuPont Asian Group, steering committee member, editor of newsletter, 1991-; Winterthur Museum, volunteer editor, 1993-; Science Alliance, volunteer, 1989-. **SPECIAL ACHIEVEMENTS:** Ullmann's Encyclopedia of Industrial Chemistry, senior editor; invention disclosures: Novel pH Sensitive Antihalation Dyes, Novel Dye Intermediates for the Preparation of Solubilized Dyes; Cooperative Education: Academic Involovement, section, 1980. **BUSINESS ADDRESS:** Editor, DuPont, PO Box 80016, BMP 16/1216, Wilmington, DE 19880-0016, (302)892-8879.

YAMAMOTO, YUTAKA

Educator. Japanese American. **PERSONAL:** Born May 17, 1935, Petaluma, CA; son of Roy Eiichi Yamamoto and Hisano Yamamoto; divorced. **EDUCATION:** University of California, Berkeley, BS, 1957; University of Michigan, Ann Arbor, MA, PhD, 1973. **CAREER:** Purdue University, instructor, 1969-73; Kobe University, Japan, visiting professor, 1982-84; University of Hawaii, Manoa, visiting professor, 1988; University of Calif, UCLA, visiting professor, 1970, 1971-81; University of New Hampshire, associate professor, chairman, 1973-. **ORGANIZATIONS:** University of New Hampshire, Dept of Philo, chairman, 1979-; Advisory Board to Multicultural Affairs, chairman, 1993-; US Japan Society of New Hampshire, founding member, 1988-; New Hampshire Advisory Committee to US Commission Civil Rights, 1992-; American Philosophical Association, 1970-; American Association of University Professors, 1990-. **HONORS/AWARDS:** NSF and NEH grants. **SPECIAL ACHIEVEMENTS:** Articles on ethics and Japanese morality; work in progress; books: A Portrait of an American as a Duck-Rabbit, Communitarianism and Japanese Morality; two screenplays: The Texas Diary, The Bookie; proficient in Japanese. **MILITARY SERVICE:** US Army Intelligence, first lt, 1958-60, reserves, 1960-63. **BUSINESS ADDRESS:** Professor & Chairman, Dept of Philosophy, University of New Hampshire, Hamilton Smith 27, Durham, NH 03824, (603)862-1040.

YAMANISHI, HENRY KAZUO
Landscape contractor. Japanese American. **PERSONAL:** Born Jul 4, 1930, San Juan Batista, CA; son of Frank & Masako Yamanishi; married Tayeko Grace Yamanishi, Oct 17, 1959; children: Mark Kaz, Joannie Ruth. **CAREER:** US Army, 1951-53; Solomone & Hoy Landscape Contractors, foreman, 1953-61; self-employed, landscaper, 1961-. **ORGANIZATIONS:** California Landscape Contractor Association. **MILITARY SERVICE:** US Army, corporal, 1951-53; United Nation & Korean Ribbon, Combat Infantry Badge. **BUSINESS ADDRESS:** Owner/President, Henry Yamanishi Landscaping Inc, 2046 Sunset Dr, Pacific Grove, CA 93950, (408)373-1636.

YAMASAKI, GEORGE, JR.
Attorney. Japanese American. **PERSONAL:** Born Mar 21, 1935, Honolulu, HI; son of George Yamasaki and Nobuko Hino; married Anne Y Sakamaki, Nov 28, 1985; children: Emily Judith, Paul Richard. **EDUCATION:** Stanford University, AB, 1957, JD, 1959. **CAREER:** Harold D Kline, attorney at law, 1963-65; self employed attorney at law, 1965-. **ORGANIZATIONS:** City & County of San Francisco Social Services Commission, 1975-, president, 1977, 1980, 1985-87, 1992-; San Francisco Japanese American Citizens League, president, 1971-72; Japanese American Citizens League, national legal counsel, 1974-75; San Francisco Cherry Blossom Festival, co-chairman, 1974, 1977, 1978; American Cancer Society, San Francisco Unit, president, 1981-83, California Division, director & member of executive committee; Japanese Chamber of Commerce of Northern California, director; Japanese Society of Northern California, director; United States District Court for the Northern District of California, director; Friends of Redevelopment, treasurer. **BUSINESS ADDRESS:** Attorney at Law, Law Offices of George Yamasaki, Jr, 500 Sansome, Ste 612, San Francisco, CA 94111-3222, (415)391-3000.

YAMASAKI, MITCH
Educator. Japanese American. **PERSONAL:** Born Apr 7, 1952, Tokyo, Japan; son of Hisao & Fusako Yamasaki. **EDUCATION:** University of Hawaii, BA, 1974, MA, 1977, PhD, 1989. **CAREER:** State Dept of Social Services, research statistician, 1979-84; Hawaii State Judiciary, senior research analyst, 1984-88; Chaminade University, associate professor, 1988-. **ORGANIZATIONS:** National History Day, executive board, 1993-96; Organization of American Historians, committee on teaching, 1994-97; American Historical Association, committee on history in the classroom; Hawaii State Judiciary History Center, board member; National Organization for Historic Preservation. **HONORS/AWARDS:** Sears Roebuck & Co, Outstanding Teacher of the Year, 1990-91. **SPECIAL ACHIEVEMENTS:** Author of: "Martial Law in Hawaii," Hawaii Committee for the Hum, 1991; "Hawaii's Trade with the People's Republic of China 1982," 1983; language proficiency: Japanese-speaking, Russian-reading. **BUSINESS ADDRESS:** Associate Professor of History, Chaminade University of Honolulu, 3140 Waialae Avenue, Honolulu, HI 96816, (808)735-4824.

YAMASHIROYA, HERBERT MITSUGI
Microbiologist, educator, educational administrator. Japanese American. **PERSONAL:** Born Sep 14, 1930, Honolulu, HI; son of Midori Yamashiroya and Yasue Yamashiroya; married Kiyoka Yamashiroya, Jun 3, 1957; children: Gail Paskind, Eliot, Eric, Gary. **EDUCATION:** University of Hawaii, BA, 1953; University of Illinois, MS, 1962, PhD, 1965. **CAREER:** National Acad Sciences, Atomic Bomb Casualty Comm, supervisor of clinical labs, 1956-58; IIT Research Institute, associate to senior bacteriologist, 1964-71; University of Illinois, Chicago, research and teaching assistant in microbiology, 1960-64, associate professor of pathology, head of virology, director of grad studies, 1971-. **ORGANIZATIONS:** American Society for Microbiology; American Society for Investigative Pathology; American Association for Advancement of Science; Society of the Sigma Xi; Illinois Society for Microbiology. **HONORS/AWARDS:** Illinois Society for Microbiology, Tanner-Shaughnessy Merit Award, 1982; Institute for Advanced Biotech, senior fellow, 1991. **SPECIAL ACHIEVEMENTS:** Co-author of book: Essentials of Medical Virology, WB Saunders, 1975; two chapters in Medical Microbiology, Little, Brown, 1980; over 25 publications in scientific journals; member of State of Illinois Clin Lab and Blood Bank Advisory Board, 1980-92; lecturer and consultant in medical virology, VA West Side Hospital, Chicago, 1982-. **MILITARY SERVICE:** US Army, captain, 1953-55; National Defense Service Medal, Korean Service Medal, UN Service Medal. **BUSINESS ADDRESS:** Associate Professor, Dept of Pathology, University of Illinois at Chicago, 808 S Wood, M/C 847, Chicago, IL 60612, (312)996-2954.

YAMASHITA, FRANCIS ISAMI
Judge. Japanese American. **PERSONAL:** Born May 14, 1949, Hilo, HI; son of Yuji Yamashita and Sadako Hirayama Yamashita; married Alexa Denise Mariko Fujise, Feb 26, 1983. **EDUCATION:** Pacific University, BA, 1971; The University of Chicago Law School, JD, 1974. **CAREER:** Circuit Court of the First Circuit, State of Hawaii, law clerk, 1975-76; Ikazaki, Devens, Lo, Youth & Nakano, associate, 1979-82; Department of the Prosecuting Attorney, City & County of Honolulu, deputy prosecuting attorney, 1976-79, 1982-87; Department of the Prosecuting Attorney, White Collar Crime Unit, head, 1985-87; District Court of the First Circuit, State of Hawaii, district judge, 1987-92; US District Court, District of Hawaii, US magistrate judge, 1992-. **BUSINESS ADDRESS:** US Magistrate Judge, US District Court, District of Hawaii, 300 Ala Moana Blvd, PO Box 50122, Prince Jonah Kuhio Kalanianaole Federal Bldg, Rm C-340, Honolulu, HI 96850, (808)541-1308.

YAMASHITA, KENNETH AKIRA
Librarian. Japanese American. **PERSONAL:** Born Sep 11, 1945, Topaz, UT; son of Susumu Yamashita and Kiyoko Kitano Yamashita. **EDUCATION:** Rutgers University, BA, 1967, MLS, 1972; Indiana University, MA candidate, 1970; Simmons College, DA, 1982. **CAREER:** Montclair Free Public Library, reference/outreach librarian, 1970-73; Decatur Public Library, extension services supervisor, 1973-75; Chicago Public Library, assistant to the commissioner, 1975-78; CLSI, Inc, marketing representative for S California public libraries, 1978-79; Stockton-San Joaquin County Public Library, branch/bookmobile supervisor, 1982-90, library division manager for branch services, 1990-93, library division manager for central library services, 1993-. **ORGANIZATIONS:** American Library Association, reviewer, ref/subscrip bks rev comm, 1975-78, consultant, chair, office for library outreach services adv comm, 1982-91, council committee on minority concerns, 1985-87, ex-officio member, ALA/OLOS, minority fellow advisory board, 1988-90, OLOS, Director Search Committee, chair, 1986, 1987; ALA Public Library Association, division and metro libs sec comms, 1986-93; California Library Association, councilor/assemblyman, 1987-93; California State Library, Multi-Ethnic Schol, PFC eval, adv comms, 1990-93. **HONORS/AWARDS:** Rutgers University, English dept honors program, 1964-65; Indiana University, Asian studies comm fellow, Carnegie Grant fellow, 1967-70; Montclair Free Pub Lib, board of trustees fellow to Rutgers University, 1971; Beta Phi Mu, 1972; Simmons College, HEA title II-B fellowship, 1979-80. **SPECIAL ACHIEVEMENTS:** Author, "Asian American Pub Librns" Opportunities for Minorities in Librarianship, Scarecrow, 1977; ALA, Booklist, reviews/notes, Ref & Subscrip Bks Rev Comm, 1975-78; case study contributor, Probs in Lib Management, Libraries Unlimited, 1981; doctoral field research, Minority Librns in Upper Mgt of Urban US Pub Libs, 1982; advisor to library professional; publications: monographs/books/manuals: University of Wisconsin, ALA/ACRL, Gale Research, CA State Library Foundation, 1989-90. **HOME ADDRESS:** 1209 West Downs St, Stockton, CA 95207. **BUSINESS ADDRESS:** Library Division Manager, Central Library Services, Stockton-San Joaquin County Public Library, 605 North El Dorado St, Stockton, CA 95202, (209)937-8467.

YAMASHITA, PEARL NOBUKO
Educator (retired). Japanese American. **PERSONAL:** Born Nov 14, 1920, Honolulu, HI; daughter of Toichi and Toyo Kaneshige; married Paul Toshio Yamashita, Jun 17, 1949; children: Margaret, Allen, David, Bruce. **EDUCATION:** University of Hawaii, BEd, 1942, 5th yr diploma, 1943; University of Iowa, MA, 1947. **CAREER:** State Dept of Education, teacher, 1942-48; University of Hawaii, instructor, asst professor, associate professor, 1948-51, 1961-93. **ORGANIZATIONS:** Student Council for Exceptional Children, faculty advsr, 1977-93; Pi Lambda Theta, Beta Zeta Chapter, faculty advsr, 1987-; Opportunities for the Retarded, bd mbr, 1980-; Hawaii State Advisory Committee for Gifted & Talented, 1989-; Autistic Vocational Education Center, bd secretary, 1989-; Cottington Trust for Gifted & Talented, 1990-; Na Pua No'lou, Center for Gifted Hawaiian Students, University of Hawaii Hilo, 1990-. **HONORS/AWARDS:** Intl Council for Exceptional Children, Susan Gorin Award, 1989; Pi Lambda Theta, Regional Award for Outstanding Faculty, 1990; Star Bulletin, 10 Persons in the State Who Made a Difference, honoree, 1988; Pearl N Yamashita Scholarship for Special Education Students, University of Hawaii Manoa. **SPECIAL ACHIEVEMENTS:** Lecturer, workshop coordinator, seminar leader for: early childhood educators from Japan; special education faculties from Japan. **BIOGRAPHICAL SOURCES:** "The New Volunteers: America's Unsung Heroes," Newsweek Magazine, Jul 10, 1989; "Headstart in Hawaii," Educational Horizons (Pi Lambda Theta); "Be-

ginning Teacher Programs in Hawaii," *Educational Perspectives*. **HOME ADDRESS:** 1436 St Louis Dr, Honolulu, HI 96816, (808)734-6401.

YAMAUCHI, TOSHIO
Pediatrician. Japanese American. **PERSONAL:** Born Feb 13, 1945, Newell, CA; son of Steve Hiroshi Yamauchi and Marie Okamura Yamauchi; married Joyce Reiko Yamauchi, Jun 12, 1976; children: Kyle Hiromi, Tyler Shigeo. **EDUCATION:** Northwestern University, BA, 1966, PhD, 1972; University of Texas Medical School, Houston, MD, 1979. **CAREER:** UT MD Anderson, research associate, 1972-76; self employed pediatrician, 1982-. **ORGANIZATIONS:** American Academy of Pediatrics, fellow, 1982-; American Medical Association, 1982-. **HONORS/AWARDS:** Alpha Omega Alpha, 1979-. **SPECIAL ACHIEVEMENTS:** Board certified in pediatrics, 1984. **BIOGRAPHICAL SOURCES:** Nurses Rate the Doctors, Houston Metropolitan Magazine, p 37-41, Nov 1992. **BUSINESS ADDRESS:** Pediatrician, First Colony Pediatrics, 3425 Hwy Six, Ste 107, Sugar Land, TX 77478, (713)980-1020.

YAN, CHIOU-SHUANG JOU
Educator. Taiwanese American. **PERSONAL:** Born Oct 7, 1934, Tainan, Taiwan. **EDUCATION:** National Taiwan University, BA, 1960; Purdue University, MS, 1962, PhD, 1966. **CAREER:** Mobil Research, economic consultant, 1964, 1968; Haverford College, assistant professor of economics, 1965-67; Drexel University, assistant professor of economics, 1967-75, associate professor of economics, 1975-82, professor of economics, 1982-. **ORGANIZATIONS:** Pennsylvania Economic Association, vice president, program, 1992; Economic & Business History Society, 1985-; SWSE, 1985-. **HONORS/AWARDS:** Freedoms Foundation, Valley Forge, Leavey Award, 1988. **SPECIAL ACHIEVEMENTS:** Introduction to Input Output Economics; Trade Patterns & Deviation of Exchange Rate from PPP; Distribution of Producers' Goods in China; Import Contents of Final Demands; Interindustry Interrelatedness. **BUSINESS ADDRESS:** Professor of Economics, Drexel University, 32nd & Chestnut St, Philadelphia, PA 19104-6297, (215)895-6972.

YAN, HAIPING (SANG SHI)
Educator, writer. Chinese American. **PERSONAL:** Born in Shanghai, People's Republic of China; daughter of Ciqin Yan & Xiulan Chen; married Zhigang Yang, Jun 28, 1990. **EDUCATION:** Fudan University, Shanghai, China, BA, 1982; Cornell University, MA, 1987, PhD, 1990. **CAREER:** Children's Performing Arts Center, China, instructor, artistic director, 1973-78; Fudan University, assistant professor of Chinese literature, 1982; Cornell University, teaching assistant in modern languages, 1984-85, teaching assistant in Asian studies, 1989; Oberlin College, visiting assistant professor of theatre & comparative literature, 1991-. **ORGANIZATIONS:** Modern Language Association; Theatre in Higher Education; Chinese Dramatists' Association; Ohio Chinese Academic and Professional Association. **HONORS/AWARDS:** Chinese Dramatists' Association, First Prize for Excellence, 1982, for drama, 1980-81; Cornell University, Sage Scholarship, 1983-84, Martin M McVoy Jr Trust Scholarship, 1984-88. **SPECIAL ACHIEVEMENTS:** Author, Li Shi-min, Prince of Qin, a ten-part historical drama, published and performed, 1981; "Modern Chinese Drama & Its Western Models: A Critical Reconstruction of Chinese Subjectivity," 1992; "Images of Women in Three Traditional Chinese Music Dramas," 1993. **BIOGRAPHICAL SOURCES:** Modern Drama, p 185, March 1992; Literature and History, p 254-258, March 1992; Asian Theatre Journal, Univ of Hawaii, p 90, spring 1994; Journal of Dramatic Theory and Criticism, Univ of Kansas, p 61, fall 1993; A History of Contemporary Chinese Dramatic Literature, pp 40, 167, 265, 266, 322, Guangxi People's Publishing House, PPC, Dec 1990. **BUSINESS ADDRESS:** Assistant Professor, Theatre & Dance Program, Oberlin College, Hall Annex, Oberlin, OH 44074-1019.

YAN, HONG-CHENG
Educator. Chinese American. **PERSONAL:** Born May 28, 1947, Fuzhou, Fujian, China; son of Ziqi Yan & Ruiting Xu; divorced; children: Qijia. **EDUCATION:** Harbin Polytechnic University, China, BS, 1970; Graduate School of Chinese Academy of Sciences, MScE, 1982; Clarkson University, PhD, engineering science, 1987; Purdue University, PhD, electrical engineering, 1993. **CAREER:** Fujian Longyan Iron and Steel Company, China, electrical engineer, 1970-82; UK Patent Office, trainee & practitioner, 1980-81; Institute of Petroleum Exploration and Development, China, applied software engineer, 1982-83; Clarkson University, teaching assistant, 1983-85; Purdue University, research assistant, 1986-88; Missouri Western State College, assistant professor, 1989-. **ORGANIZATIONS:** IEEE, 1985-; Missouri Vocational Association, 1993-. **HONORS/AWARDS:** World Intellectual Property Orga-

nization, UN, fellowship, 1980; Purdue University, School of Engineering, Dean's Graduate Engineering Award, 1988. **SPECIAL ACHIEVEMENTS:** "On Controlling Generalized State Space (descriptor) Systems," International Journal of Control, April 1986; "A Note on Optimal Control of Generalized State-Space (descriptor) Systems," International Journal of Control, Sept 1986; 7 papers in Proceedings of IEEE International Conferences, 1987-93. **HOME ADDRESS:** 3029 Bristol St, Saint Joseph, MO 64506-1159. **BUSINESS PHONE:** (816)271-5823.

YAN, JOSEPH GEA-GUE
Educator. Taiwanese American. **PERSONAL:** Born Sep 24, 1958, Miao-Li, Taiwan; son of Shyue-You Yan and Min-Feng Hou; married Gloria C Yan, Apr 29, 1988; children: Jessica J, Jason J. **EDUCATION:** National Cheng-Kung University, BS, math, 1980; SUNY, Buffalo, MS, math, 1985, PhD, math, 1988. **CAREER:** Thunderbird Video Inc, Taiwan, computer programmer, 1982-83; SUNY, Buffalo, teaching assistant, 1983-87, lecturer, 1987-88; University of North Carolina, Wilmington, assistant professor, 1988-93, associate professor, 1993-. **ORGANIZATIONS:** American Mathematics Association, 1983-; Mathematics Association of America, 1989-; Pi Mu Epsilon, 1988-; Upsilon Pi Epsilon, 1990-; Asian American Faculty Society, UNCW, secretary, 1992-. **HONORS/AWARDS:** North Carolina Board of Science and Technology, research grant, 1989; UNCW, Faculty Development Fund, 1990, Research Initiative Award, 1992, Cahill Research Award, 1993; North Carolina Supercomputer Center, research grant, 1989-. **MILITARY SERVICE:** Military Police, Army, Taiwan, 1980-82. **HOME PHONE:** (910)395-4480. **BUSINESS ADDRESS:** Associate Professor, Dept of Mathematical Sciences, University of North Carolina, Wilmington, 601 S College Rd, Wilmington, NC 28403-3201, (910)395-3820.

YAN, MARTIN
Chef, television show host, author. Chinese American. **PERSONAL:** Born 1952?, Guangzhou, People's Republic of China; children: two. **EDUCATION:** Chinese restaurants in China, Hong Kong, US, apprenticeship; Overseas Institute of Cookery, Hong Kong, diploma, 1967; University of California, Davis, master's degree, food science, 1975. **CAREER:** Sun Wong Kee Restaurant, Hong Kong, asst cook, 1966-69; Black Pagoda Restaurant, cook, 1970-72; Amoy Canning Corp, Hong Kong, product manager, 1976-77; Gourmet Cooking Institute, Alberta, Canada, director, 1977-80; Lee's Garden Restaurant, Alberta, Canada, manager, head cook, 1977; major food companies & restaurants, consultant, 1980-; host of 700 cooking shows in US, Canada, Asia, 1978-; Yan Can Intl Cooking School, founder, 1985; many professional chef's programs, including California Culinary Academy, University of San Francisco, chef instructor, 1978-; "Yan Can Cook Show," natl public television, host, 1983-. **ORGANIZATIONS:** AFTRA/ACTRA, US/Canada, 1983-; American Author's Guild, 1982-; Institute of Food Technologists, 1973-; Intl Assn of Culinary Professionals, professional member, 1980-; American Culinary Federation, 1982-, culinary diplomat; Assn of Chinese Cooking Teachers, 1983-; San Francisco Professional Food Soc, 1983-; American Institute of Wine & Food, 1985-; Chef's Assn of the Pacific Coast, 1985-; Chinese Cuisine Research Institute, 1988-; Kaiser's Project Lean, board member. **HONORS/AWARDS:** Chef's Assn of the Pacific Northwest, Antonin Careme Award, 1989; Johnson and Wales University, Distinguished Visiting Chef's Chair, 1990; Courvoisier Leadership Award, 1991; Golden West College Pillar Award, 1992. **SPECIAL ACHIEVEMENTS:** Author, books: Yan Can Cook Book; Joy of Wokking; Martin Yan, the Chinese Chef; A Wok for All Seasons; Everybody's Woking; The Well-Seasoned Wok; participant, A Taste of Asia, fundraiser for Self-Help for the Eldery organization, San Francisco, 1992. **BUSINESS ADDRESS:** Host, Yan Can Cook, KQED Public Television, C 9, 2601 Mariposa St, San Francisco, CA 94110, (415)341-5133.

YAN, SAU-CHI BETTY
Research biochemist. Chinese American. **PERSONAL:** Born Nov 25, 1954, Hong Kong; daughter of Ming Yan & Choo Chen Woo; married Victor J Chen, Feb 29, 1980; children: Heidi I. **EDUCATION:** Central Missouri State University, BS, 1975; Iowa State University, PhD, 1980. **CAREER:** Eli Lilly & Co, Cardiovascular Research, senior biochemist, 1985-88, senior scientist, senior research scientist, 1989-. **ORGANIZATIONS:** American Society for Biochemistry and Molecular Biology, 1988-; The Protein Society, 1988-, chairman travel grant section, 1990; Sigma Xi, 1986-90; American Association for the Advancement of Science, 1986-; Society of Chinese Bioscientists in America, 1986-; American Chemical Society, 1973-82; Chinese Student Association, executive committee, 1976-77. **HONORS/AWARDS:** Robert A Welch Foundation Fellowship, 1982-84; Edwards Memorial Trust Fellowship, 1980-82;

ISU, Graduate Student Teaching Award, 1978; Central Missouri State University, Outstanding Senior Woman of the Year, 1975. **SPECIAL ACHIEVEMENTS:** Co-author of numerous papers, including: "Novel oligosaccharide structures on recombinant human Protein C expressed in human kidney 293 cells," J Cell Biochemistry, vol 16D, p 151, 1992; lecturer, The Protein Society annual meeting, section on post-translational modifications of proteins, 993; reviewer for Hematology, BioTechnology; holder of 5 US end European patents including: purification of human Protein C, US, 1991, Canadian, 1993. **BUSINESS ADDRESS:** Sr Research Scientist, Cardiovascular Research, Eli Lilly & Co, DC 1543, 307 E McCarty St, Indianapolis, IN 46285, (317)276-6689.

YAN, TSOUNG-YUAN
Consultant. Taiwanese American. **PERSONAL:** Born Sep 17, 1933, Tainan, Taiwan; son of Yong-mu Yan and Huei-o Chang Yan; married Chiou-shuang Jou Yan, Dec 15, 1960; children: Kay, Roy. **EDUCATION:** National Taiwan University, BE, 1959; Purdue University, MS, 1962, PhD, 1963. **CAREER:** Mobil Research & Development Corp, research engineer, 1962-65, senior research engineer, 1965-70, research associate, 1970-78, senior research associate, 1978-82, research scientist, 1982-91, senior research consultant, 1991-. **ORGANIZATIONS:** Energy International Journal, associate editor, 1988-; Industrial Technology Research Institute, advisory board, 1989-; American Chemical Society, 1970-; Sigma Xi, 1961-. **SPECIAL ACHIEVEMENTS:** Petroleum refining research; uranium leaching process development; environmental control process; coal utilization processes; natural gas processing technology; 162 US patents; 70 refereed papers. **BUSINESS ADDRESS:** Senior Research Consultant, Mobil Research & Develop Corp, PO Box 1025, Princeton, NJ 08540, (609)737-4284.

YAN, XIAO-HAI
Educator. Chinese American. **PERSONAL:** Born May 23, 1952, Shanghai, People's Republic of China; son of De Lian Yan and Wu Su Jin. **EDUCATION:** Tong Chi University, BS, 1977; Academy Sinica, MS, 1981; SUNY, Stony Brook, PhD, 1989; UCSD, Scripps Institute of Oceanography, post doctoral, 1990. **CAREER:** Academia Sinica, remote sensing physics, 1977-85; SUNY-Stony Brook, research assistant, 1985-89; University of California, post doc, 1989-90; University of Delaware, assistant professor, 1990-93, associate professor, 1993-. **ORGANIZATIONS:** American Geophysical Union, 1985-; American Meteorological Society, 1989-; Oceanography Society, 1992-; IEEE Society, 1993-; Space Society, council member. **HONORS/AWARDS:** State Oceanic Administration of China, honorary professor, 1993; Rockefeller Institute, Research Award, 1987; NASA, Graduate Research Award, 1989; AGU, Travel Award, 1988; NSF, International Travel Award, 1991. **SPECIAL ACHIEVEMENTS:** Year Book, 1993; Science Year, 1993; paper in science: "Temperature and Size Variabilities of the Western Pacific Warm Pool," 1992, Science 258, 5088: 1643 & 645; paper in JGR, 1992 97, C12: 20201-20226. **BIOGRAPHICAL SOURCES:** The New York Times, page C4, April 28, 1992; National Geographic, Dec, 1992. **BUSINESS ADDRESS:** Professor, University of Delaware, Graduate College of Marine Studies, Robinson Hall 209, Newark, DE 19716, (302)831-3694.

YANAGISAWA, SAMUEL TSUGUO
Electronics company executive (retired). Japanese American. **PERSONAL:** Born Feb 18, 1922, Berkeley, CA; son of George Jusaku Yanagisawa and Mitsuyo Yanagisawa; married Fern Renar; children: Shane, Steven, Ian. **EDUCATION:** University of California, Berkeley, BSEE, 1942. **CAREER:** Machlett Laboratories, Inc, product mgr, 1943-63; Warnecke Electron Tubes, exec vp, 1963-67; Varo Inc, chmn, pres, CEO, 1967-87. **ORGANIZATIONS:** US Night Vision Mfrs Association, president, 1983-93; US Army Science Board, 1986-90; Air Force Studies Board, 1991-; American Defense Prep Association, 1970-; Association of US Army, 1970-; McDonald Observatory, board of visitors chairman, 1986-88; U Texas-Austin, College of Natural Sciences, exec council advisory council, 1992-; Sigma Xi, 1985; Tau Beta Pi, 1940; Eta Kappa Nu, 1940. **HONORS/AWARDS:** Phi Beta Kappa, 1942. **SPECIAL ACHIEVEMENTS:** First to develop first & second generations of night vision tubes & equipment, 1960-85. **MILITARY SERVICE:** US Infantry, 2nd lt, 1944-46. **BIOGRAPHICAL SOURCES:** History of Night Vision, Dr Robert Wiseman. **HOME ADDRESS:** 7708 Chalkstone Drive, Dallas, TX 75248, (214)239-3202.

YANG, ALBERT C.
Business executive, educator. Chinese American. **PERSONAL:** Born Jun 13, 1951, Taipei, Taiwan; son of Ching-Chuan Yang and Hsing-Chiu Lee Yang;

married Jean Yang, Aug 20, 1977; children: Angela, Andrew. **EDUCATION:** Tunghai University, Taiwan, BA, 1975; MIT, MAAS, 1979; Northeastern University, MSIS, 1985. **CAREER:** Eduardo Catalano A&E, associate architect, 1979-85; Prime Computer Inc, senior engineer, 1985-88; Computervision, senior engineer, 1988-91; Sigma Design Inc, director, r&d, 1991-; Northeastern University, professor, 1991-. **ORGANIZATIONS:** Registered architect, Massachusetts; AIA; IEEE; Lexington Chinese Language School, general manager, spokesman parent representatives. **BUSINESS ADDRESS:** Director, Research and Development, Sigma Design Inc, One Van de Graaff Dr, Burlington, MA 01803, (617)270-1000.

YANG, ANAND ALAN
Educator, educational administrator. Chinese American. **PERSONAL:** Born Jan 12, 1949, Shantineketan, Bengal, India; son of Yun Yuan & Loheng Yang; children: Sandrine. **EDUCATION:** Swarthmore College, BA, 1970; University of Virginia, PhD, 1976. **CAREER:** Sweet Briar College, visiting instructor, 1974; University of Utah, professor and chair, 1975-. **ORGANIZATIONS:** Association of Asian Studies, assistant editor, Journal of Asian Studies, 1993-; American Historical Association, professional division, 1991-93; Association of Asian Studies, board of directors, 1991-92; Association of Asian Studies, chair, council on conferences, 1991-92; American Historical Association, program committee, 1987; Repertory Dance Theater, national board, 1986-. **HONORS/AWARDS:** NEH, Travel to Collections, 1991; SSRC/ACLS, grant, 1989; Fulbright-Hays, faculty grant, 1983-84, Doctoral Dissertation Award, 1972-74. **SPECIAL ACHIEVEMENTS:** Editor, Peasant Studies, 1980-; author, The Limited Raj: Agrarian Relations in Colonial India, 1989; editor, Crime and Criminality in British India, 1986. **BUSINESS ADDRESS:** Professor, Dept of History, University of Utah, 211 Carlson Hall, Salt Lake City, UT 84112, (801)581-8596.

YANG, BAO-WEN
Research center administrator. Taiwanese American. **PERSONAL:** Born Oct 22, 1956, Taiwan; son of Chou-Ming Yang and Chin-Li Wei Yang; married Shu-Yi Hsiao, Jul 14, 1982; children: Eric, Stephanie H. **EDUCATION:** Tamkang University, Taiwan, BS, 1979; SUNY at Syracuse, MS, 1985; Columbia University, PhD, 1988. **CAREER:** Con-Edison, process engr, 1985, 1986; Columbia University, mgr, 1993-, group lead research engr, 1988-91, project mgr, 1991-93. **ORGANIZATIONS:** AIChE; ANS; TAPPI, 1982-85. **SPECIAL ACHIEVEMENTS:** Author, more than 35 papers and reports published in intl conferences and journals in the areas of thermal hydraulics, heat transfer, two-phase measurement, nuclear safety, flow instability/control/optimization including: "Optimal Control of Periodic Processes," 1988. **BUSINESS ADDRESS:** Manager, Heat Transfer Research Facility, Columbia University, 632 W 125th St, New York, NY 10027, (212)280-4163.

YANG, BINGEN
Educator. Chinese American. **PERSONAL:** Born Mar 4, 1955, Beijing, People's Republic of China; son of Chengzhong Yang and Yi-Ai Chen; married Haiyan Wang, Oct 20, 1958; children: Sonia Suyu. **EDUCATION:** Dalian Institute of Technology, China, BS, 1982; Michigan State University, MS, 1985; University of California at Berkeley, PhD, 1989. **CAREER:** Dalian Institute of Technology, research assistant, 1981-83; Michigan State University, research assistant, 1984; University of California, Berkeley, research assistant, 1985-89; University of Southern California, assistant professor, 1989-. **ORGANIZATIONS:** ASME, 1988-, design engr tech committee on vibration & sound, 1991-; AIAA, 1993-. **HONORS/AWARDS:** University of California, Regent Fellowship, 1985; Charles Lee Powell Foundation, Research Award, 1989; USC, Faculty Research and Innovation Award, 1990; NSF, Research Inititation Award, 1990; US Army Research Office, ARO Research Award, 1993. **SPECIAL ACHIEVEMENTS:** Author of 40 publications including: "Active Vibration Control of the Axially Moving String in the S Domain," JAM, 1991; "Eigenvalue Inclusion Principles for Distributed Gyroscopic Systems," JAM, 1992; "On Time Delay in Noncolorated Control of Flexible Mechanical Systems," JDSMC, 1992; "Transfer Functions of One-Dimensional Distributed Parameter Systems," JAM, 1992; "Exact Receptances of Non-Proportionally Dynamic Systems," J Vib & Acoust, 1993. **BUSINESS ADDRESS:** Asst Professor, Dept of Mechanical Engineering, University of Southern California, OHE 430, Los Angeles, CA 90089-1453, (213)740-7082.

YANG, CHEN NING
Educator, physicist. Chinese American. **PERSONAL:** Born Sep 22, 1922, Hofei, Anhwei, China; son of Meng Hwa Lo and Ke Chuan; married Chih Li

Tu, Aug 26, 1950; children: Franklin, Eulee, Gilbert. **EDUCATION:** National SW Assoc University, China, BS, 1942; University of Chicago, PhD, 1948. **CAREER:** University of Chicago, instructor, 1948-49; Princeton University, Institute for Advanced Study, member, 1949-55, professor, 1955-66; SUNY, Stony Brook, Albert Einstein Professor, 1966-, Institute for Theoretical Physics, director, 1966-. **ORGANIZATIONS:** Salk Institute, trustee, 1978-; Ben Gurion University, trustee, 1980-; American Physical Society; National Academy of Sciences; Royal Spanish Academy of Sciences; American Philosophical Society; Sigma Xi. **HONORS/AWARDS:** Nobel Prize, physics, 1957; Rumford Prize, 1980; National Medal of Science, 1986; Liberty Award, 1986; honorary DSc degrees: Princeton University, 1958; Brooklyn Poly Institute, 1956; University of Wroclaw, Poland, 1974; Gustavus Adolphus College, 1975; University of Maryland, 1979; University of Durham, England, 1979; Fudan University, 1984; Eldg Technische Hochschule, Switzerland, 1987. **BUSINESS ADDRESS:** Director/Albert Einstein Professor, Institute for Theoretical Physics, State University of New York, Stony Brook, Stony Brook, NY 11794-3840, (516)632-7980.*

YANG, CHIA CHI
Educator. Chinese American. **PERSONAL:** Born Aug 19, 1926, Wuhan, China; married Kathy Feng Yang. **EDUCATION:** National Chen Kung University, Taiwan, BS, 1949; Georgia Institute of Technology, MS, 1967, PhD, 1979. **CAREER:** Chen Kung University, Taiwan, instructor, 1949-57; Tunghai University, Taiwan, associate professor, chmn, dept of chemistry, 1957-70; Knox College, instructor, 1976-78; Middle Tennessee State University, assistant professor, 1978-80; Arkansas Tech University, professor of chemistry, 1980-. **ORGANIZATIONS:** American Chemical Society, 1980-; Chinese Chemical Engineer Society, 1949-70; Phi Delta Kappa Educator Society, 1989-; Arkansas Academy of Science, 1980-. **HONORS/AWARDS:** Arkansas Tech University, Annual Outstanding Faculty Award, 1993; Taiwan Provincial Government, Outstanding Undergraduate Junior Award, 1948. **HOME ADDRESS:** 12 Tanglewood Drive, Russellville, AR 72801, (501)968-6777. **BUSINESS ADDRESS:** Professor of Chemistry, Arkansas Tech University, N Arkansas Avenue, Russellville, AR 72801-2222, (501)968-0363.

YANG, CHIA HSIUNG
Educator, educational administrator. Taiwanese American. **PERSONAL:** Born Sep 24, 1940, Peikong, Taiwan; son of Shing Yang and Jing Tsay Yang; married Su-Ling Shih Yang, Jan 4, 1970; children: Susan, Candace, Chris. **EDUCATION:** Tunghai University, Taichung, Taiwan, BS, 1962; Tsing Hua University, Taiwan, MSc, 1965; Washington University, St Louis, MA, 1967, PhD, 1971. **CAREER:** Washington University, research associate, 1971; Southern University, assistant professor, 1971-76, associate professor, 1976-80, professor, 1980-87, professor and chairman, 1987-. **ORGANIZATIONS:** American Physical Society, 1965-; Sigma Xi, 1967-; Sigma Pi Sigma, 1971-; Taiwanese Association, Baton Rouge, 1972-, president, 1974-75. **HONORS/AWARDS:** Dept of Physics, SUBR, Outstanding Teacher, 1984, 1987; Faculty Senate, SUBR, Outstanding Physics Teacher, 1984; NASA, research grants, 1972-79; PDRC, research grants, 1991-. **SPECIAL ACHIEVEMENTS:** Author, "Cluster-Variation Calculations for Extended Nuclear Systems," Nuclear Phys, 1976; "Effects of Polarization on Superfluidity in Low Density Neutron Matter," Physics Lett, 1976; "Proton Superfluidity in Neutron Star Matter," Nuclear Physics, 1972; "Thermodynamic Critical Field of Superconducting Neutron Star Matter," Physics Letter al Nuovo Cimento, 1972. **MILITARY SERVICE:** ROC Air Force, 2nd lieutenant, 1962-63. **HOME ADDRESS:** 1062 Stoneliegh Dr, Baton Rouge, LA 70808. **BUSINESS ADDRESS:** Professor and Chairman, Dept of Physics, Southern University and A&M College, Wm James Hall, Rm 155, Harding Blvd, Baton Rouge, LA 70813, (504)771-4130.

YANG, CHIH TED
Government official. Chinese American. **PERSONAL:** Born Jan 23, 1940, Chung King, China; son of Tsui-Yi Yang and Amy Yao Yang; married Eveline Liu Yang, Nov 28, 1969; children: Michael, David. **EDUCATION:** National Cheng Kung University, BS, 1962; Colorado State University, MS, 1965, PhD, 1968. **CAREER:** Illinois State Water Survey, associate hydrologist, 1968-74; US Army Corps of Engineers, hydraulic engineer, 1974-78; University of Colorado, adjunct professor, 1982-; US Bureau of Reclamation, technical review staff, 1979-88, international & special projects coordinator, 1988-93, international & technical assistance program manager, 1993-. **ORGANIZATIONS:** American Society of Civil Engineers, fellow, Sedimentation Committee, chairman, 1987-88; American Geophysical Union; International Association of Hydraulic Research; International Association of Hydrological

Sciences; US Committee on Large Dams; Denver Federal Center Professional Engineers Group, president, 1990-91. **HONORS/AWARDS:** American Geophysical Union, Robert E Horton Award, 1972; American Society of Civil Engineers, Walter L Huber Prize, 1973, JC Stevens Award, 1980; National Society of Professional Engineers, Federal Engineer of the Year, 1983; Pakistan Engineering Congress, Gold Medal, 1986. **SPECIAL ACHIEVEMENTS:** Three books and more than 90 technical papers. **BUSINESS ADDRESS:** International and Technical Assistance Program Manager, US Bureau of Reclamation, PO Box 25007, Mail Code D-3240, Building 67, Denver Federal Center, Denver, CO 80225, (303)236-8541.

YANG, CHUN-YEONG
Attorney. Korean American. **PERSONAL:** Born Jul 18, 1968, Seoul, Republic of Korea; son of Se Wook Yang & Kyung Ja Kim; married Sun Hye Yang, Jun 3, 1989. **EDUCATION:** Harvard College, AB (cum laude), physics, 1989; Harvard Law School, JD (cum laude), 1992. **CAREER:** Fish & Neave, associate attorney, 1992-. **SPECIAL ACHIEVEMENTS:** Specializing in intellectual property law patents, copyright, trademarks; proficiency in Korean & Japanese. **HOME PHONE:** (201)226-4655. **BUSINESS ADDRESS:** Associate Attorney, Fish & Neave, 1251 Ave of the Americas, New York, NY 10020, (212)596-9151.

YANG, CHUNG S.
Educator, educational administrator. Taiwanese American. **PERSONAL:** Born Aug 8, 1941, Beijing, China; son of Su-Chuan Yang and Su-Fen Li Yang; married Sue Pei Y Yang, Jun 25, 1966; children: Arlene, Jenny. **EDUCATION:** National Taiwan University, BS, 1962; Cornell University, MS, 1965, PhD, 1967. **CAREER:** UMDNJ-Medical School, assistant professor, 1971-75, associate professor, 1975-79, professor, 1979-87; Rutgers University, professor II, associate chair, 1987-. **ORGANIZATIONS:** American Society of Biochemistry and Molecular Biology; American Society for Pharmacology and Experimental Therapeutics; American Institute of Nutrition; American Association for Cancer Research; Intl Society for the Study of Xenobiotics; NIH Chemical Pathology Study Section; US NCI & Cancer Institute, China, consultant, collaborator, 1980-; US NCI & Beijing Cancer Institute, consultant, 1987-; Shanghai Cancer Institute, China, consultant, 1985-; AICR, Grant Review Panel, 1991-93; ACS, Advisory Committee on Carcinogens and Nutrition, 1992-; AACRNJ Legislative Committee, 1990-; Basic Science Advisory Committee, 1991-; SCBA, president, 1994-95. **HONORS/AWARDS:** American Cancer Society, Faculty Research Award, 1971; Nutrition Foundation, Future Leaders Award, 1973; International Union Against Cancer, Technology Transfer Award, 1979; National Cancer Institute, Merit Award, 1987; NJ Association for Biomed Research, Distinguished Researcher Award, 1990; Rutgers University, Board of Trustees Award, 1991. **SPECIAL ACHIEVEMENTS:** Published more than 190 scientific papers. **BIOGRAPHICAL SOURCES:** "Research Diet's Role in Cancer Fight," New York Times, April 29, 1990; "Tea and Garlic May Stop Cancer, Researcher Says," The Courier News, 1992. **BUSINESS ADDRESS:** Professor II, Associate Chair, College of Pharmacy, Rutgers University, Frelinghuysen Rd, Laboratory for Cancer Research Bldg, Piscataway, NJ 08855, (908)932-5360.

YANG, CHYAN
Educator. Chinese American. **PERSONAL:** Born Jul 17, 1948, Jingchiang, Fukien, China; son of Dern Yang and Larnfoon Chen; married Anna Yang, Feb 12, 1977; children: Minnie, Conna, Camerdy. **EDUCATION:** National Chiao Tung University, Taiwan, MS, 1977; Georgia Institute of Technology, MS, 1980; University of Washington, PhD, 1987. **CAREER:** Burnham Van Service, system analyst, 1980-83; University of Washington, predoctoral research assistant, 1983-87; Naval Postgraduate School, assistant professor, 1987-92; National Chiao Tung University, associate professor, 1992-. **ORGANIZATIONS:** IEEE, senior member, 1990-; ACM, 1983-; Computer Simulation Society, committee, Taiwan, 1993-. **HONORS/AWARDS:** Phi Tau Phi, 1977. **SPECIAL ACHIEVEMENTS:** IEEE Transactions, Conferences, 1985-. **MILITARY SERVICE:** Army, Republic of China, second lieutenant, 1973-75. **HOME ADDRESS:** 7133 Bark Lane, San Jose, CA 95129. **BUSINESS ADDRESS:** Associate Professor, Institute of Information Management, National Chiao Tung University, 1001 TaHseuh Road, Hsinchu, Taiwan, 01188635.

YANG, DA-PING
Medical research scientist. Chinese American. **PERSONAL:** Born Oct 5, 1933, Beijing, China; son of Yu-Chang Yang and Hsin-Shiu Ho; married Augustina Yang, Sep 2, 1967; children: Yvonne, Victor. **EDUCATION:** Na-

tional Taiwan University, Taipei, BS, 1956; University of Ottawa, Canada, MSc, 1964, PhD, 1969. **CAREER:** University of Ottawa, instructor, 1965-68; National Research Council of Canada, postdoctoral fellow, 1968-70; Wyeth-Ayerst Labs, principal scientist, 1971-. **ORGANIZATIONS:** Tissue Culture Association, 1965-; International Association of Biological Standardization, 1991-. **HONORS/AWARDS:** National Institutes of Health, Principal Investigator, 1971-74; Food and Drug Administration, Principal Investigator, 1972-74. **MILITARY SERVICE:** Chinese Army, Taiwan, Republic of China, 2nd lt, 1956-58. **BUSINESS ADDRESS:** Principal Scientist, Wyeth-Ayerst Laboratories Inc, 145 King of Prussia Rd, Radnor, PA 19087, (215)341-2435.

YANG, DAVID C.

Educator. Taiwanese American. **PERSONAL:** Born Nov 7, 1954, Tainan, Taiwan; son of Wen-Shen Yang & Lee Chin-Huei Yang. **EDUCATION:** National Taiwan University, BA, economics, 1977; University of California, Berkeley, MBA, 1979; Columbia University, MPH, accounting, 1983, PhD, accounting, 1985. **CAREER:** Columbia University, Accounting Research Center, research associate, 1981-84; University of Hawaii, School of Accountancy, assistant professor, 1985-91, associate professor, 1991-, director, 1992-. **ORGANIZATIONS:** American Accounting Association, International Accounting Section, membership committee, chair, 1993-94; EDP Auditors Association, Hawaii chapter, treasurer, 1989, program director, 1988, publicity director, 1991-92; American Accounting Association, 1985-; Institute of Internal Auditors, Hawaii chapter, College Relations & University Committee, chair, 1986-88. **HONORS/AWARDS:** College of Business Administration University of Hawaii, Dennis Ching/First Interstate Memorial Teaching Award, 1993, Teaching Excellence Award, 1989; Beta Alpha Psi-Delta chapter, Outstanding Professor Award, 1992. **SPECIAL ACHIEVEMENTS:** Fluent in Chinese & Taiwanese; books published: Western Contemporary Finance Management; The Association between SFAS 33 Information and Bond Ratings; consultant, CIEC CPA firm in Beijing, China, Shanghai Academy of Social Science CPA firm in Shanghai. **BUSINESS ADDRESS:** Director, University of Hawaii, School of Accountancy, 2404 Maile Way, Honolulu, HI 96822, (808)956-6975.

YANG, DONGPYO (DON)

Certified public accountant. Korean American. **PERSONAL:** Born Dec 1, 1944, Kwangju, Chunnam, Republic of Korea; son of Bosung Yang and Soonsik Yang; married Chungae, Jun 7, 1969; children: Christopher Euyul. **EDUCATION:** Yonsei University, BA, 1968; University of Texas at Austin, MA, 1977, MPA, 1979. **CAREER:** The Dong-A Ilbo Newspaper, reporter, 1967-73; Deloitte & Touche, tax partner, 1980-. **ORGANIZATIONS:** Korean Chamber of Commerce NY, advisor, 1992-; Korean Traders Representatives NY, advisor, 1987-92. **SPECIAL ACHIEVEMENTS:** Taxation in the United States, 1987; US Tax Topics, 1990. **BIOGRAPHICAL SOURCES:** Featured in Korean Economic Daily. **BUSINESS ADDRESS:** Tax Partner, Deloitte & Touche, 1633 Broadway, New York, NY 10019, (212)492-4311.

YANG, EMIKO

Nurse, health administrator. Japanese American. **PERSONAL:** Born Oct 5, 1927, Waikapa, HI; daughter of Kazao Kamasaki and Shimoyo; divorced; children: Byron Duke, Leonard Reid, Lloyd Nelson. **EDUCATION:** University of Hawaii, 1947; Queen's Hospital School of Nursing, 1950. **CAREER:** Queen's Hospital, asst head nurse, 1950-55; Methodist Medical Center, OR nurse, 1956-66, Healthcare Services, clinical nursing supervisor, 1966-. **ORGANIZATIONS:** Illinois Nursing Administrators; United Way, panel mbr, 1978-; Planned Parenthood, board member, 1988-92; Community Partnership, focus group, 1992; Wildlife Prairie, volunteer, 1993; Sierra Club, volunteer. **HONORS/AWARDS:** Chicago Marathon, 4th in age group, 1990; Columbus Marathon, 3rd in age group, 1990; Houston Marathon, 2nd in age group, 1991. **SPECIAL ACHIEVEMENTS:** Study abroad: healthcare, People's Republic of China and the Philippines, 1982; Soviet Union, 1983; peak erosion, Ireland; archeological digs, Copan, Honduras; comparative study of national healthcare system, England, Scotland, 1984; medical missions to Haiti, 1980-83. **BIOGRAPHICAL SOURCES:** Peoria Journal Star, 1986, 1991. **HOME ADDRESS:** 6606 N Allen Rd, #92, Peoria, IL 61614, (309)691-5213. **BUSINESS ADDRESS:** Clinical Nursing Supervisor, Methodist Medical Center Healthcare Services, 221 NE Glen Oak Ave, Peoria, IL 61636, (309)672-5525.

YANG, HAN-JIANG (JOHN YOUNG)

Computer programmer, entrepreneur. Chinese American. **PERSONAL:** Born Oct 23, 1956, Guiyang, Guizhou, People's Republic of China; son of De-zeng Yang and Jin-xia Wang; married Ge-jin Wang, Aug 26, 1984; children: Yang

Yang, Franklin Young. **EDUCATION:** Guilford Tech Comm College, certificate, 1990; South China Institute of Technology, diploma, 1980; North Carolina A&T State University, MSEE, 1992. **CAREER:** Guiyang Quenjiang Mfg, engr, 1980-84; Guizhow Mech & Electronics Institute, engr, 1984-87; NC A&T State University, teaching asst, 1988-90, research asst, 1990-91; T W Service, programmer, 1991-92; Cotton Inc, programmer, 1992-93; Sunshine Enterprises, president, 1993-. **ORGANIZATIONS:** IEEE, 1989-91. **HONORS/AWARDS:** NC A&T State University, assistantship, 1988-91. **SPECIAL ACHIEVEMENTS:** Author: computer software packages, 1991-93; research papers, 1991; system design and research: projects for US Space Station PPS, 1990; system design and manufacturing: projects for hospital and residential heating, 1984-87. **HOME ADDRESS:** 320 S Walker St, #9, Cary, NC 27511, (919)469-5789. **BUSINESS PHONE:** (919)380-0299.

YANG, HEE K.

Dentist. Korean American. **PERSONAL:** Born Nov 19, 1955, Seoul, Republic of Korea; son of In Suk Yang and Kyung Ae Yang; married Joe Ming Kay Fung, Dec 25, 1979. **EDUCATION:** University of Texas, Health Science Center, Houston, Dental Branch; Baylor University. **CAREER:** Hee K Yang DDS, Inc, dentist, owner, currently. **ORGANIZATIONS:** American Dental Assn; Texas Dental Assn; Greater Dental Society; Academy of General Dentistry. **BUSINESS ADDRESS:** Dentist, Owner, Hee K Yang, DDS, Inc, 12403-C Scarsdale Blvd, Houston, TX 77089, (713)481-4777.

YANG, HENRY TZU-YOW

Educator, educational administrator. Chinese American. **PERSONAL:** Born Nov 29, 1940, ChungKing, Sichuan, China; son of Chen-pei Yang & Wei-gin Gee; married Dilling Teh-lin Tsui Yang, Sep 2, 1967; children: Maria, Martha. **EDUCATION:** National Taiwan University, BSCE, 1962; West Virginia University, MSCE, 1965; Cornell University, PhD, 1968. **CAREER:** Gilbert Associates, Reading, PA, structural engineer, 1968-69; Air Force Flight Dynamics Lab, visiting scientist, 1976; Space Industries International, board of dirs, 1993; Purdue University, School of Aeronautics & Astronautics, asst professor, 1969-72, associate professor, 1972-76, professor, 1976-, head, 1979-84, Schools of Engineering, dean, 1984-. **ORGANIZATIONS:** American Institute of Aeronautics & Astronautics, fellow, 1985; American Society of Mechanical Engineers; Society of Civil Engineers; American Society of Engineering Education; Tau Beta Pi; National Academy of Engineering, 1991; Academia Sinica, 1992. **HONORS/AWARDS:** Neil A Armstrong Distinguished Professor of Engineering, 1988; Governor Orr of the State of Indiana, Sagamore of the Wabash, 1988; US Air Force, Meritorious Civilian Service Award, 1989; Socitty of Engineering Education, Centennial Medal, 1993. **SPECIAL ACHIEVEMENTS:** Over 200 publications in the field of engineering. **BUSINESS ADDRESS:** Dean, Schools of Engineering, Purdue University, 1280 ENAD Bldg, West Lafayette, IN 47907-1280, (317)494-5346.

YANG, IN CHE

Government official. Chinese American. **PERSONAL:** Born Feb 7, 1934, Hsinchu, Taiwan; son of Ho Mu Yang and Hwang Tsin Yang; married Lih Huey Yang, Oct 6, 1966; children: Bayard, George Daniel, Norman Daniel. **EDUCATION:** National Taiwan University, BSc, engineering, 1956; Carleton University, MSc, 1966; University of Washington, PhD, 1971. **CAREER:** University of Washington, College of Fisheries, post-doctoral fellow, 1972-73, Dept of Geological Sciences, research associate, 1973-74, research assistant professor, 1974-78; US Geological Survey, Central Lab, section chief, radiochemistry, 1978-83, project chief, hydrochemistry, 1983-. **ORGANIZATIONS:** Standard Methods, American Water Work Association, Joint Task Group, 16th, 17th, 18th and 19th editions of Standard Methods, 1978-; National Handbook of Recommended Methods for Water-Data Acquisition, Work Group on Radioactivity, 1978-; American Geophysical Union, 1982-. **HONORS/AWARDS:** Department of Energy, contributions to the Yucca Mountain Public Outreach Program, 1992, 1993; US Geological Survey, Special Achievement Award, 1993, 1992, 1991, Group Cash Award on analyses of Mt St Helen erupted ashes, 1981; National Science Foundation, Travel Award to New Zealand, 1976. **SPECIAL ACHIEVEMENTS:** Author and co-author of more than 40 papers published in professional scientific journals, 1973-93. **BIOGRAPHICAL SOURCES:** Holt Earth Science, Holt, Rinehart and Winston Inc, 1994. **BUSINESS ADDRESS:** Project Chief, Hydrologic Investigation Program, US Geological Survey, MS 421, Denver Federal Center, PO Box 25046, Lakewood, CO 80225, (303)236-5178.

YANG, JEFFREY CHIH-HO
Publishing executive, editor, columnist. Taiwanese American. **PERSONAL:** Born Mar 14, 1968, Brooklyn, NY; son of David C Yang and Bailing Yang. **EDUCATION:** Harvard University, BA, psychology, 1989. **CAREER:** Asian Cinevision, publicist, 1991; Village Voice, columnist, 1993; A Magazine, The Asian American Quarterly, editor-in-chief, founder, 1989-; Metro East Publications, Inc, president & CEO, 1989-. **ORGANIZATIONS:** Asian American Journalists Association, 1989-; Asian American Writers Workshop, founding member, 1992. **BIOGRAPHICAL SOURCES:** New York Times, March 23, 1993. **BUSINESS ADDRESS:** President and Chief Executive Officer, Metro East Publications, Inc, 296 Elizabeth St, Ste 2F, New York, NY 10012, (212)505-1416.

YANG, JEN TSI
Educator. Chinese American. **PERSONAL:** Born Mar 18, 1922, Shanghai, China; son of Dao Kai Yang and Ho Ching Yu Yang; married Yee-Mui Lee Yang, Aug 8, 1949; children: Janet N, Frances A. **EDUCATION:** National Central University, China, BS, 1944; Iowa State University, PhD, 1952. **CAREER:** Iowa State University, research associate, 1952-54; Harvard University, research fellow, 1954-56; American Viscose Corp, research chemist, 1956-59; Dartmouth Medical School, associate professor, 1959-60; University of California, San Francisco, associate professor, 1960-64, professor, 1964-92, professor emeritus, 1992-. **ORGANIZATIONS:** American Chemical Society; American Society for Biochemistry & Molecular Biology; Biophysical Society; Protein Society; Sigma Xi. **HONORS/AWARDS:** John Simon Guggenheim Foundation, fellow, 1959-60; Commonwealth Fellow, 1967; Japan Society for the Promotion of Science, fellow, 1975. **SPECIAL ACHIEVEMENTS:** Research: Chiroptical Phenomena of Biopolymers; Structure-Function Relationship of Proteins. **MILITARY SERVICE:** Chinese Army, interpreter, 1944-45. **HOME PHONE:** (415)564-6213. **BUSINESS ADDRESS:** Professor, University of California, Cardiovascular Research Institute, San Francisco, CA 94143-0130.

YANG, JIANN-SHIOU
Educator. Taiwanese American. **PERSONAL:** Born Jul 30, 1954, Taiwan; married Liang-Pi Yang, Dec 29, 1986; children: Kevin. **EDUCATION:** National Chiao Tung University, Taiwan, BS, 1976, MS, 1978; University of Maryland, College Park, MS, 1983, PhD, 1988. **CAREER:** Naval Communications & Electronics Technology School, Taiwan, ensign, 1979-80; National Chiao Tung University, Taiwan, instructor, 1980-81; University of Maryland, College Park, teaching assistant, 1981-83, research asst, 1983-84 IBM fellow, 1985-86, Systems Research Center, fellow, 1986-87, research assistant, 1987-88; University of Minnesota, Duluth, assistant professor, 1988-. **ORGANIZATIONS:** IEEE Control System Society, 1987-, Robotics & Automation Society, 1992-; Phi Tau Phi Scholastic Honor Society, 1978-. **HONORS/AWARDS:** National Engineering Consortium, NEC Information Industry University Faculty Grants, 1991, 1992, 1993; University of Minnesota, Twin Cities, Faculty Summer Research Fellowships, 1989, 1991, Faculty Travel Grants, 1991, 1993, GIA Research Award, 1992; IBM, IBM Fellowship, 1985; University of Maryland, Systems Research Center, Fellowship, 1986; invited conference session chair, IASTED Intl Conf on Robotics and Manufacturing, 1993, American Control Conference, 1993. **SPECIAL ACHIEVEMENTS:** Technician license of electric power, national-wide exam for professionals & technicians, 1977; author, "H-Infinity Robust Control Design for Linear Feedback Systems," Journal of Guidance, Control and Dynamics, vol 16, no 6, p 1131-37, 1993; "An H-∞finity Method for the Design of LTI Multivariable Sampled-Data Control Systems," lecture notes, Control and Info Sciences, vol 111, Springer-Verlag, p 89-100, 1988, numerous others. **MILITARY SERVICE:** Chinese Navy, reserve officer, 1979-80. **BIOGRAPHICAL SOURCES:.** **BUSINESS ADDRESS:** Assistant Professor, Dept of Computer Engineering, University of Minnesota, 10 University Dr, 271 Marshall W Alworth Hall, Duluth, MN 55812.

YANG, JOHN ERIC
Newspaper editor. Chinese American. **PERSONAL:** Born Feb 10, 1958, Chillicothe, OH; son of Yih-Chang and Cynthia Poon Yang. **EDUCATION:** Wesleyan University, BA (cum laude), 1980. **CAREER:** The Boston Globe, staff writer, 1980-81; Time Magazine, correspondent, 1981-86; The Wall Street Journal, staff reporter, 1986-90; The Washington Post, staff writer/assistant financial editor, 1990-. **ORGANIZATIONS:** Asian American Journalists Association, national board of directors. **BUSINESS ADDRESS:** Assistant Financial Editor, Washington Post, 1150 15th St NW, Washington, DC 20071, (202)334-7454.

YANG, JOSEPH CHI-HOUNG
Dentist. Taiwanese American. **PERSONAL:** Born Jan 26, 1955, Taipei, Taiwan; son of Yi-Fung Yang and Chen-Yen Yang; married Li-Li Ma Yang, Aug 8, 1988; children: James, Joshua. **EDUCATION:** Washington University, DMD, 1988. **CAREER:** Yang's Dental Office, dentist, currently. **BUSINESS ADDRESS:** Dentist, Yang's Dental Office, 11851 E South St, Cerritos, CA 90701, (310)809-8911.

YANG, JULIE CHI-SUN
Industrial consultant. Chinese American. **PERSONAL:** Born Jun 10, 1928, Beijing, China; daughter of Shao T Yang and Chung-Yu Liu Yang. **EDUCATION:** National Tsing Hua University, Beijing, China, BS, 1949; Indiana University, MS, 1952; University of Illinois, Urbana, PhD, 1955. **CAREER:** University of Indiana, teaching assistant, 1950-52; University of Illinois, research assistant, 1952-53; Johns-Manville, senior research chemist, 1955-67, research associate, 1967-72; W R Grace & Co, senior group leader, 1972-74, research manager, 1974-92, consultant, 1992-. **ORGANIZATIONS:** American Chemical Society, 1955-, Tropical Group, officer, 1964-66; American Mineral Society, 1958-92; ASTM, 1985-. **HONORS/AWARDS:** Johns-Manville, Achievement Award, 1960, cash award for patent, 1965. **SPECIAL ACHIEVEMENTS:** 8 technical publications, 1961-70; 70-80 American and foreign patents, 1963-92. **HOME ADDRESS:** 6 Foster Rd, Lexington, MA 02173, (617)861-8360.

YANG, KAI
Educator. Chinese American. **PERSONAL:** Born Jun 18, 1956, Beijing, People's Republic of China; son of Kuan Hua Yang and Yishi Sun; married Jide Jin, Aug 4, 1982; children: Fan, Kevin J. **EDUCATION:** East China Petroleum Institute, BS, 1981; University of Michigan, MS, 1985, PhD, 1990. **CAREER:** University of Michigan, research assistant, 1984-90; Wayne State University, assistant professor, 1990-. **ORGANIZATIONS:** Institute of Industrial Engineers, senior member, 1991; ORSA/TIMS; south eastern Michigan, vice president; American Statistical Association. **HONORS/AWARDS:** East China Petroleum Institute, Honor Roll Scholarship, 1979. **SPECIAL ACHIEVEMENTS:** 14 journal papers in quality, reliability and optimization area; 5 sponsored research projects; 5 PhD students. **BUSINESS ADDRESS:** Asst Professor, Dept of Industrial & Manufacturing Engineering, Wayne State University, 5050 Anthony Wayne Dr, Rm 3160, Detroit, MI 48202-4095, (313)577-3858.

YANG, KARL L.
Physician, educator. Taiwanese American. **PERSONAL:** Born Oct 26, 1958, Taichung, Taiwan; son of Norman Y P Yang and Joyce Chi-Yuin Yang; married Wei Chen Yang, Jul 15, 1990. **EDUCATION:** West Virginia University, BS, 1980; University of Texas Medical School, San Antonio, MD, 1984. **CAREER:** Baylor College of Medicine, resident, 1984-87; University of Texas Medical School, Houston, fellow, 1987-90, assistant professor, 1990-. **ORGANIZATIONS:** American Thoracic Society, 1988-; American College of Chest Physicians, fellow, 1992-; Harris County Medical Society, 1993-; American Medical Association, 1984-. **SPECIAL ACHIEVEMENTS:** American Board of Internal Medicine, diplomate, 1987; American Board of Subspecialty-Pulmonary, diplomate, 1990. **BIOGRAPHICAL SOURCES:** "A Prospective Study of Indexes Predicting the Outcome of Wearing Trials," New England Journal of Medicine, pp 324:1445-50, 1991; "Reproductibility of Wearing Parameters, Chest," 102:1829-32, 1992. **HOME ADDRESS:** 7626 Westwind Ln, Houston, TX 77071, (713)272-9322.

YANG, KICHOON
Educator. Korean American. **PERSONAL:** Born Apr 12, 1955, Pusan, Republic of Korea; son of Mooyong Yang and Kyungsik Lee Yang; married Heejin Kim Yang, Aug 9, 1979; children: Eli. **EDUCATION:** University of North Carolina, BS, 1977; Washington University, PhD, 1982. **CAREER:** Arkansas State University, mathematics, assistant professor, 1982-86, associate professor, 1986-91, professor, 1991-. **ORGANIZATIONS:** American Mathematical Society, 1977-; Korean Mathematical Society, 1984-. **HONORS/AWARDS:** National Science Foundation Grant, 1983-86; ASU Faculty Research Grant, 1988-90; invited lectures in China, Korea & numerous US universities. **SPECIAL ACHIEVEMENTS:** Books published: Almost Complex Homogeneous Spaces and Their Submanifolds, 1987; Compact Riemann Surfaces and Algebraic Curves, 1988; Complete and Compact Minimal Surfaces, 1989; Complex Algebraic Geometry: an Introduction to Curves and Surfaces, 1991; Exterior Differential Systems and Equivalence Problems, 1992; Complete Minimal Surfaces of Finite Total Curvature, forthcoming. **BUSINESS ADDRESS:**

Professor, Dept of Mathematics, Arkansas State University, PO Box 70, State University, AR 72467, (501)972-3090.

YANG, LANG
Loss prevention agent. Laotian American/Hmong American. **PERSONAL:** Born Feb 12, 1968, Xieng Khouang, Lao People's Democratic Republic; son of Chia Kee Yang and May H Yang; married Phoua H Yang, Aug 15, 1987; children: Fouachee C, Gaoxee S. **EDUCATION:** Isothermal Community College, certificate, jailer certification, 1990; Mayland Community College, AAS (honors graduate), criminal justice, 1990; McDowell Technical Community College, AA, general education, 1990; Gardner-Webb University, BSCJ, 1992. **CAREER:** Lowes Food, grocery mgr, 1984-87; Frisbee's Super Market, asst mgr, 1987-88; Bi-Lo, dairy clerk, 1988-89; McDowell County Sheriff, jailer, 1989-90; Food Lion Inc, loss prevention agent, currently. **ORGANIZATIONS:** McDowell Technical Community College, SGA, vice pres, 1989. **SPECIAL ACHIEVEMENTS:** Language proficiency: English, Hmong; first Hmong police officer in North Carolina, 1989; recording artist: SAB NYOB Tom Tsev, 1990. **HOME ADDRESS:** Rt 1, Box 620, Nebo, NC 28761, (704)652-8242. **BUSINESS PHONE:** (704)633-8250.

YANG, NIEN-CHU C.
Educator. Chinese American. **PERSONAL:** Born May 1, 1928, Shanghai, China; son of Yu-Long Yang and Lan-Xi Cao Yang; married Ding-Djung Hwang Yang, Apr 24, 1954; children: Charles Chi-kang, Julia Ann C Yang Snyder, Morris Chi-hsin Yang. **EDUCATION:** St John's University, Shanghai, BS, 1948; University of Chicago, PhD, 1952. **CAREER:** MIT, research associate, 1952-55; Harvard University, research fellow, 1955-56; University of Chicago, assistant professor, 1956-61, associate professor, 1961-63, professor, 1963-92, Gustavus F & Ann M Swift Distinguished Service Professor, 1992-. **ORGANIZATIONS:** Institute of Organic Chemistry Academia Sinica, academic council, 1980-; Institute of Photographic Chemistry, Academia Sinica, honorary professor, 1979-; Institute of Chemistry, Taipei, advisory committee, 1985-; Chinese University of Hong Kong, external examiner, 1974-. **HONORS/AWARDS:** Academia Sinica, Taipei, 1982-; AAAS, fellow, 1993; New York Academy of Sciences, Gregory & Freda Halpern Award, 1981; Guggenheim Foundation, fellow, 1974; Sigma Xi, 1951; University of Chicago, Quantrell Prize for Excellence in Undergraduate Teaching, 1965, AMOCO Award for Distinguished Contribution to Undergraduate Teaching, 1992; Inter-American Photochemical Society, fellow, 1994-. **SPECIAL ACHIEVEMENTS:** Over 150 scientific publications in international scientific journals. **HOME ADDRESS:** 5729 S Blackstone Avenue, Chicago, IL 60637. **BUSINESS ADDRESS:** Gustavus F & Ann M Swift Distinguished Service Professor, Dept of Chemistry, University of Chicago, 5735 S Ellis Avenue, Chicago, IL 60637-1403, (312)702-7064.

YANG, QING
Educator. Chinese American. **PERSONAL:** Born Oct 8, 1957, Xifeng, Liaoning, People's Republic of China; son of Yitian Yang & Guifang Lu; married Liping Wu, Sep 8, 1983; children: Alicia W, Kerry F. **EDUCATION:** Huazhong University of Science & Technology, BS, 1982; University of Toronto, MASc, 1985; University of SW Louisiana, PhD, 1988. **CAREER:** University of Toronto, teaching assistant, 1983-85; University of SW Louisiana, research assistant, 1986-88; University of Rhode Island, assistant professor, 1988-93, associate professor, 1993-. **ORGANIZATIONS:** HUAAN, alumni association, president, 1993; IEEE, 1988-; ACM, 1989-. **HONORS/AWARDS:** National Science Foundation, Research Initiation Award, 1989, Research Award, 1992, Research Opportunity Award, Travel Award to Australia, 1992; University of Rhode Island, Faculty Excellence Award, 1993; University of SW Louisiana, dean's honor list, 1988. **SPECIAL ACHIEVEMENTS:** Over 40 refereed articles published in journals & proceedings, 1988-93; 5 book chapters, 1990; several patents and technical reports, 1988-92. **BUSINESS ADDRESS:** Associate Professor, Dept of Electrical Engineering, University of Rhode Island, Kelley Hall, Kingston, RI 02881, (401)792-5880.

YANG, RALPH TZU-BOW
Educator. Chinese American. **PERSONAL:** Born Sep 18, 1942, Chung King, China; son of Chen Pei Yang and Wei Jin Gee; married Frances Chang Yang, Dec 23, 1972; children: Michael, Robert. **EDUCATION:** National Taiwan University, BS, 1964; Yale University, MS, 1968, PhD, 1971. **CAREER:** Aluminum Co of America, scientist, 1973-74; Brookhaven National Lab, group leader, 1974-78; National Science Foundation, program director, 1987-88; State University of New York, associate professor, 1978-82, professor, 1982-, Dept of Chem Engineering, chairman, 1989-, Praxair Chair Professor, 1993-.

ORGANIZATIONS: American Institute of Chem Eng, Separations Division, director, 1992-, Adsorption Comm, chairman, 1989-91; American Carbon Society, advisory board, 1985-91; Industrial Engineering Chemistry Journal, advisory board, 1991-93; American Chem Society, 1972-; Adsorption Sci & Tech, advisory board, 1988-; American Society Eng Education, 1980-; J Adsorption, advisory board, 1993-. **HONORS/AWARDS:** American Institute of Chemical Engineers, William H Walker Award, Excellence in Contr to Chem Eng Literature, 1991; Alcoa, Tech Achievement Award, 1974. **SPECIAL ACHIEVEMENTS:** Author of two books on gas separation, 1987, 1989; author of 180 refereed journal publications; author of 10 US patents. **HOME ADDRESS:** 19 Pine Court, Williamsville, NY 14221. **BUSINESS ADDRESS:** Praxair Endowed Chair Professor, Dept of Chem Eng, State University of New York, Buffalo, NY 14260, (716)645-2909.

YANG, SCHUMAN CHUO
Educator (retired). Chinese American. **PERSONAL:** Born Dec 28, 1924, Canton, Kwantung, China; daughter of Shou-Kiu Lee and Chun-Sing Chuo; married Johann Y Yang, Jan 1, 1949; children: Johann Jr. **EDUCATION:** Wheaton College, BM, 1953; American Conservatory of Music, MM, 1958; George Peabody College, EdS, 1964, PhD, 1973. **CAREER:** Ohio County (Kentucky) State School System, music teacher, 1961-64; East Texas Baptist College, assistant professor, 1966-68; Louisiana Tech University, professor, 1968-93. **ORGANIZATIONS:** National Association of Teachers of Singing, 1966-, president, North Louisiana, 1979-80; National Opera Association, 1981-; Sigma Alpha Iota, 1963-. **HONORS/AWARDS:** American Association of University Women, College Faculty Fellowship Award, 1964-65; Association of Women Students, Louisiana Tech University, Outstanding Faculty, 1977; National Endowment of Humanities, Summer Seminar Award, 1979; Louisiana Tech University, Faculty Research Award, 1989. **SPECIAL ACHIEVEMENTS:** Lecture-recital on the development of "20th Century Chinese Songs," 1970-80; Louisiana Tech University Opera Workshop, director-producer, 1974-93. **HOME ADDRESS:** 2804 Belcara Dr, Ruston, LA 71270, (318)255-6022.

YANG, SHANG FA
Educator. Taiwanese American. **PERSONAL:** Born Nov 10, 1932, Tainan, Taiwan; son of Chiang-Zuei Yang; married Eleanor S Yang, Sep 16, 1965; children: Abert, Bryant. **EDUCATION:** National Taiwan University, BS, 1956, MS, 1958; Utah State University, PhD, 1962. **CAREER:** NYU Medical School, research associate, 1963-64; University of California, San Diego, research associate, 1964-66; University of California, Davis, research associate, 1962-63, assistant professor, 1966-69, associate professor, 1969-74, professor, 1974-. **ORGANIZATIONS:** Plant Physiology, editorial board member, 1974-92; Plant Physiology and Biochemistry, editorial board member, 1988-; Plant Cell Physiology, editorial board member, 1988-91; Journal of Plant Growth Regulation, associate editor, 1988-93. **HONORS/AWARDS:** Wolf Prize in Agriculture, 1991; JS Guggenheim Foundation, fellowship, 1983; International Plant Growth Substances Association, research award, 1986; National Academy of Sciences, 1990; Academia Sinica, Taipei, 1992. **SPECIAL ACHIEVEMENTS:** Published about 200 scientific articles, 1958-. **BUSINESS ADDRESS:** Professor, Mann Laboratory, University of California-Davis, 1118 Villanova Dr, Davis, CA 95616, (916)752-1414.

YANG, SHI-TIEN
Nuclear engineer. Taiwanese American. **PERSONAL:** Born Jul 9, 1946, Hsinchu, Hsinchu, Taiwan; son of Ssu-sung Yang and Li-ching Lin; married Yufen Yang, Sep 6, 1970; children: Justine, Jeffrey. **EDUCATION:** Tunghai University, BS, 1968; Massachusetts Institute of Technology, PhD, 1975. **CAREER:** Nuclear Services Corp, senior engineer, 1976-78; Science Applications Inc, senior scientist, 1978-79; Argonne National Laboratory, nuclear engineer, 1979-89; Commonwealth Edison, technical expert, nuclear design, 1989-. **ORGANIZATIONS:** American Nuclear Society, 1973-; North American Taiwanese Professors Association, 1984-. **HONORS/AWARDS:** Commonwealth Edison, Edison Outstanding Achievement Awards, 1991. **HOME ADDRESS:** 1113 Timber Ln, Darien, IL 60561. **BUSINESS PHONE:** (312)394-3879.

YANG, SONG
Educator. Chinese American. **PERSONAL:** Born Aug 14, 1961, Santai, Sichuan, People's Republic of China; son of Suzhen Yang; married Chunxiao Zhao, Aug 6, 1991. **EDUCATION:** Sichuan University, China, BS, 1982; Michigan State University, PhD, 1988. **CAREER:** Texas Tech University, assistant professor, 1988-. **ORGANIZATIONS:** Institute of Mathematical

Statistics, currently. **BUSINESS ADDRESS:** Assistant Professor, Texas Tech University, Lubbock, TX 79401, (806)742-1504.

YANG, SONG-YU
Scientist. Chinese American. **PERSONAL:** Born Oct 27, 1938, Wu-Xi City, Jiangsu, China; son of Rong-Geng Zong and Su-Fei Yang; married Xue-Ying He Yang, Jan 30, 1965; children: Ying-Zi, Yu-Xiao. **EDUCATION:** Peking Medical College, MD, 1960; City College of New York, MA, 1982; Graduate School of CUNY, PhM, 1983; City University of New York, PhD, 1984. **CAREER:** Peking Medical College, instructor, 1960-75; Shanghai Institute of Cell Biology, Academia Sinica, assistant professor, 1975-80; City College of City University of New York, teaching assistant, 1981-84; Research Foundation of CUNY, research associate, 1984-88; NYS Institute for Basic Research in Develomental Disabilities, research scientist, 1988-. **ORGANIZATIONS:** America Society for Biochemistry and Molecular Biology, 1985; AAAS, 1983; Sigma Xi, 1983. **HONORS/AWARDS:** City College of New York, L J Curtman Prize, 1984; American Heart Association, Wall Street Run Fellowship Award, 1991; Natl Institutes of Health, Public Health Service Grant Award, 1994. **SPECIAL ACHIEVEMENTS:** Contributed many articles to professional journals and books. **BUSINESS ADDRESS:** Research Scientist, NYS Institute for Basic Research in Developmental Disabilities, 1050 Forest Hill Rd, Staten Island, NY 10314, (718)494-5317.

YANG, SUN HYE
Accountant. Korean American. **PERSONAL:** Born Jan 9, 1966, Seoul, Republic of Korea; daughter of Chang Joo & Kyung Ja Yang; married Chun-Yeong Yang, Jun 3, 1989. **EDUCATION:** Harvard College, BA, 1988; Northeastern University, MS, 1991. **CAREER:** Harvard Law School, East Asian Legal Studies, staff, 1989-90; Arthur Andersen & Co, staff accountant, 1991-. **SPECIAL ACHIEVEMENTS:** Certified public accountant. **HOME ADDRESS:** 4 Rosemont Court, North Caldwell, NJ 07006, (201)226-4655. **BUSINESS ADDRESS:** Accountant, Arthur Andersen & Co, 1345 Avenue of the Americas, New York, NY 10105, (212)708-6349.

YANG, SUSAN Y.
Architecture/construction company associate. Chinese American. **PERSONAL:** Born Jan 28, 1955, Manila, Philippines; daughter of Yu Kim Giang and Chua Gim Land; married Thomas S Yang, Aug 9, 1981. **EDUCATION:** University of Philippines, Quezon City, BS, arch, 1977; University of Colorado at Denver, master's, urban and regional planning, 1981. **CAREER:** Chapa, draftsman, 1979; City of Denver, planning intern, 1980; City of Northglenn, planning technician, 1980-82; Kunz Construction Co, project designer, 1982-88; Karl W Schmidt & Associates, project manager, 1988-93; TSY Enterprises, currently. **ORGANIZATIONS:** American Business Womens Assn, 1992-; Sogetsu School of Flower Arranging, 1990-. **BUSINESS ADDRESS:** TSY Enterprises, 2877 Xenon St, Lakewood, CO 80215-7029, (303)238-3336.

YANG, SZE CHENG
Educator. Chinese American. **PERSONAL:** Born Mar 6, 1946, Nanking, China; son of Chialo Yang & Hui-ke L Yang; married Shiao-Lien Yang, 1970. **EDUCATION:** National Taiwan University, BS, 1967; Columbia University, PhD, 1973. **CAREER:** University of Iowa, post-doctoral fellow, 1973-75; National Taiwan University, associate professor, 1975-79; University of Rhode Island, professor, 1980-. **ORGANIZATIONS:** Rhode Island American Chinese Association, trustee, 1992-93; Department of Energy Housing Energy Conservation, Program Review Committee, 1990-92; American Chemical Society, 1973-; Materials Research Society, 1990-. **SPECIAL ACHIEVEMENTS:** Author: "Conducting Polymer as Electrochromic Material," part 7, in Large-Area Chromogenics: Materials and Devices for Transmittance Control, edited by C M Lampert, C G Granqvist, SPIE Press, 1990; 40 publications in professional journals. **BUSINESS ADDRESS:** Professor, Dept of Chemistry, University of Rhode Island, Pastore Chemical Laboratories, Kingston, RI 02881, (401)792-5081.

YANG, TAH-TEH
Educator, researcher. Chinese American. **PERSONAL:** Born Aug 15, 1927, Shanghai, China; married Jeffery Ann S Yang, Feb 24, 1963; children: Nanci Cathaci Yang Salzer, Timothy T. **EDUCATION:** Shanghai Institute, 1948; Oklahoma State University, MS, 1957; Cornell University, PhD, 1961. **CAREER:** Curtis & Wright Corp, Wright Aeronautical Div, project engineer, 1960-62; chief project engineer, 1962; Clemson University, Mechanical Engineering Dept, assistant professor, 1962-63, associate professor, 1963-69, professor, 1969-. **ORGANIZATIONS:** International Gas Turbine Institute, edu-

cational comm, vice chairman, 1990-92, chairman, 1992-94. **HONORS/AWARDS:** Strom Thurmond Institute, senior fellow, 1991-, fellow, 1990-; American Society of Mechanical Engineers, fellow, 1981-. **SPECIAL ACHIEVEMENTS:** Extensive experience in internal flow research, principal investigator for 28 projects over 31 years, specialized in diffuser flows in gas turbines, received funds externally for research totaling over 4 million dollars.

YANG, TIMOTHY C.
Engineer. Chinese American. **PERSONAL:** Born Jul 1, 1965, Stamford, CT; son of Jackson Yang and Monica Yang; married Elise Yang, Jul 14, 1990. **EDUCATION:** Michigan State University, BSEE (w/high honors), 1987; Cornell University, MSEE, 1988. **CAREER:** IBM-FSC, Owego, engineer, 1988-. **ORGANIZATIONS:** IEEE, 1986-; Phi Kappa Phi, 1986-; Eta Kappa Nu, 1984-. **SPECIAL ACHIEVEMENTS:** Drawing, painting, electronic repair, antique radio restoration. **BUSINESS ADDRESS:** Systems Engineer, IBM-FSC, Owego, 1801 Route 17C, MS 0200, Owego, NY 13827, (607)751-4298.

YANG, TSU-JU (THOMAS J.)
Educator, educational administrator. Taiwanese American. **PERSONAL:** Born Aug 14, 1932, Fengshang, Taiwan; son of Fu-Su Yang and Mon-Tau Hsu-Yang; married Sue N Yang, Jul 2, 1961; children: Kai H, Andrew T, Michael B. **EDUCATION:** National Taiwan University, BVM, 1955; Ministry of Examination, Taiwan, DVM, 1959; McGill University, PhD, 1971. **CAREER:** Academia Sinica, Taipei, Taiwan, associate member, 1961-64; University of Pennsylvania, research associate, 1964-66; University of Minnesota, research fellow, 1966-67; McGill University, demonstrator, 1968-71; University of Tennessee, assistant professor, 1971-75; Hall Institute of Medical Res, Melbourne, Australia, visiting fellow, 1983; National Taiwan University, Taipei, Taiwan, visiting professor, 1990; University of Connecticut, associate professor, 1975-78, professor, assistant head, 1978-. **ORGANIZATIONS:** American Association of Immunologists, currently; American Association for Cancer Research, currently; American Society for Microbiology, currently; American Association for the Advancement of Science, currently. **HONORS/AWARDS:** Ralston Purina Co, St Louis, MO, Animal Research Award, 1988; NIH, USA, research grants, 1973-85; USDA, USA, research grants, 1980-; National Dairy Council, USA, research grants, 1989-; American Kennel Club, New York, research grants, 1989-93. **SPECIAL ACHIEVEMENTS:** 110 journal articles on immunology, cancer research, hematology, cell biology, pathobiology, and veterinary science, 1962-. **BUSINESS ADDRESS:** Professor, Assistant Head, Dept of Pathobiology, University of Connecticut, U-89, 61 N Eagleville Road, Atwater Building, Room A160, Storrs Mansfield, CT 06269-3089, (203)486-3739.

YANG, TUEN-PING
Movie producer and director. Taiwanese American. **PERSONAL:** Born Dec 6, 1945, WuHan, Hubei, China; son of Chi Yang and Hsia-Yuen Y Yang; married Anna D Yang, Feb 22, 1977; children: Christina. **EDUCATION:** The School of Visual Arts, BA, 1973; University of California, Los Angeles, MFA, 1976. **CAREER:** Movie director, 25 years; Central Motion Picture Co, director/producer, 1985-88; Motech, vp, 1988-92; Cinema Systems Inc., president, currently. **ORGANIZATIONS:** UCLA Alumni Association; Taiwan Film Director's Association; Taiwan Cinematographer's Society; International Amusement Park Association; San Marino Chinese Club; Alhambra Rotary Club. **HONORS/AWARDS:** Taiwan National Film Festival, Golden Horse Award, Best Documentary Director, 1972, 1980; Taiwan TV Commercial Award, Best TV Commercial Director, 1977; Taiwan Cinematographic Society, Best Achievements Award, 1990. **SPECIAL ACHIEVEMENTS:** Tom Bradley, Mayor of Los Angeles, 1984; Dianne Feinstein, Mayor of San Francisco, 1984; Daniel Wong, Mayor of City of Cerritos, 1984; March Fong Eu, Secretary of State of California, 1993. **MILITARY SERVICE:** Taiwan Military Service, one year. **BUSINESS ADDRESS:** President, Cinema Systems, Inc, 616 S Del Mar Ave, Ste D, San Gabriel, CA 91776, (818)286-8648.

YANG, VICTOR CHI-MIN
Educator. Chinese American. **PERSONAL:** Born Jul 2, 1949, Shanghai, Jiangsu, People's Republic of China; son of Pei-Nan Yang and Wen-Ke Pang Yang; married Iris Sun Yun Yang, Aug 25, 1979; children: Joseph Li-Han, Emily Shi-Han. **EDUCATION:** Tamkang College, Taiwan, BS, 1972; East Texas State University, MS, 1977; Brown University, PhD, 1983; MIT, post-doctoral, 1985. **CAREER:** East Texas State University, research asst, 1975-77; Brown University, teaching/research asst, 1978-82; MIT, postdoctoral fellow, 1983-85, co-lecturer, 1984; University of Michigan, asst professor, 1986-90,

associate professor, 1990-. **ORGANIZATIONS:** American Chemical Society, 1986-; Biomedical Engineering Society, 1987-; American Society for Artificial Internal Organs, 1987-; AAAS, 1987-; American Assn of Pharmaceutical Scientists, 1988-; BioTechniques, editor, 1988-. **HONORS/AWARDS:** American Assn of Medical Instrumentation, Most Outstanding Manuscript Award, 1989; American Chemical Society, Arthur Doolittle Award, 1990; Whitaker Foundation, Biomedical Engineering Grant, 1987; NIH, FIRST Award, 1986, Heart Lung & Blood Institute Grant, 1993. **SPECIAL ACHIEVEMENTS:** Published over 50 scientific papers; editor, Cosmetic and Pharmaceutical Applications of Polymers; 8 US patents; developed first electrochemical sensor for heparin; developed first biofeedback heparin removing system. **MILITARY SERVICE:** Taiwanese Army, second lt, 1972-74. **BUSINESS ADDRESS:** Assoc Professor, The University of Michigan, College of Pharmacy, 428 Church St, Pharmacy Bldg, Rm 3056, Ann Arbor, MI 48109-1065, (313)764-4273.

YANG, WEITAO
Educator. Chinese American. **PERSONAL:** Born Mar 31, 1961, Chaozhou, Guangdong, China; son of Baoru Yang and Xunhua Li. **EDUCATION:** Peking University, Beijing, BS, 1982; University of North Carolina, PhD, 1986, postdoctoral, 1986-87; University of California, Berkeley, postdoctoral, 1988-89. **CAREER:** Duke University, assistant professor, 1989-. **ORGANIZATIONS:** American Physical Society, 1985-; American Chemical Society, 1988-; North Carolina Super Computing Center Research Institute, fellow, 1992-. **HONORS/AWARDS:** North Carolina Board of Science and Technology, North Carolina Science and Engineering Development Award, 1990; Alfred P Sloan Foundation, Sloan Research Fellow, 1993-95. **SPECIAL ACHIEVEMENTS:** Co-author with R G Parr, "Density-Functional Theory of Atoms and Molecules," Oxford University Press, 1989. **BUSINESS ADDRESS:** Professor, Department of Chemistry, Duke University, Durham, NC 27708, (919)660-1562.

YANG, WEN-CHING
Engineer. Taiwanese American/Chinese American. **PERSONAL:** Born Nov 11, 1939, Taipei, Taiwan; son of Ting-Lien Yang and Ho Lee Yang; married Rae Tien Yang, Aug 24, 1968; children: Evonne R, Peter T. **EDUCATION:** National Taiwan University, BS, 1962; University of California, Berkeley, MS, 1965; Carnegie Mellon University, PhD, 1968. **CAREER:** Westinghouse Electric Corp, senior engineer, 1968-75, fellow engineer, 1976-92, advisory engineer, 1993-. **ORGANIZATIONS:** American Institute of Chemical Engineers, chair & vice chair, Area 3b, fluidization and fluid/particle systems, 1983-87, chair, Group 3, contacting of particulates, operations and processes, 1992-; Particle Technology Forum, secretary, 1992-; American Chemical Society, 1976-; Chinese American Chemical Society, 1992-. **HONORS/AWARDS:** American Institute of Chemical Engineers, Fellow, 1992, Fluidized Processes Recognition Award, 1993. **SPECIAL ACHIEVEMENTS:** Published more than 75 papers on pneumatic transport fluidization and fluid/particle systems; 4 patents; edited 3 AIChE Symposium Series & a special issue of Powder Technology Journal; contributed 2 chapters to Encyclopedia of Fluid Mechanics. **HOME ADDRESS:** 236 Mount Vernon Avenue, Export, PA 15632, (412)327-3011. **BUSINESS ADDRESS:** Advisory Engineer, Westinghouse Electric Corporation, Science and Technology Center, 1310 Beulah Road, Pittsburgh, PA 15235, (412)256-2207.

YANG, WEN-JEI
Educator. Taiwanese American. **PERSONAL:** Born Oct 14, 1931, Kaohsiung, Taiwan; son of Shui-Lai Yang and Chin-Tsa Lin Yang; married Shu-Yuan Lin Yang, May 31, 1960; children: Ling-Hsiang, Mimi Ling-Ing, Paul Po-Tsang. **EDUCATION:** National Taiwan University, BS, 1954; University of Michigan, MS, 1956, PhD, 1960. **CAREER:** Ford Motor Company, research engineer, 1957-58; Mitsui Shipbuilding Co, research engineer, 1960-61; Westinghouse Electric Corp, fellow engineer, 1967; University of Michigan, lecturer, 1961-62, assistant professor, 1962-65, associate professor, 1965-70, mechanical engineering professor, 1970-. **ORGANIZATIONS:** Pacific Center of Thermal-Fluid Engineering, president, 1990-; International Conferences on Mechanics in Medicine and Biology, coordinator, 1978-; Michigan Academy of Science, Arts and Letters, Academy Council, 1972-74. **HONORS/AWARDS:** Japan Society for the Promotion of Science, Senior Scholar, 1982; American Soc Mech Engrs, Heat Transfer Memorial Award, 1984; International Flow Visualization Society, C Strouhal Award, 1989; Council for International Exchange of Scholars, J W Fulbright Award, 1991; Japan Society Mech Engrs, Thermal Engineering Memorial Award, 1992. **SPECIAL ACHIEVEMENTS:** Handbook of Flow Visualization, ed, 1989; Biothermal Fluid Sciences—Principles and Applications, 1989; Flow Visualization III, ed, 1985; Computer-Assisted Flow Visualization—Principles and Applications, 1993; over 380 articles and 15 books. **BUSINESS ADDRESS:** Professor, Mechanical Engineering & Applied Mechanics, University of Michigan, 2150 G G Brown Building, Ann Arbor, MI 48105, (313)764-9910.

YANG, WILLIAM C. T.
Educator. Chinese American. **PERSONAL:** Born Nov 30, 1922, Peking, Hopei, China; son of M L Yang & Hwa Ru Chao; married Ben-yi Yang, Nov 11, 1964. **EDUCATION:** Soochow University, BS, 1942; University of Southern California, MS, 1950, PhD, 1956. **CAREER:** Soochow University, instructor, 1946-48; University Southern California, teaching assistant, 1948-51, research assistant, 1951-55, post-doctoral fellow, 1955-56, instructor, 1956-89, professor emeritus, 1989-. **HONORS/AWARDS:** Soochow University, Phi Tau Phi, 1946; University of Southern California, Phi Sigma Award for Excellence in Biological Science, 1950; Best Teacher Award, 1967, 1970, 1974, 1976. **SPECIAL ACHIEVEMENTS:** Research in: culture of protozoans, metabolism of cardiac mitochondria, and the function of cardiac creatine phosphokinase. **BUSINESS ADDRESS:** Professor Emeritus, University of Southern California, School of Medicine, 2033 Zonal Ave, Keith Bldg, Los Angeles, CA 90033, (213)342-1781.

YANG, WINSTON L.
Educator, educational administrator. Chinese American. **PERSONAL:** Born Jun 1, 1933, Nanking, China; son of Chu-yi Yang; married Teresa Yang, Jun 1, 1968; children: David, Elaine. **EDUCATION:** National Taiwan University, BA, 1958; Stanford University, PhD, 1970. **CAREER:** San Francisco State University, Department of Asian Studies, lecturer; Winthrop College, Department of Asian Studies, associate professor, chair, 1968-69; Seton Hall University, Department of Asian Studies, professor, 1972-, chair, 1984-. **ORGANIZATIONS:** Royal Asiatic Society, fellow, 1974-. **HOME ADDRESS:** 32 Spring Rd, Livingston, NJ 07039, (201)994-2094. **BUSINESS ADDRESS:** Professor, Chair, Dept of Asian Studies, Seton Hall University, South Orange, NJ 07079-2697, (201)761-9464.

YANG, XIAOWEI
Electrical engineer, educator. Chinese American. **PERSONAL:** Born Jul 19, 1954, Shanghai, China; son of Yi-Fang Yang and Yi-Min Wang Yang; married Diming Wan, Jul 22, 1983; children: Yuan, Jessica Lin. **EDUCATION:** Wuhan University, China, BS, 1978; East China Normal University, Shanghai, MS, 1982; University of Maryland, College Park, MS, 1988, PhD, 1989. **CAREER:** East China Normal University, lecturer, 1982-83; University of Maryland, College Park, teaching asst, 1984-86, research asst, 1986-89, research associate, 1989-92; Multichannel Concepts, Inc, manager for product development, 1990-93; University of Maryland University College, adjunct asst professor, 1993-; Cambridge Research Associates, Inc, senior systems engineer, 1993-. **ORGANIZATIONS:** IEEE, 1987-, Signal Processing Society, 1987-, Communication Society, 1987-, Neural Network Society, 1990-. **HONORS/AWARDS:** NIH, SBIR Grant, 1991; China Education Ministry, Study Abroad Fellowship, 1983. **SPECIAL ACHIEVEMENTS:** Publications: IEEE Transaction on Information Theory, 1992; Biological Cybernetics, 1991; Biophysical Journal, 1990; IEEE Transactions on Biomedical Engineering, 1988; Electronics Technology, 1984. **BUSINESS ADDRESS:** Senior Systems Engineer, Cambridge Research Associates, Inc, 1430 Spring Hill Road, Ste 200, Mc Lean, VA 22102, (703)790-0505.

YANG, YIH-MING
Physician, educator. Taiwanese American. **PERSONAL:** Born Jul 13, 1947, Hualien, Taiwan; son of Sol Yang and Si-Mei Yang; married Yia-Mei Yang, Jun 15, 1974; children: David M, Mark L. **EDUCATION:** China Medical College, MD, 1972. **CAREER:** Charity Hospital of Louisiana, staff pediatrician, 1977-88; LSU School of Medicine, instructor of pediatrics, 1978-80; Children's Hospital of New Orleans, staff pediatrician, 1978-80; The Mennonite Christian Hospital, Department of Pediatrics, head, 1980-86; China Medical College, Taiwan, associate professor of pediatrics, 1982-86; University of South Alabama, assistant professor of pediatrics, 1981-88, associate professor of pediatrics, 1991-. **ORGANIZATIONS:** American Medical Association, 1975-; American Academy of Pediatrics, 1980-; Pediatric Society of Republic of China, 1981-; Taipei Childhood Leukemia Study Group, TCL841 Study Protocol, coordinator, 1984-86; American Society of Pediatric Hematology/Oncology, 1982-; American Society of Clinical Oncology, 1984-; American Society of Hematology, 1987-; Medical Association of the State of Alabama, 1988-; Hualien Childhood Leukemia Foundation, Taiwan, founder, 1982.

HONORS/AWARDS: University of South Alabama, Department of Pediatrics, Ped House Staff, Best Role Model, 1989, Excellence in Resident Teaching, 1990-91, Best Resident Teaching, 1991-92, Resident Advocate Award, 1992-93; Hualien County Medical Assn, Taiwan, Outstanding Physician's Award, 1986. **BUSINESS ADDRESS:** Associate Professor, Dept of Pediatrics, University of South Alabama, 2451 Fillingim St, #1065 MCSB, Mobile, AL 36617, (205)471-7335.

YANG, YISONG
Educator. Chinese American. **PERSONAL:** Born May 3, 1958, Beijing, People's Republic of China; daughter of Zhaoqi Yang and Hua Han; married Sheng Wang, Jan 12, 1985; children: Peter Huayue. **EDUCATION:** Henan University, BS, 1982; Chinese Academy of Sciences, MS, 1985; University of Massachusetts, PhD, 1988. **CAREER:** University of Minnesota, postdoctoral member, 1988-89; University of New Mexico, assistant professor, 1989-92, associate professor, on leave of absence, 1993-; Carnegie Mellon University, assistant professor, 1992-93; Institute for Advanced Study, 1993-94. **ORGANIZATIONS:** American Mathematical Society, 1985-; London Mathematical Society, 1991-. **HONORS/AWARDS:** University of Massachusetts, University Graduate Fellowship, 1986; University of New Mexico, Efroymson Award, 1991. **SPECIAL ACHIEVEMENTS:** More than thirty published research articles on applied mathematics, theoretical physics, and numerical methods. **BUSINESS ADDRESS:** Professor, Dept of Mathematics, Carnegie Mellon University, Wean Hall 6211, Pittsburgh, PA 15213, (412)268-6471.

YANG, ZHANBO
Educator. Chinese American. **PERSONAL:** Born Feb 3, 1958, Harbin, Heilongjiang, People's Republic of China; son of Baozhi Yang & SuQing Li; married Liping Peng, Apr 13, 1985; children: Brenda Wei. **EDUCATION:** Heilougjiang University, Harbin, China, BS, 1982, MS, 1985; Auburn University, Auburn, Alabama, PhD, 1989. **CAREER:** Shawnee State University, mathematics, associate professor, 1989-. **ORGANIZATIONS:** American Mathematics Society; Mathematics Association of America; South Central Ohio Council of Teachers of Mathematics. **SPECIAL ACHIEVEMENTS:** Publication of research papers; grants for teaching innovation with technologies. **BUSINESS ADDRESS:** Associate Professor of Mathematics, Shawnee State University, 940 2nd St, Business Annex, Rm 121, Portsmouth, OH 45662, (614)355-2363.

YANO, FLEUR B.
Educator. Chinese American. **PERSONAL:** Born Sep 26, 1934, Beijing, China; daughter of Charles K A Wang and Flora Belle Jan; married Alva F Yano, 1959; children: Robert William. **EDUCATION:** Columbia University, BS, 1954, University of Southern California, MA, 1958; University of Rochester, PhD, 1966. **CAREER:** California State University, Los Angeles, professor, 1964-. **ORGANIZATIONS:** American Physical Society, 1964-; Chinese Engineers & Scientists Society of Southern California, 1979-. **BUSINESS ADDRESS:** Professor, California State University, Los Angeles, Department of Physics and Astronomy, 5151 State University Dr, Los Angeles, CA 90032, (213)343-2100.

YANO, RONALD MAKOTO
Controller, chief financial officer. Japanese American. **PERSONAL:** Born May 22, 1945, Denver, CO; son of Mr & Mrs Thomas Yano; married Julia K Yano, Aug 14, 1971; children: Jason, Adam. **EDUCATION:** Los Angeles City College, AA, 1966; University of Southern California, BS, 1971. **CAREER:** Arthur Young & Company, auditor, 1971-74; Fluor Corporation, division controller, 1974-88; Orrick, Herrington, controller, 1988-93; Loeb and Loeb, chief financial officer, 1993-. **ORGANIZATIONS:** Members in Industry, California Society of Certified Public Accountants, San Francisco Chapter, co-char, 1991-93. **BIOGRAPHICAL SOURCES:** US Navy, E-5, 1966-68. **BUSINESS ADDRESS:** Chief Financial Officer, Loeb and Loeb, 1000 Wilshire Blvd, Suite 1800, Los Angeles, CA 90017, (213)688-3400.

YAO, DAVID D.
Educator. Chinese American. **PERSONAL:** Born Jul 14, 1950, Shanghai, People's Republic of China; son of Kang-Fu Yao & Yun-Lan Lu; married Helen Chen Yao, Jan 31, 1979; children: Henry J, John J. **EDUCATION:** Fudan University, BS, 1979; University of Toronto, MASc, 1981, PhD, 1983. **CAREER:** Columbia University, industrial engineering and operations research, assistant professor, 1983-86; Harvard University, systems engineering, associate professor, 1986-88; Yale University, operations research, visting professor, 1991-92; Columbia University, industrial engineering and opera-

tions, research professor, 1988-, Thomas Alva Edison Professor, 1992-. **ORGANIZATIONS:** IEEE, senior member; Operations Research Society of America; Society of Industrial and Applied Mathematics. **HONORS/AWARDS:** Guggenheim Foundation, Guggenheim fellow, 1991-92; National Science Foundation, Presidential Young Investigator, 1987-92; Operations Research Society of America, George E Nicholson Jr Memorial Award, 1983. **SPECIAL ACHIEVEMENTS:** Over 80 archival publications in scientific journals; co-author, Monotone Structure in Discrete-Event Systems, Wiley, 1993; associate editor, eight scientific journals. **BUSINESS ADDRESS:** Thomas Alva Edison Professor, IEOR Dept, Columbia University, 302 Mudd Bldg, New York, NY 10027-6699, (212)854-2934.

YAO, DENNIS ALDEN
Government official, educator. Chinese American. **PERSONAL:** Born Aug 29, 1953, Urbana, IL; son of Alden K Yao & Josephine Shen Yao; married Jane Morley, Mar 23, 1985. **EDUCATION:** Princeton University, BSE, 1975; University of California, Berkeley, MBA, 1977; Stanford University, PhD, 1984. **CAREER:** Ford Motor Co, product planning group analyst/chief analyst, 1977-79; University of Pennsylvania, Wharton School, assistant professor, 1980-90, Wharton School, associate professor, 1990-. **ORGANIZATIONS:** Strategic Management Journal, editorial board, 1992-. **HONORS/AWARDS:** University of Pennsylvania, MA (honorary), 1990; Huntsman Center, Wharton School, fellow, 1990; CitiFellowship, Snider Entrepreneurial Center, Wharton, 1989; Fishman-Davidson Center, Wharton, fellow, 1985. **SPECIAL ACHIEVEMENTS:** Articles in the American Economic Review, Quarterly Journal of Economics, American Journal of Political Science, Public Choice, Journal of Policy Analysis and Management, Strategic Management Journal, Journal of Industrial Economics, and the RAND Journal of Economics. **BUSINESS ADDRESS:** Commissioner, US Federal Trade Commission, 6th & Pennsylvania Ave, NW, Rm 326, Washington, DC 20580, (202)326-2175.

YAO, DORCAS C.
Physician. Taiwanese American. **PERSONAL:** Born in Taipei, Taiwan; daughter of John & Grace Yao. **EDUCATION:** Massachusetts Institute of Technology, SB, 1986; University of Pennsylvania School of Medicine, MD, 1990. **CAREER:** Cooper Hospital, University Medical Center, medical intern, 1990-91; Yale-New Haven Hospital, radiology resident, 1991-93; University of California San Francisco School of Medicine, radiology resident, currently. **ORGANIZATIONS:** American Roentgen Ray Society, 1991-; American Association for Women Radiologists, 1991-. **HONORS/AWARDS:** Alpha Omega Alpha Medical Honor Society, 1990; American Women Medical Association, Scholastic Citation, 1990; Phi Beta Kappa, 1986. **BUSINESS ADDRESS:** Radiology Resident, Dept of Radiology, University of California San Francisco, 505 Parnassus Avenue, San Francisco, CA 94143-0628.

YAO, LUN-SHIN
Educator. Chinese American. **PERSONAL:** Born Oct 25, 1943, China; son of Shao-Yung and Ya-Yun Yau; married Jeannie, Nov 4, 1987; children: Mike, Dwight, Alice. **EDUCATION:** Cheng-Kung University, Tainan, Taiwan, BSE, 1966; University of Texas, Austin, MSE, 1968; University of California, Berkeley, PhD, 1974. **CAREER:** Rand Corporation, research staff, 1975; University of Illinois, assistant professor, 1978; Arizona State University, Dept of Mech Engineering, professor, 1981-. **BUSINESS ADDRESS:** Professor, Dept of Mechanical Engineering, Arizona State University, Tempe, AZ 85287-0001, (602)965-5914.

YAO, SHI CHUNE
Educator. Chinese American. **PERSONAL:** Born Dec 31, 1946, Taipei, Taiwan; son of S C Yao; married Taiti Yas, 1972; children: S H, S D. **EDUCATION:** University of California, Berkeley, PhD, 1974. **CAREER:** Carnegie Mellon University, assistant professor, 1977-80, associate professor, 1980-83, professor, 1983-. **ORGANIZATIONS:** ASME, Combustion Committee, vice chairman, 1992-, Heat Transfer Division, 1974-; Combustion Institute, 1980-. **HONORS/AWARDS:** ASME, life fellow, 1989. **SPECIAL ACHIEVEMENTS:** Published 4 books; more than 100 articles in technical publications on heat transfer and combustions. **BUSINESS ADDRESS:** Professor, Dept of Mechanical Engineering, Carnegie Mellon University, Scaife Hall 205, Pittsburgh, PA 15213, (412)268-2508.

YAP, STACEY G. H.
Educator. Singaporean American. **PERSONAL:** Born 1955, Singapore; daughter of Yap Twee (deceased) and Kok Ho Tan; married Peng-Khuan Chong, 1984; children: Raina Ee-Leng Chong. **EDUCATION:** Northeastern

University, Boston, BS, BA, 1977; Boston University, MA, 1979, PhD, 1983. **CAREER:** Marketing Institute of Singapore, lecturer, 1983-84; Consensus Marketing Research SE Asia Ltd, research director, 1983-84; University of New Hampshire, School for Lifelong Learning, adjunct faculty, 1985-88; New Hampshire College, adjunct faculty, 1985-86; Plymouth State College, adjunct faculty, 1986-88, assistant professor, 1988-92, associate professor, 1993-. **ORGANIZATIONS:** Plymouth State Colleges, Women Studies Council, chair, 1991-; American Sociological Association; Association of Asian Studies, National and New England Chapter; Association for Asian American Studies; National Womens Studies Association; Association for Women in Development; Wellesley College, Center for Research on Women, associate; Pi Gamma Mu Society; New Hampshire Women in Higher Education, 1984-. **SPECIAL ACHIEVEMENTS:** Book: Gather Your Strength, Sisters: The Emerging Role of Chinese Women Community Workers, New York: AMS Press Inc, 1989; published articles: "Have You Ever Heard of Asian American Feminism?" in Women's Images and Reality: A Multicultural Anthology About Women, Mayfield Pub, 1994; Chinese American Families, co-author, Ethnic Families, McGraw-Hill, 1994. **BUSINESS ADDRESS:** Associate Professor, Social Science Dept, Plymouth State College, Rounds Hall, Plymouth, NH 03264-1600, (603)535-2333.

YASUMURA, SEIICHI
Educator. Japanese American. **PERSONAL:** Born Sep 28, 1932, New York, NY; son of Jobu & Rae Ota Yasumura; married Lee, Feb 13, 1963; children: Lyn, Robert. **EDUCATION:** Occidental University, BA, 1958; University of Cincinnati, PhD, 1962. **CAREER:** State University of New York-Health Science Center, Brooklyn, assistant professor, beginning 1964, professor of physiology, currently. **HONORS/AWARDS:** Fulbright Scholar, 1992. **MILITARY SERVICE:** US Army, 1954-56. **BUSINESS ADDRESS:** Professor of Physiology, State University of New York, Health Science Center, 450 Clarkson Ave, Box 31, Brooklyn, NY 11203, (718)270-3102.

YAU, CHEUK CHUNG
Chemist. Chinese American/Hong Kong American. **PERSONAL:** Born Apr 21, 1950, Hong Kong; son of To Sang Yau and Kowk Yung Yau; married Karen Yuen Tam Yau, Dec 27, 1977; children: Vincent Han Young, Stephen Han Chiu, Warren Han Dung. **EDUCATION:** University of Hawaii, BS, 1974; Georgia Institute of Technology, PhD, 1979. **CAREER:** Tennessee Eastman Co, development chemist, 1979-84, Eastman Chemical Co, senior research chemist, 1986-89, principal research chemist, 1989-91, research associate, 1991-. **ORGANIZATIONS:** American Chemical Society, 1979-. **SPECIAL ACHIEVEMENTS:** Co-author, "Perhydroazulenes, The 2-t-tert-butylperhydroazulen-4-one system", 1979; "Chemistry of Carbanions, Formation of the Perhydroazulene System by Intramolecular Alkylation", 1978; "Chemistry of Carbanions, Cyclization of the Metal Enolates from Omega-bromo Ketones", 1978; "Synthesis of Omega-bromo Ketones", 1977; "Photochemistry of Polyenes, VIII, Preparation of Sterically Hindered Geometric Isomers of 7-cis-beta-ionyl and Beta-ionylidene Derivatives in the Vitamin A Series", 1975; patent granted: US005145742, 1992. **HOME ADDRESS:** 313 Highridge Road, Kingsport, TN 37660.

YAU, KING-WAI
Educator. Chinese American. **PERSONAL:** Born Oct 27, 1948, Canton, China; son of Tin-Man Yau & Wai-Hing Chan; married Crystal L Yau, Dec 27, 1975; children: Emily, Jason. **EDUCATION:** University of Hong Kong, Faculty of Medicine, 1967-68; University of Minnesota, Minneapolis, 1968-69; Princeton University, AB, 1971; Harvard University, PhD, 1976. **CAREER:** Stanford University School of Medicine, post-doctoral fellow, 1976-79; University of Cambridge, England, post-doctoral fellow, 1979-80; University of Texas, Medical Branch at Galveston, assistant professor, professor, 1980-86; Howard Hughes Medical Institute, investigator, 1986-; Johns Hopkins School of Medicine, professor of neuroscience, 1986-. **ORGANIZATIONS:** Society of Neuroscience; Biophysical Society; Association for Research in Vision and Ophthalmology; Society of General Physiologists; The Physiological Society, England. **HONORS/AWARDS:** Rank Prize Funds, Rank Prize in Optoelectronics, 1980; ARVO, Friedenwald Award, 1993. **BUSINESS ADDRESS:** Professor of Neuroscience, Johns Hopkins School of Medicine, 725 N Wolfe St, Baltimore, MD 21205, (410)955-1260.

YAU, STEPHEN SHING-TOUNG
Educator. Hong Kong American. **PERSONAL:** Born Apr 12, 1952, Hong Kong; son of Ching Ying Yau and Yeuk Lam Leung; married Eileen Lai-Wing Yau, Jul 5, 1985; children: Andrew Duh-Wah. **EDUCATION:** The Chinese

University of Hong Kong, 1970-73; State University of New York, Stony Brook, MA, 1974, PhD, 1976. **CAREER:** Institute of Advanced Study, School of Mathematics, 1976-77, 1981-82; Harvard University, assistant professor, 1977-80; Yale University, visiting professor of mathematics, 1984-85; Johns Hopkins University, visiting professor of mathematics, 1989-90; University of Illinois, Chicago, associate professor of mathematics, 1980-84, professor of math stat & comp science, 1984-, control & information lab director, 1993-. **ORGANIZATIONS:** Institute of Electrical & Electronic Engineers, senior member, 1993-; Society for Industrial and Applied Mathematics, 1989-; American Mathematical Society, 1981-; University Press, Journal of Algebraic Geometry, managing editor, 1991-. **HONORS/AWARDS:** Alfred P Sloan Foundation, Research Fellowship, 1980-82; University of Illinois, University Scholar, 1987-90; American Mathematical Society, invited one-hour address at Worchester, MA, 1985; Swedish Mathematical Society, invited one-hour address at annual meeting, 1987. **SPECIAL ACHIEVEMENTS:** Solution to Complex Plateau problem; classification of isolated hypersurface singularities; establishing theory connecting isolated hypersurface singularities & solvable Lie Algebras; establishing the most general kind of finite dimensional filters; explicit closed form solution to Kolmogorov equation. **BUSINESS ADDRESS:** Professor of Mathematics, Director of Control and Information Laboratory, University of Illinois, Chicago, 851 S Morgan, SEO 322 m/c 249, Chicago, IL 60607, (312)996-3065.

YAZAKI, TOYU
Translator, interpreter. Japanese American. **PERSONAL:** Born Feb 18, 1954, Tokyo, Japan; son of Chiharu Yazaki; married Junko Yazaki; children: Anthony Yu. **EDUCATION:** North Seattle Community College, 1972-73; Claremont Men's College, 1973-75; Stanford University, 1975-76, 1982-83. **CAREER:** Self-employed interpreter, translator, currently. **ORGANIZATIONS:** ATA; NCTA. **BUSINESS ADDRESS:** Translator, Interpreter, 391 Sutter St, Ste 601, San Francisco, CA 94108, (415)391-9308.

YE, JOSE
Accounting assistant. Filipino American/Chinese American. **PERSONAL:** Born Aug 25, 1934, Iloilo City, Philippines; son of Kui Ye and Choi Yung Ham; married Nilda Ye, Mar 24, 1963; children: Wilson Chu, Helen. **EDUCATION:** University of Iloilo, Philippines, BSc, 1963; Lincoln University, MBA, 1974; Vancouver Community College, realty appraisal, 1979-81. **CAREER:** Sampaguita Bakery, manager, 1963-72; Three Spirits Liquor, manager, 1972-74; Kripps Pharmacy, cashier, 1974-75; United Warehouse Equipment, office manager, 1975-82; Welco-Beales Corp, supervisor of costing dept, 1982-87; REH Wholesale Supply, accounting assistant, 1988-. **ORGANIZATIONS:** Yee Fung Chai Association. **SPECIAL ACHIEVEMENTS:** Language proficiency in Mandarin, Cantonese, Folkanese, English, Ilongo & Tagalog. **HOME ADDRESS:** 921 Rivera St, San Francisco, CA 94116, (415)665-0648.

YEE, ALFRED ALPHONSE
Consulting engineering company executive. Chinese American. **PERSONAL:** Born Aug 5, 1925, Honolulu, HI; son of Yun Sau and Kam Ngo Yee; married Elizabeth Wong Yee, Jun 24, 1975; children: Alethea Lailan Yee Fell, Mark K K, Eric K S, Malcolm K O, Ian K P, Suling Victoria, Trevor K M, I'Ling Noela. **EDUCATION:** Rose-Hulman Institute of Technology, BA, civil engineering, 1948; Yale University, MS, structural engineering, 1949. **CAREER:** Alfred A Yee & Associates Inc, president, 1960-82, Leo A Daly Division, vice president, technical administrator, 1982-89; Applied Technology Corporation, president, 1984-. **ORGANIZATIONS:** American Society of Civil Engineers, fellow; American Concrete Institute, fellow; Earthquake Engineering Research Institute; Florida Engineering Society; International Association for Bridge and Structural Engineering; National Society of Professional Engineers; Post-Tensioning Institute; Prestressed Concrete Institute; Society of Naval Architects and Marine Engineers; Structural Engineering Association of Hawaii; Yale Engineering Association, fellow. **HONORS/AWARDS:** Prestressed Concrete Institute, Martin P Korn Award, 1965, PCI Journal, Robert J Lyman Award, 1984; Hawaii Society of Professional Engineers, Engineer of the Year, 1969; Rose-Hulman Institute of Technology, Honorary Doctor of Engineering, 1976. **SPECIAL ACHIEVEMENTS:** Author of: "Prestressed Concrete for Buildings," PCI Journal, Sept/Oct, 1976; "Honeycomb Units for Barges and Floating Platforms," Structural Engineering Practice: Analysis, Design, Management, volume 1, no 1, 1982; "One Hundred Washington Square: Structural Design and Construction," coauthor with Chang Nai Kim, PCI Journal, Jan/Feb, 1984; "Design Considerations for Precast Prestressed Concrete Building Structures in Seismic Areas," PCI Journal, volume 36, no 3, May/June, 1991. **MILITARY SERVICE:** US Army, pvt first class, 1946-47. **BUSINESS AD-**

DRESS: President, Applied Technology Corporation, 1441 Kapiolani Boulevard, Suite 810, Honolulu, HI 96814, (808)973-1800.

YEE, ALLEN Y.
Pharmacist. Chinese American. **PERSONAL:** Born Nov 14, 1958, Chicago, IL; son of William Yee and Joanne Yee. **EDUCATION:** University of Illinois, pre-pharmacy, College of Pharmacy, BS, 1981, Business College. **CAREER:** Bethany Methodist Hospital, staff pharmacist; St Joseph Hospital, staff pharmacist; Walgreens Drugs, staff pharmacist, currently. **ORGANIZATIONS:** National Pharmacists Assn, steward; American Pharmaceutical Assn; American Society of Hospital Pharmacists; National Assn of Retail Druggists; Illinois Pharmaceutical Assn. **BUSINESS ADDRESS:** Registered Pharmacist, Walgreens Drugs, 1130 S Main St, Antioch, IL 60002.

YEE, ANGELINA CHUN-CHU
Educator. Chinese American. **PERSONAL:** Born Jan 8, 1949, Guangzhou, China; daughter of Swa-ching Yee & Ying-har Siu; married Bei-Lok B Hu, Jun 24, 1972; children: Tung-Hui Victor Hu, Tung-Hui Amelia Hu. **EDUCATION:** University of California, Berkeley, BA, comparative literature, 1969; Harvard University, MA, comparative literature, 1971, PhD, comparative literature, 1986. **CAREER:** Self-employed, consultant, 1980-; United Nations, simultaneous interpreter, 1972-80; University of Pennsylvania, lecturer, 1986-87; University of Maryland, visiting assistant professor, 1987-88, assistant professor, 1990-; Cornell University, Mellon postdoctoral fellow, 1989-90. **ORGANIZATIONS:** Modern Languages Association, 1990-; Association for Asian Studies, 1986-; Association for Asian American Studies, 1992-; Traditional China Colloqium of Greater Washington, 1986-; Association of Chinese Comparatists, 1990-; Committee on East Asia, 1987-; Friendship Chorus, conductor, 1973-79. **HONORS/AWARDS:** Mellon Foundation, Mellon Postdoctoral Fellowship for the Humanities, 1989; Lilly Foundation, Lilly Teaching Fellowship, 1990; Danforth Foundation, Danforth Fellowship, 1969-72; Harvard University, Harvard Graduate Prize Fellowship, 1969-72; University of California, Phi Beta Kappa, Regents Scholarship, 1968-69. **SPECIAL ACHIEVEMENTS:** Language proficiency: Cantonese, Mandarin, English, French, Latin, Japanese; "Counterpoise in the Honglou Meng," Harvard Journal of Asiatic Studies, 1990; Art, Politics and Self: Litertaure of Resistance in Colonial Taiwan, 1993; Sympathy, Counterpoise & Symbolism in Dream of Red Chamber, 1986; conductor of Friendship Chorus, numerous performances in New York, Princeton & Washington DC, 1973-79; producer, Harvard-MIT Chinese Drama Club, performances in Cambridge, Boston, and New York, 1970-72. **BUSINESS ADDRESS:** Professor, East Asian Languages & Literatures, University of Maryland, 2106 Jimenez Hall, College Park, MD 20742-0001, (301)405-4541.

YEE, BARBARA W. K.
Psychologist, educator. Chinese American. **PERSONAL:** Born May 20, 1952, Honolulu, HI; daughter of Henry L S Yee and Florence L Yee; married David A Chiriboga, Mar 25, 1986; children: Carlos Danny Chiriboga, David A Chiriboga II. **EDUCATION:** University of Hawaii, BA, 1974; University of Denver, MA, 1979, PhD, 1982. **CAREER:** University of Denver, aging specialist, 1979-81; Miami University, minority research associate, 1981-82; University of Oklahoma, asst professor, 1982-85; San Jose State University, instructor, 1985; University of Texas Medical Branch, assistant professor, 1986-92, associate professor, 1992-. **ORGANIZATIONS:** Gerontological Society of America, 1979-, BSS Executive Committee Minority Taskforce, 1992-96; American Psychological Assn, 1978-, Minority Fellowship Comm, 1990-93; Asian American Psychological Assn, 1989, vice president, 1993-95; Texas Consortium of Geriatric Education Centers, Minority Taskforce, chair, 1991-; National Asian Women's Health Organization, board member, 1993-; Journal of Ethnicity and Aging, editorial board, 1994-. **HONORS/AWARDS:** Administration on Aging, Minority Aging Fellow, 1979-80; American Psychological Assn, Minority Fellow, 1976-79; University of Hawaii, Phi Beta Kappa, Phi Kappa Phi, 1972-74; Noon Optimist of Galveston, Community Service Award, 1989. **SPECIAL ACHIEVEMENTS:** Author, works include: "Markers of Successful Aging Among Vietnamese Refugee Women," Women and Therapy, 13 (3), p 221-238, 1992; "Gender and Family Issues in Minority Groups," Generations, 14 (3), p 39-42, 1990; "Elders in Southeast Asian Refugee Families," A New Look at Minority Families and the Elderly, Generations, vol 17, no 3, p 24-27, 1992; Variations in Aging: Older Minorities, Geriatrics/Gerontology Curriculum Module, 4th ed, 1994; "Risk Taking and Abusive Behaviors Among Ethnic Minority Individuals," Health Psychology, 1994; several others forthcoming. **BUSINESS ADDRESS:** Associate Professor, Dept of Health Promotion and Gerontology, University of Texas - Medical

Branch, School of Allied Health Sciences, RT J28, Galveston, TX 77555-1028, (409)772-3038.

YEE, CARLTON S.
Educator. Chinese American. **PERSONAL:** Born May 25, 1941, Morenci, AZ; son of Joe Yee and Laura Woo; married Judith Rocha Yee, Mar 18, 1989. **EDUCATION:** Humboldt State University, BS, 1964; Yale University, MF, forestry, 1965; Oregon State University, PhD, 1975. **CAREER:** Humboldt State University, department of forestry, professor, 1970-. **ORGANIZATIONS:** Society of American Foresters, 1964-; California Licensed Foresters Assoc, 1991-; California State Board of Forestry, chairman, 1983-91. **SPECIAL ACHIEVEMENTS:** Commercial pilot, flight instructor, 1978-. **MILITARY SERVICE:** US Army, Lt, 1960-61. **BIOGRAPHICAL SOURCES:** California Forest Practice Program, by E F Martin, p 54, 82, 92, 98, et al, 1989. **BUSINESS ADDRESS:** Professor, Forestry Dept, Humboldt State University, Arcata, CA 95521, (707)826-4100.

YEE, DARLENE
Educator. Chinese American. **PERSONAL:** Born Sep 19, 1958, New York, NY; daughter of Jimmy Tow and Yuen Hing Yee. **EDUCATION:** Barnard College, Columbia University, BA, 1980; College of New Rochelle, MS, 1981; Teachers College, Columbia University, MS, 1984, EdD, 1985. **CAREER:** Teachers College, Columbia University, research associate, Safety Research and Education Project, 1983-85; Barnard College, Columbia University, asst director, biology laboratories, 1980-83; York College, CUNY, asst professor, health education, 1985-88; University of Texas Medical Branch, associate professor, graduate studies, 1988-90; San Francisco State University, professor, gerontology and health education, 1990-. **ORGANIZATIONS:** Sigma Xi-SFSU Club, pres/pres-elect, 1990-93; American Society on Aging, research committee, 1991-; Barnard College, board of directors, AABC, 1991-; Assn of Geront in Higher Education, publications committee, 1990-91; National Council on the Aging, delegate-at-large, Health Promotion Institute, 1990-; AAHPERD-Southern District, Texas representative, Council on Adult Development, 1989-90; American Public Health Assn, Asian American Caucus and Geront Health Sec, 1988-; Gerontological Society of America, chair, chair-elect, new professional & student section, 1984-86, fellow, 1994. **HONORS/AWARDS:** San Francisco State University, Certificate of Outstanding Instruction, 1991; University of Texas Medical Branch, Outstanding Award for Teaching, 1989, 1990; York College, CUNY, Outstanding Faculty Member of the Year, 1988; Gerontological Society of America, International Travel Award, 1989; Alcohol and Drug Abuse Problems Assn, North American Congress Scholarship, 1986. **SPECIAL ACHIEVEMENTS:** Certified Health Education Specialist, National Commission for Health Education Credentialing, 1989; numerous presentations and publications in peer-reviewed conferences and journals. **HOME ADDRESS:** 40 Meadow Park Circle, Belmont, CA 94002-2947, (415)593-4076. **BUSINESS ADDRESS:** Professor, San Francisco State University, 1600 Holloway Ave, San Francisco, CA 94132, (415)338-7568.

YEE, DONALD H.
Educator. Chinese American. **PERSONAL:** Born Aug 29, 1953, Flagstaff, AZ; son of William Yee & Ann Yee. **EDUCATION:** Northern Arizona University, BS, 1975, MA, 1977; Arizona State University, 1985-. **CAREER:** Flagstaff Public Schools, instructor, 1976-85; Northern Arizona University, instructor, 1976-85; Arizona State University, graduate assistant, 1985-89; US Forest Service, survey technician, 1979-; Mesa Community College, faculty, 1985-. **ORGANIZATIONS:** Epsilon Pi Tau, 1975-. **BUSINESS ADDRESS:** Engineering Science Instructor, Mesa Community College, 1833 W Southern Ave, Physical Science, PS3WC, Mesa, AZ 85202-4866, (602)461-7014.

YEE, DONALD POY
Educational administrator. Chinese American. **PERSONAL:** Born Mar 29, 1941, New York, NY; son of Yee Chee-Poy and Phyllis M Yee; married Kathleen S Yee, Dec 23, 1981; children: Otsu H, Tsuya H, Jason Ashcroft. **EDUCATION:** Rutgers University, BA, 1963; New York University, MS, 1967. **CAREER:** New Jersey Institute of Technology, mathematics, assistant professor, 1963-69; Essex County College, mathematics and computer science, professor, 1969-, Computer and Information Sciences Dept, chair, 1983-86, dean of science and technology, 1986-91, dean of institutional computing, 1991-. **ORGANIZATIONS:** Liberty State Park Public Advisory Commission, NJ, commissioner, 1993-; NJ Mathematics Coalition, board of governors, 1990-; Mathematical Association of America, 1980-; Association of Computing Machinery, 1983-; Institute of Electrical and Electronics Engineers Com-

puter Society, 1986-. **BUSINESS ADDRESS:** Dean of Institutional Computing, Essex County College, 303 University Ave, Newark, NJ 07102-1798, (201)877-3528.

YEE, EDMOND
Educator. Chinese American. **PERSONAL:** Born Jan 11, 1938, Guangdong, China; son of Wing Fook Yee and Fung San Chan Yee; married Katharine R Yee; children: Peter Edmond, Timothy Richard. **EDUCATION:** Midland Lutheran College, BA, 1963; Pacific Lutheran Theological Seminary, MDIV, 1967; San Francisco State University, MA, 1972; University of California, Berkeley, C Phil, 1975, PhD, 1977. **CAREER:** Pacific Lutheran Theological Seminary, professor, 1978-. **ORGANIZATIONS:** Association for Asian Studies; International Center for Asian Studies; Society for Asian and Comparative Philosophy. **HONORS/AWARDS:** Graduate Theological Union, Newhall Fellowship, 1989-92. **SPECIAL ACHIEVEMENTS:** Augsburg Publishing House/Fortress Press: Eternal River: An Asian Cultural Awareness Resource, two vols, 1988; Wo Xin Shangdi, 1989; Jidutu Shenghuo, 1989; Jidu Jiaohui, 1989; numerous others. **BUSINESS ADDRESS:** Prof of Multicultural Studies, Pacific Lutheran Theological Seminary, 2770 Marin Ave, Berkeley, CA 94708, (510)524-5264.

YEE, FRANKLIN
Educator, business executive. Chinese American. **PERSONAL:** Born Mar 1, 1942, Taylor, TX; son of Mr and Mrs David Yee; married Darleen Jean Yee, Aug 22, 1981; children: Heather Starr, Alissa Noel, Lisa Murphy. **EDUCATION:** Mt San Antonio College, AA, 1963; California Poly, Pomona, BA, 1965; California State University, Long Beach, MA, 1983. **CAREER:** Los Angeles School Dist, voc agric teacher, 1969-76; Cerritos College, professor, 1976-; Quest Design and Associates, owner/president, currently. **ORGANIZATIONS:** FAAC. **HONORS/AWARDS:** Cerritos College, Science, Engineering, Math Teacher of Year, 1988; Most Outstanding Teacher of the Year, 1992. **SPECIAL ACHIEVEMENTS:** "Non-Traditional Learning Modes of Mature Adults," 1983, Masters Thesis; certified by the Feng Shui Institute. **MILITARY SERVICE:** US Army E-5, 1967-69; Good Conduct Medal, 1968; Army Medal of Commendation, 1969. **HOME ADDRESS:** 1907 Park St, Huntington Beach, CA 92648. **BUSINESS ADDRESS:** Professor, Cerritos College, 11110 E Alondra Blvd, Norwalk, CA 90650.

YEE, JAMES
Television executive. Chinese American. **EDUCATION:** MIT. **CAREER:** ITVS (Independent Television Service), executive director, currently. **ORGANIZATIONS:** Natl Asian American Telecommunications Assn, 1982-, former executive director; San Francisco Film Commission, 1992. **HONORS/AWARDS:** Asian CineVision, Asian American Media Award; Visual Communications, Tatsukawa Award. **SPECIAL ACHIEVEMENTS:** Producer for "The Kiss," by Philip Gotanda. **BUSINESS ADDRESS:** Executive Director, ITVS, 190 E 5th #200, St Paul, MN 55101, (612)225-9035.*

YEE, JIMMIE N.
City council member. Chinese American. **PERSONAL:** Born Feb 10, 1960. **CAREER:** Sacramento City Council, council member, currently. **BUSINESS ADDRESS:** Council Member, Sacramento City Council, 915 I St, Rm 205, Sacramento, CA 95814, (916)264-5407.*

YEE, JOANNE
City government official. **CAREER:** City of Sacramento, Board of Education, board member, currently. **BUSINESS ADDRESS:** Board Member, Board of Education, City of Sacramento, 1619 N St, Sacramento, CA 95814, (916)264-4310.*

YEE, JOHN DAVID (JODY)
Auditor. Chinese American. **PERSONAL:** Born Jan 27, 1961, Aberdeen, MD; son of George S Yee and Patricia P Yee; married Pamela M Yee, Mar 14, 1987; children: Courtney E. **EDUCATION:** Harding University, BS, public administration, 1986; Cannon Financial Institute Audit School I, II, graduate, 1990; Cannon Financial Institute Trust Audit/Compliance School I, II, III, graduate, 1993. **CAREER:** Farmers and Mechanics National Bank, courier, ATM clerk, floating teller, vault/senior teller, staff auditor, sr staff auditor, audit officer, 1984-. **ORGANIZATIONS:** Institute of Internal Auditors, 1991-; Natl Assn of Trust Auditors and Compliance Professionals, 1993-. **BUSINESS ADDRESS:** Audit Officer, Farmers and Mechanics National Bank, 110 Thomas Johnson Dr, Frederick, MD 21701, (301)694-4121.

YEE, LAWRENCE K.
Educator, educational administrator. Chinese American. **PERSONAL:** Born Feb 7, 1948, Oakland, CA; son of Albert S Yee and Evelyn L Yee; married Kathleen H Yee, Jul 5, 1970; children: Ryan H, Erin K. **EDUCATION:** University of California, Davis, BS, biological science, 1969; University of Santa Clara, MBA, 1983. **CAREER:** University of California, Cooperative Extension, 4-H youth development adviser, 1975-86, county director, 1986-. **ORGANIZATIONS:** AAAS, 1991-; American Management Association, 1987-91; Institute for Alternative Agriculture, 1989-; National Association of Extension 4-H Agents, 1976-88. **HONORS/AWARDS:** Resources for the Future, Kellogg Fellow, 1987; Extension Service, USDA, NELD Intern, 1992; National Business Honor Society, 1983; University of California, Distinguished Service Award for Administration, 1993. **HOME ADDRESS:** 306 Del Norte Rd, Ojai, CA 93023. **BUSINESS PHONE:** (805)645-1451.

YEE, LELAND
Educational administrator. **CAREER:** San Francisco Board of Education, president, currently. **BUSINESS ADDRESS:** President, San Francisco Board of Education, 135 Van Ness Ave Rm 120, San Francisco, CA 94102, (415)241-6000.*

YEE, MELINDA C.
Government official. Chinese American. **PERSONAL:** Born 1963?; daughter of Peter and Helen Yee. **EDUCATION:** University of California, San Diego; University of Southern California, MPA. **CAREER:** Democratic National Committee, Washington, DC, director of constituencies, 1990; Clinton/Gore '92 Committee, Asian Pacific American Political Affairs, national director; White House Office of Presidential Personnel, special assistant; US Department of Commerce, special assistant to Secretary Ronald H Brown, senior advisor on the Pacific Rim, 1993-. **ORGANIZATIONS:** National Network Against Anti-Asian Violence, founder; Organization of Chinese Americans, former executive director; Conference on Asian Pacific American Leadership, founder. **SPECIAL ACHIEVEMENTS:** Coordinated first national Asian Pacific American Democratic Summit, 1991. **BUSINESS ADDRESS:** Senior Advisor, Pacific Rim, US Department of Commerce, Minority Business Development Agency, 14th & Constitution Ave, NW, Room 5055, Washington, DC 20230, (202)482-5061.

YEE, NANCY J.
Dentist. Chinese American. **PERSONAL:** Born Jun 23, 1952, San Francisco, CA; daughter of Robert W Yee and Charlene Yee; married Richard Kudo, Apr 29, 1984; children: Brandon, Jennifer. **EDUCATION:** CCSF, AA, 1975; University of California-Berkeley, BS (with honors), 1978; UCLA, doctorate, 1983. **CAREER:** Private practice, dentist, currently. **ORGANIZATIONS:** UCLA Asian Pacific Alumni, board of directors, 1989-93; Asian Pacific Centre Theater Gp Pacific, board of directors, 1989-; UCLA School of Dentistry, treasurer, 1982, 1983; American Assn of Women Dentists, treasurer, 1982-83. **BUSINESS ADDRESS:** Dentist, 620 Arizona Ave, Santa Monica, CA 90403, (310)395-7221.

YEE, ROBERT DONALD
Educator. Chinese American. **PERSONAL:** Born Feb 21, 1945, Beijing, China; son of James Yee and Marian Y M Li; married Linda Margaret Yee; children: Jillian Neil, Allison Bertram. **EDUCATION:** Harvard College, AB (summa cum laude), 1966; Harvard Medical School, MD (cum laude), 1970. **CAREER:** UCLA School of Medicine, professor of ophthalmology, 1976-87; Indiana University School of Medicine, Department of Ophthalmology, professor, chairman, 1987-. **ORGANIZATIONS:** American Academy of Ophthalmology, fellow, 1976-; American Board of Ophthalmology, fellow, 1975-; American College of Surgeons, fellow, 1988-; Chinese American Ophthalmological Society, 1988-; Association of Research in Vision and Ophthalmology, 1975-; Frank B Walsh Neuro-ophthalmology Society, vice president, 1989-91; North American Neuro-ophthalmological Society, 1991-; American Ophthalmological Society, 1990-. **HONORS/AWARDS:** Harvard College, Phi Beta Kappa, 1966; Harvard Medical School, Alpha Omega Alpha, 1970; Fulbright Fellowship, 1966; UCLA School of Medicine, endowed chair, Charles K Feldman Professorship, 1983-87. **SPECIAL ACHIEVEMENTS:** Medical research on normal and abnormal eye movements, 1971-. **MILITARY SERVICE:** USPHS, lt commander, 1974-76. **BUSINESS ADDRESS:** Professor and Chairman of Ophthalmology, Indiana University School of Medicine, 702 Rotary Circle, Room 344, Indianapolis, IN 46202-5135, (317)274-7101.

YEE, SHIRLEY JO-ANN
Educator. Chinese American. **PERSONAL:** Born Mar 6, 1959, New York, NY; daughter of Audrey J Wong Yee and Donald Y Yee; partner: Arline L Garcia. **EDUCATION:** University of Scranton, AB, 1981; Ohio State University, MA, 1983, PhD, 1987. **CAREER:** Indiana-Purdue University, Ft Wayne, visiting assistant professor, 1987-88; University of Washington, assistant professor, 1988-. **ORGANIZATIONS:** American Ethnic Studies Association, 1991-; Organization of American Historians, 1986-; National Women Studies Association, 1986-. **SPECIAL ACHIEVEMENTS:** Black Women Abolitionists: A Study in Activism, 1828-1860, Knoxville, University of Tennessee Press, 1992. **BUSINESS ADDRESS:** Professor, Women Studies Program, University of Washington, Padelford Hall, B 110 Q, GN-45, Seattle, WA 98195-0001, (206)543-6984.

YEE, STANLEY C.
State government administrator. Chinese American. **PERSONAL:** Born Dec 25, 1939, Honolulu, HI; son of Tin Yau Yee and Kwai Git Wong Yee; children: Kevin W H, Aaron W G, Sera-Lyn S H. **EDUCATION:** University of Hawaii, Manoa, BFA, 1963, MSW, 1969. **CAREER:** State Dept of Health, Chn's Health Services Div, family planning social worker, 1971, Waimano Training School & Hospital, social services supervisor, social worker V, 1972-74, HIP director, social worker VI, 1974-75, branch chief, 1975-79, Community Services for Developmentally Disabled Branch, sec supervisor, 1979-88, Dev Disabilities Div, branch chief, social services manager I, 1988-91, division chief, DD administrator, 1991-. **ORGANIZATIONS:** National Association of State Directors of DD Services Inc, 1991-; State Special Education Advisory Council, 1991-; State Board of Vocational Rehabilitation, 1990-; Governor's Family Together Initiative Council, 1992-; State Developmental Disabilities Council, ex-officio, 1991-; Hawaii Early Intervention Council, 1991-; Respite Care Advisory Committee, chair, 1990-; Hawaii State Cluster on Severe Emotionally Handicapped & Developmentally Disabled Children, 1991-. **SPECIAL ACHIEVEMENTS:** Co-author: "A Cytogenetic Study of a Population of MR Males with Sp Marker (X) Syndrome," Human Genetics, 1983; "A Cytogenetic Study of a Population of Retarded Females with Special Ref to Fragile (X) Syndrome," Human Genetics, 1985; "Comm Placement Success Based on Client Behavior Preferences of Care Providers," MR, 1981; "Comparison of Successful & Unsuccessful CP MR Person," Am Journal of Mental Deficiency, 1980. **MILITARY SERVICE:** Army, specialist 5, 1963-67. **HOME ADDRESS:** 91-126 'Aipo'ola Place, Ewa Beach, HI 96706, (808)681-0223. **BUSINESS ADDRESS:** Developmental Disabilities Administrator, Developmental Disabilities Div, State Department of Health, 2827 Waimano Home Road, Pearl City, HI 96782, (808)453-6406.

YEE, VIRGINIA BOW SUE
Nurse. Chinese American. **PERSONAL:** Born Oct 23, 1938, Boise, ID; daughter of Yick Yee and Chow Lun Wong. **EDUCATION:** University of Colorado, BSN, 1960; University of Washington, MN, 1965. **CAREER:** San Mateo County Department of Public Health, public health nurse, 1960-63; University of Washington Child Study and Premature Follow Up, 1964-65; Imperial County Health Department, director of nursing, 1965-68; City & County of San Francisco, Department of Public Health, acting district health officer, 1967-90, supervising public health nurse, 1968-93, Tom Waddell Clinic, public health nurse, 1993-. **ORGANIZATIONS:** Sigma Theta Tau, 1964-; American Nurses Association, House of Delegates, 1980, 1990, 1992; California Nurses Association House of Delegates, 1987, 1989, 1991, 1993; OMI Pilgrim Community Center, board of directors, 1989-92; AIDS Health Project Community Advisory Board, 1989-; San Francisco Childrens' Council, board of directors, 1990-, board president, 1993, 1994. **SPECIAL ACHIEVEMENTS:** State of California Board of Nursing Education and Nurse Registration, board president, 1969, 1967-71. **HOME ADDRESS:** 200 Colon Ave, San Francisco, CA 94112, (415)333-5331. **BUSINESS ADDRESS:** Public Health Nurse, Tom Waddell Clinic, 50 Ivy St, San Francisco, CA 94102, (415)554-2662.

YEE, WALTER
Physician. Chinese American. **PERSONAL:** Born Jan 28, 1955, New York, NY; married. **EDUCATION:** Columbia University, BA, 1977; Albert Einstein College of Medicine, MD, 1981. **CAREER:** Queens-Long Island Medical Group, physician, currently. **ORGANIZATIONS:** American Academy of Family Physicians, 1984-. **BUSINESS ADDRESS:** Physician, Queens-Long Island Medical Group, 86-15 Queens Blvd, James Rudel Center, Elmhurst, NY 11373, (718)899-6600.

YEE, WILFRED WEE BIN
Physician. Chinese American. **PERSONAL:** Born Dec 17, 1949, Honolulu, HI; son of Yat Kwai Yee and Wei Sit Yee; married Gilda Yee, Mar 18, 1978. **EDUCATION:** University of Hawaii, BA, 1971; Cornell University Medical College, MD, 1975. **CAREER:** Reade Medical Associates, attending physician, 1986-. **ORGANIZATIONS:** Chirurgio Society, 1981-; American College of Emergency Physicians, 1986-. **HONORS/AWARDS:** American Board of Surgery, board certification, 1982; American Board of Emergency Medicine, board certification, 1988. **HOME ADDRESS:** 11 Edna Drive, Hyde Park, NY 12538.

YEE, WONG HERBERT
Graphic artist, writer. Chinese American. **PERSONAL:** Born Aug 19, 1953, Detroit, MI; son of Gee Hing & Toy Wun Yee; married Judy Anne, Dec 19, 1975; children: Ellen. **EDUCATION:** Wayne State University, BFA, 1975. **CAREER:** Graphic artist, writer, currently. **SPECIAL ACHIEVEMENTS:** Author: EEK! There's a Mouse In the House, Houghton Mifflin, 1992; Big Black Bear, Houghton Mifflin, 1993; Fireman Small, Houghton Mifflin, 1994. **BIOGRAPHICAL SOURCES:** "Silly Rhymes Plus Bright Pictures = Fun, "Detroit Free Press, pg 3C, Feb 24, 1993; "EEK! Troy Artist Turns Over New Leaf Writing Kids Books," Detroit News, pg 1F, July 2, 1993.

YEH, BILLY KUO-JIUN
Physician, scientist. Chinese American. **PERSONAL:** Born Aug 28, 1937, Foochow, Fukien, China; son of Shin-Hwa Yeh & Gui-Lu Yeh; married Lydia L P Yeh, Aug 21, 1965; children: Elizabeth Shih-I, Brian Shih-Heng, William Shih-Tseng. **EDUCATION:** National Taiwan University, MD, 1961, University of Oklahoma, MS, 1963; Columbia University, PhD, 1967. **CAREER:** Columbia University College of Physicians and Surgeons, teaching assistant, 1963-67; University of Miami School of Medicine, assistant professor, 1970-76, clinical associate professor of medicine, 1976-. **ORGANIZATIONS:** American College of Physicians, fellow, 1973; American College of Cardiology, fellow, 1973; American Heart Association, Council on Clinical Cardiology, fellow, 1980; American College of Chest Physicians, fellow, 1983. **SPECIAL ACHIEVEMENTS:** Author/co-author, more than one hundred scientific publications. **BUSINESS ADDRESS:** Clinical Associate Professor, University of Miami School of Medicine, 315 Palermo Ave, Coral Gables, FL 33134, (305)445-3739.

YEH, CHAI
Educator. Chinese American. **PERSONAL:** Born Sep 21, 1911, Hangzhou, Zhejiang, China; son of Yunqing Yeh & Ayehwa Ho; married Ida Shu-Yen Chiang, Jun 20, 1936; children: Yin, Jen. **EDUCATION:** Zhejiang University, China, BSEE, 1931; Harvard University, PhD, 1936. **CAREER:** Peiyang University, China, professor, 1936-37; Tsinghua University, China, professor, 1937-48, chairman, 1945-47; Southwestern Association University, China, professor, 1938-45; University of Kansas, visiting professor, 1948-56; University of Michigan, professor, 1956-81, emeritus professor, 1981-. **ORGANIZATIONS:** Tau Beta Pi, 1934-; Sigma Xi, 1948-; Institute of Electrical & Electronic Engineers, 1948-, senior member, 1956-. **HONORS/AWARDS:** UNV of Shanghai, Science & Technology, Honorary Professor, 1983. **SPECIAL ACHIEVEMENTS:** 51 published articles in Chinese and American scientific magazines, 1937-; author: Handbook of Fiber Optics, Academic Press, 1990; Applied Photonics, 1994. **HOME ADDRESS:** 1821 Alhambra Dr, Ann Arbor, MI 48103, (313)662-5961. **BUSINESS ADDRESS:** Professor Emeritus, University of Michigan, 1213 EECS Bldg, Ann Arbor, MI 48109, (313)763-1156.

YEH, CHIEN JO (JOSEPH)
Company executive, engineer. Chinese American. **PERSONAL:** Born Jun 6, 1930, Shanghai, China; son of Xiang-Ting Yeh and Qui-Zhen Chow; married Katherine K So, Sep 6, 1983; children: Patricia T, Paul Lee. **EDUCATION:** National Taiwan University, BSChE, 1952; University of Orono, MS, pulp & paper technology, 1954; University of Michigan, MSChE, 1955; Syracuse University, MSEE, 1966. **CAREER:** University of Akron, Institute of Rubber Research, research assistant, 1955-56; Endura Corp, research chemist, 1956-58; IBM Corp, staff engineer, 1958-66; Moore Business Forms Inc, manager, process engineering, 1966-92; Ecostar International Inc, Manufacturing, vice president, 1992-. **ORGANIZATIONS:** American Chemical Society. **SPECIAL ACHIEVEMENTS:** Language proficiency: Chinese, read, write, speak; Japanese, read, speak, 50% - 75%; experience/areas of specialization: environmental affairs: policy, regulation, audit, program, 10 years; business planning and ROI evaluation; scale up, from bench, pilot to production:

magnetic tape, latex paper, release coating, carbon paper, carbonless paper, printing ink. **MILITARY SERVICE:** ROTC, Taiwan, lt, 1952-53. **BUSINESS ADDRESS:** Vice President, Manufacturing, Ecostar International, Inc, 181 Cooper Avenue, Tonawanda, NY 14150, (716)874-8696.

YEH, EDWARD H. Y. (HSIN-YANG)
Physicist. Taiwanese American. **PERSONAL:** Born Jan 1, 1930, Hsin-chu, Taiwan; son of Sung-teh Yeh and Shiang-hua Tsai; married Gretchen C Yeh, Jun 14, 1967; children: Henry T, Daniel N. **EDUCATION:** National Taiwan University, BS, 1952; Kyushu University, Japan, MS, 1957; University of North Carolina, Chapel Hill, PhD, 1960. **CAREER:** Nuclear Data Group, National Academy of Sciences, National Research Council, research physicist, 1960-61; EG&G Inc, senior scientist, 1961-63; Dublin Institute for Advanced Studies, Ireland, visiting scholar, 1963-66; Moorhead State University, professor of physics and astronomy, 1966-87; Naval Air Warfare Center, code C2818 Weapons Division, physicist, 1984-. **ORGANIZATIONS:** American Physical Society; Sigma Psi Sigma; Reviewer of Mathematical Reviews; International Society of General Relativity and Gravitation, New York; Academy of Science Society, Photo-Optical Industrial Engineers. **HONORS/AWARDS:** New York Academy of Science, participating scholar for the scientist-in-residence program, Dublin Institute of Advanced Studies, visiting scholarships, 1963-66; University of North Carolina, fellowships, 1958-60. **SPECIAL ACHIEVEMENTS:** Published over 30 papers in professionals journals in physics and mathematics such as Nuclear Physics, Physical Reviews, Physics Letters, Journal of Mathematical Physics and Mathematical Reviews. **BUSINESS ADDRESS:** Physicist, Weapons Division, Naval Air Warfare Center, China Lake, CA 93555.

YEH, GREGORY S. Y.
Educator, researcher. Chinese American. **PERSONAL:** Born Apr 11, 1933, Shanghai, China; son of Clement & Wilma Wong. **EDUCATION:** Holy Cross College, BS, 1957; Cornell University, MS, 1960; Case Institute Tech, PhD, 1966. **CAREER:** Goodyear Tire, physical, 1960-61; General Tire, senior scientist, 1961-64; University of Michigan, professor, 1967-; East West Technology, CEO, currently. **HONORS/AWARDS:** Fulbright, 1973, 1983-84; Humboldt, Senior Scientist Award. **SPECIAL ACHIEVEMENTS:** One hundred publications of original scientific work, 1960-. **BUSINESS ADDRESS:** Professor, Dept of Chemical Eng, University of Michigan, Bldg 3042, Ann Arbor, MI 48109.

YEH, HEN-GEUL
Educator. Chinese American. **PERSONAL:** Born Jan 15, 1957, Taiwan; married. **EDUCATION:** University of California, Irvine, PhD, EE, 1982. **CAREER:** Parker-Hannifin Corp, engineering specialist, 1979-81; Magnavox, scientist, 1987-91; California State University, Long Beach, professor, 1983-; Jet Propulsion Lab, member of technical staff, 1992-. **ORGANIZATIONS:** IEEE, senior member, 1988-. **HONORS/AWARDS:** NASA, New Technology Award, 1987, Space Act Technology Brief Award, 1987. **SPECIAL ACHIEVEMENTS:** US patent, systolic VLSI array for implementing the Kalman Filter Algorithm, patent no 4823299, April 1989. **BIOGRAPHICAL SOURCES:** IEEE Trans on ASSP, vol 36, September 1988, p 1514-1517; IEEE, Trans on IE, vol 38, no 4, p 298-302, August 1991. **HOME ADDRESS:** 24306 Carlene Lane, Lomita, CA 90717. **BUSINESS PHONE:** (310)985-4899.

YEH, HENRY
Educator. Taiwanese American. **PERSONAL:** Born Dec 29, 1958, Taiwan; son of Wei-Ching Yeh; married Rachel Yeh, May 12, 1983. **EDUCATION:** National Tsing-Hwa University, BS, 1981; Columbia University, MS, 1985; City University of New York, Baruch College, MBA, 1988, PhD, 1992. **CAREER:** College of Staten Island/CUNY, instructor, 1986-89; Trans World Airline, operating research analyst, 1989-90; Wagner College, assistant professor, 1990-91; St John's University, assistant professor, 1991-. **SPECIAL ACHIEVEMENTS:** Published 6 papers in various journals. **HOME ADDRESS:** 164 Harold St, Staten Island, NY 10314, (718)698-8005.

YEH, HSI-HAN
Engineer. Chinese American. **PERSONAL:** Born Nov 10, 1935, Shanghai, China; son of Ching-Hwa Yeh and Yu-Zhi Yeh; married Lily Y Bao, Jun 18, 1966; children: Anita R, Sharon R. **EDUCATION:** National Taiwan University, BSc, EE, 1956; National Chiao-Tung University, Taiwan, MSc, EE, 1961; University of New Brunswick, MSc, EE, 1963; Ohio State University, PhD, EE, 1967. **CAREER:** University of Kentucky, assistant professor, 1967-73;

associate professor, 1973-85; Wright Laboratory, U.S. Air Force, engineer, 1986-. **ORGANIZATIONS:** IEEE, 1966-; Sigma Xi, 1966-; AIAA, 1992-. **HONORS/AWARDS:** U.S. Air Force, General Foulois Award, 1989, Scientific Achievement Awards, 1988, 1989, Invention Award, 1991. **SPECIAL ACHIEVEMENTS:** 40 technical publications; 2 patents: US Patent nos 4,949,236, 4,970,138, 1989-90. **BIOGRAPHICAL SOURCES:** Who's Who in Technology, Gale Research Inc, 1988. **HOME ADDRESS:** 1181 Mint Springs Dr, Fairborn, OH 45324.

YEH, HSIEN-YANG
Educator. Chinese American. **PERSONAL:** Born Jun 26, 1947, Herng Yang, Henan, China; son of Jih-Min Yeh and Huey-Ru Kao Yeh; married Ching-Hwan Yeh, Apr 28, 1972; children: Shi-Kun Karl, Shi-Pong Norman. **EDUCATION:** National Cheng-Kung University, BSE, 1969; Brown University, MS, 1972; Columbia University, MS, 1975; University of Southern California, PhD, 1987. **CAREER:** Stone & Webster Engineering Corp, design engineer, 1972-76; Bechtel Power Corp, structural engineer, 1976-78; TRW, staff engineer, 1978-81; Hughes Aircraft Co, senior staff engineer, 1981-86; California State University, Long Beach, professor, 1986-. **ORGANIZATIONS:** ASME, 1983-; ASCE, 1981-; ASEE, 1985-; SAMPE, 1992-; Sigma Xi, 1987-. **HONORS/AWARDS:** NASA-ASEE, Summer Faculty Fellowship, 1987-89, 1991; California State University, Long Beach, Meritorious Performance and Professional Promise Award, 1988. **SPECIAL ACHIEVEMENTS:** Numerous journal articles in the field of mechanical failure analysis and composite materials; founder of Torrance Chinese School, a nonprofit, weekend Chinese culture school, 1989. **MILITARY SERVICE:** Army, ROTC, 1969-70. **BUSINESS ADDRESS:** Professor, Dept of Mechanical Engineering, California State University, Long Beach, 1250 Bellflower Blvd, Long Beach, CA 90840, (310)985-4611.

YEH, IDA SHUYEN CHIANG
Educator, artist (retired). Chinese American. **PERSONAL:** Born Apr 8, 1912, Pingyang, Zhejiang, China; daughter of Beirui & Shiuyun Chang; married Chai Yeh, Jun 20, 1936; children: Yin, Jen. **EDUCATION:** Nankai University, BA, 1934; Radcliffe College, MA, 1936. **CAREER:** Southwestern Association University, China, instructor, 1943-46; National Chekiang University, China, lecturer, 1946-49; Bendix System Division, engineer programmer, 1959-61; University of Michigan, Ann Arbor, School of Public Health, programmer analyst, 1961-71; water colour artist, 1973-82. **ORGANIZATIONS:** Ann Arbor Art Association, 1973-80. **HONORS/AWARDS:** Radcliffe College, scholarship, 1934-35. **SPECIAL ACHIEVEMENTS:** Statistical computer programs, STCP 01, 02 . . . 12, stored at University of Michigan Computing Center, 1970; water color paintings exhibited at Genesee County Community Health Center, Flint, Michigan, Rackham Gallery, University of Michigan, Platt Rd Gallery, Ann Arbor Art Association, 1973-75. **HOME ADDRESS:** 1821 Alhambra Dr, Ann Arbor, MI 48103-5006, (313)662-5961.

YEH, JAMES TEHCHENG
Chemical engineer. Chinese American. **PERSONAL:** Born Apr 19, 1933, Fuzhou, Fujian, China; son of Shusheng Yeh and Huihua Wu Yeh; married Diana Hou Yeh, Nov 18, 1967; children: Theresa Ling. **EDUCATION:** National Cheng Kung University, Taiwan, BS, 1956; University of Detroit, MS, 1961; Stevens Institute of Technology, PhD, 1970. **CAREER:** Singer Simulation Products, staff engr-systems, 1974; US Dept of Energy, project leader, chemical engr, 1974-. **ORGANIZATIONS:** American Institute of Chemical Engineers, mem, sessions chmn during natl mtgs, 1974-; American Chemical Society; Air & Waste Management Assn, 1980-, short course lecturer. **HONORS/AWARDS:** Federal Laboratory Consortium, Award for Excellence in Technology Transfer, 1993. **SPECIAL ACHIEVEMENTS:** US Patent: #4878442, area of air pollution control; contributing author: Air Pollution Control and Design Handbook, Dekker Publishing, 1974. **HOME ADDRESS:** 5705 Glenhill Dr, Bethel Park, PA 15102. **BUSINESS PHONE:** (412)892-5737.

YEH, LEE-CHUAN CAROLINE
Educator. Chinese American. **PERSONAL:** Born Jan 3, 1954, Taipei, Taiwan. **EDUCATION:** Fu-Jen Catholic University, BS, 1976; University of Georgia, MS, 1978; Oregon State University, PhD, 1984. **CAREER:** University of Texas Health Science Center, San Antonio, Department of Biochemistry, postdoctoral fellow, instructor, currently. **BUSINESS ADDRESS:** Instructor, Dept of Biochemistry, University of Texas Health Science Center, 7703 Floyd Curl Dr, San Antonio, TX 78284-7760, (210)567-3778.

YEH, MICHELLE M.
Educator. Chinese American/Taiwanese American. **PERSONAL:** Born Jan 6, 1955, Taipei, Taiwan; daughter of Hsing-chu Sun and Shu-chuang Hsi; married Kwang Yeh, Jun 15, 1980; children: Jonathan. **EDUCATION:** National Taiwan University, Taipei, BA, English, 1976; University of Southern California, MA, comparative lit, 1978, PhD, comparative lit, 1983. **CAREER:** California State University, Long Beach, assistant professor of Chinese & Comparative Literature, 1983-88; University of California, Davis, assistant professor of Chinese, 1988-90, associate professor of Chinese, 1990-. **ORGANIZATIONS:** Association for Asian Studies; Council for International Exchange of Scholars, Fulbright Awards Committee; American Association of Chinese Comparative Literature, executive board. **HONORS/AWARDS:** Chiang Ching-kuo Foundation for International Scholarly Exchange, Research Grant, 1993-95; Council for Cultural Planning & Development, Taiwan, Translation Grant, 1991-92; Pacific Cultural Foundation, Taiwan, Writing Grant, 1991. **SPECIAL ACHIEVEMENTS:** Modern Chinese Poetry: Theory and Practice since 1917, Yale University Press, 1991; Anthology of Modern Chinese Poetry, Yale University Press, 1992. **BUSINESS ADDRESS:** Associate Professor, Dept of Chinese and Japanese, University of California, Davis, Davis, CA 95616-8560, (916)752-4995.

YEH, PU-SEN
Educator. Chinese American. **PERSONAL:** Born Jul 7, 1935, Hualien, Taiwan; son of Fa-Eang Yeh and Chin-Mei L Yeh; married Chun-Chih C Yeh, Jun 6, 1964; children: Flora M, Felice H, Gilbert C. **EDUCATION:** National Taiwan University, BS, 1958; University of Illinois, MS, 1962; Rutgers University, PhD, 1967. **CAREER:** University of Illinois, research and teaching assistant, 1961-64; Rutgers University, research and teaching assistant, 1964-66, research associate, 1966-67; Jacksonville State University, associate professor, 1967-83, department of engineering and computer science, head, 1978-83, department of engineering, head, 1983-88, professor, 1983-. **ORGANIZATIONS:** American Society of Mechanical Engineers, 1972-; American Society for Engineering Education, 1971-. **HONORS/AWARDS:** Jacksonville State University, researcher of the year, 1990. **SPECIAL ACHIEVEMENTS:** Total of 13 research articles, 1965-; author, Engineering Methods, 1990, 1992; read and speak Chinese and Japanese. **MILITARY SERVICE:** Chinese Army, second lieutenant, 1958-60. **BUSINESS ADDRESS:** Professor, Jacksonville State University, 700 Pelham Rd, North, 340 Martin Hall, Jacksonville, AL 36265, (205)782-5229.

YEH, SUSAN S. WANG
Educator. Chinese American. **PERSONAL:** Born Feb 18, 1961, Taipei, Taiwan; daughter of Ho-Hsiang Wang & Hsiao-Yun Wang; married Michael T C Yeh; children: Stephanie. **EDUCATION:** Massachusetts Institute of Technology, BS, 1983; Princeton University, MA, 1985, PhD, 1989. **CAREER:** IBM, Tokyo Research Lab, post-doctoral fellow, 1988-89; Princeton University, instructor, 1990; Mills College, assistant professor, currently. **ORGANIZATIONS:** ACM, 1984-; IEEE, 1984-. **BUSINESS ADDRESS:** Assistant Professor, Mills College, 5000 MacArthur Blvd, Oakland, CA 94613, (510)430-2138.

YEH, THOMAS Y.
Librarian, educator. Chinese American. **PERSONAL:** Born Sep 27, 1936, Nanking, China; married May Y Yeh, Jun 19, 1965; children: Edna, Emily. **EDUCATION:** Soochow University, Taiwan, BA, 1958; University of Minnesota, MA, 1962, MALS, 1965. **CAREER:** Central Washington University Library, professor, head, docs dept, 1965-. **ORGANIZATIONS:** American Library Association, 1965-; Pacific Northwest Library Association, 1979-; Washington Library Association, Doc-Ser, chair, 1988-91, AARL, chair, 1988-89. **SPECIAL ACHIEVEMENTS:** Author of: "A Profile of Academic Libraries in China," College and Research Libraries, v 46, no 6, p 499-503, November, 1985; "Government Publications in the People's Republic of China," Government Publications Review, v 14, no 4, p 405-410, 1987. **HOME ADDRESS:** 2019 Mt Daniels Drive, Ellensburg, WA 98926, (509)925-9257. **BUSINESS ADDRESS:** Professor & Head, Documents Dept, Central Washington University Library, Library, Room 301B, Ellensburg, WA 98926, (509)963-1542.

YEH, TIMOTHY S.
Physician. **PERSONAL:** Born Dec 9, 1950, Jersey City, NJ; son of Shu Tze Yeh and Wan Yuan Yeh; divorced. **EDUCATION:** Massachusetts Institute of Technology, BS, 1972; University of California, Davis, MD, 1976. **CAREER:** Children's Hospital of San Francisco, dir pediatric critical care, 1981-87; Children's Hospital of Oakland, dir pediatric critical care, 1987-. **ORGANIZATIONS:** Society of Critical Care Medicine, 1981-; Pediatric Intensive Care Network of Northern and Central California, 1981-; American Academy of Pediatrics, fellow, 1983-; American College of Critical Care Medicine, fellow, 1989-. **HONORS/AWARDS:** University of California, Davis, Department of Pediatrics, Resident of the Year, 1979; Children's Hospital of San Francisco, Department of Pediatrics, Teacher of the Year, 1981. **SPECIAL ACHIEVEMENTS:** "Use of Scoring Systems in the Pediatric ICU," Problems in Critical Care-Scoring Systems, 1989; guest editor: Critical Care Outlook; guest editor: Pediatric Trauma and Acute Care, 1991; co-author: "Because It's the Right Thing To Do," Critical Care Medicine, 1992; numerous others. **BUSINESS ADDRESS:** Director, Pediatric Critical Care, Children's Hospital Oakland, 747 52nd St, Oakland, CA 94609, (510)428-3714.

YEN, ALFRED CHUEH-CHIN
Educator. Chinese American/Taiwanese American. **PERSONAL:** Born Dec 6, 1958, Boston, MA; son of I-Kuen Yen & Chen-wan Yen; married Karin Jane, Jun 23, 1984; children: Julie. **EDUCATION:** Stanford University, BS, 1980, MS, 1980; Harvard Law School, JD, 1983. **CAREER:** Sheppard, Mullin, Richter Hampton, associate attorney, 1983-87; Boston College Law School, assistant professor, 1987-91, associate professor, 1991-. **ORGANIZATIONS:** Association of American Law Schools, committee on recruitment & retention of minority law teachers, 1992-, executive committee, 1991-94, chair-elect, section on minority groups, 1991-94; American Bar Association, section on intellectual property, 1988-; Coypright Society of USA, 1990-; Asian American Lawyers Association of Massachusetts, 1987-; Volunteer Lawyers for the Arts, Massachusetts, board of directors, 1993-; Boston Bar Association, 1992-. **SPECIAL ACHIEVEMENTS:** "Judicial Review of the Zoning of Adult Entertainment: A Search for the Purposeful Suppression of Protected Speech," 12 Pepperdine Letters Review, vol 651, 1985; "It's Not that Simple: An Unnecessary Elimination of Strict Liability and Presumed Damages in Libel Law," 23 Harv CR-CL Law Review, vol 593, 1988; "A First Amendment Perspective on the Idea/Expression Dichotomy and Copyright in a Work's, Total Concept and Feel," 38 Emory Law Journal, vol 393, 1989; "Restoring the Natural Law: Copyright as Labor and Possession," 51 Ohio State Law Journal, vol 517, 1990; "The Legacy of Feist: The Consequences of a Weak Connection Between Copyright and the Economics of Public Goods," 52 Ohio State Law Journal, vol 1343, 1991; "When Authors Won't Sell: Parody, Fair Use and Efficiency in Copyright law," 62 University Colorado Law Review, vol 79, 1991. **BUSINESS ADDRESS:** Associate Professor of Law, Boston College Law School, 885 Centre St, Newton, MA 02159-1157, (617)552-4395.

YEN, BEN CHIE
Educator, engineer. Chinese American. **PERSONAL:** Born Apr 14, 1935, Canton, China; son of T T Yen and J Yeh Yen; married Ruth H Chao Yen, Mar 6, 1993. **EDUCATION:** National Taiwan University, BS, 1956; University of Iowa, MS, 1959, PhD, 1965. **CAREER:** Water Resources Planning and Development Commission, Taiwan, junior engineer, 1958; Iowa Institute of Hydraulic Research, research associate, 1960-64; Princeton University, research associate, 1964-66; University of Virginia, professor of civil engineering, Center for Advanced Studies, 1988-91; University of Illinois, assistant professor of civil engineering, 1966-70, associate professor of civil engineering, 1970-76; professor of civil engineering, 1976-. **ORGANIZATIONS:** American Society of Civil Engineers, fellow, Journal of Hydraulic Engineering, associate editor, 1985-94, chairman, numerous committees, 1974-; International Association for Hydraulic Research, chairman, numerous committees, 1980-, Journal of Hydraulic Research, editorial board, 1985-; International Joint Committee on Urban Drainage, founding chairman, 1982-86; Journal of Engineering Mechanics, editorial board, 1978-80; American Geophysical Union, life member, several committees, 1961-; Fulbright Scholar Awards, CIES Engineering Discipline Committee, 1991-94. **HONORS/AWARDS:** Department of the Environment (UK), Research Fellowship, 1975; Fulbright Distinguished Senior Lecturer Award, 1988; National Science Council, Taiwan, Distinguished Senior Lecturer Chair, 1989; Korea Society of Civil Engineers, Korean Hydraulic Engineering Lecturer, 1988. **SPECIAL ACHIEVEMENTS:** Author/co-author of over 180 articles, 1959-; editor/co-author of 9 books, 1981-; director of 3 international conferences, 7 workshops; keynote speaker of 7 major international conferences; invited professor, distinguished guest professor at universities and institutes in Germany, UK, Sweden, China, Belgium, Switzerland, Taiwan and Australia. **MILITARY SERVICE:** Army Engineers Branch, Taiwan, 2nd lt, 1956-58. **BUSINESS ADDRESS:** Professor, Dept of Civil Engineering, University of Illinois, 205 N Mathews Avenue, Urbana, IL 61801, (217)333-4934.

YEN, CHEN-WAN L.
Physicist. **PERSONAL:** Born Jan 26, 1932, Tainan, Taiwan; daughter of Mau Yun and Mei Chen Liu; married I-Kuen, Feb 4, 1958; children: Alfred, Albert. **EDUCATION:** National Taiwan University, BS, 1954; Massachusetts Institute of Technology, PhD, 1964. **CAREER:** Jet Propulsion Laboratory, member of tech staff, 1972-. **ORGANIZATIONS:** AIAA. **BUSINESS ADDRESS:** Member-Technical Staff, Jet Propulsion Lab, 4800 Oak Grove Dr, Pasadena, CA 91108, (818)354-4899.

YEN, CHI-CHUNG DAVID
Educator. Taiwanese American. **PERSONAL:** Born Nov 15, 1953, Taichung, Taiwan; son of I-King Yen and Chi-Ann Lo; married Wen-Yawn Yen, Jul 3, 1981; children: Keeley Ju, Caspar Lung, Christopher Lung. **EDUCATION:** Central State University, Edmond, Oklahoma, BS, 1982, MBA, 1982; University of Nebraska, Lincoln, MS, comp sci, 1985, PhD, MIS, 1985. **CAREER:** University of Nebraska, Lincoln, instructor/graduate assistant, 1982-85; Miami University, assistant professor, 1985-89, associate professor, 1989-93, assistant chair, 1993-. **ORGANIZATIONS:** Decision Sciences Institute, ad hoc committee for international scholars, 1992-94; International Business Computer User Association, executive director, 1987-90; Data Processing Management Association, 1985-; IEEE, 1985-; Association for Computer Machinery, 1985-; Association of North American Chinese Management Educator, 1988-; North American Chinese MIS Professor Association, 1989-, secretary, 1991, president-elect, 1992. **HONORS/AWARDS:** Delta Sigma Pi, 1993 Professor of the Year, 1993; Beta Upsilon Sigma, Honor Member, 1992; Miami University, Alumni Teaching Scholar, 1987, Senior Faculty for Teaching Excellence, 1993. **SPECIAL ACHIEVEMENTS:** More than ninety publications including: Communication of the ACM, Information & Management, Journal of Information Management, European Journal of Information Systems, etc; language proficiency in Chinese, English & Japanese. **MILITARY SERVICE:** Chinese Navy, Keelung Brank, lieutenant, 1978-80. **BUSINESS ADDRESS:** Asst Chairman, Dept of Decision Sciences, Miami University, 302 Upham Hall, Oxford, OH 45056, (513)529-4827.

YEN, I-KUEN (IKE)
Engineer. Taiwanese American. **PERSONAL:** Born May 29, 1930, Singapore; son of Shang and Juei-Hung Yen; married Chen-Wan, Feb 4, 1958; children: Alfred, Albert. **EDUCATION:** National Taiwan University, BS, 1954; Massachusetts Institute of Technology, SM, 1956, ScD, 1960. **CAREER:** Occidental Research Corp, manager, 1968-83; Ike Yen Associates, principal, 1983-. **ORGANIZATIONS:** AIChE; ACS; New York Academy of Sciences; American Academy of Industrial Hygiene. **BUSINESS ADDRESS:** Principal, Ike Yen Associates, 867 Marymount Ln, Claremont, CA 91711.

YEN, JOAN JUE
Art educator. Chinese American. **PERSONAL:** Born Sep 25, 1930, Los Angeles, CA; daughter of Santong Jue & Rosemary Chung; married Richard Yen, Jul 16, 1950; children: Richard Scott, Robert, Jennifer Pang. **EDUCATION:** University of California, Los Angeles, 1948-50; Arizona State University, BA, 1969, MA, 1975. **CAREER:** Glendale Union High School, art teacher, 1970-75; Scottsdale Community College, art professor, 1975-. **ORGANIZATIONS:** Desert Jade, Chinese Women's Club, Arizona, charter member, 1969-90. **HONORS/AWARDS:** Arizona State Fair, Popular Appeal Award, 1960; Maricopa County Fair, honorary mention, 1977; Scottsdale Festival of Arts, charity auction, 1979. **SPECIAL ACHIEVEMENTS:** Slide show of 500 slides of China and display of 30 art works inspired by trip to China during sabbatical, 1984; art displayed: Phoenix Art Museum, Heard Art Museum. **BIOGRAPHICAL SOURCES:** Scottsdale Progress, Phoenix Gazette Newspaper, 1978-84; Arizona Republic, Newspaper Extra, 1982. **BUSINESS ADDRESS:** Professor, Scottsdale Community College, 9000 E Chapparal Rd, AB 114, Scottsdale, AZ 85250-2614, (602)423-6340.

YEN, JOHN (CHIA-HWEI)
Educator. Taiwanese American. **PERSONAL:** Born Oct 14, 1958, Hsin-Chu, Taiwan; son of Francis Yen & Bernedette Fong; married Tai-Yu Lu, Jul 7, 1985; children: Philip, Angela. **EDUCATION:** National Taiwan University, BS, electrical engineering, 1980; University of Santa Clara, MS, computer science, 1982; University of California, Berkeley, PhD, computer science, 1986. **CAREER:** Information Sciences Institute, University of Southern California, research scientist, 1986-89; Texas A&M University, assistant professor, 1989-93, director, Center for Fuzzy Logic and Intelligent Systems Research, 1991-, associate professor, 1993-. **ORGANIZATIONS:** North American Fuzzy Information Processing Society, board member, 1992-; IEEE Transac-

tions on Fuzzy Systems, associate editor, 1992-; International Journal of Intelligent and Fuzzy Systems, associate editor, 1992-; International Journal of Artificial Intelligence, editorial board, 1992-; Program Committee of IEEE Conf on Tools with AI, vice-program chair, 1992-93; Program Committee of International Conference on Industrial Applications of Fuzzy Control and Intelligent Systems, chair, 1991-93. **HONORS/AWARDS:** National Science Foundation, NSF Young Investigator Award (NYI), 1992; Texas A&M University, TEES Select Young Faculty Award, 1992; Association of Computing Machinery, Texas A&M Student Chapter, Faculty Achievement Award, 1991. **SPECIAL ACHIEVEMENTS:** Coeditor: "Industrial Applications of Fuzzy Control and Intelligent Systems," IEEE Press, 1994; "Generalizing Dempster-Shafer Theory to Fuzzy Sets," IEEE Transactions on Systems, Men, and Cybernetics, vol 20, no 3, pp 559-570, May 1990; "CLASP: Integrating Term Subsumption Systems and Production Systems," IEEE Transactions on Knowledge and Data Engineering, vol 3, No 1, pp. 25-32, March, 1991. **BIOGRAPHICAL SOURCES:** Fuzzy Logic, by Daniel McNeil and Paul Frieberger, Simon & Schuster, 1993; Windows, published by Texas Engineering Experiment Station, p 7, Spring 1992. **BUSINESS ADDRESS:** Associate Prof, Dept of Computer Sci, Texas A&M University, Harvey R Bright Bldg, MS 3112, College Station, TX 77843, (409)845-5466.

YEN, KANG KENNETH
Educator. Chinese American. **PERSONAL:** Born Jun 15, 1952, Tai-Chung, Taiwan; son of Sih-Fu Yen & Yen-Fen Yen; married Siulan M Yen, Nov 19, 1989; children: Hung-Liang, Hung-Hsin. **EDUCATION:** National Central University, BS, physics, 1974; University of Virginia, MEE, 1979; Vanderbilt University, PhDEE, 1985. **CAREER:** Florida International University, assistant professor, 1985-91, associate professor, 1991-. **ORGANIZATIONS:** State of Florida, registered professional engineer, 1989-; IEEE, sr member, 1993-, Miami section, chairperson, 1991-93, Florida Council, 1991-93; Chinese American Scholars Association of Florida, secretary in general, 1992-93; Organization of Chinese Americans, Miami chapter, board of directors, 1993-; American Biographical Institute, research board of advisors, 1991-; Dade County Science and Engineering Fair, judge, 1986-. **HONORS/AWARDS:** Tau Beta Pi, 1983; Eta Kappa Nu, 1979; Chinese American Scholars Association of Florida, Presidential Award for Service, 1993. **SPECIAL ACHIEVEMENTS:** Publication of more than 60 technique papers; promotion of Engineering Study among Minority Student Groups. **MILITARY SERVICE:** Combined Forces Services of ROC, 2nd lt, 1974-76. **BUSINESS ADDRESS:** Associate Prof, Dept of Elec and Compt Engineering, Florida International University, University Park, Miami, FL 33199, (305)348-3037.

YEN, MATTHEW MING-SHIH
Educator. Chinese American. **PERSONAL:** Born Nov 15, 1950, Kaoshiung, Taiwan; son of Honda Yen and Mann-Hwa Chou; married Elaine Yen, Jun 4, 1977; children: Richard, Jonathan, Irene. **EDUCATION:** National Taiwan University, BS, 1973; University of Idaho, MS, 1976; Purdue University, PhD, 1979. **CAREER:** Household International Corp, engineer, 1980-83; Imperial Metal Inc, project manager, 1983-85; St Cloud State University, professor, 1985-86; University of St Thomas, professor, 1986-89; California State University, Fresno, professor, 1989-. **ORGANIZATIONS:** Society of Manufacturing Engineers, senior member, 1986-; Institute of Electrical & Electronics Engineers, 1992; International Neural Networks Society, 1990-92; Association of Computing Machinery, 1986-90; American Society of Heating & Refrigeration Air/Conditioning, 1982-86; American Society of Mechanical Engineers, 1976-85; National Management Association, program chair, 1979-81. **HONORS/AWARDS:** Office of Naval Research, research recognition, 1990; National Association of Industrial Technology, service appreciation, 1990. **SPECIAL ACHIEVEMENTS:** Grape Drying Process Control with Back-propagation Net, 1991; Feature Based Weight Vectors for Spatiotemporal Pattern Recognition, 1990; Software Development for a Spatiotemporal Pattern Recognition, 1990; Performance of a Pulse Combustion Gas-fired Heater, 1980; An Equation of State for Air. **BUSINESS ADDRESS:** Professor, Industrial Technology, California State University, Fresno, 2255 E Barstow Ave, MS #9, Fresno, CA 93740-0009, (209)278-4201.

YEN, NAI-CHYUAN (NATE)
Physicist. Chinese American. **PERSONAL:** Born Apr 12, 1936, Shaoxing, Zhejiang, China; son of Chia-Hong Yen and Lin-Hsing Wang Yen; married Molly Mu-Lyan Kao Yen, Sep 2, 1967; children: Adelina Huey-Ru, Beatrice Huey-Ching, Clarette Huey-Chung. **EDUCATION:** Cheng Kung University, BS, electrical engineering, 1957; University of Rhode Island, MS, electrical engineering, 1962; Harvard University, PhD, applied physics, 1971. **CA-**

REER: University of Rhode Island, research assistant, associate, 1960-62; Bendix Corp, electronic engineer, 1962-66; Harvard University, teaching fellow, research assistant, 1966-72; AM International, senior engineer, 1972; Naval Underwater Systems Center, research physicist, 1972-80; US Coast Guard Research and Development Center, branch chief, 1980-82; Naval Research Laboratory, research physicist, 1982-; Yale University, visiting fellow, 1993-94. ORGANIZATIONS: Acoustical Society of America, 1967-, fellow, 1980-; Chinese Culture Society of Southeastern Connecticut, president, 1979; Sigma Xi, 1967-; Institute of Electrical and Electronic Engineers, 1962-; American Association for the Advancement of Science, 1962-; Association of Computing Machinery, 1985-; Phi Kappa Phi, 1962; Tau Beta Pi, 1962. HONORS/AWARDS: NRL, Berman Publication Award, 1989, Invention Award, 1993. SPECIAL ACHIEVEMENTS: Contributed more than 80 research papers and reports, 1962-; team leader for Joint Ocean Experiment at Pacific Ocean with Australia, New Zealand, 1978. BIOGRAPHICAL SOURCES: Who's Who in Technology Today, p 2080, 1981. HOME ADDRESS: 2109 Ramport Dr, Alexandria, VA 22308. BUSINESS ADDRESS: Research Physicist, NRL, 4555 Overlook Avenue, SW, Washington, DC 20375-5320, (202)767-2367.

YEN, PETER T.
Educator. Chinese American. PERSONAL: Born Sep 22, 1937, China; son of Paul S P Yen and Maria H Yen; married Selina Y Yen, Sep 2, 1967; children: Vevey E. EDUCATION: National Chung-Hsing University, BA, 1958; Advanced Studies: University of Louvain, Belgium, certificate, 1959; California State University, Fullerton, MA, 1966; University of Fribourg, Switzerland, PhD, 1969; University of California, Riverside, 1975; UCLA, post doc, 1979; MIT, certificate, 1983. CAREER: National University, Chung-Hsing, chair/professor, 1967-79; United Export & Import Co, vp, 1969-74; University of California, Riverside, lecturer, 1970-75; Virginia Polytechnic Institute, asst professor, 1975-76; University of West Florida, visiting prof, 1979-80; UCLA, Visiting Scholar Program, visiting scholar, 1980; St Bonaventure University, School of Business, professor/chairman, 1980-. ORGANIZATIONS: American Marketing Assn, 1975; Management Science Assn, 1976; Marketing Research Assn, board of directors, 1976-88; Academic of Intl Business, 1980-; Delta Epsilon Sigma & Pi Omega Pi, 1985-; Intl Academy of Management, fellow, 1979-. HONORS/AWARDS: The Small Business Community, Public Service Award, 1980; State of Florida, Culture Exchange Award, 1980; City of Pensacola, FL, Honorary Citizen, 1981; National Science Council, Grant, 1976-78; Switzerland Government, Fellowship, 1961-67. SPECIAL ACHIEVEMENTS: The Modern Management Organizational Behavior Theories, 1979; Business Strategic Planning, 1982; New Principles of Marketing, 1985; Dictionary of Marketing Terms, 1985; editor-in-chief, The PACCIOS Newsletter, 1983-85. BUSINESS ADDRESS: Professor/Chairman, School of Business, St Bonaventure University, West State Rd, PO Box 29, Mecom Academic Center, Room 218, St Bonaventure, NY 14778, (716)375-2111.

YEN, SHERMAN M. Y.
Educator, company executive. Chinese American. PERSONAL: Born Aug 4, 1934, Peking, China; son of C H Yen & Wang Peng Yen. EDUCATION: Bethel College, BA, 1960; Wichita State, MS, 1963; Catholic University of America, PhD, 1969; The Johns Hopkins University, postdoctoral. CAREER: Essex Community College, professor, 1970; Alcohol & Drug Treatment, executive director, 1989; Applied Research & Management, president, 1987-. ORGANIZATIONS: Association for Behavior Analysis, 1970; American Psychological Association, 1965. HONORS/AWARDS: State of Maryland, Salute to Excellent Service Award, 1993. SPECIAL ACHIEVEMENTS: Specialized in applied behavior analysis treatment of substance abusers; published more than 30 articles and 2 chapters in related books. BUSINESS ADDRESS: President, Applied Research & Management Inc, PO Box 133, Owings Mills, MD 21117.

YEN, STEVEN T.
Educator. Taiwanese American. PERSONAL: Born Jul 10, 1954, Tainan, Taiwan; son of Sen-ho Yen and Shan Yen; married Shew-Jiuan Su, Dec 25, 1991. EDUCATION: National Taiwan University, BS, 1977; University of Minnesota, Twin Cities, PhD, 1987. CAREER: University of Alaska, Fairbanks, assistant professor, 1987-89; Nicholls State University, Louisiana, assistant professor, 1989-. ORGANIZATIONS: American Agricultural Economics Association, 1983-93; American Economic Association, 1989-93; American Statistical Association, 1989-93; Southern Economic Association, 1989-93; Western Economic Association, 1989-93. SPECIAL ACHIEVEMENTS: Research in consumer economics, public economics, and natural resource economics; published in American Journal of Agricultural Economics, Southern Economics Journal, European Economic Review, Review of Agricultural Economics. MILITARY SERVICE: Taiwanese Navy, ensign, 1977-79. BIOGRAPHICAL SOURCES: "Estimation of Two-Level Demand System. . .," American Journal of Agricultural Economics vol 71, pp 85-98, 1989; Southern Economic Journal, vol 58, pp 988-101, 1992; American Journal of Agricultural Economics, 1993. HOME PHONE: (504)447-1817. BUSINESS ADDRESS: Asst Professor of Economics, Nicholls State University, PO Box 2015, 102D White Hall, Thibodaux, LA 70310, (504)448-4238.

YEN, TEH FU
Educator. Chinese American. PERSONAL: Born Jan 9, 1927, Kunming, Yunnan, China; son of Guang Pu Yen; married Shiao Ping S Yen, May 30, 1959. EDUCATION: Huachung (Central China) University, BS, 1949; West Virginia University, MS, 1953; Virginia Polytechnic Institute, PhD, 1955. CAREER: Goodyear Tire and Rubber, senior research chemist, 1955-59; Mellon Institute, fellow, 1959-66, senior fellow, 1965-66; Carnegie-Mellon University, senior fellow, 1966-68; California State University, associate professor, 1968-69; University of Southern California, associate professor, 1969-80, professor, 1980-. ORGANIZATIONS: American Chemical Society, councilor, 1979-; Institute of Petroleum Exploration and Development, honorary consultant, 1982-; Chinese American Chemical Society, board of directors, 1992-; Institute of Petroleum (London), fellow, 1959-; Chinese Academy of Science, standing committee, 1990-. HONORS/AWARDS: Pepperdine University, Honorary DSc, 1982; University of Petroleum, Beijing, honorary professor, 1986-; Government of Iran, Imperial Crown Gold Medal, 1977; Phi Kappa Phi, Diploma of Honor, 1982; Southern California Engineering and Science Association, Achievement Award, 1977; American Institute of Chemists, fellow, 1972. SPECIAL ACHIEVEMENTS: Over four hundred publications and twenty books; 20 US patents. BUSINESS ADDRESS: Professor of Environmental and Civil Engineering, University of Southern California, 3620 S Vermont Ave, 224A Kapprielian Hall, Los Angeles, CA 90089-2531, (213)740-0586.

YEN, TIEN-SZE BENEDICT
Pathologist, educator. Taiwanese American. PERSONAL: Born Oct 15, 1953, Taipei, Taiwan; son of Yen-Chen Yen and Er-Ying Chi; married Maria, Mar 26, 1983; children: Cecilia, Brian. EDUCATION: Stanford University, BS, 1973; Duke University, MD, PhD, 1982. CAREER: University of California, assistant professor, 1985-, associate professor, 1991-. HONORS/AWARDS: SCBA, Cathay Hepatitis Award, 1990; Duke University, Markey Anatomy Award, 1974; Stanford University, Phi Beta Kappa, 1973. SPECIAL ACHIEVEMENTS: More than 50 papers in scientific journals. BUSINESS ADDRESS: Associate Professor, University of California, 4150 Clement St, Anatomic Pathology 113B, San Francisco, CA 94121, (415)476-5334.

YEN, WEN-HSIUNG
Educator, composer. Chinese American. PERSONAL: Born Jun 26, 1934, Tainan, Taiwan; son of Xian-Chi Yen and Jin-Zhi Yen; married Yuan Yuan Yen, Jan 6, 1961; children: Tin-ju, Tin-jen, Tin-tao. EDUCATION: National Taiwan Normal University, BA, 1960; Chinese Culture University, MA, 1964; UCLA, MA, 1971; University of MD, UCLA, PhD candidate. CAREER: Chinese Culture University, professor, 1964-69; Los Angeles Community College, lecturer, 1978-82; Los Angeles City College, instructor, 1983-85; California State University, Northridge, Chinese professor, 1987-88; California State University, LA, lecturer, 1985-; UCLA, teaching associate, 1992-. ORGANIZATIONS: Society for Ethnomsicology, 1978-; International Council for Traditional Music, 1980-; Alumni Association of Chinese Culture University of Southern California, president, 1969-77, adviser, currently; Taiwan Benevolent Association of America, 1987-88, adviser, 1989-; Taiwan Benevolent Association of California, president , 1988-89, adviser, currently; Chinese American Musician Association of South Carolina, president; Chinese Writers Association of Southern California, board member, 1992-. HONORS/AWARDS: California Museum Foundation, board of trustees, 1976; Confucius Commemorative Day Deremony LA, Outstanding Teacher, 1984; Recipient Commendation from President George Bush and President Lee Teng-hui, Representative of China, 1989; National Taiwan University, Joint Teacher College and Normal University, Southern California, Award of Outstanding Achievement, 1992. SPECIAL ACHIEVEMENTS: Taiwan Folk Songs, vol 1, 1967, vol 2, 1969; A Collection of Wen-Hsiung Yen's Songs, 1968, vol 2, 1987; Chinese Musical Culture and Folk Songs, 1989; Conductor: Chinese Music Orchestra of Southern California, 1974-. HOME ADDRESS: 1116 Drake Rd, Arcadia, CA 91007, (818)447-3823.

YEN, WILLIAM MAO-SHUNG
Educator. Chinese American. **PERSONAL:** Born Apr 5, 1935, Nanking, Jiangsu, China; son of Wan Li Yen and Jane Hsung-Lin Jing Yen; married Laurel Frances Curtis Yen, Aug 18, 1978; children: Jan Luhsan Bess. **EDUCATION:** University of Redlands, BS, 1956; Washington University, PhD, 1962. **CAREER:** Washington University, research associate, 1962; Stanford University, research associate, 1962-65; University of Wisconsin, Madison, assistant professor, 1965-68, associate professor, 1968-72, professor, 1972-90; University of Georgia, Graham Perdue Professor, 1986-. **ORGANIZATIONS:** American Physical Society, 1957-77; Optical Society of America, 1978-79; American Association for the Advancement of Science, 1972-80; Electrochemical Society of America, chair elect of luminescence and display divison, 1981-; Sigma Xi, 1958-; Phi Beta Delta, 1989-. **HONORS/AWARDS:** Washington University, fellow, 1956-61; APS, fellow, 1977; OSA, fellow, 1979; AAS, fellow, 1980; JS Guggenheim, felow, 1979-80; A von Humboldt Sr US Scientist Award, 1985, 1990; University of San Antonio Abad, Peru, Honorary Professor, 1982. **SPECIAL ACHIEVEMENTS:** Editor, co-editor, "Laser Spectroscopy of Solids I & II," 1980, 1985; over 200 articles in scientific journals on optical & magnetic properties of solids; fluency: Chinese, Spanish, French, German. **BUSINESS ADDRESS:** Graham Perdue Professor, Dept of Physics & Astronomy, University of Georgia, Physics Bldg, Rm 215, Athens, GA 30602-2451, (706)542-2491.

YEN, YANG
Educator, geneticist. Chinese American. **PERSONAL:** Born Dec 4, 1952, Chendu, Sichuan, People's Republic of China; son of Chi Yen and Jiun-Liang Yang; married Xiao-dong Liu, Feb 14, 1984; children: Pei. **EDUCATION:** Sichuan Teachers College, diploma, 1978; Nanjing Agricultural University, MS, 1986; University of Missouri-Columbia, PhD, 1989. **CAREER:** Sichuan Agricultural University, research geneticist, 1986-87; University of Missouri, research assistant, 1987-89; Michigan State University, research associate, 1990-91; University of Nebraska, research associate, 1991-92, assistant professor, 1992-. **ORGANIZATIONS:** American Society of Agronomy, 1991-; Crop Science Society of America, 1991-; The International Society of Plant Molecular Biology, 1991-; The Genetics Society of Canada, 1992-. **HONORS/AWARDS:** University of Missouri, The Sears-Longwell Award, 1990; Gamma Sigma Delta, 1992. **SPECIAL ACHIEVEMENTS:** Published: 19 journal articles and 1 book chapter. **BUSINESS ADDRESS:** Assistant Professor, Dept of Agronomy, University of Nebraska-Lincoln, PO Box 830915, 308 Keim Hall, Lincoln, NE 68583-0915, (402)472-9613.

YEN-KOO, HELEN CHIANG-YING
Government official (retired). Chinese American. **PERSONAL:** Born May 8, 1925, Shanghai, Jiangsu, China; daughter of Mr & Mrs W G Yen; married John K Koo, Aug 30, 1958; children: Robin. **EDUCATION:** Franco-Chinese University, BS, 1945; Ohio State University, MS, 1951; George Washington University, PhD, 1955. **CAREER:** Rosewell Park Research Institute, cancer research scientist, 1955-56; Johnson and Johnson Company, neuropharmacologist, 1956-60; Ciba-Geigy company, group leader, neuropharmacologist, 1960-64; DuPont Company, group leader, neuropharmacologist, 1964-66; FDA, group leader and acting chief, psychopharmacology and toxicoloy lab, 1966-92. **ORGANIZATIONS:** Chinese Medical and Health Association, president, 1980. **HONORS/AWARDS:** Society of Experimental Biology and Medicine, Scientist Emeritus Award, 1993. **SPECIAL ACHIEVEMENTS:** Photography. **HOME ADDRESS:** 5310 Danbury Rd, Bethesda, MD 20814.

YENSON, EVELYN PHOEBE
Government administrator. Chinese American. **PERSONAL:** Born Dec 20, 1944, Johannesburg, Republic of South Africa; daughter of Phoebe Fisher and Tommy Yenson; divorced; children: Megan V Sun, Elliot Sun. **EDUCATION:** College of New Rochelle, BA, history, 1967; University of Wisconsin, MA, urban affairs, 1968; Cornell University, Summer Institute of Design, 1969; Harvard University, JFK School of Government, 1988. **CAREER:** City of Rye, NY, city planner, 1970-71; Seattle Public Schools, program planner & evaluator, 1971-73; City of Seattle, various planning & mgmt positions, 1973-84; consultant, 1984-85; Washington Pavilion, Expo '86, director, deputy commissioner, 1985-86; Washington State Lottery, director, 1987-. **ORGANIZATIONS:** North American Association of State & Provincial Lotteries, president, 1992-; Bumbershoot Festival Commission, vice-chair, 1991-; Seattle Arts Commission, 1989-; Washington World Affairs Fellows Program, fellow, 1992-93; Municipal League, board member, 1989-92; Council for the Prevention of Child Abuse and Neglect, 1984-88. **HONORS/AWARDS:** Women

Executives in State Government, RJR Nabisco Fellow, JFK School of Govt, 1988. **SPECIAL ACHIEVEMENTS:** Monthly columns in Public Gaming Magazine, 1992-93; columns in international magazines; speaker at national & international conferences. **BUSINESS ADDRESS:** Director, Washington State Lottery, 814 4th Avenue, PO Box 43001, Olympia, WA 98506, (206)753-3330.

YEO, YUNG KEE
Educator. Korean American. **PERSONAL:** Born Apr 24, 1938, Song Jook-Ri, Kyungbuk, Republic of Korea; son of Nam Jin Yeo & Jong Soon Eom; married Young Ok Yeo, May 31, 1964; children: Song Mi, Lami. **EDUCATION:** Seoul National University, Korea, BS, 1961, graduate school, 1961-64; University of Southern California, PhD, 1972. **CAREER:** University of Southern California, postdoc, 1972; Develco Inc, physicist, 1973-74; University of Oregon, postdoc, 1974-77; AF Wright Aeronautical Laboratories, resident scientist, 1977-78; Systems Research Laboratories Inc, senior physicist, 1978-80; Universal Energy Systems Inc, principal investigator, 1980-84; Air Force Institute of Technology, professor of physics, 1984-. **ORGANIZATIONS:** American Physical Society; Materials Research Society; Korean Scientists and Engineers Association in America; Association of Korean Physicists in America. **HONORS/AWARDS:** Air Force Institute of Technology, Professor Kotcher Award, 1990, Gage H Crocker Outstanding Professor Award, 1992. **SPECIAL ACHIEVEMENTS:** Conducted electrical and optical characterization studies on various electronic and optoelectronic semiconductors; published over 40 archival journal articles; presented over 90 papers at professional conferences; reviewer for Applied Physics Letters, Journal of Applied Physics, and Air Force Office of Scientific Research. **MILITARY SERVICE:** Korean Army, 1962-63. **BUSINESS ADDRESS:** Professor, Dept of Engineering Physics, Air Force Institute of Technology, 2950 P St, Bldg 640, Rm 134B, Wright-Patterson Air Force Base, Dayton, OH 45433-7765, (513)255-4498.

YEP, LAWRENCE MICHAEL
Writer. Chinese American. **PERSONAL:** Born Jun 14, 1948, San Francisco, CA; son of Thomas Gim Yep & Franche Lee Yep; married Joanne Ryder, Feb 14, 1989. **EDUCATION:** UC, Santa Cruz, BA, 1970; SUNY, Buffalo, PhD, 1975. **CAREER:** San Jose City College, instructor, 1975-76; Foothill College, Mountain View, instructor, 1975; UC, Berkeley, visiting lecturer, 1987-89. **HONORS/AWARDS:** ALA, Newbery Honor, 1976; IRA, Children's Book Award, 1976; NCSS, Carter G Woodson Award, 1976; Horn Book, Boston Globe, award, 1978; Commonwealth Club, Children's Book Award, 1979; Christopher Society, Christopher Medal, 1992. **SPECIAL ACHIEVEMENTS:** Author: Sweetwater, 1973; Dragonwings, 1975; Child of the Owl, Seademons, 1977; Sea Glass, 1979; The Mark Twain Murders, 1981; Kind Hearts & Gentle Monsters, 1982; Liar, Liar, Dragon of the Lost Sea, 1983; Serpent's Children, Shadow Lord, The Tom Sawyer Fires, 1984; Dragon Steel, Montain Light, 1985; Monster Makers Inc, 1986; Curse of the Squirrel, 1987; Rainbow People, 1989; Dragon Cauldron, 1991; The Lost Garden, 1991; The Star Fisher, 1991; Tongues of Jade, 1991; forthcoming: The Boy Who Swallowed Snakes; The Dragon Prince; Hiroshima; Later, Gator; The Shepherd; The Starmaker; When Dragons Weep; American Dragons, 1993; Dragon's Gate, 1993; The Ghost Fox, 1993; The Man Who Tricked A Ghost, 1993; Shell Woman and the King, 1993; The Tiger Woman, 1993; numerous others.

YEP, RALPH LEE
Physician, educator. Chinese American. **PERSONAL:** Born Dec 12, 1957, Oakland, CA; son of Robert Lai Yep and Lena Yep; married Lori Yep Kam, Aug 25, 1984; children: Melinda Kam, Daniel Kam. **EDUCATION:** UC-Riverside, BS, biomedical sciences, 1979; UCLA School of Medicine, MD, 1983. **CAREER:** Southern California Permanente Medical Group, staff physician, 1986-; UCLA School of Nursing, asst clinical professor, 1987-; USC School of Medicine, clinical instructor, 1990-. **ORGANIZATIONS:** American Academy of Family Physicians, 1983-; California Academy of Family Physicians, 1983-. **HONORS/AWARDS:** American Board of Family Practice, Diplomate, 1986, 1992; American Academy of Family Physicians, Fellow, 1989. **BUSINESS ADDRESS:** Family Practitioner, Southern California Permanente Medical Group, 12001 W Washington Blvd, Los Angeles, CA 90066, (310)915-5000.

YEUNG, CHUN W.
State government official. Chinese American. **PERSONAL:** Born Feb 27, 1949, Los Angeles, CA; son of Shang Sung Young and Chow Q Lam; married Susan Yeung, Jun 6, 1974; children: Ernest. **EDUCATION:** California State University, Los Angeles, BA, economics, 1973; St John's University, MBA,

accounting, 1980. **CAREER:** Worldwide Shipping Co, Hong Kong, junior executive, 1973-76; Worldwide Marine, Inc, assistant chartering manager, 1976-80; Sino Am Marine, Inc, shipbroker, 1981-84; Florida Department of Revenue, audit group supervisor, 1985-. **HONORS/AWARDS:** St John's University Chapter, Beta Gamma Sigma, 1981; Florida Board of Accountancy, CPA, 1988. **SPECIAL ACHIEVEMENTS:** Proficient in Chinese (Mandarin & Cantonese); seminars to: Chinese delegation on Beijing Tax Bureau; Audit Branch of Department of Commerce, 1993. **HOME ADDRESS:** 16627 Chariot Pl, Hacienda Heights, CA 91745, (818)330-0528.

YEUNG, RONALD WAI-CHUN (R. W.)
Educator. Chinese American. **PERSONAL:** Born Jul 19, 1945, Hong Kong; son of Foo and Pui-Fong Yeung; married Grace Y Chow, Sep 5, 1970; children: Brian Hao-Wen. **EDUCATION:** University of California, Berkeley, BS, mech engineering, 1968, MS, naval arch, 1970, PhD, 1973. **CAREER:** Litton Ship Systems, Culver City, CA, naval architect, 1970-71; MIT, Dept of Ocean Engineering, assistant professor, 1973-78, associate professor, 1978-82; University of Hamburg, West Germany, Institut fur Schiffbau, Humboldt Professor, 1988-89; University of California, Berkeley, Dept of Naval Architecture & Offshore Engineering, professor of hydromechanics, 1982-, dept chair, 1989-. **ORGANIZATIONS:** Society of Naval Architects & Marine Engineers, H-5 Technical Panel, Analytical Ship-Wave Relations, 1975-; American Society of Engineering Education, 1974-; Society of Naval Architects of Japan, 1989-; International Society of Offshore & Polar Engineering, 1992-; Phi Beta Kappa, Tau Beta Pi, Pi Tau Sigma, 1968-; Journal of Ship Research, editorial board, 1978-; Intl Journal of Computers & Fluids, editorial board, 1984-; Journal of Engineering Mathematics, editorial board, 1988-. **HONORS/AWARDS:** American Society of Mech Engineers, Best Paper Award for Originality & Significance, OMAE Div, 1992; Alexander v Humboldt Foundation, Germany, US Distinguished Scientist Award, 1988; University of Adelaide, S Australia, Dept of Applied Math, Fulbright-Hays Foundation, US Australian Education Foundation, Senior Fulbright Fellowship, 1981; University of California, Berkeley, University Gold Medal, 1968. **SPECIAL ACHIEVEMENTS:** Expert in ship & ocean related hydromechanics, numerical fluid mechanics, surface wave phenomena, and wave-vorticity interaction; published over 50 articles in technical journals & conference proceedings; research work has been supported by Sea Grant/NOAA, NSF, Office of Naval Research & Ocean Industry. **BIOGRAPHICAL SOURCES:** Oakland Tribune, p1, column 1, June 15, 1968. **HOME ADDRESS:** 27 Indian Wells, Moraga, CA 94556. **BUSINESS ADDRESS:** Prof & Dept Chairman, Dept of Naval Architecture & Offshore Engineering, University of California, Berkeley, 300A Naval Arch Bldg, Berkeley, CA 94720, (510)642-5464.

YI, GANG
Educator. Chinese American. **PERSONAL:** Born Mar 5, 1958, Beijing, People's Republic of China; son of Zhen Yi and Zhao An; married Jingping Guo, May 10, 1985; children: Justin. **EDUCATION:** Peking University, China, 1978-80; Hamline University, BA (cum laude), business, 1982; University of Illinois, Urbana, MS, economics, 1984, PhD, economics, 1986. **CAREER:** Indiana University, Indianapolis, assistant professor, 1986-92, associate professor of economics, 1992-. **ORGANIZATIONS:** Chinese Economists Society, president, 1992-93; American Economic Association, 1987-; Association for Comparative Economic Studies, 1987-. **HONORS/AWARDS:** Chinese Economists Society, fellow, 1993; Hamline University, full scholarship, 1980-82. **SPECIAL ACHIEVEMENTS:** Money, Banking and Financial Markets in China, Westview Press, 1993; Chinese Economic Reform: Retrospect and Comtemplation, special issue of China Economic Review, JAI Press, 1991; Introduction to Money and Banking, in Chinese, Shanghai People's Press, 1993; published many articles in refereed journals on Chinese economy and econometrics. **BUSINESS ADDRESS:** Professor, Dept of Economics, Indiana University, 425 University Blvd, Indianapolis, IN 46202-5140, (317)274-7217.

YI, XIAOXIONG
Educator. Chinese American. **PERSONAL:** Born Jul 8, 1953, Beijing, People's Republic of China; son of Lirong Yi & Xin Yu. **EDUCATION:** Beijing Normal University, BA, 1982; Pennsylvania State University, MA, 1985; American University, PhD, 1993. **CAREER:** Beijing 123 Senior High School, teacher, 1982-83; Dickinson College, instructor, 1988-89; Marietta College, associate professor, 1989-. **ORGANIZATIONS:** American Political Science Association, 1993-; Association for Asian Studies, 1989-. **HONORS/AWARDS:** John Fletcher Hurst Fellowship, 1985-88. **SPECIAL ACHIEVEMENTS:** Publication: "China's Korea Policy," Global Affairs, winter 1993; "China and the Two Koreas," Korea and World Affairs, spring 1994. **BUSI-**

NESS ADDRESS: Assistant Professor, Marietta College, 105 Thomas Hall, Marietta, OH 45750-3031, (614)374-7502.

YIEN, JEAN MAY
Architect. Chinese American. **PERSONAL:** Born Dec 29, 1952, Lincoln, NE; daughter of Chen Hwa Yien and Tan Ju-Lu Yien; married Paul R Riley, Dec 29, 1992. **EDUCATION:** University of Nebraska, 1971-73; Kansas State University, BA, 1977. **CAREER:** Architects & Planners International, drafter, 1977-78; Slater-Paull & Associates, drafter, 1978-79; Stearns-Roger Architects, Ltd, specifications writer, 1979-80; CM, Inc/Constructors & Managers, estimator, sched, 1981; Stearns-Catalytic, architect, 1981-89; City of Aurora, Colorado, plans examiner, 1989-90; Raytheon Engineers & Constructors, consulting architect, 1990-. **ORGANIZATIONS:** International Council of Building Officials, 1991-; Construction Specifications Institute, membership chairman, 1991-92. **HONORS/AWARDS:** International Naginata Federation, 2nd, 3rd Goodwill Tournaments, third place team comp, 1992; US Naginata Federation, national tournament, second place Shiai, sparring, 1991, 1993, second place Engi comp, form, 1991, second place team comp, 1993; Certified Plans Examiner; Certified Special Inspector Spray Applied Fireproofing; Int Fire Code Inst, Certified Uniform Fire Code Insp. **BUSINESS ADDRESS:** Consulting Architect, Raytheon Engineers & Constructors, 5555 Greenwood Plaza Blvd, Englewood, CO 80111, (303)843-3330.

YIH, CHIA-SHUN
Educator (retired). Chinese American. **PERSONAL:** Born Jul 25, 1918, Guiyang, Guizhou, China; son of Ting-Jian Yih and Wan-Lan Shao Yih; married Shirley A Yih, Feb 17, 1949; children: Yiu-Yo, Yuen-Ming David, Weiling Katherine. **EDUCATION:** National Central University, BS, 1942; University of Iowa, MS, 1947, PhD, 1948. **CAREER:** University of Wisconsin, instructor of mathematics, 1948-49; University of British Columbia, lecturer of mathematics, 1949-50; State University of Colorado, associate professor of civil engineering, 1950-52; University of Iowa, associate research eng, associate professor, 1952-56; University of Michigan, associate professor, 1956-58, professor, 1958-68, S P Timoshenko Distinguished University Professor, 1968-88; University of Florida, graduate research professor, 1988-90. **ORGANIZATIONS:** American Physical Society, fellow, 1959-; American Physical Society, Fluid Dynamics Division, chairman of the executive committee, 1973-74; Intl Assn of Hydraulic Research, 1956-82, chairman of the committee on fundamentals, 1979-82; Academia Sinica, 1970-; US Natl Academy of Engineering, 1980-. **HONORS/AWARDS:** University of Michigan, Henry Russel Lecturer, 1974; Alexander von Humboldt Foundation, Senior Scientist Award, 1977; American Society of Civil Engineers, Theodore von Karman Medal, 1981; American Physical Society, Fluid Dynamics Prize, 1985, Otto Laporte Award, 1989; University of Florida, Sir Geoffrey Taylor Lecturer, 1992. **SPECIAL ACHIEVEMENTS:** Dynamic of Nonhomogeneous Fluids, Macmillan Co, 1965; Fluid Mechanics, McGraw-Hill Co, 1969, West River Press, 1979, 1984, 1988; Stratified Flows, Academic Press, 1980; selected papers, in two volumes, World Scientific, 1991; 120 scientific papers in professional journals.

YIH, ROY YANGMING
Research department manager. Chinese American. **PERSONAL:** Born Oct 5, 1931, Changsha, Hunan, China; married Madeline W Yih, Oct 21, 1960; children: Ann, Jean Yih Kingston, John. **EDUCATION:** Taiwan National Normal University, BS, 1956; University of South Carolina, MS, 1959; Rutgers University, PhD, 1963. **CAREER:** Rohm and Haas Company, senior scientist, 1962-64, group leader, 1965-71, lab head, 1972, project leader, 1973-82, research department manager, 1982-. **ORGANIZATIONS:** American Chemical Society, 1965-. **SPECIAL ACHIEVEMENTS:** More than 20 articles published in scientific journals, including Science, Journal of Agr and Food Chemistry, Weed Science; more than 30 patents for herbicides. **MILITARY SERVICE:** Chinese Air Force, lieutenant, 1954-55. **BUSINESS ADDRESS:** Research Dept Manager, Rohm and Haas Company, 727 Norristown Road, Spring House, PA 19477, (215)619-5531.

YIH, YUEHWERN
Educator, engineer. Chinese American. **PERSONAL:** Born Dec 16, 1962, Keelung, Taiwan; daughter of Ren-Ku Yih and Cheng Gwey-Rong Yih; married Jong-I Mou, Jan 11, 1987. **EDUCATION:** National Tsing Hua University, Taiwan, BSIE, 1984; University of Wisconsin-Madison, PhD, 1988. **CAREER:** University of Wisconsin-Madison, teaching assistant, 1985-88; Purdue University, assistant professor, 1989-. **ORGANIZATIONS:** Institute of Industrial Engineers, Chapter 35, 1987-, secretary, 1990-92, vice president, 1992-93,

president, 1993-94; The Institute of Management Science, 1988-; American Assn of Artificial Intelligence, 1992-; America Chinese Management Educators Assn, 1987-; Artificial Intelligence Committee of the Indiana Corporation for Science and Technology, 1990-. **HONORS/AWARDS:** National Science Foundation, Young Investigator Award, 1993; NEC Corporation, Faculty Fellow, 1993; General Electric Foundation, Junior Faculty Fellow, 1992; Pacific Region Management International Conference, Best Paper Award, 1992; Omega Rho Honor Society, 1990; National Tsing Hua University, Dr Y C May Leadership Scholarship, 1983. **SPECIAL ACHIEVEMENTS:** Published: fourteen refereed archival journal papers on artificial intelligence and production control, 1990-93; fifteen research conference proceeding papers, 1987-93; gave twenty-four presentations in research conferences, invited seminars, workshops and short courses in Taiwan, Hong Kong, Germany, Japan, and the USA, 1986-93; co-editor with Y C Lee and W T Chen, Manufacturing Aspects in Electronic Packaging, 1993. **BUSINESS ADDRESS:** Assistant Professor, Purdue University, School of Industrial Engineering, 1287 Grissom Hall, Rm 228-A, West Lafayette, IN 47907-1287, (317)494-0826.

YIM, CHI-KIN BENNETT
Educator. Chinese American. **PERSONAL:** Born Jul 14, 1961, Hong Kong; son of Chun Kwok Yim and Siu Yin Chan; married Yin-Mei Ng-Yim; children: Rebecca L. **EDUCATION:** Chinese University of Hong Kong, BBA, marketing, 1983; Purdue University, PhD, management, 1989. **CAREER:** Chinese University of Hong Kong, teaching assistant, 1983-84; Purdue University, teaching assistant, 1984-89; Rice University, assistant professor, 1989-. **ORGANIZATIONS:** The Institution of Management Science, 1984-. **HONORS/AWARDS:** Rice University, Jones Graduate School, Teaching Excellence Award, 1993. **SPECIAL ACHIEVEMENTS:** "A Price Expectations Model of Customer Brand Choice," Journal of Marketing Research, 1990; "Consumer Price and Promotion Expectations: An Experimental Study," Journal of Marketing Research, 1992. **BUSINESS ADDRESS:** Assistant Professor, Jesse H Jones Graduate School of Administration, Rice University, PO Box 1892, Houston, TX 77251-1892, (713)285-5392.

YIM, SOLOMON C. S.
Educator. Hong Kong American. **PERSONAL:** Born Sep 11, 1952, Hong Kong; son of S C Leung-Yim and F C Yim; married Lenore S Hata, Aug 27, 1983; children: Rachel, Joshua. **EDUCATION:** Rice University, BS (summa cum laude), 1976; University of California, Berkeley, MS, 1977, MA, 1981, PhD, 1983. **CAREER:** University of California, Berkeley, research engineering assistant, 1983-84; visiting lecturer, 1983-84; Exxon Production Research Company, research engineer, 1984-85, senior research engineer, 1986-87; University of California, Berkeley, visiting associate professor, 1993-; Oregon State University, assistant professor, 1987-91, associate professor, 1991-. **ORGANIZATIONS:** ASCE; ASME; ASEE; ISOPE; American Society of Civil Engineers, EMD Dynamics Committee, 1988-; Dept of Defense, Science and Engineering Graduate Fellowship Committee, 1989-; ASCE Structural Engineering Div, Reliability of Offshore Structures committee, 1992-, Journal of Waterway, Port Coastal and Ocean Engr, Publication Committee, 1991-; International Society of Offshore and Polar Engineers, Student Activities Committee, chairman, 1991-; National Research Council, Ship Structures Committee, Design Work Group, International Society of Offshore and Polar Engineers, International Conference Technical Program Committee, 1992-. **HONORS/AWARDS:** Tau Beta Pi, 1975; Phi Beta Kappa, 1976; University of California, Earle C Anthony Fellowship, 1976; Xi Epsilon, 1977; US Navy/ONR, ONR Young Investigator, 1988-91; US Navy/ASEE, Senior Faculty Research Fellow, 1993; Norwegian Science and Engineering Faculty Visiting Research Fellow, 1994. **SPECIAL ACHIEVEMENTS:** Research in earthquake engineering, 1977-; research in offshore structural dynamics, 1984-; research in chaos theory and applications in engineering, 1987-; research in nonlinear stochastic systems theory and applications, 1984-; over 60 books, journals, conference proceedings, and reports published; over 40 seminars and workshops. **BIOGRAPHICAL SOURCES:** OSU College of Engineering Research Activities Annual Report, vol no 63, p 2, 1987-88. **BUSINESS ADDRESS:** Associate Professor, Dept of Civil Engineering, Oregon State University, Apperson Hall 202, Corvallis, OR 97331-2302, (503)737-6894.

YIM, SOO JUNG
Lawyer. Korean American. **PERSONAL:** Born Aug 15, 1966, Seoul, Republic of Korea; daughter of Am Im & Bongim Im; married Seong-Jae Yim, Oct 12, 1991. **EDUCATION:** Harvard College, BA (magna cum laude), 1989; Harvard Law School, JD (magna cum laude), 1992. **CAREER:** World Bank, Legal Department, Ford Fellow, 1992-93; Wilmer, Cutler & Pickering, associate,

1993-. **ORGANIZATIONS:** Phi Beta Kappa, 1989-. **HONORS/AWARDS:** Harvard Law School, Ford Fellowship in International Law, 1990. **SPECIAL ACHIEVEMENTS:** Author: "Privatization in the Former Soviet Union," World Bank, 1993; "Emerging Stock Markets," ICSID Review, 1993; "Recent Securities Regulations in the European Community," Harvard International Law Journal, 1991. **BIOGRAPHICAL SOURCES:** Korean Economic Daily, July, 1992. **BUSINESS ADDRESS:** Associate Attorney, Wilmer, Cutler & Pickering, 2445 M St, NW, Washington, DC 20037-1420, (202)663-6000.

YIN, GANG GEORGE
Educator. Chinese American. **PERSONAL:** Born Aug 26, 1954, Beijing, People's Republic of China; son of Yi-Xin Yin & Wan-Zhen Zhu. **EDUCATION:** University of Delaware, BS (magna cum laude), mathematics, 1983; Brown University, MS, applied mathematics, 1984, MS, electric engineering, 1987, PhD, applied mathematics, 1987. **CAREER:** Institute for Mathematics & Its Appl, visiting member, 1988-90; Exxon Res Eng Co, visiting scholar, 1991; Brown University, visiting assistant professor, 1991; University of Toronto, visiting assistant professor, 1991; Wayne State University, lecturer, 1987-89, assistant professor, 1990-92, associate professor, 1992-. **ORGANIZATIONS:** Mathematical Review Comm for Reviewing the Content of the MR data base, 1992-; International Association on Untraditional Optim Methods, 1991-; Stochastic Optim & Design, journal editorial board, 1991-; American Mathematical Society, 1984-; Institute of Elect & Electronics Eng, 1987-; Society for Industrial & Applied Mathematics; ESD, the Engineering Society, 1992-; Sigma Xi; SIAM Activity Group in Control and Systems Theory Newsletter, editor, 1993-. **HONORS/AWARDS:** Wayne State University, Career Development Chair Award, 1993; Brown University, University Fellowship, 1983; University of Delaware, William D Clark Prize, 1983; Pi Mu Epsilon; Phi Kappa Phi. **SPECIAL ACHIEVEMENTS:** Published over 30 papers in refereed journals such as IEEE Transactions on Automatic Control, IEEE Transaction on Information Theory, Journal of Mathematical Analysis and Applications, SIAM Journal on Control and Optimization, Stochastic Processes and Applications, Stochastics etc, and over 20 papers in conference proceedings; books: Introduction to Systems Analysis, Russian Academy of Sciences and Engineering Siberia Branch, 1993; dissertation: Asymptotic Properties of Decentralized Stochastic Approximation Alogrithms, 1987. **BUSINESS ADDRESS:** Associate PRO, Dept of Mathematics, Wayne State University, Detroit, MI 48202.

YIN, GEORGE KUO-MING
Educator. Chinese American. **PERSONAL:** Born Mar 14, 1949, New York, NY; son of Paul Huo-Chun Yin and Loo-Yuin How Yin; married Mary J Walter, May 11, 1974; children: Elizabeth Pei-Hua, Laura Hsiao-Yuin. **EDUCATION:** University of Michigan, BA, 1970; University of Florida, MEd, 1972; George Washington University, JD, 1977. **CAREER:** US Court of Claims, judicial law clerk, 1977-78; Sutherland, Asbill & Brennan, attorney, 1978-83; US Senate Finance Comm, tax counsel, 1983-85; University of Pennsylvania, visiting assoc prof, 1988; US Joint Comm on Taxation, visiting professor, 1990; Brigham Young University, visiting professor of law, 1992; University of Virginia, visiting professor of law, 1993; University of Florida, associate professor, 1986-91, professor of law, 1991-. **ORGANIZATIONS:** American Law Institute, consultant, 1987-93; US House Ways & Means Comm, consultant, 1988-; American Tax Policy Institute, bd of trustees, 1991-; Florida Tax Review, bd of editors, 1992-; IRS Contin Prof Educ Pgrm, bd of advisers, 1991-93; DC Bar, 1977-; ABA Tax Section, 1978-; Life Skills Center, bd of directors, president, 1982-83, vp, 1977-80. **SPECIAL ACHIEVEMENTS:** Corporate Tax Integration and the Search for the Pragmatic Ideal, 47 Tax L Rev, 431, 1992; Redesigning the Earned Income Tax Credit Program to Provide More Effective Assistance for the Working Poor, 59 Tax Notes 951, 1993; Of Indianapolis Power & Light and the Definition of Debt: Another View, 11 Va Tax Rev, 467, 1991; A Different Approach to the Taxation of Corporate Distributions: Theory & Implementation of a Uniform Corporate-Level Distributions Tax, 78 Georgetown LJ 1837, 1990. **BIOGRAPHICAL SOURCES:** ABA Section of Taxation Newsletter, vol 10, no 1, Fall, 1990, p11; Gainesville Sun, September 16, 1990, p1-G. **BUSINESS ADDRESS:** Professor, College of Law, University of Florida, Holland Hall, Gainesville, FL 32611, (904)392-1081.

YIN, LO I.
Physicist (retired). Chinese American. **PERSONAL:** Born Apr 19, 1930, Wuchang, Hubei, China; married Won Ok Yin, Jul 7, 1958; children: Way, Hwei. **EDUCATION:** Central China University, Wuchang, BA, English,

1949; Carleton College, BA, music, 1951; Eastman School of Music, MA, music, 1952; University of Rochester, BS, 1956; University of Michigan, Ann Arbor, MS, physics, 1959, PhD, physics, 1963. **CAREER:** Bendix Research Lab, research physicist, 1964-67; NASA Goddard Space Flight Center, astrophysicist, 1967-90; University of Maryland, adjunct professor, chemistry, 1977-87. **ORGANIZATIONS:** American Physical Society, 1963-; American Association for the Advancement of Science, 1968-; American Nuclear Society, 1975-89; Society of Photo-Optical Engineers, 1975-89. **HONORS/ AWARDS:** Industrial Research Magazine, IR-100, 100 most significant new technology, 1979; NASA, Inventor of the Year, 1980, Goddard Space Flight Center, Outstanding Service Award, 1979, 10 certificates of recognition for science, technology & invention, 1977-83. **SPECIAL ACHIEVEMENTS:** Inventor of the Lixiscope, miniature x-ray imaging device, 1977; 5 US patents on x-ray and gamma-ray imaging devices, 1979-88; 90 publications on nuclear, atomic and chemical physics; electron, x-ray and gamma-ray spectroscopy; x-ray and gamma-ray imaging. **HOME ADDRESS:** 1207 Downs Dr, Silver Spring, MD 20904, (301)622-0296.

YIN, MARK Y. Q.
Educator. Chinese American. **PERSONAL:** Born Jul 12, 1930, Shenyang, China; son of Shochen; married; children: Yin Yin, Zhong Yin. **EDUCATION:** University of Pittsburgh, PhD, 1985. **CAREER:** China University of Science and Tech, professor, 1962-81; University of Arizona, assistant professor, 1985-88; University of Massachusetts, Lowell, professor, 1988-. **HONORS/AWARDS:** National Science Foundation, 1987, 1989. **SPECIAL ACHIEVEMENTS:** Forty articles published in refereed journals, including: Annals of Probability; Probability Theory and Applications; Probability Theory and Related Fields. **BUSINESS ADDRESS:** Professor, Dept of Math, University of Massachusetts, 218 Olsen, Lowell, MA 01854, (508)934-2431.

YIN, RONALD L.
Attorney. Chinese American. **PERSONAL:** Born Jul 23, 1947, Shanghai, China; son of Homer and Virginia Yin; married Peggy. **EDUCATION:** MIT, BS, 1969; Cornell University, MS, 1970; Georgetown University Law School, JD, 1974. **CAREER:** RCA Corp, patent counsel, 1974-76; Measurex Corp, corporate legal counsel, 1976-80; Limbach & Limbach, partner, 1980-. **ORGANIZATIONS:** California Bar, exec comm of IP section, 1990-93; Asian-American Bar Assn, 1981-; Asian-Business League, 1983-; American Bar Association, 1980-. **BIOGRAPHICAL SOURCES:** California Lawyer, p 30, Mar 1992; Martindale-Hubbell Law Directory-AV Rating, 1992. **BUSINESS ADDRESS:** Partner, Limbach & Limbach, 2001 Ferry Bldg, San Francisco, CA 94111, (415)433-4150.

YIN, XIAO-HUANG
Educator, scholar. Chinese American. **PERSONAL:** Born Aug 25, 1954, Yangzhou, People's Republic of China; married. **EDUCATION:** Nanjing University, China, BA, 1979; Harvard University, AM, 1987, PhD, 1991. **CAREER:** Nanjing University, lecturer, 1981-85; Occidental College, assistant professor, 1991-. **ORGANIZATIONS:** Harvard University, Center for East Asian Research, associate, 1991-; Paragon House Publishers, corresponding editor, 1988-; American Historical Association, 1991-. **HONORS/ AWARDS:** Natl Endowment for the Humanities, 1993; Massachusetts Historical Society, Andrew Mellon Fellowship, 1992; Whiting Foundation, fellowship, 1990-91; Smithsonian Institution, Predoctoral Fellowship, 1989; Harvard-Yenching Fellowship, 1985-86. **SPECIAL ACHIEVEMENTS:** "Between East and West," Arizona Quarterly, vol 47, no 4, 1991; "Progress and Problems: American Studies in China in the Post-Mao Era," As Others Read Us, University of Mass Press, 1991; "The Scarlet Letter in China," American Quarterly, vol 39, no 4, 1987; co-translator: Secret Speeches of Chairman Mao, Harvard University Press, 1989; A Documentary History of the Communist Party of China, 1994; "A Land of Opportunity and Uncertainty: China Revisited," Atlantic Monthly, April 1994. **BUSINESS ADDRESS:** Professor, Occidental College, 1600 Campus Road, Los Angeles, CA 90041, (213)259-2578.

YIN, ZENONG
Educator. Chinese American. **PERSONAL:** Born Jun 9, 1960, Zhengzhon, Henan, People's Republic of China; son of Guaishan Yin and Yuqing Lin; married Yun Wang, 1989. **EDUCATION:** Beijing Institute of Physical Education, China, BEd, 1981; University of Southern California, MA, 1985, PhD, 1990. **CAREER:** University of Southern California, Department of Physical Education, instructor, 1984-88; Brown University, Athletic Department, assistant head swimming coach, instructor, 1988-91; University of Texas, Hispanic Research Center, faculty associate, 1992-, Division of Education, assistant

professor, 1991-. **ORGANIZATIONS:** American Alliance for Health, Physical Education, Recreation and Dance, 1987-; North American Society for Psychology of Sport and Physical Activity, 1988-; Texas Association for Health, Physical Education, Recreation and Dance, Region 20 Rep, 1991-. **HONORS/AWARDS:** Brown University Athletic Department, Florence Filippo Award, 1988-89, 1990-91. **SPECIAL ACHIEVEMENTS:** Co-author, "Correlates of Learned Helplessness in Youth Sport and Physical Activity," Applied Research in Coaching and Athletics Annual, 1993; co-author, "Ten Questions about Mainstreaming," Strategies: A Journal for Sport and Physical Educators, 1993; Olympic Organizing Committee, 1984; certified official interpreter: Mandarin, Chinese. **BUSINESS ADDRESS:** Assistant Professor, Division of Education, University of Texas, San Antonio, 6900 NW Loop 1604, San Antonio, TX 78249-0600, (210)691-5642.

YIU, ERIC. *See* YIU, PAO ON.

YIU, PAO ON (ERIC YIU)
Manufacturing company executive. Chinese American. **EDUCATION:** Hong Kong Polytechnic, 1971-72; Golden Gate University, MBA, 1987. **CAREER:** GTE Sylvania Far East Ltd, cost accountant, 1976-78; National Semiconductor, Hong Kong, cost accounting manager, 1978-80, financial controller, 1981-83, Singapore, financial controller, 1983-84, senior product line controller, 1985-89; Matel Toys Hong Kong Ltd, assistant financial controller, 1980-81; Dyna-Craft Inc, director of finance, 1989-. **ORGANIZATIONS:** Chartered Institute of Management Accountants, associate member, 1977-. **BUSINESS ADDRESS:** Director of Finance, Dyna-Craft Inc, 2919 San Ysidro Way, Santa Clara, CA 95051, (408)721-2754.

YOH, JOHN K.
Scientist. Chinese American. **PERSONAL:** Born Oct 9, 1944, Shanghai, China; son of Joseph Yoh & Esther Way; married Hua Zheng, Jun 23, 1984; children: Kathryn E. **EDUCATION:** Cornell University, BA, 1964; Cal Tech, MS, 1966, PhD, 1970. **CAREER:** CERN, European Centre for Nuclear Research, NATO postdoctoral fellow, 1970-71, visiting scientist, 1971-73; Columbia University, research associate, 1973-77, assistant professor, 1977-80; FermiLab, scientist, 1980-. **SPECIAL ACHIEVEMENTS:** Co-discoverer of Upsilon Particle, Bottom Quark, 1977, B-Mesons, 1978-81. **BUSINESS ADDRESS:** Scientist, FermiLab, PO Box 500, MS 223, Batavia, IL 60510.

YONAMINE, HENRY KIYOSHI
Survey technician. Japanese American. **PERSONAL:** Born Dec 15, 1935, Keaau, HI; son of Matsuzo Yonamine (deceased) and Uta Arakaki (deceased); married Evelyn Miyoko Maru Yonamine, Jun 12, 1965; children: Clint K, Don K, Roy K. **EDUCATION:** Hono Community College, 1957-58; Honolulu Community College, 1982. **CAREER:** US Army Corp of Engineers, PODED, survey technician, permanent, 1982-. **ORGANIZATIONS:** Walter P Thompson, party chief, 1979-81; Parsons Hawaii, party chief, 1975-79; Towill Shigeoka & Associates, party chief, 1973-75; R M Towill Corp, party chief, 1970-73; Sam O Hirota Inc, instrument man, 1966-70. **HONORS/AWARDS:** Corps of Engineers, Special Act of Service Award, 1988, 1989, 1991, 1992, 1993. **MILITARY SERVICE:** US Army, sp3, 1953-56; National Defense Service Medal, Good Conduct Medal. **HOME ADDRESS:** 2924 Kolomona Pl, Honolulu, HI 96822, (808)988-6400.

YOO, CHAI HONG (JAY)
Educator. Korean American. **PERSONAL:** Born Sep 16, 1939, Seoul, Republic of Korea; son of Chong Ryul Yoo & Kwi Rhe Lim Yoo; married Chum Sook Lee Yoo, Jun 19, 1970; children: Anna, Laura. **EDUCATION:** Seoul National University, BS, 1962; University of Maryland, MS, 1969, PhD, 1971. **CAREER:** Pacific Architects & Engrs, engineer, 1966-67; University of Maryland, graduate research assistant, 1968-71; faculty research associate, 1972-73; visitng assistant professor, 1973-74; McGaughy, Marshall & McMillan Associates, str engineer, 1971-72; Marquette University, asst professor, assoc professor, 1975-81; Auburn University, assoc professor, professor, 1981-. **ORGANIZATIONS:** American Society of Civil Engineers, Comm Flexural Members, chairman, 1980-84; Structural Stability Research Council, Task Group #14, chairman, 1981-87; Korean Scientists & Engineers in America. **HONORS/ AWARDS:** NSF Grantee, 1979-81, 1983-86; NASA, New Technology Award, 1985. **SPECIAL ACHIEVEMENTS:** Co-author, Analysis and Design of Horizontally Curved Steel Bridges, McGraw Hill, 1988; author/co-author of over 30 refereed journal papers; generated over $2M of research funding. **BUSINESS ADDRESS:** Professor, Dept of Civil Engineering, Auburn Uni-

versity, 238 Harbert Engineering Center, Auburn, AL 36849-5337, (205)844-6279.

YOO, TAI-JUNE

Educator. Korean American. **PERSONAL:** Born Mar 7, 1935, Seoul, Republic of Korea; son of H J Yoo; married Marie Ann Yoo; children: Christine, Stephanie, Kathy. **EDUCATION:** Seoul National University, Korea, BS, 1955; Seoul National School of Medicine, Korea, MD, 1959; University of California, Berkeley, PhD, 1963. **CAREER:** University of California, Berkeley, teaching assistant, 1960-61; Niagara University, New York, research professor, 1967-69; University of Iowa, Iowa City, A/I research lab, director, assistant and associate professor of medicine, 1972-80; University of Tennessee, professor of medicine, professor of Microbiology & Imunology Neurosciences, chief division of allergy-imunology, 1980-. **ORGANIZATIONS:** American Association Adv of Science, 1969; American Association Immunologists, 1969; Association Research Otolaryngology, 1982; New York Academy of Science, 1969; Biophysical Society, 1966; American Association for Cancer Research, 1976; American Society Exp Pathology, 1976; American Academy of Allergy, 1972. **HONORS/AWARDS:** Korea Atomic Energy Office, post-doctoral research fellowship; NIH, post-doctoral fellowship; Clinical Investigatorship, VA, 1972-75. **SPECIAL ACHIEVEMENTS:** Molecular biology of collagen autoimmune injury; autoimmune sensorineural hearing loss, inner ear immunology; ultrastructure of collagen in the inner ear; molecular biology of cochlea and TCR transgene; genomic structure of 11q for the atopy and asthma gene. **MILITARY SERVICE:** ARCOM Surgeon, 125th Army Reserve Command, colonel, 1968-; selected for the master list for general officer, 1990. **BUSINESS ADDRESS:** Professor of Medicine, Microbiology & Immunology, University of Tennessee, Memphis, 956 Court Ave, Rm H300, Coleman Bldg, Memphis, TN 38163, (901)448-6663.

YOON, CHONGYUL JOHN

Educator, engineer. Korean American. **PERSONAL:** Born Sep 8, 1958, Seoul, Republic of Korea; son of Dae Kyun Yoon and Sung Do Yoon. **EDUCATION:** Massachusetts Institute of Technology, BSc, 1980, MSc, 1982; University of California at Berkeley, PhD, 1990. **CAREER:** Massachusetts Institute of Technology, instructor, 1982-83; Northeastern University, lecturer, 1983-84; PMB Engineering, senior engineer, consultant, 1989-90; Polytechnic University, Dept of Civil Engineering, asst professor, 1990-. **ORGANIZATIONS:** American Society of Civil Engineers, 1982-; American Institute of Steel Construction, faculty member, 1990-; American Society of Engineering Education, 1991-; Institute of Electrical and Electronic Engineers, 1991-; National Society of Professional Engineers, 1993-; Korean Society of Engineers in America, 1992-; Society for International Development, 1980-; Structural Engineers Assn of Northern California, 1987-. **HONORS/AWARDS:** NASA/ASEE, Summer Faculty Fellowship, 1991; University of California at Berkeley, tuition scholarship, 1985-90; Korean Government, Korean Honor Graduate Scholarship, 1987-89; Chi Epsilon, 1979-; Sigma Xi, 1979-. **SPECIAL ACHIEVEMENTS:** "An Object Oriented Design and Implementation of a Finite Element and Graphics Data Translation Facility," ASCE Journal of Computing in Civil Engineering, p 302-322, June 1992; "Object Oriented Development of Large Engineering Software Using CLIPS," Microcomputers in Civil Engineering, vol 18, 1993; "Application of Neural Networks to Solve Simple Truss Problems," Proceedings of the 2nd Canadian Conference on Computing in Civil Engineering, Ottawa, Canada, p 182-192, Aug 1992; licensed professional engineer, State of New York, 1993; language proficiency: Korean. **HOME PHONE:** (718)651-5744. **BUSINESS ADDRESS:** Assistant Professor, Dept of Civil and Environmental Engineering, Polytechnic University, Six Metrotech Center, 526 Rogers Hall, Brooklyn, NY 11201, (718)260-3016.

YOON, DAVID HWA HYUN

Educator. Korean American. **PERSONAL:** Born Aug 10, 1942, Seoul, Republic of Korea; son of Jae-il Yoon; married Young Oak Yoon, Dec 25, 1991. **EDUCATION:** SUNY, Buffalo, BA, 1975; Wayne State University, MA, 1980, PhD, 1989. **CAREER:** University of Michigan, Dearborn, assistant professor, 1989-. **ORGANIZATIONS:** Association for Computing Machinery; Institute of Electrical and Electronic Engineers. **SPECIAL ACHIEVEMENTS:** "The Categorical Framework of Object-Oriented Concurrent Systems," Computer & Mathematics with Applications: An International Journal, vol 25, no 2, p 33-38, 1993; "Basis Functions in Computer Aided Geometric Modeling," Mathematical Modelling and Scientific Computing, vol 2, section A, p 199-202. **BUSINESS ADDRESS:** Assistant Professor, University of Michigan, Dearborn, 4901 Evergreen Rd, 126 ELB, Dearborn, MI 48128-1491.

YOON, HYO-CHUN

Educator. Korean American. **PERSONAL:** Born Feb 13, 1959, Seoul, Republic of Korea; son of Samuel & Esther Yoon; married Katherine K Uyeda, Apr 7, 1990; children: Ian Yoshiro. **EDUCATION:** Harvard University, AB, 1981; UCLA, School of Medicine, MD, 1987, Molecular Biology Institute, PhD, 1988. **CAREER:** UCLA, Medical Center, Cardiovascular Interventional Radiology, assistant professor, 1993-. **BUSINESS ADDRESS:** Asst Professor, Dept of Radiological Sciences, University of California, Los Angeles, 10833 Le Conte Ave, CHS, Los Angeles, CA 90024.

YOON, KWANGSUN PAUL

Educator. Korean American. **PERSONAL:** Born Jul 19, 1947, Seoul, Republic of Korea; son of Se-Chang Yoon and Ki-In Lee; married Soon Young Park, Aug 21, 1976; children: Justin, Mark. **EDUCATION:** Seoul National University, Korea, BS, 1971; Kansas State University, MS, 1977, PhD, 1980. **CAREER:** Fairleigh Dickinson University, assistant professor, 1980-84, associate professor, 1984-93, professor, 1993-, deputy chairperson, 1990-. **ORGANIZATIONS:** Institute of Industrial Engineering, senior member, 1983-; Production and Operations Management Society, 1990-. **SPECIAL ACHIEVEMENTS:** Articles published in various journals, including The Engineering Economist, Intl Journal of Operations and Production Management; Journal of the Operational Research Society; Transactions of Institute of Industrial Engineering; Intl Journal of Production Research; author, Multiple Attribute Decision Making, Springer-Verlag, 260p, 1980; Methods for Multiple Attribute Decision Making, Sage, 90p, 1994. **HOME ADDRESS:** 645 Fairview Place, Wyckoff, NJ 07481. **BUSINESS ADDRESS:** Professor, Deputy Chairperson, Dept of Information Systems and Sciences, Fairleigh Dickinson University, Madison, NJ 07940, (201)593-8870.

YOON, MYUNG-HO

Educator. Korean American. **PERSONAL:** Born May 3, 1954, Seoul, Republic of Korea; son of Il-Kyun Yoon and Sook-Ja Chung Yoon; married Il-Sun Yoon, Jun 16, 1982; children: Haewon, Jinwoo, Michelle. **EDUCATION:** Houston Baptist University, BA, 1981; University of Houston, MBA, 1983, PhD, 1988. **CAREER:** Kytex Engineering Co Inc, accountant, 1979-80; Northeastern Illinois University, professor, 1989-; Felix Enterprises Inc, vice president, 1991-. **ORGANIZATIONS:** American Accounting Association, 1985-; Institute of Management Accountants, 1991-; Korean American Accounting Professors Association, 1990-. **HONORS/AWARDS:** Beta Gamma Sigma, 1989. **SPECIAL ACHIEVEMENTS:** Certified Tae Kwon Do instructor, 1976; Certified Accupuncture/Accupressurer, 1976. **HOME ADDRESS:** 3954 Dundee Rd, Northbrook, IL 60062, (708)205-9083. **BUSINESS ADDRESS:** Professor, Dept of Accounting & Finance, Northeastern Illinois University, 5500 N St Louis Ave, Chicago, IL 60625, (312)794-2551.

YOON, PETER HAESUNG

Physicist. Korean American. **PERSONAL:** Born Apr 3, 1958, Seoul, Republic of Korea; son of Doo-Hyuk Yoon and Ok-Hyun Koh; married Aeseun Loh Yoon, May 30, 1987; children: Elias Wonbin, Kate Wonmi. **EDUCATION:** Yonsei University, Seoul, Korea, BS, 1980; Massachusetts Institute of Technology, PhD, 1987. **CAREER:** Massachusetts Institute of Technology, postdoctoral research associate, 1987-89; University of Maryland, research associate, 1989-90, assistant research scientist, 1990-. **ORGANIZATIONS:** American Physical Society, 1987-; American Geophysical Union, 1987-; Sigma Xi, 1987-. **SPECIAL ACHIEVEMENTS:** Publication of more than 30 articles in international journals. **HOME ADDRESS:** 8920 Pembrook Woods, Laurel, MD 20723, (301)604-8815. **BUSINESS ADDRESS:** Assistant Research Scientist, University of Maryland, Institute for Physical Science and Technology, College Park, MD 20742, (301)405-4826.

YOON, PETER JIUNG

County official. Korean American. **PERSONAL:** Born Dec 9, 1961, Seoul, Republic of Korea; son of Bok Myung Yoon and Hae Sook Kang; married Bok Hee Kwon, May 6, 1989; children: Grace Sung Eun, Daniel Sung Hyun. **EDUCATION:** UC, Davis, 1980-82. **CAREER:** Applied Materials, computer specialist; County of Santa Clara, eligibility worker III, currently. **SPECIAL ACHIEVEMENTS:** Language proficiency: Korean. **HOME ADDRESS:** 2762 Kesey Lane, San Jose, CA 95132, (408)254-1908.

YOON, STEVEN ILSANG

Curator. Korean American. **PERSONAL:** Born Feb 9, 1931, Wonju, Republic of Korea; son of Tae Wan Yoon and Man Bong Whang; married Julia Hyun, Sep 27, 1961; children: Karen, Joyce, Peter. **EDUCATION:** Yonsei University, Seoul, Korea, BA, 1959, MMus, 1961; University of Pittsburgh, MSLS, 1967, PhD, 1977; Howard University, MA, education, 1969. **CAREER:** Kyun Myung High School, Seoul, Korea, music teacher, 1959-61; Martin Luther King Library, cataloger, 1967-70; Howard University, reference librarian, 1973-76, Technical Services, cataloger, 1976-80, Founders Library, curator, 1981-. **ORGANIZATIONS:** Korean American Scholarship Foundation, board of directors, 1980-; Korean Baptist Church of Washington, deacon, 1961-. **BUSINESS ADDRESS:** Curator, Founders Library, Howard University, 500 Howard Pl NW, Washington, DC 20059.

YOON, WON Z.
Educator, educational administrator. Korean American. **PERSONAL:** Born Oct 15, 1932, Pyongyang, Korea; son of Taesup & Haksil Yoon; married Young Sook Yoon, Aug 25, 1957; children: Merry, Mercy, David Tochin. **EDUCATION:** Friends University, BA, history, 1959; Wichita State University, MA, history, 1961; New York University, PhD, history, 1971. **CAREER:** New York State University, College at Geneseo, assistant professor, 1963-71; Siena College, Dept of History, associate professor, 1971-74, professor, 1974-, chairman, 1989-. **ORGANIZATIONS:** American-Asian Educational Exchange Inc, Publication Committee, reader, 1969; Journal of SE Asian Studies, reader, 1978-; National Endowment for Humanities, reviewer for research grant proposals, 1973-; Program Committee, World War II Conference at Siena College, 1987-; State University of New York, Albany, New York Conference on Asian Studies, Steering Committee, General Committee, Program Committee, 1988. **HONORS/AWARDS:** Friends University, Faith Scholarship, 1956; New York University, Founders' Day Award, 1971; Institute of SE Asian Studies, Singapore, visiting fellow, 1978; Japan-US Friendship Commission, research grant, 1987; Siena College, Faculty Research Grant, 1989. **SPECIAL ACHIEVEMENTS:** Burma: Japanese Military Administration, Selected Documents, 1941-45; Japan's Scheme for the Liberation of Burma and the Role of the Minami Kikan; "Manchukuo"; "Mukden Incident of 1931"; "The Marco Polo Bridge Incident of 1937"; "The Panay Incident of 1937"; "Military Expediency—A Determining Factor in the Japanese Policy Regarding Burmese Independence," Journal of Southeast Asian Studies; "Konosuke Matsushita," Great Lives from History, Twentieth Century. **BUSINESS ADDRESS:** Chairman and Professor, Dept of History, Siena College, Loudonville, NY 12211-1462, (518)783-4271.

YOON, YOUNGOHI CHOI (YOUNGOHI CHOI)
Educator. Korean American. **PERSONAL:** Born Apr 22, 1957, Republic of Korea; daughter of Byung R Choi and Eun S Lee; married Young J Yoon, Aug 13, 1983; children: Ruth S. **EDUCATION:** Chung-Ang University, BS, 1979; University of Pittsburgh, MS, 1982; University of Texas at Arlington, PhD, 1989. **CAREER:** University of Texas at Arlington, asst instructor, 1988-89, visiting asst prof, 1989; Southwest Missouri State University, asst prof, 1990-. **ORGANIZATIONS:** Decision Sciences Institutes, 1988-; American Assn for Artificial Intelligence, 1986-; Assn for Computing Machinery, 1990-. **BUSINESS ADDRESS:** Assistant Professor, Southwest Missouri State University, 901 S National Ave, Springfield, MO 65804, (417)836-4837.

YORITA, FRANK KAZUO
Orthodontist. Japanese American. **PERSONAL:** Born Jan 2, 1945, Tokyo, Japan; son of Tatsuo Yorita and Yoshi Yorita; divorced; children: Claire, Rachel. **EDUCATION:** University of California, Los Angeles, pre-dentistry, 1962-65; University of California, San Francisco Medical Center, BS, DDS, 1969; University of Southern California, certificate of specialization in orthodontics, 1972. **CAREER:** University of Southern California, Orthodontic Dept, asst clinical professor, 1972-84; private practice, orthodontist, currently. **ORGANIZATIONS:** California Dental Assn, 1969-; American Dental Assn, 1969-; American Assn of Orthodontists, 1972-; Pacific Coast Society of Orthodontists, 1972-; Orange County Dental Society, 1972-, editor, 1982-; Japanese-American Dental Society, 1972-; USC Dental Alumni Assn, 1971-, editor, 1982-; USC Orthodontic Alumni Assn, secretary-treasurer, president, 1972-; Orthodontic Research Foundation, 1974-; American Assn of Functional Orthodontics, 1980-; American Equilibration Society, 1982-; Orange County Performing Arts Center, founder, 1982-; Mothers and Others Against Child Abuse, bd member, 1988; Health Volunteers Overseas, 1989; Japanese-American National Museum, charter member, 1992-. **HONORS/AWARDS:** UCLA, Honors at Entrance, Alumni Scholarship, 1962; UCSF, Omicron Kappa Upsilon, 1969; Orange County Dental Society, Distinguished Service Award, 1988; Mothers and Others Against Child Abuse, Community Service Award, 1988, 1991; California Dental Assn, Journalism Award, 1981, 1989, 1992; Intl College of Dentists, Journalism Award, 1985; American College of Dentists,

Fellowship, 1990; Intl College of Dentists, 1991; Academy of Dentistry Intl, Fellowship, 1988; American Society of Dentistry for Children, Fellowship, 1985; Pierre Fauchard Academy, Fellowship, 1989. **SPECIAL ACHIEVEMENTS:** Certification, American Board of Orthodontics, 1981. **BUSINESS ADDRESS:** Dentist, 12777 Valley View St, Suite 222, Garden Grove, CA 92645, (714)893-7539.

YOROZU, WILLIAM S.
Landscape/irrigation contractor. Japanese American. **PERSONAL:** Born Jan 28, 1914, Thomas, WA; son of Tokisaburo Yorozu and Hatsu Yorozu; married Yae A Yorozu, Apr 8, 1945; children: Joyce A Larson, Christine, Kenneth T, David S. **EDUCATION:** Washington State University, BS, 1942. **CAREER:** T Yorozu Gardening Co, owner, 1935-. **ORGANIZATIONS:** Associate Landscape Contractors of America, member of board, 1965; Seattle Japanese Gardeners Association, advisor, currently; Washington Association of Landscape Professionals. **HONORS/AWARDS:** National Nurseryman Association, national award given by Nancy Reagan for waterfall garden in Seattle, WA, 1981; Seattle Realtors Association, Children's International Garden, 1985. **SPECIAL ACHIEVEMENTS:** University of Washington, aboretum, general contractor, 1961; Waterfall Garden, Seattle Washington, general contractor, 1980. **BUSINESS ADDRESS:** Owner, T Yorozu Gardening Co, 13335 32nd Ave S, Seattle, WA 98168-3957, (206)242-7700.

YOSHIDA, AKIRA
Scientist. Japanese American. **PERSONAL:** Born May 10, 1924, Okayama, Japan; son of Isao Yoshida & Etsu Yoshida; married Michiko Yoshida, Nov 10, 1954; children: Emmy. **EDUCATION:** University of Tokyo, faculty of sciences, MS, 1947, graduate school, 1954. **CAREER:** University of Tokyo, associate professor, 1952-60; University of Pennsylvania, senior research scientist, 1960-62; National Institutes, of Health, res sci, 1962-64; University of Washington, res prof, 1964-72; City of Hope Medical Center, director, Dept of Bioch Genetics, 1972-. **ORGANIZATIONS:** American Society Bio & Mol Biology; American Society Human Genet; American Society Hematol; Res Soc Alcoholism; Japan Society Bioch; New York Academy Sci; American Society Adv Sci. **HONORS/AWARDS:** Rockefeller Foundation, scholarship, 1956, international res grant, 1959; Japanese Society Human Genet, merit award, 1980; City of Hope Medical Center, achievement award, 1981; National Institutes of Health, merit grant award, 1988. **SPECIAL ACHIEVEMENTS:** Over 250 articles in professional journals and books. **BUSINESS ADDRESS:** Director, Dept of Biochemical Genetics, City of Hope Medical Center, 1450 E Duarte Rd, Duarte, CA 91010, (818)359-8111.

YOSHIDA, ALAN K.
Dentist. Japanese American. **PERSONAL:** Born Nov 1, 1954, Honolulu, HI; son of Kiyoshi & Doris Yoshida. **EDUCATION:** University of Hawaii, BS, 1976; University of the Pacific, DDS, 1979. **CAREER:** Strong-Carter Dental Clinic, staff dentist; Kalihi-Palama Dental Clinic, staff dentist; self-employed, dentist, currently. **ORGANIZATIONS:** Hawaii Dental Association, chairman political action committee, 1993-; Honolulu County Dental Assn, 1979-; Southshore Dental Society, past prefabricateds, 1981-; Academy of General Dentistry, 1990-; Queen's Medical Center, active staff, 1980-; State Health Planning & Development Agency, past chairman/co-chairman, 1980-85; UOP Dental Alumni, Hawaii Chapter, president, 1993-94. **HONORS/AWARDS:** Tau Kappa Omega, 1979. **BUSINESS ADDRESS:** President, Alan K. Yoshida DDS Inc, 1001 Bishop St, Ste 350, Pauahi Tower, Honolulu, HI 96813, (808)537-4404.

YOSHIDA, KANETAKA
Banking executive. Japanese American. **PERSONAL:** Born 1938?, Fukuoka, Japan. **EDUCATION:** Tokyo University School of Law, JD. **CAREER:** Bank of Tokyo, 31 years of service including: Jakarta office, Project Finance Division, general manager, Corporate Banking, Securities, Capital Markets, and Foreign Exchange Divisions, manager, 1983-90; California First Bank (now Union Bank), Corporate Banking Group, senior vice president, 1978-83, vice chairman, chief financial officer, until 1993, president, CEO, currently. **BUSINESS ADDRESS:** President, CEO, Union Bank, 350 California St, San Francisco, CA 94120, (415)445-0200.∗

YOSHIDA, RAY KAKUO
Educator, artist. Japanese American. **PERSONAL:** Born Oct 3, 1930, Kapaa, Kauai, HI; son of Kazuyo Yoshida and Kichizo Yoshida. **EDUCATION:** School of the Art Institute of Chicago, BAE, 1953; Syracuse University, MFA, 1958. **CAREER:** School of the Art Institute of Chicago, Frank Harrold Sellers

Professor, 1960-. **ORGANIZATIONS:** American Association of University Professors, 1980-; Arts Club of Chicago; Japanese American Citizens League. **HONORS/AWARDS:** Natl Endowment for the Arts, Grant, 1989; Illinois Arts Council, Grant, 1985. **SPECIAL ACHIEVEMENTS:** Awarded numerous awards and prizes in various art exhibitions; paintings in the permanent collections of the Art Institute of Chicago, Everson Museum, Syracuse, New York, Smithsonian Institution National Collection, Washington, DC, Museum des 20th Jarhunderts, Vienna, Museum of Contemporary Art, Chicago, Contemporary Art Center, Honolulu. **MILITARY SERVICE:** US Army, spec 2, 1954-56. **BIOGRAPHICAL SOURCES:** "Ray Yoshida: A Review," NAME Gallery, 1984; "Fantastic Images," Franze Schulze, Chicago, p 208, 209, 221, 1972. **HOME ADDRESS:** 1944 N Wood St, Chicago, IL 60622.

YOSHIDA, ROLAND K.
Educational administrator, educator. Japanese American. **PERSONAL:** Born May 3, 1948, Los Angeles, CA; son of Robert M Yoshida and Yoshiye Yoshida; married Sharon A Stirler Yoshida, Oct 13, 1984. **EDUCATION:** University of Southern California, BA, 1970, MSED, 1971, PhD, 1974. **CAREER:** US Dept of Education, education program specialist, 1975-82; Fordham University, assoc prof, 1982-85, prof, 1985-87; Queens College, professor, 1987-, dean of education, 1990-. **ORGANIZATIONS:** American Psychological Assn, fellow, 1975-; Council for Exceptional Children, 1971. **HONORS/AWARDS:** Phi Beta Kappa, 1970; Phi Delta Kappa, 1974; Kappa Delta Pi, 1991. **SPECIAL ACHIEVEMENTS:** "A Matter of Different Priorities," Contemporary Psychology, 1989; co-author, "The Influences of Social Psychological Variables in the Evaluation of School Children," 1992; co-author, "Type of Instruction and the Relationship of Classroom Behavior to Achievement among Learning Disabled Children," Journal of Classroom Interaction, 1993; numerous others. **BUSINESS ADDRESS:** Dean, School of Education, Queens College, CUNY, 65-30 Kissena Blvd, Flushing, NY 11367, (718)997-5220.

YOSHIDA, RONALD YUTAKA
Aerospace engineer. Japanese American. **PERSONAL:** Born Oct 11, 1927, San Francisco, CA; son of Albert Misao Yoshida and Tokuko Uchihara Yoshida; married Miye Yoshimori Yoshida, Aug 27, 1960; children: Ronald Y, Douglas K, Karen E Leib. **EDUCATION:** Massachusetts Institute of Technology, BS, 1952; University of California at Los Angeles, MS, 1960. **CAREER:** Marquardt Corporation, project manager, 1952-71; Jet Propulsion Laboratory, technical manager, 1971-. **ORGANIZATIONS:** Japanese American Citizens League, board member, 1960-; San Fernando Valley Nikkei Village, board member, 1985-; State of California, Registered Professional Engineer, 1961-. **HONORS/AWARDS:** National Aeronautics and Space Admin, Exceptional Service Medal, 1993, Apollo Achievement Award, 1969, Voyager, Viking, Electric Vehicle Projects, Numerous Group Achievement Awards, 1977-82; MIT, Admiral Luis de Florez Award in Machine Design, 1952. **SPECIAL ACHIEVEMENTS:** "Management Experience of an International Venture in Space-The Ulysses Mission," presented at the 15th International Symposium on Space Technology and Science Tokyo, Japan, 1966. **MILITARY SERVICE:** US Army, Military Intelligence, tech/4th grade, 1946-48. **HOME ADDRESS:** 10836 Des Moines Ave, Northridge, CA 91326, (818)363-5198.

YOSHIKAMI, SANDRA
Marketing director. Japanese American. **PERSONAL:** Born Sep 23, 1960, New York, NY; daughter of Saddaharo and Midori Yoshikami. **EDUCATION:** Harvard University, MBA, marketing, 1981. **CAREER:** Procter and Gamble, brand manager, 1981-86; International Plastics, marketing director, 1986-. **ORGANIZATIONS:** Society of Plastics Engineers, 1990-. **BUSINESS ADDRESS:** Director of Marketing, International Plastics Company, 1950 Third Avenue, New York, NY 10029.

YOSHIKAWA, HERBERT HIROSHI
Manager. Japanese American. **PERSONAL:** Born May 13, 1929, South Dos Palos, CA; son of Ichiji Yoshikawa and Chiyo Morita Yoshikawa; married Helen Sadataki Yoshikawa, Sep 24, 1960. **EDUCATION:** University of Chicago, PhB, 1948, MS, 1951; University of Pennsylvania, PhD, 1958. **CAREER:** General Electric, senior scientist, 1958-64; Battelle Northwest, manager, 1964-70; Westinghouse Hanford Co, strategic planning, manager, 1970-. **ORGANIZATIONS:** American Nuclear Society, 1960-; National Management Association, 1985-; Sigma Xi, 1958-; American Association for the Advancement of Science, 1958-. **MILITARY SERVICE:** US Army Chemical Corp, pfc, 1951-53. **BUSINESS ADDRESS:** Manager, Strategic Planning, Westinghouse Hanford Company, PO Box 1970, Richland, WA 99352.

YOSHIKAWA, SHOICHI
Physicist, educator. Japanese American. **PERSONAL:** Born Apr 9, 1935, Tokyo, Japan; son of Haruhisa Yoshikawa & Eiko Inouye Yoshikawa; married Elinor D Yoshikawa, Oct 20, 1984; children: Yoko, Machiko, Aiko. **EDUCATION:** University of Tokyo, BS, 1958; MIT, MS, 1960, PhD, 1961. **CAREER:** University of Tokyo, professor, 1973-75; Princeton University, principal research physicist, professor, 1961-. **ORGANIZATIONS:** American Physical Society, fellow, 1960. **HONORS/AWARDS:** Mainichi Newspaper Co, Mainichi Publication Award, 1974. **SPECIAL ACHIEVEMENTS:** Scientific publications include books in Japanese: Introduction to Nuclear Fusion, Challenge to Nuclear Fusion, Challenge to Energy. **HOME PHONE:** (609)921-1723. **BUSINESS ADDRESS:** Principal Research Physicist, Plasma Physics Lab, Princeton University, PO Box 451, Princeton, NJ 08543, (609)243-2497.

YOSHIMOTO, WATSON TOSHINORI
Company executive. Japanese American. **PERSONAL:** Born Nov 21, 1909, Punaluu, Oahu, HI; son of Yoshinosuke Yoshimoto and Kou Nagawa Yoshimoto; married Katherine Katsuyo Yoshimoto, Nov 2, 1951; children: Watson Jr, Geneveve, Maxine. **CAREER:** W T Yosimoto Corp, Oahu Construction Co, president, 1940-; Classic Bowling Center, 1965-; Mak Bowl Inc, president, CEO, 1967-; W T Yoshimoto Oahu Inc, 1980-; W T Yoshimoto Foundation, World Wildlife Museum, 1992. **ORGANIZATIONS:** Safari Club Intl, life member; Game Conservation Intl, life member; Natl Rifle Assn, life member; Foundation of North American Wild Sheep, life member; North American Hunting Club, life member, Society for the Conservation of Bighorn Sheep, life member; Intl Sheep Hunters Assn, life member; The One Shot Antelope Hunt Foundation, life member; Mzuri Wildlife Foundation, life member; Natl Skeet Shooting Assn, life member; Bishop Museum Assn of Honolulu, life member; Hawaiiian Humane Society, life member; Arizona Desert Bighorn Sheep Society, life member; Grand Slam Club, life member; Explorers Club of New York; Adventurers Club of Honolulu; Shikar Safari Club Intl. **HONORS/AWARDS:** Roy E Weatherby Foundation, Big Game Trophy Award, 1980; Safari Club International, Hunting Hall of Fame, 1982; American Field Publishing Co, Field Trial Hall of Fame, 1991; numerous other big game awards. **SPECIAL ACHIEVEMENTS:** Organized Oahu Construction Co; of more than 40,000 registered Hawaiian businesses, Oahu Construction was included as one of the top 250 largest public and private corporations in Hawaii, 1984; Selection Committee, Weatherby Big Game Trophy Award, 1990; Selection Committee, Safari Club International Hall of Fame, 1982. **BIOGRAPHICAL SOURCES:** Biographical Record of Japanese Ancestry, p 126-133; Gun Dog Book, p 47-52. **BUSINESS ADDRESS:** President, W T Yoshimoto Corp, PO Box 4234, Honolulu, HI 96812-4324, (808)842-6164.

YOSHIMURA, EVELYN
Association administrator, activist. Japanese American. **PERSONAL:** Born in Denver, CO; married Bruce Iwasaki; children: Naomi. **EDUCATION:** California State University, Long Beach. **CAREER:** Little Tokyo People's Rights Organization, administrative assistant, currently. **ORGANIZATIONS:** Amerasia Bookstore, co-founder; GIDRA, staff; National Coalition for Redress and Reparations. **HONORS/AWARDS:** Visual Communications, Tatsukawa Award, 1992. **SPECIAL ACHIEVEMENTS:** Numerous contributions toward: Rainbow Coalition; Jesse Jackson presidential campaign; Free South Africa Movement; UNITY LA; numerous others. **BUSINESS ADDRESS:** Administrative Assistant, Little Tokyo People's Rights Organization, 244 S San Pedro St #44, Los Angeles, CA 90012, (213)680-3729. *

YOSHIMURA, MICHAEL AKIRA
Educator. Japanese American. **PERSONAL:** Born May 30, 1948, Honolulu, HI; son of Lester T Yoshimura and Sadako Yoshimura; married Mary Joyce Yoshimura, Feb 17, 1973; children: Emi Lynn, Gwen Mieko. **EDUCATION:** Stanford University, BA, 1970; University of Hawaii, MS, 1972; University of Arizona, PhD, 1975. **CAREER:** University of Hawaii, research assistant, 1971-72; University of Arizona, research assistant, 1972-75; California Polytechnic State University, professor, 1975-. **ORGANIZATIONS:** American Phytopathological Society, 1971-. **SPECIAL ACHIEVEMENTS:** The Occurrence and Effect of a Protozoan Parasite on Overwintering Monarch Butterflies, 1992; Low Susceptibility of Overwintering Monarch Butterflies to Bacillus Thuringiensis, 1992; Entomogenous Nematodes for Biological Control of the Western Spotted Cucumber Beetle, 1989; Etiology and Control of Alternaria Blight of Poinsettia, 1986; Etiology and Control of Poinsettia Blight Caused by Phytophthora Nicotiana and P Drechsleri, 1985. **MILITARY SERVICE:** Air Force National Guard, ssgt, 1970-76. **BUSINESS ADDRESS:**

Professor, Biological Sciences Dept, California Polytechnic State University, San Luis Obispo, CA 93407-0001, (805)756-2466.

YOSHIMURA, YOSHIKO
Librarian. Japanese American. **PERSONAL:** Born Oct 21, 1933, Tokyo, Japan; daughter of Shigeru Yoshimura and Jun Yoshimura. **EDUCATION:** Tsuda College, BA, English, 1956; Syracuse University, MSLS, 1960; Harvard University, AM, regional studies, East Asia, 1970. **CAREER:** Toyo Bunko, oriental library, library assistant, 1956-58; Syracuse University Library, cadet, 1958-60; Harvard-Yenching Library, cataloger/senior cataloger, 1960-71; Library of Congress, cataloger/senior cataloger, 1971-82, Japan area specialist, 1982-. **ORGANIZATIONS:** Association for Asian Studies. **HONORS/ AWARDS:** Japan Foundation Scholarship, 1959; Beta Phi Mu. **SPECIAL ACHIEVEMENTS:** Guide to Japanese Reference Books, co-editor, 1979; Japanese Govt Documents and Censored Publications, 1992; Japanese Censored Serials, in press. **HOME ADDRESS:** 2311 Pimmit Dr #1215, Falls Church, VA 22043, (703)560-0512. **BUSINESS ADDRESS:** Area Specialist, Library of Congress, 2nd St & Independence Ave SE, LA 133B, Washington, DC 20540, (202)707-5431.

YOSHINAGA, GEORGE
Writer. Japanese American. **PERSONAL:** Born Jul 19, 1925, Redwood City, CA; son of Usaburo and Tsuru Yoshinaga (deceased); married Yoshiko, Dec 17, 1955; children: Paul, Robin, Mark, Tim. **EDUCATION:** Los Angeles City College, AA, 1948; UCLA Ext, 1950. **CAREER:** Kashu Mainichi, English section editor, 1957-90; Rafu Shimpo, columnist, 1990-. **ORGANIZATIONS:** LA County Commission on Physical Fitness, director, 1991-; VFW, Post 1961, 1991-; JACL, 1990-; California State Athletic Commission, asst chief executive official, 1986-91. **SPECIAL ACHIEVEMENTS:** Founded Japan Bowl College All-Star Game; promoted first world heavy weight boxing title in Japan. **MILITARY SERVICE:** US Army CIC, s sgt, 1943-46. **BUSINESS ADDRESS:** Columnist, Rafu Shimpo Newspaper, 259 S Los Angeles St, Los Angeles, CA 90012, (213)629-2231.

YOSHINO, KOUICHI
Physicist. Japanese American. **PERSONAL:** Born Jan 1, 1931, Matsuyama, Ehime, Japan; son of Kazuo Yoshino and Katsura Yoshino; married Shizuko Yoshino, Nov 7, 1957; children: Mika, Miki, Makoto. **EDUCATION:** Tokyo University of Education, BA, 1953, MA, 1955, PhD, 1972. **CAREER:** Industrial Institute of Kanagawa, physicist, 1953; Tokyo Industrial Research Institute, physicist, 1958; Air Force Cambridge Research Laboratories, physicist, 1965; Harvard-Smithsonian Center for Astrophysics, senior physicist, 1976-. **ORGANIZATIONS:** Physical Society of Japan, 1953; Optical Society of America, 1976; Japanese Association of Greater Boston, president, 1965. **BUSINESS ADDRESS:** Senior Physicist, Harvard-Smithsonian Center for Astrophysics, 60 Garden St, MS-50, Cambridge, MA 02138, (617)495-2796.

YOSHINO, RONALD WARREN
Educator. Japanese American. **PERSONAL:** Born May 18, 1946, Merced, CA; son of William Biyo and Reiko; married Diana; children: Brooke, Jason, Mathew, Erin. **EDUCATION:** California State University, Fresno, BA, 1968, MA (with distinction), 1975; Claremont Graduate School, PhD, 1985. **CAREER:** Riverside Community College, associate professor, department chairperson, 1986-. **ORGANIZATIONS:** Alpha Gamma Sigma, advisor, 1986-. **HONORS/AWARDS:** Riverside Community College, Distinguished Faculty Lecturer, 1991; Claremont Graduate School, History Graduate Teaching Fellowship, 1976-78. **SPECIAL ACHIEVEMENTS:** Major contributor, 17 articles, to Charles Bright, editor, Historical Dictionary of the US Air Force, 1993; author, Lightning Strikes-the 475th Fighter Group in the Pacific War, 1943-45, 1988; co-author with S H H Chang and Sharon Lloyd, Method and Form for Writing Papers: A Manual, 1977. **BUSINESS ADDRESS:** Professor, Riverside Community College, 4800 Magnolia Ave, Riverside, CA 92506-1299, (909)684-3240.

YOSHINO, WILLIAM
Association administrator. Japanese American. **PERSONAL:** Born Oct 4, 1946. **CAREER:** Japanese American Citizen League, Midwest regional director, currently. **HONORS/AWARDS:** Illinois Ethnic Consultation, American Pluralism Award, 1992. **BUSINESS ADDRESS:** Midwest Regional Director, Japanese American Citizens League, 5415 N Clark St, Chicago, IL 60640, (312)728-7171.*

YOSHITOMI, KAREN
Association administrator. Japanese American. **PERSONAL:** Born Nov 1963?. **CAREER:** Japanese American Citizens League, Seattle, regional director, currently. **BUSINESS ADDRESS:** Regional Director, Japanese American Citizens League, Seattle Chapter, 671 S Jackson, No 206, Seattle, WA 98104, (206)623-5088.*

YOUN, HEE YONG
Educator. Korean American. **PERSONAL:** Born Jun 27, 1955, Seoul, Republic of Korea; son of Kang Jin Youn & Jeong Joo Youn; married Joo Young Youn, Oct 28, 1981; children: Soo Kyung, Soo Jin, Susie. **EDUCATION:** Seoul National University, BS, 1977, MS, 1979; University of Massachusetts, Amherst, PhD, 1988. **CAREER:** Gold Star Precision, Central Research Lab, senior researcher, 1979-84; University of Massachusetts, Amherst, teaching assistant, research assistant, 1985-88; University of North Texas, assistant professor, 1988-91; University of Texas, Arlington, assistant professor, 1991-93, associate professor, 1993-. **ORGANIZATIONS:** IEEE Computer Society; Association for Computing Machinery. **HONORS/AWARDS:** IEEE Supercomputing '92, Best Student Paper Award, 1992; IEEE Computer Society, co-author, Outstanding Paper Award, 1988; Korean Government, Presidential Best Development Award, 1983. **SPECIAL ACHIEVEMENTS:** Lecturer, Association for Computing Machinery; author: "Performance Analysis of Finite Buffered Multistage Interconnection Networks," IEEE Trans on Computer, p 1, Jan 1994; "A Comprehensive Performance Evaluation of Crossbar Network," IEEE Trans on Parallel and Distributed Systems, p 481, May 1993; "An Efficient Algorithm-Based Fault Tolerance Design with Extended Rearranged Hamming Checksum," in IEEE DFT, 1992; "Performance Enhancement of Multistage Interconnection Network with Noncuneiform Traffic," SPDP, 1991; "A Fault Tolerant Binary Tree Architecture for VLSI with Short Limbs," IEEE Trans on Computer, p 882, July 1991; "On Implementing Large Binary Tree Architectures in VLSI and WSI," IEEE Trans on Computer, p 37, April 1989. **HOME PHONE:** (817)572-1839. **BUSINESS ADDRESS:** Associate Professor, Dept of Computer Science Engineering, University of Texas, Arlington, PO Box 19015, Arlington, TX 76019-0015, (817)273-3602.

YOUN, LUIS TAI-OH
Educator. Korean American. **PERSONAL:** Born Jan 6, 1956, Seoul, Republic of Korea; son of Bock Hyun Youn and Kyung Soon Youn; married Hyeh Young Youn, Aug 17, 1982; children: Ariana M. **EDUCATION:** University of Sao Paulo, BS, 1980; University of Houston, MS, 1982, PhD, 1985. **CAREER:** Asea Electrica, design engineer, 1980; Southern Illinois University at Edwardsville, associate professor, 1985-. **ORGANIZATIONS:** Institute of Electrical and Electronic Engineers, 1985-; Illinois State Academy of Science, 1986-. **SPECIAL ACHIEVEMENTS:** Author, Planning Model for Small Power Producing Facilities, Electric Power Systems Research, 1993; Optimal Long Range Generation Expansion Planning for Hydro-Thermal Systems, IEEE Transaction, 1987; New Analytical Approach for Long-Term Generation Expansion Planning, IEEE Transaction, 1985. **BUSINESS ADDRESS:** Associate Professor, Southern Illinois University at Edwardsville, Box 1801, Edwardsville, IL 62026-1801, (618)692-2809.

YOUNG, ALICE
International corporate lawyer. Chinese American. **PERSONAL:** Born Apr 7, 1950, Washington, DC; daughter of John Young & Elizabeth Ren; married Thomas Leonard Shovtall, Sep 22, 1984; children: Amanda Young Shovtall, Stephen Young Shovtall. **EDUCATION:** Yale University, AB, 1971; Harvard Law School, JD, 1974. **CAREER:** Office for Civil Rights, 1972-73; Coudert Brothers, associate, 1974-81; Graham & James, founding and resident partner, 1981-87; Milbank, Tweed, Hadley, & McCloy, partner and head of Japan Corporate Group, 1987-93; Kaye, Scholer, Fierman, Hays & Handler, partner, chair of Asia Pacific Practice, 1994-. **ORGANIZATIONS:** Aspen Institute, board of trustees, 1988; Japan Society, secretary, 1989; Metropolitan Museum of Art, business committee, 1989; Asia Society, president's council, 1984; Council on Foreign Relations, 1977; National Committee on US-China Relations, 1993-; Harvard University Board of Overseers Visitation Committee; Harvard Law School Association, trustee, 1990; Committee of 100, 1993-. **HONORS/AWARDS:** New York Women's Agenda, Star Award, 1992; Crain's 40 Outstanding Achievers Under 40, 1988; Dewar's, New York Doers Award, 1989. **SPECIAL ACHIEVEMENTS:** Japanese and Chinese language proficiency, written French. **BIOGRAPHICAL SOURCES:** Working Women for the 21st Century, Williamson, 1991, p212-217; Where They Are Now: Women at Harvard Law 1974, Doubleday, 1986; New York Times Magazine, November 12, 1989. **BUSINESS ADDRESS:** Partner, Chair of

Asia Pacific Practice, Kaye, Scholer, Fierman, Hays & Handler, 425 Park Ave, New York, NY 10022, (212)836-8047.

YOUNG, BING-LIN
Educator. Chinese American. **PERSONAL:** Born Feb 3, 1937, Louyang, Henan, China; married Theresa F Y Young, Sep 12, 1964; children: Rowena Y-H. **EDUCATION:** National Taiwan University, BS, 1959; University of Minnesota, PhD, 1966. **CAREER:** Indiana University, research associate, 1966-68; Brookhaven National Laboratory, research associate, 1968-70; Iowa State University, professor, currently. **ORGANIZATIONS:** Overseas Chinese Physics Association, chair, 1993-94; American Physical Society, 1965-; Henan Fundamental and Applied Sciences Research Institute, China, director, currently; Center of Theoretical Physics, Jilin University, China, International Academy Council, chair, currently. **HONORS/AWARDS:** Zhengfhou University, China, honorary professor; Henan Normal University, China, honorary professor; Jilin University, China, guest professor; Zhejiang University, China, guest professor; Dalian University of TEC, China, guest professor. **SPECIAL ACHIEVEMENTS:** Publication of research articles on theoretical high energy physics; book, Introduction to Quantum Field Theory, English edition, 1987, Chinese edition, 1988. **BUSINESS ADDRESS:** Professor, Dept of Physics and Astronomy, Iowa State University, Ames, IA 50011.

YOUNG, FRANKLIN
Educator. Chinese American. **PERSONAL:** Born Feb 1, 1928, Beijing, Hopeh, China; son of Andrew Young & Helen Loh Young; married Kathlina Patanella, Dec 21, 1982. **EDUCATION:** University of Shanghai, China, 1946-48; Mercer University, AB, 1951; University of Florida, BSA (magna cum laude), 1952, MAgr, 1954, PhD, 1960. **CAREER:** University of Florida, post-doctoral research fellow, 1960-61; Bowman Gray School of Medicine, research associate, 1961-65, research associate instructor, 1965-66; University of Hawaii, associate professor, 1966-83, chair, graduate faculty, 1969-73; University of Utah, professor, department chair, 1983-85; West Chester University, professor, 1985-. **ORGANIZATIONS:** American Institute of Nutrition, 1961-; American Chemical Society, 1961-; New York Academy of Sciences, 1984-90; Hawaii Academy of Sciences, 1968-80; Hawaii Heart Association, 1967-80; Order Sons of Italy of America, 1985-, elected orator, 1987-88. **HONORS/AWARDS:** Phi Kappa Phi, 1952; Sigma Xi, 1961, charter member, Wake Forest College Chapter, 1965; Gamma Sigma Delta, 1960, Hawaii Chapter, charter member, 1968, executive comm, 1969-70, awards comm, 1969-70, treasurer, 1970-71; Phi Sigma. **SPECIAL ACHIEVEMENTS:** Conducted research in Vibrio fetus, Newcastle disease vaccination, parasitism and visceral lymphomatosis in turkeys, erysipelas in porpoises, atherosclerosis and lipid metabolism in squirrel monkeys and pigeons, and blood pressure and electrolyte excretion in humans, resulting in the publication of 18 scientific papers in refereed journals; manuscript reviewer of the textbook, Decisions in Nutrition, by Vincent Hegarty, Mosby; reviewer of grant proposals for NIH and USDA; reviewer of scientific manuscripts for journal publishers. **BUSINESS ADDRESS:** Professor, Dept of Health, West Chester University, West Chester, PA 19383, (215)436-2113.

YOUNG, HOA PHAM
Community liaison representative. Vietnamese American. **PERSONAL:** Born Jul 30, 1941, Hanoi, Vietnam; daughter of Binh D Pham (deceased) & Nhu T Ta; married Stephen B Young, Mar 22, 1970; children: Ian, Warren, Antonia. **EDUCATION:** University of Saigon, 1965-67; University of Hawaii, East West Center, 1968-69. **CAREER:** Harvard University-East Asia Research Center, library, 1971-74; Avon Products, secretary to the manager of marketing, 1976-78; Family Service of Boston, family educator, 1979-81; Family Service of St Paul, family educator, 1981-86; realtor and coordinator for the newly arrived Vietnamese refugees, 1986-88; State of MN, Council on A-P Minnesotans, community liaison representative, 1988-. **ORGANIZATIONS:** St Paul Public Library, trustee, 1988-; St Paul/Nagasaki Sister Cities Committee, 1988-; Family Service of St Paul, 1990-93; MN Center for Women in Government, advisory board, 1991-; Ordway Music Theater/Asian Pacific Cultural Advisors, chair, 1993-; Cultural Diversity & Childcare System Steering Comm, co-chair, 1993-; Asian-American Renaissance, 1992-; People of Color Concerned with Child Protection, 1991. **HONORS/AWARDS:** BIHA in Action, Award of Merit, 1990; WISE, A Minnesota Treasure, 1991. **SPECIAL ACHIEVEMENTS:** Co-author of a curriculum on survival skills & home management, Family Service, Boston, 1980; designed a teaching curriculum on family/career counseling for southeast Asian youth, 1984-85; review funding proposals for DHS, State Arts Board, United Way, yearly; cross-cultural instructor/consultant/trainer; fluent in English, French, Vietnamese. **BUSI-**

NESS ADDRESS: Community Liaison Representative, State Council on Asian-Pacific Minnesotans, Meridian National Bank Bldg, 205 Aurora Ave, Ste 100, St Paul, MN 55103, (612)296-0538.

YOUNG, JACQUELINE EURN HAI
State representative, educator. **PERSONAL:** Born May 20, 1934, Honolulu, HI; daughter of Paul Bai Young and Martha Cho Young; married Harry Valentine Daniels, Dec 25, 1954 (divorced 1978); children: Paula, Harry, Nani, Laura; married Everett Kleinjans, Jun 4, 1988. **EDUCATION:** University of Hawaii, BS, speech pathology, audiology; Old Dominion University, MEd, special education; Loyola College, advanced certificate; Union Institute, PhD, communications, women's studies. **CAREER:** Maryland School for the Blind, Dept Speech and Hearing, director, 1975-77; Easter Seal Society, Oahu, Deaf-Blind Project, director, 1977-78; Hawaii State Dept of Education, Equal Educational Opportunity Programs, project director, 1978-85, state educational specialist, 1978-90; Hawaii State Legislature, state representative, 1990-; Hawaii Pacific University, adjunct professor of communication, anthropology, and management, currently. **ORGANIZATIONS:** National Women's Political Caucus, first vice president; Hawaii Women's Political Caucus, chair, 1987-89; YWCA Oahu, board of directors; Honolulu County Committee on the Status of Women, appointee, 1986-87; numerous others. **SPECIAL ACHIEVEMENTS:** US Department of Education, Guam, American Samoa, Ponape, Palau, Marshall Islands, consultant on special education, 1977-85; consultant to various organizations regarding workplace diversity; Station KGMB-TV, guest moderator. **BUSINESS ADDRESS:** Representative, District #51, 235 South Beretania St, Room 1309, Honolulu, HI 96813, (808)586-6540.*

YOUNG, JOHN. *See* YANG, HAN-JIANG.

YOUNG, LLOYD YEE
Educator, author, director. Chinese American. **PERSONAL:** Born Aug 25, 1944, Macao; son of Nathan & Lucy Young; married. **EDUCATION:** University of California, San Francisco, PharmD, 1969. **CAREER:** Washington State University, clinical pharmacy, associate professor, 1972-90, adjunct professor, 1990-; Southwest Washington Medical Center, Pharmacy/IV Services, director, 1990-. **ORGANIZATIONS:** Washington State Board of Pharmacy, 1984-93; numerous professional organizations. **HONORS/AWARDS:** Numerous professional honors. **SPECIAL ACHIEVEMENTS:** Writer, editor, author. **BUSINESS ADDRESS:** President, Applied Therapeutics Inc, PO Box 5077, Vancouver, WA 98668, (206)253-7123.

YOUNG, PETER R.
Librarian, federal administrator. Chinese American. **PERSONAL:** Born Aug 13, 1944, Washington, DC; son of Ju Chin Young & Jane Katherine Young; married Mary Townsend, Mar 25, 1978; children: Kathryn, Timothy. **EDUCATION:** College of Wooster, AB, philosophy, 1966; George Washington University, graduate study, philosophy, 1967; Columbia University, MSLS, 1968. **CAREER:** American University Library, admin librarian, 1968; Franklin & Marshall College Lib, head cataloger, 1971, ref librarian, 1971-74; Rice University Libraries, asst librarian for public services, 1974-76; Grand Rapids Public Lib, asst director, 1978; CL Systems, sales support librarian, 1976-78, library sys analyst, 1978-80; Library of Congress, Cataloging Distr Svc, customer services officer, 1980-84, MARC Editorial Div, asst chief, 1984-85, Copyright Cataloging Div, chief, 1985-88; Faxon Co, Academic Info Services, dir, 1988-89; Faxon Institute for Advanced Studies in Scholarly & Scientific Communication, dir, 1989-90; US Natl Commn on Libraries & Info Sci, executive director, 1990-. **ORGANIZATIONS:** American Library Assn, comm on research & statistics, 1990-, Public Library Assn, public policy for public libraries comm, 1993-; Federal Library & Info Ctr Comm, executive bd, 1993-; Highsmith Press, advisory bd, 1991-; Natl Standards Info Office, library statistics standard revision comm, co-chair, 1989-93; Serials Review, editorial bd, 1990-; US Office Educ Research & Improvement, Natl Ctr for Educ Statistics, advisory council on educ statistics, 1990-. **SPECIAL ACHIEVEMENTS:** Author, "Global Knowledge Network Infrastructure Development," proceedings of Intl Conference on Natl Libraries: Toward the 21st Century, Taiwan, Natl Central Library, 1993; professional addresses & progs: Association of College & Research Libraries, New England Chapter, "Future Support for Academic Libraries" Mar 1993; Delaware State Conference on Library & Info Services, "Role of NCLIS in Fulfilling the Vision of WHCLIS," Nov 1992. **MILITARY SERVICE:** US Army Infantry Division, specialist, 5th class, 1968-70, 3 bronze star medals. **BUSINESS ADDRESS:** Executive Director, US Natl Commission on Libraries & Information Science, 1110 Vermont Ave NW, Ste 820, Washington, DC 20005, (202)606-9200.

YOUNG, SHIRLEY

Corporate executive. Chinese American. **PERSONAL:** Born May 25, 1935, Shanghai, China; daughter of Juliana Wellington Koo & Clarence Young; divorced; children: David Hsieh, William Hsieh, Douglas Hsieh. **EDUCA-TION:** Wellesley College, BA, economics, 1955; New York University Graduate School of Arts & Sciences. **CAREER:** Alfred Politz Research Organization, project director, 1955-58; Hudson Paper Corp, market research manager, 1958-59; Grey Advertising, executive vice president, 1959-83; Grey Strategic Marketing, president, 1983-88, chairman, 1988-90; General Motors Corp, Consumer Market Development, consultant, 1983-88, vice president, 1988-. **OR-GANIZATIONS:** Junior Achievement Inc, board of directors, 1993-; Bell Atlantic, board of directors, 1987-; Promus Companies, board of directors, 1984-; Harvard Business School, board of directors of the associates; Wellesley College, trustee; WTVS, Channel 56, board of directors; Detroit Symphony Orchestra, board of directors; Detroit Institute of Arts, Founders Society, board of trustees; Interlochen Corporate Council; Greening of Detroit, commissioner; Committee of 100, chair; numerous others. **HONORS/AWARDS:** National Women's Economic Alliance, Director's Choice Award; Chinese American Planning Council, Woman of the Year; Catalyst Award; Women's Equity Action Award; American Advertising Federation, Advertising Woman of the Year; Russell Sage College, Honorary Doctorate of Letters, 1986. **HOME ADDRESS:** 771 Fisher Rd, Grosse Pointe, MI 48230. **BUSINESS AD-DRESS:** Vice President, Consumer Market Development, General Motors Corporation, 3044 W Grand Blvd, 14 117 GM Bldg, Detroit, MI 48202, (313)556-2801.

YOUNG, SHUN CHUNG

Surgeon. Chinese American. **PERSONAL:** Born Oct 7, 1937, Canton, China; son of Chuck-Chung-Young; married Le, 1964; children: Sally, Mimi, Alex. **EDUCATION:** Natl Taiwan University, MD, 1962. **CAREER:** Mt Carmel Mercy Hospital, attending surgeon, 1969-75; Pontiac State Hospital, consulting surgeon, 1969-77; American Cancer Soc, Michigan Division, chm, district 14, house of delegates, 1979-81, pres, 1981-82; Dept of Health, Taiwan, China, consultant of medical services, 1983; Samaritan Health Center, medical director, surgical education, 1985-; Metropolitan Detroit Cancer Control Program, medical advisory panel, section of head & neck cancer, currently; American College of Surgeons, Michigan Chapter, prog comm, currently, Commission on Cancer, field liaison fellow, currently; Providence Hospital, attending surgeon, 1969-, assoc chm, dept of general surgery, 1978-82, prog director, surgical education, 1970-, surgical exec comm, 1978-, assoc chm, cancer comm, 1978-, dept of general surgery, chm, 1982-. **ORGANIZATIONS:** Wayne Medical Soc; Michigan State Medical Soc; Roswell Park Surgical Soc; Soc of Head & Neck Surgeons; American Board of Surgery, diplomate; American College of Surgeons, fellow; Southwest Oncology Group; Detroit Surgical Assn; Surgical Academy of Detroit; Detroit Gastroenterology Soc; Assn of Program Directors in Surgery. **SPECIAL ACHIEVEMENTS:** Licenses: Taiwan Medical Soc, China; Hong Kong Medical Council; Canadian Medical Council; General Medical Council of England; Michigan State Board; New York State Board; California State Board; "Fluorescein Dye Tested in Viability of Colon," Oakland County Medical Soc Bulletin; coauthor, "Heterolytic Spleen Implants," OHEP Research Forum, 1984; coauthor, "Hepatic Arterial & Systemic Chemotherapy for the Treatment of Primary & Secondary Malignancies of the Liver," Cancer Drug Delivery, 2:2, 1985. **BUSINESS ADDRESS:** Chairman, Dept of Surgery, Providence Hospital, 22250 Providence Dr, Southfield, MI 48075, (313)557-5717.

YOUNG, TZAY Y.

Educator. Chinese American. **PERSONAL:** Born Jan 11, 1933, Shanghai, China; son of Chao-Hsiung Young and Chiu-Ming Chu Young; married Lily Liu Young, Dec 27, 1965; children: Debbie Chai-Pei, Arthur Chin-Kai. **EDU-CATION:** National Taiwan University, BS, 1955; University of Vermont, MS, 1958; Johns Hopkins University, DEngr, 1962. **CAREER:** Johns Hopkins University, research assoc, 1962-63; Bell Laboratories, technical staff, 1963-64; NASA Goddard Space Flight Ctr, sr res assoc, 1972-73; Carnegie-Mellon University, assistant professor, 1964-68, associate professor, 1968-74; University of Miami, professor, 1974-, acting chair, 1988-91, chair, 1991-. **ORGANI-ZATIONS:** IEEE Computer Soc, Trans Computers, associate editor, 1974-76, editorial board, 1979-84, Trans PAMI, advisory board, 1984-90, conference general chair, 1985, conference technical program, chair, 1982; IEEE Region 3, conference technical program, co-chair, 1994; Sigma Xi; Eta Kappa Nu. **HONORS/AWARDS:** IEEE, Fellow, 1988. **SPECIAL ACHIEVEMENTS:** Co-author: Classification, Estimation & Pattern Recognition, 1974; co-editor, Handbook of Pattern Recognition & Image Processing, 1986; editor, Handbook of Pattern Recognition & Image Processing, vol 2, Computer Vision, 1994; Numerous articles in technical journals and for conferences. **BUSINESS AD-DRESS:** Professor and Chair, Dept of Electrical & Computer Engineering, University of Miami, EB 406, Coral Gables, FL 33124, (305)284-3291.

YU, ALICE L.

Educator. Taiwanese American. **PERSONAL:** Born May 8, 1943, Taipei, Taiwan; daughter of Chiun Lin Chen and Chien Siu Su; married John Yu, Aug 2, 1969; children: Timothy, Elaine. **EDUCATION:** National Taiwan University, MD, 1968; Yale University, MS, 1973. **CAREER:** National Taiwan University Hospital, rotating intern, 1967-68; University of Chicago, pediatric level I, 1973-74; Harvard Medical School, Children's Hospital, fellow in immunology, 1974-76; Boston University, School of Medicine, pediatric level II, 1976-77; UCSD Medical Center, Pediatrics, assistant professor, 1977-84, associate professor, 1984-. **ORGANIZATIONS:** National Cancer Institute, Clinical Cancer Investigational Review Committee; American Society of Clinical Oncology; American Association for Cancer Research; American Society of Hematology; Pediatric Oncology Group; American Academy of Pediatrics, fellow; Society for Pediatric Research; Western Society for Pediatric Research. **SPECIAL ACHIEVEMENTS:** 45 articles in peer-reviewed scientific journals; treatment of childhood cancers; research activities: novel approaches to therapy of neuroblastoma and T-cell Acute Lymphoblastic Leukemia (T-ALL); language proficiency: Taiwanese, Mandarin. **BUSINESS ADDRESS:** Associate Professor, Pediatric Hematology/Oncology, University of California at San Diego Medical Center, 200 West Arbor Drive, San Diego, CA 92103-8447, (619)543-6844.

YU, BYUNG PAL

Educator, association executive. Korean American. **PERSONAL:** Born Jun 27, 1931, Ham Hung, Republic of Korea; son of Hong Soon Yu and Ok Soon; married Kyung Hi, May 9, 1959; children: Victor Sung Hwan. **EDUCATION:** Central Missouri State University, BS, 1960; University of Illinois, Urbana, PhD, 1965. **CAREER:** Woman's Medical College, assistant professor, 1965-71; Medical College of Pennsylvania, associate professor, 1971-73; University of Texas Health Science Center, associate professor, 1973-78, professor, 1978-. **ORGANIZATIONS:** American Aging Association, president, 1992-; Gerontological Society of American, Biological Sciences, chair, 1993-94, fellow, 1989-. **HONORS/AWARDS:** American Diabetes Research Development Award, 1969; Henry L Moss Award, 1973; Republic of Korea, National Merit Medal (Presidential Aedal), 1983, Merit Award (Minister of Education), 1981. **SPECIAL ACHIEVEMENTS:** Free Radicals in Aging, 1993; over 200 research articles published. **MILITARY SERVICE:** Army, captain, 1951-56. **HOME ADDRESS:** 9427 Callaghan Road, San Antonio, TX 78230, (210)349-2291.

YU, CHANG-AN

Educator. Taiwanese American. **PERSONAL:** Born Oct 19, 1937, Taiwan; married Linda S Chang Yu, Aug 1968; children: Wayne, Jeanne. **EDUCA-TION:** Taiwan University, BS, 1961, MS, 1964; University of Illinois, PhD, 1969. **CAREER:** State University of New York, assistant professor, 1974-78, associate professor, 1978-81; Oklahoma State University, associate professor, 1981-82, professor, 1982-85, regents professor, 1985-. **ORGANIZATIONS:** American Society of Biochemistry and Molecular Biology; Biophysical Society; American Association for the Advancement of Science; American Chemical Society; Society of Chinese Bioscientists in American. **HONORS/AWARDS:** NIH, member of biophysical chemistry study section, 1987-91. **SPECIAL ACHIEVEMENTS:** Author and co-author of over two hundred biochemical journal articles in bioenergetic or related fields. **BUSINESS AD-DRESS:** Regents Prof, Dept of Biochemistry & Molecular Biology, Oklahoma State University, Noble Research Center, Rm 255, Stillwater, OK 74078, (405)744-6198.

YU, CHI KANG

Educator, biologist, geneticist. Chinese American. **PERSONAL:** Born Jun 28, 1924, Shanghai, China; son of Kwang Yu and Hsu Yu; married Hsiu Kuei Yu, Jan 10, 1981. **EDUCATION:** University of Toronto, MSA, 1956; University of Ottawa, PhD, 1959. **CAREER:** Argonne National Laboratory, radiation biologist, geneticist, cell biologist; University of South California, educator, currently. **ORGANIZATIONS:** The Genetics Society of Canada, 1957-. **SPE-CIAL ACHIEVEMENTS:** Published 85 scientific papers in various journals including: Science, Nature, Radiation Research, Canadian Journal of Genetics, Journal of Cellular Physiology, Argonne Periodicals, Nuclear Science. **HOME ADDRESS:** 300 El Camino Lane, Placentia, CA 92670, (714)993-2717.

YU, CLARA
Educational administrator. Chinese American. **PERSONAL:** Born in Nanjing, People's Republic of China. **EDUCATION:** University of Illinois, PhD, 1978. **CAREER:** Middlebury College, vice president for languages, director of language schools, 1993-. **ORGANIZATIONS:** Northeast Conference on the Teaching of Foreign Languages, board member. **BUSINESS ADDRESS:** Vice President for Languages, Director of Language Schools, Middlebury College, Sunderland, Middlebury, VT 05753-6000, (802)388-3711.

YU, CLEMENT TAK
Educator. Chinese American. **PERSONAL:** Born Aug 31, 1948, Hong Kong; son of Ching Hang Yu and Chen Chun Sheit; married Teresa Chan, May 30, 1975; children: Victor, Christine. **EDUCATION:** Columbia University, BSc, 1970, Cornell University, MSc, 1972, PhD, 1973. **CAREER:** University of Alberta, Canada, asst professor, 1973-77, assoc professor, 1977-78; University of Illinois at Chicago, assoc professor, 1978-84, professor, 1984-. **ORGANIZATIONS:** Assn for Computing Machinery, Special Interest Group on Info Retrieval, chmn, 1985-87, treasurer, 1983-85; IEEE, Intl Workshop on Data Eng, chmn, 1992; NSF, Workshop on Heterogeneous Database, prgm committee chmn, 1989; ACM, SIGIR Conference, prgm committee chmn, 1987; Distributed and Parallel Databases, Journal, editorial board, 1993. **HONORS/AWARDS:** Assn for Computing Machinery, Service Award, 1987; NSF, research grants, 1979-93; Omron Corp, research grants, 1992-93; Hughes Aircraft, research grants, 1990-93; Argonne Lab, research grant, 1987-88. **SPECIAL ACHIEVEMENTS:** Author: over 100 technical papers in various journals and conference proceedings, 1973-. **BUSINESS ADDRESS:** Professor, University of Illinois at Chicago, Dept of Electrical Engineering & Computer Science, 1109 SEO, Chicago, IL 60680.

YU, DAVID C.
Educator. Taiwanese American. **PERSONAL:** Born Dec 12, 1955, Kaohsiung, Taiwan; son of H C Yu and C F Ma; married Ellen Liou, Jan 17, 1981; children: Jamie M, Jonathan D. **EDUCATION:** Chung-Yuan University, BS, 1977; University of Oklahoma, MS, 1979, PhD, 1983. **CAREER:** University of Wisconsin, Milwaukee, associate prof, 1984-, dept of EECS, associate prof, co-chair, 1993-. **ORGANIZATIONS:** IEEE, 1984. **SPECIAL ACHIEVEMENTS:** Author: "A Graphical User Interface for Design, Simulation and Analysis of Power Plant . . .," IEEE Trans on PWRS, 1993; "Weather Sensitive Short-term Load Forecastry Using Nonfully Conected ANN," IEEE Trans on PWRS, 1992; "An Interactive Graphic Interface to Illustrate Sparse Matrix/Vector Methods," IEEE Trans on PWRS, 1991; "A New Parallel LU Decomposition Method," IEEE Trans on PWRS, 1990; "A PC Oriented Interactive Graphical Simulation and Analysis Package," IEEE Trans on PWRS, 1990. **BUSINESS ADDRESS:** Associate Professor, University of Wisconsin, Milwaukee, PO Box 784, Milwaukee, WI 53201, (414)229-6885.

YU, FU-LI
Educator, educational administrator. Chinese American. **PERSONAL:** Born May 2, 1934, Peking, China; son of Ling-Ko Yu & Ying Chang Yu; married Jie Feng Yu, Apr 20, 1980; children: Chan-Ching, Chan Mei. **EDUCATION:** Chung Shing University, Taiwan, BS, 1956; University of Alabama, MS, 1962; University of California, PhD, 1965. **CAREER:** Columbia University, research associate, 1966-72; Thomas Jefferson University, assistant professor, 1973-79; University of Illinois, College of Medicine, Dept of Biomedical Sciences, assistant professor, 1979-80, associate professor, 1980-85, professor, 1985-, professor, acting head, 1988-90, professor, head, 1990-. **ORGANIZATIONS:** American Association for Cancer Research, 1976-; American Society for Biochemistry and Molecular Biology, 1976-; American Chemical Society, 1970-; Harvey Society, 1970-; Sigma Xi, 1974-; American Association for the Advancement of Science, 1970-; Society of Chinese Bioscientists in America, life member, 1985-. **HONORS/AWARDS:** National Cancer Institute, Principal Investigator, 1974-90; American Cancer Society, Principal Investigator, 1978-81. **SPECIAL ACHIEVEMENTS:** Author, with P Feigelson, Proc Natl Acad Sci, USA, vol 68, p 2177-2180, 1971, vol 69, p 2833-2837, 1972; Nature, vol 251, p 344-346, 1974; with others, Carcinogenesis, vol 11, p 475-78, 1990, vol 12, p 997-1002, 1991. **BUSINESS ADDRESS:** Professor/Head, Dept of Biomedical Sciences, University of Illinois, Rockford, 1601 Parkview Ave, Rockford, IL 61107, (815)395-5680.

YU, GANG
Educator. Chinese American. **PERSONAL:** Born Jun 2, 1959, Datong, Shanxi, People's Republic of China; son of Deqian Yu and Junxiu Zhang; married Xiaomei Song. **EDUCATION:** Wuhan University, BS, 1982; Cornell University, MS, 1986; University of Pennsylvania, Wharton School, PhD, 1990. **CAREER:** University of Pennsylvania, Wharton School, research assistant, 1986-89; United Airlines, consultant, 1989-91; IBM, consultant, 1991-93; UC Berkeley, Department of IEOR, consultant, 1992-; American Airlines, consultant, 1992-; Center for Cybernetic Studies, associate director, 1993-; University of Texas at Austin, asst professor, 1989-. **ORGANIZATIONS:** 3 intl societies, member, 1987-. **HONORS/AWARDS:** Cornell University, Hartman Fellowship, 1986; Wuhan University, Student Excellence Award, 1978, 1979, 1980, 1981; received research grants from NSF, ONR, IBM, URI, CBA. **SPECIAL ACHIEVEMENTS:** Author: Over 20 publications in international journals, 1989-; over 60 presentations in national and international conferences, 1989-; author, reviewer of many articles, books, manuscripts, 1989-; dissertation supervisor of 6 PhD students, 1990-. **BUSINESS ADDRESS:** Professor, Dept of MSIS, University of Texas, CBA 5-202, Austin, TX 78712-1104, (512)471-1677.

YU, JAMES H.
Educator. Chinese American. **PERSONAL:** Born Aug 27, 1943, Hsin-Chu, Taiwan; son of Shuei-Deh Yu and Jule-Mei Yu-Fang; married Susan W Yu, Nov 24, 1968; children: Jerry J, Constance C, Andrew J. **EDUCATION:** National Taiwan Normal University, BEd, 1966; University of Wisconsin, Platteville, MS, 1971; University of Wisconsin, Milwaukee, MSEE, 1978; Ohio State University, PHD, 1987. **CAREER:** Ren-Ai Junior High, Taipei, teacher, 1967-69; Union Grove High School, Wisconsin, electronics instructor, 1970-78; Moraine Park Technical College, Wisconsin, chair/lead instructor, 1978-87; San Jose State University, professor, 1987-, graduate coordinator, 1993-. **ORGANIZATIONS:** Society of Manufacturing Engineers, 1989-; Chinese Institute of Engineers-USA, life member, 1990-; National Association of Industrial Technology, 1987-; American Vocational Association, 1978-; Institute of Electrical & Electronics Engineers, 1985-92; California Association of Industrial Technology, president, 1991-92, vice president, 1990-91, secretary, 1989-90. **HONORS/AWARDS:** San Jose State University, Meritorious Performance Professional Promise Award, 1989; Moraine Park Technical College, Wisconsin, Outstanding Adult Educator of the Year Award, 1981. **SPECIAL ACHIEVEMENTS:** Research papers, technical workbooks, presentations at national and international conferences and symposiums; fluent in Mandarin and two other Chinese dialects. **BUSINESS ADDRESS:** Professor & Graduate Coordinator, San Jose State University, One Washington Sq, San Jose, CA 95192-0061, (408)924-3215.

YU, JEN
Medical doctor, educator. Taiwanese American. **PERSONAL:** Born Jan 23, 1943, Taipei, Taiwan; son of Chin Chuan Yu and Shiu Lan Lin; married Janet Chen, Jun 16, 1973; children: Benjamin P, Christopher C. **EDUCATION:** National Taiwan University, MD, 1968; University of Pennsylvania, PhD, 1972. **CAREER:** University of Pennsylvania, School of Medicine, Dept of Physical Medicine & Rehabilitation, assistant professor, 1975-76; University of Texas Health Science Center at San Antonio, Dept of Physical Medicine & Rehabilitation, assistant professor, 1976-79, associate professor, 1979-81; University of California Irvine, College of Medicine, Dept of Physical Medicine & Rehabilitation, professor, 1981-82, professor & chair, 1982-. **ORGANIZATIONS:** American Academy of Physical Medicine & Rehabilitation; American Congress of Rehabilitation Medicine; Association of Academic Physiatrists; American Association of Anatomists; Society for Neuroscience; International Rehabilitation Medicine Association. **HONORS/AWARDS:** American Congress of Rehabilitation Medicine, Essay Contest, Winner, 1974, Elizabeth & Sidney Licht Award for Excellence in Scientific Writing, 1988. **SPECIAL ACHIEVEMENTS:** Publications on research in neuroscience and physical medicine & rehabilitation. **BUSINESS ADDRESS:** Professor & Chair, Dept of Physical Medicine & Rehabilitation, University of California Irvine Medical Center, 101 The City Drive, Orange, CA 92668, (714)456-6504.

YU, JIA-HUEY
Educator. Taiwanese American. **PERSONAL:** Born May 16, 1941, Taipei, Taiwan; daughter of Te-Fang Lin and Chin-len Chang Lin; married Henry H Yu; children: Deborah, Tyson. **EDUCATION:** National Taiwan University, DDS, 1966; University of Alberta, MSc, 1968; University of Michigan, PhD, 1973. **CAREER:** University of Michigan, lecturer, 1973-74; University of Alabama, research assistant professor, 1979-83; FDA, reviewing pharmacologist, 1989-90, expert pharmacologist, 1990-; Georgetown University Medical Center, research assistant professor, 1983-86, research associate professor, 1986-. **ORGANIZATIONS:** International Association for Dental Research, 1974-. **HONORS/AWARDS:** National Institute of Dental Research, modulat-

ing role of prostaglandins in salivary glands, 1980-89, xerostomia-inducing mechanisms of psychotropic drugs, 1987-. **SPECIAL ACHIEVEMENTS:** Author, "Effects of Chronic Amituphyline Administration on Saliva from the Parotid and Submandibular Glands of Rates," Clin Auto Res, 2:5-15, 1992; "Effects of Chronic Clonidine Administration on Parasympatheic-Evoked Rat Saliva," Life Sciences, 51:1493-1499, 1992; "The Influence of Varying the Electrical-frequency of Sympathetic Nerve Stimulation on Fluid and Calcium Secretion of Rat Parotid Gland," Arch Oral Biol, 35:639-643, 1992; "The Uptake and Metabolism of 3h- 5-Hydroxytptamine in Brain Slices and Ileum from Rats," 1973. **BUSINESS ADDRESS:** Associate Professor, Georgetown University, DVA Medical Center, 50 Irving St NW, Washington, DC 20422, (202)745-8489.

YU, JIMMY CHAI-MEI
Educator. Chinese American. **PERSONAL:** Born Feb 24, 1956, Nan An, Fujian, People's Republic of China; son of Yan-Po Yu and Hung-Hai Cheng; married Joan Yin-Ping, Jul 23, 1980; children: Alfred B, Conrad J, Vincent E. **EDUCATION:** Saint Martin's College, BS, 1980; University of Idaho, PhD, 1985. **CAREER:** University of Puget Sound, assistant professor, 1984-85; Central Missouri State University, assistant professor, 1985-90, associate professor, 1990-. **ORGANIZATIONS:** Sigma Xi, 1983-; American Chemical Society, 1983-; Missouri Academy of Science, 1987-. **HONORS/AWARDS:** Sigma Zeta, Outstanding Faculty Award, 1988; College of A&S, Performance Recognition Award, 1989. **SPECIAL ACHIEVEMENTS:** Author: "Extraction of Gold and Mercury from Seawater," 1983; "Dithiocarbamate Extraction of Gallium," 1985; "Semiconductor-Olefin Adducts: Photoluminescent Properties," 1989; "Flow Injection Chemiluminescent Immunoassay," 1991; "A First Experiment in Analytical Chemistry," 1992. **BUSINESS ADDRESS:** Associate Professor, Dept of Chemistry, Central Missouri State University, WCM 410, Warrensburg, MO 64093, (816)543-4948.

YU, JOHN K.
Hydrologist. Chinese American. **PERSONAL:** Born Jul 10, 1944, Tsingtao, Shantung, China; son of Wen-Hao Yu and Ming-Yueh Sun Yu; married Gloria C Yu, Oct 10, 1971; children: Mu-Han Samuel, Mu-Chieh Anne. **EDUCATION:** Taiwan Chunghsing University, BS, 1968; The University of Arizona, MS, 1974, PhD, 1977. **CAREER:** VTN Consolidated, senior hydrologist, 1977-80; Tera Corp, senior geohydrologist, 1980; Morrison-Knudsen Co, senior hydrologist, 1980-81; Soil Exploration Co, senior hydrologist, 1981-84; US Air Force, chief/environmental restoration branch, 1984-90; Roy F Weston Inc, technical director, 1990-91; Engineering-Science Inc, manager/department of hydrogeology, 1991-. **ORGANIZATIONS:** American Geophysical Union, 1974-; Association of Ground Water Scientists and Engineers, 1981-. **HONORS/AWARDS:** San Antonio Federal Executive Association, supervisor of the year finalist, 1988; USAF Occupational and Environmental Health Laboratory, civilian employee of the year, 1989. **SPECIAL ACHIEVEMENTS:** Published 17 papers in journals, proceedings, and handbooks; fluent in Chinese. **MILITARY SERVICE:** Infantry, Republic of China, second lieutenant, 1968-69. **HOME ADDRESS:** 702 Golfcrest Dr, Windcrest, TX 78239-2623.

YU, K. TIMOTHY. *See* YU, KAR YUK.

YU, KAI-BOR
Electrical engineer. Hong Kong American. **PERSONAL:** Born Apr 20, 1953, Canton, China; son of Cheung Yu and Wai Chun Lau; married Wen-Li Fan, Aug 28, 1982; children: Christina, Anna. **EDUCATION:** Yale University, BS, 1977; Brown University, MS, 1979; Purdue University, PhD, 1982. **CAREER:** Virginia Tech, assistant professor, 1982-88; GE, electrical engineer, 1988-. **ORGANIZATIONS:** IEEE Signal Processing Society, 1979-, Aerospace & Electronic Systems, 1985-, Virginia Mountain Section, Publicity Committee Chairman, 1986-88. **HONORS/AWARDS:** GE, Whitney Gallery of Technical Achievers, 1991; IEEE National Radar Conf, Best Poster Paper, 1993, Outstanding Paper, 1991; Virginia Tech, DuPont Assistant Professor, 1985-87. **SPECIAL ACHIEVEMENTS:** Over 50 publications on signal processing, radar, and ECCM. **HOME ADDRESS:** 789 Red Oak Dr, Schenectady, NY 12309, (518)374-2253. **BUSINESS ADDRESS:** Electrical Engineer, GE Research & Development Center, PO Box 8, KW-C606, Schenectady, NY 12301, (518)387-5228.

YU, KAI FUN
Mathematical statistican. Chinese American. **EDUCATION:** Dartmouth College, AB, 1973; Columbia University, PhD, 1978. **CAREER:** Yale University,

assistant professor, 1978-84; University of South Carolina, associate professor, 1984-90; National Institutes of Health, mathematical statistician, 1990-. **BUSINESS ADDRESS:** Mathematical Statistican, National Institutes of Health, BMSB, DESPR, NICHD, Bldg 6100, Room 7B13, Bethesda, MD 20892, (301)496-6811.

YU, KAR YUK (K. TIMOTHY YU)
Consulting firm executive. Chinese American. **PERSONAL:** Born Sep 19, 1948, Canton, China; son of Wah Sheh Yu (deceased) and Sui Fa Ng; married Cecilia L Yu, May 12, 1974; children: Brandon, Cameron, Ashlin. **EDUCATION:** University of California, BS, 1972; University of Wisconsin, MS, 1974; University of Southern California, PhD, 1979. **CAREER:** Jacobs Engineering, sr engineer, 1978; TRW, section head, 1978-83; CKY Inc, president, 1983-93. **ORGANIZATIONS:** Association of Hazardous Waste Professionals, 1988; Sigma Xi, 1972. **HONORS/AWARDS:** TRW, Outstanding Supplier, 1990; Southern California Regional Purchasing Council, Supplier of the Year, 1990; National Supplier Development Council, Supplier of the Year, 1990. **BIOGRAPHICAL SOURCES:** "Making It," KTLA-Los Angeles, Channel 5, Dec 5, 1992. **BUSINESS ADDRESS:** President, CKY Inc Environmental Services, 630 Maple Ave, Torrance, CA 90503, (310)618-8889.

YU, LARRY
Educator. Chinese American. **PERSONAL:** Born May 11, 1957, Tianjin, Hebei, People's Republic of China; son of Ruiyun Yu and Huiling Zhang; married Sarah Chen, Mar 14, 1983; children: Gordon. **EDUCATION:** Hangzhou University, BA, 1980; Boston University, EdM, 1984; University of Oregon, PhD, 1988. **CAREER:** China Express International, managing director, 1989; Northern Arizona University, assistant professor, 1990-. **ORGANIZATIONS:** Arizona Asian American Association, Northern Arizona Chapter, founding member, 1992-; Society of Travel and Tourism Educators, 1991-; Travel and Tourism Research Association, Arizona Chapter, 1992-; Council on Hotel, Restaurant, and Institutional Education, 1993-. **HONORS/AWARDS:** Northern Arizona University, Leadership Development Programs Recognition Award, 1992; Northern Arizona University, School of Hotel and Restaurant Management, Outstanding Scholar Award, 1993. **SPECIAL ACHIEVEMENTS:** Publications: "Teaching International Hospitality Management," Hospitality and Tourism Educators, 1992; "Hotel Rating System in China," Cornell Quarterly, 1992; "Hotel Development & Structures in China," International Journal of Hospitality Management, 1992; "Emerging Markets for China's Tourism Industry," Journal of Travel Research, 1992; "Referral Associations in the Hospitality Industry," Hospitality Management: An Introduction to the Industry, 1993. **HOME ADDRESS:** 2761 N Eddy Dr, Flagstaff, AZ 86001, (602)779-1205. **BUSINESS ADDRESS:** Assistant Professor, Northern Arizona University, School of Hotel and Restaurant Management, Box 5638, Flagstaff, AZ 86011, (602)523-1705.

YU, LINDA
Television news anchor. Chinese American. **PERSONAL:** Born Dec 1, 1946, Xian, China; daughter of Stanley Yu and Roberta Yu; married Richard Baer, Jun 12, 1982; children: Rick, Francesca. **EDUCATION:** University of Southern California, BA, 1968. **CAREER:** KABC-TV, Los Angeles, writer, 1974; KTLA-TV, Los Angeles, writer, 1974-75; KATV-TV, Portland, reporter, 1975; KGO-TV, San Francisco, reporter, 1976-79; WMAQ-TV, Chicago, anchor, 1979-84; WLS-TV, anchor, 1984-. **BUSINESS ADDRESS:** Anchor, WLS-TV, 190 N State Street, Chicago, IL 60610, (312)750-7884.

YU, MELVIN JOSEPH
Chemist. Korean American/Japanese American. **PERSONAL:** Born Sep 21, 1956, Tacoma, WA. **EDUCATION:** Massachusetts Institute of Technology, BS, 1979; Harvard University, MA, 1983, PhD, 1985. **CAREER:** Eli Lilly and Co, research scientist, 1985-92; Eisai Research Institute, senior scientist, 1992-. **ORGANIZATIONS:** New York Academy of Sciences, 1993-; Society for Neuroscience, 1992-93; American Chemical Society, associate member, 1979-. **SPECIAL ACHIEVEMENTS:** Co-author: "Benzylamine Antioxidants: Relationship Between Structure, Peroxyl Scavenging, Lipid Peroxidation Inhibition and Cytoprotection," Journal of Medical Chemistry, 1993; "Stucturally Novel Antiarrhythmic/Antioxidant Quinazolines," BioMed Chem Letter, 1992; numerous others. **BUSINESS ADDRESS:** Senior Scientist, Eisai Research Institute, 4 Corporate Dr, Andover, MA 01810.

YU, PAUL KIT-LAI
Educator. Chinese American. **PERSONAL:** Born Jul 12, 1957, Hong Kong; son of Kwai Lau (deceased) and Chiu Ying Yu; married De De Yu, Dec 26,

1986; children: Lea S, Elton, Stephen. **EDUCATION:** California Institute of Technology, BSc, 1979, MSc, 1979, PhD, 1983. **CAREER:** California Institute of Tech, research assistant, 1979-83; University of California Regents, assistant professor, 1983-88, associate professor, 1988-93, professor, 1993-. **ORGANIZATIONS:** IEEE, 1991-, chapter officer, MTT/AP/EDS, secretary at San Diego, 1991-; Optical Society of America, 1984-; Society of Photo-Electrical Engineers, 1984-; American Physical Society, 1982-92. **HONORS/AWARDS:** IEEE, senior member, 1990; Tau Beta Pi, 1977. **SPECIAL ACHIEVEMENTS:** Published over 70 technical papers over the last 14 years in various technical journals; contributed 4 chapters to handbooks on fiber optics and semiconductors. **BUSINESS ADDRESS:** Associate Professor, Dept of Electrical & Computer Engineering, University of California San Diego, M/S 0407, La Jolla, CA 92093-0407, (619)534-6180.

YU, PETER TAT-KONG
Hotel/real estate executive. Macanese American/Chinese American. **PERSONAL:** Born Nov 20, 1948, Macao; son of Keng Sau Yu and Mai Kit Man Yu; married Isabelle Lafforgue Yu, Apr 26, 1980; children: Jeffrey, Cedric, Melanie. **EDUCATION:** University of Manitoba, BS, 1968-71; University of British Columbia, MBA, 1971-73; Canadian Chartered Accountant, 1978. **CAREER:** University of Singapore, lecturer business administration, 1973-75; Thorne Ernst & Whinney, public accountant, 1975-79; Kaiser Resources Ltd, assistant to chairmen, 1979-82; Universal Matchbox, CFO, 1982-85; Century City Holdings Ltd, director, 1985-89; Richfield Hotel Management Inc, president, CEO, director, 1989-. **ORGANIZATIONS:** American Hotel & Motel Association, IREFAC Committee; Denver Chamber of Commerce; Asian American Hotel Owners Association, honorary board of advisors; American Hotel & Motel Association Educational Institute, board of regents. **BIOGRAPHICAL SOURCES:** Various trade publications articles. **BUSINESS ADDRESS:** President, CEO, Richfield Hotel Mangement, Inc, 4600 S Ulster St, Ste 1200, Denver, CO 80237, (303)220-2034.

YU, PRISCILLA C.
Librarian. Chinese American. **PERSONAL:** Born in New York, NY; daughter of Tsechang Kent Chang & Yeuh-Hai Kwan Chang; married George Tzuchiao Yu; children: Anthony J, Phillip C. **EDUCATION:** University of California, Berkeley, BA; Columbia University, MLS. **CAREER:** University of California, Berkeley, general reference assistant librarian, 1957-61; University of North Carolina, Chapel Hill, chemistry librarian, head, 1962-63; University of Illinois, Urbana, gifts & exch div, head, 1976-78, documents bibliographer, 1980-84, asst history librarian, 1984-92, acting asst to the director of departmental lib serv, 1992-. **ORGANIZATIONS:** American Library Association, Gifts & Exchange Discussion Grp, chair, 1983-84, Duplicates Exchange Union Comm, 1983-85, Books to China Comm, CALA chair, 1984-85, Esther J Piercy Award Jury, 1985-86, Nominating Comm, International Rel Round Table, chair, 1990, Women's Studies sec, Tech Serv Comm, 1991-93, LAMA Publns Comm, 1993-95. **HONORS/AWARDS:** Council on Library Resources, Collection Dev of Western Language Materials in Chinese Libraries, 1985-86; University of Illinois, Scholars Travel Fund, Arthur E Bostwick & Chinese Library Development: A Chapter in International Cooperation, 1993; University of Illinois, Urbana, Research & Publication Comm, Chinese Academic & Research Libraries, 1993. **SPECIAL ACHIEVEMENTS:** "Berkeley's Exchange Program: A Case Study," Journ of Lib Hist, 1982; "Taiwan's International Exchange Program: A Study in Cultural Diplomacy," Asian Affairs, an American Review, 1985; "The Development of Foreign Language Collections at Peking University Library," Library Acquisitions: Practice & Theory, 1991. **BUSINESS ADDRESS:** Professor, University of Illinois Library at Urbana-Champaign, 1408 West Gregory Drive, 246A Main Library, Urbana, IL 61801, (217)333-0317.

YU, ROBERT KUAN-JEN
Educator, educational administrator. Chinese American. **PERSONAL:** Born Jan 27, 1938, Chungking, China; son of Shen-cheng Yu and June Tsao Yu; married Helen Yu, Jul 1972; children: David S, Jennifer S. **EDUCATION:** Tunghai University, Taichung, Taiwan, BS, 1960; University of Illinois, Urbana, PhD, 1967. **CAREER:** Albert Einstein College of Med, postdoctoral, beginning 1967 instructor, until 1973; Yale University, assistant professor, beginning 1973, prof, until 1988; Medical College of Virginia, professor and chairman, 1988-. **ORGANIZATIONS:** ASBMB, 1973-; International Soc Neurochem, 1973-; American Soc Neurochem, council, 1986, 1989, 1991-; American Chem Society; NY Acad Sci; AAAS; Society of Neuroscience. **HONORS/AWARDS:** University Tokyo, Hon Doc Med Sci, 1980; Yale University, honorary MA, 1985; Alexander Von Humboldt Award, 1990; Jacob

Javits Neuroscience Award, 1984-91; Josiah Macy Award, 1979; honorary professor at three universities. **SPECIAL ACHIEVEMENTS:** Publication of 2 books, 1984, 1988; publication of 240 full papers in scientific journals; publication of 180 abstracts and notes in science. **BUSINESS ADDRESS:** Professor and Chairman, Dept of Biochemistry and Molecular Biophysics, Medical College of Virginia, Virginia Commonwealth University, Box 614, Richmond, VA 23298-0614, (804)786-9762.

YU, SHIAO-LING S.
Educator. Chinese American. **PERSONAL:** Born Dec 16, 1936, Nanking, China; daughter of Yueh Sheng and Mei-ying Ching; married Yun-sheng Yu, Apr 17, 1960; children: Larry, Mike, Mark, David. **EDUCATION:** Caldwell College, BA, chemistry, 1958; Boston College, MS, chemistry, 1961; University of Kansas, MA, Chinese literature, 1977; University of Wisconsin-Madison, PhD, Chinese literature, 1983. **CAREER:** Ohio State University, visit asst prof of Chinese, 1983-84; University of Kansas, visit asst prof of Chinese, 1984-86; Oregon State University, asst prof of Chinese, 1987-91, assoc prof of Chinese, 1991-. **ORGANIZATIONS:** Association for Asian Studies; Modern Languages Association; Association for Asian Performance; International Society for Chinese Language Teaching, based in Beijing. **HONORS/AWARDS:** Newcombe/Woodrow Wilson, Dissertation Fellowship, 1982; National Endowment for the Arts, Translation Fellowship, 1994. **SPECIAL ACHIEVEMENTS:** Publications on post-Mao Chinese literature and traditional Chinese drama have appeared in: Renditions, China Quarterly, Journal of Chinese Philosophy, Asian Theatre Journal, and three anthologies: Post-Mao Chinese Literature (M E Sharpe, 1985); A Writer at the Crossroads: The Short Stories of Chen Ruoxi (Edwin Mellen, 1992); Nativism Overseas: Contemporary Chinese Women Writers (SUNY, 1993). **BUSINESS ADDRESS:** Associate Professor, Oregon State University, Kidder Hall 235, Corvallis, OR 97331, (503)737-2146.

YU, SHIU YEH
Educator. Taiwanese American. **PERSONAL:** Born Jun 1, 1926, Chang Hwa, Formosa; son of Cheh Yu and Su Eng Yu; married Noriko M, Feb 28, 1958; children: Kiyoshi. **EDUCATION:** National Chung Hsing University, Taichung, Formosa, China, BS, 1951; Oklahoma State University, Stillwater, MS, 1955; St Louis University, School of Medicine, PhD, 1963. **CAREER:** Jewish Hospital of St Louis, research associate, 1955-62; Washington University School of Medicine, St Louis, assistant professor in medicine, 1972-78; St Louis University School of Medicine, assistant clinical professor, 1978-82, associate research professor, 1982-90; St Louis VA Hospital, Clinical Laboratory, director, 1988-90; National VA Environmental Laboratory, consultant, 1990-; University of Rochester School of Medicine, assistant professor, 1990-. **ORGANIZATIONS:** Sigma Xi, 1961-; Council of Atherosclerosis, American Heart Association, fellow, 1962-90; American Association of Investigative Pathology, 1964-; Biochemical Society of London, England, 1972-87; American Institute of Chemistry, fellow, 1972-74; American Society of Electron Microscopists, 1964-72; American Gerontological Society, 1959-80; New York Academy of Science, 1965-72. **HONORS/AWARDS:** NIH Grantee, 1958, 1989; Graduate Scholarship Awardee, 1952, 1961. **SPECIAL ACHIEVEMENTS:** Contributed articles for professional journals; more than 100 papers about pathology and medicine; publications on asbestos analysis. **HOME ADDRESS:** 1004 Amsterdam Dr, Manchester, MO 63011. **BUSINESS ADDRESS:** Asst Prof, Dept of Obstetrics and Gynecology, Rochester General Hospital, 1425 Portland Ave, Rochester, NY 14621, (716)338-4808.

YU, THOMAS H.
Engineer. Taiwanese American. **PERSONAL:** Born Mar 20, 1957, Taipei, Taiwan; married Bang-Huei Yen, Jul 1, 1982; children: Frank C, Alice J. **EDUCATION:** National Taiwan University, BS, chem eng, 1980; University of Rochester, PhD, chem eng, 1987; Cleveland State University, MBA, 1993. **CAREER:** GE Lighting, development engineer, 1986-88, advance engineer, 1988-91, sr advance engineer, 1991-92, team leader, automotive halogen, 1992-. **ORGANIZATIONS:** GE Elfun Society, 1992-; American Institute of Chemical Engineers, 1982-; Chinese Academy of Cleveland, board of directors, 1982-. **HONORS/AWARDS:** GE Lighting, Managerial Award, 1988. **SPECIAL ACHIEVEMENTS:** Author of eleven technical papers, 1983-. **BUSINESS ADDRESS:** Team Leader, Automotive Halogen, GE Lighting, Nela Park, Bldg 323, East Cleveland, OH 44112, (216)266-3490.

YU, VICTOR LIN-KAI
Physician. Chinese American. **PERSONAL:** Born Jan 9, 1943, Minneapolis, MN; son of Robert Si-Hsuin Yu and Victoria Hsiao; married Deborah, Feb 4,

1971; children: Chen, Kwan-Ting. **EDUCATION:** Carleton College, BA, 1965; University of Minnesota, MD, 1970; University of Colorado Med Ctr, intern, 1970-72; Stanford University, fellow, 1974-77. **CAREER:** University of Pittsburgh, professor of medicine, 1978-. **ORGANIZATIONS:** Organization of Chinese Americans; American Society of Microbiology, National Library of Medicine, board scientific counselors; National Institutes of Health, VA Infectious Disease Field Advisory Group, 1983-; Pitt Asian Medical Student Association, faculty advisor, 1993-. **HONORS/AWARDS:** National Institutes of Health, Distinguished Service Award, 1992; American Legion, Distinguished Research Award, 1982; Health Research & Services Foundation, Outstanding Contribution to Health Research, 1984; American Society of Microbiology, Distinguished Lecturer, 1988. **SPECIAL ACHIEVEMENTS:** Published 300 papers, scientific abstracts, book chapters on infectious diseases and medicine; 50 visiting professorships and invited lectureships. **HOME ADDRESS:** 87 Longuevue Drive, Pittsburgh, PA 15228, (412)343-7429. **BUSINESS ADDRESS:** Professor of Medicine, University of Pittsburgh, School of Medicine, 968 Scaife Hall, Pittsburgh, PA 15261, (412)683-3189.

YU, WEN C.

Business executive. Chinese American. **PERSONAL:** Born Jan 1, 1942, Taiwan; son of Ping & June Yu; married Jenny S Yu, Sep 9, 1971; children: Jessen, Jessica. **EDUCATION:** Taipei Institute of Technology, BS, 1962; University of Rhode Island, MS, 1968, PhD, 1971; Harvard University, MS, 1974. **CAREER:** Exxon, project engineer, 1974-78; TRW, project engineer, 1978-82; UOP, senior engineer, 1982-85; Fair East Group, president, CEO, 1985-. **ORGANIZATIONS:** AIChE; NAR; AOIHA. **HONORS/AWARDS:** Sigma Xi. **BUSINESS ADDRESS:** President, Fair East Group, 8212-B Old Courthouse Road, Vienna, VA 22182, (703)827-0520.

YU, WINNIE Y.

Educator. Hong Kong American. **PERSONAL:** Born May 5, 1960, Hong Kong; daughter of Poon Yin Yu and Yu Wan Mui Yu; married Jeffrey C F Ng, May 16, 1987; children: Thaddeus Alexander Ng, Thomas Antony Ng. **EDUCATION:** Monmouth College, BS (cum laude), 1983; Columbia University, MS, 1985. **CAREER:** Southern Connecticut State University, asst professor, 1985-. **ORGANIZATIONS:** Association for Computing Machineries. **HONORS/AWARDS:** Connecticut Dept of Higher Education, co-recepient of high-technology grant, 1987. **BUSINESS ADDRESS:** Asst Professor, Computer Science, Southern Connecticut State University, 501 Crescent St, Morrill Hall Rm 121, New Haven, CT 06515, (203)397-4514.

YU, YEOU-CHONG SIMON

Electronics company manager. Taiwanese American. **PERSONAL:** Born Nov 11, 1958, Taipei Hsien, Taiwan; son of Sheng-Shun Yu and I-Liang Jeng Yu; married Shumei Chiu Yu, May 30, 1987. **EDUCATION:** National Chiao Tung University, BSEE, 1981; Case Western Reserve University, MSEE, 1984. **CAREER:** Tektronix Inc, project leader, 1984-88; Aspen Semiconductor Corp, senior technology engineer, 1988-89; California Micro Devices Corp, manager, BICMOS, 1989-91; Monolith Technologies Corp, manager, technology, 1991-. **HONORS/AWARDS:** IEEE Electron Devices Society, Paul Rappaport Award, 1989. **SPECIAL ACHIEVEMENTS:** Publications: 17 papers in major technical journals, 1986-91; US patents: 4,994,400, Method of Fabricating a Semiconductor Device Using a Tri-Layer Structure and Conductive Sidewalls, 1991; 4,876,400, 1989. **BIOGRAPHICAL SOURCES:** IEEE Transactions on Electron Devices, vol 35, no 8, p 1247, 1988. **BUSINESS ADDRESS:** Engineering Manager, Monolith Technologies Corporation, 5620 N Kolb Rd, Ste 100, Tucson, AZ 85715, (602)577-8292.

YU, YUN-SHENG

Educator. Chinese American. **PERSONAL:** Born Nov 21, 1926, I-Hsing, Jiangsu, China; son of Wen-Wei Yu & Shieh-shi Yu; married Lucy Shiao-Ling Yu, Apr 17, 1960; children: Lawrence Hsioa-Yun, Michael Xiao-Feng, Mark Hsiao-Lan, David Hsioa-Tien. **EDUCATION:** National Taiwan University, BS, civil engineering, 1953; University of Iowa, MS, 1956; Massachusetts Institute of Technology, ScD, civil engineering, 1960. **CAREER:** Taiwan Power Company, engineer, 1953-54; Iowa Institute of Hydraulic Research, research associate, 1956-57; MIT Hydrodynamics Laboratory, research associate, 1959-60; University of Kansas, associate professor, 1960-65; US Army Tank-Automotive Center, research mechanical engineer, 1966; University of Michigan, visiting professor, 1967; University of Kansas, professor of civil engineering, 1966-. **ORGANIZATIONS:** American Society of Civil Engineers; American Geophysical Union; American Association of Water Resources; American Mathematical Association; International Association of Wa-

ter Resources. **HONORS/AWARDS:** Li Foundation, Li Foundation Fellow, 1954-56; Hehai University, Nanjing, China, Honorary Professorship, 1992. **SPECIAL ACHIEVEMENTS:** Published more than 100 publications and 10 book reviews. **BUSINESS ADDRESS:** Professor, Dept of Civil Engineering, University of Kansas, 1039 Learned Hall, Lawrence, KS 66045, (913)864-3807.

YUAN, JIAN-MIN

Educator, researcher. Taiwanese American/Chinese American. **PERSONAL:** Born Aug 31, 1944, Chung king, Sichuan, China; son of Wen-Kai Yuan and Wen-Ming Liao; married Barbara O-Ching Chen Yuan, Dec 19, 1971; children: Jean W, Conan W. **EDUCATION:** National Taiwan University, BS, 1966, MS, 1968; University of Chicago, PhD, 1973. **CAREER:** University of Chicago, teaching assistant, research assistant, 1968-73; University of Florida, postdoctoral fellow, 1973-75; University of Rochester, instructor, research associate, 1975-78; Drexel University, professor, 1978-. **ORGANIZATIONS:** American Physical Society, 1970-; American Chemical Society, 1970-. **HONORS/AWARDS:** Drexel University, University Research Scholar Award, 1981. **SPECIAL ACHIEVEMENTS:** Published more than 85 professional papers in the fields of molecular & chemical physics, atomic physics, molecule-radiation interaction, chaos, nonlinear dynamics, and reaction dynamics; languages: fluent in reading, German & French; proficient in Chinese. **HOME ADDRESS:** 140 S Spring Mill Rd, Villanova, PA 19085, (215)525-5742. **BUSINESS ADDRESS:** Professor, Dept of Physics & Atmospheric Science, Drexel University, 32nd and Chestnut Sts, Disque Hall 811, Philadelphia, PA 19104, (215)895-2722.

YUAN, LUKE CHIA-LIU

Physicist. Chinese American. **PERSONAL:** Born Apr 5, 1912, An-Yang, Henan, China; son of Ke-Wen Yuan (deceased) and Dan Liu Yuan (deceased); married Chien-Shiung Wu, May 31, 1942; children: Vincent. **EDUCATION:** Yenching University, BS, MS; California Institute of Technology, PhD. **CAREER:** California Institute of Technology, graduate assistant, 1937-40, research fellow, 1940-42; RCA Lab, research physicist, 1942-47; Princeton University, research associate, 1947-49; Centre d'Etudes Nucleaires de Saclay, Paris, France, and CERN, Geneva, Switz, visiting professor, 1972-75; Institute for High Energy Physics, Serpukhov, USSR, visiting professor, 1979; University of Paris, France, visiting professor, 1982; Brookhaven National Lab, associate physicist, physicist, senior physicist, 1949-78; Synchrotron Radiation Center, Taiwan, chairman board of directors, 1983-; Adelphi University, adjunct professor, 1989-. **ORGANIZATIONS:** American Physical Society, fellow; Adelphi University Research Center, board of directors, 1983-86; Sigma Xi, 1942-. **HONORS/AWARDS:** Honorary Professor: China University of Science & Technology, Nankai University, Henan University, Southeastern University; Henan Acad of Sci, China, honorary member; numerous honorary degrees & professorships; Academia Simica; New York Acad of Sci; Guggenheim Fellow, 1957; Chingyun Presidential Medal, 1994. **SPECIAL ACHIEVEMENTS:** Establishment of the existence of a maximum in the neutron distribution in the atmosphere as a function of altitude showing that neutrons in the atmosphere originate inside the earth's atmosphere, of the existence of a resonance state in the pion-nucleon interaction; experimental verification of the important characteristics of transition radiation produced by high energy particles, establishment of its application as high energy detectors; introduction of superheated superconducting granules as high energy detector capable of energy determination. **HOME ADDRESS:** 15 Claremont Ave, New York, NY 10027, (212)662-8064.

YUAN, ROBIN TSU-WANG

Plastic surgeon. Chinese American. **PERSONAL:** Born Jul 2, 1954, Boston, MA; son of Grace I Chen and Robert Hsun-Piao Yuan. **EDUCATION:** Harvard College, AB, 1974; Harvard Medical School, MD, 1978. **CAREER:** Private practice, plastic surgeon, 1987-; Cedars-Sinai Medical Center, Division of Plastic Surgery, vice-chief, 1993. **ORGANIZATIONS:** Los Angeles County Medical Association, district 1, board of governors, 1991-93; California Medical Association, delegate, 1991-93; Cedars-Sinai Craniofacial Clinic, surgical coordinator/founder, 1990-93; Family of Independent Reconstructive Surgery Teams, founder/president, 1991-93. **HONORS/AWARDS:** Newton High School, Charles Dana Merserve Award, 1971; Harvard University, Harvard Award, 1971-74. **BUSINESS ADDRESS:** 150 N Robertson Blvd, #315, Beverly Hills, CA 90211, (310)652-8425.

YUAN, SIDNEY W. K.
Aerospace engineer. Chinese American. **PERSONAL:** Born Jul 30, 1957, Hong Kong; son of Chia Chi Yuan and Tso Tak Wong Yuan; married Katherine K Y Dai, Sep 8, 1981; children: Jacquelyn Kate, Chrystal Sidney. **EDUCATION:** University of California, Los Angeles, BSc, 1980, MSc, 1981, PhD, 1985. **CAREER:** Lockheed Missiles & Space Co, research scientist, 1985-; Toyo Sanso KK, Japan, consultant, 1990-; Applied Aerotek Inc, consultant, 1991-; Compliance Engineering & Technology, consultant, 1992-. **ORGANIZATIONS:** Tau Beta Pi, 1983-; American Institute of Chemical Engineers, 1984-; American Institute of Aeronautics & Astronautics, senior member, 1985-; Sigma Xi, 1985-. **HONORS/AWARDS:** The Space Foundation, National Excellence Recognition Award, 1985; Lockheed Missiles & Space Co, Superior Performance Team Award, 1990; American Institute of Aeronautics & Astronautics, Engineer of the Year Award, 1991. **SPECIAL ACHIEVEMENTS:** Published more than 32 papers in professional journals; University of California, Los Angeles, short course lecturer; proficient in Chinese. **HOME ADDRESS:** 4964 Adagio Ct, Fremont, CA 94538, (510)659-0138. **BUSINESS ADDRESS:** Research Scientist, Lockheed Missiles and Space Co, 3251 Hanover St, Bldg 205, Organization 92-40, Palo Alto, CA 94304, (415)424-3398.

YUASA, JOJI
Composer, educator. Japanese American. **PERSONAL:** Born Aug 12, 1929, Koriyama, Japan; son of Daitaro Yuasa and Otoe Yuasa; married Reiko Yuasa, Nov 12, 1958; children: Rena, Ryuhei Rex. **EDUCATION:** Keio University, BA. **CAREER:** Tokyo College of Music, visiting professor, 1981; Kunitachi College of Music, visiting professor, 1988; University of California, San Diego, professor of music, 1981-. **ORGANIZATIONS:** ISCM, executive committee, 1979-80; Japan Federation of Composers, vp, 1980-81, ICMC 93, chairman of jury, 1993. **HONORS/AWARDS:** Odaka Prize, Chronoplastic for Orchestra, 1972; Odaka Prize, Revealed Time for Viola & Orchestra, 1988; Prix Italia, Comet Ikeya, 1966; Prix Italia, Love and Hate (stereophonic musical), 1967. **SPECIAL ACHIEVEMENTS:** Orchestral concert by the Tokyo Metropolitan Symphony Orchestra, 1994; orchestral concert by Suntory Music Foundation, 1986; concert for chamber music, by Music Today 92 Festival. **HOME ADDRESS:** 1517 Shields Ave, Encinitas, CA 92024, (619)436-3775.

YUCHENGCO, MONA LISA SYCIP
Publisher. Filipino American. **PERSONAL:** Born Oct 15, 1950, Manila, Philippines; daughter of Alfonso T Yuchengco and Paz Sycip; married Danilo C Goquingco, Sep 27, 1992; children: Jose Paolo Y Abaya, Carlos Miguel Y Abaya. **EDUCATION:** Assumption College, BS, education, liberal arts, 1971; Ateneo De Manila University, MBA, 1979; University of California, Berkeley, creative writing, publishing, 1988-92; Stanford University, professional publishing course, 1993. **CAREER:** Rizal Commercial Banking Corp, vice president, 1973-82; Hi-Am Inc, president, 1983-; Filipinas Publishing Inc, publisher, editor-in-chief, 1992-. **ORGANIZATIONS:** Philippine International Aid, founder, chair, executive director, 1986-; Asian Business League; Filipino American Chamber of Commerce of San Francisco; Assumption Alumnae Association. **HONORS/AWARDS:** Saint Paul the Shipwreck Church, Martin Luther King Award, 1993; Philippine Arts, Letters & Media, short story writing contest, third place, 1990. **SPECIAL ACHIEVEMENTS:** Author: weekly column entitled, "Heart to Heart," Philippine News, San Francisco, 1990-91; "The Changing Face of the Filipino Woman," a three part series on domestic helpers, migrant workers and mail-order brides, Filipinas Magazine, 1992. **BUSINESS ADDRESS:** Publisher, Editor-in-Chief, Filipinas Publishing Inc, 5222 Diamond Heights Blvd, San Francisco, CA 94131, (415)824-0735.

YUE, CHINNY
Consulting company executive. Chinese American. **PERSONAL:** Born Aug 22, 1965, Hong Kong; daughter of Wing-Yip Yue and Shui-Chee Law. **EDUCATION:** Boston University, 1983-84; MIT, BSME, 1987, MSME, 1988. **CAREER:** Boston Edison Company, intern, 1985-86; MIT, research assistant, 1986-88; AT&T Bell Laboratories, member of technical staff, 1988-92; Yue International, president, 1992-. **ORGANIZATIONS:** Tau Beta Pi, chairman of career planning committtee, 1986-87; Pi Tau Sigma, publicity director, 1986-87; IEEE, 1988-; ASME, 1986-92; SME, 1986-92. **HONORS/AWARDS:** AT&T Bell Labs, Presidential Quality Award, 1990; Academic All-American Collegiate Award, 1987; MIT grant, 1984-87; Boston University, dean's list w/ honors, 1984. **SPECIAL ACHIEVEMENTS:** Co-author, "Alternate Control Laws for Automotive Active Suspensions," Journal of Dynamic Systems, Measurements and Controls, Transactions of the ASME, vol 112, no 2, June, 1989; soprano soloist at MIT, 1987; Tanglewood Festival Chorus, member,

performed with Boston Symphony Orchestra and Boston Pops, 1987; soloist, Monmouth Civic Chorus, NJ, 1989. **BUSINESS ADDRESS:** President, Yue International, 1004 Maple Hill Dr, Woodbridge, NJ 07095, (908)843-7971.

YUE, DAVID T.
Medical researcher, educator. Chinese American. **PERSONAL:** married Nancy Nai Hun Chang; children: Michael David Tzeruen. **EDUCATION:** Harvard University, BA, 1983; Johns Hopkins Medical Institutions, MD, PhD, 1987. **CAREER:** Johns Hopkins Medical Institutions, Biomedical Engineering Dept, assistant professor, currently. **BUSINESS ADDRESS:** Assistant Professor, Dept of Biomedical Engineering, Johns Hopkins Medical Institutions, Baltimore, MD 21287.

YUE, ROBERT HON-SANG
Biochemist. Chinese American. **PERSONAL:** Born Sep 9, 1937, Canton, Kwongtung, China; son of Paak C Yue and Shui-Ching Yue; married Noel Sung-Mei Yue, Jun 6, 1970; children: Jennifer Arleen, Alana Frances, Sylvia Irene. **EDUCATION:** East Texas Baptist College, BS, chemistry, 1961; University of Minnesota, 1961-63; University of Utah, PhD, biological chemistry, 1968. **CAREER:** University of Minnesota, teaching fellow, 1961-63; University of Utah, research associate, assistant to postdoctoral associate, 1963-70; New York University Medical Center, associate research scientist to research associate professor, 1970-81; Revlon Health Care Group, research associate fellow, 1981-85; Enzon Inc, director of product development to senior director of product development, 1985-93; Clinical Research Associates, quality assurance officer, 1994-. **ORGANIZATIONS:** American Chemical Society, 1960-; American Association for the Advancement of Sciences, 1961-; New York Academy of Sciences, 1970-; International Society on Thrombosis and Haemostasis, 1971-; American Heart Association, 1970-; New York Heart Association, 1970-; Council on Thrombosis, 1971-; Parenteral Drug Association, 1985-. **HONORS/AWARDS:** East Texas Baptist University, W T Tardy Award for Outstanding Service, 1979. **SPECIAL ACHIEVEMENTS:** US Patent No 4,478,829, Pharmaceutical Preparation Containing Purified Fibronectin, 1984; 19 publications in leading scientific journals, 1965-84. **HOME ADDRESS:** 259-15 86th Ave, Floral Park, NY 11001-1023, (718)347-0183. **BUSINESS ADDRESS:** Quality Assurance Officer, Clinical Research Associates, 50 Madison Ave, New York, NY 10010, (212)685-8788.

YUE, XIAODONG
Psychologist. Chinese American. **PERSONAL:** Born Jul 7, 1959, Beijing, People's Republic of China; son of Shaoxian Yue and Hongliang Sun; married X H Zhang, Sep 1985; children: Serena. **EDUCATION:** Beijing Second Foreign Languages Institute, China, BA, 1982; Canberra College of Advanced Education, Australia, MA, 1983; Tufts University, MA, 1987; Harvard University, EdD, 1993. **CAREER:** Harvard University, Graduate School of Education, instructor/therapist, currently. **ORGANIZATIONS:** American Psychology Association, 1990-; American Counseling Association,1991-. **HONORS/AWARDS:** Tsai Shao-Hua Scholarship Foundation, Dissertation Award, 1991; Run Run Shao Scholarship Foundation, scholarship, 1990-91; Harvard Institute of International Development, Dissertation Grant, 1991; Harvard University Scholarship Foundation, John Thayer Fellowship, 1988-90; Beijing Second Foreign Language Institute, Outstanding Graduate Award, 1982. **SPECIAL ACHIEVEMENTS:** College Counseling in the US (in Chinese), 1993; Psychological Features of Adolescents, 1992; On Principles of Counseling, 1992; Cultural Issues in Counseling Chinese Students, 1991; Introduction of Counseling Center at Harvard University, 1990. **HOME ADDRESS:** 255 Beacon St, #1C, Somerville, MA 02143.

YUEN, CALVIN N.
Actuarial firm executive. Chinese American. **PERSONAL:** Born Dec 16, 1928, Los Angeles, CA; son of Ora Helene Tom and Ng Sing Yuen; married Elaine Wong Yuen, Mar 24, 1951; children: Keith N, Cherri E Houser. **EDUCATION:** LACC, 1947-48; Cal State, 1948-49; UCLA, 1949-52. **CAREER:** ANICO, staff supervisor, 1955-58; American National Insurance Co, asst general agent, 1958-71; Advance Benefits Systems Corp, vice president, 1971-93. **ORGANIZATIONS:** American Society of Pension Actuaries, 1979-88; Chartered Life Underwriters, 1967-88; National Eagle Scout Assn, currently. **SPECIAL ACHIEVEMENTS:** California L-D License and Casualty License Holder, Securities license, NASDAC, 1968. **MILITARY SERVICE:** US Army, sgt, 1952-54.

YUEN, PAUL C.

Educator. Chinese American. **PERSONAL:** Born Jun 7, 1928, Hilo, HI; son of James Anee Yuen & Elsie Chun (both deceased); married Janice K Ogasawara Yuen, Mar 15, 1952; children: Sandra Harano, Marcia Ito. **EDUCATION:** University of Chicago, BS, physics, 1952; Illinois Institute of Technology, MS, electrical engineering, 1955, PhD, electrical engineering, 1960. **CAREER:** University of Hawaii, Manoa, associate dean, College of Engg, 1970-79, assistant to the chancellor, 1971-72, director, Hawaii Natural Energy Inst, 1977-81, dean, College of Engg, 1981-; Pacific International Center for High Tech Res, acting president, 1983-88; University of Hawaii, senior vice president for academic affairs, 1989-, acting president, 1992-93. **HONORS/AWARDS:** Hawaii Chapter of National Society of Professional Engineers, Hawaii Engineer of the Year, 1983; IEEE, Centennial Medal, 1984. **BUSINESS ADDRESS:** Senior Vice President, University of Hawaii, 2444 Dole Street, Bachman Hall 202, Honolulu, HI 96822, (808)956-7486.

YUEN, STEVE CHI-YIN

Educator. Chinese American. **PERSONAL:** Born Jun 8, 1953, Hong Kong; son of Kok-Ming Yuen & Yiu-Oi Cheng; married Patrivan Kongvej, Aug 11, 1984; children: Anthony Ka-Leung, Alyssa Wai-Ting. **EDUCATION:** National Taiwan Normal University, BEd, 1979; East Tennessee State University, MA, 1981; Pennsylvania State University, PhD, 1984. **CAREER:** Cho Po Sin Primary School, teacher, 1972-74; Pui Ying College, instructor, 1978-79; East Tennessee State University, teaching assistant, 1979-81; The Pennsylvania State University, research assistant, 1981-84; National Kaohsiung Normal University, Fulbright Professor, 1992-93; University of Southern Mississippi, associate professor, 1984-. **ORGANIZATIONS:** Occupational Education Forum, editorial board, 1993-; American Vocational Association, 1981-; American Vocational Education Research Association, 1981-89; International Technology Education Association, 1988-; Iota Lamba Sigma, secretary, treasurer, 1983-84; Mississippi Association of Vocational Educators, 1984-; American Society for Quality Control, 1981-92; Society of Manufacturing Engineers, 1981-. **HONORS/AWARDS:** J William Fulbright Foreign Scholarship Board, Fulbright Scholar Lecturing Award, 1992; Oversea Chinese Affairs Commission, Outstanding Oversea Chinese Student Scholarship, 1976, 1977. **SPECIAL ACHIEVEMENTS:** Author, "Incorporating CAD Instruction into the Drafting Curriculum," The Technology Teacher, vol 50, no 3, pp30-32, 1990; "An Assessment of Diversified Technology Programs," Journal of Industrial Teacher Education, vol 27, no 4, p31-45, 1990; "How Vocational Teachers Perceive Microcomputers," Journal of Research on Computing in Education, vol 20, no 4, p 375-383, 1988; "The Challenge of Microcomputer Technology," Journal of Studies in Technical Careers, vol 10, no 1, p49-59, 1988; "Attitude of Teachers Toward the use of Computers," Journal of Vocational Research, vol 10, no 2, 1951-64, 1985. **BUSINESS ADDRESS:** Associate Professor, University of Southern Mississippi, SS Box 5036, Hattiesburg, MS 39406-5036, (601)266-4670.

YUEN-TERRY, KAIMAY

Business executive. Hong Kong American. **PERSONAL:** Born Jun 4, 1940, Hong Kong; daughter of Mr & Mrs Ha-Kong Yuen; married Joseph M Terry, Feb 8, 1975; children: Amanda. **EDUCATION:** Oberlin College, BA, 1962; University of Chicago, School of Social Service Administration, MA, 1964; Johns Hopkins University, MPH, 1997. **CAREER:** Cambridge Model Cities Mental Health Program, 1964-68; Tufts University Medical Center, chief, ambulatory/social services, 1968-75; George Washington University, researcher, 1973-76; United Way of Minneapolis, senior health planner, 1979-82; Videomed Inc, owner, president, 1983-. **ORGANIZATIONS:** Citizen League of Minneapolis, 1983-; Academy of Certified Social Workers, 1966-83; American Public Health Assn, 1977-83; Chinese Americans of Minneapolis, 1988-; Organization of Chinese Americans, 1988-. **BUSINESS ADDRESS:** President, Owner, Videomed, Inc, 5109 Ridge Rd, Minneapolis, MN 55436, (612)938-6994.

YUH, JAI K.

Investment specialist. Korean American. **PERSONAL:** Born Nov 11, 1938, Seoul, Republic of Korea; son of Wan Chang Yuh; married Kim Unyoung Yuh, May 30, 1967; children: Leighanne. **EDUCATION:** Harvard University, BS, 1962. **CAREER:** Santa Barbara Research Center, program manager, 1969-87; INCO, partner, currently. **ORGANIZATIONS:** Optical Society, 1965-87; IEEE. **SPECIAL ACHIEVEMENTS:** Various scientific research papers for journals, 1965-87. **HOME ADDRESS:** 813 Paseo Alicante, Santa Barbara, CA 93103, (805)964-8987.

YUKAWA, MASAKO

Librarian, educator. Japanese American. **PERSONAL:** Born May 5, 1931, Odawara City, Japan; daughter of Miya and Shinzaburo Yukawa. **EDUCATION:** Tsuda College, BA, English lit, 1954; Long Island University, MLS, 1963. **CAREER:** Tsuda College, Tokyo, librarian; United States Inf Agency, American Cultural Center, Yokohama, librarian; Long Island University, librarian, professor, currently. **ORGANIZATIONS:** American Library Association; ACRL; GODORT; New York Library Association, Governmental Information Roundtable, pres; Nassau County Library Association, academic/special library division; US Japan Fulbright Association, vice pres. **HONORS/AWARDS:** Fulbright Commission, Fulbright Graduate Scholarship, 1961-62; Nassau County, District Service Award. **SPECIAL ACHIEVEMENTS:** Publications on subjects of government documents; fluent in Japanese; public speeches on government publications; lectures on library instructions. **BIOGRAPHICAL SOURCES:** Directory of Library and Information Professionals, Research Publication Inc, Woodbridge, Connecticut, c 1988. **BUSINESS ADDRESS:** Professor/Head Librarian, Government Documents Dept, C W Post Campus Library, Long Island University, Greenvale, NY 11548, (516)299-2142.

YUN, CHUNG-HEI K. (NAN-HAE YUN)

Educator. Korean American. **PERSONAL:** Born Mar 26, 1932, Pyungyang, Pyung-an Do, Republic of Korea; daughter of Chong-Pil Kim and Kyung-Sil Hahn; married Suk-Koo Yun, Jul 20, 1957; children: Stephen Tae-Young, Elise Hae-Ryung, Christina Ae-Ryung. **EDUCATION:** San Francisco State University, BA, English, 1956; University of Chicago, MA, English, 1959; Syracuse University, PhD, English, 1979. **CAREER:** Western Michigan University, instructor in humanities, 1974-78; Saginaw Valley State University, adjunct faculty in English, 1978-80; Notre Dame College, NH, assistant/associate professor of English, 1980-87; Shawnee State University, associate professor of English, 1988-91, professor of English, 1991-. **ORGANIZATIONS:** Modern Language Association; Association for Asian American Studies; Association for Canadian Studies in the US. **HONORS/AWARDS:** NEH, Summer Seminar for College/University Teachers, 1986. **SPECIAL ACHIEVEMENTS:** "Beyond 'Clay Walls': Korean American Literature," Reading the Literatures of Asian America, Temple University Press, 1992; languages include Korean, Japanese, and French. **HOME ADDRESS:** 6109 Partridge Ln, Midland, MI 48640, (517)631-3508.

YUN, NAN-HAE. *See* YUN, CHUNG-HEI K.

YUN, SEUNG SOO

Educator. Korean American. **PERSONAL:** Born Mar 1, 1932, Kangwond-Do, Republic of Korea; married Jeung Soo Yun, Jun 15, 1957; children: Philip, Juanita, John. **EDUCATION:** Seoul National University, 1951-54; Clark University, BS, 1957; Brown University, MS, 1960, PhD, 1963. **CAREER:** Ohio University, professor of physics, currently. **ORGANIZATIONS:** Acoustical Society of America, 1963-. **BUSINESS ADDRESS:** Professor of Physics, Dept of Physics & Astronomy, Ohio University, Athens, OH 45701-2979, (614)593-1694.

YUN, SUK KOO

Educator, educational administrator. Korean American. **PERSONAL:** Born Nov 10, 1930, Seoul, Republic of Korea; son of Il Sun Yun and Margaret Cho Yun; married Jul 20, 1957; children: Stephen T, Elise H, Christina A. **EDUCATION:** Seoul National University, BA, physics, 1955; University of Chicago, MS, physics, 1957; Boston University, PhD, physics, 1967. **CAREER:** Clarkson University, instructor, 1959-63; Syracuse University, research associate, 1967-69; Saginaw Valley State University, assistant professor, beginning 1969, associate professor, Natural Science Department, chairman, 1972-74, Physics Department, chairman, 1977-. **ORGANIZATIONS:** Sigma Xi; American Physical Society; Association of Korean Physicists in America; Korean Scientists and Engineers in America. **HONORS/AWARDS:** Harvard University, honorary research fellow, 1975-76; E L Warrick Award for Excellence in Research, 1987; State of Michigan, Distinguished Faculty Award, 1988; Saginaw Valley State University, NSF, Frederick Gardner Cottrell grantee, 1988. **SPECIAL ACHIEVEMENTS:** Visiting scientist: Fermi National Accelerator Laboratory, 1978-92; MIT, 1980, 1984-89; author: A Vision of Beauty in Order, 1972. **BUSINESS ADDRESS:** Chairman, Professor, Physics Dept, Saginaw Valley State University, University Center, MI 48710.

YUN, XIAOPING
Educator. Chinese American. **PERSONAL:** Born Feb 15, 1962, Gansu, People's Republic of China. **EDUCATION:** Northeastern University, China, BS, 1982; Washington University, St Louis, MS, 1984, DSc, 1987. **CAREER:** Washington University, research assistant, 1982-87; University of Pennsylvania, assistant professor, 1987-. **ORGANIZATIONS:** IEEE, 1986-. **BUSINESS ADDRESS:** Prof, Dept of Compt and Info Sci, University of Pennsylvania, 200 South 33rd St, Philadelphia, PA 19104, (215)898-6783.

YUNE, HEUN YUNG (HEARN)
Physician, educator. Korean American. **PERSONAL:** Born Feb 1, 1929, Seoul, Republic of Korea; son of Sun-Wook & Won Eun Lee Yune; married Kay Kim Yune, Apr 12, 1956; children: Jeanny K Wildi, Helen K Bolles, Marc E. **EDUCATION:** Severance Medical College, MD, 1956. **CAREER:** Presbyterian Medical Center, chief of radiology, 1964-66; Vanderbilt University, assistant to associate professor, 1966-71; Indiana University, professor of radiology, 1971-, professor of otolaryngology, head and neck surgery, 1993-, director, radiology residency program, 1985-. **ORGANIZATIONS:** Radiological Society of North America, manuscript reviewer, 1969-; American Roentgen Ray Society, manuscript reviewer, 1972-; Association of University Radiologists, 1974-; American Society of Head & Neck Radiology, 1978-; American Medical Association, 1972-; Association of Radiology Residency Program Directors, 1993-; Presbyterian Church in the USA, elder, elected-ordained, 1979-. **HONORS/AWARDS:** AOA Medical Honor Society, elected member, 1975; American College of Radiology, elected fellow, 1982; Indiana University, endowed professorship: John A Campbell Professor, 1991; State of Tennessee, Honorary Citizen, 1961. **SPECIAL ACHIEVEMENTS:** Scientific papers and book chapters, 163 scientific exhibits, 1960-; visiting professor, invited lecturer, 1964-; reading, writing and speaking proficiency in Korean and Japanese. **MILITARY SERVICE:** Army, Republic of Korea, captain, 1951-55; Hwarang Medal of Military Valor, 1953; Bronze Star, USA, 1955. **BUSINESS ADDRESS:** The John A Campbell Professor of Radiology, Professor of Otolaryngology, Head and Neck Surgery, Indiana University School of Medicine, 550 N University Blvd, University Hospital 0279, Indianapolis, IN 46202-5253, (317)274-1846.

YUNG, CHRISTOPH YINGWAI
Psychiatrist, educator. Macanese American. **PERSONAL:** Born Aug 21, 1935, Macao; married Carol, 1964. **EDUCATION:** National Taiwan University School of Medicine, MD, 1963; Wayne State University School of Medicine, 1968; McGill University, School of Medicine, psychiatry diploma, 1970; State University of NY, Downstate Medical Center, fellowship, 1972. **CAREER:** Texas Tech University Health Science Centre, assoc professor, 1978-; Chinese University of Hong Kong, senior lecturer, 1984-90. **ORGANIZATIONS:** College of Physician & Surgeons of Canada, fellow, 1970; American Psychiatric Association, 1965-; American Board of Medical Hypnosis, diplomatic, 1993; Pacific Rim College of Psychiatrists, fellow, 1985-; Hong Kong College of Psychiatrists, founding fellow, 1991-. **HONORS/AWARDS:** Open University of Sri Lanka, MD, 1986. **SPECIAL ACHIEVEMENTS:** Area of specialization: psychotherapy. **BUSINESS ADDRESS:** Associate Professor, Texas Tech University Health Sciences Center, 3601 4th St, Lubbock, TX 79430-0001, (806)743-2800.

YUNG, KENNETH KWOKHUNG
Educator. Hong Kong American. **PERSONAL:** Born Aug 7, 1957, Hong Kong; son of Yung Kam Wah; married Grace, 1989. **EDUCATION:** University of Hong Kong, BS, social science, 1980; State University of New York at Buffalo, MBA, 1984; George State University, PhD, 1989. **CAREER:** Mobil Oil Corportion, financial planner, 1984-85; Old Dominion University, professor, 1989-. **ORGANIZATIONS:** American Finance Association, 1989-; Financial Management Association, 1989-; Southern Finance Association, 1989-; Eastern Finance Association, 1989-; Western Finance Association, 1989-. **HONORS/AWARDS:** Beta Sigma Gamma, 1990. **SPECIAL ACHIEVEMENTS:** Published work in Journal of Financial Economics, Journal of Financial Research, Journal of Futures Market, Journal of Business Finance and Accounting, Journal of Multinational Financial Management, Journal of International Securities, American Real Estate and Urban Economics Journal. **BUSINESS ADDRESS:** Professor, Dept of Finance, Old Dominion University, College of Business Administration, Norfolk, VA 23529-0001, (804)683-3573.

YUNG, RINGO
Educator. Hong Kong American. **PERSONAL:** Born Oct 23, 1934, Hong Kong; son of Yung Tak-Ming & Choung See Yu; married Christine, Jul 11, 1971; children: Jason, Edwin. **EDUCATION:** Tientsin University, China, BArch, 1961; Kansas University, MFA, design, 1970. **CAREER:** H M Chau Architects, assistant architect, 1963-65; Takming College, instructor, 1964-65; Takwah & Co, Hong Kong, interior & furniture designer, 1965-67; Hong Kong University, instructor, 1967-68; Virginia Commonwealth University, assistant professor, 1970-75, associate professor, 1975-82, professor, 1982-. **ORGANIZATIONS:** IDEC, active member, 1972-; IBD, associate member, 1975. **HONORS/AWARDS:** IESNA, Summer Workshop for Teaching of Lighting, 1987; IWM & FSF, Recognition Award for Furniture Design Education, 1978. **BUSINESS ADDRESS:** Professor, Dept of Interior Design, Virginia Commonwealth University, School of the Arts, 325 N Harrison St, 426 Pollak Bldg, Richmond, VA 23284-2519, (804)367-1713.

YUNG, W. K. ALFRED
Neuro-oncologist, educator. Hong Kong American. **PERSONAL:** Born Apr 8, 1948, Hong Kong; married Suzie; children: Kathy, Karen, Joshua. **EDUCATION:** University of Minnesota, Minneapolis, BSc, 1971; University of Chicago Pritzker School of Medicine, MD, 1975. **CAREER:** University of Texas Medical School, M D Anderson Cancer Center, Depts of Neuro-oncology and Tumor Biology, asst prof, 1985-86, assoc prof, 1986-92, prof, 1992-, Dept of Neurology, assoc prof, 1986-92, prof, 1992-. **ORGANIZATIONS:** NIH Path A study section, national committee, charter member, 1991-95; RTOG, Brain Medical Oncology Subcomittee, chairman, Brain Committee, co-chair; NCI/NIH Site Visit Committee; American Academy of Neurology; American Neurological Association; American Society for Cell Biology; American Association for the Advancement of Science; American Association for Cancer Research; American Society of Clinical Oncology; The Society for Neuroscience; American Medical Association; Texas Medical Association. **HONORS/AWARDS:** American Academy of Neurology, fellow, 1985; PHS National Research Service Award, Cancer Chemotherapy Grant, 1979-81; University of Chicago, Franklin McLean Research Award, 1975; University of Minnesota, Best Senior Award in Biochemistry, 1971; Best Doctor in America, 1992, 1994. **BUSINESS ADDRESS:** Professor of Medicine, M D Anderson Cancer Ctr, University of Texas, 1515 Holcombe Blvd PO Box 100, Houston, TX 77030, (713)794-1285.

YUVARAJAN, SUBBARAYA
Educator. Indo-American. **PERSONAL:** Born Sep 15, 1941, Sowdhapuram, Tamil Nadu, India; son of Mr and Mrs Subbaraya Gounder; married Annapoorani Yuvarajan, May 23, 1973; children: Chudar, Elil. **EDUCATION:** American College, Madurai (Madras University), BSc, 1961; Government College of Technology, Coimbatore (Madras University), BE (honors), 1966; Indian Institute of Technology, Madras, India, MTech, 1969, PhD, 1981. **CAREER:** P S G College of Technology, Coimbatore, lecturer, 1969-74; Indian Institute of Technology, Madras, assistant professor/lecturer, 1974-83; North Dakota State University, associate professor, 1983-. **ORGANIZATIONS:** IEEE, senior member, 1984-; ASEE, 1985-; Sigma Xi, 1985-. **SPECIAL ACHIEVEMENTS:** Published over 25 technical papers in journals and conference proceedings. **BUSINESS ADDRESS:** Associate Professor, Electrical Engineering, North Dakota State University, North University Drive, Fargo, ND 58105, (701)237-7365.

Z

ZAMORA, MARIO DIMARUCUT
Educator. Filipino American. **PERSONAL:** Born Jul 27, 1935, Angeles, Pampanga, Philippines; son of Leon B Zamora and Caridad Dimarucut (deceased); married Maria Luz Mercado, 1982; children: Gregory Ronald, Nerissa Caridad, Morris Edward, Lili, Sarah, Jovito Jose, Maria Gracia. **EDUCATION:** University of the Philippines, AB, 1956, MA, 1959; Delhi University, India, Research, 1957-58; Cornell University, PhD, 1963. **CAREER:** University of the Philippines, Diliman, Anthropology Dept, chairman, 1965-69; University of the Philippines, Baguio, dean of the college, 1969-72; Adlai Stevenson Fellow to UNITAR, United Nations, New York, 1969; Eastern Montana College, visiting foreign professor, 1972-73; University of Trondheim, Norway, visiting Fulbright prof, 1986; College of William and Mary, visiting professor, 1973-1975, professor of anthropology, 1975-. **ORGANIZATIONS:** Assn of Third World Studies, vice-pres, pres-elect, 1994-95; International Union of Anthropological and Ethnological Sciences, exec member, 1983-88,

vice-pres, 1988-93; American Anthropological Association; Association of Asian Studies; Ethnographic and Folk Culture Society; Indian Institute of Public Adm; Association for Anthropological Diplomacy, founding chair; US Association of Philippine Anthropologists, founding chair; Virginia Social Science Association, pres, 1987. **HONORS/AWARDS:** Philippine Jaycees, Ten Outstanding Young Men of Philippines, 1969, Ten Outstanding Filipinos Overseas, 1979; Association of Third World Studies, Presidential Award, 1992; UP Alumni Association, Distinguished Service Award, 1991; VA Social Science Association, Distinguished Service Award, 1991. **SPECIAL ACHIEVEMENTS:** Author: The Panchayat Tradition, New Delhi, India, 1990; Los Indigenas Delas Islas Filipinas, Madrid, Spain, 1992; Perspectives on Cultural Change and Development, India, 1993; editor/author: with VJ Rohrl and Mer Nicholson, The Anthropology of Peace, essays in honor of E Qadamson Hoebel, Virginia, 1992; author and editor of books and articles in journals of 20 or more nations. **HOME ADDRESS:** 3009 E Brittington, Williamsburg, VA 23185. **BUSINESS PHONE:** (804)221-1064.

ZAVERI, PRAD S.
Engineer. Indo-American. **PERSONAL:** Born May 11, 1938, Bombay, Maharashtra, India; son of Shantilal G Zaveri and Rupabai S Zaveri; married Dhanlaxmi P Zaveri, May 24, 1967; children: Khushali P, Pavan P. **EDUCATION:** Birla Engineering College, India, BSME, 1960, BSEE, 1961; Michigan State University, MSEE, 1970 . **CAREER:** Premier Automobiles, senior engineer, 1961-69; Lorain Product Corp, product engineer, 1970-75; North Elect Co, product engineer, 1975-77; General Electric, senior engineer, 1977-81; Martin Marietta, senior engineer, 1981-84; AT&T Bell Labs, DMTS, engineer, 1984-. **ORGANIZATIONS:** IEEE; Professional Engineers Society of India. **HOME ADDRESS:** 5829 Broadwell Dr, Plano, TX 75093, (214)608-0400. **BUSINESS ADDRESS:** Engineer,DMTS, AT&T Bell Labs, 3000 Skyline Dr, Mesquite, TX 75149, (214)284-2764.

ZEE, TEDDY
Motion picture executive. Chinese American. **PERSONAL:** married Elizabeth; children: Katherine, Mia. **EDUCATION:** Cornell University, industrial and labor relations, 1979; Harvard Business School, 1984. **CAREER:** NBC, management associates program, 1979; Los Angeles, accountant; Paramount, creative executive, senior vice president, 1985-90; Sony/Columbia Pictures, executive vice president of production, 1990-. **BUSINESS ADDRESS:** Executive Vice President, Production, Sony/Columbia Pictures, 10202 W Washington Blvd, Thalberg Room 3218, Culver City, CA 90232, (310)280-6718. *

ZEN, E-AN
Educator, geologist. Chinese American. **PERSONAL:** Born May 31, 1928, Peking, China; son of Hung-chun Zen and Heng-chi'h Chen Zen. **EDUCATION:** Cornell University, AB, 1951; Harvard University, MA, 1952, PhD, 1955. **CAREER:** Woods Hole Oceanographic Institute, research fellow, 1955-56, research associate, 1956-58; University of North California, assistant professor, 1958-59; US Geological Survey, geologist, 1959-80, research geologist, 1981-89; University of Maryland, adjunct research professor, geology, 1990-. **ORGANIZATIONS:** Geological Society of America, councillor, 1985-88, vice president, 1991, president, 1992; Mineral Society of America, councillor, 1975-77, president, 1975-76; National Academy of Science; numerous others. **HONORS/AWARDS:** California Institute of Technology, visiting associate professor, 1962; MIT, Crosby visiting professor, 1973; Princeton University, Harry H Hess senior visiting fellow, 1981; numerous others. **SPECIAL ACHIEVEMENTS:** Author of numerous articles in professional journals. **BUSINESS ADDRESS:** Adjunct Professor, Dept of Geology, University of Maryland, College Park, College Park, MD 20742. *

ZETTERLUND, YOKO KARIN
Volleyball player, receptionist. Japanese American. **PERSONAL:** Born Mar 24, 1969, San Francisco, CA; daughter of Lars W Zetterlund & Masako Horie-Zetterlund. **EDUCATION:** Waseda University, Japan, department of human science, BS, 1991. **CAREER:** Automobile Club of Southern California, receptionist, 1993-; USA Volleyball Team, member, currently. **HONORS/AWARDS:** Judy Bellomo Players' Award, 1993. **SPECIAL ACHIEVEMENTS:** Summer Olympics, bronze medalist, volleyball, 1992. **BUSINESS ADDRESS:** Member, USA Volleyball Team, 4510 Executive Dr, Plaza 1, San Diego, CA 92121, (619)625-8200.

ZHANG, JOHN Z. H.
Educator. Chinese American. **PERSONAL:** Born Feb 15, 1961, Shanghai, People's Republic of China; son of X B Zhang & Q F Sun; married Wendy W Zhu, Jun 18, 1988; children: Michael H. **EDUCATION:** East China Normal University, BS, 1982; University of Houston, PhD, 1987. **CAREER:** University of Houston, research assistant, 1982-87; University of California, Berkeley, research associate, 1987-90; New York University, assistant professor of chemistry, 1990-. **ORGANIZATIONS:** American Chemical Society, 1990-; American Physical Society, 1990-. **HONORS/AWARDS:** R E Welch, predoctoral fellow, 1985; Camille & Henry Dreyfus, New Faculty Award, 1990. **SPECIAL ACHIEVEMENTS:** Author or co-author of: "L2 Amplitude Density Method. . .," J Chem Phys, 1988; "Quantum Reactive. . .," J Chem Phys, 1989; "Quantum Reactive. . .," Chem Phys Lett, 1988; "New Method in Time-. . .," J Chem Phys, 1990; "Total and Partial. . .," J Chem Phys, 1993. **BUSINESS ADDRESS:** Asst Professor, Dept of Chemistry, New York University, 4 Washington Place, Room 514, New York, NY 10003, (212)998-8412.

ZHANG, LONGXI
Educator. Chinese American. **PERSONAL:** Born Jun 10, 1947, Chengdu, Sichuan, China; son of Zhang Xidu & Guan Yufang; married Weilin Tang, Jan 23, 1978; children: Celia Youhuan Zhang. **EDUCATION:** Peking University, MA, 1981; Harvard University, PhD, 1989. **CAREER:** University of California, associate professor, 1989-. **ORGANIZATIONS:** Modern Language Association, 1989-; Association for Asian Studies, 1989-. **HONORS/AWARDS:** University of California, President's Research Fellowship in Humanities, 1991-92; University of California, Riverside, Humanist Achievement Lecturer, 1993; Harvard University, Hoopes Teaching Prize, 1989. **SPECIAL ACHIEVEMENTS:** The Tao and the Logos: Literary Hermeneutics, East and West, 1992; A Critical Introduction to 20th Century Theories of Literature, 1986. **BUSINESS ADDRESS:** Associate Professor of Comparative Literature, University of California, Riverside, Humanities 3317, Riverside, CA 92521.

ZHANG, WENXIAN
Librarian. Chinese American. **PERSONAL:** Born Aug 27, 1963, Zhengzhou, Henan, People's Republic of China; son of Jiatai Zhang & Sufen Cao; married Qun Du, Oct 10, 1987. **EDUCATION:** Beijing University, BA, 1985; Southern Connecticut State University, MLS, 1990, MS, business, 1993. **CAREER:** Yellow River University, librarian, 1985-86, acting director, 1986-88; Southern Connecticut State University, graduate assistant, 1988-89; Ansonia Library, assistant director, 1990-91, director, 1991-. **ORGANIZATIONS:** American Library Association, 1989-; Connecticut Library Association, 1989-; Association for Information Studies, 1990-. **HONORS/AWARDS:** H W Wilson, Scholarship Award, 1989; President's List of Beijing University, Merit Student Award. **SPECIAL ACHIEVEMENTS:** Author, "Fire & Blood: Censorship of Books in China," International Library Review, March 1990; language proficiency: Chinese. **HOME ADDRESS:** 188 Goffe Terrace, New Haven, CT 06511, (203)624-7226. **BUSINESS ADDRESS:** Library Director, Ansonia Library, 53 S Cliff St, Ansonia, CT 06401, (203)734-6275.

ZHAO, QUANSHENG
Educator, educational administrator. Chinese American. **EDUCATION:** Peking University, BA, international politics, 1981; University of California-Berkeley, MA, political science, 1982, PhD, political science, 1987. **CAREER:** University of California, Berkeley, teaching/research assistant, 1981-85, 1986-87; Oxford University, senior research associate, 1984; University of Tokyo, visiting research fellow, 1985-86; Cleveland State University, assistant professor, 1987-88; University of Hawaii, adjunct professor of political science, 1990-; East-West Center, Honolulu, research fellow, 1989-90; United States Institute of Peace, peace fellow, 1991; Virginia Consortium for Asian Studies, vice president, 1992-93; Fletcher School of Law and Diplomacy, Tufts University, international politics, adjunct associate professor, currently; Old Dominion University, director of the Institute of Asian Studies, associate professor of political science, 1988-. **ORGANIZATIONS:** American Asian Review, Editorial Advisory Board; Conference Group on China Studies, American Political Science Association, program organizer. **HONORS/AWARDS:** Harvard University, Pacific Basin Research Fellowship, 1993-94; Pacific Culture Foundation, research grant, 1992; United States Institute of Peace, Peace Fellowship, 1991; Harvard-Yenching Library, research grant, 1991; Ohira Memorial Foundation, Pacific Basin Academic Grant, 1990. **SPECIAL ACHIEVEMENTS:** Author of numerous publications, including: Japanese Policymaking: The Politics Behind Politics—Informal Mechanisms and the Making of China Policy, book, 1993; "Patterns and Choices of Chinese

Foreign Policy," Asian Affairs: An American Review, vol 20, no 1, spring 1993; language proficiency in Chinese and Japanese. **HOME ADDRESS:** 409 Connecticut Ave, Norfolk, VA 23508. **BUSINESS ADDRESS:** Associate Professor, Dept of Political Science, Old Dominion University, Norfolk, VA 23529-0088, (804)683-3852.

ZHENG, YUAN FANG
Educator. Chinese American. **PERSONAL:** Born Jul 2, 1946, Shanghai, China; son of Xian Yun Zheng and Gui Qing Zhang; married Yu-Lu Zhang, Sep 13, 1977; children: Julia Rui. **EDUCATION:** Tsinghua University, Beijing, China, BS, 1970; Ohio State University, MS, 1980, PhD, 1984. **CAREER:** Clemson University, assistant professor, 1984-87, associate professor, 1987-89; Ohio State University, associate professor, 1989-92, professor, 1992-. **ORGANIZATIONS:** IEEE, senior member, 1991-; Robotics and Automation Society of IEEE, Mobile Robots Technical Committee, chairman, 1992-, Administrative Committee, 1994-96. **HONORS/AWARDS:** National Science Foundation, Presidential Young Investigator Award, 1987; Ohio State University, College of Engineering, Research Award, 1993. **SPECIAL ACHIEVEMENTS:** Published over 100 papers in archival journals and conference proceedings on robotics research, 1984-93. **BUSINESS ADDRESS:** Professor, Ohio State University, 2015 Neil Avenue, 664 Dreese Laboratory, Columbus, OH 43210, (614)292-2981.

ZIA, HELEN
Editor. Chinese American. **CAREER:** Ms Magazine, former executive editor, contributing editor, currently; World View Systems, vice president, currently. **ORGANIZATIONS:** San Francisco State University, Center for Integration and Improvement of Journalism/Asian American Journalists Assn, Project Zinger Advisory Board, 1992. **HONORS/AWARDS:** Asian Pacific Women's Network, Woman Warrior Award, 1992. **SPECIAL ACHIEVEMENTS:** Numerous articles, including: "Not Black, Not White," Essence, May 1993, p2; "Women in Hate Groups," Ms Magazine, March-April 1991, p20; "Midwives: Talking about a Revolution," Ms Magazine, November-December 1990, p 91; "Donna Red Wing," The Advocate, December 29, 1992, p42. **BUSINESS ADDRESS:** VP, World View Systems, 114 Sansome St, Ste 700, San Francisco, CA 94104, (415)391-7100.*

ZIA, HOYT HANSON
Attorney. Chinese American. **PERSONAL:** Born Apr 24, 1953, Newark, NJ; son of Yee Chen & Beilin Woo Zia; married Leigh-Ann Kiyo Miyasato, Apr 30, 1988; children: Emily Shizue, Rory Hajime. **EDUCATION:** Dartmouth College, AB, 1975; UCLA, JD, 1981. **CAREER:** US Marine Corps, officer, 1975-78; Bronson, Bronson & McKinnon, associate, 1981-84; Lee & Hui, associate, 1984; Motorola Inc, senior division counsel, 1984-91; AMFAC/JMB

Hawaii Inc, vice president, associate general counsel, 1991-. **ORGANIZATIONS:** Japanese American Citizens League, Honolulu Chapter, board of directors, 1991-; Council on Legal Education Opportunity, board of directors, 1990-; ABA House of Delegates, delegate from California, 1988-91; National Asian Pacific American Bar Association, founder, president, 1989-90; State Bar of California, committee of bar examiners, 1986-88, ethnic minority relations committee, chair, 1984-86; Chinatown Youth Center, board of directors, 1983-89; Asian Pacific Bar of California, president, 1987-88; Asian American Bar Association of the Greater Bay Area, president, 1986-87. **MILITARY SERVICE:** US Marine Corps Reserves, captain, 1975-81. **BUSINESS ADDRESS:** Vice President & Assoc Gen Counsel, Amfac/JMB Hawaii Inc, 700 Bishop St, 20th Fl, Honolulu, HI 96813, (808)543-8521.

ZIEN, TSE-FOU
Government official. Chinese American. **PERSONAL:** Born Aug 9, 1937, Shanghai, China; son of Yih Zien and Mon-Mei Chang; married Suzy Shen Zien, Jul 7, 1962; children: Livia, Conroy. **EDUCATION:** National Taiwan University, BSME, 1958; Brown University, MS, engineering, 1963; California Institute of Technology, PhD, aeronautics, 1967. **CAREER:** Case Western Reserve University, post doctoral fellow, 1967-70; Naval Surface Warfare Center, research aerospace engineer, 1970-80, Mathematics and Computation Branch, branch head, 1980-; George Washington University, professorial lecturer of engineering, 1977-; Catholic University of America, adjunct professor of engineering, 1990-. **ORGANIZATIONS:** American Institute of Aeronautics and Astronautics, associate fellow, 1964-; Washington Academy of Sciences, fellow, 1978-; American Physical Society, 1968-; Society of Industrial and Applied Mathematics, 1984-; AIAA, Flood Dynamics Technology Committee, 1979-82, Thermophysics Technical Committee, 1982-85, Applied Aerodynamics Technology Committee, 1990-93; National Taiwan University, Alumni Association, president, 1977-78; Rho Psi Society, IOTA Chapter, president, 1987-88. **HONORS/AWARDS:** Washington Academy of Sciences, Scientific Achievements in Engineering Sciences, 1978; National Taiwan University, Shu-Cheon Award for Scholastic Achievements, 1955-58, Sir Lin's Fellowship for Scholastic Achievements, 1956-58; Brown University, University Scholar, 1960-63; California Institute of Technology, Institute Scholar, 1963-67. **SPECIAL ACHIEVEMENTS:** Scientific/professional journal articles on fluid dynamics and heat transfer in: AIAA Journal, International Journal of Heat and Mass Transfer, AIAA Progress Series, Journal of Biomechanics, Bulletin of Mathematical Biophysics, etc; Developmed optimization methodologies to find optimal aerodynamic configurations of hypersonic vehicles, approximate methods for predicting friction and heating, and method in holographic interferometry. **BUSINESS ADDRESS:** Branch Head, Math & Computation, Naval Surface Warfare Center, White Oak Detachment, 10901 New Hampshire Ave, Bldg 427, Rm 542, Silver Spring, MD 20903.

OBITUARIES

FANG, JOHN TA-CHUAN

Publisher. Chinese American. **PERSONAL:** Born 1925; died Apr 27, 1992. **CAREER:** San Francisco Independent, founder; Asian Week, founding publisher. **SPECIAL ACHIEVEMENTS:** San Francisco State University has set up a scholarship fund in memory of John Fang. **BUSINESS ADDRESS:** Publisher, Asian Week, 809 Sacramento St, San Francisco, CA 94108.

FANG, MING M.

Educator. Chinese American. **PERSONAL:** Born Nov 27, 1955, Qingdao, Shandong, People's Republic of China; died Dec 10, 1993; son of Tsung-Ci Fang & Nai E Kiang; married Mei P Pang Fang, Aug 17, 1990; children: Gary N. **EDUCATION:** Shandong College of Oceanography, BS, acoustics, 1981; Western Illinois University, MS, solid state physics, 1983; Iowa State university, PhD, explt solid state phys, 1986. **CAREER:** Shandong College of Oceanography, electronics technician, 1976-77; Western Illinois University, teaching assistant, 1982-83, assistant professor, 1986-89, associate professor, 1989-93, professor, 1993-; Iowa State University, teaching assistant, 1983-86. **ORGANIZATIONS:** American Physical Society, 1988-; Overseas Chinese Physics Association; Society of Physics, 1983-86; Sigma Pi Sigma, 1983; Western Illinois University, University Personnel Committee, chairman, 1993. **HONORS/AWARDS:** Illinois Dept of Energy and Natural Resources, research awards, 1989-91; Western Illinois University, Faculty Excellence Award, 1987-92; several research grants and awards, 1987-. **SPECIAL ACHIEVEMENTS:** Author: Magnetic Flux Expulsion from Superconducting Shields, 1987; Free Energy of Thallium-based Superconductors, Phys Rev B, 1989; lecturer: Physics Department Seminar at Bradley University, 1989; Physics Department Seminar at the University of Missouri-Columbia, 1992; TV Presentation, NSF Career Awareness Experiences in Sci and Math, 1993. **HOME ADDRESS:** 302 N Sherman Avenue, Macomb, IL 61455, (309)833-4756. **BUSINESS ADDRESS:** Professor, Physics Dept, Western Illinois University, Macomb, IL 61455, (309)298-1462.

HAYAKAWA, S. I. (SAMUEL ICHIYE)

Former US senator, educator. Japanese American. **PERSONAL:** Born Jul 18, 1906, British Columbia; died Feb 27, 1992, Green Brae, CA; married Margedant Peters, 1937; children: Alan Romer, Mark, Wynne. **EDUCATION:** University of Manitoba, BA, 1927; McGill University, MA, 1928; University of Wisconsin, PhD, 1935. **CAREER:** Univ of Wisconsin, instructor of English, 1936-39; Illinois Inst of Tech, instructor to assoc prof of English, 1939-47; Univ of Chicago, lecturer, 1950-55; San Francisco State University, prof of English, 1955-68, president, 1968-73, president emeritus, 1973-92; US Senator, 1977-83. **ORGANIZATIONS:** American Psychol Assn, fellow; Modern Lang Assn; AAAS; Bohemian Club; Athenian Nile Club. **HONORS/AWARDS:** Honorary Degrees: California Coll of Arts & Crafts, DFA; Grinnell Coll, DLitt; Pepperdine Univ, LHD; The Citadel, LLD. **SPECIAL ACHIEVEMENTS:** Author, Language in Thought and Action, 1949; Symbol, Status and Personality, 1963; Through the Communication Barrier, 1978.

HAYASHIDA, CHARLEY TAKETOSHI

Agribusiness grower, shipper. Japanese American. **PERSONAL:** Born Jul 22, 1918, Fort Lupton, CO; died Dec 9, 1993, Victorville, CA; son of Takematsu & Kiyono Hayashida; married Sadako Hayashida, Dec 27, 1942; children: Larry, Beverly Chien, Marilynn Hikiji. **CAREER:** First National Bank of Alamosa,

board member, 1989-93; Charley Hayashida Farms Inc, president, owner, 1942-93. **ORGANIZATIONS:** Rotary International, 1955-93, club president, 1959; United Fruit & Vegetable Association, 1956-93; Produce Marketing Association, 1957-93; Soil Conservation District, 1962-78; Japanese American Citizens League, 100 club member, 1951-93, chapter president, 1957. **HONORS/AWARDS:** American Vegetable Grower, National Top 100 Growers, 1990-92. **HOME ADDRESS:** PO Box 8, Blanca, CO 81123, (719)379-3499.

HSIAO, SIDNEY C.

Educator, author. Chinese American. **PERSONAL:** Born Oct 24, 1905, Wuchang, China; died Oct 9, 1989, Honolulu, HI; married Erica Karawina. **EDUCATION:** Shanghai University, BS, 1928; Yenching University, MA, 1933; Harvard University, marine zoology, PhD, 1938. **CAREER:** Central China University, Coll of Natural Science, dean, 1941-44; Yale University, Seessel Fellow, 1946-48; University of Hawaii, zoology prof, 1957-71; National Taiwan University, Fulbright lecturer, 1962-63, 1968-69; Natl Normal University, China, visiting prof; Cuttington University, Liberia, visiting prof of biology, 1975-77. **ORGANIZATIONS:** Member of many scientific and professional organizations. **HONORS/AWARDS:** Research grants: US Atomic Energy Commission; Natl Institutes of Health; Natl Science Foundation. **SPECIAL ACHIEVEMENTS:** Author of books and research on radiation effects on marine life.

IKUHARA, AKIHIRO (IKE)

Professional baseball executive. Japanese American. **PERSONAL:** died Oct 1992. **CAREER:** Promoted intl baseball, 26 years; Los Angeles Dodgers, intl asst to president, until 1992. **SPECIAL ACHIEVEMENTS:** Intl Baseball Assn established the Akihiro "Ike" Ikuhara Award, for outstanding athletes who participate in the annual IBA youth programs; instrumental in his efforts to see baseball spread worldwide & become an official Olympic sport; collection of his Dodger uniform and championship ring exhibited in the Japanese Hall of Fame. **BUSINESS ADDRESS:** Asst to Pres Peter O'Malley, Los Angeles Dodgers, 1000 Elysian Park Ave, Los Angeles, CA 90012.

KANEMITSU, MATSUMI

Artist. Japanese American. **PERSONAL:** Born 1922, Ogden, UT; died May 11, 1992, Los Angeles, CA. **EDUCATION:** Art Students League, New York, studied with Japanese painter, Yasuo Kuniyoshi; associated with leading figures at the school such as: Willem de Kooning, Franz Kline and Jackson Pollack; studied with Fernando Leger. **CAREER:** Artist, works include paintings, sumi ink drawings, watercolors, and lithographs; taught at Chouinard, Otis Art Institute. **HONORS/AWARDS:** Ford Foundation grant, Tamarind Lithography Workshop; Longview Foundation Awards (2); American Federation of the Arts, Artist-in-Residence Award. **SPECIAL ACHIEVEMENTS:** Four memorable solo exhibitions: Gene Thaw's New Gallery; Widdifield; Stephen Radich (2); work exhibited as numerous museums including: Museum of Modern Art, New York; Philadelphia Museum; Natl Museum of Modern Art, Tokyo, numerous others. **MILITARY SERVICE:** US Army, 1941-46.

KITAGAWA, JOSEPH MITSUO

Theologian, educator. Japanese American. **PERSONAL:** Born Mar 8, 1915, Osaka, Japan; died Oct 7, 1992, Chicago, IL; son of Chiyokichi and Kumi

Kitagawa; married Evelyn Mae Rose, Jul 22, 1946; children: Anne Rose. **CAREER:** University of Chicago, history of religion, assoc prof, 1959-64, prof, beginning 1964, dean, Divinity School, 1970-80, professor emeritus, until 1992. **ORGANIZATIONS:** American Coin Learned Socs; American Soc Study Religions, pres, 1969-72; American Acad Religion; Intl Assn History Religions, vp, 1975-; Assn Religious Studies in Japan. **SPECIAL ACHIEVEMENTS:** Religions of the East, 1960; Spiritual Liberation and Human Freedom in Contemporary Asia, 1990; Christian Tradition: Beyond Its European Captivity; founding editor, History of Religions, 1960.

KOBAYASHI, KEY K.

Library administrator (retired), organization administrator. Japanese American. **PERSONAL:** Born 1922?, Fresno, CA; died Nov 15, 1992, Burke, VA; married Kyoko; children: Frances Varner, Forrest, Teresa Oelkers, Turner, Arleen Walton, Baylor, Beverly (deceased). **EDUCATION:** University of California, Berkeley, bachelor's degree; Columbia University, master's degree, foreign study. **CAREER:** State Dept, political analyst, Japanese specialist; Library of Congress, asst head, Japanese section, 1955-80. **ORGANIZATIONS:** Japanese American Citizens League, Washington, DC chapter, president; Natl Veterans Assn, Go For Broke; Kiwanis Club, Falls Church, VA; Little League, 30-year volunteer. **MILITARY SERVICE:** US Army, Intelligence Service, World War II; postwar stationed in Japan and Korea.

KOCHIYAMA, WILLIAM

Association executive. Japanese American. **PERSONAL:** Born May 10, 1921, Washington, DC; died Oct 25, 1993, New York, NY; married Mary Yuri Kochiyama; children: Eddie, Jim, Tom, Audee Holman. **EDUCATION:** Long Island Univ, journalism degree. **CAREER:** Japan Intl Christian University Foundation, public relations officer; Tamblyn & Brown, public relations officer; New Jersey Inst of Technology, assoc director for public & institute relations, until 1981. **ORGANIZATIONS:** Asian Community Center, founder. **MILITARY SERVICE:** Member of 442nd Regimental Combat Team, most decorated unit in US military history.

KOHASHI, ETHEL TSUKIKO

Community activist. Japanese American. **PERSONAL:** Born 1910?; died Apr 15, 1993. **CAREER:** Japanese American Cultural and Community Center, charter member, exec secretary. **ORGANIZATIONS:** Montebello Japanese Women's Club; Little Tokyo Service Center; Southern California Japanese Women's Society; Japanese American Republicans; Friends of the Japanese Philharmonic Ladies Auxiliary; Tuesday Niters.

LAIGO, VALERIANO EMERCIANO MONTANTE (VAL)

Educator, painter, lecturer. Filipino American. **PERSONAL:** Born Jan 23, 1930, Naguilian, La Union, Philippines; died Dec 11, 1992, Seattle, WA; married Austreberta Garrido; children: Adrian, Rene. **EDUCATION:** Seattle University, BEd, 1954; Mexico City College, postgraduate studies, 1956-57; University of Washington, MFA, 1964. **CAREER:** Seattle Post-Intelligencer, Editorial Dept, artist, 1950; Boeing Research Labs, art director, staff artist, 1959-63; Seattle University, Dept of Fine Arts, faculty member, 1965-92 (on medical leave since 1985). **ORGANIZATIONS:** Asian American Education Assn; Filipino American Natl Historical Soc; Asian Multi-Media Center; New Horizons for Learning. **SPECIAL ACHIEVEMENTS:** Public art works include: Seattle University's Lemieux Library Mural; Dr Jose Rizal Park Double Triptych Mural, 1981; exhibits in Mexico City, Los Angeles, Tucson, New York, Portland, Santa Barbara, Spokane, Tacoma, Gig Harbor, Bellevue, Kirkland, Auburn, and Seattle; vocalist: Lloyd Lindroth Show; KYAC-AM; The Art Barduhn-Stan Boreson Show; KING-TV; Gentlemen of Rhythm Orchestra.

LEE, BRANDON

Actor. Chinese American. **PERSONAL:** Born 1964?, Oakland, CA; died Mar 31, 1993, Wilmington, NC; son of Linda & Bruce Lee. **EDUCATION:** Emerson College, theater arts; Strasberg Academy. **CAREER:** Actor, movies include: Laser Mission, 1990; Showdown in Little Tokyo, 1992; Rapid Fire, 1992; The Crow, 1993; television appearance: Kung Fu: The Movie, 1986. **BIOGRAPHICAL SOURCES:** "Who Killed Brandon Lee?," Transpacific, June 1993, p40; "Brandon Lee: Movie Star in the Making Cruelly Cut Down at

28," Asian Week, April 9, 1993, p32. **BUSINESS ADDRESS:** Actor, c/o William Morris Agency, 151 El Camino Dr, Beverly Hills, CA 90212.

LEE, GUY

Business owner, talent agent. Chinese American. **PERSONAL:** Born 1927?; died Nov 22, 1993. **CAREER:** Actor; East West Players, cofounder, 1965; Guy Lee & Associates (formerly Bessie Loo Agency), owner, 1973-93. **ORGANIZATIONS:** Asian Pacific American Artists, board mem, co-founder; Media Image Coalition. **SPECIAL ACHIEVEMENTS:** Actor: Hong Kong; Keys of the Kingdom; Smugglers Island Blue Hawaii; Girls! Girls! Girls!; regular on "The Islander"; as a talent agent he guided the careers of hundreds of Asian actors including Keye Luke, Joan Chen, John Lone, B D Wong, James Hong, Soon Teck Oh, Ernest Harada; spent his entire career trying to make things better for Asian and Pacific Islander Americans in the entertainment industry. **BUSINESS ADDRESS:** Board Member, Association of Asian Pacific American Artists, 3518 Cahuenga Blvd, W Ste 302, Los Angeles, CA 90068.

MAENO, JOHN Y.

Attorney. Japanese American. **PERSONAL:** Born Mar 2, 1908; died Feb 4, 1993, Los Angeles, CA; married Tomi Maeno; children: John Rey, Vivian Moyer, Mary Jo Glynn. **EDUCATION:** Occidental Coll, Phi Beta Kappa; Univ of Southern California, law degree, 1932. **CAREER:** Self-employed attorney, over 50 years. **ORGANIZATIONS:** California Bar Assn, 1932-93. **SPECIAL ACHIEVEMENTS:** First Japanese American to practice law in Los Angeles.

MAKHIJANI, SRICHAND (JOHN)

Television producer, businessman. Pakistani American. **PERSONAL:** Born Oct 6, 1939, Nawabshah, Sind, Pakistan; died Apr 21, 1993, Glen Cove, NY; married Vidya; children: Shawn Rajil, John Sanjil. **EDUCATION:** Jai Hind College, interscience degree; University of Hubli, degree, mechanical engineering, 1958; University of Arizona, Tucson, master's degree. **CAREER:** Kemet Electronics, 11 years; AVX Corp, 1976-84; INI, president, 1985-87; UNITEC, owner, 1987-89; Shearson, 1992; Indo-American Enterprises, "Namaste America," chmn, producer.

POONI, AMARDEEP SINGH

Soccer association founder. **PERSONAL:** Born 1963?, Ba, Fiji; died Mar 2, 1993, Sacramento, CA; son of Mr & Mrs Chenchal Singh Pooni; married Maggie; children: Shaleen. **CAREER:** Fiji Khalsa Soccer Association, cofounder; Vallejo Fiji Khalsa Soccer Team, founder, player.

RIVERS, MAVIS

Singer. Pacific Islander American. **PERSONAL:** Born 1929?, Samoa; died May 29, 1992, Los Angeles, CA. **CAREER:** Jazz vocalist: joined father's band, World War II; sang with Red Norvo combo, George Shearing and Andre Previn. **SPECIAL ACHIEVEMENTS:** Recordings include: Take a Number; Hooray for Love; The Simple Live; Mavis; with Red Norvo: We Remember Mildred Bailey.

SARKER, BIMAL

Engineer. Indo-American. **PERSONAL:** Born Nov 4, 1939, Purulia, Bihar, India; died Mar 15, 1993, Pleasanton, CA; married Aparna; children: Falguni, Arnab. **EDUCATION:** Bihar Univ, BSCE; Calcutta Univ, master's degree, structural eng; Univ of California, Berkeley, master's degree, structural eng and structural mechanics, 1971. **CAREER:** Libyan Government, civil engineer, 1966-70; Bechtel Corp, engineer, 18 years; Pacific Gas & Electric Co, 1992-93. **ORGANIZATIONS:** Assn of Indians in America, vice president of programs,

1977-82; Prabasi, founding member; Berkeley Bangla School, past president; Founder of Antara, a singing group.

SHIM, SANG KYU
Businessman. Korean American. **PERSONAL:** Born 1939?, Republic of Korea; died Nov 21, 1992, Detroit, MI; married Young; children: Ben, Wesley, John. **EDUCATION:** Wayne State University, graduate, 1960s. **CAREER:** YMCA, teacher of tae kwon do; United Tae Kwon Do, owner, 1987-92. **ORGANIZATIONS:** World Martial Arts Assn, founder. **SPECIAL ACHIEVEMENTS:** Ninth-degree blackbelt; author, The Making of a Martial Artist; editor-in-chief, Tae Kwon Do Times.

SINGH, NATASHA
Journalist. Indo-American. **PERSONAL:** Born 1964?, Jhansi, India; died Apr 16, 1993, Afghanistan; daughter of Kartar and Jit Sidhu Singh. **EDUCATION:** San Jose State University, BA, journalism, 1987. **CAREER:** Freelance reporter for: Asia Now (Tokyo), San Francisco Chronicle, Miami Herald, United Press Intl, Pioneer (Bombay). **SPECIAL ACHIEVEMENTS:** Accomplished freelancer who travelled around the world working for major newspapers, radios and television stations in the US.

UCHIDA, YOSHIKO
Author. Japanese American. **PERSONAL:** Born Nov 24, 1921, Alameda, CA; died Jun 21, 1992, Berkeley, CA; daughter of Dwight Takashi and Iku Umegaki Uchida. **EDUCATION:** University of California, Berkeley, AB (cum laude), 1942; Smith College, MEd, 1944. **CAREER:** Elementary school teacher, Utah, beginning 1942; Frankford Friends' School, teacher, 1944-45; Inst of Pacific Relations, mem secretary, 1946-47; United Student Christian Council, secretary, 1947-52; full-time writer, 1952-57; University of California, Berkeley, secretary, 1957-62; full-time writer, 1962-92. **HONORS/AWARDS:** American Library Assn Notable Book Citation, 1972; Children's Choices award; Commonwealth Club of California Medal, 1972, 1982; Bay Area Book Reviewers Citation, 1985; numerous others. **SPECIAL ACHIEVEMENTS:** Author of 30 children's books, articles and short stories including: The Dancing Kettle, 1949; Journey to Topaz, 1971; Journey Home, 1978; Jar of Dreams, 1981; The Best Bad Thing, 1983; The Happiest Ending, 1985; The Invisible Thread, 1991; also wrote books for adult readers: Desert Exile: The Uprooting

of a Japanese American Family; We Do Not Work Alone: The Thoughts of Kanjiro Kawai; Picture Bride.

WATANABE, ROBERT
Surgeon. Japanese American. **PERSONAL:** Born 1926?, San Luis Obispo, CA; died Sep 30, 1992, Los Angeles, CA; children: Craig. **CAREER:** Self-employed orthopedic surgeon, about 40 years; Watanabe Orthopedic Systems Inc, president. **SPECIAL ACHIEVEMENTS:** Invented a video arthroscope, a diagnostic instrument which allows surgeons to look into a joint via a television screen; UCLA Track Team, 1948-51; TAC/USA Natl Masters Track and Field Championship, winner of 100-meter dash for age group, 1991; ran the 100-yard dash in 9.6 seconds; winner of numerous other track & field competitions.

WU, SAM *See* WU, SHIEN-MING.

WU, SHIEN-MING (SAM WU)
Educator. Chinese American. **PERSONAL:** Born Oct 28, 1924, Hangzhou, China; died Oct 28, 1992; married Daisy Tsui Wu, Oct 3, 1959; children: Benjamin T, Elaine I. **EDUCATION:** Chiao-Tung University, Shanghai, China, BS, financial administration, 1945; University of Pennsylvania, Wharton School, MBA, transportation, 1956; University of Wisconsin, Madison, BS, mechanical engineering, 1958, PhD, mechanical engineering, 1962. **CAREER:** University of Wisconsin, Madison, assistant professor, 1962-65, associate professor, 1965-68, production engineering division, chairman, 1966-74, professor, 1968-80, research professor, 1981-87; University of Michigan, J Reid and Polly Anderson Professor of Manufacturing Technology, 1987-92. **ORGANIZATIONS:** American Society of Mechanical Engineers, fellow, 1983; Society of Manufacturing Engineers; American Society for Engineering Education; Phi Tau Phi; Pi Tau Sigma; Sigma Xi. **HONORS/AWARDS:** University of Michigan, Distinguished Faculty Achievement Award, 1992; Chiang Industrial Charity Foundation, Chiang Technology Achievement Award, 1991; Fulbright-Hays distinguished professorship, USSR, 1988, Yugoslavia, 1975; Academia Sinica, 1982. **BUSINESS ADDRESS:** J Reid and Polly Anderson Professor of Manufacturing Technology, Dept of Mechanical Engineering & Applied Mechanics, University of Michigan, 2351 Herbert, 3424 G G Brown Laboratory, Ann Arbor, MI 48109-2125, (313)763-5299.

GEOGRAPHIC INDEX

ALABAMA

Auburn
Chang, Kai-Hsiung
Chiba, Lee I.
Chin, Bryan Allen
Govil, Narendra Kumar
Lau, Tin Man
Liao, Ming
Min, Hokey
Rao, Sadasiva Madiraju
Varma, Vishwa K.
Wang, Yong Tai
Yoo, Chai Hong

Birmingham
Bhown, Ajit Singh
Cheung, Herbert Chiu-Ching
Chow, Louise Tsi
Krishna, N. Rama
Liu, Ray H.
Nanda, Navin Chandar
Sani, Brahma P.
Shin, Myung Soo

Huntsville
Abbas, Mian M.
Aggarwal, Manmohan D.
Chang, Mou-Hsiung
Fu, Peter K.
Hung, Ru J.
Li, Jia
Park, Ounyoung
Srinivas, Ramachandra
Sung, Chi Ching
Vikram, Chandra Shekhar
Wu, Shi Tsan

Jacksonville
Yeh, Pu-Sen

Mobile
Bhatnagar, Yogendra Mohan
Lanewala, Mohammed Ali
Shah, Ahmer
Yang, Yih-Ming

Montgomery
Chang, Moon K.
Huang, Cheng-Chi
Kim, Ki Hang
Lieu, George Y.
Lu, John Y.
Mathew, Saramma T.
Sharma, Udhishtra Deva
Shih, Stephen Chingyu

Normal
Aggarwal, Manmohan D.
Hung, Chih-Cheng
Sharma, Govind Chandra

Selma
Chapatwala, Kirit D.

Troy
Mathew, Saramma T.

Tuscaloosa
Lin, Kai-Ching
Park, Duk-Won
Wu, Zhijian

Tuskegee
Dalvi, Ramesh R.
Lieu, George Y.

ALASKA

Eagle River
Nakazawa, Anthony Tadashi

Fairbanks
Sharma, Ghanshyam D.

ARIZONA

Chandler
Hom, Peter Wah
Hoque, Enamul

Flagstaff
Lew, Alan August
Merchant, Vasant V.
Yu, Larry

Florence
Don, James E.

Glendale
Fong, Glenn Randall
Kadomoto, Thomas
Takiguchi, Masako

Mesa
Singhal, Avinash Chandra
Wong, Willie
Yee, Donald H.

Phoenix
Ariza, Yasumi
Cheng, Eddy
Chung, Catherine L.
Jeevanandam, Malayappa
Kedia, Ullas V.
Lui, Wai Ming
Premraj, A. N.
Tang, Thomas
Ullah, M. Rifat

Scottsdale
Aikawa, Jerry Kazuo
Dao, Hong T.
Jeevanandam, Malayappa
Yamamori, Tetsunao
Yen, Joan Jue

Tempe
Chen, Kangping
Ching, Anthony B.
Ching, Chee
Culp, Mae Ng
Gupta, Sanjay
Hom, Peter Wah

Hotelling, Katsuko Tsurukawa
Inaba, Jeffrey Norihisa
Kim, Joochul
Kulkarni, Uday Ravindra
Lai, Richard Tseng-yu
Ren, Shang Yuan
Singhal, Avinash Chandra
So, Ronald Ming Cho
Wang, Alan P.
Yao, Lun-Shin

Tucson
Chan, Cho Lik
Chandra, Abhijit
Desai, Chandrakant S.
Fan, Chang-Yun
Ganguly, Jibamitra
Hu, Paul Y.
Kwan, Simon Hing-Man
Lim, Nancy Wong
Mishra, Shitala P.
Soo Hoo, Eric Randolph
Wang, Fei-Yue
Yu, Yeou-Chong Simon

ARKANSAS

Camden
Ishikawa, Ishi

Conway
Mehta, Rahul

Decatur
Reddy, Ramakrishna P.

Fayetteville
Huang, Feng Hou
Singh, Surendra Pal

Little Rock
Chang, Louis Wai-Wah
Tai, C. Stephen

Pine Bluff
Reddy, Pannala Sathyanahayana
Tai, C. Stephen

Russellville
Mori, John P.
Yang, Chia Chi

Siloam Springs
Kim, Young-Gurl

State University
Yang, Kichoon

CALIFORNIA

Alameda
Chang, Yen Fook
Louie, Gilman G.
Ohno, Peter Takeshi
Sakamoto, Katsuyuki

Albany
Lin, Jiann-Tsyh

Alhambra
Ting, Shih-Fan
Wong, Sophie Chao

Aliso Viejo
Ting Cang-Kim, Donna Marie

Altadena
Koga, Toyoki
Krishnaswamy, Rukmini

Anaheim
Chen, Tai
Kariya, Paul
Sumida, Kenneth Dean
Sun, Richard C.

Arcadia
Ho, Chin Chih
Ko, William Weng-Ping
Nakatani, Corey
Wang, Charles Chiming
Yen, Wen-Hsiung

Arcata
Gotera, Vicente Ferrer
Lee, Sue Ying
Yee, Carlton S.

Bakersfield
Fang, Fabian Tien-Hwa
Wang, Huaqing

Baldwin Park
Cruzada, Rodolfo Omega

Barstow
Jiang, Zhenying

Belmont
Louie, Alan C.
Yee, Darlene

Belvedere Tiburon
Chan, Gary Lee

Berkeley
Chan, Sham-Yuen
Chang, Shih-Ger
Chiang, Chin Long
Ching, Hugh
Chu, William Tongil
Chua, Leon O.
Horiuchi, Glenn
Hsu, Chieh-Su
Hu, Chenming
Kato, Tosio
Kuan, Kah-Jin
Kuh, Ernest Shiu-Jen
Lee, Pamela Tau
Lee, Yuan Tseh
Lin, Patricia Yu
Lin, Robert Peichung
Louie, Steven Gwon Sheng
Ma, Fai

Mei, Kenneth K.
Min, Kyung Ho
Miyasaki, George Joji
Mukherjee, Bharati
Nagano, Kent George
Sasaki, Ruth A.
Shen, Hsieh Wen
Shen, Yuen-Ron
Song, Choan-Seng
Sung, Zinmay Renee
Takaki, Ronald
Tanouye, Mark Allen
Tien, Chang-Lin
Wang, William S-Y.
Wong, Eugene
Wong, Nicole Anna
Wu, Hung-Hsi
Yee, Edmond
Yeung, Ronald Wai-Chun

Beverly Hills
Chao, Jowett
Chen, Joan
Chin, Katherine M.
Chong, Rae Dawn
Fung, Sui An
Lee, Brandon
Lee, Jason Scott
Nair, Mira
Reeves, Keanu
Salonga, Lea
Wang, Wayne
Yuan, Robin Tsu-Wang

Bodega Bay
Chang, Ernest Sun-Mei

Bolinas
Okamura, Arthur Shinji

Brea
Oh, Chan Soo
Woo, P. T.

Brisbane
Leung, Ka-Wing
Tsui, Cheryl Wai-Kuen

Buena Park
Jain, Naresh C.
Minnig, William Paul

Burbank
Ho, Alexander Kitman
Nakamoto, Donald Jiro
Su, Tuhuei
Tao, Stephen G.
Tokuda, Wendy
Wong, Kenneth P.

Burlingame
Pati, A. Kumar

Campbell
Shimomura, Yukio
Tokunaga, Katsumi

713

Canyon Country
Uda, Robert Takeo

Carlsbad
Chang, Jennie C. C.

Carmel
Chong, Tommy

Carmichael
Tanaka, James Junji

Carson
Fajardo, Peter
Hata, Donald Teruo, Jr.
Hosokawa, Fumiko
Landero, Reynaldo Rivera, II
Mitoma, Mike
Moy, Naomi Ogawa

Castro Valley
Honda, Allen Shigeru
Teramoto, Yoshitsugu
Wang, Ging-Long

Cerritos
Chhim, Him S.
Chiu, Jim
Yang, Joseph Chi-Houng

Chatsworth
Wong, Clark Chiu-Yuen

Chico
Gee, Arthur
Huang, George Wenhong

China Lake
Yeh, Edward H. Y.

Chino
Hsu, George Chi-Yung

Chula Vista
Gil, Libia Socorro

City of Industry
Fong, Matthew K.
Hwu, Peter S.
Nagaoka, Michael M.
Tanaka, Eddy Sei
Tang, America

Claremont
Kim, Chan-Hie
Kubota, Mitsuru
Kuwahara, Steven Sadao
Yen, I-Kuen

Compton
Hom, Rose
Suzukawa, Steven
Wang, Charles Ping
Wang, Lily L.

Concord
Iwahashi, Satoshi
Loor, Rueyming

Corona
Chao, Allen Y.

Costa Mesa
Parekh, Navnit M.

Covina
Ito, Noriaki

Culver City
Kashyap, Pankaj Kumar
Lee, Christopher
Nakano, Frank Hiroshi
Shah, Mayank H.

Singh, Kim
Wong, Evelyn
Zee, Teddy

Cupertino
Chang, Michael S.
Chou, Timothy C.
Wang, Gene

Cypress
Mathews, Peter
Pham, Danny

Daly City
Cheng, Carlos
Guingona, Michael Patrick
Santos, Mario Alban

Danville
Leung, Dennis B.

Davis
Chang, Chia-ning
Doi, Roy Hiroshi
Fong, Mary Helena
Fujimoto, Isao
Geng, Shu
Hsieh, You-Lo
Ishida, Andrew
Kaneda, Hiromitsu
Ko, Winston T.
Lagura, Franklin Sasutana
Lakshmanan, Chithra
Lin, Wen Chun
Luh, Bor Shiun
Ogawa, Joseph Minoru
Peng, Ying-shin Christine
Ryu, Dewey Doo Young
Sen, Arun Kumar
Wang, Shih-Ho
Yang, Shang Fa
Yeh, Michelle M.

Diamond Bar
Kuo, Wayne Wen-Long
Wu, Hofu

Downey
Furuta, Harry
Uda, Robert Takeo
Wasserman, Fumiko Hachiya

Duarte
Chou, Chung-Kwang
Ikeda, Kazuo
Itakura, Keiichi
Kuwahara, Steven Sadao
Yoshida, Akira

El Cajon
Chow, Bob Ching-Hong
Kapur, Kamal K.

El Cerrito
Aoki, Haruo
Gouw, Cynthia Gie-Kiok
Miyawaki, Kiyoshi
Nozaki, Kenzie
Wong, Anna Clara

El Monte
Au, Andrew T.
Louie, Marvin Kim

El Segundo
Chang, Juang-Chi
Gupta, Madhu Sudan

El Sobrante
Lin, Jennifer Jen-Huey

Elk Grove
Tsukamoto, Mary Tsuruko

Emeryville
Cheng, Carlos
Lee, Juwan

Encinitas
Kang, Chang-Yuil
Yuasa, Joji

Fair Oaks
Kim, Jong H.

Folsom
Rao, Mahesh K.

Fontana
Hoang, Frank H.

Foothill Ranch
Tran, Tuyet-Nhung T.

Foster City
Chinn, Roger
Lin, Felix

Fremont
Chan, Steven D.
Chang, Paul Peng-Cheng
Jain, Ashit
Japra, Romesh K.
Kaul, Maharaj Krishen
Kee, Willie
Khan, Mahbub R.
Mammen, Thomas
Nguyen, An H.
Raimundo, Cris C.
Tran, Thinh Quy
Wong, Steven W.
Wong, William Wai-Lun
Wu, Nan-Ray
Yamaguchi, Kristine Tsuya
Yuan, Sidney W. K.

Fresno
Brahma, Chandra Sekhar
Chang, Hsu Hsin
Chen, Kuang Chung
Lee, Karen
Leung, Chi Kin
Nakaguchi, Richard T.
Ong, Beng Soo
Pham, Kien Trung
Sidhu, Gurmel Singh
Sun, Hugo Sui-Hwan
Sy, Jose
Tong, Lee M.
Wang, Jia
Wong, Kin-Ping
Yen, Matthew Ming-Shih

Fullerton
Chan, Peng S.
Chan, Su Han
Kagiwada, Harriet H. Natsuyama
Lai, Tsong-Yue
Matsumoto, Keiji
Wang, Ko
Wong, Dorothy Pan

Garden Grove
Chung, Ho Young
Tam, Henry
Yorita, Frank Kazuo

Gardena
Fukai, Masani
Hu, Steve Seng-Chiu
Kaji, Jonathan T.
Kawahara, Lindon Ken
Sakamoto, Lynn
Sakurai, Fred Yutaka

Gilroy
Hashmi, Mohammed Zafar

Lai, Kai Sun
Sumisaki, Roy

Glendale
Hayashi, Seigo
Shah, Amar M.

Glendora
Umali, Filemon J.

Hacienda Heights
Gee, Montgomery M.
Hsiao, Tyzen
Yeung, Chun W.

Hawthorne
Tin, Bo

Hayward
Jun, Jong S.
Kam, Vernon T.
Lin, You-An Robert
Munakata, Grace Megumi
Pan, Fung-Shine
Pannu, Dave S.
Ramachandra, Srinivas R.

Hillsborough
Kwong, Bill Wai Lam

Huntington Beach
Bai, Shen Hum
Hwang, Chong F.
Matsui, Keiko
Miura, Nolan A.
Yee, Franklin

Inglewood
Castro, Marissa Barbers
Sharma, Satanand

Irvine
Chan, Robert T. P.
Chew, Kenneth Sze-Ying
Cho, Zang-Hee
Chu, Timothy Scott
Dang, Phu Ngoc
Dutt, Nikil D.
Fitzpatrick, Eileen Tabata
Hamamoto, Darrell Yoshito
Hayashi, Masato
Hu, Can Beven
Huang, C.-T. James
Li, Peter Wai-Kwong
Mathur, Raghu P.
Min, Yong Soon
Murata, Margaret K.
Nomura, Masayasu
Suda, Tatsuya
Tong, Sun-De
Tong, Wen-How
Tseng, Beatrice Shan-Yi
Yamada, Mitsuye May

La Canada
Kobayashi, William N., Jr.

La Jolla
Chang, Shen Chie
Cheng, Chung-Kuan
Cheng, Lanna
Fung, Yuan-Cheng Bertram
Kishimoto, Yasuo
Lin, James Peicheng
Lin, Ting-Ting Yao
Nguyen-huu, Xuong
Ramanathan, Veerabhadran
Sham, Lu Jeu
Sinha, Yagya Nand
Subramani, Suresh
Tu, Charles W.
Wong, David Yue
Yildiz, Alaettin

Yu, Paul Kit-Lai

La Mirada
Patel, Ramesh V.

La Palma
Patel, Pratibha A.

La Verne
Chen, James

Lafayette
Chen, Carl Wan-Cheng
Chu, William Tongil
Sasaki, Hideo

Laguna Hills
Tsutsui, James Haruo, Jr.

Laguna Niguel
Wong, Gregory Dean

Lake Forest
Ting Cang-Kim, Donna Marie
Wu, Frank I.

Lakewood
Jeong, Wallace Dun

Livermore
Damria, Mulkh Raj
Lin, Wunan
Saito, Theodore Teruo

Loma Linda
Silao, Ray A.

Lomita
Yeh, Hen-Geul

Long Beach
Anand, Rajen S.
Blanco, Paul De La Cruz
Chan, Kwan M.
Chen, Hsin-Piao Patrick
Domondon, Oscar
Fung, Henry C.
Gamblin, Noriko
Hirano-Nakanishi, Marsha Joyce
Ho, Ju-shey
Iwasaki, Ronald Seiji
Jung, John R.
Kashyap, Moti Lal
Kong, Chhean
Li, San-pao
Lim, Paulino Marquez, Jr.
Lu, Kau U.
Nakamoto, Donald Jiro
Oh, Taesung
Tana, Phongpan
Tang, Paul Chi Lung
Wan, James X.
Yeh, Hsien-Yang

Los Alamitos
Shim, Jae K.

Los Altos
Divakaruni, Chitra Banerjee
Kim, Kristin Imsoo
Lam, Eppie C. F.
Wong, Rita F.

Los Altos Hills
Ni, Preston C.

Los Angeles
Abarquez-Delacruz, Prosy
Aki, Keiiti
Au, Wilkie Wai Kee
Castro, Marissa Barbers
Chan, Anthony Kit-Cheung
Chang, Alice Ching

Chang, Ben
Chang, Henry C.
Chang, Howard F.
Chang, Tim P.
Chao, Rosalind
Chen, Francis F.
Chen, Wun-ee Chelsea
Cheng, Hsien K.
Chew, Richard Franklin
Chin, George K. W.
Chin, Pamela Grace
Ching, Deborah F.
Chiu, Thomas Chee-Wang
Choi, Richard Yungho
Choo, Marcia
Chopra, Inder Jit
Chung, Harold
Chung, T. S.
Chung, Thomas Yongbong
Chuong, Cheng-Ming
Dang, Tim
Davino, Carmencita Fernandez
Dong, Arthur
Ebata, Duane
Embrey, Sue Kunitomi
Fischer, Takayo
Fong, Herbert S.
Fong, J Craig
Fong, Thomas Y. K.
Frey, Francesca
Furukawa, Larry Kiyoshi
Furuta, Karin L.
Furutani, Warren
Gee, Dolly M.
Goishi, Dean M.
Goo, Edward Kwock Wai
Gotanda, Philip Kan
Greenberg, Asha Saund
Hamasaki, Les
Hanami, Clement S.
Hill, Amy
Hirano, Irene Yasutake
Hiroshige, Ernie
Ho, Chih-Ming
Hoang, Giao
Hokoyama, J. D.
Hong, George K.
Hur, John Chonghwan
Hwang, Henry Y.
Hwang, Xochitl
Iko, Momoko Marlene
Ikuhara, Akihiro
Imai, Douglas Scott
Ito, Lance A.
Iwataki, Miya
Jayaram, Mysore
Kaji, Bruce
Kan-Mitchell, June
Kano, Sachio
Kao, Tai-Wu
Kashiwagi, Soji Charles
Kataoka, Muneo
Kato, Dean M.
Kawafuchi, Glenn Misaki
Kawasaki, Lillian Y.
Khorasanee, Barker M.
Khurana, Krishan Kumar
Kikumura, Akemi
Kim, Bong Hwan
Kim, Chin Hui
Kim, Eun Mee
Kim, Il Young
Kim, Jay Chul
Kim, Joseph K.
Kim, Michael Yong
Kim, Neung Jip
Kita, Sadao
Koga, Rokutaro
Komai, Michael Mikio
Koo, Ja Hung
Kuo, Chung-Chieh Jay
Kurup, Shishir Ravindran
Kuwahara, Frank

Kuwayama, George
Kwan, Catherine Ning
Kwoh, Stewart
Kwon, Jeffrey Young
Lai, Michael Ming-Chiao
Lee, Guy
Lee, Robert Terry
Leong, Russell C.
Leung, Margaret W.
Leung, Yuen-Sang
Lew, Ronald S. W.
Li, Victor On-Kwok
Liu, Alan Fong-Ching
Loui, Warren R.
Louie, Dickson Lew
Louie, Emma Woo
Louie, Paul
Lum, Gene
Ma, Stephen K.
Mahajan, Anoop Kumar
Mak, Chi Ho
Makinodan, Takashi
Matsumoto, Donald Michiaki
Matsumoto, Nancy K.
Miura, Nolan A.
Miyoshi, David Masao
Murakami, Jeffrey Hisakazu
Murakami, Richard M.
Nagatani, Scott A.
Nakanishi, Don Toshiaki
Nakano, Francis
Ng, Rebecca P.
Nietes, Linda Maria
Nishikawa, Dennis
Nishioka, Hayward H.
Ochi, Rose Matsui
Ogawa, Patrick
Okamoto, Shari Akiko
Okazaki, James
Ono, Kanji
Ota, Henry Yasushi
Ota, Mabel Takako
Pal, Pratapaditya
Park, Chan Ho
Park, Laura Heyong
Patel, Chandra Kumar Naranbhai
Patel, Kevin R.
Quismorio, Francisco P., Jr.
Ramchandani, Raj S.
Rasheed, Suralya
Recana, Mel Red
Roy-Burman, Pradip
Ru, Wesley
Saito, Thomas E.
Sathyavagiswaran, Lakshmanan
Senzaki, Miyo
Seto, Joseph Tobey
Seto, Theodore Paul
Sheu, Bing J.
Singh, Kim
Suzuki, Paul Ted
Tagashira, Gail S.
Tagawa, Cary-Hiroyuki
Takahashi, George Masara
Takahashi, Masato
Takasugi, Robert M.
Takei, George Hosato
Takimoto, Hideyo Henry
Tam, Simon M. W.
Tan, Lawrence W.
Tan, Zoe
Tang, Alex Ying Ho
Tashima, A. Wallace
Ting, Sandra
Todd, Kathryn Doi
Tomita, Tamlyn Naomi
Van Houten, David J.
Villa-Real, Olivia Canchela
Wakabayashi, Ron
Wang, David Edward
Wang, Robert T.
Watai, Madge S.
Watanabe, Mike

Wong, Bryan Allen
Wong, Henry Sik-Yin
Wong, Kent Douglas
Wong, Linda J.
Wong, Wing Y.
Woo, Michael K.
Wu, Chivey Dragenson Lung
Wu, Julia Li
Yamaki, Michael Roger
Yang, Bingen
Yang, William C. T.
Yano, Fleur B.
Yano, Ronald Makoto
Yen, Teh Fu
Yep, Ralph Lee
Yin, Xiao-huang
Yoon, Hyo-Chun
Yoshimura, Evelyn
Yoshinaga, George

Los Gatos
Chiang, Ping-Wang
Leung, Charles Cheung-Wan

Malibu
Kagy, Tom
Louganis, Greg E.
Mow, Chao-chow
Shohara, Sei

Martinez
Rao, Ananda G.

Menlo Park
Iyer, Hariharaiyer Mahadeva
Lau, Regina
Lee, David C.
Maruyama, Takashi

Merced
Kobayashi, Deanna Hasuye
Taniguchi, Robert Iwao

Mill Valley
Kobayashi, Yoshiko

Milpitas
Chen, Winston H.
Chua, Conrad E.
Desaigoudar, Chan
Huang, Ian
Lee, David Sen-Lin
Nakujima, Hideyuki
Wang, Xiaohan

Mission Viejo
Sim, John Kim-Chye
Tan, Eric Tuanlee

Modesto
Doo, Jack P., Jr.
Sen, Karabi

Moffett Field
Sharma, Surendra P.

Monrovia
Pang, Chap Aik

Montebello
Nomura, Masae Goto

Monterey
Bhaskar, Surindar Nath
Chan, Carl Chiang
Chu, Peter Cheng
Jayachandran, Toke
Kang, Keebom
Kwon, Young Wuk
Lam, Alex W.
Sohn, So Young
Wu, C. Thomas
Yamada, David Takao

Monterey Park
Chen, Simon Ying
Chong, Pek-Ean
Chu, Judy M.
Foong, Nicolai Yein
Lau, David T.
Ting, Ying Ji
Uyeda, Roger Makoto
Wong, Clifford S.

Moorpark
Kim, Edward J.

Moraga
Wu, Diana Ting Liu
Yeung, Ronald Wai-Chun

Morgan Hill
Jain, Rakesh

Mountain View
Chiou, Wun C.
Chu, Nhan V.
Koo, George P.
Ong, Georgina

Napa
Shin, Ernest Eun-Ho
Tanada, Takuma

Newbury Park
Bak, Chan Soo

Newport Beach
Chan, John
Chen, Yen-Hsu
Chiu, John T.
Jung, Soon J.
Lin, James Chow

North Hollywood
Jao, Radmar Agana
Kim, Paul Myungchyun

Northridge
Chan, Kenyon S.
Chen, Chao
Chen, Tung-Shan
Chow, Paul Chuan-Juin
Kwan, Kian M.
Lee, Yow-Min R.
Su, Zhixin
Tsai, Mark F.
Uba, George R.
Wang, I-Shou
Wong, Clark Chiu-Yuen
Yoshida, Ronald Yutaka

Norwalk
Banada-Tan, Leticia
Yee, Franklin

Novato
Tam, Bing Kwong

Oakland
Chan, Glenn
Ch'en, Lena B.
Cheng, Norman Alan
Cheung, Fernando C. H.
Cho, David
Darling, Ron
Hayslip, Le Ly
Hotta, Gina H.
Ishi, Tomoji
Isokawa, Ned
Kawaichi, Ken M.
Kelly, Darlene Okamoto
Ko, Kathleen Lim
Krishnan, Kalliana R.
Lo, Suzanne J.
Lu, Janet Y. H.
Nakadegawa, Roy

Nguyen, Long
Ogawa, Frank Hirao
Ohashi, Alan Joseph
Ong, Edward Frank
Ong, James M.
Patel, Kanti L.
Sato, William K.
Sayaphupha, Robert Bouakham
Shin, Young
Suzuki, Masao Fred
Wong, Charles Foo, Jr.
Wong, Donald N. F.
Wong, Karl
Wong, William
Yeh, Susan S. Wang
Yeh, Timothy S.

Ojai
Yee, Lawrence K.

Ontario
Kim, Edward Ik Hwan

Orange
Chung, Ling Jia
Ishii, Robert Frank
Murata, Yuji
Yu, Jen

Pacific Grove
Yamanishi, Henry Kazuo

Pacific Palisades
Sato, Gary Teruo

Pacoima
Takimoto, Mabel Yayoko

Palo Alto
Chan, David S.
Chang, Edmund Z.
Chin-Lee, Cynthia Denise
Chiu, Martha Li
Chow, Kao Liang
Eng, Lawrence Fook
Gin, Jerry B.
Hingorani, Narain G.
Jue, Francis
Kishimoto, Yoriko
Lee, Chiho
Nag, Ronjon
Okano, Yuji
Oshiro, Roy C.
Tahiliani, Vasu Hariram
Tsai, Chuang Chuang
Yuan, Sidney W. K.

Palos Verdes
Wong, Angela Ma

Palos Verdes Peninsula
Wang, H. E. Frank

Paramount
Kimura, Kolin M.

Pasadena
Chang, Yang-Shim
Choi, Raymond Yoonseok
Higa, Walter Hiroichi
Huynh, Emmanuelle
Kim, Joanne Young
Kinaga, Patricia Anne
Kong, Stanley Young
Konishi, Masakazu
Le, Tieng Quang
Mitchell-Onuma, Susan C.
Rhee, Chase Chonggwang
Shimada, Katsunori
Trinh, Eugene
Wang, Wei
Wing, Charmeen Hah-Ming
Wu, Theodore Yao-Tsu

Yen, Chen-wan L.

Petaluma
Uyeda, Arthur Asa

Pico Rivera
Shimamoto, Scott Seiya

Pittsburg
Chin, Stanley H.
Hsieh, Durwynne

Placentia
Wong, Morton Min-Fong
Yu, Chi Kang

Pleasant Hill
Chow, Ivan S.
Rao, Ananda G.
Wu, Christopher N.

Pleasanton
Choy, Antonio J.
Lin, Chien-Chang

Pomona
Awakuni, Gene I.
Dolor, Deogracias Asuncion, Jr.
Kapoor, Tarun
Kumar, Ramesh
Lee, Chung
Liu, Hsun Kao
Nguyen, Thuan Ke
Shieh, John Ting-Chung
Suzuki, Bob H.
Wu, Hofu

Presidio of Monterey
Chan, Carl Chiang

Rancho Dominguez
Hee, Edward K. Y.

Rancho Palos Verdes
Chi, Cheng-Ching
Kim, Byong-Kon
Lal, Dhyan
Morizumi, S. James
Song, John D.
Ubhayakar, Shivadev K.

Rancho Santa Fe
Chang, Wayne Wei

Rancho Santa Margarita
Chu, Warren

Redlands
Rio-Jelliffe, Rebecca
Wong, Frank F.

Redondo Beach
Lao, Binneg Y.
Tamaki, Jeanne Keiko

Redwood City
Chen, Henry J.
Kung, Frank F. C.
Villanueva, Marianne Del
    Rosario

Reseda
Rawn, Byung Soon

Richmond
Rao, Nagaraja R.
Takeuchi, Esther Kiyomi

Riverside
Chang, Andrew C.
Chang, Edward Taehan
Chang, Sylvia Tan
Fung, Sun-Yiu

Hwang, Enoch Oi-Kee
Kim, Michael Wooyung
Lee, Tien-Chang
Liao, Woody M.
Lin, Yuet-Chang Joseph
Sasaki, Chiyo Katano
Takano, Mark Allan
Wu, Yenna
Yoshino, Ronald Warren
Zhang, Longxi

Rohnert Park
Shinagawa, Larry

Roseville
Goto, George
Liu, Edmund K.

Rowland Heights
Chi, Bo Kyung
Lang, David C.
Tsai, Michael Ming-Ping
Wang, Sue S.

Sacramento
Aoki, Thomas T.
Chan, Thomas O.
Chatterjee, Satya N.
Cheung, Luke P.
Chung, Robert
Enomoto, Jiro
Eu, March Fong
Fong, Eva Chow
Fung, Dennis Lung
Furukawa, Fred M.
Ha, Chong W.
Hwang, John C.
Jain, Bimla Agarwal
Kim, Jong H.
Lee, Ming-Tung
Leung, Peter
Liu, Edmund K.
Lum, Doman
Mukai, Robert L.
Ogata, Jeffery Morimasa
Satow, Stuart Alan
Soo Hoo, William Fong
Takasugi, Nao
Tom, Leland B.
Wong, Steven Dale
Yamada, Yozo
Yee, Jimmie N.
Yee, Joanne

San Anselmo
Ng, David

San Bernardino
Liu, Anne W.
Wang, Ching-Hua

San Diego
Bulsara, Ardeshir Ratan
Chang, Albert
Chang, Wayne Wei
Chen, Audrey Huey-Wen
Chen, Ding-Bond
Chen, Kao
Chin, Marilyn Mei Ling
Chou, Hsin-Pei
Chu, Elizabeth Chan
Chun, Aulani
Dirige, Ofelia Villa
Higuchi, Clayton T.
Hwang, Guann-Jiun
Inoue, Michael Shigeru
Iwanaga-Penrose, Margaret
Jung, Kwan Yee
Jung, Yee Wah
Kang, Chang-Yuil
Kim, Chin
Kim, Jinchoon
Kim, Leo

Kim, Yoonchung Park
Kobayashi, Bert Nobuo
Krishnamoorthy, Govindarajalu
Kumar, Meera
Kumar, Ram Sakthi
Li, Shing Ted
Lin, Ting-Ting Yao
Malhotra, Manohar Lal
McCarty, Faith B.
Mizuno, Nobuko Shimotori
Mong, Seymour
Ng, Michael Wai-Man
Parke, Keol-bai
Partido, Rousalyn Bautista
Pinto, James J.
Sinha, Yagya Nand
Soo Hoo, Karen
Tran, Myluong Thi
Wang, Kuo Chang
Yu, Alice L.
Zetterlund, Yoko Karin

San Dimas
Yamaguchi, Ko

San Francisco
Akiyoshi, Mike M.
Aoki, Brenda Jean
Aoki, Kathryn Kiku
Bhandari, Sanjiv
Bloch, Julia Chang
Chan, Angela
Chan, Timothy T.
Chang, Ming
Chang, Patricia W.
Chau, Peter
Chen, John L.
Chen, Yea-Mow
Chen, Yu-Charn
Chew, Wellington Lum
Chin, Helen
Chin, Ming William
Chin, Steven Alexander
Chinn, Roger
Chong, Frank
Chu, Kuang Han
Chung, Anni Yuet-Kuen
Chung, Lisa A.
Collier, Irene Dea
Cuajao, Tracy Lee
Deng, Ming-Dao
Der, Henry
de Vera, Federico
Eng, Jamie Pearl
Fa, Angie
Fang, Florence
Fang, James
Fang, John Ta-Chuan
Fong, Kevin Murray
Fong-Torres, Shirley
Fu, Karen K.
Funabiki, Jon
Fung, Gordon L.
Geaga, Jaime V.
Gee, Virginia Catherine
Goto, Yukihiro
Govindarajulu, Zakkula
Guillermo, Tessie
Hiramoto, Joni T.
Hironaka, Steve
Holl, Julie Kawahara
Hong, Carl
Hong, S. K.
Horn, Jennie A.
Hsia, Judo Jeoudao
Hsiao, Julia
Hsieh, Tom
Hu, Wayne
Huey, Jolene W.
Igasaki, Paul
Iiyama, Chizu
Ito, Caryl
Jamero, Peter M.

Jang, Dennis
Jang, Jon
Jimenez, Josephine Santos
Kam, James T.-K.
Kan, Yuet Wai
Kaneko, William Masami
Kennard, Joyce L.
Kikuchi, George Susumu
Kim, Myung Mi
Kim, Wendell Kealohopauloe
Kingman, Dong
Kishimoto, Richard Noriyuki
Kobashigawa, Ben
Kobayashi, Yoshiko
Kong, William T.
Koo, Michelle E. M.
Kwok, Joseph
Lam, Dick
Lau, Edward C. Y.
Lau, Fred H.
Lee, Miko
Lee, Vic Ling
Lew, Eugene
Lin, Eva I.
Lin, Jennifer Jen-Huey
Lin, Tung Yen
Liou, Shy-Sheng P.
Liu, Edwin H.
Liu, Gerald Hanmin
Liu, Thomas
Lock, Chuck Choi
Louie, David A.
Louie, Sammy G.
Low, Harry William
Low, Randall
Lowe, Rolland Choy
Lum, George
Maniwa, Kaz
Mar, William David
Masaoka, Miya Joan
Miyahara, Paul Masayoshi
Mori, Sandy Ouye
Moy, Stan Yip
Munroe, Tapan
Muriera, Helen Bautista
Nakagawa, Cressey
Nakajo, Steve
Nakayama, Randall Shige
Ng, Thomas
Nishimura, Tom
Noguchi, John Takeo
Okazaki, Steven
Ong, Cynthia
Paek, Min
Pang, Wilma
Park Li, Gimmy
Pham, Hung Do
Quan, Katie
Raju, Solomon Nalli, Sr.
Renge, I. Beth
Rodis, Rodel E.
Senzaki, Randall Kiyomi
Seto, Benjamin S. F.
Seto, Thelma G.
Shimizu, Taisuke
Sing, Lillian K.
Soriano, Lee G.
Tai, William P.
Takahashi, Rita
Tang, Julie Mong-See
Teng, Mabel Sik Mei
Tom, Angelo C.
Tonai, Rosalyn
Tong, Benjamin Robert
Tsang, Chiu
Uyeda, Clifford I.
Vyas, Girish N.
Wada, Patricia
Wang, Ching Chung
Wang, William Kai-Sheng
Wong, Anna Clara
Wong, Bernard P.
Wong, Byron F.

Wong, Charles Foo, Jr.
Wong, Chin Siong
Wong, Harold H.
Wong, Janet S.
Wong, Nellie
Wong, Pablo Jose
Woo, Celeste Kimberlee
Wu, Christopher N.
Wu, William Gay
Yamaguchi, Michael J.
Yamakawa, David Kiyoshi, Jr.
Yamamoto, Keith Robert
Yamamoto, Michael Toru
Yamasaki, George, Jr.
Yan, Martin
Yang, Jen Tsi
Yao, Dorcas C.
Yazaki, Toyu
Ye, Jose
Yee, Darlene
Yee, Leland
Yee, Virginia Bow Sue
Yen, Tien-Sze Benedict
Yin, Ronald L.
Yoshida, Kanetaka
Yuchengco, Mona Lisa Sycip
Zia, Helen

San Gabriel
Labasan, Alejandro B.
Uyeshima, Mary
Yang, Tuen-Ping

San Jose
Batra, Rajeev
Chan, Ted W.
Chang, Helen Kuang
Chang, Simon
Chen, Gong
Chin, Edwin, Jr.
Choi, Eunhye Jenni
Dedhia, Navin Shamji
Fong, Charlen
Hinoki, George
Hiura, Alan
Honda, Michael M.
Hsu, Ping
Hu, Albert Ke-Jeng
Jethanandani, Ashok
Jiang, William Yuying
Kimura, Brian
Kong, Dongsung
Kong, Ronald A.
Kumar, Arvind
Kumar, Mythili
LaCuesta, Lloyd R.
Lakkaraju, Harinarayana Sarma
Lam, Alex W.
Lam, An Ngoc
Lam, Lui
Lee, Bradford Young
Leung, Kai-Cheong
Lin, Chaote
Liu, Mengxiong
Liu, Susana Juh-mei
Louie, Eugene H.
Luu, Lang Van
Mai, Hugh D.
Mai, Marianne Vu
Mihara, Nathan
Miura, Irene Takei
Nguyen, Mike Chi
Okita, George Torao
Patel, Arvindkumar Motibhai
Quon, Shun Wing
Rao, Kameswara Kolla
Respicio, Elsa Toje
Sasaki, Dale I.
Seid, Allan
Shigemasa, Thomas Ken
Shimomura, Yukio
Shirakawa, George
Tokunaga, Howard Taira

Tsai, Kuei-wu
Uchida, Yoshihiro
Wang, Jen-Yu
Wang, Louisa Ho-Ching
Wang, Stanley
Wong, Steven W.
Wu, Hsiu-ying
Wu, Kim
Yang, Chyan
Yoon, Peter Jiung
Yu, James H.

San Leandro
Fong, Joshua
Ong, Edward Frank
Wang, Carl C. T.

San Luis Obispo
Hsieh, Carl Chia-Fong
Jen, Joseph Jwu-Shan
Kato, Goro
Lau, Frederick C.
Liu, Hong-Ting
Lo, Chien-kuo
Nakamura, Royden
Tokuuke, Terrance Katsuki
Tseng, James H. W.
Yoshimura, Michael Akira

San Marcos
Hwang, Nen-chen Richard
Kang, Byung I.
Kang, Eun Chul
Nguyen, Chuong Van

San Marino
Ko, Cheng Chia Charles
Wong, Kenneth P.

San Mateo
Aoyama, Calvin Takeo
Chin, Charlie William David
Ching, Joseph Yu Nun
Hsu, Albert Yutien
Tanouye, Mark Allen

San Pedro
Arikawa, Norman

San Rafael
Lee, Robert

San Ramon
Hironaka, Steve
Parikh, Rupesh N.
Tam, Eric Tak-Keung

Santa Ana
Cheng, Nancy C.
Hsia, Yukun
Kang, James Jyh-Huei
Shinsato, Francis G.
Tran, Nhut Van
Wang, Hai-Tao
Wong, Maywood

Santa Barbara
Chen, Chi-yun
Hauh, Paul-Thomas B.
Hsu, Immanuel C. Y.
Hu, Daniel Ching
Jammalamadaka, Sreenivasa Rao
Li, Charles N.
Lim, Shirley Geok-Lin
Narayanamurti, Venkatesh
Oka, Christine Kazuko
Wong, Raymond Y.
Yuh, Jai K.

Santa Clara
Chan, Marsha J.
Cheng, Kenneth
De, Suranjan

Feng, Guofu Jeff
Fugita, Stephen Susumu
Han, Anna M.
Li, Qiang
Ma, Alan King-Yan
Ng, Patrick
Nguyen, Luu Thanh
Rao, Kameswara Kolla
Rhee, Young Eun
Tseng, Huan-Chi Chris
Tu, Samson W.
Yiu, Pao On

Santa Cruz
Chang, Peter Asha, Jr.
Fukurai, Hiroshi
Houston, Jeanne Wakatsuki
Kimura, Donna Junko
Sugano, Katsuhito
Takagi, Dana Y.
Wang, Howard H.
Wei, Wei
Wong, Mel

Santa Monica
Aoki, Guy Miki
Chan, Edwin Y.
Chang, Howard F.
Chow, Brian Gee-Yin
Chu, Julia Nee
Fukuhara, Henry
Fukuyama, Francis
Houston, Velina Hasu
Ito, Henry M.
Johnston, George Toshio
Lei, Shau-Ping
Tran, Tuan Anh
Wu, Sylvia Cheng
Yee, Nancy J.

Santa Rosa
Ho, Xuan Michael
Shimizu, Gordon Toshio

Saratoga
Fasang, Patrick Pad
Shimizu, Tak
Tseng, Rose Y. L.
Wong, Henry H.

Sausalito
Wong, John Lap

Sebastopol
Nakano, Mei Takaya

Selma
Hatayama, Rodney Ken

Sepulveda
Fujikawa, Denson Gen

Simi Valley
Mow, Bill

South Gate
Louie, Ruby Ling

South Pasadena
Iwataki, Miya
Lum, Albert C.
Sato, Irving Shigeo
Whang, Sukoo Jack

South San Francisco
Aono, Isamu
Esclamado, Alejandro A.
Khatwani, Mahesh
Querol Moreno, Cherie M.

Stanford
Aziz, Khalid
Bai, Taeil Albert

Chang, Gordon H.
Dev, Parvati
Feng, Jonathan Lee
Hing, Bill Ong
Lai, Tze Leung
Lau, Lawrence Juen-Yee
Okimoto, Daniel Iwao
Tsai, Stephen Wei-Lun
Tu, Samson W.
Whang, Seungjin
Wu, Ho-Mou

Stanton
Okada, Tony Manabu

Stockton
Gatdula, Francisco Ric
Hirata, Henry Minoru
Hong, Frances
Lau, Estelle Pau On
Minnick, Sylvia Sun
Nagai, Nelson Kei
Nakamura, Patricia Akemi Kosugi
Nguyen, Caroline P.
Shen, Xiao-Yan
Yamashita, Kenneth Akira

Sun Valley
Wu, George K.

Sunnyvale
Araki, Minoru S.
Chan, Marsha J.
Fan, Chien
Kong, Eric Siu-Wai
Kung, Alice How Kuen
Lee, Lester Hsin-Pei
Singh, Prithipal

Sylmar
Fujimoto, Jack

Thousand Oaks
Chattopadhyay, Kallol
Hsu, Robert Ying
Shahzad, Farhat

Torrance
Chang, Juang-Chi
Fu, Paul Chung, Jr.
Hata, Nadine Ishitani
Hoshi, Mineo
Hsieh, Brian
Huang, Chaofu
Kiriyama, Iku
Kwon, Jeffrey Young
Lin, James Y.
Louie, James Sam
Malhotra, Vijay K.
Matsumoto, Ryujiro
Nakano, George
Nojima, Darren F.
Subramanya, Shiva
Tanaka, Kouichi Robert
Wong, Tom
Wong, Wendell P.
Yu, Kar Yuk

Trabuco Canyon
Li, Chia-Chuan

Twin Peaks
Chan, Mason C.

Ukiah
Louie, George Chang

Vallejo
Marasigan, Rogelio U.
Villanueva, Chris

Valley Center
Lau, Gilbert Minjun

Van Nuys
Shih, John Chau
Takei, Richard
Uyematsu, Amy

Venice
Cheng, Fu-Ding

Ventura
Liu, Louis F.

Vernon
Tiangco, Eddie Eugenio

Victorville
Chang, Henry C.

Walnut
Sato, Frederick Akira
Tan, Colleen Woo

Walnut Creek
Au, Tung
Lee, Chi-Hang
Maedjaja, Daniel

Watsonville
Murakami, Pamela S.

West Covina
Liu, Hanjun
Miyakawa, Edward T.
Shah, Mayank H.
Tiangco, Eddie Eugenio

Westminster
Anand, A. Angela
Lam, Tony

Whittier
Hsia, Yuchuek
Kaneko, Ryoji Lloyd
Mohan, Chandra

Wilmington
Mukai, Yoshiko

Winnetka
Varma, Rakesh

Woodland
Singh, Sharon

Woodland Hills
Lam, Leo Kongsui
Law, H. David

Yorba Linda
Chen, Tai
Ikuta, Takatoshi
Wang, John Chiang

COLORADO

Aspen
Aoyama, Yasutaka Barron

Aurora
Ahn, Steve Fitzgerald
Pham, Henry Tuoc Van

Blanca
Hayashida, Charley Taketoshi

Boulder
Chan, Suitak Steve
Chow, Chuen-Yen
Datta, Subhendu K.
Hirabayashi, Lane Ryo

Kashiwa, Hank Charles
Koh, Kilsan
Kompala, Dhinakar S.
Lee, Byung-Joo
Low, Boon-Chye
Ma, Mark T.
Mahajan, Roop L.
Mahanthappa, Kalyana T.
Pak, Ronald Yu-Sang
Wei, William

Colorado Springs
Chen, Di
Fujimura, Robert Kiyoshi
Gupta, Rajiv Kumar
Lee, Gus Chien-Sun
Patel, Jay M.

Denver
Abo, Ronald K.
Chan, Laurence Kwong-Fai
Chang, Jack H. T.
Chen, Alan Keith
Cho, Frank Fulai
Cho, Kang Rae
Choi, Soonok
Chugh, Ashok Kumar
Fang, Louis Li-Yeh
Goto, Leo K.
Hennessy, Sumiko Tanaka
Kao, Yasuko W.
Kubota, Gerald K.
Kulkarni, Kishore G.
Mitamura, Ron W.
Nakayama, Harvey Kiyoshi
Poc, Sorya
Pouw, Stanley Siong-In
Siddiqui, Aleem Abdul
Takeda, Yasuhiko
Vovan, Ba
Yang, Chih Ted
Yu, Peter Tat-kong

Englewood
Kuo, Feng Yang Kuo
Wong, Earl Gar, Jr.
Yien, Jean May

Fort Collins
Chiu, Shean-Tsong
Ozawa, Terutomo
Tsai, Theodore F.
Woody, A-Young Moon

Golden
Chung, Jin Soo
Fujimoto, Robert I.
Jha, Mahesh Chandra
Sakagawa, Richard Masaru

Greeley
Dong, John W.

Lakewood
Chandramouli, S.
Chugh, Ashok Kumar
Ohtake, Takeshi
Yang, In Che
Yang, Susan Y.

Louisville
Lee, Byung-Joo

Pueblo
Cheng, Joseph Kwang-Chao
Mo, Suchoon
Shah, Abhay

Sedalia
Iwata, Paul Yoshio

US Air Force Academy
Dhillon, Joginder Singh

Wheat Ridge
Ng, Rita Mei-Ching

Windsor
Dominh, Thap

CONNECTICUT

Ansonia
Zhang, Wenxian

Branford
Shankar, Srinivasan

Bridgeport
Chang, Craig

Cheshire
Arif, Shoaib
Wong, James H.

Danbury
Akkapeddi, Prasad Rao
Chen, Chin
Fong, Jack Sun-Chik

Darien
Lim, Ralph Wei Hsiong

East Hartford
Lai, Jai-Lue Leon
Tanaka, Richard I.

East Lyme
Huang, Liang Hsiung

Fairfield
Tong, Lik Kuen
Wu, Wei-ping

Farmington
Nanda, Ravindra

Glastonbury
Lai, Jai-Lue Leon

Greenwich
Wong, John Bullitt

Groton
Huang, Liang Hsiung
Kiron, Ravi
Wang, Tixiang

Hartford
Chaturvedi, Rama Kant

Middletown
Rajasekhar, Amar

New Britain
Kim, Ki Hoon

New Canaan
Peii, Ahmad Osni

New Haven
Chua, Amy Lynn
Hsu, Yu Chu
Ikeda, Naomi Ruth
Kim, Kathleen M.
Lee, K. J.
Ma, Tso-Ping
Oh, Tae Hee
Rajendran, Vazhaikkurichi M.
Sreenivasan, Katepalli Raju
Wang, Shaoguang
Wei, Kuo-Yen
Yu, Winnie Y.
Zhang, Wenxian

New London
Ching, Stanton Sakae Hong Yat

Newington
Ng, Vincent W.
Patel, Bhupen N.

North Haven
Hsu, Yu Chu

Norwalk
Chang, Nelson

Old Saybrook
Kiron, Ravi

Orange
Luh, Yuhshi
Sabnis, Suman Trimbak

Redding
Shah, Mirza Mohammed

Ridgefield
Liu, Qing-Huo
Ramakrishnan, Terizhandur S.
Sen, Pabitra Narayan

Shelton
Singh, Ajaib

South Norwalk
Patel, Kishor N.

Southbury
Syed, Karamat A.

Stamford
Abraham, Thomas
Chien, Gary K.
Gupta, Dharam V.
Hwa, Jesse Chia-Hsi
Mayell, Jaspal Singh
Pai, Venkatrao K.
Patel, Bharat R.
Sood, Ravinder Singh

Storrs
Ghosh, Chinmoy
Hahn, Yukap
Kim, Soon-Kyu
San Juan, E.
Tanaka, John

Storrs Mansfield
Cheo, Peter K.
Kim, Ilpyong J.
Lee, Tsoung-Chao
Omori, Yoshiaki
Ting, T. C.
Yang, Tsu-Ju

Trumbull
Chang, Robert C.
Vaidya, Kirit Rameshchandra

West Hartford
Vohra, Ranbir

West Haven
Hsiung, Gueh Djen
Sharma, Ramesh

Willimantic
Fu, Tina C.

Woodbridge
Hasegawa, Jack Koichi

DELAWARE

Centreville
Dwivedy, Ramesh Chandra

Dover
Ho, Dennis
Hu, Chao Hsiung
Sheth, Kishor C.

Hockessin
Kwok, Wo Kong
Singh, Gurdial
Uy, William C.

New Castle
Iqbal, S. Mohammed

Newark
Advani, Suresh Gopaldas
Borgaonkar, Digamber Shankarrao
Cheng, Alexander H-D.
Chou, Tsu-Wei
Dwivedy, Ramesh Chandra
Huang, Chin-pao
Ih, Charles Chung-Sen
Jain, Mahendra K.
Kikuchi, Shinya
Kobayashi, Nobuhisa
Lam, Gilbert Nim-Car
Leung, Chung-Ngoc
Quon, Check Yuen
Wang, Margaret K.
Woo, S. B.
Yan, Xiao-Hai

Rockland
Myoda, Toshio Timothy

Wilmington
Bahal, Surendra Mohan
Chen, Harry W.
Chen, Jyh-Hong Eric
Chu, Terence
Hsiao, Benjamin S.
Nair, K. M.
Patel, Jitendra B
Tam, Sang William
Tong, Douglas L.
Un, Howard Ho-Wei
Uy, William C.
Wu, Dan Qing
Yamamoto, Y. Stephen

DISTRICT OF COLUMBIA

Washington
Aggarwal, Ishwar D.
Ahluwalia, Balwant S.
Ahn, Jaehoon
Akaka, Daniel Kahikina
Allen, Susan Au
Asano, Izumi
Bagasao, Paula Y.
Banik, Sambhu Nath
Benavides, Vida
Bhagat, Nazir A.
Blaz, Ben
Caoile, Gloria T.
Chan, Arthur H.
Chan, Tsze Hau
Chan, Wai-Yee
Chang, Amy Lee
Chang, Michael
Chen, John Shaoming
Chen, Pamela Ki Mai
Cheong, Fiona
Cherian, Joy
Chiang, Asuntha Maria Ming-Yee
Chiang, Erick
Chiang, Sie Ling
Chin, Cecilia Hui-hsin
Chin, Michelle Lorraine
Chin, Steven Han-Hoy
Ching, Theodora Lam
Chiu, Lue-Yung Chow
Choi, Songsu
Chopra, Joginder
Chow, Barbara A.
Chu, David S. C.
Chu, Patricia Pei-chang
Chung, David Yih
Chung, Ed Baik
Cua, Antonio S.
Dinh, Thuy Tu Bich
Efurd, Laura L.
Faleomavaega, Eni Faauaa Hunkin, Jr.
Feng, Theo-dric
Finucane, Matthew H.
Fugh, John L.
Gandhi, Natwar Mohan
Garg, Rajinder P.
Gawande, Atul A.
Gramm, Wendy Lee
Gupta, Om Prakash
Gupta, Raj Kumar
Haley, Maria Luisa Mabilangan
Han, In-Sop
Haque, M. Shamsul
Hayashi, Dennis Wayne
Hayashi, Fumihiko
Hernandez, Tomas C.
Ho, Daniel F.
Ho-González, William
Hom, Kathleen B.
Hou, William Chen-Nan
Hsu, Evelyn
Ihm, Tysun
Inouye, Daniel K.
Isaki, Cary T.
Ishaq, Ashfaq M.
Jiang, Xixiang
Jung, Louise Rebecca
Kawata, Paul Akio
Kim, Jay C.
Konoshima, Joji
Kwok, Daphne
Lam, Fat C.
Lê, Hy Xuân
Le, Xuan Khoa
Lee, Arthur Richard
Lee, Che-Fu
Lee, Jeff S.
Lew, Susie Q.
Lin, Liang-Shiou
Liu, Alfred H.
Liu, Eric P.
Liu, Lin Chun
Liu, Su-Feng
Liu, Wei-Ying
Loo, Ti Li
Lu, David Yun-Chen
Maeda, Sharon
Mao, Ho-Kwang
Marshall, Thurgood, Jr.
Marumoto, William Hideo
Mathur, Krishan D.
Matsui, Doris Kazue Okada
Matsui, Robert Takeo
Mehta, Amarjit
Mineta, Norman Yoshio
Mink, Patsy Takemoto
Misra, Prabhakar
Moy, Edmund
Nakashima, Tom Vincent
Nash, Philip Tajitsu
Natividad, Irene
Nayak, Tapan Kumar
Ngai, Kia Ling

Nguyen, Charles C.
Nguyen, Xe V.
Ninomiya, Calvin
Nishimura, Miwa
Nishioka, David Jitsuo
Noga, Al
Okabe, Hideo
Pandya, Amit Anant
Pang, Keum Y.
Parikh, Kirit Girishchandra
Park, Ted S.
Pindiprolu, Manjula
Rai, Arti K.
Rai, Vijai Narain
Ramachandran, Nadaraja
Rao, Potarazu Krishna
Rao, Venigalla Basaveswara
Sagawa, Shirley Sachi
Sayala, Chhaya
Seto, Robert Mahealani Ming
Shah, Bhupendra P.
Shah, Dhiren Bhawanji
Shen, I-Yao
Shih, Arnold Shang-Teh
Sibal, Nicolas Villadolid
Singpurwalla, Nozer Darabsha
Sison, Fredilyn
Sreevalsan, Thazepadath
Sugawara, Sandra Lee
Sundaresan, Gloria Marquez
Sung, Lawrence M.
Suzuki, Michio
Takakoshi, William K.
Trieu, Phong L.
Tsai, Frank Y.
Tsui, Pauline Woo
Tsukamoto, Jack Toru
Uemoto, Karen
Underwood, Robert Anacletus
Van, Thanhtan C.
Verma, Ajay
Wada, Debra Sadako
Wang, Charles Pei
Wang, George Hung-Kai
Wang, Yan
Wong, Alfred
Wong, Harry Yuen Chee
Wong, Jacqueline Jeanne
Wong, Kin Fai
Woo, Chung S. H.
Woo, Michael T.
Wu, Angela Yuen
Wu, Jeremy S.
Yang, John Eric
Yao, Dennis Alden
Yee, Melinda C.
Yen, Nai-Chyuan
Yim, Soo Jung
Yoon, Steven Ilsang
Yoshimura, Yoshiko
Young, Peter R.
Yu, Jia-Huey

FLORIDA

Boca Raton
Chow, Wen Lung
Han, Chingping Jim
Hung, Chao-Shun
Su, Tsung-chow Joe
Wu, Jie

Bradenton
Haramaki, Chiko

Canal Point
Tai, Peter Y. P.

Clearwater
Lee, Ming T.

Coral Gables
Fung, Kee-Ying
Lian, Maria Z. N.
Liu, Peter Chi-Wah
Sharma, Arun
Wu, Ying-Chan Fred
Yeh, Billy Kuo-Jiun
Young, Tzay Y.

Daytona Beach
Gupta, Tej R.

Deerfield Beach
Wang, Gary S. H.

Fort Lauderdale
Liou, K. T.
Toyota, Michael Douglas
Tsai, James H.

Fort Meade
Fujioka, Takashi

Fort Myers
Virji, Nazneen

Gainesville
Chakravarthy, Upendranath Sharma
Chang, Myron N.
Chang, Weilin P.
Chen, Chao Ling
Fu, LiMin
Gupta, Santosh
Gupta, Virendra K.
Hsu, Chen-Chi
Huang, Shih-Wen
Iwata, Brian A.
Lee, Chung-Yee
Li, Sheng S.
Mahajan, Jayashree
Mehta, Jawahar L.
Miyamoto, Michael Masao
Moudgil, Brij Mohan
Sah, Chih-Tang
Shah, Dinesh Ochhavlal
Sun, Chang-Tsan
Suzuki, Howard Kazuro
Wu, Jin Zhong
Yin, George Kuo-Ming

Jacksonville
Lee, Chew-Lean
Lee, Ker-Fong

Lakeland
Choe, Sun Tok

Lauderhill
Pande, Gyan Shanker
Wong, George

Melbourne
Alota, Ruben Villaruel
Kung, Jeffrey

Miami
Aoki, Rocky
Chang, Chun-Hao
Lee, Marietta Y. W. T.
Lian, Eric Chun-Yet
Liu, Tally C.
Roy, Dev Kumar
Santhanam, Radhika
Sawhney, Gurjeet Singh
Shaikh, Saeed Ahmad
Siu, Nancy
Wang, Ton-Lo
Wong, Albert
Wong, Kau Fui
Yen, Kang Kenneth

Naples
Wei, Chao Hui

New Port Richey
Patel, Jayanti R.

North Miami
Simunek, Linda A.

Orlando
Asuncion, Gary Raymond Espejo
Desai, Vimal H.
Foshee, Thuong Nguyen
Huang, William H.
Kuo, Shiou-San
Lee, Byung-Moon
Sabharwal, Kulbir
Shah, Mubarak Ali
Ting, Robert Yen-Ying

Panama City
Trinh, Nam Ky

Pembroke Pines
Toyota, Michael Douglas

Pensacola
Chang, Clifford Wah Jun
Li, Kuiyuan

Pompano Beach
Kapoor, Harish K.

Sarasota
Mahadevan, Kumar
Vedamuthu, Ebenezer Rajkumar

St. Petersburg
Lai, Patrick Kinglun
Shon, Kyo Kwa
Tran, Dorothy N.

Tallahassee
Kim, HeeMin
Krishnamurti, T. N.
Lee, Henry Joung
Lin, Pi-Erh
Shih, Chiang
Tam, Christopher Kwong-Wah
Wang, Ben

Tampa
Chen, Tsong-Ming
Choksi, Jayendra C.
Kulkarni, Arun P.
Liang, Diana F.
Lim, Daniel V.
Mukherjea, Arunava
Rao, Papineni S.

Tarpon Springs
Patel, Jayanti R.

Temple Terrace
Dan, Phan Quang

Winter Park
Chow, Balance Tin-Ping
Kuo, Shiou-San

Winter Springs
Park, Hoon
Wang, K. P.

GEORGIA

Albany
Chang, Edward C.

Alpharetta
Chang, Chin Hao

Americus
Gupta, Arun Premchand

Athens
Chu, Chung Kwang
Jun, Hung Won
Lu, Donghao Robert
Srivastava, Prakash Narain
Yen, William Mao-Shung

Atlanta
Agrawal, Pradeep K.
An, Nack Young
Chen, Bessie B.
Chen, David W.
Chen, Ye-Hwa
Cheung, Shun Yan
Chou, Mei-Yin
Chu, Kong
Ghim, Thad T.
Han, Grace Yang
Higa, Kunihiko
Hong, Shuguang
Hsu, Frank H.
Huang, Wei-Sung Wilson
Huynh, Boi-Hanh
Kabir, Abulfazal M. Fazle
Kadaba, Prasanna Venkatarama
Kale, Jayant R.
Kim, Chulwan
Kim, Suzy Linda
Ku, David Nelson
Lee, Kok-Meng
Lee, Susan H.
Liang, Steven Yuehsan
Murty, Komanduri Srinivasa
Narasimhan, Sridhar
Panlilio, Adelisa Lorna
Park, Byungwoo
Parthasarathy, Sampath
Shah, Nagambal Deepak
Ueng, Charles En-Shiuh
Woo, Robert Ken, Jr.
Wu, De Ting

Augusta
Gulati, Adarsh Kumar
Huang, Denis K.
Joe, Clarence
Mahesh, Virendra Bhushan
Shaikh, Abdul Hamid

Carrollton
Barron, Purificacion C.
Hahn, Hwa Suk
Sinha, Uday K.

Columbus
Chang, David W.

Covington
Gupta, Rakesh Kumar

Decatur
Chin, Susan Ho
Luong, Son N.
Vanchiasong, Siong Koua

Doraville
Patel, Sanjay Vrajlal

Fort Valley
Gupta, Ratanlal N.

Macon
Kapadia, Bharat S.
Shih, Ko-Ming

Marietta
Chen, Ming
Jain, Arun K.
Liang, Steven Yuehsan
Sumartojo, Jojok

Martinez
Iyer, Prem Shankar

Norcross
Lee, Kok-Meng
Nanda, Vir A.
Patel, Bhulabhai C.
Shankar, Subramonian

Roswell
Lau, Jark C.

Savannah
Lee, Richard Fayao
Liu, Ying
Raut, Kamalakar Balkrishna
Singh, Harpal

Smyrna
Kadaba, Prasanna Venkatarama

Statesboro
Li, Ming

Stone Mountain
Chen, David W.

Tucker
Woo, Robert Ken, Jr.

HAWAII

Aiea
Kawaguchi, Stanley Kenji

Ewa Beach
Ling, Christine N.
Yee, Stanley C.

Hilo
Chan, Harvey Thomas, Jr.
Chan, John G.
Chang, Deanna BauKung
Chang, Jerry Leslie
Fujii, Jack Koji
Higashi, Kerwin Masuto
Ito, Philip Jitsuo
Kimura, Gwen C.
Kimura, Kongo
Ko, Wen-hsiung
Kohara, David Noboru
Miyamoto, Wayne Akira
Sugano, Miyoko
Wang, James C. F.

Honokaa
Mahilum, Benjamin C.

Honolulu
Cayetano, Benjamin J.
Chang, Anthony K. U.
Chang, Jerry Leslie
Chang, Mervin Henry
Chang, Sen-dou
Chen, Yi-Leng
Cheng, Ping
Ching, Gale Lin Fong
Chiu, Arthur Nang Lick
Chou, James C. S.
Choy, Herbert Y. C.
Chu, Victor Fu Hua
Chun, Joe Y. F.
Chung, Chin Sik
Chung, Hyun S.
Dayao, Firmo Salvador
Doi, Stanley T.
Doo, Leigh-Wai
Fan, Carol C.
Fok, Agnes Kwan
Fok, Yu-Si
Fong, Bernard Wah Doung
Fong, Harold Michael

Fong, Hiram Leong
Go, Mateo Lian Poa
Goto, Unoji
Hara-Nielsen, Sylvia Ann
Hihara, Lloyd Hiromi
Ho, Edwin Soon Hee
Ho, Reginald C. S.
Hokama, Yoshitsugi
Hu, Joseph Kai Ming
Ing, Malcolm Ross
Ishida, Dianne N.
Iwase, Randall Y.
Iwata, Jerry T.
Izumigawa, Wallace Minoru
Joe, Karen Ann
Kam, Thomas K. Y.
Kawaguchi, Stanley Kenji
Kawashima, Edith T.
Khan, Mohammad Asad
Kim, Donald Chang Won
Kim, Donna Mercado
Kim, Karl Eujung
Kim, Robert
Kim, Uichol
Kobayashi, Bertrand
Koga, Yoshi Tanji
Koide, Frank Takayuki
Kono, Hideto
Kudo, Eigo H.
Kuroda, Yasumasa
Kwock, Francis T. W.
Kwok, Daniel W. Y.
Kwok, Reginald Yin-Wang
Laskar, Devi Sen
Lau, Bennett M. K.
Lau, Jenni Meili
Lee, Clarence Kim Mun
Lee, Yeu-Tsu Margaret
Leong, Jack Y. H.
Leung, Louis W.
Leung, PingSun
Li, Bichuan
Liao, Shun-Kwung
Lin, Yu-Chong
Liu, Juanita Ching
Liu, Leighton Kam Fat
Loo, Cyrus W.
Lum, Jean L. J.
Mak, James
Martin, Abraham Nguyen
Matsuda, Fujio
Matsumoto, Randall Itsumi
Matsuo, Paul T.
Mirikitani, Andy
Moon, Ronald Tae-yang
Morita, John Takami
Mukai, Francis Ken
Nakamura, Karen Tsuneko
Nakamura, Michael S.
Nakasato, George
Nakatani, Henry Masatoshi
Nip, Wai-Kit
Nishimura, Wendy Natsue
Nishina, Clifford M.
Nomura, Jerry Kazuto
Odo, Blair M. T.
Omori, Alvin I.
Oshiro, Kathleen F.
Ota, Isaac I.
Pai, Gregory Gi Yong
Pakvasa, Sandip
Ramil, Mario R.
Sagawa, Yoneo
Saito, Walter Masao
Sakai, Victoria K.
Sasaki, Raymond Toshiaki, Jr.
Sharma, Santosh Devraj
Shim, Walton Kenn Tsung
Sinco, Victor
Sugihara, Jared Genji
Suh, Dae-Sook
Sun, Samuel Sai-Ming
Tahara, Mildred Machiko

Taira, Masa Morioka
Takasaki, Richard Sadaji
Takumi, Roy M.
Tan, S. Y.
Tanabe, George Joji, Jr.
Tang, Chung-Shih
Toda, Harold Keiji
Toyama, Jean Yamasaki
Tuan, San Fu
Waihee, John David
Wang, Bin
Wang, Jaw-Kai
Watumull, Indru
Whang, Robert
Wong, Alvin C. P.
Wong, Bradley D.
Wong, Eugene G. C.
Wong, Henry L.
Wong, Terry Chen Yi
Wong, Vernon D. B.
Wong, William K. C.
Woo, Vernon Ying-Tsai
Yamada, Kay Matayoshi
Yamaga, Chester Kiyoshi
Yamamoto, Eric K.
Yamamoto, John Hiroshi
Yamasaki, Mitch
Yamashita, Francis Isami
Yamashita, Pearl Nobuko
Yang, David C.
Yee, Alfred Alphonse
Yonamine, Henry Kiyoshi
Yoshida, Alan K.
Yoshimoto, Watson Toshinori
Young, Jacqueline Eurn Hai
Yuen, Paul C.
Zia, Hoyt Hanson

Kahului
Sakamoto, Clyde Mitsuru

Kailua
Tom, Melvin Gee Lim

Kalaheo
Nakashima, Mitsugi

Kaneohe
Ching, Harvey Cho Wing
Furukawa, Theodore Paul
Lim, Chhorn E.
Shishido, Calvin M.

Laie
Furuto, Sharlene Bernice Choy Lin
Han, Sherman Hsiao-min

Lihue
Kikuchi, William Kenji
Lai, Waihang
Nakamura, Russell Koichi

Pearl City
Higa, Ross Rikio
Kajiwara, Kenneth Kyo
Kaya, Douglas Hifuto, Jr.
Shimokihara, Stanley Shigeo
Takayama, Gregg
Uchida, Richard Noboru
Yee, Stanley C.

Wailuku
Ing, Lawrence N. C.
Kwon, Ronald Chi-Oh
Sato, Tommy M.
Ueoka, Meyer Masato

Waipahu
Tsuha, Wallace Koichi

IDAHO

Idaho Falls
Chan, Mei-Mei
Oh, Chang H.
Sato, Walter N.

Lewiston
Fong, Kai Meng

Moscow
Chang, Kang-Tsung

Pocatello
Chang, Jane Yueh
Inouye, Richard Saburo
Rao, Bhamidipaty Kameswara
Yokota, Ronnie Yoshiteru

ILLINOIS

Abbott Park
Chu, Daniel Tim-Wo
Kim, Ki Hwan
Lee, Jang Yun
Tanaka, S. Ken

Addison
Kato, Theodore Toshihiko
Lakshman, Govind

Antioch
Yee, Allen Y.

Argonne
Chang, Yoon Il
Chen, Shoei-sheng
Inokuti, Mitio
Kimura, Mineo
Kumar, Romesh
Marr, William Wei-Yi
Teng, Lee Chang-Li

Arlington Heights
Patel, Deepak M.
Teraji, Thomas Shuichi

Barrington
Tomomatsu, Hideo

Bartlett
Desai, Ashok Govindji

Batavia
Raja, Rajendran
Yoh, John K.

Bellwood
Thakore, Kirit Jamiyatram

Bolingbrook
Chandran, Ravi

Brookfield
Lee, Albert W.

Buffalo Grove
Gupta, Kamla P.

Burr Ridge
Pai, Sadanand V.

Carbondale
Banerjee, Chandra Madhab
Chen, Juh Wah
Chu, Tsuchin Philip
Desai, Uday
Hoshiko, Michael
Kim, Alan Hyun-Oak
Mathur, Ike
Rai, Arun

Sharma, Subhash C.
Takayama, Akira

Champaign
Chew, Weng Cho
Chou, Chen-Lin
Iyer, Ravishankar Krishnan
Kapoor, Shiv G.
Kim, Michael Kyong-il
Liu, Ben Shaw-Ching
Park, Hun Young
Tang, Ming-Je

Charleston
Dao, Minh Quang
Hsu, Nai-chao
Liu, Ping

Chicago
Abe, Makoto
Agarwal, Gyan Chand
Baldonado, Ardelina Albano
Belbis, Manuel Emuslan
Bhattacharya, Pradeep Kumar
Bhatti, Rashid A.
Cabana, Veneracion Garganta
Cha, Soyoung Stephen
Chan, Kawei
Chandran, Satish Raman
Chandrasekhar, Subrahmanyan
Chang, Carl Kochao
Chen, Chong-Tong
Chen, Donald S.
Chen, Jackson W.
Chen, Wai-Kai
Chen, Xiangming
Chin, William Nigel
Cho, Wonhwa
Choi, Jin Wook
Choi, Paul Lee
Chun, Shinae
Chung, Paul Myungha
Chung, Simon Lam-Ying
Dhaliwal, Amrik Singh
Fong, Harry H. S.
Fujimoto, James Randall
Gandhi, Vikram H.
Gangwal, Rakesh
Gupta, Rajat Kumar
Harano, Ross Masao
Hashimoto, Steven George
Hayashi, James Akira
Hayashi, William Yasuo
Hayashida, Frank
Hong, Sung Ok
Hori, Yutorio Claude
Hsieh, Cynthia C.
Iqbal, Zafar
Iyer, Ananth. V.
Kang, Shin T.
Khan, Mohammed Abdul Quddus
Kim, Byung Suk
Kim, Chung-Sook Charlotte
Kim, Jong Koo
Kitahata, Stacy Dee
Ko, Steven W.
Koga, Mary H.
Kumar, Sudhir
Kuo, Ken Nan
Lam, Chow-Shing
Lau, Yvonne M.
Lazo, Douglas T.
Lee, Chung
Lee, Nan-Nan
Lee, Suk Hun
Leighton, Veronica V.
Liao, Shutsung
Lin, Chin-Chu
Lin, James Chih-I
Liu, Ben Chieh
Ma, Tai-Loi
Ma, Yan

Mehta, Rajendra G.
Mian, Waqar Saeed
Murad, Sohail
Naito, Michael K.
Najita, Tetsuo
Narahashi, Toshio
Nayyar, Sarv P.
Nguyen, Bao Gia
O, San Luong
Okita, Dwight Holden
Ozaki, Yoji
Papasani, Subbaiah Venkata
Park, Chung I.
Patel, Hiren S.
Pillay, Mullayil K. G.
Prasad, Rameshwar
Punwani, Dharam Vir
Rajan, Frederick E. N.
Rajan, Raghuram Govind
Reyes, Hernan M.
Rhim, Aesop
Rikhiraj, Sadhu Singh
Saxena, Satish Chandra
Sen, Ashish Kumar
Song, John S.
Song, Shin-Min
Soni, Narendra
Soo, Charlie H.
Sood, Mohan K.
Taura, Richard Bill
Thadhani, Kaloo C.
Ting, Thomas Chi Tsai
Tom, Ping
Tran, Loi Huu
Tripathi, Ramesh Chandra
Tripathi, Satish Chandra
Tsai, Jeffrey J. P.
Tsukuno, Paul
Tun, Harry T.
Vu, Joseph
Whang, Un-Young
Wong, Kenneth K.
Wong, Paul Wing Kon
Wu, Anna Fang
Yamashiroya, Herbert Mitsugi
Yang, Nien-chu C.
Yau, Stephen Shing-Toung
Yoon, Myung-Ho
Yoshida, Ray Kakuo
Yoshino, William
Yu, Clement Tak
Yu, Linda

Chicago Heights
Chow, Edmund Chun-Ying

Danville
Mehta, Bharat V.
Prabhudesai, Mukund M.

Darien
Kumar, Sudhir
Wasan, Darsh T.
Yang, Shi-tien

De Kalb
Das, Man Singh
Hong, Yoopyo
Huang, Samuel T.
Kuo, Yih-Wen
Lin, Chhiu-Tsu
Ling, Hsin Yi
Song, Xueshu

Des Plaines
Kim, Anna Charr
Li, Norman N.
Nguyen, Ngoc-Diep Thi
Omura, Mark Christopher

Downers Grove
Atoji, Masao
Moy, Donald

Srinivasan, Thiru R.
Su, Cheh-Jen

Edwardsville
Ho, Chung-Wu
Lee, Heungsoon Felix
Youn, Luis Tai-Oh

Elgin
Agrawal, Brijmohan
Nandkumar, Nuggehalli Balmukund

Elizabeth
Sharma, Brij Lal

Elk Grove Village
Kalra, Bhupinder Singh
Wong, Ovid K.

Elmhurst
Eng, Ana Mar

Evanston
Barot, Navnit Manilal
Chang, Darwin
Chang, Sookyung
Cheng, Herbert S.
Chiou, Wen-An
Chung, Yip-Wah
Dutta, Pulak
Kim, Anna Charr
Kim, Chang Kyu
Kung, Harold H.
Lee, Der-Tsai
Liu, Wing Kam
Mah, Richard Sze Hao
Meshii, Masahiro
Miura, Ken-ichi
Mura, Toshio
Takahashi, Joseph S.
Tamhane, Ajit C.
Wang, Sylvia
Wu, Tai Te

Flossmoor
Chandran, Satish Raman

Frankfort
Mothkur, Sridhar Rao

Glen Ellyn
Agnihotri, Newal K.
Rhee, Susan Byungsook

Glencoe
Sasahara, Arthur Asao

Glendale Heights
Fajardo, Ben
Patel, Vipin A.

Glenview
Lin, Juiyuan William

Granite City
Chen, William Hok-Nin
Kato, Masatoshi

Grayslake
Kim, Helen

Highland
Myint, Than Htun

Highland Park
Meshii, Masahiro

Hinsdale
Liu, Yung Y.
Teng, Lee Chang-Li

Hoffman Estates
Barot, Navnit Manilal
Mirchandani, Arjun Sobhraj

Homewood
Malik, Zafar A.
Pai, K. Vasanth

Huntley
Hayakawa, Noboru

Itasca
Moy, Donald
Patel, Jayant P.

Jacksonville
Tong, Ts'ing H.

Joliet
Desai, Vijay
Shah, Pravin M.
Thiruvathukal, Kris V.

La Grange
Inokuti, Mitio

Lake Bluff
Kim, Helen

Lake Forest
Tung, John

Libertyville
Li, Conan K. N.
Mehta, Ujjwal J.
Woo, Lecon

Lisle
Liu, Ben Chieh

Lockport
Shah, Shirish

Macomb
Chu, Felix T.
Fang, Ming M.
Lee, Jai Hyon
Lee, Tzesan David
Made Gowda, Netkal M.
Park, Siyoung
Rao, Vaman
Ting, Lee Hsia

Maywood
Louie, Eric K.

Mc Gaw Park
Udani, Kanak H.

Melrose Park
Pai, Sadanand V.
Rao, Gopal Subba

Morton Grove
Hong, Lily Toy
Kim, Yong Bok

Naperville
Desai, Vikram J.
Jindal, Om P.
Kumar, Romesh
Punwani, Dharam Vir
Sato, Paul Toshio
Sethi, Naresh Kumar
Singh, Madan Mohan

Niles
Gandhi, Mukesh P.
Kalra, Bhupinder Singh

Normal
Chang, Sukjeong J.
Chitgopekar, Sharad S.

Jayaswal, Raoheshyam K.
Lim, Billy Lee

North Chicago
Chang, Kwang-Poo
Singh, Sant P.
Sze, Paul Y.

Northbrook
Noojibail, Eshwar
Sato, Paul Toshio
Yoon, Myung-Ho

Oak Brook
Sha, William T.

Oak Park
Hayashi, William Yasuo
Mehrotra, Prem N.
Shima, John David

Palatine
Uchimoto, Dennis D.

Park Ridge
Choi, Sung Sook

Peoria
Andrada, Wilmer Vigilia
Ho, Andrew Kong-Sun
Liu, Jiang Bo
Safdari, Yahya Bhai
Wu, Ying Victor
Yang, Emiko

Plainfield
Chakrabarti, Subrata Kumar

Quincy
Okamoto, Kenneth Wayne

Rockford
Yu, Fu-Li

Rolling Meadows
Patel, Roger

Roselle
Ahmed, Wase U.

Rosemont
Leu, Dennis Thomas

Round Lake
Lin, Lawrence I-Kuei

Schaumburg
Bijlani, Chandur Kishinchand
Mehrotra, Prem N.
Moy, James Yee Kin
Patil, Pralhad T.

Skokie
Chang, Shi-Kuo
Hsu, Charles Fu-Jen
Saxena, Satish Chandra
Shah, Chimanlal Keshavlal
Tripathi, Satish Chandra

South Barrington
Patel, Bhagvan H.

Springfield
Lee, Tony J. F.

St. Charles
Wang, Bee-Lan Chan

Tinley Park
Anand, Rakesh

University Park
Kong, Ana C.

Wei, Anthony Yueh-shan
Wong, K. C.

Urbana
Banerjee, Prithviraj
Chang, Shau-Jin
Chang, Yia-Chung
Chao, Bei Tse
Cheryan, Munir
Govindjee
Hsui, Albert Tong-Kwan
Iyer, Ravishankar Krishnan
Kachru, Braj B.
Kapoor, Shiv G.
Kumar, Panganamala Ramana
Lo, Kwok-Yung
Lo, Yuen-Tze
Tang, Wilson Hon-chung
Tripathy, Deoki N.
Wang, Lawrence Kongpu
Yen, Ben Chie
Yu, Priscilla C.

West Chicago
Ozaki, Yoji

Westmont
Cabana, Veneracion Garganta
Cheng, David
Manankil, Norma Ronas

Wheaton
Cha, Soyoung Stephen
Desai, Suresh A.
Hsieh, Jeanette L.
Pun, Pattle Pak-Toe

Wilmette
Bhavnani, Pratap Gagumal
Chiou, Wen-An
Mura, Toshio

Wood Dale
Shah, Nitin J.

INDIANA

Angola
Kumar, Sushil
Lin, Ping-Wha

Bloomington
Azumaya, Goro
Choksy, Jamsheed Kairshasp
Gupta, Anil K.
Sha, Ji-Ping

Carmel
Ku, Wen-Chi

Columbus
Thakkar, Pravin Asharam

East Chicago
Ranade, Madhukar G.

Elkhart
Kotani, Shigeto
Kuo, Charles Chang-Yun

Evansville
Choe, Sang Tae
Khan, Walayet A.
Sharma, Ravindra Nath
Wu, Yao Hua

Fort Wayne
Chowdhury, Dipak Kumar
Shah, Nagin B.

Franklin
Ling, Yu-long

Gary
Bhattacharya, Pradeep Kumar
Gupta, Omprakash K.

Granger
Kumar, Vijay A.

Hammond
Choi, Young Dong

Highland
Kim, Bong Yohl

Indianapolis
Chen, Jie
Chen, Victor John
Daryanani, Michael
Gidda, Jaswant Singh
Han, Xianming Lance
Ho, Peter Peck Koh
Liu, Wei-Min
Ly, Kieu Kim
Matsumoto, Ken
Nagarajan, Ramakrishnan
Ng, Anastacio C.
Patel, Ramesh D.
Sato, Masahiko
Sharma, Saroj
Su, Julie Chu-chu
Vohra, Indu
Wong, David Taiwai
Yan, Sau-Chi Betty
Yee, Robert Donald
Yi, Gang
Yune, Heun Yung

Jeffersonville
Ohta, Shirley Mae

Lafayette
Sharma, Hari Chand

Logansport
Shih, Philip C.

Michigan City
Mothkur, Sridhar Rao

Mishawaka
Hagiwara, Kokichi

Muncie
Ali, Mir Masoom
Bagga, K. Jay Singh
Cheng, Chu-Yuan
Gupta, Jatinder Nath Dass
Gupta, Naim C.
Kuo, Ming-ming Shen

New Albany
Wong, Alan S.

Notre Dame
Biswas, Nripendra Nath
Chen, Houn-Gee
Garg, Umesh
Huang, Nai-Chien
Kobayashi, Francis Masao
Tripathi, Gorakh Nath Ram

Richmond
Matsui, Noriatsu

Schererville
Chen, Wayne Y.

South Bend
Chen, Linda
Doshi, Bipin N.
Garg, Umesh
Liu, Nancy Shao-Lan
Sen, Mihir

Terre Haute
Ghosh, Swapan Kumar
Liu, Karen Chia-Yu

West Lafayette
Abhyankar, Shreeram Shankar
Chang, Ching-jer
Chang, Tien-Chien
Chao, Kwang-Chu
Chen, Chin-Lin
Chen, Li-Fu
Chen, Wai Fah
Fukunaga, Keinosuke
Furuta, Otto K.
Hong, Gong-Soog
Lin, Pen-Min
Lin, Poping
Mathur, Aditya P.
Ong, Chee-Mun
Ramadhyani, Satish
Rao, Singiresu Sambasiva
Sharma, Hari Chand
Shibata, Edward Isamu
Shieh, Yuch-Ning
Shin, Yung C.
SooHoo, Leo, Jr.
Sun, Wen-Yih
Tsai, Chia-Yin
Tsao, George T.
Tse, John Yung Dong
Wang, Jin-Liang
Wu, Kingsley K.
Yang, Henry Tzu-yow
Yih, Yuehwern

IOWA

Ames
Chan, Chiu Shui
Hsu, Cathy H. C.
Lee, Dah-Yinn
Liu, Donald Jiann-Tyng
Min, K. Jo
Pak, Yong Chin
Shen, Sheldon Shih-Ta
Wong, Johnny S.
Young, Bing-Lin

Cedar Falls
Chang, James C.
Chao, Paul W. F.
Chung, Ronald Aloysius
Lew, William W.

Des Moines
Lu, Min Zhan
Ng, May-May Donna Lee
Song, Joseph M.

Dubuque
Kang, Wi Jo

Iowa City
Chan, Kai Chiu
Chandran, Krishnan Bala
Chen, Lea Der
Chiang, Chao-Kuo
Choi, Kyung Kook
Chyung, Dong Hak
Higa, Leslie Hideyasu
Kim, Chong Lim
Kim, Yong-Gwan
Lim, Ramon Khe-Siong
Min, David Ilki
Park, Joon B.
Patel, Virendra Chaturbhai
Shih, Ming-Che
Wu, Chun-Fang
Wu, Shih-Yen

Le Mars
Li, Ya

Pella
Chia, Ning
Huang, Ko-Hsing

West Des Moines
Krishna, Gopal T. K.
Shen, Sheldon Shih-Ta

KANSAS

Kansas City
Gonzalez-Pardo, Lillian
Hung, Kuen-Shan
Lee, Kyo Rak
Melookaran, Joseph
Suzuki, Tsuneo

Lawrence
Gee, Norman F.
Kuo, Joseph C.
Lan, Chuan-Tau Edward
Li, Chu-tsing
Lim, Paul Stephen
Yu, Yun-Sheng

Manhattan
Chang, Shing I.
Fung, Daniel Yee Chak
Huang, Chi-Lung Dominic
Hwang, Ching-Lai
Lee, E. Stanley
Liang, George Hsueh-Lee
Minocha, Harish C.
Muthukrishnan, Subbaratnam
Ohno, Mitsugi
Park, Jinwoo
Ranhotra, Gurbachan S.
Wong, Peter P.

Mission Hills
Lee, King Y.

Overland Park
Caoile, John Anthony
Lee, Kyo Rak
Mathiprakasam, Balakrishnan
Melookaran, Joseph

Pittsburg
Lee, Choong Yang

Prairie Village
Arakawa, Kasumi

Salina
Tran, Loc Binh

Shawnee
Patel, Anil J.

Shawnee Mission
Lee, King Y.

Wichita
Choi, In-Chan
Chopra, Dharam Vir
Giri, Jagannath
Ho, Lop-Hing
Hong, Il Sik
Jong, Mark M. T.
Liu, Ming Cheng
Mathur, Balbir Singh
Wong, John D.

KENTUCKY

Bowling Green
Hong, Ilyoo Barry
Pan, Wei-Ping

Frankfort
Lee, Dae Sung

Lexington
Bhapkar, Vasant P.
Chan, Lois Mai
Chen, Linda Li-yueh
Chung, Chen Hua
Govindarajulu, Zakkula
Li, Bing An
Liu, Keh-Fei Frank
Man, Chi-Sing
Moon, Chung-In
Subbaswamy, Kumble Ramarao
Tai, Hsin-Hsiung
Urano, Muneyasu
Wang, Shien Tsun
Wang, Yi-Tin
Wu, Ting-Wen

Louisville
Bhatnagar, Kunwar P.
Huang, Kee Chang
Huang, Weifeng
Liu, Pinghui Victor
Rangaswamy, Thangam
Tran, Long Trieu
Viswanadham, Ramamurthy K.

Murray
Cheng, Louis Tsz-Wan

Paducah
Ghosh, Bivas Kanti

Richmond
Matsuoka, Matthew S.

Russell
Choudhury, Pinak

LOUISIANA

Baton Rouge
Chen, Jianhua
Chen, Ye-Sho
Cheng, Benjamin Shujung
Hu, John Nan-Hai
Kak, Subhash Chandra
Kamo, Yoshinori
Kumar, Devendra
Liao, T. Warren
Murai, Norimoto
Pang, Su-Seng
Raman, Aravamudhan
Rau, A. Ravi Prakash
Sarker, Bhaba Ranjan
Singh, Vijay P.
Tang, Kwei
Vora, Narendra Mohanlal
Yang, Chia Hsiung

Belle Chasse
Arimura, Akira

Grambling
Agarwal, Arun Kumar
Naidu, Seetala Veeraswamy
Sharma, Parashu Ram

Gretna
Viet-Chau, Nguyen Duc

Kenner
Pandit, Grish Roy
Thakore, Killol J.

Lafayette
Chan, Chiu Yeung
Fang, Cheng-Shen
Im, Young-Ai
Kim, Jung Hwan

Rao, Spuma M.
Shang, Weijia

Lake Charles
Bose, Pratim

Metairie
Kuan, Shia Shiong
Wan, Peter J.

Monroe
Hwang, Hsin-Ginn

Natchitoches
Banerjee, Debasish
Durlabhji, Subhash
Lin, James C.

New Orleans
Agrawal, Krishna Chandra
Bhatnagar, Deepak
Bhattacharyya, Ashim Kumar
Chacko, Harsha E.
Das, Shovan
Dhurandhar, Nina R.
Im, Jin-Hyouk
Kokatnur, Mohan Gundo
Kumar, Atul
Lim, Rodney Gene
Ling, Jack Chieh-Sheng
Mui, Constance L.
Nakamoto, Tetsuo
Puri, Pratap
Radhakrishnamurthy, Bhandaru
Sharma, Bhudev
Shih, Fred F.
Subramaniam, Pramilla N.
Thakore, Killol J.
Tu, Shengru
Walia, Jasjit Singh

Ruston
Yang, Schuman Chuo

Shreveport
Lin, Binshan

Thibodaux
Yen, Steven T.

West Monroe
Chin, David

MAINE

Bar Harbor
Lim, Chong C.

Farmington
Wong, Eugene Hanlai

Orono
Cheng, Hsiang-tai

Waterville
Sasaki, Betty Gail

MARYLAND

Aberdeen Proving Ground
Cheng, Tu-chen
Shih, Tsung-Ming Anthony

Annapolis
Barve, Kumar P.
Hsin, Chen-Chung
Kiang, Robert L.
Valderrama, David Mercado
Wu, Chih

Baltimore
Chan, Cheung M.
Chang, Chein-I
Chang, Yung-Feng
Chen, Henry
Chien, Chia-Ling
Chien, Chih-Yung
de la Peña, Violeta R.
Fung, Hung-Gay
Hashmi, Sayed A.
Hosmane, Ramachandra S.
Huang, Shan-Jen Chen
Kattakuzhy, George Chacko
Kim, Chung Wook
Kuan, David A.
Leu, Rong-Jin
Lin, Diane Chang
Lin, Shin
Shah, Shirish K.
Song, Yangsoon
Tang, Mark Giakhy
Thakor, Nitish Vyomesh
Tsai, Stanley
Ts'o, Paul On Pong
Wu, Tung
Yau, King-Wai
Yue, David T.

Beltsville
Bhathena, Sam Jehangirji
Durrani, Sajjad Haidar
Raina, Ashok K.
Tso, Tien Chioh
Wang, Chien Yi

Bethesda
Alvares, Alvito P.
Chen, Benjamin Yun-Hai
Cheng, Sheue-yann
Cheung, David F.
Chuang, De-Maw
Dhir, Surendra Kumar
Dighe, Shrikant Vishwanath
Dubey, Satya Deva
Hayase, Joshua Yoshio
Ito, Yoichiro
Kan, Kit-Keung
Krishna, Darshan
Kumaroo, K.
Kwon-Chung, Kyung Joo
Lee, Chi-Jen
Malkani, Roma V.
Minamoto, Jennifer Noriko
Moon, Jung Suk
Oka, Takami
Ozato, Keiko
Ramachandran, Nadaraja
Rhim, Johng Sik
Seto, Belinda P.
Shivanandan, Kandiah
Sung, Lawrence M.
Tsai, Lin
Tsukahira, Toshio George
Uyehara, Cecil H.
Wang, Shou-Ling
Whang, Benjamin
Wu, Roy S.
Yagi, Haruhiko
Yen-Koo, Helen Chiang-ying
Yu, Kai Fun

Bowie
Kumar, Surendra Mohan
Misra, Prabhakar
Srivastava, Sadanand
Wu, Wei-hsiung

Brunswick
Kao, Kung-Ying Tang

Catonsville
Krishnan, Radha
Wu, En Shinn

Cheverly
Rustagi, Ravinder Kumar

Chevy Chase
Cheng, David Keun
Kajioka, June J.

Clarksburg
Gupta, Ramesh K.
Pande, Krishna P.

Cockeysville
Leu, Rong-Jin

College Park
Chang, Chia-Cheh
Chang, Peter C.
Chao, Lin
Chellappa, Rama
Fu, Michael Chung-Shu
Gupta, Ashwani Kumar
Hu, Bei-Lok Bernard
Kundu, Mukul Ranjan
Lin, Hung Chang
Liu, Chuan Sheng
Malhotra, Anju
Mohanty, Sashi B.
Mohapatra, Rabindra N.
Paik, Ho Jung
Shen, I-Yao
Singh, Amarjit
Sumida, Jon Tetsuro
Tripathi, Satish K.
Tsai, Lung-Wen
Vernekar, Anandu Devarao
Wang, Nam Sun
Wang, Orrin Nan Chung
Wu, Ching-Sheng
Yee, Angelina Chun-chu
Yoon, Peter Haesung
Zen, E-an

Columbia
Go, Howard T.
Huang, Joseph T.
Kerkar, Awdhoot Vasant
Khare, Mohan
Kochhar, Man Mohan
Pien, Edward H.

Cumberland
Dhillon, Neil

Ellicott City
Kattakuzhy, George Chacko
Kawaja, Kaleem U.

Forestville
Wong, Alexius Yu-Ming

Fort George G Meade
Chaudhari, Anshumali

Frederick
Liu, Ching-Tong
Miura, George Akio
Seth, Arun K.
Yee, John David

Frostburg
Sharma, Anil F.
Shin, Hung Sik
Tam, Francis Man Kei

Gaithersburg
Chang, Ren-Fang
Chiang, Chwan K.
Chuang, Tze-jer
Fang, Jin Bao
Hahn, Youngja Choi
Hsu, Stephen M.
Jagadeesh, G.
Kacker, Raghu Nath

Kim, Yong-Ki
Misra, Dwarika Nath
Pande, Krishna P.
Parikh, Kirit Girishchandra
Prabhakar, Arati
Shah, Narendra M.
Sohn, David Youngwhan
Tung, Ming Sung
Wang, Francis Wei-Yu
Wang, Shu-Hsia

Germantown
Kaul, Pradaman
Seth, Arun K.

Greenbelt
Choi, Michael Kamwah
Rao, Gopalakrishna M.
Sakimoto, Philip Jon
Singh, Amarjit

Hagerstown
Patel, Ramesh P.
Rhee, Hang Yul

Hyattsville
Chen, Siu Loong

Lanham
Tran, Thang Nhut

Laurel
Cheng, Andrew F.
Kitahara, David James
Sundaresan, P. Ramnathan
Yoon, Peter Haesung

Lutherville
Varma, Usha

Millersville
Omata, Robert Rokuro

Morningside
Canlas, John Hicks

North Potomac
Chan, Wai-Yee
Parkhie, Mukund R.

Owings Mills
Yen, Sherman M. Y.

Oxon Hill
Cabrera, Cesar Trinidad

Pasadena
Park, Kap Yung

Potomac
Alvares, Alvito P.
Chandersekaran, Achamma C.
Gong, Ginny
Hu, Jane H.
Huang, Joseph Chi Kan
Jiang, Xixiang
Malkani, Roma V.
Park, Young Whan
Rhim, Johng Sik
Sha, Shung-tse
Whang, Yun Chow

Princess Anne
Gupta, Gian Chand

Rockville
Chang, Richard
Chiu, Yuan-yuan H.
Choi, Jai Won
Dubey, Satya Deva
Duong, Duc Hong
Fang, Florence S.
Fujimura, Robert Kanji

Hajiyani, Mehdi Hussain
Jagadeesh, G.
Joshi, Sewa Ram
Kochhar, Man Mohan
Kothari, Ajay P.
Kumar, Jatinder
Lao, Chang S.
Lim, David J.
Oh, Harry K.
Parkhie, Mukund R.
Patel, Appasaheb R.
Shroff, Arvin P.
Taira, Toy-Ping Chan
Vadlamudi, Sri Krishna
Wing, James

Salisbury
Gupta, Gian Chand

Severna Park
Kapoor, Jagmohan

Silver Spring
Chen, John Shaoming
Chiogioji, Melvin H.
Choy, Simon
Hsueh, Chun-tu
Jan, Han S.
Jen, Chih Kung
Kaneko, William Masami
Kundu, Mukul Ranjan
Lee, Sheng Yen
Li, Bob Cheng-Liang
Liu, Chuan Sheng
Malik, Sadiq R.
Rao, Venigalla Basaveswara
Sabnis, Gajanan M.
Shah, Bhupendra P.
Song, Yo Taik
Wongananda, Boondharm
Yin, Lo I.
Zien, Tse-Fou

St. Mary's City
Nguyen, Ho Ngoc

Timonium
Kim, Soon Jin

Towson
Huang, Jacob Wen-Kuang
Lee, Kangoh

University Park
Singha, Nabaghana Shyam

Washington Grove
Kim, Vivian C.

Wheaton
Bhathena, Sam Jehangirji
Chow, Alexander Wing-Yat
Kumaroo, K.
Wang, Kung-Lee

MASSACHUSETTS

Acton
Lee, Shih Ying
Li, Yao Tzu
Teng, Henry Shao-lin

Amherst
Chang, Briankle G.
Chang, Edward Shih-Tou
Chen, Weihang
Han, Susan S.
Hsu, Shaw Ling
Iyer, Easwar S.
Ku, Mei-Chin Hsiao
Tan, Barrie
Wu, En-Fuh

Andover
Fan, Ada Mei
Goela, Jitendra Singh
Soo Hoo, Richard
Wang, Dora Chia-Chi
Yu, Melvin Joseph

Arlington
Ono, Richard Dana

Bedford
Chang, Shin-Jyh Frank
Gangulee, Amitava

Belmont
Sihag, Ram K.

Boston
Ahmed, A. Razzaque
Chakrabarti, Supriya
Chang, Caroline J.
Chao, Stanley K.
Chatterjee, Lata Roy
Chen, Ching-chih
Chen, Yi-Shon
Cheng, Jill Tsui
Cheng, Lawrence Kai-Leung
Chien, Arnold Jensen
Chin, Alice L.
Chishti, Athar Husain
Choo, Arthur C. S.
Chou, Iih-Nan
Chu, Adam
Chu, Jonathan Moseley
Chung, Chai-sik
Dang, Harish C.
Fen, Allan Ming
Honda, Maya
Hsieh, Chung-cheng
Hsueh, Yi-Fun
Huang, Thomas W.
Khaw, Ban-An
Kiang, Peter Nien-chu
Kim, Chan-Wung
Kim, Jason Jungsun
Kim, Jay S.
Kim, Yunghi
Lau, Albert Kai-Fay
Lee, Paul Wah
Lee, Wei-ping Andrew
Li, Vivien
Liang, Matthew H.
Lim, Poh C.
Lui, MeiZhu
Ma, Ching-To Albert
Nagano, Paul Tatsumi
Oshima, Harold H.
Ozawa, Seiji
Patel, Dinesh
Pei, Lowry Cheng-Wu
Rha, ChoKyun
Sanadi, D. R.
Say, Allen
Sze, Chia-Ming
Takenaka, Makoto B.
Tam, Leo
Tan, Cheng Imm
Tsai, Jen-San
Tseng, Louisa
Wang, Dora Chia-Chi
Wang, Guo-Hua
Wang, Helen Hai-ling
Wang, Ping H.
Watanabe, Paul Yashihiko
Wong, David Tai Wai
Wong, Liliane R.
Wu, Fa Yueh
Wu, George
Wu, Norman B.

Braintree
Nayak, Bhagchand D.

Bridgewater
Rao, Madhusudana N.
Tu, Shu-chen H.

Brockton
Tsuang, Ming T.

Brookline
Ta, Tai Van

Burlington
Chia, David
Gopikanth, M. L.
Hsing, Rodney W.
Tsang, Dean Zensh
Tse, Ming-Kai
Yang, Albert C.

Cambridge
An, Myoung Hee
Bhagat, Hitesh Rameshchandra
Chun, Hon Ming
Dixit, Sudhir Sharan
Fan, Angela P.
Fujimoto, James G.
Ho, Yu-Chi
Hsiao, William C.
Inouye, Charles Shiro
Jen, Lillian C.
Khorana, Har Gobind
Kung, H. T.
Kung, Patrick Chung-Shu
Kwon, Young Ha
Lee, Harvey Shui-Hong
Liem, Karel Frederik
Lin, Chia Chiao
Liu, Jun S.
Masamune, Satoru
Mei, Chiang Chung
Mitter, Sanjoy K.
Moodera, Jagadeesh Subbaiah
Muni, Indu A.
Nguyen, Nghia Van
Pian, Theodore Hsueh-Huang
Poon, Chi-Sang
Rao, Ramgopal P.
Rha, ChoKyun
Shen, Hao-Ming
Shlang, Elaine
Siu, Yum-Tong
Suh, Nam Pyo
Ta, Tai Van
Ting, Samuel C. C.
Tonegawa, Susumu
Wang, Daniel I.-Chyau
Wong, Liliane R.
Wu, George
Yoshino, Kouichi

Carlisle
Bedi, Sandeep

Chelsea
Chung, Frank Huan-Chen

Chestnut Hill
Pan, Yuh-Kang
Saito, Yoshio
Soo, Billy S.

Concord
Wu, Yau

Danvers
Reddy, Pradeep K.

Dorchester
Chang, Caroline J.
Honda, Maya
Nguyen, Hue Thi

Foxboro
Chung, Eugene

Framingham
Sheikh, Ghafoor A.

Grafton
Ng, Frank Mang Leang
Ng, Jeanne H.

Hanscom AFB
Annamalai, Nagappan K.

Ipswich
Hashimoto, Akira

Jamaica Plain
Lee, Vivian Wai-fun

Lancaster
Chopra, Deepak

Lexington
Aggarwal, Roshan Lal
Chin, Thomas
Sahni, Sham L.
Tsang, Dean Zensh
Tse, Charles Jack-Ching
Wang, Chi-Hua
Wang, Christine A.
Wang, Nancy Y.
Wong, Doris Ning
Yang, Julie Chi-Sun

Lincoln
Wu, Michael Ming-Kun

Lowell
Kim, Byung Guk
Lee, Siu-Lam
Pho, Hai B.
Tang, Wen
Tong, Benjamin
Yin, Mark Y. Q.

Lynn
Kakkar, Subash

Maynard
Lam, Thomas Manpan

Medford
Ch'en, Li-li
Chew, Frances Sze-Ling
Gupta, Tapan K.
Inouye, Charles Shiro
Ko, Bing H.
Mistry, Jayanthi
Verma, Dhani Ram
Vo, Van Toi

Millbury
Anand, Charanjit S.

Natick
Hong, Glenn Thomas
Korten, Geraldine B.

Needham
Guen, Amy Chin
Pandya, Deepak N.
Rao, Ramgopal P.
Vu, Liem T.
Wang, Chih-Chung
Wang, Frederick Andrew

Needham Heights
Shah, Amit

Newton
Lam, Thomas Manpan
Pian, Carlson Chao-Ping
Yen, Alfred Chueh-Chin

North Andover
Ho, Benson P.

Nguyen, Kim-Oanh Thi

North Dartmouth
Chen, Chi Hau
Hsu, Jong-Ping
Kim, Saeja Oh
Liu, Hong
Su, Timothy C.
Wong, Janine Mei-Chiao

Northampton
Lim, Richard

Norwood
Dixit, Sudhir Sharan

Pittsfield
Mehta, Mahendra

Quincy
Choo, Arthur C. S.
Ling, Paul Kimberley
Moy, Jeffery Fei

Revere
Wong, Doris Ning

Shrewsbury
Jen, James A.

Shutesbury
Kim, Richard E.

Somerville
Barat, Kahar
Lim, Joo Kun
Shah, Amit
Wan, Sze-kar
Wong, Po Kee
Yue, Xiaodong

South Hadley
Peterson, Indira Viswanathan

South Lancaster
Wada, Toshimasa Francis

South Lee
Mehta, Mahendra

South Walpole
Leung, Woon-Fong

South Weymouth
Watanabe, Paul Yashihiko

Southbridge
Chu, Nori Yaw-Chyuan

Springfield
Chen, Chuan Ju
Lee, Kang In

Stoneham
Krishnan, Sundaram

Tewksbury
Hong, Glenn Thomas

Wakefield
Chen, Robert Chia-Hua

Waltham
Chang, Shin-Jyh Frank
Hahn, Bessie King
Jungalwala, Firoze Bamanshaw
Maeda, Robert J.

Watertown
Lin, Sin-Shong
Patel, Kiran K.
Wong, Philip

Wayland
Wong, Backman

Wellesley
Ho, Richard H.

Westfield
Wang, Shujen

Weston
Chen, Stephen C.
Kim, Sang Phill
Kulkarni, Dilip

Westwood
Wu, Christine A.

Wilmington
Chen, Helen T. W.
Mehta, Mahesh

Winchester
Kakkar, Rita
Ou, Shukong

Woburn
Chiang, Tsung Ting
Goela, Jitendra Singh

Woods Hole
Lin, Jian
Ramakrishna, Kilaparti
Shimizu, Nobumichi

Worcester
Chou, Arthur W.
Ghosh, Kalyan K.
Jung, Lawrence Kwok Leung
Keshavan, Krishnaswamiengar
Lingappa, Banadakoppa
    Thimmappa
Lingappa, Yamuna
Ma, Yi Hua
Patel, Mukesh M.
Wen, Wen-Yang

MICHIGAN

Allegan
Hsiao, Margaret Sheng-Mei

Allen Park
Desai, Sudhir G.

Allendale
Chen, Hong Chyi

Ann Arbor
Chang, Byung Jin
Chen, Michael M.
Hashimoto, Ken
Hayashi, Robert H.
Hsu, Timothy
Huang, Yasheng
Khanna, Naveen
Kim, Jong-Jin
Kshirsagar, Anant M.
Li, Shin-Hwa
Li, Victor C.
Lin, Fred Reggie
Liu, Warren Kuo-Tung
Murty, Katta Gopalakrishna
Phan, Sem Hin
Swaroop, Anand
Tai, Chen To
Wang, Henry Yee-Neen
Wu, Alfred Chi-Tai
Wu, Shien-Ming
Yang, Victor Chi-Min
Yang, Wen-Jei
Yeh, Chai
Yeh, Gregory S. Y.

Yeh, Ida Shuyen Chiang

Battle Creek
Takasaki, William Yoshi Tsugu

Berrien Springs
Wong, Peter Alexander

Big Rapids
Rao, Taramanohar B.
Shin, Kilman

Birmingham
Mehta, Mehul Mansukh

Bloomfield Hills
Kim, Chaesik

Dearborn
Chen, Yubao
Kumar, Kamalesh
Lin, Paul Kuang-Hsien
Ling, Paul
Mallick, Pankaj K.
Shah, Parth J.
Tai, Julia Chow
Yoon, David Hwa Hyun

Dearborn Heights
Desai, Sudhir G.
Narayanaswamy, Onbathiveli S.

Detroit
Chang, Jhy-Jiun
Ho, Birong A.
Kan, Michael
Kushida, Toshimoto
Patel, Indravadan R.
Sarkar, Fazlul H.
Sengupta, Dipak Lal
Sethi, Ishwar Krishan
Tan, Chin An
Tsai, Bor-sheng
Tse, Harley Yau-Shuin
Wei, Wei-Zen
Woo, Benson K.
Yang, Kai
Yin, Gang George
Young, Shirley

East Lansing
Chang, Timothy S.
Chao, Georgia Tze-Ying
Chen, Bang-Yen
Chen, Kun-Mu
Chou, Ching-Chung
Honma, Shigemi
Koo, Anthony Ying Chang
Koul, Hira Lal
Kuan, Wei Eihn
Kumar, Ashir
Lee, Shyu-tu
Lew, Gloria Maria
Li, Tien-Yien
Reddy, Chilekampalli
    Adinarayana
Rivera, Evelyn Margaret
Tien, H. Ti
Tsai, Chester
Tung, Wu-Ki

Farmington Hills
Bautista, Veltisezar Bal

Flint
Arora, Madan Lal
Chakravarthy, Srinivasaraghavan
D'Souza, Harry J.
Gupta, Rajeshwar Kumar
Marur, Hanuman
Reddy, Nallapu Narayan
Wong, Victor Kenneth

Franklin
Wang, Charles Chen-ding

Grand Blanc
D'Souza, Harry J.
Reddy, Nallapu Narayan

Grand Rapids
Chung, Douglas Kuei-Nan
Le, Christine Dung

Grosse Pointe
Young, Shirley

Holland
Kim, Pilkyu

Houghton
Cho, Peck
Huang, Eugene Yuching
Kulkarni, Anand K.
Lee, Sung Mook
Ling, Zhi-Kui
Moon, Kee Suk
Pandit, Sudhakar Madhavrao

Kalamazoo
Bhuyan, Bijoy Kumar
Cho, Christopher Sang Kyu
Chou, Kuo-Chen
Gupta, Ajay Kumar
Hsiao, Margaret Sheng-Mei
Hsieh, Philip Po-Fang
Huang, Wei-chiao
Jaglan, Prem S.
Jariwala, Sharad Lallubhai
Joshi, Mukund Shankar
Lin, Chiu-Hong
Sun, Frank F.
Tang, Andrew Hing-Yee
Tang, Roger Y. W.
Tsuji, Kiyoshi
Uchimura, Bruce Jiro

Lambertville
Shah, Arvind K.

Lansing
Hwang, Roland
Liu, Lily Pao-Ih
Takahashi, Abraham Tomio

Livonia
Evangelista, Stella
Rab, Mirza M.
Tang, Kin Ling

Madison Heights
Shah, Jayprakash Balvantrai

Midland
Chau, Henry Chun-Nam
Chen, Catherine W.
Hyun, Kun Sup
Lee, Do Ik
Sarkar, Nitis
So, Ying Hung
Yun, Chung-Hei K.

Mount Pleasant
Chen, Meanshang
Ong, Sing-Cheong

Northville
Hwang, Roland

Novi
Ng, Richard Yut

Okemos
Kumar, Kusum
Liu, Lily Pao-Ih
Wong, Pui Kei

Perry
Takahashi, Abraham Tomio

Plymouth
Koh, Kwang K.

Port Huron
Wu, Harry Pao-Tung

Portage
Jariwala, Sharad Lallubhai
Kuo, Ming-Shang

Richville
Hang, Tru

Rochester
Chaudhry, G. Rasul
Cheng, Charles Ching-an
Moudgil, Virinder K.
Unakar, Nalin Jayantilal
Usui, Kiichi
Wang, Stuart Sui-Sheng

Rochester Hills
Mital, Naveen Kumar
Tsuha, Wallace K., Jr.

Royal Oak
Diokno, Ananias Cornejo
Shetty, Anil N.

Saline
Iyengar, Doreswamy
    Raghavachar
Panjwani, Vishnu

Sodus
Kumar, Vijay A.

Southfield
Young, Shun Chung

St. Clair Shores
Brown, Julie
Chen, Ming Chih

Sterling Heights
Hong, Ryang H.

Tecumseh
Seki, Akiro

Troy
Inatome, Joseph T.
Inatome, Rick
Jain, Jitender K.
Shetty, Anil N.
Shimoura, James
Tan, Chin An
Wang, Dazong

University Center
Yun, Suk Koo

Vandalia
Green, Yoshiko Okada

Walled Lake
Sawatari, Takeo

Warren
Mital, Naveen Kumar

West Bloomfield
Tse, Harley Yau-Shuin

Westland
Shah, Sarju S.

Wixom
Gupta, Chitranjan J.

Woodhaven
Virk, Muhammad Yaqub

Wyoming
Kim, Roderick Sungwook

Ypsilanti
Chung, Young-Iob
Garg, Ramesh Chandra
Lin, Su-Chen Jonathon
Rinpoche, Gelek

MINNESOTA

Bloomington
Rao, Gundu H. R.

Burnsville
Winick, Tranquilina Rios

Coon Rapids
Chang, Clement C.

Duluth
Chee, Cheng-Khee
Cheung, Philip
Liu, Zhuangyi
Tsai, Bilin Paula
Yang, Jiann-Shiou

Eagan
Phommasouvanh, Banlang

Edina
Dash, Sita K.

Golden Valley
Bhatt, Gunvant R.

Mankato
Wu, Hai-Sheng

Maple Grove
Chang, Clement C.
Vu, Quang

Maplewood
Dam, Quy T. T.

Minneapolis
Amphavannasouk, Eng
Berssenbrugge, Mei-mei
Chang, Tsan-Kuo
Chin, Frank Chew, Jr.
Gam, Paul Jonathan
Hsu, Mei-Ling
Huang, Cheng-Cher
Huang, Victor Tsangmin
Hwang, Ange
Iwasaki, Iwao
Kubota, Yuichi
Kumar, Vipin
Lee, Chin-Chuan
Leung, Benjamin Shuet-Kin
Li, Shuhe
Liu, Benjamin Y. H.
Motilall, Makeshwar Fip
Paz, Jennifer C.
Pong, Ting-Chuen
Rahman, Yueh-Erh
Rao, Gundu H. R.
Shimooka, Russell
Sinha, Akhouri A.
Suryanarayanan, Raj Gopalan
Takemori, Akira Eddie
Tandon, Rajiv
Thao, Christopher Teng
Wang, Yang
Wang, Yijiang
Woo, Edward D.
Yuen-Terry, Kaimay

Moorhead
Chan, Henry Y. S.
Chan, Kam Chuen
Gunaratne, Dhavalasri Shelton
  Abeywickreme
Hwang, Hi Sook
Kalra, Rajiv

New Brighton
Chandan, Ramesh Chandra

Rochester
Hazama, Chuck
Jiang, Nai-Siang
Phan, Trung Huynh
Siy, James Andrew
Takekawa, Thomas Tsuyoshi

Shakopee
Thangaraj, Sandy

St. Paul
Cheng, H. H.
Chiang, Huai C.
Hsiao, Feng
Hwang, Ange
Lee, Chin-Chuan
Li, Shuhe
Lo, Yao
Moy, Robert Carl
Nam, Sehyun
Park, Chang Ho
Patel, Ray L.
Sasaki, Ruth A.
Uemura, Joseph Norio
Wong, Gregory Sterling
Xiong, Lee Pao
Yee, James
Young, Hoa Pham

MISSISSIPPI

Clarksdale
Pang, Seng Puang

Hattiesburg
Khanna, Rajive Kumar
Pandey, Ras Bihari
Shang, Bernard Y.
Yuen, Steve Chi-Yin

Holly Springs
Kulkarni, Krishnaji Hanamant

Jackson
Chan, Albert
Chao, Ching Yuan
Raju, Seshadri

Mississippi State
Shim, Jung P.

Oxford
Jung, Mankil
Sadana, Ajit

Starkville
Kim, Moon G.

University
Chen, Wei-Yin
George, K. P.
Jung, Mankil
Sadana, Ajit

MISSOURI

Arnold
Shahzad, Farhat

Ballwin
Banakar, Umesh Virupaksh
Wang, Victor Sheng

Branson
Tabuchi, Shoji

Cape Girardeau
Gong, Jin Kang
Park, Kang H.
Tikoo, Mohan L.

Chesterfield
Agarwal, Ramesh Kumar
Ku, William H.

Clayton
Park, Tae Sung

Columbia
Bajpai, Rakesh Kumar
Basu, Asit Prakas
Chang, Won Ho
Huang, Jiann-Shiun
Jen, Philip HungSun
Khanna, Ramesh
Lin, Yuyi
Liu, Henry
Rhee, Hahn-Kyou
Sehgal, Om Parkash
Shukla, Shivendra D.

Creve Coeur
Li, Guodong

Hazelwood
Mak, Sioe Tho

Jefferson City
Chi, Myung Sun
Park, Chung Uk
Su, Kwei Lee

Joplin
Wang, May X.

Kansas City
Cheng, Kuang Lu
Ching, Wai-Yim
Hasan, Syed E.
Mathiprakasam, Balakrishnan
Reddy, Eashwer K.

Kirksville
Lin, Jason Jia-Yuan

Manchester
Yu, Shiu Yeh

New Haven
Gow, Haven Bradford

Portageville
Anand, Satish Chandra

Rolla
Batra, Romesh Chander
Chen, Ta-Shen
Chen, Yih-Wen David
Cheng, Franklin Yih
Huang, Ju-Chang
Liou, Fue-Wen
Prakash, Shamsher

Springfield
Chen, Wenxiong
Hom, Harry Lee, Jr.
Liu, Yuan Hsiung
Yoon, Youngohi Choi

St. Joseph
Lin, Charles Fley-Fung
Shah, Narendra N.

Shah, Sheila
Yan, Hong-Cheng

St. Louis
Agarwal, Ramesh Kumar
Banakar, Umesh Virupaksh
Chang, Tony H.
Chen, Su-chiung
Cheng, Ta-Pei
Dai, Liyi
Domoto, Douglass T.
Gupta, Surendra K.
Hsieh, Winston Wen-sun
Ikeda, Shigemasa
Jain, Savitri
Kim, Yee S.
Kwak, No Kyoon
Lee, Angel Wai-Mun
Lee, Soo See
Lin, Hsiu-San
Lin, Yeong-Jer
Liu, Maw-Shung
Lum, Sharon Shou Jen
Mukai, Hiroaki
Nahm, Moon H.
Obata, Gyo
Ozawa, Martha Naoko
Palamand, Krishna
Park, Tae Sung
Peng, Dachung Pat
Rana, Mohammed Waheed-uz-
  Zaman
Rao, Dabeeru C.
Rao, Gandikota Venkata
Rath, Nigam Prasad
Shen, Chung Yu
Takano, Masaharu
Woo, William Franklin

Warrensburg
Oshima, Eugene Akio
Yu, Jimmy Chai-Mei

MONTANA

Missoula
Chin, Beverly Ann
Ikeda, Elizabeth Rae
Nakamura, Mitsuru James

NEBRASKA

Kearney
Chen, Xiangning

Lincoln
Cheng, Nelly Ching-yun
Cho, Jang Youn
Kim, Bonn-Oh
Lee, Sang Moon
Leung, Joseph Yuk-Tong
Liou, Sy-Hwang
Lu, Janet C.
Wang, C. H.
Yen, Yang

Omaha
Fong, Nelson C.
Kwak, Wikil
Lau, Yuen-Sum
Mei, Wai-Ning
Nair, Chandra K.
Peng, Chang-Shyh
Tran, Phuoc Huu
Tu, Harold Kai
Ueda, Clarence Tad

NEVADA

Carson City
Lau, Cheryl Ann
Ozawa, Galen M.

Las Vegas
Chiang, Theresa Yi-Chin Tung
Chung, Sue Fawn
Hoang, Ba Hong
Kwon, Myoung-ja L.
Lee, Ju-Cheon
Liu, Stephen Shu-Ning
Nitta, Sandra Haruye
Prabhu, R. D.
Sharma, Satish

Nellis AFB
Que, Nestor Agoo

North Las Vegas
Wong, Buck W.

Reno
Cabanting, George Paul
Chang, Maria Hsia
Hsu, Liang-Chi
Luo, Shen-Yi
Rawat, Banmali Singh
Wu, Ishiung J.

NEW HAMPSHIRE

Bow
Kundu, Bejoy B.

Concord
Kundu, Bejoy B.

Durham
Tso, L. Hilary
Yamamoto, Yutaka

Hanover
Gupta, Vijay
Watanabe, John Mamoru

Lyme
Chin, Raymond J.

Nashua
Chow, Michael Hung-Chun
Lu, Michael Y.
Raghavan, Sridhar A.

Peterborough
Chatterjee, Lata Roy

Plymouth
Chong, Peng-Khuan
Yap, Stacey G. H.

Portsmouth
Sze, Morgan Chuan-Yuan

Salem
Misra, Alok C.

NEW JERSEY

Annandale
Fung, Shun C.
Huang, John Shiao-Shih
Sinha, Sunil Kumar

Belleville
Kumar, Saran Kandakuri

Bergenfield
Shah, Pradyumna R.

Berkeley Heights
Chand, Naresh

Blackwood
Kapadia, H. Viren

Bloomfield
Kimura, Lillian C.

Branchburg
Hsu, Merlin

Bridgewater
Capoor, Asha
Chen, S. Steve
Ghosh, Amal K.
Kapoor, Sanjiv
Lim, Antonio Lao
Ling, Hubert

Camden
Krishnan, Gopal
Kuroda, Koson
Vora, Pramathesh S.

Carteret
Mustafa, Shams

Chatham
Goyal, Suresh
Ong, Owh Kian

Cherry Hill
Farouk, Bakhtier
Gandhi, Prashant P.
Kuan, Jenny W.
Wang, Yu

Clifton
Eng, Henry
Wang, Tsuey Tang

Clinton
Cho, Soung Moo

Collingswood
Cueto, Alex

Convent Station
Murthy, A. Kumaresa S.

Cranbury
Trivedi, Nayan B.

Cresskill
Kim, Youn-Suk

Dayton
Chatterjee, Pronoy Kumar
Nguyen, Hien Vu
Patel, Ashok R.

Deepwater
Chen, Karl A.

Demarest
Jotwani, Chandru

East Brunswick
Balachandran, Kashi
Ramamurthi
Chang, Stephen S.
Lai, Dennis Fu-hsiung

East Hanover
Chen, Rong Yaw
Hsu, Kenneth Hsuehchia
Tse, Francis Lai-Sing

Edison
Choi, Paul W.
Lee, Wooyoung
Modi, Shailesh
Shah, Shailesh R.

Englewood Cliffs
Kang, Yung C.

Florham Park
Hemrajani, Ramesh Relumal

Fords
Shah, Nilesh D.

Fort Lee
Chen, Nai-Ni
Choi, Ye-Chin
Kusumoto, Sadahei
Leung, Kok Ming

Fort Monmouth
Behl, Wishvender K.
Dutta, Mitra

Franklin Lakes
Chiu, Tin-Ho

Glassboro
Lee, Jooh

Glen Ridge
Desai, Suresh A.

Glen Rock
Gandhi, Homi D.
Sankaran, Aiylam P.

Great Meadows
Parikh, Paresh Manilal

Hillsdale
Jain, Sushil C.

Hoboken
Prasad, Marehalli Gopalan

Holmdel
Chai, David
Kam, Lit-Yan
Li, Tingye
Malik, Naeem
Tien, Ping King

Howell
Halemane, Thirumala Raya
Sood, Devinder Kumar

Jersey City
Chopra, Jasbir
Kuroda, Teruhisa
Reyes, Adelaida

Kearny
Sheng, Tony L.

Kenilworth
Ahn, Ho-Sam

Lake Hiawatha
Lo, Samuel E.

Lambertville
Chung, Thomas D.

Lawrenceville
Tang, Charles Chau Ching

Liberty Corner
Rajani, Prem Rajaram

Livingston
Chan, Chun Kin

Lin, Chengmin Michael
Oishi, Satoshi
Pai, David Hsien-Chung
Yang, Winston L.

Madison
Lee, Jung Young
Yoon, Kwangsun Paul

Mahwah
Hayashida, Ronald Hideo

Manalapan
Chen, Le Chun
Kaita, Robert

Marlton
Iyer, Ram Ramaswamy

Matawan
Patel, Nagin K.

Metuchen
Srivastava, Om P.

Middletown
Bhojwani, Ram J.

Millburn
Chiu, Tin-Ho

Millington
Hemrajani, Ramesh Relumal

Montclair
Chao, Xiuli
Ho, Ting

Montville
Das Dasgupta, Shamita

Moonachie
Mittal, Kamal

Moorestown
Maheshwari, Arun K.

Morris Plains
Bulusu, Suryanarayana

Morristown
Cheng, Joe Zen
Dalal, Siddhartha Ramanlal

Mountain Lakes
Sen, Tapas K.

Mountain View
Murthy, Srinivasa

Murray Hill
Bhandarkar, Suhas D.
Chin, Patrick K.
Chu, Sung Nee George
Goyal, Suresh
Han, Byung Joon
Lo, Chi-Yuan
Matsuoka, Shiro
Miyamoto, Lance
Mondal, Kalyan
Quan, Xina
Shen, Tek-Ming
Sheu, Lien-Lung
Takahashi, Ken M.

New Brunswick
Chan, Yeung Yu
Chen, Tseh An
Ho, Chi-Tang
Kim, Dongcheol
Li, Marjorie H.
Liao, Mei-June
Shah, Hasmukh N.

Shih, Chilin
Tu, Ching-I
Wang, Shaw S.

Newark
Ahluwalia, Daljit Singh
Ahmed, Shaikh Sultan
Cheng, Mei-Fang Hsieh
Chin, Ken K.
Chung, Tae-Soo
Fu, Shou-Cheng Joseph
Hsieh, Hsin-Neng
Huang, Xun-Cheng
Humayun, M. Zafri
Leu, Ming C.
Leung, Christopher Chung-Kit
Ng, Peter A.
Patel, Rakesh
Ravindra, Nuggehalli Muthanna
Sawhney, Ajay
Wang, Jason T. L.
Yee, Donald Poy

North Branch
Reddy, Pratap P.

North Caldwell
Yang, Sun Hye

Northvale
Sachdev, Ramesh Kumar

Oakland
Ngo, Wilbur

Ocean
Behl, Wishvender K.
Mahajan, Y. Lal

Old Bridge
Nahata, Suparas M.

Paramus
Nakasone, Robert C.

Park Ridge
Narita, George M.

Piscataway
Balaguru, Perumalsamy N.
Chae, Yong Suk
Chaudhary, Ved P.
Chen, Kuang Yu
Chen, Yu
Chien, Yie W.
Jaluria, Yogesh
Lai, Kuo-Yann
Langrana, Noshir A.
Wong, Suk Yee
Woo, Henry
Wu, Xian Connie
Yang, Chung S.

Plainsboro
Biswas, Dipak R.

Princeton
Cai, Jin-Yi
Chang, Kern K. N.
Chen, Nai Y.
Cheng, Charmian S.
Cheng, Sin I.
Cho, Dong-il Dan
Erramilli, Shyamsunder
Hirata, Hosea
Hsu, Stephen Charles
Ito, Mark Mitsuo
Kaita, Robert
Kripalani, Kishin J.
Lam, Sau-Hai
Lau, Ngar-Cheung
Ling, Hung Chi
Manabe, Syukuro

Manne, Veeraswamy
Miyakoda, Kikuro
Ong, Nai-Phuan
Purohit, Milind Vasant
Shinozuka, Masanobu
Singhvi, Sampat M.
Tsui, Daniel Chee
Wei, James
Wong, King-Lap
Yan, Tsoung-Yuan
Yoshikawa, Shoichi

Princeton Junction
Lee, Lihsyng Stanford
Makino, Seiichi

Randolph
Lem, Kwok Wai
Ling, Hubert

Raritan
Kanojia, Ramesh Maganlal

Red Bank
Chang, Chuan Chung
Lai, Ming-Yee
Liao, Paul Foo-Hung
Lin, Chinlon
Ramaswami, Vaidyanathan

Ridgewood
Kamiyama, Osamu

River Edge
Thadani, Raju

Rivervale
Patnaik, Amiya K.

Saddle Brook
Brillantes, Hermogenes Bilgera

Sewell
Vora, Pramathesh S.

Short Hills
Aviado, Domingo M.

Shrewsbury
Louie, Ai-Ling M.

Somerdale
Bhatt, Kiran Chandrakant

Somerset
Horng, John Jang-Ji
Lee, Wei-Kuo

Somerville
Kanojia, Ramesh Maganlal

South Orange
Leung, Edwin Pak-Wah
Yang, Winston L.

South Plainfield
Chung, Jesse Y. W.
Lan, Dong Ping

Spotswood
Prakash, Vinod

Stirling
Biswas, Dipak R.

Teaneck
Abraham, John
Chandy, Varughese Kuzhiyath
Wang, Hsueh-Hwa

Tenafly
Ahmed, Shaikh Sultan
Chang, Hyong Koo

726

Wang, Shih-Chun

Tinton Falls
Murthy, Srinivasa

Trenton
Dhruv, Arvind B.
Liu, Chao-Nan
Liu, James P.

Union
Hiraoka, Leslie Satoshi
Kim, Youn-Suk
Patel, Dilipkumar Z.

Union Beach
Huang, Jennming Stephen

Upper Montclair
Desai, Suresh A.
Lee, Lee Hwang
Pai, Anna Chao
Wang, Dajin

Voorhees
Varghese, Raju Molethu

Warren
Chiao, Yu-Chih
Huang, Charles
Tang, Wallace T. Y.

Watchung
Hwang, Cherng-Jia

Wayne
Anandan, Munisamy
Cheng, David Hong
Cheo, Li-hsiang S.
Parikh, Hemant Bhupendra
Takagi, Norio

West Caldwell
Kaul, Balkrishena

West Long Branch
Mahajan, Y. Lal
Naik, Datta Vittal

West Paterson
Maj, Naweed K.

Whippany
Nagoshi, Douglas N.

Woodbridge
Mustafa, Shams
Ong, Owh Kian
Sood, Devinder Kumar
Yue, Chinny

Wyckoff
Kim, Kwang-Shin
Yoon, Kwangsun Paul

NEW MEXICO

Albuquerque
Ahluwalia, Harjit Singh
Chen, Er-Ping
Cheng, Yung-Sung
Doddapaneni, Narayan
Fukushima, Eiichi
Hahn, Liang-Shin
Hsi, David C.
Ju, Frederick D.
Lee, David Oi
Lee, William Wai-Lim
Ng, Tang-Tat Percy
Park, Su-Moon
Suelto, Teem D.
Wong, Siu G.

Carlsbad
Wu, Chuan-Fu

Las Cruces
Bhada, Rohinton Khurshed
Chen, Tuan Wu

Las Vegas
Wang, George Maosue

Los Alamos
Hsu, Albert Hsueh-Li
Mudundi, Ramakrishna Raju
Peng, Jen-Chieh
Pillay, Sivasankara K. K.
Sinha, Dipen N.

Tyrone
Chen, Wai Jun

NEW YORK

Albany
Han, Jaok
Kim, Sung Bok
Miyashiro, Akiho
Myer, Yash Paul
Sun, Chih Ree
Tsan, Min-Fu
Vemula, Subba Rao
Wang, Sho-Ya

Alfred
Takeuchi, Takao
Tang, Jianxin
Wang, Xingwu

Amherst
Kwok, Hoi-Sing
Rao, Raghav H.

Annandale
Cheng, Amy I.

Ardsley
Dinh, Steven M.

Auburn
Verma, Anil K.

Bardonia
Chen, Anne Chi

Barrytown
Kim, David Sang Chul

Bay Shore
Rao, Barry

Bayside
Chao, Tim
Cheng, Hsueh-Jen
Min, Pyong-Gap
Verma, Ram Sagar

Beaver Falls
Shah, Minal J.

Bedford Hills
Bora, Sunder S.

Bellerose
Barnabas, Mathews Mar

Bethpage
Cheung, Lim H.

Binghamton
Chang, Yu Lo Cyrus
Chatterjee, Monish Ranjan
Huie, Carmen Wah-Kit
Morisawa, Marie Ethel

Wu, Francis Taming

Brockport
Chan, Stephen W.
Li, Yu-ku

Bronx
Biradavolu, Kaleswara Rao
Chang, Mabel Li
Chen, David Ting-Kai
Collantes, Augurio L.
Doyle, Ruth Narita
Gupta, Sanjeev
Hirano, Asao
Lai, Richard Thomas
Lee, John Jongjin
Lim, Josefina Paje
Pe, Maung Hla
Shah, Syed M.
Shang, Stella I-Hua
Wang, Molly M.
Wong, Frank Van

Brooklyn
Chin, Winifred C.
Hu, Jimmy
Kwei, Ti-Kang
Lee, Myung-Soo
Leung, Kok Ming
Lin, Feng-Bao
Ma, Tsu Sheng
Mak, Paul P.
Nguyen, Cuong Phu
Pillai, Unnikrishna S.
Rao, T. K. Sreepada
Sahni, Viraht
Saito, Seiji
Shen, Wu-Mian
Shevde, Ketan
Verma, Ram Sagar
Yasumura, Seiichi
Yoon, Chongyul John

Brookville
Lu, Linyu Laura
Rao, Srikumar S.

Buffalo
Bahl, Om Parkash
Chadha, Kailash Chandra
Chan, Arthur Wing Kay
Chang, Winston Wen-Tsuen
Chen, Stuart S.
Cho, Kah-Kyung
Choi, Dosoung Philip
Choi, Namkee Gang
Choi, Tai-Soon
Chung, Deborah Duen Ling
Dutta, Shib Prasad
Fung, Ho-Leung
Gao, Jiali
Hata, Hiroaki
Ho, John Ting-Sum
Hong, Suk Ki
Hui, Sek Wen
Jain, Piyare Lal
Kim, Yung Mo
Kuramitsu, Howard K.
Lau, Joseph T. Y.
Matsumoto, Mark R.
Park, Seung-Kyoon
Rao, Tejaswini
Shin, In-Sook Jeong
Takeuchi, Kenneth James
Trivedi-Doctor, Minakshi Dipak
Vaidhyanathan, Vishnampet S.
Yang, Ralph Tzu-Bow

Carmel
Shen, Chia Theng

Cedarhurst
Moon, Inso John

Clifton Park
Gajjar, Jagdish Trikamji
Gupta, Pradeep Kumar

Clinton
Li, Cheng

Clinton Corners
Leung, Ida M.

Commack
Lieu, Hou-Shun
Rao, Srikumar S.

Cortland
Chaturvedi, Ram Prakash

Delmar
Narahara, Hiromichi T.
Shen, Thomas T.
Ting, Joseph K.

East Amherst
Kuo, James K. Y.

East Hampton
Li-lan

East Hills
Collantes, Augurio L.

Elmhurst
Chan, Ting Y.
Jhun, Ki Yung
Yee, Walter

Elmira
Daga, Raman Lall

Far Rockaway
Chopra, Rajbir Singh

Farmingdale
Chiang, Yuen-Sheng
Lu, I-Tai
Malhotra, Om P.

Floral Park
Patel, Chandu M.
Patel, Mitesh K.
Yue, Robert Hon-Sang

Flushing
Ghosh, Nimai Kumar
Goh, David S.
Gupta, Anil S.
Han, Jinchen
Hsu, Konrad Chang
Kam, Mei-Ki F. P.
Kang, Weon Hi
Kwan, Franco Chang-Hong
Lee, Hak-Kwon
Madan, Dwarka Nath
Meng, Jimmy Z.
Nori, Dattatreyudu
Rathbone, Susan Wu
Sy, Bon Kiem
Tchen, John Kuo Wei
Wang, Molly M.
Xu, Chia-Yi
Yoshida, Roland K.

Forest Hills
Choy, Wanda Wai Ying

Fredonia
Chan, Tat-Hung
Ma, Chen-Lung Ringo

Garden City
Rao, Gottipaty N.

Geneseo
Joshi, Bhairav D.

Geneva
Desai, Manisha
Huang, Chi-chiang
Rao, Mentreddi Anandha

Glen Cove
Tseng, Mou-sien

Glendale
Kumar, Narinder M.

Grand Island
Shah, Dhiraj Harilal

Grandview
Menon, Gopinath K.

Great Neck
Kawano, Arnold H.

Greenvale
Yukawa, Masako

Hempstead
Jaiswal, Gopaljee
Wong, Daniel W.

Hicksville
Das, Mohan N.

Highland
Sheth, Renuka R.

Highland Mills
Leung, Pak Sang

Hopewell Junction
Saji, Kiyotaka
Srinivasan, Gunumakonda
    Ramaswamiengar

Howard Beach
Tam, Thomas Kwai-Sang

Hyde Park
Yee, Wilfred Wee Bin

Inwood
Seshadri, Rajagopal

Irvington
Sikand, Chander Kumari

Islandia
Wang, Charles B.

Ithaca
Hsu, John Tseng-Hsiu
Khare, Bishun Narain
Kinoshita, Toichiro
Lee, Ocksoo Kim
Lee, Soo-Young
Li, Che-Yu
Okihiro, Gary Yukio
Shen, Shan-Fu
Sudan, Ravindra Nath
Tang, Chung Liang
Tye, Bik-Kwoon Yeung
Tye, Sze-Hoi Henry
Wang, Kuo King

Jackson Heights
Mammen, Abraham
Thadani, Raju

Jamaica
Chao, Chiang-nan
Chen, Augustine Cheng-Hsin
Haldar, Dipak
Liu, Si-kwang

Patel, Narendra D.
Reddy, Indra Karan
Tang, Sherman
Wong, Kwok-Fai Matthew

Johnson City
Siddiqui, Ehtisham Uddin
  Ahmad

Kings Park
Datta, Vijay K.

Lewiston
Kagetsu, Tadashi Jack

Lockport
Shah, Ramesh Keshavlal

Long Island City
Pulijal, Madhu V.

Loudonville
Yoon, Won Z.

Lowville
Shah, Minal J.

Lynbrook
Chen, Tony Young

Maplecrest
Truong Thi, Hoa-Dien

Massena
Hung, Stephen Chifeng

Melville
Chan, Jack-Kang

Middletown
Dass, Edgar Sushil
Langit, Ralph P., Jr.

Mineola
Kwan, Yuen-yin Kathy

Montrose
Shah, Naren N.

Mount Kisco
Bora, Sunder S.

Mount Vernon
Chen, Kenny T.

New City
Chin, Chew
Grewal, Perminder Singh

New Hyde Park
Metha, Pradipkumar D.

New Paltz
Ho, Hon Hing

New Rochelle
Huang, Ming-Hui
Tan, Chor Weng

New York
Ahmad, Jameel
Alejandro, Reynaldo Gamboa
Arai, Tomie
Arora, Samir Chandra
Bajaj, Harjit Singh
Balachandran, Kashi
  Ramamurthi
Bhattacharya, Purna
Chacko, Kurian
Chacko, Varkki P.
Chai, Jay
Chan, Lo-Yi C. Y.
Chandra Sekhar, Hosakere K.

Chang, David Hsiang
Chang, Douglas Howe
Chang, Marian S.
Chang, Ngee-Pong
Chaudhri, Rajiv Jahangir
Chen, Amy L.
Chen, Bernard Shao-Wen
Chen, Derrick A.
Chen, Paul Kuan Yao
Chen, Thomas K. S.
Chen, Virginia L.
Chew, Denley Y.
Chia, Swee Lim
Chiang, Oscar C. K.
Chiang, Yung Frank
Chien, Alan Shueshih
Chin, Connie Frances
Chin, John Way
Chin, Kathy Hirata
Chin, Tamera Ann
Chin, Yee Wah
Cho, Renee
Choe, Kenneth
Choi, Frederick D. S.
Choi, Hyungmoo
Choi, Tony Sung
Chong, Ping
Chou, Ting-Chao
Chow, Peter Chi-Yuan
Chow, Russell W.
Choy, Christine
Chu, David
Chu, Franklin Janen
Chun, Wei Foo
Chung, Connie
Compas, Lolita Burgos
Doyle, Ruth Narita
Duong, Cambao De
Ebron, Betty Liu
Eng, Patricia
Eng, William
Fong, Dewey
Fong, Raymond
Francia, Luis H. F.
Fujiki, Marjorie
Fujimatsu, Tadao
Gupta, Sunil
Gupta, Udayan
Hanafusa, Hidesaburo
Hattori, James
Hayashi, Mie May
Hirano, Kyoko
Ho, David D.
Ho, Fred Wei-han
Ho, Ping Pei
Ho, Thierry
Hong, John Song Yook
Hsia, Lisa
Hsu, Charles Jui-cheng
Huang, Alice Shih-Hou
Hwang, David Henry
Hwang, Ivy
Hwang, Suein Lim
Ishikawa-Wolf, Ana Yoshiko
Iyer, Siddharth Pico
Jin, Morgan
Jotwani, Chandru
Kadohata, Cynthia Lynn
Kaku, Michio
Kakutani, Michiko
Kam, William
Kan, Diana
Kan, Yue-Sai
Kang, Heesook Sophia
Kawano, Arnold H.
Kim, Augustine H.
Kim, David Doyung
Kim, Kunsoo
Kim, Kwang-Shin
Koide, Samuel Saburo
Krist, Elizabeth Cheng
Kulkarni, Ravi S.
Kuo, Nina L.

Lee, Ang
Lee, Bing
Lee, Kimyeong
Lee, Marie Grace
Lee, Myung-Soo
Lee, Tsung-Dao
Lee, Wol Sue
Lee, Wonyong
Leung, Kenneth Ch'uan-k'ai
Leung, Som-Lok
Lewis, Loida Nicolas
Li, Ivan C.
Li, Lily Elizabeth
Liem, Ronald Kian Hong
Lim, Josefina Paje
Limb, Ben Quincy
Lin, James P.
Lin, Joseph Pen-Tze
Lin, Maya Ying
Lin, Xiao-Song
Ling, Matthew S.
Liu, Mini
Louie, David Wong
Ma, Yo-Yo
Maeyama, Kikuko
Magdamo, Patricia L.
Mahajan, Harpreet
Makino, Yasuko
Malik, Tirlok N.
Mathai, Anish
Mathai-Davis, Prema
Matsuda, Fay Chew
Mehta, Ajai Singh
Mehta, Ved
Mehta, Zubin
Mei, June Y.
Merchant, Ismail Noormohamed
Mian, Athar S.
Midori
Mo, Hugh H.
Mura, David
Nambiar, Madhavan
Narasimhan, Subha
Natori, Josie Cruz
Ng, Jeffrey C. F.
Ngor, Haing S.
Nguyen, Dung Dang
Noda, Takayo
O, Cao Kinh
Ohashi, Wataru
Onishi, Hironori
Ono, Yoko
Oshiro, Rene Katsuko
Pak, Nam S.
Parikh, Rohit J.
Park, Jeannie
Park, Sung-Il
Patel, Kantilal P.
Patnaik, Amiya K.
Pei, I. M.
Ramachandran, Rita
Roser, Ce
Saeki, Hiroko Yoda
Sagami, Kim
Sakita, Bunji
Sassa, Shigeru
Saxena, Brij B.
Sheng, Bright
Shimada, Yoshiki
Shin, SoonMi
Shirai, Akiko
Shum, William
Sogi, Francis Y.
Somasundaran, Ponisseril
Soong, Arthur J.
Subramanian, Sribala
Sui, Anna
Sumii, Takao
Sun, Tung-Tien
Sundaram, Kalyan
Sung, Betty Lee
Takami, Hideki
Takeshita, Kenichi

Tana, Akira
Thakur, Manish
Tong, Jennie S.
Tran, La Dinh
Tsai, Jir-Shiong
Tsang, Bion Yu-Ting
Tse, Sau P.
Tseng, Muna Siu-Chuk
Tsui, Annie
Tsusaka, Jun
Tung, Ko-Yung
Ueno, Takemi
Vyas, Gaurang Rajnikant
Wan, David A.
Wan, Stephen Samkong
Wang, George H.
Wang, N. T.
Watanabe, Yuki
Weglyn, Michi Nishiura
White, Cedina Miran Kim
Wong, B. D.
Wong, Frederick
Wong, Jade Snow
Wong, Paul K.
Wong, Samuel T.
Yang, Bao-Wen
Yang, Chun-Yeong
Yang, Dongpyo
Yang, Jeffrey Chih-Ho
Yang, Sun Hye
Yao, David D.
Yoshikami, Sandra
Young, Alice
Yuan, Luke Chia-Liu
Yue, Robert Hon-Sang
Zhang, John Z. H.

Niagara Falls
Shah, Dhiraj Harilal

North Tarrytown
Chen, Henry

Northport
Hwang, Wei-Yuan

Norwich
Huang, Chau-Ting
Pong, Schwe Fang

Nyack
Lum, Tammy Kar-Hee

Oakdale
Suh, Bernadyn Kim

Old Westbury
Collantes, Lourdes Yapchiongco
Lu, Steven Zhiyun
Wu, Konrad T.

Oneonta
Chiang, Joseph F.
Kang, Sugwon
Malhotra, Ashok K.
Singh, Madho

Orangeburg
Hsu, Donald K.

Owego
Yang, Timothy C.

Ozone Park
Shah, Ramesh V.

Palisades
Ou, Hsien-Wang
Shah, Uma
Takahashi, Taro

Pearl River
Lee, Ving J.

Tsai, Gow-Jen

Pelham Manor
Datta, Ranajit Kumar

Penfield
Shiao, Daniel Da-Fong

Pomona
Jin, Morgan

Port Jefferson
Kato, Walter Y.

Port Washington
Sato, Shigetada

Potsdam
Lee, Jong Seh
Li, Yuzhuo
Lin, Sung P.

Poughkeepsie
Chin, Yin-lien Chen
Sharma, Onkar Prasad

Rego Park
Gupta, Ram Bihari

Ridgewood
Wong, Kwok-Fai Matthew

Riverdale
Hashimoto, Rentaro
Jan, Kung-ming

Rochester
Chang, Jack Che-Man
Deol, Harjyot
Farhataziz
Ko, Kei-Yu
Li, James C. M.
Liang, Chang-seng
Mehra, Ravinder C.
Ravindran, Nair N.
Yu, Shiu Yeh

Roslyn
Patel, Narendra D.

Roslyn Heights
Esguerra, Arturo Sazon
Gupta, Saroj Lata
Gupta, Surendra Kumar
Jen, Serena

Rye
Datta, Ranajit Kumar

Schenectady
Chan, David So Keung
Gajjar, Jagdish Trikamji
Liu, Yung Sheng
Yu, Kai-Bor

Selden
Huang, Zhen
Kong, Corita Shuk Sinn

Setauket
Ishida, Takanobu

South Richmond Hill
Patel, Kantilal P.

Southfields
Godsay, Madhu P.

St. Bonaventure
Parikh, Rajeev N.
Yen, Peter T.

Staten Island
Mody, Mukund V.
Nizami, Shafiq Ahmed
Yang, Song-Yu
Yeh, Henry

Stony Brook
Chu, Benjamin
Krishnan, Chirakkal
Ojima, Iwao
Tewarson, Reginald P.
Wang, Dong-Ping
Yang, Chen Ning

Suffern
Ahuja, Satinder

Syracuse
Asuncion, Alfredo, Jr.
Bhatia, Tej K.
Chan, Samuel H. P.
Chen, Chung
Hoo, Joe-Jie
Hsu, Robert Ying
Kim, Moon Kyu
Li, Wen-Hsiung
Liu, Zhuang
Mehrotra, Kishan Gopal
Moon, Young B.

Tarrytown
Chaudhari, Shobhana Ashok

Thornwood
Mittal, Kashmiri Lal
Wu, Joseph M.

Tonawanda
Yeh, Chien Jo

Troy
Ghandhi, Sorab K.
Hajela, Prabhat
Lee, Daeyong
Li, Ching James
Mukhopadhyay, Nimai C.
Wang, Gwo-Ching

Tuxedo
Godsay, Madhu P.

Upton
Kato, Walter Y.
Mane, Sateesh Ramchandra
Rohatgi, Upendra Singh
Subudhi, Manomohan
Tuli, Jagdish K.
Weng, Wu-Tsung

Valhalla
Ahluwalia, Brij Mohan Singh
Chang, Pei K.
Gupta, Krishan L.
Reddy, Bandaru S.
Tan, Sinforosa G.
Tse Dinh, Yuk-Ching
Wu, Joseph M.

Valley Stream
Eng, Mamie

Vestal
Huie, Carmen Wah-Kit

Victor
Dixit, Sudhakar Gajanan

Webster
Garg, Devendra
Hwang, Shyshung
Lin, George H. Y.

Westbury
Ghosh, Nimai Kumar

White Plains
Furuta, Soichi
Mian, Athar S.

Williamsville
Bahl, Om Parkash
Chadha, Kailash Chandra
Cho, Kah-Kyung
Jain, Piyare Lal
Kim, Jonathan Jang-Ho
Kim, Yung Mo
Yang, Ralph Tzu-Bow

Woodside
Javed, Mohd S.

Yorktown Heights
Chaudhari, Praveen
Fang, Frank F.
Maruyama, Kiyoshi
Ning, Tak Hung
Tong, Franklin Fuk-Kay

NORTH CAROLINA

Apex
Shendrikar, Arun D.

Boiling Springs
Chang, Jeffrey Chit-Fu

Boone
Land, Ming Huey

Carrboro
Huh, Billy K.

Cary
Tang, Yingchan Edwin
Yang, Han-Jiang

Chapel Hill
Huang, Jamin
Kim, Young Chan
Lee, Kuo-Hsiung
Ma, Tsu Sheng

Charlotte
Chou, Ernest Yen
Kim, Rhyn H.
Parikh, Pravin P.
Pradhan, Shekhar
Sarkar, Santanu Kumar
Shah, Nandlal Chimanlal

Durham
Han, Moo-Young
LaCuesta, Wesley Ray, Sr.
Ma, Wenhai
Parikh, Indu
Rao, Koneru Ramakrishna
Trivedi, Kishor S.
Wang, Jing
Wani, Mansukhlal Chhaganlal
Yang, Weitao

Elizabeth City
Chou, Leland L. C.
Choudhury, A. Latif

Fayetteville
Liu, Shia-Ling

Greensboro
Kumar, Jothi V.
Reddy, Gudigopuram Bhaskar
Wang, Jie

Wang, Shih-Liang
Greenville
Chia, Rosina Chih-Hung
Chin, Robert Allen
Hsu, Yuan-Hsi
Lee, Tung-Kwang
Li, Chia-yu
Wang, Veronica C.

Hickory
Chou, David Yuan-Pin

Kinston
Ho, Yuh Jyue Agnes Wang

Mars Hill
Hong, Weihu

Morganton
Lo, Tou Ger

Nebo
Yang, Lang

Pisgah Forest
Dixit, Ajit S.

Raleigh
Agrawal, Dharma Prakash
Baliga, Jayant
Chan, Po Chuen
Chow, Mo-yuen
Chung, Kwong T.
Gupta, Bhupender S.
Huang, Barney Kuo-Yen
Ji, Chueng Ryong
Kim, Youngsoo Richard
Lin, Yuh-Lang
Lu, Jye-Chyi
Luh, Jiang
Pao, Chia-Ven
Park, Jae Young
Qureshi, Muquarrab Ahmed
Rhee, Sang Foon
Shih, Jason Chia-Hsing
Tang, Yingchan Edwin
Whangbo, Myung-Hwan

Research Triangle Park
Chan, Po Chuen
Huang, Jamin
Lee, Yue-Wei
Li, Steven Shoei-lung
Wani, Mansukhlal Chhaganlal
Wu, Julian Juh-Ren
Yamamoto, Toshiaki

Rocky Mount
Navangul, Himanshoo Vishnu Bhat

Salisbury
Hung, Yen-Wan
Tseng, S. C.

Wilmington
Wang, Li-Shing
Yan, Joseph Gea-Gue

Winston-Salem
Chen, Michael Y. M.
Hayashi, Elmer Kinji
Lee, Wei-chin
Sharma, Deva Datta
Vyas, Udaykumar Dayalal
Wu, Wallace C.

NORTH DAKOTA

Fargo
Chang, Kow-Ching

Lee, Yur-Bok
Sugihara, James Masanobu
Yuvarajan, Subbaraya

Grand Forks
Wang, Jun

OHIO

Akron
Cheng, Stephen Z. D.
Choy, Fred Kat-Chung
Kim, Il-Woon
Lee, Sunggyu
Ma, Laurence J. C.
Nakajima, Nobuyuki
Rana, Gurinder Mohan Singh
Reddy, Narender Pabbathi

Athens
Chen, Hollis Ching
Gupta, Ashok K.
Hikida, Robert Seiichi
Jain, Surender K.
Kaneshige, Harry Masato
Lee, Hwa-Wei
Lin, Julia C.
Wen, Shih-liang
Yun, Seung Soo

Bay Village
Ling, Alexander

Beavercreek
Parthasarathy, Triplicane Asuri

Bowling Green
Gupta, Arjun K.
Kim, Kyoo Hong
Rohatgi, Vijay K.
Shih, Wei

Brecksville
Lai, Ying-San

Canton
Desai, Chandra
Lee, Peter Wankyoon

Centerville
Chong, Timothy

Cincinnati
Dave, Janak
Garg, Prem
Hashimoto, Eiji
Jain, Sulekh Chand
Lee, Sooncha A.
Ma, Michael
Mehta, Raj B.
Shah, Chandu M.
Sharma, Shri C.
Tan, Henry S. I.
Wang, I-chih

Cleveland
Aggarwal, Raj
Banerjee, Amiya Kumar
Chai, An-Ti
Chatterjee, Pranab
Chatterjee, Sayan
Flores, Susan Gumabao
Gopalakrishna, K. V.
Gorla, Rama S. R.
Gupta, Manjula K.
Hayashi, Masumi
Khosla, Mahesh Chandra
Ko, Wen Hsiung
Lee, Jae-won
Li, George S.
Liu, Chung-Chiun
Lo, Howard H.

Naito, Herbert K.
Reddy, Dhanireddy Ramalinga
Saha, Gopal Bandhu
Sharma, Jandhyala L.
Tung, Theodore H.
Wang, ShiQing
Wei, Robert

Columbus
Atoji, Masao
Chandrasekaran, Balakrishnan
Cruz, Jose Bejar, Jr.
Fu, Paul S.
Gupta, Bhagwandas
Jalil, Mazhar
Kim, Moon H.
Kim, Myung-Hye
Lal, Rattan
Lee, June Key
Ling, Ta-Yung
Liou, Ming Jaw
Morita, Ichiko T.
Nahata, Milap Chand
Patil, Popat N.
Pham, Viet Van
Sandhu, Ranbir Singh
Satyapriya, Coimbatore K.
Sharma, Hari M.
Singh, Rajendra
Somani, Pitambar
Tsai, Ming-Daw
Zheng, Yuan Fang

Dayton
Bajpai, Praphulla Kumar
Bhattacharya, Rabi Sankar
Chen, C. L. Philip
Cheng, Songlin
Chitkara, Vijay Kumar
Chuang, Henry Ning
Fu, Jyun-Horng
Honda, Shigeru Irwin
Ismail, Amin Rashid
Li, Peter Tu
Liang, Tehming
Lu, Luo
Mantil, Joseph Chacko
Nam, Sangboo
Park, Won J.
Parthasarathy, Triplicane Asuri
Rai, Amarendra Kumar
Ramalingam, Mysore Loganathan
Shenoi, B. A.
Tsui, Susan Lee
Wu, Richard L. C.
Yeo, Yung Kee

Dublin
Chen, Moon Shao-Chuang, Jr.
Singh, Rajendra

East Cleveland
Yu, Thomas H.

Fairborn
Yeh, Hsi-Han

Findlay
Bhalla, Vipan Kumar

Franklin
Mehta, Kailash

Granville
Chang, Che-Gil

Highland Heights
Lee, Jae-won

Kent
Kumar, Satyendra
Kwong, Eva

Tuan, Debbie Fu-tai

Kenton
Bhalla, Vipan Kumar

Kettering
Mantil, Joseph Chacko

Lima
Lee, Sun-Young Won

Maple Heights
Sakai, Michael H.

Marietta
Yi, Xiaoxiong

Maumee
Rawat, Arun Kumar

Medina
Woo, James T. K.

Miamisburg
Chong, Clyde Hok Heen

Milford
Chiu, Victor

Oberlin
Nee, Michael Wei-Kuo
Yan, Haiping

Oxford
Bhattacharjee, Jnanendra Kumar
Chi, Jacob
Lim, Kam Ming
Yen, Chi-Chung David

Portsmouth
Yang, Zhanbo

Powell
Suzawa, Naoko M.

Rootstown
Caldito, Gloria Cruz
Chan, Phillip Paang

Seven Hills
Kim, Jungnam Ego
Moinuddin, Masood A.

Sidney
Hsieh, Franklin

Strongsville
Gorla, Rama S. R.
Patel, Chandu K.
Reddy, Dhanireddy Ramalinga

Toledo
Chakraborty, Joana
Chang, Gene Hsin
Fu, Kuan-Chen
Guo, Hua
Gupta, Jiwan D.
Kadowaki, Joe George
Kim, Ken I.
Kim, Kitai
Kim, Wun Jung
Koo, Benjamin Hai-Chang
Kumar, Ashok
Lau, Peter Man-Yiu
Lee, Kai-Fong
Oh, Keytack Henry
Rawat, Arun Kumar
Shah, Arvind K.

Upper Arlington
Lee, June Key

Warren
Mathur, Harbans B.

West Chester
Shah, Chandu M.

West Worthington
Satyapriya, Coimbatore K.

Wilberforce
Nam, Wonki Kim

Worthington
Fu, Paul S.
Pham, Viet Van
Sinha, Nirmal K.

Youngstown
Chen, Haiyang
Huang, Pei
Kim, Hong Yung
Kim, Hyun Wang
Lateef, Abdul Bari
Lim, Soon-Sik

OKLAHOMA

Edmond
Godhania, Laxman P.
Jung, Byung Il
Li, Xiao-Bing

Langston
Lim, Kwee-Eng Lyn

Norman
Cheung, John Yan-Poon
Fung, Bing M.
Gollahalli, Subramanyam
  Ramappa
Kim, Changwook

Oklahoma City
Chaturvedi, Arvind Kumar
Chung, Kyung Won
Lee, Diana Mang
Li, Xiao-Bing
Nguyen, Cu D.
Varghese, Thomas K.
Vo, Jimmy
Wang, Chi-Sun

Ponca City
Ho, Thomas Tong-Yun

Stillwater
Ho, Chrwan-Jyh
Hsu, Paul
Lau, Hon-Shiang
Ramakumar, Ramachandra
  Gupta
Yu, Chang-An

Tulsa
Bhat, Shankar U.
Chew, Pamela Christine
Chin, Alexander Foster
Joshi, Sada D.
Lin, Chi Yung
Musapeta, Hari
Sheth, Ketankumar Kantilal
Viswanath, Rampur S.

OREGON

Albany
Ko, Hon-Chung

Ashland
Inada, Lawson Fusao

Aumsville
Chen, David Ta-Fu

Beaverton
Miya, Wayne
Wong, John A.

Corvallis
Cauthorn, James Daniel
Liu, Xingwu
Morita, Richard Yukio
Tripathi, Vijai Kumar
Wang, Chih H.
Yim, Solomon C. S.
Yu, Shiao-ling S.

Eugene
Deshpande, Nilendra Ganesh
Ho, Vernon S. C.
Hongo, Garrett Kaoru
Kim, Hee-Jin
Rhee, Song Nai

Forest Grove
Lu, Lina

Gresham
Lim, John K.

Klamath Falls
Shih, Hong-Yee

Lake Oswego
Cho, Hyong W.

Monmouth
Ando, Koichi
Liu, Jie

Portland
Azumano, George Ichiro
Chen, Stanford
Dozono, Sho G.
Fong, April Ann
Gn, Thye-Wee
Ha, Joseph Man-Kyung
Hata, David M.
Hisatomi, John A.
Kao, Timothy Tieh-Hsiung
Katagiri, George
Krishnamurthy, Gerbail T.
Lau, Leslie
Leung, Pui-Tak
Lin, Kuan-Pin
Liu, Tsu-huei
Louie, David H.
Matsushima, Charles Hiroshi
Naito, Samuel Teruhide
Nishiura, Wayne Iwao
So, Magdalene Yee-Huen
Soohoo, Richard Allen
Szeto, Erik K.
Tan, Nady
Tran, Hong-Y Thi
Vo, D. Brian
Watanabe, Suwako

Salem
Hsin, Liang Yih
Rohila, Pritam Kumar
Tran, Huyen Lam

PENNSYLVANIA

Abington
Le, Binh P.

Alcoa Center
Chen-Tsai, Charlotte Hsiao-yu
Ray, Siba Prasad

Allentown
Kumar, Ashok
Mao, Chung-Ling
Nakahara, Shohei
Roy, Pradip Kumar

Ambler
Hong, Kenneth

Annville
Liu, Thomas Jyhcheng

Ardmore
Chi, Yinliang

Audubon
Patel, Mukul B.

Bala Cynwyd
Chiu, S. M.

Bethel Park
Tang, Lillian Y. D.
Tang, Yu-Sun
Yeh, James Tehcheng

Bethlehem
Chen, Edward C. H.
Ghosh, Bhaskar Kumar
Gupta, Parveen P.
Hong, Daniel Chonghan
Jain, Himanshu
Lu, Le-Wu
Tzeng, Kenneth Kai-Ming
Wu, David

Bloomsburg
Hsieh, Li-Ping
Hwang, Dennis B. K.
Liu, Hsien-Tung

Breinigsville
Nakahara, Shohei

Bristol
Siddiqui, Habib

Bryn Mawr
Albano, Alfonso M.
Wang, Albert S. D.
Wu, Jean Yu-Wen Shen

California
Kiang, Clyde Y.

Center Valley
Kumar, Ashok

Chadds Ford
Chuang, Strong C.

Cheltenham
Paik, Woon Ki

Chester
Mansur, Iqbal

Collegeville
Singh, Baldev

Downingtown
Deb, Arun Kumar
Hong, S. Theodore

Doylestown
Nair, K. M.

East Stroudsburg
Cheng, Cheng-Yin
Shwe, Hla
Xia, Yun

Elkins Park
Dalal, Fram R.

Export
Yang, Wen-Ching

Exton
Patel, Mukul B.

Ford City
Rishi, Satchidanand Raam

Frazer
Shenoy, Narasimha B.

Gettysburg
Viswanathan, Byravan

Gibsonia
Mehta, Kishor Singh

Grove City
Mehta, Sunil Kumar

Havertown
Choi, Eung Ryong
Mehta, Krishnakant Hiralal

Hershey
Cheung, Joseph Y.
Ng, Yuk-Chow
Tan, Tjiauw-Ling

Hummelstown
Tan, Tjiauw-Ling

Indiana
Jen, Horatio H.
Kulkarni, Gopal S.

Kennett Square
Chowdhry, Vinay

Kingston
Mitra, Grihapati

Kutztown
Gupta, Venu Gopal

Lancaster
Duong, Ngo Dinh

Landenberg
Mao, James Chieh-Hsia

Langhorne
Hsu, Samuel

Lansdale
Shah, Harikrishna D.

Lewisburg
Meng, Xiannong

Lincoln University
Bhat, K. Ramachandra

Linwood
Iyer, Ram Ramaswamy

Lock Haven
Biswas, Renuka
Chang, Shirley Lin
Chu, Tien Lu

Malvern
Pak, Koon Yan

Mansfield
Kim, Youngsuk

Media
Idnani, Kamal M.

Mansur, Iqbal

Melrose Park
Banerji, Ranan Bihari

Middletown
Chen, Yohchia

Milford
Dass, Edgar Sushil

Monroeville
Vijayendran, Bhima R.

Morgantown
Nguyen, Anh Mai

Morrisville
Miyakoda, Kikuro
Sen, Arun

Murrysville
Chun, Sun Woong
Ray, Siba Prasad

Newtown
Chang, Kelvin Yau-Min
Tsai, Betty L.

Newtown Square
Soh, Joong Min

Norristown
Chang, Charles Hung

Olyphant
Syal, Shanta

Penndel
Sen, Arun

Perkasie
Sum, Grace C. K.

Philadelphia
Aggarwal, Lalit Kumar
Ang, Charles C.
Bagasra, Omar
Chang, Farland H.
Ch'ih, John Juwei
Chow, Shirley Chin-Ping
Chu-Andrews, Jennifer
Chung, Edward K.
Dai, Hai-Lung
Dalal, Fram R.
Das, Shyam
Farouk, Bakhtier
Gupta, Pardeep K.
Hayashi, Midori
Hom, Mei-Ling
Hong, Jin Sung
Hong, Kenneth
Hsu, Samuel
Hung, Paul P.
Hyun, Bong Hak
Kaji, Akira
Kim, Haewon Chang
Kochhar, Devendra M.
Kumar, Prasanna K.
Lee, Chen Lok
Lee, Ying K.
Lim, Teck-Kah
Liu, Richard Chung-Wen
Liu, Te-Hua
Lu, Ponzy
Matsumoto, Teruo
Nath, Amar
Ohnishi, Tomoko
Patel, Kalyani
Patel, Narayan G.
Rao, Angara Koneti
Sato, Keiko
Shen, Benjamin Shih-Ping

Shih, Joan Fai
Shim, Eun Sup
Singh, Jagbir
Song, Il-Yeol
Suh, Byungse
Takashima, Shiro
Tang, Chik-Kwun
Ting, Jan C.
Uchimoto, William Warren
Wang, Albert S. D.
Wei, Susanna
Wei, William Wu-Shyong
Wei, Yen
Wong, Anthony Joseph
Wong, Deborah Anne
Wong, Peter M. C.
Wu, Chung-Hsiu
Yan, Chiou-Shuang Jou
Yuan, Jian-Min
Yun, Xiaoping

Phoenixville
Hsieh, Dean Shui-Tien
Ng, Richard

Pittsburgh
Au, Leo Yuin
Au, Patrick Siu-Kee
Bhagavatula, Vijayakumar
Chen, Xinfu
Chiang, Shiao-Hung
Chiu, Chao-Lin
Dixit, Balwant N.
Fung, John
Guo, David
Gupta, Rajiv
Hayashikawa, Doris S.
Ho, Chien
Hsu, Tse-Chi
Hung, Tin-Kan
Hwang, Charles C.
Jhon, Myung S.
Kang, Joonhee
Khan, Shakil Ahmad
Kim, Hyong Sok
Kim, Yong Ik
Ko, Edmond Inq-Ming
Kokan, Ghiasuddin
Lai, Ralph Wei-meen
Li, C. C.
Li, Ching-Chung
Li, Hanna Wu
Li, Ling-Fong
Li, William Wei-Lin
Liu, Frank Yining
Mehta, Kishor Singh
Mirchandani, Prakash
Paek, Chisun Jim
Quimpo, Rafael Gonzales
Rajagopal, Kumbakonam
  Ramamani
Reddy, Raj
Saluja, Jagdish Kumar
Shih, Tom I-Ping
Shin, Doug Yong
Takeuchi, Kenji
Todo, Satoru
Tsai, Chon-Kwo
Venkataramanan, Raman
Wang, Yi T'ung
Wing, Jeannette M.
Wu, Ching-Yong
Yang, Wen-Ching
Yang, Yisong
Yao, Shi Chune
Yu, Victor Lin-Kai

Quakertown
Shah, Piyush A.

Radnor
Chiang, Soong T.
Mizutani, Satoshi

Yang, Da-Ping

Sayre
Choi, John Haetak

Scranton
Chien, Ying I.
Hussain, Riaz

Shady Grove
Patel, Ramesh P.

Shippensburg
Hsu, Margaretha

Somerset
Nair, V. Krishnan

Spring House
Wu, Wu-Nan
Yih, Roy Yangming

State College
Chang, Shirley Lin
Debroy, Chitrita

Swarthmore
Li, Lillian M.
Siddiqui, Faruq Mahmud Anam

Towanda
Choi, John Haetak

Trafford
Rao, K. L. Seshagiri

University Park
Ashtekar, Abhay Vasant
Chung, Tze-Chiang
Debroy, Chitrita
Haramaki, Chiko

Villanova
Chi, Yinliang
Malik, Hafeez
Yuan, Jian-Min

Warminster
Varma, Asha

Waynesburg
Moribayashi, Mikio

West Chester
Chu, Hung Manh
Deb, Arun Kumar
Gupta, Pardeep K.
Kim, James Joo-Jin
Young, Franklin

Wexford
Au, Leo Yuin

Whitehall
Gupta, Parveen P.

Wilkes-Barre
Arora, Vijay K.
Lee, Taehee
Mitra, Grihapati
Wong, Bing K.

Wyncote
Lee, Chen Lok

Wyomissing
Gupta, Ron Singh

Yardley
Ghosh, Sujan
Patel, Mukund R.
Patel, Sarla M.

PUERTO RICO

Mayaguez
Banerjee, Jayanta Kumar
Goyal, Megh R.

RHODE ISLAND

Barrington
Sakoda, James Minoru

Bristol
Joe, Alexander H.

Cranston
Fang, Pen Jeng

Kingston
Kang, Jun-Koo
Kim, Hesook Suzie
Kim, Yong Choon
Lee, Yul W.
Shaikh, Zahir A.
Yang, Qing
Yang, Sze Cheng

Newport
Joe, Alexander H.
Kim, David U.
Meng, James Cheng-Sun
Tang, Assumpta

Portsmouth
Meng, James Cheng-Sun

Providence
Anderson, Wanni W.
Cha, Sungman
Teng, Anthony Yung-yuan

Warwick
Bhatt, Jagdish J.

SOUTH CAROLINA

Aiken
Lee, Si Young

Clemson
Hon, David Nyok-Sai
Kumar, Ranganathan
Wang, Samuel T. M.

Columbia
Au, Chi-Kwan
Bhatia, Sharmila
Chao, Yuh J.
Hwang, Te-Long
Kobayashi, Hideaki
Kwok, Chuck Chun-yau
Pujara, Subhash Somabhai
Shah, Harnish V.
Sy, Francisco S.
Wu, Xian

Conway
Saxena, Subhash Chandra
Song, Ralph H.

Greenville
Choudhary, Subodh Kumar
Gandhi, Vikram Ijatrai

Myrtle Beach
Saxena, Subhash Chandra

Orangeburg
Hwang, Shoi Yean
Mathur, Kailash V.

Sandhu, Shingara Singh
Sandrapaty, Ramachandra Rao

Rock Hill
Lee, Heakyung

Union
Wang, Jih Ming

SOUTH DAKOTA

Brookings
Dwivedi, Chandradhar
Kim, Bang Ja

Rapid City
Han, Kenneth N.

Vermillion
Chang, Hui-Ching
Margallo, Lucio N., II

TENNESSEE

Antioch
Escueta, Arthur V.

Blountville
Wang, Xiaoping

Brentwood
Wong, David Craig

Chattanooga
Wang, Ling Jun

Cookeville
Choi, Kyung-Ju
Deivanayagam, Subramaniam
Liu, Yung-Way
Mahajan, Satish Murlidhar
Rajan, Periasamy Karivaratha
Sundaram, Meenakshi R.
Wang, Louie Kehluh

Cordova
Chung, King-Thom
Lau, Shuk-fong

East Ridge
Desai, Hiren Sharad

Germantown
Kumar, Suresh A.
Tan, Wai-Yuan

Johnson City
Chi, David Shyh-Wei
Huang, Thomas Tao-Shing
Kao, Race L.
Mehta, Ashok V.
Miyamoto, Michael Dwight
Sakhare, Vishwa M.

Kingsport
Kuo, Chung Ming
Wang, Richard Hsu-Shien
Yau, Cheuk Chung

Knoxville
Bose, Bimal Kumar
Chen, Chung-Hsuan
Chen, James Pai-fun
Hung, James Chen
Kim, Young-Bae
Lin, Dennis Kon-Jin
Malik, Anand Kumar
Sachan, Dileep Singh
Shih, Chia C.
Tanaka, Ty Skip

Trivedi, Mohan Manubhai
Trivedi, Nayana Mohan

Livingston
Maeda, Yutaka

Martin
Kim, Choong Soon
Kim, HakLin

Maryville
Kim, Young-Bae

Memphis
Achar, Narahari B. N.
Chan, Kwok Hung
Cheung, Wai Yiu
Chiang, Thomas Minghung
Ching, Marvin K. L.
Chung, King-Thom
Gandhi, Arun Manilal
Huang, Ken Shen
Kuo, Chao Ying
Lau, Shuk-fong
Lin, L. Yu
Pui, Ching-Hon
Tan, Wai-Yuan
Wu, Lyn Xiling
Yoo, Tai-June

Murfreesboro
Aggarwal, Rajesh
Kim, Jwa Keun
Tang, Thomas Li-Ping

Nashville
Banerjee, Mukul R.
Dao, Anh Huu
Das, Salil Kumar
Escueta, Arthur V.
Gupta, Brij Mohanlal
Hara, Saburo
Inagami, Tadashi
Kang, Weng Poo
Kawamoto, Brian Michio
Kono, Tetsuro
Kumar, Kusum Verma
Reddy, Churku Mohan
Shieh, Wun-Ju
Surti, Tarun Natwarlal
Tam, James Pingkwan
Wong, David Craig
Wong, Ray G. L.

Oak Ridge
Arakawa, Edward Takashi
Bowman, Kimiko O.
Chen, Chung-Hsuan
Phung, Doan Lien
Wang, Xun-Li

Tullahoma
Reddy, Kapuluru
  Chandrasekhara
Sheth, Atul Chandravadan
Wu, Y. C. L. Susan

TEXAS

Abilene
Kim, Thomas Kunhyuk

Allen
Nguyen, Tony C.

Arlington
Han, Chien-Pai
Huang, Tseng
Lu, Frank Kerping
Patel, Anil S.
Qasim, Syed Reazul
Shieh, Tsay-Jiu Brian

Tung, Hsi-tang
Vyas, Niyanta N.
Wakamatsu, Don
Youn, Hee Yong

Austin
Banerjee, Sanjay K.
Chakravarty, Indranil
Chang, Sung-sheng Yvonne
Chen, Wayne G.
Garg, Vijay Kumar
Gavande, Sampat A.
Gee, Robert W.
Lam, Simon Shin-Sing
Lee, Chong Sung
Lee, Wei-Na
Ling, Hao
Liu, Min
Mahajan, Vijay
Parate, Natthu Sonbaji
Puligandla, Viswanadham
Rao, Ramesh K. S.
Sakamoto, Arthur, Jr.
Shah, Rajani C.
Sharma, Mukul Mani
Tajima, Toshiki
Taniguchi, Alan Y.
Tong, Alvin H.
Tran, Thomas
Tseng, Wan Chi
Varghese, Philip Leslie
Vasan, Srini Varadarajan
Wang, Kuan
Wong, Martin Ding-Fat
Wong, Pat Chung
Yu, Gang

Baytown
Chen, Michael Chia-Chao

Beaumont
Chiou, Paul C. J.
Choi, Jai-Young
Ma, Li-Chen

Bellaire
Chien, Sze-Foo
Sarathy, Partha R.
Tang, Klairon Kit-ling

Big Spring
Tan, Cheng-Pheng
Tan, Mary

Carrollton
Husain, Mustafa Mahmood

College Station
Bhattacharyya, Shankar P.
Chang, Kai
Chang, Ping
Chui, Charles K.
Chung, H. Michael
Das, Phanindramohan
Furuta, Richard K.
Han, Je-Chin
Hu, Chia-Ren
Huang, Garng Morton
Kim, Junguk Lawrence
Kinra, Vikram Kumar
Kuo, Way
Liu, Jyh-Charn Steve
Lu, Mi
Mahajan, Arvind
Nguyen, Cam
Reddy, Junuthula N.
Rhee, Khee Choon
Tang, Eugenia C. G.
Tang, Yi-Noo
Vaid, Jyotsna
Wang, Suojin
Wu, Hsin-i
Yen, John

Commerce
Chopra, Dev Raj
Ho, Michael Shiukeung

Corpus Christi
Gupta, Ajay
Ochiai, Shinya
Park, Sung-won Sam

Dallas
Aslam, Nasim Mohammed
Batra, Ravi
Chang, Cheng-Hui
Chen, Andrew Houng-Yhi
Chu, Ting L.
Desai, Kantilal Panachand
Hwang, Shin Ja Joo
Lam, Chun H.
Li, Jennifer L. H.
Matsui, Machiko
Nguyen, Bong Van
Song, Yong Chol
Tandon, Anand
Teng, Hsi Ching
Tong, Alex Wai Ming
Wu, Nancy Nan-hwa
Yanagisawa, Samuel Tsuguo

Denton
Pillai, Vijayan K.
Wong, Benedict Ding Chung
Wu, Frederick H.

Duncanville
Sheth, Ashvin C.

Edinburg
Farooqui, Mohammed Y. H.
Hwang, Mark I.

El Paso
Chang, Yi-Chieh
Miyamoto, Seiichi
Singh, Vijay Pal
Wang, Paul Weily
Wong, Albert Y.
Wu, Kung Chris

Fort Sam Houston
Shum, Alex C.

Fort Worth
Ali, Yusuf
Bapatla, Krishna M.
Bhatia, Ramesh
Kai, Robert T.
Patel, Anil S.
Trinh, Hoang Huy

Galveston
Chan, Lee-Nien Lillian
Chen, Victoria Liu
Dinh, Tung Van
Gan, José C.
Giam, Choo Seng
Hsie, Abraham Wuhsiung
Suen, Ching-Yun
Yee, Barbara W. K.

Garland
Choe, Timothy Songsik
Kim, Yongshik

Grand Prairie
Mahinay, Lily C.
Tung, Hsi-tang

Houston
Aggarwal, Bharat Bhushan
Chacko, Mariam Renate
Chacko, Ranjit C.
Chan, Chong B.
Chan, Pui Kwong

Chang, Benjamin Tai-An
Chang, Helen T.
Chang, James Wan Chie
Chang-Diaz, Franklin Ramon
Chen, Guanrong
Chen, Terry
Chen, Yi-Chao
Chiao, Leroy
Chiu, Wah
Chowdhury, Nazmul A.
Chu, Ching-Wu
Chu, Paul Ching-Wu
Chu, Wei-Kan
Chuang, Vincent P.
Dinh, Nicholas Nguyen
Gupta, Samir
Hingorani, Bhagwan V.
Hirasaki, George Jiro
Hsi, Bartholomew P.
Hsu, Laura Ling
Hu, Bambi
Huang, Huey-Wen
Huang, Jung-chang
Huang, Wuu-Liang
Hussain, Fazle
Kashiwagi, Brian Rio
Kim, Han-Seob
Kumar, V.
Lee, Wea Hwa
Li, Ke Wen
Liang, Edison Park-tak
Lin, Ilan S.
Mahadevan, Dev
Mathew, Valsa
Mehta, Mohinder Paul
Moy, Mamie Wong
Newaz, S. S.
Ng, Martin K.
Nguyen, Benjamin Ban
Nguyen, Nam Van
Ou, Ching-Nan
Pan, Dawning
Patel, Chandrakant B.
Patel, Ray J.
Patel, Shailesh R.
Pathak, Sen
Sarin, Harry C.
Sehgal, Raj K.
Shah, Harish S.
Sharma, Puneet
Shen, Grace Liu
Shen, Liang Chi
Sohal, Harjit Singh
Srinivasan, Ramachandra Srini
Talwani, Manik
Tan, Jack Sim Eddy
Tu, Shiao-Chun
Turek, Laura Kim
Vyas, Premila Hariprasad
Wang, Chao-Cheng
Wang, Don J.
Wang, Su-Su
Wong, Martha
Wong, Norman Zaw
Wong, William Wai-Lun
Woo, Savio Lau-Ching
Wu, Tiee-Jian
Yang, Hee K.
Yang, Karl L.
Yim, Chi-Kin Bennett
Yung, W. K. Alfred

Irving
Chang, Elden T.

Kerrville
Tran, Qui-Phiet

League City
Nakazono, Benito Lopez

Lubbock
Chatterjee, Sankar

Goh, Ben K.
Le, Vy Phuong
Lodhi, M. A. K.
Nguyen, Henry Thien
Peng, George Tso Chih
Yang, Song
Yung, Christoph Yingwai

Mesquite
Zaveri, Prad S.

Missouri City
Patel, Chandrakant B.
Patel, Shirish A.

Nacogdoches
Chang, Mingteh

New Braunfels
Sugioka, Michael Hiroyuki

Odessa
Seth, Shyam S.

Pharr
Liu, David Ta-ching

Plano
Bawa, Mohendra S.
Long, Grace Fan
Patel, Chandrakant J.
Qureshi, Qadeer Ahmad
Shimizu, Scott Edward
Walia, Harjeet Rosie
Zaveri, Prad S.

Port Arthur
Patel, Bhagwandas Mavjibhai

Prairie View
Chang, Ann Han-Chih
Lin, Shield B.
Wang, Fa-chung

Richardson
Huynh, Dung Thiet
Tsen, May F.

San Antonio
Dung, Hou Chi
Ghosh, Amitava
Hsu, Jong-Pyng
Lee, John Chung
Mehta, Kamlesh T.
Nguyen, Vung Duy
Nishimura, Jonathan Sei
Park, Myung Kun
Pemmaraju, Narasimha Rao
Yeh, Lee-Chuan Caroline
Yin, Zenong
Yu, Byung Pal

San Marcos
Meng, Qing-Min

Seabrook
Krishen, Kumar

Sheppard AFB
Sampang, Conrado Carriedo

Sherman
Chen, Terry Li-Tseng

Sugar Land
Chan, James C.
Chang, Robert Huei
Yamauchi, Toshio

The Woodlands
Varma, Rajender S.

Tyler
Kulkarni, Arun Digambar
Yaden, Senka Long

Wichita Falls
Mathur, Achint P.

Windcrest
Yu, John K.

UTAH

Bountiful
Hori, Tom Nichi
Kim, Yun

Layton
Lim, Kap Chul

Logan
Kim, Yun
Salunkhe, Dattajeerao K.
Sharma, Raghubir Prasad
Wang, Zhi Qiang

Midvale
Lam, Toan Hoang
Nadkarni, Sudhir V.

Ogden
Kumar, Raj
Wang, Shi-Hwa

Provo
Lee, Tsaifeng Mazie

Salt Lake City
Chan, Gary M.
Cho, Weol D.
Chong, Richard David
Kim, Sung Wan
Kuo, Wen Hsiung
Liou, Kuo-Nan
Loh, Eugene C.
Mitsunaga, Jimi
Ong, Cynthia K. Char
Sohn, Hong Yong
Tran, Thuan Van
Wong, Kuang Chung
Yang, Anand Alan

Sandy
Lee, Min-Shiu

VERMONT

Bennington
Yamamoto, Roger Masaaki

Burlington
Chen, Hongda
Lin, Roxanne Veronica
Wang, Deane
Wu, Jun-Ru

Middlebury
Yu, Clara

VIRGINIA

Alexandria
Chao, Elaine Lan
Cheng, Tung Chao
Do, Toa Quang
Huang, H. T.
Nguyen, Xe V.
Okuda, Yasuyori
Tang, Victor K. T.
Watanabe, Clyde Kazuto

Yen, Nai-Chyuan

Annandale
Chen, Angela Tzu-Yau
Khim, Jay Wook
Mehta, Gurmukh Dass
Seto, Robert Mahealani Ming
Wu, Yen

Arlington
Briggs, Tracey Wong
Chacko, George Kuttickal
Chang, William Y. B.
Chi, Lotta C. J. Li
Chong, Ken P.
Endo, Paula Sayoko Tsukamoto
Hayakawa, Sidney Akira
Kim, Yong K.
Mehta, Gurmukh Dass
Mukherjee, Tapan Kumar
Ng, Kam Wing
Shah, Mowahid Hussain
Uno, Anne Quan

Blacksburg
Liu, Yilu
Mo, Luke W.
Ng, Wing

Charlottesville
Chan, Donald P. K.
Ghosh, Subhas
Kaul, Sanjiv
Lee, Jen-Shih
Wang, Gwo-Jaw

Chesapeake
Li, Diane Dai
Montero, Juan Murillo, II

Colonial Heights
Chiu, Ming S.

Fairfax
Cao, Le Thi
Nguyen, Manh-Hung
Nguyen, Tri Huu
Shrivastava, Satyendra P.
Sudarshan, T. S.
Wu, Anna Chaoying
Wu, Chien-yun

Falls Church
Bhagat, Nazir A.
Chen, Zhong-Ying
Kan, Victor
Kikuchi, Carl H.
Kim, David Ho-Sik
Outhuok, T.
Yoshimura, Yoshiko

Glen Allen
Dwivedy, Keshab K.

Gloucester Point
Kuo, Albert Yi-shuong

Great Falls
Aulakh, Kay

Hampton
Chaudhuri, Tapan K.
Joshi, Suresh Meghashyam
Leung, Wing Hai
Mehrotra, Sudhir Chandra

Harrisonburg
Ma, Sheng-mei

Herndon
Choi, Michael Kamwah
Goel, Subhash Chand
Islam, Nurul

Tsang, Wai Lin

Lynchburg
Kim, Changyup Daniel

Mc Lean
Chang, Paul Keub
Chuang, De-Maw
Chung, Y. David
Ganguly, Suman
Hwang, William Gaong
Kuttan, Roger
Lee, Cheng-Chun
Patel, Kamla
Pei, Richard Y.
Rhee, Jhoon Goo
Teng, Tsuchi Paul
Yang, Xiaowei

Midlothian
Jaisinghani, Rajan A.

New Kent
Ito, Michael Shuji

Newport News
Chen, Jizeng
Park, Sang Oh

Norfolk
Li, Wu
Wang, Leon Ru-Liang
Wei, Benjamin Min
Yung, Kenneth Kwokhung
Zhao, Quansheng

Oakton
Shieh, Rong Chung

Petersburg
Reddy, C. Subba

Reston
Chao, Edward C. T.
Dharamsi, Manoj T.
Sayala, Dash

Richmond
Chan, James C. M.
Chiou, Minshon J.
Hsu, Hsiu-Sheng
Jena, Purusottam
Jung, Audrey Moo Hing
Kalimi, Mohammed Yahya
Khanna, Shiv Narain
Lee, Hyung Mo
Miah, Abdul J.
Narula, Subhash Chander
Nuon, Samuel
Park-Taylor, Sonya Sunnah
Sheth, Navin D.
Wu, Fang-Sheng
Yu, Robert Kuan-jen
Yung, Ringo

Shawsville
Ijaz, Lubna Razia

Springfield
Lee, Siani
Malik, Saied Ahmad

Sweet Briar
Chang, Claudia

Vienna
Chung, Luke Tsun
Jimenez, Christina Lee
Ke, Gang
Kuttan, Appu
Nguyen, Bao T.
Oettinger, Reena
Shah, Yogesh K.

Yu, Wen C.

Virginia Beach
Cheng, Richard Tien-Ren

Williamsburg
Ito, Michael Shuji
Ito, Satoshi
Zamora, Mario Dimarucut

Woodbridge
Choy, Simon

WASHINGTON

Bellevue
Falaniko, Frank, Jr.
Gulrajani, Robert B.
Lee, Conrad
Mak, Stanley M.
Oki, Scott D.
Pang, Rubye-Huey

Bellingham
Hung, Ken
Kim, Robert Hyung-chan

Bothell
Chen, Sam W.
Hara, Lloyd
McNeely, June
Ng-Breckwoldt, May Sue
Valmonte, Arnel Elvambuena

Burien
Jhaveri, Arunkumar Ganpatlal

College Place
Kim, Jae Won

Edmonds
Chia, Kai

Ellensburg
Lin, Cen-Tsong
Yeh, Thomas Y.

Federal Way
Asahara, David J.
Chin, Warren

Kennewick
Hon, Andrew
Ranade, D. G.

Kent
Shah, Amitkumar L.

Lacey
Liddell, Gene Canque

Mercer Island
Pai, Kenneth Y.

Monroe
Guloy, Pompeyo B., Jr.

Moses Lake
Tse, Stephen

Olympia
Cai, Shelton Xuanqing
Flemming, Stanley Lalit Kumar
Miyahara, Bruce
Moriwaki, Clarence
Shin, Paull H.
Veloria, Velma Rosete
Wang, Arthur C.
Yenson, Evelyn Phoebe

Port Townsend
Nomura, Kaworu Carl

Pullman
Chen, Bintong
Dong, Zheng-Min
Gupta, Yogendra Mohan
Ichiye, Takashi
Kim, Kwan Hee
Mahalingam, R.
Nakata, Herbert Minoru
Wong, Paul

Puyallup
Doi, Stan Sumio

Redmond
Arakawa, Minoru
Myung, John Y.
Nakatani, Roy Eiji
Quan, William Chun
Yagi, Fumio

Renton
Go, Daniel Y.
Kanaya, Barbara J.

Richland
Desai, Sharad P.
Yoshikawa, Herbert Hiroshi

Seattle
Alcantara, Larry James
Bacho, Peter
Basu, Sutapa
Campbell, Phyllis J. Takisaki
Chan, Anthony Bernard
Chen, Shi-Han
Cheng, Josephine
Chew, Ronald A.
Chin, Donald G.
Chin, Henry Han
Cho, Andrew Byong-Woo
Choe, Martha C.
Chow, Cheryl
Chung, Jong Rak Philip
Dao, Tuan Anh
Della, David J.
Djao, Angela Wei
Domingo, Cynthia Garciano
Dow, Faye Lynn
Francisco, Emiliano Alonzo
Fujimoto, Wilfred Yorio
Fujiwara, Theresa
Hu, Shiu-Lok
Huang, Arnold
Huang, Zhen-Fen
Ikeda, Tsuguo
Imamura, Lawrence Junji
Isaki, Paul
Ishimaru, Akira
Iwamoto, Satori
Juanitas, Cyril E. B., Jr.
Kawahara, William T.
Kay, Helen
Kim, Jae Hoon
Kirchner, Bharti
Ko, Ada
Ko, Elaine Ikoma
Kobayashi, Albert Satochi
Kobayashi, John M.
Kobayashi, Koichi
Kondo, C. Kimi
Ku, Peter
Kubota, Carole Ann
Kubota, Kenneth R.
Kumata, Gerald Hiroshi
Kurose, Ruthann
Lachica, Edward Anthony
Laly, Amy
Leong, Robin Yee
Lin, Nina S. F.
Liu, Chen-Ching
Liu, LiLi
Liu, Nora M.
Locke, Gary F.

Loh, Wallace D.
Louie, Cliff
Low, Loh-Lee
Lum, Dean Scott
Ly, Tam Minh
Mamidala, Ramulu
Mamiya, Ron
Mar, Dan K.
Miyata, Keijiro
Nakatani, Roy Eiji
Narayanan, A. Sampath
Ng, Assunta C. M.
Ohta, Masao
Okada, Connie Tokiye
Pang, Martin S.
Ragudos, John L.
Rao, Yalamanchili Krishna
Rawlings, Noella A.
Shigihara, Patricia
Shimizu, Toru
Somani, Arun K.
Su, Judy Ya-Hwa Lin
Sugiyama, Alan
Takami, David A.
Tang, David Kwong-Yu
Venkata, Subrahmanyam
 Saraswati
Wan, Frederic Yui-Ming
Wang, Ji-Ping
Wang, Rita
Warashina, M. Patricia
Wong, Barry
Wong, Benson D.
Wong, Dorothy
Wong, Kar-yiu
Wong, Kwan P.
Wong, Shawn Hsu
Wu, Jennifer Lee
Wu, Stan
Yakasujin, Maxine Toshiko
Yee, Shirley Jo-Ann
Yorozu, William S.
Yoshitomi, Karen

Selah
Toba, Hachiro Harold

Spokane
Bertrand, Mieko
Kuroiwa, George Masaharu
Matsumoto, Iku
Wang, Ming-Yu Rachel

Tacoma
Bacho, Norris V.
Corpuz, Ray E., Jr.
Oh, Joseph
Wang, Arthur C.

Vancouver
Young, Lloyd Yee

Woodinville
Somani, Arun K.
Venkata, Subrahmanyam
 Saraswati

Yakima
Baldoz, Gerald L.
Toba, Hachiro Harold

WEST VIRGINIA

Dunbar
Das Sarma, Basudeb

Fairmont
Shan, Robert Kuocheng
Wang, Shen K.

Institute
Das Sarma, Basudeb

Morgantown
Ahluwalia, Rashpal S.
Chang, William Wei-Lien
Chen, Hung-Liang
Chen, Ping-fan
Chiang, Yi-ling F.
Das, Kamalendu
Kim, Hong Nack
Li, Dening
Nath, Joginder
Peng, Syd S.
Seshadri, Kal S.

New Martinsville
Gangal, Shiva Shanker

Vienna
Kartha, Mukund K.

WISCONSIN

Appleton
Dugal, Hardev S.
Tannan, Ashok

Beloit
Moy, Henry

Brookfield
Lai, Ching-San

Brown Deer
Ishii, Thomas Koryu

Jain, Rajeev K.

Eau Claire
Chan, Lung S.
Chen, Steve S.
Ho, Yui Tim
Huang, Jin
Suh, Yung-Ho

Franklin
Chughtai, Shahid H.

Kenosha
Chen, Chong-Maw

La Crosse
Ma, Xiaoyun

Madison
Bhargava, Ashok
Bhattacharyya, Gouri Kanta
Chang, Chawnshang
Chow, Tse-tsung
Chun, Raymond W. M.
Dong, Wei
Gupta, Amit
Lai, Albert Wenben
Lin, Yü-sheng
Ling, Amy
Moy, James S.
Mukerjee, Pasupati
Narayan, Kirin
Takahashi, Lorey K.
Uno, Hideo
Verma, Ajit K.
Wang, Pao-Kuan

Milwaukee
Chan, Adrian
Chan, Carlyle Hung-lun
Chan, Shih-Hung
Cheng, Eugene Y.
Chong-Gottinger, Ivy Wok
 Kuong
Feng, Xin
Garg, Arun
Ho, Khang-cheng
Jain, Rajeev K.
Kumaran, A. Krishna
Lai, Ching-San
Lee, Kwang K.
Liu, John J.
Naik, Tarun Ratilal
Rohatgi, Pradeep K.
Sieu, Benny Lou
Singh, Ajaib
Tang, Thomas Tze-Tung
Tseng, Leon F.
Wang, Luoyong

Xiong, William Joua
Yu, David C.

Oshkosh
Chang, David Wen-Wei
Chiang, Berttram
Rouf, Mohammed Abdur

River Falls
Kim, Young-Jin
Wang, Qun

Rothschild
Lin, Stephen Yaw-rui

Sheboygan
Hsieh, Wen-jen

Shorewood
Chan, Adrian

Stevens Point
Kim, Hyun Kap
Lee, Chen Hui
Wang, Jin

Tomah
Shim, Sook Chin

Waukesha
Moy, George S.
Shah, Ghulam Mohammad

Wauwatosa
Naik, Tarun Ratilal

Whitewater
Huang, I-Ning
Huang, Joyce L.

WYOMING

Laramie
Cha, Chang-Yul
Ji, Inhae
Ji, Taehwa
Kim, Quee-Young
Sharma, M. P.
Tung, Yeou-Koung
Wang, Junping
Wang, Lih-Jau

CANADA

Edmonton, Alberta
Hirabayashi, Gordon

Toronto, Ontario
Lin, Elizabeth

HONG KONG

Kowloon
Chang, Eric Chieh
Huang, Ju-Chang
Kung, Shain-dow
Sheng, Ping

ITALY

Rome
Ting, Sandra

JAPAN

Nagasaki-shi
Hayashi, Tetsumaro

Sapporo
Takahashi, Kozo

Tokyo
Akebono
Makino, Shojiro

PHILIPPINES

Makati
Denton, Victoria Villena-

SINGAPORE
Liu, Warren Kuo-Tung

SWITZERLAND

Geneva
Wu, Sau Lan Yu

TAIWAN

Hsinchu
Yang, Chyan

Taipei
Huang, Jack J. T.

TaoYuan
Huang, Laura Yueh-Guey

OCCUPATION INDEX

**ACCOUNTING/
AUDITING
(SEE ALSO
MANAGEMENT/
ADMINISTRATION—
ACCOUNTING/
FINANCIAL)**
Arikawa, Norman
Asano, Izumi
Bedi, Sandeep
Cao, Le Thi
Chandy, Varughese Kuzhiyath
Chen, Chong-Tong
Chen, Tai
Chen, Victoria Liu
Chin, Thomas
Chitkara, Vijay Kumar
Cho, Jang Youn
Choi, Eunhye Jenni
Choi, Frederick D. S.
Chung, Anni Yuet-Kuen
Gandhi, Homi D.
Gulrajani, Robert B.
Gupta, Brij Mohanlal
Gupta, Parveen P.
Gupta, Sanjay
Haque, M. Shamsul
Hong, S. Theodore
Hwang, Dennis B. K.
Hwang, Nen-chen Richard
Jaiswal, Gopaljee
Jang, Dennis
Joe, Alexander H.
Kadomoto, Thomas
Kam, Thomas K. Y.
Kam, Vernon T.
Kapadia, Bharat S.
Kato, Theodore Toshihiko
Khorasanee, Barker M.
Kim, Il-Woon
Kim, Neung Jip
Ko, Steven W.
Kudo, Eigo H.
Kwak, Wikil
Lai, Richard Thomas
Leung, Margaret W.
Li, Yu-ku
Liao, Woody M.
Lin, Juiyuan William
Lin, You-An Robert
Ly, Kieu Kim
Marasigan, Rogelio U.
McNeely, June
Mehta, Krishnakant Hiralal
Melookaran, Joseph
Modi, Shailesh
Ng, May-May Donna Lee
Nguyen, Benjamin Ban
Nguyen, Bong Van
Nishina, Clifford M.
Ong, Cynthia K. Char
Ong, James M.
Parikh, Pravin P.
Park, Sung-Il
Patel, Chandu M.
Patel, Jay M.
Patel, Kantilal P.
Patel, Sanjay Vrajlal

Patel, Shailesh R.
Respicio, Elsa Toje
Sato, Tommy M.
Shim, Eun Sup
Shin, Doug Yong
Siu, Nancy
Soo, Billy S.
Soo Hoo, Richard
Soohoo, Richard Allen
Suelto, Teem D.
Tang, Alex Ying Ho
Tang, Roger Y. W.
Toda, Harold Keiji
Tran, Thang Nhut
Tran, Tuyet-Nhung T.
Varghese, Thomas K.
Wong, Gregory Dean
Wong, Steven W.
Wu, Frederick H.
Yamada, Yozo
Yang, David C.
Yang, Dongpyo
Yang, Sun Hye
Yee, John David
Yiu, Pao On
Yoon, Myung-Ho

ACTING
Aoki, Brenda Jean
Chao, Rosalind
Chen, Joan
Cheung, Cindy Siu-Whei
Chong, Rae Dawn
Chong, Tommy
Choudhury, Sarita
Dang, Tim
Fischer, Takayo
Florentino, Leila San Jose
Goto, Yukihiro
Hill, Amy
Jao, Radmar Agana
Jue, Francis
Kothari, Ajay P.
Kuroda, Emily
Kurup, Shishir Ravindran
Kwan, Nancy Kashen
Lee, Brandon
Lee, Guy
Lee, Jason Scott
Lee, Miko
Lee, Robert Terry
Leong, Robin Yee
Louganis, Greg E.
Mako
McCarthy, Nobu
Morita, Pat
Nakazono, Benito Lopez
Ngor, Haing S.
Nishioka, Hayward H.
Paz, Jennifer C.
Reeves, Keanu
Rhee, Phillip
Salonga, Lea
Sunaida, Mari
Tagawa, Cary-Hiroyuki
Takei, George Hosato
Tomita, Tamlyn Naomi

Wang, Luoyong
Wong, B. D.

**ACTIVISM, POLITICAL/
CIVIL/SOCIAL
RIGHTS**
Basu, Sutapa
Chang, Patricia W.
Chen, Pamela Ki Mai
Chuang, Strong C.
Das Dasgupta, Shamita
de la Peña, Violeta R.
Domingo, Cynthia Garciano
Embrey, Sue Kunitomi
Finucane, Matthew H.
Fong, J Craig
Gee, Dolly M.
Gupta, Raj Kumar
Hotta, Gina H.
Iiyama, Chizu
Ishi, Tomoji
Iwataki, Miya
Kawata, Paul Akio
Kiang, Peter Nien-chu
Konoshima, Joji
Krishna, Gopal T. K.
Kwok, Daphne
Lee, Pamela Tau
Lee, Vivian Wai-fun
Ling, Christine N.
Liu, Richard Chung-Wen
Lui, MeiZhu
Murakami, Jeffrey Hisakazu
Murase, Mike
Nash, Philip Tajitsu
Natividad, Irene
Ono, Yoko
Ozaki, Yoji
Park, Laura Heyong
Prabhu, R. D.
Ratti, Rakesh Kumar
Seid, Allan
Senzaki, Randall Kiyomi
Singh, Kim
Sundaresan, Gloria Marquez
Szeto, Erik K.
Tsukamoto, Mary Tsuruko
Weglyn, Michi Nishiura
Wong, Linda J.
Wong, Nellie
Wu, Christopher N.
Yoshimura, Evelyn
Young, Hoa Pham

ACTUARIAL SCIENCE
Li, Guodong
Patel, Dilipkumar Z.
Shih, Fred F.
Yuen, Calvin N.

**ADVERTISING/
PROMOTION
(SEE ALSO
MANAGEMENT/
ADMINISTRATION—
ADVERTISING/
MARKETING/PUBLIC
RELATIONS)**
Jen, Serena
Kong, Ana C.
Lee, Wei-Na
Liu, Richard Chung-Wen
Maeyama, Kikuko
McCarty, Faith B.
Mitchell-Onuma, Susan C.
Ng, Assunta C. M.
Taura, Richard Bill
Tong, Jennie S.

AEROSPACE
SEE ENGINEERING—
AEROSPACE

AGRIBUSINESS
Fukuhara, Henry
Hayashida, Charley Taketoshi
Kuwahara, Frank
Lau, Gilbert Minjun
Matsuo, Paul T.
Mustafa, Shams
Oshiro, Kathleen F.
Sabharwal, Kulbir
Wu, Lyn Xiling

**AGRICULTURAL
SCIENCE**
Anand, Satish Chandra
Chan, Harvey Thomas, Jr.
Chandan, Ramesh Chandra
Chang, Ernest Sun-Mei
Chang, Kow-Ching
Chen, Tseh An
Cheng, H. H.
Chiang, Huai C.
Chong, Pek-Ean
Fujii, Jack Koji
Gavande, Sampat A.
Geng, Shu
Gupta, Santosh
Gupta, Virendra K.
Han, Susan S.
Haramaki, Chiko
Hayashi, Fumihiko
Honma, Shigemi
Huang, Feng Hou
Huang, Jamin
Islam, Nurul
Ito, Philip Jitsuo
Jain, Rakesh
Jen, Joseph Jwu-Shan
Joshi, Jagmohan
Kim, Kwang-Shin
Kim, Leo
Kuan, Shia Shiong
Kumar, Ramesh

Lal, Rattan
Leung, PingSun
Liang, George Hsueh-Lee
Lim, Chhorn E.
Lu, John Y.
Luh, Bor Shiun
Mahilum, Benjamin C.
Miyamoto, Seiichi
Nguyen, Henry Thien
Nip, Wai-Kit
Ogawa, Joseph Minoru
Patel, Narayan G.
Peng, Ying-shin Christine
Qureshi, Muquarrab Ahmed
Raina, Ashok K.
Reddy, Gudigopuram Bhaskar
Reddy, Ramakrishna P.
Rhee, Khee Choon
Sehgal, Om Parkash
Sen, Arun Kumar
Shah, Syed M.
Sharma, Govind Chandra
Sharma, Hari Chand
Shih, Jason Chia-Hsing
Sidhu, Gurmel Singh
Sun, Samuel Sai-Ming
Tai, Peter Y. P.
Tan, Kim Howard
Tang, Chung-Shih
Toba, Hachiro Harold
Tsai, Chia-Yin
Tsai, James H.
Wan, Peter J.
Wang, Chien Yi
Wang, Jaw-Kai
Wang, Jen-Yu
Yang, Shang Fa
Yee, Lawrence K.
Yen, Yang
Yih, Roy Yangming

AIRLINE INDUSTRY
Chacko, Kurian
Fujimatsu, Tadao
Gangwal, Rakesh
Oh, Taesung
Oshiro, Roy C.
Shimokihara, Stanley Shigeo
Thadani, Raju
Wong, Clifford S.

ANTHROPOLOGY
Anderson, Wanni W.
Chang, Claudia
Chang, Kwang-chih
Chia, Ning
Hirabayashi, Lane Ryo
Kikumura, Akemi
Kim, Choong Soon
Kim, Myung-Hye
Liu, Xingwu
Narayan, Kirin
Rhee, Song Nai
Watanabe, John Mamoru
Wong, Bernard P.
Zamora, Mario Dimarucut

ARCHAEOLOGY
Chang, Claudia
Chang, Kwang-chih
Kikuchi, William Kenji
Rhee, Song Nai

ARCHITECTURE
Abo, Ronald K.
Bhandari, Sanjiv
Chan, Chiu Shui
Chan, Edwin Y.
Chan, Lo-Yi C. Y.
Chen, John Shaoming
Ch'en, Lena B.
Chen, Paul Kuan Yao
Cheng, Lawrence Kai-Leung
Cheng, Tung Chao
Chien, Alan Shueshih
Chin, Grace Y.
Chinn, Roger
Chong, Richard David
Chou, Hsin-Pei
Chow, Ivan S.
Chun, Wei Foo
Gupta, Ron Singh
Han, Jinchen
Hata, Hiroaki
Hoang, Frank H.
Hori, Tom Nichi
Hsiao, Tony An-Jen
Hsieh, Tom
Hsu, Merlin
Inaba, Jeffrey Norihisa
Jeong, Wallace Dun
Kajiwara, Kenneth Kyo
Kim, Jong-Jin
Kim, Michael Kyong-il
Kubota, Kenneth R.
Kumata, Gerald Hiroshi
Lam, Thomas Manpan
Lee, Jeff S.
Lew, Eugene
Lim, Joo Kun
Lin, Jennifer Jen-Huey
Lin, Maya Ying
Liu, Alfred H.
Liu, Nora M.
Matsumoto, George
Moy, Stan Yip
Nayak, Bhagchand D.
Ng, Jeffrey C. F.
Obata, Gyo
Ohashi, Alan Joseph
Park, Young Whan
Patel, Ray J.
Pei, I. M.
Peng, George Tso Chih
Pouw, Stanley Siong-In
Sasaki, Hideo
Sato, Shigetada
Sibal, Nicolas Villadolid
Sinco, Victor
Sze, Chia-Ming
Taniguchi, Alan Y.
Thakore, Kirit Jamiyatram
Valmonte, Arnel Elvambuena
Whang, Benjamin
Wong, Janine Mei-Chiao
Wong, Liliane R.
Wu, Hofu
Yang, Albert C.
Yang, Susan Y.
Yien, Jean May
Yung, Ringo

ART, VISUAL—COMMERCIAL ART/GRAPHIC DESIGN
Bertrand, Mieko
Chan, Phillip Paang
Chan Costa, Vivian Rhoda

Emura, Cynthia Sanae
Furuta, Soichi
Gee, Zand F.
Gn, Thye-Wee
Huang, Ken Shen
Ishikawa-Wolf, Ana Yoshiko
Kong, Stanley Young
Lagura, Franklin Sasutana
Lee, Clarence Kim Mun
Lim, Chong C.
Liu, Leighton Kam Fat
Liu, Lily Pao-Ih
Mar, William David
Nakaguchi, Richard T.
Patel, Mitesh K.
Rhim, Aesop
Shirai, Akiko
Taura, Richard Bill
Tolentino, Virginia Cantor
Wong, Albert Y.

ART, VISUAL—ILLUSTRATION
Arai, Tomie
Chan Costa, Vivian Rhoda
Chavan, Sangita D.
Chen, Tony Young
Hong, Lily Toy
Kingman, Dong
Li, San-pao
Lim, Edward Hong
Ma, Wenhai
Nakaguchi, Richard T.
Say, Allen
Tang, Charles Chau Ching
Tseng, Mou-sien
Yee, Wong Herbert

ART, VISUAL—PAINTING
Chee, Cheng-Khee
Chen, Hilo C. H.
Cheng, Amy I.
Cheng, Fu-Ding
Chin, Grace Y.
Chu, Julia Nee
Chung, Ling Jia
Deng, Ming-Dao
Djao, Angela Wei
Fukuhara, Henry
Gee, Norman F.
Goto, Joseph N.
Huang, Ken Shen
Ikegawa, Shiro
Jung, Kwan Yee
Jung, Yee Wah
Kam, Mei-Ki F. P.
Kan, Diana
Kan, Kit-Keung
Kanemitsu, Matsumi
Kim, Poe
Kingman, Dong
Kuo, James K. Y.
Kuo, Nina L.
Lagura, Franklin Sasutana
Lai, Waihang
Laigo, Valeriano Emerciano Montante
Lee, Bing
Lee, Sun-Young Won
Li-lan
Lim, Edward Hong
Liu, Nancy Shao-Lan
Maeda, Robert J.
Meng, Qing-Min
Miyasaki, George Joji
Miyata, Keijiro
Munakata, Grace Megumi
Nagano, Paul Tatsumi
Nakashima, Tom Vincent
Nguyen, Long

Okamura, Arthur Shinji
Ono, Yoko
Roser, Ce
Shih, Joan Fai
Tang, Charles Chau Ching
Tse, Stephen
Tseng, Mou-sien
Tsutakawa, George
Usui, Kiichi
Wang, Victor Sheng
Wong, Frederick
Wong, Mel
Wong, Paul K.
Yeh, Ida Shuyen Chiang
Yen, Joan Jue
Yoshida, Ray Kakuo

ART, VISUAL—SCULPTING
Chin, Grace Y.
Ching, Theodora Lam
Goto, Joseph N.
Hom, Mei-Ling
Kim, Yoonchung Park
Kwong, Eva
Lin, Maya Ying
Miyata, Keijiro
Mori, John P.
Nguyen, Long
Niizuma, Minoru
Peii, Ahmad Osni
Saito, Seiji
Tsutakawa, George
Tsutakawa, Gerard K.
Warashina, M. Patricia

ART, VISUAL—NOT ELSEWHERE CLASSIFIED
Arai, Tomie
Brillantes, Hermogenes Bilgera
Chen, Ming
Chew, Richard Franklin
Chin, Alice L.
Chung, Y. David
Endo, Paula Sayoko Tsukamoto
Fong, Mary Helena
Fulbeck, Kip
Hanami, Clement S.
Hom, Mei-Ling
Horiuchi, Chikamasa Paul
Ikegawa, Shiro
Kimura, Risaburo
Koga, Mary H.
Kuo, Yih-Wen
Kwong, Eva
Lee, Chen Lok
Lew, William W.
Li, Chu-tsing
Lin, Ilan S.
Liu, Lily Pao-Ih
Min, Yong Soon
Miyamoto, Wayne Akira
Morita, John Takami
Murakami, Pamela S.
Noda, Takayo
Ohno, Mitsugi
Pal, Pratapaditya
Saeki, Hiroko Yoda
Saito, Yoshio
Sakoda, James Minoru
Shirai, Akiko
Suzuki, Howard Kazuro
Wong, Paul K.

ASSOCIATION MANAGEMENT
Allen, Susan Au
Aoki, Guy Miki
Banik, Sambhu Nath

Barve, Kumar P.
Blanco, Paul De La Cruz
Caoile, Gloria T.
Chan, Cheung M.
Chan, Lo-Yi C. Y.
Chang, Amy Lee
Chang, Warren W.
Chao, Elaine Lan
Chhim, Him S.
Chiang, Chao-Kuo
Chin, Helen
Chinn, Daisy Wong
Choi, Sung Sook
Chung, Anni Yuet-Kuen
Chung, Lisa A.
Das Dasgupta, Shamita
de la Peña, Violeta R.
Der, Henry
Ebata, Duane
Eng, Patricia
Evangelista, Stella
Fong, J Craig
Fujimura, Robert Kiyoshi
Geaga, Jaime V.
Goishi, Dean M.
Guillermo, Tessie
Guloy, Pompeyo B., Jr.
Hahn, Youngja Choi
Harano, Ross Masao
Hauh, Paul-Thomas B.
Hayashi, Tetsumaro
Hennessy, Sumiko Tanaka
Hoang, Giao
Hokoyama, J. D.
Hong, Carl
Hong, S. K.
Hsi, David C.
Hsiao, Julia
Hsu, Evelyn
Igasaki, Paul
Iiyama, Chizu
Ito, Caryl
Iwanaga-Penrose, Margaret
Japra, Romesh K.
Kabadi, Balachandra Narayan
Kaneko, William Masami
Kano, Sachio
Kashiwagi, Soji Charles
Kawata, Paul Akio
Ke, Gang
Kim, Bong Hwan
Kim, Chang Kyu
Kim, Vivian C.
Kiriyama, Iku
Kita, Sadao
Ko, Elaine Ikoma
Kobayashi, Key K.
Kochiyama, William
Konoshima, Joji
Kumar, Narinder M.
Kuttan, Appu
Kuwahara, Frank
Kwok, Daphne
Lau, Regina
Le, Xuan Khoa
Lee, Guy
Li, Marjorie H.
Limb, Ben Quincy
Lingappa, Yamuna
Liu, Gerald Hanmin
Lo, Yao
Lowe, Rolland Choy
Magdamo, Patricia L.
Mak, Paul P.
Mammen, Thomas
Maniwa, Kaz
Masaoka, Miya Joan
Mathai-Davis, Prema
Mathur, Balbir Singh
Moy, Edmund
Nakajo, Steve
Nakasato, George
Nishimura, Tom

O, Cao Kinh
O, San Luong
Oh, Angela
Ohashi, Wataru
Oki, Scott D.
Paek, Min
Phan, Trung Huynh
Pillay, Mullayil K. G.
Ragudos, John L.
Rhee, Jhoon Goo
Rinpoche, Gelek
Saito, Walter Masao
Seid, Allan
Senzaki, Miyo
Shah, Uma
Shin, Ernest Eun-Ho
Shin, Young
Singh, Kim
Sogi, Francis Y.
Song, John D.
Soo, Charlie H.
Sum, Grace C. K.
Takahashi, Abraham Tomio
Takiguchi, Masako
Takimoto, Mabel Yayoko
Tan, Chor Weng
Tan, Nady
Tazoi, Norma
Tonai, Rosalyn
Tsui, Annie
Tsui, Pauline Woo
Vanchiasong, Siong Koua
Wada, Patricia
Wang, Rita
Watanabe, Mike
Wing, Charmeen Hah-Ming
Wong, Byron F.
Wong, Kent Douglas
Wong, Linda J.
Yoshino, William
Yoshitomi, Karen
Young, Peter R.
Yu, Byung Pal

ASTRONOMY
SEE PHYSICS/ASTRONOMY

ATHLETICS
SEE SPORTS—AMATEUR; SPORTS—PROFESSIONAL/SEMIPROFESSIONAL; SPORTS—NOT ELSEWHERE CLASSIFIED; SPORTS COACHING/TRAINING/MANAGING/OFFICIATING

AUDITING
SEE ACCOUNTING/AUDITING

AUTOMOBILE INDUSTRY
SEE MANUFACTURING—MOTOR VEHICLES; RETAIL TRADE—MOTOR VEHICLES, PARTS, AND SERVICES; WHOLESALE TRADE—MOTOR VEHICLES AND PARTS

AVIATION
SEE **AIRLINE INDUSTRY**

BANKING/FINANCIAL SERVICES
Aoyama, Yasutaka Barron
Arora, Samir Chandra
Au, Leo Yuin
Bhatt, Kiran Chandrakant
Bhattacharya, Purna
Bloch, Julia Chang
Campbell, Phyllis J. Takisaki
Chacko, Varkki P.
Chan, Angela
Chan, Su Han
Chandersekaran, Achamma C.
Chang, Elden T.
Chang, Ming
Chang, Nelson
Chau, Peter
Chaudhri, Rajiv Jahangir
Chen, Andrew Houng-Yhi
Chen, Bernard Shao-Wen
Chen, Chao
Chen, David Ta-Fu
Chen, Derrick A.
Chen, John L.
Chen, Thomas K. S.
Chen, Victoria Liu
Chen, Yea-Mow
Cheng, Hsueh-Jen
Chin, George K. W.
Ching, Hugh
Ching, Joseph Yu Nun
Choe, Kenneth
Choi, Paul W.
Choi, Songsu
Choi, Tony Sung
Chopra, Jasbir
Chow, Brian Gee-Yin
Chu, Franklin Janen
Chu, Terence
Chua, Conrad E.
Chung, Harold
Datta, Ranajit Kumar
Dayao, Firmo Salvador
Fen, Allan Ming
Fong, Hiram Leong
Fong, Joshua
Fung, Hung-Gay
Gandhi, Homi D.
Hayashida, Charley Taketoshi
Hsia, Yukun
Hsiao, Joan Hsi-Min
Hsu, George Chi-Yung
Huang, Arnold
Hwang, Henry Y.
Hwang, Ivy
Jang, Dennis
Jimenez, Josephine Santos
Kalra, Rajiv
Kapadia, H. Viren
Kawano, Arnold H.
Ku, William H.
Kulkarni, Dilip
Kuttan, Roger
Kwok, Chuck Chun-yau
Kwok, Joseph
Lam, Dick
Lam, Nelson Jen-Wei
Lau, Gloria J.
Lee, Juwan
Leung, Ida M.
Leung, Som-Lok
Li, Bob Cheng-Liang
Li, Conan K. N.
Li, Ivan C.
Li, Lily Elizabeth
Lin, Juiyuan William
Liu, Dwight Davidson
Liu, Wei-Ying

Mahajan, Y. Lal
Marasigan, Rogelio U.
Maruyama, Kiyoshi
Mathai, Anish
Ng, May-May Donna Lee
Nguyen, Xe V.
Oettinger, Reena
Oshima, Harold H.
Park, Jinwoo
Parke, Keol-bai
Patel, Hiren S.
Ramachandran, Rita
Renge, I. Beth
Sankaran, Aiylam P.
Santos, Mario Alban
Shimizu, Taisuke
Shin, Hung Sik
Shum, William
Siu, Nancy
Takei, George Hosato
Tang, Alex Ying Ho
Thakur, Manish
Tse, Sau P.
Tsusaka, Jun
Tung, John
Tung, Theodore H.
Uchida, Yoshihiro
Varghese, Raju Molethu
Varghese, Thomas K.
Virk, Muhammad Yaqub
Wang, Don J.
Wang, George Hung-Kai
Wang, Tsuey Tang
Wong, Alvin C. P.
Wong, James H.
Wong, Philip T.
Wong, Sophie Chao
Wong, Wing Y.
Wu, Frank I.
Yee, John David
Yoshida, Kanetaka
Yu, Wen C.
Yuh, Jai K.

BIOCHEMISTRY
Aggarwal, Bharat Bhushan
Ahluwalia, Balwant S.
Ahn, Ho-Sam
Bahl, Om Parkash
Banerjee, Amiya Kumar
Bhathena, Sam Jehangirji
Bhatnagar, Deepak
Bhown, Ajit Singh
Bhuyan, Bijoy Kumar
Bora, Sunder S.
Cabana, Veneracion Garganta
Cha, Sungman
Chan, David S.
Chan, Pui Kwong
Chan, Samuel H. P.
Chandan, Ramesh Chandra
Chang, Chawnshang
Chang, Sookyung
Chang, Yung-Feng
Chaturvedi, Arvind Kumar
Chaudhari, Anshumali
Chaudhry, G. Rasul
Chen, Chong-Maw
Chen, Harry W.
Chen, James Pai-fun
Chen, Kuang Yu
Chen, Victor John
Cheung, Herbert Chiu-Ching
Cheung, Wai Yiu
Chi, Myung Sun
Chiang, Thomas Minghung
Ch'ih, John Juwei
Chishti, Athar Husain
Chiu, Wah
Chiu, Yuan-yuan H.
Cho, Wonhwa
Choi, Ye-Chin

Chou, Iih-Nan
Chou, Kuo-Chen
Chow, Louise Tsi
Chowdhry, Vinay
Chung, Ronald Aloysius
Chung, Thomas D.
Das, Salil Kumar
Dixit, Balwant N.
Dutta, Shib Prasad
Dwivedi, Chandradhar
Eng, Lawrence Fook
Fu, Shou-Cheng Joseph
Fujimura, Robert Kanji
Gan, José C.
Haldar, Dipak
Hanafusa, Hidesaburo
Hayashi, Fumihiko
Hayashi, James Akira
Ho, Chien
Ho, Peter Peck Koh
Hosmane, Ramachandra S.
Hsie, Abraham Wuhsiung
Hsieh, Durwynne
Hsu, Robert Ying
Huang, Chau-Ting
Huang, H. T.
Hui, Sek Wen
Humayun, M. Zafri
Inagami, Tadashi
Iqbal, Zafar
Jaglan, Prem S.
Jain, Mahendra K.
Jeevanandam, Malayappa
Ji, Inhae
Ji, Taehwa
Jungalwala, Firoze Bamanshaw
Kaji, Akira
Kan-Mitchell, June
Kao, Kung-Ying Tang
Kaul, Balkrishena
Kim, Helen
Kim, Kwan Hee
Kiron, Ravi
Kishimoto, Yasuo
Kobayashi, Yutaka
Koide, Samuel Saburo
Kokatnur, Mohan Gundo
Kompala, Dhinakar S.
Kono, Tetsuro
Kripalani, Kishin J.
Krishna, N. Rama
Kuan, Shia Shiong
Kulkarni, Arun P.
Kumaroo, K.
Kuramitsu, Howard K.
Kuwahara, Steven Sadao
Lai, Michael Ming-Chiao
Lau, Joseph T. Y.
Lee, Angel Wai-Mun
Lee, Chi-Jen
Lee, Diana Mang
Lee, John Chung
Lee, Lihsyng Stanford
Lee, Marietta Y. W. T.
Lee, Richard Fayao
Lei, Shau-Ping
Leung, Benjamin Shuet-Kin
Li, Conan K. N.
Li, Steven Shoei-lung
Lian, Eric Chun-Yet
Liang, Tehming
Liao, Mei-June
Liao, Shutsung
Liem, Ronald Kian Hong
Lim, Ramon Khe-Siong
Lin, Diane Chang
Lin, Jiann-Tsyh
Loor, Rueyming
Louis, Lawrence Hua-Hsien
Lu, John Y.
Lu, Ponzy
Mahesh, Virendra Bhushan
Manne, Veeraswamy

Mao, James Chieh-Hsia
Mathur, Kailash V.
Mehta, Rajendra G.
Mizuno, Nobuko Shimotori
Moudgil, Virinder K.
Muni, Indu A.
Murai, Norimoto
Muthukrishnan, Subbaratnam
Myer, Yash Paul
Myoda, Toshio Timothy
Nguyen-huu, Xuong
Nomura, Masayasu
Oh, Chan Soo
Ohnishi, Tomoko
Oka, Takami
Ou, Ching-Nan
Paik, Woon Ki
Pak, Koon Yan
Papasani, Subbaiah Venkata
Parikh, Indu
Parthasarathy, Sampath
Phan, Sem Hin
Prasad, Rameshwar
Radhakrishnamurthy, Bhandaru
Raj, Harkisan D.
Rao, Ananda G.
Rao, Gundu H. R.
Reddy, Bandaru S.
Reddy, Chilekampalli Adinarayana
Roy-Burman, Pradip
Sanadi, D. R.
Sani, Brahma P.
Sarkar, Fazlul H.
Sassa, Shigeru
Sayala, Chhaya
Seth, Arun K.
Siddiqui, Aleem Abdul
Sihag, Ram K.
Singh, Prithipal
Srivastava, Prakash Narain
Subramani, Suresh
Sun, Frank F.
Sun, Tung-Tien
Sundaram, Kalyan
Sundaresan, P. Ramnathan
Suzuki, Tsuneo
Sy, Jose
Sze, Paul Y.
Tai, Hsin-Hsiung
Takashima, Shiro
Tang, Chung-Shih
Thadhani, Kaloo C.
Tong, Sun-De
Tripathi, Satish Chandra
Tsai, Lin
Tsao, Francis Hsiang-Chian
Tse Dinh, Yuk-Ching
Tsen, May F.
Ts'o, Paul On Pong
Tu, Shiao-Chun
Tye, Bik-Kwoon Yeung
Verma, Ajay
Verma, Ajit K.
Wang, Chi-Sun
Wang, Ching Chung
Wang, Howard H.
Wang, Kuan
Wang, Nancy Y.
Wei, Robert
Wong, David Taiwai
Wong, Dorothy Pan
Wong, Peter M. C.
Wong, Peter P.
Woody, A-Young Moon
Wu, Joseph M.
Wu, Roy S.
Wu, Ying Victor
Yagi, Haruhiko
Yamamoto, Keith Robert
Yan, Sau-Chi Betty
Yang, Chung S.
Yang, Jen Tsi

Yang, Shang Fa
Yang, Song-Yu
Yeh, Lee-Chuan Caroline
Yen, Tien-Sze Benedict
Yih, Roy Yangming
Yoon, Hyo-Chun
Yoshida, Akira
Young, Franklin
Yu, Chang-An
Yu, Fu-Li
Yu, Robert Kuan-jen
Yu, Shiu Yeh
Yue, Robert Hon-Sang

BIOLOGY/ MICROBIOLOGY
Aggarwal, Bharat Bhushan
Banerjee, Amiya Kumar
Bhatnagar, Deepak
Bhattacharjee, Jnanendra Kumar
Bhattacharya, Pradeep Kumar
Borgaonkar, Digamber Shankarrao
Chan, James C.
Chan, John G.
Chan, Lee-Nien Lillian
Chan, Po Chuen
Chan, Sham-Yuen
Chan, Stephen W.
Chandran, Satish Raman
Chang, Amy Lee
Chang, Jennie C. C.
Chang, Kwang-Poo
Chang, Te-Wen
Chang, Timothy S.
Chao, Jowett
Chao, Lin
Chapatwala, Kirit D.
Chaudhry, G. Rasul
Chen, Anne Chi
Chen, Chong-Maw
Cheng, Lanna
Cheng, Sheue-yann
Cheng, Tu-chen
Chi, Lotta C. J. Li
Chin, Edwin, Jr.
Choi, Sung Sook
Choi, Ye-Chin
Chou, Iih-Nan
Chung, King-Thom
Chung, Simon Lam-Ying
Debroy, Chitrita
Dhaliwal, Amrik Singh
Doi, Roy Hiroshi
Fok, Agnes Kwan
Fong, April Ann
Fung, Daniel Yee Chak
Fung, Henry C.
Ghosh, Swapan Kumar
Gulati, Adarsh Kumar
Gupta, Sanjeev
Hanafusa, Hidesaburo
Hikida, Robert Seiichi
Ho, Chien
Ho, David D.
Ho, Yui Tim
Hokama, Yoshitsugi
Honda, Shigeru Irwin
Hsi, David C.
Hsu, Hsiu-Sheng
Hsu, Konrad Chang
Hu, Shiu-Lok
Huang, Alice Shih-Hou
Huang, Chau-Ting
Huang, H. T.
Huang, Liang Hsiung
Humayun, M. Zafri
Hung, Kuen-Shan
Hung, Paul P.
Itakura, Keiichi
Jalil, Mazhar
Jayaswal, Raoheshyam K.

Jen, Philip HungSun
Ji, Inhae
Ji, Taehwa
Jung, Lawrence Kwok Leung
Kaji, Akira
Kang, Chang-Yuil
Kartha, Mukund K.
Khan, Mohammed Abdul
  Quddus
Kim, Byung Suk
Kim, Kwang-Shin
Kiron, Ravi
Ko, Wen-hsiung
Kobayashi, Bert Nobuo
Koide, Samuel Saburo
Kompala, Dhinakar S.
Konishi, Masakazu
Kumar, Kusum Verma
Kumaran, A. Krishna
Kumaroo, K.
Kung, Patrick Chung-Shu
Kung, Shain-dow
Kuo, Chao Ying
Kuramitsu, Howard K.
Kwon-Chung, Kyung Joo
Lachica, Edward Anthony
Lai, Michael Ming-Chiao
Lai, Patrick Kinglun
Lau, Joseph T. Y.
Lee, Chung
Lee, Lee Hwang
Lee, Marietta Y. W. T.
Lee, Siu-Lam
Li, Steven Shoei-lung
Liem, Karel Frederik
Lim, Daniel V.
Lin, James C.
Lin, Shin
Ling, Hubert
Lingappa, Banadakoppa
  Thimmappa
Lingappa, Yamuna
Liu, Pinghui Victor
Loor, Rueyming
Mai, Marianne Vu
Manne, Veeraswamy
Mizutani, Satoshi
Morita, Richard Yukio
Myoda, Toshio Timothy
Nakamura, Mitsuru James
Nakata, Herbert Minoru
Nath, Joginder
Nishioka, David Jitsuo
Omata, Robert Rokuro
Pai, Anna Chao
Park, Chung Uk
Pun, Pattle Pak-Toe
Raj, Harkisan D.
Rajendran, Vazhaikkurichi M.
Raju, Solomon Nalli, Sr.
Rao, Venigalla Basaveswara
Reddy, Chilekampalli
  Adinarayana
Rha, ChoKyun
Rouf, Mohammed Abdur
Ryu, Dewey Doo Young
Sadana, Ajit
Sato, Masahiko
Shah, Dhiren Bhawanji
Shah, Syed M.
Sharma, Udhishtra Deva
Shih, Jason Chia-Hsing
Shih, Ming-Che
Siddiqui, Aleem Abdul
Singh, Ajaib
Singh, Baldev
Singh, Balwant
Singh, Harpal
Singh, Madho
Sinha, Akhouri A.
So, Magdalene Yee-Huen
Subramani, Suresh
Suzuki, Tsuneo

Sze, Paul Y.
Takahashi, Joseph S.
Takahashi, Lorey K.
Takeshita, Kenichi
Tam, James Pingkwan
Tanaka, S. Ken
Tanouye, Mark Allen
Thadhani, Kaloo C.
Tonegawa, Susumu
Tripathi, Satish Chandra
Tse, Harley Yau-Shuin
Tsen, May F.
Tsuji, Kiyoshi
Tung, Hsi-tang
Tye, Bik-Kwoon Yeung
Uchida, Richard Noboru
Unakar, Nalin Jayantilal
Urano, Muneyasu
Vedamuthu, Ebenezer Rajkumar
Verma, Ram Sagar
Vyas, Girish N.
Wang, James Chou
Wang, Sho-Ya
Wei, Wei-Zen
Whang, Sukoo Jack
Wong, Peter M. C.
Wong, Peter P.
Wu, Chun-Fang
Wu, Fang-Sheng
Wu, William Gay
Yaden, Senka Long
Yamashiroya, Herbert Mitsugi
Yang, Da-Ping
Yang, Tsu-Ju
Yen, Yang
Yoshimura, Michael Akira
Yu, Chi Kang

BOTANY

Bhattacharya, Pradeep Kumar
Choi, Young Dong
Falaniko, Frank, Jr.
Ho, Hon Hing
Kwon-Chung, Kyung Joo
Lin, Liang-Shiou
Ling, Hubert
Murai, Norimoto
Sagawa, Yoneo
Shih, Ming-Che
Sidhu, Gurmel Singh
Sung, Zinmay Renee
Tanada, Takuma

BUILDING/
CONSTRUCTION
(*SEE ALSO* RETAIL
TRADE—BUILDING/
CONSTRUCTION
MATERIALS;
WHOLESALE TRADE—
BUILDING/
CONSTRUCTION
MATERIALS)

Akiyoshi, Mike M.
Aulakh, Kay
Barot, Navnit Manilal
Cauthorn, James Daniel
Chang, Weilin P.
Chiogioji, Melvin H.
Datta, Vijay K.
Falaniko, Frank, Jr.
Higuchi, Clayton T.
Hsiao, Feng
Huang, William H.
Iwahashi, Satoshi
Iwata, Paul Yoshio
Krishnan, Kalliana R.
Lam, Eppie C. F.
Lim, Antonio Lao
Liu, Alfred H.
Mar, Dan K.

Martin, Abraham Nguyen
Matsumoto, Randall Itsumi
Meng, Jimmy Z.
Nakamura, Karen Tsuneko
Noojibail, Eshwar
Pai, Kenneth Y.
Patel, Kanti L.
Shah, Pravin M.
Shah, Ramesh V.
Sheth, Navin D.
Tanaka, James Junji
Tang, America
Wang, Charles Chiming
Yamamoto, John Hiroshi
Yang, Susan Y.
Yoshimoto, Watson Toshinori

CABLE
BROADCASTING
INDUSTRY
SEE TELEVISION/
CABLE
BROADCASTING
INDUSTRY

CHEMISTRY

Aggarwal, Ishwar D.
Ahuja, Satinder
Atoji, Masao
Behl, Wishvender K.
Bulusu, Suryanarayana
Chan, Harvey Thomas, Jr.
Chang, Charles Hung
Chang, Ching-jer
Chang, Clifford Wah Jun
Chang, Jack Che-Man
Chang, James C.
Chang, Kelvin Yau-Min
Chang, Shih-Ger
Chang, Sookyung
Chatterjee, Pronoy Kumar
Chaturvedi, Rama Kant
Chen, Chung-Hsuan
Chen, Kuang Yu
Chen, Michael Chia-Chao
Chen, S. Steve
Chen, Xiangning
Chen, Yih-Wen David
Cheng, Brian Kai-Ming
Cheng, Cheng-Yin
Cheng, Kuang Lu
Cheng, Stephen Z. D.
Chiang, Chao-Kuo
Chiang, Joseph F.
Chiao, Yu-Chih
Ching, Stanton Sakae Hong Yat
Chiu, Lue-Yung Chow
Chiu, Tin-Ho
Chiu, Yuan-yuan H.
Cho, Wonhwa
Choi, John Haetak
Chong, Clyde Hok Heen
Chou, David Yuan-Pin
Chowdhry, Vinay
Chu, Chung Kwang
Chu, Daniel Tim-Wo
Chu, Nori Yaw-Chyuan
Chu, Victor Fu Hua
Chun, Hon Ming
Chung, Frank Huan-Chen
Chung, Tze-Chiang
Dai, Hai-Lung
Dalal, Fram R.
Das, Kamalendu
Das Sarma, Basudeb
Dighe, Shrikant Vishwanath
Dixit, Ajit S.
Doddapaneni, Narayan
Dominh, Thap
Dutta, Shib Prasad
Fang, Fabian Tien-Hwa

Farhataziz
Fung, Bing M.
Fung, Shun C.
Furuta, Otto K.
Gao, Jiali
Giam, Choo Seng
Gong, Jin Kang
Guo, Hua
Gupta, Manjula K.
Hajiyani, Mehdi Hussain
Han, Grace Yang
Ho, Chi-Tang
Hosmane, Ramachandra S.
Hsiao, Benjamin S.
Hsieh, You-Lo
Hsu, Jong-Pyng
Hu, Can Beven
Huang, Jamin
Huang, Shan-Jen Chen
Huang, Thomas Tao-Shing
Huang, Victor Tsangmin
Huie, Carmen Wah-Kit
Hung, Yen-Wan
Hwa, Jesse Chia-Hsi
Inokuti, Mitio
Ishida, Takanobu
Ito, Yoichiro
Iyengar, Doreswamy
  Raghavachar
Jaglan, Prem S.
Jain, Bimla Agarwal
Jain, Naresh C.
Joshi, Bhairav D.
Jung, Mankil
Kanojia, Ramesh Maganlal
Kaul, Balkrishena
Khanna, Rajive Kumar
Khare, Mohan
Khorana, Har Gobind
Khosla, Mahesh Chandra
Kim, Moon G.
Ko, Hon-Chung
Kong, Eric Siu-Wai
Kripalani, Kishin J.
Krishnan, Chirakkal
Kubota, Mitsuru
Kumar, Devendra
Kumar, Jothi V.
Kuo, Chung Ming
Kwei, Ti-Kang
Kwok, Wo Kong
Lai, Kuo-Yann
Lateef, Abdul Bari
Lee, Chi-Hang
Lee, Henry Joung
Lee, Kang In
Lee, Ker-Fong
Lee, Kuo-Hsiung
Lee, Lihsyng Stanford
Lee, Min-Shiu
Lee, Sheng Yen
Lee, Ving J.
Lee, Yuan Tseh
Lee, Yue-Wei
Leung, Pak Sang
Leung, Wing Hai
Li, Chia-yu
Li, George S.
Li, Yongji
Li, Yuzhuo
Lin, Chhiu-Tsu
Lin, Chien-Chang
Lin, Chiu-Hong
Lin, Jiann-Tsyh
Lin, Ming-Chang
Lin, Sin-Shong
Liu, Edmund K.
Liu, Hanjun
Liu, Ray H.
Louis, Lawrence Hua-Hsien
Luh, Yuhshi
Ma, Tsu Sheng
Made Gowda, Netkal M.

Mak, Chi Ho
Mao, Chung-Ling
Masamune, Satoru
Mathur, Raghu P.
Matsumoto, Ken
Mayell, Jaspal Singh
Mehta, Mahendra
Mehta, Prakash V.
Misra, Dwarika Nath
Mitra, Grihapati
Mittal, Kashmiri Lal
Moy, Mamie Wong
Myer, Yash Paul
Nagarajan, Ramakrishnan
Naik, Datta Vittal
Nair, K. M.
Nath, Amar
Navangul, Himanshoo Vishnu
  Bhat
Nee, Michael Wei-Kuo
Newaz, S. S.
Ngai, Kia Ling
Nozaki, Kenzie
Oh, Chan Soo
Ohta, Masao
Ojima, Iwao
Okabe, Hideo
Pai, Sadanand V.
Pan, Yuh-Kang
Pande, Gyan Shanker
Park, Su-Moon
Patel, Anil J.
Patel, Bhagvan H.
Patel, Bhagwandas Mavjibhai
Patel, Indravadan R.
Patel, Kiran K.
Patel, Kishor N.
Patel, Shirish A.
Pemmaraju, Narasimha Rao
Puligandla, Viswanadham
Rao, Gopalakrishna M.
Rath, Nigam Prasad
Raut, Kamalakar Balkrishna
Ravindran, Nair N.
Saha, Gopal Bandhu
Sanadi, D. R.
Sandhu, Shingara Singh
Sarkar, Nitis
Sayala, Chhaya
Seshadri, Kal S.
Sethi, Naresh Kumar
Shah, Chandu M.
Shah, Harikrishna D.
Shah, Nitin J.
Shah, Shirish
Shah, Shirish K.
Shah, Syed M.
Shendrikar, Arun D.
Shiao, Daniel Da-Fong
Shih, Fred F.
Shroff, Arvin P.
Singh, Ajaib
Singh, Baldev
So, Ying Hung
Su, Kwei Lee
Su, Timothy C.
Sugihara, James Masanobu
Sun, Frank F.
Sundaresan, Gloria Marquez
Sy, Jose
Tai, Julia Chow
Takeuchi, Kenneth James
Takimoto, Hideyo Henry
Tam, Eric Tak-Keung
Tan, Barrie
Tan, Henry S. I.
Tanaka, John
Tang, Yi-Noo
Ting, Shih-Fan
Tong, Sun-De
Toy, Madeline Shen
Tripathi, Gorakh Nath Ram
Tsai, Bilin Paula

Tsai, Lin
Tsai, Ming-Daw
Tso, Tien Chioh
Tsuji, Kiyoshi
Tuan, Debbie Fu-tai
Tung, Ming Sung
Un, Howard Ho-Wei
Vaidhyanathan, Vishnampet S.
Varma, Rajender S.
Vijayendran, Bhima R.
Viswanath, Rampur S.
Vora, Narendra Mohanlal
Walia, Jasjit Singh
Wang, C. H.
Wang, Chi-Hua
Wang, Chih H.
Wang, Francis Wei-Yu
Wang, Jih Ming
Wang, Jin-Liang
Wang, Ming-Yu Rachel
Wang, Nancy Y.
Wang, Richard Hsu-Shien
Wani, Mansukhlal Chhaganlal
Wei, Chao Hui
Wei, Yen
Wen, Wen-Yang
Whangbo, Myung-Hwan
Wing, James
Wong, Albert
Wong, Dorothy Pan
Wong, Peter Alexander
Wong, William Wai-Lun
Woo, James T. K.
Woody, A-Young Moon
Wu, Ching-Yong
Wu, Dan Qing
Wu, Konrad T.
Wu, Richard L. C.
Wu, Tung
Wu, Wu-Nan
Wu, Yao Hua
Wu, Ying Victor
Yagi, Haruhiko
Yamamoto, Y. Stephen
Yang, Chia Chi
Yang, In Che
Yang, Julie Chi-Sun
Yang, Nien-chu C.
Yang, Sze Cheng
Yang, Weitao
Yau, Cheuk Chung
Yu, Chang-An
Yu, Jimmy Chai-Mei
Yu, Melvin Joseph
Yuan, Jian-Min
Yue, Robert Hon-Sang
Zhang, John Z. H.

CHIROPRACTIC
Sato, Gary Teruo

CHOREOGRAPHY
SEE DANCE/
CHOREOGRAPHY

**CIVIL RIGHTS
ACTIVISM**
SEE ACTIVISM,
POLITICAL/CIVIL/
SOCIAL RIGHTS

CLERGY—BUDDHIST
Ito, Noriaki
Ly, Tam Minh
Nishimura, Tom
Rinpoche, Gelek
Shen, Chia Theng
Shohara, Sei
Sircar, Rina Schyamcharan

Tan, Cheng Imm

CLERGY—CATHOLIC
Au, Wilkie Wai Kee
Viet-Chau, Nguyen Duc

**CLERGY—MOSLEM/
MUSLIM**
Haque, M. Shamsul

**CLERGY—
PROTESTANT**
Chan, Glenn
Cheng, Hsueh-Jen
Ching, Harvey Cho Wing
Choi, Jai-Keun
Chow, Ivan S.
Kang, Wi Jo
Kim, Chan-Hie
Kim, Changyup Daniel
Kim, David Sang Chul
Kim, Edward Ik Hwan
Kim, Jonathan Jang-Ho
Kim, Yongshik
Kitagawa, Joseph Mitsuo
Kitahata, Stacy Dee
Kuan, Kah-Jin
Kwan, Franco Chang-Hong
Lee, Hak-Kwon
Lee, Jung Young
Lo, Samuel E.
Louie, Paul
Lum, Doman
Maedjaja, Daniel
Moon, Byung Hwa
Moy, James Yee Kin
Ng, David
Nuon, Samuel
Rajan, Frederick E. N.
Sim, John Kim-Chye
Song, Choan-Seng
Thiruvathukal, Kris V.
Yee, Edmond

**CLERGY—NOT
ELSEWHERE
CLASSIFIED**
Barnabas, Mathews Mar
Emura, Cynthia Sanae
Godsay, Madhu P.
Mammen, Thomas
Pang, Rubye-Huey
Patel, Indravadan R.
Tan, Cheng Imm
Tokuuke, Terrance Katsuki

COMMUNITY SERVICE
Alcantara, Larry James
Bhavnani, Pratap Gagumal
Blanco, Paul De La Cruz
Cabrera, Cesar Trinidad
Castro, Marissa Barbers
Chao, Elaine Lan
Cheng, Lawrence Kai-Leung
Chien, Alan Shueshih
Chin, Donald G.
Ching, Deborah F.
Chinn, Daisy Wong
Cho, David
Choi, Sung Sook
Choo, Marcia
Chung, Anni Yuet-Kuen
Cruzada, Rodolfo Omega
Dayao, Firmo Salvador
Fitzpatrick, Eileen Tabata
Fujimoto, Isao
Guen, Amy Chin
Haque, M. Shamsul

Hayashi, Seigo
Hoang, Giao
Hom, Kathleen B.
Hyun, Bong Hak
Jalil, Mazhar
Jung, Emma
Kanegai, Toy
Kang, Heesook Sophia
Kim, Hyung J.
Ko, Elaine Ikoma
Kochiyama, William
Kohashi, Ethel Tsukiko
Li, Marjorie H.
Li, Vivien
Liu, LiLi
Liu, Mini
Lo, Yao
Lowe, Rolland Choy
Manankil, Norma Ronas
Marur, Hanuman
Ng, Rita Mei-Ching
Ozaki, Yoji
Park, Kap Yung
Pillay, Mullayil K. G.
Querol Moreno, Cherie M.
Rathbone, Susan Wu
Saito, Walter Masao
Shen, Grace Liu
Shigemasa, Thomas Ken
Singh, Kim
Sugiyama, Alan
Suzuki, Paul Ted
Takeuchi, Esther Kiyomi
Tan, Cheng Imm
Teng, Mabel Sik Mei
Uyeshima, Mary
Vanchiasong, Siong Koua
Verma, Dhani Ram
Wong, Anna Clara
Wong, Dolores
Wong, Linda J.
Wong, Sophie Chao
Wu, Hsiu-ying
Yoshimura, Evelyn
Young, Hoa Pham

**COMPUTER SCIENCE—
PROGRAMMING/
SOFTWARE
DEVELOPMENT**
Arakawa, Minoru
Bagga, K. Jay Singh
Banerjee, Debasish
Banerjee, Prithviraj
Banerji, Ranan Bihari
Chakravarty, Indranil
Chan, Tat-Hung
Chang, Jeffrey Chit-Fu
Chen, Bernard Shao-Wen
Chen, C. L. Philip
Chen, Henry
Chen, Robert Chia-Hua
Chen, Rong Yaw
Chen, Steve S.
Cheng, Charles Ching-an
Cheo, Li-hsiang S.
Cheung, David F.
Cheung, John Yan-Poon
Chin, David
Ching, Hugh
Chiou, Wun C.
Chiu, Victor
Chou, Timothy C.
Chow, Paul Chuan-Juin
Chu, Nhan V.
Chung, Luke Tsun
Dalal, Siddhartha Ramanlal
Desaigoudar, Chan
Gandhi, Vikram Ijatrai
Goel, Subhash Chand
Goyal, Suresh
Gupta, Ajay Kumar

Gupta, Arun Premchand
Gupta, Rajiv Kumar
Halemane, Thirumala Raya
Hayashi, Masato
Ho, Edwin Soon Hee
Hong, Shuguang
Hsu, John Y.
Huynh, Dung Thiet
Ishikawa, Ishi
Jen, James A.
Kan, Victor
Kapoor, Sanjiv
Kim, HakLin
Kim, Junguk Lawrence
Kulkarni, Krishnaji Hanamant
Kumar, Ashok
Kumar, Atul
Kuroda, Teruhisa
Lam, An Ngoc
Lee, Chung
Li, Ivan C.
Lim, Poh C.
Lin, Chi Yung
Liu, Hsun Kao
Liu, Thomas Jyhcheng
Liu, Tsu-huei
Liu, Warren Kuo-Tung
Liu, Ying
Lo, Chi-Yuan
Louie, Gilman G.
Lum, Vincent Y.
Mei, Kenneth K.
Misra, Alok C.
Mitamura, Ron W.
Mondal, Kalyan
Murad, Sohail
Nag, Ronjon
Nguyen, Nghia Van
Pang, Chap Aik
Patel, Chandrakant J.
Pham, Danny
Pong, Ting-Chuen
Sato, Frederick Akira
Sato, Paul Toshio
Shih, John Chau
Song, Xueshu
Teng, Henry Shao-lin
Ting, T. C.
Tong, Benjamin
Tsai, Jeffrey J. P.
Tu, Samson W.
Tu, Shengru
Wang, Charles B.
Wang, Charles Chiming
Wang, Gene
Wang, Jason T. L.
Wang, Sue S.
Wang, Xiaohan
Wei, Susanna
Wong, Benedict Ding Chung
Wong, Suk Yee
Wong, William Wai-Lun
Woo, Henry
Wu, Jie
Wu, Jin Zhong
Wu, Ying-Chan Fred
Yang, Albert C.
Yang, Chyan
Yang, Han-Jiang
Yeh, Pu-Sen
Yen, John
Yu, Clement Tak

**COMPUTER SCIENCE—
SYSTEMS ANALYSIS/
DESIGN**
Aggarwal, Rajesh
Banerjee, Debasish
Bedi, Sandeep
Bhojwani, Ram J.
Chakravarty, Indranil
Chang, Shin-Jyh Frank

Chang, Yu Lo Cyrus
Chaudhary, Ved P.
Chen, Henry
Chen, Steve S.
Cheng, Norman Alan
Cheung, David F.
Chin, David
Chiou, Wun C.
Chiu, Jim
Chong, Pek-Ean
Chu, Warren
Chung, H. Michael
Dev, Parvati
Dixit, Sudhir Sharan
Do, Toa Quang
Feng, Tse-Yun
Gajendar, Nandigam
Gandhi, Vikram Ijatrai
Gupta, Ajay Kumar
Hayase, Joshua Yoshio
Higa, Kunihiko
Ho, Edwin Soon Hee
Hong, Shuguang
Huang, Garng Morton
Huang, Ian
Khim, Jay Wook
Kim, Jay Chul
Kim, Junguk Lawrence
Kung, H. T.
Lam, Simon Shin-Sing
Li, Qiang
Liu, James P.
Liu, Jyh-Charn Steve
Liu, Min
Liu, Ying
Louie, Gilman G.
Ly, Kieu Kim
Mak, Sioe Tho
Mehta, Gurmukh Dass
Nahata, Suparas M.
Ng-Breckwoldt, May Sue
Pang, Chap Aik
Parikh, Rupesh N.
Pham, Danny
Sato, Frederick Akira
Sawhney, Gurjeet Singh
Shankar, Subramonian
Shih, John Chau
Somani, Arun K.
Song, Il-Yeol
Sy, Antonio Ngo, Jr.
Tran, Thinh Quy
Tran, Thomas
Trivedi, Kishor S.
Trivedi, Mohan Manubhai
Tsai, Bor-sheng
Tsai, Jeffrey J. P.
Tu, Shengru
Van Houten, David J.
Wang, Fei-Yue
Wang, Louisa Ho-Ching
Watanabe, Yuki
Yang, Han-Jiang
Yen, Chi-Chung David
Yoon, Youngohi Choi
Yun, Xiaoping

**COMPUTER SCIENCE—
NOT ELSEWHERE
CLASSIFIED**
Banerji, Ranan Bihari
Cai, Jin-Yi
Chakravarthy, Upendranath
  Sharma
Chan, Chiu Shui
Chan, Kwok Hung
Chan, Ted W.
Chandramouli, S.
Chang, Carl Kochao
Chang, Simon
Chen, David Ting-Kai

Chen, Di
Chen, Jianhua
Chen, Kenny T.
Cheung, Shun Yan
Chiang, Joseph F.
Chiang, Yi-ling F.
Chien, Arnold Jensen
Ching, Chee
Chin-Lee, Cynthia Denise
Chua, Leon O.
De, Suranjan
Dutt, Nikil D.
Fu, LiMin
Fu, Paul Chung, Jr.
Furuta, Richard K.
Gupta, Rajiv
Huang, Jung-chang
Hung, Chih-Cheng
Jiang, Zhenying
Kak, Subhash Chandra
Kaneko, Ryoji Lloyd
Khatwani, Mahesh
Kim, Changwook
Kim, HakLin
Krishnan, Radha
Kulkarni, Arun Digambar
Kulkarni, Ravi S.
Kumar, Romesh
Kumar, Vipin
Leung, Joseph Yuk-Tong
Li, Ching-Chung
Li, Kai
Lim, Billy Lee
Liu, Hong
Liu, Jie
Lu, Michael Y.
Mathur, Aditya P.
Mehrotra, Kishan Gopal
Meng, Xiannong
Mitter, Sanjoy K.
Ng, Peter A.
Ohno, Peter Takeshi
Parekh, Navnit M.
Parikh, Rohit J.
Peng, Chang-Shyh
Raghavan, Sridhar A.
Reddy, Raj
Sethi, Ishwar Krishan
Shah, Mubarak Ali
Shah, Shirish
Sharma, Onkar Prasad
Sohn, David Youngwhan
Srivastava, Sadanand
Suda, Tatsuya
Suh, Yung-Ho
Sy, Bon Kiem
Tan, Jack Sim Eddy
Tanaka, Richard I.
Tripathi, Satish K.
Wang, Dajin
Wang, Frederick Andrew
Wang, Huaqing
Wang, Jie
Wang, Junping
Wing, Jeannette M.
Wong, Chin Siong
Wong, Johnny S.
Wong, K. C.
Wong, Martin Ding-Fat
Wu, Angela Yuen
Yee, Donald Poy
Yoon, David Hwa Hyun
Youn, Hee Yong
Young, Tzay Y.
Yu, Clement Tak
Yuen, Steve Chi-Yin

COMPUTER SERVICES
(SEE ALSO MANAGEMENT/ ADMINISTRATION— COMPUTER SYSTEMS/ DATA PROCESSING)

Au, Andrew T.
Chen, Ye-Sho
Chiu, Jim
Fajardo, Ben
Ha, Chong W.
Hayashi, Midori
Ho, Daniel F.
Ho, Yu-Chi
Huang, Ian
Hwang, Enoch Oi-Kee
Inatome, Joseph T.
Ismail, Amin Rashid
Iyer, Ravishankar Krishnan
Jen, James A.
Kan, Victor
Kim, Yong K.
Lanewala, Mohammed Ali
Lau, Albert Kai-Fay
Lee, Der-Tsai
Maheshwari, Arun K.
Mehrotra, Sudhir Chandra
Mitamura, Ron W.
Nanda, Vir A.
Ohno, Peter Takeshi
Ou, Shukong
Patel, Chandu M.
Sawhney, Gurjeet Singh
Shah, Nilesh D.
Shrivastava, Satyendra P.
Soo Hoo, Richard
Thadani, Raju
Tong, Alvin H.
Tran, Nhut Van
Tran, Tri K.
Vu, Quang
Wang, Charles B.
Wong, Buck W.
Wong, Henry Sik-Yin
Wong, John A.

CONSTRUCTION
SEE BUILDING/ CONSTRUCTION; RETAIL TRADE— BUILDING/ CONSTRUCTION MATERIALS; WHOLESALE TRADE— BUILDING/ CONSTRUCTION MATERIALS

CONSULTING
Ang, Charles C.
Asuncion, Gary Raymond Espejo
Balachandran, Kashi Ramamurthi
Banerjee, Chandra Madhab
Bawa, Mohendra S.
Bhargava, Ashok
Bhatt, Kiran Chandrakant
Biradavolu, Kaleswara Rao
Brillantes, Hermogenes Bilgera
Chacko, George Kuttickal
Chai, David
Chan, Cheung M.
Chan, Tsze Hau
Chandra, Abhijit
Chandramouli, S.
Chang, Clifford Wah Jun
Chang, Kern K. N.
Chang, Paul Peng-Cheng
Chang, Stephen S.
Chang, Yia-Chung
Chao, Chiang-nan

Chen, Chi Hau
Chen, Ching-chih
Chen, Di
Chen, Karl A.
Chen, Wayne G.
Chen, Yohchia
Chen, Zhong-Ying
Cheng, Sin I.
Cherian, Joy
Chien, Gary K.
Chinn, Thomas Wayne
Chiu, Jim
Cho, Frank Fulai
Chong, Clyde Hok Heen
Chong, Pek-Ean
Choudhury, Pinak
Chow, Philip Yeong-Wai
Chu, Kuang Han
Chu, Ting L.
Chun, Wei Foo
Chung, Tae-Soo
Datta, Ranajit Kumar
Deb, Arun Kumar
Do, Toa Quang
Dugal, Hardev S.
Enomoto, Jiro
Fajardo, Ben
Fang, Pen Jeng
Fok, Samuel Shiu-Ming
Fong, Eva Chow
Fukuyama, Francis
Ghosh, Chinmoy
Go, Howard T.
Gupta, Rajat Kumar
Gupta, Rajiv Kumar
Hamasaki, Les
Hasegawa, Jack Koichi
Ho, Vernon S. C.
Hsu, Donald K.
Huang, Barney Kuo-Yen
Huang, Joseph T.
Hwa, Jesse Chia-Hsi
Ikeda, Tsuguo
Ishaq, Ashfaq M.
Iyengar, Doreswamy Raghavachar
Jiang, Nai-Siang
Kagetsu, Tadashi Jack
Kang, James Jyh-Huei
Kawaguchi, Stanley Kenji
Kawamoto, Brian Michio
Ke, Gang
Khare, Mohan
Kim, Robert Hyung-chan
Kim, Sang Phill
Kishimoto, Yoriko
Kobayashi, Yoshiko
Kulkarni, Kishore G.
Kumar, Jatinder
Kumar, V.
Kuroda, Teruhisa
Kwan, Simon Hing-Man
Lai, Dennis Fu-hsiung
Lam, Chun H.
Lam, Dick
Lanewala, Mohammed Ali
Lang, David C.
Law, H. David
Leu, Rong-Jin
Leung, Margaret W.
Leung, Som-Lok
Li, Kai
Lim, Billy Lee
Lim, Joo Kun
Lim, Ralph Wei Hsiong
Lin, Felix
Lin, Fred Reggie
Lin, James Chow
Lin, James Y.
Lin, Ting-Ting Yao
Liu, Ben Chieh
Liu, Gerald Hanmin
Liu, John J.

Louie, George Chang
Louie, Paul
Lu, Frank Kerping
Luh, Yuhshi
Ma, Tsu Sheng
Ma, Yi Hua
Mahajan, Arvind
Mahilum, Benjamin C.
Marumoto, William Hideo
Maruyama, Kiyoshi
Matsuoka, Shiro
Mehrotra, Prem N.
Mei, June Y.
Melookaran, Joseph
Merchant, Vasant V.
Misra, Alok C.
Miyamoto, Lance
Miyamoto, Seiichi
Moy, Edmund
Myoda, Toshio Timothy
Naik, Tarun Ratilal
Narayanaswamy, Onbathiveli S.
Ng, Richard
Nishikawa, Dennis
O, San Luong
Oishi, Satoshi
Oki, Scott D.
Ong, Cynthia K. Char
Ou, Shukong
Pai, K. Vasanth
Pan, Dawning
Parikh, Kirit Girishchandra
Patel, Ramesh D.
Rao, Ramesh K. S.
Rao, Srikumar S.
Rao, Vaman
Rikhiraj, Sadhu Singh
Rohatgi, Vijay K.
Ru, Wesley
Safdari, Yahya Bhai
Saji, Kiyotaka
Saluja, Jagdish Kumar
Sasaki, Raymond Toshiaki, Jr.
Sato, Irving Shigeo
Shah, Abhay
Shah, Amar M.
Shah, Bhupendra P.
Sharma, Anil F.
Sheikh, Ghafoor A.
Shen, Thomas T.
Shenoy, Narasimha B.
Shiao, Daniel Da-Fong
Shim, Jae K.
Shimada, Katsunori
Shimizu, Tak
Singh, Balwant
Soo, Charlie H.
Su, Cheh-Jen
Suelto, Teem D.
Sugihara, Jared Genji
Syed, Karamat A.
Tahiliani, Jamnu H.
Takano, Masaharu
Tandon, Rajiv
Tien, H. Ti
Tsai, Kuei-wu
Tsukahira, Toshio George
Uyehara, Cecil H.
Varma, Vishwa K.
Wang, Kung-Lee
Wing, Jeannette M.
Wong, Angela Ma
Wong, Chin Siong
Wong, Morton Min-Fong
Wong, Rita F.
Wong, Wendell P.
Woo, Lecon
Wu, Jun-Ru
Wu, Lyn Xiling
Wu, Wei-ping
Yamaga, Chester Kiyoshi
Yamakawa, David Kiyoshi, Jr.
Yang, Dongpyo

Yang, Julie Chi-Sun
Yang, Tah-teh
Yap, Stacey G. H.
Yee, Alfred Alphonse
Yee, Angelina Chun-chu
Yeh, Gregory S. Y.
Yeh, Hen-Geul
Yu, Kar Yuk
Yuan, Sidney W. K.
Yuh, Jai K.

CORRECTIONS
SEE CRIMINOLOGY/ CORRECTIONS

COUNSELING— CAREER/ PLACEMENT
Chan, Mason C.
Culp, Mae Ng
Fujiwara, Theresa
Poc, Sorya

COUNSELING— MARRIAGE/FAMILY
Bhuyan, Bijoy Kumar
Her, Chou
Hong, George K.
Hosokawa, Fumiko
Rathbone, Susan Wu
Vyas, Premila Hariprasad

COUNSELING— MENTAL HEALTH
Chiu, Martha Li
Iqbal, S. Mohammed
Kong, Chhean
Merchant, Vasant V.
Yamamoto, Eric K.
Yen, Sherman M. Y.
Yue, Xiaodong

COUNSELING— REHABILITATION
Hayashi, Seigo
Lam, Chow-Shing
Shah, Nandlal Chimanlal
Shon, Kyo Kwa
Wong, Daniel W.

COUNSELING— SCHOOL/ACADEMIC
Chang, Yang-Shim
Chia, Rosina Chih-Hung
Chong-Gottinger, Ivy Wok Kuong
Fan, Ada Mei
Feng, Xin
Kim, Anna Charr
Kim, Edward J.
Lin, Chin-Chu
Mathur, Kailash V.
Phommasouvanh, Banlang
Rhee, Susan Byungsook
Shimizu, Gordon Toshio
Wu, Jean Yu-Wen Shen
Xiong, William Joua

COUNSELING—NOT ELSEWHERE CLASSIFIED
Au, Wilkie Wai Kee
Chan, Adrian
Culp, Mae Ng
Ikeda, Tsuguo
Wu, Wei-ping

CRIMINOLOGY/ CORRECTIONS
Enomoto, Jiro
Huang, Wei-Sung Wilson
Joe, Karen Ann
Moy, George S.
Murty, Komanduri Srinivasa

DANCE/ CHOREOGRAPHY
Alejandro, Reynaldo Gamboa
Chen, Nai-Ni
Cho, David
Chong, Ping
Chun, Aulani
Jung, Audrey Moo Hing
Kumar, Mythili
Sagami, Kim
Singha, Nabaghana Shyam
Srirama, Malini
Tseng, Muna Siu-Chuk
Wong, Mel

DENTISTRY
Bhaskar, Surindar Nath
Chan, Kai Chiu
Chan, Steven D.
Chang, Richard
Chen, Jie
Chen, William Hok-Nin
Chin, Henry Han
Choi, Raymond Yoonseok
Chow, Michael Hung-Chun
Domondon, Oscar
Go, Daniel Y.
Gupta, Om Prakash
Higa, Leslie Hideyasu
Hiura, Alan
Kang, Yung C.
Kawahara, Lindon Ken
Kim, Jungnam Ego
Kitahara, David James
Nakamoto, Tetsuo
Nanda, Ravindra
Patel, Narendra D.
Shigihara, Patricia
Song, Yong Chol
Tung, Ming Sung
Wang, Shu-Hsia
Wong, David Tai Wai
Yang, Hee K.
Yang, Joseph Chi-Houng
Yee, Nancy J.
Yorita, Frank Kazuo
Yoshida, Alan K.
Yu, Jia-Huey

DIRECTING/ PRODUCING (PERFORMING ARTS)
Chan, Anthony Bernard
Chang, Douglas Howe
Chang, Marian S.
Cheng, Fu-Ding
Chong, Ping
Chong, Tommy
Choy, Christine
Dang, Tim
Dong, Arthur
Goto, Yukihiro
Ho, Alexander Kitman
Hsia, Lisa
Jao, Radmar Agana
Kaya, Douglas Hifuto, Jr.
Kinaga, Patricia Anne
Kurup, Shishir Ravindran
Laly, Amy
Lee, Ang
Lee, Miko
Makhijani, Srichand

McCarthy, Nobu
Merchant, Ismail Noormohamed
Nair, Mira
Okazaki, Steven
Ono, Yoko
Rhee, Phillip
Sasaki, Raymond Toshiaki, Jr.
Wang, Wayne
Yang, Tuen-Ping
Yee, James

ECOLOGY
Chen, Carl Wan-Cheng
Cheng, Lanna
Chew, Frances Sze-Ling
Choi, Young Dong
Dwivedy, Ramesh Chandra
Geng, Shu
Giam, Choo Seng
Inouye, Richard Saburo
Lee, Jeff S.
Liu, Edwin H.
Mahalingam, R.
Nakatani, Roy Eiji
Reddy, Gudigopuram Bhaskar
Shan, Robert Kuocheng
Shendrikar, Arun D.
Tom, Melvin Gee Lim
Wang, Deane

ECONOMICS
Aono, Isamu
Batra, Ravi
Bhargava, Ashok
Chan, Anthony Kit-Cheung
Chan, Arthur H.
Chang, Eric Chieh
Chang, Gene Hsin
Chang, Mabel Li
Chang, Winston Wen-Tsuen
Cheng, Benjamin Shujung
Cheng, Chu-Yuan
Cheng, Hsiang-tai
Choi, Jai-Young
Choi, Jin Wook
Choi, Songsu
Chow, Peter Chi-Yuan
Chu, David S. C.
Chu, Kong
Chung, Young-Iob
Dao, Minh Quang
Desai, Suresh A.
Fung, Hung-Gay
Gramm, Wendy Lee
Haque, M. Shamsul
Ho, Chin Chih
Hoang, Giao
Hsiao, William C.
Hsieh, Wen-jen
Hsu, Albert Yutien
Hsu, Yu Chu
Huang, Wei-chiao
Hung, Chao-Shun
Ishaq, Ashfaq M.
Jun, Joosung
Kaneda, Hiromitsu
Khim, Jay Wook
Kim, Ki Hoon
Kim, Kyoo Hong
Kim, Vivian C.
Kim, Yong-Gwan
Kim, Youn-Suk
Kim, Yung Mo
Koo, Anthony Ying Chang
Kulkarni, Kishore G.
Lau, Lawrence Juen-Yee
Lee, Byung-Joo
Lee, Dae Sung
Lee, Kangoh
Lee, Tsoung-Chao
Leung, PingSun

Li, Bob Cheng-Liang
Li, Shuhe
Lieu, George Y.
Lieu, Hou-Shun
Lin, Jason Jia-Yuan
Lin, Kuan-Pin
Lin, Yuet-Chang Joseph
Liu, Ben Chieh
Liu, Chao-Nan
Liu, Donald Jiann-Tyng
Liu, Peter Chi-Wah
Liu, Su-Feng
Lu, Linyu Laura
Ma, Ching-To Albert
Mahajan, Y. Lal
Mak, James
Matsui, Noriatsu
Munroe, Tapan
Nagai, Nelson Kei
Nguyen, Ho Ngoc
Omori, Yoshiaki
Ozawa, Terutomo
Pai, Gregory Gi Yong
Park, Hun Young
Park, Kang H.
Park, Sang Oh
Ramachandran, Nadaraja
Rao, Vaman
Reddy, Nallapu Narayan
Respicio, Elsa Toje
Shah, Parth J.
Sharma, Jandhyala L.
Shieh, John Ting-Chung
Shin, Doug Yong
Shin, Kilman
Suzuki, Masao Fred
Takayama, Akira
Tang, Assumpta
Tung, Theodore H.
Wang, Jin
Wang, Kung-Lee
Wang, Yan
Wang, Yijiang
Wong, Henry L.
Wong, Kar-yiu
Wong, Kwok-Fai Matthew
Wu, Ho-Mou
Wu, Lyn Xiling
Wu, Shih-Yen
Wu, Wei-ping
Yan, Chiou-Shuang Jou
Yen, Steven T.
Yi, Gang

EDITING
SEE WRITING/ EDITING—FICTION; WRITING/EDITING— NONFICTION; WRITING/EDITING— PLAYS, SCREENPLAYS, TV SCRIPTS; WRITING/ EDITING—POETRY; WRITING/EDITING— NOT ELSEWHERE CLASSIFIED

EDUCATION—ADULT/ VOCATIONAL
Chan, Robert T. P.
Cheng, Chung-Kuan
Dirige, Ofelia Villa
Embrey, Sue Kunitomi
Gandhi, Arun Manilal
Go, Daniel Y.
Govindjee
Hsu, Laura Ling
Kim, Vivian C.
Kimura, Gwen C.
Liu, Karen Chia-Yu
Matsumoto, Iku

Nakatani, Henry Masatoshi
O, San Luong
Oshiro, Rene Katsuko
Pang, Seng Puang
Pang, Wilma
Pham, Kien Trung
Sen, Karabi
Shah, Harish S.
Shon, Kyo Kwa
Teng, Mabel Sik Mei
Tran, Myluong Thi
Uno, Anne Quan
Wang, Rita

EDUCATION— COLLEGE/ UNIVERSITY
Abe, Makoto
Abhyankar, Shreeram Shankar
Achar, Narahari B. N.
Advani, Suresh Gopaldas
Agarwal, Arun Kumar
Agarwal, Gyan Chand
Agarwal, Ramesh Kumar
Aggarwal, Bharat Bhushan
Aggarwal, Lalit Kumar
Aggarwal, Manmohan D.
Aggarwal, Raj
Aggarwal, Rajesh
Aggarwal, Roshan Lal
Agrawal, Dharma Prakash
Agrawal, Krishna Chandra
Agrawal, Pradeep K.
Ahluwalia, Brij Mohan Singh
Ahluwalia, Daljit Singh
Ahluwalia, Harjit Singh
Ahluwalia, Rashpal S.
Ahmed, A. Razzaque
Ahmed, Shaikh Sultan
Ahuja, Satinder
Aikawa, Jerry Kazuo
Aki, Keiiti
Albano, Alfonso M.
Ali, Mir Masoom
Alvares, Alvito P.
An, Nack Young
Anand, Rajen S.
Anand, Satish Chandra
Anderson, Wanni W.
Ando, Koichi
Annamalai, Nagappan K.
Aoki, Haruo
Aoki, Thomas T.
Arakawa, Kasumi
Arimura, Akira
Arora, Madan Lal
Arora, Vijay K.
Ashtekar, Abhay Vasant
Au, Chi-Kwan
Au, Tung
Au, Wilkie Wai Kee
Aziz, Khalid
Azumaya, Goro
Bagasra, Omar
Bagga, K. Jay Singh
Bahl, Om Parkash
Bajpai, Praphulla Kumar
Bajpai, Rakesh Kumar
Balachandran, Kashi Ramamurthi
Balaguru, Perumalsamy N.
Baliga, Jayant
Banakar, Umesh Virupaksh
Banerjee, Chandra Madhab
Banerjee, Debasish
Banerjee, Jayanta Kumar
Banerjee, Mukul R.
Banerjee, Prithviraj
Banerjee, Sanjay K.
Basu, Asit Prakas
Batra, Ravi
Batra, Romesh Chander

Bhada, Rohinton Khurshed
Bhagavatula, Vijayakumar
Bhapkar, Vasant P.
Bhargava, Ashok
Bhat, K. Ramachandra
Bhathena, Sam Jehangirji
Bhatia, Tej K.
Bhatnagar, Kunwar P.
Bhatnagar, Yogendra Mohan
Bhatt, Jagdish J.
Bhattacharjee, Jnanendra Kumar
Bhattacharyya, Ashim Kumar
Bhattacharyya, Gouri Kanta
Bhattacharyya, Shankar P.
Bhatti, Rashid A.
Bhown, Ajit Singh
Biradavolu, Kaleswara Rao
Biswas, Nripendra Nath
Biswas, Renuka
Bolen, Jean Shinoda
Borgaonkar, Digamber Shankarrao
Bose, Bimal Kumar
Bowman, Kimiko O.
Brahma, Chandra Sekhar
Cabana, Veneracion Garganta
Cai, Jin-Yi
Caldito, Gloria Cruz
Cao, Le Thi
Cha, Chang-Yul
Cha, Soyoung Stephen
Cha, Sungman
Chacko, George Kuttickal
Chacko, Harsha E.
Chacko, Mariam Renate
Chacko, Ranjit C.
Chadha, Kailash Chandra
Chae, Yong Suk
Chakrabarti, Supriya
Chakraborty, Joana
Chakravarthy, Balaji Srinivasan
Chakravarthy, Srinivasaraghavan
Chakravarthy, Upendranath Sharma
Chan, Adrian
Chan, Albert
Chan, Anthony Bernard
Chan, Anthony Kit-Cheung
Chan, Arthur Wing Kay
Chan, Carlyle Hung-lun
Chan, Chiu Shui
Chan, Chiu Yeung
Chan, Cho Lik
Chan, Gary M.
Chan, Henry Y. S.
Chan, James C.
Chan, James C. M.
Chan, John G.
Chan, Kai Chiu
Chan, Kam Chuen
Chan, Kenyon S.
Chan, Kwan M.
Chan, Kwok Hung
Chan, Laurence Kwong-Fai
Chan, Lee-Nien Lillian
Chan, Lo-Yi C. Y.
Chan, Lois Mai
Chan, Lung S.
Chan, Marsha J.
Chan, Mason C.
Chan, Peng S.
Chan, Phillip Paang
Chan, Pui Kwong
Chan, Robert T. P.
Chan, Samuel H. P.
Chan, Shih-Hung
Chan, Stephen W.
Chan, Su Han
Chan, Sucheng
Chan, Suitak Steve
Chan, Tat-Hung
Chan, Wai-Yee
Chandra, Abhijit

Chandran, Krishnan Bala
Chandran, Satish Raman
Chandrasekaran, Balakrishnan
Chandra Sekhar, Hosakere K.
Chandrasekhar, Subrahmanyan
Chang, Albert
Chang, Andrew C.
Chang, Briankle G.
Chang, Carl Kochao
Chang, Chawnshang
Chang, Chein-I
Chang, Cheng-Hui
Chang, Chia-Cheh
Chang, Chia-ning
Chang, Chin Hao
Chang, Ching-jer
Chang, Chun-Hao
Chang, Clement C.
Chang, Clifford Wah Jun
Chang, Darwin
Chang, David Hsiang
Chang, David W.
Chang, Deanna BauKung
Chang, Edmund Z.
Chang, Edward C.
Chang, Edward Shih-Tou
Chang, Edward Taehan
Chang, Eric Chieh
Chang, Gene Hsin
Chang, Gordon H.
Chang, Howard F.
Chang, Hsu Hsin
Chang, Hui-Ching
Chang, James C.
Chang, Jane Yueh
Chang, Jeffrey Chit-Fu
Chang, Jhy-Jiun
Chang, Kai
Chang, Kai-Hsiung
Chang, Kang-Tsung
Chang, Kow-Ching
Chang, Kwang-chih
Chang, Kwang-Poo
Chang, Louis Wai-Wah
Chang, Mabel Li
Chang, Maria Hsia
Chang, Michael S.
Chang, Mingteh
Chang, Moon K.
Chang, Mou-Hsiung
Chang, Myron N.
Chang, Ngee-Pong
Chang, Paul Keub
Chang, Peter C.
Chang, Ping
Chang, Robert C.
Chang, Robert Huei
Chang, Sen-dou
Chang, Shau-Jin
Chang, Shen Chie
Chang, Shing I.
Chang, Shirley Lin
Chang, Stephen S.
Chang, Sukjeong J.
Chang, Sung-sheng Yvonne
Chang, Sylvia Tan
Chang, Tien-Chien
Chang, Tsan-Kuo
Chang, Weilin P.
Chang, William Wei-Lien
Chang, William Y. B.
Chang, Winston Wen-Tsuen
Chang, Won Ho
Chang, Yang-Shim
Chang, Yi-Chieh
Chang, Yia-Chung
Chang, Yu Lo Cyrus
Chang, Yung-Feng
Chao, Bei Tse
Chao, Chiang-nan
Chao, Ching Yuan
Chao, Georgia Tze-Ying
Chao, Kwang-Chu

Chao, Lin
Chao, Tim
Chao, Xiuli
Chao, Yuh J.
Chapatwala, Kirit D.
Chatterjee, Lata Roy
Chatterjee, Monish Ranjan
Chatterjee, Pranab
Chatterjee, Sankar
Chatterjee, Sayan
Chaturvedi, Ram Prakash
Chau, Peter
Chaudhry, G. Rasul
Chaudhuri, Tapan K.
Chee, Cheng-Khee
Chellappa, Rama
Chen, Alan Keith
Chen, Andrew Houng-Yhi
Chen, Audrey Huey-Wen
Chen, Augustine Cheng-Hsin
Chen, Bang-Yen
Chen, Bintong
Chen, C. L. Philip
Chen, Catherine W.
Chen, Chao
Chen, Chao Ling
Chen, Chi Hau
Chen, Chi-yun
Chen, Chin
Chen, Chin-Lin
Chen, Ching-chih
Chen, Chong-Maw
Chen, Chong-Tong
Chen, Chung
Chen, David Ting-Kai
Chen, Donald S.
Chen, Francis F.
Chen, Gong
Chen, Guanrong
Chen, Haiyang
Chen, Hollis Ching
Chen, Hong Chyi
Chen, Hongda
Chen, Houn-Gee
Chen, Hsin-Piao Patrick
Chen, Hung-Liang
Chen, James Pai-fun
Chen, Jianhua
Chen, Jie
Chen, John Shaoming
Chen, Juh Wah
Chen, Jyh-Hong Eric
Chen, Kuang Chung
Chen, Kun-Mu
Chen, Lea Der
Chen, Li-Fu
Ch'en, Li-li
Chen, Linda
Chen, Linda Li-yueh
Chen, Meanshang
Chen, Michael M.
Chen, Ming
Chen, Moon Shao-Chuang, Jr.
Chen, Ping-fan
Chen, Rong Yaw
Chen, Shi-Han
Chen, Simon Ying
Chen, Stuart S.
Chen, Su-chiung
Chen, Ta-Shen
Chen, Thomas Shih-Nien
Chen, Tseh An
Chen, Tsong-Ming
Chen, Tuan Wu
Chen, Tung-Shan
Chen, Wai Fah
Chen, Wai-Kai
Chen, Wei-Yin
Chen, Weihang
Chen, Wenxiong
Chen, Xiangming
Chen, Xiangning
Chen, Xinfu

Chen, Ye-Hwa
Chen, Ye-Sho
Chen, Yea-Mow
Chen, Yi-Chao
Chen, Yi-Leng
Chen, Yohchia
Chen, Yu
Chen, Yu-Charn
Chen, Yubao
Cheng, Alexander H-D.
Cheng, Amy I.
Cheng, Benjamin Shujung
Cheng, Charles Ching-an
Cheng, Cheng-Yin
Cheng, Chu-Yuan
Cheng, Chung-Kuan
Cheng, David Hong
Cheng, David Keun
Cheng, Franklin Yih
Cheng, H. H.
Cheng, Herbert S.
Cheng, Hsiang-tai
Cheng, Hsien K.
Cheng, Joseph Kwang-Chao
Cheng, Kuang Lu
Cheng, Louis Tsz-Wan
Cheng, Mei-Fang Hsieh
Cheng, Nancy C.
Cheng, Nelly Ching-yun
Cheng, Ping
Cheng, Richard Tien-Ren
Cheng, Sin I.
Cheng, Songlin
Cheng, Stephen Z. D.
Cheng, Ta-Pei
Cheng, Ying-wan
Cheo, Li-hsiang S.
Cheo, Peter K.
Cheong, Fiona
Cheryan, Munir
Cheung, Herbert Chiu-Ching
Cheung, Julian F. Y.
Cheung, Philip
Cheung, Shun Yan
Cheung, Wai Yiu
Chew, Frances Sze-Ling
Chew, Kenneth Sze-Ying
Chew, Pamela Christine
Chew, Weng Cho
Chi, David Shyh-Wei
Chi, Jacob
Chi, Myung Sun
Chi, Yinliang
Chia, Kai
Chia, Ning
Chia, Rosina Chih-Hung
Chia, Swee Lim
Chiang, Berttram
Chiang, Chin Long
Chiang, Huai C.
Chiang, Joseph F.
Chiang, Shiao-Hung
Chiang, Yung Frank
Chiao, Jen Wei
Chiba, Lee I.
Chien, Chia-Ling
Chien, Chih-Yung
Chien, Yie W.
Chien, Ying I.
Ch'ih, John Juwei
Chin, Alexander Foster
Chin, Beverly Ann
Chin, Henry Han
Chin, Ken K.
Chin, Marilyn Mei Ling
Chin, Robert Allen
Chin, Steven Han-Hoy
Chin, William Nigel
Chin, Winifred C.
Chin, Yin-lien Chen
Ching, Chee
Ching, Harvey Cho Wing
Ching, Marvin K. L.

Ching, Stanton Sakae Hong Yat
Ching, Wai-Yim
Chiou, Paul C. J.
Chiou, Wen-An
Chishti, Athar Husain
Chitgopekar, Sharad S.
Chiu, Arthur Nang Lick
Chiu, Chao-Lin
Chiu, Lue-Yung Chow
Chiu, S. M.
Chiu, Shean-Tsong
Chiu, Wah
Cho, Alfred Yi
Cho, Christopher Sang Kyu
Cho, Dong-il Dan
Cho, Eun-Sook
Cho, Jang Youn
Cho, Kah-Kyung
Cho, Kang Rae
Cho, Peck
Cho, Soung Moo
Cho, Weol D.
Cho, Wonhwa
Cho, Zang-Hee
Choe, Sang Tae
Choe, Sun Tok
Choi, Dosoung Philip
Choi, Frederick D. S.
Choi, In-Chan
Choi, Jai-Young
Choi, Jin Wook
Choi, Kyung-Ju
Choi, Kyung Kook
Choi, Namkee Gang
Choi, Paul W.
Choi, Soonok
Choi, Tai-Soon
Choi, Ye-Chin
Choi, Young Dong
Chong, Peng-Khuan
Chopra, Dev Raj
Chopra, Dharam Vir
Chou, Arthur W.
Chou, Ching-Chung
Chou, David Yuan-Pin
Chou, Iih-Nan
Chou, James C. S.
Chou, Leland L. C.
Chou, Mei-Yin
Chou, Ting-Chao
Chou, Tsu-Wei
Choudhury, A. Latif
Chow, Balance Tin-Ping
Chow, Bob Ching-Hong
Chow, Chuen-Yen
Chow, Kao Liang
Chow, Louise Tsi
Chow, Mo-yuen
Chow, Paul Chuan-Juin
Chow, Peter Chi-Yuan
Chow, Tse-tsung
Chowdhury, Dipak Kumar
Choy, Fred Kat-Chung
Chu, Benjamin
Chu, Ching-Wu
Chu, Chung Kwang
Chu, Elizabeth Chan
Chu, Felix T.
Chu, Hung Manh
Chu, Jonathan Moseley
Chu, Judy M.
Chu, Kong
Chu, Patricia Pei-chang
Chu, Paul Ching-Wu
Chu, Peter Cheng
Chu, Shirley S.
Chu, Tien Lu
Chu, Ting L.
Chu, Tsuchin Philip
Chu, Wei-Kan
Chua, Leon O.
Chu-Andrews, Jennifer
Chuang, Henry Ning

Chui, Charles K.
Chun, Aulani
Chun, Joe Y. F.
Chun, Raymond W. M.
Chung, Chai-sik
Chung, Chen Hua
Chung, Chin Sik
Chung, David Yih
Chung, Deborah Duen Ling
Chung, Douglas Kuei-Nan
Chung, Ed Baik
Chung, H. Michael
Chung, Hyun S.
Chung, Jin Soo
Chung, Jong Rak Philip
Chung, King-Thom
Chung, Kyung Won
Chung, Ling Jia
Chung, Paul Myungha
Chung, Simon Lam-Ying
Chung, Sue Fawn
Chung, Tze-Chiang
Chung, Yip-Wah
Chung, Young-Iob
Chuong, Cheng-Ming
Chyung, Dong Hak
Collantes, Augurio L.
Cua, Antonio S.
Dai, Hai-Lung
Dai, Liyi
Dalvi, Ramesh R.
Dao, Anh Huu
Dao, Minh Quang
Das, Man Singh
Das, Phanindramohan
Das, Salil Kumar
Dass, Edgar Sushil
Das Sarma, Basudeb
Datta, Subhendu K.
Dave, Janak
De, Suranjan
Debroy, Chitrita
Deivanayagam, Subramaniam
Desai, Chandrakant S.
Desai, Manisha
Desai, Sudhir G.
Desai, Suresh A.
Desai, Vimal H.
Deshpande, Nilendra Ganesh
Dev, Parvati
Dhaliwal, Amrik Singh
Dhurandhar, Nina R.
Dinh, Tung Van
Diokno, Ananias Cornejo
Dirige, Ofelia Villa
Divakaruni, Chitra Banerjee
Dixit, Balwant N.
Djao, Angela Wei
Doi, Roy Hiroshi
Domoto, Douglass T.
Dong, Wei
Dong, Zheng-Min
Doyle, Ruth Narita
D'Souza, Harry J.
Dung, Hou Chi
Durlabhji, Subhash
Dutt, Nikil D.
Dutta, Pulak
Dwivedi, Chandradhar
Endo, Paula Sayoko Tsukamoto
Eng, Jamie Pearl
Eng, Lawrence Fook
Eng, William
Erramilli, Shyamsunder
Fa, Angie
Fan, Carol C.
Fan, Chang-Yun
Fan, Chien
Fan, Liang-Shih
Fang, Cheng-Shen
Fang, Fabian Tien-Hwa
Fang, Ming M.
Farouk, Bakhtier

Feng, Tse-Yun
Feng, Xin
Fok, Agnes Kwan
Fok, Yu-Si
Fong, April Ann
Fong, Bernard Wah Doung
Fong, Glenn Randall
Fong, Harry H. S.
Fong, Jack Sun-Chik
Fong, Mary Helena
Fong, Nelson C.
Fu, Jyun-Horng
Fu, Karen K.
Fu, Kuan-Chen
Fu, LiMin
Fu, Michael Chung-Shu
Fu, Shou-Cheng Joseph
Fugita, Stephen Susumu
Fujii, Jack Koji
Fujimoto, Isao
Fujimoto, James G.
Fujimoto, Wilfred Yorio
Fukunaga, Keinosuke
Fukurai, Hiroshi
Fulbeck, Kip
Funabiki, Jon
Fung, Bing M.
Fung, Daniel Yee Chak
Fung, Dennis Lung
Fung, Gordon L.
Fung, Henry C.
Fung, Ho-Leung
Fung, Hung-Gay
Fung, Kee-Ying
Fung, Sun-Yiu
Fung, Yuan-Cheng Bertram
Furukawa, Fred M.
Furuta, Richard K.
Furuto, Sharlene Bernice Choy
  Lin
Gajendar, Nandigam
Gajjar, Jagdish Trikamji
Gan, José C.
Gandhi, Natwar Mohan
Gandhi, Prashant P.
Gandhi, Vikram H.
Gangopadhyay, Chitta R.
Ganguly, Jibamitra
Gao, Jiali
Garg, Arun
Garg, Ramesh Chandra
Garg, Umesh
Garg, Vijay Kumar
Gee, Arthur
Gee, Norman F.
Geng, Shu
George, K. P.
Ghim, Thad T.
Ghosh, Bhaskar Kumar
Ghosh, Chinmoy
Ghosh, Subhas
Ghosh, Swapan Kumar
Giam, Choo Seng
Gidda, Jaswant Singh
Gnanadesikan, Ramanathan
Go, Howard T.
Goh, Ben K.
Goh, David S.
Gollahalli, Subramanyam
  Ramappa
Gong, Jin Kang
Gonzalez-Pardo, Lillian
Goo, Edward Kwock Wai
Gorla, Rama S. R.
Gotera, Vicente Ferrer
Goto, George
Goto, Yukihiro
Govil, Narendra Kumar
Govindarajulu, Zakkula
Goyal, Megh R.
Green, Yoshiko Okada
Gulati, Adarsh Kumar

Gunaratne, Dhavalasri Shelton
  Abeywickreme
Guo, Hua
Gupta, Ajay Kumar
Gupta, Amit
Gupta, Anil K.
Gupta, Arjun K.
Gupta, Arun Premchand
Gupta, Ashok K.
Gupta, Bhupender S.
Gupta, Gian Chand
Gupta, Jatinder Nath Dass
Gupta, Jiwan D.
Gupta, Krishan L.
Gupta, Madhu Sudan
Gupta, Manjula K.
Gupta, Naim C.
Gupta, Om Prakash
Gupta, Omprakash K.
Gupta, Pardeep K.
Gupta, Parveen P.
Gupta, Rajeshwar Kumar
Gupta, Rajiv
Gupta, Ramesh K.
Gupta, Ratanlal N.
Gupta, Sanjay
Gupta, Sanjeev
Gupta, Santosh
Gupta, Sunil
Gupta, Tapan K.
Gupta, Tej R.
Gupta, Venu Gopal
Gupta, Vijay
Gupta, Virendra K.
Gupta, Yogendra Mohan
Ha, Joseph Man-Kyung
Hahn, Hwa Suk
Hahn, Liang-Shin
Hahn, Yukap
Hajela, Prabhat
Hajiyani, Mehdi Hussain
Haldar, Dipak
Halemane, Thirumala Raya
Hamamoto, Darrell Yoshito
Han, Anna M.
Han, Chien-Pai
Han, Chingping Jim
Han, Grace Yang
Han, Jaok
Han, Je-Chin
Han, Kenneth N.
Han, Moo-Young
Han, Sherman Hsiao-min
Han, Susan S.
Han, Xianming Lance
Hanami, Clement S.
Haque, M. Shamsul
Haque, Zahur U.
Hara, Saburo
Haramaki, Chiko
Hasan, Syed E.
Hashimoto, Eiji
Hashimoto, Ken
Hashimoto, Rentaro
Hata, David M.
Hata, Donald Teruo, Jr.
Hata, Hiroaki
Hata, Nadine Ishitani
Hayakawa, S. I.
Hayashi, Elmer Kinji
Hayashi, James Akira
Hayashi, Masato
Hayashi, Masumi
Hayashi, Robert H.
Hayashi, Tetsumaro
Hayashi, William Yasuo
Hayashida, Frank
Hayashida, Ronald Hideo
Higa, Kunihiko
Higa, Leslie Hideyasu
Higa, Ross Rikio
Hihara, Lloyd Hiromi
Hikida, Robert Seiichi

Hing, Bill Ong
Hirabayashi, Lane Ryo
Hirano, Kyoko
Hirano-Nakanishi, Marsha Joyce
Hiraoka, Leslie Satoshi
Hirasaki, George Jiro
Hirata, Hosea
Ho, Andrew Kong-Sun
Ho, Chi-Tang
Ho, Chien
Ho, Chih-Ming
Ho, Chrwan-Jyh
Ho, Chung-Wu
Ho, David D.
Ho, Hon Hing
Ho, John Ting-Sum
Ho, Ju-shey
Ho, Khang-cheng
Ho, Ping Pei
Ho, Ting
Ho, Xuan Michael
Ho, Yu-Chi
Ho, Yui Tim
Hokama, Yoshitsugi
Hom, Mei-Ling
Hom, Peter Wah
Hon, David Nyok-Sai
Honda, Maya
Honda, Shigeru Irwin
Hong, Daniel Chonghan
Hong, George K.
Hong, Gong-Soog
Hong, Ilyoo Barry
Hong, John Song Yook
Hong, S. Theodore
Hong, Shuguang
Hong, Suk Ki
Hong, Weihu
Hongo, Garrett Kaoru
Honma, Shigemi
Hoo, Joe-Jie
Hoshiko, Michael
Hosmane, Ramachandra S.
Hosokawa, Fumiko
Houston, Velina Hasu
Hsi, Bartholomew P.
Hsi, David C.
Hsia, Judith Ann
Hsiao, Sidney C.
Hsiao, William C.
Hsie, Abraham Wuhsiung
Hsieh, Carl Chia-Fong
Hsieh, Chung-cheng
Hsieh, Durwynne
Hsieh, Hsin-Neng
Hsieh, Jeanette L.
Hsieh, Philip Po-Fang
Hsieh, Wen-jen
Hsieh, Winston Wen-sun
Hsieh, You-Lo
Hsu, Albert Yutien
Hsu, Cathy H. C.
Hsu, Chen-Chi
Hsu, Frank H.
Hsu, Hsiu-Sheng
Hsu, Immanuel C. Y.
Hsu, John Tseng-Hsiu
Hsu, John Y.
Hsu, Jong-Ping
Hsu, Liang-Chi
Hsu, Margaretha
Hsu, Mei-Ling
Hsu, Nai-chao
Hsu, Paul
Hsu, Ping
Hsu, Robert Ying
Hsu, Samuel
Hsu, Shaw Ling
Hsu, Tse-Chi
Hsu, Yu Chu
Hsu, Yuan-Hsi
Hsueh, Chun-tu
Hsui, Albert Tong-Kwan

Hu, Albert Ke-Jeng
Hu, Bambi
Hu, Bei-Lok Bernard
Hu, Chao Hsiung
Hu, Chenming
Hu, Chi Yu
Hu, Chia-Ren
Hu, Shiu-Lok
Hu, Steve Seng-Chiu
Huang, Alice Shih-Hou
Huang, Barney Kuo-Yen
Huang, C.-T. James
Huang, Cheng-Cher
Huang, Cheng-Chi
Huang, Chi-chiang
Huang, Chi-Lung Dominic
Huang, Chin-pao
Huang, Garng Morton
Huang, George Wenhong
Huang, Huey-Wen
Huang, I-Ning
Huang, Jacob Wen-Kuang
Huang, Jiann-Shiun
Huang, Jin
Huang, Joseph T.
Huang, Ju-Chang
Huang, Jung-chang
Huang, Kee Chang
Huang, Ko-Hsing
Huang, Ming-Hui
Huang, Nai-Chien
Huang, Samuel T.
Huang, Shan-Jen Chen
Huang, Shih-Wen
Huang, Thomas Tao-Shing
Huang, Tseng
Huang, Wei-chiao
Huang, Wei-Sung Wilson
Huang, Weifeng
Huang, Xun-Cheng
Huang, Yasheng
Huang, Zhen
Hui, Sek Wen
Huie, Carmen Wah-Kit
Humayun, M. Zafri
Hung, Chao-Shun
Hung, Chih-Cheng
Hung, James Chen
Hung, Ken
Hung, Kuen-Shan
Hung, Paul P.
Hung, Ru J.
Hung, Yen-Wan
Husain, Mustafa Mahmood
Hussain, Fazle
Hussain, Riaz
Huynh, Boi-Hanh
Huynh, Dung Thiet
Hwang, Charles C.
Hwang, Ching-Lai
Hwang, Dennis B. K.
Hwang, Hi Sook
Hwang, Hsin-Ginn
Hwang, John C.
Hwang, Mark I.
Hwang, Nen-chen Richard
Hwang, Shin Ja Joo
Hwang, Te-Long
Ih, Charles Chung-Sen
Iiyama, Chizu
Ikeda, Elizabeth Rae
Ikeda, Shigemasa
Im, Jin-Hyouk
Im, Young-Ai
Inaba, Jeffrey Norihisa
Inada, Lawson Fusao
Inagami, Tadashi
Ing, Malcolm Ross
Inouye, Charles Shirō
Inouye, Richard Saburo
Iqbal, Zafar
Ishaq, Ashfaq M.
Ishi, Tomoji

Ishida, Andrew
Ishida, Dianne N.
Ishida, Takanobu
Ishii, Thomas Koryu
Ishikawa, Ishi
Ishikawa-Wolf, Ana Yoshiko
Ishimaru, Akira
Ismail, Amin Rashid
Ito, Mark Mitsuo
Ito, Philip Jitsuo
Ito, Satoshi
Iwasaki, Iwao
Iwata, Brian A.
Iyer, Ananth. V.
Iyer, Easwar S.
Iyer, Prem Shankar
Iyer, Ravishankar Krishnan
Jain, Himanshu
Jain, Mahendra K.
Jain, Naresh C.
Jain, Piyare Lal
Jain, Surender K.
Jaluria, Yogesh
Jammalamadaka, Sreenivasa Rao
Jayaswal, Raoheshyam K.
Jen, Horatio H.
Jen, Philip HungSun
Jhon, Myung S.
Ji, Chueng Ryong
Ji, Inhae
Ji, Taehwa
Jiang, Nai-Siang
Jiang, William Yuying
Jiang, Xixiang
Jiang, Zhenying
Joe, Clarence
Jong, Mark M. T.
Joshi, Bhairav D.
Joshi, Jagmohan
Ju, Frederick D.
Jun, Hung Won
Jun, Jong S.
Jung, Audrey Moo Hing
Jung, Byung Il
Jung, John R.
Jung, Mankil
Kabir, Abulfazal M. Fazle
Kachru, Braj B.
Kadaba, Prasanna Venkatarama
Kagiwada, George
Kagiwada, Harriet H. Natsuyama
Kaita, Robert
Kaji, Akira
Kak, Subhash Chandra
Kaku, Michio
Kale, Jayant R.
Kalra, Rajiv
Kam, Thomas K. Y.
Kam, Vernon T.
Kamo, Yoshinori
Kan, Yuet Wai
Kaneda, Hiromitsu
Kaneshige, Harry Masato
Kang, Eun Chul
Kang, Jun-Koo
Kang, Keebom
Kang, Sugwon
Kang, Weng Poo
Kang, Wi Jo
Kang, Yung C.
Kao, Race L.
Kao, Tai-Wu
Kapoor, Jagmohan
Kapoor, Shiv G.
Kapoor, Tarun
Kapur, Kamal K.
Kashyap, Moti Lal
Kato, Goro
Kato, Tosio
Kaul, Sanjiv
Kawafuchi, Glenn Misaki
Kaya, Douglas Hifuto, Jr.
Ke, Gang

Keshavan, Krishnaswamiengar
Khan, Mohammad Asad
Khan, Mohammed Abdul
  Quddus
Khan, Walayet A.
Khanna, Naveen
Khanna, Rajive Kumar
Khanna, Ramesh
Khanna, Shiv Narain
Khaw, Ban-An
Khorana, Har Gobind
Kiang, Clyde Y.
Kiang, Peter Nien-chu
Kikuchi, Shinya
Kikuchi, William Kenji
Kim, Alan Hyun-Oak
Kim, Anna Charr
Kim, Bang Ja
Kim, Bonn-Oh
Kim, Byong-Kon
Kim, Byung Guk
Kim, Byung Suk
Kim, Chan-Hie
Kim, Chan-Wung
Kim, Changwook
Kim, Changyup Daniel
Kim, Chin
Kim, Chin Hui
Kim, Chong Lim
Kim, Choong Soon
Kim, Chulwan
Kim, Chung Wook
Kim, David Ho-Sik
Kim, David U.
Kim, Dongcheol
Kim, Edward Ik Hwan
Kim, Eun Mee
Kim, Haewon Chang
Kim, HakLin
Kim, Han-Seob
Kim, Hee-Jin
Kim, HeeMin
Kim, Hesook Suzie
Kim, Hong Nack
Kim, Hong Yung
Kim, Hyong Sok
Kim, Hyun Kap
Kim, Hyun Wang
Kim, Il-Woon
Kim, Ilpyong J.
Kim, Jae Won
Kim, Jay S.
Kim, Joanne Young
Kim, Jong H.
Kim, Jong-Jin
Kim, Joochul
Kim, Jung Hwan
Kim, Junguk Lawrence
Kim, Jwa Keun
Kim, Karl Eujung
Kim, Kathleen M.
Kim, Ken I.
Kim, Ki Hang
Kim, Kitai
Kim, Kunsoo
Kim, Kwan Hee
Kim, Kyoo Hong
Kim, Michael Kyong-il
Kim, Michael Wooyung
Kim, Moon Kyu
Kim, Myung-Hye
Kim, Myung Mi
Kim, Neung Jip
Kim, Paul Myungchyun
Kim, Pilkyu
Kim, Quee-Young
Kim, Rhyn H.
Kim, Robert Hyung-chan
Kim, Saeja Oh
Kim, Sang Phill
Kim, Soon Jin
Kim, Soon-Kyu
Kim, Sung Bok

Kim, Suzy Linda
Kim, Uichol
Kim, Wun Jung
Kim, Yee S.
Kim, Yong Choon
Kim, Yong-Gwan
Kim, Yongshik
Kim, Yoonchung Park
Kim, Youn-Suk
Kim, Young-Bae
Kim, Young Chan
Kim, Young-Gurl
Kim, Young-Jin
Kim, Youngsoo Richard
Kim, Youngsuk
Kim, Yun
Kim, Yung Mo
Kimura, Brian
Kimura, Gwen C.
Kimura, Mineo
Kingman, Dong
Kingston, Maxine Hong
Kinoshita, Jin H.
Kinoshita, Toichiro
Kinra, Vikram Kumar
Kishimoto, Yasuo
Ko, Ada
Ko, Edmond Inq-Ming
Ko, Wen Hsiung
Ko, Wen-hsiung
Ko, Winston T.
Kobashigawa, Ben
Kobayashi, Albert Satochi
Kobayashi, Bert Nobuo
Kobayashi, Francis Masao
Kobayashi, Hideaki
Kobayashi, Koichi
Kobayashi, Nobuhisa
Kobayashi, Yoshiko
Kochhar, Devendra M.
Kochhar, Man Mohan
Koide, Frank Takayuki
Kompala, Dhinakar S.
Kong, Ana C.
Kong, Corita Shuk Sinn
Kong, Dongsung
Kong, Stanley Young
Konishi, Masakazu
Koo, Anthony Ying Chang
Koo, Benjamin Hai-Chang
Koo, Delia
Koul, Hira Lal
Krishnamoorthy, Govindarajalu
Krishnamurti, T. N.
Krishnan, Chirakkal
Krishnan, Radha
Kshirsagar, Anant M.
Ku, Mei-Chin Hsiao
Kuan, Wei Eihn
Kubota, Carole Ann
Kubota, Mitsuru
Kuh, Ernest Shiu-Jen
Kulkarni, Anand K.
Kulkarni, Arun Digambar
Kulkarni, Arun P.
Kulkarni, Gopal S.
Kulkarni, Kishore G.
Kulkarni, Krishnaji Hanamant
Kulkarni, Ravi S.
Kulkarni, Uday Ravindra
Kumar, Ashir
Kumar, Ashok
Kumar, Ashok
Kumar, Atul
Kumar, Devendra
Kumar, Jothi V.
Kumar, Kamalesh
Kumar, Kusum
Kumar, Kusum Verma
Kumar, Meera
Kumar, Panganamala Ramana
Kumar, Raj
Kumar, Ramesh

Kumar, Ranganathan
Kumar, Satyendra
Kumar, Sudhir
Kumar, Sushil
Kumar, V.
Kumaran, A. Krishna
Kundu, Mukul Ranjan
Kung, H. T.
Kung, Harold H.
Kung, Shain-dow
Kuo, Albert Yi-shuong
Kuo, Chao Ying
Kuo, Chung-Chieh Jay
Kuo, Feng Yang Kuo
Kuo, James K. Y.
Kuo, Joseph C.
Kuo, Ken Nan
Kuo, Ming-ming Shen
Kuo, Shiou-San
Kuo, Way
Kuo, Wen Hsiung
Kuramitsu, Howard K.
Kuroda, Yasumasa
Kurup, Shishir Ravindran
Kushida, Toshimoto
Kwak, No Kyoon
Kwak, Wikil
Kwan, Catherine Ning
Kwan, Kian M.
Kwan, Simon Hing-Man
Kwei, Ti-Kang
Kwoh, Stewart
Kwok, Chuck Chun-yau
Kwok, Daniel W. Y.
Kwok, Hoi-Sing
Kwok, Reginald Yin-Wang
Kwon, Young Wuk
Lai, Albert Wenben
Lai, Michael Ming-Chiao
Lai, Patrick Kinglun
Lai, Richard Thomas
Lai, Richard Tseng-yu
Lai, Tsong-Yue
Lai, Tze Leung
Lai, Waihang
Laigo, Valeriano Emerciano
  Montante
Lal, Rattan
Lam, Alex W.
Lam, Chow-Shing
Lam, Chun H.
Lam, Fat C.
Lam, Sau-Hai
Lam, Simon Shin-Sing
Land, Ming Huey
Landero, Reynaldo Rivera, II
Langrana, Noshir A.
Lateef, Abdul Bari
Lau, Estelle Pau On
Lau, Frederick C.
Lau, Hon-Shiang
Lau, Ngar-Cheung
Lau, Peter Man-Yiu
Lau, Tin Man
Lau, Yuen-Sum
Lê, Hy Xuân
Le, Tieng Quang
Lee, Byung-Joo
Lee, Che-Fu
Lee, Chen Hui
Lee, Chen Lok
Lee, Chew-Lean
Lee, Chin-Chuan
Lee, Chong Sung
Lee, Choong Yang
Lee, Chung
Lee, Chung
Lee, Chung-Yee
Lee, Daeyong
Lee, Dah-Yinn
Lee, Der-Tsai
Lee, E. Stanley
Lee, Hak-Kwon

Lee, Heakyung
Lee, Henry Joung
Lee, Heungsoon Felix
Lee, Hwa-Wei
Lee, Jae-won
Lee, Jai Hyon
Lee, Jen-Shih
Lee, John Chung
Lee, Jong Seh
Lee, Jooh
Lee, June Key
Lee, Jung Young
Lee, K. J.
Lee, Kai-Fong
Lee, Kangoh
Lee, Ker-Fong
Lee, Kimyeong
Lee, King Y.
Lee, Kok-Meng
Lee, Kuo-Hsiung
Lee, Kwang K.
Lee, Kyo Rak
Lee, Lee Hwang
Lee, Marietta Y. W. T.
Lee, Ming-Tung
Lee, Myung-Soo
Lee, Nan-Nan
Lee, Ocksoo Kim
Lee, Pamela Tau
Lee, Richard Fayao
Lee, Robert
Lee, Sang Moon
Lee, Shih Ying
Lee, Siu-Lam
Lee, Soo See
Lee, Soo-Young
Lee, Sue Ying
Lee, Suk Hun
Lee, Sun-Young Won
Lee, Sung Mook
Lee, Sunggyu
Lee, Taehee
Lee, Tien-Chang
Lee, Tony J. F.
Lee, Tsaifeng Mazie
Lee, Tsoung-Chao
Lee, Tsung-Dao
Lee, Tung-Kwang
Lee, Tzesan David
Lee, Wei-chin
Lee, Wei-Na
Lee, Wonyong
Lee, Yeu-Tsu Margaret
Lee, Yow-Min R.
Lee, Yuan Tseh
Lee, Yul W.
Lee, Yur-Bok
Leu, Ming C.
Leung, Benjamin Shuet-Kin
Leung, Chi Kin
Leung, Christopher Chung-Kit
Leung, Chung-Ngoc
Leung, Edwin Pak-Wah
Leung, Joseph Yuk-Tong
Leung, Kai-Cheong
Leung, Kok Ming
Leung, Louis W.
Leung, Pui-Tak
Leung, Wing Hai
Leung, Yuen-Sang
Lew, Alan August
Lew, Gloria Maria
Lew, Susie Q.
Lew, William W.
Li, Bichuan
Li, Bing An
Li, C. C.
Li, Charles N.
Li, Che-Yu
Li, Cheng
Li, Chia-yu
Li, Ching-Chung
Li, Ching James

Li, Dening
Li, Hanna Wu
Li, James C. M.
Li, Jia
Li, Kai
Li, Kuiyuan
Li, Lillian M.
Li, Ling-Fong
Li, Ming
Li, Peter Wai-Kwong
Li, Qiang
Li, San-pao
Li, Sheng S.
Li, Shuhe
Li, Tien-Yien
Li, Victor C.
Li, Victor On-Kwok
Li, Wen-Hsiung
Li, Wu
Li, Xiao-Bing
Li, Ya
Li, Yao Tzu
Li, Yongji
Li, Yu-ku
Li, Yuzhuo
Liang, Bruce T.
Liang, Chang-seng
Liang, Edison Park-tak
Liang, George Hsueh-Lee
Liang, Matthew H.
Liang, Steven Yuehsan
Liang, Tehming
Liao, Ming
Liao, Shutsung
Liao, T. Warren
Liao, Woody M.
Liem, Karel Frederik
Liem, Ronald Kian Hong
Lieu, George Y.
Lieu, Hou-Shun
Lim, Billy Lee
Lim, Daniel V.
Lim, Kam Ming
Lim, Kap Chul
Lim, Kwee-Eng Lyn
Lim, Paul Stephen
Lim, Paulino Marquez, Jr.
Lim, Ralph Wei Hsiong
Lim, Ramon Khe-Siong
Lim, Richard
Lim, Rodney Gene
Lim, Shirley Geok-Lin
Lim, Soon-Sik
Lim, Teck-Kah
Lin, Binshan
Lin, Cen-Tsong
Lin, Chaote
Lin, Chhiu-Tsu
Lin, Chi Yung
Lin, Chin-Chu
Lin, Dennis Kon-Jin
Lin, Diane Chang
Lin, Feng-Bao
Lin, Hsiu-San
Lin, Hung Chang
Lin, James C.
Lin, James Chih-I
Lin, James Peicheng
Lin, Jason Jia-Yuan
Lin, Joseph Pen-Tze
Lin, Julia C.
Lin, Kai-Ching
Lin, Kuan-Pin
Lin, L. Yu
Lin, Ming-Chang
Lin, Patricia Yu
Lin, Paul Kuang-Hsien
Lin, Pen-Min
Lin, Pi-Erh
Lin, Ping-Wha
Lin, Poping
Lin, Robert Peichung
Lin, Roxanne Veronica

Lin, Shield B.
Lin, Shin
Lin, Su-Chen Jonathon
Lin, Sung P.
Lin, Ting-Ting Yao
Lin, Wen Chun
Lin, Xiao-Song
Lin, Yeong-Jer
Lin, You-An Robert
Lin, Yu-Chong
Lin, Yü-sheng
Lin, Yuet-Chang Joseph
Lin, Yuh-Lang
Lin, Yuyi
Ling, Amy
Ling, Christine N.
Ling, Hao
Ling, Hsin Yi
Ling, Jack Chieh-Sheng
Ling, Ta-Yung
Ling, Yu-long
Ling, Zhi-Kui
Lingappa, Banadakoppa
   Thimmappa
Liou, Fue-Wen
Liou, K. T.
Liou, Sy-Hwang
Liou, Yihwa Irene
Liu, Anne W.
Liu, Ben Chieh
Liu, Ben Shaw-Ching
Liu, Benjamin Y. H.
Liu, Chao-Nan
Liu, Chen-Ching
Liu, Chuan Sheng
Liu, Chung-Chiun
Liu, Donald Jiann-Tyng
Liu, Frank Yining
Liu, Gerald Hanmin
Liu, Henry
Liu, Hong
Liu, Hong-Ting
Liu, Hsun Kao
Liu, James P.
Liu, Jiang Bo
Liu, Jie
Liu, John J.
Liu, Juanita Ching
Liu, Jun S.
Liu, Jyh-Charn Steve
Liu, Karen Chia-Yu
Liu, Keh-Fei Frank
Liu, Leighton Kam Fat
Liu, Lily Pao-Ih
Liu, Maw-Shung
Liu, Mengxiong
Liu, Min
Liu, Ming Cheng
Liu, Peter Chi-Wah
Liu, Ping
Liu, Pinghui Victor
Liu, Ray H.
Liu, Shia-Ling
Liu, Stephen Shu-Ning
Liu, Susana Juh-mei
Liu, Te-Hua
Liu, Thomas Jyhcheng
Liu, Wei-Min
Liu, Xingwu
Liu, Yilu
Liu, Ying
Liu, Yuan Hsiung
Liu, Zhuangyi
Lo, Chien-kuo
Lo, Kwok-Yung
Lo, Samuel E.
Lo, Yuen-Tze
Lodhi, M. A. K.
Loh, Eugene C.
Loh, Wallace D.
Loo, Ti Li
Louie, David Wong
Louie, Eric K.

Louie, James Sam
Louie, Sammy G.
Louie, Steven Gwon Sheng
Lowe, Rolland Choy
Lu, Donghao Robert
Lu, Frank Kerping
Lu, I-Tai
Lu, Janet C.
Lu, John Y.
Lu, Jye-Chyi
Lu, Kau U.
Lu, Le-Wu
Lu, Lina
Lu, Linyu Laura
Lu, Luo
Lu, Mi
Lu, Min Zhan
Lu, Ponzy
Lu, Steven Zhiyun
Luh, Bor Shiun
Luh, Jiang
Lum, Tammy Kar-Hee
Lum, Vincent Y.
Luo, Shen-Yi
Luong, Son N.
Ma, Chen-Lung Ringo
Ma, Ching-To Albert
Ma, Fai
Ma, Laurence J. C.
Ma, Li-Chen
Ma, Michael
Ma, Sheng-mei
Ma, Stephen K.
Ma, Tso-Ping
Ma, Wenhai
Ma, Xiaoyun
Ma, Yan
Ma, Yi Hua
Made Gowda, Netkal M.
Maeda, Robert J.
Magdamo, Patricia L.
Mah, Richard Sze Hao
Mahajan, Anoop Kumar
Mahajan, Arvind
Mahajan, Harpreet
Mahajan, Jayashree
Mahajan, Roop L.
Mahajan, Satish Murlidhar
Mahajan, Vijay
Mahajan, Y. Lal
Mahalingam, R.
Mahanthappa, Kalyana T.
Mahesh, Virendra Bhushan
Mak, Chi Ho
Mak, James
Makino, Seiichi
Makinodan, Takashi
Malhotra, Anju
Malhotra, Ashok K.
Malhotra, Om P.
Malhotra, Vijay K.
Malik, Anand Kumar
Malik, Hafeez
Malik, Sadiq R.
Malik, Zafar A.
Mallick, Pankaj K.
Mamidala, Ramulu
Man, Chi-Sing
Mansur, Iqbal
Mantil, Joseph Chacko
Margallo, Lucio N., II
Masamune, Satoru
Mathew, Saramma T.
Mathews, Peter
Mathur, Aditya P.
Mathur, Harbans B.
Mathur, Kailash V.
Mathur, Krishan D.
Matsui, Machiko
Matsui, Noriatsu
Matsumoto, Donald Michiaki
Matsumoto, George
Matsumoto, Mark R.

Matsumoto, Teruo
Matsuoka, Shiro
Mehrotra, Kishan Gopal
Mehta, Jawahar L.
Mehta, Kamlesh T.
Mehta, Mahesh
Mehta, Mehul Mansukh
Mehta, Mohinder Paul
Mehta, Prakash V.
Mehta, Rahul
Mehta, Raj B.
Mehta, Ved
Mei, Chiang Chung
Mei, Kenneth K.
Mei, Wai-Ning
Meng, Xiannong
Merchant, Vasant V.
Meshii, Masahiro
Min, David Ilki
Min, Hokey
Min, K. Jo
Min, Kyung Ho
Min, Pyong-Gap
Min, Yong Soon
Minocha, Harish C.
Mirchandani, Gagan
Mirchandani, Prakash
Mishra, Shitala P.
Misra, Prabhakar
Mistry, Jayanthi
Mitra, Grihapati
Mitter, Sanjoy K.
Miura, Irene Takei
Miura, Ken-ichi
Miyakoda, Kikuro
Miyamoto, Michael Dwight
Miyamoto, Michael Masao
Miyamoto, Seiichi
Miyamoto, Wayne Akira
Miyasaki, George Joji
Miyashiro, Akiho
Miyata, Keijiro
Mo, Luke W.
Mo, Suchoon
Mohan, Chandra
Mohapatra, Rabindra N.
Montero, Juan Murillo, II
Moon, Chung-In
Moon, Kee Suk
Moon, Young B.
Mori, John P.
Morisawa, Marie Ethel
Morita, Richard Yukio
Mothkur, Sridhar Rao
Moudgil, Brij Mohan
Moudgil, Virinder K.
Moy, Henry
Moy, James S.
Moy, Mamie Wong
Moy, Naomi Ogawa
Moy, Robert Carl
Mui, Constance L.
Mukai, Hiroaki
Mukerjee, Pasupati
Mukherjea, Arunava
Mukherjee, Bharati
Munakata, Grace Megumi
Mura, Toshio
Murai, Norimoto
Murakami, Pamela S.
Murata, Margaret K.
Murata, Yuji
Murty, Katta Gopalakrishna
Murty, Komanduri Srinivasa
Muthukrishnan, Subbaratnam
Nagai, Nelson Kei
Nahata, Milap Chand
Nahm, Moon H.
Naidu, Seetala Veeraswamy
Naik, Datta Vittal
Naik, Tarun Ratilal
Nair, Chandra K.
Najita, Tetsuo

Nakajima, Nobuyuki
Nakamoto, Tetsuo
Nakamura, Mitsuru James
Nakamura, Patricia Akemi
   Kosugi
Nakamura, Royden
Nakanishi, Don Toshiaki
Nakashima, Tom Vincent
Nakata, Herbert Minoru
Nakatani, Roy Eiji
Nakayama, Randall Shige
Nakazawa, Anthony Tadashi
Nam, Sangboo
Nambu, Yoichiro
Nanda, Navin Chandar
Nanda, Ravindra
Narahara, Hiromichi T.
Narahashi, Toshio
Narasimhan, Sridhar
Narasimhan, Subha
Narayan, Kirin
Narayanan, A. Sampath
Narula, Subhash Chander
Nath, Amar
Nath, Joginder
Navangul, Himanshoo Vishnu
   Bhat
Nayak, Tapan Kumar
Nee, Michael Wei-Kuo
Newaz, S. S.
Ng, David
Ng, Peter A.
Ng, Rita Mei-Ching
Ng, Tang-Tat Percy
Ng, Wing
Nguyen, An H.
Nguyen, Bao Gia
Nguyen, Cam
Nguyen, Charles C.
Nguyen, Chuong Van
Nguyen, Henry Thien
Nguyen, Ho Ngoc
Nguyen, Luu Thanh
Nguyen, Manh-Hung
Nguyen, Ngoc-Diep Thi
Nguyen, Thuan Ke
Nguyen, Tri Huu
Nguyen, Vung Duy
Nguyen-huu, Xuong
Ni, Preston C.
Nip, Wai-Kit
Nishimura, Jonathan Sei
Nishimura, Miwa
Nishioka, David Jitsuo
Nishioka, Hayward H.
Nomura, Masayasu
Nori, Dattatreyudu
Odo, Blair M. T.
Odo, Franklin Shoichiro
Ogawa, Joseph Minoru
Oh, Keytack Henry
Oh, Tae Hee
Ohnishi, Tomoko
Ohtake, Takeshi
Ojima, Iwao
Okabe, Hideo
Okamura, Arthur Shinji
Okihiro, Gary Yukio
Okita, George Torao
Omori, Yoshiaki
Ong, Beng Soo
Ong, Chee-Mun
Ong, Nai-Phuan
Ong, Sing-Cheong
Onishi, Hironori
Ono, Kanji
Oshima, Eugene Akio
Ou, Ching-Nan
Ou, Hsien-Wang
Ozawa, Martha Naoko
Ozawa, Terutomo
Pai, Anna Chao
Paik, Ho Jung

Paik, Woon Ki
Pak, Ronald Yu-Sang
Pak, Yong Chin
Pakvasa, Sandip
Pan, Fung-Shine
Pan, Wei-Ping
Pan, Yuh-Kang
Pandey, Ras Bihari
Pandit, Sudhakar Madhavrao
Pandya, Deepak N.
Pang, Keum Y.
Pang, Seng Puang
Pang, Su-Seng
Pao, Chia-Ven
Papasani, Subbaiah Venkata
Parate, Natthu Sonbaji
Parikh, Rajeev N.
Parikh, Rohit J.
Park, Byungwoo
Park, Chang Ho
Park, Chung I.
Park, Chung Uk
Park, Duk-Won
Park, Hun Young
Park, Jae Young
Park, Jinwoo
Park, Joon B.
Park, Kang H.
Park, Myung Kun
Park, Ounyoung
Park, Sang Oh
Park, Seung-Kyoon
Park, Siyoung
Park, Su-Moon
Park, Sung-won Sam
Park, Tae Sung
Park, Won J.
Patel, Dinesh
Patel, Nagin K.
Patel, Virendra Chaturbhai
Pathak, Sen
Patil, Popat N.
Pei, Lowry Cheng-Wu
Peng, Chang-Shyh
Peng, George Tso Chih
Peng, Syd S.
Peng, Ying-shin Christine
Peterson, Indira Viswanathan
Pham, Kien Trung
Phan, Sem Hin
Pho, Hai B.
Pian, Theodore Hsueh-Huang
Pillai, Unnikrishna S.
Pillai, Vijayan K.
Pong, Ting-Chuen
Poon, Chi-Sang
Prabhudesai, Mukund M.
Prasad, Marehalli Gopalan
Prasad, Rameshwar
Pui, Ching-Hon
Pun, Pattle Pak-Toe
Puri, Pratap
Purohit, Milind Vasant
Qasim, Syed Reazul
Quimpo, Rafael Gonzales
Quismorio, Francisco P., Jr.
Qureshi, Muqarrab Ahmed
Radhakrishnamurthy, Bhandaru
Raghavan, Sridhar A.
Rahman, Yueh-Erh
Rai, Arun
Rai, Gauri S.
Raj, Harkisan D.
Rajagopal, Kumbakonam
   Ramamani
Rajan, Periasamy Karivaratha
Rajan, Raghuram Govind
Raju, Seshadri
Raju, Solomon Nalli, Sr.
Ramadhyani, Satish
Ramakumar, Ramachandra
   Gupta
Raman, Aravamudhan

745

Ramanathan, Veerabhadran
Ramchandani, Raj S.
Rana, Mohammed Waheed-uz-Zaman
Rao, Angara Koneti
Rao, Bhamidipaty Kameswara
Rao, Gandikota Venkata
Rao, Gottipaty N.
Rao, Gundu H. R.
Rao, K. L. Seshagiri
Rao, Kameswara Kolla
Rao, Madhusudana N.
Rao, Mentreddi Anandha
Rao, Papineni S.
Rao, Raghav H.
Rao, Ramesh K. S.
Rao, Sadasiva Madiraju
Rao, Singiresu Sambasiva
Rao, Spuma M.
Rao, Srikumar S.
Rao, T. K. Sreepada
Rao, Taramanohar B.
Rao, Tejaswini
Rao, Venigalla Basaveswara
Rasheed, Suraiya
Rath, Nigam Prasad
Raut, Kamalakar Balkrishna
Ravindra, Nuggehalli Muthanna
Rawat, Arun Kumar
Rawat, Banmali Singh
Reddy, C. Subba
Reddy, Chilekampalli Adinarayana
Reddy, Churku Mohan
Reddy, Gudigopuram Bhaskar
Reddy, Junuthula N.
Reddy, Pannala Sathyanahayana
Reddy, Pratap P.
Reddy, Raj
Reyes, Adelaida
Reyes, Hernan M.
Rha, ChoKyun
Rhee, Chase Chonggwang
Rhee, Hahn-Kyou
Rhee, Hang Yul
Rhee, Khee Choon
Rhee, Song Nai
Rhee, Susan Byungsook
Rio-Jelliffe, Rebecca
Rivera, Evelyn Margaret
Rohatgi, Pradeep K.
Rouf, Mohammed Abdur
Roy, Dev Kumar
Roy-Burman, Pradip
Ryu, Dewey Doo Young
Sabnis, Gajanan M.
Sachan, Dileep Singh
Sadana, Ajit
Safdari, Yahya Bhai
Sagawa, Yoneo
Sah, Chih-Tang
Sahni, Viraht
Saito, Yoshio
Sakamoto, Arthur, Jr.
Sakamoto, Clyde Mitsuru
Sakamoto, Katsuyuki
Sakhare, Vishwa M.
Sakita, Bunji
Salunkhe, Dattajeerao K.
Sanadi, D. R.
Sandhu, Ranbir Singh
Sandhu, Shingara Singh
San Juan, E.
Santhanam, Radhika
Sarkar, Fazlul H.
Sarker, Bhaba Ranjan
Sasahara, Arthur Asao
Sasaki, Betty Gail
Sasaki, Chiyo Katano
Sato, Paul Toshio
Sato, William K.
Saxena, Brij B.
Saxena, Satish Chandra

Saxena, Subhash Chandra
Sehgal, Om Parkash
Sen, Ashish Kumar
Sen, Karabi
Sen, Mihir
Sen, Pabitra Narayan
Sengupta, Dipak Lal
Sethi, Ishwar Krishan
Seto, Joseph Tobey
Seto, Theodore Paul
Sha, Ji-Ping
Sha, Shung-tse
Shah, Bhupendra P.
Shah, Dinesh Ochhavlal
Shah, Mubarak Ali
Shah, Nagambal Deepak
Shah, Nilesh D.
Shah, Parth J.
Shah, Shirish K.
Shaikh, Abdul Hamid
Shaikh, Saeed Ahmad
Shaikh, Zahir A.
Sham, Lu Jeu
Shang, Bernard Y.
Shang, Weijia
Sharma, Anil F.
Sharma, Arun
Sharma, Bhudev
Sharma, Deva Datta
Sharma, Ghanshyam D.
Sharma, Govind Chandra
Sharma, Jandhyala L.
Sharma, M. P.
Sharma, Mukul Mani
Sharma, Onkar Prasad
Sharma, Parashu Ram
Sharma, Raghubir Prasad
Sharma, Ramesh
Sharma, Santosh Devraj
Sharma, Saroj
Sharma, Satish
Sharma, Subhash C.
Sharma, Udhishtra Deva
Shen, Benjamin Shih-Ping
Shen, Hsieh Wen
Shen, I-Yao
Shen, Liang Chi
Shen, Shan-Fu
Shen, Sheldon Shih-Ta
Shen, Thomas T.
Shen, Xiao-Yan
Shen, Yuen-Ron
Shenoi, B. A.
Sheth, Ashvin C.
Sheth, Atul Chandravadan
Sheth, Kishor C.
Sheu, Bing J.
Shibata, Edward Isamu
Shieh, John Ting-Chung
Shieh, Rong Chung
Shieh, Tsay-Jiu Brian
Shieh, Yuch-Ning
Shih, Chia C.
Shih, Chiang
Shih, Chilin
Shih, Hong-Yee
Shih, Joan Fai
Shih, Ko-Ming
Shih, Ming-Che
Shih, Stephen Chingyu
Shih, Tom I-Ping
Shih, Wei
Shim, Eun Sup
Shim, Jae K.
Shim, Jung P.
Shim, Walton Kenn Tsung
Shimizu, Gordon Toshio
Shin, Doug Yong
Shin, Hung Sik
Shin, In-Sook Jeong
Shin, Kilman
Shin, Myung Soo
Shin, Paull H.

Shin, Yung C.
Shinagawa, Larry
Shinozuka, Masanobu
Shirai, Akiko
Shukla, Shivendra D.
Shwe, Hla
Siddiqui, Aleem Abdul
Siddiqui, Faruq Mahmud Anam
Sidhu, Gurmel Singh
Sihag, Ram K.
Simunek, Linda A.
Singh, Harpal
Singh, Madho
Singh, Rajendra
Singh, Sant P.
Singh, Surendra Pal
Singh, Vijay P.
Singh, Vijay Pal
Singhal, Avinash Chandra
Singpurwalla, Nozer Darabsha
Sinha, Akhouri A.
Sircar, Rina Schyamcharan
Siu, Yum-Tong
So, Magdalene Yee-Huen
So, Ronald Ming Cho
Sohn, Hong Yong
Sohn, So Young
Somani, Arun K.
Somasundaran, Ponisseril
Song, Choan-Seng
Song, Il-Yeol
Song, Joseph M.
Song, Shin-Min
Song, Xueshu
Song, Yangsoon
Soo, Billy S.
Sood, Devinder Kumar
Sreenivasan, Katepalli Raju
Sreevalsan, Thazepadath
Srirama, Malini
Srivastava, Prakash Narain
Su, Judy Ya-Hwa Lin
Su, Timothy C.
Su, Tsung-chow Joe
Su, Tuhuei
Su, Zhixin
Subbaswamy, Kumble Ramarao
Subramani, Suresh
Subramaniam, Pramilla N.
Suda, Tatsuya
Sudan, Ravindra Nath
Suen, Ching-Yun
Sugano, Miyoko
Sugihara, James Masanobu
Suh, Bernadyn Kim
Suh, Byungse
Suh, Dae-Sook
Suh, Nam Pyo
Suh, Yung-Ho
Sumida, Jon Tetsuro
Sun, Chang-Tsan
Sun, Chih Ree
Sun, Hugo Sui-Hwan
Sun, Tung-Tien
Sun, Wen-Yih
Sundaram, Meenakshi R.
Sung, Betty Lee
Sung, Chi Ching
Sung, Zinmay Renee
Suryanarayanan, Raj Gopalan
Suzuki, Masao Fred
Swaroop, Anand
Sy, Bon Kiem
Sy, Francisco S.
Tahara, Mildred Machiko
Tai, C. Stephen
Tai, Chen To
Tai, Hsin-Hsiung
Tai, Julia Chow
Taira, Toy-Ping Chan
Tajima, Toshiki
Takagi, Dana Y.
Takahashi, Joseph S.

Takahashi, Kozo
Takahashi, Lorey K.
Takahashi, Rita
Takahashi, Taro
Takaki, Ronald
Takasaki, William Yoshi Tsugu
Takashima, Shiro
Takayama, Akira
Takeda, Yasuhiko
Takemori, Akira Eddie
Takenaka, Makoto B.
Takeshita, Kenichi
Takeuchi, Kenneth James
Talwani, Manik
Tam, Christopher Kwong-Wah
Tam, Francis Man Kei
Tam, James Pingkwan
Tamhane, Ajit C.
Tan, Barrie
Tan, Cheng-Pheng
Tan, Chin An
Tan, Chor Weng
Tan, Colleen Woo
Tan, Henry S. I.
Tan, Jack Sim Eddy
Tan, Kim Howard
Tan, S. Y.
Tan, Sinforosa G.
Tan, Tjiauw-Ling
Tan, Wai-Yuan
Tanabe, George Joji, Jr.
Tanaka, John
Tanaka, Kouichi Robert
Tandon, Rajiv
Tang, Assumpta
Tang, Chik-Kwun
Tang, Chung Liang
Tang, Chung-Shih
Tang, Jianxin
Tang, Julie Mong-See
Tang, Kin Ling
Tang, Kwei
Tang, Mark Giakhy
Tang, Ming-Je
Tang, Paul Chi Lung
Tang, Roger Y. W.
Tang, Thomas Li-Ping
Tang, Wen
Tang, Wilson Hon-chung
Tang, Yi-Noo
Tang, Yingchan Edwin
Tang, Yu-Sun
Taniguchi, Alan Y.
Taniguchi, Robert Iwao
Tanouye, Mark Allen
Teng, Anthony Yung-yuan
Teng, Henry Shao-lin
Tewarson, Reginald P.
Thakor, Nitish Vyomesh
Thiruvathukal, Kris V.
Tien, Chang-Lin
Tien, H. Ti
Tikoo, Mohan L.
Ting, Joseph K.
Ting, Lee Hsia
Ting, Robert Yen-Ying
Ting, Samuel C. C.
Ting, Shih-Fan
Ting, T. C.
Ting, Thomas Chi Tsai
Todo, Satoru
Tokunaga, Howard Taira
Tonegawa, Susumu
Tong, Alex Wai Ming
Tong, Benjamin Robert
Tong, Lik Kuen
Tong, Ts'ing H.
Toyama, Jean Yamasaki
Tran, Loc Binh
Tran, Myluong Thi
Tran, Phuoc Huu
Tran, Qui-Phiet
Tripathi, Gorakh Nath Ram

Tripathi, Ramesh Chandra
Tripathi, Satish K.
Tripathi, Vijai Kumar
Tripathy, Deoki N.
Tsai, Betty L.
Tsai, Bilin Paula
Tsai, Bor-sheng
Tsai, Chester
Tsai, Chia-Yin
Tsai, James H.
Tsai, Jeffrey J. P.
Tsai, Jir-Shiong
Tsai, Kuei-wu
Tsai, Lung-Wen
Tsai, Ming-Daw
Tsai, Stephen Wei-Lun
Tsao, George T.
Tse, Harley Yau-Shuin
Tse, John Yung Dong
Tse, Stephen
Tse Dinh, Yuk-Ching
Tsen, Meng Chi
Tseng, Beatrice Shan-Yi
Tseng, Huan-Chi Chris
Tseng, James H. W.
Tseng, Leon F.
Tseng, S. C.
Tso, L. Hilary
Ts'o, Paul On Pong
Tsuang, Ming T.
Tsui, Daniel Chee
Tsui, Susan Lee
Tsukahira, Toshio George
Tsukamoto, Jack Toru
Tsutakawa, George
Tu, Charles W.
Tu, Ching-I
Tu, Harold Kai
Tu, Shengru
Tu, Shiao-Chun
Tuan, Debbie Fu-tai
Tuan, San Fu
Tung, Wu-Ki
Tung, Yeou-Koung
Tye, Bik-Kwoon Yeung
Tye, Sze-Hoi Henry
Tzeng, Kenneth Kai-Ming
Uba, George R.
Uchimura, Bruce Jiro
Ueda, Clarence Tad
Uemura, Joseph Norio
Ueng, Charles En-Shiuh
Ullah, M. Rifat
Unakar, Nalin Jayantilal
Underwood, Robert Anacletus
Vaid, Jyotsna
Vaidhyanathan, Vishnampet S.
Varghese, Philip Leslie
Varma, Rajender S.
Venkata, Subrahmanyam Saraswati
Venkataramanan, Raman
Verma, Ajit K.
Verma, Ram Sagar
Vernekar, Anandu Devarao
Vikram, Chandra Shekhar
Villa-Real, Olivia Canchela
Vo, Van Toi
Vohra, Indu
Vohra, Ranbir
Vovan, Ba
Vu, Joseph
Vyas, Premila Hariprasad
Wada, Toshimasa Francis
Walia, Jasjit Singh
Wan, Frederic Yui-Ming
Wan, James X.
Wan, Sze-kar
Wang, Alan P.
Wang, Albert S. D.
Wang, Ben
Wang, C. H.

Wang, Chao-Cheng
Wang, Chi-Hua
Wang, Ching Chung
Wang, Ching-Hua
Wang, Dajin
Wang, Daniel I.-Chyau
Wang, Deane
Wang, Dong-Ping
Wang, Fa-chung
Wang, Fei-Yue
Wang, George Maosue
Wang, Gwo-Jaw
Wang, Helen Hai-ling
Wang, Henry Yee-Neen
Wang, Hsueh-Hwa
Wang, Huaqing
Wang, I-chih
Wang, I-Shou
Wang, James C. F.
Wang, James Chou
Wang, Jason T. L.
Wang, Jaw-Kai
Wang, Jen-Yu
Wang, Jia
Wang, Jie
Wang, Jih Ming
Wang, Jing
Wang, Jun
Wang, Ko
Wang, Kuan
Wang, Kuo Chang
Wang, Kuo King
Wang, Leon Ru-Liang
Wang, Li-Shing
Wang, Lih-Jau
Wang, Ling Jun
Wang, Louie Kehluh
Wang, Luoyong
Wang, Margaret K.
Wang, May X.
Wang, Ming-Yu Rachel
Wang, N. T.
Wang, Nam Sun
Wang, Orrin Nan Chung
Wang, Pao-Kuan
Wang, Paul Weily
Wang, Qun
Wang, Samuel T. M.
Wang, Shaw S.
Wang, Shi-Hwa
Wang, Shien Tsun
Wang, Shih-Chun
Wang, Shih-Ho
Wang, Shih-Liang
Wang, ShiQing
Wang, Sho-Ya
Wang, Shujen
Wang, Stuart Sui-Sheng
Wang, Suojin
Wang, Sylvia
Wang, Tixiang
Wang, Ton-Lo
Wang, Tsuey Tang
Wang, Veronica C.
Wang, Victor Sheng
Wang, William Kai-Sheng
Wang, William S-Y.
Wang, Xiaoping
Wang, Xue-Sen
Wang, Xuefeng
Wang, Yan
Wang, Yang
Wang, Yi-Tin
Wang, Yi T'ung
Wang, Yijiang
Wang, Yong Tai
Wang, Zhi Qiang
Warashina, M. Patricia
Wasan, Darsh T.
Watanabe, John Mamoru
Watanabe, Paul Yashihiko
Watanabe, Suwako
Wei, Anthony Yueh-shan

Wei, Benjamin Min
Wei, James
Wei, Kuo-Yen
Wei, Robert
Wei, Susanna
Wei, William
Wei, William Wu-Shyong
Wei, Yen
Wen, Shih-liang
Wen, Wen-Yang
Whang, Benjamin
Whang, Robert
Whang, Seungjin
Whang, Un-Young
Whang, Yun Chow
Whangbo, Myung-Hwan
Wing, Jeannette M.
Wong, Alan S.
Wong, Albert Y.
Wong, Benedict Ding Chung
Wong, Bernard P.
Wong, Bing K.
Wong, Bradley D.
Wong, Chin Siong
Wong, Daniel W.
Wong, David Tai Wai
Wong, David Yue
Wong, Deborah Anne
Wong, Dorothy Pan
Wong, Eugene
Wong, Eugene Hanlai
Wong, Frank F.
Wong, Frank Van
Wong, Frederick
Wong, Janine Mei-Chiao
Wong, John D.
Wong, Johnny S.
Wong, K. C.
Wong, Kar-yiu
Wong, Kenneth K.
Wong, Kent Douglas
Wong, Kin-Ping
Wong, Kuang Chung
Wong, Kwok-Fai Matthew
Wong, Martin Ding-Fat
Wong, Mel
Wong, Pat Chung
Wong, Paul
Wong, Paul Wing Kon
Wong, Peter Alexander
Wong, Peter M. C.
Wong, Peter P.
Wong, Raymond Y.
Wong, Rita F.
Wong, Siu G.
Wong, Steven W.
Wong, Victor Kenneth
Wong, William Wai-Lun
Wong, William Wai-Lun
Woo, Michael K.
Woo, S. B.
Woo, Savio Lau-Ching
Woody, A-Young Moon
Wu, Alfred Chi-Tai
Wu, Angela Yuen
Wu, Anna Fang
Wu, Chien-yun
Wu, Chih
Wu, Ching-Sheng
Wu, Chivey Dragenson Lung
Wu, Chun-Fang
Wu, Chung-Hsiu
Wu, David
Wu, De Ting
Wu, Diana Ting Liu
Wu, En Shinn
Wu, Fa Yueh
Wu, Fang-Sheng
Wu, Francis Taming
Wu, Frederick H.
Wu, George
Wu, Hai-Sheng
Wu, Ho-Mou

Wu, Hofu
Wu, Hsin-i
Wu, Hung-Hsi
Wu, Jean Yu-Wen Shen
Wu, Jennifer Lee
Wu, Jeremy S.
Wu, Jie
Wu, Jun-Ru
Wu, Kingsley K.
Wu, Konrad T.
Wu, Kung Chris
Wu, Nan-Ray
Wu, Nancy Nan-hwa
Wu, Sau Lan Yu
Wu, Shi Tsan
Wu, Shien-Ming
Wu, Shih-Yen
Wu, Tai Te
Wu, Theodore Yao-Tsu
Wu, Tiee-Jian
Wu, Ting-Wen
Wu, Tung
Wu, Wallace C.
Wu, Wei-hsiung
Wu, Wei-ping
Wu, William Gay
Wu, Xian
Wu, Xian Connie
Wu, Y. C. L. Susan
Wu, Yau
Wu, Yen
Wu, Yenna
Wu, Ying-Chan Fred
Wu, Zhijian
Xia, Yun
Xu, Chia-Yi
Yaden, Senka Long
Yagi, Fumio
Yamada, David Takao
Yamada, Kay Matayoshi
Yamada, Mitsuye May
Yamamori, Tetsunao
Yamamoto, Keith Robert
Yamamoto, Yutaka
Yamasaki, Mitch
Yamashiroya, Herbert Mitsugi
Yamashita, Pearl Nobuko
Yan, Chiou-Shuang Jou
Yan, Haiping
Yan, Hong-Cheng
Yan, Joseph Gea-Gue
Yang, Albert C.
Yang, Anand Alan
Yang, Bingen
Yang, Chen Ning
Yang, Chia Chi
Yang, Chia Hsiung
Yang, Chih Ted
Yang, Chung S.
Yang, Chyan
Yang, David C.
Yang, Henry Tzu-yow
Yang, Jen Tsi
Yang, Jiann-Shiou
Yang, Kichoon
Yang, Nien-chu C.
Yang, Qing
Yang, Schuman Chuo
Yang, Shang Fa
Yang, Song
Yang, Sze Cheng
Yang, Tah-teh
Yang, Tsu-Ju
Yang, Victor Chi-Min
Yang, Weitao
Yang, Wen-Jei
Yang, William C. T.
Yang, Winston L.
Yang, Xiaowei
Yang, Yih-Ming
Yang, Yisong
Yang, Zhanbo
Yano, Fleur B.

Yao, David D.
Yao, Dennis Alden
Yao, Lun-Shin
Yao, Shi Chune
Yap, Stacey G. H.
Yasumura, Seiichi
Yau, King-Wai
Yau, Stephen Shing-Toung
Yee, Angelina Chun-chu
Yee, Barbara W. K.
Yee, Carlton S.
Yee, Darlene
Yee, Donald H.
Yee, Donald Poy
Yee, Edmond
Yee, Franklin
Yee, Robert Donald
Yee, Shirley Jo-Ann
Yeh, Billy Kuo-Jiun
Yeh, Chai
Yeh, Gregory S. Y.
Yeh, Henry
Yeh, Ida Shuyen Chiang
Yeh, Lee-Chuan Caroline
Yeh, Michelle M.
Yeh, Pu-Sen
Yeh, Susan S. Wang
Yeh, Thomas Y.
Yen, Alfred Chueh-Chin
Yen, Ben Chie
Yen, Chi-Chung David
Yen, Joan Jue
Yen, John
Yen, Kang Kenneth
Yen, Matthew Ming-Shih
Yen, Peter T.
Yen, Sherman M. Y.
Yen, Steven T.
Yen, Teh Fu
Yen, Tien-Sze Benedict
Yen, Wen-Hsiung
Yen, William Mao-Shung
Yen, Yang
Yeo, Yung Kee
Yep, Ralph Lee
Yeung, Ronald Wai-Chun
Yi, Gang
Yi, Xiaoxiong
Yih, Chia-Shun
Yih, Yuehwern
Yim, Chi-Kin Bennett
Yim, Solomon C. S.
Yin, Gang George
Yin, George Kuo-Ming
Yin, Mark Y. Q.
Yin, Xiao-huang
Yin, Zenong
Yoo, Chai Hong
Yoo, Tai-June
Yoon, Chongyul John
Yoon, David Hwa Hyun
Yoon, Hyo-Chun
Yoon, Kwangsun Paul
Yoon, Myung-Ho
Yoon, Peter Haesung
Yoon, Won Z.
Yoon, Youngohi Choi
Yoshida, Ray Kakuo
Yoshida, Roland K.
Yoshikawa, Shoichi
Yoshimura, Michael Akira
Yoshino, Ronald Warren
Youn, Hee Yong
Youn, Luis Tai-Oh
Young, Bing-Lin
Young, Franklin
Young, Jacqueline Eurn Hai
Young, Lloyd Yee
Yu, Alice L.
Yu, Byung Pal
Yu, Chang-An
Yu, Chi Kang
Yu, Clement Tak

Yu, David C.
Yu, Fu-Li
Yu, Gang
Yu, James H.
Yu, Jen
Yu, Jia-Huey
Yu, Jimmy Chai-Mei
Yu, Larry
Yu, Paul Kit-Lai
Yu, Robert Kuan-jen
Yu, Shiao-ling S.
Yu, Shiu Yeh
Yu, Victor Lin-Kai
Yu, Winnie Y.
Yu, Yun-Sheng
Yuan, Jian-Min
Yuasa, Joji
Yue, David T.
Yue, Xiaodong
Yuen, Paul C.
Yuen, Steve Chi-Yin
Yukawa, Masako
Yun, Chung-Hei K.
Yun, Seung Soo
Yun, Suk Koo
Yun, Xiaoping
Yune, Heun Yung
Yung, Christoph Yingwai
Yung, Kenneth Kwokhung
Yung, Ringo
Yung, W. K. Alfred
Yuvarajan, Subbaraya
Zamora, Mario Dimarucut
Zen, E-an
Zhang, John Z. H.
Zhang, Longxi
Zhao, Quansheng
Zheng, Yuan Fang
Zien, Tse-Fou

EDUCATION—ELEMENTARY/SECONDARY

Berssenbrugge, Mei-mei
Chen, Ivan Mao-Chang
Chong-Gottinger, Ivy Wok Kuong
Chopra, Rajbir Singh
Collier, Irene Dea
Dam, Quy T. T.
Fan, Ada Mei
Furukawa, Larry Kiyoshi
Gong, Ginny
Green, Yoshiko Okada
Jain, Bimla Agarwal
Kalra, Bhupinder Singh
Katagiri, George
Kimura, Kongo
Koo, Ja Hung
Kwong, Bill Wai Lam
Lal, Dhyan
Lim, Nancy Wong
Louie, Ruby Ling
Lu, Janet Y. H.
Manankil, Norma Ronas
Matsumoto, Iku
Matsushima, Janie Mitsuye
Nakano, Francis
Ota, Mabel Takako
Pham, Henry Tuoc Van
Pham, Viet Van
Phommasouvanh, Banlang
Rhee, Jhoon Goo
Shang, Bernard Y.
Takano, Mark Allan
Teraji, Thomas Shuichi
Tran, Dorothy N.
Tran, Huyen Lam
Uyematsu, Amy
Vovan, Ba
Wong, Albert
Wong, Alexius Yu-Ming

Yamashita, Pearl Nobuko

EDUCATION—NOT ELSEWHERE CLASSIFIED
Chan, Adrian
Chan, Tsze Hau
Chang, Moon K.
Chen, Weihang
Choe, Sun Tok
Chuang, Vincent P.
Compas, Lolita Burgos
Davino, Carmencita Fernandez
Dugal, Hardev S.
Fong, Eva Chow
Gupta, Kamla P.
Horn, Jennie A.
Hsueh, Chun-tu
Jang, Jon
Kamiyama, Osamu
Katagiri, George
Kawahara, Lindon Ken
Kim, Alan Hyun-Oak
Kitahata, Stacy Dee
Koga, Yoshi Tanji
Krishna, Darshan
Kuan, Kah-Jin
Kuttan, Appu
Lakshmanan, Chithra
Lau, Edward C. Y.
Lee, Hyung Mo
Lee, Vivian Wai-fun
Leong, Robin Yee
Liu, Ray H.
Louie, Sammy G.
Matsumoto, Donald Michiaki
Saji, Kiyotaka
SooHoo, Leo, Jr.
Takeuchi, Esther Kiyomi
Tan, Cheng-Pheng
Tang, Paul Chi Lung
Tolentino, Virginia Cantor
Tran, Huyen Lam
Tsukamoto, Mary Tsuruko
Wu, Anna Fang
Yee, Edmond
Yuen-Terry, Kaimay

EDUCATIONAL ADMINISTRATION
Aggarwal, Raj
Ahmad, Jameel
Anderson, Wanni W.
Ando, Koichi
Aoki, Thomas T.
Awakuni, Gene I.
Baliga, Jayant
Basu, Sutapa
Bhada, Rohinton Khurshed
Bhatia, Tej K.
Bhatt, Gita
Chae, Yong Suk
Chakraborty, Joana
Chan, Anthony Bernard
Chan, Carlyle Hung-lun
Chan, James C. M.
Chan, Kenyon S.
Chan, Sucheng
Chan, Ting Y.
Chang, Albert
Chang, Edward C.
Chang, Henry C.
Chang, Mervin Henry
Chang, Mou-Hsiung
Chang, Shau-Jin
Chang, Weilin P.
Chang, William Y. B.
Chang, Won Ho
Chatterjee, Sayan
Chaturvedi, Rama Kant
Chen, Catherine W.

Chen, Chong-Tong
Chen, Juh Wah
Chen, Lea Der
Chen, Linda Li-yueh
Chen, Simon Ying
Chen, Tseh An
Cheng, Chu-Yuan
Cheng, David Keun
Cheng, Mei-Fang Hsieh
Cheng, Ping
Cheo, Peter K.
Cheung, Herbert Chiu-Ching
Chew, Wellington Lum
Chiang, Theresa Yi-Chin Tung
Chien, Yie W.
Chin, Bryan Allen
Chin, Helen
Chin, Stanley H.
Chin, Thomas
Chong, Frank
Chou, Leland L. C.
Chu, Hung Manh
Chun, Joe Y. F.
Chung, Paul Myungha
Chung, Simon Lam-Ying
Cruz, Jose Bejar, Jr.
Desai, Uday
Duong, Cambao De
Eng, William
Fa, Angie
Fong, Eva Chow
Fong, Mary Helena
Fu, Tina C.
Fujii, Jack Koji
Fujimoto, Jack
Fung, Dennis Lung
Fung, Henry C.
Furutani, Warren
Gangopadhyay, Chitta R.
Ghosh, Kalyan K.
Gil, Libia Socorro
Goh, Ben K.
Gong, Ginny
Goto, George
Gupta, Ashok K.
Hara, Saburo
Hasegawa, Jack Koichi
Hashimoto, Ken
Hata, David M.
Hata, Nadine Ishitani
Hayashi, William Yasuo
Hayashida, Frank
Hirabayashi, Lane Ryo
Hirano, Kyoko
Hirano-Nakanishi, Marsha Joyce
Hiraoka, Leslie Satoshi
Ho, Daniel F.
Ho, Hon Hing
Ho, John Ting-Sum
Ho, Xuan Michael
Honda, Allen Shigeru
Hong, Kenneth
Hong, Sung Ok
Horn, Jennie A.
Hsi, Bartholomew P.
Hsieh, Jeanette L.
Hsu, Donald K.
Hsu, Laura Ling
Hu, Steve Seng-Chiu
Huang, Alice Shih-Hou
Huang, Jacob Wen-Kuang
Huang, Jung-chang
Hung, Chao-Shun
Hung, Yen-Wan
Hwang, Dennis B. K.
Hwang, Enoch Oi-Kee
Jammalamadaka, Sreenivasa Rao
Jayachandran, Toke
Jen, Joseph Jwu-Shan
Jiang, Xixiang
Jong, Mark M. T.
Jun, Jong S.
Kang, Shin T.

Kao, Timothy Tieh-Hsiung
Kao, Yasuko W.
Kim, Chin Hui
Kim, David Ho-Sik
Kim, David Sang Chul
Kim, Ilpyong J.
Kim, Sung Bok
Kim, Sung Wan
Kim, Thomas Kunhyuk
Kitagawa, Joseph Mitsuo
Kobayashi, Francis Masao
Kong, Ronald A.
Kono, Hideto
Krishna, Darshan
Ku, Peter
Kumar, Atul
Kumar, Ramesh
Kung, Harold H.
Kung, Shain-dow
Kuo, Albert Yi-shuong
Kuo, Joseph C.
Kuo, Way
Kurose, Ruthann
Kwon, Myoung-ja L.
Lakshmanan, Chithra
Lal, Dhyan
Lam, Simon Shin-Sing
Land, Ming Huey
Lau, Albert Kai-Fay
Lau, David T.
Lau, Yvonne M.
Lazo, Douglas T.
Lee, Bing
Lee, Dae Sung
Lee, Daeyong
Lee, Lester Hsin-Pei
Lee, Robert
Lee, Sung Mook
Leung, Benjamin Shuet-Kin
Li, Charles N.
Lian, Maria Z. N.
Liddell, Gene Canque
Liem, Karel Frederik
Lin, James Chih-I
Lin, Shin
Ling, Yu-long
Liu, Chuan Sheng
Liu, Frank Yining
Liu, Hsien-Tung
Loh, Wallace D.
Lu, Janet Y. H.
Lu, Lina
Ma, Yi Hua
Mahajan, Harpreet
Malhotra, Om P.
Mathur, Ike
Mathur, Raghu P.
Matsuda, Fujio
Mehta, Ashok V.
Mehta, Kamlesh T.
Mehta, Mohinder Paul
Miah, Abdul J.
Mishra, Shitala P.
Moy, James Yee Kin
Mukai, Hiroaki
Murakami, Jeffrey Hisakazu
Nakajima, Nobuyuki
Nakanishi, Don Toshiaki
Nakano, Francis
Nakashima, Mitsugi
Narayanamurti, Venkatesh
Nguyen, Henry Thien
Nguyen, Ho Ngoc
Nguyen, Ngoc-Diep Thi
Odo, Blair M. T.
Odo, Franklin Shoichiro
Okihiro, Gary Yukio
Ota, Mabel Takako
Parate, Natthu Sonbaji
Parikh, Rajeev N.
Park, Sang Oh
Park, Seung-Kyoon
Patel, Chandra Kumar Naranbhai

Peterson, Indira Viswanathan
Phan, Trung Huynh
Pradhan, Shekhar
Raimundo, Cris C.
Rajan, Periasamy Karivaratha
Rao, Gandikota Venkata
Rao, Koneru Ramakrishna
Rao, Srikumar S.
Reddy, Gudigopuram Bhaskar
Reddy, Kapuluru Chandrasekhara
Rhee, Song Nai
Rodis, Rodel E.
Roy, Dev Kumar
Sakamoto, Clyde Mitsuru
Sampang, Conrado Carriedo
Sandhu, Shingara Singh
Sato, Irving Shigeo
Senzaki, Randall Kiyomi
Sha, Shung-tse
Shaikh, Abdul Hamid
Shaikh, Zahir A.
Sharma, Onkar Prasad
Shen, Chia Theng
Shirakawa, George
Shwe, Hla
Simunek, Linda A.
Somasundaran, Ponisseril
Sood, Devinder Kumar
Sood, Mohan K.
Su, Zhixin
Subbaswamy, Kumble Ramarao
Sugihara, James Masanobu
Sugioka, Michael Hiroyuki
Sugiyama, Alan
Sung, Betty Lee
Suzuki, Bob H.
Takahashi, Joseph S.
Takasaki, Richard Sadaji
Tanabe, George Joji, Jr.
Tanaka, Kouichi Robert
Tchen, John Kuo Wei
Teraji, Thomas Shuichi
Tien, Chang-Lin
Tripathi, Satish K.
Tsang, Chiu
Tseng, James H. W.
Tseng, Rose Y. L.
Tu, Ching-I
Ueda, Clarence Tad
Villanueva, Marianne Del Rosario
Wang, Howard H.
Wang, I-Shou
Wang, Jing
Wang, Li-Shing
Wasan, Darsh T.
Wei, James
Wen, Shih-liang
Whang, Robert
Wong, David Yue
Wong, Evelyn
Wong, Frank F.
Wong, Frank Van
Wong, Kent Douglas
Wong, Kin-Ping
Wong, Nellie
Wong, Ovid K.
Wong, Paul
Wong, Pui Kei
Wong, Shawn Hsu
Wong, Victor Kenneth
Wu, Diana Ting Liu
Wu, Frederick H.
Wu, Jean Yu-Wen Shen
Wu, Julia Li
Wu, Shi Tsan
Yamada, Yozo
Yamamoto, Keith Robert
Yamashiroya, Herbert Mitsugi
Yang, Anand Alan
Yang, Chen Ning
Yang, Chia Hsiung

Yang, Henry Tzu-yow
Yang, Ralph Tzu-Bow
Yang, Tsu-Ju
Yee, Donald Poy
Yee, Joanne
Yee, Lawrence K.
Yee, Leland
Yoon, Won Z.
Yoshida, Roland K.
Yu, Clara
Yu, Fu-Li
Yu, Jen
Yu, Robert Kuan-jen
Yun, Suk Koo
Zhao, Quansheng

ELECTRONICS
SEE COMPUTER SCIENCE—PROGRAMMING/ SOFTWARE DEVELOPMENT; COMPUTER SCIENCE—SYSTEMS ANALYSIS/DESIGN; COMPUTER SCIENCE—NOT ELSEWHERE CLASSIFIED; ENGINEERING—ELECTRICAL/ ELECTRONICS; RETAIL TRADE—ELECTRICAL/ ELECTRONICS PRODUCTS; WHOLESALE TRADE—ELECTRICAL/ ELECTRONICS PRODUCTS

ENGINEERING—AEROSPACE
Agarwal, Ramesh Kumar
Araki, Minoru S.
Chai, An-Ti
Chang, Juang-Chi
Chang, Paul Keub
Chang-Diaz, Franklin Ramon
Chen, Hsin-Piao Patrick
Chen, Kangping
Chen, Ming Chih
Cheng, Hsien K.
Cheng, Sin I.
Cheung, Lim H.
Chi, Cheng-Ching
Choi, Michael Kamwah
Chong, Timothy
Chow, Chuen-Yen
Chow, Wen Lung
Chun, Hon Ming
Dao, Tuan Anh
Durrani, Sajjad Haidar
Fang, Louis Li-Yeh
Fong, Herbert S.
Fung, Kee-Ying
Ganguly, Suman
Giri, Jagannath
Gollahalli, Subramanyam Ramappa
Gupta, Ashwani Kumar
Gupta, Tej R.
Hajela, Prabhat
Han, Je-Chin
Hee, Edward K. Y.
Hirasuna, Alan Ryo
Ho, Benson P.
Ho, Chih-Ming
Hong, Jin Sung
Hsin, Chen-Chung
Hsu, Chen-Chi

Hsu, Chieh-Su
Hu, Steve Seng-Chiu
Huang, Nai-Chien
Hung, Ru J.
Hussain, Fazle
Iyer, Ram Ramaswamy
Joshi, Suresh Meghashyam
Kim, Jae Hoon
Kinra, Vikram Kumar
Kobayashi, Francis Masao
Kothari, Ajay P.
Kumar, Ranganathan
Lai, Jai-Lue Leon
Lai, Kai Sun
Lam, Leo Kongsui
Lam, Sau-Hai
Lan, Chuan-Tau Edward
Lau, Jark C.
Lee, Arthur Richard
Leung, Woon-Fong
Lin, James Chow
Liu, Alan Fong-Ching
Liu, Edmund K.
Mehrotra, Sudhir Chandra
Meng, James Cheng-Sun
Morizumi, S. James
Nguyen, Caroline P.
Nguyen, Nghia Van
Pande, Krishna P.
Park, Chul
Patel, Jayanti R.
Patel, Mukund R.
Patel, Sarla M.
Pei, Richard Y.
Pian, Carlson Chao-Ping
Pian, Theodore Hsueh-Huang
Premraj, A. N.
Rajasekhar, Amar
Ramalingam, Mysore
　　Loganathan
Rao, Bhamidipaty Kameswara
Rao, Gopalakrishna M.
Reddy, Dhanireddy Ramalinga
Reddy, Junuthula N.
Reddy, Kapuluru
　　Chandrasekhara
Sharma, Surendra P.
Shen, Shan-Fu
Shieh, Rong Chung
Siddiqui, Ehtisham Uddin
　　Ahmad
So, Ronald Ming Cho
Srinivas, Ramachandra
Subramanya, Shiva
Sun, Chang-Tsan
Tam, Henry
Tamaki, Jeanne Keiko
Trinh, Eugene
Trinh, Hoang Huy
Tsai, Stephen Wei-Lun
Tsang, Wai Lin
Tse, Charles Jack-Ching
Uda, Robert Takeo
Valmonte, Arnel Elvambuena
Varghese, Philip Leslie
Vo, Jimmy
Wang, H. E. Frank
Wang, Hai-Tao
Wang, Kuo Chang
Wang, Kuo King
Whang, Yun Chow
Wong, Buck W.
Wong, Po Kee
Wu, Y. C. L. Susan
Wu, Yau
Yagi, Fumio
Yan, Xiao-Hai
Yang, Henry Tzu-yow
Yeh, Hsien-Yang
Yen, Chen-wan L.
Yoshida, Ronald Yutaka
Yu, Kai-Bor
Zien, Tse-Fou

ENGINEERING— CHEMICAL

Agrawal, Pradeep K.
Ali, Yusuf
Bajpai, Rakesh Kumar
Bawa, Mohendra S.
Bhada, Rohinton Khurshed
Bhandarkar, Suhas D.
Cha, Chang-Yul
Chan, Yeung Yu
Chang, Ren-Fang
Chang, Shih-Ger
Chao, Kwang-Chu
Chen, Chuan Ju
Chen, Juh Wah
Chen, Nai Y.
Chen, Wei-Yin
Cheng, Carlos
Cheng, Yung-Sung
Cheryan, Munir
Chi, Bo Kyung
Chiang, Ping-Wang
Chiang, Shiao-Hung
Chiou, Minshon J.
Choi, Kyung-Ju
Choudhury, Pinak
Chu, Vincent Hao-Kwong
Chun, Sun Woong
Desai, Vikram J.
Dinh, Steven M.
Duong, Ngo Dinh
Fan, Liang-Shih
Fang, Cheng-Shen
Fang, Jin Bao
Fung, Shun C.
Ghosh, Sujan
Gopikanth, M. L.
Goswami, Pankaj P.
Gupta, Ajay
Gupta, Rajeshwar Kumar
Han, Byung Joon
Hemrajani, Ramesh Relumal
Hirasaki, George Jiro
Hon, David Nyok-Sai
Hong, Glenn Thomas
Hsiao, Margaret Sheng-Mei
Hsu, George Chi-Yung
Hsu, Stephen M.
Hu, John Nan-Hai
Huang, Denis K.
Huang, Jennming Stephen
Huh, Billy K.
Hyun, Kun Sup
Jaisinghani, Rajan A.
Jariwala, Sharad Lallubhai
Jha, Mahesh Chandra
Jhon, Myung S.
Joshi, Mukund Shankar
Kagetsu, Tadashi Jack
Kang, James Jyh-Huei
Kashiwagi, Brian Rio
Kerkar, Awdhoot Vasant
Ko, Bing H.
Ko, Edmond Inq-Ming
Kompala, Dhinakar S.
Krishnan, Sundaram
Kumar, Romesh
Kung, Harold H.
Kuo, Charles Chang-Yun
Lanewala, Mohammed Ali
Lee, Do Ik
Lee, Min-Shiu
Lee, Sunggyu
Lee, Wei-Kuo
Lee, Wooyoung
Lem, Kwok Wai
Leung, Woon-Fong
Li, Ke Wen
Li, Norman N.
Li, Yao Tzu
Lim, Soon-Sik
Liu, Chung-Chiun
Liu, Hanjun

Ma, Yi Hua
Mah, Richard Sze Hao
Mahalingam, R.
Mao, Chung-Ling
Murad, Sohail
Murthy, A. Kumaresa S.
Nakazono, Benito Lopez
Nam, Sehyun
Nguyen, Caroline P.
Nguyen, Hien Vu
Nguyen, Kim-Oanh Thi
Nguyen, Thuan Ke
Ochiai, Shinya
Oh, Chang H.
Pai, Venkatrao K.
Parikh, Hemant Bhupendra
Park, Chang Ho
Patel, Bhagvan H.
Punwani, Dharam Vir
Quan, Xina
Ramakrishnan, Terizhandur S.
Ryu, Dewey Doo Young
Sabnis, Suman Trimbak
Sadana, Ajit
Sarathy, Partha R.
Sarin, Harry C.
Saxena, Satish Chandra
Shah, Chandu M.
Shah, Dinesh Ochhavlal
Shah, Hasmukh N.
Sharma, Mukul Mani
Sharma, Parashu Ram
Sharma, Puneet
Shen, Chung Yu
Sheth, Atul Chandravadan
Sheu, Lien-Lung
Siddiqui, Habib
Somasundaran, Ponisseril
Song, Yo Taik
Sze, Morgan Chuan-Yuan
Takahashi, Ken M.
Tang, Yu-Sun
Thangaraj, Sandy
Tien, H. Ti
Tsai, Gow-Jen
Tsai, Stanley
Tsao, George T.
Uy, William C.
Vasan, Srini Varadarajan
Vijayendran, Bhima R.
Vora, Pramathesh S.
Vu, Liem T.
Wang, Daniel I.-Chyau
Wang, Henry Yee-Neen
Wang, Jih Ming
Wang, Lawrence Kongpu
Wang, Nam Sun
Wang, Shaw S.
Wasan, Darsh T.
Wei, James
Wong, Kin Fai
Woo, P. T.
Yan, Tsoung-Yuan
Yang, Bao-Wen
Yang, Ralph Tzu-Bow
Yang, Wen-Ching
Yeh, Chien Jo
Yeh, James Tehcheng
Yen, I-Kuen
Yen, Teh Fu
Yu, Thomas H.
Yu, Wen C.

ENGINEERING—CIVIL

Ahmad, Jameel
Ang, Charles C.
Au, Patrick Siu-Kee
Au, Tung
Balaguru, Perumalsamy N.
Barot, Navnit Manilal
Batra, Rajeev
Bhatt, Kiran Chandrakant

Brahma, Chandra Sekhar
Chae, Yong Suk
Chang, Chin Hao
Chang, Paul Peng-Cheng
Chang, Peter C.
Chang, Wayne Wei
Chen, Benjamin Yun-Hai
Chen, Carl Wan-Cheng
Chen, Hung-Liang
Chen, Shoei-sheng
Chen, Stuart S.
Chen, Wai Fah
Chen, Yen-Hsu
Chen, Yi-Shon
Cheng, Alexander H-D.
Cheng, Franklin Yih
Cheng, Joseph Kwang-Chao
Chiang, Sie Ling
Chiang, Tsung Ting
Chiu, Arthur Nang Lick
Chiu, Chao-Lin
Chiu, Thomas Chee-Wang
Chong, Ken P.
Choo, Arthur C. S.
Chow, Philip Yeong-Wai
Chu, Kuang Han
Chuang, Tze-jer
Chugh, Ashok Kumar
Darji, Bhuleshwar S.
Deb, Arun Kumar
Desai, Chandrakant S.
Dwivedy, Keshab K.
Fang, Pen Jeng
Fok, Yu-Si
Fu, Kuan-Chen
Fujimoto, Robert I.
Fukushima, Eiichi
Gangopadhyay, Chitta R.
Garg, Prem
George, K. P.
Go, Mateo Lian Poa
Godhania, Laxman P.
Gupta, Jiwan D.
Hingorani, Bhagwan V.
Ho, Dennis
Hoque, Enamul
Hori, Tom Nichi
Hsieh, Carl Chia-Fong
Hsieh, Hsin-Neng
Hu, Chao Hsiung
Huang, Ju-Chang
Huang, Tseng
Hung, Stephen Chifeng
Hung, Tin-Kan
Hwang, Guann-Jiun
Hwang, Shoi Yean
Iwata, Paul Yoshio
Kam, James T.-K.
Kaneshige, Harry Masato
Kapadia, H. Viren
Kaul, Maharaj Krishen
Kawaguchi, Stanley Kenji
Keshavan, Krishnaswamiengar
Kikuchi, Shinya
Kim, Donald Chang Won
Kim, Youngsoo Richard
Kobayashi, Nobuhisa
Koo, Benjamin Hai-Chang
Krishnamoorthy, Govindarajalu
Ku, Wen-Chi
Kumar, Sushil
Kuo, Shiou-San
Kuo, Wayne Wen-Long
Lai, Dennis Fu-hsiung
Lee, Arthur Richard
Lee, Conrad
Lee, Dah-Yinn
Lee, Jong Seh
Lee, Kwang K.
Lee, Ming T.
Li, Victor C.
Li, Wen-Hsiung
Lin, Feng-Bao

Lin, Ping-Wha
Lin, Tung Yen
Liu, Henry
Liu, Hong-Ting
Liu, Wing Kam
Lo, Chien-kuo
Lu, Le-Wu
Marur, Hanuman
Matsumoto, Mark R.
Matsumoto, Randall Itsumi
Matsuo, Paul T.
Mei, Chiang Chung
Metha, Pradipkumar D.
Mura, Toshio
Naik, Tarun Ratilal
Nakadegawa, Roy
Nayyar, Sarv P.
Ng, Michael Wai-Man
Ng, Tang-Tat Percy
Oishi, Satoshi
Pai, David Hsien-Chung
Pai, Kenneth Y.
Pak, Ronald Yu-Sang
Pannu, Dave S.
Pao, Chia-Ven
Parikh, Kirit Girishchandra
Patel, Chandu K.
Patel, Ramesh D.
Patel, Vipin A.
Prakash, Shamsher
Qasim, Syed Reazul
Quimpo, Rafael Gonzales
Rana, Gurinder Mohan Singh
Rangaswamy, Thangam
Rikhiraj, Sadhu Singh
Sabnis, Gajanan M.
Sandhu, Ranbir Singh
Sarker, Bimal
Satyapriya, Coimbatore K.
Shah, Amar M.
Shah, Arvind K.
Shah, Chimanlal Keshavlal
Shah, Jayprakash Balvantrai
Shah, Ramesh V.
Shen, Hsieh Wen
Shinozuka, Masanobu
Siddiqui, Faruq Mahmud Anam
Singh, Madan Mohan
Singh, Vijay P.
Singhal, Avinash Chandra
Su, Tsung-chow Joe
Tahiliani, Jamnu H.
Tang, Wilson Hon-chung
Teng, Tsuchi Paul
Tong, Wen-How
Tsai, Frank Y.
Tsai, Kuei-wu
Tsutsui, James Haruo, Jr.
Tung, Yeou-Koung
Ueng, Charles En-Shiuh
Van, Thanhtan C.
Vemula, Subba Rao
Wang, Lawrence Kongpu
Wang, Leon Ru-Liang
Wang, Shien Tsun
Wang, Shou-Ling
Wang, Ton-Lo
Wang, Yi-Tin
Wong, Benedict Ding Chung
Wu, Yen
Yamamoto, John Hiroshi
Yen, Ben Chie
Yim, Solomon C. S.
Yoo, Chai Hong
Yoon, Chongyul John
Yu, Yun-Sheng

ENGINEERING— ELECTRICAL/ ELECTRONICS

Agarwal, Gyan Chand
Agnihotri, Newal K.

Akkapeddi, Prasad Rao
An, Myoung Hee
Anandan, Munisamy
Annamalai, Nagappan K.
Arora, Vijay K.
Baliga, Jayant
Banerjee, Sanjay K.
Bhagavatula, Vijayakumar
Bhattacharyya, Shankar P.
Bijlani, Chandur Kishinchand
Bose, Bimal Kumar
Chan, Chun Kin
Chan, David So Keung
Chan, Jack-Kang
Chand, Naresh
Chandrasekaran, Balakrishnan
Chang, Byung Jin
Chang, Chein-I
Chang, Chuan Chung
Chang, Juang-Chi
Chang, Kai
Chang, Kai-Hsiung
Chang, Kern K. N.
Chang, Shen Chie
Chang, Yi-Chieh
Chatterjee, Monish Ranjan
Chaudhri, Rajiv Jahangir
Chellappa, Rama
Chen, C. L. Philip
Chen, Chin-Lin
Chen, Di
Chen, Ding-Bond
Chen, Francis F.
Chen, Guanrong
Chen, Hollis Ching
Chen, Kao
Chen, Kun-Mu
Chen, Robert Chia-Hua
Chen, Stephen C.
Chen, Tsong-Ming
Cheng, David Keun
Cheng, Joe Zen
Cheng, Richard Tien-Ren
Cheo, Peter K.
Cheung, John Yan-Poon
Cheung, Julian F. Y.
Chew, Weng Cho
Chin, Alexander Foster
Chin, Steven Han-Hoy
Chiogioji, Melvin H.
Cho, Alfred Yi
Choe, Timothy Songsik
Chou, Chung-Kwang
Chou, Timothy C.
Chow, Mo-yuen
Chu, Nhan V.
Chu, Shirley S.
Chu, Sung Nee George
Chu, Ting L.
Chua, Leon O.
Chui, Charles K.
Chyung, Dong Hak
Cruz, Jose Bejar, Jr.
Dao, Tuan Anh
Dedhia, Navin Shamji
Desai, Ashok Govindji
Dharamsi, Manoj T.
Dixit, Sudhir Sharan
Dolor, Deogracias Asuncion, Jr.
Durrani, Sajjad Haidar
Dutt, Nikil D.
Dutta, Mitra
Fasang, Patrick Pad
Feng, Guofu Jeff
Feng, Tse-Yun
Fu, Jyun-Horng
Fu, Peter K.
Fujimoto, James G.
Gajjar, Jagdish Trikamji
Gandhi, Mukesh P.
Gandhi, Prashant P.
Gangal, Shiva Shanker
Ganguly, Suman

Garg, Vijay Kumar
Gatdula, Francisco Ric
Gee, Arthur
Ghandhi, Sorab K.
Gupta, Madhu Sudan
Gupta, Rajiv
Gupta, Ramesh K.
Gupta, Samir
Gupta, Tapan K.
Hata, David M.
Hayase, Joshua Yoshio
Hingorani, Narain G.
Ho, Benson P.
Ho, Ping Pei
Ho, Yu-Chi
Hsia, Yukun
Hsu, Ping
Hsu, Stephen Charles
Hu, Chenming
Huang, Chaofu
Huang, Charles
Huang, Garng Morton
Hung, James Chen
Hwang, Cherng-Jia
Hwang, William Gaong
Ih, Charles Chung-Sen
Ishii, Thomas Koryu
Ishimaru, Akira
Ismail, Amin Rashid
Iyer, Prem Shankar
Iyer, Ravishankar Krishnan
Jain, Arun K.
Jen, Chih Kung
Jong, Mark M. T.
Joshi, Suresh Meghashyam
Kak, Subhash Chandra
Kang, Joonhee
Kang, Weng Poo
Kao, Tai-Wu
Kapoor, Harish K.
Kim, Byung Guk
Kim, Chaesik
Kim, Hyong Sok
Kim, Jae Hoon
Kim, Jung Hwan
Kim, Yong Bok
Ko, Kei-Yu
Ko, Wen Hsiung
Kobayashi, Hideaki
Koga, Rokutaro
Koide, Frank Takayuki
Krishen, Kumar
Krishna, Gopal T. K.
Kuh, Ernest Shiu-Jen
Kulkarni, Anand K.
Kumar, Panganamala Ramana
Kumar, Ram Sakthi
Kung, Jeffrey
Kwok, Hoi-Sing
Lan, Dong Ping
Lao, Binney Y.
Lee, Kai-Fong
Lee, Soo-Young
Li, Chia-Chuan
Li, Ching-Chung
Li, Sheng S.
Li, Shin-Hwa
Li, Shing Ted
Li, Tingye
Li, Victor On-Kwok
Lin, Chinlon
Lin, Hung Chang
Lin, James Chih-I
Lin, James Chow
Lin, James P.
Lin, Pen-Min
Lin, Wen Chun
Ling, Hao
Liou, Shy-Sheng P.
Liu, Chen-Ching
Liu, Jyh-Charn Steve
Liu, Qing-Huo
Liu, Tsu-huei

Liu, Yilu
Liu, Yung Sheng
Lo, Chi-Yuan
Lo, Yuen-Tze
Lock, Chuck Choi
Lu, I-Tai
Lu, Mi
Ma, Alan King-Yan
Ma, Mark T.
Ma, Tso-Ping
Maedjaja, Daniel
Mahajan, Satish Murlidhar
Mak, Sioe Tho
Malik, Naeem
Mathur, Harbans B.
Mian, Athar S.
Minnig, William Paul
Mitter, Sanjoy K.
Mo, Luke W.
Mondal, Kalyan
Mukai, Hiroaki
Murthy, Srinivasa
Narayanamurti, Venkatesh
Nguyen, An H.
Nguyen, Cam
Nguyen, Charles C.
Nguyen, Cuong Phu
Nguyen, Mike Chi
Oh, Harry K.
Ong, Chee-Mun
Park, Sung-won Sam
Patel, Arvindkumar Motibhai
Patel, Mukul B.
Patel, Mukund R.
Patel, Ramesh V.
Patel, Sarla M.
Patil, Pralhad T.
Pillai, Unnikrishna S.
Poon, Chi-Sang
Prabhakar, Arati
Pradhan, Shekhar
Quan, Hanson Wayne
Qureshi, Qadeer Ahmad
Rab, Mirza M.
Rajan, Periasamy Karivaratha
Ramakumar, Ramachandra
  Gupta
Ramchandani, Raj S.
Rao, Kameswara Kolla
Rao, Mahesh K.
Rao, Ramgopal P.
Rao, Sadasiva Madiraju
Rawat, Banmali Singh
Ren, Shang Yuan
Roy, Pradip Kumar
Sah, Chih-Tang
Sengupta, Dipak Lal
Shah, Ahmer
Shah, Bhupendra P.
Shah, Narendra M.
Shah, Yogesh K.
Shaikh, Saeed Ahmad
Shang, Weijia
Sharma, Brij Lal
Shen, Hao-Ming
Shen, Tek-Ming
Shen, Wu-Mian
Shenoi, B. A.
Shenoy, Narasimha B.
Sheu, Bing J.
Shieh, Tsay-Jiu Brian
Shih, Ko-Ming
Shimada, Katsunori
Singh, Amarjit
Singh, Vijay Pal
Sinha, Dipen N.
Sohal, Harjit Singh
Somani, Arun K.
Srinivasan, Gunumakonda
  Ramaswamiengar
Srivastava, Om P.
Subramanya, Shiva
Sudan, Ravindra Nath

Sy, Bon Klem
Tahiliani, Vasu Hariram
Tai, Chen To
Tang, Chung Liang
Tang, Jianxin
Tang, Wallace T. Y.
Thakkar, Pravin Asharam
Tien, Ping King
Tong, Benjamin
Tong, Franklin Fuk-Kay
Tran, Thinh Quy
Tran, Thomas
Trinh, Hoang Huy
Tripathi, Vijai Kumar
Trivedi, Kishor S.
Trivedi, Mohan Manubhai
Tsang, Dean Zensh
Tsang, Wai Lin
Tseng, James H. W.
Tsuha, Wallace K., Jr.
Tsui, Daniel Chee
Tu, Charles W.
Tun, Harry T.
Tzeng, Kenneth Kai-Ming
Venkata, Subrahmanyam
  Saraswati
Vo, D. Brian
Vo, Van Toi
Wang, Christine A.
Wang, Jun
Wang, Lily L.
Wang, Shih-Ho
Wang, Xingwu
Watanabe, Clyde Kazuto
Wong, Eugene
Wong, Henry Sik-Yin
Wu, George K.
Wu, Nan-Ray
Wu, Ying-Chan Fred
Yamakawa, Kazuo Alan
Yan, Hong-Cheng
Yanagisawa, Samuel Tsuguo
Yang, Jiann-Shiou
Yang, Qing
Yang, Timothy C.
Yang, Xiaowei
Yau, Stephen Shing-Toung
Yeh, Chien Jo
Yeh, Edward H. Y.
Yeh, Hen-Geul
Yeh, Hsi-Han
Yen, Kang Kenneth
Yen, Nai-Chyuan
Youn, Luis Tai-Oh
Young, Tzay Y.
Yu, David C.
Yu, James H.
Yu, Kai-Bor
Yu, Paul Kit-Lai
Yu, Yeou-Chong Simon
Yuen, Paul C.
Yun, Xiaoping
Yuvarajan, Subbaraya
Zaveri, Prad S.
Zheng, Yuan Fang

ENGINEERING— INDUSTRIAL

Ahluwalia, Rashpal S.
Chang, Shing I.
Chang, Tien-Chien
Chao, Xiuli
Chen, Houn-Gee
Chen, Yubao
Choi, In-Chan
Choy, Antonio J.
Chu, Chung-Yu Chester
Deivanayagam, Subramaniam
Desai, Sharad P.
Gupta, Jatinder Nath Dass
Han, Chingping Jim
Hwang, Ching-Lai

Inoue, Michael Shigeru
Iyer, Ananth. V.
Jain, Sushil C.
Kang, Keebom
Kim, Jason Jungsun
Kim, Michael Wooyung
Kuo, Way
Lee, Chung-Yee
Lee, E. Stanley
Lee, Heungsoon Felix
Lee, Taehee
Liao, T. Warren
Liu, Ming Cheng
Min, K. Jo
Minamoto, Jennifer Noriko
Moon, Young B.
Murty, Katta Gopalakrishna
Nahata, Suparas M.
Ngo, David
Oh, Keytack Henry
Ordanza, Bonagrace Francisco
Rhee, Hahn-Kyou
Sandrapaty, Ramachandra Rao
Sarker, Bhaba Ranjan
Seth, Shyam S.
Shih, Stephen Chingyu
Shum, Alex C.
Singpurwalla, Nozer Darabsha
Sohn, So Young
Sundaram, Meenakshi R.
Tin, Bo
Tran, Long Trieu
Wang, Ben
Wong, Benedict Ding Chung
Wu, David
Wu, Kung Chris
Yang, Kai
Yih, Yuehwern

ENGINEERING— MECHANICAL

Advani, Suresh Gopaldas
Aulakh, Kay
Bai, Shen Hum
Banerjee, Jayanta Kumar
Batra, Romesh Chander
Bhalla, Vipan Kumar
Bhatt, Gunvant R.
Cha, Soyoung Stephen
Chakrabarti, Subrata Kumar
Chan, Cho Lik
Chan, Kawei
Chan, Shih-Hung
Chandran, Krishnan Bala
Chao, Bei Tse
Chao, Yuh J.
Chen, Benjamin Yun-Hai
Chen, Hsin-Piao Patrick
Chen, Jie
Chen, Kangping
Chen, Lea Der
Chen, Meanshang
Chen, Michael M.
Chen, Rong Yaw
Chen, Shoei-sheng
Chen, Ta-Shen
Chen, Ye-Hwa
Chen, Yi-Chao
Chen, Yu
Cheng, David Hong
Cheng, Herbert S.
Cheng, Ping
Chi, Bo Kyung
Chi, Cheng-Ching
Chien, Sze-Foo
Cho, Christopher Sang Kyu
Cho, Dong-il Dan
Cho, Peck
Cho, Soung Moo
Choi, Kyung Kook
Choi, Michael Kamwah
Chou, James C. S.

Chou, Tsu-Wei
Chow, Wen Lung
Choy, Fred Kat-Chung
Chu, Chung-Yu Chester
Chu, Tsuchin Philip
Chuang, Henry Ning
Chuang, Strong C.
Chung, Jin Soo
Chung, Paul Myungha
Datta, Subhendu K.
Dave, Janak
Desai, Chandra
Dhir, Surendra Kumar
Dolor, Deogracias Asuncion, Jr.
Dong, John W.
Dwivedy, Keshab K.
Fan, Chien
Fang, Jin Bao
Farouk, Bakhtier
Fukushima, Eiichi
Fung, Sui An
Garg, Rajinder P.
Gee, Montgomery M.
Giri, Jagannath
Goela, Jitendra Singh
Gollahalli, Subramanyam
   Ramappa
Gorla, Rama S. R.
Goyal, Suresh
Gupta, Ashwani Kumar
Gupta, Chitranjan J.
Gupta, Pradeep Kumar
Gupta, Vijay
Han, Je-Chin
Hihara, Lloyd Hiromi
Ho, Chih-Ming
Hong, Jin Sung
Hong, Ryang H.
Horng, John Jang-Ji
Hsieh, Franklin
Hsu, Chen-Chi
Hsu, Chieh-Su
Hu, Paul Y.
Huang, Chi-Lung Dominic
Huang, Nai-Chien
Hussain, Fazle
Hwang, Charles C.
Hwang, Shoi Yean
Hwang, Shyshung
Iyer, Ram Ramaswamy
Jain, Sulekh Chand
Jaluria, Yogesh
Jhaveri, Arunkumar Ganpatlal
Ju, Frederick D.
Kadaba, Prasanna Venkatarama
Kam, Lit-Yan
Kam, William
Kaul, Maharaj Krishen
Kawaja, Kaleem U.
Kiang, Robert L.
Kim, Hyun Wang
Kim, Rhyn H.
Kim, Young-Gurl
Kobayashi, Albert Satochi
Kotani, Shigeto
Krishnan, Radha
Ku, David Nelson
Kumar, Jatinder
Kumar, Ranganathan
Kumar, Sudhir
Kuo, Wayne Wen-Long
Kwon, Young Wuk
Lai, Ying-San
Langrana, Noshir A.
Lau, Jark C.
Lee, Daeyong
Lee, David Oi
Lee, Harvey Shui-Hong
Lee, June Key
Lee, Kok-Meng
Lee, Lester Hsin-Pei
Lee, Shih Ying
Lee, Si Young

Leu, Ming C.
Leung, Woon-Fong
Li, Ching James
Liang, Steven Yuehsan
Lin, James Chow
Lin, Shield B.
Lin, Su-Chen Jonathon
Lin, Sung P.
Lin, Yuyi
Ling, Paul
Ling, Zhi-Kui
Liou, Fue-Wen
Liu, Alan Fong-Ching
Liu, Benjamin Y. H.
Liu, Ping
Liu, Wing Kam
Lu, Steven Zhiyun
Luo, Shen-Yi
Ma, Fai
Mahadevan, Dev
Mahajan, Roop L.
Mallick, Pankaj K.
Mamidala, Ramulu
Marr, William Wei-Yi
Mathiprakasam, Balakrishnan
Mathur, Achint P.
Mehra, Ravinder C.
Mehrotra, Prem N.
Mehta, Amarjit
Meng, James Cheng-Sun
Mital, Naveen Kumar
Moon, Kee Suk
Mow, Chao-chow
Nandkumar, Nuggehalli
   Balmukund
Narayanaswamy, Onbathiveli S.
Ng, Kam Wing
Ng, Wing
Nguyen, Anh Mai
Nguyen, Cu D.
Nguyen, Luu Thanh
Noojibail, Eshwar
Oh, Harry K.
Pandit, Sudhakar Madhavrao
Pang, Su-Seng
Park, Ounyoung
Patel, Jayanti R.
Patel, Virendra Chaturbhai
Pei, Richard Y.
Prasad, Marehalli Gopalan
Premraj, A. N.
Rajagopal, Kumbakonam
   Ramamani
Ramadhyani, Satish
Ramalingam, Mysore
   Loganathan
Rao, Bhamidipaty Kameswara
Rao, Singiresu Sambasiva
Reddy, C. Subba
Reddy, Junuthula N.
Reddy, Narender Pabbathi
Rishi, Satchidanand Raam
Rohatgi, Upendra Singh
Safdari, Yahya Bhai
Sandrapaty, Ramachandra Rao
Sarin, Harry C.
Sarkar, Santanu Kumar
Sato, Walter N.
Sen, Mihir
Seth, Shyam S.
Sha, William T.
Shah, Mirza Mohammed
Shah, Pravin M.
Shah, Ramesh Keshavlal
Shen, Shan-Fu
Sheth, Ketankumar Kantilal
Shih, Chiang
Shih, Hong-Yee
Shih, Tom I-Ping
Shin, Yung C.
Singh, Rajendra
Sinha, Nirmal K.
So, Ronald Ming Cho

Soh, Joong Min
Song, Shin-Min
Song, Xueshu
Sreenivasan, Katepalli Raju
Subudhi, Manomohan
Suh, Nam Pyo
Takeuchi, Kenji
Tan, Chin An
Tan, Chor Weng
Tannan, Ashok
Tien, Chang-Lin
Ting, Joseph K.
Ting, Thomas Chi Tsai
Trinh, Nam Ky
Tsai, Lung-Wen
Tsai, Stephen Wei-Lun
Tse, Ming-Kai
Tsuei, Y. G.
Ubhayakar, Shivadev K.
Ullah, M. Rifat
Vemula, Subba Rao
Wang, Albert S. D.
Wang, Chao-Cheng
Wang, Charles Ping
Wang, Dazong
Wang, I-chih
Wang, Kuo King
Wang, Shih-Liang
Wang, Su-Su
Wang, Yu
Whang, Yun Chow
Wong, Backman
Wong, Earl Gar, Jr.
Wong, Kau Fui
Wu, Chih
Wu, Chivey Dragenson Lung
Wu, Julian Juh-Ren
Wu, Kung Chris
Wu, Shien-Ming
Wu, Theodore Yao-Tsu
Wu, Ting-Wen
Wu, Yau
Yamamoto, Toshiaki
Yang, Bingen
Yang, Wen-Jei
Yao, Lun-Shin
Yao, Shi Chune
Yeh, Hsien-Yang
Yeh, Pu-Sen
Yen, Matthew Ming-Shih
Yeung, Ronald Wai-Chun
Yih, Chia-Shun
Yoshida, Ronald Yutaka

ENGINEERING—METALLURGICAL/CERAMIC/MATERIALS

Abraham, Thomas
Agarwala, Vinod Shanker
Aggarwal, Ishwar D.
Ahmed, Wase U.
Atoji, Masao
Bhattacharya, Rabi Sankar
Biswas, Dipak R.
Chan, Cho Lik
Chang, Benjamin Tai-An
Chang, Chuan Chung
Chen, Jyh-Hong Eric
Chen, Wai Jun
Chen, Wayne Y.
Chen-Tsai, Charlotte Hsiao-yu
Chin, Bryan Allen
Chiou, Wen-An
Cho, Weol D.
Choi, Kyung-Ju
Chou, Tsu-Wei
Chu, Paul Ching-Wu
Chu, Sung Nee George
Chuang, Tze-jer
Chung, Deborah Duen Ling
Chung, Yip-Wah

Daga, Raman Lall
Desai, Vimal H.
Gangulee, Amitava
Ghandhi, Sorab K.
Goela, Jitendra Singh
Goo, Edward Kwock Wai
Gupta, Chitranjan J.
Gupta, Yogendra Mohan
Han, Kenneth N.
Hihara, Lloyd Hiromi
Hsiao, Benjamin S.
Hsu, Stephen M.
Hu, Can Beven
Iwasaki, Iwao
Jain, Himanshu
Jha, Mahesh Chandra
Kerkar, Awdhoot Vasant
Khan, Mahbub R.
Kim, Jonathan Jang-Ho
Kulkarni, Anand K.
Kumai, Motoi
Kumar, Vijay A.
Kuo, Charles Chang-Yun
Lai, Ralph Wei-meen
Lee, Peter Wankyoon
Li, Che-Yu
Li, Chia-Chuan
Li, James C. M.
Li, Shin-Hwa
Lin, Sin-Shong
Ling, Hung Chi
Liu, Thomas Jyhcheng
Liu, Yung Y.
Malhotra, Manohar Lal
Matsuoka, Shiro
Meshii, Masahiro
Mittal, Kashmiri Lal
Moudgil, Brij Mohan
Mukherjee, Tapan Kumar
Naidu, Seetala Veeraswamy
Nair, K. M.
Nakahara, Shohei
Nam, Sehyun
Nguyen, Hien Vu
Ono, Kanji
Pang, Su-Seng
Park, Byungwoo
Parthasarathy, Triplicane Asuri
Puligandla, Viswanadham
Rai, Amarendra Kumar
Raman, Aravamudhan
Ranade, Madhukar G.
Rao, Yalamanchili Krishna
Ray, Siba Prasad
Rohatgi, Pradeep K.
Roy, Pradip Kumar
Sarkar, Nitis
Sen, Arun
Shah, Rajani C.
Shankar, Srinivasan
Sinha, Uday K.
Sohn, Hong Yong
Somasundaran, Ponisseril
Srinivasan, Gunumakonda
   Ramaswamiengar
Sudarshan, T. S.
Sun, Richard C.
Ting, Robert Yen-Ying
Tu, Charles W.
Viswanadham, Ramamurthy K.
Wang, Christine A.
Wang, Francis Wei-Yu
Wang, Hai-Tao
Wang, K. P.
Wang, Paul Weily
Wang, ShiQing
Wang, Su-Su
Wang, Xingwu
Wang, Xun-Li
Wong, Morton Min-Fong
Wong, Philip
Woo, Lecon
Wu, Richard L. C.

ENGINEERING—MINING
(*SEE ALSO* MINING/QUARRYING)

Chang, Tim P.
Chen, Wai Jun
Ghosh, Amitava
Kim, Kunsoo
Park, Duk-Won
Peng, Syd S.
Reddy, Nallapu Narayan
Saluja, Jagdish Kumar
Singh, Madan Mohan
Sumartojo, Jojok
Wang, K. P.
Wu, Ishiung J.

ENGINEERING—NUCLEAR

Chan, Kawei
Chang, Yoon Il
Chao, Yuh J.
Datta, Vijay K.
Hon, Andrew
Kato, Walter Y.
Kim, Jinchoon
Lee, Si Young
Lin, Chien-Chang
Lin, James Chow
Liu, Yung Y.
Lui, Wai Ming
Mehta, Amarjit
Phung, Doan Lien
Pillay, Sivasankara K. K.
Rohatgi, Upendra Singh
Saluja, Jagdish Kumar
Sha, William T.
Siddiqui, Habib
Song, Yo Taik
Subudhi, Manomohan
Takeuchi, Kenji
Tsai, Chon-Kwo
Wang, Chih H.
Wang, Xiaohan
Wang, Yu
Wu, Chuan-Fu
Yang, Bao-Wen
Yang, Shi-tien
Yoshikawa, Herbert Hiroshi

ENGINEERING—PETROLEUM

Aziz, Khalid
Chien, Sze-Foo
Desai, Kantilal Panachand
Hemrajani, Ramesh Relumal
Joshi, Sada D.
Le, Vy Phuong
Lee, Wooyoung
Leung, Woon-Fong
Patel, Bhagwandas Mavjibhai
Ramakrishnan, Terizhandur S.
Sharma, Ghanshyam D.
Sharma, M. P.
Sharma, Mukul Mani
Shen, Liang Chi
Woo, P. T.
Yan, Tsoung-Yuan

ENGINEERING—NOT ELSEWHERE CLASSIFIED

Aggarwal, Ishwar D.
Agrawal, Dharma Prakash
Asuncion, Gary Raymond Espejo
Bhat, Shankar U.
Bhatt, Gunvant R.
Biswas, Dipak R.
Chakrabarti, Subrata Kumar
Chandran, Krishnan Bala

Chang, Andrew C.
Chang, Carl Kochao
Chang, Chin Hao
Chen, Chuan Ju
Chen, Er-Ping
Chen, Hongda
Chen, Yi-Shon
Cheng, Yung-Sung
Cheryan, Munir
Chia, David
Chiao, Leroy
Choi, In-Chan
Choo, Arthur C. S.
Chu, Warren
Chung, Jin Soo
Das, Mohan N.
Dedhia, Navin Shamji
Dwivedy, Ramesh Chandra
Fok, Samuel Shiu-Ming
Fujimoto, Robert I.
Gavande, Sampat A.
Goyal, Megh R.
Gupta, Bhupender S.
Gupta, Ron Singh
Han, Jinchen
Hon, Andrew
Hori, Tom Nichi
Hsieh, Franklin
Hsu, Kenneth Hsuehchia
Huang, Barney Kuo-Yen
Huang, Chin-pao
Huang, Jennming Stephen
Huang, Weifeng
Hung, Tin-Kan
Hwang, Wei-Yuan
Hyun, Kun Sup
Jimenez, Christina Lee
Kam, William
Krishnan, Kalliana R.
Kumar, Ashok
Kumar, Ramesh
Lee, Albert W.
Lee, David Oi
Lee, Jen-Shih
Lee, June Key
Lee, Shyu-tu
Lee, Sunggyu
Lee, William Wai-Lim
Leu, Rong-Jin
Lin, Dennis Kon-Jin
Lin, Ping-Wha
Liu, Henry
Lo, Chien-kuo
Mahalingam, R.
Man, Chi-Sing
Mathiprakasam, Balakrishnan
Mehra, Ravinder C.
Mehta, Gurmukh Dass
Mehta, Kishor Singh
Nakajima, Nobuyuki
Nakatani, Henry Masatoshi
Ng, Richard
Ong, Edward Frank
Ordanza, Bonagrace Francisco
Pannu, Dave S.
Parikh, Kirit Girishchandra
Park, Joon B.
Park, Young Whan
Patel, Anil S.
Patel, Chandrakant B.
Peng, Dachung Pat
Pian, Carlson Chao-Ping
Rangaswamy, Thangam
Reddy, Narender Pabbathi
Roy, Pradip Kumar
Saito, Theodore Teruo
Sarker, Bhaba Ranjan
Satyapriya, Coimbatore K.
Sawatari, Takeo
Shah, Hasmukh N.
Sharma, Puneet
Sheikh, Ghafoor A.
Shen, Thomas T.

Shimomura, Yukio
Srinivasan, Ramachandra Srini
Thakor, Nitish Vyomesh
Ubhayakar, Shivadev K.
Varma, Vishwa K.
Vikram, Chandra Shekhar
Vo, Van Toi
Wang, Carl C. T.
Wang, Jaw-Kai
Wang, Shou-Ling
Wang, Yi-Tin
Whang, Benjamin
Wong, William K. C.
Woo, Edward D.
Wu, Hsin-i
Wu, Shi Tsan
Wu, Xian Connie
Yee, Alfred Alphonse
Yen, I-Kuen
Yeung, Ronald Wai-Chun
Yonamine, Henry Kiyoshi
Youn, Hee Yong
Yu, Kar Yuk
Yuan, Sidney W. K.
Yun, Xiaoping

ENTERTAINMENT/ RECREATION—NOT ELSEWHERE CLASSIFIED
(SEE ALSO ACTING; DANCE/ CHOREOGRAPHY; DIRECTING/ PRODUCING (PERFORMING ARTS); MUSIC—COMPOSING/ SONGWRITING; MUSIC— CONDUCTING/ DIRECTING; MUSIC— INSTRUMENTAL; MUSIC—VOCAL; MUSIC—NOT ELSEWHERE CLASSIFIED; SPORTS— AMATEUR; SPORTS— PROFESSIONAL/ SEMIPROFESSIONAL; SPORTS—NOT ELSEWHERE CLASSIFIED)*

Aoki, Guy Miki
Chew, Richard Franklin
Hagedorn, Jessica Tarahata
Hsia, Judo Jeoudao
Jung, Emma
Lee, Guy
Malik, Tirlok N.
Okuda, Yasuyori
Posey, Sandra Mizumoto
Shahzad, Farhat
Tabuchi, Shoji
Tao, Stephen G.
Ting, Sandra
Zee, Teddy

FASHION DESIGN
Chavan, Sangita D.
Chu, David
Fitzpatrick, Eileen Tabata
Natori, Josie Cruz
Oshiro, Rene Katsuko
Sasaki, Raymond Toshiaki, Jr.
Shah, Amitkumar L.
Sui, Anna
Weglyn, Michi Nishiura
Wu, Christine A.

FINANCIAL SERVICES
SEE BANKING/ FINANCIAL SERVICES; MANAGEMENT/ ADMINISTRATION— ACCOUNTING/ FINANCIAL

FIRE PREVENTION AND CONTROL
Ng, Thomas
Wong, Henry Sik-Yin

FOOD AND BEVERAGE INDUSTRY
SEE MANUFACTURING— FOOD/BEVERAGES; RESTAURANT/FOOD SERVICE INDUSTRY; RETAIL TRADE—FOOD AND BEVERAGES; WHOLESALE TRADE— FOOD AND BEVERAGES

FOREIGN SERVICE
Bloch, Julia Chang
Tsukahira, Toshio George

FORESTRY/FOREST INDUSTRIES
Doi, Stan Sumio
Hon, David Nyok-Sai
Hsin, Liang Yih
Huang, Feng Hou
Kim, Moon G.
Lee, Chen Hui
Lin, Stephen Yaw-rui
Yee, Carlton S.

GALLERY/MUSEUM ADMINISTRATION/ EDUCATION
Chatterjee, Sankar
Chew, Ronald A.
Cho, Frank Fulai
de Vera, Federico
Gamblin, Noriko
Hanami, Clement S.
Hirano, Irene Yasutake
Hsu, Liang-Chi
Jayaram, Mysore
Kaji, Bruce
Kan, Michael
Kay, Helen
Kikumura, Akemi
Kubota, Carole Ann
Kuwayama, George
Matsuda, Fay Chew
Moy, Henry
Oki, Scott D.
Ota, Henry Yasushi
Pal, Pratapaditya
Taira, Masa Morioka
Usui, Kiichi
Wong, Jade Snow

GEOGRAPHY
Chang, Kang-Tsung
Chang, Sen-dou
Chatterjee, Lata Roy
Chiang, Erick
Hsu, Mei-Ling
Jung, Byung Il
Kulkarni, Gopal S.
Leung, Chi Kin

Lew, Alan August
Ma, Laurence J. C.
Park, Siyoung
Rao, Madhusudana N.
Tang, Assumpta
Wang, I-Shou

GEOLOGY/ GEOPHYSICS
Ahmed, Wase U.
Aki, Keiiti
Bhatt, Jagdish J.
Caoile, John Anthony
Chan, Lung S.
Chang, Edmund Z.
Chao, Edward C. T.
Chatterjee, Sankar
Chen, Chin
Chen, Ping-fan
Cheng, Songlin
Chiou, Wen-An
Chou, Chen-Lin
Chowdhury, Dipak Kumar
Desai, Kantilal Panachand
Ganguly, Jibamitra
Hasan, Syed E.
Ho, Thomas Tong-Yun
Hsu, Liang-Chi
Hsui, Albert Tong-Kwan
Huang, Wuu-Liang
Iyer, Hariharaiyer Mahadeva
Kam, James T.-K.
Khan, Mohammad Asad
Khurana, Krishan Kumar
Lee, Tien-Chang
Lin, Jian
Lin, Wunan
Ling, Hsin Yi
Liu, Qing-Huo
Lo, Howard H.
Mao, Ho-Kwang
Mei, Chiang Chung
Miyashiro, Akiho
Morisawa, Marie Ethel
Patel, Chandrakant B.
Rai, Vijai Narain
Rao, Yalamanchili Krishna
Sayala, Dash
Sharma, Ghanshyam D.
Shieh, Yuch-Ning
Shimizu, Nobumichi
Singh, Vijay P.
Sood, Mohan K.
Sumartojo, Jojok
Takahashi, Taro
Talwani, Manik
Wei, Kuo-Yen
Wu, Francis Taming
Wu, Ishiung J.
Yan, Xiao-Hai
Yang, In Che
Yu, John K.
Zen, E-an

GEOPHYSICS
SEE GEOLOGY/ GEOPHYSICS

GOVERNMENT SERVICE (ELECTED OR APPOINTED)/ GOVERNMENT ADMINISTRATION— CITY
Abraham, John
Alcantara, Larry James
Bacho, Norris V.
Batra, Rajeev
Blanco, Paul De La Cruz
Chang, Helen T.

Chang, Patricia W.
Chinn, Roger
Choe, Martha C.
Chou, Hsin-Pei
Chow, Cheryl
Chu, Judy M.
Chung, Ho Young
Corpuz, Ray E., Jr.
Damria, Mulkh Raj
Do, Toa Quang
Doo, Leigh-Wai
Fajardo, Ben
Fajardo, Peter
Fang, James
Fong, Dewey
Fujiwara, Theresa
Fukai, Masani
Greenberg, Asha Saund
Guingona, Michael Patrick
Hashmi, Sayed A.
Hayashi, Midori
Hazama, Chuck
Hom, Kathleen B.
Hong, Frances
Hsia, Yuchuek
Hsieh, Tom
Jhaveri, Arunkumar Ganpatlal
Juanitas, Cyril E. B., Jr.
Kang, Heesook Sophia
Kawasaki, Lillian Y.
Khorasanee, Barker M.
Kim, Donna Mercado
Kinaga, Patricia Anne
Kondo, C. Kimi
Kuwahara, Frank
Lai, Kai Sun
Lam, Tony
Lee, Conrad
Li, Jennifer L. H.
Liddell, Gene Canque
Liu, Richard Chung-Wen
Louie, Marvin Kim
Metha, Pradipkumar D.
Minnick, Sylvia Sun
Mirikitani, Andy
Mitoma, Mike
Mori, Sandy Ouye
Mukai, Yoshiko
Nakano, George
Nishikawa, Dennis
Noguchi, John Takeo
Ochi, Rose Matsui
Ogawa, Frank Hirao
Okazaki, James
Patel, Bhupen N.
Rao, Nagaraja R.
Sakamoto, Lynn
Shirakawa, George
Takami, David A.
Takasugi, Nao
Villanueva, Chris
Vyas, Gaurang Rajnikant
Wakabayashi, Ron
Wong, Anthony Joseph
Wong, Kwan P.
Wong, Martha
Wong, Willie
Woo, Michael K.
Wu, Norman B.
Wu, Stan
Yamaki, Michael Roger
Yamashita, Kenneth Akira
Yee, Jimmie N.

GOVERNMENT SERVICE (ELECTED OR APPOINTED)/ GOVERNMENT ADMINISTRATION— COUNTY
Baldoz, Gerald L.
Blanco, Paul De La Cruz

Domingo, Cynthia Garciano
Duong, Duc Hong
Hirata, Henry Minoru
Honda, Michael M.
Huynh, Emmanuelle
Kong, Chhean
Lau, David T.
Locke, Gary F.
Ochoa, Gloria Megina
Ogawa, Patrick
Omori, Alvin I.
Ozawa, Galen M.
Tanaka, Eddy Sei
Trivedi, Nayana Mohan
Wong, Anna Clara
Yeung, Chun W.
Yoon, Peter Jiung

GOVERNMENT SERVICE (ELECTED OR APPOINTED)/ GOVERNMENT ADMINISTRATION— STATE

Abarquez-Delacruz, Prosy
Barve, Kumar P.
Blanco, Paul De La Cruz
Castro, Marissa Barbers
Cayetano, Benjamin J.
Chang, Alice Ching
Chang, Anthony K. U.
Chang, Jerry Leslie
Chin, Connie Frances
Chou, Chen-Lin
Chun, Shinae
Chung, Robert
Cung, Tien Thuc
Dam, Quy T. T.
Della, David J.
Der, Henry
Eu, March Fong
Flemming, Stanley Lalit Kumar
Fong, Matthew K.
Gee, Virginia Catherine
Gupta, Brij Mohanlal
Ha, Chong W.
Hara-Nielsen, Sylvia Ann
Ho, Dennis
Ho, Richard H.
Hu, Chao Hsiung
Hur, John Chonghwan
Hwang, Roland
Iwanaga-Penrose, Margaret
Iwase, Randall Y.
Iwata, Jerry T.
Jalil, Mazhar
Kaji, Jonathan T.
Katagiri, George
Kennard, Joyce L.
Kobayashi, Bertrand
Kobayashi, John M.
Kurose, Ruthann
Lau, Cheryl Ann
Lee, Shyu-tu
Leung, Peter
Liddell, Gene Canque
Lim, John K.
Locke, Gary F.
Minnick, Sylvia Sun
Miyahara, Bruce
Moriwaki, Clarence
Mukai, Robert L.
Murakami, Richard M.
Nakatani, Henry Masatoshi
Nakatsuka, Lawrence Kaoru
Nakayama, Harvey Kiyoshi
Nakazawa, Anthony Tadashi
Ong, Cynthia
Parikh, Pravin P.
Park-Taylor, Sonya Sunnah
Partido, Rousalyn Bautista
Poc, Sorya

Ramil, Mario R.
Saiki, Patricia F.
Sen, Arun Kumar
Shigihara, Patricia
Shin, Paull H.
Shishido, Calvin M.
Sinha, Nirmal K.
Somani, Pitambar
Soo Hoo, William Fong
Takahashi, Abraham Tomio
Takasaki, Richard Sadaji
Takasugi, Nao
Takayama, Gregg
Takumi, Roy M.
Tang, David Kwong-Yu
Tom, Leland B.
Tran, Thang Nhut
Tsukuno, Paul
Valderrama, David Mercado
Veloria, Velma Rosete
Vemula, Subba Rao
Virk, Muhammad Yaqub
Vohra, Indu
Waihee, John David
Wang, Arthur C.
Wong, Maywood
Wong, Pablo Jose
Wong, Steven Dale
Wong, William K. C.
Yang, Song-Yu
Yee, Stanley C.
Yenson, Evelyn Phoebe
Young, Hoa Pham
Young, Jacqueline Eurn Hai

GOVERNMENT SERVICE (ELECTED OR APPOINTED)/ GOVERNMENT ADMINISTRATION— FEDERAL

Abbas, Mian M.
Agarwala, Vinod Shanker
Aggarwal, Ishwar D.
Akaka, Daniel Kahikina
Bagasao, Paula Y.
Benavides, Vida
Bhagat, Nazir A.
Blaz, Ben
Chan, Harvey Thomas, Jr.
Chandersekaran, Achamma C.
Chang, Caroline J.
Chang, Deborah I-Ju
Chao, Edward C. T.
Chen, David Ta-Fu
Cherian, Joy
Chiang, Asuntha Maria Ming-Yee
Chiang, Erick
Chiang, Sie Ling
Chiang, Thomas Minghung
Chin, Michelle Lorraine
Chiu, Yuan-yuan H.
Choi, Jai Won
Chong, Ken P.
Chow, Barbara A.
Chuang, De-Maw
Chuang, Tze-jer
Chugh, Ashok Kumar
Chun, Sun Woong
Culp, Mae Ng
Dhillon, Neil
Dhir, Surendra Kumar
Dighe, Shrikant Vishwanath
Dow, Faye Lynn
Dubey, Satya Deva
Faleomavaega, Eni Faauaa Hunkin, Jr.
Fujimura, Robert Kanji
Gandhi, Natwar Mohan
Garg, Rajinder P.
Gawande, Atul A.

Gramm, Wendy Lee
Gupta, Raj Kumar
Haley, Maria Luisa Mabilangan
Han, In-Sop
Hara, Lloyd
Hayakawa, S. I.
Hayashi, Dennis Wayne
Hayashi, Fumihiko
Hiramoto, Joni T.
Hironaka, Steve
Ho-González, William
Hon, Andrew
Hsu, Stephen M.
Huang, Joseph Chi Kan
Inouye, Daniel K.
Islam, Nurul
Iyer, Hariharaiyer Mahadeva
Jagadeesh, G.
Jhaveri, Arunkumar Ganpatlal
Joshi, Sewa Ram
Jung, Louise Rebecca
Kacker, Raghu Nath
Kikuchi, Carl H.
Kikuchi, George Susumu
Kim, Jay C.
Kim, Vivian C.
Ko, Hon-Chung
Kubota, Gerald K.
Lao, Chang S.
Lee, Arthur Richard
Lee, Chi-Jen
Lee, Susan H.
Li, Shing Ted
Lim, Chhorn E.
Lim, David J.
Lin, Liang-Shiou
Liu, Ben Chieh
Liu, Edwin H.
Liu, Eric P.
Liu, Lin Chun
Liu, Thomas
Ma, Mark T.
Maeda, Sharon
Makinodan, Takashi
Marshall, Thurgood, Jr.
Matsui, Doris Kazue Okada
Matsui, Robert Takeo
Meng, James Cheng-Sun
Mineta, Norman Yoshio
Mink, Patsy Takemoto
Miyahara, Paul Masayoshi
Mukherjee, Tapan Kumar
Ng, Kam Wing
Nguyen, Bao T.
Nguyen, Xe V.
Ninomiya, Calvin
Outhuok, T.
Pandya, Amit Anant
Parkhie, Mukund R.
Patel, Appasaheb R.
Patel, Kamla
Patel, Kantilal P.
Pindiprolu, Manjula
Prabhakar, Arati
Rai, Vijai Narain
Rao, Potarazu Krishna
Sagawa, Shirley Sachi
Sakimoto, Philip Jon
Sato, Walter N.
Sayala, Chhaya
Seto, Robert Mahealani Ming
Shah, Dhiren Bhawanji
Shah, Yogesh K.
Sharma, Surendra P.
Shroff, Arvin P.
Shum, Alex C.
Singh, Sharon
Sison, Fredilyn
Song, Yo Taik
Sundaresan, P. Ramnathan
Suzuki, Michio
Taira, Toy-Ping Chan
Takasaki, William Yoshi Tsugu

Takasugi, Robert M.
Takei, Richard
Tanada, Takuma
Tashima, A. Wallace
Teng, Tsuchi Paul
Toba, Hachiro Harold
Tom, Angelo C.
Tsai, Frank Y.
Tsai, Lin
Tsai, Theodore F.
Uemoto, Karen
Underwood, Robert Anacletus
Van, Thanhtan C.
Varma, Asha
Wada, Debra Sadako
Wan, Peter J.
Wang, Charles Pei
Whang, Robert
White, Cedina Miran Kim
Wong, Alfred
Wong, Kin Fai
Wong, Siu G.
Woo, Michael T.
Wu, Roy S.
Yamaguchi, Michael J.
Yamashita, Francis Isami
Yang, Chih Ted
Yang, In Che
Yao, Dennis Alden
Yee, Melinda C.
Yoshino, Kouichi
Young, Peter R.

GOVERNMENT SERVICE (ELECTED OR APPOINTED)/ GOVERNMENT ADMINISTRATION— NOT ELSEWHERE CLASSIFIED (SEE ALSO JUDICIARY)

Chang, Michael S.
Jun, Jong S.
Ling, Jack Chieh-Sheng
Soo, Charlie H.
Takano, Mark Allan
Tan, Nady
Wong, Sophie Chao
Woo, Chung S. H.

GRAPHIC DESIGN SEE ART, VISUAL— COMMERCIAL ART/ GRAPHIC DESIGN

HEALTH CARE—NOT ELSEWHERE CLASSIFIED (SEE ALSO CHIROPRACTIC; DENTISTRY; HEALTH SERVICES ADMINISTRATION; MEDICINE—SPECIFIC CATEGORIES, E.G. MEDICINE— ANESTHESIOLOGY; NURSING; NUTRITION; OPTOMETRY; PHARMACY; PODIATRY)

Abarquez-Delacruz, Prosy
Ahluwalia, Balwant S.
Ahmed, Shaikh Sultan
Andrada, Wilmer Vigilia
Bhatti, Rashid A.
Chang, Alice Ching
Chang, Cheng-Hui
Chang, David W.
Chang, Deborah I-Ju

Chang, Helen T.
Chen, Gong
Chen, Karl A.
Cho, David
Choi, Tai-Soon
Choy, Simon
Dan, Phan Quang
Das, Salil Kumar
Dirige, Ofelia Villa
Gupta, Ram Bihari
Hsi, Bartholomew P.
Hsu, Charles Fu-Jen
Ikeda, Elizabeth Rae
Ito, Henry M.
Jain, Naresh C.
Jiang, Zhenying
Kapoor, Harish K.
Kartha, Mukund K.
Kim, Ki Hwan
Kim, Moon H.
Kochhar, Man Mohan
Kumar, Ashir
Kung, Frank F. C.
Lee, Pamela Tau
Liao, Shun-Kwung
Lin, Elizabeth
Lingappa, Yamuna
Louie, George Chang
Park, Ted S.
Patel, Anil J.
Patel, Narayan G.
Quon, Check Yuen
SooHoo, Leo, Jr.
Sy, Francisco S.
Tang, Wallace T. Y.
Udani, Kanak H.
Umali, Filemon J.
Uyeda, Roger Makoto
Vadlamudi, Sri Krishna
Viswanathan, Byravan
Yang, Karl L.
Yen-Koo, Helen Chiang-ying
Yoo, Tai-June
Young, Franklin
Yuen-Terry, Kaimay

HEALTH SERVICES ADMINISTRATION

Aikawa, Jerry Kazuo
Anand, A. Angela
Barron, Purificacion C.
Bhatt, Gita
Bora, Sunder S.
Chang, Patricia W.
Chang, Sylvia Tan
Choi, Tai-Soon
Chopra, Deepak
Chou, Chung-Kwang
Fang, Florence S.
Fong, Bernard Wah Doung
Furukawa, Theodore Paul
Geaga, Jaime V.
Gupta, Ram Bihari
Hayashi, Robert H.
Holl, Julie Kawahara
Hsu, Timothy
Huey, Jolene W.
Ito, Michael Shuji
Iwataki, Miya
Izumigawa, Wallace Minoru
Jamero, Peter M.
Japra, Romesh K.
Kakkar, Rita
Kao, Timothy Tieh-Hsiung
Ko, Kathleen Lim
Li, Yongji
Lim, Josefina Paje
Ling, Christine N.
Mantil, Joseph Chacko
Mori, Sandy Ouye
Ng, Vincent W.
Nori, Dattatreyudu

Omata, Robert Rokuro
Padre, Marc Cruz
Pai, K. Vasanth
Park-Taylor, Sonya Sunnah
Rawat, Arun Kumar
Sakurai, Fred Yutaka
Seto, Belinda P.
Singh, Balwant
Singh, Sant P.
Somani, Pitambar
Soo Hoo, Eric Randolph
Sugihara, Jared Genji
Tana, Phongpan
Teramoto, Yoshitsugu
Tom, Leland B.
Uyeda, Roger Makoto
Varma, Rakesh
Wang, Bee-Lan Chan
Wong, Dorothy
Wong, Siu G.
Yang, Emiko
Yee, Stanley C.
Young, Shun Chung

HISTORY

Barat, Kahar
Chan, Henry Y. S.
Chang, Hsu Hsin
Chen, Chi-yun
Cheng, Ying-wan
Chia, Kai
Chia, Ning
Chin, Charlie William David
Chinn, Thomas Wayne
Chiu, S. M.
Choksy, Jamsheed Kairshasp
Chong, Peng-Khuan
Chow, Tse-tsung
Chu, Jonathan Moseley
Chung, Sue Fawn
Dan, Phan Quang
Fan, Carol C.
Hata, Donald Teruo, Jr.
Hsieh, Winston Wen-sun
Huang, Chi-chiang
Huang, Pei
Kim, Sung Bok
Kong, Corita Shuk Sinn
Kwok, Daniel W. Y.
Kwon, Myoung-ja L.
Lee, Yur-Bok
Leung, Yuen-Sang
Li, Chu-tsing
Li, Lillian M.
Li, San-pao
Li, Xiao-Bing
Lim, Richard
Lin, Patricia Yu
Lin, Yü-sheng
Odo, Franklin Shoichiro
Okihiro, Gary Yukio
Sha, Shung-tse
Shen, I-Yao
Shin, Paull H.
Sumida, Jon Tetsuro
Takaki, Ronald
Teng, Anthony Yung-yuan
Vohra, Ranbir
Wang, Yi T'ung
Wei, William
Wu, Wei-ping
Yamasaki, Mitch
Yang, Anand Alan
Yin, Xiao-huang
Yoon, Won Z.
Yoshino, Ronald Warren

HORTICULTURE
SEE **LANDSCAPE/**
HORTICULTURAL
SERVICES

HOTEL/MOTEL
INDUSTRY

Cabrera, Cesar Trinidad
Chacko, Harsha E.
Chen, Sam W.
Choy, Simon
Hsu, Cathy H. C.
Kapoor, Tarun
Patel, Bhulabhai C.
Patel, Jay M.
Patel, Kanti L.
Tran, La Dinh
Truong Thi, Hoa-Dien
Wang, John Chiang
Yu, Peter Tat-kong

INDUSTRIAL DESIGN

Kawahara, William T.
Kimura, Brian
Lau, Tin Man
Liu, Yuan Hsiung
Quan, William Chun

INFORMATION
SCIENCE
SEE **LIBRARY/**
INFORMATION
SCIENCE

INSURANCE

Aoyama, Calvin Takeo
Azumano, George Ichiro
Chow, Alexander Wing-Yat
Chung, Ho Young
Datta, Ranajit Kumar
Dinh, Nicholas Nguyen
Esguerra, Arturo Sazon
Fong, Hiram Leong
Fukai, Masani
Hisatomi, John A.
Hu, Joseph Kai Ming
Iwasaki, Ronald Seiji
Kai, Robert T.
Kawamoto, Brian Michio
Kim, Hyung J.
Maheshwari, Arun K.
Moinuddin, Masood A.
Moy, Donald
Myung, John Y.
Ng, May-May Donna Lee
Sakagawa, Richard Masaru
Santos, Mario Alban
Sawhney, Ajay
Soriano, Lee G.
Tam, Leo
Tanaka, Ty Skip
Toda, Harold Keiji
Tokunaga, Katsumi
Tseng, Wan Chi
Wong, John Bullitt
Yuen, Calvin N.

INTERIOR DESIGN

Dong, Wei
Kajioka, June J.
Kim, Michael Yong
Langit, Ralph P., Jr.
Liu, Alfred H.
Ohashi, Alan Joseph
Wu, Kingsley K.
Yung, Ringo

INTERPRETATION
SEE **TRANSLATION/**
INTERPRETATION

JOURNALISM—
BROADCAST

Ahn, Jaehoon
Chan, Anthony Bernard
Chang, Farland H.
Chang, Helen T.
Chen, Amy L.
Cheng, Josephine
Chung, Connie
Denton, Victoria Villena-
Gouw, Cynthia Gie-Kiok
Hattori, James
Hotta, Gina H.
Hsia, Lisa
Hwang, John C.
LaCuesta, Lloyd R.
Lee, Chin-Chuan
Lee, Karen
Lee, Siani
Lee, Vic Ling
Leighton, Veronica V.
Leung, Ka-Wing
Louie, David A.
Nguyen, Tri Huu
Outhuok, T.
Paek, Min
Satow, Stuart Alan
Shimamoto, Scott Seiya
Shimooka, Russell
Sumii, Takao
Tan, Zoe
Tokuda, Wendy
Tong, Jennie S.
Tsui, Cheryl Wai-Kuen
Yu, Linda

JOURNALISM—
PHOTOJOURNALISM
(SEE ALSO
PHOTOGRAPHY)

Endo, Paula Sayoko Tsukamoto
Gow, Haven Bradford
Imai, Douglas Scott
Kang, Hyungwon
Kee, Willie
Kim, Yunghi
Krist, Elizabeth Cheng
Lau, Jenni Meili
Louie, Eugene H.
Morita, John Takami
Sieu, Benny Lou
Wong, Barry

JOURNALISM—PRINT
(SEE ALSO **WRITING/**
EDITING—
NONFICTION)

Ahn, Jaehoon
Aoki, Guy Miki
Aoki, Kathryn Kiku
Bautista, Veltisezar Bal
Bhavnani, Pratap Gagumal
Briggs, Tracey Wong
Chan, Mei-Mei
Chang, Tsan-Kuo
Chen, Jizeng
Chen, Simon Ying
Chen, Stanford
Chew, Ronald A.
Chiang, Asuntha Maria Ming-Yee
Chiang, Oscar C. K.
Chin, Charlie William David
Chin, Steven Alexander
Cho, Andrew Byong-Woo
Chung, Lisa A.
Denton, Victoria Villena-
Doo, Jack P., Jr.
Ebron, Betty Liu
Fan, Ada Mei
Fong-Torres, Ben

Francia, Luis H. F.
Funabiki, Jon
Gunaratne, Dhavalasri Shelton Abeywickreme
Guo, David
Gupta, Udayan
Hosokawa, William K.
Hsieh, Cynthia C.
Hsieh, Wen-jen
Hsu, Evelyn
Hwang, Suein Lim
Iyer, Siddharth Pico
Jayaram, Mysore
Johnston, George Toshio
Kakutani, Michiko
Kee, Willie
Kim, David Doyung
Kim, Soon Jin
Kimura, Donna Junko
Kishimoto, Yoriko
Kong, William T.
Kumar, Arvind
Laskar, Devi Sen
Lau, Jenni Meili
Lee, Chin-Chuan
Lee, Jae-won
Lee, Jai Hyon
Lee, Kyung Won
Leighton, Veronica V.
Liu, Eric P.
Liu, Nancy Shao-Lan
Lord, Bette Bao
Louie, Cliff
Matsumoto, Nancy K.
Nakamoto, Donald Jiro
Nakatsuka, Lawrence Kaoru
Okamoto, Shari Akiko
Park, Jeannie
Querol Moreno, Cherie M.
Rhee, Sang Foon
Rodis, Rodel E.
Seto, Benjamin S. F.
Shah, Amit
Shah, Mowahid Hussain
Singh, Natasha
Subramanian, Sribala
Sugawara, Sandra Lee
Sunoo, Brenda Paik
Tagashira, Gail S.
Thakur, Manish
Van Houten, David J.
Vu, Quang
Watanabe, Mark Hisashi
Wong, Gregory Sterling
Wong, Nicole Anna
Wong, Ray G. L.
Wong, William
Woo, William Franklin
Yamamoto, Michael Toru
Yang, Jeffrey Chih-Ho
Yang, John Eric
Yoshinaga, George
Zia, Helen

JOURNALISM—NOT
ELSEWHERE
CLASSIFIED

Ahn, Jaehoon
Ling, Jack Chieh-Sheng
Louie, Eugene H.
Malik, Saied Ahmad
Nishimura, Wendy Natsue
Tang, Lillian Y. D.
Wang, Shujen
Wong, Wing Y.

JUDICIARY

Chin, Ming William
Choy, Herbert Y. C.
Don, James E.
Fong, Harold Michael

Fong, Thomas Y. K.
Fujimoto, James Randall
Hiroshige, Ernie
Hom, Rose
Ing, Lawrence N. C.
Ito, Lance A.
Kawaichi, Ken M.
Kennard, Joyce L.
Kwoh, Stewart
Lew, Ronald S. W.
Low, Harry William
Mamiya, Ron
Mihara, Nathan
Moon, Ronald Tae-yang
Ramil, Mario R.
Recana, Mel Red
Seto, Robert Mahealani Ming
Sing, Lillian K.
Suzukawa, Steven
Takasugi, Robert M.
Tang, Julie Mong-See
Tang, Thomas
Tashima, A. Wallace
Todd, Kathryn Doi
Wasserman, Fumiko Hachiya
Watai, Madge S.
Woo, Vernon Ying-Tsai
Yamashita, Francis Isami

LABOR RELATIONS
SEE **LABOR UNION**
ADMINISTRATION;
MANAGEMENT/
ADMINISTRATION—
PERSONNEL/
TRAINING/LABOR
RELATIONS

LABOR UNION
ADMINISTRATION

Caoile, Gloria T.
Finucane, Matthew H.
Jin, Morgan
Lui, MeiZhu
Minamoto, Jennifer Noriko
Miyakawa, Edward T.
Nakamoto, Donald Jiro
Quan, Katie
Rao, Nagaraja R.
Takumi, Roy M.

LANDSCAPE/
HORTICULTURAL
SERVICES

Ariza, Yasumi
Asahara, David J.
Damria, Mulkh Raj
Foshee, Thuong Nguyen
Hong, Il Sik
Hsu, Paul
Iwahashi, Satoshi
Kobayashi, Koichi
Kohara, David Noboru
Koo, Michelle E. M.
Lee, Jeff S.
Ogawa, Frank Hirao
Sasaki, Hideo
Wong, John Lap
Yamanishi, Henry Kazuo
Yee, Franklin
Yorozu, William S.

LAW ENFORCEMENT

Fong, Dewey
Hayakawa, Sidney Akira
Hironaka, Steve
Ho-González, William
Kim, Paul Myungchyun
LaCuesta, Wesley Ray, Sr.

Lau, Fred H.
Liu, Ray H.
Miyahara, Paul Masayoshi
Nagaoka, Michael M.
Naito, Michael K.
Nakamura, Michael S.
Omura, Mark Christopher
Sayaphupha, Robert Bouakham
Shigemasa, Thomas Ken
Shishido, Calvin M.
Sumisaki, Roy
Ting, Jan C.
Wong, Anthony Joseph
Wong, Bryan Allen
Wong, Clifford S.
Yang, Lang

LAW/LEGAL SERVICES

Ahn, Steve Fitzgerald
Allen, Susan Au
Bacho, Peter
Cayetano, Benjamin J.
Chan, Ted W.
Chang, Howard F.
Chang, James Wan Chie
Chang, Peter Asha, Jr.
Chang, Tim P.
Chen, Alan Keith
Chen, Pamela Ki Mai
Chen, Wun-ee Chelsea
Chiang, Yung Frank
Chin, Kathy Hirata
Chin, Ming William
Chin, Pamela Grace
Chin, Yee Wah
Ching, Anthony B.
Ching, Gale Lin Fong
Choi, Hyungmoo
Choi, Paul Lee
Chu, Adam
Chu, Terence
Chua, Amy Lynn
Chung, T. S.
Cruzada, Rodolfo Omega
Das, Shyam
Dhillon, Joginder Singh
Dinh, Thuy Tu Bich
Doo, Leigh-Wai
Fong, J Craig
Fong, Kevin Murray
Fong, Matthew K.
Frey, Francesca
Fu, Paul S.
Fugh, John L.
Fujiki, Marjorie
Fukurai, Hiroshi
Gee, Dolly M.
Greenberg, Asha Saund
Guingona, Michael Patrick
Gupta, Raj Kumar
Han, Anna M.
Hayashi, Dennis Wayne
Hing, Bill Ong
Hinoki, George
Hiramoto, Joni T.
Ho, Peter Peck Koh
Ho-González, William
Hong, John Song Yook
Hou, William Chen-Nan
Hsueh, Yi-Fun
Huang, Jack J. T.
Huang, Thomas W.
Huynh, Emmanuelle
Hwang, Ivy
Hwang, Roland
Hwu, Peter S.
Igasaki, Paul
Ihm, Tysun
Ing, Lawrence N. C.
Isokawa, Ned
Jaiswal, Gopaljee
Jung, Louise Rebecca

Kato, Dean M.
Kawaichi, Ken M.
Kawano, Arnold H.
Kim, Augustine H.
Kim, Chin
Kim, Joseph K.
Kim, Yung Mo
Kinaga, Patricia Anne
Ko, Ada
Kwan-Gett, Mei Lin
Lai, Richard Thomas
Lau, Edward C. Y.
Lee, David C.
Lee, Gus Chien-Sun
Lee, Paul Wah
Lewis, Loida Nicolas
Limb, Ben Quincy
Ling, Yu-long
Liu, Frank Yining
Loh, Wallace D.
Loui, Warren R.
Lum, Albert C.
Lum, Dean Scott
Maeno, John Y.
Maniwa, Kaz
Marshall, Thurgood, Jr.
Matsui, Robert Takeo
Matsumoto, Takashi
Mink, Patsy Takemoto
Mirikitani, Andy
Mitsunaga, Jimi
Miyoshi, David Masao
Mo, Hugh H.
Moy, Robert Carl
Mukai, Francis Ken
Mukai, Robert L.
Murase, Mike
Myung, John Y.
Nakagawa, Cressey
Narasimhan, Subha
Nash, Philip Tajitsu
Nguyen, Benjamin Ban
Ninomiya, Calvin
Ochi, Rose Matsui
Ochoa, Gloria Megina
Ogata, Jeffery Morimasa
Oh, Angela
Ong, Cynthia
Ota, Henry Yasushi
Pai, Lisa Koonghui Kim
Pandya, Amit Anant
Park, Laura Heyong
Rai, Arti K.
Ramakrishna, Kilaparti
Rawlings, Noella A.
Rodis, Rodel E.
Sagawa, Shirley Sachi
Saito, Thomas E.
Sakai, Michael H.
Sasaki, Dale I.
Seto, Theodore Paul
Shah, Mowahid Hussain
Shimada, Yoshiki
Shimoura, James
Sison, Fredilyn
Sogi, Francis Y.
Soong, Arthur J.
Sung, Lawrence M.
Suzuki, Paul Ted
Ta, Tai Van
Tan, S. Y.
Tanaka, Wayne D.
Tang, David Kwong-Yu
Tang, Thomas
Thao, Christopher Teng
Ting, Jan C.
Tran, Thuan Van
Tsukuno, Paul
Tung, Ko-Yung
Uchimoto, William Warren
Ueno, Takemi
Ueoka, Meyer Masato
Wang, Arthur C.

Wang, David Edward
Wang, George H.
Wang, William Kai-Sheng
White, Cedina Miran Kim
Wong, Benson D.
Wong, Byron F.
Wong, Charles Foo, Jr.
Wong, Jacqueline Jeanne
Wong, John D.
Wong, Kent Douglas
Wong, Nicole Anna
Woo, Chung S. H.
Woo, Robert Ken, Jr.
Woo, Vernon Ying-Tsai
Wu, Christopher N.
Yamaguchi, Michael J.
Yamakawa, David Kiyoshi, Jr.
Yamaki, Michael Roger
Yamamoto, Eric K.
Yamasaki, George, Jr.
Yang, Chun-Yeong
Yen, Alfred Chueh-Chin
Yim, Soo Jung
Yin, George Kuo-Ming
Yin, Ronald L.
Young, Alice
Zia, Hoyt Hanson

LIBRARY/ INFORMATION SCIENCE

Banada-Tan, Leticia
Bhatia, Sharmila
Chan, Carl Chiang
Chan, Lois Mai
Chang, Ann Han-Chih
Chang, Che-Gil
Chang, Henry C.
Chang, Robert Huei
Chang, Shirley Lin
Chang, Tony H.
Chen, Ching-chih
Chen, David W.
Cheng, Charmian S.
Chin, Cecilia Hui-hsin
Chu, Felix T.
Chu, Tien Lu
Chung, Catherine L.
Collantes, Augurio L.
Collantes, Lourdes Yapchiongco
Eng, Mamie
Fu, Paul S.
Fu, Tina C.
Gupta, Saroj Lata
Hahn, Bessie King
Hayashi, Midori
Hayashikawa, Doris S.
Ho, Birong A.
Ho, Michael Shiukeung
Ho, Yuh Jyue Agnes Wang
Hotelling, Katsuko Tsurukawa
Hsieh, Cynthia C.
Huang, George Wenhong
Huang, Joyce L.
Huang, Samuel T.
Ikeda, Naomi Ruth
Jung, Soon J.
Kabir, Abulfazal M. Fazle
Kalra, Bhupinder Singh
Kang, Byung I.
Kao, Yasuko W.
Kiang, Clyde Y.
Kim, Bang Ja
Kim, Chung-Sook Charlotte
Kim, David U.
Kim, Joanne Young
Kobayashi, Deanna Hasuye
Kobayashi, Key K.
Kuan, David A.
Kuan, Jenny W.
Kuo, Ming-ming Shen
Kwan, Yuen-yin Kathy

Kwon, Myoung-ja L.
Lau, Shuk-fong
Le, Binh P.
Lee, Hwa-Wei
Lee, John Jongjin
Lee, Ocksoo Kim
Lee, Sooncha A.
Lee, Wol Sue
Li, Diane Dai
Li, Marjorie H.
Liang, Diana F.
Lim, Josefina Paje
Lin, Poping
Liu, David Ta-ching
Liu, Frank Yining
Liu, Mengxiong
Liu, Susana Juh-mei
Lo, Suzanne J.
Louie, Ai-Ling M.
Louie, Ruby Ling
Lu, Janet C.
Ma, Tai-Loi
Ma, Yan
Maeyama, Kikuko
Makino, Yasuko
Miah, Abdul J.
Morita, Ichiko T.
Motihar, Kamla Mansharamani
Moy, Naomi Ogawa
Nam, Wonki Kim
Ng, Rebecca P.
Oka, Christine Kazuko
Okada, Connie Tokiye
Park, Chung I.
Saito, Thomas E.
Shah, Syed M.
Shang, Stella I-Hua
Sharma, Ravindra Nath
Shen, I-Yao
Shen, Xiao-Yan
Shih, Philip C.
Srirama, Malini
Su, Julie Chu-chu
Takahashi, Rita
Tang, Eugenia C. G.
Tang, Klairon Kit-ling
Tang, Sherman
Ting, Lee Hsia
Ting, Ying Ji
Tolentino, Virginia Cantor
Tsai, Betty L.
Tsai, Bor-sheng
Tseng, Louisa
Tsui, Susan Lee
Tsukamoto, Jack Toru
Tsuneishi, Warren Michio
Tu, Shu-chen H.
Verma, Dhani Ram
Wang, George Maosue
Wang, Guo-Hua
Wang, Margaret K.
Wang, Molly M.
Wei, Anthony Yueh-shan
Wei, Wei
Wong, Clark Chiu-Yuen
Wu, Anna Chaoying
Wu, Harry Pao-Tung
Wu, Jennifer Lee
Wu, Xian Connie
Xia, Yun
Yamashita, Kenneth Akira
Yeh, Thomas Y.
Yoon, Steven Ilsang
Yoshimura, Yoshiko
Young, Peter R.
Yu, Priscilla C.
Yukawa, Masako
Zhang, Wenxian

MANAGEMENT/ ADMINISTRATION— ACCOUNTING/ FINANCIAL (*SEE ALSO* ACCOUNTING/ AUDITING)

Chacko, Varkki P.
Chan, John
Chandran, Ravi
Chandy, Varughese Kuzhiyath
Chang, Chun-Hao
Chang, Craig
Chang, Robert C.
Chang, Sukjeong J.
Chen, Amy L.
Chen, Chao
Chen, Haiyang
Chen, Terry
Cheng, Louis Tsz-Wan
Chiang, Yuen-Sheng
Choi, Dosoung Philip
Chow, Shirley Chin-Ping
Gangwal, Rakesh
Garg, Devendra
Ghosh, Bivas Kanti
Haque, M. Shamsul
Ho, Thierry
Hoshi, Mineo
Hsiao, Feng
Hwang, Dennis B. K.
Izumigawa, Wallace Minoru
Joe, Alexander H.
Kale, Jayant R.
Kang, Jun-Koo
Kedia, Ullas V.
Khan, Walayet A.
Khanna, Naveen
Kim, Dongcheol
Kim, Jong H.
Kim, Moon Kyu
Lam, Chun H.
Lee, Suk Hun
Lee, Yow-Min R.
Lee, Yul W.
Leung, Kenneth Ch'uan-k'ai
Li, Jennifer L. H.
Liao, Woody M.
Lim, Ralph Wei Hsiong
Louie, Marvin Kim
Mansur, Iqbal
Mathur, Ike
Mehta, Ujjwal J.
Melookaran, Joseph
Miura, Nolan A.
Ng, Frank Mang Leang
Ngo, David
Nishina, Clifford M.
Ong, Owh Kian
Padre, Marc Cruz
Pan, Fung-Shine
Park, Sung-Il
Patel, Chandu M.
Raimundo, Cris C.
Rajan, Raghuram Govind
Rao, Barry
Rao, Spuma M.
Sachdev, Ramesh Kumar
Sawhney, Ajay
Shah, Pradyumna R.
Sheth, Navin D.
Shim, Jae K.
Shin, Hung Sik
Shinsato, Francis G.
Shum, William
Syed, Karamat A.
Tai, William P.
Tam, Simon M. W.
Tandon, Anand
Tiangco, Eddie Eugenio
Tom, Leland B.
Tse, Sau P.
Tseng, S. C.

Tseng, Wan Chi
Uchimoto, Dennis D.
Varma, Rakesh
Vu, Joseph
Wan, David A.
Wang, Louie Kehluh
Winick, Tranquilina Rios
Wong, Desmond C.
Wong, Janet S.
Wong, John Bullitt
Woo, Benson K.
Yamamoto, Roger Masaaki
Yano, Ronald Makoto
Ye, Jose

MANAGEMENT/ ADMINISTRATION— ADVERTISING/ MARKETING/PUBLIC RELATIONS (*SEE ALSO* ADVERTISING/ PROMOTION)

Abe, Makoto
Bhatia, Tej K.
Chang, David Hsiang
Chang, Helen Kuang
Chia, Swee Lim
Chin, Katherine M.
Choe, Sang Tae
Chow, Russell W.
Esguerra, Arturo Sazon
Fong, Charlen
Gn, Thye-Wee
Gupta, Ashok K.
Gupta, Sunil
Hong, Kenneth
Iyer, Easwar S.
Javed, Mohd S.
Jiang, Xixiang
Kaneko, William Masami
Kim, Chulwan
Kishimoto, Richard Noriyuki
Kobayashi, William N., Jr.
Kumar, V.
Lee, Ming-Tung
Lee, Myung-Soo
Lin, Chengmin Michael
Lin, Felix
Liu, Ben Shaw-Ching
Mahajan, Jayashree
Mahajan, Vijay
Mak, William K.
Malik, Naeem
Mian, Athar S.
Moriwaki, Clarence
Mustafa, Shams
Nagoshi, Douglas N.
Nguyen, Tony C.
Nishimura, Wendy Natsue
Ohno, Peter Takeshi
Oki, Scott D.
Patel, Ramesh P.
Phan, Trung Huynh
Pindiprolu, Manjula
Rao, Mahesh K.
Shah, Abhay
Sheth, Kishor C.
Shin, SoonMi
Siddiqui, Ehtisham Uddin Ahmad
Tan, Zoe
Tang, Thomas Li-Ping
Tang, Yingchan Edwin
Tong, Douglas L.
Trivedi-Doctor, Minakshi Dipak
Wang, Dora Chia-Chi
Wang, Gary S. H.
Wu, Christine A.
Yen, Peter T.
Yim, Chi-Kin Bennett
Yoshikami, Sandra

Young, Shirley
Yue, Chinny

MANAGEMENT/ ADMINISTRATION— COMPUTER SYSTEMS/DATA PROCESSING

Banerjee, Debasish
Cabanting, George Paul
Cao, Hoang-Yen Thi
Chang, Yen Fook
Chen, Houn-Gee
Chong, Pek-Ean
Chu, Nhan V.
Gangulee, Amitava
Hong, Ilyoo Barry
Hsin, Chen-Chung
Hwang, Enoch Oi-Kee
Hwang, Mark I.
Im, Jin-Hyouk
Jaisinghani, Rajan A.
Jayachandran, Toke
Kim, Yong K.
Kulkarni, Uday Ravindra
Kuo, Feng Yang Kuo
Lee, Shyu-tu
Lin, Binshan
Ly, Kieu Kim
Mahajan, Harpreet
Malkani, Roma V.
Maruyama, Kiyoshi
Mathai, Anish
Mehta, Ujjwal J.
Melookaran, Joseph
Murthy, Srinivasa
Nakayama, Harvey Kiyoshi
Ng, Martin K.
Nguyen, Bao T.
Patel, Jayant P.
Rai, Arun
Rao, Raghav H.
Santhanam, Radhika
Shim, Jung P.
Shrivastava, Satyendra P.
Suh, Yung-Ho
Tam, Simon M. W.
Tang, Mark Giakhy
Tran, Thinh Quy
Wu, Michael Ming-Kun
Yu, Gang

MANAGEMENT/ ADMINISTRATION— CONSULTATION/ ANALYSIS (*SEE ALSO* CONSULTING)

Aggarwal, Raj
Banerjee, Debasish
Bhalla, Vipan Kumar
Chakravarthy, Balaji Srinivasan
Chan, John
Chan, Peng S.
Chandramouli, S.
Chang, Shin-Jyh Frank
Chang, Yen Fook
Chau, Henry Chun-Nam
Chen, Haiyang
Choe, Kenneth
Choi, Jin Wook
Chopra, Joginder
Desai, Sharad P.
Do, Toa Quang
Gangulee, Amitava
Ghosh, Amitava
Ghosh, Sujan
Goishi, Dean M.
Gupta, Amit
Hauh, Paul-Thomas B.
Hiraoka, Leslie Satoshi

Ho, Vernon S. C.
Hsieh, Daniel Sebastian
Hsu, Albert Yutien
Isaki, Paul
Kim, Jae Won
Kim, Jay S.
Koo, George P.
Kumar, V.
Kuo, Feng Yang Kuo
Kuttan, Appu
Kuwahara, Steven Sadao
Lai, Albert Wenben
Lai, Ming-Yee
Lee, Sang Moon
Lee, Ving J.
Lian, Maria Z. N.
Lim, Kwee-Eng Lyn
Lin, Paul Kuang-Hsien
Mehta, Kamlesh T.
Mirchandani, Prakash
Mital, Naveen Kumar
Moy, Jeffery Fei
Ong, Beng Soo
Parate, Natthu Sonbaji
Patel, Chandu M.
Patel, Kamla
Phung, Doan Lien
Ranade, Madhukar G.
Sarathy, Partha R.
Shim, Jung P.
Shimizu, Tak
Tang, Kwei
Tang, Ming-Je
Tsen, Meng Chi
Tsutsui, James Haruo, Jr.
Yoshikawa, Herbert Hiroshi
Young, Shirley

MANAGEMENT/ ADMINISTRATION— GENERAL

Aggarwal, Anil K.
Au, Patrick Siu-Kee
Batra, Rajeev
Bhatia, Ramesh
Bhatia, Salim A. L.
Capoor, Asha
Chai, Jay
Chang, Elden T.
Chang, Jack Che-Man
Chang, William Y. B.
Chao, Allen Y.
Chen, Nai-Ni
Chen, Wayne Y.
Chen, Winston H.
Cheng, Andrew F.
Cheng, Carlos
Chiang, Erick
Chiang, Yuen-Sheng
Cho, Frank Fulai
Cho, Hyong W.
Chou, Ernest Yen
Chowdhry, Vinay
Choy, Fred Kat-Chung
Chu, Hung Manh
Chung, Jesse Y. W.
Deivanayagam, Subramaniam
Doi, Stanley T.
Eng, Henry
Fasang, Patrick Pad
Fujimatsu, Tadao
Ganguly, Suman
Garg, Prem
Gupta, Anil S.
Gupta, Pradeep Kumar
Gupta, Ron Singh
Gupta, Samir
Hagiwara, Kokichi
Hamasaki, Les
Hee, Edward K. Y.
Hirasuna, Alan Ryo
Hom, Peter Wah

Hsia, Judo Jeoudao
Hu, Daniel Ching
Hu, Jimmy
Hur, John Chonghwan
Hwang, Cherng-Jia
Inoue, Michael Shigeru
Iyer, Hariharaiyer Mahadeva
Jan, Han S.
Jha, Mahesh Chandra
Joshi, Sada D.
Kadowaki, Joe George
Kakkar, Subash
Kan, Yue-Sai
Khan, Shakil Ahmad
Kim, Bonn-Oh
Kim, Yongshik
Kita, Sadao
Kobayashi, Jerry T.
Koh, Kwang K.
Kokan, Ghiasuddin
Koo, George P.
Kotani, Shigeto
Kumar, Kamalesh
Kung, Alice How Kuen
Kung, Patrick Chung-Shu
Kusumoto, Sadahei
Lai, Ying-San
Lau, Gilbert Minjun
Le, Vy Phuong
Lee, Byung-Moon
Lee, David Sen-Lin
Leung, Charles Cheung-Wan
Li, Diane Dai
Lim, Rodney Gene
Lin, Charles Fley-Fung
Lin, Stephen Yaw-rui
Liu, Warren Kuo-Tung
Louie, Alan C.
Maeda, Yutaka
Mak, Stanley M.
Mar, William David
Martin, Abraham Nguyen
Marur, Hanuman
Matsuoka, James Toshio
Matsuoka, Matthew S.
Matsushima, Charles Hiroshi
McCarty, Faith B.
Mehta, Gurmukh Dass
Miyoshi, David Masao
Moon, Inso John
Moribayashi, Mikio
Mow, Bill
Muni, Indu A.
Murthy, A. Kumaresa S.
Musapeta, Hari
Naito, Samuel Teruhide
Nakasone, Robert C.
Nakujima, Hideyuki
Nietes, Linda Maria
Nomura, Kaworu Carl
O, Cao Kinh
Oh, Joseph
Ota, Dean
Ota, Isaac I.
Pai, David Hsien-Chung
Park, Ted S.
Patel, Ashok R.
Patel, Bhagvan H.
Patel, Bhulabhai C.
Patel, Dilipkumar Z.
Patel, Ray L.
Peng, Dachung Pat
Rajan, Frederick E. N.
Rajasekhar, Amar
Rao, Ramgopal P.
Rawn, Byung Soon
Reddy, Dhanireddy Ramalinga
Shah, Piyush A.
Sharma, Shri C.
Shen, Chung Yu
Sheng, Tony L.
Shih, Wei
Shim, Sang Kyu

Shima, John David
Singh, Ajaib
Sohal, Harjit Singh
Song, John S.
Srinivas, Ramachandra
Srivastava, Om P.
Surti, Tarun Natwarlal
Tahiliani, Vasu Hariram
Takagi, Norio
Takei, George Hosato
Tam, Eric Tak-Keung
Tan, Lawrence W.
Tan, Nady
Tanaka, James Junji
Tandon, Anand
Tong, Alvin H.
Trivedi, Nayan B.
Tse, John Yung Dong
Tsuha, Wallace K., Jr.
Uchida, Yoshihiro
Virk, Muhammad Yaqub
Wang, Charles Pei
Wang, Charles Ping
Wang, Frederick Andrew
Wing, Charmeen Hah-Ming
Wong, Dorothy
Wong, John A.
Wong, Kenneth P.
Wong, Norman Zaw
Wu, Harry Pao-Tung
Wu, Kim
Yamaguchi, Ko
Yanagisawa, Samuel Tsuguo
Ye, Jose
Yeh, Henry
Zee, Teddy

MANAGEMENT/ ADMINISTRATION— OPERATIONS/ MAINTENANCE

Bose, Pratim
Chang, Hyong Koo
Chitgopekar, Sharad S.
Chow, Shirley Chin-Ping
Chung, Chen Hua
Desai, Hiren Sharad
Doi, Stan Sumio
Duong, Ngo Dinh
Fujioka, Takashi
Garg, Rajinder P.
Gopikanth, M. L.
Gupta, Omprakash K.
Ho, Chrwan-Jyh
Hung, Stephen Chifeng
Ito, Henry M.
Kawaja, Kaleem U.
Lai, Jai-Lue Leon
Lee, Jooh
Luu, Lang Van
Mehta, Kailash
Min, Hokey
Mukai, Yoshiko
Murakami, Richard M.
Park, Kap Yung
Patel, Mukesh M.
Patel, Rakesh
Shah, Arvind K.
Sohn, So Young
Song, Yangsoon
Tan, Eric Tuanlee
Tang, Mark Giakhy
Thakkar, Pravin Asharam
Tom, Melvin Gee Lim
Weng, Wu-Tsung
Wong, Vernon D. B.
Wu, Y. C. L. Susan

MANAGEMENT/ ADMINISTRATION— PERSONNEL/ TRAINING/LABOR RELATIONS

Bagasao, Paula Y.
Chang, Chuan Chung
Choy, Simon
Gatdula, Francisco Ric
Gee, Virginia Catherine
Haley, Maria Luisa Mabilangan
Hara-Nielsen, Sylvia Ann
Huey, Jolene W.
Jiang, William Yuying
Kawafuchi, Glenn Misaki
Kohara, David Noboru
Lau, David T.
Le, Christine Dung
Lee, Robert Terry
Lin, Nina S. F.
Miya, Wayne
Miyamoto, Lance
Okamoto, Kenneth Wayne
Rhee, Susan Byungsook
Sen, Tapas K.
Shimomura, Yukio
Tokunaga, Howard Taira
Wong, Clark Chiu-Yuen
Wong, Richard Gene
Yamamoto, Roger Masaaki
Yuen-Terry, Kaimay

MANAGEMENT/ ADMINISTRATION— PURCHASING

Furuta, Otto K.
Hsiao, Margaret Sheng-Mei
Kim, Bong Yohl
Okano, Yuji
Patel, Rakesh
Sachdev, Ramesh Kumar
Song, Yangsoon

MANAGEMENT/ ADMINISTRATION— SALES

Anand, Charanjit S.
Chen, Le Chun
Chen, Stephen C.
Chow, Russell W.
Chua, Conrad E.
Dang, Harish C.
Domondon, Oscar
Hoang, Frank H.
Hsing, Rodney W.
Idnani, Kamal M.
Javed, Mohd S.
Jin, Morgan
Kung, Alice How Kuen
Lin, Nina S. F.
Moribayashi, Mikio
Nishiura, Wayne Iwao
Nizami, Shafiq Ahmed
Santos, Mario Alban
Shimizu, Scott Edward
Shin, SoonMi
Srinivasan, Thiru R.
Tiangco, Eddie Eugenio
Ting Cang-Kim, Donna Marie
Tong, Douglas L.
Tsen, Meng Chi
Un, Howard Ho-Wei

MANAGEMENT/ ADMINISTRATION— NOT ELSEWHERE CLASSIFIED
(SEE ALSO ASSOCIATION MANAGEMENT; EDUCATIONAL ADMINISTRATION; HEALTH SERVICES ADMINISTRATION; LABOR UNION ADMINISTRATION; SPORTS COACHING/ TRAINING/ MANAGING/ OFFICIATING)

Chao, Paul W. F.
Chhim, Him S.
Chung, Robert
Dalal, Siddhartha Ramanlal
Dinh, Steven M.
Do, Toa Quang
Gam, Paul Jonathan
Gin, Jerry B.
Hayakawa, Noboru
Huang, John Shiao-Shih
Hwang, Wei-Yuan
Jimenez, Josephine Santos
Lee, K. J.
Liou, Yihwa Irene
Liu, Edmund K.
Marumoto, William Hideo
Mehta, Amarjit
Mohanty, Sashi B.
Ni, Preston C.
Park, Hoon
Patel, Deepak M.
Patel, Ray L.
Rhee, Chase Chonggwang
Shah, Rajani C.
Sheu, Lien-Lung
Singh, Amarjit
Sohn, David Youngwhan
Teng, Lee Chang-Li
Trivedi-Doctor, Minakshi Dipak
Wang, Jia
Yang, Lang

MANUFACTURING— APPAREL

Chang, Elden T.
Chu, David
Fitzpatrick, Eileen Tabata
Mow, Bill
Shah, Amitkumar L.
Tran, Hong-Y Thi

MANUFACTURING— CHEMICALS AND ALLIED PRODUCTS

Advani, Suresh Gopaldas
Arif, Shoaib
Belbis, Manuel Emuslan
Bose, Pratim
Chan, David S.
Chang, Kelvin Yau-Min
Chang, Pei K.
Chen, George Chi-Ming
Chen, Michael Chia-Chao
Chen, Yih-Wen David
Chu, Nori Yaw-Chyuan
Chung, Frank Huan-Chen
Chung, Jesse Y. W.
Desai, Vikram J.
Dixit, Ajit S.
Fujioka, Takashi
Ghosh, Sujan
Gin, Jerry B.
Gupta, Rakesh Kumar
Gupta, Surendra K.

Iyengar, Doreswamy Raghavachar
Kashiwagi, Brian Rio
Khan, Shakil Ahmad
Kuo, Chung Ming
Kwok, Wo Kong
Lakshman, Govind
Lee, Ying K.
Leu, Dennis Thomas
Li, Ke Wen
Lin, Stephen Yaw-rui
Makino, Shojiro
Nguyen, Bong Van
Nguyen, Duc Ba
Pai, Venkatrao K.
Parikh, Hemant Bhupendra
Shah, Harnish V.
Shah, Nitin J.
Syal, Shanta
Tomomatsu, Hideo
Wei, Chao Hui
Wu, Ching-Yong
Yan, Tsoung-Yuan
Yau, Cheuk Chung
Yeh, Chien Jo

MANUFACTURING— DRUGS AND TOILETRIES

Arif, Shoaib
Banakar, Umesh Virupaksh
Bapatla, Krishna M.
Chao, Allen Y.
Chin, Tamera Ann
Chu, Daniel Tim-Wo
Dhruv, Arvind B.
Hsieh, Dean Shui-Tien
Hung, Paul P.
Jariwala, Sharad Lallubhai
Joshi, Mukund Shankar
Kumar, Saran Kandakuri
Matsumoto, Ken
Mong, Seymour
Patel, Kishor N.
Sharma, Shri C.
Singhvi, Sampat M.
Tsai, Gow-Jen
Tse, Francis Lai-Sing
Tung, Hsi-tang

MANUFACTURING— ELECTRICAL/ ELECTRONICS PRODUCTS

Chan, Chong B.
Chao, Stanley K.
Chen, Kenny T.
Chen, Wayne G.
Chen, Winston H.
Chiang, Ping-Wang
Chu, Nhan V.
Dang, Phu Ngoc
Das, Mohan N.
Dong, John W.
Higa, Walter Hiroichi
Hsu, Charles Jui-cheng
Hu, Daniel Ching
Huang, Charles
Kokan, Ghiasuddin
Lee, David Sen-Lin
Leung, Charles Cheung-Wan
Ling, Hung Chi
Liou, Ming Jaw
Liu, Yung Sheng
Lock, Chuck Choi
Ng, Patrick
Patel, Jayant P.
Patel, Mukesh M.
Patel, Roger
Pinto, James J.
Rao, Gopal Subba

Shankar, Subramonian
Sharma, Brij Lal
Shen, Hao-Ming
Shinsato, Francis G.
Takagi, Norio
Takahashi, Ken M.
Toyama, Frank Kenichi
Tran, Long Trieu
Wang, Stanley
Wong, Henry H.
Wu, George K.
Yiu, Pao On

MANUFACTURING— FOOD/BEVERAGES

Agrawal, Brijmohan
Chang, Pei K.
Chen, Li-Fu
Chowdhry, Vinay
Ghosh, Nimai Kumar
Hsu, Kenneth Hsuehchia
Huang, Victor Tsangmin
Kirchner, Bharti
Kobayashi, Jerry T.
Krishnaswamy, Rukmini
Lee, Chi-Hang
Lewis, Loida Nicolas
Ling, Matthew S.
Luh, Bor Shiun
Nguyen, Chris Cuong Manh
Pulijal, Madhu V.
Sabharwal, Kulbir
Sharma, Shri C.
Shim, Sook Chin
Tan, Lawrence W.
Tom, Ping
Tomomatsu, Hideo
Udani, Kanak H.
Vedamuthu, Ebenezer Rajkumar
Vora, Pramathesh S.
Wong, Karl

MANUFACTURING— FURNITURE/ FIXTURES

Labasan, Alejandro B.

MANUFACTURING— INDUSTRIAL/ COMMERCIAL MACHINERY

Bhatia, Ramesh
Hsieh, Brian
Kimura, Kolin M.
Koh, Kwang K.
Matsuoka, James Toshio
Myint, Than Htun
Patel, Mukul B.
Sinha, Nirmal K.
Wang, Lily L.

MANUFACTURING— METALWORKING INDUSTRIES

Bai, Shen Hum
Desai, Chandra
Desai, Suresh A.
Doshi, Bipin N.
Gupta, Kamla P.
Hagiwara, Kokichi
Hoang, Frank H.
Jain, Sulekh Chand
Kakkar, Subash
Kato, Masatoshi
Kumar, Vijay A.
Lee, Peter Wankyoon
Ling, Paul
Lo, Tou Ger
Mathur, Achint P.

Nandkumar, Nuggehalli Balmukund
Ohta, Shirley Mae
Palamand, Krishna
Sakai, Michael H.
Saluja, Jagdish Kumar
Seki, Akiro
Shankar, Srinivasan
Sun, Richard C.
Tang, America
Toyama, Frank Kenichi
Wang, Charles Chen-ding
Wang, Chih-Chung

MANUFACTURING— MOTOR VEHICLES

Brown, Julie
Cabanting, George Paul
Chen, Ming Chih
Chowdhury, Nazmul A.
Hang, Tru
Hayakawa, Noboru
Kaul, Pradaman
Wang, Dazong
Wong, Backman
Woo, Benson K.

MANUFACTURING— PAPER AND ALLIED PRODUCTS

Dixit, Ajit S.
Ghosh, Bivas Kanti
Godsay, Madhu P.
Huang, Denis K.
Jain, Sushil C.
Kawahara, William T.
Mehta, Kailash
Mehta, Mahendra
Rao, Barry

MANUFACTURING— TEXTILE MILL PRODUCTS

Abraham, John
Chang, David Hsiang
Chen, Le Chun
Dixit, Sudhakar Gajanan

MANUFACTURING— NOT ELSEWHERE CLASSIFIED

Akiyoshi, Mike M.
Chang, Byung Jin
Chang, Charles Hung
Chung, Jesse Y. W.
Daga, Raman Lall
Desai, Hiren Sharad
Desai, Suresh A.
Doi, Stanley T.
Eng, Henry
Garg, Devendra
Hashimoto, Akira
Hsu, Charles Jui-cheng
Kadowaki, Joe George
Kashiwa, Hank Charles
Kawashima, Edith T.
Kim, James Joo-Jin
Lai, Kuo-Yann
Lee, Albert W.
Lin, Chengmin Michael
Maeda, Yutaka
Matsuoka, Matthew S.
Mehra, Ravinder C.
Motilall, Makeshwar Fip
Ong, Owh Kian
Ota, Dean
Pande, Gyan Shanker
Ru, Wesley
Sehgal, Raj K.

Singh, Prithipal
Song, John S.
Syal, Shanta
Thangaraj, Sandy
Tse, Ming-Kai
Vora, Narendra Mohanlal
Wang, Chih-Chung
Wang, Dora Chia-Chi
Wang, Stanley

MARKETING
SEE ADVERTISING/
PROMOTION;
MANAGEMENT/
ADMINISTRATION—
ADVERTISING/
MARKETING/PUBLIC
RELATIONS

MATHEMATICS
Abhyankar, Shreeram Shankar
Agarwal, Arun Kumar
Ahluwalia, Daljit Singh
An, Myoung Hee
Azumaya, Goro
Bagga, K. Jay Singh
Bowman, Kimiko O.
Cai, Jin-Yi
Chakravarthy, Srinivasaraghavan
Chan, Chiu Yeung
Chan, Jack-Kang
Chan, Kwok Hung
Chan, Tat-Hung
Chang, Jane Yueh
Chang, Jeffrey Chit-Fu
Chang, Mou-Hsiung
Chen, Bang-Yen
Chen, Bintong
Chen, Guanrong
Chen, Wenxiong
Cheng, Charles Ching-an
Cheo, Li-hsiang S.
Chiang, Yi-ling F.
Chin, William Nigel
Choi, Jai Won
Chopra, Dharam Vir
Chou, Arthur W.
Chow, Bob Ching-Hong
Chui, Charles K.
Dalal, Siddhartha Ramanlal
D'Souza, Harry J.
Fu, Jyun-Horng
Ghosh, Bhaskar Kumar
Govil, Narendra Kumar
Govindarajulu, Zakkula
Hahn, Hwa Suk
Hahn, Liang-Shin
Hayashi, Elmer Kinji
Hayashi, Masato
Ho, Chung-Wu
Ho, Lop-Hing
Hong, Weihu
Hong, Yoopyo
Hsieh, Philip Po-Fang
Hsu, Nai-chao
Huang, Cheng-Chi
Huang, Jiann-Shiun
Huang, Xun-Cheng
Jain, Surender K.
Jayachandran, Toke
Jen, Horatio H.
Kapoor, Jagmohan
Kato, Goro
Kato, Tosio
Kattakuzhy, George Chacko
Katti, Shriniwas K.
Kim, Ki Hang
Kim, Saeja Oh
Kim, Soon-Kyu
Ku, Mei-Chin Hsiao
Kuan, Wei Eihn

Kulkarni, Krishnaji Hanamant
Kulkarni, Ravi S.
Kumar, Ashok
Lam, Fat C.
Lao, Chang S.
Lee, Heakyung
Lee, Tzesan David
Li, Dening
Li, Guodong
Li, Jia
Li, Kuiyuan
Li, Peter Wai-Kwong
Li, Tien-Yien
Li, Wu
Li, Ya
Liao, Ming
Lin, Chia Chiao
Lin, James Peicheng
Lin, Kai-Ching
Lin, Xiao-Song
Liu, Jun S.
Liu, Thomas Jyhcheng
Liu, Wei-Min
Liu, Yung-Way
Lu, Kau U.
Luh, Jiang
Luong, Son N.
Ma, Xiaoyun
Malhotra, Vijay K.
Man, Chi-Sing
Morizumi, S. James
Mukherjea, Arunava
Nam, Sangboo
Nguyen, Bao Gia
Nguyen, Chuong Van
Ong, Sing-Cheong
Onishi, Hironori
Pao, Chia-Ven
Park, Won J.
Peng, Chang-Shyh
Puri, Pratap
Ramaswami, Vaidyanathan
Reddy, Pannala Sathyanahayana
Roy, Dev Kumar
Sakhare, Vishwa M.
Saxena, Subhash Chandra
Sha, Ji-Ping
Shah, Ghulam Mohammad
Sharma, Bhudev
Sharma, Ramesh
Sharma, Saroj
Shieh, Rong Chung
Siu, Yum-Tong
Srivastava, Sadanand
Suen, Ching-Yun
Sun, Hugo Sui-Hwan
Tam, Christopher Kwong-Wah
Tan, Cheng-Pheng
Tan, Sinforosa G.
Tewarson, Reginald P.
Tikoo, Mohan L.
Tong, Ts'ing H.
Tsai, Chester
Vyas, Udaykumar Dayalal
Wan, Frederic Yui-Ming
Wan, James X.
Wang, Alan P.
Wang, Dajin
Wang, Junping
Wang, Stuart Sui-Sheng
Wang, Tixiang
Wang, Xuefeng
Wang, Zhi Qiang
Wen, Shih-liang
Wong, Bing K.
Wong, James H.
Wong, Pui Kei
Wong, Raymond Y.
Wong, William Wai-Lun
Wu, De Ting
Wu, Hung-Hsi
Wu, Julian Juh-Ren
Wu, Tiee-Jian

Wu, Xian
Wu, Zhijian
Xu, Chia-Yi
Yan, Joseph Gea-Gue
Yang, Kichoon
Yang, Song
Yang, Yisong
Yang, Zhanbo
Yau, Stephen Shing-Toung
Yee, Donald Poy
Yin, Gang George
Yin, Mark Y. Q.
Yu, Kai Fun

MEDICINE—
ANESTHESIOLOGY
Arakawa, Kasumi
Chen, Bessie B.
Chen, Henry
Cheng, Eugene Y.
Deol, Harjyot
Fung, Dennis Lung
Gupta, Bhagwandas
Huh, Billy K.
Ikeda, Shigemasa
Lau, Leslie
Oh, Tae Hee
Patel, Kalyani
Shah, Narendra N.
Shevde, Ketan
Su, Judy Ya-Hwa Lin
Vaidya, Kirit Rameshchandra
Wong, Kuang Chung
Wu, Nancy Nan-hwa

MEDICINE—
CARDIOLOGY
Ahmed, Shaikh Sultan
Arakawa, Kasumi
Chen, Henry J.
Chung, Edward K.
Fong, Bernard Wah Doung
Fukushima, Eiichi
Fung, Gordon L.
Goto, Unoji
Grewal, Perminder Singh
Han, Jaok
Hsia, Judith Ann
Jain, Ashit
Jain, Savitri
Jan, Kung-ming
Kao, Race L.
Kashyap, Moti Lal
Kaul, Sanjiv
Khaw, Ban-An
Kim, Il Young
Liang, Bruce T.
Liang, Chang-seng
Liu, Maw-Shung
Liu, Si-kwang
Louie, Eric K.
Low, Randall
Lu, David Yun-Chen
Maj, Naweed K.
Mehta, Ashok V.
Mehta, Jawahar L.
Nair, Chandra K.
Nair, V. Krishnan
Nakano, Frank Hiroshi
Nanda, Navin Chandar
Pak, Peter Hui-Mun
Reddy, Pradeep K.
Rustagi, Ravinder Kumar
Sasahara, Arthur Asao
Shah, Naren N.
Subramaniam, Pramilla N.
Takahashi, Masato
Wang, Yang
Yeh, Billy Kuo-Jiun

MEDICINE—
DERMATOLOGY
Ahmed, A. Razzaque
Chen, Virginia L.
Chow, Edmund Chun-Ying
Eng, Ana Mar
Hashimoto, Ken
Iwamoto, Satori
Kim, Robert
Liang, Tehming
Loo, Cyrus W.
Sun, Tung-Tien
Uno, Hideo

MEDICINE—FAMILY
PRACTICE
Anand, Rakesh
Flemming, Stanley Lalit Kumar
Kumar, Surendra Mohan
Liu, Mini
Muriera, Helen Bautista
Ng, Richard Yut
Patel, Bharat R.
Shah, Sarju S.
Szeto, Erik K.
Walia, Harjeet Rosie
Yee, Walter
Yep, Ralph Lee

MEDICINE—INTERNAL
MEDICINE
Arora, Madan Lal
Chan, Laurence Kwong-Fai
Chang, Te-Wen
Chaudhari, Shobhana Ashok
Chiu, Ming S.
Chopra, Inder Jit
Chopra, Rajbir Singh
Chou, Ching-Chung
Choy, Wanda Wai Ying
Chung, Edward K.
Desai, Sudhir G.
Domoto, Douglass T.
Flores, Susan Gumabao
Fong, Bernard Wah Doung
Fu, LiMin
Fujimoto, Wilfred Yorio
Gopalakrishna, K. V.
Goto, Unoji
Gupta, Krishan L.
Gupta, Sanjeev
Gupta, Surendra Kumar
Hayashi, Mie May
Jain, Ashit
Jain, Jitender K.
Jain, Rajeev K.
Jain, Savitri
Jan, Kung-ming
Kashyap, Moti Lal
Kaul, Sanjiv
Khanna, Ramesh
Kim, Jong Koo
Kim, Suzy Linda
Ko, Bing H.
Koide, Samuel Saburo
Krishnamurthy, Gerbail T.
Kundu, Bejoy B.
Kwon, Ronald Chi-Oh
Lai, Amy
Landero, Reynaldo Rivera, II
Lew, Susie Q.
Li, William Wei-Lin
Lian, Eric Chun-Yet
Liang, Matthew H.
Liu, Pinghui Victor
Louie, Eric K.
Louie, James Sam
Low, Randall
Mai, Hugh D.
Mantil, Joseph Chacko
Margallo, Lucio N., II

Mehta, Sunil Kumar
Mian, Waqar Saeed
Nakano, Frank Hiroshi
Narahara, Hiromichi T.
Nguyen, Dung Dang
Pandya, Deepak N.
Quismorio, Francisco P., Jr.
Rao, Angara Koneti
Rao, T. K. Sreepada
Sasahara, Arthur Asao
Sathyavagiswaran, Lakshmanan
Shah, Minal J.
Shiang, Elaine
Silao, Ray A.
Singh, Sant P.
Siy, James Andrew
Somani, Pitambar
Subramaniam, Pramilla N.
Sugihara, Jared Genji
Suh, Byungse
Takeshita, Kenichi
Tan, S. Y.
Tanaka, Kouichi Robert
Teng, Hsi Ching
Trivedi, Nayana Mohan
Tsai, Jir-Shiong
Tsai, Mark F.
Tsan, Min-Fu
Wang, Ping H.
Wang, Robert T.
Whang, Robert
Wu, Anna Fang
Wu, Wallace C.
Yang, Karl L.
Yeh, Billy Kuo-Jiun
Yu, Victor Lin-Kai
Yung, W. K. Alfred

MEDICINE—
NEUROLOGY
Ahluwalia, Brij Mohan Singh
Chow, Kao Liang
Fujikawa, Denson Gen
Gonzalez-Pardo, Lillian
Hirano, Asao
Ho, Khang-cheng
Hwang, Te-Long
Iqbal, Zafar
Kishimoto, Yasuo
Ling, Alexander
Pandya, Deepak N.
Shin, In-Sook Jeong
Verma, Ajay
Yung, W. K. Alfred

MEDICINE—
OBSTETRICS/
GYNECOLOGY
Dinh, Tung Van
Foong, Nicolai Yein
Hayashi, Robert H.
Kim, Moon H.
Ko, Cheng Chia Charles
Lin, Chin-Chu
Sharma, Santosh Devraj
Umali, Filemon J.
Varma, Usha
Wan, Stephen Samkong
Wu, Chung-Hsiu

MEDICINE—
OPHTHALMOLOGY
Chin, Patrick K.
Fong, Raymond
Ing, Malcolm Ross
Kinoshita, Jin H.
Ko, William Weng-Ping
Kwon, Young Ha
Lee, King Y.
Patel, Anil S.

Tripathi, Ramesh Chandra
Wong, Wendell P.
Yau, King-Wai
Yee, Robert Donald

MEDICINE— PATHOLOGY
Ahmed, A. Razzaque
Asuncion, Alfredo, Jr.
Bagasra, Omar
Bhaskar, Surindar Nath
Chang, Louis Wai-Wah
Chang, William Wei-Lien
Chen, Thomas Shih-Nien
Cho, Eun-Sook
Chung, Ed Baik
Chuong, Cheng-Ming
Dalal, Fram R.
Dao, Anh Huu
Dhurandhar, Nina R.
Dinh, Tung Van
Eng, Lawrence Fook
Hirano, Asao
Ho, Khang-cheng
Hokama, Yoshitsugi
Hsu, Konrad Chang
Hyun, Bong Hak
Joshi, Sewa Ram
Kan-Mitchell, June
Kim, Han-Seob
Kim, Kitai
Krishnan, Gopal
Kumar, Kusum
Lau, Peter Man-Yiu
Lee, Shuishih Sage
Lee, Tung-Kwang
Liu, Si-kwang
Nahm, Moon H.
Omori, Alvin I.
Ou, Ching-Nan
Patnaik, Amiya K.
Phan, Sem Hin
Prabhudesai, Mukund M.
Prasad, Rameshwar
Quismorio, Francisco P., Jr.
Rao, Angara Koneti
Rao, Gundu H. R.
Rasheed, Suraiya
Roy-Burman, Pradip
Sarkar, Fazlul H.
Sathyavagiswaran, Lakshmanan
Shah, Sheila
Sharma, Hari M.
Shieh, Wun-Ju
Song, Joseph M.
Takeda, Yasuhiko
Tang, Chik-Kwun
Tang, Thomas Tze-Tung
Tripathi, Ramesh Chandra
Uno, Hideo
Venkataramanan, Raman
Vyas, Girish N.
Wang, Helen Hai-ling
Wei, Wei-Zen
Whang, Sukoo Jack
Wong, David Tai Wai
Yen, Tien-Sze Benedict

MEDICINE— PEDIATRICS
Chacko, Mariam Renate
Chan, Gary M.
Chan, James C. M.
Chang, Albert
Chaudhari, Shobhana Ashok
Chen, Su-chiung
Chopra, Joginder
Chun, Raymond W. M.
Deol, Harjyot
Evangelista, Stella
Fong, Jack Sun-Chik

Fu, Paul Chung, Jr.
Ghim, Thad T.
Gonzalez-Pardo, Lillian
Hara, Saburo
Hoo, Joe-Jie
Huang, Shih-Wen
Jung, Lawrence Kwok Leung
Kim, Haewon Chang
Kumar, Ashir
Lam, Toan Hoang
Lee, Susan H.
Mehta, Ashok V.
Mody, Mukund V.
Park, Myung Kun
Patel, Pratibha A.
Pui, Ching-Hon
Reddy, Churku Mohan
Shim, Walton Kenn Tsung
Soo Hoo, Karen
Takahashi, Masato
Tang, Thomas Tze-Tung
Tsai, Theodore F.
Uyeda, Clifford I.
Wong, Doris Ning
Wong, Paul Wing Kon
Yamauchi, Toshio
Yang, Yih-Ming
Yeh, Timothy S.
Yu, Alice L.

MEDICINE— PSYCHIATRY
Bolen, Jean Shinoda
Chacko, Ranjit C.
Chan, Carlyle Hung-lun
Choksi, Jayendra C.
Chuang, De-Maw
Hsu, Timothy
Husain, Mustafa Mahmood
Iwamoto, Satori
Kim, Kathleen M.
Kim, Wun Jung
Pang, Keum Y.
Park, Seung-Kyoon
Sikand, Chander Kumari
Tan, Tjiauw-Ling
Tsai, Michael Ming-Ping
Tsuang, Ming T.
Verma, Anil K.
Wang, Ging-Long
Yung, Christoph Yingwai

MEDICINE— RADIOLOGY
Chaudhuri, Tapan K.
Chen, Michael Y. M.
Cheung, Luke P.
Cho, Zang-Hee
Chuang, Vincent P.
Ho, Xuan Michael
Joe, Clarence
Kartha, Mukund K.
Kumar, Prasanna K.
Kuroda, Koson
Lee, Kyo Rak
Lee, Tung-Kwang
Lin, Eva I.
Lin, Hsiu-San
Lin, Joseph Pen-Tze
Liu, Te-Hua
Mothkur, Sridhar Rao
Ng, Anastacio C.
Nguyen, Vung Duy
Pak, Koon Yan
Pien, Edward H.
Pujara, Subhash Somabhai
Reddy, Eashwer K.
Rishi, Satchidanand Raam
Shah, Dhiraj Harilal
Shetty, Anil N.
Shin, Myung Soo

Thakore, Killol J.
Urano, Muneyasu
Yao, Dorcas C.
Yoon, Hyo-Chun
Yune, Heun Yung

MEDICINE—SURGERY
Chan, Donald P. K.
Chandra Sekhar, Hosakere K.
Chang, Jack H. T.
Chatterjee, Satya N.
Diokno, Ananias Cornejo
Kao, Race L.
Koh, Kilsan
Ku, David Nelson
Kuo, Ken Nan
Lee, Bradford Young
Lee, Hyung Mo
Lee, K. J.
Lee, Wei-ping Andrew
Lee, Yeu-Tsu Margaret
Liao, Shun-Kwung
Ling, Alexander
Lowe, Rolland Choy
Lum, Sharon Shou Jen
Maj, Naweed K.
Matsumoto, Teruo
Mehta, Mehul Mansukh
Montero, Juan Murillo, II
Patel, Dinesh
Raju, Seshadri
Ramachandra, Srinivas R.
Reyes, Hernan M.
Rhee, Young Eun
Sakurai, Fred Yutaka
Sharma, Mutyam V.
Shim, Walton Kenn Tsung
Teramoto, Yoshitsugu
Todo, Satoru
Tu, Harold Kai
Turek, Laura Kim
Wang, Gwo-Jaw
Wang, Shen K.
Watanabe, Robert
Wong, Bradley D.
Wongananda, Boondharm
Young, Shun Chung
Yuan, Robin Tsu-Wang

MEDICINE—NOT ELSEWHERE CLASSIFIED (*SEE ALSO* PHARMACY; VETERINARY MEDICINE)
Agrawal, Krishna Chandra
Aoki, Thomas T.
Aviado, Domingo M.
Bhatnagar, Kunwar P.
Cai, Shelton Xuanqing
Chan, Arthur Wing Kay
Chan, Wai-Yee
Chang, Paul Steven
Chaudhuri, Tapan K.
Chen, Edward C. H.
Chen, Jackson W.
Cheng, Eugene Y.
Cheung, Joseph Y.
Chi, David Shyh-Wei
Chin, Donald G.
Chiu, John T.
Chiu, Tin-Ho
Choi, Eung Ryong
Chopra, Deepak
Chu-Andrews, Jennifer
Chung, Tae-Soo
Chuong, Cheng-Ming
Cueto, Alex
Datta, Syamal K.
Desai, Sudhir G.

Desai, Vijay
Domoto, Douglass T.
Dung, Hou Chi
Farhataziz
Fu, Karen K.
Gandhi, Vikram H.
Gopalakrishna, K. V.
Gupta, Manjula K.
Gupta, Surendra Kumar
Ho, Reginald C. S.
Hoo, Joe-Jie
Huang, Shih-Wen
Inagami, Tadashi
Jain, Jitender K.
Jain, Rajeev K.
Jiang, Nai-Siang
Kartha, Mukund K.
Kashyap, Pankaj Kumar
Kaul, Balkrishena
Kim, Sung Wan
Kim, Young Chan
Kobayashi, John M.
Krishnamurthy, Gerbail T.
Kumar, Narinder M.
Kumar, Vipin
Kwon, Ronald Chi-Oh
Landero, Reynaldo Rivera, II
Lau, Bennett M. K.
Lee, Bradford Young
Lee, Chi-Jen
Lee, Ju-Cheon
Lee, Susan H.
Lee, Yeu-Tsu Margaret
Leung, Peter
Liang, Matthew H.
Lim, David J.
Loo, Ti Li
Louie, Emma Woo
Maj, Naweed K.
Mehta, Bharat V.
Mehta, Rajendra G.
Mudundi, Ramakrishna Raju
Naito, Herbert K.
Narahara, Hiromichi T.
Narahashi, Toshio
Ngor, Haing S.
Nori, Dattatreyudu
Ohashi, Wataru
Panlilio, Adelisa Lorna
Park, Tae Sung
Patel, Appasaheb R.
Patel, Bharat R.
Patel, Dinesh
Prabhu, R. D.
Pujara, Subhash Somabhai
Ramachandra, Srinivas R.
Rana, Mohammed Waheed-uz-Zaman
Reddy, Bandaru S.
Rhim, Johng Sik
Saha, Gopal Bandhu
Seth, Arun K.
Seto, Belinda P.
Seto, Joseph Tobey
Shah, Nandlal Chimanlal
Shaikh, Abdul Hamid
Shaikh, Zahir A.
Sharma, Hari M.
Sharma, Mutyam V.
Sharma, Satanand
Shevde, Ketan
Shih, Tsung-Ming Anthony
Shukla, Shivendra D.
Soo Hoo, Eric Randolph
Suzuki, Howard Kazuro
Sy, Francisco S.
Tan, Mary
Tang, Andrew Hing-Yee
Tsai, Jen-San
Tsai, Mark F.
Tu, Samson W.
Urano, Muneyasu
Verma, Ram Sagar

Wang, Carl C. T.
Wang, Ching-Hua
Wang, Hsueh-Hwa
Wang, Ping H.
Wong, Eugene G. C.
Wong, Terry Chen Yi
Yee, Wilfred Wee Bin
Yu, Jen
Yu, Victor Lin-Kai
Yue, David T.

METEOROLOGY
Chang, Ping
Chen, Yi-Leng
Das, Phanindramohan
Huang, Joseph Chi Kan
Krishnamurti, T. N.
Kumai, Motoi
Lau, Ngar-Cheung
Lin, Yeong-Jer
Lin, Yuh-Lang
Liou, Kuo-Nan
Manabe, Syukuro
Miyakoda, Kikuro
Ohtake, Takeshi
Ou, Hsien-Wang
Ramanathan, Veerabhadran
Rao, Gandikota Venkata
Sun, Wen-Yih
Tam, Francis Man Kei
Tang, Wen
Vernekar, Anandu Devarao
Wang, Bin
Wang, Jen-Yu
Wang, Pao-Kuan

MICROBIOLOGY
SEE BIOLOGY/ MICROBIOLOGY

MILITARY—AIR FORCE
Chong, Timothy
Dhillon, Joginder Singh
Sampang, Conrado Carriedo
Sheikh, Ghafoor A.
Tran, Tri K.
Tun, Harry T.
Wong, Harry Yuen Chee

MILITARY—ARMY
Chang, Paul Steven
Fugh, John L.
Miura, George Akio
Takakoshi, William K.
Yonamine, Henry Kiyoshi

MILITARY—COAST GUARD
Watanabe, Clyde Kazuto

MILITARY—MARINE CORPS
Wong, David Craig
Wong, George

MILITARY—NATIONAL GUARD
Chin, Robert Allen

MILITARY—NAVY
Alota, Ruben Villaruel

MILITARY—NOT ELSEWHERE CLASSIFIED
Omata, Robert Rokuro

MINING/QUARRYING
(*SEE ALSO* ENGINEERING— MINING)
Ghosh, Amitava

MOTOR VEHICLE INDUSTRY
SEE MANUFACTURING— MOTOR VEHICLES; RETAIL TRADE— MOTOR VEHICLES, PARTS, AND SERVICES; WHOLESALE TRADE— MOTOR VEHICLES AND PARTS

MOVING SERVICES
SEE TRANSPORTATION/ MOVING SERVICES

MUSEUM ADMINISTRATION/ EDUCATION
SEE GALLERY/ MUSEUM ADMINISTRATION/ EDUCATION

MUSIC—COMPOSING/ SONGWRITING
Chang, Marian S.
Chin, Charlie William David
Cung, Tien Thuc
Hashimoto, Steven George
Ho, Fred Wei-han
Ho, Ting
Horiuchi, Glenn
Hsiao, Tyzen
Hsieh, Durwynne
Iwataki, David Michael
Jang, Jon
Kim, Byong-Kon
Liu, Zhuang
Masaoka, Miya Joan
Matsui, Keiko
Nagatani, Scott A.
Ono, Yoko
Sheng, Bright
Shimamoto, Scott Seiya
Tana, Akira
Villa-Real, Olivia Canchela
Yen, Wen-Hsiung
Yuasa, Joji

MUSIC—CONDUCTING/ DIRECTING
Chang, Warren W.
Chen, Donald S.
Chi, Jacob
Dang, Harish C.
Hsiao, Tyzen
Hsu, John Tseng-Hsiu
Huang, Zhen-Fen
Kim, Byong-Kon
Mehta, Zubin
Nagano, Kent George
Nagatani, Scott A.
Ozawa, Seiji

Sheng, Bright
Wada, Toshimasa Francis
Wong, Samuel T.

MUSIC— INSTRUMENTAL
Chan, Timothy T.
Chi, Jacob
Hashimoto, Eiji
Hashimoto, Steven George
Ho, Fred Wei-han
Horiuchi, Glenn
Hsieh, Li-Ping
Hsu, Samuel
Iwataki, David Michael
Jang, Jon
Lau, Frederick C.
Li, Bichuan
Li, Hanna Wu
Long, Grace Fan
Lum, Tammy Kar-Hee
Ma, Yo-Yo
Masaoka, Miya Joan
Matsui, Keiko
Midori
Nagatani, Scott A.
Sato, Keiko
Sheng, Bright
Singha, Nabaghana Shyam
Sumida, Jon Tetsuro
Tabuchi, Shoji
Takenaka, Makoto B.
Tana, Akira
Tanaka, Ty Skip
Tsang, Bion Yu-Ting
Uchimura, Bruce Jiro
Villa-Real, Olivia Canchela
Wang, Shi-Hwa
Wang, Sylvia
Whang, Un-Young
Wong, Alexius Yu-Ming

MUSIC—VOCAL
Florentino, Leila San Jose
Hsieh, Li-Ping
Kaneko, Ryoji Lloyd
Kim, Youngsuk
Ono, Yoko
Pang, Wilma
Rivers, Mavis
Salonga, Lea
Shimamoto, Scott Seiya
Tanaka, Ty Skip
Villa-Real, Olivia Canchela
Wang, Sue S.
Yang, Schuman Chuo

MUSIC—NOT ELSEWHERE CLASSIFIED
Chou, Leland L. C.
Furuta, Karin L.
Jang, Jon
Lau, Frederick C.
Murata, Margaret K.
Tsang, Bion Yu-Ting
Watanabe, Yuki
Wong, Deborah Anne

NURSING
Aslam, Nasim Mohammed
Baldonado, Ardelina Albano
Barron, Purificacion C.
Chen, Angela Tzu-Yau
Cheng, Nancy C.
Compas, Lolita Burgos
Ishida, Dianne N.
Kim, Hesook Suzie
Kokatnur, Mohan Gundo

Louie, Emma Woo
Lum, Jean L. J.
Mathew, Valsa
Pang, Keum Y.
Pang, Seng Puang
Sasaki, Chiyo Katano
Shim, Sook Chin
Simunek, Linda A.
Tana, Phongpan
Tran, Dorothy N.
Wu, Chien-yun
Yang, Emiko
Yee, Virginia Bow Sue
Yep, Ralph Lee

NUTRITION
Bhathena, Sam Jehangirji
Bhattacharyya, Ashim Kumar
Chan, Gary M.
Chang, Kow-Ching
Chen, Linda Li-yueh
Chen, Tung-Shan
Cheryan, Munir
Chi, Myung Sun
Chiba, Lee I.
Chopra, Joginder
Chu, Elizabeth Chan
Chung, Ronald Aloysius
Dash, Sita K.
Fung, Daniel Yee Chak
Ho, Chi-Tang
Jeevanandam, Malayappa
Kakkar, Rita
Lim, Chhorn E.
Lingappa, Banadakoppa Thimmappa
Mathur, Kailash V.
Mohan, Chandra
Nakamoto, Tetsuo
Ranhotra, Gurbachan S.
Rao, Ananda G.
Sachan, Dileep Singh
Sakai, Victoria K.
Salunkhe, Dattajeerao K.
Sundaresan, P. Ramnathan
Taira, Masa Morioka
Tan, Barrie
Tseng, Rose Y. L.
Verma, Ajit K.
Wong, William Wai-Lun
Wu, Yao Hua
Yang, Chung S.
Young, Franklin

OCEANOGRAPHY
Bhatt, Jagdish J.
Chan, Kwan M.
Chang, Ping
Chen, Chin
Chu, Peter Cheng
Huang, Joseph Chi Kan
Ichiye, Takashi
Kuo, Albert Yi-shuong
Lee, Richard Fayao
Lin, Jian
Mahadevan, Kumar
Miyakoda, Kikuro
Morita, Richard Yukio
Ono, Richard Dana
Ou, Hsien-Wang
Takahashi, Kozo
Takahashi, Taro
Wang, Bin
Wang, Dong-Ping

OPTOMETRY
Fong, Joshua
Mai, Marianne Vu
Matsumoto, Donald Michiaki
Wong, Siu G.

PERSONNEL MANAGEMENT
SEE MANAGEMENT/ ADMINISTRATION— PERSONNEL/ TRAINING/LABOR RELATIONS

PHARMACOLOGY
Ahn, Ho-Sam
Alvares, Alvito P.
Aviado, Domingo M.
Chiang, Soong T.
Dwivedi, Chandradhar
Farooqui, Mohammed Y. H.
Hsieh, Dean Shui-Tien
Jagadeesh, G.
Kulkarni, Arun P.
Kuwahara, Steven Sadao
Lee, Chiho
Lee, Jang Yun
Lee, Tony J. F.
Liu, Ching-Tong
Nuon, Samuel
Okita, George Torao
Parikh, Indu
Parkhie, Mukund R.
Pong, Schwe Fang
Shih, Tsung-Ming Anthony
Su, Judy Ya-Hwa Lin
Tam, Sang William
Yu, Jia-Huey

PHARMACY
Agrawal, Brijmohan
Banakar, Umesh Virupaksh
Bapatla, Krishna M.
Bhagat, Hitesh Rameshchandra
Chang, Ching-jer
Chattopadhyay, Kallol
Chiang, Chao-Kuo
Chien, Yie W.
Chin, John Way
Choi, Sung Sook
Chu, Chung Kwang
Dinh, Steven M.
Dwivedi, Chandradhar
Fong, Harry H. S.
Fung, Ho-Leung
Gupta, Pardeep K.
Hsieh, Dean Shui-Tien
Jindal, Om P.
Jun, Hung Won
Kabadi, Balachandra Narayan
Kanojia, Ramesh Maganlal
Khaw, Ban-An
Kim, Sung Wan
Kumar, Saran Kandakuri
Kwon, Jeffrey Young
Lam, Gilbert Nim-Car
Lee, Jang Yun
Lee, Soo See
Lu, Donghao Robert
Min, David Ilki
Mong, Seymour
Nahata, Milap Chand
Pai, Sadanand V.
Patel, Jitendra B
Patel, Nagin K.
Patil, Popat N.
Pham, Hung Do
Quon, Shun Wing
Rahman, Yueh-Erh
Reddy, Indra Karan
Sehgal, Raj K.
Shaikh, Zahir A.
Sharma, Shri C.
Suryanarayanan, Raj Gopalan
Tai, Hsin-Hsiung
Tan, Henry S. I.
Tang, Lillian Y. D.

Tran, Thuan Van
Tse, Francis Lai-Sing
Ueda, Clarence Tad
Venkataramanan, Raman
Wang, Ji-Ping
Winick, Tranquilina Rios
Wong, David Taiwai
Wu, Wu-Nan
Yang, Victor Chi-Min
Yee, Allen Y.
Young, Lloyd Yee

PHILANTHROPY
Hayslip, Le Ly
Mathur, Balbir Singh
Matsui, Doris Kazue Okada
Natividad, Irene
Yamamori, Tetsunao
Yuchengco, Mona Lisa Sycip

PHOTOGRAPHY
(*SEE ALSO* JOURNALISM— PHOTOJOURNALISM)
Chin, Alice L.
Dominh, Thap
Endo, Paula Sayoko Tsukamoto
Gee, Zand F.
Hayashi, Masumi
Koga, Mary H.
Kuo, Nina L.
Ohtake, Takeshi
Quan, Hanson Wayne
Ravindran, Nair N.
Tsuha, Wallace Koichi
Wang, Samuel T. M.

PHYSICS/ASTRONOMY
Abbas, Mian M.
Achar, Narahari B. N.
Aggarwal, Ishwar D.
Aggarwal, Manmohan D.
Aggarwal, Roshan Lal
Ahluwalia, Harjit Singh
Akkapeddi, Prasad Rao
Albano, Alfonso M.
Anandan, Munisamy
Arakawa, Edward Takashi
Ashtekar, Abhay Vasant
Atoji, Masao
Au, Chi-Kwan
Bai, Taeil Albert
Bak, Chan Soo
Bhattacharya, Rabi Sankar
Biswas, Nripendra Nath
Bulsara, Ardeshir Ratan
Chai, An-Ti
Chakrabarti, Supriya
Chan, Chun Kin
Chandrasekhar, Subrahmanyan
Chang, Cheng-Hui
Chang, Chia-Cheh
Chang, Chuan Chung
Chang, Darwin
Chang, Edward Shih-Tou
Chang, Jhy-Jiun
Chang, Kern K. N.
Chang, Ngee-Pong
Chang, Ren-Fang
Chang, Shau-Jin
Chang, Yia-Chung
Chaturvedi, Ram Prakash
Chaudhari, Praveen
Chen, Augustine Cheng-Hsin
Chen, Chung-Hsuan
Chen, Francis F.
Chen, Tuan Wu
Chen, Zhong-Ying
Cheng, Andrew F.
Cheng, Ta-Pei

Cheung, Lim H.
Chiang, Chwan K.
Chien, Chia-Ling
Chien, Chih-Yung
Chin, Ken K.
Ching, Wai-Yim
Chiu, Victor
Cho, Zang-Hee
Chopra, Dev Raj
Chou, Mei-Yin
Choudhury, A. Latif
Chow, Brian Gee-Yin
Chow, Paul Chuan-Juin
Chowdhury, Dipak Kumar
Chu, Ching-Wu
Chu, Paul Ching-Wu
Chu, Wei-Kan
Chu, William Tongil
Chuang, Tze-jer
Chung, David Yih
Chung, Kwong T.
Das, Phanindramohan
Deshpande, Nilendra Ganesh
Dutta, Mitra
Dutta, Pulak
Erramilli, Shyamsunder
Fan, Chang-Yun
Fang, Frank F.
Fang, Ming M.
Feng, Guofu Jeff
Feng, Jonathan Lee
Fukushima, Eiichi
Fung, Sun-Yiu
Garg, Umesh
Ghosh, Amal K.
Gupta, Yogendra Mohan
Hahn, Yukap
Halemane, Thirumala Raya
Han, Moo-Young
Han, Xianming Lance
Higa, Walter Hiroichi
Ho, John Ting-Sum
Hong, Daniel Chonghan
Hsu, Frank H.
Hsu, Jong-Ping
Hsu, Shaw Ling
Hu, Bambi
Hu, Bei-Lok Bernard
Hu, Chia-Ren
Huang, Cheng-Cher
Huang, Huey-Wen
Huang, Jacob Wen-Kuang
Huang, Jin
Huang, John Shiao-Shih
Huang, Ming-Hui
Huang, Weifeng
Hussain, Riaz
Huynh, Boi-Hanh
Ijaz, Lubna Razia
Inokuti, Mitio
Ito, Mark Mitsuo
Iyer, Prem Shankar
Jain, Piyare Lal
Jen, Chih Kung
Jena, Purusottam
Ji, Chueng Ryong
Kagiwada, Harriet H. Natsuyama
Kaita, Robert
Kaku, Michio
Kan, Kit-Keung
Kang, Joonhee
Kartha, Mukund K.
Kato, Walter Y.
Khan, Mahbub R.
Khanna, Shiv Narain
Kim, Chung Wook
Kim, Jinchoon
Kim, Yong-Ki
Kimura, Mineo
Kinoshita, Toichiro
Ko, Kei-Yu
Ko, Winston T.
Koga, Rokutaro

Koga, Toyoki
Kumar, Satyendra
Kundu, Mukul Ranjan
Kushida, Toshimoto
Lakkaraju, Harinarayana Sarma
Lam, Leo Kongsui
Lao, Binneg Y.
Lee, Chew-Lean
Lee, Ker-Fong
Lee, Kimyeong
Lee, Sung Mook
Lee, Tsung-Dao
Lee, Wonyong
Leung, Chung-Ngoc
Leung, Kok Ming
Leung, Pui-Tak
Li, Bing An
Li, Ling-Fong
Li, Yongji
Liang, Edison Park-tak
Lim, Teck-Kah
Lin, Robert Peichung
Lin, Sung P.
Ling, Ta-Yung
Liou, Sy-Hwang
Liu, Chuan Sheng
Liu, Keh-Fei Frank
Liu, Samuel Hsi-Peh
Lo, Kwok-Yung
Lodhi, M. A. K.
Loh, Eugene C.
Louie, Steven Gwon Sheng
Low, Boon-Chye
Ma, Michael
Mahanthappa, Kalyana T.
Malhotra, Manohar Lal
Malik, Sadiq R.
Mane, Sateesh Ramchandra
Maruyama, Takashi
Mehta, Rahul
Mei, Wai-Ning
Misra, Prabhakar
Mo, Luke W.
Mohapatra, Rabindra N.
Moodera, Jagadeesh Subbaiah
Mukhopadhyay, Nimai C.
Naidu, Seetala Veeraswamy
Naik, Datta Vittal
Nam, Sangboo
Nambu, Yoichiro
Navangul, Himanshoo Vishnu
    Bhat
Ngai, Kia Ling
Ning, Tak Hung
Nomura, Kaworu Carl
Ong, Nai-Phuan
Paik, Ho Jung
Pakvasa, Sandip
Pandey, Ras Bihari
Park, Byungwoo
Park, Jae Young
Patel, Chandra Kumar Naranbhai
Pe, Maung Hla
Peng, Jen-Chieh
Purohit, Milind Vasant
Rai, Amarendra Kumar
Raja, Rajendran
Rao, Gottipaty N.
Rau, A. Ravi Prakash
Ravindra, Nuggehalli Muthanna
Ren, Shang Yuan
Sahni, Viraht
Saito, Theodore Teruo
Sakimoto, Philip Jon
Sakita, Bunji
Sawatari, Takeo
Sen, Pabitra Narayan
Sham, Lu Jeu
Sharma, Deva Datta
Shen, Benjamin Shih-Ping
Shen, Wu-Mian
Shen, Yuen-Ron
Sheng, Ping

Shetty, Anil N.
Shibata, Edward Isamu
Shih, Arnold Shang-Teh
Shih, Chia C.
Shin, Ernest Eun-Ho
Shivanandan, Kandiah
Shwe, Hla
Singh, Surendra Pal
Sinha, Dipen N.
Sinha, Sunil Kumar
Subbaswamy, Kumble Ramarao
Sudan, Ravindra Nath
Sugano, Katsuhito
Sun, Chih Ree
Sung, Chi Ching
Tajima, Toshiki
Takeuchi, Takao
Tam, Francis Man Kei
Ting, Robert Yen-Ying
Ting, Samuel C. C.
Tran, Loc Binh
Tripathi, Gorakh Nath Ram
Tsai, Chuang Chuang
Tsai, Jen-San
Tuan, San Fu
Tuli, Jagdish K.
Tung, Wu-Ki
Tye, Sze-Hoi Henry
Vaidhyanathan, Vishnampet S.
Wang, C. H.
Wang, Charles Chen-ding
Wang, Fa-chung
Wang, Gwo-Ching
Wang, Ling Jun
Wang, ShiQing
Wang, Xue-Sen
Wang, Xun-Li
Weng, Wu-Tsung
Whangbo, Myung-Hwan
Wong, David Yue
Wong, King-Lap
Wong, Po Kee
Wong, Victor Kenneth
Woo, S. B.
Wu, Alfred Chi-Tai
Wu, Chien-Shiung
Wu, Ching-Sheng
Wu, Dan Qing
Wu, En Shinn
Wu, Fa Yueh
Wu, Hai-Sheng
Wu, Hsin-i
Wu, Jin Zhong
Wu, Jun-Ru
Wu, Sau Lan Yu
Yamakawa, Kazuo Alan
Yang, Chen Ning
Yang, Chia Hsiung
Yano, Fleur B.
Yeh, Edward H. Y.
Yen, Chen-wan L.
Yen, Nai-Chyuan
Yen, William Mao-Shung
Yeo, Yung Kee
Yin, Lo I.
Yoh, John K.
Yoon, Peter Haesung
Yoshikawa, Shoichi
Yoshino, Kouichi
Young, Bing-Lin
Yuan, Jian-Min
Yun, Seung Soo
Yun, Suk Koo
Zhang, John Z. H.

PHYSIOLOGY
Anand, Rajen S.
Bajpai, Praphulla Kumar
Banerjee, Chandra Madhab
Banerjee, Mukul R.
Bhattacharyya, Ashim Kumar
Chakraborty, Joana

Chan, Stephen W.
Chaudhari, Anshumali
Chen, Chao Ling
Cheung, Joseph Y.
Chin, Edwin, Jr.
Chou, Ching-Chung
Chow, Kao Liang
Chung, Kyung Won
Farooqui, Mohammed Y. H.
Fukushima, Eiichi
Gidda, Jaswant Singh
Hong, Suk Ki
Hu, Jane H.
Huang, Kee Chang
Ikeda, Kazuo
Jen, Philip HungSun
Kalimi, Mohammed Yahya
Koide, Frank Takayuki
Kono, Tetsuro
Lee, Cheng-Chun
Lee, Chung
Lee, Diana Mang
Lin, James C.
Lin, Yu-Chong
Liu, Ching-Tong
Liu, Maw-Shung
Lu, Luo
Mahesh, Virendra Bhushan
Nakamoto, Tetsuo
Rajendran, Vazhaikkurichi M.
Rao, Papineni S.
Srinivasan, Ramachandra Srini
Su, Judy Ya-Hwa Lin
Sumida, Kenneth Dean
Sundaram, Kalyan
Tanouye, Mark Allen
Tsan, Min-Fu
Wang, Kuan
Wang, Shih-Chun
Wong, Harry Yuen Chee
Wu, Michael Ming-Kun
Yang, William C. T.
Yasumura, Seiichi
Yau, King-Wai
Yee, Robert Donald
Yu, Byung Pal

PODIATRY
Choudhary, Subodh Kumar

**POLITICAL RIGHTS
ACTIVISM**
SEE ACTIVISM,
POLITICAL/CIVIL/
SOCIAL RIGHTS

POLITICAL SCIENCE
Abraham, John
An, Nack Young
Bhagat, Nazir A.
Chan, Suitak Steve
Chang, David Wen-Wei
Chang, Maria Hsia
Chen, Linda
Chong, Peng-Khuan
Desai, Uday
Fong, Glenn Randall
Gupta, Ratanlal N.
Hayashida, Ronald Hideo
Huang, Ko-Hsing
Kang, Sugwon
Kim, Chong Lim
Kim, HeeMin
Kim, Hong Nack
Kim, Ilpyong J.
Kim, Pilkyu
Kim, Young-Bae
Kuroda, Yasumasa
Le, Binh P.
Lee, Wei-chin

Lee, Yur-Bok
Li, Cheng
Lin, Chi Yung
Liu, Hsien-Tung
Liu, Shia-Ling
Ma, Stephen K.
Mahajan, Harpreet
Malik, Hafeez
Mathews, Peter
Nguyen, Manh-Hung
Okimoto, Daniel Iwao
Pho, Hai B.
Suh, Dae-Sook
Tai, C. Stephen
Vohra, Indu
Vohra, Ranbir
Wang, James C. F.
Wang, Shaoguang
Watanabe, Paul Yashihiko
Wong, Kenneth K.
Yamada, David Takao
Zhao, Quansheng

PRINTING
SEE PUBLISHING/
PRINTING

**PRODUCING/
DIRECTING
(PERFORMING ARTS)**
SEE DIRECTING/
PRODUCING
(PERFORMING ARTS)

PROMOTION
SEE ADVERTISING/
PROMOTION

PSYCHOLOGY
Banik, Sambhu Nath
Chan, Kenyon S.
Chang, Edward C.
Chen, Audrey Huey-Wen
Chen, Hong Chyi
Cheng, Mei-Fang Hsieh
Chia, Rosina Chih-Hung
Chiu, Martha Li
Das Dasgupta, Shamita
Feng, Theo-dric
Fugita, Stephen Susumu
Goh, David S.
Gupta, Naim C.
Gupta, Venu Gopal
Hayashi, William Yasuo
Hom, Harry Lee, Jr.
Honda, Maya
Hong, George K.
Hoshiko, Michael
Huang, I-Ning
Iqbal, S. Mohammed
Ito, Michael Shuji
Iwata, Brian A.
Jung, John R.
Kim, Jwa Keun
Kim, Uichol
Lê, Hy Xuân
Lim, Kam Ming
Ling, Paul Kimberley
Mathew, Saramma T.
Merchant, Vasant V.
Mistry, Jayanthi
Miura, Irene Takei
Mo, Suchoon
Rao, Koneru Ramakrishna
Rao, Taramanohar B.
Ratti, Rakesh Kumar
Rohila, Pritam Kumar
Sakamoto, Katsuyuki
Seid, Allan

Sharma, Satanand
Song, Ralph H.
Takahashi, Lorey K.
Tokunaga, Howard Taira
Tong, Benjamin Robert
Uyeda, Arthur Asa
Vaid, Jyotsna
Wang, May X.
Wong, Eugene Hanlai
Yee, Barbara W. K.
Yin, Zenong
Yoshida, Roland K.
Yue, Xiaodong

PUBLIC ADMINISTRATION
SEE GOVERNMENT SERVICE (ELECTED OR APPOINTED)/ GOVERNMENT ADMINISTRATION— CITY; GOVERNMENT SERVICE (ELECTED OR APPOINTED)/ GOVERNMENT ADMINISTRATION— COUNTY; GOVERNMENT SERVICE (ELECTED OR APPOINTED)/ GOVERNMENT ADMINISTRATION— STATE; GOVERNMENT SERVICE (ELECTED OR APPOINTED)/ GOVERNMENT ADMINISTRATION— FEDERAL; GOVERNMENT SERVICE (ELECTED OR APPOINTED)/ GOVERNMENT ADMINISTRATION— NOT ELSEWHERE CLASSIFIED

PUBLIC UTILITIES
Gee, Robert W.
Miya, Wayne
Myint, Than Htun
Parikh, Kirit Girishchandra
Rao, Nagaraja R.
Sawhney, Gurjeet Singh
Sinha, Nirmal K.

PUBLISHING/PRINTING
Agnihotri, Newal K.
Cheng, Jill Tsui
Chinn, Thomas Wayne
Cho, Renee
Dominh, Thap
Esclamado, Alejandro A.
Fang, Florence
Fang, John Ta-Chuan
Fong, Charlen
Francisco, Emiliano Alonzo
Hori, Yutorio Claude
Horng, John Jang-Ji
Hwang, Shyshung
Hwang, Xochitl
Jethanandani, Ashok
Jin, Morgan
Kagy, Tom
Kim, David Sang Chul
Kishimoto, Richard Noriyuki
Komai, Michael Mikio
Lee, Robert
Lee, Sheng Yen
Lee, Wea Hwa
Li, Peter Ta

Liu, Louis F.
Liu, Tally C.
Louie, Dickson Lew
Mehta, Ajai Singh
Minnick, Sylvia Sun
Mirchandani, Arjun Sobhraj
Nakaguchi, Richard T.
Nakano, Mei Takaya
Narita, George M.
Ng, Assunta C. M.
Patel, Mitesh K.
Pati, A. Kumar
Shah, Syed M.
Song, John D.
Uchimoto, Dennis D.
Wan, David A.
Wang, Molly M.
Wong, Angela Ma
Yuchengco, Mona Lisa Sycip

RADIO BROADCASTING INDUSTRY
Aoki, Guy Miki
Chen, Amy L.
Choi, Richard Yungho
Feng, Theo-dric
Fong-Torres, Ben
Han, In-Sop
Kobayashi, William N., Jr.
Maeda, Sharon
Mak, Stanley M.
Park Li, Gimmy

REAL ESTATE
Andrada, Wilmer Vigilia
Chan, Timothy T.
Chang, Jerry Leslie
Chen, Angela Tzu-Yau
Chen, Siu Loong
Cheng, Jill Tsui
Chua, Conrad E.
Chung, Jong Rak Philip
Hsia, Yukun
Hu, Jimmy
Hu, Wayne
Ishii, Robert Frank
Iwata, Jerry T.
Kaji, Jonathan T.
Kelly, Darlene Okamoto
Kim, Edward J.
Lam, Eppie C. F.
Lim, Edward Hong
McNeely, June
Menon, Gopinath K.
Mirchandani, Arjun Sobhraj
Moon, Jung Suk
Mow, Chao-chow
Patel, Vipin A.
Shirakawa, George
Su, Cheh-Jen
Tam, Thomas Kwai-Sang
Tan, Eric Tuanlee
Tanaka, Gary Alan Shinichi
Tse, Charles Jack-Ching
Tse, John Yung Dong
Tung, John
Virk, Muhammad Yaqub
Vyas, Gaurang Rajnikant
Wang, Ko
Wong, Harold H.
Wong, Kenneth P.
Wong, Pablo Jose
Wong, Philip T.
Wong, Sophie Chao
Woo, Celeste Kimberlee
Xiong, William Joua
Yamamoto, John Hiroshi
Yang, Susan Y.
Yu, Peter Tat-kong

REGIONAL PLANNING
SEE URBAN/REGIONAL PLANNING

RELIGION
SEE CLERGY— BUDDHIST; CLERGY— CATHOLIC; CLERGY— MOSLEM/MUSLIM; CLERGY— PROTESTANT; CLERGY—NOT ELSEWHERE CLASSIFIED

RESTAURANT/FOOD SERVICE INDUSTRY
(SEE ALSO RETAIL TRADE—FOOD AND BEVERAGES)
Aoki, Rocky
Chen, Sam W.
Chen, Siu Loong
Chen, Terry Li-Tseng
Goto, Leo K.
Higashi, Kerwin Masuto
Hwang, Chong F.
Kapoor, Tarun
Lam, Tony
Louie, Sammy G.
Malik, Tirlok N.
Mammen, Abraham
Sahni, Sham L.
Soni, Narendra
Takami, Hideki
Truong Thi, Hoa-Dien
Wu, Sylvia Cheng
Yan, Martin

RETAIL TRADE— APPAREL AND ACCESSORIES
Chiu, Jim
Fitzpatrick, Eileen Tabata
Kanaya, Barbara J.
Madan, Dwarka Nath
Natori, Josie Cruz
Nizami, Shafiq Ahmed
Takimoto, Mabel Yayoko
Tran, Loi Huu
Wong, Desmond C.

RETAIL TRADE— BUILDING/ CONSTRUCTION MATERIALS
Kumar, Suresh A.
Sen, Arun
Toyota, Michael Douglas

RETAIL TRADE— DRUGS AND TOILETRIES
Srinivasan, Thiru R.

RETAIL TRADE— ELECTRICAL/ ELECTRONICS PRODUCTS
Arakawa, Minoru
Inatome, Rick
Jan, Han S.
Kim, James Joo-Jin
Nadkarni, Sudhir V.
Rab, Mirza M.

RETAIL TRADE—FOOD AND BEVERAGES
Cho, Frank Fulai
Chu, Hung Manh
Lewis, Loida Nicolas
Park, Kap Yung
Takami, Hideki
Tiangco, Eddie Eugenio

RETAIL TRADE— FURNITURE/HOME FURNISHINGS
Imamura, Lawrence Junji
Labasan, Alejandro B.
Langit, Ralph P., Jr.
Shimizu, Scott Edward

RETAIL TRADE— GENERAL MERCHANDISE
Chai, Jay
Chandran, Ravi
Chin, Alice L.
Moy, Jeffery Fei
Wu, Kim

RETAIL TRADE— HARDWARE
Moon, Inso John

RETAIL TRADE— MOTOR VEHICLES, PARTS, AND SERVICES
Hashmi, Mohammed Zafar
Ota, Isaac I.
Tran, Dorothy N.

RETAIL TRADE— SERVICE INDUSTRY
Chowdhury, Nazmul A.
Choy, Antonio J.
Korten, Geraldine B.
Kuroiwa, George Masaharu
Lin, Nina S. F.
Louie, David H.
Nagoshi, Douglas N.
Ong, Georgina
Uno, Anne Quan

RETAIL TRADE—NOT ELSEWHERE CLASSIFIED
Asahara, David J.
Chacko, Kurian
Chin, Alice L.
Chung, Thomas Yongbong
Daryanani, Michael
Fong-Torres, Shirley
Hong, Gong-Soog
Kapadia, Bharat S.
Khatwani, Mahesh
Lee, Byung-Moon
Lim, Chong C.
Nakasone, Robert C.
Nietes, Linda Maria
Nomura, Masae Goto
Pandit, Grish Roy
Shah, Shailesh R.
Sheth, Kishor C.
Xiong, William Joua

SALES MANAGEMENT
SEE MANAGEMENT/ ADMINISTRATION— SALES

SCIENCE—NOT ELSEWHERE CLASSIFIED
(SEE ALSO AGRICULTURAL SCIENCE; BIOLOGY/ MICROBIOLOGY; BOTANY; CHEMISTRY; ECOLOGY; OCEANOGRAPHY; PHYSIOLOGY; ZOOLOGY)
Alvares, Alvito P.
Arimura, Akira
Asuncion, Gary Raymond Espejo
Bahal, Surendra Mohan
Bak, Chan Soo
Behl, Wishvender K.
Bhat, K. Ramachandra
Borgaonkar, Digambar Shankarrao
Bulusu, Suryanarayana
Chacko, George Kuttickal
Chadha, Kailash Chandra
Chan, Albert
Chan, Po Chuen
Chang, Mingteh
Chang-Diaz, Franklin Ramon
Chatterjee, Pronoy Kumar
Chaudhari, Praveen
Chen, Anne Chi
Chen, Shi-Han
Cheng, Lanna
Cheng, Mei-Fang Hsieh
Cheng, Tu-chen
Chen-Tsai, Charlotte Hsiao-yu
Cheung, Herbert Chiu-Ching
Chiang, Erick
Chiao, Jen Wei
Chin, Raymond J.
Chou, Chung-Kwang
Chou, Ting-Chao
Chow, Louise Tsi
Chu, Benjamin
Dalvi, Ramesh R.
Datta, Syamal K.
Dixit, Padmakar Kashinath
Fong, Jack Sun-Chik
Fung, Ho-Leung
Govindjee
Gulati, Adarsh Kumar
Gupta, Dharam V.
Gupta, Gian Chand
Ho, Andrew Kong-Sun
Ho, Ju-shey
Hsieh, Chung-cheng
Hsiung, Gueh Djen
Hsu, Charles Fu-Jen
Hsu, Shaw Ling
Huang, C.-T. James
Huang, Liang Hsiung
Ishida, Andrew
Ito, Yoichiro
Jen, Joseph Jwu-Shan
Jungalwala, Firoze Bamanshaw
Khare, Bishun Narain
Khaw, Ban-An
Khurana, Krishan Kumar
Kim, Helen
Kim, Ki Hwan
Kim, Yee S.
Kochhar, Devendra M.
Koga, Yoshi Tanji
Krishna, N. Rama
Kung, Shain-dow
Kuo, Chao Ying
Kuo, Ming-Shang
Kwei, Ti-Kang
Lachica, Edward Anthony
Lai, Ching-San
Lam, Gilbert Nim-Car
Lam, Lui
Lau, Yuen-Sum

Lee, Chong Sung
Lee, Chung
Lee, Do Ik
Lee, Ying K.
Leung, Benjamin Shuet-Kin
Leung, Christopher Chung-Kit
Leung, Peter
Li, C. C.
Liao, Paul Foo-Hung
Lin, Elizabeth
Lin, George H. Y.
Lin, Hsiu-San
Liu, LiLi
Lo, Howard H.
Low, Loh-Lee
Makinodan, Takashi
Miura, George Akio
Miyamoto, Michael Dwight
Mizutani, Satoshi
Mukherjea, Arunava
Nahm, Moon H.
Nair, K. M.
Nakamura, Royden
Nakatani, Roy Eiji
Narayanan, A. Sampath
Nath, Joginder
Ng, Yuk-Chow
Nishimura, Jonathan Sei
Oka, Takami
Ozato, Keiko
Pe, Maung Hla
Pillay, Sivasankara K. K.
Raman, Aravamudhan
Ranade, D. G.
Rao, Dabeeru C.
Rasheed, Suraiya
Ravindran, Nair N.
Reddy, Gunda
Rhim, Johng Sik
Sasahara, Arthur Asao
Sayala, Dash
Shen, Benjamin Shih-Ping
Shendrikar, Arun D.
Shih, Chilin
Shih, Tsung-Ming Anthony
Sihag, Ram K.
Singh, Gurdial
Sinha, Yagya Nand
Srinivasan, Ramachandra Srini
Sun, Samuel Sai-Ming
Swaroop, Anand
Takahashi, Joseph S.
Takemori, Akira Eddie
Tam, James Pingkwan
Teng, Lee Chang-Li
Toba, Hachiro Harold
Tong, Alex Wai Ming
Trivedi, Nayan B.
Tse, Harley Yau-Shuin
Tseng, Leon F.
Uchida, Richard Noboru
Viswanath, Rampur S.
Wang, Charles Chiming
Wang, Charles Ping
Wang, Ji-Ping
Wang, Jin-Liang
Wang, Yong Tai
Woo, Savio Lau-Ching
Wu, Chuan-Fu
Wu, Tai Te
Yang, Chia Chi
Yang, In Che
Yuan, Luke Chia-Liu

**SOCIAL RIGHTS
ACTIVISM**
SEE ACTIVISM,
POLITICAL/CIVIL/
SOCIAL RIGHTS

SOCIAL WORK
Amphavannasouk, Eng
Biswas, Renuka
Chatterjee, Pranab
Cheung, Fernando C. H.
Choi, Namkee Gang
Chung, Douglas Kuei-Nan
Domingo, Cynthia Garciano
Furukawa, Theodore Paul
Furuto, Sharlene Bernice Choy
  Lin
Goishi, Dean M.
Guen, Amy Chin
Ho, Richard H.
Jamero, Peter M.
Jotwani, Chandru
Kimura, Lillian C.
Kwan, Franco Chang-Hong
Le, Christine Dung
Liu, Richard Chung-Wen
Lum, Doman
Ly, Tam Minh
Matsuda, Fay Chew
Moy, George S.
Nguyen, Hue Thi
O, Cao Kinh
O, San Luong
Rai, Gauri S.
Sharma, Satish
Shen, Grace Liu
Suzuki, Michio
Takekawa, Thomas Tsuyoshi
Wang, Rita
Watanabe, Mike
Wong, Dolores
Wong, Pat Chung
Wu, Hsiu-ying
Wu, Norman B.
Xiong, Lee Pao
Yee, Stanley C.

SOCIOLOGY
Chang, Deanna BauKung
Chatterjee, Pranab
Chen, Xiangming
Chew, Kenneth Sze-Ying
Das, Man Singh
Desai, Manisha
Doyle, Ruth Narita
Fukurai, Hiroshi
Hirabayashi, Gordon
Ito, Satoshi
Joe, Karen Ann
Kamo, Yoshinori
Kim, Eun Mee
Kim, Quee-Young
Kim, Yun
Kuo, Wen Hsiung
Kwan, Kian M.
Lee, Che-Fu
Ma, Li-Chen
Malhotra, Anju
Matsui, Machiko
Min, Pyong-Gap
Pillai, Vijayan K.
Rai, Gauri S.
Sakamoto, Arthur, Jr.
Sakoda, James Minoru
Takagi, Dana Y.
Wong, Paul

SPORTS—AMATEUR
Aoki, Rocky
Fujimura, Robert Kiyoshi
Kuttan, Roger
Louganis, Greg E.
Nitta, Sandra Haruye
Okada, Tony Manabu
Shim, Sang Kyu
Tam, Henry
Yien, Jean May

**SPORTS—
PROFESSIONAL/
SEMIPROFESSIONAL**
Briggs, Tracey Wong
Chang, Michael
Chung, Eugene
Darling, Ron
Jiang, Zhenying
Kariya, Paul
Kashiwa, Hank Charles
Nakatani, Corey
Noga, Al
Paek, Chisun Jim
Park, Chan Ho
Pooni, Amardeep Singh
Uyeda, Roger Makoto
Wakamatsu, Don
Wang, Wei
Yamaguchi, Kristine Tsuya
Zetterlund, Yoko Karin

**SPORTS—NOT
ELSEWHERE
CLASSIFIED**
Chen, Gong
Endo, Frank
Furukawa, Fred M.
Kamiyama, Osamu
Li, Ming
Pak, Yong Chin
Tong, Alvin H.
Yin, Zenong

**SPORTS COACHING/
TRAINING/
MANAGING/
OFFICIATING**
Choe, Sun Tok
Fong, Kai Meng
Goto, George
Ikuhara, Akihiro
Isaki, Paul
Kim, Wendell Kealohopauloe
Kuttan, Appu
Lin, Fred Reggie
Min, Kyung Ho
Nitta, Sandra Haruye
Rhee, Jhoon Goo
Sato, Gary Teruo
Shima, John David
Uchida, Yoshihiro
Wang, Wei

STATISTICS
Aggarwal, Lalit Kumar
Ahluwalia, Daljit Singh
Ali, Mir Masoom
Basu, Asit Prakas
Bhapkar, Vasant P.
Bhattacharyya, Gouri Kanta
Bowman, Kimiko O.
Caldito, Gloria Cruz
Chakravarthy, Srinivasaraghavan
Chang, Jane Yueh
Chang, Myron N.
Cheng, Hsiang-tai
Chiang, Chin Long
Chiou, Paul C. J.
Chitgopekar, Sharad S.
Chiu, Shean-Tsong
Choi, Jai Won
Chopra, Dharam Vir
Dalal, Siddhartha Ramanlal
Dubey, Satya Deva
Eng, Jamie Pearl
Fong, Nelson C.
Fu, Michael Chung-Shu
Ghosh, Bhaskar Kumar
Gnanadesikan, Ramanathan
Govindarajulu, Zakkula

Gupta, Arjun K.
Han, Chien-Pai
Hsi, Bartholomew P.
Hsu, Margaretha
Huang, Cheng-Chi
Hung, Ken
Isaki, Cary T.
Jammalamadaka, Sreenivasa Rao
Kacker, Raghu Nath
Kattakuzhy, George Chacko
Katti, Shriniwas K.
Kim, Yun
Koul, Hira Lal
Kshirsagar, Anant M.
Kuo, Way
Lai, Tze Leung
Lao, Chang S.
Lee, Tzesan David
Lem, Kwok Wai
Lin, Dennis Kon-Jin
Lin, Lawrence I-Kuei
Lin, Paul Kuang-Hsien
Lin, Pi-Erh
Liu, Jun S.
Lu, Jye-Chyi
Mehrotra, Kishan Gopal
Narula, Subhash Chander
Nayak, Tapan Kumar
Nguyen, Bao Gia
Park, Won J.
Rao, Dabeeru C.
Reddy, Ramakrishna P.
Rohatgi, Vijay K.
Saji, Kiyotaka
Shah, Ghulam Mohammad
Shah, Nagambal Deepak
Shinagawa, Larry
Singh, Jagbir
Singpurwalla, Nozer Darabsha
Sohn, So Young
Tamhane, Ajit C.
Tan, Wai-Yuan
Tang, Victor K. T.
Wan, James X.
Wang, George Hung-Kai
Wang, Suojin
Wei, William Wu-Shyong
Wong, Paul
Wu, Jeremy S.
Wu, Tiee-Jian
Yeh, Henry
Yi, Gang
Yin, Mark Y. Q.
Yu, Kai Fun

TELEGRAPH INDUSTRY
SEE TELEPHONE/
TELEGRAPH
INDUSTRY

**TELEPHONE/
TELEGRAPH
INDUSTRY**
Chai, David
Chand, Naresh
Chang, Chuan Chung
Chang, Shin-Jyh Frank
Chaudhary, Ved P.
Choe, Timothy Songsik
Lai, Ming-Yee
Lee, David Sen-Lin
Liao, Paul Foo-Hung
Lin, Chinlon
Louie, Alan C.
Patel, Chandrakant J.
Ramaswami, Vaidyanathan
Ting Cang-Kim, Donna Marie
Wang, Gary S. H.
Wong, Henry Sik-Yin
Woo, Henry
Yan, Martin

**TELEVISION/CABLE
BROADCASTING
INDUSTRY**
Chin, Katherine M.
Choi, Richard Yungho
Dong, Arthur
Furuta, Harry
Hwang, Ange
Kan, Yue-Sai
Laly, Amy
Lee, Christopher
Leung, Ka-Wing
Leung, Louis W.
Louie, David A.
Lum, George
Makhijani, Srichand
Su, Tuhuei
Sumii, Takao
Ting, Sandra
Wong, Tom

**TRANSLATION/
INTERPRETATION**
Ahn, Steve Fitzgerald
Chen, Angela Tzu-Yau
Ch'en, Li-li
Chen, Yung
Dong, Zheng-Min
Kobayashi, Yoshiko
Lee, Cheng-Chun
O, San Luong
Poc, Sorya
Suzawa, Naoko M.
Tran, Qui-Phiet
Wu, Yenna
Yazaki, Toyu

**TRANSPORTATION/
MOVING SERVICES**
Das, Shovan
Rajani, Prem Rajaram
Uemoto, Karen

TRAVEL INDUSTRY
Azumano, George Ichiro
Bajaj, Harjit Singh
Chang, Helen Kuang
Dozono, Sho G.
Jimenez, Christina Lee
Jotwani, Chandru
Kimura, Kongo
Korten, Geraldine B.
Liu, Juanita Ching
Sahni, Sham L.
Shah, Mayank H.
Soni, Narendra
Takano, Masaharu
Wong, Jade Snow
Yu, Larry

**URBAN/REGIONAL
PLANNING**
Chia, David
Choi, Songsu
Chou, Hsin-Pei
Kim, Joochul
Kim, Karl Eujung
Kwok, Reginald Yin-Wang
Lai, Richard Tseng-yu
Leung, Chi Kin
Lew, Alan August
Liu, Alfred H.
Ng, Jeffrey C. F.
Park, Siyoung
Peng, George Tso Chih
Sen, Ashish Kumar
Sze, Chia-Ming
Wong, John Lap
Woo, Michael K.

VETERINARY MEDICINE

Banerjee, Mukul R.
Chang, Timothy S.
Chen, Chao Ling
Chughtai, Shahid H.
Dalvi, Ramesh R.
Dash, Sita K.
Debroy, Chitrita
Hatayama, Rodney Ken
Lee, Cheng-Chun
Minocha, Harish C.
Mohanty, Sashi B.
Nuon, Samuel
Parkhie, Mukund R.
Patnaik, Amiya K.
Sharma, Udhishtra Deva
Singh, Ajaib
Sinha, Yagya Nand
Tripathy, Deoki N.
Vadlamudi, Sri Krishna
Yang, Tsu-Ju

WHOLESALE TRADE— APPAREL, PIECE GOODS, AND NOTIONS

Au, Calvin K.
Chang, Hyong Koo
Matsumoto, Ryujiro
Mittal, Kamal

WHOLESALE TRADE— BUILDING/ CONSTRUCTION MATERIALS

Kumar, Suresh A.
Panjwani, Vishnu

WHOLESALE TRADE— CHEMICALS AND ALLIED PRODUCTS

Chou, Ernest Yen
Cuajao, Tracy Lee
Mittal, Kamal
Woo, P. T.

WHOLESALE TRADE— DRUGS AND TOILETRIES

Gupta, Samir
Mong, Seymour
Nagarajan, Ramakrishnan

WHOLESALE TRADE— ELECTRICAL/ ELECTRONICS PRODUCTS

Chan, Chong B.
Chen, James
Law, H. David
Leong, Jack Y. H.
Liou, Ming Jaw
Mak, Stanley M.
Minnig, William Paul
Nadkarni, Sudhir V.
Sabnis, Suman Trimbak

WHOLESALE TRADE— FOOD AND BEVERAGES

Alejandro, Reynaldo Gamboa
Chan, Angela
Chan, Thomas O.
Chin, Chew
Ghosh, Nimai Kumar
Lewis, Loida Nicolas
Mak, William K.
Matsushima, Charles Hiroshi
Matsushima, Janie Mitsuye
Nakamura, Russell Koichi
Panjwani, Vishnu
Shimizu, Toru
Tom, Ping

WHOLESALE TRADE— HARDWARE

Leong, Jack Y. H.
Shah, Nagin B.

WHOLESALE TRADE— INDUSTRIAL MACHINERY, EQUIPMENT, AND SUPPLIES

Hu, Jimmy
Ijaz, Lubna Razia
Lee, Ming-Tung
Panjwani, Vishnu

WHOLESALE TRADE— MOTOR VEHICLES AND PARTS

Hashmi, Mohammed Zafar

WHOLESALE TRADE— NOT ELSEWHERE CLASSIFIED

Capoor, Asha
Chang, Ben
Chen, Helen T. W.
Chung, Thomas Yongbong
Jen, Serena
Kaji, Jonathan T.
Kuroiwa, George Masaharu
Leung, Dennis B.
Matsushima, Charles Hiroshi
Ng, Jeanne H.
Panjwani, Vishnu
Patel, Shailesh R.
Saeki, Hiroko Yoda
Sheth, Ashvin C.
Sood, Ravinder Singh
Su, Kwei Lee
Virji, Nazneen
Wang, K. P.
Yamaguchi, Ko

WRITING/EDITING— FICTION

Bacho, Peter
Berssenbrugge, Mei-mei
Chen, Yung
Chin, Frank Chew, Jr.
Chin-Lee, Cynthia Denise
Chong, Tommy
Dass, Edgar Sushil
Divakaruni, Chitra Banerjee
Hagedorn, Jessica Tarahata

Hong, Lily Toy
Hongo, Garrett Kaoru
Hosokawa, William K.
Houston, Jeanne Wakatsuki
Iko, Momoko Marlene
Inouye, Charles Shirō
Jen, Lillian C.
Kadohata, Cynthia Lynn
Kapur, Kamal K.
Kim, Richard E.
Kim, Yong Ik
Kingston, Maxine Hong
Krishnaswamy, Rukmini
Lee, Gus Chien-Sun
Lee, Marie Grace
Leong, Russell C.
Lim, Paulino Marquez, Jr.
Lord, Bette Bao
Louie, Ai-Ling M.
Louie, David Wong
Lu, Min Zhan
Mehta, Ved
Mukherjee, Bharati
Mura, David
Nakano, Mei Takaya
Narayan, Kirin
Pei, Lowry Cheng-Wu
Posey, Sandra Mizumoto
Ratti, Rakesh Kumar
Sasaki, Ruth A.
Say, Allen
Seto, Thelma G.
Tan, Amy Ruth
Uchida, Yoshiko
Villanueva, Marianne Del Rosario
Wong, Shawn Hsu
Yan, Haiping
Yee, Wong Herbert
Yep, Lawrence Michael

WRITING/EDITING— NONFICTION (SEE ALSO JOURNALISM—PRINT)

Batra, Ravi
Bautista, Veltisezar Bal
Bolen, Jean Shinoda
Chatterjee, Monish Ranjan
Chen, Ching-chih
Chen, Helen T. W.
Ch'en, Li-li
Chen, Tony Young
Chen, Yung
Chia, Kai
Chin, Steven Alexander
Chin-Lee, Cynthia Denise
Chopra, Deepak
Deng, Ming-Dao
Dinh, Thuy Tu Bich
Doo, Jack P., Jr.
Fukuyama, Francis
Gandhi, Arun Manilal
Gow, Haven Bradford
Gupta, Omprakash K.
Hamamoto, Darrell Yoshito
Hayslip, Le Ly
Hori, Yutorio Claude
Hosokawa, William K.
Hsiao, Sidney C.
Hsieh, Winston Wen-sun
Ito, Thomas Hiroshi
Iyer, Siddharth Pico
Kikumura, Akemi
Kim, David Doyung

Kim, Richard E.
Kirchner, Bharti
Lee, Gus Chien-Sun
Lee, Marie Grace
Lee, Robert
Leong, Russell C.
Lewis, Loida Nicolas
Lim, Shirley Geok-Lin
Lord, Bette Bao
Lu, Min Zhan
Mehta, Ved
Mukherjee, Bharati
Mura, David
Nakano, Mei Takaya
Nakayama, Randall Shige
Narita, George M.
Ngor, Haing S.
Ohashi, Wataru
Park, Chung I.
Rao, K. L. Seshagiri
San Juan, E.
Sasaki, Raymond Toshiaki, Jr.
Shah, Amit
Shah, Syed M.
Shim, Jae K.
Sung, Betty Lee
Ta, Tai Van
Takaki, Ronald
Takami, David A.
Tan, Amy Ruth
Viet-Chau, Nguyen Duc
Wang, Bee-Lan Chan
Weglyn, Michi Nishiura
Wong, Jade Snow
Wong, Ovid K.
Wong, Shawn Hsu

WRITING/EDITING— PLAYS, SCREENPLAYS, TV SCRIPTS

Chang, Douglas Howe
Chen, Joan
Chin, Charlie William David
Chin, Frank Chew, Jr.
Gotanda, Philip Kan
Hayashida, Frank
Hill, Amy
Houston, Jeanne Wakatsuki
Houston, Velina Hasu
Hwang, Ange
Hwang, David Henry
Iko, Momoko Marlene
Kapur, Kamal K.
Kashiwagi, Soji Charles
Kurup, Shishir Ravindran
Lim, Paul Stephen
Mako
Moy, James S.
Mukherjee, Bharati
Okazaki, Steven
Okita, Dwight Holden
Sunaida, Mari
Wong, B. D.
Yan, Haiping
Yep, Lawrence Michael

WRITING/EDITING— POETRY

Berssenbrugge, Mei-mei
Bhandari, Sanjiv
Chin, Marilyn Mei Ling
Chow, Tse-tsung
Francia, Luis H. F.

Furuta, Soichi
Gotera, Vicente Ferrer
Hongo, Garrett Kaoru
Hu, Jane H.
Inada, Lawson Fusao
Kanojia, Ramesh Maganlal
Kapur, Kamal K.
Kikuchi, Carl H.
Kim, Myung Mi
Leong, Russell C.
Lim, Shirley Geok-Lin
Liu, Stephen Shu-Ning
Ma, Sheng-mei
Marr, William Wei-Yi
Mura, David
Okita, Dwight Holden
Pham, Henry Tuoc Van
Seto, Thelma G.
Shahzad, Farhat
Sun, Hugo Sui-Hwan
Toyama, Jean Yamasaki
Tse, John Yung Dong
Uba, George R.
Uyematsu, Amy
Wong, Nellie
Yamada, Mitsuye May

WRITING/EDITING— NOT ELSEWHERE CLASSIFIED

Aoki, Guy Miki
Barnabas, Mathews Mar
Chang, Helen Kuang
Chaturvedi, Arvind Kumar
Chen, Moon Shao-Chuang, Jr.
Cheong, Fiona
Chin, Winifred C.
Chinn, Daisy Wong
Chow, Balance Tin-Ping
Collier, Irene Dea
Datta, Ranajit Kumar
Divakaruni, Chitra Banerjee
Fong-Torres, Shirley
Furuta, Karin L.
Kak, Subhash Chandra
Kumar, Prem
Liu, Xingwu
Malik, Saied Ahmad
Pang, Rubye-Huey
Wang, Ling Jun
Wang, Qun
Yamamoto, Y. Stephen

ZOOLOGY

Chang, Ernest Sun-Mei
Chao, Lin
Chong, Pek-Ean
Gupta, Santosh
Gupta, Virendra K.
Ho, Ju-shey
Lee, Sue Ying
Lew, Gloria Maria
Liem, Karel Frederik
Mathur, Krishan D.
Miyamoto, Michael Masao
Ono, Richard Dana
Reddy, Gunda
Rivera, Evelyn Margaret
Shan, Robert Kuocheng
Shen, Sheldon Shih-Ta
Singh, Madho
Yaden, Senka Long

ETHNIC/CULTURAL HERITAGE INDEX

BANGLADESH

Ali, Mir Masoom
Banerjee, Jayanta Kumar
Basu, Asit Prakas
Bhattacharjee, Jnanendra Kumar
Chatterjee, Monish Ranjan
Chatterjee, Pronoy Kumar
Choudhury, A. Latif
Chowdhury, Nazmul A.
Das, Kamalendu
Das, Phanindramohan
Farouk, Bakhtier
Haque, M. Shamsul
Haque, Zahur U.
Hoque, Enamul
Hussain, Fazle
Islam, Nurul
Kabir, Abulfazal M. Fazle
Khan, Mahbub R.
Malik, Sadiq R.
Mansur, Iqbal
Miah, Abdul J.
Newaz, S. S.
Rouf, Mohammed Abdur
Saha, Gopal Bandhu
Sarker, Bhaba Ranjan
Siddiqui, Faruq Mahmud Anam
Siddiqui, Habib
Ullah, M. Rifat

CAMBODIA

Chhim, Him S.
Kong, Chhean
Lim, Chhorn E.
Ly, Tam Minh
Ngor, Haing S.
Nuon, Samuel
Outhuok, T.
Poc, Sorya
Tan, Nady

CHINA

Allen, Susan Au
Ang, Charles C.
Aoki, Brenda Jean
Au, Chi-Kwan
Au, Leo Yuin
Au, Patrick Siu-Kee
Au, Tung
Au, Wilkie Wai Kee
Bai, Shen Hum
Barat, Kahar
Berssenbrugge, Mei-mei
Bloch, Julia Chang
Briggs, Tracey Wong
Brillantes, Hermogenes Bilgera
Cai, Jin-Yi
Cai, Shelton Xuanqing
Chai, An-Ti
Chai, David
Chan, Adrian
Chan, Albert
Chan, Anthony Bernard
Chan, Arthur Wing Kay
Chan, Carl Chiang
Chan, Carlyle Hung-lun

Chan, Cheung M.
Chan, Chiu Shui
Chan, Cho Lik
Chan, Chong B.
Chan, Chun Kin
Chan, David So Keung
Chan, Donald P. K.
Chan, Edwin Y.
Chan, Gary M.
Chan, Glenn
Chan, Harvey Thomas, Jr.
Chan, Henry Y. S.
Chan, Jack-Kang
Chan, John
Chan, John G.
Chan, Kai Chiu
Chan, Kawei
Chan, Kenyon S.
Chan, Laurence Kwong-Fai
Chan, Lee-Nien Lillian
Chan, Lo-Yi C. Y.
Chan, Lois Mai
Chan, Marsha J.
Chan, Mason C.
Chan, Mei-Mei
Chan, Peng S.
Chan, Phillip Paang
Chan, Po Chuen
Chan, Pui Kwong
Chan, Robert T. P.
Chan, Samuel H. P.
Chan, Stephen W.
Chan, Steven D.
Chan, Su Han
Chan, Sucheng
Chan, Suitak Steve
Chan, Tat-Hung
Chan, Ted W.
Chan, Thomas O.
Chan, Timothy T.
Chan, Ting Y.
Chan, Wai-Yee
Chan, Yeung Yu
Chan Costa, Vivian Rhoda
Chang, Albert
Chang, Alice Ching
Chang, Amy Lee
Chang, Andrew C.
Chang, Anthony K. U.
Chang, Benjamin Tai-An
Chang, Briankle G.
Chang, Carl Kochao
Chang, Caroline J.
Chang, Charles Hung
Chang, Cheng-Hui
Chang, Chia-ning
Chang, Chin Hao
Chang, Claudia
Chang, Clement C.
Chang, Clifford Wah Jun
Chang, Craig
Chang, David Hsiang
Chang, David W.
Chang, David Wen-Wei
Chang, Deanna BauKung
Chang, Deborah I-Ju
Chang, Douglas Howe
Chang, Edmund Z.

Chang, Edward C.
Chang, Edward Shih-Tou
Chang, Elden T.
Chang, Eric Chieh
Chang, Ernest Sun-Mei
Chang, Farland H.
Chang, Gene Hsin
Chang, Gordon H.
Chang, Helen T.
Chang, Henry C.
Chang, Howard F.
Chang, Hsu Hsin
Chang, Jack Che-Man
Chang, Jack H. T.
Chang, James C.
Chang, James Wan Chie
Chang, Jeffrey Chit-Fu
Chang, Jennie C. C.
Chang, Jerry Leslie
Chang, Jhy-Jiun
Chang, Juang-Chi
Chang, Kai
Chang, Kern K. N.
Chang, Kwang-chih
Chang, Kwang-Poo
Chang, Louis Wai-Wah
Chang, Luke
Chang, Mervin Henry
Chang, Michael
Chang, Michael S.
Chang, Ming
Chang, Mingteh
Chang, Mou-Hsiung
Chang, Myron N.
Chang, Nelson
Chang, Patricia W.
Chang, Paul Peng-Cheng
Chang, Paul Steven
Chang, Pei K.
Chang, Ping
Chang, Ren-Fang
Chang, Robert C.
Chang, Robert Huei
Chang, Sen-dou
Chang, Shau-Jin
Chang, Shen Chie
Chang, Shi-Kuo
Chang, Shin-Jyh Frank
Chang, Simon
Chang, Stephen S.
Chang, Sylvia Tan
Chang, Te-Wen
Chang, Tien-Chien
Chang, Tim P.
Chang, Timothy S.
Chang, Tony H.
Chang, Warren W.
Chang, Wayne Wei
Chang, Weilin P.
Chang, William Wei-Lien
Chang, William Y. B.
Chang, Yen Fook
Chang-Diaz, Franklin Ramon
Chao, Allen Y.
Chao, Bei Tse
Chao, Chiang-nan
Chao, Ching Yuan
Chao, Edward C. T.

Chao, Elaine Lan
Chao, Georgia Tze-Ying
Chao, Jowett
Chao, Kwang-Chu
Chao, Lin
Chao, Paul W. F.
Chao, Rosalind
Chao, Stanley K.
Chao, Tim
Chao, Xiuli
Chau, Henry Chun-Nam
Chee, Cheng-Khee
Chen, Alan Keith
Chen, Amy L.
Chen, Andrew Houng-Yhi
Chen, Anne Chi
Chen, Augustine Cheng-Hsin
Chen, Benjamin Yun-Hai
Chen, Bernard Shao-Wen
Chen, Bessie B.
Chen, Bintong
Chen, Carl Wan-Cheng
Chen, Catherine W.
Chen, Chao
Chen, Chi Hau
Chen, Chi-yun
Chen, Chin
Chen, Chin-Lin
Chen, Ching-chih
Chen, Chung
Chen, David Ta-Fu
Chen, David W.
Chen, Di
Chen, Er-Ping
Chen, Francis F.
Chen, George Chi-Ming
Chen, Gong
Chen, Guanrong
Chen, Haiyang
Chen, Helen T. W.
Chen, Henry
Chen, Henry
Chen, Henry J.
Chen, Hollis Ching
Chen, Hongda
Chen, Ivan Mao-Chang
Chen, James
Chen, Jianhua
Chen, Jie
Chen, Jizeng
Chen, Joan
Chen, John Shaoming
Chen, Juh Wah
Chen, Kangping
Chen, Kao
Chen, Karl A.
Chen, Kuang Yu
Chen, Le Chun
Ch'en, Lena B.
Ch'en, Li-li
Chen, Linda
Chen, Michael Chia-Chao
Chen, Michael M.
Chen, Michael Y. M.
Chen, Ming
Chen, Ming Chih
Chen, Moon Shao-Chuang, Jr.
Chen, Nai-Ni

Chen, Nai Y.
Chen, Pamela Ki Mai
Chen, Paul Kuan Yao
Chen, Ping-fan
Chen, Robert Chia-Hua
Chen, Sam W.
Chen, Shi-Han
Chen, Simon Ying
Chen, Siu Loong
Chen, Stanford
Chen, Stephen C.
Chen, Steve S.
Chen, Stuart S.
Chen, Tai
Chen, Thomas K. S.
Chen, Thomas Shih-Nien
Chen, Tony Young
Chen, Tseh An
Chen, Tung-Shan
Chen, Victoria Liu
Chen, Virginia L.
Chen, Wai Fah
Chen, Wai Jun
Chen, Wai-Kai
Chen, Wei-Yin
Chen, Weihang
Chen, Wenxiong
Chen, William Hok-Nin
Chen, Xiangming
Chen, Xiangning
Chen, Xinfu
Chen, Ye-Hwa
Chen, Yi-Chao
Chen, Yu
Chen, Yu-Charn
Chen, Yubao
Chen, Yung
Chen, Zhong-Ying
Cheng, Amy I.
Cheng, Andrew F.
Cheng, Brian Kai-Ming
Cheng, Carlos
Cheng, Charles Ching-an
Cheng, Chu-Yuan
Cheng, David Hong
Cheng, David Keun
Cheng, Eugene Y.
Cheng, Franklin Yih
Cheng, Fu-Ding
Cheng, H. H.
Cheng, Herbert S.
Cheng, Hsien K.
Cheng, Jill Tsui
Cheng, Joseph Kwang-Chao
Cheng, Kuang Lu
Cheng, Lanna
Cheng, Louis Tsz-Wan
Cheng, Nancy C.
Cheng, Norman Alan
Cheng, Ping
Cheng, Richard Tien-Ren
Cheng, Sheue-yann
Cheng, Sin I.
Cheng, Stephen Z. D.
Cheng, Ta-Pei
Cheng, Tu-chen
Cheng, Tung Chao
Cheng, Ying-wan

Chen-Tsai, Charlotte Hsiao-yu
Cheo, Li-hsiang S.
Cheo, Peter K.
Cheung, Cindy Siu-Whei
Cheung, David F.
Cheung, Fernando C. H.
Cheung, Herbert Chiu-Ching
Cheung, Joseph Y.
Cheung, Julian F. Y.
Cheung, Luke P.
Cheung, Philip
Cheung, Shun Yan
Cheung, Wai Yiu
Chew, Frances Sze-Ling
Chew, Kenneth Sze-Ying
Chew, Pamela Christine
Chew, Richard Franklin
Chew, Ronald A.
Chew, Wellington Lum
Chew, Weng Cho
Chi, Cheng-Ching
Chi, Jacob
Chi, Lotta C. J. Li
Chi, Yinliang
Chia, David
Chia, Kai
Chia, Ning
Chia, Rosina Chih-Hung
Chiang, Asuntha Maria Ming-Yee
Chiang, Berttram
Chiang, Chin Long
Chiang, Chwan K.
Chiang, Erick
Chiang, Huai C.
Chiang, Joseph F.
Chiang, Oscar C. K.
Chiang, Ping-Wang
Chiang, Shiao-Hung
Chiang, Sie Ling
Chiang, Soong T.
Chiang, Theresa Yi-Chin Tung
Chiang, Tsung Ting
Chiang, Yi-ling F.
Chiang, Yuen-Sheng
Chiao, Jen Wei
Chiao, Leroy
Chien, Alan Shueshih
Chien, Arnold Jensen
Chien, Chia-Ling
Chien, Chih-Yung
Chien, Gary K.
Ch'ih, John Juwei
Chin, Alexander Foster
Chin, Alice L.
Chin, Beverly Ann
Chin, Bryan Allen
Chin, Cecilia Hui-hsin
Chin, Charlie William David
Chin, Chew
Chin, Connie Frances
Chin, David
Chin, Donald G.
Chin, Edwin, Jr.
Chin, Frank Chew, Jr.
Chin, Grace Y.
Chin, Helen
Chin, Henry Han
Chin, John Way
Chin, Katherine M.
Chin, Ken K.
Chin, Marilyn Mei Ling
Chin, Michelle Lorraine
Chin, Ming William
Chin, Pamela Grace
Chin, Patrick K.
Chin, Raymond J.
Chin, Robert Allen
Chin, Stanley H.
Chin, Steven Alexander
Chin, Steven Han-Hoy
Chin, Tamera Ann
Chin, Thomas

Chin, William Nigel
Chin, Winifred C.
Chin, Yee Wah
Chin, Yin-lien Chen
Ching, Anthony B.
Ching, Chee
Ching, Deborah F.
Ching, Gale Lin Fong
Ching, Harvey Cho Wing
Ching, Hugh
Ching, Joseph Yu Nun
Ching, Marvin K. L.
Ching, Stanton Sakae Hong Yat
Ching, Theodora Lam
Ching, Wai-Yim
Chin-Lee, Cynthia Denise
Chinn, Daisy Wong
Chinn, Roger
Chinn, Thomas Wayne
Chiou, Wen-An
Chiou, Wun C.
Chiu, Arthur Nang Lick
Chiu, Lue-Yung Chow
Chiu, Martha Li
Chiu, S. M.
Chiu, Thomas Chee-Wang
Chiu, Tin-Ho
Chiu, Victor
Chiu, Yuan-yuan H.
Cho, Alfred Yi
Cho, David
Cho, Frank Fulai
Cho, Renee
Choe, Martha C.
Choi, Michael Kamwah
Chong, Clyde Hok Heen
Chong, Frank
Chong, Ken P.
Chong, Pek-Ean
Chong, Ping
Chong, Rae Dawn
Chong, Richard David
Chong, Timothy
Chong, Tommy
Chong-Gottinger, Ivy Wok Kuong
Choo, Arthur C. S.
Chou, Arthur W.
Chou, Chen-Lin
Chou, Chung-Kwang
Chou, David Yuan-Pin
Chou, Ernest Yen
Chou, Iih-Nan
Chou, James C. S.
Chou, Kuo-Chen
Chou, Leland L. C.
Chou, Mei-Yin
Chou, Timothy C.
Chou, Tsu-Wei
Chow, Balance Tin-Ping
Chow, Barbara A.
Chow, Bob Ching-Hong
Chow, Brian Gee-Yin
Chow, Cheryl
Chow, Chuen-Yen
Chow, Edmund Chun-Ying
Chow, Ivan S.
Chow, Kao Liang
Chow, Louise Tsi
Chow, Paul Chuan-Juin
Chow, Philip Yeong-Wai
Chow, Russell W.
Chow, Shirley Chin-Ping
Chow, Tse-tsung
Chow, Wen Lung
Choy, Antonio J.
Choy, Christine
Choy, Fred Kat-Chung
Choy, Simon
Choy, Wanda Wai Ying
Chu, Adam
Chu, Benjamin
Chu, Ching-Wu

Chu, Chung-Yu Chester
Chu, Daniel Tim-Wo
Chu, David S. C.
Chu, Elizabeth Chan
Chu, Felix T.
Chu, Franklin Janen
Chu, Jonathan Moseley
Chu, Judy M.
Chu, Julia Nee
Chu, Kong
Chu, Kuang Han
Chu, Patricia Pei-chang
Chu, Paul Ching-Wu
Chu, Peter Cheng
Chu, Shirley S.
Chu, Sung Nee George
Chu, Terence
Chu, Tien Lu
Chu, Ting L.
Chu, Tsuchin Philip
Chu, Victor Fu Hua
Chu, Vincent Hao-Kwong
Chu, Warren
Chu, Wei-Kan
Chua, Amy Lynn
Chua, Conrad E.
Chua, Leon O.
Chuang, Henry Ning
Chui, Charles K.
Chun, Aulani
Chun, Hon Ming
Chun, Joe Y. F.
Chun, Raymond W. M.
Chun, Wei Foo
Chung, Anni Yuet-Kuen
Chung, Connie
Chung, David Yih
Chung, Frank Huan-Chen
Chung, Harold
Chung, King-Thom
Chung, Kwong T.
Chung, Ling Jia
Chung, Lisa A.
Chung, Robert
Chung, Ronald Aloysius
Chung, Simon Lam-Ying
Chung, Sue Fawn
Chung, Yip-Wah
Collier, Irene Dea
Cua, Antonio S.
Culp, Mae Ng
Dai, Hai-Lung
Dai, Liyi
Deng, Ming-Dao
Der, Henry
Dinh, Steven M.
Djao, Angela Wei
Don, James E.
Dong, Arthur
Dong, John W.
Dong, Wei
Dong, Zheng-Min
Doo, Jack P., Jr.
Doo, Leigh-Wai
Duong, Cambao De
Ebron, Betty Liu
Eng, Ana Mar
Eng, Henry
Eng, Jamie Pearl
Eng, Lawrence Fook
Eng, Mamie
Eng, William
Eu, March Fong
Fa, Angie
Fan, Ada Mei
Fan, Carol C.
Fan, Chang-Yun
Fan, Chien
Fang, Fabian Tien-Hwa
Fang, Florence
Fang, Frank F.
Fang, James
Fang, John Ta-Chuan

Fang, Ming M.
Fen, Allan Ming
Feng, Guofu Jeff
Feng, Jonathan Lee
Feng, Theo-dric
Feng, Tse-Yun
Feng, Xin
Fok, Agnes Kwan
Fok, Samuel Shiu-Ming
Fok, Yu-Si
Fong, April Ann
Fong, Bernard Wah Doung
Fong, Charlen
Fong, Dewey
Fong, Eva Chow
Fong, Glenn Randall
Fong, Harold Michael
Fong, Harry H. S.
Fong, Herbert S.
Fong, Hiram Leong
Fong, J Craig
Fong, Jack Sun-Chik
Fong, Joshua
Fong, Kai Meng
Fong, Kevin Murray
Fong, Mary Helena
Fong, Matthew K.
Fong, Nelson C.
Fong, Raymond
Fong, Thomas Y. K.
Fong-Torres, Ben
Fong-Torres, Shirley
Foong, Nicolai Yein
Frey, Francesca
Fu, Karen K.
Fu, Kuan-Chen
Fu, Michael Chung-Shu
Fu, Paul Chung, Jr.
Fu, Paul S.
Fu, Shou-Cheng Joseph
Fu, Tina C.
Fugh, John L.
Fulbeck, Kip
Fung, Bing M.
Fung, Daniel Yee Chak
Fung, Dennis Lung
Fung, Gordon L.
Fung, Henry C.
Fung, Ho-Leung
Fung, Hung-Gay
Fung, Kee-Ying
Fung, Shun C.
Fung, Sui An
Fung, Sun-Yiu
Fung, Yuan-Cheng Bertram
Furuto, Sharlene Bernice Choy Lin
Gam, Paul Jonathan
Gao, Jiali
Gee, Arthur
Gee, Dolly M.
Gee, Montgomery M.
Gee, Norman F.
Gee, Robert W.
Gee, Virginia Catherine
Geng, Shu
Gil, Libia Socorro
Gin, Jerry B.
Gn, Thye-Wee
Go, Daniel Y.
Go, Howard T.
Go, Mateo Lian Poa
Goh, Ben K.
Goh, David S.
Gong, Ginny
Gong, Jin Kang
Goo, Edward Kwock Wai
Gouw, Cynthia Gie-Kiok
Gow, Haven Bradford
Guen, Amy Chin
Guo, David
Guo, Hua
Hahn, Bessie King

Han, Anna M.
Han, Chien-Pai
Han, Chingping Jim
Han, Jinchen
Han, Xianming Lance
Hang, Tru
Hee, Edward K. Y.
Hing, Bill Ong
Ho, Benson P.
Ho, Chi-Tang
Ho, Chien
Ho, Chih-Ming
Ho, Chung-Wu
Ho, Daniel F.
Ho, David D.
Ho, Dennis
Ho, Edwin Soon Hee
Ho, Fred Wei-han
Ho, Hon Hing
Ho, John Ting-Sum
Ho, Lop-Hing
Ho, Peter Peck Koh
Ho, Ping Pei
Ho, Reginald C. S.
Ho, Richard H.
Ho, Thierry
Ho, Ting
Ho, Vernon S. C.
Ho, Yu-Chi
Ho, Yuh Jyue Agnes Wang
Ho-González, William
Hom, Harry Lee, Jr.
Hom, Kathleen B.
Hom, Mei-Ling
Hom, Peter Wah
Hom, Rose
Hon, Andrew
Hong, Carl
Hong, Frances
Hong, Glenn Thomas
Hong, Lily Toy
Hong, Shuguang
Hong, Weihu
Hoo, Joe-Jie
Horn, Jennie A.
Hou, William Chen-Nan
Hsi, Bartholomew P.
Hsi, David C.
Hsia, Judith Ann
Hsia, Judo Jeoudao
Hsia, Lisa
Hsia, Yuchuek
Hsia, Yukun
Hsiao, Benjamin S.
Hsiao, Feng
Hsiao, Joan Hsi-Min
Hsiao, Julia
Hsiao, Margaret Sheng-Mei
Hsiao, Sidney C.
Hsiao, Tony An-Jen
Hsiao, William C.
Hsieh, Brian
Hsieh, Daniel Sebastian
Hsieh, Durwynne
Hsieh, Franklin
Hsieh, Jeanette L.
Hsieh, Li-Ping
Hsieh, Tom
Hsieh, Winston Wen-sun
Hsieh, You-Lo
Hsin, Chen-Chung
Hsing, Rodney W.
Hsiung, Gueh Djen
Hsu, Albert Yutien
Hsu, Cathy H. C.
Hsu, Charles Fu-Jen
Hsu, Chen-Chi
Hsu, Chieh-Su
Hsu, Donald K.
Hsu, Frank H.
Hsu, Hsiu-Sheng
Hsu, Immanuel C. Y.
Hsu, John Tseng-Hsiu

Hsu, John Y.
Hsu, Konrad Chang
Hsu, Laura Ling
Hsu, Liang-Chi
Hsu, Margaretha
Hsu, Mei-Ling
Hsu, Ping
Hsu, Robert Ying
Hsu, Samuel
Hsu, Shaw Ling
Hsu, Stephen M.
Hsu, Timothy
Hsu, Tse-Chi
Hsu, Yu Chu
Hsu, Yuan-Hsi
Hsueh, Chun-tu
Hsueh, Yi-Fun
Hsui, Albert Tong-Kwan
Hu, Albert Ke-Jeng
Hu, Bambi
Hu, Bei-Lok Bernard
Hu, Can Beven
Hu, Chenming
Hu, Chi Yu
Hu, Chia-Ren
Hu, Daniel Ching
Hu, Jane H.
Hu, Jimmy
Hu, John Nan-Hai
Hu, Joseph Kai Ming
Hu, Paul Y.
Hu, Shiu-Lok
Hu, Steve Seng-Chiu
Hu, Wayne
Huang, Alice Shih-Hou
Huang, Arnold
Huang, Barney Kuo-Yen
Huang, C.-T. James
Huang, Chaofu
Huang, Chau-Ting
Huang, Chi-chiang
Huang, Chi-Lung Dominic
Huang, Denis K.
Huang, Eugene Yuching
Huang, Garng Morton
Huang, H. T.
Huang, I-Ning
Huang, Ian
Huang, Jacob Wen-Kuang
Huang, Jennming Stephen
Huang, Jiann-Shiun
Huang, Jin
Huang, John Shiao-Shih
Huang, Joseph Chi Kan
Huang, Joseph T.
Huang, Joyce L.
Huang, Kee Chang
Huang, Ko-Hsing
Huang, Nai-Chien
Huang, Pei
Huang, Samuel T.
Huang, Shan-Jen Chen
Huang, Thomas Tao-Shing
Huang, Thomas W.
Huang, Tseng
Huang, Weifeng
Huang, Xun-Cheng
Huang, Yasheng
Huang, Zhen
Huang, Zhen-Fen
Huey, Jolene W.
Hui, Sek Wen
Huie, Carmen Wah-Kit
Hung, James Chen
Hung, Ken
Hung, Tin-Kan
Hung, Yen-Wan
Huynh, Boi-Hanh
Huynh, Dung Thiet
Hwa, Jesse Chia-Hsi
Hwang, Ange
Hwang, Charles C.
Hwang, David Henry

Hwang, Enoch Oi-Kee
Hwang, Guann-Jiun
Hwang, Henry Y.
Hwang, John C.
Hwang, Roland
Hwang, Shoi Yean
Hwang, Te-Long
Hwang, Wei-Yuan
Hwang, William Gaong
Ih, Charles Chung-Sen
Ing, Malcolm Ross
Jan, Han S.
Jan, Kung-ming
Jang, Dennis
Jang, Jon
Jao, Radmar Agana
Jen, Chih Kung
Jen, Horatio H.
Jen, James A.
Jen, Joseph Jwu-Shan
Jen, Lillian C.
Jen, Philip HungSun
Jeong, Wallace Dun
Jiang, Nai-Siang
Jiang, William Yuying
Jiang, Xixiang
Jiang, Zhenying
Jimenez, Christina Lee
Jin, Morgan
Joe, Alexander H.
Joe, Clarence
Joe, Karen Ann
Ju, Frederick D.
Jue, Francis
Jung, Audrey Moo Hing
Jung, Emma
Jung, John R.
Jung, Kwan Yee
Jung, Lawrence Kwok Leung
Jung, Louise Rebecca
Jung, Yee Wah
Kam, James T.-K.
Kam, Lit-Yan
Kam, Mei-Ki F. P.
Kam, Thomas K. Y.
Kam, Vernon T.
Kam, William
Kan, Diana
Kan, Kit-Keung
Kan, Michael
Kan, Victor
Kan, Yue-Sai
Kang, Weng Poo
Kao, Kung-Ying Tang
Kao, Race L.
Kao, Tai-Wu
Kao, Timothy Tieh-Hsiung
Kay, Helen
Ke, Gang
Kee, Willie
Kennard, Joyce L.
Kiang, Peter Nien-chu
Kiang, Robert L.
Kim, Thomas Kunhyuk
Kingman, Dong
Kingston, Maxine Hong
Ko, Ada
Ko, Bing H.
Ko, Elaine Ikoma
Ko, Hon-Chung
Ko, Kathleen Lim
Ko, Kei-Yu
Ko, Steven W.
Ko, Wen Hsiung
Ko, Winston T.
Kong, Ana C.
Kong, Corita Shuk Sinn
Kong, Eric Siu-Wai
Kong, Ronald A.
Kong, Stanley Young
Kong, William T.
Koo, Anthony Ying Chang
Koo, Benjamin Hai-Chang

Koo, Delia
Koo, George P.
Krist, Elizabeth Cheng
Ku, David Nelson
Ku, Wen-Chi
Kuan, David A.
Kuan, Jenny W.
Kuan, Kah-Jin
Kuan, Shia Shiong
Kuan, Wei Eihn
Kuh, Ernest Shiu-Jen
Kung, Alice How Kuen
Kung, Frank F. C.
Kung, H. T.
Kung, Harold H.
Kung, Jeffrey
Kung, Patrick Chung-Shu
Kung, Shain-dow
Kuo, Chao Ying
Kuo, Charles Chang-Yun
Kuo, Chung Ming
Kuo, James K. Y.
Kuo, Joseph C.
Kuo, Ming-ming Shen
Kuo, Nina L.
Kuo, Yih-Wen
Kwan, Catherine Ning
Kwan, Franco Chang-Hong
Kwan, Kian M.
Kwan, Simon Hing-Man
Kwan, Yuen-yin Kathy
Kwan-Gett, Mei Lin
Kwei, Ti-Kang
Kwoh, Stewart
Kwok, Daniel W. Y.
Kwok, Daphne
Kwok, Hoi-Sing
Kwok, Joseph
Kwok, Reginald Yin-Wang
Kwok, Wo Kong
Kwong, Bill Wai Lam
Lai, Amy
Lai, Dennis Fu-hsiung
Lai, Jai-Lue Leon
Lai, Kai Sun
Lai, Kuo-Yann
Lai, Patrick Kinglun
Lai, Richard Thomas
Lai, Richard Tseng-yu
Lai, Tze Leung
Lai, Waihang
Lam, Alex W.
Lam, Chow-Shing
Lam, Chun H.
Lam, Eppie C. F.
Lam, Fat C.
Lam, Gilbert Nim-Car
Lam, Lui
Lam, Nelson Jen-Wei
Lam, Sau-Hai
Lam, Simon Shin-Sing
Lam, Thomas Manpan
Lan, Chuan-Tau Edward
Lan, Dong Ping
Lang, David C.
Lao, Binney Y.
Lao, Chang S.
Lau, Albert Kai-Fay
Lau, Bennett M. K.
Lau, Cheryl Ann
Lau, David T.
Lau, Edward C. Y.
Lau, Estelle Pau On
Lau, Fred H.
Lau, Gilbert Minjun
Lau, Gloria J.
Lau, Jark C.
Lau, Jenni Meili
Lau, Lawrence Juen-Yee
Lau, Leslie
Lau, Ngar-Cheung
Lau, Peter Man-Yiu
Lau, Yuen-Sum

Lau, Yvonne M.
Law, H. David
Lee, Albert W.
Lee, Ang
Lee, Arthur Richard
Lee, Bing
Lee, Bradford Young
Lee, Brandon
Lee, Che-Fu
Lee, Chen Lok
Lee, Cheng-Chun
Lee, Chew-Lean
Lee, Chi-Hang
Lee, Chin-Chuan
Lee, Christopher
Lee, Chung
Lee, Clarence Kim Mun
Lee, Conrad
Lee, Dah-Yinn
Lee, David C.
Lee, David Oi
Lee, David Sen-Lin
Lee, Diana Mang
Lee, E. Stanley
Lee, Gus Chien-Sun
Lee, Guy
Lee, Harvey Shui-Hong
Lee, Hwa-Wei
Lee, Jason Scott
Lee, Jen-Shih
Lee, John Chung
Lee, K. J.
Lee, Kai-Fong
Lee, Karen
Lee, Ker-Fong
Lee, King Y.
Lee, Kwang K.
Lee, Lee Hwang
Lee, Lester Hsin-Pei
Lee, Lihsyng Stanford
Lee, Marietta Y. W. T.
Lee, Miko
Lee, Min-Shiu
Lee, Ming-Tung
Lee, Nan-Nan
Lee, Pamela Tau
Lee, Paul Wah
Lee, Richard Fayao
Lee, Robert
Lee, Robert Terry
Lee, Sheng Yen
Lee, Shih Ying
Lee, Shuishih Sage
Lee, Siu-Lam
Lee, Sue Ying
Lee, Susan H.
Lee, Tsaifeng Mazie
Lee, Tsoung-Chao
Lee, Tsung-Dao
Lee, Tung-Kwang
Lee, Tzesan David
Lee, Vic Ling
Lee, Ving J.
Lee, Vivian Wai-fun
Lee, Wea Hwa
Lee, Wei-Kuo
Lee, Wei-ping Andrew
Lee, William Wai-Lim
Lee, Yeu-Tsu Margaret
Lee, Ying K.
Lee, Yow-Min R.
Lee, Yuan Tseh
Lee, Yue-Wei
Lem, Kwok Wai
Leong, Jack Y. H.
Leong, Robin Yee
Leong, Russell C.
Leu, Dennis Thomas
Leung, Benjamin Shuet-Kin
Leung, Chi Kin
Leung, Christopher Chung-Kit
Leung, Chung-Ngoc
Leung, Dennis B.

Leung, Edwin Pak-Wah
Leung, Ida M.
Leung, Ka-Wing
Leung, Kenneth Ch'uan-k'ai
Leung, Kok Ming
Leung, Louis W.
Leung, Pak Sang
Leung, Peter
Leung, Pui-Tak
Leung, Woon-Fong
Lew, Alan August
Lew, Eugene
Lew, Gloria Maria
Lew, Ronald S. W.
Lew, Susie Q.
Lew, William W.
Li, Bichuan
Li, Bing An
Li, C. C.
Li, Charles N.
Li, Che-Yu
Li, Cheng
Li, Chia-yu
Li, Ching-Chung
Li, Chu-tsing
Li, Conan K. N.
Li, Dening
Li, Diane Dai
Li, George S.
Li, Guodong
Li, Hanna Wu
Li, James C. M.
Li, Jennifer L. H.
Li, Jia
Li, Kai
Li, Kuiyuan
Li, Lillian M.
Li, Lily Elizabeth
Li, Ling-Fong
Li, Marjorie H.
Li, Ming
Li, Norman N.
Li, Peter Ta
Li, Peter Wai-Kwong
Li, Qiang
Li, San-pao
Li, Shing Ted
Li, Shuhe
Li, Tien-Yien
Li, Tingye
Li, Vivien
Li, Wen-Hsiung
Li, William Wei-Lin
Li, Wu
Li, Xiao-Bing
Li, Ya
Li, Yao Tzu
Li, Yongji
Li, Yu-ku
Li, Yuzhuo
Lian, Eric Chun-Yet
Lian, Maria Z. N.
Liang, Bruce T.
Liang, Chang-seng
Liang, Diana F.
Liang, Edison Park-tak
Liang, George Hsueh-Lee
Liang, Matthew H.
Liao, Ming
Liao, Paul Foo-Hung
Liao, Shun-Kwung
Liem, Karel Frederik
Liem, Ronald Kian Hong
Lieu, Hou-Shun
Li-lan
Lim, Antonio Lao
Lim, Billy Lee
Lim, Daniel V.
Lim, Edward Hong
Lim, Joo Kun
Lim, Josefina Paje
Lim, Kwee-Eng Lyn
Lim, Nancy Wong

Lim, Paul Stephen
Lim, Ralph Wei Hsiong
Lim, Ramon Khe-Siong
Lim, Richard
Lim, Rodney Gene
Lim, Shirley Geok-Lin
Lim, Teck-Kah
Lin, Cen-Tsong
Lin, Chhiu-Tsu
Lin, Chia Chiao
Lin, Chinlon
Lin, Dennis Kon-Jin
Lin, Diane Chang
Lin, Elizabeth
Lin, Felix
Lin, George H. Y.
Lin, Hung Chang
Lin, Ilan S.
Lin, James C.
Lin, James Chih-I
Lin, James Chow
Lin, James P.
Lin, James Peicheng
Lin, Jian
Lin, Joseph Pen-Tze
Lin, Julia C.
Lin, Kuan-Pin
Lin, Lawrence I-Kuei
Lin, Liang-Shiou
Lin, Maya Ying
Lin, Nina S. F.
Lin, Pen-Min
Lin, Pi-Erh
Lin, Ping-Wha
Lin, Poping
Lin, Robert Peichung
Lin, Sin-Shong
Lin, Stephen Yaw-rui
Lin, Sung P.
Lin, Ting-Ting Yao
Lin, Tung Yen
Lin, Wen Chun
Lin, Xiao-Song
Lin, You-An Robert
Lin, Yü-sheng
Lin, Yuyi
Ling, Alexander
Ling, Amy
Ling, Christine N.
Ling, Hao
Ling, Hubert
Ling, Hung Chi
Ling, Jack Chieh-Sheng
Ling, Paul
Ling, Paul Kimberley
Ling, Ta-Yung
Ling, Yu-long
Ling, Zhi-Kui
Liou, Kuo-Nan
Liou, Shy-Sheng P.
Liu, Alan Fong-Ching
Liu, Alfred H.
Liu, Anne W.
Liu, Ben Chieh
Liu, Benjamin Y. H.
Liu, Ching-Tong
Liu, Chuan Sheng
Liu, Chung-Chiun
Liu, David Ta-ching
Liu, Dwight Davidson
Liu, Edmund K.
Liu, Edwin H.
Liu, Eric P.
Liu, Gerald Hanmin
Liu, Hanjun
Liu, Henry
Liu, Hong
Liu, Hong-Ting
Liu, Hsien-Tung
Liu, Hsun Kao
Liu, James P.
Liu, Jiang Bo
Liu, Jie

Liu, John J.
Liu, Juanita Ching
Liu, Jun S.
Liu, Karen Chia-Yu
Liu, Keh-Fei Frank
Liu, Leighton Kam Fat
Liu, Lily Pao-Ih
Liu, Mengxiong
Liu, Min
Liu, Mini
Liu, Nancy Shao-Lan
Liu, Nora M.
Liu, Ping
Liu, Pinghui Victor
Liu, Qing-Huo
Liu, Samuel Hsi-Peh
Liu, Shia-Ling
Liu, Stephen Shu-Ning
Liu, Susana Juh-mei
Liu, Te-Hua
Liu, Thomas
Liu, Tsu-huei
Liu, Warren Kuo-Tung
Liu, Wei-Min
Liu, Wei-Ying
Liu, Xingwu
Liu, Yilu
Liu, Ying
Liu, Yung Sheng
Liu, Yung-Way
Liu, Yung Y.
Liu, Zhuang
Liu, Zhuangyi
Lo, Chi-Yuan
Lo, Chien-kuo
Lo, Howard H.
Lo, Kwok-Yung
Lo, Suzanne J.
Lo, Yuen-Tze
Lock, Chuck Choi
Locke, Gary F.
Loh, Eugene C.
Loh, Wallace D.
Long, Grace Fan
Loo, Cyrus W.
Loo, Ti Li
Lord, Bette Bao
Loui, Warren R.
Louie, Ai-Ling M.
Louie, Alan C.
Louie, Cliff
Louie, David A.
Louie, David H.
Louie, David Wong
Louie, Dickson Lew
Louie, Emma Woo
Louie, Eric K.
Louie, Eugene H.
Louie, George Chang
Louie, Gilman G.
Louie, James Sam
Louie, Marvin Kim
Louie, Paul
Louie, Ruby Ling
Louie, Sammy G.
Louie, Steven Gwon Sheng
Louis, Lawrence Hua-Hsien
Low, Harry William
Low, Loh-Lee
Low, Randall
Lowe, Rolland Choy
Lu, David Yun-Chen
Lu, Donghao Robert
Lu, Frank Kerping
Lu, I-Tai
Lu, Janet C.
Lu, Janet Y. H.
Lu, John Y.
Lu, Kau U.
Lu, Le-Wu
Lu, Lina
Lu, Linyu Laura
Lu, Luo

Lu, Mi
Lu, Michael Y.
Lu, Min Zhan
Lu, Ponzy
Lu, Steven Zhiyun
Luh, Bor Shiun
Luh, Jiang
Lui, MeiZhu
Lui, Wai Ming
Lum, Albert C.
Lum, Dean Scott
Lum, Doman
Lum, George
Lum, Jean L. J.
Lum, Sharon Shou Jen
Lum, Tammy Kar-Hee
Lum, Vincent Y.
Luo, Shen-Yi
Ly, Kieu Kim
Ma, Chen-Lung Ringo
Ma, Ching-To Albert
Ma, Fai
Ma, Laurence J. C.
Ma, Li-Chen
Ma, Mark T.
Ma, Stephen K.
Ma, Tai-Loi
Ma, Tso-Ping
Ma, Tsu Sheng
Ma, Wenhai
Ma, Xiaoyun
Ma, Yan
Ma, Yi Hua
Ma, Yo-Yo
Mah, Richard Sze Hao
Mak, James
Mak, Sioe Tho
Mak, Stanley M.
Mak, William K.
Man, Chi-Sing
Mao, Chung-Ling
Mao, Ho-Kwang
Mao, James Chieh-Hsia
Mar, Dan K.
Mar, William David
Marr, William Wei-Yi
Matsuda, Fay Chew
McNeely, June
Mei, Chiang Chung
Mei, June Y.
Mei, Kenneth K.
Mei, Wai-Ning
Meng, James Cheng-Sun
Meng, Jimmy Z.
Meng, Qing-Min
Meng, Xiannong
Minnick, Sylvia Sun
Minnig, William Paul
Mo, Hugh H.
Mo, Luke W.
Mong, Seymour
Mow, Bill
Mow, Chao-chow
Moy, Donald
Moy, Edmund
Moy, George S.
Moy, Henry
Moy, James S.
Moy, Jeffery Fei
Moy, Mamie Wong
Moy, Robert Carl
Moy, Stan Yip
Mui, Constance L.
Nee, Michael Wei-Kuo
Ng, Assunta C. M.
Ng, David
Ng, Frank Mang Leang
Ng, Jeanne H.
Ng, Jeffrey C. F.
Ng, Michael Wai-Man
Ng, Patrick
Ng, Rebecca P.
Ng, Richard

Ng, Richard Yut
Ng, Tang-Tat Percy
Ng, Vincent W.
Ng, Yuk-Chow
Ngai, Kia Ling
Ng-Breckwoldt, May Sue
Ni, Preston C.
Ning, Tak Hung
Nip, Wai-Kit
O, Cao Kinh
O, San Luong
Omura, Mark Christopher
Ong, Cynthia K. Char
Ong, Edward Frank
Ong, Georgina
Ong, James M.
Ong, Nai-Phuan
Ong, Owh Kian
Ong, Sing-Cheong
Ou, Hsien-Wang
Ou, Shukong
Ozawa, Seiji
Pai, Anna Chao
Pai, David Hsien-Chung
Pak, Koon Yan
Pak, Ronald Yu-Sang
Pan, Dawning
Pan, Yuh-Kang
Pang, Rubye-Huey
Pang, Seng Puang
Pang, Wilma
Pao, Chia-Ven
Park Li, Gimmy
Pei, I. M.
Pei, Lowry Cheng-Wu
Pei, Richard Y.
Peng, Dachung Pat
Peng, George Tso Chih
Peng, Jen-Chieh
Peng, Syd S.
Peng, Ying-shin Christine
Pham, Henry Tuoc Van
Phan, Sem Hin
Pian, Carlson Chao-Ping
Pian, Theodore Hsueh-Huang
Pien, Edward H.
Pong, Ting-Chuen
Pouw, Stanley Siong-In
Pun, Pattle Pak-Toe
Quan, Hanson Wayne
Quan, Katie
Quan, William Chun
Quan, Xina
Quon, Check Yuen
Rahman, Yueh-Erh
Rathbone, Susan Wu
Reeves, Keanu
Ren, Shang Yuan
Roser, Ce
Ru, Wesley
Sah, Chih-Tang
Sato, Gary Teruo
Seto, Belinda P.
Seto, Robert Mahealani Ming
Sha, Ji-Ping
Sha, Shung-tse
Sha, William T.
Sham, Lu Jeu
Shan, Robert Kuocheng
Shang, Stella I-Hua
Shang, Weijia
Shen, Benjamin Shih-Ping
Shen, Chia Theng
Shen, Chung Yu
Shen, Grace Liu
Shen, Hao-Ming
Shen, Hsieh Wen
Shen, I-Yao
Shen, Liang Chi
Shen, Shan-Fu
Shen, Sheldon Shih-Ta
Shen, Tek-Ming
Shen, Thomas T.

Shen, Wu-Mian
Shen, Xiao-Yan
Shen, Yuen-Ron
Sheng, Bright
Sheng, Ping
Sheng, Tony L.
Shiang, Elaine
Shiao, Daniel Da-Fong
Shieh, John Ting-Chung
Shih, Arnold Shang-Teh
Shih, Chia C.
Shih, Chiang
Shih, Chilin
Shih, Fred F.
Shih, Hong-Yee
Shih, Jason Chia-Hsing
Shih, Joan Fai
Shih, Philip C.
Shih, Tom I-Ping
Shih, Tsung-Ming Anthony
Shih, Wei
Shim, Walton Kenn Tsung
Shum, William
Shwe, Hla
Sieu, Benny Lou
Sing, Lillian K.
Siu, Nancy
Siu, Yum-Tong
Siy, James Andrew
So, Magdalene Yee-Huen
So, Ying Hung
Song, John S.
Song, Xueshu
Soo, Billy S.
Soo, Charlie H.
Soo Hoo, Eric Randolph
Soo Hoo, Karen
SooHoo, Leo, Jr.
Soo Hoo, Richard
Soohoo, Richard Allen
Soo Hoo, William Fong
Soong, Arthur J.
Su, Judy Ya-Hwa Lin
Su, Julie Chu-chu
Su, Timothy C.
Su, Zhixin
Suen, Ching-Yun
Sui, Anna
Sum, Grace C. K.
Sun, Chang-Tsan
Sun, Chih Ree
Sun, Frank F.
Sun, Hugo Sui-Hwan
Sun, Richard C.
Sun, Samuel Sai-Ming
Sung, Betty Lee
Sung, Chi Ching
Sung, Zinmay Renee
Sy, Antonio Ngo, Jr.
Sy, Francisco S.
Sy, Jose
Sze, Chia-Ming
Sze, Morgan Chuan-Yuan
Sze, Paul Y.
Szeto, Erik K.
Tai, Chen To
Tai, Julia Chow
Tai, Peter Y. P.
Taira, Toy-Ping Chan
Takayama, Gregg
Tam, Christopher Kwong-Wah
Tam, Eric Tak-Keung
Tam, Henry
Tam, Leo
Tam, Sang William
Tam, Thomas Kwai-Sang
Tan, Amy Ruth
Tan, Barrie
Tan, Cheng Imm
Tan, Chin An
Tan, Chor Weng
Tan, Colleen Woo
Tan, Henry S. I.

Tan, Jack Sim Eddy
Tan, Lawrence W.
Tan, Sinforosa G.
Tan, Tjiauw-Ling
Tan, Wai-Yuan
Tan, Zoe
Tang, America
Tang, Andrew Hing-Yee
Tang, Assumpta
Tang, Charles Chau Ching
Tang, Chik-Kwun
Tang, Chung Liang
Tang, Chung-Shih
Tang, David Kwong-Yu
Tang, Eugenia C. G.
Tang, Jianxin
Tang, Kin Ling
Tang, Klairon Kit-ling
Tang, Lillian Y. D.
Tang, Mark Giakhy
Tang, Ming-Je
Tang, Paul Chi Lung
Tang, Roger Y. W.
Tang, Sherman
Tang, Thomas
Tang, Thomas Tze-Tung
Tang, Victor K. T.
Tang, Wen
Tang, Yi-Noo
Tang, Yu-Sun
Tao, Stephen G.
Tchen, John Kuo Wei
Teng, Anthony Yung-yuan
Teng, Henry Shao-lin
Teng, Hsi Ching
Teng, Lee Chang-Li
Teng, Mabel Sik Mei
Teng, Tsuchi Paul
Thao, Christopher Teng
Tien, Chang-Lin
Tien, H. Ti
Tien, Ping King
Ting, Jan C.
Ting, Joseph K.
Ting, Lee Hsia
Ting, Robert Yen-Ying
Ting, Samuel C. C.
Ting, Sandra
Ting, Shih-Fan
Ting, T. C.
Ting, Thomas Chi Tsai
Ting, Ying Ji
Ting Cang-Kim, Donna Marle
Tom, Angelo C.
Tom, Leland B.
Tom, Melvin Gee Lim
Tom, Ping
Tong, Alvin H.
Tong, Benjamin Robert
Tong, Douglas L.
Tong, Franklin Fuk-Kay
Tong, Jennie S.
Tong, Lik Kuen
Tong, Sun-De
Tong, Ts'ing H.
Tong, Wen-How
Toy, Madeline Shen
Tran, Tri K.
Tsai, Bilin Paula
Tsai, Bor-sheng
Tsai, Chester
Tsai, Chon-Kwo
Tsai, Frank Y.
Tsai, James H.
Tsai, Kuei-wu
Tsai, Lin
Tsai, Michael Ming-Ping
Tsai, Ming-Daw
Tsai, Stanley
Tsai, Stephen Wei-Lun
Tsai, Theodore F.
Tsang, Bion Yu-Ting
Tsang, Chiu

Tsang, Dean Zensh
Tsang, Wai Lin
Tsao, Francis Hsiang-Chian
Tsao, George T.
Tse, Charles Jack-Ching
Tse, Francis Lai-Sing
Tse, Harley Yau-Shuin
Tse, John Yung Dong
Tse, Ming-Kai
Tse, Sau P.
Tse Dinh, Yuk-Ching
Tsen, May F.
Tseng, James H. W.
Tseng, Mou-sien
Tseng, Muna Siu-Chuk
Tseng, Rose Y. L.
Tso, Tien Chioh
Tsuei, Y. G.
Tsui, Annie
Tsui, Daniel Chee
Tsui, Pauline Woo
Tsui, Susan Lee
Tu, Ching-I
Tu, Harold Kai
Tu, Shengru
Tu, Shiao-Chun
Tuan, Debbie Fu-tai
Tuan, San Fu
Tun, Harry T.
Tung, John
Tung, Ko-Yung
Tung, Theodore H.
Tung, Wu-Ki
Tung, Yeou-Koung
Tye, Bik-Kwoon Yeung
Tye, Sze-Hoi Henry
Tzeng, Kenneth Kai-Ming
Ueng, Charles En-Shiuh
Un, Howard Ho-Wei
Uno, Anne Quan
Uy, William C.
Wan, David A.
Wan, Frederic Yui-Ming
Wan, James X.
Wan, Peter J.
Wan, Stephen Samkong
Wan, Sze-kar
Wang, Alan P.
Wang, Albert S. D.
Wang, Arthur C.
Wang, Bee-Lan Chan
Wang, Ben
Wang, Bin
Wang, Carl C. T.
Wang, Chao-Cheng
Wang, Charles B.
Wang, Charles Chen-ding
Wang, Charles Pei
Wang, Charles Ping
Wang, Chi-Hua
Wang, Chi-Sun
Wang, Chih-Chung
Wang, Chih H.
Wang, Ching Chung
Wang, Ching-Hua
Wang, Christine A.
Wang, Dajin
Wang, Daniel I.-Chyau
Wang, David Edward
Wang, Dazong
Wang, Deane
Wang, Don J.
Wang, Dong-Ping
Wang, Dora Chia-Chi
Wang, Fa-chung
Wang, Fei-Yue
Wang, Frederick Andrew
Wang, Gene
Wang, George H.
Wang, George Hung-Kai
Wang, Guo-Hua
Wang, Gwo-Ching
Wang, Gwo-Jaw

Wang, H. E. Frank
Wang, Hai-Tao
Wang, Helen Hai-ling
Wang, Henry Yee-Neen
Wang, Howard H.
Wang, Hsueh-Hwa
Wang, Huaqing
Wang, I-chih
Wang, I-Shou
Wang, James C. F.
Wang, James Chou
Wang, Jaw-Kai
Wang, Jen-Yu
Wang, Ji-Ping
Wang, Jia
Wang, Jie
Wang, Jih Ming
Wang, Jin
Wang, Jing
Wang, Jun
Wang, Junping
Wang, K. P.
Wang, Kuan
Wang, Kung-Lee
Wang, Kuo Chang
Wang, Kuo King
Wang, Lawrence Kongpu
Wang, Leon Ru-Liang
Wang, Lily L.
Wang, Ling Jun
Wang, Louie Kehluh
Wang, Louisa Ho-Ching
Wang, Luoyong
Wang, Margaret K.
Wang, May X.
Wang, Ming-Yu Rachel
Wang, N. T.
Wang, Nam Sun
Wang, Nancy Y.
Wang, Orrin Nan Chung
Wang, Paul Weily
Wang, Qun
Wang, Richard Hsu-Shien
Wang, Rita
Wang, Robert T.
Wang, Samuel T. M.
Wang, Shaoguang
Wang, Shaw S.
Wang, Shen K.
Wang, Shien Tsun
Wang, Shih-Chun
Wang, Shih-Ho
Wang, Shih-Liang
Wang, ShiQing
Wang, Shou-Ling
Wang, Shu-Hsia
Wang, Stanley
Wang, Stuart Sui-Sheng
Wang, Su-Su
Wang, Suojin
Wang, Sylvia
Wang, Tixiang
Wang, Veronica C.
Wang, Victor Sheng
Wang, Wayne
Wang, Wei
Wang, William Kai-Sheng
Wang, William S-Y.
Wang, Xiaohan
Wang, Xiaoping
Wang, Xingwu
Wang, Xue-Sen
Wang, Xuefeng
Wang, Xun-Li
Wang, Yan
Wang, Yang
Wang, Yi-Tin
Wang, Yi T'ung
Wang, Yijiang
Wang, Yong Tai
Wang, Yu
Wang, Zhi Qiang
Wei, Anthony Yueh-shan

Wei, Benjamin Min
Wei, Chao Hui
Wei, James
Wei, Kuo-Yen
Wei, Wei
Wei, Wei-Zen
Wei, William
Wei, Yen
Wen, Shih-liang
Whang, Yun Chow
Wing, Charmeen Hah-Ming
Wing, James
Wing, Jeannette M.
Wong, Alan S.
Wong, Albert
Wong, Albert Y.
Wong, Alfred
Wong, Alvin C. P.
Wong, Angela Ma
Wong, Anna Clara
Wong, Anthony Joseph
Wong, B. D.
Wong, Backman
Wong, Barry
Wong, Benson D.
Wong, Bernard P.
Wong, Bing K.
Wong, Bradley D.
Wong, Bryan Allen
Wong, Buck W.
Wong, Byron F.
Wong, Charles Foo, Jr.
Wong, Clark Chiu-Yuen
Wong, Clifford S.
Wong, Daniel W.
Wong, David Craig
Wong, David Tai Wai
Wong, David Taiwai
Wong, David Yue
Wong, Deborah Anne
Wong, Desmond C.
Wong, Dolores
Wong, Doris Ning
Wong, Dorothy
Wong, Dorothy Pan
Wong, Earl Gar, Jr.
Wong, Eugene
Wong, Eugene G. C.
Wong, Evelyn
Wong, Frank F.
Wong, Frank Van
Wong, Frederick
Wong, George
Wong, Gregory Dean
Wong, Gregory Sterling
Wong, Harold H.
Wong, Harry Yuen Chee
Wong, Henry Sik-Yin
Wong, Jacqueline Jeanne
Wong, Jade Snow
Wong, James H.
Wong, Janet S.
Wong, Janine Mei-Chiao
Wong, John Bullitt
Wong, John D.
Wong, John Lap
Wong, Kar-yiu
Wong, Karl
Wong, Kau Fui
Wong, Kenneth P.
Wong, Kent Douglas
Wong, Kin Fai
Wong, Kin-Ping
Wong, King-Lap
Wong, Kuang Chung
Wong, Kwan P.
Wong, Liliane R.
Wong, Linda J.
Wong, Martha
Wong, Martin Ding-Fat
Wong, Maywood
Wong, Mel
Wong, Morton Min-Fong

Wong, Nellie
Wong, Nicole Anna
Wong, Ovid K.
Wong, Pablo Jose
Wong, Pat Chung
Wong, Paul
Wong, Paul K.
Wong, Paul Wing Kon
Wong, Peter Alexander
Wong, Peter P.
Wong, Philip
Wong, Philip T.
Wong, Po Kee
Wong, Pui Kei
Wong, Ray G. L.
Wong, Raymond Y.
Wong, Richard Gene
Wong, Rita F.
Wong, Shawn Hsu
Wong, Siu G.
Wong, Sophie Chao
Wong, Steven Dale
Wong, Steven W.
Wong, Terry Chen Yi
Wong, Tom
Wong, Vernon D. B.
Wong, Victor Kenneth
Wong, Wendell P.
Wong, William
Wong, William K. C.
Wong, Willie
Wong, Wing Y.
Woo, Benson K.
Woo, Celeste Kimberlee
Woo, Edward D.
Woo, Henry
Woo, James T. K.
Woo, Lecon
Woo, Michael K.
Woo, Michael T.
Woo, P. T.
Woo, Robert Ken, Jr.
Woo, S. B.
Woo, William Franklin
Wu, Alfred Chi-Tai
Wu, Angela Yuen
Wu, Anna Chaoying
Wu, Anna Fang
Wu, Chien-Shiung
Wu, Chien-yun
Wu, Chih
Wu, Ching-Sheng
Wu, Chivey Dragenson Lung
Wu, Christine A.
Wu, Christopher N.
Wu, Chun-Fang
Wu, Dan Qing
Wu, De Ting
Wu, Diana Ting Liu
Wu, En Shinn
Wu, Fa Yueh
Wu, Francis Taming
Wu, Frank I.
Wu, George
Wu, Harry Pao-Tung
Wu, Ho-Mou
Wu, Hsin-i
Wu, Hung-Hsi
Wu, Jean Yu-Wen Shen
Wu, Jennifer Lee
Wu, Jeremy S.
Wu, Jie
Wu, Jin Zhong
Wu, Joseph M.
Wu, Julia Li
Wu, Julian Juh-Ren
Wu, Jun-Ru
Wu, Kingsley K.
Wu, Konrad T.
Wu, Lyn Xiling
Wu, Nan-Ray
Wu, Nancy Nan-hwa
Wu, Norman B.

Wu, Roy S.
Wu, Shi Tsan
Wu, Shien-Ming
Wu, Shih-Yen
Wu, Stan
Wu, Sylvia Cheng
Wu, Tai Te
Wu, Theodore Yao-Tsu
Wu, Ting-Wen
Wu, Tung
Wu, Wallace C.
Wu, Wei-hsiung
Wu, Wei-ping
Wu, William Gay
Wu, Xian
Wu, Xian Connie
Wu, Y. C. L. Susan
Wu, Yao Hua
Wu, Yau
Wu, Yen
Wu, Yenna
Wu, Ying Victor
Wu, Zhijian
Xia, Yun
Xiong, William Joua
Xu, Chia-Yi
Yan, Haiping
Yan, Hong-Cheng
Yan, Martin
Yan, Sau-Chi Betty
Yan, Xiao-Hai
Yang, Albert C.
Yang, Anand Alan
Yang, Bingen
Yang, Chen Ning
Yang, Chia Chi
Yang, Chih Ted
Yang, Chyan
Yang, Da-Ping
Yang, Han-Jiang
Yang, Henry Tzu-yow
Yang, In Che
Yang, Jen Tsi
Yang, John Eric
Yang, Julie Chi-Sun
Yang, Kai
Yang, Nien-chu C.
Yang, Qing
Yang, Ralph Tzu-Bow
Yang, Schuman Chuo
Yang, Song
Yang, Song-Yu
Yang, Susan Y.
Yang, Sze Cheng
Yang, Tah-teh
Yang, Timothy C.
Yang, Victor Chi-Min
Yang, Weitao
Yang, Wen-Ching
Yang, William C. T.
Yang, Winston L.
Yang, Xiaowei
Yang, Yisong
Yang, Zhanbo
Yano, Fleur B.
Yao, David D.
Yao, Dennis Alden
Yao, Lun-Shin
Yao, Shi Chune
Yau, Cheuk Chung
Yau, King-Wai
Ye, Jose
Yee, Alfred Alphonse
Yee, Allen Y.
Yee, Angelina Chun-chu
Yee, Barbara W. K.
Yee, Carlton S.
Yee, Darlene
Yee, Donald H.
Yee, Donald Poy
Yee, Edmond
Yee, Franklin
Yee, James

Yee, Jimmie N.
Yee, John David
Yee, Lawrence K.
Yee, Melinda C.
Yee, Nancy J.
Yee, Robert Donald
Yee, Shirley Jo-Ann
Yee, Stanley C.
Yee, Virginia Bow Sue
Yee, Walter
Yee, Wilfred Wee Bin
Yee, Wong Herbert
Yeh, Billy Kuo-Jiun
Yeh, Chai
Yeh, Chien Jo
Yeh, Gregory S. Y.
Yeh, Hen-Geul
Yeh, Hsi-Han
Yeh, Hsien-Yang
Yeh, Ida Shuyen Chiang
Yeh, James Tehcheng
Yeh, Lee-Chuan Caroline
Yeh, Michelle M.
Yeh, Pu-Sen
Yeh, Susan S. Wang
Yeh, Thomas Y.
Yen, Alfred Chueh-Chin
Yen, Ben Chie
Yen, Joan Jue
Yen, Kang Kenneth
Yen, Matthew Ming-Shih
Yen, Nai-Chyuan
Yen, Peter T.
Yen, Sherman M. Y.
Yen, Teh Fu
Yen, Wen-Hsiung
Yen, William Mao-Shung
Yen, Yang
Yen-Koo, Helen Chiang-ying
Yenson, Evelyn Phoebe
Yep, Lawrence Michael
Yep, Ralph Lee
Yeung, Chun W.
Yeung, Ronald Wai-Chun
Yi, Gang
Yi, Xiaoxiong
Yien, Jean May
Yih, Chia-Shun
Yih, Roy Yangming
Yih, Yuehwern
Yim, Chi-Kin Bennett
Yin, Gang George
Yin, George Kuo-Ming
Yin, Lo I.
Yin, Mark Y. Q.
Yin, Ronald L.
Yin, Xiao-huang
Yin, Zenong
Yiu, Pao On
Yoh, John K.
Young, Alice
Young, Bing-Lin
Young, Franklin
Young, Lloyd Yee
Young, Peter R.
Young, Shirley
Young, Shun Chung
Young, Tzay Y.
Yu, Chi Kang
Yu, Clara
Yu, Clement Tak
Yu, Fu-Li
Yu, Gang
Yu, James H.
Yu, Jimmy Chai-Mei
Yu, John K.
Yu, Kai Fun
Yu, Kar Yuk
Yu, Larry
Yu, Linda
Yu, Paul Kit-Lai
Yu, Peter Tat-kong
Yu, Priscilla C.

Yu, Robert Kuan-jen
Yu, Shiao-ling S.
Yu, Victor Lin-Kai
Yu, Wen C.
Yu, Yun-Sheng
Yuan, Jian-Min
Yuan, Luke Chia-Liu
Yuan, Robin Tsu-Wang
Yuan, Sidney W. K.
Yue, Chinny
Yue, David T.
Yue, Robert Hon-Sang
Yue, Xiaodong
Yuen, Calvin N.
Yuen, Paul C.
Yuen, Steve Chi-Yin
Yun, Xiaoping
Zee, Teddy
Zen, E-an
Zhang, John Z. H.
Zhang, Longxi
Zhang, Wenxian
Zhao, Quansheng
Zheng, Yuan Fang
Zia, Helen
Zia, Hoyt Hanson
Zien, Tse-Fou

HMONG

Lo, Tou Ger
Thao, Christopher Teng
Vanchiasong, Siong Koua
Xiong, Lee Pao
Xiong, William Joua
Yang, Lang

HONG KONG

Au, Andrew T.
Au, Calvin K.
Chan, Angela
Chan, Anthony Kit-Cheung
Chan, Arthur H.
Chan, Arthur Wing Kay
Chan, Chiu Yeung
Chan, David S.
Chan, James C.
Chan, James C. M.
Chan, Kam Chuen
Chan, Kwan M.
Chan, Kwok Hung
Chan, Laurence Kwong-Fai
Chan, Lung S.
Chan, Sham-Yuen
Chan, Tsze Hau
Chan, Wai-Yee
Chan, Yeung Yu
Chang, Mabel Li
Chang, Maria Hsia
Chang, Michael S.
Chang, Peter C.
Chau, Henry Chun-Nam
Chau, Peter
Chen, Terry
Chen, Victor John
Cheng, Brian Kai-Ming
Cheng, Lawrence Kai-Leung
Cheng, Louis Tsz-Wan
Cheung, Fernando C. H.
Cheung, John Yan-Poon
Cheung, Lim H.
Chin, George K. W.
Chiu, Wah
Cho, David
Choi, Michael Kamwah
Chow, Alexander Wing-Yat
Chow, Balance Tin-Ping
Chow, Michael Hung-Chun
Chow, Mo-yuen
Chung, Anni Yuet-Kuen
Chung, Catherine L.
Chung, Deborah Duen Ling

Chung, Jesse Y. W.
Chung, Simon Lam-Ying
Dow, Faye Lynn
Fu, Peter K.
Ho, Alexander Kitman
Ho, Andrew Kong-Sun
Ho, Michael Shiukeung
Ho, Yui Tim
Hong, George K.
Hsu, Evelyn
Huie, Carmen Wah-Kit
Kan, Yuet Wai
Kan-Mitchell, June
Ko, Edmond Inq-Ming
Ko, Kei-Yu
Kung, Alice How Kuen
Kwan, Nancy Kashen
Kwan, Simon Hing-Man
Kwok, Chuck Chun-yau
Kwong, Eva
Lam, Alex W.
Lam, Chun H.
Lam, Dick
Lam, Leo Kongsui
Lau, David T.
Lau, Frederick C.
Lau, Joseph T. Y.
Lau, Ngar-Cheung
Lau, Regina
Lau, Shuk-fong
Lau, Tin Man
Law, H. David
Lee, Angel Wai-Mun
Leung, Charles Cheung-Wan
Leung, Edwin Pak-Wah
Leung, Joseph Yuk-Tong
Leung, Kai-Cheong
Leung, Margaret W.
Leung, PingSun
Leung, Pui-Tak
Leung, Som-Lok
Leung, Wing Hai
Leung, Yuen-Sang
Li, Ivan C.
Li, Victor C.
Li, Victor On-Kwok
Liang, Edison Park-tak
Lin, Shin
Lin, Yuet-Chang Joseph
Liu, Peter Chi-Wah
Liu, Wing Kam
Lui, Wai Ming
Lum, Tammy Kar-Hee
Ma, Alan King-Yan
Ma, Ching-To Albert
Ma, Michael
Mak, Chi Ho
Mak, Paul P.
Moy, James Yee Kin
Ng, Kam Wing
Ng, Martin K.
Ng, May-May Donna Lee
Ng, Patrick
Ng, Rita Mei-Ching
Ng, Wing
Ng, Yuk-Chow
Poon, Chi-Sang
Pui, Ching-Hon
Quon, Shun Wing
Shen, Tek-Ming
Shum, Alex C.
So, Ronald Ming Cho
Sy, Bon Kiem
Tam, James Pingkwan
Tam, Simon M. W.
Tan, Chin An
Tang, Alex Ying Ho
Tang, Charles Chau Ching
Tang, Julie Mong-See
Tang, Wallace T. Y.
Tang, Wilson Hon-chung
Tong, Alex Wai Ming
Tong, Franklin Fuk-Kay

Tong, Jennie S.
Tse, Stephen
Tsen, Meng Chi
Ts'o, Paul On Pong
Tsui, Cheryl Wai-Kuen
Tye, Bik-Kwoon Yeung
Tye, Sze-Hoi Henry
Wong, Benedict Ding Chung
Wong, Daniel W.
Wong, David Tai Wai
Wong, Eugene Hanlai
Wong, Henry H.
Wong, John Lap
Wong, Johnny S.
Wong, Kenneth K.
Wong, Kwan P.
Wong, Kwok-Fai Matthew
Wong, Peter M. C.
Wong, Samuel T.
Wong, Suk Yee
Wong, William Wai-Lun
Wong, William Wai-Lun
Woo, Edward D.
Woo, Savio Lau-Ching
Wu, Sau Lan Yu
Wu, Wallace C.
Yau, Cheuk Chung
Yau, Stephen Shing-Toung
Yim, Solomon C. S.
Yu, Kai-Bor
Yu, Winnie Y.
Yuen-Terry, Kaimay
Yung, Kenneth Kwokhung
Yung, Ringo
Yung, W. K. Alfred

INDIA

Abhyankar, Shreeram Shankar
Abraham, John
Abraham, Thomas
Achar, Narahari B. N.
Advani, Suresh Gopaldas
Agarwal, Arun Kumar
Agarwal, Gyan Chand
Agarwal, Ramesh Kumar
Agarwala, Vinod Shanker
Aggarwal, Anil K.
Aggarwal, Bharat Bhushan
Aggarwal, Ishwar D.
Aggarwal, Lalit Kumar
Aggarwal, Manmohan D.
Aggarwal, Raj
Aggarwal, Rajesh
Aggarwal, Roshan Lal
Agnihotri, Newal K.
Agrawal, Brijmohan
Agrawal, Dharma Prakash
Agrawal, Krishna Chandra
Agrawal, Pradeep K.
Ahluwalia, Balwant S.
Ahluwalia, Brij Mohan Singh
Ahluwalia, Daljit Singh
Ahluwalia, Harjit Singh
Ahluwalia, Rashpal S.
Ahmed, A. Razzaque
Ahuja, Satinder
Akkapeddi, Prasad Rao
Ali, Yusuf
Anand, A. Angela
Anand, Charanjit S.
Anand, Rajen S.
Anand, Rakesh
Anand, Satish Chandra
Anandan, Munisamy
Annamalai, Nagappan K.
Arora, Madan Lal
Arora, Samir Chandra
Arora, Vijay K.
Ashtekar, Abhay Vasant
Aslam, Nasim Mohammed
Aulakh, Kay
Bagasra, Omar

Bagga, K. Jay Singh
Bahal, Surendra Mohan
Bahl, Om Parkash
Bajaj, Harjit Singh
Bajpai, Praphulla Kumar
Bajpai, Rakesh Kumar
Balachandran, Kashi
  Ramamurthi
Balaguru, Perumalsamy N.
Baliga, Jayant
Banakar, Umesh Virupaksh
Banerjee, Amiya Kumar
Banerjee, Chandra Madhab
Banerjee, Debasish
Banerjee, Jayanta Kumar
Banerjee, Mukul R.
Banerjee, Prithviraj
Banerjee, Sanjay K.
Banerji, Ranan Bihari
Banik, Sambhu Nath
Bapatla, Krishna M.
Barnabas, Mathews Mar
Barot, Navnit Manilal
Barve, Kumar P.
Basu, Sutapa
Batra, Rajeev
Batra, Ravi
Batra, Romesh Chander
Bawa, Mohendra S.
Bedi, Sandeep
Behl, Wishvender K.
Bhada, Rohinton Khurshed
Bhagat, Hitesh Rameshchandra
Bhagat, Nazir A.
Bhagavatula, Vijayakumar
Bhalla, Vipan Kumar
Bhandari, Sanjiv
Bhandarkar, Suhas D.
Bhapkar, Vasant P.
Bhargava, Ashok
Bhaskar, Surindar Nath
Bhat, K. Ramachandra
Bhat, Shankar U.
Bhathena, Sam Jehangirji
Bhatia, Ramesh
Bhatia, Salim A. L.
Bhatia, Sharmila
Bhatia, Tej K.
Bhatnagar, Deepak
Bhatnagar, Kunwar P.
Bhatnagar, Yogendra Mohan
Bhatt, Gita
Bhatt, Gunvant R.
Bhatt, Jagdish J.
Bhatt, Kiran Chandrakant
Bhattacharjee, Jnanendra Kumar
Bhattacharya, Pradeep Kumar
Bhattacharya, Purna
Bhattacharya, Rabi Sankar
Bhattacharyya, Ashim Kumar
Bhattacharyya, Gouri Kanta
Bhavnani, Pratap Gagumal
Bhojwani, Ram J.
Bhown, Ajit Singh
Bhuyan, Bijoy Kumar
Bijlani, Chandur Kishinchand
Biradavolu, Kaleswara Rao
Biswas, Dipak R.
Biswas, Nripendra Nath
Biswas, Renuka
Bora, Sunder S.
Borgaonkar, Digamber
  Shankarrao
Bose, Bimal Kumar
Bose, Pratim
Brahma, Chandra Sekhar
Bulsara, Ardeshir Ratan
Bulusu, Suryanarayana
Capoor, Asha
Chacko, George Kuttickal
Chacko, Harsha E.
Chacko, Kurian
Chacko, Mariam Renate

Chacko, Ranjit C.
Chacko, Varkki P.
Chadha, Kailash Chandra
Chakrabarti, Subrata Kumar
Chakrabarti, Supriya
Chakraborty, Joana
Chakravarthy, Balaji Srinivasan
Chakravarthy, Srinivasaraghavan
Chakravarthy, Upendranath
  Sharma
Chakravarty, Indranil
Chand, Naresh
Chandan, Ramesh Chandra
Chandersekaran, Achamma C.
Chandra, Abhijit
Chandramouli, S.
Chandran, Krishnan Bala
Chandran, Ravi
Chandran, Satish Raman
Chandrasekaran, Balakrishnan
Chandra Sekhar, Hosakere K.
Chandrasekhar, Subrahmanyan
Chandy, Varughese Kuzhiyath
Chapatwala, Kirit D.
Chatterjee, Lata Roy
Chatterjee, Monish Ranjan
Chatterjee, Pranab
Chatterjee, Pronoy Kumar
Chatterjee, Sankar
Chatterjee, Satya N.
Chatterjee, Sayan
Chattopadhyay, Kallol
Chaturvedi, Arvind Kumar
Chaturvedi, Ram Prakash
Chaturvedi, Rama Kant
Chaudhari, Anshumali
Chaudhari, Praveen
Chaudhari, Shobhana Ashok
Chaudhary, Ved P.
Chaudhri, Rajiv Jahangir
Chaudhuri, Tapan K.
Chavan, Sangita D.
Chellappa, Rama
Cherian, Joy
Cheryan, Munir
Chiang, Asuntha Maria Ming-
  Yee
Chishti, Athar Husain
Chitgopekar, Sharad S.
Chitkara, Vijay Kumar
Choksi, Jayendra C.
Choksy, Jamsheed Kairshasp
Chopra, Deepak
Chopra, Dev Raj
Chopra, Dharam Vir
Chopra, Inder Jit
Chopra, Jasbir
Chopra, Joginder
Chopra, Rajbir Singh
Choudhary, Subodh Kumar
Choudhury, Pinak
Choudhury, Sarita
Chowdhry, Vinay
Chowdhury, Dipak Kumar
Chugh, Ashok Kumar
Daga, Raman Lall
Dalal, Fram R.
Dalal, Siddhartha Ramanlal
Dalvi, Ramesh R.
Damria, Mulkh Raj
Dang, Harish C.
Darji, Bhuleshwar S.
Daryanani, Michael
Das, Man Singh
Das, Phanindramohan
Das, Salil Kumar
Das, Shovan
Das, Shyam
Das Dasgupta, Shamita
Dash, Sita K.
Dass, Edgar Sushil
Das Sarma, Basudeb
Datta, Ranajit Kumar

Datta, Subhendu K.
Datta, Syamal K.
Datta, Vijay K.
Dave, Janak
De, Suranjan
Deb, Arun Kumar
Debroy, Chitrita
Dedhia, Navin Shamji
Deivanayagam, Subramaniam
Deol, Harjyot
Desai, Ashok Govindji
Desai, Chandra
Desai, Chandrakant S.
Desai, Hiren Sharad
Desai, Kantilal Panachand
Desai, Manisha
Desai, Sharad P.
Desai, Sudhir G.
Desai, Suresh A.
Desai, Suresh A.
Desai, Uday
Desai, Vijay
Desai, Vikram J.
Desai, Vimal H.
Desaigoudar, Chan
Deshpande, Nilendra Ganesh
Dev, Parvati
Dhaliwal, Amrik Singh
Dharamsi, Manoj T.
Dhillon, Joginder Singh
Dhillon, Neil
Dhir, Surendra Kumar
Dhruv, Arvind B.
Dhurandhar, Nina R.
Dighe, Shrikant Vishwanath
Divakaruni, Chitra Banerjee
Dixit, Ajit S.
Dixit, Balwant N.
Dixit, Padmakar Kashinath
Dixit, Sudhakar Gajanan
Dixit, Sudhir Sharan
Doddapaneni, Narayan
Doshi, Bipin N.
D'Souza, Harry J.
Dubey, Satya Deva
Dugal, Hardev S.
Durlabhji, Subhash
Dutt, Nikil D.
Dutta, Mitra
Dutta, Pulak
Dutta, Shib Prasad
Dwivedi, Chandradhar
Dwivedy, Keshab K.
Dwivedy, Ramesh Chandra
Erramilli, Shyamsunder
Farhataziz
Farooqui, Mohammed Y. H.
Flemming, Stanley Lalit Kumar
Gajendar, Nandigam
Gajjar, Jagdish Trikamji
Gandhi, Arun Manilal
Gandhi, Homi D.
Gandhi, Mukesh P.
Gandhi, Natwar Mohan
Gandhi, Prashant P.
Gandhi, Vikram H.
Gandhi, Vikram Ijatrai
Gangal, Shiva Shanker
Gangopadhyay, Chitta R.
Gangulee, Amitava
Ganguly, Jibamitra
Ganguly, Suman
Gangwal, Rakesh
Garg, Arun
Garg, Devendra
Garg, Prem
Garg, Rajinder P.
Garg, Ramesh Chandra
Garg, Umesh
Garg, Vijay Kumar
Gavande, Sampat A.
Gawande, Atul A.
George, K. P.

Ghandhi, Sorab K.
Ghosh, Amal K.
Ghosh, Amitava
Ghosh, Bhaskar Kumar
Ghosh, Bivas Kanti
Ghosh, Chinmoy
Ghosh, Kalyan K.
Ghosh, Nimai Kumar
Ghosh, Subhas
Ghosh, Sujan
Ghosh, Swapan Kumar
Gidda, Jaswant Singh
Giri, Jagannath
Gnanadesikan, Ramanathan
Godhania, Laxman P.
Godsay, Madhu P.
Goel, Subhash Chand
Goela, Jitendra Singh
Gollahalli, Subramanyam
  Ramappa
Gopalakrishna, K. V.
Gopikanth, M. L.
Gorla, Rama S. R.
Goswami, Pankaj P.
Govil, Narendra Kumar
Govindarajulu, Zakkula
Govindjee
Goyal, Megh R.
Goyal, Suresh
Greenberg, Asha Saund
Grewal, Perminder Singh
Gulati, Adarsh Kumar
Gulrajani, Robert B.
Gupta, Ajay
Gupta, Ajay Kumar
Gupta, Amit
Gupta, Anil K.
Gupta, Anil S.
Gupta, Arjun K.
Gupta, Arun Premchand
Gupta, Ashok K.
Gupta, Ashwani Kumar
Gupta, Bhagwandas
Gupta, Bhupender S.
Gupta, Brij Mohanlal
Gupta, Chitranjan J.
Gupta, Dharam V.
Gupta, Gian Chand
Gupta, Jatinder Nath Dass
Gupta, Jiwan P.
Gupta, Kamla P.
Gupta, Krishan L.
Gupta, Madhu Sudan
Gupta, Manjula K.
Gupta, Naim C.
Gupta, Om Prakash
Gupta, Omprakash K.
Gupta, Pardeep K.
Gupta, Parveen P.
Gupta, Pradeep Kumar
Gupta, Raj Kumar
Gupta, Rajat Kumar
Gupta, Rajeshwar Kumar
Gupta, Rajiv
Gupta, Rajiv Kumar
Gupta, Rakesh Kumar
Gupta, Ram Bihari
Gupta, Ramesh K.
Gupta, Ratanlal N.
Gupta, Ron Singh
Gupta, Samir
Gupta, Sanjay
Gupta, Sanjeev
Gupta, Santosh
Gupta, Saroj Lata
Gupta, Sunil
Gupta, Surendra K.
Gupta, Surendra Kumar
Gupta, Tapan K.
Gupta, Tej R.
Gupta, Udayan
Gupta, Venu Gopal
Gupta, Vijay

Gupta, Virendra K.
Gupta, Yogendra Mohan
Hajela, Prabhat
Hajiyani, Mehdi Hussain
Haldar, Dipak
Halemane, Thirumala Raya
Hasan, Syed E.
Hashmi, Sayed A.
Hemrajani, Ramesh Relumal
Hingorani, Bhagwan V.
Hosmane, Ramachandra S.
Humayun, M. Zafri
Idnani, Kamal M.
Iqbal, Zafar
Ismail, Amin Rashid
Iyengar, Doreswamy
  Raghavachar
Iyer, Ananth. V.
Iyer, Easwar S.
Iyer, Hariharaiyer Mahadeva
Iyer, Prem Shankar
Iyer, Ram Ramaswamy
Iyer, Ravishankar Krishnan
Iyer, Siddharth Pico
Jagadeesh, G.
Jaglan, Prem S.
Jain, Arun K.
Jain, Ashit
Jain, Bimla Agarwal
Jain, Himanshu
Jain, Jitender K.
Jain, Mahendra K.
Jain, Naresh C.
Jain, Piyare Lal
Jain, Rajeev K.
Jain, Rakesh
Jain, Savitri
Jain, Sulekh Chand
Jain, Surender K.
Jain, Sushil C.
Jaisinghani, Rajan A.
Jaiswal, Gopaljee
Jalil, Mazhar
Jaluria, Yogesh
Jammalamadaka, Sreenivasa Rao
Japra, Romesh K.
Jariwala, Sharad Lallubhai
Javed, Mohd S.
Jayachandran, Toke
Jayaram, Mysore
Jayaswal, Raoheshyam K.
Jeevanandam, Malayappa
Jena, Purusottam
Jethanandani, Ashok
Jha, Mahesh Chandra
Jhaveri, Arunkumar Ganpatlal
Jindal, Om P.
Joshi, Bhairav D.
Joshi, Jagmohan
Joshi, Mukund Shankar
Joshi, Sada D.
Joshi, Sewa Ram
Joshi, Suresh Meghashyam
Jotwani, Chandru
Jungalwala, Firoze Bamanshaw
Kabadi, Balachandra Narayan
Kachru, Braj B.
Kacker, Raghu Nath
Kadaba, Prasanna Venkatarama
Kak, Subhash Chandra
Kakkar, Rita
Kakkar, Subash
Kale, Jayant R.
Kalimi, Mohammed Yahya
Kalra, Bhupinder Singh
Kalra, Rajiv
Kanojia, Ramesh Maganlal
Kapadia, Bharat S.
Kapadia, H. Viren
Kapoor, Harish K.
Kapoor, Jagmohan
Kapoor, Sanjiv
Kapoor, Shiv G.

Kapoor, Tarun
Kapur, Kamal K.
Kartha, Mukund K.
Kashyap, Moti Lal
Kashyap, Pankaj Kumar
Kattakuzhy, George Chacko
Katti, Shriniwas K.
Kaul, Balkrishena
Kaul, Maharaj Krishen
Kaul, Pradaman
Kaul, Sanjiv
Kawaja, Kaleem U.
Kedia, Ullas V.
Kerkar, Awdhoot Vasant
Khanna, Naveen
Khanna, Rajive Kumar
Khanna, Ramesh
Khanna, Shiv Narain
Khare, Bishun Narain
Khare, Mohan
Khatwani, Mahesh
Khorana, Har Gobind
Khosla, Mahesh Chandra
Khurana, Krishan Kumar
Kinra, Vikram Kumar
Kirchner, Bharti
Kiron, Ravi
Kochhar, Devendra M.
Kochhar, Man Mohan
Kokan, Ghiasuddin
Kokatnur, Mohan Gundo
Kompala, Dhinakar S.
Kondo, C. Kimi
Kothari, Ajay P.
Koul, Hira Lal
Kripalani, Kishin J.
Krishen, Kumar
Krishna, Darshan
Krishna, Gopal T. K.
Krishna, N. Rama
Krishnamoorthy, Govindarajalu
Krishnamurthy, Gerbail T.
Krishnamurti, T. N.
Krishnan, Chirakkal
Krishnan, Gopal
Krishnan, Kalliana R.
Krishnan, Radha
Krishnan, Sundaram
Krishnaswamy, Rukmini
Kshirsagar, Anant M.
Kulkarni, Anand K.
Kulkarni, Arun Digambar
Kulkarni, Arun P.
Kulkarni, Dilip
Kulkarni, Gopal S.
Kulkarni, Kishore G.
Kulkarni, Krishnaji Hanamant
Kulkarni, Ravi S.
Kulkarni, Uday Ravindra
Kumar, Arvind
Kumar, Ashir
Kumar, Ashok
Kumar, Ashok
Kumar, Atul
Kumar, Devendra
Kumar, Jatinder
Kumar, Jothi V.
Kumar, Kamalesh
Kumar, Kusum
Kumar, Kusum Verma
Kumar, Mythili
Kumar, Narinder M.
Kumar, Panganamala Ramana
Kumar, Prasanna K.
Kumar, Prem
Kumar, Raj
Kumar, Ram Sakthi
Kumar, Ramesh
Kumar, Ranganathan
Kumar, Romesh
Kumar, Saran Kandakuri
Kumar, Satyendra
Kumar, Sudhir

Kumar, Suresh A.
Kumar, Sushil
Kumar, V.
Kumar, Vijay A.
Kumar, Vipin
Kumaran, A. Krishna
Kumaroo, K.
Kundu, Bejoy B.
Kundu, Mukul Ranjan
Kurup, Shishir Ravindran
Kuttan, Appu
Kuttan, Roger
Lakkaraju, Harinarayana Sarma
Lakshman, Govind
Lakshmanan, Chithra
Lal, Rattan
Laly, Amy
Lanewala, Mohammed Ali
Langrana, Noshir A.
Laskar, Devi Sen
Lingappa, Banadakoppa
  Thimmappa
Lingappa, Yamuna
Lodhi, M. A. K.
Madan, Dwarka Nath
Made Gowda, Netkal M.
Mahadevan, Dev
Mahadevan, Kumar
Mahajan, Anoop Kumar
Mahajan, Arvind
Mahajan, Harpreet
Mahajan, Jayashree
Mahajan, Roop L.
Mahajan, Satish Murlidhar
Mahajan, Vijay
Mahajan, Y. Lal
Mahalingam, R.
Mahanthappa, Kalyana T.
Mahesh, Virendra Bhushan
Maheshwari, Arun K.
Malhotra, Anju
Malhotra, Ashok K.
Malhotra, Manohar Lal
Malhotra, Om P.
Malhotra, Vijay K.
Malik, Anand Kumar
Malik, Saied Ahmad
Malik, Tirlok N.
Malik, Zafar A.
Malkani, Roma V.
Mallick, Pankaj K.
Mamidala, Ramulu
Mammen, Abraham
Mammen, Thomas
Manne, Veeraswamy
Mansur, Iqbal
Mantil, Joseph Chacko
Marur, Hanuman
Mathai, Anish
Mathai-Davis, Prema
Mathew, Saramma T.
Mathew, Valsa
Mathews, Peter
Mathiprakasam, Balakrishnan
Mathur, Achint P.
Mathur, Aditya P.
Mathur, Balbir Singh
Mathur, Harbans B.
Mathur, Ike
Mathur, Kailash V.
Mathur, Krishan D.
Mathur, Raghu P.
Mayell, Jaspal Singh
Mehra, Ravinder C.
Mehrotra, Kishan Gopal
Mehrotra, Prem N.
Mehrotra, Sudhir Chandra
Mehta, Ajai Singh
Mehta, Amarjit
Mehta, Ashok V.
Mehta, Bharat V.
Mehta, Gurmukh Dass
Mehta, Jawahar L.

Mehta, Kailash
Mehta, Kamlesh T.
Mehta, Kishor Singh
Mehta, Krishnakant Hiralal
Mehta, Mahendra
Mehta, Mahesh
Mehta, Mehul Mansukh
Mehta, Mohinder Paul
Mehta, Prakash V.
Mehta, Rahul
Mehta, Raj B.
Mehta, Rajendra G.
Mehta, Sunil Kumar
Mehta, Ujjwal J.
Mehta, Ved
Mehta, Zubin
Melookaran, Joseph
Menon, Gopinath K.
Merchant, Ismail Noormohamed
Merchant, Vasant V.
Metha, Pradipkumar D.
Minocha, Harish C.
Mirchandani, Gagan
Mirchandani, Prakash
Mishra, Shitala P.
Misra, Alok C.
Misra, Dwarika Nath
Misra, Prabhakar
Mistry, Jayanthi
Mital, Naveen Kumar
Mitra, Grihapati
Mittal, Kamal
Mittal, Kashmiri Lal
Mitter, Sanjoy K.
Modi, Shailesh
Mody, Mukund V.
Mohan, Chandra
Mohanty, Sashi B.
Mohapatra, Rabindra N.
Moinuddin, Masood A.
Mondal, Kalyan
Moodera, Jagadeesh Subbaiah
Mothkur, Sridhar Rao
Motihar, Kamla Mansharamani
Motilall, Makeshwar Fip
Moudgil, Brij Mohan
Moudgil, Virinder K.
Mudundi, Ramakrishna Raju
Mukerjee, Pasupati
Mukherjea, Arunava
Mukherjee, Bharati
Mukherjee, Tapan Kumar
Mukhopadhyay, Nimai C.
Muni, Indu A.
Munroe, Tapan
Murthy, A. Kumaresa S.
Murthy, Srinivasa
Murty, Katta Gopalakrishna
Murty, Komanduri Srinivasa
Musapeta, Hari
Muthukrishnan, Subbaratnam
Myer, Yash Paul
Nadkarni, Sudhir V.
Nag, Ronjon
Nagarajan, Ramakrishnan
Nahata, Milap Chand
Nahata, Suparas M.
Naidu, Seetala Veeraswamy
Naik, Datta Vittal
Naik, Tarun Ratilal
Nair, Chandra K.
Nair, K. M.
Nair, Mira
Nair, V. Krishnan
Nanda, Navin Chandar
Nanda, Ravindra
Nanda, Vir A.
Nandkumar, Nuggehalli
  Balmukund
Narasimhan, Sridhar
Narasimhan, Subha
Narayan, Kirin
Narayanamurti, Venkatesh

Narayanan, A. Sampath
Narayanaswamy, Onbathiveli S.
Narula, Subhash Chander
Nath, Amar
Nath, Joginder
Navangul, Himanshoo Vishnu
  Bhat
Nayak, Bhagchand D.
Nayak, Tapan Kumar
Nayyar, Sarv P.
Noojibail, Eshwar
Nori, Dattatreyudu
Oettinger, Reena
Pai, K. Vasanth
Pai, Sadanand V.
Pai, Venkatrao K.
Pakvasa, Sandip
Pal, Pratapaditya
Palamand, Krishna
Pande, Gyan Shanker
Pande, Krishna P.
Pandey, Ras Bihari
Pandit, Grish Roy
Pandit, Sudhakar Madhavrao
Pandya, Amit Anant
Pandya, Deepak N.
Panjwani, Vishnu
Pannu, Dave S.
Papasani, Subbaiah Venkata
Parate, Natthu Sonbaji
Parekh, Navnit M.
Parikh, Hemant Bhupendra
Parikh, Indu
Parikh, Kirit Girishchandra
Parikh, Pravin F.
Parikh, Rajeev N.
Parikh, Rohit J.
Parikh, Rupesh N.
Parkhie, Mukund R.
Parthasarathy, Sampath
Parthasarathy, Triplicane Asuri
Patel, Anil J.
Patel, Anil S.
Patel, Appasaheb R.
Patel, Arvindkumar Motibhai
Patel, Ashok R.
Patel, Bhagvan H.
Patel, Bhagwandas Mavjibhai
Patel, Bharat R.
Patel, Bhulabhai C.
Patel, Bhupen N.
Patel, Chandra Kumar Naranbhai
Patel, Chandrakant B.
Patel, Chandrakant J.
Patel, Chandu K.
Patel, Chandu M.
Patel, Dilipkumar Z.
Patel, Dinesh
Patel, Hiren S.
Patel, Indravadan R.
Patel, Jay M.
Patel, Jayant P.
Patel, Jayanti R.
Patel, Jitendra B
Patel, Kalyani
Patel, Kamla
Patel, Kanti L.
Patel, Kantilal P.
Patel, Kiran K.
Patel, Kishor N.
Patel, Mitesh K.
Patel, Mukesh M.
Patel, Mukul B.
Patel, Mukund R.
Patel, Nagin K.
Patel, Narayan G.
Patel, Narendra D.
Patel, Pratibha A.
Patel, Rakesh
Patel, Ramesh D.
Patel, Ramesh P.
Patel, Ramesh V.
Patel, Ray J.

Patel, Ray L.
Patel, Roger
Patel, Sanjay Vrajlal
Patel, Sarla M.
Patel, Shailesh R.
Patel, Shirish A.
Patel, Vipin A.
Patel, Virendra Chaturbhai
Pathak, Sen
Pati, A. Kumar
Patil, Popat N.
Patil, Pralhad T.
Patnaik, Amiya K.
Pemmaraju, Narasimha Rao
Peterson, Indira Viswanathan
Pillai, Unnikrishna S.
Pillai, Vijayan K.
Pillay, Mullayil K. G.
Pillay, Sivasankara K. K.
Pindiprolu, Manjula
Pinto, James J.
Prabhakar, Arati
Prabhu, R. D.
Prabhudesai, Mukund M.
Pradhan, Shekhar
Prakash, Shamsher
Prakash, Vinod
Prasad, Marehalli Gopalan
Prasad, Rameshwar
Premraj, A. N.
Pujara, Subhash Somabhai
Puligandla, Viswanadham
Pulijal, Madhu V.
Punwani, Dharam Vir
Puri, Pratap
Purohit, Milind Vasant
Qasim, Syed Reazul
Rab, Mirza M.
Radhakrishnamurthy, Bhandaru
Raghavan, Sridhar A.
Rai, Amarendra Kumar
Rai, Arti K.
Rai, Arun
Rai, Gauri S.
Rai, Vijai Narain
Raina, Ashok K.
Raj, Harkisan D.
Raja, Rajendran
Rajagopal, Kumbakonam
  Ramamani
Rajan, Frederick E. N.
Rajan, Periasamy Karivaratha
Rajan, Raghuram Govind
Rajani, Prem Rajaram
Rajasekhar, Amar
Rajendran, Vazhaikkurichi M.
Raju, Seshadri
Raju, Solomon Nalli, Sr.
Ramachandra, Srinivas R.
Ramachandran, Rita
Ramadhyani, Satish
Ramakrishna, Kilaparti
Ramakrishnan, Terizhandur S.
Ramakumar, Ramachandra
  Gupta
Ramalingam, Mysore
  Loganathan
Raman, Aravamudhan
Ramanathan, Veerabhadran
Ramaswami, Vaidyanathan
Ramchandani, Raj S.
Rana, Gurinder Mohan Singh
Rana, Mohammed Waheed-uz-
  Zaman
Ranade, D. G.
Ranade, Madhukar G.
Rangaswamy, Thangam
Ranhotra, Gurbachan S.
Rao, Ananda G.
Rao, Angara Koneti
Rao, Barry
Rao, Bhamidipaty Kameswara
Rao, Dabeeru C.

Rao, Gandikota Venkata
Rao, Gopal Subba
Rao, Gopalakrishna M.
Rao, Gottipaty N.
Rao, Gundu H. R.
Rao, K. L. Seshagiri
Rao, Kameswara Kolla
Rao, Koneru Ramakrishna
Rao, Madhusudana N.
Rao, Mahesh K.
Rao, Mentreddi Anandha
Rao, Nagaraja R.
Rao, Papineni S.
Rao, Raghav H.
Rao, Ramesh K. S.
Rao, Ramgopal P.
Rao, Sadasiva Madiraju
Rao, Singiresu Sambasiva
Rao, Spuma M.
Rao, Srikumar S.
Rao, T. K. Sreepada
Rao, Taramanohar B.
Rao, Tejaswini
Rao, Vaman
Rao, Venigalla Basaveswara
Rao, Yalamanchili Krishna
Rath, Nigam Prasad
Ratti, Rakesh Kumar
Rau, A. Ravi Prakash
Raut, Kamalakar Balkrishna
Ravindra, Nuggehalli Muthanna
Ravindran, Nair N.
Rawat, Arun Kumar
Rawat, Banmali Singh
Ray, Siba Prasad
Reddy, Bandaru S.
Reddy, C. Subba
Reddy, Chilekampalli
  Adinarayana
Reddy, Churku Mohan
Reddy, Dhanireddy Ramalinga
Reddy, Eashwer K.
Reddy, Gudigopuram Bhaskar
Reddy, Gunda
Reddy, Indra Karan
Reddy, Junuthula N.
Reddy, Kapuluru
  Chandrasekhara
Reddy, Nallapu Narayan
Reddy, Pannala Sathyanahayana
Reddy, Pradeep K.
Reddy, Pratap P.
Reddy, Raj
Reddy, Ramakrishna P.
Rikhiraj, Sadhu Singh
Rishi, Satchidanand Raam
Rohatgi, Pradeep K.
Rohatgi, Upendra Singh
Rohatgi, Vijay K.
Rohila, Pritam Kumar
Roy, Dev Kumar
Roy, Pradip Kumar
Roy-Burman, Pradip
Rustagi, Ravinder Kumar
Sabharwal, Kulbir
Sabnis, Gajanan M.
Sabnis, Suman Trimbak
Sachan, Dileep Singh
Sachdev, Ramesh Kumar
Sadana, Ajit
Safdari, Yahya Bhai
Sahni, Sham L.
Sahni, Viraht
Sakhare, Vishwa M.
Saluja, Jagdish Kumar
Salunkhe, Dattajeerao K.
Sanadi, D. R.
Sandhu, Shingara Singh
Sandrapaty, Ramachandra Rao
Sani, Brahma P.
Sankaran, Aiylam P.
Santhanam, Radhika
Sarathy, Partha R.

Sarkar, Fazlul H.
Sarkar, Nitis
Sarkar, Santanu Kumar
Sarker, Bimal
Sathyavagiswaran, Lakshmanan
Satyapriya, Coimbatore K.
Sawhney, Ajay
Sawhney, Gurjeet Singh
Saxena, Brij B.
Saxena, Satish Chandra
Saxena, Subhash Chandra
Sayala, Chhaya
Sayala, Dash
Sehgal, Om Parkash
Sehgal, Raj K.
Sen, Arun
Sen, Arun Kumar
Sen, Ashish Kumar
Sen, Karabi
Sen, Mihir
Sen, Pabitra Narayan
Sen, Tapas K.
Sengupta, Dipak Lal
Seshadri, Kal S.
Seth, Arun K.
Seth, Shyam S.
Sethi, Ishwar Krishan
Sethi, Naresh Kumar
Shah, Abhay
Shah, Amar M.
Shah, Amit
Shah, Amitkumar L.
Shah, Arvind K.
Shah, Bhupendra P.
Shah, Chandu M.
Shah, Chimanlal Keshavlal
Shah, Dhiraj Harilal
Shah, Dhiren Bhawanji
Shah, Dinesh Ochhavlal
Shah, Ghulam Mohammad
Shah, Harikrishna D.
Shah, Harish S.
Shah, Harnish V.
Shah, Hasmukh N.
Shah, Jayprakash Balvantrai
Shah, Mayank H.
Shah, Minal J.
Shah, Mirza Mohammed
Shah, Nagambal Deepak
Shah, Nagin B.
Shah, Nandlal Chimanlal
Shah, Naren N.
Shah, Narendra M.
Shah, Narendra N.
Shah, Nilesh D.
Shah, Nitin J.
Shah, Parth J.
Shah, Piyush A.
Shah, Pradyumna R.
Shah, Pravin M.
Shah, Rajani C.
Shah, Ramesh Keshavlal
Shah, Ramesh V.
Shah, Sarju S.
Shah, Shailesh R.
Shah, Sheila
Shah, Shirish
Shah, Shirish K.
Shah, Uma
Shah, Yogesh K.
Shahzad, Farhat
Shankar, Srinivasan
Shankar, Subramonian
Sharma, Anil F.
Sharma, Arun
Sharma, Bhudev
Sharma, Brij Lal
Sharma, Deva Datta
Sharma, Ghanshyam D.
Sharma, Hari Chand
Sharma, Jandhyala L.
Sharma, M. P.
Sharma, Mukul Mani

Sharma, Mutyam V.
Sharma, Onkar Prasad
Sharma, Parashu Ram
Sharma, Puneet
Sharma, Raghubir Prasad
Sharma, Ramesh
Sharma, Ravindra Nath
Sharma, Santosh Devraj
Sharma, Saroj
Sharma, Satanand
Sharma, Satish
Sharma, Shri C.
Sharma, Subhash C.
Sharma, Surendra P.
Sharma, Udhishtra Deva
Sheikh, Ghafoor A.
Shendrikar, Arun D.
Shenoi, B. A.
Shenoy, Narasimha B.
Sheth, Ashvin C.
Sheth, Atul Chandravadan
Sheth, Ketankumar Kantilal
Sheth, Kishor C.
Sheth, Navin D.
Shetty, Anil N.
Shevde, Ketan
Shrivastava, Satyendra P.
Shroff, Arvin P.
Shukla, Shivendra D.
Siddiqui, Aleem Abdul
Sidhu, Gurmel Singh
Sihag, Ram K.
Sikand, Chander Kumari
Singh, Ajaib
Singh, Ajaib
Singh, Amarjit
Singh, Baldev
Singh, Balwant
Singh, Gurdial
Singh, Harpal
Singh, Jagbir
Singh, Kim
Singh, Madan Mohan
Singh, Madho
Singh, Natasha
Singh, Prithipal
Singh, Rajendra
Singh, Sant P.
Singh, Sharon
Singh, Surendra Pal
Singh, Vijay P.
Singh, Vijay Pal
Singha, Nabaghana Shyam
Singhal, Avinash Chandra
Singhvi, Sampat M.
Singpurwalla, Nozer Darabsha
Sinha, Akhouri A.
Sinha, Dipen N.
Sinha, Nirmal K.
Sinha, Sunil Kumar
Sinha, Uday K.
Sinha, Yagya Nand
Sircar, Rina Schyamcharan
Sohal, Harjit Singh
Somani, Arun K.
Somani, Pitambar
Somasundaran, Ponisseril
Soni, Narendra
Sood, Devinder Kumar
Sood, Mohan K.
Sood, Ravinder Singh
Sreenivasan, Katepalli Raju
Sreevalsan, Thazepadath
Srinivas, Ramachandra
Srinivasan, Gunumakonda
  Ramaswamiengar
Srinivasan, Ramachandra Srini
Srinivasan, Thiru R.
Srirama, Malini
Srivastava, Om P.
Srivastava, Prakash Narain
Srivastava, Sadanand
Subbaswamy, Kumble Ramarao

Subramani, Suresh
Subramaniam, Pramilla N.
Subramanian, Sribala
Subramanya, Shiva
Subudhi, Manomohan
Sudan, Ravindra Nath
Sudarshan, T. S.
Sundaram, Kalyan
Sundaram, Meenakshi R.
Sundaresan, P. Ramnathan
Surti, Tarun Natwarlal
Suryanarayanan, Raj Gopalan
Swaroop, Anand
Syal, Shanta
Syed, Karamat A.
Tahiliani, Jamnu H.
Tahiliani, Vasu Hariram
Talwani, Manik
Tamhane, Ajit C.
Tandon, Anand
Tandon, Rajiv
Tannan, Ashok
Tewarson, Reginald P.
Thadani, Raju
Thakkar, Pravin Asharam
Thakor, Nitish Vyomesh
Thakore, Killol J.
Thakore, Kirit Jamiyatram
Thakur, Manish
Thangaraj, Sandy
Thiruvathukal, Kris V.
Tikoo, Mohan L.
Tripathi, Gorakh Nath Ram
Tripathi, Ramesh Chandra
Tripathi, Satish Chandra
Tripathi, Satish K.
Tripathi, Vijai Kumar
Tripathy, Deoki N.
Trivedi, Kishor S.
Trivedi, Mohan Manubhai
Trivedi, Nayan B.
Trivedi, Nayana Mohan
Trivedi-Doctor, Minakshi Dipak
Tuli, Jagdish K.
Ubhayakar, Shivadev K.
Udani, Kanak H.
Unakar, Nalin Jayantilal
Vadlamudi, Sri Krishna
Vaid, Jyotsna
Vaidhyanathan, Vishnampet S.
Vaidya, Kirit Rameshchandra
Varghese, Philip Leslie
Varghese, Raju Molethu
Varghese, Thomas K.
Varma, Asha
Varma, Rajender S.
Varma, Rakesh
Varma, Usha
Varma, Vishwa K.
Vasan, Srini Varadarajan
Vedamuthu, Ebenezer Rajkumar
Vemula, Subba Rao
Venkata, Subrahmanyam
  Saraswati
Venkataramanan, Raman
Verma, Ajay
Verma, Ajit K.
Verma, Anil K.
Verma, Dhani Ram
Verma, Ram Sagar
Vernekar, Anandu Devarao
Vijayendran, Bhima R.
Vikram, Chandra Shekhar
Virji, Nazneen
Viswanadham, Ramamurthy K.
Viswanath, Rampur S.
Viswanathan, Byravan
Vohra, Indu
Vohra, Ranbir
Vora, Narendra Mohanlal
Vora, Pramathesh S.
Vyas, Gaurang Rajnikant
Vyas, Girish N.

Vyas, Premila Hariprasad
Vyas, Udaykumar Dayalal
Walia, Harjeet Rosie
Walia, Jasjit Singh
Wani, Mansukhlal Chhaganlal
Wasan, Darsh T.
Watumull, Indru
Yaden, Senka Long
Yuvarajan, Subbaraya
Zaveri, Prad S.

INDONESIA

Hoo, Joe-Jie
Kennard, Joyce L.
Liem, Karel Frederik
Liem, Ronald Kian Hong
Maedjaja, Daniel
Peii, Ahmad Osni
Sumartojo, Jojok
Tan, Henry S. I.
Tan, Kim Howard
Tan, Mary
Tan, Tjiauw-Ling

JAPAN

Abe, Makoto
Abo, Ronald K.
Aikawa, Jerry Kazuo
Aki, Keiiti
Akiyoshi, Mike M.
Ando, Koichi
Aoki, Brenda Jean
Aoki, Guy Miki
Aoki, Haruo
Aoki, Kathryn Kiku
Aoki, Rocky
Aoki, Thomas T.
Aono, Isamu
Aoyama, Calvin Takeo
Aoyama, Yasutaka Barron
Arai, Tomie
Arakawa, Edward Takashi
Arakawa, Kasumi
Arakawa, Minoru
Araki, Minoru S.
Arikawa, Norman
Arimura, Akira
Ariza, Yasumi
Asahara, David J.
Asano, Izumi
Atoji, Masao
Awakuni, Gene I.
Azumano, George Ichiro
Azumaya, Goro
Bertrand, Mieko
Bolen, Jean Shinoda
Bowman, Kimiko O.
Campbell, Phyllis J. Takisaki
Chang, Jerry Leslie
Chang, Tim P.
Chiba, Lee I.
Chin, Kathy Hirata
Ching, Stanton Sakae Hong Yat
Chiogioji, Melvin H.
Doi, Roy Hiroshi
Doi, Stan Sumio
Doi, Stanley T.
Domoto, Douglass T.
Doyle, Ruth Narita
Dozono, Sho G.
Ebata, Duane
Embrey, Sue Kunitomi
Emura, Cynthia Sanae
Endo, Frank
Endo, Paula Sayoko Tsukamoto
Enomoto, Jiro
Finucane, Matthew H.
Fischer, Takayo
Fitzpatrick, Eileen Tabata
Fugita, Stephen Susumu
Fujii, Jack Koji

Fujikawa, Denson Gen
Fujiki, Marjorie
Fujimatsu, Tadao
Fujimoto, Isao
Fujimoto, Jack
Fujimoto, James G.
Fujimoto, James Randall
Fujimoto, Robert I.
Fujimoto, Wilfred Yorio
Fujimura, Robert Kanji
Fujimura, Robert Kiyoshi
Fujioka, Takashi
Fujiwara, Theresa
Fukai, Masani
Fukuhara, Henry
Fukunaga, Keinosuke
Fukurai, Hiroshi
Fukushima, Eiichi
Fukuyama, Francis
Funabiki, Jon
Furukawa, Fred M.
Furukawa, Larry Kiyoshi
Furukawa, Theodore Paul
Furuta, Harry
Furuta, Karin L.
Furuta, Otto K.
Furuta, Richard K.
Furuta, Soichi
Furuto, Sharlene Bernice Choy Lin
Gamblin, Noriko
Goishi, Dean M.
Gotanda, Philip Kan
Goto, George
Goto, Joseph N.
Goto, Leo K.
Goto, Unoji
Goto, Yukihiro
Green, Yoshiko Okada
Hagiwara, Kokichi
Hamamoto, Darrell Yoshito
Hamasaki, Les
Hanafusa, Hidesaburo
Hanami, Clement S.
Hara, Lloyd
Hara, Saburo
Haramaki, Chiko
Hara-Nielsen, Sylvia Ann
Harano, Ross Masao
Hasegawa, Jack Koichi
Hashimoto, Akira
Hashimoto, Eiji
Hashimoto, Ken
Hashimoto, Rentaro
Hashimoto, Steven George
Hata, David M.
Hata, Donald Teruo, Jr.
Hata, Hiroaki
Hata, Nadine Ishitani
Hatayama, Rodney Ken
Hattori, James
Hayakawa, Noboru
Hayakawa, S. I.
Hayakawa, Sidney Akira
Hayase, Joshua Yoshio
Hayashi, Dennis Wayne
Hayashi, Elmer Kinji
Hayashi, Fumihiko
Hayashi, James Akira
Hayashi, Masato
Hayashi, Masumi
Hayashi, Midori
Hayashi, Mie May
Hayashi, Robert H.
Hayashi, Seigo
Hayashi, Tetsumaro
Hayashi, William Yasuo
Hayashida, Charley Taketoshi
Hayashida, Frank
Hayashida, Ronald Hideo
Hayashikawa, Doris S.
Hazama, Chuck
Higa, Karin

Higa, Kunihiko
Higa, Leslie Hideyasu
Higa, Ross Rikio
Higa, Walter Hiroichi
Higashi, Kerwin Masuto
Higuchi, Clayton T.
Hihara, Lloyd Hiromi
Hikida, Robert Seiichi
Hill, Amy
Hinoki, George
Hirabayashi, Gordon
Hirabayashi, Lane Ryo
Hiramoto, Joni T.
Hirano, Asao
Hirano, Irene Yasutake
Hirano, Kyoko
Hirano-Nakanishi, Marsha Joyce
Hiraoka, Leslie Satoshi
Hirasaki, George Jiro
Hirasuna, Alan Ryo
Hirata, Henry Minoru
Hirata, Hosea
Hironaka, Steve
Hiroshige, Ernie
Hisatomi, John A.
Hiura, Alan
Hokama, Yoshitsugi
Hokoyama, J. D.
Holl, Julie Kawahara
Honda, Allen Shigeru
Honda, Maya
Honda, Michael M.
Honda, Shigeru Irwin
Hongo, Garrett Kaoru
Honma, Shigemi
Hori, Tom Nichi
Hori, Yutorio Claude
Horiuchi, Chikamasa Paul
Horiuchi, Glenn
Hoshi, Mineo
Hoshiko, Michael
Hoshino, Takao
Hosokawa, Fumiko
Hosokawa, William K.
Hotelling, Katsuko Tsurukawa
Hotta, Gina H.
Houston, Jeanne Wakatsuki
Houston, Velina Hasu
Ichiye, Takashi
Igasaki, Paul
Iiyama, Chizu
Ikeda, Elizabeth Rae
Ikeda, Kazuo
Ikeda, Naomi Ruth
Ikeda, Shigemasa
Ikeda, Tsuguo
Ikegawa, Shiro
Iko, Momoko Marlene
Ikuhara, Akihiro
Imai, Douglas Scott
Imamura, Lawrence Junji
Inaba, Jeffrey Norihisa
Inada, Lawson Fusao
Inagami, Tadashi
Inatome, Joseph T.
Inatome, Rick
Inokuti, Mitio
Inoue, Michael Shigeru
Inouye, Charles Shiro
Inouye, Daniel K.
Inouye, Richard Saburo
Isaki, Cary T.
Isaki, Paul
Ishi, Tomoji
Ishida, Andrew
Ishida, Dianne N.
Ishida, Takanobu
Ishihara, Akinobu
Ishii, Robert Frank
Ishii, Thomas Koryu
Ishikawa, Ishi
Ishikawa-Wolf, Ana Yoshiko
Ishimaru, Akira

Isokawa, Ned
Itakura, Keiichi
Ito, Caryl
Ito, Henry M.
Ito, Lance A.
Ito, Mark Mitsuo
Ito, Michael Shuji
Ito, Noriaki
Ito, Philip Jitsuo
Ito, Satoshi
Ito, Thomas Hiroshi
Ito, Yoichiro
Iwahashi, Satoshi
Iwamoto, Satori
Iwasaki, Iwao
Iwasaki, Ronald Seiji
Iwase, Randall Y.
Iwata, Brian A.
Iwata, Jerry T.
Iwata, Paul Yoshio
Iwataki, David Michael
Iwataki, Miya
Izumigawa, Wallace Minoru
Johnston, George Toshio
Kadohata, Cynthia Lynn
Kadomoto, Thomas
Kadowaki, Joe George
Kagetsu, Tadashi Jack
Kagiwada, George
Kagiwada, Harriet H. Natsuyama
Kai, Robert T.
Kaita, Robert
Kaji, Akira
Kaji, Bruce
Kaji, Jonathan T.
Kajioka, June J.
Kajiwara, Kenneth Kyo
Kaku, Michio
Kakutani, Michiko
Kamiyama, Osamu
Kamo, Yoshinori
Kanaya, Barbara J.
Kaneda, Hiromitsu
Kanegai, Toy
Kaneko, Ryoji Lloyd
Kaneko, William Masami
Kanemitsu, Matsumi
Kano, Sachio
Kao, Yasuko W.
Kariya, Paul
Kashiwa, Hank Charles
Kashiwagi, Brian Rio
Kashiwagi, Soji Charles
Katagiri, George
Kato, Dean M.
Kato, Goro
Kato, Masatoshi
Kato, Theodore Toshihiko
Kato, Tosio
Kato, Walter Y.
Kawafuchi, Glenn Misaki
Kawaguchi, Stanley Kenji
Kawahara, Lindon Ken
Kawahara, William T.
Kawaichi, Ken M.
Kawamoto, Brian Michio
Kawano, Arnold H.
Kawasaki, Lillian Y.
Kawashima, Edith T.
Kawata, Paul Akio
Kaya, Douglas Hifuto, Jr.
Kelly, Darlene Okamoto
Kikuchi, Carl H.
Kikuchi, George Susumu
Kikuchi, Shinya
Kikuchi, William Kenji
Kikumura, Akemi
Kimura, Brian
Kimura, Donna Junko
Kimura, Gwen C.
Kimura, Kolin M.
Kimura, Kongo
Kimura, Lillian C.

Kimura, Mineo
Kimura, Risaburo
Kinaga, Patricia Anne
Kinoshita, Jin H.
Kinoshita, Toichiro
Kiriyama, Iku
Kishimoto, Richard Noriyuki
Kishimoto, Yasuo
Kishimoto, Yoriko
Kita, Sadao
Kitagawa, Joseph Mitsuo
Kitahara, David James
Kitahata, Stacy Dee
Ko, Elaine Ikoma
Kobashigawa, Ben
Kobayashi, Albert Satochi
Kobayashi, Bert Nobuo
Kobayashi, Bertrand
Kobayashi, Deanna Hasuye
Kobayashi, Hideaki
Kobayashi, Jerry T.
Kobayashi, John M.
Kobayashi, Key K.
Kobayashi, Koichi
Kobayashi, Nobuhisa
Kobayashi, William N., Jr.
Kobayashi, Yoshiko
Kobayashi, Yutaka
Kochiyama, William
Koga, Mary H.
Koga, Rokutaro
Koga, Toyoki
Koga, Yoshi Tanji
Kohara, David Noboru
Kohashi, Ethel Tsukiko
Koide, Frank Takayuki
Koide, Samuel Saburo
Komai, Michael Mikio
Konishi, Masakazu
Kono, Hideto
Kono, Tetsuro
Konoshima, Joji
Kotani, Shigeto
Kubota, Carole Ann
Kubota, Gerald K.
Kubota, Kenneth R.
Kubota, Mitsuru
Kudo, Eigo H.
Kumai, Motoi
Kumata, Gerald Hiroshi
Kuramitsu, Howard K.
Kuroda, Emily
Kuroda, Koson
Kuroda, Teruhisa
Kuroda, Yasumasa
Kuroiwa, George Masaharu
Kuroiwa, Hiromi
Kurose, Ruthann
Kushida, Toshimoto
Kusumoto, Sadahei
Kuwahara, Frank
Kuwahara, Steven Sadao
Kuwayama, George
Kwon, Ronald Chi-Oh
Maeda, Robert J.
Maeda, Sharon
Maeda, Yutaka
Maeno, John Y.
Maeyama, Kikuko
Makino, Seiichi
Makino, Shojiro
Makino, Yasuko
Makinodan, Takashi
Mako
Mamiya, Ron
Manabe, Syukuro
Maniwa, Kaz
Marumoto, William Hideo
Maruyama, Kiyoshi
Maruyama, Takashi
Masamune, Satoru
Masaoka, Miya Joan
Matsuda, Fujio

Matsui, Doris Kazue Okada
Matsui, Keiko
Matsui, Machiko
Matsui, Noriatsu
Matsui, Robert Takeo
Matsumoto, Donald Michiaki
Matsumoto, George
Matsumoto, Iku
Matsumoto, Ken
Matsumoto, Mark R.
Matsumoto, Nancy K.
Matsumoto, Randall Itsumi
Matsumoto, Ryujiro
Matsumoto, Takashi
Matsuo, Paul T.
Matsuoka, James Toshio
Matsuoka, Matthew S.
Matsuoka, Shiro
Matsushima, Janie Mitsuye
McCarthy, Nobu
Meshii, Masahiro
Midori
Minamoto, Jennifer Noriko
Mineta, Norman Yoshio
Mink, Patsy Takemoto
Mirikitani, Andy
Mitamura, Ron W.
Mitchell-Onuma, Susan C.
Mitoma, Mike
Mitsunaga, Jimi
Miura, George Akio
Miura, Irene Takei
Miura, Ken-ichi
Miura, Nolan A.
Miya, Wayne
Miyahara, Bruce
Miyahara, Paul Masayoshi
Miyakawa, Edward T.
Miyakoda, Kikuro
Miyamoto, Lance
Miyamoto, Michael Dwight
Miyamoto, Michael Masao
Miyamoto, Seiichi
Miyamoto, Wayne Akira
Miyasaki, George Joji
Miyashiro, Akiho
Miyata, Keijiro
Miyoshi, David Masao
Mizuno, Nobuko Shimotori
Mizutani, Satoshi
Mori, John P.
Mori, Sandy Ouye
Moribayashi, Mikio
Morisawa, Marie Ethel
Morita, Ichiko T.
Morita, John Takami
Morita, Pat
Morita, Richard Yukio
Moriwaki, Clarence
Morizumi, S. James
Moy, Naomi Ogawa
Mukai, Francis Ken
Mukai, Hiroaki
Mukai, Robert L.
Mukai, Yoshiko
Munakata, Grace Megumi
Mura, David
Mura, Toshio
Murai, Norimoto
Murakami, Jeffrey Hisakazu
Murakami, Pamela S.
Murakami, Richard M.
Murase, Mike
Murata, Margaret K.
Murata, Yuji
Myoda, Toshio Timothy
Nagai, Nelson Kei
Nagano, Kent George
Nagano, Paul Tatsumi
Nagaoka, Michael M.
Nagatani, Scott A.
Nagoshi, Douglas N.
Naito, Herbert K.

Naito, Michael K.
Naito, Samuel Teruhide
Najita, Tetsuo
Nakadegawa, Roy
Nakagawa, Cressey
Nakaguchi, Richard T.
Nakahara, Shohei
Nakajima, Nobuyuki
Nakajo, Steve
Nakamoto, Donald Jiro
Nakamoto, Tetsuo
Nakamura, Karen Tsuneko
Nakamura, Michael S.
Nakamura, Mitsuru James
Nakamura, Patricia Akemi Kosugi
Nakamura, Royden
Nakamura, Russell Koichi
Nakanishi, Don Toshiaki
Nakano, Francis
Nakano, Frank Hiroshi
Nakano, George
Nakano, Mei Takaya
Nakasato, George
Nakashima, Mitsugi
Nakashima, Tom Vincent
Nakasone, Robert C.
Nakata, Herbert Minoru
Nakatani, Corey
Nakatani, Henry Masatoshi
Nakatani, Roy Eiji
Nakatsuka, Lawrence Kaoru
Nakayama, Harvey Kiyoshi
Nakayama, Randall Shige
Nakazawa, Anthony Tadashi
Nakazono, Benito Lopez
Nakujima, Hideyuki
Nambu, Yoichiro
Narahara, Hiromichi T.
Narahashi, Toshio
Narita, George M.
Nash, Philip Tajitsu
Niizuma, Minoru
Ninomiya, Calvin
Nishikawa, Dennis
Nishimura, Jonathan Sei
Nishimura, Miwa
Nishimura, Tom
Nishimura, Wendy Natsue
Nishina, Clifford M.
Nishioka, David Jitsuo
Nishioka, Hayward H.
Nishiura, Wayne Iwao
Nitta, Sandra Haruye
Noda, Takayo
Noguchi, John Takeo
Nomura, Kaworu Carl
Nomura, Masae Goto
Nomura, Masayasu
Nozaki, Kenzie
Obata, Gyo
Ochi, Rose Matsui
Ochiai, Shinya
Odo, Blair M. T.
Odo, Franklin Shoichiro
Ogawa, Frank Hirao
Ogawa, Joseph Minoru
Ogawa, Patrick
Ohashi, Alan Joseph
Ohashi, Wataru
Ohnishi, Tomoko
Ohno, Mitsugi
Ohno, Peter Takeshi
Ohta, Masao
Ohta, Shirley Mae
Ohtake, Takeshi
Oishi, Satoshi
Ojima, Iwao
Oka, Christine Kazuko
Oka, Takami
Okabe, Hideo
Okada, Connie Tokiye
Okada, Tony Manabu

Okamoto, Kenneth Wayne
Okamoto, Shari Akiko
Okamura, Arthur Shinji
Okano, Yuji
Okazaki, James
Okazaki, Steven
Oki, Scott D.
Okihiro, Gary Yukio
Okimoto, Daniel Iwao
Okita, Dwight Holden
Okita, George Torao
Okuda, Yasuyori
Omata, Robert Rokuro
Omori, Alvin I.
Omori, Yoshiaki
Omura, Mark Christopher
Onishi, Hironori
Ono, Kanji
Ono, Richard Dana
Ono, Yoko
Oshima, Eugene Akio
Oshima, Harold H.
Oshiro, Kathleen F.
Oshiro, Rene Katsuko
Oshiro, Roy C.
Ota, Dean
Ota, Henry Yasushi
Ota, Isaac I.
Ota, Mabel Takako
Ozaki, Yoji
Ozato, Keiko
Ozawa, Galen M.
Ozawa, Martha Naoko
Ozawa, Terutomo
Posey, Sandra Mizumoto
Rawlings, Noella A.
Renge, I. Beth
Saeki, Hiroko Yoda
Sagami, Kim
Sagawa, Shirley Sachi
Sagawa, Yoneo
Saiki, Patricia F.
Saito, Seiji
Saito, Theodore Teruo
Saito, Thomas E.
Saito, Walter Masao
Saito, Yoshio
Saji, Kiyotaka
Sakagawa, Richard Masaru
Sakai, Michael H.
Sakai, Victoria K.
Sakamoto, Arthur, Jr.
Sakamoto, Clyde Mitsuru
Sakamoto, Katsuyuki
Sakamoto, Lynn
Sakimoto, Philip Jon
Sakita, Bunji
Sakoda, James Minoru
Sakurai, Fred Yutaka
Sasahara, Arthur Asao
Sasaki, Betty Gail
Sasaki, Chiyo Katano
Sasaki, Dale I.
Sasaki, Hideo
Sasaki, Raymond Toshiaki, Jr.
Sasaki, Ruth A.
Sassa, Shigeru
Sato, Frederick Akira
Sato, Gary Teruo
Sato, Irving Shigeo
Sato, Keiko
Sato, Masahiko
Sato, Paul Toshio
Sato, Shigetada
Sato, Tommy M.
Sato, Walter N.
Sato, William K.
Satow, Stuart Alan
Sawatari, Takeo
Say, Allen
Seki, Akiro
Senzaki, Miyo
Senzaki, Randall Kiyomi

Seto, Benjamin S. F.
Seto, Joseph Tobey
Seto, Thelma G.
Seto, Theodore Paul
Shibata, Edward Isamu
Shigemasa, Thomas Ken
Shima, John David
Shimada, Katsunori
Shimada, Yoshiki
Shimamoto, Scott Seiya
Shimizu, Gordon Toshio
Shimizu, Nobumichi
Shimizu, Scott Edward
Shimizu, Taisuke
Shimizu, Tak
Shimizu, Toru
Shimokihara, Stanley Shigeo
Shimomura, Yukio
Shimooka, Russell
Shimoura, James
Shin, In-Sook Jeong
Shinagawa, Larry
Shinozuka, Masanobu
Shinsato, Francis G.
Shirai, Akiko
Shirakawa, George
Shishido, Calvin M.
Shohara, Sei
Sogi, Francis Y.
Suda, Tatsuya
Sugano, Katsuhito
Sugano, Miyoko
Sugawara, Sandra Lee
Sugihara, James Masanobu
Sugihara, Jared Genji
Sugioka, Michael Hiroyuki
Sugiyama, Alan
Sugiyama, Glenn
Sumida, Jon Tetsuro
Sumida, Kenneth Dean
Sumii, Takao
Sumisaki, Roy
Sunaida, Mari
Suzawa, Naoko M.
Suzukawa, Steven
Suzuki, Bob H.
Suzuki, Howard Kazuro
Suzuki, Masao Fred
Suzuki, Michio
Suzuki, Paul Ted
Suzuki, Tsuneo
Tabuchi, Shoji
Tagashira, Gail S.
Tagawa, Cary-Hiroyuki
Tahara, Mildred Machiko
Taira, Masa Morioka
Tajima, Toshiki
Takagi, Dana Y.
Takagi, Norio
Takahashi, Abraham Tomio
Takahashi, Joseph S.
Takahashi, Ken M.
Takahashi, Kozo
Takahashi, Lorey K.
Takahashi, Masato
Takahashi, Rita
Takahashi, Taro
Takaki, Ronald
Takakoshi, William K.
Takami, David A.
Takami, Hideki
Takano, Mark Allan
Takano, Masaharu
Takasaki, Richard Sadaji
Takasaki, William Yoshi Tsugu
Takashima, Shiro
Takasugi, Nao
Takasugi, Robert M.
Takayama, Akira
Takayama, Gregg
Takeda, Yasuhiko
Takei, George Hosato
Takei, Richard

Takekawa, Thomas Tsuyoshi
Takemori, Akira Eddie
Takenaka, Makoto B.
Takeshita, Kenichi
Takeuchi, Esther Kiyomi
Takeuchi, Kenji
Takeuchi, Kenneth James
Takeuchi, Takao
Takiguchi, Masako
Takimoto, Hideyo Henry
Takimoto, Mabel Yayoko
Takumi, Roy M.
Tamaki, Jeanne Keiko
Tana, Akira
Tanabe, George Joji, Jr.
Tanada, Takuma
Tanaka, Eddy Sei
Tanaka, Gary Alan Shinichi
Tanaka, James Junji
Tanaka, John
Tanaka, Kouichi Robert
Tanaka, Richard I.
Tanaka, Ty Skip
Tanaka, Wayne D.
Taniguchi, Alan Y.
Taniguchi, Robert Iwao
Tanouye, Mark Allen
Tashima, A. Wallace
Taura, Richard Bill
Tazoi, Norma
Teraji, Thomas Shuichi
Teramoto, Yoshitsugu
Ting, Joseph K.
Ting Cang-Kim, Donna Marie
Toba, Hachiro Harold
Toda, Harold Keiji
Todd, Kathryn Doi
Todo, Satoru
Tokuda, Kip
Tokuda, Wendy
Tokunaga, Howard Taira
Tokunaga, Katsumi
Tokuuke, Terrance Katsuki
Tomita, Tamlyn Naomi
Tomomatsu, Hideo
Tonai, Rosalyn
Tonegawa, Susumu
Toyama, Frank Kenichi
Toyama, Jean Yamasaki
Toyota, Michael Douglas
Tsai, Bilin Paula
Tsuha, Wallace K., Jr.
Tsuha, Wallace Koichi
Tsuji, Kiyoshi
Tsukahira, Toshio George
Tsukamoto, Jack Toru
Tsukamoto, Mary Tsuruko
Tsukuno, Paul
Tsuneishi, Warren Michio
Tsusaka, Jun
Tsutakawa, George
Tsutakawa, Gerard K.
Tsutsui, James Haruo, Jr.
Uba, George R.
Uchida, Richard Noboru
Uchida, Yoshihiro
Uchida, Yoshiko
Uchimoto, Dennis D.
Uchimoto, William Warren
Uchimura, Bruce Jiro
Uda, Robert Takeo
Ueda, Clarence Tad
Uemoto, Karen
Uemura, Joseph Norio
Ueno, Takemi
Ueoka, Meyer Masato
Uno, Hideo
Urano, Muneyasu
Usui, Kiichi
Uyeda, Arthur Asa
Uyeda, Clifford I.
Uyeda, Roger Makoto
Uyehara, Cecil H.

Uyematsu, Amy
Uyeshima, Mary
Wada, Debra Sadako
Wada, Patricia
Wada, Toshimasa Francis
Wakabayashi, Ron
Wakamatsu, Don
Warashina, M. Patricia
Wasserman, Fumiko Hachiya
Watai, Madge S.
Watanabe, Clyde Kazuto
Watanabe, John Mamoru
Watanabe, Mark Hisashi
Watanabe, Mike
Watanabe, Paul Yashihiko
Watanabe, Robert
Watanabe, Suwako
Watanabe, Yuki
Weglyn, Michi Nishiura
Yagi, Fumio
Yagi, Haruhiko
Yamada, David Takao
Yamada, Kay Matayoshi
Yamada, Mitsuye May
Yamada, Yozo
Yamaga, Chester Kiyoshi
Yamaguchi, Ko
Yamaguchi, Kristine Tsuya
Yamaguchi, Michael J.
Yamakawa, David Kiyoshi, Jr.
Yamakawa, Kazuo Alan
Yamaki, Michael Roger
Yamamori, Tetsunao
Yamamoto, Eric K.
Yamamoto, John Hiroshi
Yamamoto, Keith Robert
Yamamoto, Michael Toru
Yamamoto, Roger Masaaki
Yamamoto, Toshiaki
Yamamoto, Y. Stephen
Yamamoto, Yutaka
Yamanishi, Henry Kazuo
Yamasaki, George, Jr.
Yamasaki, Mitch
Yamashiroya, Herbert Mitsugi
Yamashita, Francis Isami
Yamashita, Kenneth Akira
Yamashita, Pearl Nobuko
Yamauchi, Toshio
Yanagisawa, Samuel Tsuguo
Yang, Emiko
Yano, Ronald Makoto
Yasumura, Seiichi
Yazaki, Toyu
Yonamine, Henry Kiyoshi
Yorita, Frank Kazuo
Yorozu, William S.
Yoshida, Akira
Yoshida, Alan K.
Yoshida, Kanetaka
Yoshida, Ray Kakuo
Yoshida, Roland K.
Yoshida, Ronald Yutaka
Yoshikami, Sandra
Yoshikawa, Herbert Hiroshi
Yoshikawa, Shoichi
Yoshimoto, Watson Toshinori
Yoshimura, Evelyn
Yoshimura, Michael Akira
Yoshimura, Yoshiko
Yoshinaga, George
Yoshino, Kouichi
Yoshino, Ronald Warren
Yoshino, William
Yoshitomi, Karen
Yu, Melvin Joseph
Yuasa, Joji
Yukawa, Masako
Zetterlund, Yoko Karin

KOREA
Ahn, Ho-Sam

Ahn, Jaehoon
Ahn, Steve Fitzgerald
An, Myoung Hee
An, Nack Young
Bai, Taeil Albert
Bak, Chan Soo
Cauthorn, James Daniel
Cha, Chang-Yul
Cha, Soyoung Stephen
Cha, Sungman
Chae, Yong Suk
Chai, Jay
Chang, Byung Jin
Chang, Che-Gil
Chang, Edward Taehan
Chang, Hyong Koo
Chang, Marian S.
Chang, Moon K.
Chang, Paul Keub
Chang, Peter Asha, Jr.
Chang, Sookyung
Chang, Sukjeong J.
Chang, Won Ho
Chang, Yang-Shim
Chang, Yoon Il
Chi, Bo Kyung
Chi, Myung Sun
Cho, Andrew Byong-Woo
Cho, Christopher Sang Kyu
Cho, Dong-il Dan
Cho, Eun-Sook
Cho, Hyong W.
Cho, Jang Youn
Cho, Kah-Kyung
Cho, Kang Rae
Cho, Peck
Cho, Soung Moo
Cho, Weol D.
Cho, Wonhwa
Cho, Zang-Hee
Choe, Sang Tae
Choe, Sun Tok
Choe, Timothy Songsik
Choi, Dosoung Philip
Choi, Eung Ryong
Choi, Eunhye Jenni
Choi, Frederick D. S.
Choi, Hyungmoo
Choi, In-Chan
Choi, Jai-Keun
Choi, Jai Won
Choi, Jai-Young
Choi, Jin Wook
Choi, John Haetak
Choi, Kyung-Ju
Choi, Kyung Kook
Choi, Namkee Gang
Choi, Paul Lee
Choi, Paul W.
Choi, Raymond Yoonseok
Choi, Richard Yungho
Choi, Songsu
Choi, Soonok
Choi, Sung Sook
Choi, Tai-Soon
Choi, Tony Sung
Choi, Ye-Chin
Choi, Young Dong
Choo, Marcia
Choy, Christine
Choy, Herbert Y. C.
Chu, Chung Kwang
Chu, William Tongil
Chun, Shinae
Chun, Sun Woong
Chung, Chai-sik
Chung, Chin Sik
Chung, Ed Baik
Chung, Edward K.
Chung, Eugene
Chung, H. Michael
Chung, Ho Young
Chung, Hyun S.

Chung, Jin Soo
Chung, Jong Rak Philip
Chung, Kyung Won
Chung, Paul Myungha
Chung, T. S.
Chung, Tae-Soo
Chung, Thomas D.
Chung, Thomas Yongbong
Chung, Y. David
Chung, Young-Iob
Chyung, Dong Hak
Ghim, Thad T.
Gramm, Wendy Lee
Ha, Chong W.
Ha, Joseph Man-Kyung
Hahn, Hwa Suk
Hahn, Youngja Choi
Hahn, Yukap
Han, Byung Joon
Han, In-Sop
Han, Jaok
Han, Kenneth N.
Han, Moo-Young
Hauh, Paul-Thomas B.
Hong, Daniel Chonghan
Hong, Gong-Soog
Hong, Il Sik
Hong, Ilyoo Barry
Hong, Jin Sung
Hong, John Song Yook
Hong, Kenneth
Hong, Ryang H.
Hong, S. K.
Hong, S. Theodore
Hong, Suk Ki
Hong, Yoopyo
Huh, Billy K.
Hur, John Chonghwan
Hwang, Chong F.
Hwang, Hi Sook
Hwang, Shin Ja Joo
Hwang, Suein Lim
Hwang, Xochitl
Hyun, Bong Hak
Hyun, Kun Sup
Ihm, Tysun
Im, Jin-Hyouk
Im, Young-Ai
Jhon, Myung S.
Ji, Chueng Ryong
Ji, Inhae
Ji, Taehwa
Jun, Hung Won
Jun, Jong S.
Jun, Joosung
Jung, Byung Il
Jung, Mankil
Jung, Soon J.
Kang, Byung I.
Kang, Chang-Yuil
Kang, Eun Chul
Kang, Heesook Sophia
Kang, Hyungwon
Kang, Joonhee
Kang, Jun-Koo
Kang, Keebom
Kang, Sugwon
Kang, Wi Jo
Kang, Yung C.
Khim, Jay Wook
Kim, Alan Hyun-Oak
Kim, Anna Charr
Kim, Augustine H.
Kim, Bang Ja
Kim, Bong Hwan
Kim, Bong Yohl
Kim, Bonn-Oh
Kim, Byong-Kon
Kim, Byung Guk
Kim, Byung Suk
Kim, Chaesik
Kim, Chan-Hie
Kim, Chan-Wung

Kim, Chang Kyu
Kim, Changwook
Kim, Changyup Daniel
Kim, Chin
Kim, Chin Hui
Kim, Chong Lim
Kim, Choong Soon
Kim, Chulwan
Kim, Chung-Sook Charlotte
Kim, Chung Wook
Kim, David Doyung
Kim, David Ho-Sik
Kim, David Sang Chul
Kim, David U.
Kim, Donald Chang Won
Kim, Dongcheol
Kim, Donna Mercado
Kim, Edward Ik Hwan
Kim, Edward J.
Kim, Eun Mee
Kim, Haewon Chang
Kim, HakLin
Kim, Han-Seob
Kim, Hee-Jin
Kim, HeeMin
Kim, Helen
Kim, Hesook Suzie
Kim, Hong Nack
Kim, Hong Yung
Kim, Hyong Sok
Kim, Hyun Kap
Kim, Hyun Wang
Kim, Hyung J.
Kim, Il-Woon
Kim, Il Young
Kim, Ilpyong J.
Kim, Jae Hoon
Kim, Jae Won
Kim, James Joo-Jin
Kim, Jason Jungsun
Kim, Jay C.
Kim, Jay Chul
Kim, Jay S.
Kim, Jinchoon
Kim, Joanne Young
Kim, Jonathan Jang-Ho
Kim, Jong H.
Kim, Jong-Jin
Kim, Jong Koo
Kim, Joochul
Kim, Joseph K.
Kim, Jung Hwan
Kim, Jungnam Ego
Kim, Junguk Lawrence
Kim, Jwa Keun
Kim, Karl Eujung
Kim, Kathleen M.
Kim, Ken I.
Kim, Ki Hang
Kim, Ki Hoon
Kim, Ki Hwan
Kim, Kitai
Kim, Kunsoo
Kim, Kwan Hee
Kim, Kwang-Shin
Kim, Kyoo Hong
Kim, Leo
Kim, Michael Kyong-il
Kim, Michael Wooyung
Kim, Michael Yong
Kim, Moon G.
Kim, Moon H.
Kim, Moon Kyu
Kim, Myung-Hye
Kim, Myung Mi
Kim, Neung Jip
Kim, Paul Myungchyun
Kim, Pilkyu
Kim, Poe
Kim, Quee-Young
Kim, Rhyn H.
Kim, Richard E.
Kim, Robert

Kim, Robert Hyung-chan
Kim, Saeja Oh
Kim, Sang Phill
Kim, Soon Jin
Kim, Soon-Kyu
Kim, Sung Bok
Kim, Sung Wan
Kim, Suzy Linda
Kim, Uichol
Kim, Vivian C.
Kim, Wendell Kealohopauloe
Kim, Wun Jung
Kim, Yee S.
Kim, Yong Bok
Kim, Yong Choon
Kim, Yong-Gwan
Kim, Yong Ik
Kim, Yong K.
Kim, Yong-Ki
Kim, Yongshik
Kim, Yoonchung Park
Kim, Youn-Suk
Kim, Young-Bae
Kim, Young Chan
Kim, Young-Gurl
Kim, Young-Jin
Kim, Youngsoo Richard
Kim, Youngsuk
Kim, Yun
Kim, Yung Mo
Kim, Yunghi
Koh, Kilsan
Koh, Kwang K.
Kong, Dongsung
Koo, Ja Hung
Koo, Michelle E. M.
Kwak, No Kyoon
Kwak, Wikil
Kwon, Jeffrey Young
Kwon, Myoung-ja L.
Kwon, Ronald Chi-Oh
Kwon, Young Ha
Kwon, Young Wuk
Kwon-Chung, Kyung Joo
Lee, Byung-Joo
Lee, Byung-Moon
Lee, Chong Sung
Lee, Choong Yang
Lee, Chung
Lee, Dae Sung
Lee, Daeyong
Lee, Do Ik
Lee, Hak-Kwon
Lee, Heakyung
Lee, Henry Joung
Lee, Heungsoon Felix
Lee, Hyung Mo
Lee, Jae-won
Lee, Jai Hyon
Lee, Jang Yun
Lee, Jeff S.
Lee, John Jongjin
Lee, Jong Seh
Lee, Jooh
Lee, Ju-Cheon
Lee, Jung Young
Lee, Juwan
Lee, Kang In
Lee, Kangoh
Lee, Kimyeong
Lee, Kyo Rak
Lee, Kyung Won
Lee, Marie Grace
Lee, Myung-Soo
Lee, Ocksoo Kim
Lee, Peter Wankyoon
Lee, Sang Moon
Lee, Si Young
Lee, Siani
Lee, Soo-Young
Lee, Sooncha A.
Lee, Suk Hun
Lee, Sun-Young Won

Lee, Sung Mook
Lee, Sunggyu
Lee, Taehee
Lee, Wol Sue
Lee, Wonyong
Lee, Wooyoung
Lee, Yul W.
Lee, Yur-Bok
Lieu, George Y.
Lim, Chong C.
Lim, David J.
Lim, John K.
Lim, Kap Chul
Lim, Soon-Sik
Limb, Ben Quincy
Min, David Ilki
Min, Hokey
Min, K. Jo
Min, Kyung Ho
Min, Pyong-Gap
Min, Yong Soon
Minnig, William Paul
Mo, Suchoon
Moon, Byung Hwa
Moon, Chung-In
Moon, Inso John
Moon, Jung Suk
Moon, Kee Suk
Moon, Ronald Tae-yang
Moon, Young B.
Myung, John Y.
Nahm, Moon H.
Nam, Sangboo
Nam, Sehyun
Nam, Wonki Kim
Oh, Angela
Oh, Chan Soo
Oh, Chang H.
Oh, Harry K.
Oh, Joseph
Oh, Keytack Henry
Oh, Tae Hee
Oh, Taesung
Ong, Cynthia
Paek, Chisun Jim
Paek, Min
Pai, Gregory Gi Yong
Pai, Lisa Koonghui Kim
Paik, Ho Jung
Paik, Woon Ki
Pak, Peter Hui-Mun
Pak, Yong Chin
Pang, Keum Y.
Park, Byungwoo
Park, Chan Ho
Park, Chang Ho
Park, Chul
Park, Chung I.
Park, Chung Uk
Park, Duk-Won
Park, Hoon
Park, Hun Young
Park, Jae Young
Park, Jeannie
Park, Jinwoo
Park, Joon B.
Park, Kang H.
Park, Kap Yung
Park, Laura Heyong
Park, Myung Kun
Park, Ounyoung
Park, Sang Oh
Park, Seung-Kyoon
Park, Siyoung
Park, Su-Moon
Park, Sung-Il
Park, Sung-won Sam
Park, Tae Sung
Park, Ted S.
Park, Won J.
Park, Young Whan
Parke, Keol-bai
Park-Taylor, Sonya Sunnah

Rawn, Byung Soon
Rha, ChoKyun
Rhee, Chase Chonggwang
Rhee, Hahn-Kyou
Rhee, Hang Yul
Rhee, Jhoon Goo
Rhee, Khee Choon
Rhee, Phillip
Rhee, Sang Foon
Rhee, Song Nai
Rhee, Susan Byungsook
Rhee, Young Eun
Rhim, Aesop
Rhim, Johng Sik
Ryu, Dewey Doo Young
Shim, Eun Sup
Shim, Jae K.
Shim, Jung P.
Shim, Sang Kyu
Shim, Sook Chin
Shin, Doug Yong
Shin, Ernest Eun-Ho
Shin, Hung Sik
Shin, In-Sook Jeong
Shin, Kilman
Shin, Myung Soo
Shin, Paull H.
Shin, SoonMi
Shin, Yung C.
Shon, Kyo Kwa
Soh, Joong Min
Sohn, David Youngwhan
Sohn, Hong Yong
Sohn, So Young
Song, Il-Yeol
Song, John D.
Song, Joseph M.
Song, Ralph H.
Song, Yangsoon
Song, Yo Taik
Song, Yong Chol
Suh, Bernadyn Kim
Suh, Byungse
Suh, Dae-Sook
Suh, Nam Pyo
Suh, Yung-Ho
Sunoo, Brenda Paik
Tai, C. Stephen
Turek, Laura Kim
Van Houten, David J.
Wei, Robert
Whang, Benjamin
Whang, Robert
Whang, Seungjin
Whang, Sukoo Jack
Whang, Un-Young
Whangbo, Myung-Hwan
White, Cedina Miran Kim
Woo, Celeste Kimberlee
Woo, Chung S. H.
Woody, A-Young Moon
Yang, Chun-Yeong
Yang, Dongpyo
Yang, Hee K.
Yang, Kichoon
Yang, Sun Hye
Yeo, Yung Kee
Yim, Soo Jung
Yoo, Chai Hong
Yoo, Tai-June
Yoon, Chongyul John
Yoon, David Hwa Hyun
Yoon, Hyo-Chun
Yoon, Kwangsun Paul
Yoon, Myung-Ho
Yoon, Peter Haesung
Yoon, Peter Jiung
Yoon, Steven Ilsang
Yoon, Won Z.
Yoon, Youngohi Choi
Youn, Hee Yong
Youn, Luis Tai-Oh
Yu, Byung Pal

Yu, Melvin Joseph
Yuh, Jai K.
Yun, Chung-Hei K.
Yun, Seung Soo
Yun, Suk Koo
Yune, Heun Yung

LAOS
Amphavannasouk, Eng
Hang, Tru
Her, Chou
Lo, Tou Ger
Lo, Yao
Phommasouvanh, Banlang
Sayaphupha, Robert Bouakham
Vanchiasong, Siong Koua
Xiong, Lee Pao
Xiong, William Joua
Yang, Lang

MACAO
Cheng, Tu-chen
Cheung, Fernando C. H.
Chiu, John T.
Tam, Francis Man Kei
Yu, Peter Tat-kong
Yung, Christoph Yingwai

MALAYSIA
Chan, Su Han
Chen, Sam W.
Chia, Swee Lim
Chong, Pek-Ean
Chong, Peng-Khuan
Chong, Timothy
Chong-Gottinger, Ivy Wok
   Kuong
Choy, Simon
Goh, Ben K.
Hon, David Nyok-Sai
Kuan, David A.
Lee, Chew-Lean
Lee, Ker-Fong
Lee, Soo See
Lim, Billy Lee
Lim, Kam Ming
Lim, Kwee-Eng Lyn
Lim, Poh C.
Lim, Shirley Geok-Lin
Lim, Teck-Kah
Ling, Matthew S.
Low, Loh-Lee
Mane, Sateesh Ramchandra
Ng, Peter A.
Ong, Beng Soo
Ong, Chee-Mun
Ong, Nai-Phuan
Ong, Sing-Cheong
Pang, Seng Puang
Shivanandan, Kandiah
Tan, Cheng Imm
Tan, Cheng-Pheng
Wang, Bee-Lan Chan
Wang, Shen K.
Wang, Sylvia
Wong, Alexius Yu-Ming
Wong, Chin Siong
Wong, Kau Fui
Wong, Wing Y.

MYANMAR
Bhattacharyya, Shankar P.
Chatterjee, Monish Ranjan
Chu-Andrews, Jennifer
Khorasanee, Barker M.
Magdamo, Patricia L.
Myint, Than Htun
Pe, Maung Hla
Shwe, Hla

Sircar, Rina Schyamcharan
Tin, Bo
Tsai, Stanley
Wong, Henry L.
Wong, Norman Zaw

PACIFIC ISLANDS
Akaka, Daniel Kahikina
Blaz, Ben
Chun, Aulani
Falaniko, Frank, Jr.
Faleomavaega, Eni Faauaa
   Hunkin, Jr.
Hamamoto, Darrell Yoshito
Hokama, Yoshitsugi
Ikeda, Naomi Ruth
Izumigawa, Wallace Minoru
Kim, Wendell Kealohopauloe
Labasan, Alejandro B.
Lal, Dhyan
Lee, Jason Scott
Liu, Edwin H.
Louganis, Greg E.
Nakamura, Royden
Noga, Al
Oshiro, Roy C.
Reeves, Keanu
Rivers, Mavis
Ruiz-Conforto, Tracie
Seto, Robert Mahealani Ming
Tomita, Tamlyn Naomi
Underwood, Robert Anacletus
Waihee, John David
Wong, Clifford S.

PAKISTAN
Abbas, Mian M.
Ahmad, Jameel
Ahmed, Shaikh Sultan
Ahmed, Wase U.
Arif, Shoaib
Aziz, Khalid
Bhatti, Rashid A.
Chaudhry, G. Rasul
Chughtai, Shahid H.
Dass, Edgar Sushil
Durrani, Sajjad Haidar
Farhataziz
Hashmi, Mohammed Zafar
Hingorani, Narain G.
Husain, Mustafa Mahmood
Hussain, Riaz
Ijaz, Lubna Razia
Iqbal, S. Mohammed
Ishaq, Ashfaq M.
Khan, Mohammad Asad
Khan, Mohammed Abdul
   Quddus
Khan, Shakil Ahmad
Khan, Walayet A.
Krishna, Darshan
Lateef, Abdul Bari
Lodhi, M. A. K.
Madan, Dwarka Nath
Maj, Naweed K.
Makhijani, Srichand
Malik, Hafeez
Malik, Naeem
Malik, Saied Ahmad
Mathur, Ike
Miah, Abdul J.
Mian, Athar S.
Mian, Waqar Saeed
Murad, Sohail
Mustafa, Shams
Nizami, Shafiq Ahmed
Qureshi, Muquarrab Ahmed
Qureshi, Qadeer Ahmad
Rana, Mohammed Waheed-uz-
   Zaman
Rasheed, Suraiya

Shah, Ahmer
Shah, Mowahid Hussain
Shah, Mubarak Ali
Shah, Syed M.
Shaikh, Abdul Hamid
Shaikh, Saeed Ahmad
Shaikh, Zahir A.
Sheikh, Ghafoor A.
Siddiqui, Ehtisham Uddin
   Ahmad
Syed, Karamat A.
Thadhani, Kaloo C.
Virk, Muhammad Yaqub

PHILIPPINES
Abarquez-Delacruz, Prosy
Albano, Alfonso M.
Alcantara, Larry James
Alejandro, Reynaldo Gamboa
Alota, Ruben Villaruel
Andrada, Wilmer Vigilia
Asuncion, Alfredo, Jr.
Asuncion, Gary Raymond Espejo
Aviado, Domingo M.
Bacho, Norris V.
Bacho, Peter
Bagasao, Paula Y.
Baldonado, Ardelina Albano
Baldoz, Gerald L.
Banada-Tan, Leticia
Barron, Purificacion C.
Bautista, Veltisezar Bal
Belbis, Manuel Emuslan
Benavides, Vida
Blanco, Paul De La Cruz
Brillantes, Hermogenes Bilgera
Cabana, Veneracion Garganta
Cabanting, George Paul
Cabrera, Cesar Trinidad
Caldito, Gloria Cruz
Caoile, Gloria T.
Caoile, John Anthony
Castro, Marissa Barbers
Cayetano, Benjamin J.
Chua, Conrad E.
Collantes, Augurio L.
Collantes, Lourdes Yapchiongco
Compas, Lolita Burgos
Corpuz, Ray E., Jr.
Cruz, Jose Bejar, Jr.
Cruzada, Rodolfo Omega
Cuajao, Tracy Lee
Cueto, Alex
Davino, Carmencita Fernandez
Dayao, Firmo Salvador
de la Peña, Violeta R.
Della, David J.
Denton, Victoria Villena-
   de Vera, Federico
Diokno, Ananias Cornejo
Dirige, Ofelia Villa
Dolor, Deogracias Asuncion, Jr.
Domingo, Cynthia Garciano
Domondon, Oscar
Esclamado, Alejandro A.
Esguerra, Arturo Sazon
Evangelista, Stella
Fajardo, Ben
Fajardo, Peter
Florentino, Leila San Jose
Flores, Susan Gumabao
Francia, Luis H. F.
Francisco, Emiliano Alonzo
Gan, José C.
Gatdula, Francisco Ric
Geaga, Jaime V.
Gonzalez-Pardo, Lillian
Gotera, Vicente Ferrer
Guillermo, Tessie
Guingona, Michael Patrick
Hagedorn, Jessica Tarahata
Haley, Maria Luisa Mabilangan

Hernandez, Tomas C.
Jamero, Peter M.
Jao, Radmar Agana
Jimenez, Josephine Santos
Juanitas, Cyril E. B., Jr.
Kim, Donna Mercado
Korten, Geraldine B.
Labasan, Alejandro B.
Lachica, Edward Anthony
LaCuesta, Lloyd R.
LaCuesta, Wesley Ray, Sr.
Lagura, Franklin Sasutana
Laigo, Valeriano Emerciano
   Montante
Landero, Reynaldo Rivera, II
Langit, Ralph P., Jr.
Lazo, Douglas T.
Leighton, Veronica V.
Lewis, Loida Nicolas
Liddell, Gene Canque
Lim, Antonio Lao
Lim, Josefina Paje
Lim, Paul Stephen
Lim, Paulino Marquez, Jr.
Lim, Ramon Khe-Siong
Linsangan, Renato
Mahilum, Benjamin C.
Manankil, Norma Ronas
Marasigan, Rogelio U.
Margallo, Lucio N., II
Marshall, Thurgood, Jr.
McCarty, Faith B.
Montero, Juan Murillo, II
Muriera, Helen Bautista
Natividad, Irene
Natori, Josie Cruz
Ng, Anastacio C.
Nietes, Linda Maria
Ochoa, Gloria Megina
Ordanza, Bonagrace Francisco
Padre, Marc Cruz
Panlilio, Adelisa Lorna
Partido, Rousalyn Bautista
Paz, Jennifer C.
Querol Moreno, Cherie M.
Quimpo, Rafael Gonzales
Quismorio, Francisco P., Jr.
Ragudos, John L.
Raimundo, Cris C.
Ramil, Mario R.
Recana, Mel Red
Respicio, Elsa Toje
Reyes, Adelaida
Reyes, Hernan M.
Rio-Jelliffe, Rebecca
Rivera, Evelyn Margaret
Rodis, Rodel E.
Salonga, Lea
Sampang, Conrado Carriedo
San Juan, E.
Santos, Mario Alban
Sato, Gary Teruo
Sibal, Nicolas Villadolid
Silao, Ray A.
Simunek, Linda A.
Sinco, Victor
Sison, Fredilyn
Siy, James Andrew
Soo, Billy S.
Soriano, Lee G.
Suelto, Teem D.
Sugioka, Michael Hiroyuki
Sundaresan, Gloria Marquez
Suzuki, Masao Fred
Sy, Antonio Ngo, Jr.
Sy, Francisco S.
Tiangco, Eddie Eugenio
Ting, Joseph K.
Ting Cang-Kim, Donna Marie
Tolentino, Virginia Cantor
Tomita, Tamlyn Naomi
Umali, Filemon J.
Valderrama, David Mercado

Ethnic/Cultural Heritage Index

Valmonte, Arnel Elvambuena
Veloria, Velma Rosete
Villanueva, Chris
Villanueva, Marianne Del
  Rosario
Villa-Real, Olivia Canchela
Winick, Tranquilina Rios
Ye, Jose
Yuchengco, Mona Lisa Sycip
Zamora, Mario Dimarucut

SINGAPORE
Chang, Ngee-Pong
Cheng, Lanna
Cheong, Fiona
Choe, Kenneth
Chow, Ivan S.
Giam, Choo Seng
Hwang, Ivy
Kashyap, Moti Lal
Lau, Hon-Shiang
Lee, Kok-Meng
Lu, Frank Kerping
Pang, Chap Aik
Sim, John Kim-Chye
Tan, Eric Tuanlee
Tan, Jack Sim Eddy
Tan, S. Y.
Wang, Gary S. H.
Yap, Stacey G. H.

SRI LANKA
Choksy, Jamsheed Kairshasp
Gunaratne, Dhavalasri Shelton
  Abeywickreme
Ramachandran, Nadaraja

TAIWAN
Chan, Shih-Hung
Chang, Ann Han-Chih
Chang, Ben
Chang, Chawnshang
Chang, Chein-I
Chang, Chia-Cheh
Chang, Ching-jer
Chang, Chuan Chung
Chang, Chun-Hao
Chang, Darwin
Chang, Helen Kuang
Chang, Hui-Ching
Chang, Jane Yueh
Chang, Kai-Hsiung
Chang, Kang-Tsung
Chang, Kelvin Yau-Min
Chang, Kow-Ching
Chang, Richard
Chang, Shih-Ger
Chang, Shing I.
Chang, Shirley Lin
Chang, Sung-sheng Yvonne
Chang, Tien-Chien
Chang, Tsan-Kuo
Chang, William Wei-Lien
Chang, Winston Wen-Tsuen
Chang, Yi-Chieh
Chang, Yia-Chung
Chang, Yu Lo Cyrus
Chang, Yung-Feng
Chao, Yuh J.
Chen, Angela Tzu-Yau
Chen, Anne Chi
Chen, Audrey Huey-Wen
Chen, Bang-Yen
Chen, C. L. Philip
Chen, Carl Wan-Cheng
Chen, Chao Ling
Chen, Chong-Maw
Chen, Chong-Tong
Chen, Chuan Ju
Chen, Chung-Hsuan

Chen, David Ting-Kai
Chen, Derrick A.
Chen, Ding-Bond
Chen, Donald S.
Chen, Edward C. H.
Chen, Harry W.
Chen, Hilo C. H.
Chen, Hong Chyi
Chen, Houn-Gee
Chen, Hsin-Piao Patrick
Chen, Hung-Liang
Chen, Jackson W.
Chen, James Pai-fun
Chen, John L.
Chen, Jyh-Hong Eric
Chen, Kenny T.
Chen, Kuang Chung
Chen, Kun-Mu
Chen, Lea Der
Chen, Li-Fu
Chen, Linda Li-yueh
Chen, Meanshang
Chen, Rong Yaw
Chen, S. Steve
Chen, Sam W.
Chen, Shoei-sheng
Chen, Su-chiung
Chen, Ta-Shen
Chen, Terry Li-Tseng
Chen, Tsong-Ming
Chen, Tuan Wu
Chen, Wayne G.
Chen, Wayne Y.
Chen, Winston H.
Chen, Wun-ee Chelsea
Chen, Ye-Sho
Chen, Yea-Mow
Chen, Yen-Hsu
Chen, Yi-Leng
Chen, Yi-Shon
Chen, Yih-Wen David
Chen, Yohchia
Chen, Yu-Charn
Cheng, Alexander H-D.
Cheng, Benjamin Shujung
Cheng, Charmian S.
Cheng, Cheng-Yin
Cheng, Hsiang-tai
Cheng, Hsueh-Jen
Cheng, Joe Zen
Cheng, Josephine
Cheng, Mei-Fang Hsieh
Cheng, Nelly Ching-yun
Cheng, Songlin
Cheng, Yung-Sung
Chi, David Shyh-Wei
Chiang, Chao-Kuo
Chiang, Thomas Minghung
Chiang, Yung Frank
Chiao, Yu-Chih
Chien, Yie W.
Chien, Ying I.
Chin, Tamera Ann
Chiou, Minshon J.
Chiou, Paul C. J.
Chiou, Wen-An
Chiu, Chao-Lin
Chiu, Jim
Chiu, Ming S.
Chiu, Shean-Tsong
Chou, Ching-Chung
Chou, Hsin-Pei
Chou, Ting-Chao
Chow, Peter Chi-Yuan
Chu, David
Chu, Nori Yaw-Chyuan
Chuang, De-Maw
Chuang, Strong C.
Chuang, Tze-jer
Chuang, Vincent P.
Chung, Chen Hua
Chung, Douglas Kuei-Nan
Chung, Luke Tsun

Chung, Tze-Chiang
Chuong, Cheng-Ming
Dung, Hou Chi
Fan, Liang-Shih
Fang, Cheng-Shen
Fang, Jin Bao
Fang, Louis Li-Yeh
Fang, Pen Jeng
Fu, Jyun-Horng
Fu, LiMin
Hahn, Liang-Shin
Han, Grace Yang
Han, Je-Chin
Han, Sherman Hsiao-min
Han, Susan S.
Ho, Birong A.
Ho, Chin Chih
Ho, Chrwan-Jyh
Ho, Ju-shey
Ho, Khang-cheng
Ho, Thomas Tong-Yun
Horng, John Jang-Ji
Hsiao, Margaret Sheng-Mei
Hsiao, Tyzen
Hsie, Abraham Wuhsiung
Hsieh, Brian
Hsieh, Carl Chia-Fong
Hsieh, Chung-cheng
Hsieh, Cynthia C.
Hsieh, Dean Shui-Tien
Hsieh, Hsin-Neng
Hsieh, Philip Po-Fang
Hsieh, Wen-jen
Hsin, Liang Yih
Hsu, Albert Yutien
Hsu, Cathy H. C.
Hsu, Charles Jui-cheng
Hsu, George Chi-Yung
Hsu, Jong-Ping
Hsu, Jong-Pyng
Hsu, Kenneth Hsuehchia
Hsu, Liang-Chi
Hsu, Merlin
Hsu, Nai-chao
Hsu, Paul
Hsu, Stephen Charles
Hsu, Tse-Chi
Hu, Chao Hsiung
Huang, Barney Kuo-Yen
Huang, C.-T. James
Huang, Charles
Huang, Chau-Ting
Huang, Cheng-Cher
Huang, Cheng-Chi
Huang, Chin-pao
Huang, Feng Hou
Huang, George Wenhong
Huang, Huey-Wen
Huang, Jack J. T.
Huang, Jamin
Huang, Jennming Stephen
Huang, Joseph T.
Huang, Ju-Chang
Huang, Jung-chang
Huang, Ken Shen
Huang, Liang Hsiung
Huang, Ming-Hui
Huang, Shan-Jen Chen
Huang, Shih-Wen
Huang, Victor Tsangmin
Huang, Wei-chiao
Huang, Wei-Sung Wilson
Huang, William H.
Huang, Wuu-Liang
Hung, Chao-Shun
Hung, Chih-Cheng
Hung, Kuen-Shan
Hung, Paul P.
Hung, Ru J.
Hung, Stephen Chifeng
Hwang, Ange
Hwang, Cherng-Jia
Hwang, Ching-Lai

Hwang, Dennis B. K.
Hwang, Hsin-Ginn
Hwang, Mark I.
Hwang, Shyshung
Hwu, Peter S.
Jen, Serena
Jong, Mark M. T.
Kang, James Jyh-Huei
Kao, Timothy Tieh-Hsiung
Kiang, Clyde Y.
Ko, Cheng Chia Charles
Ko, Wen-hsiung
Ko, William Weng-Ping
Ku, Mei-Chin Hsiao
Ku, Peter
Ku, William H.
Kuo, Albert Yi-shuong
Kuo, Chao Ying
Kuo, Chung-Chieh Jay
Kuo, Feng Yang Kuo
Kuo, Ken Nan
Kuo, Ming-Shang
Kuo, Shiou-San
Kuo, Way
Kuo, Wayne Wen-Long
Kuo, Wen Hsiung
Kuo, Yih-Wen
Lai, Albert Wenben
Lai, Amy
Lai, Ching-San
Lai, Jai-Lue Leon
Lai, Michael Ming-Chiao
Lai, Ming-Yee
Lai, Ralph Wei-meen
Lai, Ying-San
Land, Ming Huey
Lee, Chen Hui
Lee, Chi-Jen
Lee, Chiho
Lee, Chung-Yee
Lee, Der-Tsai
Lee, Kuo-Hsiung
Lee, Kwang K.
Lee, Ming T.
Lee, Shyu-tu
Lee, Tien-Chang
Lee, Tony J. F.
Lee, Wei-chin
Lee, Wei-Na
Lei, Shau-Ping
Leu, Ming C.
Leu, Rong-Jin
Li, Bob Cheng-Liang
Li, Chia-Chuan
Li, Ching James
Li, Ke Wen
Li, Sheng S.
Li, Shin-Hwa
Li, Steven Shoei-lung
Liang, Steven Yuehsan
Liang, Tehming
Liao, Mei-June
Liao, Shun-Kwung
Liao, Shutsung
Liao, T. Warren
Liao, Woody M.
Lin, Binshan
Lin, Cen-Tsong
Lin, Chaote
Lin, Charles Fley-Fung
Lin, Chengmin Michael
Lin, Chi Yung
Lin, Chien-Chang
Lin, Chin-Chu
Lin, Chinlon
Lin, Chiu-Hong
Lin, Dennis Kon-Jin
Lin, Eva I.
Lin, Felix
Lin, Feng-Bao
Lin, Fred Reggie
Lin, Hsiu-San
Lin, James Y.

Lin, Jason Jia-Yuan
Lin, Jennifer Jen-Huey
Lin, Jiann-Tsyh
Lin, Juiyuan William
Lin, Kai-Ching
Lin, Kuan-Pin
Lin, L. Yu
Lin, Liang-Shiou
Lin, Ming-Chang
Lin, Patricia Yu
Lin, Paul Kuang-Hsien
Lin, Roxanne Veronica
Lin, Shield B.
Lin, Sin-Shong
Lin, Su-Chen Jonathon
Lin, Wunan
Lin, Yeong-Jer
Lin, Yu-Chong
Lin, Yuh-Lang
Ling, Hao
Ling, Hsin Yi
Liou, Fue-Wen
Liou, K. T.
Liou, Kuo-Nan
Liou, Ming Jaw
Liou, Sy-Hwang
Liou, Yihwa Irene
Liu, Ben Shaw-Ching
Liu, Chao-Nan
Liu, Chen-Ching
Liu, Donald Jiann-Tyng
Liu, Jyh-Charn Steve
Liu, LiLi
Liu, Lin Chun
Liu, Louis F.
Liu, Maw-Shung
Liu, Ming Cheng
Liu, Ray H.
Liu, Richard Chung-Wen
Liu, Si-kwang
Liu, Su-Feng
Liu, Thomas Jyhcheng
Liu, Yuan Hsiung
Liu, Yung-Way
Lo, Howard H.
Lo, Samuel E.
Loor, Rueyming
Lu, Frank Kerping
Lu, Jye-Chyi
Luh, Yuhshi
Ma, Sheng-mei
Ng, May-May Donna Lee
Ni, Preston C.
Ou, Ching-Nan
Pai, Kenneth Y.
Pan, Fung-Shine
Pan, Wei-Ping
Pang, Su-Seng
Peng, Chang-Shyh
Peng, Dachung Pat
Pong, Schwe Fang
Shang, Bernard Y.
Sheu, Bing J.
Sheu, Lien-Lung
Shieh, Rong Chung
Shieh, Tsay-Jiu Brian
Shieh, Wun-Ju
Shieh, Yuch-Ning
Shih, John Chau
Shih, Ko-Ming
Shih, Ming-Che
Shih, Stephen Chingyu
Song, Choan-Seng
Song, Shin-Min
Su, Cheh-Jen
Su, Kwei Lee
Su, Tsung-chow Joe
Su, Tuhuei
Sun, Tung-Tien
Sun, Wen-Yih
Sung, Lawrence M.
Tai, Hsin-Hsiung
Tai, William P.

Tang, Kwei
Tang, Thomas Li-Ping
Tang, Yingchan Edwin
Teng, Tsuchi Paul
Tsai, Betty L.
Tsai, Bor-sheng
Tsai, Chia-Yin
Tsai, Chuang Chuang
Tsai, Gow-Jen
Tsai, Jeffrey J. P.
Tsai, Jen-San
Tsai, Jir-Shiong
Tsai, Lung-Wen
Tsai, Mark F.
Tsai, Ming-Daw
Tsan, Min-Fu
Tseng, Beatrice Shan-Yi
Tseng, Huan-Chi Chris
Tseng, Leon F.
Tseng, Louisa
Tseng, S. C.
Tseng, Wan Chi
Tso, L. Hilary
Tsuang, Ming T.
Tu, Charles W.
Tu, Samson W.
Tu, Shu-chen H.
Tung, Hsi-tang
Tung, Ming Sung
Tung, Yeou-Koung
Wang, Ben
Wang, C. H.
Wang, Charles Chiming
Wang, Chien Yi
Wang, Francis Wei-Yu
Wang, George Maosue
Wang, Ging-Long
Wang, Gwo-Jaw
Wang, Jason T. L.
Wang, Jin-Liang
Wang, John Chiang
Wang, Ko
Wang, Li-Shing
Wang, Lih-Jau
Wang, Molly M.
Wang, Pao-Kuan
Wang, Ping H.
Wang, Shi-Hwa
Wang, Shih-Ho
Wang, Sho-Ya
Wang, Shujen

Wang, Stanley
Wang, Sue S.
Wang, Ton-Lo
Wang, Tsuey Tang
Wei, Susanna
Wei, Wei-Zen
Wei, William Wu-Shyong
Wen, Wen-Yang
Weng, Wu-Tsung
Wong, K. C.
Wu, Ching-Yong
Wu, Chuan-Fu
Wu, Chun-Fang
Wu, Chung-Hsiu
Wu, David
Wu, Fang-Sheng
Wu, Frederick H.
Wu, George K.
Wu, Hai-Sheng
Wu, Hofu
Wu, Hsiu-ying
Wu, Ishiung J.
Wu, Kim
Wu, Kung Chris
Wu, Michael Ming-Kun
Wu, Richard L. C.
Wu, Tiee-Jian
Wu, Wu-Nan
Wu, Ying-Chan Fred
Yan, Chiou-Shuang Jou
Yan, Joseph Gea-Gue
Yan, Tsoung-Yuan
Yang, Bao-Wen
Yang, Chia Hsiung
Yang, Chung S.
Yang, David C.
Yang, Jeffrey Chih-Ho
Yang, Jiann-Shiou
Yang, Joseph Chi-Houng
Yang, Karl L.
Yang, Shang Fa
Yang, Shi-tien
Yang, Tsu-Ju
Yang, Tuen-Ping
Yang, Wen-Ching
Yang, Wen-Jei
Yang, Yih-Ming
Yao, Dorcas C.
Yeh, Edward H. Y.
Yeh, Henry
Yeh, Michelle M.

Yen, Alfred Chueh-Chin
Yen, Chi-Chung David
Yen, I-Kuen
Yen, John
Yen, Steven T.
Yen, Tien-Sze Benedict
Yu, Alice L.
Yu, Chang-An
Yu, David C.
Yu, Jen
Yu, Jia-Huey
Yu, Shiu Yeh
Yu, Thomas H.
Yu, Yeou-Chong Simon
Yuan, Jian-Min

THAILAND
Anderson, Wanni W.
Chan, Angela
Chen, Kenny T.
Chiang, Asuntha Maria Ming-Yee
Fasang, Patrick Pad
Sukantarat, Wichada
Tana, Phongpan
Wongananda, Boondharm

TIBET
Rinpoche, Gelek

VIETNAM
Brown, Julie
Cao, Hoang-Yen Thi
Cao, Le Thi
Chan, Anthony Bernard
Ch'en, Lena B.
Chu, Hung Manh
Chu, Nhan V.
Cung, Tien Thuc
Dam, Quy T. T.
Dan, Phan Quang
Dang, Phu Ngoc
Dao, Anh Huu
Dao, Minh Quang
Dao, Tuan Anh
Dinh, Nicholas Nguyen
Dinh, Thuy Tu Bich
Dinh, Tung Van

Do, Toa Quang
Dominh, Thap
Duong, Cambao De
Duong, Duc Hong
Duong, Ngo Dinh
Foshee, Thuong Nguyen
Hayslip, Le Ly
Ho, Xuan Michael
Hoang, Frank H.
Hoang, Giao
Huynh, Dung Thiet
Huynh, Emmanuelle
Lam, An Ngoc
Lam, Toan Hoang
Lam, Tony
Le, Binh P.
Le, Christine Dung
Lê, Hy Xuân
Le, Tieng Quang
Le, Vy Phuong
Le, Xuan Khoa
Luong, Son N.
Luu, Lang Van
Ly, Kieu Kim
Ly, Tam Minh
Mai, Hugh D.
Mai, Marianne Vu
Ngo, David
Nguyen, An H.
Nguyen, Anh Mai
Nguyen, Bao Gia
Nguyen, Bao T.
Nguyen, Benjamin Ban
Nguyen, Bong Van
Nguyen, Cam
Nguyen, Caroline P.
Nguyen, Charles C.
Nguyen, Chris Cuong Manh
Nguyen, Chuong Van
Nguyen, Cu D.
Nguyen, Cuong Phu
Nguyen, Duc Ba
Nguyen, Dung Dang
Nguyen, Henry Thien
Nguyen, Hien Vu
Nguyen, Ho Ngoc
Nguyen, Hue Thi
Nguyen, Kim-Oanh Thi
Nguyen, Long
Nguyen, Luu Thanh
Nguyen, Manh-Hung

Nguyen, Mike Chi
Nguyen, Nghia Van
Nguyen, Ngoc-Diep Thi
Nguyen, Thuan Ke
Nguyen, Tony C.
Nguyen, Tri Huu
Nguyen, Vung Duy
Nguyen, Xe V.
Nguyen-huu, Xuong
O, San Luong
Pham, Danny
Pham, Henry Tuoc Van
Pham, Hung Do
Pham, Kien Trung
Pham, Viet Van
Phan, Trung Huynh
Pho, Hai B.
Phung, Doan Lien
Ta, Tai Van
Tong, Benjamin
Tran, Dorothy N.
Tran, Hong-Y Thi
Tran, Huyen Lam
Tran, La Dinh
Tran, Loc Binh
Tran, Loi Huu
Tran, Long Trieu
Tran, Myluong Thi
Tran, Nhut Van
Tran, Phuoc Huu
Tran, Qui-Phiet
Tran, Thang Nhut
Tran, Thinh Quy
Tran, Thomas
Tran, Thuan Van
Tran, Tri K.
Tran, Tuyet-Nhung T.
Trinh, Eugene
Trinh, Hoang Huy
Trinh, Nam Ky
Truong Thi, Hoa-Dien
Van, Thanhtan C.
Viet-Chau, Nguyen Duc
Vo, D. Brian
Vo, Jimmy
Vo, Van Toi
Vovan, Ba
Vu, Joseph
Vu, Liem T.
Vu, Quang
Young, Hoa Pham